The New Encyclopædia Britannica

Volume 29

MACROPÆDIA

Knowledge in Depth

FOUNDED 1768
15 TH EDITION

Encyclopædia Britannica, Inc.
Robert P. Gwinn, Chairman, Board of Directors
Charles E. Swanson, President
Philip W. Goetz, Editor-in-Chief

Chicago
Auckland/Geneva/London/Manila/Paris/Rome
Seoul/Sydney/Tokyo/Toronto

The Encyclopædia Britannica is published with the
editorial advice of the faculties of the University of Chicago;
a committee of persons holding academic appointments
at the universities of Oxford, Cambridge, London, and Edinburgh;
and committees drawn from members of the faculties of the
University of Tokyo and the Australian National University.

 THE UNIVERSITY OF CHICAGO

"Let knowledge grow from more to more
and thus be human life enriched."

First Edition	1768–1771
Second Edition	1777–1784
Third Edition	1788–1797
Supplement	1801
Fourth Edition	1801–1809
Fifth Edition	1815
Sixth Edition	1820–1823
Supplement	1815–1824
Seventh Edition	1830–1842
Eighth Edition	1852–1860
Ninth Edition	1875–1889
Tenth Edition	1902–1903

Eleventh Edition
© 1911
By Encyclopædia Britannica, Inc.

Twelfth Edition
© 1922
By Encyclopædia Britannica, Inc.

Thirteenth Edition
© 1926
By Encyclopædia Britannica, Inc.

Fourteenth Edition
© 1929, 1930, 1932, 1933, 1936, 1937, 1938, 1939, 1940, 1941, 1942, 1943,
   1944, 1945, 1946, 1947, 1948, 1949, 1950, 1951, 1952, 1953, 1954,
   1955, 1956, 1957, 1958, 1959, 1960, 1961, 1962, 1963, 1964,
   1965, 1966, 1967, 1968, 1969, 1970, 1971, 1972, 1973
By Encyclopædia Britannica, Inc.

Fifteenth Edition
© 1974, 1975, 1976, 1977, 1978, 1979, 1980, 1981, 1982, 1983, 1984, 1985,
   1986
By Encyclopædia Britannica, Inc.

© 1986
By Encyclopædia Britannica, Inc.

Printed in U.S.A.

Library of Congress Catalog Card Number: 85-80367
International Standard Book Number: 0-85229-434-4

CONTENTS

CONTENTS

United Kingdom

The United Kingdom of Great Britain and Northern Ireland is the official title of the political union of England, Scotland, Wales, and Northern Ireland. The country is situated in northwestern Europe, separated from the continent proper by the English Channel and the North Sea and lying to the north of France and the west of The Netherlands and Denmark. The total area of the United Kingdom (known popularly, if not quite accurately, as Britain) is 94,512 square miles (244,786 square kilometres), including numerous small islands and 1,189 square miles of inland waters.

The effective union of the principality of Wales with England dates from 1301, when Edward I's son was created prince of Wales, although Wales was not enfranchised until the reign of Henry VIII (acts of 1536 and 1543). The name Great Britain was used in a royal proclamation of 1604, when James VI of Scotland, having succeeded to the throne of England as James I, determined to give expression to the fact that he was sovereign of an undivided island and not only of England or of Scotland. The name Great Britain was formally adopted in the Act of Union of 1707 that united the Parliaments of England and Scotland. Ireland was similarly joined to Great Britain by the Act of Union of 1801, and the official title then became the United Kingdom of Great Britain and Ireland.

In 1922, 26 Irish counties were severed from the United Kingdom as the Irish Free State (later Eire; since 1949 the Republic of Ireland), and from then onward the title of the United Kingdom of Great Britain and Northern Ireland was frequently used in official documents to designate those parts of the British Isles that were represented in the Imperial Parliament, meeting at Westminster.

On May 13, 1927, under the Royal and Parliamentary Titles Act of that year, it was proclaimed that "Parliament shall hereafter be known as and styled the Parliament of the United Kingdom of Great Britain and Northern Ireland."

Finally, on May 29, 1953, under the Royal Titles Act, a proclamation was issued by which the Queen adopted the title of "Elizabeth II, by the Grace of God, of the United Kingdom of Great Britain and Northern Ireland and of her other Realms and Territories Queen, Head of the Commonwealth, Defender of the Faith." The form of the title is varied for those independent Commonwealth member nations that owe allegiance to the crown, to suit the particular circumstances of each.

Although there is a single Parliament at Westminster for the whole of Great Britain and Northern Ireland, three of the original constituent kingdoms (Scotland, Wales, and Northern Ireland) retain autonomy in different degrees. A secretary of state for Scotland was appointed in 1885, and separate departments in Edinburgh now deal with such areas as home and health, agriculture and fisheries, education, and development. Scotland also has its own separate legal system. From 1964 the secretary of state for Wales and the Welsh Office provided an increased amount of specialized treatment in matters affecting Wales. By the Government of Ireland Act (1920) it was provided that Northern Ireland would continue to be represented at Westminster but that it should also have its own parliament (Stormont) for home affairs. In 1972 Westminster suspended Stormont.

(Ed.)

The article is divided into the following sections:

PHYSICAL AND HUMAN GEOGRAPHY

The land

Great Britain, the island comprising England, Scotland, and Wales, forms, together with numerous smaller islands, an archipelago that is as irregular in shape as it is diverse in its natural heritage. This latter circumstance stems largely from the nature and disposition of the underlying rocks, which are westward extensions of European structures, with the shallow waters of the Strait of Dover and the North Sea concealing former land links. Northern Ireland—which politically completes the United Kingdom— is a westward extension of the rock structures of Scotland. These common rock structures are breached by the narrow North Channel. Northern Ireland, too, has a very diverse natural environment.

On a global scale, this natural endowment covers a small area—approximating that of Oregon, in the United States, or the African nation of Guinea—and its internal diversity, accompanied by rapid changes of often beautiful scenery, may perhaps convey to visitors from larger countries a striking sense of compactness and consolidation. The peoples who, over the centuries, have made their way to, and hewed an existence from, this Atlantic extremity of Eurasia have put their own imprint on the environment, with the ancient and distinctive palimpsest of their field patterns and settlements complementing the natural diversity.

RELIEF

The traditional division of Great Britain into a Highland and Lowland zone is still meaningful. A line running from the mouth of the River Exe, in the southwest, to that of the Tees, in the northeast, is a crude expression of this division. The course of the 700-foot (213-metre) contour, or of the boundary separating the generally older rocks of the north and west from the younger southeastern strata, provide more appropriate indications of the extent of the Highlands.

The Tees–Exe Line

The Highland zone. The creation of the Highlands was a long process, yet altitudes, compared with European equivalents, are low, with the highest summit, Ben Nevis, only 4,406 feet (1,342 metres) above sea level. In addition, the really mountainous areas above 2,000 feet often lie in smooth profiles against the changing skies, reminders of the effects of former periods of erosion.

Scotland's three main topographic regions follow the northeast to southwest trend of the ancient underlying rocks. The northern Highlands and the Southern Uplands are separated by the intervening rift valley, or subsided structural block, of the Central Lowlands. The core of the Highlands is the elevated, worn-down surface of the Grampians, 2,000–3,000 feet above sea level, with the Cairngorm Mountains rising to over 4,000 feet. This majestic mountain landscape is furrowed by numerous wide valleys, or straths, and occasional large areas of lowland, often fringed with long lines of sand dunes, add variety to the east. The Buchan peninsula, the Moray Firth estuarine flats, and the plain of Caithness—all low-lying areas—contrast sharply with the mountain scenery and show more mellow outlines than do the glacier-scoured landscapes of the west, where northeasterly-facing hollows, or corries, separated by knife-edge ridges and deep glens, sculpture the surfaces left by erosion. The many freshwater lochs further enhance a landscape of wild beauty. The linear Glen More, where the Caledonian Ship Canal now threads a chain of lakes, is the result of a vast structural sideways tear in the whole mass of the Northwest Highlands. To the northwest of Glen More stretch most of the counties given over to agricultural small holdings, or crofts; settlement is intermittent and mostly coastal, a pattern clearly reflecting the pronounced dissection of a highland massif that has been scored and plucked by the Ice Age glaciers. Many sea-drowned, glacier-widened, river valleys (fjords) penetrate deeply into the mountains, the outliers of which rise from the sea in stately, elongated peninsulas or emerge in hundreds of offshore islands.

Landscapes of the Scottish Highlands

In comparison with the northern Highlands of Scotland, the Southern Uplands present a more subdued relief, the land nowhere rising above 2,790 feet. The main hill masses are the Cheviots, which rise to 2,676 feet, while Merrick and Broad Law reach just above the 2,700-foot contour line. Broad plateau surfaces, separated by numerous dales, are again characteristic of these uplands, and in the west most of the rivers flow across the prevailing northeast-southwest trend, following the general slope of the plateau, toward the Solway Firth. Bold masses of granite and the rugged imprint of former glaciers occasionally impart a mountainous quality to the scenery. In the east, the valley network of the Tweed and its many tributaries forms a broad lowland expanse between the Lammermuir and Cheviot Hills.

The Central Lowlands are bounded by great regular structural faults. The northern boundary with the Highlands is a wall-like feature, but the boundary with the Southern Uplands exhibits a linear topographic form only near the coast. This vast trench is by no means a continuous plain, for high ground—often formed of sturdy, resistant masses of volcanic rock—meets the eye in all directions, rising above the low-lying areas that flank the rivers and the deeply penetrating estuaries of the Firth of Clyde and the Firth of Forth.

Northern Ireland extensions of the Scottish Highlands

In Northern Ireland, structural extensions of Scottish Highland geomorphology reappear in the generally rugged mountain scenery and in the peat-covered summits of the 2,240-foot Sperrin Mountains. The uplands of County Down and County Armagh in Northern Ireland are the western continuation of the Southern Uplands but rise over 500 feet only in limited areas, the one important exception being the Mourne Mountains, a lovely cluster of granite summits, the loftiest of which, Slieve Donard, rises to 2,796 feet within two miles of the sea. Compared with that of the Scottish Central Lowlands, Northern Ireland's structure has been complicated by the outpouring of basaltic lavas to form a huge plateau, much of which is occupied by the shallow Lough Neagh, the largest freshwater lake in the British Isles.

The Highland zone of England and of Wales consists, from north to south, of four broad upland masses: the Pennines, the Lake District, Wales, and the South West Peninsula. The Pennines are usually considered to end in the north along the River Tyne gap, but the surface features of the Northumberland Fells are in many ways similar to those of the northern Pennines. The general surface of the asymmetrically arched backbone (anticline) of the Pennines is remarkably smooth, because many of the valleys, though deep, occupy such a small portion within the total area that the windswept moorland between them appears almost featureless. This is particularly true of the landscape around Alston, in Cumberland, which, cut off by faults on its north, west, and south sides, stands out as an almost rectangular block of high moorland plateau with isolated peaks (known to geographers as monadnocks), rising up above it. Farther south, the Pennine plateau is cut into by deep and scenic dales, their craggy sides formed of Millstone Grit, beneath which lie streams stepped by waterfalls. The most southerly part of the Pennines is a grassy upland, in places over 2,000 feet above sea level, but it is characterized by the dry valleys, steep-sided gorges, and underground streams and caverns of a limestone-drainage system rather than the bleak moorland that might be expected at this altitude. At lower levels, the larger dales are more richly wooded, the trees standing out against a background of rugged cliffs of white-gray rocks. On both Pennine flanks, older rocks disappear beneath younger layers, and the uplands merge into flanking coastal lowlands.

The famous Lake District, celebrated in poetry by William Wordsworth and the other "Lake poets," is an isolated, compact mountain group to the west of the Pennines. The tough slate rocks of the northern portion have been cut into many deep gorges, separated by narrow ridges and sharp peaks. Greater expanses of level upland, formed from thick beds of lava and the ash thrown out by ancient volcanoes, are found to the south. Although Scafell Pike, at 3,210 feet, and Helvellyn, at 3,117 feet, are high for

Britain, the volcanic belt is largely an irregular upland, traversed by deep, narrow valleys. Nine rivers, flowing out in all directions from the centre of this uplifted dome, form a classic radial drainage pattern. The valleys, often occupied by long, narrow lakes, have been widened to a U-shape by glacial action, which has also etched corries from the mountainsides and deposited the heaps of debris known as moraines. Glacial action also created a number of "hanging valleys" by truncating former tributary valleys.

The Welsh Massif

The core of the principality of Wales is formed by a highland block, clearly defined by the sea except on its eastern side, where a sharp break of slope often marks the transition to the English plain. Cycles of erosion have several times worn down its ancient and austere surfaces; many topographic features may be attributed to glacial processes; some of the most striking scenery owes much to former vulcanism. The mountain areas above 2,000 feet are most extensive in North Wales, in Snowdonia and its southward extensions, Cader Idris and the Berwyn mass. With the exception of Plynlimon and the Forest of Radnor, central Wales lacks similar high areas, but the monadnocks of South Wales—notably the Black Mountains and the Brecon (Brecknock) Beacons—again stand out in solitary splendour above the upland surfaces. Three of these are distinguishable: a high plateau of 1,700 to 1,800 feet; a middle peneplain, or worn-down surface, of 1,200 to 1,600 feet; and a low peneplain of 700 to 1,100 feet. These smooth, rounded, grass-covered moorlands present a remarkably even skyline. Below 700 feet lies a further series of former wave-cut surfaces. Several valleys radiate from the highland core to the coastal regions. In the west these lowlands have provided a haven for traditional Welsh culture, but the deeply penetrating eastern valleys have channelled anglicizing influences into the highland. A more extensive lowland—physically and structurally an extension of the English plain—in the southeast borders the Bristol Channel. The irregularities of the 600-mile Welsh coast exhibit differing adjustments to the pounding attack of the sea.

The South West—England's largest peninsula—has six locally conspicuous uplands: Exmoor, where Dunkery Beacon reaches 1,707 feet; the wild, granite uplands of Dartmoor (High Willhays; 2,039 feet); Bodmin Moor; St. Austell (Hensbarrow); Carnmenellis; and the spectacular extremity of Land's End. Granite reappears above the sea in the Isles of Scilly, 28 miles further southwest. Despite this variation in general elevation, the landscape, like that of so many other parts of the United Kingdom, has a quite marked uniformity of summit heights, with a high series occurring between 1,000 and 1,400 feet; a middle group between 700 and 1,000 feet; and coastal plateaus ranging between about 200 and 400 feet. A network of deep, narrow valleys alternates with flat-topped, steplike areas rising inland. The South West derives much of its renowned physical attraction from its peninsular nature, for, in addition to magnificent drowned estuaries created by sea-level changes, the coastline is unsurpassed for its diversity.

The South West peninsula

The Lowland zone. Gauged by the 700-foot contour, the Lowland zone starts around the Solway Firth in the northwest, with a strip of low-lying ground extending up the fault-directed Vale of Eden. Southward, the narrow coastal plain bordering the Lake District broadens into the flat, glacial-drift-covered Lancastrian lowlands, with their slow-flowing rivers. East of the Pennine ridge, the lowlands are continuous, save for the limestone plateau north of the River Tees and, to the south, the North York Moors, with large, exposed tracts over 1,400 feet. South again lies the wide Vale of York, which the broad lower Trent Valley links to the younger rocks of the Midland Plain, terminating against the Welsh Massif on the west. The lowland continues southward along the flat landscapes bordering the lower River Severn, becomes constricted by the complex Bristol–Mendip upland, and opens out once more into the extensive and flat plain of Somerset. The eastern horizon of much of the Midland Plain is the scarp face of the Cotswolds, part of the discontinuous outcrop of limestones and sandstones that arcs from the Dorset coast across the heart of England, continuing in

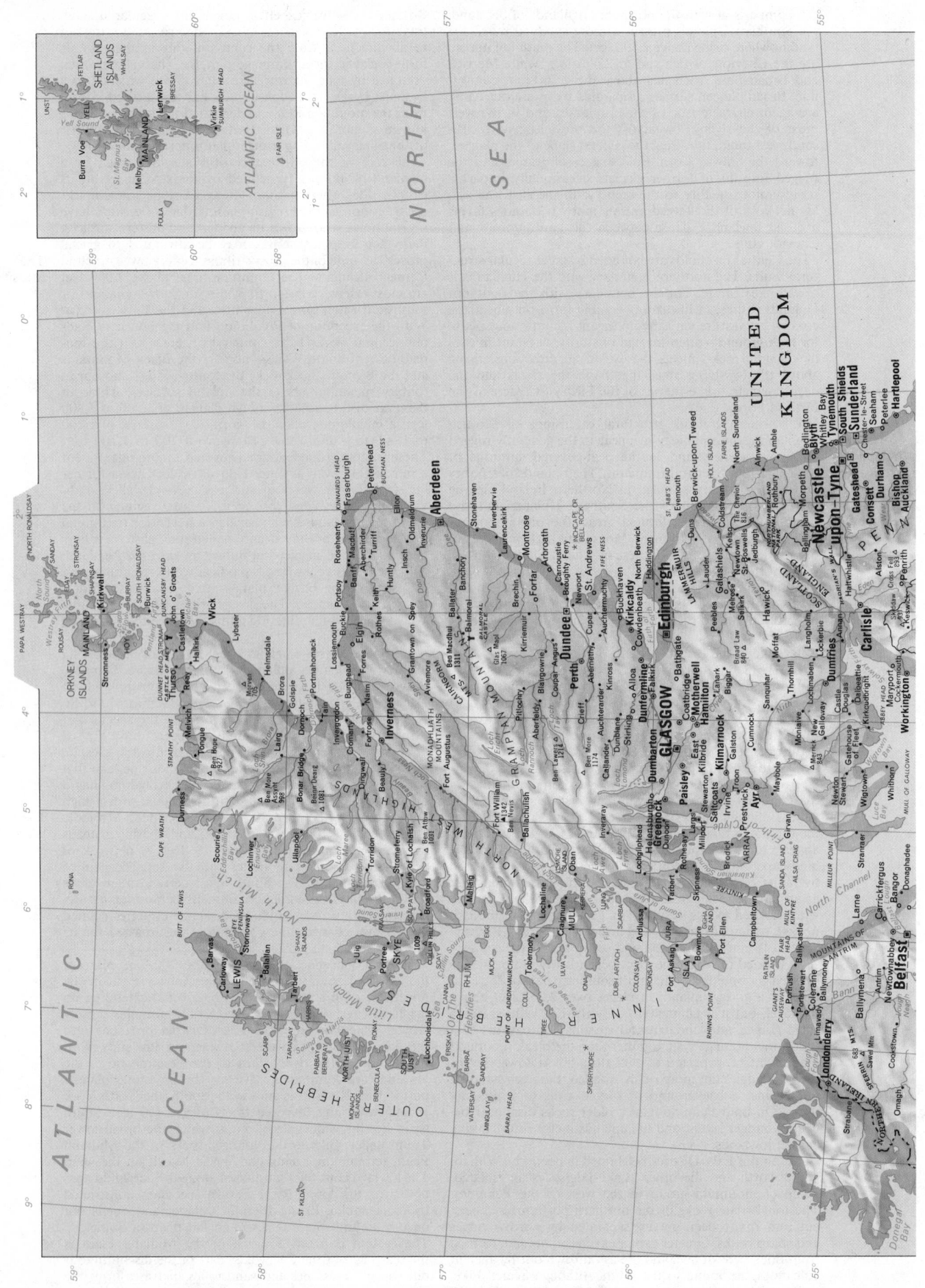

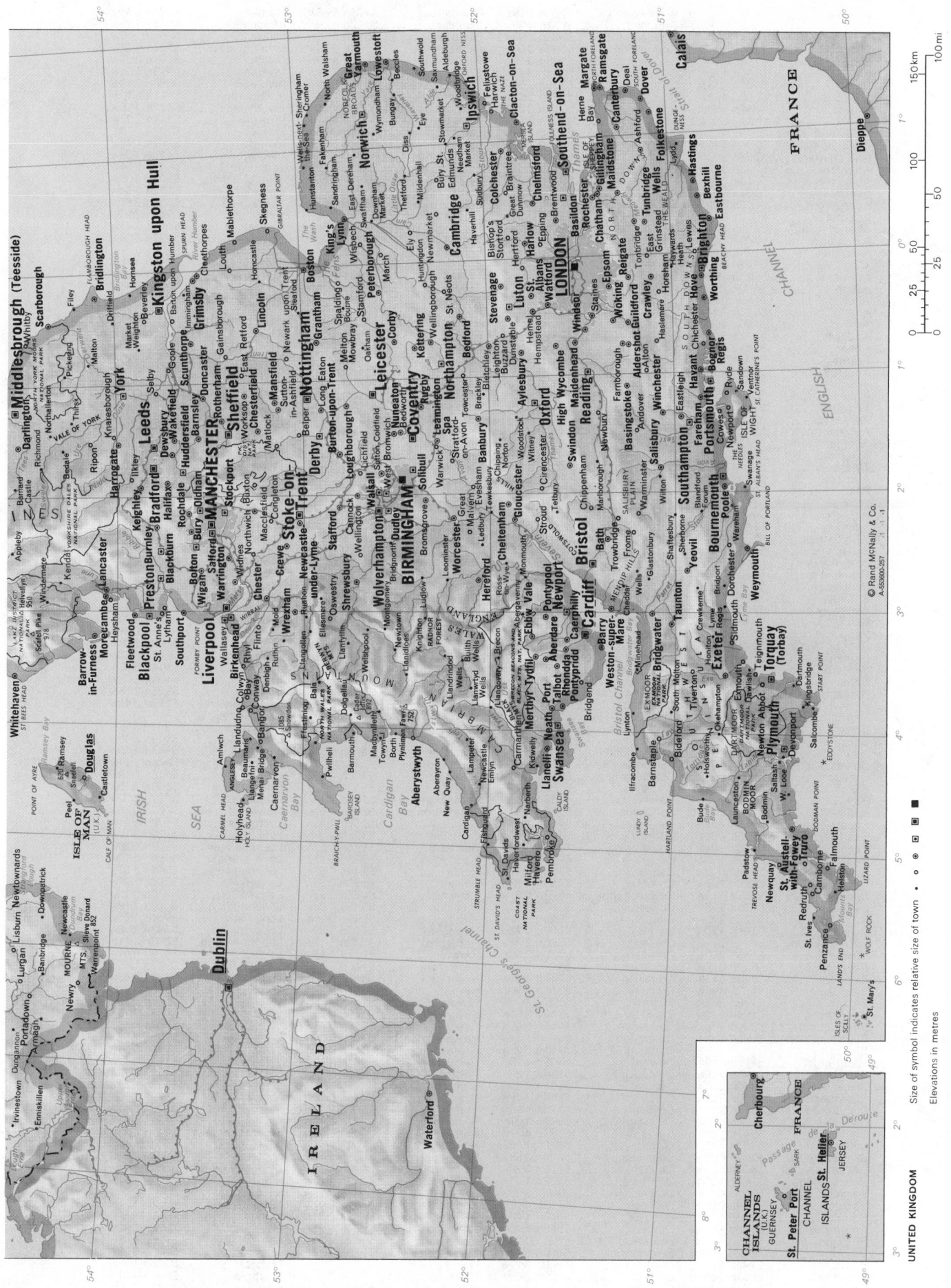

UNITED KINGDOM

Size of symbol indicates relative size of town

Elevations in metres

© Rand McNally & Co.
A-565000-257

MAP INDEX

Political subdivisions

the Cleveland Hills as far as the north Yorkshire coast. The more massive limestones and sandstones give rise to noble, 1,000-foot-high escarpments, yet the dip slope is frequently of such a low angle that the countryside resembles a dissected plateau, passing gradually on to the clay vales of Oxford, White Horse, Lincoln, and Pickering. The flat, often reclaimed landscapes of the Fenlands are also underlain by these clays, and the next scarp, the western-facing chalk outcrop (cuesta), undergoes several marked directional changes in the vicinity of the Wash, a shallow arm of the North Sea.

The chalk outcrop is a more conspicuous and continuous feature than its sandstone and limestone predecessor: it begins in the north with the open rolling country known as the Yorkshire Wolds, where heights of 750 feet are reached; is breached by the River Humber; and then continues in the Lincolnshire Wolds. East of the Fens the outcrop, or cuesta, is very low, barely attaining 150 feet, but it then rises gradually to the 807 feet reached in the attractive Chilterns, a ridge interrupted by several wind gaps, or former river courses; the Thames alone actually cuts through it, in the Goring Gap. Where the dip slope of the chalk is almost horizontal, as is the case in the open Salisbury Plain, the landscape is that of a large dissected plateau, of 350 to 500 feet. Only the main valleys contain rivers, and most of the tributary valleys are dry.

The chalk outcrop continues into Dorset, but in the south the chalk has been folded along west-to-east lines.

Eastern chalklands and vales

Down-folds, subsequently filled in by geologically recent sands and clays, now floor the London and Hampshire basins. The former, an asymmetrical synclinal, or structurally down-warped, lowland rimmed by chalk, is occupied mainly by gravel terraces and valley-side benches and has relatively little floodplain; the latter is similarly cradled by a girdle of chalk, but the southern rim, or monocline, has been cut by the sea in two places to form the scenic Isle of Wight.

Between these two synclinal areas rises the anticlinal, or structurally upwarped, dome of the Weald region of Kent and East Sussex. The arch of this vast geological upfold has long since been eroded away, and the bounding chalk escarpments of the North and South Downs (uplands so named because of their open, rolling, treeless grassland) are therefore inward facing and enclose a concentric series of exposed clay vales and sandstone ridges. Eaten into by the waters of the English Channel, a dazzling succession of chalk cliffs faces the European mainland, 21 miles distant at the narrowest point.

DRAINAGE

The main water parting in Great Britain runs from north to south, keeping well to the west until the basin of the River Severn. Westward-flowing streams attain the Atlantic in relatively short reaches, and the Clyde in Scotland, the Eden and Mersey in northwest England, and the Welsh Dee, Teifi, and Tywi are the only significant rivers.

The main watershed

The drainage complex that debouches into the Severn Estuary covers a large area in central and eastern Wales and the greater part of seven English counties. Thereafter, the Bristol Avon and the Parret catchments take the water parting somewhat to the east, but subsequently, with the exception of the Taw–Torridge valleys, it runs very close to the west coast in Devon and Cornwall.

The rivers draining east from the main water parting are longer, several coalescing into wide estuaries. The fast-flowing Spey, Don, Tay, Forth, and Tweed of eastern Scotland run generally across impermeable rocks, and their discharges increase rapidly after rain. From the northern Pennines, the Tyne, Wear, and Tees flow independently to the North Sea, but thereafter significant estuary groupings occur. A number of rivers drain into the Humber, including, after it leaves the Pennines, the important Trent. To the south, another group of rivers enters the Wash after sluggishly draining a large flat countryside. The big drainage complex of the Thames dominates South East England; its source is in the Cotswolds, and, after being joined by many tributaries as it flows over the Oxford Clay, the mainstream breaches the chalk escarpment in the Goring Gap. A number of tributaries add their discharges farther downstream, and the total drainage converging on the Thames Estuary exceeds 4,000 square miles. The rivers flowing into the English Channel are mainly short, as are those in Northern Ireland, with the exceptions of the Erne, Foyle, and Bann.

SOILS

The regional pattern of soil formation can be correlated usefully with local variations of relief and climate. Although changes are gradual and can be complicated by local factors, a division of Britain into four climatic regimes (see below *Climate*) goes far to explain the distribution of soils.

On those loftier parts of the Highland zone, particularly in Scotland, experiencing a cold, wet regime of more than 40 inches (1,000 millimetres) rainfall and less than 47° F (8° C) mean temperature annually, blanket peat and peaty podzol soils, the organic surface layer of which rests on a gray, leached base, are found. A similarly wet regime, but with a mean annual temperature exceeding 47° F, obtains over most of the remainder of the Highland zone, particularly on the lower parts of the Southern Uplands, the Solway Firth–Lake District area, the peripheral plateaus of Wales, and most of South West England. These areas are covered by acid brown soils and weakly podzolized associates. On the lower lying areas within the Highland zone, more particularly in eastern Scotland and the eastern flanks of the Pennines, a relatively cold, dry regime gives rise to soils intermediate between the richer brown earths and the podzols.

Over the whole of the Lowland zone, which also has a mean annual temperature above 47° F (8° C) but less than 40 inches of rain, leached brown soils are characteristic. Calcareous, and thus alkaline, parent materials are widespread, particularly in the southeast, and so acid soils and podzols are confined to the most quartz-laden parent materials. In Northern Ireland, above about 460 feet, brown earths are replaced by semipodzols, and these grade upslope into more intensively leached podzols. This is particularly the case in the Sperrins and the Mournes, but, between them in the Lough Neagh lowland, rich brown earth soils are extensively developed.

CLIMATE

The climate of the United Kingdom, a perennial topic of conversation within the country, is broadly determined by its setting within the pattern of the atmosphere's general circulation and its position in relation to the form and distribution of land and sea. Regional diversity does exist, but the boundaries of major world climatic systems do not pass through the country. Britain's marginal position between the European land-mass to the east, and the ever-present, relatively warm Atlantic waters to the west, ensures the modification of both the thermal and moisture characteristics of the principal types of air reaching British shores. These, according to their source regions, are Arctic,

Air-mass charac- teristics

polar, and tropical, and, by their route of travel, may in each case be maritime or continental. For much of the year the weather is dominated by the sequence of disturbances within the mid-latitude Westerlies that bring in mostly polar-maritime, and, occasionally, tropical-maritime air. In winter, occasional high-pressure areas to the east allow biting Arctic or polar-continental air to sweep over Britain. All of these atmospheric systems tend to fluctuate rapidly in their paths and to vary both in frequency and intensity throughout the seasons of the year and also from year to year for any given season. Variability contributes much to the character of British weather, and extreme conditions, though rare, can be very important for the life of the country.

The westerly maritime origin of so much of the air reaching the country in winter creates a temperature distribution that does not reflect latitudinal differences. Thus the north-to-south run of the 40° F (4° C) January isotherm, or line of equal temperature, from the coast in northwest Scotland down to the Isle of Wight betrays the moderating influence of the winds blowing off the Atlantic Ocean. In summer, polar-maritime air is less common, and a nine-degree difference of latitude and distance from the sea assume more importance, with temperatures increasing from north to south and from the coast inland. Above-average temperatures are usually associated with tropical-continental air, particularly in anticyclonic, or high-pressure, conditions. These southerly or southeasterly airstreams can bring to southern England heat waves with temperatures of more than 90° F (32° C). In spring and autumn a variety of airstreams and temperature conditions may be experienced, and changing patterns of sunlight and shadow enhance the natural seasonal beauty of the landscape.

Rain-producing atmospheric systems arrive from a westerly direction, and some of the bleak summits of the highest peaks of the Highland zone can receive as much as 200 inches (5,100 millimetres) of driving rainfall a year. East Anglia and the Thames Estuary, in contrast, can expect as little as 20 inches (500 millimetres). Rain is fairly well distributed throughout the year: June, on the whole, is the driest month all over Britain; May is the next driest in the east and centre of England, but April is drier in parts of the west and north. The wettest months are usually October, December, and August, but in any particular year almost any month can prove to be the wettest, and the association of Britain with seemingly perpetual rainfall (a concept popularly held among foreigners) is based on a germ of truth. Some precipitation falls as snow, and the average number of days with snow falling can vary from as many as 30 in blizzard-prone northeast Scotland to as few as five in South West England.

Rainfall patterns

PLANT AND ANIMAL LIFE

Except for northern Scotland, the highest hills of the north and west, the saturated fens and marshes, and the seacoast fringes, the natural vegetation of the British Isles was deciduous summer forest dominated by oak. The hand of man has, however, lain long and heavy on this heritage, and only scattered woodlands and areas of wild or semi-natural vegetation lie outside the enclosed cultivated fields. Few of these fine moorlands and heathlands, wild though they may appear, can lay claim to any truly natural plant communities: nearly all show varying degrees of adjustment to grazing, swaling (controlled burning), or other activities. Woodland now covers only a small portion of the country, and, because the Forestry Commission has been active since its creation in 1919, only about half of this woodland remains in private hands. The largest areas of woodland are now to be found in northeast Scotland; Kielder in Northumberland; South East England; Gwent; and Breckland in Norfolk.

The moorlands and heathlands occupy about a third of the total area of the United Kingdom. They consist of the possibly true Arctic–Alpine vegetation on some mountain summits in Scotland and the much more extensive peat moss, heather, bilberry, and the thin *Molinia* and *Nardus* grass moors of the Highland zone. A similar vegetation exists on high ground in eastern Northern Ireland and

Flora of the moor- lands and heathlands

on the Mournes, with considerable areas of peat moss vegetation on the mountains of Antrim. In the Lowland zone, where light sandy soils are found, the vegetation is dominated typically by the common heather—the deep purple of which adds a splash of colour to the autumn countryside—but sometimes by bilberry or bell heather. A strip of land immediately bordering the coastline has also largely escaped the attention of man and his animals, so that patches of maritime vegetation can frequently be found in approximately their natural state.

The survival of the wild mammals, amphibians, and reptiles of the United Kingdom depends on their ability to come to terms with the changing environment and to protect themselves from attacks by their enemies—the most dangerous being man. British mammals survive in a greater range of habitats than do amphibians and reptiles. Most of the former larger mammals have become extinct, but red deer survive in the Scottish Highlands and on Exmoor, and roe deer in the wooded areas of Scotland and southern England. The carnivorous mammals (badgers, otters, foxes, stoats, and weasels) thrive in most rural areas; also widely distributed are the rodents (rats, squirrels, mice) and the insectivores (hedgehogs, moles, shrews). Rabbits are widespread and their numbers are again increasing despite the outbreak, in the 1950s, of the disease known as myxomatosis. The other nocturnal vegetarian, the brown hare, is found in open lowland country, while the mountain hare is native to Scotland. The amphibians are represented by three species of newt and five species of frogs and toads, while reptiles consist of three species of snakes, of which only the adder is venomous, and three species of lizard. There are no snakes in Northern Ireland.

SETTLEMENT PATTERNS

Traditional regions.   When a long view is taken of the slow possession of Britain by its peoples, it seems an inescapable conclusion that the man–land relationship probably reached its greatest intimacy late in the 18th century: communications at this time were good enough to bind the community into a unity but were not yet so good as to destroy the sense of belonging to a specific locality, as well as to a particular nation, Scotland, England, Wales, or Ireland. Generations of toiling hands had won the necessities of life from the landscape, and generations of tongues had shaped the national languages and dialects for the expression of local things. The regional character of British life is still recognizable, but its heyday has passed. The consciousness of being a Northern Irelander, a Scot, a Welshman, or a Cornishman—to say nothing of the rivalry between a North and South Walian, or a Highland and Lowland Scot—is as marked as is the obvious geographical identity of these parts of the Highland zone.

Within England nine traditional regions may be distinguished. The North Country province—including the present counties of Durham, Northumberland, Cumbria, Tyne and Wear, and Cleveland—formed, after the Anglo-Saxon settlement of the mid-5th to late 6th century AD, the central part of the Anglian Kingdom of Northumbria. Later, it became an area whose life, over a period of centuries, was dominated by border warfare with Scotland; this strengthened its regional traditions and folklore. With the coming of the Industrial Revolution, the region's wealth in coal and iron gave it great advantages that later were to enhance its traditions of independence and initiative. The county of Yorkshire, finally dismembered in the administrative reorganization of 1974, had existed as a northern unit in various forms from Roman times, and the cohesion given to it when it became the Danish Kingdom of York was maintained until the Council of the North—a prerogative court established in Tudor times to ensure the fair administration of English common law—was abolished in 1641. The growth of the wool-textile industry in the former West Riding wrought major changes in the rural economy, but, despite this and the variety in the landscape, the sense of being a Yorkshireman is still a reality. Across the Pennines, on the other hand, it would be difficult to find a time before the Industrial Revolution when Lancaster formed a unit, yet there now exists a Lancastrian tradition and dialect, as well as a provincial

The conditions of regional awareness

entity. These stem from a certain physical unity and the cohesion imposed by the long dominion of the cotton industry. The English Midlands are really divisible into two regions: a West Midland province, which has become much more conscious of its identity since the emergence of Birmingham as a regional capital, and, in contrast, the East Midland province, which has a greater physical and historic—but much less economic—unity.

Norfolk, Suffolk, and Cambridgeshire and Isle of Ely make up what was the ancient Kingdom of East Anglia. This is an agricultural province. In this respect it forms a marked contrast with its London-dominated neighbour, South East England, which in size and density of population is the largest region in all England. The Hampshire Downs form the core of Wessex, a province with that well-marked regional consciousness and patriotism that is so vividly depicted in the writings of the novelist Thomas Hardy. The eastern side of the Severn Estuary, together with the Somerset Levels, has become known as the West of England, a province which tends to look to the old city of Bristol as its centre. The completion of the elegant Severn Bridge, as part of the national motorway system, has tended to unify both sides of the Severn Estuary into a Severnside region.

Rural settlement.   The forms and patterns of settlement are remarkably varied in the United Kingdom and reflect not only the physical variety of the landscape but also the successive movements of peoples arriving as settlers, refugees, conquerors, or traders from continental Europe. The social and economic advantages that led folk to cluster and, on the other hand, the equally strong desire for separateness on the part of some individuals are apparent in settlement forms from very early times, and so regional contrasts in the degree of dispersion and nucleation are frequent.

The single farmstead, together with many survivals of the old clachan (cluster or hamlet), interspersed with the occasional village and small town, is still characteristic of much of the Highland zone. Radical alteration has nevertheless occurred in some nucleated settlement patterns: in Wales the breakup of hamlets began in the late Middle Ages as a result of the related processes of consolidation and enclosure that accompanied the late medieval decline in the numerical strength of the bond (feudally tied) population. This trend was reinforced by the Black Death of 1349, which spread quickly among the inhabitants of lowly status. Many surviving bondsmen took advantage of the turmoil caused by the nationalistic uprising led by Owen Glendower (Welsh Owain Glyndŵr) to escape their servile obligations by flight, and thus many Welsh hamlets fell into decay by 1410, when the rebellion was crushed. In Scotland great changes accompanied the Highland clearances in the mid-18th century; in Northern Ireland, as late as the 1880s, many clachans disappeared as part of a deliberate policy of reallocating land to new dispersed farmsteads. Great changes have also occurred in the Lowland zone, where the swing to individual ownership or tenancy from the medieval custom of landholding in common brought about not only dispersion and deserted villages but also the enclosure of fields by hedges and walls. Nucleations remain remarkably stable features of the rural landscape of Britain, and linear, round, oval, and ring-shaped villages survive, many with their ancient greens still held in common by the community.

Urban settlement.   By any standards Britain must be regarded as the most urbanized of countries, for towns are not only particularly expressive of the national way of life but are also unusually significant elements in the geography of the country. The greatest overall change in settlement was, in fact, the massive urbanization that accompanied Britain's early industrial development. The increasing percentage of employees in offices and service industries ensures continued contemporary urban growth. Of every 10 people in the United Kingdom, almost eight live in towns, four of them in one of the eight major urban groups, or conurbations. The Greater London conurbation—the greatest port, the largest centre of industry, the most important centre of office employment, and the capital city—is by far the largest of these. The need for

Highland-zone hamlets

The role of Greater London

accommodating business premises has involved the displacement of population from inner London, and this, in part, has led to the designation of nine New Towns outside the 10-mile-wide Green Belt, which surrounds London's built-up area, and two more distant "overspill" towns.

Large conurbations have also formed on or near the exposed coalfields. The extensive built-up area of the West Midlands conurbation is dominated by Birmingham, but the industrial Black Country—named for its formerly polluted skies and grimy buildings—also has several large and flourishing towns. In the Manchester conurbation, with an equivalent number of inhabitants, urbanization accompanied the mechanization of the cotton-textile industry. Across the Pennines similar mechanization of wool textiles created the West Yorkshire conurbation, with Leeds and Bradford as its twin centres. Tyne and Wear and the Central Clydeside conurbation are also located on coalfields, the latter housing about one-third of Scotland's people. Merseyside is not on the Lancashire coalfield, but it has close economic links with it. In Northern Ireland only Belfast may be considered a major conurbation.

In addition to these large metropolitan areas, there are also a number of other minor conurbations and large towns, a large number of which are strung out along the coast.

With so much urban and suburban concentration, the problems of air, water, and noise pollution have become subjects of much concern in the United Kingdom. Considerable progress has been made in controlling air pollution as a result of changes in fuel usage and the operation of clean-air legislation, which has led to the establishment of smoke-control areas in most cities and towns. Pollution of the rivers remains a large problem, particularly in the highly industrialized parts of the United Kingdom, but vigilance and control on the part of the river authorities, research done by the Water Pollution Research Laboratory, and general public concern for the environment are encouraging features of contemporary Britain. Several statutory and voluntary organizations support measures to protect the environment; they have as their aim the conservation of the natural amenity and beauty not only of the countryside but also of the towns and cities.

The people

LINGUISTIC AND ETHNIC GROUPS

All the traditional languages spoken in the United Kingdom are descended from a common Aryan, or Indo-European, original, a tongue so ancient that, over the centuries, it has split into a variety of languages, each with its own peculiarities in sounds, grammar, and vocabulary. A separate idiom in what became the United Kingdom was initiated when peoples from the Continent were cut off, in their new homes, from regular intercourse with their continental kindred.

Of the surviving languages the earliest to arrive were the two forms of Celtic: the Goidelic (from which Irish Gaelic, Manx, and Scottish Gaelic are derived) and Brythonic, from which are descended the old Cornish language and modern Welsh. Among the contemporary Celtic languages Welsh is the strongest: more than a quarter of the total population of Wales are able to speak it, and there are extensive interior upland areas and regions facing the Irish Sea where the percentage rises to 70 percent and more. Scottish Gaelic is at its strongest among the inhabitants of the Islands and is still heard in the nearby Northwest Highlands. Because only about 1.6 percent of the Scottish people are able to speak it, it has long since ceased to be a national language, and even in the northwest, where it remains the language of religion, business, and social activity, Gaelic is losing ground. In Northern Ireland very little Gaelic is spoken; similarly Manx is now used by very few individuals indeed, although as late as 1870 it was spoken by about half the people of the Isle of Man. Cornish became extinct in the early 18th century.

Germanic language links The second link with Indo-European is through the ancient Germanic language group, two branches of which, the North Germanic and the West Germanic, were destined to make contributions to the English language.

Modern English is derived mainly from the four Germanic dialects spoken by the Angles, Saxons, and Jutes (who all arrived in Britain in the 5th century AD) and by the Danes, whose long series of raids began about 790. The Humber became an important linguistic as well as geographical boundary, and the English-speaking portion of what became England was divided into a Northumbrian and a Southumbrian province (in which the most important kingdoms were Mercia, Wessex, and Kent). In the 8th century, Northumbria was foremost in literature and culture, followed, for a short time, by Mercia; finally Wessex remained the linguistic centre until the time of King Edward the Confessor. The Normans, although also of Viking stock, were at first regarded as much more of an alien race than the Danes. Under the Norman and Angevin kings, England formed part of a continental empire; and the prolonged connection with France retained by its new rulers and landlords made a deep impression on the English language. An Anglo-French hybrid speech developed and remained the official language, sometimes even displacing Latin in public documents, until the mid-14th century. Many additions to the English language have been made since that date, but the Normans were the last important linguistic group to enter Britain.

RELIGIOUS GROUPS

The various Christian denominations in the United Kingdom have emerged from the schisms that divided the church. The greatest of these occurred in England in the 16th century, when Henry VIII rejected the absolute supremacy of the pope. This break with Rome facilitated the adoption of some Protestant tenets and was the foundation of the Anglican Church, still the established church of England. In Scotland, the Reformation gave rise to a church governed by a presbytery—a body composed of ministers and laymen—rather than by bishops, as was the case in England. Roman Catholicism in Ireland as a whole was almost undisturbed by these events, but what became Northern Ireland came strongly under the influence of the Anglican and Presbyterian churches. In the 17th century further schisms divided the Church of England; these were associated with the rise of the Puritan movement, which, with its desire for simpler forms of worship and government, led to a proliferation of nonconformist churches, such as those of the Baptists and the Congregationalists; the Society of Friends (Quakers) also originated at that time. Religious revivals of the mid-18th century gave to Wales a form of Protestantism closely linked with the Welsh language; Calvinistic Methodism is still the most powerful religious influence in the principality. The great evangelical revivals of the 18th century, associated with John Wesley and others, led to the foundation of Methodist churches, particularly in the industrial areas; northeastern England and Cornwall still have the largest percentages of adherents to this denomination. In the 19th century the Salvation Army and various fundamentalist sects grew from minor schisms. That century also saw the introduction of sects from the United States as well as a marked increase in the number of Jews in Britain. The first Jewish community in Britain after their expulsion in 1290 was that established in London during the 17th century, and in the 19th century Jews also settled in many of the large provincial cities. More than half of the British Jews live in London, and the rest are essentially members of urban communities. In the 20th century, immigrants from India and Pakistan have introduced various Eastern religions into the United Kingdom, but their places of worship are, for the most part, found only in the largest cities.

The Judaic and Eastern traditions

It is difficult to characterize and describe this variety of beliefs and their distribution in the United Kingdom, since the statistics for the various denominations are collected separately and on widely differing bases. The generalized description of England as Anglican, Scotland as Presbyterian, Wales as Calvinistic Methodist, and Northern Ireland as Protestant remains useful so long as it is remembered that each country contains large minority groups adhering to other Christian denominations and that a large proportion of the population is, in effect, agnostic.

At any time, the basic factors governing population changes are the relation of births to deaths and of immigration to emigration. Since the making, in 1086, of the Domesday Survey, a detailed compilation that enables the earliest reasonable estimate of population to be made, at least of England's population (the survey did not cover other areas), the number of people has been increasing. This growth has continued despite some setbacks, by far the most serious of which was the Black Death in the mid-14th century, in which it is estimated that about one-third of the population died. There is little concrete information, however, concerning variation in these rates until 1801, when the first official census was taken. The assumption is that a population of about 2,000,000 lived in what became the United Kingdom at the end of the 11th century and that this figure had increased to about 12,000,000 by 1801. This slow growth rate, in contrast with that of more modern times, resulted mainly from the fact that a high birth rate was accompanied by an almost equally high death rate. Family monuments in old churches show many examples of men whose "quivers were full" but whose hearths were not crowded. It is estimated that, in the first half of the 18th century, three-quarters of the children born in London died before they reached puberty. Despite the appalling living conditions it produced, the Industrial Revolution resulted in an acceleration of the birth rate; gradually the greater medical knowledge, improved nutrition, and concern for public health that characterized the 19th and 20th centuries bore fruit in a lower mortality rate and an overall increase in population.

Although historical records make reference to emigration to North America in the 17th and 18th centuries, there is little quantitative information about such movements before the middle of the following century. The greatest numbers appear to have left Great Britain in the 1880s and between 1900 and the outbreak of World War I. Emigration, particularly to Canada and Australia, continued at a high rate after the war until 1930, when unfavourable economic conditions in the British Empire and in the United States reversed the movement. During the same years there also was an influx of refugees from Europe. After World War II both inward and outward movements reached considerable dimensions. Emigration to the countries of the Commonwealth and, to a smaller degree, to the United States continued, but, until 1951, the net migration balance of the United Kingdom with the rest of the world was not large.

After 1957 the immigration of nonwhite ("New Commonwealth") people from such developing nations as India, Pakistan, and the countries of the West Indies became significant, and, from that year until 1962, there was a net migration gain. The immigrants came chiefly to find work. Despite efforts to achieve racial integration, both the white and nonwhite communities in Britain have tended to see themselves as distinct and different, but not necessarily separate—a neutral relationship for which the term "social pluralism" was coined. As in many other countries, race relations in the United Kingdom nevertheless continued to present problems throughout the late 20th century. About 60 percent of these immigrants from all sources have moved into the Greater London and the Birmingham conurbations, where opportunities for employment are greatest.

Migration within the United Kingdom has at times reached sizable dimensions. Until 1700 the small population was sparsely distributed and largely rural and agricultural, much as it had been in medieval times. From the mid-18th century, scientific and technological innovations created the first modern industrial state, while, at the same time, agriculture was undergoing technical and tenurial changes, and revolutionary improvements in transport made easier the movement of materials and people. As a result, by the first decade of the 19th century, a previously mainly rural population had been largely replaced by a nation that was made up of industrial workers and town dwellers.

The rural exodus was a long process; the breakdown of communal farming started before the 14th century; and, subsequently, enclosures advanced steadily, especially after 1740, until, a century later, open fields had virtually disappeared from the landscape. Many of the landless agricultural labourers so displaced were attracted to the better opportunities for employment and the higher wage levels existing in the growing industries; their movements, together with those of the surplus population produced by the contemporary rapid rise in the birth rate, resulted in a high volume of internal migration that took the form of a movement toward town.

Industry, as well as the urban centres that inevitably grew up around it, was increasingly located near the coalfields, while the railway network, which grew rapidly after 1830, enhanced the commercial importance of many towns. The migration of people, especially young people, from the country to industrialized towns took place at an unprecedented rate in the early railway age, and such movements were relatively confined geographically. Migration from agricultural Ireland provided an exception, for, when the disastrous potato disease of 1845–46 led to widespread famine, large numbers moved to Britain to become the urban workers of Lancashire, Clydeside, and London. The rural exodus continued, but on a greatly reduced scale, after 1901.

Soon after World War I, new interregional migration flows commenced when the formerly booming 19th-century industrial and mining districts lost much of their economic momentum. Declining or stagnating heavy industry in Clydeside, northeastern England, South Wales, and parts of Lancashire and Yorkshire swelled the ranks of the unemployed, and the consequent outward migration became the drift south to the relatively more prosperous Midlands and south of England. This movement of people continued until it was arrested by the relatively full employment conditions that obtained soon after the outbreak of World War II.

In the 1950s, opportunities for employment in the United Kingdom improved with government-sponsored diversification of industry, and this did much to reduce the magnitude of the prewar drift to the south. The decline of certain northern industries—coal mining, shipbuilding, and cotton textiles in particular—had nevertheless reached a critical level by the late 20th century, and the emergence of new growth points in the West Midlands and southeastern England made the drift to the south a continuing feature of British economic life. In addition, population has increased significantly in the East Midlands and around the great estuaries such as the Bristol Channel, Southampton Water, Merseyside, and Teesside. (W.Ra./Ed.)

The economy

The United Kingdom occupies a unique position in the world economy. The dominant industrial nation of the 19th century, it has, during the 20th century, seen its markets and its position in the world whittled away by other developed countries, especially by the United States, other nations of western Europe, and, more recently, Japan. Part of this relative decline has been due to the increasing industrialization of other countries, but a more fundamental reason has been the maintenance of the national role as sterling-area banker, necessitating restrictions on any domestic growth that might precipitate balance-of-payments deficits, loss of confidence in sterling, and consequent outflows of currency. The United Kingdom's growth rate has thus compared poorly with that of other industrial countries. This slow growth rate in the United Kingdom has, in turn, retarded the standard of living, as measured in terms of disposable income per capita.

Given favourable conditions, the potential for the United Kingdom's growth, relative to that of other countries, is nevertheless large. An increasing proportion of world trade is in manufactured goods, and thus the British industrial sector, already providing a larger proportion of such trade relative to its population size than any other country except Japan, is in a favourable position to take advantage of increased growth in world trade. By the late 20th century, exports to other countries of western Europe already

First official census

The drift south

Slow economic growth

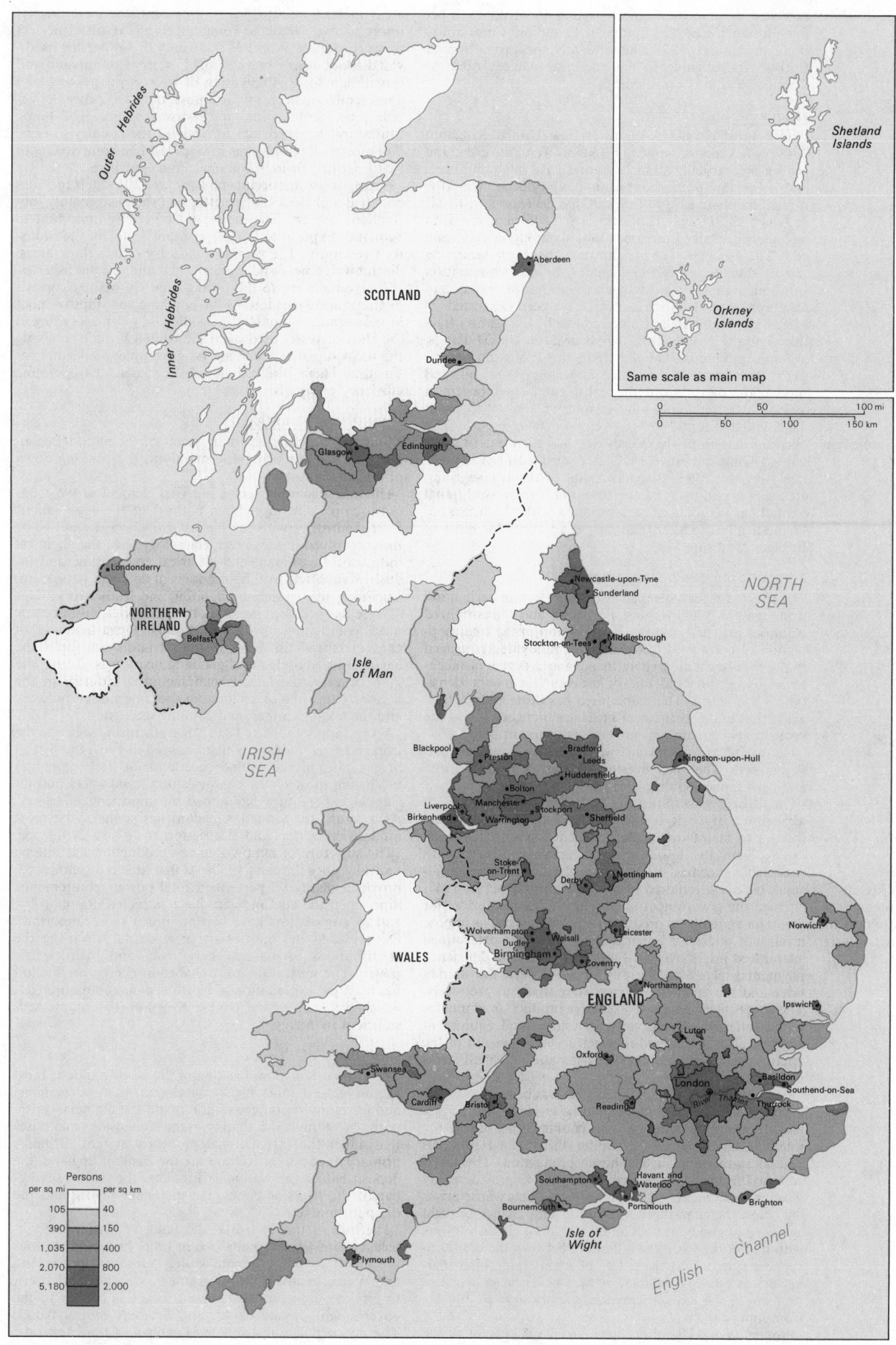

Orkney Islands

Same scale as main map

per sq mi	per sq km
105	40
390	150
1,035	400
2,070	800
5,180	2,000

Persons

Population density of the United Kingdom.

exceeded those to the Commonwealth countries, even before Britain joined the European Economic Community (EEC) in January 1972. Subsequently the proportion of British exports going to the EEC rose, while exports to Commonwealth countries dropped.

RESOURCES

Unlike most developed countries, the United Kingdom has very few natural mineral resources. With the exception of iron ore, virtually all metallic ores have to be imported, and even the proportion of home-produced iron ore, mined mainly in eastern England, has decreased. Minerals in which the United Kingdom is self-sufficient are sand and gravel, chalk, limestone, salt, slate, china clay, and coal. The production of coal, however, has been decreasing rapidly since the early 1950s, mainly because competition from other energy sources, such as oil, has increased, and also because easily worked seams have been exhausted.

Of all the crude oil consumed annually, only a tiny fraction, coming mainly from small fields in the Midlands, is home produced. The search in the 1960s for natural gas in the North Sea revealed large reserves of oil, and production of oil from the continental shelf began in 1975. The estimated North Sea reserves amount to about 4,075,000,000 tons.

Natural gas   Natural gas from the North Sea has been entering the United Kingdom since 1962. A controlled licensing system over the 100,000 square miles of the British claim area is operated by the Department of Energy. Additional natural gas is produced in association with North Sea oil. Domestically produced natural gas accounts for most of Britain's total supplies.

AGRICULTURE, FORESTRY, AND FISHING

The two main features that distinguish British agriculture from that of other western European and industrialized countries are, first, the small proportion of the total population (2 percent of those in civil employment) engaged in the industry and, second, its advanced degree of mechanization. Britain has one of the heaviest tractor densities in the world. The arable area has decreased slightly, while that under permanent grass has increased—changes brought about mainly by government-support policies.

The main farm crops are wheat, barley, potatoes, and sugar beets. The chief livestock output consists of cattle and calves, pigs, poultry, and sheep and lambs.

The British government is intimately concerned with agriculture, since it is considered a matter of national interest to maintain a stable, efficient food-producing industry, with the lowest possible prices consistent with reasonable incomes for those involved. An agricultural-support policy, required by the Agricultural Act of 1947, enabled the government to provide guaranteed prices for the main agricultural products and, if necessary, to impose minimum prices for imports. Annual reviews determined guaranteed prices over a 12-month period, and deficiency payments, related to the difference between the market price and the guaranteed price, were made to producers. The government also gave extensive production grants for improvements to land, crops, livestock, and equipment and was also empowered to meet up to 50 percent of the approved costs of voluntary amalgamation of small farms into commercial units.

By the late 20th century, this system was being changed to one whereby import duties would be levied on temperate-zone foodstuffs coming into the country, thus raising the internal-market prices for similar British food products and so stimulating further home production. The funds collected from the levies were to be used to provide price-deficiency payments on those home products whose prices fell below the guaranteed minimum. This change brought agricultural policy in the United Kingdom closer into line with that of the EEC. The difference between the old farm-support system and the policy of maintaining high market prices followed in the EEC was nevertheless a major problem in the United Kingdom's application to join the Common Market.

Productive woodland occupies about 6.5 percent of the total United Kingdom land area; scrub and old felled

Government support for agriculture

areas increase this to nearly 9 percent, the large area of unproductive woodland being largely the result of neglect of work during World Wars I and II. Ownership is divided about evenly between the Forestry Commission and private landlords. Replanting of trees is progressing at a considerable rate, mostly in forests of Sitka spruce, lodgepole pine, Scotch pine, and Norway spruce. The home timber industry provides for little of the country's needs, and most of its produce is low-grade when compared with that imported from Scandinavia and elsewhere.

Fishing is an important industry, and the catch includes cod, haddock, mackerel, plaice, and shellfish, mainly lobsters and oysters. The industry is especially important to Scotland. Exports of fish are a minor factor in the industry's economy. The whitefish industry covers three areas: distant water, near and middle water, and inshore fisheries.

Government aid to the fishing industry mainly consists of grants and loans toward the purchase and improvement of vessels and equipment. Subsidies are given according to the class of vessel used, with the whitefish trade receiving the most support. There are no government subsidies for shellfish. There is also a subsidy related to the operating efficiency of vessels.

MINING AND INDUSTRY

Mining is a rapidly declining sector of the national economy, the decline being due mainly to the running down of the coal industry.

The manufacturing sector is a vital element in the economy, employing more than a third of the total labour force. Industries with the highest growth rates tend to be those involved in advanced technology; *e.g.,* the chemical industries, instrument and electrical engineering, and industries involved with by-products of coal and petroleum. Declining sectors are shipbuilding and leatherwork. This decline has occurred because other countries have become more competitive, primarily through the availability of cheaper labour. In terms of output and work force, the engineering and electrical-goods industry was, in the late 20th century, the largest manufacturing industry in the nation. Other major sectors are the automotive industry and the textile, leather, and clothing industries.

A key supply industry to the manufacturing sector is the iron and steel industry. Renationalized in 1967, the British Steel Corporation combines several major steel companies producing most of the country's total crude-steel output. Capital expenditure has aimed at improving efficiency. As a result, the United Kingdom has some of the most modern converter- and electric-furnace plants in Europe.

Iron and steel industry

The structure of national energy production has altered radically since the early 1950s. At that time indigenous coal provided nearly 90 percent of total power requirements. Since then the coal industry has contracted dramatically, and its competitors have become much more important. Oil provided the bulk of the new output, dwarfing the contributions of nuclear energy, gas, and hydroelectric power. The most significant change in energy production has been the exploitation of North Sea oil and natural gas, which has enabled the United Kingdom to become self-sufficient in energy.

FINANCE

The United Kingdom has one of the world's oldest, most extensive, and most highly developed financial systems, and for many purposes London is still the financial centre of the Western world, sharing in the convulsions and crises that afflict the international monetary system. Britain's primary financial institutions are the Bank of England, the deposit banks, the National Girobank, the trustee savings banks, the overseas banks, the merchant banks, and the discount market.

The hub of this system is the Bank of England, established in 1694 and nationalized in 1946. Its main functions are to act as the sole note-issuing authority in England and Wales, to advise the government on financial matters, to execute monetary policy, and to act as banker to the government, private banks, and overseas central banks. The major policy instrument is control of the bank rate, the rate at which the bank lends money as lender of last

The Bank of England

resort to the discount houses. The country's interest-rate structure is based either on a fixed relationship to the bank rate or on expectations about its possible movements. In many circumstances movements in the bank rate can have considerable effect on the money supply and on the cost of borrowing. The Bank of England also manipulates the supply of money by open-market operations on the money and gilt-edged (government stock) markets. It can affect the policy of the commercial banks by issuing directives on the level of lending and credit regarded as permissible, and it can extract from them special deposits over and above those already held at the bank as liquid assets.

The commercial bank group consists of London clearing banks, which carry on virtually all commercial banking in England and Wales, Scottish clearing banks, and Northern Ireland banks. All have numerous branches. The Banking Act of 1979 requires all deposit-taking institutions to receive authorization in the form of recognition or licensing from the Bank of England. Once authorized, institutions are subject to continuing supervision.

Banking in the City

This comprehensive banking system is integrated with complex and sophisticated capital and discount markets, which are based in the City of London, a small area of old London that retains its global preeminence as a commercial and financial centre. The continuing importance of the City is based on the United Kingdom's position as banker for the sterling area; this means that substantial funds are held in the City for overseas sterling countries and are used, together with funds from many nonsterling countries, in various financial transactions that are to the advantage of the City and its customers. A major trend is for London banks to receive large deposits of dollars, which are then re-lent, creating the Eurodollar market.

The Stock Exchange

Many other important institutions operate in the City, among them the amalgamated stock exchanges of the United Kingdom and Irish Republic, commonly known as the Stock Exchange. Also located there are numerous insurance companies, dominated by the international insurance market of Lloyds; shipping companies; the merchant banks and discount houses; foreign banks; life assurance offices; building societies; and many of the world's major commodity markets. The various activities of the City make a large contribution to the United Kingdom's favourable balance on invisible trade transactions.

TRADE

With less than 2 percent of the world's population, the United Kingdom is one of the world's largest trading nations. With few natural resources of its own, the United Kingdom relies on imports for nearly half of its food and for most of its raw materials. In order to earn the foreign exchange needed to pay for these commodities, exports make up a good percentage of the country's total GNP. Almost three-quarters of the total exports are in manufactured goods. Machinery, both electrical and mechanical, vehicles, tractors, and scientific instruments are the major components of this sector, while chemicals are a rapidly growing export. Sectors in relative decline include textiles and metal manufactures other than machinery.

The sources and destinations of United Kingdom trade include every country in the world; but, since Britain's entry into the EEC, the trend is for a relatively larger percentage of all trade to be carried out with other countries of western Europe. Because of increased importance of western Europe in the country's trade, the United States, formerly Britain's major single customer, has come to share that role with West Germany.

MANAGEMENT OF THE ECONOMY

The private sector. The British economy is a good example of a mixed economic system, for the public and private sectors claim almost equal shares of the GNP. The relationship between government and the private sector varies to some extent, according to whether a Conservative or a Labour government is in power; the former tends to allow the private sector to succeed or fail according to its own resources and energy, while the latter usually intervenes more actively, bolstering failing sectors and also initiating new projects. Within such a system,

and given an international situation beyond its control, a government can clearly impose no overall plan, but it is able to indicate to private industry the lines of expansion that it believes necessary and, to some extent, force it to act along them. The main ways in which a government influences industry are by its fiscal and monetary policies, by its control of the level of public expenditure, and by provision of government contracts, services, information, and advice. These operate mainly to affect aggregate demand, supply, investment, and savings. Equally effective is the two-pronged policy of encouraging investment and counteracting relatively high unemployment in the more depressed areas, forcing development away from the prosperous and congested areas of the Midlands and the South East.

Among the government bodies concerned with the private sector is the National Economic Development Council, which organizes committees to study and promote productivity in some 21 separate industries. The Monopolies Commission and the Restrictive Practices Court (Department of Employment and Productivity) operate to ensure that agreements entered into by companies do not jeopardize the public interest.

The public sector and the role of government. Less than 10 percent of the total British labour force works for statutory bodies directly controlling public corporations, which operate major industries and services in the public interest. These include the Bank of England, the Post Office, the British Broadcasting Corporation (BBC), the major airlines, the Atomic Energy Authority, the coal, gas, electricity, and steel industries, and the railway, docks, waterway, and freight services. Although not part of government departments, these bodies are under varying degrees of control by them. Responsibility for management nevertheless lies with the boards and staff of each public corporation, not with the minister of the government department concerned. Some bodies are self-supporting, while others receive Exchequer grants. The minister appoints the chairman and members of the board and can direct the general running of the corporation, but he does not interfere in day-to-day operations.

Taxation. Government revenues are produced by three major forms of taxation: on income, on capital, and on expenditure. Considerable reform of the structure of taxation was effected in the late 20th century.

Although accurate comparisons are not feasible because of differences in taxation methods, costs of living, and social security benefits and payments, personal taxation in the United Kingdom is generally considered among the highest in the world. Income taxes include the personal income tax, surtax, and corporation tax. Taxes on capital are estate duties, popularly called death duties, and capital gains tax, both estimated to account for about 1 percent of the United Kingdom's total tax receipts. Taxes on expenditures including customs and excise duties, apply mainly to tobacco, hydrocarbon oil, and alcoholic drinks. Other taxes on expenditures include betting taxes and motor-vehicle-license charges.

In 1973 a value-added tax was placed on the supply of goods and services and on the importation of goods, subject to certain exceptions. This tax is levied at each stage of production and distribution, with the final tax borne by the consumer. The account of tax collected by customs and excise is the difference between the initial product tax and the tax paid by the consumer. A tax on new and imported cars is also levied.

Employers' associations and trade unions. The main employers' organization is the Confederation of British Industry (CBI), which deals with all industrial matters affecting employers. In close contact with the government, the public, and other interested parties, it includes more than 1,400 different employers' organizations. These are the bodies that negotiate most of the important collective agreements with trade unions.

Labour in nearly all industries and occupations in the United Kingdom is organized, to a varying extent, into trade unions. The largest unions include the Transport and General Workers Union, the Amalgamated Union of Engineering Workers, the General and Municipal Workers

Trades
Union
Congress

Union, and the National and Local Government Officers Association. Most unions belong to the Trades Union Congress (TUC), the central body of the labour movement. The TUC is empowered to mediate between unions, to comment on wage claims, and to deal with unauthorized or unconstitutional strikes. It is nonpolitical, but individual unions may set up a political fund that is financed by a membership levy, from which any member may opt out. Most unions have such a fund, which is used to support the Labour Party.

Voluntary consultation and negotiation is the foundation of British industrial relations. The Advisory Conciliation and Arbitration Service (ACAS) promotes improved industrial relations by voluntary means, emphasizing the extension of collective bargaining and development and reform in bargaining procedures. The ACAS itself conciliates public and private sector disputes and, in arbitration, appoints a single arbitrator or refers the dispute to the Central Arbitration Committee (CAC). The CAC is an independent body that provides arbitration boards for settling disputes and adjudicated claims made under various legislative acts that deal with employment protection and fair wages. Wages in small industries and in trades in which employees and employers are well organized for successful voluntary bargaining are set by wage-regulating bodies called wage councils. Each of these councils comprises equal numbers of employers and employees from industry, along with three independent members.   (E.I.U./Ed.)

TRANSPORTATION

Most of the heaviest British passenger and freight loads travel along the main English commercial axis running from London, through Birmingham, to Liverpool and Manchester. Along this route, that of the Roman Watling Street and the Scottish civil engineer Thomas Telford's London to Holyhead Road, lie the principal electrified trunk rail line, the M.1 and M.6 motorways, the Grand Union Canal, the principal internal air corridor, and the main natural-gas and petroleum pipelines. This axis has three extensions: northward as the west coast route to Scotland; westward through North Wales to Holyhead, the principal port for travel to Dublin; and southward from London to the southern coast and the prospective Channel Tunnel. London and Liverpool–Manchester are by far the largest freight ports, as well as the largest centres of population and industry in the United Kingdom. Major transport arteries have developed that link them with other cities and regions in Britain.

Apart from traffic covering the main intercity routes, most urban and interurban public transportation of both people and freight is in decline. Despite the growing population and the consequent increase of production and consumption, the amount of freight and number of passengers moved by railways fell during the 20th century. Although urban populations have steadily increased in the United Kingdom, public passenger traffic in towns and cities had been declining by a few percent per annum for many years even before the 1960s, when spiralling fare increases and diminished services accelerated the annual falloff rate.

Ownership of private cars in the United Kingdom has been increasing consistently since the 1920s, except during World War II and periods of economic depression. By the late 20th century more than 80 percent of total passenger mileage was made in privately owned vehicles.

The near-crisis conditions that have developed for the publicly owned road, rail, and waterways transportation systems in the United Kingdom and the seriously congested state of most main roads in the country have brought the problem of transportation under closer public scrutiny. The need to maintain some form of passenger-transport services, despite declining demand and consequent increasing losses, has resulted in practical attempts to cut costs, especially labour costs. Some one-man buses have been introduced; in London the Underground Victoria Line has automated trains, and automated ticket collection has been introduced in underground stations.

Government policy for the national transport undertakings varies according to whether the government is Conser-

The English commercial transport axis

Automation in urban transport

vative or Labour. The Conservatives practice a fairly strict commercialism. Labour, on the other hand, has tended to recognize the social value of many of the country's public transport services and, when in power, has paid considerable subsidies to the British Railways Board.

A policy statement that preceded the 1968 Transport Act showed government acceptance of the movement away from rail traffic and from public transport in general. It cleared the way for the railways to concentrate on providing the services for which they are best suited: intercity passenger trains, city commuter services, and trainload freight. By the terms of the act, previously competing bus and rail passenger services in many city regions were placed under the operational control of unified passenger transport authorities, which were required to coordinate services and balance operating costs against revenues supplemented by local taxation. The act incorporated most of the bus undertakings that were not municipally owned into a National Bus Company. In 1969 the control of London Transport (buses and underground railways) was vested in the Greater London Council.

The increasing demand for oil and oil products in the United Kingdom, coupled with the growing congestion in road transport and the discovery of natural gas in the North Sea, led during the late 20th century to the development of pipelines for the transport of oil and gas. Two major systems are operated: one by the British Gas Corporation for the distribution of natural gas, and the other by the petroleum industry for that of oil and oil products.

Ownership of the majority of commercial seaports in Britain was vested in the British Transport Docks Board by the 1962 Transport Act. Half of Britain's imports and exports are nevertheless handled by the major independent ports, particularly those on the Rivers Mersey and Thames. The traffic of the docks of the British Transport Docks Board is mainly of the cross-Channel, short-haul variety, serving Ireland, the offshore islands, and the closer continental ports, as well as British coastwise traffic.

The association of shipping lines with individual ports has led to a tendency for traffic with particular parts of the world to become associated with one particular port. Thus, Tilbury, part of the Port of London, is associated with the Australasian passenger trade, Liverpool with that to Canada, West Africa, and the Far East, and Southampton with the North and South American and South African trades. During the 1960s, however, much of the deep-sea passenger-liner traffic was transferred to Southampton, which is exceptional among ports of the British Transport Docks Board in that it has developed a major traffic role comparable with that of Liverpool and London. Much of its success is due to its geographical location, its peculiar double-crested tide, which obviates the need for enclosed water docks, and to a history of good labour relations. Although other major ports have made considerable investments to equip themselves to handle container-freight traffic, it appears that much of this trade will also go through Southampton.

Britain is linked with the rest of Europe and other continents by state-owned airlines. A number of subsidiary and independent companies also operate airlines. Most world airlines use London's Heathrow Airport, making it one of the busiest in the world. It is supported by the smaller subsidiary airports of Gatwick to the south, Southend on the east, and Luton and Stanstead to the north.

Domestic air traffic is comparatively light, since distances between the principal cities are small, and air travel offers scant savings in travel time. Each major city region, nevertheless, has its own airport, with passenger services to and from London accounting for most of the traffic. Special networks serve the offshore islands and some cross-country routes. Few of the provincial airports have significant international links other than cross-Channel, the exceptions being Manchester and Prestwick (Glasgow), which both have a moderate level of traffic services to North America.

The British Airport Authority administers seven airports: Heathrow, Gatwick, and Stanstead in England and Glasgow, Edinburgh, Aberdeen, and Prestwick in Scotland.

(J.Pro./Ed.)

The role of Southampton

The role of Heathrow Airport

Administrative and social conditions

GOVERNMENT

Britain is a constitutional monarchy and a parliamentary democracy. The country's permanent head of state is the reigning king or queen, and the head of government is the prime minister, who derives that position from the fact that the prime minister is the leader of the political party that at any given time possesses, or can command, a majority of votes in the House of Commons.

Sources of the constitution

The British constitution is partly unwritten and wholly flexible. Its basic sources are legislative enactments of Parliament, such as the Act of Settlement (1701) and decisions made by courts of law. Matters for which there is no formal law, as, for instance, the resignation of office by a government, are determined by important conventions of the constitution, based on precedent, but always open to development or modification.

The main elements in the constitution are the legislature, the executive, and the judiciary; and government, in the most general sense, involves all three, with many functions overlapping, since there is no separation of powers. Sovereignty resides in Parliament, which comprises the monarch, referred to as the Crown, the hereditary and appointive House of Lords, and the elected House of Commons acting in concert; the sovereignty of Parliament is expressed in its legislative enactments. These are therefore binding on all, although the liberty of the individual subject, secured in essence by the rule of law, is, in practice, exemplified by the right of the private individual to contest in the courts the legality of any action under a specific statute.

All political power is concentrated in the prime minister and the Cabinet, and the monarch must act on their advice. Members of the Cabinet are chosen by the prime minister from among his own political party in Parliament. Most Cabinet ministers are heads of such government departments as the Home Office or the Foreign Office. The prime minister's authority over the Cabinet has tended to increase, and some decisions previously within the competence of the Cabinet as a whole are now made by the prime minister alone. A clear example of this development occurred in 1918, when the right to request the monarch to dissolve Parliament and fix the date of an election passed by tacit consent from Cabinet to prime minister. The prime minister can also, on occasion, alone or with one or two colleagues, make decisions without consulting the Cabinet. A prime minister has nevertheless been overruled by the Cabinet on many occasions, and, in order to exercise fully his enhanced powers, the prime minister must, as a rule, have the support of the Cabinet. The prime minister also appoints about 25 ministers who are not members of the Cabinet, as well as about 50 junior ministers.

Powers of the Cabinet

The Cabinet exercises the sovereignty of Parliament because, as it is drawn from, and supported by, the party that has a majority in the House of Commons, it can effectively control legislation. The royal right of veto has not been exercised since the early 18th century, and the once coequal legislative power of the hereditary House of Lords was reduced in 1911 to a mere right of temporary delay. The Cabinet plans, drafts, and lays before Parliament all important bills, including the budget, using its majority to get them through Parliament with reasonable dispatch. While the Cabinet thus controls the lawmaking machinery, it is also subject to Parliament, in the sense that it must expound and defend its policy in parliamentary debate.

Administrative decisions of the Cabinet are implicitly and immediately obeyed and carried out by the entire executive apparatus, both civil and military. The Cabinet secretariat, which developed after World War I, is the mechanism by which the Cabinet's decisions, always in exercise of already existing statutory powers or of the reserve powers of the Crown or, exceptionally, requiring retrospective parliamentary authorization, are converted into executive action. Besides preparing the agenda of the Cabinet and circulating all relevant papers to members, the secretariat records the conclusions of the Cabinet in such a form that the government departments concerned can speedily carry them into effect.

Within the United Kingdom, Scotland has a distinct legal system based on Roman law; much of Wales is bilingual, and in some parts Welsh is the first language. Both regard themselves as nations on a par with England. England itself is divided by dialect and sentiment into regions that are in varying degree conscious of their own identity. Until 1973 Northern Ireland had a Parliament (located at Stormont) and a Cabinet that, under a United Kingdom act of 1920, had autonomy in purely domestic affairs. The Stormont Parliament was abolished by the Northern Ireland Constitution Act of 1973 and was replaced by an Assembly for about one year. In July 1974, however, Northern Ireland became subject to "direct rule" by the British secretary of state for Northern Ireland.

Compared with other countries (and despite the differences between England, Scotland, and Wales), the United Kingdom is, to a high degree, homogeneous. Practically everyone speaks English; the electoral system is uniform; the same legal system prevails throughout England, Wales, and Northern Ireland; and three-quarters of the population lives within daily travelling distance of the centres of six conurbations.

Local government is also homogeneous. Although its roots stretch back to a period before the Norman Conquest in 1066, it was first established on a uniform basis between 1835 and 1888, and it remained unchanged until the present system was adopted in 1973–75. Until 1973 local authorities were subordinate corporations formed by acts of Parliament or by charters. Their powers, which were executive as well as legislative and which included the levying and appropriating of financial rates, derived both from statute and from judicial interpretation.

Local government bodies in England, Wales, Northern Ireland, and Scotland included county (shire) councils, whose area of jurisdiction in the main followed that of the corresponding geographical counties but excluded county-borough areas; county borough councils, established in some large boroughs having a population of 100,000 upward; ordinary borough (or, in Scotland, burgh) councils; and urban district or rural district councils (in Scotland, district councils). County councils and county borough councils consisted of a chairman, aldermen, and councillors; borough councils of a mayor, aldermen, and councillors; and urban and rural district councils of a chairman and councillors. In Scotland burgh councils consisted of a provost, bailies, and councillors.

Local government officials

Many local-government responsibilities were subsidized, and to some extent supervised, by the central government, but local authorities are proud and careful of their independence. They are organized into national associations capable of making potent representations to the government of the day.

A royal commission set up in 1966 to examine the system of local government issued a report in 1969 that formed the basis of government proposals issued in 1971 for a reorganization of local government that took effect in Northern Ireland in 1973, in England and Wales in 1974, and in Scotland in 1975. First, an almost uniform two-tier system largely extinguished the existing extensive powers previously wielded by borough councils. A large reduction in the number of local government authorities was then effected, and 62 new larger areas, called counties in England (45) and Wales (8) and called regions in Scotland (9), were created. These, in turn, were subdivided into 402 districts. The new English county areas, in the main, follow the historic county boundaries, but each new Scottish region took in two or more of the original shires. Under the reorganization both counties and districts have separate elected councils, and, although the reorganization left parish councils undisturbed, some additional powers were granted.

Districts are responsible for local services, such as housing and refuse collection, and counties for major services, such as police, education, and social works; but, in the six English metropolitan counties formed in areas of extensive urban development, responsibility for education and social services was given to the district councils. This fol-

London
govern-
ment

lows a practice adopted when the government of Greater London was reformed in 1963 and its boundaries were enlarged to include 610 square miles and a population of about 7,750,000. Governmental responsibilities were divided between the Greater London Council and 32 London borough councils at that time and were not further altered. Through the reorganization of local government many boroughs or burghs, including the Scottish cities of Edinburgh, Glasgow, Aberdeen, and Dundee, often with a long history of civic autonomy, thus lost to their respective county or region the control of services such as education.

POLITICS

Elections. Voters in Britain vote both in parliamentary and in local government elections. The former are either general elections, in which an entirely new House of Commons is chosen, or there are by-elections, which occur when a sitting member has died or has resigned. All other public posts are filled by appointment.

Each member of the House of Commons represents one parliamentary constituency. Constituency boundaries are drawn so that they are all approximately the same size in population—about 88,000 people. The constituencies are divided into wards and other units for the election of local government councillors. Periodically, a commission recommends to Parliament any boundary changes that may seem necessary because of shifts that have occurred in the population.

Registration of electors is compulsory and is carried out annually by the state. Candidates for election to Parliament or a council are chosen by the local parties. There is no primary system on the United States model, and there could not well be any, since the timing of general elections is unpredictable.

Duration
of
Parliament

The House of Commons is elected, not for a fixed term but for a maximum term—reduced in 1911 from seven to five years. At any time during this five years, the prime minister has the right to dissolve Parliament and call a general election. The use of this power for party advantage is checked by the probability of public resentment at such a manoeuvre. A government returned with a majority is expected to govern for the major part of the five-year life of Parliament. It is accepted, nonetheless, that Parliament may be dissolved at any time in about the last year and a half of its life, and it rarely runs its full five years.

An early election is, however, acceptable if the prime minister and Cabinet emerge from a general election with less than a working majority—that is, one of about 20 seats—in which case the paramount need for effective government is considered to justify an election. This is especially so if the government majority is so slim that it might be lost should by-elections run against the government.

Only three weeks' notice of a general election need by law be given, and expenses of parliamentary candidates are strictly limited by law. These provisions and the uncertainty about the timing of an election produce campaigns of unusual brevity and inexpensiveness.

Political parties. A two-party political system has existed in Britain since the late 17th century, and the two rival groups have always respectively embodied, in some form related to the main issues of the day, the conservative and progressive elements in human character. This two-

The
two-party
system

party system—which predominates despite the existence of minority parties such as the extremely small Communist Party, the rump of the historic Liberal Party, or the Social Democratic Party (formed in 1981 by disaffected members of the Labour Party)—is one of the most outstanding features of British politics and has done much to produce a history of firm and decisive government.

The political system and the nature of the great parties themselves have been shaped by the special role of the Cabinet as the centre of political authority. Control of the Cabinet has long been the prize and object of British politics, fought for from the early 18th century by Whigs against Tories, later by Liberals against Conservatives, and now by Labour against Conservatives. The practice of simple majority voting, which has always prevailed, and the final establishment of single-member constituencies of uniform population size have tended to exaggerate the

majority of the winning party and thus to eliminate third parties. On occasions when the two-party system has been disturbed, these factors have helped to restore it. If one of the major parties has been, temporarily, in abeyance, two rival groups have thus usually developed among members of the predominant party and have contended for control of the Cabinet. A new party only rises to power by displacing another, as happened when Labour superseded the Liberals in the first half of the 20th century.

Progressive widening of the franchise from the early 19th century (the vote is now given to all at the age of 18) made it increasingly necessary to organize mass parties in the country in order to win a clear and firm majority of parliamentary seats in a general election. But, equally, the parties in the country depended on their representatives in Parliament and, in particular, on those who, as members of the Cabinet, drafted and introduced bills to carry through the parties' legislative programs. Thus the parliamentary parties not only became indissolubly linked with the national parties but also inevitably dominated them.

There grew up in the 20th century one of the most distinctive features of the British party system, namely the choice by the parliamentary parties of leaders who were then automatically accepted as the leaders of the national parties.

The growth and maintenance of a mass two-party system, together with the uncertainty of the timing of a general election, produced the British phenomenon of the Opposition. Each party when out of office has to organize and conduct itself so as, if possible, to win the next general election. The decisive characteristic of the Opposition is that it is a viable alternative government, ready at any time to take office. The leader of the Opposition is paid an official salary as such.

The
Opposition

Government and Opposition are ranged against each other in daily battle in Parliament. The perpetual conflict between them has caused national political issues to dominate, increasingly, local elections, while ensuring that the two main parties themselves remain continuously alert and disciplined. In the last resort the two-party system depends upon its acceptance by the British voters and upon their readiness to find satisfaction in and through one of the two major parties and to reject independent candidates or those of third parties.

The participation of the citizen. Fundamentally, the right of citizens to participate in public affairs is exercised when they cast their votes in parliamentary or local elections. They can also participate in the political field by becoming paid-up members or voluntary workers for the party of their choice. Further participation in affairs of state can take the form of support of particular causes and attempts to urge Parliament to further them, or, more often effective, of protest outside the field of electoral politics against actions or proposed actions of the government. Vested interests and pressure groups nevertheless play a relatively small part in British parliamentary life. The disciplined two-party system means that the members' loyalty to a party normally transcends loyalty to an interest and that the members are more conscious of the authority of the party whips than of the influence of pressure groups or of vocal minorities. Party members are not subjected to massive campaigns of letters and telegrams.

Movements of protest have been endemic in British history and have been associated with many major reforms. In the 20th century, although no less frequent in occurrence, they have perhaps been more fragmented and less likely to be effective. Movements of protest against nuclear weapons have developed. Supporters of the Welsh movement have organized protests to further the use of the Welsh language, and have on rare occasions resorted to sabotage, such as the blowing up of pipelines carrying water from Welsh lakes to English cities. In Northern Ireland a civil rights movement has in recent years worked for the ending of discrimination against the Roman Catholic minority. The result of civil violence led to the dispatch of troops by the British government.

Political
protest
movements

Trade unions directly challenged the authority of the state in the general strike of 1926. That experience convinced them that strikes for political ends would always be defeated by the government, backed by considerable popular support. They also realized that such strikes were incompatible with parliamentary democracy, in that they would usurp or frustrate the electoral processes that make possible the constant criticism and ultimate replacement of a government. Since 1926 the trade unions, which participate in politics by supporting the Labour Party with their funds, have thus used industrial action solely in furtherance of the economic interests of their members.

Britain has a long history of participation by the private citizen in voluntary work outside party politics. Unpaid justices of the peace, besides hearing cases, discharge many administrative functions such as the annual licensing of public houses (bars) and betting shops. The welfare services run by central and local government are reinforced by a great deal of voluntary help.

THE ARMED FORCES

Supreme responsibility for national defense rests with the prime minister and the Cabinet. The secretary of state for defense formulates and proposes defense policy. His ministry, created in 1970 by a merger of the three original service ministries (Admiralty, War, and Air), has responsibility for the armed forces. The secretary of state is advised by the chief of defense staff aided by the three service chiefs.

JUSTICE

Judges in the United Kingdom are irremovable and appointed. There is no election to judicial office. The Bench, as it is known, is recruited from practicing lawyers and never from people in public or elected office. The courts alone declare the law; but any act of Parliament is accepted by the courts as part of the law. No court can declare a statute invalid.

An accused person is presumed innocent until proved guilty. The courts strictly enforce the law of contempt to prevent newspapers or television from prejudicing by comment the trial of the accused before a jury. Accused persons and litigants in civil actions are entitled to legal aid paid by the state on a scale varying with their income. Two-thirds or more of persons in criminal cases are granted legal aid.

Legal aid

About 90 percent of criminal cases are tried and determined by justices of the peace, who act as unpaid magistrates, or in towns and some other places by stipendiary (paid) magistrates who are trained lawyers. Magistrates' courts sit in about 700 places in England and Wales and are therefore within comparatively easy reach of everyone. The remaining 10 percent of more serious crimes also come in the first place before a magistrate's court. The police must bring an arrested person within 24 hours before a magistrate, who alone decides whether he shall be remanded on bail or in custody. If they so find, they commit him for trial by a judge and jury. In 1967 an act of Parliament enabled jurors to give a majority verdict in criminal cases; the majority must be at least 10–2. Hanging for murder was abolished in 1965.

The vast majority of civil actions are tried in local county courts before paid judges. Their jurisdiction is limited by the nature of the action and by the amount of money at stake. In both these respects the jurisdiction of the courts has been steadily widened.

Partly in an effort to reduce delays in the hearing of criminal cases, which had been running at about four and one-half months, the higher courts in the United Kingdom were radically reorganized by an act of Parliament in 1971. As a result, the Supreme Court of Judicature now consists of the Appeal Court; the High Court of Justice with civil jurisdiction; and the Crown Court, for criminal work above the level handled by the magistrates' courts. The High Court and Crown Court move between the major centres of the country's population. The High Court hears the most important and difficult criminal and civil cases; criminal cases of less importance are tried by the Crown Court.

Appeals

Appeals in both civil and criminal matters lie from the High and Crown Courts to the Appeal Court. This court can give leave, in cases of great legal importance, for a final appeal to the judges in the House of Lords.

EDUCATION

The government operates no schools, employs no teachers, prescribes no textbooks or curricula; nor does it control universities. There is, however, a central Department of Education and Science headed by a minister who is responsible to Parliament and who is usually in the Cabinet.

The prime responsibility for managing schools is in the hands of elected local education authorities, which allocate children among schools and appoint and pay teachers. Head teachers (principals) enjoy a high measure of independence; they cannot be given instructions on textbooks or teaching methods. Local education authorities plan and build schools, and they also meet the greater part of the cost of voluntary schools—those maintained by religious bodies. The authorities incur four-fifths of education expenditures, with government grants covering the remainder.

The Education Act of 1944 established free and compulsory secondary education for those from 11 to 15 years of age. In 1972 the school-leaving age was raised to 16. By the terms of the act, children were allocated by examination at the age of 11 either to grammar schools, which prepared them for universities, or to secondary modern schools, from which they generally went into industry. In 1964 the Labour government reorganized secondary education on comprehensive lines to end this segregation. All children were to go to comprehensive schools.

Comprehensive schools

Independent schools exist outside the government system. Chief of these are about 450 fee-paying private schools (called public schools), half of which are for girls.

Some 30 percent of the United Kingdom's 18–20-year-olds go on to some form of higher education. Almost the whole cost is met by the government. The money is given to the University Grants Committee, an independent body that deals directly with the universities.

Universities are wholly independent; they arrange their own courses of study and research and appoint their own staff. They also decide about the admission of students. Students in some universities have achieved some measure of representation on the governing councils. Universities in the United Kingdom are relatively small: none except London has more than 15,000 students; many have fewer.

Most of those who fail to gain entry to a university go to some other form of higher education. Local education authorities maintain about 800 colleges that provide mainly technical and commercial courses: some of these institutions award degrees of university level. There are also nearly 170 colleges of education for the training of teachers, who can also gain degrees.

In January 1971 the Open University—something unique of its kind in the world—was begun. It provides for adults who missed the chance of university education, and it uses television, radio, and local study and lecture courses. Applicants to the Open University have to be accepted for a number of places limited at any one time by the availability of teachers. Degrees are awarded as at any university.

The Open University

HEALTH AND WELFARE SERVICES

The National Health Service. A complete national health service began to operate in the United Kingdom on July 5, 1948. Every man, woman, and child is entitled to medical treatment of every kind, free at the moment of need. The only exceptions are a number of charges that meet part of the cost of dental work, spectacles, and prescribed medicines. All these charges are remitted for children, old-age pensioners, and people below a certain income level. The charges meet about 10 percent of the cost of the National Health Service. The service is voluntary: doctors may, if they wish, take only fee-paying patients, but 98 percent of general practitioners in the nation participate in the service, as do almost all of the dentists. Some 2,500 hospitals provide entirely free treatment. A small number of hospitals have opted out of the service—most of them run by religious orders or maintained for special groups, as in the case of the Italian, Jewish, and trade-union hospitals. Private nursing homes are permitted, but they must be registered.

The normal doctor–patient relationship is maintained. A patient can freely choose or change the doctor with whom he is registered, and a doctor may decline to have a patient on his list. A doctor receives from the state a basic practice allowance, payments for ancillary staff, and a capitation grant for each patient on his list, limited to a maximum of 3,500. Doctors receive a higher fee for every patient they have who is over 65, for night visits, and for practicing in an undoctored area. They can also take private patients.

Some of the total cost of the National Health Service comes from the central or local government.

The general management and discipline of the family practitioner service in the United Kingdom is exercised by about 150 local bodies, half of the members of which are appointed by doctors, dentists, and pharmacists. Hospitals are supervised by 20 regional boards, which receive government grants and are responsible for planning and building hospitals.

The local authorities have a legal obligation to provide maternity and child-welfare services, home nursing, health visiting, domestic help for those in need, and the care and aftercare of illness, including mental disorders. They organize ambulance services and build and maintain health centres.

Social security. The social security system in the United Kingdom makes up a vital part of the welfare services. It, too, was established in 1948 and is based on compulsory insurance. Employees pay, by law, a weekly contribution, which is supplemented by a charge upon the employer. The state meets the balance of the cost.

Retirement pension In return for their contributions employees are entitled to retirement pensions (at 65 for men and at 60 for women) and to cash benefits in unemployment or sickness. The duration of these benefits depends on the number of contributions paid. Should these be exhausted, employees can draw a supplementary benefit, as can all whose incomes fall below a certain level, even if they are employed. The supplementary benefit depends upon a means test, and the cost is borne wholly by the state. The benefit also meets the entire cost of family allowances for all children after the first so long as they remain in full-time education. The system of flat contributions and flat benefits was in the process of being changed in the early 1980s to one based on a percentage of wages.

In 1965 a statutory system of redundancy or severance pay was introduced. An employee who loses his job through no fault of his own receives a lump-sum payment. The cost of the payment is met in part by his employer and in part out of a fund made up by a levy on all employers.

Local authorities have a legal obligation to see that housing in their area is adequate. This they fulfill mainly by building houses and apartments (flats) for rent. The central government lays down mandatory minimum standards, and local authorities maintain waiting lists and allocate houses according to need. The cost of the housing program is met in part by government subsidies, in part by rents collected from the tenants, and in part by contributions from local taxation. Since 1971 local authorities have had a statutory duty to operate rent rebates. They must charge their tenants the true economic rent and make rebates to those whose incomes fall below a certain level. Local authorities can make grants of up to 50 percent of the cost, up to a certain limit, of improving privately owned houses.

The whole country is subject to town and country planning by eight regional boards, which control where new building or the substantial alteration of existing structures may be undertaken.

POLICE SERVICES

There is in Britain no national police force nor any minister exclusively responsible for the police. Each provincial police force is maintained by a police authority—a committee elected by a number of local authorities—which determines the establishment of the force and provides and maintains buildings, vehicles, and other equipment. The police authority also appoints and dismisses the chief constable, who, however, has the sole right of appointment, promotion, discipline, and deployment of his force and who alone decides police action in individual cases.

The home secretary is the police authority for the Metropolitan Police in London. Broadly, the commissioner in charge of the Metropolitan Police has status similar to that of a chief constable. The famous Scotland Yard (the criminal investigation department of the Metropolitan Police) helps other police forces on request and handles the British business of the International Criminal Police Organization (Interpol).

The supervisory powers of the home secretary over the police forces of the country have been steadily extended by acts of Parliament. In 1856 the secretary was empowered to appoint officials to inspect all police forces; those forces certified by the Home Office to be efficient received a government grant, which amounts to 50 percent. In 1919 the home secretary was given the right to make regulations dealing with such matters as pay, pensions, and conditions of service. In 1964 he was further empowered to compel the amalgamation of police forces. The police forces are grouped into eight regions for the provision of forensic-science laboratories, wireless services, criminal records, and crime squads.

In addition to the regular police force, chief constables may appoint special constables, unpaid volunteers who can be called upon to act as auxiliaries to the police. Police authorities appoint and pay traffic wardens, who have limited powers in relation to parking offenses and the direction of traffic.

Traffic wardens

The British police wear a uniform that is nonmilitary in appearance. Their only regular weapon is a short wooden truncheon, which they keep out of sight and which may not be employed except in self-defense or to restore order. Police engaged on dangerous missions may carry firearms for that specific occasion. (P.G.W./Ed.)

Cultural life

Widespread changes in the United Kingdom's cultural life have occurred since 1945. The most remarkable was perhaps the emergence first of Liverpool and then of London in the 1960s as a world centre of popular culture. The capital soon became a mecca for pleasure-seekers of all varieties, replacing, for many of them, the perennial popularity of Paris.

The new cultural milieu

The Beatles were only the first and best known of the many British rock-music groups to bring new dimensions to the musical tastes of Europe and the Americas. British clothing designers for a time led the world as innovators of new styles of dress for both men and women, and the brightly coloured, often extreme, outfits sold in Carnaby Street and King's Road shops perhaps became more symbolic of Britain than the traditionally staid tailoring of Savile Row and neighbouring streets, while flea markets as sources of bizarre clothing flourished in many large towns, particularly London. The long-established addiction of the British to betting and gambling was recognized in the easing of legal restrictions during the 1960s, which led to the establishment of casino-style gambling in London and other large cities, as well as to a boom in horse-racing betting shops.

More traditional fields also have experienced renewed vigour. In the decade after World War II the British motion picture industry came of age and set a standard of excellence that, by and large, it has continued to maintain. The steady stream of productions on London and provincial stages includes many new works by a large group of dramatists who are nearly as well represented on stages from New York City to Melbourne. Beginning in the 1930s, Britain has enjoyed an eminence as well in the visual arts, most notably in sculpture, in which a sense of the organic unity of form and material asserted itself.

Underlying these changes were several important social developments. Most evident was the rising standard of education. Increasingly large numbers of pupils are going on to higher education with a major expansion in the number of universities and other institutions of higher education. Within the schools, especially since the early

The social settings of the arts

1960s, emphasis was placed on creative activity and play. In society in general there was an increase in leisure.

During this same period, successive governments have shifted their policies toward the arts. The Arts Council, formed in 1946, provides widespread support for many kinds of contemporary creative and performing arts. This has coincided with a great expansion of the cultural market, mainly commercial, and of audiences and viewers for the arts generally. The ordinary person's life has been greatly changed by the more sophisticated standards of design that have developed in domestic equipment and home furnishing and decoration—as well as by the impact of television and radio. These changes have been accompanied by continuous argument about their nature and bearings and about the effects on the arts of a greatly expanded audience. A clash of tastes and values between generations and, to some extent, between social classes has been sharp, and the quality of the national life increasingly has been judged—favourably and unfavourably—in terms of current work in the arts. By comparison with any earlier period, this is a unique situation in Britain.

A notable postwar development in the United Kingdom has been proliferation of festivals involving one or several of the arts, of which the Edinburgh International Festival is the most ambitious. Other festivals are devoted to specialized art forms; these include the Three Choirs Festival in Gloucester and the Cheltenham Festival of contemporary music.

LITERATURE
Since World War II, the novel, social reporting, and criticism have attracted major attention. The several new movements in poetry have included vigorous revival of live readings for audiences, a movement perhaps sparked largely by the Welsh poet Dylan Thomas. Commercially, however, the many new little magazines that have appeared in Britain often have had difficulty in surviving, and the financial situation of all but a few best-selling authors has not improved in the proportion that might be expected from an enlarged readership.

THEATRE AND FILM

The performing arts

During the 20th century the number of theatres in Britain has fallen to less than one-half of those existing in 1900, and the financial situation of the living theatre remains precarious. At the same time, there has been continuous dramatic experiment, principally in the "little theatres" and in independent experimental companies, from the revival of verse drama in the 1930s and 1940s, through Joan Littlewood's Theatre Workshop in the 1950s and early 1960s, and to the English Stage Company at the Royal Court Theatre, London, from the 1950s onward. Many writers have turned back to the theatre or have developed through it: the work of John Arden, Arnold Wesker, John Osborne, and Harold Pinter is only the best known. In the 1950s a number of writers—playwrights, novelists, and critics—who were dubbed collectively as the Angry Young Men brought a new thrust of social criticism to British letters, perhaps most clearly evident in Osborne's *Look Back in Anger* (performed 1956). In 1968, after theatre censorship by the lord chamberlain ended, for a time the most obvious beneficiary of the new freedom was eroticism, though the resulting wave of staged nudity, often gratuitous, often proved unarousing.

The National Theatre Company began in 1963, and a National Theatre was built on the south bank of the Thames in Central London. The Royal Shakespeare Company, based at Stratford-upon-Avon and in London, has been vigorous and generally successful and, like other new developments, is supported by the Arts Council. More than 150 professional theatres, each seating at least 200 persons, operate as commercial or as nonprofit distributing companies, most of which receive Arts Council subsidies. Some three score of these theatres are located in or near London, though many operate touring productions to other areas. The many provincial theatres and companies, the growth of amateur drama groups, the support of theatre for young people, and sound dramatic training in academies and universities all provide further assur-

ance of the continued vitality of this traditionally richest of British arts.

In the late 1940s and early 1950s a series of social comedies made by Ealing Studios, such as *Kind Hearts and Coronets* and *Passport to Pimlico,* brought international acclaim to the British film industry. The most valuable new work has come, however, from relatively short-lived independent companies. Among important directors have been Tony Richardson, Lindsay Anderson, Joseph Losey, Karel Reisz, John Schlesinger, and Ken Russell. The nearness of film studios to the London stages has allowed directors and actors to pursue careers in both mediums to an extent unknown in the United States. A new school of actors emerged in the production of genre films based on working-class and provincial life, a movement that was at its finest in the late 1950s and early 1960s. Important films have also been made in Britain by major foreign directors, including the Italian Michelangelo Antonioni and the Frenchman Jean-Luc Godard. Organizational difficulties have severely restricted British filmmakers, however, and many of the younger generation have turned to the experimental work of the underground cinema, which is exhibited mainly by the many thriving British film societies or on television.

MUSIC
Music has gained a vast new public in Britain since the 1930s, at first through the influence of radio and, more recently, through the great expansion of record buying. Concerts draw substantial audiences in many of the larger towns, but the financial situation of orchestras has remained precarious and requires regular subsidies. There is also a continuing shortage of adequate concert halls in many towns. In the same period, there has been a remarkable expansion of popular music. In the 1960s British rock groups acquired international fame, providing models for similar groups in virtually every city of the world.

Covent Garden

Before 1945 it had proved very difficult to establish a permanent English opera company, and most singers and even choruses had come from abroad. Arrangements for a national opera theatre were developed at Covent Garden in London, between 1945 and 1947, and since that time it has become a world-renowned resident company. In addition to the international repertory, modern English-language operas by such composers as Benjamin Britten, Sir William Walton, and Michael Tippett have been performed. Though audiences are substantial, the heavy deficit has to be met partly by an Arts Council grant. Standards of performance and production have made Covent Garden one of the world's great opera houses. The Sadler's Wells Company, usually performing in English and undertaking more extensive tours both in Britain and abroad, in 1968 moved to a larger London theatre, the Coliseum. The English Opera Group, which is associated with the Royal Opera Company, presents works of smaller scale, a number of them new and experimental.

English ballet enjoys a high international esteem for both its direction and its dancing. In 1956 the Sadler's Wells Ballet, formed in 1931 under Ninette de Valois, became the Royal Ballet. From 1945 it was based at Covent Garden, where it is backed up by a Theatre Ballet and the Royal Ballet School. The company has won the highest reputation, both in the classical repertory and in the production of new works by English choreographers and composers. London's Festival Ballet has a mainly classical repertory, while the Ballet Rambert, a leading pioneer in English ballet since 1930, has returned to the experimental role of its earlier years. In spite of a shortage of suitable provincial theatres in the United Kingdom, a limited touring program is maintained by most British ballet companies.

VISUAL ARTS
The revival of the visual arts in Britain that began in the 1930s was effected largely through the work of the generation of painters born between 1890 and 1910: Ben Nicholson, Ivon Hitchens, Victor Pasmore, Sir Stanley Spencer, John Piper, and Graham Sutherland. They were followed by such artists as Francis Bacon, John Minton,

John Craxton, John Bratby, David Hockney, and Bridget Riley. Among sculptors, Henry Moore and Barbara Hepworth were followed by Reg Butler, Kenneth Armitage, Lynn Chadwick, Elisabeth Frink, and Anthony Caro. Public interest has been stimulated by sponsored exhibitions both in the national galleries and throughout the country and by the acquisition of new works of art for many public buildings and developments. Public sponsorship of individual artists has been undertaken, but commissions and purchases are more common. The Arts Council supports painting and sculpture by providing maintenance and purchase grants to galleries, commissions and awards to artists, grants for art education, and guarantees for exhibitions. Experimentation among the younger generation of artists has been not only in the pop-art field and in the expanded use of new materials but also in the interaction between art and industrial design.

A wide field of design, ranging from architecture to dress fashions, has experienced a remarkable growth of confidence and experiment. Though most apparent in inexpensive everyday objects—gaily coloured paper bags, for example—it shows up as well in furniture, textiles, pottery, toys, and, above all, clothes. Many young artist-designers choose to work not only in the industrial field but also in that part of it producing for the mass market. Since the late 1950s the look of Britain, not only in the capital but also very widely in the provinces, has been changed quite remarkably by their efforts, though a heavy legacy of bleak and dull industrial townscape still survives. Glass and steel skyscrapers owing their genesis to the modern international style of architecture have risen virtually alongside buildings echoing a centuries-older Britain.

Much of the excitement of this new work has been reflected in the art colleges of Britain, where controversies about the relations between art and design and about the proper place of art and design in the educational complex date at least from the 19th century. Public interest in design is fostered by the Council of Industrial Design, a government-grant-aided body established in 1944, which runs selective and changing displays of well-designed domestic products in London and Glasgow, maintains a Design Index of well-designed products, and promotes good design standards in industrial equipment.

Marginal note: Industrial and commercial arts

THE MASS MEDIA

The communications media—press, publishing, broadcasting, and entertainment—provide mass coverage in Great Britain, but their scale varies from the multi-million audiences for television, radio, and national newspapers to the small minority audiences for local papers, specialist periodicals, or experimental theatre and film that may count their following in a few thousands or even hundreds. Though the mass media in the United Kingdom have been subject to the economic trends toward concentration in large single-ownership groups, variety has been preserved in the expression of political views and the satisfaction of cultural tastes.

A tradition of editorial independence is recognized in newspaper groups, which give substantial freedom to the running of each of their newspapers and periodicals. This philosophy of independence extends to the state-owned British Broadcasting Corporation (BBC) and also to the Independent Television News (ITN), the news service that supplies the commercial television companies. It is well understood that broadcasting and the press, whether publicly or privately owned, will resist political pressures from government. The BBC, with a monopoly of radio until 1972, and with two out of four television channels, has been in practice as critically independent of government as have privately owned broadcasting media. A similar philosophy animates the work of the Arts Council, to which the government allocates a flat sum to cover all its work—with no strings attached. The Arts Council chooses its beneficiaries and distributes funds to a large number of organizations and individuals, so that creative independence may be preserved.

Marginal note: The tradition of editorial independence

The press. The structure of the British newspaper industry is derived from the dense population and the availability of a closely knit rail network, which has enabled newspapers published in London to sell all over the country the next morning. Hence a sharp division has emerged between national newspapers and the regional and local press.

Both in sales and reputation, the national papers dominate. Within the national-newspaper business in the United Kingdom, a distinction has grown up between popular papers with multi-million circulation and quality papers with relatively small sales. Four populars account for about 85 percent of the total morning paper circulation. In both groups, competition for circulation and advertising has been acute in a market in which total sales have been declining since the late 1950s, and some advertising has been diverted to television. With continuously escalating labour costs in the printing industry, the financial viability of some of the most prestigious papers, such as *The Times, The Guardian,* and *The Observer,* has been precarious. Both *The Times* and *The Guardian* have been run at a heavy loss, covered by the profits of other papers in their respective companies.

The variety of the newspaper and periodical press has been sustained by some of the newer and relatively cheap printing techniques. These have made it possible for fringe interests to publish their own papers cheaply and have provided scope for the "underground press," which has been probably rather more successful in outraging conventional opinion than influential in spreading its views of a "dropout," or alternative, society.

Broadcasting. A monopoly of both radio and television broadcasting was in the hands of the BBC, which had been established as an independent public corporation in 1927, until the establishment of the Independent Television Authority (ITA) in 1954. The ITA was intended to provide the facilities for a number of commercial television program companies. In 1972 the ITA became the Independent Broadcasting Authority (IBA) with responsibility also for commercial radio.

Marginal note: The BBC and ITA

The BBC draws its revenue from license fees (on a scale fixed by the government) from persons owning receiving sets. The IBA owns transmitters that it leases to the commercial program companies, which obtain their revenue from selling advertising time. The BBC operates two television channels, and the IBA operates one (with a second operated via a subsidiary that began operations in 1982). Since 1970 all channels have been in colour. Until 1972 the BBC had a monopoly of radio, but in that year Parliament authorized the creation of local commercial radio stations to be financed by advertising. The BBC's four programs are Radio 1 (mostly popular music), Radio 2 (mostly light music), Radio 3 (mostly classical music, and some programs of an intellectual content in the tradition of the BBC's famous Third Programme), and Radio 4 (mostly news, current affairs, and speech programs). In its second television channel the BBC has tended to put programs of above-average intellectual and cultural interest—competition that the IBA commercial channel meets with its own cultural programs. The BBC also operates a comprehensive external service, broadcasting around the world in 40 languages, as well as a world service in English 24 hours a day.

The BBC has won an international reputation for the impartiality and objectivity of its news services. The concept of public-service broadcasting requires the BBC to inform, to educate, and to entertain. As a public service, the BBC must maintain a fair balance in political argument and must not express political views of its own. Similar requirements have been placed on the IBA. Both the BBC and the IBA supply educational programs for schools and for adult studies. The Open University, offering degree courses to people who are without formal academic qualifications, is based on educational programs that are broadcast by the BBC; these programs are backed by correspondence courses.

Both the BBC and IBA are public bodies that in the last resort can be controlled by the government, and Parliament can alter the terms of their authority. The government has the statutory power to veto a broadcast, but this power has never been exercised, and the BBC and the IBA program companies are not interfered with in the day-today management of their affairs. Furthermore, on such rare occasions as the Suez crisis of 1956, when governmental pressure has been brought to bear on the BBC, the broadcasters successfully have asserted their independence. There have been complaints by politicians, however, that individual broadcasting producers sometimes have mis-

used their power, and objections by politicians may partly account for the disappearance of political satire, which floundered during the mid-1960s, from the BBC. Some viewers have complained persistently about what they consider to be the BBC's "permissive" attitude toward sex.   (Ed.)

HISTORY OF ENGLAND AND GREAT BRITAIN

Ancient Britain

Apart from a few short references in the classics, knowledge of Britain before the Roman conquest (begun AD 43) is derived entirely from archaeological research. It is thus lacking in detail, for archaeology can rarely identify personalities, motives, or exact dates. All that is available is a picture of successive cultures and some knowledge of economic development. But even in Roman times, Britain lay on the periphery of the civilized world, and Roman historians, for the most part, provide for that period only a framework into which the results of archaeological research can be fitted. Britain emerged into the light of true history only after the Saxon settlements in the 5th century AD.

Until late in the Mesolithic (Middle Stone) Age, Britain formed part of the continental landmass and was easily accessible to migrating hunters. The cutting of the landbridge, c. 6000–5000 BC, had important effects: migration became more difficult and remained for long impossible to large numbers. Thus Britain developed insular characteristics, absorbing and adapting rather than fully participating in successive continental cultures. And within the island geography worked to a similar end; the fertile southeast was more receptive of influence from the adjacent continent than were the less accessible hill areas of the west and north. Yet in certain periods the use of sea routes brought these too within the ambit of the continent.

From the end of the Ice Age (c. 11,000 BC), there was a gradual amelioration of climate leading to the replacement of tundra by forest and of reindeer hunting by that of red deer and elk. Valuable light on contemporary conditions was gained by the excavation of a lakeside settlement at Star Carr, Yorkshire, which was occupied for about 20 successive winters by hunting people in the 8th millennium BC.

PRE-ROMAN BRITAIN

Neolithic Age. A major change occurred c. 4000 BC with the introduction of agriculture by Neolithic immigrants from the coasts of western and possibly northwestern Europe. They were pastoralists as well as tillers of the soil. Tools were commonly of flint, which toward the close of the period was won by mining, but axes of volcanic rock were also traded by prospectors exploiting distant outcrops. The dead were buried in communal graves of two main kinds: in the west, tombs were built out of stone and concealed under mounds of rubble; in the stoneless eastern areas the dead were buried under long barrows (mounds of earth), which normally contained timber structures. Other evidence of religion comes from campsites (*e.g.,* Windmill Hill, Wiltshire), which are now believed to have been centres of ritual and of seasonal tribal feasting. From them developed, late in the 3rd millennium, more clearly ceremonial ditch-enclosed earthworks known as henge monuments. Some, like Durrington Walls, Wiltshire, are of great size and enclose subsidiary timber circles. British Neolithic culture thus developed an individuality of its own.

Bronze Age. Early in the 2nd millennium or perhaps even earlier, from c. 2300 BC, changes were introduced by the Beaker folk from the Low Countries and the middle Rhine. These people, whose round skulls differentiate them from the long-headed Neolithic people, buried their dead in individual graves, often with the drinking vessel that gives their culture its name. The earliest of them still used flint; later groups, however, brought a knowledge of metallurgy and were responsible for the exploitation of

gold and copper deposits in Britain and Ireland. They may also have introduced an Indo-European language. Control of the trade routes was soon taken over by the chieftains of Wessex, whose rich graves testify to their success as middlemen. Commerce was farflung, in one direction to Ireland and Cornwall and in the other to central Europe and the Baltic, whence amber was imported. Amber bead spacers from Wessex have been found in the shaft-graves at Mycenae in Greece. It was, perhaps, this contact which enabled the Wessex chieftains to construct the remarkable monument of shaped sarsens (large sandstones) known as Stonehenge III. Originally a late Neolithic henge, Stonehenge was uniquely transformed in Beaker times with a circle of large bluestone monoliths transported from southwest Wales.

Little is known in detail of the Middle Bronze Age and the Late Bronze Age. Because of present ignorance of domestic sites, these periods are mainly defined only by technological advances and changes in tools or weapons. In general, the southeast of Britain continued in close contact with the continent and the north and west with Ireland.

From about 1200 BC there is clearer evidence for agriculture in the south; the farms consisted of circular huts in groups with small oblong fields and stock enclosures. This type of farm became standard in Britain down to and into the Roman period. From the 8th century, expansion of continental Urnfield and Hallstatt groups brought new people (mainly the Celts) to Britain; at first, perhaps, these were small prospecting groups, but soon new settlements developed. Some of the earliest hill forts in Britain were constructed in this period (*e.g.,* Beacon Hill, near Ivinghoe, of Buckinghamshire; or Finavon, Angus); though formally belonging to the Late Bronze Age, they usher in the succeeding period.

Iron Age. The introduction of knowledge of iron was in fact merely incidental: it does not signify a change of population. The centuries 700–400 BC saw a succession of small migrations; the newcomers mingled easily with existing inhabitants. Yet the greater availability of iron facilitated land clearance and the growth of population. The earliest ironsmiths made daggers of the Hallstatt type but of distinctively British form; and the settlements were also of a distinctively British type with the traditional round house, the "Celtic" system of farming with its small fields, and storage pits for grain. Thus Britain absorbed the newcomers.

Conditions in the 4th century grew more disturbed. By the year 300 BC, swords were being made once more in place of daggers; hill forts grew more numerous and elaborate. Finally, from the 3rd century, a British form of La Tène Celtic art was developed to decorate warlike equipment such as scabbards, shields, and helmets, and eventually also bronze mirrors and even domestic pottery. During the 2nd century, the export of Cornish tin, noted before 300 by Pytheas of Massilia, a Greek explorer, continued; evidence of its destination is provided by the Paul (Cornwall) hoard of north Italian silver coins. In the 1st century BC this trade was in the hands of the Veneti of Brittany; their conquest (56 BC) by Julius Caesar, who destroyed their fleet, seems to have put an end to it.

By 200 Britain had fully developed its insular Celtic character. The emergence, however, of the British tribes known to Roman historians was due to a further phase of settlement, by tribesmen from Belgic Gaul. Coin finds suggest that the earliest movements of this migration began before the end of the 2nd century; the decisive settlements were made in the 1st century probably as a result of pressures

Stonehenge

Celtic field system

Ritual centres

in Gaul created by Germanic and Roman expansion. The result was a distinctive culture in southeast Britain (especially in Kent and north of the Thames), that represented a later phase of the continental Celtic La Tène culture. Its people used coins and the potter's wheel, cremated their dead, and their better equipment enabled them to begin the exploitation of heavier soils for agriculture.

ROMAN BRITAIN

The conquest. Caesar's description of Britain at the time of his invasions of 55 or 54 BC is the first coherent account extant, and it was his conquest of Gaul that brought the island into close contact with the Roman world. From about 20 BC it is possible to distinguish two principal powers: the Catuvellauni north of the Thames led by Tasciovanus, successor of Caesar's adversary Cassivellaunus, and, south of the river, the kingdom of the Atrebates ruled by Commius and his sons Tincommius, Eppillus, and Verica. Tasciovanus was succeeded in about AD 5 by his son Cunobelinus, who, during a long reign, established a paramount power all over the southeast, which he ruled from Camulodunum (Colchester). Beyond these kingdoms lay the Iceni in what is now Norfolk, the Coritani in the Midlands, the Dobuni (Dobunni) in the area of Gloucestershire, and the Durotriges in that of Dorset, all of whom issued coins and probably had Belgic rulers. Behind these again lay further independent tribes—the Dumnonii of Devon, the Brigantes of Yorkshire, the Silures and Ordovices in Wales. It was the Belgic and semi-Belgic tribes who later formed the civilized nucleus of the Roman province: the Belgic contribution to Roman Britain is great.

The client relationships that Caesar had established with certain British tribes were extended by Augustus. In particular, the Atrebatic kings welcomed Roman aid in their resistance to Catuvellaunian expansion. The decision of the emperor Claudius to conquer the island was the result partly of his personal ambition, partly of British aggression. Verica had been driven from his kingdom and appealed for help, and it may have been calculated that a hostile Catuvellaunian supremacy would endanger stability across the Channel. Under Aulus Plautius an army of four legions was assembled, together with a number of auxiliary regiments consisting of cavalry and infantry raised among warlike tribes subject to the empire. After delay caused by the troops' unwillingness to cross the ocean, which they then regarded as the boundary of the human world, a landing was made at Richborough, Kent, in AD 43. The British under Togodumnus and Caratacus, sons and successors of Cunobelinus, were taken by surprise and defeated. They retired to defend the Medway crossing near Rochester but were again defeated in a hard battle. The way to Camulodunum lay open, but Plautius halted at the Thames to await the arrival of the emperor, who took personal command of the closing stages of the campaign. In one short season, the main military opposition had been crushed: Togodumnus was dead and Caratacus fled to Wales. The rest of Britain was by no means united, for Belgic expansion had created tensions. Some tribes submitted, and the overrunning of the rest remained the task for the year 44. For this purpose smaller expeditionary forces were formed consisting of single legions or parts of legions with their *auxilia* (subsidiary allied troops). The best documented campaign is that of Legion II under its legate Vespasian starting from Chichester, where the Atrebatic kingdom was restored; the Isle of Wight was taken, and the hill forts of Dorset reduced. Legion IX advanced into Lincolnshire, and Legion XIV probably across the Midlands toward Leicester. Colchester was the chief base, but the fortresses of individual legions at this stage have not yet been identified.

By the year 47, when Plautius was succeeded as com-

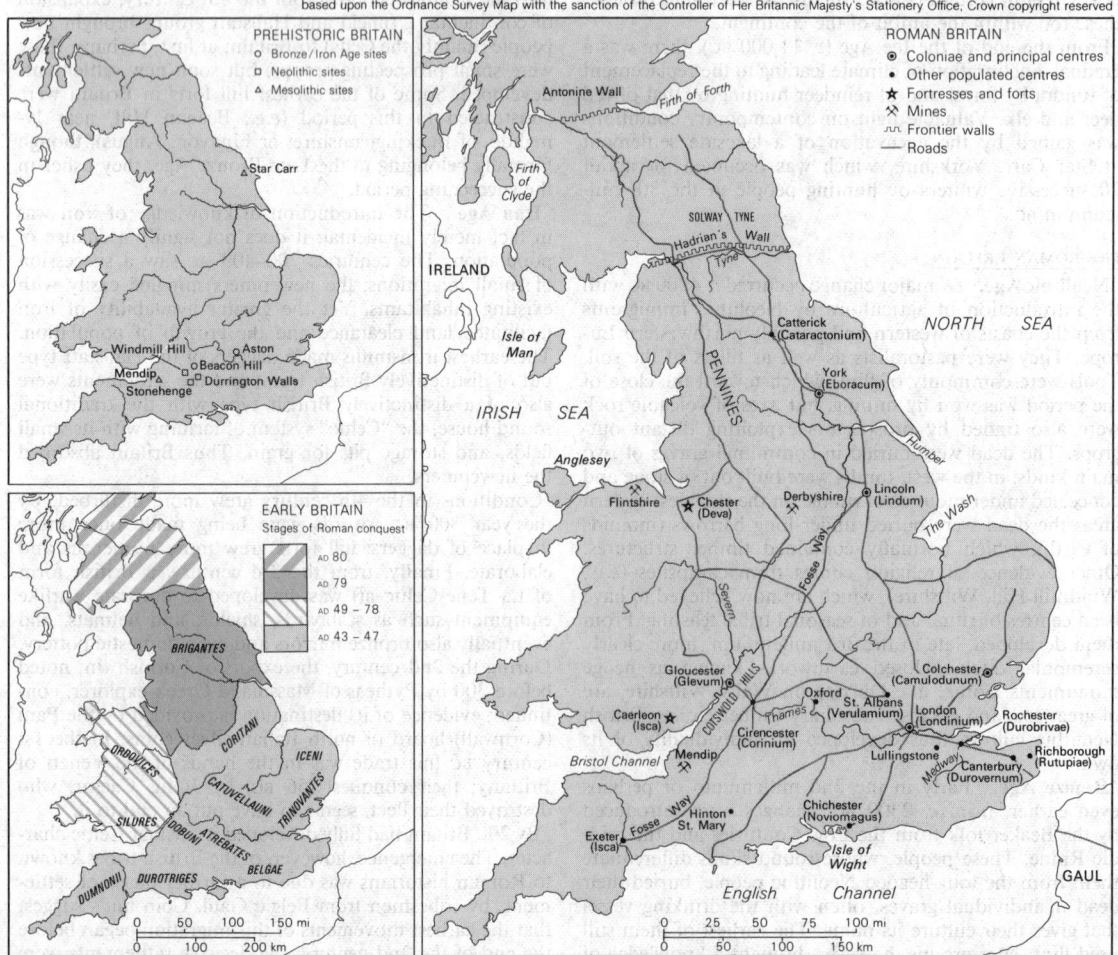

Ancient Britain.

manding officer by Ostorius Scapula, a frontier had been established from Exeter to the Humber based on the road known as the Fosse Way; from this fact it appears that Claudius did not plan the annexation of the whole island but only of the arable southeast. The intransigence of the tribes of Wales spurred on by Caratacus, however, caused Scapula to occupy the lowlands beyond the Fosse Way up to the River Severn and to move forward his forces into this area for the struggle with the Silures and Ordovices; they were strengthened by the addition of Legion XX, released for this purpose by the foundation of a veteran settlement (*colonia*) at Camulodunum in the year 49. The *colonia* would form a strategic reserve as well as setting the Britons an example of Roman urban organization and life. A provincial centre for the worship of the emperor was also established. Scapula's right flank was secured by the treaty relationship that had been established with Cartimandua, queen of the Brigantes. Hers was the largest kingdom in Britain, occupying the whole area between Derbyshire and the Tyne; unfortunately it lacked stability, nor was it united behind its queen, who lost popularity when she surrendered the British resistance leader, Caratacus, to the Romans. Nevertheless, with occasional Roman military support, Cartimandua was maintained in power down to 69 against the opposition led by her husband, Venutius, and this enabled Roman governors to concentrate on Wales.

By AD 60 much success had been achieved; Suetonius Paulinus, governor from 59 to 61, was invading the island of Anglesey, the last stronghold of independence, when a serious setback occurred: this was the rebellion **Boudicca's** of Boudicca, queen of the Iceni. This tribe had enjoyed **rebellion** a position of alliance and independence under its king Prasutagus; but on his death (60) the territory was forcibly annexed and outrages occurred. Boudicca was able to rally other tribes to her assistance; chief of these were the Trinovantes of Essex, who had many grievances against the settlers of Camulodunum for their arrogant seizure of lands. Roman forces were distant and scattered; and, before peace could be restored, the rebels had sacked Camulodunum, Verulamium (St. Albans), and London, the three chief centres of Romanized life in Britain. Paulinus acted harshly after his victory, but the procurator of the province, Julius Classicianus, with the revenues in mind and perhaps also because, as a Gaul by birth, he possessed a truer vision of provincial partnership with Rome, brought about his recall.

In the first 20 years of occupation, some progress had been made in spreading Roman civilization. Towns had been founded, the imperial cult had been established, and merchants were busily introducing the Britons to material benefits. It was not, however, until the Flavian Period, AD 69–96, that real advances were made in this field. With the occupation of Wales by Julius Frontinus (governor from 74 to 78) and the advance into northern Scotland by Gnaeus Julius Agricola (78–84), troops were removed from southern Britain, and self-governing *civitates,* administrative areas based for the most part on the indigenous tribes, took over local administration. This involved a large program of urbanization and also of education, which continued on into the 2nd century; Tacitus, in his biography of Agricola, emphasizes the encouragement given to it. The conquest of Wales was complete by 78, but Agricola's invasion of Scotland failed through shortage of manpower to complete the occupation of the whole island, and when the British garrison was reduced (c. AD 90) by a legion because of continental needs, it became evident that a frontier would have to be maintained in the north. After several experiments, the Solway–Tyne isthmus was chosen, and there the emperor Hadrian built his stone wall (c. 122–130).

Condition of the province. There was a marked contrast in attitude toward the Roman occupation between the lowland Britons and the inhabitants of Wales and of the hill country of the north. The economy of the former was that of settled agriculture, and they were largely of Belgic stock; they soon accepted, and appreciated, the Roman way of life. The economy of the hill dwellers was pastoral; to them the urban civilization of Rome

threatened their freedom of life. Resistance in Wales was stamped out by the end of the 1st century AD, but even so, Roman influences were weak except in the plain of Glamorgan. In the Pennines until the beginning of the 3rd century there were repeated rebellions, the more dangerous because of the threat of assistance from free Scotland.

Army and frontier. After the emperor Domitian had reduced the garrison in about the year 90, three legions remained; their permanent bases were established at York, Chester, and Caerleon. The legions formed the foundation of Roman military power, but they were supplemented in garrison duty by numerous smaller auxiliary regiments both of cavalry and infantry, either 1,000 or 500 strong. These latter garrisoned the wall and were stationed in a network of other forts established for police work in Wales and northern England. With 15,000 legionaries, and about 40,000 auxiliaries, the army of Britain was very powerful; its presence had economic as well as political results. Hadrian's Wall was the most impressive frontier-work in **Hadrian's** the Roman empire. Despite a period in the following two **Wall** reigns when another frontier was laid out on the Glasgow–Edinburgh line—the Antonine Wall, built of turf— the wall of Hadrian came to be the permanent frontier of Roman Britain. The northern tribes only twice succeeded in passing it, and then at moments when the garrison was fighting elsewhere. In the late Roman period, when searaiding became prevalent, the wall lost its preeminence as a defense for the province, but it was continuously held until the end of the 4th century. But although they withdrew to Hadrian's line not later than the year 196, the Romans never abandoned interest in southern Scotland. In the 2nd century their solution was military occupation. In the 3rd, after active campaigning (208–211) by the emperor Septimius Severus and his sons during which permanent bases were built on the east coast of Scotland, the solution adopted by the emperor Caracalla was regulation of relationship by treaties. These, perhaps supported by subsidies, were enforced by supervision of the whole Lowlands by patrols based on forts beyond the wall. During the 4th century, more and more reliance was placed on friendly native states, and patrols were withdrawn.

Administration. Britain was an imperial province. The governor represented the emperor, exercising supreme military as well as civil jurisdiction. As commander of three legions, he was a senior general of consular rank. From the late 1st century, he was assisted on the legal side by a *legatus juridicus.* The finances were in the hands **Finance** of the provincial procurator, an independent official of **and** equestrian status whose staff supervised imperial domains **taxation** and the revenues of mines in addition to normal taxation. In the early 3rd century, Britain was divided into two provinces in order to reduce the power of its governor to rebel as Albinus had done in 196: Britannia Superior had its capital at London and a consular governor in control of two legions and a few auxiliaries; Britannia Inferior, with its capital at York, was under a praetorian governor with one legion but many more auxiliaries.

Local administration was of varied character. First came the chartered towns. By the year 98, Lincoln and Gloucester had joined Camulodunum as *coloniae,* and by 237 York had become a fourth. *Coloniae* of Roman citizens enjoyed autonomy with a constitution based on that of republican Rome, and Roman citizens had various privileges before the law. It is likely that Verulamium was chartered as a Latin *municipium* (free town); in such a town the annual magistrates were rewarded with Roman citizenship. The remainder of the provincials ranked as *peregrini* (subjects). In military districts control was in the hands of fort prefects responsible to legionary commanders; but, by the late 1st century, local self-government, as already stated, was granted to *civitates peregrinae,* whose number tended to increase with time. These also had republican constitutions, being controlled by elected councils and annual magistrates and having responsibility for raising taxes and administering local justice. In the 1st century there were also client kingdoms whose rulers were allied to Rome; Cogidubnus, Verica's successor, who had his capital at Chichester, is the best known. But Rome regarded these as temporary expedients, and none outlasted the Flavian Period (69–96).

Society. Pre-Roman Celtic tribes had been ruled by kings and aristocracies; the Roman *civitates* remained in the hands of the rich because of the heavy expense of office. But since trade and industry now yielded increasing profits, and the old aristocracies no longer derived wealth from war but only from large estates, it is likely that new men rose to power. Roman citizenship was now an avenue **Roman** of social advancement, and it could be obtained by 25 **citizenship** years' service in the auxiliary forces as well as (more rarely) by direct grants. Soldiers and traders from other parts of the empire significantly enhanced the cosmopolitan character of the population, nor should the large number of legionaries be forgotten: they were already citizens and many must have settled locally. The population of Roman Britain at its peak amounted perhaps to about 2,000,000.

Economy. Even before the conquest, according to the Greek geographer Strabo, Britain exported gold, silver, iron, hides, slaves, and hounds in addition to grain. A Roman gold mine is known in Wales, but its yield was not outstanding. Iron was worked in many places but only for local needs; silver, obtained from lead, was of more significance, but the basis of the economy was agriculture, and the conquest greatly stimulated production because of the requirements of the army. According to Tacitus, grain to feed the troops was levied as a tax; correspondingly more had to be grown before a profit could be made. The pastoralists in Wales and the north probably had to supply leather, which the Roman army needed in quantity for tents, boots, uniforms, and shields. A military tannery is known at Catterick. A profit could, nonetheless, be won from the land because of the increasing demand from the towns, and at the same time the development of a system of large estates (villas) relieved the ancient "Celtic" farming system of the necessity of shouldering the whole burden. Small peasant farmers tended to till the lighter, less productive, easier-worked soils. Villa estates were established on heavier richer soils, sometimes on land recently won by forest clearance, itself a result of the enormous new demand for building timber from the army and the new towns and for fuel for domestic heating and for public baths. The villa owners had access to the precepts of classical farming manuals and also to the improved equipment made available by Roman technology. Their growing prosperity is vouched for by excavation: there are few villas that did not increase in size and luxury as corridors and wings were added or mosaics and bath blocks provided. At least by the 3rd century, some landowners were finding great profit in wool; Diocletian's price edict (AD 301) shows that at least two British cloth products had won an empire-wide reputation. Archaeological evidence indicates that the Cotswold district was one of the centres of this industry.

Trade in imported luxury goods ranging from wine to table wares and bronze trinkets was vastly increased as traders swarmed in behind the army to exploit new markets. The profits of developing industries went similarly at first to foreign capitalists. This is clearly seen in the exploitation of silver-lead and even in the pottery industry. The Mendip lead-field was being worked under military control as early as the year 49, but under Nero (54–68) both there and in Flintshire, and not much later also in the Derbyshire lead-field, freedmen—the representatives of Roman capital—were at work. By Vespasian's reign (69–79) organized companies (*societates*) of prospectors are attested. Roman citizens, who must in the context be freedmen, are also found organizing the pottery industry in the late 1st century. Large profits were made by continental businessmen in the first two centuries not only from such sources but also by the import on a vast scale of high-class pottery from Gaul and the Rhineland, and on a lesser scale of glass vessels, luxury metalware, and Spanish oil and wine. A large market existed among the military, and the Britons themselves provided a second. Eventually this adverse trade balance was rectified by the gradual capture of the market by British products. Much of the exceptional prosperity of 4th-century Britain must have been due to its success in retaining available profits at home.

A final important point is the role of the Roman army in the economic development of the frontier regions. The presence as consumers of large forces in northern Britain created a revolution in previous patterns of trade and civilized settlement. Cereal production was encouraged in regions where it had been unknown, and large settlements grew up in which many of the inhabitants must have been retired soldiers with an interest in the land as well as in trade and industry.

Towns. Belgic Britain had large centres of population but not towns in the Roman sense, which meant not merely streets and public buildings but also the amenities and local autonomy of a city. In Britain these had therefore to be provided if Roman civilization and normal methods of provincial administration were to be introduced. Thus an urbanizing policy existed in which the assistance of the **Urbaniza-** legions, as the nearest convenient source of architects and **tion** craftsmen, played an organizing role. The earlier towns consisted of half-timbered buildings; before AD 100 only public buildings seem to have been of stone. The administrative capitals had regular street grids, a forum with basilica (public hall), public baths, and temples; a few had theatres and amphitheatres, too. With few exceptions they were undefended. Town walls were provided in the 3rd century, not so much as a precaution in unsettled times as a means of keeping operational the earthwork defenses already provided to meet a crisis at the end of the 2nd century. In size these towns grew to about 100–130 acres with populations of about 5,000; a few were twice this size. The majority of towns in Roman Britain seem to have developed out of traders' settlements in the vicinity of early garrison-forts: those that were not selected as administrative centres remained dependent on economic factors as centres of trade or manufacture or else as markets for the agricultural peasantry. They varied considerably in size. In the north, where garrisons were permanently established, quite large trading settlements grew up in their vicinity, and at least some of these would rank as towns.

Villas. Apart from the exceptional establishment at Fishbourne, in West Sussex, whose Italian style and luxurious fittings show that it was the palace of King Cogidubnus, the houses of Roman-British villas had simple beginnings and were of a provincial type. A few were prosperous enough in the 2nd century to afford mosaics; but the great period of villa prosperity lay in the 4th century, when many villas grew to impressive size. Their importance was economic and has already been described. Much remains to be learnt from full excavation of their subsidiary work buildings. Larger questions of tenure and organization are probably insoluble in the absence of documentary evidence, for it is dangerous to draw analogies from classical sources since conditions in Celtic Britain were very different from those of the Mediterranean world.

Religion and culture. A great variety of religious cults were to be found, for, in addition to numerous Celtic deities of local or wider significance, the gods of the classical pantheon were introduced and were often identified with their Celtic counterparts. In official circles the worship of the state gods of Rome and of the imperial cult was duly observed. In addition merchants and soldiers introduced oriental cults, among them Christianity. The latter, however, made little headway until the late 4th century, though the frescoes at Lullingstone in Kent and the mosaics at Hinton St. Mary in Dorset attest its presence among villa owners. Classical temples are sometimes found in towns, but the normal temple was of the Romano-Celtic type with a small square shrine and surrounding portico; these are found in town and country alike.

Romanization was strongest in the towns and among the upper classes, as would be expected; there is evidence that in the countryside Celtic continued to be spoken, though it was not written. Many people were bilingual: graffiti prove that even artisans wrote Latin. Evidence of the classical education of the villa owners is provided by their mosaics, which prove an acquaintance with classical mythology and even with the *Aeneid* of Virgil. Sculpture and wall painting were both novelties in Roman Britain. Statues or busts in bronze or marble were imported from Gaulish or Mediterranean workshops, but British sculptors

Mosaics

soon learned their trade and at their best produced attractive works in a provincial idiom, very often for votive purposes. Many cruder works were also executed: their interest lies in the proof they afford that the conventions of the classical world had penetrated even to the lower classes. Mosaic floors are found in towns and villas, at first, as at Fishbourne, laid by imported craftsmen; there is evidence that by the middle of the 2nd century a local firm was at work at Colchester and Verulamium, and in the 4th century, a number of local mosaic workshops can be recognized by their styles. One of the most skilled of these was based in Cirencester.

Roman civilization thus took root in Britain. The resulting growth was more obvious in urban circles than among the agricultural peasants and weakest in the resistant highland zone. It was a provincial version of Roman culture, but one with recognizably British traits.

The decline of Roman rule. The reforms of Diocletian ended the chaos of the 3rd century and ushered in the late imperial period. Britain, however, for a short period became a separate empire through the rebellion (286/287) of Carausius. This man had commanded against the Saxon pirates in the Channel and by his naval power was able to maintain his independence. His main achievement was to complete the new system of Saxon Shore forts around the southeastern coasts. At first he sought recognition as co-emperor, but this was refused; in 293 the fall of Boulogne to Roman forces led to his murder and the accession of Allectus, who, however, fell in his turn when Constantius I invaded Britain in 296. Allectus had withdrawn troops from the north to oppose the landing, and Hadrian's Wall seems to have been attacked, for Constantius had to restore the frontier as well as to reform the administration. He divided Britain into four provinces, and in the same period the civil power was separated from the military. Late Roman sources show three separate commands respectively under the *dux Britanniarum* (commander of the Britains), the *comes litoris Saxonici* (count of the Saxon Shore), and the *comes Britanniarum,* though the dates of their establishment are unknown and may not have been identical. The 4th century was a period of great prosperity in towns and countryside alike. Britain had escaped the invasions of the 3rd century and may have seemed a safe refuge for wealthy continentals. Its weakness lay in the fact that its defense was ultimately controlled by distant rulers rather than by local responsibility. The garrison was perhaps weakened by withdrawals for the civil war of Magnentius (350–351); at any rate in 367 there was a military disaster due to concerted sea-borne attacks from the Picts of Scotland and the Scots of Ireland. But, though the frontier and forts behind it suffered severely, there is little trace of damage to towns or villas. Count Theodosius in 369 restored the situation and strengthened the defenses of the towns with external towers designed to mount artillery. Prosperity continued, but there were ominous withdrawals of troops by Magnus Maximus in 383 and again at the end of the century by Stilicho. Thus, when in 407 Constantine III was declared emperor by the army in Britain and took further troops to Gaul, the forces remaining in the island were insufficient to provide protection against increasing Pictish and Saxon raids. The Britons appealed to the legitimate emperor, Honorius, who was unable to send assistance but authorized the cities to provide for their own defense (410). This marks the end of Roman Britain, for the central government never re-established control: but for a generation there was little other outward change.

The rise of tyrants

Power fell gradually into the hands of tyrants. Chief of these was Vortigern (*c.* 425), but he, unlike earlier usurpers, made no attempt to become Roman emperor, being content with power in Britain. Independence was producing separate interests. By this date Christianity had made considerable headway in the island, but the leaders followed the heretical teaching of Pelagius, himself a Briton, who had emphasized the importance of the human will over divine grace in the achievement of salvation. It has been held that the self-reliance shown in the maintenance of national independence was inspired by this philosophy. Yet there was also a powerful Catholic party

anxious to reforge the links with Rome, in support of whom St. Germanus of Auxerre visited Britain in 429. It may have been partly to thwart the plans of this party that Vortigern made the mistake (*c.* 430; the "traditional" date given by Bede is between 446 and 454) of inviting Saxons to settle and garrison strategic areas of the east coast, though he certainly also had in mind the need to ward off sea-borne raids by Picts, which at this time were troublesome. Planned settlement of this sort is the best explanation for the earliest Saxon settlements found around the mouths of the east coast estuaries and also in the central-southeast region around Oxford. For a time the system worked successfully; but when, in 442, these Saxon *foederati* ("allies") rebelled and called in others of their race to help them, it was found that they had been given a stranglehold on Britain. A long period of warfare and chaos was inaugurated that was economically disastrous. It was probably this period that saw the disintegration of the majority of the villa estates; with the breakdown of markets and the escape of slaves, villas ceased to be viable and must have gradually fallen into ruin, though the land itself did not cease to be cultivated. A few villas met a violent end. The towns, under the protection of their strong defenses, at first provided refuge at any rate for the rich who could leave their lands; but by degrees decay set in as trade declined and finally the supply of food was itself threatened. In about 446 the British made a vain appeal for help to the Roman general Aetius (the "Groans of the Britons" mentioned in the *De excidio et conquestu Britanniae* of the British writer Gildas). For several decades they suffered reverses; many emigrated to Brittany. In the second half of the 5th century Ambrosius Aurelianus and the shadowy figure of Arthur began to turn the tide by the use of cavalry against the ill-armed Saxon infantry. A great victory was won at Mons Badonicus (a site not identifiable) toward 500: now it was Saxons who emigrated, and the British lived in peace all through the first half of the 6th century, as Gildas records. But in the second half the situation slowly worsened.

(S.S.F.)

Anglo-Saxon England

THE INVADERS AND THEIR EARLY SETTLEMENTS

Germanic tribes began to settle in Britain from about the middle of the 5th century AD. The first arrivals, according to the 6th-century British writer Gildas, were invited by a British king to defend his kingdom against the Picts and Scots. A tradition reached the historian Bede that the first settlers were from three tribes—the Angles, Saxons, and Jutes—which he locates on the Cimbric Peninsula and the coastlands of northwestern Germany, though the Jutes should perhaps be connected with the Rhineland rather than with Jutland, where Bede, by implication, puts them. Early settlements, near the coasts and the basins of navigable rivers in eastern and southern Britain, were halted about 500 by the Britons at the Battle of Mons Badonicus at an unidentified location; but a new Germanic drive began about 550, and before the century had ended the Britons had been driven west to the borders of Dumnonia (Cornwall and Devon) and to the Welsh Marches, while invaders were advancing west of the Pennines and northward into Lothian.

The distinction between the three Germanic tribes soon lost significance; certainly by the end of the 7th century men regarded themselves as "the nation of the English," though divided into several kingdoms. They were conscious of their kinship with the continental Germans and were little influenced by the civilization of the previous inhabitants (thus forming a striking contrast to the Germanic tribes that settled in Gaul); few Britons in England were above servile condition. This sense of unity was strengthened during long periods when all kingdoms south of the Humber acknowledged the overlordship (called by Bede an *imperium*) of a single ruler, known as a *bretwalda,* a word first recorded in the 9th century.

The first such overlord was Aelle of Sussex, in the late 5th century; the second was Ceawlin of Wessex, who died in 593. The third overlord, Aethelberht of Kent, held this power in 597 when the monk Augustine led a mission from Rome to Kent; Kent was the first English kingdom to be converted to Christianity. The Christian Church provided another unifying influence, overriding political divisions, although it was not until 669 that the church in England acknowledged a single head.

The social system.   When Aethelberht set a code of laws down in writing, under Christian influence, the system underlying the laws was already old, in its main lines

Adapted from R. Treharne and H. Fullard (eds.), *Muir's Historical Atlas: Ancient, Medieval and Modern*, 9th ed. (1965); George Philip & Son Ltd., London

Anglo-Saxon England.

brought over from the Continent. Its strongest bond was that of kinship; every free man depended on his kindred for protection, and the social classes were distinguished by the amount of their wergild (the sum that the kindred could accept in place of vengeance if a man were killed). The normal free man was the *ceorl*, an independent peasant landowner; below him in Kent were persons with lower wergilds, who were either freedmen or, as were similar persons in Wessex, members of a subject population; above the *ceorls* were the nobles—some perhaps noble by birth but more often men who had risen by service as companions of the king—with a wergild three times that of a *ceorl* in Kent, six times that of a *ceorl* elsewhere. The tie that bound a man to his lord was as strong as that of the kindred. Both nobles and *ceorls* might possess slaves, who had no wergild and were regarded as chattels.

The rights of the king   The king had special rights—compensations for offenses committed in his presence or his home or against anyone under his protection; rights to hospitality, which later became a food rent charged on all land; and rights to various services. He rewarded his followers with grants of land, probably at first for their lifetime only; but the need to provide permanent endowment for the church brought into being a type of land free from most royal dues and that did not revert to the king. From the latter part of the 7th century such land was sometimes conferred by charter. It became common to make similar grants by charter to laymen, with power to bequeath; but three services—the building of forts and bridges and service in the army—were almost invariably excepted from the immunity. The king received fines for various crimes; but a man's guilt was established in an assembly of freemen, where the accused tried to establish his innocence by his oath—supported by oath helpers—and, if this failed, by ordeal.

On matters of importance, the king normally consulted his *witan* (wise men).

There were local variations in the law. And over a period of time the law developed to meet changed circumstances. As kingdoms grew larger, for example, an official called an "ealdorman" was needed to administer part of the area, and, later, a sheriff was needed to look after the royal rights in each shire. The acceptance of Christianity made it necessary to fit the clergy into the scale of compensations and assign a value to their oaths and to fix penalties for offenses such as sacrilege, heathen practices, and breaches of the marriage law. But the basic principles were little changed.

The conversion to Christianity.   Place-names containing the names of gods or other heathen elements are plentiful enough to prove the vitality of heathenism and to account for the slow progress of conversion in some areas. In Kent, the first kingdom to accept Christianity, King Wihtred's laws in 695 contained clauses against heathen worship. The conversion renewed relations with Rome and the Continent; but the full benefit of this was delayed by the conversion of much of England by the Celtic Church, which had lost contact with Rome.

Augustine's mission in 597 converted Kent; but it had only temporary success in Essex, which reverted to heathenism in 616. A mission sent from Kent under Paulinus to Northumbria that, in 627, converted King Edwin and many of his subjects in Northumbria and Lindsey received a setback in 632 when Edwin was killed and Paulinus withdrew to Kent. About 630 Archbishop Honorius of Canterbury sent a Burgundian, Felix, to convert East Anglia, and the East Anglian church thenceforth remained faithful to Canterbury. Soon after, the West Saxons were converted by Birinus, who came from Rome. Meanwhile, King Oswald began to restore Christianity in Northumbria, bringing Celtic missionaries from Iona. And it was the Celtic Church that began in 653 to spread the faith among the Middle Angles, the Mercians, and the peoples of the Severn Valley; it also won back Essex.

At first there was little friction between the Roman and Celtic missions. Oswald of Northumbria joined with Cynegils of Wessex in giving Dorchester-on-Thames as seat for Birinus' bishopric; the Irishmen Maildubh in Wessex and Fursey in East Anglia worked in areas converted by the Roman Church; and James the Deacon continued Paulinus' work in Northumbria. Later, however, differences in usage—especially in the calculation of the date of Easter—caused controversy, which was settled in favour of the Roman party at the Synod of Whitby in 664. The adherents of Celtic usage conformed or withdrew, and advocates of Roman practice became active in the north, the Midlands, and Essex. Theodore of Tarsus (arrived 669), the first archbishop to be acknowledged all over England, was active in establishing a proper diocesan system, whereas in the Celtic Church bishops tended to move freely without fixed sees and settled boundaries; he held the first synod of the English church at Hertford in 672, and this forbade a bishop to interfere in another's diocese or any priest to move into another diocese without his bishop's permission. Sussex and the Isle of Wight—the last outposts of heathenism—were converted by Bishop Wilfrid and his followers from 681 to 687 and thenceforth followed Roman usages.

The Anglo-Saxons attributed their conversion to Pope Gregory I, "the Apostle of the English," who had sent Augustine. This may seem less than fair to the Celtic mission, but modern scholars have tended to undervalue the work of the Roman Church. The Celtic Church made a great impression by its asceticism, fervour, and simplicity, and it had a lasting influence on scholarship. Yet the period of Celtic dominance was only 30 years. The decision at Whitby reunited the English to the universal church and made possible a form of organization better fitted for permanent needs than the looser system of the Celtic Church.

The conversion of the English was hardly completed before they began to take the faith to the continental Germans. The earliest missionaries were Northumbrians who worked in Frisia. Wilfrid converted some Frisians in the winter of 677 on his way to Rome, but the permanent

Early Northumbrian missionaries

conversion began about 690 with the work of Willibrord, a Northumbrian missionary.

Willibrord converted Frankish Frisia and founded the see of Utrecht. He was joined by the West Saxon Wynfrith (better known as Boniface), who worked with him from 718 to 721. Boniface's main missionary work was in Thuringia and Hesse. The Pope consecrated him bishop to the Germans in 722, archbishop in 732. In addition to his success as a missionary and his founding of sees among the Germans, Boniface reorganized the church of Bavaria and helped the Frankish leaders Pippin and Carloman to reform the Frankish church, bringing it into relations with the papacy and thus profoundly affecting Frankish history. He was joined by many men and women from England, mainly from Wessex. Boniface was martyred by the heathens in northern Frisia in 754.

The "Golden Age" of Bede. Within a century of Augustine's landing, England was in the forefront of scholarship. This high standard arose from a combination of influences: that from Ireland, which had escaped the decay caused elsewhere by the barbarian invasions, and that from the Mediterranean, which reached England mainly through Archbishop Theodore and his companion, the abbot Adrian. Under Theodore and Adrian, Canterbury became a famous school, and men trained there took their learning to other parts of England. One of these was Aldhelm, who had been a pupil of Maildubh (the Irish founder of Malmesbury); under Aldhelm, Malmesbury became an influential centre of learning. Aldhelm's own works, in Latin verse and prose, reveal a familiarity with many Latin authors; his writings became popular among admirers of the ornate and artificial style he had learned from his Celtic teachers. Before long a liberal education could be had at such other West Saxon monasteries as Nursling and Wimborne.

The finest centre of scholarship was Northumbria. There Celtic and classical influences had met: missionaries brought books from Ireland, and many Englishmen went to Ireland to study. Other Northumbrians went abroad, especially to Rome; among them was Benedict Biscop. Benedict returned from Rome with Theodore (668–669) and spent some time in Canterbury, and he brought the learning acquired there to Northumbria. He founded the monasteries at Wearmouth (674) and Jarrow (682), where Bede spent his life. Benedict and Ceolfrith, abbot of Jarrow, brought books from the Continent and assembled the fine library that was available to Bede.

Bede (c. 672–735) is remembered as a great historian whose work has never lost its value; but he was also a theologian regarded throughout the Middle Ages as second only to the Church Fathers. Though he was outstanding, he did not work in isolation. Other Northumbrian houses—Lindisfarne, Whitby, and Ripon—produced saints' lives, and Bede was in touch with many learned men, not only in Northumbria; there are also signs of scholarly activity in London and in East Anglia.

Moreover, in this period religious poetry was composed in the diction and technique of the older vernacular, secular poetry. *Beowulf,* considered the greatest Old English poem, is sometimes assigned to this age, but the dating is uncertain. Art flourished, with a combination of native elements and of influences from Ireland and the Mediterranean. The Hiberno-Saxon (or Anglo-Irish) style of illumination was evolved, its greatest example—the Lindisfarne Gospels—also showing classical influence. Masons from Gaul and Rome built stone churches. In Northumbria stone monuments with figure sculpture and vine-scroll patterns were set up. Churches were equipped with precious objects—some from abroad, some of native manufacture (even in heathen times the English had been skilled metalworkers). Manuscripts and works of art were taken abroad to churches founded by the English missions, and these churches, in turn, became centres of production.

Visual arts and architecture

THE HEPTARCHY

The supremacy of Northumbria and the rise of Mercia. When Northumbria became eminent in scholarship, its age of political importance was over. This political dominance had begun when Aethelfrith, ruling over the united Northumbrian kingdoms of Bernicia and Deira, defeated the Dalriadic Scots at Degsastan in 603 and the Welsh at Chester in 613–616. Aethelfrith was himself defeated and killed in 616 by Edwin, the exiled heir to Deira, with the help of Raedwald of East Anglia, then overlord of the southern peoples.

Edwin continued to defeat the Welsh and became the acknowledged overlord of all England except Kent: he annexed the British kingdom of Elmet, invaded North Wales, and captured Anglesey and the Isle of Man. But he fell at Hatfield in 632 before the forces of Cadwallon, king of Gwynedd, and of Penda, a Mercian chieftain. A year later Aethelfrith's son Oswald destroyed Cadwallon and restored the kingdom of Northumbria, and he became overlord of all the lands south of the River Humber. But Mercia was becoming a serious rival; originally a small kingdom in the northwest midlands, it had absorbed the peoples of the Severn Valley, including the Hwicce, a West Saxon people annexed in 628 after a victory by Penda at Cirencester.

Penda threw off Northumbrian control when he defeated and killed Oswald in 641. He drove out Cenwalh of Wessex, who took refuge in East Anglia from 645 to 648. Penda's control of Middle Anglia, where he made his son subking in 653, brought him to the East Anglian frontier; and he invaded this kingdom three times, killing three of their kings. He was able to draw an army from a wide area, including East Anglia, when he invaded Northumbria in 654; nevertheless, he was defeated and killed by Oswiu, Oswald's successor.

For a short time Oswiu was overlord of southern England; but a Mercian revolt put Penda's son Wulfhere on the throne in 657, and he greatly extended Mercian power to the southeast and south. Wulfhere became overlord of Essex, with London, and of Surrey; he held the West Saxon lands along the middle Thames and blocked any eastward advance of the West Saxons by capturing the Isle of Wight and the mainland opposite and giving them to his godson, Aethelwalh of Sussex. Yet Wulfhere's reign ended in disaster; the Kentish monk Aedde, in his *Life of St. Wilfrid,* said Wulfhere roused all the southern peoples in an attack on Ecgfrith of Northumbria in 674 but was defeated and died soon after.

Ecgfrith took possession of Lindsey, a section of modern Lincolnshire, but he lost it to Aethelred of Mercia after the Battle of the Trent in 678. Thenceforward Northumbria was no threat to Mercian dominance; it was occupied in fighting the Picts in the north, and after Ecgfrith was slain by them in 685, his successors took little part in external affairs.

Yet Mercian power was threatened from the south. Though Aethelred invaded Kent in 676 and though part of Kent was ruled after 686 in subordination to him by a member of the royal house of Essex, Caedwalla of Wessex also obtained some power in Kent. Caedwalla had added Surrey, Sussex, and the Isle of Wight to the West Saxon kingdom and thus came near to uniting all lands south of the Thames into a single kingdom, which might have held its own against Mercia. But this kingdom was short-lived (it was left to Egbert of Wessex to make such a kingdom a reality in 825). Kent became free from foreign interference in 694, two years after the accession of Wihtred, who re-established the Kentish royal line. Sussex appears again as an independent kingdom; and Caedwalla's successor, Ine, was mainly occupied in extending his territory to the west. After Wihtred's death in 725 and Ine's abdication in 726, both Kent and Wessex had internal troubles and could not resist the Mercian kings Aethelbald and Offa.

The great age of Mercia. Aethelbald succeeded in 716 to the rule of all the midlands and to the control of Essex and London. By 731 all provinces south of the Humber were subject to him. Some of his charters use a regnal style suited to this dignity, such as "king not only of the Mercians but also of all provinces . . . of the South English" and "rex Britanniae" (a Latinization of "bretwalda"). Aethelbald held this position, with only occasional warfare, until his death, in 757—far longer than any previous holder of the *imperium.* St. Boniface praised the good order he maintained in his kingdom, though complaining of his immoral life and his encroachment on church privileges. Aethelbald was murdered by his own household, perhaps suborned by Beornred, a rival who was driven out by Offa before the end of the year.

Offa did not at once attain the powerful position that later caused Charles the Great (Charlemagne) to treat with him on equal terms; Cynewulf of Wessex recovered West Saxon lands by the middle Thames and did not submit until 779. Offa was overlord in Kent by 764, in Sussex and the district of Hastings by 771; he apparently lost his authority in Kent after the Battle of Otford in 776 but recovered it in 785. His use of an East Anglian mint shows him supreme there. He claimed greater powers than earlier overlords—subkings among the Hwicce and in Sussex dropped their royal titles and appeared as ealdormen, and he referred to a Kentish king as his thegn. The English scholar Alcuin spoke of the blood shed by Offa to secure the succession of his son, and fugitives from his kingdom sought asylum with Charles the Great. Charles treated Offa as if he were sole king of England, at least of the region south of the Humber; the only other king he acknowledged was the Northumbrian ruler. Offa seemed not to have claimed authority beyond the Humber but instead allied himself with King Aethelred of Northumbria by giving him his daughter in 794.

Offa appears on the continental scene more than had any previous English king. Charles wrote to him as "his dearest brother" and wished for a marriage between his own son Charles and Offa's daughter. Offa's refusal unless Charles let one of his daughters marry Offa's son Ecgfrith led to a three-year quarrel in which Charles closed his ports to traders from England. This and a letter about regulating trade, written when the quarrel was over, provide evidence for the importance of cross-Channel trade, which was one reason for Offa's reform of the coinage.

Imitating the action of Pepin in 755, Offa took responsibility for the coinage, and thenceforward the king's name normally appeared on coins. But the excellent quality in design and workmanship of his coins, especially those with his portrait, served an additional purpose: they had a propaganda value in bringing home the preeminence of the Mercian king not only to his English subjects but also on the Continent. Pope Adrian I regarded Offa with awe and respect.

Because Offa's laws are lost, little is known of his internal government, though Alcuin praises it. Offa was able to draw on immense resources to build a dike to demarcate his frontier against Wales. In the greatness of its conception and the skill of its construction, the dike forms a fitting memorial to him. It probably belongs to his later years, and it secured Mercia from sudden incursions.

The church and scholarship in Offa's time. The missionary activities of Willibrord and Boniface were continued after their deaths by Lull, Boniface's successor at Mainz, and by the Northumbrians Willehad and Aluberht, who converted the Old Saxons. Northumbria was still preeminent in scholarship, and the fame of the school of York, founded by Bede's pupil Archbishop Egbert, attracted students from the Continent and from Ireland. Eventually it supplied Alcuin to take charge of the revival of learning inaugurated by Charles the Great; Alcuin's writings exercised great influence on theological, biblical, and liturgical studies, and his pupils carried on his work well into the 9th century.

Learning was not confined to Northumbria; one Latin work was produced in East Anglia, and recent attribution of manuscripts to Lichfield suggests that Mercian scholarship has been underestimated. Offa himself took an interest in education, and men from all areas corresponded with the missionaries. The Mercian schools that supplied Alfred with scholars in the 9th century may go back to this period. Vernacular poetry was composed, perhaps including *Beowulf* and the poems of Cynewulf.

A steady advance was made in the creation of parishes, and monasticism flourished and received support from Offa. A great event in ecclesiastical history was the arrival of a papal legation in 787, the first since the conversion. It drew up reforming statutes, which were accepted by the

two ecclesiastical provinces, meeting separately under the presidency of Offa and Aelfwald of Northumbria. Offa used the visit to secure the consecration of his son—the first recorded coronation ceremony in England—and also to have Mercia made into a metropolitan province with its see at Lichfield. The latter was because of Offa's dislike of the Kentish archbishop of Canterbury, Jaenberht, but it would also seem fitting to him that the leading kingdom should be free from external interference in ecclesiastical affairs. This move was unpopular with the church, and in 802, when improved relations with Canterbury had been established, the archbishopric of Lichfield was abolished.

The decline of Mercia and the rise of Wessex. Offa died in 796, and his son died a few weeks later. Cenwulf, their successor, suppressed revolts in Kent and East Anglia, but he never attained Offa's position. Cenwulf allowed Charles to intervene in Northumbria in 808 and restore Eardwulf (who had been driven from his kingdom) to the throne—a unique incident in Anglo-Saxon history. Mercian influence in Wessex was ended when Egbert became king there in 802, though there is no recorded warfare between the kingdoms for many years, during which Egbert conquered Cornwall and Cenwulf fought in Wales. But in 825 Egbert defeated Beornwulf of Mercia and then sent an army into Kent, with the result that he was accepted as king of Kent, Surrey, Sussex, and Essex. In that same year the East Angles threw off the Mercian yoke, killing Beornwulf. In 829 Egbert became ruler of Mercia and all south of the Humber, which caused the chronicler to add his name to Bede's list of kings who held the *imperium*, calling him *bretwalda*. The Northumbrians accepted Egbert without fighting. Yet he held this proud position only one year; then Wiglaf recovered the Mercian throne and ruled without subjection to Egbert.

By this time Danish Viking raids were a grave menace, and Aethelwulf, who succeeded his father Egbert in 839, had the wisdom to see that Mercia and Wessex must combine against the Vikings. Friendly relations between them were established by marriage alliances and by a peaceful settlement of boundaries; this paved the way for the acceptance in 886 of Alfred, king of Wessex, as lord of all the English who had not fallen under Danish rule.

THE PERIOD OF THE SCANDINAVIAN INVASIONS

Viking invasions and settlements. Small scattered Viking raids began in the last years of the 8th century; in the 9th century, large-scale plundering incursions were made in Britain and in the Frankish empire as well. Though Egbert defeated, in 838, a large Viking force that had combined with the Britons of Cornwall, and Aethelwulf won a great victory in 851 over a Viking army that had stormed Canterbury and London and put the Mercian king to flight, it was difficult to deal with an enemy that could attack anywhere on a long and undefended coastline. Destructive raids are recorded for Northumbria, East Anglia, Kent, and Wessex.

A large Danish army came to East Anglia in the autumn of 865, apparently intent on conquest. By 871, when it first attacked Wessex, it had already captured York, been bought off by Mercia, and had taken possession of East Anglia. Many battles were fought in Wessex, including a Danish defeat at Ashdown in 871, before Alfred the Great, a son of Aethelwulf, who succeeded to the throne in the course of the year, made peace; this gave him a respite until 876. Meanwhile the Danes drove out Burgred of Mercia, putting a puppet king in his place, and one division of them made a permanent settlement in Northumbria.

Alfred was able to force the Danes to leave Wessex in 877, and they settled northeastern Mercia; but a Viking attack in the winter of 878 came near to conquering Wessex. That it did not is to be attributed to Alfred's tenacity. He retired to the Somerset marshes, and in the spring he secretly assembled an army that routed the Danes at Edington. Their king, Guthrum, accepted Christianity and took his forces to East Anglia, where they settled.

The importance of Alfred's victory cannot be exaggerated. It prevented the Danes from becoming masters of the whole of England. Wessex was never again in such danger, and from Wessex, in the next century, the Danish

Margin notes:

The spread of missionary activities and learning

The papal legation of 787

Mercian–West Saxon alliance

Alfred's defense of Wessex

areas were reconquered. Alfred's capture of London in 886, and the resultant acceptance of him by all the English outside the Danish areas, was a preliminary to this reconquest. That Wessex stood when the other kingdoms had fallen must be put down to Alfred's courage and wisdom, to his defensive measures in reorganizing his army, to his building fortresses and ships, and to his diplomacy, which made the Welsh kings his allies. Renewed attacks by Viking hosts in 892–896, supported by the Danes resident in England, caused widespread damage but had no lasting success.

Alfred's government and his revival of learning. Good internal government contributed to Alfred's successful resistance to the Danes. He reorganized his finances and the services due from thegns, issued an important code of laws, and scrutinized carefully the exercise of justice. Alfred saw the Viking invasions as a punishment from God, especially because of a neglect of learning, without which men could not know and follow the will of God. He deplored the decay of Latin and enjoined its study by those destined for the church; but he also wished all young free men of adequate means to learn to read English, and he aimed at supplying men with "the books most necessary for all men to know," in their own language.

Alfred had acquired an education despite great difficulties, and he translated some books himself, with the help of scholars from Mercia, the Continent, and Wales. Among them they made available works of Bede and Orosius, Gregory and Augustine, and the *De consolatione philosophiae* of Boethius. Compilation of the Anglo-Saxon Chronicle began in his reign. The effects of Alfred's educational reforms can be glimpsed in succeeding reigns, and his works continued to be copied. Only in an attempt to revive monasticism did he achieve little, for the monastic idea had lost its appeal—in England as well as on the Continent—during the Viking Age.

THE ACHIEVEMENT OF POLITICAL UNITY

The reconquest of the Danelaw. When Alfred died in 899 his son Edward succeeded him. Edward had to deal with a rival, his cousin Aethelwold, who obtained support from the Northumbrian and East Anglian Danes; but Aethelwold and the Danish king of East Anglia fell before Edward's forces in 902. A large-scale incursion by the Danes of Northumbria ended in their crushing defeat at Tettenhall in 910. Edward completed his father's plan of building a ring of fortresses round Wessex, and his sister Aethelflaed took similar measures in Mercia. In 912 Edward was ready to begin the series of campaigns by which he relentlessly advanced into the Danelaw (Danish territory in England), securing each advance by a fortress, until he won back Essex, East Anglia, and the east-midland Danish areas. Aethelflaed moved similarly against the Danish territory of the Five Boroughs (Derby, Leicester, Nottingham, Lincoln, and Stamford). She obtained Derby and Leicester and gained a promise of submission from the Northumbrian Danes before she died in 918. Edward had by then reached Stamford, but he broke off his advance to secure his acceptance by the Mercians at Tamworth and to prevent their setting up an independent kingdom. Then he took Nottingham, and all the Danes in Mercia submitted to him.

Meanwhile another danger had arisen: Norsemen from Ireland had been settling for some time west of the Pennines, and Northumbria was threatened by Raegnald, a Norse leader from Dublin, who made himself king at York in 919. Edward built fortresses at Thelwall and Manchester, and in 920 he received Raegnald's submission, along with that of the Scots, the Strathclyde Welsh, and all the Northumbrians. Yet Norse kings reigned at York intermittently until 954.

The Kingdom of England. Athelstan succeeded his father Edward in 924. He made terms with Raegnald's successor Sihtric and gave him his sister in marriage. When Sihtric died in 927, Athelstan took possession of Northumbria, thus becoming the first king to have direct rule of all England. He received the submission of the kings of Wales and Scotland and of the English ruler of Northumbria beyond the Tyne.

Athelstan was proud of his position, calling himself "king of all Britain" on some of his coins and using in his charters flamboyant styles with the same meaning; he held great courts attended by dignitaries from all over England and by Welsh kings; he subjected the Welsh to tribute and quelled a revolt of the Britons of Cornwall. His sisters were married to continental princes—Charles the Simple, king of the Franks; Otto, son of Henry the Fowler; Hugh, duke of the Franks. Among those brought up at his court were Louis, Charles's son; Alan of Brittany, Athelstan's godson; and Haakon, son of Harald Fairhair of Norway; they all returned to win their respective inheritances with his support. He received spectacular embassies from Harald Fairhair and Duke Hugh, and he was a generous donor to continental and English churches. But Athelstan is remembered chiefly as the victor at Brunanburh, against a combine of Olaf Guthfrithson, king of Dublin; Owain of Strathclyde; and Constantine, king of the Scots, whom Athelstan had defeated in 934. They invaded England in 937, and their defeat is celebrated by a poem in the Anglo-Saxon Chronicle.

Immediately after Athelstan's death in 939, Olaf seized not only Northumbria but also the Five Boroughs. By 944 Athelstan's successor, his younger brother Edmund, had retrieved the situation, and in 945 Edmund conquered Strathclyde and gave it to Malcolm of Scotland. But Edmund's successor, Eadred, lost control of Northumbria for part of his reign to the Norse kings Erik Bloodax (son of Harald Fairhair) and Olaf Sihtricson. When Erik was killed in 954 Northumbria became a permanent part of the kingdom of England.

By becoming rulers of all England, the West Saxon kings had to administer regions with variant customs, governed under West Saxon, Mercian, or Danish law. In some parts of the area of Danish occupation, especially in Yorkshire and the district of the Five Boroughs, the evidence of place-names, personal names, and dialect proves a dense Danish settlement; but Danish law also prevailed in such other regions as Essex, Middlesex, and Buckinghamshire, with differences from the rest of England in procedure and in the system of fines, including much higher fines for serious crimes. There were other differences. Money was calculated in marks and ores instead of shillings in Danish areas, and arable land was divided into plowlands and oxgangs instead of hides and virgates in the northern and northeastern parts of the Danelaw; most important was the presence in some areas of a number of small landholders with a much greater degree of independence than their counterparts elsewhere where many *ceorls* had so suffered under the Danish ravages that they had bought a lord's support by sacrificing some of their independence.

The kings did not try to eradicate these local peculiarities. King Edgar (reigned 959–975) expressly granted local autonomy to the Danes. But from Athelstan's time it was decreed that there was to be one coinage over all the king's dominion, and a measure of uniformity in administrative divisions was gradually achieved. Mercia became divided into shires on the pattern of those of Wessex. It is uncertain how early the smaller divisions of the shires were called "hundreds," but they now became universal (except in the northern Danelaw, where an area called a *wapentake* carried on their fiscal and jurisdictional functions); an ordinance of the mid-10th century laid down that the court in each hundred (called "hundred courts") must meet every four weeks to handle local legal matters, and Edgar enjoined that the shire courts must meet twice a year, the borough courts three times. This pattern of local government survived the Norman Conquest.

The church and the monastic revival. To those who judged the church solely by the state of its monasteries, the first half of the 10th century seemed a period of inertia. In fact, the great tasks of converting the heathen settlers, restoring ecclesiastical organization in Danish areas, and repairing the damages of the invasions elsewhere must have absorbed much energy. Even so, learning and book production were not at so low an ebb as monastic reformers claimed. Moreover, new monasteries were founded and benefactions were made to older ones, even though, by post-revival standards, none of these was lead-

(margin notes)

Edward's successes in England

Athelstan's ascendancy over all England

Variant laws and customs within the kingdom

Movement for monastic reform

ing a strict monastic life and several were held by secular priests. Alfred had failed to arouse much enthusiasm for monasticism. The movement for reform began in England about 940 and soon came under the influence of reforms in Fleury and Lorraine. King Edgar, an enthusiastic supporter, promoted the three chief reformers to important positions—Dunstan to Canterbury, Aethelwold to Winchester, and Oswald to Worcester and later to York. The secular clergy were violently ejected from Winchester and some other places; Oswald gradually replaced them with monks at Worcester. All three reformers founded new houses, including the great monasteries in the Fenlands, where older houses had perished in the Danish invasion; but Oswald had no success in Northumbria. The reformers, however, were concerned with more than monasticism—they paid great attention to other needs of their dioceses; the scholars Abbot Aelfric and Archbishop Wulfstan, trained by the reformers, directed much of their writings to improving the education and morals of the parish clergy and, through them, of the people.

The monastic revival resulted in a great revival of both vernacular and Latin literature, of manuscript production and illumination, and of other forms of art. It reached its zenith in the troubled years of King Ethelred II (reigned 978–1016), after a brief, though violent, reaction to monasticism following Edgar's death. In the 11th century, monasteries continued to be productive and new houses were founded; there was also a movement to impose a communal life on bodies of secular priests and to found houses of secular canons.

THE ANGLO-DANISH STATE

The Danish conquest and the reigns of the Danish kings. Ethelred succeeded as a child in 978, after the murder of his stepbrother Edward. He took the throne in an atmosphere of insecurity and distrust, which partly accounts for the incompetence and treachery rife in his reign. Viking raids began in 980 and steadily increased in intensity.

Revival of Danish attacks

They were led by formidable leaders: from 991 to 994 by Olaf Tryggvason, later king of Norway, and frequently from 994 by Sweyn, king of Denmark. Ethelred's massacre of the Danes in England on St. Brice's Day, 1002, called for vengeance by Sweyn and, from 1009 to 1012, by a famous Viking, Thorkell the Tall. In 1013 the English, worn out by continuous warfare and heavy tributes to buy off the invaders, accepted Sweyn as king. Ethelred, his wife Emma, and his younger sons sought asylum with Richard, duke of Normandy, brother of Emma. Ethelred was recalled to England after Sweyn's death in 1014; but Sweyn's son Canute (Cnut) renewed the invasions and, in spite of valiant resistance by Ethelred's son and successor, Edmund, obtained half of England after a victory at Ashingdon in October 1016 and the rest after Edmund's death that November.

Canute rewarded some of his followers with English lands, and he made the Viking leader Erik of Hlathir earl of Northumbria and Thorkell the Tall, earl of East Anglia. He ruthlessly got rid of some prominent Englishmen, among them Edmund's brother Edwy, but Edmund's infant sons were carried away to safety in Hungary. Yet Canute's rule was not tyrannical, and his reign was remembered as a time of good order. The Danish element in his entourage diminished; and the Englishmen, Leofric, earl of Mercia, and Godwine, earl of Wessex, became the most powerful magnates. Canute married Ethelred's widow, Emma, thus removing the danger of Norman support for her sons by Ethelred. Canute fought a successful campaign in Scotland in 1031, and Englishmen were drawn into his wars in Scandinavia, which made him lord of Norway. But at home there was peace. Probably under the influence of Archbishop Wulfstan, he became a stout supporter of the church, which in his reign had the vitality to engage in missionary work in Scandinavia. Religious as well as political motives may have caused his pilgrimage to Rome in 1027, to attend the coronation of the emperor Conrad; from the Pope, the Emperor, and the princes whom he met he obtained concessions for English pilgrims and traders going to Rome. Canute's laws, drafted

by Archbishop Wulfstan, are mainly based on those of earlier kings, especially Edgar.

Already in 1018 the English and Danes had come to an agreement "according to Edgar's law." No important changes were made in the machinery of government except that small earldoms were combined to make great earldoms, which placed much power in the hands of their holders. No attempt was made to restore the English line when Canute died in 1035; he was followed by his sons Harold and Hardecanute, whose reigns were unpopular. Denmark passed to Sweyn, son of Canute's sister Estrith, in 1043. Meanwhile the Norwegians in 1035 had driven out another Sweyn, the son whom Canute had set to rule over them with his mother, Aelfgifu, and had elected Magnus.

Canute's successors

The close links with Scandinavia had benefitted English trade, but they left one awkward heritage: Hardecanute and Magnus made an agreement that if either died without a son, the survivor was to succeed to both kingdoms. Hardecanute died without a son in 1042, and he was succeeded by Ethelred's son Edward, who was known as the "Confessor" or the "Saint" because of his reputation for chastity. Magnus was prevented by trouble with Denmark from invading England as he intended in 1046; but Harold Hardraada inherited Magnus' claim to the English throne, and he came to enforce it in 1066.

The reign of Edward the Confessor and the Norman Conquest. It is easy to regard the years of Edward's rule simply as a prelude to the catastrophe of 1066, yet there are other aspects of his reign. Harrying caused by political disturbances or by incursions of the Scots or Welsh was only occasional and localized; friendly relations were usually maintained with Malcolm of Scotland, whom Earl Siward of Northumbria had supported against Macbeth in 1054; and in 1063 the victories of Harold, earl of Wessex, and his brother Tostig ended the trouble from Wales. The normal course of administration was maintained, with efficient mints, writing office, taxation system, and courts of justice. Trade was prosperous. The church contained several good and competent leaders, and bad appointments—like those of the Normans, Ulf to Dorchester and Robert to London and Canterbury, and of Stigand to Winchester—were the exception. Scholarship was not decadent, and manuscripts were produced in great number. English illumination and other forms of art were admired abroad.

The troubles of the reign came from the excessive power concentrated in the hands of the rival houses of Leofric of Mercia and Godwine of Wessex and from resentment caused by the King's introduction of Norman friends, though their influence has sometimes been exaggerated. A crisis arose in 1051 when Godwine defied the King's order to punish the men of Dover, who had resisted an attempt by Eustace of Boulogne to quarter his men on them by force. The support of Earl Leofric and Earl Siward enabled Edward to secure the outlawry of Godwine and his sons; and Duke William of Normandy paid Edward a visit during which Edward may have promised William succession to the English throne, if this Norman claim was not mere propaganda. Godwine and his sons came back the following year with a strong force, and the magnates were not prepared to engage them in civil war but forced the king to make terms. Some unpopular Normans were driven out, including Archbishop Robert, whose archbishopric was given to Stigand; this act supplied one excuse for the papal support of William's cause.

Harold succeeded his father Godwine as earl of Wessex in 1053; Tostig was made earl of Northumbria in 1055; and their younger brothers were also provided with earldoms. To settle the question of succession, negotiations were begun in 1054 to bring Edward, Edmund's son (nephew of Edward the Confessor), from Hungary; but he died in 1057, leaving a son, Edgar Aetheling, then a child, who was passed over in 1066. In about 1064 Harold of Wessex, when visiting Normandy, swore to support William's claim; only Norman versions of the incident survive and the true circumstances cannot be ascertained, but William used Harold's broken oath to help secure papal support later. In 1065 Harold had to acquiesce in the appointment of Morcar, brother of Earl Edwin of Mercia, to replace Tostig when the Northumbrians revolted against him, and thus Harold turned his brother into an enemy. King Edward when dying named Harold to succeed him, and he was universally accepted after he had overcome Northumbrian reluctance with the help of Bishop Wulfstan of Worcester.

Harold might have proved an effective ruler, but the forces against him were too strong. The papacy, without hearing the defense, gave its blessing to an invasion of a people who had always been distinguished for their loyalty to Rome, and this helped William to collect his army widely. The threat from Harold III Hardraade, who was joined by Tostig, prevented Harold from concentrating his forces in the south and took him north at a critical moment. He fought at Hastings only 24 days after the armies of Mercia and Northumbria had been put out of action by enormous losses at Fulford and only 19 days after he had defeated and killed Harold III Hardraade and Tostig at Stamford Bridge. Harold was slain at Hastings, and on Christmas Day, 1066, William of Normandy was crowned king of England. Unwise decisions and out-of-date methods of fighting may have played a part in Harold's defeat at Hastings, but it is not difficult to understand the English chronicler's view that God was angry with the English people. (D.W.)

The crowning of William

The Normans (1066–1154)

WILLIAM I (1066–87)

Scholars argue endlessly about the significance of the Norman Conquest: whether the results were good or bad, whether there was more continuity than change, whether feudalism existed in England before the Conquest, to what extent Anglo-Saxon institutions survived the Conquest, and so forth. No one doubts that there was change and also continuity, but on balance the argument seems to be in favour of change.

The introduction of feudalism. The major change was the subordination of England to a Norman aristocracy. William distributed estates to his followers on a piecemeal basis as the lands were conquered. Fewer than 180 great tenants in chief were given large parcels of land distributed about the country. Most of these, however, held concentrations of land in some one part of the country, where they centred their "honours," or feudal states. From these centres, usually fortified by a castle, the Norman tenants in chief conducted their administration and organized their military power. They held their land from the Conqueror in return for units of knight service; that is, in return for supplying a certain number of knights to the king's feudal army—which had no necessary relationship to the quantity or quality of land held. In the beginning of the reign, many tenants in chief maintained their quotas of knights out of their own households, but before the end of the reign they had subinfeudated portions of their lands to rear vassals. Private warfare, endemic in Normandy despite efforts of the Duke to suppress it, was, however, successfully prohibited in England. Castles could be built only with the King's license, and the only feudal army permitted was that of the King himself. As an added precaution, rear vassals were required to take an oath of fealty directly to the King. With the Conquest, England became that anomaly, a unified and centralized feudal state.

Distribution of land

Government and justice. William professed a desire to govern England as it had been ruled by his Anglo-Saxon predecessors, and he tried to fulfill his promise. Under William the Anglo-Saxon *witenagemot,* the assemblage of the wise men of the realm, became the King's Curia Regis, an assemblage of the King's ecclesiastical and lay tenants in chief, called together in part or in full when occasion required. Three times in the year—at Christmas, Easter, and Whitsuntide—William was alleged by contemporary chroniclers to have held especially full and solemn assemblages of his court, to which were summoned all the great men of the realm and at which he wore his crown. Inevitably, because of the great number of disputes about land, the Curia Regis became a court for the administration of justice to the King's great tenants in chief. William tried to learn English in order to better his administration

of justice, and he is said to have sat one Sunday "from morn to eve" to hear a plea between William de Braose and the Abbot of Fécamp.

William also tried at first to preserve Anglo-Saxon administrative organization. The central administration under Edward the Confessor had probably been quite similar to that of Normandy, except for the titles of the officers. At first, even the personnel did not change. But, by the end of William's reign, all important administrative officers were Norman, and their titles corresponded to the titles in the duchy administration. There were a steward, a butler, a chamberlain, a constable, a marshall, and, finally, a head of the royal scriptorium (or chancellor). The royal scriptorium was the source from which all writs (*i.e.,* written royal commands) were issued. At the beginning of William's reign the writs were in English, by the end of the reign in Latin.

In local government the Anglo-Saxon shire and hundred courts continued to function as units of administration and of justice but with important changes. Bishops and earls ceased to preside over the shire courts. Bishops henceforth were to have their own ecclesiastical courts. Earls exercised feudal jurisdiction in their honour courts but took as a prerequisite a third of the proceeds of the shire court. But the new earls created by the Conqueror did not wield the vast local power of their pre-Conquest counterparts.

Local government

The office of shire-reeve (or sheriff) was continued under William, as were many of the English incumbents in the early part of the reign. But soon the native sheriffs were replaced by men of the new Norman aristocracy, and the office came to resemble the office of the Norman *vicomte,* a title that also appears in English documents. Their duties remained those that they had exercised before the Conquest. Royal officers exercising the king's will, they were responsible for collecting the royal revenue, for administering local justice, and for keeping the castles that had been built to subdue and protect the country.

William made the most of the financial system that he inherited. In addition to customary dues, the revenues from justice, and the proceeds from their own estates, his predecessors had been able to levy a geld, or tax, distributed over the whole realm. This has been called the "first system of national taxation known to western Europe." William levied a geld at least four times during his reign. He was also able to levy extensive duties on trade with the Continent. Trade had been temporarily disrupted by the Conquest, but it recovered rapidly and proved to be an important source of revenue.

The Conqueror strengthened immensely the administration of justice in his new realm. He occasionally appointed justiciars to preside over local administration of justice and occasionally also sent down commissioners from the central administration. There were a number of great trials during the reign. The most famous of them was the trial at Pinnenden Heath of a case between Lanfranc, archbishop of Canterbury, and the King's half-brother, Odo, bishop of Bayeux and earl of Kent. To this trial came not only all of the Frenchmen of the shire but also a great number of Englishmen, especially those learned in the customary law. In these trials held before the king's officers, jurors were sometimes summoned to give a collective verdict under oath. It is debated among historians whether this institution of the jury was introduced by the Danish kings or was drawn from the Carolingian kings through the Normans. The important point, however, is that the jury came into common use under the Normans.

Church–state relations. The upper ranks of the clergy were Normanized and feudalized following the pattern of lay society. Bishops received their temporal estates and the symbols of spiritual office from the king. They owed service of knights in return for tenure of their temporal estates, and they were brought under firm royal control. In time, all the leading bishoprics were held by continental clergy. In 1070 Lanfranc replaced Stigand as archbishop of Canterbury. Ecclesiastical lawyer, teacher, and statesman of the church, Lanfranc was Italian in origin and had been a monk at Bec and abbot of Saint-Étienne's at Caen. Lanfranc and William understood each other and worked together to introduce discipline and order into the English church. The see of York was definitively subordinated to Canterbury, and the ecclesiastical affairs of Ireland and Scotland were brought under Lanfranc's control—this despite the fact that papal policy of the period was to bring each province directly under the control of Rome. Several church councils were held in England to legislate for the English church as similar councils did in Normandy. William refused to give homage to the pope for the realm of England, although he acknowledged papal support in winning the new realm. To further implement his headship of the English church, William laid down some general rules where disputes might arise. No pope was to be recognized in England without his decision. Without William's consent no papal letter was to be received, no ecclesiastical council was to legislate, and no baron or officer of the realm was to be excommunicated. William and Lanfranc resisted Gregory VII's claim to papal supremacy but based their resistance on English tradition. During William's reign the controversy over the right of lay rulers to invest ecclesiastics with the symbols of their spiritual offices did not affect England, as it did other parts of Latin Christendom.

William's accomplishments.   In 1085 William, after "deep speech" with his assembled barons, ordered a general survey of the land, manor by manor and vill by vill. Historians have debated the purpose of this "Domesday" survey, some putting more emphasis on its usefulness for tax purposes, some emphasizing its importance as a basis for feudal rights and duties. It was probably, in fact, a multipurpose document with the main emphasis on resources for taxation. It constitutes a unique record for the time and offers rich materials for research.

The Domesday survey

One innovation of the Norman kings that caused deep resentment under William I and even more hatred under William II Rufus was the taking over of vast tracts of land for the king's forests. In some areas, whole villages were destroyed and the people driven out; elsewhere, people living in the forest areas were not necessarily removed, but drastic penalties were imposed for poaching.

William the Conqueror is presented in contemporary chronicles as a ruthless tyrant who rigorously put down rebellion and devastated vast areas, especially in his pacification of the north. He was, however, an able administrator. Perhaps his greatest contribution to England's future was the linking up of England with continental affairs. If the country had been conquered again by the Danes, it might well have remained in a kind of backwater of European development. As it happened, England was linked in economic and cultural development with France and the Mediterranean states, with a common Latin language and a common church organization.

THE SONS OF WILLIAM I

William II Rufus (1087–1100).   Under William's two sons William II and Henry I strong, centralized government continued in a feudalized society. Under William II, a rebellion of Norman barons led by the King's two half-uncles, Odo of Bayeux and Robert of Mortain, was put down with the help of the fyrd. The King promised good government, relief from taxation and from the severity of the forest laws in return for this valuable support and won a quick victory. Odo of Bayeux was banished, and William of St. Carilef, bishop of Durham, was tried for treason. As an ecclesiastic he refused jurisdiction of the king's court. But Lanfranc pointed out that it was not as bishop but as lord of his temporal fiefs that he was tried. William threatened to take the case to Rome, but the matter was ultimately compromised by the permission given him to leave the country in return for surrender of his fiefs.

The King forgot his promise and became a notoriously tyrannical ruler. His main preoccupation during his reign was the endeavour to recover Normandy and rejoin it with England. William I had given Normandy to Robert, the eldest and least able of his three sons, Robert, William, and Henry. William II preferred to use peaceful methods if possible.

After brief skirmishes in which he won from Robert the southern part of the duchy, William II joined Robert in warfare against Henry. William's plans were interrupted by a second rebellion of the Norman earls in 1095 but were furthered by Robert's decision to go on Crusade in 1096. Robert mortgaged his Norman lands to William for 10,000 marks. William raised the money in England by drastic and unpopular taxation but died before he achieved his ambition. His death was the result of an "accident" in the New Forest in which he was shot through the back with an arrow. Henry, who was conveniently of the hunting party, rode posthaste to Winchester, seized the treasury, and was chosen king the next day.

Henry I (1100–35).   A good politician and a competent administrator, Henry I was the ablest of the Conqueror's sons. At his coronation on August 5, 1100, he issued a charter intended to win the support of the nation. In general this was a propaganda document, but it does show the extent to which feudal institutions had come to stay. Henry promised not to exploit church vacancies as his brother had done. He remitted debts due his brother as well as penalties for killing Normans due at the time of William's death. He promised a return to those practices of his Anglo-Saxon predecessors that had been superseded under his father and brother. He promised return to the laws of Edward the Confessor with only such amendments as had been made with the counsel of the barons in his father's time. The main provisions of the charter guaranteed feudal custom as it had developed in England and Normandy. Reliefs to be paid by feudal vassals to the king when they took over the estates of their fathers were to be "just and legitimate." Henry certainly did not mean this charter to be enforced literally. He did not return to the laws of Edward the Confessor nor did he afterward adhere rigorously to feudal law and custom.

Henry's coronation charter

Henry inherited from William II a quarrel with the church that became part of the Europe-wide Investiture Controversy. After Lanfranc's death, William had delayed appointing a successor, presumably for the privilege of wasting the resources of the province. After four years, during a bout of illness, he appointed Anselm of Bec, one of the greatest scholars of his time (1093). Anselm did homage for his temporalities but, in keeping with the decrees of Pope Gregory VII, refused to receive the symbols of his spiritual office from the King. Papal confirmation was complicated by the fact that there were two popes: Urban II, a reform pope in the tradition of Gregory VII, and Clement III, an antipope nominated by the Holy Roman emperor Henry IV. A church council was held to decide whether Anselm should go to Rome for confirmation. Anselm refused to accept a decision given by the King's supporters, and he finally got his pallium from a cardinal legate sent by Urban. Conflict between King and Archbishop flared up again in 1097 over what William considered to be an inadequate Canterbury contingent for the Welsh war. The upshot of this was that Anselm went into exile until William's death.

Anselm supported Henry I's bid for the throne and returned from exile at Henry's accession in 1100. But he quarrelled almost immediately with Henry over the homage for his temporal estates. After various ineffectual appeals to Rome, Anselm again went into exile. A compromise was finally arranged with the help of Ivo of Chartres in 1107. Although no authoritative text has survived of the terms of this compromise, it appears to have been agreed that the king would surrender investiture with the symbols of spiritual office in return for an agreement that the king should supervise the election and take homage for the temporalities before investiture with the spiritual symbols. The compromise, in fact, changed very little the king's power in ecclesiastical elections.

Henry continued and extended the administrative reforms of his father. He appointed a justiciar to be a kind of deputy king when he himself was occupied in Normandy. In his reign, the writ, or sealed royal letter of command, became the normal method of initiating judicial action. The Exchequer became organized as a department of government dealing with royal revenues and independent of the meetings of the Curia Regis. Justices in eyre (*i.e.,* itinerant justices) began to be sent out into the counties to inquire concerning crown pleas, the king's revenues, and other matters of interest to the king. This was a kind of extension of the procedure of the Domesday inquest, especially in its use of the jury procedure.

Henry's conquest of Normandy

Henry's most spectacular success was his conquest of Normandy. His reign opened with a rebellion of Robert, newly returned from the First Crusade. Henry reissued his coronation charter, called out the shire levies to defeat the invading army, and, in two years of war, captured all the important castles in England. By Holy Week 1105, he was ready to take the offensive and began a severe onslaught on the Cotentin, the maritime province of Normandy. In September 1106 he won a decisive battle at Tinchebrai (modern Tinchebray) that gave him control of the whole of Normandy. Robert was captured and spent the remainder of his 80 years in castle dungeons. His son, William Clito, escaped and remained until his death in 1128 a thorn in Henry's flesh. Henry had won the support of the French king Philip I against Robert, but he was not so successful in winning the support of Philip's son and successor, Louis VI. A coalition of rebellious Norman barons with Louis VI, Fulk of Anjou, and the Count of Flanders temporarily kept Henry out of the county of Maine. But by 1120 Henry was everywhere successful both in diplomacy and war. He had arranged a marriage for William, his only legitimate son, to Matilda, daughter of Fulk of Anjou, and had received Fulk's homage for Maine. Pope Calixtus I, his cousin, gave him support for his control of Normandy on condition that his son William do homage to the French king.

During the last 15 years of his reign, the most important question was the succession. William, Henry's only legitimate son, died in 1120, leaving Henry's daughter Matilda, wife of the Holy Roman emperor Henry V, as heir. When Henry V died in 1125, Matilda returned to England. Henry persuaded his barons to take an oath in her support in 1127 but did not consult them concerning her second marriage to Geoffrey Plantagenet of Anjou.

Geoffrey was 14, the Empress 25, and they took an instant dislike to one another. Geoffrey repudiated her within a year but was persuaded to take her back, just long enough for her to bear him three children. Henry spent his declining years doting on his grandchildren and died, probably of a heart attack, on December 1, 1135.

THE PERIOD OF ANARCHY (1135–54)

Matilda and Stephen. Henry's death precipitated a 20-year crisis. No one was very enthusiastic about accepting Matilda as queen, especially since her husband, Geoffrey, was tied in friendship to Henry's Norman enemies and was actually at war with Henry at the time of his death. Robert, earl of Gloucester, one of Henry's illegitimate sons, was an impressive candidate.

Then there were Henry's two nephews, Thibaut and Stephen of Blois. The matter took an unexpected turn: while Thibaut was receiving the homage of the continental vassals in Normandy, Stephen took ship for England and claimed the kingship. On December 22, having first secured the treasury at Winchester, he was crowned. The Pope confirmed him early in 1136, thus relieving the English barons of their oath to support Matilda.

Stephen's clash with King David

Stephen had shown himself quick in decision and resolute in securing the crown. But, after the first flush of victory, he seems to have expected to win support by concessions. King David of Scotland was an earl in England with respect to the honour of Huntingdon. When he heard the news of Stephen's accession, he crossed the border and took Carlisle and other northern fortresses. Stephen, surprisingly in view of his lack of feudal support, assembled an army consisting mainly of Flemish mercenaries and marched north. David was persuaded to negotiate an agreement under which Stephen surrendered Doncaster and Carlisle. King David's son was to have Huntingdon on the condition of doing homage to Stephen. To the church Stephen granted a charter forbidding simony and granting that all clerics should be tried under canon law.

Stephen's first concern in governing England seems to have been to get his own men into the main posts in central government, replacing Henry I's administrators. He increased the number of earls from seven to 16. These earls were evidently intended to exercise real power and to undermine that of the sheriffs. In the central government, power had become concentrated in the hands of Roger, bishop of Salisbury, and his family. Roger had been justiciar under Henry; his son Roger le Poer was chancellor, his nephew Nigel, bishop of Ely, was treasurer, and his nephew Alexander was bishop of Lincoln. The Beaumont earl of Leicester and his family on both sides of the Channel were jealous of this power and pressed Stephen to end it. The question was how to do so without incurring obloquy for attacking bishops of the church. An incident was planned for the Oxford meeting of the great council of magnates and prelates in June 1139. A street brawl broke out between Alan of Brittany's men and Bishop Roger's men. The King summoned the bishops before him to make satisfaction for the disturbance of the peace. They were to surrender their castles as a sign of their good faith. Nigel of Ely took refuge in Devizes Castle and prepared for a siege until the King appeared and threatened to hang the Chancellor if Nigel refused to surrender.

This whole episode constituted a turning point for Stephen. Henceforth he was in disfavour with the clergy. He had already forfeited the favour of his brother, Henry of Blois, bishop of Winchester, by failing to make him archbishop of Canterbury when the position fell open in 1137. Henry was papal legate throughout the pontificate of Innocent II and was the most influential member of the clergy in the realm.

Civil war. War for the succession in England did not begin until the landing of Matilda at Arundel in 1139, supported by her half-brother Robert of Gloucester. They established themselves in the southwest, seizing various castles. Stephen fought back in desultory fashion, besieging castles, then abandoning siege. He finally sent the Empress to Bristol under escort. The decisive year in the early part of the war was 1141, when Stephen, acting on information from the citizens of Lincoln that the castle there was lightly guarded, attempted to win it back from Ranulf of Chester and William of Roumare, his half-brother, who had seized it by strategy. Unfortunately for Stephen, Ranulf escaped and brought up troops to attack the royal army. Many of the great magnates deserted Stephen in the course of the battle. He was defeated and taken prisoner along with many lesser barons.

Matilda took advantage of the victory by going to Winchester, where, on March 3, 1141, she was received in state and then, on April 8, given the title *domina Anglorum*. Her great mistake, which ultimately turned the tide of war against her, was her treatment of the Londoners. When she demanded their allegiance and a tallage (tax) as well, they flew to arms "like a swarm of bees from a hive" and forced her to leave the city. Meanwhile, Stephen's queen had rallied the King's forces in Kent and moved into London. Stephen was exchanged for Robert of Gloucester, who had been captured at Winchester, and Stephen was again in the ascendant. He was supported by a church council and wore his crown at Westminster for the second time. Matilda's fortunes waned from this event on, although she continued to dominate the southwest. The deaths of Miles, earl of Hereford, in 1143 and of Robert, earl of Gloucester, in 1147 deprived her of two royal and able supporters. A brief and rash invasion on her behalf by her 14-year-old son, Henry, in 1147 did nothing to change the balance of forces. Henry lacked both troops and money. Early in 1148 Matilda left England for Normandy, never to return.

The revolt of London against Matilda

Her son Henry did return in 1153 and carried on a vigorous and successful campaign. This, the sudden death of his elder son, Eustace, and his precarious hold over the magnates persuaded Stephen to a compromise peace at the end of 1153. Stephen was to continue as king so long as he lived and to receive Henry's homage. In turn, Stephen was to recognize Henry as his heir. Certain of Stephen's castles were to be surrendered to castellans who took oath to turn them over to Henry at Stephen's death. The most difficult questions to be settled after the long period of "the Anarchy" were the titles to land of various members of the nobility. The general principle that was accepted was that whoever had held the titles in the time of Henry

I had the best right. Clearly what was intended was that the feudal principle of succession should prevail. But this principle was not easy to enforce because so much land had changed hands during the reign of Henry I and after. In the last year of Stephen's reign many of the "adulterine castles" (those castles built during the Anarchy without royal license) were destroyed. They are said to have disappeared in 1154 like "wax before a flame," except for certain castles that Stephen continued to hold, somewhat to the distrust of his recognized heir.

The Anarchy was chiefly important in its effect on government. Henry I had left a tightly governed country in which a royally appointed bureaucracy carried on the functions of central government and supervised local government. Under Stephen this had broken down. And local offices such as that of sheriff and castellan had changed hands frequently with the change in the fortunes of war. On the other hand, it cannot be shown that the Exchequer or the regular administration of justice in the county and hundred courts had broken down. Power seems to have been fragmented and decentralized as in a typically feudal state, but order did not disappear altogether.

The early Plantagenets

HENRY II (1154–89)

Matilda's son Henry Plantagenet, the first and greatest of three Angevin kings of England, succeeded Stephen in 1154. At age 21, he was in the prime of life and already possessed a reputation for restless energy and decisive action. He was heir to a vast feudal empire. As heir to his mother and to Stephen, he held England and Normandy; as heir to his father, he held Anjou (hence Angevin) and Touraine; as heir to his brother Geoffrey he got Brittany; as husband of Eleanor, divorced wife of Louis VII of France, he held Aquitaine, the major part of southern France. Altogether his holdings in France were far larger than those of the French king. From the beginning Henry showed himself determined to assert and maintain his rights in all these lands and to reassert in England the centralized power of his grandfather, Henry I. His success in these aims is the measure of his greatness.

Henry's reforms. After completing the destruction of the adulterine castles, Henry carried through certain changes in the military and in government administration. In 1166 he issued writs commanding his tenants in chief to disclose the number of knights they had subinfeudated on their lands in excess of their quotas of service owed to the king. Henry's intent was to demand the excess either in service or scutage (money payment in lieu of service). In principle, barons did not need feudal military vassals for private warfare because it was forbidden. The evidence is that Henry preferred scutage to service because mercenaries were more efficient than feudal contingents. In the Assize of Arms of 1181, Henry required of every free man that he have and maintain arms appropriate to his rank based on his income from land. This measure was intended to provide the basis for the maintenance of the fyrd, which could be called to repress rebellion or meet invasion. Henry, no more than his Norman predecessors, depended on a feudal army for his wars. He did, however, try to make sure that he could tap all the existing sources of men or money to constitute his army.

The Inquest of Sheriffs
A major administrative reform of his reign was the so-called Inquest of Sheriffs in 1170. Inquiries were instituted into the details of local administration. Many sheriffs were dismissed, especially those in shires in which local barons had become too great in the control of the office. Henry revived the device of his grandfather of sending out itinerant justices to check on local administration and to hold the possessory assizes (see below). Royal writs were used, as in Henry I's time, to begin actions in the royal courts.

Henry greatly expanded royal powers of justice by bringing all land held in feudal tenure under royal jurisdiction. Sometime in his reign or earlier the grand assize was introduced. In order to call a grand assize, the plaintiff went to the chancery and got a writ to the sheriff calling on him to demand the attendance of the possessor of the land that the plaintiff claimed and to call four men who would

then choose 12 men to determine the case. An alternative of this writ merely called on the lord of the complainant to do justice to him or appear before the king's officers. Various other actions less formidable in character than the writ of right and the grand assize were available to parties in land disputes at this time. These were the so-called possessory assizes. They determined who had the right to immediate possession of land rather than who had the best fundamental right. The result of these measures was that no freeman could be brought to answer for his freehold save in a royal court. The acceptance of these innovations indicates that feudal land tenure and feudal jurisdiction over land tenure were already on their way out.

Struggle with Thomas Becket. Henry attempted also to restore the close relationship between church and state that had existed under the Norman kings. His first move in this direction was the appointment in 1162 of Thomas Becket as archbishop of Canterbury. Becket had served as Henry's chancellor from 1155 and had proved to be an unusually efficient royal servant as well as the King's boon companion. Henry assumed that Thomas, as archbishop, would continue in these roles. Becket disappointed him. As soon as he was appointed archbishop, Becket became a militant defender of the church against royal encroachments and a champion of Pope Gregory VII's program of ecclesiastical supremacy over the lay world. Becket recognized the need for better church discipline but thought that reform should be carried out by the church itself. The struggle between Henry and Becket reached a crisis at the Council of Clarendon in 1164, the main issue proving to be the jurisdiction over "criminous clerks" (members of the clergy who had committed crimes). The King maintained that clergy should be subject to the same penalties as laymen. After accusation in the king's court, they should be turned over to the bishop's officers, tried in ecclesiastical court, and, if found guilty, should be returned to the king's officers to be punished. Other important principles laid down at Clarendon included the following: disputes concerning the right to present to ecclesiastical office were to be tried in royal courts; appeals to the papal Curia should be undertaken only with royal permission; disputes as to whether land was of lay fee or free alms should be decided in royal courts. A clause concerning ecclesiastical elections simply reiterated current custom: elections were to be free, but the king was to have the revenues during vacancy.

The Council of Clarendon

Becket accepted this document verbally and led the other bishops to accept it also, but he later refused to seal it. In expiation of his previous consent, he suspended himself from office for the sin of yielding to royal will in the matter. He applied to the Pope for absolution, and Alexander III ultimately came to his support against the Constitutions. Later in the same year, the Archbishop was charged with peculation of royal funds during his chancellorship. Becket appeared briefly at the Council of Northampton but took flight to France when he became convinced that the King intended to destroy him. Henry confiscated the revenues of the province, exiled Becket's friends, and confiscated their revenues. And, most serious of his offenses, Henry had his eldest son crowned in 1170 by the archbishop of York, rather than by the archbishop of Canterbury, as was customary. Becket, in exile, appealed to Rome and excommunicated the clergy who had taken part in the offensive ceremony. A reconciliation between Becket and Henry at the end of the same year settled none of the points at issue. But when Becket returned to England he took further measures against those clergy who had taken part in the coronation. In Normandy the enraged King, hearing the news, burst out with the fateful words that incited four of his knights to take ship for England to murder the Archbishop.

Almost overnight the martyred Thomas became a saint in the eyes of the people. Henry repudiated responsibility for the murder and reconciled himself with the church at the expense of promising to go on a crusade, to allow appeals from English courts to Rome, to restore the possessions of Canterbury, and to renounce practices of his time that were detrimental to the church. He seems to have made no formal withdrawal of the Constitutions of Clarendon. But henceforth criminous clerks were to be tried in ecclesiastical courts except for treason, breach of forest laws, or petty misdemeanours. Disputes between laymen and ecclesiastics over land or over presentation to church offices were to be tried by lay courts. Finally, Henry did penance at Canterbury, allowing the monks to scourge him.

Rebellions of Henry's sons and Eleanor of Aquitaine. Henry's sons, urged on by their mother and by a coalition of his enemies, took advantage of Henry's weakness in public opinion as a result of the Becket murder and in 1173 raised a rebellion throughout his domains. The lack of cooperation among the rebels allowed Henry to defeat them one at a time. Eleanor was retired to polite imprisonment for the remainder of Henry's life. The King's sons and his baronial rebels were treated with leniency. There followed a brief period of amity between Henry and Louis of France, and the years between 1175 and 1182 marked the zenith of Henry's prestige and power. In 1183 the younger Henry again tried to organize opposition to his father, but he died in June of that year. Henry spent the last years of his life locked in combat with the new French king, Philip II Augustus, with whom his son Richard had entered into alliance.

RICHARD I THE LION-HEART (1189–99)

Henry II died in 1189, an embittered old man. He was succeeded by his son Richard I, nicknamed the Lion-Heart. Richard was mainly interested in the crusade to recover Jerusalem and in the struggle to maintain his French holdings against Philip Augustus. During his ten-year reign Richard spent only about six months in England. During his frequent absences he left a committee in charge of the realm. Inevitably one or another of the group became Richard's dominant. Chancellor William Longchamp, bishop of Ely, ministers dominated the early part of the reign until 1191, when a rebellion of the barons forced him into exile. Walter of Coutances, archbishop of Rouen, succeeded Longchamp and took the title of justiciar. But the most important and able of Richard's ministers was Hubert Walter, archbishop of Canterbury, justiciar from 1193 to 1198, and also chancellor from 1199 to 1205. These strong ministers kept government without the King from being catastrophic. A revolt led by Richard's brother John was put down with severe measures in 1193 by Hubert Walter and Eleanor, the King's mother. An oath of allegiance was required of all freemen and the royal castles were strengthened. The fyrd was called out, and John's supporters were outlawed or excommunicated. But when Richard returned from abroad, he forgave John and promised him the succession.

Richard was responsible for some innovations in taxation and for an attempt at military reorganization. At the beginning of his reign, a tax levied by Henry II to support his proposed crusade had to be collected. This so-called Saladin Tithe was levied on personal property rather than real estate and was collected from both clergy and laity and on spiritual as well as temporal revenues. On his Richard's return from the crusade Richard was captured by Leopold capture of Austria and held for a high ransom. According to the and chroniclers, the 150,000 marks demanded was five times ransom the King's annual revenue, and its collection created a financial crisis. Traditional feudal revenues were insufficient. Heavy taxes levied on towns and on demesne serfs caused protests against its incidence on the poor of London. A general levy of one-quarter of all revenue on land in 1194 was more successful. And in 1198 a carucage, or a levy on all plowlands, was tried. The ransom, though never paid in full, caused Richard's government to become highly unpopular.

Richard also aroused opposition by attempting to put an army on permanent standing. He found it increasingly difficult to maintain an army consisting of feudal contingents and foreign mercenaries. Daily wages for a knight had risen from eightpence a day in Henry II's time to one shilling, and other costs rose correspondingly. The English baronage began to resist the demand that they serve abroad. In order to deal with these problems, Richard tried to set up a standing army of 300 knights who were expected to serve a whole year. This was to be accomplished by asking each holder of a knight's fee to contribute enough to pay for such an army. The barons, led by the bishops of Lincoln and Salisbury, opposed Richard's scheme, preventing the most serious threat yet conceived against the feudal organization of society.

JOHN (1199–1216)

Richard, killed during a siege operation in France in 1199, was succeeded by his brother John, one of the most unpopular and unfortunate of English kings. John bears the main responsibility for his misfortunes, but it is only fair to recognize that he inherited some resentments built up against his brother and father. Henry had encroached on feudal jurisdictions, and Richard had drained England of money for his crusade, his ransom, and his war in France. John inherited also claims to the large and heterogeneous Angevin empire. In England and Normandy, he was recognized as heir to Richard. Brittany, Anjou, Maine, and Touraine recognized Arthur, son of John's brother Geoffrey, as heir. Arthur's mother, Constance of Brittany, saw to it that her 12-year-old son went to do his homage to his suzerain, Philip II. John's mother, Eleanor, held Aquitaine as dowager duchess, but the province would devolve upon John at her death.

Loss of French possessions. John had nothing like the military ability or reputation of his brother, although he could sometimes win a battle in a fit of energy, only to lose his advantage in a spell of indolence. Richard's ally, the Count of Flanders, decided that John was a bad risk. John alienated some of his vassals in Aquitaine by repudiating his first wife, Isabella of Gloucester, and then carrying off the fiancée of Hugh de Lusignan, one of his vassals in Poitou. For this offense he was summoned to answer to Philip II, John's feudal overlord for his holdings in France. He refused to attend. For the disobedience his lands in France were declared forfeit. John, in a brilliant spurt of energy, marched 80 miles (130 kilometres) in 48 hours, captured young Arthur near Poitiers along with 200 Poitevins, and retired to Rouen. There, if contemporaries can be believed, he murdered Arthur in anger during a bout of drunkenness. John failed to follow up his advantage, and he let a strategic castle, the Château Gaillard, fall to the enemy in March 1204. By 1206 all that was left of the inheritance of the Norman kings was the Channel Islands.

Struggle with the papacy. John returned to England and, unlike any king since the Conquest, devoted his undivided attention to the realm for the next few years. Immediately he became involved in a conflict with Pope Innocent III over the choice of an archbishop. At Hubert Walter's death in 1205, the monks of Canterbury had resorted to a secret election in the night in order to avoid participation of the clergy of the province and the interference of the King's officers. They elected the subprior and sent him to Rome to receive the pallium from the Pope. The secret got out, and John went angrily to Canterbury to force the monks to elect John de Gray, bishop of Norwich and one of John's close confidants. He, too, was sent to Rome. Pope Innocent III could not be expected to miss so good an opportunity to demonstrate the plenitude of papal power. He quashed both elections and persuaded a delegation of Canterbury monks sent by his command to Rome to elect the learned and talented Stephen Langton, an English cardinal. John refused to receive Stephen, who retired to Pontigny, where Archbishop Thomas before him had taken refuge. John seized the revenues of Canterbury. He had already quarrelled with his half brother Geoffrey, archbishop of York, over Geoffrey's leadership in 1207 of resistance to a tax on movables. Geoffrey fled to the Continent, where he died in 1212. England was without either archbishop. In March 1208 Innocent placed England under an interdict, or ban forbidding the administration of the sacraments and certain religious rites. All but five of the 16 bishops either died or fled to the Continent. In November 1209 Innocent excommunicated John. In John's response, the bishops of Bath, Salisbury, and Rochester excommu- left their posts. Peter des Roches of Winchester and John nication de Gray of Norwich remained the sole support of John's power in the church, and John made the most of the opportunity to gather in the revenues of the vacant ecclesiastical sees.

John's excommunication freed his vassals from their oaths of fealty to him. Strangely, however, there was no immediate revolt. Indeed, the interdict seems to have had some popular support, perhaps because the King, by taking over ecclesiastical property, temporarily relieved the laity of burdensome taxes. John was able to conduct highly successful expeditions to Scotland, Wales, and Ireland in the period. It was not until 1212, when John's plans for the reconquest of his former French possessions began to reach the boiling point, that rebellion flared up. Ever since the loss of Normandy, John had been busy building up a coalition of German rulers to assist him against the French king. His chief ally was Otto of Saxony, claimant to the German throne, who became the Holy Roman emperor Otto IV. Meanwhile, John issued writs to the leading towns of England, demanding contingents for war on the Continent, and he ordered an inquest of fees under which each of his tenants in chief was required to report the service due from his fiefs.

At this point the Welsh raised a revolt with the support of Philip of France, and John's troops had to be diverted to Wales. But before he could take punitive measures against the Welsh, a plan of the barons to depose him was rumoured, and Robert Fitzwalter and Eustace de Vesci fled the country to the King's enemies. John's brilliant solution of the problem of multiple threats was to effect a reconciliation with the papacy. He agreed to receive Stephen Langton as archbishop, to reinstate the clergy in exile, and to compensate the church for his depredations on revenues. In addition, without papal prompting, John resigned his kingdoms in England and Ireland and received them back as fiefs from the Pope in return for an annual contribution of 1,000 marks. He now had an able ally against his adversaries at no great cost in terms of concessions on his own part.

John now made a second attempt to set out for Poitou. This time it was the northern barons who revolted and prevented him from going. John was furious and marched north to the attack. Only Stephen Langton's persuasion finally effected a reconciliation and made possible the Poitou venture. The campaign in Poitou failed when John's painfully assembled allies were decisively defeated at Bouvines on July 27, 1214. John was forced to withdraw from France and to return home to face his disgruntled barons.

Revolt of the barons and Magna Carta. Even so, rebellion developed slowly. Stephen Langton is alleged to have read to the barons a copy of Henry I's coronation charter as early as August 14, 1214, presumably to stir them to action. It was not until the spring of the following year that the opposition to John took shape, and the so-called Unknown Charter was drawn up. It was based on Henry I's charter but reflected more recent grievances. Resistance to the King came chiefly from the northern barons who had rebelled against service in Poitou, but by the spring of 1215 many others had joined to support the protest against the scutage for Poitou and John's abuse or disregard of feudal law and custom.

On June 15, 1215, the rebellious barons met John at Runnymede on the Thames near Windsor (modern New Windsor), and, on the basis of the Articles of the Barons presented to the King, Magna Carta was drawn up. For a document hallowed in history during more than 750 years and frequently cited as a forerunner of the Declaration of Independence and the Declaration of the Rights of Man and of the Citizen, Magna Carta is a singularly undramatic document. It is thorny with problems of a feudal age that are largely untranslatable into modern idiom. Read in its historical context, the charter was a guarantee against the sort of arbitrary disregard of feudal right that the three Angevin kings had made familiar. The main importance of Magna Carta derives first from the fact that it was agreed upon between the King's party and the baronial party and therefore has the character of a contract, and second that, even though John was released by the Pope from his obligations under it, the charter was reissued under John's son and so became a part of the permanent law of the land. The King's repudiation and the barons' reluctance to fulfill their part of the agreement of June 1215 led to renewal of civil war. The barons announced their *diffidatio* and chose Louis, son of Philip Augustus, as their king. But John's death in October of 1216 brought an end to the civil war.

The 13th century

The 13th century was an important formative period in the history of England. It was during that century that the concept of the community of the realm developed in sufficient strength to provide the foundation for parliamentary government. Something like the phrase had first been used formally in clause 61 of Magna Carta. The barons, in devising a method of enforcement for the provisions of the charter, had provided that if grievances occurred they should be carried to a committee of four barons among 25 who were to enforce the charter, and that if the king or his justiciar, on being duly advised of the problem, did not provide a remedy, the 25 chosen barons "with the commune of all the land" were to distrain and distress the king in every possible way until he should offer remedy.

The notion that the realm was a community and that it was governed by representatives of that community perhaps got its start in the period following Magna Carta in which a council of regency ruled on behalf of a child-king not yet able to govern in his own right. The phrase community of the realm used to mean just the totality of the baronage. Yet the representative idea had made some headway. In a writ of 1237 for the collection of a tax earlier granted to the King, the earls, barons, knights, and freemen are said to have acted "for themselves and their villeins." But it is in the conflict that broke out between the King and a party among the barons in the latter part of the reign that all these terms acquire some sophistication.

The notion of the community of the realm

HENRY III (1216–72)

Early reign. The issue on which conflict centred in Henry III's reign was whether the King should be allowed to choose his own counsellors or whether he was bound to consult his barons. The King himself pointed out that the barons denied him the right of free choice of his servants that they exercised in conducting their own affairs. Men of the 13th century realized that the kingship was different from any other feudal lordship, but it was not clear to contemporaries in what precise way it differed.

So long as Henry was under tutelage the question did not become a critical one. Henry declared himself of age in 1227, but he did not immediately take control. After the death of the regent, William Marshal, in 1219, Hubert de Burgh, the justiciar, dominated the group of officers surrounding the King. Hubert was the King's chief minister until two others among Henry's close advisers engineered his fall. A subsequent revolt of the barons led by Richard, son of William Marshal, ended in tragedy. Richard was killed in Ireland, and Henry found that he had unknowingly signed an authorization for the killing. In 1236 Henry married Eleanor of Provence and introduced her relatives as a new element in English politics.

Simon de Montfort and the Barons' War. In all the crises of his younger years, Henry showed himself to be naïve; on the one hand he was overtrustful, and on the other bitter against those who betrayed his trust. The main crisis of his reign came in 1258, when he asked for taxes to pay the 135,000 marks he had promised the Pope as the price of making his second son king of Sicily. Henry had already made himself unpopular by asking for taxes to pay the costs of expeditions to Gascony in which he showed his incompetence as a military leader and failed to gain either vassals or prestige on the Continent.

The crisis began in May 1258, when the King was persuaded to agree to the meeting of a "parliament" and to the appointment of a joint committee of the dissident barons and of his own supporters. Twelve were to be elected by each side and were to recommend the necessary measures for the reform of the kingdom. Simon de Montfort, the King's brother-in-law, was the able but fanatical leader of the opposition party.

The
Provisions
of Oxford

The Provisions of Oxford, which the 24 drew up by mid-June, would have made the king a constitutional monarch if they had been permanently effective. The 24 were to choose four: two on the king's side, two on the barons' side. These four were to choose a 15-member council that would supervise the king's government. There were to be three "parliaments" a year—at Michaelmas, Candlemas, and the first of June—to which were to come the 15 of the king's council and 12 to be elected by the "community" (*le commun* in the original French). The community was to accept as established what the 12 should do. The office of justiciar was to be revived, and this officer was to account at the end of his term of office before the council. The treasurer and the chancellor were likewise to account before the council, and the chancellor was to seal nothing merely by the king's will but was to act by advice of the council. The households of the king and queen were to be reformed. Sheriffs were to be knights of the shire and to hold office for one year only.

The Provisions of Oxford led to two years in which the King was again under tutelage, less even than a *primus inter pares* because he was not free to choose his own councillors. A Welsh truce was arranged against the opposition of the King's party. The King's men were dismissed from their positions as castellans and banished from the country. Discussions of aid broke down because the Sicilian project fell through and the King no longer needed the money. Peace with France had been arranged in November 1258 so that Henry was free of financial necessity for war in France. In October 1259 the *communitas bacheleriae* (a group of lesser vassals of the barons) petitioned for fulfillment of the promises of the magnates and King to remedy their grievances. The results were embodied in the Provisions of Westminster, mainly reforms of the common law in the interest of the knights bachelors of England—that is, the tenants of the magnates who had imposed the Provisions of Oxford on the King.

Break-
down of
the Oxford
settlement

The Oxford settlement began to break down in 1260. Henry became suspicious that his eldest son, Edward, had come to some agreement with the rebels. A reconciliation was arranged, and Edward, aged 21, went off to the Continent on a jousting expedition intending eventually to settle down to deal with the problems of governing Gascony. Odo Rigaud, archbishop of Rouen, arrived in the summer of 1260 intent on reconciling Simon de Montfort and the King, and peace was temporarily restored. Then in April 1261 the Pope sent a bull absolving Henry from his oath to support the Oxford Provisions. The King, encouraged by this release, dismissed the baronial sheriffs, castellans, and other officers imposed on him by his council. Simon de Montfort returned from abroad and again raised rebellion against the King. In January 1264 Henry appealed to Louis IX of France, his fellow sovereign and his overlord with respect to his French holdings, to decide the case between him and his barons. In the Mise of Amiens, Louis released Henry from his commitments, insisting on Henry's right to appoint his own ministers. Louis incorporated a saving clause in favour of "charters, liberties, establishments, and praiseworthy customs . . . existing before the time of such provisions."

Inevitably war broke out, in April 1264. In the first phase of the war, Simon and his supporters were successful. Near Lewes, in May, Simon captured the King, the King's son Edward, and the entire leadership of the royal party. Henry was forced to agree to govern by the Charters and Provisions of Oxford, and in the King's name a "parliament" was called for June in which four knights from each shire were to assist in setting up a new form of government to control the King. Simon governed in the King's name, though still considering himself to be the King's loyal subject. Early in 1265 he called a second parliament, this time to include representative burgesses of the boroughs as well as knights of the shire. Simon's motivation was undoubtedly political, to win support from elements in the community of the realm below the baronage, especially the moneyed class in the towns. Peace negotiations with the royal party failed, despite the efforts of the papal legates, Gui and Ottobuono. But in May, young Edward escaped by collusion with his captors, and the war became

Edward's war. He rallied the royal forces, particularly the Marcher earls, whom Simon had allowed to go free after Lewes, and in August he defeated Simon by turning against him his own tactics. Simon himself was killed.

Later reign. The rest of Henry's reign was spent in settling the problems created by the rebellion. Simon's supporters were deprived of their lands, and as "the Disinherited" they fought back from redoubts in forest or fens. The original of the Robin Hood legends may have been one of them. The Statute of Marlborough (1267) was the final document of the reign. It was a confirmation, restatement, and implementation of the Provisions of Westminster and of the peace terms ending the war. With it went a confirmation of the charters. The parliament that adopted it included representatives of the lower classes as well as the barons. It granted a subsidy for the crusade, and "Lord Edward" went off to war against the Muslims, not to return until two years after his father's death.

"The Dis-
inherited"

EDWARD I (1272–1307)

Lord Edward, who became King Edward I in 1272, was in many ways the ideal medieval king. He had learned early in life, in the conflict with Earl Simon de Montfort and his followers, how to command an army and something about strategy and tactics. He was a good fighter, according to one contemporary "the best lance in the world." He had learned from his father's experience something about the mistakes a medieval king must avoid. He enjoyed both war and statecraft and had a gift for leadership. He looked on kingship as good management of the king's possessions and prerogatives.

Statute law. In his reign, statute law began to take shape as a kind of supplement to the common law. Statutes remedied deficiencies in the "law and custom of the realm" either in protection of the king's rights or in remedy of grievances of his subjects. To protect his own rights, for example, there were the *quo warranto* proceedings under the Statute of Gloucester of 1278 and the Statute of Quo Warranto of 1290. Under these statutes, the king's subjects were asked by what warrant they claimed possession of royal franchises. Edward's object was not so much to recover such franchises as to discover which of them were held legitimately. It was found that over half the hundred courts were in private hands. By the Statute of Mortmain of 1279, it was provided that no more land might be given into the hands of the church without royal license. The Statute of Quia Emptores of 1290 had the effect of forbidding further subinfeudation of land. Two great statutes of Westminster, one of 1275 and one a decade later, remedied deficiencies in the common law and provided improvements in legal procedures on behalf of the king's subjects. These conservative and definitory measures ushered in a new era in British government.

Edward also established an alliance between the king and the merchant class. He offered the merchants his protection in return for a grant of export duties on wool, woolfells, and hides, payable at London and 12 other ports to royal customs officials. The tax brought in a good income—an average of £8,800 in a good year. In return for this new source of income, Edward granted royal favour to the merchants. The Statute of Acton Burnell (the name of a castle of Edward's chancellor, Robert Burnell) facilitated the collection of merchants' debts by establishing debtors' prisons. Finally, in 1303, Edward negotiated with the foreign merchants the so-called *Carta Mercatoria,* whereby he granted them freedom of trade in England in return for additional customs revenues. Despite this assured income from trade, Edward, in the critical period of the 1290s, seized the whole output of wool to support his wars in Wales or in France.

Edward's
encourage-
ment of
merchants

The growth of Parliament. Edward also fostered the concept of the *communitas regni* and the practice of calling representative knights of the shire and burgesses of the borough. Of the 45 parliaments called during Edward's reign, knights and burgesses attended 17 of them. In 1295 Edward called the gathering that older historians have called the "Model Parliament," because it contained all the elements later associated with the word parliament and because the writs to the sheriffs to call knights

The
"Model
Parliament"

and burgesses expressed the representative principle very clearly. They were to be summoned

> so that the said knights shall then and there have full and sufficient authority on behalf of themselves and the community of the county aforesaid, and the said citizens and burgesses on behalf of themselves and the respective communities of the cities and boroughs aforesaid, to do whatever in the aforesaid matters may be ordained by common counsel; and so that through default of such authority, the aforesaid business shall by no means remain unfinished.

So this parliament to Edward was representative of local communities and of the whole community of the realm.

Edward's wars. Edward aimed to be as successful in war as he was in peace, but only in relation to Wales did he succeed fully. There Llywelyn ap Gruffudd, prince of Snowdonia, had taken advantage of the Barons' War against Henry III to try to make himself ruler of all Wales. In 1277 Edward conducted a short and methodical war against Llywelyn. Using a fleet from the Cinque Ports and a paid army combined with feudal contingents from the Marcher lords, Edward won a quick victory and exacted from Llywelyn the Treaty of Conway, whereby Llywelyn agreed to take an oath of fealty, pay homage for his lands, surrender to Edward certain northern districts of Wales, hold all his other lands subject to Edward's justice, and pay a large indemnity.

David, the younger brother of Llywelyn, was responsible for the breach of the Treaty of Conway. He waged war against Edward and was joined by Llywelyn in 1282. David was captured and executed as a traitor; Llywelyn was killed in battle. In the peace following, North Wales was organized into counties and the whole realm was to become the appanage of Edward's son, Edward of Caernarvon, who was given the title Prince of Wales—a title borne ever since by the heir to the English throne. Edward built four great castles (Conway, Caernarvon, Criccieth, and Harlech) at strategic points in North Wales; founded merchant settlements that he colonized with English craftsmen and merchants; and revised Welsh law. Archbishop Pecham reorganized the Welsh church and brought it more fully under the sway of Canterbury. A final revolt in 1294–95 was quickly quelled, and Wales became the *communitas Walliae,* which granted its share of subsidies in support of the king.

Edward also tried to bring Ireland into closer relationship to England and to enforce some sort of peace and order there. The outcome was the establishment of the English Pale, an area in which English law, customs, and speech were enforced, and the establishment of an Irish Parliament on the model of the English Parliament, which met in 1297 to consider Edward's demands for troops for war in France.

Attempts to secure Scotland

Edward's efforts to bring Scotland under English suzerainty met with only temporary success. Alexander III (1249–86) had married Margaret, Edward's sister. During his reign, peaceful relations prevailed, and parliaments, or assemblies of prelates and magnates, met to consider the problems of the king and the kingdom. A crisis developed only when Alexander rode off a cliff in a wild storm in 1286, leaving as his only immediate heir his three-year-old granddaughter, Margaret, the "Maid of Norway." A regency council was set up and ruled the realm until 1290, when Margaret was brought from Norway to become queen. Edward had negotiated a marriage for her with his son Edward, and all seemed auspicious for a friendly and close relation between the two kingdoms. These plans were defeated by Margaret's death in September 1290. The whole question was thrown open to challenge and conflict. Edward claimed and received the right of arbitration. There were three main candidates, all descendants of David, earl of Huntingdon, the brother of William the Lion, king of Scotland from 1165 to 1214. John de Balliol was the grandson of David's eldest daughter; Robert de Bruce was the son of David's second daughter; and John de Hastings was the grandson of David's youngest daughter. A commission consisting of one-half chosen by Bruce and one-half by Balliol designated Balliol as king. Balliol took an oath of fealty and did homage to Edward and was accepted in Scotland.

This settlement by no means ended the problem of Scotland. In 1294 the Scottish lords' committee set up a system of restraints on the king modelled on the Provisions of Oxford. In 1295 a treaty was negotiated with France that provided for the marriage of John de Balliol's son Edward to the French king's niece. The king of England then demanded the surrender of three border castles and, on John's refusal, summoned him to his court. John did not appear and war became inevitable. Edward conquered the country in five months in 1296-97. But he appointed inept agents to enforce peace in Scotland. Revolt broke out again when William Wallace, a free tenant of the Scottish king's steward, slew an English official. Wallace was eventually captured and executed. Meanwhile, Robert Bruce, grandson of the original claimant to the throne, had taken over the leadership of the rebel party. War continued into the new reign when Edward II succeeded his father in 1307.

French campaign

In his war against Philip the Fair of France, Edward I encountered opposition both in raising men and money and he achieved little success. In the last years of the reign, a peace with France was negotiated based on a double marriage agreement: Edward himself was to marry Philip's sister Margaret, and the Prince of Wales was to marry Philip's daughter Isabella. This peace freed Edward for a stronger effort against Scotland. He died on campaign in the North.

The 14th century

The 14th century in English history is a difficult century to characterize. At the beginning and end of the century two kings' reigns ended in tragic failure. In between there was the 50-year reign of Edward III, the most popular with his contemporaries of England's medieval kings. Certain general themes are clear. There was continuous development during the century of the importance of the Commons in Parliament. War between England and France continued intermittently throughout the century, and that part of it from 1337 on is called the Hundred Years' War. The Black Death struck in 1348–49, remained endemic, and recurred several times during the latter part of the century, bringing with it profound economic and social change.

EDWARD II (1307–27)

Edward II's reign was an almost unmitigated disaster. He inherited some of his problems from his father. The most important were a treasury deficit of £60,000 and the Scottish war. He inherited none of his father's strengths and seems to have developed his own weaknesses in rebellion against his father. Surrounded with a ruling class strongly tied to his family by blood and service, he rejected the company of his peers, seeking that of the lower orders of society. He enjoyed swimming, ditch digging, thatching, theatricals, but not swordplay or tournaments. His "dear friend" Piers Gaveston, the son of a Gascon knight, was a man of simple birth and no claim to breeding. Edward's father had exiled Gaveston in an attempt to quash the friendship. Edward, the son, recalled him and conferred on him the highest honours he had to bestow; that is, the earldom of Cornwall and marriage with Margaret de Clare, sister of the Earl of Gloucester. Edward also recalled Archbishop Winchelsey and Bishop Bek of Durham, whom his father had banished. He dismissed one of his father's most trusted servants, Walter Langton, the treasurer.

Edward's ministers

Edward II failed as king, but his reign is important for a new attempt of the barons to set up a system of checks on the king's exercise of power similar to the system set up to control his grandfather. At the beginning of the reign, in the coronation oath—which he took in French rather than Latin—he was asked, in addition to the promises extracted from his ancestors, to promise to keep such laws "as the community of your realm shall have chosen."

From the beginning of the reign the hostility of the barons toward Edward was strong. The barons came armed to the 1308 Parliament and warned the king that "homage and the oath of allegiance are stronger and bind more by reason of the crown than by reason of the person of the king" and that "if the king by chance be not guided by reason, in relation to the estate of the crown, his liege subjects are bound by the oath made to the crown to guide the king back to reason and amend the estate of the crown." To the Parliament of 1310 they again came armed and forced the king to allow the election of 21 lords ordainers, "prelates, earls and barons," to make ordinances for the betterment of the estate of the realm.

Apart from a third banishment of Gaveston and the demotion of the Frescobaldi family from control over collection of the wool customs, the main provisions of the ordinances had as their object a reduction of the king's control over his own ministers. A long list of officers, including the chancellor, the treasurer, and the justices of both benches, were to be chosen with the advice and consent of the barons in Parliament. Parliament was to meet twice a year. Consent of the baronage was also required for participation in foreign war and in the appointment of a keeper of the realm in the king's absence. Letters of the king under privy seal were to be null and void if they interfered with justice. The ordinances, like the earlier Provisions of Oxford, if they had been fully enforced, would have created a constitutional monarchy.

The middle years of Edward's reign were a period of uneasy truce between King and barons. Thomas of Lancaster, leader of the opposition, had supervised the capture and execution of Piers Gaveston in 1312. He maintained a kind of surly enforcement of the ordinances. In 1314 the King went off to Scotland with an army raised by county muster and therefore not dependent on the barons for consent. In the Battle of Bannockburn, the Scots were victorious with an army consisting of pikemen and bowmen, giving the English a lesson they did not forget in the French war. The Scottish war continued in somewhat desultory fashion until 1323, when a truce was arranged. In 1315–17 there were torrential rains that destroyed the crops. In the ensuing famine, the government could think of no better remedy than trying to enforce maximum prices of wheat without any apparatus for enforcement.

In 1321 conflict again erupted between King and the opposition barons. The King's ablest ministers, Hugh Despenser, father and son, were banished in 1321 by act of Parliament. Civil war ensued in which the King was victorious. He got his revenge against Thomas of Lancaster by executing him after a pretended trial. Popular sympathy was with Lancaster, who was spontaneously canonized, though he had been anything but saintly in his life. In 1322 at York, Parliament repealed the ordinances and got from the king a promise

> that matters which are to be determined with regard to the estate of our lord the king and of his heirs or with regard to the estate of the kingdom and of the people shall be considered, granted, and established in parliament by our lord the king with the consent of the prelates, earls, and barons, and of the community of the kingdom, as has been accustomed in times past.

The meaning of this Statute of York has been much debated, the main problem being whether to give to the term parliament its later meaning of lords and representatives of the community of the realm, or to give it the narrower meaning of earlier times. There was clearly some notion of limiting the king's powers.

The final period of the reign was one in which the Despensers, restored to power, carried out various administrative reforms, ably assisted by Walter Stapledon, the treasurer. The reign ended with a renewal of conflict. Isabella, the king's French wife, with the assistance of Roger Mortimer, earl of March, landed in England with a force of only 700 men and, with popular support, especially in London, overthrew the government. The Despensers were tried and hanged, and the King was imprisoned. Parliament was called in his name, Edward II was charged with breaking his coronation oath and was persuaded to abdicate in favour of his son, Edward III. After two conspiracies to release him, the King was killed and his body was exhibited publicly to avoid further attempts on his behalf.

EDWARD III (1327–77)

Outbreak of the Hundred Years' War. Edward III's long reign was relatively uneventful in terms of politi-

cal and constitutional crises. He was crowned at 14 and overthrew his mother's and Mortimer's dominance when he was 17. Mortimer was tried and condemned by the Lords in Parliament. Edward's mother was retired to her estates; she later repented her sins and died a sister of the Poor Clares. Her son began his fortunate military career by winning the Battle of Halidon Hill against the Scots (1333). From then until 1337, it was just a matter of time until Edward took up war against his French overlord, Philip IV, beginning over a century of Anglo-French warfare known as the Hundred Years' War. The causes of the war were several. Friction over allegiances in Gascony had been chronic since 1294. Both sides had built *bastides,* or new fortified towns, to try to keep one another at bay. English and French seamen had long engaged in acts of piracy along the coasts. The Count of Flanders was a vassal of the French king, but the livelihood of his state depended on wool from England, as the livelihood of England did on selling the wool in Flanders. The rulership of Brittany was in dispute, and both the English and French kings had their candidates. Finally, there was the matter of the French throne itself. Edward, through his mother, was closer in blood to the last of the Capetians than was Philip of Valois. Edward did not present his claim to the French throne in dead seriousness, but he used to the full its propaganda value. The French complained that he had not done liege homage to Philip for his possessions in Gascony in accordance with the agreement of Saint-Germain-en-Laye (1331). War began in somewhat desultory fashion in 1337.

Domestic achievements. In the domestic history of Edward III's reign there is little of interest except for a crisis in 1341–43 over the King's finances in the conduct of the war and a critical period at the end of the reign, when Edward was in his dotage. Edward received generous grants for the war in the years from 1336 to 1340, but he found himself short in 1340 because of his grants and promises of grants to his allies. He seized the wool exports and had recourse to reckless borrowing from Italian merchants in anticipation of future parliamentary grants. In 1341 he returned from France and charged John Stratford, archbishop of Canterbury, with working against him and delaying the grant and collection of subsidies. In the Parliament of April–May 1341, various statutes were passed that were reminiscent of the kind of restraints put on earlier and less popular kings. Officers of state and the king's household were to be appointed and sworn in Parliament. Commissioners were to be sworn in Parliament to audit the king's accounts. Peers of the realm were to be arraigned and tried only before their peers in Parliament. Breaches of the charters were to be reported in Parliament and tried there. Stratford was summoned before a committee of two bishops and four earls who were to hear the charges against him, but the charges were dropped, and in 1343 the record of the case was annulled. Also in 1343, the King repudiated the statutes. Only the Commons protested, and they did not persist. The chief lesson of the crisis was that it illustrated the great extent of the king's dependence on Parliament, particularly his dependence on the Commons, for supply.

The later legislation of Edward III's reign had to do with matters that had for some time needed remedy or were related to the social and economic crisis that followed in the wake of the Black Death. The Statute of Treasons (1352) had as its object the clear definition of great treason, that is, treason against the king involving forfeiture of land and goods, as against petty treason against a lesser lord, in which case forfeiture to the crown was not involved. The Statute of Provisors gave statutory authority to measures already in use to prevent papal provisors from usurping the right of Englishmen to present to church offices in England. The Statute of Praemunire (1353) introduced better procedures for checking appeals to the papal courts in cases involving rights of Englishmen to present candidates to church offices. These acts were accepted by the King only with reservations on his side about enforcement. Many of his ministers and clerks were clerics, and it was often to his advantage to negotiate with the pope concerning appointments. The Statute of Labourers

The lords ordainers

The Statute of York

Edward's deposition

Edward's claim to the French throne

Later legislation

(1351) attempted to fix wages during the labour shortage following the devastation of the Black Death. In 1362 Parliament passed an act to make English rather than French the official language of pleadings in the law courts. This measure failed because of resistance of the lawyers, who complained that they could not state their cases properly in English. In parliamentary rolls and statutes on the other hand, the English language made its way slowly, so that English ultimately became the official language.

The crises of Edward's later reign. The last ten years of Edward III's reign were a time of suppressed crisis. The king was in his dotage and, since the death of his wife, Philippa, in 1369, in the clutches of Alice Perrers, the rather unscrupulous wife of a London citizen. Edward, the Black Prince, heir to the throne, was ill and dying. Lionel, duke of Clarence, the next eldest son, died in 1368, leaving a daughter, Phillippa, as heiress. Her husband, Edmund Mortimer, would not arrive at his majority until 1373. John of Gaunt, the fourth son, was occupied with his claims to Castile, his inheritance from his second wife, Constance of Castile, whom he had married in 1371. Edmund of Langley, the fifth son, earl of Cambridge, later duke of York, was a man of no ability and had nothing to offer toward establishing good and responsible government. Thomas of Woodstock, the King's youngest son, was not yet of age. John of Gaunt was the only real leader among the King's sons, and after 1373 he was under a cloud because of an ineffectual and fruitless campaign in France. A parliament met in 1371 and dismissed William of Wykeham, the chancellor, a notorious curialist and pluralist, and demanded the appointment of laymen to state offices. This proved to be a not very practical manoeuvre. It mainly illustrates the anticlericalism of the times, a spirit already illustrated by the Statutes of Provisors and Praemunire.

No parliaments were held in 1374 or 1375, and by the time the Good Parliament of 1376 was elected there was an accumulation of grievances to be dealt with. Petitions and protests included a demand for annual parliaments, for the election of sheriffs and knights of the shire by the better people of the county, reform of local government, measures to deal with "rogues, vagabonds, and sturdy beggars," a check to the peculations of royal officers (Gaunt's following especially), reform of the navy, and improvement in the protection of the borders of the realm. As in previous crises, a committee consisting of four bishops, four earls, and four barons was set up to take the responsibility for the reforms. Then, under the leadership of the speaker, Peter de la Mare, steward in the household of the Earl of March, the Commons stumbled onto a new procedure. They impeached Alice Perrers and the royal officers who profited personally from administration of the royal finances. The Commons took the role of prosecutors before the Lords as judges.

The achievement of the Good Parliament was ephemeral. John of Gaunt soon recovered his power in the government. Peter de la Mare was jailed in Nottingham. William of Wykeham was attacked for alleged peculations as chancellor, and Alice Perrers was restored to court. The Parliament of 1377 reversed all the important acts of the Good Parliament. But Richard, son of Edward, the Black Prince, was created prince of Wales, duke of Cornwall, and earl of Chester, allaying suspicions that John of Gaunt aimed at the throne. Richard was asked to make peace between John and the citizens of London. So the reign ended in truce if not peace.

RICHARD II (1377–99)

Richard II's reign was fraught with crises—economic, social, political, and constitutional. Richard was ten years old when his grandfather died, and the first problem that had to be dealt with was the King's minority. A "continual council" was set up to "govern the king and his kingdom." John of Gaunt was still clearly the dominant figure in the royal family, but neither he nor his brothers were included in the council.

The Peasants' Revolt (1381). Immediately the matter of finances for the war in France came up. In the last Parliament of Edward III's reign, a poll tax of fourpence

per head had been introduced. It had not been a great success. The 1379 Parliament introduced a graduated tax based on rank in society. This, too, was a failure, and crown jewels had to be sold to meet expenses. In 1380 the tax was set up at one shilling per head with the proviso that the rich should help the poor in paying it. This was obviously an inequitable and impractical tax, and trouble developed rapidly when the government tried to speed up its collection in the spring of 1381. By May the whole of southeast England was on the verge of rebellion. The poll tax was the immediate cause of unrest, but the deeper origins of the so-called Peasants' Revolt of 1381 go back to earlier developments, particularly to the demographic crisis caused by the Black Death in 1348 and 1349.

This outbreak of bubonic and pneumonic plague had carried off from one-third to one-half of the population and had been particularly severe among the lower social levels. The result was a labour crisis. Hired labourers, being fewer, asked for higher wages and better food, and peasant tenants, also fewer, asked for better conditions of tenure when they took up land. Some landlords, in trying to come to terms with the new conditions, attempted to reassert labour services where they had been commuted. They ran into strong opposition from the peasants. An Ordinance of Labourers (1349) and a Statute of Labourers (1351) had tried to set maximum wages at the levels of the years before the Black Death, but strict enforcement was impossible. Still the friction and the frustration provided by the acts persisted, and the peasants resented the efforts to prevent them from making the most of their new opportunities. Meanwhile, popular poor preachers were spreading subversive ideas about relations among the ranks of English society. A popular slogan asked:

When Adam delved and Eve span
Who was then the gentleman?

Sharper than the attacks on the gentlemen were the attacks on the clergy. A proposal widely accepted was that all the lands held by the clergy be confiscated and distributed among the peasantry.

Government policies that added coal to the fire were the fostering of the expanding powers of the justices of the peace at the expense of local courts and manorial courts and the attempts at levying the poll tax. Attempts at levying back taxes in Essex and Kent were the immediate signal for revolt. A royal justice on a special commission in Essex was seized and forced to swear not to hold further sessions of his court. The appearance of a tax collector in Kent was the signal for revolt there. Widespread outbreaks occurred in the southeastern part of the country: attacks on landlords and their manor houses and the destruction of documentary evidence of villein status, assaults on royal officers trying to collect taxes, and attacks on lawyers because of their association with the landed classes. Attacks on religious houses were particularly severe, perhaps because they had been the most conservative among the landlords about commuting labour services.

Meanwhile, men of Essex and men of Kent were moving on London to attack the King's evil councillors and to demand from him redress for their grievances. In this curiously spontaneous revolt, the men of Essex and the men of Kent arrived outside London at approximately the same time. By June 11 the men of Essex were assembled outside the northeast gates of the city. The Kentishmen gathered at Blackheath on June 13 and attacked the Marshalsea Prison and Lambeth Palace, both on the south side of the Thames. The rebels were let into London by sympathizers among the citizenry and attacked the Fleet-street Prison and the town house of John of Gaunt, duke of Lancaster. On June 14 the young King rode out to Mile End to meet the rebels and, in default of sufficient available force to turn them back, promised them charters of liberation from serfdom. Meanwhile, rebels broke into the Tower and killed Sudbury, the chancellor, Hales, the treasurer, and two other ministers of the King. On the next day, Richard met the rebels at Smithfield. The rebel leader Wat Tyler presented the rebels' demands in the presence of the royal party and his own followers drawn up in battle array. During a parley with the King's forces Tyler was attacked and fatally wounded by the Mayor of

The rise of John of Gaunt

Imposition of the poll tax

The attack on London

London and a follower. The young King rode forward to reassure Tyler's men, who had not clearly seen the murder, and asked them to follow him to Clerkenwell. This proved to be the turning point of the rebellion. Having exhausted their supplies and got promises regarding their grievances, the rebels began to make their way home. Disorders in the countryside continued, although retaliatory measures were taken by the government. On June 23 the King and Sir Robert Tresilian began a tour of the eastern counties and trial of the ringleaders. When challenged about his promises at Mile End, the King replied: "Villeins ye are and villeins ye shall remain." Special commissions continued to act until August 30, when the King ordered all further arrest and executions to cease. In November a Parliament confirmed the King's revocation of charters but demanded amnesty except for a few special offenders.

The results of the uprising, though not spectacular, were important. The government never again attempted to collect a poll tax. The landlord class learned to fear the peasants. The London uprising would probably not have succeeded to the extent that it did if it had not been for the support of London citizens, but the march on London was bound to fail in the end because the peasants had no practical program to present to the King, in whom they placed their entire trust for the improvement of their condition. Richard seems to have derived a rather exalted idea of his own powers and prerogatives from the appeal to him and his success in meeting the peasants at Smithfield. But the very real improvement in the position of the peasants—the abandonment of labour services and the leasing out of the demesne lands to them—seems to have occurred not so much as a consequence of the revolt as of changes in the economy that would have occurred anyhow.

John Wycliffe. Religious unrest was another subversive factor in the reign of Richard II. John Wycliffe, a priest and an Oxford scholar, began his career as a religious reformer with two treatises on divine and civil *dominium* in 1375–76. According to him, *dominium*, that is, the power of possession and of government, was a gift of God to those who were in his grace, that is, those who served him faithfully. He conceived *dominium* in feudal terms as power and possession granted in return for service, not in the hierarchical terms of contemporary feudalism. *Dominium* was exercised not mediately through kings or popes but immediately by anyone who was in God's grace. Everyone standing in God's grace has all the gifts of God. And, contrariwise, no one who is not in the grace of God has any sort of *dominium*. Priests, therefore, have no power to administer the sacraments unless they are in a state of grace. The pope himself has no power except through grace.

This doctrine brought Wycliffe into direct conflict with the church hierarchy. In the next years he was twice summoned before an assembly of bishops, first at St. Paul's (February 1377), then at Lambeth (March 1378). Both times, the trial was effectively interrupted by an outbreak of hostility between the London citizens and the retinue of John of Gaunt, Wycliffe's patron and protector. The beginnings of the Great Schism in 1378 gave Wycliffe further opportunities for attack on the papacy. And in 1379, in a treatise on the Eucharist, he espoused heresy. Christ, he said, was present in the bread and wine, not literally as the result of a miracle performed by the priest, but spiritually as the result of the faith of the believer. The miracle is God's miracle, not that of some sinful priest.

Wycliffe was tried twice again and, after the second trial, was banished from Oxford. He retired to his parish at Lutterworth, in Leicestershire, which became the centre of the so-called Lollard movement. Two of Wycliffe's followers translated the Bible into English and others went out as missionaries in London and Leicestershire and in the West Country. Wycliffe died in 1384, but the movement continued to expand despite the loss of the founder and despite the government's attempts to destroy it.

Political struggles and Richard's deposition. Richard's reign is of great interest from the political and constitutional point of view as well as for economic and social developments. Soon after his success in putting down the peasant rebels, the King began to build up a court

party. He used the signet for warranty of royal actions as against the Privy Seal and the Great Seal. He got control of the treasurership, the keepership of the Privy Seal, the subchamberlainship, the chamberlainship, and, eventually, the chancellorship itself. There was ground for thinking that these measures were in part directed against the King's uncle, John of Gaunt. But even the Londoners who hated Gaunt withdrew their support from Richard when he appointed the young and inexperienced Robert de Vere, earl of Oxford, as lieutenant of Ireland. A crisis was precipitated in 1386, when Parliament was asked for a subsidy to finance an expedition to France. Parliament demanded dismissal of the King's favourites, and the King withdrew to Eltham. Richard defied Parliament, threatened to enlist the King of France in his cause, and said that he would not dismiss so much as a scullion in his kitchen at the request of Parliament. In the end, however, he was forced by the impeachment of his ministers to agree to the appointment of a council to reform the King and the kingdom. He withdrew from London and made an appeal to the country. He also called the judges before him at Shrewsbury and asked them to pronounce the illegality of Parliament's actions. The King's appeal to the people and the judges failed, and a pitched battle at Radcot Bridge was needed to settle the matter of ascendancy. In the "Merciless Parliament" of 1388 five lords accused the King's friends of treason under a very expansive definition of the crime.

Richard was chastened. He pardoned those lords who had made the accusations and proceeded to rule with moderation for the few years until 1394, when Anne of Bohemia, his queen, died. He put down a rebellion in Ireland and was, for a time, almost popular. Then, after Anne's death, he began to implement his personal policy and to rebuild a royal party. He made a 25-year peace with France and married the seven-year-old daughter of the French king as security for the treaty. He built up a household of faithful servants, including the notorious Sir John Bussy, Sir William Bagot, and Sir Henry Green. He enlisted household troops wearing his personal badge, the white hart.

In January 1397 a Parliament met. Thomas Haxey, a clerical proctor, submitted a long bill of complaints concerning maladministration, extravagance in the royal household, and the inadequate defense of the Scottish border. Haxey was arrested and adjudged in Parliament a traitor, thus extending the definition of treason even beyond the scope adopted in the Merciless Parliament. The lords appellant, who had accused the King's friends in 1388, were taken into custody—that is, those who could be found. A second Parliament in September 1397 repealed the pardons of the lords who had accused the King's friends in 1388. Three of them were now accused. One was beheaded on Tower Hill; one was exiled; the third was secretly murdered. Parliament annulled all the acts of the Parliament of 1388, granted the customs on wool for the King's life, and delegated the powers of Parliament to a committee that was to continue to sit and finish the business after the Parliament was dissolved. After this other events followed quickly. The Duke of Norfolk and Henry, son of John of Gaunt, duke of Hereford, quarrelled, accusing each other of treason. They were both banished, the former for life and the latter for ten years. Following this, John of Gaunt, duke of Lancaster, died and Richard confiscated his estates instead of allowing his son, Henry, to return to claim them. Richard went off to Ireland seemingly secure.

Richard was unduly confident. Henry landed at Ravenspur in Yorkshire, as he said, to claim his father's estates and the hereditary stewardship. The Percys, the chief lords of the north, welcomed him and promised their aid. Popular support was far more than Henry had expected. Richard returned from Ireland to negotiate first with Archbishop Arundel at Conway, then with Henry at Flint. According to Lancastrian history, he abdicated at Flint. Other evidence is that he tried to keep his estate and his life and that Henry demanded only his father's lands and the stewardship. The historian is at a disadvantage in reconstructing events because the official records were

Wycliffe's denial of transubstantiation

"The Merciless Parliament"

altered and even the chroniclers were given an official version after the fact. The end was swift. A Parliament was called for September 30 in Richard's name. Before this body had fully assembled, its members, the "estates of the realm," and the *populus* of London were presented with Richard's alleged abdication and Henry's claim as legitimate descendant of Henry III and by right of conquest.

Richard's deposition

Thirty-three articles of deposition were set forth against Richard, accusing him of misgovernment. The abdication and deposition were accepted, and Henry sent out writs for Parliament to meet on October 6.

Richard made a last futile appeal based on the sacred character of the power conferred on him. He was taken from the Tower and transferred to Pontefract Castle, where he either died of self-starvation or was murdered by smothering. Thus ended the last attempt of a medieval king to assert arbitrary power. Whether Richard had been motivated by an ideal of medieval monarchy or, as his accusers said, by new ideas about monarchy, he failed in the practical measures necessary to sustain his power.

Lancaster and York

HENRY IV (1399–1413)

Henry of Lancaster seemed to promise better rapport with his people. He was a warrior of great renown. He had travelled to Jerusalem and had fought in Prussia against infidels. He had a reputation for affability and for statesmanlike self-control. But he had won his crown with the support of "the estates of the realm." It did not matter much whether that meant Parliament or something more vague and symbolic. His parliaments, from the first, expected him to govern with the advice and consent of his council and to listen in Parliament with respect to requests for money to carry on his government. And Henry himself, in order to demonstrate his superiority to Richard, emphasized his desire to govern with council and Parliament.

The rebellions.   Henry's immediate task after his acceptance as king was to put down a rebellion threatening to restore Richard. The earls of Rutland, Kent, and Huntingdon, degraded from their former dukedoms but nonetheless members of the new king's council, supported by the former bishop of Carlisle, planned an attack on the King and his son at Windsor. Warned by Rutland's confession of the details to his father, the Duke of York, Henry went up to London, successfully raised an army there, and defeated the rebels near Cirencester. This event was followed by Richard's death at Pontefract. But though Richard's body was exhibited publicly in London and elsewhere, sentiment in his favour continued to crop up until well into Henry V's reign.

Owen Glendower's rebellion

A more serious rebellion was levied by Owen Glendower in 1402. He was the descendant of Welsh princes and a man of statesmanlike abilities. He sought an alliance with the French king and received some small contingents of raiders. He captured Edmund Mortimer, uncle of another Edmund, who was the only legitimate heir to Richard. He also won the valuable support of the northern barons of England including, first and foremost, the Percys of Northumberland. They had enormous prestige in the north and were connected to most of the other baronial families. Henry defeated the coalition at Shrewsbury in July 1403, and the younger Henry Percy ("Hotspur") was killed in battle. The elder Percy was pardoned on condition of surrendering his castles.

Owen Glendower meanwhile seized castles in Wales, renewed the alliance with the elder Percy, and got the support of Richard Scrope, archbishop of York. This new alliance had to be broken up in 1405. Henry won a victory at Shipton Moor and executed Scrope in a barley field without trial and over the protests of the Archbishop of Canterbury. He then defeated the elder Percy at Bramham Moor. The traitor's head was displayed on London Bridge, and his body was quartered, pickled, and sent for public exhibition to various parts of England. The war in Wales continued for some time because Henry had not enough resources to support the garrisons in the Welsh castles. But Glendower was pushed into the mountains of North

Wales, and Henry was vastly more secure after 1408, although Glendower was never captured.

Henry and Parliament.   Henry's relations with his Parliaments were uneasy. The main problem, of course, was money. Henry, as duke of Lancaster, was a wealthy man, wealthier than any private landlord in England. But, as king, he had forfeited some of his income by repudiating Richard's tactics. Richard had had an annual income of over £115,000, whereas Henry had only £90,000, and his income was diminished by his gifts of royal lands and revenues to his supporters. But his needs were as great as or greater than Richard's. He was threatened by rebellion at home and war from France. He borrowed as heavily as Richard but was slower in paying back. His first Parliament began the attack on royal extravagance.

They asked that he submit to the council the grants he had made to his supporters. They also asked for resumption of lands granted since 1327. Henry agreed to be advised concerning these matters but would not agree to a general resumption. On the other hand, issue was clearly joined, and the slogan that the "king should live of his own" had been introduced.

In Henry's second Parliament (1401), the Commons fired a salvo at the beginning, asking for redress of grievances before grant of supply. The King promised to confer with the Lords but in the end turned down the proposition as "unprecedented." Nonetheless, the grant of funds in the form of tenths and fifteenths and of customs is recorded in the Parliament roll as of March 10, the last day of the session. In this Parliament also, King, Lords, and Commons cooperated in a bill that required secular officers to assist ecclesiastical authorities in wiping out the Lollard heresy.

Henry called ten Parliaments in his 13 years as king. The main issues between him and these Parliaments were the demand for the resumption of crown lands so that the king might "live of his own," the demand for supervision of grants of crown lands and of expenditure generally, and finally the organization and personnel of the king's and queen's household.

The Parliament of 1406

The critical year in Henry's relations with Parliament was 1406. The Parliament of that year, the longest of the medieval period, met for 159 days and lasted from March to December. The grant of a subsidy was discussed early in the session but was promised only on condition that grants should be expended with the advice of "Lords and officers named and elected in the present parliament for defense of the realm and safeguard of the seas," except for £6,000 to be spent "as the king wishes." A grant of tonnage and poundage for safeguard of the seas was made to the merchants, but when they asked for an advance of £4,000 to deal with immediate problems, the King's reply was "Il n'y a de quoi" ("There is no money"). The second session of the Parliament demanded nomination of the King's council in Parliament. The King agreed but in no spirit of allowing interference with his choices of men to serve on the council. It was also agreed that warrants for payments from the subsidy after the safeguard of the seas had been provided for should be endorsed and made by the advice of the council. Audit of account was agreed to on the last day of the session. The third and final session of the Parliament dealt with household matters. A subsidy was granted as had been promised at the beginning of Parliament, and the Parliament broke up for Christmas on December 22.

The later Parliaments of Henry brought up no new issues, but Henry became less active in government as he was more and more incapacitated by illness. Archbishop Arundel and Henry, the King's eldest son, conducted the government until 1411, when young Henry was dismissed because of his father's suspicions concerning his loyalty. These uneasy relations between the Prince and his father lasted for the rest of the reign and kept young Henry from taking part in a campaign in France. Henry IV died on March 20, 1413. There was no question about Prince Henry's succession despite the fact of his father's usurpation.

HENRY V (1413–22)

Henry V's brief reign is important mainly for the glorious victories in the war with France, which visited on his infant son the enormous and not so glorious burden of governing both France and England. Two rebellions troubled the security of the realm in the first two years of the reign. The first was organized by Sir John Oldcastle, a Lollard and a former confidant of the new king. Oldcastle was tried by the archbishop's court and condemned to excommunication for heresy. He was handed over to the secular authorities and imprisoned in the Tower of London. He escaped with the help of two London citizens and formulated a plot against the life of the King and his brothers to take place during the Christmas celebrations in 1413–14. Some 38 of his supporters were caught and sentenced to execution. Oldcastle himself escaped arrest until 1417. Another plot against Henry's life gathered around Richard, earl of Cambridge, a younger brother of the Duke of York. Richard had married Anne Mortimer, daughter of Roger Mortimer and sister to Edmund Mortimer, the nearest legitimate claimant to the throne by descent from Lionel, duke of Clarence, second son to Edward III. Edmund gave the plot away, and the leading conspirators were tried and executed on the eve of the King's departure for France.

In general, after these early disorders, the reign was internally a peaceful one. The King appointed a council to carry on the government in his absence but kept the seals in his own hands abroad. The Parliaments of the reign granted the subsidies requested.

The Treaty of Troyes marks the high point of Henry's greatest achievement; that is, his conquest of northern France. Under its terms, Henry was to marry Catherine, daughter of Charles VI. He was to be heir to the French throne, and that throne was to descend to his heirs in perpetuity. Charles VI's son, the Dauphin, was not party to the treaty, and so the war continued. Henry tried to make his possessions in France pay for their own upkeep, but he still needed money for the war. Reluctant to ask for subsidies at a time when he needed all the support he could get for the treaty, he asked for loans. That they were forthcoming as readily as they were is an indication of his popularity. Meanwhile, he contracted dysentery at the siege of Meaux on the Marne and died on August 31, 1422, just six weeks before the death of his father-in-law, Charles VI. He left as his heir a son less than a year old. There could be no immediate question of the accession of that infant to the French throne. On the other hand, no question was raised about the infant's title to the English throne even though the dynasty was of dubious legitimacy and was relatively new to tenure of the throne. Under the terms of Henry V's will a council of nine was set up in which Humphrey, duke of Gloucester and second brother to Henry V, was to be the protector and defender of the realm and the Church of England, and John Plantagenet, duke of Bedford, Henry's third brother, was to take over the rule of Normandy and of France also if the Duke of Burgundy would not accept the latter responsibility.

HENRY VI (1422–61 AND 1470–71)

Henry VI, whose long reign lasted from 1422 to 1461 with a brief revival of his power in 1470–71, was never a ruler in his own person. Until 1437 he was a child under the regency of a council of nobles dominated by his uncles of Lancaster and his Beaufort kin. When he was declared of age in 1437, John, duke of Bedford, had died, and the Beauforts were the real rulers of England. In 1445, through the initiative of the Duke of Suffolk, he married Margaret of Anjou, who with Suffolk dominated the King. Finally, in the period from 1450 to 1461, he suffered two bouts of mental illness. During these crises Richard, duke of York, ruled the kingdom as protector.

Domestic rivalries and the loss of France. In the first period of the reign, the Duke of Bedford proved to be as able a commander in the French war as his brother, Henry. He pushed the French back everywhere south of the Loire except at Orléans. Then, in 1429, Joan of Arc appeared and revitalized French resistance. Orléans was relieved, and Joan persuaded the Dauphin to go deep into Anglo-Burgundian country, to Reims (the traditional city for French coronations) to be crowned. Joan's brief career as charismatic leader of the French army ended in

May 1430, when she was captured by the Burgundians and sold to the English. She was tried as a heretic and a witch by an Inquisition court and burned at the stake in May 1431. John, duke of Bedford, died in 1435, and the Congress of Arras, an effort at general peace settlement, failed. Philip of Burgundy deserted the English alliance and came to terms with Charles VII. From then on the war was one of attrition until the English had lost all their possessions save Calais.

At home there were no great political issues. The main problem was the financing of the war. The country was ruled by a council of magnates with the increasingly reluctant financial support of the Parliament. Humphrey, duke of Gloucester, and Henry Beaufort, bishop of Winchester (cardinal from 1426), were the main figures in the government. The Bishop was supported by his nephew John, duke of Somerset. He was enormously wealthy and effectively increased his wealth by lending money to the king and getting control of the customs for repayment. Gloucester was completely unscrupulous and irresponsible where his own interests were engaged.

In 1447 both the Cardinal and the Duke died, the latter under circumstances that suggested the possibility of murder by poison. The Duke of Suffolk, who had arranged the King's marriage with Margaret of Anjou, was in the ascendant. He was the leader of the so-called peace party, but his peace lasted only two years, from 1444 to 1446. Margaret proved to be a high-spirited, determined, and ambitious young woman of 16 who dominated King Henry throughout the rest of his reign and fought for her son's right long after the Lancastrian cause was lost.

Though the Duke of Suffolk was in the ascendant, he was blamed for the failure of the French peace and held accountable for rumours that Maine and Anjou had been surrendered. He was impeached in the Parliament of March 1450. The King tried to save him by exiling him for five years. But when he took ship for France, the ship "Nicholas de la Tour" waylaid him. "And thanne a knave of Yrlong smot of his hed" with six strokes of a rusty sword. Suffolk was succeeded by Edmund, duke of Somerset, as the leader of the court party.

Cade's rebellion. Less than three months later, in the southeast of England, Jack Cade, who sometimes styled himself as Mortimer, presumably to associate himself with the Yorkist claimant to the throne, led a rebellion against the government. Unlike the rising of 1381, this was not a peasant movement; Cade's followers were mainly middle class, from the rank of knight down, and their complaints were mainly about the want of governance rather than of economic repression. The rebels protested feigned indictments under forest law, failure of justice, excessive bail, those who endeavoured to teach the King that he was above the law, and rigged elections to Parliament. The remedies they proposed were political: they advocated reclamation of the King's land so that he might live off his own, the removal of his corrupt councillors, and improved methods of collecting taxes. Lord Saye and Sele, the treasurer, and Crowmer, sheriff of Kent, were singled out for special attack and were captured and executed after a military victory by Cade's forces near Sevenoaks. At the end of June the rebels brutally murdered Bishop Ayscogh of Salisbury, a friend of Suffolk. The revolt was put down in early July by troops under Lord Scales. He seized London Bridge from the rebels, and with the capture at Rochester of Cade, mortally wounded, the rebellion was over.

The beginning of the Wars of the Roses. Cade's rebellion was the signal for the beginning of the so-called Wars of the Roses—the struggle between the Lancastrian and the Yorkist descendants of Edward III for control of the crown and of local government. Richard, duke of York and heir apparent, claimed under two lines of descent. His mother was great-granddaughter of Lionel, duke of Clarence, second son of Edward III. His father was son of Edmund of Langley, duke of York, fourth son of Edward III. According to feudal principle he had a better hereditary right than anyone of the Lancastrian line. Henry VI was great-grandson to John of Gaunt, duke of Lancaster, third son of Edward III.

Richard returned from Ireland with 4,000 men in 1450

Marginal notes:

Sir John Oldcastle

The Treaty of Troyes

Joan of Arc

The Duke of York's claim to the throne

to assert his right to participate in the King's council and to counter the machinations of the court party, especially Edmund, duke of Somerset. Somerset was recalled from France to meet Richard's charges. In the Parliament of 1450 Richard supported a measure for rigorous reclamation of the King's grants, and Thomas Young, member of the Commons from Bristol, urged the recognition of Richard as heir apparent. Young was committed to the Tower, and Richard was not called to the council until 1453. That August the King fell into insanity. The Queen and the court party attempted to conceal this, but in March 1454 Richard was made protector; he represented himself as leader of a reform faction. Early in 1455 Henry recovered his wits. During Henry's illness, on October 13, 1454, there had been born to him a son, Edward; this changed the balance of politics because Richard of York was no longer the heir apparent.

Battle of
St. Albans

Richard went north to gather his forces, alleging that he could not safely attend a council summoned to meet at Leicester without the support of his troops. He met the King near St. Albans and first tried to prefer his charges against Somerset. But the King would neither listen nor have those whom Richard designated as traitors arrested. A brief battle followed, and York's forces, larger than the King's, won a decisive victory. As a result, a Yorkist regime was set up with York as constable of England and the Earl of Warwick, emerging as the strong support of the Yorkist cause, as captain of Calais. Somerset was killed in the battle and was succeeded in the title by his son, Henry. The King fell ill again in the autumn of 1455, and York was again protector for a brief period; the King recovered early in 1456.

Hostilities were renewed in 1459. The Yorkists were defeated at Ludford Bridge, giving the Lancastrians an opportunity to recover their influence. The latter failed to meet the challenge. Demands for money, purveyances, and commissions of array increased the burdens but not the benefits of Lancastrian rule. A brief battle at Northampton on July 10, 1460, went overwhelmingly for the Yorkists, and the King was captured. Parliament was summoned to meet at Westminster on October 7. There Richard showed unwarranted self-confidence; he put his hand on the cushion of the empty throne as if he intended to sit there. When the Archbishop asked if he wanted to see the King, Richard replied with a claim to the realm of England as heir to Richard II. The Commons and judges refused to consider a matter so high, leaving it to the Lord's decision. During the fortnight of debate, the Lancastrians had an opportunity to re-form their forces.

The death
of York

When Richard finally met them at Wakefield (December 30) in Yorkshire, he was defeated and killed.

The Yorkist cause would have been lost if not for Richard's son, Edward, earl of March, who defeated the Lancastrian forces at Mortimer's Cross (February 3, 1461) and marched on to an enthusiastic reception in London. The Lancastrians retreated northward. At Towton Moor on March 29, Edward won a victory that put the Lancastrians decisively to flight into Scotland. Edward was crowned king on June 28, but he dated his reign from March 4, the day the London citizens and soldiers recognized his title as king.

EDWARD IV (1461–70 AND 1471–83)

During the early years of his reign, from 1461 to 1470, Edward was chiefly concerned with putting down the opposition to his rule. He was occupied with trying to keep order and defeating Lancastrian plots against him. He was also involved with France and with Burgundy because Margaret of Anjou's chief hope of recovering Lancastrian fortunes lay in the support of the French king; but Louis XI was miserly in his aid to Margaret. Edward's main internal problem lay in his relations with Warwick, who had been his chief supporter in 1461. Richard Neville, earl of Warwick and Salisbury, called the "Kingmaker," was cousin to the King and was related to much of the English nobility. But Edward refused to let himself be dominated, particularly with respect to his marriage. When the crucial moment came in Warwick's negotiations for the French king's sister-in-law, Edward disclosed his secret marriage

Warwick,
the "King-
maker"

in 1464 to Elizabeth Woodville, a commoner. In addition, Edward conducted his own negotiations for the marriage of his sister, Margaret, to Charles the Bold of Burgundy in 1467. Warwick now allied himself with the Duke of Clarence, Edward's younger brother, basing the alliance in part on the marriage to Clarence of Warwick's daughter, Isabel; but he seemed to have no clear objective except to re-establish his authority with Edward. Ultimately, through the machinations of Louis XI, Warwick joined forces with Margaret of Anjou, deposed Edward in October 1470, and brought back Henry VI. The old king was from time to time exhibited to the London citizens in worn and unregal clothing, while Warwick conducted the government. Edward went into a brief exile in the Netherlands, but with the help of his brother-in-law, Charles, duke of Burgundy, he recovered his throne in the spring of 1471. Henry VI was put to death in the Tower, and his son was killed in battle.

The second half of Edward's reign, 1471–83, was a period of relative order, peace, and security. A council with extensive judicial and military powers was set up to govern the marches of Wales on behalf of the Prince of Wales; and Edward's brother, Richard of Gloucester, ruled ably in the north, presiding over a council that became the model for the Tudor Council of the North. Edward was popular. He levied few subsidies; in fact, he called Parliament only six times during his 25-year reign, and Parliament made only four grants of direct taxes. Early in his reign Edward had agreed to acts of resumption of royal estates, and he had also invested his personal fortune in trade; he thus had a considerable personal income, which allowed him more independence of parliamentary grants than his predecessors. Nonetheless, he levied benevolences, or supposedly voluntary gifts, from his subjects. In 1475 he took an army to France, but he accepted a pension from the King of France for not fighting. This increased Edward's financial independence and enabled him to leave a sizable fortune to his son. "False, fleeting, perjured Clarence," his eldest living brother, was attainted in Parliament in 1478 for involvement in a plot to depose Edward (Louis XI had planned for Clarence to marry Mary of Burgundy, the greatest heiress in Christendom, to stir up enmity between the two brothers). Clarence died in the Tower in 1478, reportedly executed by drowning in his bath.

Edward died in 1483, at age 40, worn out, it was said, by his sexual excesses. He left two sons, Edward and Richard, to the protection of his brother Richard, duke of Gloucester, although young Edward was actually at Ludlow with Earl Rivers, his maternal uncle. After a series of skirmishes with the Queen's party, the Duke domiciled both young princes in the Tower. The Queen took sanctuary in Westminster Abbey; her second son (by a previous marriage) and a brother were arrested and later killed. Young Edward's coronation was set for June 24. Meanwhile, Richard eliminated those who opposed his function as protector and defender of the realm and guardian to the young King. Eventually, even William, Lord Hastings, who had sent Richard word of Edward IV's death and had warned him against the Queen's party, was accused of treachery and summarily executed. Then on the day after the date originally set for Edward V's coronation, Lords and Commons summoned to Parliament unanimously adopted a petition requesting Richard to take over the crown and royal dignity. Richard accepted and rode to Westminster to sit on the royal throne in the King's Bench. Richard was crowned on July 6, taking the oath in English.

Accession
of Richard
III

RICHARD III (1483–85)

Richard was readily accepted no doubt because of his reputed ability and because people feared the insecurity of a long minority. The tide began to turn against him, however, in October 1483, when it began to be rumoured that he had murdered or connived at the murder of his nephews. Whether this was true or not mattered less than that it was thought to be true and that it obscured the King's able governance during his brief tenure of the royal estate. Legislation against benevolences and protection for English merchants and craftsmen did little to counteract his reputation as a treacherous friend and a wicked uncle;

and in the summer of 1485, when Henry Tudor, sole male claimant to Lancastrian ancestry and the throne, landed at Milford Haven, Richard's supporters widely deserted him and he was defeated and killed at the Battle of Bosworth Field.

ENGLAND IN THE LATE MIDDLE AGES

Bosworth Field has traditionally been taken as the date of the end of the Middle Ages in English history. Recently, however, a strong case has been made for setting the division between medieval and modern at 1536 or 1540. Henry Tudor did not bring to England any unique concept of monarchy, nor did he bring new order and peace to the country until toward the end of his reign. Yet he was the first of a dynasty under which, in the course of a century, English society and culture took on the peculiarly national characteristics that account for England's place in the modern world.

The emergence of the English nationality

The outstanding change in late medieval England was the emergence of an English nationality, largely because of the adoption of English as the language not only of everyday speech but also of documents and literature. An attempt as early as 1362 to legislate English into use in the law courts failed because the lawyers contended that they could not accurately plead in English. But in spite of this failure, English began to creep into public documents and records, including a City of London proclamation in 1384, Henry of Lancaster's claiming of the throne in 1399, royal letters of Henry V, some parliamentary petitions, and some 15th-century chronicles. Chaucer wrote his great work in English, and 15th-century writers followed his example, even though there was as yet no standard form of the language. The printer William Caxton set up his press in 1476 to publish English works for the growing reading public.

Sir Thomas More estimated, perhaps optimistically, that in his time (the early 16th century) more than half the people of England could read. The 15th century was a great period in the foundation of song schools, English reading schools, grammar schools, and colleges. Some schools were set up as adjuncts to chantries, some by guilds or by collegiate churches. Henry VI founded Eton College in 1440 and King's College in the University of Cambridge in 1441. His wife founded Queens' College in 1448. St. Catharine's was founded in 1473. By midcentury Lincoln, All Souls, and Magdalen had all been founded at Oxford.

The academies of English law (*i.e.,* the Inns of Court) expanded their membership and systematized their teaching of the law in this period. Many gentlemen's sons became members of the inns though not necessarily lawyers; many attended to learn the rudiments of the law in order to be able to defend and extend their estates. Two lawyers—Sir John Fortescue and Sir Thomas Littleton—wrote treatises on law and government that are studied down to the present day. Fortescue, a Lancastrian supporter, wrote while in exile a book in Latin in praise of English law; later, returning to England, he wrote in English a book titled *The Governance of England.* Littleton wrote in law French a learned treatise on tenures.

Change in the economy

Basic to all social change in the 15th century was change in the economy. Though England remained a predominantly agrarian society, it had begun to manufacture woollen cloth, which by the end of the 15th century had become an important source of wealth and a major export. As early as the 13th century the woollen industry had begun moving from the guild-ridden towns to the country, where waterpower could be harnessed. This movement had by the 15th century reduced the population of many formerly prosperous towns and contributed to the growth of new villages and towns. Oxford, Winchester, and Lincoln, for example, declined; Halifax and Leeds grew at the expense of York, and the West Riding at the expense of the eastern parts of Yorkshire; Suffolk and the Cotswolds region became important in the national economy.

In England's agrarian society, towns remained intricately involved with the countryside surrounding them. Land was still the most conspicuous form of wealth, and even money gained by trade or by plunder and rich ransoms in war was invested in land. But land ceased to be the main basis of feudal relationships. Money fiefs, in the form of annual stipends, increasingly took the place of landed fiefs in interconnections among the ruling classes. A great lord's power was no longer judged by the number of landed vassals who owed him service but by the number of liveried retainers he could call out to accompany him on important journeys. Contracted by indenture, a great man's retinue could be used to intimidate sheriffs or other local officers, to "labour" juries (to use prestige or force to persuade a jury to a verdict), and to assert rights of possession over land. This late medieval feudalism in England has been called bastard feudalism, because instead of acting as a substitute for public power in maintaining order it became on the part of the powerful lord a means of subverting it. When public power was weak, as it was in the latter part of Henry VI's reign, great lords implemented their rivalries in struggles for control of land and local offices.

On the lower social levels, villein labour service largely disappeared and serfdom or villeinage declined. Many serfs had taken up holdings deserted by victims of the Black Death at advantageous terms; others had escaped into the agrarian wage-labour force or taken refuge in towns. By the end of the 14th century many landlords had begun to see their best interest in letting out demesne lands formerly cultivated by villein or wage labour to tenants who would pay them a settled rent. Copyhold tenure (tenure by copy of the record of the manorial court) replaced villein tenure. In a time of falling prices, leaseholders were not necessarily better off financially than they had been as villeins, but they probably had more food. There was an active land market among peasants, some of whom managed to rise above their neighbours and began to constitute a class called yeomen. By the end of the 15th century villein status had ceased to have any importance.

Scholars disagree about what happened to the level of population in the century after the Black Death. An increase in the level of wages in a time of declining prices, extending well into the 15th century, can best be explained by a decline in population. But population figures for particular regions raise questions about this generalization. Part of the difficulty arises because there was in some areas a change in land use. Many landlords solved the problem of labour shortage and decline of food prices by converting their holdings to sheep pasture; this often involved displacement of peasant agriculturists. Some peasant cultivators also converted their lands to pasture. More land was enclosed for sheep pasture in the north, and there was a shift of population density to the southwest and southeast.

The main development in England's trade in the late Middle Ages was the increasing participation of Englishmen and the shift from trade in raw wool to trade in woollens. Edward III ruined the Italian bankers by failing to repay loans for conduct of the war. He then gave English merchants a monopoly of the wool export in return for their support. Many of these merchants were also ruined, but families like the de la Poles of Hull made lasting fortunes and eventually joined the ranks of the nobility. The Merchants of the Staple, who held a monopoly on raw wool exports, were more or less permanently established at Calais from the mid-14th century. As the cloth trade grew, a new association, the Merchant Adventurers, grew in power and wealth. Their chief export was cloth, and their chief market was the Netherlands, where they had their headquarters. In spite of xenophobia in England, which led to outbreaks in London against foreign merchants, the Italians reached their zenith of prosperity in Yorkist England, and Edward IV had to make important concessions to the Hanseatic merchants who helped him regain his throne in 1471.

Culturally, in the 15th century monastic chronicles came to an end and the writing of history declined. Thomas Walsingham (died 1422) was the last of the St. Albans chroniclers. There were some English chronicles written by citizens of London, and two lives of Henry V, but no great work of history came until later. Neither were there great works of philosophy or theology, although Reginald Pecock wrote an English treatise against the Lollards and

Art and architecture in the 15th century

various other works emphasizing the rational element in the Christian faith; he was judged guilty of heresy for his pains. No great poets succeeded to Chaucer, perhaps partly because there was no standard English language in which to express thought. The influence of the Italian Renaissance scarcely affected England before 1485. The full impact of the new learning was not felt until the 16th century.

In architecture alone, England showed originality. The 15th century was a great period of building of parish churches. Especially in the areas where the woollen industry had produced wealth, large churches were built in the peculiarly English Perpendicular style. The tomb of Richard Beauchamp at Warwick and King's College Chapel in Cambridge show what heights could be reached in English architecture and sculpture in the period.

England in the 15th century presents a confused picture politically and socially, and the economy is still something of an enigma. But as more work is done to elucidate their mysteries, these "scrambling and unquiet times" seem to promise a rich period to come.   (M.Has.)

England under the Tudors

HENRY VII (1485–1509)

When Henry Tudor, earl of Richmond, seized the throne on August 22, 1485, leaving the Yorkist Richard III dead upon the field of battle, few Englishmen would have predicted that 118 years of Tudor rule had begun. Six sovereigns had come and gone, and at least 15 major battles had been fought between rival contenders to the throne since that moment in 1399 when the divinity that "doth hedge a king" was violated and Richard II was forced to abdicate. Simple arithmetic forecast that Henry VII would last no more than a decade. Bosworth Field appeared to be nothing more than another of the erratic swings of the military pendulum in the struggle between the houses of York and Lancaster, and further evidence that the English crown had become a political football to be kicked about by overmighty magnates who captained semimercenary armies financed largely by foreign sources. What gave Henry Tudor victory in 1485 was not so much personal charisma as the fact that key noblemen deserted Richard III at the moment of his greatest need, that Thomas Stanley, 2nd Baron Stanley (later 1st earl of Derby), and his brother, Sir William, stood aside during most of the battle in order to be on the winning team, and that Louis XI of France supplied the Lancastrian forces with 1,000 mercenary troops.

The weakness of Henry's claim to the throne

The desperateness of the new monarch's gamble was equalled only by the doubtfulness of his claim. Henry VII's Lancastrian blood was tainted by bastardy, for he was descended on his mother's side from the Beaufort family, the offspring of John of Gaunt and his mistress Catherine Swynford, and though their children had been legitimized by act of Parliament, they had been specifically barred from the succession. His father's genealogy was equally suspect: Edmund Tudor, earl of Richmond, was born to Catherine of Valois, widowed queen of Henry V, by her clerk of the wardrobe, Owen Tudor; and the precise marital status of their relationship has never been established. Had quality of Plantagenet blood, not military conquest, been the essential condition of monarchy, Edward, earl of Warwick, the ten-year-old nephew of Edward IV, would have sat upon the throne. Might, not soiled right, had won out on the high ground at Bosworth Field, and Henry VII claimed his title by conquest. The new king, however, wisely sought to fortify his doubtful genealogical pretension first by parliamentary acclamation and then by royal marriage. The Parliament of November 1485 did not confer regal power on the first Tudor monarch—victory in war had already done that; but it did acknowledge Henry as "our new sovereign lord." Then on January 18, 1486, Henry VII married Elizabeth of York, the eldest daughter of Edward IV, thereby uniting "the white rose and the red" and launching England upon a century of "smooth-fac'd peace with smiling plenty and fair prosperous days."

"God's fair ordinance," which Shakespeare and later generations so clearly observed in the events of 1485–86, was

not limited to military victory, parliamentary sanction, and a fruitful marriage; the hidden hand of economic, social, and intellectual change was also on Henry's side. The day was coming when the successful prince would be more praised than the heroic monarch and the solvent sovereign more admired than the pious one. Henry Tudor was probably no better or worse than the first Lancastrian, Henry IV; they both worked diligently at their royal craft and had to fight hard to keep their crowns; but the seventh Henry achieved what the fourth had not—a secure and permanent dynasty—because England in 1485 was moving into a period of unprecedented economic growth and social change.

Economy and society. Long before 1485 the kingdom had begun to recover from the demographic catastrophe of the Black Death and the agricultural depression of the late 14th century; but as the 15th century came to a close, the rate of revival increased. The population in 1400 may have dropped as low as 2,500,000; by 1500 it was back up to at least 3,000,000, and a century later it was over 4,000,000. More people meant more mouths to feed, more backs to cover, and more vanity to satisfy. In response, yeoman farmers, gentleman sheep growers, urban cloth manufacturers, and merchant adventurers produced a social and economic revolution. With extraordinary speed the export of raw wool gave way to the export of woollen cloth manufactured at home, and the wool clothier or entrepreneur was soon buying fleece from sheep raisers, transporting the wool to cottagers for spinning and weaving, paying the farmer's wife and children by the piece, and collecting the finished article for shipment to Bristol, London, and eventually Europe. By the time Henry VII seized the throne, the Merchant Adventurers, an association of London wool exporters, were controlling the London–Antwerp market, replacing in economic importance the Staplers who dealt in raw wool. By 1496 they were a chartered organization with a legal monopoly of the woollen cloth trade, and largely as a consequence of their political and international importance, Henry successfully negotiated the Intercursus Magnus, a highly favourable commercial treaty between England and the Low Countries.

Revolution in the wool industry

As landlords increased the size of their flocks to the point that ruminants outnumbered human beings three to one, and as clothiers such as John Winchcombe (better known as Jack of Newbury) grew so rich that they could afford to entertain kings, inflation injected new life into the economy. England was caught up in a vast European spiral of rising prices, declining real wages, and cheap money. Inflation was largely the result of the growing abundance of gold and silver that flooded in upon the European economy from the New World and drove down the value and purchasing power of the traditional coinage, forcing up the cost of services and supplies. Between 1500 and 1540 prices in England doubled, and they doubled again in the next generation. In 1450 the cost of wheat had been what it was in 1300; by 1550 it had tripled.

Inflation and the wool trade together created an economic and social upheaval. Land plenty, labour shortage, low rents, and high wages, which had prevailed throughout the early 15th century as a consequence of economic depression and reduced population, were replaced by land shortage, labour surplus, high rents, and declining wages. The landlord, who a century before could find neither tenants nor labourers for his land and had left his fields fallow, could now convert his meadows into sheep runs. His rents and profits soared; his need for labour declined, for one shepherd and his dog could do the work of half a dozen men who had previously tilled the same field. Slowly the medieval system of land tenure and communal farming broke down. The common land of the manor was divided up and fenced in, and the peasant farmer who held his tenure either by copy (a document recorded in the manor court) or by unwritten custom was evicted. The total extent of enclosure and eviction is difficult to assess, but between 1455 and 1607 in 34 counties 516,573 acres (208,954 hectares), or 2.76 percent of the total, were enclosed, and some 50,000 persons were forced off the land. Statistics, however, are deceptive both as to emotional impact and extent of change. The most disturbing aspect

Enclosures

of the land revolution was not the emergence of a vagrant and unemployable labour force for whom society felt no social responsibility but an unprecedented increase in what men feared most—change. Farming techniques were transformed, the gap between rich and poor increased, the timeless quality of village life was upset, and on all levels of society old families were being replaced by new.

The beneficiaries of change, as always, were the most grasping, the most ruthless, and the best educated segments of the population: the landed country gentlemen and their socially inferior cousins, the merchants and lawyers. By 1500 the essential economic basis for the landed country gentleman's future political and social ascendancy was taking shape—the 15th-century knight of the shire was changing from a desperate and irresponsible land proprietor, ready to support the baronial feuding of the Wars of the Roses, into a respectable landowner desiring strong, practical government and the rule of law. The gentry did not care whether Henry VII's royal pedigree could bear close inspection; their own lineage was not above suspicion, and they were willing to serve the prince "in parliament, in council, in commission and other offices of the commonwealth."

Dynastic threats. It is no longer fashionable to call Henry VII a "new monarch," and indeed if the first Tudor had a model for reconstructing the monarchy it was the example of the great medieval kings. Newness, however, should not be totally denied Henry Tudor; his royal blood was very "new," and the extraordinary efficiency of his regime introduced a spirit into government that had rarely been present in the medieval past. It was, in fact, "newness" that governed the early policy of the reign, for the Tudor dynasty had to be secured and all those with a better or older claim to the throne liquidated. Elizabeth of York was deftly handled by marriage; the sons of Edward IV had already been removed from the list, presumably murdered by their uncle Richard III; the Earl of Warwick was promptly imprisoned; but the descendants of Edward IV's sister and daughters remained a threat to the new government. Equally dangerous was the persistent myth that the younger of the two princes murdered in the Tower had escaped his assassin and that the Earl of Warwick had escaped his jailers. The existence of pretenders acted as a catalyst for further baronial discontent and Yorkist aspirations, and in 1487 John de la Pole, a nephew of Edward IV by his sister Elizabeth, with the support of 2,000 mercenary troops paid for with Burgundian gold, landed in England to support the pretensions of Lambert Simnel, who passed himself off as the authentic Earl of Warwick. Again Henry Tudor was triumphant in war; at the Battle of Stoke, de la Pole was killed and Simnel captured and demoted to a scullery boy in the royal kitchen. Ten years later Henry had to do it all over again, this time with a handsome Flemish lad named Perkin Warbeck, who for six years was accepted in Yorkist circles in Europe as the real Richard IV, brother of the murdered Edward V. Warbeck tried to take advantage of Cornish anger against heavy royal taxation and increased government efficiency and sought to lead a Cornish army of social malcontents against the Tudor throne. It was a measure of the new vigour and popularity of the Tudor monarchy, as well as the support of the gentry, that social revolution and further dynastic war were total failures, and Warbeck found himself in the Tower along with the Earl of Warwick. In the end both men proved too dangerous to live, even in captivity, and in 1499 they were executed.

The policy of dynastic extermination did not cease with the new century. Under Henry VIII, the Duke of Buckingham was destroyed in 1521; the Earl of Warwick's sister, the Countess of Salisbury, was beheaded in 1541 and her descendants harried out of the land; and in 1546 the poet Henry Howard, earl of Surrey, the grandson of Buckingham, was put to death. By the end of Henry VIII's reign the job had been so well done that the curse of Edward III's fecundity had been replaced by the opposite problem—the Tudor line proved to be infertile when it came to producing healthy male heirs. Henry VII sired Arthur, who died in 1502, and Henry VIII in turn produced only

margin note: The threats of pretenders

one legitimate son, Edward VI, who died at the age of 16, thereby ending the direct male descent.

Financial policy. It was not enough for Henry VII to secure his dynasty; he also had to re-establish the financial credit of his crown and reassert the authority of royal law. Feudal kings had traditionally lived off four sources of nonparliamentary income: rents from the royal estates, revenues from import and export taxes, fees from the administration of justice, and moneys extracted on the basis of a vassal's duty to his overlord. The first Tudor was no different from his Yorkist or medieval predecessors; he was simply more ruthless and successful in demanding every penny that was owed him. Henry's first move was to confiscate all the estates of Yorkist adherents and to restore all property over which the crown had lost control since 1455 (in some cases as far back as 1377). To these essentially statutory steps he added efficiency of rent collection. In 1485 income from crown lands had totalled £29,000; by 1509 land revenues had risen to £42,000 and the profits from the Duchy of Lancaster had jumped from £650 to £6,500. At the same time, the Tudors profited from the growing economic prosperity of the realm, and custom receipts rose from over £20,000 to an average of £40,000 by the time Henry died.

The increase in custom and land revenues was applauded, for it meant fewer parliamentary subsidies and fitted the medieval formula that kings should live on their own, not parliamentary, income. But the collection of revenues from feudal sources and from the administration of justice caused great discontent and earned for Henry his reputation as a miser and extortionist. Generally, Henry demanded no more than his due as the highest feudal overlord, and a year after he became sovereign he established a commission to look into land tenure to discover who held property by knight's fee—that is, by obligation to perform military services. Occasionally he overstepped the bounds of feudal decency and abused his rights. In 1504, for instance, he levied a feudal aid (tax) to pay for the knighting of his son—who had been knighted 15 years before and had been dead for two. Henry VIII continued his father's policy of fiscal feudalism, forcing through Parliament in 1536 the Statute of Uses to prevent landowners from escaping "relief" and wardship (feudal inheritance taxes) by legal trickery and establishing the Court of Wards and Liveries in 1540 to handle the profits of feudal wardship. The howl of protest was so great that in 1540 Henry VIII had to compromise, and by the Statute of Wills a subject who held his property by knight's fee was permitted to bequeath two-thirds of his land without feudal obligation.

To fiscal feudalism Henry VII added rigorous administration of justice. As law became more effective it also became more profitable, and the policy of levying heavy fines as punishment upon those who dared break the king's peace proved to be a useful whip over the mighty magnate and a welcome addition to the King's exchequer. Even war and diplomacy were sources of revenue, and one of the major reasons why Henry VII wanted his second son, Henry, to marry his brother's widow was that the King was reluctant to return the dowry of 200,000 crowns that Ferdinand and Isabella of Spain had given for the marriage of their daughter, Catherine of Aragon. Generally Henry believed in a good neighbour policy—alliance with Spain by the marriage of Arthur and Catherine in 1501 and peace with Scotland by the marriage of his daughter Margaret to James IV in 1503—on the grounds that peace was cheap and trade profitable. In 1489, however, he was faced with the threat of the union of the Duchy of Brittany with the French crown; and England, Spain, the empire, and Burgundy went to war to stop it. Nevertheless, as soon as it became clear that nothing could prevent France from absorbing the duchy, Henry negotiated the unheroic but financially rewarding Treaty of Étaples in 1492, whereby he disclaimed all historic rights to French territory (except Calais) in return for an indemnity of £159,000. By fair means or foul, when the first Tudor died, his total nonparliamentary annual income had risen at least twofold and stood in the neighbourhood of £113,000 (some estimates are as high as £142,000). From land alone the King received £42,000, while the greatest landlord in the

margin note: Henry's sources of revenue

margin note: Income from the law courts and from marriage arrangements realm had to make do with less than £5,000; economically speaking, there were no longer any overmighty magnates.

The administration of justice. Money could buy power, but really successful kings, be they medieval or Tudor, had to earn the respect of their subjects by enforcing and administering the law. The problem for Henry VII was not to replace an old system of government with a new—no Tudor was consciously a revolutionary—but to make the ancient system work tolerably well. He had to tame but not destroy the nobility, develop organs of administration directly under his control, and wipe out provincialism and privilege wherever they appeared. In the task of curbing the old nobility, the King was immeasurably helped by the high aristocratic death rate during the Wars of the Roses; but where war left off, policy took over. Within three years of Bosworth Field, Thomas Howard, earl of Surrey, who had fought for Richard III, was liberated from the Tower of London and his estates restored; six years later Sir William Stanley, whose betrayal of Richard had helped Henry win his crown, was executed for high treason. The former was willing to become a devoted Tudor workhorse; the latter persisted in the anachronistic code of the divine right of nobility. Commissions of Array composed of local notables were appointed by the crown for each county in order to make use of the power of the aristocracy in raising troops but to prevent them from maintaining private armies (livery) with which to intimidate justice (maintenance) or threaten the throne.

Previous monarchs had sought to enforce the laws against livery and maintenance, but the first two Tudors, though they never totally abolished such evils, built up a reasonably efficient machine for enforcing the law, based on the historic premise that the king in the midst of his council was the fountain of justice. Traditionally the royal council had heard all sorts of cases, and very rapidly its members began to specialize. The Court of Chancery had for years dealt with civil offenses, the Court of Star Chamber evolved to handle criminal cases, the Court of Requests for poor men's suits, and the Court of Admiralty to cope with piracy. The process by which the conciliar courts developed was largely accidental, and the Court of Star Chamber acquired its name from the star-painted ceiling of the room in which the councillors sat, not from the statute of 1487 that simply recognized its existence. Conciliar justice was popular because the ordinary courts where common law prevailed were slow, cumbersome, favoured the rich and mighty, and tended to break down when asked to deal with riot, maintenance, livery, perjury, and fraud. The same search for efficiency applied to matters of finance. The traditional fiscal agency of the crown, the exchequer, was burdened down with archaic procedures and restrictions, and Henry VII turned to the more intimate and flexible departments of his personal household—specifically to the treasurer of the chamber, whom he could supervise directly—as the central tax-raising, rent-collecting, and money-disbursing segment of government.

The Tudors sought to enforce law in every corner of their kingdom, and step by step the blurred medieval profile of a realm shattered by semi-autonomous franchises, in which local law and custom were obeyed more than the king's law, was transformed into the clear outline of a single state filled with loyal subjects obeying the king's decrees. By 1500 royal government had been extended into the northern counties and Wales by the creation of a Council of the North and a Council for the Welsh Marches. The Welsh principalities had always been difficult to control, and it was not until 1536 that Henry VIII brought royal law directly into Wales and incorporated the 136 self-governing lordships into a greater England with five new shires.

If the term "new monarchy" was inappropriate in 1485, the same cannot be said for the year of Henry VII's death, for when he died in 1509, after 24 years of reign, he bequeathed to his son something quite new in English history: a safe throne, a full treasury, a solvent government, a prosperous land, and a united kingdom. Only one vital aspect of the past remained untouched, the independent Catholic Church, and it was left to the second Tudor to destroy this remaining vestige of medievalism.

Conciliar government

Henry VII's achievements

HENRY VIII (1509–47)

Cardinal Wolsey. A prince of 18 inherited his father's throne, but the son of an Ipswich butcher carried on the first Tudor's administrative policies. While the young sovereign enjoyed his inheritance, Thomas Wolsey collected titles—archbishop of York in 1514, lord chancellor and cardinal legate in 1515, and papal legate for life in 1524. He exercised a degree of power never before wielded by king or minister, for as lord chancellor and cardinal legate he united in his portly person the authority of church and state. He sought to tame both the lords temporal and spiritual, administering to the nobility the "new law of the Star Chamber," protecting the rights of the underprivileged in the poor men's Court of Requests, and teaching the abbots and bishops that they were subjects as well as ecclesiastical princes. Long before Henry assumed full power over his subjects' souls as well as their bodies, his servant had marked the way. The cardinal's administration, however, was stronger on promise than performance, and for all his fine qualities and many talents he exposed himself to the accusation that he prostituted policy for pecuniary gain and personal pride. Together, the King and Cardinal plunged the kingdom into international politics and war and helped make England one of the centres of Renaissance learning and brilliance; had Henry VIII died before 1529 he would have had to share the accolades with his chief minister. The King, however, lived on for 17 crucial years, and three interrelated factors brought Wolsey's career to an end—England's weakness as an international power, Henry's "Great Matter," and the growth of heresy.

Both the sovereign and his chief servant overestimated England's international position in the continental struggle between Francis I of France and the emperor Charles V. Militarily, the kingdom was of the same magnitude as the papacy—the English king had about the same revenues and could field about the same size army—and, as one contemporary noted, England with its back door constantly exposed to Scotland and with its economy dependent upon the Flanders wool trade was a mere "morsel among those choppers" of Europe. Nevertheless, Wolsey's diplomacy was based on the expectation that England could swing the balance of power either to France or to the empire and by holding that position could maintain the peace of Europe. The hollowness of the cardinal's policy was revealed in 1525 when Charles disastrously defeated and captured Francis at the Battle of Pavia. Italy was overrun with the Emperor's troops, the Pope became an imperial chaplain, all of Europe bowed before the conqueror, and England sank from being the fulcrum of continental diplomacy to the level of a second-rate power just at the moment when Henry had decided to rid himself of his wife, the 42-year-old Catherine of Aragon.

The divorce question. It is still a subject of debate whether Henry's decision to seek an annulment of his marriage and wed Anne Boleyn was a matter of state, of love, or of conscience. Quite possibly all three operated; Catherine was fat, seven years her husband's senior, incapable of bearing further children, and Anne was everything that the Queen was not—pretty, vivacious, and fruitful. Catherine had produced only one child and that was a girl, Princess Mary, and it seemed ironic indeed that the first Tudor should have solved the question of the succession only to expose the kingdom to an even greater peril in the second generation: a female ruler. The need for a male heir was paramount, for the last queen of England, Matilda, in the 12th century, had been a disaster, and there was no reason to believe that another would be any better. Finally, there was the question of the King's conscience. Henry had married his brother's widow, and though the Pope had granted a dispensation, the fact of the matter remained that every male child born to Henry and Catherine had died, and it was clearly written in Leviticus: "If a man takes his brother's wife, it is impurity; he has uncovered his brother's nakedness, they shall be childless" (20:21).

Unfortunately, Henry's divorce was not destined to stand or fall upon the theological issue of whether a papal dis-

Foreign policy

pensation could set aside such a prohibition, for Catherine was not simply the King's wife, she was also the aunt of the emperor Charles V, the most powerful sovereign in Europe. Both Henry and his cardinal knew that the divorce would never be granted unless the Emperor's power in Italy could be overthrown by an Anglo-French military alliance and the Pope rescued from imperial domination, and for three years Wolsey worked desperately to achieve this diplomatic and military end. Caught between an all-powerful emperor and a truculent English king, Clement VII procrastinated and offered all sorts of doubtful solutions short of divorce, including the marriage of Princess Mary and the King's illegitimate son, Henry Fitzroy, duke of Richmond; the legitimizing of all children begotten of Anne Boleyn; and the suggestion that Catherine go into a nunnery so that the King could be given permission to remarry. Wolsey's purpose was to have the divorce trial held in London, but in 1529, despite the arrival of Cardinal Lorenzo Campeggio to set up the machinery for a hearing, Wolsey's plans exploded. In July the Pope ordered Campeggio to transfer the case to Rome, where a decision against the King was a foregone conclusion; and in August Francis and the Emperor made peace at the Treaty of Cambrai. Wolsey's policies were a failure, and he was dismissed from office in October 1529. He died on November 29, just in time to escape trial for treason.

The fall of Wolsey

The Reformation background. Henry now began groping for new means to achieve his purpose. At first he contemplated little more than blackmail to frighten the Pope into submission; but slowly, reluctantly, and not realizing the full consequences of his actions, he moved step by step to open defiance and a total break with Rome. Wolsey in his person and his policies had represented the past. He was the last of the great ecclesiastical statesmen who had been as much at home in the cosmopolitan world of European Christendom, with its spiritual centre in Rome, as in a provincial capital such as London. By the time of Henry's divorce, Christendom was dissolving. Not only were feudal kingdoms assuming the character of independent nation-states but the spiritual unity of Christ's seamless cloak was also being torn apart by heresy. Possibly Henry would never have won his divorce had there not existed in England men who desired a break with Rome, not because it was dynastically expedient but because they regarded the Pope as the "whore of Babylon."

The medieval church had become an anachronism out of touch with the 16th-century reality of changing economic practices, governmental structure, and social values. More and more, God was French or German or English, and his representative in Rome was having ever greater difficulty in speaking so many languages and in persuading his international flock that he was the spiritual leader of all Christians and not simply a petty Italian potentate motivated by family ambition and political aggrandizement. The church was also withering from within. Historically, it was a state within a state—an independent clerical body possessed of special rights and privileges because of the fundamental division of man into body and soul. In the eyes of many, however, the church's duties in matters spiritual had been superseded by matters temporal. Absenteeism and pluralism were rife, and by 1520 in Oxfordshire alone 58 percent of the county's 192 parish priests were absentees. Bishops and high ecclesiastics were meant to tend to the cure of souls, but in fact they were engrossed in worldly affairs. Wolsey himself, as the greatest and richest clerical statesman, seemed to epitomize the worst aspects of that worldliness and corruption. Men continued to go to church, but it was increasingly difficult, especially for the landed gentleman and the wealthy merchant, to respect the old church. A sure sign that zeal for the ancient structure was flagging was the economic decline of the monasteries: in Norfolk, Yorkshire, and Buckinghamshire the capital wealth of the religious foundations rose only 1.13 percent between 1480 and 1540, which was not enough to offset normal depreciation, let alone keep up with inflation. More and more surplus wealth was being directed into other than religious channels; in the 15th century, the wool merchant Thomas Paycocke of Coggeshall had used the proceeds of trade to found a chantry to sing masses for his soul; a century later, William Sanderson of London invested the profits of fishmongering into two small ships to carry Capt. John Davis over the top of the world in search of the Northwest Passage to Cathay.

Abuses within the church

As the old church lived on in a fossilized condition, Christians looked elsewhere for inner contentment, and all over Europe men like Martin Luther, the German monk in Saxony, and Thomas Bilney, the Cambridge scholar in England, sought spiritual meaning and relief from ritualism, worldliness, and religious apathy. Luther in his monastery and Bilney in his college turned to the Bible, and each stumbled across the knowledge that even in the midst of despair, faith in God's mercy could save sinners. The new religious ideas flowed into England largely in the form of Lutheran doctrines, but they found a receptive audience not only because there were upper-class individuals who could find no spiritual satisfaction in the old religious formulas and who were looking for exactly what Luther and Bilney had to offer but also because there existed in England a religious subculture in the form of Lollardy. Its existence was always officially denied by the established church, but the ideas of John Wycliffe (died 1384) had never been exterminated. They lived on just below the surface, and by the time of the Reformation Lollardy was once again becoming respectable. Though Henry himself was never a Protestant, and during the first 20 years of his reign was a zealous persecutor of religious nonconformity, be it Lutheran or Lollard, the King would never have been able to push through the break with Rome simply on the basis of anticlericalism or apathy within the existing church. If his headship of an independent English church was to live in "the hearts of his subjects" and not "post alone hidden in acts of parliament," he had to call upon the support of the "zely people" (Protestant zealots) who viewed the political and constitutional steps by which Henry's divorce was legalized as being the prelude to a thorough spiritual reformation.

Lollardy

The break with Rome. With Wolsey and his papal authority gone, Henry turned to the authority of the state to obtain his divorce, and the so-called Reformation Parliament that first met in November 1529 was unprecedented—it lasted seven years, enacted 137 statutes (32 of which were of vital importance), and legislated in areas that no feudal Parliament had ever dreamed of entering. "King in Parliament" became the revolutionary instrument by which the medieval church was destroyed. The first step was to intimidate the church, and in 1531 Convocation was forced under threat of praemunire (a statute prohibiting the operation of the legal and financial jurisdiction of the pope without royal consent) to grant the sovereign a gift of £119,000 and to acknowledge him supreme head of the church "as far as the law of Christ allows." Then the government struck at the papacy, threatening to cut off its revenues; the Annates Statute of 1532 empowered Henry, if he saw fit, to abolish payment to Rome of the first year's income of all newly installed bishops. The implied threat had little effect on the Pope; and time was running out, for by December 1532 Anne Boleyn was pregnant, and on January 25, 1533, she was secretly married to Henry. If the King was to be saved from bigamy and his child born in wedlock, he had less than eight months to get rid of Catherine of Aragon. Archbishop William Warham conveniently died in August 1532, and in March 1533 a demoralized and frightened pontiff sanctioned the installation of Thomas Cranmer as primate of the English church. Cranmer was a friend of the divorce, but before he could oblige his sovereign the Queen's right of appeal from the archbishop's court to Rome had to be destroyed; and this could be done only by cutting the constitutional cords holding England to the papacy. Consequently, in April 1533 the crucial statute was enacted; the Act of Restraint of Appeals boldly decreed that "this realm of England is an empire." A month later an obliging archbishop heard the divorce case and adjudged the King's marriage to be null and void. On June 1 Anne was crowned rightful queen of England, and three months and a week later, on September 7, 1533, the royal child was born. To "the great shame and confusion" of astrologers, it turned out to be Elizabeth Tudor.

Thomas Cranmer and the divorce

Henry was mortified; he had risked his soul and his crown for yet another girl, but Anne had proved her fertility and it was hoped that a male heir would shortly follow. In the meantime it was necessary to complete the break with Rome and rebuild the Church of England. By the Act of Succession of March 1534, subjects were ordered to accept the King's marriage to Anne as "undoubted, true, sincere and perfect." A second Annate's Statute severed most of the financial ties with Rome, and in November the constitutional revolution was solemnized in the Act of Supremacy, which announced that Henry Tudor was and always had been "Supreme Head of the Church of England"; not even the qualifying phrase "as far as the law of Christ allows" was retained.

The consolidation of the Reformation. The medieval tenet that church and state were separate entities with divine law standing higher than human law had been legislated out of existence; the new English Church was in effect a department of the Tudor state. The destruction of the Catholic Church led inevitably to the dissolution of the monasteries. As monastic religious fervour and economic resources began to dry up, it was easy enough for the government to build a case that monasteries were centres of vice and corruption. In the end, however, what destroyed them was neither apathy nor abuse but the fact that they were contradictions within a national church, for religious foundations by definition were international, supranational organizations that traditionally supported papal authority. Though they bowed to the royal supremacy, the government continued to view them with suspicion, arguing that they had obeyed only out of fear, and their destruction got underway early in 1536. In the name of fiscal reform and efficiency, foundations with endowments of under £200 a year (nearly 400 of them) were dissolved on the grounds that they were too small to do their job effectively. By late 1536 confiscation had become state policy, for the Pilgrimage of Grace, a Catholic-inspired uprising in the north, seemed to be clear evidence that all monasteries were potential nests of traitors. By 1539 the foundations, both great and small, were gone, and property worth possibly £2,000,000 was nationalized and incorporated into the crown lands, thereby almost doubling the government's normal peacetime, nonparliamentary income. Had those estates remained in the possession of the crown, English history might have been very different, for the kings of England would have been able to rule without calling upon Parliament, and the constitutional authority that evolved out of the crown's fiscal dependence on Parliament would never have developed. For better or for worse, Henry and his descendants had to sell the profits of the Reformation; and by 1603 three-fourths of the monastic loot had passed into the hands of the landed gentry. The legend of a "golden shower" is false. Monastic property was never given away at bargain prices, nor was it consciously presented to the kingdom in order to win the support of the ruling elite. Instead, most of the land was sold at its fair market value to pay for Henry's wars and foreign policy. The effect, however, was crucial—the most powerful elements within Tudor society now had a vested interest in protecting their property against papal Catholicism.

The divorce, the break with Rome, and even the destruction of the monasteries went through with surprisingly little opposition. It had been foreseen that the royal supremacy might have to be enacted in blood, and the Act of Supremacy (March 1534) and the Act of Treason (December) were designed to root out and liquidate the dissent. The former was a loyalty test requiring subjects to take an oath swearing to accept not only the matrimonial results of the break with Rome but also the principles on which it stood; the latter extended the meaning of treason to include all those who did "maliciously wish, will or desire, by words or writing or by craft imagine" the King's death or slander his marriage. Sir Thomas More (who had succeeded Wolsey as lord chancellor), Bishop John Fisher (who almost alone among the episcopate had defended Catherine during her trial), and a handful of monks suffered death for their refusal to accept the concept of a national church. Even the Pilgrimage of Grace of 1536–37

The dissolution of the monasteries

The acts of Supremacy and Treason

was a short-lived eruption. The uprisings in Lincolnshire in October and in Yorkshire during the winter were without doubt religiously motivated, but they were also as much feudal and social rebellions as revolts in support of Rome. Peasants, landed country gentlemen, and feudal barons could unite in defense of the monasteries and the old religion, and for a moment the rebels seemed on the verge of toppling the Tudor state. The nobility were angered that they had been excluded from the King's government by men of inferior social status, and they resented the encroachment of bureaucracy into the northern shires. The gentry were concerned by rising taxes and the peasants by threatened enclosure; but the three elements had little in common outside religion, and the uprisings fell apart from within. The rebels were soon crushed and their leaders—including Robert Aske, one of the most pleasing figures of the century—brutally executed.

Henry's last years. Henry was so securely seated upon his throne that the French Ambassador announced that he was more an idol to be worshipped than a king to be obeyed, and the King successfully survived four more matrimonial experiments, the enmity of every major power in Europe, and an international war. On May 19, 1536, Anne Boleyn's career was terminated by the executioner's ax. She had failed in her promise to produce further children to secure the succession. The King's love had turned to hatred, but what sealed the Queen's fate was the death of her rival, Catherine of Aragon, on January 8, 1536. From that moment it was clear that should Henry again marry, whoever was his wife, the children she might bear would be legitimate in the eyes of Catholics and Protestants alike. How much policy, how much repulsion for Anne, how much attraction for Jane Seymour played in the final tragedy is beyond analysis, but 11 days after Anne's execution Henry married Jane. Sixteen months later the future Edward VI was born. The mother died as a consequence, but the father finally had what it had taken a revolution to achieve, a legitimate male heir.

Henry married thrice more, once for reasons of diplomacy, once for love, and once for peace and quiet. Anne of Cleves, his fourth wife, was the product of Reformation international politics. For a time in 1539 it looked as if Charles V and Francis would come to terms and unite against the schismatic King of England, and the only allies Henry possessed were the Lutheran princes of Germany. In something close to panic, he was stampeded into marriage with Anne of Cleves, but the following year, the moment the diplomatic scene changed, he dropped both his wife and the man who had engineered the marriage, his vicar general in matters spiritual, Thomas Cromwell. Anne was divorced July 12, Cromwell was executed July 28, and Henry married Catherine Howard the same day. The second Catherine did not do as well as her cousin, the first Anne; she lasted only 18 months. Catherine proved to be neither a virgin before her wedding nor a particularly faithful damsel after her marriage. With the execution of his fifth wife, Henry turned into a sick old man, and he took as his last spouse Catherine Parr, who was as much a nursemaid as a wife. During those final years, the King's interests turned to international affairs. Henry's last war (1543–46) was fought not to defend his church against resurgent European Catholicism but to renew a much older policy of military conquest in France. Though he enlarged the English Pale at Calais by seizing the small French port of Boulogne, the war had no lasting diplomatic or international effects except to assure that the monastic lands would pass into the hands of the gentry.

By the time Henry died (January 28, 1547) medievalism had nearly vanished. The crown stood at the pinnacle of its power, able to demand and receive a degree of obedience from both great and small that no feudal monarch had been able to achieve. The measure of that authority was threefold: (1) the extent to which Henry had been able to thrust a very unpopular divorce and supremacy legislation down the throat of Parliament; (2) his success in raising unprecedented sums of money through taxation; and (3) his ability to establish a new church on the ashes of the old. It is difficult to say whether these feats were the work of the King or his chief minister, Thomas Cromwell. The

Birth of Edward VI

The achievements of Henry VIII

will was probably Henry's, the parliamentary means his minister's, but whoever was responsible, by 1547 England was a long way along the road of Reformation. The crown had assumed the authority of the papacy without as yet fundamentally changing the old creed, but the ancient structure was severely shaken. Throughout England men were arguing that because the pontiff had been proved false, the entire Catholic creed was suspect; and the cry went up to "get rid of the poison with the author." It was not long before every aspect of Catholicism was under attack—the miracle of the mass whereby the bread and wine were converted into the body and blood of Christ, the doctrine of purgatory, the efficacy of saints and images, the concept of an ordained priesthood with miraculous powers, and the doctrine of the celibacy of the clergy. The time had come for Parliament and the supreme head to decide what constituted the "true" faith for Englishmen. Henry never worked out a consistent religious policy: the Ten Articles of 1536 and the *Bishop's Book* of the following year tended to be somewhat Lutheran in tone; the Six Articles of 1539, or the Act for Abolishing Diversity of Opinion, and the *King's Book* of 1543 were mildly Catholic. Whatever the religious colouring, Henry's ecclesiastical *via media* was based on obedience to an authoritarian old king and on subjects who were expected to live "soberly, justly and devoutly." Unfortunately for the religious, social, and political peace of the kingdom, both these conditions disappeared the moment Henry died and a nine-year-old boy sat upon the throne.

EDWARD VI (1547–53)

Seymour's protectorate

Henry was legally succeeded by his son Edward VI, but power passed to his brother-in-law, Edward Seymour, earl of Hertford, who became duke of Somerset and lord protector shortly after the new reign began. Seymour ruled *in loco parentis;* the divinity of the crown resided in the boy king, but authority was exercised by an uncle who proved himself to be more merciful than tactful, more idealistic than practical. Sweet reason and tolerance were substituted for the old King's brutal laws. The treason and heresy acts were repealed or modified, and the result came close to destroying the Tudor state. The moment idle tongues could speak with impunity, the kingdom broke into a chorus of religious and social discord. To stem religious dissent, the Lord Protector introduced the Prayer Book of 1549 and an act of uniformity to enforce it. Written by Thomas Cranmer, the Prayer Book was a literary masterpiece but a political flop, for it failed in its purpose. It sought to bring into a single Protestant fold all varieties of middle-of-the-road religious beliefs by deliberately obscuring the central issue of the exact nature of the mass—whether it was a miraculous sacrament or a commemorative service. The Prayer Book succeeded only in antagonizing Protestants and Catholics alike.

Somerset was no more successful in solving the economic and social difficulties of the reign. Rising prices, debasement of the currency, and the cost of war had produced an inflationary crisis in which prices doubled between 1547 and 1549. A false prosperity ensued in which the wool trade boomed, but so also did enclosurers with all their explosive potential. The result was social revolution. Whether Somerset deserved his title of "the good duke" is a matter of opinion. Certainly the peasants thought that he favoured the element in the House of Commons that was anxious to tax sheep raisers and curb enclosures and that section of the clergy that was lashing out at economic inequality. In the summer of 1549 the peasantry in Cornwall and Devonshire revolted against the Prayer Book in the name of the good old religious days under Henry VIII, and almost simultaneously the humble folk in Norfolk rose up against the economic and social injustices of the century. At the same time that domestic rebellion was stirring, the

The fall of Seymour

protector had to face a political and international crisis, and he proved himself to be neither a far-sighted statesman nor a shrewd politician. He embroiled the country in war with Scotland that soon involved France and ended in total defeat, and he earned the enmity and disrespect of the members of his own council. In the eyes of the ruling elite, he was responsible for governmental inepti-

tude and social and religious revolution. The result was inevitable: a palace revolution in October 1549 ensued in which Seymour was arrested and deprived of office, and two and a half years later he was executed on trumped-up charges of treason.

The protector's successor and the man largely responsible for his fall was John Dudley, earl of Warwick, who became duke of Northumberland. The Duke was a man of action who represented most of the acquisitive aspects of the landed elements in society and who allied himself with the extreme section of the Protestant reformers. Under Northumberland, England pulled out of Scotland and in 1550 returned Boulogne to France; social order was ruthlessly re-established in the countryside, the more conservative of the Henrician bishops were imprisoned, the wealth of the church was systematically looted, and uncompromising Protestantism was officially sanctioned. The Ordinal of 1550 transformed the divinely ordained priest into a governmental appointee, the new Prayer Book of 1552 was avowedly Protestant, altars were turned into tables, clerical vestments gave way to plain surplices, and religious orthodoxy was enforced by a new and more stringent Act of Uniformity. How long a kingdom still attached to the outward trappings of Catholicism would have tolerated doctrinal radicalism and the plundering of chantry lands and episcopal revenues under Somerset and Northumberland is difficult to say, but in 1553 the ground upon which Northumberland had built his power crumbled: Edward was dying of consumption. To save himself from Catholic Mary, who was Edward's legal heir as established both by Parliament and her father's will, the Duke tried his hand at kingmaking. He persuaded Edward to declare his sister illegitimate and to bequeath his throne to Lady Jane Grey, the granddaughter of Henry VIII's sister (Mary, duchess of Suffolk), and incidentally Northumberland's daughter-in-law. The gamble failed, for when Edward died on July 6, 1553, the kingdom rallied to the daughter of Catherine of Aragon. Whatever their religious inclinations, Englishmen preferred a Tudor on the throne to a kingmaker ruling behind a puppet queen; in nine days the interlude was over, and Northumberland and his daughter-in-law were in the Tower.

Lady Jane Grey

MARY I (1553–58)

The new Catholic Queen had many fine qualities, and contemporaries announced that she was "a prince of heart and courage more than commonly is in womanhood"; but she was hopelessly outdated. She envisioned the return of a Catholic Church that had long since ceased to exist anywhere in Europe. The worldly and pliable church of pre-Reformation days had been destroyed by the fire of religious war and extremism, and both Catholic and Protestant now denied the tolerant humanistic principle that "men who live according to equity and justice shall be saved" no matter what their creed. By 1553 salvation was strictly a matter of right belief. For Mary it was a sacred obligation to return England to the Catholic fold, and it was almost as great a duty to marry Philip of Spain, her Habsburg cousin and the son of Charles V, the man who had defended her mother's marital rights. She married Philip on July 25, 1554, and six months later, after the landed elements had been assured that their monastic property would not be taken from them, Parliament repealed the Act of Supremacy, reinstated the heresy laws, and petitioned for reunion with Rome. In the end both achievements proved sterile. Her marriage was without love or children, and by associating Catholicism in the popular mind with Spanish arrogance, it triggered a rebellion that almost overthrew the Tudor throne. In January 1554, under the leadership of Sir Thomas Wyat, the peasants of Kent rose up against the Queen's Catholic and Spanish policies, and 3,000 men marched on London. The rebellion was crushed, but it revealed to Mary and her chief minister, Cardinal Reginald Pole, that the kingdom was filled with disloyal hearts who placed Protestantism and nationalism higher than their obedience to the throne.

The tragedy of Mary's reign was the belief not only that the old church of her mother's day could be restored but also that it could be best served by fire and blood. Some

300 men and women were martyred in the Smithfield Fires during the last three years of her reign; compared to the Continent, the numbers were not large, but the emotional impact was great. Among the first half-dozen martyrs were the Protestant leaders Cranmer, Ridley, Latimer, and Hooper, and they were burned to strike terror into the hearts of lesser men. Their deaths, however, had the opposite effect; their bravery encouraged others to withstand the flames, and the Smithfield Fires continued to burn because nobody could think of what to do with heretics except to put them to death. The law required it, the prisons were overflowing, and the martyrs themselves offered the government no way out except to enforce the grisly laws.

Mary's reign was a study in failure. Her husband, who was ten years her junior, remained in England as little as possible; the war between France and the Habsburg Empire, into which her Spanish marriage had dragged the kingdom, was a disaster and resulted in the loss of England's last continental outpost, Calais; her subjects learned to call her "bloody," and Englishmen greeted the news of her death and the succession of her sister Elizabeth on November 17, 1558, with ringing bells and bonfires.

ELIZABETH I (1558–1603)

No one in 1558, any more than in 1485, would have predicted that despite the social discord, political floundering, and international humiliation of the past decade, the kingdom again stood on the threshold of an extraordinary reign. Elizabeth had much in common with her grandfather; in both cases their pedigrees were suspect and the political omens unfavourable, and to make matters worse the new monarch was the wrong sex. Englishmen knew that it was unholy and unnatural that "a woman should reign and have empire above men." At 25, however, Elizabeth was better prepared than most women to have empire over men. She had survived the palace revolutions of her brother's reign and the Catholicism of her sister's; she was the product of a fine Renaissance education, and she had learned the need for strong secular leadership devoid of religious bigotry. Moreover, she possessed her father's magnetism without his egotism or ruthlessness. She was also her mother's daughter, and the offspring of Anne Boleyn had no choice but to reestablish the royal supremacy and once again sever the ties with Rome. Elizabeth herself would have preferred a variety of her father's Catholicism without the pope, but she needed the support of the "zely people" and had to take her religious stand well to the left of centre. Her religious settlement was based on the Protestant Prayer Book of 1552. Many of the ceremonial trappings of Catholicism, however, were retained, and the tone of the document was softened to allow the communion service to become a mass for those Catholics who were looking for a way of conforming with the new settlement. The compromise worked largely because the Queen and her advisers correctly argued that Catholics were better losers than Protestants and that the structure of the new religious establishment should be large, comfortable, and popular, with authority stemming from the royal prerogative. The ecclesiastical history of Elizabeth's reign was, in fact, a long debate with the radicals over the source of divine power—whether it was hierarchical and ultimately emanated from the crown itself or whether it was democratic and was centred in the congregation of all believers.

The Tudor ideal of government. The religious settlement was part of a larger social arrangement that was authoritarian to its core. Elizabeth was determined to be queen in fact as well as in name. She tamed the House of Commons with tact combined with firmness, and she carried on a love affair with her kingdom in which womanhood, instead of being a disadvantage, became her greatest asset. The men she appointed to help her run and stage-manage the government were *politiques* like herself: William Cecil (later Lord Burghley), her principal secretary and in 1572 her lord treasurer; Matthew Parker, her archbishop of Canterbury; and a small group of other moderate and secular men.

In setting her house in order, the Queen followed the hierarchical assumptions of her day. All creation was presumed to be a Great Chain of Being, running from the tiniest insect to the godhead itself, and the universe was seen as an organic whole in which each part played a divinely prescribed role. In politics every element was expected to obey "one head, one governor, one law" in exactly the same way as all parts of the human body obeyed the brain. The crown was divine and gave leadership, but it did not exist alone, nor could it claim a monopoly of divinity, for all parts of the body politic had been created by God. The organ that spoke for the entire kingdom was not the king alone, but "King in Parliament," and when Elizabeth sat in the midst of her Lords and Commons it was said that "every Englishman is intended to be there present from the prince to the lowest person in England." The Tudors needed no standing army in "the French fashion" because God's will and the monarch's decrees were enshrined in acts of Parliament, and this was society's greatest defense against rebellion. The controlling mind within this mystical union of crown and Parliament belonged to the Queen. The Privy Council, acting as the spokesman of royalty, planned and initiated all legislation, and Parliament was expected to turn that legislation into law. Inside and outside Parliament the goal of Tudor government was benevolent paternalism in which the strong hand of authoritarianism was masked by the careful shaping of public opinion, the artistry of pomp and ceremony, and the deliberate effort to tie the ruling elite to the crown by catering to the financial and social aspirations of the landed country gentleman. Every aspect of government was intimate because it was small and rested on the support of probably no more than 5,000 key persons. The bureaucracy consisted of a handful of privy councillors at the top and at the bottom possibly 500 paid civil servants—the 15 members of the secretariat, the 265 clerks and custom officials of the treasury, a staff of 50 in the judiciary, and approximately 150 more scattered in other departments. Tudor government was not predominantly professional. Most of the work was done by unpaid amateurs: the sheriffs of the shires, the lord lieutenants of the counties, and above all the Tudor maids-of-all-work—the 1,500 or so justices of the peace.

Smallness did not mean lack of government, for the 16th-century state was conceived of as an organic totality in which the possession of land carried with it duties of leadership and service to the throne, and inferior social position bore the obligation to accept the decisions of elders and betters. The Tudors were essentially medieval in their economic and social philosophy. The usurer and capitalist were considered as dangerous to the commonweal as the overmighty magnate. The aim of government was to curb competition and regulate life so as to attain an ordered and stable society in which all could share according to status. The Statute of Apprentices of 1563 embodied this concept, for it assumed the moral obligation of all men to work, the existence of divinely ordered social distinctions, and the need for the state to define and control all occupations in terms of their utility to society. The same assumption operated in the famous Elizabethan Poor Law of 1601—the need to assure a minimum standard of living to all men within an organic and noncompetitive society. By 1600 poverty, unemployment, and vagrancy had become too widespread for the church to handle, and the state had to take over, instructing each parish to levy taxes to pay for poor relief, and to provide work for the able-bodied, punishment for the indolent, and charity for the sick, the aged, and the disabled. The Tudor social ideal was to achieve a static class structure by guaranteeing a fixed labour supply, restricting social mobility, curbing economic freedom, and creating a kingdom in which subjects could fulfill their ultimate purpose in life—spiritual salvation, not material well-being.

Elizabethan society. Social reality, at least for the poor and powerless, was probably a far cry from the ideal, but for a few years Elizabethan England seemed to possess an extraordinary internal balance and external dynamism. In part the Queen herself was responsible. She demanded no windows into men's souls, and she charmed both great and small with her artistry and tact. In part, however, the

Elizabethan age was a success because men had at their disposal new and exciting areas into which to channel their energy. From a kingdom that had once been known for its "sluggish security," Englishmen suddenly turned to the sea and the world that was opening up around them. The first hesitant steps had been taken under Henry VII when John Cabot in 1497 sailed in search of a Northwest Passage to China and as a consequence discovered Cape Breton Island. The search for Cathay became an economic necessity in 1550 when the wool trade collapsed and merchants had to find new markets for their cloth. In response, the Muscovy Company was established to trade with Russia, and by 1588 a hundred vessels a year were visiting the Baltic. Martin Frobisher during the 1570s made a series of voyages to northern Canada in the hope of finding gold and a shortcut to the Orient; John Hawkins encroached upon Spanish and Portuguese preserves and sailed in 1562 for Africa in quest of slaves to sell to West Indian plantation owners; and Sir Francis Drake circumnavigated the globe (December 13, 1577–September 26, 1580) in search not only of the riches of the East Indies but also of Terra Australis, the great southern continent, and new worlds to open up to English trade and colonization. Suddenly Englishmen were on the move: Sir Humphrey Gilbert and his band of settlers set forth for Newfoundland (1583); Sir Walter Raleigh organized the equally ill-fated "lost colony" at Roanoke (1587–91); John Davis in his two small ships, the "Moonshine" and the "Sunshine," reached 72° north, the farthest north any Englishman had ever been (1585–87); and the honourable East India Company was founded to organize the silk and spice trade with the Orient on a permanent basis. The outpouring was certainly inspired by the urge for riches, but it was also religious—the desire to labour in the Lord's vineyard and to found in the wilderness a new and better nation. As it was said, Englishmen went forth "to seek new worlds for gold, for praise, for glory." The same dynamism was manifest in art and culture. Elizabeth's reign was the age of Shakespeare, Marlowe, Spenser, Raleigh, Sidney, Bacon, Donne, and a host of lesser literary lights. It was also the century of stately homes, when the houses of the great were no longer fortresses to defend a man's retainers and dependents but were unprotected residences open to the sunshine. They were designed to reflect man's rational control over nature and were built by gentlemen with enormous confidence in England's future as well as their own. Even the dangers of the reign—the precariousness of Elizabeth's throne and the struggle with Catholic Spain—somehow contrived to generate a self-confidence that had been lacking under "the little Tudors."

Mary, Queen of Scots. The first decade of Elizabeth's reign was relatively quiet, but after 1568 three interrelated matters set the stage for the crisis of the century: the Queen's refusal to marry, the various plots to replace her with Mary of Scotland, and the religious and economic clash with Spain. Elizabeth Tudor's virginity was the cause of great international discussion, for every bachelor prince of Europe hoped to win a throne through marriage with Gloriana, and the source of even greater domestic concern, for everyone except the Queen herself was convinced that Elizabeth should marry and produce heirs. The issue was the cause of her first major confrontation with the House of Commons, which was informed that royal matrimony was not a subject for commoners to discuss. Elizabeth preferred maidenhood; it was politically safer and her most useful diplomatic weapon, but it gave poignancy to the intrigues of her cousin Mary, Queen of Scots. Mary had been an unwanted visitor-prisoner in England ever since 1568, after she had been forced to abdicate her Scottish throne in favour of her 13-month-old son, James VI. She was Henry VIII's grandniece and, in the eyes of many Catholics and a number of political malcontents, the rightful ruler of England, for Mary of Scotland was a Catholic. As the religious hysteria mounted, there was steady pressure put on Elizabeth to rid England of this dangerous threat, but the Queen delayed a final decision for almost 19 years. In the end, however, she had little choice. Jesuit priests were entering the kingdom to harden the hearts of the Queen's subjects against her, forcing the government to introduce

harsher and harsher recusancy laws (the fine for failure to attend Anglican service on Sundays was raised from one shilling a week to £20 a month). Puritans were thundering for even stiffer penalties, and Mary played into the hands of her religious and political enemies by involving herself in a series of schemes to unseat her cousin. One plot helped to trigger the rebellion of the northern earls in 1569. Another, the Ridolfi plot of 1571, called for an invasion by Spanish troops stationed in the Netherlands and resulted in the execution in 1572 of the Duke of Norfolk, the ranking peer of the realm. Yet another, the Babington plot of 1586, was in fact a carefully arranged government trap to gain sufficient evidence to have Mary tried and executed for high treason.

The clash with Spain. Mary was executed on February 8, 1587; by then England had moved from cold war to open war against Spain. Philip II was the colossus of Europe and leader of resurgent Catholicism. His kingdom was strong; Spanish troops were the best in Europe, Spain itself had been carved out of territory held by the infidel and still retained its crusading zeal, and the wealth of the New World poured into the treasury at Madrid. Spanish pre-eminence was directly related to the weakness of France, which ever since the accidental death of Henry II in 1559 had been torn by factional strife and civil and religious war. In response to this diplomatic and military imbalance, English foreign policy underwent a fundamental change. By the Treaty of Blois in 1572 England gave up its historic enmity with France, accepting by implication that Spain was the greater danger. It is difficult to say at what point a showdown between Elizabeth and her former brother-in-law became unavoidable—there were so many areas of disagreement—but the two chief points were the refusal of English merchants-cum-buccaneers to recognize Philip's claims to a monopoly of trade wherever the Spanish flag flew throughout the world, and the military and financial support given by the English to Philip's rebellious and heretical subjects in the Netherlands.

The most blatant act of English poaching in Spanish imperial waters was Drake's circumnavigation of the earth, during which Spanish shipping was looted, Spanish claims to California ignored, and Spanish world dominion proved to be a paper empire. But the encounter that really poisoned Anglo-Iberian relations was the Battle of San Juan de Ulúa in September 1568. It concerned John Hawkins' third and final slaving expedition to the Caribbean. After a highly successful voyage in which he exchanged African slaves for West Indian sugar, gold, and hides in defiance of Spanish commercial regulations, Hawkins' fleet of ten vessels put in for repairs at San Juan de Ulúa on the Mexican coast. The next day the Spanish Caribbean fleet appeared, and on the Spanish commander's written statement of peaceful intentions, Hawkins made room in the crowded harbour. No sooner were the Spanish anchored than they launched a surprise attack; only Hawkins in the "Minion" and Drake in the "Judith" escaped. The English cried foul treachery, the Spanish dismissed the action as sensible tactics when dealing with pirates. Drake and Hawkins never forgot or forgave, and it was Hawkins who, as treasurer of the navy, began to build the revolutionary ships that destroyed the old-fashioned galleons of the Spanish Armada.

If the English never forgave Philip's treachery at San Juan de Ulúa, the Spanish never forgot Elizabeth's interference in the Netherlands, where Dutch Protestants were in full revolt. At first, aid had been limited to money and the harbouring of Dutch ships in English ports; but after the assassination of the Protestant leader, William of Orange, in 1584, the position of the rebels became so desperate that Elizabeth in August 1585 sent over an army of 6,000 under the command of the Earl of Leicester. Reluctantly, Philip decided on war against England as the only way of exterminating heresy and disciplining his subjects in the Netherlands. Methodically, he began to build a fleet of 130 vessels, 31,000 men, and 2,431 cannons to hold naval supremacy in the Channel long enough for the Duke of Parma's army, stationed at Dunkirk, to cross over to England. Nothing Elizabeth could do seemed to be able to stop the *Armada Catholica*. She sent Drake to

The English explorers

The question of the Queen's marriage

Plots on Mary's behalf

The harassment of Spain at sea

Spain in April 1587 in a spectacular strike at that portion of the fleet forming at Cádiz, but it succeeded only in delaying the sailing date. That delay, however, was important, for Philip's Admiral of the Ocean Seas, the veteran Marqués de Santa Cruz, died, and the job of sailing the Armada was given to the Duque de Medina-Sidonia, who was invariably seasick and confessed that he knew more about gardening than war. What ensued was not the new commander's fault. He did the best he could in an impossible situation, for Philip's Armada was invincible in name only. It was technologically and numerically outclassed by an English fleet of close to 200. Worse, its strategic purpose was grounded on a fallacy: that Parma's troops could be conveyed to England; for the Spanish controlled no deep-water port in the Netherlands in which the Armada's great galleons and Parma's light troop-carrying barges could rendezvous. Even the deity seemed to be more English than Spanish, and in the end the fleet, buffeted by gales, was dashed to pieces as it sought to escape home via the northern route around Scotland and Ireland. Of the 130 ships that left Spain, only 76 crept home; 10 had been captured, sunk, or driven aground by English guns, 24 were sacrificed to wind and storm, and 20 others were "lost, fate unknown."

Internal discontent. When the Armada died during the first weeks of August 1588, the crisis of Elizabeth's reign was reached and successfully passed. The last years were an anticlimax, for the moment the international danger was surmounted, domestic strife ensued. There were moments of great heroism and success—as when Essex, Raleigh, and Howard made a second descent on Cádiz in 1596, seized the city, and burned the entire West Indian treasure fleet—but the war so gloriously begun deteriorated into a costly campaign in the Netherlands and France and an endless guerrilla action in Ireland, where Philip discovered he could do to Elizabeth what she had been doing to him in the Low Countries. Even on the high seas, the days of fabulous victories were over, for the King of Spain soon learned to defend his empire and his treasure fleets. Both Drake and Hawkins died in 1596 on the same ill-conceived expedition into Spanish Caribbean waters—symbolic proof that the good old days of buccaneering were gone forever. At home the cost of almost two decades of war (£4,000,000) raised havoc with the Queen's finances. It forced her to sell her capital (about £800,000, or roughly one-fourth of all crown lands) and increased her dependence upon parliamentary sources of income, which rose from an annual average of £35,000 to over £112,000 a year.

Elizabeth's financial difficulties were a symptom of a mounting political crisis which under her successors would destroy the entire Tudor system of government. The 1590s were years of depression—bad harvests, soaring prices, peasant unrest, high taxes, and increasing parliamentary criticism of the Queen's economic policies and political leadership. Imperceptibly, the House of Commons was becoming the instrument through which the will of the landed classes could be heard and not an obliging organ of royal control. In Tudor political theory this was a distortion of the proper function of Parliament, which was meant to beseech and petition, never to command or initiate. Three things, however, forced theory to make way for reality. First was the government's financial dependence on Commons, for the organ that paid the royal piper eventually demanded that it also call the governmental tune. Second, under the Tudors, Parliament had been summoned so often and forced to legislate on such crucial matters of church and state—legitimizing and bastardizing monarchs, breaking with Rome, proclaiming the supreme headship (governorship under Elizabeth), establishing the royal succession, and legislating in areas that no Parliament had ever dared enter before—that Commons got into the habit of being consulted. Inevitably a different constitutional question emerged: if Parliament is asked to give authority to the crown, can it also take away that authority? Finally, there was the growth of a vocal, politically conscious, and economically dominant gentry; and the increase in the size of the House of Commons reflected the activity and importance of that class. In Henry

VIII's first Parliament there were 74 knights who sat for 37 shires, and 224 burgesses who represented the chartered boroughs of the kingdom. By the end of Elizabeth's reign, borough representation had been increased by 135 seats. Commons was replacing the Lords in importance because the social element it represented had become economically and politically more important than the nobility. Should the crown's leadership falter, there existed by the end of the century an organization that was quite capable of seizing the political initiative, for as one disgruntled contemporary noted: "the foot taketh upon him the part of the head and commons is become a king." Elizabeth had sense enough to avoid a showdown with Commons, and she retreated under parliamentary attack on the issue of her prerogative rights to grant monopolies regulating and licensing the economic life of the kingdom, but on the subject of her religious settlement she refused to budge.

By the last decade of the reign, Puritanism was on the increase. During the 1570s and '80s "cells" had sprung up to spread God's word and rejuvenate the land, and Puritan strength was centred in exactly that segment of society that had the economic and social means to control the realm—the gentry and merchant classes. What set a Puritan off from other Protestants was the literalness with which he held to his creed, the discipline with which he watched his soul's health, the militancy of his faith, and the sense that he was somehow apart from the rest of corrupt humanity. This disciplined spiritual elite clashed with the Queen over the purification of the church and the stamping out of the last vestiges of Catholicism. The controversy went to the root of society: was the purpose of life spiritual or political, was the role of the church to serve God or the crown? In 1576 two brothers, Paul and Peter Wentworth, led the Puritan attack in Commons, criticizing the Queen for her refusal to allow Parliament to debate religious issues. The crisis came to a head in 1586, when Puritans called for legislation to abolish the episcopacy and the Anglican Prayer Book. Elizabeth ordered the bills to be withdrawn, and when Peter Wentworth raised the issue of freedom of speech in Commons, she answered by clapping him in the Tower of London. There was emerging in England a group of religious idealists who derived their spiritual authority from a source that stood higher than the crown and who thereby violated the concept of the organic society and endangered the very existence of the Tudor paternalistic monarchy. As early as 1573 the threat had been recognized:

> At the beginning it was but a cap, a surplice, and a tippet [over which Puritans complained]; now, it is grown to bishops, archbishops, and cathedral churches, to the overthrow of the established order, and to the Queen's authority in causes ecclesiastical.

James I later reduced the problem to one of his usual *bon mots*—"no bishop, no king." Elizabeth's answer was less catchy but more effective; she appointed as archbishop John Whitgift, who was determined to destroy Puritanism as a politically organized sect. Whitgift was only partially successful, but the Queen was correct: the moment the international crisis was over and a premium was no longer placed on loyalty, Puritans were potential security risks.

The final years of Gloriana's life were difficult both for the theory of Tudor kingship and for Elizabeth herself. She began to lose hold over the imaginations of her subjects, and she faced the only palace revolution of her reign when her favourite, Robert Devereux, earl of Essex, sought to touch her crown. There was still fight in the old Queen, and Essex ended on the scaffold in 1601, but his angry demand could not be ignored:

> What! Cannot princes err? Cannot subjects receive wrong? Is an earthly power or authority infinite? Pardon me, pardon me, my good Lord, I can never subscribe to these principles.

When the old Queen died on March 24, 1603, it was as if the critics of her style of rule and her concept of government had been waiting patiently for her to step down. It was almost with relief that men looked forward to the problems of a new reign, a new dynasty, and a new century.

(La.B.S.)

Defeat of the Armada

Elizabeth and Parliament

The growth of Puritanism

The early Stuarts and the Commonwealth

THE CONDITION OF ENGLAND IN 1603

Social classes

In 1603 England was a nation of some 4,000,000–4,500,-000 people, mostly living in the south and east, who were divided into social classes based, as Shakespeare observed in *Troilus and Cressida* (1609), upon "degree, priority, and place." At the top of the social hierarchy was the Stuart royal family, headed by King James I (1603–25), whose hereditary claim to the English throne came from his mother, Mary, Queen of Scots. Also, as James VI of Scotland, the King represented a personal union between the two kingdoms. Advising the King were his privy councillors, men of lesser political stature than those who had served under Elizabeth and, consequently, far less successful in managing the houses of Parliament. The ablest of them was Robert Cecil, 1st earl of Salisbury, son of Elizabeth's great minister Lord Burghley. After Salisbury's death in 1612, two young men captured James's affections: Robert Carr, earl of Somerset, who fell from power after his lovely young wife caused a court scandal by poisoning her detractor, Sir Thomas Overbury; and George Villiers, who rose from a gentleman of the bedchamber to become the 1st duke of Buckingham (1623). The King's fondness for young men can be seen in his statement to the Privy Council in 1617: "I love the Earl of Buckingham more than anyone else. . . . Christ had his John, and I have my George."

Below the royal family came some 60 hereditary members of the nobility or aristocracy, ranging in descending order from dukes, marquesses, earls, viscounts, and barons who, together with 26 nonhereditary bishops, sat in the House of Lords. The doubling of the number of lay nobles as a result of "bargain and sale" by Buckingham not only brought the monarchy into disrepute but also brought a loss of prestige to the nobility. This crisis of confidence in the nobility, aggravated by its conspicuous consumption and the slow decay of its military power, greatly weakened the effectiveness of the Lords as a mediating body between the King and the House of Commons. The decline in the prestige of the nobility had been preceded by a financial crisis among the aristocracy from about 1590 to 1610 as a result of the shrinkage of their landed wealth. A member of the nobility claimed in 1628 that the Commons, which was made up mostly of gentry, could buy up the Lords three times over. By 1640 the aristocracy had probably recovered from its financial crisis.

Below the nobility came the gentry, who numbered less than 5 percent of the population. They were technically those large landowners to whom the College of Arms had granted the right of gentility—*i.e.*, the right to bear a coat of arms—but a small number of them held nonhereditary titles (either baronetcies or knighthoods), which, like the titles of the nobility, were sold by the crown or its ministers. Nearly 1,000 knights were created in James's first year on the throne. A fairly high turnover in the ownership of land, because of the inflation of prices, resulted in some changes in the composition of the gentry: some new families rose to the top (a few becoming peers), whereas some older families either died out or declined, sometimes falling into the social category of yeomen, or chief farmers, who were only one step above the husbandmen, or petty farmers. Some members of both the gentry and the nobility engaged in careful estate management in order to meet the price squeeze, and a number of these improving landlords sought positions at court. These officeholders were part of the Court Party in the House of Commons. At the local county level, the justices of the peace—unpaid administrative officers of the crown—tended to be Country, or opposition, gentry, whereas the lords lieutenant—the unpaid military officers of the crown—frequently were Court, or government, peers. The conflict between the Court and Country parties was one of the long-range causes of the English Civil War later in the century, but it would be a mistake to assume that the difference, either at the national or local level, was as simple as an affluent rising Court Party and a poverty-stricken declining Country Party.

Although the economy of England was predominantly tied to land, there was a commercial society of financiers, manufacturers, merchants, shopkeepers, tradesmen, and artisans who lived in the cities and towns, the largest of which was London, with a population of about 250,000; Norwich, Norfolk, with 15,000, was the second largest. There were four times as many borough seats in the Commons as County seats, but the merchants comprised only a small fraction of the Commons. Many successful merchants acquired landed estates and married their daughters into the gentry and aristocracy. Conversely, the younger sons of gentry families who could not succeed to the family estate under the law of primogeniture frequently turned to trade and commerce in order to make their livings. As a result, there was a horizontal social mobility between town and country in addition to the vertical mobility within the town and country hierarchies that gave a certain vigour and freedom of opportunity to English society that tended to offset its rigid social structure.

The economy

JAMES I (1603–25)

Religious policy. When James travelled south from Edinburgh in April 1603 to take up his duties at Westminster, he was presented with the Millenary Petition (so called because it was allegedly supported by 1,000 ministers) calling for reforms of the Anglican Church.

The King, though a Calvinist in his theology, was an Erastian in church government, advocating state supremacy in ecclesiastical affairs; he responded to the Millenary Petition by calling a conference at Hampton Court in London to which he invited moderate Puritan divines and Anglican bishops. The Puritans presented their case for recasting the Thirty-Nine Articles along more Calvinist lines, for revitalizing popular preaching, and for excluding the "relics of popery" from the Anglican prayer book. The Puritans also proposed that religious questions should be settled by episcopal synods made up of a bishop and a presbytery (or a group of elders) rather than by the bishops alone. But James erroneously assumed that the Puritan proposal for a "reduced episcopacy" was in fact a proposal for a "Scottish presbytery," which, as he knew from personal experience in Scotland, tried to subordinate the state to the church. After all, it had been in reaction to this hierocratic view that the King had exhumed the medieval notion of divine-right monarchy in order to counteract the clerical demands of both Scottish Presbyterians and Roman Catholics. As James had written in his *Trew Law of Free Monarchies* (1598), "Kings are called Gods . . . because they sit upon GOD his Throne in the earth, and have the count of their administration to give unto [H]im." The King regarded any diminution of episcopal power as having the same effect, as stated in his often-quoted political aphorism: "no bishop, no king." The bishops were instrumental in getting the Convocation of the clergy to pass the Canons of 1604, which provided for the excommunication of anyone who impugned the royal supremacy, the Anglican prayer book, or the Thirty-nine Articles. Shortly afterward a group of Puritan Separatists—separatists because they no longer felt a binding tie with the Anglican Church—were forced to leave England, settling in Holland until their transatlantic crossing as Pilgrims to Plymouth Rock in 1620. Perhaps some of them were attracted by stories they had heard about an earlier English settlement at Jamestown, Virginia, in 1607. The only significant Puritan accomplishment to come out of the Hampton Court conference was the authorization for a new translation of the Bible—the King James Version used by all English-speaking Protestants until well into the 20th century. The King's experience with English Catholics was about as bad as it had been with Scottish Catholics, especially when a group of them, including Guy Fawkes, was caught in an abortive plot on November 5, 1605, to blow up the houses of Parliament. The Gunpowder Plot, which provoked Parliament to require an oath of allegiance to the King from Catholic recusants, jeopardized the Catholic cause for a number of years.

The Gunpowder Plot

James and Parliament. The first session of James's first Parliament in 1604 was primarily concerned with several questions of parliamentary privilege, which set the tone for the constitutional struggle with the crown. In a disputed parliamentary election case (*Goodwin* v. *Fortescue*), it was decided that in the future the Commons, rather than the Court of Chancery, was the proper judge of election returns. In a dispute over the parliamentary privilege of freedom from arrest, it was decided that a member of Parliament, Sir Thomas Shirley, who had been imprisoned for a private debt, should not be molested while Parliament was in session. Both of these privileges, together with that of freedom of speech (especially in matters of religion), were eloquently set forth at the end of the session by some of the members in *The Form of Apology and Satisfaction*. The *Apology* was a lecture to a foreign king on how parliamentary privileges were "our right and due inheritance," not something bestowed by the grace of the crown. Although the extremist language of the *Apology*—"the voice of the people, in the things of their knowledge, is said to be as the voice of God"—kept it from coming to a vote in the Commons and although James probably never received the intended instruction, it was a shadow of things to come.

The most important difference between the King and his parliaments arose over the question of money. James's conventional sources of revenue were several: the income from crown lands, feudal dues (especially wardship, or the right to collect income from estates left to minors), purveyance (buying at less than the market price), monopolies, and customs duties called tonnage and poundage on imported wine and exported wool. Since all of these fiscal sources were inadequate to handle the extravagance of the court, the rising costs, and the debt from the recently concluded war with Spain, the crown decided to levy impositions (additional customs duties). The legality of impositions had been upheld in 1606 in the trial of John Bates, a merchant who had refused to pay an imposition on currants. Chief Baron Thomas Fleming had ruled that impositions fell under the king's "absolute power," which, unlike his "ordinary power," could not be changed by Parliament. The new Book of Rates of 1608 increased impositions, but in the parliamentary session of 1610, when James had forbidden the members to discuss that subject, once again the Commons claimed the privilege of free speech. Salisbury's proposal in that session for a

The Great Contract

Great Contract (1610)—by which the King would give up his feudal dues and purveyance in exchange for an annual parliamentary grant of £200,000—was never completed because of the King's dissolution of Parliament. The short-lived "Addled" Parliament of 1614 was no more successful in solving the crown's financial problems. In that same year a syndicate formed by a London alderman, William Cockayne, tried to increase James's revenue by substituting the export of finished woollen cloth (with its higher duties) for the export of undyed woollen cloth previously handled by the monopoly company of the Merchant Adventurers. But the Dutch boycotted the new product, and, as a result, the woollen-cloth industry, the largest after agriculture, suffered severe dislocation, drastically reducing the King's revenue from customs.

According to Attorney General Francis Bacon, the king's judges were supposed to be "lions *under* the throne," but Chief Justice Edward Coke, who disagreed with the decision in the Bates case, thought that the judges, as interpreters of the common law, should be mediators between the prerogative of the king and the rights of Parliament. In the case of Dr. Thomas Bonham (1606), Coke stated: "when an act of Parliament is against common right and reason, or repugnant, or impossible to be performed, the common law will control it, and judge such an act to be void." American scholars in particular have regarded the "higher law background" of this case as an important precedent for the American doctrine of judicial review, whereby a supreme court may annul legislation or executive acts as contrary to a constitution. In the matter of prohibitions, whereby the common-law courts would take over proceedings in the Anglican Church courts dealing with the collection of tithes, Coke told James, much to the joy of the Puritans, that matters of property were not to be decided by "natural reason," which the king and the bishops admittedly possessed, but by "artificial reason,"

which only common lawyers possessed. In a dispute between the King and Parliament over the use, or abuse, of royal proclamations in 1610, Coke and his colleagues told James that the king had no prerogative except that which the law allowed him. The final showdown between James and Coke came in the case of *Commendams* (1616), when Bacon requested the 12 judges to delay their decision until the King—who said that, in cases involving the prerogative, he was a party to the suit—had spoken with them, but Coke alone, while lying prostrate before the throne, contended for the independence of the judiciary. Coke was dismissed as a judge but later joined the Country opposition in Parliament. Bacon became lord chancellor, only to be impeached by Parliament for bribery the year after he published his scientific treatise, *Novum Organum* (1620).

Foreign policy. In matters of foreign policy, James was anxious to marry his surviving son, Charles, to the Spanish princess Donna Maria (in order to obtain a large dowry) and to become a peacemaker for Europe. But, at the same time, the German Catholic League, which Spain supported, toppled James's son-in-law, Frederick of the Palatinate, from his newly acquired kingdom of Bohemia and invaded the Upper Palatinate in what were to be the opening moves of the Thirty Years' War. Said James: "I like not to marry my son with my daughter's tears." The King reluctantly called his third Parliament in 1621 for funds to aid Frederick. The Commons continued to encroach upon the Stuart royal prerogative by criticizing the Spanish marriage and by urging a naval war with Spain, but James ordered them to desist from such "deep matters of State." At once the Commons issued the Protestation stating that foreign policy was a proper subject for the exercise of free speech in Parliament; the King, in turn, promptly tore the Protestation out of the journal of the House of Commons and dissolved Parliament. Even though the Rhenish Palatinate was occupied by Spanish troops in 1622, Prince Charles and Buckingham journeyed to Madrid the following year in an attempt to sweep the Princess off her feet. But they were so humiliated by their treatment there—Charles's leap over a wall to see the Princess was a fiasco—that they returned to England calling for war against Spain and the impeachment in Parliament of the pro-Spanish privy councillor, Sir Lionel Cranfield. At this, James told Buckingham that he was "making a rod with which you will be scourged yourself." England went to war with Spain in 1624, and negotiations were opened with France for a marriage between Charles and the French Catholic princess Henrietta Maria.

The Spanish marriage

The economy. One of the results of the Thirty Years' War was a severe slump in the woollen-cloth trade in 1620, just after Cranfield had been successful in bringing about a temporary recovery following the disastrous Cockayne project. The most important cause of the slump was a devaluation of currencies in Germany and eastern Europe that made it difficult for the Merchant Adventurers and the Eastland Company to export cloth profitably. The ensuing unemployment and poverty in the West Country and Suffolk, the home of the Old Draperies, or broadcloths, together with bad harvests beginning in 1621 that sent food prices spiralling, produced the worst depression of the first half of the century. The parish register of Ashton-under-Lyne, Lancashire, indicates a possible famine condition during the bad harvest year of 1623–24, when burials were up 250 percent and births fell 43 percent from the previous year. The development of New Draperies, or worsted cloths, in East Anglia, which were sold in Spain and the semitropical climates by the Levant Company, did not offset the loss from the older markets. The King, who insisted that the regulation of economic affairs (not in any mercantile sense but as a part of his concern for public order and economic stability) was part of the royal prerogative, appointed a Commission of Trade, the precursor of the Board of Trade, to look into the whole matter. On its recommendation the Parliament of 1624 was able to get the Privy Council to loosen the grip of the Merchant Adventurers on trade to the Low Countries and Germany by allowing any merchant to join the export trade in the cheaper varieties of the Old Draperies and in the New Draperies. But Sir

Economic depression of 1620s

Edward Coke drew up a bill that prevented the granting of monopolies to individuals by the crown on the grounds that these monopolies constituted only a different form of taxation. Even though specific exemptions were made for charters of trading companies and town corporations and for patents on inventions, the Monopolies Act was a clear blow to the royal prerogative. By 1625 the stabilization of the foreign currencies permitted the cloth trade to return almost to normal, but the problem of Dutch competition remained, as was indicated by the massacre of East India Company traders in 1623 by the Dutch at Amboina in the Dutch East Indies.

CHARLES I (1625–49)

Charles and Parliament. Unlike his father, Charles I (1625–49) was shy and nervous but handsome and dignified, as can be seen in portraits by Van Dyck, whom, with Rubens, he brought to England. Like James, Charles was an advocate of divine right, and, as James had warned, he was to have his "bellyfull of Parliament." Charles's immediate problem was to get Parliament to pay for the war against Spain. His first Parliament, in 1625, refused to grant him tonnage and poundage duties for life, so he dissolved this Parliament without getting any money to fight the war. From the King's rapidly dwindling resources, Buckingham was able to finance an expedition to attack the Spanish port of Cádiz. The venture failed disastrously, and Charles was again forced to turn to Parliament for funds. Charles's second Parliament, under the leadership of Sir John Eliot, demanded (as James had predicted) the impeachment of Buckingham. Charles again dissolved Parliament, still without money, because of the attack on his favourite. Instead, Charles and Buckingham resorted to the collection of forced loans and began to billet troops under martial law in private homes. Moreover, they foolishly went to war with the Catholic monarchy in France in addition to the ongoing war with Spain. The militant Puritans in Parliament were delighted with the opportunity to aid the rebelling French Calvinists (Huguenots), but Buckingham's military operations at La Rochelle in their behalf ended in failure, as at Cádiz. Five knights from the Country gentry, who were imprisoned for refusing to pay forced loans in 1627, obtained a writ of habeas corpus, but Chief Justice Nicholas Hyde ruled that their arrest, which had been at the special command of the King, was for "matters of state." In Charles's third Parliament of 1628 (the fifth Parliament in eight years), Coke, Eliot, and Sir Thomas Wentworth, somewhat incorrectly claiming the precedent of Magna Carta, drew up a petition asking the King not to levy taxes without the consent of Parliament, not to imprison his subjects without due cause being shown, not to billet soldiers in private homes, and not to put civilians under martial law. Charles reluctantly agreed to the Petition of Right, thereby receiving the money he needed to fight Spain and France. Within a few months, however, Buckingham was dead from an assassin's knife.

In addition to the problems of finance and constitutional privilege, Charles's first three Parliaments also were greatly concerned with the growth of Arminianism within the Anglican Church. Beginning in the 17th century, many followers of the Dutch theologian Jacobus Arminius modified the Calvinist doctrine of predestination and election. The Arminians moved in the direction of free will and good works for the salvation of all men, not merely a few elect. An international synod was held at Dort (Dordrecht, in the Netherlands) in 1618–19, at which the orthodox followers of Calvin refused to alter their position. Nevertheless, several Anglican churchmen opted for Arminianism. Among them was the archdeacon of Hereford, Herefordshire, Richard Montagu, whose book *Appello Caesarem* (1625) won him a bishopric from the King. Another Arminian was William Laud, bishop of London (1628), who introduced innovations in the church service—for example, placing the communion table "altarwise" at the east end of the chancel—and who stressed the divine right of bishops, a view that tended to erode the royal supremacy. Laud shared the anti-Calvinist theology but not the Erastianism of the Dutch Arminians, since he believed, as did many Puritans, that the king should

be merely a member, not the supreme governor (a tenet to which he only paid lip service), of the church. Because these innovations in theology, liturgy, and episcopacy were so close to Roman Catholicism, the Arminians, as high churchmen, were in effect Anglo-Catholics. In an eloquent speech before the Commons in 1629, the Puritan Francis Rous called Arminianism "an Error that makes the Grace of God Lackey it after the will of man," a "Trojan Horse . . ready to open the Gates to *Romish* Tyranny, and Spanish Monarchy." Apparently other members agreed with Rous, for the Commons passed Eliot's three resolutions against Arminianism and tonnage and poundage duties, with the Speaker held in his chair to prevent adjournment. (The King had continued to collect the duties because he believed they were not included in the Petition of Right.) In this instance, at least, the Puritan and Country opposition were united against Anglo-Catholicism and the court.

The years of personal rule. By 1629 Charles had had enough of Parliament, and for the next 11 years he conducted a policy of personal rule, sometimes with the aid of the "Thorough" policy of Laud and Wentworth, the latter having defected from the Country opposition. Thorough is the name applied to the governmental policies of these two ministers, who called for strong and efficient central government under the King. In order to cut down on his expenses, Charles terminated the wars with France (1629) and with Spain (1630), but the immediate advantages to the nation's economy from the return to peace were offset by a temporary slump in the cloth trade, especially the New Draperies of East Anglia, plus two consecutive harvest failures. The Privy Council's attempt to meet the crisis, particularly with a rigorous enforcement of the Elizabethan Poor Law, or Statute of Poor Relief (1601), was to give rise to a limited policy of state paternalism. Some paternalistic projects, such as the monopoly of pin making, were designed to inaugurate new industries, but others, such as the London Society of Soap Boilers, had the effect of an embryonic excise tax. The King attempted to raise revenue from the commercial classes by obtaining long-term loans from London financiers who managed the traditional customs revenue (though he did add some impositions), but he milked the gentry through the absurd revival of obsolete feudal dues (fines on forest lands once owned by the crown and fines on those who refused to buy knighthoods) and Ship Money. As late as 1626 writs for Ship Money, in the form of either ships or cash, had been temporarily levied on all of the commercial ports in order to raise a navy to protect commerce from pirates or to provide for the national defense. When the King, against the advice of Laud and Wentworth, extended the writs to the whole country, thereby making it a regular assessment like the future land tax, John Hampden, a Puritan gentleman from an inland county, refused to pay. In the Hampden Ship Money case (1637), Attorney General John Bankes, arguing for the King's "absolute power" as promulgated in Bate's case, stated that there was no such "King-yoking" policy requiring parliamentary consent. A bare majority of the common-law judges found Hampden guilty, a decision that alienated many Country gentry.

Although there was an appearance of a Catholic revival in England during the mid-1630s—Laud himself was twice offered a cardinal's hat but refused "til Rome were other than it is"—the period is better characterized as the Laudian counterreformation. With the appointment of Laud as archbishop of Canterbury (1633) and Bishop William Juxon as lord treasurer (1636), it was the highest point of clerical influence since the days of Cardinal Wolsey. As Laud said: "a bishop may preach the Gospel more publicly, and to far greater edification, in a court of judicature, or at a council table." The persecution of the Puritans now began in the Courts of High Commission and Star Chamber. When Charles reissued James's Book of Sports (1618), permitting lawful recreations on Sundays, a Puritan lawyer named William Prynne published his *Histrio-Mastix* (1633), an attack upon stage plays, mixed dancing, lewd pictures, face makeup, and long hair, among other things. An index entry listed women actors, which the Queen aspired to be, as "notorious whores." Prynne was found guilty of seditious libel in the Court of Star Chamber, a royal prerogative court made up of Laudian bishops. His sentence consisted of imprisonment for life, expulsion from the law profession, a fine of £5,000, a session in the pillory, and the hacking off of both ears (the stumps of which he could cover, ironically, only by growing long hair). In prison Prynne was joined by a Puritan clergyman, Henry Burton, and a Puritan physician, John Bastwick, and all of them busied themselves by writing vitriolic pamphlets attacking the bishops for their Arminianism. All three were brought before Star Chamber for libel and given the usual severe punishments, Prynne being specially branded on both cheeks with an *SL* (seditious libeler). From Ireland, where he was serving as lord deputy, Wentworth (now earl of Strafford) wrote to Laud: "these men do but begin with the Church, that they might have freer access to the State." Laud's harassment of the Puritans, with an assist from the depressed cloth industry in East Anglia, contributed greatly to that exodus of Puritans to New England in the 1630s that is sometimes called the Great Migration.

Religious reform in Scotland.   With the nation at peace, trade recovering, a revenue coming into the crown, and the bishops seemingly in control of the Puritans, Charles conceivably could have carried on for some time, if not indefinitely, without calling Parliament into session. A turning point in the fortunes of the monarchy, however, was reached when the King and the Archbishop decided to bring the Scottish Presbyterian Church, or Kirk, into closer accord with the Anglican Church. Accordingly, a new prayer book was prepared by the Scottish bishops, who had been reinstituted by James I (1610). When the new liturgy was first read in Edinburgh (1637), rioting broke out against what many Scots considered popery. Large numbers of Scots drew up the National Covenant (1638), a civil compact to resist all of the innovations in worship. The General Assembly of the Scottish Kirk quickly rejected the new prayer book and the Scottish episcopacy. Faced by such defiance to the royal prerogative, Charles made his fateful decision to send an army into Scotland. The English troops, lacking money and discipline, ended the First Bishops' War (1639) without fighting by signing a truce. At the advice of Laud and Strafford, in 1640 Charles summoned his first Parliament in 11 years, with its concomitant Convocation of the clergy. Although the proposed agreement in this Short Parliament for the King to abandon Ship Money in exchange for 12 subsidies fell through, Convocation did give him six benevolences (gifts of money) plus a new set of canons defining the church liturgy. The Canons of 1640 were severely criticized by the Puritans in Parliament for enshrining Arminian practices as well as requiring of all clergy and selected laymen the Etcetera Oath never to alter the Anglican hierarchy of archbishops, bishops, etc. Without having learned the obvious lesson from these events, Charles opened the Second Bishops' War (1640), but this time the Scottish Covenanters encamped on English soil with a large army, charging Charles £850 per day for its upkeep until their demands were met. The King could not tolerate such ignominy, and, since loans were not forthcoming from the London financiers, a new Parliament, the most eventful in all of English history, had to be called, this time to sit for 13 years.

The meeting of the Long Parliament.   The first session of the Long Parliament met from November 1640 to September 1641 with the support of the Scottish army. The new Parliament, under the leadership of John Pym, immediately set about redressing its grievances against what it considered the arbitrary authority of the royal government. The first order of business was to release the political prisoners—including Prynne, Burton, and Bastwick—and to impeach both Laud and Strafford for treason, the latter allegedly having advised Charles that he had an army in Ireland with which he could overawe Parliament. When impeachment proceedings by Pym against Strafford looked doubtful, both Houses passed a Bill of Attainder—*i.e.,* an arbitrary political sentence of death without trial. The King, fearful for the Queen's life from a London mob, reluctantly signed the bill. Laud remained imprisoned in

the Tower of London until his execution in 1645. Action was next taken to guarantee Parliament's own existence against future periods of "personal rule"; the Triennial Act stated that there should be no more than three years between Parliaments, and another act—in many ways the most significant of all—stated that the present Parliament could not be adjourned without its own consent. The constitutional revolution continued with statutes abolishing the courts of Star Chamber and High Commission and abolishing Ship Money, forest and knighthood fines, and tonnage and poundage duties, except with parliamentary consent. On the matter of religious reform, all agreed that the Canons of 1640 were invalid, but it was soon apparent that there was considerable division of thought among the Country opposition. Some radical Puritans in the Commons, such as Henry Vane the Younger, thought that the Anglican form of church government should be destroyed "root and branch"; some moderate Puritans and Low Church Anglicans, such as Edward Hyde, only wished to trim branches by removing the bishops and clergy from all secular offices. A bill containing the moderate proposal passed the Commons overwhelmingly, but it was rejected by the Lords. In the Lords the Calvinist archbishop James Ussher advocated a reduced episcopacy, as advanced at Hampton Court, conjoining episcopal and presbyterian church government. The only agreement came in a protestation by the Lords and Commons, reminiscent of the Scottish National Covenant, to defend the "*true reformed Protestant Religion . . . against all Popery and Popish innovations.*" Just before a six weeks' autumn recess, both houses voted sufficient funds to send the Scottish army back home since it was no longer useful or necessary.

The outbreak of rebellion in Ireland during the autumn recess (with the attendant question as to who should control the army needed to quell it) only added to the differences about religion already existing within the Country opposition. These differences became even more apparent in November with the slim 11-vote majority given to the Grand Remonstrance, creating new royalist and parliamentary parties in place of the old parties. The Grand Remonstrance, which demanded that the King should appoint only advisors approved by Parliament and that an international synod of divines should be called to resolve the religious question, contained a long list of political and religious grievances that later became a model for Jefferson's Declaration of Independence. Had the Remonstrance not passed, Oliver Cromwell is supposed to have said that he would leave England—perhaps for Massachusetts. At Christmastime the Commons impeached, and the Lords sequestered, 12 bishops who had the audacity to claim that Parliament was "not free" after they had been jostled by a London mob while en route to the House of Lords. Charles panicked at the mob and at the Lords' about-face on the bishops; yet, in an uncharacteristically bold but ill-advised counterrevolutionary act, he attempted to arrest five members of Parliament, including Pym and Hampden, on January 4, 1642. Shortly before the King's arrival in the Commons' chamber with troops, the five members sought refuge in the City of London, the new government of which was sympathetic to them. When Charles asked where they had gone, the Speaker of the House boldly spoke: "I have neither eyes to see nor tongue to speak . . . but as this house is pleased to direct me." The Speaker's independence from the crown dates from this occasion. The King's violent breach of parliamentary privilege against arrest, as established in Shirley's case, had so backfired that he and the Queen left Westminster on January 10, he not to return for seven years and she for 18.

From mid-January through mid-August, Charles and Parliament seemed to be playing out the last few scenes of a tragic drama the climax of which had already taken place. The Lords, with their numbers now decimated by royalist defections, gave their assent to the Bishops' Exclusion Bill, which prevented all clergymen from holding secular office and all bishops from sitting in the Lords. On February 5 the King reluctantly signed the bill, either to save the bishops from a worse fate or, more likely, to gain time for effective military resistance. The final break

The Bishops' Wars

Laud's fall

The Grand Remonstrance

The Militia Ordinance

came with the passage of the Militia Ordinance without Charles's signature. From that moment until 1660 all parliamentary legislation was technically illegal. The Militia Ordinance, which seemed directed more toward Parliament's self-preservation than toward the reconquest of Ireland, gave control over the militia to lords lieutenant appointed by Parliament rather than by the king. Some members of Parliament now claimed that the person of the king should be distinguished from the office and that the office could be better administered by them. In June 1642, Parliament issued its Nineteen Propositions, terms for Charles's surrender that called for acceptance of the Militia Ordinance and a church synod, as well as approval by Parliament of the King's ministers and the education and marriage of his children. Charles of course refused, but his response, written by the moderate Lord Falkland, surprisingly set forth a "mixed" theory of government by king, Lords, and Commons. The events of the preceding year and a half had clearly shown that the Parliamentary Party had become just as arbitrary as Charles, if not more so. But on August 22 at the small county town of Nottingham, the King, in a rebel-like action, raised his military standard against Parliament. Ireland was practically forgotten for ten years.

THE CIVIL WARS

The causes. The various reasons that historians have given for the cause(s) of the English Civil Wars indicate that there is no simple explanation. Some contemporaries, such as Richard Baxter, observed that the nobility, gentry, and the "poorest of the people" followed the King, whereas tradesmen, freeholders, and the "middle sort of men" followed Parliament. Recent research, however, indicates that there were no important economic or social differences within the leadership of the two parties; about two-thirds of the nobles became royalists; almost three-fifths of the gentry became parliamentarians. The gentry of some northern and western counties, such as Yorkshire and Cheshire (agricultural areas of traditional royal power), were predominantly royalist, whereas the gentry

of some eastern and southeastern counties, clothmaking areas accessible to European trade, were predominantly parliamentarian. Cities such as London, Bristol, and Norwich tended to be parliamentarian, but other cities, such as Newcastle upon Tyne and Chester had a majority of royalists. Textile areas such as East Anglia and the West Riding of Yorkshire also tended to be centres of Puritanism, partly because these areas had once been the home of the Lollard heresy, partly because of the Calvinist ethic of work (emphasizing public service but not profit-making acquisitiveness), and partly, perhaps, because of the relief provided by the Calvinist doctrine of election from the anxiety that characterized an urban and commercial milieu such as London. Although the religious issue had been divisive in the summer of 1641, the parliamentary leaders had kept it to a minimum in the debate over the Grand Remonstrance, and, with the Bishops' Exclusion Act, it temporarily lost some of its importance. Nevertheless, religion was a determining factor in the selection of sides, because the men who stayed at Westminster at the outbreak of hostilities were mostly Puritan in sympathy. The decisive issue—one that had been building up for several decades and reached its peak with the impeachment of Strafford, the Grand Remonstrance, the attempted arrest of the five members, and, above all, in the Militia Ordinance—was constitutional in nature: who should have the sovereign power in the kingdom? Only a civil war would determine the answer to that question.

Parliamentary victory. The early Civil War began on August 22, 1642, when Charles, like the feudal barons of old, erected his standard before only a few hundred followers and onlookers at Nottingham, an unimportant county town. The King controlled most of the north and west of England, including Wales, and had the advantage of a well-trained cavalry led by his nephew, Prince Rupert of the Palatinate. Parliament, on the other hand, possessed London and most of the east and southeastern England and had the advantage of more regular sources of revenue and manpower. The inconclusive outcome of the Battle of Edgehill (1642) accentuated the political di-

Adapted from R. Treharne and H. Fullard (eds.), *Muir's Historical Atlas: Ancient, Medieval and Modern,* 9th ed. (1965). George Philip & Son Ltd., London

England during the Civil Wars.

visions within the Parliamentary Party. In the Commons a war group wanted the unconditional surrender of the King before negotiations; a middle group, led by Pym, wanted to negotiate only from a position of strength; a peace group wanted immediate negotiations, which shortly resulted in the Oxford Propositions, a document more conciliatory on constitutional matters than the Nineteen Propositions, although demanding ("root and branch") on religion. But Charles rejected them. Some royalist victories in the summer of 1643 forced Pym to obtain military assistance from the Scots, but the price—Scotland's revenge for Laud's imposition of the prayer book—was agreement to the Solemn League and Covenant, which called for the complete reformation of the Anglican Church "according to the Word of God [Vane's phrase] and the example of the best reformed churches," obviously meaning Scottish Presbyterianism. At long last the synod of Puritan divines called for in the Grand Remonstrance met at Westminster. The Scottish and English divines of the Westminster Assembly drew up a Calvinistic confession of faith and agreed to substitute the Scottish Directory for Public Worship for the Anglican prayer book.
The adoption by Parliament of the Directory, plus the victory by an East Anglian cavalry leader, Oliver Cromwell,

Marston Moor

over Prince Rupert at Marston Moor (1644), produced the stronger Uxbridge Propositions to the King in 1645, constitutional proposals similar to the Nineteen Propositions but, in addition, requiring agreement to the Solemn League and Covenant. Again Charles refused. On matters of church government and church discipline in the Assembly, the Presbyterian majority called for a compulsory national church with a hierarchy of church courts that would suspend scandalous members from the Sacrament, but a group of "dissenting brethren" called Independents advocated voluntary congregational churches, independent of any higher ecclesiastical authority, the visible saints of which covenanted together on the basis of a conversion experience. By 1645 the members of the peace group in Parliament were called the Presbyterian Party because they sometimes overlapped with that kind of Puritanism, and for a similar reason the members of the war group were called the Independent Party. The middle group tended to ally with the Independent Party. The religious Presbyterians in Parliament were successful in replacing the bishops of the Anglican Church with a Presbyterian form of church government, but the Scottish Presbyterians in the assembly called it a "lame Erastian Presbytery" since the Erastians from all parliamentary groups or parties had made sure that Parliament rather than the church would have control over religious affairs. Lieutenant General Cromwell, an Independent in religion and a radical member of the middle group in Parliament, was able, with a corps of Independent chaplains, to establish his religious imprint on the parliamentary forces, which, under the leadership of Sir Thomas Fairfax (later 3rd Baron Fairfax of Cameron), the commander in chief, was remodelled into a well-disciplined fighting unit. The New Model Army—with the motto "If God be for us, who

Naseby

can be against us?"—defeated the King's forces at Naseby (1645). With the King's flight to the Scots in May and the surrender of Oxford to the New Model Army in June 1646, the first phase of the Civil Wars came to an end.

The King, the army, and Parliament. The Scots, Parliament, and the army made successive attempts during the next two years to come to terms with an evasive King determined to play off one suitor against the others. After the failure of negotiations between Charles and the Scots, they turned him over to Parliament. Parliament presented the King with the Newcastle Propositions (very similar to the Uxbridge Propositions), and on May 31 he finally agreed to accept Presbyterianism for a period of three years and to surrender control of the militia to Parliament for ten years. The agreement did not come into effect because the New Model Army seized Charles on June 4. On the following day, disturbed at Parliament's desire to reduce its numbers and send a force to Ireland, the New Model Army issued its Solemn Engagement not to disband until its grievances, including pay in arrears, were redressed. While the quarrel between Parliament and the army pro-

gressed, some army officers, especially Cromwell's son-in-law, Commissary General Henry Ireton, made some new proposals to Charles on August 1. The officers' Heads of the Proposals called for a council of state and biennial Parliaments that would control the militia for ten years and a limited toleration as a defense against Presbyterianism. Charles liked the Heads better than the Newcastle Propositions because of the implied admission of episcopacy, but he finally rejected them. Within the New Model Army's rank and file were the Agitators, who drew up an Agreement of the People based upon the views of the Leveller Party leaders: men such as John Lilburne, William Walwyn, and Richard Overton.

The Agreement of the People

Lilburne was influenced by the fundamental law of Coke, whereas Walwyn and Overton stemmed from a Christian Humanist tradition. The Agreement set forth ideas that were to be realized in the U.S. Constitution: legislative power as a trusteeship from the people (who are sovereign) and civil and religious rights, based upon natural laws, reserved by the people from the legislature. Although some Levellers, such as Lilburne, wanted to limit voting privileges only to freemen (excluding servants and alms takers), other Levellers, such as Col. Thomas Rainborow, wished to include everyone. For instance, at the army debates over the Agreement at Putney (October 1647), Rainborow said: "The poorest hee that is in England hath a life to live as the greatest hee." To this, Ireton (no Leveller) responded that no one should vote except those with "a permanent fixed interest in the kingdom." However much Puritan Independency may have provided a training ground for Leveller ideas through the election of ministers, the church covenant, and the equality of the saints, the chaplains of the New Model Army preached an Antinomianism (the complete assurance of salvation for God's elect solely through the free gift of the Holy Spirit), which stressed a millennial holy commonwealth ruled over by the lay saints.

While the army was debating the Agreement, Charles fled from its custody to the Isle of Wight, where on December 26 he signed the secret Treaty of Newport with the Scots that was to lead to his undoing. In the treaty the King agreed to eradicate Independency and to establish Presbyterianism for three years, and the Scots agreed to send an army to England to settle a lasting peace should the King, Parliament, and themselves fail to do so. The treaty virtually made a second civil war a certainty. In a huge prayer meeting at New Windsor, Berkshire, the army agreed to bring Charles Stuart, "that man of blood," to account. This took place just before the army defeated the Scots at Preston in mid-August. "Surely," wrote Cromwell, "this is nothing but the hand of God." After Preston the Commons passed the final ordinance establishing the Erastian Presbyterianism. When it appeared that the King and Parliament at long last would sign a peace treaty, Col. Thomas Pride arrested or imprisoned 231 M.P.'s from the Presbyterian Party and the moderate majority of the middle group that previously had been tied to the Independent Party. Pride's Purge left a small Rump Parliament made up of the Independent Party and the radical minority of the middle group, some of whom were religious Presbyterians. The Rump Parliament proceeded to create a wholly unprecedented High Court of Justice to bring Charles to trial for high treason and other crimes. High treason, according to the law, was a crime performed against, not by, the king, but something of a case could be made that Charles had levied war against his subjects. The army, having reached the point where it no longer trusted the King, was determined to show that kings had to be responsible to their subjects. At his trial in late January, Charles refused to recognize the jurisdiction of the court, but he did say, without his usual stammer: "if Power without Law may make Lawes . . . I do not know what subject he is in England, that can be sure of his life or any thing that he calls his own." The King's guilt was a foregone conclusion. On January 30 at Whitehall, Charles Stuart—unlike Edward II, Richard II, and Henry VI, who were deposed before they were killed—was executed as a reigning king. Cromwell attributed the Court's action to "Providence and necessity."

Flight of Charles

Trial of the King

THE COMMONWEALTH (1649–60)

With the abolition of the office of monarchy and the House of Lords in 1649, the Rump proclaimed the "Commonwealth and Free-State," a republican form of government to be directed by the Council of State for the next four years. As Latin secretary for the Council, it was the task of John Milton, the poet, to defend the regicide to the rest of Europe. With Cromwell as commander in chief, the army, after suppressing a Leveller mutiny, weakened the Presbyterian Church settlement by defeating the Scots at Dunbar, East Lothian (1650), and at Worcester (1651). Also, it finally ended the Irish revolt by slaughtering the survivors (including women and children) of the besieged garrisons of Drogheda and Wexford in accordance with contemporary practice. As a result Scotland and England achieved a temporary political union, as James I had wished, and many English landowners acquired property in Ireland, a situation somewhat related to the confiscation and sale of sizable church, crown, and royalist lands in England. The Commonwealth's navy took command of the English Channel in the first of three trade wars fought with the Dutch in the mid-17th century. On matters of religion, the Rump produced no major ecclesiastical changes, but a spate of legislation, including the Blasphemy Act of 1650, dealt with moral and doctrinal laxity, especially in such Puritan sects as the Ranters, Diggers, Muggletonians, and Quakers. The Rump delayed enacting the army's program to abolish tithes, to reform the law, and to hold free elections, so Cromwell entered St. Stephen's Chapel with troops, as Charles I had done, and dissolved the remnant of the Long Parliament (1653). At the advice of Maj. Gen. Thomas Harrison, who was sympathetic to the political millennialism of another Puritan sect known as the Fifth Monarchy Men, Cromwell convoked a small Parliament of 140 Puritan saints chosen by the army with nominations by some Independent churches. The radical millenarians of this Barebones Parliament (named after a member, Praise-God Barbon) abolished the Court of Chancery and planned to abolish ecclesiastical patronage and tithes, so Cromwell, always a conservative in social reform, got the moderate Independents to dissolve the experiment in saintly rule after six months.

The Protectorate. For the next few years the form of government was to be called a Protectorate, as provided by the Instrument of Government (1653), a written constitution (England's first) drawn up by Maj. Gen. John Lambert from Ireton's Heads of Proposals. In addition to making Cromwell the lord protector (an office subsequently to be elective) and commander in chief of the army, the Instrument provided for a council and a single-chamber, triennial Parliament, the redrawn constituencies of which contained a much larger percentage of county seats held by Country gentry. The Instrument designated Christianity as the "public profession" of the nation, but religious toleration was to be extended only to such Puritan groups as the Independents, Presbyterians, Baptists, and some Puritan sectarians (not to Catholics, Anglicans, and licentious people). Cromwell, who allowed the Jews to return to England, was somewhat more tolerant than his two Parliaments, which prosecuted the Socinian (Unitarian) John Biddle for heresy and the Quaker James Nayler for blasphemy. The Protector's preference for Independency was revealed in his personal ordinances to regulate the ministry: a central committee of Triers to admit new ministers and county committees of Ejectors to remove scandalous ministers. Peace with Holland (1654) and a war with Spain (1655), which resulted in the capture of Jamaica, suited the Protector's notion of a Protestant crusade, but he did make an alliance with the France of Cardinal Mazarin. Cromwell also differed with his Parliaments, both of which he purged, over the control and payment of the army, even though taxes, including the excise begun in the 1640s and a new assessment levied directly on property, were higher than they had been under Charles I. In response to a royalist uprising in 1655, the Protector instituted the Rule of the Major Generals, a scheme dividing England into 11 military districts to keep down plots and to enforce the Commonwealth's repressive blue laws. The resentment inspired by the major generals caused Parliament to issue a modified version of the Instrument known as the Humble Petition and Advice (1657). This new constitution would have made Cromwell a king, but, under heavy republican pressure from the army, which he had hoped to reduce in size, he refused the crown while accepting its other provisions providing for the restoration of the "Other House" (*i.e.*, an upper chamber), a hereditary protectorate, and further restrictions on liberty of conscience. On September 3, 1658, Cromwell died, and with him went all hope for a permanent Puritan commonwealth. He had been a brilliant commander of troops, but he had never been able to find a lasting settlement for church and state. "I am as much for government by consent as any man," he once said, "but where will you find that consent?"

The Instrument of Government

The return of the monarchy. The next two years brought about the restoration of the monarchy through a continuation of the steps, in reverse order, by which it had been dismantled. In January 1659 Richard Cromwell, who succeeded his father as lord protector, called his only Parliament, elected by the pre-Instrument constituencies, but in April he dissolved it under pressure from ambitious army officers whose allegiance his inexperience and indecision could not command. Richard resigned as protector, and the army, in need of some legitimate authority, decided to restore the surviving members of the Rump Parliament whom they had expelled in 1653. The Protectorate had come to an end. Despite the appearance of a large number of tracts by Milton, James Harrington, and others in behalf of the "good old cause" of republicanism, an alliance between royalists and Presbyterians was formed. Lambert, acting on behalf of the republicans in the army, dismissed the Rump Parliament in October, but Gen. George Monck, commander of the army in Scotland, decided to intervene. Meanwhile, the Rump, which had been expelled twice, was restored in December for the second time. Lambert's troops were unable to stop Monck's entrance into London in February 1660, whereupon Monck enlarged the Rump Parliament to include all of those surviving members who had been purged by Colonel Pride. This restored Long Parliament, with its Presbyterian party majority, proceeded to implement Presbyterianism and to reaffirm the Treaty of Newport of 1647 as the basis for peace with the crown. After 20 years it finally voted to dissolve itself, as the law prescribed, in favour of a Convention Parliament that called for the return of the Stuarts in the person of Charles II, the son of the executed king. The Convention Parliament accepted without any conditions Charles II's Declaration of Breda (April 4), promising his consent to parliamentary bills relating to land purchases and army arrears in pay, a general pardon to all except those specified by Parliament, and liberty of conscience for all men unless there was a disturbance to the peace of the kingdom. There was something in the declaration for everyone. Because of Richard Cromwell's weakness and lack of experience, because of the differences between the various Parliaments and the army, and because of the divisions within Parliament (at first between republicans and Cromwellians and later between republicans and Presbyterians), Charles II (ruled 1660–85) could safely return to England, which he did on May 25, 1660, never to embark on his travels again.

The Declaration of Breda

The later Stuarts

CHARLES II (1660–85)

The Restoration settlement. Charles II quickly addressed himself to the promises in the Declaration of Breda: the crown, the Anglican Church (including bishops in England and Scotland), and some royalist lands in England were restored; a large part of the army was demobilized with full pay in arrears; and only a handful of Independent and sectarian regicides, including Vane and Harrison, were executed. But the liberty of conscience did not come into effect despite the King's efforts. The Sion House Proposals of some leading Presbyterians, including Richard Baxter, for a comprehensive church through Ussher's 1641 plan for a reduced episcopacy were firmly rejected by the 11 surviving Anglican bishops. Charles's

Religious policies

Worcester House Declaration, drafted by Edward Hyde (soon to be earl of Clarendon), called for suffragan bishops and Presbyters plus the calling of a national synod on the Anglican prayer book. But these concessions, the most generous ever offered by Anglicans to Puritans, were rejected by the Convention Parliament, some Independent members voting with the majority. The only salve for the Presbyterians was the King's call for a conference to be held at the Savoy (in London) between Presbyterian and Anglican divines, but, before any agreement was reached, the Convention Parliament was superseded by the Cavalier Parliament (1661–79), which was overwhelmingly Anglican. The failure of the Presbyterians at the Savoy Conference was similar to that of their forefathers at Hampton Court.

The Cavalier Parliament set the tone for forthcoming legislation by welcoming the bishops back to the House of Lords with the repeal of the Bishops' Exclusion Act of 1642. This repeal was followed by the passage of the Corporation Act (1661) restricting local political office to Anglicans. Meanwhile, the Convocation of the clergy, after taking over from the Savoy Conference, drafted a new prayer book making slight concessions to the Savoy Presbyterians and to the Laudian Anglicans that became the basis for a new Act of Uniformity (1662). The Caroline Uniformity Act required subscription by the clergy to the new prayer book, the Thirty-nine Articles, the oaths of supremacy and allegiance, and a new oath of nonresistance to the crown. The expulsion of nearly 2,000 ministers (about 20 percent) from their livings meant the end of comprehension, or the policy of including diverse religious groups within the Anglican Church. In the Conventicle Act (1664) the Nonconformists, or Dissenters, as the Puritan community was now called, were prevented, largely out of fear of subversion, from assembling in groups of five or more persons. In the Five Mile Act (1665) they were forbidden from coming within five miles of where they had once preached. The Great Fire of London (1666) destroyed Dissenter meeting houses and Anglican churches, and from the ruins of the city, Inigo Jones developed the Palladian style of church architecture, which ultimately found its way into Christopher Wren's St. Paul's Cathedral.

The foregoing pieces of legislation, inaccurately referred to as the Clarendon Code, had one important consequence: together with the Test Acts of the 1670s, they cut off Dissenters from all avenues of professional advancement—church, politics, education, and the professions—except for business. It may well be that the affinity between Dissent and the business world, so characteristic of the age of the Industrial Revolution, can be explained more by this exclusion than by the Calvinist ethic of Puritan theology. Nor does there seem to have been much affinity between Puritan theology and the "new science," as some historians have claimed, in the founding of the Bacon-inspired Royal Society by Charles II in 1662. Such scientists as William Harvey, Robert Boyle, Isaac Newton, and John Wilkins were latitudinarian in their religious views, tending to gravitate toward the natural theology of the Cambridge Platonists, who reacted strongly against the Puritan doctrines of predestination and election. The policies of the government in economic affairs at the Restoration were an acceleration, rather than a reversal (as in religious affairs) of those underway during the Interregnum. On the question of the king's revenue, for example, Charles agreed to give up purveyance and the feudal dues, abolished during the Interregnum, in exchange for Parliament's retention of the excise started by Pym and continued by Cromwell. A new hearth tax and the traditional tonnage and poundage duties for life did not bring the King up to the proposed annual income of £1,200,000 per year, and he was constantly in debt, as his father had been. Charles II, therefore, was not able to resist Parliament as strongly as he might have wished. In matters of overseas trade, including that with Scotland and Ireland, the government's policy of protectionism was reflected in the Corn Laws, which were to protect producers—instead of consumers, as under earlier acts—through import duties on grain from abroad during bad harvests and by

Economic policies

means of bounties on exports to foreign countries during good harvests. Thomas Mun's book *England's Treasure by Forraign Trade* (written earlier but published in 1664), in which he said that the rule is "to sell more to strangers yearly than we consume of theirs in value," reflected the mercantilist idea of the Navigation Acts (1660–63). Patterned after the Cromwellian ordinance of 1651, the Navigation Acts provided for the transportation of all goods to and from the colonies in English or English colonial ships. The exceptions to this principle were (1) certain colonial enumerated commodities that were first to be shipped directly to England and (2) all commodities produced in Europe for the colonies, which were first to be shipped to England, either in ships of England, her colonies, or the originating European country. The Navigation Acts, designed to give the mother country a favourable balance of trade with the colonies, stood for the triumph of the national interest over the special interests of the trading companies. They were also designed to damage the Dutch carrying trade by giving shipping a monopoly, and they contributed heavily to the commercial rivalry, especially in the New Draperies, that was a basic cause of the second Dutch war in 1665. The capture and burning of English naval ships by the Dutch in the Thames in 1667 terminated the war but not before the English capture of New Amsterdam (renamed New York). It also led to the fall of Charles's chief minister, the Earl of Clarendon.

The Cabal. After the fall of Clarendon in 1667, government power passed into the hands of a group of five men, all non-Anglicans, whose initial letters formed the word cabal. Although a Triple Alliance had been signed with Holland and Sweden in 1668, Charles was more interested in a treaty with the France of Louis XIV, whom he admired. Accordingly, the Treaty of Dover was signed in 1670, in which Charles promised to support France in a war with Holland in exchange for a subsidy during the war. But a secret provision, known only to the Cabal's Catholic sympathizers, Thomas Clifford and Lord Arlington, provided for the King, in exchange for another subsidy and troops if necessary, to declare himself a Roman Catholic—a step his brother James, duke of York, had taken the preceding year. A Stop of the Exchequer in 1672, by which the government halted payment to its banker creditors, indicated that the royal treasury was almost bankrupt, so Charles declared war on Holland, gaining the annual subsidy from Louis XIV. Charles did not announce any conversion to Catholicism, but he did resume his attempts at religious toleration with the issuance of a Declaration of Indulgence (1672). As a result the Dissenter John Bunyan was freed from Bedford jail, where he had written most, if not all, of *Pilgrim's Progress* (1678). The Indulgence suspended the penal laws, including the Clarendon Code, in ecclesiastical matters, but it was greeted with reservations by some Dissenters, partly because they questioned this extension of the royal prerogative and partly because they feared that the King's ultimate goal was the advancement of popery. The Cavalier Parliament strongly opposed the Indulgence, largely for the same reasons, so Charles, anxious to get a subsidy from Parliament, cancelled the Indulgence on the advice of a Cabal Dissenter (Lord Ashley, by then earl of Shaftesbury). Not content to stop there, Parliament passed a Test Act (1673) requiring any civil or military officeholder at the national level to take the Anglican holy sacrament and to denounce the Roman Catholic doctrine of transubstantiation. The latter excluded all Catholics, and the former excluded all Dissenters. The King reluctantly signed the bill, and the Duke of York resigned as lord high admiral. The Test Act began the breakup of the Cabal that was completed with the appointment of the Earl of Danby as chief minister (1674).

The Popish Plot. Danby represented a change from the Cabal, for he was pro-Dutch and pro-Anglican in his sympathies. Although he brought the war with Holland to a close and although he was able to arrange the marriage of Mary, the Duke of York's elder Protestant daughter, to William (later King William III of England), the Protestant stadtholder of the United Provinces of the Netherlands, he was obliged to conduct a pro-French foreign policy, including the handling of the French subsidy, in order to

Treaty of Dover

remain in office. In the summer of 1678 Titus Oates, a habitual liar, "informed" the Privy Council of an alleged Popish Plot to kill the King and to replace him with his brother, the Duke of York. In September Oates made depositions to this effect before a popular London magistrate, Sir Edmund Godfrey, who in turn revealed them to Edward Coleman, the secretary to the Duchess of York. The arrest of Coleman, who had had a long correspondence of a treasonable nature with the Jesuit confessor to Louis XIV, gave some credence to the plot, but it was raised to near panic proportions with the discovery of Godfrey's body on Primrose Hill in Hampstead. His death still remains a mystery. On the day after Coleman was found guilty of treason (November 28), Oates accused Catherine, Charles's Catholic queen, of treason before the bar of the House of Lords; but Charles, who had sired numerous children by several mistresses throughout his entire marriage, remained cool throughout the whole proceedings and stood loyally behind the Queen. Meanwhile, Parliament passed a second Test Act (1678) requiring all members of either house of Parliament, the Duke of York excepted, to be members of the Anglican Church. In December, Danby was impeached by the House of Commons for arranging a French subsidy for Charles, but the King responded by dissolving the Cavalier parliament in 1679, 18 years after it had begun.

The Exclusion Controversy. The anti-Catholic atmosphere of the Popish Plot led directly into the Exclusion Controversy. Three short Parliaments during the years 1679–81 were primarily occupied with the efforts of Shaftesbury to exclude the Duke of York from succeeding Charles on the throne. The issue, which caused men to form embryonic political parties, was quite simple: should the future supreme governor of the church and state be a Roman Catholic? The exclusionist supporters of Shaftesbury, who were Dissenter (and frequently Low Anglican) critics of the royal prerogative, were called Whigs. The anti-exclusionist supporters of the Duke of York, who were Anglican, especially High Church (but not Catholic) backers of the royal prerogative, were known as Tories. Even though the situation was by no means as serious as 1641, Charles II, unlike his father when confronted by a Country opposition, made some conciliatory moves: he took Shaftesbury into the government as part of a new Court group, and he offered to place limitations on James. The Whigs, however, would settle only for exclusion in the Parliament of 1679, so the King dissolved it after signing a bill that strengthened procedures in the use of writs of habeas corpus, which safeguarded Englishmen from arbitrary arrest and imprisonment. In the Parliament of 1680, the Whig candidate for the succession was Charles's illegitimate son, the Duke of Monmouth—"that Absalom, ambitious of the Crown" in John Dryden's biblical allegory—but the Whigs failed again with their exclusion bill, mostly because of the opposition in the Lords. The Parliament of 1681 at Oxford, where the King had posted troops, was dissolved within a week, but there was no repetition of the events of January 1642. It was just after the Exclusion Controversy that the philosopher John Locke wrote his book *Two Treatises of Government* (published in 1690), stating that a government could be changed if it no longer represented the interests of the people; Locke's work was later used to justify the overthrow of James II in 1688. For his unflinching support of James and the Catholic succession, Charles was able to obtain another subsidy from Louis XIV, making it unnecessary for him to call any more Parliaments during the remaining four years of his reign, even though this action violated the Triennial Act of 1664, based upon that of 1641. On his deathbed Charles received the last rites of the Catholic Church, at long last fulfilling his promise in the secret Treaty of Dover.

Political parties

JAMES II (1685–88) AND THE GLORIOUS REVOLUTION

When the Duke of York succeeded his brother Charles as James II (1685–88), he promised both the Privy Council and his only Parliament to preserve the church and state "as it is now by law established," but it was soon apparent that he wanted to re-establish the Catholic religion. An attempt by Monmouth to raise a rebellion in the southwest was crushed a few months later, and Chief Justice George Jeffreys exacted a fearful retribution from Monmouth's Protestant supporters in the "Bloody Assizes." Monmouth himself was put to death. James, determined not to be without Catholic officers in the future, could not get Parliament to repeal the Test Act of 1673. In a court test of the issue in 1686 (*Godden* v. *Hales*), the judges upheld the royal dispensing power for army commissions, clearing the path for James to appoint Catholics elsewhere. Although he did not appoint any Catholics to the episcopal bench, James did create a Commission for Ecclesiastical Causes (somewhat different from the old Court of High Commission), which suspended Bishop Henry Compton, among other clergymen, for disobedience. At the instigation of William Penn, who had introduced religious toleration to the colony of Pennsylvania, James pardoned 1,200 Quakers, and he issued, as Charles II had done, a Declaration of Indulgence (1687). In the preface, James frankly admitted: "We cannot but heartily wish, as it will be easily believed, that all the people of our dominions were members of the Catholic Church." The Earl of Halifax spoke for most Dissenters: "You are therefore to be hugged now, only that you may be squeezed at another time." James's success in appointing Catholics as president and fellows of Magdalen College, Oxford, may have offset any support he may have gained from the Indulgence.

The "Bloody Assizes"

The negative response the King got from county justices of the peace and prominent gentry to questions posed by the lords lieutenant, asking if they would vote to repeal the penal laws and Test Acts if elected to a new Parliament, was the first of several defeats. James issued a second Declaration of Indulgence (April 1688), but this time he required the bishops to have it read in all churches. Seven bishops stated their "averseness" to the Indulgence in a petition to the King because they believed the suspending power was illegal. James brought them to trial for seditious libel. The bishops finally had abandoned nonresistance and passive obedience. During the course of their trial, the Queen gave birth to a male heir, which assured the continuance of a Roman Catholic monarchy. On the same day that the seven bishops were acquitted, seven Whig and Tory peers, including Bishop Compton and Lord Danby, invited William of Orange to assume the throne of England. Some last minute concessions by James came too late. Aided by the so-called Protestant wind, William landed at Torbay (the modern Tor Bay) on November 5, while Louis XIV, hopeful of another long English civil war, sent troops to his eastern border. Unlike the time of Monmouth's invasion, James's army experienced wholesale desertions. Even his old comrade-in-arms, John Churchill (later 1st duke of Marlborough and ancestor of the 20th century's Winston Churchill), deserted his post as lieutenant general of the army for William because, as he put it, "our religion and country were in danger of being destroyed." On December 11 James burned the writs for a new Parliament (already overdue) and fled to France. Although captured, James was allowed to escape, since William had no intention of making James the martyr his father had become. For the second time in 40 years, a king had been toppled from the throne; this time, however, the Church of England had been saved rather than destroyed.

Landing of William and flight of James

WILLIAM III (1689–1702) AND MARY II (1689–94)

The revolutionary settlement. From the various plans put forward for the settlement of the kingdom by Whigs and Tories, the one adopted for political affairs was the moderate Whig plan. The throne was declared vacant because of the King's abdication, and a Convention Parliament offered the throne to William III and Mary II as joint sovereigns subject to certain conditions set forth in a Bill of Rights. A hereditary succession was replaced by a parliamentary succession. With the exception of a few articles guaranteeing individual rights against royal power, the Bill's main provisions were directed toward the king and Parliament. The Bill affirmed free speech, free elections, and frequent meetings of Parliament; it prohibited the levying of taxes or the keeping of a standing army except

The Bill of Rights

with the consent of Parliament; and it proscribed ecclesiastical commissions, or courts, and the royal suspending and dispensing power. Subsequent legislation, some of which was sponsored by a new Country Party made up of Old Whigs and New Tories, enlarged upon this essentially conservative settlement by ensuring Parliament's control over the army with a system of courts-martial (1689), regularizing the election of Parliament triennially (1694), permitting a freer press through the lapse of the Licensing Act (1695), providing for the testimony of two witnesses in all treason trials (1696), and creating from the excise tax a fixed Civil List for both the crown's household and administrative expenditures (1698), the latter an enlargement upon the Long Parliament's distinction between the private man and the public office. When the Bill of Rights was enacted into law (1689), Parliament added a provision requiring oaths of fidelity and true allegiance (replacing the old oaths of supremacy and allegiance) to William and Mary, which several bishops (including, ironically, five of the "seditious" seven) refused to take. It also added a provision preventing the sovereign from being a Catholic. Even the new coronation oath required the sovereign to uphold the "protestant reformed religion established by law." A large group of Tory members agreed to support a religious toleration bill when the Whigs agreed to drop a comprehension bill to unite Anglicans and Dissenters in one church. The decline of rigid Calvinism, the weariness with religious strife, and the desire to reward Dissenters for their obedience to the law produced the Toleration Act (1689), which permitted everyone except Catholics, Jews, and Unitarians to worship as he pleased. In 1690 the Scottish Parliament removed the bishops from the Kirk, ratified the Westminster Confession, and set up the Presbyterian form of church government once again.

The revolutionary settlement brought an end to innovative attempts by Charles II and James II to rule without Parliament and to reintroduce the Catholic religion by religious toleration. In short, it was a vindication of the old Whig policy of exclusion. The Bill of Rights made it obligatory for the king to rule with the assistance of Parliament, and the Toleration Act outlawed Catholicism for all Englishmen. Monumental as the Toleration Act was, it did not repeal the Test and Corporation Acts, which would have allowed Dissenters access to the political and professional life of the nation. The Bill of Rights was neither a forward-looking guarantee of individual rights against the power of a legislative body nor a statement of the natural rights of man, as in the United States and France, respectively, 100 years later. Rather, it had much in common with the medieval charters that set out the rights and privileges of a particular group in society. As Magna Carta had guaranteed the rights of the barons against the crown, so did the Bill of Rights guarantee the rights of the nobility and gentry against the crown. By his interference with voting privileges, army commissions, church benefices, and university fellowships, James II had not only restricted the freedom of the upper orders in English society, but he had also tampered with their freeholds, the privileged social position they regarded as a property right like the ownership of land. Free elections and free speech meant free from influence by the king and the lower orders of society but not free from influence by the nobility or the gentry. Although the revolutionary settlement reasserted that the king was under the law, as Magna Carta had done, by preventing the suspending and dispensing power, it would be a mistake to assume that it effectively transferred sovereign power from the king to Parliament. While it did make Parliament a partner on the important questions of revenue and the army, other aspects of the royal prerogative remained, for the most part, untouched: the waging of war and the making of peace, the conduct of foreign policy, and, above all, the appointment and dismissal of the crown's ministers. The increasing costs of postrevolutionary warfare would increasingly bring even these aspects into the orbit of Parliament's concern.

William's campaign against France. William's central purpose in assuming the throne of England was to use its men and resources in his life's work of defending Holland against the aggrandizement of France under Louis XIV.

Effect of the revolutionary settlement on Parliament

As carried out, it meant a sharp reversal in the traditional pro-French and anti-Dutch foreign policy. William's forces, including some 70,000 English troops, lost border fortresses, such as Namur in the Spanish Netherlands, to France during the early years of the War of the League of Augsburg (1689–97), but in Ireland they were successful at the Battle of the Boyne (1690), crushing James II's last hope of regaining his throne. The scale of such operations could not be financed from the tonnage and poundage duties that William's second parliament (1690–95) had granted for four years. The hearth tax was repealed and replaced by a general land tax, but even that was insufficient. In 1693–94 the Junto group of Court Whigs joined the Cabinet Council (also called the Lords of the Committee when the monarch was absent). The Cabinet Council, or Cabinet, which was smaller than the ungainly Privy Council and designed to handle the daily business of the war, took steps to handle the growing debt—about £14,000,000 from 1688 to 1702. Investors were able to place their money not only with trading companies, which were engaged in war profiteering and speculation, but also with the government. The means to do the latter was the newly chartered Bank of England (1694), a Whig joint-stock company. The Bank raised £1,200,000 in 12 days from the public and loaned it to the government (not the King) at 8 percent interest in exchange for the right to issue bank notes and to discount bills. The loan did not have to be repaid as long as the interest, about £100,000 annually, was raised by import duties. Here was the origin of a funded national debt. The debt precluded future Stops of the Exchequer, as in 1672, and the Bank's loan paid for the recapture of Namur in 1695. The Bank's issuance of notes in excess of deposits, however, led to an inflation that, combined with a depreciated currency through the clipping of silver coins and the need to pay the troops in the Spanish Netherlands, led to a financial crisis in 1696 almost as severe as that of the early 1620s. Some 60 or 70 joint-stock companies, including the Scots' Darién Scheme in Spanish Central America, collapsed. The bank survived through the wealth of its directors; a huge pamphlet debate on monetary policy led to recoinage, rather than devaluation, under the Warden of the Mint, Isaac Newton; the Board of Trade was re-created (1696), after brief starts in 1660 and 1670, to regulate overseas trade; and the war with France was terminated by the Treaty of Rijswijk in 1697. The economy snapped back because it was more diversified and broadly based than in the 1620s, but William was only waiting for the opportunity to form an alliance once more against France.

Establishment of the Bank of England

The last few years of William's life were absorbed with the problem of the succession to the throne of Spain and, to a lesser extent, with the succession to the throne of England. When the new Country Party, together with the Tories, forced out the Whig Junto after the election of 1698, the King's armed forces were drastically reduced; even his Dutch guards were dismissed. William, disgusted with an ungrateful people, threatened to abandon England. His main concern was that the Spanish Netherlands might fall to France upon the death of the childless Spanish King, Charles II the Sufferer. The dying Spanish king's last will provided that his throne and empire should go to Louis's second grandson (Philip V) if the crowns of France and Spain would remain separate. Louis at once accepted the will. In September 1701 the French king's prohibition of imports to France and Spain from England, plus his recognition of the 13-year-old pretender, James III, upon the death of James II, as king of England, swung public opinion behind William's new Grand Alliance against France (1701).

The Spanish succession

The Act of Settlement. Meanwhile, the last surviving child of Princess Anne, the younger daughter of James II, also had died, leaving the English throne—except for Anne—without a successor, since William and Mary had had no children. After the first of two elections in 1701, both won by Tories, including Robert Harley (who had made the passage from Old Whig to New Tory), Parliament passed the Act of Settlement (1701). The act designated the granddaughter of James I, the electress Sophia of Hanover, as Anne's heir and required all future sovereigns to be members of the Anglican Church. Other clauses, which were as much New Tory and Country Party criticism of William as they were to be restrictions upon the Hanoverians, stated that foreign-born kings should not defend their continental possessions without parliamentary consent; that no king should leave the country without parliamentary consent; that all governmental transactions should be handled only in the Privy Council and signed by all who consented (repealed in 1706, thereby continuing the life of the Cabinet); that foreigners could not sit in Parliament and the Privy Council or hold civil or military office; that officeholders could not sit in the Commons (modified in 1706 so that members of the Commons, when appointed to high office, must resign but could be re-elected); that no king could pardon men impeached by the Commons; and that judges held their commissions solely on good behaviour. The last provision gave judges independence from the crown, but it did not give them the right to declare parliamentary legislation unconstitutional. When William died in 1702, the Tory party leaders had assumed the mantle of the Old Whigs as the chief critics of the royal prerogative, whereas the Whig leaders (to a lesser extent with the Junto) had assumed the mantle of the Old Tories as the chief proponents of the royal prerogative.

ANNE (1702–14)

The dull, dowdy, and devout princess Anne succeeded William as sovereign, but John Churchill (now earl of Marlborough), whose witty, beautiful, and free-thinking wife, Sarah, was an intimate friend of the new queen, succeeded William as military commander of the English and Dutch forces in the Grand Alliance. After the parliamentary election of July 1702, Marlborough and Sidney (Lord Godolphin) formed a Tory Cabinet. This election was the third in 20 months and the fifth of nine held between 1695 and 1713. While these frequent and strongly contested elections may have given a certain instability to the English political process, they also provided a healthy polarization of the two parties over issues of the royal prerogative, the war, and the church. As a High Anglican, the Queen supported the efforts of the high Tories, including the Earl of Nottingham and her uncle the Earl of Rochester to pass an Occasional Conformity Bill. Such an act would have prevented Dissenters from qualifying for political office by their occasional attendance at Anglican communion services. Some Latitudinarian bishops regarded occasional conformity as a "healing custom"—a substitute for comprehension, although Daniel Defoe thought it hypocrisy—"playing bopeep with God Almighty." But Anne's support was withdrawn when they tried unsuccessfully to win over moderate Tories to their bill by tacking it on to the land tax measure, Lord Treasurer Godolphin's means to support the European campaigns of Marlborough. The high Tories subsequently were defeated in the election of 1705. Even though the Tories still outnumbered the Whigs by 30 votes in the new Commons, Godolphin wanted the Queen to bring more Whigs into the Cabinet, since they gave stronger support than the Tories to the war, at least in the Spanish Netherlands. The Whigs, together with 100 Queen's Servants—courtiers holding pensions and placemen holding offices—formed the war majority in the Commons. Against the advice of the Tory Harley, who had joined the Cabinet, the Queen reluctantly appointed a few Whigs to her Cabinet because she did not wish to jeopardize the military successes against France. Gibraltar had been captured in 1704, and Marlborough had won two brilliant victories: at Blenheim in 1704, which saved the Grand Alliance, and at Ramillies in 1706, which removed the French from the Spanish Netherlands. For the first time since the Hundred Years' War, England was a triumphant military power in Europe.

The Act of Union.   Godolphin also called on the Whigs to help him carry through Parliament an incorporating union with Scotland that William had recommended on his deathbed. The Scottish Parliament had passed an Act of Security (1703) providing for a Protestant Stuart succession, upon Anne's death, unless the Scottish government was freed from "English or any foreign influence." The English Parliament retaliated with an Aliens Act (1705)

prohibiting all Scottish imports to England unless the Scots accepted the Hanoverian succession. In 1706 agreement was reached to an Act of Union passed by both Parliaments the following year. The Scots gained the advantage of free trade within the new British common market of some 7,000,000 people; the English gained increased security, because Scotland could no longer be used by European powers as a base for an attack on England. The Scots were allowed to keep their legal system and the Presbyterian Kirk, but they gave up their Parliament. In return, they received 45 seats in the English House of Commons and could elect 16 lords to the English House of Lords. The Act of Union provided a constitutional means whereby the crown's influence in Parliament could be strengthened through a distribution of patronage to the Scots.

Whigs and Tories.   The strong backing of the Whigs for the Act of Union gave them an even stronger claim for additional appointments to the Cabinet. A kinswoman of Harley (and of the Duchess of Marlborough), Abigail Hill, a lady of the bedchamber for Queen Anne, gave the Tory leader some influence over the Queen, but Harley's attempt in February 1708 to oust Marlborough and Godolphin, who in effect had become Whigs, only resulted in his own resignation from the Cabinet. An invasion scare in March, through Scotland, helped the Whigs in their May election victory even though many people were tiring of the war. In July at Oudenarde, Marlborough defeated a French army, which was saved from annihilation only by darkness, and the navy seized Minorca. The death in October of the prince consort, George of Denmark, opened up additional offices to the Whigs. By the beginning of 1709 the war against France had been won, but the peninsular war against Spain had only endeared Philip V to his subjects. The Whigs entered into peace negotiations with Louis on the slogan "No peace without Spain," but when Louis agreed to all of the Allies' terms except removing Philip V from the throne by force, the English broke off the negotiations. In September Marlborough won the last of his important battles at Malplaquet, but it was with such a heavy loss of life that the French spirit was restored. On November 5 Henry Sacheverell, a High Anglican who had no use for the increasing rationalism in religion, preached an inflammatory sermon against Godolphin, the Whigs, and the settlement of 1689. The Whig leaders of the Commons impeached Sacheverell for high crimes and misdemeanours, but it was a Pyrrhic victory, like Malplaquet, since the Lords convicted him only by 17 votes and gave him a light sentence. With the cry of "Sacheverell and Peace," the Tories won the election of October 1710, but Godolphin had been dismissed from the Cabinet the previous August without any thanks from the Queen, and the Duchess of Marlborough had left the Queen's service in a burst of hysterics the previous April. Only Marlborough, who had been denied his request to be captain general for life, remained at his post.

The efforts of the Tory Cabinet under Harley and Henry St. John were concentrated on a peace settlement. Because the Tories believed, with some truth, that the war's high tax on land was depleting the landed interest, which was predominantly Tory, and that wartime investments were enriching the moneyed interest, which was predominantly Whig, they passed a Parliamentary Property Qualification Act requiring possession of land worth £600 for county members and £300 for borough members. In October, St. John, much to the disgust of George of Hanover (the future George I), negotiated with French diplomats the preliminaries for a separate peace settlement that would leave Philip V on the Spanish throne, give Gibraltar, Minorca, Hudson Bay, Newfoundland, and Nova Scotia to Britain, and provide Britain with certain trading rights with the Spanish colonies in the Americas. While the Whig views on the peace found an outlet in the coffee shops through the journalistic efforts of Joseph Addison (*The Spectator*) and Richard Steele (*The Tatler*), the Tory leaders engaged an Irish Anglican churchman, Jonathan Swift, who defended a "Peace without Spain" in his *Conduct of the Allies* (1711). In the Lords the High Tory, Nottingham, agreed to support an amendment opposing "Peace without Spain" if the Whigs agreed to an Occasional Conformity bill. The

Whig ascendancy

Marlborough's victories

Whigs sacrificed the Dissenters in order to overthrow the government, the bill becoming law and the amendment carrying by eight votes. This blow to the Tory government by the Whig lords was overcome by Anne's appointment of 12 Tory peers. The dismissal of Marlborough and the withdrawal of English troops from the field finally brought their Dutch allies to the conference table at Utrecht in 1713. At Utrecht the preliminaries were adopted, plus a line of barrier fortresses for Holland and a guarantee from Louis that the thrones of France and Spain would not be united.

Problem of succession Although the Tories were able to present a united front to win the election of 1713, on the matter of the succession to the throne there had been growing division, especially between the lord treasurer, Harley (now earl of Oxford) and the secretary of state, St. John (now Viscount Bolingbroke), who became bitter rivals for power in the Tory Party. The serious illness of the Queen in December caused both men to make overtures to the Pretender, the more serious commitment being made by Bolingbroke, but by March it was clear that the Pretender would not give up his Catholicism. In April, suspicious of the policies of their party leaders, a group known as the Hanover, or "Whimsical," Tories, voted with the Whigs against a governmental motion that the Hanoverian succession was not in danger, a sure sign that the Tories were in trouble. With the death of Sophia, her son George became the heir to the throne, and Oxford, now favouring the Hanoverian succession, made a speech in favour of a large reward for the capture of the Pretender. In an effort to embarrass Oxford, who had a Dissenter's background, Bolingbroke brought forward a Schism Bill designed to put an end to all Dissenting academies, the nesting area for future Whigs. The Schism Act passed the Commons by more than a 100-vote majority, but in the Lords, where Oxford could not bring himself to oppose it, it passed by only five votes. Oxford failed in an attempt to bring corruption charges against Bolingbroke, and on July 27 the Queen dismissed Oxford as lord treasurer, but Bolingbroke did not get the coveted post. When the Queen died on August 1, the bitter struggle for power in the Tory Party was dangerous but far from hopeless.

THE ACHIEVEMENT OF THE STUARTS

Queen Anne's death followed by two years that of the Earl of Rochester, whose father, the Earl of Clarendon, had been born six years after James I came to the throne. The two men had witnessed (as had Oliver Cromwell, who was born in 1599, and his son Richard, who died in 1712) the whole succession of Stuart rulers. What were the main outlines of the struggles they had seen? Political and constitutional matters took on a fairly recognizable pattern of development. The struggle for control of the state by the king and Parliament, neither of which had a concern for anything resembling manhood suffrage, was characterized by the increasing claims of both the royal prerogative and parliamentary rights (the latter more than the former) until the 1640s when the office, as well as the holder, of the crown was eliminated and Parliament became the sovereign power in the realm. The reestablishment of the monarchy at the Restoration, foreshadowed in the Cromwellian Protectorate, was not altogether different from what it had been under James I, but the absolutist tendencies of Charles II and particularly James II brought limitations upon the crown through the revolutionary settlement, which laid the basis for the "mixed" government of the 18th century. A somewhat similar pattern can be found in religious matters. The struggle for control of the church by Puritans and Anglicans, both of which had extremists who wanted to put down the royal supremacy, was characterized by Calvinist and Arminian modifications (the former perhaps more than the latter) upon the Elizabethan church settlement until the 1640s, when the Anglican Church was abolished and the Puritans came to power—at first under a state-controlled Presbyterianism and, later, under Cromwell's theocratic establishment. The revival of the Anglican Church at the Restoration, largely along the non-Arminian and Erastian lines of Elizabeth's day, was reinforced by the monopoly of political privileges

given only to Anglicans, but the move toward Catholicism under Charles II and James II, together with the enforced separation of the Dissenters from the Anglican Communion, culminated in 1689 in a policy of religious toleration (but not political privileges) for Dissenters that was to remain until the 19th century.

In social and economic matters the pattern is broken. There was no struggle between the various classes in English society at the time of the Civil War; instead, there were divisions to varying degrees within the aristocracy, gentry, and merchants, when it came to choosing sides. Although many aristocrats and some gentry lost political and economic influence during the Interregnum, partly because of the composition of Parliament and the confiscation of lands, after the Restoration they regained their earlier privileged positions. Also, there is some evidence that these social classes were not as strongly represented among the Dissenters as they had been among their Puritan predecessors; conversely, Dissent became more associated with trade and finance. Finally, there is some evidence that the bankers and the merchants after 1689 were to be found more in the Whig Party, which embraced many Dissenters, than in the Tory Party, which embraced the High Anglicans. (L.F.S.)

Great Britain under the early Hanoverians

THE DEVELOPMENT OF PARLIAMENTARY GOVERNMENT (1714–60)

When Queen Anne died, George Louis, elector of Hanover, became George I of Great Britain and Ireland under the Act of Settlement. The Revolution of 1688 gave legitimacy to the Hanoverian succession. The Jacobite Party—a few thousand country squires, High Anglicans, and Roman Catholics—were committed to the Stuarts under the doctrine of indefeasible hereditary succession discredited by the Revolution of 1688. Most politicians and place seekers showed acceptance of George I by courting Baron Johann Caspar von Bothmer, the Hanoverian envoy. Immediately upon Anne's death, Caspar revealed to the Privy Council the list of regents; 14 of the 18 were known as Whigs. The liveliest question was not who would oppose the new king but whom he would prefer as his ministers.

The old order crumbled before the King's arrival from Hanover in September. George I had already dismissed the Tory leaders Henry St. John, 1st Viscount Bolingbroke, and James Butler, duke of Ormonde, and had excluded John Churchill, duke of Marlborough, from the regency. Preferring known loyalty, the King sought it among Whigs. Only Charles Howard, 1st earl of Nottingham, and George Talbot, duke of Shrewsbury, represented the ideal of a "mixed ministry" of Whigs and Tories. Charles Viscount Townshend and James Stanhope, 1st Earl Stanhope, secretaries of state, headed the ministry. Passing time and royal decisions virtually eliminated the leaders of the revolutionary generation of both parties.

The changeover went smoothly. The King enjoyed the prerogative right of appointment and dismissal; the only grounds for challenging his appointments were political. The Whigs, led by such men as Charles Spencer, 3rd earl of Sunderland, James Stanhope (after 1717, Earl Stanhope), Lord Townshend, and Robert Walpole, 1st earl of Orford, identified themselves with the security of the Hanoverian succession; and the election of 1715 gave the Whigs a majority of about 150 in the House of Commons. Because Bolingbroke obligingly fled to France, the government did not proceed beyond a resolution of impeachment against former ministers responsible for the unpopular Treaty of Utrecht ending English participation in the War of the Spanish Succession. Ormonde followed Bolingbroke into exile a few months later; the Earl of Oxford remained in the Tower of London; the Tory minority was leaderless. In France, Bolingbroke became secretary of state to James II's son, James III, the Stuart pretender who was preparing an invasion of Great Britain. The Jacobite Rebellion of 1715–16 (the "Fifteen") and the Whig success in identifying the Tories with it frustrated Tory hopes of recovery. The romantics who surrounded the Pretender in France

The Whig leaders

persuaded him to undertake an invasion that his able half brother Marshal Berwick and Bolingbroke opposed. Stanhope and Townshend were prepared when John Erskine, earl of Mar, led a premature rising in Scotland and an invasion of England. Mar was in retreat even before the Pretender arrived in Scotland in December. A month later they left for France, where the regency encouraged James to go on to Italy. The "Fifteen" was Mar's rebellion, mixed with Scottish politics and religious antipathies, as much as it was a Jacobite rising.

The establishment of Whig supremacy. The rising blasted Tory ambitions. The government treated actual rebels with moderation but took political vengeance upon politicians of doubtful loyalty, and, by the spring of 1716, the ministry was purely Whig. Robert Walpole, formerly paymaster of the forces, became first lord of the treasury and chancellor of the exchequer. The Septennial Act of 1716 extended the life of "this present Parliament" four years, postponed the unsettling effects of an early election, and, by providing legal lives of seven years for subsequent Parliaments, gave winners more time to consolidate victories. All politicians would enjoy the benefit of fewer elections and economies in election expenses. The act did not abolish the king's prerogative of dissolution, but it did inaugurate the septennial convention, which during the 18th century was clearly violated only once, in the election of 1784.

Whig factionalism succeeded a long generation of Whig–Tory warfare. After a decade of doubt, scholars again believe that the last two Stuart reigns knew a two-party system based on significant distinctions between the parties. Under the Whig supremacy after 1715, the differences among Whig politicians did not go to the bedrock of English life as had earlier Whig–Tory ones. Between the Townshend–Walpole and Stanhope–Sunderland factions, personal rivalries as well as disagreements over foreign policy created ill feeling, leading to Townshend's demotion and Walpole's resignation in April 1717. In foreign affairs, Stanhope pursued a vigorous continental policy. In 1717 he concluded a Triple Alliance with France and the Dutch that minimized foreign support for the Jacobites and gained for England the valuable diplomatic influence and organization of France in northern Europe. Stanhope's treaty with France was a constant of British policy for 15 years. His forward policy in the Baltic area exposed the controversial question of England's responsibilities toward Hanover, unavoidable in any case. Russia's presence in Europe after its victory over Sweden in the Great Northern War (1700–21) was less threatening to England than to Hanover; England and Russia were able to resolve commercial problems.

During his three years of office, Walpole engaged in factious opposition. In particular, he and Townshend courted the Prince of Wales. During the 18th century, the Hanoverian kings were nearly always at odds with the heir apparent, who constituted a "reversionary interest": unemployed politicians might cluster around the Prince of Wales, especially if the king was old. The game, however, was risky, as the Georges looked suspiciously at the reversionary principle. In 1719 Walpole helped defeat the Peerage Bill, which aimed at restricting the prerogative power to create new peers. The King himself favoured the bill because, if he died, it would prevent his successor from using the prerogative against Stanhope, whom he liked.

By 1720 Stanhope reached the height of his power. He had converted the Elector of Hanover into the king of Great Britain by winning for English ministers that part of the King's confidence formerly given to Hanoverian advisers. The King and the Prince of Wales were reconciled, and Walpole and Townshend accepted Stanhope's foreign policy. By April 1720 an era of good feeling prevailed among Whigs, marked by Walpole's return to the paymastership and Townshend's acceptance of the lord presidency of the council. All of this occurred on the eve of Walpole's accession to leadership. He had political luck as well as ability.

No sooner was Walpole back in office than the government was embroiled in a frenzy of speculation associated with the South Sea Company. Sunderland, first lord of

the treasury, sponsored a plan whereby the company took over three-fifths of the national debt in return for trading privileges and a payment to the government of £7,000,000. Anticipations of profits inflated imaginations, and by September 1720 the boom in company shares collapsed. An indignant public opinion and ruined speculators blamed the company and the government. Walpole, however, who had not sponsored the scheme, escaped criticism. In December his plan of salvation, endorsed by the Bank of England and the company, revived public confidence and raised Walpole's prestige. Sunderland and John Aislabie, chancellor of the exchequer, had to resign. Then Stanhope's death in February 1721 vacated the northern secretaryship of state. The successions were predictable. Walpole, with Townshend, did not acquire full control, however, until Sunderland died a year later and until John, Lord Carteret, the other secretary of state, resigned in 1724 after offending the King's mistress, the Duchess of Kendal. (The office of secretary of state was divided between the northern and southern departments until 1782, when the southern department became the Home Office and the northern department became the Foreign Office.) With Townshend and Thomas Pelham-Holles, 1st duke of Newcastle, as secretaries of state, with disaffected Whigs such as William Pulteney, 1st earl of Bath, and John Carteret (later Earl Granville) powerless, with the Tories in the wilderness, with the ministry united and strong in Parliament and enjoying the King's favour, Walpole by 1725 inaugurated the age of political stability.

Political stability in the 18th century. The English historian J.H. Plumb has defined this stability as "the acceptance by society of its political institutions, and of those classes of men or officials who control them." Three conditions making for stability prevailed by 1725: single-party government; executive control of the legislature; and a sense of identity among those people who possessed social, economic, and political power. The completeness of the Whig monopoly was unprecedented. Besides losing parliamentary seats, Tories suffered purges from local offices and governmental services. Family allegiances became Whig. That politics was a Whig preserve was clear in 1733 when Walpole created a furor of popular protest by his attempt to impose an excise tax on wine and tobacco. But despite the unpopularity of the measure, a Tory government was not a conceivable alternative to Walpole's. At his fall in 1742, the Whigs continued in power; the aristocrats were nearly all Whig, and the hard-core Tories, mainly gentry and squires, numbered only 150 in Parliament. Until the 1780s and the beginning of a new two-party system, the Whigs predominated; ministerial changes were mere Whig reshufflings.

Control of the legislature. Walpole was the first minister to control the legislature with a one-party executive. His steadfast supporters were government officeholders and placeholders whose influence joined with his own, with the King's, and with others', such as the powerful Duke of Newcastle, to manage the electoral system. Walpole, Henry Pelham, and Frederick North, Lord North, who had the longest tenures as heads of ministries until the younger William Pitt—21, 11, and 12 years, respectively—had time to perfect this kind of management, which in turn prolonged their tenures of office.

In the 18th century, a ministry needed the king's support. With the exceptions of Charles James Fox and Edmund Burke, who in the political turmoil of 1783–84 were 50 years ahead of their time in asserting the primacy of the House of Commons, politicians accepted the king's prerogative power of appointment and dismissal. Kings, like politicians, distinguished between constitutional and political precepts, conceding the importance of political realities when considering the makeup of ministries. Besides his ultimate powers, the king's patronage power and influence were available to a ministry he favoured. Good relations between ministers and courtiers who could influence the king were also important to ministerial security. George II's queen, Caroline of Ansbach, gave powerful aid, for example, to Walpole. Yet Carteret exaggerated in saying that the crown alone could keep a minister in power. Henry Pelham said more correctly that, in single

Peace with France

The South Sea bubble

The three conditions of stability

instances, the king's support could get what a minister wanted; steady control required the support of both king and Parliament.

The king sometimes farmed out his patronage powers to others, such as the Duke of Newcastle, who became known as the "ecclesiastical minister" because of his control over church appointments. Under George II, however, no one mistook the fount of patronage: government, as it had always been, was the king's. The delegation of local administrative work to parish officials and justices of the peace did not lessen the numbers of royal officials. Wars being more costly, more people were needed to collect and manage the growing revenues. Besides money for the debt service (the interest payment on the national debt) and the armed services, Parliament provided the civil list, or the annual payment to the crown, increasing it for George II from £700,000 a year to £800,000. It came in a lump sum, and with it the king paid the costs of the civil side of government, pensions, household support, and the secret service. The political use of the civil list was not so great, however, as gossip had it.

Influence and patronage did not necessarily bribe members of Parliament. Generally, placeholders as well as independent country gentlemen recognized an obligation to support the government in office because it was the king's. In any given House of Commons, two-thirds of the 200 placemen were holdovers free of obligation to the ministry in office. The total consisted of some 40 ministers and administrative officials, 50 court and household officials, 60 officers in the armed service, and the remainder sinecurists and pensioners. The king had 26 ecclesiastical appointments to the House of Lords. Political considerations entered into them, and generally the incumbents supported the government.

The electoral system. Management of the electoral system was the other requisite for control of Parliament. The peers sat in the House of Lords by hereditary right, bishops by virtue of their offices; Scotland was represented in the House of Lords by 16 members elected by their own Scottish peers. The first two Georges used sparingly their prerogative power of creating peers. The House of Lords remained at about 220 members until the 1780s, when George III tried to offset the reduction of his patronage by increasing the appointment to peerages. Some peers were active politicians, and 18th-century cabinets were predominantly aristocratic.

Parliament had taken control of the ancient electoral system in the late 17th century. The politicians preferred to manage the system rather than to tamper with it. The list of borough constituencies and franchise qualifications remained virtually unchanged until the Reform Bill of 1832 (see below). The property-based franchise was fixed by statute in 1430 for the counties and by local custom or charter in the boroughs. The electorate numbered about 400,000 voters distributed unevenly among some 300 constituencies. In only 19 boroughs besides Westminster, London, and Bristol did the electorate exceed 1,000. Yet the management of elections was neither easy nor cheap. Each borough and county had a unique character, history, and personality. Management also meant arrangements for avoiding electoral contests. A general election was a varying number of contests, normally on local issues or personalities, and not a national electorate's judgment on national issues. In the last half of the 18th century, the largest number of contested counties in any election was 11. The absence of contests, as much as electoral victories, attested to good management.

After 1770, radicals increasingly stirred the question of parliamentary reform. They desired a Parliament more representative of the number and distribution of voters, and they hoped to achieve this by more frequent elections, by the redistribution of seats in accord with population, and by adding personal (*i.e.,* not landed) property to the electoral qualifications. The basic complaint was against the preponderance of land in the electoral structure.

Land was only one of the several interests deserving representation. In 1770 Edmund Burke in his *Thoughts on the Causes of the Present Discontents* identified other

Management of elections (margin)

interests—commercial, official, professional, military, and naval. Actually, close-knit family and political relationships guaranteed representation of the other interests in themselves and through land. The propertyless—the poor, the wage labourers, the people who lacked free agency— were thought to deserve no voice in public affairs. The national consensus on the connection between property and political participation underlay the political stability of the 18th century. In the "balanced" constitution mixing democracy, aristocracy, and monarchy, and resting upon a property base, England enjoyed a closer union of political, constitutional, and social systems than perhaps any other European nation.

The growth of the Cabinet. Stability after 1725, however, was not synonymous with dullness or predictability in politics. The life of every government depended upon good working relations among king, ministers, and Parliament. The appearance of the institution of the Cabinet after the Revolution of 1688 did not solve the problem. Politicians were uncertain of the status or even the name of the executive group that took over the work of the Privy Council, which by 1715 had been reduced to honorary status. A committee of the Privy Council, the Cabinet or Cabinet Council met with the sovereign in its early days. Responsible individually to the king for the business of their offices, ministers only slowly developed a sense of corporate responsibility.

The Cabinet's membership fluctuated and was often too large for effectiveness. It included upward of 20 household and state officers, heads of administrative departments, and prominent persons such as the archbishop of Canterbury. This "nominal" Cabinet lasted into the 1760s. Walpole preferred to work with an inner cabinet made up of the two secretaries of state, the lord chancellor, the lord privy seal, the lord president of the council, and himself as first lord of the treasury and chancellor of the exchequer. But instead of creating the cabinet system, Walpole might have checked its growth had his preference prevailed. His opponents accused him of concentrating authority too narrowly, and later first ministers learned from his experience. After 1762 the "nominal" Cabinet yielded to the "effective" Cabinet, the membership of which, made up out of the Privy Council, for practical and political reasons stabilized at about nine until the 1790s, when it grew to some 12. The composition also became more fixed. By the 1780s the household officers were gone, and the Cabinet consisted of the three great officers of state and heads of administrative departments.

Yet uncertainties remained. The Cabinet had no legal status, but it was politically important and soon became a part of the working constitution. After 1718, George I, who did not speak English, ceased to attend its meetings; the next two kings followed his precedent almost without exception and did not thereby diminish the Cabinet's growing constitutional authority. Historians are cautious against dogmatism on details of Cabinet development and practice, because the sources are sometimes contradictory and seldom full.

The lack of a clearly defined party structure and the uncertain status of the Cabinet left unclear the role of the first, or prime, minister. Politicians said they feared the rise of an all-powerful subject. After the eclipse of the Tories and the prevalence of Whig factionalism, no one person was head of the Whig Party and thus the indubitable first minister. Yet the head of the government was usually identifiable. From Walpole onward he was normally the first lord of the treasury or, if in the House of Commons, chancellor of the exchequer. The term prime minister gradually took hold. The important thing was the substance, not the name, and Walpole provided an example of strong leadership of a relatively well knit government. No 18th-century head of a ministry could be a prime minister in the modern sense, because there was not a disciplined party opposition whose leader was the alternative prime minister. Nevertheless, the difference between Walpole's government after 1724 and its predecessors was striking. The contrast encouraged exaggerations of the maturity of Cabinet, party, and prime ministership and tempted historians in the 19th century to see George III

The role of the prime minister (margin)

trying to subvert a developed parliamentary government. None could have existed until the 19th century.

Walpole's ministry. *Domestic affairs.* Walpole became first minister after 20 years in Parliament. A proud House of Commons man who mastered its ways, he understood the prejudices and sensitivities of its members. During the first decade of his administration, he concentrated upon domestic matters, leaving foreign affairs to Townshend. Some substance and much political opportunism informed his harassment of Jacobites. Bolingbroke returned from exile in France in 1723 more interested in politics (though excluded from the House of Lords) than in the Pretender. Gathering about him disaffected politicians, notably William Pulteney and the old Tory Sir William Wyndham, and speaking through the newspaper *The Craftsman,* Bolingbroke attacked Walpole. Just as vocal were the "Patriots"—an ironic name given to a group of Whigs whom Walpole had alienated, among them Carteret, Lord Chesterfield (Philip Dormer Stanhope), Lord Cobham (Richard Temple), William Pitt, and Archibald Campbell, 3rd duke of Argyll. Soon after the accession of George II in 1727, the opposition swarmed around Frederick Louis, Prince of Wales, on the reversionary principle. His establishment, Leicester House, was also—in addition to being a centre of political opposition to Walpole—the centre of fashion, and attracted such leading authors as Jonathan Swift, Alexander Pope, John Gay, and Henry Fielding, along with important ladies, including Carteret's mother, Lady Granville.

The opposition was a varied, interesting group, but Walpole had the votes. The parliamentary elections of 1727 and 1734 were his victories. His parliamentary strength had a core of about 150 men, some of them placeholders, who faithfully attended sessions of Parliament. There were times of stress, like the storm over "Wood's Halfpence" in 1723–25, when an English ironmaster, William Wood, was granted a patent to mint a debased coinage for Ireland. The Irish complained that they had not been consulted and also feared that the new coins would drive out good currency. Swift's "Drapier's Letters" powerfully attacked the deal. Walpole revoked the patent in 1725. The main effect was upon Ireland, where the furor contributed to a political awakening.

The fiasco revealed two of Walpole's weaknesses—stubbornness, as contrasted with persistence, and secretiveness. His conduct over the excise in 1733 also showed these traits. Walpole desired to convert certain customs duties into excises, payable after the sale of goods released from bonded warehouses. Before he revealed his plan, the opposition and *The Craftsman* spread rumours of a general excise the merits of which were not as self-evident as Walpole thought. When he finally introduced a plan for a tobacco excise, the opposition had already misled the public. Though the government retained a majority in the House of Commons, Walpole gave up the scheme in April. "Coerced by clamor and opinion," he retreated, not because he had lost his majority but because he feared he might. But electoral success in 1734 showed that the storm had done no fatal damage.

These two episodes are better known than Walpole's solid accomplishments in national finance and commercial policy. Politicians accepted the principles underlying the protectionist commercial system; but Walpole improved its workings. He lowered many import duties, notably on raw materials, in the interest of British manufacturing and exports. Walpole's work on national finances was technical and administrative. He diverted the sinking fund to uses other than debt retirement, thus keeping down taxes. The national debt in 1739, when war began with Spain, was £46,000,000, reflecting a reduction of only £8,000,000 since 1714. But he halved the annual debt service charge by reducing the interest rate. Had he retired the debt, many holders of securities would have been unhappy. Walpole taught England that it could live and prosper with a national debt; he made it a permanent part of the nation's financial structure and of the domestic economy of many private citizens.

Foreign policy. Townshend continued Stanhope's policy of friendship with France against the empire. An al-

liance in 1725 between Austria and Spain justified distrust of Austria. Fearful for the European balance of power and for British interests in the Mediterranean, Townshend tried unsuccessfully to supplement the old Triple Alliance by new arrangements with Prussia and the northern countries. Walpole's desire for agreement with Austria, however, caused Townshend to resign in 1730 and meant the abandonment of the Stanhope policy. The Treaty of Vienna (1731) was a return to cooperation with the emperor and implied conflict of English-French interests. Commercial, colonial issues between them were growing more tense. The Treaty of Vienna proved immediately useful for Walpole, who found in it an excuse for staying out of the War of the Polish Succession, which erupted in Europe in 1733.

In the 1730s, when England had no staunch continental ally, relations with Spain deteriorated. Both sides complained of violations of trade treaties. English merchants poached upon Spain's protectionist system in the West Indies, and English opinion supported them. In 1738 Capt. Robert Jenkins, who had earlier had his ear cut off by the Spanish coastal patrol, exhibited his severed ear to Parliament. Against his will Walpole had to agree to war against Spain because Parliament, the merchants, and the nation wanted it. The Anglo-Spanish War (the so-called War of Jenkins' Ear) soon blended with the War of the Austrian Succession, a wider European war that broke out after the death of Emperor Charles VI. As a guarantor of the Pragmatic Sanction intended to safeguard the Habsburg patrimony of Charles's daughter Maria Theresa, England granted a subsidy to Austria. Walpole survived the election of 1741 with a reduced majority. He was becoming an anachronism. When he resigned in February 1742, he left the nation in good economic condition, but with military and naval establishments unprepared for war.

The attacks of the "Patriots" during the preceding decade were against Walpole personally and the concentration of authority in himself, rather than against the ministry. Neither the King nor the opposition expected or desired a clean sweeping. The new ministry was a reshuffling of Whig politicians. The opposition leader, Pulteney, tried to bring the King and Leicester House together and promoted Spencer Compton, earl of Wilmington, for first lordship of the treasury. The King and Newcastle brought in Carteret as secretary of state but kept out Pitt, Chesterfield, and the Grenvilles. "Patriot" stock fell even further when the King and the Prince of Wales made peace. The new government was strong enough to stall attempts to inquire into Walpole's conduct as minister.

The Pelhams. The times at first favoured Carteret. Content to manage foreign affairs, he refused to be angry then, after the death of Wilmington in 1743, the King replaced the latter with Henry Pelham, the brother of Newcastle, instead of Pulteney (now earl of Bath). Carteret, a Europeanist, rejected the Patriots' emphasis upon the colonial–maritime war. His search for a German settlement appeared to the Patriots to be oriented toward Hanover, and Pitt protested vigorously. English aid to Austria helped it regain ascendancy in Italy, which displeased Frederick II of Prussia. His alliance with France shattered Carteret's diplomatic structure. Pelham and Newcastle thought him a political liability. The King's protection was not enough, and Carteret resigned in November 1744.

Pelham tried to make the ministry his own. He brought in some of the Patriots, but the King balked at Pitt, without whom Pelham had trouble controlling Parliament. In February 1746, when the King rejected Pelham's request to appoint Pitt to office, the ministry resigned. It says much for Pelham's success in monopolizing political talent that only Carteret (now Earl of Granville) and Bath were available to the King. When they failed to form a government, Pelham came back on his own terms. In one of his finer moments as king, George II agreed to give his confidence to Pelham and appointed Pitt as paymaster general. For the first time there was a "broad bottomed" Whig ministry, which included all factions.

The ministerial crisis of 1746 occurred against the background of the Jacobite Rebellion of 1745, not because of it. The Young Pretender, Charles Edward, hoped that suc-

Marginal notes:
Opposition to Walpole

Walpole's financial achievements

The War of Jenkins' Ear

The Jacobite Rebellion

cess in Scotland would bring French reinforcements. The enterprise was hopeless in spite of the Stuart mystique. Charles landed in western Scotland with a few friends and gathered support as he moved eastward. In September 1745 he occupied Edinburgh. He invaded England, reaching Derby unopposed. But his officers, seeing signs of gathering English strength, forced him to withdraw. The Duke of Cumberland's forces backed Charles into northern Scotland and, on April 16, 1746, destroyed his army at Culloden. Charles then wandered in the Highlands, a refugee, until he left for France in September, committing his cause to romance and dwindling Jacobite sentimentality.

Cumberland and his successor in Scotland, William Keppel, earl of Albemarle, enforced loyalty, or at least submission, to the Hanoverian succession in Scotland. The Lowlands were by now accommodated to the Act of Union of 1707 and the new dynasty. The Highlands had remained apart, dominated by a feudal regime. Clan chieftains enjoyed medieval judicial and military privileges that were frequently in conflict with sterner conceptions of public order. Upheld by acts of Parliament, the government now extended the royal system of shires and judges, as had been done centuries before in Wales. A statute abolished the chieftains' authority to require military service from tenants. Still, the chieftains did not suffer economically; they became landlords over estates formerly held in trust for their clans. The change in the basis of landholding worked a social revolution, to the detriment of the crofters, or tenant farmers. Scottish emigration to the empire increased greatly thereafter. Other statutes required oaths of allegiance from the Episcopalian clergy, forbade the wearing of kilts and tartans, and disarmed the Scots. After the Forty-five Rebellion, Highland Scotland became a part of the United Kingdom and knew peace.

English politics were not peaceful despite the Pelham–Newcastle victory in the 1747 election. Unable to accuse Pelham of acting like Walpole, the opposition instead criticized the excessive influence of the Pelhams and the great Whig families. The opposition took up the idea, advocated by Bolingbroke, of a "patriot king," who would rule above faction and party strife. Never reliable, Pitt courted the Prince of Wales at Leicester House, while Newcastle muttered about Cumberland's influence upon the King. As George II grew older, the reversionary interest became more intriguing. Ironically, however, the Prince of Wales died first, in 1751. Pitt returned to the safety of the ministry in time to support the Regency Act that checked the ascendancy of Cumberland and before Bolingbroke's death completed the discomfiture of Pelham's opponents.

Pelham's
last years

Pelham's ministry accomplished a good deal. The Treaty of Aix-la-Chapelle in 1748 ended the war but left colonial issues unsettled. During Pelham's last six years (he died in March 1754), England was officially at peace, and Pelham, an able finance minister, reduced the annual budget from the wartime peak of £10,000,000 to just over £2,500,000. He further reduced the cost of debt service by converting most of the debt to "three per cents." The Gin Act of 1751 took distillers out of retailing. Contemporaries thought the consequent reduction in gin consumption caused a decline of drunkenness, disorder, and crime. Other legislative reforms included the adoption of the Gregorian calendar in 1752 and the Hardwicke Marriage Act of 1753, which checked the racket in secret marriages, whereby younger sons in the aristocracy could inveigle a young heiress into a quick marriage. Against these measures prejudiced and uninformed opinions protested, but never so effectively as in 1753, when, with an election pending (1754), the government repealed its own measure permitting naturalization of Jews.

More than the politicians, George II in his commonsense way had appreciated Pelham's abilities, and he feared political troubles when Pelham died. Newcastle, who overrated his own abilities as much as he underrated his brother's and who confused electioneering with statesmanship, went to the Treasury as head of the ministry. Refusing to pay the price (patronage control) demanded by Henry Fox, 1st Baron Holland, or to meet Pitt's insincere conditions, he entrusted leadership in the House

of Commons to two second-rate men, Thomas Robinson, 1st Baron Grantham, and Henry Legge. In 1755, Newcastle brought in Fox as secretary of state, passing over Pitt, whose discomfiture was the greater because he disliked Newcastle's foreign policies. Pitt attacked the Newcastle–Fox combination and was dismissed from his post of paymaster general in 1755.

Pitt and the Seven Years' War. Like the King, Newcastle did not understand the importance of the imperial issue with France, and both were anti-Prussian and pro-Austrian. Anglo-French colonial rivalry came to a head in 1754 over conflicting claims to the Ohio Valley in North America. Already Pitt could point to Gen. Edward Braddock's defeat at Ft. Duquesne in July 1755, by French and Indian forces, as indicative of French strength. Yet Newcastle managed to arrange a system of treaties that was to serve as the base in Europe for Pitt's global strategy. After arranging subsidies for Bavaria, Saxony, and Hesse, Newcastle in September 1755 made a subsidy treaty with Russia. Frederick of Prussia felt the pressure and in January 1756 agreed with England to the Convention of Westminster, providing for mutual territorial guarantees. France completed this "diplomatic revolution" by accepting Austria's overtures. Russia, realizing the incompatibility between England's treaties with Prussia and itself, joined France and Austria. In May 1756, after a French attack on the British in Minorca, Great Britain declared war; within a year all of Europe was plunged into war.

The "dip-
lomatic
revolu-
tion"

Pitt saw the potentialities of these treaties more clearly than Newcastle. News of disasters in India, North America, and Minorca added substance to attacks upon the government, which he was freer to make after dismissal from office in November 1755. Fox resigned as secretary of state in October 1756, forcing Newcastle to tell the King that only Pitt could save the government. Pitt, who hated Newcastle, thought he could save England without Newcastle's help. The King yielded in November. The government, nominally headed by William Cavendish, 4th duke of Devonshire, had support in the nation, where Pitt, secretary of state, was popular; but it lacked the King's confidence and the support of the House of Commons. The King dismissed it in April 1757. The weakness of the patchwork ministry that replaced it made possible the obvious solution. Pitt contributed his own popularity and the support of Lord John Stuart Bute and Leicester House. Newcastle offered his patronage support, his personal influence, and his political skill. Fox contributed nothing, but as paymaster he could make a fortune, and the government need not worry about him. Pitt as secretary of state controlled the war effort; Newcastle at the Treasury devoted himself to political management.

When he took over Newcastle's treaty structure, Pitt redirected it from Hanoverian to global ends. Pitt was not unique in his theoretical understanding of the relation between the German war and the imperial conflict with France. But he was foremost in determination and ability to act according to his assessment of priorities. Sea power enabled the British navy to put France upon the defensive throughout the world, preparing the way for the victories that made 1759 the "year of miracles." French naval strength was great enough, however, to threaten invasion of England until the English victory of Quiberon Bay in November 1759. This was two months after the fall of Quebec and one month after the French fleet left India, where the English dominated Bengal and were winning in the Carnatic. These victories followed upon the capture of Guadeloupe and a British surge in the West Indies. English successes continued in 1760. Pitt had united the nation in the greatest war effort in its history. At the close of the war in 1763, Great Britain had become a major world power.

Quiberon
Bay victory

George II died on October 25, 1760, in the middle of the war. His last were his best years, in that at crucial moments he subordinated personal preferences to national needs. Whether he chose freely or was a prisoner of the Whig politicians is a much debated question. The accession of his grandson, George III, who at age 22 was far from mature, made everyone ask whether a new king meant new men.

The answer was self-evident because the ministry was a patchwork of factions, and the King's opinions on politics and the war were well-known. Newcastle and his Old Whigs, wearing the Pelham mantle, were the largest active faction, allied with the Court during the late years of George II. Pitt, supported at the moment by his wife's brothers, Richard Grenville-Temple, 1st Earl Temple, and George Grenville, was popular with the Country and in the city of London but lacked parliamentary strength. He had lately neglected Leicester House, where Lord Bute and the Princess Dowager dominated. Under the reversionary principle, both Newcastle and Pitt could expect unfriendly treatment. John Russell, 4th duke of Bedford, headed a growing faction that as a peace party would soon be at odds with Pitt. The hard-working civil servant types by definition were loyal to the King and were ready on the same principle to join with politicians who naturally gravitated toward the King and were known as King's Friends. The Duke of Cumberland, though Fox followed him, was not a factional leader but a political influence in his own right. The politicians feared most Lord Bute's capacity for intrigue and his influence upon the King. Together they represented the old cant of Leicester House, namely, throw the rascals out, eliminate factions, and establish a regime of purity and high-mindedness under a king who was devoted to the public good and an enemy of evil. The program of unemployed politicians was also the substance of the idea of a patriot king, and had Bolingbroke never written the book of that title, George III would have possessed the idea, having been under the moralizing tutelage of Bute.

There were also differences of opinion among the factions over the war. George III desired to end what he called "this bloody and expensive war"; Bute thought England should consolidate its gains before concluding peace; Pitt insisted upon continuing the war vigorously, though he consented to preliminary peace talks with France. Pitt found himself in the minority in favouring immediate war against Spain when its alliance with France became known. Not only the Bedford faction but also Newcastle and Lord George Anson, the talented first lord of the admiralty, opposed him. Pitt resigned. His successor, Lord Bute, as secretary of state with the responsibility for a Cabinet he could not control, had the powerful support of the King and the Princess Dowager. Though England declared war on Spain in January 1762, the government refused to renew the Prussian subsidy treaty and resumed peace talks with France. The Bedford peace party grew in influence as war weariness spread. Newcastle, old and tired, gave way to Bute, who formed a ministry in May 1762. In Paris, Bedford reached agreement on peace terms with France. Pitt opposed these terms violently in the House of Commons in November because he thought they threw away England's war gains. But he had the sense neither of the nation nor of Parliament. The opposition was adrift, and waverers supported the government in the absence of a reversionary interest. The government's victory (319–65) indicated not steady strength but, rather, the absence of a desirable alternative policy. Nonetheless, the nation did not think the less of Pitt for losing on the peace. Contemporaries gave him credit for leading England to heights it had never before attained, and posterity has agreed.

Treaty of Paris

THE REIGN OF GEORGE III TO 1789

Political instability, 1760–70. George III had support from country gentlemen and independent members, from placeholders, from ambitious young men who aspired to political careers and government service, and from factional leaders eager to replace the Old Whigs. Newcastle had no political future, and other Old Whigs such as Devonshire and Hardwicke soon died off. A corps of younger Old Whigs maintained some cohesion and by 1764 looked to the 34-year-old Charles Watson-Wentworth, 2nd marquess of Rockingham, as their leader. Though neither a dynamic personality nor a parliamentary speaker, Rockingham had patience and a character that inspired loyalty.

The national debt and taxes were the most pressing postwar problems. The debt of £114,000,000 continued to increase. The land tax met only one-half of the annual debt service. The government's excise tax on cider was a political blunder and, as a financial expedient, not worth a furor. Pitt and the Old Whigs feared for the liberties of the subject. Though the measure passed easily, Bute quailed. He was too thin-skinned for a front-rank politician. He resigned in April 1763; neither he nor the King saw political danger in a private advisory relationship. The King's alternatives reduced to one—Sir George Grenville, whom he personally disliked. Grenville saw his constitutional duty in serving the King and protecting him from political pressures. Though honest and an able lawyer, Grenville was rigid, dogmatic, and haughty—in short, a poor politician. Grenville's Cabinet, however, was an abler one than Bute's, if for no other reason than that Grenville replaced Bute as first lord of the treasury and the incompetent Sir Francis Dashwood as chancellor of the exchequer.

Miscalculation, bad luck, and his own poor judgment of people doomed Grenville. His measures, such as the Sugar Act of 1764 and the Stamp Act of 1765, to improve the customs service and revenue collections were fiscally sound but as politically explosive as the Proclamation of 1763, a well-intentioned, temporary arrangement for the territories in America newly acquired in the Seven Years' War. The most damaging effects of these measures beset Grenville's successors. Grenville was unlucky enough to be in office when the political agitator John Wilkes, who supported Pitt, burst into prominence. Wilkes, a London demagogue, gave virulent journalistic support to Pitt and the opposition in his newspaper the *North Briton.* Wilkes was given financial assistance by Richard Grenville-Temple, 1st Earl Temple, Grenville's brother, who was, however, hostile to the new ministry. Temple encouraged Wilkes to issue the famous "No. 45" (April 23, 1763) of the *North Briton,* which attacked the King's speech defending the Treaty of Paris. The government reacted by issuing a general warrant under which 48 persons, in addition to Wilkes, were arrested. Sir Charles Pratt, chief justice of common pleas and a friend of Pitt, checkmated the government's assault upon Wilkes by affirming his privilege as a member of Parliament. Later Pratt ruled illegal the "general warrant" under which the government first proceeded against Wilkes. In Parliament the government fared better. The House of Commons voted "No. 45" a seditious libel; the House of Lords declared Wilkes's "Essay on Woman" an obscenity. After Wilkes fled to Paris to escape proceedings under an indictment in the Court of King's Bench, that court outlawed him. The House of Commons expelled Wilkes and overruled Pratt's decision on general warrants. The Rockingham Whigs and Pitt again cried that liberty was in danger and nearly beat the government on the question of general warrants.

Agitation of John Wilkes

Grenville's financial and administrative measures began to take effect by 1765. Wartime finance gave way to peacetime finance. But Grenville embarrassed the King's mother by mishandling the Regency Bill (necessitated by the King's illness). Then Grenville asked the King to keep away from Bute. After dismissing Grenville and failing to enlist Pitt's help, the King had to turn to Rockingham. The Marquess accepted some "king's friends," but his major appointments were from a Rockingham party independent of Pitt's patriots, the Grenvilles, and the Bedford gang. Rockingham appointed Edmund Burke as his secretary, and Burke won election to Parliament in December 1765.

The Rockingham government early met reactions to the Stamp Act. American discontent mingled with English mercantile complaints of declining trade. Though from substantial people, these protests were extramural (*i.e.,* outside Parliament), and they added a new dimension to parliamentary politics. When Parliament assembled in January 1766, Pitt thundered for repeal of the Stamp Act, which he claimed violated the rights of Englishmen by taxing colonials without their consent. Grenville upheld Parliament's right to tax the colonies and demanded enforcement of it. The Rockingham compromise accepted something from each. It repealed the Stamp Act as impolitic and passed the Declaratory Act of 1766 asserting Parliament's right to legislate "in all cases whatsoever." The principle of the Declaratory Act continued to frustrate the empire. Americans, who rejected the principle, eventually ceased to talk about their rights as Englishmen; in 1776 they based their claim to independence upon their rights as men. The British constitution, as most members of Parliament understood it, did not admit autonomy of subordinate assemblies in the empire. The debate on the Stamp Act showed that on questions of constitutional rights, English and American claims were antithetical.

Achievements of Rockingham's ministry

During its short life, the Rockingham ministry accomplished much. It repealed the Cider Act, declared general warrants illegal, and amended the Navigation Acts. Reduction of the levies on West Indian molasses helped the trade and produced a handsome revenue. But the King's open distaste for the ministry encouraged disaffection within it. The nation and some politicians continued to look to Pitt. The King surprised no one when he dismissed the ministry, and the nation learned joyously in midsummer of 1766 that Pitt had consented to save it. At his best, Pitt could not have imposed his reading of the constitution upon Parliament and would have met difficulties in conciliating American opinion. He was at his worst, physically and mentally, after a few months in office. He failed to provide the "patriotic," nonpartisan government the nation expected. Sitting in the House of Lords as the earl of Chatham, Pitt lost touch with the House of Commons. When he was in the country, ill and at times deranged, ministers went their several ways. Prussia and Russia repelled England's advances. Chatham's plan for asserting crown sovereignty over East India Company territories in India became a temporary arrangement whereby the company paid money to the government and continued to expand its responsibilities in India. The Americans found arguments against the quartering of troops in Massachusetts and New York. The chancellor of the exchequer, Charles Townshend, persuaded Parliament in 1767 to levy duties on certain imports into America, which he asserted were palatable as commercial regulations. This casuistry provoked an American challenge to indirect taxation and made tea a symbol of the imperial tyranny.

The Townshend duties

By autumn 1768, when a pitiful Chatham resigned along with his discouraged secretary of state, the 2nd Earl of Shelburne, the ministry lost whatever Chathamite tinge had lasted beyond Townshend's death and the entry of the Bedfords—except for Augustus, 3rd duke of Grafton, who agreed to carry on the government. John Wilkes continued to embarrass the government. Wilkes had returned from France in March to win election for the county of Middlesex. The Court of King's Bench reversed his outlawry on a technicality, but Wilkes had to spend 22 months in the Tower on other charges. There he lived happily during the storm created by government's efforts to keep him out of the House of Commons. Middlesex re-elected him each time the House of Commons expelled him, until after the fourth election the House of Commons resolved that his opponent, Col. Henry Luttrell, ought to have won and seated him.

The Rockinghams, Grenvilles, and Chathamites supported a petitioning campaign asserting the rights of electors and asking redress of grievances. The King gave them, instead, a new prime minister in January 1770. This was Lord North, a charming man and a skillful parliamentarian but a man who lacked, as Burke said, the "spirit of command that the time required." But in 1770 this deficiency was not yet apparent. North had, at any rate, strong parliamentary support and the King's confidence. Though in time he acquired a following, he never welded into a party the factions that supported him. North did not control the government tightly; each department head had access to the King.

Radical movements and the loss of America. Until the election of 1774, which seated North's government firmly, the ministry survived a sequence of embarrassments. The petitioning movement was followed by a squabble over publication of parliamentary debates. Without conceding the right of publication, the government ceased to prosecute offenders. Wilkes became active in London politics, serving as lord mayor in 1774, the year he won the election to the House of Commons. He contributed to English political history the beginnings of extramural radicalism and the movement for parliamentary reform. When Burke's

Agitation outside Parliament

Thoughts on the Causes of the Present Discontents (1770) decried the court's influence over Parliament, it offered as remedy only the Rockingham party as "trustees" for the people. But the radicals, mostly middle class and strongly Protestant Dissenter in tone, preferred parliamentary reform. The Society for the Defence of the Bill of Rights, founded in 1769 to aid Wilkes, was the first in the long history of reform associations. The radicals disagreed on details; most of them connected property with political participation. In 1776 Maj. John Cartwright's pamphlet *Take Your Choice!* demanded universal manhood suffrage. James Burgh's *Political Disquisitions* (1774–75), advocating popular associations for reform, became a source book for radicals.

The radicals, rather than the Rockingham Whigs, were the true friends of America in England. Between the Dissenters and the American Puritans was an especially close communion. Richard Price, a Dissenting clergyman, wrote a best selling pamphlet, *Observations on the nature of Civil Liberty* (1776), linking freedom with autonomy. By that test America was not free. Neither the Rockingham Whigs nor the Chathamites could go so far. The Rockingham party, stuck with the Declaratory Act, hoped that men of goodwill might somehow adjust imperial differences. Burke made it seem that the tax on tea was the problem. Chatham denounced the right to tax but defended the imperial protectionist system. His ideas were out of date by the time the Americans declared their independence.

For the first six years the nation supported the war against America. After France entered the war in 1778 and Spain joined France in 1779, the war took on a new character. The opposition had to support it as a foreign war and could only criticize the government's conduct of it. When North fell in 1782, it was because England had lost the war, not because the country had gotten into it in the first place.

The British Empire in India was another of North's problems. The East India Company exercised sovereign powers in the country. Its financial crises inflamed bitter rivalries within the court of directors and invited parliamentary concern. Between 1770 and 1773 Parliament hardly mentioned American affairs, giving its attention to the Indian question. Two temporary acts passed in 1773. One granted a loan to the company, along with trade concessions that angered American merchants and led to the Boston Tea Party. The Regulating Act altered administrative arrangements in India. The statute's ambiguities, as well as the personalities of the people who directed company affairs in India, produced contentions between the governor general, Warren Hastings, and members of the Bengal council, notably Sir Philip Francis.

The East India Company

By 1780 England's fortunes sank low. High taxes, a mounting debt, talk of financial mismanagement, and the dreary continuation of the war in America worried the country gentlemen whose support North needed. The parliamentary opposition and the radicals outside criticized bitterly. Ireland stirred as the "Volunteers," formed to defend the nation against invasion, changed into a political organization. Concessions to Roman Catholics and to Irish trade in 1778 encouraged demands for more, and in 1779 the government granted them. In April 1780 Henry Grattan in the Irish House of Commons demanded an independent legislature for Ireland. Men saw similarities between America and Ireland. In England the parliamentary reformers revived. In Yorkshire in December 1779, an Anglican clergyman, Christopher Wyvill, led a meeting to endorse a mild parliamentary reform and the idea of corresponding societies to agitate for it nationwide. Edmund Burke announced his plan to reform the king's household and the executive establishment to reduce expenditures and the political influence of the crown. Burke's bill was defeated in March 1780, but on April 6 the House of Commons demanded reduction of the influence of the crown. In the metropolis the Westminster Committee asked for radical parliamentary reform. The Society for Constitutional Information began its effort to educate England to the need for reform to recover "lost rights." In the late spring of 1780, the anti-Catholic feeling mounted. The Protestant Association under Lord George Gordon

The Gordon riots

protested to Parliament against concessions to Catholics. The demonstrations degenerated into mobs, and, during the first two weeks of June, men feared for the very existence of London. Before troops restored order, much property was destroyed.

The Gordon riots temporarily discredited extramural associations. Lord North therefore asked for an election. Without much altering the political status quo, it gave North's government a new lease on life.

The country remained troubled. Late in 1781 came news of Cornwallis' surrender at Yorktown. Independent members began to desert North. On March 15, 1782, his majority fell to nine votes, and a few days later he resigned. The angry King accused North of deserting him; in fact, an angry Parliament had overturned a ministry enjoying the King's confidence. Parliament forced upon the King a new ministry under Rockingham and a reform program he did not want. Rockingham held over only one man from North's Cabinet. George III salvaged something by using Shelburne, secretary of state for home and colonial affairs, as royal confidant. Few politicans trusted Shelburne, but Rockingham had to tolerate him because he led the Chathamites who had opposed North. Parliament passed Rockingham's reform program. Burke's economical reform marked an important stage in transferring control of the executive and all but the most intimate parts of the household to parliamentary supervision. Other reform measures disfranchised revenue officers, excluded holders of government contracts from Parliament, and changed the paymaster's office from a private sinecure to a public trust. The grant of legislative independence to Ireland did not terminate England's political control of the Irish administration or oligarchical management of the Irish Parliament.

The Fox–North coalition. Peace negotiations in Paris split the government. Shelburne hoped to hold America within the empire under a revised commercial system. Rockingham's death on July 1 gave George III an opening. Burke and Fox were alone in wanting to fight him for
Reform movement
control of appointments to the new ministry. Rather than serve under Shelburne, the King's choice, some Rockingham ministers resigned. The possibility of a drastic change of the constitution disappeared. Shelburne, with his chancellor of the exchequer, the young William Pitt, extended the administrative reforms begun by Rockingham. Shelburne also reached peace terms with France and America, which Parliament rejected as overgenerous in February 1783. The Rockingham Whigs (now headed by William Bentinck, 3rd duke of Portland, and led in the House of Commons by Fox) and Lord North's party, after defeating the treaty, went on to form a government. Again the King had to surrender. The Old Whigs dominated the government headed by Portland, with Fox and North as secretaries of state. Contemporaries established a caricature of an unholy, unnatural coalition, which historians accepted. The coalition had substance. The American Revolution was now history; Fox and North agreed to act independently on parliamentary reform; they agreed on most other current issues; they were personal friends and both hated Shelburne. Among possible combinations, the Fox–North coalition was the most likely.

The coalition survived the embarrassment of passing a peace treaty like the one they had defeated to force Shelburne's resignation. But there was a difference. Shelburne hoped to supplement the treaty with generous trading concessions to the United States. The coalition, like England, revered the protectionist system.

Apart from American affairs, England was looking to the East, where the problem of India was paramount. It had been under study since the acts of 1773. The reports of Burke's Select Committee and the secret committee of Henry Dundas, 1st Viscount Melville, appeared in 1782–83 as mines of information and indictments of company administration. The coalition brought in two bills. The opposition saw the provisions for a board of commissioners, named in the bill and after four years to be appointed by the King, as a coalition effort to monopolize Indian patronage. The bill to tighten English supervision over the administration in India was called unworkable. Fought by

the East India interest and the younger Pitt's followers, the bills passed the House of Commons only to meet defeat in the House of Lords on December 17, 1783. Ignoring the coalition's victory in the House of Commons, the King dismissed it and called upon Pitt.

Pitt's ministry. The King's action was irregular and dangerous, but events vindicated him. Pitt hung on throughout the winter as a minority minister, but the minority grew. On March 25, 1784, the King dissolved Parliament in disregard of the septennial convention. Pitt's victory was not that of a homogeneous party but of varied groups and hatred of the coalition. Pitt was not a party leader until 1789, though the Portland Whigs acted steadily in opposition along with a dwindling number of North's men.

Pitt dealt masterfully with accumulated business, aided by able men who had their first chance to lead. Pitt's India Act of 1784 created a Board of Control nominated by the King from among privy councillors. The extent of the board's domination over the company could not be specified, but under Dundas' presidency the board was vigorous. Burke and his opposition friends led the prosecution of Warren Hastings for alleged high crimes and misdemeanours in India. Pitt voted for one crucial charge as a matter for impeachment. Burke won his greatest parliamentary victory when the House of Commons voted for impeachment. In 1788 the trial opened before the House of Lords in Westminster Hall. It went on intermittently until 1795, when the House of Lords acquitted Hastings. If the evidence did not support a conviction, it supported the need for some kind of proceedings to settle doubts.
Pitt's India Act

Pitt pursued administrative and fiscal reform more vigorously than parliamentary reform. He owed an election debt to the parliamentary reformers and brought in a bill in 1785. Not a test of loyalty to him, the bill lost, 248 votes to 174; thereafter Pitt was done with the subject. His commercial reforms went as far as contemporary protectionist sentiment permitted. He carried a commercial treaty with France but failed to win lower duties on American and Irish trade. His customs reforms improved revenue collections and simplified customs administration. Advised by Richard Price, he altered methods of managing the national debt with a new sinking fund. The substantial increase of trade increased the annual revenue by one-half during Pitt's peacetime ministry. Had not war intervened in 1793, his sinking fund could have fulfilled its purpose of orderly debt retirement.

In foreign affairs Pitt raised England from the depths of the early 1780s. In 1788 he engineered a triple alliance with Holland and Prussia against France. Pitt took a strong line in two diplomatic crises. Under threat of war, Spain conceded British fishing and settlement rights on Vancouver Island and thus opened England's future interests in that region. Pitt could not force Russia in 1791 to give up Oczakov on the Black Sea. But this was so far removed that only Turkey was disturbed; in western Europe England's prestige was high. Just before the war of the French Revolution began, Pitt said England was secure and the future looked stable.

By 1789 the political future also appeared secure. The King's illness and mental derangement in the winter of 1788 (according to the latest studies, as the result of porphyria, a hereditary blood disorder) caused a crisis. As regent, the Prince of Wales might use the prerogative powers to replace Pitt with Fox. Pitt hoped by statute to restrict the regent's (not the royal) powers, but the King's recovery halted proceedings on the bill. The bitter partisanship of the debates thoroughly discredited the parliamentary opposition. Pitt emerged a Galahad with a larger and more closely knit majority. The election of 1790 renewed his political strength.

England, celebrating the King's recovery, reacted initially with mixed feelings toward the French Revolution. Enthusiasts, including survivors of the earlier reform movement, welcomed the fall of the Bastille as heralding an era of freedom and brotherhood among men. Speaking to the Revolution Society commemorating the Revolution of 1688, Dr. Price called the French Revolution an example to England and a warning to fulfill the promise of 1688 by reforming Parliament. Few people openly opposed the Revolution. The government, officially neutral, thought France too beset with internal troubles to disturb the peace of Europe. Two months after Pitt recommended a reduction in army appropriations because the future promised peace, France, in April 1792, declared war on Austria, plunging Europe into war.

THE ERA OF THE FRENCH REVOLUTION (1789–1815)

The end of reform.   By this time English opinion had become divided. Burke's *Reflections on the Revolution in France* (November 1790) condemned the English reformers and warned of the Revolution's threat to the Christian social order of Europe. Thomas Paine, whose *Rights of Man* (1791) was written in reply to Burke, represented to upholders of the established order the dangers from revived English radicalism and French Jacobinism. Burke and Paine were the extremists in the controversy over the related questions of reform, the Revolution, and war. Pitt and his foreign secretary, William Wyndham Grenville, Baron Grenville, found no English vital interest at stake in the continental war until the winter of 1792–93, when France executed its king, and its Revolutionary armies threatened the independence of the Low Countries and the European balance of power. France spared Pitt a decision by declaring war on England, February 1, 1793.

Fear of
Jacobinism

The Revolution and the war strongly affected politics and the movement for parliamentary reform. The old reform societies were middle class and property conscious. The London Corresponding Society, however, founded in 1792 with the shoemaker Thomas Hardy its secretary, brought the lower middle class and the working class into politics. This society, with its affiliates throughout England and Scotland, had organization and a sense of public purpose to distinguish it from mobs of 18th-century England. The Corresponding Societies, unlike the Society for Constitutional Information, asked for universal manhood suffrage. The number of active reformers never numbered more than a few thousand; the established order retained its credit with the nation; it is doubtful that England was on the verge of revolution. But panic spread among some of the governing class and the propertied, encouraged by reformers' indiscretions and excesses of zeal. The Association for the Preservation of Liberty and Property, founded in the winter of 1792–93 in London, had affiliates throughout the country. Authorities broke up reform conventions in Scotland in 1792–93, and the courts sentenced a few of the leaders harshly. English radicals' talk of a convention, for purposes never made quite clear, stimulated the government to act. In May 1794 it seized 12 reform leaders. After the jury acquitted the first three to be tried for high treason, the remaining cases were dropped. Some prosecutions succeeded, but the number before magistrates has never been determined. Parliament enacted some repressive statutes. By 1795 the reform agitation virtually ended, to be revived toward the end of the Napoleonic Wars.

Wartime politics.   Like England, the parliamentary opposition divided over reform and war. Fox led the liberal minority—the New Whigs—whom Burke accused of deserting the principles of 1688. The Old Whigs, fearful of splitting the Portland party, only slowly came to accept Burke's views. In 1794 they crossed over. Portland, William Wentworth, 2nd Earl Fitzwilliam, and Burke's disciple William Windham took Cabinet offices. The coalition of 1794 did not essentially change Pitt's policy. Relying on alliances and subsidies, he aimed to preserve the balance of power and England's vital interests rather than overthrow the Revolutionary government. Burke desired a Bourbon restoration in France. The abortive peace negotiations of 1796–97 showed Pitt's willingness to treat with the Revolutionary regime.

The Irish problem flared up in the 1790s. Legislative independence was a mockery when the Lord Lieutenant of Ireland and Pitt's Cabinet leagued with the Irish junto to block reforms, control patronage, and preserve the Protestant ascendancy. Although another extension of civil rights was granted to the Irish in 1793, Catholics were still forbidden to sit in Parliament. Catholic hopes

rose late in 1794, when Earl Fitzwilliam became lord lieutenant. His hasty dismissal of junto politicians and his advocacy of Catholic emancipation so alarmed the government that Portland, his superior, recalled him. Ireland drifted toward civil war, as the recently formed Society of United Irishmen took a militant lead. The Rebellion of 1798 was not as dangerous as it was dramatic. French aid supported only a small effort in the northwest of Ireland, while elsewhere English forces quickly suppressed risings. Pitt saw the solution to the Irish problem in a legislative union combined with Catholic emancipation. Cornwallis, the lord lieutenant, agreed. Both parliaments enacted legislative union in 1801, adding 100 Irish seats to the House of Commons and 28 Irish peers and four bishops to the House of Lords at Westminster. The King broadcast his opposition to Catholic emancipation, and Pitt's Cabinet rejected it. For a month in February–March 1801, the King was again deranged. Pitt could not accept responsibility for both the government of the empire and the King's health. He resigned, promising never again to bring up emancipation.

The Irish
Rebellion

Besides the Irish business, Pitt resigned because he was weary after 17 strenuous years in office. The contrast between his successes before the war and failures afterward encouraged the judgment that he was only a great peacetime minister. Yet he laid down the lines of war policy that England followed to the end.

Henry Addington (later 1st Viscount Sidmouth) formed a government in March 1801. Country gentlemen in Parliament and a nation anxious for peace supported him. Englishmen persuaded themselves that peace with Napoleon, who had recently come to power, was peace with a stable France. By the Treaty of Amiens (1802), England recognized the republican regime in France and restored all conquests except Trinidad and Ceylon. The election of 1802 registered satisfaction with both the Irish Union and the peace. But relations with France quickly deteriorated. When England declared war in May 1803, men looked to Pitt for leadership. Pitt recommended a nonpartisan ministry. George III detested Fox, but he could accept Grenville, who had deserted Pitt over Catholic emancipation. Pitt reconsidered, dropped Grenville, and formed a conservative government including only ministers personally desirable to the King. The second Pitt ministry, in May 1804, came largely from its immediate predecessor, excluding Addington. The parliamentary opposition was uncomfortably strong just when French invasion threatened and the Third Coalition was forming against Napoleon. When, in August 1805, Austria allied with England and Russia, the danger of invasion had passed, for Admiral Nelson had frustrated Napoleon's plans for controlling the Channel. Nelson's victory at Trafalgar in October 1805 gave England mastery of the seas. Napoleon, however, smashed the Third Coalition after invading Austria.

Battle of
Trafalgar

Pitt's death on January 23, 1806, confused English politics. The Cabinet refusing to go on, George III was forced to accept the Fox–Grenville "Ministry of All the Talents," less comprehensive than the name suggests. It was mainly Foxite, if returned Whigs like Fitzwilliam and Windham are so considered, but hardly homogeneous with its inclusion of Addington (Lord Sidmouth) and Thomas Lord Erskine, counsel for the defendants in the treason trials of 1794. Before his death in September 1806, Fox failed to achieve the peace with France that he had always thought men of goodwill could make. Grenville carried on, strengthened by the election of October 1806. With strong radical support, the government abolished the slave trade in March 1807, ending a 20-year campaign that had worn down the opposition. The King, encouraged by Sidmouth, frustrated Grenville's desire to open army careers to Catholics by dismissing the government before Parliament seriously took up the bill. The Duke of Portland was called upon to form a ministry. There was no place in Portland's government for Sidmouth because George Canning would not serve with him. Portland's strong Cabinet included Canning, Spencer Perceval, Lord Hawkesbury (Robert Banks Jenkinson), and Viscount Castlereagh. But personal dislikes and disagreements over the conduct of the war betrayed the ideological harmony. After Canning and Castlereagh resigned, Portland yielded to Perceval in October 1809; the Whigs could only observe. Perceval carried on until an assassin's bullet killed him in May 1812.

Yet through this period cabinets were remarkably stable. Like Perceval, Lord Liverpool (Hawkesbury) as prime minister continued his predecessor's Cabinet. Canning and Castlereagh were the main problems. With Canning choosing to remain out of office, Castlereagh returned as foreign secretary before Perceval died and continued under Liverpool. Two other men contributed to the stability. The Prince of Wales, regent because of his father's incapacity, wisely gave his confidence to Liverpool. After his powers as regent were made permanent, he broke with his former Whig friends. The choice of Liverpool was a happy one. Considered a man of second-rate abilities in his own time and nearly ever since, Liverpool has recently been recognized for one great talent. He held his government together as a conciliator rather than as a powerful personality. Prime minister until 1827, he molded a party out of the elements that Pitt, Portland, and Perceval had gathered. More than Pitt, Liverpool left a party behind him, having identified with conservatism the Tory party he inherited.

The conduct of the war. The steady war effort also reveals the continuity of the period of 1807–15. The standoff between French land power and British sea power persuaded Napoleon to try economic warfare against England. By his Continental System he aimed to exclude English goods from European markets. England, in turn, blockaded ports its ships could not enter. This warfare hurt England; the trade statistics show that in 1811 England exported to northern European ports goods of only one-sixth the value of exports in 1805. Unemployment grew. The increase in England's Latin American trade only partially made up for the decline in trade with Europe and the United States. The Americans boycotted British goods in retaliation against England's interference with their shipping and neutral rights. The War of 1812 with the United States followed; a central event in American history, the war is only peripherally treated in British history.

Europe also suffered from Napoleon's economic war, and in 1810 he replaced exclusion with high tariffs. His economic policy needed political–military support; Napoleon invaded Russia and the Iberian Peninsula in part to complete his economic system. But England found entry to the Continent in Portugal, where its forces landed in 1808. The Peninsular War culminated in Wellington's invasion of France over the Pyrenees in 1813–14. This occurred as the allies penetrated from the east. Never before had Napoleon faced such universal and united opposition. Stressing the need for unity to win victory and a peace settlement imposed by the great powers, Castlereagh avoided piecemeal treaties lacking the force of general agreement. The government and Parliament supported generously the subsidy policy undergirding Castlereagh's diplomacy. The Treaty of Chaumont (March 9, 1814), his great edifice, clarified allied war aims (including the expulsion of Napoleon), tightened allied unity, and promised a general European settlement under supervision of the great powers for 20 years. Napoleon's return from Elba, the Hundred Days ending at Waterloo, and his exile to St. Helena did not interrupt the peacemakers at Vienna or change England's policy. The Vienna Congress settlement of 1815 was the concrete manifestation of Castlereagh's definition of British policy: to assure the peaceful conduct of France by not mistreating her, while providing security against her for the Netherlands and northern Italy; to stabilize Germany by strengthening Prussian and Austrian influence in central Europe and the Rhineland; to check the extension of Russian influence westward; and to safeguard England's commercial and colonial interests.

The end of a long generation of war found in office a Tory government proud of England's contribution to war and the peace, secure in its parliamentary strength, but uncertain of its domestic course. A vastly different England than had entered the war in 1793 faced problems only partly to be understood as marking the transition from war to peace. They were also those of the first modern nation to experience the change from rural and agrarian to industrial and urban nationhood.

ECONOMIC, SOCIAL, AND CULTURAL LIFE

Population. The dearth of reliable demographic and economic statistics for 18th-century England contrasts with the abundance of contemporary writings on "political arithmetic." A lexicographer in 1710 described its content as the extent and value of land, population, public revenues, commerce, and manufactures, or whatever related to the strength and riches of a nation. Concern with the well-being of the state thus showed a mercantilist bias. The earliest official national census (1801) produced the first dependable population statistics for England, Wales, and Scotland. For the first two the population was 8,893,000 and for Scotland 1,608,000. In 1811 the numbers were 10,164,000 and 1,806,000—a remarkable growth. Just over a century earlier, the statistician Gregory King estimated the population of England and Wales as 5,500,000. Attempts to explain the near doubling of the population during the century produced disputes about numbers and statistical methodology. The population grew slowly, if at all, until the 1740s, rapidly after 1780.

Demographers and economic historians disagree on the reasons for population growth and its effect upon economic growth. The declining death rate, increasing birthrate, improved medical science, and a rise in the standard of living, all offered as explanation, have been challenged. None by itself explains the growth but taken together they mean multiple causation for a complex phenomenon. Statistical evidence is impeachable, contemporary opinions were impressionistic, yet together they suggest a rise in general well-being, whatever the hardships of life.

Equally complex is the relationship between economic and population growth. To say that the latter caused the other oversimplifies and hardly explains increased output per person. Population growth helps account for increased labour supply and consumer demand. Expansion of overseas trade stimulated demand and production. The overall impression is of a growing population and expanding economy buoyed by a confident spirit.

The Industrial Revolution. The word revolution is used to describe economic changes of the past two centuries. Though a few historians place the beginnings in the mid-16th century, most hold that the "takeoff," or the dramatic upturn, of industrial growth began about 1780, with the social impact coming later.

During the 18th century, English society was preindustrial, an agricultural and commercial rural society with one metropolis, London. After 1780 migration to cities increased as manufacturing acquired a factory, power-driven character, especially in the cotton-textile industry. This industry was the bellwether of the Industrial Revolution; by 1815 exports of cotton cloth exceeded woollen by three times. Yet the population, 85 percent in the country or in communities under 5,000 persons during the century, remained officially rural until the census of 1851. In the 18th century the structure of society and distribution of population among classes remained preindustrial. Contrary to older views, the enclosure of common lands to increase efficiency did not depopulate the countryside. Population growth supplied the surplus from rural areas for the factory system. Migration was toward the towns and industry; in the midlands and north of England, new industry attracted people to once thinly populated areas. Not until the 19th century did the industrial–urban complex exist, emphasizing textiles, iron, and coal. Besides London, the population of which nearly doubled from 1700 to 1801 to a total of 1,000,000 persons, the considerable towns (though none exceeded 80,000) were Liverpool, Birmingham, Sheffield, Norwich, Bristol, and Glasgow. Birmingham doubled between 1770 and 1801.

Much of the rural population engaged in domestic manufactures of textiles or in supplying agricultural, mining, or building needs. Occupational classification was therefore difficult; the census of 1841 was the first to attempt it. Gregory King's groupings were socio-occupational. He thought 70 percent of the population was primarily agricultural, with the family the unit of production. King distinguished between families (511,586) who "increas[ed] to the Wealth of the Kingdom" and the majority (849,000) who decreas[ed] the Wealth of the Kingdom because the cost of living exceeded their incomes. Supplements deriving ultimately from the productive minority made up the difference, for England had an annual economic surplus and more than fed itself.

In King's groupings, the margins of the upper and middle classes and of the lower middle class and the lower class overlapped. Some great traders were wealthier than some peers and most gentlemen. Rich merchants often owned land and almost always aspired to it because land conferred status. Ownership of land was an eligibility requirement for the House of Commons. Below the nobility and gentry, King listed officeholders, merchants, clergy, professional men, freeholders, and farmers. Shopkeepers and artisans occupied the borderland above the lower class. The lower orders—common soldiers and sailors, labourers and servants, cottagers, paupers, and vagrants—constituted the majority who "diminished the wealth of the kingdom." Contemporaries nevertheless considered England a rich nation whose people were better off than any Europeans except the Dutch. Estimates of per capita income—£9 at the beginning of the century, £13 at mid-century, and £22 at the end—suggest a level comparable to that in the wealthier underdeveloped countries in mid-20th century.

Agricultural revolution   By 1815 English agriculture had changed in important ways within a nation becoming an urban and industrial community. Increasing consumer demand stimulated the agricultural revolution and an increasing supply of capital assisted improvement. New techniques of cultivation and of land usage and management as well as new crops not only made land more productive but brought new land into tillage. Between 1700 and 1760, some 300,000 acres were enclosed, and ten times that amount between 1760 and 1800. Under the General Act of 1801, which eliminated the need for private enclosure acts, the transformation to closed fields was nearly complete by 1820. Enclosure facilitated more effective use of arable land and encouraged improvement of breeding by the segregation of livestock. The social effects of enclosure have been debated vigorously and emotionally. Recent studies show that enclosure did not depopulate rural districts. The need for agricultural labour did not decline. The citywide migration was that of the rural surplus. Nor did enclosure eliminate the smallholders. If enclosure costs forced out some, compensation for surrender of ancient common rights often enabled cottagers to acquire small holdings. The post-1815 agricultural depression hurt the smallholders severely. The agricultural revolution, important in itself, sustained and encouraged the Industrial Revolution, providing food for the growing nonagricultural population and supplying some of the capital for industrial expansion.

Commercial revolution   The term commercial revolution usually refers to the preceding centuries, but important changes occurred in the 18th century. Commerce became securely interlocked with agricultural and industrial expansion. The volume of trade, which increased sevenfold during the century and doubled between 1750 and 1800, also shifted regionally. Domestic exports to Europe declined from 85 to 30 percent of Britain's total, while those to North America increased from 6 to 30 percent and to the West Indies from 5 to 25 percent, all between the opening and the end of the century. Meanwhile imports from Europe declined from 66 to 43 percent of a total of which the West Indies and the East Indies each sent 25 percent. Europe took 85 percent of England's re-exports both at the beginning and the end of the century, but the total was much larger at the end. England was the primary supplier of colonial products to Europe. The monetary gains of the re-export trade were great because British merchants made a profit on the average of about 15 percent on the value of the goods traded. Commerce aided English manufacturing by stimulating domestic and foreign demand, assisting other countries to buy English goods, bringing raw materials to British industry, and contributing to the stock of investment capital.

The Industrial Revolution of the 18th and early 19th

centuries was a British phenomenon. Manufacturing increased in Europe but the use of power-driven machinery concentrated in factories was strikingly particular to Britain and especially to the cotton and iron industries. If the history of the cotton industry is not quite the history of the Industrial Revolution from about 1780 to 1840, it is illustrative. The traditional textile industry was woollen; cotton manufacturing became important in the last third of the 18th century. In 1815 England exported £22,000,000 worth of cotton cloth, three times as much as woollen cloth, and over 100 times the value of cotton cloth exports in the early 1760s. This was the result of a sequence of technological innovations in spinning and weaving, beginning in the 1730s. The most sophisticated machine, Edmund Cartwright's power loom (1787), did not come into general use until after 1815. The cotton industry, new and unrestrained by tradition, became the example par excellence of machine work in the factory.

The iron industry was also amenable to technological change. Use of coke for smelting, shown to be practicable by Abraham Darby in 1709, was widespread by midcentury. Henry Cort's puddling process for making bar iron, patented in 1783, increased the supply of wrought iron. James Watt's improvement of the steam engine in 1775 marked the beginning of the machine age. The iron industry was as productive in the reign of Charles I as in 1760. Then came Watt and Cort and the "takeoff." In 1800 England produced 1,000,000 tons of pig iron, of which 60,000 were exported. The export figure alone was twice the total production of 1760. The statistics of coal production, so closely related, are 6,000,000 tons in 1770 and 15,000,000 in 1815.

Growth of transport   Inland transport responded to economic necessity and stimulated industrial growth. The canal age began in 1759, when Francis Egerton, 3rd duke of Bridgwater, linked his Worsley coal mines by canal with Manchester. By the 1820s local capital organized corporately, and ingenious engineers, such as the canal builder James Brindley and the highway builders Thomas Telford and John MacAdam, laced England with canals and improved roads. The history of the Wedgwood potteries, a striking story of entrepreneurial genius, reveals the dependence of manufacturing growth upon safer, cheaper, and faster transportation. New manufacturing techniques increased production, salesmanship and promotion spread the demand for Wedgwood ware, and improved transport brought raw materials to the potteries and carried the ware to consumers. When the age of canal building ended, England had invested £20,000,000 in a system of navigation vital especially to heavy industries but inadequate for the future needs of industry. The railways were to meet the need in the next age.

Effects of industrialization.   To the usual list of physical, social, and political causes of the economic revolution should be added a psychological one. England in the 18th and early 19th centuries was as buoyant and confident as Holland in the 17th century or the United States after the American Civil War. Englishmen responded to challenges, risking loss of capital should an invention prove impracticable, an enterprise be mismanaged, or any number of unforeseen calamities occur. This happened despite the fact that the principle of unlimited liability prevailed, whereby all shareholders were held responsible for any debts incurred by the company. Often the people who suffered worst when a joint-stock enterprise collapsed were small investors, and many were the unhappy partners in failing enterprises. The first 75 years of the Industrial Revolution were years when the spirit of adventure was keen.

The standard of living   The growth of wealth suggests the potential for amelioration of life in this period. Judgments have been influenced by emotional involvement and political opinions. No one denies the existence of poverty and hardship, but some historians stress improvement throughout the period. Economic growth helped the worker directly and made possible greater indirect aid from private and group philanthropy. Parish officials and the magistrates were responsible for enforcement of the Poor Laws, which was spotty in the absence of central supervision; a zealous local official, however, might send the poor to the workhouse, where paupers, sick or well, young or old, were thrown together indiscriminately. The Poor Laws also forbade the destitute to settle outside their own parishes, but these laws were not rigorously enforced, permitting mobility of labour. Economic growth and increased concern for the poor existed together; whether there was merely heightened awareness or an actual increase of poverty, the statistics show a sixfold growth in the amount of poor-rate collections between 1775 and 1825. Part of the increased expenditures went for wage supplements to bring incomes among the poor up to a minimum cost of living. The practice, called the Speenhamland system, spread widely after 1795, when a group of Berkshire magistrates adopted it. To attribute the apparently growing magnitude of the problem of the poor to industrialization and urbanization is to oversimplify the problem and to slight the problem of the poor in preindustrial England. The population trebled between 1700 and 1821, and the urban poor made the problem more visible.

The growth of industry and towns created a serious psychological problem. The pattern of life governed by the seasons, the sun and moon, and the weather gave way to the discipline of the clock and the rhythms of the machines. Neither the laws of nature nor of Parliament, but the laws of the marketplace, determined the times for operating machines. Workers had no preparation for the new industrial discipline. In addition to physical adjustment, they had to make within two generations a radical mental and moral adjustment to a new way of life.

Religion. Religion probably offered less consolation to the labouring poor and the paupers than some might like to think. The churches and organized religion did not deal adequately with problems arising from new urban and industrializing trends. But the churches were not meeting social problems in preindustrial England, and the poor often shirked churchgoing. Statistics are lacking except in scattered localities. Contemporary literature shows the churches as the preserves of the upper and middle classes. Among Protestant Dissenters, the Baptists were thought of as the poorer sort. Quakers, not strictly Dissenters, were in the middle ranks of society, along with Presbyterians, Independents, and Unitarians. The Roman Catholics, a small minority, cut across all ranks of the social structure, as did the Established Church of England.

One of the traditional explanations for the rise of Methodism is that it filled a gap in religious life. This was particularly true in Wales, despite the prominence there of Protestant Dissent. Neither Dissent nor the Church of England reached certain areas and groups in England and Wales. Dissent was notoriously intellectual and held "enthusiasm" (which in the 18th century connoted fanaticism) in disfavour as much as did the Established Church. Launched by the brothers Charles and John Wesley and by George Whitefield in 1739, Methodism sought out the neglected and underprivileged. Emotionally and enthusiastically, itinerant preachers offered "the glad tidings of salvation," as John Wesley put it, often in the open air. Edmund Gibson, bishop of London, called Methodists "Rabble." Methodism was not a socially revolutionary force, except by the implication of equality in its teachings about salvation, but it felt the disapproval of the religious establishment. Separation from the Church of England did not come until just after John Wesley's death in 1791, and then on technical grounds. But in spirit and form Methodism was nonconformist long before the separation.

Methodism influenced some earnest Anglicans, the Evangelicals, who deplored the decline of manners in society and the religious lethargy in the Church of England. The Evangelicals promoted social but not political reforms; they worked for the abolition of the slave trade and of slavery; and as social superiors they desired the amelioration of the hard lot of the poor and the oppressed. But Evangelicalism did not try to abolish deference among the lower orders. Sunday schools would teach people to read the Bible and Hannah More's popular tracts that offered patience in this world and the expectation of rewards in Heaven. Literacy was not for absorbing the doctrines of Thomas Paine's *Rights of Man* or his *Age of Reason*.

Dissenters were prominent out of proportion to their

Methodism

numbers in the political-reform movements. The Test and Corporation acts (1673 and 1661) limited the civil rights of non-Anglicans, and Dissenters, often well-educated and prosperous, resented the discrimination. They disliked the preference for land in determining political qualifications, and they abhorred restrictions imposed upon them merely because they were Dissenters. They desired to open careers to men of talent, but they thought especially of opportunities for the middle class. Their campaign for repeal of the Test and Corporation acts lasted a century before it succeeded in the 1820s. It joined that for parliamentary reform to form an important chapter in the history of political and constitutional change in modern England.

The Church of England remained secure in its position of establishment, less torpid than tradition has it, but less vital intellectually than in the 17th century. Its legal position guaranteed involvement of the clergy in politics, if nothing more than in patronage. Deism did not become a strong influence in England, in part because, in its benevolently placid faith in reason, it was not far removed from the Latitudinarianism so prominent in the church.

The Enlightenment. Faith in the power of human reason has been emphasized into a cliché suggesting a monolithic character for 18th-century thought. Recent writings on the Enlightenment qualify this exaggeration. René Descartes, Sir Isaac Newton, and John Locke bequeathed a conception of man's capacity to discover the laws governing the universe and similarly his capacity to understand and apply the laws governing the social order. England enjoyed a reputation, spread by Voltaire and Montesquieu, for having devised a political order that was the envy of Europeans. Englishmen were proud that their "happy constitution" combined freedom with good order, protected property, and responded to the country's needs. It was a unique political system; the great powers of Europe knew only monarchical absolutism even in the later period of Enlightened Despotism.

The Philosophes desired freedom above all, for it was fundamental to human improvement or any concept of perfectibility. They did not seek a particular organization for society, nor were they uniformly optimistic about the powers of human reason to create a perfect social order. English writers, already enjoying freedom, had less at stake than continental Philosophes. England's two most important contributors to the Enlightenment were George Berkeley and the Scot David Hume, whose writings, by demonstrating the limitation of human reason, ironically did much to undermine the Rationalism upon which the Enlightenment was built. There were other anti-Rationalist elements in 18th-century England. The novels of Samuel Richardson contributed to a "cult of sensibility." Edmund Burke wrote on the sublime in an anti-Rationalist approach to aesthetics and art and directly attacked Rationalism in other writings. Burke's emphasis upon history and experience in the development of society, law, and government placed him among the precursors of Romanticism. Jeremy Bentham denied the existence of natural law so prominent in Enlightenment thought and replaced it with utility (the principle of the greatest good for the greatest number) as the guiding principle of the legislator. Thus England contributed to the Enlightenment and exemplified the freedom it desired but at the same time prepared the way for Romanticism and Utilitarianism.

(C.B.Co.)

The growth of the British Empire

The beginnings of the British Empire are usually located in the 16th century, when an urge toward overseas trade and settlement developed out of the pioneering voyages of Elizabethan seamen. A succession of voyages followed John Cabot's discovery of Newfoundland in 1497 and the establishment of a flourishing fishing trade there. At first the objects were trade and plunder; settlement had to wait until the beginning of the 17th century, although there were earlier abortive attempts to settle Newfoundland and Virginia. The expansion of Britain's maritime strength, however, paved the way for the establishment of settlements in North America and the West Indies.

Beginnings of the empire

In later centuries, exploration again stimulated imperial expansion, notably through the discoveries of Capt. James Cook in the South Pacific in the latter part of the 18th century and those of David Livingstone, Richard Burton, John Hanning Speke, and other travellers in Africa in the 19th. Apart from these notable cases, however, the 18th- and 19th-century development of the empire was due much more to conquest, international rivalry, and the search for favourable trading opportunities than to direct discovery.

ORIGINS OF BRITISH EXPANSION

British expansion in the Americas, India, and Africa began in earnest in the 17th century. North America and the Caribbean were the scenes of what is sometimes called "the first British Empire," terminating in the loss of the colonies that became the United States. In nearly all cases, the early settlements arose from the enterprise of particular companies and magnates rather than from any effort on the part of the crown.

In the first half of the 17th century, when Virginia, Maryland, and the colonies of New England were set up, there were also settlements in Nova Scotia, Barbados, the Bermudas, Honduras, Antigua, and certain other West Indian islands. Jamaica was obtained by conquest in 1655. The Hudson's Bay Company established itself in what became northwestern Canada from the 1670s onward. The hold of the crown over these colonies, obtained through the issue of a charter, was slight but greater than that of the British Parliament. As late as 1732, the parliamentary leader Robert Walpole objected to the discussion by Parliament of the charter for Georgia, since it was regarded as part of the royal prerogative.

The crown exercised some rights of appointment and supervision, but the colonies were essentially self-managing, the form of their management depending on the character of those who had established them. No attempt was made to establish a uniform administration, although it was usual for the colonies to have some sort of local legislature and to reproduce the English legal system.

In India the beginnings of British influence were similar, though they did not involve settlement. The East India Company, granted its charter in 1600, was content for a long time to establish trading posts without controlling territory. Not until the authority of the Mogul Empire began to disintegrate at the beginning of the 18th century and other European powers, especially France, began actively to look for gains in India did the company set about the series of treaties and conquests that led to the consolidation of the Indian Empire. The Straits Settlements (Penang, Singapore, Malacca, and Labuan) became British through an extension of the East India Company's activities.

The British became involved in Africa later than in the Americas and India, though the first permanent British settlement on the African continent was established on James Island in the Gambia River as early as 1661. Sierra Leone was the scene of Sir John Hawkins' successful slave-trading ventures in 1562, but it did not become a British possession until 1787, after which it was used to resettle slaves from other British colonies. The Gold Coast (later Ghana) was a further example of 17th-century British trading effort, but it did not develop into an administered territory until the 19th century, when Nigeria, by various stages, also became British.

Whereas the main British interest in these western African territories was in trade, in the southern tip of Africa it was in settlement, following the acquisition of the Cape in 1806; the interior was opened up by Boer and British pioneers, ultimately under British control. British administration of what are now Kenya and Uganda, on the eastern coast, did not begin until the 1880s.

Thus the motives that led to British control of great areas far from Britain itself were various. The commercial motive was undoubtedly the strongest at the start, and it remained important; but as time went on, it was augmented by missionary influence and by strategic considerations. It is important to emphasize, however, how unorganized was the extension of the empire. Only rarely was there strong sentiment in Britain in favour of the acquisition of territory as such (the last two decades of the 19th century were one such period). The British tradition was of piecemeal acquisition, each case being treated on its merits, sometimes with the British government being the least willing partner in the enterprise.

THE EMPIRE OF OUTPOSTS, TO 1763

The sphere in which the crown exercised most control over the colonies in the 17th and 18th centuries was trade and shipping.

Trade in goods and slaves. In accordance with the mercantilist philosophy of the time—also adhered to by other European colonial powers—the colonies were regarded as a source of necessary supplies for England and were granted monopolies for their products, such as tobacco and sugar, in the British market. In return, they were expected to conduct all their trade by means of English ships. The Navigation Act of 1651 and further acts after the Restoration provided that no other country could carry goods to or from the colonies, that the main colonial products could be exported only to England, and that only those foreign products that had been brought to England first could be imported into the colonies. This closed economic system caused objections from some of the colonies but guaranteed others that their distinctive products would find a sheltered market in Britain and not be subject to competition from other powers' sugar colonies, especially those of Spain. This arrangement lasted until the combined effects of the Scottish economist Adam Smith's *Wealth of Nations* (1776), the loss of the American colonies, and the growth of a free-trade movement in Britain slowly brought it to an end; but the last Navigation Act was not repealed until 1849.

In the 18th century, most of the colonial economic systems in the Americas rested on the Navigation Acts, on the one hand, and slavery, on the other. The slave trade, begun by Hawkins, had become an economic necessity for the Caribbean colonies and the southern parts of what later became the United States. It was not confined to these British colonies but was common to those of France and Spain, with which the British colonists were in competition. Movements for the ending of the slave trade and of slavery itself had begun in Britain before the loss of the colonies on the eastern American seaboard; they came to fruition in British possessions long before the similar movement in the United States. The trade was abolished in 1807, slavery in 1833. It left behind it, however, many people of African stock who still form the bulk of the populations of the independent states of Jamaica, Trinidad, Barbados, and other Caribbean islands that remain British dependencies.

British sea power and conquests. In the 18th century, the Caribbean colonies were important to Britain not only as suppliers of sugar and buyers of slaves but also as strategic possessions in deciding the issue of naval supremacy between Britain, France, and Spain. The admirals George Rodney and Horatio Nelson were as familiar with the waters of the Indies as with those of Europe. Indeed, as hostility continued between Britain and France, colonial possessions became not only bases but also prizes. In the process, Britain gained two of the most important parts of its empire—Canada and India.

Fighting between the French and British colonies in North America was endemic in the first half of the 18th century. It was especially fierce during the Seven Years' War (1756–63), which was ended by the Peace of Paris in 1763, whereby British control of Canada became undisputed, with expansion into the west and northwest no longer threatened by a chain of French forts stretching southward from Quebec to Louisiana. Control of a large population of French descent, language, and culture in Quebec was a new experience for Britain, but this did not prevent an eventual consolidation of Canada.

In India, the East India Company was confronted by the French Compagnie des Indes. Under the governor general Joseph-François Dupleix, French influence and conquest flourished while British influence diminished. The balance was redressed in favour of the British by the military genius of Robert Clive and by a change in French policy,

Relations between England and the empire

which recalled Dupleix. Clive and Eyre Coote went on to further victories against the French and against the rulers of Bengal, thus providing the East India Company with its first massive accession of territory and ensuring that no other European power would challenge British supremacy in India.

Clive's victory at Plassey in India was in 1757; James Wolfe's at Quebec, in 1759. By this time Britain was, of necessity, showing more governmental concern for the colonies. Although the New England colonists in America and the East India Company in India might fight the French on local ground, their doing so was part of the larger struggle between Britain and France and had to be taken into account—sometimes assisted, sometimes muted—by the government in London. For strategic reasons, the government displayed a great interest in acquiring territory at the Treaty of Aix-la-Chapelle in 1748 and the Treaty of Paris in 1763. Yet it could not be said that any great colonial design was manifest in the British demands; the fact that Lord Bute's Cabinet in 1763 discussed whether it would be better to retain the conquered sugar island of Guadeloupe than to keep the French out of Canada indicates the short-term considerations that often governed policy.

LOSSES AND GAINS, 1763–1815

Changes in the empire

The loss of the American colonies. Britain lost the 13 colonies in North America because it attempted to interfere in their affairs but lacked the military skill and organization to bring them to heel when they revolted. The war in America dragged on from 1775 until 1783 and was enlarged by the entry of France, Spain, and Holland against Britain. Apart from the loss of the colonies in revolt, some Caribbean islands were lost temporarily to France, and Tobago and Minorca were no longer British after the peace settlement. The blow to British pride was considerable; but the British Empire was soon to show further vitality through the spectacular growth of Upper Canada after the emigration there of loyalists from what had become the United States and through the establishment of new colonies of settlement in the South Pacific.

The first settlements in Australia. In 1770 Capt. James Cook sailed along the previously unknown eastern coast of Australia and around New Zealand, bringing back reports that formed the basis of later settlement. New Zealand did not come under formal British control until 1840; but the settlement of Australia began in New South Wales in 1788, in part due to the loss of the American colonies, which were no longer available as a repository for some of Britain's convicts. Australia's period of transportation lasted only about 60 years, however, and the main mass of the population was derived from free settlement. Tasmania (1803) and Queensland (1824) were convict settlements, and Western Australia, after its inception as a freemen's colony, took convicts for labour from 1849 until 1868; but Victoria (1834) and South Australia (1836) were never convict colonies.

Conquests during the Napoleonic Wars. The Napoleonic Wars (1799–1815) provided further additions of territory to the empire, although only one acquisition—the Cape of Good Hope—became an area of substantial British settlement. By the Treaty of Amiens in 1802 Britain gained Trinidad and Ceylon. By the first Treaty of Paris in 1814 gains included Tobago, Mauritius, St. Lucia, and Malta—each of which had strategic value. At the Cape, however, Britain made its most fateful acquisition. The Dutch had been settling there since 1652, reinforced by French Huguenots. The Boer farmers had developed a distinctive society and an ethos of their own. Britain's interest in retaining the Cape was at first a naval one because of the route to India, but this was soon augmented by the wish to anglicize the Boers through the use of the English language and through added immigration from Britain. Many of the Boers proved recalcitrant.

Certain other additions, made early in the 19th century, were of great future importance. They included Malacca, which came into British hands in 1795; and Singapore—a mudbank with few inhabitants when Sir Thomas Stamford Raffles took it over for the East India Company in

1819, but later a trading port of growing importance. The future shape of Canada was being determined with the settlement of Alberta, Manitoba, and British Columbia. These, like Australia, New Zealand, and the Cape, were fertile and comparatively empty; they were to become areas of substantial British migration. The War of 1812 with the United States provided an impetus to Canadian unity and strengthened Canadian disinclination to become part of the U.S.

In India, the period of the Napoleonic Wars was notable—not for fighting with France but for local wars against French influence and for the acquisition by the East India Company, through conquest and treaty, of the United Provinces of Agra and Oudh and the Central Provinces; East Bengal and Assam were to follow before long.

(J.D.B.M./Ed.)

Great Britain, 1815–1914

BRITAIN AFTER THE NAPOLEONIC WARS

The end of the long wars against Napoleon did not usher in a period of peace and contentment. Although both agricultural and industrial production had greatly, if unevenly, increased during the wars, the total national debt had nearly quadrupled since 1793. Of the total annual public revenue after 1815, more than half had to be employed to pay interest on this debt. The abolition of Pitt's income tax in 1816 meant that the debt burden fell on consumers—many of them with low incomes—and on industrialists. The archaic and regressive nature of the national taxation system, associated as it was with a mounting scale of locally levied poor-law rates, provoked widespread anxiety and criticism.

The postwar economy and society. The peace was followed, indeed, by open social conflicts, most of them exacerbated by a postwar slump. As the long-run process of industrialization continued, with a rising population and a cyclical pattern of relative prosperity and depression, many social conflicts centred on questions of what contemporaries called "corn and currency." Others were directly related to the growth of factories and towns and to the parallel development of middle class and working class consciousness.

The agriculturalists, who were predominant in Parliament, attempted to safeguard their wartime economic position by securing, in 1815, a new Corn Law designed to keep up grain prices and rents by taxing imported grain. Their political power enabled them to acquire economic protection. Yet many of them suffered, particularly after 1819, from a serious fall of agricultural prices. Debts contracted during the wars became more onerous as prices fell. There were many complaints of agricultural distress during the early 1820s.

The Corn Law of 1815

Many of the industrialists, an increasingly vociferous group outside Parliament, resented the passing of the Corn Law. Others objected to the return of gold, agreed to by Parliament in 1819 and put into effect in 1821. Whatever their outlook, industrialists were beginning to demand a voice in Parliament. The term middle class began to be used more frequently in social and political debate.

Town and village labourers were also unrepresented in Parliament, and it was they who bore the main brunt of the postwar difficulties. Bad harvests and high food prices left them hungry and discontented, and in the worst years, when bad harvests and industrial unemployment coincided, discontent assumed a political shape. The creation of the sense of a working class followed the emergence of a steam-driven factory system with new rhythms of work and new disciplines of control, a breakdown in traditional family relationships, and the growth of towns with structures of communication quite different from those of villages or preindustrial urban communities. There were radical riots in 1816, 1817, and particularly in 1819, the year of the Peterloo Massacre, when there was a clash in Manchester between workers and troops of the yeomanry, or local citizenry.

Local magistrates, with no adequate police forces at their disposal, were often unsure how to deal either with secret "conspiracy" or with open challenges to authority, while Lord Liverpool's government, with only rudimentary administrative machinery at its disposal, tended to follow a policy of repression. The Six Acts of 1819, associated with Viscount Sidmouth, the home secretary, were designed to reduce disturbances and to check the extension of radical propaganda and organization. They provoked sharp criticism from Whigs as well as from radicals, and they did not dispel the fear and suspicion that were threatening the stability of the whole social order.

There was a revival of confidence after 1821, as economic conditions improved and the government itself embarked on a program of economic reform. Sidmouth retired, to be succeeded by Sir Robert Peel; and Viscount Castlereagh, the foreign secretary, committed suicide. Even the king, George IV (1820–30), who had been drawn into the heart of politics when his discarded queen, Caroline, returned to England in 1820 and for a time became a radical heroine, ceased to be the target for continual radical abuse. Liverpool was a sufficiently able and sensible prime minister to work with new men and to move in new directions. Between 1821 and 1825, duties on raw material imports were reduced and tariff schedules were simplified; and in 1828, one year after Liverpool resigned, the fixed Corn Law of 1815 was replaced with a sliding scale. During this same period, Peel was reforming the law. Even after the collapse of the economic boom of 1824–25, no attempt was made to return to negative policies of repression.

Foreign policy. There was a change of tone if not of principle in foreign policy, as in home affairs, after Castlereagh's suicide. Castlereagh himself, who had represented Britain at the Congress of Vienna in 1815, had refused to follow up the peace settlement he had signed by converting the Quadruple Alliance of the victorious wartime allies into an instrument of police action to suppress liberalism and nationalism anywhere in Europe. His policy was one of nonintervention. His successor at the Foreign Office, George Canning, propounded the British viewpoint in more colourful language and with a strong appeal to British public opinion and emphasized differences between British viewpoints and those of the European great powers as much as their common interests. In 1824 he recognized the independence of Spain's American colonies, declaring in a famous phrase that he was calling "the New World into existence to redress the balance of the Old." In 1826 he used British force to defend constitutional government in Portugal, while, in the tension-ridden area of the eastern Mediterranean, he supported the cause of Greek independence. Although he died in 1827, before the new Greek state came into existence, after having served for a few months as Lord Liverpool's successor as prime minister, his policies and styles were reasserted by Palmerston, who became foreign minister in 1830.

The beginning of political reform. Between the death of Canning and Palmerston's acceptance of office in a government presided over by the aristocratic Whig leader Earl Grey, there had been a major shift in British politics. Canning's weak successor as prime minister, Viscount Goderich, who had been a successful chancellor of the exchequer under Liverpool, was unable to deal adequately with the increasingly complicated tangle of Tory and Whig factions, and he was soon replaced by Wellington, the military hero of the Napoleonic Wars. It was the Wellington ministry that introduced the new Corn Law of 1828 and presented Peel, the Prime Minister's chief henchman, with the renewed opportunity of reforming the law and, in 1829, with the chance of creating a new model police force for London. Yet Wellington, more soldier than politician, had to tackle two very difficult tasks—coping with Irish disorders and holding together in the same government Tories who had supported and opposed Canning.

The issue of Catholic emancipation Irish disorders centred, as they had since 1801, on the issue of Catholic emancipation, a favourite cause of the Whigs, who had been out of power since 1807. During the 18th century, Catholics in England had achieved a large measure of unofficial toleration, but, in Ireland, restrictions against Catholics' holding office were still rigorously enforced. In 1823 Daniel O'Connell, a Dublin Roman-Catholic lawyer, had founded the Catholic Association, the object of which was to give Roman Catholics in Ireland the same political and civil freedoms as Protestants. Employing impressive techniques of organization, he galvanized opinion in Ireland while at the same time mobilizing all his allies in England. In 1828 he won an election in County Clare, Ireland, so convincingly that Wellington, who—like the king—had always opposed Catholic emancipation, came to the conclusion that the government would have to push a measure for emancipation, which Canning had supported, through a Tory-dominated British Parliament. With difficulty he persuaded Peel, who had been tempted to resign, and the king, who had to be bullied, that an emancipation act was necessary and inevitable. Yet 128 "ultra-Tories" voted against the 1829 measure. Tory divisions left an opening for the Whigs, who were themselves divided on tactics if not on objectives. Some of them had joined the Canning ministry, but others had stayed aloof, biding their time. They had considerable support from financial interests and from religious dissenters, whose civil rights were recognized in 1828.

The death of George IV, in June 1830, speeded up events. After the accession of William IV (1830–37) and an inconclusive general election, Wellington, beset by many enemies, was defeated in November on a relatively unimportant motion on royal expenditure. In a year of renewed economic distress and of revolution in France, when the political reform issue was being raised again at public meetings in different parts of the country, Wellington had not made matters easier for himself by expressing complete confidence in the constitution as it stood. He decided, therefore, to resign, and the king went on to send for Earl Grey, who had been *persona non grata* with George IV, to ask him to form a new ministry. The government Grey assembled was predominantly aristocratic—and it included Canningites as well as Whigs—but the new Prime Minister, like most of his colleagues, was committed to introducing a measure of parliamentary reform. For this reason, 1830 marked a real parting of the ways. At last there was a break in the continuity of regime that led back to Pitt's victory over Fox in the 1780s and that had only temporarily been interrupted in 1806–07. Moreover, the new government, aristocratic or not, was the parent of most of the Whig–Liberal administrations of the next 35 years.

The year 1830 was also one of economic and social grievances, with religion still being thrown into the melee. In many parts of the southern countryside, village labourers, backed, if not instigated, by the popular radical leader William Cobbett, were engaged in acts of violence against landlords and property (the "Captain Swing" disturbances), while in the midland and northern towns and cities, political reform movements were winning the support of the crowds. The Whigs were as afraid of rural riot as the Tories and almost as suspicious of new urban radical leaders in cities like Birmingham. Corn laws, currency laws, poor laws, and game laws were all being attacked, while, in the industrial north, the demand was growing for new laws to protect factory labour. It was in such an atmosphere that the new Whig-led government prepared its promised reform bill.

THE POLITICS OF REFORM

Whig interest in parliamentary reform went back to the 18th century, and Grey himself provided a link between two separate periods of public agitation. Yet, in the country as a whole, there were at least three approaches to the reform question. Middle class "reformers" were anxious to secure representation for commercial and industrial interests and for towns and cities, like Birmingham and Manchester, that had no direct voice in Parliament. "Popular radicals," middle class or working class, were concerned with asserting rights as well as with relieving distress. "Philosophic radicals," the followers of the utilitarian philosophy of Jeremy Bentham, were strong ideological protagonists of parliamentary reform but deeply hostile both to the arguments and the tactics of the popular radicals, unless they felt that they were in a position to deploy or control them. It was agitation in the country that kept the reform question on the boil between 1830

Three approaches to reform

and 1832, while Grey, aloof from all forms of agitation, faced unprecedented constitutional difficulties with both the King and Parliament.

The Reform Act of 1832.   A Whig reform bill was introduced in March 1831 and was carried, in its first form in the Commons, by one vote. In mid-April, however, after an opposition amendment had been successfully pressed, Grey induced a reluctant King to dissolve Parliament. At the ensuing general election, the government won a clear majority on the single cry "the bill, the whole bill and nothing but the bill." A second reform bill passed the Commons with no difficulty but was defeated in October in the Lords. Immediately there was a public outcry, with mass meetings of "political unions" and, in some cities, riots. A third bill was then passed by the Commons, only to be thrown out again—on an amendment—in the Lords in May 1832. William refused Grey's request to create a number of new peers who would carry the bill in the Lords, and, in consequence, Grey resigned and Wellington was called in. Such was the public mood, however, that he could not form a ministry, and Grey had to be reappointed, this time with a royal pledge that peers would be created if necessary. The threat was sufficient, and the bill passed, receiving the royal assent on June 7.

Membership change, by county, in the House of Commons as a result of the Reform Act of 1832 (England only).

*Achieve-
ment of
the Re-
form Act*

The Reform Act was in no sense a democratic measure. It was concerned with giving the middle classes a stake in responsible government rather than with changing the basis of government. Yet it entailed a substantial redistribution of constituencies and a change in the conditions of the franchise. The total electorate was increased by 217,000, but the artisans, the working classes, and some sections of the lower middle classes still remained outside "the pale of the constitution." No radical demands were met, even if the manner of the passing of the bill had demonstrated the force of organized opinion in the country. Those Tories who had prophesied that it would mean revolution were wrong, since the composition of the new House of Commons differed little from the old. It continued, indeed, for many years to reflect property

rather than population, and landed interests remained by far the largest interests represented there. The Tories were nonetheless right in arguing that in the long run there would be a change of system. The Whigs, for their part, were wise in recognizing that if a reform bill were not passed, there might well be real pressure for revolution but unrealistic in arguing that it would satisfy reformers as a final measure.

Further Whig reforms.   In fact, the Whigs, returned with a huge majority at the general election of December 1832, carried out a number of other important reforms. A statute in 1833 ended slavery in the British colonies; in the same year the East India Company lost its monopoly of the China trade and became a purely governing body with no commercial functions. In 1834 a new Poor Law, recommended by a royal commission appointed in 1832, was passed; this law grouped parishes into unions and placed the unions under the control of elected boards of guardians, with a national Poor Law Board in London. In 1835 the Municipal Corporations Act was passed, which swept away old oligarchies in local government. Elected councils were to appoint town clerks and treasurers, and many unincorporated industrial communities were to be granted their first governmental powers. In some towns, religious dissenters became the new governing class, though the Whigs did not satisfy their demands nationally.

The end of slavery was the final act in a long campaign in which a number of Tories had always played an important part, and the other reforming Whig measures owed much to the ideas of the philosophic radicals. The new Poor Law turned out to be an unpopular measure in the country and led to outbreaks of disturbance. Its basic principle—that outdoor poor relief should cease and that conditions in workhouses should be "less eligible" than the worst conditions in the labour market outside—was attacked by writers like Thomas Carlyle and Charles Dickens as much as by workingmen themselves. In fact, procedures of inquiry and inspection, associated with this and later reform measures, marked a change in the conduct of government at least as significant in the long run as the political reform of 1832. Public servants like Sir Edwin Chadwick, a disciple of Bentham, played an increasingly important, if controversial, part in administration, turning naturally from questions of poor relief to public health, education, and social reform. Inspired less by philanthropy than by belief in efficiency and economy, they extended the preoccupations of government at the very time when businessmen were seeking to demolish the apparatus of economic control. Much administrative change in the 19th century was to have a momentum of its own, but its origins were in new forms of social awareness in an increasingly industrialized society.

*The new
Poor Law*

The Whigs were not at ease in this changing context. Nor were they united in dealing with the problems either of England or of Ireland. Indeed, Grey's successor, Viscount Melbourne, was for a time pushed out of office in 1834, to return in 1835. He was adept in his dealings with the young Queen Victoria, who came to the throne in 1837, but incapable of finding effective answers to any of the pressing financial, economic, and social questions of the day. All of these questions multiplied after 1836, when a financial crisis ushered in a period of economic depression accompanied by a series of bad harvests. Social conflicts, never far from the surface, became more open and dramatic. Early Victorian England was turbulent and excited, and if it had not been for Robert Peel, who succeeded Melbourne as prime minister after the general election of 1841 had returned to power the "Conservatives" (as Peel liked to think of his party), there might well have been even greater disorder. The achievements of his Conservative ministry must be considered both within the context of the immediate social and political disturbance and within the perspectives of 19th-century British history as a whole.

SOCIAL CLEAVAGE AND SOCIAL CONTROL IN THE EARLY VICTORIAN YEARS

Chartism and the Anti-Corn Law League.   As the economic skies darkened after 1836 and prophets like Carlyle anticipated cataclysmic upheaval, the two most disgruntled groups in society were the industrial workers and their employers. Each group developed new forms of organization and each turned from local to national extraparliamentary action. The two most important organizations were the Chartists and the Anti-Corn Law League. Chartism drew on a multiplicity of working class grievances, extending working class consciousness as it grew; the Anti-Corn Law League, founded as a national organization in Manchester in 1839, was the spearhead of middle class energies, and it enjoyed the advantage not only of lavish funds but also of a single-point program—the repeal of the restrictive Corn Laws.

Chartism, which aimed at parliamentary reform, took its name from the People's Charter published in London in May 1838, containing six points, all of them political and all with a radical pedigree—annual parliaments; universal male suffrage; the ballot; no property qualifications for members of Parliament; payment of members; and equal electoral districts. Behind the political demands, however, was a fierce social discontent and a desire to establish working class political power. The new Poor Law of 1834 was a main source of grievance in the provinces; so, too, in Lancashire and Yorkshire, were long working hours in the factories. Earlier localized agitations centring on such grievances were subsumed in Chartism. In addition, the failure to create effective trade unions during the early 1830s directed efforts toward national political action. The Chartists failed to secure any of the six points during the course of their mostly uncoordinated agitation that continued with fluctuating fortunes until the early 1850s. Problems of organization, local differences, disagreements about tactics (including the use of force), arguments about leadership (particularly about the leadership of Feargus O'Connor), and an improvement in economic conditions—first between 1844 and 1846 and then after 1848—dictated the details of the story. One of the few violent incidents was the small "rising" at Newport on the Welsh border in November 1839, like many of the other demonstrations, a demonstration that got out of hand before it failed. In Scotland "moral force" Chartism was particularly strong. In discontented Ireland, which might have provided support for Chartism, it was only after O'Connell's death in 1847 that the Chartists found allies.

Disagreement among Chartists

The middle class Anti-Corn Law League, led by Richard Cobden and John Bright, attempted to secure the repeal of the duties on imported grain, which were believed to raise the price of food for the workingman and benefit only the landowning classes. The League also had its difficulties, particularly at the outset, but it employed every device of propaganda, including the use of new media of communication, such as the penny post, introduced in 1840. The formula of the League was a simple one, designed to secure working class as well as middle class support. Repeal of the Corn Laws, it was argued, would settle the two great issues that faced Britain in the "hungry forties"—securing the prosperity of industry and guaranteeing the livelihood of the poor. The only barrier to salvation was the landlord. Most Chartists were unconvinced by this logic, but, in a landed Parliament, a few Anti-Corn Law Leaguers, led by Richard Cobden, told Peel firmly that he would be "a criminal and a poltroon" if he did not repeal what they regarded as an immoral as well as an economically restrictive piece of legislation.

Peel and the Peelite heritage. Much depended on the nature of Peel's response to the problems of the time. Between 1832 and 1841 he had built up a disciplined party, most members of which accepted 1832 as a *fait accompli*. He himself, though brought up as a Tory, was a child of the Lancashire cotton industry and accepted industrialization as beneficial as well as inevitable. Afraid of violence, he sought, with a strong sense of public duty, to discover practical solutions to the complex issues of an industrializing society. He was the presiding genius of a powerful administration, strictly supervising the business of each separate branch of government, some of which were managed by very able lieutenants. From the start Peel attached top priority to financial reform. Beginning with his budget of 1842, he set about simplifying and reducing tariff restrictions on trade and in the same year

Peel's reforms

he reintroduced income tax. In 1844 his Bank Charter Act laid the foundations of a sound national banking and credit system centred on the Bank of England. Finally, in 1846 he repealed the Corn Laws.

In this sequence of changes he alienated many of his followers, and repeal brought all the conflicts within his party to a head. The squirearchy rebelled, roused by the brilliant speeches of an exotic young politician, Benjamin Disraeli, who in his writings had already approached the "condition of England question" in a totally different style from that of Peel. During the crisis, Peel put his sense of duty to his sovereign, to posterity, and to his own conscience first and his obligations to his party second.

The results of repeal were important politically as well as economically. Party boundaries remained blurred until 1859, with the "Peelites" retaining a sense of identity even after Peel's premature death following a riding accident in 1850. Some of them, particularly Gladstone, eventually became leaders of the late-19th-century Liberal Party, which emerged from the midcentury confusion. The protectionists, most of whom abandoned protection after 1852, formed the nucleus (around the Earl of Derby and Disraeli) of the later Conservative Party, but they were unable to secure a majority at any election until 1874. The minority governments they formed in 1852, 1858, and 1866 lacked any secure sense of authority. The Whigs, themselves divided into factions, returned to office in 1847 and held it for most of the midcentury years, but they were often dependent on radical and Irish support. Leadership in these years rested with strong or persuasive personalities, of whom Viscount Palmerston was the most prominent.

There was no time between 1846 and 1866, however, when extraparliamentary agitation assumed the dimensions it had done between 1838 and 1846; and, when revolutions spread throughout Europe in 1848, Britain remained almost immune. Only a fierce outburst of Chartism, this time Chartism with an injection of socialism and of Irish nationalism, disturbed the year. Ireland, positively or negatively, played an important part in the politics of crisis, for it was the failure of the Irish potato crop in 1845–46 and the threat of famine in Ireland that helped sway Peel to repeal the Corn Laws. Unfortunately, disaster was not averted in Ireland itself, and in the course of a few terrible famine years, about 500,000 Irish died and 1,000,000 Irish emigrated. Peel's Whig successor, Lord Russell, had no command over this situation, which challenged all the economic, administrative, and political assumptions of the time.

Irish famine

Social legislation and social control. In Britain, by contrast, steps were taken before and after Peel to assume an increasing measure of social control. The question of public health, raised in the late 18th century and given a high degree of urgency during the 1830s, was the subject of several widely discussed reports before the passing of the first national Public Health Act in 1848. Chadwick was the leading spokesman of "the sanitary idea," which was canvassed vigorously by the novelists Charles Dickens and Charles Kingsley and which was to inspire George Eliot. Industrial questions also figured prominently in the social novels of the 1840s, including those of Disraeli; and statisticians, treated warily by most novelists, provided a different form of ammunition in the social debate. A report on conditions in the mines was followed by legislation, in 1842, forbidding the employment underground of children under ten and of all women. Meanwhile, the reports of factory inspectors, appointed under an act of 1833, were attracting widespread interest; and in 1847, after earlier attempts had proved abortive, a Factory Act was passed, limiting the hours of work of children in textile factories to ten: it was the first of many acts amending abuses and extending the principle of intervention.

In education there were significant new departures, limited in scope by the rivalry between churchmen and dissenters. In 1833 the first government grants had been made to the two main voluntary organizations sponsoring primary education, and in 1839 the first school inspectors had been appointed. J.P. Kay (later Sir James Kay-Shuttleworth), secretary of the Committee of Council on

Developments in education

Education, did everything he could to make the most of an admittedly inadequate system of provision, which was extended further with the first grants for teacher training and salaries in 1846. Kay's main object was to encourage the use of education as a means of introducing a measure of order and discipline into the working class population, when older and more traditional methods of wielding authority through subordination had broken down. Yet just as the operation of the deterrent Poor Law directed attention in the long run to the need for more complex welfare policies, so the extension of educational provision, limited and belated though it was, involved the interplay of more varied motives and purposes. That there was no revolution in Britain in 1848, as there was in most countries in Europe, was owing to the character of Britain's social structure. Yet the contemporary prophets of revolution, whether for or against, tended to overlook the effort, local as well as national, to influence conditions of life through conscious policies.

The evolution of such policies was difficult for a number of reasons: first, there were entrenched vested interests, particularly obvious in questions of public health; second, there was a shortage of professional expertise, particularly in engineering and medicine; third, most radicals were highly suspicious of all forms of state intervention, particularly if they involved spending large sums of money or interfering with local freedoms; fourth, the orthodox economic policies of the day stressed the need for private rather than for public initiative. Yet there were aspects of the social structure that encouraged social action. Industrialists were sometimes especially sensitive to the problems of the workers in the countryside, particularly during the heyday of the Anti-Corn Law League, when the Leaguers were attacking "feudalism"; and some landlords, notably the evangelical philanthropist Lord Ashley, were especially sensitive throughout the 1830s and '40s to the problems of town workers. In such circumstances, it was difficult to rest content with things as they were. In the words of one of Disraeli's characters, this was a "high-pressure" age. For the statistician G.R. Porter, whose *Progress of the Nation* (1836–43) went through many editions, all "the elements of improvement" in the country were "working with incessant and increasing energy." He added that in his own lifetime he had seen "the greatest advances in civilisation that can be found recorded in the annals of mankind."

The pace of economic change. Not all of Porter's contemporaries would have agreed about the phrase "the greatest advances in civilisation," for some of them criticized the quality of life in the new society, and others pointed to the social contrasts reflected, for example, in the unequal distribution of incomes. There was a debate between "optimists" and "pessimists," the latter suggesting that the condition of the working classes was actually deteriorating as national wealth increased. Most people were concerned, too, about the rise in population. At the first (defective) census of 1801, the population of England and Wales was around 9,000,000 and that of Scotland around 1,500,000. By 1851 the comparable figures were 18,000,-000 and 3,000,000. At its peak between 1811 and 1821, the growth rate for Britain as a whole was 17 percent for the decade. It took time to realize that the fears expressed so eloquently by Malthus that population would outrun subsistence were exaggerated and that, as population grew, national production would grow also.

Indeed, national income at constant prices increased nearly threefold between 1801 and 1851, substantially more than the increase in population, and the share of manufacturing, mining, and building in the national accounts of wealth increased sharply, as compared with the share of agriculture. In 1801 agriculture accounted for 34 percent and manufacturing, mining, and building for 28 percent. The comparable figures for 1851 were 21 percent and 40 percent. Cotton textiles remained the dominant new industry, with the cotton factory being thought of by one of its contemporary admirers, Edward Baines, as "the most striking example of the dominion obtained by human science over the powers of nature of which modern times can boast." There were 1,800 cotton factories in 1851. Raw cotton imports had increased unevenly from

101,000,000 pounds in 1815 to 757,000,000 pounds in 1851 and exports of manufactured cotton piece goods from 253,000,000 yards in 1815 to 1,543,000,000 yards in 1851. Similar steam-driven technology accounted for the expansion of the woollen textiles industry over the same period, with Australia, which provided no raw wool for Britain in 1815, providing 30,000,000 pounds in 1851. It was the textiles industry more than any other that illustrated Britain's dependence on international trade, a trade that it commanded not only through the size of the import bill or of manufacturing output but through the strength of its banking and other financial institutions and the extent of its shipping industry. Despite the advance of steam (registered steamship tonnage in 1815, 1,000, and in 1851, 187,000), the tonnage of sailing ships also increased. There was no problem comparable to that of the displaced handloom weavers, the victims of technological progress.

The new technology rested on coal, iron, and steam; it reached its peak in the age of the railway and the steamship. Coal production, about 13,000,000 tons in 1815, increased five times during the next 50 years, and, by 1850, Britain was producing over 2,000,000 tons of pig iron, half the world's output. Both coal and iron exports increased dramatically, with coal exports amounting to 3,300,000 tons in 1851, as against less than 250,000 tons at the end of the French wars. Coal mining was scattered in the coal-producing districts, with few large towns and with miners living a distinctive life with their own patterns of work and leisure. Iron production was associated with larger plants and considerable urbanization. In South Wales, for example, one of the areas of industrial expansion, the Dowlais works were employing 6,000 people and turning out 20,000 tons of pig iron each year during the 1840s. Birmingham, Britain's second largest city, was the centre of a broad range of metallurgical industries, mainly organized in small workshops, very different in character from the huge textile mills of Lancashire and Yorkshire.

Industrialization preceded the coming of the railway, but the railway did much to lower transport costs, to consume raw materials, to stimulate investment through an extended capital market, and to influence the location of industry. The railway age may be said to have begun in 1830, when the line from Liverpool to Manchester was opened, and to have gone through its most hectic phases during the 1840s, when contemporaries talked of a "railway mania." By 1851, 6,800 miles of railway were open, some of them involving engineering feats of great complexity. There was as much argument among contemporaries about the impact of railways as there was about the impact of steam engines in factories, but there was general agreement about the fact that the coming of the railway marked a great divide in British social history. The novelist William Thackeray put it succinctly, when he compared the last years of the stagecoach with the railway age. "Your railroad starts the new era, and we of a certain age belong to the new time and the old one." It was not until the 1870s and '80s that steamships brought this "new time" to its full realization, and by then British engineers and workmen had been responsible for building railways in all parts of the world. By 1890 Britain had more registered shipping tonnage than the rest of the world put together.

The Great Exhibition of 1851. By 1890 it had become apparent that the British industrial revolution, far from being unique, was merely the first in a sequence of industrial revolutions and that Britain's early lead was becoming something of a handicap. In 1851, however, Britain was not only the workshop of the world but the main influence on the industrialization of other nations as well as its own. The Great Exhibition of 1851, in London, symbolized this economic supremacy. The exhibition was housed in a huge glass and iron building called—with a touch of romance—"the Crystal Palace." Here, people from all parts of the world could examine machines of every kind, which Thackeray, once again catching the mood for posterity, described as "England's arms of conquest . . . the trophies of her bloodless war." Part of the success of the exhibition was political as much as economic. Many of the visitors who flocked to London came from European cities that

*"Opti-
mists" and
"pessi-
mists"*

Impact
of the
railroads

had been racked with revolution only three years before.

The exhibition was a triumph not only for the economy but also for Victoria and her German husband, Albert, whom she had married in 1840. "In England," wrote a continental observer, "loyalty is a passion." Despite outbursts of opposition to Albert, particularly in 1855, the family life of the Victorian court began to be considered increasingly as a model for the whole country. The fact that Albert had appreciated the significance of Peel's achievement and that he put his trust in the advancement of industry and science was as important as the fact that Victoria herself established monarchy on respectable foundations of family life. It was during the 1850s that the word "Victorian" began to be employed to express a new self-consciousness, both in relation to the nation and to the period through which it was passing. The death of Albert in 1861 and the subsequent withdrawal of the Queen from public life led to a decline in the popularity of the court, but in time the Queen's subjects, both at home and overseas, came once again to consider both her developed virtues and her obvious limitations as the very essence of "Victorianism" itself.

MID-VICTORIAN SOCIETY AND CULTURE

After the excitements of the 1830s and 1840s, mid-Victorian England was relatively quiet, with the family being regarded by most mid-Victorians as the central institution in society. In national social life, a kind of balance was struck between the busy industrial north and midlands and the sleepy countryside described in the novels of Anthony Trollope. A kind of balance was also struck between the traditional ideal of "the gentleman" and the new ideal of the hero of "self-help," with a place being left both for deference and dependence, on the one hand, and for individual advancement and acquisitiveness, on the other. There was far more talk during this period of self-help than there was of class conflict; indeed, the most comfortable social theory of the period rested on the assumption that class dividing lines could and should stay, provided that individuals in each class could move. Social discipline was strong, counting for more, perhaps, than the extension of the local police forces by an act of 1856.

Victorian attitudes. All kinds of balance rested, however, on economic as well as on psychological and sociological factors. From the early 1850s to the early 1870s, with occasional years of high unemployment and business failure (bad harvests counted for less as food imports increased), almost all sections of the population seemed to be benefitting from relative prosperity. Profits rose, as did wages and incomes from land. Indeed, those supporters of protection who had argued in the 1840s that free trade would ruin British agriculture were mocked by the mid-Victorian prosperity of agriculture in a golden age of high arable farming. There seemed to be little need in such a society for strong government, and it was only during the Crimean War (1854–56), when even many radicals looked for enemies abroad rather than at home and when the war itself was managed with obvious inefficiency, that either society or government seemed to be under great strain.

It was during these years, when great individual creative power was tapped, that Victorianism, perhaps the only "ism" in history attached to the name of a sovereign, came to represent a cluster of restraining moral attributes—earnestness, respectable comportment and behaviour, "character," "duty," hard work, and thrift. All these were virtues extolled and related to each other in the many books of Samuel Smiles, author of the best seller *Self-Help* (1859). Later in the century, they were to be taken apart and criticized, even lampooned, one by one in the course of a late-Victorian revolt. It is too simple, however, to dismiss them as bourgeois virtues, since many of them were shaped more by religion than by class, and all of them made an appeal, for a time at least, to nonmiddle-class sections of the population, aristocratic or trade unionist. All of them, moreover, were subjected to contemporary criticism. In the same year as Smiles's *Self-Help,* there appeared John Stuart Mill's essay, *On Liberty,* a powerful attack on conformity and a classic liberal statement of freedom of discussion. Charles Dickens frequently

made fun of the Victorian smugness and unwillingness to face unpleasant facts, as represented by Mr. Podsnap in *Our Mutual Friend;* the critics Matthew Arnold and John Ruskin, each arguing from a different point of departure, questioned many of the accepted beliefs and prejudices of the age. Minority communicators in the widely read reviews were often extremely critical, and even Smiles himself, writing for a bigger public, thought that none of the virtues he was extolling came to men naturally nor could any of them be taken for granted in the middle of the 19th century. There was always a Victorian underworld. Belief in the family was accompanied by a high incidence of prostitution, and in every large city there were districts where every Victorian virtue was ignored or flouted. Mill's London was also the London of Henry Mayhew, whose *London Labour and the London Poor* was published in book form in 1862.

Religion. The critical sense of many of the great Victorians—at least as far as opinions were concerned—inevitably involved questions of religion as much as of society or politics, and Victorian doubt was as much an acknowledged theme of the period as Victorian belief. During the year of the Great Exhibition, the poet Tennyson's *In Memoriam* considered the triumphs of 50 years of economic advance against the background of the whole story of man and of the earth. Geology and biology continued to challenge all accepted views of religion handed down from the past. Darwin's *Origin of Species* was another of the great books of the remarkable year 1859. A year later *Essays and Reviews* was published; a lively appraisal of fundamental religious questions by a number of liberal-minded religious thinkers, it provoked the sharpest religious controversy of the century.

Yet, behind such controversies, there were many signs of a confident belief on all sides that inquiry itself, if freely and honestly pursued, would do nothing to dissolve the ideals of conduct that were generally shared. Even those writers who were "agnostic" sought the "religion of humanity" or tried to be good "for good's sake, not God's." There was also a dutiful acceptance of the importance of standards in institutional as well as in private life. These were years when the extension of the civil service involved the development of a remarkable code of institutional morality. Following a report by Sir Charles Trevelyan and Sir Stafford Northcote in 1853–54, a civil service commission was set up. Recruitment and promotion in most parts of the service were to depend on competitive examination. An order-in-council of 1870 made this system mandatory, except for the Foreign Office. The extended civil service that took shape owed little to political patronage and was almost completely free from corruption.

Emphasis on conduct was, of course, related to religion. The English religious spectrum was of many colours. The Church of England was flanked on one side by Rome and on the other by religious dissent. Both were active forces to be reckoned with. The Roman Catholic Church was growing in importance not only in the Irish sections of the industrial cities but also among university students and teachers. Dissent had a grip on the whole culture of large sections of the middle classes, dismissed too abruptly by Arnold as "mutilated and incomplete men." Sometimes the local battle between Church of England and Dissent was bitterly contested, with Nonconformists acting as a militant group, opposing church rates (taxes), challenging closed foundations, and preaching total abstinence and educational reform. A whole network of local voluntary bodies, led either by Anglicans or Dissenters, usually in rivalry, came into existence, a tribute to the energies of the age and to its fear of state intervention.

The Church of England itself was a divided family, with different groups contending for positions of influence. The High Church movement (which emphasized the "Catholic" side of Anglicanism) was given a distinctive character, first by the Oxford Movement, or Tractarianism, which had grown up in the 1830s as a reaction against the new liberal theology, and then by the often provocative and always controversial ritualist agitation of the 1850s and '60s. The fact that prominent members of the Church of England flirted with "Romanism" and even crossed the

Victoria and Albert

Effects of economic prosperity

Self-criticism and doubt

The Oxford Movement

Rubicon often raised the popular Protestant cry of the "church in danger." Peel's conversion to free trade in 1846 scarcely created any more excitement than John Henry Newman's conversion to Rome the previous year, while, in 1850, Lord John Russell, Peel's successor as prime minister, tried to capitalize politically on violent antipapal feelings stimulated by the Pope's decision to create Roman Catholic dioceses in England.

The Evangelicals, in many ways the most influential as well as the most distinctively English religious group, were suspicious both of ritual and of appeals to any authority other than that of the Bible. Their concern with individual conduct was a force making for social conformity during the middle years of the century rather than for that depth of individual religious experience that the first advocates of "vital religion" had preached in the 18th century. Yet leaders like Ashley were prepared to probe some of the difficult questions of the social order and to stir men's consciences, even if their preoccupation was with saving souls, and their missionary zeal influenced overseas as well as domestic development. There were some members of the church, usually not evangelicals, who urged the cause of what they called "Christian Socialism." Their intellectual leader was the outstanding Anglican theologian Frederick Denison Maurice.

Beyond the influence of both church and chapel there were thousands of people in mid-Victorian England who were ignorant of, or indifferent toward, the message of Christianity, a fact demonstrated by England's one religious census in 1851. Although movements like the Salvation Army, founded by William Booth in 1865, attempted to rally the poor of the great cities, there were many signs of apathy or even hostility. There was also a small but active secularist agitation. The great religious controversies of mid-Victorian England were not so much settled as shelved.

The Church of Scotland In Scotland, where the Church of Scotland had been fashioned by the people against the crown, there was a revival of Presbyterianism in the 1820s and '30s. A complex and protracted controversy, centring on the right of congregations to exclude candidates for the ministry whom they thought unsuitable, ended in schism. In 1843, 474 ministers left the Church of Scotland and established a free church. Within four years they had raised over £1,250,000 and built 654 churches. This was a remarkable effort, even in a great age of church and chapel building. It left Scotland with a religious pattern even more different from that of England and Wales than it had been in 1815. Yet many of the most influential voices in mid-Victorian Britain, including Thomas Carlyle and Samuel Smiles, were Scottish voices, and the conception of the gospel of work, in particular, owed much in content and tone, even if often indirectly, to Scottish Calvinism.

MID-VICTORIAN POLITICS

Religious questions helped divide the limited electorate, with the dissenters encouraging, from their local bases, the development of liberalism, and churchmen often—but by no means universally—supporting the Conservative Party. Party divisions were based on customary allegiance as much as on careful scrutiny of issues, and there was still considerable scope for bribery at election times. The civil service might be pure, but the electors often were not. The Corrupt Practices Act of 1854 provided a more exact definition of bribery than there had been before, but it was not until a further act of 1883 that election expenses were rigorously controlled. During the mid-Victorian years, the way to Parliament often led through the pigsty.

The prestige of the individual member of Parliament was high, and the fragmentation of parties after 1846 allowed him considerable independence. Groups of members supporting particular economic interests, especially the railways, could often determine parliamentary strategies. Contemporaries feared such interests less than they feared what was often called the most dangerous of all interests, executive government. Powerful government and large-scale "organic" reform were considered dangerous, and even those radicals who supported organic reform, like Cobden and Bright, were suspicious of powerful govern-

ment. For most politicians, politics was identified not with theories or even programs but with pragmatic leadership.

In his interesting analysis of the English constitution (1867), Walter Bagehot considered the cabinet as "a board of control chosen by the legislature, out of persons whom it trusts and knows, to rule the nation." Its primary task was to administer, not to legislate. There was little legislation dealing with public health or trade unions or Irish agrarian problems until the late 1860s, although the Company Act of 1862 consolidated limited liability legislation passed during the 1850s. A judge told a number of men who were convicted of illegal activities during a strike of 1867,

> Everybody knows that the total aggregate happiness of mankind is increased by every man being left to the unbiased, unfettered determination of his own will and judgement as to how he will employ his industry and other means of getting on in the world.

Palmerston. Palmerston, an aristocrat born in 1784, stood out as the dominant political personality in mid-Victorian Britain, precisely because he was opposed to dramatic change and because he knew through long experience how to manoeuvre politics within the half-reformed constitution. In a period when it was difficult to collect parliamentary majorities, he often forced decisions, as at the general election of 1857, on the simple question, "are you for or against me?" He was skillful also in using the growing power of the press in order to reinforce his influence. At a time of party confusion, when the Queen might well have played a key part in politics, Palmerston found the answer to royal opposition in popular prestige, carefully stage-managed. His chief preoccupation was with foreign affairs, and his approach was diametrically opposed to that of the court on several occasions.

There was no contradiction between his views on domestic and foreign policy. He preferred the English system of constitutional government, resting on secure social foundations, to continental absolutism, but, like Canning before him, he was anxious above all else to advance the interests of England as he saw them. The supremacy of British sea power, British economic ascendancy, and political divisions inside each of the main countries of Europe before and after the revolutions of 1848 gave him his opportunity. He liked to appear active. In 1850 he sent a blockading squadron to Greece to enforce payments of debts due to Don Pacifico, a Gibraltar-born British subject, and restated the doctrine of *civis Romanus sum* ("I am a Roman citizen," by which an ancient Roman could proclaim his rights throughout the empire) in a Victorian setting. In 1852, when he helped overturn Russell's shaky government, he had his revenge on Russell, who had dismissed him from his post as foreign secretary in December 1851 for welcoming Napoleon III's coup d'etat in France. In January 1855, after Lord Aberdeen, a Peelite, had shown his incompetence as a war leader during the Crimean War, Palmerston was made prime minister for the first time. His interventions were not confined to Europe. In 1840–41 he forced the China ports open to foreign trade and, by the Treaty of Nanking (1842), acquired Hong Kong for Britain. In 1857 he went to war in China again and, when defeated in Parliament, appealed triumphantly to the country. Although his government was defeated in 1858, he was back again as prime minister, for the last time, a year later.

During the remarkable ministry of 1859–65, which included Russell as foreign secretary and the Peelite Gladstone as chancellor of the exchequer, it was impossible for Britain to dominate the international scene as effectively as in previous periods of Palmerstonian power. With efficient military power at his disposal, the Prussian prime minister, Otto von Bismarck, proved more than a match for him. The union of modern Italy, which Palmerston supported; the American Civil War, in which his sympathies were with the South; and the rise of Bismarck's Germany, which he did not understand, were reshaping the world in which he had been able to achieve so much by forceful opportunism. When he died, in October 1865, it was clear that, in foreign relations as well as in home

The Don Pacifico affair

politics, there would have to be what Gladstone described as "a new commencement."

In home politics it had been only the continued influence of Palmerston as prime minister that had delayed overdue reforms. In the large urban constituencies, the demand for a new and active liberalism was gaining ground, and at Westminster itself Gladstone was beginning to identify himself not only with the continued advance of free trade but with the demand for parliamentary reform. In 1864 he forecast new directions in politics when he stated that the burden of proof concerning the case for reform rested not with the reformers but with their opponents. A year later he lost his seat at Oxford University and was returned "unmuzzled" as representative for a populous Lancashire constituency. The death of Palmerston was followed by the reopening of the question of parliamentary reform and by the passing of the Second Reform Bill in 1867.

The Reform Bill of 1867.　Yet it was Disraeli and not Gladstone who claimed the credit for the act of 1867. On Palmerston's death, Russell and Gladstone had introduced a modest and colourless bill that was severely mauled both by Conservatives and reform Liberals. The government resigned, and Derby and Disraeli took office. It was difficult to shelve the demand for reform, and the government decided to "dish the Whigs" and "take a leap in the dark." Agitation in the country was more vociferous on the issue than it had been since the days of the Chartists, and organizations, notably the Reform League, were engaged in stirring the public, alongside prominent individuals, notably John Bright. In a Parliament where Disraeli was in a minority, his only chance lay in accepting amendments, however radical, to the bill that he had introduced and in claiming them as his own. All reserves and safeguards were dropped, and, although he lost some of his own supporters, he eventually carried a bill very different from the one he had introduced. It added 938,000 new names to the register, almost a doubling of the electorate, and gave the vote to many workingmen in the towns and cities. The county franchise was not substantially changed, but 45 new seats were created by taking one member from existing borough constituencies with a population of less than 10,000. Disraeli hoped that, in return for passing this measure, urban workingmen would vote for him—he believed rightly that many of them were Conservatives already by instinct and allegiance—but, at the first general election under the new system, it was Gladstone who was returned as prime minister.

GLADSTONE AND DISRAELI

The choice between Gladstone and Disraeli was the first of many similar choices offered to an extended electorate—the choice between two men who were completely different in temperament and political outlook. Gladstone had made his mark first and lived on far longer (1898) than did his rival (1881). He saw politics in terms of moral principles and, in his ministry of 1868–74, introduced some of the most important Liberal legislation of the 19th century. Disraeli, who combined opportunism and political imagination, carried through an impressive program of social reform and embarked upon an active foreign policy both in Europe and overseas. Yet much of the Liberal legislation was the product of compromise rather than of principle, and much of the significant social legislation of the Conservatives was considered sufficiently politically unimportant by them, at the time, for them to neglect it when they appealed to the electorate in 1880. In both parties, there were new forces stirring at the local level and energetic efforts to organize the electorate and the political parties along new lines. With the development of central party machinery and local organization, the role of the crown was reduced during this period to that of merely ratifying the result of general elections. Although the Queen greatly preferred Disraeli to Gladstone, she could not keep Gladstone out. Her obvious partisanship made some of her acts look unconstitutional, but they would not have been deemed unconstitutional in any previous period of history. The public during this period was more interested in the political leaders than in the Queen, who

lived in retirement and was sharply criticized in sections of the press.

Gladstone's first administration.　The achievements of Gladstone's first administration were several: the disestablishment and partial disendowment of the Irish Church, accomplished in 1869 in face of the opposition of the House of Lords; the Irish Land Act of 1870, providing some safeguards to Irish tenant farmers; William Edward Forster's Education Act of the same year, the first national act dealing with primary education; the Trade-Union Act of 1871, legalizing unions and giving them the protection of the courts; and the Ballot Act of 1872, introducing secret voting. There were many other important reforms, most of which were designed to broaden the span of individual opportunity or to reform cumbersome administrative machinery. In 1871, for example, the universities of Oxford and Cambridge were opened to Dissenters, while between 1868 and 1873 the cumbrous military machine was renovated by Gladstone's secretary for war, Edward Cardwell. The system of dual responsibility of commander in chief and secretary for war was abolished, and the subordination of the former to the latter was asserted. In 1873 the Judicature Act, amended in 1876, simplified the tangle of legal institutions and procedures.

Many of these reforms did not satisfy affected interests. The Irish Church Disestablishment Act failed to placate the Irish and alarmed many English churchmen, while the Education Act was passed only in face of bitter Nonconformist opposition. The Dissenters objected that Forster's system did not break the power of the church over primary education, and, although the act was extended in 1880 when primary education was made compulsory and in 1891 when it became free, there were often noisy struggles between churchmen and Dissenters in the new school boards set up locally under the Forster Act. If the Education Act alienated many Dissenters, the Licensing Bills of 1871 and 1872 alienated their enemies, the brewers. At the general election of 1874, therefore, months after Disraeli had described the Liberal leaders in one of his many memorable phrases as a "range of exhausted volcanoes," the brewers threw all their influence behind the Conservatives. "We have been borne down in a torrent of gin and beer," Gladstone complained.

Disraeli's second administration.　Disraeli's ministry embarked upon a sizable program of social legislation. Gladstone, throughout his life, preferred free and cheap government to expensive and socially committed government. He was anxious, indeed, in 1873 to abolish income tax, on which the public finances of the future were to depend. Disraeli had always been interested in "the condition of England question" and, with the assistance of men like Richard Cross, the home secretary, justified at last his reputation as a social reformer. By the Employers and Workmen Act of 1875, "masters" and "men" were put on an equal footing as regards breaches of contract, while by a Trade-Union Act of 1875 that went much further than the Liberal act of 1871, trade unionists were allowed to engage in peaceful picketing and to do whatever would not be criminal if done by an individual. The Public Health Act of 1875, a consolidating piece of legislation, created a public health authority in every area; the Artizans' and Labourers' Dwellings Improvement Act of the same year enabled local authorities to embark upon schemes of slum clearance; a factory act of 1878 fixed a 56-hour week; while further legislation dealt with Friendly Societies (private societies for mutual-health and old-age insurance), the protection of seamen, land improvements carried out by tenants, and the adulteration of food. There was no similar burst of social legislation until after 1906.

Foreign policy.　If there were significant, if not fully acknowledged, differences between the records of the two governments on domestic issues, there were open, even strident differences on questions of foreign policy. Gladstone had never been a Palmerstonian. He was always anxious to avoid the resort to force, and he put his trust not in national prejudices but in an enlightened public opinion in Europe as well as England. His object was justice rather than power. In practice, however, he often gave the impression of a man who vacillated and could

The "leap in the dark"

Administrative reforms

not act firmly. Disraeli was willing to take risks to enhance British prestige and to seek to profit from, rather than to moralize about, foreign dissensions. His first ventures in "imperialism"—a speech at the Crystal Palace in 1872, the purchase of the Suez Canal shares in 1875, and the proclamation of the Queen as "Empress of India"—showed that he had abandoned the view, popular during the middle years of the century, that colonies were millstones around the mother country's neck. But these moves did not involve him in any European entanglements, nor did the costly if brilliantly led campaigns of Major General Roberts in Afghanistan (1878–80) and the annexation of the Transvaal in South Africa in 1877.

It was the Near Eastern crisis of 1875–78 that produced the liveliest 19th-century debate on foreign policy issues. In May 1876, Disraeli rejected overtures made by Russia, Austria-Hungary, and Germany to deal jointly with the Turks, who were faced with revolt in Serbia. His pro-Turkish sympathies irritated many Liberals, and, after the Turks had gone on to suppress with great violence a revolt in Bulgaria in 1876, the Liberal conscience was stirred and mass meetings were held in many parts of the country. Gladstone, who had gone into retirement as Liberal leader in 1875, was slower to respond to the issue than many of his followers, but, once roused, he emerged from retirement, wrote an immensely influential pamphlet on the atrocities, and led a public campaign on the platform and in the press. For him the Turks were "inhuman and despotic," and, whatever the national interests involved, Britain, in his view, should do nothing to support them. Disraeli's calculations concerned strategic and imperial necessities rather than ideals of conduct, and his suspicions were justified when the Russians attacked Turkey in April 1877. Opinion swung back to his side, and in 1878 Disraeli sent a British fleet to the Dardanelles. There was a war fever in London—the term jingoism was used to describe it—that was intensified when news reached London that a peace treaty had been signed at San Stefano whereby the Turks accepted maximum Russian demands. Reservists were mobilized in Britain, and Indian troops were sent to the Mediterranean. Disraeli's Foreign Minister, who disapproved of such action, resigned, to be succeeded by Lord Salisbury, who was eventually to serve as prime minister in the last Conservative administrations of the 19th century. The immediate crisis passed, and, at an international conference held in Berlin in June and July 1878, which Disraeli attended, the inroads into Turkish territory were reduced, Russia was kept well away from Constantinople, and Britain acquired Cyprus. Disraeli brought back "peace with honour." But the swings of public opinion continued, and in 1879 Gladstone, starting at Midlothian in Scotland, fought a nationwide political campaign of unprecedented excitement and drama. At the general election of April 1880, the Liberals returned to power triumphantly, with a majority of 137 over the Conservatives. Disraeli, who had moved to the House of Lords in 1876, died in 1881.

LATE VICTORIAN POLITICS

Gladstone and Chamberlain.   Yet the second Gladstone administration (1880–85) did not live up to the promise of the election victory. The Cabinet that Gladstone assembled was neither compact nor united. Eight of the members were Whigs, but, of the other three, one—Joseph Chamberlain—was representative of a new and aggressive urban radicalism, less interested in orthodox statements of liberal individualism than in the uncertain aspirations and strivings of the different elements in the mass electorate. Already, as mayor of Birmingham (1873–76), he had embarked upon large-scale schemes of civic improvement, which he did not scruple to call "municipal socialism." At the opposite end of the spectrum, the Whigs were the largest group in the Cabinet, but the smallest in the country. Many of them were already abandoning the Liberal Party; all of them were nervous about the kind of radical program that Chamberlain and the newly founded National Liberal Federation (1877) were advocating and about the kind of caucus-based organization that Chamberlain favoured locally and nationally. In terms of political logic, it seemed likely in 1880 that the Gladstonian

Liberal Party would eventually split into Whig and radical components, the latter led by Chamberlain. For the moment, however, Gladstone was the man of the hour, and Chamberlain himself conceded that he was indispensable.

The government carried a number of important reforms culminating in the Third Reform Bill of 1884, which continued the trend toward universal male suffrage by giving the vote to agricultural labourers, thereby tripling the electorate, and the Redistribution Act of 1885, which robbed 79 towns with populations under 15,000 of their separate representation. For the first time, the franchise reforms ignored the claims of the traditional influences of property and wealth and rested firmly on the democratic principle that the vote ought to be given to people as a matter of right and not of expediency.

The most difficult problems continued to arise in relation to foreign affairs and, above all, to Ireland. When, in 1881, the Boers defeated the British at Majuba Hill and Gladstone abandoned the attempt to hold the Transvaal, there was considerable public criticism. And in the same year, when he agreed to the bombardment of Alexandria in a successful effort to break a nationalist revolt in Egypt, he lost the support of the aged radical, Bright. In 1882 Egypt was occupied, thereby adding, against Gladstone's own inclinations, to British imperial commitments. A rebellion in the Sudan, which led to the sending out of British troops in 1883, was the occasion of one of the most terrible tragedies of the decade. Gen. Charles Gordon, who was dispatched to Khartoum, was killed in 1885, two days before the arrival of a mission to relieve him. Large numbers of Englishmen held Gladstone personally responsible, and, in June 1885, he resigned after a defeat on an amendment to the budget.

The Irish Question.   The Irish question had loomed ominously as soon as Parliament had assembled in 1880, for there was now an Irish nationalist group of more than 60 members led by Charles Stewart Parnell, most of them committed to Irish Home Rule; in Ireland itself, the Land League, founded in 1879, was struggling to destroy the power of the landlord. Parnell himself embarked on a program of agrarian agitation in 1881, at the same time that his followers at Westminster were engaged in various kinds of parliamentary obstructionism. Gladstone's response was an Irish Land Act, based on guaranteeing "three fs"—fair rents, fixity of tenure, and free sale—and a tightening up of the rules of closure in parliamentary debate. The Land Act did not go far enough to satisfy Parnell, who continued to make speeches couched in violent language; a coercion act was passed by Parliament against Irish agitators and Parnell was arrested. He was released, however, in April 1882 after an understanding had been reached that he would abandon the land war and the government would abandon coercion. Lord Frederick Charles Cavendish, a close friend of Gladstone and brother of the Whig leader, Lord Hartington, was sent to Dublin as chief secretary on a mission of peace, but the whole policy was undermined when Cavendish, along with the permanent undersecretary, was murdered in Phoenix Park, Dublin, within a few hours of landing in Ireland.

Between 1881 and 1885, Gladstone coupled a somewhat stiffer policy in Ireland with minor measures of reform, but in 1885, when the Conservatives returned to power under Salisbury, the Irish question forced itself to the forefront again. Lord Carnarvon, the new lord lieutenant of Ireland, was a convert to Home Rule and followed a more liberal policy than his predecessor. At the general election of November 1885, Parnell secured every Irish seat but one outside Ulster and urged Irish voters in British constituencies—a large group mostly concentrated in a limited number of places like Lancashire and Clydeside in Scotland—to vote Conservative. The result of the election was a Liberal majority of 86 over the Conservatives, almost exactly balanced by the Irish group, who thus controlled the balance of power in Parliament. The Conservatives stayed in office, but when, in December 1885, the newspapers reported a confidential interview with Gladstone's son, in which he had stated (rightly) that his father had been converted to Home Rule, Salisbury made it clear that he himself was not a convert,

Disraeli's "imperialism"

Third Reform Bill

The Phoenix Park Murders

and Carnarvon resigned. All Conservative contacts with Parnell ceased, and a few weeks later, in January 1886, after the Conservatives had been defeated in Parliament on a radical amendment for agrarian reform, Salisbury resigned, and Gladstone returned to power.

Split of the Liberal Party. Gladstone's conversion had been gradual but profound, and it had more far-reaching political consequences for Britain than for Ireland. It immediately alienated him further from most of the Whigs and from a considerable number of radicals led by Joseph Chamberlain. He had hoped at first that Home Rule would be carried by an agreement between the parties, but Salisbury had no intention of imitating Peel. Gladstone made his intentions clear by appointing John Morley, a Home Rule advocate as Irish secretary, and in April 1886 he introduced a Home Rule bill. The Liberals remained divided, and 93 of them united with the Conservatives to defeat the measure. Gladstone appealed to the country and was decisively beaten at the general election, in which 316 Conservatives were returned to Westminster along with 78 Liberal Unionists, the new name chosen by those Liberals who refused to back Home Rule. The Liberals mustered only 191, and there were 85 Irish nationalists. Whigs and radicals, who had often seemed likely to split Gladstone's 1880 government on left–right lines, were now united against the Gladstonians, and all attempts at Liberal reunion failed.

Chamberlain, the astute radical leader, like many others of his class and generation, ceased to regard social reform as a top priority and worked in harness with Hartington, his Whig counterpart. In 1895 they both joined a Salisbury government. The Liberals were, in effect, pushed into the wilderness, although they held office briefly and unhappily from 1892 to 1895. Gladstone, 82 years old when he formed his last government, actually succeeded in carrying a Home Rule bill in the Commons in 1893, with the help of Irish votes (Parnell's power had been broken as a result of a divorce case in 1890, and he died in 1891), but the bill was thrown out by the Lords. He

Rise of the Conservatives

resigned in 1894, to be succeeded by Lord Rosebery, who further split the party; at the general election of 1895, the Conservatives could claim that they were the genuinely popular party, backed by the urban as well as the rural electorate. Although Salisbury always stressed the defensive aspects of Conservatism, both at home and abroad, Chamberlain and his supporters were able to mobilize considerable working class as well as middle class support for a policy of crusading imperialism.

Imperialism and British politics. The word imperialism was the key word of the 1890s, just as Home Rule had been in the critical decade of the 1880s, and the cause of empire was associated not merely with the economic interests of businessmen, looking for materials and markets, and the enthusiasm of crowds, excited by the adventure of empire, but with the traditional lustre of the crown. Disraeli had emphasized the last of these associations, just as Chamberlain emphasized the first. When Chamberlain deliberately chose to take over the Colonial Office in 1895, he was acknowledging the opportunities, both economic and political, afforded by a vast "undeveloped estate." The same radical energies that he had once devoted to civic improvement were now directed toward imperial problems, with every effort being made at the same time to make the empire meaningful and attractive to children at school and to the newspaper-reading mass electorate.

In fact, however, it was difficult to pull the empire together politically or constitutionally, certainly to move toward federation, since the interests of different parts were already diverging, and in the last resort only British power—above all, sea power—held it together. The processes of imperial expansion were always complex, and there was neither one dominant theory of empire nor one single explanation of why it grew. White colonies, like Canada or New Zealand and the states of Australia, had been given substantial powers of self-government since the Durham Report of 1839 and the Canada Union Act of 1840. Yet India, "the brightest jewel in the British crown," was held not by consent but by conquest. The Indian "mutiny" of 1857 was suppressed, and a year later

the East India Company was abolished; thereafter, given the strategic importance of India to the military establishment, attempts were made to justify British rule in terms of benefits of law and order said to accrue to Indians. "The white man's burden," as the poet Rudyard Kipling saw it, was a burden of responsibility.

It was difficult for the British voter to understand or to appreciate this network of motives and interests. Chamberlain himself was always far less interested in India than the white "kith-and-kin dominions" and in the new tropical empire that was greatly extended in area between 1884 and 1896, when 2,500,000 square miles of territory fell under British control. Even he did not fully understand either the rival aspirations of different dominions or relationship between economic development in the "formal" empire and trade and investment in the "informal" empire where the British flag did not fly.

Victoria's jubilees in 1887 and 1897 involved both imperial pageantry and imperial conferences, but, between 1896 and 1902, public interest in problems of empire was intensified not so much by pageantry as by crisis. British–Boer relations in South Africa, always tense, were further worsened after the Jameson raid of December 1895, and, in October 1899, war began. The early stages of the struggle were favourable to the Boers, and it was not until spring 1900 that superior British equipment began to count. British troops entered Pretoria in June 1900 and Paul Kruger, the Boer president, fled to Europe, where most governments had given him moral support against the British. Thereafter the Boers followed guerrilla tactics, and the war did not end until May 1902. It was the most expensive of all the 19th-century "little wars," with the British employing 450,000 troops, of whom 22,000 never returned. Just as the Crimean War had focussed attention on "mismanagement," so the South African (Boer) War led to demands not only for greater "efficiency" but for more enlightened social policies in relation to health and education.

The South African War

While the war lasted, it emphasized the political differences within the Liberal Party and consolidated Conservative–Unionist strength. Rosebery's Liberal imperialism was totally uncongenial to young pro-Boer Liberals like Lloyd George. A middle group of Liberals emerged, but it was not until after 1903 that party rifts were healed. The Unionists won the "khaki election" of 1900 and secured a new lease of power for nearly six years, but their unity also was threatened after the Peace of Vereeniging in May 1902. Salisbury retired in 1902, to be succeeded by his nephew, Arthur Balfour, a brilliant man but a tortuous and insecure politician. There had been an even bigger break in January 1901 when the Queen died, after a brief illness, in her 82nd year. She had ruled for 64 years and her death seemed to mark not so much the end of a reign as the end of an age.

EDWARDIAN AND PREWAR BRITAIN

Victoria's successor, Edward VII, 59 years old, had never been on good terms with his mother, whose ways of life were sharply different from his. He, too, gave his name to an age: flamboyant, ostentatious, at times vulgar and strident, with picturesque contrasts of fortune and circumstance. Yet the sharpness of the contrast between "Edwardian" and "late Victorian" should not be exaggerated. The last decade of the 19th century and the first decade of the 20th century had much in common, and there had been bigger breaks in mood and preoccupation between the high-Victorian years and the 1890s.

Darwin's disciple, Thomas Huxley, an influential popularizer of science, had noted during the 1870s that everything was in question—opinions, institutions, and conventions—and the questioning thereafter never stopped. "The disintegration of opinion is so rapid," one writer put it in the 1880s, "that wise men and foolish are equally ignorant where the close of this waning century will find us." The writers of the last decades of the 19th century included iconoclasts like George Bernard Shaw and deviants like Oscar Wilde; for both, as for many others like them, all that was established was now suspect. Some commentators wrote of "a general revolt" against the accepted canons of the midcentury, a revolt influenced by thinkers outside Britain and challenging not only political or social assumptions (for example, about law and will or self-help and respectability) but also 19th-century culture as a whole, the culture of an industrialized society transformed through individual enterprise.

The economy. Changes in economic conditions during the last decades of the century were obviously of crucial importance. Mid-Victorian prosperity had reached its peak in a boom that collapsed in 1873. Thereafter, although national income continued to increase (nearly four times at constant prices between 1851 and 1911), there was a persistent pressure on profit margins, with a price fall that lasted until the mid-1890s. Contemporaries talked mis-leadingly of a "great depression," but however misleading the phrase was as a description of the movement of economic indexes, the period as a whole was one of doubt and tension. There was anxious concern about both markets and materials, and the fact that there was a retardation in the national rate of growth to below 2 percent per annum was even harder to bear when the growth rates of competitors were rising, sometimes in spectacular fashion.

The interests of different sections of the community diverged between 1870 and 1900 as they had diverged before the mid-Victorian period of equipoise. In particular, arable and meat-producing farmers felt the full weight of foreign competition in cereals, and many, though not all, industrialists felt the growing pressure of foreign competition both in old and new industries. As a result of improved transport, including storage and refrigeration facilities, and the application of improved agricultural machinery, overseas cereal producers fully penetrated the British market. In 1877 the price of English wheat stood at 56s. 9d. a quarter (1846: 54s. 6d); for the rest of the century it never again came within 10s. of that figure. During the 1890s, therefore, there was a sharp fall of rents, a shift in land ownership, and a challenge to the large estate in the cereal-growing and meat-producing areas of the country. The fact that dairy and fruit farmers flourished did not relieve the pessimism of most spokesmen of the threatened landed interests.

In industry, where there were new forms of power and a trend toward bigger plants and more impersonal organization, there were also moves throughout the period to increase cartels and amalgamations. Britain was never as strong or as innovatory in the age of steel as in the earlier age of iron—by 1896 British steel output was less than that of either the United States or Germany—while the textile industry was declining absolutely. Exports fell between 1880 and 1900 from £105,000,000 to £95,000,000. There were many explanations of what was happening, psychological as well as economic, but none of them was encouraging. Yet the country's economic position would have been completely different, had it not been for Britain's international economic strength as banker and financier. During years of economic challenge at home, capital exports greatly increased, until they reached a figure of almost £200,000,000 per annum before 1914, and investment income poured in to rectify adverse balances on visible trade accounts. During the last 20 years of peace before 1914, when Britain's role as *rentier* was at its height, international prices began to rise again, continuing to rise, with fluctuations, until after the end of World War I.

The rise of labour. Meanwhile, whether prices were falling or rising, labour in Britain was increasingly discontented, more articulate, and more highly organized. Throughout the period, national income per head grew faster than the continuing population growth (which stayed at above 10 percent per decade until 1911, although the birth rate fell sharply after 1900), but neither the growth of income nor the falling level of retail prices until the mid-1890s made for industrial peace. By the end of the century, when pressure on real wages was once again increasing, there were 2,000,000 trade unionists in unskilled unions as well as in skilled unions of the midcentury type, and by 1914 the figure had doubled.

There were also significant political changes. Some of the new union leaders were confessed socialists, anxious to use political as well as economic power to secure their objectives, and a number of socialist organizations emerged between 1880 and 1900—all conscious, at least intermittently, that, whatever their differences, they were part of a "labour movement." The Social Democratic Federation, influenced by Marxism, was founded in 1884; it was never more than a tiny and increasingly sectarian organization. The Independent Labour Party, founded in Bradford in 1893, had a more general appeal, while the Fabian Society, founded in 1883–84, included intellectuals who were to play a big part in 20th-century labour politics. In February 1900 a labour representation conference was held in London at which trade unionists and socialists agreed to found a committee, with Ramsay MacDonald as first secretary, to promote the return of Labour members to Parliament. This conference marked the beginning of the 20th-century Labour Party, which, with Liberal support, won 29 seats at the general election of 1906. Although until 1914 the party at Westminster for the most part supported the Liberals, in 1909 it secured the allegiance of the "Lib-Lab" miners' members. Financially backed by the trade unions, it was eventually to take the place of the Liberal Party as the second party in the state.

The return of the Liberals. The Liberals returned to power in December 1905 after Balfour had resigned. Between the end of the South African War and this date, they had become more united as the Conservatives had disintegrated. In 1903 Chamberlain had taken up the cause of protection, thereby disturbing an already uneasy balance within Balfour's cabinet. He failed to win large-scale middle class or working class support outside Parliament as he had hoped, and the main effect of his propaganda was to draw rival groups of Liberals together to protect free trade. At the general election of 1906 the Liberals won 377 seats, which gave them an enormous majority of 84 over all other parties combined. Their leader was Sir Henry Campbell-Bannerman, a cautious Scot, who had stayed clear of the extreme factions during the South African War. He formed an able cabinet that included radicals and Liberal imperialists, and when he retired in 1908, H.H. Asquith moved from the Home Office to become prime minister.

Social reform had not been the chief cry at the general election, which was fought mainly on the old issues of free trade, temperance reform, and education. In many constituencies there was evidence of Nonconformist grievances against a Balfour education act of 1902 that abolished the school boards, transferred educational responsibilities to the all-purpose local authorities, and laid the foundations of a national system of secondary education. Yet local and national inquiries, official and unofficial, into the incidence of poverty had pointed to the need for public action to relieve distress, and, from the start, the new Liberal government embarked upon a program of social legislation. In 1906 free school meals were made available to poor children; in 1907 a school medical service was founded; in 1908 a Children's Act was passed, along with an Old Age Pensions Act granting pensions under prescribed conditions to people over 70; in 1908 the miners were given a statutory working day of eight hours; and in 1909 trade boards were set up to fix wages in designated industries where there was little or no trade-union strength, and labour exchanges were created to try to reduce unemployment (a subject that was also being investigated locally and nationally) and to increase mobility. The vigour of these reforms owed much to a partnership between Winston Churchill at the Board of Trade and Lloyd George, chancellor of the exchequer.

Lloyd George's budget of 1909 set out deliberately to raise money to "wage implacable warfare against poverty and squalidness." The money was to come in part from supertax on high incomes and from capital gains on land sales. The budget so enraged Conservative opinion, inside and outside Parliament, that the Lords, already hostile to the trend of Liberal legislation, rejected it, thereby turning a political debate into a constitutional one. Passions were as strong as they had been in 1831, yet, at the ensuing general election of January 1910, the Liberal majority was greatly reduced and the balance of power in Parliament was now held by Labour and Irish Nationalist members.

Slowing of growth rate

Labour and politics

The Parlia-
ment Act
of 1911

The death of Edward in May 1910 and the succession of the politically inexperienced George V added to the confusion, and it proved impossible to reach agreement between the parties on the outlines of a Parliament bill to define or to curb the powers of the House of Lords. After a Liberal Parliament bill had been defeated, a second general election in December 1910 produced similar political results to those earlier in the year, and it was not until August 1911 that the peers eventually passed the Parliament Act by 131 votes to 114. The act provided that money bills could become law without the assent of the Lords and that other bills would also become law if they passed in the Commons and failed in the Lords three times within two years. The act was finally passed only after the Conservative leadership had repudiated the "diehard peers" who refused to be intimidated by a threat to create more peers.

In the course of the struggle over the Parliament bill, strong, even violent, feelings had been roused among lords who had seldom bothered hitherto to attend their house. Their intransigence provided a keynote to four years of equally fierce struggle on many other issues in the country, with different sectional groups turning to noisy direct action. The Liberals remained in power, carrying important new legislation, but they faced so much opposition from extremists, who cared little either about conventional political behaviour or the rule of law, that these years have been called by the American historian, George Dangerfield, "the strange death of Liberal England." The most important legislation was once more associated with Lloyd George—the National Insurance Act of 1911, which provided, on a contributory basis, for limited unemployment and health insurance for large sections of the population.

The National Insurance Act, which Parliament accepted without difficulty, was the subject of much hostile criticism in the press and was bitterly opposed by doctors and duchesses. Nor did it win unanimous support from labour. The parliamentary Labour Party itself mattered less during these years, however, than extraparliamentary trade-union protests, some of them violent in character— "a great upsurge of elemental forces." There was a wave of strikes in 1911 and 1912, some of them tinged with syndicalist ideology, all of them asserting, in difficult economic circumstances for the workingman, claims that had never been made before. Old-fashioned trade unionists were almost as unpopular with the rank and file as capitalists. In June 1914, less than two months before the outbreak of World War I, a "triple alliance" of transport workers, miners, and railwaymen was formed to buttress labour solidarity. In parallel to labour agitation, the suffragettes, fighting for women's rights, resorted to militant tactics that not only embarrassed Asquith's government but tested the whole local and national machinery for maintaining order. The Women's Social and Political Union, founded in 1903, was prepared to encourage illegal acts, including bombing and arson, which led to sharp police retaliation, severe sentences, harsh and controversial treatment in prison, and even martyrdom.

Irish
difficulties

The issue that created the greatest difficulties, however, was one of the oldest: Ireland. In April 1912, armed with the new powers of the Parliament Act, Asquith introduced a new Home Rule bill. Conservative opposition to it was reinforced on this occasion by a popular Protestant movement in Ulster; and the new Conservative leader Bonar Law, who had replaced Balfour in 1911, gave his covert support to army mutineers in Ulster. No compromises were acceptable, and the struggle to settle the fate of Ireland was still in full spate when war broke out in August 1914. Most ominously for the Liberals, the Irish Home Rule supporters at Westminster were losing ground in southern Ireland, where in 1913 a militant working class movement entered into close alliance with the nationalist forces of Sinn Féin. Ireland was obviously on the brink of civil war.

The international crisis. The seeds of international war, sown long before 1900, were nourished between the resignation of Salisbury and August 1914. Two intricate systems of agreements and alliances—the Triple Alliance of Germany, Austria-Hungary, and Italy, and the Triple Entente of France, Russia, and Britain—faced each other in 1914. Both were backed by military and naval apparatus (Britain had been building a large fleet, and Richard Haldane had been reforming the army), and both could appeal to half-informed or uninformed public opinion. The result was that a war that was to break the continuities of history started as a popular war cheered by the crowds.

The Liberal government under Asquith faced a number of diplomatic crises from 1908 onward. Throughout a period of recurring tension, its foreign minister, Sir Edward Grey, often making decisions that were not discussed by the Cabinet as a whole, strengthened the understanding with France that had been initiated by his Conservative predecessor in 1903. An alliance had already been signed with Japan in 1902, and in 1907 agreements were reached with Russia. Meanwhile, naval rivalry with Germany familiarized Englishmen with the notion that if war came, it would be with Germany. The 1914 crisis began in the Balkans, an old storm centre, where the heir to the Austro-Hungarian throne was assassinated in June 1914. Soon Austria, backed by Germany, and Russia, supported by France, were arrayed against each other. The British Cabinet was divided, but after the Germans invaded Belgium on August 4, thereby violating a neutrality that Britain was committed by treaty to support, Britain and Germany went to war. Bonar Law pledged full support, as did John Redmond, the Irish leader at Westminster; only a few pacifists, radicals, and socialists stood on one side. Few foresaw a war of attrition or had any intimation of the profound economic, social, and political changes that lay in store. (As.B.)

The British Empire, 1815–1921

EXPANSION IN THE 19TH CENTURY

The Crimean War (1854–56) made little or no difference to the British Empire, and Britain had no other wars with European powers between 1815 and 1914. During this long period, British wars were either in India or in the colonial empire—notably in pacification programs in Africa—but also against the Maoris in New Zealand. The most serious conflicts were with the Boers (in 1881 and 1899–1902) and with the Mahdi (1884) in the Sudan. For the most part, 19th-century development was a matter of consolidating existing colonies and of extending into new areas, especially in Africa.

Further
spread of
British
influence

Colonial administration and policy. Administration and policy changed during the century from the haphazard arrangements inherited from the 17th and 18th centuries to the relatively sophisticated system characteristic of Joseph Chamberlain's tenure in the Colonial Office (1895–1900). That office, the distinct existence of which can be traced from 1801, was first an appendage of the Home Office and Board of Trade, and then linked with the secretary for war. By the 1850s, it had become a separate department with an increasing staff and something of a continuing policy; it was the means by which discipline and pressure were exerted on the colonial governments (though not upon the East India Company) when such action was considered necessary.

In the main, however, colonial governments were left largely to themselves. In the areas of new settlement in North America, South Africa, and the Pacific, local self-government was soon granted to the settlers. In the Caribbean, however, an opposite movement took place; the powers of most of the long-established legislative bodies were reduced and those of the governors increased so that these became "crown colonies," subject to direct rule. The reason for this was the condition of the islands after the repeal of slavery in 1833. Emancipation, combined with the effects of the withdrawal of the sugar monopoly in Britain after the triumph of Free Trade, made government in the interests of the tiny minority of planters no longer acceptable. When expansion took place in Africa and the Pacific, the crown colony system was again applied.

New Zealand and Oceania. In the Pacific, New Zealand became officially British in 1840, following pressure from the missionaries who were alarmed at the impact on the Christianized Maoris of the small collection of white rogues and vagabonds who had established themselves there. Systematic colonization followed rapidly. Land disputes between the settlers and the Maoris led to the Maori Wars of the 1840s and 1860s; but the eventual settlement satisfied both sides, and British troops were withdrawn. Late in the century British control was extended to other islands in the Pacific—often again because of missionary pressure and sometimes because of international rivalry. Fiji was ceded in 1874. A British High Commission for the Western Pacific Islands was established in 1877. A protectorate was declared over Papua in 1884, following pressure from Queensland, and over Tonga in 1900. Other groups of islands were also taken over. Some of these acquisitions later became the responsibility of Australia and New Zealand.

Asia. The situation in 19th-century India was one of slow but constant extension, first of the East India Company's territory, and then, after the replacement of the company's authority by that of the crown following the Indian Mutiny (1857), of the Indian Empire. The greatest acquisition was that of Burma, completed in 1886; but the conquest of the Punjab (1849) and of British Baluchistan (1854–76) provided substantial territory in the Indian subcontinent itself. The importance of a new route to India, after the opening of the Suez Canal, was signified by the growth of Aden (originally captured by the East India Company in 1839), by a protectorate in Somaliland, and by the extension of British influence among the sheikhdoms of southern Arabia and the Persian Gulf. Cyprus—a link, like Gibraltar and Malta, in the chain of communication with India through the Mediterranean— was occupied by treaty with the Ottoman Empire in 1878.

British influence in the Far East expanded with the development of the Straits Settlements and the federated Malay states. In the 1880s Britain became established in Borneo, with a chartered company at work in British North Borneo and protectorates over Brunei and Sarawak. Hong Kong island became British in 1841, and adjacent territories on the Chinese mainland were acquired in 1860 and 1896. The British also obtained special rights in Shanghai, another great trading port through which Britain's "informal empire" in China operated; this was not a matter of sovereignty, however, and mention of it in the context of the British Empire, while realistic in a sense, is more doubtful in legal terms.

Africa. The greatest development of 19th-century British imperial power took place in Africa. In Egypt, Britain was the acknowledged ruling force from 1882 onward, following a naval bombardment of Alexandria; in The Sudan, formerly a nominal Egyptian province, British control was exercised under the guise of an Anglo–Egyptian joint administration established in 1899. The idea that British power might extend "from the Cape to Cairo" fascinated many people in Britain in the 1880s and '90s— a period of great enthusiasm for the empire, marked by Queen Victoria's two jubilees, by colonial conferences, by the re-establishment of chartered companies to seek out new areas of opportunity, and by mining discoveries and wars in South Africa. On the western coast the Royal Niger Company began the extension of British influence in Nigeria. The Imperial British East Africa Company operated in what are now Kenya and Uganda, and the British South Africa Company in the areas now called Rhodesia, Zambia, and Malawi. Again, missionary influence was strong in the eventual transfer of some of these territories to the crown.

After the South African War (Boer War, 1899–1902), British influence spread northward from the Cape. Natal had become British in 1843. The Orange Free State and the Transvaal swayed back and forth between independence and British suzerainty, but they were annexed after the South African War. Meanwhile, the activities of the British South Africa Company, north of the Transvaal, had ensured a British presence in Southern and Northern Rhodesia. South Africa was the principal source of argument between imperialists and anti-imperialists. To many, British policies there epitomized the misuse of imperial power.

For better or worse, the spread of the British Empire had been so great during the 19th century that it comprised nearly a quarter of the land surface and included more than a quarter of the population of the world. The term empire, however, was obviously used rather for convenience than in any sense equivalent to the older or despotic empires of history. This was due to the high degrees of self-government obtained by the white-dominated colonies.

GROWTH OF SELF-GOVERNMENT
IN THE COLONIES AND DOMINIONS

The beginnings of the self-government movement probably lie with Lord Durham's *Report on the Affairs of British North America* (1839). Following minor rebellions in both Upper Canada (Ontario) and Lower Canada (Quebec), John George Lambton, 1st earl of Durham, was sent out as governor general to investigate. Durham's report recommended that responsible government (*i.e.*, the acceptance of the advice of local ministers by governors) be granted to the two Canadas, which should be merged in one. The merger took place immediately, but Durham's advice on responsible government was not accepted until put into effect by his son-in-law Lord Elgin, governor general in 1847. Thereafter, the pattern was applied to other Canadian provinces and to the Australian colonies. The British government's willingness to let the colonies of settlement manage their own affairs was very much in line with its contemporary disavowal of the mercantilist philosophy and with its withdrawal of colonial privileges in the British market.

New South Wales, Tasmania, South Australia, and Victoria had responsible government by the end of 1855, having been invited to draw up their own constitutions by the Australian Colonies Government Act of 1850. Queensland followed in 1859. Western Australia had to wait until 1890. In New Zealand and South Africa, the position of the local colonists was not so strong as in Canada and Australia because in both cases they were still dependent on British troops for protection against natives; moreover, the existence of large native populations in both was an argument used by the Colonial Office (often subject to humanitarian pressure in London) against a too rapid advance toward local autonomy. New Zealand obtained responsible government in all but native matters in 1856; by 1870, when the British troops went home after the Maori Wars, even these reservations had disappeared, and the local settlers were in full charge of the country's affairs. The Cape Colony achieved responsible government in 1872, and Natal in 1893.

Meanwhile, British North America experienced further development in self-government. The union of Upper and Lower Canada developed many stresses by the 1860s. In addition, the maritime colonies were seeking new forms of association with one another and with Upper and Lower Canada. The result, after local conferences, was the British North America Act of 1867, whereby Ontario, Quebec, New Brunswick, and Nova Scotia were brought together in a confederation known as the Dominion of Canada. Manitoba joined in 1870, British Columbia in 1871, and Prince Edward Island in 1873. The continuing development of the prairies brought in Alberta and Saskatchewan in 1905. Of the British North American colonies, this left only Newfoundland outside the confederation—a situation finally adjusted by Newfoundland's entrance in 1949.

The Australian colonies formed a federation in 1901. There was a union of the South African colonies in 1910. In the latter, the defeated Transvaal and Orange Free State were added to the Cape and Natal. By means of these arrangements, each of the three countries (including Canada) obtained a national government that operated in full control of its own affairs, as did that of New Zealand. Britain retained minor powers of veto, which amounted to very little. Its influence lay in its provision of naval defense and its position as a buyer of local products and an investor in local enterprises. In 1907 the countries' special position was recognized by their designation as "dominions," not colonies; by the creation of a special Dominions division in the Colonial Office; and by the regular institution of an Imperial Conference, which they, with Newfoundland, would attend.

Growth of national governments

In World War I, the contribution of the dominions was so substantial that they were given representation in an "imperial cabinet" that, while it did not survive the war, emphasized the degree of autonomy they had attained. At the peace settlement some of the dominions acquired mandatory responsibilities, and all became members of the League of Nations. In the 1920s Canada, South Africa, and the Irish Free State (which had been given the status of a dominion in 1921) applied pressure for a clearer definition of dominion status.   (J.D.B.M./Ed.)

Britain from 1914 to 1945

WORLD WAR I

In the political and constitutional areas, the war witnessed many significant modifications in parliamentary and administrative practices required for transforming democratic processes designed for peace into an efficient machine for waging war. Thus, to avoid partisan division on war issues, no elections were held during the war—the general election, provided by law at the latest in 1915, was postponed by parliamentary resolution. There were, nevertheless, shifts in power. The first formal change came in May 1915, when the Liberal government under Asquith, weakened by criticism of the War Office and the munitions shortage and suffering from controversy over strategy between Churchill at the Admiralty and John Fisher, the first sea lord, was reorganized as a "Coalition" government, including Conservatives and one Labourite.

Wartime govern-ment

But continued discontent in Parliament over the conduct of the war, distrust of Asquith's capacity as a war leader, and the weakening of his control over the Cabinet forced his hand in December 1916, and he was replaced as prime minister by David Lloyd George. Political power became largely concentrated in the War Cabinet of five, with parliamentary support taken for granted. As political processes, these changes were hardly revolutionary—well before 1914, party organization controlling the electorate and tighter discipline within parliamentary parties were elevating the roles of prime minister and Cabinet.

While intervention of the state in economic and social questions had been increasing since the late Victorian era and accelerated after 1906, during 1914–18 governmental controls were greatly expanded in marshalling resources for the war effort. DORA (Defence of the Realm Acts), though usually administered with caution and discretion, authorized regulations "for public safety and defence," control of armament plants, the requisitioning of factories, and the control of production and distribution. But authority was exercised through advisory commissions and was usually limited to establishing priorities. In munitions, coal, and railroads, controls came closest to outright government ownership. Various measures encouraged home food production and regulated prices and wages, but rationing of foodstuffs came only in 1918, and to a limited degree.

The prolongation of the war beyond all initial expectations complicated these problems and added to them. When voluntary enlistment proved insufficient to replace the thinning ranks of the armed forces, after long debate, in May 1916, came military conscription of all males between 18 and 41—the first such in English history. Labour unrest, at a peak at the outbreak of the war and further aroused by fears of the consequences of a war economy, was a constant concern, with serious strikes and stoppages in 1917 and 1918, but government and industry managed to maintain, without compulsion, a fairly satisfactory degree of order. In all ranks of society the tragedy of long casualty lists (of 6,000,000 in uniform from the United Kingdom some 750,000 lost their lives and 1,700,000 others were wounded) made heavy inroads on national morale. With the Lloyd George government a policy of "war to the finish" terminated any prospects for an early end to the war by negotiation, and in some circles, particularly the literary and the intellectual, patriotic support of the war effort turned to one of horror and despair at man's inhumanity to man.

Deteriora-tion of morale

Public morale, however, was periodically fortified by talk of reconstruction, social reform, "a better world." There were indeed winds of change during the war. What peace

had not secured for women, the war did: women's suffrage in 1918, and inevitably so because of their role in the war—in the auxiliaries of the armed forces, in the nurses corps, and particularly in industry—in offices, in shops, on the farms, on trams and buses. Because of the heavy reliance on home production of foodstuffs, the status of the farmer and the agricultural labourer attained a respectability unknown for two generations. In general, class lines, so pronounced in Victorian and Edwardian days, were becoming blurred, particularly in matters of dress. Economic inequalities were lessened. There was a sharp decline in servant keeping. A salaried and professional "middle class" grew apace, and the traditional cleavage between landowners and men of commerce disappeared for good. Nonetheless, distinct class lines remained in education, in accent, in class consciousness, and in life style generally.

Lloyd George, always sensitive to public opinion, took the lead in establishing by statute the Ministry of Reconstruction in 1917; investigations of industry, public health, transport, and housing were soon underway. An education act set the school-leaving age at 14, envisioned raising it to 15, and provided for part-time schooling until 16.

The power structure that waged and won the war began as a Liberal government in 1914 and ended as a Coalition dominated by Conservatives, though still under the leadership of a Liberal, Lloyd George. The split in 1916 between those Liberals supporting Asquith and those supporting Lloyd George was widened in May 1918 by Asquith's motion for a committee of inquiry in the Commons to investigate divergent statements of the Prime Minister and the director of military operations in the War Office over the strength of the army. Asquith's motion was defeated, with 100 Liberals voting for his motion and 71 against. But even more important, the composition of the constituencies of the major parties was uncertain, as well as the issues that would divide them after the war.

One matter became increasingly clear. The Labour Party under the leadership of J. Ramsay MacDonald and Arthur Henderson, though still small in numbers in the Commons, was becoming a stronger voice for social democracy. Labour, though somewhat divided by issues of war and peace, managed to maintain its solidarity as a parliamentary party, while moving to the left in social and economic matters. By 1918 Labour had established unity on certain essentials: (1) reorganization of its structure to provide for active membership through individuals, as well as through trade unions and socialist societies; (2) a restatement of purpose in socialist terms—"a new social order based . . . on deliberately planned cooperation in production and distribution for the benefit of all who participate by hand or brain"; (3) a decision to leave the Coalition at the end of the war and contest the next general election as an independent party.

Growth of the Labour Party

BETWEEN THE WARS

Aftermath of the war (1918–24). World War I ended November 11, 1918. England's mood was one of profound relief and a sense of triumph but also one of optimism for the future. It was perhaps unfortunate that the general election came so promptly (polling day was December 14)—unfortunate in its revival of party bitterness, revelation of personal animosities, and demands for revenge against Germany. But an immediate election was essential; the existing Parliament had been elected in 1910. In the campaign the significant factor was Lloyd George's decision to maintain the Coalition with both Conservative and Liberal support and the arrangement that no Conservative candidate would oppose a Liberal pledged to the Coalition. This divided the Liberal vote, rendering it unlikely that anything approaching proportional representation would result. The main issue was this: should Lloyd George and the Coalition continue? The result was their stunning triumph with some 478 seats out of 707, though the popular vote for their candidates was slightly in excess of their opponents. Asquith Liberals were crushed and Labour emerged, with 59 seats, as the official opposition.

The Coalition continued in power until October 1922. Its tasks and those of the British people were formidable:

to negotiate a durable peace mindful of British interests; to restore a peacetime economy favourable to British production and world trade; to absorb the returning armed forces in a changing economy and society; and to solve the problem of Irish national aspirations. These problems were compounded by a conflict of generations (especially between those returning from the trenches and the high seas, and their elders), by an almost irrational desire to forget the war and return to "normalcy," and, thus, by a breakdown of morale.

So it was that the peace treaty negotiated at Versailles was debated in England in a partisan spirit and increased the difficulty of the government in clarifying and achieving policies in the national interest: limited disarmament designed to slow down the arms race; diplomacy by negotiation to relieve international tension; general rehabilitation of Germany. In these years, in spite of some 23 international conferences, questions of disarmament and German reparations seemed without solution.

The postwar economy

As to the economy, no one seemed prepared for the situation that developed. A brief postwar boom rather encouraged the business world in its inclination to return to prewar policies and methods: free trade abroad and laissez-faire at home; restoration of the gold standard, which had been temporarily suspended in 1919; reduction of wages and other costs of production, if necessary to meet foreign competition. But when European markets were opened to the expanding economies of the United States and Asia, Britain suffered a decided decline in production and foreign trade relative to its prewar status. The chief consequence was an alarming rise in unemployment—reaching, in July 1921, 22.4 percent of all insured workers (who comprised nearly the entire work force).

Politics, influenced by uncertainties at home and abroad, tended to become motivated by fear—fear of the other side—and to polarize political groups. A new "Right" sought to erase the old distinction between Liberal and Conservative and to advocate a limited role of the state in society and the economy, to stabilize Europe as a British market, to keep a safe distance from Russia, and to strengthen imperial ties. The "Left," composed of Labour and dissident Liberals, urged nationalization of key industries and government housing, supported collective security and disarmament, encouraged ties with Russia, and was increasingly skeptical about the empire.

Resignation of Lloyd George

The Lloyd George government met the crisis in the coal industry with temporary subsidies, extended unemployment insurance, and established the Irish Free State. But the Coalition steadily weakened; in October 1922 Conservatives voted their independence and Lloyd George resigned. There followed three governments in three years. The first, a Conservative government under Bonar Law, sought to capitalize on the cry for "tranquility"; Law's serious illness soon brought about his replacement (May 1923) not by Lord Curzon, his logical successor, but by Stanley Baldwin, a member of the cabinet only since 1921. He successfully reunited the Conservative Party but failed in his attempt to get party and national support for a protective tariff. As a result of the general election of December 1923, Labour, with 191 seats in the Commons, formed with Liberal support the first Labour government in British history. In its short rule of ten months the only significant change in domestic policy was in legislation establishing new procedures for government housing. MacDonald, foreign minister as well as prime minister, was more active abroad, where he helped set in motion the Dawes Plan for German reparations, which brought evacuation of the Ruhr. Soviet Russia was recognized. But it was its policy toward Russia, including matters of trade, that lost Labour Liberal support; and in the general election of October 1924 Stanley Baldwin and the Conservatives returned to office with 48 percent of the popular poll and 419 seats in the Commons. Labour more than held its own in the popular vote, but the Liberals collapsed, polling but 18 percent of the vote.

Stanley Baldwin as prime minister

Stability and crisis (1924–31). It was perhaps logical that Stanley Baldwin was prime minister, 1924–29. He was fairly typical of Britishers of the 1920s—plain-spoken, rather modest in manner, honest, patient. He did not profess to know all the answers and was committed to no policy. But he did seek stability, tranquility, peace of mind, good will among men; in such an atmosphere, he insisted, problems would find solutions. So it was, to a degree. By mutual consent among parties British armaments were drastically reduced. Austen Chamberlain, foreign secretary, received good marks for his part in deliberations leading to the Pact of Locarno (1925), providing for arbitration of disputes in western Europe. There was little dissent to the creation of the British Broadcasting Corporation as a monopoly in 1926. National health insurance, unemployment insurance—these, in principle, ceased to divide the nation. Under Neville Chamberlain at the Ministry of Health, more social legislation was enacted than by either the Labour government that had preceded or the one that followed. This included implementation of Chamberlain's Housing Act of 1923, with over 400,000 new dwellings, and the Local Government Act of 1929, which abolished the Boards of Guardians.

In the economy, production went beyond prewar figures and unemployment levelled off at 10 percent. But such favourable signs were illusory; the significant fact was that Britain lagged behind the rest of the industrial world—by 1929 the volume of exports was still below the 1913 figure, and the annual value of exports declined after the return to the gold standard in 1925. That problems of production and of labour were out of control was evident in the General Strike of 1926. This came from the crisis in coal—the largest single industry—where royal commissions produced but temporary measures to deal with rising costs of production. An end to governmental subsidies supplementing wages led to the owners' insistence on wage reductions. Rejection of the new wage scale by the Miners' Federation of Great Britain brought lockout notices, closing down the mines on May 1, 1926. An overwhelming vote of unions affiliated with the national Trades Union Congress (TUC) approved a general strike in support of the miners. In actuality, the General Strike affected about 70 percent of union members and has been aptly described as "a strike under wraps." Most of the strikers had served in the armed forces during the war, and few of them had revolutionary intent. The strike was conducted with little violence and no loss of life. The government's attitude, however, was one of firmness; it declared the strike "unconstitutional" and "illegal" and soon persuaded the general council of the TUC to accept revision of the wage scale after reorganization of the industry. The strike ended May 12, and Baldwin broadcast a message calling for a general reconciliation. It was his greatest hour.

The General Strike of 1926

The aftermath of the strike was less successful. The government took no action to bring about reorganization of the coal industry and passed in 1927 a statute that declared sympathetic strikes illegal. Furthermore, the Baldwin government produced no program for dealing with general unemployment and did nothing to revitalize other basic industries such as steel and textiles or to assist agriculture, again in difficulties. Treasury economies stalled advances in secondary education. In foreign policy nothing was done to implement the spirit of Locarno. In imperial affairs, largely due to L.S. Amery at the Colonial Office, policy was more progressive. The Imperial Conference of 1926 adopted Balfour's report calling for abrogation of all British legislative control in the dominions—this became the Statute of Westminster in 1931. In 1927 was created the Simon Commission to review the political situation in India since 1919, when dyarchy had been adopted.

In the general election of May 1929, Labour profited by the inaction of the Baldwin government in many areas and emerged with a plurality in Parliament. The Liberals, now under Lloyd George, who had replaced Asquith as party leader in 1926, made a gigantic effort in support of state action to solve the problems of the economy and finished respectably with 23 percent of the popular vote and 59 seats. Nevertheless, they came in a poor third.

MacDonald's government

MacDonald formed a moderate Labour Cabinet the major accomplishments of which were again in foreign affairs. Philip Snowden, chancellor of the exchequer, helped implement the Young Plan for German payment of reparations; Arthur Henderson, foreign secretary, presided over the commission at The Hague that brought allied evacuation from the Rhineland. Thanks in large part to MacDonald himself, progress was made on naval reduction at the London Naval Conference in 1930. The Round Table Conference was a step toward a federated India. But the record in domestic affairs was found "meagre" by the usually objective British periodical *The Economist*. The Great Depression compounded all of England's problems. Escalating unemployment (23 percent of the insured workers by mid-1931) brought such demands on the Unemployment Insurance Fund that a budgetary and financial crisis threatened the country's international credit. Proposals for drastic cuts in unemployment insurance and other social services divided the Cabinet, and MacDonald resigned in August 1931. Neither Baldwin nor Sir Herbert Samuel (now Liberal leader) were anxious to assume responsibility alone, and MacDonald was persuaded to form a coalition, the so-called National Government (August 24).

The National Government: crisis and recovery (1931–39). The necessary financial credits were secured abroad, and the National Government, formed to deal with an emergency, was overwhelmingly confirmed in office in the general election in October 1931. The Parliamentary Labour Party had, however, repudiated MacDonald and fought the election independently; the result was disastrous—every former cabinet member save one was defeated, and only 52 Labourites were returned. In the election, the National Government made a virtue of the division of opinion in its ranks—voters were merely asked to support "Safety and the Union Jack." Whether diversity of opinion could produce action was soon tested. To meet the problems of finance and trade, the government pushed through a general protective tariff—the Liberal and Labour free traders in the Cabinet were allowed to "differ" both in the debate and in the poll. But the extension of the tariff to imperial preference brought resignation of the free traders.

Continued effects of depression

As to economic matters in general, the Depression continued until 1933 (the drop in production from 1929 to 1932 was 16 percent), with substantial recovery thereafter (by 1937 production was 50 percent above that of 1932). British industry turned to the home market with housing (average annual construction of 270,000 houses) and new industries—automobiles, electrical appliances, industrial chemistry. Recovery, however, was only in relation to the 1920s, for the United Kingdom's share in world trade continued to decline. Unemployment, though reduced, was concentrated in certain areas and trades. The very significant Unemployment Act of 1934 reorganized the system of relief, and for the working classes life was, in general, somewhat better in the 1930s than in the 1920s.

In June 1935 Baldwin replaced MacDonald as prime minister. And a few months later a general election confirmed the National Government, but with considerable gains for Labour. George Lansbury, Labour leader since 1931, but now at odds with his party on foreign policy, resigned; Clement Attlee, who had proved himself as a parliamentarian, became Labour leader. In domestic affairs the most important episode for Baldwin was the abdication crisis. The death of George V in January 1936 led to the succession of Edward VIII. For many months, few outside official circles knew of his friendship with an American-born lady, Mrs. Simpson, already twice married and once divorced. Her second divorce was granted in October. The government, with Labour support, opposed her marriage to the King and held firm against a "King's Party" forming around a strange nucleus including Winston Churchill, Sir Oswald Mosley, and George Bernard Shaw. In a message to Parliament (December 10), Edward VIII abdicated and his brother was proclaimed King George VI. But it soon became clear that the institution of monarchy had not suffered.

Abdication of Edward VIII

After the coronation of George VI in May 1937, Baldwin was replaced as prime minister by Neville Chamberlain, whose administration was largely concerned with meeting the social and economic problems of the late 1930s. The 1930s as a whole were preoccupied with "planning." PEP (Political and Economic Planning) was a nonpartisan agency for research—beginning in 1933

a series of significant reports dealt with iron and steel, cotton, coal, international trade, public health, housing, the press, and other areas of public concern. *Plan or No Plan* (1934), by Barbara Wootton of London University, urged a planned economy. *Reconstruction: A Plan for a National Policy* (1933) and *The Middle Way* (1938), by Harold Macmillan, a Conservative and a future prime minister, urged a minimum wage and partial nationalization of industry. B. Seebohm Rowntree, studying poverty in the city of York, found that 19 percent of the population was existing on a substandard diet. The distribution of national income came in for careful study and led to scholarly studies of unemployment and "the depressed areas." Implementation of some of the ideas did not have to wait. Some 120 railway companies were amalgamated into four systems. The Central Electricity Board purchased current and distributed it through "a grid"—of incalculable importance when war came. With the creation of the Exchange Equalization Fund (1932), the Bank of England was all but nationalized, and the nationalization of coal royalties in 1938 was a long step toward nationalization of that industry. As to steel, a committee from the industry and a committee from the government determined prices and controlled production. Altogether, "nationalization" was well under way before World War II.

Beginning of nationalization

Foreign policy and appeasement. In July 1931 each of the party leaders paid pious tribute to the League of Nations, to disarmament, and to the renunciation of war. But statesmanship did not bridge the gap between piety and circumstance. The carefully prepared World Disarmament Conference that convened at Geneva in February 1932 proved a disappointment. Any decisive action to break the deadlock of French and German demands depended on a military commitment that Britain refused to give. On questions of war and peace, the climate of thought in England was negative. A vague pacifism did not consider how peace was to be maintained. Collective security through the League of Nations was generally supported—as long as no obligations were incurred. This seemed to be the purport of the so-called Peace Ballot of 1934, a house-to-house canvass organized by the League of Nations Union, in which 40 percent of those polled favoured disarmament.

In his successful election campaign of 1935, Baldwin advocated collective action by the League in the border dispute between Italy and Abyssinia but added that war was not anticipated. But while government spokesmen were endorsing the League, Sir Samuel Hoare and Pierre Laval, foreign ministers for England and France, were drafting in private the proposal to settle the dispute by handing over half of Abyssinia to Italy. Its disclosure (December 9) brought a flood of protest in the press, the pulpit, and the electorate that forced the government to repudiate the agreement. Hoare resigned, to be succeeded by Anthony Eden. But there was still no will to impose sanctions on Italy, which completed without interference the conquest of Abyssinia.

The year 1936 was one of crisis. There was the abdication at home, and abroad the unfolding of Nazi policy in Europe and the outbreak of the Spanish Civil War. The usually placid *Annual Register* described British policy as hesitant, indecisive, apologetic, content to drift. The German military occupation of the Rhineland (March 1936) in violation of Versailles was accepted by the British government, with little dissent from Labour, as a *fait accompli;* few favoured sanctions against Germany and many thought Germany was justified. This was the beginning of appeasement.

The Spanish Civil War

British policy toward Spain in the civil war between the Loyalists to the Republic and the "nationalist rebels" led by Francisco Franco was hardly more forthright. Britain was the chief sponsor of "nonintervention" by the powers, which was something of a farce since Fascist Italy and Nazi Germany sent military aid to the rebels, and the Soviet Union the same, on smaller scale, to the Republic. In actuality, Britain did take sides—the government sympathized with the rebels, the Labour opposition with the Loyalists. But in public opinion generally, cleavage cut across party lines. In general, the Spanish Civil War marked the end of pacifism as a fashionable attitude.

Neville Chamberlain, as prime minister, dominated foreign policy from May 1937; the subordinate role assigned the Foreign Office contributed to Eden's resignation early in 1938. Policy, determined by Chamberlain and a few advisers, put little faith in collective security and sought direct negotiation with Hitler and Mussolini—compromise and appeasement where necessary—to reduce tensions that might lead to war. In an important interview in November 1937 Lord Halifax told Hitler that Britain would not oppose boundary changes in central Europe if they came by "peaceful evolution." But Chamberlain was not without a strategy of his own: he would settle differences with Mussolini and thus strengthen his hand against Hitler.

Munich conference

But in the event, negotiation tempered by appeasement merely brought a succession of crises. In March 1938 Austria was absorbed into the German *Reich*. In August 1938 the "Runciman mission" failed in its attempt to mediate between Germany and Czechoslovakia over the status of German-speaking Sudetenland, a part of Czechoslovakia. In September, at Munich, Chamberlain, along with the French premier Édouard Daladier, Mussolini, and Hitler, agreed to the cession of the Sudetenland to Germany but accompanied with a guarantee of the integrity of the remainder of Czechoslovakia. When Chamberlain returned to London he proclaimed that the agreement meant "peace for our time." Six months later, however, the Nazis invaded Czechoslovakia and seized control. Now at last Chamberlain denounced Hitler; rearmament was stepped up and policy reversed. Guarantees of support were given to Poland, Romania, and Greece, but Chamberlain's patient efforts to include the Soviet Union in the security system ended abruptly with the signing (August 23) of the German-Soviet Nonaggression Pact. Germany invaded Poland on September 1, and when an ultimatum to Germany calling for a cessation of hostilities went unanswered, Chamberlain broadcast to the nation, Sunday morning, September 3, that Britain was at war.

WORLD WAR II

World War II was "total war" and, as such, was in many ways a conflict in which the civilian and the man in uniform shared dangers and hardships in common. Air raid warnings began the Battle of London on the first day of the war. Two days before, on September 1, began the evacuation from danger zones, and in three days 1,473,000 persons were relocated. Two million others had already removed themselves privately, some to the country, some to the dominions, others to the United States. Schooling for a time was demoralized, and it is estimated that by the following January 1,000,000 children had not yet been placed in classrooms. Construction began at once on a program of 2,500,000 outdoor household steel shelters designed to protect 10,000,000 persons against air attack. They sold for £5 but were distributed free to low-income families.

Chamberlain broadened his government to include Winston Churchill at his old post in the Admiralty and also Anthony Eden. Hitler's Polish campaign quickly over in September, there followed six months of the "Phony War," with land operations almost at a standstill and national morale in Britain diminished. The British consoled themselves with the conviction that if it were to be an endurance contest control of the seas and blockade of Germany would eventually bring victory. But any complacency was suddenly jolted in April 1940 by the German invasion of Denmark and Norway; the collapse of Norway led to an angry Commons' debate in which some 100 Conservatives refused continued support of Chamberlain, who forthwith resigned (May 10). King George was inclined to Halifax as prime minister, but on Chamberlain's advice he sent for Churchill, who formed a coalition government, with a five-member war cabinet including the Labour leader, Attlee, who became in effect leader of the Commons. Another key appointment was that of Ernest Bevin, a trade union official, as minister of labour and national service. An inspired Churchill led the country in the "miracle of

The wartime government

Dunkirk"; at the end of May, 338,000 Allied troops were evacuated to Britain after the Germans had smashed their way to the French coast. But this episode was soon overshadowed by the Battle of Britain in August and September 1940—the most critical period of the war. Germany threatened invasion, and for that to succeed it must first cripple British defenses—air fields, radar stations, London docks—and attain air supremacy. But the Royal Air Force stood up against all attacks and by September 15 was having the better of it. Some of the most stirring narratives of the war relate the experience of "the Blitz." For a time in the metropolitan area one out of every seven was sleeping in a public shelter—a basement, a railway arch, a "tube" station. From July to December 1940 civilian casualties in air raids numbered 23,000 dead—more than in the armed forces.

The war at home remained grim in the spring of 1941 with aerial attacks on Plymouth (600 killed in five days), in Liverpool (death toll of 1,900 in a week), in London (1,400 deaths in two days and the destruction of the chamber of the Commons), and elsewhere. But 1941 was also the year in which Britain found the answer to the manpower problem in the Registration for Employment Order, which eventually mobilized into the services or into industry 94 percent of all males between the ages of 14 and 64. And in 1941 came "lend-lease" for war supplies from the United States, the Nazi invasion of the Soviet Union, and the Japanese attack on Pearl Harbor. The Grand Alliance was formed, and by the end of 1942—with allied landings in North Africa, the rout of the Germans in Libya, and the counterattack against the Germans in Russia—Churchill could speak of "the end of the beginning."

By 1943 it was clear that the war was bringing change at home. World War II was undoubtedly the most socially levelling experience in modern English history—in the risks of war, in food and shelter, in clothing and amusement, and to a degree in taxation. "Planning," in vogue in the 1930s, now became more systematically applied, for war, of course, but also for peace. Commissions drafted proposals for the use of land in town and country. And the Beveridge Report, December 1942 (Sir William Beveridge was chairman of an interdepartmental committee), outlined a program of social insurance embracing in theory all persons but in application classified according to need, with a "national minimum" of income guaranteed to all. Impressive as it was, the report was merely "welcomed" and not endorsed by the Commons and had to await the end of the war for serious consideration. The most significant piece of legislation not directly associated with the war effort was the Education Act of 1944—for the most part the work of R.A. Butler—which created the Ministry of Education with effective power for developing a national educational policy, raised the school-leaving age (after the war) to 15, and provided for a full range of educational services—primary, secondary, and "further" without fees.

The Beveridge Report

Even as the war was approaching its end, civilians still confronted grave danger. In June 1944, soon after the Allied invasion of Normandy, the first of the "flying bombs"—the V-1s—fell on England; there were nearly 5,500 dead from this weapon by September. And then came the rockets, the V-2s. When the conflict ended September 2, 1945, one day short of six years, civilian casualties numbered about 60,000. Of the armed forces of the United Kingdom, 300,000 lost their lives. And Britain lost one-fourth of its national wealth.   (A.F.H.)

Britain since 1945

THE DECLINE OF THE BRITISH EMPIRE

The Commonwealth. The Imperial Conference of 1926, held in London, had taken account of the mounting nationalist aspirations of the British dominions and territories and produced a milestone in the evolution of the Commonwealth: the report of the Inter-Imperial Relations Committee, known as the Balfour Report. This document formally recognized that Great Britain and the dominions were "autonomous communities within the British Empire, equal in status, in no way subordinate one to another

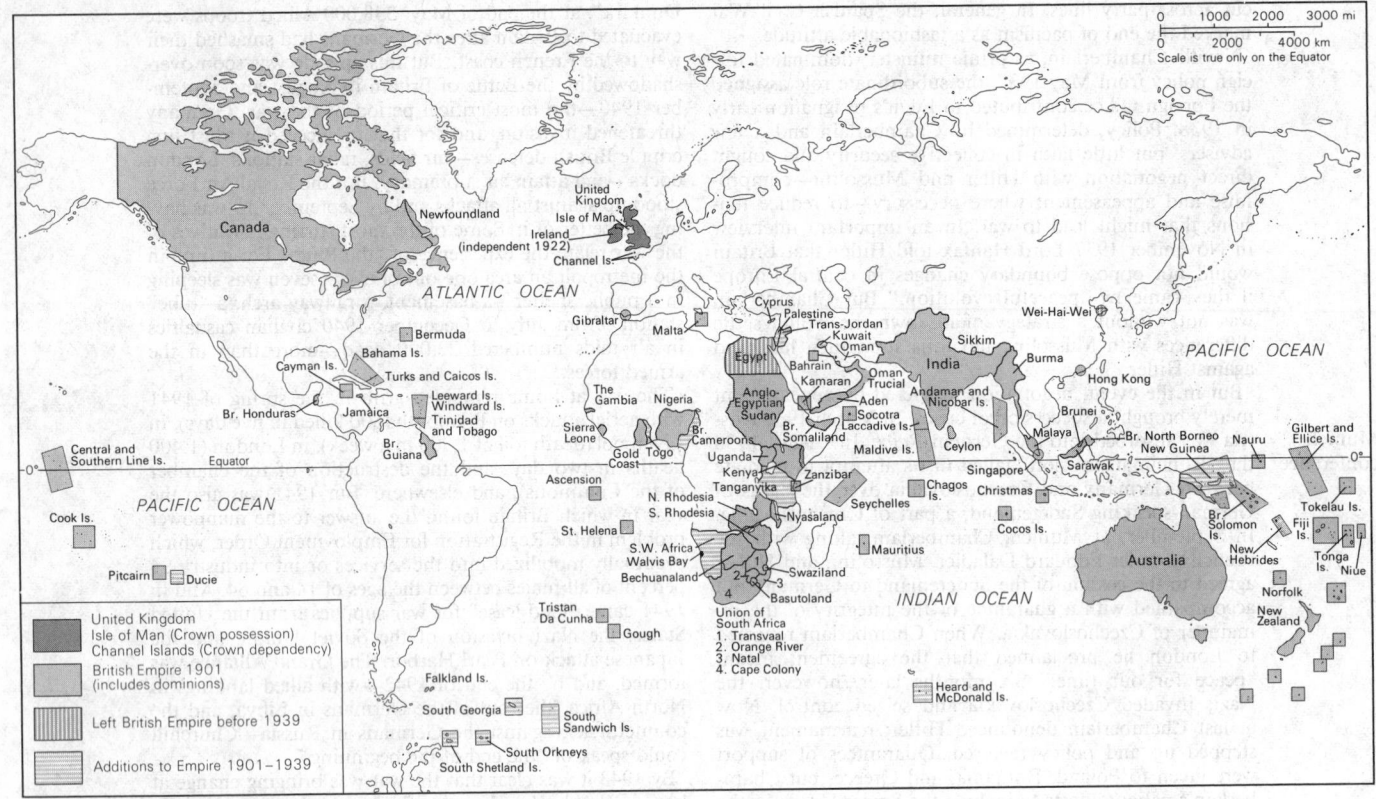

The British Empire, 1901 and 1939.

in any aspect of their external or domestic affairs, though united by a common allegiance to the Crown and freely associated as members of the British Commonwealth of Nations." Parliament passed the Statute of Westminster in 1931, which embodied this declaration in a self-denying ordinance, whereby legislation concerning the dominions would be enacted only with their consent.

The 1926 definition of dominion status, while immediately satisfying to those who had pressed for it, left a number of questions unanswered: Could a dominion secede from the Commonwealth? Did "common allegiance" mean a single crown, or was the crown divisible? Could and should there be more than one foreign policy in the Commonwealth? Could one dominion be at peace while others were at war? These questions were much discussed in the 1930s; they were answered effectively in World War II, when Canada and South Africa made separate, delayed declarations of war, and Ireland remained neutral. As in World War I, there was considerable support for Britain's war effort from the belligerent dominions, though the dispersed nature of the war—especially its Pacific aspect—led to more active diplomacy by some of them. When the war ended, their independence was no longer in question.

India's independence.   At this stage (1945), dominion status still applied only to settler communities. For some time, however, the possibility of India's achieving dominion status had been actively canvassed. India was a special case within the British Empire; by title an empire in its own right, it had a viceroy, a separate secretary of state in London, its own army, and even, to a certain degree, its own foreign policy. Its size alone made it unique—the most notable of Britain's possessions. Since the beginning of the century, however, there had been agitation for greater local autonomy, even though India's communal divisions made this hard for many Englishmen to envisage.

Indian contributions in World War I had led to reforms in 1919, whereby British India was governed under a system called "dyarchy," which gave a good deal of experience to provincial legislatures but stopped far short of self-government. The viceroy still held the keys of power. In the 1920s and '30s, the Indian National Congress, led by Mahatma Gandhi and Jawaharlal Nehru, agitated for independence. The exigencies of World War II led to explicit British promises of dominion status; this entailed

splitting the formerly undivided India into two dominions—India and Pakistan—when the move took place in 1947. Ceylon and Burma also obtained their independence at this time, but Burma chose independence outside the Commonwealth.

Changes in Commonwealth relations.   The appearance of Asian dominions led to changes of tone and character in the Commonwealth of Nations. No longer was its British quality stressed; even the adjective British was tacitly dropped by British spokesmen when they referred to it. The large-scale Imperial Conferences of the interwar years, intended to display imperial unity, gave way to briefer and more intimate gatherings of prime ministers. The Dominions Office, which had been detached from the Colonial Office in 1925, was amalgamated with the India Office to form a Commonwealth Relations Office with its own secretary of state. The network of diplomatic posts within the Commonwealth grew rapidly, under high commissioners with the status of ambassadors; but the previous assumption of a common foreign policy disappeared. Consultation, not unity, was assumed to be the essence of the Commonwealth tie.

This loosening of the previous connections was taken a stage further in 1949, when India stated its wish to assume the status of a republic but to remain within the Commonwealth. The other members gave approval. The crown thus became an institution applicable to individual Commonwealth countries, which remained realms, but not to the Commonwealth as a whole. Instead, the British monarch, in his or her person, was recognized as "Head of the Commonwealth," a ceremonial position without functions.

The rush toward independence.   In the 1950s the remaining British colonies in Africa, Asia, the Caribbean, and the Mediterranean moved at varying speeds toward further self-government. The process was at first hesitant, but it gained speed as international pressure mounted (notably at the United Nations), as the notion of independence spread in the colonies themselves, and as the British public, no longer actively imperial in its sentiments, accepted the idea of independence as a foregone conclusion. The British political parties no longer argued about whether independence should be granted or not, but about its pace and structure. In some cases—such as Aden, Singapore, Cyprus, and Malta—strategic considerations made independence difficult to contemplate at first; but these concerns were overcome either by special arrangements after independence or by the abandonment of the strategic assumptions that had previously been held. In such other cases as The Gambia and the former High Commission territories of southern Africa (Basutoland, Bechuanaland, and Swaziland), smallness of size and poverty of resources seemed at first to prevent independence; but these considerations, too, were displaced. The experiences of other European colonial powers and the pressure of American opinion also hastened the policy of independence. In nearly all cases, except those in which the complex politics of the Middle East made it impossible (The Sudan, Somaliland, South Arabia, and Palestine), former colonies chose membership in the Commonwealth. Increasingly in the 1960s and afterward, they chose also the status of republics, not realms.

Problems within the Commonwealth

The process of colonial independence was not, however, altogether smooth. Kenya, Cyprus, British Guiana, and Malaya experienced violence beforehand. The white settlers of Africa, alarmed not only by the speed of British decolonization but also by the example of the Belgian Congo and French Algeria, saw the Commonwealth increasingly as a means whereby Britain was pushed into granting independence to peoples who were not ready for it, who would misuse it, and who might, through example and subversion, threaten others' privileged position. Such feelings by the settlers of Kenya were successfully overcome. But in Southern Rhodesia they became dominant when the former Federation of Rhodesia and Nyasaland—set up in 1953 and involving, in practice, domination by the Rhodesian settlers—was dissolved in 1963 because of African pressure. The government of Rhodesia made a unilateral declaration of independence in 1965 and in spite of British, Commonwealth, and UN opposition, maintained its position. The independent black African states had been powerless to displace the white Rhodesians, despite the Commonwealth's "multiracial" character.

Even more markedly, the white government of South Africa survived a long campaign against it by African and Asian states. South Africa left the Commonwealth in 1961, following what it regarded as interference in its racial policy from other members. (This was not the first resignation, or the last: Ireland had done the same in 1948, and Pakistan did in 1972.)

Members' influence on each other

It was clear that while the Commonwealth ostensibly rested upon the complete independence of its members and had no right of censure of any majority upon individual members, pressure could be exerted to try to make a member change its policies. Because Britain remained the most powerful state in the Commonwealth, with the most extensive range of policies likely to affect other members, it was natural that most pressure should be exerted upon it—as over the Suez crisis of 1956, the British decision to seek entry into the European Economic Community in 1961, and various British decisions to restrict the immigration of Commonwealth citizens into the United Kingdom after 1962.

Links with Britain. The achievement of independence by the members did not, in itself, change a number of their traditional and informal links with Britain, though these were subject to erosion by the forces of world change generally. British investment remained a significant factor in some members' economies, and British trade did in most (although the widespread but not universal system of preferential trade, set up at a conference in Ottawa in 1932, was greatly eroded by war and postwar changes); the wartime organization of the Sterling Area (countries with most of their exchange reserves in the Bank of England) continued in the 1950s but proved less important in the late 20th century. Migration was considerable from Britain to Australia, New Zealand, and Canada and was matched by a flow into Britain from these countries and from India, Pakistan, and the West Indies. British educational, sporting, publishing, legal, and professional influence continued to be felt in countries that had been part of the empire.

The formal organization of colonial and Commonwealth affairs changed under the pressure of accelerated independence. The Colonial Office, which had grown in the 1940s and '50s, as the colonies were provided with more elaborate assistance in development and welfare, shrank in the 1960s and was incorporated in the Commonwealth Relations Office (renamed the Commonwealth Office). The Commonwealth Office, in turn, was merged with the Foreign Office, a small section continuing to administer the affairs of the few remaining dependent territories, of which by the mid-1980s there were none in Africa, only Hong Kong in Asia, Gibraltar in the Mediterranean, and certain islands in the Pacific, Indian, and Atlantic oceans, together with some islands in the Caribbean.

Before 1965 there had been no executive for the Commonwealth as such. The British government normally arranged the meetings of Commonwealth prime ministers; otherwise, contacts were at the diplomatic level, with a network of ad hoc bodies in such spheres as scientific and educational cooperation. In 1965 a Commonwealth Secretariat was established in London, with a secretary general and a staff drawn from and supported by the member states. Its duties were the promotion of Commonwealth cooperation and the conduct of Commonwealth meetings, which continued to take place at various levels, from those of prime ministers to those of officials concerned with particular activities such as finance and the promotion of trade and tourism. There was also a certain amount of intra-Commonwealth economic aid, although most aid was bilateral between donors and recipients.

Commonwealth Secretariat

The Commonwealth became only one of a growing band of international bodies to which its members belong. The British Empire, from which the Commonwealth grew, is a vestigial survival, further attenuated each year.

(J.D.B.M./Ed.)

THE UNITED KINGDOM

Labour and the welfare state (1945–51). World War II, like World War I, was followed immediately by a general election; and Churchill, like Lloyd George, sought to perpetuate the wartime coalition. But here the parallel ends. In 1945 all parties contested the election independently. During the war, Labour maintained its organization. In 1941 it had issued "Labour in Government: A Record of Social Legislation in War Time," and in 1942, "The Old World and the New Society," a statement of postwar policy. In contrast, the Conservatives had not redefined their policies.

The postwar election

The European war was at an end May 8. Angry with Labour for breaking away from the Coalition, Churchill would not await the end of the Japanese war and resigned May 23. Polling day was set for July 5. The heart of the campaign was a series of evening broadcasts. The British Broadcasting Corporation estimated that on the average 45 percent of the adult population listened, with Churchill's audiences only slightly larger than the others. In his opening broadcast Churchill sought to associate Labour with Socialism and thereby show it to be dangerous. Attlee refused to take this seriously, for Socialism as an ideology was hardly an issue. Nor was the achievement of the war coalition, despite its emphasis by the Conservatives. The important question seemed to be: What of the future? Labour had a comprehensive program; the Conservatives did not. The outcome was a stunning victory for Labour, beyond all prediction, with 393 members of Parliament, a clear majority of 146 over all other parties. Attlee formed a strong cabinet with Bevin at the Foreign Office, Hugh Dalton at the Exchequer, and Herbert Morrison as leader of the Commons.

Labour promptly implemented its program. First came nationalization of the Bank of England, of coal, of electrical power, and of inland transport (railroads, road transport, inland waterways, docks and harbours). Only transport was seriously contested. No private interest was confiscated, and management usually remained in the hands of those who directed the industry when privately owned. As to agriculture, war legislation guaranteeing prices and markets was continued, rendering farming a respected occupation and one that provided a good livelihood. Labour created "the welfare state," or, more accurately, extended in dramatic fashion social services by the state. Legislation provided insurance against unemployment, sickness, industrial injury, old age; supplementary grants were provided for emergencies—pregnancy and maternity care, widowhood, burial. The National Assistance Act provided a weekly benefit for minimum needs. The National Health Service Act (1946)—which did not go into effect until July 1948—provided medical care for all, regardless of ability to pay; as such the act was the outcome of 35 years of piecemeal social legislation. Though all assumed that some kind of national health service was required, the problem was to enact legislation that would satisfy the medical profession without their active participation in its formulation. In the controversy, the medical profession was rent asunder. But by 1950 it was clear that Britain's health service was there to stay—95 percent of the population were enrolled on lists of doctors in the service, who numbered 88 percent of all medical practitioners.

National Health Service

In order to implement the Education Act of 1944, the government by 1951 had trained 35,000 new teachers (one-sixth of those in service), had established 6,300 temporary school rooms and constructed 1,000 new buildings, had extended the school-leaving age to 15 (1947), had expanded part-time technical training schools to nearly 300,000 workers, and had underwritten higher education (73 percent of students in universities were receiving grants-in-aid).

In the economy, Britain's task was clear: to restore and if possible to improve upon its prewar standard of living; to achieve a rate of production that would satisfy consumer demands at home and provide a surplus for export to pay for imported foodstuffs and raw materials; to bolster up sterling. Labour sought to achieve these goals by maintaining controls and powers exercised by the government during the war. While there was full employment, production was unimpressive. And in 1947, partly because the severe winter of 1946–47 interfered with production and transportation, but more especially because of slowdowns in mines and factories from discontented labour, there came a severe economic crisis, British exports falling sharply and the stability of sterling challenged.

But economic policy can hardly be separated from foreign policy, for it became apparent soon after the end of the war that Britain would depend on the United States for economic aid. It was agreed that on the lend-lease war account, Britain incurred no obligation for American aid actually consumed during the war; and, more importantly, outright financial aid through the Marshall Plan began in 1948. But before the end of 1945 it was just as clear that British and Soviet interests in Europe were irreconcilable. From the Baltic to the Adriatic, said Churchill at Fulton, Missouri, March 5, 1946, "an iron curtain has descended across the continent." Eastern European states, including East Germany, became Soviet satellites, and by 1947–48 a state of "cold war" existed between the Soviet Union and the West. In its search for economic recovery and national security, Britain apparently had to choose between Commonwealth or imperial ties or European cooperation. It moved cautiously toward Europe. The Dunkirk Treaty of Alliance (1947) allied Britain and France against a possible revival of German militarism, and with them were associated Belgium, The Netherlands, and Luxembourg in the Brussels Treaty (1948). The crowning event, for security in "the free world" and for containing the Soviet Union, came with the North Atlantic Treaty Organization (NATO) in April 1949, which bound the signatories at Brussels with Canada and the United States in a military alliance.

NATO

In Commonwealth affairs (see above) there began a veritable revolution. Labour had long pledged self-determination to India. Delayed and complicated almost beyond human understanding, independence came, but with it partition. In August 1947 India and Pakistan, as independent dominions within the Commonwealth, came into being. In 1949 Ireland proclaimed itself a republic and left the Commonwealth. In 1946 Britain terminated its mandate over Transjordan, and in 1948, over Palestine. In Egypt, native nationalism forced British policy into the withdrawal of all military forces, save in the Suez, by March 1947.

At the end of 1949, Labour was confronted with a general election. The party's limited success at nationalization and other controls to strengthen the economy and an "austerity" program limiting consumption had somewhat broken Labour's hold on the electorate. Further, there was disaffection in Labour's ranks, particularly against policy at the Foreign Office. The Conservatives had, meanwhile, effectively reorganized. In the poll of February 1950, with 84 percent of the electorate voting, Labour's vote was cut sharply by the still active Liberals, and the Labour majority in the Commons was reduced to a mere six—hardly a mandate. Parliamentary government became a sparring engagement. The steel industry was nationalized, but its methods of operation remained much as before. The economy improved somewhat. United Nations support for South Korea brought modest rearmament, but this further alienated leftists in the Labour party. Britishers found a brief diversion from their problems in the summer of 1951 in the Festival of Britain on the south bank of the Thames. Reality returned in autumn, when, to no one's surprise, Attlee announced a general election. The Conservatives, in Churchill's words, made "one more heave," which brought them a majority of 17, a modest victory, but significant in ending the postwar rule of Labour.

The Conservative response to postwar change (1951–64). The Conservative comeback proved genuine, the party winning three elections in succession (1951, 1955, 1959), each with a larger majority. Leadership of the party changed, first in April 1955 in the shift from Churchill, then 80 years old, to Anthony Eden and then in January 1957 from Eden to Harold Macmillan. At Buckingham Palace there was also a change—King George VI died in February 1952. Elizabeth II was proclaimed in June 1953 with coronation ceremonies in Westminster Abbey that were televised all over the world.

Coronation of Elizabeth

The Conservatives dominated the 1950s primarily because their domestic program proved more dynamic than that of Labour, which was slow to appreciate the need for new goals and new slogans to replace "full employment," "fair shares," and "nationalization," nearly all of which, as defined by Labour, had been achieved by 1951. Furthermore, on foreign policy Labour was seriously divided, with Aneurin Bevan and Harold Wilson leading a strong minority opposed to rearmament.

But at first the Churchill government, with its slender control in the Commons, moved slowly, tampering little with Labour legislation, save for denationalizing steel and road transport. But R.A. Butler at the Exchequer produced measures designed to reverse the unfavourable balance of international payments—curtailing imports, raising the bank rate for borrowing, and cutting tourist allowances abroad 50 percent. With these measures and favourable conditions abroad, the dollar account in foreign trade by 1953 was on even terms for the first time since the war, the volume of exports steadily increased and domestic consumption advanced—an increase between 1951 and 1954 of 12 percent, especially noticeable in automobiles and television sets. A matter of great popular interest was the creation in 1954 of the Independent Television Authority (in 1972 renamed the Independent Broadcasting Authority) which ended the British Broadcasting Corporation monopoly. On the strength of this record, the Conservatives in the election of 1955 increased their majority in the Commons to 58.

The economy

There was now talk of an "affluent society." But actual growth remained modest. A threat of inflation of prices and wages caused the government to turn again in 1957 to fiscal control—raising the bank rate to 7 percent, increasing purchase taxes, reducing food subsidies, and restricting installment buying. The economy accordingly improved; 1959 was an impressive year, with industrial production up 13 percent from 1954 and with exports doubling in volume those of 1938. By 1960 the rate of growth in production was about 3 percent annually. The advances in the 1950s came, not in the nationalized industries, which under public ownership were only a little more prosperous than under private, but rather in new industries—especially automobile and aircraft production but also chemicals, scientific instruments, and electrical equipment. During the decade, real wages rose 40 percent, and the average family could possess an automobile, a refrigerator, and a television set. By 1959, 70 percent of British households had television sets. The Conservatives again scored at the polls, in 1959 polling 50 percent of the electorate against Labour's 44 percent and achieving a majority in the Commons of 100.

In the 1950s, in external affairs, decisions even more momentous than those of the immediate postwar years were forced upon Britain. A great task and a great achievement was the liquidation of the empire—accomplished without violence and, with few exceptions, the newly independent states choosing to remain in the Commonwealth. After India and Pakistan came the Anglo-Egyptian Sudan, the Somali Republic, the Federation of Malaya, Malta, a host of states in Africa. Only in Rhodesia was the movement for independence marred by intransigence—this over the status of the vast African majority. But the same issue— that of white supremacy—along with national consciousness caused South Africa to proclaim itself a republic and to sever ties with the Commonwealth.

Foreign policy in the 1950s While World War II had once more made clear that Britain was not a part of Europe, interests of national security had persuaded the country to abandon its traditional policy of temporary international agreements for immediate ends and to associate in permanent military union with those who shared its dangers. In Europe, NATO, with the admission of the Federal Republic of Germany in 1955, became the Western European Union. And in 1954 in the Far East, Britain associated itself with SEATO (Southeast Asia Treaty Organization) to resist aggression in the Southwest Pacific.

Such arrangements were made with dignity. It was otherwise in the Middle East, where Britain did not have sufficient power to implement policy in its own interests. This it was slow in realizing. As in Palestine so in Suez British policy failed. According to Eden, an Anglo-Egyptian treaty of 1954, by which British troops were to be evacuated in stages, was to create close military cooperation with Egypt. In 1956 Britain as well as the United States hoped through loans for the construction of the Aswān High Dam to counter influence of the Communist bloc with the Egyptian leader, Gamal Abdel Nasser. But Nasser's recognition of the People's Republic of China and his encouragement of a Soviet proposal to finance the dam caused the United States and Britain to withdraw their offers. Nasser's answer (July 26) was immediate nationalization of the Suez Canal. An Israeli attack across the Egyptian border brought Anglo-French intervention (perhaps by French collusion with Israel) in force. Opinion in the United Nations and throughout the world was so generally hostile to the Anglo-French action that they soon halted operations. This abortive intervention made Nasser an Arab hero and cost Britain what remained of Arab confidence. And in the next few years it was evident that the Middle East had ceased to be a British "sphere of influence."

In domestic affairs, the early 1960s stand in some contrast to the 1950s. The economy, which had been growing, if somewhat unsteadily, came to a standstill. From 1960 to 1962 three chancellors of the exchequer sought to stimulate the economy by old measures (higher bank rates and higher taxes) and new ("a pay pause"; *i.e.,* restraints in wages and salaries, and an "incomes policy"). These measures were neither popular nor successful. While British production lagged behind that of other industrial countries, wages and prices rose. For many the future looked brighter when Britain in October 1961 formally applied for membership in the European Economic Community (the Common Market). There was, to be sure, opposition in Britain, from agricultural interests and from concern over the Commonwealth as well as from an important section of the Labour Party. But negotiations were actually ended (January 1963) by France, or more exactly by Gen. Charles de Gaulle, who declared that Britain's geography, economy, and trade made it impossible, at least for the present, for Britain to join the Common Market.

The year 1963 brought other surprises, and some tragedies. First came the sudden and untimely death in January of Hugh Gaitskell, the leader of the Labour Party

since 1955—a person very much respected in all political circles. His successor was Harold Wilson, another academic, around whom leftists in the party had gathered, but no extremist himself. After failure with the Common Market the Conservative government turned to the National Economic Development Council and to the National Incomes Commission for guidance in a planned economy that would stimulate production and control inflation. Progress in both directions was limited. And the Beeching Report on British railways, calling for the discontinuance of service on one-third of the route miles, while rational, was unpopular.

Macmillan and the Conservatives also suffered in public esteem in the "Profumo Affair." John Profumo, war secretary, was involved in an unsavory situation that included a call girl and a naval attaché at the Soviet embassy. A judicial inquiry found no breach of security but censured the government for failing to make prompt and adequate investigation. Macmillan suffered acute embarrassment in the Commons (June) but made a good comeback in his contributions to the Nuclear Test-Ban Treaty (July). In October, however, after being hospitalized for a major operation, he resigned. His exit left the Conservatives divided. On his advice, Lord Home, foreign secretary, who had revealed surprising strength as a second choice, was chosen by the Queen. The "Profumo Affair"

The Peerage Act, just enacted (July 1963), permitted Home to renounce his peerage, and as Sir Alec Douglas-Home he won a vacant seat in Scotland and took his place in the Commons. Of Cabinet rank only since 1957, he soon demonstrated that he was well able to govern. But in 1964 current events were in any case overshadowed by the prospect of a general election called for by law.

The return of Labour (1963–70, 1974–79). The expected election did not come until October; thus there was a long preelection campaign. Douglas-Home's task was to make himself known, while that of Wilson was to overcome complacency within his party, which expected an easy victory. But though Labour's popularity was waning, the feeling of "time for a change" prevailed with enough voters to give Labour a majority of four in the Commons. Wilson formed the first Labour Cabinet since 1951.

Despite its slender majority, it started vigorously with an emergency budget but was considerably embarrassed when the foreign-secretary designate, Patrick Gordon Walker, was defeated in a by-election in January 1965. Also in that month came the death of Sir Winston Churchill, aged 90, a solemn moment for Britain and much of the world.

Labour made a determined effort through the National Board for Prices and Incomes to control inflation and in September 1965 unveiled a master plan for attaining a 25 percent increase in production by 1970. With by-elections favourable to Labour, Wilson, in an effort to enlarge his majority, called for a general election in March 1966. Edward Heath, the new (since July 1965) leader of the Conservatives, declared that his party would "lead England into Europe" and through free enterprise would restore the economy. In a low poll, Labour emerged with a solid majority of 97. One factor was certainly Heath's unknown and uncertain quality. Election of 1966

In the years 1966–69 Labour's economic and financial policy was energetic and often bold—with severe budgets, a six-month freeze on wages in 1966 and restraints thereafter, a 14.3 percent devaluation of sterling in November 1967, a firm tone toward labour unions, and proposals for shifting from the principle of universality in welfare to that of selectivity. But it was a policy that achieved little success and that alienated the trade unions and much of Labour's working-class following.

The 1960s proved to be an important decade in education. The school-leaving age was scheduled to rise to 16 in 1970–71, and the "comprehensive school," offering all types of secondary education, was expanding. Goals set by the Robbins Report (1963)—60 universities by 1973–74 as against 32 in 1963, and 390,000 student places in higher education—were being pursued. And, prodded by the Franks Report (1966), Oxford and Cambridge, bulwarks of tradition, were undergoing change.

By the end of the decade the Labour government was

not winning high marks for its success in dealing with the economy. On the other hand, Heath had hardly made himself credible as a future prime minister. For him a major problem was Enoch Powell, a former Conservative Cabinet member, who thrust the racial issue into politics in 1968 with a demand for a halt to nonwhite immigration from Commonwealth lands. Powell was dismissed from the shadow Cabinet, but his popularity grew.

By 1969 industrial stability seemed threatened by a series of wildcat strikes, democratic processes were being questioned, and student demonstrations illustrated a general social discontent. Wilson's government was forced to abandon two major measures on its agenda: reform of the House of Lords and reform of trade unions. But an unforeseen improvement in the nation's foreign trade, and modest gains by Labour in by-elections and in public opinion polls led Wilson to call for a general election in June 1970. With only 72 percent of the electorate voting, the lowest since 1945, it is likely that many normally Labour voters stayed away from the polls. The result was an unexpected victory for the Conservatives, with a popular swing to its ranks of 4.6 percent and a majority of 30 in the Commons.

(A.F.H.)

The new Heath government had to deal with the highest unemployment since 1939 and a series of crippling strikes. Meanwhile, unrest continued in Northern Ireland and violence increased (see below *The history of Ireland: Northern Ireland after 1921*). Prime Minister Heath temporarily balanced his difficulties with dramatic success when Britain formally entered the European Economic Community (EEC) on January 1, 1973, but the debate over this step was by no means over.

Common Market entrance

Economic problems continued to trouble Britain—low growth rate, record trade deficits, the oil crisis, demands for higher wages, rising prices (the rate of inflation reached 25 percent in 1975)—despite strong measures by the Heath (and later the Wilson) government, which included, in 1973, the declaration of a state of emergency, the imposition of a three-day workweek, and an emergency budget. Lack of confidence in the government was reflected by Conservative Party losses in the local elections of that year, and the Prime Minister called for a general election on February 28, 1974. This gave Labour five more seats in Parliament than the Conservatives, and Harold Wilson (whose party had pledged to renegotiate the terms of British membership in the EEC) was again asked to form a government on March 4. The state of emergency was ended and the five-day workweek resumed. Because Labour's lead in Parliament was so flimsy, another general election was held on October 10. Though it again failed to produce a clear majority for Labour, it did give the party 43 more seats than the Conservatives.

Still striving to cope with the recurrent economic crises, the government in December announced plans to cut defense spending by reducing military manpower, ending new programs, and bringing overseas forces home. In a national referendum on June 5, 1975, the British voted 2:1 to remain in the EEC, ending a debate that had raged for more than two decades.

In the mid-1960s petroleum deposits began to be discovered in the North Sea, from which natural gas was already being recovered. Though their size could not be determined accurately, by 1975 it was estimated that they amounted to about 2 percent of the world's total petroleum reserves, and by the end of the decade Britain would become self-sufficient in petroleum.

North Sea petroleum

In March 1976 Wilson resigned, and he was succeeded in April by the foreign secretary, James Callaghan. Britain's financial woes continued to worsen; the value of sterling dropped below $1.60 in October. In December the International Monetary Fund (IMF) began a rescue operation that sparked a dramatic economic recovery in 1977 and 1978. The increased production of North Sea oil, which by mid-1977 was supplying half of Britain's requirements, was prominent in the recovery. The Labour government, however, had never enjoyed a strong majority in Parliament and was forced to rely on smaller parties, especially the Liberals, to stay in power. Several by-election defeats in 1977, labour unrest in 1978, strikes and layoffs early in 1979, and defeat of the referenda on devolution in Scotland and Wales (see below) led to a no-confidence vote in the House of Commons on March 28, 1979, the first such defeat of a government since 1924. In the general election held May 3 the Conservative Party won a parliamentary majority, and Margaret Thatcher became Britain's first woman prime minister.

The Thatcher years. In her first budget Thatcher embarked on a policy of stringent monetarism, characterized by tight control of the money supply; tax cuts, especially to the wealthy; reliance on free-market forces; and heavy cuts in government services, especially housing and education. By the early 1980s Britain was suffering from record interest rates, numerous business foreclosures, and unemployment exceeding 11 percent. A significant political development was the emergence of the Social Democratic Party (SDP) in 1981. Drawn from Labour Party members and former members of Parliament—including former Labour Cabinet ministers Roy Jenkins, David Owen, and Shirley Williams, who were disgruntled with Labour's shift to the left—the SDP proclaimed a centrist and pro-European policy that the public appeared eager to support. By the end of the year the SDP had 25 members in Parliament, including Williams, its first elected member. In March 1982 Jenkins won a seat in Glasgow, thus officially becoming the SDP leader.

The nonwhite population of 1,000,000 in 1968 had more than doubled by the late 20th century, and racial tensions exploded. Anger was felt most deeply by the West Indians. There were outbreaks of racial violence in London and in several other cities. During this unrest, however, Britons twice joined together in unified adulation of the monarchy and unabashed displays of national pride. During the summer of 1977 the entire nation played host to a Silver Jubilee marking the 25th anniversary of Queen Elizabeth II's accession to the throne. The Queen made hundreds of public appearances and also visited several Commonwealth countries. The festivities were repeated on July 29, 1981, when Charles, prince of Wales, married Lady Diana Spencer in an internationally televised ceremony. Their first son, Prince William of Wales, a new heir to the throne, was born on June 21 of the following year.

(As.B./Ed.)

ENGLAND

England is the predominant part of the United Kingdom, yet constitutionally it no longer exists. It is not mentioned in the title of its sovereign. Elizabeth II is queen of "the United Kingdom of Great Britain and Northern Ireland and Her other Realms and Territories." Scotland and Wales have their own departments of state and Cabinet ministers, while Northern Ireland has self-government in domestic affairs. But England has no such special rights, not even a separate set of official statistics, which are conventionally compiled either for the United Kingdom, in which the administration embraces the whole country—as in overseas trade, taxation, and defense—or for

England and Wales, as in the administration of the law, education, and various social services (where Scotland exercises an independent authority). It is rare for institutions to operate for England alone. A notable exception is the Church of England, the Anglican Communion having separate churches in Wales and Scotland. Otherwise, England retains its separate identity only in such activities as sport. Cricket is strictly a matter for England and English counties (apart from the Glamorgan County Cricket Club in Cardiff, South Glamorgan, Wales), and England fields its own teams in rugby and soccer football. But in its institutions, England gives the appearance of having been swallowed up in the larger mass of Great Britain since the Act of Union of 1707. It sometimes seems that Scotland and Wales have been more successful in retaining or securing their own special institutions. Thus, the British Broadcasting Corporation (BBC) has set up national broadcasting councils for Scotland and Wales but none for England, and there are other such examples of apparently preferential treatment.

England's dominance in the United Kingdom, nevertheless, is unquestionable. Occupying a little more than half of the landmass, England has more than four-fifths of the population. The bulk of the most fertile lowlands and six of the U.K.'s seven major metropolitan areas, or conurbations, are in England, which also has a higher proportion of wealth and natural resources than the rest of the U.K. Population and wealth increase with proximity to London, the national capital. London, in turn, with its ring of densely populated home counties in an area up to 50 or 60 miles (80 to 95 kilometres) in radius, dominates England, as England dominates Great Britain (England, Scotland, and Wales). There are good historical grounds for this being so. London was the biggest town in Roman Britain and has been the capital of a unified England since the Norman Conquest of 1066. Roman control of England fanned out with a network of roads based on London— a radial pattern that persists today. The Romans extended their rule approximately to the Welsh and Scottish borders of today, driving the Brythons back into the far southwest and the mountains of Wales and holding off the Scottish clans in the north. The frontiers of Roman rule in Britain were close to those of England today. In the subsequent 1,500 years, England has retained its frontiers short of most of upland Britain. The hill and mountain people of Wales and Scotland retain their sense of identity, and the English theirs, though they share a common language (although Welsh is still the common tongue in many rural areas of the principality) and a single sovereignty.

The "Englishness" of England is a quality hard to define, yet there is no doubt that it exists. Most institutions are British, but poets have very rarely saluted Britain (Britannia who rules the waves in the patriotic song with words by a Scottish poet being the exception). But poets by the score have celebrated England and the English, from William Langland in the medieval English of the 14th century onward. Shakespeare is self-consciously English and for England. The art historian Nikolaus Pevsner has written of "The Englishness of English Art." Yet this is not an insular character. It has been continually enriched from abroad. The English of Anglo-Saxon England were able to absorb the Danish and Norse invaders and their Norman French conquerors. And when the English went on to conquer first the remainder of the British Isles and then a worldwide empire, they did so without the dilution or dispersal of their essential character. The dominant role of the English is recognized implicitly in the numerous histories of Britain and the British Empire that are called "A History of England." A remarkable capacity to absorb and transmute alien elements can be seen in English literature, which in the 20th century has been able to take into the mainstream of its tradition poets as Irish as William Butler Yeats, as Welsh as Dylan Thomas, or as securely in the classic line as the U.S. expatriates T.S. Eliot and Henry James.

One other fundamental English characteristic is diversity within a small compass. England occupies about one-thousandth of the world's land area but contains about one-eightieth of the world's population and is, therefore, one of the most densely populated countries in the world. Even the farthest points of England are no more than a day's journey from London. Some approximate road distances from London are: to Dover, for the Channel crossing to France, 72 miles; to Southampton, the port for Atlantic routes, 77 miles; to Land's End, the farthest southwesterly point, 289 miles; to the southwestern port of Bristol, 116 miles; to the northwestern port of Liverpool, 197 miles; to the Scottish border at Carlisle, 300 miles; and to Berwick-upon-Tweed, 337 miles. In addition, it might be noted that no place in England is more than 75 miles from the sea.

Extent of Roman rule (margin note)

Physical and human geography

THE LAND

Relief. The diversity of England is based on a geological structure of remarkable complexity, spanning 600,-000,000 years. Almost every phase of geological history is illustrated in the intricate patterns of the geological map of England, from the oldest igneous rocks, to be found at the western extremities in Cornwall and Cumbria, to the most recent alluvial soils of reclaimed fenland in East Anglia. Between lie bands of sandstones and limestones of different geological periods, witness to primeval times when large parts of central and southern England were submerged below warm seas. In the period of Alpine mountain building, these sedimentary rocks were lifted and folded, so that they now run from southwest to northeast, to yield chains of low hills rising to about 800 feet (245 metres) and fanning out from the Channel coast into the North and South Downs, the Wiltshire and Berkshire downs, and the Cotswolds and the Chilterns, extending through Lincolnshire and North Yorkshire to the sea. In more recent geological times these hills were rounded into characteristic plateaus with west-facing escarpments by the great glaciers of three successive Ice Ages, the glaciers extending as far south as the northern outskirts of London. When the ice melted, the landscape was further altered by deep deposits of sand, gravel, and glacial mud.

Hills and downs (margin note)

Subsequently, the processes of erosion by rain, river, and tides and subsidence in parts of the east of England have further shaped the hills and the coastline. A more substantial chain of hills, the Pennines, with moorland tops rising to between 2,000 and 3,000 feet, split the north of England into northwest and northeast. These hills of limestone, grit stone, and carboniferous strata are associated with major coalfields, some outcropping to the surface, others deeply buried. This geological history underlies the characteristic variety of the English landscape, for in journeys of only a few miles it is possible to pass through a succession of different soil structures—such as from chalk down to alluvial river valley, from limestone to sandstone and acid heath, and from clay to sand—each type of soil bearing its own special class of vegetation. The geological complexity of England is strikingly illustrated in the cliff structure of its shoreline. Along the south coast from the ancient granite cliffs of Land's End in the extreme southwest are found a succession of sandstones of different colours and of limestones of different ages, culminating in the white chalk from the Isle of Wight to Dover.

These main groups are cut into by coves, bays, and beaches of particular local identity. A constantly changing panorama of cliffs, bays, and river estuaries distinguishes the whole of the English coastline, which, with its many indentations, is some 2,000 miles long.

Climate. The diversity of the English landscape is accentuated by its weather. In a temperate maritime zone, it does not run to extremes but is certainly one of the most erratic climates in the world. The averages are moderate enough, ranging in the Thames Valley from about 40° F (4° C) for the coldest month to 62° to 64° F (17°–18° C) for the warmest; but the extremes recorded in England go below 0° F (−18° C) and above 90° F (32° C). The Roman historian Tacitus recorded that the climate was "objectionable, with frequent rains and mists, but no extreme cold." Yet the winter of 1962–63 saw most of England heavily snowbound for nearly ten weeks, and snow cover may be expected in the higher parts of England on about 50 days a year. Though it is thought of as a wet country, lowland England has less than 40 inches (1,000 millimetres) of rainfall annually, and it frequently suffers from drought, the rising demand on water supplies becoming an increasing cause of official concern. In parts of Southeast England, the annual rainfall averages as little as 20 inches. Charles II expressed a judicious view when he said that the English climate was the best in the world—"a man can enjoy outdoor exercise in all but five days of the year." But no one would dispute that it is unpredictable: hence Dr. Samuel Johnson's observation that "when two Englishmen meet their first talk is of the weather." This changeability of the weather, not only season by season

Rainfall (margin note)

but day by day and even hour by hour, has had a profound effect on English art and literature.

The English painters John Constable and J.M.W. Turner were precursors of Impressionism in their exploration of the constantly changing light of English skies, and Constable painted cloudscape for its own sake. English poets down the centuries can be found constantly referring to the weather, from William Langland in the 14th century opening his poem *Piers Plowman* with the line, "In a somer seson whan soft was the sonne," to Shakespeare in the 16th century commenting on "the uncertain glory of an April day," and W.H. Auden in the 20th century with his "traffic of magnificent cloud."

Plant and animal life. England shares with the rest of Britain a below-average range of vegetation and living creatures, partly because the island was separated from the mainland of Europe soon after much of it had been swept bare by the last Ice Age (about 10,000 years ago) and partly because the land has been so industriously worked by its dense population. Predatory wild animals, such as the wolf, disappeared centuries ago. More recently birds of prey have suffered at the hands of farmers protecting their stock and their game birds. Under new protective laws, including a law restricting the collecting of birds' eggs, some of the less common birds have been reestablishing themselves. The bird life of England is unusually varied mainly because the country lies along the line of bird migrations and provides winter feeding grounds for some species and summer breeding habitats for others. Some birds have found town gardens, in which they are likely to be fed, a favourable environment, and in London about 100 different species are recorded annually. London has also been found a favourable habitat by foxes, which in small numbers have colonized woods and heaths within a few miles of the city centre. Though the species of plants may not be so great in number as those of the European mainland, they span a wide range and include some rarities. Certain Mediterranean species are to be found in the sheltered and almost subtropical valleys of the Southwest, while vestiges of the Ice Age tundra survive in parts of the moorland of the Northeast. England has been noted for a profusion of summer wild-flowers in its fields, lanes, and hedgerows. In some parts these have been severely reduced by the use of herbicides on farms and roadside verges. Cultivated gardens account for much of the varied vegetation of the country, being enriched by the importation of many species of trees, shrubs, and flowering plants from all over the world.

Settlement patterns. Though the significance of the natural changes in England can hardly be exaggerated, the landscape as it is seen today has been significantly changed by man. Only the remotest moorland and mountain tops have been untouched; even the bleak Pennine moors of the north are crisscrossed by dry stone walls, and their vegetation modified by the cropping of mountain sheep. There is virtually no genuine wilderness left in England. The face of the country has been constantly worked over for centuries, acre by acre, and the marks of its exploitation and use dominate the contemporary landscape. The oldest traces are the antiquarian survivals, such as the Bronze Age forts studding the chalk downs of the southwest, the little rectangular Celtic fields of Cornwall, and the corrugations left by the strip farming of medieval open fields.

Towns and villages

More significant is the structure of town and village, which was established in Roman-British and Anglo-Saxon times and which has persisted as the basic pattern. The English live in scattered groups of high-density occupation, whether in village, or town, or, in modern times, in cities. The effect is to make England even in the 20th century look still a rural country, though 90 percent of its people are urban dwellers and less than 3 percent are engaged in agriculture. Despite a large amount of badly managed urban sprawl, as cities spilled out into conurbations, England, as seen from the air or from any number of hilltop viewpoints, is notable for extensive tracts of farming countryside that lie between its towns, its smaller villages often engulfed in the vegetation of trees, copses, hedgerows and fields: in a phrase of the poet Gerard Manley Hopkins,

"the sweet especial rural scene," which occupies so large a place in English literature and English art.

The quality of the English scene is deeply rooted in its geology. Local building materials account for the traditional look of the Cotswold village, built of silvery limestone with slate roofs. The colour of the stone also often identifies the locality. A honey-coloured stone (which weathers badly) was much used in Oxford, and a rusty ironstone is typical in northern Oxfordshire and Northamptonshire, along the line of an ironstone belt. The Pennine gritstone adds a special severity to the moorland villages of the north. Timber frame and thatch are the building materials of the river valleys, and excellent clay provides the warm red brick of southern England. In recent years the easy transport of cheap but alien materials is to be blamed for many jarring intrusions into the harmonious towns and villages originally built mainly of local materials.

The visual impact of a mostly green and pleasant land can, however, be seriously misleading. England is primarily an industrial country, built up in the second half of the 18th century, during the first few generations of the Industrial Revolution, by ruthless exploitation of the coalfields and equally ruthless exploitation of cheap labour, especially in the cotton-textile areas of Lancashire, in the woollen-textiles areas of Yorkshire, and in the engineering centres of the Midlands and the Northeast. England has large tracts of dismally ugly derelict areas, scarred by the spoil heaps of the coal mines, by quarries and clay pits, by abandoned industrial plants, and rundown slums. About 100,000 acres (40,000 hectares) have been officially listed as derelict, and the figure is probably an underestimate.

Conservation efforts. The landscape has been seriously threatened by rising population, increasing urbanization, and increased wealth that has led to greater personal mobility. More and more townspeople seek recreation in the countryside and, by sheer numbers, are destroying what they look for. This dilemma has come to be known as the "leisure explosion." Not only England is affected, of course, but it was in England that these pressures first led to active intervention, to start with by individual action and later by action by public authorities, to set up a system of institutions and law to preserve the heritage of the past. One of the earliest of such initiatives was the establishment of the National Trust, a private organization dedicated to the permanent preservation of beautiful countryside and fine buildings. The largest single private landowner in the country, it has holdings that cover more than 600 square miles and that include some notable beauty spots, which in total are visited by 2,000,000 to 3,000,000 people annually. Although the National Trust extends to Wales and Northern Ireland, there is a separate National Trust for Scotland. In a similar spirit, the Civic Trust was established in 1957 with the object of preserving and enhancing the best "townscape." Many hundreds of local societies dedicated to the protection of the urban environment have been set up, and there are many other voluntary organizations working to protect and improve the English scene, among them the Council for the Protection of Rural England; the Commons, Open Spaces and Footpaths Preservation Society; and the Historic Churches Preservation Trust. Here the law has been extended and strengthened. The Town and Country Planning Acts of 1947 and 1968 require local government planning authorities to prepare development plans and to control development. Buildings of architectural and historic interest are listed and may not be demolished or altered without authority. The Civic Amenities Act of 1967 provided for areas of distinguished urban architecture to be designated "conservation areas." Local authorities may issue tree preservation orders to prevent indiscriminate felling. "Green belts" of countryside protected from building development have been mapped out in the plans for London and other conurbations. The quality of town life has been improved by smoke control and checks on river pollution, so effectively that the recorded sunshine in London and other major urban centres has been greatly increased and the "pea soup" fogs that occurred in London in the early 1950s have become memories of the past. Fish are returning to reaches of rivers such as the Thames, the Tyne, and the Tees

The "leisure explosion"

from which they had been driven by industrial pollution. Among a number of governmental institutions concerned with the environment is the Countryside Commission for England and Wales, which exists to promote recreation in the countryside, to protect designated areas of outstanding natural beauty, and to manage the national parks, seven of which are in England. It also manages long-distance footpaths, among them the Pennine Way, which runs for 250 miles over the summits of the moorland spine of northern England; some 80 miles of the South Downs Way; and a North Downs equivalent that runs, in part, along the route that Chaucer and his pilgrims took to Canterbury. Government recognition of the importance of these policies was indicated by the appointment in 1969 of a cabinet minister responsible for the environment and the founding of a Department of the Environment headed by a cabinet minister by the Conservative government in 1970. A Royal Commission was set up in 1969 to keep a continuous watch on pollution of the environment. While these and subsequent measures applied to Great Britain as a whole, they were of particular relevance to England with its high-density urban development.

THE PEOPLE

Ethnic background. By ethnic origin the English are a mongrel breed. Their language is polyglot, drawn from a variety of sources, and its vocabulary has been augmented by importations from all over the world. The English language does not serve to identify the English, for it is the main language of Wales, Scotland, Ireland, many Commonwealth countries, and the United States. The primary source of the language, however, is the main ethnic stem of the English. The Anglo-Saxons who invaded and colonized England in the 5th and 6th centuries have a record of continuous occupation since. It was their language that has prevailed and provides about half the words in modern English vocabulary.

In the millennia following the last Ice Age, the British Isles were peopled by migrant tribes from the continent of Europe and, later, by traders from the countries of the Mediterranean area. In the time of the Roman occupation, England was inhabited by Celtic Brythons, but the Celts withdrew before the Teutonic Angles, Saxons, and Jutes (from northwest Germany) into the mountain areas of the west and north. The Anglo-Saxons neither preserved nor absorbed the Roman-British culture they found in the 5th century. There are remarkably few traces of Celtic or Roman Latin in the early English of the Anglo-Saxons, though some words survive in place-names, such as the Latin *castra* for camp providing the suffix "cester" and *combe* and *tor*, Celtic words for "valley" and "hill." Old Norse, the language of the Danes and Norsemen, has left more extensive traces, partly because it was a language with closer affinities to Anglo-Saxon and because the Danish occupation of large tracts of eastern and northern England was for a time quite deeply rooted, as some place-names show.

The history of the centuries before the Norman Conquest is poorly documented, but what stands out is the tenacity of the Anglo-Saxons in surviving a succession of invasions. They united most of what is now England at different times in the 9th, 10th, and 11th centuries, only to be overthrown by the Normans in 1066. For two centuries French became the language of the court and the ruling nobility; yet English prevailed and, by the middle of the 13th century, had re-established itself as the predominant tongue, to become an official language again in 1362. The characteristic English way of life prevailed too. What evidence comes down from the Dark Ages suggests that the Anglo-Saxons were stolid, industrious, and persistent colonizers, clearing the forests and opening up new land for farming. They were neither migrants nor mere piratical marauders but settlers.

Both before and after the Norman Conquest, the English showed a notable capacity for absorbing and transmuting outside influences. Church Latin and Norman French were incorporated into the language during the Middle Ages. It was then enriched by the Latin and Greek of the educated scholars of the Renaissance. The seafarers,

Roman and Anglo-Saxon occupation

explorers, and empire builders of the modern history have imported words from all corners of the globe, most copiously from Europe but also from Asia. These foreign words have been so completely absorbed into the language that they pass unselfconsciously as English. The English, it might be said, are great anglicizers.

The English have also absorbed and anglicized people of alien race, from Scandinavian pillagers and Norman conquerors to Latin churchmen. In the royal line, a Welsh dynasty of monarchs, the Tudors, was succeeded by the Scottish Stuarts, to be followed by the Dutch William of Orange and the German Hanoverians. For the Scots, the Welsh, and the Irish, English became their main language, and many moved into England to seek their fortunes and to settle down as English by adoption. England provided a haven for refugees from the time of the Huguenots in the 17th century to the totalitarian persecutions of the 20th century. Jews, too, have settled in England in large numbers. In recent decades there has been large-scale immigration of non-white peoples from India and Pakistan, Africa, and the Caribbean, posing seemingly more difficult problems of assimilation, and restrictive immigration regulations have been successively imposed that are out of key with the open-door policy that had been accepted as an English tradition for many generations. To be counted English, it has never been necessary to be of purebred English stock, and indeed, there can be few English who are.

Immigration of non-white peoples

Traditional regions. Though a small and homogeneous country bound together by law, administration, and a comprehensive transport system, distinctive regional differences persist in England. These arise from geography and history. It was natural for different groups of the population to establish themselves in recognizable physical areas. In the north, for example, the east and west are separated by the Pennines, which rise to more than 2,000 feet, and the estuaries of the Humber, the Thames, and the Severn form natural barriers. The regions that have been defined for administrative purposes have some arbitrary boundaries but nevertheless reflect true regional feeling. There are eight of them: the Southwest, the Southeast, the West Midlands, the East Midlands, East Anglia, the Northwest, Yorkshire and Humberside, and Northern England.

The Southwest. The Southwest contains the last stronghold of Celtic Britain, Cornwall, where a Celtic language was spoken until the 18th century and where the countryside is dotted with some 300 Celtic stone crosses. There is even a small nationalist movement, *Mebyon Kernow* (Sons of Cornwall), seeking to revive the old language. Though it has, as yet, no political significance, it reflects the disenchantment of a declining area, with the exhaustion of mineral deposits toward the end of the 19th century. The neighbouring county of Devon also shares this economic decline. On the other hand, these southwestern counties have a large share of the rapidly expanding tourist industry, with a splendid coastline and the Dartmoor and Exmoor national parks. Farther east and closer to the economic magnet of the London area, the counties of Dorset, Hampshire, Wiltshire, and Gloucestershire have a greater variety of new industry.

The Southeast. The Southeast, centred upon London, is of a size and wealth to match many nation states. This is the dominant area of England and the most rapidly growing one despite planning controls directed toward restricting its growth. London itself is a victim of urban sprawl that has been checked too late. It is the administrative headquarters not only of government but of many of Britain's industrial and commercial undertakings. The area as a whole has an extensive range of manufacturing industry, though not in great concentrations apart from east London and the Thames Estuary. There is an above-average concentration of science-based industry and research around London. An effectively enforced green-belt policy has slowed down the expansion of London, and the region as a whole still has one-third of its area devoted to farming or horticulture. London is the focus of the nation's transport system, with the mainline railway network based on the London termini, two international airports, at Heathrow and Gatwick, and a third proposed at Foul-

The expansion of London

ness at the mouth of the Thames. The Port of London is the largest and commercially most important in Britain. Eight new towns have been established in the Southeast, and five existing towns have been expanded to take the overflow of London population, the scarcity of housing in inner London being particularly acute. With its theatres, concert halls, museums, and art galleries, London is emphatically the cultural capital of the country. Whether the people of the Southeast feel a regional identity is questionable. The Sussex Downs and the Bedfordshire plain or Oxford and Canterbury have nothing much in common apart from being within the magnetic pull of London. Loyalties are more specifically to towns, such as Oxford, Cambridge, or Brighton, and within London there is a sense of belonging more to localities—such as Chelsea or Hampstead, which acquire something of the character of urban villages—than to the metropolis as a whole.

The West Midlands. Regional characteristics are stronger outside the Southeast. The West Midlands, centred upon Birmingham, includes the Black Country (an urban agglomeration whose name accurately reflects the coating of grime and soot afflicting the buildings of the region), with some 1,500 different industrial trades, mainly in the metal industries. The major industry is automobile manufacture, with a wide range of component suppliers. With a long history going back to the beginnings of the Industrial Revolution, the West Midland towns are ugly but prosperous. It is an area in which there is a remarkable specialization place by place: locks and keys in Willenhall; needles and hooks in Redditch; the bulk of the country's pottery and china in five towns grouped around Stoke-upon-Trent; chocolate at Bournville; and carpets at Kidderminster. The region is not exclusively industrial, however, with the Shakespeare country around Stratford-on-Avon, the fruit-growing orchards of the Vale of Evesham, and hill country on the Welsh border.

The East Midlands. The East Midlands are less coherent as a region, taking in the manufacturing towns of Northampton (footwear); Leicester (hosiery and knitwear); Nottingham (hosiery, lace, bicycles, pharmaceuticals, tobacco); and Derby (engineering, aero-engines). The region also includes some of the most productive coalfields, iron-stone mining, and much of England's best farmland in broad swathes between the industrial towns.

East Anglia. This region retains an air of remoteness that belongs to its history. With the North Sea on its northern and eastern flanks, it was at one time almost cut off by fenland to the west (now drained) and forest (long ago cleared) to the south. In medieval times it was one of the richest of the wool regions and, in some parts, was depopulated to make way for sheep. The traces of deserted villages can still be seen. Now it is the centre of some of the most industrialized farming in England. Vast fields are put down to cereals and sugar beet. It is the most thinly populated of the English regions but is beginning to be industrialized, with North Sea gas and petroleum being brought ashore on the Norfolk coast.

> Industrialized agriculture

The Northwest. The qualities of the regions become more distinctive the farther they are from London. The Northwest is in essence Lancashire, with the conurbations of Manchester and Liverpool, traditionally wet and murky, home of the declining cotton-textiles industry—rapidly being replaced by diversified engineering—but still much ravaged by the Industrial Revolution. It is a region that expresses itself in an accent of its own, with strongly flavoured variety-hall humour (of which George Formby and Gracie Fields were classic examples). It gave birth to British rock music with the Beatles and other groups in Liverpool and still celebrates an earthy community life in wakes weeks (the factory holidays) and trips to Blackpool, the epitome of the north country seaside. It is a region still painfully breaking into the new territories of modern industry, its old cotton towns symbolically overshadowed by the grim gritstone Pennine escarpments, which have been stripped of their trees by the pollution of generations of industrial smoke.

Yorkshire and Humberside. A similar character belongs to industrial Yorkshire, on the east side of the Pennines watershed, where the valley mills are engaged in the man- ufacture of woollen textiles and clothing. Here too there is a strong accent to the regional style of speech and a rugged independence of character expressed in a tough style of humour. The conurbations of Leeds and Bradford take in the woollen and commercial centres. Farther south, steel is concentrated at Sheffield, world-famous for its cutlery. West Yorkshire based its prosperity on coal, but, like other parts of the country, it has been diversifying into other industries, notably chemicals and engineering. Here, too, industrialism has left ugly scars. But Yorkshire is not only industry. There are extensive areas of farming, the deep-sea-fishing industry operating from Hull, and tourist country along a fine coast and in the beautiful valleys of the Yorkshire Dales, with an exceptional repertoire of church architecture and country mansions.

Northern England. The official northern region extends to the Scottish border, taking in both North Yorkshire and the Lake District, and is therefore more than usually anomalous. The Lake District—a highly distinctive region of igneous mountains, the highest in England, rising to just over 3,000 feet—is so shut off that it retains a strong sense of local identity quite unlike the Northeast, which, from the river Tees to the Scottish border, is by cultural climate a region of its own. Here there are more concentrations of declining 19th-century industry, notably in the Durham coalfields and some of the Tyneside shipyards. It is at the same time a region in which modernization is going on rapidly, particularly in the complex of chemical industries on Teesside, one of the largest concentrations of chemical industries in Europe. The local flavour of life can be found in the folk songs of Tyne and Wear (Tyneside) and the coal-mining villages and in the dialect known as Geordie. The smallest of the designated conurbations is centred at Newcastle upon Tyne. The region also contains some of the most deserted land in England, in the Cheviot Hills along the Scottish border.

> The Lake District

Regional disparities. The regional differences of England invite comparisons that re-emphasize the predominance of the south and particularly of the London area. The regions of the North and the Southwest may be more distinctive in character, but they are significantly poorer in wealth and social resources. The Southeast and the West Midland regions, on the other hand, are above the national average for incomes and the proportion of high-income earners. The worst parts of the North have a much higher mortality rate than the best parts of the Southeast, and this can be explained both by the bad housing, the higher level of unemployment, and the worse poverty of the North. There is a greater concentration of social services in the Southeast, especially in the London area: a wider choice of schools, hospitals, doctors, dentists, and medical specialists. The best professional and managerial jobs are to be found in London and the Southeast; there are more school pupils staying on after the minimum school-leaving age, more university students, and more universities. The attractions of this area and also of the southern parts of the Midlands are much greater for the setting up of new industries than places in the North that have a greater need of them. Hence the drift away from declining areas far from London into the already overcrowded Southeast has continued regardless of planning controls and incentives to industrialists to go to designated development areas in less favoured parts of the country.

ADMINISTRATIVE AND SOCIAL CONDITIONS

Government and politics. It is hard to identify a specifically English role in contemporary government and politics, for these operate on a nationwide British basis. Historically, the English may be credited with the evolution of Parliament, which, in its medieval form, was related to the Anglo-Saxon practice of regular gatherings of notables; and the English may also be credited with the glory of the 1688 Revolution, which affirmed the rule of law, parliamentary control of taxation and of the army, freedom of speech, and religious toleration. Freedom of speech and opinion with proper opportunities for reasonable debate form part of the continuing English tradition, but the development of party and parliamentary government in its modern forms took place after the Act of Union of 1707, since when, in politics, the history of England has been the history of Britain. There have been prime ministers as robustly English as Robert Walpole, William Pitt, or Winston Churchill, but they are in a line that includes the Jew Benjamin Disraeli, the Welshman David Lloyd George, and the Scots Harold Macmillan and Alec Douglas-Home.

In government the English legacy remains conspicuous in local affairs, which are still largely administered on a county base that can be traced back to the Anglo-Saxon shires. The separation of county and town in local government was the principle underlying the late Victorian reorganization of local government, but the reforms of the 1970s, while retaining an exclusively urban base for local government in the conurbations, reunite county and town elsewhere with a minimum of disturbance to county boundaries that in many places date back 900 years.

Law. The English have given the world, notably North America and much of the Commonwealth, the system of English law that has acquired a status and universality to match Roman law. This, too, had its origins in Anglo-Saxon times, and two of its hallmarks are its preference for customary law (the common law) rather than statute law and its system of application by locally appointed part-time magistrates or justices of the peace, locally chosen juries, and by the travelling judges going from one county town to another on circuit. Under the Normans, the Anglo-Saxon system was retained but formalized; for example, by the recording of case law to provide uniform precedents. This began toward the end of the 13th century. In modern times there has been a greater reliance upon the statute law contained in about 3,000 acts of Parliament, but there are over 300,000 recorded cases to turn to for precedent. Other aspects of the English law are the fundamental assumption that an accused person is deemed innocent until proved guilty and the independence of the judiciary from intervention by crown or government in the judicial process.

Religion. Increasingly, England is a secular country. Though more than one-half the population are baptized in an Anglican church and for form-filling purposes would say they belonged to the Church of England, fewer than one in ten of the baptized are communicant churchgoers. The Church of England still has 18,000 churches, but it has been in financial difficulties, and it has closed down underused churches and sold off redundant sites. The nonconformist Free Churches have nominally fewer members, but there is probably greater dedication among them, as with the Roman Catholic Church. Apart perhaps from some isolated centres of Irish settlement in the Northwest, there is complete religious tolerance in England and no overt prejudice against Catholics; it is quite usual for 30 or 40 members of Parliament to be Catholic, with a few of them government ministers. The decline in churchgoing has been thought to be an indicator of decline in religious belief, but opinion polls substantiate the view that belief in God and the central tenets of Christianity survives the flagging fortunes of the churches.

CULTURAL LIFE

England's contribution to the culture of the United Kingdom and of the world is too vast for anything but a random sampling. There is the complicating factor that in the contemporary cultural scene, England is not always distinguishable from Wales and Scotland or even Northern Ireland. Furthermore, what may count as mainly English achievements have often been shared with people from other countries.

Science. In the sciences, for example, the splitting of the atom was first accomplished in the Cavendish Laboratory in Cambridge by Ernest Rutherford, a New Zealander. The deoxyribonucleic acid (DNA) molecule was unravelled in Cambridge by two English geneticists, Francis Crick and Maurice Wilkins, and an American, James Watson. Radar detection of aircraft was perfected at a research station in Suffolk by a team headed by a Scot, Robert Watson-Watt. Penicillin was discovered in a London hospital by Alexander Fleming, a Scot, and developed as a medical drug by Howard Florey, an Australian, in Oxford. In the sciences the English are sometimes said to be

better at fundamental theory than at its application. Certainly Isaac Newton on gravitation and Charles Darwin on evolution have changed the history of scientific thought. But William Harvey on the circulation of the blood and Joseph Lister on antiseptic surgery were working as practical surgeons. The innovating engineers of the early Industrial Revolution were highly practical men. The choice of the Greenwich meridian as the base line for measuring longitude reflects the practicality of English astronomers, navigators, and geographers. The practical application of highly sophisticated new techniques to fundamental research is seen in the radio telescopes at Jodrell Bank and at Cambridge. In the design of nuclear power plants, research institutions in England have been abreast or ahead of the rest of the world. England has also been ahead with the design of advanced aircraft. One of the first jet engines was designed by Frank Whittle and flown in England in 1941, and the Anglo-French supersonic airliner Concorde is built in England at Bristol and powered by Rolls-Royce engines made in Derby.

Architecture. England, however, is still most famous for its architecture and its literature, both reflecting the regional diversity of the country. Architecture has been much influenced from abroad, but foreign styles take on an English aspect. So the Gothic architecture of France was transformed into a characteristically English style by the delicate use of stone to provide a framework for walls that were almost all glass, culminating in triumphs of the perpendicular style, such as King's College Chapel at Cambridge. European Renaissance influences can be seen in the buildings of Christopher Wren, yet his many London churches seem essentially English. The magnificent country houses of the 18th century are likewise not mere importations of a foreign fashion but fit their own landscape; and many such landscapes were designed by the great English garden and park designers, William Kent, Lancelot ("Capability") Brown, and Humphry Repton. Small-scale domestic architecture is often just as commendable for its fitness to its situation, and an intimate, friendly urbanity is to be found in the best of England's town centres and villages, this being partly the result of using local materials, whether stone, brick, tile, or thatch. The bulk of the building of the last 100 years excites much less enthusiasm. Many industrial slums have been condemned for demolition, but much contemporary building that is adequate for habitation or work is drearily uninspired. The reconstruction of the war-damaged city areas of England provided opportunities for notable new architecture, and some original design and construction was undertaken; for example, the Barbican scheme in a large bombed area north of St. Paul's, London, and the group of concert halls with an art gallery and the new National Theatre on the south bank of the Thames. Outside London, notable projects include the Coventry precinct and cathedral by Sir Basil Spence; a batch of new universities founded during the 1960s, among them those near Brighton, Canterbury, Colchester, Norwich, and York; and a number of local-authority housing developments, including new towns.

Literature. In literature, regional influences have often strongly affected English writers—such as Wordsworth in the Lake District, the Brontë sisters on the Yorkshire moors, Thomas Hardy in Dorset, D.H. Lawrence in the Midlands coalfields, and Charles Dickens in London. It is a characteristic that persists, in J.B. Priestley, a Yorkshireman, in Evelyn Waugh, a west-country squire, and John Betjeman, a Londoner, whose poetry is a record of his passion for English towns and landscape.

Visual arts. Regional attachments are also to be found in the visual arts. The sculptors Henry Moore and Barbara Hepworth both come from Yorkshire, and something of the quality of moorland stone can be seen in their work. Hepworth's later work has echoes of the granite coastline of Cornwall, where she settled, and Cornwall has become the chosen working place of a number of English artists. Even in music the landscape intrudes, as in Benjamin Britten's opera *Peter Grimes*, based as it is on a story of the fishing village in Suffolk where Britten lived.

Institutionally, the arts in Britain have grown in both scope and vigour since World War II. Publishers break records for the numbers of books produced; the sale of paperbacks has spread from established bookshops to newsagents and tobacconists. London theatres play to full houses, and many new repertory theatres have been established in the provinces. Music flourishes as never before in England, and visiting conductors have said that they find the English concert audience one of the most appreciative in the world. Long-playing records are sold by the tens of millions annually. Attendance at art galleries and museums has grown. Subsidies to support the arts and literature in Britain are administered by the Arts Council, a considerable proportion of them being devoted to maintaining and extending the arts in regional centres outside London. Arts Council subsidies have also been used to develop the international fame of companies such as the Royal Opera and the Royal Ballet (both of Covent Garden) and of leading London orchestras, which make regular foreign tours.

The Arts Council

Leisure. Though England has a lively intellectual and artistic life, its characteristic pursuits are of a more popular kind. The exploitation of leisure is increasingly the concern of commerce: holiday camps, foreign holiday package tours, gambling of many kinds from bingo to horse-race betting and football (soccer) pools, and the transformation of the traditional English pub by trendy interior decoration and the introduction of new kinds of beer allegedly more palatable to women. The English weekend, accorded to most of the population, is the occasion for trips into the countryside and for outdoor activities ranging from fishing to mountaineering. England gave to the world the sports of cricket, association football, and rugby football, but team and spectator sports tend to be giving way to more individualistic activities. In spite of persistent commercial tempting to do something else, the English remain a stay-at-home people. The Englishman's home is still his castle, and gardening the most frequent pastime, except for watching television, which absorbs nearly a quarter of the average person's leisure time. The English prefer living in houses to apartments, and about three out of four have gardens. They keep pets, they "do-it-yourself" in house maintenance and many other odd jobs, and their desire for privacy still mystifies foreign onlookers.

(W.H.Th./Ed.)

History

The history of England is given in the section above, *History of England and Great Britain.*

SCOTLAND

Scotland, the most northerly of the four parts of the United Kingdom—England, Scotland, Wales, and Northern Ireland—is a generally cool, hilly, and, in the west, wet country that occupies about one-third of the island of Great Britain (England, Scotland, and Wales). Scotland is bounded by England in the south and on the other three sides by sea: by the Atlantic Ocean on the west and north and by the North Sea on the east. Its mainland area is 29,794 square miles (77,167 square kilometres); including inhabited islands, it has an area of 30,414 square miles. Scotland is fringed by numerous islands of various sizes on the west coast, and the island clusters of the Orkneys and the Shetlands lie to the north; but the east coast has only a few islands, and those are relatively less significant. At its greatest length, measured from Cape Wrath to the Mull of Galloway, the mainland of Scotland extends to 274 miles (441 kilometres), while the maximum breadth, measured from Applecross, in the western Highland region, to Buchan Ness, in the eastern Grampian region, is 154 miles. But, because of the deep penetration of the sea in the fjords, or narrow, deep inlets, of the west coast and in the estuaries of the Tay and Forth rivers in the east, most places are within 40 to 50 miles of the sea, and only 30 miles of land separate the Firth of Clyde and the Firth of Forth, the two great estuarine inlets on the west and east coasts, respectively.

The country was originally known as Caledonia. The name Scotland originated in the 11th century, when the name Scotia was given to the southwestern tract settled by the tribe of Scots who had migrated from Ireland. After being independent until 1707, Scotland became an integral part of the United Kingdom, though something of a political curiosity. It has no separate legislature, executive, or political power, and, constitutionally, it is less than a state or province in a federal union. Yet it retains vestiges of ancient sovereignty in its own legal and educational systems, a national church, and a separate administration. Scotland's economy is integrated with that of the rest of Britain, and it has no separate diplomatic or consular representation in other countries, but it has managed, nevertheless, to preserve its identity in the international scene by export trade and by cultural exchanges. Some of its products, especially whisky, tartan, and tweeds, are internationally known, and generations of emigrant Scots have spread the awareness of a distinctively Scottish culture. The image cherished by foreigners is often odd, but even romantic notions of stern and wild Caledonia, of Mary, queen of Scots, and of Bonnie Prince Charlie (Charles Edward Stuart) prevent Scotland from being eclipsed in the comity of nations.

Physical and human geography

THE LAND

Relief. Scotland is traditionally divided into three geographical areas, the Highlands, the Lowlands, and the Southern Uplands. The coastal plain, stretching from eastern Grampian region round the Moray Firth to the flat expanse of northeastern Highland region, is distinctive enough, however, to constitute a separate Northeast area. The Highlands are bisected by the fault line of the Great Glen (Glen More nan Albin), which is occupied by a series of lochs (lakes), the largest of which is Loch Ness, famous for its probably mythical monster. North of the Great Glen is an ancient plateau, which, through long erosion, has been cut into a series of peaks of fairly uniform height separated by glens (valleys) carved out by glaciers. The northwestern fringe of the mainland is particularly barren, the granulated and layered rocks having been worn down by severe glaciation to produce a hummocky landscape, dotted by small lochs and rocks protruding from thin, acidic soil. Farther inland are spectacular sandstone mountains, weathered into sheer cliffs, rock terraces, and pinnacles. South of the Great Glen, the Grampian Mountains were also formed by continuous denudation and glaciation of metamorphic rocks, though there are intrusions of granitic masses in the Cairngorm Mountains. The Grampians are less rugged and rocky than the mountains of the northwest, being rounded and grassy, with more of the appearance of a plateau. There are large basins between mountain groups, the most striking being the moor of Rannoch, a bleak expanse of bogs and granitic rocks, with narrow, deep lochs, such as Loch Rannoch and Loch Ericht. The boundary of the Highlands is clearly marked by a fault (the Caledonian trend) running southwest to northeast from Helensburgh, on the River Clyde, to Stonehaven, on the east coast. The southern boundary of the Lowlands is not such a continuous escarpment, but the fault beginning in the northeast with the Lammermuir and Moorfoot hills and extending to Glen App, in the southwest, is a distinct dividing line. In some ways the label Lowlands is a misnomer, for, although this part of Scotland is low by comparison with adjoining areas, it is by no means flat. The landscape is varied by series of hills such as the Sidlaws, the Ochils, the Campsies, and the Pentlands, composed of igneous rocks rising as high as 1,898 feet (579 metres) and following the Caledonian trend. Most of the area is above 400 feet, but the lowlands in Lothian and Fife regions in the east, the rich plain in Tayside region in the northeast, and the Clyde Valley in Strathclyde region in the west are Scotland's best areas

The Great Glen

for arable farming. The Southern Uplands are not so high and fractured as the Highlands. Glaciation has resulted in narrow, flat valleys separating table mountains. To the east of Nithsdale (Valley of Nith) in the Borders region, the hills are rounded, gently sloping, and grass covered, providing excellent grazing for sheep. To the west of the Nith the landscape is rougher, with granitic intrusions around Loch Doon, and the soil more peaty and wet. The high moorlands and hills, of which Merrick (2,764 feet) is the highest, are also suitable for sheep farming. Toward the southeast the uplands open out into the Tweed Valley, which broadens into rich farming land, and to the southwest they slope toward the Galloway Peninsula.

Soil and drainage. With Scotland's diversity in geological structure, relief, and weather, the character of the soil varies greatly. In the northwest, the Hebrides, and the Shetlands, where the geological substratum is ancient rock, resistant to weather, the soil is poor, and cultivation is possible only at river mouths, glens, and coastal strips. On the west coast of some Hebridean islands, however, there are plains of calcareous sand (the machair) suitable for farming. On moors and hills between 1,000 and 2,500 feet, a peat covering is widespread because of high rainfall and poor drainage. Peat is estimated to cover some 2,600 square miles. It occurs also on lower ground, and northeastern Highland region has large peat deposits. Where there is good soil for arable farming, as in the Orkneys, the eastern Highland region, the northeastern coastal plain, and the Lowlands, it has been derived from old red sandstone and younger rocks. Though the sea lochs, or fjords, of the west are supposed to be remnants of a river system submerged by the Minch Channel, the present drainage system runs toward the east. In the northern Highlands the watershed runs from north to south, close to the west coast, so that rivers running to the west are very short and those to the east longer and less rapid. In the central Highlands the rivers meander more, but the longest, the Spey, Don, and Dee, drain the area toward the east, as do the Tay and the Forth in the Lowlands. The Clyde and the Tweed both rise in the Southern Uplands, the one flowing to the west and the other to the east coast, while the Nith and a few other small rivers run south into the Solway Firth. Lochs are useful for drainage, for reservoirs, and as sources of power. They are numerous in the Highlands, ranging from moraine-dammed lochans (pools) in mountain corries (hollows) to large and deep lochs filling rock basins. Many of the bigger lochs have been dammed and enlarged to provide a flow of water to generate electricity in stations at lower levels. In the Lowlands and Southern Uplands, lochs are shallower and less numerous, though some, notably Loch Lomond, are extensive.

Climate. Scotland has a temperate oceanic climate, milder than might be expected from its latitude. Despite its small area, there are considerable variations in climate. Rainfall is greatest in the mountainous areas of the west, as prevailing winds blow from the southwest and come laden with moisture from the Atlantic. East winds are common only in winter and spring, when cold, dry continental air masses envelop the east coast. Hence, the west tends to be milder in winter, with less frost and with snow seldom lying long, but it is damper and cloudier than the east in summer. Tyree (Tiree), in the Hebrides off the west coast, has a mean temperature in winter of 41° F (5° C) in the coldest month (as high as southeastern England), whereas Dundee, on the east coast, has 37° F (2.8° C). Dundee's mean temperature in the warmest month is 59° F (15° C) and Tyree's 57° F (13.9° C). There is a smaller range of temperatures over the year in Scotland than in southern England. Rainfall varies remarkably. In the flat Outer Hebrides it does not exceed 40 inches (1,000 millimetres) a year, the average rainfall in Britain. Some two-thirds of the surface of Scotland, however, has more than 40 inches. In the mountains of Highland region, rainfall exceeds 100 inches. Most of the east coast has below-average rainfall, less than 25 inches in the Moray Firth lowlands and 27 inches in Dundee. Sunshine averages 3½ hours per day over the year.

Plant and animal life. Lower ground, up to about 1,500 feet, was once covered with natural forests, which have been cleared in the course of centuries and replaced by introduced trees, plants, and crops. Survivals of the original forest are found in the pinewoods of Rothiemurchus, in Highland region. Grass and heather cover most of the Grampians and Southern Uplands, where the soil is not so wet and dank as in the northwestern Highlands. On boggy soil, shrubs such as bearberry, crowberry, and blueberry grow, as does bog cotton. Alpine and Arctic species flourish on the highest slopes and plateaus of the Grampians, including saxifrages, creeping azalea, and dwarf willows. Ben Lawers is noted for the wealth of its mountain flora.

For its size, Scotland is rich in animal life. Herds of red deer graze in the corries and remote glens, and their population is estimated at nearly 500,000. Lower down in wooded country the more elusive roe deer are found. Foxes and badgers are widespread, and the number of wildcats is thought to be increasing. Rabbits were decimated but not eliminated by the disease of myxomatosis. Pine marten, otters, and mountain and brown hares are among other wild animals. A few ospreys nest in Scotland, and golden eagles, buzzards, and kestrels are the most notable of resident birds of prey. Capercaillie (a species of grouse) have been successfully reintroduced. Seabirds, such as gannets, fulmars, and guillemots, and various types of gull abound on cliffs and the isolated rocks known as stacks around the magnificent coasts. The largest mammal in Scottish waters is the Atlantic gray seal, which breeds on the island of North Rona, off the west coast; the common seal is also numerous.

Settlement patterns. In early times, mountains, rivers, and seas divided the people into self-sufficient communities, which developed a strong sense of identity. This sense has been eroded by social mobility and by modern transport, broadcasting, and other standardizing influences. Yet vestiges of regional consciousness linger. The Shetland islanders speak of Scotland with detachment. The Galloway area in the southwest, cut off by hills from the rest of the country, has a vigorous regional patriotism. The Gaelic-speaking people of the Hebrides and western Highlands find their language a bond of community. A distinct dialect may differentiate some communities from others, as in the case of the Aberdeen area. Borderers celebrate their local festivals with fervour. This feeling of community survives to a varying degree in many areas, but it has no economic basis now and tends, like clan loyalty, to be a sentimental bond rather than a force of social cohesion. The most thickly populated rural areas are those with the best farming land, such as in Lothian region and in the Northeast. The Highlands nourished a large population before sheep farming led to continuous emigration. Now settlements in the Highlands are mostly crofting townships; that is, small farms of a few acres grouped together in an irregular manner. The old pattern of crofting was one of communities practicing a kind of cooperative farming, with strips of common land allotted annually to individuals. Examples of the old system survive, but now crofters have their own arable land fenced in, while they share the common grazing land. In Lothian region and other areas of high farming, the communal farm has long been replaced by single farms with steadings (farmsteads) and workers' houses. Scotland is noticeably lacking in those old villages that evolved in England from medieval hamlets of joint tenants. Some planned villages were built by enterprising landowners in the 18th century. Burghs, often little bigger than villages, were mostly set up as trading centres, ports, or river crossings or to command entrances to mountain passes. Around the east and northeast coast, there are many surviving small towns that were once obliged to be self-contained in consumer industries and burghal institutions because of poor land transport. Some coastal towns have preserved a dual character, the fishing community being grouped around the harbour, while other inhabitants occupy the higher ground. Growth of industry and transport has produced urbanization. Edinburgh, Dundee, and Aberdeen are centres of administration, commerce, and industry for their areas, but only Central Clydeside, including Glasgow with its satellite burghs, is large enough to deserve the official title of conurbation. Depopulation of city centres is occur-

Peat

Rainfall

Crofting

ring in Scotland, as elsewhere, while that of surrounding areas is rising. In Glasgow the reduction has been due to a planned overspill program, but elsewhere the trend has been due to the growth in commuting.

THE PEOPLE

Despite their diverse origins, including Celts, Angles, and Normans, the Scots in time have been fused into a fairly homogeneous population. In the 19th century there was heavy Irish immigration, which some feared would form an alien element, with different social and educational standards and religion. The Irish have settled, however, without provoking marked social conflict.

Church of
Scotland

Scotland is remarkably free from racial and religious strife. The Church of Scotland is the established religion and largest communion, though membership has been steadily declining. It is presbyterian in structure and evangelical in doctrine. Its well-articulated organization begins with the parish church or congregation, governed by a kirk session composed of minister and elders. The kirk session sends representatives to the presbytery (a group of parishes), and the presbyteries in turn are represented in the synod, which has declined in status. At the apex is the General Assembly, to which presbyteries send clerical and lay commissioners in equal numbers and which is the supreme court and legislature of the church. It meets annually and reviews the reports of numerous committees. It is perhaps the most representative body in Scotland and makes its voice heard on current moral, social, and international issues. The Roman Catholic Church is organized into two archdioceses and six bishoprics. The Episcopal Church in Scotland is also significant, and there are congregations of other denominations, such as the Free Church of Scotland, Baptists, Congregationalists, Methodists, and Unitarians. The ecumenical spirit and perhaps growing indifference have taken bitterness out of religious differences, though little progress has been made with church unity. Roman Catholics have their own schools, built and staffed from public funds on the same terms as the state schools.

THE ECONOMY

Scotland's economy compares unfavourably with that of European countries of similar size except Ireland. Scotland's growth is slower, unemployment higher, and per capita gross domestic product (GDP) lower than other nations. Even in the context of the United Kingdom it is economically backward. Its unemployment rate in postwar years has been almost consistently twice that of Britain as a whole. Male unemployment is one of the most disquieting features of the economy. Most parts of Scotland are scheduled as development areas, eligible for special state incentives to attract new enterprises.

Resources. Coal is Scotland's chief mineral resource, but the Lanark coalfields are almost exhausted, and the main mining areas are now in Lothian and Fife regions and in western Strathclyde region. The industry reached its peak production of 43,000,000 tons in 1913 but has since declined drastically. Many uneconomic collieries have been closed, and production has been concentrated on large, mechanized pits. Other minerals that have been worked intermittently include gold, silver, lead, chromite, diatomite, and dolomite, but none has been successfully exploited. At Muirshiels and Gass Water, both in Strathclyde region, barite (barium sulfate, used in paint manufacture) is produced. Though peat is available to a depth of two feet or more over some 1,700,000 acres, its economic value is limited. Some communities in the Highlands still burn it for fuel, but the time and labour involved in cutting and drying peat in an uncertain climate have led to decreasing use. Experiments in using peat as fuel for generating electricity proved it uneconomical.

During the 1970s a new Scottish resource, North Sea oil, was developed. The oil fields lie mostly in Scottish waters, North Sea but the British government holds their ownership and receives all the revenue yield. The oil has been located and extracted by large companies, most with the aid of U.S. technology. Aberdeen is the centre of the oil industry, and the Shetlands have also benefitted from discoveries in adjacent waters. Tens of thousands of jobs have been cre-

ated in Scotland by onshore oil-related enterprises, such as building oil production platforms and servicing North Sea operators. Natural gas from North Sea wells has replaced manufactured gas in Scotland.

Water is a valuable resource, especially for generating electricity. The North of Scotland Hydro-Electric Board (NSHEB) was set up in 1943 to build dams and power stations. The NSHEB operates several hydroelectric stations and has pumped storage schemes by which electricity generated in off-peak periods may be used to pump water to a higher dam, from which it descends at peak periods to operate the turbogenerators. The NSHEB has also coal- and oil-fired stations. The South of Scotland Electricity Board relies mainly on coal-fired stations.

Agriculture, forestry, and fishing. As an economic resource wild animals, birds, and river fishes are of minor importance, though deer stalking, grouse shooting, and fishing provide employment in parts of the Highlands in which other activities are hardly possible. Venison is exported to the European mainland, and game birds, salmon, and trout are delicacies, as well as objects of sport.

Fishing. Sea fishing is still a major industry, though it has faced serious difficulties in recent years. The extension of fishery limits has excluded Scottish trawlers from traditional fishing grounds like those around Iceland and the Faeroe Islands. Overfishing has depleted stocks, and bans on herring fishing have been imposed at various periods. The fishing fleet is contracting in numbers, but it has become better equipped and more efficient. The inshore fleet has been modernized, and boats have been equipped for both netting herring and catching whitefish by seine nets. Aberdeen and Moray Firth ports are the busiest centres for landing and processing whitefish, but Lerwick, in the Shetland Islands, Ullapool and Mallaig, both on the west coast of the mainland, and Stornoway, on the island of Lewis, are also important. Catches naturally fluctuate from year to year, but Scottish vessels generally account for more than half of all U.K. landings by weight and by value. Twice the number of workers are employed in fish processing as in fishing.

Agriculture. In terms of productivity, no industry has made greater progress than agriculture in postwar years. Owing to mechanization, the labour force has fallen from about 88,000 in 1951 to barely a third of that number, though some casual and part-time workers are also employed. In the Southern Uplands and the Highlands there are hill sheep farms, while in the Northeast livestock rearing combined with crops for animal feeding predominates. In the southwest, dairy farming suits the damp, mild climate, and the Central Clydeside conurbation is a convenient market. Wheat and barley are grown in Lothian, Principal
crops Fife, and Borders regions. Specialized kinds of farming flourish in certain areas, such as market gardens in eastern Lothian region, raspberry growing in Tayside region, and tomato growing under glass in the upper Clyde Valley. Early potatoes are a specialty of the southwest coast. Barley, used for distilling among other things, has become the principal crop. Wheat is grown only in the most fertile areas, but production is tending to rise, whereas the output of oats has markedly declined. While production of turnips and potatoes has fallen, that of hay and grass silage has substantially increased. In animal production the most striking feature has been the rise in the number of cattle. Sheep and pigs have also tended to become more numerous over the long term. Crofting is a special section of the agricultural scene. It has to be supplemented by other work, such as forestry, road work, catering for tourists, and weaving. Though there are thousands of crofts in the northern areas, many of them are not cultivated. The Crofters Commission gives crofters advice, and it channels grants to them for the improvement of land and houses.

Forestry. Forestry is an expanding industry, which has helped retain the population in rural areas. It is managed by the Forestry Commission, a public body, and by private landowners. Although the Forestry Commission plants throughout the country, it plays a particularly important role in Highland development. The trees it grows are conifers, including Scotch pine, Norway spruce, European larch, Sitka spruce, and Douglas fir.

Industry. In its industrial heyday Scotland's prosperity was based on such heavy industries as coal, steel, shipbuilding, and engineering. In more recent times these have been the industries most exposed to foreign competition and to changes of demand. The task of correcting Scotland's industrial balance by reducing dependence on heavy industries and replacing them with high-technology enterprises and those making consumer goods has been slow and laborious, but considerable progress has been made in diversifying the structure of industry and in modernizing it. As with coal, the history of steel and shipbuilding is one of a reduction in the number of plants and employees. Scottish steel plants now belong to the British Steel Corporation, and shipyards are under the control of another state industry, British Shipbuilders. Scotland has shared in the drastic reduction of British Steel's operations; obsolescent plants were closed. Most of the well-known names on Clydeside have vanished, and the remaining yards are Govan Shipbuilders, Yarrow, mostly engaged in naval shipbuilding, and the Scott Lithgow group on the lower reaches of the Clyde, which is capable of building anything from oil tankers to submarines. Small yards belonging to British Shipbuilders in Aberdeen, Leith, and Troon build trawlers and cargo vessels.

There is now a wide range of manufacturing industries in Scotland. The electronics and computer industries have expanded remarkably in recent years, especially in Fife and Lothian regions and in the Glasgow area. Most of the companies engaged in electronics and computers are branches of U.S. and English undertakings and include leading international firms like IBM and Hewlett-Packard. Manufacture of clocks, watches, cash registers, earth-moving machinery, precision instruments, and other modern products, introduced since World War II, has also helped to diversify the industrial structure. Old-established industries such as textiles in the Borders region towns of Hawick, Galashiels, Selkirk, and Peebles have retained their vitality. Carpet making flourishes in Glasgow and Ayr. Dundee's characteristic jute industry has been contracted and modernized and turned to the production of other fibres as well. Automobiles were made in Scotland in the pioneering days of motoring, but the industry faded away until it was revived on a considerable scale in the early 1960s through government encouragement. The industry, however, failed to grow as much as had been expected.

Printing and brewing are well-established industries in Edinburgh and Glasgow. The distilleries in the Highlands and the Northeast produce the whisky for which Scotland is internationally famous. Despite crushing taxation on home consumption, whisky sales have continued to increase, and its appeal in foreign countries remains high. Separate records of Scotland's exports are not kept, but it is known that whisky's contribution to the U.K. overseas trade is substantial. Whisky is the chief earner of foreign currency, but the textile industries of the Borders region and the Harris tweed industry of the Hebrides also have a large export business. Mechanical- and electrical-engineering industries also export much of their output.

Finance. Scotland had eight joint-stock banks until the 1950s, but, as a result of mergers, the number was reduced to three: the Bank of Scotland, the Royal Bank of Scotland, and the Clydesdale Bank. The Scottish banks have their own notes, they have introduced computers and new accounting methods, and they have moved into hire purchase (installment purchase), merchant banking, and insurance broking. Scotland formerly had been conspicuously lacking in merchant-bank facilities, but several native merchant banks have been established, in addition to branches of London banks. Investment trusts are among the most distinctive of Scottish financial institutions. One-third of Britain's investment trusts are managed in Edinburgh, Glasgow, and Dundee. They have large investments in North America and specialized knowledge of conditions there. Unit trusts are represented in Edinburgh, where some leading British insurance companies also have their headquarters.

Economic problems. It is a common complaint that Scotland's economic problems are aggravated by the poli-

cies of successive Westminster governments, framed to suit populous and prosperous regions in the Southeast and the Midlands of England. On the other hand, governments do try to compensate for the handicaps of distance and high transport costs by applying regional policies. Grants and loans for buildings and machinery are offered to industrialists willing to set up business in development areas, as those most afflicted with heavy unemployment are called. Especially attractive incentives are available in the most blighted areas like those devastated by the closings of mines or factories. The Scottish Development Agency attempts to attract foreign industrialists, to help native enterprises with financial and marketing problems, to manage industrial estates, and generally to stimulate growth.

Transportation. Most public transport in Scotland is owned by state companies or local authorities. There is a certain amount of coordination; in 1968, for example, the Scottish Transport Group was created to bring under common control steamer services in the Clyde and the Western Isles and omnibus services throughout the country. Other forms of transport—rail, road haulage, and airlines—retain their own structure. Proliferation of automobiles has made it difficult for omnibus companies to maintain profitable services in rural areas, where they are being either subsidized by local authorities and the government or withdrawn. The pattern of steamship services has greatly altered. Services from mainland ports to island towns have been curtailed and replaced by car ferries using short crossings; such ferries operate from several west coast towns to the Hebrides and other islands and from north and east coast ports to the Orkneys and Shetlands.

Despite improvement, much of the road system, especially single-track roads in the Highlands, is inadequate for rapidly growing traffic. Since 1964 the Forth Road Bridge, the Tay Road Bridge, and the Kingston and Erskine bridges over the Clyde have been opened. Main roads, such as Carlisle–Glasgow, Edinburgh–Glasgow, Glasgow–Stirling, and Edinburgh–Inverness, have been reconstructed as motorways or dual carriageways. Road improvement has been speeded up by the traffic requirements of North Sea oil production.

Railway services have been severely reduced since 1948, when more than 3,000 miles of track were open to passenger and freight traffic. Many branch lines and stations have been closed, and the route mileage has shrunk to less than two-thirds of the former total. Diesel engines have replaced steam locomotives, and some lines have been electrified. Suburban lines from Glasgow on both sides of the Clyde and to Airdrie in the east have been electrified, as has the main line from Crewe to Glasgow.

Scottish ports handle many more imports than exports, a large proportion of which is sent abroad via English ports. Glasgow, the largest port, is under the administration of the Clyde Port Authority. The Forth ports, including Grangemouth and Leith, are grouped under the Forth Ports Authority, while Dundee and Aberdeen are independent. Greenock and Grangemouth are equipped for container traffic, and extensive improvement schemes have been carried out at Leith and other ports. Coastal trade has dwindled because of the competition of motor transport, and inland waterways have never been a commercial success.

Air transport is growing steadily. The major airports are Glasgow, Edinburgh, and Prestwick, all operated by the British Airports Authority. Transatlantic services fly from Prestwick, on the west coast, which is remarkably fog-free, and Glasgow and Edinburgh are used for domestic services in the United Kingdom and to a lesser extent for flights to European cities. The Highlands and islands have several airfields, but the services to them from Edinburgh, Glasgow, and Aberdeen are unprofitable and are operated by British Airways for social reasons.

ADMINISTRATIVE AND SOCIAL CONDITIONS

Government. Scotland is represented in the United Kingdom House of Commons, and since the election of 1964 all Scottish peers have been entitled to sit in the House of Lords. The secretary of state for Scotland is responsible to Parliament for departments under his ju-

Side notes:

Steel and shipbuilding

Other industries

Incentives for development

Major ports

risdiction. These consist of the departments of Home and Health, Education, Agriculture and Fisheries, Economic Planning, and Development. In his multifarious functions the secretary of state is assisted by a minister of state and three parliamentary undersecretaries. In the House of Commons, bills relating solely to Scotland are referred to the Scottish Grand Committee, which consists of all Scottish MP's. The Grand Committee has a general debate on a bill and usually sends it for detailed examination to the Scottish Standing Committee, a smaller body of Scottish MP's. The Select Committee on Scottish Affairs, composed of Scottish MP's, investigates specific administrative or economic issues.

The two major British parties, Labour and Conservative, have separate organizations in Scotland, hold annual conferences, and take notice of Scottish problems and grievances. They hardly have distinctive policies for Scotland but rather adapt general proposals to Scottish purposes. Devolution, or self-government, became a lively issue during the late 20th century, though the question had agitated the political scene in earlier years. The Scottish National Party (SNP) advocates independence, including control of defense and foreign policy.

The local government structure of Scotland was reorganized in 1975. The number of local authorities was reduced and a two-tier system created. In place of the rather complex pattern of cities, burghs, and counties, the country was divided into nine regions: Borders, Central, Dumfries and Galloway, Fife, Grampian, Highland, Lothian, Strathclyde, and Tayside. Three island authorities—Orkney Islands, Shetland Islands, and Western Isles—have separate status. Power is distributed between the regions and the 53 districts into which they are divided. The regional authorities are responsible for planning, transport, education, police, and fire services, while the districts deal with such matters as housing, sanitation, libraries, and recreation facilities. Elections to these authorities are held every four years; most local contests are fought on party lines. Labour controls Strathclyde, the largest region, and is the predominant party in local as in parliamentary politics. Regional and district councils are financed partly by government grants and partly by the yield of rates, local taxes levied on householders, commercial properties, and industrial plants. Government grants normally cover two-thirds of the expenditure of local authorities, but they are the subject of annual negotiations. The reform of local government cannot be said to have satisfied its critics. It is felt by many of them to have become even more bureaucratic and more out of touch with local feelings. Persistent increases in the tax rates, mainly due to inflation, also fuel discontent with the system, while conflict between local authorities and the central government is apt to be keen when different parties are in power at Westminster and in the Scottish local councils.

Justice. In law Scotland has preserved its own system and courts. The lord advocate and the solicitor general for Scotland are the ministers responsible for justice; they advise the government on legal affairs and help to draft legislation. The country is divided into 12 sheriffdoms, each with a sheriff principal and a varying number of sheriffs substitute. Offenses triable by jury are reserved for the High Court of Justiciary, the supreme court for criminal cases. The judges are the same as those of the Court of Session, the supreme court for civil cases. An appeal may be directed to the House of Lords from the Court of Session, but not from the High Court of Justiciary. The Court of Session, consisting of the lord president, the lord justice clerk, and 19 other judges, sits in Edinburgh and is divided into Inner and Outer houses. The Outer House judges hear cases at first instance. The Inner House, of which there are two divisions, each of four judges, hears appeals from the Outer House and from inferior courts. The sheriff courts have a wide jurisdiction in civil cases, but certain actions, such as divorce, are reserved for the Court of Session. The police investigate cases of crime discovered by or made known to them, but the decision whether or not to prosecute is made by the lord advocate in the High Court and by procurator fiscals in the sheriff courts.

Move for self-government

High Court of Justiciary

Education. In Scotland, education is supervised by the Education Department and administered by the education committees of the regional authorities. Unlike the English system, fee-charging, independent "public schools" play only a minor role in Scottish education. Direct-grant schools, located mostly in Edinburgh and Glasgow, get a government grant to supplement the fees paid by pupils. Though education authorities were informed in 1971 that they were no longer required to organize secondary education on comprehensive lines (*i.e.*, in schools providing several types of secondary education—academic, vocational, technical—in one building), this system has been widely adopted, especially in urban areas. Teachers, many of them university graduates, get their professional training in colleges of education.

Universities emphasize research and the training of students. They give increasing attention to the study of Scottish history, literature, and politics, though the extent varies from university to university. There are now eight universities; in 1960 there were only four. The University of Strathclyde in Glasgow and the Heriot-Watt University in Edinburgh, formerly technological colleges, were upgraded to universities, retaining their scientific and technological emphasis. The University of Dundee was separated from the University of St. Andrews, which had some departments in Dundee. The University of Stirling, the only completely new foundation, was opened in 1967. The new universities do not teach law and divinity but place most emphasis on science and technology and have close links with science-based industries in their neighbourhoods. Edinburgh, famous for its medical school, is the largest of the universities. Though the constitutions of the universities vary, nearly all have rectors, elected by the students, and student representative councils.

Health and welfare services. Health and welfare services and housing are the joint responsibility of government departments and local authorities. The National Health Service is administered in Scotland by several Health Boards and the Common Services Agency; local authorities provide for the welfare of mothers, children, and the aged. Incomes are lower in Scotland than in the United Kingdom as a whole. Average weekly earnings of manual workers have caught up with those of British workers in general. But incomes from profits and professional services are below the U.K. levels, and there are more people in the lower income groups and fewer in the higher ones than in the United Kingdom as a whole. Only in investment income is Scotland almost on equal terms.

Income differentials

Police forces. Since the secretary of state has a general responsibility for law and order, he shares control of the police forces with local authorities. The police committees provide the buildings and equipment needed by the forces. The secretary of state, assisted by the chief inspector of constabulary, is concerned with efficiency and discipline; he approves the appointment of chief constables and can make regulations on conditions of service.

CULTURAL LIFE

Scotland's culture is in an indeterminate state. It could be argued that there is not a national culture but only a regional variation of a wider British culture. Scotland's culture does have stirrings of independence. Although it is perhaps dominated by the intellectual and artistic influences of London, its cultural institutions and achievements transcend the provincial level. The Edinburgh International Festival of Music and Drama in scale and quality is an outstanding event in the cultural calendar. Scotland's own contribution to it is modest but creditable, and it has probably had a good effect in raising the standards of artistic performance. The Scottish National Orchestra, Scottish Opera, and Scottish Ballet have earned high reputations, though they rely much on imported talent. These and other enterprises are subsidized by the Scottish Arts Council, which supports theatres, concerts, and exhibitions, besides giving grants or scholarships to individual artists. Scottish writers have the choice of three languages: Gaelic, Lallans (or Scots vernacular), and English. Gaelic is understood by a small minority; there are only about 90,-000 Gaelic speakers, mostly in western Highland region,

The use of Gaelic

the Hebrides, and Glasgow, but the Gaelic poets Sorley Maclean and George Campbell Hay are highly esteemed. Hugh MacDiarmid, the poet, nationalist, and Marxist, achieved an international reputation for his Scots poetry, and Robert Garioch wrote in Scots with humour and craftsmanship; but the Lallans revival has faded. English is the tongue of most poets, such as Norman MacCaig, and of popular novelists and dramatists. Scottish painting and sculpture are flourishing, as the annual exhibition of the Royal Scottish Academy proves. Folk songs and music are popular and are collected by the School of Scottish Studies, which is attached to the University of Edinburgh; it is also responsible for two great works of scholarship, *A Dictionary of the Older Scottish Tongue* and *The Scottish National Dictionary,* the latter of which has been completed. Edinburgh houses cultural institutions of notable prominence, such as the National Library of Scotland, which has a statutory right to receive copies of all books published in Britain. The National Gallery of Scotland has paintings by many famous European artists in addition to works by Allan Ramsay, Sir Henry Raeburn, and other Scottish painters. The National Portrait Gallery portrays the principal personages in Scotland's history, and the Scottish National Gallery of Modern Art has works by contemporary European painters and sculptors, as well as those of native artists. The National Museum of Antiquities contains archaeological and later evidence for the development of the material and domestic aspects of Scottish society. The Royal Scottish Museum, perhaps the most popular of all, has extensive collections in its departments of art and archaeology, natural history, technology, and geology. The galleries and museums are the responsibility of the secretary of state and are maintained by public funds.

Scottish newspapers

The Scottish press has tended to shrink in size because of rising costs and competition, but newspapers survive in sufficient variety of quality and popular appeal. There are Scottish editions printed in Manchester of London's *Daily Express* and the *Sunday Express,* and northern editions of other London newspapers are imported. Among indigenous newspapers, *The Scotsman* and the *Glasgow Herald* rank highest in antiquity and influence, giving a sound coverage of Scottish and international news and well-informed explanations and comment. Glasgow also has the *Daily Record,* a Scottish version of the London *Daily Mirror,* while Dundee and Aberdeen have well-established morning papers. There are evening papers in Glasgow, Edinburgh, Dundee, and Aberdeen. The *Sunday Post* is something of an institution, owing to its individual features, especially cartoons, and its somewhat conservative views. The 150 weekly newspapers published in Scotland have a local range, but the venerable *People's Journal* has many local editions and circulates throughout the country. Among illustrated periodicals, two monthly magazines—*Scottish Field* and *Scots Magazine*—vividly display Scotland's scenic beauty and provide a wealth of interest for outdoor enthusiasts.

Television and radio are probably more influential media than the press. The British Broadcasting Corporation (BBC) broadcasts Gaelic news, music, and church services, perhaps more than the number of Gaelic speakers would warrant. There is a good deal of Scottish dance music, songs, gardening talks, sport, and religious services on the radio and Scottish news, sport, and occasional features on television. The BBC is well disposed toward Scottish culture, but its Scottish material hardly does more than flavour programs supplied for the greater part from London. Scottish Television Ltd., a commercial company, scarcely ventures beyond sport and discussions in its specifically Scottish program content, and its contribution to Scottish culture is insignificant.

The Highland Games

Summer sports, many unique to Scotland, are provided by the Highland Games. Strong men toss the caber (a heavy pole) and perform other feats of strength; pipers play, and agile men and girls do Highland dances. The colour of the tartan and the panache of kilted pipe bands fascinate tourists, and the Braemar Gathering, in Grampian region, always attended by a royal party from Balmoral Castle, is the culmination of these displays.

Many Scots find these games and other traditions, such as Burns suppers (after Robert Burns, the 18th-century national poet) and eating haggis (a delicacy consisting of offal boiled in a sheep's stomach), a self-conscious parade of legendary characteristics that have little to do with ordinary Scottish life—a show put on, like national costumes, to gratify the expectations of tourists. This objection can hardly be levelled against the National Mod, a musical festival run annually by An Comunn Gaidhealach, a society that hopes to keep Gaelic alive by competition among choirs and soloists in singing Gaelic songs and by bards in composing Gaelic verses.   (Ma.J.M./Ed.)

History

ANCIENT TIMES

Evidence of human settlement in the area later known as Scotland dates from the 3rd millennium BC. The earliest people, Mesolithic (Middle Stone Age) hunters and fishermen, were to be found on the west coast, near Oban, and as far south as Kirkcudbright, where their settlements are marked by large deposits of discarded mollusk shells. There were also settlements in the Forth estuary, where, in the area of Stirling, they obtained meat from stranded whales. These were followed, early in the 2nd millennium BC by Neolithic (New Stone Age) farmers who knew the use of cereals and of cattle and sheep. They made settlements on the west coast and as far north as Shetland. Many built collective chamber tombs, that at Maeshowe in Orkney being the finest in Britain. A settlement of such people at Skara Brae in Orkney consists of a cluster of seven self-contained huts connected by covered galleries or alleys. The "Beaker folk," so called from the shape of their drinking vessels, came to east Scotland from northern Europe, probably from about 1800 BC on. They buried their dead individually and were pioneers in bronze working. The most impressive monuments of Bronze Age Scotland are the stone circles, presumably for religious ceremonies, like those at Callanish in Lewis and Brodgar in Orkney, the latter being over 300 feet (91 metres) in diameter.

From about 700 BC onward there was a distinct final period in Scottish prehistory. This period is the subject of current archaeological controversy, with somewhat less stress than in the past being placed on the importance of the introduction of iron using or on the impact of large new groups of iron-using settlers. One key development in the middle of the 1st millennium was the change from a relatively warm and dry climate to one that was cooler and wetter. Another was the appearance of hill forts, having stone ramparts with an internal frame of timber: a good example is at Abernethy near the Tay. Some of these forts have recently been dated to the 7th and 6th centuries BC, and this might suggest that they were adopted by already established tribes rather than introduced by incomers, whose presence at this early date has yet to be proved. Massive decorated bronze armlets with Celtic ornamentation, found in northeastern Scotland and dated to the period AD 50–150, suggest that chieftains from outside may have come to these tribes at this period, displaced from farther south by fresh settlers from the Continent and then by the advent of the Romans in AD 43. From 100 BC the "brochs" appeared in the extreme north of Scotland and the northern isles. These were high, round towers, that at Mousa in Shetland stand almost 50 feet (15 metres) in height. The broch dwellers may have carried on intermittent warfare with the fort builders of farther south. On the other hand, the two types of structures may not represent two wholly distinct cultures, and the two peoples may have together comprised the ancestors of the people later known as the Picts.

The "brochs"

The houses of this people were circular, sometimes standing alone, sometimes in groups of 15 or more, as at Hayhope Knowe in the Cheviot Hills on the border between modern Scotland and England. Some single steadings, set in bogs or on lakesides, are called crannogs. Corn growing was probably of minor importance in the economy; the people were pastoralists and food-gatherers. They were ruled by a warrior aristocracy whose bronze and iron parade equipment has, in a few instances, survived.

Roman penetration and the Dark Age peoples. Gnaeus Julius Agricola, the Roman governor of Britain (AD 77–84), was the first Roman general to operate extensively in Scotland. He defeated the natives at Mons Graupius, possibly in Banffshire, probably in AD 84. In the following year he was recalled, and his policy of containing the hostile tribes within the Highland zone, which he had marked by building a legionary fortress at Inchtuthil in Strathmore, was not continued. His tactics were logical, if Scotland was to be subdued, but probably required the commitment of more troops than the overall strategy of the Roman Empire could afford. The only other period that a forward policy was attempted was between about 144 and about 190, when a turf wall, the Antonine Wall (named after the emperor Antoninus Pius), was manned between the Forth and the Clyde.

The still-impressive stone structure known as Hadrian's Wall had been built between the Tyne and Solway Firth in the years 122–128, and it was to be the permanent northern frontier of Roman Britain. After a northern rising, the emperor Severus supervised the restoring of the Hadrianic line in the years 209–211, and thereafter southeast Scotland seems to have enjoyed almost a century of peace. In the 4th century there were successive raids from north of the Wall and periodic withdrawals of Roman troops to the Continent. Despite increasing use of native buffer-states in front of the Wall, the Romans found their frontier indefensible by the end of the 4th century.

At Housesteads, at about the midpoint of Hadrian's Wall, archaeologists have uncovered a market where northern natives exchanged cattle and hides for Roman products: in this way some Roman wares, and possibly more general cultural influences, found their way north, but the scale of this was probably small. Roman civilization, typified by the towns and villas, or country houses, of southern Britain, was unknown in Scotland. Thus Scotland as a whole was never dominated by the Romans, nor even strongly influenced by them.

The peoples of early Scotland

From about AD 400 there was a long period for which written evidence is scanty. Four peoples—the Picts, the Scots, the Britons, and the Angles—were eventually to merge and thus form the kingdom of Scots.

The Picts occupied Scotland north of the Forth. Their identity has been much debated, but they possessed a distinctive culture, seen particularly in their carved symbol stones. Their original language, presumably non-Indo-European, has disappeared: some Picts probably spoke a Brythonic Celtic language. Pictish unity may have been impaired by their custom of succession to the throne, which is thought to have been matrilinear.

The Scots, from Dalriada in northern Ireland, colonized the Argyll area, probably in the late 5th century. Their continuing connection with Ireland was a source of strength to them, and Scots and Irish Gaelic (Goidelic Celtic languages) did not become distinct from one another until the late Middle Ages. Scottish Dalriada soon extended its cultural as well as its military sway east and south, though one of its greatest kings, Aidan, was, in 603, defeated by the Angles at Degsastan near the later Scottish border.

The Britons, speaking a Brythonic Celtic language, colonized Scotland from farther south, probably from the first century BC onward. They lost control of southeastern Scotland to the Angles in the early 7th century AD. The British heroic poem *Gododdin* describes a stage in this process. The British kingdom of Strathclyde in southwestern Scotland remained, with its capital at Dumbarton.

The Angles were Teutonic-speaking invaders from across the North Sea. Settling from the 5th century, they had by the early 7th century created the kingdom of Northumbria, stretching from the Humber to the Forth. A decisive check to their northward advance was administered in 685 by the Picts at the Battle of Nechtansmere in Angus.

Christianity. Christianity was introduced to Scotland in late Roman times, and traditions of St. Ninian's evangelizing in the southwest have survived. He is a shadowy figure, and it is doubtful if his work extended very far north.

Christianity was firmly established throughout Scotland by the Celtic clergy, coming with the Scots settlers from Ireland, and possibly giving the Scots a decisive cultural advantage in the early unification of Scotland. The Celtic Church lacked a territorial organization of parishes and dioceses and a division between secular and regular clergy: its communities of missionary monks were ideal agents of conversion. The best known figure, possibly the greatest, is St. Columba who founded his monastery at Iona, an island of the Inner Hebrides, in 565: his life was written by Adamnan, abbot of Iona, within a century of his death. Columba is believed to have been influential in converting the Picts, and he certainly did much to support the Scots king Aidan politically. St. Columba

St. Aidan brought the Celtic Church to Northumbria in the 630s, establishing his monastery at Lindisfarne. At the Synod of Whitby in 664 the king of Northumbria had to decide between the Celtic and the Roman styles of Christianity: he chose the latter. There had been differences over such observances as the dating of Easter, but there was no question of the Celtic monks being regarded as schismatics. The *Ecclesiastical History of the English People,* by Bede, a monk of Jarrow in Northumbria (died 735) is a first-rate source for the history of Dark Age Scotland and shows remarkable sympathy with the Celtic clergy, though Bede was a Roman monk.

In the early 8th century the church among the Picts and Scots accepted Roman usages on such questions as Easter. Nevertheless, the church in Scotland remained Celtic in many ways until the 11th century: still dominated by its communities of clergy (who were called Célidé or Culdees), it clearly corresponded well to the tribal nature of society.

The Norse influence. Viking raids on the coasts of Britain began at the end of the 8th century, Lindisfarne and Iona being pillaged in the 790s. By the mid-9th century, Norse settlement of the western and northern isles and of Caithness and Sutherland had begun: the main cause was probably overpopulation on the west coast of Norway. During the 10th century, Orkney and Shetland were ruled by Norse earls nominally subject to Norway. In 1098 Magnus II Barefoot, king of Norway, successfully asserted his authority in the northern and western isles and made an agreement with the king of Scots on their respective spheres of influence. A mid-12th-century earl of Orkney, Ragnvald, built the great cathedral at Kirkwall in honour of his martyred uncle St. Magnus.

The Norse legacy to Scotland was long lasting. In the mid-12th century there was a rising against the Norse in the west under a native leader, Somerled, who drove them from the greater part of mainland Argyll. A Norwegian expedition of 1263 under King Haakon IV failed to maintain the Norse presence in the Hebrides, and three years later they were ceded to Scotland by the Treaty of Perth. In 1468–69 the northern isles of Orkney and Shetland were pawned to Scotland as part of a marriage settlement with the crown of Denmark-Norway. A Scandinavian language, the Norn, was spoken in these Viking possessions, and some Norse linguistic influence is discernible in Shetland to the present day.

THE UNIFICATION OF THE KINGDOM

In 843 Kenneth I MacAlpin, king of Scots, also became king of the Picts and crushed resistance to his assuming the throne. Kenneth may have had a claim on the Pictish throne through the matrilinear law of succession: probably the Picts, too, had been weakened by Norse attacks. The Norse threat helped to weld together the new kingdom of Alba and to cause its heartlands to be located in eastern Scotland, the former Pictland, with Dunkeld becoming its religious capital. But within Alba it was the Scots who established a cultural and linguistic supremacy, no doubt merely confirming a tendency seen before 843.

As the English kingdom was consolidated, its kings, in the face of Norse attacks, found it useful to have an understanding with Alba. In 945 Edmund of England is said to have leased to Malcolm I of Alba the whole of Cumbria, probably an area including land on both sides of the western half of the later Anglo-Scottish border. In the late 10th century a similar arrangement seems to have been made for Lothian, the corresponding territory to the east. The Scots confirmed their hold on Lothian, from the Forth to the Tweed, when, about 1016, Malcolm II de- Ascendancy of the Scots feated a Northumbrian army at Carham. About the same time, Malcolm II placed his grandson Duncan I upon the throne of the British kingdom of Strathclyde. Duncan succeeded Malcolm in 1034 and brought Strathclyde into the kingdom of Scots. During the next two centuries the Scots kings pushed their effective power north and west—William I was successful in the north and Alexander II in the west—until mainland Scotland became one political unit. Less discernible but as important was the way the various peoples grew together, though significant linguistic and other differences remained.

According to the Celtic system of succession, known as tanistry, a king could be succeeded by any male member of the *derbfine,* a family group of four generations: members of collateral branches seem to have been preferred to descendants, and the successor, or tanist, might be named in his predecessor's lifetime. This system, in practice, led to many successions by the killing of one's predecessor. Thus Duncan I was killed by his cousin Macbeth in 1040, and Macbeth was killed by Malcolm III Canmore, Duncan I's son, in 1057. Shakespeare freely adapted the story of Macbeth, who historically seems to have been a successful king and who may have gone on pilgrimage to Rome.

Up to the 11th century the unification was the work of a Scots Gaelic-speaking dynasty, and there is place-name evidence of the penetration of Gaelic south of the Forth. But from then on, the Teutonic English speech that had come to Scotland from the kingdom of Northumbria began to attain mastery, and Gaelic began its slow retreat north and west. This is not obscured by the fact that, from the 12th century onward, Anglo-Norman was for a time the speech of the leaders of society in England and Scotland alike. By the later Middle Ages, Old English had evolved into two separate languages, Middle English and Middle Scots, the latter with the court of the Stewart (Stuart) kings of Scots as its focus. After 1603, the increasing political and cultural assimilation of Scotland to England checked the further development of Scots as a separate language.

The royal succession

The persistence of distinctively Celtic institutions in post-12th-century Scotland is a more complex question, as will be seen from the way in which primogeniture replaced tanistry as the system of royal succession. It can be argued, however, that a Celtic stress on the family bond in society persisted throughout the Middle Ages and beyond—and not only in the Highlands, with its clan organization of society.

The development of the monarchy. Malcolm III Canmore (1058–93) came to the throne by disposing of his rivals and thereafter sought, in five unsuccessful raids, to extend his kingdom into northern England. Whereas his first wife, Ingibjorg, was the daughter of a Norse earl of Orkney, his second, Margaret, came from the Saxon royal house of England. With Margaret and her sons, Scotland entered a phase of being particularly receptive to cultural influence from the south. Margaret was a great patroness of the church but without altering its organization as her sons were to do.

On the death of Malcolm III on his last English raid, sustained attempts were made to prevent the application of the southern custom of succession by primogeniture. Both Malcolm's brother and Malcolm's son by his first marriage held the throne for short periods: but it was the three sons of Malcolm and Margaret who eventually established themselves—Edgar (1097–1107), Alexander I (1107–24), and David I (1124–53). The descendants of Malcolm III's first marriage continued to trouble the ruling dynasty until the early 13th century, but the descendants of his second retained the throne. It happened that until the late 13th century, the heir to the throne by primogeniture was always the obvious candidate. It is noteworthy that in charters of about 1145, David I's son Henry (who was to die before his father) is described as *rex designatus,* very much like the tanist of the Celtic system. It is thus very hard to date precisely the acceptance of southern custom as exemplified by primogeniture.

Such was the force of Celtic reaction against southern influence that Edgar and Alexander I could be said to owe their thrones solely to English aid and were feudally subject to the English king.

David I (1124–53). David I was by marriage a leading landowner in England and was well-known at the English court: he was, nevertheless, an independent monarch, making Scotland strong by drawing on English cultural and organizational influences. Under him and his successors many Anglo-Norman families came to Scotland, and their members were rewarded with lands and offices. Among the most important were the Bruces in Annandale, the de Morvilles in Ayrshire and Lauderdale, and the Fitzalans, who became hereditary High Stewards and who, as the Stewart dynasty, were to inherit the throne, in Renfrewshire. (After the 16th century the Stewart dynasty was known by its French spelling, "Stuart," the French language having no "w.") Such men were often given large estates in outlying areas to bolster the king's authority where it was weak.

Anglo-Norman settlement in Scotland

The decentralized form of government and society that resulted was one of the many variants of what is known as "feudalism," with tenants in chief holding lands, with jurisdiction over their inhabitants, from the king, in return for the performance of military and other services. An essentially new element in Scottish society was the written charter, setting out the rights and obligations involved in landholding. But the way in which the Anglo-Norman families, in their position as tenants in chief, were successfully grafted onto the existing society suggests that the Celtic and feudal social systems, although one stressed family bonds and the other legal contracts, were by no means mutually incompatible. The clan system of Highland Scotland became tinged with feudal influences, whereas Lowland Scottish feudalism retained a strong emphasis on the family.

David began to spread direct royal influence through the kingdom by the creation of the office of sheriff (*vicecomes*), a royal judge and administrator ruling an area of the kingdom from one of the royal castles. Centrally, a nucleus of government officials, such as the chancellor, the chamberlain, and the justiciar, was created by David and his successors: these officials, with other tenants in chief called to give advice, made up the royal court (Curia Regis). This body became formalized in various ways: by the mid-13th century it might meet as the king's council to discuss various types of business; and before the Wars of Independence (see below) the royal court in its capacity as the Supreme Court of Law was already being described as a Parliament. The almost total loss of all of the Scottish governmental records from before the early 14th century should not lead one to underestimate the efficiency of the Scots kings' government in this period; historians in recent years have done much to assemble the surviving royal documents from scattered sources.

Medieval economy and society. From David's time onward, the burghs, or incorporated towns, were created as centres of trade and small-scale manufacture in an overwhelmingly agrarian economy. At first, all burghs probably had equal rights. Later, however, royal burghs had, by their charters, the exclusive right of overseas trade, though tenants in chief could create burghs with local trade privileges. Burghs evolved their own law to govern trading transactions, and disputes could be referred to the Court of the Four Burghs (originally Berwick, Edinburgh, Roxburgh, and Stirling). Many of the original townspeople, or burgesses, were newcomers to Scotland. At Berwick, the great trading town of the 13th century, exporting the wool of the border monasteries, Flemish merchants had their own Red Hall, which they defended to the death against English attack in 1296. Besides commercial contacts with England, there is evidence of Scottish trading with the Low Countries and with Norway in the period before the Wars of Independence.

David's reorganization of the church

The church was decisively remodelled by David I and his successors. A clear division emerged between secular and regular clergy according to the normal western European pattern. A complete system of parishes and dioceses was established. But the system of "appropriating" the revenue of parish churches to central religious institutions meant that the top-heaviness in wealth and resources of the church in Scotland was a built-in feature of its existence until the Reformation. Kings and other great men vied in setting up monasteries. Alexander I had founded houses of Augustinian canons at Scone and Inchcolm, while among David's foundations were the Cistercian houses of Melrose and Newbattle and the Augustinian houses of Cambuskenneth and Holyrood. Augustinian canons might also serve as the clergy of a cathedral, as they did at St. Andrews. Prominent foundations by the magnates included Walter Fitzalan's Cluniac house at Paisley, and Hugh de Morville's Premonstratensian house at Dryburgh. Later royal foundations included that of the Benedictine house at Arbroath, established by William I.

From the standpoint of a later age, when the monasteries had lost their spiritual force, the piety of David I especially seemed a misapplication of royal resources. But the original monasteries, with their supply of trained manpower for royal service, their hospitality, and their learning, epitomized that stability which it was royal policy to achieve.

From at least 1072, the English Church, particularly the Archbishop of York, sought some control over the Scottish Church: the Scottish Church was weakened in face of such a threat through having no metropolitan see. But, probably in 1192, the Pope by the bull *Cum Universi* declared the Scottish Church to be subject only to Rome; and in 1225 the bull *Quidam Vestrum* permitted the Scottish Church, lacking a metropolitan see, to hold provincial councils by authority of Rome. Such councils, which might have served to check abuses, were, however, seldom held.

It has been argued that the cultural developments encouraged by the church in pre-Reformation Scotland were not as great as might be expected, but this may be a false impression created because the manuscript evidence has failed to survive. The monasteries of Melrose and Holyrood had each a chronicle, and Adam of Dryburgh was an able theologian of the late 12th century. Surviving Romanesque churches show that Scotland partook of the common European architectural tradition of the time: good small examples are at Dalmeny, near Edinburgh, and at Leuchars, in Fife. Glasgow and Elgin cathedrals are noteworthy, and St. Andrews Cathedral is impressive even in its ruined state. There are also distinguished examples of castle architecture, such as Bothwell in Lanarkshire; and the castles of Argyll may reflect a distinctive mixture of influences, including Norse ones.

David's successors. Malcolm IV (1153–65) was a fairly successful king, defeating Somerled when the latter, who had been triumphant over the Scandinavians in Argyll, turned against the kingdom of Scots. Malcolm's brother, William I the Lion (1165–1214) subdued much of the north, and established royal castles there. After his capture on a raid into England, he was forced to become feudally subject to the English king by the Treaty of Falaise (1174); he was able, however, to buy back his kingdom's independence by the Quitclaim of Canterbury in 1189, though it should be emphasized that this document disposed of the Treaty of Falaise and not of the less precise claims of superiority over Scotland that English kings had put forward over the previous century. William's son, Alexander II (1214–49), subdued Argyll and was about to proceed against the Hebrides at the time of his death. His son, Alexander III (1249–86), brought these islands within the Scottish kingdom in 1266, adroitly fended off English claims to overlordship, and brought to Scotland the peace and prosperity typified by the commercial growth of Berwick. In the perspective of the subsequent Wars of Independence, it was inevitable that men should look back on his reign as a golden age.

THE WARS OF INDEPENDENCE

Competition for the throne. With the death, in 1286, of Alexander III and of his young granddaughter Margaret, the "Maid of Norway," four years later, almost two centuries of relatively amicable Anglo-Scottish relations came to an end. A complete uncertainty as to the proper succession to the throne provided Edward I of England and his successors with a chance to intervene in and then to assimilate Scotland. Though the two countries were feudal monarchies of a largely similar type, the English attempt was, in practice, too tactless to have any hope of success.

Besides, the struggle for independence disclosed that a marked degree of national unity had arisen among the different peoples of Scotland. The Anglo-Scottish conflict thus begun gave Scotland a basic tendency—to seek self-sufficiency and at the same time to look to continental Europe for alliances and inspiration—that persisted at least until 1560.

Before the death of the Maid of Norway, the Scottish interim government of "guardians" had agreed (by the Treaty of Birgham, 1290) that she should marry the heir of Edward I of England, though Scotland was to be preserved as a separate kingdom. After her death, 13 claimants for the Scottish crown emerged, most of them Scottish magnates. The Scots had initially no reason to suspect the motives of Edward I in undertaking to judge the various claims. It emerged, however, that Edward saw himself not as an outside arbitrator but as the feudal superior of the Scots monarch and, therefore, able to dispose of Scotland as a fief. That Edward's interpretation was disingenuous is suggested by the fact that he had not invoked the old and vague English claims to superiority over Scotland while the Maid of Norway was still alive and had made a treaty with Scotland on a basis of equality, not as a feudal superior claiming rights of wardship and marriage over the Maid.

The leading competitors, who had much to lose by antagonizing Edward, agreed to acknowledge his superior lordship over Scotland. But a different answer to his claim to lordship was given by the "community of the realm" (the important laymen and churchmen of Scotland as a group), who declined to commit whoever was to be king of Scots on this issue and thus displayed a sophisticated sense of national unity.

Robert Bruce and John Balliol, descendants of a younger brother of Malcolm IV and William, emerged as the leading competitors, and in 1292 Edward I named the latter as king. When Edward sought to exert his overlordship by taking law cases on appeal from Scotland and by summoning Balliol to do military service for him in France, the Scots determined to resist. In 1295 they concluded an alliance with France, and in 1296 Edward's army marched north, sacking Berwick on its way.

Edward forced the submission of Balliol and of Scotland with ease. National resistance to English government of Scotland grew slowly thereafter and was led by William Wallace, a knight's son, in the absence of a lead from the magnates: Wallace defeated the English at Stirling Bridge in 1297 but lost at Falkirk the next year. He was executed in London in 1305, having shown that heroic leadership without sufficient social status was not enough. When Robert Bruce, grandson of the competitor, rose in revolt in 1306 and had himself crowned Robert I, he supplied the focus necessary for the considerable potential of national resistance.

Robert I the Bruce (1306–29). In several years of mixed fortunes thereafter, Robert had both the English and his opponents within Scotland to contend with. Edward I's death, in 1307, and the dissension in England under Edward II were assets that Bruce took full advantage of. He excelled as a statesman and as a military leader specializing in harrying tactics: it is ironic that he should be remembered best for the atypical set-piece battle that he incurred and won at Bannockburn in 1314. The Declaration of Arbroath of 1320 is perhaps more informative about his methods. Ostensibly a letter from the magnates of Scotland to the Pope, pledging their support for King Robert, it seems in reality to have been framed by Bernard de Linton, Robert's chancellor. In committing Robert to see the independence struggle through, it likewise committed those who set their seals to it. Some of them were waverers in the national cause, whether or not Robert had proof of this at the time, and his hand was now strengthened against them.

Robert I secured from England a recognition of Scotland's independence by the Treaty of Northampton in 1328; 1329 saw the Pope's granting to the independent kings of Scots the right to be anointed with holy oil, but it also saw the death of Bruce. By the appropriate standards of medieval kingship his success had been total; but by the

[margin notes:]
David's successors

The "Maid of Norway"

Bruce and Balliol

nature of medieval kingship, his successor was left with the same struggle to wage all over again.

David II (1329–71). Robert I's son, David II, has perhaps received unfair treatment from historians through having been contrasted with his illustrious father. Just over five years of age at his accession, he was soon confronted with a renewal of the Anglo-Scottish war, exacerbated by the ambitions of those Scots who had been deprived of their property by Robert I or otherwise disaffected. In the 1330s Edward Balliol, pursuing the claim to the throne of his father John, overran southern Scotland. In return for English help, he gave away to England southern lands and strongpoints not recaptured fully by the Scots for a century. After the Scots defeat at Halidon Hill near Berwick in 1333, David was forced to flee to France in the following year. Berwick itself fell to the English and was never again in Scots hands except in the period 1461–82.

The Scots gradually regained the initiative, and in 1341 David was able to return to Scotland. But in 1346 David II himself was captured at the Battle of Neville's Cross near Durham. He was released in 1357 for a ransom of 100,000 merks. This ransom, if paid (and three-quarters of it eventually was), would constitute a serious burden on Scotland, and there is evidence of Parliament's using this national emergency to establish some checks on the actions of the crown. In addition, the representatives of the royal burghs, which were important as an accessible source of finance, established a continuing right to sit in Parliament with the magnates and churchmen from the 1360s on, thus constituting the third of the "Three Estates."

Complex evidence relating to these transactions has been uniformly interpreted in a way discreditable to David. Another interpretation is possible. That he collected revenues more assiduously than he made ransom payments may indicate a reasoned attempt to strengthen the crown financially; and his negotiations, especially of 1363, whereby a member of the English royal house was to succeed him on the Scottish throne, may have been a diplomatic charade. Whatever his faults, David left Scotland with both its economy and its independence intact.

The long wars with England necessarily took their toll, retarding Scotland's economy and weakening the authority of her government. The buildings that have survived from this era are inferior to earlier work, much of which, of course, suffered damage at this time. War was increasingly expensive, and taxation was increased drastically to pay David II's ransom. But again, a rosier alternative picture can be painted, suggesting that the burgesses were able to meet the increased taxation because of increased prosperity through the still-continuing trade with England.

SCOTLAND IN THE 15TH CENTURY

The early Stewart kings. David was succeeded by Robert II (1371–90), previously the high steward and son of Robert I's daughter Marjory. The next king was Robert II's son John, restyled Robert III (1390–1406). It may be that Robert II's conduct was responsible for dissension in Scotland during David II's reign, particularly during his captivity in England. At any rate, neither Robert II nor his son Robert III were strong kings and some nobles regarded both as upstarts, and the latter as of doubtful legitimacy. There thus began a long period of monarchical weakness in Scotland, accentuated by a series of royal minorities in the 15th and 16th centuries. Historians have made much of the turbulence of these times, but there were comparable periods of governmental weakness in contemporary England and France: and "bonds of manrent" and other alliances made by the magnates with each other and with their social inferiors should be seen as much as attempts to secure political stability in their own localities as threats to the overall peace of the kingdom.

Robert III's younger brother, Robert Stewart, 1st duke of Albany, more than once was given powers to rule in his brother's name, and Robert's son James may have been sent to France in 1406 in order to keep him out of Albany's clutches. But James was captured at sea by the English, and shortly afterward Robert III died. Albany (died 1420) and then his son Murdac misgoverned the realm until 1424, when James I, then 29, was ransomed.

The Douglas family was becoming particularly powerful at this time. They had been rewarded with the gift of the royal forest of Selkirk and other lands in south and southwest Scotland for loyal service to Robert I. But the growing power of the Douglases in this vital border area posed by the end of the 14th century a growing threat to the crown, no longer able to count on the direct personal loyalty of the Douglas family. At the same time the Lords of the Isles had attained a stature in the western Highlands that overtopped that of the kings of Scots.

One notable event was the founding of Scotland's first university at St. Andrews. The Wars of Independence led Scots students to go to Paris rather than to Oxford or Cambridge. But universities were the training grounds of the clergy, and when, in the period 1408–18, Scotland recognized the anti-Pope Benedict XIII after he had been abandoned by France, it became expedient for Scotland to have its own university. The bulls of foundation from Benedict XIII reached St. Andrews in 1414.

James I (1406–37) was an active and able king, keen to make the crown wealthy and powerful again. Perhaps he was overimpatient to make up for time lost in his captivity, and thus he prompted the opposition to him that led to his death. New posts, those of the comptroller and treasurer, were created to gather royal revenues more efficiently. Murdac, 2nd duke of Albany, was executed in 1425, and other powerful men were overawed, even in the far north. The laws were to be revised, and in 1426 a court for civil cases was set up, presaging the later Court of Session.

Possibly to balance the power of the magnates, it was enacted in 1426 that all tenants in chief should attend Parliament in person. More realistically, they were, from 1428, permitted to send representatives from each shire. Even this system did not operate until the late 16th century. If James had been inspired during his captivity by the English House of Commons, he was unable to transplant that institution to Scotland. The Scots Parliament, like that of many other European countries, remained throughout the medieval period the feudal court of the kings of Scots: not undergoing the distinctive development of the English Parliament, it did not differ essentially in kind from the feudal court of any great magnate. Despite, or perhaps because of, his innovative vigour, James made enemies for himself. His murder in 1437 was part of an attempt to seize the throne for Walter Stewart, earl of Atholl, but the conspirators were executed and James's young son succeeded him.

James II (1437–60) was six at the time of his accession. His minority was marked by struggles between the Crichton and Livingston families. During this minority and that of James III, James Kennedy, bishop of St. Andrews, played a statesmanlike part in seeking to preserve peace. James II took a violent line against overmighty subjects. In 1452 he stabbed William Douglas, 8th earl of Douglas to death, and in 1455 James Douglas, 9th earl, was attainted. The main line of the Douglas family never regained its position, though a younger, or cadet, branch of the family, the earls of Angus, was important in the late 15th century. James II, like his father, thus sought manfully to reassert royal authority, and Scotland lost an able king when he was killed by the bursting of a cannon at the siege of Roxburgh Castle, one of the last Scottish strongpoints in English hands. Roxburgh was subsequently captured by the Scots. Among the cultural advances of the reign was the founding, in 1451, by Bishop William Turnbull of the University of Glasgow, Scotland's second university.

James III (1460–88), James's son, was eight years old at his accession. During his minority he was for a time the pawn of the Boyd family. The so-called Treaty of Westminster-Ardtornish of 1462 showed that John, Lord of the Isles, and the exiled Douglas were prepared to try to carve Scotland into two vassal states of England for themselves. The alliance came to nothing, but the Lords of the Isles were a threat to the territorial integrity of Scotland until their final forfeiture in 1493. On the other hand, the power vacuum left by their removal was responsible for much of the unrest in the western Highlands thereafter. It was in James III's reign that the territory of Scotland

[margin notes:]
Battle of Halidon Hill

The reign of James I

attained its fullest extent with the acquisition of Orkney and Shetland in 1468–69.

As James III came of age, he seems to have given grave offense to his nobles by shunning their company for that of artistic people. It has been suggested that his fine sensibility did him credit, but this is probably an anachronistic view. When it is seen what political disorder could follow from the absence of an adult male ruler in later medieval Scotland, it may be thought correspondingly important that such a ruler, when present, should have cultivated the nobles who were his natural companions and political associates and who tended to support a ruler who combined tact with good government. So serious was James's lack of authority that Berwick fell in 1482, when the nobles, led by Archibald Douglas, 5th earl of Angus, chose—rather than defend it against the English—to seize their opportunity to hang some of James's favourites. In 1488 James was murdered while fleeing from a battle against his opponents at Sauchieburn, though it seems that the death of the king was not intended, and he was succeeded without trouble by his son.

15th-century society. There is evidence of economic recovery in Scotland in this period, despite the continuing war and unrest. Castle-building and the extending of monasteries and cathedrals were widespread: work was done on the royal residences at Linlithgow and Stirling. The building of collegiate churches and of fine burgh churches is additional evidence of prosperity. Royal burghs with their share in international trade and baronial burghs with their rights in their own locality were alike flourishing. The craftsmen threatened to rival the merchants in the running of burgh affairs, but an act of 1469 gave the merchants the majority on the town councils: this allowed self-perpetuating cliques to misapply the assets of the burghs, an abuse not remedied until the 19th century. Accompanying the prosperity general in Scotland at this time was a tendency to inflation, and a debasement of the coinage added to the troubles of James III's reign.

From the late 14th century onward, interesting Scottish writing, both in the vernacular and in Latin, has survived. John Barbour (1316?–95) wrote a verse life of Robert I in Scots. A Latin history of Scotland was compiled by John of Fordun and continued by Walter Bower, abbot of Inchcolm, in his *Scotichronicon.* Andrew of Wyntoun wrote a history of Scotland in Scots verse.

Little is left of the corpus of medieval writings in Scottish Gaelic. But the sophistication of the west Highland stone carvings of the later Middle Ages suggests that a strong literary culture, too, was associated with the courts of the Lords of the Isles and other chiefs. The *Book of Deer,* containing the Gospels, has in its margins an 11th-century Gaelic account of Columba's foundation of the monastery of Deer in Aberdeenshire, and a series of *notitiae,* or lists of church rights, which provide clues to the nature of Celtic society. The early-16th-century *Book of the Dean of Lismore* (the seat of the Bishop of Argyll) contains over 60 Gaelic poems. From the quality of the architecture that has survived from the 15th century, one can infer the existence of paintings and other objects, such as church furnishings, that have largely disappeared. An outstandingly intricate collegiate church is that at Roslin near Edinburgh, founded by Sir William Sinclair, 3rd earl of Orkney, about 1450. There are fine burgh churches, such as St. John's in Perth and the Church of the Holy Rood in Stirling. Perhaps the outstanding piece of evidence of royal patronage of the arts is the altarpiece for James III's Trinity College Church in Edinburgh: the altarpiece is almost certainly the work of the great Flemish painter Hugo van der Goes.

In the 14th century the papacy had built up its claims to appoint to the higher offices in the church and in Scotland had established a system of "provisions," or papal appointments, to vacant offices. This cut not merely across the rights of rulers who used the church to provide their loyal bureaucrats with a living and the rights of other local patrons; it also meant a drain to Rome of money in the form of the tax payable by a cleric "provided" to a vacant post by the pope. James I resisted these developments, and at the same time, in the Council of Basel (1431–49), the "conciliarists" were seeking to curb papal power in the church: a distinguished member of the Council of Basel was the Scot Thomas Livingston, one of the first St. Andrews graduates.

James also sought to revive the monastic ideal in its early purity and established a house of the strict Carthusians at Perth. A compromise between James I and the Pope was probably pending when James was murdered, and his successors tended to let the popes collect their money as long as they "provided" to church offices along lines acceptable to the monarchy. In 1487 James III was granted the concession that the Pope would delay promotions to the higher offices for eight months so that the king could propose his nominee.

St. Andrews was made the seat of an archbishopric in 1472, in itself a desirable step. But the first archbishop of St. Andrews secured the honour by supporting the papacy against the king, and there was, as a result, no welcome for it in Scotland. Glasgow also became an archbishopric in 1492.

SCOTLAND IN THE 16TH AND EARLY 17TH CENTURIES

James IV (1488–1513) and James V (1513–42). James IV was well equipped for kingship, being physically impressive, cultured, generous, and active in politics and war alike. He eliminated a potential rival by carrying out the forfeiture of the last Lord of the Isles, in 1493, and dealt severely with unrest on the English border and elsewhere. James and Bishop William Elphinstone of Aberdeen founded King's College, Scotland's third university, in Aberdeen in 1495. This was the great age of Scots poetry, and while one of the leading "makars," or poets, Robert Henryson (1430?–1506?), author of the *Testament of Cresseid,* was a burgh schoolmaster, the others were members of the court circle: Gavin Douglas (1474–1522), bishop of Dunkeld and kinsman to the earls of Angus, translated Virgil's *Aeneid* splendidly into Scots, and William Dunbar (1460?–1520), a technically brilliant poet, showed the versatility of which Scots was capable.

After initial disharmony with England, James concluded a "treaty of perpetual peace" with Henry VII in 1502 and married Margaret, Henry's daughter, in 1503. But Henry VIII of England became involved in the anti-French schemes of Pope Julius II, and in 1512 France and Scotland renewed their "auld alliance" as a counterbalance. In 1513 Henry VIII invaded France: James IV, consequently, invaded England; there he died, along with thousands of his army, in the rashly fought and calamitous Battle of Flodden.

James's efficiency at home was thus offset by his excessive international ambitions. And both had cost money—for artillery; for a navy whose greatest ship, the "Great Michael," cost £30,000; for embassies. The crown granted lands in feu-ferme tenure, which gave heritable possession in return for a substantial down payment and an unchangeable annual rent thereafter. In the great European price rise of the 16th century, this policy in the long term weakened the crown.

James V (1513–42) was in his second year at his accession. The factional struggles of his minority were given shape by the division between those who adhered to Scotland's pro-French alignment, and those who were determined that the price Scotland paid at Flodden should not be repeated. John Stewart, duke of Albany, was regent until 1524, and favoured France: Archibald Douglas, 6th earl of Angus, then maintained a pro-English policy until 1528 when James began his personal rule. James now found Scotland's support in international politics being sought on all sides. In the 1530s he obtained papal financial help in establishing a College of Justice, and he concluded two successive French marriages, each bringing a substantial dowry: his second wife was Mary, daughter of the duc de Guise and mother of Mary, Queen of Scots. James's support for the papacy and France alienated some of his subjects, however, and his rule was not simply strict and financially vigorous but rather avaricious and vindictive. Lack of noble support seems to have caused the rout at Solway Moss in November 1542 of a force invading England. This, and the deaths of his infant sons, led to the death of James, probably from nervous prostration, in December, a week after the birth of his daughter Mary.

Mary (1542–67) and the Scottish Reformation. The church in 16th-century Scotland may not have had more ignorant or immoral priests than in previous generations, but restiveness at their shortcomings was becoming more widespread. And the power structure of the church seemed to preclude the possibility of reform without revolution. The church made a poor showing at the parish level, since by 1560 the bulk of the revenues of nearly nine parishes in every ten was appropriated to monasteries and other central institutions. The papacy, in return for receiving its share of this wealth, abandoned spiritual direction of the Scottish Church: from 1487, royal control over appointments to the higher church offices grew steadily. All this, at a time when the church's annual revenue—reckoned at £400,000 in 1560—was ten times that of the crown, readily explains the attraction of church office for unspiritual career-seeking nobles. Church lands were feued to laymen, who also became collectors of church revenues and were given abbeys as benefices. Church property, particularly monastic property, was effectively being secularized, and if Protestantism offered to the nobles and lairds of Scotland a more spiritually alive church—and one with lay participation—it probably also appealed to them as a system under which they would not have to hand back what they had grabbed.

Particular laymen were as pious as ever, endowing collegiate churches as they had once endowed monasteries, and trenchant criticism of church abuses was expressed in the play *Ane Pleasant Satyre of the Thrie Estaitis* by Sir David Lyndsay (*c. 1490–c.* 1555). But reform from within was probably almost impossible: Archbishop John Hamilton, for instance, a would-be reformer who gave his name to a vernacular catechism (1552), belonged to the family who had most to lose if the careerists were curbed.

Mary, Queen of Scots

Mary (1542–67) began her reign as another Stewart child ruler in the hands of factions: the pro-French party upheld the old church, while the pro-English desired reform. By the Treaties of Greenwich (1543), Mary was to marry Edward, Henry VIII's heir. Cardinal David Beaton and Mary of Guise, the queen mother, had this policy rescinded, and the murder of Beaton (1546) and English punitive raids culminating in the Scots defeat at Pinkie (1547) did not cause Scotland to love England more. France helped Scotland to expel the English but only in return for such a hold over the country that by the time of young Mary's marriage to the Dauphin in 1558 it was France that appeared to be about to absorb Scotland.

Anti-French feeling combined with Protestant preaching to bring about revolt. In 1559 the reformers took up arms to forestall Mary of Guise's action against them. Despite the preaching of John Knox and others and the plundering of the monasteries, the decisive issues were political and military: Queen Elizabeth of England sent troops to check French plans in Scotland. Mary of Guise died in June 1560, and by the Treaty of Edinburgh in July, both France and England undertook to withdraw their troops. With Scotland thus neutralized, England had the important advantage over France of relative nearness.

The Scots Parliament in August 1560 abolished papal authority and adopted a reformed Confession of Faith, but Mary, still in France, did not ratify this legislation. Still, the organization of local congregations, which had been going on for some years, continued, and the General Assembly emerged as the central legislative body for the church. In the *First Book of Discipline* (1560), John Knox and other ministers proposed for the church a striking social program, providing education and poor relief. But laymen had not despoiled the old church to enrich the new, and, as an interim settlement secured by Mary's government in 1562, the church and crown were together to share but one-third of the old church's revenue.

John Knox

Mary's husband died in 1560, and in 1561 she returned to Scotland. As a Catholic in a Protestant land and as nearest heir, by descent from Henry VII's daughter, to Elizabeth of England, she had many enemies. Her personal reign was brief and dramatic—she married her cousin Darnley (1565); their son James was born (1566); Darnley was murdered (1567); Mary married the adventurer James Hepburn, 4th earl of Bothwell; was imprisoned and forced to abdicate (1567); escaped and fled to England (1568). Her task as a ruler was hard, and the harder for her own errors of judgment, but she essayed it bravely and was a truly tragic rather than a pathetic figure.

James VI (1567–1625). James lived through the usual disrupted minority to become one of Scotland's most successful kings. In a civil war between his and his mother's followers, laird (landed proprietor) and merchant support for James may have been decisive in his eventual victory. Elizabeth detained Mary in England and assisted James Douglas, 4th earl of Morton, regent from 1572, to achieve stability in Scotland.

James's government ratified the reformed church settlement, and more permanent measures of church endowment were taken. The Concordat of Leith (1572) allowed the crown to appoint bishops with the church's approval. As in Mary's reign, the crown was intervening to prevent the wealth of the old church from being entirely laicized. And if the bishopric revenues were saved from going the same way as the monastic wealth, the crown expected a share in them for its services.

A new presbyterian party in the church, whose members wanted parity of all ministers and freedom from state control, rejected this compromise. Led by Andrew Melville, a rigid academic theorist, they demanded, in the *Second Book of Discipline* (1578), that the new church should receive all the wealth of the old, that it be run by a hierarchy of courts, not one of bishops, and that the state should leave the church alone but be prepared to take advice from it. Many historians have seen these demands, as James undoubtedly did, as an attempt to achieve full-blown theocracy. James was not strong enough for out-and-out resistance immediately, and he sometimes made concessions, as in the Golden Act of 1592, which gave parliamentary sanction to the system of presbyterian courts. But he gradually showed his determination to run the church his own way, through the agency of his bishops, who were brought into Parliament in 1600. From 1606 Melville was detained in London and later banished. By 1610 the civil and ecclesiastical status of the bishops was secure. The continued existence of church courts—kirk sessions, presbyteries, synods, and the General Assembly—show James's readiness for compromise; and he showed a wise cautiousness toward liturgical reform after encountering hostility over his Five Articles of Perth (1618), which imposed kneeling at communion, observance of holy days, confirmation, infant Baptism, and other practices.

In the 1580s James, as he became personally responsible for royal policy, faced the need to control unruly subjects at home, nobles and kirkmen alike, and to win friends abroad. He concluded a league with England in 1586, and when Elizabeth executed his mother in the following year, he acquiesced in what he could not prevent. He thus inherited his mother's claim to the English throne, and his efforts thereafter to keep in the good graces of Elizabeth and her minister William Cecil were successful. He succeeded peacefully to the English throne in 1603, though his two monarchies, despite his own personal inclinations, remained distinct from one another.

Accession to English throne

His policy was one of overall insurance: he avoided giving offense to Catholic continental rulers, and, while he dealt effectively with lawbreakers on the border and elsewhere, he showed marked leniency to his Catholic nobles, even when the discovery of letters and blank documents (the "Spanish Blanks" affair, 1592) showed that several of them were in treasonable conspiracy with a foreign power. Neither a heroic king, like James IV, nor the pedantic and cowardly buffoon depicted in Sir Walter Scott's *The Fortunes of Nigel,* James VI was a supple and able politician. His theories of Divine Right monarchy were a scholar-king's response to an age when the practice and theory of regicide were fashionable. Except perhaps at the very end of his life, James was too realistic to let his theories entirely govern his conduct.

James excelled in picking good servants from among the lairds and burgesses: they were his judges and privy councillors, and sat on the Committee of Articles, with which he dominated Parliament. After 1603 they governed Scotland smoothly in his absence. From 1587 Parliament was made more representative by the admission of shire commissioners to speak for the lairds, thus realizing the program of James I. The privy council had judicial as well as legislative and administrative functions: there were, in addition, the Court of Session for civil cases (it had evolved from the council in the early 16th century and, as the College of Justice, had been endowed with church funds in the 1530s) and justice courts for criminal cases. Local justice and administration continued, however, despite James VI's efforts, to be largely the prerogative of the landowners.

Scotland still had a subsistence economy, exporting raw materials and importing finished goods, including luxuries. But such luxury imports showed that the greater landowners and merchants were gaining in prosperity. Despite the absence of adequate endowment, the reformed church began to create a network of parish schools and there was advance in the universities: Andrew Melville brought discipline and the latest scholarship to Glasgow and St. Andrews in turn, and there were new foundations at Edinburgh (the Town's College, 1582) and Aberdeen (Marischal College, 1593).

Scotland and England were drawing closer together, as the period of continual strife between them receded in time. Though the two national churches were not identical in structure, they shared a common desire to protect and preserve the Reformation. James VI's accession to the English throne in 1603 as James I encouraged further cultural and economic assimilation. It was far from guaranteeing further political assimilation, but a century of the barely workable personal union of the crowns was continually to sharpen for the Scots the dilemma of choosing between complete union and complete separation.   (J.M.S.)

THE AGE OF REVOLUTION (1625–89)

Charles I (1625–49).   James VI's son, Charles I, grew up in England, lacking any understanding of his Scottish subjects and their institutions. He soon fell foul of a nobility restless in a Scotland that lacked the natural focal point of a royal court. The king also caused widespread anger by high taxation, by the special demands made on Edinburgh to build a Parliament House and to provide a cathedral for the bishopric founded there in 1633, and by a Spanish and a French war that were intended to further English diplomacy but also disrupted Scottish trading ties. The aristocratic leaders of the opposition found ideal material on which to build clerical and popular support. Charles and his Scottish bishops were fond enough of ritual and splendour in church services to make plausible the (wholly incorrect) suggestion that they were ready for compromise with Rome. The new Book of Canons (1635–36) and Liturgy (1637) therefore offended by their content, as well as by being authorized by royal prerogative alone. The National Covenant (1638) astutely collected national support for the opposition's pledge to resist Charles's innovations. Condemnation of popery was written into it for the benefit of those who feared that Charles might be a crypto-Catholic; others, more sophisticated, welcomed its implicit condemnation of a royal arbitrariness with religion and private rights that was contrary to all Scottish precedent.

Religious and political opposition

The Covenanters humbled Charles in two almost bloodless campaigns, the Bishops' Wars (1639–40), and left him with no alternative to asking for money from an English Parliament in which his opponents were strongly represented. Charles had authorized a general assembly of the Scottish Church (1638) and a Scottish Parliament (1639); the Covenanters packed these meetings, scrapped all the king's innovations, and abolished episcopacy. There was, therefore, by 1641 a revolutionary situation in both kingdoms, and in August 1642 war broke out between Charles and his English opponents. Both sides sought Scots help, which was soon accorded to the English parliamentary opposition. By the Solemn League and Covenant (1643) the English promised, in return for military aid, to help preserve Presbyterian Church government in Scotland and, so at least the Scots believed, to set it up in England. James Graham, 1st marquess of Montrose, and others who

then left the Covenanting side argued that by this second Covenant, and by certain constitutional constraints they had placed upon the crown, the Scots had gone unwarrantably far beyond the aims of the first Covenant. But those of the Scots who were prepared to make common cause with the English opposition, even if the English did have a more deep-seated quarrel with their king than the Scots, had reasoned justification; for it was realistic to expect that Charles, as soon as it proved possible, would withdraw concessions made to men whom he regarded as his enemies. Personal antipathies also helped to split the ranks of the original Covenanters—notably the antipathy between Montrose and Archibald Campbell, 1st marquess of Argyll, sincerely devoted to the cause but equally devoted to the advancement of his family. Montrose's military efforts for Charles in Scotland were crushed in 1645, and by 1646 Charles had lost the war in England too. When Charles surrendered to the Scots Army in England, the Scots failed to reach agreement with him and handed him over to the English. The Scots contribution to the English war effort had been substantial, but not spectacular enough to leave a sense of obligation; and the English Army under Oliver Cromwell, now eclipsing Parliament in English politics, preferred Independency to Presbyterianism in the church and did not propose to honour the Solemn League and Covenant. A conservative element among the Covenanters in 1647 reached a compromise, or "Engagement," with Charles by which they promised him help in return for the establishment of Presbyterianism in both kingdoms for three years and went to war on his behalf: their ill-planned campaign was crushed at Preston in 1648. The clerics, who had bitterly opposed this compromise, were now able, under the leadership of a few nobles such as Argyll, to purge the Scots Parliament and Army of all tainted with collaboration with the king. The execution of Charles by the English in 1649 genuinely shocked most Scots, who were prepared to fight for his son, Charles II, once he had been constrained to accept the Covenants and once Montrose had been executed (1650). Cromwell's victory over the Scots at Dunbar (1650) gave more moderate Scots the ascendancy again, but this brought no better military result. Another, and decisive, defeat at Cromwell's hands came to a Scottish royalist army at Worcester in 1651.

Execution of Charles

Cromwell.   Cromwell imposed on Scotland a full and incorporating parliamentary union with England (1652). This could not enjoy the popularity of a union by consent, maintained as it was by an army of occupation, but Cromwell's administration of Scotland was efficient, and his judges, some of them Englishmen, achieved an admired impartiality. Public order was well maintained, even in the Highlands after the collapse of royalist resistance in 1654. Cromwell did not overturn Presbyterianism but ensured toleration for others, save Catholics and Episcopalians.

The Restoration monarchy.   The restoration in 1660 of Charles II (1660–85) was welcomed by many moderate men of both his kingdoms. Charles had learned much from his father's fate and was prepared to forget many injuries, though his government executed some Scots, including the marquess of Argyll.

In 1662 Charles formally restored church government by bishops, but they were to act in association with synods and presbyteries, much as under James VI's compromise. Charles seems not to have been moved by rancour toward the Covenanters, who had bullied him in the early 1650s, but merely by a desire to achieve the system that satisfied most people. Many laymen accepted his system, and few nobles opposed it. Approximately 270 ministers, however—just over a quarter of the total—were deprived of their parishes for noncompliance. The Pentland Rising (1666) was easily put down and was countered by an experimental period of tolerance by the government. Persons who still persisted in attending conventicles were strong only in the southwest and to some extent in Fife and among the small lairds and common people. These men adhered to the "Protester" position, regarding Scotland as still bound by the Covenants. In another trial of strength with the government, they were defeated at Bothwell Bridge (1679). The remnant of Cameronians (from Richard Cameron, a leading Covenanter) remained in being, meeting governmental violence with further violence, and in 1690 refused to join a Presbyterian but uncovenanted Church of Scotland. Their brave and fanatical "thrawnness" endeared them to later generations of Scots.

James VII When Charles's brother succeeded as James VII of Scots and James II of Great Britain and Ireland (1685–88), most Scots showed that they were prepared to support him despite his Catholicism. But he showed his ineptitude by requesting Parliament to grant toleration to Catholics (1686); this stirred up unprecedented opposition to royal wishes in the Scottish Parliament. Nevertheless, although many exiled Scots were at the court of William of Orange in Holland, the collapse (1688–89) of James's regime in Scotland was entirely a result of the Revolution of 1688 in England and the landing there of William.

THE ERA OF UNION

The Revolution settlement. James VII having fled to France, a Convention of Estates (really the same assembly as Parliament, but meeting less formally) gave the crown jointly to William (II of Scots; 1689–1702) and his wife Mary II (1689–94), James's daughter. A series of crises throughout William's reign exposed his total lack of interest in Scotland and placed a strain on the system that had developed whereby the Scottish ministry took orders not only from the monarch but also from the English ministry. But William's first major decision was probably right: episcopacy was abolished in 1689, and Presbyterianism reestablished the following year.

The Union and its results. William fought one war against France (1689–97) and on his death in 1702 bequeathed another (1701–13) to his successor, his wife's sister Anne (1702–14). These circumstances made a Union of Scotland and England seem strategically as well as economically desirable. That Union was achieved in 1707 is at first sight surprising, since intervening sessions of the Scots Parliament had been in a mood to break the English connection altogether. But by 1707 England's appreciation of its own strategic interests, and of the nuisance value of the Scots Parliament, was lively enough for it to offer statesmanlike concessions to Scotland and material inducements to Scots parliamentarians to accept Union.

The Union was an incorporating one: the Scots Parliament was ended and the Westminster Parliament increased by 45 commoners and 16 peers representing Scotland. Scotland benefited by gaining free trade with England and its colonies, by the grant of a money "Equivalent" of the share of the English national debt that Scotland would assume, and by the explicit safeguarding of its national church and legal system. After Queen Anne's death in 1714, when the Jacobites missed their best opportunity, the worst crises of the Union were past.

Jacobitism: the Highlands. The Jacobites were seldom more than a nuisance in Britain. An expedition from France in 1708 and a West Highland rising with aid from Spain in 1719 were abortive; bad leadership in the rebellion in 1715 (known as "the Fifteen") of James VII's son, James Edward, the Old Pretender, and divided counsels in that of 1745 ("the Forty-Five") led by the Old Pretender's son Charles Edward, the Young Pretender, crippled invasions originating in France which had in any case less than an even chance of success. The government was not always sufficiently prepared agained invasions, but the generalship of John Campbell, 2nd duke of Argyll, at Sheriffmuir in 1715 sufficed to check, and that of William Augustus, duke of Cumberland, at Culloden in 1746 to give the coup de grace to, a Jacobite army. The Jacobites never had full French naval and military assistance, and support in Scotland itself was limited: not many more Lowland Scots than Englishmen loved the Stuarts enough to die for them. Many politicians, especially before 1714, corresponded with the royal exiles simply as a matter of insurance against their return, and in the dying days of Stuart hopes there were fewer people than there have been since who were struck by the romantic aura surrounding Prince Charles Edward, the "bonny Prince Charlie." In the main the Stuarts had to rely on the clans of the Gaelic-speaking regions, and Highland support in itself

The Fifteen and the Forty-five

alienated Lowlanders. Not all Highlanders were "out" in the Fifteen or the Forty-Five: such clans as the Campbells and Munros, Macleods, and Macdonalds of Sleat were Hanoverian because Presbyterian, or through their chiefs' personal inclinations. Many clans were, however, Catholic or Episcopalian, and favoured a Catholic monarch: they were legitimists and reasonably so, since both James VII and his son James Edward, the Old Pretender, appreciated Highland problems. These were the problems of an infertile land, overpopulated with fighting men who owed personal allegiance to their chiefs and were partly dependent on plunder to maintain their standard of living. It is hard to see what in the end could have happened to this society, other than what did happen: a series of attempts by the chiefs in the late 18th, and particularly in the early 19th, century to emulate the new capitalist agriculture of the Lowlands, thus creating an impersonal cash relationship with their tenants and leaving those who were redundant in the new economy no alternative to moving south or overseas. But the catastrophe of the Fifteen and Forty-Five made this process more rapid and more painful. This is the central fact of the situation, even though the atrocities of government soldiers and the repressiveness of government legislation did very much less than economic and social forces to usher in the new order.

The Scottish Enlightenment. No straightforward connection can be drawn between the Union and the exceptional 18th-century flowering of intellectual life known as the "Scottish Enlightenment." Absence of civil strife, however, permitted the best minds to turn, if they chose, from politics and its 17th-century twin, religion; and few of the best minds from 1707 onward were in fact directly concerned with politics. Philosophy, in which 18th-century Scotland excelled, was a proper concern for a country where for generations minds had been sharpened by theological debate. Scottish culture remained distinctive, and distinctively European in orientation. The historian and philosopher David Hume sought to remove Scotticisms from his speech, and the architect Robert Adam gained extra experience as well as income from being able to design buildings in London as well as in Edinburgh. Nevertheless, Adam drew most of his stylistic inspiration from the classical architecture he had studied in Italy, and Hume, "le bon David," was an honoured member of continental polite and intellectual society. Hume's *History of England* (1754–62) made his literary reputation in his lifetime; but it is his philosophical works, such as his *Treatise of Human Nature* (1739–40), which have caused the continuous growth of his reputation since his death. Adam Smith, author of *The Wealth of Nations* (1776), was the philosopher of political economy. Henry Home, Lord Kames, may be singled out from many other significant figures to illustrate the versatility characteristic of the times. He was a judge, interested in legal theory and history; an agricultural reformer in theory and practice; a Commissioner of the Forfeited Estates (of the rebels of 1745); and a member of the Board of Trustees for Manufactures (which encouraged Scottish industries, notably linen). In poetry there was a reaction, possibly against Union, and certainly against assimilation, with England; revived interest in Scots vernacular poetry of the past was the herald of a spate of new vernacular poetry, culminating in the satires of Robert Fergusson and the lyrics of Robert Burns. Some of the greatest Gaelic poets, such as Alexander MacDonald, were writing at this time too.

The Scots educational system, its foundations so securely laid throughout the previous century, made possible, though neither it nor any other single factor could be held to explain, this extraordinary cultural outpouring. The Scottish universities enjoyed their heyday, with Edinburgh notable for medicine and preeminent in most other subjects. Gradually the regents who taught students throughout their university course were replaced by professors specializing in single subjects. That students seldon troubled to graduate was little disadvantage in an age when appointments depended on patronage; and, not being bound by a rigid curriculum, they were able to indulge the Scot's traditionally wide intellectual curiosity by attending lectures in a variety of subjects. Scientific study

Scottish universities

was encouraged, and practical application of discoveries given due place. Francis Home, professor of *Materia Medica* at Edinburgh, studied bleaching processes and plant nutrition; and James Watt, instrument-maker to Glasgow University for a time, was there encouraged to work on the steam engine, to which he was to make crucial improvements.

19TH-CENTURY SCOTLAND

Agitation for constitutional change was considered treasonable by many conservatives during the years (1793–1815) when Britain was fighting revolutionary France. Several advocates of universal suffrage, including a young Glasgow lawyer, Thomas Muir of Huntershill, were sentenced to transportation in 1793. After repression had broken this first radical wave, postwar industrial depression produced another—the "Radical War" of 1820, an abortive rising of some workers in the Glasgow area. Intellectual campaigning of a more moderate sort had greater short-term success and the *Edinburgh Review,* founded in 1802 by a group of young lawyers led by Francis Jeffrey and Henry Brougham, was influential in radical politics and in literature. Edinburgh life was particularly brilliant during the years of the war with France, when Englishmen as well as Scots, unable to study abroad, found Edinburgh University more attractive than ever. Outstanding in this *Novels of* period was Sir Walter Scott, although not until 1827 was *Sir Walter* he known to be the author of the Waverley novels. Scott's *Scott* greatness as a novelist lay in the way he took Scottish society as a whole for his main character; and his best books are a lament for an era that he knew was dying, the organic society of preindustrial Scotland.

The Industrial Revolution. The Scottish Industrial Revolution was in full swing from the 1820s. Linked with this, partly as cause and partly as effect, in a way historians have not altogether disentangled, was a dramatic upsurge of population. There were perhaps about 1,000,-000 people in Scotland in 1700. By 1800 there were more than 1,500,000 and by 1900 nearly 4,500,000. The manufacturing towns showed spectacular increases. Hundreds of thousands of Irish emigrants went to Scotland in the 19th century, notably during the Irish potato famine of 1846–50. In some country regions there was a population decrease as people moved to the towns, to England, or overseas. Part of the overall increase was the result of improved medical care that had lessened the ravages of epidemic diseases by the mid-19th century. Much of the food for the increased population was supplied by progressive Scottish agriculture: farming in the southeast was celebrated throughout Britain for its efficiency in the early 19th century, and the northeast became famous for its beef cattle, Ayrshire for its milking herds.

But the key advance was in heavy industry, which from about 1830 took the industrial primacy from textiles, at a time when industry as a whole had replaced agriculture as the nation's chief concern. Coal production rose, as did that of iron, with James Beaumont Neilson's hot-blast process (1828) making Scottish ores cheaper to work. Major canals, like the Forth and Clyde, completed in 1790, enjoyed a short boom before being rendered obsolescent by the railways, of which the Glasgow to Garnkirk (1831) was noteworthy for using steam locomotives (rather than horses) from the start. Above all, Scottish international trade was catered to, and Clydeside's reputation made, by the building of ships. Robert Napier was the greatest of many great Scots marine engineers.

Politics. An installment of parliamentary (1832) and burgh (1833) reform ended fictitious county votes and corrupt burgh caucuses but disillusioned the working classes by failing to give them the vote. As in England, they had to await the 1867 and subsequent Reform Acts. But the great bulk of the Scots middle classes were delighted with the Whigs (whose lord advocate from 1830 until 1834 was Francis Jeffrey), who had brought the reforms. The Whig Party, or Liberal Party (as it became known in the 1860s), dominated Scottish mid-19th century politics; and William Ewart Gladstone, of Scots parentage, was the great Liberal hero, whose moral dynamism and fire far outweighed in Scottish eyes his High Church Episcopalianism.

Trade unions of skilled workers had had an uninterrupted existence since the early 19th century. By the 1880s groups of unskilled workers were being organized. Various factors delayed the permanent organization of the miners until this period too, when there emerged from their ranks a major leader, James Keir Hardie. Failing to engage the Liberals sufficiently in support of organized labour, he helped form the Scottish Labour Party in 1888. In 1893 he created the Independent Labour Party (ILP) for Britain as a whole, and this body in 1900 federated with the trade unions for the purpose of running the Labour Party (given its present name in 1906). Scottish political opinion moved left in the years before 1914, with Liberal fortunes reviving—partly due to the leadership (1899–1908) of Sir Henry Campbell-Bannerman, a Scot—and three Labour MP's elected.

The Highlands. By about 1800 a sharp population rise had made the Highlands overpopulated relative to the means of subsistence. Many lairds, seeking to support their tenantry by encouraging the kelp industry, were ruined when it collapsed in the decade 1815–25. Other landowners introduced sheep, sometimes violently removing their tenants in the "Highland Clearances," as agents of the Sutherland family did in Strathnaver, Sutherland, about 1810–20. The potato famine of the mid-1840s caused distress. By the 1880s Highland tenants or "crofters" faced a new problem. Deer forests had replaced sheep runs as the most immediately profitable land use open to landowners; and high rents were asked for the land that was still worked as crofts, though common grazings might at the same time be taken away. Parliamentary agitation by the crofters, who voted for the first time in 1885, and by their Lowland sympathizers, as well as sporadic outbursts of violence beginning in 1882 (the "Crofters' War"), secured *The* an act of 1886 which gave the crofters security of tenure *"Crofters'* and empowered a Crofters' Commission to fix fair rents. *War"* Unlike their Irish counterparts, the Highlanders sought not ownership of their land but the imposition of certain standards of conduct and responsibility upon their landlords. The crofting agitation of the 1880s soon died down, but it was a key stage in the forging of a modern Scottish consciousness in that Highlanders and Lowlanders had been united in the struggle.

MODERN SCOTLAND

World War I and after. The war of 1914–18 had a great impact on Scots society, with 74,000 lives lost, and industry mobilized as never before in a coordinated national effort. Clyde shipbuilding and engineering were crucial, and Clydeside was the key munitions centre in Britain. This expansion of heavy industry, however, seemed in the 1920s to have been an overexpansion. The collapse of the wartime boom in 1920 began a period of economic depression in Britain, in which Scotland was one of the worst-affected regions.

Economic distress bred political radicalism. The Liberals were eclipsed, and in most seats the real contest was between the Unionists and Labour, which became Scotland's biggest single party for the first time in the election of 1922. Willie Gallacher, Scotland's only notable Communist member of Parliament and an able political theorist strongly influenced by Lenin, was at the same time a radical belonging to a revered Scots tradition. The death (1930) of John Wheatley, who had been minister of health in the first Labour government (1924) and the author of an important housing act, deprived left-wingers in the Labour Party of a skilled leader, and counsels of moderation in the party prevented its taking any very distinctive initiative on the economic crisis. Ramsay MacDonald, a Scot who had led two minority Labour governments, agreed to form a national government in 1931. The Labour Party refused to participate, disowned MacDonald, and was heavily defeated at the polls, in Scotland as elsewhere.

Another political development that was partly the result of economic distress was the formation in 1934 of the Scottish National Party, a merger of two previous parties. It had some distinguished supporters, especially literary men, but it was suspected, sometimes unfairly, of political extremism and made little electoral impact before World

War II. The National government of the 1930s was dominated by the conservatives: among the prominent Scots conservatives was the greatly respected Walter Elliot, minister of agriculture. While opposed to any suggestion of an independent Scottish legislature, this government furthered the extension of the Scottish administrative system, in 1939 installing it in St. Andrew's House in Edinburgh.

World War II and after. During World War II Scotland sustained some 34,000 deaths in action and 6,000 civilians killed, many in air attacks on Clydeside. The outstanding Scot on the home front was Tom Johnston, a Labour MP who acted as secretary of state for Scotland in the wartime national government. He was active in setting up the North of Scotland Hydro-Electric Board in 1943.

The postwar Labour government contained no Scots of the calibre of Wheatley or Johnston, nor did the Unionists make the impact on Scottish politics that might have been expected from the frequent Conservative dominance in England. The Scottish National Party enjoyed no electoral success until the 1970s.   (J.M.S./Ed)

WALES

Wales—or, to give the principality its Welsh name, Cymru—is a squat peninsula, with an area of just over 8,000 square miles (21,000 square kilometres), jutting westward from England into the Irish Sea. It is thus an integral part of the island of Britain, with whose development—and hence with that of the European continent beyond—its character and destiny have been intimately linked. In addition, the location of Wales on that extreme western fringe often characterized as Atlantic Europe has given the country a distinctive endowment in terms of environment and landscape and, since the dawn of European history, has been responsible for a unique cultural, social, and economic development. The effects of this dual, and often uneasy, heritage continues to permeate much of its national life. It exhibited many of the problems encountered by the smaller nations of the world while lacking—as it has for the past seven centuries—their politically independent status.

On three sides the boundaries of Wales are natural, with the shores of the Dee estuary and Liverpool Bay to the north, the Irish Sea to the west, and the coastline of the Severn estuary and its development into the Bristol Channel on the south. The extent of the country from north to south is about 130 miles (210 kilometres) and its width varies, reaching 90 miles across in the north, narrowing to about 40 miles in the centre, and widening again to over 100 miles across the southern portion. The eastern boundary, that with England, is an administrative, though not political, frontier, created in 1536 as part of the Act of Union finally and effectively linking England and Wales. This boundary, being purely administrative in origin, does not, in detail, conform to any specific topographical characteristics or features. It runs, in general, from north to south through the region where the upland massif of Wales gives way to the lowlands of the west and northwest Midlands of England. Though not perhaps a natural frontier, it is one that separates distinctive regions, and, over the centuries, the borderland zone through which it runs has developed a marked character of its own.

Wales in 1974 was divided into eight administrative counties, which are subdivided into 37 districts. One of the districts, Ynys Môn–Isle of Anglesey, though physically an island off the northwest coast, is linked with the mainland by road and rail bridges. Cardiff was designated the country's capital city in 1955.

Physical and human geography

THE LAND

Relief. There are four major elements in the relief features of Wales, namely, mountains (above 2,000 feet), dissected plateaus and hills (600 feet to 2,000 feet), coastal areas, and valley lowlands. The two mountain areas, Snowdonia in the northwest and the Brecon Beacons in the south, have both been dominated by the effects of mountain glaciation. In Snowdonia, which contains the highest peak, 3,560 feet (1,085 metres), in the country, these effects have been accentuated by resistant rock, often volcanic in origin, and the magnificent scenery is much more stark and rugged than the softer outlines of the Beacons.

The two mountain areas are both joined and surrounded by a region of plateaus and hills, consisting of a number of distinct upland massifs that are themselves partially fragmented by river action. These rolling, river-cut upland surfaces, with an accordance of summit levels and broken by valley lands that tongue in toward the centre, form a backbone dominating the entire relief pattern of Wales.

The upland plateaus are themselves girdled on the seaward side by a series of coastal plateaus ranging from 100 feet to 700 feet in height and also well cut into by the erosive action of rivers. They are sometimes broken by the "steps" of fossil cliff lines, and where they do not end in spectacular sea-pounded cliffs they are replaced by coastal flats that are estuarine in origin.

The fourth relief element in the landscape, that of valley land, is made up of the larger river valleys originating in the central upland mass and broadening westward near the sea or eastward as they merge into the lowland plains of the English border.

Drainage and soils. Wales has an essentially radial drainage pattern, the main watershed running approximately from north to south along the backbone of the country. Fragmentation of drainage is therefore the characteristic feature, and, apart from the Severn and the Dee, river systems either reach the sea or debouch upon the English plain before they have an opportunity of becoming fully developed. Natural lake development in Wales is almost entirely glacial in origin and in no way controls the drainage pattern.

The country is dominated by older rocks, ranging from those of Precambrian time, the earliest geological era, to representatives of the Jurassic, some 180,000,000 years ago. Glaciation has blanketed most of the landscape with boulder clay, scraped up and carried along by the underside of the great former ice sheets, so that rarely can soils be directly related to parent rock. Brown earth and podzol soils predominate, all of them acid in nature and not fully developed.

Climate. Because of its location, Wales enjoys a maritime climate dominated by Atlantic air masses with a considerable variety of character and a relative unpredictability of occurrence. It is therefore weather, rather than climate, that influences the life of the country. Rainfall is frequent and often more than adequate, the annual average being 53 inches (1,350 millimetres), with 3 inches (81 millimetres) in April and 6 inches (149 millimetres) in January, and winter snowstorms in the uplands can be among the most severe in Britain. The annual mean temperature is 50.7° F (10.4° C) ranging from 37° F (5° C) in January to about 61° F (16° C) in July and August. These figures completely mask the very considerable internal variations that, at any one time, result from the varied character and location of relief.

Plant and animal life. The combination of physical conditions and centuries of human activity has led to a vegetation coverage in which induced grassland and plantation woodland currently predominate. Grassland varies from mountain grasses and heather to lowland agrostis–ryegrass pastures, while woodlands are either mixed parkland, boundary and private plantation, or Forestry Commission in origin.

The remoter parts of Wales shelter some mammals and birds extinct or rare elsewhere in Britain. The polecat is fairly common in central Wales though hardly known elsewhere; the pine marten occurs in a few places; a few pairs of kites represent the sole British survivors, and the chough breeds inland as well as at some coastal sites.

The upland core

Various sea-and shore-birds occur in large numbers as might be expected in a country with about 600 miles (965 kilometres) of varied coastline.

Settlement patterns. *Traditional regions.* The French name for Wales is the "Pays de Galles" (the "Region of Wales"), and in many ways Wales as a whole can be regarded as a natural or geographical region, in the fullest sense of the word *pays.* More detailed examination, however, reveals the existence of six traditional or popular regions.

The "heartland"

The first is that of the upland and mountain "heartland," a region bounded by the approximately coincident lines marking off altitudes of 700 feet (210 metres), annual rainfall of 60 inches, and the limits of mountain grassland and vegetation. Pastoral in economy and sparse in population, the region has retained most of the traditional cultural characteristics of Wales, particularly that of language. With the shadows of clouds racing across the wild moorlands in the bright afternoon sunlight, it can possess great natural beauty.

This core is girdled on the north and northwest by a coastal fringe that includes the North Wales coast and Anglesey, together with the Lleyn Peninsula. Scenic attractions and accessibility from English population centres make the whole region a popular tourist area, but, in addition, the peninsula has a small-scale farming economy supporting a society with a strongly traditional cast.

To the west of the heartland lie the coastlands of Cardigan Bay, a region of scattered and relatively prosperous farming settlements, with a superimposed element of tourism. This western-facing region, by its more isolated location, has also been able to preserve many essentially Welsh elements in its social life.

To the southwest the heartland gives way to low-lying areas. This is a rich dairy farming region, with its own coastal tourist attractions, as well as oil terminals and refineries along the vast natural harbour of Milford Haven.

South of the heartland lies the South Wales coalfield, with the Vale of Glamorgan and the Gower Peninsula providing a narrow southern agricultural and coastal fringe. The coalfield was developed in the 19th century as one of the premier mining regions of Britain, and such urban settlements as the Rhondda, with bleak, tightly packed rows of terraced housing strung out along the narrow valleys, are perhaps among the most widely known characteristics of Wales. The region, badly hit by a series of economic depressions in the period between World Wars I and II, is now less of a coalfield proper and more of a diversified industrial complex.

Finally, to the east of the heartland lies the Welsh borderland, known historically as a marcher, or patrolled frontier region. This is characterized by an amalgam of two cultures, Welsh and English. The north is dominated by the North Wales coalfield and its associated industries, often linked with Liverpool and the Merseyside region; the south is orientated toward the Severn estuary, while the agricultural middle borderland has attempted, by diversifying its economy, to halt the depopulation from which it has long suffered.

Rural settlement. Contemporary Welsh rural settlement shows a dominant pattern of scattering, or dispersion, with nucleation, or a clustering of buildings, playing a secondary role. Isolated whitewashed stone cottages and farm buildings, dotted all over the cultivated areas, are a striking feature of the rural landscape and remain a strong element underlying the Welsh social fabric. The initial element involved in achieving this pattern was the Welsh tribal economy, of seminomadic pastoral origin, which, by medieval times, had become stabilized enough to produce a settlement pattern dispersed around blocks of suitable land, with very limited nucleation on some of the larger tribal domains. The individual monastic or cell habitations of the Celtic Saints, who carried a tradition of civilization and learning northward through the Atlantic fringe of Europe during the centuries following the collapse of the Roman Empire, increased this dispersion, though some of them, because of favourable site or position, became subsequent growth points. The Anglo-Norman manorial system was introduced into Wales after the conquest of

1282, but, because of physical and political conditions, only in the eastern and southern peripheries of the country did the traditional nucleated village become significant. Post-medieval developments have increased scatter as a result of the farm settlement of former common grazings at the higher altitudes and also added to nucleation in the lowlands at route junctions and crossing places.

Urban settlement. Prior to the Anglo-Norman Conquest, there were scarcely any traces of urban development in Wales, but the Conquest introduced the bastide, or castle town, that still dominates the contemporary urban landscape, in number if not in size. Today these are the nonindustrial market and county towns of the country, commercial, administrative, and social in function. Their physical appearance, however, often betrays their military and colonial origins. Superimposed upon this urban pattern was that generated by the Industrial Revolution. In Wales this simply initiated the growth of unplanned, overcrowded urban settlements resulting from mining activities in the two coalfields. In South Wales it was also linked with development of a steel and tinplate industry and with ports designed for the export of coal. More recent developments have been those of packet stations, for traffic to Ireland, and of resort towns in some of the coastal areas. Although two-thirds of the population of Wales is urban, towns are not a part of the country's native culture.

THE PEOPLE

Although there was some Paleolithic (Old Stone Age) occupation in coastal caves, dating back some 200,000 years, and although traces of Mesolithic inhabitants (8,000–3,000 BC) remain, it was not until the Neolithic and Bronze Age periods, from the 3rd millennium BC onward, that Wales received its basic, and still important, ethnic stock, namely, that of the dark, short Mediterranean type. This western-and coastal-based entry of peoples, part of movements along the whole of Atlantic Europe, was paralleled on the east by migrations of people who had stronger links with lowland Britain and thence with continental Europe. Throughout the whole history of its ethnic and linguistic development, Wales has shared in, and sometimes been a battleground for, these two cultural elements, the one Atlantic and the other continental in origin.

It was this latter element, in the form of an immediate pre-Roman invasion of a western-based Iron Age people, that first brought a Celtic language to Wales and that introduced a Nordic element into the population. The basic culture of these peoples survived the Roman occupation, and it continued to develop, strengthened and broadened by immigrations of similar culture from other parts of Britain in the immediate post-Roman era. It was the language of these people, a Brythonic branch of Celtic speech, that formed the basis of modern Welsh. Their heroic poetry, dating from the 6th century AD, forms the basis of one of the oldest literary traditions of Europe. Subsequent developments included a considerable absorption of Latin elements.

Introduction of Celtic language

Apart from limited seaborne Dark Age Scandinavian influences upon some coastal fringes, eastern trends, namely, those of Anglo-Saxon and Anglo-Norman penetrations from the English border, have subsequently dominated the ethnic and linguistic story of the country. The effect of the Industrial Revolution in attracting immigrants from outside Wales to the developing coalfields was offset by its effect in attracting to those coalfields people from other parts of the principality. The end result was therefore not so much an influx but rather an internal redistribution of population.

As the result of this history of influence and counterinfluence, which continues in the contemporary life of the country, there are in Wales two elements, the one of which can be regarded as "native," although embracing in that term a considerable variety of type, and the other as "intrusive." The division between them is not clearcut and frequently does not coincide with any particular cultural characteristics. The influence of history has nevertheless been to produce two cultures in Wales. The contemporary problem is whether the differences between them will be sharpened or whether they may retain their respective identities while at the same time combining to form a third. Traces of the latter may already be discerned in the "Anglo-Welsh" tradition, which has made its own distinctive contribution, especially in the arts.

The people living in Wales in the late 20th century are unevenly distributed throughout the country. The pattern of settlement is largely determined by five elements.

The first of these is the mountain and upland core of the country, which is either very sparsely populated or uninhabited. Surrounding this core, and occasionally entering into it along the river valleys, is a girdle where the population is sparsely distributed. This girdle is, in turn, itself fringed by a peripheral zone reaching on three sides to the coasts and on the fourth to the English border, where the population density reaches the "normal-rural" and occasionally "dense-rural" levels for Britain. This concentric pattern, which is, of course, a reflection of the agricultural economy, has superimposed upon it two further elements, those of nonindustrial and industrial urban settlements. The former of these is represented by commercial, marketing, and residential towns. These are, in the main, confined to the peripheral zone, where they act as population "condensation points" in areas of normal-rural settlement density. The latter consists of industrial settlements deriving from the coalfields of northeast and of South Wales and their associated industrial developments. In these two areas only can the population distribution be regarded as dense urban. Approximately two-thirds of the total population of Wales is to be found in the South Wales industrial zone.

Density of industrial settlement

THE ECONOMY

Because of the complete political and economic integration of Wales with the remainder of the United Kingdom, the national economy simply reflects the trends and patterns of the larger unit. Certain specific characteristics of the economy can, however, be recognized, of which the first is that the proportion of capital-intensive industries is relatively high. This means that, since World War II, the rise in the per capita product of the economy has exceeded the U.K. average; but, because so much of this is due to capital contribution, the trend is not reflected in the level of personal income, which remains below the average for Britain. The other two individual features are that the economy does not generate sufficient capital for its needs, necessitating a net inflow from other areas, while the most unsatisfactory characteristic of all is that unemployment figures for Wales remain consistently above the national British average.

Resources. Coal remains the one major mineral resource of Wales. Nonferrous ores occur in small quantities, which are not now economically viable; while iron-ore deposits, though important during the early development of the industrial regions, are now exhausted. The two coalfields are in the northeast and in South Wales; the field in the latter is by far the largest and includes some higher grade anthracite. Following state ownership in 1946, modernization and the closure of uneconomic pits made coal mining as a whole a declining industry, but a stable economic level of activity is being achieved.

Apart from coal and, of course, agriculture, the only other natural resources of Wales are water and woodlands, with the Forestry Commission (a government department) owning and operating on a commercial basis estates of a few hundred thousand acres. Although there are three hydroelectric undertakings in Wales, water resources are mainly exploited by impounding for domestic and industrial purposes. About half of the output of waterworks in Wales serve areas in England.

Industry and agriculture. Despite the fact that coal is a major raw material in Wales, it is the energy-producing industries of gas and electricity, and also metal manufacturing (mainly of iron, steel, and tinplate), that lead in the table of total income produced per person employed. Mining, well down the list, is exceeded by agriculture, by general manufacturing, and by transport, distribution, and construction. In terms of proportions of the labour force employed, pride of place goes to services (including construction) followed by general manufacturing, distributive

trades, metal manufacture, and mining. The various other economic activities are of less significance.

A problem of particular significance in Wales is that of restructuring industry to meet contemporary economic conditions and requirements. In an attempt to diversify industrial development and to overcome the heritage of heavy industries whose general conditions no longer make them viable, various government acts have provided incentives for new industries to move into the older "depressed-area" or "development-area" industrial regions.

Diversification of industry

Transportation. For physical, economic, and historical reasons, the main lines of movement in Wales have been lateral, from west to east—that is, along the respective northern and southern coastal belts and across the centre, where they follow the Severn Valley into the English Midlands. Subsidiary lines have been from north to south, along the west coast and the English border. Cross-country links have always been poor, and even with increased road modernization they leave much to be desired. There is thus no internally integrated system of transportation, and movement into or out of the country is much more easy than movement within it.

Within Wales there is a close and well-developed network of general or all-purpose roads, but those of motorway standard are confined to the links between South Wales and the English Midlands, on the one hand, and between South Wales and London and the Bristol area, on the other.

As part of the rationalization policy of British Rail, Wales experienced a very high rate of closure of branch lines during the late 1950s and in the 1960s. By the late 20th century the end pattern was similar to that of the roads, with through routes following the north and south coasts, each of them providing a link with sea routes to Ireland, the former via Holyhead and the latter via Fishguard. Other routes are minor. Wales has also a number of picturesque narrow gauge railways that are now operated only during the tourist season, some of them run by private groups of enthusiasts.

Railway closures

Wales has no commercial inland waterways, but there are three categories of ports, all of them, except the Anglesey port of Holyhead, on the south and southwest coasts. In the first category are Holyhead and Fishguard, the two packet stations for the Irish traffic; while the second consists of the South Wales ports whose former coal-exporting functions have been replaced by those of importing iron ore, oil, and general cargo. The third category consists of one port—Milford Haven, which has become one of the major oil-importing and oil-refining centres in western Europe.

Rhoose Airport, situated near Cardiff, has domestic flights to other parts of the United Kingdom and international flights to several other countries. Smaller airports are situated at Swansea and at Hawarden.

ADMINISTRATIVE AND SOCIAL CONDITIONS

Government. The Principality of Wales is governed from Whitehall, the name by which the United Kingdom's political and administrative centre in London is known, but devolution of administration has become an accepted policy of all the major British political parties. The post of secretary of state for Wales was created in 1964, and by the late 20th century there had been considerable growth of the Welsh Office, an administrative department of government situated in Cardiff with a section also located in London.

In April 1974, as part of an administrative reorganization throughout the United Kingdom, the administrative structure of Wales was simplified. Many of the former 13 counties, four county boroughs, and numerous smaller units were too limited in extent, population, and resources to be economically feasible under modern conditions. Wales was therefore divided into eight new counties: Clwyd (incorporating the former Flintshire and a large part of Denbighshire), Dyfed (incorporating the former Cardiganshire, Carmarthenshire, and Pembrokeshire), Gwent (incorporating the former county borough of Newport and parts of Monmouthshire and Breconshire); Gwynedd (incorporating the former Anglesey, Merionethshire, and Caernarvonshire and part of Denbighshire), South Glamorgan (incorporating the southern part of the former Glamorgan, part of Monmouthshire, and the county borough of Cardiff, which retained its status as a city and capital of Wales), Mid Glamorgan (incorporating the former county borough of Merthyr Tydfil, the northern part of Glamorgan, and parts of Breconshire and Monmouthshire), West Glamorgan (incorporating the former county borough of Swansea and the western part of Glamorgan), and Powys (incorporating the former Montgomeryshire and Radnorshire and part of Breconshire). The eight counties are subdivided into a total of 37 districts.

In politics, Wales has always had a strong leaning toward radicalism. During the 19th and early 20th centuries, this was evidenced by the country's overall electoral adherence to the Liberal Party, but the industrial regions soon transferred their allegiance to Socialism. Keir Hardie, for example, the British Labour leader and the first independent Labour member of Parliament, represented the constituency of Merthyr, in the heart of the South Wales coalfield. The strong political awareness of the population is evidenced by the fact that the percentage turnout at the polls is consistently higher on average in Wales than it is for Britain as a whole.

The radical tradition in politics | The Welsh Nationalist Party (Plaid Cymru), founded in 1925, is committed to achieving, by democratic and constitutional methods, a measure of political independence that envisages Wales with its own parliament as part of a federal United Kingdom. The party first won a parliamentary seat in a by-election in 1966 and, since that time, has won additional seats in Parliament. On the fringe of this nationalist, separatist movement, and completely disassociated from Plaid Cymru, there are more extremist movements. These have as their aim the realization of political independence based upon cultural and linguistic differentiation. Some of the movements, notably the Welsh Language Society, have been prepared to use various methods of civil disobedience to further these ends.

Unlike Scotland, Wales has no separate system of justice, and the country has no independent defense arrangements. Three army regiments, however, the Welsh Guards, the Royal Welch Fusiliers, and the Royal Regiment of Wales, have particular associations with the nation.

Education. With its rich cultural heritage, Wales has maintained a tradition of quality education at all levels. Responsibility for the administration of primary and secondary education lies with the secretary of state for Wales and the education department of the Welsh Office, operating through the county Local Education Authorities and the Welsh Joint Education Committee, a body with certain statutory duties and powers. As the name implies, all Local Education Authorities in Wales contribute to and share in the work of this national organization. Higher education in Wales, apart from the University of Wales, also comes under the Welsh Office. The university is financed largely by the Treasury in London operating through the University Grants Committee.

Health and welfare. As with primary and secondary education, responsibility for health and social services rests with the secretary of state for Wales. The Welsh Office, working in partnership with the local authorities, is responsible for the planning and execution of the housing policy of the government of the day. These responsibilities embrace the provision of new housing as well as the improvement of existing housing conditions, an activity that is of particular importance in the older industrial areas of Wales.

Police services in Wales are the responsibility of the Home Office in Whitehall. They are operated and administered through local police forces or constabularies.

CULTURAL LIFE

The Welsh cultural identity | Wales has been united politically, administratively, and economically with England ever since the Act of Union in 1536; yet during that period, Wales has been able to preserve, maintain, and develop a cultural identity that, while sharing in that of its larger neighbour, is nevertheless in some important aspects quite different from it. It is the interplay between these two elements, sometimes united,

sometimes independent, and sometimes in conflict, that characterizes contemporary cultural life in Wales.

The traditional culture was oral and aural in its manifestation and nonmaterial, even unworldly, in its philosophy. It developed into a uniquely blended culture, in which great stress was laid on the spoken and the written word in poetry and in prose; in which vocal music, particularly choral singing, played a great part; and one whose rural, domestic, and noncommercial standards were strengthened and made more austere by the spread of a puritan, religious nonconformity, itself intensified by its associated 19th-century religious revival movements. This ascetic and often erudite culture, essentially of the spirit, sensitive but not sensual, and with no traditional visual expression, now finds itself struggling to maintain its identity in the face of a more material culture that is propagated by ease of communication, including the effects of the mass media, not merely from England but from the whole of the English-speaking world.

The most obvious manifestation of this native culture is that of the Welsh language, and many, though by no means all, culturally and politically conscious Welshmen link the preservation of the culture with that of the language. There are, of course, regional variations in the Welsh-speaking population, ranging from less than 10 percent in the eastern and southern fringes to more than 90 percent in northwestern Wales. One interesting development during the late 20th century was the increase in the number of adults, particularly in the commercial and administrative fields, who wished to learn Welsh; and the University of Wales now has a special unit for the teaching of Welsh to adults.

Although the formal adoption of bilingualism in education and in government is intended to arrest the decline in the Welsh-speaking percentage that has been a feature of this century, the present situation, in the view of an educated and vocal element in Wales, is far from satisfactory.

Government assistance for the arts is operated through the Welsh Arts Council. Funds for literature, art, music, and drama are allocated by the council. Literary activities involve the financial support of publications in both Welsh and English and the granting of bursaries to writers to enable them to undertake specific projects. Tours of Wales by British and foreign orchestras are arranged through the council, and support is given to amateur music-making societies and to a number of music festivals, particularly in respect to commissioning new works. The Welsh National Opera Company, one of the leading companies in Britain, also operates under the aegis of the council. Support is given to art exhibitions, to design, and, through the Welsh Theatre Company, to drama. The council also sponsors the formation of regional arts associations, which command financial support from the relevant local authorities.

Cultural institutions | The National Library of Wales, like the British Museum, is a copyright library, receiving, by law, copies of virtually all books published in the United Kingdom. Situated at Aberystwyth and receiving a government grant, it is not merely the national reference library but also a repository of documents and manuscripts relating to Wales from earliest times to the present day.

Another government-aided institution is the National Museum of Wales, situated in Cardiff, with the Welsh Folk Museum in the castle and grounds of nearby St. Fagans. The museum proper embraces the antiquities and the natural history of Wales with, in addition, a very full art collection, while examples of Welsh material culture, such as scenes of rural buildings, have been transported to, and re-erected in, the grounds of the Folk Museum.

The University of Wales is a federal university with seven constituent institutions, including the Welsh National School of Medicine. These constituents are situated at Aberystwyth, Bangor, Swansea, Cardiff (three), and Lampeter.

The above institutions are all on permanent sites, but the National Eisteddfod, or competitive festival, perhaps the most individual of Welsh cultural institutions, is peripatetic in that it is held annually but alternately in North and South Wales. The actual venue results from the invitation of a particular town or area, and the festival is housed in a transportable hall or pavilion. It is always sited on open ground that, for the duration of the Eisteddfod, becomes a campus on which most of the cultural, and some of the commercial, organizations of Wales also hold exhibitions illustrating their activities. The Eisteddfod itself is held for one week in August and consists of competitions in all aspects of music, literature, drama, and art, together with a series of dramatic performances and concerts, all held through the medium of the Welsh language. During the period of the Eisteddfod, and associated with it, the bardic circle, or Gorsedd, holds its ceremonies. For this week, the Eisteddfod field is the gathering ground for the nation, but local Eisteddfodau are held in towns and villages throughout the year.

The Welsh region of the BBC, which has always had considerable independence, provides service in both English and Welsh. Harlech television, a commercial company, covers Wales and the west country of England.

(J.G.Th./Ed.)

History

WALES BEFORE THE NORMAN CONQUEST

The Roman influence. The early history of Wales (Cymru, Gwalia, Cambria) is largely gleaned from what is known of the withdrawal of Roman authority from the land by the end of the 4th century AD. Wales in the Roman period had shared broadly the experience of the other parts of highland Britain, and the Welsh evidence can often be better understood by analogy with that of other areas. The Latin element in the Welsh language and some features of the literary tradition, such as the legends associated with the Roman emperor Magnus Maximus (Maxen Wledig in Welsh legend), suggest that the Celtic, and largely Brythonic, population of Wales assimilated some aspects of Roman culture and that the memory of imperial governance was cherished. Brythonic refers to one of the two major divisions of Celtic languages, the other being Goidelic. The former comprises Welsh, Cornish, and Breton; the latter, Irish, Scots Gaelic, and Manx.

The extent of Roman influence on political and social organization is difficult to assess. Roman authors provide the names of some of the "tribes" that occupied parts of Wales, such as the Silures in the southeast and the Demetae in the southwest, but the precise boundaries of these "tribal" territories and their relationship to the political entities that emerged in the following centuries present problems not easily resolved. With others—tribes such as the Ordovices, located roughly in central and northwest Wales—the difficulties are even more pronounced. Archaeological evidence suggests that the civilizing influence of Rome, best exemplified in the Roman town of Caerwent, was most potent along the eastern borderland and the southeast. There is certainly a marked contrast between the Roman villas of the southeast and the enclosed homesteads of the northwest. But even in those areas in which the military aspects of imperial governance are predominant, the evidence indicates increasingly that a more general infusion of Roman culture had been at work. The question of the extent of Roman influence is complicated, however, by the effects both of late migrations into Wales and the processes by which Christianity was established in the land.

The *Historia Brittonum* of Nennius, a compilation of historical and geographical lore dating from about AD 800, records a tradition that a certain Cunedda Wledig and his sons migrated to northwest Wales from Manaw, a small province round the head of the Firth of Forth in the land of Gododdin, one of the Brythonic kingdoms of north Britain, in order to expel the Irish who had occupied the area. The tradition, which may be authentic in its essentials, points to a movement about AD 400 by an aristocratic group drawn from an area of strong Romano-British traditions. It would seem that Cunedda brought stability to the area that was later to be known as Gwynedd and that he was the founder of its royal dynasty. His descendants were to rule as kings, the assumption of a royal estate being inferred from the inscribed stone at Llangadwaladr, Anglesey, which commemorates his 7th-

Cunedda Wledig's migration

century descendant Catamanus Rex (Cadfan the King). The ostensible reason for Cunedda's intervention in Wales was the presence of an Irish population, and independent evidence does indicate the existence of Goidelic features in the northwest. In southwest Wales the Irish influences were particularly marked; this was due to an immigration of Goidelic people from the land of the Deisi in southern Ireland, probably in the late 4th and 5th centuries. The royal dynasty that emerged in the southwestern kingdom of Dyfed was distinctly Irish in origin, but the adoption of some Romano-British characteristics is suggested in the inscribed stone commemorating a 6th-century ruler styled "Voteporix the Protector." Irish connections are discernible, too, in the dynasty of the inland kingdom of Brycheiniog. In the southeast, where the Roman *civitas,* or urban community, had perhaps been most firmly established, the consolidation of stable kingdoms was probably accomplished later than elsewhere. Here the territories of Glywysing and Gwent emerged to be united, though not permanently, in the 7th century and called Morgannwg. Finally, among the major divisions, an area in north-central Wales was stabilized to form the kingdom of Powys (Powis), the name being derived from the *paganses,* or country people, of the *civitas* of the Cornovii upon the Welsh borderland. It was this once large kingdom, centred at Pengwern upon the Severn, that bore the brunt of Anglo-Saxon penetration of Wales.

Early Christianity. The extent of the Romano-British inheritance is again problematical in considering the origins of the Christian Church in Wales, for direct literary and archaeological evidence is slight. Traces of Romano-British Christian influence have been detected in the southeast, the area in closest cultural contact with romanized southern Britain. But Wales as a whole was undoubtedly affected by a western reorientation of trade and cultural connections that occurred in the 5th century. Wales and Ireland participated in renewed trade with the Mediterranean and reopened traditional culture routes that had exercised a powerful influence in prehistoric times. The early Christian stone inscriptions point to the strength of the Christian influences derived from Gaul and transmitted along the western seaways. Epigraphic studies reveal, in the script and in the formulas employed upon the stones, a fusion of Gallic Christian and Celtic influences. The stones, especially numerous in southwest Wales, which bear inscriptions in the ogham script (an alphabet comprised of notches), reflect the mingling of Christian with what were essentially Goidelic influences. In its forms, the church revealed a monastic character due both to its Gallic origins and to the needs of a Celtic society that did not possess important urban centres. Major monasteries were established in Wales by the 6th century, associated with figures such as St. Illtud at Llantwit Major or St. Cadog at Llancarfan. The founding of these centres was probably followed by a secondary movement, characterized by intense activity within the church, associated particularly with the names of St. David in south Wales and St. Beuno in north Wales. An examination of the distribution of the dedications of the churches and of the evidence of place-names in which the *llan* element (signifying a sacred enclosure) is often coupled with a personal name has served to suggest the spheres of influence of the Christian missionaries, or "saints," and to illustrate the close contacts with other Celtic lands that were maintained by means of the western seaways in this creative period. During the 6th century, in fact, the characteristics of the pre-Norman church were well established. Church organization was based upon a monastic church, or *clas,* akin to a minster, with which lesser churches were associated.

Relations with the Anglo-Saxons. The settlement of Anglo-Saxon peoples along the Welsh borderland separated the Brythonic people of Wales from their compatriots in the north and southwest of Britain, and the name Cymry ("compatriots"; *i.e.,* the Welsh) dates from this period. The campaign waged by Cadwallon, king of Gwynedd, in Northumbria early in the 7th century represents a late involvement of a Welsh king in the conflict between the Brythonic kingdoms of northern Britain and the English. That conflict in the north had already provided the sub-

Westward orientation

ject matter of the earliest poetry in the Welsh language, the work of Taliesin and Aneirin. The conflict upon the Welsh border itself is echoed in the Llywarch Hen poems, which, though probably dating from the 9th century, have their setting two centuries earlier in the contest between Powys and Mercia. The gradual colonization of the approaches to Wales by English peoples, a process marked by short dikes still visible upon the landscape, led to a final demarcation of the line of Mercian penetration with the construction in the time of King Offa (died 796) of the great linear earthwork known as Offa's Dyke.

Attempts at unity   Attempts during the next two centuries to bring the Welsh kingdoms west of the dike into a political unity proved to be only partially successful and impermanent. Rhodri Mawr ("the Great"; died 878), the king of Gwynedd who provided stern resistance to the Viking attacks, brought Powys within his dominion and then briefly extended his sway over two areas in the southwest (lying north and east of Dyfed), namely Ceredigion and Ystrad Tywi, which had previously been united to form the kingdom of Seisyllwg. The period following Rhodri's death proved to be of far-reaching significance. The outlying kingdoms of Wales—Dyfed, Brycheiniog, Glywysing, and Gwent— being subjected to pressure exerted by Rhodri's sons or by Mercia, turned to the kingdom of Wessex and by a formal commendation entered into that allegiance, ultimately expressed in homage and fealty, which each of the kings of Wales owed, individually and directly, to the English monarchy. Anarawd (died 916), a son of Rhodri, and his brothers, who shared the governance of their father's lands, subsequently submitted to Alfred (died 899) and completed the theoretical subjection of the Welsh kingdoms to the English sovereign. Rhodri's grandson, Hywel ap Cadell (Hywel Dda, "the Good"; died 950), starting from a patrimony in Seisyllwg, secured Dyfed by marriage, thereby creating the kingdom of Deheubarth. Eventually Gwynedd and Powys also came under his rule. Hywel accepted the position of a *sub-regulus,* or under-king, of the king of Wessex and seems to have endeavoured to emulate the advanced institutions of the contemporary West Saxon kingdom. Hywel's appeasement of Athelstan of Wessex (died 939) provoked a reaction expressed in the poem *Armes Prydein,* which envisages the formation of an alliance of Celtic peoples to oppose the Anglo-Saxon *mechdeyrn,* or overlord.

The conflicting impulses that were to be a feature of Welsh medieval political history were already discernible by the 10th century. Before its close, Maredudd ap Owain (died 999), a grandson of Hywel Dda, brought the northern and western kingdoms once more into a transitory unity. But his death opened a period of prolonged turmoil in which internal conflicts were complicated and intensified by Anglo-Saxon and Norse intervention. The established dynasties were challenged by men who asserted themselves within the kingdoms and exercised ephemeral supremacies. Of these, the most successful was Gruffudd **Tempo-** ap Llywelyn (died 1063), who brought Gwynedd, then De- **rary unity** heubarth, and finally (though briefly) the whole of Wales **under** under his dominion. The devastation wrought upon the **Gruffudd** English borderland, still not erased at the time of the making of Domesday Book (1086), was probably in large measure due to him. His death in 1063 meant that the most powerful ruler of independent Wales was destroyed only a few years before the coming of Norman forces to the Anglo-Welsh frontier.

Early Welsh society.   The endeavours of the dynasties in the 9th and 10th centuries, though only partially successful with regard to the problem of Welsh unification, had important and lasting consequences. Scholarly activity such as that represented in the *Historia Brittonum* and in annals and genealogies, material relating both to north Britain and to Wales, may well reflect the attempt of the descendants of Rhodri Mawr to consolidate their position and enhance their prestige. In creative literature it is likely that the origins of some texts preserved in medieval manuscripts, including some material in triad form (triple groupings of legal, literary, historical, and other materials), may be traced back to this period. The earliest Welsh law texts, though they date from the late

12th century onward, attribute the original codification of law to Hywel Dda; and the possibility that a significant development in Welsh jurisprudence took place under the aegis of that ruler is not improbable. The presence not only of a stratum of early indigenous law but of Anglo-Saxon influences (reflected, for instance, in the use of the term *edling* for the heir to the throne) points to a conscious adoption by the Welsh kings of some Anglo-Saxon concepts and procedures. These indications accord well with others, including that of the late inscribed stones, which point to an eastward reorientation of Welsh culture in this period.

The law texts, studied in association with other materials, reveal an early society ruled by kings (*brenhinoedd*) of independent kingdoms who possessed an authority, notably a recognized function in the public enforcement of legal obligations, that stood in contrast to traditional **Organiza-** Celtic custom. The kingdoms were normally divided for **tion of the** purposes of royal administration into *cantrefs.* These in **kingdoms** turn consisted of groups of *maenors* occupied by the bond or free elements of which Welsh society was composed. The bond population, which was probably larger than was at one time thought and which was concentrated in fairly compact *maenors* in lowland areas favourable to an agrarian economy, was organized on conventional manorial principles. In the economy of the upland areas the emphasis was upon a pastoral economy practiced by free communities, which were accorded more extensive *maenors.* The *maenor* organization as a whole represents a stage in the economic organization of Welsh society that was to be gradually superseded as a result of changes, quickened considerably in the 12th century, designed to ensure a more intensive exploitation of the soil. A smaller unit, the *tref,* or township, then replaced the *maenor.* In the sphere of royal administration the *cantref,* by a process probably well advanced on the eve of the first Norman invasions, was largely replaced by a small unit, the *commote,* which was to remain, under Welsh and alien lords, the basic unit of administration and jurisdiction throughout the medieval period.

WALES IN THE MIDDLE AGES

Norman infiltration.   The Norman conquest of England saw the establishment upon the Welsh border of the three earldoms of Chester, Shrewsbury, and Hereford, and from each of these strongpoints advances were made into Wales. Norman progress in southern Wales in the reign of William I (1066–87) was limited to the colonization of Gwent in the southeast. Domesday Book contains evidence suggesting that King William and Rhys ap Tewdwr, king of Deheubarth (died 1093), made a compact that recognized the Welsh ruler's authority in his own kingdom and perhaps also his influence in those other areas of southern Wales outside Deheubarth, particularly Morgannwg and Brycheiniog, that still lay outside Norman control. Meanwhile, from Chester and Shrewsbury, the Normans had penetrated more deeply into Wales, so that at Domesday, though the area colonized was limited, Norman lordship had been asserted over numerous *cantrefs* and *commotes* that had previously formed portions of the kingdoms of Gwynedd and Powys. The political situations in the northern and southern parts of the country were reversed during a period of renewed conflict in the reign (1087–1100) of William II who invaded Wales three times, unsuccessfully. The death of Rhys ap Tewdwr in 1093, opposing the Norman advance into Brycheiniog, was quickly followed by the invasion of virtually the whole of southern Wales. Advances from several bases along the Welsh border enabled Norman lords to establish the major lordships of Cardigan, Pembroke, Brecon, and Glamorgan. This advance constituted the decisive stage in the creation **Creation of** of the March of Wales (that portion of Wales under the **the March** authority of the English Crown). In each lordship of the March, the Norman lord, who was himself responsible for the conquest of the land, assumed the wide range of powers previously exercised there by the Welsh kings. These indigenous rights, enlarged and given definition during the course of the following centuries, formed the basis of the Custom of the March. This was a regality that enabled the lords to exercise extensive jurisdictional powers over the largely Welsh communities of their lordships and afforded them an extraordinary degree of autonomy in their relations with the English monarchy.

Gwynedd, Powys, and Deheubarth. The crucial years after 1093 saw also the initiation in northern Wales of a period of conflict by which the area was gradually recovered from Norman rule and the kingdoms of Gwynedd and Powys reconstituted as major political entities. Gwynedd, first under Gruffudd ap Cynan (died 1137) and then under his son Owain Gwynedd (died 1170), gained a firm governance that enabled the younger ruler, controlling a kingdom extending from the Dyfi to the Dee, to withstand foreign pressure, which was particularly severe during the reign (1154–89) of Henry II. In Powys the rule of Madog ap Maredudd (died 1160) likewise proved to be a period of stability and of expansion eastward beyond Offa's Dyke into lands that had been subjected to alien settlement in both the Anglo-Saxon and Norman periods. In southwest Wales, too, representatives of the dynasty of Deheubarth for over 30 years waged a campaign that finally enabled Rhys ap Gruffudd (died 1197), a grandson of Rhys ap Tewdwr, to win from Henry II a recognition of his position. Rhys ruled a land that was not as extensive as the ancient kingdom, for Norman control of the lordship of Pembroke and of other lordships along the southern coastline was conceded, but it nevertheless constituted a considerable dominion. The three kingdoms of Gwynedd, Powys, and Deheubarth formed by the third quarter of the 12th century a well-defined sphere of Welsh political influence (Wallia, or Pura Wallia) in contradistinction to the sphere of Norman influence (Marchia Wallie). Throughout the remainder of the period of Welsh independence there remained a memory that Wales, outside the March, had consisted historically of three kingdoms ruled from the three principal seats of Aberffraw in Gwynedd, Mathrafal in Powys, and Dinefwr in Deheubarth. The evidence, especially that of Welsh jurisprudence as revealed in texts dating from the late 12th century onward, reflects an endeavour on the part of these rulers to formulate a concept of Welsh kingship in which indigenous elements were blended with the new influences at work in the feudal monarchies. Each ruler, still known as a king (*rex, brenin*) but later to be styled prince (*princeps, tywysog*) or lord (*dominus, arglwydd*), governed an autonomous kingdom. The kings' relationship with the English monarchy was formalized in the homage and fealty that was done by each ruler in respect of his patrimony.

The stability provided by these rulers enabled their territories to recover from the depredations suffered during the conflicts of the Norman period. There are strong indications that the kings effected changes in social organization designed to increase the resources of the royal demesne, or crown land, and to promote generally a more intensive exploitation of the agrarian resources of their territories. The rulers deployed, especially on the coastal lowlands, communities characterized by personal servitude and the obligation to provide labour services. The organization of the large bond element in the population was in some areas adjusted to provide more favourable tenurial conditions as an incentive to the colonization of marginal lands. The agrarian changes also involved the settlement upon the soil of kindred groups of freemen. Stemming from a primary settlement of a single family in a shareland, the combined effect of successive divisions—the result of partible inheritance and of the expansion of the cultivated area—produced a pattern of dispersed settlement, in contrast to the nucleated (clustered) settlement of the bond communities. The endowment of some privileged free proprietors with substantial estates facilitated the growth of a class of landowners, who, linked to the royal lineages by ties of service, supplied the Welsh rulers with the personnel of their increasingly sophisticated administration. A renewed cultural vitality is revealed in Latin scholarship and in a flowering of the literary tradition.

In ecclesiastical affairs, the early Norman period saw the inauguration of a process by which the *clas* organization was replaced by arrangements consonant with the practice of the reformed church. The four territorial dioceses of

Welsh kings outside the March

Ecclesiastical affairs in the Norman period

Bangor, St. David's, Llandaff, and St. Asaph were created, and a parochial organization was gradually established. The church structure was a creation of the Normans, and the bishops appointed to Welsh sees owed a profession of obedience to Canterbury. Even so, Bernard, bishop of St. David's in 1115–48, claimed the status of an archbishop and, in furthering his campaign, appealed to the historical legacy of an early independent Welsh church. His bid was revived at the end of the century by Giraldus Cambrensis, but more significant was the resistance of the clergy of Bangor, who, acting under the protection of Owain Gwynedd at a time of national resistance toward the end of his reign, steadfastly refused to meet the demands of Thomas Becket, archbishop of Canterbury, that the newly elected bishop should swear fealty to Canterbury. The lay powers found adherents in the Cistercian Order. Houses such as Margam and Tintern, situated in the March, had close associations with their marcher patrons. The offshoots of the Cistercian monastery of Whitland, notably Strata Florida and Aberconway, were handsomely endowed by the Welsh rulers, who in return were supported in their political endeavours.

Llywelyn ap Iorwerth. In each of the three kingdoms of Gwynedd, Powys, and Deheubarth, the death of its powerful ruler was followed by a contested succession. The resulting conflicts portended a furthering of the fractionization characteristic of Welsh political history. In Powys and Deheubarth the unity of the kingdom was never restored; but with the emergence to power in the late 12th century of Llywelyn ap Iorwerth (died 1240), a grandson of Owain Gwynedd, Gwynedd was united once more under the strong hand of a single ruler. Llywelyn's aggression against neighbouring territories incurred resistance, which King John turned to his advantage in a campaign in 1211 whereby the Prince of Gwynedd was subjected to humiliating terms. But availing himself of a general Welsh reaction to John's measures for the permanent subjugation of the country, Llywelyn directed a sustained campaign in which his former adversaries participated. Llywelyn achieved a dominant position among the princes, which, while the contest with John persisted, augured the forging of a Welsh polity by bonds of homage and fealty to himself. But though he remained a powerful influence over the other Welsh princes and thereby minimized the crown's involvement in the affairs of Wales, Llywelyn was unable to secure a formal royal recognition of the territorial and conceptual achievements of the period of conflict. Llywelyn's aspirations for a wider Welsh principality based upon the supremacy of Gwynedd then centred upon David (later David II), his son by Joan, daughter of King John. David was designated as Llywelyn's heir in preference to his elder but bastard son, Gruffudd, and the Welsh dynasty looked to the English monarchy to ensure an unchallenged succession. In the event, the crown was able to use the dissension between the two sons and the disparate ambitions of the other Welsh princes to restrict David's power to Gwynedd alone. During the war of 1244–46 David contended for a broader influence, but his promising endeavour was cut short by his early death in 1246, without heir.

In the following year his nephews Owain and Llywelyn, two of the four sons of Gruffudd, entered into a treaty obligation by which the crown decreed the partition of a truncated Gwynedd into two parts, with the prospect of further division to provide for the younger brothers. But between 1255 and 1258 Llywelyn ap Gruffudd (died 1282), one of the four brothers, asserted his supremacy first in Gwynedd and then farther afield. Helped by the preoccupation of the English crown with the baronial conflict, the Prince secured a hegemony formally acknowledged by Henry III in 1267 by the Treaty of Montgomery, when Llywelyn's style, "prince of Wales," first assumed in 1258, and his right to the homage and fealty of the Welsh lords of Wales were recognized. Llywelyn had thereby brought into being a Principality of Wales comprised of the lands that had formed the 12th-century kingdoms of Gwynedd, Powys, and Deheubarth as well as parts of the March. Historically, this meant the reversal of a situation, for which there were several centuries of precedent, whereby the increasingly fragmented territories under Welsh rule had been fiefs held directly from the king of England. The opportunity to consolidate the governance of the principality proved to be brief. Friction between Llywelyn and Edward I led in 1277 to a war in which the Prince, isolated by the withdrawal of his vassals' fealty and confronted with the great resources and superior organization of England, was forced to accept terms that restricted his power to Gwynedd west of the Conway. By 1282 a deterioration in relations between Edward and a number of Welsh princes resulted in renewed conflict, which, widespread and vigorous, became a true war of Welsh independence. Although sustained even after the death of Llywelyn in December 1282, the resistance finally collapsed in the summer of the following year.

The Edwardian settlement. Edward I provided for the security of his conquests by means of a program of castle building, initiated after the war of 1277 and subsequently extended to include the great structures of Conway, Caernarfon, Harlech, and, later, Beaumaris. Each castle sheltered a borough where English colonists were settled. The king's arrangements for the governance of Llywelyn's former lands in northwest Wales were embodied in the Statute of Wales (1284). Three counties—Anglesey, Caernarfon, and Merioneth—were created and placed under the custody of a justice of North Wales. In northeast Wales a fourth county, Flint, was attached to the earldom of Chester. In southwest Wales the counties of Cardigan and Carmarthen, under the custody of the justice of West Wales, were formed out of lands over which royal power had been gradually extended by a process completed upon the failure, in 1287, of the revolt of Rhys ap Maredudd, the last of the princes of the dynasty of Deheubarth. Structurally, the shires that formed the Principality of Wales were similar to those of England, and certain common-law procedures were introduced into their courts, but the shires remained outside the jurisdiction of the central courts of Westminster, and they did not elect representatives to Parliament. The March of Wales was extended through the creation by royal charters, out of parts of Gwynedd and Powys, of the lordships of Denbigh, Ruthin, Bromfield and Yale, and Chirk. In his relations with two of the major barons of the older March, Gilbert de Clare of Glamorgan and Humphrey de Bohun of Brecon, Edward showed a determination to assert the sovereignty of the crown over the March and to eradicate abuses of the Custom of the March such as the claim, defiantly expressed by Gilbert, to the right to wage war in the March. But neither Edward nor his successors attempted any far-reaching changes in the organization of the March, and political fractionization persisted over the next two centuries.

Rebellion and annexation. Both the crown and the marcher lords employed in the administration of their lands Welshmen drawn from an administrative class that had been fostered by the princes themselves. Those of the principality revealed a particular loyalty to Edward II in the political crises of his reign, and their continued attachment to his cause even after his deposition created a tense situation in 1327. During the 14th century there were occasional variances, but the identity of interest established between the crown and the leading Welshmen proved durable. Even so, the community endured both the economic difficulties encountered over wide areas of Europe at this time and the specifically Welsh problems created by the fact that an important phase in the transition from early medieval social arrangements coincided with the pressures exerted by an alien and fiscally extractive administration. At the very end of the century, the deposition of Richard II, who had influential Welshmen among his partisans, released from allegiance to the monarchy a group that, associated with Owain Glyndwr (Owen Glendower), raised a great rebellion that drew its strength from the community as a whole. In the period 1400–07 the royal government lost control of the greater part of Wales, and in some areas the insurrection remained unextinguished several years later.

The rebellion, however, quickened certain processes that were to lead ultimately to the enfranchisement provided by Tudor legislation. In northern Wales particularly, the availability of civil actions by English law led to an early but unrequited demand for English land law. After the rebellion the disabilities incurred by reason of Welsh nationality were underlined. Though often expressed in literature in militant terms and, during the years of dynastic conflict, manipulated by the protagonists of York and Lancaster, the aspirations of the community were focussed in a demand for English denizenship. First individual petitioners looked for enfranchisement and then whole communities in northern Wales secured from Henry VII, by negotiation and payment, charters conferring upon them English land law and other advantages. A realization by the crown of its inability to reverse a decline in the financial yield of its Welsh lands, an experience shared by the marcher lords, contributed to Henry VII's policy.   (J.B.Sm.)

WALES FROM THE 16TH TO 19TH CENTURY

Union with England. No event marks more clearly the transition from the Middle Ages to the modern period in the history of Wales than the act passed in 1536 uniting Wales with England. Nevertheless, it was probably not until the union of England and Scotland was mooted early in the reign of James I that the Tudor settlement of Wales in 1536 came to be regarded as a union with England. The act of 1536 was essentially an administrative measure devised by the ministers of Henry VIII to clear up the confused pattern of law and jurisdiction in Wales resulting from the piecemeal manner of the country's conquest between 1093 and 1283. Its principal objective was the division into shires of the Welsh Marches, the enclave of semi-independent lordships lying between the principality of Wales and the counties of England.

The measure was part of the administrative reforms carried out by Thomas Cromwell abolishing feudal franchises and absorbing outlying areas of the king's dominions within the realm of England. Dictated by the critical situation arising from Henry VIII's break with Rome, these reforms were also inspired by the concept of national sovereignty then becoming dominant in Europe. The incorporation of Wales into England may be compared with the absorption of Brittany into France four years earlier.

The act of 1536, together with a subsequent act passed in 1543, transformed the polity of Wales. From being a country with a system of government imposed upon it in the course of, and for the purpose of maintaining, a military conquest, Wales became politically and administratively an integral part of England, with Welshmen enjoying the same status before the law as Englishmen. This has remained the constitutional position of Wales, though certain administrative differences have from time to time distinguished Wales from England, not least in the 20th century. The union legislation provided Wales with a system of local government similar to that of England, gave representation in Parliament to Welsh shires and boroughs, abolished Welsh law relating to land tenure, extended English law to all parts of Wales, and made English the official language of courts in Wales.

The act of 1543, settling in detail the new arrangements for Wales, modified to some extent the intention implicit in the earlier act of making the administration of Wales entirely uniform with that of England. For purposes of administrative convenience, it continued and thereby gave statutory recognition to the Council in the Marches, originally set up by Edward IV and revived by Henry VII. It also established the Courts of Great Sessions as higher courts of justice in Wales but attached Monmouthshire to the Oxford circuit in England; from this arose the distinction between Wales and Monmouthshire. The Council, its powers curtailed by the Long Parliament in 1641, fell into abeyance during the English Civil War. It was revived in 1660 but abolished in 1689. The Great Sessions were not abolished until 1830. The historical concept of the principality of Wales was preserved, despite these changes, because the title of prince of Wales was retained for the heir apparent to the throne.

The drastic changes introduced in 1536 and 1543 would not have been possible if Wales had not been made ready for them by a long process of political, social, and economic assimilation to England. With the growth of landed

(Left margin:) War with Edward I

(Right margin:) The Act of 1536

estates and of the cattle and wool trade in the later Middle Ages, the economy of Wales had become integrated into that of England.

16th to 18th century. Until the Industrial Revolution, Wales was poor, sparsely populated, and largely pastoral. Its population was not more than 250,000 in the 16th century and hardly more than 400,000 at the beginning of the 18th. Towns were small and few in number. Communications were rudimentary. Despite its isolation, this rural society was by no means static. Two developments in particular became more pronounced from the mid-17th century: the continued growth of the larger estates and the anglicization of the gentry.

In the Tudor and early Stuart periods the gentry, derived mainly from the native military class of medieval Wales, were relatively numerous and merged imperceptibly into the lower orders. The small, scattered communities in which the people lived were closely knit units; and differences of rank, though real enough, were usually not conspicuous. Many of the gentry, too, were hardly more than substantial freeholders whose claim to gentryhood rested more upon their pedigrees than upon their wealth. The Tudor gentry, though turning more to the use of the English language, were far from losing their Welsh; and they tended to regard themselves as "Cambro-British" subjects of the crown. Changes already at work in this society were greatly accelerated by the English Civil Wars (1642–51). Impoverished by the wars and unable to keep pace with rising costs, the smaller gentry were losing status and sometimes land. The larger estates continued to

Social changes among the gentry

expand at the expense of the lesser. The gentry became a smaller and more exclusive class, consisting only of the wealthier families. Entering more into London society after the Restoration of Charles II in 1660, these families intermarried increasingly with English families. With the transfer of power from the monarchy to Parliament they also identified themselves politically with the English upper class represented in Parliament. They became almost entirely English in speech and outlook. A marked division—economic, social, and linguistic—thus emerged between the gentry and the lower orders in Wales.

In the Civil Wars, Wales was royalist, though some support for Parliament existed, mainly in areas in the southwest and northeast having close commercial ties with England. Welsh peasants formed part of Charles I's infantry, and Wales was strategically important for the King in 1643–44 as a landing base for his troops from Ireland and in 1645 as a retreating ground after his defeat at Naseby. In 1646 Wales was occupied by the parliamentary forces.

In 1650, at the behest of Welsh Puritan leaders, the Commonwealth government passed an act for the better propagation of the gospel in Wales. It was an attempt to convert the Welsh to Puritanism by providing them with a Puritan ministry and some form of popular education. The 60 or so schools set up under the act were the first state schools in England and Wales. The act lapsed in 1653. Puritan rule, imposed upon Wales by English parliamentary troops, was highly unpopular with the Welsh people, who welcomed the restoration of the monarchy in 1660.

Because the English system of law and government had been extended to Wales, there was no later problem of absorbing alien institutions into the English system as was the case in Scotland in 1707. Wales was a part of the English system when the Reformation occurred, and the religious history of Wales moved along with that of England. Welsh political history in the 18th century was either a part of national history or, as in the English counties, local history. Wales felt the same influences as England in that period, most notably in religion and in economic life. Nonconformity of the Dissenting and then the Methodist variety played a more important part in the intellectual and social life of Wales than of England. Along with England, Wales would participate in the agricultural and industrial revolutions. The Welsh terrain and mineral endowments made the raising of livestock, the woollen industries, and later the production of coal and iron of first importance. The history of Wales in the 18th century can be written in the histories of religion and of

the economic revolution more meaningfully than as an attempt at separate national political history.

Industrial developments. Mineral deposits in Wales, notably the veins of lead ore in Cardiganshire, had been extracted on a rudimentary scale since the 16th century. The exploitation of Welsh mineral resources on an industrial scale began in the late 18th century with the establishment, mainly by English industrialists, of iron works in Northeast Wales at Bersham, near Wrexham, and in South Wales on the northern rim of the coalfield in the neighbourhood of Merthyr Tydfil. A rich copper deposit discovered near Amlwch, in Anglesey, in 1768 gave Wales for a time a leading position in the world copper trade, but the Anglesey mines were exhausted by the beginning of the 19th century, as were the Cardiganshire lead mines by 1870. Copper works at Swansea, however, where Cornish copper was brought for smelting, continued to expand. Growing demand for roofing slates led to the development of slate quarries in Northwest Wales from the 1780s.

Coal mining in Wales was subsidiary to the iron industry until smokeless coal (dry steam), discovered in the Aberdare district in the 1830s, began to be exported from Cardiff for domestic consumption in London and elsewhere. The coal industry in South Wales expanded enormously in the later 19th century as the growth of the railways and the changeover from sail to steam created a world demand for coal. Coal also kept the iron and steel industry in South Wales despite the exhaustion of local iron ore, but the import of ore caused the steel works to be moved to the southern rim of the coalfield near the coast.

Expansion of the coal industry

The quickening tempo of industrial development brought a marked improvement in communications between 1850 and 1870. Hitherto inadequately served by roads and still less so by canals, the industrial areas of Wales were linked by rail with England. The Chester and Holyhead Railway, built for the Irish traffic and completed in 1850, opened the North Wales coast to middle-class holidaymakers and tourists, mainly from Lancashire; and the development of seaside resorts began.

Social and political developments in the 19th century. During the 18th century the population of Wales (including Monmouthshire) increased by 40 percent, reaching 587,128 in 1801. By 1851 it had risen to 1,186,697, mostly by a natural increase but partly by immigration of workers from Ireland and England. This period of rapid population growth and industrialization brought dislocation and upheaval in the settled pattern of a society hitherto almost entirely rural. The peasantry were subject to much privation and misery until the late 1840s, when the results of industrialization began to show in an amelioration of their material conditions. In the years following 1815, economic depression caused a crisis in the overpopulated countryside. There were constant disturbances and widespread discontent, but the worst consequences were avoided by the migration of unemployed labourers to the industrial centres. The only major outbreaks of violence occurred in 1839 and 1842, when small farmers in West Wales, made desperate by their poverty, destroyed turnpike gates and tollhouses in a series of attacks known as the Rebecca Riots.

The early decades of the century also saw much turbulence in the industrial areas. Crudely organized strikes against wage reductions and stoppages were frequent and were enforced by violent bands of strikers known as Scotch Cattle (so called because of their adoption of a bull's head and horns as their symbol). In the early 1830s trade unionism spread from England into the Welsh industrial areas but failed to take root. Chartism also spread from England in 1838 and 1839, chiefly among unemployed textile workers in the mid-Wales woollen towns and the ironworkers of Monmouthshire. Following the collapse of Chartism and the advent of comparative prosperity by midcentury, the working class in Wales turned from political agitation and began their long struggle to build a trade-union movement.

At the same time, the nonconformist middle classes in Wales, expanding in numbers as a result of industrialization, began to be politically militant. Radicalism, derived from the old dissent, had been gradually spreading among them since the revival of the agitation for parliamentary reform after 1815. During the 1830s radical periodicals in Welsh were beginning to appear. Methodism, however, remained politically apathetic, especially in the rural areas. In 1847 a government report on education in Wales displayed a strong bias against Welsh Nonconformity. The Nonconformists, their numbers and resources now greatly increased, were roused to fury. Radicalism, with its demand for the removal of the disabilities under which Nonconformists laboured, became henceforth the political creed of Welsh dissent. In the 1850s the London-based Liberation Society advocating the disestablishment of the church sought to enlist the support of Welsh Nonconformity and set up branches in Wales. Welsh Nonconformist radicalism was thus politically organized with disestablishment fixed as its principal objective. The county families who had hitherto exclusively controlled the parliamentary representation of Wales found their political ascendancy challenged in the elections of 1859 and 1868. The Reform Acts of 1867 and 1884, by extending the franchise, assisted in bringing about a transformation in the representation of Wales at Westminster. The Whig and Tory members and nominees of the old county families were almost entirely deposed and their places taken by Welsh Nonconformist radicals.

In 1885 they formed a Welsh parliamentary party which, profiting by divisions within the Liberal Party, exercised considerable influence. Among other things, it succeeded in 1914 in securing an act for the disestablishment of the Anglican Church in Wales. This came into effect in 1920. In the conflict in which the Anglican Church and the anglicized squirearchy supported the Conservative Party, on the one side, and the Welsh-speaking, nonconformist middle and working classes supported the Liberal Party, on the other, Welsh radicalism developed into political nationalism.

Nation-
alism
Already in 1865 this nationalism had motivated the foundation of a Welsh settlement in Patagonia in South America. Between 1886 and 1896 it inspired an abortive campaign for Home Rule for Wales, launched by a movement called Cymru Fydd, or Young Wales, in which David Lloyd George took a leading part.

Nationalism developed not only from radicalism but also from a growing consciousness of nationality. This consciousness was rooted in the Welsh language, which alone at the beginning of the 19th century marked an essential difference between England and Wales. The growth of this consciousness began with the Romantic Movement and the revival of interest in Welsh literature and history. It was stimulated by national movements in Europe and fostered by Welsh communities in London and other English cities. The sentiment of nationality made the Eisteddfod of Wales in the late 19th century a great national cultural festival. Above all, it inspired a movement that between 1849 and 1906 succeeded in creating a largely autonomous system of elementary, secondary, and university education in Wales. Outstanding events in the movement were the foundation of university colleges at Aberystwyth (1872), Cardiff (1883), and Bangor (1884); their incorporation into the University of Wales in 1893; the Welsh Interme-

diate Education Act (1889) setting up secondary schools and the creation of the Central Welsh Board (1896) for the control of these schools; the establishment of a Welsh department of the Board of Education in 1907; and finally the foundation by royal charter in 1907 of the National Library of Wales at Aberystwyth and of the National Museum at Cardiff.

The national movement failed to arrest the decline of the Welsh language, which was increasingly evident after 1870, partly because of immigration into Wales and compulsory elementary education and the use of English in schools. The proportion of Welsh speakers fell from 54.4 percent of the total population in 1891, to 37.2 percent in 1921, to less than 20 percent in the late 20th century.

WALES IN THE 20TH CENTURY

The election of James Keir Hardie at Merthyr Tydfil in 1900 as the first Labour MP representing a Welsh constituency marked the entry of the industrial working class in Wales into politics on their own account. Enthusiastic support for one of their own, Prime Minister David Lloyd George, leader of the radicals in the Liberal Party, continued for a while after World War I. But the Labour Party gained increasing support, especially during the long economic depression following the war and in the 1930s; and the advance of labour continued into the rural areas after World War II. Meanwhile, the idea of a Welsh state revived with the formation in 1925 of the Welsh Nationalist Party, later called Plaid Cymru (Party of Wales). By the 1950s it had some 210 local branches, and in 1966 amid much excitement, in a by-election in Carmarthenshire, returned to Parliament its winning candidate, the party president, Gwynfor Evans. Indeed, in the 1960s issues of devolution and federation were much discussed. In 1968 a poll indicated that 59 percent favoured some kind of Welsh parliament. These developments did not go unnoticed at Westminster—the minister for Welsh affairs, appointed in 1951, became a secretary of state in 1964, and in 1960 a Welsh grand committee was established in the Commons.

The Welsh have been interested in cultural revival, although, with strong differences between the rural north and the industrial south, this concern has not always been unifying. The University of Wales has stimulated Celtic scholarship. Welsh poets use their native tongue. The annual festival, the Eisteddfod, held alternately in North Wales and South, stimulates interest in Welsh poetry and choral singing. Nevertheless, by 1980 the issue of limited home rule (termed "devolution" by Westminster) in Wales appeared to be dead. Referenda that would have given Wales an elected assembly with limited powers were defeated in March 1979. The pressure of anglicizing influences, reinforced by press, radio, and television, had become greater than ever before.

Revival of
Welsh
culture

The attention of much of the world focussed on Wales on July 1, 1969, with the investiture of Prince Charles as prince of Wales by his mother, the Queen, in bilingual ceremonies at Caernarvon (Caernarfon) Castle. The Prince gave his pledge "to associate myself in word and deed with as much of the life of the principality as possible."

(W.O.W./Ed.)

NORTHERN IRELAND

The geographical position of Northern Ireland holds the key to much of its unique social, economic, and political development—a process beset by such deep-rooted antagonisms as to make the strife-torn nation globally significant in the late 20th century, perhaps because it seemed to mirror, in microcosm and in the Northern Hemisphere, many of the problems then afflicting evolving nation-states in other areas of the world.

The country—created a self-governing state within the United Kingdom by the Government of Ireland Act of 1920—lies in the northeast of the island of Ireland, itself located on that western continental periphery often characterized as Atlantic Europe. Northern Ireland is often referred to as the province of Ulster (and its inhabitants as

Ulstermen), though it includes only six of the nine counties which made up that historic Irish entity. It occupies 5,452 square miles (14,120 square kilometres) of land, about a sixth of the whole of the island, and is separated from Scotland, another constituent country of the United Kingdom, by the narrow North Channel, which is at one point only 13 miles (21 kilometres) wide. Historically, this channel has been a link rather than a barrier, and from the earliest times it has witnessed a constant coming and going of peoples. This interchange gave the northern part of the island a distinctive regional character, which was confirmed during the Industrial Revolution when the province emerged as a linen-manufacturing region and later was strengthened when a shipbuilding and engineering industry, based on imported raw materials, made Belfast a major city. The intrusive influences that brought about this cultural and economic transformation were attenuated in the west and south, and the political border with the Republic of Ireland is more of a compromise conveniently based on long-existing country borders than a clear-cut regional boundary. The political separation of Northern Ireland has merely confirmed its economic position as a region existing within the framework of the United Kingdom as a whole, serving as an extension of the larger unit's industrial resources. Although the cultural links of some of the people of Northern Ireland with the Republic of Ireland are strong—and much in evidence politically since 1968—it seems as though these ties are likely to suffer increasing erosion as state legislation follows economic trends, and progressively caters to educational and social needs along lines similar to those introduced in England, Scotland, and Wales.

Physical and human geography

THE LAND

Topography

Relief. Northern Ireland can be thought of topographically as a saucer centred on Lough (lake) Neagh, the upturned rim of which forms the province's highlands. Five of the six former counties—Antrim, Down, Armagh, Tyrone, and Londonderry—met at the Lough, and each had a highland region on the saucer's rim. To the north and east the Antrim Plateau tilts upward toward the coast. It reaches heights of between 1,000 and 1,500 feet (300 and 450 metres), terminating in an impressive cliff coastline of basalts and chalk, broken by a series of the glaciated valleys known as glens, which face Scotland and are rather isolated from the remainder of the province. The rounded landscape of drumlins—smooth mounds left by the ice of the final glaciation—in the southeast (former County Down) is punctuated by Slieve Croob (1,755 feet [535 metres]) and culminates in the Mourne Mountains, which rise to Slieve Donard (2,796 feet [852 metres]) within two miles of the sea. This impressive landscape of granite peaks is bounded by Carlingford Lough to the south.

The scenery in the region of former County Armagh is gentler, but the land rises to 1,894 feet in Slieve Gullion near the border with the Republic. West of Lough Neagh the land rises gently to the more rounded Sperrin Mountains, shared by the former counties of Londonderry and Tyrone: Sawel (2,240 feet [683 metres]) is the highest of several hills over 2,000 feet. The sixth county, Fermanagh, was focussed geographically on its own lake basin, occupied by Lough Erne, in a drumlin-strewn area ringed by hills more than 1,000 feet high.

Drainage and soils. Much of the Northern Ireland landscape is gentle and, in most low-lying areas, is covered with swarms of drumlins that have played havoc with the local drainage and are interspersed with marshy hollows. Glaciation also gave the land its main valleys, the River Bann—draining Lough Neagh to the north—the Blackwater to the southwest, and the River Lagan to the east. All of these valleys have been important routeways but none more important than the Lagan, penetrating from Belfast Lough to the very heart of Ulster.

Soils are varied. Although much glacially transported material covers the areas below 700 feet, the nature of the soil is predominantly influenced by the nature of the underlying parent rock. Brown earth soils, forming arable loams, are extensive, and are derived from the ancient Silurian rocks of the southeast and from the basalts of the northeast. There are some ash-like podzols in the Sperrins, and the impeded drainage of much of the southwest gives acidic soil. Peat soils are common, particularly in the hollows lying between the drumlins, and hill peat is widespread over the province. Although it is of no great commercial value, peat traditionally has been a source of fuel for the peasant farmer and is still cut extensively.

Climate. Northern Ireland's climate is temperate and maritime: most of its weather comes from the southwest in a series of lows bringing the rain and cloud that often lend character to the landscape. As the country is near the central track of such lows, it often experiences high winds,

Maritime influences

and in the north and on the wild northeast (Antrim) coast, particularly, severe westerly gales are common. Above the 800-foot level, distorted trees and windbreaks testify to the severity of the weather. Rainfall decreases from west to east, but the hills accentuate the amount to some 80 inches (2,000 millimetres) in parts of former Tyrone, and as little as 32.5 inches (825 millimetres) at Lough Neagh and the extreme southeast. A relatively dry spring gives way to a wet summer and a wetter winter. Conditions generally are very changeable, but there are no extremes of heat or cold. Normal temperatures vary between means of 41° and 50° F (5° and 10° C). These mild and humid climatic conditions have, in sum, made Northern Ireland a green country in all seasons.

Plant and animal life. The general features of the plant and animal life of the province are similar to those in the northwest of Britain. The imprint of man is heavy on the landscape and is particularly evident in the absence of trees. Most of the land has been plowed and drained and cultivated for centuries. Above the limit of cultivation, rough pastures have been grazed extensively and beyond them lies a zone of mountain vegetation. Only about 5 percent of the land is now under forest, and more than half of this has been planted by the state. Young trees in these plantations are economically unimportant, but locally they are helping to diversify the landscape.

Settlement patterns. The traditional regions of Northern Ireland correspond closely to the main topographical elements, although they are also the outcome of the cultural evolution of the province. In the north and east (former County Antrim and the Bann Valley, north County Down, and north County Armagh), the influence of the Scots and English has been paramount. West of Lough Neagh and in the fastness of the Mourne Mountains and of Slieve Gullion or in the more distant Lough Erne region indigenous elements have maintained a distinctiveness that is still apparent. Such relatively isolated pockets as the Antrim glens and Kilkeel have retained a local consciousness that gives colour and interest to the human geography of the province.

The predominant impression of Northern Ireland's landscape is of scattered and isolated farms. Occasional relics of tiny hamlets, or clachans, show that peasant crofts once were huddled together in kinship groups who worked their strips in an open-field system. Between the end of the 18th century and the middle of the 19th most of the land was enclosed and the scattered strips consolidated, partly as a policy of the landlords but finally because of the effect on the population of the potato famines of the 1840s. The end result was the orderly, small square fields that dominate the contemporary landscape. Some landlords rearranged their tenants' land in narrow ribbons, from valley bottom to mountain pasture, giving a characteristic ladder of fields, with the farms strung along the road on the valley side. Drumlins also have had an effect on siting; houses are found away from the peaty bottom lands but below the windswept skyline. Most farmhouses are small and a few are still thatched. The occasional larger farm often has a Georgian house—simple and dignified and a reflection of the age of consolidation.

Small market towns rather than villages are frequent. Built by the English and Scots planters or by the landlords of the 18th century, they have a foreign touch of orderliness and urbanity. Many are grouped around a "diamond" (meeting place), or square, which is used as a marketplace. Some of them acquired a mill in the 19th century, but in few cases has this changed the essentially rural context.

Market towns

Few of the market centres have grown into substantial towns. In the western half of the province, regional services and administration have enlarged Omagh and Enniskillen. Some towns have grown with the introduction of industry, notably Dungannon, specializing in fabrics, and Carrickfergus, noted for rayon. Armagh is an ecclesiastical centre with two cathedrals, while Lisburn, Portadown, and Lurgan, all in the Lagan Valley, form an extension of the Belfast industrial complex, their size based on the textile industry. Bangor is a resort and a residential outlier of Belfast. Londonderry is a centre for shirtmaking and textiles. It was the centre of the Lough Foyle lowlands until the hinterland that it served was split by the partition of Ireland, but it remains the main focus of the west. The size of Belfast, at the head of Belfast Lough on the northeast coast, underlines its dominance of the region, as well as its significance as an industrial centre and major port. Its economic bases are linen and engineering and, notably, shipbuilding; textile machinery is also important, and the city is the centre of provincial government, finance, and education. Reflecting the city's 19th-century origin, most of the streets are inextricably and bleakly mixed with mills and factories, while the reclaimed land at the head of the Lough is given over entirely to industry.

THE PEOPLE

The cultural differences that underlie many of Northern Ireland's contemporary social problems have a long and troubled history. The province has had lasting links with parts of western Scotland, strengthened by constant population movements. After the Tudor invasions and particularly after the forced settlements, or plantations, of the early 17th century, the English and Scots elements were further differentiated from the native Irish by their Protestant faith. Two distinct and often antagonistic elements—the indigenous Roman Catholic Irish and the intrusive Protestant English and Scots—date from that period, and have played a significant role in molding the province's development. The intrusive element dominated former County Antrim and north Down, controlled the Lagan corridor toward Armagh, and also formed powerful minorities elsewhere. This situation contributed to the decline of spoken Gaelic, and it is reflected in the contemporary distribution of religions. Gaelic is now only occasionally heard at a traditional entertainment. The accents given to English, however, are regionally distinctive. The northeastern dialect, dominating the former countries of Antrim, Londonderry, and parts of Down, is an offshoot of central Scots dialect and reflects the latter in almost all of its features. The remainder of the province, including the Lagan Valley, has accents derived from England, more particularly from Cheshire, Merseyside, Greater Manchester, and southern Lancashire, and the "west country" counties of Gloucester, Avon, Somerset, and Devon. The towns show more of a mixture and an overlay of standard English.

Dialects

About one-third of the population is Roman Catholic, about one-fourth Presbyterian, and more than one-fifth Episcopalian (Church of Ireland); Methodists and members of other sects make up the remainder. The distribution of Roman Catholics and Protestants is, however, very uneven. In country districts, the latter are in a majority in the north and east. Elsewhere, they are in a minority, though fairly highly localized. Most towns have a Protestant majority: this is the case in Belfast, where Roman Catholics comprise less than 30 percent of the population. Towns remote from Belfast—Newry and Londonderry—have higher percentages. In the towns there is a high degree of segregation of the sects and mixing is minimal. Industrial west Belfast is split into two sectors along two axial roads. The Falls Road is as exclusively Roman Catholic as the Shankill Road is Protestant. In many streets adjoining the boundary line, segregation is 100 percent. East Belfast has an exclusively Roman Catholic core, but segregation is less apparent in the middle-class suburbs. Segregation increases as socioeconomic status decreases. Civil disturbances are almost confined to locations in which segregation is highest. The proportions of the sects are changing slightly because of a differential in birth rate. In Belfast, for example, fertility ratios in Roman Catholic districts are very much higher than in Protestant areas. There has been a relative decline of Protestants in the last half century, though they have remained more or less stable in absolute numbers, and a relative and absolute increase of Roman Catholics.

THE ECONOMY

Economically, Northern Ireland is an integral part of the United Kingdom. Its trade is dominated by imports from the United Kingdom and exports to the United Kingdom, though some of the latter are reexported directly from England or are the bases of manufactured goods that are subsequently exported. Trade with the Republic of Ireland accounts for a small percentage of the total, and there are lesser links with parts of the Commonwealth and of Europe.

Compared with its southern neighbour, Northern Ireland is an industrialized country; and the mass of its exports is made up of manufactured goods. This situation, however, has placed a heavy reliance on the import of raw materials, and the Belfast region might well be thought of as an extension of the industrial regions of northwest England and the Clyde. Its own mineral resources are extremely meagre: coal must be imported from Great Britain, although local chalk, clays, limestones, and gravels are used to produce lime, bricks, and cement. Northern Ireland's power resources, too, depend on imported coal and oil.

Agriculture. Northern Ireland does possess considerable agricultural resources, which it is developing as a major part of its economy. Fundamentally, it is still a country of peasant farmers; but in the late 20th century this situation began to change. The number of farms decreased, giving a substantial increase in average size of farms. Consolidation has meant a better livelihood for fewer farmers.

Consolidation of farms

Almost all farms now have electricity, and there has been a great increase in the number of tractors and combine harvesters in use. The frequent rain, the high humidity, and the prospect of wet harvests discourage arable farming, but local conditions produce good grass and rich pasture: nearly all grassland is plowed and there is very little "rough grazing." Mixed farming predominates, with a seven-year rotation—four years of grass or hay, two of oats, with a root crop, such as potatoes, intervening. About 85 percent of farming income comes from livestock and their produce. The production of grass seed and seed potatoes for export is also important. To the south of Lough Neagh lies a rich orchard country, and apples and market gardening are constant features of the landscape. Most of the agricultural land is held by the occupiers in fee simple, but there persists the peculiar feature of conacre, a system of short (11-month) lets, which still accounts for a portion of the agricultural land. Conacre enables farmers to extend their holdings and provides an income for elderly and nonfarming owners of land without loss of ownership.

Industry. Although farming dominates the landscape of the country, it provides a livelihood for only one in 10 of Northern Ireland's inhabitants, and the real wealth lies in manufacturing—engineering; shipbuilding; vehicle manufacture; the textile industry; food, beverage, and tobacco-processing industries; and the clothing industry. Locally grown flax and a plentiful supply of soft water originally stimulated the growth of the textile industry, and spinning still flourishes in many inland towns. The other industries were more a product of foresight, as raw materials, capital, and even skills were drawn into Belfast to make them possible.

Flax is now imported, and linen is still synonymous with Northern Ireland, though cotton and artificial fibres, as well as woollen fabrics, carpets, and clothing, are now important. Although all these activities are dominated by Belfast, Londonderry is well-known for shirt and pajama manufacturing. Belfast's shipyards are world-famed, and some of the skills developed there have been diverted into the aircraft and automobile industries. Engineering grew largely to meet the demands of the textile and shipbuilding industries. Belfast also has chemical plants, rope-making factories, and a large percentage of the food-processing work of the province; tobacco also plays a leading role.

The industrial structure of Northern Ireland is a vulnerable one, and unemployment in the province is considerably higher than in the remainder of the United Kingdom, with a much higher rate among men than women. For more than two decades the government has actively encouraged the growth of manufacturing and such economic diversification as broadening the base of the textile industry by introducing man-made fibres. A series of government acts has tempted new enterprises into the country by providing factory space and making grants toward capital expenditure. In relation to the remainder of the United Kingdom, Northern Ireland is peripheral and partially isolated. This adds to the difficulty of maintaining local

Development programs

growth. The organization of labour is strongly oriented to Britain: local trade unions are affiliated to the Trades Union Congress, but, in fact, a vast majority of its members belong to English- or Scottish-based unions. Several thousand workers are members of unions controlled from the Irish Republic.

Finance. Northern Ireland is unified fiscally with the United Kingdom. It has three sources of revenue: first, a share of United Kingdom revenue from customs and excise, income, value-added, and capital gains taxes and the national insurance surcharge; second, non-tax revenue collected locally, such as rates (contributions toward the cost of local government services) and land annuities; and third, specific and nonspecific payments from the United Kingdom to bridge the gap between income and expenditure.

Transportation. One of the more noteworthy features of the countryside of Northern Ireland is a close network of well-maintained roads. The majority are very minor, but all parts of the province are accessible. Public-road transport outside the Belfast municipal service has been nationalized since 1935, and since 1948 the Ulster Transport Authority (since 1967 the Northern Ireland Transport Holding Company) has also controlled the railways. The latter have diminished rapidly—from 824 miles to 200 miles—in the economic reorganization following railway nationalization; a link with Londonderry and the line to Dublin, via Newry, were all that remained by the late 20th century. Inland waterways have almost disappeared, although a little commercial traffic still uses the Lower Bann Navigation to Coleraine, and there is some recreational sailing.

The province's links with Britain by sea and air are of paramount importance. Belfast is one of the major ports of the British Isles. Its eight miles of quays now contain modern container-handling facilities. Larne and Londonderry are the other ports of significance; Coleraine and Warrenpoint handle some freight. Larne and Belfast handle passenger transport. All services handle car ferries, an important factor in the province's increasing tourist trade. The main civil airport for Northern Ireland is at Aldergrove, which has regular air service to major cities in Britain and to North America.

ADMINISTRATIVE AND SOCIAL CONDITIONS

Government. Under the Government of Ireland Act (1920) separate parliaments were planned for both northern and southern Ireland, but the plan became effective only for the north, where a Parliament was formally opened in 1921. When the Irish Free State emerged in 1922, Northern Ireland opted to continue its form of government, which was marked by strong ties with the central government of the United Kingdom at Westminster; a commission eventually confirmed a boundary with the south that would contain the six counties. When the Irish Free State seceded from the Commonwealth in 1949, the union of Northern Ireland with the United Kingdom was further confirmed. Paradoxically, its measure of self-government is the result of its determination to preserve union with Britain, and its links with London are safeguarded by the election to Westminster of 17 members; this number was raised from 12 in 1979, to bring the size of constituencies more in line with those in the remainder of the United Kingdom. Northern Ireland elects three members to the European Parliament.

Until 1972, the crown exercised all legislative power in Northern Ireland through a governor who held office for six years. The Parliament of Northern Ireland consisted of a Senate and a House of Commons. The former had 24 members elected by the Commons for eight years, and the lord mayor of Belfast was an ex officio member. The House of Commons had 52 members and a maximum life of five years, and in all ways was closely modelled on Westminster, which was responsible for matters relating to the crown, war and peace, the armed forces, and foreign powers, as well as trade, navigation, coinage, and many others. Northern Ireland could make no laws interfering with religious equality. In almost all internal matters it followed Westminster policy.

Political links with the United Kingdom

In March 1972 years of political violence, accompanied by increased terror, led the British Parliament to suspend Northern Ireland's Parliament and government and place the country under direct rule from London. Eventually the administration was taken over by the secretary of state for Northern Ireland.

The former two-tier system of local government—six counties and a county borough, and 24 urban and 26 rural districts—was replaced in 1973 by a single-tier system, paralleling similar changes in the remainder of the United Kingdom. Based on the main population centres, 26 districts were created, each with an elected council. The status of Belfast and Londonderry was maintained in their designation as city councils, and 12 other councils—Antrim, Ards, Ballymena, Ballymoney, Carrickfergus, Castlereagh, Coleraine, Craigavon, Larne, Lisburn, Newtownards, and North Down—have borough status. Each borough council has a mayor, Belfast has a lord mayor, and each of the remainder has a chairman. The councils' direct functions are centred on local services; they have a representative function concerning regional services such as education and health, and a consultative function in planning, roads, and conservation.

Politics since the country's inception has been dominated by the issue of union or separation, and this split has followed religious lines. Protestants have been Unionists, and have always had a majority in Parliament. Roman Catholics traditionally support the Nationalist Party, advocating reunion with the Republic of Ireland, and have always been in opposition. The Labour Party in the late 20th century made some advances in representing labour, irrespective of religious affiliation. Electoral geography followed almost exactly a map of the distribution of religious majorities, the west being a stronghold of Nationalism, the east of Unionism: the concentration of people in and around Belfast assured an overall Unionist majority. Periodically, political and religious antagonisms have flared into civil disorder, most severely in 1921–22, but again from 1968. The main issues were discrimination in housing and employment, and the fact that franchise for local government, based on property ownership, favoured Protestants. An increasing diversity of political views produced a plethora of political parties, from the extremely conservative Protestant Volunteer Party to the revolutionary People's Democracy. Most support still lies in the Social Democratic and Labour Party, which supports unification with Ireland; the Ulster Unionist Party, which had members in Westminster; and the Unionist Party of Northern Ireland, which supports complete coalition with the U.K.

Religious antagonism

Civil order is maintained by the Royal Ulster Constabulary (RUC). In 1972 regular troops of the British Army entered the country to quell civil strife and thereafter continued to be deployed in the province. They are assisted by the locally recruited Ulster Defence Regiment.

Education. The social services in Northern Ireland are closely patterned on those of the United Kingdom, although there is sometimes delay in implementing policy, partly because of historic inertia and partly because of the dual nature of the society. Nowhere is this more apparent than in education. The 1947 Education Act parallels the 1944 act of England and Wales, but its implementation is hampered by the traditional tenacious denominational control of education, which the population is generally reluctant to abandon. Northern Ireland has two universities. The Queen's University, established in 1845 as one of three in Ireland, has had a charter since 1908; the New University of Ulster is at Coleraine.

Denominational education

Health and welfare. In health services, as in education, Northern Ireland follows the United Kingdom. The Queen's University has a large medical faculty that supports the health service. Ulster is also known for its export of doctors and nurses.

As in other regions of Britain, one of the major social problems in Northern Ireland is housing. There is a legacy of much poor rural housing in the countryside, exacerbated by the isolation of many of the small dispersed farms, while in Belfast the province suffers from a grim legacy of 19th-century industrial housing.

Social conditions and standards of living in the province have not yet entirely overcome a rural tradition of subsistence farming and low cost of living. Nor has this been offset by conditions among industrial workers, whose employment, as a result of the province's peripheral status in the United Kingdom economy, has felt every depression early and has always been slow to recover. High unemployment and more marked differentials between skilled and unskilled workers' wages have aggravated social problems. Generally speaking, although the standard of incomes and living in Northern Ireland and in England and Wales is roughly comparable, there are still many in Northern Ireland who do not achieve those standards.

Unemployment [margin note]

CULTURAL LIFE

In the arts and in cultural life generally it is difficult—as is the case with most aspects of life in Northern Ireland—to distinguish between native and imported. Few traces remain of any culture predating the Protestant Ascendancy: the occasional *caley,* or traditional Irish group entertainment, is only the faintest echo of a past that faded with the language. Gone, too, are the strolling players and rhyming weavers. Folk participation and recreation are periodically focussed on religious ceremonies and processions— colourful, noisy, and (in recent years) tragically violent demonstrations of sectarian feelings. This fundamental division has also given rise to the nearest approach to folk art, the painting of William of Orange crossing the Boyne, a deeply symbolic representation, adorning the gable end of many a Protestant terrace. In the name of religion, paint, bunting, flags, and arches briefly splash colour over drab gray streets.

In other respects, the cultural milieu of the province is one shared with the remainder of the British Isles and has few distinctive regional characteristics. With the exception of a few country mansions—a legacy of 18th-century English architects—the buildings of Northern Ireland are undistinguished, though this same influence has lent a dignity of proportion and urbanity to some larger farmhouses and to the occasional terrace of houses in the towns. For the most part, however, the industrial growth of the 19th century has completely overshadowed the previous planned phase of growth without contributing any buildings of distinction. It remains to be seen how far larger projects—university buildings and hospitals, for example—have improved the situation.

Arts and music [margin note]

Northern Ireland has an Arts Council, which successfully encourages all aspects of the arts. Its activities tend to be concentrated in Belfast because this city alone can provide for ballet and opera. Belfast has two theatres, and there is also a touring company based on the New University of Ulster at Coleraine. Music is mainly imported, but Belfast has a symphony orchestra and a youth orchestra and has fostered one of the largest festivals in Britain. The council also sponsors art exhibitions. Belfast has a permanent gallery, and so does Londonderry, though some exhibitions tour the entire province. The 19th century saw little development in the visual arts, but a new interest in landscape emerged briefly at the beginning of the 20th. A provincial school of painting may now be emerging for the first time and some recognize a school of poetry. But the province is only slowly shaking off the utilitarian, no-nonsense approach to life that underlay its Victorian growth.

The British Broadcasting Corporation has a near-total monopoly in sound broadcasting, but Ulster Television, Ltd., representing the Independent Broadcasting Authority, vies with the British Broadcasting Corporation. Northern Ireland also shares the British press.

The Ulster Museum is the national museum. The Ulster Folk and Transport Museum provides a particularly interesting link with peasant origins in Northern Ireland and includes an open-air folk museum. This is another reflection of an appreciation of the past that is also shown by the state's care of ancient monuments, both historic and prehistoric.

Of other cultural institutions perhaps the most notable is the observatory at Armagh. Founded by Archbishop Robinson in 1790, it has remained an independently governed institution, though it now receives considerable state aid. It has links with observatories in South Africa and also has one of the few astronomy libraries in the British Isles.

(E.J./Ed.)

History

ULSTER

Ulster (Old Irish: Ulaid) was the name of an ancient northern Ireland kingdom that extended south to near what is now the village of Dromiskin in County Louth and westward to the Atlantic in County Donegal. Owing to the Ulster Cycle of Irish literature, which gives the exploits of Cú Chulainn and many other Ulster heroes, Ulster has a place of great prominence in Irish literature. Its capital then was Emain Macha, near Armagh. Attacks from the midland kingdom of Mide (Meath) led to its disintegration in the 4th and 5th centuries AD. In mid-Ulster there appeared the new kingdom of Airgialla (Oriel), and in western Ulster the dynasties descended from Eogan and Conall, two sons of Niall of the Nine Hostages. Their chief fortress was at Ailech, near Derry, and their power in Ulster was overwhelming from the 5th century to the 12th. The name Ulster survived but, during this period, was applied to a subordinate state in what was later the counties of Antrim, Down, and Louth; and in a yet more restricted sense the name applied to a small area along the coast of Down, "the Ards of Ulster," whence the original dynasty that ruled over all Ulster had come. When the Anglo-Norman John de Courci (d. 1219) invaded this region successfully in the last quarter of the 12th century, he was referred to by contemporaries as "Princeps Ulidiae."

The earldom of Ulster, created by England's King John in 1205, was held by the Connaught Anglo-Norman family of Burgh from about 1264 to 1333, passing then to an heiress who married the royal prince Lionel, duke of Clarence. Through his descendants the title passed ultimately (1461) to the crown. In the 16th century Ulster was divided into shires (or counties), nine in all, but one of these was Cavan, which until then had been regarded as part of Connaught. Under James I thousands of new Protestant settlers were introduced into Ulster from England and Scotland. Their descendants prospered and multiplied and, in at least the six counties of Antrim, Down, Armagh, Londonderry, Tyrone, and Fermanagh, came to constitute a large majority of the population. Thus did the "Ulster problem" become a live issue in Irish politics in the general Roman Catholic Irish drive for Home Rule.

Protestant settlers under James I [margin note]

ULSTER AND HOME RULE

The Irish movement for Home Rule, or autonomy within the British Empire, began in the 19th century and succeeded in having a series of Home Rule bills introduced into the British Parliament beginning in 1886. All failed and were climaxed by a Home Rule bill introduced by Prime Minister H.H. Asquith in 1912. It passed the House of Commons in January 1913 (367 to 267) but was rejected by the House of Lords. The bill included Ulster and, if passed again in three successive sessions by the House of Commons, would automatically, pursuant to the provisions of the Parliament Act of 1911, become law without the assent of the House of Lords. Protestant Ulster prepared to resist it, and the Ulster Volunteers, cofounded and headed by Sir Edward Carson (later Baron Carson), aided and abetted by many prominent men in both countries, armed themselves and undertook, in a solemn Covenant of Resistance to Home Rule (1912), to set up a separate government in Belfast should the bill become law. The bill passed the House of Commons in May 1914; the Lords excluded the six Protestant-led counties of Ulster; an attempt at accommodation by King George V at a conference held in July failed. The outbreak of World War I altered the whole situation. The bill, without resistance, passed and became law for all Ireland in September 1914; but a contemporaneous act was passed which provided that it should not come into force until after the war, the Government giving an undertaking to bring in a bill dealing with the Ulster situation. The bill never came into operation.

The enrollment and overt military drilling of the Ulster Volunteers in resistance to Home Rule angered the south of Ireland. The impunity accorded to an unconstitutional and illegal movement emboldened and stimulated the young Home Rulers. This, among other factors, helped inspire the rebellion and Anglo-Irish conflict of the war years and postwar years. Dublin and the south of Ireland were the scene of perhaps the worst terrorism on the part of both the Irish Catholics and the British Black and Tans; but the events of the south had their repercussions in the violent religious disturbances in the north. From July 1920 to June 1922 the city of Belfast was the scene of many shocking murders.

The open competition in violence soon brought deep discredit upon British rule; and Prime Minister David Lloyd George made another attempt at a constructive solution by carrying the Government of Ireland Act of 1920, which was to establish two Irish parliaments, with equal though very limited powers, one for southern Ireland and one for the six counties of northern Ireland. The Northern Ireland Parliament was indeed brought into being, though the Ulster Unionists protested that they preferred to remain within the union. King George V went to Belfast and formally opened the new parliament on June 22, 1921.

The southern Irish still fervently resisted, and negotiations between Lloyd George and Eamon de Valera, the Sinn Féin leader, led to the Anglo-Irish Treaty of December 1921. The treaty gave Ireland the political status of the dominion of Canada—with liberty, however, to the Ulster Parliament to opt out of the measure. Ulster did opt out.

NORTHERN IRELAND

In the first parliament of Northern Ireland opened in 1921 the prime minister was Sir James Craig, who took office at the head of a Unionist government that had to deal with a disturbed country troubled by bombings, shootings, and incendiarism. From the close of 1921 there was civil war in the Irish Free State, and this overflowed into Northern Ireland, making the years 1922 and 1923 very turbulent. During 1922, 232 persons were killed in Northern Ireland in these disturbances, including two Unionist members of Parliament; nearly 1,000 were wounded, and extensive damage was done to property.

A tripartite agreement was signed in 1925 between the governments of the United Kingdom, the Irish Free State, and Northern Ireland, agreeing to maintain the existing frontier. A new phase in political affairs opened, however, in 1932 with the advent of de Valera to power in the Free State. Progressively dissociating the Free State from the United Kingdom and the Commonwealth, he substantially repudiated the agreement of 1925 and made emphatic irredentist claims upon Northern Ireland. His policy of protectionist tariffs made the frontier between Northern Ireland and the Free State into a formidable economic barrier and rendered particularly alarming any prospect of drawing Northern Ireland, with its flourishing export trade, into the Free State, or Eire as it came to be called.

With other areas of the United Kingdom, Northern Ireland suffered serious industrial depression and much unemployment in the early 1930s. The Unionist Party, standing for the maintenance of the union with Great Britain, had a strong majority at each general election, whether for the Parliament of Northern Ireland or for the province's representation at Westminster. Though united on this issue, the Unionist Party allowed and experienced differing opinions in its ranks on many other issues and may be said to have had its right and left wings. Sir James Craig (created Viscount Craigavon in 1927) was prime minister until his death on Nov. 24, 1940. Under successive prime ministers the Unionist Party ruled the six counties continuously thereafter.

In 1949 Eire, as the Republic of Ireland, withdrew from the Commonwealth. To meet consequent legal effects, the U.K. Parliament passed the Ireland Act, 1949, which contained the following provision: "It is hereby declared that Northern Ireland remains part of His Majesty's Dominions and of the United Kingdom and it is hereby affirmed that in no event will Northern Ireland or any part thereof cease to be part of His Majesty's Dominions and of the

United Kingdom without the consent of the Parliament of Northern Ireland."

During these years the two main political factions became identified with the religious affiliations of their adherents. Unionist support came from two Protestant groups, the Presbyterians (who made up 30 percent of the population) and members of the Church of Ireland (25 percent); opposition centred in the Roman Catholics (35 percent), most of whom were Irish Nationalists resentful of the partition of Ireland and of their second-class social and economic status.

From the early 1960s more active opposition arose among the younger Catholics, and successive British governments urged Ulster to endorse equality in housing, public employment, and opportunities in general. Militant Protestant groups, proclaiming the dangers of popery, secured a strong following among the poorer elements. Upon the launching of a civil-rights campaign in 1968, violence erupted in Belfast and Londonderry. At first, British troops contained the strife, but later they seemed to aggravate it. Bitterness was increased in August 1971 by the internment without trial of several members of the terrorist Irish Republican Army (IRA) who were suspected of playing leading roles in the uprising. Bombings and shootings increased in frequency for the rest of the year, and in January 1972, after British soldiers shot 13 demonstrators in Londonderry, an angry crowd burned the British embassy in Dublin. In March the British prime minister, Edward Heath, suspended the constitution of Northern Ireland, replaced the provincial government by appointing William Whitelaw secretary of state for Northern Ireland, and sent in more regular troops of the British Army to police the country. Violence continued for the rest of the decade and beyond. (Ed.)

BIBLIOGRAPHY

British land and people: E.H. BROWN, *The Relief and Drainage of Wales* (1960), is one of the classics of landscape interpretation. W.G. EAST (ed.), *Regions of the British Isles* (1961–), complete, well-illustrated surveys of the major regions. C.B. FAWCETT, *Provinces of England,* rev. ed. (1960), presents familiar material from a novel standpoint. T.W. FREEMAN, *The Conurbations of Great Britain* (1959), stresses the growth and character of Britain's cities. G.M. HOWE, *National Atlas of Disease Mortality in the United Kingdom,* rev. ed. (1970), shows a number of interesting distributions of mortality from certain specific causes. The *Registrar General's Annual Estimates of the Population of England and Wales* are important sources of data for between-census years. L.D. STAMP, *The Land of Britain: Its Use and Misuse,* 3rd ed. (1962), is a basic reference work that provides a view of the human ecology of the whole of Britain. J.A. STEERS (ed.), *Field Studies in the British Isles* (1964), are narratives of the itineraries and regions covered on the field-study tours arranged for the 20th International Geographical Congress. A.G. TANSLEY, *The British Islands and Their Vegetation,* 2 vol. (1949), is a monumental work that demonstrates the vast extension of ecological knowledge of British vegetation. J.W. WATSON and J.B. SISSONS (eds.), *The British Isles: A Systematic Geography* (1964), is an inventory of British geography written by 20 leading authorities. E.A. WRIGLEY and R.S. SCHOFIELD, *The Population History of England, 1541–1871: A Reconstruction* (1982), is an important demographic history.

British economy: Among the many studies on the British economy, the following are particularly recommended— RICHARD E. CAVES *et al., Britain's Economic Prospects* (1968); PHYLLIS DEANE and W.A. COLE, *British Economic Growth, 1688– 1959: Trends and Structure,* 2nd ed. (1967); ELY DEVONS, *An Introduction to British Economic Statistics* (1956); J.H. DUNNING and C.J. THOMAS, *British Industry: Change and Development in the Twentieth Century,* 2nd ed. (1963); ROY F. HARROD, *The British Economy* (1963); GRAHAM TURNER, *Business in Britain,* rev. ed. (1971); G.D.N. WORSWICK and P.H. ADY (eds.), *The British Economy in the Nineteen-Fifties* (1962); and A.J. YOUNGSON, *The British Economy, 1920–1957* (1960). MINISTRY OF TRANSPORT, *Transport Policy,* Cmnd. 3057 (1966–67), the White Paper in which the Government first outlined its proposals that led to the 1968 Transport Act; DEPARTMENT OF TRANSPORT, *Transport Statistics Great Britain* (annual), statistics relating to travel by road, rail, and domestic airline; *The Atlas of Britain and Northern Ireland* (1963), includes sections on transport, population, and industry; A.W.J. THOMSON and L.C. HUNTER, *The Nationalized Transport Industries* (1973), examines the history, rationale, and interaction of all the nationalized transport industries, and their performances and prospects.

Marginalia:
Civil war in the Irish Free State

Political and religious factions

British administrative and social conditions: On the constitutional framework of the structure of government, see I.H.J. GILMOUR, *The Body Politic,* rev. ed. (1971); P.C. GORDON WALKER, *The Cabinet: Political Authority in Britain* (1970); SIR W.I. JENNINGS, *Cabinet Government,* 3rd ed. (1959); J.P. MACKINTOSH, *The British Cabinet,* 3rd ed. (1977); and H.S. MORRISON, *Government and Parliament* (1954). On regional variations and local government, see R.M. JACKSON, *The Machinery of Local Government,* 2nd ed. (1965); R.E.C. JEWELL, *Central and Local Government,* rev. ed. (1970); and the *Royal Commission Report on Local Government in England,* Cmnd. 4040 (1969). Information on the political process in the United Kingdom may be found in D.E. BUTLER, *The Electoral System in Britain, 1918–1951* (1953); and R. ROSE, *Politics in England* (1964), two works on elections in Britain; R.T. MACKENZIE, *British Political Parties* (1955); and on participation of the citizen in A.M. POTTER, *Organized Groups in British National Politics* (1961). (*Justice*): *Royal Commission Report on Assizes and Quarter Sessions,* Cmnd. 4153 (1969); H.G. HANBURY, *English Courts of Law,* 5th ed. prepared by D.C.M. YARDLEY (1979). (*Armed forces*): Annual Defence White Papers and information from the Ministry of Defence. (*Educational services*): *Royal Commission Report on Higher Education,* Cmnd. 2154 (1963); TYRRELL BURGESS, *Guide to English Schools,* 3rd ed. (1972). (*Health and welfare services*): P. GREGG, *The Welfare State: An Economic and Social History of Great Britain from 1945 to the Present Day* (1967); R.M. TITMUSS, *Essays on "the Welfare State,"* 2nd ed. (1963). (*Housing*): J.B. CULLINGWORTH, *Housing and Local Government in England and Wales* (1966); and *Town and Country Planning in England and Wales* (1964). (*Police services*): T.A. CRITCHLEY, *A History of Police in England and Wales, 900–1966* (1967). (*Wages and cost of living*): CENTRAL STATISTICAL OFFICE, *Annual Abstract of Statistics* and the *Monthly Digest of Statistics.* (*Health conditions*): C.F. BROCKINGTON, *A Short History of Public Health,* 2nd ed. (1966); J. MOSS, *Health and Welfare Services Handbook,* 3rd rev. ed. (1962).

British cultural life: JOHN S. HARRIS, *Government Patronage of the Arts in Great Britain* (1970), is a general and authoritative work of reference. On particular media, see P.E.P., *The British Film Industry, 1958* (1958); and FRANCIS WILLIAMS, *Dangerous Estate: The Anatomy of Newspapers* (1957). For independent accounts, see STUART HALL and PADDY WHANNEL, *The Popular Arts* (1964); and RICHARD BOSTON (ed.), *The Press We Deserve* (1970). On effects of the media in Britain, see JAMES HALLORAN (ed.), *The Effects of Television* (1970). For a general cultural analysis, see RICHARD HOGGART, *The Uses of Literacy* (1957). For history, see RAYMOND WILLIAMS, *The Long Revolution,* rev. ed. (1966), especially ch. 2; and for origins of institutions in the media, see the same author's *Communications,* rev. ed. (1966). HUGH CUNNINGHAM, *Leisure in the Industrial Revolution* (1980), covers the period 1780–1880; SUSAN LASDUN, *Victorians at Home* (1981), a look at some aspects of Victorian family life.

General history: The 15 volumes of the *Oxford History of England,* under the editorship of SIR G.N. CLARK (3rd–4th ed., 1934–65), provide a comprehensive survey, with excellent bibliographies. Other multivolume histories include the "Pelican History of England" series, 8 vol., particularly valuable for social history; *The Political History of England,* 12 vol. (1905–10), somewhat antiquated but informative; and CHRISTOPHER BROOKE and D.M. SMITH (eds.), *A History of England,* 8 vol. (1960–). GEORGE MACAULAY TREVELYAN, *History of England,* 2nd ed. (1937; reprinted with minor corrections, 1966), is a beautifully written but highly patriotic survey. A.B. ERICKSON and M.J. HAVRAN, *England: Prehistory to the Present* (1968), is a good one-volume textbook.

Ancient Britain: S.S. FRERE, *Britannia* (1967), a full-scale history of Roman Britain with discussions of the archaeological remains; S. PIGGOTT, *Ancient Europe* (1965), a modern account of the archaeology and prehistory of Europe from the introduction of agriculture to the beginning of the Roman period; A.L.F. RIVET (ed.), *The Roman Villa in Britain* (1969), a collection of six essays describing various aspects of the Roman villas of Britain and the agricultural system and way of life they represent; A. BIRLEY, *Life in Roman Britain* (1964), a short description of the light thrown by archaeology and the ancient historians upon the government, institutions, life, and religions of Roman Britain; E. BIRLEY, *Roman Britain and the Roman Army* (1953), a collection of essays dealing with the organization of the Roman army based on the evidence of inscriptions; P.H. BLAIR, *Introduction to Anglo-Saxon England* (1956), a short history of Anglo-Saxon England from the end of the Roman period; JOHN MORRIS, *Londinium* (1982), an account of the Roman province of Britannia; H.H. SCULLARD, *Roman Britain* (1979), a history with many maps and illustrations.

The Anglo-Saxon period: (*Sources*): BEDE, *Historia ecclesiastica; Anglo-Saxon Chronicle.* For a translation of and commentary on essential record and narrative material, see DOROTHY WHITELOCK (ed.), *English Historical Documents,* vol. 1 (1955). (*General histories*): F.M. STENTON, *Anglo-Saxon England,* 3rd ed. (1971); P. HUNTER BLAIR, *An Introduction to Anglo-Saxon England,* 2nd ed. (1956); R.H. HODGKIN, *A History of the Anglo-Saxons,* 3rd ed. (1952); H.R. LOYN, *Anglo-Saxon England and the Norman Conquest* (1962); R.I. PAGE, *Life in Anglo-Saxon England* (1970); DOROTHY WHITELOCK, *The Beginnings of English Society,* rev. ed. (1966). (*Works on specific topics*): T.D. KENDRICK, *A History of the Vikings* (1930, reprinted 1968); L.M. LARSON, *Canute the Great* (1912); W.R.W. STEPHENS and W. HUNT (eds.), *A History of the English Church,* vol. 1 (1899); WILHELM LEVISON, *England and the Continent in the Eighth Century* (1946); DAVID KNOWLES, *The Monastic Order in England,* 2nd ed. (1963); J. ARMITAGE ROBINSON, *The Times of Saint Dunstan* (1923); FRANK BARLOW, *The English Church, 1000–1066* (1963); JAMES TAIT, *The Medieval English Borough* (1936, reprinted 1968); R.H.M. DOLLEY (ed.), *Anglo-Saxon Coins* (1961) and *Anglo-Saxon Pennies* (1964); C.S. and C.S. ORWIN, *The Open Fields,* 3rd ed. (1967); C.T. CHEVALLIER and DOROTHY WHITELOCK et al., *The Norman Conquest: Its Setting and Impact* (1966).

England from 1066 to 1485: (*Sources*): CARL STEPHENSON and F.G. MARCHAM (eds.), *Sources of English Constitutional History* (1937), devotes about a third of its coverage to the medieval period. In the new "English Historical Documents Series," see D.C. DOUGLAS and G.W. GREENAWAY (eds.), *English Historical Documents, 1042–1189* (1953); and A.R. MYERS (ed.), *English Historical Documents, 1327–1485* (1969). BERTIE WILKINSON, *The Constitutional History of England, 1216–1399,* 3 vol. (1948–58) and his *Constitutional History of England in the Fifteenth Century, 1399–1485* (1964), are anthologies of documents with extensive commentary by the author. (*General works*): HELEN M. CAM, *England Before Elizabeth,* 2nd rev. ed. (1960); CHRISTOPHER BROOKE, *From Alfred to Henry III, 871–1272* (1961); GEORGE HOLMES, *The Later Middle Ages, 1272–1485* (1962); F.M. STENTON, *English Society in the Early Middle Ages (1066–1307)* (1952), and A.R. MYERS, *England in the Late Middle Ages* (1952), two works that emphasize social history; A.L. POOLE, *From Domesday Book to Magna Carta, 1087–1216,* 2nd ed. (1955); F.M. POWICKE, *The Thirteenth Century, 1216–1307* (1953); MAY MCKISACK, *The Fourteenth Century, 1307–1399* (1959); E.F. JACOB, *The Fifteenth Century, 1399–1485* (1961). (*Special topics*): J.H. CLAPHAM, *A Concise Economic History of Britain, from Earliest Times to 1750* (1949); *The Cambridge Economic History of Europe,* ed. by J.H. CLAPHAM et al., 3 vol. (1941–63; 2nd ed., 1966–); H.C. DARBY (ed.), *An Historical Geography of England Before A.D. 1800* (1936), includes several essays on the medieval period; DAVID KNOWLES, *The Religious Orders in England,* 3 vol. (1948–59), a comprehensive and definitive account; C.H. LAWRENCE (ed.), *The English Church and the Papacy in the Middle Ages* (1965), a volume of essays by specialists; WILLIAM STUBBS, *The Constitutional History of England,* 6th ed. (1897, reprinted 1967), not altogether superseded by modern works such as BRYCE D. LYONS, *A Constitutional and Legal History of Medieval England* (1960). (*1066–1307*): FRANK BARLOW, *The Feudal Kingdom of England, 1042–1216,* 2nd ed. (1961); R. ALLEN BROWN, *The Normans and the Norman Conquest* (1968); STEPHEN MEDCALF, *The Later Middle Ages* (1981), introduces the literature, art, architecture, philosophy, and social history of the period 1330–1450. C.R. CHENEY, *From Becket to Langton: English Church Government, 1170–1213* (1956); H.W.C. DAVIS, *England Under the Normans and Angevins, 1066–1272* (1905), an old but not completely superseded work; R.H.C. DAVIS, *King Stephen, 1135–1154* (1967), sheds new light on the period of the anarchy; D.C. DOUGLAS, *William the Conqueror* (1964), the best single source on the conquest of England by the Normans; V.H. GALBRAITH, *The Making of Domesday Book* (1961), discusses the Conquest in an analytical statement about the survey of 1086; J.C. HOLT, *Magna Carta* (1965), the latest and most readable scholarly book on the Great Charter; J.E.A. JOLLIFFE, *Angevin Kingship,* 2nd ed. (1963), a challenging thesis that England might have developed into an absolute state in the medieval period if it had not been for the barons who fought John; REGINALD LENNARD, *Rural England, 1086–1135* (1959); H.R. LOYN, *The Norman Conquest* (1965), gives special emphasis to the social and economic impact of the Conquest; F.W. MAITLAND, *Domesday Book and Beyond* (1897), a seminal classic by a great historian; F.M. POWICKE, *King Henry III and the Lord Edward,* 2 vol. (1947); SIR FRANK STENTON, *The First Century of English Feudalism, 1066–1166,* 2nd ed. (1961), not superseded despite a great deal of discussion of the subject in later work; G.O. SAYLES, *The Medieval Foundations of England,* 2nd rev. ed. (1950), an excellent introduction to the history and the primary sources to the time of Edward I. (*The 14th and 15th centuries*): A.R. BRIDBURY, *Economic Growth: England in the Later Middle Ages* (1962); F.R.H. DU BOULAY, *An Age of Ambition* (1970); V.H.H. GREEN, *The Later Plantagenets*

(1955), a useful general textbook; P.M. KENDALL, *Richard the Third* (1955) and *Warwick the Kingmaker* (1957); E.F. JACOB, *Henry V and the Invasion of France* (1947), a critical modern treatment; GEORGE MACAULAY TREVELYAN, *England in the Age of Wycliffe*, new ed. (1909), a social and political history of Richard II's reign; R.L. STOREY, *The End of the House of Lancaster* (1966), the best book on the Wars of the Roses; H.E. HALLAM, *Rural England: 1066–1348* (1981), a social and economic history.

England in the 16th century: Standard bibliographies for 16th-century England are CONYERS READ (ed.), *Bibliography of British History: Tudor Period, 1485–1603,* 2nd ed. (1959); and MORTIMER LEVINE's shorter compilation, *Tudor England 1485–1603* (1968). The best political and social surveys are S.T. BINDOFF, *Tudor England* (1950); and G.R. ELTON, *England Under the Tudors* (1955). For the personalities of the sovereigns, see CHRISTOPHER MORRIS, *The Tudors* (1955); and for the European setting, L.B. SMITH, *The Elizabethan World* (1966). Constitutional and institutional development can be studied in CHRISTOPHER MORRIS' short but brilliant *Political Thought in England: Tyndale to Hooker* (1953); JOHN NEALE's classic works on Parliament, *Elizabeth I and Her Parliaments,* 2 vol. (1953–57), and *The Elizabethan House of Commons* (1949); and G.R. ELTON's controversial *The Tudor Revolution in Government* (1953). Social and intellectual change is best sampled in four provocative but important works: W.K. JORDAN, *Philanthropy in England, 1480–1660* (1959); LAWRENCE STONE, *The Crisis of the Aristocracy, 1558–1641* (1965); R.H. TAWNEY, *Religion and the Rise of Capitalism* (1926, reprinted 1962); and E.M.W. TILLYARD, *The Elizabethan World Picture* (1943). The religious crisis of the century is neatly summarized in A.G. DICKENS, *The English Reformation,* rev. ed. (1967); and treated in greater length from a Catholic point of view by PHILIP HUGHES, *The Reformation in England,* rev. 5th ed., 3 vol. (1963). The best works on the Elizabethan period are PATRICK COLLINSON, *The Elizabethan Puritan Movement* (1967); and W.R. TRIMBLE, *The Catholic Laity in Elizabethan England, 1558–1603* (1964), whereas a fine book on religion in pre-Reformation England is HERBERT MAYNARD SMITH, *Pre-Reformation England* (1938). Foreign policy is surveyed by R.B. WERNHAM in *Before the Armada: The Growth of English Foreign Policy, 1458–1588* (1966). Overseas expansion is handled in A.L. ROWSE, *The Expansion of Elizabethan England* (1955).

Britain in the 17th century: The starting points for a detailed study of Stuart England from 1603 to 1656 and from 1685 to 1702 are still, for all their Whiggish faults, the respective multivolume studies of two great 19th-century historians, SAMUEL RAWSON GARDINER (continued to 1660 by CHARLES H. FIRTH and GODFREY DAVIES) and T.B. MACAULAY. The best one-volume surveys of the 17th century are GEOFFREY AYLMER, *The Struggle for the Constitution, 1603–1689,* 2nd ed. (1968); CHRISTOPHER HILL, *The Century of Revolution, 1603–1714* (1961); MAURICE ASHLEY, *England in the Seventeenth Century,* 3rd ed. (1961); and JOHN P. KENYON, *The Stuarts* (1958). The best one-volume study of the causes of the English Civil War is PEREZ ZAGORIN, *The Court and the Country* (1969); and of the interregnum, IVAN ROOTS, *The Great Rebellion: 1642–1666* (1966). There are several good three-volume studies: C.V. WEDGWOOD for the reign of Charles I from 1637 to 1649 (1956–66); DAVID OGG for later Stuarts from 1660 to 1702 (1955); and GEORGE MACAULAY TREVELYAN (1930–34) for the reign of Queen Anne. There are fine biographies: DAVID HARRIS WILLSON, *King James VI and I* (1956); CATHERINE DRINKER BOWEN, *The Lion and the Throne: The Life and Times of Sir Edward Coke* (1957) and *Francis Bacon* (1963); HUGH R. TREVOR-ROPER, *Archbishop Laud, 1573–1645,* 2nd ed. (1962); and C.V. WEDGWOOD, *Strafford, 1593–1641* (1935). There have been several important historiographical controversies on the Stuart period in recent years. The Max Weber thesis on the relationship between Puritanism and economic matters was recast by R.H. TAWNEY in *Religion and the Rise of Capitalism* (1926, reprinted 1962), but it has been challenged in two articles in *Church History* by WINTHROP S. HUDSON (1949) and CHARLES H. GEORGE (1958). For the controversy over the rise of the gentry, see R.H. TAWNEY, *Economic History Review,* 11:1–38 (1941); HUGH R. TREVOR-ROPER, *Economic History Review Supplement* (1953); and JACK H. HEXTER, "Storm over the Gentry," *Encounter,* 10:22–34 (1958); LAWRENCE STONE has analyzed *The Crisis of the Aristocracy, 1588–1641* (1965); and PETER LASLETT has examined the lower orders of society in *The World We Have Lost* (1965). The relationship between Puritanism and democracy has been set forth by WILLIAM HALLER in *The Rise of Puritanism* (1938) and *Liberty and Reformation in the Puritan Revolution* (1955); and A.S.P. WOODHOUSE (ed.), *Puritanism and Liberty,* 2nd ed. (1951), but some of their conclusions have been questioned by MICHAEL WALZER, *The Revolution of the Saints* (1965); and LEO F. SOLT, *Saints in Arms* (1959). The relationship between Puritanism and the New Science was first developed by ROBERT

K. MERTON, *Science, Technology and Society in Seventeenth Century England* (1938); and more recently by J.E.C. HILL, *The Intellectual Origins of the English Revolution* (1965), but they have come under attack in articles by HUGH F. KEARNEY and THEODORE K. RABB in *Past and Present* (1964–66) and by the latter in the *Journal of World History,* 7:46–67 (1962). The traditional interpretation of a two-party system in Queen Anne's reign given by WILLIAM T. MORGAN, *English Political Parties and Leaders in the Reign of Queen Anne, 1702–1710* (1920); KEITH FEILING, *A History of the Tory Party, 1640–1714* (1924); and Trevelyan were challenged by the biographical studies of ROBERT WALCOTT, *English Politics in the Early Eighteenth Century* (1956), but the earlier view has been stressed by J.H. PLUMB, *The Growth of Political Stability in England: 1675–1725* (1967); and GEOFFREY S. HOLMES, *British Politics in the Age of Anne* (1967).

Britain, 1714–1815: T.S. ASHTON, *An Economic History of England: The Eighteenth Century* (1955), a readable introduction for the general reader, and *The Industrial Revolution, 1760–1830* (1948), a classic brief overview; JOHN M. BEATTIE, *The English Court in the Reign of George I* (1967), combines administrative with political history—aids understanding of later Hanoverian reigns; LEWIS B. NAMIER, *The Structure of Politics at the Accession of George III,* 2 vol. (1929; 2nd ed., 1 vol., 1957), an analytical study that destroyed traditional views on 18th-century political history—the starting point for all modern studies of 18th-century politics; JOHN BROOKE, *The Chatham Administration, 1766–1768* (1956), a detailed political history in the Namierite manner; HERBERT BUTTERFIELD, *George III and the Historians,* rev. ed. (1959), historiographical study with extended criticism of Namierite treatment of politics; IAN CHRISTIE, *The End of North's Ministry, 1780–1782* (1958); CARL B. CONE, *Burke and the Nature of Politics,* 2 vol. (1957–64), political biography based on recently available corpus of Burke papers; *The English Jacobins* (1968), narrative account of parliamentary reform before and during the French Revolution; PHYLLIS DEANE, *The First Industrial Revolution* (1965), topically organized work stressing the concept of economic growth; JOHN EHRMAN, *The Younger Pitt* (1969), standard biography; A.S. FOORD, *His Majesty's Opposition, 1714–1830* (1964), on the growth and acceptance of the idea and practice of a formed parliamentary opposition; DEREK JARRETT, *Britain, 1688–1815* (1965), the best short history, mainly political; D.L. KEIR, *The Constitutional History of Modern Britain Since 1485,* 9th ed. (1968), a balanced narrative treatment of this period; W.E.H. LECKY, *A History of England in the Eighteenth Century,* 7 vol. (1899–1901), good on social history but outdated in many respects; DOROTHY MARSHALL, *English People in the Eighteenth Century* (1956), emphasis on social history; RICHARD PARES, *King George III and the Politicians* (1953), a highly regarded analysis that modifies some Namierite interpretations; J.H. PLUMB, *The Growth of Political Stability in England, 1675–1725* (1967), a conceptual study showing how and why stability replaced instability; *Sir Robert Walpole,* 2 vol. (1956–61; vol. 3 in prep.), the definitive biography; NORMAN SYKES, *Church and State in England in the Eighteenth Century* (1934), corrects older views of torpor and inadequacy of the church; J.S. WATSON, *The Reign of George III, 1760–1815* (1960); R.J. WHITE, *The Age of George III* (1968), readable, brief, interpretative, and comprehensive in its coverage; BASIL WILLIAMS, *The Whig Supremacy, 1714–1760,* 2nd ed. (1962); E.N. WILLIAMS (ed.), *The Eighteenth Century Constitution, 1688–1815* (1960), a collection of well-selected documents; PAMELA HORN, *The Rural World, 1780–1850: Social Change in the English Countryside* (1981), a descriptive social history of rural labourers.

Britain, 1815–1914: ELIE HALEVY, *Histoire du peuple anglais au XIXᵉ siècle,* 5 vol. (1912–32; Eng. trans., *A History of the English People in the Nineteenth Century,* 2nd ed., 6 vol., 1949–52), is the best general account, although the second half of the century is only partially and sketchily covered. G.M. YOUNG, *Victorian England: Portrait of an Age,* 2nd ed. (1960), is a brilliant essay, as is GEOFFREY BEST, *Mid-Victorian Britain, 1851–1875* (1971); E.L. WOODWARD, *The Age of Reform, 1815–1870,* 2nd ed. (1962); see also his *Victorian People* (1954) and *Victorian Cities* (1963). R.C.K. ENSOR, *England, 1870–1914* (1936), is a good standard study. ASA BRIGGS, *The Age of Improvement* (1959), is the fullest account of the period from the Industrial Revolution to the Second Reform Bill in all its aspects; and R.K. WEBB, *Modern England: From the 18th Century to the Present* (1969), is the most valuable recent textbook; but also of interest is WALTER HOUGHTON, *The Victorian Frame of Mind, 1830–1870* (1957). There is much that cannot be found elsewhere in *Edwardian England, 1901–1914,* ed. by SIMON H. NOWELL-SMITH (1964). Among a large number of studies of economic history, W.H.B. COURT, *A Concise Economic History of Britain, from 1750 to Recent Times* (1954), provides the most useful introduction, while for Britain's overseas relationships, R.W.

SETON-WATSON, *Britain in Europe, 1789–1914* (1937, reprinted 1968); and C.E. CARRINGTON, *The British Overseas,* 2nd ed. (1968), deal with both continental and imperial relationships. On World War I, see ARTHUR MARWICK, *The Deluge* (1965).

Great Britain since 1914: Several works deal in a fairly comprehensive manner with British history since 1914: W.N. MEDLICOTT, *Contemporary England, 1914–1964* (1967); T.O. LLOYD, *Empire to Welfare State: English History 1906–1967* (1970); ALFRED F. HAVIGHURST, *Twentieth-Century Britain,* 2nd ed. (1966). Medlicott emphasizes political and diplomatic history, while the other two are somewhat broader in scope. More detailed is A.J.P. TAYLOR, *English History, 1914–45* (1965), at times extraordinarily perceptive and provocative. The best work on the interwar years is CHARLES LOCH MOWAT, *Britain Between the Wars, 1918–1940* (1955). SIDNEY POLLARD, *The Development of the British Economy, 1914–1967,* 2nd ed. rev. (1969), is reliable; and F.S. NORTHEDGE, *The Troubled Giant: Britain Among the Great Powers, 1916–1939* (1966) and *British Foreign Policy: The Process of Readjustment, 1945–1961* (1962), provide consecutive treatment of diplomatic history. The period may be approached in an interesting manner through diaries and memoirs—*e.g.,* three volumes by HAROLD MACMILLAN: *Winds of Change, 1914–1939* (1966), *The Blast of War 1939–1945* (1968), and *Tides of Fortune, 1945–1955* (1969). Excellent biographies include: HAROLD NICOLSON, *King George the Fifth: His Life and Reign* (1952); ALAN BULLOCK, *The Life and Times of Ernest Bevin,* 2 vol. (1960–67); RANDOLPH CHURCHILL, *Life of Winston S. Churchill,* 2 vol. (1966–67), vol. 3 by MARTIN GILBERT (1971). *The Annual Register of World Events* provides a useful and reliable summary of British and Commonwealth affairs. As a reference book, D.E. BUTLER and JENNIE FREEMAN, *British Political Facts, 1900–1967* (1968), is the best of its kind.

England: Many of the most useful sources deal with the United Kingdom rather than with England exclusively. An official handbook, *Britain* (HMSO, annual), surveys contemporary British life and institutions, and includes an extensive up-to-date bibliography. Other important official sources are the *Census 1971* and *Census 1981* reports and *Social Trends,* a statistical analysis periodically brought up to date. Among recent histories are the *Oxford History of England,* 15 vol. (1936–65), whose last volume, A.J.P. TAYLOR, *English History, 1914–45,* has a discursive bibliography; and *The Pelican History of England,* 8 vol. (1955–65), whose last volume, DAVID THOMSON, *England in the Twentieth Century, 1914–63,* also has a helpful bibliography. For social history, G.M. TREVELYAN, *English Social History: A Survey of Six Centuries, Chaucer to Queen Victoria* (1946), is classic but somewhat conventional; the interconnections of social and cultural history are examined by RAYMOND WILLIAMS, *Culture and Society, 1780–1950* (1958) and *The Long Revolution* (1961). RICHARD HOGGART, *The Uses of Literacy* (1957), deals with the impact of mass media on working class culture; the structure and role of newspapers is examined by COLIN SEYMOUR-URE in *The Press, Politics, and the Public* (1968). Regional differences are surveyed in B.E. COATES and E.M. RAWSTRON, *Regional Variations in Britain* (1971), and D. ELLISTON ALLEN, *British Tastes* (1968). Some other studies of 20th-century English life and attitudes are GEORGE ORWELL, *The English People* (1947); ROBERT GRAVES and ALAN HODGE, *The Long Weekend: A Social History of Great Britain, 1918–1939* (1963); MALCOLM MUGGERIDGE, *The Thirties,* new ed. (1967); R. LEWIS and A. MAUDE, *The English Middle Classes* (1949); GEOFFREY GORER, *Exploring English Character* (1955) and *Sex and Marriage in England Today* (1971); and E.J.B. ROSE, *Colour and Citizenship: A Report on British Race Relations* (1969). England's place in contemporary British politics can be judged from D.E. BUTLER, with various associates, in *The British General Election* (separate volumes on the elections of 1950, 1951, 1955, 1959, 1964, 1966, and 1970); D.E. BUTLER and D. STOKES, *Political Change in Britain* (1969); D.E. BUTLER and J. FREEMAN, *British Political Facts 1900–1967* (1968); D.E. BUTLER, *The Electoral System in Britain* (1953); and MARTIN J. WIENER, *English Culture and the Decline of the Industrial Spirit: 1850–1980* (1981). *The Royal Commission Report on Reform of English Local Government* (1969) is the most valuable and thorough recent study even though its proposals were not adopted. For geology, geography, and natural history, the "New Naturalist Series" provides authoritative studies for the general reader, among them DUDLEY STAMP, *British Structure and Scenery,* 2nd ed. (1947); GORDON MANLEY, *Climate and the British Scene* (1952); and J.A. STEERS, *The Sea Coast* (1953). Another work by J.A. STEERS, *The English Coast and the Coast of Wales* (1966), is a paperback associated with a campaign to preserve the coastline. A brief introduction to wildlife, with useful book lists, is R.S.R. FITTER, *Wildlife in Britain* (1963). For conservation of the landscape and of the human environment, recent history is summarized in DUDLEY STAMP, *The Land of Britain: Its Use*

and Misuse, 3rd ed. (1962), and *Nature Conservation in Britain* (1969). W.G. HOSKINS, *The Making of the English Landscape* (1955), is based on original field research; COLIN BUCHANAN, *Traffic in Towns* (1964), is a seminal official study; NAN FAIRBROTHER, *New Lives, New Landscapes: Planning for the 21st Century* (1970), deals with agriculture in an urban society; ROBERT ARVILL, *Man and Environment* (1967); and JOHN BARR, *Derelict Britain* (1969), study the impact of industrialism. There are useful book lists in H.E. BRACEY, *People and the Countryside* (1970); and VICTOR BONHAM-CARTER, *The Survival of the English Countryside* (1971). Trends in urban development are examined in R.H. BEST and J.T. COPPOCK, *The Changing Use of Land in Britain* (1962); FREDERICK GIBBERD, *Town Design* (1967); F. OSBORN and A. WHITTICK, *The New Towns* (1969); J.B. CULLINGWORTH, *Housing and Local Government* (1966); and D.V. DONNISON, *The Government of Housing* (1967). England's historic architecture is cataloged with lively commentary in NIKOLAUS PEVSNER, *The Buildings of England,* 37 vol. (1951–70), county by county; and its local characteristics are the theme of A. CLIFTON-TAYLOR, *The Pattern of English Building* (1962). W. GAUNT, *A Concise History of English Painting* (1964), is a reliable guide; NIKOLAUS PEVSNER, *The Englishness of English Art* (1956), expands a series of broadcasts. A. SAMPSON, *Anatomy of Britain* (1971), is a breezy, informative work on the world of public institutions, politics, and business.

Scotland: The *Reader's Guide to Scotland,* a bibliography published by the NATIONAL BOOK LEAGUE (1968), provides annotated lists of works on history, education, administration, law, the economy, sport, and other subjects. A similar bibliography for *The Highlands and Islands of Scotland* was produced by the NATIONAL BOOK LEAGUE in 1967. Excellent articles on the geography of Scottish regions appear in J.B. MITCHELL (ed.), *Great Britain: Geographical Essays* (1962). I.G. MCINTOSH and C.B. MARSHALL, *The Face of Scotland,* 3rd ed. (1977), is an introductory geography. Among innumerable books on topography, MORAY MCLAREN, *The Shell Guide to Scotland* (1977), an informative gazetteer; CALUM MACLEAN, *The Highlands* (1959), written by a Gaelic-speaking Highlander; and W.H. MURRAY, *The Hebrides* (1966), are notable for text and illustrations. F. FRASER DARLING and J. MORTON BOYD, *The Highlands and Islands* (1964); and J.B. WHITTOW, *Geology and Scenery in Scotland* (1977), are written with impressive authority. Political history since 1870 is surveyed in J.G. KELLAS, *Modern Scotland* (1968), and *The Scottish Political System,* 2nd ed. (1975). The self-government debate has inspired a prolific literature, including H.J. PATON, *The Claim of Scotland* (1968), which puts a philosopher's case for self-government. Other works on the same theme are H.J. HANHAM, *Scottish Nationalism* (1969); J.P. MACKINTOSH, *The Devolution of Power* (1968); C. HARVIE, *Scotland and Nationalism: Scottish Society and Politics 1707–1977* (1977); H.M. DRUCKER and G. BROWN, *The Politics of Nationalism and Devolution* (1980); and D.A. HEALD, *Financing Devolution Within the United Kingdom* (1980). The title of W.H. MARWICK, *A Short History of Labour in Scotland* (1967), is self-explanatory, as is that of J. BRAND, *Parties and Politics in Scotland* (1977). The *Scottish Government Yearbook,* edited by H.M. DRUCKER and published annually since 1977, provides surveys and analyses of Scottish politics. A study of the economy by T.L. JOHNSTON, N.K. BUXTON, and D. MAIR, *Structure and Growth of the Scottish Economy* (1971), is a useful textbook. G. MCCRONE, *Scotland's Economic Progress, 1951–1960* (1965), covers the 1950s; the same author's *Scotland's Future: The Economics of Nationalism* (1969), discusses the financial problems of devolution. The Scottish Office has issued booklets describing the work of its departments; the subject is treated more fully in SIR DAVID MILNE, *The Scottish Office and Other Scottish Government Departments* (1957), and more recently by M. MACDONALD and A. REDPATH, *The Scottish Office, 1954–79* (1980). The *Scottish Abstract of Statistics,* produced yearly by the Scottish Office, and its twice-yearly *Scottish Economic Bulletin* are mines of information on the economy. The Fraser of Allander Institute publishes research and quarterly projections in its *Economic Commentary.* Census reports and the annual reports of the Registrar General for Scotland, of the government departments, and of the boards of state industries are also useful sources. On family history, R.W. MUNRO, *Kinsmen and Clansmen* (1971), is a handy reference book; and ROBERT BAIN, *The Clans and Tartans of Scotland,* rev. ed. (1964), is a standard work, as is J. TELFER DUNBAR, *The History of Highland Dress* (1962). J.B. KIRKWOOD, *The Regiments of Scotland* (1949), is a general account, and there are histories of individual regiments. On the arts, IAN FINLAY, *Scottish Crafts* (1948); and S. CURSITER, *Scottish Art to the Close of the Nineteenth Century* (1949), are concise introductions. FRANCIS COLLINSON, *The Traditional and National Music of Scotland* (1966); MAURICE LINDSAY, *History of Scottish Literature* (1977); F.R. HART, *The Scottish Novel* (1978); and the publications of the Association of Scottish Literary Studies may be recommended. The best general histories are w.c. DICKINSON, *Scotland from the Earliest Times to 1603,* 2nd rev. ed. (1965); and ROSALIND MITCHISON, *A History of Scotland* (1970), which also contain bibliographies. (*Prehistoric and Roman times*): STUART PIGGOTT, *Scotland Before History* (1958), is a good introduction. I.A. RICHMOND (ed.), *Roman and Native in North Britain* (1958), is helpful. (*Dark Age peoples*): ISABEL HENDERSON, *The Picts* (1967), is authoritative. (*Unification and the development of the monarchy*): A.O. ANDERSON, *Early Sources of Scottish History,* 2 vol. (1922), supplies the sources; see also the Scottish chapters in G.W.S. BARROW, *Feudal Britain* (1956). (*The Wars of Independence*): G.W.S. BARROW, *Robert Bruce and the Community of the Realm of Scotland* (1965), is balanced and important. (*The Reformation and the 16th century*): GORDON DONALDSON, *The Scottish Reformation* (1960); and the early chapters of T.C. SMOUT, *A History of the Scottish People, 1560–1830* (1969).

Wales: UNIVERSITY OF WALES, *National Atlas of Wales* (1980); E.G. BOWEN (ed.), *Wales* (1957), a composite general physical, historical, and regional geography with extensive bibliographies; D. WILLIAMS, *History of Modern Wales, 1485–1939* (1950), political, religious, economic, and social history; E.H. BROWN, *The Relief and Drainage of Wales* (1960), an account of the physiographical evolution of the Welsh landscape; H. CARTER, *The Towns of Wales* (1965), a study of the growth, functions, and morphology of towns in Wales; T.M. THOMAS, *The Mineral Wealth of Wales and Its Exploitation* (1961), a survey of the extent and economics of known mineral resources in Wales; B. THOMAS (ed.), *The Welsh Economy* (1962), a study of postwar economic trends and developments in Wales; D.A. REES and E. DAVIES (eds.), *Welsh Rural Communities* (1960), composite sociological studies of selected rural communities; J.A. ANDREWS (ed.), *Welsh Studies in Public Law,* ch. 2–4 (1970), a historical and contemporary account of government in Wales. Additional information may also be found in the following government reports: *Report on the Welsh Language Today* (1963), and *Digest of Welsh Statistics* (annual). Two standard historical surveys are DAVID WILLIAMS, *A History of Modern Wales* (1950; reprint, 1965); and WILLIAM REES, *An Historical Atlas of Wales from Early to Modern Times,* new ed. (1959). See also KENNETH O. MORGAN, *Rebirth of a Nation: Wales, 1880–1980* (1981), a definitive history. J.E. LLOYD, *A History of Wales from the Earliest Times to the Edwardian Conquest,* 3rd ed., 2 vol. (1939), remains a valuable survey of the history of Wales to 1282. The results of more recent investigations into the early history of Wales are reflected in I.L. FOSTER and G. DANIEL (eds.), *Prehistoric and Early Wales* (1965); N.K. CHADWICK (ed.), *Studies in Early British History* (1954) and *Studies in the Early British Church* (1958). V.E. NASH-WILLIAMS, *The Roman Frontier in Wales,* rev. ed. by M.G. JARRETT (1969), and *The Early Christian Monuments of Wales* (1950); and E.G. BOWEN, *Saints, Seaways and Settlements in the Celtic Lands* (1969), are major studies. J.G. EDWARDS, "The Normans and the Welsh March," *Proceedings of the British Academy,* 42:155–177 (1956), is of fundamental importance for an understanding of the effect of the Norman invasion. The narrative account of the age of the princes in Lloyd's *History of Wales* has not been superseded; but J.G. EDWARDS, *Littere Wallie* (1940); THOMAS JONES, *Brut y Tywysogyon; or, the Chronicle of the Princes, Peniarth MS. 20 Version* (1955); and H.D. EMANUEL (ed.), *The Latin Texts of the Welsh Laws* (1967), provide key source materials and important critical studies. Chapters relating to Wales are included in F.M. POWICKE, *King Henry III and the Lord Edward,* 2 vol. (1947) and *The Thirteenth Century, 1216–1307* (1953). T. JONES PIERCE, *Medieval Welsh Society: Selected Essays* (1972); or WILLIAM REES, *South Wales and the March, 1284–1415* (1924), are indispensable studies of social and agrarian history. J. CONWAY DAVIES, *Episcopal Acts Relating to Welsh Dioceses,* 2 vol. (1948–53); and GLANMOR WILLIAMS, *The Welsh Church from Conquest to Reformation* (1962), cover ecclesiastical history. J.E. LLOYD, *Owen Glendower* (1931), describes the early-15th-century rebellion; and GLYN ROBERTS, *Aspects of Welsh History* (1969), includes essays dealing with the later Middle Ages. KENNETH O. MORGAN, *Wales in British Politics, 1868–1922,* rev. ed. (1970), treats the principality in its United Kingdom context. *The Dictionary of Welsh Biography down to 1940* (1959) is valuable. *A Bibliography of the History of Wales* (1958; 2nd ed., 1962), with supplements in *The Bulletin of the Board of Celtic Studies,* vol. 20, 22, 23, provides a comprehensive guide to primary and secondary sources, including numerous important essays whose conclusions are not as yet reflected in general works.

Northern Ireland: General background on Ireland as a whole is found in G.L. HERRIES–DAVIES and N. STEPHENS, *Ireland* (1978), and A.R. ORME, *Ireland (World's Landscapes)* (1970); a treatment of the province in particular is R. COMMON (ed.), *Northern Ireland from the Air* (1964). A brief but masterly summary is E. ESTYN EVANS, "The Personality of Ulster," *Trans.*

Inst. Br. Geogr., 51:1–20 (1970), and the character of one part of the province is admirably portrayed in the same author's *Mourne Country* (1951). The best background to the cultural and political history of Ulster is M.W. HESLINGA, *The Irish Border as a Cultural Divide* (1962). D.P. BARRITT and C.F. CARTER, *The Northern Ireland Problem* (1962), deals with the social and political prelude to the current situation; and T. WILSON, *Economic Development in Northern Ireland* (1965), provides the economic background. The details of the capital city are dealt with in E. JONES, *A Social Geography of Belfast* (1960), which discusses the historical and environmental background to the social situation. Useful factual material is found in the *Ulster Year Book* (annual), as well as in the government reports for the censuses of 1961, 1971, and 1981, *Social and Economic Trends in Northern Ireland* (annual). Discussions of the contemporary political situation are found in R. ROSE, *Northern Ireland: Time of Choice* (1976), and J. OLIVER, *Ulster Today and Tomorrow* (1978). See also SEAN CRONLIN, *Irish Nationalism: A History of its Roots and Ideology* (1981).

The British Empire to 1914: The Cambridge History of the British Empire, 8 vol. (1929–36; 2nd ed., 1963–), is still fundamental, supported by V.T. HARLOW, *The Founding of the Second British Empire, 1763–1793,* 2 vol. (1952–64); L.A. HARPER, *The English Navigation Laws* (1939, reprinted 1964); and A.B. KEITH, *The Constitutional History of the First British Empire* (1930). See also H.T. MANNING, *British Colonial Government After the American Revolution, 1782–1822* (1933, reprinted 1966); and J.H. PARRY and P.M. SHERLOCK, *A Short History of the West Indies,* 3rd ed. (1971). R.L. SCHUYLER, *Parliament and the British Empire* (1929, reprinted 1963), starts from the 16th century in its account. See also the same author's *The Fall of the Old Colonial System: A Study in British Free Trade, 1770–1870* (1945). MARTIN WIGHT, *The Development of the Legislative Council, 1606–1945* (1946), covers the evolution of colonial government from England during 1606–1945, while L.H. GIPSON, *The Coming of the Revolution, 1763–1775* (1954), relates the loss of the American colonies. J.C. MILLER, *Origins of the American Revolution,* rev. ed. (1959), is also useful. For material on India, see S.R. MEHROTRA, *India and the Commonwealth, 1885–1929* (1965), who deals with India's role in defining and enlarging the Commonwealth concept, and *The Oxford History of India,* 3rd ed. (1958). Other parts of the empire are covered in RONALD ROBINSON, JOHN GALLAGHER, and ALICE DENNY, *Africa and the Victorians* (1961); and C.P. LUCAS (ed.), *Lord Durham's Report on the Affairs of British North America,* 3 vol. (1912). Nineteenth-century opinions are treated in W.P. MORRELL, *British Colonial Policy in the Age of Peel and Russell* (1930, reprinted 1966); and C.A. BODELSEN, *Studies in Mid-Victorian Imperialism,* 2nd ed. (1960). See also J.E. TYLER, *The Struggle for Imperial Unity, 1868–1895* (1938).

The Commonwealth: R.M. DAWSON (ed.), *The Development of Dominion Status 1900–1936* (1937, reprinted 1965); J.A. WILLIAMSON, *A Notebook of Commonwealth History,* 3rd ed. (1967), which deals with the Old Colonial Empire, then the Modern Empire and Commonwealth; COLIN CROSS, *The Fall of the British Empire: 1918–1968* (1968), describing the change from empire to commonwealth; J.B. WATSON, *Empire to Commonwealth 1919 to 1970* (1971); A.L. BURT, *The Evolution of the British Empire and Commonwealth, from the American Revolution* (1956); and MAX BELOFF, *Imperial Sunset,* vol. 1, *Britain's Liberal Empire, 1897–1921* (1969), all trace the Commonwealth's emergence. Supplementary works include A.B. KEITH, *Responsible Government in the Dominions,* 2nd ed., 2 vol. (1928), and *The Governments of the British Empire* (1935); and W.K. HANCOCK, *Survey of British Commonwealth Affairs,* 2 vol. (1937–42). ALEXANDER BRADY, *Democracy in the Dominions,* 3rd ed. (1958), examines administration in the countries concerned in their position as dominions. H.J. HARVEY, *Consultation and Co-operation in the Commonwealth* (1952), examines the ways Commonwealth countries can communicate and coordinate. Other useful works on the organization's machinery are G.W. KEETON (ed.), *The British Commonwealth: The Development of Its Laws and Constitutions,* 12 vol. (1952–64); P.N.S. MANSERGH, *The Multi-Racial Commonwealth* (1955) and *Survey of British Commonwealth Affairs,* 2 vol. (1952–58); K.C. WHEARE, *The Statute of Westminster and Dominion Status,* 5th ed. (1953), and *The Constitutional Structure of the Commonwealth* (1960); CLIVE PARRY, *Nationality and Citizenship Laws of the Commonwealth and of the Republic of Ireland* (1957); and GEOFFREY MARSHALL, *Parliamentary Sovereignty and the Commonwealth* (1957). Geographical aspects of the Commonwealth are treated in DENNIS AUSTIN, *West Africa and the Commonwealth* (1957); and A.A. MAZRUI, *The Anglo-African Commonwealth* (1967), covering Africa's impact on the Commonwealth's evolution. P.N.S. MANSERGH *et al., Commonwealth Perspectives* (1958); THE ECONOMIST, *Economic Geography of the Commonwealth* (1957); and C.B. HOOVER (ed.), *Economic Systems of the Commonwealth*

(1962), deal with the Commonwealth's differing components. The more recent Commonwealth is covered in M.S. RAJAN, *The Post-War Transformation of the Commonwealth* (1963); S.A. DE SMITH, *The New Commonwealth and Its Constitutions* (1964); J.D.B. MILLER, *The Commonwealth in the World,* 3rd ed. (1965), and *Britain and The Old Dominions* (1966); ZELMAN COWEN, *The British Commonwealth of Nations in a Changing World* (1965); and W.B. HAMILTON, KENNETH ROBINSON, and C.D.W. GOODWIN (eds.), *A Decade of the Commonwealth, 1955–1964* (1966). Recent developments are covered in H. DUNCAN HALL, *Commonwealth: A History of the British Commonwealth of Nations* (1971), a standard work of the 1920s and 1930s. The CENTRAL OFFICE OF INFORMATION, *The Commonwealth in Brief,* 5th ed. (1970), a short but comprehensive summary, and

NICHOLAS MANSERGH, *The Commonwealth Experience* (1968), a critical account of the Commonwealth's development from mid-19th century to the 1970s. RICHARD BAILEY, *Promoting Commonwealth Development* (1970), suggests the Commonwealth can raise living standards of developing countries; while PAUL STREETEN and HUGH CORBET (eds.), *Commonwealth Policy in a Global Context* (1971), contains collected essays from various sources. See also DEREK INGRAM, *The Commonwealth at Work* (1969); R.F. HOLLAND, *Britain and the Commonwealth Alliance: 1918–1939* (1981); ARNOLD SMITH, *Stiches in Time: The Commonwealth in World Politics* (1981).

(W.Ra./J.Pro./P.G.W./S.S.F./D.W./M.Has./ La.B.S./L.F.S./C.B.Co./As.B./A.F.H./J.B.Sm./ J.M.S./W.H.Th./Ma.J.M./J.G.Th./E.J./J.D.B.M.)

United Nations

The name United Nations was used during World War II to denote the nations allied against Germany, Italy, and Japan and later was adopted as the name of the postwar world organization. The Declaration of the United Nations, signed by 26 states on January 1, 1942, set forth the war aims of the Allied powers.

The first major step toward the formulation of a permanent organization was taken at the Dumbarton Oaks Conference, a meeting of diplomatic experts of the Big Four powers (the United States, the United Kingdom, the Soviet Union, and China) held August 21–October 7, 1944, at Dumbarton Oaks, an estate in Washington, D.C. Though substantial progress was made, there was disagreement on two essential issues: on the voting system of the proposed Security Council, which later became famous as the "veto problem"; and on membership, because the Soviet Union demanded seats in the General Assembly for all of its constituent republics. Roosevelt, Churchill, and Stalin finally resolved these two issues at the Yalta Conference and also agreed that the new agency would include a trusteeship system to succeed the League of Nations mandate system.

The Dumbarton Oaks proposals, as modified at the Yalta Conference, thus formed the basis of negotiations at the United Nations Conference on International Organization (UNCIO), which convened at San Francisco on April 25, 1945, and drafted the Charter of the United Nations (UN). The Charter was signed on June 26 and entered into force on October 24, 1945, by which time the Big Four, France, and a majority of the other signatories had deposited their ratifications.

The San Francisco Conference was attended by representatives of the 26 states that had signed the Declaration of the United Nations and the 20 others that had declared war against the Axis powers by March 1945. Four other states (the Ukrainian S.S.R., the Belorussian S.S.R., Argentina, and Denmark) were admitted during the conference. Poland, not present at the conference, was permitted to become an original member of the UN, which thus began with 51 members.

The San Francisco Conference was the first major international conference for two millennia that was not dominated by the nations of Europe. Not only was the conference remote from Europe in a geographical sense, but only nine continental European states west of the Soviet Union were represented. The 21 American republics, seven Near Eastern states, six Commonwealth nations, three Soviet republics, two Far Eastern nations, and two African states that convened with the European states at San Francisco represented all geographical areas of the world.

The international Secretariat provided interpreters and translators and distributed documents and speeches daily in the five official languages (English, French, Spanish, Russian, and Chinese). The chairmanship of the plenary sessions rotated among the Big Four. The private consultations of the Big Four, to which France was later added, exerted a greal deal of influence. The rule of unanimity, usually adopted by political conferences, was abandoned. Measures under consideration could be carried in committees, commissions, and plenary sessions by a two-thirds vote.

Political issues arose, especially between the Western powers and the Soviet Union, over the admission of the Ukrainian S.S.R., the Belorussian S.S.R., and Argentina; the recognition of a government of Poland; and the extension of the great-power veto in the Security Council to discussion as well as to recommendations and decisions. These controversies were settled by compromises. The issues concerning domestic jurisdiction versus international competence for the protection of human rights and the promotion of economic and social welfare, the status of colonial areas and of regional and defense arrangements, and great-power dominance versus the equality of states involved other groupings. In these matters the small states, the Asian states, and the Latin-American states succeeded in obtaining modifications of the Dumbarton Oaks proposals. (Q.W./E.Lu.)

The article is divided into the following sections:

Organization of the United Nations

PURPOSES AND MEMBERSHIP

The first article of the Charter outlines the purposes of the organization, declaring that the primary objective of the United Nations is the maintenance of international peace and security. The organization is also dedicated to the development of friendly relations among nations, based on the principle of equal rights and self-determination of peoples; to the achievement of international cooperation in solving international economic, social, cultural, or humanitarian problems; and to serving as a centre for harmonizing the actions of nations in the attainment of these common ends. Some of the basic principles of the United Nations, as outlined in Article 2 of the Charter, are the following: the United Nations is based on the sovereign equality of its members; disputes are to be settled by peaceful means; members undertake not to use force or the threat of force in contravention of the purposes of the United Nations; each member must assist the organization in any action it takes under the Charter; and states that are not members of the United Nations are required to act in accordance with these principles insofar as necessary for the maintenance of international peace and security. Article 2 also stipulates that, except to take enforcement measures, the organization shall not intervene in matters within the domestic jurisdiction of any state.

Original members The original members of the United Nations were Argentina, Australia, Belgium, the Belorussian S.S.R., Bolivia, Brazil, Canada, Chile, the Republic of China, Colombia, Costa Rica, Cuba, Czechoslovakia, Denmark, the Dominican Republic, Ecuador, Egypt, El Salvador, Ethiopia, France, Greece, Guatemala, Haiti, Honduras, India, Iran, Iraq, Lebanon, Liberia, Luxembourg, Mexico, The Netherlands, New Zealand, Nicaragua, Norway, Panama, Paraguay, Peru, the Philippines, Poland, Saudi Arabia, South Africa, Syria, Turkey, the Ukrainian S.S.R., the Soviet Union, the United Kingdom, the United States, Uruguay, Venezuela, and Yugoslavia.

New members are admitted to the United Nations on recommendation of the Security Council and by a two-thirds vote of the General Assembly. They must be peace-loving states that accept, and are able and willing to carry out, the obligations contained in the Charter. The requirement of concurrence of the permanent members of the Security Council was for 10 years a serious obstacle to the admission of new members. By 1950 only nine of 31 applicants had been admitted: Afghanistan, Iceland, Sweden, and Thailand (all in 1946); Pakistan and Yemen (1947); Burma (1948); Israel (1949); and Indonesia (1950).

A number of efforts had been made by the General Assembly to break the deadlock. In the 10th assembly session (1955) there was wide support for a "package deal" sponsored by 29 members under the leadership of Canada. Though it became necessary to drop Japan and Mongolia from the package, the proposal was approved by the Security Council in modified form, and the General Assembly voted to admit 16 new members (Albania, Austria, Bulgaria, Cambodia [now Kampuchea], Ceylon [now Sri Lanka], Finland, Hungary, Ireland, Italy, Jordan, Laos, Libya, Nepal, Portugal, Romania, and Spain). Thereafter, new members were admitted almost yearly as nations became independent and sought membership.
(L.M.G./A.Va.)

Questions of representation The question of China's representation in the UN was before the General Assembly at every session from 1950, when India introduced a resolution declaring that the Communist regime was entitled to representation in the assembly. This resolution failed by a vote of 33 to 16, with 10 abstentions—largely because of the opposition led by the United States. For 20 years efforts to bring the People's Republic of China into the organization and, concurrently, to expel the representatives of Nationalist China (Taiwan) were consistently frustrated. Finally, in 1971, the United States acquiesced to the idea of admitting Communist China to the Security Council and General Assembly if, at the same time, Nationalist China could retain a seat in the General Assembly. This compromise failed. The General Assembly on October 25, 1971, voted 76 to 35, with 17 abstentions and three members absent, to admit the representatives of the People's Republic and to remove the Nationalist representatives. Nationalist China's permanent Security Council seat was also given to Communist China. A conflict concerning the representation of Kampuchea—the majority supporting the claims of the former Khmer Rouge government—arose following the establishment in that country of a Vietnam-supported government in 1979.
(L.M.G./A.Va./E.Lu.)

PRINCIPAL ORGANS

The United Nations has six principal organs: the General Assembly, Security Council, Economic and Social Council, Trusteeship Council, International Court of Justice, and Secretariat.

General Assembly. The General Assembly is the only body in which all of the UN members are represented. A member may send as many as five representatives, but each member has only one vote. Decisions on substantive questions are taken by a majority or by a two-thirds vote, depending on the importance of the matters involved. Procedural questions are decided by majority vote.

Through its deliberative, supervisory, financial, and elective functions the General Assembly occupies a central position in the functioning of the United Nations. Its role as a deliberative organ is based in Articles 10–14 of the Charter. Article 10 states that the General Assembly may discuss and make recommendations on "any questions or any matters within the scope of the present Charter or relating to the powers and functions of any organs provided for in the present Charter."

Article 10 and the role of the General Assembly

In performing its supervisory functions, the General Assembly exercises control over the activities of UN organs in the economic and social fields and in dealing with the problems of non-self-governing territories. It receives annual reports from the secretary general, Security Council, Economic and Social Council, and Trusteeship Council and may make recommendations to these organs. The Economic and Social Council and the Trusteeship Council operate under the authority of the General Assembly. The assembly approves trust agreements and through the Trusteeship Council supervises the administration of trust territories. It exercises general supervision and control over the operations of the Secretariat. The financial power of the assembly is exercised through its control over the budget of the United Nations and the scale of assessments levied on members.

In its elective capacity, the General Assembly chooses all the members of the Economic and Social Council and the elective members of the Security Council and Trusteeship Council. Along with the Security Council, it also participates in the election of judges of the International Court of Justice and the appointment of the secretary general. The assembly shares with the Security Council the power to propose amendments to the Charter, as well as the right to convene a conference for the purpose of revising the Charter.

During its first 10 years the General Assembly progressively increased in importance as an organ of deliberation and political influence. At the same time, the influence and the effectiveness of the Security Council declined because of the inability of the permanent members to cooperate. The broad language of Articles 10, 11, and 14 of the Charter permitted the role of the General Assembly to increase far beyond what was originally envisaged, and most of its members encouraged this increase. Members consequently became more and more concerned with ways and means of strengthening the assembly, in organization and procedure, so that it could more effectively handle its growing responsibilities.

The assembly convenes annually, but its rules also permit the calling of special sessions on short notice. It works through a complex structure of main committees, procedural committees, standing committees, and subsidiary and ad hoc bodies.

Security Council. The Charter assigns the Security Council primary responsibility for the maintenance of international peace and security. The council consisted originally of 11 members—five permanent members (the

Republic of China, France, the United Kingdom, the Soviet Union, and the United States) and six nonpermanent members elected by the General Assembly for two-year terms. From the beginning, nonpermanent members of the Security Council were elected with a view to giving representation to certain regions or groups of states. This practice ran into increasing difficulty as the number of UN members increased and there were not enough seats on the Security Council to distribute among the groups and regions desiring representation. In 1965, when an amendment to the Charter was ratified, the council became a 15-member body consisting of the original five permanent members and 10 nonpermanent members. The latter were to be chosen as follows: five from African and Asian states, one from eastern European states, two from Latin-American states, and two from western European and other states. The presidency is held by each member in turn for one month. In selecting nonpermanent members, the General Assembly must not only strive for an equitable geographical distribution but must also consider the contribution of members to the maintenance of international peace and security.

Under the Charter members of the United Nations agree to carry out the decisions of the Security Council. This agreement refers primarily to decisions pertaining to the maintenance of international peace and security under Chapter VII of the Charter. The council may investigate any dispute that might threaten international peace and security, but it can make recommendations only for its peaceful settlement. The council may, however, require members of the UN to apply various sanctions against any state that the council has found guilty of a threat to the peace, breach of the peace, or act of aggression (Article 39), or of failing to "perform the obligations incumbent upon it under a judgment" of the International Court of Justice (Article 94). Recommendations for the regulations of national armaments may also be made by the council (Article 26).

Procedural and substantive voting in the Security Council   On procedural matters decisions by the Security Council are made by an affirmative vote of any nine (seven until 1965) of its members. On substantive matters, including the investigation of a dispute and the application of sanctions, nine (seven until 1965) affirmative votes (including those of the five permanent members) are required, but in practice a permanent member may abstain without impairing the validity of the decision. A vote on whether a matter is procedural or substantive is itself a substantive question. Because the council is required to function continuously, each member is represented at all times at UN headquarters.   (L.M.G./A.Va.)

Economic and Social Council.   The Economic and Social Council is charged with directing and coordinating the complex system of economic, social, humanitarian, and cultural activities of the United Nations. Its 54 members (originally 18) are elected by the General Assembly for three-year terms with the possibility of reelection. Although the Economic and Social Council has no permanent members, states are regularly reelected if their participation is considered necessary to its work.

The Economic and Social Council meets at least twice a year; it is directed by the Charter to carry on studies and make recommendations for the promotion of international cooperation in economic and social matters. It may prepare draft conventions for submission to the General Assembly and call international conferences.

The council is assisted in its work by commissions organized on functional or geographical bases. The functional commissions, including an economic, a social, and a human rights commission, carry out studies in their fields and otherwise assist the council in the performance of its duties. They formulate resolutions, recommendations, and international conventions on which the council and General Assembly take action. Four regional commissions—for Europe, Asia and the Far East, Latin America, and Africa—that were established to deal with specific regional economic problems have assumed roles of considerable importance both as advisory organs and as organs with important operational responsibilities.

Trusteeship Council.   The Trusteeship Council was established to supervise, under the authority of the General Assembly, the administration of trust territories by the administering states. It is composed of UN members who administer trust territories, the permanent members of the Security Council not administering trust territories, and as many other nonadministering members elected by the General Assembly for three-year terms as are necessary to ensure an equal number of administering and nonadministering members in total membership. The Trusteeship Council is authorized to send visiting inspection missions into the trust territories, to receive and examine petitions, to consider reports submitted to it annually by the administering authorities, and to make recommendations. All trust territories except one—the Trust Territory of the Pacific Islands under U.S. administration—had secured independence by 1980. The task of the Trusteeship Council was, therefore, almost completed.

International Court of Justice.   The International Court of Justice, popularly known as the World Court, is the principal judicial organ of the United Nations, and its statute is an integral part of the Charter. The 15 judges of the court are elected by the General Assembly and the Security Council voting independently. No two judges may be nationals of the same state. The main forms of civilization and the major legal systems of the world are to be represented. Judges serve for nine years and are eligible for reelection. The seat of the World Court is The Hague, The Netherlands.   *The World Court*

The jurisdiction of the World Court comprises "all cases which parties refer to it and all matters specially provided for in the Charter of the United Nations or in treaties and conventions in force." By formal declaration states may accept the compulsory jurisdiction of the World Court in specified categories of disputes. The World Court may give advisory opinions at the request of the General Assembly or the Security Council or at the request of other organs and specialized agencies authorized by the General Assembly.

Secretariat.   The Secretariat is headed by the secretary general, who is appointed by the General Assembly upon the recommendation of the Security Council. At the beginning of its first session in 1946, the General Assembly chose Trygve Lie of Norway for a term of five years, which was extended in 1950 for three more years. This extension was bitterly opposed by the Soviet Union, and in November 1952 Lie resigned. Dag Hammarskjöld of Sweden succeeded him in April 1953 and was reelected in 1957. In September 1961 Hammarskjöld was killed in an airplane crash in Northern Rhodesia (now Zambia). After a period of controversy, during which the Soviet Union proposed that the Secretariat be headed by a three-member committee, the powers agreed upon the choice of U Thant of Burma. In December 1966 Thant was unanimously elected to a second term. Kurt Waldheim of Austria was elected at the end of 1971 and served two terms. He was succeeded in 1982 by Javier Pérez de Cuéllar of Peru.

In addition to being the chief administrative officer of the United Nations, the secretary general also has important political functions, being specifically charged with bringing before the organization any matter that threatens international peace and security (see below *Administration*).   *The UN secretary general*

(L.M.G./A.Va./E.Lu.)

Functions of the United Nations

MAINTENANCE OF INTERNATIONAL PEACE AND SECURITY

Settlement of disputes.   The preamble to the Charter begins with the declaration that the peoples of the United Nations are determined "to save succeeding generations from the scourge of war." Article 1 places the maintenance of international peace and security first among the purposes of the organization, followed by the development of "friendly relations among nations" and the achievement of "international cooperation in solving international problems of an economic, social, cultural, or humanitarian character." In the long run the secondary purposes may be more important than the first, but it is only in peace that the United Nations can function to achieve them.

The primary responsibility for the maintenance of international peace and security is placed on the Security Council. The founders realized that without basic agreement among the great powers on important international issues there could be no effective cooperation in the maintenance of peace or the application of sanctions against an aggressor. For this reason the Charter provided that substantive decisions would require the unanimous vote of the five permanent members of the Security Council. But this requirement means that when there is disagreement on substantive matters among the great powers the Security Council is unable to act. It was assumed by those who drafted the Charter that the five great powers who were given permanent membership in the council would cooperate in most such matters. This assumption proved false. Almost immediately there developed a sharp rift between the Soviet Union and the Western powers; and the Soviet Union, being in a minority, resorted to frequent use of the veto to prevent what it considered adverse action by the council.

Articles 11 and 12 and the role of the General Assembly

With a stalemate in the Security Council, members of the United Nations began to look to the General Assembly. Article 11, paragraph 2, of the Charter authorizes the General Assembly to "discuss any questions relating to the maintenance of international peace and security" and to "make recommendations with regard to any such questions to the state or states concerned or to the Security Council or to both." This broad authorization is restricted somewhat by the provision of Article 12, that, "while the Security Council is exercising in respect of any dispute or situation the functions assigned to it in the present Charter, the General Assembly shall not make any recommendations with regard to that dispute or situation unless the Security Council so requests." Whereas these provisions grant the assembly a broad secondary role, there exists a very important difference between the two bodies. The Security Council can make decisions that bind all the members, whereas the General Assembly can only make recommendations.

Because the Soviet representative was absent from the Security Council in protest against the allegedly illegal representation of China on that body by the Nationalist government, the Security Council was able to take prompt action against the North Korean forces when they attacked South Korea in June 1950. After a few weeks, however, the Soviet representative returned to the council, and further action by that body to deal with the Korean situation was impeded by Soviet vetoes. To enable it to carry out its peacekeeping function more effectively, the General Assembly in November 1950 adopted the Uniting for Peace Resolution proposed by the United States. It provided for immediate consideration by the General Assembly of a threat to the peace, breach of the peace, or act of aggression, with a view to recommending collective measures, including the use of armed force when necessary "if the Security Council, because of lack of unanimity of the permanent members, fails to exercise its primary responsibility." The resolution established a Peace Observation Commission to "observe and report on the situation in any area where there exists international tension the continuance of which is likely to endanger the maintenance of international peace and security." It also established a Collective Measures Committee to "study and report on methods which the Assembly might use in strengthening international peace and security."

1950 Uniting for Peace Resolution

In carrying out its responsibility the Security Council must first seek to bring about a pacific settlement of disputes, in accordance with Chapter VI of the Charter. If the parties to a dispute that threatens the peace fail to settle it by peaceful means of their own choice, the Security Council must call upon them to settle it. The council may investigate any dispute or situation in order to determine whether its continuance is likely to endanger international peace and security. Any state, whether it is a member of the UN or not, may bring any such dispute or situation to the attention of the Security Council or the General Assembly. At any stage of the dispute or situation the Security Council may recommend appropriate procedures or methods of adjustment, and if the parties fail to settle the dispute by peaceful means the Security Council may recommend terms of settlement.

Whenever the Security Council determines that a threat to the peace exists or that a breach of the peace or act of aggression has taken place, it may decide upon measures to be taken to meet the situation. The Charter envisages the application of graduated measures, from economic and diplomatic sanctions to action by air, sea, and land forces. By subscribing to the Charter, all the members undertook to place at the disposal of the Security Council armed forces and facilities for military sanctions against aggressors or disturbers of the peace; but this provision did not become operative because no agreements to give it effect were concluded.

During the first 35 years of its life, a large number of disputes and situations involving the maintenance of peace have come before the Security Council and the General Assembly, reflecting the unsettled conditions in the world since World War II. The United Nations has succeeded in helping to settle some of them, such as the removal of Soviet troops from northern Iran in 1946; others have remained unsolved and have been a continuing concern of the Security Council and the General Assembly. Because most of these disputes have involved actions taken by nations acting outside, as well as within, the United Nations, the detailed histories of each are not given in this article.

Regulation of armaments. The Charter places responsibility on the Security Council for preparing and submitting plans for the regulation of armaments. The General Assembly may discuss and recommend principles governing "disarmament and the regulation of armaments." The word regulation has been interpreted to include making armaments available for United Nations purposes as well as limiting or reducing armaments used for national purposes. The development of the atomic bomb during World War II created a situation in which it seemed to the United States and other governments that the international control of atomic energy demanded consideration even in advance of any perfection of collective security arrangements. Consequently, the first act of the United Nations was to establish the Atomic Energy Commission in January 1946 to prepare plans for the control of atomic energy. In December 1946 the General Assembly adopted a resolution providing for the urgent consideration of the control of atomic weapons and other weapons of mass destruction and for the regulation and reduction of all armaments and armed forces.

Atomic Energy Commission

The Atomic Energy Commission began its deliberations in June 1946. It soon became apparent that there was complete disagreement between the United States and the Soviet Union. The commission submitted reports to the Security Council in 1946, 1947, and 1948. The majority of the members of the commission called for international managerial control or ownership of atomic-energy facilities, international inspection by a proposed international atomic development authority, and the elimination of the veto from enforcement provisions of the agreement. The majority also insisted that the control system should be in operation before the existing stockpile of atomic bombs was destroyed. The Soviet Union, however, took an opposite view. It refused to agree to international ownership and to the kind of international inspection demanded by the majority; it demanded that the veto be applicable to enforcement measures under the plan and that the destruction of atomic stockpiles accompany the establishment of a control system. The commission recorded an impasse in negotiations in its 1948 report, though some agreement had been reached on matters of detail.

To deal with armaments other than weapons of mass destruction, the Security Council organized the Commission for Conventional Armaments, but progress in this field was also blocked by disagreement between the Soviet Union and the Western powers. Although the commission and the General Assembly in 1949 approved a plan whereby each state would submit full information to the commission on its conventional armaments and armed forces, the refusal of the Soviet Union to accept the plan prevented any implementation. By early 1950 it was clear that a hopeless deadlock had been reached.

In January 1952 the General Assembly voted to merge the Atomic Energy Commission and the Conventional

**Disarm-
ament
Commis-
sion**

Armaments Commission into a Disarmament Commission, thus recognizing the interdependence of the various elements of the problem. The Disarmament Commission, which consisted of the members of the Security Council and Canada, was directed to prepare proposals for the regulation, limitation, and balanced reduction of all the armed forces and armaments; for the elimination of major weapons adaptable to mass destruction; and for the effective international control of atomic energy to ensure its use for peaceful purposes only. The development of atomic and hydrogen weapons by the Soviet Union fundamentally altered the terms of the problem of the regulation and reduction of armaments and resulted in important changes in national positions. In spite of vigorous efforts to achieve constructive results both through the commission and through the General Assembly itself, little progress was made.

In his annual report to the 12th General Assembly, which convened in 1957, Secretary General Hammarskjöld stated that the year had witnessed "most sustained and intensive efforts by the members of the disarmament subcommittee to find common ground." Instead of attempting to work out a comprehensive, detailed general disarmament plan there was a shift toward efforts to obtain a limited "first step" agreement. After more than a decade of stalemate there was some hope that a limited agreement might be possible. Much attention was devoted to means of preventing surprise attacks; the United States urged acceptance of the Eisenhower "open skies" proposal for aerial inspection and exchange of military blueprints; the Soviet Union supported the Bulganin plan of ground observation posts at strategic centres. No agreement resulted. In 1957, however, the International Atomic Energy Agency was established to promote the peaceful uses of atomic energy.

World public opinion, as expressed in the General Assembly, continued to exert pressure on the great powers to resume negotiations for disarmament. A Ten-Nation Disarmament Committee, composed of five members from eastern Europe and an equal number from the West, began deliberations in March 1959, but negotiations soon reached an impasse. The committee was enlarged to 18 members by the addition of neutral countries, but one member, France, did not participate. Both the Soviet Union and the Western powers declared that general and complete disarmament was their goal, but little agreement was reached on how to achieve that goal. The Western approach was primarily military: a step-by-step movement toward a carefully inspected and controlled system of disarmament. The Soviet approach was primarily political: an agreement for complete and total disarmament within a few years. The General Assembly in 1961 adopted a resolution declaring the use of nuclear or thermonuclear weapons to be contrary to international law, to the UN Charter, and to the laws of humanity.

An important step toward disarmament was achieved by the Nuclear Test-Ban Treaty signed on August 5, 1963, by the Soviet Union, the United Kingdom, and the United States. This agreement—to which more than 100 states later adhered—prohibited nuclear tests or explosions in the atmosphere, in outer space, and underwater, but not underground. (China and France, both atomic powers, did not sign the treaty.)   (L.M.G./A.Va.)

In 1966 the General Assembly unanimously approved a treaty prohibiting the placement of nuclear arms or other weapons of mass destruction in orbit, on the Moon, or on other celestial bodies, and recognizing the use of outer space for peaceful purposes only. In January 1968 the assembly approved the draft of a "nonproliferation treaty" that banned the spread of nuclear weapons from nuclear to nonnuclear powers; the treaty has not, however, been ratified by most of the near-nuclear powers, such as Argentina, Brazil, Egypt, Israel, Pakistan, and South Africa. In 1971 the assembly approved a treaty banning the emplacement of weapons of mass destruction on the seabed.

Since 1962 negotiations on disarmament questions have taken place in Geneva: in 1962–68, by the Eighteen-Nation Committee on Disarmament; in 1968–78, by the Conference of the Committee on Disarmament; and since then, by the Committee on Disarmament. In 1978 and

1982 the UN also organized two special sessions of the General Assembly on disarmament. The first of these sessions agreed on a general statement of organizational changes and a program of negotiations; the second broke down with little agreement.   (E.Lu.)

Revision of the Charter. In accordance with Article 109, a proposal to call a conference to review the Charter was placed on the agenda of the General Assembly at its 10th session in 1955. The assembly decided that such a conference should be held at some appropriate time in the future, but no date was set. Three specific proposals for Charter amendment were urged by a number of Latin-American states as early as 1956: to increase the number of nonpermanent members of the Security Council, to increase the membership of the Economic and Social Council, and to increase the number of judges on the International Court of Justice. As the membership of the United Nations rose to more than 100, the demand for enlargement of the councils became more insistent; some regions, particularly Africa, felt they were not given adequate representation.

The General Assembly adopted, on December 17, 1963, a resolution proposing an amendment to the Charter to enlarge the Security Council to 15 (by increasing the number of nonpermanent members to 10) and to raise the membership of the Economic and Social Council to 27. Under the proposed revision, decisions of the Security Council on procedural matters would require an affirmative vote of any nine members, and decisions on all other matters would require nine affirmative votes, including those of the five permanent members. The proposed amendment provided for the geographic distribution of the seats of the nonpermanent members as follows: Africa and Asia, five; eastern Europe, one; Latin America, two; and western Europe and other regions, two. The Soviet Union, which previously had opposed any amendment to the Charter so long as China was barred from the United Nations, changed its position, and by September 1965 the two amendments had come into effect. There has been no agreement to hold conferences to discuss Charter amendment generally.

DEVELOPMENT OF INTERNATIONAL LAW

In November 1947 the General Assembly established the International Law Commission of 15 members to make recommendations for the progressive development and codification of international law. In setting up the commission, the General Assembly directed it to formulate the principles of international law recognized at the Nürnberg trial of Nazi war criminals and to prepare a draft code of offenses against the peace and security of mankind.

In 1950 the commission submitted its formulation of the Nürnberg principles, which covered crimes against the peace, war crimes, and crimes against humanity. The commission presented to the assembly in 1951 draft articles on offenses against the peace and security of mankind, which enumerated 12 crimes against international law, including any act of aggression, threat of or preparation for aggression, annexation of territory, and genocide. The commission also prepared a draft declaration on the rights and duties of states.

The commission made studies of the possibility of codifying certain branches of international law, giving priority to the law of treaties and the law of the sea (see INTERNATIONAL LAW). It also prepared a study on the legal aspects of reservations to multilateral conventions. Draft conventions were prepared on statelessness, the peaceful settlement of disputes, the law of the sea, diplomatic relations, consular relations, and the law of treaties. The commission was also concerned about the subjects of arbitral procedure and international criminal jurisdiction. After the commission has completed a draft convention it submits it to the General Assembly, which may either convene an international conference to draw up formal conventions based on the draft or merely commend the text to the states. A conference to consider the draft convention on the law of the sea was held at Geneva in 1958; conferences held at Vienna in 1961 and 1963 completed conventions on diplomatic relations and optional proto-

**Interna-
tional Law
Commis-
sion**

cols on the acquisition of nationality and the compulsory settlement of disputes and on consular relations. The commission in 1966 completed a draft convention on the law of treaties, which was placed before a conference meeting in split sessions in 1968 and 1969. The commission has since drafted conventions on special missions and on state succession and discussed the law relating to watercourses, the relations between states and international organizations, and other questions.

Prolonged attempts to arrive at a definition of aggression, undertaken both by the commission and by special committees set up by the General Assembly, eventually resulted in agreement on such a definition, passed without dissent in 1974. In 1970 the General Assembly passed a Declaration on Friendly Relations among States, which set out certain principles that should govern relations between states. In 1968 the UN Commission on International Trade Law (UNCITRAL) was established to discuss the harmonization and unification of international trade law.

ECONOMIC AND SOCIAL COOPERATION

A major purpose of the United Nations is "to achieve international cooperation in solving international problems of an economic, social, cultural, or humanitarian character, and in promoting and encouraging respect for human rights and for fundamental freedoms for all without distinction as to race, sex, language, or religion." The General Assembly, the Economic and Social Council, the Secretariat, and the specialized agencies are the organs primarily responsible for action in this field. An important part of this aspect of UN activity consists of research, publication of reports, and technical assistance to governments. The United Nations has no authority to legislate or to enforce measures of economic and social cooperation; it can only make recommendations, which the member governments may or may not follow.

Major UN annual publications

The United Nations has rendered a valuable service by publishing carefully prepared statistical data and surveys of economic and social developments. Among the more significant of its yearly publications are the *World Economic Survey,* the *Statistical Yearbook,* the *Demographic Yearbook,* and the *Yearbook on Human Rights.*

Economic reconstruction. The devastation of large areas of the world and the dislocation of normal economic relations during World War II resulted in the need for concerted measures of relief, rehabilitation, and reconstruction. The United Nations Relief and Rehabilitation Administration, established in 1943, did much to alleviate the situation. To assist in dealing with regional problems the Economic and Social Council in 1947 established the Economic Commission for Europe and the Economic Commission for Asia and the Far East. Similar commissions were established for Latin America in 1948 and for Africa in 1958.

Technical assistance. A modest program of technical assistance to the less developed countries was undertaken in 1946, when the General Assembly passed a resolution calling for the establishment of machinery in the Secretariat for giving such aid. The Expanded Program of Technical Assistance was approved by the General Assembly in 1949. It is financed by voluntary contributions from members. Pledges are made at an annual conference.

Financing economic development. The United Nations gave a great deal of consideration to ways and means of making capital available to less developed countries for financing projects that were not self-liquidating or that did not meet the International Bank's requirements for loans. In 1954 the General Assembly recommended that both capital-importing and capital-exporting countries examine their policies and practices with a view to encouraging the flow of private capital. In April 1955 the bank submitted to its members the draft charter of the International Finance Corporation, to come into operation as soon as ratified by 30 states and as soon as 75 percent of the $100,000,000 capital had been subscribed. The corporation was to make direct loans to private enterprises without government guarantees and was to be allowed to make loans for other than fixed returns. The charter entered into force on July 20, 1956.

In 1960 the International Development Association was established as an affiliate of the International Bank. It was created to make loans to less developed countries on terms that were more flexible than bank loans. It was authorized to finance any project "which will make an important contribution to the development of an area or areas concerned, whether or not the project is revenue producing or directly productive."

To assist in the financing of non-self-liquidating development projects a proposal was submitted to the General Assembly for a Special United Nations Fund for Economic Development (SUNFED). The General Assembly in 1957 unanimously adopted a resolution to set up a separate fund to provide systematic assistance in fields essential to technical, economic, and social development of less developed countries. The special fund began operations in 1959.

The expanded program and the special fund had similar goals, but they were different in structure and operation. The special fund put greater emphasis on the pre-evaluation of projects for subsequent investment, but because of their closely related goals the two were merged in 1965 to become the UN Development Programme (UNDP). The funds available to the UNDP, which are provided by voluntary donations from governments, had progressively expanded to more than $500,000,000 a year by the early 1980s.

Trade and development. Because they were dissatisfied with the existing international trading system and because they believed that the General Agreement on Tariffs and Trade (GATT) was primarily interested in the trade problems of rich countries, developing countries demanded the establishment of a new organization to consider their trade problems. In 1964 a United Nations Conference on Trade and Development (UNCTAD) took place in Geneva and decided to establish the discussions on a continuing basis. There would be full conferences every three or four years, a Trade and Development Board of 55 members elected by the conference, a permanent secretariat under a secretary general (to be appointed by the UN secretary general, with the confirmation of the General Assembly), and committees to discuss specialized topics.

UNCTAD

Discussion in these bodies resulted in agreements on a "generalized system of preferences," providing for lower tariff rates for some exports of poorer countries, and on the creation of a Common Fund to help finance buffer stocks for commodity agreements. UNCTAD has also discussed questions relating to shipping, including the operation of liner conferences, and insurance, commodities, the transfer of technology, and ways of assisting the exports of developing countries.

Refugees. The International Refugee Organization (IRO) was established in 1946 to take over the refugee functions of the United Nations Relief and Rehabilitation Administration, which expired in 1947. The IRO was successful in resettling, repatriating, transporting, and maintaining more than 1,000,000 European refugees. Because the IRO was conceived as a short-term emergency organization, it was abolished in 1952 and replaced by a new refugee structure. A United Nations high commissioner for refugees was appointed and was directed to act under the Convention Relating to the Status of Refugees, drawn up by the Economic and Social Council and approved by the General Assembly in 1951. An Advisory Committee on Refugees was appointed by the council in 1951 to assist the high commissioner. The assembly in 1957 voted to continue the office of UN high commissioner for refugees for five years from January 1959, and in 1963 and 1968 voted to extend it for five-year periods. The commission has undertaken major operations to help refugees in western Europe, Hong Kong, The Sudan, the Congo (now Zaire), and many other areas. The scale of its work has increased greatly since 1970, with major crises affecting refugees from Bangladesh and Indochina and in Central America. A separate organization, the UN Relief and Works Agency (UNRWA), is responsible for aiding refugees in the Middle East.

Human rights. The General Assembly in 1948 adopted the Universal Declaration of Human Rights, which was prepared by the Commission on Human Rights. In 1948

Commission on Human Rights

the commission began to draft a Covenant of Human Rights that, upon ratification by governments, would become legally binding upon them. Wide differences in economic and social philosophies hampered efforts to achieve agreement on a common text, but finally the Covenants on Economic, Social, and Cultural Rights and the Covenant on Civil and Political Rights were agreed upon by the General Assembly in 1966. Ten years later the latter, having been ratified by 35 states, entered into force, including provisions for regular cross-examination of ratifying countries concerning their implementation of the covenant. The General Assembly has adopted a Convention on the Elimination of all Forms of Racial Discrimination, which has come into force, and has passed declarations on this and many other human rights questions.

The UN Commission on Human Rights and its subcommission meet regularly in Geneva to consider a wide range of human rights issues. Since the early 1970s, under the confidential 1502 procedure, these bodies have examined the human rights situations in particular countries, and in many cases they have passed resolutions concerning violations of human rights in the countries concerned. They have also considered such questions as slavery, religious intolerance, detention without trial, and forcible incarceration in mental hospitals. The General Assembly has established a Special Committee on Apartheid, concerned with the violations of human rights in South Africa. Long-standing proposals to create a post of UN high commissioner for human rights had not been adopted by the required majority by the early 1980s.

Commission on Narcotic Drugs

Control of narcotics. The Commission on Narcotic Drugs was authorized by the General Assembly in 1946 to carry out the functions entrusted by international conventions to the League of Nations Advisory Committee on Traffic in Opium and Other Dangerous Drugs. The agreements, conventions, and protocols on the control of narcotic drugs concluded in 1912, 1925, 1931, and 1936 were amended in a draft protocol approved by the assembly in November 1946 and subsequently came into force among its signatories. In addition to reestablishing the pre-World War II system of narcotics control, which had suffered from the dislocations of the war, the UN concerned itself with new problems resulting from the development of synthetic drugs. Efforts were made to simplify the system of control by drafting one convention incorporating all the agreements in force. (L.M.G./A.Va./E.Lu.)

Specialized agencies. The League of Nations provided a focal point for intergovernmental organizations and also for the growing network of nongovernmental agencies. Following World War II the United Nations became a kind of "roof organization" for the major enterprises in systematic international cooperation. In accordance with its Charter, the UN entered into coordinating agreements with intergovernmental agencies operating in economic, social, cultural, educational, health, and related fields. By the 1980s the roster of specialized agencies affiliated with the United Nations included the following: the International Maritime Organization (IMO; until 1982 known as the Inter-Governmental Maritime Consultative Organization); International Labour Organisation (ILO); United Nations Educational, Scientific and Cultural Organization (UNESCO); Food and Agriculture Organization (FAO); International Civil Aviation Organization (ICAO); International Bank for Reconstruction and Development (World Bank); World Health Organization (WHO); International Telecommunication Union (ITU); Universal Postal Union (UPU); World Meteorological Organization (WMO); International Atomic Energy Agency (IAEA); World Intellectual Property Organization (WIPO); and the UN Industrial Development Organization (UNIDO). The Economic and Social Council maintains a consultative relationship with about 300 nongovernmental organizations.

General structure of UN agencies

The general structure of each specialized agency follows a common pattern. Each agency has a general conference in which all the members are represented, and the conference elects an executive council that is charged with initiating proposals and carrying out decisions of the general conference. Each agency also has a permanent secretariat headed by a director. Many agencies have re-

gional subcommissions operating in various parts of the world. Some of the specialized agencies were in existence before the United Nations was organized; some were in the process of establishment during World War II; and some agencies were organized under the auspices of the United Nations. (Ed./E.Lu.)

International Labour Organisation. The ILO is an example of an official international institution in existence before World War II and now affiliated with the UN. In 1919 the Peace Conference of Paris, fearful of social revolution, set up a commission for international labour legislation headed by Samuel Gompers, president of the American Federation of Labor. The commission put aside the more ambitious claims for a body with legislative authority and proposed a body with powers of recommendation to national governments for action by them, in composition a tripartite body in which half the representation would be by governments, and one-fourth each by labour and by employers. The peace conference adopted these proposals and, by inserting them in the Treaty of Versailles, set up the ILO.

In its first decade the ILO was concerned primarily with its research efforts; with the definition and promotion of proper minimum standards of labour legislation for adoption by member states; and with "mutual education" and some forms of collaboration among worker, employer, and government delegates and the office professional staff. During the 1930s the ILO sought ways to combat worldwide unemployment and economic depression. Its proposals of extensive international public works never influenced national decision makers.

After 1945 the "Cold War," the breakup of European colonial empires, and the claims of the developing nations placed new tasks in the foreground for an organization the membership of which was no longer chiefly that of European, economically developed states but increasingly that of the less developed states. The ILO's major emphases shifted therefore to the area of human rights and to technical assistance and other work of an operating character in the interest of the less developed countries of Asia, Africa, Latin America, and Europe itself. The ILO's ideal has been universality of membership. It admitted Germany in 1919, long before the League of Nations did. Some nations— Brazil and, for a time, Japan—remained in the ILO after resigning from the League. Others became members of the ILO without joining the League or the UN. The United States, which remained aloof from the League, joined the ILO in 1934; it withdrew in 1977 but rejoined in 1980. After World War II the ILO admitted the Federal Republic of Germany and in 1951, Japan. But South Africa was practically forced out of the organization because of its racial policies. Post-World War II amendments made it easier to join the ILO. Members of the UN do not have automatic membership in the ILO, as did League members, but they may become members simply by filing a declaration accepting the obligations of the ILO constitution. Nonmembers of the UN must be accepted by a vote of two-thirds of the conference, including that of two-thirds of the government delegates. By 1982 the ILO had 150 members.

Membership of the ILO

The International Labour Office is the secretariat of the organization and its research staff. By 1970 it had international civil servants from more than 90 nations, including technical-assistance experts on temporary missions, working in Geneva, or in the field, all over the world. Their work was made possible by the ILO's own budget plus funds from other sources, chiefly UN Development Programme funds. Some idea of the ILO's manifold activities may be gleaned from its *Catalogue of Publications;* most widely used are the monthly *International Labour Review* and the *Year Book of Labour Statistics.*

In 1962 the ILO helped to establish the International Institute for Labour Studies at Geneva. In 1965, in cooperation with the Italian government, it opened an International Centre for Technical and Vocational Training in Turin. During the 1970s the ILO launched its "World Employment Programme," designed to encourage all countries, especially poor ones, to adopt development and industrial strategies likely to maximize employment for their populations. (V.R.L./E.Lu.)

International Bank for Reconstruction and Development and International Monetary Fund. Two complementary, but separate, organizations, the International Bank (better known as the World Bank) and the International Monetary Fund (IMF), had their origin in wartime preparations for postwar international financial and economic cooperation that culminated in the United Nations Monetary and Financial Conference held in July 1944 at Bretton Woods, New Hampshire, and attended by 44 nations. The principal purposes of the World Bank, set forth in its articles of agreement (charter), may be summarized as follows: to assist in the reconstruction and development of its member countries by facilitating the investment of capital for productive purposes, thereby promoting the long-range growth of international trade and improvement of standards of living; to promote private foreign investment by guarantees of and participation in loans and other investments made by private investors; and to make loans for productive purposes out of its own resources or funds borrowed by it when private capital is not available on reasonable terms.

The World Bank came into existence on December 27, 1945, when its articles of agreement were signed by 29 governments. The bank officially began operations at its headquarters in Washington, D.C., in June 1946. By 1982 the bank had 142 member countries. It had an executive board of 20 states, most of them representing a group of members, and a managing director. Voting in the bank is on a weighted basis according to initial contributions to the bank's capital: in 1982 roughly 60 percent of the votes were held by developed countries, 10 percent by oil-producing countries, and the remaining 30 percent by developing countries.

The World Bank's charter authorized it to engage in the following types of financing: it may lend funds directly, either from its capital funds or from funds that it borrows in private investment markets; it may guarantee loans made by others; or it may participate in such loans. Loans may be made to member countries directly or to any of their political subdivisions or to private business or agricultural enterprises in the territories of members. When the member government in whose territory the project is located is not itself the borrower, however, this member government must guarantee the loan.

The World Bank obtains its funds for loans from paid-in capital subscription, from borrowings in the capital markets of the world, and from net earnings. Sales to investors of portions of the bank's loan portfolio and repayments of loans to the bank, while representing only a recovery of funds originally derived from one of the above sources, have the same effect as new capital in that they reduce the amount the bank would otherwise have to obtain from other sources. The capital markets of the world provide the largest amount of funds for loans. By the late 1960s the bank's outstanding funded debt amounted to more than $4,000,000,000. By the early 1980s the bank was agreeing to lend about $10,000,000,000–$12,000,000,000 a year and had become the largest single source of development finance. Its soft-loan affiliate, the International Development Association (IDA), lends to low-income countries on favourable terms, free of interest except for a small service charge. The International Finance Corporation (IFC), another affiliate of the bank, provides loans to private business in developing countries.

Most of the World Bank's loans at first went for large-scale infrastructure projects—roads, railways, ports, power projects, and telecommunications. Since about 1970 an increasing proportion of World Bank lending has been for agricultural, educational, and population programs.

The International Monetary Fund was designed to stabilize international monetary rates. It came into existence in March 1946 after the ratification and appropriation of funds by national governments had been completed, but the IMF was not actually opened until March 1947, and the first transactions were made in May of that year. Operating funds of the IMF are subscribed by member governments. Each member has a quota, of which an amount equal either to 25 percent of the quota or 10 percent of the member's holdings of gold and U.S. dol-

lars, whichever is smaller, is subscribed in gold and the remainder in national currency. The IMF was designed to stabilize exchange rates by assisting members over temporary difficulties in their international balance of payments. It does so partly by consultation and technical advice, but also by allowing members to purchase from it with their own national currencies the gold or foreign exchange they need. In principle, not more than 25 percent of the member's quota may be purchased in any one year, but in an emergency this limit may be, and often is, waived. Not more than 125 percent of the quota may be purchased in all. Charges begin at 0.5 percent for the first 25 percent for the first year, rising by 0.5 percent for each additional year, with a limit of 5 percent. Members may arrange standby credits to use as and if necessary. The IMF's lending is intended to be for short-term purposes while the borrower overcomes balance of payment problems. Most lending is to developing countries, which—with the increasing cost of imports, uncertain export markets, and heavy debt burdens—have become especially dependent on this help. The IMF has created a number of "facilities" under which it provides loans for countries facing particular difficulties. Members are required to repurchase the excess of their own currencies over their quotas within an agreed period as their balances improve. Members agree not to alter the exchange value of their currencies (except once by no more than 10 percent) without prior IMF agreement.

The expansion of world trade, however, coupled with a succession of international financial crises, created a demand for additional reserves that could be used in settlement of international balances. In October 1969 the IMF voted to distribute a total of $9,500,000,000 in Special Drawing Rights. These served, in effect, to enlarge members' quotas without any additional subscription either in gold or in national currencies, and thus to create a base for new credit expansion. But demands upon international liquidity continued to increase. A realignment of currencies agreed upon in December 1971 included an effective 11-percent devaluation of the U.S. dollar and the upvaluation of other major currencies. Another realignment came after the United States announced a new devaluation of 10 percent in February 1973. A number of countries allowed their currencies to "float"—*i.e.,* to change in value according to market conditions and without formal announcement. (J.H.A./J.B.C./E.Lu./Ed.)

Food and Agriculture Organization. The FAO, first of the permanent specialized agencies of the United Nations to be founded after World War II, came into formal being in October 1945 with the signing of its constitution at a conference held in Quebec. The immediate factor leading to its foundation was the Conference on Food and Agriculture convened at the request of U.S. Pres. Franklin D. Roosevelt at Hot Springs, Virginia, in 1943. In 1951 the organization was transferred from its temporary headquarters in Washington, D.C., to a permanent seat in Rome.

The ideas underlying the foundation of the new organization came from two sources. First was the International Institute of Agriculture founded in Rome in 1905. The IIA had been designed to protect farmers against the effects of sudden slumps and gluts and was, therefore, concerned with information about market trends and agricultural statistics. Second was the League of Nations, which in the period immediately before World War II had been interested in problems of nutrition and their relationship to health. Both the IIA and the League, however, had been principally concerned with the more advanced countries, whereas in the foundation of the FAO several of the new and developing countries took great interest and played an active part.

Because the FAO was in part an answer to the question of feeding vast populations in the countries the economics of which had been seriously disrupted by World War II, it was natural that the first few years should be mainly devoted to trying to help bring about a rapid increase in the world's overall supplies of food. At the same time, the FAO's member countries had an eye on the possible emergence of surpluses of some commodities in certain countries should the distribution system break down or should needy governments not be able to pay for the food

World Bank (margin label)

International Monetary Fund (margin label)

Basis of FAO (margin label)

they required. Finally, an appreciation of the rapid rise in population in virtually all parts of the world in the immediate postwar period added urgency to the organization's work.

With the creation of the United Nations Expanded Programme of Technical Assistance, further extrabudgetary sums became available for the FAO's field operations and from 1950 onward an increasing number of countries received technical assistance from the FAO under the terms of that fund. The range of projects covered all of the FAO's activities in agriculture, nutrition, forestry, fisheries, and economics.

Most of the experts working under the technical-assistance program were on individual assignments, advising governments concerned on specific problems. The FAO also helped its member governments through regional projects, including widespread plant and animal disease control schemes, such as the desert locust-control program in the Arabian Peninsula; projects for the eradication of rinderpest; and creation of a European commission for the control of foot-and-mouth disease. A broad educational program was also in continual operation, with training centres and seminars in many subjects and a fellowship program run in connection with the assignment of technical-assistance experts.

These programs were implemented by various publications and reports of a technical nature, including the *Plant Protection Bulletin,* comprising the work of a worldwide reporting service on plant diseases and quarantine regulations. A parallel informational service for animal diseases included an annual overall summary of developments in the subject field as well as periodical reports. The FAO-sponsored monthly bulletin of agricultural statistics and allied yearbooks on production and trade in agriculture, fisheries, and forest products became standard works in their fields.

United Nations Educational, Scientific and Cultural Organization. The historical roots of UNESCO lie in the intellectual cooperation efforts of the League of Nations and in the 1945 UN founding conferences at San Francisco and London, at which scholars who wanted to help increase the flow and exchange of knowledge drafted the organization's program.

UNESCO's activities were intended to be facilitative; through conferences, seminars, and publications, through the promotion of research and exchange of information and knowledge, and through technical advisory services, it was to assist, support, and seek to complement national efforts of member states. The significance of its activities in the life of any individual nation is limited. Even the allocation of the total budget among the neediest members would provide small amounts compared to what is spent by the countries themselves. The real effect is to be measured by the influence of internationally formulated standards of excellence, by the effectiveness of scholarly communication and exchanges, and by the quality of technical assistance provided.

Administration of UNESCO

UNESCO is administered by a director general and an international civil service of about 1,500 persons, subject to advice and direction from an executive board of 30 (originally 18) members elected by the General Conference and designated by individual member states. Its permanent headquarters are in Paris. The constitution provides for national citizen advisory commissions in member states. The activities of UNESCO are coordinated with those of other UN agencies by the UN Economic and Social Council and by the policies of their respective member states. UNESCO's membership, 44 in 1945, had reached 158 by 1982.

Emphasis has been placed upon strengthening international professional (nongovernmental) organizations in education, science, and culture; establishing clearinghouses for the exchange of information; promoting international professional conferences, symposia, and seminars; and publishing scholarly abstracts. A Universal Copyright Convention and an Agreement on the Importation of Educational, Scientific, and Cultural Materials were drafted and submitted for ratification by member states. Since 1960 an increasing proportion of UNESCO's work has consisted of programs to assist developing countries, for example, in eliminating illiteracy, training teachers, and developing educational institutions. Part of this is financed by funds from the UN Development Programme. UNESCO has also provided assistance in developing library resources, fellowships for study in more highly developed areas of the world, and some pilot projects in so-called fundamental education.

Although UNESCO's contributions have been mainly indirect, exceptions have been the annual *Study Abroad,* a comprehensive index to foreign study opportunities; seminars for teachers on methods to increase international understanding; some modest promotion of social science research into national character and the nature of race; a project urging member states to increase understanding between Asia and the West; and some efforts to promote international exchanges in the arts.

United Nations Children's Fund. The General Assembly established the United Nations International Children's Emergency Fund (later styled the UN Children's Fund but still officially called UNICEF) in December 1946 to provide for the emergency needs of children in devastated areas. Financed by contributions from member states, UNICEF was effective in helping to feed destitute children in more than 100 countries; preventing such diseases as tuberculosis, whooping cough, and diphtheria; and providing for children's clothing and other needs. It was made a permanent UN organization in 1953.   (Ed./E.Lu.)

UNICEF

World Health Organization. WHO, established in 1948, is a specialized agency of the United Nations designed to further international cooperation for improved health conditions. WHO inherited various international duties from the Health Organization of the former League of Nations, set up in 1923, and from the International Office of Public Health at Paris, established in 1909. These duties included epidemic control, quarantine measures, and the standardization of drugs. Under its constitution, however, WHO is given a much broader mandate—to promote the attainment of "the highest possible level of health" by all peoples. Health is defined positively as "a state of complete physical, mental, and social well-being and not merely the absence of disease or infirmity," and good health is held to be fundamental to world peace and security.

The membership of WHO consists of sovereign states and non-self-governing territories, their number growing from 26 in 1948 to 158 in 1982. The organization is financed primarily from annual contributions made by member governments on the basis of relative capacity to pay. The regular annual budget expanded from $5,000,000 in the first year to $234,000,000 by 1982, the largest contributor being the United States, which at first provided approximately one-third of the total. In addition, after 1951 WHO was allocated substantial resources from the expanded technical-assistance program of the UN. Grants for special purposes have been also made to WHO from time to time by private foundations and individual governments.

The work of WHO embraces three fairly distinct categories of activities:

1. The provision of central clearinghouse and research services. As an example, information about the occurrence of pestilential disease anywhere in the world is broadcast over an international radio network to national health authorities, seaports, airports, and ships at sea. In 1952, 13 outdated international sanitary agreements were replaced by a codified set of international sanitary regulations designed to standardize quarantine measures without interfering unnecessarily with trade and air travel across national boundaries. The central WHO secretariat also issues numerous publications, sets statistical standards, and keeps member countries informed of the latest developments in use of vaccines, cancer research, nutritional discoveries, control of drug addiction, and health hazards of nuclear radiation.

2. Measures for the control of epidemic and endemic disease. This category consists chiefly of mass campaigns promoted by WHO against communicable diseases. These campaigns have been successful in eliminating smallpox from the world, largely eliminating plague, and reducing the incidence of several other diseases. The organization

Activities of WHO

launched a worldwide campaign for the complete eradication of malaria. Considerable progress also has been made by the organization in attacking such diseases as cholera, yellow fever, yaws, and trachoma. Among the techniques employed in these campaigns are nationwide vaccination programs, instruction in the use of antibiotics and insecticides, the improvement of laboratory and clinical facilities for early diagnosis and prevention of disease, assistance in providing pure water supplies and adequate sanitation systems, and health education for rural communities. The World Health Organization has promoted the use of paramedics and primary health care in developing countries and has published a code of practice concerning the advertisement of baby foods and a list of simple generic drugs that can be substituted for the relatively more expensive proprietary medicines.

3. Efforts to strengthen and expand the public health administrations of member nations. As its program developed, the World Health Organization set as its most important task the strengthening of national and local health services, especially in nations of Africa, Asia, and Latin America. In furthering this vital objective, a wide variety of devices is utilized. The organization provides technical advice to governments on request in the preparation of long-term national health plans; sends out to the field international teams of experts to conduct surveys and demonstration projects; helps plan and set up local health centres; offers aid in the development of national training institutions for medical and nursing personnel; makes available teachers for on-the-spot short-course training experiments; and makes travelling fellowship awards to doctors, public health administrators, nurses, sanitary inspectors, and laboratory technicians. (W.R.S./E.Lu.)

DEPENDENT AREAS

The United Nations has maintained concern for people living in non-self-governing territories on two different levels: under principles and procedures developed for making administering states internationally accountable for the treatment of their non-self-governing territories, and under the United Nations trusteeship system.

Non-self-governing territories. Under Article 73 of the Charter, members of the United Nations responsible for administering non-self-governing territories agreed to ensure the people of such territories just treatment, protection against abuses, and advancement toward self-government. They also agreed to transmit to the secretary general technical information concerning the economic, social, and educational conditions in their territories. In 1947 the General Assembly created a special committee to receive and analyze information on these territories and to make recommendations to the administering authorities on the basis of information received. Attempts of the committee to obtain political information on territories from the administering states met with resistance in many instances. Only Australia, The Netherlands, New Zealand, and the United States transmitted such information; the other administering states declined, contending that the Charter did not formally require the transmission of political information.

There was considerable controversy over the questions of which territories were non-self-governing and when they ceased to be non-self-governing. France soon stopped transmitting information on a number of territories on the ground that they had either become self-governing or had become an integral part of France. Later, Great Britain ceased to send information on Malta and Ghana, the United States on the Panama Canal Zone and Puerto Rico, Denmark on Greenland, and The Netherlands on Surinam (now Suriname) and the Antilles. Administering states claimed the sole right to decide whether Article 73 (e) did or did not apply to one of their territories, but this position was challenged by the General Assembly, which in 1952 adopted a resolution containing a list of factors to serve as a guide in deciding whether a territory had obtained a full measure of self-government. In 1947 the committee received information on 74 territories with about 215,000,000 inhabitants; by 1956 this had declined to 55 territories with 115,000,000 inhabitants. In 1963

the committee was dissolved and its functions were transferred to a Special Committee on Colonialism that had been created in 1961.

The anticolonial movement in the United Nations reached a high point in 1960, when the General Assembly adopted a resolution sponsored by 43 African and Asian states. This resolution, called the Declaration on the Granting of Independence to Colonial Countries and Peoples, condemned "the subjection of peoples to alien subjugation, domination, and exploitation" and declared that "immediate steps shall be taken . . . to transfer all powers" to the peoples in the colonies "without any conditions or reservations, in accordance with their freely expressed will and desire . . . in order to enable them to enjoy complete independence and freedom . . ." The declaration was adopted by a vote of 89 for and zero against (with nine abstentions).

Spain, Portugal, South Africa, and Southern Rhodesia (whose unilateral declaration of independence in 1965 as Rhodesia was not recognized by the UN) were the chief targets of the anticolonial drive. Spain and Portugal had refused to transmit information on their overseas territories on the ground that they were not dependencies but provinces enjoying constitutional equality with the provinces in the homeland. Southern Rhodesia was a peculiar case; the situation in South Africa was somewhat similar, except that South Africa was completely independent. Hostility toward South Africa, Southern Rhodesia, and Portugal on the part of the other African countries became intense. In the 1970s the Portuguese territories won their independence, and in 1980 Southern Rhodesia was recognized as the independent nation of Zimbabwe. There remained only about 20 dependent territories, mostly small, often isolated islands, many of which did not want independence. Whether or how the principle of decolonization would be applied in these cases appeared uncertain. (L.M.G./A.Va./E.Lu.)

Trusteeship system. The trusteeship system of the UN, the successor to the mandates system of the League of Nations, was established on the principle that colonial territories wrested from defeated enemies should not be annexed by any victorious nation but should be administered by mandatory or trust power under international supervision until they were able to determine their own future status.

Eleven such territories taken from Germany, Italy, and Japan were brought under the trusteeship system after 1945. Other colonial territories could have been voluntarily brought under the system by Article 77 of the UN Charter, but no such action was taken. With the attainment of independence by Togo, the British Cameroons (part of which joined Nigeria, the remainder becoming part of Cameroon), the French Cameroons (now Cameroon), Somalia, Tanganyika (now Tanzania), Western Samoa, Ruanda-Urundi (which became the separate countries of Rwanda and Burundi), New Guinea (now part of Papua New Guinea), and Nauru, by 1980 only the Trust Territory of the Pacific Islands remained under trusteeship. Failure to utilize the trusteeship system for other colonial areas was attributed for the most part to two principal developments. First, after 1945 many colonies attained independence without being made subject to the trusteeship system. Second, the colonial powers were reluctant to bring their colonial territories under the system because of the critical and even hostile attitude shown in the debates of the United Nations toward any form of colonial relationship.

The UN trusteeship system differed in two important respects from the mandate system of the League of Nations. The first difference was the provision that facilitated the submission of petitions from inhabitants of the trust territory or from any other source. In addition, the Charter provided that a petitioner might appear in person to present his case orally before the Trusteeship Council or the General Assembly. Tens of thousands of written petitions were submitted to the United Nations. Indeed, the flood of petitions was sometimes so great that it was difficult to work out a procedure for handling them efficiently and expeditiously. The second basic innovation

[margin note:] Declaration on the Granting of Independence to Colonial Countries and Peoples (1960)

[margin note:] Differences between the mandate and trusteeship systems

that differentiated the trusteeship system from the mandate system was the Charter provision for periodic visits by UN missions to the trust territories. In practice, each territory was visited by such a mission every three years. The purpose of the missions was to supplement information provided in the annual reports of the administering authorities and to provide what were regarded as objective and impartial evaluations of the conditions observed in each territory. Each visiting mission was composed of two persons drawn from administering countries and two selected from nonadministering countries, accompanied by five or six members of the UN Secretariat. The two members from administering countries were not drawn from among the nationals of the country administering the territory to be visited.

The Trusteeship Council was established by the Charter under the authority of the UN General Assembly. The council was empowered to consider reports made to it by the administering authorities, accept and examine petitions in consultation with the appropriate administering authority, provide for periodic visiting missions to the respective trust territories, and take such other actions as might be in conformity with the terms of trusteeship agreements between each administering authority and the General Assembly or, in the case of a strategic trust territory, with the Security Council.

The Trusteeship Council was to consist of an equal number of members administering trust territories and members not administering such territories, provided all of the permanent members of the Security Council were also to be members of the Trusteeship Council. To keep the council in balance there were to be as many nonadministering members elected for three-year terms as would be necessary to ensure that the council was equally divided between the administering and nonadministering members.   (O.B.G.)

All of the former mandatory powers entered into UN trusteeship agreements after 1945 except South Africa, which refused to enter into such an agreement for the mandated territory of South West Africa. The United States became a member of the Trusteeship Council both by virtue of the fact that it was a permanent member of the Security Council and because it negotiated an agreement with the UN regarding the Pacific Islands territories, which it had taken from Japan during World War II. The territories placed in trusteeship were almost all former League of Nations mandated territories once under German control, together with two territories controlled by Italy and Japan. The council supervised the arrangements made in the territories under its authority, sent occasional visiting missions, and issued reports about the progress made in each case. Because the essential decisions were made by the administering powers, however, the transition to independence was not significantly different from that which took place in the colonies. Most of the trust territories secured independence by 1970, and all except the Trust Territory of the Pacific Islands by 1980.

Strategic areas

(O.B.G./E.Lu.)

The UN Charter (Article 82) provided that certain areas, which might include part or all of a trust territory, could be designated as strategic areas. This provision was placed in the Charter in 1945 on the initiative of the United States, and in 1947 a strategic trusteeship agreement was concluded between the United States and the United Nations that placed the Pacific Islands (the Marshalls, Marianas, and Carolines) under the trusteeship system. All of the other trust agreements were made between the administering authority and the General Assembly, but that for the Pacific Islands was made with the Security Council. In practice, however, there was no appreciable difference in the way the two types of territories were handled within the system. In the agreement with the Security Council the United States provided that it might close off any area for security reasons. This provision was never put into effect, and the United States freely permitted UN visiting missions to go through the territory and agreed that the Trusteeship Council should examine the annual reports on political, economic, and social conditions in the territory.   (O.B.G.)

Administration

FINANCES

The secretary general must submit an annual budget including estimated expenditures to the General Assembly for approval. The Charter stipulates that the expenses of the organization shall be borne by members as apportioned by the General Assembly. The Committee on Contributions prepares a scale of assessments for each member, based on the general economic level and capacity of each state, and this scale is submitted to the General Assembly for approval. The United States is the largest contributor, but other members make a larger per capita contribution. The U.S. assessment began at 49 percent of the total, but, at the request of the United States government, this figure was steadily reduced until in 1982 it was 25 percent.

The normal operating expenses of the United Nations increased from $19,000,000 in 1946 to more than $600,000,-000 in 1982. When the cost of the special programs, specialized agencies, and peacekeeping operations was added to the regular budget, the total annual cost of the United Nations system became much greater. The special programs are financed by voluntary contributions of the members of the United Nations, and the specialized agencies have their own budgets. The rapid increase in membership after 1955 did not help UN finances, for most of the new members were economically weak. Nearly all of them needed help, and their financial contributions to the UN were minimal.

SECRETARIAT

The organization is served by a substantial Secretariat, which is responsible for preparing numerous reports, studies, and investigations, in addition to the major tasks of providing services for large numbers of meetings, translating, interpreting, and other work. Under the Charter the staff is to be recruited mainly on the basis of merit, but "due regard is to be paid to the importance of recruiting the staff on as wide a geographical basis as possible." Some members of the Secretariat are engaged on permanent contracts, while others serve on temporary secondment from their national governments. In both cases, they must take an oath of loyalty to the UN and are not to receive instructions from member governments.

A United Nations Field Service and a United Nations Panel of Field Observers were organized by the General Assembly in 1949. The Field Service looks after the safety of UN missions in many parts of the world, and the Panel of Field Observers assists the various missions in supervising truces and observing plebiscites. Both are under the supervision of the secretary general.

PRIVILEGES AND IMMUNITIES

A General Convention on Privileges and Immunities of the United Nations, approved by the General Assembly in February 1946 and accepted by most of the members except the United States, asserted that the UN possesses juridical personality. The convention also provided for such matters as immunity from legal process of the property and officials of the United Nations. An agreement between the UN and the United States, signed in June 1947, defined the privileges and immunities of the UN headquarters in New York City.

HEADQUARTERS

The General Assembly decided during the second part of its first session in New York City to locate its permanent headquarters there. John D. Rockefeller, Jr., gave land for a building site in Manhattan. Temporary headquarters were established at Lake Success on Long Island, New York. The permanent Secretariat building was completed and occupied in 1951. The building providing accommodations for the General Assembly and the councils was completed and occupied in early 1952.

The design of the UN flag, adopted in 1947, consists of the official emblem of the UN in white centred on a light-blue background. The Assembly designated October 24 as United Nations Day.   (L.M.G./A.Va./E.Lu.)

BIBLIOGRAPHY. ROBERT E. ASHER *et al., The United Nations and Promotion of the General Welfare* (1957); INIS L. CLAUDE, *Swords into Plowshares: The Problems and Progress of International Organization,* 4th ed. (1971), and *The Changing United Nations* (1967); ERNEST A. GROSS, *The United Nations: Structure for Peace* (1962); HERBERT G. NICHOLAS, *The United Nations as a Political Institution,* 5th ed. (1975); MAURICE WATERS, *The United Nations: International Organization and Administration* (1967); LEON GORDENKER, *The UN Secretary-General and the Maintenance of Peace* (1967); ROSALYN HIGGINS, *United Nations Peacekeeping: Documents and Commentary,* 4 vol. (1969–81); MARK W. ZACHER, *Dag Hammarskjöld's United Nations* (1970); PETER I. HAJNAL, *Guide to United Nations Organization, Documentation & Publishing for Students, Researchers, Librarians* (1978); EVAN LUARD, *International Agencies: The Emerging Framework of Interdependence* (1977), and *The United Nations:*

How It Works and What It Does (1979); UNITED NATIONS. DEPARTMENT OF PUBLIC INFORMATION, *Everyman's United Nations,* 8th ed. (1968), and *Everyone's United Nations,* 9th ed. (1979). Contemporary information is found in the *Yearbook of the United Nations;* the *UN Chronicle* (monthly); and the *Report of the Secretary-General on the Work of the Organization* (annual). See also *Your United Nations: The Official Guidebook* (1982); *United Nations, Image and Reality: Questions and Answers About Management, Finance, and People* (1981); EVAN LUARD, *A History of the United Nations: The Years of Western Domination, 1945–1955* (1982); JOHN F. MURPHY, *The United Nations and the Control of International Violence: A Legal and Political Analysis* (1982); HANNA NEWCOMBE, *Design for a Better World* (1983); PETER I. HAJNAL, *Guide to UNESCO* (1983); and TOBY TRISTER GATI (ed.), *The US, the UN, and the Management of Global Change* (1983).

United States of America

The foremost country in the Western Hemisphere in population and economic development, the United States of America is a federal republic composed of 50 states. It is often referred to simply as the United States or, colloquially, as America. The 48 conterminous states, which occupy the central one-third of North America, are bounded on the west by the Pacific Ocean, on the north by Canada, on the east by the Atlantic Ocean, and on the south by Mexico and arms of the Atlantic and Pacific. The newest states, Alaska and Hawaii, lie at the northwestern extremity of the continent and in the mid-Pacific, respectively.

The total area of the country is 3,615,122 square miles (9,363,123 square kilometres), making it the fourth largest in the world in area (after the Soviet Union, Canada, and China). Such outlying possessions as the Virgin Islands, the United Nations Trust Territory of the Pacific Islands, and the U.S. unincorporated territories in the Pacific and such politically related entities as the Commonwealth of Puerto Rico add approximately 13,000 square miles to this figure.

The major characteristic of the United States is probably its great variety. Its physical environment ranges from the Arctic to the subtropical, from the moist rain forest to the arid desert, from the bald mountain peak to the flat prairie. Its people probably embrace a wider range of racial, ethnic, and cultural types than any other country in the world. Quite apart from the presence of surviving American Indians and the descendants of slaves brought from Africa, the United States shows the effects of having taken in about 35,000,000 immigrants from around the world between the declaration of national independence in 1776 and the imposition of immigration quotas in 1921. Its natural resources, though increasingly depleted or seriously polluted in some areas, continued to sustain an economic life that is more diversified than any other on Earth, providing the majority of its people with a high standard of living. Although the United States still offers its residents opportunities for unparalleled personal advancement and wealth, it also contains areas of poverty and blight that have become an increasing threat to the social and political fabric of the country.

The article is divided into the following sections:

PHYSICAL AND HUMAN GEOGRAPHY

The land

The two great sets of elements that mold the physical environment of the United States are, first, the geologic, which determines the main patterns of landforms, drainage, and mineral resources and influences soils to a lesser degree, and, second, the atmospheric, which dictates not only climate and weather but also in large part the distribution of soils, plants, and animals. Although geologic and atmospheric processes are not entirely independent of one another, each produces on a map patterns that are so profoundly different that essentially they remain two separate geographies. (Since this portion of the article covers only the conterminous United States, see also the sections in this article on *Alaska* and *Hawaii*.)

RELIEF

The grand geological pattern

The centre of the conterminous United States is a great sprawling interior lowland, reaching from the ancient shield of central Canada on the north to the Gulf of Mexico on the south. To east and west this lowland rises first gradually, then abruptly, to mountain ranges that divide it from the sea on both sides. The two mountain systems differ drastically. The Appalachians on the east are low, almost unbroken, and in the main set well back from the Atlantic. From New York City to the Mexican border stretches the low Coastal Plain; its swampy and convoluted shoreline merges almost imperceptibly with the ocean. Southward the plain grows wider, swinging westward in Georgia and Alabama to truncate the Appalachians along their southern extremity and separate the interior lowland from the Gulf.

West of the Central Lowlands is the mighty Cordillera, part of the global mountain system that entirely rings the Pacific Basin. The Cordillera encompasses fully one-third of the United States, with an internal variety commensurate with its size. At its eastern margin lie the Rocky Mountains, a high, diverse, and discontinuous chain that stretches all the way from New Mexico to the Canadian border. The Cordillera's western edge is a Pacific coastal chain of rugged mountains and inland valleys, the whole rising spectacularly from the sea without benefit of a coastal plain. Pent between the Rockies and the Pacific chain is a vast intermontane complex of basins, plateaus, and isolated ranges, so large and remarkable that they merit recognition as a region separate from the Cordillera itself.

These regions—the Interior Lowlands and their upland fringes, the Appalachian Mountain system, the Atlantic Plain, the Western Cordillera, and the Western Intermontane Region—contain so much variety that they require further division into 24 major subregions (see map).

The Interior Lowlands and their upland fringes.   Andrew Jackson is supposed to have remarked that the United States begins at the Alleghenies, implying that only west of the mountains, in the isolation and freedom of the great Interior Lowlands, could people finally escape Old World influences. Whether or not the lowlands constitute the country's cultural core is debatable, but there can be no doubt that they comprise its geological core and in many ways its geographical core as well.

This enormous region rests upon an ancient, much-eroded platform of complex crystalline rocks that have lain undisturbed by major orogenic (mountain-building) activity for more than 600,000,000 years. Over much of central Canada, these old rocks are exposed at the surface and form the continent's single largest topographic region, the formidable and ice-scoured Canadian Shield.

The midcontinent of the nation

In the United States most of the crystalline platform is concealed under a deep blanket of sedimentary rocks. In the far north, however, the naked shield extends into the United States far enough to form two small but distinctive landform regions: the rugged and occasionally spectacular Adirondack Mountains of northern New York; and the more subdued but austere Superior Uplands of northern Minnesota, Wisconsin, and Michigan. As in the rest of the shield, glaciers have stripped soils away, strewn the surface with boulders and other debris, and obliterated preglacial drainage systems. Most attempts at farming in these regions have been abandoned, but the combination of a comparative wilderness in a northern climate, clear lakes, and white-water streams have turned both areas into seasonal vacationlands.

Mineral wealth in the Superior Uplands is legendary. Iron lies near the surface and close to the deepwater ports of the lower Great Lakes. Iron is mined both north and south of Lake Superior, but most famous are the colossal deposits of Minnesota's Mesabi Range, known for more than a century as one of the world's richest and a vital element in America's rise to industrial power. In spite of depletion, the Minnesota and Michigan mines still yield about 80 percent of the country's iron and a significant percentage of the world's supply.

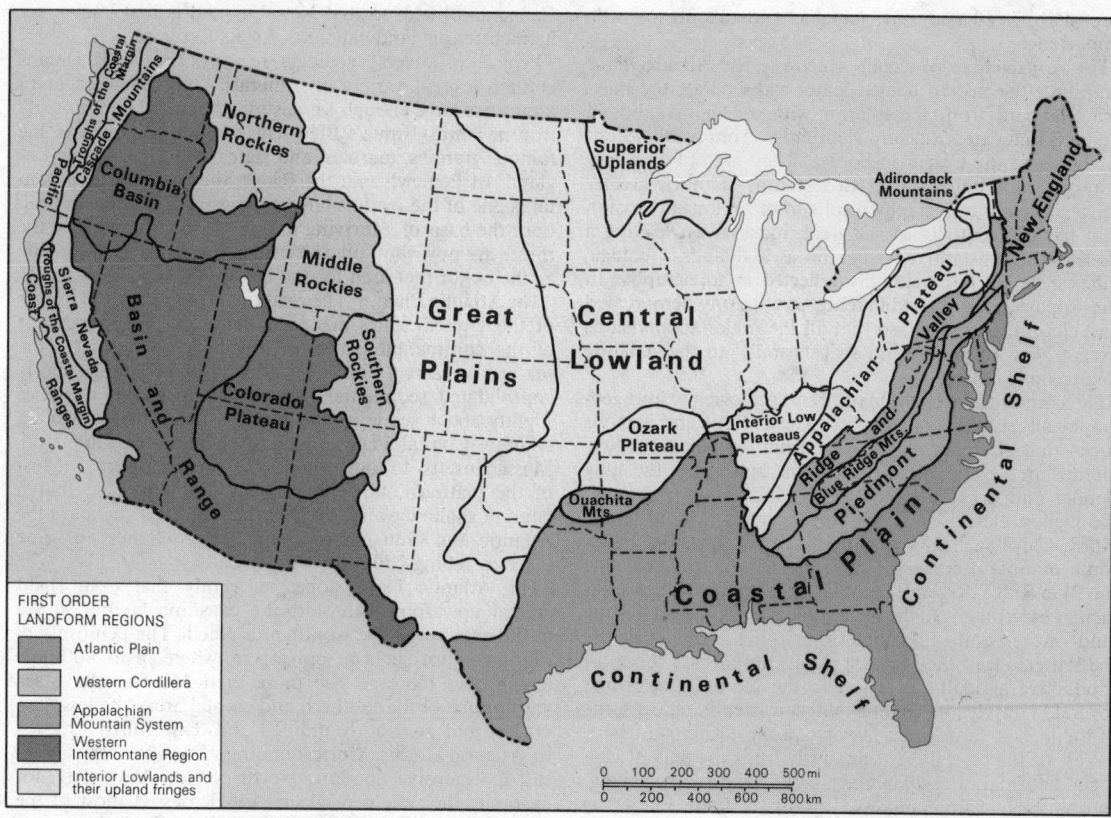

Physiographic regions of the United States.

South of the Adirondacks and Superior Uplands lies the boundary between crystalline and sedimentary rocks; abruptly, everything is different. The core of this sedimentary region—quite literally the heartland of the United States—is the great Central Lowland, which stretches for 1,500 miles (2,400 kilometres) from New York to central Texas and north another 1,000 miles to the Canadian province of Saskatchewan. To some, the landscape may seem dull, for heights of more than 2,000 feet (600 metres) are unusual, and truly rough terrain is almost unknown. Landscapes are varied, however, largely as the result of glaciation that directly or indirectly affected most of the region. North of the Missouri–Ohio river line, the advance and readvance of continental ice left an intricate mosaic of boulders, sand, gravel, silt, and clay and a complex pattern of lakes and drainage channels, some abandoned, some still in use. The southern part of the Central Lowland is quite different, covered mostly with wind-borne loess that subdued the already low relief to nearly billiard-table flatness. Elsewhere, especially near major rivers, postglacial streams carved the loess into rounded hills, and visitors have aptly compared their billowing shapes to the waves of the sea. Above all, the loess produces soil of extraordinary fertility. As the Mesabi iron is a major source of America's industrial wealth, its agricultural prosperity is in large part rooted in Midwestern loess.

The Central Lowland resembles a vast saucer, rising gradually to higher lands on all sides. Southward and eastward, the land climbs gradually to three major plateaus. Beyond the reach of glaciation to the south, the sedimentary rocks have been raised into two broad upwarps, separated from one another by the great valley of the Mississippi River. The Ozark Plateau lies west of the river and occupies most of southern Missouri and northern Arkansas; on the east the Interior Low Plateaus dominate central Kentucky and Tennessee. Except for two nearly circular patches of rich limestone country—the Nashville Basin of Tennessee and the fabled racehorse country of the Kentucky Bluegrass—most of both plateau regions is sandstone uplands, intricately dissected by streams. Local relief runs to several hundreds of feet in most places, and visitors to the region must travel winding roads along narrow stream valleys. The soils there are poor, and mineral resources are scanty.

Eastward from the Central Lowland the Appalachian Plateau—a narrow band of dissected uplands that strongly resembles the Ozark Plateau and Interior Low Plateaus in steep slopes, wretched soils, and endemic poverty—forms a transition between the interior plains and the Appalachian Mountains. Usually, however, the Appalachian Plateau is considered a subregion of the Appalachian Mountains, partly on grounds of location, partly because of geologic structure. Unlike the other plateaus, where rocks are warped upward, the rocks there form a long narrow basin, wherein bituminous coal has been preserved from erosion. This Appalachian coal, like the Mesabi iron that it complements in U.S. industry, is extraordinary. Extensive, thick, and close to the surface, it has stoked the furnaces of northeastern steel mills for decades and helps explain the huge concentration of heavy industry along the lower Great Lakes.

The western flanks of the Interior Lowlands are the Great Plains, a region of awesome bulk that spans the full distance between Canada and Mexico in a swath nearly 500 miles wide. The Great Plains were built by successive layers of poorly cemented sand, silt, and gravel—debris laid down by parallel east-flowing streams from the Rocky Mountains. Seen from the east, the surface of the Great Plains rises inexorably from about 2,000 feet near Omaha, Nebraska, to more than 6,000 feet at Cheyenne, Wyoming, but the climb is so gradual that popular legend holds the Great Plains to be flat. True flatness is rare, although the High Plains of western Texas, Oklahoma, Kansas, and eastern Colorado come close. More commonly, the land is broadly rolling, and parts of the northern plains are sharply dissected into "badlands."

The main mineral wealth of the Interior Lowlands derives from fossil fuels, scarcely surprising in a region underlain by sedimentary rocks. Coal occurs in structural basins protected from erosion—high-quality bituminous in the Appalachian, Illinois, and western Kentucky basins; and poorer bituminous and lignite in the eastern and northwestern Great Plains. Petroleum and natural gas have been found in nearly every state between the Appalachians and the Rockies, but the Midcontinent Fields of western Texas, the Texas Panhandle, Oklahoma, and Kansas surpass all others in the Interior Lowlands. Aside from small

The plateaus surrounding the midcontinent

The Great Plains

deposits of lead and zinc, metallic minerals are of little importance.

The Appalachian Mountain system.   The Appalachians dominate the eastern United States and separate the Eastern Seaboard from the interior with a belt of subdued uplands that extends nearly 1,500 miles from northeastern Alabama to the Canadian border. They are old and very complex mountains, the eroded stumps of much greater ranges. Present topography results from prolonged erosion that has differentially carved weak rocks away, leaving a skeleton of resistant rocks behind as highlands. Geologic differences are thus faithfully reflected in topography. In the Appalachians these differences are sharply demarcated and elegantly arranged, so that all the major subdivisions except New England lie in strips parallel to the Atlantic and to one another.

The core of the Appalachians, both geologically and geographically, is a belt of complex metamorphic and igneous rocks that stretches all the way from Alabama to New Hampshire. The western side of this belt forms the long slender rampart of the Blue Ridge Mountains, containing the highest elevations in the Appalachians (Mt. Mitchell, North Carolina, 6,684 feet) and some of its most handsome mountain scenery. On its eastern, or seaward, side the Blue Ridge descends in an abrupt and sometimes spectacular escarpment to the Piedmont, a well-drained, rolling land—never quite hills, but never quite a plain. Before the settlement of the Midwest the Piedmont was the most productive agricultural region in the United States, and several Pennsylvania counties still consistently report some of the highest farm yields per acre in the entire country.

West of the crystalline zone, away from the axis of geologic deformation, sedimentary rocks have escaped metamorphism but are compressed into tight folds, like a rug that has slid and crumpled on a slippery floor. Erosion has carved the upturned edges of these folded rocks into the remarkable Ridge and Valley country of the western Appalachians. Seen from the air, this region looks as if some cosmic rake had been dragged for more than 1,000 miles along the length of the Appalachian system. Long linear ridges characteristically stand about 1,000 feet from base to crest and run for tens of miles, paralleled by broad open valleys of comparable length. In Pennsylvania ridges run unbroken for great distances, occasionally turning abruptly in a zigzag pattern; by contrast, the southern ridges are broken by faults and form short parallel segments that are lined up like magnetized iron filings. By far the largest valley—and one of the most important routes in North America—is the Great Valley, an extraordinary trench of shale and limestone that runs nearly the entire length of the Appalachians. It provides a lowland passage from the middle Hudson Valley to Harrisburg, Pennsylvania, and on southward where it forms the Cumberland and Shenandoah valleys, one of the main paths through the Appalachians since pioneer times. In New England it is floored with slates and marbles and forms the Valley of Vermont, one of the few fertile areas in an otherwise mountainous region.

Topography much like that of the Ridge and Valley is found in the Ouachita Mountains of western Arkansas and eastern Oklahoma, an area generally thought to be a detached continuation of Appalachian geologic structure, the intervening section buried beneath the sediments of the lower Mississippi Valley.

The New England mountain systems

The glaciated New England section of the Appalachians is divided from the rest of the chain by an indentation of the Atlantic. Although almost completely underlain by crystalline rocks, New England is laid out in north–south bands, reminiscent of the southern Appalachians. The rolling, rocky hills of southeastern New England are not dissimilar to the Piedmont, while, farther northwest, the rugged and lofty White Mountains are an obvious New England analogue to the Blue Ridge. (Mt. Washington, New Hampshire, at 6,288 feet is the highest peak in the northeastern United States.) The westernmost ranges—the Taconics, Berkshires, and Green Mountains—show a strong north–south lineation like the Ridge and Valley. Unlike the rest of the Appalachians, however, glaciation has scoured the crystalline rocks much like those of the

Canadian Shield, so that New England is best known for its picturesque landscape, not for its fertile soil.

Typical of diverse geologic regions, the Appalachians contain a great variety of minerals. Only a few occur in quantities large enough for sustained exploitation, notably iron in Pennsylvania's Blue Ridge and Piedmont and the famous granites, marbles, and slates of northern New England. In Pennsylvania the Ridge and Valley region contains one of the world's largest deposits of anthracite coal, once the basis of a thriving mining economy; many of the mines are now shut, oil and gas having replaced anthracite as the major fuel used for the heating of U.S. homes.

The Atlantic Plain.   The eastern and southeastern fringes of the United States are part of the outermost margins of the continental platform, repeatedly invaded by the sea and veneered with layer after layer of young, poorly consolidated sediments. Part of this platform now lies slightly above sea level and forms a nearly flat and often swampy Coastal Plain, which stretches from Cape Cod, Massachusetts, to and beyond the Mexican border. Most of the platform, however, is still submerged, so that a band of shallow water, the Continental Shelf, parallels the Atlantic and Gulf coasts of the United States, in some places reaching 250 miles out to sea.

Coastal uplifts and depressions

The Atlantic Plain slopes so gently that even slight crustal upwarping can shift the coastline far out to sea at the expense of the Continental Shelf. The peninsula of Florida is just such an upwarp; nowhere in its 400-mile length does the land rise more than 350 feet above sea level; much of the southern and coastal areas rise less than 10 feet and are poorly drained and dangerously exposed to Atlantic storms. Correspondingly, downwarps can result in extensive flooding. North of New York City, for example, the weight of glacial ice depressed most of the Coastal Plain beneath the sea, and the Atlantic now beats directly against New England's rock-ribbed coasts. Cape Cod, Long Island, and a few offshore islands are all that remain of New England's drowned Coastal Plain. Another downwarp lies perpendicular to the Gulf coast and guides the course of the Lower Mississippi. The river, however, has filled with alluvium what otherwise would be an arm of the Gulf, forming a great inland salient of the Coastal Plain called the Mississippi Embayment.

South of New York the Coastal Plain gradually widens, but ocean water has invaded the lower valleys of most of the coastal rivers and has turned them into estuaries. The greatest of these is Chesapeake Bay, merely the flooded lower valley of the Susquehanna and its tributaries, but there are literally hundreds of others. Offshore a line of sandbars and barrier beaches stretches intermittently the length of the Coastal Plain, hampering entry of shipping into the estuaries but providing the crowded eastern United States with a marine playground that is more than 1,000 miles long.

Poor soils are the rule on the Coastal Plain, though rare exceptions have formed some of America's most famous agricultural regions—for example, the citrus country of central Florida's limestone uplands and the Cotton Belt of the Old South, once centred on the alluvial plain of the Mississippi and belts of chalky black soils of eastern Texas, Alabama, and Mississippi. The Atlantic Plain's greatest natural wealth derives from petroleum and natural gas trapped in domal structures that dot the Gulf coast of eastern Texas and Louisiana. Onshore and offshore drilling have revealed colossal reserves, and Louisiana alone produces almost one-seventh of the country's crude oil and one-eighth of the natural gas in the world.

The Western Cordillera.   West of the Great Plains the United States seems to become another world, a craggy land whose skyline is rarely without mountains—totally different from the open plains and rounded hills of the East. On a map the alignment of the two main chains—the Rockies on the east, the Pacific ranges on the west—tempts one to assume a certain geologic and hence topographic homogeneity. Nothing could be farther from the truth, for each chain is divided into widely disparate sections.

The Rockies are typically diverse. The Southern Rockies are composed of a disconnected series of lofty elongated

Diversity
of the
Rocky
Mountain
chains

upwarps, their cores made of granitic basement rocks, stripped of sediments, and heavily glaciated at high elevations. In New Mexico and along the western flanks of the Colorado ranges, widespread volcanism and deformation of colourful sedimentary rocks have produced rugged and picturesque country, but the characteristic central Colorado or southern Wyoming range is impressively austere rather than spectacular. The Front Range west of Denver is prototypical, rising abruptly from its base to rolling alpine meadows between 11,000 and 12,000 feet. Peaks appear as low hills perched on this high-level surface, so that Colorado, for example, boasts 53 mountains over 14,000 feet but not one over 14,500 feet.

The Middle Rockies cover most of west central Wyoming. Most of the ranges resemble the granitic upwarps of Colorado, but thrust faulting and volcanism have produced varied and spectacular country to the west, some of which is included in Grand Teton and Yellowstone national parks. Much of the region, however, is not mountainous at all but consists of extensive intermontane basins and plains—largely floored with enormous volumes of sedimentary waste eroded from the mountains themselves. Whole ranges have been buried, producing the greatest gap in the Cordilleran system, the Wyoming Basin—which is an intermontane peninsula of the Great Plains. As a result, the Rockies have never posed an important barrier to east–west transportation in the United States; all major routes, from the Oregon Trail to interstate highways, funnel through the basin, essentially circumventing the Rockies.

The Northern Rockies contain the most varied mountain landscapes of the Cordillera, reflecting a corresponding geologic complexity. The region's backbone is a mighty series of batholiths—huge masses of molten rock that slowly cooled below the surface and were later uplifted. The batholiths are eroded into rugged granitic ranges, which, in central Idaho, compose the most extensive wilderness country in the conterminous United States. East of the batholiths and opposite the Great Plains, sediments have been folded and thrust-faulted into a series of linear north–south ranges, a southern extension of the spectacular Canadian Rockies. Although elevations run 2,000 to 3,000 feet lower than the Colorado Rockies (most of the Idaho Rockies lie well below 10,000 feet), increased rainfall and northern latitude have encouraged glaciation—there as elsewhere a sculptor of handsome alpine landscape.

The Pacific
mountain
chains

The western branch of the Cordillera directly abuts the Pacific Ocean. This coastal chain, like its Rocky Mountain cousins on the eastern flank of the Cordillera, conceals bewildering complexity behind a facade of apparent simplicity. At first glance the chain consists merely of two lines of mountains with a discontinuous trough between them. Immediately behind the coast is a line of hills and low mountains—the Pacific Coast Ranges. Farther inland, averaging 150 miles from the coast, the line of the Sierra Nevada and the Cascade Range includes the highest elevations in the conterminous United States. Between these two unequal mountain lines is a discontinuous trench, the Troughs of the Coastal Margin.

The apparent simplicity disappears under the most cursory examination. The Pacific Coast Ranges actually contain five distinct sections, each of different geologic origin, and each with its own distinctive topography. The Transverse Ranges of southern California are a crowded assemblage of barren island-like ranges, with peak elevations of more than 10,000 feet but sufficiently separated by plains and low passes so that travel through them is easy. From Point Conception to the Oregon border, however, the main California Coast Ranges are entirely different, resembling the Appalachian Ridge and Valley region, with low linear ranges that result from erosion of faulted and folded rocks. Major faults run parallel to the low ridges, and the greatest—the notorious San Andreas Fault—was responsible for the earthquake that all but destroyed San Francisco in 1906. Along the California–Oregon line, everything changes again. In this region, the wildly rugged Klamath Mountains represent a western salient of interior structure reminiscent of the Idaho Rockies and the northern Sierra Nevada. In western Oregon and southwestern Washington

the Coast Ranges are also different—a gentle, hilly land carved by streams from a broad arch of marine deposits interbedded with tabular lavas. In the northernmost part of the Coast Ranges and the remote northwesternmost corner of the conterminous United States, a domal upwarp has produced the Olympic Mountains; its serrated peaks tower nearly 8,000 feet above Puget Sound and the Pacific, and its upper slopes still support the largest active glaciers in the United States outside of Alaska.

East of these Pacific Coast Ranges the Troughs of the Coastal Margin contain the only extensive lowland plains of the Pacific margin—California's Central Valley, Oregon's Willamette Valley, and the half-drowned basin of Puget Sound in Washington. Parts of an inland trench that extends for great distances along the east coast of the Pacific, similar valleys occur in such diverse areas as Chile and the Alaska Panhandle. These valleys are blessed with superior soils, easily irrigated, and very accessible from the Pacific. They have enticed settlers for more than a century and have become the main centres of population and economic activity for much of the United States West Coast.

Still farther east rise the two highest mountain chains in the conterminous United States—the Cascades and the Sierra Nevada. Aside from elevation, geographical continuity, and spectacular scenery, however, the two ranges differ in almost every important respect. Except for its northern section, where sedimentary and metamorphic rocks occur, the Sierra Nevada is largely made of granite, part of the same batholithic chain that creates the Idaho Rockies. The range is grossly asymmetrical, the result of massive faulting that has gently tilted the western slopes toward the Central Valley but has uplifted the eastern side to confront the interior with an awesome escarpment nearly two miles high. At high elevation glaciers have scoured the granites to an astonishing gleaming white, while on the west the ice has carved spectacular valleys such as the Yosemite. The loftiest peak in the Sierras is Mt. Whitney, which, at 14,494 feet, is the highest mountain in the coterminous states. The upfaulting that produced Mt. Whitney is accompanied by downfaulting that formed nearby Death Valley, at 282 feet below sea level the lowest point in North America.

The Cascades are made of volcanic rock; those in northern Washington contain granite like the Sierras, but the rest are formed from relatively recent lava outpourings of dun-coloured basalt and andesite. The Cascades are in effect two ranges. The lower, older range is a long belt of upwarped lava, rising unspectacularly to elevations between 6,000 and 8,000 feet. Perched above the "low Cascades" is a chain of lofty quiescent (until Mt. St. Helens' 1980 eruption) volcanoes that punctuate the horizon with magnificent glacier-clad peaks. The highest is Mt. Rainier, whose 14,410 feet are all the more dramatic for rising from near sea level.

The
Cascades
and Sierras

The Western Intermontane Region. The Cordillera's two main chains enclose a vast intermontane region of arid basins, plateaus, and isolated mountain ranges that stretches from the Mexican border nearly to Canada and extends 600 miles from east to west. This enormous territory contains three huge subregions, each with a distinctive geologic history and its own striking topographic personality.

The Colorado Plateau, nestled against the western flanks of the Southern Rockies, is an extraordinary island of geologic stability set in the turbulent sea of Cordilleran tectonic activity. Stability was not absolute, of course, so that parts of the plateau are warped and injected with volcanics, but in general the landscape results from the erosion by streams of nearly flat-lying sedimentary rocks. The result is a mosaic of angular mesas, buttes, and steplike canyons intricately cut from rocks that often are vividly coloured. Large areas of the plateau are so improbably picturesque that they have been set aside as national preserves. The Grand Canyon of the Colorado River is the most famous of several dozen such areas.

West of the plateau and abutting the Sierra Nevada's eastern escarpment lies the barren, arid Basin and Range, among the most remarkable topographic provinces of the United States. Rocks of great complexity have been bro-

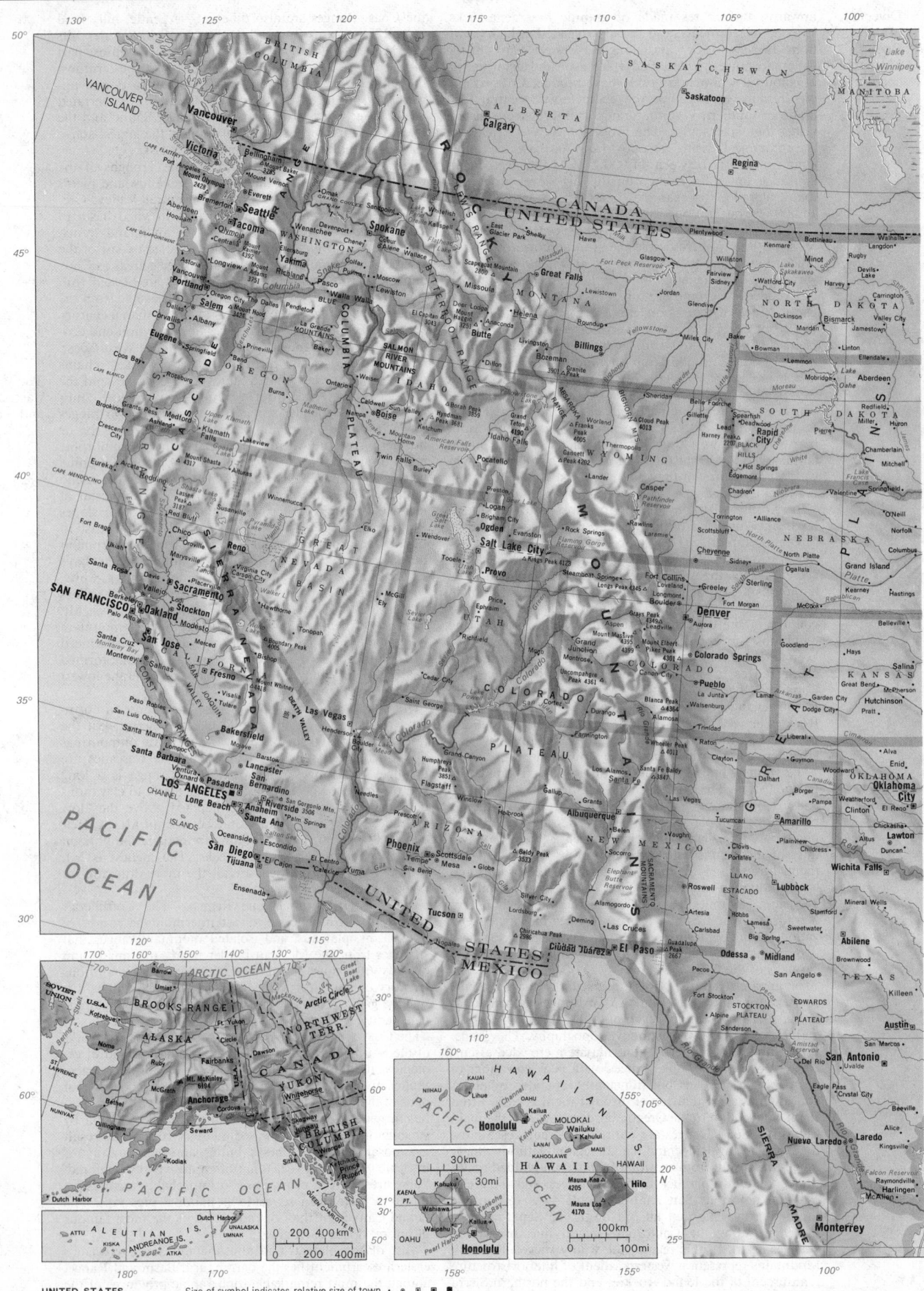

UNITED STATES   Size of symbol indicates relative size of town • ▫ ⊡ ■ ▪

Elevations in metres

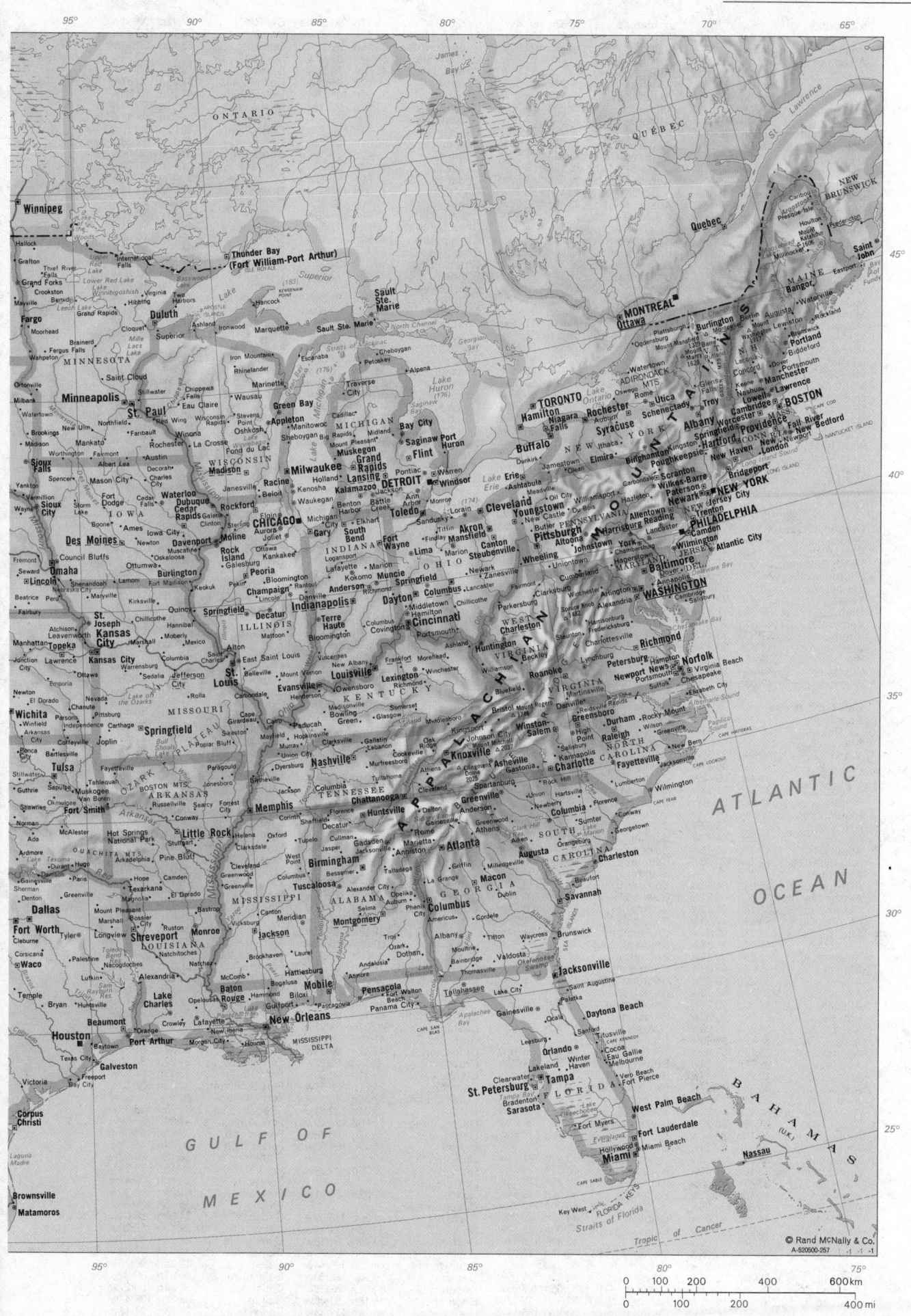

95°　　90°　　85°　　80°　　75°　　70°　　65°

ONTARIO

QUÉBEC

NEW BRUNSWICK

Winnipeg

Thunder Bay
(Fort William-Port Arthur)

45°

Duluth

Saint John

Fargo

MINNESOTA

Minneapolis
St. Paul

WISCONSIN

Green Bay

MICHIGAN

MONTREAL

Ottawa

MAINE

Bangor

TORONTO

Hamilton

Rochester

Syracuse

BOSTON

Sioux Falls

Madison

Milwaukee

Grand Rapids

Lansing

DETROIT

Buffalo

NEW YORK

Albany

40°

IOWA

Des Moines

Rockford

CHICAGO

Gary

South Bend

Fort Wayne

Cleveland

PENNSYLVANIA

Pittsburgh

NEW YORK

Philadelphia

Omaha

Lincoln

ILLINOIS

Peoria

INDIANA

OHIO

Columbus

Dayton

Cincinnati

WEST VIRGINIA

WASHINGTON

Baltimore

Kansas City

Topeka

St. Louis

Louisville

Lexington

KENTUCKY

VIRGINIA

Richmond

35°

Wichita

MISSOURI

Springfield

Nashville

TENNESSEE

Knoxville

Asheville

Charlotte

NORTH CAROLINA

Tulsa

ARKANSAS

Memphis

Chattanooga

Atlanta

SOUTH CAROLINA

Columbia

ATLANTIC

Little Rock

Birmingham

GEORGIA

Charleston

OCEAN

Dallas

Fort Worth

MISSISSIPPI

ALABAMA

Montgomery

Columbus

Savannah

30°

Shreveport

LOUISIANA

Jackson

Mobile

Pensacola

Jacksonville

Houston

Baton Rouge

New Orleans

FLORIDA

Orlando

Tampa

St. Petersburg

West Palm Beach

BAHAMAS
(U.K.)

25°

Corpus Christi

GULF OF

Fort Lauderdale

Miami

Nassau

Brownsville

Matamoros

MEXICO

Key West

Straits of Florida

Tropic of Cancer

© Rand McNally & Co.
A-520500-257

95°　　90°　　85°　　80°　　75°

0　100　200　400　600 km

0　100　200　400 mi

MAP INDEX

Political subdivisions

Alabama	32·50n	86·30w
Alaska	65·00n	153·00w
Arizona	34·00n	112·00w
Arkansas	34·50n	93·40w
California	37·30n	119·30w
Colorado	39·30n	105·30w
Connecticut	41·45n	72·45w
Delaware	39·10n	75·30w
District of Columbia	38·54n	77·01w
Florida	28·00n	82·00w
Georgia	32·50n	83·15w
Hawaii	20·00n	157·45w
Idaho	45·00n	115·00w
Illinois	40·00n	89·00w
Indiana	40·00n	86·15w
Iowa	42·15n	93·15w
Kansas	38·45n	98·15w
Kentucky	37·30n	85·15w
Louisiana	31·15n	92·15w
Maine	45·15n	69·15w
Maryland	39·00n	76·45w
Massachusetts	42·15n	71·50w
Michigan	44·00n	85·00w
Minnesota	46·00n	94·15w
Mississippi	32·50n	89·30w
Missouri	38·30n	93·30w
Montana	47·00n	110·00w
Nebraska	41·30n	100·00w
Nevada	39·00n	117·00w
New Hampshire	43·35n	71·40w
New Jersey	40·15n	74·30w
New Mexico	34·30n	106·00w
New York	43·00n	75·00w
North Carolina	35·30n	80·00w
North Dakota	47·30n	100·15w
Ohio	40·15n	82·45w
Oklahoma	35·30n	98·00w
Oregon	44·00n	121·00w
Pennsylvania	40·45n	77·30w
Rhode Island	41·40n	71·30w
South Carolina	34·00n	81·00w
South Dakota	44·15n	100·00w
Tennessee	35·50n	85·30w
Texas	31·30n	99·00w
Utah	39·30n	111·30w
Vermont	43·50n	72·45w
Virginia	37·30n	78·45w
Washington	47·30n	120·30w
West Virginia	38·45n	80·30w
Wisconsin	44·45n	89·30w
Wyoming	43·00n	107·30w

Cities and towns

Aberdeen, S. Dak.	45·28n	98·29w
Aberdeen, Wash.	46·59n	123·50w
Abilene	32·27n	99·44w
Ada	34·46n	96·41w
Aiken	33·34n	81·43w
Akron	41·05n	81·31w
Alamogordo	32·54n	105·57w
Alamosa	37·28n	105·52w
Albany, Ga.	31·35n	84·10w
Albany, N.Y.	42·39n	73·45w
Albany, Oreg.	44·38n	123·06w
Albert Lea	43·39n	93·22w
Albuquerque	35·05n	106·40w
Alexander City	32·56n	85·57w
Alexandria, La.	31·18n	92·27w
Alexandria, Va.	38·48n	77·03w
Alice	27·45n	98·04w
Allentown	41·07n	76·54w
Alliance	42·06n	102·52w
Alpena	45·04n	83·26w
Alpine	30·22n	103·40w
Alton	38·54n	90·10w
Altoona	40·30n	78·24w
Alturas	41·29n	120·32w
Altus	34·38n	99·20w
Alva	36·48n	98·40w
Amarillo	35·13n	101·49w
Americus	32·04n	84·14w
Ames	42·02n	93·37w
Anaconda	46·08n	112·57w
Anaheim	33·51n	117·57w
Anchorage	61·13n	149·53w
Andalusia	31·19n	86·29w
Anderson, Ind.	40·10n	85·41w
Anderson, S.C.	34·31n	82·39w
Annapolis	38·59n	76·30w
Ann Arbor	42·18n	83·45w
Anniston	33·40n	85·50w
Appleton	44·16n	88·25w
Arcata	40·52n	124·05w
Ardmore	34·10n	97·08w
Arkadelphia	34·07n	93·04w
Arkansas City	37·04n	97·02w
Arlington	38·52n	77·05w
Artesia	32·51n	104·24w
Asheville	35·34n	82·33w
Ashland, Ky.	38·28n	82·38w
Ashland, Oreg.	42·12n	122·42w
Ashland, Wis.	46·35n	90·53w
Ashtabula	41·52n	80·48w
Aspen	39·11n	106·49w
Astoria	46·11n	123·50w
Atchison	39·34n	95·07w
Athens, Ga.	33·57n	83·23w
Athens, Tenn.	35·27n	84·36w
Atlanta	33·45n	84·23w
Atlantic City	39·22n	74·26w
Atmore	31·02n	87·29w
Auburn, Ala.	32·36n	85·29w
Auburn, N.Y.	42·56n	76·34w
Augusta, Ga.	33·29n	81·57w
Augusta, Maine	44·19n	69·47w
Aurora, Colo.	39·44n	104·52w
Aurora, Ill.	42·46n	88·19w
Austin, Minn.	43·40n	92·59w
Austin, Tex.	30·16n	97·45w
Bainbridge	30·54n	84·34w
Baker, Mont.	46·22n	104·17w
Baker, Oreg.	44·47n	117·50w
Bakersfield	35·23n	119·01w
Baltimore	39·17n	76·37w
Bangor	44·49n	68·47w
Barre	44·12n	72·30w
Barrow	71·17n	156·47w
Barstow	34·54n	117·01w
Bartlesville	36·45n	95·59w
Bastrop	32·47n	91·55w
Baton Rouge	30·23n	91·11w
Battle Creek	42·19n	85·12w
Bay City, Mich.	43·36n	83·53w
Bay City, Tex.	28·59n	95·58w
Baytown	29·44n	94·58w
Beatrice	40·16n	96·44w
Beaufort	32·26n	80·40w
Beaumont	30·05n	94·06w
Beeville	28·24n	97·45w
Belen	34·40n	106·46w
Belleville, Ill.	38·31n	90·00w
Belleville, Kans.	39·49n	97·38w
Belle Fourch	44·40n	103·51w
Bellingham	48·46n	122·29w
Beloit	42·31n	89·02w
Bemidji	47·29n	94·53w
Bend	44·03n	121·19w
Benton Harbor	42·06n	86·27w
Berkeley	37·57n	122·18w
Berlin	44·29n	71·10w
Bessemer	33·25n	86·57w
Bethel	60·48n	161·46w
Biddeford	43·30n	70·26w
Big Rapids	43·42n	85·29w
Big Spring	32·15n	101·28w
Billings	45·47n	118·27w
Biloxi	30·24n	88·53w
Binghamton	42·08n	75·54w
Birmingham	33·31n	86·49w
Bishop	37·22n	118·24w
Bismarck	46·48n	100·47w
Bloomington, Ill.	40·29n	88·60w
Bloomington, Ind.	39·10n	86·32w
Bluefield	37·16n	81·13w
Blytheville	35·56n	89·55w
Bogalusa	30·47n	89·52w
Boise	43·37n	116·13w
Boone	42·04n	93·53w
Borger	33·39n	101·24w
Bossier City	32·31n	93·43w
Boston	42·21n	71·04w
Bottineau	48·50n	100·27w
Boulder	40·01n	105·17w
Boulder City	35·59n	114·50w
Bowling Green	37·00n	86·27w
Bowman	46·11n	103·24w
Bozeman	45·41n	111·02w
Bradenton	27·29n	82·34w
Brainerd	46·21n	94·12w
Bremerton	47·34n	122·38w
Bridgeport	41·11n	73·11w
Brigham City	41·31n	112·01w
Bristol	36·36n	82·11w
Brookhaven	31·35n	90·26w
Brookings, Oreg.	42·02n	124·17w
Brookings, S. Dak.	44·19n	96·48w
Brownsville	25·54n	97·30w
Brownwood	31·43n	98·59w
Brunswick, Ga.	31·10n	81·29w
Brunswick, Maine	43·55n	69·58w
Bryan	30·40n	96·22w
Burley	42·32n	113·48w
Burlington, Iowa	40·49n	91·14w
Burlington, N.J.	40·04n	74·49w
Burns	43·35n	119·03w
Butler	40·52n	79·54w
Butte	46·00n	112·32w
Cadillac	44·15n	85·24w
Cairo	37·00n	89·11w
Caldwell	43·40n	116·14w
Cambridge, Md.	38·34n	76·04w
Cambridge, Mass.	42·22n	71·06w
Camden, Ark.	33·35n	92·50w
Camden, N.J.	39·57n	75·07w
Canon City	38·27n	105·14w
Canton, Miss.	32·37n	90·02w
Canton, Ohio	40·48n	81·22w
Cape Girardeau	37·19n	89·32w
Carbondale, Ill.	37·44n	89·13w
Carbondale, Pa.	41·35n	75·30w
Caribou	46·52n	68·01w
Carlsbad	32·25n	104·14w
Carrington	47·27n	99·08w
Carson City	39·10n	119·46w
Carthage	37·11n	94·19w
Casper	42·51n	106·19w
Cedar City	37·41n	113·04w
Cedar Falls	42·32n	92·27w
Cedar Rapids	41·59n	91·40w
Centralia	46·43n	122·58w
Chadron	42·50n	102·60w
Chamberlain	43·49n	99·20w
Chambersburg	39·56n	77·39w
Champaign	40·07n	88·12w
Chanute	37·41n	95·27w
Charles City	43·04n	92·40w
Charleston, S.C.	32·48n	79·57w
Charleston, W. Va.	38·21n	81·38w
Charlotte	35·14n	80·50w
Charlottesville	38·02n	78·29w
Chattanooga	35·03n	85·19w
Cheboygan	45·39n	84·29w
Cheney	47·29n	117·34w
Chesapeake	36·43n	76·15w
Cheyenne	41·08n	104·49w
Chickasha	35·02n	97·58w
Chicago	41·53n	87·38w
Chico	39·44n	121·50w
Childress	34·25n	100·13w
Chillicothe, Mo.	39·48n	93·33w
Chillicothe, Ohio	39·20n	82·59w
Chippewa Falls	44·56n	91·24w
Circle	65·50n	144·04w
Cincinnati	39·06n	84·31w
Clarksburg	39·17n	80·21w
Clarksdale	34·12n	90·34w
Clarksville	36·32n	87·21w
Clayton	36·27n	103·11w
Clearwater	27·58n	82·48w
Cleburne	32·21n	97·23w
Cleveland, Miss.	33·45n	90·50w
Cleveland, Ohio	41·30n	81·41w
Cleveland, Tenn.	35·10n	84·53w
Clinton, Iowa	41·51n	90·12w
Clinton, Okla.	35·31n	98·59w
Cloquet	46·43n	92·28w
Clovis	34·24n	103·12w
Cocoa	28·21n	80·44w
Coeur d'Alene	47·41n	116·46w
Coffeyville	37·02n	95·37w
Colfax	46·53n	117·22w
Colorado Springs	38·50n	104·49w
Columbia, Mo.	38·57n	92·20w
Columbia, S.C.	34·00n	81·03w
Columbia, Tenn.	35·37n	87·02w
Columbus, Ga.	32·29n	84·59w
Columbus, Ind.	39·13n	85·55w
Columbus, Miss.	33·30n	88·25w
Columbus, Nebr.	41·25n	97·22w
Columbus, Ohio	39·57n	83·00w
Concord	43·12n	71·32w
Conway, Ark.	35·05n	92·26w
Conway, S.C.	33·50n	79·03w
Cookeville	36·10n	85·31w
Coos Bay	43·22n	124·13w
Cordele	31·58n	83·47w
Cordova	60·33n	145·46w
Corinth	34·56n	88·31w
Corpus Christi	27·48n	97·24w
Corsicana	32·06n	96·28w
Cortez	37·21n	108·35w
Corvallis	44·34n	123·16w
Council Bluffs	41·16n	95·52w
Covington	40·07n	84·21w
Crescent City	41·45n	124·12w
Crookston	47·47n	96·37w
Crowley	30·13n	92·22w
Crystal City	28·41n	99·50w
Cullman	34·11n	86·51w
Cumberland	37·30n	78·15w
Dalhart	36·04n	102·31w
Dallas, Oreg.	44·55n	123·19w
Dallas, Tex.	32·47n	96·48w
Dalton	34·47n	84·58w
Danville, Ill.	40·08n	87·37w
Danville, Va.	36·35n	79·24w
Davenport, Iowa	41·32n	90·41w
Davenport, Wash.	47·39n	118·09w
Davis	38·33n	121·44w
Dayton	39·45n	84·15w
Daytona Beach	29·12n	80·60w
Deadwood	44·23n	103·44w
Decatur, Ala.	34·36n	86·59w
Decatur, Ill.	39·51n	89·32w
Decorah	43·18n	91·48w
Deer Lodge	46·24n	112·44w
Del Rio	29·22n	100·54w
Deming	32·16n	107·45w
Denison	33·45n	96·33w
Denton	33·13n	97·08w
Denver	39·43n	105·01w
Des Moines	41·35n	93·37w
Detroit	42·20n	83·03w
Devils Lake	48·01n	98·52w
Dickinson	46·53n	102·47w
Dillingham	59·02n	158·29w
Dillon	45·13n	112·38w
Dodge City	37·45n	100·01w
Dothan	31·13n	85·24w
Dover, Del.	39·10n	75·32w
Dover, Mass.	42·15n	71·17w
Dublin	32·32n	82·54w
DuBois	41·07n	78·46w
Dubuque	42·30n	90·41w
Duluth	46·47n	92·06w
Duncan	34·30n	97·57w
Dunkirk	42·29n	79·20w
Durango	37·16n	107·53w
Durant	33·60n	96·23w
Durham	35·59n	78·54w
Dutch Harbor	53·53n	166·32w
Dyersburg	36·03n	89·23w
Eagle Pass	28·43n	100·30w
East Glacier Park	48·27n	113·13w
Eastport	44·54n	66·60w
East Saint Louis	38·38n	96·08w
Eau Claire	44·49n	91·31w
Eau Gallie	28·08n	80·38w
Edgemont	43·18n	103·50w
El Cajon	32·48n	116·58w
El Centro	32·48n	115·34w
El Dorado, Ark.	33·13n	92·40w
El Dorado, Kans.	37·49n	96·52w
Elgin	42·02n	88·17w
Elizabeth City	36·18n	76·14w
Elkhart	41·41n	85·58w
Elko	40·50n	115·46w
Ellendale	46·06n	98·32w
Ellensburg	46·60n	120·32w
Elmira	42·06n	76·49w
El Paso	31·45n	106·29w
El Reno	35·32n	97·57w
Ely	39·15n	114·53w
Emporia	38·24n	96·11w
Enid	36·19n	97·48w
Ephraim	39·22n	111·35w
Erie	42·08n	80·04w
Escanaba	45·45n	87·04w
Escondido	33·07n	117·05w
Eugene	44·02n	123·05w
Eureka	40·47n	124·09w
Evanston	41·16n	110·58w
Evansville	37·58n	87·35w
Everett	47·59n	122·13w
Fairbanks	64·51n	147·43w
Fairbury	40·08n	97·11w
Fairmont, Minn.	43·39n	94·28w
Fairmont, W. Va.	39·29n	80·09w
Fairview	47·51n	104·03w
Fall River	41·43n	71·08w
Fargo	46·52n	96·48w
Faribault	44·18n	93·16w
Farmington	43·24n	71·04w
Fayetteville, Ark.	36·04n	94·10w
Fayetteville, N.C.	35·03n	78·54w
Fergus Falls	46·17n	96·04w
Findlay	41·02n	83·39w
Flagstaff	35·12n	111·39w
Flint	43·01n	83·41w
Florence, Ala.	34·49n	87·40w
Florence, S.C.	34·12n	79·46w
Fond du Lac	43·47n	88·27w
Forrest City	35·01n	90·47w
Fort Bragg	39·26n	123·48w
Fort Collins	40·35n	105·05w
Fort Dodge	42·30n	94·10w
Fort Lauderdale	26·07n	80·08w
Fort Madison	40·38n	91·27w
Fort Morgan	40·15n	103·48w
Fort Myers	26·37n	81·54w
Fort Pierce	27·27n	80·20w
Fort Smith	35·23n	94·25w
Fort Stockton	30·53n	102·53w
Fort Walton Beach	30·25n	86·36w
Fort Wayne	41·04n	85·09w
Fort Worth	32·45n	97·20w
Fort Yukon	66·34n	145·17w
Frankfort	38·12n	84·52w
Fredericksburg	38·18n	77·29w
Freeport	40·40n	79·41w
Fremont	41·26n	96·30w
Fresno	36·45n	119·45w
Gadsden	34·02n	86·02w
Gainesville, Fla.	29·40n	82·20w
Gainesville, Ga.	34·18n	83·50w
Gainesville, Tex.	33·37n	97·08w
Galena	42·25n	90·26w
Galesburg	40·57n	90·22w
Gallatin	36·24n	86·27w
Gallup	35·32n	108·44w
Galveston	29·18n	94·48w

ken by faulting, and the resulting blocks have tumbled, eroded, and been partly buried by alluvial debris that has accumulated in the desert basins at their feet. The eroded blocks form mountain ranges that are characteristically dozens of miles long; several thousand feet from base to crest, with peak elevations that only occasionally rise to more than 10,000 feet; and almost always aligned roughly north–south. The basins are typically floored with alluvium and sometimes salt.

The third intermontane region, the Columbia Basin, is literally the last, for in some parts its rocks are still being formed. Its entire area is underlain by innumerable tabular lava flows that have flooded the basin between the Cascades and Northern Rockies to undetermined depths. The volume of lava must be measured in thousands of cubic miles, for the flows blanket large parts of Washington, Oregon, and Idaho and in southern Idaho have drowned the Northern Rocky Mountains in a basaltic sea. Where the lavas are fresh, as in southern Idaho, the surface is often nearly flat, but more often the floors have been trenched by rivers—conspicuously the Columbia and the Snake—or by glacial floodwaters that have carved an intricate system of braided canyons in the remarkable Channeled Scablands of eastern Washington. In surface form the eroded lava often resembles the topography of the Colorado Plateau, but the gaudy colours of the Colorado are replaced by the black and brown of basalt.

Most large mountain systems are sources of varied min-

eral wealth, and the American Cordillera is no exception. Metallic minerals have been taken from most crystalline regions and have furnished the United States with both romance and wealth—the Sierra gold that provoked the 1849 Gold Rush, the fabulous silver lodes of western Nevada's Basin and Range, and gold strikes all along the Rocky Mountain chain. Industrial metals, however, are far more important now; copper and lead are among the base metals, and the more exotic molybdenum, vanadium, and cadmium are mainly useful in alloys.

Minerals of the Cordillera

In the Cordillera, as elsewhere, the greatest wealth stems from fuels. Most major basins contain oil and natural gas, conspicuously the Wyoming Basin, the Central Valley of California, and the Los Angeles Basin. The Colorado Plateau, however, has yielded some of the most interesting discoveries—considerable deposits of uranium and colossal occurrences of oil shale. Oil from the shale, however, probably could not be economically removed without widespread strip mining, and correspondingly large-scale damage to the environment. Wide exploitation of low-sulfur bituminous coal has been initiated in the Four Corners area of the Colorado Plateau, and open-pit mining has already devastated parts of this once pristine country as completely as it has in West Virginia.

DRAINAGE

As befits a nation of continental proportions, the United States has an extraordinary network of rivers and lakes, including some of the largest and most useful in the world. In the humid East they provide an enormous mileage of cheap inland transportation; westward, most rivers and streams are unnavigable but are heavily used for irrigation and power generation. Both East and West, unfortunately, have traditionally used lakes and streams as public sewers, and most large waterways are laden with vast, poisonous volumes of industrial, agricultural, and human wastes.

The Eastern systems. Chief among U.S. rivers is the Mississippi, which, with its great tributaries, the Ohio and the Missouri, drains most of the midcontinent. It is one of the world's great inland waterways, navigable to Minneapolis nearly 1,200 airline miles from the Gulf of Mexico. Its eastern branches, chiefly the Ohio and the Tennessee, are also navigable for great distances. From the west, however, many of its numerous Great Plains tributaries are too seasonal and choked with sandbars to be used for shipping. The Missouri, for example, though longer than the Mississippi itself, was essentially without navigation until the mid-20th century, when a combination of large dams, locks, and continual dredging opened the river to considerable barge traffic.

The Great Lakes–St. Lawrence system forms the second half of the world's greatest network of inland waterways, for it is connected to the Mississippi–Ohio by canals. No description of the Great Lakes is possible without superlatives, for the five lakes (four of which are shared with Canada) constitute by far the largest freshwater lake group in the world and carry a larger tonnage of shipping than any other. The three main barriers to navigation—the St. Marys Rapids, at Sault Ste. Marie; Niagara Falls; and the rapids of the St. Lawrence—are all bypassed by locks, whose 27-foot draft lets ocean vessels penetrate 1,300 miles into the continent, to Duluth, Minnesota, and Chicago.

The third group of Eastern rivers drains the coastal strip along the Atlantic Ocean and the Gulf of Mexico. Except for the Rio Grande, which rises west of the Rockies and flows about 1,900 circuitous miles to the Gulf, few of these coastal rivers measure more than 300 miles, and most flow in an almost straight line to the sea. Except in glaciated New England and in arid southwestern Texas, most of the larger coastal streams are navigable for some distance.

The Pacific systems. West of the Rockies, nearly all of the rivers are strongly influenced by aridity. In the deserts and steppes of the intermontane basins, most of the scanty runoff disappears into interior basins only one of which, the Great Salt Lake, holds any substantial volume of water. Aside from a few minor coastal streams, only three large river systems manage to reach the sea—the Columbia, the Colorado, and the San Joaquin–Sacramento system of California's Central Valley. All three of these river systems are exotic: that is, they flow for considerable distances across dry lands from which they receive no water. Both the Columbia and the Colorado have carved awesome gorges, the former through the sombre lavas of the Cascades and the Columbia Basin, the latter through the brilliantly coloured rocks of the Colorado Plateau. These gorges lend themselves to easy damming, and the once wild Columbia has been turned into a stairway of placid lakes whose waters irrigate the arid plateaus of eastern Washington and power one of the world's largest hydroelectric networks. The Colorado is less extensively developed, and proposals for new dam construction have met fierce opposition from those who want to preserve the spectacular natural beauty of the river's canyon lands.

CLIMATE

Climate affects human habitats both directly and indirectly through its influence on vegetation, soils, and wildlife. In the United States, however, the natural environment has been altered drastically by nearly four centuries of European settlement, as well as thousands of years of Indian occupancy.

Wherever land is abandoned, however, "wild" conditions return rapidly, achieving over the long run a dynamic equilibrium among soils, vegetation, and the inexorable strictures of climate. Thus, though Americans have created an artificial environment of continental proportions, the United States still can be divided into a mosaic of

bioclimatic regions, each of them distinguished by peculiar climatic conditions and each with a potential vegetation and soil that eventually would return in the absence of man. The main exception to this generalization applies to fauna, so drastically altered that it is almost impossible to know what sort of animal geography would redevelop in the areas of the United States if humans were removed from the scene.

Climatic controls. The pattern of U.S. climates is largely set by the location of the conterminous United States almost entirely in the middle latitudes, by its position with respect to the continental landmass and its fringing oceans, and by the nation's gross pattern of mountains and lowlands. Each of these geographic controls operates to determine the character of air masses and their changing behaviour from season to season.

The conterminous United States lies entirely between the Tropic of Cancer and 50° N latitude, a position that confines Arctic climates to the high mountaintops and genuine tropics to a small part of southern Florida. By no means, however, is the climate literally temperate, for the middle latitudes are notorious for extreme variations of temperature and precipitation.

The great size of the North American landmass tends to reinforce these extremes. Since land heats and cools more rapidly than water, places distant from an ocean tend to have "continental" climates; that is, they alternate between extremes of hot summers and cold winters, in contrast to the "marine" climates, which are more equable. Most U.S. climates are markedly continental, the more so because the Cordillera effectively confines the moderating Pacific influence to a narrow strip along the West Coast. Extremes of continentality occur near the centre of the continent, and in North Dakota temperatures have ranged between a summer high record of 121° F (49° C) and a winter low of −60° F (−51° C). Moreover, the general eastward drift of air over the United States carries continental temperatures all the way to the Atlantic coast. Bismarck, North Dakota, for example, has a great annual temperature range. Boston, on the Atlantic but largely exempt from its influence, has a lesser but still continental range, while San Francisco, which is under strong Pacific influence, has only a small summer–winter differential.

The Western Cordillera confines Pacific temperatures and rainfall to the coastal margin. The Pacific Coast Ranges are high enough to make a local rain shadow in their lee, but the main barrier is the great rampart formed by the Sierra Nevada and Cascade ranges. Rainy on their western slopes and barren on the east, this mountain crest forms one of the sharpest climatic divides in the United States.

The rain shadow continues east to the Rockies, leaving the entire Intermontane Region either arid or semiarid, except where isolated ranges manage to capture leftover moisture at high altitudes. East of the Rockies the westerly drift brings mainly dry air, and as a result, the Great Plains are semiarid. Still farther east, humidity increases owing to the frequent incursion from the south of warm, moist, and unstable air from the Gulf of Mexico, which produces more precipitation in the United States than the Pacific and Atlantic oceans combined.

Although the landforms of the Interior Lowlands have been termed dull, there is nothing dull about their weather conditions. Air from the Gulf of Mexico can flow northward across the Great Plains, uninterrupted by topographic barriers, but continental Canadian air flows south by the same route, and, since these two air masses differ in every important respect, the collisions often produce disturbances of monumental violence. Plainsmen and Midwesterners are accustomed to unexpected displays of furious weather—tornadoes, blizzards, hailstorms, precipitous drops and rises in temperature, and a host of other spectacular meteorological displays, sometimes dangerous but seldom boring.

The change of seasons. Most of the United States is marked by sharp differences between winter and summer. In winter, when temperature contrasts between land and water are greatest, a huge mass of frigid, dry Canadian air spreads far south over the midcontinent, bringing cold, sparkling weather to the interior and generating great cy-

The Mississippi and Great Lakes waters

Climatic impact of latitude, landforms, and oceans

clonic storms where its leading edge confronts a shrunken mass of warm Gulf air to the south. Although such cyclonic activity occurs throughout the year, it is most frequent and intense during the winter, parading eastward out of the Great Plains to bring the Eastern states practically all their winter precipitation. Temperatures differ widely, depending largely on latitude. Thus, New Orleans, at 30° N latitude, and International Falls, Minnesota, at 49° N, have respective January temperature averages of 55° F (13° C) and 3° F (−16° C). In the north, therefore, precipitation often comes as snow, often driven by furious winds; farther south, cold rain alternates with sleet and occasional snow. Southern Florida is the only dependably warm part of the East, though "polar outbursts" have been known to bring temperatures below 0° F (−18° C) as far south as Tallahassee. The main uniformity of Eastern weather in wintertime is the expectation of continual change.

Winter climate on the West Coast is very different. A great spiralling mass of relatively warm, moist air spreads south from the Aleutian Islands of Alaska, its semipermanent front producing gloomy overcast and drizzles that hang over the Pacific Northwest all winter long, occasionally reaching southern California, which receives nearly all of its rain at this time of year. This Pacific air brings mild temperatures along the whole coast; the average January day in Seattle, Washington, ranges between 33° and 44° F (1° and 7° C), in Los Angeles between 45° and 64° F (7° and 18° C). In southern California, however, rains are separated by long spells of fine weather, and the whole region is a winter haven for those seeking refuge from less agreeable weather in other parts of the country. The Intermontane Region is similar to the Pacific coast, but with much less rainfall and a somewhat wider range of temperatures.

During the summer there is a reversal of the air masses, and east of the Rockies the change resembles the summer monsoon of Southeast Asia. As the midcontinent heats up, the cold Canadian air mass weakens and retreats, pushed north by an aggressive mass of warm, moist air from the Gulf. The great winter temperature differential between North and South disappears as the hot, soggy blanket spreads from the Gulf coast to the Canadian border. Heat and humidity are naturally most oppressive in the South, but there is little comfort in the more northern latitudes. In Houston, Texas, the temperature on a typical July day reaches 92° F (33° C), with relative humidity averaging near 75 percent, but Minneapolis, Minnesota, more than 1,000 miles north, is only slightly cooler and less humid.

Since the Gulf air is unstable as well as wet, convectional and frontal summer thunderstorms are endemic east of the Rockies, accounting for a majority of total summer rain. These storms usually drench small areas with short-lived, sometimes violent downpours, so that crops in one Midwestern county may prosper, those in another shrivel in drought, and those in yet another are flattened by hailstones. Relief from the humid heat comes in the north from occasional outbursts of cool Canadian air; small, but more consistent relief is found through influences from the Great Lakes and high elevations in the Appalachians. East of the Rockies, however, U.S. summers are distinctly uncomfortable, and air conditioning is viewed as a desirable amenity in any Eastern city.

Again, the Pacific regime is different. The moist Aleutian air retreats northward, to be replaced by mild, stable air from over the cool subtropical Pacific, and except in the mountains the Pacific coast is nearly rainless, though often foggy. Meanwhile, a small but potent mass of dry hot air raises temperatures to blistering levels over much of the intermontane Southwest. In Yuma, Arizona, for example, the normal temperature in July reaches 108° F (42° C), while nearby Death Valley, California, holds the national record, 134° F (57° C). During its summer peak this scorching air mass spreads from the Pacific margin as far as Texas on the east and Idaho to the north, turning the whole interior basin into a summer desert.

Over most of the United States, as in most continental climates, spring and autumn are agreeable but disappointingly brief. Autumn is particularly idyllic in the East, with

a romantic Indian summer of ripening corn and brilliantly coloured foliage and of mild days and frosty nights. The shift in dominance between marine and continental air masses, however, spawns furious weather in some regions. Along the Atlantic and Gulf coasts, for example, autumn is the season for hurricanes—the American equivalent of Southeast Asian typhoons—which rage northward from the Gulf and Caribbean to create havoc along the East Coast as far north as New England. The Mississippi Valley holds the dubious distinction of recording more tornadoes than any other area on Earth. These violent storms usually occur over relatively small areas and are confined largely to springtime.

The bioclimatic regions. Three first-order bioclimatic zones encompass most of the conterminous United States—regions in which climatic conditions are similar enough to dictate similar conditions of mature (zonal) soil and potential climax vegetation (*i.e.,* the assemblage of plants that would grow and reproduce indefinitely given stable climate and average conditions of soil and drainage). These are the Humid East, the Humid Pacific Coast, and the Dry West. In addition, the boundary zone between the Humid East and the Dry West is so large and important that it constitutes a separate region, the Humid–Arid Transition. Finally, because the Western Cordillera contains an intricate mosaic of climatic types, largely determined by local elevation and exposure, it is useful to distinguish the Western Mountain Climate. The first three zones, however, are very diverse and require further breakdown, producing a total of 10 main bioclimatic regions. For two reasons, the boundaries of these bioclimatic regions are much less distinct than boundaries of landform regions. First, climate obviously varies from year to year, especially in boundary zones, whereas landforms do not. Second, regions of climate, vegetation, and soils coincide generally but sometimes not precisely. Boundaries, therefore, should be interpreted as zonal and transitional, and rarely should be considered as sharp lines in the landscape. *Indistinctness of climatic boundaries*

For all of their indistinct boundaries, however, these bioclimatic regions have strong and easily recognized identities. Such regional identity is strongly reinforced when a particular area falls entirely within a single bioclimatic region and at the same time a single landform region. The result—as in the Piedmont South, the central Midwest, or the western Great Plains—is a landscape with an unmistakable regional personality.

The Humid East. The largest and in some ways the most important of the bioclimatic zones, the Humid East was where the Europeans first settled, tamed the land, and adapted to American conditions. In early times much of this territory was forested, a fact of central importance in American history that profoundly influenced both soils and wildlife. As in most of the world's humid lands, soluble minerals have been leached from the earth, leaving a great family of soils called pedalfers, rich in relatively insoluble iron and aluminum compounds.

Both forests and soils, however, differ considerably within this vast region. Since rainfall is ample and summers are warm everywhere, the main differences result from the length and severity of winters, which determine the length of growing season. Winter, obviously, differs according to latitude, so that the Humid East is sliced into four great east–west bands of soils and vegetation, with progressively more amenable winters as one travels southward. These changes occur very gradually, however, and the boundaries therefore are extremely subtle.

The Sub-Boreal Forest Region is the northernmost of these bands. It is only a small and discontinuous part of the United States, representing the tattered southern fringe of the vast Canadian taiga—a scrubby forest dominated by evergreen needle-leaf species that can endure the ferocious winters and reproduce during the short, erratic summers. Average growing seasons are less than 120 days, though Newberry, Michigan, has recorded frost-free periods lasting as long as 161 days and as short as 76 days. Soils of this region that survived the scour of glaciation are miserably thin podzols—heavily leached, highly acid, and often interrupted by extensive stretches of bog. Most attempts at farming in the region long since have been abandoned. *Climatic sub-regions of the Eastern United States*

Nationwide seasonal variations

Farther south lies the Humid Microthermal Zone of milder winters and longer summers. Large broadleaf trees begin to crowd out the evergreens, producing a mixed forest of greater floristic variety and economic value that is famous for its brilliant autumn colours. As the forest grows richer in species, sterile podzols give way to more productive gray-brown podzolic soils, stained and fertilized with humus. Although winters are warmer than in the Sub-Boreal zone, and although the Great Lakes help temper the bitterest cold, January temperatures ordinarily average below freezing, and a winter without a few days of subzero temperatures is uncommon. Everywhere, the ground is solidly frozen and snow covered for several months of the year.

Still farther south are the Humid Subtropics. The region's northern boundary is one of the country's most portentous climatic lines, the approximate northern limit of a 180–200-day growing season, the outer margin of cotton growing, and, hence, of the Old South. Most of the South lies in the Piedmont and Coastal Plain, for higher elevations in the Appalachians cause a peninsula of Northern mixed forest to extend as far south as northern Georgia. The red-brown podzolic soil, once moderately fertile, has been severely damaged by overcropping and burning. Thus much of the region that once sustained a rich, broadleaf-forest flora now supports poor pinewoods. Throughout the South, summers are hot, muggy, long, and disagreeable; Dixie's "frosty mornings" bring a welcome respite in winter.

The southern margins of Florida contain the only real tropics in the conterminous United States; it is an area in which frost is almost unknown. Hot, rainy summers alternate with warm and somewhat drier winters, with a secondary rainfall peak during the autumn hurricane season—altogether a typical monsoonal regime. Soils and vegetation are mostly immature, however, since southern Florida rises so slightly above sea level that substantial areas, such as the Everglades, are swampy and often brackish. Peat and sand frequently masquerade as soil, and much of the vegetation is either salt-loving mangrove or sawgrass prairie.

The Humid Pacific Coast. The western humid region differs from its eastern counterpart in so many ways as to be a world apart. Much smaller, it is crammed into a narrow littoral belt to the windward of the Sierra–Cascade summit, dominated by mild Pacific air, and chopped by irregular topography into an intricate mosaic of climatic and biotic habitats. Throughout the region rainfall is extremely seasonal, falling mostly in the winter half of the year. Summers are droughty everywhere, but the main regional differences come from the length of drought—from about two months in humid Seattle to nearly five months in semiarid San Diego.

Western Washington, Oregon, and northern California lie within a zone that climatologists call Marine West Coast. Winters are raw, overcast, and drizzly—not unlike northwestern Europe—with subfreezing temperatures restricted mainly to the mountains, upon which enormous snow accumulations produce local alpine glaciers. Summers, by contrast, are brilliantly cloudless, cool, and frequently foggy along the West Coast and somewhat warmer in the inland valleys. This mild marine climate produces some of the world's greatest forests of enormous straight-boled evergreen trees that furnish the United States with much of its commercial timber. Mature soils are typical of humid midlatitude forestlands, a moderately leached gray-brown podzol.

A Mediterranean-like climate

Toward the south, with diminishing coastal rain the moist marine climate gradually gives way to California's tiny but much publicized Mediterranean regime. Although mountainous topography introduces a bewildering variety of local environments, scanty winter rains are quite inadequate to compensate for the long summer drought, and much of the region has a distinctly arid character. For much of the year, cool, stable Pacific air dominates the West Coast, bringing San Francisco its famous fogs and Los Angeles its infamous smoggy temperature inversions. Inland, however, summer temperatures reach blistering levels, so that in July, while Los Angeles expects a normal

daily maximum of 76° F (24° C), Fresno expects 100° F (38° C) and is climatically a desert. As might be expected, Mediterranean California contains a huge variety of vegetal habitats, but the commonest perhaps is the chaparral, a drought-resistant, scrubby woodland of twisted hard-leafed trees, picturesque but of little economic value. Soils are similarly varied, but most of them are light in colour and rich in soluble minerals, qualities typical of subarid soils.

The Dry West. In the United States, to speak of dry areas is to speak of the West. It covers an enormous region beyond the dependable reach of moist oceanic air, occupying the entire Intermontane area and sprawling from Canada to Mexico across the western part of the Great Plains. To Americans nurtured in the Humid East, this vast territory across the path of all transcontinental travellers has been harder to tame than any other—and no region has so gripped the national imagination as this fierce and dangerous land.

In the Dry West nothing matters more than water. Thus, though temperatures may differ radically from place to place, the really important regional differences depend overwhelmingly on the degree of aridity, whether an area is extremely dry and hence desert or whether it is semiarid and therefore steppe.

Americans of the 19th century were preoccupied by the myth of a Great American Desert, which supposedly occupied more than one-third of the entire country. True desert, however, is confined to the Southwest, with patchy outliers elsewhere, all without exception located in the lowland rain shadows of the Cordillera. Vegetation in these desert areas varies between nothing at all (a rare circumstance confined mainly to salt flats and sand dunes) to a low cover of scattered woody scrub and short-lived annuals that burst into flamboyant bloom after rains. Soils are usually thin, light coloured, and very rich with mineral salts. In some areas wind erosion has removed fine-grained material, leaving behind desert pavement, a barren veneer of broken rock.

The Great American Desert

Most of the West, however, lies in the semiarid region, in which rainfall is scanty but adequate to support a thin cover of short bunchgrass, commonly alternating with scrubby sagebrush. Here, as in the desert, soils fall into the large family of the pedocals, rich in calcium and other soluble minerals, but in the slightly wetter environment of the West, they are enriched with humus from decomposed grass roots. Under the proper type of management, these chestnut-coloured steppe soils have the potential to be very fertile.

Weather in the West resembles that of other dry regions of the world, often extreme, violent, and reliably unreliable. Rainfall, for example, obeys a cruel natural law: as total precipitation decreases, it becomes more undependable. John Steinbeck's novel *The Grapes of Wrath* describes the problems of a family enticed to the arid frontier of Oklahoma during a wet period, only to be driven out by the savage drought of the 1930s that turned the western Great Plains into the great American Dust Bowl. Temperatures in the West also fluctuate convulsively within short periods, and high winds are infamous throughout the region.

The Humid–Arid Transition. East of the Rockies, all climatic boundaries are gradational. None, however, is so important nor so imperceptibly subtle as the boundary zone that separates the Humid East from the Dry West and that alternates unpredictably between arid and humid conditions from year to year. Stretching approximately from Texas to North Dakota in an ill-defined band between the 95th and 100th meridians, this transitional region deserves separate recognition, partly because of its great size, and partly because of the fine balance between surplus and deficit rainfall, which produces a unique and valuable combination of soils, flora, and fauna. The native vegetation, insofar as it can be reconstructed, was prairie, the legendary sea of tall, deep-rooted grass now almost entirely tilled and planted to grains. Soils, often of loessial derivation, include the enormously productive chernozem (black earth) in the north, with reddish prairie soils of nearly equal fertility in the south. Throughout the region temperatures are severely continental, with bitterly cold winters in the north and scorching summers everywhere.

The prairies

The western edge of the prairie fades gradually into the shortgrass steppe of the High Plains, the change a function of diminishing rainfall. The eastern edge, however, represents one of the few major discordances between a climatic and biotic boundary in the United States, for the grassland penetrates the eastern forest in a great salient across humid Illinois and Indiana. Many scholars believe this part of the prairie was artificially induced by repeated Indian burning and consequent destruction of the forest margins.

The Western Mountain Climate. Throughout the Cordillera and Intermontane regions, irregular topography shatters the grand bioclimatic pattern into an intricate mosaic of tiny regions that differ drastically according to elevation and exposure. No small- or medium-scale map can accurately record such complexity, and mountainous parts of the West are said, noncommittally, to have a "mountain climate." Lowlands are usually dry, but increasing elevation brings lower temperature, decreased evaporation, and—if a slope faces prevailing winds—greater precipitation. Soils vary wildly from place to place, but vegetation is fairly predictable. From the desert or steppe of intermontane valleys, a climber typically ascends into parklike savanna, then through an orderly sequence of increasingly humid and boreal forests until, if the range is high enough, he reaches timberline and Arctic tundra. The very highest peaks are snow-capped, although permanent glaciers rarely occur outside the cool humid highlands of the Pacific Northwest. (P.F.L.)

PLANT LIFE

The dominant features of the vegetation are indicated by the terms forest, grassland, desert, and alpine tundra. A coniferous forest of white and red pine, hemlock, spruce, jack pine, and balsam fir extends interruptedly in a narrow strip near the Canadian border from Maine to Minnesota and southward along the Appalachian Mountains. There may be found smaller stands of tamarack, spruce, paper birch, willow, alder, and aspen or poplar. Southward, a transition zone of mixed conifers and deciduous trees gives way to a hardwood forest of broad-leaved trees. This forest, with varying mixtures of maple, oak, ash, locust, linden, sweet gum, walnut, hickory, sycamore, beech, and the more southerly tulip tree, once extended uninterruptedly from New England to Missouri and eastern Texas. Pines are prominent on the Atlantic and Gulf coastal plain and adjacent uplands, often occurring in nearly pure stands called pine barrens. Pitch, longleaf, slash, shortleaf, Virginia, and loblolly pines are commonest. Hickory and various oaks combine to form a significant part of this forest, with magnolia, white cedar, and ash often seen. In the frequent swamps, bald cypress, tupelo, and white cedar predominate. Pines, palmettos, and live oaks are replaced at the southern tip of Florida by the more tropical royal and thatch palms, figs, satinwood, and mangrove.

The grasslands occur principally in the Great Plains area and extend westward into the intermontane basins and benchlands of the Rocky Mountains. Numerous grasses such as buffalo, grama, side oat, bunch, needle, and wheat grass, together with many kinds of herbs, make up the plant cover. Coniferous forests cover the lesser mountains and high plateaus of the Rocky Mountains, Cascades, and Sierra Nevada. Yellow pine, Douglas fir, western larch, white pine, lodgepole pine, several spruces, coast hemlock, grand fir, red fir, and the lofty redwood are the principal trees of these forests. The densest growth occurs west of the Cascade and Coast ranges in Washington, Oregon, and northern California, where the trees are often 100 feet (30 metres) or more in height. There the forest floor is so dark that only ferns, mosses, and a few shade-loving shrubs and herbs may be found.

The alpine tundra, located in conterminous United States only in the mountains above the limit of trees, consists principally of small plants that bloom brilliantly for a short season. Sagebrush is the commonest plant of the arid basins and semideserts west of the Rocky Mountains, but juniper, nut pine, and mountain mahogany are often on the slopes and low ridges. The desert, extending from southeastern California to Texas, is noted for the many cacti, some of

which grow to the height of trees, and for the Joshua tree and other yuccas, creosote bush, mesquite, and acacias.

The United States is rich in the variety of its native forest trees, some of which, as the species of sequoia, are the most massive known. More than 1,000 species and varieties have been described, of which almost 200 are of economic value, either because of the timber and other useful products that they yield or by reason of their importance in forestry.

Besides the native flowering plants, estimated at between 20,000 to 25,000 species, many hundreds of species introduced from other regions—chiefly Europe, Asia, and tropical America—have become naturalized. A large proportion of these are common annual weeds of fields, pastures, and roadsides. In some districts these naturalized "aliens" comprise 50 percent or more of the total plant population. (P.H.O./R.C.R.)

ANIMAL LIFE

With most of North America, the United States lies in the Nearctic faunistic realm, a region containing an assemblage of species similar to Eurasia and North Africa but sharply different from the tropical and subtropical zones to the south. Main regional differences correspond roughly with primary climatic and vegetal patterns. Thus, for example, the animal communities of the Dry West differ sharply from those of the Humid East and from those of the Pacific coast. Because animals tend to range over wider areas than plants, faunal regions are generally coarser than vegetal regions and harder to delineate sharply.

The animal geography of the United States, however, is far from a natural pattern, for European settlement produced a series of environmental changes that grossly altered the distribution of animal communities. First, many species were hunted to extinction or near extinction, most conspicuously, perhaps, the American bison, which ranged by the millions nearly from coast to coast but now lives only in zoos and wildlife preserves. Second, habitats were upset or destroyed throughout most of the country—forests cut, grasslands plowed and overgrazed, and migration paths interrupted by fences, railroads, and highways. Third, certain introduced species found hospitable niches and, like the English sparrow, spread over huge areas, often preempting the habitats of native animals. Fourth, though their effects are not well understood, chemical biocides such as DDT were used for so long and in such volume that they are believed at least partly responsible for catastrophic mortality rates among large mammals and birds, especially predators high on the food chain. In consequence, many native animals have been reduced to tiny fractions of their former ranges or exterminated completely, while other animals, both native and introduced, have found the new anthropocentric environment well suited to their needs, with explosive effects on their populations. The coyote and several species of deer are among the animals that now occupy much larger ranges than they once did. (P.F.L.)

Excluding from consideration the tropical and Arctic elements, the fauna of the United States falls into a well-marked pattern, associated with the more conspicuous botanical and geological formations. The southeastern region of hardwood and pine, a rich mixed forest, extends somewhat beyond the Mississippi, contrasting sharply with the Sonoran Desert of the southwest. The great central grasslands from the Dakotas to the Gulf contrast as sharply with the transcontinental coniferous forest at the north; this forest sends great "peninsulas" southward in the Appalachian and Rocky mountains, accompanied by northern types of animals.

The Rocky Mountains, with other western ranges, supply a suitable environment for various rock-dwelling types, whose relatives are found in the mountain ranges of Eurasia. The more western ranges, the Cascades and the Sierra Nevada and the Pacific coastal region, have a distinctive fauna with a mixture of unique elements and of forms related to those of the southeastern forest region. The Pacific region has a varied fauna, mostly sharply distinct from that of the southeastern forest.

Arrangement of the account of the distribution of the

Disruption of natural patterns of animal life

fauna according to these regional provinces has the merit that it can be compared further with the distribution of insects and of other invertebrates, some of which may be expected to fall into the same patterns as the vertebrates, while others, with different modes or different ages of dispersal, will have geographic patterns of their own.

The transcontinental zone of coniferous forest at the north, the taiga, and the tundra zone into which it merges at the northern limit of tree growth are strikingly paralleled by similar zones in the Rockies, and on Mt. Washington in the east, where the area above timberline and below snow line is a kind of tundra, often with tundra animals like the ptarmigan and the white *Parnassius* butterflies, while the spruce and other conifers below timberline form a belt sharply set off from the grassland or hardwood forest or desert at still lower altitudes.

A whole series of important types of animals spread beyond the limits of such regions or zones, sometimes over most of the continent. Aquatic animals, in particular, may live equally in forest and plains, in the Gulf states, and at the Canadian border. Such widespread animals include the white-tailed (Virginia) deer and black bear, the puma (though only in the remotest parts of its former range) and bobcat, the river otter (though now rare in inland areas, south of the Great Lakes) and mink, and the beaver and muskrat. The distinctive coyote ranges over all of western North America and eastward as far as Maine. The snapping turtle ranges from the Atlantic coast to the Rocky Mountains.

Widespread fauna

At the north, in the coniferous forest zone, the relations of animals with European or Eurasian representatives are numerous, and this zone, often referred to under the Siberian name of taiga, is also essentially circumpolar. The relations are less close than in the Arctic forms, but the moose, beaver, hare, red fox, otter, wolverine, and wolf are recognizably related to Eurasian animals. Even some fishes, like the whitefishes (Coregonidae), the yellow perch, and the pike, exhibit this kind of Old World-New World relation. A distinctively North American animal in this taiga assemblage is the Canadian porcupine.

The hardwood forest area of the east and the southeastern pinelands compose the most important of the faunal regions within the United States. A great variety of fishes, amphibians, and reptiles of this region have related forms in eastern Asia, and this pattern of representation is likewise found in the flora. This area is rich in catfishes, minnows, and suckers. The curious ganoid fishes, the bowfin and the gar, are ancient types. The "spoon-billed cat," a remarkable type of sturgeon in the lower Mississippi, is represented elsewhere in the world only in the Yangtze in China. The Appalachian region is headquarters for the salamanders of the world, with no less than seven of the eight families of this large group of amphibians represented; no other continent has more than three of the eight families together. The eellike sirens and amphiumas are confined to the southeastern states. The lungless salamanders of the family Plethodontidae exhibit a remarkable variety of genera and a number of species centring in the Appalachians. There is a great variety of frogs, and these include tree frogs whose main development is South American and Australian. The emydid freshwater turtles of the southeast parallel those of eastern Asia to a remarkable degree, though the genus *Clemmys* is the only one represented in both regions. Much the same is true of the water snakes, pit vipers, rat snakes, and green snakes, though still others are peculiarly American. The familiar alligator is a form with an Asiatic relative, the only other living true alligator being a species in central China.

In its mammals and birds the southeastern fauna is less sharply distinguished from the life to the north and west and is less directly related to that of eastern Asia. The forest is (or was) the home of the Virginia deer, the black bear, the gray fox, the raccoon, and the common opossum. The wild turkey and the extinct hosts of the passenger pigeon were characteristic. There is a remarkable variety of woodpeckers. The bird life in general tends to differ from that of Eurasia in the presence of birds, like the tanagers, American orioles, and hummingbirds, that belong to South American families. Small mammals abound with types of the worldwide rodent family Cricetidae, and with distinctive moles and shrews.

The western grasslands merge by insensible degrees into semidesert and desert toward the Great Basin and the Sonoran Desert. Most distinctive of the grassland animals proper is the American bison, whose nearly extinct European relative, the wisent, is found in the forest. The most distinctive of the American hoofed animals is the pronghorn, or prongbuck, which represents a family intermediate between the deer and the true antelopes in that it sheds its horns like a deer but retains the bony horn cores. The pronghorn is perhaps primarily a desert mammal, but it formerly ranged widely into the short-grass plains. Everywhere in open country in the West there are conspicuous and distinctive rodents. The burrowing pocket gophers are peculiarly American, rarely to be seen, but making their presence known by their pushed-out mounds of earth. The ground squirrels of the genus *Citellus* are related to those of central Asia, and resemble them in habit; in North America the gregarious prairie dog is a closely related form. The American badger, not especially related to the badger of Europe, has its headquarters in the grasslands. The prairie chicken is a bird distinctive of the plains region, which is invaded everywhere by birds from both the east and the west.

The Sonoran Desert of the southwest, which may be regarded as including southeastern California, southern Nevada and Arizona, a corner of Utah, parts of New Mexico, and extreme western Texas, is a paradise for reptiles. Distinctive lizards abound, and the rattlesnakes, of which only a few species are found elsewhere in the United States, have their headquarters there. Among lizards the poisonous Gila monster is wholly Sonoran, though with a Mexican relative. Sonoran types range to the Pacific coast and northward in the Great Basin. Noteworthy mammals are the graceful bipedal kangaroo rats (almost exlusively nocturnal), the ring-tailed cat, a relative of the raccoons, and the piglike peccary.

The Rocky Mountains and other western ranges afford distinctive habitats for rock- and cliff-dwelling hoofed animals and rodents. The little pikas, related to the rabbits, live in the rock-slides at high altitudes as they do in the mountain ranges of eastern Asia. Marmots live in the Rockies as in the Alps. Every west American range formerly had its own race of mountain sheep. At the north the Rocky Mountain goat lives at high altitudes—it is more properly a goat antelope, related to the takin of the mountains of western China. The dipper, remarkable for its habit of feeding in swift-flowing streams, though otherwise a bird without special aquatic adaptations, is a Rocky Mountain form with relatives in Asia and Europe.

In the Pacific region, the extremely distinctive primitive frog *Ascaphus*, which inhabits icy mountain brooks, represents a family by itself, perhaps more nearly related to the frogs of New Zealand than to more familiar types. The Cascades and Sierras form centres for salamanders of the families Ambystomidae and Plethodontidae second only to the Appalachians, and there are also distinctive newts. The burrowing lizards, of the well-defined family Anniellidae, are found only in a limited area in coastal California. The only family of birds distinctive of North America, that of the wren tits, Chamaeidae, is found in the chaparral of California. The mountain beaver, or sewellel (which is not at all beaverlike), is likewise a type peculiar to North America, confined to the Cascades and Sierras; and there are distinct kinds of moles in the Pacific area.

The mammals of the two coasts are strikingly different, though true seals (the harbour seal and the harp seal) are found on both. The sea lions, with longer necks and with projecting ears, are found only in the Pacific—the California sea lion, the more northern Steller's sea lion, and the fur seal. On the East Coast the larger rivers of Florida are inhabited by the Florida manatee or sea cow, a close relative of the more widespread and more distinctively marine West Indian species. (K.P.S.)

SETTLEMENT PATTERNS

Although the land was occupied and much affected by diverse Indian cultures over many millennia, these pre-

European settlement patterns have had virtually no impact upon the contemporary nation—except locally, as in parts of New Mexico. A benign habitat permitted a huge contiguous tract of settled land to materialize across nearly all the eastern half of the United States and within lesser, but still substantial, patches of the West. The vastness of the land, the scarcity of labour, and the abundance of migratory opportunities in a land replete with raw physical resources contributed to exceptional human mobility and a quick succession of ephemeral forms of land use and settlement. Human endeavours have greatly transformed the landscape, but such efforts have been largely destructive. Most of the pre-European landscape in the United States was so swiftly and radically altered that it is difficult to conjecture intelligently about its earlier appearance.

(For further details on settlement and cultural patterns, see the sections on the individual U.S. states and the articles on the major cities.)

The overall impression of the settled portion of the U.S. landscape, rural or urban, is one of disorder and incoherence, even in areas of strict geometric survey. The individual landscape unit is seldom in visual harmony with its neighbour, so that, however sound in design or construction the single structure may be, the general effect is untidy. These attributes have been intensified by the acute individualism of the American, vigorous speculation in land and other commodities, a strongly utilitarian attitude toward the land and the treasures above and below it, and government policy and law. The landscape is also remarkable for its extensive transportation facilities, which have greatly influenced the configuration of the land.

Another special characteristic of U.S. settlement, one that became obvious only by the mid-20th century, is the convergence of rural and urban modes of life. The farmsteads—and rural folk in general—have become increasingly urbanized, and agricultural operations have become more automated, while the metropolis grows more gelatinous, unfocussed, and pseudo-bucolic along its margins.

Rural settlement. Patterns of rural settlement indicate much about the history, economy, society, and minds of those who created them as well as about the land itself. The essential design of rural activity in the United States bears a strong family resemblance to that of other neo-European lands, such as Canada, Australia, New Zealand, South Africa, Argentina, or czarist Siberia—places that have undergone rapid occupation and exploitation by immigrants intent upon short-term development and enrichment. In all such areas, under novel social and political conditions and with a relative abundance of territory and physical resources, ideas and institutions derived from a relatively stable medieval or early-modern Europe have undergone major transformation. Further, these are nonpeasant countrysides, alike in thus far having failed to achieve the intimate symbiosis of people and habitat, the humanized rural landscapes characteristic of many relatively dense, stable, earthbound communities in parts of Asia, Africa, Europe, and Latin America.

Early models of land allocation. From the beginning the prevalent official policy of the British (except between 1763 and 1776) and then of the U.S. government was to promote agricultural and other settlement—to push the frontier westward as fast as physical and economic conditions permitted. The British crown's grants of large, often vaguely specified tracts to individual proprietors or companies enabled the grantees to draw settlers by the sale or lease of land at attractive prices or even by outright gift.

Of the numerous attempts at group colonization, the most notable effort was the theocratic and collectivist New England town that flourished, especially in Massachusetts, Connecticut, and New Hampshire, during the first century of settlement. The town, the basic unit of government and comparable in area to townships in other states, allotted both rural and village parcels to single families by group decision. The residences of farmers and all others were concentrated in a central village. This quasi-communal system broke down before the end of the colonial era, although the village persisted as an amoeba-shaped entity straggling along converging roads, neither fully rural nor agglomerated in form. The only latter-day

settlement experiment of notable magnitude to achieve enduring success was a series of Mormon settlements in the Great Basin region of Utah and adjacent states, with their tightly concentrated farm villages reminiscent of the New England model. Other efforts have been made along ethnic, religious, or political lines, but success has been at best brief and fragile.

Creating the national domain. With the coming of independence and after complex negotiations, the original 13 states surrendered to the new national government nearly all their claims to the unsettled western lands beyond their boundaries. Some tracts, however, were reserved for disposal to particular groups. Thus, the Western Reserve of northeastern Ohio gave preferential treatment to natives of Connecticut, while the military tracts in Ohio and Indiana were used as bonus payments to veterans of the American Revolution.

A federally administered national domain was created, to which the great bulk of the territory acquired in the 1803 Louisiana Purchase and later beyond the Mississippi and in 1819 in Florida was consigned. The only major exceptions were the public lands of Texas, which were left within that state's jurisdiction; such earlier French and Spanish land grants as were confirmed, often after tortuous litigation; and some Indian lands. In sharp contrast to the slipshod methods of colonial land survey and disposal, the federal land managers expeditiously surveyed, numbered, and mapped their territory in advance of settlement, beginning with Ohio in the 1780s, then sold or deeded it to settlers under inviting terms at a number of regional land offices.

The design universally followed in the new survey system (except within the French, Spanish, and Indian grants) was a simple, efficient rectangular scheme. Townships were laid out as blocks, each six by six miles in size, oriented with the compass directions. Thirty-six sections, each one square mile, or 640 acres (260 hectares), in size, were designated within each township; and public roads were established along section lines and, where needed, along half-section lines. At irregular intervals, offsets in survey lines and roads were introduced to allow for the Earth's curvature. Individual property lines were coincident with, or parallel to, survey lines, and this pervasive rectangularity generally carried over into the geometry of fields and fences or into the townsites later superimposed upon the basic rural survey.

This all-encompassing checkerboard pattern is best appreciated from an airplane window over Iowa or Kansas. There, one sees few streams or other natural features or few diagonal highways or railroads interrupting the overwhelming squareness of the landscape. A systematic rectangular layout, rather less rigorous in form, also appears in much of Texas and those portions of Maine, western New York and Pennsylvania, and southern Georgia that were settled since the 1780s.

Distribution of rural lands. Since its formation, Congress has enacted a series of complex schemes for distribution of the national domain. The most famous of these plans was the Homestead Act of 1862, which offered title to 160 acres to individual settlers, subject only to residence for a certain period of time and to the making of minimal improvements to the land thus acquired. The legal provisions of such acts have varied with time as the nature of farming technology and of the remaining lands have changed, but their inspiration has been to create the Jeffersonian ideal of a republic in which yeoman farmers own and till self-sufficient properties.

The program was successful in providing private owners with almost all choice lands, aside from parcels reserved for schools and various township and municipal uses. More than one-third of the national territory, however, is still owned by federal and state governments, with most of this land in forest and wildlife preserves. A large proportion of this land is in the West and is unsuited for intensive agriculture or grazing because of the roughness, dryness, or salinity of the terrain; much of it is leased out for light grazing or for timber cutting.

Patterns of farm life. During the classic period of U.S. rural life, around 1900, the typical American lived or

Marginal notes:

Factors affecting use of the land

Comparative rural patterns: United States and elsewhere

The establishment of townships

The U.S.
farm
around
1900

worked on a farm or was economically dependent upon farmers. In contrast to rural life in many other parts of the world, the farm family lived on an isolated farmstead some distance from town and often from farm neighbours; its property averaged less than one-quarter square mile. This farmstead would vary in form and content with local tradition and economy. In particular, barn types were localized—for example, the tobacco barns of the South, the great dairy barns of Wisconsin, or the general-purpose forebay barns of southeastern Pennsylvania—as were modes of fencing. In general, however, the farmstead contained dwelling, barn, storage and sheds for small livestock and equipment, a small orchard, and a kitchen garden. A woodlot might be found in the least accessible or least fertile part of the farm.

Successions of such farms were connected with one another and with the towns by means of a dense, usually rectangular lattice of roads, largely unimproved at the time. The hamlets, villages, and smaller cities were arrayed at relatively regular intervals, with size and affluence determined in large part by the presence and quality of rail service or status as the county seat. But, among people who have been historically rural, individualistic, and antiurban in bias, many services normally located in urban places might be found in rustic settings. Thus much retail business was transacted by means of itinerant peddlers, while small shops for the fabrication, distribution, or repair of various items were often located in isolated farmsteads, as were the post offices.

Social activity also tended to be widely dispersed among numerous rural churches, schools, or grange halls; and the climactic event of the year might well be the county fair, political rally, or religious encampment—again on a rural site. Not the least symptomatic sign of the strong tendency toward spatial isolation are the countless family burial plots or community cemeteries so liberally distributed across the countryside.

Regional small-town patterns. There has been much regional variation among smaller villages and hamlets. Unfortunately, such phenomena have received relatively little attention from students of U.S. culture or geography. The distinctive New England village, of course, is generally recognized and cherished: it consists of a loose clustering of white-frame buildings, including a church (usually Congregationalist or Unitarian), town hall, shops, and stately homes with tall shade trees around the central green, or commons—a grassy expanse that may contain a bandstand and monuments or flowers. Derivative village forms were later carried westward to sections of the northern Midwest.

Town
morphol-
ogies in
the rural
United
States

Less widely known but equally distinctive is the town morphology characteristic of the Midland, or Pennsylvanian, culture area and most fully developed in southeastern and central Pennsylvania and Piedmont Maryland. It differs totally from the New England model in density, building materials, and general appearance. Closely packed, often contiguous buildings—mostly brick, but sometimes stone, frame, or stucco—abut directly on a sidewalk, which is often paved with brick and usually thickly planted with maple, sycamore, or other shade trees. Such towns are characteristically linear in plan, have only one or two principal streets, and may radiate outward from a central square lined with commercial and governmental structures.

The most characteristic U.S. small town was the one whose pattern evolved in the Midwest. Its simple scheme was usually based on the grid plan. Functions are rigidly segregated spatially, with the central business district, consisting of closely packed two- or three-story brick buildings, limited exclusively to commercial and administrative activity. The residences, generally set well back within spacious lots, are peripheral in location, as are most rail facilities, factories, and warehouses.

Even the modest urbanization of the small town came late to the South. Most urban functions long were spatially dispersed—almost totally so in the early Chesapeake Bay country or North Carolina—or were performed entirely by the larger plantations dominating the economic life of much of the region. When city and town began to mate-

alize in the 19th and 20th centuries, they tended to follow the Midwestern model in layout.

Although quite limited in geographical area, the characteristic villages of the Mormon and Hispanic-American districts are of considerable interest. The Mormon settlement uncompromisingly followed the ecclesiastically imposed grid plan composed of square blocks, each with perhaps only four very large house lots, and the block surrounded by extremely wide streets. Those villages in New Mexico in which population and culture were derived from Old Mexico were often built according to the standard Latin-American plan. The distinctive feature is a central plaza dominated by a Roman Catholic church and encircled by low stone or adobe buildings.

The rural–urban transition. *Weakening of the agrarian ideal.* The United States has had little success in achieving or maintaining the family-farm ideal. Through purchase, inheritance, leasing, and other means, some of dubious legality, smaller properties have been merged into much larger entities. In 1978, when average farm size had grown to 444 acres, farms containing 2,000 or more acres accounted for almost half of all farmland and 17 percent of cropland harvested, although comprising less than 3 percent of all farms. At the other extreme were those 60 percent of all farms that contained fewer than 180 acres and reported less than 14 percent of cropland harvested. Succeeding years have intensified this trend toward fewer but larger farms.

The huge, heavily capitalized "neoplantation," essentially a factory in the field, is especially conspicuous in parts of California, Arizona, and the Mississippi Delta, but examples can be found in any state. There are also many smaller but intensive operations that call for large investments and advanced managerial skills. This trend toward large-scale, capital-intensive farm enterprise has been paralleled by a sharp drop in rural farm population—a slump from the all-time maximum of about 32,000,000 in the early 20th century to 7,553,000 in 1979; but even in 1940, when farm folk still numbered more than 30,000,000, nearly 40 percent of farm operators were tenants, and another 10 percent were only partial owners.

As the agrarian population has dwindled, so too has its immediate impact lessened, though less swiftly, in economic and political matters. The rural United States, however, has been the source of many of the nation's values and images. The United States has become a highly urbanized, technologically advanced society far removed in daily life from cracker barrel, barnyard, corral, or logging camp. Although Americans have gravitated, sometimes reluctantly, to the big city, in the daydreams and assumptions that guide many sociopolitical decisions, the memory of a rapidly vanishing agrarian America is well noted. This is revealed not only in the works of contemporary novelists, poets, and painters but also throughout the popular arts: in movies, television, soap operas, folklore, country-and-western music, political oratory, and in much leisure-time activity.

The
mythology
of small-
town
America

Impact of the motor vehicle. Since about 1920 more genuine change has occurred in U.S. rural life than during the preceding three centuries of European settlement in North America. Although the basic explanation is the profound social and technological transformations engulfing most of the world, the most immediate agent of change has been the internal-combustion engine. The automobile, truck, bus, and paved highway have more than supplanted a moribund passenger-railroad system. While many local rail depots have been boarded up and scores of secondary lines have been abandoned, hundreds of thousands of miles of old dirt roads have been paved, and a vast system of interstate highways has been constructed to connect major cities in a single nonstop network. The net result has been a shrinking of the mile and more travel for the individual driver, rural or urban.

High-
ways and
human
settle-
ment

Small towns have undergone a number of changes. Before 1970 towns near highways and urban centres generally prospered; while in the less fortunate towns, where the residents lingered on for the sake of relatively cheap housing, downtown businesses often became extinct. Since 1970, however, the rural and small-town population has grown at a faster rate than the metropolitan population, reversing more than 100 years of urban growth.

As Americans have become increasingly mobile, the visual aspect of rural America has altered drastically. The highway has become the central route, and many of the functions once confined to the local town or city now stretch for many miles along major roads.

Reversal of the classic rural dominance. The metropolitanization of life in the United States has not been limited to city, suburb, or exurb; it now involves most of the rural area and population. The result has been the decline of local crafts and regional peculiarities, quite visibly in such items as farm implements, fencing, silos, and housing and in many commodities such as clothing or bread. In many ways, the countryside is now economically dependent on the city.

The city dweller is the dominant consumer for products other than those of field, quarry, or lumber mill; and city location tends to determine patterns of rural economy rather than the reverse. During weekends and the vacation seasons, swarms of city folk stream out to second homes in the countryside, to campgrounds, ski trails, beaches, boating areas, or hunting and fishing tracts. For many large rural areas, recreation is the principal source of income and employment; and such areas as northern New England and Upstate New York have become playgrounds and sylvan refuges for many urban residents.

The larger cities reach far into the countryside for their vital supplies of water and energy. There is an increasing reliance upon distant mine-mouth power plants for electrical power, and cities have gone far afield in seeking out rural dumps for their ever-growing garbage and trash.

The majority of the rural population now lives within daily commuting range of a sizable city. This enables many farm residents to operate the farm while working part- or full-time at a city job and prevents the drastic decline in rural-farm population that has occurred in remoter parts of the country. Similarly, many small towns within the shadow of the metropolis, with fewer and fewer farmers to service, have become dormitory satellites, serving residents from nearby cities and suburbs.

Urban settlement. The United States has moved from a predominantly rural settlement into an urban society. In so doing, it has followed the general path that other advanced nations have travelled and one along which developing nations have begun to hasten. About three-fourths of the population live clustered within officially designated urban places and "urbanized areas," which account for less than 2 percent of the national territory. At least another 15 percent live in dispersed residences that are actually urban in economic or social orientation.

Classic patterns of siting and growth. Although more than 95 percent of the population was rural during the colonial period and for the first years of independence, cities were crucial elements in the settlement system from the earliest days. Boston; New Amsterdam (New York City); Jamestown; Charleston; and Philadelphia were founded at the same time as the colonies they served. Like nearly all other North American colonial towns of consequence, they were ocean ports. Until at least the beginning of the 20th century the historical geography of U.S. cities has been intimately related with that of successive transportation systems. The location of successful cities with respect to the areas they served, as well as their internal structure, was determined largely by the nature of these systems.

The colonial cities acted as funnels for the collection and shipment of farm and forest products and other raw materials from the interior to trading partners in Europe, the Caribbean, or Africa and for the return flow of manufactured goods and other locally scarce items, as well as immigrants. Such cities were essentially marts and warehouses and only minimal attention was given to social, military, educational, or religious functions. The inadequacy and high cost of overland traffic dictated sites along major ocean embayments or river estuaries; the only pre-1800 nonports worthy of notice were Lancaster and York, both in Pennsylvania, and Williamsburg, Virginia. With the populating of the interior and the spread of a system

Evolving functions of U.S. cities

of canals and improved roads, such new cities as Pittsburgh, Cincinnati, Buffalo, and St. Louis mushroomed at junctures between various routes or at which modes of transport were changed. Older ocean ports, such as New Castle, Delaware; Newport, Rhode Island; Charleston, South Carolina; Savannah, Georgia; and Portland, Maine, whose locations prevented them from serving large hinterlands, tended to stagnate.

From about 1850 to 1920 the success of new cities and the further growth of older ones in large part were dependent on their location within the new steam railroad system and on their ability to dominate a large tributary territory. Such waterside rail hubs as Buffalo, Toledo (Ohio), Chicago, and San Francisco gained population and wealth rapidly, while such offspring of the rail era as Atlanta, Georgia; Indianapolis, Indiana; Minneapolis, Minnesota; Fort Worth, Texas; and Tacoma, Washington, also grew dramatically. Much of the rapid industrialization of the 19th and early 20th centuries occurred in places already favoured by water or rail transport systems; but in some instances, such as in the cities of northeastern Pennsylvania's anthracite region, some New England mill towns, and the textile centres of the Carolina and Virginia Piedmont, manufacturing brought about rapid urbanization and the consequent attraction of transport facilities. The extraction of gold, silver, copper, coal, iron, and in the 20th century, gas and oil led to rather ephemeral centres—unless these places were able to capitalize on local or regional advantages other than minerals.

A strong early start, whatever the inital economic base may have been, was often the key factor in competition among cities. With sufficient early momentum, urban capital and population would tend to expand almost automatically. The point is illustrated perfectly by the larger cities of the northeastern seaboard, from Portland (Maine) through Baltimore. The nearby physical wealth is poor to mediocre, and they are now far off-centre on the national map; but a prosperous mercantile beginning, good land and sea connections with distant places, and a rich local accumulation of talent, capital, and initiative were sufficient to bring about the growth of one of the world's largest concentrations of industry, commerce, and people.

New factors in municipal development. The pre-1900 development of the U.S. city was almost completely a chronicle of the economics of the production, collection, and distribution of physical commodities and basic services dictated by geography, but there have been striking deviations from this pattern. The physical determinants of urban location and growth have given way to social factors. Increasingly, the most successful cities are oriented toward the more advanced modes for the production and consumption of services, specifically the knowledge, managerial, and recreational industries. The largest cities have become more dependent upon corporate headquarters, communications, and the manipulation of information for their sustenance. Washington, D.C., is the most obvious example of a metropolis in which government and ancillary activities have been the spur for vigorous growth; but almost all of the state capitals have displayed a similar demographic and economic vitality. Further, urban centres that contain a major college or university often have enjoyed remarkable expansion.

With the coming of relative affluence and abundant leisure to the population and a decrease of labour input in industrial processes, a new breed of cities has sprouted across the land: those that cater to the pleasure-seeker, vacationer, and the retired—for example, the young, flourishing cities of Florida or Nevada and many locations in California, Arizona, and Colorado.

The automobile as a means of personal transportation was developed about the time of World War I, and the U.S. city was catapulted into a radically new period, both quantitatively and qualitatively, in the further evolution of physical form and function. The size, density, and internal structure of the city were previously constrained by the limitations of the pedestrian and early mass-transit systems. Only the well-to-do could afford horse and carriage or a secluded villa in the countryside. Cities were relatively small and compact, with a single clearly defined centre, and grew by accretion along their edges, without any significant spatial hiatuses, except where commuter railroads linked outlying towns to the largest of metropolises. Workers living beyond the immediate vicinity of their work had to locate within reach of the few horse-drawn omnibuses or the later electric street railways.

Effect of the automobile on urban development

The universality of the automobile, even among the less affluent, and the parallel proliferation of service facilities and highways greatly loosened and fragmented the U.S. city, which spread over surrounding rural lands. Older, formerly autonomous towns grew swiftly. Many towns became satellites of the larger city or were absorbed. Many suburbs and subdivisions arose with single-family homes on lots larger than had been possible for the ordinary householder in the city. These communities were almost totally dependent on the highway for the flow of commuters, goods, and services, and many were located in splendid isolation, separated by tracts of farmland, brush, or forest from other such developments. At the major interchanges of the limited-access highways, a new form of agglomerated settlement sprung up: the service station, motel, restaurant, and other establishments for a mobile clientele. Such satellite communities are especially noteworthy in the environs of such larger cities as Philadelphia, New York City, Detroit, and Chicago.

The new look of "the metropolitan area." The outcome has been a broad, ragged, semiurbanized belt of land surrounding each city, large or small, and quite often blending imperceptibly into the suburban–exurban halo encircling a neighbouring metropolitan centre. There is a great similarity in the makeup and general appearance of all such tracts: the planless intermixture of scraps of the rural landscape with the fragments of the scattered metropolis; the randomly distributed subdivisions or single homes; the vast shopping centres, the large commercial cemeteries, drive-in theatres, junkyards, and golf courses and other recreational enterprises; and the regional or metropolitan airport, often with its own cluster of factories, warehouses, or travel-oriented businesses. The traditional city—unitary, concentric in form, with a single well-defined middle—was replaced by a relatively amorphous, polycentric metropolitan sprawl.

The inner cities

The inner city of the larger U.S. metropolitan area displays some traits that are common to the larger centres of all advanced nations. A central business district, almost always the oldest section of the city, is surrounded by a succession of roughly circular zones, each distinctive in economic and social-ethnic character. The symmetry of this scheme is distorted by the irregularities of surface and drainage or the effects of radial highways and railroads. Land is most costly, and hence land use is most intensive, toward the centre. Major business, financial and governmental offices, department stores, and specialty shops dominate the downtown which is usually fringed by a band of factories and warehouses. The outer parts of the city, like the suburbs, are mainly residential.

With some exceptions—*e.g.,* large apartment complexes in downtown Chicago—people do not reside in the downtown areas, and there is a steady downward gradient in population density per unit area (and more open land and single-family residences) as one moves from the inner city toward the open country. Conversely, there is a general rise in income and social status with increasing distance from the core. The sharply defined immigrant neighbourhoods of the 19th century generally persist in a somewhat diluted form, though specific ethnic groups may have shifted their location. Later migrant groups, notably Southern blacks and Latin Americans, generally dominate the more rundown neighbourhoods of the inner cities.

Individual and collective character of U.S. cities. American cities, more so than the small-town or agrarian landscape, are more the product of a particular period than of location. The relatively venerable centres of the Atlantic Seaboard—Boston; Philadelphia; Baltimore; Albany, New York; Chester, Pennsylvania; Alexandria, Virginia; or Georgetown (a district of Washington, D.C.), for example—are virtual replicas of the fashionable European models of their early period rather than the fruition of a regional culture, unlike New Orleans and Santa Fe,

New Mexico, which reflect other times and regions. The townscapes of Pittsburgh, Detroit, Chicago, and Denver, Colorado, depict national modes of thought and the technological development of their formative years, just as Dallas, Texas; Las Vegas, Nevada; San Diego, California; Tucson, Arizona; and Albuquerque, New Mexico, proclaim contemporary values and gadgetry more than any local distinctiveness. When strong-minded city founders instituted a highly individual plan and their successors managed to preserve it—as, for example, in Savannah, Georgia; Washington, D.C.; and Salt Lake City, Utah—or when there is a happy combination of a spectacular site and appreciative residents—as in San Francisco or Seattle, Washington—a genuine individuality does seem to emerge. Such an identity also may develop where immigration has been highly selective, as in such places as Miami; Phoenix, Arizona; and Los Angeles.

As a group, U.S. cities differ from cities in other countries in both type and degree. The national political structure, the social inclinations of the people, and the strong outward surge of urban development have led to the political fragmentation of metropolises that socially and economically are relatively cohesive units. The fact that a single metropolitan area may sprawl across numerous incorporated towns and cities, several townships, and two or more counties and states has a major impact upon both its appearance and the way it functions. Not the least of these effects is a dearth of overall physical and social planning (or its ineffectuality when attempted), and the rather chaotic, inharmonious appearance of both inner-city and peripheral zones painfully reflects the absence of any effective collective action concerning such matters.

Political fragmentation and lack of planning

The U.S. city is a place of sharp transitions. Construction, demolition, and reconstruction go on almost ceaselessly, though increasing thought has been given to preserving monuments and buildings. From present evidence, it would be impossible to guess that New York City and Albany date from the 1620s or that Detroit was founded in 1701. Preservation and restoration do occur, but often only when it makes sense in terms of tourist revenue. Physical and social blight has reached epidemic proportions in the slum areas of the inner city; but, despite the wholesale razing of such areas and the subsequent urban-renewal projects (sometimes as apartment or commercial developments for the affluent), the belief has become widespread that the ills of the U.S. city are incurable, especially with the increasing flight of capital, tax revenue, and the more highly educated, affluent elements of the population to suburban areas and the spatial and political polarization of whites and nonwhites.

In the central sections of U.S. cities, there is little sense of history or continuity; instead, one finds evidence of the dominance of the engineering mentality and of the credo that the business of the city is business. Commercial and administrative activities are paramount, and usually there is little room for the church buildings or for parks or other nonprofit enterprises. The role of the cathedral, so central in the medieval European city, is filled by a U.S. invention serving both utilitarian and symbolic purposes, the skyscraper. Some cities have felt the need for other bold secular monuments; hence the Gateway Arch looming over St. Louis, Seattle's Space Needle, and Houston's Astrodome. Future archaeologists may well conclude from their excavations that American society was ruled by an oligarchy of highway engineers, architects, and bulldozer operators. The great expressways converging upon, or looping, the downtown area and the huge amount of space devoted to parking lots and garages are even more impressive than the massive surgery executed upon U.S. cities a century ago to hack out room for railroad terminals and marshalling yards.

Altered land-forms and land-scapes of the city

Within many urban sites there has been such radical physical transformation of shoreline, drainage systems, and land surface as would be difficult to match elsewhere in the world. Thus, in their physical lineaments, Manhattan and inner Boston bear scant resemblance to the landscapes seen by their initial settlers. The surface of downtown Chicago has been raised several feet above its former swamp level, the city's lakefront extensively reshaped, and the flow of the Chicago River reversed. Even Los Angeles, notorious for its disregard of the environment, has its concrete arroyo bottoms, terraced hillsides and landslides, and its own artificial microclimate.

The super-cities of the United States. The unprecedented outward sprawl of U.S. urban settlement has created some novel settlement forms, for the quantitative change has been so great as to induce qualitative transformation. The conurbation—a territorial coalescence of two or more sizable cities whose peripheral zones have grown together—may have first appeared in early-19th-century Europe. There are major examples in Great Britain, the Low Countries, and West Germany, as well as in Japan.

Nothing elsewhere, however, rivals in size and complexity the aptly named megalopolis, that super-city stretching along the Atlantic from Boston to Richmond, Virginia. Other large conurbations include, in the Great Lakes region, one centred on Chicago and containing large slices of Illinois, Wisconsin, and Indiana; another based in Detroit, embracing large parts of Michigan and Ohio and reaching into Canada; and a third stretching from Buffalo through Cleveland and back to Pittsburgh. All three are reaching toward one another and may form another megalopolis that, in turn, may soon be grafted onto the seaboard megalopolis by a corridor through central New York state.

Another example of a growing megalopolis is the huge southern California conurbation reaching from Santa Barbara, through a dominating Los Angeles, to the Mexican border. The solid strip of urban territory that lines the eastern shore of Puget Sound is a smaller counterpart. Quite exceptional in form is the slender linear multicity occupying Florida's Atlantic coastline, from Jacksonville to Miami, and the loose swarm of medium-sized cities clustering along the Southern Piedmont, from south central Virginia to Atlanta.

One of the few predictions that seem safe in so dynamic and innovative a land as the United States is that, unless severe and painful controls are placed on land use, the shape of the urban environment will be increasingly megalopolitan: a small set of great constellations of polycentric urban zones, each complexly interlocked socially and physically with its neighbours.

Traditional regions. The differences among U.S. "traditional regions," or "culture areas," tend to be slight and shallow as compared with such areas in most older, more stable countries. The muted, often subtle nature of interregional differences can be ascribed to the relative newness of U.S. settlement, a perpetually high degree of mobility, a superb communications system, and the galloping centralization of economy and government. It might even be argued that some of these regions are quaint vestiges of a vanishing past, of interest only to antiquarians.

Yet, in spite of the nationwide standardization in many areas of U.S. thought and behaviour, the lingering effects of the older culture areas do remain potent. In the case of the South, for example, the differences helped to precipitate the gravest political crisis and bloodiest military conflict in the nation's history. More than a century after the Civil War, the South remains a powerful entity in political, economic, and social terms, and its peculiar status is recognized in religious, educational, athletic, and literary circles.

Even more intriguing is the appearance of a series of essentially 20th-century regions. Southern California is the largest and perhaps the most distinctive region, and its special culture has attracted large numbers of immigrants to the state. Similar trends are visible in southern Florida; in Texas, whose mystique has captured the national imagination; and to a certain degree in the more ebullient regions of New Mexico and Arizona as well. At the metropolitan level, it is difficult to believe that such distinctive cities as San Francisco, Las Vegas, Dallas, Tucson, and Seattle have become like all other American cities. A detailed examination, however, would show significant if sometimes subtle interregional differences in terms of language, religion, diet, folklore, folk architecture and handicrafts, political behaviour, social etiquette, and a number of other cultural categories.

A multitiered hierarchy of culture areas might be postulated for the United States; but the most interesting levels are, first, the nation as a whole and, second, the five to 10 large subnational regions, each comprising parts or entire states. There is a remarkably close coincidence between the political United States and the cultural United States. Crossing into Mexico, the traveller passes across a cultural chasm. If the contrasts are less dramatic between the two sides of the U.S.–Canadian boundary, they are nonetheless real, especially to the Canadian. Erosion of the cultural barrier has been largely limited to the area that stretches from northern New York state to Aroostook County, Maine. There, a vigorous demographic and cultural immigration by French-Canadians has gone far toward eradicating international differences.

While the international boundaries act as a cultural container, the interstate boundaries are curiously irrelevant. Even when the state had a strong autonomous early existence—as happened with Massachusetts, Virginia, or Pennsylvania—subsequent economic and political forces have tended to wash away such initial identities. Actually, it could be argued that the political divisions of the 48 conterminous states are anachronistic in the context of contemporary socioeconomic and cultural forces. Partially convincing cases might be built for equating Utah and Texas with their respective culture areas because of exceptional historical and physical circumstances, or perhaps Oklahoma, given its very tardy European occupation and its dubious distinction as the territory to which exiled Indian tribes of the East were relegated. In most instances, however, the states either contain two or more distinctly different culture and political areas or fragments thereof or are part of a much larger single culture area. Thus sharp North–South dichotomies characterize California, Missouri, Illinois, Indiana, Ohio, and Florida, while Tennessee advertises that there are really three Tennessees. In Virginia the opposing cultural forces were so strong that actual fission took place in 1863 (with the admission to the Union of West Virginia) along one of those rare interstate boundaries that approximate a genuine cultural divide.

Much remains to be learned about the cause and effect relations between economic and culture areas in the United States. If the South or New England could at one time be correlated with a specific economic system, this is no longer easy to do. Cultural systems appear to respond more slowly to agents of change than do economic or urban systems. Thus the Manufacturing Belt, a core region for many social and economic activities, now spans parts of four traditional culture areas—New England, the Midland, the Midwest, and the northern fringes of the South. The great urban sprawl, from southern Maine to central Virginia, blithely ignores the cultural slopes that are still visible in its more rural tracts.

The culture areas of the United States are generally European in origin, the result of importing European colonists and ways of life and the subsequent social groups to new habitats. The aboriginal cultures have had relatively little influence on the nation's modern culture. In the Southwestern and the indistinct Oklahoman subregions, the Indian element merits consideration only as one of several ingredients making up the regional mosaic. With some exceptions, the map of U.S. culture areas in the East can be explained in terms of the genesis, development, and expansion of the three principal colonial cultural hearths along the Atlantic Seaboard. Each was basically British in character, but their personalities remain distinct because of, first, different sets of social and political conditions during the critical period of first effective settlement and, second, local physical and economic circumstances. The cultural gradients between them tend to be much steeper and the boundaries more distinct than is true for the remainder of the nation.

New England. New England was the dominant region during the century of rapid expansion following the American Revolution and not merely in terms of demographic or economic expansion. In social and cultural life—in education, politics, theology, literature, science, architecture, and the more advanced forms of mechanical and social technology—the area exercised its primacy. New England was the leading source of ideas and styles for the nation

Megalopolis: concept and forms

Relation of political and cultural boundaries

Amorphous relation of cultures and economies

from about 1780 to 1880; it furnishes an impressive example of the capacity of strongly motivated communities to rise above the constraints of a harsh environment.

During its first two centuries, New England had an unusually homogeneous population. With rare exceptions, the British immigrants shared the same religion (Congregationalist), language, social organization, and general outlook. A distinctive regional culture took form, most noticeably in terms of dialect, town morphology, and folk architecture. The personality of the people also took on a regional coloration both in folklore and in actuality; there is sound basis for the belief that the traditional New England Yankee is self-reliant, thrifty, inventive, and enterprising. The influx of foreign-born immigrants that began in the 1830s diluted and altered the New England identity, but much of its early personality survived.

By virtue of location, wealth, and seniority, the Boston metropolitan area has become the cultural economic centre of New England. This sovereignty is shared to some degree, however, with two other old centres, the lower Connecticut Valley and the Narragansett Bay region of Rhode Island.

The early westward demographic and ideological expansion of New England was so influential that it is justifiable to call New York, northern New Jersey, northern Pennsylvania, and much of the Upper Midwest "New England Extended." Further, the energetic endeavours of New England whalers, merchants, and missionaries had a considerable impact on the cultures of Hawaii, various other Pacific isles, and several points in the Caribbean. New Englanders also were active in the Americanization of early Oregon and Washington, with results that are still visible. Later, the overland diffusion of New England natives and practices meant a recognizable New England character not only for the Upper Midwest, from Ohio to the Dakotas, but also in the Pacific Northwest in general, though to a lesser degree.

The South. By far the largest of the three original Anglo-American culture areas, the South is also the most idiosyncratic with respect to national norms—or slowest to accept them. The South was once so distinct from the non-South in almost every observable or quantifiable feature and so fiercely proud of its peculiarities that for some years the question of whether it could maintain political and social unity with the non-South was in serious doubt. These differences are still observable in almost every realm of human activity, including rural economy, dialect, diet, costume, folklore, politics, architecture, social customs, and recreation. Only during the 20th century can an argument be made that it has achieved a decisive convergence with the rest of the nation, at least in terms of economic behaviour and material culture.

A persistent deviation from the national mainstream probably began in the first years of settlement. The first settlers of the South were almost purely British, not outwardly different from those who flocked to New England or the Midland, but almost certainly distinct in terms of motives and social values and more conservative in retaining the rurality and the family and social structure of premodern Europe. The vast importation of African slaves was also a major factor, as was a degree of contact with the Indians that was less pronounced farther north. In addition, the unusual pattern of economy (much different from that of northwestern Europe), settlement, and social organization, which were in part an adaptation to a starkly unfamiliar physical habitat, accentuated the South's deviation from other culture areas.

In both origin and spatial structure, the South has been characterized by diffuseness. In the search for a single cultural hearth, the most plausible choice is the Chesapeake Bay area and the northeastern corner of North Carolina, the earliest area of recognizably Southern character. Early components of Southern population and culture also arrived from other sources. A narrow coastal strip from North Carolina to the Georgia–Florida border and including the Sea Islands is decidedly Southern in character, yet it stands apart self-consciously from other parts of the South. Though colonized directly from Great Britain, it had also significant connections with the West Indies,

in which relation the African cultural contribution was strongest and purest. Charleston and Savannah, which nurtured their own distinctive civilizations, dominated this subregion. Similarly, French Louisiana received elements of culture and population—to be stirred into the special Creole mixture—not only, putatively, from the Chesapeake Bay hearth area but also indirectly from France, French Nova Scotia, the French West Indies, and Africa. In south central Texas, the Germanic and Hispanic influx was so heavy that a special subregion can be designated.

It would seem, then, that the Southern culture area may be an example of convergent, or parallel, evolution of a variety of elements arriving along several paths but subject to some single general process that could mold one larger regional consciousness and way of life.

Because of its slowness in joining the national technological mainstream, the South can be subdivided into a much greater number of subregions than is possible for any of the other older traditional regions. Those described above are of lesser order than the two principal Souths, variously called Upper and Lower (or Deep) South, Upland and Lowland South, or Yeoman and Plantation South.

The Upland South, which comprises the southern Appalachians, the upper Appalachian Piedmont, the Cumberland and other low interior plateaus, and the Ozarks and Ouachitas, was colonized culturally and demographically from the Chesapeake Bay hearth area and the Midland; it is most emphatically white Anglo-Saxon Protestant (WASP) in character. The latter area, which contains a large black population, includes the greater part of the South Atlantic and Gulf coastal plains and the lower Appalachian Piedmont. Its early major influences came from the Chesapeake Bay area, with only minor elements from the coastal Carolina–Georgia belt, Louisiana, and elsewhere. The division between the two subregions remains distinct from Virginia to Texas, but each region can be further subdivided. Within the Upland South, the Ozark region might legitimately be detached from the Appalachian; and, within the latter, the proud and prosperous Kentucky Bluegrass, with its emphasis on tobacco and thoroughbreds, certainly merits special recognition.

Toward the margins of the South, the difficulties in delimiting subregions become greater. The outer limits themselves are a topic of special interest. There seems to be more than an accidental relation between these limits and various climatic factors. The fuzzy northern boundary, definitely not associated with the conventional Mason and Dixon Line or the Ohio River, seems most closely associated with length of frost-free season or with temperature during the winter. As the Southern cultural complex was carried to the West, it not only retained its strength but became more intense, in contrast to the influence of New England and the Midland. But the South finally fades away as one approaches the 100th meridian, with its critical decline in annual precipitation. The apparent correlation between the cultural South and a humid subtropical climatic regime is in many ways valid.

The Texas subregion is so large, distinctive, vigorous, and self-assertive that it presents some vexing classificatory questions. Is Texas simply a subregion of the Greater South, or has it acquired so strong and divergent an identity that it can be regarded as a major region in its own right? It is likely that a major region has been born in a frontier zone in which several distinct cultural communities confront one another and in which the mixture has bred the vigorous, extroverted, aggressive Texas personality so widely celebrated in song and story. Similarly, peninsular Florida may be considered either within or juxtaposed to the South but not necessarily part of it. In the case of Florida, an almost empty territory began to receive significant settlement only after about 1890, and if, like Texas, most of it came from the older South, there were also vigorous infusions from elsewhere.

The Midland. The significance of this region has not been less than that of New England or the South, but its characteristics are the least conspicuous to outsiders as well as to its own residents—reflecting, perhaps, its centrality in the course of U.S. development. The Midland (a term not to be confused with Midwest) comprises portions of

The character of early New England

Southern deviation from the U.S. mainstream

The two Souths

Southern culture and climate

Middle Atlantic and Upper Southern states: Pennsylvania, New Jersey, Delaware, and Maryland. Serious European settlement of the Midland began a generation or more after that of the other major cultural centres and after several earlier, relatively ineffectual trials by the Dutch, Swedes, Finns, and British. But once begun late in the 17th century by William Penn and his associates, the colonization of the area was a success. Within southeastern Pennsylvania this culture area first assumed its distinctive character: a prosperous, sober, industrious agricultural society that quickly became a mixed economy as mercantile and later industrial functions came to the fore. By the mid-18th century much of the region had acquired a markedly urban character, resembling in many ways the more advanced portions of the North Sea countries. In this respect, at least, the Midland was well ahead of neighbouring areas to the north and south.

Polyglot nature of the Midland culture

It differed also in its polyglot ethnicity. From almost the beginning, the various ethnic and religious groups of the British Isles were joined by immigrants from the European mainland. This diversity has grown and is likely to continue. The mosaic of colonial ethnic groups has persisted in much of Pennsylvania, New York, New Jersey, and Maryland, as has the remarkable variety of more nationalities and churches in coalfields, company towns, cities and many rural areas. Much of the same ethnic heterogeneity can be seen in New England, the Midwest, and a few other areas, but the Midland stands out as perhaps the most polyglot region of the nation. The Germanic element has always been notably strong, if irregularly distributed, in the Midland, accounting for more than 70 percent of the population of many towns. Had the Anglo-American culture not triumphed, the area might well have been designated Pennsylvania German.

Physiography and migration carried the Midland culture area into the Maryland Piedmont. Although its width tapers quickly below the Potomac, it reaches into parts of Virginia and West Virginia, with traces legible far down the Appalachian zone and into the South.

The northern half of the greater Midland region (the New York subregion, or New England Extended) cannot be assigned unequivocally to either New England or this Midland. Essentially it is a hybrid formed mainly from two regional strains of almost equal strength: New England and the post-1660 British element moving up the Hudson Valley and beyond. There has also been a persistent, if slight, residue of early Dutch culture and some subtle filtering northward of Pennsylvanian influences. Apparently within the New York subregion occurred the first major fusion of American regional cultures, especially within the early 19th-century "Burned-Over District," around the Finger Lakes and Genesee areas of central and western New York. This locality, the seedbed for a number of important social innovations, was a major staging area for westward migration and possibly a major source for the people and notions that were to build the Midwestern culture area.

Toward the west the Midland retains its integrity for only a short distance—certainly no further than eastern Ohio—as it becomes submerged within the Midwest. Still, its significance in the genesis of the Midwest and the national culture should not be minimized. Its success in projecting its image upon so much of the country may have drawn attention away from the source area. As both name and location suggest, the Midland is intermediate in character in many respects, lying between New England and the South. Its residents are much less concerned with, or conscious of, a strong regional identity (excepting the "Pennsylvania Dutch" caricatures) than is true for other regions, and, in addition, the Midland lacks their strong political and literary traditions, though it is unmistakable in its distinctive townscapes and farmsteads.

The Midwest. There is no such self-effacement in the Midwest, that large triangular region justly regarded as the most nearly representative of the national average. Everyone within or outside of the Midwest knows of its existence, but no one is certain where it begins or ends. The older apex of the eastward-pointing triangle appears to rest around Pittsburgh, while the two western corners

melt away somewhere in the Great Plains, possibly in southern Manitoba in the north and southern Kansas in the south. The eastern terminus and the southern and western borders are broad, indistinct transitional zones.

This historical geography of the Midwest remains largely unstudied, but it seems likely that this culture region was the combination of all three colonial regions and that this combination first took place in the upper Ohio Valley. The early routes of travel—the Ohio and its tributaries, the Great Lakes, and the low, level corridor along the Mohawk and the coastal plains of Lake Ontario and Lake Erie—converge upon Ohio. There, the people and cultural traits from New England, the Midland, and the South were first funnelled together. There seems to have been a fanlike widening of the new hybrid area into the West as settlers worked their way frontierward.

Two major subregions are readily discerned, the Upper and Lower Midwest. They are separated by a line, roughly approximating the 41st parallel, that persists as far west as Colorado in terms of speech patterns and indicates differences in regional provenance in ethnic and religious terms as well. Much of the Upper Midwest retains a faint New England character, although Midland influences are probably as important. A rich mixture of German, Scandinavian, Slavic, and other non-WASP elements has greatly diversified a stock in which the British element usually remains dominant and the range of church denominations is great. The Lower Midwest, except for the relative scarcity of blacks, tends to resemble the South in its predominantly Protestant and British makeup. There are some areas with sizable Roman Catholic and non-WASP populations, but on the whole the subregion tends to be more WASP in inclination than most other parts of the nation. Contrasts of Upper and Lower Midwest

The problem of "the West." The foregoing culture areas account for roughly the eastern half of the conterminous United States. There is a genuine dilemma in classifying the remaining half. The concept of an "American West," strong in the popular imagination, is reinforced constantly by romanticized cinematic and television images of the cowboy. It is facile to accept the widespread Western livestock complex as somehow epitomizing the full gamut of Western life, but, although the cattle industry may have once accounted for more than one-half of the active Western domain as measured in acres, it employed only a relatively small fraction of the total population. As a single subculture, it cannot bear the burden of representing the total regional culture.

It is not clear whether there is a genuine, single, grand Western culture region. Unlike the East, where virtually all the land is developed and culture areas and subregions abut and overlap in splendid confusion, the eight major and many lesser nodes of population in the western United States resemble oases, separated from one another by wide expanses of nearly unpopulated mountain or arid desert. The only obvious properties these isolated clusters have in common are, first, the intermixture of several strains of culture, primarily from the East but with additions from Europe, Mexico, and East Asia, and, second, except for one subregion, a general modernity, having been settled in a serious way no earlier than the 1840s. Some areas may be viewed as inchoate, or partially formed cultural entities; the others have acquired definite personalities but are difficult to classify as first-order or lesser order culture areas.

There are several major tracts in the western United States that reveal a genuine cultural identity: the Upper Rio Grande region; the Mormon region; southern California; and, by some accounts, northern California. To this group one might add the anomalous Texan and Oklahoman subregions, which have elements of both the West and the South.

The term Upper Rio Grande region was coined to denote the oldest and strongest of the three sectors of Hispanic-American activity in the Southwest, the others being southern California and portions of Texas. Although covering the valley of the Upper Rio Grande, the region also embraces segments of Arizona and Colorado as well as other parts of New Mexico. European communities and culture have been present there, with only one interruption, since the late 16th century. The initial sources Upper Rio Grande and Mormon regions were Spain and Mexico, but after 1848 at least three distinct strains of Anglo-American culture were increasingly well represented—the Southern, Mormon, and a general undifferentiated northeastern U.S. culture—plus a distinct Texan subcategory. For once this has occurred without obliterating the Indians, whose culture endures in various stages of dilution, from the strongly Americanized or Hispanicized to the almost undisturbed.

The general mosaic is a fabric of Indian, Anglo, and Hispanic elements, and all three major groups, furthermore, are complex in character. The Indian component is made up of Navajo, Pueblo, and several smaller groups, each of which is quite distinct from the others. The Hispanic element is also diverse—modally Mexican mestizo, but ranging from pure Spanish to nearly pure pre-Spanish aboriginal.

The Mormon region is expansive in the religious and demographic realms, though it has ceased to expand territorially as it did in the decades after the first settlement in the Salt Lake Valley in 1847. Despite its Great Basin location and an exemplary adaptation to environmental constraints, this cultural complex appears somewhat non-Western in spirit: the Mormons may be in the West, but they are not entirely of it. Their historical derivation from the Midwest and from ultimate sources in New York and New England is still apparent, along with the generous admixture of European converts to their religion.

As in New England, the power of the human will and an intensely cherished abstract design have triumphed over an unfriendly habitat. The Mormon way of life is expressed in the settlement landscape and economic activities within a region more homogeneous internally than any other U.S. culture area.

In contrast, northern California has yet to gain its own strong cultural coloration. From the beginning of the great 1849 Gold Rush the area drew a diverse population from Europe and Asia as well as the older portions of the United States. Whether the greater part of northern California has produced a culture amounting to more than the sum of the contributions brought by immigrants is questionable. San Francisco, the regional metropolis, may have crossed the qualitative threshold. An unusually cosmopolitan outlook that includes an awareness of the Orient stronger than that of any other U.S. city, a fierce self-esteem, and a unique townscape may be symptomatic of a genuinely new, emergent local culture.

Southern California is the most spectacular of the Western regions, not only in terms of economic and population growth but also for the luxuriance, regional particularism, and general avant-garde character of its swiftly evolving cultural pattern. Until the coming of a direct transcontinental rail connection in 1885, the region was remote, rural, and largely inconsequential. Since then, the invasion by persons from virtually every corner of North America and by the world has been massive and did not slow down until the late 1960s. A loosely articulated series of conurbations has encroached upon what little is left of arable or habitable land in the Coast Ranges and valleys from Santa Barbara to the Mexican border.

Although every major ethnic and racial group and every other U.S. culture area is amply represented in southern California, there is reason to suspect that a process of selection for certain types of people, attitudes, and personality traits may have been at work at both source and destination. The region is distinct from, or perhaps in the vanguard of, the remainder of the nation. One might view southern California as the super-American region or the outpost of a postindustrial future; but its cultural distinctiveness is very evident in landscape and social behaviour. Southern California in no way approaches being a "traditional region," or even the smudged facsimile of such, but rather the largest, boldest experiment in creating a "voluntary region," one built through the self-selection of immigrants and their subsequent interaction.

The remaining identifiable Western regions—the Willamette Valley of Oregon, the Puget Sound region, the Inland Empire of eastern Washington and adjacent tracts of Idaho and Oregon, central Arizona, and the Colorado Piedmont—can be treated jointly as potential, or emer-

gent, culture areas, still too close to the national mean to display any cultural distinctiveness. In all of these regions is evident the arrival of a cross section of the national population and the growth of regional life around one or more major metropolises. A New England element is noteworthy in the Willamette Valley and Puget Sound regions, while an Hispanic-American component appears in the Colorado Piedmont and central Arizona. Only time and further study will reveal whether any of these regions, so distant from the historic sources of U.S. population and culture, have the capacity to become an independent cultural area. (W.Ze.)

The people

By the late 20th century the majority of the U.S. population had achieved a relatively high level of material comfort, prosperity, and security. They appeared to be, however, in a pessimistic and divided mood. They were concerned about crime, racial injustice, urban decay, nuclear proliferation, environmental pollution, drug abuse, unemployment, and the high cost of living.

Economic uncertainty and social tensions and divisions among its citizens were the major causes of discontentment, according to several surveys. Many Americans perceived these problems as caused by the failure of society to extend what is traditionally called the "American dream" equally to all its people, particularly to those who were members of minority groups. The traditional ideal of U.S. society had characterized the nation as a democratic "land of opportunity," in which social, political, economic, and religious freedom prevail, one person is as good as another, and individuals can achieve their goals if only they work hard enough. A shared belief in such egalitarian ideals is often seen as being perhaps the strongest bond that has united Americans, and the fact that the ethnic groups had not achieved equality troubled many Americans.

The population of the United States is probably the most widely diverse of any nation in the world. It is possible to create pictures of statistically "typical" Americans—an average voter, for example, might be a 47-year-old housewife who lives in the outskirts of Dayton, Ohio, and whose husband works as a machinist. Far more typical, however, is the scenario in which, on a summer Sunday in Chicago, three queens might be crowned: one by the Polish National Alliance, another by the Scandinavian Midsummer Night Festival, and a third to lead the annual Puerto Rican Independence Day parade. The United States is not homogeneous; it is a pluralistic society, a nation of groups. The long cherished belief that the United States has been a great "melting pot" in which people from all nations and cultures have blended into what are called "Americans" is in many respects a myth. During the late 20th century a strong trend among minorities (primarily among blacks and white ethnics) to organize groups to press for social change made the American people increasingly conscious of the characteristics of the various ethnic and racial groups that make up the national population.

ETHNIC DISTRIBUTION

The "old-stock" Americans. Until about 1860 the population of the United States was relatively homogeneous. It was overwhelmingly WASP (the majority had come originally from the British Isles). Of the 5,000,000 European immigrants who had entered the United States between 1820 and 1860, nine out of 10 were from England, Ireland, or Germany. With the exception of some of the Irish Roman Catholics, these early immigrants, many of whom were barely distinguishable from the native stock, were easily assimilated by the English Protestants.

After the Civil War, however, larger numbers of immigrants began to arrive from the countries of central and southeastern Europe: Italy, the Balkans, Poland, and Russia. This vast group of newcomers, some 30,000,000 of them from 1860 to 1920, flooded the U.S. cities. Most were non-English, non-Protestant, and markedly different in culture and language from the earlier Americans. The immigrants established their own neighbourhoods and rapidly developed ethnic societies, clubs, newspapers, and

Northern and southern California

Emergent culture areas of the West

Social pluralism and the "melting-pot" myth

theatres; and their living areas became distinctive cultural and social enclaves within the larger society.

The immigrants, however separate, in large part were not denied access to the mainstreams of U.S. life. Those with ability and intelligence usually achieved success— and some achieved greatness.

The old-stock English Protestants who remained the dominant cultural group came, in time, to be defined by the fact that they were not the descendants of immigrants. The term WASP is frequently used to describe all those—including such groups as the Dutch and Scots-Irish—whose assimilation has become so complete that the national origins of their families have become merely a memory. They make up a significant proportion of the U.S. population, though the nonwhite population is growing more rapidly than the white population in general, and the WASP population in particular.

The "Yankee Patricians" among them still retain a firm grip on the U.S. social order. They are prominent in the headquarters of large corporations, banks, insurance companies, law offices, and educational, cultural, and philanthropic institutions. Many other less affluent old-stock white Protestants are concentrated in the rural areas of the United States and in the South.

The "ethnics."   The name ethnics was used in the early 1970s to describe the Americans of Polish, Italian, Lithuanian, Bohemian, Slovakian, and other extraction, most of whom live in the northern and Midwestern cities. They tend to be Roman Catholic and middle-class. Most workers are either part of the blue-collar labour force or holders of low-level white-collar jobs. The neighbourhoods in which many of them live have their roots in the "Little Italys" and "Polish Hills" established by the immigrants. Their strong ethnic ties are apparent in the pattern of their lives: spouses, friends, neighbours, fellow churchmembers, and even co-workers often are also Polish, Italian, or Slovakian.

Their ethnic group identity is not, however, merely a holdover from the era of mass immigration. It is based not only upon a common cultural heritage but also on the common interests, needs, and problems they face in the present-day United States. White ethnics are concentrated in the inner cities, though increasingly less so, and are affected by high crime rates, deteriorating municipal services, inferior schools, and urban unrest. They fear losing their jobs and neighbourhoods to other minority groups. Neither rich nor poor, they anxiously watch their purchasing power being diminished by inflation and rising taxes.

As the children and grandchildren of immigrants, they have been taught to believe that the road to success in the United States is achieved through individual effort. They believe in equality of opportunity and self-improvement, and they attribute poverty to the failing of the individual and not to inequities in society. This attitude makes them largely unsympathetic to the demands of blacks, to student protest (which they tend to view as the antics of spoiled children of the rich), and during the Vietnam war, to the peace movement, which they regarded as un-American, especially since their own sons, many of whom did not attend college, made up a large percentage of the fighting force in Vietnam.

As the ethnics became more vocal in the late 20th century the public became aware of the problems and concerns of the urban ethnic minorities and stopped dismissing them as merely "racist" or "uneducated." Ethnic groups began to be included in the planning and administration of social-welfare programs of government or foundations, and an ethnic identity was no longer looked upon as somehow un-American and vaguely shameful. It had become legitimate to be an "ethnic."

The blacks.   The civil rights movement that gained momentum in the early 1960s awakened the nation's conscience to the plight of black Americans, who had long been denied first-class citizenship. By the late 20th century, despite government poverty programs and equal-opportunity laws that outlawed discrimination in education, housing, and employment, blacks clearly remained unequal partners in U.S. society. Their median income and education were far below those of whites, and their

average rate of unemployment was far greater. The black population nonetheless has made important advances. Their share of higher paying jobs, their median income, and their college enrollment have increased dramatically.

The civil rights movement prior to the mid-1960s was largely middle-class and interracial; it used nonviolence and passive resistance to change discriminatory laws and practices, primarily in the South. It aimed for an integration of blacks into U.S. life. For the militants who later arose from the urban poor in the North and West, separatism replaced integration as the primary objective. The militants rejected the U.S. cultural mainstream and spoke instead of black pride, of "soul," of Afro-American history and culture. Instead of attempting to bring change through the moral persuasion of white governmental bodies and institutions, the militants aimed for black autonomy and community control. They turned their attention to developing black political organizations that would give them a position of bargaining strength and political control over their own communities. Most frightening to whites, the militants rejected nonviolence and proclaimed the need for self-defense to protect themselves from police harassment in the urban ghettoes.

There were strong indications that the majority of blacks generally supported the more militant posture. The militants' concern with the daily problems of ghetto living spoke directly to the three out of five black households that live in inner-city areas. Moreover, sociological studies and public-opinion polls made subsequent to riots and demonstrations indicated that, though deploring violence and destruction, blacks generally viewed militant-type activities as useful and legitimate forms of protest.

The Hispanics.   Persons with Spanish surnames make up more than 6 percent of the U.S. population. More than half of them are of Mexican origin, the descendants of ancestors who settled in areas that were once part of Mexico. A majority still live in Arizona, California, Colorado, New Mexico, and Texas. Another 15 percent of the Hispanics are of Puerto Rican origin; they are concentrated in New York City. Nearly 6 percent are Cuban immigrants who have settled in or near Miami.

Although the Hispanics have experienced less outright discrimination than blacks, they, like the blacks, have a generally lower economic and educational level than the rest of the population. They are far less likely to hold white-collar jobs as the rest of the population and are much more likely to be unemployed; and their average education is less. Although four out of five Hispanics were born in the United States or Puerto Rico, Spanish is the main language in about half of the homes. The continued use of Spanish indicates the strength of the bonds that tie Hispanics together.

After generations of quiet acceptance and near-invisibility, Mexican-Americans began to organize in the late 20th century. Following the example of black activism, Mexican-Americans formed groups in the barrios of such large cities as Los Angeles and Denver and in the southern Texas towns in which they often constituted a majority. Their major goals were greater political representation through which they might gain better health, housing, and municipal services, bilingual school programs, and a better education for their children.

The Indians.   The American Indians, the only Americans who can truly be called native, are the group that has been least integrated into U.S. society. The Indian population is concentrated in Oklahoma, Arizona, New Mexico, California, and North Carolina.

The Indian reservations, on which more than half of all Indians live, are often enclaves of deep poverty and social distress. The median Indian family income is far below the national average; and, since Indian families tend to be large, most live near destitution. A large proportion of Indian children do not finish high school, and many of those who do graduate often lag behind the national educational norms by several years. Substandard, unsanitary, and overcrowded housing conditions contribute to the high death rates from tuberculosis and from dysentery, which are, respectively, nearly six times and twice that of the nation as a whole. Their infant mortality rate is higher

Group
identity of
the white
"ethnics"

Militancy
among the
blacks

Cultural
isolation
of the
American
Indian

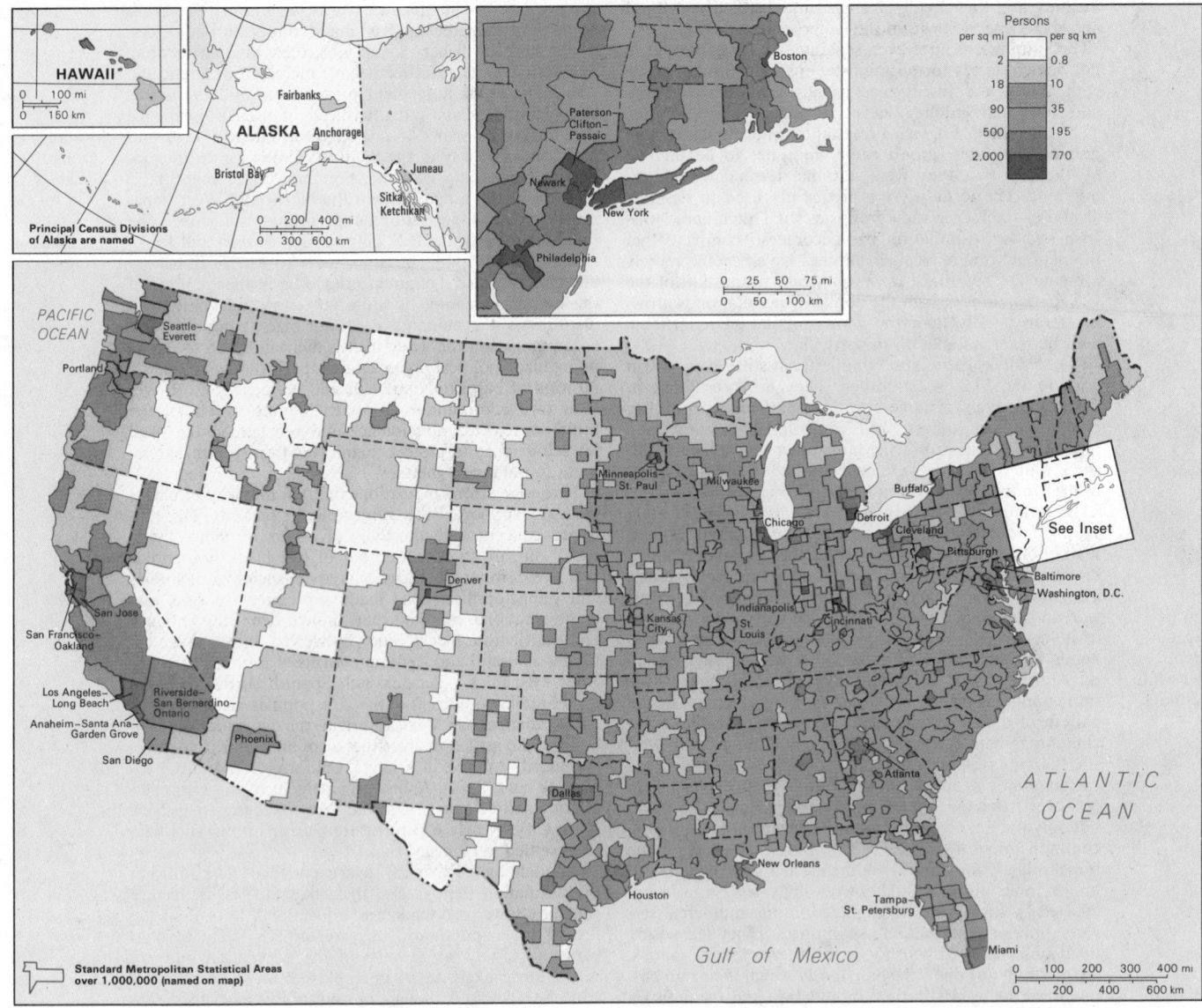

Population density of the United States.

than the national figure, and their average age at death is much younger than the rest of the population.

The physical and social isolation of the reservation has caused a cultural hiatus that has left Indians unprepared educationally and culturally to take part in the urbanized, technical United States. The poverty and frustration of life on the reservation prompted many Indians to migrate to large cities, especially Los Angeles and Chicago. In such environments they possessed neither the occupational skills nor the cultural background necessary to sustain themselves, and social workers reported a high percentage of family disintegration, alcoholism, and suicide among them. A few "red-power" Indian groups had begun to organize to call attention to their condition and press for change through political and legal action.

The Oriental Americans. The Oriental population of the United States consists primarily of Japanese, Chinese, and Filipinos, the great majority of whom live in the cities of California and in Hawaii. Like other ethnic groups, the Oriental Americans have established their own urban neighbourhoods, the most famous of which is San Francisco's Chinatown. The Oriental Americans are not "problem minorities": strong family ties, cultural pride, respect for authority, and an emphasis on education have brought them extraordinary success in the United States. Despite severe discrimination and internment during World War II the Japanese Americans have achieved educational and employment levels that are substantially higher than those of the white population.

RELIGIOUS GROUPS

Nearly a quarter of the U.S. population are Roman Catholics, and about 6,000,000 are Jews. Nine out of 10 churches in the United States, however, are Protestant, with the largest groups being the Baptists, Methodists, Lutherans, and members of the Churches of Christ. Many of the others can be grouped into such families as Adventist, Brethren, Churches of God, Churches of the New Jerusalem, Eastern, Friends, Latter Day Saints, Mennonite, Moravian, Old Catholic, Pentecostal, Presbyterian, Reformed, River Brethren, and United Brethren.

There are well over 1,200 religious bodies within the United States. A number of them, however, including the Disciple of Christ (1809), Mormons (1830), Seventh-Day Adventists (1863), Jehovah's Witnesses (1872) and Christian Scientists (1875) have been called uniquely American.

IMMIGRATION

The era of mass immigration came to an abrupt end soon after World War I, when the Immigration Act of 1924 established an annual quota, later fixed at 150,000 immigrants (1929). The act also established the national-origins system, which was to characterize national immigration policy until 1968. Under it, quotas were established for each country based on the number of persons of that national origin who were living in the United States in 1920. The quotas reduced drastically the flow of immigrants from southeastern Europe—who, since they were still relatively new arrivals in the United States, formed

Quota
system of
immigra-
tion

only a small percentage of the population in 1920—and discriminated in favour of the countries of northwestern Europe. Under this system Great Britain, Ireland, and Germany were allotted more than 70 percent of the quota, an allotment that rarely was filled.

The quota system was liberalized in December 1965, and in 1968 it was finally abolished in favour of a first-come, first-served policy. An annual ceiling of 170,000 immigrant visas for nations outside the Western Hemisphere was established, with 20,000 the maximum allowed to any one nation. A ceiling of 120,000 was set for persons from the Western Hemisphere.

The new policy radically changed the pattern of immigration. In 1965, the last year during which the old national-origins system was still in effect, Mexico, Canada, and Great Britain topped the list of countries sending immigrants to the United States. By the late 20th century the last two had been displaced by a number of other countries. (Jo.N./T.K.F./Ed.)

The economy

Economic
power of
the United
States

The United States is the world's greatest economic power, measured in terms both of gross national product (GNP) and of GNP per capita. The nation's wealth is partly a reflection of its rich natural resources. In the late 20th century the United States, with 5 percent of the world's population, produced one-fourth of the world's output of coal and copper, almost one-fifth of its crude petroleum, and one-tenth of its iron ore. The agricultural sector produced half of the world's corn (maize); more than a fifth of its beef, pork, mutton, and lamb; and more than a tenth of its wheat. The United States owes more, however, to its developed industry.

Despite its relative self-sufficiency, the United States is the most important single factor in world trade by virtue of the sheer size of its economy. Its exports represent more than 10 percent of the world total. The United States impinges on the economy of the rest of the world not only as a trading power but also as a source of investment capital. Direct investment abroad by U.S. firms was a dominant factor in the economies of Canada and many Latin-American countries; U.S. investments in Europe were concentrated in manufacturing.

RESOURCES

Oil and
gas reserves

Mineral resources. The United States is the world's third largest petroleum-producing nation, accounting for almost one-seventh of world output. The major reserves have been in the offshore fields of Texas, Louisiana, and California, but to these have been added those discovered in Alaska. Important reserves of natural gas are found in Louisiana, Texas, New Mexico, and Alaska.

Coal deposits are concentrated largely in eastern parts of the country. About half of the bituminous coal and lignite is mined in West Virginia, Kentucky, and Pennsylvania—the last-named state also producing the country's only anthracite. Illinois and Ohio also produce coal. Iron ore is mined predominantly in the Great Lakes region; there has been a long-term shift away from the mining of hematite toward the mining of magnetite.

The United States also has important reserves of copper, lead, and zinc. Copper production is concentrated in the mountainous states of the West, in Arizona, Utah, Montana, Nevada, and New Mexico. Zinc is more scattered, being mined in Tennessee, Missouri, Idaho, and New York. Lead mining is concentrated in Missouri. Other metals mined in the United States are gold, silver, molybdenum, manganese, tungsten, bauxite, uranium, vanadium, and nickel. Important nonmetallic minerals produced are phosphates, potash, and sulfur.

Land and
water
resources

Biological resources. Of the total land area, somewhat less than half is devoted to farming. Tobacco is produced in the Southeast and cotton in the South and Southwest; California is noted for its vineyards, citrus groves, and truck gardens; the Midwest is the centre of corn and wheat farming, while dairy herds are concentrated in the Northern states. The Southwestern and Rocky Mountain states support large herds of livestock.

More than two-thirds of the vast forestlands are in commercial forestland, defined as economically available land producing or capable of producing industrial timber. The area with the most forestland was the West, including Alaska; but there are large areas also in the South and the North. Almost half of the hardwood was located in the North. Of total commercial forestland, more than 70 percent was in private ownership. About 20 percent was owned or controlled by the federal government, the remainder being under the control of state and local administrations.

Hydroelectric resources. Hydroelectric resources are heavily concentrated in the Pacific and Mountain regions, which together account for almost three-fifths of the nation's installed capacity. Alaska is estimated to have nearly one-fifth of the nation's unrealized potential capacity.

SOURCES OF NATIONAL INCOME

Changing
structure of
agriculture

Agriculture, forestry, and fishing. Despite the enormous output of U.S. agriculture, the sector of agriculture, forestry, and fishing altogether produces less than 3 percent of the net national income. Farm productivity has grown at a very rapid rate, enabling a smaller labour force to produce more than ever before. Farm manpower has fallen, while mechanization and concentration of farm holdings has increased. Among the most important crops are corn (maize), wheat, oats, grain sorghums, cotton, rice, soybeans, and tobacco. The general improvement in yields over the years has been accompanied by a large increase in the use of commercial fertilizers, pesticides, and herbicides.

The United States is second only to the Soviet Union as a producer of timber. More than 80 percent of the production was made up of softwoods and the remainder of hardwoods; the principal trees cut in the first category were Douglas fir and southern yellow pine, and, in the second category, oak. Domestic consumption of timber products has been growing faster than national production; imports have risen greatly.

The United States is one of the most important countries in the world in fishing, along with Japan, the Soviet Union, China, and Peru. Fish for human consumption accounts for more than half of the tonnage landed. Nearly half of the annual catch consists of shellfish.

Mining and quarrying. Less than 2 percent of the national income comes from mining and quarrying, despite the fact that the United States is a major world producer of a number of metals and of coal and petroleum.

Industry. Manufacturing output has grown at approximately the same rate as the economy as a whole. The increase in productivity over the years has been in part a function of the increased level of capital investment. Manufacturing accounts for about a fourth of the net national income.

Leading
sectors in
manufac-
turing

One of the most important sectors in terms of value added has been the manufacture of transportation equipment, including passenger cars, trucks, and buses. Other important sectors include nonelectrical machinery, electrical machinery, fabricated metal products, primary metals, and motor-vehicle parts.

Steel-mill products go largely to the automotive industry and to the construction industry. The chemical industry has shown good growth, as have the industries for textiles, food and kindred products, and apparel.

Ownership of many industries in the United States, as in other countries, is highly concentrated. In the production of motor vehicles and parts, most of the value added by the industry has been accounted for by the largest four producers. In aircraft two-thirds of the value added was accounted for by the largest four companies in the industry. Corresponding figures occur in the aircraft engines and parts industry, oil refining, paper mills, production of radio and television receivers, cigarette production, and the pharmaceutical industry. Litigation by the federal government under the antitrust laws may have helped to prevent significant increases in concentration in individual industries, but the rise of "conglomerates"—corporations with interests in diverse industries—increased the concentration of ownership overall.

Military orders have been of considerable importance to industry, and thus many industries and geographic areas are particularly sensitive to reductions in defense spending.

Finance. Under the Federal Reserve System, central banking functions are exercised by 12 Federal Reserve banks, each serving an important area of the country, supervised by the Board of Governors in Washington, D.C. The governors are appointed by the president, subject to confirmation by the Senate, but are by no means invariably in accord with the administration's views on economic policy—in contrast to the formal dependence of the Bank of England on the treasury in the United Kingdom. The Federal Reserve System regulates bank credit and the money supply by changes in the rediscount rate charged on loans to member banks, by changes in the reserve requirements imposed on commercial banks, and by open-market operations in government securities. The Treasury is not, however, without influence on the working of the monetary system; it influences market interest rates through its management of the national debt, while, by changing its own deposits with the Federal Reserve banks, it can affect the volume of credit.

The capital market

Laws hindering the formation of branch banks have led to a proliferation of individual domestic commercial banks, of which a third, accounting for some 80 percent of total deposits with commercial banks, are members of the Federal Reserve System. Banks incorporated under national charter must be members of the system, while banks incorporated under state charters may become members. Member banks must maintain minimum legal reserves with a Federal Reserve bank and must deposit between 3 and 10 percent of their time (savings) deposits with a Federal Reserve bank.

In addition to commercial banks, there are a few hundred noninsured banks and a few thousand savings and loan associations or building societies. Other financial intermediaries include insurance companies, with enormous assets, and finance companies dealing mainly in consumer credit. The federal government sponsors other credit agencies in the fields of housing and farming.

New York has two organized stock exchanges, the New York Stock Exchange and the American Stock Exchange. There are, however, subsidiary New York markets: one in which members of the two exchanges sell unlisted stocks across the counter; another in which firms that are not members sell listed stocks across the counter without commission, taking a jobber's profit rather than a broker's; and a third in which institutions bypass the exchanges and deal directly with one another.

Foreign trade. International trade plays an increasingly important part in the U.S. economy, as in other major industrial countries. Indeed, in both exports and imports the United States is the most important single trading country.

MANAGEMENT OF THE ECONOMY

Government and private enterprise. Government plays only a small direct part in economic activity in the United States, where it is restricted to the U.S. Postal Service, the uranium enrichment facilities of the federal Nuclear Regulatory Commission, and market activities such as those of the Tennessee Valley Authority. Enterprises that are often in public hands in other countries, such as airlines and telephone systems, are run privately in the United States.

A principal effort of the government has been the fostering of competition through enforcement of the antitrust laws. These are designed to combat collusion among companies with respect to prices, output levels, or market shares and, where feasible, to prevent mergers that significantly reduce competition. The 1969 merger between The Standard Oil Co. (Ohio) (Sohio) and a subsidiary of The British Petroleum Co. Ltd., for example, was challenged by the government and allowed to go through only when Sohio agreed to exchange stations in Ohio for others elsewhere in the country, thus fostering competition in gasoline retailing. So-called conglomerate mergers, between corporations in unrelated industries, have not come within the purview of the antitrust laws. There has been some sentiment for opposing such mergers among the 200 largest manufacturing companies or any merger by one

of them with a leading producer in a highly concentrated industry. This opposition arises in part because conglomerates are able to switch the profits of one market to subsidize price wars in others, thus reducing competition in the long run. Conglomerates also are able to require suppliers of one industry in the group to buy from others, on the principle of reciprocity, thus again potentially excluding competitors.

The major area of government regulation of economic activity is through fiscal and monetary policy. The government also exerts considerable leverage on certain sectors of the economy as a purchaser of goods, notably in the aircraft and aerospace industries. Proposals for governmental controls of prices and incomes have been a frequent source of much controversy.

Fiscal and monetary policy

Another field in which the government strongly influences private economic activity is farming. It endeavours to support farm incomes through payments to farmers, controls on output, price supports, and the provision of storage and marketing facilities. One disadvantage of the system is that payments are related to farm output, so that the benefit has often gone to the larger commercial farms rather than to those the income level of which was originally the main object of governmental concern.

Taxation. Nearly all of the federal government's revenues come from taxes. By far the most important source of tax revenue is the personal income tax. Gross receipts from corporate income taxes yield a far smaller percentage of total federal receipts. Excise duties yield another small percentage of the total federal revenue, but this is offset by the fact that individual states levy their own excise and sales taxes. Federal excises rest heavily on alcohol, gasoline, and tobacco. Another major source of revenue is social-insurance taxes and contributions; estate and gift taxes yield a tiny percentage of the total.

Rates of income taxation

Trade unions. The labour force in the United States is not highly organized. More than 80 percent of those belonging to unions are affiliated with the American Federation of Labor-Congress of Industrial Organizations (AFL-CIO), the nationwide federation of unions. The biggest unions are the International Brotherhood of Teamsters, Chauffeurs, Warehousemen, and Helpers of America; the United Automobile Workers; and the United Steelworkers of America. Most unions in manufacturing bargain on a plant- or company-wide scale, although the older unions, such as those of the carpenters and the electricians, bargain by crafts. Settlements negotiated by the unions do not necessarily set the pattern for the movement of wage rates in general. There have been periods when negotiated settlements secured wage increases rather lower than the rate at which wage rates were rising overall.

Although the freedom to strike is hedged about with legislative provisions for "cooling-off" periods and in some cases compulsory arbitration, major unions are able and willing to embark on long strikes. (E.I.U./Ed.)

TRANSPORTATION

The economic and social complexion of life in the United States mirrors the nation's extraordinary mobility. It may be that no other people on Earth allocate so many resources and so much of their time and attention to moving and getting things moved. A pervasive transportation network has helped bring together in the vast geographic expanse of the country a surprisingly homogeneous and close-knit social and economic environment. This freedom to move explains in large measure the dynamism of the U.S. economy. Mobility has made possible vast metropolises, spreading suburbs, a lengthening radius of commuter travel, dispersal of shops and industry, and the growing millions of nonfarm rural residents who constitute a new kind of urbanization without a strong centre. Mobility has also had destructive effects. It has accelerated the decay of older urban areas, multiplied traffic congestion, intensified pollution of the environment, undermined public-transportation systems, and made recluses of those who lack automobiles.

The mobility of the population

The most spectacular part of the transportation network has been the 42,000-mile Interstate Highway System, a national network of multiple-lane dual expressways con-

Elevations and depressions are given in feet

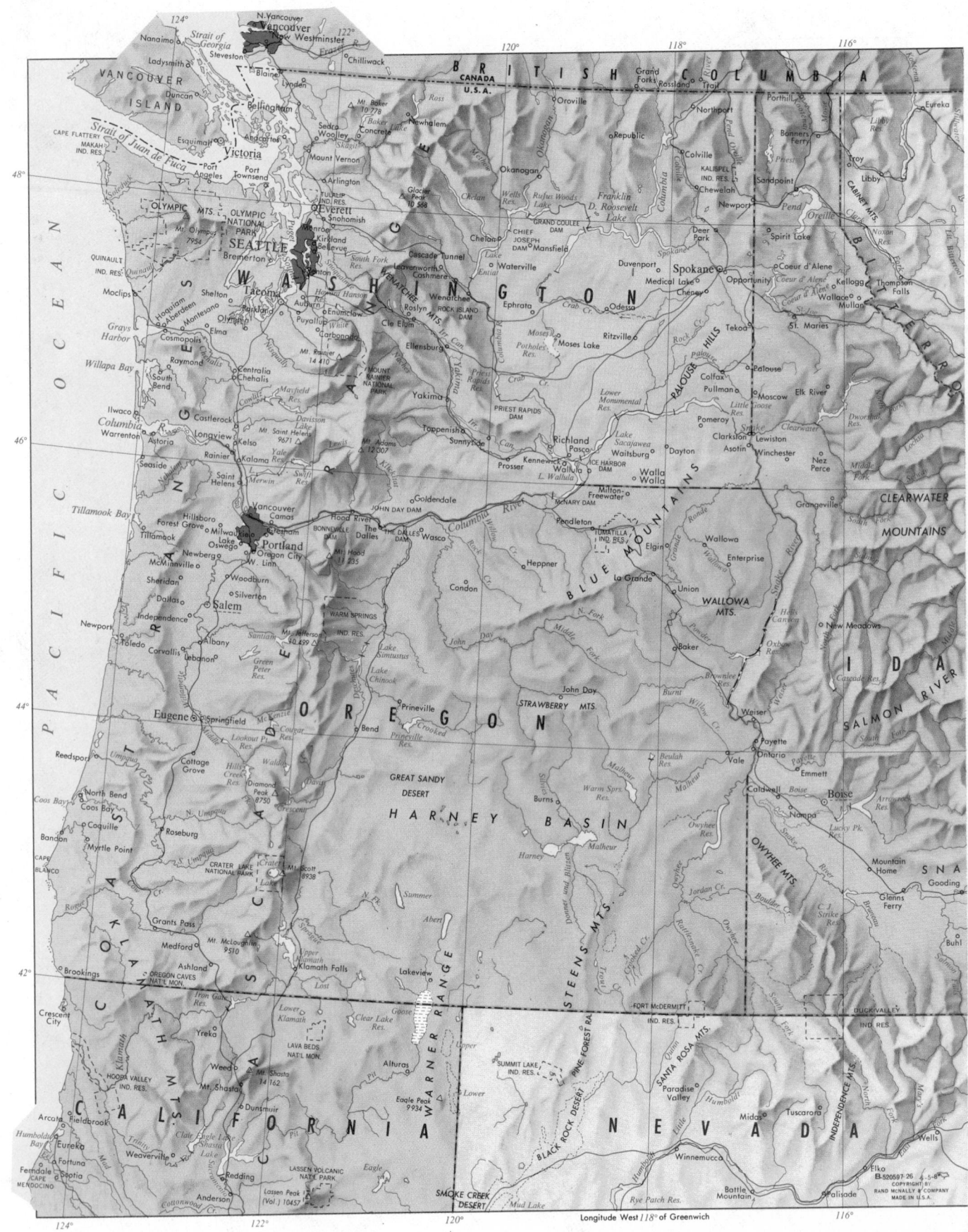

Longitude West *118°* of Greenwich

Elevations and depressions are given in feet

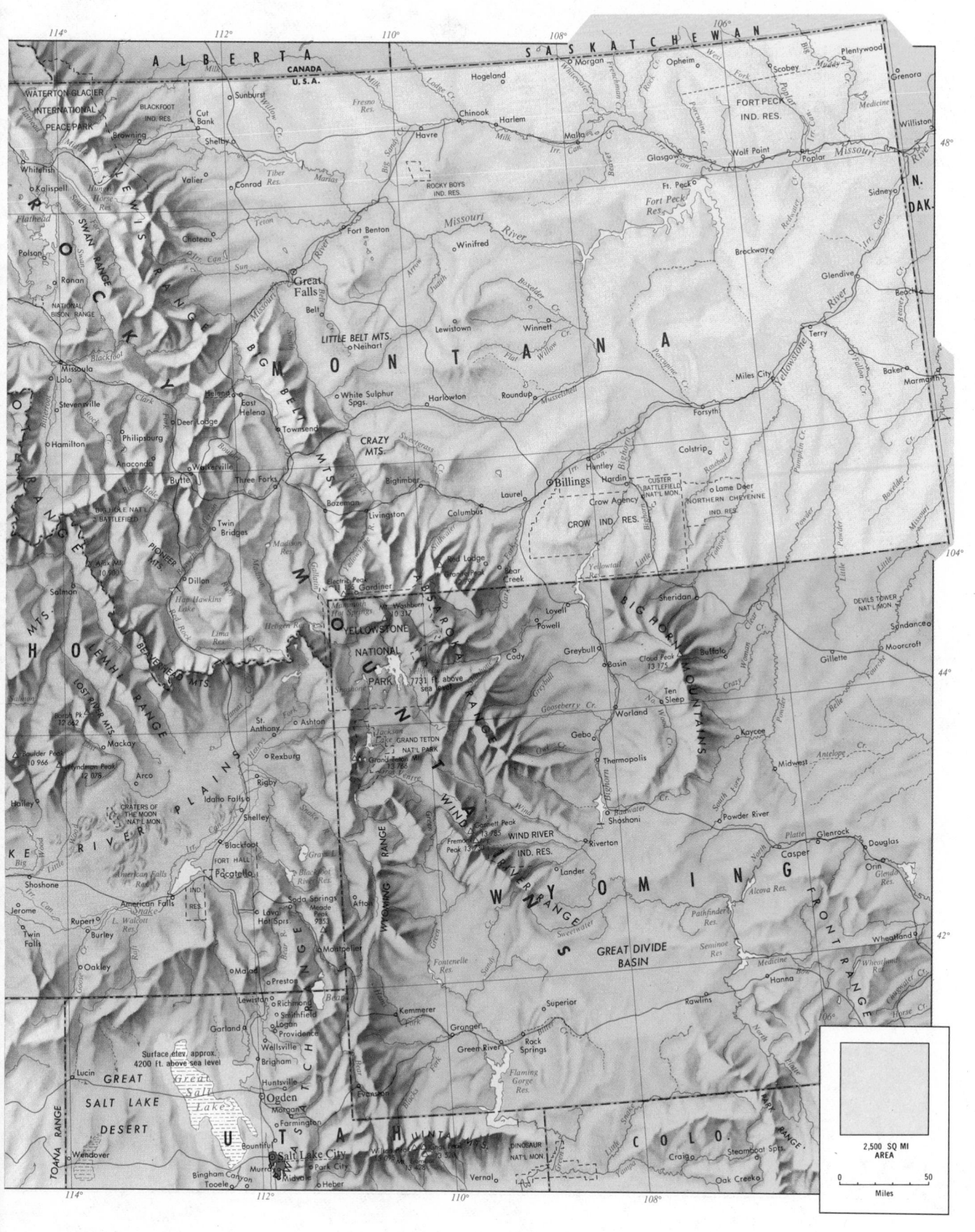

2,500 SQ MI
AREA

0   50
Miles

0 20   40   60   80   100   120 Miles
0 20 40 60 80 100 120 140 160 180 200 Kilometers

2,500 SQ MI
AREA

0   50
Miles

POINT
ARENA

Anderson
Cottonwood
Westwood
Red Bluff
Lassen Peak (Vol.) 10,457
LASSEN VOLCANIC NATL. PARK
Susanville
SMOKE CREEK DESERT
Mud
Battle Mountain
Palisade
Franklin
RUBY MTS.
Ruby

Chico
Willows
Black Butte Res.
Oroville Res.
Downieville
PYRAMID LAKE
Pyramid
Lovelock
Winnemucca
HUMBOLDT RA.
Pine
Honey

Gridley
Oroville
Portola
INDIAN RESERVATION
Wadsworth
Sparks
Humboldt Sink
STILLWATER RA.
Humboldt Salt Marsh
Carson Sink
Austin
Eureka
Mc Gill

Ukiah
Lakeport
Cloverdale
Colusa
Yuba City
Marysville
Nevada City
Grass Valley
Truckee
Reno
Virginia City
Carson City
Fallon
RANGE
Ruth
Ely

POINT ARENA
Healdsburg
Clear
Lincoln
Roseville
Auburn
Placerville
Yerington
WASSUK RANGE
Walker Lake
Hawthorne
Coaldale
Tonopah
Duckwater Pk. 11,493

COAST RANGES
Sebastopol
Santa Rosa
Napa
Woodland
Folsom City
Folsom
Sacramento
Jackson
Angels Camp
Sonora Pk. 11,429
TOIYABE RANGE
Arc Dome 11,775

Petaluma
Vallejo
Benicia
Lodi
San Andreas
Sonora
YOSEMITE NATIONAL PARK
Mt. Lyell 13,095
Dana Mtn. 13,055
Boundary Peak 13,145
Goldfield
Alamo

POINT REYES
San Rafael
MUIR WOODS NATL. MON.
Sausalito
San Francisco
Daly City
Burlingame
Richmond
Berkeley
Oakland
Alameda
Stockton
Oakdale
Modesto
Turlock
Merced
Tuolumne
DEVILS POSTPILE N.M.
White Mt. Peak 14,246

San Mateo
Redwood City
Palo Alto
Santa Clara
San Jose
Los Gatos
Tracy
Livermore
Mariposa
Bishop

Santa Cruz
Watsonville
Hollister
Madera
Pine Flat Res.
Benton

Pacific Grove
Monterey
Salinas
PINNACLES NATL. MON.
Fresno
Sanger
Reedley
Selma
Dinuba
KINGS CANYON NATL. PARK
Lone Pine
Mt. Whitney 14,494
Owens
DEATH VALLEY
Beatty
FRENCHMAN FLAT
MOAPA RIVER IND. RES.

King City
Coalinga
Visalia
Hanford
Tulare
Exeter
SEQUOIA NATL. PARK
Telescope Peak 11,045
DEATH VALLEY 282 ft. below sea level
SPRING MTS.
Las Vegas
Henderson

Paso Robles
Atascadero
Tulare Basin
Porterville
TULE RIVER IND. RES.
Inyokern
Trona
Searles
NATL. MON.
HOOVER DAM
Boulder City

Estero Bay
San Luis Obispo
Delano
Bakersfield
Buena Vista Lake Reservoir
Mojave
Aqueduct
Mohave
FORT MOHAVE IND. RES.
Goffs
Needles

Santa Maria
Lompoc
POINT ARGUELLO
POINT CONCEPTION
Taft
MOJAVE DESERT
Barstow
Daggett
Cadiz

Santa Barbara
Ventura
Oxnard
Santa Paula
Burbank
Glendale
Pasadena
Monrovia
San Bernardino
SAN BERNARDINO MTS.
JOSHUA TREE NATL. MON.
Aqueducts
Rice

SAN MIGUEL
SANTA CRUZ
SANTA ROSA
LOS ANGELES
Santa Monica
Inglewood
Redondo Beach
SAN PEDRO
Alhambra
Huntington Park
Compton
Pomona
Redlands
Riverside
Orange
MORONGO IND. RES.
Palm Springs
AGUA CALIENTE IND. RES.
Blythe
Colorado

SANTA BARBARA CHANNEL ISLANDS NATL. MON.
SANTA CATALINA
Avalon
Long Beach
Huntington Beach
Santa Ana
Newport Beach
Elsinore
SANTA ROSA IND. RES.
TORRES MARTINEZ IND. RES.
Salton Sea Bottom 235 ft. below sea level

SAN NICOLAS
SAN CLEMENTE
Oceanside
Escondido
LA JOLLA IND. RES.
SANTA YSABEL IND. RES.
Calipatria
Brawley
IMPERIAL VALLEY
Holtville
FT. YUMA IND. RES.

Gulf of Santa Catalina
SAN DIEGO
Coronado
National City
Chula Vista
Tijuana
INAJA IND. RES.
CUYAPAIPE IND. RES.
CAMPO IND. RES.
El Centro
Calexico
Mexicali
Somerton
Laguna Salada

BAJA CALIFORNIA NORTE

B-520599-26°-67-10
COPYRIGHT BY
RAND McNALLY & COMPANY
MADE IN U.S.A.

NEVADA
CALIFORNIA
SIERRA NEVADA
COAST RANGES
SAN JOAQUIN VALLEY
PACIFIC OCEAN
Monterey Bay
San Luis Obispo Bay
Santa Barbara Channel
SANTA BARBARA ISLANDS

Longitude West of Greenwich

Elevations and depressions are given in feet

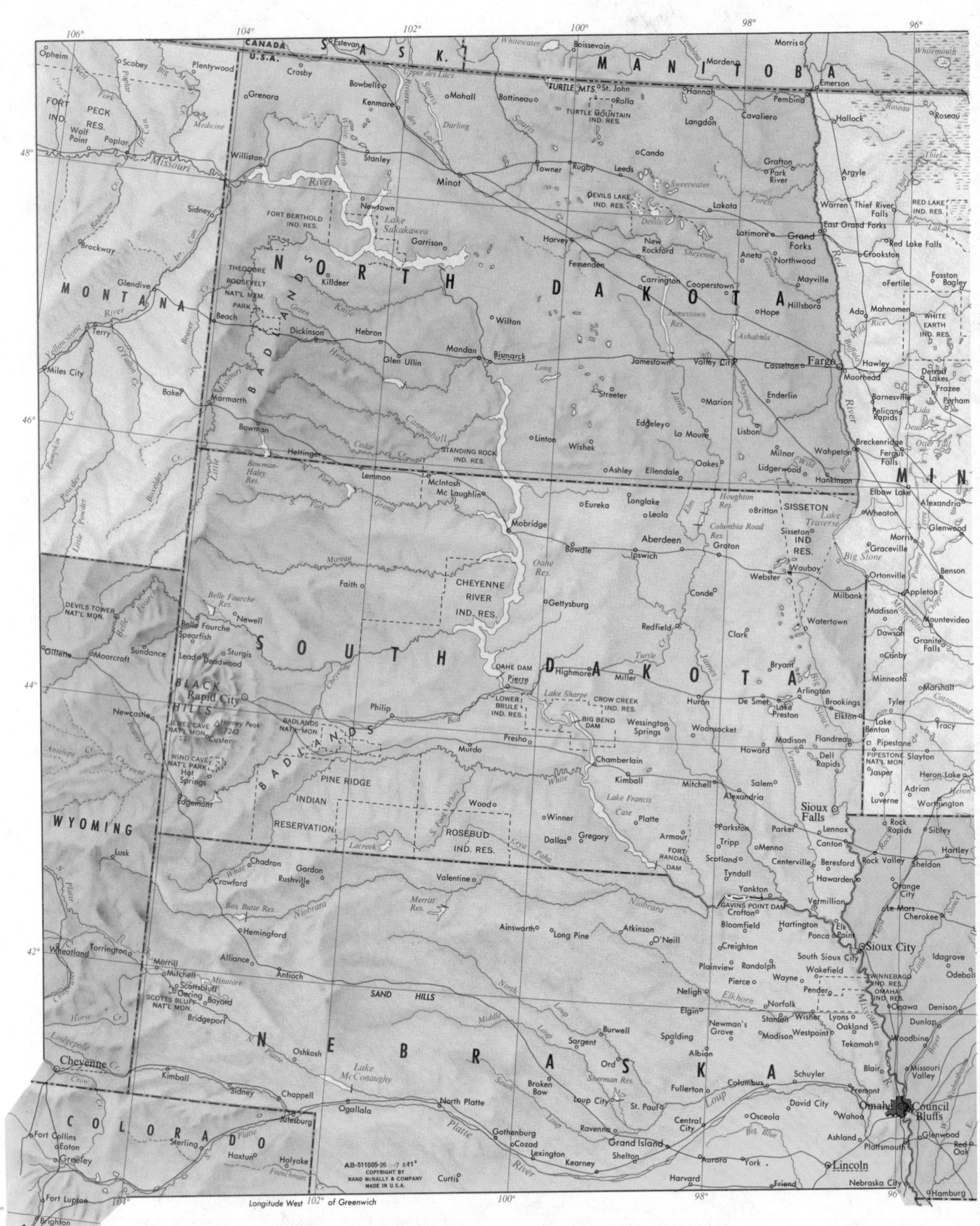

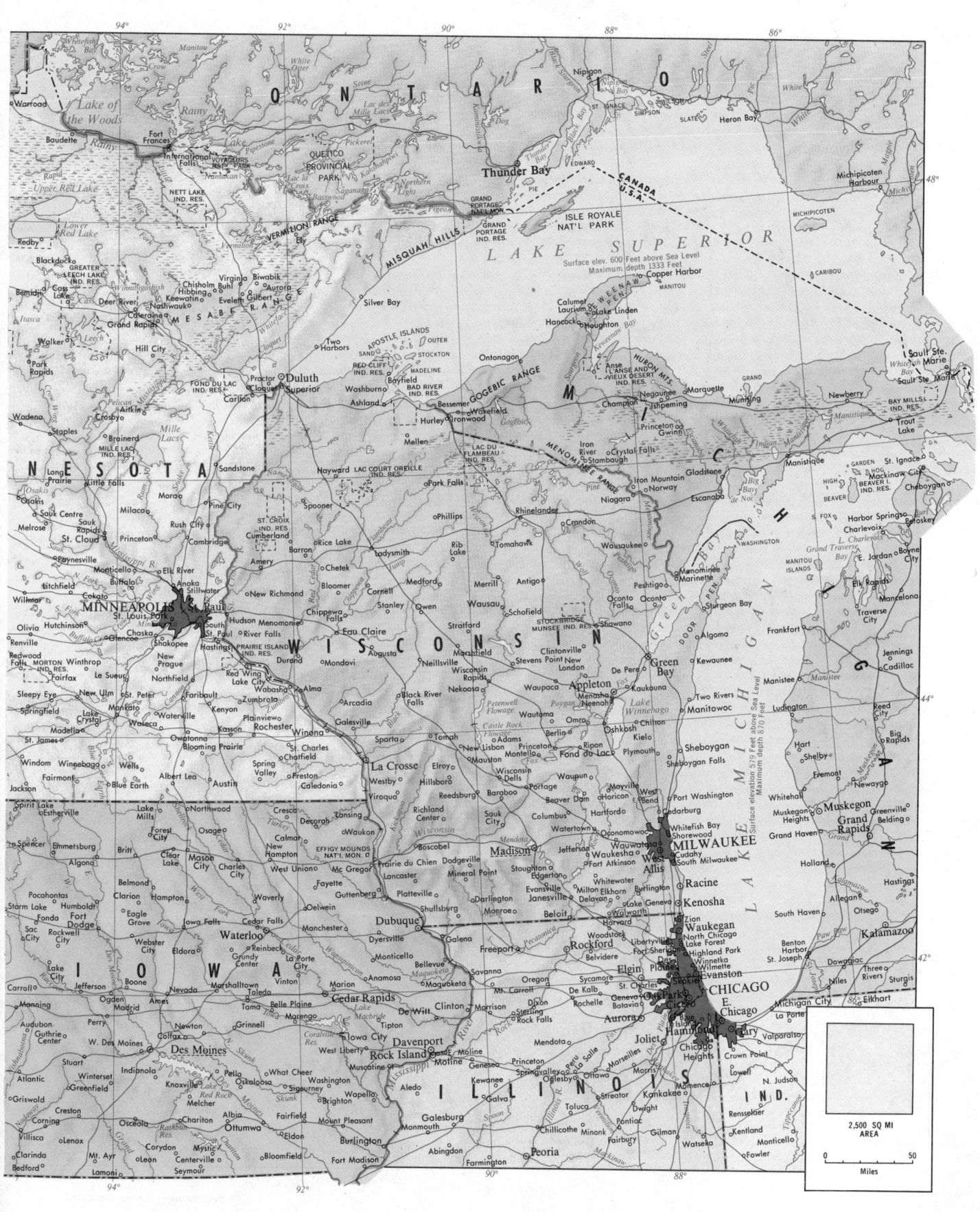

2,500 SQ MI
AREA

0   50
Miles

0   20   40   60   80   100   120 Miles
0   20 40 60 80 100 120 140 160 180 200 Kilometers

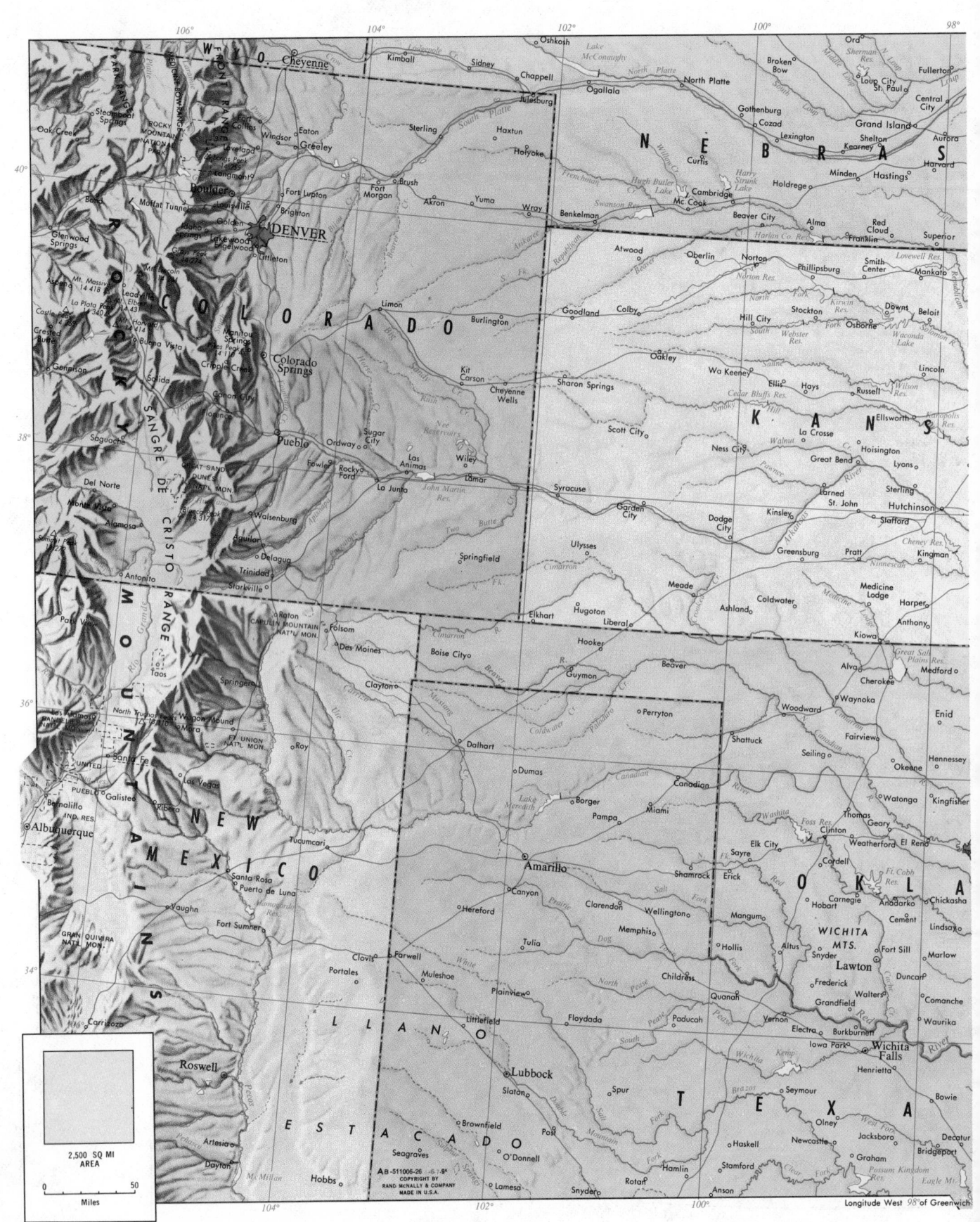

2,500 SQ MI
AREA

0   50

Miles

A-B-511006-26 -6-7-9*
COPYRIGHT BY
RAND McNALLY & COMPANY
MADE IN U.S.A.

Longitude West 98° of Greenwich

Elevations and depressions are given in feet.

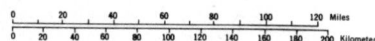

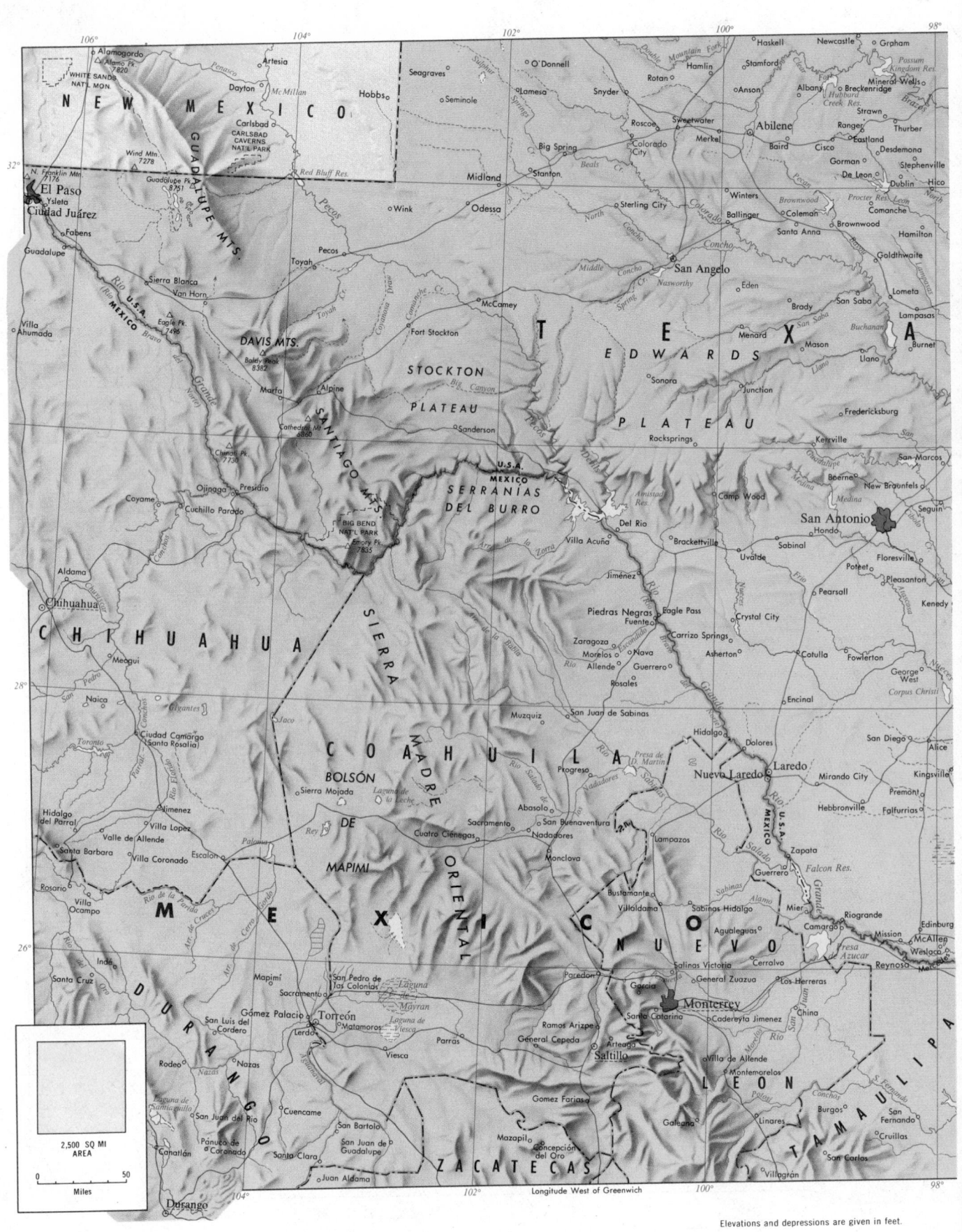

Elevations and depressions are given in feet.

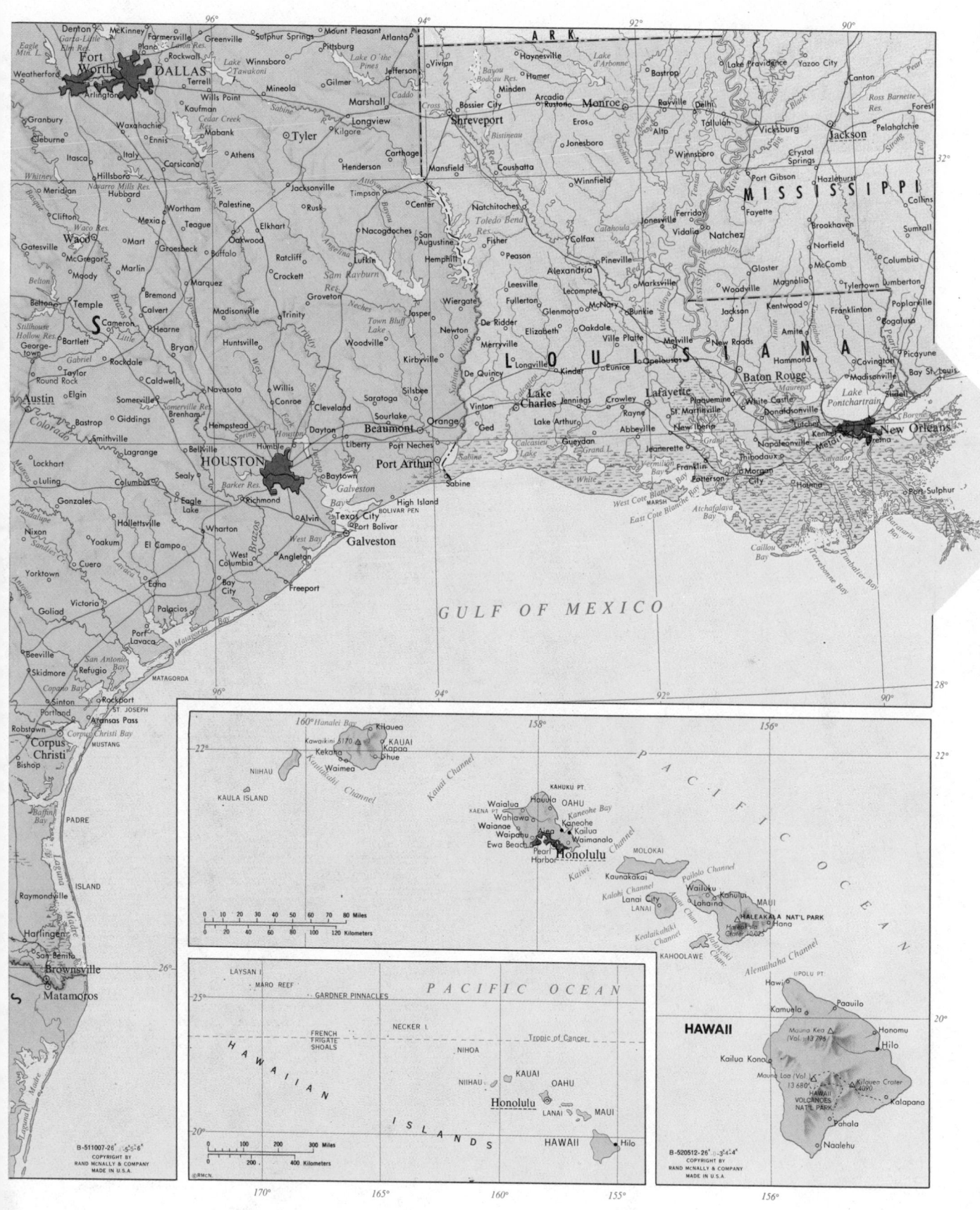

ARK.

MISSISSIPPI

LOUISIANA

GULF OF MEXICO

PACIFIC OCEAN

HAWAII

HAWAIIAN ISLANDS

PACIFIC OCEAN

B-511007-26
COPYRIGHT BY
RAND McNALLY & COMPANY
MADE IN U.S.A.

B-520512-26
COPYRIGHT BY
RAND McNALLY & COMPANY
MADE IN U.S.A.

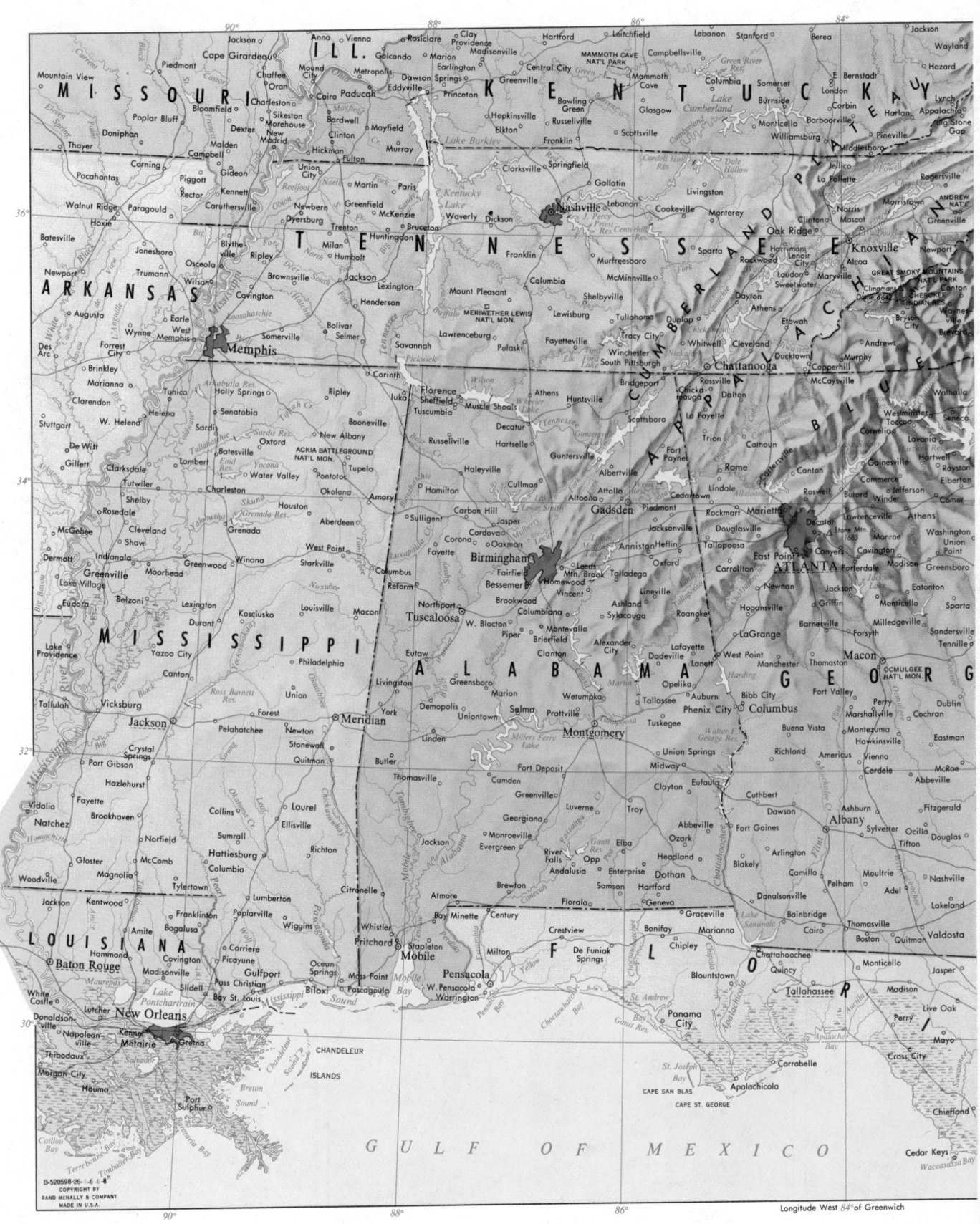

Elevations and depressions are given in feet.

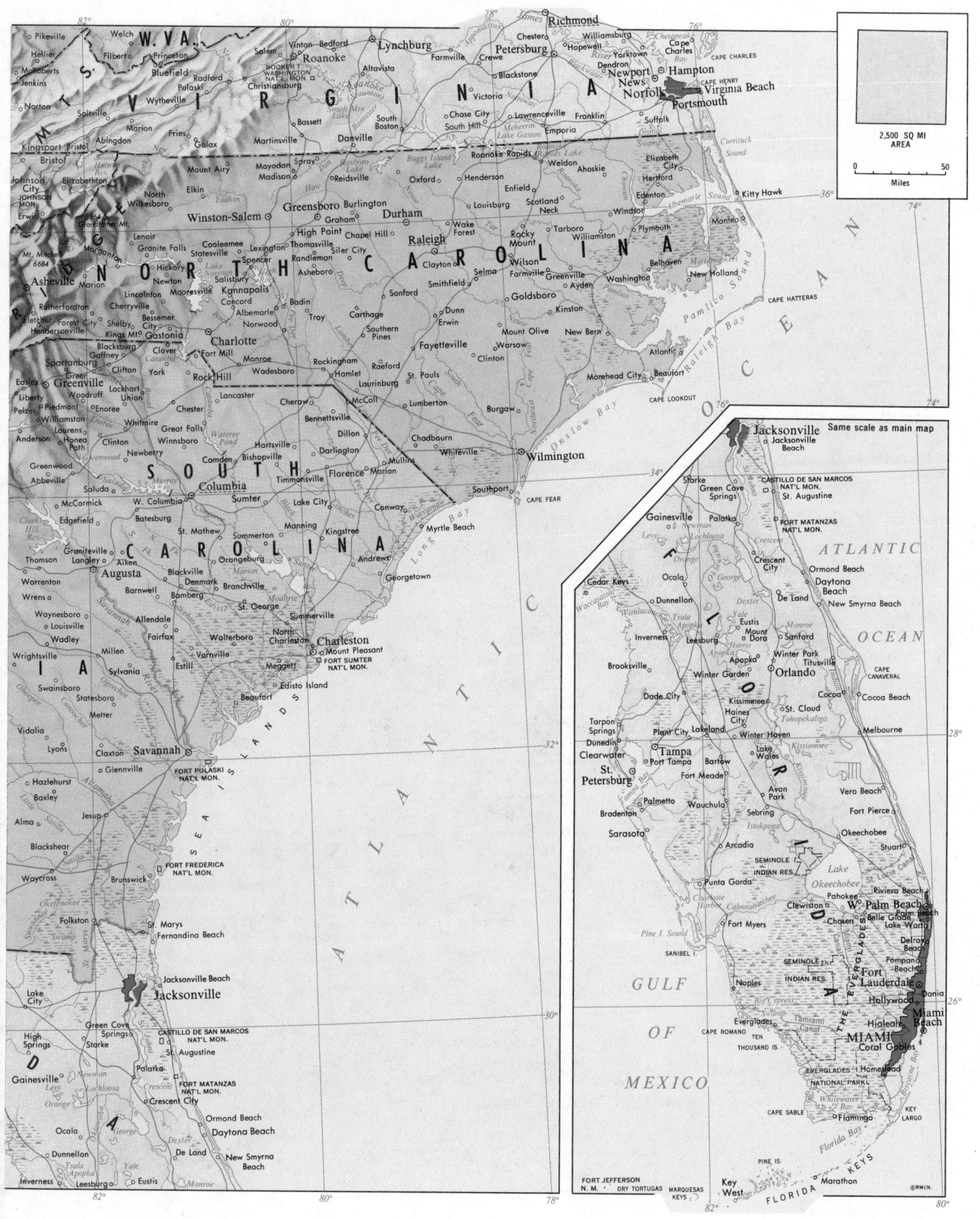

2,500 SQ MI
AREA

0   50
Miles

Same scale as main map

0 10 20 30 40 50 60 70 80 90 100 110 120 Miles
0   20   40   60   80   100 120 140 160 180 200 Kilometers

Elevations and depressions are given in feet

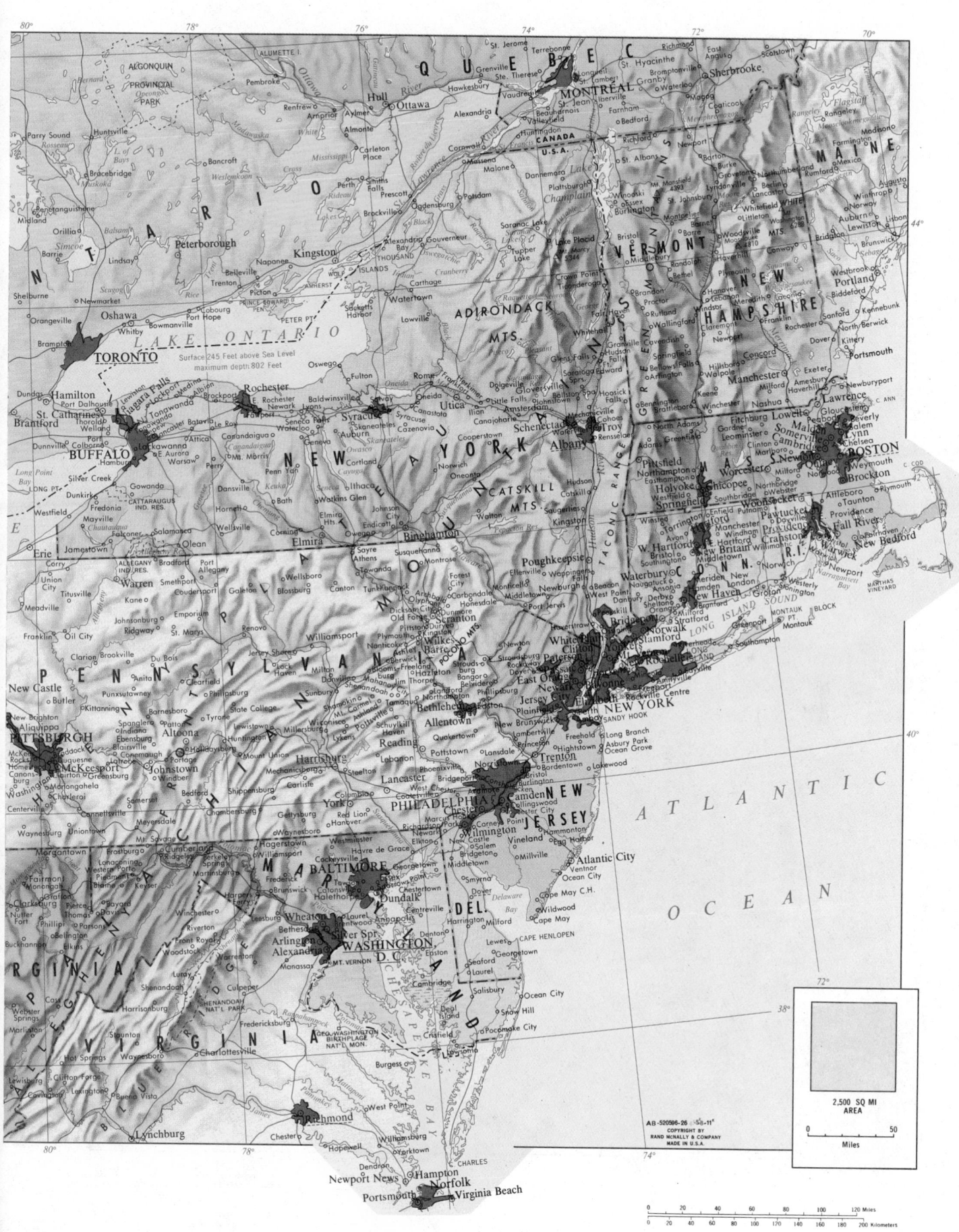

2,500 SQ MI
AREA

0   50
Miles

AB-520596-26   58-11°
COPYRIGHT BY
RAND McNALLY & COMPANY
MADE IN U.S.A.

0   20   40   60   80   100   120 Miles
0 20 40 60 80 100 120 140 160 180 200 Kilometers

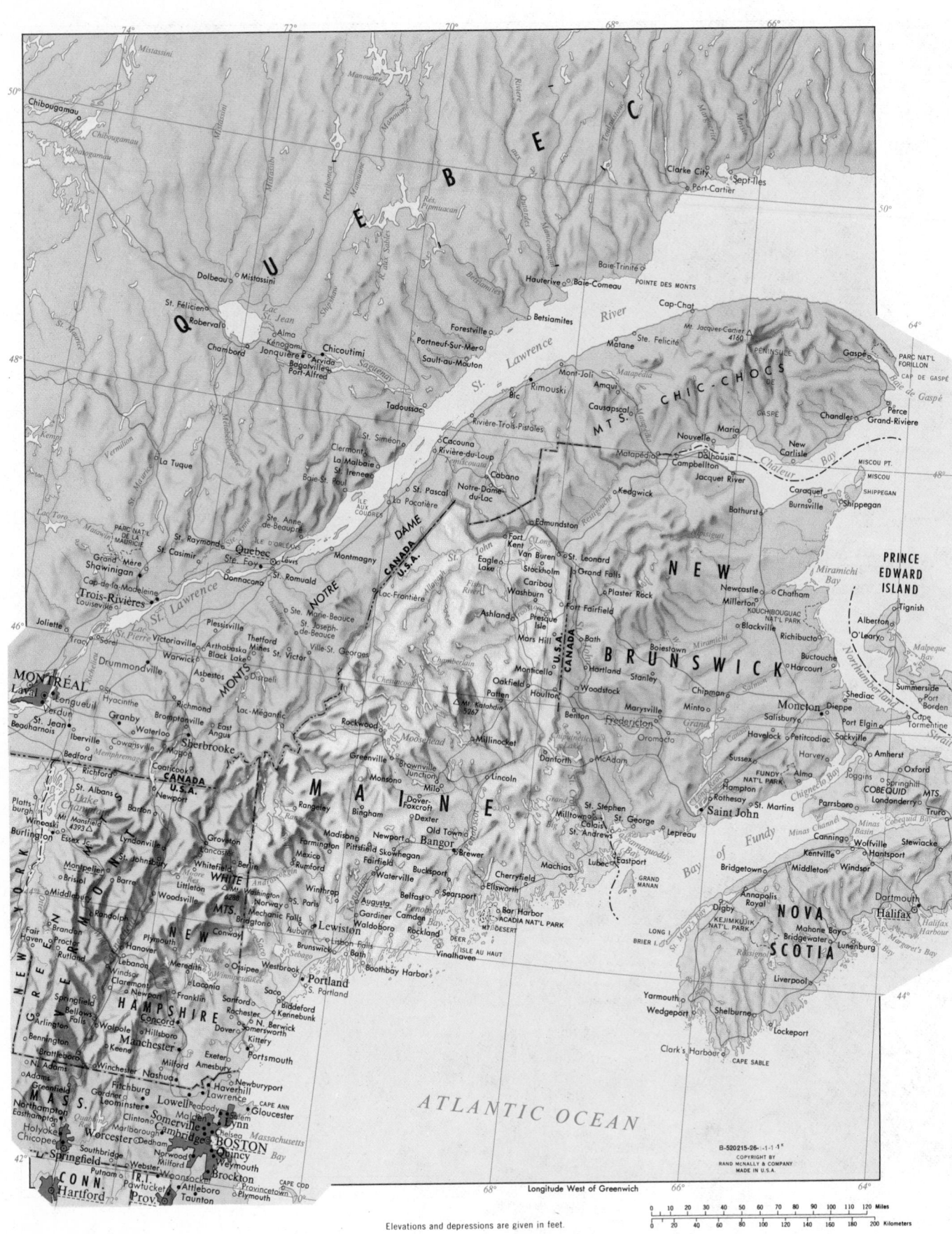

ATLANTIC OCEAN

B-520215-26-i-1-1*
COPYRIGHT BY
RAND McNALLY & COMPANY
MADE IN U.S.A.

Longitude West of Greenwich

Elevations and depressions are given in feet.

0 10 20 30 40 50 60 70 80 90 100 110 120 Miles

0 20 40 60 80 100 120 140 160 180 200 Kilometers

necting 48 states and 90 percent of all cities of 50,000 population or more. This system, begun in the 1950s, was almost complete by late 20th century, when it carried nearly 14 percent of the nation's motor traffic. It is possible to drive from coast to coast on the interstate network without stopping for a traffic light. The network of roads is densest on the Eastern Seaboard, along the Mississippi and Ohio valleys, and on the West Coast. In addition, there are railway lines, interstate pipelines, airways, and navigable waterways on the rivers and Great Lakes. The number of persons employed in motor-vehicle services and in their supporting equipment and supply industries is huge.

The overriding factor in the nation's mobility is the automobile. More than 80 percent of all households own at least one car or truck, and many own two or more. It is possible to eat a meal, attend the theatre, or make a bank deposit without getting out of one's car, and only slightly more effort is required to spend the night at a motel or to visit a shopping centre. Millions work in suburban factories far from any means of public transportation, where getting the job requires having a car.

Importance of the automobile

The increase in car ownership has sometimes exceeded the rising output of goods and services and has continued to outstrip the growth of population. At the same time, the city transit systems have undergone a sharp decline: bus and subway rides have decreased despite a large increase in the urban population of some areas.

The purposes of automobile riding are fairly evenly distributed among work, personal business, and recreation. About one-third of all trips are for the purpose of getting to work, and another one-third are for personal and family businesses. Shopping and social or recreational travel account for the remaining proportion.

While most trips in metropolitan areas are made by car, public transit and rail commuter lines play an important role in the most populous cities. The majority of home-to-work travel in the rush hours is by public carrier in such large centres as Boston, Philadelphia, Chicago, and New York City.

Railroads as bulk carriers

Railroads still play an important part in freight transportation between cities, carrying a preponderance of heavy bulk materials, while commercial vehicles tend to carry the lighter and more valuable goods.

The automobile age has brought some unpleasant consequences, including traffic congestion and air pollution. Some efforts have been made at various governmental levels to adapt the transportation system to the changing needs of society. These have included programs of aid for urban transit in hope of providing an attractive alternative for automobile commuters. Various federal safety requirements for passenger cars are aimed at reducing the highway death toll, and new engines and fuels have helped to reduce air pollution. Efforts have been increasingly directed to making transportation investment decisions more responsive to community desires. Bans have been imposed on cars on certain downtown streets in some large cities.

The U.S. Congress gave recognition to the urgency of transportation problems in 1965 by establishing the federal Department of Transportation. The country has entered a new era of jumbo jets, vertical- and steep-takeoff airplanes, high-speed ground transport, computerized freight systems, automated highways, and new power sources. Further improvement of urban mass-transit systems is uncertain, however, as governments have become increasingly unable or reluctant to subsidize them.   (W.O.)

Administrative and social conditions

GOVERNMENT

The national government. The U.S. Constitution sets up and defines a federal system of government in which certain powers are delegated to the national government and all other powers fall to the states. The national government consists of executive, legislative, and judicial branches designed to check and balance each other, all interrelated and overlapping yet each quite distinct.

Since the Constitution was ratified in 1788, there have been 26 amendments to it. The first 10, known as the Bill of Rights, established a number of individual liberties.

Notable among the other amendments are the 13th, 14th, and 15th, which abolished slavery and declared former slaves citizens with the right to vote; the 19th, which effected female suffrage; and the 17th, which provided for the direct election of U.S. senators. Amending the Constitution requires a proposal by a two-thirds vote in Congress or by a national convention, followed by ratification by three-fourths of the state legislatures or state conventions.

The executive and legislative branches

The executive branch of the government is headed by the president, who must be a natural-born citizen of the United States, at least 35 years old, and a resident of the country for at least 14 years. The formal responsibilities of the president include those of chief executive, treaty maker, commander in chief of the army, and head of state. In practice, they have grown to include the drafting of legislation, the formulation of foreign policy, personal diplomacy, and leadership of his political party. The members of the president's Cabinet—the secretaries of State; Treasury; Defense; Interior; Agriculture; Commerce; Labor; Health and Human Services; Housing and Urban Development; Transportation; Education; Energy; and the Attorney General—are defined in the 25th amendment as "the principal officers of the executive departments," but much power has come to be exercised by presidential aides who are not in the Cabinet. Thus, the president's Executive Office includes the Office of Management and Budget, the Council of Economic Advisers, and the National Security Council.

The legislative branch of the government is the Congress, which has two houses: the Senate and the House of Representatives. Powers granted Congress under the Constitution include the power to levy taxes, borrow money, regulate interstate commerce, declare war, seat members, discipline its own membership, and determine its rules of procedure.

The House of Representatives is chosen by direct vote of the electorate in each state, the number of representatives allotted to each state being based on population and the overall total never exceeding 435. Members must be 25 years old, residents of the states from which they are elected, and previously citizens of the United States for at least seven years. It has become practically imperative, though not constitutionally required, that they be inhabitants of the districts that elect them. They serve for a two-year period. The speaker of the House, who is chosen by the majority party, presides over debate, appoints members of select conference committees, and performs other leading duties. The parliamentary leaders of the two parties are the majority floor leader and the minority floor leader; they are helped by party whips who maintain contact between the leadership and the members of the House. Bills introduced by members in the House of Representatives are received by the standing committees, which meet in private executive session and can amend, expedite, delay, or kill the bills. The committee chairmen attain their positions on the basis of seniority, a criterion that is increasingly challenged. Among the most important committees are those on Appropriations, Ways and Means, and Rules. The Rules Committee, traditionally conservative, has great power to determine which bills will be brought to the floor of the House for consideration.

Each state elects two senators. Senators must be at least 30 years old, residents of the state from which they are elected, and previously citizens of the United States for at least nine years. Each term of service is for six years, and terms are so arranged that one-third of the members are elected every two years.

The Senate has 16 standing committees, among which the most prominent are those on Foreign Relations, Finance, Appropriations, and Government Operations. Debate is almost unlimited and may be used to delay the vote on a bill indefinitely. Such a delay is known as a filibuster and can be brought to an end only if two-thirds of the Senate agree. Treaties made by the president with other governments must be ratified by a two-thirds vote of the Senate.

The judicial branch

The U.S. Supreme Court, the third, or judicial, branch of the government, interprets the meaning of the Constitution and of federal laws. It consists of nine justices (including the chief justice) appointed for life by the president with the consent of the Senate. It has appellate jurisdiction for the lower federal courts and from state courts of last resort if a federal question is involved. It has original jurisdiction over cases involving foreign ambassadors, ministers, consuls, and cases to which a state is a party.

Three types of cases commonly reach the Supreme Court: cases involving litigants of different states, cases involving the interpretation of federal law, and cases involving the interpretation of the Constitution. Six judges consider each case, and a majority vote of the whole court is decisive; a tie vote sustains a lower-court decision. Often the minority judges will write a dissenting report.

The Supreme Court has often been criticized for its decisions. In the 1930s a conservative court overturned much of Pres. Franklin D. Roosevelt's New Deal legislation. In the area of civil rights it has received criticism from various groups at different times. After a 1954 ruling against school segregation, Southern political leaders attacked it harshly. Later, they were joined by Northern conservatives. During the late 20th century a number of decisions involving the pretrial rights of prisoners came under attack on the ground that the court had made it difficult to convict criminals.

Below the Supreme Court is the U.S. Court of Appeals. Special courts handle property and contract damage suits against the United States (U.S. Court of Claims), review customs rulings (U.S. Customs Court), and apply the uniform Code of Military Justice (U.S. Court of Military Appeals). Each state has at least one federal district court and at least one federal judge. District judges are appointed for life by the president with Senate consent. Appeals from district-court decisions are carried to the Court of Appeals.

State and municipal governments.   The governments of the 50 states have structures closely paralleling those of the federal government. Each state has a governor, a legislature, and a judiciary. Each state has its own constitution.

All state legislatures but one have two houses, Nebraska's being unicameral. Traditionally, state legislatures have been dominated by rural representatives who are not always sympathetic to the needs of growing urban areas. State judicial systems are based upon elected justices of the peace, above whom come the major trial courts, often called district courts, and appellate courts. In addition, there are probate courts concerned with wills, estates, and guardianships. Most state judges are elected.

State governments have a wide array of functions, encompassing agriculture and conservation, highway and motor-vehicle supervision, public safety and correction, professional licensing, regulation of intrastate business and industry, and certain aspects of education, public health, and welfare. These activities require a large administrative organization, headed by the governor. In most states there is also a lieutenant governor, not always of the same party as the governor, who serves as the presiding officer of the Senate. Other elected officials include the secretary of state, state treasurer, state auditor, attorney general, and superintendent of public instruction.

Municipal governments are more diverse in structure than state governments. There are three basic types: *The three* mayor–council governments, commission governments, *types of* and council–manager governments. In the first type, the *municipal* mayor and the council are elected; the council is nomin- *govern-* inally responsible for formulating city ordinances, which *ment* the mayor enforces; often the mayor controls the actions of the council. Boston, New York City, Philadelphia, Chicago, and Seattle have the mayor–council type of city government. In the commission type, voters elect a number of commissioners each of whom serves as head of a city department; the presiding commissioner is generally the mayor. Des Moines, Iowa, and New Orleans have council–manager governments. In the council–manager type, an elected council hires a city manager to administer the city departments. The mayor, elected by the council, simply chairs it and officiates at important functions.

Political parties.   There are two major political parties, *The* the Democratic Party and the Republican Party. Other *political* parties have occasionally challenged these two but without *process* permanent success. One reason for their failure is that in

order to win a national election, a party must appeal to a broad base of voters and a wide spectrum of interests. The two major parties tend to be moderate in their programs, and there is often little difference between them. Each has a conservative wing, and each has a wing that is considered liberal. The conservative Democrats tend to be more conservative on racial issues than their Republican counterparts; the liberal Democrats are more radical on economic issues than the liberal Republicans. The national parties sometimes seem to exist mainly to contest presidential elections every four years, and, in between their quadrennial national conventions, they are often little more than loose alliances of state and local party organizations.

In elections for president, voters actually choose among electors committed to the support of a particular candidate. Each state is allotted one electoral vote for each senator and representative in Congress. This is called the electoral-college system.

At the state level, political parties reflect the diversity of the population. Large urban centres are likely to support a Democratic ticket, whereas rural areas, small cities, and suburban areas tend to vote Republican. In many states the rural areas and smaller towns control the state legislatures, even though the more populous city areas provide the greater proportion of tax revenue. A Supreme Court ruling in 1964 sought to remedy this situation by ordering states to reapportion their legislatures more according to population. Some states have traditionally given majorities to one particular party. The 11 Southern states of the old Confederacy have until the mid-20th century voted almost solidly for Democratic candidates; in Maine and South Dakota the Republicans are more likely to win.

Municipal political parties have a pyramidal structure based, at the lowest level, on districts or precincts. The leaders of these units are responsible to ward leaders, who form the governing body of the municipal party. All of these party functionaries are responsible for getting their voters to the polls at election time, often on the basis of a return for services rendered. It is to them, after all, that voters have gone with requests for better municipal services, jobs, and assistance in minor difficulties. One route to political office for the ordinary citizen has been through the organization: belonging to a neighbourhood party club, helping to raise funds, getting out the vote, watching the polls, and gradually rising through the system to committeeman, city councilman, representative to the state legislature, or—depending on chance, talent, political expediency, and a host of other factors—to higher positions.

As society has become increasingly urban, politics and government have become more and more complex. Many *Decline* problems of the cities, including the problems of trans- *of local* portation, housing, education, health, and welfare, can *autonomy* no longer be handled entirely on the local level. Since even the states do not have the necessary resources, the cities have been forced to turn to the federal government for assistance.

Armed forces.   The military forces of the United States consist of the Army, Navy (including the Marine Corps), and the Air Force, under the umbrella of the Department of Defense with its headquarters in the Pentagon building in Arlington, Virginia. (A related force, the Coast Guard, is governed by the Department of Transportation.) The armed services also maintain reserve forces that may be called upon in time of war. Each state has a National Guard consisting of reserve groups subject to call at any time by the governor of the state.

Since a large part of the military budget is spent on matériel and research and development, military programs have considerable economic and political impact. The influence of the military also extends to other countries through a variety of multilateral and bilateral treaties for mutual defense and military assistance. The United States has military bases in Africa, Asia, Europe, and Latin America.

SOCIAL SERVICES

Education.   The interplay of local, state, and national programs and policies is particularly evident in the field

Colleges and universities

of education. Historically, education has been considered the province of the state and local governments. Of the more than 3,000 colleges and universities, the academies of the armed services are the only notable federal institutions. (The United States also administers, among others, the College of the Virgin Islands.) For years, however, the federal government has been involved in education at all levels, beginning in 1872 with the grant of public lands to the states for the purpose of establishing agricultural and mechanical arts colleges, called land-grant colleges. Additionally, the federal government supports school lunch programs, administers Indian education, makes research grants to universities, underwrites loans to college students, finances education for veterans, and prepares teaching materials. Whether the government should also give assistance to private and parochial (religious) schools has been widely debated. The Supreme Court has ruled that direct assistance to parochial schools is barred by the First Amendment to the Constitution, which states that "Congress shall make no law respecting an establishment of religion," although this has not been extended to the use of textbooks and so-called "supplementary educational centres."

Although responsibility for elementary education still rests primarily with local government, it is increasingly affected by state and national policies. The 1964 Civil Rights Act, for example, required federal agencies to cut off financial aid to school districts that are not racially integrated. This has raised difficult problems for many school systems where blacks live in largely segregated enclaves, requiring children to be transported long distances to nonsegregated schools.

Trends in education have been toward meeting the needs of a complex society: preschool programs; nongraded, multilevel classrooms; classes in the community; summer and night schools; increased facilities for exceptional children; and a general restructuring of traditional mores to improve the education of the culturally deprived and the disaffected student. The results of such programs, however, have been only partially fruitful.

The poor

Health and welfare. For all its wealth, poverty remains a reality for many persons in the United States—more than one-tenth of the population. About half of the poor were in homes in which the householder was a full- or part-time wage earner. Of the others, most were too old or disabled to work, while about a tenth of the householders were mothers of young children. The states provide assistance to the poor in varying amounts. The U.S. Department of Agriculture subsidizes the distribution of low-cost food and food stamps to the poor through the state and local governments.

Increasing public concern with poverty and welfare led to new federal legislation in the 1960s. Work, training, and rehabilitation programs were established in 1962 for welfare recipients. Between 1965 and 1969 the Office of Economic Opportunity set in motion a host of programs: the Head Start program for preschool children, the Neighborhood Youth Corps, the Teacher Corps, and the Manpower Training and Development program for unemployed workers.

Persons who have been employed are eligible for retirement pensions under the federal social security program established in the 1930s. Many employers also provide additional retirement benefits, as well as health insurance and life insurance, usually based on contributions by both the employer and the worker. Almost all employees are covered by Social Security, whose solvency, however, is increasingly uncertain. In addition, 30,000,000 persons were covered by private pension plans.

The provision of medical and health care is one of the largest industries in the United States. There were, nevertheless, many inadequacies in medical services, particularly in rural and poor areas. About one-sixth of the population, including members of the armed forces and their families, receive medical care paid for or subsidized by the federal government. Many people are not covered by any form of health insurance.

The federal Department of Health and Human Services through its National Institutes of Health supports much of the biomedical research in the United States. Grants are made also to researchers in clinics and medical schools.

Housing. More than two-thirds of the housing units in the United States are single-family houses, and a majority of the remainder are in structures containing two, three, or four units. Most houses in the United States are of wood construction, though often covered with shingles or brick veneer.

Quality of housing

Housing, like health, was long considered a private rather than public concern. The growth of urban slums led many municipal governments to enact stricter building codes and sanitary regulations. In 1934 the Federal Housing Administration was established to make loans to institutions that would build low-rent dwellings. Efforts to reduce the slums in large cities by developing low-cost housing in other areas frequently have been resisted by property owners. For many years the restrictive covenant, by which property owners pledged not to sell to certain racial or religious groups, served to bar those groups from many communities. A 1948 Supreme Court decision declared covenants unenforceable; a 1962 executive order by President Kennedy prohibited discrimination in housing built with federal aid; and many states and cities have adopted fair-housing laws and set up fair-housing commissions. These efforts, however, have had relatively little effect upon the black ghettos in large cities.

Law enforcement. The enforcement of law in the United States has traditionally been centred in the hands of local police officials. The bulk of the work is done by the police and detectives in the cities and by sheriffs and constables in rural areas. Many of the state governments also have law-enforcement agencies, and all of them have highway-patrol systems for traffic-law enforcement. Crimes that come under federal jurisdiction (for example, those committed in more than one state) are the responsibility of the Federal Bureau of Investigation (FBI), which also provides assistance through fingerprint identification and technical laboratory services to state and local law-enforcement agencies.

Crime rates have risen and law enforcement continues to be a major political issue. In 1966 the federal government began encouraging state coordinating councils composed of local police, prosecutors, courts, and corrective officers—a trend that was strengthened by the omnibus Crime Control and Safe Streets Act (Public Law 90–351). Other measures taken to combat crime included enlarging police departments and raising the level of competence in police work.   (J.T.H./Ed.)

Cultural life

THE CULTURAL MILIEU

The dominant fact of cultural life in the United States during the 20th century has been rapid and continual change brought about by such factors as population growth, technological development, urbanization, and the press of world events. By the middle decades of the 20th century the principal question was whether change was producing a more unified, homogeneous, and standardized culture or a culture increasingly divided and fragmented into sometimes conflicting parts.

Trends toward uniformity. With the advent of commercial television at midcentury, it was generally believed that U.S. cultural life would be increasingly shaped by the techniques and requirements of the mass cultural institutions. According to this view, the major media of communications—television, radio, motion pictures, national magazines, and record companies, operating principally in New York City and Los Angeles—would produce an overwhelming proportion of the entertainment and information that was available to the public. Such cultural production, it was argued, would inevitably be controlled by the commercial need to appeal to the largest possible audience and to sell advertised goods and services. The result of this would be a growing cultural uniformity throughout the entire country at a level of lowest-common-denominator mediocrity, wiping out ethnic and regional differences and confining the creation and preservation of "high culture"—literature, the fine arts, classical

Homogenizing influences of mass communications and institutions music and opera, philosophy and social thought—to a small, educated elite.

Some of these pessimistic predictions have come true in U.S. cultural life. In a period of rapid communications and nationwide consolidation of corporate industry, regional variations in such facets of cultural life as architecture, language, popular entertainment, and style of dress have unquestionably diminished. It is possible to travel west across the country in a few hours and find in Arizona or Oregon shops and restaurants with the same names, buildings, and products, as well as television channels and movie theatres with the same programs, that are in Virginia or Connecticut. Few other countries had attained such unity of cultural life over so vast a territory and so large a population.

The countercultures. During this period of increasing standardization of cultural life, however, a countertrend began that opposed the process of unification with a process of fragmentation. In its origins, this countermovement was essentially not a conscious effort to resist the development of mass culture, in the form, for example, of a bohemian colony of nonconformists. Rather, its sources came from movements of social change and political opposition, including the various civil rights movements.

The fragmentation of cultural life took new forms. Black power for blacks became red power for American Indians, brown power for Chicanos and other Spanish-speaking people, women's liberation as a new form of feminism, and gay liberation for homosexuals. In all these cases the rhetoric of "power" and "liberation" implied a pride and self-confidence in racial, ethnic, sexual, and ultimately cultural differences. It marked a new form of consciousness among minority groups in the cultural life of the United States, a militancy arising from the assertion of group solidarity and the distinctive traits and appearances of the group. Only a few years before, members of minority groups had been striving to adapt themselves as much as possible to a unified mode of cultural behaviour in grooming, dress, work habits, and recreation. By the late 20th century such efforts at acculturation had proven so effective that many of the old ethnic, nationality, and religious distinctions among white Americans had lost their emotional force. White Americans of the middle classes, whatever their country of origin or form of worship, were described as "middle Americans," marked by an increasing resistance to social and cultural change. But it remained to be seen how much cohesion this group possessed, whether political or economic differences would take on growing importance as cultural differences waned. There were signs, moreover, that the new minority consciousness also was affecting the older European ethnic allegiances, causing a revival of ethnic awareness and assertion among groups nominally part of the undifferentiated "middle Americans."

The roots of the startling and unexpected trend toward cultural differentiation have been traced to several causes. One useful explanation centres on the practical impossibility of attaining a single standardized cultural life in the United States. This viewpoint holds that differences in ethnic and racial background and in sexual and cultural experience are real and that the effort to deny them led to social and cultural tensions that exploded in cultural conflict and self-assertion. It would be better, according to this view, to foster cultural pluralism in the United States and encourage groups and individuals to create their own cultural lives based on their differences and also their inevitable relation within the shared activities of national life.

Another explanation finds the cause of cultural divergence paradoxically in the very technologies that make a unified culture possible. This view asserts that the new electronic technologies of computers, artificial Earth satellites, and television have created a revolution in communications and in culture. They make possible an instantaneous transmission of information to any part of the world. Instant communications thereby pose a double challenge to traditional centralized and large-scale organizations. People are learning to think in global terms, as part of a single Earth system. At the same time, transnational

technologies encourage people to reexamine their cultural identities. One result has been the desire to reformulate cultural life in smaller, more distinctive units.

Such theories may help to explain many of the contradictory features of new cultural movements in the United States. The distinctive styles and languages of the minority cultures were projected across the nation through the media and were adopted, imitated, or commercialized for mass cultural use. Information made available by the new technologies has convinced many that technological growth is leading the society to great ecological problems. An ecology movement has developed that opposes further technological expansion and fosters the trend toward smaller cultural units. Cultural life in the United States continues to be marked by rapid change, emphasizing new relationships among people and between people and their environment.

THE ARTS

Forms. The technological, economic, social, and intellectual factors underlying cultural change obviously affect the work of artists and entertainers in the United States, as well as the audiences and status of the various arts. But the relationship of the arts to the structure of culture has always been an ambiguous one, with artists sometimes anticipating or prefiguring cultural change in their works and at other times reflecting or documenting such changes. In either case, the arts have been deeply involved in the transformations shaping cultural life in the United States.

Literature. This involvement may be readily seen in literature, the form of artistic expression in which U.S. artists first received worldwide recognition. Fiction and poetry have traditionally been mediums that members of minority groups have used to express their sense of life in the United States. Burdened and blessed with a double consciousness, at once insider and outsider to the mainstream of cultural life in the United States, the minority-group writer has a special perspective that can illuminate aspects of the national culture inaccessible to others. After World War II writers from regional and ethnic minorities thus played important roles in sensing and interpreting U.S. life through fiction and poetry. Southerners were prominent among U.S. writers, including William Faulkner, Eudora Welty, Robert Penn Warren, Katherine Anne Porter, Flannery O'Connor, and Walker Percy. Beginning in the 1950s, Jewish writers came to the fore in literary life, among them Saul Bellow, Norman Mailer, Bernard Malamud, Philip Roth, and Allen Ginsberg.

Such black novelists as James Baldwin and Ralph Ellison also became prominent, and Ellison's *Invisible Man* (1952) was considered by many critics to be the outstanding U.S. novel of the quarter century following World War II. But, as the civil rights movement turned to black power, writers who expressed the black perspective on U.S. culture were not novelists but militant activists who wrote essays, memoirs, and polemics. Such works as *The Autobiography of Malcolm X* (1965), Eldridge Cleaver's *Soul on Ice* (1968), and George Jackson's *Soledad Brother* (1970) claimed for nonfiction the imaginative force and depth that the literary public had been accustomed to finding only in poetry and fiction. Among the outstanding black novelists of the late 20th century were Maya Angelou, who established her reputation with *I Know Why the Caged Bird Sings* (1970), and Toni Morrison, whose *Song of Solomon* (1977) won her the National Book Critics Circle Award.

The prominence of nonfiction among black writers was one part of a general movement in the U.S. literary community to reassess the traditions and future of literature. The feminist novel came to the fore. Erica Jong's *Fear of Flying* (1973) created a sensation with its blend of feminism and sexual adventure, while John Irving, *The World According to Garp* (1978), and Leonard Michaels, *The Men's Club* (1981), explored the impact of feminism on men.

In the late 20th century many of the functions of literature as a source of description and information seemed to have been taken over by the communications media and the social sciences. The question was asked, "Is the novel dead as an art form?" Some writers responded to the challenge by proclaiming a new form, the "nonfiction novel,"

Impulses toward increased cultural fragmentation

Literary perspectives of the U.S. minorities

Literature of cultural alienation and protest

and at least one masterwork was produced in this form, Norman Mailer's *The Armies of the Night* (1968). Other writers, such as John Barth and Donald Barthelme, experimented with new forms, emphasizing fiction as a source of fantasy rather than fact. Such genre forms as the science-fiction novels of Kurt Vonnegut, Jr., were taken more seriously, but so too were novels of social realism such as those of Joyce Carol Oates. Literature, like other aspects of cultural life during this period, was in a state of change.

The visual arts. While the perspectives of minority groups helped to shape the development of U.S. literature, the advance of technology played a similar role for painting and sculpture. Until around 1960, however, trends in general cultural life, technological or otherwise, seemed to bear little relation to the practice of the visual arts in the United States. In the aftermath of World War II, U.S. painting came for the first time to take a dominant position in the world art scene in the style of abstract expressionism, which took as its subject matter not a rendering of natural forms but rather the formal properties of the artistic mediums—line and colour; the textures of paint, wood, or stone; purely geometric form; and the like—and the subjectivity of the artist. Allied to this style was one that came to be called Pop art, a style that was inspired by the banal objects of U.S. commercial, technological, and popular culture that included comic strips, advertisements, soda bottles, soup cans, trademarks, billboards, hamburgers, automobiles, and telephones. Such pop artists as Andy Warhol, Roy Lichtenstein, or Claes Oldenburg turned to everyday life and the objects around them, making abstractions of such objects from their environment and presenting them almost as icons.

The abstract tradition was carried forward more directly in Minimal art, a style of stark geometric forms, shapes, and colours practiced by such older artists of the New York school as Barnett Newman and Mark Rothko and carried forward by younger painters such as Frank Stella. Many artists became increasingly interested not only in the products of modern technology as subject matter but also in technology itself as a medium for artistic creation. An exhibition at the Museum of Modern Art in New York City, "The Machine as Seen at the End of the Mechanical Age," publicized the ways in which 20th-century artists depicted and used technology in their work. The Los Angeles County Museum of Art carried the process a step further, developing collaboration between artists and business firms specializing in advanced technology.

Sculptors pioneered in outdoor works that were designed to take art outside the museum and to involve the public more actively in art. Alexander Liberman's *In* (1973), for example, encouraged the viewer to walk inside a structure composed of large tubes. Tony Smith, Claes Oldenburg, Louise Nevelson, Alexander Calder, and Beverly Pepper were also active in the creation of large-scale public works. Javacheff Christo's *Running Fence* (1976) stretched nylon for 24 miles outside San Francisco and was perhaps the most publicized of the outdoor works.

The theatre. Much of the expressionism and subjectivity that was excluded from painting and sculpture was channelled into new forms of theatre, sometimes called "happenings" or "assemblages." These were performances involving several mediums, including music, film, sound and light effects, materials, live acting, and often the audience as well. Arising from the works and teachings of the composer John Cage, the new theatre practiced an aesthetic of chance and indeterminacy, aiming at times toward the elimination of distinctions between art and life. One composition by Cage called for musicians to maintain four minutes and 33 seconds of silence, allowing incidental sounds, coughing in the audience, or outdoor noises to become the "music."

Similar innovations occurred in the drama, though not quite through such extreme breaks with traditional forms. The dominance of Broadway over conventional theatrical production of drama, comedy, and musicals continued to give way to regional theatre as well as to Off-Broadway theatre in New York, a development of the 1950s, and Off-Off-Broadway, a more experimental theatre that emerged in the 1960s. Many of the new playwrights expressed the

same fascination as the Pop artists with the artifacts and myths of popular culture and the U.S. past, and they tried to infuse them with a similar iconographic objectivity and mystery. Two plays presenting such themes, Arthur Kopit's *Indians* and Howard Sackler's *The Great White Hope,* were first produced at the Arena Stage in Washington, D.C., and later moved to Broadway; other works, such as Jean-Claude van Italie's *America Hurrah* and the short plays of Sam Shepard, originated Off-Off-Broadway under the auspices of the La Mama Experimental Theatre Company and other small theatres. The coming together of high culture and popular culture in the theatre reached a new level in the late 1960s with *Hair,* the first rock musical, followed in 1971 by *Jesus Christ Superstar,* a rock musical based on a rock-opera record album.

Motion pictures. The movies had dominated the popular arts and entertainment from the 1920s until shortly after World War II, when the advent of television and new uses of leisure time for sports and recreation began to compete with their audience. Rapidly increasing production costs; the breakup of the studio system, with its emphasis on star performers and its virtual control of production and distribution of films; and the retirement of important creative workers continued to weaken the Hollywood-based motion-picture industry in the late 20th century, although the work of a new generation of filmmakers developed an audience for movies as a form of high culture.

Audiences. If the arts and entertainment were deeply implicated in forms of cultural change, perhaps nowhere was this more apparent than in the way culture was disseminated to the general population. In the long run, it may be recognized that the latter half of the 20th century in the United States was characterized by cultural revolution brought about by communications technology. Beginning with television by 1950, followed rapidly by paperbound books, long-playing records, multiple reproductions of art works, transistors, tape recorders, and other innovations, technology made possible an unprecedented inexpensive mass production of art and entertainment products. A steadily increasing enrollment in colleges and universities during these years brought a far greater proportion of the population into contact with instruction in the history, criticism, and techniques of the arts and also, for the first time, with professional performances of music, dance, and drama and exhibitions of painting and sculpture.

The consequences of such a historic democratization of culture remain a subject of much debate. Some critics see largely negative results, pointing to the commercialization of "high culture" and a concomitant turning of artists into celebrities and art styles into fads and fashions that change before they can develop; to continuing weaknesses in the educational system, suggesting that culture has not penetrated much beyond its usual minority audience; and to the precarious survival of many cultural institutions. Others, recognizing such criticisms, nevertheless contend that democratization of culture, spreading information about society and the arts to new sectors of the population, belies the prediction that mediocrity and homogeneity would be the result and lead to the dramatic transformation of attitude and expectation affecting U.S. society at all its levels.

Mass culture, with its opposing tendencies toward standardization and differentiation, has remained a major force in artistic life in the United States. Some artists and entertainers are directly employed in mass-culture industries—motion pictures, recording, and television. Others use the technology of mass culture—audiotape and videotape, film, and electronics—in their artistic creation. In all fields, the artifacts and myths of mass popular culture are a common subject of artistic exploration and treatment. Historically, the boundary between folk traditions and commercial culture has always been ambiguous in the United States, and artists have found a new modern folklore emerging from earlier manifestations of commercial mass culture.

CULTURAL INSTITUTIONS

Leadership and support for such cultural institutions as museums, symphony orchestras, and theatres in the United States has come traditionally from individual and private

Theatrical investigations of U.S. mythologies

Deification of technology and banality

The democratization of the arts

sources. In the late 20th century, however, local, state, and federal government began to play a larger role in the planning and financing of cultural institutions. Nowhere was this public expenditure more significant for cultural life than in the expansion and transformation of colleges and universities.

In response to the growing need for a skilled work force, state legislatures and the federal government contributed to a swift development of higher education in the United States. Older public universities added new departments and schools; teacher-training colleges became full-scale universities; and two-year junior colleges became four-year institutions. Hundreds of new junior colleges were founded and many new four-year and graduate institutions as well. States such as New York and Massachusetts developed almost entirely new systems of public higher education, and states such as California, with a traditionally strong system, vastly expanded their institutions and resources. The number of students attending degree-granting institutions more than doubled.

Universities continue to function as institutions in which the cultural heritage is preserved and transmitted to a new generation, but, during this period of growth, a large number of universities also took on new roles as centres in which the arts were performed, exhibited, and created. As part of their task of teaching skills as well as knowledge, universities added active writers, composers, musicians, painters, sculptors, and other artists and performers to their teaching staffs. A number of universities established or expanded museum, music, and theatre programs as the means of training students and also of improving the cultural environments of their cities and states. Among the most notable examples of such programs was the Tyrone Guthrie Theater associated with the University of Minnesota, which became nationally known for the high quality of its stagings and performances. The new cultural activities of universities served in important ways to decentralize cultural production in the United States and make live performances of the arts available to a far wider audience.

Government support for the arts also took the form of aid and planning for new cultural centres in the nation's cities. In the course of extensive urban renewal many cities sought to concentrate or revive their cultural institutions by constructing centres for cultural activity in inner-city locations. New York City established the Lincoln Center for the Performing Arts, with facilities for opera, theatre, music, film, and other arts, and Los Angeles developed its Music Center. In 1971 the federally sponsored John F. Kennedy Center for the Performing Arts was opened, to mixed critical reception, in Washington, D.C.

Both privately and publicly supported cultural institutions have become increasingly involved in the cultural and social issues of society as a whole. Although the cultural activities of universities were not directly affected by the political controversies and turmoil on many college campuses, the resulting cutbacks in state aid and private donations placed a strain on the financing of higher education that curtailed the growth or sometimes even threatened the survival of many cultural programs. Museums and cultural centres in inner cities suffered declines in attendance and revenues because patrons became reluctant to enter high-crime areas in which these centres were located.

Above all, the problem for cultural institutions is one of finding continued financial support. At a time when the resources of cultural institutions have reached their highest levels of quality and breadth in the history of the United States, many such institutions are plagued by financial difficulties that can only be solved by changes in national economic conditions that are beyond their control.

COMMUNICATIONS MEDIA

The development of media for communicating news, entertainment, and commercial advertising since the middle of the 20th century has been primarily shaped by the two dominant factors of contemporary cultural life: technological change and the emergence of minority cultures. Television has become the major medium, surpassing newspapers, magazines, and radio and profoundly influencing the structure of their institutions. With its production mostly

Expanding role of the university in the arts

Declining financial support for the arts

centralized in three commercial networks, television has been less affected by minority interests than the other mediums, but technological innovations within television itself are providing more opportunities for minority and community expression.

Printed media and radio.   The impact of television struck newspapers at the same time that the growth of suburbs and satellite cities around urban centres reshaped the needs and desires of newspaper readers. With the loss of advertising revenue to television and of readership to suburban newspapers, the big-city dailies have been seriously hurt. Since the 1950s scores of major urban newspapers have ceased operation, leaving most large U.S. cities with no more than one morning and one afternoon newspaper. Since the ownership is often in one company, a diversity in editorial point of view or content often has been lacking. At the same time, the growing number of suburban papers has led to a small net gain in the number of newspapers in the United States. Most of these, however, are smaller and often less ambitious, and observers note a trend toward less independent reporting and an increasing reliance on nationwide press services for national and international news.

Television had similar effects on general magazines and radio. Those magazines that were edited for a broad common denominator of readers tended to suffer from competition with television, and *Collier's, The Saturday Evening Post,* and *Look* were among the major general-readership periodicals that ceased publication. At the same time, smaller magazines that were edited for a specialized audience thrived by reaching audiences and providing services that competing media could not offer. Radio was most directly affected by television, giving up almost entirely its drama and variety programming and concentrating on music for teenage audiences. A new trend in radio broadcasting that developed during the late 1960s was the "talk show," featuring conversations between listeners and announcers or guests in the studio. Thus, the development of television had the long-range effect of loosening the structure of other media and permitting increasing diversity of communications—although increases in printing costs and postal rates pose difficulties for periodical publishers and threaten to reduce the number of specialized and minority magazines.

Television.   Within the television industry itself, however, just the opposite development occurred. Television production rapidly became concentrated in three major networks, whose uniformity of programming seemed to bear out the fears of the critics of mass culture that standardization and the lowest common denominator of cultural communication would result from the growth of mass media.

Almost every U.S. home has a television receiver, and the very size of the potential audience—virtually the entire U.S. population—has made television a medium different from any other in history. Commercial advertisers pay large sums of money to advertise their products in the evening "prime-viewing" time, and a one-half-hour network entertainment show costs several hundred thousand dollars to produce. These high costs of production and advertising time have led the television industry to place great emphasis on national ratings, which indicate the number of persons believed to be watching a show. Shows that do not get high ratings tend to be cancelled after a few weeks or a season, and successful shows are widely copied. Original and innovative programming has given way to a standard television schedule featuring movies, sports, celebrity talk shows, and genre programs adapted from other media—soap operas, comedies, adventures, and mysteries.

Efforts have been made to increase the variety and quality of programming through the U.S. Corporation for Public Broadcasting network. An important trend was cable television, carried to homes on wires rather than through the atmosphere. Cable television has vastly increased the number of channels available to viewers, and, according to regulations of the Federal Communications Commission, it is expected to provide opportunities for community-controlled channels and programming. For statistical data, see the "Britannica World Data" section in the current *Britannica Book of the Year.*   (R.Sk./Ed.)

Realignments within newspaper and magazine publishing

Counterbalances to commercial mediocrity

HISTORY

The territory represented by the continental United States had, of course, been discovered, perhaps several times, before the voyages of Columbus. When Columbus came, he found the New World inhabited by peoples who in all likelihood had originally come from the continent of Asia. Probably these first inhabitants had arrived 10,000 to 30,000 years before in a series of migrations from Asia to North America by way of the Bering Strait. By the time the white man appeared, the aborigines had spread and occupied all portions of the New World.

The foods and other resources available in each physiographic region largely determined the type of culture prevailing there. Fish and sea mammals, for example, contributed the bulk of the food supply of coastal tribes, although the acorn was a staple for California Indians; plant life and wild game (especially the American bison, or buffalo) were sources for the plains Indians; small-game hunting and fishing (depending again on local resources) provided for middle-western and eastern tribes. These foods were supplemented by corn, which was a staple food for the Indians of the southwest. The procurement of these foods called for the employment of fishing, hunting, plant and berry gathering, and farming techniques, the application of which depended, in turn, upon the food resources utilized in given areas.

Foods and other raw materials likewise conditioned the material culture of the respective regional groups. All Indians transported goods by human carrier; the use of dogs to pull sleds or travois was widespread; and rafts, boats, and canoes were used where water facilities were available. The horse was the white man's importation (by the Spanish in the early 16th century), but it was quickly adopted by the Indians once it had made its appearance. The horse became widely used by the buffalo-hunting Indians of the plains.

Indian culture groups are distinguished among other things by house types. The dome-shaped ice houses were developed by the Eskimos; rectangular plank houses were produced by the northwest Indians; earth and skin lodges and tepees by plains and prairie tribes; flat-roofed and often multistoried houses by some of the Pueblo Indians of the southwest; barrel houses by the natives in the northeast. Clothing, or the lack of it, likewise varied with native groups, as did crafts, weapons, and tribal economic, social, and religious customs.

At the time of Columbus' arrival there were probably roughly 1,500,000 Indians in what is now the continental United States, although estimates vary greatly. In order to assess the role and the impact of the American Indian upon the subsequent history of the United States in any meaningful way, one must understand the differentiating factors, such as those mentioned above. Generally speaking it may be said, however, that the American Indians as a whole exercised an important influence upon the white civilization transplanted from Europe to the New World. Indian foods and herbs, articles of manufacture, methods of raising some crops, war techniques, words, a rich folklore, and racial infusions are among the more obvious general contributions of the Indians to their white conquerors. Indian resistance to the white man's advance, taking the form of a protracted brutal conflict on the westward-moving frontier of white settlement, constitutes one of the most tragic chapters in the history of the United States.   (Ed.)

Colonial America to 1763

THE EUROPEAN BACKGROUND

The English colonization of North America was but one chapter in the larger story of European expansion throughout the globe. The Portuguese, beginning with a voyage to Porto Santo off the coast of West Africa in 1418, were the first Europeans to promote overseas exploration and colonization. By 1487 the Portuguese had travelled all the way to the southern tip of Africa, establishing trading stations at Arguin, Sierra Leone, and El Mina. In 1497 Vasco da Gama rounded the Cape of Good Hope and sailed up the eastern coast of Africa, laying the groundwork for Portugal's later commercial control of India. By 1500, when Pedro Álvares Cabral stumbled across the coast of Brazil en route to India, Portuguese influence had expanded to the New World as well.

Though initially lagging behind the Portuguese in the arts of navigation and exploration, the Spanish quickly closed that gap in the decades following Columbus' (see COLUMBUS) voyages to America. First in the Caribbean and then in spectacular conquests of New Spain and Peru, they captured the imagination, and the envy, of the European world.

France, occupied with wars in Europe to preserve its own territorial integrity, was not able to devote as much time or effort to overseas expansion as Spain and Portugal. Beginning in the early 16th century, however, French fishermen established an outpost in Newfoundland, and in 1534 Jacques Cartier began exploring the Gulf of St. Lawrence. By 1543 the French had ceased their efforts to colonize the northwest portion of the New World. In the last half of the 16th century, France attempted to found colonies in Florida and Brazil; but each of these efforts failed, and by the end of the century Spain and Portugal remained the only two European nations to have established successful colonies in America. **French settlement**

The English, although anxious to duplicate the Spanish and Portuguese successes, nevertheless lagged far behind in their colonization efforts. The English possessed a theoretical claim to the North American mainland by dint of the 1497 voyage of John Cabot off the coast of Nova Scotia, but in fact they had neither the means nor the desire to back up that claim during the 16th century. Thus it was that England relied instead on private trading companies, which were interested principally in commercial rather than territorial expansion, to defend its interests in the expanding European world. The first of these commercial ventures began with the formation of the Muscovy Company in 1554. In 1576–78 the English mariner Martin Frobisher undertook three voyages in search of a Northwest Passage to the East. In 1577 Sir Francis Drake made his famous voyage around the world, plundering the western coast of South America en route. A year later Sir Humphrey Gilbert, one of the most dedicated of Elizabethan imperialists, began a series of ventures aimed at establishing permanent colonies in North America. All of his efforts met with what was, at best, limited success. Finally, in September 1583, on what would prove to be his final voyage, Gilbert, with five vessels and 260 men, disappeared in the North Atlantic. With the failure of Gilbert's voyage, the English turned to a new man, Sir Walter Raleigh, and a new strategy—a southern rather than a northern route to North America—to advance England's fortunes in the New World. Raleigh's efforts to found a permanent colony off the coast of Virginia, although they did finally fail with the mysterious destruction of the Roanoke Island colony in 1587, awakened popular interest in a permanent colonizing venture. **The voyages of Sir Humphrey Gilbert**

During the years separating the failure of the Roanoke colony and the establishment in 1607 of the English settlement in Jamestown, English propagandists worked hard to convince the public that a colony in America would yield instant and easily exploitable wealth. Even men like the English geographer Richard Hakluyt were not certain that the Spanish colonization experience could or should be imitated but hoped nevertheless that the English colonies in the New World would prove to be a source of immediate commercial gain. There were, of course, other motives for colonization. Some hoped to discover the much sought after route to the Orient in North America. English imperialists thought it necessary to settle in the New World in order to limit Spanish expansion. Once it was proven that America was a suitable place for settlement, some Englishmen would travel to those particular colonies that promised to free them from religious persecution. There were also Englishmen, primarily of lower and middle class origin, who hoped the New World would provide them with increased economic opportunity in the form of free or inexpensive land. These last two motives, while they have been given considerable attention by historians, appear not to have been so much original motives for English colonization as they were shifts of attitude once colonization had begun.

SETTLEMENT

Virginia. The leaders of the Virginia Company of London, a joint-stock company in charge of the Jamestown enterprise, were for the most part wealthy and wellborn commercial and military adventurers eager to find new outlets for investment. During the first two years of its existence, the Virginia colony, under the Charter of 1607, proved an extraordinarily bad investment. This was principally due to the unwillingness of the early colonizers to do the necessary work of providing for themselves and to the chronic shortage of capital for supply of the venture.

A new charter in 1609 significantly broadened membership in the Virginia Company, thereby increasing temporarily the supply of capital at the disposal of its directors; but most of the settlers continued to act as though they expected the Indians to provide for their existence, a notion that the Indians fiercely rejected. As a result, the enterprise still failed to yield any profits and the number of investors again declined.

The crown issued a third charter in 1612 authorizing the company to institute a lottery to raise more capital for the floundering enterprise. In that same year John Rolfe harvested the first crop of a high-grade and therefore potentially profitable strain of tobacco. At about the same time, with the arrival of Sir Thomas Dale in the colony as governor in 1611, the settlers gradually began to practice the discipline necessary for their survival, though at an enormous personal cost.

The administration of Sir Thomas Dale

Dale carried with him the "Laws Divine, Morall and Martial," which were intended to supervise nearly every aspect of the settlers' lives. Each person in Virginia, including women and children, was given a military rank, and his duties were spelled out in minute detail. Penalties imposed for violating these rules were severe: those who failed to obey the work regulations were to be forced to lie neck and heels together all night for the first offense, whipped for the second, and sent to a year's service in the galleys for the third. The settlers could hardly protest against the harshness of the code, for that might be deemed slander against the company—an offense punishable by service in the galleys or by death.

Dale's Code brought order to the Virginia experiment, but it hardly served to attract new settlers. To increase incentive the company, beginning in 1618, offered 50 acres of land to those settlers who could pay their transportation to Virginia and a promise of 50 acres after seven years of service to those who could not pay their passage. Concurrently, the new governor of Virginia, Sir George Yeardley, issued a call for the election of representatives to a House of Burgesses, which was to convene in Jamestown in July 1619. In its original form, the House of Burgesses was little more than an agency of the governing board of the Virginia Company, but it would later expand its powers and prerogatives and become an important force for colonial self-government.

Virginia made a crown colony

Despite the introduction of these reforms, the years from 1619 to 1624 proved fatal to the future of the Virginia Company. Epidemics, an Indian massacre in 1622, and internal disputes took a heavy toll on the colony. In 1624 the crown finally revoked the charter of the company and placed the colony under royal control. The introduction of royal government into Virginia, while it was to have important long-range consequences, did not produce an immediate change in the character of the colony. The economic and political life of the colony continued as it had in the past. The House of Burgesses, though its future under the royal commission of 1624 was uncertain, continued to meet on an informal basis; by 1629 it was officially re-established. The crown also grudgingly acqui-

esced to the decision of the Virginia settlers to continue to direct most of their energies to the growth and exportation of tobacco. By 1630 the Virginia colony, while not prosperous, at least showed signs that it was capable of surviving without royal subsidy.

Maryland. Maryland, Virginia's neighbour to the north, was the first English colony to be controlled by a single proprietor rather than by a joint-stock company. George Calvert (Lord Baltimore) had been an investor in a number of colonizing schemes before being given a grant of land from the crown in 1632. Baltimore was given a sizable grant of power to go along with his grant of land; he had control over the trade and political system of the colony so long as he did nothing to deviate from the laws of England. Baltimore's son Cecilius Calvert took over the project at his father's death and promoted a settlement at St. Mary's on the Potomac. Supplied in part by Virginia and buoyed by their own crop of corn in the very first year, the Maryland colonists managed to prosper from the beginning.

The colony was intended to serve at least two purposes. Lord Baltimore, a Roman Catholic, was anxious to found a colony where Catholics could live in peace, but he was also eager to see his colony yield him as large a profit as possible. From the outset Protestants outnumbered Catholics, although a few prominent Catholics tended to own an inordinate share of the land in the colony. Despite this favouritism in the area of land policy, Lord Baltimore was for the most part a good and fair administrator.

Following the accession of William and Mary to the English throne, however, control of the colony was taken away from the Calvert family and entrusted to the royal government. Shortly thereafter the crown decreed that Anglicanism would be the established religion of the colony. In 1715, after the Calvert family had renounced Catholicism and embraced Anglicanism, the colony reverted back to a proprietary form of government.

The New England Colonies. Although lacking a charter, the founders of Plymouth in Massachusetts were, like their counterparts in Virginia, dependent upon private investments from profit-minded backers to finance their colony. The nucleus of that settlement was drawn from an enclave of English émigrés in Leyden, Holland. These religious "Separatists" believed that the true church was a voluntary company of the faithful under the "guidance" of a pastor and tended to be exceedingly individualistic in matters of church doctrine. Unlike the settlers of Massachusetts Bay, the Pilgrims chose to "separate" from the Church of England rather than to reform it from within.

In 1620, the first year of settlement, nearly half the settlers died of disease. From that time forward, however, and despite decreasing support from English investors, the health and the economic position of the colonists improved. The Pilgrims soon secured peace treaties with most of the Indians around them, enabling them to devote their time to building a strong, stable economic base rather than diverting their efforts toward costly and time-consuming problems of defending the colony from attack. Although none of their principal economic pursuits—farming, fishing, and trading—promised them lavish wealth, the Pilgrims in America were, after only five years, self-sufficient.

Mayflower Compact

Although the Pilgrims were always a minority in Plymouth, they nevertheless controlled the entire governmental structure of their colony during the first four decades of settlement. Before disembarking from the "Mayflower" in 1620, the Pilgrim founders, led by William Bradford, demanded that all 41 adults aboard sign a compact promising obedience to the laws and ordinances drafted by the leaders of the enterprise. Although the Mayflower Compact has been interpreted as an important step in the evolution of democratic government in America, it is a fact that the compact represented a one-sided arrangement, with the settlers promising obedience and the Pilgrim founders promising very little. Although nearly all the male inhabitants were permitted to vote for deputies to a provincial assembly and for a governor, the colony, for at least the first 40 years of its existence, remained in the tight control of a few men. After 1660 the people of Plymouth gradually gained a greater voice in both their church and civic affairs, and by 1691, when Plymouth colony was annexed to Massachusetts Bay, the Plymouth settlers had distinguished themselves by their quiet, orderly ways.

The Puritans of Massachusetts Bay, like the Pilgrims, sailed to America principally to free themselves from religious restraints. Unlike the Pilgrims, the Puritans did not desire to "separate" themselves from the Church of England but, rather, hoped by their example to reform it. Nonetheless, one of the recurring problems facing the leaders of the Massachusetts Bay Colony was to be the tendency of some, in their desire to free themselves from the alleged corruption of the Church of England, to espouse "separatist" doctrine. When these tendencies or any other hinting of deviation from orthodox Puritan doctrine developed, those holding them were either quickly corrected or expelled from the colony. The leaders of the Massachusetts Bay enterprise never intended their colony to be an outpost of toleration in the New World; rather, they intended it to be a "Zion in the wilderness," a model of purity and orthodoxy, with all backsliders subject to immediate correction.

John Winthrop and Massachusetts Bay

The civil government of the colony was guided by a similar authoritarian spirit. Men like John Winthrop, the first governor of Massachusetts Bay, believed that it was not the duty of the governors of society to act as the direct representatives of their constituents but rather to decide, independently, what measures were in the best interests of the total society. The original charter of 1629 gave all power in the colony to a General Court composed of only a small number of shareholders in the company. On arriving in Massachusetts, many disenfranchised settlers immediately protested against this provision and caused the franchise to be widened to include all church members. These "freemen" were given the right to vote in the General Court once each year for a governor and a Council of Assistants. Although the Charter of 1629 technically gave the General Court the power to decide on all matters affecting the colony, the members of the ruling elite initially refused to allow the freemen in the General Court to take part in the lawmaking process on the grounds that their numbers would render the court inefficient.

In 1634 the General Court adopted a new plan of representation whereby the freemen of each town would be permitted to select two or three delegates and assistants, elected separately but sitting together in the General Court, who would be responsible for all legislation. There was always tension existing between the smaller, more prestigious group of assistants and the larger group of deputies. In 1644, as a result of this continuing tension, the two groups were officially lodged in separate houses of the General Court, with each house reserving a veto power over the other.

Despite the authoritarian tendencies of the Massachusetts Bay Colony, a spirit of community developed there as perhaps in no other colony. The same spirit that caused the residents of Massachusetts to report on their neighbours for deviation from the true principles of Puritan morality also prompted them to be extraordinarily solicitous about their neighbours' needs. Although life in Massachusetts was made difficult for those who dissented from the prevailing orthodoxy, it was marked by a feeling of attachment and community for those who lived within the enforced consensus of the society.

Many New Englanders, however, refused to live within the orthodoxy imposed by the ruling elite of Massachusetts, and both Connecticut and Rhode Island were founded as a by-product of their discontent. The Rev. Thomas Hooker, who had arrived in Massachusetts Bay in 1633, soon found himself in opposition to the colony's restrictive policy regarding the admission of church members and to the oligarchic power of the leaders of the colony. Motivated both by a distaste for the religious and political structure of Massachusetts and by a desire to open up new land, Hooker and his followers began moving into the Connecticut Valley in 1635. By 1636 they had succeeded in founding three towns—Hartford, Windsor, and Wethersford. In 1638 the separate colony of New Haven was founded, and in 1662 Connecticut and Rhode Island merged under one charter.

Connecticut and Rhode Island

Roger Williams, the man closely associated with the founding of Rhode Island, also fled Massachusetts because of his objections to the arbitrary nature of Massachusetts government. Williams, however, was in some ways more rigid in his approach to religious polity than those Puritans he criticized. His own strict criteria for determining who was regenerate, and therefore eligible for church membership, finally led him to deny any practical way to admit anyone into the church. Once he recognized that no church could insure the purity of its congregation, he ceased using purity as a criterion for membership. Though this train of logic ultimately led him to adopt a position that subsequent generations labelled "democratic," the fact is that the principal source of Williams' policy of religious libertarianism was his very extremism in Calvinist orthodoxy.

The unpopularity of Williams' views forced him to flee Massachusetts Bay for Providence in 1636. In 1639 William Coddington, another dissenter in Massachusetts, settled his congregation in Newport. Four years later Samuel Gorton, another minister banished from Massachusetts Bay because of his differences with the ruling oligarchy, settled in Shawomet (later renamed Warwick). In 1644 these three communities joined with a fourth in Portsmouth under one charter to become one colony called Providence Plantation in Narragansett Bay. The early settlers of New Hampshire and Maine were also ruled by the government of Massachusetts Bay. New Hampshire was permanently separated from Massachusetts in 1692, although it was not until 1741 that it was given its own royal governor. Maine remained under the jurisdiction of Massachusetts until 1820.

The Middle Colonies. New Netherland, founded in 1624 on Manhattan Island by the Dutch West India Company, was but one element in a wider program of Dutch expansion in the first half of the 17th century. The English captured New Netherland in 1664; it was renamed New York, after James, duke of York, brother of Charles II, and was placed under the proprietary control of the Duke. In return for an annual gift to the King of 40 beaver skins, the Duke of York and his resident Board of Governors were given extraordinary discretion in the ruling of the colony. Although the grant to the Duke of York made mention of a representative assembly, the Duke was not legally obliged to summon it and in fact did not summon it until 1683. The Duke's interest in the colony was chiefly economic, not political, but most of his efforts to derive economic gain from New York proved futile. Indians, foreign interlopers (the Dutch actually recaptured New York in 1673 and held it for more than a year), and the success of the colonists in evading taxes made the proprietor's job a frustrating one.

In February 1685 the Duke of York found himself not only proprietor of New York but also king of England, a fact that changed the status of New York from that of a proprietary to a royal colony. The process of royal consolidation was accelerated when, in 1688, the colony was made part of the ill-fated Dominion of New England. In 1691, Jacob Leisler, a German merchant living on Long Island, led a successful revolt against the rule of the deputy governor, Francis Nicholson. The revolt, which was a product of dissatisfaction with a small aristocratic ruling elite and a more general dislike of the consolidated scheme of government of the Dominion of New England, served to hasten the demise of the dominion.

Dominion of New England

Pennsylvania, in part because of the liberal policies of its founder, William Penn, was destined to become the most diverse, dynamic, and prosperous of all the North American Colonies. Penn himself was a liberal, but by no means radical, English Whig. His Quaker faith was marked not by the religious extremism of some Quaker leaders of the day but rather by an adherence to certain dominant tenets of the faith—liberty of conscience and pacifism—and by an attachment to some of the basic tenets of Whig doctrine. William Penn sought to implement these ideals in his "holy experiment" in the New World.

Penn received his grant of land along the Delaware River in 1681 from Charles II. The "first frame of government" proposed by Penn in 1682 provided for a council and an assembly, each to be elected by the freeholders of the colony. The council was to have the sole power of initiating legislation; the lower house could only approve or veto bills submitted by the council. After numerous objections about the "oligarchic" nature of this form of government, Penn issued a second "frame of government" in 1682 and then a third in 1696, but even these did not wholly satisfy the residents of the colony. Finally, in 1701, a Charter of Privileges, giving the lower house all legislative power and transforming the council into an appointive body with advisory functions only, was approved by the citizens. The Charter of Privileges, like the other three frames of government, continued to guarantee the principle of religious toleration to all Protestants.

Pennsylvania prospered from the outset. Although there was some jealousy between the original settlers (who had received the best land and important commercial privileges) and the later arrivals, economic opportunity in Pennsylvania was on the whole greater than in any other colony. Beginning in 1683 with the immigration of Germans into the Delaware Valley and continuing with an enormous influx of Irish and Scots-Irish in the 1720s and 1730s, the population of Pennsylvania increased and diversified. The fertile soil of the countryside, in conjunction with a generous government land policy, kept immigration at high levels throughout the 18th century. William Penn's sons, John, Richard, and Thomas, although they ultimately converted back to Anglicanism, continued their father's policies of religious toleration after his death in 1718.

New Jersey

New Jersey remained in the shadow of both New York and Pennsylvania throughout most of the colonial period. Part of the territory ceded to the Duke of York by the English crown in 1664 lay in what would later become the colony of New Jersey. The Duke of York in turn granted that portion of his lands to John Berkeley and George Carteret, two close friends and allies of the King. In 1665 Berkeley and Carteret established a proprietary government under their own direction. Constant clashes, however, developed between the New Jersey and the New York proprietors over the precise nature of the New Jersey grant. The legal status of New Jersey became even more tangled when Berkeley sold his half interest in the colony to two Quakers, who in turn placed the management of the colony in the hands of three trustees, one of whom was William Penn. The area was then divided into East Jersey, controlled by Carteret, and West Jersey, controlled by Penn and the other Quaker trustees. In 1682 the Quakers bought East Jersey. A multiplicity of owners and an uncertainty of administration caused both colonists and colonizers to feel dissatisfied with the proprietary arrangement, and in 1702 the crown united the two Jerseys into a single royal province.

When the Quakers purchased East Jersey, they also acquired the tract of land that was to become Delaware, in order to protect their water route to Pennsylvania. That territory remained part of the Pennsylvania colony until 1704, when it was given an assembly of its own. It remained under the Pennsylvania governor, however, until the Revolution.

The Carolinas and Georgia. The English crown had issued grants to the Carolina territory as early as 1629, but it was not until 1663 that a group of eight proprietors—most of them men of extraordinary wealth and power even by English standards—actually began colonizing the area. The proprietors hoped to grow silk in the warm climate of the Carolinas, but all efforts to produce that valuable commodity failed. Moreover, it proved difficult to attract settlers to the Carolinas; it was not until 1718, after a series of violent Indian wars had subsided, that the population began to increase substantially. The pattern of settlement, once begun, followed two paths. North Carolina, which was largely cut off from the European and Caribbean trade by its unpromising coastline, developed into a colony of small to medium farms. South Carolina, with close ties to both the Caribbean and Europe, produced rice and, after 1742, indigo for a world market. The early settlers in both areas came primarily from the West Indian colonies. This pattern of migration was not,

however, as distinctive in North Carolina, where many of the residents were part of the spillover from the natural expansion of Virginians southward.

The original frame of government for the Carolinas, the Fundamental Constitutions, drafted in 1669 by Anthony Ashley Cooper (Lord Shaftesbury) with the help of the philosopher John Locke, was largely ineffective because of its restrictive and feudal nature. The Fundamental Constitutions was abandoned in 1693 and replaced by a frame of government diminishing the powers of the proprietors and increasing the prerogatives of the provincial assembly. In 1729, primarily because of the proprietors' inability to meet the pressing problems of defense, the Carolinas were converted into the two separate royal colonies of North and South Carolina.

The

Funda-

mental

Constitu-

tions

The proprietors of Georgia, led by James Oglethorpe, were wealthy philanthropic English gentlemen. It was Oglethorpe's plan to transport imprisoned debtors to Georgia where they could rehabilitate themselves by profitable labour and make money for the proprietors in the process. Those who actually settled in Georgia—and by no means all of them were impoverished debtors—encountered a highly restrictive economic and social system. Oglethorpe and his partners limited the size of individual landholdings to 500 acres, prohibited slavery, forbade the drinking of rum, and instituted a system of inheritance that further restricted the accumulation of large estates. The regulations, though noble in intention, created considerable tension between some of the more enterprising settlers and the proprietors. Moreover, the economy did not live up to the expectations of the colony's promoters. The silk industry in Georgia, like that in the Carolinas, failed to produce even one profitable crop.

The settlers were also dissatisfied with the political structure of the colony; the proprietors, concerned primarily with keeping close control over their utopian experiment, failed to provide for local institutions of self-government. As protests against the proprietors' policies mounted, the crown in 1753 assumed control over the colony; subsequently, many of the restrictions that the settlers had complained about, notably that prohibiting slavery, were lifted.

IMPERIAL ORGANIZATION

British policy toward the American Colonies was inevitably affected by the domestic politics of England; since the politics of England in the 17th and 18th centuries were never wholly stable, it is not surprising that British colonial policy during those years never developed along clear and consistent lines. During the first half century of colonization, it was even more difficult for England to establish an intelligent colonial policy because of the very disorganization of the Colonies themselves. It was nearly impossible for England to predict what role Virginia, Maryland, Massachusetts, Connecticut, and Rhode Island would play in the overall scheme of empire because of the diversity of the aims and governmental structures of those colonies. By 1660, however, England had taken the first steps in reorganizing her empire in a more profitable manner. The Navigation Act of 1660, a modification and amplification of a temporary series of acts passed in 1651, provided that goods bound to England or to English colonies, regardless of origin, must be shipped only in English vessels; that three-fourths of the personnel of those ships be Englishmen; and that certain "enumerated articles," such as sugar, cotton, and tobacco, be shipped only to England, with trade in those items with other nations prohibited. This last provision hit Virginia and Maryland particularly hard; although those two colonies were awarded a monopoly over the English tobacco market at the same time that they were prohibited from marketing their tobacco elsewhere, there was no way that England alone could absorb their tobacco production.

Navigation

Acts

The 1660 act proved inadequate to safeguard the entire British commercial empire and in subsequent years other navigation acts were passed strengthening the system. In 1663 Parliament passed an act requiring all vessels with European goods bound for the Colonies to pass first through English ports to pay customs duties. In 1673 Parliament, in order to prevent merchants from shipping

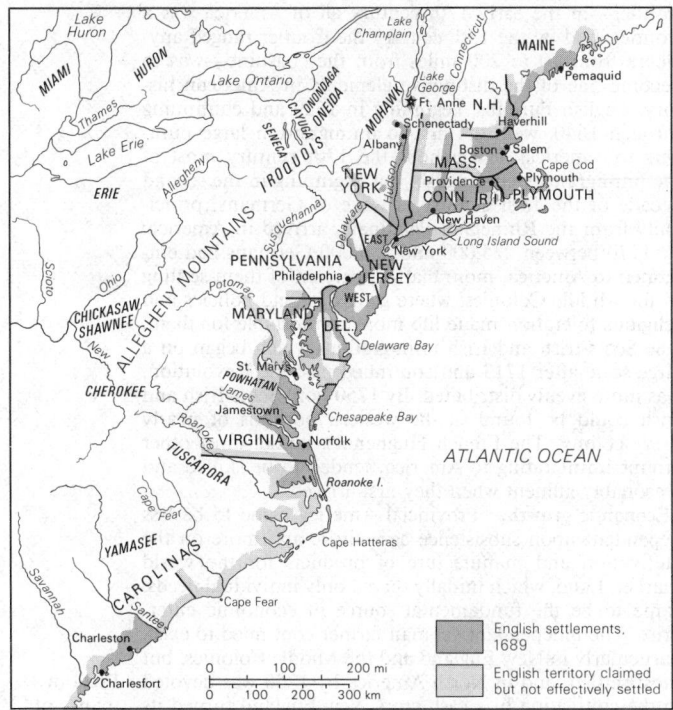

Seventeenth-century English colonies in North America.

Adapted from R. Treharne and H. Fullard (eds.), *Muir's Historical Atlas:
Medieval and Modern*, 9th ed. (1962); George Philip and Son, Ltd., London

the enumerated articles from colony to colony in the coastal trade and then taking them to a foreign country, required that merchants post bond guaranteeing that those goods be taken only to England. Finally, in 1696 Parliament established a Board of Trade to oversee Britain's commercial empire, instituted mechanisms to insure that the colonial governors aided in the enforcement of trade regulations, and set up vice admiralty courts in America for the prosecution of those who violated the Navigation Acts. The effectiveness of Britain's commercial policy is not altogether clear. It is certain that a significant amount of trade occurred in violation of that policy. The most recent investigations suggest, however, that by the end of the 17th century the Navigation Acts were being enforced successfully and that these acts did, in fact, constitute a significant economic burden for the American colonists.

In addition to the agencies of royal control in England, there were a number of royal officials in America responsible not only for aiding in the regulation of England's commercial empire but also for overseeing the internal affairs of the Colonies. The weaknesses of royal authority in the politics of provincial America were striking. In some areas, particularly in the corporate colonies of New England during the 17th century and in the proprietary colonies throughout their entire existence, direct royal authority in the person of a governor responsible to the crown was nonexistent. The absence of a royal governor in those colonies had a particularly deleterious effect on the enforcement of trade regulations. In fact, the lack of royal control over the political and commercial activities of New England prompted the Board of Trade to overturn the Massachusetts Bay Charter in 1684 and to consolidate Massachusetts, along with the other New England colonies and New York, into the Dominion of New England. After the colonists, aided by the turmoil of the Revolution of 1688 in England, succeeded in overthrowing the dominion scheme, the crown installed a royal governor in Massachusetts to protect its interests.

Powers of the royal governors

In those colonies with royal governors—the number of those colonies grew from one in 1650 to eight in 1760—the crown possessed a mechanism by which to ensure that royal policy was enforced. The Privy Council issued each royal governor in America a set of instructions carefully defining the limits of provincial authority. The royal governors were to have the power to decide when to call the provincial assemblies together, to prorogue, or dissolve,

the assemblies, and to veto any legislation passed by those assemblies. The governor's power over other aspects of the political structure of the colony was just as great. In most royal colonies he was the one official primarily responsible for the composition of the upper houses of the colonial legislatures and for the appointment of important provincial officials, such as the treasurer, attorney general, and all colonial judges. Moreover, the governor had enormous patronage powers over the local agencies of government. The officials of the county court, who were the principal agents of local government, were appointed by the governor in most of the royal colonies. Thus, the governor had direct or indirect control over every agency of government in America.

THE GROWTH OF PROVINCIAL POWER

Political growth. The distance separating England and America, the powerful pressures exerted on royal officials by Americans, and the inevitable inefficiency of any large bureaucracy all served to weaken royal power and to strengthen the hold of provincial leaders on the affairs of their respective colonies. During the 18th century, the colonial legislatures gained control over their own parliamentary prerogatives, achieved primary responsibility for legislation affecting taxation and defense, and ultimately took control over the salaries paid to royal officials. Provincial leaders also made significant inroads into the governor's patronage powers. Although theoretically the governor continued to control the appointments of local officials, in reality he most often automatically followed the recommendations of the provincial leaders in the localities in question. Similarly, the Governor's Councils, theoretically agents of royal authority, came to be dominated by prominent provincial leaders who tended to reflect the interests of the leadership of the lower house of assembly rather than those of the royal government in London.

Thus, by the mid-18th century most political power in America was concentrated in the hands of provincial rather than royal officials. These provincial leaders undoubtedly represented the interests of their constituents more faithfully than any royal official, but it is clear that the politics of provincial America were hardly democratic by modern standards. In general, both social prestige and political power tended to be determined by economic standing; and the economic resources of colonial America, though not as unevenly distributed as in Europe, were nevertheless controlled by relatively few men.

In the Chesapeake societies of Virginia and Maryland, and particularly in the regions east of the Blue Ridge Mountains, a planter class came to dominate nearly every aspect of those colonies' economic life. These same planters, joined by a few prominent merchants and lawyers, dominated the two most important agencies of local government—the county courts and the provincial assemblies. This extraordinary concentration of power in the hands of a wealthy few occurred in spite of the fact that a large percentage of the free adult male population (some have estimated as high as 80 to 90 percent) was able to participate in the political process. The ordinary citizens of the Chesapeake society, and those of most colonies, nevertheless continued to defer to those whom they considered to be their "betters." Although the societal ethic that enabled power to be concentrated in the hands of a few was hardly a democratic one, there is little evidence, at least for Virginia and Maryland, that the people of those societies were dissatisfied with their rulers. For the most part they believed that their local officials ruled responsively.

In the Carolinas a small group of rice and indigo planters monopolized much of the wealth. As in Virginia and Maryland, the planter class came to constitute a social elite. As a rule the planter class of the Carolinas did not have the same long tradition of responsible government as did the ruling oligarchies of Virginia and Maryland, and, as a consequence, they tended to be absentee landlords and governors, often passing much of their time in Charleston, away from their plantations and their political responsibilities.

The western regions

The western regions of both the Chesapeake and Carolina societies displayed distinctive characteristics of their own. Ruling traditions were fewer, accumulations of land and wealth less striking, and the social hierarchy less rigid in the west. In fact, in some western areas antagonism toward the restrictiveness of the east and toward eastern control of the political structure led to actual conflict. In both North and South Carolina armed risings of varying intensity erupted against the unresponsive nature of the eastern ruling elite. As the 18th century progressed, however, and as men accumulated more wealth and social prestige, the societies of the west came more closely to resemble those of the east.

New England society was more diverse and the political system less oligarchic than that of the South. In New England the mechanisms of town government served to broaden popular participation in government beyond the narrow base of the county courts.

New England town meetings

The town meetings, which elected the members of the provincial assemblies, were open to nearly all free adult males. Despite this, a relatively small group of men dominated the provincial governments of New England. As in the South, men of high occupational status and social prestige were closely concentrated in leadership positions in their respective colonies; in New England, merchants, lawyers, and to a lesser extent clergymen made up the bulk of the social and political elite.

The social and political structure of the Middle Colonies was more diverse than any region in America. New York, with its extensive system of manors and manor lords, often displayed genuinely feudal characteristics. The tenants on large manors often found it impossible to escape the influence of their manor lords. The administration of justice, the election of representatives, and the collection of taxes often took place on the manor itself. As a consequence, the large land-owning families exercised an inordinate amount of economic and political power. The "Great Rebellion of 1766," a short-lived outburst directed against the manor lords, was a symptom of the widespread discontent among the lower and middle classes. By contrast, Pennsylvania's governmental system was more open and responsive than that of any other colony in America. A unicameral legislature, free from the restraints imposed by a powerful governor's council, allowed Pennsylvania to be relatively independent of the influence of both the crown and the proprietor. This fact, in combination with the tolerant and relatively egalitarian bent of the early Quaker settlers and the subsequent immigration of large numbers of Europeans, made the social and political structure of Pennsylvania more democratic but more faction ridden than that of any other colony.

The "Great Rebellion of 1766"

Population growth. The increasing political autonomy of the American Colonies was a natural reflection of their increased stature in the overall scheme of the British Empire. In 1650 the population of the Colonies had been about 52,000; in 1700 it was perhaps 250,000, and by 1760 it was approaching 1,700,000. Virginia had increased from about 54,000 in 1700 to approximately 340,000 in 1760. Pennsylvania had begun with about 500 settlers in 1681 and had attracted at least 250,000 people by 1760. And America's cities were beginning to grow as well. By 1765 Boston had reached 15,000; New York City, 16,000–17,000; and Philadelphia, the largest city in the Colonies, 20,000.

Part of that population growth was the result of the involuntary immigration of African slaves. During the 17th century, slaves remained a tiny minority of the population. By the mid-18th century, after Southern colonists discovered that the profits generated by their plantations could support the relatively large initial investments needed for slave labour, the volume of the slave trade increased markedly. In Virginia the slave population leaped from about 2,000 in 1670 to perhaps 23,000 in 1715 and reached 150,000 on the eve of the Revolution. In South Carolina it was even more dramatic. In 1700 there were probably no more than 2,500 blacks in the population; by 1765 there were 80,000–90,000, with blacks outnumbering whites by about two to one.

African slaves

One of the principal attractions to the immigrants who moved to America voluntarily was the availability of inexpensive arable land. The westward migration to America's frontier—in the early 17th century all of America was a frontier, and by the 18th century the frontier ranged anywhere from 10 to 200 miles from the coastline—was to become one of the distinctive elements in American history. English Puritans, beginning in 1629 and continuing through 1640, were the first to immigrate in large numbers to America. Throughout the 17th century most of the immigrants were English; but beginning in the second decade of the 18th century, a wave of Germans, principally from the Rhineland Palatinate, arrived in America: by 1770 between 225,000 and 250,000 Germans had emigrated to America, more than 70 percent of them settling in the Middle Colonies, where generous land policies and religious toleration made life more comfortable for them. The Scots-Irish and Irish immigration, which began on a large scale after 1713 and continued past the Revolution, was more evenly distributed. By 1750 both Scots-Irish and Irish could be found in the western portions of nearly every colony. The French Huguenots, unlike most other groups immigrating to America, tended to be skilled and reasonably affluent when they first arrived.

Economic growth. Provincial America came to be less dependent upon subsistence agriculture and more on the cultivation and manufacture of products for the world market. Land, which initially served only individual needs, came to be the fundamental source of economic enterprise. The independent yeoman farmer continued to exist, particularly in New England and the Middle Colonies, but most settled land in North America by 1750 was devoted to the cultivation of a cash crop. New England turned its land over to the raising of meat products for export. The Middle Colonies were the principal producers of grains. By 1700 Philadelphia exported more than 350,000 bushels of wheat and more than 18,000 tons of flour annually. The Southern Colonies were, of course, even more closely tied to the cash crop system. South Carolina, aided by British incentives, turned to the production of rice and indigo. North Carolina, although less oriented toward the market economy than South Carolina, was nevertheless one of the principal suppliers of naval stores. Virginia and Maryland steadily increased their economic dependence on tobacco and on the London merchants who purchased that tobacco; and for the most part they ignored those who recommended that they diversify their economies by turning part of their land over to the cultivation of wheat. Their near-total dependence upon the world tobacco price would ultimately prove disastrous, but for most of the 18th century Virginia and Maryland soil remained productive enough to make a single-crop system reasonably profitable.

Predominance of cash crops

As America evolved from subsistence to commercial agriculture, an influential commercial class increased its power in nearly every colony. Boston was the centre of the merchant elite of New England, who not only dominated economic life but also wielded social and political power as well. Merchants like James De Lancey and Philip Livingston in New York and Joseph Galloway, Robert Morris, and Thomas Wharton in Philadelphia exerted an influence far beyond the confines of their occupations. In Charleston the Pinckney, Rutledge, and Lowndes families controlled much of the trade that passed through that port. Even in Virginia, where a strong merchant class was nonexistent, those people with the most economic and political power were those commercial farmers who best combined the occupations of merchant and farmer. And it is clear that the commercial importance of the Colonies was increasing. During the years 1700–10, approximately £265,000 sterling was exported annually to Great Britain from the Colonies, with roughly the same amount being imported by the Americans from Great Britain. By the decade 1760–70, that figure had risen to more than £1,000,000 sterling of goods exported annually to Great Britain and £1,760,000 annually imported from Great Britain.

CULTURAL AND RELIGIOUS DEVELOPMENT

Colonial culture. America's intellectual attainments during the 17th and 18th centuries, while not inferior to those of the nations of Europe, were nevertheless of a decidedly different character. It was the techniques of applied science that most excited the minds of Americans, who, faced with the problem of subduing an often wild and unruly land, saw in science the best way to explain, and eventually to harness, those forces around them. Ultimately this scientific mode of thought might be applied to the problems of civil society as well, but for the most part the emphasis in colonial America remained on science and technology, not politics or metaphysics. Typical of America's peculiar scientific genius was John Bartram of Pennsylvania, who collected and classified important botanical data from the New World. The American Philosophical Society, founded in 1744, is justly remembered as the focus of intellectual life in America. Men like David Rittenhouse, an astronomer who built the first planetarium in America; Cadwallader Colden, the lieutenant governor of New York, whose accomplishments as a botanist and as an anthropologist probably outmatched his achievements as a politician; and Benjamin Rush, a pioneer in numerous areas of social reform as well as one of colonial America's foremost physicians, were among the many active members of the Society. At the centre of the American Philosophical Society was one of its founders, Benjamin Franklin, who (in his experiments concerning the flow of electricity) proved to be one of the few American scientists to achieve a major theoretical breakthrough but who was more adept at the kinds of applied research that resulted in the manufacture of more efficient fireplaces and the development of the lightning rod.

American cultural achievements in nonscientific fields were less impressive. American literature, at least in the traditional European forms, was nearly nonexistent. The most important American contribution to literature was neither in fiction nor in metaphysics but rather in such histories as Robert Beverley's *History and Present State of Virginia* (1705) or William Byrd's *History of the Dividing Line* (1728–29, but not published until 1841). The most important cultural medium in America was not the book but the newspaper. The high cost of printing tended to eliminate all but the most vital news, and thus local gossip or extended speculative efforts were sacrificed so that more important material such as classified advertisements and reports of crop prices could be included. Next to newspapers, almanacs were the most popular literary form in America, Franklin's *Poor Richard's* being only the most famous among scores of similar projects. Not until 1741 and the first installment of Franklin's *General Magazine* did literary magazines begin to make their first appearance in America. Most of the 18th-century magazines, however, failed to attract subscribers, and nearly all of them collapsed after only a few years of operation.

Art and drama, though flourishing somewhat more than literature, were nevertheless slow to achieve real distinction in America. America did produce one good historical painter in Benjamin West and two excellent portrait painters in John Copley and Gilbert Stuart; but it is not without significance that all three men passed much of their lives in London, where they received more attention and higher fees.

The Southern Colonies, particularly Charleston, seemed to be more interested in providing good theatre for their residents than did other regions, but in no colony did the theatre approach the excellence of that of Europe. In New England, Puritan influence was a roadblock to the performance of plays, and even in cosmopolitan Philadelphia the Quakers for a long time discouraged the development of the dramatic arts.

If Americans in the colonial period did not excel in achieving a high level of traditional cultural attainment, they did manage at least to disseminate what culture they had in a manner slightly more equitable than that of most nations of the world. Newspapers and almanacs, though hardly on the same intellectual level as the Encyclopédie produced by the European Philosophes, probably had a wider audience than any European cultural medium. The New England Colonies, although they did not always manage to keep pace with population growth, pioneered in the field of public education. Outside of New England, education remained the preserve of those who could afford to send their children to private schools. The existence of privately supported but tuition-free charity schools and of some of the more inexpensive "academies" made it possible for the children of the American middle class to receive at least some education. The principal institutions of higher learning—Harvard (1636), William and Mary (1693), Yale (1701), Princeton (1747), Pennsylvania (a college since 1755), King's College (1754, now Columbia), Rhode Island College (1764, now Brown), Queen's College (1766, now Rutgers), and Dartmouth (1769)—served the upper class almost exclusively.

The "Great Awakening." A series of religious revivals known collectively as the "Great Awakening" swept over the Colonies in the 1730s and the 1740s. Its impact was first felt in the Middle Colonies, where Theodore J. Frelinghuysen, a minister of the Dutch Reformed Church, began preaching in the 1720s. In New England, in the early 1730s, men such as Jonathan Edwards, perhaps the most learned theologian of the 18th century, were responsible for a reawakening of religious fervour. By the late 1740s the movement had extended into the Southern Colonies, where itinerant preachers such as Samuel Davies and George Whitefield exerted considerable influence, particularly in the backcountry.

The Great Awakening represented a reaction against the increasing secularization of society and against the corporate and materialistic nature of the principal churches of American society. By making conversion the initial step on the road to salvation and by opening up the conversion experience to all who recognized their own sinfulness, the ministers of the Great Awakening, some intentionally and others unwittingly, democratized Calvinist theology. The technique of many of the preachers of the Great Awakening was to inspire in their listeners a fear of the consequences of their sinful lives and a respect for the omnipotence of God. This sense of the ferocity of God was often tempered by the implied promise that a rejection of worldliness and a return to faith would result in a return to grace and an avoidance of the horrible punishments of an angry God. There was a certain contradictory quality about these two strains of Great Awakening theology, however. Predestination, one of the principal tenets of the Calvinist theology of most of the ministers of the Great Awakening, was ultimately incompatible with the promise that man could, by a voluntary act of faith, achieve salvation by his own efforts. Furthermore, the call for a return to complete faith and the emphasis on the omnipotence of God was the very antithesis of Enlightenment thought, which called for a greater questioning of faith and a diminishing role for God in the daily affairs of man. On the other hand, Jonathan Edwards, one of the principal figures of the Great Awakening in America, explicitly drew on the thought of men like John Locke and Isaac Newton in an attempt to make religion rational. Moreover, in attacking the leadership of the prevailing religious sects of the time, the ministers of the Great Awakening fostered a questioning of many forms of institutional authority and helped break up the oligarchic control of a few wealthy, traditionalist-minded men on organized religion in America.

AMERICA, ENGLAND, AND THE WIDER WORLD

The American Colonies, though in many ways isolated from the nations of Europe, were nevertheless continually subject to diplomatic and military pressures from abroad. In particular, Spain and France were always nearby, waiting to exploit any signs of English weakness in America to increase their commercial and territorial designs on the North American mainland. The Great War for the Empire, or the French and Indian War as the Americans called it (see EUROPE), was but another round in a century of warfare between the major European powers. First in King William's War (1689–97), then in Queen Anne's War (1702–13), and in King George's War (1744–48; the American phase of the War of the Austrian Succession), Englishmen and Frenchmen had vied for control over the Indians, for possession of the territory lying to the north of the North American Colonies, for access to the trade

(Margin labels: American Philosophical Society; Art and drama; Public education)

in the Northwest, and for commercial superiority in the West Indies. In most of these encounters France had been aided by her ally, Spain. Because of its own holdings immediately south and west of the British colonies and in the Caribbean, Spain realized that it was in its own interest to join with the French in limiting British expansion. The culmination of these struggles came in 1754 with the Great War for the Empire. Whereas previous contests between Great Britain and France in America had been mostly provincial affairs, with American colonists doing most of the fighting for the British, the Great War for the Empire saw sizable commitments of English troops to America. The strategy of the English under William Pitt was to allow their ally, Prussia, to carry the brunt of the fighting in Europe, thus freeing the English to concentrate their troops in America.

The French, despite the fact that they were outnumbered 15 to one by the English colonial population in America, were nevertheless well-equipped to hold their own against the British. They had a larger military organization in America than did the English, their troops were better trained, and they were more successful than the British in forming military alliances with the Indians. The early engagements of the war went to the French; the surrender of George Washington to a superior French force at Ft. Necessity, the annihilation of Gen. Edward Braddock at the Monongahela River, and French victories at Oswego and Ft. William Henry all made it seem as if the war would be a short and unsuccessful one for the British. Even as these defeats took place, however, the English were able to increase their supplies of both men and material in America. By 1758, with its strength finally up to a satisfactory level, England began to implement its larger strategy, which involved sending a combined land and sea force to gain control of the St. Lawrence and a large land force aimed at Ft. Ticonderoga to eliminate French control of Lake Champlain. The first expedition against the French at Ticonderoga was a disaster, as Gen. James Abercrombie led about 15,000 British and colonial troops in an attack against the French before his forces were adequately prepared. The English assault on Louisburg, the key to the St. Lawrence, was more successful. In July 1758 Lord Jeffrey Amherst led a naval attack in which his troops landed on the shores from small boats, established beachheads, and then captured the fort at Louisburg.

The capture of Quebec In 1759, after several months of sporadic fighting, the forces of James Wolfe captured Quebec from the French army led by the Marquis de Montcalm. This was probably the turning point of the war. By the fall of 1760 the British had taken Montreal, and England possessed practical control of all of the North American continent. It took another two years for England to defeat her rivals in other parts of the world, but the contest for control of North America had been settled.

In the Treaty of Paris of 1763, England took possession of all of Canada, East and West Florida, all territory east of the Mississippi in North America, and St. Vincent, Tobago, and Dominica in the Caribbean. The British victory had not come cheaply, however. British government expenditures, which had amounted to nearly £6,500,000 annually before the war, rose to about £14,500,000 annually during the war. The cost of winning the war, and of maintaining the spoils of war, would be very high indeed—so high, in fact, that most Englishmen thought that the American Colonies should help pay the costs. The American colonists in 1763, freed for the first time in the 18th century from the threat posed by the French and the Indians, were more reluctant than ever before to be taxed to pay for a burdensome military establishment. The British, at least in part to pay the costs of the Great War for the Empire, would institute a program reorganizing the structure of the empire and imposing taxes on the Colonies to pay for that reorganization. The American Colonies, now economically powerful, culturally distinct, and steadily becoming more independent politically, would ultimately rebel before submitting to the English plan of empire.

(R.R.B.)

The American Revolution

PRELUDE TO REVOLUTION

Effects of the French and Indian War. Although the immediate results of the war had been to secure and greatly expand Britain's empire in North America, the longer range results were to achieve just the opposite; for in winning the war, Britain had dissolved the empire's most potent material adhesives. What had held the empire together were common interests and common enemies, along with a common reverence for the "rights of Englishmen" and for an imperial constitution that all parties had scrupulously avoided defining. Subjects in the parent country and in the Colonies alike had profited from the maintenance of a vast enclosed common market; and, when colonials had wanted or needed to trade outside the empire, lax law enforcement usually made illicit trade possible. Similarly, the presence of Spanish and French colonies to the south, west, and north of the British colonies had produced interdependence of military and political interests between England and America. Removal of the French after 1760 destroyed Anglo-American strategic interdependence and (though this was slower to become visible) thoroughly disrupted the community of economic interests. Assorted conflicts between Britain and the various colonies began to arise; and, as they arose, spokesmen for all sides arose also, demanding their "rights" and defining the imperial constitution as they understood it. For 13 years definition followed conflict and conflict followed definition until the only thing remaining clear was that the empire could no longer be held together in peace.

Even before the end of the war, two ominous developments had indicated that Americans and Englishmen were not of one mind in their understanding of the constitution. These were the celebrated Writs of Assistance case in Massachusetts (1761), protesting general search warrants, and the case of the Parson's Cause in Virginia (1763), in which James Otis and Patrick Henry successfully challenged, on "constitutional" grounds, the authority of both Parliament and royal officials. Otis argued in terms of John Locke's concept of a higher law, and Henry in terms of Viscount Bolingbroke's concept of the king as father to his subjects; but the significance of their arguments was that they won the support of the local populace and jury and were worlds away from attitudes current in London. *Constitutional differences with Britain*

But the warning implicit in these cases was lost in the wave of euphoria and myopia that swept Britain and the Colonies at the war's end. Military victory and the Peace of Paris seemed an unmixed blessing; indeed, a large part of what went wrong in the 1760s was that everyone behaved as if only his own circumstances and opportunities had been altered and failed to perceive that anything fundamental had gone wrong or even changed.

Officers of the government in London, to the extent that they concerned themselves with America at all, were interested primarily from a military point of view. They proposed to make various minor reforms in the administration of the old empire, to require the colonials to bear a share of the cost of running the expanded territory that was acquired for their own protection, to ignore as much as possible the civil administration of the former French colonies, and to devote careful attention only to the changed military situation in America.

The most important part of the latter involved relations with the Indians, who had long been taught by the French to fear and despise the English. Prudently, in the Proclamation of 1763, London ordered that Anglo-Americans remain east of the crest of the Appalachians and allowed dealings with the Indians for land or goods only through London-appointed commissioners. Rather less prudently, the British refused to pacify the Indians with either an overwhelming show of force or a systematic program of bribes, both of which the French had long found necessary to comfortable and profitable relations with the red men. The immediate consequence was that in 1763 the Indians, under the Ottawa chief Pontiac, rose in a series of "guerrilla" attacks. The professional British military men were helpless until Col. Henry Bouquet—borrowing a technique that Anglo-Americans had earlier discovered—learned to *Proclamation of 1763* wipe out the home bases of the Indians by burning their villages and fields and killing their women and children. By 1765 the Indians were willing to acknowledge defeat, and most British officials expected relations between England and America to reach a state of harmony.

Local grievances. Local activities, however, sometimes in interplay with actions in London, produced turbulence instead. In the Middle Colonies—Pennsylvania, New York, New Jersey, and Delaware—there was general economic prosperity but also social and political friction and disagreement with the mother country. Production of wheat and flour boomed, bringing good times for farmers and merchants; and the output of the area's second major product, ironware, expanded steadily. But the arrival of hordes of immigrants—especially New Englanders, Ulstermen, and Highland Scots—created social tensions in each of the Middle Colonies. Each, moreover, was rent by the efforts of land speculators to gain political power so as to profit from the immigration.

Aristo-
cratic
factions
in New
York

In New York this took the form of rivalry between aristocratic family connections, the De Lanceys and the Livingstons, and was purely local until a new issue intruded: Parliament's Sugar Act of 1764, imposing taxes and new commercial regulations, squeezed New York's West Indies merchants and their artisan adjuncts; the De Lanceys gained popular support and power by assuming a stance as defenders of American liberties against parliamentary encroachments. (Their most important defiance of Parliament was their refusal to obey the Quartering Act, requiring colonies to support the imperial soldiers stationed in America.) In Pennsylvania a clique headed by Joseph Galloway and Benjamin Franklin made a popular issue out of efforts to secure revocation of the Penn family's proprietary charter, secretly expecting that under a royal charter they could gain for themselves the vast tracts of land they sought; their opponents, led by John Dickinson, opposed a royal charter and, by logical extension, assumed a stance comparable to that of the De Lanceys in New York.

In the lower South—the Carolinas and Georgia—the situation was somewhat similar to that in the Middle Colonies. The economy, based on the production of rice, indigo, and naval stores, was booming; but the social order was strained. Indians were strong and hostile in South Carolina and Georgia, and in the backcountry of both Carolinas the frontiersmen, mainly Scots-Irish immigrants, were demanding overhaul of local government. In the middle and late 1760s, when so-called frontier Regulators rose in armed defiance of the authority of the low-country aristocrats, they sought imperial intervention; the aristocrats for that and other reasons opposed the extension of imperial authority.

In the upper South, in the tobacco colonies of Virginia and Maryland, everything was awry. Tobacco prices were erratically downward and crop failures were common. One faction of tidewater planters, led by the speaker of the House of Burgesses, remained afloat through fraudulent manipulations of paper currency, in violation of Parliament's Currency Act of 1764, requiring the extinction of such currency. Another pair of factions, one southwestern and the other Potomac-based, hoped to survive by land speculation that could succeed only through circumvention of the Proclamation of 1763.

Finally, there was New England, socially more or less calm and politically harmonious, except in Massachusetts, but economically depressed and afoul of the mother country and the other colonies in various ways. With rare exceptions, the complex New England economy failed to perform well after 1763. The Yankees blamed their troubles variously on the Sugar Act and other tightened commercial regulations, the Currency Act, the Proclamation of 1763, and malice in London. Meanwhile, settlers from overcrowded Connecticut, backed by the colony's government, invaded Pennsylvania; and, less officially but more numerously, colonials from Massachusetts invaded upper New York.

The Stamp Act and Townshend Duties. In sum, by the mid-1760s the colonists were sharply divided against one another, and objection to several parliamentary acts was strong though diffuse. Then, in 1765, Parliament passed the Stamp Act, designed to produce colonial revenues and thus reduce the heavy tax burden in England—which many Englishmen thought stemmed from the cost of maintaining the enlarged colonial establishment. In several American ports (notably Boston, where Samuel Adams formed and led a widely copied organization called the Sons of Liberty), opposition to collecting the Stamp Tax was violent; in Virginia legislative opposition (under Patrick Henry) was based on a radical constitutional position; and in many places colonists refused to import any British goods until the tax should be repealed. For the most part, however, the resistance, though firm, was more moderate. In October 1765, nine colonies sent delegates to New York for an extralegal congress that protested the Stamp Act mainly on the ground that it violated the ancient principle that taxes were a voluntary gift from the people to the sovereign.

The
Stamp Act
Congress

Much misunderstanding ensued. Parliament repealed the act, largely at the behest of London merchants suffering from the American boycott, but it saved face by pretending to bow to a distinction between acceptable "external" taxes and unacceptable "internal" taxes—a distinction suggested by Franklin, then pursuing his land schemes in London, but actually held by virtually no colonists. Colonial spokesmen cheered the repeal and failed, almost unanimously, to notice the Declaratory Act—passed along with the Stamp Act's repeal—asserting Parliament's right to legislate for the Colonies "in all cases whatsoever." Fifteen months later (June 1767) Parliament passed the Townshend Duties (Acts), imposing external taxes on lead, glass, paint, paper, and tea imported into America. Disregarding Franklin's misleading distinctions, John Dickinson penned a series of articles (*Letters from a farmer in Pennsylvania*) that galvanized a new colonial resistance. Dickinson's position was quickly adopted as the majority position in America; Parliament could tax the Colonies, but only incidentally to the power to regulate trade and other relations within the empire—and not at all for purposes of revenue.

Though all the Townshend Duties except that on tea were shortly repealed, partly in response to a new colonial non-importation policy and partly in response to political pressures inside England, three positions besides Dickinson's soon became manifest. Britain's position, apart from what was based on practical political considerations, was one of bewilderment; for, since the Glorious Revolution of 1688, chasing James II from the throne, the only limitation on the power of Parliament, as most Englishmen understood things, was Parliament's own self-restraint. Rather to the right of this position was that held by the Virginia Burgesses, who professed allegiance only to the crown, felt not even that, and regarded Parliament as being at best co-equal with the assembly of Virginia. Far to the left were the Yankees, especially those of Massachusetts, who regarded themselves as the heirs of 17th-century Puritanism, beyond the reach of crown and the corrupt 18th-century Parliament.

Repeal of
Town-
shend
Duties

After the repeal of the Townshend Duties, however, everything cooled for awhile. A tide of credit-based prosperity, engendered by fraudulent banking activities in Scotland, swept the empire. Swollen revenues lulled royal government officials, and in New England and Virginia the more dissident elements succumbed to the lure of unexpected credit and prosperity. In Pennsylvania and in the lower South, the sudden and unexpected boom was enough to create the illusion that internal strains (from frontiersmen and Indians) were not so potent as had been imagined. In New York the De Lanceyites, given special exemption from the Currency Act and favourable treatment with regard to Indian land titles, abandoned all opposition to Parliament. In Massachusetts, Sam Adams found himself a radical leader virtually without a following.

The Tea Act and "Intolerable Acts." But late in 1772 the bubble burst. The effects of the collapse were slow to be felt, but in the spring of 1773 the most volatile groups in the Colonies felt them severely: radicals in Boston suddenly found themselves supported by the normally conservative farmers of the interior of Massachusetts, who had gotten themselves deeply into debt during the credit boom; the tobacco planters of Virginia, long trembling on the brink of insolvency, suddenly found themselves deeper in debt than farmers in New England could possibly imagine. Operators in Parliament, lately encouraged by speculative profits to ignore colonial problems, suddenly found themselves with a colonial problem in an unexpected area. The East India Company, the grandest speculation of them all, was tottering on the verge of bankruptcy. To save the company, Parliament passed (May 10, 1773) a complicated act giving it various new privileges, including a refund of import duties already paid on tea stored in London if it were reshipped to America. Consequently, high-quality English-India tea could, despite the Townshend Duties, be sold in America cheaper than inferior Dutch tea, which Americans habitually consumed because of its lower price.

The Tea Act reunited dissident elements in America. Merchants in New York, Philadelphia, and the New England outports, long accustomed to profits from illicit tea trade and now doubly squeezed by the financial collapse, financed and supported a new resistance. Propagandists, both opportunistic and idealistic, denounced the act as a dangerous "innovation" by Parliament and as an insidious plot to subvert American liberties by bribery—that is, by inducing Americans to buy taxed tea because it was cheaper. Radicals in Boston and Charleston capitalized on the furore, the former (in the Boston Tea Party) destroying and the latter confiscating cargoes of tea; tea consignments were turned back elsewhere. Virginia land speculators and planters sought any advantage they could find in the confusion.

The Boston Tea Party

Parliament, succumbing to an almost paranoid fear that the Americans were plotting independence, responded by cracking down on what most Englishmen regarded as the main source of trouble. In a series of acts passed in 1774, Parliament imposed a strangulating set of commercial restrictions on the port of Boston. Coincidentally, Parliament also passed an act, long in the making, providing for the government of the recently acquired French province of Quebec. The act provided, among other things, for retaining French law and the Roman Catholic establishment in the province and extended the province's jurisdiction to the trans-Appalachian area north of the Ohio River—thereby convincing New Englanders that the whole affair was a Catholic conspiracy aimed against Yankee Puritans along with the Boston Port Act and incidentally cutting Virginians off from the possibility of profitable land dealings in the Ohio country. Thus New England Yankees and Virginia plantation aristocrats, distrustful of one another since the Roundhead–Cavalier struggles of the English Civil War more than a century earlier, were thrust into the same radical camp in 1774.

General American response to the "Intolerable Acts"—as the restrictive parliamentary legislation was promptly dubbed in America—resulted in the calling of a Continental Congress in October. Despite the radicalism of the Yankees and Virginians, the dominant voice in the Congress was that of John Dickinson, a thoroughgoing conservative in the sense later identified with Edmund Burke. Dickinson, steeped in British history and law but oblivious to constitutional developments since 1689, insisted that recent acts of Parliament were innovations that, if persisted in, could destroy the excellent British constitution and insisted also that colonial resistance was justified by history and tradition. He was supported by most delegates from the Middle Colonies and the lower South, where, despite inner tensions, imperial regulation had been advantageous, at least to the dominant groups.

The move toward independence. Radical voices were distinctly in the minority, and that fact did not change much though violence was soon forthcoming. In April of 1775 British troops clashed with colonial militiamen in Lexington and Concord, Massachusetts, and at the suggestion of Congress the several colonial militias prepared themselves for more conflict. Brilliant young propagandists—notably Thomas Jefferson, John Adams, James Wilson, and Alexander Hamilton—penned persuasive tracts that essentially denied all power of Parliament over the Colonies, placed the burden of conflict upon the crown, and came perilously close to advocating independence; but still, despite everything, anger on neither side was sufficient to cause many to contemplate seriously the dismemberment of the empire. Then in December Thomas Paine wrote "Common Sense," a masterpiece of sledgehammer logic couched in the near-poetry of the King James Bible, dissolving every claim that had been advanced for loyalty to kings.

Thomas Paine's "Common Sense"

Early in 1776 resistance hardened into war, and advocates of independence grew in numbers. Until the very end, however, congressional delegates and popular majorities in the Middle Colonies and the lower South opposed independence, for the empire had been good to them and revolution could unleash a host of troubles from Indians, slaves, and frontiersmen. New England and Virginia, less blessed by the fruits of empire and socially far more stable—and also, unlike the other colonies, having matured in the 17th century, when rebellion and even regicide were common—were willing to take the risk. On July 2, 1776, Congress voted for independence. Two days later it published the Declaration of Independence, written by Jefferson and addressed "to the opinions of mankind."

(F.McD.)

WAR OF INDEPENDENCE

Until early in 1778 the War of Independence, also known as the American Revolution, was a civil war within the British Empire; afterward it became an international war as France in 1778, Spain in 1779, and the Netherlands in 1780 joined the colonies against Britain. From the beginning sea power was vital in determining the course of the war, lending to British strategy a flexibility that helped compensate for the comparatively small numbers of troops sent to America and ultimately enabling the French to help bring about the final British surrender at Yorktown.

Land campaigns. Americans fought the war on land essentially with two types of organization, the Continental (national) Army and the state militias. The total number of the former provided by quotas from the states throughout the conflict was 231,771 men; the militia totalled 164,087. At any given time, however, the American forces seldom numbered over 20,000; in 1781 there were only about 29,000 insurgents under arms throughout the country. The war was therefore one of small field armies. Militia, poorly disciplined and with elected officers, were summoned for periods usually not exceeding three months. The terms of Continental Army service were only gradually increased from one to three years, and not even bounties and the offer of land kept the army up to strength. Reasons for the difficulty in maintaining an adequate Continental force included the colonists' traditional antipathy to regular armies, the objections of farmers to being away from their fields, the competition of the states with Congress to keep men in the militia, and the wretched and uncertain pay in a period of inflation.

By contrast, the British Army was a reliable, steady force of professionals. Since it numbered only about 42,000, heavy recruiting programs were introduced. Many of the enlisted men were farm boys, like most of the Americans. Others were unemployed persons from the urban slums. Still others joined the army to escape fines or imprisonment. The great majority became efficient soldiers owing to sound training and ferocious discipline. The officers, who were fairly competent, were drawn largely from the gentry and the aristocracy and obtained their commissions and promotions by purchase. Though they received no formal training, they were not so dependent on a book knowledge of military tactics as were many of the Americans. British generals, however, tended toward a lack of imagination and initiative, while those who demonstrated such qualities often were rash.

Because troops were still few and conscription unknown, the British government, following a traditional policy, purchased about 30,000 troops from various German princes. Approximately three-fifths of this total were furnished by the Landgrave of Hesse. Few acts by the crown roused so much antagonism in America as this use of foreign mercenaries.

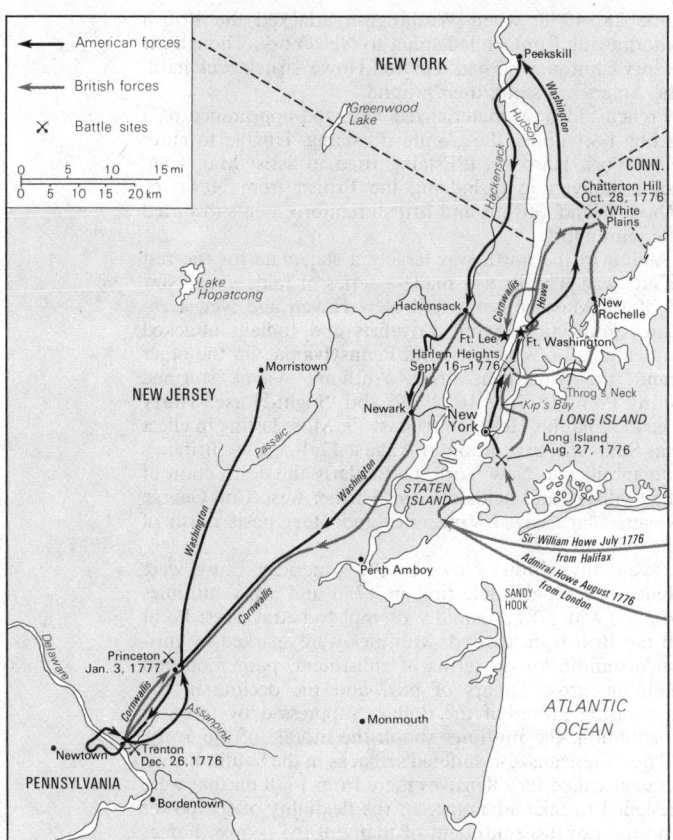

New York–New Jersey Campaign of 1776–77.

Adapted from *The American Heritage Pictorial Atlas of United States History*;
copyright © 1966 by American Heritage Publishing Co., Inc.

Opening engagements

The war began in Massachusetts when Gen. Thomas Gage sent a force from Boston to destroy rebel military stores at Concord. Fighting occurred at Lexington and Concord on April 19, 1775, and only the arrival of reinforcements saved the British original column. Rebel militia then converged on Boston from all over New England, besieging the British-held city. Their entrenching on Breed's Hill led to a British frontal assault on June 17 under Gen. William Howe, who won the hill but at the cost of more than 40 percent of the assault force.

Gen. George Washington was appointed commander in chief of the American forces by the Continental Congress. Not only did he have to contain the British in Boston but he had also to recruit a Continental army. During the winter of 1775–76 recruitment lagged so badly that fresh drafts of militia were called up to help maintain the siege. The balance was shifted in late winter, when General Henry Knox arrived with artillery from Ft. Ticonderoga in New York, which had been captured from the British in May 1775. Mounted on Dorchester Heights, above Boston, the guns forced Howe, who had replaced Gage in command, to evacuate the city on March 17.

While Howe sailed from Halifax to prepare for an invasion of New York and Washington moved units southward for its defense, action flared in the north. In the fall of 1775 the Americans invaded Canada. One force under Gen. Richard Montgomery captured Montreal on November 13. Another under Benedict Arnold made a remarkable march through the Maine wilderness to Quebec. Unable to take the city, Arnold was presently joined by Montgomery, many of whose troops had gone home because their enlistments had expired. An attack on the city the last day of the year failed, Montgomery was killed, and many troops were captured. The Americans maintained a siege of the city but withdrew with the arrival of British reinforcements in the spring. Pursued by the British and decimated by smallpox, the Americans fell back to Ticonderoga. General Guy Carleton's hopes of moving quickly down Lake Champlain, however, were frustrated by Arnold's construction of a fighting fleet. Forced to build one of his own, Carleton destroyed most of the American fleet

in October 1776 but considered the season too advanced to bring Ticonderoga under siege.

As the Americans suffered defeat in Canada, so did the British in the South. North Carolina patriots trounced a body of Loyalists at Moore's Creek Bridge on February 27, 1776. Charleston, South Carolina, was successfully defended against a British assault in June.

Having made up its mind to crush the rebellion, the British government sent General Howe and his brother, Adm. Lord Richard Howe, with a large fleet and 34,000 British and German troops to New York. It also gave the Howes a commission to treat with the Americans. Congress, which had proclaimed the independence of the colonies, at first thought the Howes empowered to negotiate peace terms but discovered they were authorized only to accept submission and assure pardons.

Their peace efforts getting nowhere, the Howes turned to force. Under his brother's guns, General Howe landed troops on Long Island, and on August 27 scored a smashing victory. Washington evacuated his army from Brooklyn to Manhattan that night under cover of a fog. On September 15, Howe followed up his victory by invading Manhattan. Though checked at Harlem Heights the next day, he drew Washington off the island in October by a move to Throg's Neck and then to New Rochelle, northeast of the city. Leaving garrisons at Ft. Washington on Manhattan and at Ft. Lee on the opposite shore of the Hudson River, Washington hastened to block Howe. The latter, however, defeated him on October 28 at Chatterton Hill near White Plains. Howe slipped between the American Army and Ft. Washington and stormed the fort on November 16, seizing nearly 3,000 prisoners, guns, and supplies. Lord Cornwallis then took Ft. Lee and on November 24 started to drive the American Army across New Jersey. Though Washington escaped to the west bank of the Delaware, his army nearly disappeared. Howe then put his army into winter quarters, with outposts at such towns as Bordentown and Trenton.

On Christmas night Washington struck back with a brilliant riposte. Crossing the ice-strewn Delaware with 4,000 men he fell upon the Hessian garrison at Trenton at dawn, taking nearly 1,000 prisoners. Though almost trapped by Cornwallis, who recovered Trenton on January 2, 1777, Washington made a skillful escape during the night, won a battle against British reinforcements at Princeton the next day, and went into winter quarters in the defensible area around Morristown. The Trenton–Princeton campaign, which roused the country, saved the struggle for independence from collapse.

Britain's strategy in 1777 aimed at driving a wedge between New England and the other colonies. An army under Gen. John Burgoyne was to march south from Canada and join forces with Howe on the Hudson. But Howe seems to have concluded that Burgoyne was strong enough to oper-

British seizure of New York

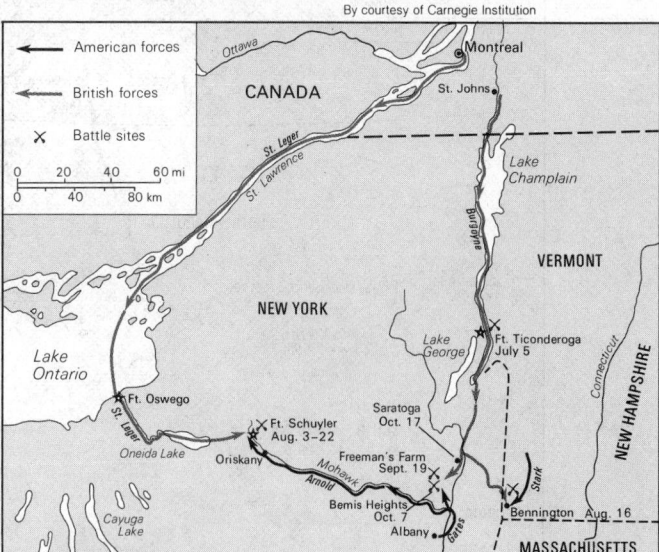

By courtesy of Carnegie Institution

Northern Campaign of 1777.

ate on his own and left New York in the summer, taking his army by sea to the head of Chesapeake Bay. Once ashore, he defeated Washington badly but not decisively at Brandywine Creek on September 11. Then, feinting westward, he entered Philadelphia, the American capital, on September 25. The Congress fled to York. Washington struck back at Germantown on October 4 but, compelled to withdraw, went into winter quarters at Valley Forge.

In the north the story was different. Burgoyne was to move south to Albany with a force of about 9,000 British, Germans, Indians, and American Loyalists; a smaller force under Lieut. Colonel Barry St. Leger was to converge on Albany through the Mohawk Valley. Burgoyne took Ticonderoga handily on July 5, then, instead of using Lake George, chose a southward route by land. Slowed by the terrain and trees cut down by American axmen under Gen. Philip Schuyler and needing horses, he sent a force of Germans to collect them at Bennington, Vermont. The Germans were nearly wiped out on August 16 by New Englanders under Gen. John Stark and Col. Seth Warner. Meanwhile, St. Leger besieged Ft. Schuyler (present Rome, New York), ambushed a relief column of American militia at Oriskany on August 6, but retreated as his Indians gave up the siege and an American force approached under Arnold. Burgoyne himself reached the Hudson, but the Americans, now under Gen. Horatio Gates, checked him at Freeman's Farm on September 19 and decisively defeated him at Bemis Heights on October 7. Ten days later, unable to get help from New York, Burgoyne surrendered his army at Saratoga.

The most significant result of Burgoyne's capitulation was the entrance of France into the war. The French had secretly furnished financial and material aid since 1776. Now they prepared fleets and armies, though they did not formally declare war until June 1778.

Meanwhile, the Americans survived a hungry winter at Valley Forge, made worse by quartermaster and commissary mismanagement, grafting contractors, and the unwillingness of farmers to sell produce for paper money. The situation was improved by the arrival of Baron Friedrich Wilhelm von Steuben, a Prussian officer in the service of France. Von Steuben instituted a training program in which he emphasized drilling by officers and marching in column, while he drastically reduced the number of motions for loading and firing weapons.

The program paid off at Monmouth, New Jersey, on June 28, 1778, when Washington attacked the British withdrawing from Philadelphia to New York. Though Sir Henry Clinton, who had replaced Howe, struck back hard, the Americans stood their ground.

French aid now materialized with the appearance of a strong fleet under the Comte d'Estaing. Unable to enter New York Harbour, d'Estaing tried to assist Maj. Gen. John Sullivan in dislodging the British from Newport, Rhode Island. Storms and British reinforcements thwarted the joint effort.

Action in the north was largely a stalemate for the rest of the war. The British made a series of raids upon New Bedford, Massachusetts, and New Haven and New London, Connecticut, while Loyalists and Indians attacked settlements in New York and Pennsylvania. On the other hand, the Americans under Anthony Wayne stormed Stony Point on July 16, 1779, and "Light-Horse" Harry Lee took Paulus Hook on August 19. More lasting in effect was Sullivan's expedition of August 1779 against Britain's Indian allies in New York, particularly the destruction of their villages and fields of corn. Farther west, Col. George Rogers Clark seized Vincennes and other posts north of the Ohio in 1778.

Potentially serious blows to the American cause were Benedict Arnold's defection in 1780 and army mutinies in 1780 and 1781. Arnold's attempt to betray West Point to the British miscarried. Mutinies were sparked by misunderstandings over terms of enlistment, poor food and clothing, gross arrears of pay, and the decline in the purchasing power of the dollar. Suppressed by force or negotiation, the mutinies shook the morale of the army.

The Americans also suffered setbacks in the South. British strategy called for offensives there from 1778 on that were designed to take advantage of the flexibility of sea power and the Loyalist sentiment of many of the people. Forces from New York and St. Augustine occupied Georgia by the end of January 1779 and successfully defended Savannah in the fall against d'Estaing and a Franco-American army. Clinton, having withdrawn his Newport garrison, captured Charleston and an American army of 5,000 under Gen. Benjamin Lincoln in May 1780. Learning that Newport was threatened by a French expeditionary force under the Comte de Rochambeau, he returned to New York, leaving Cornwallis at Charleston.

Cornwallis, however, took the offensive. On August 16 he shattered General Gates' army at Camden, South Carolina.

The Battles of Saratoga

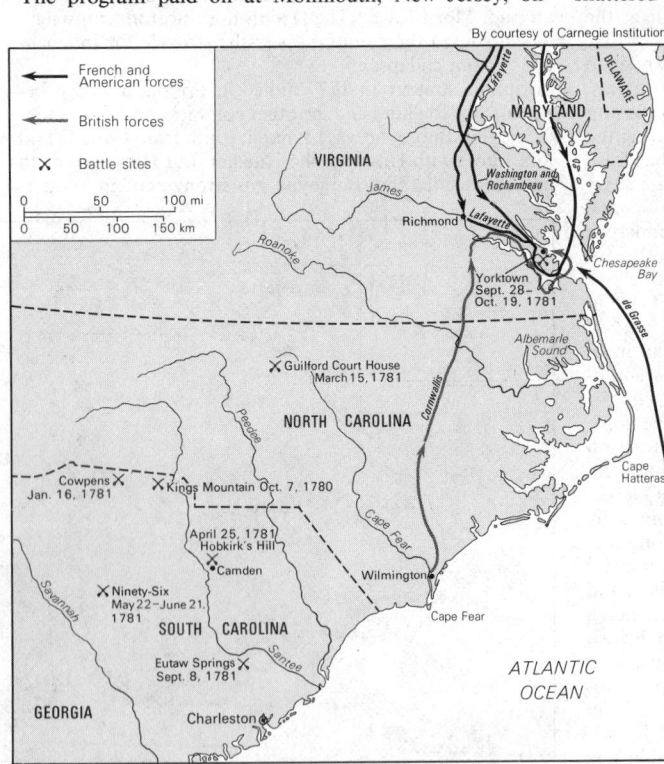

By courtesy of Carnegie Institution

Final campaigns in the South.

The destruction of a force of Loyalists at Kings Mountain on October 7 led him to move against the new American commander, Nathanael Greene. When Greene put part of his force under Gen. Daniel Morgan, Cornwallis sent his cavalry leader, Banastre Tarleton, after Morgan. At Cowpens on January 17, 1781, Morgan destroyed practically all of Tarleton's column. Subsequently, on March 15, Greene and Cornwallis fought at Guilford Court House, North Carolina. Cornwallis won but suffered heavy casualties. After withdrawing to Wilmington, he marched into Virginia to join British forces sent there by Clinton.

Greene then moved to South Carolina, where he was defeated at Hobkirk's Hill on April 25, at Ninety-Six in June, and at Eutaw Springs on September 8. In spite of this, the British, harassed by partisan leaders like Francis Marion, Thomas Sumter, and Andrew Pickens, soon retired to the coast and remained locked up in Charleston and Savannah until the end of the war.

The final campaign

Meanwhile Cornwallis entered Virginia. Sending Tarleton on raids across the state, he started to build a base at Yorktown, at the same time fending off American forces under Wayne, von Steuben, and the Marquis de Lafayette.

Learning that the Comte de Grasse had arrived in the Chesapeake with a large fleet and 3,000 French troops, Washington and Rochambeau moved south to Virginia. By mid-September the Franco-American forces had placed Yorktown under siege, and British rescue efforts proved fruitless. Cornwallis surrendered his army of more than 7,000 men on October 19. Thus, for the second time during the war the British had lost an entire army.

Thereafter, land action in America died out, though the war persisted in other theatres and on the high seas. Eventually Clinton was replaced by Sir Guy Carleton. While the peace treaties were under consideration and afterward, Carleton evacuated thousands of Loyalists from America, including many from Savannah on July 11, 1782, and others from Charleston on December 14. The last British forces finally left New York on November 25, 1783. Washington then re-entered the city in triumph.

Historians' judgments

In explaining the outcome of the war, scholars have pointed out that the British never contrived an overall general strategy for winning it. Also, even if the war could have been terminated by British power in the early stages, the generals during that period, notably Howe, declined to make a prompt, vigorous, intelligent application of that power. They acted, to be sure, within the conventions of their age, but in choosing to take minimal risks (for example, Carleton at Ticonderoga and Howe at Brooklyn Heights and later in New Jersey and Pennsylvania) they lost the opportunity to deal potentially mortal blows to the rebellion. There was also a grave lack of understanding and cooperation at crucial moments (as with Burgoyne and Howe in 1777). Finally, the British counted too strongly on Loyalist support they did not receive.

But British mistakes alone could not account for the success of the United States. Feeble as their war effort occasionally became, the Americans were able generally to take advantage of their enemies' mistakes. The Continental Army, moreover, was by no means an inept force even before von Steuben's reforms. The militia, while usually unreliable, could perform admirably under the leadership of men who understood them, like Arnold, Greene, and Morgan, and often reinforced the Continentals in crises. Furthermore, Washington, a rock in adversity, learned slowly but reasonably well the art of generalship. The supplies and funds furnished by France from 1776 to 1778 were invaluable, while French military and naval support after 1778 was essential. The outcome, therefore, resulted from a combination of British blunders, American efforts, and French assistance.

The war at sea. Though the colonists ventured to challenge Britain's naval power from the outbreak of the conflict, the war at sea in its later stages was mainly fought between Britain and America's European allies, the American effort being reduced to privateering.

The importance of the sea was recognized early. In October 1775, the Continental Congress authorized the creation of the Continental Navy and established the Marine Corps in November. Taking its direction from the naval and marine committees of the Congress, the Navy was only occasionally effective. In 1776 it had 27 ships as against Britain's 270; by the end of the war, the British total had risen close to 500, the Americans dwindled to 20. Many of the best seamen available went off privateering, and both Continental Navy commanders and crews suffered from a lack of training and discipline.

The first significant blow by the navy was struck by Commo. Esek Hopkins, who captured New Providence (Nassau) in the Bahamas in 1776.

Other captains such as Lambert Wickes, Gustavus Conyngham, and John Barry also enjoyed successes, but the former Scot, John Paul Jones, was especially notable. As captain of the "Ranger," Jones scourged the British coasts in 1778, capturing the man-of-war "Drake." As captain of the "Bonhomme Richard" in 1779, he intercepted a timber convoy and captured the British frigate "Serapis."

More injurious to the British were the raids by American privateers on their shipping. American ships swarmed about the British Isles furnished with letters of marque by the Congress or the states. By the end of 1777 they had taken 560 British vessels, and by the end of the war they had probably seized 1,500. More than 12,000 British sailors also were captured. One result was that by 1781 British merchants were clamouring for an end to hostilities.

Though most of the naval action occurred at sea, the significant exception was Benedict Arnold's battles against General Carleton's fleet on Lake Champlain at Valcour Island on October 11 and off Split Rock on October 13, 1776. Arnold lost both battles, but his construction of his fleet of tiny vessels, mostly gundalows and row galleys, had forced the British to build a larger one and hence delayed their attack on Ft. Ticonderoga until the following spring.

The entrance of France into the war, followed by Spain in 1779 and the Netherlands in 1780, was an important factor in the naval aspect of the war. The Spanish and Dutch were not particularly active, but their role in keeping British naval forces tied down in Europe was significant. The British Navy could not maintain an effective blockade of both the American coast and the enemies' ports. Owing to years of economy and neglect, Britain's ships of the line were neither modern nor sufficiently numerous. An immediate result was that France's Toulon fleet under d'Estaing got safely away to America where it appeared off New York and later assisted General Sullivan in the unsuccessful siege of Newport. A fierce battle off Ushant in July 1778 between the Channel fleet under Adm. Augustus Keppel and the Brest fleet under the Comte d'Orvilliers proved inconclusive. Had Keppel won decisively, French aid to the Americans would have diminished and Rochambeau might never have been able to lead his expedition to America.

The following year England was in real danger. Not only did it have to face the privateers of the United States, France, and Spain off its coasts, as well as the raids of John Paul Jones, but it also lived in fear of invasion. Its fleet at home was too inferior to face the combined fleets of France and Spain, which acquired command of the Channel. Meanwhile, a French army of 50,000 waited for the propitious moment to board their transports. Luckily for the British, storm, sickness among the Allied crews, and changes of plans terminated the threat.

The planned invasion of England

Despite Allied supremacy in the Channel in 1779, the threat of invasion, and the loss of islands in the West Indies, the British maintained control of the North American seaboard for most of 1779 and 1780, which made possible their Southern land campaigns. They also reinforced Gibraltar, which the Spaniards had brought under siege in the fall of 1779, and sent a fleet under Adm. Sir George Rodney to the West Indies in early 1780. After fruitless manoeuvring against the Comte de Guichen, who had replaced d'Estaing, Rodney sailed for New York.

While Rodney had been in the West Indies, a French squadron slipped out of Brest and sailed to Newport with Rochambeau's army. Rodney, instead of trying to block the approach to Newport, returned to the West Indies, where, upon receiving instructions to attack Dutch possessions, he seized St. Eustatius, the Dutch island that served as the principal depot for war materials shipped from Europe and transshipped into American vessels. He became so involved in the disposal of the enormous booty that he dallied at the island for six months.

In the meantime, a powerful British fleet relieved Gibraltar in 1781, but the price was the departure of the French fleet at Brest, part of it to India, the larger part under Adm. de Grasse to the West Indies. After manoeuvring indecisively against Rodney, de Grasse received a request from Washington and Rochambeau to come to New York or the Chesapeake.

Earlier, in March, a French squadron had tried to bring troops from Newport to the Chesapeake but was forced to return by Adm. Marriot Arbuthnot, who had succeeded Lord Howe. Soon afterward Arbuthnot was replaced by Thomas Graves, a conventional-minded admiral.

Informed that a French squadron would shortly leave the West Indies, Rodney sent Samuel Hood north with a powerful force while he sailed for England, taking with him several formidable ships that might better have been left with Hood.

Soon after Hood dropped anchor in New York, de Grasse appeared in the Chesapeake, where he landed troops to help Lafayette contain Cornwallis until Washington and Rochambeau could arrive. Fearful that the Comte de Barras, who was carrying Rochambeau's artillery train from Newport, might join de Grasse and hoping to intercept him, Graves sailed with Hood to the Chesapeake. Graves had 19 ships of the line against de Grasse's 24. Though the battle that began on September 5 off the Virginia capes was not a skillfully managed affair, only the leading squadrons seeing close action, Graves had the worst of it and retired to New York. He ventured out again on October 17 with a strong contingent of troops and 25 ships of the line, while de Grasse, reinforced by Barras, now had 36 ships of the line. No battle occurred, however, since off the capes Graves learned that Cornwallis had surrendered. He returned to New York.

Though Britain subsequently recouped some of its fortunes, Rodney defeating and capturing de Grasse in the Battle of the Saints off Dominica in 1782 and British land and sea forces inflicting defeats in India, the turn of events did not significantly alter the situation in America as it existed after Yorktown. A new government under Lord Shelburne (1st marquess of Lansdowne) tried to get the American commissioners to agree to a separate peace, but, ultimately, the treaty negotiated with the Americans was not to go into effect until the formal conclusion of a peace with their European allies.

Treaty of Paris. The military verdict in North America was reflected in the preliminary Anglo-American peace treaty of 1782, which was included in the Treaty of Paris of 1783. Benjamin Franklin, John Adams, John Jay, and Henry Laurens served as the American commissioners. By its terms Britain recognized the independence of the United States with generous boundaries, including the Mississippi River on the west. Britain retained Canada but ceded East and West Florida to Spain. Provisions were inserted calling for the payment of American private debts to British citizens, for American access to the Newfoundland fisheries, and for a recommendation by the Congress to the states in favour of fair treatment of the Loyalists.

Most of the Loyalists remained in the new nation. Perhaps as many as 37,000 Tories migrated to Canada, with smaller numbers going to England and the British West Indies. Many of these had served as British soldiers, and many had been banished by the American states. The less ardent and more cautious Tories, staying in the United States, accepted the separation from Britain as final and could not be distinguished from the Patriots after the passage of a generation. The Loyalists were harshly treated as dangerous enemies by the American states during the war and immediately afterward. They were commonly deprived of civil rights, often fined, and frequently deprived of their property. The more conspicuous were usually banished upon pain of death. The British government compensated more than 4,000 of the exiles for property losses, paying out almost £3,300,000. It also gave them land grants, pensions, and appointments to enable them to reestablish themselves. (W.M.Wa./Ed.)

The Battle of the Virginia capes

The Confederation and the early federal republic

THE CONFEDERATION AND THE CONSTITUTIONAL CONVENTION

As the debate on independence moved toward a climax in 1776, the internal political alignments of the various colonies began to harden around that issue. In New England, minority groups were overridden, royalists fleeing for Nova Scotia or England, while Baptists and other religious minorities were vigorously suppressed; south of the Potomac, backcountry dissenters were subdued by force, though Loyalism remained endemic in the area. In the Middle Colonies, Galloway broke with Franklin and remained Loyalist as a matter of conscience; Pennsylvania's Quakers became nonmilitarily Loyalist; New York's De Lanceyites became militantly so out of fear of the social turmoil that seemed in store; the Livingston connection became reluctant rebels.

Among those who supported independence, two broad divisions soon became manifest. The reluctant rebels of the Middle Colonies and the lower South insisted, at the last minute, that if independence was to come, it should be preceded by the creation of a strong national government. The more ardent rebels of New England and Virginia became hard-shelled "republicans"—by which they meant opponents of monarchy, central government, executive authority, and all other forms of restraint upon the power of dominant local groups. The republicans prevailed from 1776 until 1780, almost preventing victory by their hostility to central authority and ensuring the adoption of the Articles of Confederation (a "league of friendship" rather than the strong national government proposed by Dickinson and supported by nationalists).

"Republicans" versus centralists

Predictably, few internal reforms were brought about by the prevalence of republicanism: all colony-states except Rhode Island and Connecticut, which had long governed themselves under colonial charters, did adopt new constitutions, but none save those of Pennsylvania and Georgia were especially radical. The latter two established unicameral legislatures virtually unchecked by executive or judicial branches and experienced considerable political turbulence. The other nine were relatively conservative and were designed to freeze political power where it was in the summer of 1776; all emasculated the executive branch and expanded legislative authority, but few broadened the franchise, only seven provided bills of rights (none of which had the force of law), and several provided elaborate checks on direct popular rule.

Problems under the Articles of Confederation. Government under the Articles of Confederation and the new state constitutions was adequate to see the United States through to independence, but only after republicanism had been discredited by corruption and incompetence in 1781, after nationalists had seized unconstitutional powers under Superintendent of Finance Robert Morris, after Gen. George Washington's army acquired military discipline and a most unrepublican spirit, and after various British generals, notoriously the commander of the southern army, Lord Cornwallis, committed blunders that bordered on the preposterous. At Yorktown, Virginia, in October of 1781, Cornwallis was forced to surrender to Washington. A year later, a definitive treaty of peace, recognizing American independence and placing the western boundary of the United States at the Mississippi, had been signed. Britain retained Canada, Spain received Florida to the Mississippi, and everything west of the river remained Spanish. France, allied with the United States after 1778, got nothing for all its troubles.

End of the war

The Americans suddenly found themselves in an unfriendly world. Britain closed its West Indies to American shipping, Spain closed its colonies entirely and also, by closing New Orleans, deterred development of the West, though frontiersmen spilled over the mountains in great numbers. Even France imposed commercial restrictions, cutting New England fish and Virginia tobacco from profitable markets. In short, the tangible gains many expected from independence were simply not forthcoming.

Domestic tensions aggravated the difficulties of the new

republic. Congress, nearly impotent under the Articles of Confederation and weakened further by the resurgence of republicans after the peace, was unable to cope with either national or local problems. The most pressing of all domestic problems was the public debt, national and state, of about $60,000,000, incurred to finance the war. The vast domain of public lands might have been used to retire these debts—trans-Appalachia north of the Ohio River had come, by circuitous means, to be vested in Congress by 1784—but local and private greed, Spanish obstructionism, and efforts of nationalists to use public debts and lands as cements of a stronger union combined to thwart such action.

In default of effective national action, the several states attempted to service the public debts, with varying results. Most of the Southern states virtually repudiated their debts, alienating public creditors and straining the private economy. Even so, Georgia and North Carolina thrived for special local reasons, South Carolina might have flourished but for a freakish succession of crop failures, Virginia did well until 1786, and only Maryland was torn by internal political and financial problems. In the Middle states, New York and Pennsylvania handled their public affairs well, with the result that New York drifted away from nationalism, though internal dissension kept Pennsylvania divided. New Jersey and Delaware and two New England states, Connecticut and New Hampshire, were entirely unable to manage alone. Massachusetts, sorely depressed economically in the postimperial world and burdened by high taxes imposed to pay war debts, was torn in civil war (Shays's Rebellion) in 1786. In all of New England, only Rhode Island flourished, and it did so only through the kind of brigandage that Americans had come to expect from the "otherwise-minded" colony-state.

The Constitutional Convention. In sum, by the winter of 1786–87 America was in crisis. In Massachusetts, Capt. Daniel Shays, a Revolutionary War veteran, led a band of embattled farmers against the state court to prevent foreclosures on tax delinquent farmers; and in New York the state legislature defeated an amendment to the Articles of Confederation giving Congress an independent source of revenue from import duties. In desperation, Congress and all the states except Rhode Island acceded to a call—issued by nationalists at a commercial convention in Annapolis the preceding September—for a general convention to meet in Philadelphia in May 1787 and "consider the exigencies of the Union."

The Philadelphia Convention has been described, and not without merit, as the most gifted collection of statesmen ever assembled (even though Jefferson, Sam and John Adams, Richard Henry Lee, John Hancock, Patrick Henry, and other heroes of 1776 were absent). Well-versed in political theory, the delegates were nonetheless practical men of business and public affairs who addressed themselves less to the theoretical problem of what kind of national government America should have (which, given everything, could only be answered republican and federal) than to the more basic question, whether the United States would have a national government at all. On that crucial question, the 55 delegates lined up in four general camps.

A majority of delegates were strong nationalists: an unconditional nationalist group of eight or ten, led by Washington and Franklin, who preferred a limited national authority based on a separation of powers but who would have accepted almost any form approved by the other delegates; two monarchists, Dickinson and Hamilton; six or eight aristocrats, led by Gouverneur Morris of Pennsylvania and John Rutledge of South Carolina, who would accept almost any energetic national government but preferred one as "high-toned" as possible; and seven or eight rather "democratic" nationalists, led by James Wilson of Pennsylvania and James Madison of Virginia, who wanted a strong national government founded on a broad popular base.

Next came two groups of conditional nationalists. The first of these—consisting of Elbridge Gerry of Massachusetts, George Wythe, Edmund Randolph, and George Mason of Virginia, and Luther Martin and John Francis Mercer of Maryland—were ideologues, who would support a na-

tional government only if it were founded on narrowly defined republican principles. The other group, which included most of the delegates from Maryland, New Hampshire, Connecticut, New Jersey, and Delaware, shared a more tangible concern. As representatives of states without viable claims to western lands, they insisted that the lands become the common property of all the states; but, given that condition, they were willing to support an extremely strong central authority. Finally, a few delegates, notably two of the three from New York, were flatly opposed to increased national authority.

In reconciling the ideological differences, Madison and Wilson were the most important delegates; in managing the political and economic differences, Rutledge, together with Roger Sherman and Oliver Ellsworth of Connecticut, towered over the rest.

The main business began with Washington presiding and Governor Randolph of Virginia presenting 15 resolutions, probably authored by Madison. The idea of creating a national authority was quickly approved, along with the principle that the new government should be divided into executive, legislative, and judicial branches. The most heated debate concerned the makeup of the legislative branch, the "landless" states insisting on equal representation by states and their opponents demanding that representation be apportioned according to population. A compromise was reached with a bicameral legislature, one house representing population and the other representing the states equally and the latter having control over questions of public lands. This arrangement was agreed upon by mid-July, but the constitution of the other branches was left vague and unsettled. The work of the convention was then turned over to a five-man Committee of Detail, which produced (August 6) a rough draft of a constitution, retaining the compromise legislature and making executive and judiciary subordinate to it. Early in September, however, after several weeks spent mainly in haggling over special interest features, the cumbersome electoral college was proposed (probably by Franklin), making the presidency independent of the proposed Congress. That feature made the Constitution awkward but also built into it the principle of separation of powers. Following a few more days of discussion, the convention's various resolutions were turned over to a Committee on Style, under Gouverneur Morris, which drafted the final document. Morris took several liberties with the text, introducing ambiguity at key points to make the Constitution flexible and also (without the delegates noticing) injecting various features, notably the "contract clause," which had been voted down. On September 17, 1787, the Constitution was approved by 39 of the 42 delegates remaining in the convention.

Struggle for ratification. The Constitution stipulated that it should become effective when specially elected conventions in nine states ratified, despite the requirement in the Articles of Confederation that amendments be ratified by the legislatures of every state. The smallest and weakest states, most pleased with the new system, ratified quickly: Delaware, New Jersey, and Georgia all unanimously and before year's end and Connecticut early in 1788 by a majority of three to one. Meanwhile, Pennsylvania, one of the states expected to be reluctant, responded to political manipulation and high-pressure campaign techniques and ratified in December 1787 by a convention vote of 46 delegates to 23. Massachusetts, another "swing" state, ratified early in 1788 in response to clever politicking by Federalists, as proponents of the Constitution called themselves, though "Anti-Federalists" may well have been in a majority in the state.

With six states having approved and three to go, the contest came to a climax in the spring of 1788. Maryland and South Carolina (both being extremely aristocratic states that had been lukewarm toward the democratic trends implicit in independence and both being landless states that stood to gain from the pooling of the domain of public lands) ratified by sizable majorities early in the year. But New Hampshire, populated mainly by backcountrymen who were loathe to accept any change, postponed a decision; and the dominant groups in Virginia, New York,

Shays's Rebellion

Alignment of the delegates

Proposal of the electoral college

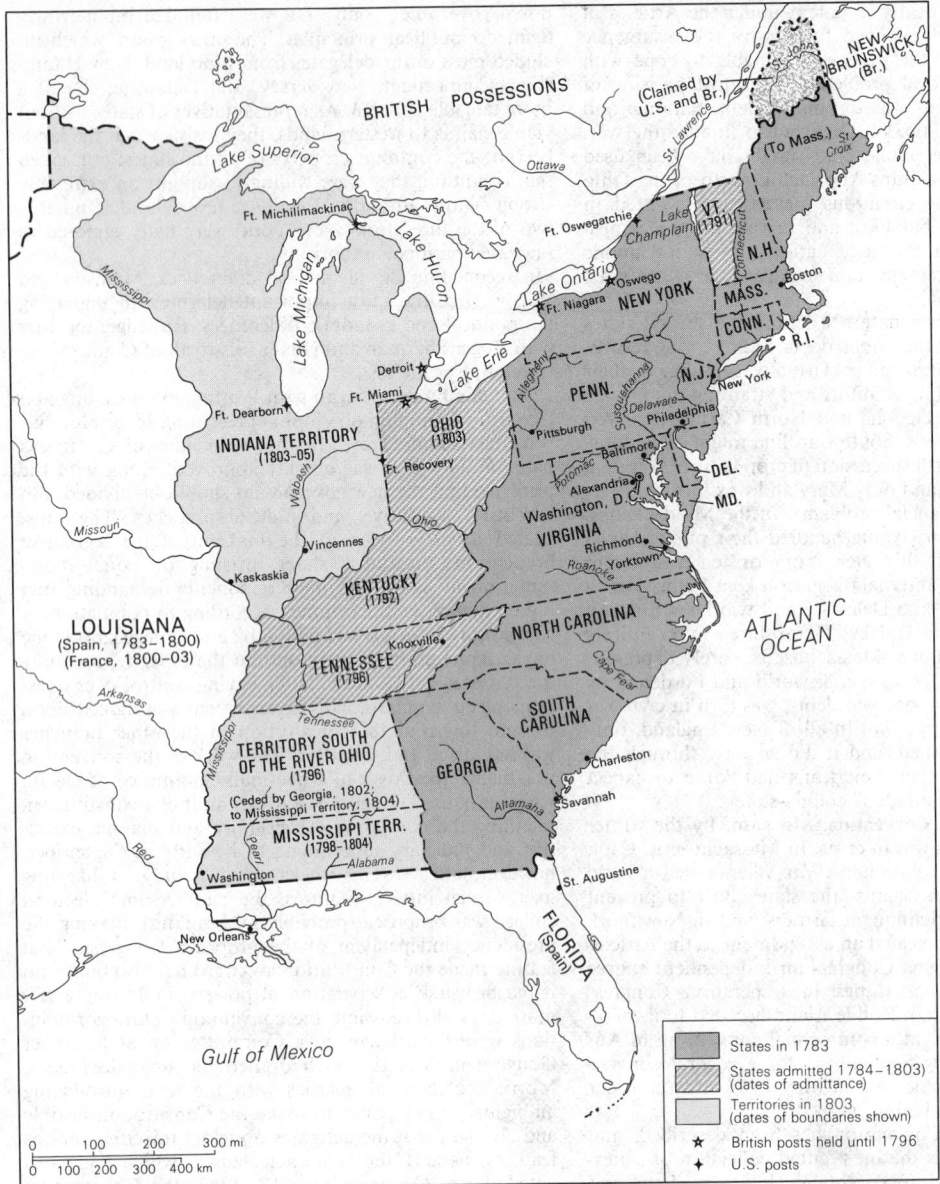

BRITISH POSSESSIONS

(Claimed by U.S. and Br.)

NEW BRUNSWICK (Br.)

Lake Superior

Ft. Michilimackinac

Ft. Oswegatchie

Ottawa

St. Lawrence

(To Mass.)

St. Croix

Lake Champlain

VT. (1791)

N.H.

Lake Huron

Lake Michigan

Lake Ontario

Oswego

Ft. Niagara

NEW YORK

Boston

MASS.

CONN.

R.I.

Detroit

Lake Erie

Allegheny

Susquehanna

New York

Ft. Dearborn

Ft. Miami

OHIO (1803)

PENN.

Delaware

Philadelphia

INDIANA TERRITORY (1803-05)

Pittsburgh

N.J.

Wabash

Ft. Recovery

Potomac

Baltimore

DEL.

Alexandria

MD.

Ohio

Washington, D.

Vincennes

VIRGINIA

Richmond

Kaskaskia

Yorktown

Roanoke

KENTUCKY (1792)

NORTH CAROLINA

Missouri

ATLANTIC OCEAN

LOUISIANA (Spain, 1783-1800) (France, 1800-03)

Arkansas

TENNESSEE (1796)

Knoxville

Cape Fear

Tennessee

SOUTH CAROLINA

TERRITORY SOUTH OF THE RIVER OHIO (1796)

GEORGIA

Charleston

(Ceded by Georgia, 1802, to Mississippi Territory, 1804)

Altamaha

Savannah

Mississippi

MISSISSIPPI TERR. (1798-1804)

Red

Pearl

Alabama

Washington

St. Augustine

New Orleans

FLORIDA (Spain)

Gulf of Mexico

	States in 1783
	States admitted 1784-1803 (dates of admittance)
	Territories in 1803 (dates of boundaries shown)
★	British posts held until 1796
✦	U.S. posts

0 100 200 300 mi
0 100 200 300 400 km

The United States, 1783–1803.

North Carolina, and Rhode Island were opposed to ratification. After considerable debate and political jockeying, however, the first three had ratified by July of 1788, despite the probable opposition of popular majorities. North Carolina finally ratified in November of 1789, several months after the new government had begun to operate, and Rhode Island ratified in May 1790.

Attitudes toward the Constitution can be accounted for on four major sets of grounds, apart from considerations already mentioned: (1) proximity to regular commerce and communication, those Americans having the broadest world view, deriving from regular contact with other places, being more favourable to national authority than those in more isolated places; (2) military vulnerability, those areas that had suffered most from the wartime fighting being the most nationalist (a striking number of the ablest pieces in favour of the Constitution, *The Federalist Papers* by Jay, Hamilton, and Madison, were concerned with the advantages for national defense that would result from ratification); (3) relative success under the Confederation, those states that had fared best as sovereign entities being least favourable toward the Constitution; and (4) ideology, the more doctrinaire republicans being cool toward the Constitution because of its ambiguity and lack of a bill of rights. Economic interests also entered the contest over ratification but won about as many enemies as friends for the new system.

NATIONAL POLITICS, 1789–1816

The first elections under the Constitution were held early in 1789. Federalists, mainly old nationalists, swept to power: Washington received every electoral vote and became president, John Adams became vice president, and only a handful of Anti-Federalists were elected to Congress. The new government wasted some time on precedents and protocol, but by early summer of 1789 it had plunged earnestly into serious business. One such concerned an issue raised during the conflict over ratification: Anti-Federalists had demanded a second convention to add a bill of rights to the Constitution, some hoping that a second convention might undo the work of the first. Madison, fighting for his political life in predominantly Anti-Federalist Virginia, sought to please his constituents by proposing a number of amendments; he was supported, for reasons of political expediency, by some Federalists who actually opposed a bill of rights and was opposed, for similar reasons, by some Anti-Federalists who favoured such amendments. Twelve amendments were finally approved by Congress and submitted to the states for ratification. Ten, which became the Bill of Rights, were ratified in December 1791. Together the amendments restricted national authority against states and individuals and guaranteed various procedural rights, but the restrictions did not apply to state governments.

Meanwhile, Congress was resolving two other major

The Bill of Rights

problems in 1789. It levied a tariff on imports, and though supplementary internal taxes were enacted from time to time, import duties would remain the major source of national revenue for more than a century. The first Congress also passed the Judiciary Act, filling a void in the Constitution by establishing a hierarchical system of appellate courts. For practical purposes this act became part of the Constitution itself.

In dealing with its remaining major tasks, Congress went only part of the way in 1789. Instead of creating new executive departments, it adopted and modified the machinery of the Confederation. The Department of Foreign Affairs became State (to head which Washington appointed Thomas Jefferson, after incumbent John Jay indicated his preference for the chief justiceship); the War Department was retained intact, including the incumbent head, Henry Knox. The Confederation's three-man Board of the Treasury was replaced by a department headed by a single secretary. Washington wanted Robert Morris, Philadelphia merchant and erstwhile "financier of the Revolution," for the post, but Morris declined and Washington appointed instead his own former aide-de-camp, the brilliant young New Yorker Alexander Hamilton. Congress promptly instructed Hamilton to produce, by the time it reconvened at year's end, a plan for retiring the public debts.

Hamilton's fiscal system. The following January, Hamilton presented his First Report on the Public Credit, a comprehensive plan modelled after the system evolved in England between the 1690s and 1730s. Instead of attempting to retire the public debt, which imposed crippling tax burdens on the nascent American economy, Hamilton proposed to "fund" it and transform it into currency. Toward that end, all obligations of the old Confederacy as well as the war debts of the states would be made exchangeable for bonds of the new national government; the new bonds would receive regular interest payments and be supported by open-market purchases by Treasury Department agents, using a "sinking fund" created for the purpose. With public bonds thus stabilized and "pegged," government obligations could form the basis of a paper currency: a national bank, quasi-public and patterned after the Bank of England, could issue notes based on the public debt.

Most Congressmen from the tobacco-growing states opposed Hamilton's plan, partly because the planters were major importers who had largely repudiated their own debts and thus stood to pay heavily for a scheme that would directly profit them little. In part, however, their antagonism arose from much deeper roots, the so-called agrarian mentality. The aristocratic republicans of the tobacco belt were by no means opposed to making profit; indeed they were so avid for profit that they were willing to enslave blacks and slaughter Indians to obtain it; but they fiercely opposed the monetization of American life, much as the Bolingbroke Tories (whom the Virginians regularly read and quoted) had opposed the monetization of England by the Walpole Whigs.

Accordingly, Hamilton's proposals met stiff resistance from the "republican interest" in Congress, led by Madison, but the plan for assuming the state debts and funding all the debts was passed in August 1790. The act creating the Bank of the United States was passed in February 1791. Washington's cabinet split on this issue, Jefferson arguing, as a "strict constructionist," that the bank was unconstitutional and Hamilton defending its constitutionality with the doctrine of implied powers. Other portions of Hamilton's program, notably his proposal for protective tariffs to promote infant American industries, were defeated.

Formation of political parties. Mainly as a result of these disputes, something resembling political parties had begun to crystallize by 1792. Republicans, led by Madison and Jefferson, founded an anti-administration newspaper, built local organizations through private clubs called Democratic-Republican societies, and tried to coordinate electioneering activities; they were strong in the upper South, on the western frontier, and among erstwhile Anti-Federalists in the Middle states. Federalists, led by Hamilton, also founded a newspaper, but for the most part their political organization consisted of Treasury Department

"Funding" the debt

employees. The prosperity attending Hamilton's program and the immense popularity of President Washington won Federalist supporters everywhere, though the "party" was strongest in New England, South Carolina, and the environs of New York City and Philadelphia.

Effects of the French Revolution. In 1793 a new issue arose, one that would dominate American affairs for 22 years: the wars of the French Revolution. American involvement began with the arrival of Citizen Edmond Genet as minister from France, claiming that the Franco-American Alliance of 1778 bound the United States in the current French war against England, Spain, and other European nations. Hamilton, recognizing that war with England would dry up revenues from imports (most of which came from Britain) and thus destroy the financial system that bound the nation together, insisted on neutrality. Republicans warmly favoured France, partly out of ideological kinship, partly because of opposition to Hamilton's system, partly because the alliance would justify seizure of Spanish territory on the southern and western frontiers. Washington followed Hamilton's advice and issued a neutrality proclamation, and Jefferson soon resigned as secretary of state.

The Republicans gained popular support in the winter of 1793–94, when the British Navy seized many American commercial vessels and impressed into its service a number of American seamen. To prevent a break with England, Washington sent John Jay to London. The resulting treaty ensured cordial Anglo-American relations, provided for the evacuation of British posts in the American Northwest, and (in conjunction with Orders in Council issued at the same time) afforded great opportunities for American commerce as the neutral carrier of belligerent goods. Meanwhile, when Jay was in London the so-called Whiskey Rebellion (actually only a limited opposition to the federal excise tax on liquor) was crushed in western Pennsylvania; and because the "rebels" were associated with Democratic-Republican societies, such societies were widely discredited. Even so, Republicans were able to organize a spirited opposition to Jay's Treaty; but its obvious advantages, together with the loss of enthusiasm for France during and as a result of the Reign of Terror (1793–94), were enough to secure senatorial ratification by the necessary two-thirds majority. A year later the Federalists scored another diplomatic gain with Pinckney's Treaty, whereby Spain opened the Mississippi, allowing Americans the right of deposit at Spanish New Orleans.

On that note, and largely because the tenor of domestic politics had grown so scurrilous, Washington decided to retire at the end of his second term (March 3, 1797). Federalist vice president John Adams was elected president, but the Republican Jefferson became vice president. Adams' administration was marked throughout by strained relations with a France that was angry over Jay's Treaty and arrogant after defeating the best armies of Europe, a France that demanded bribes and tribute as a condition to recognizing American diplomats. Incensed, the United States prepared for war. What followed was complex. There was some naval fighting in 1798–99 at a time when the infant U.S. Navy consisted mainly of a new class of super-frigates designed by Joshua Humphreys. Hamilton, retired from the Treasury but still influential among the Federalists, advocated a large army also, partly for conquest of Spanish territory in the Southwest (Spain having become an ally of France) and partly to suppress a pro-French insurrection he feared was brewing in the South. Virginia, North Carolina, and Kentucky did contemplate insurrection and armed their militias to fight if Hamilton's "invasion" materialized. Moreover, in opposition to the Alien and Sedition Acts, restrictive measures passed as part of the war preparations, Madison and Jefferson penned the so-called Virginia and Kentucky Resolutions, defying Congress and postulating the classical states-sovereignty constitutional position. (Actually, the Alien and Sedition Acts were the mildest restrictions on civil liberties ever imposed by the United States in time of war.)

In 1799, France, suddenly jeopardized by the formation of a new coalition in Europe, signified its willingness to negotiate. Adams then sent a new minister, William

The Jay Treaty

Alien and Sedition Acts

Vans Murray, who agreed to the Convention of 1800, terminating the quasi-war. France continued to have designs on America; the secret Treaty of San Ildefonso, whereby Napoleon (now ruling France) obtained Spanish Louisiana, was signed on October 1, 1800, the day after Murray's convention was signed. But Adams had avoided war and gained considerable popularity in so doing. He had also split his party by his open break with Hamilton, however, and thereby prevented his re-election in 1800. Jefferson and Aaron Burr tied for the lead in the electoral college, and only after an acrimonious contest in Congress did Jefferson become president.

Jefferson's presidency. The "Revolution of 1800," as Jefferson later described his election, reflected no popular mandate—most electors were chosen by state legislatures—and did not, in fact, bring sweeping changes to the national government. To the disappointment of Republican ideologues, Jefferson neither purged the government of Federalist employees nor destroyed the Hamiltonian system, and he abandoned the principles of strict construction and a weak executive branch. Albert Gallatin, as secretary of the treasury, introduced various administrative reforms; but otherwise the Jeffersonians, in domestic affairs, concentrated mainly on trying to rid the federal courts of Federalist judges. The President and his intimates shared a distrust of the judicial branch, were incensed by Adams' "midnight appointments" (several new judgeships created in February of 1801 and filled by Adams just before he left office in March), and were outraged when one of the late appointees, Chief Justice John Marshall, established the principle of judicial review by declaring an act of Congress unconstitutional (*Marbury* v. *Madison,* 1803). Attempts to clear the bench by impeachment reached a climax early in 1805, with the trial of Justice Samuel Chase. When Chase was acquitted, the Jeffersonians abandoned the effort.

Jefferson's main concern was with foreign affairs and especially with territorial expansion. The most successful action in that direction was the purchase of the vast Louisiana territory from France in 1803 for $15,000,000. Jefferson also sought diligently to obtain Spanish Florida, which was needed for a southern outlet to the sea. Toward that end he played up to Napoleon, who could have forced Spain to cede Florida to the United States—and who tantalized the President by hinting he might do so. Jefferson also flirted with the idea of secretly backing a private expedition against Spanish territory. One such expedition

Establishment of judicial review

was that of Aaron Burr, who in 1804 had been dumped by the Jeffersonians, ran unsuccessfully for governor of New York, and killed Hamilton in a duel and who in 1805–06 was engaged in various western conspiracies. Arrested late in 1806, he was tried for treason and acquitted in 1807.

Meanwhile, the United States had again become entangled in the European wars. In 1805 Britain reversed the orders that enabled Americans to grow rich as neutral carriers to belligerents, and the next year Britain and France imposed various orders and decrees that sorely limited American trade with Europe and confiscated hundreds of American ships for violating the new rules. As a countermeasure, Jefferson requested and Congress authorized an embargo on all American exports. This was the darkest hour in Jefferson's presidency. In the enforcement of the embargo, civil liberties were ruthlessly suppressed; the embargo's main effect was to starve slaves in the West Indies—which the Jeffersonians expected and even welcomed because it had the incidental advantage, from their point of view as slaveowners, of punishing the blacks who had fought a successful revolution in Santo Domingo; and the effect on the European belligerents was nil. When his second term ended, Jefferson retired and never participated in public affairs again.

Jefferson's embargo on exports

Madison's presidency. Jefferson's secretary of state, James Madison, succeeded him as president in 1809. Madison had been skillful in politics, both as theoretician and as practical operator, but he lacked the qualities of leadership that Jefferson had brought to the presidency. Slavishly adhering to his narrow understanding of Jefferson's policies, Madison tried with a succession of commercial restrictions to force Britain and France to respect freedom of the seas. The efforts were futile, and Britain, master of the oceans since Nelson's victory over the combined French and Spanish fleets at Trafalgar in 1805, seized American ships and seamen at will and periodically insulted the small American navy. Meanwhile, the navy was considerably reduced, out of ideological opposition to standing armed forces, and the national government was drastically weakened when the charter of the national bank expired and Republicans in Congress refused to renew it.

Thus, as 1812 approached, American relations with both Britain and France degenerated, as did America's ability to wage war. But just then a popular clamour for war began to mount. In part the clamour was born of frustration and a desire to redeem the national honour. In part it was triggered by the private conquest of a portion of Spanish Florida (Spain having rejoined Britain against France), which convinced many expansionists that the rest of Florida and all of Canada would be easy prey for American militiamen. Madison himself inched toward war, seeking no conquests but determined to win freedom of the seas. These mounting forces, compounded by bungling diplomacy, resulted in a declaration of war against England on June 18, 1812. The vote was close, 79–49 in the House and 19–13 in the Senate. North and east of the Delaware River the vote was almost unanimous for peace.

THE WAR OF 1812

The American strategy in the War of 1812 was to fight for freedom of the seas by staying ashore. The navy was to be ordered to port, to defend the major cities; Canada was to be invaded at Detroit, Ft. Niagara, and Lake Champlain by a large militia force (100,000 were authorized for six months' service) and the small regular army. British strategy was to bottle the American navy in port, blockade the coast, and ignore the militia threat as so much braggadocio.

In the first year of the war, British thinking proved eminently the sounder. American militiamen under Gen. William Hull, instead of invading Canada, made a series of blunders and on August 16 surrendered Detroit to a small detachment of British. At Ft. Niagara the militiamen, first under Gen. Stephen Van Rensselaer and then under Alexander Smyth, refused to cross the frontier into Canada. At Lake Champlain the same thing happened with the largest American force, under Henry Dearborn.

Luckily for the Americans, naval captains William Bain-

Louisiana Purchase.

bridge and Charles Stewart persuaded Madison, at the last moment, to allow the small U.S. Navy (12 ships fit for sea duty, versus more than 600 in the Royal Navy) to go to sea. There the Americans distinguished themselves. Capt. John Rodgers sailed with five ships on a cruise that, though disappointing in its haul of prizes, diverted the British for months. The Humphreys frigate USS "Constitution," first under Isaac Hull and then under Bainbridge, destroyed HMS "Guerrière" and "Java," two frigates of her own class; and the Humphreys frigate "United States," under Stephen Decatur, captured HMS "Macedonian." In smaller ship actions, USS "Wasp" took HMS "Frolic," and USS "Hornet" defeated HMS "Peacock." It had been years since an enemy had defeated a British naval vessel of its own class in single combat, and yet the Americans did so five times in succession during the first eight months of the war.

Early in 1813, however, the Royal Navy bottled the United States Navy in port, and it was ineffectual on the high seas thereafter. Then, having neutralized the Americans' fleet and being contemptuous of their fighting ability on land, the British in Canada were emboldened to attempt the conquest of the American Northwest, with a combined force of regulars and Indians. Success depended on control of the Great Lakes, however, and once again the U.S. Navy performed admirably. A naval building race on Lake Ontario was more or less a stalemate. On Lake Erie, a motley fleet under Oliver Hazard Perry defeated a similar British fleet under R.H. Barclay (September 10, 1813). That victory enabled the American western commander, Gen. William Henry Harrison, to move a force of 4,500 across the lake and, at the Battle of the Thames (October 5), rout the British and their Indian allies, killing the chief Tecumseh. Efforts to follow up this victory were futile, but at least the western frontier was secure.

Perry's
victory

Elsewhere, however, the United States was nearing calamity. The British, victorious over Napoleon (March–April 1814), prepared a massive blow to destroy the United States: diversionary naval raids on coastal cities, followed by invasions at Ft. Niagara, Lake Champlain, and New Orleans. Moreover, American public finances were chaotic, and popular morale was even worse. Having destroyed the Bank of the United States and alienated almost every merchant north of New York, the Republican administration had neither money nor credit. New Yorkers and New Englanders openly opposed the war, traded with the enemy, and talked of rejoining Britain (though at the Hartford Convention in December, secessionist proposals were rejected).

Yet in the actual fighting of 1814, the Americans were surprisingly successful. The only part of the British plan that worked was that for coastal raids: great destruction was wrought on the Connecticut River, Buzzard's Bay (Massachusetts), and Alexandria, Virginia; and Royal Marines took Washington and burned the public buildings there and then bombarded Baltimore (August–September). At Ft. Niagara, however, American militiamen and regulars repulsed the invasion attempt (July–September); and on Lake Champlain Capt. Thomas Macdonough, USN, assembled a fleet that, for the second time in the war, defeated a British fleet (September 11)—thus precluding invasion by that route. Finally, at the Battle of New Orleans (fought January 8, 1815, two weeks after the peace treaty had been signed), Americans under Andrew Jackson slaughtered the invading British army.

Meanwhile, the British government had heeded the sage advice of the Duke of Wellington. The hero of the Peninsular Campaign maintained that, in an unorganized frontier country like the United States, fighting could go on endlessly without either side "winning," despite the superiority of British resources. Accordingly, British negotiators at Ghent, Belgium (where talks with an American commission had been underway for several months), agreed to peace on December 24, 1814. The terms were status quo antebellum. The illusion of victory in the United States, plus the reestablishment of peace, strengthened Madison's administration. His handpicked successor, James Monroe—former secretary of state and war—easily won the presidential election of 1816.   (F.McD.)

The United States from 1816 to 1850

THE ERA OF MIXED FEELINGS

The years between the election to the presidency of James Monroe in 1816 and of John Quincy Adams in 1824 have long been known in American history as the "Era of Good Feelings." The phrase was conceived by a Boston editor during Monroe's visit to New England early in his first term. That a representative of the heartland of Federalism could speak in such positive terms of the visit by a Southern president whose decisive election had marked not only a sweeping Republican victory but also the demise of the national Federalist Party was dramatic testimony that former foes were inclined to put aside the sectional and political differences of the past.

Effects of the War of 1812.   Later scholars have questioned the strategy and tactics of the United States in the War of 1812, the war's tangible results, and even the wisdom of commencing it in the first place. To contemporary Americans, however, the striking naval victories and Andrew Jackson's victory over the British at New Orleans created a reservoir of "good feeling" on which Monroe was able to draw.

Abetting the mood of nationalism was the foreign policy of the United States after the war. Florida was acquired from Spain (1819) in negotiations the success of which owed more to Andrew Jackson's indifference to such niceties as the inviolability of foreign borders and the nation's evident readiness to back him up than it did to diplomatic finesse. The Monroe Doctrine (1823) was actually a few phrases inserted in a long presidential message; its immediate effect on other nations was slight, and that on its own citizenry was impossible to gauge, yet its self-assured tone in warning off the Old World from the New reflected well the nationalist mood that swept the nation. Internally, the decisions of the Supreme Court under Chief Justice John Marshall in such cases as *McCulloch* v. *Maryland* (1819) and *Gibbons* v. *Ogden* (1824) promoted nationalism by strengthening Congress and national, or federal, power at the expense of the states. The congressional decision to charter the second Bank of the United States (1816) was explained in part by the nation's financial weaknesses, exposed by the War of 1812, and in part by the intrigues of financial interests. The readiness of Southern Jeffersonians—former strict constructionists—to support such a measure indicates, too, an amazing degree of national feeling. Perhaps the clearest sign of a new sense of national unity was the victorious Republican Party, standing in solitary splendour on the national political horizon, its long-time foes the Federalists vanished without a trace (on the national level), the Republican standard bearer elected so overwhelmingly in 1820 that it was long believed that the one electoral vote denied him had been held back only in order to preserve George Washington's record of unanimous selection.

Foreign
policy

National disunity.   For all the signs of national unity and feelings of oneness, equally convincing evidence points in the opposite direction. The very Supreme Court decisions that delighted friends of strong national government infuriated its opponents, while Marshall's defense of the rights of private property was construed by critics as betraying a predilection for one kind of property over another. The growth of the West was by no means regarded as an unmixed blessing. Eastern conservatives sought to keep land prices high, speculative interests opposed a policy that would be advantageous to poor squatters, politicians feared a change in the sectional balance of power, businessmen were wary of a new section with interests unlike their own. European visitors testified that, even during the so-called Era of Good Feelings, Americans characteristically expressed scorn for their countrymen in sections other than their own.

Opponents
of
nationalism

The causes of the financial panic in 1819 are complex. Far clearer was the tendency of its victims to blame it on one or another hostile or malevolent interest—whether the second Bank of the United States, Eastern capitalists, selfish speculators, or perfidious politicians—each charge expressing the bad feeling that existed side by side with the good. If harmony seemed to reign on the level of

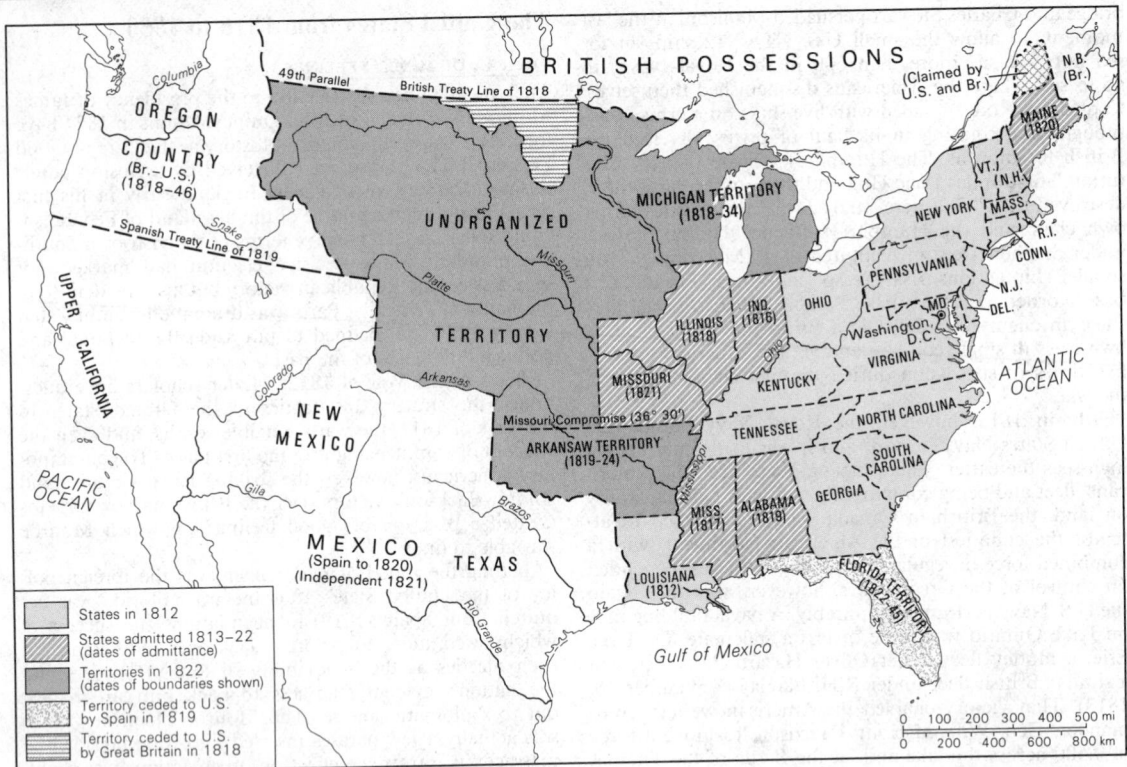

The United States, 1812–22.

national political parties, disharmony prevailed within the states. In the early-19th-century United States, local and state politics were typically waged less on behalf of great issues than for petty gain. That the goals of politics were often sordid did not mean that political contests were bland. In every section, state factions led by shrewd men waged bitter political warfare to attain or entrench themselves in power.

The most dramatic manifestation of national division was the political struggle over slavery, particularly over its spread into new territories. The Missouri Compromise of 1820 eased the threat of further disunity, at least for the time being—the sectional balance between the states was preserved; in the Louisiana Purchase, with the exception of the Territory of Missouri, slavery was to be confined to the area south of the 36° 30′ line. Yet astute men knew that this compromise did not end the crisis but only postponed it. The determination by Northern and Southern senators not to be outnumbered by one another suggests that the people continued to believe in the conflicting interests of the various great geographical sections. The weight of evidence indicates that the decade after the Battle of New Orleans was an era not of good feelings so much as it was one of mixed feelings.

THE ECONOMY

Economic growth and maturation

The American economy expanded and matured at a remarkable rate in the decades after the War of 1812. The rapid growth of the West created a great new centre for the production of grains and pork, permitting the nation's older sections to specialize in other crops. New processes of manufacture, particularly in textiles, not only accelerated an "industrial revolution" in the Northeast but, by drastically enlarging the Northern market for raw materials, helped account for a boom in Southern cotton production. If by midcentury the white South had come to regard slavery as a "positive good" rather than the "necessary evil" it had earlier held the system to be, it was due largely to the increasingly central role played by cotton in earning profits for the section; the cotton economy relied on slavery. Industrial workers organized the nation's first trade unions and even workingmen's political parties early in the period. The corporate form thrived in an era the booming capital requirements of which made older and simpler forms of attracting investment capi-

tal obsolete. Commerce became increasingly specialized, the division of labour in the disposal of goods for sale matching the increasingly sophisticated division of labour that had come to characterize production. Banks were created in unprecedented numbers, turning out quantities of paper money to meet the thriving economy's need for additional exchange. The fact that little coin or specie was actually kept in vaults to back up this paper explains both why many bank notes were discounted severely and why the state of the economy was typically unstable. A rage for speculation was widely noted by contemporaries, encouraged by an almost frighteningly rapid rise in real-estate values and in the production by state banks of large quantities of paper money on demand. Probably the most important changes occurred in the nation's system for moving people and goods. According to a number of later scholars, a "transportation revolution" was the key to almost all other economic changes in the period.

Transportation revolution. The controversial political issue of "internal improvements" focussed on a simple question: would national government finance local and state transportation projects? That some presidents hesitated, in the absence of explicit language in the Constitution urging federal support, had little effect in dampening the near-mania for such projects. More federal moneys were expended on them under Pres. Andrew Jackson (served 1829–37), who on this issue was a strict constructionist, than in the administrations of all previous presidents combined. Actually, most of the capital was raised by state governments, by private citizens, and from abroad. In their turn, turnpikes (or tollroads), canals, steamboats, and railroads inspired booms, typically featured by lack of planning, business failures, shoddy construction, profits that fell far short of expectations largely because costs exceeded anticipations, rampant corruption, and, withal, an improved transportation system that was the wonder of the world. The system did well the basic job that transportation was called on to do for a swiftly expanding region.

Waterways. Steamboats replaced rafts on the Mississippi and sharply reduced the price of Latin-American coffee in ports upstream by drastically cutting shipping time and expense. The Erie Canal, the most publicized as well as the most successful individual project constructed during the era, enabled efficient Western grain producers ultimately to undersell Eastern farmers in the distant

New York City market for similar reasons. Imitators of the Erie in Pennsylvania and throughout the South and West discovered, however, that canals were poor business propositions unless cheaply and efficiently built, heavily used, and spared from drought or flooding.

Railroads. A controversy has developed among scholars over the significance of railroads in antebellum America—one interpretation regards their development as the key to the era's industrialization, while another viewpoint holds that the West would have been developed as quickly and goods moved as cheaply without them. In any case, the speed and reliability of the "iron horse" attracted investors and, at first, passengers, seeking comfort in travel, rather than freight. By midcentury, however, the advantages of the new form, for all its expense, were luring shippers of industrial and agricultural products to use the nation's thousands of miles of railroad network.

Beginnings of industrialization. Agriculture remained an important industry in all sections, although a sectional division of labour became increasingly discernible at the era's end, spurred on by transportation and mechanical developments that permitted more productive areas to undersell their competitors even in the home markets of the latter. Nevertheless, New York and Pennsylvania in the Northeast and Kentucky and Tennessee in the South remained important producers of corn, wheat, and livestock even in the 1840s. The trend, however, was in the direction of specialization. Cotton became king, not only in the South but in the nation as a whole, because its sale overseas brought in more money than the sale of all other products combined. Slavery accordingly became more entrenched, despite the sharp rise in the price of slaves that marked the era. Econometricians have used detailed statistical evidence to challenge the ideas that slavery was unprofitable and that the South's overcommitment to cash crops was ruinous to its economy in the long run. Contemporary Southerners put ever more capital into the system that promised quick profits and a "social harmony" based on the total subordination of the slaves. Slavery was a complex system, particularly in cities, marked by the hiring out of tens of thousands of skilled slave artisans and by an amazing degree of free physical movement and personal behaviour displayed by slaves in such a city as New Orleans. When most of the country referred to slavery, however, they appeared to mean the plantation system based on the labour of hundreds of field hands, though, actually, a minority of Southern whites owned slaves.

By midcentury, factories accounted for most textile production in the northeastern states, while the factory system was beginning to spread across the states of the Ohio Valley. The labour organizations that sprang up in the nation's cities were composed not of machine hands but primarily of skilled mechanics. A major purpose of this movement was to enable their membership to withstand the spread of a system associated by labour spokesmen with speedup, the devaluation of skill, low wages, child and female labour, and a general debasement of the working class. The spread of the factory system was not to be deflected, however, not even by a movement that at its height claimed a membership of 300,000 (a claim that was undocumented and undoubtedly exaggerated). The labour movement was crushed not by industrialization but rather by a depression that followed financial panics in 1837 and 1839.

These panics, like the earlier crisis in 1819, illustrate well the erratic course of the American economy during the era. Growth was not unbroken. Overspeculation, inflation, governmental inaction in some instances or chicanery in others created an atmosphere of instability that was as characteristic of the era as were its tangible achievements. Hundreds of bank and business failures, large-scale unemployment, and hard times followed in the wake of these debacles, lasting in the latter case to the middle 1840s before the economy again moved forward, more productive than ever, to resume its upward thrust.

SOCIAL DEVELOPMENTS

In the decades before the Civil War (1861–65), the civilization of the United States exerted an irresistible pull on visitors, hundreds of whom were assigned to report back to European audiences that were fascinated by the new society and insatiable for information on every facet of the "fabled republic." What appeared to intrigue the travellers above all was the uniqueness of American society. In contrast to the relatively static and well-ordered civilization of the Old World, America seemed turbulent, dynamic, and in constant flux, its people crude but vital, awesomely ambitious, optimistic, and independent. Many well-bred Europeans were evidently taken aback by the self-assurance of lightly educated American common folk. Ordinary Americans seemed unwilling to defer to anyone on the basis of rank or status.

The people. American society was rapidly changing. Population grew at what to Europeans was an amazing rate—although it was the normal pace of American population growth for the antebellum decades—of between three-tenths and one-third a decade. After 1820 the rate of growth was not uniform throughout the country. New England and the Southern Atlantic states languished—the former region because it was losing settlers to the superior farmlands of the Western Reserve, the latter because its economy offered too few places to newcomers.

The special feature of the population increase of the 1830s and 1840s was the extent to which it was composed of immigrants. Whereas about 250,000 Europeans had come in the first three decades of the 19th century, ten times as many arrived between 1830 and 1850. The newcomers were overwhelmingly Irish and German. Travelling in family groups rather than as individuals, they were attracted by the dazzling opportunities of American life: abundant work, land, food, and freedom, on the one hand, and the absence of compulsory military service, on the other.

The German contingent did well, settling mostly on semi-improved farms and towns in the Ohio Valley, their success promoted by their relatively prosperous state on arrival and by the solid aid given newcomers by the efficient network of economic and cultural organizations founded by earlier German settlers. Irish immigrants, however, fared poorly; too poor to buy land, lacking in skills, disorganized, members of a faith considered alien and even dangerous by many native Americans, the Irish suffered various forms of ostracism and discrimination in the cities, where they tended to congregate. They provided the menial and unskilled labour needed by the expanding economy. Their low wages forced them to live in tightly packed slums, whose chief features were filth, disease, rowdyism, prostitution, drunkenness, crime, a high mortality rate, and the absence of even rudimentary toilet facilities. Adding to the woes of the first generation of Irish immigrants was the tendency of many disgruntled natives to treat the newcomers as scapegoats who allegedly threatened the future of American life and religion. In the North, only free blacks were treated worse.

Most Northern blacks possessed theoretical freedom and little else. Confined to menial occupations for the most part, they fought a losing battle against the inroads of Irish competition in northeastern cities. The struggle between the two groups erupted spasmodically into ugly street riots. The hostility shown free blacks by the general community was less violent but equally unremitting. Discrimination in politics, employment, education, housing, religion, and even in cemeteries resulted in a cruelly oppressive system. Unlike a slave, the free Northern Negro could criticize and petition against his subjugation, but this proved fruitless in preventing the continued deterioration of his situation.

Most Americans continued to live in the country. Although improved machinery had resulted in expanded farm production and had given further impetus to the commercialization of agriculture, the way of life of independent agriculturists had changed little by midcentury. The public journals put out by some farmers insisted that their efforts were unappreciated by the larger community. Private accounts kept by farmers pointed to lives marked by unremitting toil, little cash, and little leisure. To own land was an achievement beyond the expectations of their European counterparts; but in all sections of the country, much land and agricultural wealth was concentrated in the hands of a few farmers.

Marginal notes:

Trend toward industrial specialization

European interest in American life

German and Irish immigrants

Urban
expansion

Cities. Cities thrived during the era, their growth in population outstripping the spectacular growth rate of the nation as a whole. Urban expansion was not confined to New York City, Philadelphia, Charleston, or New Orleans; towns such as Syracuse, Natchez, St. Louis, Lexington, Pittsburgh, Chicago, and Cincinnati also flourished. And their importance and influence far transcended the relatively small proportions of citizens living in them. Whether on the "urban frontier" or in the older seaboard region, antebellum cities were the centres of wealth and political influence of their outlying hinterlands. New York City, with a population approaching 500,000 by midcentury, faced problems of a different order of magnitude from those confronting such cities as Poughkeepsie or Newark. Yet the pattern of change during the era was amazingly similar for eastern cities or western, old cities or new, great cities or small. The lifeblood of them all was commerce. Old ideals of economy in town government were grudgingly abandoned by the merchant, professional, and landowning elites that typically ruled. Taxes were increased in order to deal with pressing new problems and to enable the urban community of midcentury to realize new opportunities. Harbours were improved, police forces professionalized, services expanded, waste more reliably removed, streets improved, welfare activities broadened, all as the result of the statesmanship and the self-interest of property owners who were convinced that amelioration was socially beneficial.

Education and religion. Cities were also centres of educational and intellectual progress. The emergence of a relatively well-financed public educational system, free of the stigma of "pauper" or "charity" schools, and of a lively "penny press," made possible by a technological revolution, were among the most important developments. An evangelical movement that swept the Northeast and West before 1840 was largely an urban phenomenon. Cutting across Protestant denominational lines, the movement was regarded by many of its leaders as a struggle against satanic influences that thrived best in the secular atmosphere of cities. Influential merchants made generous contributions to this great "revival," which combined detailed, fiery exhortations against sin and the devil with a social message of unabashed conservatism. The urban wealthy had reason to find such a message useful.

Wealth. The brilliant French visitor Alexis de Tocqueville, in common with most contemporary observers, believed American society to be remarkably egalitarian.

Illusions
about
American
wealth

Most rich American men were thought to have been born poor; "self-made" was the term Henry Clay popularized for them. The society was allegedly a very fluid one, marked by the rapid rise and fall of fortunes, with room at the top accessible to all but the most humble; opportunity for success seemed freely available to all, and although material possessions were not distributed perfectly equally they were, in theory, dispersed so fairly that only a few poor and a few rich men existed at either end of the social spectrum.

The actuality, however, was far different. While the rich were inevitably not numerous, America by 1850 had more millionaires than all of Europe. New York, Boston, and Philadelphia had perhaps 1,000 individuals, each admitting to $100,000 or more, at a time when wealthy taxpayers kept secret from assessors the bulk of their wealth. Because an annual income of $4,000 or $5,000 enabled a man to live luxuriously, these were great fortunes indeed. Typically, the wealthiest 1 percent of urban citizens owned approximately one-half the wealth of the great cities of the Northeast, while the great bulk of their populations were worth little or nothing. In what has long been called the "Age of the Common Man," rich men were almost invariably born not into humble or poor families but into wealthy and prestigious ones. In western cities, too, class lines increasingly hardened after 1830. The common man lived in the age, but he did not dominate it. It appears that contemporaries, overimpressed with the absence of a titled aristocracy and with the democratic tone and manner of American life, failed to see the extent to which money, family, and status exerted power in the New World even as they did in the Old.

JACKSONIAN DEMOCRACY

The democratization of politics. American politics became increasingly democratic during the 1820s and 1830s. Local and state offices that had earlier been appointive became elective. The suffrage was expanded as property and other restrictions on voting were reduced or abandoned in most states. The freehold requirement that had denied voting to all but holders of real estate was almost everywhere discarded before 1820, while the taxpaying qualification was also removed, if more slowly and gradually. In many states a printed ballot replaced the earlier system of voice voting, while the secret ballot also grew in favour. Whereas in 1800 only two states provided for the popular choice of presidential electors, by 1832 only South Carolina still left the decision to the legislature. Conventions of elected delegates increasingly replaced legislative or congressional caucuses as the agencies for making party nominations. By the latter change, a system for nominating candidates by self-appointed cliques meeting in secret was replaced by a system of open selection of candidates by democratically elected bodies.

Extension
of voting
rights

These democratic changes were not engineered by Andrew Jackson and his followers, as was once believed. Most of them antedated the emergence of Jackson's Democratic Party, and in New York, Mississippi, and other states some of the reforms were accomplished over the objections of the Jacksonians. There were men in all sections who feared the spread of political democracy, but by the 1830s few were willing publicly to voice such misgivings. Jacksonians effectively sought to fix the impression that they alone were champions of democracy, engaged in mortal struggle against aristocratic opponents. The accuracy of such propaganda varied according to local circumstances. The great political reforms of the early 19th century in actuality were conceived by no one faction or party. The real question about these reforms concerns the extent to which they truly represented the victory of democracy in the United States.

Small cliques or entrenched "machines" dominated democratically elected nominating conventions as earlier they had controlled caucuses. While by the 1830s the common man—of white if not of black or red skin—had come into possession of the vote in most states, the nomination process continued to be outside his control. More importantly, the policies adopted by competing factions and parties in the states owed little to ordinary voters. The legislative programs of the "regencies" and juntos that effectively ran state politics were designed primarily to reward the party faithful and to keep them in power. State parties extolled the common people in grandiloquent terms but characteristically focussed on prosaic legislation that awarded bank charters or monopoly rights to construct transportation projects to favoured insiders. That American parties would be pragmatic vote-getting coalitions, rather than organizations devoted to high political principles, was due largely to another series of reforms enacted during the era. Electoral changes that rewarded winners or plurality gatherers in small districts, in contrast to a previous system that divided a state's offices among the several leading vote getters, worked against the chances of "single issue" or "ideological" parties while strengthening parties that tried to be many things to many men.

The status
of the
common
man

The Jacksonians. To his army of followers, Andrew Jackson was the embodiment of popular democracy. A truly self-made man of will and courage, he personified for many citizens the vast power of nature and providence, on the one hand, and the majesty of the people, on the other. His very weaknesses, such as a nearly uncontrollable temper, were political strengths. Opponents who branded him enemy to property and order only gave credence to the claim of Jackson's supporters that he stood for the poor against the rich, the plain people against the interests.

Jackson, like most of his leading antagonists, was in fact a wealthy man of conservative social beliefs. In his many volumes of correspondence he rarely referred to labour. As a lawyer and man of affairs in Tennessee prior to his accession to the presidency, he aligned himself not with have-nots but with the influential, not with the debtor but with the creditor. His reputation was created largely by astute men who propagated the belief that his party was the people's party and that the policies of his administrations were in the popular interest. Savage attacks on those policies by some wealthy critics only fortified the belief that the Jacksonian movement was radical as well as democratic.

Birth of the Democratic Party

At its birth in the middle 1820s, the Jacksonian, or Democratic Party was a loose coalition of diverse men and interests united primarily by a practical vision. They held to the twin beliefs that "Old Hickory," as Jackson was known, was a magnificent candidate and that his election to the presidency would benefit those who helped bring it about. His excellence as candidate derived in part from the fact that he appeared to have no known political principles of any sort. In this period there were no distinct parties on the national level. Jackson, Henry Clay, John C. Calhoun, John Quincy Adams, and William H. Crawford—the leading presidential aspirants—all portrayed themselves as "Republicans," followers of the party of the revered Jefferson. The National Republicans were the followers of Adams and Clay; the Whigs, who emerged in 1834, were, above all else, the party dedicated to the defeat of Jackson.

The major parties. The great parties of the era were thus created to attain victory for men rather than measures. Once in being, their leaders understandably sought to persuade the electorate of the primacy of principles. It is noteworthy, however, that former Federalists at first flocked to the new parties in largely equal numbers and that men on opposite sides of such issues as internal improvements or a national bank could unite behind Jackson. With the passage of time, the parties did come increasingly to be identified with distinctive, and opposing, political policies.

By the 1840s, Whig and Democratic congressmen voted as rival blocs. Whigs supported and Democrats opposed a weak executive, a new Bank of the United States, a high tariff, distribution of land revenues to the states, relief legislation to mitigate the effects of the depression, and federal reapportionment of House seats. Whigs voted against and Democrats approved an independent treasury, an aggressive foreign policy, and expansionism. These were important issues, capable of dividing the electorate just as they divided the major parties in Congress. Certainly it was significant that Jacksonians were more ready than their opponents to banish and use other forceful measures against the southern Indian tribes or to take punitive measures against blacks or abolitionists. But these differences do not substantiate the belief that the Democrats and Whigs were divided ideologically, with only the former somehow representing the interests of the propertyless.

Party lines earlier had been more easily broken. Jackson's firm opposition to Calhoun's policy of Nullification (*i.e.,* the right of a state to nullify a federal law) in 1828 had commanded wide support within and outside the Democratic Party. Clay's compromise solution to the crisis represented not an ideological split with Jackson but Clay's ability to conciliate and to draw political advantage from astute tactical manoeuvring.

Jackson's attack on the Bank of the United States

The Jacksonians depicted their war on the second Bank of the United States as a struggle against an alleged aristocratic monster that oppressed the West, debtor farmers, and poor people generally. Jackson's decisive re-election in 1832 was once interpreted as a sign of popular agreement with the Democratic interpretation of the bank war, but recent evidence discloses that Jackson's margin was hardly unprecedented and that Democratic success may have been due to other considerations. The second bank was evidently well thought of by many Westerners, many farmers, and even by Democratic politicians who admitted to opposing it primarily not to incur the wrath of Andrew Jackson.

Jackson's reasons for detesting the bank and Nicholas Biddle, its president, were complex. Anticapitalist ideology would not explain a Jacksonian policy that replaced a quasi-national bank as repository of government funds with dozens of state and private banks, equally controlled by capitalists and even more dedicated than was Biddle to profit making. The saving virtue of these "pet banks" appeared to be the Democratic political affiliations of their directors. Perhaps the pragmatism as well as the large degree of similarity between the Democrats and Whigs

is best indicated by their frank adoption of the "spoils system." The Whigs, while out of office, denounced the vile Democratic policy for turning lucrative custom-house and other posts over to supporters; but once in office they resorted to similar practices. It is of interest that the Jacksonian appointees were hardly more plebeian than were their so-called aristocratic predecessors.

Minor parties. The politics of principle was represented during the era not by the major parties but by the minor ones. The Anti-Masons aimed to stamp out an alleged aristocratic conspiracy. The Workingmen's Party called for "social justice." The Locofocos (so named after the matches they used to light up their first meeting in a hall darkened by their opponents) denounced monopolists in the Democratic Party and out. The variously named nativist parties accused the Roman Catholic Church of all manner of evil. The Liberty Party opposed the spread of slavery. All of these parties were ephemeral since they proved incapable of mounting a broad appeal that attracted masses of voters in addition to their original constituencies. The Democratic and Whig parties thrived not in spite of their opportunism but because of it, reflecting well the practical spirit that animated most American voters.

AN "AGE OF REFORM"

Historians have labelled the period 1830–50 an "age of reform." At the same time that the pursuit of the dollar was becoming so frenzied that some observers called it the nation's true religion, tens of thousands of Americans joined an array of movements dedicated to spiritual and secular uplift. There is not yet agreement as to why a rage for reform erupted in the antebellum decades. A few of the explanations cited, none of them conclusive, include an outburst of Protestant evangelicalism, a reform spirit that swept across the Anglo-American community, and a delayed reaction to the perfectionist teachings of the Enlightenment.

What is not in question is the amazing variety of reform movements that flourished simultaneously in the northern states—women's rights, pacifism, temperance, prison reform, abolition of imprisonment for debt, an end to capital punishment, improving the conditions of the working classes, a system of universal education, the organization of communities that discarded private property, improving the condition of the insane and the congenitally enfeebled, and the regeneration of the individual were among the causes that inspired zealots during the era.

Variety of reform movements

Abolitionism. There can be no doubt that antislavery, or "Abolition" as it came to be called, was the nonpareil reform. Abolition was a diverse phenomenon. At one end of its spectrum was William Lloyd Garrison, an "immediatist," who denounced not only slavery but the Constitution of the United States for tolerating the evil. His newspaper, *The Liberator,* lived up to its promise that it would not equivocate in its war against slavery. Garrison's uncompromising tone infuriated not only the South but many Northerners as well and was long treated as though it were typical of Abolitionism in general. Actually it was not. At the other end of the Abolitionist spectrum and in between stood such men and women as Theodore Weld, James Birney, Gerrit Smith, Theodore Parker, Julia Ward Howe, Lewis Tappan, Salmon P. Chase, and Lydia Maria Child, all of whom represented a variety of stances, all more conciliatory than Garrison's. James Russell Lowell, whose emotional balance has been cited by a recent biographer as proof that Abolitionists need not have been unstable, urged in contrast to Garrison that "the world must be healed by degrees."

Whether they were Garrisonians or not, Abolitionist leaders were scorned as cranks who were either working out their own personal maladjustments or as people using the slavery issue to restore a status that as an alleged New England elite they feared they were losing. The truth may be simpler. Few neurotics and few members of the northern socio-economic elite became Abolitionists. For all the movement's zeal and propagandistic successes, it was bitterly resented by many Northerners, and the masses of free whites were indifferent to its message. In the 1830s, urban mobs, typically led by "gentlemen of property and standing," stormed Abolitionist meetings,

The United States, 1822–54.

wreaking violence on the property and persons of blacks and their white sympathizers, evidently indifferent to the niceties distinguishing one Abolitionist theorist from another. It is a good question as to who betrayed greater emotional imbalance: those who attacked slavery with words or those whose hatred of such verbal attacks drove them to murder. That Abolition leaders were remarkably similar in their New England backgrounds, their Calvinist self-righteousness, their high social status, and the relative excellence of their educations is hardly evidence that their cause was either snobbish or elitist. Ordinary citizens were more inclined to loathe Negroes and to preoccupy themselves with personal advance within the system.

Support of reform movements.   The existence of many reform movements did not mean that a vast number of Americans supported them. Abolition did poorly at the polls. Some reforms were more popular than others, but by and large none of the major movements had mass followings. The evidence indicates that few persons actually participated in these activities. Utopian communities such as Brook Farm and those in New Harmony, Indiana, and Oneida, New York, did not succeed in winning over many followers or in inspiring many other groups to imitate their example. The importance of these and the other movements derived neither from their size nor their achievements. Reform reflected the sensitivity of a small number of persons to imperfections in American life. In a sense, the reformers were "voices of conscience," reminding their materialistic fellow citizens that the American Dream was not yet a reality, pointing to the gulf between the ideal and the actuality.

Religious-inspired reform.   A unique feature of antebellum reform was its religious character. Unlike European social critics of the same era, who were not only secular but often antireligious, American perfectionists were largely inspired by religious zeal. Not that religious enthu-

siasm was invariably identified with social uplift; many reformers were more concerned with saving souls than with curing social ills. The merchant princes who played active roles in—and donated large sums of money to—the Sunday school unions, home missionary societies, and Bible and tract societies did so in part because the latter organizations stressed spiritual rather than social improvement while teaching the doctrine of the "contented poor." In effect, conservatives who were strongly religious found no difficulty in using religious institutions to fortify their social predilections. Radicals, on the other hand, interpreted Christianity as a call to social action, convinced that true Christian rectitude could be achieved only in struggles that infuriated the smug and the greedy. Ralph Waldo Emerson was a nice example of the American reformer's insistence on the primacy of the individual. The great goal according to him was the regeneration of the human spirit, rather than a mere improvement in material conditions. Emerson and reformers like him, however, acted on the premise that consistency was indeed a hobgoblin of small minds, for they saw no contradiction in uniting with like-minded idealists to act out or argue for a new social model. The spirit was to be revived and strengthened through forthright social action undertaken by similarly independent individuals.

EXPANSIONISM AND POLITICAL CRISIS AT MIDCENTURY

Throughout the 19th century, eastern settlers kept spilling over into the Mississippi Valley and beyond, pushing the frontier farther westward. (In 1893 the historian Frederick Jackson Turner was to say that this ever-moving frontier was the most decisive influence on American civilization and values.) The Louisiana Purchase territory offered ample room to pioneers and those who came after. American wanderlust, however, was not confined to that area. Throughout the era Americans in varying numbers moved into regions south, west, and north of the Louisiana Territory. Because Mexico and Great Britain held or claimed most of these lands, dispute inevitably broke out between these governments and the United States.

Westward expansion. The growing nationalism of the American people was effectively engaged by Democratic presidents Jackson and James K. Polk (served 1845–49) and the expansionist Whig president John Tyler (served 1841–45) to promote their goal of enlarging the "empire for liberty." Each of these presidents performed shrewdly. Jackson waited until his last day in office to establish formal relations with the Republic of Texas, one year after his friend Sam Houston had succeeded in dissolving the ties between Mexico and the newly independent state of Texas. On the Senate's overwhelming repudiation of his proposed treaty of annexation, Tyler resorted to the use of a joint resolution so that each house could vote by a narrow margin for incorporation of Texas into the Union. Polk also succeeded in getting the British to negotiate a treaty (1846) whereby the Oregon Country south of the 49th latitude would revert to the United States. These were precisely the terms of his earlier proposal, which had been rejected by the British. Intent on securing the Mexican territories of New Mexico and upper California and ready to resort to almost any means to do so, Polk used a border incident as a pretext for commencing a war with Mexico. The war was not widely acclaimed and many congressmen disliked it, but few dared to oppose the appropriations that financed it.

The Mexican War

Although there is no evidence that these actions had anything like a public mandate, clearly they did not evoke widespread opposition. Nonetheless, the expansionists' assertion that Polk's election in 1844 could be construed as a popular clamour for the annexation of Texas was hardly a solid claim; Clay was narrowly defeated and would have won but for the defection from Whig ranks of small numbers of Liberty Party and nativist voters. The nationalistic idea, conceived in the 1840s by a Democratic editor, that it was the "manifest destiny" of the United States to expand westward to the Pacific undoubtedly prepared public opinion for the militant policies undertaken by Polk shortly thereafter. It has been said that this notion represented the mood of the American people; it is safer to say it reflected the feelings of many of the people.

Attitudes toward expansionism. Public attitudes toward expansion into Mexican territories were very much affected by the issue of slavery. Those opposed to the spread of slavery or simply not in favour of the institution joined Abolitionists in discerning a proslavery policy in the Mexican War. The great political issue of the postwar years concerned slavery in the territories. Calhoun and spokesmen for the slaveowning South argued that slavery could not be constitutionally prohibited in the Mexican cession. "Free Soilers" supported the Wilmot Proviso idea—that slavery should not be permitted in the new territory. Others supported the proposal that "squatter sovereignty" should prevail—settlers in the territories should decide the issue. Still others called for the extension westward of the 36°30′ line of demarcation for slavery that had resolved the Missouri controversy in 1820. Now, 30 years later, Henry Clay again pressed a compromise on the nation, supported dramatically by the aging Daniel Webster and by moderates in and out of the Congress. As the events in the California gold fields showed (beginning in 1849), many people had things other than political principles on their minds. The Compromise of 1850, as the separate resolutions resolving the controversy came to be known, infuriated those of high principle on both sides of the issue—Southerners resented California being admitted as a free state and the theoretical right given territories to deny existence to their "peculiar institution," while antislavery men deplored the same theoretical right of territories to permit the institution and abhorred the new, more stringent federal fugitive slave law. That Southern political leaders ceased talking secession shortly after the enactment of the compromise indicates who truly won the political skirmish. The people probably approved the settlement—but as subsequent events were to show, the issues had not been met but only deferred.   (E.Pe.)

Civil War

PRELUDE TO WAR, 1850–60

Before the Civil War, the United States experienced a whole generation of nearly unremitting political crisis. Underlying the problem was the fact that America in the early 19th century had been a country, not a nation. The major functions of government—those relating to education, transportation, health, and public order—were performed on the state or local level, and little more than a loose allegiance to the government in Washington, a few national institutions such as churches and political parties, and a shared memory of the Founding Fathers of the republic tied the country together. Within this loosely structured society every section, every state, every locality, every group could pretty much go its own way.

Gradually, however, changes in technology and in the economy were bringing all the elements of the country into steady and close contact. Improvements in transportation—first canals, then toll roads, and especially railroads—broke down isolation and encouraged the boy from the country to wander to the city, the farmer from New Hampshire to migrate to Iowa. Improvements in the printing press, which permitted the publication of penny newspapers, and the development of the telegraph system broke through the barriers of intellectual provincialism and made everybody almost instantaneously aware of what was going on throughout the country. As the railroad network proliferated, it had to have central direction and control; and national railroad corporations—the first true "big businesses" in the United States—emerged to provide order and stability.

Pre-Civil War changes that linked the states more closely

For many Americans the wrench from a largely rural, slow-moving, fragmented society in the early 1800s to a bustling, integrated, national social order in the midcentury was an abrupt and painful one; and they often resisted it. Sometimes resentment against change manifested itself in harsh attacks upon those who appeared to be the agents of change—especially immigrants, who seemed to personify the forces that were altering the older America. Vigorous nativist movements appeared in most cities during the 1840s; but not until the 1850s, when the huge numbers of Irish and German immigrants of the previous decade became eligible to vote, did the antiforeign fever reach its peak. Directed both against immigrants and against the Catholic Church, to which so many of them belonged, the so-called Know-Nothing movement emerged as a powerful political force in 1854 and increased the resistance to change.

Sectionalism and slavery. A more enduring manifestation of hostility toward the nationalizing tendencies in American life was the reassertion of strong feelings of sectional loyalty. New Englanders felt threatened by the West, which drained off the ablest and most vigorous members of the labour force and also, once the railroad network was complete, produced grain that undersold the products of the poor New England hill country. The West, too, developed a strong sectional feeling, blending its sense of its uniqueness, its feeling of being looked down upon as raw and uncultured, and its feeling that it was being exploited by the businessmen of the East.

Reassertion of sectional loyalty

The most conspicuous and distinctive section, however, was the South—an area set apart by climate; by a plantation system designed for the production of such staple crops as cotton, tobacco, and sugar; and, especially, by the persistence of Negro slavery, which had been abolished or prohibited in all other parts of the United States. It should not be thought that all or even most white Southerners were directly involved in the section's "peculiar institution." Indeed, in 1850 there were only 347,525 slaveholders in a total white population of about 6,000,000 in the slave states. Half of these owned four slaves or less and could not be considered planters. In the entire South there were fewer than 1,800 persons who owned more than 100 slaves.

Nevertheless, slavery did give a distinctive tone to the whole pattern of Southern life. If the large planters were few, they were also wealthy, prestigious, and powerful; often they were the political as well as the economic leaders of their section; and their values pervaded every stratum of Southern society. Far from opposing slavery, small farmers thought only of the possibility that they too might, with hard work and good fortune, some day join the ranks of the planter class—to which they were closely connected by ties of blood, marriage, and friendship. Behind this virtually unanimous support of slavery lay the universal belief—shared by many whites in the North and West as well—that blacks were an innately inferior people who had risen only to a state of barbarism in their native Africa and who could live in a civilized society only if disciplined through slavery. Though by 1860 there were in fact about 250,000 free blacks in the South, most Southern whites resolutely refused to believe that the slaves, if freed, could ever coexist peacefully with their former masters. With shuddering horror they pointed to an insurrection of blacks that had occurred in Santo Domingo, to a brief slave rebellion led by the Negro Gabriel in Virginia in 1800, to a plot of Charleston, South Carolina, blacks headed by Denmark Vesey in 1822, and, especially, to a bloody and determined Virginia insurrection led by Nat Turner in 1831 as evidence that black persons had to be kept under iron control. Facing increasing opposition to slavery outside their section, Southerners developed an elaborate "proslavery argument," defending the institution on biblical, economic, and sociological grounds.

A decade of political crises. In the early years of the republic, sectional differences had existed, but it had been possible to reconcile or ignore them because distances were great, communication was difficult, and the powerless national government had almost nothing to do. The revolution in transportation and communication, however, eliminated much of the isolation, and the victory of the United States in its brief war with Mexico left the national government with problems that required action.

Popular sovereignty. The Compromise of 1850 was an uneasy patchwork of concessions to all sides that began to fall apart as soon as it was enacted. Most unsatisfactory of all in the long run would be the principle of popular sovereignty, which was bound to make of each territory a battleground where the supporters of the South would contend with the defenders of the North and West.

The seriousness of those conflicts became clear in 1854, when Stephen A. Douglas introduced his Kansas–Nebraska bill in Congress. Unconcerned over the moral issue of slavery and desiring only to get on with the settling of the West and the construction of a transcontinental railroad, Douglas knew that the Southern senators would block the organization of Kansas as a free territory, as had been provided by the Missouri Compromise. Recognizing that the North and West had outstripped their section in population and hence in the House of Representatives, the Southerners clung desperately to an equality of votes in the Senate and were not disposed to welcome any new free states. Accordingly, Douglas thought that the doctrine of popular sovereignty, which had been applied to the territories gained from Mexico, might provide the legal justification needed to allow slavery in future states of the West that would ordinarily have become free states under the Missouri Compromise of 1820. Douglas' bill created the territories of Kansas and Nebraska out of the vast Indian reservations that lay between the Missouri River and the Rocky Mountains, but he included in his bill a provision that the territories of the United States should be allowed self-government in all matters of domestic importance including the slavery issue. This provision in effect allowed the territorial legislatures to mandate slavery in their areas and was directly contrary to the Missouri Compromise of 1820, by which slavery had been forever excluded from that part of the Louisiana Purchase lying north of 36°30′, an area that included the two new territories. With the backing of Pres. Franklin Pierce (served 1853–57), Douglas bullied, wheedled, and bluffed congressmen into passing his bill.

Polarization over slavery. Northern sensibilities were outraged. Disliking slavery, Northerners had made few efforts to change the South's "peculiar institution" so long as the republic was loosely articulated. (Indeed, when William Lloyd Garrison began his *Liberator* in 1831, urg-

Black insurrections

The Kansas–Nebraska bill

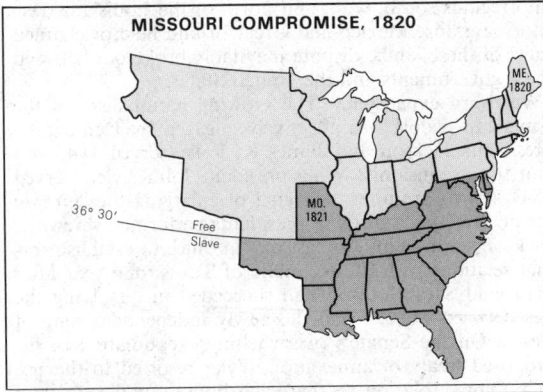

MISSOURI COMPROMISE, 1820

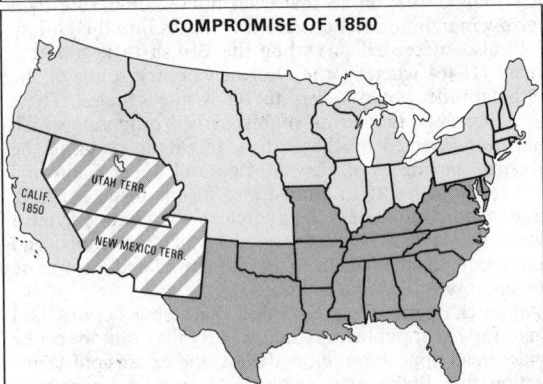

COMPROMISE OF 1850

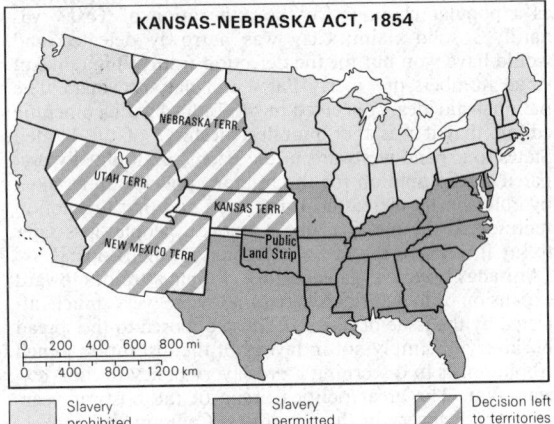

KANSAS-NEBRASKA ACT, 1854

| Slavery prohibited | Slavery permitted | Decision left to territories |

Compromises over extension of slavery into the territories.
By courtesy of Carnegie Institution

ing the immediate and unconditional emancipation of all slaves, he had only a tiny following; and a few years later he had actually been mobbed in Boston.) But with the sections, perforce, being drawn closely together, Northerners could no longer profess indifference to the South and its institutions. Sectional differences, centring on the issue of slavery, began to appear in every American institution. During the 1840s the major national religious denominations, such as the Methodists and the Presbyterians, split over the slavery question. The Whig Party, which had once allied the conservative businessmen of the North and West with the planters of the South, divided and virtually disappeared after the election of 1852. When Douglas' bill opened up to slavery Kansas and Nebraska—land that had long been reserved for the westward expansion of the free states—Northerners began to organize into an antislavery political party, called in some states the Anti-Nebraska Democratic Party, in others the People's Party, but in most places, the Republican Party.

Events of 1855 and 1856 further exacerbated relations between the sections and strengthened this new party. Kansas, once organized by Congress, became the field of battle between the free and the slave states in a contest in which concern over slavery was mixed with land speculation and office seeking. A virtual civil war broke out,

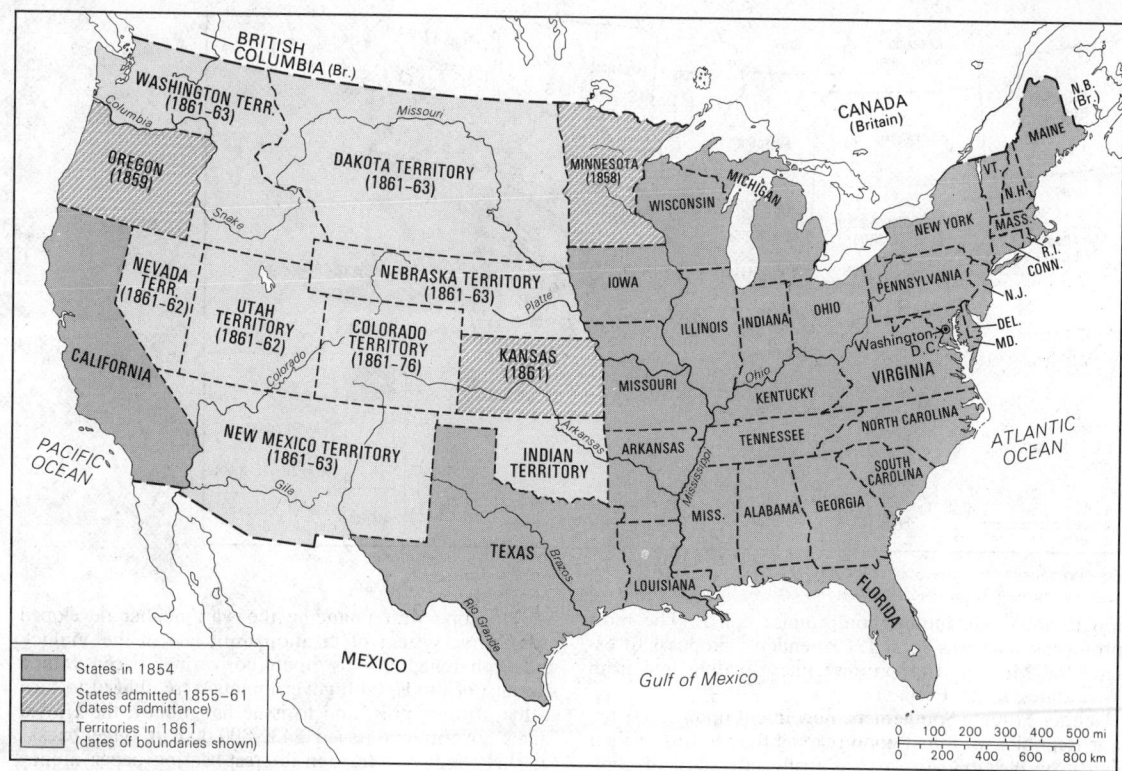

The United States, 1854–61.

with rival free-and slave-state legislatures both claiming legitimacy. During the turmoil, John Brown, a free-state partisan, on May 24–25, 1856, led a small party in a raid upon some proslavery settlers on Pottawatomie Creek, murdered five men in cold blood, and left their gashed and mutilated bodies as a warning to the slaveholders. As if to show that atrocities could be committed by both sides, almost simultaneously (May 22) a South Carolina congressman brutally attacked Sen. Charles Sumner of Massachusetts at his desk in the Senate chamber because of a speech he had given that presumably insulted the Carolinian's "honour." The 1856 presidential election made it clear that voting was becoming polarized along sectional lines. Though James Buchanan, the Democratic nominee, was elected, John C. Frémont, the Republican candidate, received a majority of the votes in the free states.

The following year the Supreme Court of the United States tried to solve the sectional conflicts that had baffled both the Congress and the President. Hearing the case **The Dred** of Dred Scott, a Missouri slave who claimed freedom on **Scott case** the ground that his master had taken him to live in free territory, the majority of the court, headed by Chief Justice Roger B. Taney, found that Negroes were not citizens of the United States and that Scott hence had no right to bring suit before the court. Taney also concluded that the U.S. laws prohibiting slavery in the territory were unconstitutional. Two Northern antislavery judges on the court bitterly attacked Taney's logic and his conclusions. Acclaimed in the South, the Dred Scott decision was condemned and repudiated throughout the North.

By this point many Americans, North and South, had come to the conclusion that slavery and freedom could not much longer coexist in the United States. For Southerners the answer was withdrawal from a Union that no longer protected their rights and interests; they had talked of it as early as the Nashville Convention of 1850, when the compromise measures were under consideration, and now more and more Southerners favoured secession. For Northerners the remedy was to change the social institutions of the South; few advocated immediate or complete emancipation of the slaves, but many felt that the South's "peculiar institution" must be contained. In 1858 William H. Seward, the leading Republican of New York, spoke of an "irrepressible conflict" between freedom and slavery; and in Illinois a rising Republican politician, Abraham

Lincoln, who unsuccessfully contested Douglas for a seat in the Senate, announced that "this government cannot endure, permanently half *slave* and half *free.*"

That it was not possible to end the agitation over slavery became further apparent in 1859 when John Brown, fresh from his crimes in Kansas, on the night of October 16, staged a raid on Harpers Ferry, Virginia (now in West Virginia), designed to free the slaves and, apparently, to help them begin a guerrilla war against the Southern whites. Though Brown was promptly captured and Virginia slaves gave no heed to his appeals, Southerners feared that this was the beginning of organized Northern efforts to undermine their social system. The fact that Brown, who may have been partially insane, was an inept strategist did not lessen Northern admiration for him.

The presidential election of 1860 occurred, therefore, in **Election** an atmosphere of great tension. Southerners, determined **of 1860** that their rights should be guaranteed by law, insisted upon a Democratic candidate willing to protect slavery in the territories; and they rejected Stephen A. Douglas, whose popular-sovereignty doctrine left the question in doubt, in favour of John C. Breckinridge. Douglas, backed by most of the Northern and border-state Democrats, ran on a separate Democratic ticket. Elderly conservatives, who deplored all agitation of the sectional questions but advanced no solutions, offered John Bell as candidate of the Constitutional Union Party. Republicans, confident of success, passed over the claims of Seward, who had accumulated too many liabilities in his long public career, and nominated Lincoln instead. Voting in the subsequent election was along markedly sectional patterns, with Republican strength confined almost completely to the North and West. Though Lincoln received only a plurality of the popular vote, he was an easy winner in the electoral college.

SECESSION AND THE POLITICS OF THE CIVIL WAR, 1860–65

The coming of the war. In the South, Lincoln's election was taken as the signal for secession, and on December 20 South Carolina became the first state to withdraw from the Union. Promptly the other states of the lower South followed. Feeble efforts on the part of Buchanan's administration to check secession failed, and one by one most of the federal forts in the Southern states were taken over by secessionists. Meanwhile, strenuous efforts in Washing-

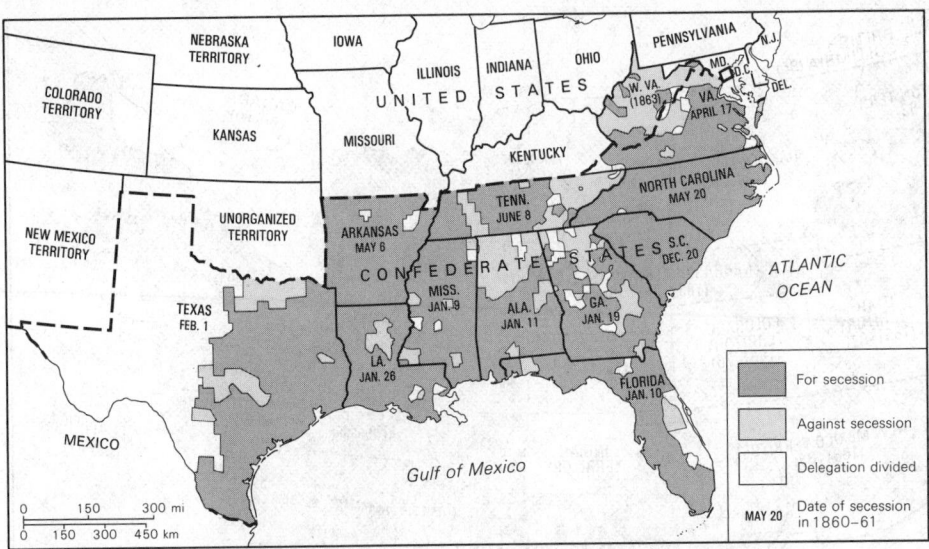

Vote on secession in the South by counties.

Adapted from R. Hofstadter, W. Miller, and D. Aaron, *The American Republic*, vol. 1, to 1865 (© 1959), by permission of Prentice-Hall, Inc.

ton to work out another compromise failed. (The most promising plan was John J. Crittenden's proposal to extend the Missouri Compromise line, dividing free from slave states, to the Pacific.)

Neither extreme Southerners, now intent upon secession, nor Republicans, intent upon reaping the rewards of their hard-won election victory, was really interested in compromise. On February 4, 1861—a month before Lincoln could be inaugurated in Washington—six Southern states (South Carolina, Georgia, Alabama, Florida, Mississippi, Louisiana) sent representatives to Montgomery, Alabama, to set up a new independent government. Delegates from Texas soon joined them. With Jefferson Davis of Mississippi at its head, the Confederate States of America came into being, set up its own bureaus and offices, issued its own money, raised its own taxes, and flew its own flag. Not until May 1861, after hostilities had broken out and Virginia had seceded, did the new government transfer its capital to Richmond.

Faced with a *fait accompli,* Lincoln when inaugurated was prepared to conciliate the South in every way but one; he would not recognize that the Union could be divided. The test of his determination came early in his administration, when he learned that the Federal troops under Maj. Robert Anderson in Ft. Sumter, South Carolina—then one of the few military installations in the South still in Federal hands—had to be promptly supplied or withdrawn. After agonized consultation with his cabinet, Lincoln determined that supplies must be sent even if doing so provoked the Confederates into firing the first shot. On April 12, 1861, just before Federal supply ships could reach the beleaguered Anderson, Confederate guns in Charleston opened fire upon Fort Sumter, and the war began.

The political course of the war. For the next four years the Union and the Confederacy were locked in conflict—by far the most titanic waged in the Western Hemisphere.

The policies pursued by the governments of Abraham Lincoln and Jefferson Davis were astonishingly similar. Both presidents at first relied upon volunteers to man the armies, and both administrations were poorly prepared to arm and equip the hordes of young men who flocked to the colours in the initial stages of the war. As the fighting progressed, both governments reluctantly resorted to conscription—the Confederates first, in early 1862, and the Federal government more slowly, with an ineffective measure of late 1862 followed by a more stringent law in 1863. Both governments pursued an essentially laissez-faire policy in economic matters, with little effort to control prices, wages, or profits. Only the railroads were subject to close government regulation in both regions; and the Confederacy, in constructing some of its own powder mills, made a few experiments in "state socialism." Neither Lincoln's nor Davis' administrations knew

how to cope with financing the war; neither developed an effective system of taxation until late in the conflict, and both relied heavily upon borrowing. Faced with a shortage of funds, both governments were obliged to turn to the printing press and to issue fiat money; the United States government issued $432,000,000 in "greenbacks" (as this irredeemable, non-interest-bearing paper money was called), while the Confederacy printed over $1,554,000,000 in such paper currency. In consequence, both sections experienced runaway inflation, which was much more drastic in the South, where, by the end of the war, flour sold at $1,000 a barrel.

Even toward slavery, the root cause of the war, the policies of the two warring governments were surprisingly similar. The Confederate Constitution, which was in most other ways similar to that of the United States, expressly guaranteed the institution of Negro slavery. Despite pressure from Abolitionists, Lincoln's administration was not disposed to disturb the "peculiar institution," if only because any move toward emancipation would upset the loyalty of Delaware, Maryland, Kentucky, and Missouri—the four slave states that remained in the Union.

Moves toward emancipation. Gradually, however, under the pressure of war, both governments moved to end slavery. Lincoln came to see that emancipation of the blacks would favourably influence European opinion toward the Northern cause, would deprive the Confederates of their productive labour force on the farms, and would add much-needed recruits to the Federal armies. In September 1862 he issued his preliminary proclamation of emancipation, promising to free all slaves in rebel territory by January 1, 1863, unless those states returned to the Union; and when the Confederates remained obdurate, he followed it with his promised final proclamation. A natural accompaniment of emancipation was the use of black troops, and by the end of the war the number of blacks who served in the Federal armies totalled 178,895. Uncertain of the constitutionality of his Emancipation Proclamation, Lincoln urged Congress to abolish slavery by constitutional amendment; but this was not done until January 31, 1865, and the actual ratification did not take place until after the war.

Meanwhile the Confederacy, though much more slowly, was also inevitably drifting in the direction of emancipation. The South's desperate need for troops caused many military men, including Robert E. Lee, to demand the recruitment of blacks; finally, in March 1865 the Confederate congress authorized the raising of Negro regiments. Though a few blacks were recruited for the Confederate armies, none actually served in battle because surrender was at hand. In yet another way Davis' government showed its awareness of slavery's inevitable end, when, in a belated diplomatic mission to seek assistance from Europe, the Confederacy in March 1865 promised to emancipate

Marginal notes:

Formation of the Confederacy

Manning and financing the armies

Lincoln's Emancipation Proclamation

the slaves in return for diplomatic recognition. Nothing came of the proposal, but it is further evidence that by the end of the war both North and South realized that slavery was doomed.

Sectional dissatisfaction. As war leaders, both Lincoln and Davis came under severe attack in their own sections. Both had to face problems of disloyalty. In Lincoln's case, the Irish immigrants to the Eastern cities and the Southern-born settlers of the Northwestern states were especially hostile to the Negro and, therefore, to emancipation, while many other Northerners became tired and disaffected as the war dragged on interminably. Residents of the Southern hill country, where slavery never had much of a foothold, were similarly hostile toward Davis. In order to wage war, both presidents had to strengthen the powers of central government, thus further accelerating the process of national integration that had brought on the war. Both administrations were, in consequence, vigorously attacked by state governors, who resented the encroachment upon their authority and who strongly favoured local autonomy.

The extent of Northern dissatisfaction was indicated in the congressional elections of 1862, when Lincoln and his party sustained a severe rebuff at the polls and the Republican majority in the House of Representatives was drastically reduced. Similarly in the Confederacy the congressional elections of 1863 went so strongly against the administration that Davis was able to command a majority for his measures only through the continued support of representatives and senators from the states of the upper South, which were under control of the Federal Army and consequently unable to hold new elections.

As late as August 1864, Lincoln despaired of his re-election to the presidency and fully expected that the Democratic candidate, Gen. George B. McClellan, would defeat him. Davis, at about the same time, was openly attacked by Alexander H. Stephens, the vice president of the Confederacy. But Federal military victories, especially William T. Sherman's capture of Atlanta, greatly strengthened Lincoln; and as the war came to a triumphant close for the North, he attained new heights of popularity. Davis' administration, on the other hand, lost support with each successive defeat, and in January 1865 the Confederate Congress insisted that he make Robert E. Lee the supreme commander of all Southern forces. (Some, it is clear, would have preferred to make the general dictator.)

(D.H.D.)

THE MILITARY BACKGROUND OF THE WAR

Comparison of North and South. At first glance it seemed that the 23 states of the Union were more than a match for the 11 seceding Southern states—South Carolina, Mississippi, Florida, Alabama, Georgia, Louisiana, Texas, Virginia, Arkansas, Tennessee, and North Carolina. There were approximately 21,000,000 people in the North compared with some 9,000,000 in the South (of whom about 3,500,000 were Negro slaves). In addition, the Federals possessed over 100,000 manufacturing plants as against 18,000 south of the Potomac River, and more than 70 percent of the railroads were in the North. Furthermore, the Union had at its command a 30-to-1 superiority in arms production, a 2-to-1 edge in available manpower, and a great preponderance in commercial and financial resources. It had a functioning government and a small but efficient regular army and navy.

But the Confederacy was not predestined to defeat. The Southern armies had the advantage of fighting on interior lines, and their military tradition had bulked large in the history of the United States before 1860. Moreover, the long Confederate coastline of 3,500 miles (5,600 kilometres) seemed to defy blockade; and the Confederate president, Jefferson Davis, hoped to receive decisive foreign aid and intervention. Finally, the gray-clad Southern soldiers were fighting for the intangible but strong objectives of home and white supremacy. So the Southern cause was not a lost one; indeed, other nations had won independence against equally heavy odds.

The high commands. Command problems plagued both sides. Of the two rival commanders in chief, most people in 1861 thought Davis to be abler than Lincoln. Davis

was a West Point graduate, a hero of the Mexican War, a capable secretary of war under Pres. Franklin Pierce, and a United States senator from Mississippi; whereas Lincoln—who had served in the Illinois state legislature and as an undistinguished one-term member of the U.S. House of Representatives—could boast of only a brief period of military service in the Black Hawk War, in which he did not do well.

As president and commander in chief of the Confederate forces, Davis revealed many fine qualities, including patience, courage, dignity, restraint, firmness, energy, determination, and honesty; but he was flawed by his excessive pride, hypersensitivity to criticism, and his inability to delegate minor details to his subordinates. To a large extent Davis was his own secretary of war, although five different men served in that post during the lifetime of the Confederacy. Davis himself also filled the position of general in chief of the Confederate armies until he named Robert E. Lee to that position on February 6, 1865, when the Confederacy was near collapse. In naval affairs—an area about which he knew little—the Confederate president seldom intervened directly, allowing the competent secretary of the navy, Stephen Mallory, to handle the Southern naval buildup and operations on the water. Although his position was onerous and perhaps could not have been filled so well by any other Southern political leader, Davis' overall performance in office left something to be desired.

To the astonishment of many, Lincoln grew in stature with time and experience, and by 1864 he had become a consummate war director. But he had much to learn at first, especially in strategic and tactical matters and in his choices of army commanders. With an ineffective first secretary of war—Simon Cameron—Lincoln unhesitatingly insinuated himself directly into the planning of military movements. Edwin M. Stanton, appointed to the secretaryship on January 20, 1862, was equally untutored in military affairs, and he was fully as active a participant as his superior.

Winfield Scott was the Federal general in chief when Lincoln took office. The 75-year-old Scott—a hero of the War of 1812 and of the Mexican War—was a magnificent and distinguished soldier whose mind was still keen in 1861. But he was physically incapacitated and had to be retired from the service on November 1, 1861. Scott was replaced by young George B. McClellan, an able and imaginative general in chief but one who had difficulty in establishing harmonious and effective relations with Lincoln. Because of this and because he had to campaign with his own Army of the Potomac, McClellan was relieved as general in chief on March 11, 1862. He was eventually succeeded on July 11 by the inept Henry W. Halleck, who held the position until replaced by Ulysses S. Grant on March 9, 1864. Halleck then became chief of staff under Grant in a long-needed streamlining of the Federal high command. Grant served efficaciously as general in chief throughout the remainder of the war.

After the initial call by Lincoln and Davis for troops and as the war lengthened indeterminately, both sides turned to raising massive armies of volunteers. Local citizens of prominence and means would organize regiments that were uniformed and accoutred at first under the aegis of the states and then mustered into the service of the Union and Confederate governments. As the war dragged on, the two governments had to resort to conscription to fill the ranks being so swiftly thinned by battle casualties.

Strategic plans. In the area of grand strategy, Davis persistently adhered to the defensive, permitting only occasional "spoiling" forays into Northern territory. Yet perhaps the Confederates' best chance of winning would have been an early grand offensive into the Union states before the Lincoln administration could find its ablest generals and bring the preponderant resources of the North to bear against the South.

Lincoln, on the other hand, in order to crush the rebellion and re-establish the authority of the Federal government, had to direct his blue-clad armies to invade, capture, and hold most of the vital areas of the Confederacy. His grand strategy was based on Scott's so-called Anaconda plan,

Margin notes:

Disloyalty to both presidents

Performances of Davis and Lincoln

Recruitment of troops

a design that evolved from strategic ideas discussed in messages between Scott and McClellan on April 27, May 3, and May 21, 1861. It called for a Union blockade of the Confederacy's littoral as well as a decisive thrust·down the Mississippi River and an ensuing strangulation of the South by Federal land and naval forces. But it was to take four years of grim, unrelenting warfare and enormous casualties and devastation before the Confederates could be defeated and the Union preserved.

THE LAND WAR

The war in 1861. The first military operations took place in northwestern Virginia, where non-slaveholding pro-Unionists sought to secede from the Confederacy. McClellan, in command of Federal forces in southern Ohio, advanced on his own initiative in the early summer of 1861 into western Virginia with about 20,000 men. He encountered smaller forces sent there by Lee, then in Richmond in command of all Virginia troops. Although showing signs of occasional hesitation, McClellan quickly won three small but significant battles: at Philippi on June 3, at Rich Mountain on July 11, and at Carrick's (or Corrick's) Ford on July 13. McClellan's casualties were light, and his victories went far toward eliminating Confederate resistance in northwestern Virginia and paving the way for the admittance into the Union of the new state of West Virginia in 1863.

Meanwhile, sizable armies were gathering around the Federal capital of Washington, D.C., and the Confederate capital of Richmond, Virginia. Federal forces abandoned Harpers Ferry on April 18, and it was quickly occupied by Southern forces, who held it for a time. The Federal naval base at Norfolk fell into enemy hands on April 20. On May 6 Lee ordered a Confederate force—soon to be commanded by Beauregard—northward to hold the rail hub of Manassas Junction, some 26 miles (42 kilometres) southwest of Washington. With Lincoln's approval, Scott appointed Irvin McDowell to command the main Federal army, being hastily collected near Washington. But

political pressure and Northern public opinion impelled Lincoln, against Scott's advice, to order McDowell's still-untrained army forward to push the enemy back from Manassas. Meanwhile, Federal forces were to hold Confederate soldiers under Joseph E. Johnston in the Shenandoah Valley near Winchester, thus preventing them from reinforcing Beauregard along the Bull Run near Manassas.

First Bull Run

McDowell advanced from Washington on July 16 with nearly 35,000 men and moved slowly toward Bull Run. Two days later a reconnaissance in force was repulsed by the Confederates at Mitchell's and Blackburn's Fords, and when McDowell finally attacked on July 21 in the First Battle of Bull Run (or Manassas), he discovered that Johnston had escaped the Federals in the Valley and had joined Beauregard near Manassas just in time, bringing the total Confederate force to around 32,000. McDowell's sharp attacks with green troops forced the equally untrained Southerners back a bit, but a strong defensive stand by Jackson (who thereby gained the nickname "Stonewall") enabled the Confederates to check and finally throw back the Federals that afternoon. The Federal retreat to Washington soon became a rout. McDowell lost 2,708 men—killed, wounded, and missing (including prisoners)—against a Southern loss of 1,981. Both sides now settled down to a long war.

The war in the East in 1862. Fresh from his victories in western Virginia, McClellan was called to Washington to replace Scott. There he began to mold the Army of the Potomac into a resolute, effective shield and sword of the Union. But personality clashes and unrelenting opposition to McClellan from the Radical Republicans in Congress hampered the sometimes tactless, conservative, Democratic general. It took time to drill, discipline, and equip this force of considerably more than 100,000 men, but as fall blended into winter loud demands arose that McClellan advance against Johnston's Confederate forces at Centreville and Manassas. McClellan, however, fell seriously ill with typhoid fever in December, and when he had recovered weeks later he found that Lincoln, desperately

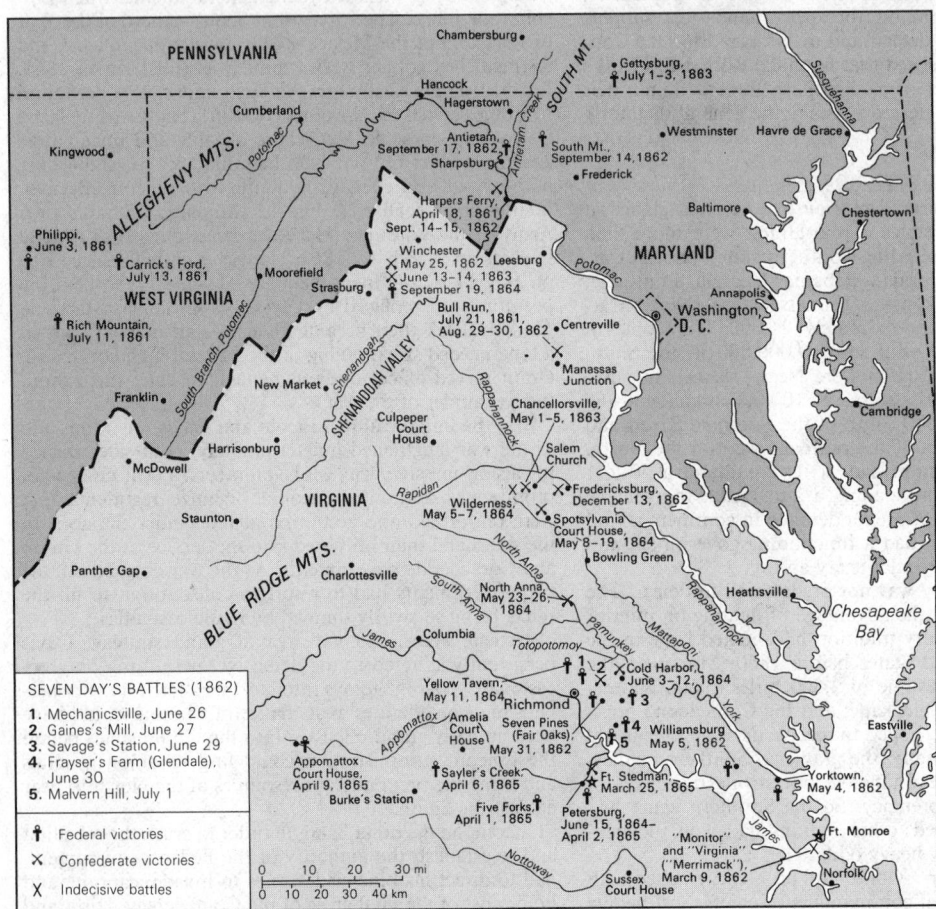

The main area of the eastern campaigns, 1861–65.

eager for action, had ordered him to advance on February 22, 1862. Long debates ensued between President and Commander. When in March McClellan finally began his Peninsular Campaign, he discovered that Lincoln and Stanton had withheld large numbers of his command in front of Washington for the defense of the capital—forces that were actually not needed there. Upon taking command of the army in the field, McClellan was relieved of the duties of general in chief.

The Peninsular Campaign. Advancing up the historic peninsula between the York and James rivers, McClellan began a month-long siege of Yorktown and captured that stronghold on May 4, 1862. A Confederate rearguard action at Williamsburg the next day delayed the blue-clads, who then slowly moved up through heavy rain to within four miles of Richmond. Striving to seize the initiative, Johnston attacked McClellan's left wing at Seven Pines (Fair Oaks) on May 31 and, after scoring initial gains, was checked; Johnston was severely wounded, and Lee, who had been serving as Davis' military adviser, succeeded Johnston in command of the Army of Northern Virginia. McClellan counterattacked on June 1 and forced the Southerners back into the environs of Richmond. The Federals suffered a total of 5,031 casualties out of a force of nearly 100,000, while the Confederates lost 6,134 of about 74,000 men.

As McClellan inched forward toward Richmond in June, Lee prepared a counterstroke. He recalled from the Shenandoah Valley Jackson's forces—which had threatened Harpers Ferry and had brilliantly defeated several scattered Federal armies—and, with about 90,000 soldiers, attacked McClellan on June 26 to begin the fighting of the Seven Days' Battles (usually dated June 25–July 1). In the ensuing days at Mechanicsville, Gaines's Mill, Savage's Station, Frayser's Farm (Glendale), and Malvern Hill, Lee tried unsuccessfully to crush the Army of the Potomac, which McClellan was moving to another base on the James River; but the Confederate chieftain had at least saved Richmond. McClellan inflicted 20,614 casualties on Lee while suffering 15,849 himself. McClellan felt he could not move upon Richmond without considerable reinforcement, and against his protests his army was withdrawn from the peninsula to Washington by Lincoln and the new general in chief, Halleck. Many of McClellan's units were given to a new Federal Army commander, John Pope, who was directed to move overland against Richmond.

Second Battle of Bull Run (Manassas) and Antietam. Pope advanced confidently toward the Rappahannock River with his army of Virginia, while Lee, once McClellan had been pulled back from near Richmond, moved northward to confront Pope before the latter could be joined by all of McClellan's troops. Daringly splitting his army, Lee sent Jackson to destroy Pope's base at Manassas, while he himself advanced via another route with James Longstreet's half of the army. Pope opened the Second Battle of Bull Run (in the South, Second Manassas) on August 29 with heavy but futile attacks on Jackson. The next day Lee arrived and crushed the Federal left with a massive flank assault by Longstreet, which, combined with Jackson's counterattacks, drove the Northerners back in rout upon Washington. Pope lost 16,054 men out of a force of more than 70,000, while Lee lost 9,197 out of about 55,000. With the Federal soldiers now lacking confidence in Pope, Lincoln relieved him and merged his forces with McClellan's Army of the Potomac.

Lee followed up his advantage with his first invasion of the North, pushing as far as Frederick, Maryland. McClellan had to reorganize on the march, a task that he performed capably. But he was beset by contradictory orders: Lincoln urged him to pursue Lee more swiftly; Halleck directed him to slow down and to stay closer to Washington. Biding his time, McClellan pressed forward and wrested the initiative from Lee by attacking and defeating a Confederate force at three gaps of the South Mountain between Frederick and Hagerstown on September 14. Lee fell back into a cramped position along the Antietam Creek, near Sharpsburg, Maryland. After a delay, McClellan struck the Confederates on September 17 in the bloodiest single-day's battle of the war. Although gaining some ground, the Federals were unable to drive the Confederate Army into the Potomac; but Lee was compelled to retreat back into Virginia. At Antietam, McClellan lost 12,410 of some 69,000 engaged, while Lee lost 13,724 of 52,000 effectives. When McClellan was unable to pursue Lee as quickly as Lincoln and Halleck thought he should, he was replaced in command by Ambrose E. Burnside, who had been an ineffective corps commander at Antietam.

Fredericksburg. Burnside delayed for a number of weeks before marching his reinforced army of 120,281 men to a point across the Rappahannock River from Fredericksburg, Virginia. On December 13 he ordered a series of 16 hopeless, piecemeal, frontal assaults across open ground against Lee's army of 78,513 troops, drawn up in an impregnable position atop high ground and behind a stone wall; the Federals were repelled with staggering losses. Burnside had lost 12,653 men, compared to Lee's 5,309. The plunging Federal morale was reflected in an increasing number of desertions. Therefore, on January 25, 1863, Lincoln replaced Burnside with a proficient corps commander, Joseph ("Fighting Joe") Hooker, who was a harsh critic of other generals and even of the President. Both armies went into winter quarters near Fredericksburg.

The war in the West in 1862. Military events, meanwhile, were transpiring in other arenas.

Trans-Mississippi theatre and Missouri. In the Trans-Mississippi theatre covetous Confederate eyes were cast on California, where ports for privateers could be seized, as could gold and silver to buttress a sagging treasury. Led by Henry Sibley, a Confederate force of some 2,600 invaded the Union's Department of New Mexico, where the Federal commander, Edward Canby, had but 3,810 men to defend the entire vast territory. Although plagued by pneumonia and smallpox, Sibley bettered a Federal force on February 21, 1862, at Valverde and captured Albuquerque and Sante Fe on March 23. But at the crucial engagement of La Glorieta Pass (known also as Apache Canyon, Johnson's Ranch, or Pigeon's Ranch) a few days later, Sibley was checked and lost most of his wagon train. He had to retreat into Texas, where he reached safety in April but with only 900 men and seven of 337 supply wagons left.

Farther eastward, in the more vital Mississippi Valley, operations were unfolding as large and as important as those on the Atlantic seaboard. Commanders there—especially on the Federal side—had greater autonomy than those in Virginia. Missouri and Kentucky were key border states that Lincoln had to retain within the Union orbit. Affairs began inauspiciously for the Federals in Missouri when Federal general Nathaniel Lyon's 5,000 troops were defeated at Wilson's Creek on August 10, 1861, by a Confederate force of more than 10,000 under Sterling Price and Benjamin McCulloch, each side losing some 1,200 men. But the Federals under Samuel Curtis decisively set back a gray-clad army under Earl Van Dorn at Pea Ridge (Elkhorn Tavern), Arkansas, on March 7–8, 1862, saving Missouri for the Union and threatening Arkansas.

Operations in Kentucky and Tennessee. The Confederates to the east of Missouri had established a unified command under Albert Sidney Johnston, who manned, with only 40,000 men, a long line running in Kentucky from near Cumberland Gap on the east through Bowling Green, to Columbus on the Mississippi. Numerically superior Federal forces cracked this line in early 1862. First, George H. Thomas smashed Johnston's right flank at Mill Springs (Somerset), Kentucky, on January 19. Then, in February, Grant, assisted by Federal gunboats commanded by Andrew H. Foote and acting under Halleck's orders, ruptured the centre of the Southern line in Kentucky by capturing Ft. Henry on the Tennessee River and Fort Donelson, 11 miles (18 kilometres) to the east on the Cumberland River. The Confederates suffered more than 16,000 casualties at the latter stronghold—most of them taken prisoner—as against Federal losses of less than 3,000. Johnston's left anchor fell when Pope seized New Madrid and Island Number Ten in the Mississippi in March and April. This forced Johnston to withdraw his remnants quickly from Kentucky through Tennessee and to reorganize them for a counterstroke. This seemingly impossible task he performed splendidly.

Federal threat to Richmond

Lee's first invasion of the North

Fighting in New Mexico

The Confederate onslaught came at Shiloh, Tennessee, near Pittsburg Landing, to which point on the west bank of the Tennessee River Grant and William T. Sherman had incautiously advanced. In a herculean effort, Johnston had pulled his forces together and, with 40,000 men, suddenly struck a like number of unsuspecting Federals on April 6. Johnston hoped to crush Grant before the arrival of Don Carlos Buell's 20,000 Federal troops, approaching from Nashville. A desperate combat ensued, with Confederate assaults driving the Unionists perilously close to the river. But at the height of success, Johnston was mortally wounded; the Southern attack then lost momentum, and Grant held on until reinforced by Buell. On the following day the Federals counterattacked and drove the Confederates, now under Beauregard, steadily from the field, forcing them to fall back to Corinth, in northern Mississippi. Grant's victory cost him 13,047 casualties, compared to Southern losses of 10,694. Halleck then assumed personal command of the combined forces of Grant, Buell, and Pope and inched forward to Corinth, which the Confederates evacuated on May 30.

Beauregard, never popular with Davis, was superseded by Braxton Bragg, one of the President's favourites. Bragg was an effective drillmaster and organizer; but he was also a martinet who was disliked by a number of his principal subordinates. Leaving 22,000 men in Mississippi under Price and Van Dorn, Bragg moved through Chattanooga with 30,000, hoping to reconquer Tennessee and carry the war into Kentucky. Some 18,000 other Confederate soldiers under Edmund Kirby Smith were at Knoxville. Buell led his Federal force northward to save Louisville and force Bragg to fight. Occupying Frankfort, Bragg failed to move promptly against Louisville. In the ensuing Battle of Perryville on October 8, Bragg, after an early advantage, was halted by Buell and impelled to fall back to a point south of Nashville. Meanwhile, the Federal general William S. Rosecrans had checked Price and Van Dorn at Iuka on September 19 and had repelled their attack on Corinth on October 3–4.

Buell—like McClellan a cautious, conservative, Democratic general—was, despite his success at Perryville, relieved of his command by Lincoln on October 24. His successor, Rosecrans, had to safeguard Nashville and to move southeastward against Bragg's army at Murfreesboro. He did so, with partial success, bringing on the bloody Battle of Stones River (or Murfreesboro, December 31, 1862–January 2, 1863). Again, after first having the better of the combat, Bragg was finally contained and forced to retreat. Of some 41,400 men, Rosecrans lost 12,906, while Bragg suffered 11,739 casualties out of about 34,700 effectives. Although it was a strategic victory for Rosecrans, his army was so shaken that he felt unable to advance again for five months, despite the urgings of Lincoln and Halleck.

The war in the East in 1863. In the East, after both armies had spent the winter in camp, the arrival of the active 1863 campaign season was eagerly awaited—especially by Hooker. "Fighting Joe" had capably reorganized and refitted his army, the morale of which was high once again. This massive host numbered around 132,000—the largest formed during the war—and was termed by Hooker "the finest army on the planet." It was opposed by Lee with about 62,000. Hooker decided to move most of his army up the Rappahannock, cross, and come in upon the Confederate rear at Fredericksburg, while John Sedgwick's smaller force would press Lee in front.

Chancellorsville. Beginning his turning movement on April 27, 1863, Hooker masterfully swung around toward the west of the Confederate Army; thus far he had apparently outmanoeuvred Lee. But Hooker was astonished on May 1 when the Confederate commander suddenly moved the bulk of his army directly against him. "Fighting Joe" lost his nerve and pulled back to Chancellorsville in the Wilderness, where the superior Federal artillery could not be used effectively.

Lee followed up on May 2 by sending Jackson on a brilliant flanking movement against Hooker's exposed right flank. Bursting like a thunderbolt upon Oliver O. Howard's 11th Corps late in the afternoon, Jackson crushed this wing; while continuing his advance, Jackson was accidentally and fatally wounded by his own men. This helped stall the Confederate advance. Lee then resumed the attack on the morning of May 3 and slowly pushed Hooker back; the latter was wounded by Southern artillery fire. That afternoon Sedgwick drove Jubal Early's Southerners from Marye's Heights at Fredericksburg, but Lee countermarched his weary troops, fell upon Sedgwick at Salem Church, and forced him back to the north bank of the Rappahannock. Lee then returned to Chancellorsville to resume the main engagement; but Hooker, though he had 37,000 fresh troops available, gave up the contest on May 5 and retreated across the river to his old position opposite Fredericksburg. The Federals suffered 17,278 casualties at Chancellorsville, while the Confederates lost 12,764.

Gettysburg. While both armies were licking their wounds and reorganizing, Hooker, Lincoln, and Halleck debated Union strategy. They were thus engaged when Lee launched his second invasion of the North on June 5, 1863. His advance elements moved down the Shenandoah Valley toward Harpers Ferry, brushing aside small Federal forces near Winchester. Marching through Maryland into Pennsylvania, the Confederates reached Chambersburg and turned eastward. They occupied York and menaced Carlisle and Harrisburg. Meanwhile, the dashing Confederate cavalryman, J.E.B. ("Jeb") Stuart, set off on a questionable ride around the Federal Army and was unable to join Lee's main army until the second day at Gettysburg.

Hooker—on unfriendly terms with Lincoln and especially Halleck—ably moved the Federal forces northward, keeping between Lee's army and Washington. Reaching Frederick, Hooker requested that the nearly 10,000-man Federal garrison at Harpers Ferry be added to his field army. When Halleck refused, Hooker resigned his command and was succeeded by George Gordon Meade, the commander of the Fifth Corps. Meade was granted a greater degree of freedom of movement than Hooker had enjoyed, and he carefully felt his way northward, looking for the enemy.

Learning to his surprise on June 28 that the Federal Army was north of the Potomac, Lee hastened to concentrate his far-flung legions. Hostile forces came together unexpectedly at the important crossroads town of Gettysburg, in southern Pennsylvania, bringing on the greatest battle ever fought in the Western Hemisphere. Attacking on July 1 from the west and north with 28,000 men, Confederate forces finally prevailed after nine hours of desperate fighting against 18,000 Federal soldiers under John F. Reynolds. When Reynolds was killed, Abner Doubleday ably handled the outnumbered Federal troops, and only the sheer weight of Confederate numbers forced him back through the streets of Gettysburg to strategic Cemetery Ridge south of town, where Meade assembled the rest of the army that night.

On the second day of battle Meade's 88,289 troops were ensconced in a strong, fishhook-shaped defensive position, running northward from the Round Tops hills along Cemetery Ridge and thence eastward to Culp's Hill. Lee, with 75,000 troops, ordered Longstreet to attack the Federals diagonally from Little Round Top northward and Richard S. Ewell to assail Cemetery Hill and Culp's Hill. The Confederate attack, coming in the late afternoon and evening, saw Longstreet capture the positions known as the Peach Orchard, Wheat Field, and Devil's Den on the Federal left in furious fighting but fail to seize the vital Little Round Top. Ewell's later assaults on Cemetery Hill failed, and he could capture only a part of Culp's Hill.

On the morning of the third day, Meade's right wing drove the Confederates from the lower slopes of Culp's Hill and checked Stuart's cavalry sweep to the east of Gettysburg in midafternoon. Then, in what has been called the greatest infantry charge of history, Lee—against Longstreet's advice—hurled 15,000 soldiers, under the immediate command of George E. Pickett, against the centre of Meade's lines on Cemetery Ridge, following a fearful artillery duel of two hours. Despite heroic efforts, only several hundred Southerners temporarily cracked the Federal centre at the so-called High-Water Mark; the rest were shot down by Federal cannoneers and musketrymen, captured, or thrown back, suffering casualties of almost

60 percent. Meade felt unable to counterattack, and Lee conducted an adroit retreat into Virginia. The Confederates had lost 28,063 men at Gettysburg, the Federals, 23,049. After indecisive manoeuvring and light actions in northern Virginia in the fall of 1863, the two armies went into winter quarters. Never again was Lee able to mount a full-scale invasion of the North with his entire army.

The war in the West in 1863. *Arkansas and Vicksburg.* In Arkansas, Federal troops under Frederick Steele moved upon the Confederates and defeated them at Prairie Grove, near Fayetteville, on December 7, 1862—a victory that paved the way for Steele's eventual capture of Little Rock the next September.

More importantly, Grant, back in good graces following his undistinguished performance at Shiloh, was authorized to move against the Confederate "Gibraltar of the West"—Vicksburg, Mississippi. This bastion was difficult to approach; Adm. David G. Farragut, Grant, and Sherman had failed to capture it in 1862. In the early months of 1863, in the so-called Bayou Expeditions, Grant was again frustrated in his efforts to get at Vicksburg from the north. Finally, escorted by Adm. David Dixon Porter's gunboats, which ran the Confederate batteries at Vicksburg, Grant landed his army to the south at Bruinsburg on April 30, 1863, and pressed northeastward. He won small but sharp actions at Port Gibson, Raymond, and Jackson, while the Confederate defender of Vicksburg, John C. Pemberton, was unable to link up with a smaller Southern force under Joseph E. Johnston near Jackson.

Turning due westward toward the rear of Vicksburg's defenses, Grant smashed Pemberton's army at Champion's Hill and the Big Black River and invested the fortress. During his 47-day siege, Grant eventually had an army of 71,000; Pemberton's command numbered 31,000, of whom 18,500 were effectives. After a courageous stand, the outnumbered Confederates were forced to capitulate on July 4. Five days later, 6,000 Confederates yielded to Nathaniel P. Banks at Port Hudson, Louisiana, to the

Grant's siege of Vicksburg

south of Vicksburg, and Lincoln could say, in relief, "The Father of Waters again goes unvexed to the sea."

Chickamauga and Chattanooga. Meanwhile, 60,000 Federal soldiers under Rosecrans sought to move out from central Tennessee against the important Confederate rail and industrial centre of Chattanooga in the southeastern corner of the state, then held by Bragg with some 43,000 troops. In a series of brilliantly conceived movements, Rosecrans manoeuvred Bragg out of Chattanooga without having to fight a battle. Bragg was then bolstered by Longstreet's veteran corps, sent swiftly by rail from Lee's army in Virginia. With this reinforcement, Bragg turned on Rosecrans and, in a vicious two-day battle (September 19–20) at Chickamauga Creek, Georgia, just southeast of Chattanooga, gained one of the few Confederate victories in the West. Bragg lost 18,454 of his 66,326 men; Rosecrans, 16,170 out of 53,919 engaged. Rosecrans fell back into Chattanooga, where he was almost encircled by Bragg.

But the Southern success was short-lived. Instead of pressing the siege of Chattanooga, Bragg sent Longstreet off in a futile attempt to capture Knoxville, then being held by Burnside. When Rosecrans showed signs of disintegration, Lincoln replaced him with Grant and strengthened the hard-pressed Federal Army at Chattanooga by sending, by rail, the remnants of the Army of the Potomac's 11th and 12th Corps, under Hooker's command. Outnumbering Bragg now 56,359 to 46,165, Grant attacked on November 23–25, capturing Lookout Mountain and Missionary Ridge, defeating Bragg's army and driving it southward toward Dalton, Georgia. Grant sustained 5,824 casualties at Chattanooga and Bragg, 6,667. Confidence having been lost in Bragg by most of his top generals, Davis replaced him with Joseph E. Johnston. Both armies remained quiescent until the following spring.

The war in 1864–65. Finally dissatisfied with Halleck as general in chief and impressed with Grant's victories, Lincoln appointed Grant to supersede Halleck and to assume the rank of lieutenant general, which Congress had

Grant's appointment as Federal general in chief

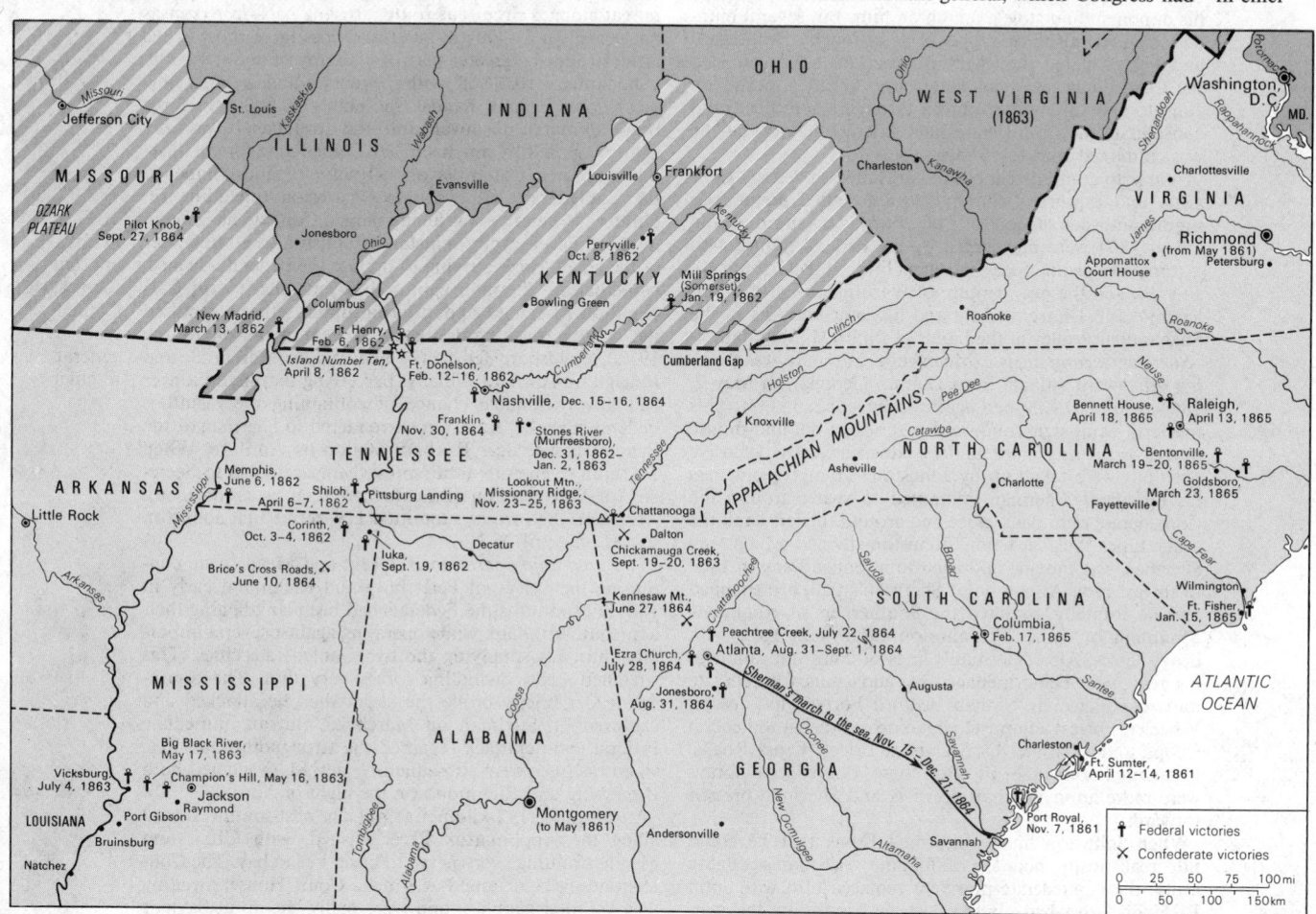

The main area of the Western and Carolinas campaigns, 1861–65.

re-created. Leaving Sherman in command in the West, Grant arrived in Washington on March 8, 1864. He was given largely a free hand in developing his grand strategy. He retained Meade in technical command of the Army of the Potomac but in effect assumed direct control of it by establishing his own headquarters with it. He sought to move this army against Lee in northern Virginia while Sherman marched against Johnston and Atlanta. Several lesser Federal armies were also to advance in May.

Grant's overland campaign. Grant surged across the Rapidan and Rappahannock rivers on May 4, hoping to get through the tangled Wilderness before Lee could move. But the Confederate leader reacted instantly and, on May 5, attacked Grant from the west in the Battle of the Wilderness. Two days of bitter, indecisive combat ensued. Although Grant had 115,000 men available against Lee's 62,000, he found both Federal flanks endangered. Moreover, Grant lost 17,666 soldiers compared to a probable Southern loss of about 8,000. Pulling away from the Wilderness battlefield, Grant tried to hasten southeastward to the crossroads point of Spotsylvania Courthouse, only to have the Confederates get there first. In savage action (May 8–19), including hand-to-hand fighting at the famous "Bloody Angle," Grant, although gaining a little ground, was essentially thrown back. He had lost 18,399 men at Spotsylvania. Lee's combined losses at the Wilderness and Spotsylvania were an estimated 17,250.

Again Grant withdrew, only to move forward in another series of attempts to get past Lee's right flank; again, at the North Anna river and at the Totopotomoy Creek, he found Lee confronting him. Finally at Cold Harbor, just northeast of Richmond, Grant launched several heavy attacks, including a frontal, near-suicidal one on June 3, only to be repelled with grievous total losses of 12,737. Lee's casualties are unknown but were much lighter.

Grant, with the vital rail centre of Petersburg—the southern key to Richmond—as his objective, made one final effort to swing around Lee's right and finally outguessed his opponent and stole a march on him. But several blunders by Federal officers, plus swift action by Beauregard and Lee's belated though rapid reaction, barely enabled the Confederates to hold Petersburg. Grant attacked on June 15 and 18, hoping to break through before Lee could consolidate the Confederate lines east of the city, but he was contained with 8,150 losses.

Unable to admit defeat but having failed to destroy Lee's army and capture Richmond, Grant settled down to a nine-month active siege of Petersburg. The summer and fall of 1864 were highlighted by the Federal failure with a mine explosion under the gray lines at Petersburg on July 30, and the near capture of Washington by the Confederate Jubal Early in July and his later setbacks in the Shenandoah Valley at the hands of Philip H. Sheridan.

Sherman's campaigns. Meanwhile, Sherman was pushing off toward Atlanta from Dalton, Georgia, on May 7, 1864, with 110,123 men against Johnston's 55,000. This masterly campaign comprised a series of cat-and-mouse moves by the rival commanders. Nine successive defensive positions were taken up by Johnston. Trying to outguess his opponent, Sherman attempted to swing around the Confederate right flank twice and around the left flank the other times, but each time Johnston divined which way Sherman was moving and each time pulled back in time to thwart him. At one point Sherman's patience snapped and he frontally assaulted the Southerners at Kennesaw Mountain on June 27; Johnston threw him back with heavy losses. Also, Sherman's lines of communication in his rear were being menaced by audacious Confederate raids conducted by Nathan Bedford Forrest and Joseph Wheeler. Forrest administered a crushing defeat to Federal troops under Samuel D. Sturgis at Brice's Cross Roads, Mississippi, on June 10. But these Confederate forays were more annoying than decisive, and Sherman pressed forward.

When Johnston finally informed Davis that he could not realistically hope to annihilate Sherman's mighty army, the Confederate president replaced him with John B. Hood, who had already lost two limbs in the war. Hood inaugurated a series of premature offensive battles at Peachtree Creek, Atlanta, Ezra Church, and Jonesboro but was repulsed in each of them. With his communications threatened, Hood evacuated Atlanta on the night of August 31–September 1. Sherman pursued only at first. Then, on November 15, he commenced his great march to the sea with more than 60,000 men, laying waste to the economic resources of Georgia in a 50-mile-wide swath of destruction. He took Savannah on December 21.

Sherman's march to the sea

Hood had sought unsuccessfully to lure Sherman out of Georgia and back into Tennessee by marching northwestward with nearly 40,000 men toward the key city of Nashville, the defense of which had been entrusted by Sherman to George H. Thomas. At Franklin, Hood was checked for a day with severe casualties by a Federal holding force under John M. Schofield. This helped Thomas to retain Nashville, where, on December 15–16, he delivered a crushing counterstroke against Hood's besieging army, cutting it up so badly that it was of little use thereafter.

Sherman's force might have been larger and his Atlanta–Savannah Campaign consummated much sooner had not Lincoln approved the Red River Campaign of Banks in the spring of 1864, aimed as much at capturing cotton as at defeating Southern forces under Kirby Smith and Richard Taylor. Accompanied by Porter's warships, Banks moved up the Red River with some 40,000 men. Not only did he fail to net much cotton but he was also checked with loss on April 8 at Sabine Cross Roads and forced to retreat. Porter lost several gunboats, and the campaign amounted to a costly debacle.

That fall Kirby Smith ordered the reconquest of Missouri. Sterling Price's Confederate army advanced on a broad front into Missouri but was set back temporarily by Thomas Ewing at Pilot Knob on September 27. Resuming the advance toward St. Louis, Price was forced westward along the south bank of the Missouri River by pursuing Federal troops under A.J. Smith, Alfred Pleasonton, and Samuel Curtis. Finally, on October 23, at Westport, near Kansas City, Price was decisively defeated and forced to retreat along a circuitous route, arriving back in Arkansas on December 2. This ill-fated raid cost Price most of his artillery and the greater part of his army of about 12,000.

On January 10, 1865, with Tennessee and Georgia now securely in Federal hands, Sherman's 60,000-man force began to march northward into the Carolinas. It was only lightly opposed by much smaller Confederate forces. Sherman captured Columbia on February 17 and compelled the Confederates to evacuate Charleston (including Ft. Sumter). When Lee was finally named Confederate general in chief, he promptly reinstated Johnston as commander of the small forces striving to oppose the Federal advance. Nonetheless, Sherman captured Fayetteville, North Carolina, on March 11 and, after an initial setback, repulsed the counterattacking Johnston at Bentonville on March 19–20. Goldsboro fell to the Federals on March 23, and Raleigh on April 13. Finally, perceiving that he no longer had any reasonable chance of containing the relentless Federal advance, Johnston surrendered to Sherman at the Bennett House near Durham Station on April 18. When Sherman's generous terms proved unacceptable to Secretary of War Stanton (Lincoln had been assassinated on April 14), the former submitted new terms that Johnston signed on April 26.

Lee's appointment as Confederate general in chief

The final land operations. Grant and Meade were continuing their siege of Petersburg and Richmond early in 1865. For months the Federals had been lengthening their left (southern) flank while operating against several important railroads supplying the two Confederate cities. This stretched Lee's dwindling forces very thin. The Southern leader briefly broke the siege when he attacked and captured Ft. Stedman on March 25. But an immediate Federal counterattack regained the strongpoint, and Lee, when his lines were subsequently pierced, evacuated both Petersburg and Richmond on the night of April 2–3.

An 88-mile (142-kilometre) pursuit west-southwestward along the Appomattox River ensued, with Grant and Meade straining every nerve to bring Lee to bay. The Confederates were detained at Amelia Court House, awaiting delayed food supplies, and were badly cut up at Sayler's Creek and Five Forks, with their only avenue of escape now cut off by Sheridan and George A. Custer. When Lee's final attempt to break out failed, he surrendered the remnants of his gallant Army of Northern Virginia at the McLean house at Appomattox Court House on April 9. The lamp of magnanimity was reflected in Grant's unselfish terms.

On the periphery of the Confederacy, 43,000 gray-clad soldiers in Louisiana under Kirby Smith surrendered to Canby on May 26. The port of Galveston, Texas, yielded to the Federals on June 2, and the greatest war in history on American soil was over.

THE NAVAL WAR

While the Federal armies actually stamped out Confederate land resistance, the increasingly effective Federal naval effort must not be overlooked. If Union sea power did not win the war, it enabled the war to be won. When hostilities opened, the United States Navy numbered 90 warships, of which only 42 were in commission, and many of these were on foreign station. Fortunately for the Federals, Lincoln had, in the person of Gideon Welles, a wise secretary of the navy and one of the President's most competent Cabinet members. Welles was ably seconded by his assistant, Gustavus Vasa Fox.

By the time of Lee's surrender, Lincoln's navy numbered 626 warships, of which 65 were ironclads. From a tiny beginning force of nearly 9,000 seamen, the Union Navy increased by war's end to about 59,000 sailors, whereas naval appropriations per year leaped from approximately $12,000,000 to perhaps $123,000,000. The blockade of about 3,500 miles of Confederate coastline was a factor of incalculable value in the final defeat of the Davis government, although the blockade did not become effective before the end of 1863.

The Confederates, on the other hand, had to start from almost nothing in building a navy. That they did so well was largely because of untiring efforts by the capable secretary of the navy, Stephen Mallory. He dispatched agents to Europe to purchase warships, sought to refurbish captured or scuttled Federal vessels, and made every effort to arm and employ Southern-owned ships then in Confederate ports. Mallory's only major omission was his delay in seeing the advantage of Confederate government control of blockade runners bringing in strategic supplies; not until later in the war did the government begin closer supervision of blockade-running vessels. Eventually, the government commandeered space on all privately owned blockade runners and even built and operated some of its own late in the war.

The naval side of the Civil War was a revolutionary one. In addition to their increasing use of steam power, of the screw propeller, of shell guns, and of rifled ordnance, both sides built and employed ironclad warships. The notable clash on March 9, 1862, between the North's "Monitor" and the South's "Virginia" (formerly the "Merrimack") was the first battle ever waged between ironclads. Also, the first sinking of a warship by a submarine occurred when, on February 17, 1864, the Confederate submersible "Hunley" sank the blockader USS "Housatonic."

Daring Confederate sea raiders preyed upon Union commerce. Especially successful were the "Sumter," commanded by Raphael Semmes, which captured 18 Northern merchantmen early in the war; the "Florida," captained by John Maffit, which, in 1863, seized 37 Federal prizes in the North and South Atlantic; the "Shenandoah," with James Waddell as skipper, which took 38 Union merchant ships, mostly in the Pacific; and the most famous of all Confederate cruisers, the "Alabama," commanded by Semmes, which captured 69 Federal ships in two years; not until June 19, 1864, was the "Alabama" intercepted and sunk off Cherbourg by the Federal warship "Kearsarge," captained by John Winslow. Not only were a great many other Federal ships captured, but marine insurance rates were driven to a prohibitive high by these Southern depredations. This led to a serious deterioration of the American merchant marine, the effects of which have lasted into the 20th century.

Besides fighting efficaciously with ironclads on the inland rivers, Lincoln's navy also played an important role in a series of coastal and amphibious operations, some in conjunction with the Federal Army. As early as November 7, 1861, a Federal flotilla under Samuel F. Du Pont seized Port Royal, South Carolina, and another squadron under Louis M. Goldsborough assisted Burnside's army in capturing Roanoke Island and New Berne on the North Carolina littoral in February–March 1862. One month later, Savannah was closed to Confederate blockade runners when the Federal Navy reduced Ft. Pulaski guarding the city; and on April 25 Farragut, running the forts near the mouth of the Mississippi, took New Orleans, which was subsequently occupied by Benjamin F. Butler's army.

But in April 1863, and again in July and August, Federal warships were repelled at Ft. Sumter when they descended upon Charleston, and a Federal army under Quincy A. Gillmore fared little better when it tried to assist. Farragut had better luck, however, when he rendered Mobile, Alabama, useless by reducing Ft. Morgan and destroying several defending Confederate ships on August 5, 1864, in the hardest fought naval action of the war. The last open Atlantic port, Wilmington, North Carolina, successfully withstood a Federal naval attack by Porter on defending Ft. Fisher when Butler's army failed to coordinate its attack properly in December 1864, but it fell one month later to Porter and an ably conducted army assault led by Alfred H. Terry. Only Galveston remained open to the Confederates in the last months of the war. In short, "Uncle Sam's web feet," as Lincoln termed them, played a decisive role in helping crush the Confederacy.

FOREIGN AFFAIRS

Davis and many Confederates expected recognition of their independence and direct intervention in the war on their behalf by Great Britain and possibly France. But they were cruelly disappointed, in part through the skillful diplomacy of Lincoln, Secretary of State William H. Seward, and the Union ambassador to England, Charles Francis Adams, and in part through Confederate military failure at a crucial stage of the war.

The Union's first trouble with Britain came when Capt. Charles Wilkes halted the British steamer, "Trent," on November 8, 1861, and forcibly removed two Confederate envoys, James M. Mason and John Slidell, bound for Europe. Only the release of the two men prevented a diplomatic rupture with Palmerston's government in London. Another crisis erupted between the Union and England when the "Alabama," built in the British Isles, was permitted upon completion to sail and join the Confederate Navy, despite Adams' protestations. And when word reached the Lincoln government that two powerful ironclad rams were being constructed in Britain for the Confederacy, Adams sent his famous "this is war" note to Palmerston and the rams were seized by the British government at the last moment.

The diplomatic crisis of the Civil War came after Lee's striking victory at Second Manassas in late August 1862 and subsequent invasion of Maryland. The British government was set to offer mediation of the war and, if this were refused by the Lincoln administration (as it would have been), forceful intervention on behalf of the Confederacy. Only a victory by Lee on Northern soil was needed, but he was stopped by McClellan in September at Antietam, the Union's most needed success. The Confederate defeats at Gettysburg and Vicksburg the following summer ensured the continuing neutrality of England and France, especially when Russia seemed inclined to favour the Northern cause. Even the growing English shortage of cotton from the Southern states did not force Palmerston's government into Davis' camp, particularly when British consuls in the Confederacy were more closely restricted toward the close of the war. In the final act, even the Confederate offer to abolish slavery in early 1865 in return for British recognition fell on deaf ears.

THE COST AND SIGNIFICANCE OF THE CIVIL WAR

On the positive side, the triumph of the North, above and beyond its superior naval forces, numbers, and industrial and financial resources, was due in part to the statesmanship of Lincoln, who by 1864 had become a masterful war leader; to the pervading valour of Federal soldiers; and to the increasing skill of their officers. On the negative side, the victory was due in part to failures of Confederate transportation, matériel, and political leadership. Only praise can be extended to the continuing bravery of Confederate soldiers and to the strategic and tactical dexterity of such generals as Lee and Joseph E. Johnston.

War casualties

While there were some desertions on both sides, the personal valour and the enormous casualties—both in absolute numbers and in percentage of numbers engaged—have not yet ceased to astound scholars and military historians everywhere. Based on the three-year standard of enlistment, about 1,556,000 soldiers served in the Federal armies, which suffered a total of 634,703 casualties (359,528 dead and 275,175 wounded). There were probably about 800,000 men serving in the Confederate forces, which sustained approximately 483,000 casualties (about 258,000 deaths and perhaps 225,000 wounded).

The cost in treasure was, of course, staggering for the embattled sections. Both governments, after strenuous attempts to finance the prosecution of the war by increasing taxes and floating loans, were obliged to resort to the printing press to make fiat money. While separate Confederate figures are lacking, the war finally cost the United States more than $15,000,000,000. In sum, although the Union was preserved and restored, the cost in physical and moral suffering was incalculable, and some spiritual wounds caused by the holocaust still have not yet been healed.

The American Civil War has been called by some the last of the old-fashioned wars; others have termed it the first of the modern wars of history. Actually it was a transitional war, and it had a profound impact, technologically, on the development of modern weapons and techniques. There were many innovations. It was the first war in history in which ironclad warships clashed; the first in which the telegraph and railroad played significant roles; the first to use, extensively, rifled ordnance and shell guns and to introduce a machine gun; the first to have widespread newspaper coverage, voting by servicemen in national elections, and photographic recordings; the first to organize medical care of troops systematically; and the first to use land and water mines and to employ a submarine that could sink a warship. It was also the first war in which armies widely employed aerial reconnaissance (by means of balloons).

The Civil War has been written about as has no other war in history. More than 60,000 books and articles give eloquent testimony to the accuracy of Walt Whitman's prediction that "a great literature will . . . arise out of the era of those four years." The events of the war left a rich heritage for future generations, and that legacy was summed up by the martyred Lincoln as showing that the reunited sections of the United States comprised "the last best hope of earth." (W.W.H.)

Reconstruction and the New South, 1865–1900

RECONSTRUCTION, 1865–77

Reconstruction under Abraham Lincoln. The original Northern objective in the Civil War was the preservation of the Union—a war aim with which virtually everybody in the free states agreed. As the fighting progressed, the Lincoln government concluded that emancipation of the slaves was necessary in order to secure military victory; and thereafter freedom became a second war aim for the members of the Republican Party. The more radical members of that party—men like Charles Sumner and Thaddeus Stevens—believed that emancipation would prove a sham unless the government guaranteed the civil and political rights of the freedmen; and equality of all citizens before the law became a third war aim for this powerful faction. The fierce controversies of the Reconstruction era raged over which of these objectives should be insisted upon and how these goals should be secured.

Northern war aims

Lincoln's plan. Lincoln himself had a flexible and pragmatic approach to Reconstruction, insisting only that the Southerners, when defeated, pledge future loyalty to the Union and emancipate their slaves. As the Southern states were subdued, he appointed military governors to super-

vise their restoration. The most vigorous and effective of these appointees was Andrew Johnson, whose success in reconstituting a loyal government in Tennessee led to his nomination as vice president on the Republican ticket with Lincoln in 1864. In December 1863 Lincoln announced a general plan for the orderly reconstruction of the Southern states, promising to recognize the government of any state that pledged to support the Constitution and the Union and to emancipate the slaves if it was backed by at least 10 percent of the number of voters in the 1860 presidential election. In both Arkansas and Tennessee loyal governments were formed under Lincoln's plan; and they sought readmission to the Union with the seating of their senators and representatives in Congress.

The Radicals' plan. Radical Republicans were outraged at these procedures, which savoured of executive usurpation of Congressional powers, which required only minimal changes in the Southern social system and which left political power essentially in the hands of the same Southerners who had led their states out of the Union. The Radicals put forth their own plan of Reconstruction in the Wade–Davis bill, which Congress passed on July 2, 1864; it required not 10 percent but a majority of the white male citizens in each Southern state to participate in the reconstruction process, and it insisted upon an oath of past, not just of future, loyalty. Finding the bill too rigorous and inflexible, Lincoln pocket-vetoed it; and the Radicals bitterly denounced him. During the 1864–65 session of Congress, they in turn defeated the president's proposal to recognize the Louisiana government organized under his 10 percent plan. At the time of Lincoln's assassination, therefore, the President and the Congress were at loggerheads over Reconstruction.

Reconstruction under Andrew Johnson. At first it seemed that Andrew Johnson might be able to work more cooperatively with Congress in the process of Reconstruction. A former representative and a former senator, he understood congressmen. A loyal Unionist who had stood by his country even at the risk of his life when Tennessee seceded, he was certain not to compromise with secession; and his experience as military governor of that state showed him to be politically shrewd and tough toward the slaveholders. "Johnson, we have faith in you," Radical Benjamin F. Wade assured the new president on the day he took the oath of office. "By the gods, there will be no trouble running the government."

Johnson's policy. Such Radical trust in Johnson proved misplaced. The new president was, first of all, himself a Southerner. He was a Democrat who looked for the restoration of his old party partly as a step toward his own re-election to the presidency in 1868. And, most important of all, Johnson shared the white Southerners' attitude toward the Negro, considering black men innately inferior and unready for equal civil or political rights. On May 29, 1865, Johnson made his policy clear when he issued a general proclamation of pardon and amnesty for most Confederates and authorized the provisional governor of North Carolina to proceed with the reorganization of that state. Shortly afterward he issued similar proclamations for the other former Confederate states. In each case a state constitutional convention was to be chosen by the voters who pledged future loyalty to the U.S. Constitution. The conventions were expected to repeal the ordinances of secession, to repudiate the Confederate debt, and to accept the Thirteenth Amendment, abolishing slavery. The President did not, however, require them to enfranchise the blacks.

"Black Codes." Given little guidance from Washington, Southern whites turned to the traditional political leaders of their section for guidance in reorganizing their governments; and the new regimes in the South were suspiciously like those of the antebellum period. To be sure, slavery was abolished; but each reconstructed Southern state government proceeded to adopt a "Black Code," regulating the rights and privileges of freedmen. Varying from state to state, these codes in general treated blacks as inferiors, relegated to a secondary and subordinate position in society. Their right to own land was restricted, they could not bear arms, and they might be bound out in servitude

for vagrancy and other offenses. The conduct of white Southerners indicated that they were not prepared to guarantee even minimal protection of Negro rights. In riots in Memphis (May 1866) and New Orleans (July 1866), black persons were brutally assaulted and promiscuously killed.

Civil rights legislation. Watching these developments with forebodings, Northern Republicans during the Congressional session of 1865–66 inevitably drifted into conflict with the President. Congress attempted to protect the rights of blacks by extending the life of the Freedmen's Bureau; but Johnson vetoed the bill. An act to define and guarantee the blacks' basic civil rights met a similar fate, but Republicans succeeded in passing it over the President's veto. While the President, from the porch of the White House, denounced the leaders of the Republican Party as "traitors," Republicans in Congress tried to formulate their own plan to reconstruct the South. Their first effort was the Fourteenth Amendment, which guaranteed the basic civil rights of all citizens, regardless of colour, and which tried to persuade the Southern states to enfranchise blacks by threatening to reduce their representation in Congress.

Conflict between Republicans and Johnson

The President, the Northern Democrats, and the Southern whites spurned this Republican plan of Reconstruction. Johnson tried to organize his own political party in the National Union Convention, which met in Philadelphia in August 1866; and in August and September he visited many Northern and Western cities in order to defend his policies and to attack the Republican leaders. At the President's urging, every Southern state except Tennessee overwhelmingly rejected the Fourteenth Amendment.

Victorious in the fall elections, Congressional Republicans moved during the 1866–67 session to devise a second, more stringent program for reconstructing the South. After long and acrimonious quarrels between Radical and moderate Republicans, the party leaders finally produced a compromise plan in the First Reconstruction Act of 1867. Expanded and clarified in three supplementary Reconstruction acts, this legislation swept away the regimes the President had set up in the South, put the former Confederacy back under military control, called for the election of new constitutional conventions, and required the constitutions adopted by these bodies to include both Negro suffrage and the disqualification of former Confederate leaders from officeholding. Under this legislation, new governments were established in all the former Confederate states (except Tennessee, which had already been readmitted); and by July 1868 Congress agreed to seat senators and representatives from Alabama, Arkansas, Florida, Louisiana, North Carolina, and South Carolina. By July 1870 the remaining Southern states had been similarly reorganized and readmitted.

Suspicious of Andrew Johnson, Republicans in Congress did not trust the President to enforce the Reconstruction legislation they passed over his repeated vetoes, and they tried to deprive him of as much power as possible. Congress limited the President's control over the army by requiring that all his military orders be issued through the general of the army, Ulysses S. Grant, who was believed loyal to the Radical cause; and in the Tenure of Office Act (1867) they limited the President's right to remove appointive officers. When Johnson continued to do all he could to block the enforcement of Radical legislation in the South, the more extreme members of the Republican Party demanded his impeachment. The President's decision in February 1868 to remove the Radical secretary of war Edwin M. Stanton from the Cabinet, in apparent defiance of the Tenure of Office Act, provided a pretext for impeachment proceedings. The House of Representatives voted to impeach the President, and after a protracted trial the Senate acquitted him by the margin of only one vote.

Impeachment of Johnson

The South during Reconstruction. Contrary to conventional stereotypes, the Southern states were relatively tranquil during the Reconstruction period. Exhausted and bankrupt after four years of war, most Southern whites wanted nothing more than to return to their farms and try to make a living. Most of the former slaves also settled down to quiet lives of labour on the farms after some initial wandering about to test their freedom. Indeed, the most important developments of the Reconstruction era were not the highly publicized political contests but the slow, almost imperceptible changes that occurred in Southern society. Blacks could now legally marry, and they set up conventional and usually stable family units; they quietly seceded from the white churches and formed their own religious organizations, which became centres for the black community. Without land or money, most freedmen had to continue working for white masters; but they were now unwilling to labour in gangs or to live in the old slave quarters under the eye of the plantation owner.

Sharecropping gradually became the accepted labour system in most of the South—planters, short of capital, favoured the system because it did not require them to pay cash wages; blacks preferred it because they could live in individual cabins on the tracts they rented and because they had a degree of independence in choosing what to plant and how to cultivate. The section as a whole, however, was desperately poor throughout the Reconstruction era; and a series of disastrously bad crops in the late 1860s, followed by the general agricultural depression of the 1870s, hurt both whites and blacks.

The governments set up in the Southern states under the congressional program of Reconstruction were, contrary to traditional clichés, fairly honest and effective. Though the period has sometimes been labelled "Black Reconstruction," the Radical governments in the South were never dominated by blacks. There were no black governors, only two black senators and a handful of congressmen, and only one legislature controlled by blacks. Those blacks who did hold office appear to have been about equal in competence and honesty to the whites. It is true that these Radical governments were expensive, but large state expenditures were necessary to rebuild after the war and to establish—for the first time in most Southern states—a system of common schools. Corruption there certainly was, though nowhere on the scale of the Tweed Ring, which was simultaneously looting New York City; but it is not possible to show that Republicans were more guilty than Democrats, or blacks than whites, in the scandals that did occur.

Southern Reconstruction governments

Though some Southern whites in the mountainous regions and some planters in the rich bottomlands were willing to cooperate with the blacks and their Northern-born "carpetbagger" allies in these new governments, there were relatively few such "scalawags"; the mass of Southern whites remained fiercely opposed to Negro political, civil, and social equality. Sometimes their hostility was expressed through such terrorist organizations as the Ku Klux Klan, which sought to punish so-called uppity Negroes and to drive their white collaborators from the South. More frequently it was manifested through support of the Democratic Party, which gradually regained its strength in the South and waited for the time when the North would tire of supporting the Radical regimes and would withdraw federal troops from the South.

The Ulysses S. Grant administrations, 1869–77. During the two administrations of President Grant there was a gradual attrition of Republican strength. As a politician the President was passive, exhibiting none of the brilliance he had shown on the battlefield. His administration was tarnished by the dishonesty of his subordinates, whom he loyally defended. As the older Radical leaders—men like Sumner, Wade, and Stevens—died, leadership in the Republican Party fell into the hands of technicians like Roscoe Conkling and James G. Blaine, men devoid of the idealistic fervour that had marked the early Republicans. At the same time, many Northerners were growing tired of the whole Reconstruction issue and were weary of the annual outbreaks of violence in the South that required repeated use of federal force.

Weakening of the Radicals

Efforts to shore up the Radical regimes in the South grew increasingly unsuccessful. The adoption of the Fifteenth Amendment (1870), prohibiting discrimination in voting on account of race, had little effect in the South, where terrorist organizations and economic pressure from planters kept blacks from the polls. Nor were three Force Acts passed by the Republicans (1870–71), giving the President the power to suspend the writ of habeas corpus and imposing heavy penalties upon terroristic organizations, in the long run more successful. If they succeeded in dispersing the Ku Klux Klan as an organization, they also drove its members, and their tactics, more than ever into the Democratic camp.

Growing Northern disillusionment with Radical Reconstruction and with the Grant administration became evident in the Liberal Republican movement of 1872, which resulted in the nomination of the erratic Horace Greeley for president. Though Grant was overwhelmingly reelected, the true temper of the country was demonstrated in the congressional elections of 1874, which gave the Democrats control of the House of Representatives for the first time since the outbreak of the Civil War. Despite Grant's hope for a third term in office, most Republicans recognized by 1876 that it was time to change both the candidate and his Reconstruction program, and the nomination of Rutherford B. Hayes of Ohio, a moderate Republican of high principles and of deep sympathy for the South, marked the end of the Radical domination of the Republican Party.

The circumstances surrounding the disputed election of 1876 strengthened Hayes's intention to work with the Southern whites, even if it meant abandoning the few Radical regimes that remained in the South. In an election marked by widespread fraud and many irregularities, the Democratic candidate, Samuel J. Tilden, received the majority of the popular vote; but the vote in the electoral college was long in doubt. In order to resolve the impasse, Hayes's lieutenants had to enter into agreement with Southern Democratic congressmen, promising to withdraw the remaining federal troops from the South, to share the Southern patronage with Democrats, and to favour that section's demands for federal subsidies in the building of levees and railroads. Hayes's inauguration marked, for practical purposes, the restoration of "home rule" for the South—*i.e.,* that the North would no longer interfere in Southern elections to protect the blacks and that the Southern whites would again take control of their state governments.

Restoration of Southern "home rule"

THE NEW SOUTH, 1877–90

The era of conservative domination, 1877–90. The Republican regimes in the Southern states began to fall as early as 1870; by 1877 they had all collapsed. For the next 13 years the South was under the leadership of white Democrats whom their critics called "Bourbons" because, like the French royal family, they supposedly had learned nothing and forgotten nothing from the revolution they had experienced. For the South as a whole, the characterization is neither quite accurate nor quite fair. To be sure, Democrats in South Carolina, led by former Confederate general Wade Hampton, seemed to desire nothing so much as the restoration of the antebellum plantation way of life. But in most Southern states the new political leaders represented less the planters than the rising Southern business community, interested in railroads, cotton textiles, and urban land speculation.

Even on racial questions the new Southern political leaders were not so reactionary as the label Bourbon might suggest. Though whites were in the majority in all but two of the Southern states, the conservative regimes did not attempt to disfranchise the Negroes. Partly their restraint was caused by fear of further federal intervention; chiefly, however, it stemmed from a conviction on the part of conservative leaders that they could control the black voters.

Indeed, Negro votes were sometimes of great value to these regimes, which favoured the businessmen and planters of the South at the expense of the small white farmers. These "Redeemer" governments sharply reduced or even eliminated the programs of the state governments that benefitted poor people. The public school system was starved for money; in 1890 the per capita expenditure in the South for public education was only 97 cents, as compared with $2.24 in the country as a whole. The care of state prisoners, the insane, and the blind was also neglected; and measures to safeguard the public health were rejected. At the same time these conservative regimes were often astonishingly corrupt, and embezzlement and

Reduced benefits for the poor

defalcation on the part of public officials were even greater than during the Reconstruction years.

The small white farmers resentful of planter dominance, residents of the hill country outvoted by Black Belt constituencies, and politicians excluded from the ruling cabals tried repeatedly to overthrow the conservative regimes in the South. During the 1870s they supported Independent or Greenback Labour candidates, but without notable success. In 1879 the Readjuster Party in Virginia—so named because its supporters sought to readjust the huge funded debt of that state so as to lessen the tax burden on small farmers—gained control of the legislature and secured in 1880 the election of its leader, Gen. William Mahone, to the United States Senate. Not until 1890, however, when the powerful Farmers' Alliance, hitherto devoted exclusively to the promotion of agricultural reforms, dropped its ban on politics, was there an effective challenge to conservative hegemony. In that year, with Alliance backing, Benjamin R. Tillman was chosen governor of South Carolina and James S. Hogg was elected governor of Texas; the heyday of Southern Populism was at hand.

Jim Crow legislation. Negro voting in the South was a casualty of the conflict between Redeemers and Populists. Though some Populist leaders, such as Tom Watson in Georgia, saw that poor whites and poor blacks in the South had a community of interest in the struggle against the planters and the businessmen, most small white farmers exhibited vindictive hatred toward the blacks, whose votes had so often been instrumental in upholding conservative regimes. Beginning in 1890, when Mississippi held a new constitutional convention, and continuing through 1908, when Georgia amended its constitution, every state of the former Confederacy moved to disfranchise blacks. Because the United States Constitution forbade outright racial discrimination, the Southern states excluded Negroes by requiring that potential voters be able to read or to interpret any section of the Constitution—a requirement that local registrars waived for whites but rigorously insisted upon when an audacious black wanted to vote. Louisiana, more ingenious, added the "grandfather clause" to its constitution, which exempted from this literacy test all of those who had been entitled to vote on January 1, 1867—*i.e.,* before Congress imposed Negro suffrage upon the South—together with their sons and grandsons. Other states imposed stringent property qualifications for voting or enacted complex poll taxes.

Discrimination in voting

Socially as well as politically, race relations in the South deteriorated as farmers' movements rose to challenge the conservative regimes. By 1890, with the triumph of Southern Populism, the black's place was clearly defined by law; he was relegated to a subordinate and entirely segregated position. And while legal sanctions were being imposed upon the Negro, informal, extralegal, and often brutal steps were being taken to keep him in his "place." From 1889 to 1899 lynchings in the South averaged 187.5 per year.

Booker T. Washington and the "Atlanta Compromise." Faced with implacable and growing hostility from Southern whites, many blacks during the 1880s and 1890s felt that their only sensible course was to avoid open conflict and to work out some pattern of accommodation. The most influential black spokesman for this policy was Booker T. Washington, the head of Tuskegee Institute in Alabama, who urged his fellow Negroes to forget about politics and college education in the classical languages and to learn how to be better farmers and artisans. With thrift, industry, and abstention from politics, he thought that Negroes could gradually win the respect of their white neighbours. In 1895, in a speech at the opening of the Atlanta Cotton States and International Exposition, Washington most fully elaborated his position, which became known as the "Atlanta Compromise." Abjuring hopes of federal intervention in behalf of the Negro, Washington argued that reform in the South would have to come from within. Change could best be brought about if blacks and whites recognized that "the agitation of questions of social equality is the extremist folly"; in the social life the races in the South could be as separate as the fingers, but in economic progress as united as the hand.

Enthusiastically received by Southern whites, Washington's program also found many adherents among Southern blacks, who saw in his doctrine a way to avoid head-on, disastrous confrontations with overwhelming white force. Whether or not Washington's plan would have produced a generation of orderly, industrious, frugal blacks slowly working themselves into middle-class status is not known because of the intervention of a profound economic depression throughout the South during most of the post-Reconstruction period. Neither poor white nor poor black had much opportunity to rise in a region that was desperately impoverished. By 1890 the South ranked lowest in every index that compared the sections of the United States—lowest in per capita income, lowest in public health, lowest in education. In short, by the 1890s the South, a poor and backward region, had yet to recover from the ravages of the Civil War or to reconcile itself to the readjustments required by the Reconstruction era.   (D.H.D.)

Economic depression in the South

The transformation of U.S. society, 1865–1900

NATIONAL EXPANSION

Growth of the nation. The population of the continental United States in 1880 was slightly above 50,000,000. In 1900 it was just under 76,000,000, a gain in 20 years of over 50 percent. Despite the arrival of more than 9,000,000 immigrants between 1880 and 1900, the rate of population increase was the lowest for any 20-year period of the 19th century. The rate of increase was unevenly distributed, ranging from less than 10 percent in northern New England to more than 125 percent in the 11 states and territories of the Far West. Most of the states east of the Mississippi reported gains slightly below the national average.

Immigration. The 9,000,000 immigrants who entered the United States in the last 20 years of the century were the largest number to arrive in any comparable period up to that time. From the earliest days of the republic until 1895, the majority of immigrants had always come from northern or western Europe. Beginning in 1896, however, the great majority of the immigrants were from southern or eastern Europe. Nervous Americans, already convinced that immigrants wielded too much political power or were responsible for violence and industrial strife, found new cause for alarm, fearing that the new immigrants could not easily be assimilated into U.S. society. Those fears gave added stimulus to agitation for legislation to limit the number of immigrants eligible for admission to the United States.

Westward migration. In 1880 about 22 percent of the American people lived west of the Mississippi. By 1900 that figure had increased to 27 percent. The development of the West continued to add new states to the Union. Nebraska became a state in 1867 and Colorado in 1876; they were followed by North and South Dakota, Washington, and Montana in 1889, by Wyoming and Idaho in 1890, and by Utah in 1896. In 1900 there were only three territories still awaiting statehood in the continental United States: Oklahoma, Arizona, and New Mexico.

New states 1867–96

Urban growth. In 1890 the Bureau of the Census discovered that a continuous line could no longer be drawn across the West to define the farthest advance of settlement. Despite the continuing westward movement of population, the frontier had become a symbol of the past. The movement of people from farms to cities more accurately predicted the trends of the future. In 1880 about 28 percent of the American people lived in communities designated by the Bureau of the Census as urban; by 1900 that figure had risen to 40 percent. In those statistics could be read the beginning of the decline of rural power in America and the emergence of a society built upon a burgeoning industrial complex.

The West. Abraham Lincoln once described the West as the "treasure house of the nation." In the 30 years after the discovery of gold in California, prospectors found gold or silver in every state and territory of the Far West.

The mineral empire. There were few truly rich "strikes" in the post-Civil War years. Of those few, the most im-

portant were the fabulously rich Comstock Lode of silver in western Nevada (first discovered in 1859 but developed more extensively later) and the discovery of gold in the Black Hills of South Dakota (1874) and at Cripple Creek, Colorado (1891).

Each new discovery of gold or silver produced an instant mining town to supply the needs and pleasures of the prospectors. If most of the ore was close to the surface, the prospectors would soon extract it and depart, leaving behind a ghost town—empty of people but a reminder of a romantic moment in the past. If the veins ran deep, organized groups with the capital to buy the needed machinery would move in to mine the subsoil wealth, and the mining town would gain some stability as the centre of a local industry. In a few instances, those towns gained permanent status as the commercial centres of agricultural areas that first developed to meet the needs of the miners but later expanded to produce a surplus that they exported to other parts of the West.

The open range. At the close of the Civil War, the price of beef in the Northern states was abnormally high. At the same time, millions of cattle grazed aimlessly on the plains of Texas. A few shrewd Texans concluded that there might be greater profits in cattle than in cotton, especially because it required little capital to enter the cattle business—only enough to employ a few cowboys to tend the cattle during the year and to drive them to market in the spring. No one owned the cattle, and they grazed without charge upon the public domain.

The one serious problem was the shipment of the cattle to market. The Kansas Pacific resolved that problem when it completed a rail line that ran as far west as Abilene, Kansas, in 1867. Abilene was 200 miles (300 kilometres) from the nearest point in Texas where the cattle grazed during the year, but Texas cattlemen almost immediately instituted the annual practice of driving that portion of their herds that was ready for market overland to Abilene in the spring. There they met representatives of Eastern packinghouses, to whom they sold their cattle.

The problem of cattle shipment

The open-range cattle industry prospered beyond expectations and even attracted capital from conservative investors in the British Isles. By the 1880s the industry had expanded along the plains as far north as the Dakotas. In the meantime, a new menace had appeared in the form of the advancing frontier of population; but the construction of the Santa Fe Railway through Dodge City, Kansas, to La Junta, Colorado, permitted the cattlemen to move their operations westward ahead of the frontier; Dodge City replaced Abilene as the principal centre for the annual meeting of cattlemen and buyers. Despite sporadic conflicts with settlers encroaching upon the high plains, the open range survived until a series of savage blizzards struck the plains with unprecedented fury in the winter of 1886–87, killing hundreds of thousands of cattle and forcing many owners into bankruptcy. Those who still had some cattle and some capital abandoned the open range, gained title to lands farther west, where they could provide shelter for their livestock, and revived a cattle industry on land that would be immune to further advances of the frontier of settlement. Their removal to these new lands had been made possible in part by the construction of other railroads connecting the region with Chicago and the Pacific Coast.

The expansion of the railroads. In 1862 Congress authorized the construction of two railroads that together would provide the first railroad link between the Mississippi Valley and the Pacific coast. One was the Union Pacific, to run westward from Council Bluffs, Iowa; the other was the Central Pacific, to run eastward from Sacramento, California. To encourage the rapid completion of those roads, Congress provided generous subsidies in the form of land grants and loans. Construction was slower than Congress had anticipated, but the two lines met, with elaborate ceremonies, on May 10, 1869, at Promontory Point, Utah.

Completion of the first transcontinental railroad

In the meantime, other railroads had begun construction westward, but the Panic of 1873 and the ensuing depression halted or delayed construction of many of those lines. With the return of prosperity after 1877, some of those railroads resumed or accelerated construction; by 1883 three more rail connections between the Mississippi Valley and the West Coast had been completed—the Northern Pacific, from St. Paul to Portland; the Santa Fe, from Chicago to Los Angeles; and the Southern Pacific, from New Orleans to Los Angeles. The Southern Pacific had also acquired, by purchase or construction, lines from Portland to San Francisco and from San Francisco to Los Angeles.

The construction of the railroads from the Middle West to the Pacific coast was the railroad builders' most spectacular achievement in the quarter century after the Civil War. No less important, in terms of the national economy, was the development in the same period of an adequate rail network in the southern states and the building of other railroads that connected virtually every important community west of the Mississippi with Chicago.

The West developed simultaneously with the building of the Western railroads, and in no part of the nation was the importance of railroads more generally recognized. The railroad gave vitality to the regions it served, but, by withholding service, it could doom a community to stagnation. The railroads appeared to be ruthless in exploiting their powerful position: they fixed prices to suit their convenience; they discriminated among their customers; they attempted to gain a monopoly of transportation wherever possible; and they interfered in state and local politics to elect favourites to office, to block unfriendly legislation, and even to influence the decisions of the courts.

Indian policy. Large tracts of land in the West were reserved by law for the exclusive use of specified Indian tribes. By 1870, however, the pressure of the frontier and the outbreak of a series of Indian wars had raised serious questions about the government's Indian policies. Many agents of the Bureau of Indian Affairs, charged with responsibility for dealing directly with the tribes, were lax, and some were corrupt in the discharge of their duties. Most Westerners and some army officers contended that the only satisfactory resolution of the Indian question was the removal of the tribes from all lands coveted by the whites.

In the immediate postwar years, reformers advocated adoption of programs designed to prepare the Indians for ultimate assimilation into American society. In 1869 the reformers persuaded Pres. Ulysses S. Grant and Congress to establish a nonpolitical Board of Indian Commissioners to supervise the administration of relations between the government and the Indians. The board, however, encountered so much political opposition that it accomplished little. The reformers then proposed legislation to grant title for specific acreages of land to the head of each family in those tribes thought to be ready to adopt a sedentary life as farmers. Congress resisted that proposal until land-hungry Westerners discovered that, if the land were thus distributed, a surplus of land would result that could be added to the public domain. When land speculators joined the reformers in support of the proposed legislation, Congress in 1887 enacted the Dawes Act, which empowered the President to grant title to 160 acres (65 hectares) to the head of each family, with smaller allotments to single members of the tribe, in those tribes believed ready to accept a new way of life as farmers. With the grant of land, which could not be alienated by the Indians for 25 years, they were to be granted United States citizenship. Reformers rejoiced that they had finally given the Indians an opportunity to have a dignified role in U.S. society, overlooking the possibility that there might be values in Indian culture worthy of preservation. Meanwhile, the land promoters placed successive presidents under great pressure to accelerate the application of the Dawes Act in order to open more land for occupation or speculation.

Programs for assimilation of Indians

INDUSTRIALIZATION OF THE U.S. ECONOMY

The growth of industry. By 1878 the United States had re-entered a period of prosperity after the long depression of the mid-1870s. In the ensuing 20 years the volume of industrial production, the number of workers employed in industry, and the number of manufacturing plants all more than doubled. A more accurate index to the scope of this industrial advance may be found in the aggregate annual value of all manufactured goods, which increased from about $5,400,000,000 in 1879 to perhaps $13,000,-000,000 in 1899. The expansion of the iron and steel industry, always a key factor in any industrial economy, was even more impressive; in 20 years, from 1880 to 1900, the annual production of steel in the United States went from about 1,400,000 to more than 11,000,000 tons. Before the end of the century, the United States surpassed Great Britain in the production of iron and steel and was providing more than one-quarter of the world's supply of pig iron.

Many factors combined to produce this burst of industrial activity. The exploitation of Western resources, including mines and lumber, stimulated a demand for improved transportation, while the gold and silver mines provided new sources of capital for investment in the East. The construction of railroads, especially in the West and South, with the resulting demand for steel rails, was a major force in the expansion of the steel industry and increased the railroad mileage in the United States from less than 93,262 miles (150,151 kilometres) in 1880 to about 190,000 miles (310,000 kilometres) in 1900. Technological advances, including the utilization of the Bessemer and open-hearth processes in the manufacture of steel, resulted in improved products and lower production costs. A series of major inventions, including the telephone, typewriter, linotype, phonograph, electric light, cash register, air brake, refrigerator car, and the automobile, became the bases for new industries, while many of them facilitated the conduct of business. The use of petroleum products in industry as well as for domestic heating and lighting became the cornerstone of the most powerful of the new industries of the period, while the trolley car, the increased use of gas and electric power, and the telephone led to the establishment of important public utilities that were natural monopolies and could operate only on the basis of franchises granted by state or municipal governments. The widespread employment of the corporate form of business organization offered new opportunities for large-scale financing of business enterprise and attracted new capital, much of it furnished by European investors. Over all this industrial activity, there presided a colourful and energetic group of entrepreneurs, who gained the attention, if not always the commendation, of the public and who appeared to symbolize for the public the new class of leadership in the United States. Of this numerous group the best known were John D. Rockefeller in oil, Andrew Carnegie in steel, and such railroad builders and promoters as Cornelius Vanderbilt, Leland Stanford, Collis P. Huntington, Henry Villard, and James J. Hill.

New class of leadership

The dispersion of industry. The period was notable also for the wide geographical distribution of industry. The Eastern seaboard from Massachusetts to Pennsylvania continued to be the most heavily industrialized section of the United States, but there was a substantial development of manufacturing in the states adjacent to the Great Lakes and in certain sections of the South.

The experience of the steel industry reflected this new pattern of diffusion. Two-thirds of the iron and steel industry was concentrated in the area of western Pennsylvania and eastern Ohio. After 1880, however, the development of iron mines in northern Minnesota (the Vermilion Range in 1884 and the Mesabi Range in 1892) and in Tennessee and northern Alabama was followed by the expansion of the iron and steel industry in the Chicago area and by the establishment of steel mills in northern Alabama and in Tennessee.

Most manufacturing in the Middle West was in enterprises closely associated with agriculture and represented expansion of industries that had first been established before 1860. Meat-packing, which in the years after 1875 became one of the major industries of the nation in terms of the value of its products, was almost a Middle Western monopoly, with a large part of the industry concentrated in Chicago. Flour milling, brewing, and the manufacture of farm machinery and lumber products were other important Middle Western industries.

The industrial invasion of the South was spearheaded

by textiles. Cotton mills became the symbol of the New South, and mills and mill towns sprang up in the Piedmont region from Virginia to Georgia and into Alabama. By 1900 almost one-quarter of all the cotton spindles in the United States were in the South, and Southern mills were expanding their operations more rapidly than were their well-established competitors in New England. The development of lumbering in the South was even more impressive, though less publicized; by the end of the century the South led the nation in lumber production, contributing almost one-third of the annual supply.

Industrial combinations. The geographical dispersal of industry was part of a movement that was converting the United States into an industrial nation. It attracted less attention, however, than the trend toward the consolidation of competing firms into large units capable of dominating an entire industry. The movement toward consolidation received special attention in 1882 when John D. Rockefeller and his associates organized the Standard Oil Trust under the laws of Ohio. A trust was a new type of industrial organization, in which the voting rights of a controlling number of shares of competing firms were entrusted to a small group of men, or trustees, who thus were able to prevent competition among the companies they controlled. The stockholders presumably benefitted through the larger dividends they received. For a few years the trust was a popular vehicle for the creation of monopolies, and by 1890 there were trusts in whiskey, lead, cottonseed oil, and salt.

Trusts, mergers, and holding companies

In 1892 the courts of Ohio ruled that the trust violated that state's antimonopoly laws. Standard Oil then reincorporated as a holding company under the more hospitable laws of New Jersey. Thereafter, holding companies or outright mergers became the favourite forms for the creation of monopolies, though the term trust remained in the popular vocabulary as a common description of any monopoly. The best known mergers of the period were those leading to the formation of the American Tobacco Company (1890) and the American Sugar Refining Company (1891). The latter was especially successful in stifling competition, for it quickly gained control of most of the sugar refined in the United States.

Foreign commerce. The foreign trade of the United States, if judged by the value of exports, kept pace with the growth of domestic industry. Exclusive of gold, silver, and re-exports, the annual value of exports from the United States in 1877 was about $590,000,000; by 1900 it had increased to approximately $1,371,000,000. The value of imports also rose, though at a slower rate. When gold and silver are included, there was only one year in the entire period in which the United States had an unfavourable balance of trade; and, as the century drew to a close, the excess of exports over imports increased perceptibly.

Agriculture continued to furnish the bulk of U.S. exports. Cotton, wheat, flour, and meat products were consistently the items with the greatest annual value among exports. Of the nonagricultural products sent abroad, petroleum was the most important, though by the end of the century its position on the list of exports was being challenged by machinery.

Despite the expansion of foreign trade, the U.S. merchant marine was a major casualty of the period. While the aggregate tonnage of all shipping flying the U.S. flag remained remarkably constant, the tonnage engaged in foreign trade declined sharply. On the eve of the Civil War, the tonnage in overseas trade had exceeded 2,400,000 tons; by 1877 it had dropped to 1,571,000 tons, and, thereafter, it continued to decline until it reached a low point in 1898 of only 726,000 tons. In 1900 only about 10 percent of the exports of the United States were sent abroad in ships of U.S. registry.

Labour. The expansion of industry was accompanied by increased tensions between employers and workers and by the appearance, for the first time in the United States, of national labour unions.

Formation of unions. The first effective labour organization that was more than regional in membership and influence was the Knights of Labor, organized in 1869. The Knights believed in the unity of the interests of all

The Knights of Labor

producing groups and sought to enlist in their ranks not only all labourers but everyone who could be truly classified as a producer. They championed a variety of causes, many of them more political than industrial, and they hoped to gain their ends through politics and education rather than through economic coercion.

The hardships suffered by many workers during the depression of 1873–78 and the failure of a nationwide railroad strike, which was broken when Pres. Rutherford B. Hayes sent federal troops to suppress disorders in Pittsburgh and St. Louis, caused much discontent in the ranks of the Knights. In 1879 Terence V. Powderly, a railroad worker and mayor of Scranton, Pennsylvania, was elected grand master workman of the national organization. Powderly supposedly favoured a program of aggressive action on behalf of labour. In practice, however, he hesitated to endorse strikes, and the effective control of the Knights shifted to regional leaders who were willing to initiate strikes or other forms of economic pressure to gain their objectives. The Knights reached the peak of their influence in 1885, when they claimed a national membership of nearly 700,000. In that year a much-publicized strike against the Wabash Railroad attracted substantial public sympathy and succeeded in preventing a reduction in wages. In that year also Congress took note of the apparently increasing power of labour and prohibited the entry into the United States of immigrants who had signed contracts to work for specific employers.

The year 1886 was a troubled one in labour relations. There were nearly 1,600 strikes, involving about 600,000 workers, with the eight-hour day the most prominent item in the demands of labour. About half of these strikes were called for May Day; some of them were successful, but the concerted action by workers on a nationwide basis turned public opinion against labour and deprived it of much of the sympathy it had enjoyed in the preceding year.

The Haymarket Riot. The most serious blow to the unions came from a tragic occurrence with which they were only indirectly associated. One of the strikes called for May Day in 1886 was against the McCormick Harvesting Machine Company in Chicago. Fighting broke out along the picket lines, and, when police intervened to restore order, several strikers were injured. Union leaders called a protest meeting at Haymarket Square for the evening of May 4; but, as the meeting was breaking up, a group of anarchists took over and began to make inflammatory speeches. The police quickly intervened, and a bomb exploded, killing seven policemen and injuring many others. Eight of the anarchists were arrested, tried, and convicted of murder. Four of them were hanged, and one committed suicide. The remaining three were pardoned in 1893 by Gov. John P. Altgeld, who was persuaded that they had been convicted in such an atmosphere of prejudice that it was impossible to be certain that they were guilty.

The public tended to blame organized labour for the Haymarket tragedy, and many persons had become convinced that the activities of unions were likely to be attended by violence. The Knights never regained the ground they lost in 1886, and, until after the turn of the century, organized labour seldom gained any measure of public sympathy. Aggregate union membership did not again reach its 1885–86 figure until 1900. Unions, however, continued to be active; and in each year from 1889 through the end of the century there were more than 1,000 strikes.

As the power of the Knights declined, the leadership in the trade union movement passed to the American Federation of Labor (AFL). This was a loose federation of local and craft unions, organized first in 1881 and reorganized in 1886. For a few years there was some nominal cooperation between the Knights and the AFL, but the basic organization and philosophy of the two groups made cooperation difficult. The AFL appealed only to skilled workers, and its objectives were those of immediate concern to its members: hours, wages, working conditions, and the recognition of the union. It relied on economic weapons, chiefly the strike and boycott, and it eschewed political activity, except for state and local election campaigns. The central figure in the AFL was Samuel Gompers, a New York cigar maker, who was its president from 1886 to his death in 1924.

The American Federation of Labor

NATIONAL POLITICS

The dominant forces in U.S. life in the last quarter of the 19th century were economic and not political. This fact was reflected in the ineffectiveness of political leadership and in the absence of deeply divisive issues in politics, except perhaps for the continuing agrarian agitation for inflation. There were colourful political personalities, but they gained their following on a personal basis rather than as spokesmen for a program of political action. No president of the period was truly the leader of his party, and none apparently aspired to that status except Grover Cleveland during his second term (1893–97). Such shrewd observers of U.S. politics as Woodrow Wilson and James Bryce agreed that great men did not become presidents; and it was evident that the nominating conventions of both major parties commonly selected presidential candidates who were "available" in the sense that they had few enemies.

In the absence of leadership from the White House, public policy was largely formulated in Congress. As a result, public policy commonly represented a compromise among the views of many congressional leaders—a situation made the more essential because of the fact that in only four of the 20 years from 1877 to 1897 did the same party control the White House, the Senate, and the House.

The Republicans appeared to be the majority party in national politics. From the Civil War to the end of the century, they won every presidential election save those of 1884 and 1892, and they had a majority in the Senate in all but three Congresses during that same period. The Democrats, however, won a majority in the House in eight of the ten Congresses from 1875 to 1895. The success of the Republicans was achieved in the face of bitter intra-party schisms that plagued Republican leaders from 1870 until after 1890 and despite the fact that, in every election campaign after 1876, they were forced to concede the entire South to the opposition. The Republicans had the advantage of having been the party that had defended the Union against secession and had freed the slaves. When all other appeals failed, Republican leaders could salvage votes in the North and West by reviving memories of the war. A less tangible but equally valuable advantage was the widespread belief that the continued industrial development of the nation would be more secure under a Republican than under a Democratic administration. Except in years of economic adversity, the memory of the war and confidence in the economic program of the Republican Party were normally enough to ensure Republican success in most of the northern and western states.

The Rutherford B. Hayes administration. President Hayes (served 1877–81) willingly carried out the commitments made by his friends to reconcile Southerners to the decisions of the electoral commission that had awarded him the disputed electoral votes in three key Southern states needed for his election. He withdrew the federal troops still in the South, and he appointed former senator David M. Key of Tennessee to his Cabinet as postmaster general. Hayes hoped that these conciliatory gestures would encourage many Southern conservatives to support the Republican Party in the future. But the Southerners' primary concern was the maintenance of white supremacy; this, they believed, required a monopoly of political power in the South by the Democratic Party. As a result, the policies of Hayes led to the virtual extinction rather than the revival of the Republican Party in the South.

Hayes's efforts to woo the South irritated some Republicans, but his attitude toward the federal civil service was a more immediate challenge to his party. In June 1877 he issued an executive order prohibiting political activity by those who held federal appointments. When two friends of Sen. Roscoe Conkling defied this order, Hayes removed them from their posts in the administration of the Port of New York. Conkling and his associates showed their contempt for Hayes by bringing about the election of one of the men (Alonzo B. Cornell) as governor of New York in 1879 and nominating the other (Chester A. Arthur) as Republican candidate for the vice presidency in 1880.

One of the most serious issues facing Hayes was that of inflation. Hayes and many other Republicans were staunch

supporters of a sound-money policy, but the issues were sectional rather than partisan. In general, sentiment in the agricultural South and West was favourable to inflation, while industrial and financial groups in the Northeast opposed any move to inflate the currency, holding that this would benefit debtors at the expense of creditors.

In 1873 Congress had discontinued the minting of silver dollars, an action later stigmatized by friends of silver as the Crime of '73. As the depression deepened, inflationists began campaigns to persuade Congress to resume coinage of silver dollars and to repeal the act providing for the redemption of Civil War greenbacks in gold after January 1, 1879. By 1878 the sentiment for silver and inflation was so strong that Congress passed, over the President's veto, the Bland–Allison Act, which renewed the coinage of silver dollars and, more significantly, included a mandate to the Secretary of the Treasury to purchase silver bullion at the market price in amounts of not less than $2,000,000 and not more than $4,000,000 each month.

The silver controversy

Opponents of inflation were somewhat reassured by the care with which Secretary of the Treasury John Sherman was making preparation to have an adequate gold reserve to meet any demands on the Treasury for the redemption of greenbacks. Equally reassuring were indications that the nation had at last recovered from the long period of depression. These factors re-established confidence in the financial stability of the government; and, when the date for the redemption of greenbacks arrived, there was no appreciable demand upon the Treasury to exchange them for gold.

Hayes chose not to be a candidate for re-election. Had he sought a second term, he would almost certainly have been denied renomination by the Republican leaders, with whom he had never been popular. His tolerant disposition and quiet dignity had won the respect of millions of his fellow countrymen, and he appeared to symbolize the amelioration of the economic and sectional tensions that had gripped the country in 1877. But the forces that molded national destiny during his administration and for 20 years thereafter were economic and social rather than political.

Three prominent candidates contended for the Republican presidential nomination in 1880: Grant, James G. Blaine, and John Sherman. Grant had a substantial and loyal bloc of delegates in the convention, but their number was short of a majority. Neither of the other candidates could command a majority, and on the 36th ballot the weary delegates nominated a compromise candidate, Congressman James A. Garfield of Ohio. To placate the "Stalwart," or pro-Grant, faction, the convention nominated Chester A. Arthur of New York for vice president.

The Democrats probably would have renominated Samuel J. Tilden in 1880, hoping thereby to gain votes from those who believed Tilden had lost in 1876 through fraud. But Tilden declined to become a candidate again, and the Democratic convention nominated Gen. Winfield S. Hancock. Hancock had been a Federal general during the Civil War, but he had no political record and little familiarity with questions of public policy.

The campaign failed to generate any unusual excitement and produced no novel issues. As in every national election of the period, the Republicans stressed their role as the party of the protective tariff and asserted that Democratic opposition to the tariff would impede the growth of domestic industry. Actually, the Democrats were badly divided on the tariff, and Hancock surprised political leaders of both parties by declaring that the tariff was an issue of only local interest.

Garfield won the election with an electoral margin of 214 to 155, but his plurality in the popular vote was a slim 9,644. The election revealed the existence of a new "solid South," for Hancock carried all the former Confederate states and three of the former slave states that had remained loyal to the Union.

The administrations of James A. Garfield and Chester A. Arthur. Garfield had not been closely identified with either of the two major factions within the Republican Party—the "Stalwarts" and the "Half-Breeds." Upon becoming president, he named James G. Blaine, the leader

Regional political differences

of the "Half-Breeds," as secretary of state. He gave even more serious offense to the pro-Grant "Stalwart" faction by appointing as collector of customs at New York a man who was unacceptable to the two senators from that state, Roscoe Conkling and Thomas Platt, who showed their displeasure by resigning their Senate seats, expecting to be re-elected triumphantly by the legislature of New York; but in this they were disappointed.

The assassination of Garfield

The tragic climax to this intraparty strife came on July 2, 1881, when Garfield was shot, in Washington, D.C., by a disappointed and mentally deranged office seeker. For two months the President lingered between life and death. He died on September 19 and was succeeded by Vice Pres. Chester A. Arthur.

The accession of Arthur to the presidency caused widespread concern. He had held no elective office before becoming vice president, and he had been closely associated with the Grant wing of the party. It was assumed that like others in that group he would be hostile to reform of the civil service, and his nomination for the vice presidency had been generally regarded as a deliberate rebuke to President Hayes. The members of Garfield's Cabinet immediately tendered their resignations, but Arthur asked them to continue in office for a time. By mid-April 1882, however, all but one of the Cabinet officers had been replaced. Among those replaced was Secretary of State Blaine.

Arthur soon surprised his critics and the country by demonstrating an unexpected independence of his former political friends. In his first annual message to Congress, in December 1881, he announced his qualified approval of legislation that would remove appointments to the federal civil service from partisan control. In January 1883 Congress passed and Arthur signed the Pendleton Civil Service Act, which established the Civil Service Commission and provided that appointments to certain categories of offices should be made on the basis of examinations and the appointees given an indefinite tenure in their positions.

The Chinese Exclusion Act

In May 1882 Congress enacted the Chinese Exclusion Act, prohibiting for a period of ten years the immigration of Chinese labourers into the United States. This act was both the culmination of more than ten years of agitation on the West Coast for the exclusion of the Chinese and an early sign of some modification of the traditional U.S. philosophy of welcoming virtually all immigrants. In response to pressure from California, Congress had passed an exclusion act in 1879, but it had been vetoed by Hayes on the ground that it abrogated rights guaranteed to the Chinese by the Burlingame Treaty of 1868. In 1880 these treaty provisions were revised to permit the United States to suspend the immigration of Chinese. The Chinese Exclusion Act was renewed in 1892 for another ten-year period, and in 1902 the suspension of Chinese immigration was made indefinite.

President Arthur hoped to be the presidential nominee of the Republicans in 1884. His administration had won the respect of many who had viewed his accession to office with misgivings. It had not, however, gained him any powerful following among the leaders of his party. The strongest candidate for the Republican nomination was James G. Blaine. Despite opposition from those who believed he was too partisan in spirit or that he was vulnerable to charges of corrupt actions while speaker of the house many years before, Blaine was nominated on the fourth ballot.

The Democratic candidate, Gov. Grover Cleveland of New York, was in many respects the antithesis of Blaine. He was a relative newcomer to politics. He had been elected mayor of Buffalo in 1881 and governor of New York in 1882. In both positions he had earned a reputation for political independence, inflexible honesty, and an industrious and conservative administration. His record made him an attractive candidate for persons who accepted the dictum that "a public office is a public trust." This was, in 1884, a valuable asset; and it won for Cleveland the support of a few outstanding Republicans and some journals of national circulation that usually favoured Republican nominees for office.

As in 1880, the campaign was almost devoid of issues

of public policy: only the perennial question of the tariff appeared to separate the two parties. Cleveland had not served in the army during the Civil War, and Republicans made an effort to use this fact, together with the power of the South in the Democratic Party, to arouse sectional prejudices against Cleveland. During the campaign it was revealed that Cleveland, a bachelor, was the father of an illegitimate son, an indiscretion that gave the Republicans a moral issue with which to counteract charges of corruption against their own candidate.

The election was very close. On the evening of the voting it was apparent that the result depended upon the vote in New York State, but not until the end of the week was it certain that Cleveland had carried New York by the narrow margin of 1,149 votes and been elected president. In the electoral college, Cleveland received 219 votes to 182 for Blaine.

Grover Cleveland's first term. Cleveland was the first Democratic president since James Buchanan a quarter of a century earlier. More than two-thirds of the electoral votes he received came from southern or border states, so that it appeared that his election marked the close of one epoch and the beginning of a new political era in which the South could again hope to have a major voice in the conduct of national affairs. Because of his brief career in politics, Cleveland had only a limited acquaintance with leaders of his own party. He accepted literally the constitutional principle of the separation of powers, and he opened his first annual message to Congress, in December 1885, with an affirmation of his devotion to "the partitions of power between our respective departments." This appeared to be a disavowal of presidential leadership, but it quickly became apparent that Cleveland intended to defend vigorously the prerogatives that he believed belonged to the executive.

Cleveland's relations with his party and politics

During his first term (1885–89) Cleveland was confronted with a divided Congress—a Republican Senate and a Democratic House. This added to the complexities of administration, especially in the matter of appointments. Cleveland was a firm believer in a civil service based on merit rather than on partisan considerations, but, as the first Democratic president in a quarter of a century, he was under great pressure to replace Republicans in appointive offices with Democrats. He followed a line of compromise. In his first two years he removed the incumbents from about two-thirds of the offices subject to his control, but he scrutinized the qualifications of Democrats recommended for appointment and in a number of instances refused to abide by the recommendations of his party leaders. He thus offended both the reformers, who wished no partisan removals, and his fellow Democrats, whose nominees he rejected. Although his handling of the patronage alienated some powerful Democrats, he scored a personal triumph when he persuaded Congress to repeal the obsolete Tenure of Office Act of 1867, which Republican senators had threatened to revive in order to embarrass him.

Cleveland was a conservative on all matters relating to money, and he was inflexibly opposed to wasteful expenditure of public funds. This caused him to investigate as many as possible of the hundreds of private bills passed by Congress to compensate private individuals, usually Federal veterans, for claims against the federal government. When, as was frequently the case, he judged these claims to be ill founded, he vetoed the bill. He was the first president to use the veto power extensively to block the enactment of this type of private legislation.

Cleveland's use of veto powers

The surplus and the tariff. The flurry of private pension bills had been stimulated, in part, by a growing surplus in the Treasury. In every year since the Civil War, there had been an excess of revenue over expenditures, a circumstance that encouraged suggestions for appropriations of public funds for a variety of purposes. The surplus also focussed attention upon the tariff, which was the principal source of this excess revenue. In 1883 Congress had reviewed the tariff and made numerous changes in the rates, increasing the tariff on some items and reducing it on others, without materially decreasing the revenue received. Cleveland believed that the surplus presented a very real problem. It hoarded in the Treasury money that could have been in circulation, and it encouraged reckless spending by the government. Like many other Democrats, he disliked the high protective tariff. After waiting in vain for two years for Congress to meet this issue boldly, Cleveland adopted the extraordinary tactic of devoting his entire annual message in 1887 to a discussion of this question and to an appeal for a lowering of the tariff. The House then passed a bill generally conforming to Cleveland's views on the tariff; but the Senate rejected it, and the tariff became a leading issue in the presidential campaign of 1888.

The public domain. After 1877 hundreds of thousands of agricultural settlers went westward to the plains, where they came into competition for control of the land with the cattlemen, who hitherto had dominated the open range. The pressure of population as it moved into the plains called attention to the diminishing supply of good arable land still open to settlement, thus presaging the day when there would no longer be a vast reservoir of land in the West awaiting the farmer. It also focussed attention on the fact that millions of acres of Western land were being held for speculative purposes and that other millions of acres had been acquired by questionable means or were still in the possession of railroads that had failed to fulfill the obligations they assumed when the land was granted to them. Upon assuming office, Cleveland was confronted with evidence that some of these claims had been fraudulently obtained by railroads, speculators, cattlemen, or lumbering interests. He ordered an investigation, and for more than a year agents of the Land Office roamed over the West uncovering evidence of irregularities and neglected obligations. Cleveland acted firmly. By executive orders and court action he succeeded in restoring more than 81,000,000 acres (33,000,000 hectares) to the public domain.

Diminish-
ing supply
of land

The Interstate Commerce Act. The railroads were vital to the economy of the nation, but because in so many regions a single company enjoyed a monopoly of rail transportation, many of the railroads adopted policies that large numbers of their customers believed to be unfair and discriminatory. Before 1884 it was clear that the Granger laws of the preceding decade (state laws prohibiting various abuses by the railroads) were ineffective, and pressure groups turned to the federal government for relief. In this, Western farm organizations were joined by influential Eastern businessmen who believed that they, too, were the victims of discrimination by the railroads. This powerful political alliance persuaded both parties to include regulation of the railroads in their national platforms in 1884 and induced Congress to enact the Interstate Commerce Act in 1887.

Interstate
Com-
merce Act

This law, designed to prevent unjust discrimination by the railroads, prohibited the pooling of traffic and profits, made it illegal for a railroad to charge more for a short haul than for a longer one, required that the roads publicize their rates, and established the Interstate Commerce Commission to supervise the enforcement of the law. The rulings of the commission were subject to review by the federal courts, the decisions of which tended to narrow the scope of the act. The commission was less effective than the sponsors of the act had hoped, but the act in itself was an indication of the growing realization that only the federal government could cope with the new economic problems of the day.

The election of 1888. Cleveland's plea for a reduction of the tariff in his annual message of 1887 made it certain that the tariff would be the central issue in the presidential campaign of 1888. The Democrats renominated Cleveland, although it was thought that he had endangered his chances of re-election by his outspoken advocacy of tariff reduction. The Republicans had their usual difficulty in selecting a candidate. Blaine refused to enter the race, and no other person in the party commanded substantial support. From among the many who were willing to accept the nomination, the Republicans selected Benjamin Harrison of Indiana, a Federal general in the Civil War and the grandson of Pres. William Henry Harrison.

Cleveland had won respect as a man of integrity and courage, but neither he nor Harrison aroused any great en-thusiasm among the voters. One feature of the campaign noted by observers was the extensive use of money to influence the outcome; this was not a new phenomenon, but the spending of money to carry doubtful states and the apparent alliance between business and political bosses had never before been so open.

The results were again close. Cleveland had a plurality of about 100,000 popular votes, but the Republicans carried two states, New York and Indiana, which they had lost in 1884, and in the electoral college Harrison won by a margin of 233 to 168.

The Benjamin Harrison administration. The Republicans also gained control of both houses of the 51st Congress. Their margin in the House of Representatives, however, was so small that it seemed uncertain whether they could carry controversial legislation through it. This obstacle was overcome by the speaker of the House, Thomas B. Reed of Maine. Reed refused to recognize dilatory motions, and, contrary to precedent, he counted as present all members who were in the chamber. Using that tactic, he ruled, on occasion, that a quorum was present even though fewer than a majority had actually answered a roll call. His iron rule of the House earned him the sobriquet Czar Reed, but only through his firm control of the House could the Republicans pass three controversial bills in the summer and early autumn of 1890. One dealt with monopolies, another with silver, and the third with the tariff.

The Sherman Anti-Trust Act. The first of these major measures declared illegal all combinations that restrained trade between states or with foreign nations. This law, known as the Sherman Anti-Trust Act, was passed by Congress early in July. It was the congressional response to evidence of growing public dissatisfaction with the development of industrial monopolies, which had been so notable a feature of the preceding decade.

Public
dissatis-
faction
with
monop-
olies

More than ten years passed before the Sherman Act was used to break up any industrial monopoly. It was invoked by the federal government in 1894 to obtain an injunction against a striking railroad union accused of restraint of interstate commerce, and the use of the injunction was upheld by the Supreme Court in 1895. Indeed, it is unlikely that the Senate would have passed the bill in 1890 had not the chairman of the Senate Judiciary Committee, George F. Edmunds of Vermont, felt certain that unions were combinations in restraint of trade within the meaning of the law. To those who hoped that the Sherman Act would inhibit the growth of monopoly, the results were disappointing. The passage of the act only three years after the Interstate Commerce Act was, however, another sign that the public was turning from state capitals to Washington for effective regulation of industrial giants.

The silver issue. Less than two weeks after Congress passed the antitrust law, it enacted the Sherman Silver Purchase Act, which required the secretary of the treasury to purchase each month 4,500,000 ounces (130,000 kilograms) of silver at the market price. This superseded the Bland–Allison Act of 1878 and had the effect of increasing the government's monthly purchase of silver by more than 50 percent. The act was adopted in response to pressure from mineowners, who were alarmed by the falling price of silver, and from Western farmers, who were always favourable to inflationary measures and who, in 1890, were also suffering from the depressed prices of their products.

The McKinley Tariff. Most Republican leaders had been lukewarm to the proposal to increase the purchase of silver and had accepted it only to assure Western votes for the measure in which they were most interested—upward revision of the protective tariff. This was accomplished in the McKinley Tariff Act of October 1890, passed by Congress one month before the midterm elections of that year. The tariff was designed to appeal to the farmers because some agricultural products were added to the protected list. A few items, notably sugar, were placed on the free list, and domestic sugar planters were to be compensated by a subsidy of two cents a pound. The central feature of the act, however, was a general increase in tariff schedules, with many of these increases applying to items of general consumption.

The new tariff immediately became an issue in the congressional elections. It failed to halt the downward spiral of farm prices, but there was an almost immediate increase in the cost of many items purchased by the farmers. With discontent already rife in the agricultural regions of the West and South, the McKinley Tariff added to the agrarian resentment. The outcome of the elections was a major defeat for the Republicans, whose strength in the House of Representatives was reduced by almost half.

The agrarian revolt. Political disaster befell the Republicans in the trans-Mississippi West, resulting from an economic and psychological depression that enveloped the region after widespread crop failures and the collapse of inflated land prices in the summer of 1887. The Western boom had begun in the late 1870s, when the tide of migration into the unoccupied farmlands beyond the Mississippi quickly led to the settlement of hitherto unoccupied parts of Iowa and Minnesota and to the pushing of the frontier westward across the plains almost literally to the shadows of the Rocky Mountains.

Westward expansion was encouraged by the railroads that served the region. It was supported by the satisfactory price and encouraging foreign market for wheat, the money crop of the plains. For ten years, from 1877 through 1886, the farmers on the plains had the benefit of an abnormally generous rainfall, leading many to assume that climatic conditions had changed and that the rain belt had moved westward to provide adequate rainfall for the plains. Confidence was followed by unrestrained optimism that engendered wild speculation and a rise in land prices. Lured on by these illusions, the settlers went into debt to make improvements on their farms while small-town leaders dreamed of prodigious growth and authorized bond issues to construct the public improvements they felt certain would soon be needed.

The collapse of these dreams came in 1887. The year opened ominously when the plains were swept by a catastrophic blizzard in January that killed thousands of head of cattle and virtually destroyed the cattle industry of the open range. The following summer was dry and hot; crops were poor; and, to compound the woes of the farmers, the price of wheat began to slide downward. The dry summer of 1887 was the beginning of a ten-year cycle of little rainfall and searingly hot summers. By the autumn of 1887 the exodus from the plains had begun; five years later, areas of western Kansas and Nebraska that had once been thriving agricultural centres were almost depopulated. The agricultural regions east of the plains were less directly affected, though there the farmers suffered from the general decline in farm prices.

Although the disaster on the plains bred a sense of distress and frustration, the lure of good land was still strong. When the central portion of the present state of Oklahoma was opened to settlement in April 1889, an army of eager settlers, estimated to have numbered 100,000, rushed into the district to claim homesteads and build homes.

The Populists. The collapse of the boom and the falling prices of agricultural products forced many farmers to seek relief through political action. In 1888 and again in 1890 this discontent was expressed through local political groups, commonly known as Farmers' Alliances, which quickly spread through parts of the West and South. The alliances won some local victories and contributed to the discomfiture of the Republicans in 1890. They were not, however, an effective vehicle for concerted political action; and in 1891 the leaders of the alliances organized the Populist (People's) Party.

The Populists aspired to become a national party and hoped to attract support from labour and from reform groups generally. In practice they continued through their brief career to be almost wholly a party of farmers, with a platform tailored to meet the wishes of Western farmers. They demanded an increase in the circulating currency, to be achieved by the unlimited coinage of silver, a graduated income tax, government ownership of the railroads, a tariff for revenue only, the direct election of United States senators, and other measures designed to strengthen polit-

ical democracy and give the farmers economic parity with business and industry. In 1892 the Populists nominated Gen. James B. Weaver of Iowa for president.

The election of 1892. The nominees of the two major parties for president in 1892 were the same as in the election of 1888. The Republicans reluctantly renominated Harrison, whose personal relations with many party leaders were distinctly cool. Before the Democratic convention there was a spirited struggle for the nomination between Cleveland and Gov. David Hill of New York, but Cleveland had far greater support among rank-and-file Democrats and was nominated on the first ballot.

The unpopularity of the McKinley Tariff gave Cleveland an advantage, as did the discontent in the West, which was directed largely against the Republican Party. From the beginning of the campaign it appeared probable that the Democrats would be successful, and Cleveland carried not only the southern states but such key northern states as New York and Illinois. His electoral vote was 277 to 145 for Harrison. Weaver carried four Western states, three of them states with important silver mines, and received 22 electoral votes.

Cleveland's second term. When Cleveland was inaugurated for his second term in March 1893, the country hovered on the brink of financial panic. Six years of depression in the trans-Mississippi West, the decline of foreign trade after the enactment of the McKinley Tariff, and an abnormally high burden of private debt were disquieting features of the situation. Most attention was centred, however, on the gold reserve in the federal Treasury. It was assumed that a minimum reserve of $100,000,000 was necessary to assure redemption of government obligations in gold. When, on April 21, 1893, the reserve fell below that amount, the psychological impact was far-reaching. Investors hastened to convert their holdings into gold; banks and brokerage houses were hard pressed; and many business houses and financial institutions failed. Prices dropped, employment was curtailed, and the nation entered a period of severe economic depression that continued for more than three years.

The causes of this disaster were numerous and complex, but the attention that focussed on the gold reserve tended to concentrate concern upon a single factor—the restoration of the Treasury's supply of gold. It was widely believed that the principal cause of the drain on the Treasury was the obligation to purchase large amounts of silver. To those who held this view, the obvious remedy was the repeal of the Sherman Silver Purchase Act.

The issue was political as well as economic. It divided both major parties, but most of the leading advocates of existing silver policies were Democrats. Cleveland, however, had long been opposed to the silver purchase policy and in the crisis he resolved upon repeal as an essential step in protecting the Treasury. He therefore called Congress to meet in special session on August 7, 1893.

The new Congress had Democratic majorities in both houses, and, if it had any mandate, it was to repeal the McKinley Tariff. It had no mandate on the silver issue, and more than half of its Democratic members came from constituencies that favoured an increase in the coinage of silver. Cleveland faced a herculean task in forcing repeal through Congress, but, by the use of every power at his command, he gained his objective. The Sherman Silver Purchase Act was repealed at the end of October by a bill that made no compensating provision for the coinage of silver. Cleveland had won a personal triumph, but he had irrevocably divided his party; and in some sections of the nation he had become the most unpopular president of his generation.

The extent to which Cleveland had lost control of his party became apparent when Congress turned from silver to the tariff. The House passed a bill that would have revised tariff rates downward in accordance with the President's views. In the Senate, however, the bill was so altered that it bore little resemblance to the original measure, and on some items it imposed higher duties than had the McKinley Act. It was finally passed in August 1894, but Cleveland was so dissatisfied that he refused to sign it; and it became law without his signature. The act contained a

Margin notes:

Farmers' resentment of the tariff

Settlement of Oklahoma

The Panic of 1893

Cleveland's splitting of the Democratic Party

provision for an income tax, but this feature was declared unconstitutional by the Supreme Court in 1895.

In the midterm elections of 1894 the Republicans recaptured control of both houses of Congress. This indicated the discontent produced by the continuing depression. It also guaranteed that, with a Democratic president and Republican Congress, there would be inaction in domestic legislation while both parties looked forward to the election of 1896.

At their convention in St. Louis the Republicans selected Gov. William McKinley of Ohio as their presidential nominee. He had served in the Federal Army during the Civil War, and his record as governor of Ohio tended to offset his association with the unpopular tariff of 1890. His most effective support in winning the nomination, however, was provided by Mark Hanna, a wealthy Cleveland businessman who was McKinley's closest friend.

The Democratic convention in Chicago was unusually exciting. It was controlled by groups hostile to Cleveland's financial policies, and it took the unprecedented step of rejecting a resolution commending the administration of a president of its own party. The debate on the party platform featured an eloquent defense of agrarian interests by William Jennings Bryan, which won him not only a prolonged ovation but also his party's presidential nomination. Bryan was a former congressman from Nebraska, and at 36 he was the youngest man ever to be the nominee for president of a major party. By experience and conviction he shared the outlook of the agrarian elements that dominated the convention and whose principal spokesman he became.

Bryan conducted a vigorous campaign. For the first time a presidential candidate carried his case to the people in all parts of the country, and for a time it appeared that he might win. The worried conservatives charged that Bryan was a dangerous demagogue, and they interpreted the campaign as a conflict between defenders of a sound economic system that would produce prosperity and dishonest radicals who championed reckless innovations that would undermine the financial security of the nation. On this interpretation they succeeded in raising large campaign funds from industrialists who feared their interests were threatened. With this money, the Republicans were able to turn the tide and win a decisive victory. Outside the South, Bryan carried only the Western silver states and Kansas and Nebraska.

Economic recovery.   Soon after taking office on March 4, 1897, McKinley called Congress into special session to revise the tariff once again. Congress responded by passing the Dingley Tariff Act, which eliminated many items from the free list and generally raised duties on imports to the highest level they had yet reached.

Although the preservation of the gold standard had been the chief appeal of the Republicans in 1896, it was not until March 1900 that Congress enacted the Gold Standard Act, which required the Treasury to maintain a minimum gold reserve of $150,000,000 and authorized the issuance of bonds, if necessary, to protect that minimum. In 1900 such a measure was almost anticlimactic, for an adequate gold supply had ceased to be a practical problem. Beginning in 1893, the production of gold in the United States had increased steadily; by 1899 the annual value of gold added to the American supply was double that of any year between 1881 and 1892. The chief source of the new supply of gold was the Klondike, where important deposits of gold had been discovered during the summer of 1896.

Increase in gold production

By 1898 the depression had run its course; farm prices and the volume of farm exports were again rising steadily, and Western farmers appeared to forget their recent troubles and to regain confidence in their economic prospects. In industry, the return of prosperity was marked by a resumption of the move toward more industrial combinations, despite the antitrust law; and great banking houses, such as J.P. Morgan and Company of New York, played a key role in many of the most important of these combinations by providing the necessary capital and receiving, in return, an influential voice in the management of the companies created by this capital.   (H.W.Br.)

Imperialism, the Progressive Era, and the rise to world power, 1896–1920

AMERICAN IMPERIALISM

The Spanish–American War.   Militarily speaking, the Spanish–American War of 1898 was so brief and relatively bloodless as to have been a mere passing episode in the history of modern warfare. Its political and diplomatic consequences, however, were enormous: it catapulted the United States into the arena of world politics and set it, at least briefly, on the new road of imperialism. To be sure, specific events drove the United States to hostilities in 1898; but the stage had already been set by profound changes in thought about the nation's mission and its destiny.

The United States in world politics

Before the 1890s, roughly speaking, most Americans had adhered stubbornly to the belief, as old as the Revolution itself, that their country should remain aloof from European affairs and offer an example of democracy and peace to the rest of the world; but slowly in the 1880s, and more rapidly in the 1890s, new currents of thought eroded this historic conviction. The United States had become a great power by virtue of its prodigious economic growth since the Civil War; numerous publicists said that it ought to begin to act like one. Propagandists of sea power argued that future national security and greatness depended upon a large navy supported by bases throughout the world. After the disappearance of the American frontier in 1890, the conviction grew that the United States would have to find new outlets for an ever-increasing population and agricultural and industrial production; this belief was particularly rife among farmers in dire distress in the 1890s. Social Darwinists said that the world is a jungle, with international rivalries inevitable, and that only strong nations could survive. Added to these arguments were those of idealists and religious leaders that Americans had a duty to "take up the white man's burden" and to carry their assertedly superior culture and the blessings of Christianity to the backward peoples of the world.

It was against this background that the events of 1898 propelled the United States along the road to war and empire. Cuban rebels had begun a violent revolution against Spanish rule in 1895, set off by a depression caused by a decline in U.S. sugar purchases from Cuba. Rebel violence led progressively to more repressive Spanish countermeasures. Cuban refugees in the United States spread exaggerated tales of Spanish atrocities, and these and numerous others were reprinted widely (particularly by William Randolph Hearst's New York *American* and Joseph Pulitzer's New York *World,* then engaged in a fierce battle for circulation). Pres. Grover Cleveland resisted the rising public demand for intervention, until by early 1898 the pressure, then on his successor, William McKinley, was too great to be defied. When an explosion—caused by a submarine mine, according to a U.S. naval court of inquiry—sank the USS "Maine" with large loss of life in Havana Harbour on February 15, 1898, events moved beyond the President's control. Though Spain was willing to make large concessions to avoid war, it adamantly resisted what had become the minimum public and official U.S. demand— Spanish withdrawal from Cuba and recognition of the island's independence. Hence Congress in mid-April authorized the President to use the armed forces to expel the Spanish from Cuba.

For Americans it was, as Secretary of State John Hay put it in a letter to Theodore Roosevelt, "a splendid little war." An American expeditionary force, after quickly overcoming the Spaniards in Cuba, turned against Spain's last island in the Caribbean, Puerto Rico. Meanwhile, on May 1, 1898, the American commodore George Dewey, with his Asiatic squadron, destroyed a decrepit Spanish flotilla in the Harbour of Manila in the Philippines.

War with Spain

The fighting was over by August 12, when the United States and Spain signed a preliminary peace treaty in Washington, D.C. Negotiators met in Paris in October to draw up a definitive agreement. Spain recognized the independence of Cuba and ceded Puerto Rico to the United States, but the disposition of the Philippines was another matter. Business interests in the United States, which had been noticeably cool about a war over Cuba, demanded the acquisition of the entire Philippine Archipelago in the hope that Manila would become the base for a great Far Eastern trade; chauvinists declaimed against lowering the flag under Spanish pressure. Concluding that he had no alternative, McKinley forced the Spanish to "sell" the Philippines to the United States for $20,000,000.

But a strong reaction in the United States against acquisition of the Philippines had already set in by the time the Treaty of Paris was signed on December 10, 1898; and anti-imperialists declared that the control and governance of distant alien peoples violated all American traditions of self-determination and would even threaten the very fabric of the republic. Though there were more than enough votes in the Senate to defeat the treaty, that body gave its consent to ratification largely because William Jennings Bryan, the Democratic leader, wanted Democrats to approve the treaty and then make imperialism the chief issue of the 1900 presidential campaign.

The new American empire.   McKinley easily defeated Bryan in 1900. The victory, however, was hardly a mandate for imperialism, and, as events were soon to disclose, the American people were perhaps the most reluctant imperialists in history. No sooner had they acquired an overseas empire than they set in motion the processes of its dissolution or transformation.

By the so-called Teller Amendment to the war resolution, Congress had declared that the United States would not annex Cuba. This pledge was kept, although Cuba was forced in 1903 to sign a treaty making it virtually a protectorate of the United States. The Hawaiian Islands, annexed by Congress on July 7, 1898, were made a territory in 1900 and were hence, technically, only briefly part of the American empire. Puerto Rico was given limited self-government in 1900; and the Jones Act of 1917 conferred full territorial status on the island, gave U.S. citizenship to its inhabitants, and limited its self-government only by the veto of a governor appointed by the president of the United States. Establishing any kind of government in the Philippines was much more difficult because a large band of Filipinos resisted American rule as bravely as they had fought the Spanish. The Philippine insurrection was over by 1901, however, and the Philippine Government Act of 1902 inaugurated the beginning of partial self-government, which was transformed into almost complete home rule by the Jones Act of 1916.

The Open Door in the Far East.   Although Americans were reluctant imperialists, the United States was an important Pacific power after 1898, and American businessmen had inflated ambitions to tap what they thought was the enormous Chinese market. The doors to that market were being rapidly closed in the 1890s, however, as Britain, France, Russia, and Japan carved out large so-called spheres of influence all the way from Manchuria to southern China. With Britain's support (the British stood to gain the most from equal trade opportunities), on September 6, 1899, Secretary of State John Hay addressed the first so-called Open Door note to the powers with interests in China; it asked them to accord equal trade and investment opportunities to all nationals in their spheres of interest and leased territories. With considerable bravado, Hay announced that all the powers had agreed to respect the Open Door, even though the Russians had declined to give any pledges. On July 3, 1900, after the Boxer Rebellion—an uprising in China against foreign influence—Hay circulated a second Open Door note announcing that it was American policy to preserve Chinese territorial and political integrity.

Such pronouncements had little effect because the United States was not prepared to support the Open Door Policy with force; successive administrations to the 1940s, however, considered it the cornerstone of their Far Eastern policy. Pres. Theodore Roosevelt reluctantly mediated the Russo-Japanese War in 1905 in part to protect the Open Door as well as to maintain a balance of power in the Far East. When Japan attempted in 1915 to force a virtual protectorate on China, Pres. Woodrow Wilson intervened sternly and in large measure successfully to protect Chinese independence. Victory for American policy seemed

to come with the Nine-Power Treaty of Washington of 1922, when all nations with interests in China promised to respect the Open Door.

Building the Panama Canal and American domination in the Caribbean.   Strategic necessity and the desire of eastern businessmen to have easy access to Pacific markets combined in the late 1890s to convince the President, Congress, and a vast majority of Americans that an isthmian canal linking the Atlantic and Pacific oceans was vital to national security and prosperity. In the Hay–Pauncefote Treaty of 1901, the British government gave up the rights to joint construction with the United States that it had gained under the Clayton–Bulwer Treaty of 1850. A French company, which had tried unsuccessfully to dig a canal across the Isthmus of Panama, was eager to sell its right of way to the United States. Thus, the only obstacle to the project was the government of Colombia, which owned Panama. When Colombia refused to cooperate, Roosevelt, in 1903, covertly supported a Panamanian revolution engineered by officials of the French company. A treaty was quickly negotiated between the United States and the new Republic of Panama; construction began, and the canal was opened to shipping on August 15, 1914.

Concern over what Americans regarded increasingly as their "lifeline" increased in proportion to progress in the construction of the canal. An early manifestation of that concern came in 1902–03, when Britain, Germany, and Italy blockaded Venezuela to force the payment of debts, and particularly when the Germans bombarded and destroyed a Venezuelan town; so agitated was American opinion that Roosevelt used a veiled threat to force Germany to accept arbitration of the debt question by the Hague Court. When the Dominican Republic defaulted on its foreign debt to several European countries in 1904, Roosevelt quickly established an American receivership of the Dominican customs in order to collect the revenues to meet the country's debt payments. Moreover, in his annual message to Congress of 1904, the President announced a new Latin American policy, soon called the Roosevelt Corollary to the Monroe Doctrine—because the Monroe Doctrine forbade European use of force in the New World, the United States would itself take whatever action necessary to guarantee that Latin American states gave no cause for such European intervention. It was, in fact, a considerable extension of the Monroe Doctrine, not a correct historical interpretation of it; but it remained the cornerstone of American policy in the Caribbean at least until 1928.

Actually, Roosevelt was reluctant to interfere in the domestic affairs of neighbouring states; his one significant intervention after 1904—the administration of the Cuban government from 1906 to 1909—was undertaken in order to prevent civil war and at the insistence of Cuban authorities. Roosevelt's successor, however, William Howard Taft, had more ambitious plans to guarantee American hegemony in the approaches to the Panama Canal. Adopting a policy called Dollar Diplomacy, Taft hoped to persuade American private bankers to displace European creditors in the Caribbean area and thereby to increase American influence and encourage stability in countries prone to revolution. Dollar Diplomacy was a total failure; its one result was to involve the United States in a civil war in Nicaragua with the effect of perpetuating a reactionary and unpopular regime.

The accession of Woodrow Wilson in 1913 seemed to augur the beginning of a new era in Latin American relations; the new president and his secretary of state, William J. Bryan, were idealists who had strongly condemned interventions and Dollar Diplomacy. But although Wilson did negotiate a treaty with Colombia to make reparation for U.S. complicity in the Panamanian revolution, it was defeated by the Senate. Moreover, Wilson tried hard to promote a Pan-American nonaggression pact; but it foundered on the opposition of certain Latin American governments.

When crises threatened the domestic stability of the Caribbean area, however, Wilson revealed that he was just as determined to protect American security as Roosevelt and Taft had been and that he was perhaps even more

Dollar
Diplomacy

willing to use force. Frequent revolutions and the fear of European intervention led Wilson to impose a protectorate and a puppet government upon Haiti in 1915 and a military occupation of the Dominican Republic in 1916. He concluded a treaty with Nicaragua making that country a protectorate of the United States. Moreover, he purchased the Danish Virgin Islands in 1916 at the inflated price of $25,000,000 in order to prevent their possible transfer from Denmark to Germany.

THE PROGRESSIVE ERA

The character and variety of the Progressive movement. The inauguration of Pres. William McKinley in 1897 had seemed to mark the end of an era of domestic turmoil and the beginning of a new period of unparalleled tranquility. Prosperity was returning after the devastating Panic of 1893. The agrarian uprising led by Bryan in the election of 1896 had been turned back, and the national government was securely in the hands of friends of big business. The Dingley Tariff of 1897 greatly increased tariff rates; the Gold Standard Act of 1897 dashed the hopes of advocates of the free coinage of silver; and McKinley did nothing to stop a series of industrial combinations in defiance of the Sherman Anti-Trust Act.

Origins of Progressivism. Never were superficial signs more deceiving than during McKinley's first term. Actually, the United States already was in the first stages of what historians came to call the Progressive Movement. Generally speaking, Progressivism was the response of various groups to problems raised by the rapid industrialization and urbanization that followed the Civil War. These problems included the spread of slums and poverty; the exploitation of labour; the breakdown of democratic government in the cities and states caused by the emergence of political organizations, or machines, allied with business interests; and a rapid movement toward financial and industrial concentration. Many Americans feared that their historic traditions of responsible democratic government and free economic opportunity for all were being destroyed by gigantic combinations of economic and political power.

Actually there was not, either in the 1890s or later, any one Progressive movement. There were numerous movements for reform and reconstruction on the local, state, and national levels that were too diverse, and sometimes too mutually antagonistic, ever to coalesce into a national crusade. But they were generally motivated by common assumptions and goals—*e.g.,* the repudiation of individualism and laissez-faire, concern for the underprivileged and downtrodden, the restoration of government to the rank and file, and the enlargement of governmental power in order to bring industry and finance under a measure of popular control.

The origins of Progressivism were as complex and are as difficult to describe as the movement itself. In the vanguard were various agrarian crusades, such as the Grangers and the Populists and Democrats under Bryan, with their demands for stringent railroad regulation and national control of banks and the money supply. At the same time a new generation of economists, sociologists, and political scientists was undermining the philosophical foundations of the laissez-faire state and constructing a new ideology to justify democratic collectivism; and a new school of social workers was establishing settlement houses and going into the slums to discover the extent of human degradation. Allied with them was a growing body of ministers, priests, and rabbis—proponents of what was called the Social Gospel—who struggled to arouse the social concerns and consciences of their parishioners. Finally, journalists called "muckrakers" probed into all the dark corners of American life and carried their message of reform through mass-circulation newspapers and magazines.

Two specific catalytic agents set off the Progressive movement—the agrarian depression of the early 1890s and the financial and industrial depression that began in 1893. Low prices drove farmers by the hundreds of thousands into the radical People's Party of 1892. Widespread suffering in the cities beginning in 1893 caused a breakdown of many social services and dramatized for the increasing

number of urban middle class Americans the wide contrast between rich and poor.

Urban reforms. A movement already begun, to wrest control of city governments from corrupt political machines, was given tremendous impetus by the Panic of 1893. The National Municipal League, organized in 1894, united various city reform groups throughout the country; corrupt local governments were overthrown in such cities as New York in 1894, Baltimore in 1895, and Chicago in 1896–97. And so it went all over the country well into the 20th century.

Despite differences among urban reformers at the beginning of their movement, by the early 1900s the vast majority of them were fighting for and winning much the same objectives—more equitable taxation of railroad and corporate property, tenement house reform, better schools, and expanded social services for the poor. Even big-city machines like Tammany Hall became increasingly sensitive to the social and economic needs of their constituents. Reformers also devised new forms of city government to replace the old mayor–city-council arrangement that had proved to be so susceptible to corrupt influences. One was the commission form, which vested all responsibility in a small group of commissioners, each responsible for a single department; another was the city-manager form, which provided administration by a professionally trained expert, responsible to a popularly elected council (these two forms were in widespread use in small and medium-sized cities by 1916).

Reform in state governments. The reform movement spread almost at once to the state level, for it was in state capitals that important decisions affecting the cities were made. Entrenched and very professional political organizations, generously financed by officeholders and businessmen wanting special privileges, controlled most state governments in the late 1890s; everywhere, these organizations were challenged by a rising generation of young and idealistic anti-organization leaders, ambitious for power. They were most successful in the Middle West, under such leaders as Robert M. La Follette of Wisconsin; but they had counterparts all over the country—*e.g.,* Charles Evans Hughes of New York, Woodrow Wilson of New Jersey, Andrew J. Montague of Virginia, and Hiram W. Johnson of California.

These young leaders revolutionized the art and practice of politics in the United States, not only by exercising strong leadership but also by effecting institutional changes such as the direct primary, direct election of senators (rather than by state legislatures), the initiative, referendum, and recall—which helped restore and revitalized political democracy. More important, perhaps, progressives to a large degree achieved their economic and social objectives—among them, strict regulation of intrastate railroads and public utilities, legislation to prevent child labour and to protect women workers, penal reform, expanded charitable services to the poor, and accident insurance systems to provide compensation to workers and their families.

Theodore Roosevelt and the Progressive movement. By 1901 the reform upheaval was too strong to be contained within state boundaries. Moreover, certain problems cried out for solution, with which only the federal government was apparently competent to deal. McKinley might have succeeded in ignoring the rising tide of public opinion, had he served out his second term. But McKinley's assassination in September 1901 brought to the presidency an entirely different kind of man—Theodore Roosevelt, at age 42 the youngest man yet to enter the White House. Roosevelt had broad democratic sympathies; moreover, thanks to his experience as police commissioner of New York City and governor of New York State, he was the first president to have an intimate knowledge of modern urban problems. Because Congress was securely controlled by a group of archconservative Republicans, the new president had to feel his way cautiously in legislative matters; but he emerged full-grown as a tribune of the people after his triumph in the presidential election of 1904. By 1906 he was the undisputed spokesman of national Progressivism and by far its best publicity agent. (The White House was, he said, "a bully pulpit.") Meanwhile, by his leadership of

[margin notes:]

Problems of industrialization and urbanization

Depressions of the early 1890s

Anti-organizational leaders

public opinion and by acting as a spur on Congress, he had revived the presidency and made it incomparably the most powerful force in national politics.

In 1901 Americans were perhaps most alarmed about the spread of so-called trusts, or industrial combinations, which they thought were responsible for the steady price increases that had occurred each year since 1897. Ever alert to the winds of public opinion, Roosevelt responded by activating the Sherman Anti-Trust Act of 1890, which had lain dormant because of Cleveland's and McKinley's refusal to enforce it and also because of the Supreme Court's ruling of 1895 that the measure did not apply to combinations in manufacturing. Beginning in 1902 with a suit to dissolve a northwestern railroad monopoly, Roosevelt moved next against the so-called Beef Trust, then against the oil, tobacco, and other monopolies. In every case the Supreme Court supported the administration, going so far in the oil and tobacco decisions of 1911 as to reverse its 1895 decision. In addition, in 1903 Roosevelt persuaded a reluctant Congress to establish a Bureau of Corporations with sweeping power to investigate business practices; the bureau's thoroughgoing reports were of immense assistance in antitrust cases. While establishing the supremacy of the federal government in the industrial field, Roosevelt, in 1902, also took action unprecedented in the history of the presidency by intervening on labour's behalf to force the arbitration of a strike by the United Mine Workers of America against the Pennsylvania anthracite coal operators.

Roosevelt moved much more aggressively after his 1904 election. Public demand for effective national regulation of interstate railroad rates had been growing since the Supreme Court had emasculated the Interstate Commerce Commission's (ICC) rate-making authority in the 1880s. Determined to bring the railroads—the country's single greatest private economic interest—under effective national control, Roosevelt waged an unrelenting battle with Congress in 1905–06. The outcome—the Hepburn Act of 1906—was his own personal triumph; it greatly enlarged the ICC's jurisdiction and forbade railroads to increase rates without its approval. By using the same tactics of aggressive leadership, Roosevelt in 1906 also obtained passage of a Meat Inspection Act and a Pure Food and Drug Act. Passage of the former was aided by the publication of Upton Sinclair's famous novel, *The Jungle* (1906), which revealed in gory detail the insanitary conditions of the Chicago stockyards and packing plants.

Meanwhile, almost from his accession to the presidency, Roosevelt had been carrying on a crusade, often independent of Congress, to conserve the nation's fast-dwindling natural resources and to make them available for exploitation under rigorous national supervision. He withdrew from the public domain some 148,000,000 acres of forest lands, 80,000,000 acres of mineral lands, and 1,500,000 acres of water-power sites. Moreover, adoption of the National Reclamation Act of 1902 made possible the beginning of an ambitious federal program of irrigation and hydroelectric development in the West.

Republican troubles under William Howard Taft. Roosevelt was so much the idol of the masses of 1908 that he could have easily gained the Republican nomination in that year. After his election in 1904, however, he had announced that he would not be a candidate four years later; adhering stubbornly to his pledge, he arranged the nomination of his secretary of war, William Howard Taft of Ohio, who easily defeated Bryan.

Taft might have made an ideal president during a time of domestic tranquility, but his tenure in the White House was far from peaceful. National progressivism was nearly at high tide; and a large group of Republican progressives, called "insurgents," sat in both houses of Congress.

The Republican insurgents. These Republicans, like a majority of Americans, demanded such reforms as tariff reductions, an income tax, the direct election of senators, and even stricter railroad and corporation regulations. Taft, who had strongly supported Roosevelt's policies, thought of himself as a progressive. Actually he was temperamentally and philosophically a conservative; moreover, he lacked the qualities of a dynamic popular leader.

In the circumstances, his ineptness, indecision, and failure to lead could only spell disaster for his party.

Taft's troubles began when he called Congress into special session in 1909 to take up the first item on his agenda—tariff reform. The measure that emerged from Congress actually increased rates. Republican insurgents and a majority of Americans were outraged, but Taft signed the bill and called it the best tariff law that the Republican Party had ever enacted.

By 1910 the Republican insurgents were clearly in the ascendancy in the Congress. Taking control of the President's railroad-regulation measure they added new provisions that greatly enlarged the ICC's authority. The following year they bitterly opposed Taft's measure for tariff reciprocity with Canada; it passed with Democratic support in Congress, only to go down to defeat at the hands of the Canadian electorate.

The 1912 election. Republican insurgents were determined to prevent Taft's renomination in 1912. They found their leader in Roosevelt, who had become increasingly alienated from Taft and who made a whirlwind campaign for the presidential nomination in the winter and spring of 1912. Roosevelt swept the presidential primaries, even in Taft's own state of Ohio; but Taft and conservative Republicans controlled the powerful state organizations and the Republican National Committee and were able to nominate Taft by a narrow margin. Convinced that the bosses had stolen the nomination from him, Roosevelt led his followers out of the Republican convention. In August they organized the Progressive Party at Chicago and named Roosevelt to lead the third-party cause.

Democrats had swept the 1910 congressional and gubernatorial elections; and after the disruption of the Republican Party in the spring of 1912, it was obvious that almost any passable Democrat could win the presidency in that year. Woodrow Wilson, former president of Princeton University, who had made a brilliant progressive record as governor of New Jersey, was nominated by the Democrats on the 46th ballot.

Taft's single objective in the 1912 campaign was to defeat Roosevelt. The real contest was between Roosevelt and Wilson for control of the progressive majority. Campaigning strenuously on a platform that he called the New Nationalism, Roosevelt demanded effective control of big business through a strong federal commission, radical tax reform, and a whole series of measures to put the federal government squarely into the business of social and economic reform. By contrast Wilson seemed conservative with a program he called the New Freedom; it envisaged a concerted effort to destroy monopoly and to open the doors of economic opportunity to small businessmen through drastic tariff reduction, banking reform, and severe tightening of the antitrust laws. Roosevelt outpolled Taft in the election, but he failed to win many Democratic progressives away from Wilson, who won by a huge majority of electoral votes, though receiving only about 42 percent of the popular vote.

The New Freedom and its transformation. A trained political scientist and historian, Wilson believed that the president should be the leader of public opinion, the chief formulator of legislative policy, and virtually sovereign in the conduct of foreign relations. With the support of an aroused public opinion and a compliant Democratic majority, he was able to put his theories of leadership into effect with spectacular success.

The first item in Wilson's program was tariff reform, a perennial Democratic objective since the Civil War; the President's measure, the Underwood Tariff Act of 1913, reduced average rates from 40 percent to 25 percent, greatly enlarged the free list, and included a modest income tax. Next came adoption of the President's measure for banking and monetary reform, the Federal Reserve Act of 1913, which created a federal reserve system to mobilize banking reserves and issue a flexible new currency—federal reserve notes—based on gold and commercial paper; uniting and supervising the entire system was a federal reserve board of presidential appointees.

The third, and Wilson thought the last, part of the New Freedom program was antitrust reform. In his first sig-

Marginal notes:

The breaking of the trusts

The high tide of Progressivism

Wilson's domestic program

nificant movement toward Roosevelt's New Nationalism, Wilson reversed his position that merely strengthening the Sherman Anti-Trust Act would suffice to prevent monopoly. Instead, he took up and pushed through Congress the Progressive-sponsored Federal Trade Commission Act of 1914. It established an agency—the Federal Trade Commission (FTC)—with sweeping authority to prevent business practices that would lead to monopoly. Meanwhile, Wilson had abandoned his original measure, the Clayton Anti-Trust Bill passed by Congress in 1914; its severe provisions against interlocking directorates and practices tending toward monopoly had been gravely weakened by the time the President signed it. The Clayton Bill included a declaration that labour unions, as such, were not to be construed as conspiracies in restraint of trade in violation of the antitrust laws; but what organized labour wanted, and did not get, was immunity from prosecution for such measures as the sympathetic strike and the secondary boycott, which the courts had proscribed as violations of the Sherman Act.

In a public letter in November 1914, the President announced that his reform program was complete. But various groups were still demanding the advanced kind of social and economic legislation that Roosevelt had advocated in 1912; also, by early 1916 the Progressive Party had largely disintegrated, and Wilson knew that he could win re-election only with the support of a substantial minority of Roosevelt's former followers. Consequently— and also because his own political thinking had been moving toward a more advanced progressive position— Wilson struck out upon a new political course in 1916. He began by appointing Louis D. Brandeis, the leading critic of big business and finance, to the Supreme Court. Then in quick succession he obtained passage of a rural-credits measure to supply cheap long-term credit to farmers; anti-child-labour and federal workmen's-compensation legislation; the Adamson Act, establishing the eight-hour day for interstate railroad workers; and measures for federal aid to education and highway construction. With such a program behind him, Wilson was able to rally a new coalition of Democrats, former Progressives, independents, social workers, and a large minority of Socialists; and he narrowly defeated his Republican opponent, Charles Evans Hughes, in the 1916 presidential election.

THE RISE TO WORLD POWER

Woodrow Wilson and the Mexican revolution. Although Wilson's consuming interest was in domestic politics, he had to deal primarily with foreign affairs while in the White House; and before the end of his presidency he had developed into a diplomatist of great skill as well as one of the commanding figures in world affairs. He was a "strong" president in the conduct of foreign policy, writing most of the important diplomatic correspondence of his government and making all important decisions himself. He usually worked well with his secretaries of state, Bryan and Robert Lansing, and often relied for advice upon his confidential counsellor, Col. Edward M. House of Texas.

Wilson served his apprenticeship by having to deal at the outset of his administration with an uprising in Mexico, set off when a military usurper, Victoriano Huerta, murdered liberal president Francisco Madero and seized the executive power in February 1913. It was difficult for the United States to remain aloof because Americans had invested heavily in Mexico and 40,000 American citizens resided there.

If Wilson had followed conventional policy and the urgings of Americans with interests in Mexico, he would have recognized Huerta (as most European governments did), who promised to respect and protect all foreign investments and concessions. But Wilson was revolted by Huerta's bloody rise to power; moreover, he believed that the revolution begun by Madero in 1910 was a glorious episode in the history of human liberty. Wilson thus not only refused to recognize Huerta but also tried to persuade the dictator to step down from office and permit the holding of free elections for a new democratic government. When Huerta refused to cooperate, Wilson gave open support to the Constitutionalists—Huerta's opponents under Madero's successor, Venustiano Carranza— and when it seemed that the Constitutionalists could not themselves drive Huerta from power, Wilson seized the port of Veracruz in April 1914 to cut off Huerta's supplies and revenues. This stratagem succeeded, and Carranza and his army occupied Mexico City in August.

The revolutionary forces then divided between Carranza's followers and those of his chief rival and most colorful general, Pancho Villa; and civil war raged for another year. Wilson refused to interfere; Carranza emerged victoriously by the summer of 1915, and Wilson accorded him de facto recognition in October. But Villa, seeking to provoke war between the United States and Mexico, raided Columbus, New Mexico, on March 9, 1916, burning the town and killing 19 inhabitants. Wilson sent a punitive expedition under Gen. John J. Pershing into Mexico in hot pursuit of Villa; but the wily bandit eluded Pershing, and the deeper the Americans penetrated into Mexican territory, the more agitated the Carranza government became. There were two serious skirmishes between regular Mexican and American troops in the spring, and full-scale war was averted only when Wilson withdrew Pershing's column some months later. Relations between the two governments were greatly improved when Wilson extended de jure recognition to Carranza's new constitutional regime in April 1917. Thereafter, Wilson adamantly rejected all further foreign and American suggestions for intervention in Mexico.

The struggle for neutrality. The outbreak of general war in Europe in August 1914 raised grave challenges to Wilson's skill and leadership in foreign affairs. In spite of the appeals of propagandists for the rival Allies and Central Powers, the great majority of Americans were doggedly neutral and determined to avoid involvement unless American rights and interests were violated. This, too, was Wilson's own feeling, and in August he issued an official proclamation of neutrality and two weeks later appealed to Americans to be "impartial in thought as well as in action."

Loans and supplies for the Allies. Difficulties arose first with the British government, which at once used its vast fleet to establish a long-range blockade of Germany. The U.S. State Department sent several strong protests to London, particularly against British suppression of American exports of food and raw materials to Germany. Anglo-American blockade controversies were not acute, however, because the British put their blockade controls into effect gradually, always paid for goods seized, argued persuasively that in a total war food and raw materials were as essential as guns and ammunition, and pointed out that they, the British, were simply following blockade precedents established by the United States itself during the Civil War. As a result of a tacit Anglo-American agreement, the United States soon became the chief external source of supply for the food, raw materials, and munitions that fed the British and French war machines. In addition, and in accordance with the strict rules of neutrality, the Wilson administration permitted the Allied governments to borrow more than $2,000,000,000 in the United States in order to finance the war trade. At the same time, the President resisted all efforts by German Americans for an arms embargo on the ground that such a measure would be grossly unneutral toward the Allies.

German submarine warfare. There was no possibility of conflict between Germany and the United States so long as the former confined its warfare to the continent of Europe; a new situation full of potential danger arose, however, when the German authorities decided to use a new weapon, the submarine, to challenge British control of the seas. The German admiralty announced in February 1915 that all Allied vessels would be torpedoed without warning in a broad area and that even neutral vessels were not safe. Wilson replied at once that he would hold Germany to "strict accountability" if submarines destroyed American ships and lives without warning. The Germans soon gave broad guarantees concerning American ships, and their safety against illegal submarine attacks was not an issue between the two countries before 1917.

An issue much more fraught with danger was the safety of

Wilson's conduct of foreign affairs

Outbreak of World War I

Americans travelling and working on Allied ships. A German submarine sank the unarmed British liner "Lusitania" without warning on May 7, 1915, killing, among others, 128 Americans. Wilson at first appealed to the Germans on broad grounds of humanity to abandon submarine warfare, but in the subsequent negotiations he narrowed the issue to one of safety for unarmed passenger liners against violent underseas attack. Momentary resolution came when a submarine sank the unarmed British liner "Arabic" in August. Wilson warned that he would break diplomatic relations if such attacks continued, and the Germans grudgingly promised not to attack unarmed passenger ships without warning. The controversy escalated to a more dangerous level when a submarine torpedoed the packet steamer "Sussex" in the English Channel with heavy loss of life in March 1916. In an ultimatum to Berlin, Wilson threatened to break diplomatic relations if the Germans did not cease attacking liners and merchantmen without warning; once again the Germans capitulated, but they threatened to resume unrestricted submarine warfare if the United States failed to force the British to observe international law in their blockade practices.

The sinking of unarmed ships

The Allies complicated the submarine controversy in late 1915 by arming many of their liners and merchantmen sailing to American ports. Wilson tried to arrange a compromise by which the Allies would disarm their ships in return for a German promise not to sink them without warning. When the British rejected the proposal, the President gave the impression that he would hold Germany accountable for American lives lost on armed ships, setting off a rebellion in Congress and the near passage of resolutions forbidding American citizens to travel on armed ships. Actually, the President had no intention of permitting armed ships to become a serious issue; their status was never a subject of serious controversy between the United States and Germany.

Arming for war. Meanwhile, the increasingly perilous state of relations with Germany had prompted Wilson, in December 1915, to call for a considerable expansion in the nation's armed forces. A violent controversy over preparedness ensued, both in Congress and in the country at large. The army legislation of 1916 was a compromise, with Wilson obtaining only a modest increase in the army and a strengthening of the National Guard; but the Naval Appropriations Act of 1916 provided for more ships than the administration had requested.

The United States enters the Great War. Wilson's most passionate desire, aside from avoiding belligerency, was to bring an end to the war through his personal mediation. He sent Colonel House to Europe in early 1915 to explore the possibilities of peace and again early in 1916 to press for a plan of Anglo-American cooperation for peace. The British refused to cooperate, and the President, more than ever eager to avoid a final confrontation with Germany on the submarine issue, decided to press forward with independent mediation. He was by this time also irritated by the intensification of British blockade practices and convinced that both sides were fighting for domination and spoils. On December 18, 1916, Wilson asked the belligerents to state the terms upon which they would be willing to make peace. Soon afterward, in secret, high-level negotiations, he appealed to Britain and Germany to hold an early peace conference under his direction.

Wilson's attempts to achieve peace

Break with Germany. Chances for peace were blasted by a decision of the German leaders, made at an imperial conference on January 9, 1917, to inaugurate an all-out submarine war against all commerce, neutral as well as belligerent. The Germans knew that such a campaign would almost certainly bring the United States into the war; but they were confident that their augmented submarine fleet could starve Britain into submission before the U.S. could mobilize and participate effectively.

The announcement of the new submarine blockade in January left the President no alternative but to break diplomatic relations with Germany, which he did on February 3. At the same time, and in subsequent addresses, the President made it clear that he would accept unrestricted submarine warfare against belligerent merchantmen and would act only if American ships were sunk. In early

March he put arms on American ships in the hope that this would deter submarine attacks. The Germans began to sink American ships indiscriminately in mid-March; and Wilson, on April 2, asked Congress to recognize that a state of war existed between the United States and the German empire. Congress approved the war resolution quickly, and Wilson signed it on April 6.

Mobilization. Generally speaking, the efforts at mobilization went through two stages. During the first, lasting roughly from April to December 1917, the administration relied mainly on voluntary and cooperative efforts. During the second stage, after December 1917, the government moved rapidly to establish complete control over every important phase of economic life. Railroads were nationalized; a war industries board established ironclad controls over industry; food and fuel were strictly rationed; an emergency-fleet corporation began construction of a vast merchant fleet; and a war labour board used coercive measures to prevent strikes. Opposition to the war was sternly suppressed under the Espionage Act of 1917 and the even severer Sedition Act of 1918. By the spring of 1918, the American people and their economy had been harnessed for total war (a near miracle, considering the lack of preparedness only a year before).

Government controls during the war

America's role in the war. The American military contribution, while small compared to that of the Allies during the entire war, was in two respects decisive in the outcome. The United States Navy, fully prepared at the outset, provided the ships that helped the British overcome the submarine threat by the autumn of 1917. The United States Army, some 4,000,000 men strong, was raised mainly by conscription under the Selective Service Act of 1917; the American Expeditionary Force of more than 1,200,000 men under General Pershing reached France by September 1918, and this huge infusion of manpower tipped the balance on the western front and helped to end the war in November 1918, a year earlier than military planners had anticipated.

Wilson's vision of a new world order. In one of the most ambitious rhetorical efforts in modern history, President Wilson attempted to rally the people of the world in a movement for a peace settlement that would remove the causes of future wars and establish machinery to maintain peace. In an address to the Senate on January 22, 1917, he called for a "peace without victory" to be enforced by a league of nations that the United States would join and strongly support. He reiterated this program in his war message, adding that the United States wanted above all else to "make the world safe for democracy." And when he failed to persuade the British and French leaders to join him in issuing a common statement of war aims, he went to Congress on January 8, 1918, to make, in his Fourteen Points Address, his definitive avowal to the American people and the world.

In his general points Wilson demanded an end to the old diplomacy that had led to wars in the past. He proposed open diplomacy instead of entangling alliances, and he called for freedom of the seas, an impartial settlement of colonial claims, general disarmament, removal of artificial trade barriers, and, most important, a league of nations to promote peace and protect the territorial integrity and independence of its members. On specific issues he demanded, among other things, the restoration of a Belgium ravaged by the Germans; sympathetic treatment of the Russians, then involved in a civil war; establishment of an independent Poland; the return of Alsace-Lorraine to France; and autonomy or self-determination for the subject peoples of the Austro-Hungarian and Ottoman empires. A breathtaking pronouncement, the Fourteen Points gave new hope to millions of liberals and moderate socialists who were fighting for a new international order based upon peace and justice.

Wilson's Fourteen Points

The Paris Peace Conference and the Versailles Treaty. With their armies reeling under the weight of a combined allied and American assault, the Germans appealed to Wilson in October 1918 for an armistice based on the Fourteen Points and other presidential pronouncements. The Allies agreed to conclude peace on this basis, except that the British entered a reservation about freedom of the seas, and Wilson agreed to an Anglo-French demand that the Germans be required to make reparation for damages to civilian property.

Wilson led the American delegation and a large group of experts to the peace conference, which opened in Paris in January 1919. He fought heroically for his Fourteen Points against the Allied leaders—David Lloyd George of Britain, Georges Clemenceau of France, and Vittorio Orlando of Italy—who, under heavy pressure from their own constituencies, were determined to divide the territories of the vanquished and make Germany pay the full cost of the war. Wilson made a number of compromises that violated the spirit if not the letter of the Fourteen Points, including the imposition of a potentially astronomical reparations bill upon Germany. Moreover, the Allies had intervened in the Russian Civil War against the dominant revolutionary Socialist faction, the Bolsheviks; and Wilson had halfheartedly cooperated with the Allies by dispatching small numbers of troops to northern Russia, to protect military supplies against the advancing Germans, and to Siberia, mainly to keep an eye on the Japanese, who had sent a large force there. But Wilson won many more of his Fourteen Points than he lost; his greatest victories were to prevent the dismemberment of Germany in the west and further intervention in Russia and, most important, to obtain the incorporation of the Covenant of the League of Nations into the Versailles Treaty. He was confident that the League, under American leadership, would soon rectify the injustices of the treaty.

The League of Nations

The fight over the treaty and the election of 1920. Public opinion in the United States seemed strongly in favour of quick ratification of the Versailles Treaty when the President presented that document to the Senate in July 1919. But traditional isolationist sentiment was beginning to revive, and a group of 16 senators, irreconcilably opposed to American membership in the League, vowed to oppose the treaty to the bitter end; but they were a small minority, helpless by themselves. A crucial controversy developed between the President and a majority of the Republican senators, led by Henry Cabot Lodge of Massachusetts. Lodge insisted upon adding 14 reservations to the treaty; the second reservation declared that the United States assumed no obligations under Article X of the Covenant, which guaranteed the integrity and independence of members of the League, and moreover it said that the president could not use the armed forces to support the Covenant without the explicit consent of Congress in every instance.

Calling this reservation a nullification of the treaty, Wilson in September made a long speaking tour of the West to build up public support for unconditional ratification. He suffered a breakdown at the end of his tour and a serious stroke on October 2. The President's illness, which incapacitated him for several months, may have increased his intransigence against the Lodge reservations; with equal stubbornness, the Massachusetts senator refused to consent to any compromise. The result was failure to obtain the necessary two-thirds majority for ratification, with or without reservations, when the Senate voted on November 19, 1919, and again on March 19, 1920.

Wilson had suggested that the ensuing presidential campaign and election should be a "great and solemn referendum" on the League. The Democratic candidate, James M. Cox of Ohio, fought hard to make it the leading issue; but the Republican candidate, Warren G. Harding of Ohio, was evasive on the subject, and a group of 31 leading Republican internationalists assured the country that Harding's election would be the best guarantee of American membership in the League of Nations. Harding swamped Cox, and his victory ended all hopes for American membership. In his inaugural Harding announced that the United States would not be entangled in European affairs; he emphasized this determination by concluding a separate peace with Germany in 1921.   (A.S.L.)

The United States from 1920 to 1945

THE POSTWAR REPUBLICAN ADMINISTRATIONS

Politics and economics. Harding assumed the presidency pledged to return to normalcy a nation suffering postwar dislocation and depression. He and his Republican administration put into effect his campaign slogan, "Less government in business and more business in government." They reversed the progressive and wartime trend toward business regulation but tried through a number of measures to foster business both large and small.

Harding's administration

Harding's cabinet, together with Republican congressional leaders, helped establish probusiness policies. Harding wanted to put the best qualified men in the cabinet and was partly successful. The distinguished secretary of state, Charles Evans Hughes, was a well-known New York lawyer who fostered American economic interests overseas. The secretary of the treasury Andrew W. Mellon, one of the nation's wealthiest men, tried to stimulate business expansion by persuading Congress to cut drastically the taxes of those with large incomes; Mellon also promoted economy within the government and sharply reduced the national debt. The secretary of commerce, Herbert Hoover, the defender of small enterprise, promoted foreign trade and, through the National Bureau of Standards, improved business efficiency; Hoover also encouraged the formation of trade associations. The secretary of agriculture, Henry C. Wallace, obtained for Midwest farmers (with progressive Republican support) legislation regulating commodity exchanges and stockyards, providing credit for distressed farmers, and encouraging farm cooperatives. The secretary of the interior, Albert B. Fall, was one of the most outspoken opponents of conservationist interference with western development. The attorney general, Harry M. Daugherty, aided railroads and mining companies by obtaining injunctions against strikes.

Capping this program to aid businessmen and farmers was a tariff act in 1922, which, although it placed a 42¢ a bushel duty on wheat, gave farmers little protection. By raising duties to cover the differential between the cost of production within the United States and that abroad, it helped manufacturers. Its effect upon other countries was to stimulate them to raise their own tariffs.

The government itself became more businesslike. The Budget and Accounting Act of 1921 established the Bureau of the Budget, which prepared a single unified budget, and also the General Accounting Office, an auditing agency.

Legislation restricting immigration reversed traditional American policy and stemmed the flow from Europe. In 1920, the year before enactment of emergency legislation, 800,000 immigrants had arrived. Added to the protests of organized labour were the objections of business leaders and patriotic organizations, who feared that some of the immigrants might be radicals. Legislation in 1924 set small quotas totalling 164,000 people yearly; it favoured immigrants from northwestern Europe and outraged the Japanese by banning all immigration from east Asia. Immigration from within the Western Hemisphere continued— 900,000 Canadians (mostly French-speaking) and 500,000 Mexicans entered the United States during the 1920s.

By 1923, with the return of prosperity, Harding was enjoying widespread popularity but was heartsick over evidence of scandal within his administration. He died of a heart attack in the summer of 1923, and in subsequent months the public learned of the corruption. The most publicized was the illegal leasing of naval oil reserves at Teapot Dome, Wyoming, which led to the conviction of Secretary Fall for accepting a bribe.

The return of prosperity

Calvin Coolidge and the progress of business. Calvin Coolidge, Harding's successor, was so impeccably honest and frugal that his administration suffered none of the stigma of the Harding scandals. "Keep cool with Coolidge," was the campaign slogan when he ran in 1924 against the conservative Democrat John W. Davis. The Republicans directed more of their campaign oratory against the third-party Progressive candidate, Sen. Robert La Follette. Coolidge received more popular votes than his opponents combined.

Through essentially negative policies, the President presided over what came to be known as the years of "Coolidge prosperity." He was considerably more conservative than Harding, and through exercise of the veto and appointment power he prevented restrictions upon business. Like his predecessor, he appointed judges and members of regulatory commissions who he felt would not interfere with the nation's economic life, and regulation did slacken. (He did not always succeed, however; Harlan F. Stone, whom he appointed to the Supreme Court, became one of its most liberal members.) Toward the end of his administration, Coolidge refused to use his influence to tighten credit or to make stock market speculation more difficult. In 1927 he vetoed a bill that would have raised prices of basic farm commodities because he considered it contrary to laissez-faire; the same day he authorized a 50 percent increase in the tariff on pig iron. In 1928 he pocket-vetoed Sen. George W. Norris' bill for the development of the federally owned dam at Muscle Shoals on the Tennessee River. On the other hand, Norris led the senators in blocking Coolidge's recommendation to sell Muscle Shoals to the industrialist Henry Ford.

Overall, the national economy was booming during the 1920s. Improvements in machinery and management brought an increase of 50 percent in industrial productivity, while labour costs dropped 9.5 percent. Production of automobiles and consumer durable goods rose dramatically; although the wealthy benefitted most, living standards of middle class and working people rose. Between 1922 and 1929 salaries increased 42 percent; wages, 33 percent; and consumer purchases, 23 percent. Corporate net profits rose 76 percent; dividends to stockholders, 108 percent. On the other hand, agriculture and several industries, such as textiles and bituminous coal mining, were seriously depressed, and after 1926 construction declined; thus the prosperity was not solidly based.

New social trends and the growth of organized crime. For millions of Americans, the sober-minded Coolidge was a more appropriate symbol for the era than the journalistic term "jazz age." Although there was stock market speculation and a real estate boom in Florida, and though there were emancipated young women with short skirts and bobbed hair—the "flappers"—dancing the Charleston to the music of jazz orchestras, playing in speakeasies, where liquor was sold illegally, most people shared in the excitement only vicariously, through several innovations of these years—through tabloid newspapers or radio or through silent motion pictures, which drew an audience of 50,000,000 a week (all these were novel, as was the automobile, in which the family went out on freshly paved highways for a Sunday outing or to spend an afternoon at the country club). They also read the novels of Sinclair Lewis, which satirized the age, and those of F. Scott Fitzgerald, which made it glamorous.

The "jazz age"

Many writers and intellectuals were sharply critical of the mass culture of the period. Nevertheless the 1920s brought improved communications, erasing differences between urban and country life; the building of highways, parkways, and parks; and spectacular improvement in education, from kindergarten through universities.

On the darker side, the 1920s were years of mass lawbreaking and the rise of organized crime. The Volstead Act, providing for the federal enforcement of the Prohibition (Eighteenth) Amendment (which prohibited the manufacture, sale, or transportation of intoxicating liquors), went into effect in January 1920. But enforcement machinery was so slight that gangsters were soon engaged in large-scale smuggling, manufacture, and sale of alcoholic beverages. Millions of otherwise law-abiding citizens drank the prohibited liquor. On the other hand, millions of mostly Protestant churchgoers hailed prohibition as a moral advance, and the liquor consumption of working people seemed to have dropped.

The presidential campaign of 1928 between the Republican nominee, Herbert Hoover, and the Democrat, Gov. Alfred E. Smith of New York, involved the twin issues of prohibition and religion. Smith was an opponent of prohibition and a Roman Catholic. His candidacy brought enthusiasm and a heavy Democratic vote in the large cities and a landslide against him in the dry and Protestant hinterlands. Some of the opposition to Smith was marshalled by the Ku Klux Klan, anti-Catholic as well as anti-Negro, which had flourished in the early 1920s. A national law enforcement commission, formed to study the flouting of prohibition and the activities of gangsters, was to report in 1931 that prohibition was virtually unenforceable; and with the coming of the Great Depression, prohibition ceased to be a key political issue. In 1933 the Twenty-first Amendment brought its repeal.

Herbert Hoover and the Great Depression. Hoover won an overwhelming victory in 1928, in part because his opponent was a "wet" Catholic but in larger part because Hoover, as the "Great Engineer," seemed best qualified to continue the prosperity of the 1920s. Yet within a few months of his inauguration in 1929, the stock market crashed and the Great Depression began; ironically Hoover had to devote his administration to trying to regain a vanished prosperity.

In the stock market crash of October 1929, stocks in a few weeks lost 40 percent of their value; the market continued an intermittent downward course through 1932. The crash had come in response to declines in industrial production, construction, and retail sales. It helped trigger a deflationary spiral that became difficult to stop as businessmen were gradually forced to curtail their activities.

The stock market crash of 1929

Anti-Depression measures. In trying to end the Depression, Hoover went further than any of his predecessors in utilizing government powers in a positive, although limited way; his administration created many of the precedents for later measures. At first he tried to restore public confidence by obtaining the voluntary cooperation of business and labour leaders, who pledged to maintain production, employment, and existing pay scales. Hoover also tried to stem deflation by liberalizing Federal Reserve credit, cutting taxes, and obtaining from Congress an unprecedented increase of $423,000,000 in the public works appropriation. Before the crash, he had already signed the Agricultural Marketing Act of 1929, creating the Federal Farm Board to bolster farm prices by purchasing surpluses. In 1930 he signed the Hawley–Smoot Tariff Bill, which raised the average ad valorem duty from 26 to 50 percent and brought retaliation from other countries.

Into 1931 these mild expedients seemed sufficient, and the Depression appeared no worse than that of 1921. Then, the threatened financial collapse of western Europe brought a new wave of deflation to the United States. In order to save the financial system of Germany, whose collapse might well take under that of other nations, Hoover agreed in June 1931 to a one-year moratorium on reparations and war debt payments. This was of relatively little help. The financial systems of England and other western European nations survived, but by September most of them had gone off the gold standard and had devalued their currency. European gold was withdrawn from the United States, and European-held securities were dumped on the U.S. stock markets. Devaluation of currency further cut the already declining foreign trade. These disasters, heightening difficulties at home, caused the Depression to become steadily worse from May 1931 to July 1932.

Democratic control of Congress. Worsening conditions forced Hoover to propose more drastic expedients to bring recovery; but as much as possible, he still wished the recovery program to be voluntary. In the 1930 elections the Democrats had won control of the House by a narrow margin and had almost won the Senate. Through a coalition with 12 Republican progressive senators, the Democrats were able to muster a majority of votes against administration measures when the 72nd Congress assembled in December 1931. Congress thus attacked many of Hoover's proposals and called for still more drastic action.

Nevertheless Congress did, as Hoover requested, in January 1932 establish a federal loan agency—the Reconstruction Finance Corporation (RFC)—with a capitalization of $2,000,000,000, empowered to make loans to banks, insurance companies, agricultural associations, railroads, and other industries. The RFC loaned $1,500,000,000 to banks and businesses during its first year. In July 1932 Hoover signed a measure allowing it to lend an additional $1,500,000,000 for self-liquidating public works and $300,000,000 for relief purposes. The RFC did much to keep the Depression from becoming even worse than it eventually became.

The Reconstruction Finance Corporation

Despite the efforts of President Hoover and Congress, the Depression continued to deepen. By 1932 banks had failed by the hundreds; mills and factories were shut down or operating only part-time. Estimates of the unemployed ranged as high as 13,000,000 (one worker in four); many of those employed received only subsistence wages. A quarter of the farmers had lost their farms. In the 1932 election, voters by a wide margin rejected Hoover and voted for the Democratic candidate, Gov. Franklin D. Roosevelt of New York, who promised them a New Deal.

THE NEW DEAL

The first New Deal. The nation was in a state of acute banking crisis when Roosevelt took office. Beginning in Michigan in mid-February 1933, runs on banks had forced state after state to close or limit the activities of its banks. This was the setting in which the new President delivered his inaugural address on March 4. Above all he tried to dispel the fright in peoples' minds; he emphatically stated, "the only thing we have to fear is fear itself."

Roosevelt's first 100 days. In the next several days Roosevelt acted quickly, and rather conservatively, to restore business confidence. In March he submitted to Congress the Emergency Banking Bill, empowering the administration to strengthen and reopen sound banks; Congress enacted the bill in four hours. Within three days three-fourths of the banks within the Federal Reserve system had reopened. There followed an economy act reducing federal salaries and veterans' pensions and legislation legalizing the sale of beer of 3.2 percent alcoholic content. The stock market went up 15 percent.

With the country enthusiastically behind him, Roosevelt kept Congress in special session and piece by piece sent it recommendations that formed the basic recovery program of his first 100 days in office. He expected later to submit to Congress proposals for long-range reform legislation to eliminate maladjustments responsible for the Depression and likely to cause future depressions. Between March 16 and May 17, 1933, he sent messages and draft bills to Congress proposing an agricultural recovery program, unemployment relief, federal supervision of investment securities, creation of a Tennessee Valley Authority, prevention of mortgage foreclosures on homes, railroad recovery legislation, and an industrial recovery program. From March 9 to mid-June 1933, Congress enacted all of Roosevelt's proposals—an unprecedented legislative achievement.

Farm recovery. The passage of the Agricultural Adjustment Act in May 1933 marked the beginning of an era in which the American farmer received aid from the Federal government to improve his economic status. It was an omnibus farm-relief bill embodying the schemes of the major farm organizations to limit crops and of agrarian radicals to inflate the currency. The Agricultural Adjustment Administration (AAA) established by the act put into effect a "domestic allotment" plan to make benefit payments to producers of seven basic commodities, including wheat, cotton, and corn, in return for cutting their output. At first a processing tax upon the commodities provided funds for the benefit payments; but after an adverse Supreme Court decision in 1936, Congress appropriated funds for crop reduction coupled with soil conservation. The AAA program was of only limited help to farmers. Drought in 1933–36 did more than production quotas to cut farm surpluses and increase commodity prices, but most farmers nonetheless favoured the early program. The cash income of farmers nearly doubled between 1932 and 1936 but did not again reach the 1929 level until 1941.

Business recovery. The New Deal sought to bring business recovery through the omnibus National Industrial Recovery Act (NIRA) of June 1933. This act, administered by the National Recovery Administration (NRA), granted businessmen government backing for agreements to stabilize production and prevent price slashing. Labour was to receive wages-and-hours protection and the right to bargain collectively. A large-scale public-works appropriation, administered through the Public Works Administration (PWA), was intended to pour sufficient money into the economy to increase consumer buying power while prices and wages went up.

In practice, the NRA program went awry. While codes were being negotiated, in the summer of 1933, manu-

facturers increased production in anticipation of higher prices and greater demand. Buying power did not keep pace, and in the fall of 1933 the boomlet collapsed. The NRA then became too complicated; by February 1934 it had negotiated far too many codes with even minor industries, covering vast intricacies of regulations—a total of 557 basic codes and 208 supplementary ones. Such a mass of detail proved almost unenforceable. Workingmen felt they obtained little from the codes, although in a few industries, like textiles, child labour was ended and working conditions were improved. The collective bargaining provision in the act led to a strong unionization movement and to numerous strikes against nonunion employers. The National Labor Board in 1933 and its successor, the National Labor Relations Board, dealt with labour disputes but had little power.

The NRA was a failure, despite some achievements in improving wages and hours and in bringing order to chaotic large industries. It was too complicated to be enforceable, it tended to create monopoly conditions, and because public works expenditures were too slow it raised prices without a comparable increase in consumer buying power. When the Supreme Court invalidated the NRA code system in 1935, Congress enacted new laws salvaging parts of it, but the experiment was basically over.

Relief. Relief programs were urgent in the New Deal to provide aid to millions of hungry people for whom states and cities were able to provide only a pittance. The Federal Emergency Relief Administration provided grants to state relief agencies; in return the state agencies had to meet federal standards. The Civilian Conservation Corps (CCC), which employed young men from families on relief in reforestation and similar projects, became one of the most popular New Deal agencies. Several laws aided farmers and homeowners threatened by mortgage foreclosures. The Farm Credit Administration (FCA) was a consolidation of several earlier federal agencies; in 1933–34 it refinanced one-fifth of all farm mortgages. A farm bankruptcy act of June 1934 enabled farmers who had lost their farms to regain them. For homeowners, the Home Owners Loan Corporation refinanced about one-sixth of the mortgages on homes. In 1934 the Federal Housing Administration (FHA), more a recovery than a relief agency, began to insure mortgages upon new construction and home repairs. The Reconstruction Finance Corporation continued to make large recovery loans.

The economic downturn in the fall of 1933 led to new relief and recovery devices. During the winter of 1933–34, the Civil Works Administration (CWA) employed about 4,000,000 people on emergency projects. Roosevelt also experimented with mild currency inflation, devaluating the gold content of the dollar to 59.06 percent of what it had been formerly and beginning in 1934 a silver purchase program (these were the beginnings of America's government management of the currency).

Reform. Early in the New Deal there was some reform legislation. The Glass–Steagall Act of 1933 created the Federal Deposit Insurance Corporation (FDIC), guaranteeing small bank deposits. Later, the Banking Act of 1935 altered and strengthened the Federal Reserve System. Two measures regulated stock exchange: the Truth-in-Securities Act of 1933, requiring corporations to file data on new securities, and the Securities Exchange Act of 1934, establishing a commission to check new securities and to police the stock markets. The most spectacular piece of conservation legislation was the establishment in 1933 of the Tennessee Valley Authority (TVA), which took over the dam at Muscle Shoals and four other existing dams; it also built 20 new dams in the next two decades, regulating floods in an area previously devastated by them, generating cheap electricity, and undertaking the general rehabilitation of a poverty-stricken area. Other power development and irrigation projects were built in the West. The Taylor Grazing Act of 1934 regulated public rangeland; the Indian Reorganization Act of 1934 protected the Indians and their lands.

The second New Deal and the Supreme Court. In reaction to pressures from the left and hostility from the right, the New Deal shifted more toward reform in 1935–36.

(margin notes:)

Roosevelt's recovery program

Failure of the NRA

Popular leaders, promising more than Roosevelt, threatened to pull sufficient votes from him in the 1936 election to bring Republican victory. Sen. Huey P. Long of Louisiana was building a national following with a "Share the Wealth" program. The poor in northern cities were attracted to the Roman Catholic priest the Rev. Charles E. Coughlin, who later switched from a program of nationalization and currency inflation to an antidemocratic, anti-Semitic emphasis. Many older people supported Dr. Francis E. Townsend's plan to provide $200 per month for everyone over age 60. At the same time, conservatives, including such groups as the American Liberty League, founded in 1934, attacked the New Deal as a threat to states' rights, free enterprise, and the open shop.

Roosevelt's response in 1935 was to propose greater aid to the underprivileged and extensive reforms. Congress created the Works Progress Administration (WPA), which replaced direct relief with work relief; between 1935 and 1941 an annual average of 2,100,000 workers were carried on WPA rolls. For younger people there was the National Youth Administration (NYA). Of long-range significance was the Social Security Act of 1935, which provided federal aid for the aged, retirement annuities, unemployment insurance, aid for persons who were blind or crippled, and aid to dependent children; the original act suffered from various inadequacies, but it was the beginning of a permanent, expanding national program. A tax reform law, labelled by newspapers as the "soak the rich tax," fell heavily upon corporations and well-to-do people. The National Labor Relations Act, or Wagner Act, reluctantly accepted by Roosevelt, gave organized labour federal protection in collective bargaining; it prohibited a number of "unfair practices" on the part of employers and created the strong National Labor Relations Board (NLRB) to enforce the law.

While the New Deal was moving toward reform in 1935, the Supreme Court was invalidating several of its earlier key measures. In *Schechter Poultry Corp.* v. *U.S.* the Court invalidated the NIRA, creating a national sensation; Roosevelt charged the justices with taking a "horse-and-buggy age view" of federal regulatory power. In 1936 Roosevelt, aided by his reform program, defeated the Republican nominee for president, Gov. Alfred ("Alf") M. Landon of Kansas, receiving over 60 percent of the popular vote and the electoral votes of every state except Maine and Vermont.

Viewing his decisive victory as an electoral mandate for continued reform, Roosevelt sought to remove the impediment the Supreme Court seemed to be placing in his way. He felt that the powers involved in such reform legislation as the Wagner Act and Social Security Act, both being challenged before the Supreme Court, were to be found in the Constitution and that the court had been interpreting it too narrowly. In February 1937 he proposed to Congress

a reorganization of the court system, which would have included giving him the power to appoint one new justice for each justice who was 70 years of age or older, but not exceeding six new justices in all. Roosevelt's proposal created a furor, especially because he did not state frankly the obvious fact that he wished the court to interpret the Constitution more broadly. Some Democrats and a few liberal Republicans in Congress supported the proposal, but a strong coalition of Republicans and conservative Democrats, backed by much public support, fought the so-called court-packing plan.

Meanwhile the court itself in a new series of decisions began upholding as constitutional measures involving both state and federal economic regulation. In April 1937 it approved the National Labor Relations Act. These decisions, which began an extensive revision of constitutional law concerning governmental regulation, made the reorganization plan unnecessary; the Senate defeated it in July 1937 by a vote of 70 to 22. Roosevelt had suffered a stinging political defeat, even though he no longer had to fear the court. Turnover on the court was rapid as older members retired or died; by 1942 all but two of the justices were Roosevelt appointees.

The culmination of the New Deal. Roosevelt lost further prestige in the summer of 1937, when the nation plunged into a sharp recession. Economists had feared an inflationary boom as industrial production moved up to within 7.5 percent of 1929. Other indices were high except for a lag in capital investment and continued heavy unemployment. Roosevelt, fearing a boom and eager to balance the budget, cut government spending, which most economists felt had brought the recovery. Between August 1937 and May 1938 the index of production fell from 117 to 76 (on a 1929 base of 100) and unemployment increased by perhaps 4,000,000 persons. Congress voted an emergency appropriation of $5,000,000,000 for work relief and public works, and by June 1938 recovery once more was under way.

Considerable legislation augmenting and consolidating earlier New Deal measures was passed during the second Roosevelt administration. There was further legislation to reduce farm production and raise crop prices and to alleviate rural poverty. For workers the Fair Labor Standards Act of 1938 established a minimum wage and maximum work week (in later years the minimum wage was repeatedly raised and coverage was broadened). Substantial construction of public housing began with establishment of the U.S. Housing Authority in 1937. Altogether this was a considerable array of legislation; but it had been vigorously opposed by many conservative Democrats in Congress, allied with the Republicans. During the congressional campaign of 1938, Roosevelt intervened in primaries, mostly in the South, trying to defeat conservative Democratic congressional leaders. For the most part he failed; throughout the country the tide of support for the New Deal was ebbing, and the Republicans gained 80 seats in the House and seven in the Senate. Nevertheless, the Democrats still controlled each house by a heavy margin.

Spectacular violence accompanying union organization drives was another factor in the New Deal's waning popularity among middle class Americans. Aided by the Wagner Act, unions had begun organizing vigorously early in the New Deal. A few months after the passage of the Wagner Act, John L. Lewis, president of the United Mine Workers of America, led in forming the Committee for Industrial Organization (CIO) to organize the great mass-production industries, which for the most part had never been unionized. The CIO came into conflict with the American Federation of Labor (AFL), which mounted its own unionization drives. The result was struggle between organizers and industrialists and at times between rival organizers. In bitter fights with the automobile companies the CIO used the sit-down strike, in which the strikers entrenched themselves in the factories and refused to work or to let others in to work; in February 1947 General Motors Corporation recognized the United Automobile Workers, and gradually other manufacturers did the same. The United States Steel Corporation signed union contracts in the spring of 1937 rather than risk strikes, but three "little steel" companies resisted vigorously before finally signing contracts with the CIO. Roosevelt, declining to take sides during the struggle, called down "a plague on both your houses." The organizing drives continued to make headway; union membership, which had been about 3,000,000 in 1932, was about 9,500,000 by 1941.

An assessment of the New Deal. The New Deal established federal responsibility for the welfare of the economy and the American people. At the time, conservative critics, among whom the most notable was former President Hoover, charged it was bringing statism or even socialism. Left-wing critics of a later generation have charged just the reverse—that it bolstered the old order and prevented significant reform. Others have suggested that the New Deal was no more than the extension and culmination of Progressivism.

In its early stages, the New Deal did begin where Progressivism left off and built upon the Hoover program for fighting the Depression. But Roosevelt soon took the New Deal well beyond Hoover and Progressivism, programs came to have more of an element of compulsion in them and were larger in scale. For the first time the federal government assumed responsibility for the social security of the nation's citizens. The Wagner Act fostered unionism, and organized labour became a vital part of the

Democratic coalition, contributing both votes and campaign dollars.

New Deal efforts to stimulate prosperity resulted in a trial-and-error approach to economic regulation. National planning failed in the NRA yet continued for decades as a means of reducing production of major farm crops. Management of currency and credit, beginning in 1933, slowly became more sophisticated and came to be a key means by which the government could control inflation or prevent deflation. Government spending, undertaken at first as a means primarily of relief, became the prime device for stimulating the economy. Social Security through automatically providing benefits in time of unemployment became another countercyclical economic stabilizer.

Roosevelt himself, though he adopted some of his proposals, never became a disciple of J.M. Keynes, the contemporary British economic theorist, who advocated spending during a recession; but many of the young New Deal economists were Keynesians by the late 1930s. The New Deal did not achieve complete economic recovery before war intervened, but it had taken the nation well in that direction. (It was also evolving economic devices which after 1945 further developed in both Democratic and Republican administrations as the means of preventing runaway inflation and depression.)

THE IMPACT OF WORLD WAR II

Isolation, neutrality, and the U.S. entry into the war. During the New Deal years the American response to threats of war in other parts of the world was to seek security through isolation. Congress, with the approval of Roosevelt and Secretary of State Cordell Hull, enacted a series of neutrality laws; in order to keep the nation out of a new conflict, these legislated against the factors that supposedly had taken the United States into World War I. As Italy prepared to invade Ethiopia, Congress passed the Neutrality Act of 1935, embargoing shipment of arms to either aggressor or victim. Stronger legislation followed the outbreak of the Spanish Civil War in 1936, even relinquishing the traditional American claim to freedom of seas in wartime.

Threats to American security. The gravest threat seemed to come from Japan. Roosevelt followed the doctrine of nonrecognition of Japan's conquests on the Asiatic mainland, and in 1934, began rebuilding the navy toward treaty strength. When Japan in 1937 began a large-scale drive into north China, Roosevelt did not proclaim neutrality; thus munitions could be sold to both sides. But in October, when Roosevelt suggested that war, like disease, was a contagion that peace-loving nations should quarantine, he created a furor and had to retreat. In December, when Japanese aviators sank the U.S. gunboat "Panay" in the Yangtze River, the United States accepted Japanese apologies and indemnities.

As war continued in Asia and threatened to break out in Europe as a result of German aggressions, Roosevelt tried to develop a policy of collective security. He encountered little opposition as long as he confined himself to working agreements for mutual defense among the nations of the Western Hemisphere—at Buenos Aires in 1936, at Lima in 1938, and with Canada in 1938.

When Germany's invasion of Poland in 1939 touched off World War II, Roosevelt called Congress into special session to revise the Neutrality Act to allow belligerents (in reality only Great Britain and France both on the Allied side) to purchase munitions on a "cash-and-carry" basis. With the fall of France to Germany in 1940, Roosevelt, with heavy public support, threw the resources of the United States behind the British, including the spectacular exchange of 50 overage U.S. destroyers in return for 99-year leases on bases stretching from Newfoundland to British Guiana. In the fall of 1940 Roosevelt also conducted a political campaign for a tradition-breaking third term, running against the Republican Wendell L. Willkie, and was re-elected with over 54 percent of the popular vote.

From the fall of France until the Japanese bombing of the American naval base at Pearl Harbor, Hawaii (December 1941), a great debate stirred the nation as isolation-

The policy of collective security

ists, especially through a group called the America First Committee, charged that Roosevelt was taking the nation into war, and interventionists complained that he was not moving rapidly enough. While the debate went on, the United States built its defenses and sent supplies to the British. The Burke–Wadsworth Act of 1940 established the first peacetime selective service, or conscription, act in the nation's history. The Lend-Lease Act of 1941, passed after vehement debate, provided the British and their allies with munitions, which could be repaid after the crisis was over. In August 1941 Roosevelt met with British prime minister Winston Churchill off the coast of Newfoundland and then announced a set of war aims known as the Atlantic Charter. It called for national self-determination, larger economic opportunities, freedom from fear and want, freedom of the seas, and disarmament.

American military involvement. In September a German submarine attacked an American destroyer, and Roosevelt issued orders to "shoot on sight." In October another destroyer was sunk, and the United States embarked on an undeclared naval war against Germany.

For a decade the relations of the United States with Japan had grown less friendly. In January 1940 the United States abrogated its commercial treaty of 1911 with Japan, yet Americans continued to sell Japan materials used in its war against China. When Japanese armies invaded French Indochina in September 1940 with the apparent purpose of establishing bases for an attack on the East Indies, the United States placed an embargo on scrap iron and steel. Japan retaliated by signing a triple alliance agreement with Germany and Italy (September 1940). Japan was close to war with the United States, but it entered into negotiations in the spring of 1941, which continued into December. The United States, to try to thwart an expected Japanese thrust into the East Indies, placed tight economic sanctions upon Japan in July. The Japanese reaction was to prepare for war in case negotiations failed. Neither nation would make serious concessions over China, and by the end of November the United States (through intercepted Japanese messages) knew that a military attack was likely. Roosevelt and his military advisers, expecting it to be against the East Indies and possibly the Philippines, were caught by surprise when Japanese planes struck at Pearl Harbor on December 7, 1941. They destroyed or damaged 15 ships and 188 airplanes and inflicted 3,435 casualties.

On December 8, 1941, Congress with only one dissenting vote declared war against Japan. Three days later Germany and Italy declared war against the United States; and Congress, voting unanimously, reciprocated. As a result of the attack on Pearl Harbor, the previously divided nation entered into the global struggle with virtual unanimity.

Declaration of war

The conduct of the war and its domestic effects. Within the United States during World War II, the American people had to produce the enormous quantities of every sort of material of war, clothing, and food with which to defeat the enemies. The war also meant great dislocations as approximately 15,000,000 men and women went into uniform and many additional millions moved to jobs in war plants. The war brought an enormous increase in productivity and a higher living standard than ever before; it also brought continued debates among the American people over the way in which the war was to be conducted and what national policies should be afterward.

Congressional controls. Congress moved to the right during the war. In the 1942 election Republicans gained 47 seats in the House and 10 in the Senate. Democrats still controlled Congress, but conservatives of both parties were able to force dismantling of several New Deal agencies. Congress used its investigatory power to keep a check on war agencies and military expenditures, especially through the Senate War Investigating Committee, headed by Harry S. Truman of Missouri. Congress also became committed to the policy of postwar American cooperation with other nations to preserve the peace.

War production. As the government tried to control war production, government agencies were organized and reorganized repeatedly. In January 1942 the War Production Board replaced an earlier agency, and in 1943 it became subsidiary to the Office of War Mobilization. Agencies established priorities to channel scarce raw materials into the most essential types of production, controlled prices (through the Office of Price Administration), and allocated war supplies to the various branches of the armed forces and to the Allies. After initial snarls and never-ending disputes, by the beginning of 1944 production was reaching astronomical totals—double those of all the enemy countries combined. The output of American factories almost doubled between 1939 and 1945. (By the end of the war the United States had produced, for example, 6,500 naval vessels, 296,400 airplanes, and 86,330 tanks.)

Much of the production was in new types of weapons, as U.S. engineers and scientists matched their ingenuity against the Germans. The Office of Scientific Research and Development directed scientists in the development of superior radar and sonar, radio-directed proximity fuses, and countless other devices. The most dramatic race was the secret one to try to build an atomic bomb more quickly than the enemy. Through the Manhattan Project, $2,000,000,000 was expended upon plants and laboratories; and on July 6, 1945, the first workable atomic bomb was tested.

Develop-
ment of
the atomic
bomb

The use of manpower. The war put manpower suddenly at a premium after years of heavy unemployment. Selective Service draft boards registered about 31,000,000 men; including volunteers, more than 15,000,000 men and women served in the armed forces during the war. At the same time, the working force at home increased from about 46,500,000 to perhaps 53,000,000, and about 6,600,000 persons moved from rural poverty to cities. Approximately 2,000,000 blacks obtained work in war industries, protected by the Fair Employment Practices Committee (FEPC), established in 1941. Although 2,000,000 families still suffered from substandard incomes, most families benefitted economically from the war; gross weekly wages increased from $25.20 to $43.39. Most workers were better off, although the cost-of-living index (1935–39 = 100) went up to 128.4 by 1945, and most workers for the first time had to pay a federal income tax. Personal incomes were a third greater than available goods and services; much of the excess buying power was drained off into purchases of war bonds and stamps.

Financing the war. Through taxes the government raised 41 percent of the cost of the war (compared with 33 percent in World War I). The Revenue Act of 1942 levied 94 percent on the largest incomes; a withholding-tax measure passed in 1943 provided for deducting tax payments from workers' pay as it was earned. The total cost of the war to the Federal government between 1941 and 1945 was about $321,000,000,000 (ten times as much as World War I), and the national debt mounted from about $49,000,000,000 in 1941 to approximately $259,000,000,000 in 1945.

Labour. Unions agreed not to strike during the war and submitted disputes to the strong National War Labor Board. Nevertheless, there were 15,000 work stoppages during the war, which created much resentment among the public and in Congress (they accounted for only one-ninth of 1 percent of total hours worked). Congress in 1943 passed over the President's veto the Smith-Connally, or War Labor Disputes, Act, requiring unions to wait 30 days before striking and giving the president the right to seize a struck war plant.

Farmers. Congress was relatively generous with farmers, granting them less than they wanted but nevertheless setting price ceilings at 100 percent of parity. Produce prices more than doubled. In good-crop years during the war, agricultural production set new records, increasing from an index figure of 108 to 123.

Japanese Americans. During the war most Americans were undisturbed in the exercise of their civil liberties. But Japanese Americans felt the brunt of public anger. In February 1942 Roosevelt authorized the removal of 117,000 of them, two thirds of whom were United States citizens, from the Pacific Coast to ten interior relocation centres. Some 17,600 Japanese Americans fought in the armed forces; some of their units established notable records for bravery.

The 1944 election. In 1944 the United States under-

went the first wartime presidential election since the Civil War. Roosevelt was nominated for a fourth term; the vice presidential nominee was Sen. Harry S. Truman. The Republican party nominated the governor of New York, Thomas E. Dewey. Roosevelt was again elected.

The end of isolation and the new U.S. role in world affairs. The United States entry into World War II brought an end to isolation. The United States as a result of conferences between President Roosevelt and Prime Minister Churchill in December 1941 formed a grand wartime alliance, the United Nations, which 46 nations ultimately joined.

In 1943 six major conferences took place. At Casablanca, Morocco, in January the Allies decided to invade Italy and declared the need for "unconditional surrender." In May, in Washington, D.C., they decided to increase the bombing of Germany. From Quebec in August came the decision to invade German-occupied France in a "second front." In October Secretary Hull in Moscow reached agreements on establishment of a United Nations organization after the war. At Cairo in November Roosevelt and Churchill, meeting with Pres. Chiang Kai-shek of the Republic of China, affirmed a postwar settlement for east Asia. Later that month at Teheran, Iran, Roosevelt, Prime Minister Joseph Stalin of the Soviet Union, and Churchill agreed upon plans for launching a second front in Europe.

Inter-
national
confer-
ences

In June 1944 a cross-channel Allied landing took place on the coast of German-occupied Normandy. By the end of August, Allied forces occupied most of France. In August, at Dumbarton Oaks in Washington, D.C., representatives of the United States, Great Britain, the Soviet Union, and China met and agreed upon a charter for a permanent international organization. In mid-September in Quebec, Roosevelt again met with Churchill, and they tentatively agreed upon plans for dealing with Germany after the war.

The year 1945 brought an end to the war. Roosevelt, in February, met with Stalin and Churchill at Yalta in the Crimea. There policies were agreed upon to enforce the unconditional surrender of Germany, to divide it into zones for occupation and policing by the respective Allied forces, and to provide democratic regimes in eastern European nations. A series of secret agreements were also made at Yalta; chief among these was the Soviet pledge to enter the war against Japan after the German surrender, in return for concessions in east Asia.

Roosevelt died on April 12 and was succeeded by Truman. In the following months, the German armed forces collapsed; and on May 7, all German forces surrendered. In the Pacific, the invasions of Iwo Jima and Okinawa in early 1945 brought Japan under a state of siege. In the summer, before an invasion could take place, the United States dropped atomic bombs on Hiroshima and Nagasaki. On September 2 the surrender of Japan was signed in Tokyo Harbour on the battleship "Missouri." (F.Fr.)

The United States since 1945

THE PEAK COLD WAR YEARS, 1945–60

The Harry S. Truman administration. Upon the sudden death of President Roosevelt on April 12, 1945, Harry S. Truman became president of the United States. Truman was aware of the nation's problems only in a general way, for he had not had close association with the administration. The conference to establish the United Nations took place as planned, opening on April 25 in San Francisco. In May the German forces surrendered, and in July Truman conferred at Potsdam, Germany, with Stalin and Churchill (later succeeded by Clement Richard Attlee) to discuss future operations against Japan and a peace settlement for Europe. The Soviets had been ignoring many of their Yalta pledges concerning eastern Europe; at Potsdam they refused to make satisfactory arrangements with Truman. These difficulties did not seem serious, because the United States held a monopoly of atomic secrets and it was thought that the Soviet Union would need U.S. help to reconstruct its vast devastated areas.

The
death of
Roosevelt

In September the war with Japan ended and extensive demobilization of United States forces began. By the end of 1946 the army was down to 1,500,000 men and the navy to 700,000; by the spring of 1950 the army numbered 500,000 men, and the United States was relying mainly on air power and atomic weapons.

In June 1946 the United States proposed a plan for international control of atomic energy through the United Nations, but the Soviet Union would not agree to such control, insisting that the United States unilaterally destroy its atomic arsenal. Meanwhile, Soviet scientists were engaged in nuclear research; in 1949 they exploded their first atomic bomb. The U.S. continued research and development in atomic energy under the control of a five-man Atomic Energy Commission (AEC), created in 1946. The U.S. armed forces were reorganized and brought under a secretary of defense by the National Security Act of 1947, which created the U.S. Air Force as an independent service. In 1949 a Department of Defense was established, and greater unification of the services took place.

The Cold War and containment. In 1946 and early 1947 the Soviet Union supported Communist guerrillas in Greece and brought pressure upon Turkey in a way that seemed to foreshadow Soviet expansion to the Mediterranean. In March 1947, after the British government declared that it could no longer afford to continue its aid to Greece and Turkey, Truman asked Congress to appropriate funds for military aid to help these two countries resist Communist aggression. "It must be the policy of the United States," he declared, "to support free peoples who are resisting attempted subjugation by armed minorities or by outside pressures." This policy came to be known as the Truman Doctrine. Congress appropriated $400,000,000, and by 1949 the Communist threat had diminished.

In June 1947 Secretary of State George C. Marshall proposed a plan for economic rehabilitation of Europe to meet the growing Communist threat. Despite Communist harassment, 16 nations (plus western Germany) participated, and in the next three years the United States spent $12,000,000,000 through the Economic Cooperation Administration. The Marshall Plan (or European Recovery Program) revitalized the economy of western Europe and cut the strength of western European Communist parties. In his inaugural address in 1949, following re-election, Truman proposed extending the same sort of aid to underdeveloped nations throughout the world. The fourth of his proposals called for giving technical assistance to underdeveloped countries and came to be known as the Point Four Program.

The United States and Great Britain set out to rebuild western Germany as an economically strong area with sovereignty over its domestic affairs. When the U.S.S.R. retaliated in June 1948 by blockading the land and waterway routes leading from eastern Germany into the western-occupied sectors of Berlin, Truman ordered military planes to fly food and supplies into the city. In the spring of 1949 the Soviet Union ended the blockade.

In June 1948 the U.S. Senate passed the Vandenberg Resolution, authorizing negotiations that led to the signing of the North Atlantic Treaty of April 1949 by 12 nations (and later also by Greece and Turkey). The treaty created a new defense force to resist Soviet aggression, the North Atlantic Treaty Organization (NATO). Its first supreme commander was Gen. Dwight D. Eisenhower.

On the other side of the world, Truman had sent General Marshall to China as early as December 1945 to prevent warfare between Nationalist and Communist forces and to form a coalition government. In the summer of 1947, after the Communists had made rapid advances, the President sent Gen. A.C. Wedemeyer to study the situation; Wedemeyer recommended sending military personnel and large quantities of supplies. The President, who was concentrating upon containment in Europe, asked for only $570,000,000 to aid Chiang Kai-shek; Congress in April 1948 voted $400,000,000, of which only $125,000,000 could be spent for military supplies. By the end of 1949 the Nationalist government had fallen and had retreated to Taiwan. The response of the United States was to inaugurate a policy of strengthening occupied Japan.

The Fair Deal. In September 1945 Truman sent a message to Congress outlining a 21-point domestic program, which later came to be known as the Fair Deal. It called for

expanded social security, new wages-and-hours and public-housing legislation, and a permanent Fair Employment Practices Act to prevent racial or religious discrimination in hiring. Congress and the country were so preoccupied with problems of reconversion and the threat of inflation, however, that Truman was unable to get his proposals enacted; one significant exception was the Employment Act of 1946, which clearly stated the government's responsibility for maintaining full employment and established a three-man Council of Economic Advisers to advise the President and issue an annual economic report.

Reconversion went smoothly and rapidly: war contracts were cancelled and settled; war agencies were curtailed; and surplus factories and property were sold. The Serviceman's Readjustment Act of 1944 (the G.I. Bill of Rights) provided aid to former members of the armed forces. Consumer buying power, including almost unlimited credit, was far greater than the output of consumer goods and put pressure on prices to rise. In addition, labour unions, no longer bound by their wartime no-strike pledge, began to strike for higher wages. Settlement of a steel strike early in 1946 allowed a large wage increase and a resulting rise in steel prices. This "bulge in the line," justified on the basis that living costs had gone up by more than 30 percent since 1941, led to a spiral of increased wages and prices throughout industry. Farmers and businessmen tried to end price controls entirely, but Congress in June 1946 passed a bill preserving limited controls; Truman vetoed the bill because it did not go far enough. Controls expired, the prices of 28 basic commodities jumped 25 percent in the first 16 days of July, and Congress passed a new price-control bill, which Truman signed. Because of price increases, real earnings dropped 12 percent below what they had been in July 1945. In 1946 Republicans won control of both houses of Congress. Truman, regarding the election as a mandate against controls, dropped most of them. Retail prices rose at the rate of 3 percent a month, leading to a second round of strikes and higher wages and prices.

The 80th Congress, dominated by conservative Republicans, ignored the Fair Deal program. It authorized a commission on the reorganization of executive departments, and Truman appointed former president Herbert Hoover as chairman. It also enacted a new basic labour law, the Taft–Hartley Labor Management Relations Act of 1947, over Truman's veto, which removed some restrictions on management and added several on labour unions.

In the 1948 campaign the Republican presidential candidate, Gov. Thomas E. Dewey of New York, seemed almost certain of victory over Truman. A third party, the Progressive Party, calling for a more conciliatory policy toward the Soviet Union, nominated former vice president Henry A. Wallace; a fourth party, the States' Rights Democrats (Dixiecrats), protesting civil-rights provisions in the Democratic platform, nominated Gov. Strom Thurmond of South Carolina. Truman embarked upon a vigorous campaign directed against the conservative congressional Republicans. Mustering the support of labour, discontented farmers, and Northern Negroes, Truman defeated Dewey by a popular vote of about 24,106,000 to about 21,970,000 and an electoral vote of 303 to 189. Thurmond received about 1,169,000 votes and 39 electoral votes; Wallace, about 1,157,000 votes. The Democrats recaptured the House (263 to 171) and the Senate (54 to 42).

In his inaugural address on January 20, 1949, Truman called for a vigorous advancement of his Fair Deal program to aid the underprivileged. Except for the Social Security Act of 1950, which added almost 10,000,000 persons to the beneficiaries of old-age insurance, only a small part of the Fair Deal was enacted into law.

During the postwar years public attention focussed more and more on charges that the federal government was infiltrated with Communists. In 1946 a Soviet spy ring was uncovered in Canada, and Truman set up a Temporary Commission on Employee Loyalty, which recommended the establishment of loyalty review boards. By 1951 these boards had dismissed 212 government employees, and more than 2,000 others had resigned; about 3,000,000 had been cleared. Over the President's veto, Congress in 1950

The
Truman
Doctrine

Truman's
21-point
domestic
program

Charges of
Communists in
government

passed the McCarran Internal Security Act, which placed numerous restrictions upon Communists throughout the nation. In 1949, under the Smith Act of 1940, which prohibited conspiring to teach the violent overthrow of the government, 11 Communist leaders were convicted and sentenced to prison. In 1951 two Communist agents, Julius and Ethel Rosenberg, were convicted of transmitting atomic secrets to the U.S.S.R.; they were executed in 1953. In 1950 Alger Hiss, formerly an employee of the Department of State, was convicted of perjury. Capitalizing upon the resulting furor, Sen. Joseph R. McCarthy of Wisconsin charged in February 1950 that he had a list of 57 (some listeners said 205) men loyal to Communism still in the State Department. A subcommittee of the Senate Foreign Relations Committee could not find even one, but McCarthy, going on to other sensational charges, built a national following.   (F.Fr.)

With the victory of the Communists in China in 1949 and the announcement that September of a Soviet atomic explosion, fear of Communist expansion and a determination to contain it became the dominant theme in U.S. foreign policy. Truman's Point Four program was motivated in large part by a desire to persuade impoverished nations to cast their lot with the United States rather than with the Soviet Union. It was matched by the announcement in January 1950 that the President had directed the U.S. Atomic Energy Commission to proceed with work on a hydrogen bomb that would be vastly more powerful than the atomic bombs used in World War II.

The Korean War. On June 25, 1950, armed forces of the Democratic People's Republic of Korea (North Korea), supported by the Soviet Union, advanced south of the 38th parallel separating the northern Communist state from the Republic of Korea (South Korea). The U.S. government immediately presented the matter to the UN Security Council, urging that military forces under UN auspices be sent to Korea to resist Communist aggression. The Security Council, acting during a Soviet boycott, adopted a resolution calling upon UN members to resist the North Korean invasion.

Under the command of Gen. Douglas MacArthur, UN forces drove the North Koreans north of the 38th parallel. As the year ended, however, the UN troops were forced into a costly and precarious retreat by overwhelming numbers of Chinese Communists, whose entrance into the struggle had been foreseen as a possibility but was not expected. The situation for the United States, as the leader against Communist aggression, now became critical, and Congress supported the President in a gigantic program for defense. On December 16, 1950, Truman declared a national emergency and outlined plans for placing the country on a war basis.

Truman's defense program

MacArthur, whose view of the conduct of the war contrasted with the policy of the administration, was recalled by Truman on April 11, 1951, and was succeeded by Gen. Matthew B. Ridgway. Armistice talks began on July 10, 1951, but not until July 27, 1953, was an armistice signed. After further negotiations, an exchange of prisoners was completed by September 6, 1953. Efforts to negotiate the unification of Korea ended in failure at Geneva in June 1954.

Peace treaties. The United States had meanwhile taken the lead in concluding a peace treaty with Japan; the treaty was signed in San Francisco on September 8, 1951, by 49 nations. Japan and the U.S. also agreed upon a bilateral security treaty, which provided that U.S. troops could be stationed in Japan for an indefinite period; the U.S. signed separate defense pacts with the Philippines, Australia, and New Zealand.

On July 1, 1952, the Senate approved a peace agreement between western Germany and the western Allies. The U.S.S.R. retained control of all territory it occupied at the end of World War II and drew an "iron curtain" between eastern and western Europe.

The election of 1952. In 1952 General Eisenhower's name was entered in Republican state presidential primaries, a number of which he won. After he retired from his military post, Eisenhower's supporters campaigned actively for his nomination, and the Republican convention

nominated him on the first ballot. Sen. Richard M. Nixon of California was named Republican vice presidential candidate. The Democratic national convention nominated Gov. Adlai E. Stevenson of Illinois as its presidential candidate.

Eisenhower charged the Truman administration with responsibility for events leading to the Korean War and promised that, if elected, he would visit Korea before his inauguration. Republican campaigners continued to make accusations of Communist infiltration in government offices. Truman supported Stevenson.

In November the popular vote of more than 61,000,000 was the largest in the nation's history. Eisenhower carried 39 states (442 electoral votes); Stevenson carried 9 (89 electoral votes). Republicans gained control of the House and won a narrow 48-to-47 margin in the Senate, not including one independent Republican. Gubernatorial contests in 30 states resulted in 20 Republican victories.

Eisenhower's landslide victory

The Dwight D. Eisenhower administration. The new president had run far ahead of his party ticket, attracting portions of the labour vote that had been consistently Democratic for 20 years, as well as a substantial Negro city vote and a widespread Middle Western farm vote.

Domestic policies. Eisenhower's middle-of-the-road policy in domestic affairs weakened the influence of labour elements in the Democratic Party and strengthened liberal elements in the Republican Party. Among his appointments were those of Gov. Earl Warren of California as Supreme Court chief justice and John Foster Dulles as secretary of state. Eisenhower was not supported by the united action of his party members in House and Senate. His differences with the right-wing elements were most marked. The President won important victories in legislation only because of Democratic support.

The Eisenhower administration was plagued throughout its first two years by the activities of the Senate subcommittee charged with investigation under the loyalty-security program. Eisenhower took the position that loyalty and security maintenance were the responsibility of the executive branch of the government; yet he did not interfere with the activities of the subcommittee, the chairman of which, Senator McCarthy, was later condemned by the Senate for conduct "contrary to Senate traditions."

The years 1953–56 were characterized by general prosperity. Confidence on the part of investment capital contributed to business development, but the Federal Reserve Board checked expansion of bank credit by adopting a tight-money policy intended to prevent inflation. The national budget was balanced, despite huge expenditures for national defense, because taxes were maintained at the necessary level and employment and earnings were moderately high.

On May 17, 1954, the Supreme Court unanimously ruled, in effect, that racial segregation in elementary and secondary public schools was unconstitutional. This decision resulted in a division of sentiment in both political parties, especially the Democratic Party. Some immediate progress toward integration of schools was made in the North and in the border states, but in the South change was less immediate.

The Supreme Court decision on racial segregation

Foreign policy. Eisenhower's attempts to improve international relations were seconded by John Foster Dulles, who travelled widely on diplomatic missions; but the administration suffered a series of defeats in promoting U.S. objectives. Following the prolonged Korean armistice discussions, a stalemate ensued in the Far East and Communist strength in that area continued to grow.

Eisenhower's Atoms for Peace plan, proposed in 1953, was a step toward using nuclear science for the welfare of the world. His proposals for international control of atomic armaments and his suggestion for open-sky inspection of military installations were not adopted, but they conferred an important initiative on the democracies in the controversy with the Soviet Union over arms limitation. The leaders of the Big Four powers met in Geneva in 1955 in the hope of lessening Cold War tensions, but the results were inconclusive.

Eisenhower's illness and re-election. The President's personal role in government was basically altered in the months following a heart attack on September 24, 1955. Although he gradually resumed the responsibilities of the presidency, the temporary disability raised concern over the increasing burden placed upon a president of the United States and the calibre of men nominated for the vice presidency. The President's gradual return to health was interrupted by a severe attack of ileitis and a surgical operation on June 9, 1956. He resumed his duties and, well in advance of the Republican convention, let it be known that he would accept the nomination for re-election. He and Vice President Nixon were nominated unanimously. Adlai E. Stevenson was again nominated by the Democrats.

World
crises in
1956

The outcome of the election was largely determined by external events. Late in October eastern Europe and the Middle East burst into flames. Protest against Soviet Communist Party domination raged in Poland and brought the Soviet army into Hungary. An invasion of Egyptian territory by Israel, claiming self-defense against border depredations, and the swift attack of Great Britain and France upon Egypt to regain control of the Suez Canal, which Egypt had seized in July, dominated the final days of the presidential campaign. The electorate voted overwhelmingly for the President, who carried all but seven states. It was more a personal than a party victory, however, for the Democrats won control of both houses of Congress.

The Democratic majority in House and Senate was divided, especially on civil rights, and there was also a wide division among the Republican minority. Eisenhower's vetoes defeated Democratic plans on public housing, enlarged social security, and deficit spending.

In the midterm elections an economic recession in 1957–58 and a continuing increase in unemployment were determining influences. The Democrats won a widespread national victory, including 32 governorships. Alaska was formally admitted to the Union on January 3, 1959. The resolution admitting Hawaii as the 50th state was signed by the President on March 18.

Racial and labour problems increased in intensity; public-school integration was contested by Southern states, and peaceful sit-in demonstrations by blacks seeking service at "white" lunch counters led to police action. In July 1959 about 500,000 steelworkers went on strike. The strike lasted 116 days before the government obtained an injunction forcing the workers back while efforts were made for government arbitration. No decision completely satisfactory to either side was reached, but work was resumed. Investigation of union leadership by committees of Congress led to passage in 1959 of the Landrum–Griffin Act, aimed at fighting corruption in labour unions and at the establishment of procedures to maintain democratic elections within unions.

The United States in world affairs. On October 4, 1957, the Soviet Union launched the first artificial Earth satellite. This achievement seemed to shift the world balance of power to the Soviet Union until, on January 31, 1958, the

Beginning
of the
space race

U.S. Army launched an Earth satellite. Within the United States the space age brought increased attention to the long-range program of education necessary for scientists and the increased costs of experimental programs.

Several crises in 1958 brought the United States to the brink of war. In July Eisenhower ordered U.S. troops to Lebanon to prevent the overthrow of the Lebanese government by elements unfriendly to the Western powers. In August, the bombardment, by Communist China, of the offshore islands of Quemoy and Matsu brought the administration face to face with its treaty commitment to Nationalist China. In November, the Soviet Union again threatened to isolate Berlin. On December 31 rebels led by Fidel Castro seized control of the government of Cuba.

The illness of Secretary of State Dulles in March 1959 led the President to increase his own activity in foreign affairs. On April 15 Eisenhower announced Dulles' resignation, and on April 18 he named Undersecretary of State Christian Herter to replace him. Dulles died on May 24.

Eisenhower's personal diplomacy. Eisenhower accepted personal diplomacy by heads of states as desirable in the Cold War. The President on August 26, 1959, flew to Europe, where he conferred with British prime minister Harold Macmillan, French president Charles de Gaulle, and West German chancellor Konrad Adenauer. On September 15 Soviet premier Nikita Khrushchev, at Eisenhower's invitation, began a tour of the United States. In December Eisenhower travelled more than 22,000 miles (35,000 kilometres) in 19 days, visiting 11 countries; early in 1960 he visited five countries in Latin America.

Khrushchev proposed that a summit conference be held in May 1960 at Paris to discuss a relaxation of world tensions. But, when the heads of state met in Paris, the conference was broken up by Khrushchev, who angrily announced that a high-altitude U.S. reconnaissance plane (U-2) had been shot down over Soviet territory on May 1. Eisenhower still pursued his plan to visit the Far East that summer. He visited Alaska, Hawaii, the Philippines, Okinawa, Taiwan, and Korea. Violent anti-American outbursts in Japan brought about cancellation of a visit to Tokyo. On his return, he restated his belief in the efficacy of personal diplomacy.

Anti-
American
outbursts
in Japan

Growth and prosperity. The decade 1950–60 was marked by a steady increase in population, which passed 179,000,000 in 1960. The shift of population from east to west continued, with a new emphasis upon movement from urban to suburban areas. Widespread prosperity, increased productivity, and higher incomes gave impetus to construction activities of all kinds. Recessions in 1953–54 and 1957–58 did not alter the generally prosperous character of the period, although agricultural income continued to lag and unemployment persisted.   (E.E.R.)

The election of 1960. The two major U.S. political parties nominated comparatively young presidential candidates at their 1960 national conventions. The Republican nominee, Vice Pres. Richard M. Nixon of California, was 47; the Democrat, Sen. John F. Kennedy of Massachusetts, was 43. A dramatic feature of the campaign was a series of television appearances (publicized as debates), during which the two candidates stated their positions and answered questions from newsmen. Kennedy defeated Nixon in the most closely contested election of the century; Kennedy won 303 electoral votes to Nixon's 219, but, in the popular vote of more than 68,000,000, Kennedy's margin was only 118,000. The Democrats retained control of both houses of Congress but with a somewhat smaller majority than before.

The
Kennedy-
Nixon
debates

THE LATE 20TH CENTURY

The John F. Kennedy administration. The population growth and westward movement continued into the 1960s, with California replacing New York as the most populous state. The economy was fairly stable and buoyant, as production, employment, and corporate profits reached new high levels. U.S. scientists and engineers made remarkable progress in space exploration in the 1960s. But numerous problems remained. In domestic affairs, racial tensions mounted, urban problems multiplied, poverty remained widespread, and air and water pollution reached alarming proportions. The predicted long-term effects of automation on employment posed fundamental questions as to the future of the nation's economy and of its educational system. In Southeast Asia a controversial war in Vietnam continued year after year with increasing U.S. involvement. In Europe, NATO, a key element in U.S. military strategy of the 1950s, suffered a severe setback in 1966 when France declared its intention of withdrawing its forces and requested the removal of all NATO installations from French soil. The proliferation of nuclear weapons, with both France and China setting off nuclear explosions during the decade, greatly complicated the prospects for disarmament and world peace.

Kennedy was inaugurated as the 35th president of the United States on January 20, 1961, the first Roman Catholic and the youngest man ever to be elected to that office. His vice president was Lyndon B. Johnson of Texas, who had been majority leader of the Senate during the Eisenhower administration. The new President set the tone of his administration in an eloquent inaugural address that called for national dedication to a worldwide struggle against tyranny, poverty, disease, and war. His Cabinet included Dean Rusk as secretary of state, Robert

F. Kennedy, the President's brother, as attorney general, and Robert S. McNamara as secretary of defense.

Foreign affairs. President Kennedy's first year in office saw an abortive invasion of Cuba, aimed at overthrowing the Castro regime by forces that had been secretly trained and supplied by the United States, a personal meeting of the President with Soviet premier Khrushchev in Vienna, and a continuation of Cold War tensions. In October 1962 the Cuban problem reached a critical point, when U.S. intelligence agencies learned that the Soviet Union had installed in Cuba ballistic missiles capable of attacking the United States. The President ordered a naval quarantine of Cuba to prevent Soviet ships from delivering additional missiles to the island. After five tense days during which the U.S. and the U.S.S.R. seemed on the verge of war, the U.S.S.R. agreed to dismantle its missile bases and to withdraw its troops.

On August 5, 1963, diplomats representing the U.S., the U.S.S.R., and the U.K. signed a nuclear test-ban treaty in Moscow. The signatories agreed to stop all testing of nuclear weapons in the atmosphere, in outer space, and under water, thus permitting only underground tests, which did not contaminate the atmosphere. Within a few months, more than 100 other nations signed the treaty. France, the only other nation then possessing a nuclear capability, did not sign, nor did China, which was soon to detonate its first nuclear device and become the world's fifth nuclear power.

Domestic affairs. President Kennedy appealed to Congress for legislation to stimulate international trade, reduce unemployment, provide medical care for the aged under social security, reduce federal income taxes, and protect the civil rights of blacks. The latter issue, which had aroused national concern in 1962 when federal troops were employed to assure the admission of a Negro at the University of Mississippi, caused further concern in 1963, when similar action was taken at the University of Alabama. Although the Democrats controlled both houses of Congress, the administration's proposals encountered strong opposition from a coalition of Republicans and Southern Democrats. Enactment of the Trade Expansion Act and a tax-reform law were the only important administration victories in 1962. The two most important bills before Congress in 1963 called for reduction of income taxes and the strengthening of civil-rights legislation.

Kennedy's assassinationOn November 22 President Kennedy was assassinated in Dallas, Texas. Lyndon Johnson took the oath of office as 36th president of the United States at the Dallas airport and flew to Washington. Hours after the assassination, the Dallas police arrested 24-year-old Lee Harvey Oswald. While the Dallas police were transferring the suspected assassin from one jail to another on November 24, Jack Ruby, owner of a Dallas nightclub, shot and killed Oswald in full view of millions of persons watching the events on television.

The Lyndon B. Johnson administration. During his first days in office, Johnson conferred with scores of leaders from other countries, who were in Washington for the funeral of President Kennedy, and assured them that there would be no basic change in U.S. foreign policy. He also appointed a commission, headed by Chief Justice Earl Warren, to investigate the events surrounding the assassination.

Domestic affairs. On November 27, before a joint session of Congress, Johnson paid tribute to his predecessor and called for prompt enactment of measures Kennedy had proposed. Johnson's skill as a parliamentary strategist helped push his legislative program through Congress. The tax-reduction bill was soon passed, but the civil-rights bill encountered opposition from Southern Democrats in the Senate, finally passing in June 1964.

In his 1964 state-of-the-union message, Johnson declared "an unconditional war on poverty." As finally passed, the Economic Opportunity Act (or antipoverty bill) provided funds for vocational training at schools and colleges, establishment of work-training camps and centres for underprivileged youths, aid to various types of community-action programs to combat poverty, loans to small businessmen and small farmers, and related projects. R. Sar-

gent Shriver, director of the Peace Corps established by President Kennedy, was named director.

In 1964 Johnson won a landslide victory over his Republican opponent, Sen. Barry Morris Goldwater of Arizona, losing only six states—Goldwater's home state of Arizona and five states of the deep South. The Democrats also strengthened their majority in the House and gained one seat in the Senate.

Johnson's Great SocietyAfter outlining his program for a "Great Society" in his 1965 state-of-the-union message, Johnson sent to Congress a series of special messages on health, immigration, disarmament, tax reduction, conservation, housing, rail transportation, crime, and voting rights. The 89th Congress passed a bill to eliminate many excise taxes at once and to reduce others gradually; it passed the "Medicare" bill, providing hospital and nursing-home care for persons over 65 under the Social Security Act, and made numerous other changes in social security; and it passed a strong right-to-vote bill that abolished literacy tests and other voting restrictions and authorized federal officials to register voters in areas where discrimination existed.

The 24th Amendment to the federal Constitution, ratified in January 1964, banned poll taxes as a requirement for voting in federal elections; in March 1966 the Supreme Court ruled that states could not make payment of a poll tax a requirement for voting in state or local elections. In 1965 Congress also voted substantial appropriations for public housing, education, the "war on poverty," aid to Appalachia, and military pay increases.

Congress added two departments to the Cabinet in 1965–66: a Department of Housing and Urban Development, to coordinate various federal agencies, and a Department of Transportation, to develop a coordinated national transportation policy. In 1965 a new immigration law, the first major change in U.S. immigration policy in 41 years, abolished the national-origins quota system favouring northern European countries and adopted a system giving priority to close relatives of U.S. residents and to persons with special skills. The act marked the first limitation placed on immigration from the Western Hemisphere.

In 1966 Congress responded to most of the President's requests for new legislation. It increased the federal minimum wage for nonfarm workers and extended coverage to agricultural workers for the first time. It enacted the Clean Waters Restoration Act, providing funds to help communities build sewage-treatment plants. The Demonstration Cities and Metropolitan Development Act of 1966 provided funds to aid 60 to 70 selected cities in rebuilding their blighted areas. Two major measures defeated in the 1966 session were proposed civil-rights legislation (providing for "open occupancy," to halt racial discrimination in the sale or rental of housing) and an attempt to repeal section 14(b) of the Taft–Hartley Act, permitting states to enact right-to-work laws that outlawed the closed shop and union shop.

Changes in presidential successionShortly after the 1966 election, in which the Democrats retained control of Congress, Johnson underwent surgery. This operation, the second within 13 months, focussed attention on the proposed 25th Amendment to the Constitution that provided procedures by which the vice president could become acting president and provided for filling the office of vice president if it became vacant. It became a part of the Constitution in February 1967.

The Democratic leadership of the 90th Congress could not count on the support of conservative Democrats, chiefly Southerners, to convert its paper majority into a voting majority. President Johnson urged Congress to increase social security benefits and levy a surcharge on corporate and individual income taxes to help meet the cost of the Vietnam War.

Riots in the slums of many large cities during the mid-1960s caused extensive property damage from arson and looting. In some cities National Guard troops were needed to restore order. After the riots of 1967 President Johnson appointed a commission, headed by Gov. Otto Kerner of Illinois, to investigate the causes of these civil disorders and to recommend a course of action. The commission's report in February 1968 placed most of the blame on "white racism" and recommended action by all levels of government to provide employment, better housing, improved education, and more adequate police protection for black ghetto residents.

In April the populace was shocked by the assassination in Memphis, Tennessee, of the black civil-rights leader Dr. Martin Luther King, Jr. The U.S. House of Representatives, spurred to action, passed a civil-rights bill forbidding discrimination in the sale or rental of homes and apartments on the basis of race, religion, or national origin. The Senate had passed the bill earlier. (James Earl Ray was convicted of the murder in 1969.)

In June 1968 Chief Justice Warren submitted his resignation. The President's nomination of Associate Justice Abe Fortas aroused strong opposition in the Senate. The appointment was criticized because Fortas, while a member of the Supreme Court, had several times served as confidential adviser to Johnson. Fortas finally asked that his name be withdrawn.

Foreign affairs. President Johnson soon gave American foreign policy his own emphasis. It was directed chiefly toward Southeast Asia, where the United States had for several years been helping South Vietnam defend itself against the Viet Cong, who were being aided by North Vietnam. During 1964 U.S. aid, initially military supplies and a large number of military advisers, rapidly increased in the face of continued Viet Cong successes. In August, when U.S. warships patrolling the Gulf of Tonkin were allegedly attacked by torpedo boats, Johnson ordered retaliatory air strikes against North Vietnamese torpedo-boat bases. Congress approved the Gulf of Tonkin resolution authorizing "all necessary measures to repel any armed attack" against U.S. forces and "to prevent further aggression." Beginning in 1965 the President sent more and more troops to Vietnam, the total reaching more than 500,000 by 1968. He also ordered the bombing of North Vietnamese military targets, while repeatedly announcing a willingness to negotiate a peace settlement with North Vietnam. Both houses of Congress approved the actions but with sharp dissent. When a Christmas truce in 1965 and a subsequent bombing halt failed to bring the North Vietnamese to the conference table, Johnson resumed the bombing and asked the UN Security Council to arrange a cease-fire agreement and a peace conference. The UN efforts failed.

In February 1966 President Johnson and his advisers conferred in Hawaii with South Vietnamese leaders and expressed a determination to continue the war and to work for democratic self-government in South Vietnam. North Vietnam declared its unwillingness to negotiate until the bombing was stopped. In October Johnson made an extensive Asian journey, and at a conference in Manila he stressed the need for social revolution in South Vietnam. He offered to withdraw all troops if "the other side" would withdraw and cease infiltration and acts of violence. North Vietnam rejected the offer.

In the United States, opposition to the Vietnam War rose sharply in the winter of 1967–68 as casualties mounted and victory on either side seemed impossible. In a nationwide address on March 31, 1968, Johnson declared that he would not seek or accept the Democratic nomination for another term. He announced conditional cessation of U.S. bombing of North Vietnam, except in an area north of the demilitarized zone, and again called upon Hanoi to negotiate. A discussion between the United States and North Vietnam began at Paris in May 1968. On November 1, all bombing of North Vietnam ceased.

The election of 1968. The Vietnam war was the major issue in 1968. The chief contenders for the Democratic presidential nomination were Sen. Eugene J. McCarthy of Minnesota, a champion of the antiwar faction, Sen. Robert F. Kennedy of New York, and Vice Pres. Hubert H. Humphrey. On June 5 Kennedy was shot by an assassin and died the following day. Humphrey was nominated at the Democratic National Convention at Chicago in August, with Sen. Edmund S. Muskie of Maine as his running mate. Violent disorders in the streets of Chicago arising from opposition to the war as well as opposition to party positions and procedures marred the convention. Earlier in August the Republicans had nominated Nixon

for president and Gov. Spiro T. Agnew of Maryland for vice president.

The election in November was close in the popular vote between Humphrey and Nixon, but Nixon won a decisive majority of the electoral votes, 301 votes to 191 for Humphrey and 46 for the former governor of Alabama, George Wallace, who led a third party. The Democrats, however, held a majority of 243 to 192 in the House and 58 to 42 in the Senate.

The Richard M. Nixon administration. *Foreign affairs.* Nixon made a round-the-world trip in July 1969, restating U.S. policy in talks with various Asian leaders. He enunciated what some observers called the "Nixon Doctrine," to the effect that the United States would maintain a presence in the Far East but that the Asian nations would have to carry the main burden of their own defense. Strategic Arms Limitation Talks (SALT) between the United States and the Soviet Union were initiated in Helsinki, Finland, in November 1969; Nixon and N.V. Podgorny, chairman of the Presidium of the Supreme Soviet of the U.S.S.R., signed the Treaty on the Non-proliferation of Nuclear Weapons on November 24.

Inconclusive fighting continued in Vietnam, and unproductive peace talks continued in Paris. The pace of the war slackened in 1969, and Nixon announced plans to reduce the number of U.S. troops. In a major address to the nation, the President reaffirmed the Johnson policy of aiding South Vietnam but promised that U.S. troops would be brought home as soon as South Vietnamese forces could be trained to take their place. In April 1970, however, the fighting spread to Cambodia.

Following the withdrawal from Cambodia in June 1970, Nixon continued his policy of "Vietnamization." Systematic withdrawal of U.S. troops reduced American ground forces in Vietnam to fewer than 70,000 by early 1972. In April, when the North Vietnamese launched an invasion of South Vietnam, Nixon temporarily broke off the Paris talks and resumed the bombing. To stop shipments of arms and supplies, North Vietnamese harbour entrances and coastal waters were mined. U.S. forces took little part in the expanding warfare on the ground, but U.S. air power was heavily employed.

Serious peace negotiations resumed between the North Vietnamese representative, Le Duc Tho, and the U.S. special adviser, Henry Kissinger, in Paris, and the long-awaited cease-fire agreement was finally signed on January 27, 1973. The agreement, which provided for exchange of prisoners of war and for U.S. withdrawal from South Vietnam without any similar commitment from the North Vietnamese, ended 12 years of U.S. military effort that had taken nearly 46,000 American lives.

Employing a policy of personal as well as traditional diplomacy, Nixon met periodically with leaders of the Western bloc. In addition, he completely reversed U.S. policy by accepting an invitation from the People's Republic of China to visit Peking in March 1972. Long-term tensions between the two nations were markedly lessened by this journey, which included several days of discussion with the Chinese leaders Mao Tse-tung and Chou En-lai. For a similar purpose, Nixon travelled to Moscow in May 1972 for discussions with Soviet leaders. On this trip, several Soviet-American accords were signed, including agreements aimed at limiting the production of strategic armaments. In July 1972 Nixon announced an agreement for the sale of large quantities of wheat, corn, and other grains to the Soviet Union over a period of three years.

In June 1973 a visit to the United States of Leonid I. Brezhnev, general secretary of the Soviet Communist Party, appeared to strengthen the détente of the previous year, but the Arab-Israeli war that broke out in October brought some strain to the relationship. Kissinger, newly appointed as U.S. secretary of state, was active in negotiations that brought about a cease-fire between Israel and Egypt in November and between Israel and Syria in mid-1974. Soon afterward, Nixon toured the Middle East and then made another visit to the Soviet Union.

Domestic affairs. Nixon's domestic policies made slow progress, partly because of opposition from a Congress that was controlled by the Democrats. On May 21, 1969,

Escalation of the war in Vietnam

Johnson's decision not to seek re-election

the President nominated Warren E. Burger to succeed Earl Warren as chief justice of the United States. The nomination was quickly approved. Prior to Burger's nomination, Associate Justice Abe Fortas had resigned from the court after disclosure that he had accepted $20,000 from a private foundation. Fortas stated that he had returned the money and denied guilt of wrongdoing. To replace him, Nixon nominated, successively, two Southern judges, both of whom were rejected by the Senate. The President's third nominee was confirmed in May 1970.

A controversy over the administration's anti-ballistic missile (ABM) program reached a climax in the summer of 1969, the administration's bill passing in the Senate by the margin of one vote; it was enacted in November. Opponents charged that it might have an adverse effect on the continuing SALT negotiations, but one result of Nixon's visit to the Soviet Union in May 1972 was an agreement to limit the two nations' ABM systems.

As a political issue the Vietnamese war had subsided until the presidential announcement in April 1970 of the U.S. military involvement in Cambodia. The announcement aroused strong protest; student demonstrations at Kent State University in Ohio led (May 4) to a confrontation with troops of the Ohio National Guard, who fired on the students without orders, killing four and wounding several others. National revulsion at this act led to serious disorders at many universities and forced some of them to close for the remainder of the term.

A U.S. Army court-martial jury on March 29, 1971, found Lieut. William L. Calley, Jr., guilty of murdering unarmed South Vietnamese civilians at My Lai 4 in March 1968. Public opinion critical of the military court's sentence of life imprisonment followed, and Nixon ordered Calley released from jail, though he was restricted to his quarters, pending a review of the case. In turn, Nixon was criticized by many for undermining the cause of justice and the military court system.

Spokesmen for the administration, notably Vice President Agnew, attacked the news media when coverage was considered inadequate or unsympathetic to the administration. The fight for minority rights continued as a major domestic issue, and the 12 black members of the U.S. House of Representatives charged the administration with reneging on past promises and turning a deaf ear to minority groups. In 1972 the Congress, with the support of the President, adopted (49 years after it was first introduced) a proposed constitutional amendment guaranteeing equal rights for women and submitted it to the states for ratification. (The Equal Rights Amendment, or ERA, as it was called, failed ultimately, however, to secure ratification in a sufficient number of states, even after an extended deadline to June 30, 1982.)

Nixon gave high priority to the control of inflation and the reduction of military expenditures. But the cost of living continued to rise, until by June 1970 it was 30 percent above the level of 1960; industrial production declined, as did the stock market. By mid-1971 unemployment had reached a 10-year peak of 6 percent, and inflation continued. Wage and price controls were instituted in various phases, the dollar was devalued twice, and the limitation on the national debt was raised three times in 1972 alone. The U.S. trade deficit improved, but inflation continued unchecked.

The 1972 election and the Watergate scandal. Sen. George McGovern of South Dakota, an early and earnest opponent of the Vietnam War who called for drastic reforms in welfare programs and cuts in military spending, won the Democratic nomination for president in 1972. The primary campaign had been marred by an assassination attempt on George Wallace that left him disabled. Sen. Thomas Eagleton of Missouri was the vice-presidential candidate but was soon replaced by R. Sargent Shriver after unfavourable publicity about the Senator's earlier psychiatric treatment. Nixon and Agnew, who were renominated by the Republicans, won a landslide victory in November, capturing every state except Massachusetts and the District of Columbia. The Democrats retained majorities, however, in both the Senate and the House.

The scandal that was to haunt Nixon's second term,

and lead to its premature end, first surfaced in June 1972, when five men were arrested for breaking into the Democratic national headquarters at the Watergate office–apartment building in Washington. It was revealed that the men were in the hire of the Committee for the Reelection of the President (CRP). The director of security and a counsel of CRP were discharged and later convicted on charges of burglary and wiretapping. John N. Mitchell, former U.S. attorney general and the campaign director of CRP, resigned.

The events had no effect on the election and roused no national attention until 1973, when it was revealed that an attempt to suppress knowledge of the connection between the Watergate affair and CRP involved highly placed members of the White House staff. In response, a Senate select committee was formed and opened hearings on May 17, 1973; Nixon appointed a special prosecutor on May 25 to investigate the scandal. Amid conflicting testimony, almost daily disclosures of further scandals, and continuing resignations of administrative personnel, a battle developed between the legislative and executive branches of government.

The Watergate affair itself was further complicated by the revelation of other irregularities. It became known that a security unit in the White House had engaged in illegal activities under the cloak of national security. Nixon's personal finances were questioned, and Vice President Agnew resigned after pleading no contest to charges of income-tax evasion. On December 6, 1973, Nixon's nominee, Congressman Gerald R. Ford of Michigan, was approved by Congress as the new vice president. The investigations, criminal indictments, and court battles initiated as a consequence of the scandals continued unabated into 1974.

The resignation. By late autumn 1973, both Democratic and Republican leaders in Congress, as well as many other public officials and many newspapers that had formerly supported the President, were beginning to talk of his resignation or impeachment. His popularity in the country, as indicated by public-opinion polls, declined steadily. On July 24, 1974, the Supreme Court ruled unanimously that Nixon must provide potential evidence (including, in this case, tapes of recorded conversations) for the criminal trial of his former subordinates, rejecting flatly his contention that he had authority to withhold such material; the court emphasized that it was ruling with specific reference to a criminal trial. The Judiciary Committee of the House of Representatives, which since May 9 had been hearing evidence relating to a possible impeachment proceeding, voted on July 27–30 to recommend that Nixon be impeached on three charges. The first article of impeachment (approved by all 21 Democrats and by six Republicans on the committee) charged that he had engaged in a course of conduct designed to obstruct justice in trying to conceal the role the White House had played in the Watergate affair. Such action had been strenuously and repeatedly denied by Nixon. But on August 5, on releasing transcripts of three of the tape-recorded conversations on which the Supreme Court had ruled, he admitted that, as evidenced in the recordings, he had indeed taken steps to direct the Federal Bureau of Investigation away from the White House when its inquiries into the Watergate burglary were leading it toward his staff.

The admission created a storm. Nixon's support in Congress vanished. It became obvious that the House would vote approval of the articles by a very large margin, and by August 6 it was estimated that no more than 20 senators would support the President in an impeachment trial; he would need 34 votes to survive. On the evening of August 8, in a television address, Nixon announced his resignation, effective the next day. He was the first man to resign the presidency. At noon on August 9, Vice President Ford was sworn in as his successor, the first president not elected to the office or to the vice presidency.

The Gerald R. Ford administration. *Domestic affairs.* Ford saw as his first duty the binding of the nation's wounds and the restoration of confidence in the presidency. He seemed ideally suited to the task, as attested by his reputation for integrity and candour, but his actions did not go unchallenged. His nomination on August 20 of Nelson A. Rockefeller to be vice president was widely acclaimed, although extensive congressional hearings delayed confirmation until December 19. But Ford's pardon of Nixon on September 8 undermined his base of support so seriously that he volunteered to appear before a subcommittee of the House of Representatives to explain his action. Watergate reappeared in the headlines in October at the beginning of the trial of five of Nixon's aides on charges of obstructing justice (four were subsequently convicted, and in the following year former attorney general John N. Mitchell was also tried and convicted and served a term in prison). Ford took an active part in the autumn election campaigns, but the Democrats gained 43 seats in the House, three in the Senate, and the governorships of four states. The new Congress took action that reduced the powers of its firmly entrenched seniority system.

Proclaiming inflation the major economic problem, Ford conducted a "summit conference" of economists and presented an anti-inflation program to Congress on October 8. His "Whip Inflation Now" (WIN) proposals contained little mandatory action and were received coolly. As increasing unemployment overtook inflation as a serious problem, a unique recession got under way, and the WIN program quietly disappeared. The pace of inflation rose to 14.4 percent per year during the final quarter of 1974 (it was 10.2 percent for the whole year) but declined to a "manageable" 5 to 6 percent in 1976; the unemployment rate reached a peak of 8.9 percent in April 1975 and remained high. The administration was criticized for inaction, but it was generally agreed that the economy was improving by the end of 1975. In the post-Watergate mood of assertiveness, the Congress passed a bill that established procedures for greater involvement of Congress in the budget-making process, and in September 1976 an extensive revision of the tax structure was enacted.

Inflation and unemployment

The growing financial plight of U.S. cities reached crisis proportions in 1975 in New York City. Expenses had exceeded tax revenues over the previous 10 years, and the city was unable to pay its maturing debt obligations. Both the state of New York and the federal government at first rejected all pleas for help, but in June 1975 the state legislature created a new agency, the Municipal Assistance Corporation (MAC), that virtually took control of the city's fiscal affairs. President Ford repeatedly refused federal help, but he changed his position after the state approved still more aid and the city showed signs of making major economies. Congress authorized restricted loans and a revision of municipal bankruptcy laws.

New York City financial crisis

Allegations made during the Watergate scandal led separate subcommittees of the Senate and House in 1975–76 to scrutinize the Central Intelligence Agency (CIA) and the Federal Bureau of Investigation (FBI), as well as the Internal Revenue Service and the army intelligence staff. The inquiries revealed numerous illegal activities, both at home and overseas, through several administrations. Tighter controls were urged; actions included the dismissal of the CIA director and the FBI associate director, issuance of an executive order outlining a new command structure and restricting activities, and selection of a Senate committee to oversee all intelligence gathering.

End of the Vietnam War

Foreign affairs. The Vietnam War came to an end in April 1975. Just a few weeks earlier the President had requested nearly $1,000,000,000 in military and humanitarian aid for South Vietnam but had been rebuffed by Congress. Only hours before the end he ordered an airlift of refugees from Indochina, and Congress later authorized expenditure of $455,000,000 for assistance to refugees. In May Ford sent the Marines to rescue a cargo ship, the "Mayaguez," from illegal seizure by Cambodia.

The policy of détente continued as the basis of relations between the U.S. and the Soviet Union, but not without incidents of strain. A five-year trade agreement was signed in October 1975, under which the U.S. would supply grain to the Soviet Union in return for petroleum; this was followed two months later by a six-year shipping agreement. The Soviet government had cancelled (January 1975) a trade agreement made in 1972, claiming internal interference in Congress' stipulation that Moscow must permit freer emigration of Jews. A treaty limiting underground nuclear explosions for peaceful purposes, signed in May 1976, complemented a treaty of July 1974. The Strategic Arms Limitation Talks (SALT) produced only limited agreements.

Henry A. Kissinger, as secretary of state, was one of only three Cabinet members retained from the Nixon administration. He dominated foreign policy in the Ford administration even more than he had under Nixon. He undertook many missions of his own, continuing his "shuttle diplomacy" in the Middle East and in 1976 adding Africa to his areas of activity. He was responsible for a five-year treaty of friendship (January 1976) between Spain and the U.S. and for Iran's plans (August 1976) to purchase U.S. arms worth approximately $10,000,000,000.

Bicentennial celebration. July 4, 1976, marked the 200th anniversary of the Declaration of Independence, the birth of the nation. A celebration began in July 1975 and continued to the end of 1976 with projects, exhibits, and activities in almost every institution and community of the country. The bicentennial inspired many varieties of commemoration, including the British Parliament's loan of one of the four first copies of Magna Carta, escorted from London by 25 members of Congress and displayed in the rotunda of the Capitol in Washington.

The election of 1976. The election of 1976 was the first to be held under provisions of a law regulating the financing of political campaigns, passed in 1974 and amended in 1976. Ford announced his candidacy for the Republican nomination in July 1975. Though he was seriously challenged by Ronald Reagan, the former governor of California, Ford won the nomination, choosing Sen. Robert J. Dole of Kansas as his running mate.

In the Democratic contest there were 10 major contenders. By June 1976, however, more than a month before the Democratic National Convention, Jimmy Carter, a former governor of Georgia, had won enough delegates to be assured of the nomination. He chose Walter F. Mondale, senator from Minnesota, as his running mate.

The most notable feature of the autumn campaign was a series of debates on television (the first in 16 years) between the two major presidential candidates and one between the vice-presidential opponents. Both Ford and Carter seemed to stand solidly in the traditions of their respective parties. Carter maintained his early lead and was elected president in November.

The Jimmy Carter administration. *Foreign affairs.* During his first year in office, Carter introduced his policy of tying the guarantee of human rights to the conduct of foreign affairs. This policy was echoed by Andrew Young, U.S. ambassador to the United Nations (1977–79), despite protests by the Soviet Union. To protest racial policies, the U.S. voted for a UN embargo of arms sales to South Africa and ended importation of chromium from Rhodesia (Zimbabwe). In May restrictions on arms sales to all nations not linked to the U.S. in defense treaties were announced. In February 1977 the U.S. extended its control of fishing rights to 200 miles offshore, giving priority to U.S. fishermen, placing restrictions on the kinds of fish caught, and limiting foreign fishing permits. This led to the first direct formal negotiations in 16 years with Cuba.

On September 7, 1977, the U.S. and Panama signed two treaties giving full control of the Panama Canal to Panama at the end of 1999 and guaranteeing the neutrality of the waterway thereafter. U.S. control of the Panama Canal Zone ended formally on October 1, 1979.

The normalization of diplomatic relations with the People's Republic of China, begun by President Nixon in 1972, was achieved on January 1, 1979. The U.S. simultaneously broke official ties with the Republic of China (Taiwan), although unofficial contact was maintained; the mutual defense treaty of 1954 between the U.S. and Taiwan was terminated on January 1, 1980.

Carter's Middle East policy

A change in U.S. Middle East policy was indicated by a joint U.S.–Soviet communiqué on October 1, 1977, calling for a guarantee of "the legitimate rights of the Palestinian people," the "withdrawal of Israeli armed forces from territories occupied in the October 1967 conflict," and the presence of Palestinians at the Geneva Conference. This was balanced, however, by U.S. support for negotiations between Egypt and Israel begun by Pres. Anwar as-Sadat and Prime Minister Menachem Begin in November 1977. On December 6–17, 1978, the U.S. sponsored a meeting at Camp David, Maryland, with Carter, Begin, and Sadat. This led to the signing on March 26, 1979, of a peace treaty between Egypt and Israel that served as the basis for ongoing negotiations between the two nations.

The major crisis of the Carter administration began in 1978 in Iran. Riots against the pro-U.S. Iranian government increased throughout the year and, on January 16, 1979, the Shah left Iran. On April 1, 1979, an Islāmic republic was declared in Iran under the leadership of the Ayatollah Ruhollah Khomeini. On November 4, militants invaded the U.S. embassy compound in Tehrān, taking the occupants hostage and demanding the return of the Shah, then in the U.S. for medical treatment. The U.S. government refused to comply and instituted economic and diplomatic sanctions. An attempt to rescue the hostages in April 1980 failed. Despite the death of the Shah in July 1980, diplomatic efforts by the UN and the U.S. and other countries, and the outbreak of war between Iran and Iraq in September, the hostages were not released until January 1981.

The Strategic Arms Limitation Talks (SALT) produced a treaty (SALT II) that was signed by Leonid Brezhnev and Carter on June 15, 1979. Ratification of the treaty by the U.S. Senate was delayed, however. Relations between the U.S. and the Soviet Union were jarred in late 1979 with the Soviet invasion of Afghanistan. Soviet troops entered that country on December 27 to support a coup and the new government of Babrak Karmal. In protest Carter announced a boycott of the Moscow Summer Olympic Games held in August 1980. The Soviet government, however, maintained its troops on Afghan soil.

Domestic affairs. The day after his inauguration on January 20, 1977, Carter granted a pardon to those who evaded the military draft between August 1964 and March 1973 (the period of the war in Indochina). He also ordered a review of the cases of deserters and of those who received qualified discharges during the same period. This was followed by other proposals for reform of the government bureaucracy and of the electoral, federal welfare, and Social Security systems.

Energy program

Carter also stressed his energy program, which met with great resistance in Congress. Aimed at reducing the U.S. dependence on imported oil, the program included gasoline and domestic oil taxes and tax incentives for the purchase of more fuel-efficient automobiles and for the discovery of new energy technologies and sources. Congress, however, blocked or greatly modified the entire program.

U.S. economic growth throughout the late 1970s was obstructed by the large deficit in foreign trade caused by petroleum imports. Inflation climbed to an annual rate of more than 13 percent in 1979, and unemployment hovered around 7 percent of the work force. The adverse effects of a second successive severe winter in 1977–78 were exacerbated by a nationwide coal strike that began in December and led to Carter's implementation of the Taft-Hartley Labor Relations Act in March 1978. An "accident" in the spring of 1979 at the Three Mile Island nuclear plant near Harrisburg, Pennsylvania, in which uranium in the reactor core was damaged, cast doubt on nuclear power as a solution to the country's energy needs. A gasoline shortage that summer again pointed to the U.S. dependence on imported oil.

The contest for the presidential elections of 1980 began in 1979, with 13 contenders for the nominations of the two major parties. Ronald Reagan, who capitalized on a conservative resurgence in the Republican Party, won the nomination from a field of 10 candidates. Carter faced a tougher challenge from two other candidates, but won the Democratic nomination. Congressman John B. Anderson of Illinois, a moderate Republican, failed to win his party's nomination and ran as an independent candidate. The elections, held on November 4, 1980, were won decisively by Reagan and his vice president, George Bush of Texas; they carried 44 states.

The Ronald Reagan administration. Reagan had campaigned against the relentless increase of big government

and for a cut in income taxes and a defense buildup. He was inaugurated under auspicious circumstances: the American hostages from the U.S. embassy in Iran were released and returned to the United States on that day. Reagan took advantage of his momentum and of Republican control of the Senate and demanded a major tax cut from Congress.

On March 30, 1981, as the measure was being debated, the President was shot in the chest during an assassination attempt outside a Washington hotel by a deranged young drifter that left his press secretary, James S. Brady, critically wounded and two security officers badly hurt. The President, who underwent two hours of emergency surgery, made a thorough recovery, in part because of his excellent physical condition. He returned to the White House on April 11 and resumed his pressures for the tax legislation. After some compromises it was delivered to him on July 29 in the form of a three-stage cut over three years, amounting to a 25 percent reduction in personal income taxes.

In the meantime the U.S. economy, which had grown buoyantly in the first quarter of 1981, had begun to slide into the recession that the rest of the developed world was already experiencing, and as it deepened it came to be recognized as the worst U.S. economic downturn since the Great Depression. Reagan's attacks on big government and big spending found widespread popular support that quickly communicated itself to Congress, and the President's New Federalism program began to take effect, actually reducing Washington's influence and control over the states, virtually for the first time. The enthusiasm with which state administrations greeted this new freedom began to pale as it became apparent that in place of abandoned federal grants there was to be no substitute source of funds. As a result, states and localities were obliged to increase taxes on their own, and indeed in 1982 alone 22 states put through tax increases aggregating more than $3,000,000,000, and in the following year some of those were among 39 that levied the highest total state tax increase in history, $7,000,000,000.

Reagan's cabinet appointments generated controversy that fed a barrage of criticism. His labour secretary was charged with various improprieties and finally exonerated. His education and energy secretaries had been appointed in the hope that they would dismantle their departments, although both continued to operate. His national security advisor was forced out over a mini-scandal over an unreported gift of little consequence. His interior secretary had been an anti-environmentalist lobbyist and set about reducing or rejecting federal controls on wilderness areas, selling mining rights briskly and cheaply, and otherwise enraging conservationists until the furor forced his resignation in 1983. His designee to head the Environmental Protection Agency loosened controls and resisted cleanups of toxic-waste sites until public clamour forced her resignation in favour of the first administrator of the agency, who had a sound reputation for supporting its mission. By 1984, Democrats were complaining of Reagan's "Teflon presidency," an invisible shield to which no stain from his aides' unsavory actions would adhere.

By 1984, also, the recession was clearly waning, and without a resurgence of inflation, which had begun its retreat from the double digits of the Carter years as early as 1981. Unemployment, having peaked in 1981, began its decline, and the U.S. economy moved into one of the strongest postwar recoveries—with interest rates, however, stubbornly refusing to drop into single digits.

In foreign affairs the Reagan luck was much less visible, once the hostages were home from Iran. His delivery of AWACS aircraft to Saudi Arabia angered Israel and its manifold U.S. supporters. His stubborn support for rightist regimes in Central America and for covert support for anti-Sandinista "Contras" in Nicaragua angered liberals. His determination to strengthen U.S. arms and his truculent attitude and rhetoric about the Soviet Union coincided with a period of introversion in Soviet leadership to depress relations between the two countries to the lowest level since the Cold War. He did prevail on Congress, however, to sustain his demand for building the cruise missile and for at least a token start on the MX missile program, the latter widely seen as a bargaining chip for arms limitation or reduction talks; and NATO did start installing U.S. cruise and Pershing missiles in Europe despite a Soviet propaganda campaign and opposition from European parties of the left. Reagan's decision to send a battalion of Marines to bolster a cease-fire in Lebanon set the stage for a 1983 attack on their unprotected garrison, killing more than 200 of them. A few months later the force was withdrawn, but the "Teflon presidency" continued to shield Reagan from effective criticism.

As 1984 dawned, a crowded field of Democrats vied for the chance to oppose Reagan, but former vice president Walter F. Mondale's organizational strength and establishment support prevailed, and he chose a three-term New York congresswoman, Geraldine Ferraro, as his vice presidential candidate, the first woman ever selected for that post by a major U.S. party. Reagan's running mate was Vice President George Bush. The sustained growth of the economy, moderating its pace enough to lower interest rates slightly, supported Reagan's campaign themes of well-being and patriotism. Record registration of blacks, stimulated by Chicago minister and activist Jesse Jackson were matched or exceeded by white registrations by the new religious right, and in the election Mondale carried only his home state of Minnesota and the District of Columbia. Reagan, already at age 73 the oldest president in U.S. history, won his second term with nearly 60 percent of the popular vote and a record electoral tally of 525–13. For current political history, see the annual issues of the *Britannica Book of the Year*. (Ed.)

NEW ENGLAND

New England, the six most northeasterly states of the United States—Maine, New Hampshire, Vermont, Massachusetts, Rhode Island, and Connecticut—received its name from Capt. John Smith, who explored its shores in 1614 for some London merchants.

Along its entire length the coastline of New England is indented with harbours, large and small. Of New England seaports Boston soon became the most important. Eastward from the coast stretches a broad continental shelf that rises in places near enough to the surface to make grounds favourable for fishing. About 80 species of edible fish live in these waters, made cold by the Labrador Current. The most important of these are haddock, redfish, flounder, cod, whiting, pollack, and hake. Inland from the coast stretches an uneven hill country that rises into rugged, forest-covered mountains. These, beginning in Maine at the Canadian border, extend into the White Mountains of New Hampshire (seen and reported by Smith in 1614) and into the Green Mountains, the giant ridge that runs north and south the length of Vermont. The Berkshire Hills in western Massachusetts and the Litchfield Hills in northwestern Connecticut form the southernmost extension in New England of this geologically ancient system. The last of the ice caps of the Glacial Age covered all of New England save for a very narrow band on Cape Cod. The receding ice left soil filled with stones and dotted in many places by great boulders. Glacial action, in overdeepening old valleys and in depositing moraines or drifts, created over the entire area a profusion of large and small lakes. The largest of these, Lake Champlain, lying in the broad lowland between the Adirondack Mountains and the Green Mountains, separates the states of Vermont and New York. Of the innumerable streams that flow from the mountains across the rolling lowlands, the Connecticut River is the largest and most important. This stream, while navigable in its lower reaches, provides access north of Massachusetts only to a region of little economic importance. In the 17th century the first settlers of New England found iron in bogs, and their successors in the 18th and 19th centuries mined small veins of copper and iron in the ancient rocks of the uplands. But granite, marble, and clay comprise the only important mineral resources of the 20th century.

Settlement. The first attempt to settle New England, that of France in 1604 at the mouth of the St. Croix River, the boundary between Maine and New Brunswick, proved abortive. The leaders took the colony to Acadia (Nova Scotia) in the spring of 1605. In 1613 an armed force of Englishmen captured a second French colony at Mt. Desert on the coast of Maine.

In 1620 a company of Separatists, who had found Holland an undesirable refuge from persecution, migrated, with the aid of some London merchants, across the Atlantic to found an English beachhead at Plymouth in New England. Ten years later the Massachusetts Bay Company, chartered to trade and to colonize in a designated portion of New England, established what its Puritan sponsors and members looked upon as a new Zion in the American wilderness. Bringing the charter to Massachusetts, John Winthrop turned the management of a trading company into the government of a colony. Persecution by the English government of the growing Puritan party caused some 20,000 persons to cross to Massachusetts between 1630 and 1640. In the New World the Puritans laid out villages whose centre of life was the parish church. Following the precedent set by the Pilgrims, the government of the church became congregational. A systematic allotment of land reinforced the close social structure of the Puritan villages.

Other Puritans from England founded New Haven Colony in 1638. Some of the Massachusetts Puritans, dissatisfied with the government of that colony, moved westward to found three towns on the Connecticut River—Hartford, Wethersfield, and Windsor. In 1662 New Haven, the Connecticut River towns, and another settlement at Saybrook united to make the colony of Connecticut. Roger Williams, pastor of the church at Salem, opposed the religious intolerance of the Massachusetts magistrates and even questioned the right of the English crown to grant territory in America that had not first been purchased from its Indian owners. Williams, circumventing a decree of banishment, led followers in the spring of 1636 to Narragansett Bay, where he founded Providence.

North of the Merrimack River, Capt. John Mason received a grant from the crown and sent settlers to the mouth of the Piscataqua River (Portsmouth). His plans for an aristocratic domain modelled on the medieval county palatine, as well as his appointment as governor general of all New England, came to naught with his death in 1635. His settlers came under the rule of the Massachusetts Bay Company until organized as a royal province (New Hampshire) in 1679. Farther northeast another royal proprietor, Sir Ferdinando Gorges, planned to colonize. Ultimately his enterprise failed in competition with Massachusetts settlers. His heirs sold their claims to Massachusetts in 1677 and the region, under the name of the district of Maine, remained a part of Massachusetts until erected into an independent state in 1820. In the latter half of the 18th century, settlers moved into the region north of Massachusetts and west of the Connecticut River and occupied land under grants from New Hampshire. But the province of New York claimed the region. In 1764 an Order in Council adjudged the country between Lake Champlain and the Connecticut River to be part of New York but without prejudice to the grants from New Hampshire. The status of the region remained in dispute and unsettled until 1790, when New York state relinquished its claim. Congress admitted Vermont to the union in 1791.

Colonial New England. New England was founded by religious refugees who were strongly influenced by the teachings of John Calvin. In America circumstances compelled them to set up a separate (Congregational) church. They were uncompromising Sabbatarians. They opposed the theatre as immoral. They replaced the ritual of the Church of England with a plain service in a plain meetinghouse. The centre of the service was the sermon and extemporaneous prayer. Puritan prudential ethics sancti-

(margin note left:) New England's hills and mountains

(margin note right:) Puritan character

fied work, insisting that faithful attention to the secular calling was, in itself, worship of God. Discouraging idleness and luxury and glorifying saving, Puritan ethics served admirably the needs of frontier communities where the work to be done was prodigious and the hands to perform it few.

Many of the leaders of the Puritans were university men, particularly from Cambridge. As a consequence, New England Puritans held learning in high esteem and insisted on an educated clergy. Massachusetts required each town to provide education for its children. To train men for service in church and state, Harvard College was founded in 1636 and Yale College in 1701. Sometimes local pastors prepared boys for admission to these institutions by teaching them Latin and Greek. Grammar schools (Boston Public Latin School and Hopkins Grammar Schools in New Haven and Hartford) arose to perform more effectively the same function.

From their beginnings, the New England colonies (like the other mainland colonies) enjoyed representative government. The towns managed their affairs through the direct democracy of the town meeting. The Fundamental Orders of Connecticut, a kind of 17th-century constitution of the three river towns—Hartford, Windsor, and Wethersfield—proclaimed the principle that government must rest on the consent of the governed and that liberty implied liberty under law. Roger Williams' Rhode Island from its beginning in 1636 guaranteed religious freedom. The charters granted to Connecticut and Rhode Island by Charles II after the Restoration were surprising documents for the 17th century in that they provided not only for representative government but for the election of the provincial governor within the colony. Save for the reserved power of the crown to disallow acts passed by their assemblies, these corporate colonies were virtually tiny independent republics. In this characteristic they differed in the 18th century from Massachusetts, which had lost its charter in 1684 and had become a royal colony.

The end of colonial status. In the 18th century, as the frontiers of New England pushed westward and northward, the greater part of the population lived by agriculture. Husbandmen cleared fields high on the slopes of hills and mountains to take advantage of the fertility of the rich mold under the primeval forest. It was the day of the self-sufficient farm. The land on which the family lived provided materials for practically all its needs—timber for house and barn (often one continuous building in northern New England), fuel, food, wool and flax for cloth, leather for harness and shoes. Primitive roads and the almost complete absence of bridges made transportation and communication difficult. Self-sufficiency was an adjustment to isolation. But colonial New England enjoyed three advantages that led to special economic developments. Shipbuilding flourished in many harbours at the mouths of rivers. On these streams logs from the forest in the interior could be floated to the yards. The making of ships began with the founding of the Massachusetts Bay Colony when Winthrop's "Blessing of the Bay" was launched in 1631. New England ships found a ready sale because the English Navigation Acts admitted colonial-built vessels to the status of English ships in the monopoly of the carrying trade of the expanding empire. Many boats were constructed for the fisheries, which from the beginning of settlement remained an important part of New England's economy, providing food for the colonials and an important item of external trade. Good harbours and available ships stimulated the growth of the sea trade. Merchants in Boston and other coast towns ventured in commerce with England and with the British and French colonies in the West Indies.

New Englanders, like other colonials, resented the increasing enforcement after 1763, when New France fell, of the principles of mercantilism on which British imperial policy was based. They looked upon a succession of parliamentary acts as denials of their traditional rights as Englishmen.

The American Revolution broke out in 1775 when New England minutemen engaged, at Lexington and Concord, in armed conflict with a detachment of British regulars

sent from Boston to destroy military stores being gathered by the colonial militia.

New England played its chief part in the American Revolution during the years 1765–75 in defining issues and precipitating hostilities. In the Continental Congress the New England colonies early supported the independence movement in 1776. After the evacuation of Boston by the British Army on March 17, 1776, New England saw only minor military actions, but Connecticut became a major source of supply for George Washington's army. After 1775 the irreconcilable temper of New England people convinced the British military leaders in America that attempts at conciliation or subjugation had a better chance of success elsewhere. Tories, while important as economic and social leaders, did not constitute a large percentage of the New England population. Many of them fled to Nova Scotia, New Brunswick, and England when the British Army left Boston. The revolt against the mother country brought less civil war between rebels and Tories in New England than occurred farther south. Control of the governments of the newly independent states fell into the hands of conservatives who assumed the political offices and the economic and social leadership vacated by the fugitive Loyalists.

New England in the new nation. The period of disorganization that followed the cessation of hostilities brought suffering to many communities. The disruption of the old courses of commerce within the British Empire, no longer supplemented by privateering and wartime trade with other countries, caused a lack of currency. The departure of British armies, which had purchased supplies in the colonies, contributed to the same deficiency. Farmers who had gone into debt in the development of their holdings found themselves facing difficulties when interest payments and taxes were due. Distress led to a demand, most successful in Rhode Island, to print paper money whose depreciation would assist the debtor and work to the disadvantage of the creditor. In the western counties of Massachusetts and New Hampshire, opposition to the tax collector and to court action against debtors was terminated by a show of force and belated remedial measures.

Although New England leaders played prominent parts in the Constitutional Convention, actual ratification proved a difficult matter in Massachusetts and New Hampshire. Rhode Island rejected the instrument until after the new federal government was organized. The creditor and mercantile sections of the population supported the stronger national government provided in the Constitution in the hope that the national credit would be established and a national currency created that would have stability. Supporters of the Constitution hoped that a national tariff might be used to persuade reluctant European governments to open their home and colonial ports to American trade. For nearly a decade after the inauguration of the new government under President Washington, the superior organization of the dominant commercial interests committed New England as a whole to the Federalist Party. But Thomas Jefferson, representing the common man and the agrarian interests, had sufficient success in organizing anti-Federalist elements to carry several representative districts in the presidential election of 1800.

The basis of New England's prosperity in the Federalist period seems to have lain in the application of Yankee energy and resourcefulness to the exploitation of the peculiar advantages of New England in foreign trade. Its ships, restricted in their enterprises in the older fields under the control of the British crown, turned to the Mediterranean and to the Pacific and Indian oceans. In 1786 Samuel Shaw established in Canton the first American mercantile house in China. In 1787 the "Grand Turk" brought to Salem the first of the many Oriental cargoes that made that port famous. In 1787–90 Capt. Robert Gray's "Columbia" carried the flag of the new republic around the world for the first time and laid the foundations for the U.S. claim not only to Oregon but also to the very profitable trade with the northwest coast. There, furs that could be exchanged in China for silks and tea were obtained. Salem became for a time the tea market of North America and Europe and the third city in the union.

Navigation and development

New England and the Federalist Party

The Napoleonic Wars shattered this prosperity. President Jefferson's embargo, continued in milder form under Pres. James Madison, struck a heavy blow at New England commercial interests. The War of 1812, strongly opposed in New England, brought opportunities for privateering and the profits of blockade-running. But commercial interests suffered. The disaster of the war—along with concern that westward expansion of the nation, made possible by the purchase of Louisiana, would seriously reduce the relative political power of New England—led to a secession movement. This came to climax in the Hartford Convention, which formulated demands for drastic changes in the U.S. Constitution. News of the signing of a peace treaty (December 1814), coming immediately after the convention adjourned, made the New England effort abortive.

The sea trade revived after the war. In the 1840s New England shipyards created the clipper ships, in their day the fastest sailing vessels afloat. By reducing materially the sailing time to the Orient, they brought large profits to their owners. In the 1830s and 1840s a large New England whaling fleet, mostly out of New Bedford and Nantucket, pursued their profitable prey in all the oceans.

Manufacturing using the machines of the Industrial Revolution began in New England near the end of the 18th century. The disaster of the embargo and the interruption of trade caused by the War of 1812 caused a shift of New England capital from commerce to manufacturing. Dams across the numerous rivers provided power. Textiles, shoes, clocks, hardware, and articles of wood entered the market in increasing amounts. Itinerant Yankee peddlers distributed "Yankee notions" in the middle states and the South and as far west as the Mississippi. The rapid expansion of the agricultural regions of the south and west from 1815 to 1850 brought into the eastern market cheaper cotton as well as cheaper foodstuffs. The former stimulated more textile activity; the latter drove the less well-situated farmers to abandon their farms and migrate to the west. In fact, New England contributed greatly to westward expansion as migrants from New England moved early to the old northwest and later to Iowa, Kansas, and Oregon. Through these pioneers on new frontiers New England continued to exert the peculiar influence of its Puritan traditions.

The growth of manufacturing bound New England to the nation because of the need for cotton and for an expanding market. Sectionalism gave way to a strong nationalism. Beginning with the tariff of 1816, New England supported protection, but after 1833 the strong opposition of the agrarian South prevented the maintenance of a strong protective policy.

New England was a pioneer in railroad experimentation. One of the first railroads in the United States was built in 1826 to carry granite blocks from the Quincy quarries to tidewater. In the 1840s short lines were built connecting Boston with Providence, Lowell, Portsmouth, Springfield, New Haven, and New York. The railroad brought to an end the period of self-sufficiency in New England farming. Husbandmen raised crops to sell in the growing industrial towns. But location excluded New England from the competition in canal, highway, and railroad building for access to the west that engrossed the attention of the states to the south. Although in 1850 Massachusetts ranked third to New York and Pennsylvania in railroad mileage, its railroads failed to secure connections with the great productive areas of the Mississippi Valley, so that Boston, as a port of export, fell behind its rivals. Yet New England had its own expansion. Its northern and eastern regions—Vermont, New Hampshire, and Maine—were losing their frontier character. The northern boundary, long subject to dispute even to the extent of an armed clash in 1839 known as the Aroostook War, was finally determined by the Webster-Ashburton Treaty in 1842. By that arrangement a large area in northern Maine came under the permanent jurisdiction of that state. The victory for New England claims stimulated the sentiment of nationalism. During the Civil War, New England, where anti-slavery sentiment was very strong, stoutly supported the cause of the Union.

The war brought to an end a phase of New England life.

Early railroads

New England commerce had suffered severely. The whaling fleet was broken up by Confederate raiders, and its monopoly of the illuminating-oil market was destroyed by the introduction of kerosene and gas. By the change from wooden to iron and then steel ships and by the rising costs of operation under the U.S. flag, all the natural advantages in construction and operation of ships that New England formerly possessed were lost.

New England in a changing America. Between 1855 and U.S. entry into World War I the country underwent its Industrial Revolution. By the end of that period the region east of the Mississippi and north of the Ohio and Potomac rivers had become thoroughly industrialized. New England, where industrialization had gotten under way late in the 18th century, kept its place in the forefront of the economic advance. Throughout the period it was a high income area. New England cities burgeoned as did those throughout the entire industrialized area. The need for labour brought a social change that has been called the "conquest of New England by the immigrant." The Irish came first to help build the railroads, to work in the mills, and to transform Yankee Boston into something approaching an Irish city. Italians, Poles, Swedes, Czechs, Slovaks, Ukrainians, Lithuanians, Hungarians, and French Canadians combined to bring about in New England a veritable ethnic revolution. In the great variety of manufacturing enterprises, they acquired the skills that enabled New England to hold fast to an old tradition. One of the most important assets of the region in the 19th century (and continuing into the 20th) was the existence of a numerous and highly skilled labour force.

In the 20th century, and particularly after World War I, New England's economic position was seriously disturbed by the impact of new trends in several fields. The demand for both granite and marble from the Maine coast and the Green Mountains of Vermont declined with the extensive use of cement and steel in construction. Lumber for the building trade, which reached its peak in the 1860s, when 60 schooners came down the Penobscot River from Bangor, was displaced by lumber from Oregon and Washington or by other materials. Most timber by mid-20th century fell into the class of pulp for paper mills and had to compete with Canadian and southern products. In the second half of the 20th century Aroostook County, Maine, the Connecticut Valley, and the area adjacent to Plymouth and Cape Cod remained the only sections where extensive agricultural operations were still profitable. There, potatoes, tobacco, onions, and cranberries are raised for export. Forests moved in to take over land no longer profitable for crops. The result was the paradox that in one of the most highly industrialized regions in the world three-quarters of the land area is occupied by forests. Though important national and state forests exist, most of the wooded country is privately owned.

After World War I some New England textile industries moved to the South where they would be nearer to raw materials and also in a lower wage area. The danger that communities, such as Manchester, New Hampshire, that had primarily depended upon textiles would become ghost towns was averted by the development of new and diversified industries. Nevertheless, as industrialization spread over much of the United States, New England lost its former preeminence. Its rate of growth became slower than that of newer industrial areas. Only in an absolute sense does progress continue. Diversification has gone beyond manufacturing. If the pre-Civil War merchant marine that sailed from New England's ports has disappeared, the region contains in Hartford, Connecticut, the "insurance capital" of the nation. New England's mountains, lakes, rivers, and seashore are not only available for the enjoyment of the people of the region but attract a sufficient number from beyond its borders to make the tourist business a major industry.

In manufacturing, no giant mass-production industries took form. Limited supplies of power and lack of local raw materials suggested to New England enterprisers that they concentrate, like their counterparts in Switzerland, on products of small bulk and of high quality and value. In an age of relative decline on the part of railroads,

Industrial change

New England built arterial highways east and west across Connecticut and Massachusetts that connected with others running north and northeast in New Hampshire and Maine. The new highway network increased the mobility of goods and persons within the area and, by being joined with the highway system of New York State, maintained for New England effective contact with the rest of the nation. If transoceanic airways and seaways bypassed New England, the busy life of the region brought about a considerable airborne and seaborne commerce. Suburbs pushed out from the major coastal cities until the "long street" from Boston to New York and beyond became almost a literal reality. If the growth of suburbia threatened parent cities with decay at the centre, New Haven's thoroughgoing destruction of obsolete downtown commercial structures and its creation of a modern city centre demonstrated community readiness to face realities and determination to keep in the vanguard of 20th-century progress.

In the arts the Boston Symphony Orchestra achieved a preeminent position. Its Berkshire Summer Festival became a national cultural event. In the same period Yale established the first school of music of graduate level in the United States. In architecture New England, while cherishing the tradition of 18th-century Georgian expressed in carefully guarded old houses and churches, welcomed the new philosophies and new forms of modern architecture. The theatre and chapel at the Massachusetts Institute of Technology and the hockey rink at Yale expressed freedom and creativity. A concentration of institutions of higher learning within its small area made New England in the 20th century a great intellectual centre. Thornton Wilder's *Our Town* summed up the region: the play's theme is universal, but "Our Town" remains a New England village.

(R.H.Ga./Ed.)

Connecticut

One of the six New England states, Connecticut is located in the northeastern corner of the United States. In area it is the third smallest state in the nation, with 5,009 square miles (12,973 square kilometres), and ranks among the most densely populated. It lies athwart the great urban-industrial complex along the Atlantic Coast, with Massachusetts on the north, Rhode Island on the east, Long Island Sound (an arm of the Atlantic Ocean) on the south, and New York on the west.

Connecticut, with its many beaches and harbours, its forest-clad hills, and its village greens that are often surrounded by houses that date from the 17th and 18th centuries, represents a special blend of modern urban life, rustic landscape, and historic sites. It is a highly industrial and service-oriented state, and its per capita income and value added by manufacture are among the highest in the nation. The strength of its economy lies in a skilled working force, much of it fabricating products that have been manufactured in Connecticut since the products were invented.

The population is heavily urban. The state has no single large city, however, and the intense crowding characteristic of many urban areas is not found in Connecticut. On a national scale, it continues its long tradition of being a prosperous state, with in-migration attracted by the good employment opportunities, excellent educational facilities, and pleasant living conditions for the majority of its people.

PHYSICAL AND HUMAN GEOGRAPHY

The land. *Relief.* Essentially a rectangle in shape, 100 miles (160 kilometres) west to east and 50 miles north to south, Connecticut covers the southern portion of the New England Upland. It contains three major regions: the Western Upland, the Central Lowland (Connecticut Valley), and the Eastern Upland. The northern part of the Western Upland, often called the Berkshire Hills, contains the highest elevations in the state, about 2,300 feet (700 metres) in the northwest corner. It is drained by one major river, the Housatonic, and numerous tributaries.

The Central Lowland is different in character, being a downfaulted block of land, approximately 20 miles wide

at the Massachusetts border and narrowing as one progresses toward the sea, which it meets at New Haven. It is filled with sandstone and shale. Periodic volcanic activity pushed immense quantities of molten rock to the surface and produced the igneous deposits of the central valley. These layers of sandstones and traprock have been faulted, broken, and tipped so that there are numerous small ridges, some reaching as high as 1,000 feet above their valleys. Within the lowland, the Connecticut and other rivers have eroded the soft sandstones into broad valleys.

The Eastern Upland resembles the Western in being a hilly region drained by numerous rivers. Their valleys come together to form the Thames River, which reaches Long Island Sound at New London. Elevations in this area rarely reach above 1,300 feet. In both uplands the hilltops tend to be level and have been cleared for agriculture.

Climate. In Connecticut's moderate climate, winters usually average slightly below the freezing level (32° F, or 0° C) and the state receives from three to five feet (one to 1.5 metres) of snow each year. Snow may remain on the ground until March, but more commonly mild spells and rains that occur during the winter melt it so that the ground is bare. Summers average between 70° and 75° F (21° to 24° C), with occasional heat waves driving the daytime temperatures above 90° F (32° C). Precipitation, averaging from three to four inches (75 to 100 millimetres) per month, is quite evenly distributed. The coastal portions have somewhat warmer winters and cooler summers than does the interior, while the northwestern uplands are high enough to have cooler and longer winters with heavier falls of snow. Perhaps the most marked characteristic of Connecticut's weather is its changeability. Cold waves and heat waves, storms and fine weather can alternate with each other weekly or even daily. The statement of Hartford resident Mark Twain "If you don't like Connecticut weather, wait a minute" has become a widely appropriated and adapted proposition.

Plant and animal life. Originally, Connecticut was a forested region. The few Indian clearings, the swampy flood plains, and the tidal marshes accounted for about five percent of the total area. It is part of the mixed deciduous and coniferous forest of the eastern United States. The southern two-thirds is largely an oak forest. The northern border belongs to the northern hardwood region of birch, beech, maple, and hemlock. A few higher elevations and some sandy sections support a coniferous forest. Virtually all of the primeval forest has been cut, and the current woodland that covers two-thirds of the state is a mixed forest.

The animal life when the first settlers arrived included deer, bear, wolves, foxes, and numerous smaller species, such as raccoon, muskrat, porcupines, weasels, and beaver. Deer are still found in the less densely settled regions, but in general the larger animals have been severely decimated. Most birds are migratory, but chickadees, blue jays, and the immigrant English sparrows are year-round residents.

Settlement patterns. Most regions in Connecticut are not clearly defined, although Fairfield County in the southwest section is uniquely oriented toward New York City, serving as a major "bedroom suburb" for many commuters. With two of the state's largest cities, Stamford and Bridgeport, the region is the fastest growing area of the state. The northwestern and northeastern quarters are less densely populated areas. They have some agriculture, but most residents there, as elsewhere in the state, work in the manufacturing cities and towns along the rivers.

Connecticut's small towns represent a territorial concept that is equivalent to a township in other parts of the country. Within each town, a town centre is surrounded by the town hall, schools, churches, usually a village green, a number of houses, and often a tiny business district with several stores. Elsewhere within the town, other hamlets may contain similar communal gatherings. If the hamlet is on a stream, the houses often cluster around a red brick factory that was erected in the 19th century to run its machinery from a waterwheel in the river. Such mill villages are to be found throughout the state, although many of the factories have been abandoned. Farmsteads and cultivated fields once lay between such small population nodes, but the roads connecting these villages have become sparsely lined with rural, nonfarm homes.

City status in Connecticut is determined not by population but by vote of the residents to change their governmental system from a town meeting to a city form. All of the larger towns and cities are manufacturing centres, some of which originated as mill towns and grew with their factories. The power source changed from water to steam and later to electricity, and often the products manufactured have changed to fill the needs of a new economic and social structure, but each city and town prides itself on the uniqueness that often is associated with its products.

The people. The Algonkin Indians, the original occupants of Connecticut, comprised about 16 separate tribes with some 5,000 to 7,000 members. The first European settlers were English, coming directly from England or by way of the Massachusetts Bay Colony. During the 17th and 18th centuries population growth occurred primarily through an excess of births over deaths; immigrants, mainly from the British Isles, arrived at a rather slow rate. At the time of the first U.S. census, in 1790, Connecticut had a homogeneous population, about 90 percent of which was of English ancestry. Blacks were a minor element in the population, accounting for about 2 percent in 1790.

Patterns of immigration

The immigration of the Irish, beginning in the 1840s, and of French Canadians after the Civil War, continued throughout the 19th century. Later in the 19th century the primary sources of foreign immigration shifted to southern and eastern Europe—Italy, Poland, the Austro-Hungarian Empire, and Russia. Each immigrant group tended to congregate in certain parts of the state. Thus New Haven and its suburbs are populated largely by descendants of Italian immigrants; Poles are concentrated in the Naugatuck Valley, and the French Canadians live in the northeast. The immigration of blacks into Connecticut after World War II showed the same tendency. In the late 20th century, most of them lived in the five largest cities. New Haven and Hartford were more than 30 percent black. Puerto Ricans have moved to Connecticut from New York City, especially into Stamford and Bridgeport.

Demography. From 1790 to 1840 the state's growth rate hovered between 4 and 8 percent per decade. Connecticut was—considering its small size and its limited agricultural resources—quite adequately filled. During the 19th century thousands of Connecticut residents, especially the young, migrated to better agricultural lands in the western part of the country; their places were taken by newcomers from Europe. The state's population growth passed the national rate in 1900 and did not fall below it until the late 20th century.

For more than 300 years the distribution of Connecticut's people has reflected the region's changing economy and resources of the land. Settlement began in the middle Connecticut Valley, where the soils were good, and on the coast, where maritime activities, trading, and fishing supplemented the living that the settlers were able to derive from the land. The upland areas were not fully occupied until the late 18th century, yet by 1790 the population was fairly evenly distributed across the state. Towns with better agricultural lands or with other resources—marine or mineral—had denser populations. During the 19th century the rise of waterpowered manufacturing attracted young people from the agricultural upland towns to the growing mill towns, and virtually all of the upland towns lost population. Towns with better assets for manufacturing grew rapidly.

The movement of people and industry into the cities dominated the population movements until 1920. Since then Bridgeport, Hartford, and New Haven, the three largest cities, have had a general movement of population to the suburbs and to the former agricultural hill towns.

The economy. *Industry and agriculture.* The foundation of Connecticut's economy is manufacturing, which employs about one-third of the state's work force. In addition to such military products as helicopters, submarines, aircraft engines, guns, and ammunition, it makes thousands of items that are sold on a worldwide basis. Among the

An economic overview

items that have been manufactured in Connecticut by long tradition are pins, clocks, silverware, sewing machines, Winchester rifles, and many brass products. Historically, mining was important; but the last iron mines closed early in the 20th century, and the state's high ranking in value added by manufacture is due mainly to the import of nearly all raw materials. Only sand, gravel, and stone are still produced within the state.

Since 1870, agriculture has declined in importance, and it is a relatively minor element in the economy. The precipitous decline in the number of farms resulted in the enactment of a farmland preservation program. Connecticut's farms produce substantial quantities of milk, eggs, poultry, and vegetables for local consumption and one important export crop, shade-grown tobacco, used mainly for cigar wrappers.

Except for the oyster industry and the historically important whaling industry, commercial fishing has never been very important in the state. The oyster industry has been attempting a comeback from the devastation that was caused by natural elements and pollution of the coastal waters.

Connecticut often is referred to as the nation's insurance centre and Hartford as The Insurance City. Marine insurance was the first concern of Connecticut companies, and eventually the coverages that they offered expanded to many forms of casualty insurance. Some of the largest insurance companies of the United States are based in Connecticut.

Management of the economy. To correct abuses in the free enterprise system, Connecticut has had to enact numerous regulations. The first child labour law was passed in 1842, but it was ineffectual; for 30 years after its passage hundreds of children continued to work long hours in the textile mills. A labour department was set up by the state government in 1873, and since then hundreds of laws and regulations have been enacted to control working conditions. The length of the working day, minimum wage rates, equal pay for equal work, and similar protective regulations have been passed. State departments supervise banks, insurance companies, and the public utilities, and in 1959 the Department of Consumer Protection was organized to consolidate several existing agencies. Labour unions are strong and may be given partial credit for the high wages and good working conditions characteristic of most factories. There is also an active association of manufacturers.

Labour legislation

Transportation. Connecticut's railroad network is a basic link in the Boston–New York City transportation pattern. The first railroads were constructed to bring the produce of the agricultural interior to Connecticut ports. Each of the larger river valleys—the Housatonic, Naugatuck, Connecticut, Willimantic, and Quinebaug—supported its own railroad. The line along the shore was completed in 1852. Until 1930 the railroads flourished with the expanding Connecticut economy, but highway competition for passengers and products reduced railroad traffic severely. Most of the river lines have dropped passenger service; freight service continues on some, but on others it has been abandoned. Service on the New York–New Haven Line has deteriorated despite its heavy use as a commuter facility between southern Connecticut and New York City. Limited-access highways crisscross the state, but they are concentrated in the densely settled coastal and Connecticut Valley regions. Connecticut pioneered this new type of road. The first section of the Merritt Parkway, from New York to near Milford, opened in 1938 and often is acclaimed as one of the most scenic and best designed of these highways.

Bradley International Airport, north of Hartford, is the major airport, but there are many other airports throughout the state that offer regional services. The port of New Haven is one of the largest in New England, and the U.S. Coast Guard Academy is located in New London.

Administrative and social conditions. *Government.* Connecticut's state government is headed by a strong governor who is elected for a four-year term. The governor initiates legislation, prepares the state budget, appoints department heads, and can veto individual items of an appropriation bill.

Connecticut's General Assembly met biennially until the adoption of a constitutional amendment in 1970 provided for annual legislative sessions. The 187 members are elected for two-year terms. The 36 senatorial districts are approximately equal in population. The House of Representatives was originally based on towns, with each town, regardless of size, having at least one representative. The 1965 constitution reapportioned the lower branch so that it also is based upon population.

The judicial system

The state's judiciary is headed by the Supreme Court. Superior courts were formed in 1978 by a merger of the courts of common pleas and the juvenile courts. The justices of the Supreme Court and of the superior courts are nominated by the governor and appointed by the General Assembly for eight-year terms. Probate judges are elected on partisan ballots for four-year terms.

Below the state government are 169 local units called towns. Legally, they are creations of the state, with their rights and responsibilities set out in state statutes. There is, nonetheless, a long-standing and intense tradition of local autonomy. These local governments maintain roads and provide elementary and secondary education and police and fire protection. Larger municipalities also provide water and sewage facilities and other services. The original form of government was based on the town meeting, at which the citizens elected selectmen to run the town between the annual meetings. As populations increased and problems of administration became more complex, other systems were substituted. Most larger communities have opted for a city form with an elected mayor and council. Some smaller communities have elected mayors; some have town or city managers. Many towns have retained the town meeting or have substituted the representative town meeting.

Education. From the earliest days, every town has been required to maintain public elementary schools and, as the town grew in size, secondary schools as well. Connecticut is renowned for its private schools and colleges. Yale University, in New Haven, is regarded as one of the world's great universities; and other institutions, such as Wesleyan University in Middletown, have national recognition. Public higher education has expanded considerably. The community college system, founded in 1965, had 12 colleges by 1980. Also under the control of the state are five technical colleges, four state colleges, and the University of Connecticut, with its main campus in Storrs.

Health and welfare. The community and the state have become increasingly involved in health and medical care. Most people live within 10 miles of hospital services, and doctors and other medical personnel are numerous. There are many community health clinics in addition to the advanced medical centres of the University of Connecticut at Farmington and of the Yale–New Haven Hospital. In relation to most states, Connecticut provides generous welfare benefits. Departments for the aged and for children and youth services have been established to meet the special needs of communities.

Despite inner-city blight and abandoned housing, progress has been made by urban redevelopment programs in Connecticut's larger cities. Urban renewal programs in New Haven during the 1950s and 1960s became a prototype for the nation. Much work in rehabilitating urban areas remains to be done, however, especially in residential neighbourhoods.

State agencies

The state government has provided increasing funds to local governments for the many social programs that are operated. Although Connecticut has an income tax, the government relies to a great extent on high sales and business taxes for revenue. In 1977 the state government was reorganized, consolidating authority in 20 executive and two administrative departments in order to make these departments and the many unaffiliated agencies more accountable to public officials.

Cultural life. Connecticut provides a variety of landscapes: rocky headlands, beaches, forested hills, and, perhaps most attractive, the small towns around their tree-dotted village greens. Throughout the towns, hundreds of houses dating from the 17th and 18th centuries are preserved by more than 100 local or national historical societies.

Numerous sites important in Connecticut's past or associated with illustrious individuals are maintained by state or private organizations. These include the Putnam Wolf Den in Pomfret, Mt. Riga Furnace in Salisbury, Ft. Griswold State Park in Groton, Old New-Gate Prison and Copper Mine in East Granby, the Mark Twain Memorial home in Hartford, the Tapping Reeve House and Law School in Litchfield, and the (William) Gillette Castle State Park in East Haddam. Perhaps the best known is Mystic Seaport in Mystic, where a small New England seaport has been recreated with all its ships and shops. The outdoorsman can tramp the many miles of trails and camp in one of the 30 state forests, covering more than 130,000 acres (52,500 hectares), or in one of 88 state parks, comprising some 30,000 acres.

Recreation in another form is provided in the fine arts. Art exhibitions are held annually in many cities, a number of which have art galleries and museums. The best known are the Yale University Art Gallery, the Wadsworth Atheneum in Hartford, and the New Britain Museum of American Art. Symphony concerts and concerts by smaller groups are presented regularly in the larger communities. Several educational institutions have public concerts throughout the year. Repertory companies operating in or near resort areas in the summer include Westport County Playhouse in Westport and the Oakdale Musical Theatre in Wallingford. The American Shakespeare theatre in Stratford, the Long Wharf Theatre in New Haven, and the Goodspeed Opera House in East Haddam are well known. The Yale School of Drama was, at its founding in 1925, the first such school at an institution of higher learning. Southwestern Connecticut is also within easy reach of the vast artistic resources of New York City.

HISTORY

Colonization. In contrast to many of the other New England areas, relations between Indians and the early settlers in Connecticut were good. Trading posts were established along the Connecticut River by the Dutch from New Amsterdam and by the English from the Plymouth Colony, but the first permanent European settlers in the state came from the Massachusetts Bay Colony to the middle Connecticut Valley during 1633–35 and to the Saybrook–New Haven coastal strip during 1635–38. In 1665 the Connecticut River settlements and the New Haven Colony were united, and the general outline of the state emerged, although its borders were not finally demarcated until 1881, more than 200 years later. The New Haven Colony was unsuccessful in an attempt to settle Delaware Bay, and the united Connecticut Colony, despite its charter provisions, lost its claim to a strip of land extending to the Pacific. Following the American Revolution settlers from Connecticut, with claims in the Midwest, were among the first to move into an area that became known as the Western Reserve, now northeastern Ohio.

Land claims

The political development of the colony began with the Fundamental Orders of Connecticut (1639), a civil covenant by the settlers establishing the system by which the river towns of Windsor, Hartford (now the capital), and Wethersfield agreed to govern themselves. The orders created an annual assembly of legislators and provided for the election of a governor. This was superseded by the royal charter of 1662, a liberal document that provided for virtual self-government. (J.B.Ho./I.J.S.)

The Revolutionary period. Connecticut took an enthusiastic part in the American Revolution. More than one-half of George Washington's army at New York in 1776 was composed of Connecticut soldiers. Yet, with the exception of isolated British movements against Stonington in 1775, Danbury in 1777, New Haven in 1779, and New London in 1781, no battles were fought in Connecticut territory.

In 1776 Connecticut was reorganized as a state, the charter of 1662 being adopted by the General Court as "the Civil Constitution of this State, under the sole authority of the people thereof, independent of any king or prince whatever." In the formation of the general government the policy of the state was national. In the Constitutional Convention of 1787 the present system of national representation in Congress was proposed by the Connecticut delegates as a compromise between the plans presented by Virginia and those presented by New Jersey.

The 19th century. For many years following the Revolution, the Federalist Party controlled the affairs of the state. The opposition to the growth of American nationality that characterized the later years of that party found expression in the prominent part taken by Connecticut in the Hartford Convention (a secret session, 1814–15, of delegates from five New England states to consider grievances against the national government and to consider revising the federal Constitution) and in the advocacy of the extensive amendments proposed by it. The development of manufactures, the discontent of nonconforming religious sects with the establishment, and the confusion of the executive, legislative, and judicial branches of government in the constitution, however, opened the way for a political revolution. All the discontented elements united with the Democratic Republican Party in 1817 and defeated the Federalists in the state election; in 1818 a constitution that remained in effect until 1965 was adopted. From 1830 until 1855 there was close rivalry between the Democratic and Whig parties for control of the state administration.

In the Civil War Connecticut was one of the most ardent supporters of the Union cause. After the war the Republicans were more frequently successful at the polls than the Democrats. Representation in the lower house of the General Assembly, by the constitution of 1818, was
Township based on the townships, each township having two rep-
representa- resentatives, except townships created after 1818, which
tion had only one each. This method constituted a serious evil when, in the transition from agriculture to manufacturing as the leading industry, the population became concentrated to a considerable degree in a few large cities and the relative importance of the various townships was greatly changed. A constitutional amendment of 1828 provided that senators should be chosen by districts and that in the apportionment regard should be paid to population. No county or township was to be divided and no part of one county was to be joined to the whole or part of another county, and each county was to have at least two senators. By 1900, however, any relation that the districts might once have had to population had disappeared. This system of representation sometimes put in power a political party representing a minority of the voters. In 1878, 1884, 1886, 1888, and 1890 the Democratic candidates for state executive offices received a plurality vote; but, because a majority was not obtained, these elections were referred to the General Assembly, and the Republican Party, in control of the lower house, secured the election of its candidates. In 1901 constitutional amendments were adopted making a plurality vote sufficient for election, increasing the number of senatorial districts, and stipulating that "in forming them regard shall be had" to population.

The growth and movement of population has greatly complicated and confused the representative system. A constitutional amendment in 1901 provided for decennial reapportionment of the Senate, if necessary, but no reapportionment was made after 1903 until 1965 (see below).

The 20th century. World War I was a period of great industrial expansion and consequent prosperity. After the Armistice, despite a recession, the state continued prosperous until the Depression of the 1930s, which was especially severe in Connecticut. Conditions, however, were improved by federal agencies, as well as by an extensive public works program undertaken by the state. A number of towns thus acquired new schools, libraries, town halls, and other public buildings at about half the cost of the work in normal times. Under the same conditions many miles of dirt roads were hard-surfaced.

With the outbreak of World War II in Europe, Connecticut firms began to receive large war contracts. Employment and production reached a new peak, with continued expansion and diversification after the war.

Many important measures of social legislation were adopted after 1930, notably: systems of unemployment compensation; old-age assistance; a fair employment prac-

tices act; an act prohibiting discrimination because of racial, religious, or national origin; and a minimum-wage bill. In 1937 the state administration was extensively reorganized by a series of legislative acts which increased the powers of the governor, established a department of finance and control, and put the employees of the executive department under the merit system.

Two laws of major importance were passed by the General Assembly in 1959. The first abolished the county governments as of October 1, 1960, the necessary county functions being transferred to the state government. The second law revised the local court systems. The Municipal Court judges and the justices of the peace were replaced on January 1, 1961, by a new Circuit Court system.

As a result of a federal court order to redistrict and reapportion the two houses of the General Assembly according to population, a constitutional convention convened July 1, 1965, and completed the drafting of a new constitution in October. On December 14 the voters approved this document. The new constitution required the House of Representatives to have from 125 to 225 members, the Senate from 30 to 50. The old system had 36 Senate districts very unequal in population. House members (294) represented towns with even greater inequalities. To prevent indefinite continuation of existing districts, the new constitution provided that the assembly at its first regular session after the decennial census redistrict each house as necessary to be "consistent with federal constitutional standards." The new constitution also introduced several other major changes. It strengthened the governor's powers by increasing from a simple majority to two-thirds the vote required to override a veto. The formerly mandatory use of party lever on the voting machines was made optional. A new article gave towns, cities, and boroughs a guarantee of home rule. A new section in the Bill of Rights prohibited segregation or discrimination in exercise of civil or political rights because of religion, race, colour, ancestry, or national origin.
(Ed.)

Maine

Maine, the largest of the six New England states in area, lies at the northeastern tip of the United States. Its 33,215 square miles (86,026 square kilometres), including 2,295 square miles of water area, represent nearly one-half of the total area of New England. Maine is bounded on Location the northwest and northeast by the Canadian provinces and of Quebec and New Brunswick, respectively, and on the general west by New Hampshire. The famed rocky coastline of character the state is angled from southwest to northeast, along the Atlantic Ocean. Maine's capital has been Augusta since its admission, in 1820, as the 23rd state of the Union.

Maine is the most sparsely populated state east of the Mississippi River. More than 80 percent of its area is under forest cover. It is also, by most statistical measures, an economically depressed state; but the rugged beauty and challenge of its climate and landscape and the character of its people have given Maine an importance beyond its economic and political power. Limited economic growth, in fact, has contributed to the preservation of much of its natural appearance. Maine's economy remains largely dependent upon the extractive industries and the recreational opportunities associated with its status as a major vacationland. The state epitomizes the increasingly difficult national choices between preservation of environmental quality or potential economic expansion. Politically, Maine was long regarded as a stronghold of the Republican Party, but it has become a two-party state in recent years.

PHYSICAL AND HUMAN GEOGRAPHY

The land. *Relief.* The Appalachian Mountain chain extends into Maine from New Hampshire, terminating in Mt. Katahdin, at 5,268 feet (1,606 metres), the state's tallest peak. The western and northwestern borders adjoining New Hampshire and Quebec have the most rugged terrain, with numerous glacier-scoured peaks, lakes, and narrow valleys. South and east of the mountain areas lie rolling hills and smaller mountains and the broad river valleys of the Saco, the Androscoggin, the Kennebec, and the Penobscot.

From Kittery, at the southern tip of the state, to Cape Elizabeth, just southwest of Portland, the state's largest city, long sand beaches are interrupted intermittently by rocky promontories. North and east of Cape Elizabeth the coastline of Maine is a series of peninsulas, narrow estuaries, bays, fjords, and coves, once mountains and valleys that glaciers of the Ice Age pushed beneath the ocean. The Camden Hills and Mount Desert Island are the largest of the coastal mountains. The tides along this famous rockbound coast are among the strongest in the world, running between 12 and 24 feet (3.7–7.3 metres). Off the coast of the state lie about 1,200 islands, some no more than rocky ledges, others topped with trees and sheltering the homes of fishermen, lobstermen, and summer residents. All told, the coast of Maine—including the bays, islands, and inlets washed by the tides—totals some 3,500 miles (5,630 kilometres).

Drainage and soils. Most of Maine's river systems flow from north to south. The St. John River and its principal tributary, the Allagash, are the major exceptions, flowing north and then east along the northern border of Maine and turning south through New Brunswick, Canada, to the sea. The state is dotted with 2,500 lakes and ponds, the largest of which is Moosehead Lake (120 square miles [311 square kilometres]). Soils in southwestern Maine were formed primarily from granite; coastal, central, and eastern soils are composed of shale, sand, and limestone; while the soils of Aroostook County, in the northeast, which are among the most productive in the state, are largely composed of caribou loam.

Climate. Maine has three relatively well-defined climatic areas: southern interior, coastal, and northern. The southern and coastal regions are influenced by air masses from the south and west. North of the land dividing the St. John and Penobscot River basins, air masses moving down the St. Lawrence River basin tend to prevail. Mean annual temperatures range from 37° to 39° F (3° to 4° C) in the north and from 43° to 45° F (6° to 7° C) in the southern interior and coastal regions. Mean temperatures are about 62° F (17° C) throughout the state during the summer and 20° F (−7° C) during the winter. About 60 percent of the days are sunny, and annual precipitation averages 40 to 46 inches (1,060 to 1,160 millimetres). Snowfall averages more than 100 inches in the northern area and the higher elevations.

Plant and animal life. Flora and fauna represent a combination of subarctic and Appalachian species. Forests include heavy stands of pine, spruce, and fir among the hardwoods. Among the fauna are the deer, moose, black bear, fox, lynx, hare, raccoon, porcupine, skunk, and woodchuck. Songbirds, lake birds, seabirds, and many game species abound throughout the state. Among the many aquatic species are the seal, whale, porpoise, lobster, shrimp, clam, haddock, cod, mackerel, and Atlantic and landlocked salmon, as well as many freshwater game fishes.

Settlement patterns. Coastal Maine is best known, from anecdotes and dialect stories, as the traditional home of the "Downeast Yankee." Many communities in the region, relatively isolated from the principal avenues of highway traffic, were once bustling centres of ocean commerce and river trade. Population movements in the state have blurred some of the regional differences; but within the coastal region there are three areas, each with its own sense of identity. The southwestern coast, predominantly a resort area, extends from Kittery to the Portland metropolitan region on Casco Bay. The midcoast region, marked by a combination of fishing and maritime activities, vacation and retirement homes, and resort centres, runs from Bath (long a shipbuilding centre) and the mouth of the Kennebec River to Belfast, on the western shore of Penobscot Bay. The eastern coastal region of Maine begins on the eastern shore of Penobscot Bay and ends at Calais, on the St. Croix River, at the New Brunswick border.

Central and southern Maine form a contiguous region covering the southern half of the state, from the New Hampshire border to the Penobscot River. It contains the bulk of the population and most of its industrial and commercial activities. The western border areas of York, Cumberland, Oxford, and Franklin counties form a subregion within the state, but increased mobility is tending to erode the distinctive community and speech patterns of those sections.

Aroostook County, a region by itself, is often referred to as "the" county. Central and southern Aroostook areas were settled by English and Irish immigrants whose speech patterns continue to resemble those of their neighbours across the border in New Brunswick more than they do the broad *a*'s and dropped *r*'s of the rest of Maine speech. The St. John Valley along the northern border of Aroostook County was settled by Acadians of French descent from Nova Scotia and New Brunswick. The communities of the valley retain their French character and speech.

Maine's rocky terrain limited the size of farms in most areas of the state. With the exception of Aroostook County and a few broad valleys in the central region, the fields are small, and, in many cases, they are marked by old stone walls or separated by wooded lots.

Interior rural communities in Maine vary according to the terrain and their economic history. Some consist only of a crossroads settlement with a store, gas station, post office, and three or four homes; others have a church, school, a few stores, and small establishments clustered around a millsite; still others have the traditional village green, often with the typical white frame, single-spired New England church, as well as such social centres as a grange hall. Communities in the state that prospered during the height of the lumber trade are marked, where the terrain permits, by broad avenues and imposing wooden homes. Coastal communities are similar, with commercial areas on the waterfront and social, cultural, and residential centres on higher ground.

Maine's largest urban communities are Portland, Lewiston–Auburn, Bangor, Augusta, Biddeford, and Waterville. Portland is the centre of a metropolitan area (population about 184,000) spreading inland and around the harbour city, which lies on Casco Bay. It is the commercial and transportation hub of the state, whose economy has a growing and diversified industrial base, including paper manufacturing, steel fabrication, light manufacturing, and assembly. Bangor (about 32,000), an old lumbering town at the head of navigation on the Penobscot River, is the commercial centre for eastern and northern Maine. Augusta (about 22,000), the state capital, lies at the head of navigation on the Kennebec River. State government is the principal source of employment for the city, but it is also the site of textile, shoe, and paper industries.

The twin cities of Lewiston and Auburn form the second largest urban centre in the state (about 64,000). Long dependent on textile and shoe manufacturing, the two communities have pursued aggressive industrial development programs and have diversified into electronics and light manufacturing. They also serve as a commercial and trade centre for the Androscoggin Valley and eastern Oxford County. Biddeford (about 20,000), south of Portland at the base of Saco Falls, is a lumbering and textile centre. Waterville (about 18,000), north of Augusta on the Kennebec, with its neighbouring communities of Winslow and Fairfield, is a pulp-and-paper and textile centre and a commercial and trade centre for the central and northern Kennebec Valley.

The people. The original "Downeast Yankees" were English–Scots–Irish Protestant immigrants who made the most substantial and persistent early European settlements in Maine. They set the style of dour and taciturn industry and dry wit that is characteristic of Maine legends and stories. Their descendants dominated the political and economic life of the state during most of its development and they comprise its largest population group, particularly in the smaller communities and rural areas.

Contrary to popular impressions, however, Yankees are not the sole inhabitants of Maine. Two groups of French descent make up the second largest ethnic bloc in the state. The Acadians, originally from Brittany and Normandy, were driven out of Nova Scotia in 1763 by the British; many of them settled in the St. John Valley, which now forms the northern border of Maine, while

Margin notes:
Lakes and ponds

Rural life

Urban communities

others made the long trip to Louisiana. The later French-Canadian migration from Quebec province began with the growth of the lumber and textile industries following the Civil War. French is the primary language in much of the St. John Valley, and it is the second language in Maine's industrial cities. Irish immigration to the state began in the 18th century, and the Irish and the French comprise the bulk of Maine's Roman Catholic population. French Huguenot and German settlements were made early near the coast. During the 1870s the state encouraged the building of a Swedish settlement in Aroostook County as part of a program for agricultural development and population growth.

French language in Maine

Among the relatively small population of the state, a number of ethnic groups of significant size are identifiable. Most of the remaining few thousand members of the original American Indian population of the area live on state reservations. The nonwhite population of Maine is less than 2 percent.

Maine's general population distribution reflects the early patterns of settlement along the coast and the river valleys, with vast sections of the interior covered with forest and virtually uninhabited, except for occasional lumber encampments. About one-half of the population is concentrated in four southwestern counties: Androscoggin, Cumberland, Kennebec, and York. Almost one-half of Maine's residents live in what are classified as urban areas, but there are only a few cities of 25,000 or more inhabitants.

The economy. Maine's forest and waterpower resources invited exploitation during the early years of the Industrial Revolution, and skilled, low-cost labour provided a long-time advantage in the textile and shoe industries. Those advantages faded as textile and shoe companies moved their operations to factories in low-wage areas of the South and overseas.

Aroostook County, where the potato is the main crop, is one of the few areas with rich agricultural soils. Terrain and soil conditions throughout most of the state are inadequate for large-scale farming. With the exception of lobster production, fishing is a marginal industry. As a result of these factors, Maine is a relatively poor state, with the second lowest per capita income in New England.

Since 1955 the state government has promoted an active economic development program through the Department of Economic Development. The state-operated Maine Industrial Building Authority, the Maine Recreation Authority, and the privately sponsored Maine Development Credit Corporation have provided both industrial and commercial loan guarantees. The state also has used the services and financial assistance of the federal Economic Development Administration and of the Small Business Administration.

State and private economic promotion

Economic resources and components. Maine's primary natural resources are timber, sand, gravel, limestone and building stone, fish, and shellfish. There are limited deposits of copper, zinc, feldspar, and semiprecious stones. Peat is mined for horticultural use. Soils and climate have contributed to the production of high-quality potatoes and of apples, blueberries, and other fruits. Dairying is also an important activity.

The services sector represents the largest component in the market value of Maine goods and services; the manufacturing sector is second, and the trade sector is third. Pulp and paper constitute the largest item in manufactured products, potatoes and poultry in farm income, and lobsters in the fishery industry. Tourists—attracted by Maine's picturesque lakes, streams, and coast and the opportunities for swimming, boating, fishing, hunting, hiking, and winter sports—account for a large portion of retail sales and service income.

Electrical power. More than three-fourths of the electrical energy generated within the state is produced in steam plants, a large percentage of which is supplied by nuclear power; hydroelectric stations and diesel and gas-turbine units provide the remainder. Most of the state's hydroelectric sites have been developed. Notable exceptions are the sites of the proposed Dickey-Lincoln School project on the Upper St. John River and the proposed joint U.S.–Canada tidal power project on Passamaquoddy and Cobscook bays at the eastern end of the state. Both projects have been opposed by private utility companies and the St. John project by conservation groups as well. Since 1972 a consortium of New England utility companies has operated the Maine Yankee atomic power plant at Wiscasset.

Hydroelectric production and potential

Transportation. Maine depends heavily on its roads for ground transportation. The 1,690 miles (2,700 kilometres) of railroad track carry freight but no longer carry passengers. Buses provide interstate, intrastate, and some suburban and urban passenger transportation. Portland and Searsport are the major seaports. State and private passenger and freight ferry services operate to many of the coastal islands; and Portland and Bar Harbor have ferry connections with Yarmouth, Nova Scotia. An airline operates from Presque Isle, Bangor, and Portland to points outside Maine; and commuter airlines provide intrastate and interstate service to other Maine communities. Some international nonscheduled air passenger and freight traffic is routed through Bangor International Airport.

Administrative and social conditions. *Government.* The constitution of the state, derived from that of the Commonwealth of Massachusetts, reflects the hangover of colonial suspicions toward royal governors. The governor, Maine's chief executive officer, is checked by a seven-member executive council elected biennially by the state legislature. Several constitutional officers, including the attorney general, the secretary of state, the auditor, and the state treasurer, are elected by the legislature, and, until 1971, state department heads, who must be confirmed by the council, were appointed for fixed terms. Repeated efforts to abolish the council have failed. In 1958 the governor's term was extended to four years, with a two-term limit.

Executive, legislature, and judiciary

The legislature, which is comprised of a 151-member house and a 33-member senate, is elected every two years. The president of the senate is the constitutional successor to the governor. Maine has a three-tiered judicial branch, including district judges, a superior court, and a supreme court. There are separate probate courts that serve at the county level.

Maine's 16 counties traditionally have provided an administrative framework for the superior court system, law enforcement, land records, and probate practice and for some road maintenance and construction functions. Town government, with the annual town meeting and a board of selectmen, prevails in most communities. More than 20 communities operate under city charters. Professional managers are used in most cities and in many towns.

Finances. Local communities depend for revenues on property, automobile excise, and poll taxes (the last a requirement for hunting, driving, and other licenses, not for voting), on state aid for education, roads, and welfare, and on federal grants-in-aid. State revenues are obtained from a corporate and personal income tax, inheritance tax, sales and use taxes, motor fuel taxes, tobacco and alcoholic beverage taxes, licenses and miscellaneous taxes, and federal grants-in-aid.

Political life. With the election of 1954, traditional Republican dominance in Maine's state offices and national representation ended. Thereafter, Democrats competed successfully with Republicans for the governorship and for federal and state legislative seats. Party officials are elected in local caucuses and state conventions. Nominations for county and state offices are obtained through primary elections, but Maine has no presidential-preference primary.

Education. Local governments are responsible for public elementary and secondary education, under the general supervision of a state board of education. Most rural areas are served by multicommunity school administrative districts. The state operates technical institutes for post-secondary-school vocational training. The University of Maine, established in 1865 in Orono as a college of agriculture and mechanic arts, has been reorganized into a seven-branch system and offers a broad range of undergraduate and graduate curricula. Private liberal arts colleges include Bowdoin College (Brunswick; 1794), Bates College (Lewiston; 1864), and Colby College (Waterville; 1813).

Welfare. Maine's chronic economic problems are reflected in the high incidence of poverty. The largest proportion of poverty is found in the rural counties of the state, particularly in the eastern coastal counties and in Aroostook County. Public awareness of Maine's poverty problems and of the particular difficulties faced by the state's small Indian and black populations has led to more vigorous efforts by community action groups, civil rights organizations, and health and housing associations to improve economic opportunity, as well as to deal with the related problems of housing, education, and health. Local communities provide some assistance to the poor, but most poverty assistance is administered by the state Department of Health and Welfare.

Cultural heritage

Cultural life. *Folk arts and artifacts.* In its culture, as in its social and economic development, Maine reveals the attributes of both a struggling frontier community and an eclectic society immersed in commerce with other cultures. Folktales, songs, local humour, and the short stories and poems of native authors are direct, earthy, and filled with a sense of the awkward absurdities of man's attempt to subdue nature.

The tools of the woodsman, farmer, and fisherman are clean and simple, as are the lines of country homes, meetinghouses, and working boats. The great mansions of the old seaports, among some of the finest memorials to an earlier America, are filled with chairs, tables, chests, books, prints, hangings, screens, pottery, and bric-a-brac gathered on the many voyages of Maine's seamen to Europe and Asia, as well as with examples of the shipbuilders' and sailors' arts of wood carving and scrimshaw. Maine has, in addition, the unique contributions of such groups as the Shakers and its own local versions of the Federal, Greek Revival, Gothic, and Victorian periods of American architecture.

Maine has had a revival in crafts production, including pottery, metalworking, block and silkscreen printing, weaving, furniture making, and carving. State agencies, historical societies, museums, and local associations are engaged in preserving historic sites and in the collection, preservation, and presentation of materials on Maine's heritage.

Fine arts. Maine has been, and continues to be, the birthplace or the permanent or seasonal home of well-known figures in the American arts. They have included such writers as Henry Wadsworth Longfellow, Harriet Beecher Stowe, Sarah Orne Jewett, Edward Arlington Robinson, and Edna St. Vincent Millay; the painters Winslow Homer, John Marin, Edward Hopper, and Andrew Wyeth; and composer Walter Piston. Active cultural programs are sponsored by the state's colleges and universities, museums, community symphonies, workshops and camps, and the numerous summer theatres.

Recreation. Maine's special attractions include Acadia National Park on Mount Desert Island, the first national park east of the Mississippi River; Baxter State Park, a wilderness area of 200,000 acres (80,940 hectares) surrounding Mt. Katahdin; the 92-mile (147-kilometre) Allagash Wilderness Waterway; and more than 100 state parks and historic sites.

HISTORY

The Indian natives

Algonkian Indians were the earliest known settlers in Maine. They lived along the river valleys and the coasts, hunting and fishing and planting crops. Few of them survived the arrival of the European settlers. But the earlier tribes are remembered in numerous place-names; in the sites of their camps and burial grounds; in ancient trails and water routes; in the use of the canoe, the snowshoe, and the toboggan; in crops such as corn (maize), beans, and squash; and in the revived concern for the natural environment.

Explorations and disputes. The first European explorations of Maine are shrouded in mystery. Evidence that the Norsemen landed on the coast is scant and disputed, and serious questions exist about some of the early British claims based on John Cabot's voyages in the late 1490s. Portuguese, Spanish, French, and English explorers did probe the islands, the bays, and the rivers of the "maine" throughout the 16th century; and by the first decade of the 17th century, summer fisheries had been established on some of the coastal islands and fur trade had begun with the Indians.

The French and English crowns claimed the same territory; and the area was an intermittent battleground between the English, the Indians, and the French from 1615 until 1675 and a constant battleground from that date until 1763, when the British conquered the French in eastern Canada.

Maine was given separate provincial status in New England under royal patents granted by Charles I. The Puritans of Massachusetts took over the territory when the proprietor, Sir Ferdinando Gorges, backed the losing side in the British Civil War. Frontier settlers in Maine chafed under Massachusetts rule; but the merchants of the coastal towns resisted the separation movement until the War of 1812, when popular resentment against the failure of the Massachusetts Commonwealth to protect the District of Maine against British raids tipped the scales in favour of separation. Maine entered the Union as a free state under the Missouri Compromise of 1820, offsetting the simultaneous admission of Missouri without restrictions on the ownership of slaves.

Boundary dispute. The northeast boundary of the state, which forms the northeast boundary of the United States, was long a matter of serious controversy between the United States and Great Britain. The Treaty of Paris of 1783 ending the Revolutionary War identified the boundary in part as extending along the middle of the St. Croix River to its source, from there due north to certain highlands and along the highlands "to the north-westernmost head of Connecticut river." The dispute concerned just what the St. Croix River was and the location of its source and which highlands were to mark the boundary. The exact location of the St. Croix and its source was established by a commission provided for by the Jay Treaty of 1794, but identifying the highlands proved to be a more difficult problem. Maine claimed that the highlands referred to overlooked the St. Lawrence River, but Great Britain contended that they were in the vicinity of Mars Hill. The King of The Netherlands was chosen as arbitrator, and in 1831 he returned a decision unfavourable to Maine, causing the federal Senate to withhold its assent. The disputed area thus became the scene of a disturbance known as the Aroostook War in 1838–39. Maine erected forts along the line it claimed, and the federal government prepared to resist British efforts to exercise exclusive jurisdiction. War seemed inevitable until Gen. Winfield Scott, who had been sent to take command on the Maine frontier, was able to arrange a truce whereby both sides withdrew their armed forces in favour of a civilian posse. Three years later the Webster-Ashburton Treaty was effected, whereby Maine and Great Britain divided the disputed territory virtually in half.

Economic growth. Maine intrigued entrepreneurs, who hoped to make their fortune in furs, fisheries, timber, and land development. The first three proved to be lucrative for a few; but the climate, border troubles, and the knowledge of the more fertile land of the newer territories to the west curtailed settlement of the area before and after statehood. The period of greatest economic growth came between 1830 and 1860, when lumber, ice, granite, lime (extracted from limestone), and fishing and shipbuilding dominated the state's economy. Coastal communities flourished and railroads developed as Maine merchants traded around the world.

The Civil War and the Industrial Revolution diverted workers and capital from Maine during the last decades of the 19th century. Textiles and paper products became the primary sources of manufacturing employment, while fisheries and agriculture continued as important but uncertain sources of income. The details of economic activity changed during the first half of the 20th century, but the overall picture remained one of precarious prosperity and extreme susceptibility to swings in the national economy.

Political development. Maine's social and political history has been dominated by struggles against the adversity of frontier life and economic limitations, coupled with strong drives within the state for social reform, including world peace, antislavery, prohibition, and women's suffrage. Jeffersonian and Jacksonian Democrats held sway from statehood until the rise of the Whigs and the emergence of the Republican Party. The Abolitionist movement gave the Republican Party its start in Maine in 1854, and the Grand Old Party dominated the state for almost a century. Democrats scored temporary gains in the elections of 1910 and 1912 and in the Depression elections of 1932 and 1934, but it was not until 1954 that sustained competition began to develop between the major parties.

(E.S.M./Ed.)

Massachusetts

Like others of the 13 British colonies along America's Atlantic Seaboard in the 17th and 18th centuries, Massachusetts was founded by people seeking in a wilderness for a new way of life involving such then untried notions as freedom of religion and self-government. These and other ideals were severely tested during more than 150 years of colonial life, but they came to provide much of the ideological underpinning of the American Revolution, from which Massachusetts emerged as one of the founding and leading members of the new United States.

Character and location of the commonwealth

One of the six New England states lying in the northeastern corner of the nation, the Commonwealth of Massachusetts, as it is known officially, is bounded on the north by Vermont and New Hampshire, on the east and southeast by the Atlantic Ocean, on the south by Rhode Island and Connecticut, and on the west by New York. It covers 8,257 square miles (21,386 square kilometres) and ranks 45th in area among the states. The residents represent an amalgamation of the prototypal Yankee spirit of an earlier America and the energies of the later immigrants who flocked to its cities in the 19th century.

Massachusetts has been, nearly from its founding, a leading force in American education. During the 19th century, Boston, its capital, became synonymous nationally with the highest attainments in America's cultural and artistic life, and the state as a whole provided industrial and financial leadership for the nation. Though these latter positions have long since been yielded to larger and faster growing states and regions, the history and people of Massachusetts have left an indelible mark on the development of the American consciousness.

PHYSICAL AND HUMAN GEOGRAPHY

The land.   A walk along the Massachusetts coast would register about 1,500 miles (2,400 kilometres), yet the cross-country distances are only 190 miles (304 kilometres) from east to west and 110 miles (176 kilometres) from north to south. The jagged coast winds from Rhode Island around Cape Cod, in and out of scenic harbours along the shore south of Boston, through Boston Harbor and up the North Shore, swinging around the painters' paradise of Cape Ann before reaching New Hampshire.

Relief.   The indented coast of Massachusetts was formed by the great glaciers that in places covered the land with several thousand feet of ice. Ocean tides licked away the last ice some 11,000 years ago, revealing massive chunks of rocks along the shore. Hard, flat land stretches out beyond, becoming stony upland pastures near the central part of the state and bulging into a gently hilly country in the west. Except toward the west, the land is rocky, often sandy, and not fertile.

Cape Cod and the offshore islands

In the southeast Cape Cod juts out into the ocean. This 65-mile-long appendage is rectangular in shape except at its easternmost point, where it hooks northward. Its offshore waters are among the most treacherous in the country. Henry David Thoreau wrote that, to the people of Provincetown, at the tip of the cape, the sea is their garden, and the dog that growls at their door is the Atlantic Ocean. Tufts of grass spring up along the sand dunes, and gnarled jack pines and scrub oaks, some only head high, grow in bunches. Off the southeastern coast lie the islands of Nantucket and Martha's Vineyard, lashed by the gray Atlantic in winter but in summer alive with thousands of tourists and longtime seasonal residents.

Central Massachusetts comprises rolling plains fed by

innumerable streams. Beyond lies the broad and fertile Connecticut Valley and then the Berkshire Hills. The now-paved Mohawk Trail crosses the Berkshires, the Taconic Range on the west and the Hoosac Range on the east. The state's highest point, 3,491 feet (1,064 metres), is Mt. Greylock on the Taconic side near Adams. In North Adams a natural bridge of white marble has been formed by the wind and water, and at nearby Sutton is a half-mile-long gorge that knifes through the rock, exposing 600,000,000 years of geological history.

Drainage.   The land is veined with rivers—19 main systems, the best known of which are the Connecticut, Charles, and Merrimack. More than 1,100 ponds or lakes lie among the hollows of the hills, one in almost every one of the 365 communities. Many bear long Indian names, most notably Lake Chargoggagoggmauchuaggagogg-chaubunagungamaugg (which, translated, means "You fish on your side; I fish on my side; nobody fish in the middle"). The best known small body of water, however, is Walden Pond, immortalized by Thoreau.

Rivers and lakes

Nearly all the rivers and many lakes have become too polluted for swimming. This has long been true of the meandering Charles, which separates Boston and Cambridge and which is favoured by college rowing crews, canoeists, and sailboat enthusiasts.

Climate.   The state has a temperate climate. The climate is colder but drier in western Massachusetts, although its winter snowfalls may be more severe than those nearer the coast. July and August are the hottest months, averaging about 70° F (21° C), in contrast to the 30° F (−1° C) average of winter.

Plant and animal life.   Despite its industrialization, Massachusetts has managed to preserve many of its forests, and it has more than 130 state forests and reservations.

Not far from downtown Boston is the Arnold Arboretum, which has one of the largest collections of trees and shrubs in the United States. Along the shores the sandpiper, blue heron, American egret, sanderling, and turnstone can be seen. Water birds include the gull, scoter, cormorant, and loon, while those most often seen on land are the kingfisher, warbler, bobwhite, brown thrasher, sparrow hawk, yellow-shafted flicker, and whippoorwill. Game birds include ruffed grouse, wild turkey, and pheasant.

Public hunting grounds amount to about 23,000 acres (9,300 hectares). Three national wildlife refuges and Cape Cod National Seashore allow further contact with nature, but few animals remain. Of the larger animals, deer, snowshoe hare, red fox, woodchuck, muskrat, otter, and chipmunk still may be seen.

Settlement patterns.   In the early days the most populated seacoast towns lay at the mouths of rivers. The settlers fanned inland along these streams, drawing on them at first for farming and later for the power to run the mills.

Today, the lure of the sea results in nearly equal popularity for all of the towns along the coast, where sunbathing, swimming, yachting, and fishing are a way of life. Among these coastal towns are Plymouth, with its long harbour; Duxbury, Marshfield, Scituate, and Cohasset, where the first suburbs sprang up in colonial days; the boating bays from Hingham to Boston; the beaches at Revere and Lynn; the famous fishing off Gloucester and Cape Ann; and Marblehead, the yachting capital of the world.

Boston is surrounded by communities many of whose residents work in the city by day, sleep in the suburbs by night, and clog the highways commuting back and forth. Other urban cores include Springfield, Worcester, Fall River-New Bedford, and Lowell-Lawrence. These cities, which grew large during the Industrial Revolution, have begun to decline in population.

The people.   *Ethnic composition.* Boston and San Francisco often are referred to as sister cities because of such similarities as busy oceanside ports, good restaurants, emphasis on culture, prominence of religion in civic and social life, fine architecture in both public and private buildings, and echoes of a colourful history. Their ethnic mix is comparable as well. The blend of peoples in Boston has spread across the state. Although Boston is heavily Irish, so too are the urban areas in western Massachusetts, and the native brogue of Ireland is more likely to be heard around Springfield, Westfield, and Holyoke than it is in Boston. In the first half of the 20th century large numbers of Italians followed the Irish immigrations of the 1800s. In the late 1960s and 1970s the newcomers to the state were mostly Spanish speaking, from Cuba and Puerto Rico; by 1980 nearly 10 percent of Boston's population was Hispanic.

The English stock that still forms the backbone of the population is intermingled with Slovaks, Poles, Canadians, Russian Jews, Greeks, Scandinavians, Syrians, Germans, French, and Chinese. Fall River and New Bedford are the homes of many Portuguese and Cape Verde Islanders. Descendants of the Indians are few, though the state was named by Capt. John Smith for the Massachuset tribe, whose name meant "near the great hill," believed to refer to the Blue Hill Range that rises south of Boston in an otherwise flat area. Blacks are concentrated mainly in the old and deteriorating Roxbury and Dorchester sections of Boston and in New Bedford and Springfield.

Religions. Massachusetts is largely Roman Catholic, though its religious foundation was solidly Protestant. The Mayflower colonists were Separatists who had fled to Amsterdam from England to practice their religion without official interference. Hardship and a desire to establish an identity that was free of Dutch influence prompted them to seek out America in 1620. The Puritans, who came to Massachusetts in 1630, believed in reform but only within the church structure. (They were not believers in religious freedom, a fact that other Protestant groups, such as the Anabaptists and Quakers, soon discovered, to their discomfort.)

Religious separatists and other dissenters

From this socioreligious framework evolved a theocracy in which government officials attempted to act as clergy, interpreting the will of God for the people. The arrangement fell short of its purpose. When in 1634 Gov. John Winthrop refused to call a meeting of the legislature, or General Court, the freemen demanded to see the charter. He acceded, divulging his infringement on the rights of the legislature, and a bill was quickly passed vesting governmental power in the people. The establishment religion was whittled at constantly by scores of radicals. Many of them were banished—including Roger Williams from Salem and Anne Hutchinson from Boston—for their independent views.

During its subsequent development Massachusetts remained very religious. Following colonial patterns, churches often are found in the most prominent places of the towns and villages, symbolizing their traditional role in social life.

Social hierarchies. All the people of Massachusetts may be created equal, but some gained an edge earlier than others. The variety of peoples in the state fails to alter the fact that the major concentration of wealth and power continues to be controlled by the 800 or so families who trace their pedigrees to the "Mayflower" and the handful who in the following centuries so successfully trod the winding avenues of commerce, finance, and culture that they came to be considered among the ranks of that still relevant cadre, the Proper Bostonians. Many descendants of later immigrants also have found their way to the top of the financial—and often political—ladder. The proud tradition of family participation in the building of the state extends also to those of less exalted position: a large proportion of the residents of small-town Massachusetts, especially in the west, can claim many generations of Yankee background.

The old families and the new

The economy. *Industry.* Massachusetts has been a manufacturing state since the early 1640s, when John Winthrop, Jr. (son of Governor Winthrop), opened a saltworks in Beverly and ironworks in Saugus and Quincy. Francis Cabot Lowell was largely responsible, however, for raising the state to its manufacturing eminence, which accounts for nearly one-half of New England's manufacturing income. Lowell went to England to study methods of textile operations and built a power loom in Waltham in 1814. He died in 1817, but his associates developed the brick city of Lowell, with its mills driven by the Merrimack River.

Yankee ingenuity fostered much early handicraft-based

industry, though the influx of unskilled, low-paid labourers from Europe during the 19th century was the necessary ingredient for the mass production that developed in the state's shoe and textile factories. One of the first and largest shoe plants in America was the United Shoe Machinery Corporation in Beverly, while the building of the Springfield armory in 1777 boosted industry in western Massachusetts at the same time that it aided the Revolutionary cause. Other well-known goods from Massachusetts factories include watches from Waltham, Salem, and Boston; rockers from Gardner; cutlery and hand tools from Greenfield; guns and motorcycles from Springfield; leather goods from Peabody; shovels (which were used by the '49ers during the California Gold Rush) from North Eaton; envelopes from Worcester; paper from Holyoke; silverware from Newburyport; and razor blades from Boston.

Today, the electronics and communications industries draw heavily upon the many educational institutions in and around Boston. The western suburbs of Boston have become world famous for their research-and-development facilities, which have contributed significantly to space technology.

Fishing and agriculture. Foreign trade, fishing, and agriculture long buoyed the economy. Salem sailors brought exotic goods from China, the West Indies, and other faraway lands. Fishing was lucrative, adventuresome, and dangerous—more than 10,000 Gloucester fishermen have lost their lives over the centuries. Fishing and shipbuilding went hand in hand. Between 1789 and 1810 the Massachusetts fleet grew 10-fold, some of it to aid in defense against British and French aggressions on the high seas. Yankee sailors also found much "black gold" in the slave trade between West Africa and Southern ports.

The golden age of the Yankee seafarers

At the height of the whaling boom in the 19th century, 329 whaling vessels sailed from New Bedford, in addition to others from Nantucket and other ports, bringing in $10,000,000 worth of cargo each year in their holds. This great industry was not to last, however, and, by the turn of the century, its contribution to the state's economy had dwindled to only a fraction of its former importance. Fishing later suffered substantial reverses, as well. A $42,-000,000 annual business in the early 1960s, fishing began to wane, late in the decade, because of foreign competition in the traditional Atlantic fishing grounds and the depletion of such species as haddock and lobster from overfishing. By the late 1970s, however, the industry was making a comeback, with the value of landings reaching $142,000,000 by 1978.

The generally rocky soils support only truck gardening, although the purple sandy bogs of southeastern Massachusetts and Cape Cod produce more than 40 percent of the U.S. cranberry supply. Poultry accounts for about 10 percent of the state's agricultural income.

Finance. Since colonial days Boston has been a financial centre. Its investments contributed heavily to developing the American West, while the shipping industry made it the first insurance capital of the nation.

Transportation. "Never, in these United States, has the brain of man conceived, or the hand of man fashioned, so perfect a thing as the clipper ship," wrote historian Samuel Eliot Morison in *Maritime History of Massachusetts.* All clipper ships were built between 1850 and 1855, and from then on a kind of World Series of ship racing began. The champion was Donald McKay's "Flying Cloud," which sailed to San Francisco in 89 days, went 374 miles (598 kilometres) in one day, and averaged 13.5 knots over four days. Records were not the only motivating factor: the clippers carried 1,700 tons of cargo. Long before this, however, in 1716, Boston Light had been built off the busy port, the first lighthouse in the United States.

Waterways and highways in the past

Water formed the Bay State's highway system for 200 years. Rivers such as the Connecticut and Merrimack and man-made canals such as the Middlesex served early needs well. The Boston Post Road and the Mohawk Trail were the most heavily travelled of the early roadways. Opened to Boston-New York mail in 1673, the Post Road consisted of three routes. The Mohawk, an Indian footpath that was converted to an ox road by the settlers, became the first interstate toll-free road, called Shunpike, in 1786.

In 1826 the nation's first railroad brought granite from the quarries of Quincy and Charlestown for the building of the Bunker Hill Monument in Charlestown. The cars were horse drawn. A steam railroad connected Springfield and Worcester in 1839, and 15 systems were shuttling freight among western Massachusetts cities by 1855. Among the most impressive feats of early railroad building was the 4½-mile Hoosac Tunnel, drilled under the Hoosac Range between 1851 and 1875. The first electric street railway began in Brockton, and Boston had the nation's first passenger subway, as well as an elevated system.

Boston's Logan International Airport, stretching parallel to the harbour, is one of the few large air terminals in close proximity to a major city. It also is the nation's only airport owned and operated by the state. In spite of the general modernity of the state's transportation system, however, the sleek high-speed trains and the supersonic jets have yet to match the aesthetic perfection of the Yankee clipper.

Administrative and social conditions. *Government.* From the Mayflower Compact, drawn up by the Pilgrims in 1620 when the concept of "the divine right of kings" dominated Europe and the idea of self-government was little more than an exotic notion, a form of government evolved of which the people could feel themselves a part. In 1630, when the Puritans of the Massachusetts Bay Company settled Boston and other surrounding towns, John Winthrop and 18 assistants formed the governing body known as the Great and General Court. In a dispute over a stray pig, the Court became bicameral in 1644, the assistants forming the Senate and two deputies elected from each town making up the House.

The state constitution

After independence was declared, the General Court drew up a state constitution. The people rejected it, however, wanting a share in the drafting, and they elected a constitutional convention. Meeting in Cambridge in 1779, it gave the writing task to John Adams, and the people ratified his work in 1780. One of its extraordinary provisions permits the governor and his council or the legislature to seek advisory opinions on questions pertaining to the scope of gubernatorial or legislative power from justices of the Supreme Judicial Court. Today, Massachusetts is the only one of the 13 original states still governed under its first constitution, though the document has been updated many times by amendment.

The first meeting of the General Court as the legislative body of the new state took place in October 1780, exactly 150 years after the first meeting of the Puritans' Great and General Court. It today comprises 40 senators and 160 representatives. The state's judiciary mainly divides into the district courts for handling minor matters, superior courts for trial by jury, and the Supreme Judicial Court.

Another political phenomenon that grew up shortly after the settlers arrived was the town meeting, which started as a forum for settling local quarrels and grew to what is in many smaller towns the community event of the year. (As the poet James Russell Lowell observed, "Puritanism, believing itself quick with the seed of religious liberty, laid without knowing it, the egg of democracy.") The first recorded meeting was in Dorchester in 1633, when citizens were summoned by the roll of a drum. A year later Charlestown organized the first Board of Selectmen, the emergence of such local government balancing the power of the colony's executive. A county system also was developed patterned after the English model, in which the greater powers reside in townships and cities rather than in the counties, which serve chiefly for judicial purposes. A major need of Massachusetts is the redefinition of the roles of municipal, county, and state governments.

The legislature tends to be dominated by Democrats, but it is not surprising for Republicans to win the governorship or seats in the U.S. Congress. The Boston Irish politician has become legendary, mostly because of Mayor James Michael Curley, a skillful orator from a lowly background who was jailed twice, once while in office. During the late 19th and early 20th centuries, politics became a means to a better life—to a place alongside the "Boston Brahmins" of Mayflower heritage—for the Irish, who were discrimi-

nated against in employment advertisements that carried the letters "N.I.N.A."—No Irish Need Apply.

Social conditions. Discrimination was practiced from time to time in Massachusetts against such groups as the Indians, religious sects, and women, but the state also provided leaders in major fights to improve social conditions: Roger Williams and Anne Hutchinson for religious freedom; William Lloyd Garrison and Horace Greeley for the abolition of slavery; Horace Mann for public secondary education; Mary Lyon for women's education; and Francis Cabot Lowell, whose brick housing near his factories, though grim by modern standards, was better than the workers' ghettos he had seen in England.

Leaders of social consciousness

Women and children were exploited at the start of the Industrial Revolution, but Massachusetts was a pioneer in devising laws to protect them. State boards, under the supervision of the governor, later grew out of the need to improve conditions in health, education, welfare, labour, banking, insurance, and prisons.

Health and welfare. Massachusetts is one of the chief medical centres of the world, particularly in the area of specialists and specialty hospitals. It also has been a leader in research, notably at Boston's Children's Cancer Research Foundation. An urgent contemporary challenge is the delivery of medical services to the poor, who have been victimized by urbanization and the gradual disappearance of the family physician. Care for the mentally ill, the alcoholic, the addict, and the juvenile delinquent remains a problem, even though the state recognized its responsibility as early as 1818, when it opened an asylum for the insane.

Welfare was the province of the cities and towns until taken over by the state in 1970. Although the new program was fraught with difficulty, it was an improvement over the system that existed in the mid-19th century, when 3,000 citizens were imprisoned annually for indebtedness. Massachusetts' welfare payments are well above the national average.

Social tensions. Except among the intellectual elite, little concern was shown for blacks before 1850 for fear of alienating Southern cotton producers. Boston had a separate school for blacks, but otherwise they were denied schooling. The Know-Nothing Party emerged in 1845 primarily to combat growing Irish immigration but also to fight slavery, which the party considered an outgrowth of indifference by the rich toward human rights.

In the 1960s the urban areas experienced racial unrest similar to that throughout the country. Blacks have made some advances through political and economic means. Bussing of school children became a serious problem in Massachusetts cities during the late 20th century.

The Yankees, meanwhile, continue to run most of the banks, most of the law firms, and many of the businesses. They still represent the rock-ribbed solidarity in the state, built up through generations and epitomized by their contributions to the entire nation.

Education. Close to the heart of Massachusetts' social and cultural life lies education. Harvard College (now Harvard University), founded in 1636 in New Towne (now Cambridge), was long the major factor, although it was designed originally to provide the wilderness colony with a continuing supply of trained clergy rather than an educated lay population. Its graduates became community leaders, and schooling soon was provided colony-wide. In 1647, towns with 50 householders were required to support an elementary school; those with 100, a secondary school.

Educational pioneering

Massachusetts became the pioneer as well in kindergarten and secondary education and developed a uniform state public-school system in 1840. The state has numerous private preparatory schools of national ranking. Roxbury Latin School, founded in 1645, is among the nation's oldest, while others are located in Andover, Groton, Milton, Mount Hermon and Northfield, and Deerfield.

Many of the nation's oldest and most prestigious institutions of higher learning, in addition to Harvard, are located in Massachusetts. Some 385,000 students were in its public and private institutions in 1978, about 177,000 in the Boston area, where Boston University (1839) and Northeastern University (1898) are the largest. Nearby are the Massachusetts Institute of Technology (Cambridge; 1861) and Tufts (Medford; 1852) and Brandeis (Waltham; 1948) universities. Amherst (Amherst; 1821) and Williams (Williamstown; 1791) colleges have perpetuated traditions of academic excellence at small schools, while Mount Holyoke (South Hadley; 1837), Wellesley (Wellesley; 1870), Smith (Northampton; 1871), and Radcliffe (Cambridge; 1879) colleges have been pioneers in women's education. Boston College (Chestnut Hill; 1863) and Holy Cross (Worcester; 1843) are major Roman Catholic institutions. The University of Massachusetts (Amherst and Boston; 1863) has raised its academic standing significantly in the 20th century.

Cultural life. The blending of an Old World heritage and a New World spirit produced a bountiful cultural environment in Massachusetts.

The arts. Literature was virtually lost in the leaden language of the early writings and sermons, though poets such as Anne Bradstreet and Edward Taylor rose well above the level of dogmatizing, and Jonathan Edwards combined taut language and a brilliant theological mind. During what has been called the American renaissance, however, beginning around the time of the Revolution and lasting through much of the 19th century, the state nourished many writers who might be said to have founded the bases of American literature—and who brought it recognition outside the new nation.

The group of writers who brought fame to Concord are an indication of the inspiration of this period. A deep sense of both community responsibility and individualism may be traced through the writings of Ralph Waldo Emerson, Henry David Thoreau, Nathaniel Hawthorne, and Louisa May Alcott, all of whom were neighbours. The eloquence of Emerson, preacher, philosopher, and poet, carried his concepts of individual spiritual freedom to faraway lands, while Hawthorne found tranquillity in the small town after growing up in the shadows of Salem witches near the House of Seven Gables.

The mountains of Pittsfield also provided a congenial working environment for Hawthorne, as well as for Herman Melville, Oliver Wendell Holmes, and Henry Wadsworth Longfellow (the latter two combining, respectively, medicine and scholarship with their writings). Among other famous writers of the era were John Greenleaf Whittier and James Russell Lowell, as well as Emily Dickinson, today generally acclaimed as one of the finest American poets of the 19th century.

The universities have become central to many of the performing arts (theatre, dance, and music) in Massachusetts, although the Boston Symphony Orchestra generally is regarded as among the finest musical ensembles in the world. Its Tanglewood concerts under the stars at Lenox in the Berkshires (begun in 1937) are, with the Jacob's Pillow Dance Festival at nearby Lee, among the major attractions of the New England summer. The museums, libraries, and historical societies of Boston are among the most distinguished in the nation. These and other cultural aspects of that city are covered in greater detail in the article BOSTON.

Monuments to history. Historical sites in Boston draw the most tourists. A Freedom Trail provides a whirl through yesteryear that includes Boston Common, the old and new (1795) state houses, Park Street Church, the Old Granary Burying Ground, Old Corner Book Store, Faneuil Hall, Paul Revere House, the Old North Church, and the USS "Constitution," better known as "Old Ironsides."

Outside the capital the past seems still alive in three villages: Plimoth Plantation, Old Sturbridge Village, and Shaker Village in Hancock, where the sect established its communal-church concept in the 1780s. Harvard Square in Cambridge is a favourite tourist stop for its potpourri of people, its proximity to Harvard and Massachusetts Institute of Technology, and the history imbedded in the cobblestone atmosphere along its narrow side streets: the Harvard Yard, Christ Church, the Fogg Art Museum, Longfellow House (one of seven making up Tory Row), and innumerable other attractions of the city.

Salem prefers to forget its witch-hunting period of the late 17th century, but visitors to the House of Seven Gables

and other "haunted houses" keep the memories alive. In the elm-shrouded Chestnut Street area are Federal-style homes that reflect the days of prosperity for merchants, shipowners, diplomats, congressmen, and writers.

Along the South Shore are Quincy, where the humble homes of the eminent Adams family are next door to one another, and Hingham, where the Old Ship Church is the oldest surviving church in the 13 colonies. The Whaling Museum in New Bedford includes a half-size reproduction of a whaling vessel and some 600 log books, and the Seamen's Bethel (chapel) there was immortalized by Melville in *Moby Dick.*

West of Boston lies Concord and its Old Manse, home of the Emersons and, for four years, of the Hawthornes.

Past the Old Mill and Longfellow's Wayside Inn in Sudbury are Worcester and then Springfield, where the armoury and arsenal are reminders of the city's famous rifle. In nearby Pelham the Town Hall complex has the oldest continuously used meeting house in the country and a monument to Capt. Daniel Shays, who led a rebellion of poor farmers in 1786. Chesterwood in Stockbridge was the site of the studio of Daniel Chester French, sculptor of the great seated Lincoln statue in Washington's Lincoln Memorial. Some of the doors of houses in Old Deerfield bear the marks of Indian tomahawks wielded during the raids of the early 18th century.

Recreation. Private clubs, both social and athletic, long have been Massachusetts institutions, especially for golf, tennis, and yachting. Among the most exclusive are the Brookline Country Club and the Longwood Cricket Club in Brookline, the Myopia Hunt Club in Hamilton, and various yacht clubs along the North Shore above Boston, particularly in Marblehead.

Athletics have come in recent decades to form a subculture among all social classes. The professional teams—Boston's Red Sox in baseball, Bruins in hockey, and Celtics in basketball and the Foxboro-based New England Patriots in football—attract the most attention, but the state gives considerable emphasis to high school and college athletic activities as well.

HISTORY

History is woven into the very fabric of life in Massachusetts and has become one of the state's most valuable resources. The Pilgrims' landing and the American Revolution were the most heralded events, but the elements of struggle and survival were the main lessons for posterity from those two eras.

Cornerstones of the colony. The landing of the Pilgrims on November 21 (November 11, old style), 1620, was significant, yet the Indians had found this corner of the country some 3,500 years earlier, and Leif Eriksson and his Norsemen may have landed somewhere in the Cape Cod region in 1003. European seafarers tapped the fertile fishing areas throughout the 1500s, the French explorer Samuel de Champlain mapped the area in 1605, and in 1614 Capt. John Smith of Virginia drafted a detailed map of the New England coast from Penobscot Bay in Maine to Cape Cod. He even fought the Indians at Plymouth, stealing their canoes and trading them back in exchange for beaver skins.

At the time of the landing at Plymouth, most of the Pilgrims were at Provincetown, where they had arrived several days earlier and where the "Mayflower" was still anchored. An expedition of a dozen Pilgrims and six crewmen was sent to scout for a suitable settling place, which they found at Plymouth. The "Mayflower" did not arrive until the day after Christmas.

The Mayflower Compact, signed five weeks earlier by 41 men while still at sea, was hardly democratic. Basically, it called for rule by the elite, but it established an elective system and a basis for limited consent of the governed as the source of authority. The Compact for "the general good of ye Colonie" agreed that the "civill body politick" would abide by "just and equall lawes." Nearly 170 years later, the framers of the U.S. Constitution adopted that theme.

During that first winter the Pilgrims lived aboard ship and suffered the loss of 47 colonists. Probably they were

(margin notes)

Place in American arts and letters

Historic Western Massachusetts

Early
struggle
for
survival

victims of the same epidemic that was believed to have killed 95,000 Indians from 1615 to 1617, leaving only about 5,000 along the coast. The "Mayflower" returned to England in the spring, leaving a hardy band atop Cole's Hill, where they buried their dead and then planted seed to conceal their tragedy.

According to tradition, in March a tall, nearly naked Indian named Samoset confronted the haggard settlers with the peace cry in English, "Much welcome, Englishmen! Much welcome, Englishmen!" Both races had been weakened by the plague and needed one another. Their common efforts at survival gave rise after the autumn harvests to the feast of Thanksgiving, the first and the most characteristic celebration of the peoples of the United States. Samoset, a Pemaquid from Maine, introduced his friend Massasoit, chief of the Wampanoags, and 20 braves. Among them was Squanto, once sold into slavery in Spain and later a resident at the home of an English gentleman, where he learned English. By a quirk of history, he became the interpreter, guide, and teacher of the first white settlers.

Settlers had feared Massachusetts for its hostile Indians, but, until 1675, relative peace prevailed because of a pact with Massasoit. This accord was ended by King Philip (Metacom), Massasoit's son. His open warfare (King Philip's War [1675–76]) ended in his own death, but only after 300 settlers had been killed, 600 dwellings levelled, and 50 towns raided in southeastern and central Massachusetts.

Revolutionary period and after. A new struggle against new obstacles was touched off 100 years later by "the shot heard 'round the world." The colonists' fight was not so much against the British Redcoats as it was for an ideal, and the struggle actually had begun several years earlier, when a new spirit grew out of years of physical sacrifice and radical ideas involving such concepts as equality, freedom, and unity.

Leadership
in foment-
ing the
Revolution

From a tragic moment of that period—the Boston Massacre of 1770, in which British soldiers killed five civilians after a snowball-throwing incident that got out of hand—came one of the finest moments in the annals of the American judicial system. John Adams, later to be president, and Josiah Quincy successfully defended the soldiers against the outcries of an enraged citizenry bent on retribution. Three years later Samuel Adams, a second cousin of John Adams, gave the signal for the raid known as the Boston Tea Party, during which chests of taxable tea were dumped into the harbour, forcing the British to close the port of Boston, and striking a kindred nerve of resistance in other colonies. Events occurred in rapid-fire sequence after that—the battles of Lexington and Concord and Bunker Hill and the evacuation of Boston, inspiring song and verse that came to typify the spirit and events of the Revolutionary era.

Two years of prosperity following the signing of peace in 1783 soon gave place to serious financial difficulty, particularly among the poor and heavily taxed farming class. Violence occurred in most counties and became especially serious in the western ones. Owing largely to the failure of the legislature either to suppress the insurrection or to redress grievances, the revolt gained headway. Many former Revolutionary soldiers and officers took part in it, among others Capt. Daniel Shays, and because of his leadership the movement became known as Shays's Rebellion. It was finally put down by aid of heavy forces under General Lincoln.

The incident was important because it frightened the moneyed classes into more readily accepting the new federal constitution. This was ratified by only a very small majority. After its adoption the state became strongly Federalist in politics.

19th century. A group of leading politicians, known as the "Essex Junto" and including such men as Fisher Ames, George Cabot, Timothy Pickering, John Lowell, and others (all opponents of democracy and strongly reactionary), long dominated the politics of the state. They were utterly out of sympathy with the principles of the party in national power after 1800 and with the policy of war against England in 1812. As a commercial community the state suffered heavily from the embargo measures preceding the war and it was characterized by extreme sectionalism and

The Essex
Junto

antinationalism during the war. Although New England held most of the currency of the country, it refused, in the main, to subscribe to the war loans. Although great numbers of its citizens supported the government, the policy of the state as a whole was distinctly obstructionist. Rumours of secession, which had been heard at intervals from 1800, seemed to find confirmation with the convening in 1814 of the Hartford Convention to consider grievances against the federal government; it was mainly dominated by Massachusetts. The convention adjourned, however, doing little harm except to the reputations of those who had attended. The state also opposed the Mexican War of 1846–48 as it had the policy leading to it.

The period 1830–40 witnessed great social changes, among others the rise of factories and the influx of imported foreign labour. It was a period of intellectual ferment and of social experiment. Utopian communities, such as Brook Farm, were undertaken, and although they all ended in failure they left their mark on the thought and idealism of the times.

In the middle and late 19th century pronounced changes took place in the state, spurred by the factories spawned by the Industrial Revolution, a golden age of literature, and immigration, particularly by the Irish. The older, established classes remained dominant during this period, taking advantage of the new, cheap work force. A large segment of the rural population migrated westward, however, where the opportunities were greater and the discrimination less.

Grass-roots agitation prompted legislation in 1820 that removed property requirements for voters, and in 1833 the church was separated from the state. This set the stage for the Jacksonian Democrats, who advocated giving more power to the people. The large immigrant voting bloc soon achieved this, mainly through the Democratic Party.

Under the lead of William Lloyd Garrison and Wendell Phillips, Massachusetts was in the van of the Abolitionist movement. Such citizens as C.F. Adams and Charles Sumner took leading parts in the formation of the Free-Soil Party, and when at last the Civil War came the state rallied to the support of the federal government in a spirit utterly different from that which had marked the two preceding ones.

Later history. After the war the Republicans maintained a fairly continuous control until 1911. The industrialization of the state and the increasing domination of the cities by newer immigrant peoples—mainly Irish, Italians, and Slavs—strengthened the Democrats, and, except for the period 1916–28, they usually dominated the state in national elections.

New England lost its textile leadership to the South and much of its shoe business to the Midwest in the first half of the 20th century, but it continued its financial, educational, and cultural prominence, while branching into the fields of electronics and communications.　(J.S.D./Ed.)

New Hampshire

New Hampshire, one of the 13 original U.S. states, is located in the New England area at the extreme northeastern corner of the nation. With an area of 9,304 square miles (24,097 square kilometres), it is bounded on the north by the Canadian province of Quebec, on the east by Maine and an 18-mile (29-kilometre) stretch of the Atlantic Ocean, on the south by Massachusetts, and on the west by Vermont. The capital is Concord, located in the south central part of the state.

Though the essence of New Hampshire may be symbolized by its underlying granite bedrock, by the stern visage of the rock profile known as the "Old Man of the Mountain" looking out from Cannon Mountain in Franconia Notch, and by its more than three centuries of staunch Yankee tradition, New Hampshire contains a number of contradictions. It is generally perceived as a rural state, but more than one-third of its residents' wages and salaries comes from manufacturing; by this measure it ranks among the most industrialized states in the nation. New Hampshire became a national pioneer in 1964, when a statewide sweepstakes went into effect, its income ear-

Stability
and
progress

marked for education. The innovation was necessitated, however, by the lack of either a general sales tax or a state individual income tax.

New Hampshire seems very much a region tied to the past, to the land, and to a conservative way of life. Many of its residents can trace their New Hampshire ancestry for generations. The names of many of its towns and 1,300 lakes and ponds—Sunapee, Winnipesaukee, and Kearsarge, for example—are picturesque reminders of the Indians who lived in northern New England before the arrival of Europeans in the 17th century. Its towns are governed by the town meeting, a last bastion of direct democracy.

PHYSICAL AND HUMAN GEOGRAPHY

The land. *Relief.* The basic physical features of New Hampshire are the result of the last glacial age (64,000 to 10,000 years ago), during which the "Wisconsin ice sheet" moved like a huge bulldozer across New England from the northwest to the southeast. Loose sand, silt, clay, and gravel were deposited as masses of glacial till that, near the town of Greenland, are 395 feet (120 metres) in depth. The mountain notches of New Hampshire—Carter, Crawford, Dixville, and Franconia—are the result of the glacial action, as are the potholes and cirques found in the state. The great glacier left deposits in the form of many deltas and hillocks of stratified deposits. New Hampshire's lakes are also the results of glacial action.

Glacier-formed topography

The mountains are the most striking feature of New Hampshire's landscape. There are about 1,500 classified elevations, including eight mountains rising more than a mile in altitude, 61 rising more than three-quarters of a mile in height, and 157 with an elevation of a half-mile or more. The best known is Mt. Washington at 6,288 feet (1,917 metres), the third highest peak in the nation east of the Mississippi River. The mean elevation of the state is about 1,000 feet above sea level.

Drainage and soils. New Hampshire has five main river-drainage basins. The largest is that of the Merrimack River in the central part of the state. Second in size is the Connecticut River drainage basin along the western border. The remaining waters flow into the Saco, Piscataqua, and Androscoggin rivers, known collectively as the coastal rivers, as well as into several smaller streams.

Climate. New Hampshire's climate is highly varied. In winter temperatures may drop below 0° F (−17° C) for days at a time. Summers are relatively cool, and the mean annual temperature is about 40° F (4.4° C). Annual precipitation is approximately 40 inches (1,000 millimetres) and is rather evenly distributed over the four seasons.

Plant and animal life. More than 80 percent of New Hampshire remains under forest cover. The majority of the trees found in the eastern United States are indigenous to the state. The most valuable single species of tree has always been the white pine, which has been characterized as "nature's chief gift to New England."

The wooded areas also support a flourishing wildlife. Whitetail deer are numerous, and moose are occasionally seen. There is a hunting season for deer each year, but the killing of moose is prohibited. Beaver, once almost exterminated, have been protected and are making a comeback. Black bear are relatively common, while smaller mammals like rabbit, squirrel, raccoon, fox, and mink are plentiful. There is an abundance of bird life, including such species as grouse, woodcock, pheasant, and duck. Many varieties of fish have been depleted from coastal and interior waters. State rearing stations keep the interior lakes and rivers well stocked for fishing. There has been much concern about the effects of pollution on the underwater world, and strenuous efforts, both public and private, are under way to prevent further contamination of lakes, streams, and coastal waters.

Settlement patterns. There are six distinctive regions, each with its roots deep in New Hampshire's history. The heavily forested White Mountain area in the north is popular with mountaineers and tourists in summer and winter alike. The lakes region around Lake Winnipesaukee is a favoured locality for summer camps and resorts and for water sports. The seacoast region, which includes

Historic regions

Portsmouth, Dover, Exeter, and Hampton, has many maritime activities. The south central, or Merrimack, region surrounds Manchester, the most heavily industrialized section of the state. The Dartmouth–Sunapee Lake region in the west central portion is dotted with educational institutions and summer homes. The area around Mount Monadnock, in the southwestern corner of the state, is noted for many small industries and such attractions as the MacDowell Colony, a residential retreat in Peterborough for artists, and for the Cathedral of the Pines in Rindge, an outdoor shrine dedicated to the nation's war dead. Each region is officially organized and finances its own promotional activities. The 11 percent of the state's area that comprises the massive White Mountain National Forest is almost uninhabited.

The people. In the first U.S. census, in 1790, New Hampshire had a population of 141,885. Since then each decennial count has recorded a growth, except for that of 1870, when there was an extensive post-Civil War exodus to the Midwest. The urban population is concentrated to a large extent in the southern and southeastern regions, and the larger urban centres are all located south of the White Mountains. In the area nearest to Boston, New Hampshire has become a "bedroom suburb" for thousands of commuters to that metropolis.

In the colonial period the majority of the people were of English origin, but a significant influx of Scots-Irish, who were largely Presbyterian in faith, began in 1719. They settled in the south central and southwestern portions of New Hampshire and named their principal towns Derry, Londonderry, Antrim, and Dublin. The Scots-Irish were energetic pioneers, excellently suited for fighting Indians, the British, or any other enemy of their adopted country. They gave yeoman service in the Revolution and all subsequent wars.

Immigration and religion

New Hampshire had a unique system of "town churches" in which any officially recognized denomination could be designated at the annual town meeting to receive public tax support. Prior to the American Revolution, there were five possible denominations from which to choose: Congregational, Baptist, Presbyterian, Quaker, and Church of England. The system was discarded in 1819 by the Toleration Act passed by the legislature. Since then all churches have been privately supported, and any denomination may function freely.

During the 19th and 20th centuries waves of immigrants came into the state from central and eastern Europe. The first Roman Catholic congregation was established in 1828, the first parochial school in 1859, and a statewide diocese in 1884. The first Jewish congregation was organized in 1892, and the first Greek Orthodox Church in 1905. One of only two Shaker communities in the nation is located in Canterbury. The Cathedral of the Pines attracts thousands of visitors each year. The New Hampshire Council of Churches, organized in 1945, has developed broad ecumenical policies to include many faiths.

By late 20th century black citizens comprised less than 1 percent of the population, and citizens of Asian origin were even fewer. The largest group not directly descended from origins in the British Isles was the French Canadian, or "Canado-Americaine," who first began to arrive in the years immediately after the Civil War, chiefly from Quebec. They were attracted mainly to such industrial cities as Manchester, Nashua, Laconia, and Berlin. By the end of World War I New Hampshire had the largest percentage of French-Canadians among the states.

French-Canadian population

The economy. The historic shoemaking, woodworking, apparel, and textile industries have declined in productivity and employment opportunities, while space-age industries have grown rapidly. Among nonmanufacturing industries that also grew significantly were public utilities, insurance and banking, medical and health-service establishments, miscellaneous business services, and wholesale and retail trades.

Agriculture, forestry, and fisheries. Agricultural acreage decreased by two-thirds in the 20th century. Dairy products are the chief source of agricultural income, followed by poultry and poultry products, and cattle. More than three-fourths of the harvested timber is used for sawlogs and the rest is used for pulpwood to supply paper and newsprint industries. The state ranks low in commercial fishing yields but has marketable catches of lobsters and deep-sea fish.

Changing industrial base

Industry. Electrical- and electronic-goods manufacturing has largely supplanted the textile and garment industry, much of which after 1945 either closed or moved to the South. Machinery and paper and wood products comprise the next largest industries. The only large industrial centre north of the White Mountains is Berlin, with large paper and pulp mills.

There are many rock quarries, chiefly of granite, throughout New Hampshire. Sand and gravel are the major minerals produced in terms of both tonnage and value. Other native minerals that have commercial value include garnet, zircon, beryl, and bog iron. In 1955 the state legislature established an Industrial Park Authority, now the Industrial Development Authority, to attract more business into New Hampshire. Supplemented by the endeavours of individual cities and towns and by various private organizations, the authority has been successful in modernizing the industrial and business life of the state. An organized effort began in 1925 to publicize New Hampshire as a tourist area, and this effort has steadily expanded. With the increase in popularity of winter sports following World War II, New Hampshire became attractive to visitors in the cold months as it had been in the summer.

Transportation. At its maximum extent, in 1920 the New Hampshire railroad network comprised 1,252 miles (2,003 kilometres) of track; it is now scarcely half that figure. Hundreds of miles of right-of-way have been abandoned, and there is no passenger service except on a six-mile (10-kilometre) cog railway on Mount Washington. The line opened in 1869, as the first construction of its kind in the world, and is used to carry tourists behind steam locomotives during the summer. As the railroad disappeared, the bus and highway systems of the state greatly increased.

Administrative and social conditions. *Government.* The constitution of New Hampshire, the second oldest among the 50 states, was adopted in 1784. Every seven years the residents may vote on the question of holding a convention to consider modifications of the basic law. Proposals that pass these conventions must be approved by two-thirds of the voters at a popular referendum. Sixteen conventions have been held in the state's history, and a large number of modifications have been adopted, but a considerable portion of the original constitution remains intact.

Constitutional development

New Hampshire has had an elected governor since 1784. The incumbency is two terms of two years each. The governor is assisted by a five-member council, an institution that is found elsewhere in the United States only in Maine and Massachusetts. Members, elected every two years from five geographical districts in the state, must approve all appointments to state offices and to judicial posts.

The state legislature, the General Court, comprises more than 400 members elected every two years. The lower body, the House of Representatives, has between 375 and 400 delegates, depending on changes in population, and in the English-speaking world is believed to be exceeded in size only by the U.S. House of Representatives and the British Parliament. The state Senate has a modest membership of 24.

The state's judicial functions take place in three levels of courts: municipal and district courts, county superior and probate courts, and the state Supreme Court. All justices are appointed by the governor and council and serve during good behaviour or until they are 70 years old. The state police, in addition to their usual duties, are at the disposal of the governor and council for emergency assignments. Local police are under the jurisdiction of the municipal authorities.

The annual town meeting

The traditional town meeting, held annually on the first Tuesday in March, is the keystone of local government in New Hampshire. The town meeting is one of the last vestiges of pure democracy in the world and is basic to community life in New Hampshire. It is presided over by an elected moderator and the voters ballot on each article in the town warrant. If adopted, these articles be-

come the guide to town action for the ensuing 12 months. The meeting chooses the executive of the town and one of three selectmen, each of whom serves for a three-year term. The meeting also selects such departmental heads as fire chief, treasurer, town clerk, and road agent, as well as the members of various special boards and commissions. In some towns the selectmen are empowered to choose a town manager, who conducts the daily affairs of the community. Cities are governed by mayor–council, council–manager, or commission systems.

New Hampshire has always been a two-party state, and third-party candidates traditionally have had little success with Granite State voters. Prior to the Civil War, New Hampshire was overwhelmingly Democratic, but from then to the Depression of the 1930s it was dominated by the Republicans. The voters, however, have opted on several occasions for Democratic presidential candidates—Woodrow Wilson, Franklin D. Roosevelt, and Lyndon B. Johnson—and have sent a number of Democrats to Congress.

Taxation and finances. Taxes in New Hampshire are unusual. New Hampshire has clung tenaciously to its distinction of having neither a general sales tax nor a comprehensive state individual income tax. Almost one-half of state income is derived from taxes on alcoholic beverages, tobacco, legalized racetrack betting, sweepstakes, and motor fuels and vehicles. Such taxes admittedly were designed to draw heavily on the immense volume of tourism. The overwhelming burden of local income is derived from property.

As a result, state aid to local units of government has become an increasing and abrasive problem. Whereas, nationally, state aid provides slightly more than one-third of all local general revenue, in New Hampshire it provides less than one-fifth. New Hampshire ranks extremely low among states in state aid to welfare services, in state aid for local education, and in support of its state university.

Financial difficulties

Education. New Hampshire has had a public school system since 1647, when, as a part of Massachusetts, it was required to provide different kinds of schools depending on community size. The statewide system is administered by a board of education headed by a commissioner. Each town is constituted a school district, with its main support coming from local property taxes. The land-grant college that became the state university was founded in 1866 in Hanover and moved to Durham in 1893. Affiliated colleges are located at Plymouth and Keene. There are six state vocational colleges and a technical institute; an educational television system at the state university has been operated since 1959.

Best known among the private institutions of higher learning is Dartmouth College at Hanover, a liberal arts college that observed its bicentennial in 1969. Other private colleges include St. Anselm's College (1889) at Manchester, Mount Saint Mary College (1934) at Hooksett, and Rivier College (1933) at Nashua; the last two are for women only. Since 1945 five liberal arts colleges, all privately financed, have been founded in the state. In addition, there are several private junior colleges, the oldest of which is Colby-Sawyer College (1837) at New London.

Cultural life. *The arts.* New Hampshire has several outstanding cultural institutions. The MacDowell Colony was founded as a memorial to the composer and Peterborough resident Edward MacDowell (1860–1908) by his widow in 1907, and it since has been a mecca for musicians and writers. The 86-acre (35-hectare) former home of the noted sculptor Augustus Saint-Gaudens (1848–1907) at Cornish was designated as a National Historic Site in 1964. The Currier Gallery of Art and an institute of arts and sciences are located in Manchester; Dartmouth College is a distinguished fine arts centre, and there is an arts and science centre in Nashua. Several towns have smaller galleries, art centres, and museums. Summer theatres flourish in a dozen or more resort areas.

Sporting and historic sites. Recreation and tourism are important parts of the cultural pattern of the state. New Hampshire has some 30 ski areas, many of which operate their lifts in the summer for sightseers. There are more than 200 youth camps and more than 70 golf courses. Historical sites throughout the state include restored colonial homes and Ft. William and Mary at New Castle. There are more than 60 state parks and more than 800,000 acres of publicly owned forest preserves.

HISTORY

The English colony. The region that was to become New Hampshire was included in a series of grants made by the English crown to John Mason and others during the 1620s. A fishing and trading settlement was established in 1623, and in 1629 the name New Hampshire, after the English county of Hampshire, was applied to a grant for a region between the Merrimack and Piscataqua rivers. The towns of Dover, Portsmouth, Exeter, and Hampton were the main settlements.

From 1641 to 1679 the region was administered by the colonial government of Massachusetts. Following territorial and religious dispute between Massachusetts and Mason's heirs, New Hampshire became a separate royal province in 1679. Bitter boundary feuds with Massachusetts and New York over that part of the New Hampshire grant that became Vermont continued almost until the American Revolution. Benning Wentworth held the post of colonial governor from 1741 to 1767, the longest tenure of any royal governor in any of the colonies.

In 1767 the colony had its first census and reported about 52,700 people. In 1769 it was divided into five counties, to which five others have been added since 1800. New Hampshire soldiers played an active part in the colonial wars between Great Britain and France from 1689 to 1763. By the end of the colonial period the seat of government was at Portsmouth, and there were 147 chartered towns in the province.

Revolution and statehood. In December 1774 there was armed resistance to the British at New Castle, where Ft. William and Mary was seized by colonists. The citizens of New Hampshire were overwhelmingly in sympathy with the aims of the revolutionary leaders. The state furnished two major generals to the Continental Army, three regiments of regular troops, and hundreds of short-term militiamen. New Hampshire officially became a state in 1776 and issued its own Declaration of Independence several weeks before the national Declaration of July 4, 1776. New Hampshire's vote was the ninth and decisive vote in ratifying the Constitution of the United States in 1788.

Following the establishment of the nation, the state grew rapidly. Agriculture, notably sheep raising, flourished, and manufacturing developed along the fast-flowing rivers, particularly in Manchester. When the railroads appeared in the northeast, an extensive rail network was constructed. Portsmouth and its surrounding towns were shipbuilding centres. In 1846 Manchester became the first incorporated city in the state. New Hampshire was also the birthplace of such noted statesmen as Daniel Webster and Pres. Franklin Pierce.

Contributions to war and politics. New Hampshire played an active part in the Civil War and, following that conflict, voted regularly for Republican candidates until the New Deal of the 1930s. The progressive movement had an impact upon the state in the early 20th century, and the economic depression of the 1930s left scars that were only slowly effaced. In World Wars I and II and in the Korean and Vietnamese conflicts, soldiers from New Hampshire played important roles, and the shipbuilding and naval facilities at Portsmouth were of special value.

Because it holds the earliest presidential primary in the nation, New Hampshire has furnished the first testing ground for many candidacies. In 1905 Portsmouth was the site of the peace conference that ended the Russo-Japanese War, and in 1944 the state was host to the Bretton Woods Conference that founded the International Bank for Reconstruction and Development and the International Monetary Fund. The U.S. Air Force constructed a huge Strategic Air Command base at Newington in 1957, and the Portsmouth Naval Shipyard, in Kittery, has continued to specialize in building and repairing submarines.

(J.D.S.)

Role in forming the nation

Rhode Island

Perhaps the most remarkable feature of Rhode Island, one of the six New England states in the northeastern corner of the United States, is its size. About 48 miles (77 kilometres) long and 37 miles (59 kilometres) wide at the maximum, it is the smallest and one of the most densely populated states in the nation. Many of the state's ample woodlands were once farms that were abandoned during the 19th century; during the 1800s migrations to the cities resulted in an urban population that by 1900 was 90 percent. Rhode Island has since become one of the most heavily industrialized areas in the world.

This extreme compactness of area and the proliferation of people and activity have tied Rhode Island closely to its neighbours, Connecticut on the west and Massachusetts on the north and east. The Atlantic Ocean, which lies to the south, cuts deep into the state as Narragansett Bay.

The major islands within the state are Block Island and Rhode Island. On the latter is the famous yachting and music centre, Newport. A popular resort since West Indian and Southern planters discovered the island as a summer home in the mid-18th century, Newport became an international symbol of wealth and elegance in the 19th century as millionaires from across the country built the many mansions that stand as memorials to a gilded past.

Historical and contemporary character

PHYSICAL AND HUMAN GEOGRAPHY

The land. *Relief.* Rhode Island's rocky soil is mostly glacial till deposited by the great ice sheets that covered the northern United States thousands of years ago. Glaciation also provided the material that the ocean later formed into the barrier beaches along the state's southern coast, where tidal ponds, open to the ocean through narrow breachways, stretch from the mouth of the Pawcatuck River at Westerly and Watch Hill to Point Judith. The best farmland is in Portsmouth, Middletown, and areas around the southern coast. There, potatoes and corn (maize) are the principal crops. Elsewhere the land is good only for pasture and dairy or poultry farming. Fields that have been cleared for farming are bounded by omnipresent stone walls. These old stone walls can still be found deep in the woods, evidence that the land once was under cultivation.

Although the western part of the state has hills rising as high as 800 feet (240 metres) above sea level, most of it is quite flat, and the average altitude is about 200 feet. The highest points are Jerimoth Hill, 812 feet, in the town of Foster and less than a mile from the Connecticut border; and Durfee Hill, 804 feet, in Glocester, a few miles farther north. The lowest part of the state, other than the ocean beaches, is in the vicinity of the Great Swamp in South Kingstown.

Climate. With a reasonably salubrious climate, the state is not normally subjected to great extremes of either heat or cold. The average mean temperature at Providence is 50° F (10° C), while the mean for summer is 70° F (21° C) and for winter 30° F (−1° C). Mean annual precipitation throughout the state is about 37 inches (940 millimetres).

Drainage. Two large river systems drain Rhode Island. Most important is the Blackstone River and its tributaries. Rising near Worcester, Massachusetts, it cuts through the northeastern part of the state and was the source of waterpower for numerous textile mills that were built in the Blackstone Valley, at Woonsocket, Pawtucket, and a dozen mill villages between the two cities. The Pawcatuck River and its main branch, the Wood, provided power for numerous other small mills. Although it drains a smaller area, the Pawtuxet River was once of comparable economic importance, and its valley is crowded with mill villages.

These mill villages, which thrived in the 19th century, give rural Rhode Island its characteristic look. Small one- and two-family houses, set out in orderly rows along a single street, are not far from the mill where the residents worked. Formerly these houses were built and owned by the mill owners, but, with the demise of many of the mills or their conversion to kinds of manufacturing other than textiles, the mill village houses were sold off to the persons who lived in them.

Waterpower and the mill villages

Before the mills Narragansett Bay was the state's great asset, providing a convenient waterway running two-thirds of the length of the state and navigable as far up the Blackstone Valley as Pawtucket Falls. The small commercial trade on which the wealth of Newport, Bristol, and Providence was founded has given way to a larger oceanborne commerce. Storage tanks for oil and gasoline dot both shores of the upper bay, and Providence has become one of the principal oil-distributing centres of the Northeast.

Role of Narragansett Bay

Narragansett Bay also has been useful in bringing U.S. Navy establishments to Rhode Island. The Naval War College has operated at Newport since the middle of the 19th century. Although before World War II the navy occupied about 500 acres (200 hectares) in Newport County, a Naval Operating Base was established and enlarged to more than 2,100 acres in 1941. The navy's presence continued to be strong through the late 1960s, when about 42,000 people were employed at Newport and other naval bases. By 1980, however, the number had been reduced to 9,500 people.

Other major waterways of the state are Mount Hope Bay, an arm of Narragansett Bay, providing navigable water to Somerset and Fall River, Massachusetts, and the Sakonnet River, a saltwater strait separating the island of Rhode Island from Little Compton and Tiverton on the east. Block Island Sound, lying between Block Island and the mainland, is highly regarded by sport fishermen seeking marlin and tuna and also yields commercial quantities of swordfish.

Settlement patterns. Rhode Island comprises five counties, eight cities, and 31 towns. It sometimes is described as a city-state, and a large proportion of its population resides in Providence or in contiguous communities, such as Pawtucket on the north, North Providence and Johnston on the west, Cranston and Warwick on the south, and East Providence across the river to the east. Except for Warwick, all of these communities are in Providence County. Warwick and Cranston are the state's second and third largest cities, respectively.

The people. Although the population of the state has undergone considerable change since World War II, with the exodus from the congested parts of such cities as Providence to the "bedroom communities" of Cranston and Warwick, much remains the same. Woonsocket still has a large population with French-Canadian ancestry whose first language is French. Pawtucket retains a large group of English whose ancestors came to work in the textile mills, and Providence has a strong Italian-American community as well as a large number of Irish-Americans. In the small towns of the western and southern parts of the state, however, the typical Yankee farmers predominate, though mixed with an increasing number of people of Portuguese, Finnish, and Polish extraction and others who have fled the cities. Providence had the greatest number of blacks and other nonwhites.

Although ethnic origins are a strong factor in political actions in Rhode Island, the state has returned to the principles of toleration on which the colony was founded. Despite much unwillingness to assimilate immigrant groups in the 19th century, the state has always clung to its ideals of religious freedom. In the 17th and early 18th centuries, Rhode Island was a refuge especially for Quakers and Jews, both of whom contributed substantially to the wealth and economic power of Newport. Touro Synagogue in Newport, a colonial building that has been carefully restored in decor and furnishings, is the oldest synagogue in the United States; it has been declared a national landmark.

Like other predominantly urban states, Rhode Island has begun to feel the effect of the flight from the cities, which leaves behind more and more of the unemployed, the economically depressed, the unskilled, and those on the public welfare rolls. At the same time the cities continue to lose much of their economic and tax base.

The economy. *Industry.* Rhode Island depends increasingly on brainpower and skilled labour to keep its economy afloat. Relying in its early years almost entirely on subsistence agriculture and seaborne trade, it became after the Revolution a pioneer manufacturing state, principally in the textile field. In the 20th century it has developed more diversified small industries, especially in the jewelry and allied industries, electronics, and such service fields as education and insurance.

The largest group of workers is engaged in the jewelry and allied trades, whereas the once dominant textile industry has fallen to second place. The manufacture of machine tools and precision-measuring instruments is an important element in the economy; coupled with the fabrication of metal products and electrical equipment, it often employs large numbers of people, although any national retrenchment in heavy industry, such as automobile manufacturing, is quickly reflected in Rhode Island's economy. Since the jewelry industry is also remarkably sensitive to fashion trends and available money supplies, employment in this trade is frequently seasonal or otherwise erratic. One of the stablest elements of the economy is the state's educational institutions.

Manufacturing employment and value

Rhode Island is not a rich state, and its per capita income places it in the middle ranks among the states. Jewelry and silverware manufacturing is Rhode Island's leading industry, with textiles second and metalworking machinery third.

Finance. Two Providence-based banks, the Industrial National and the Rhode Island Hospital Trust, through their branches throughout the state, are the dominant financial institutions, but there are several important banks of secondary rank.

Transportation. In addition to its bridges and ferries, Rhode Island has many other connections with states of the Eastern Seaboard. Providence is the centre of limited-access expressways to Boston, less than one hour away, to Cape Cod, and westward and southwestward into Connecticut. A main railroad provides the state with freight and passenger service, while interstate and intrastate bus lines run on its highways. There are several airports in Rhode Island, with most of the passenger service handled at the Theodore Francis Green State Airport, located at Hillsgrove.

Administrative and social conditions. Atop the state capitol in Providence is the statue of "The Independent Man," a symbol of so much that is characteristic of Rhode Island. Roger Williams wrote that he had founded Providence as a place of refuge for "those distressed for cause of conscience," and the principle of absolute religious freedom has been an abiding article of Rhode Island's political philosophy. Because of the nature of its first settlements, which were not bound to any one religious faith, most Rhode Island towns do not have a central common, as do many New England towns, where the houses are usually clustered around a central group of churches or a single church.

Government. Ever since its founding, the state has shown a reluctance to permit elected officials to exercise extensive powers. In the early years legislatures and elected officials served for only six months. Prior to 1854 the state had five capitals, Providence, Newport, East Greenwich, Bristol, and South Kingstown, and the General Assembly travelled from one to another. In 1900 Providence was chosen as the sole capital.

Executive, legislative, and judiciary

The governor has the power of the veto and the power to name certain department heads. Judges are elected by both houses of the General Assembly sitting as a committee of the whole, and since the 1930s they have had tenure.

Members of the General Assembly are paid by the day for 60 legislative days. A number of attempts to amend the state constitution to increase legislators' pay have been soundly beaten by the voters, who in 1968 defeated by a four-to-one margin a new constitution to replace the 126-year-old document.

In addition to the usual officers and the legislators, the state has a district court system, superior courts, a Supreme Court, which also can give advisory opinions if requested, and municipal and probate courts, the latter frequently identical with the town council in the smaller communities. There is also a Family Court, which handles both juvenile and domestic cases. In addition, a U.S. District Court sits in Providence.

Most of the cities in Rhode Island operate with a mayor and city council form of government, but some have a city manager, and the mayor is chosen from among councilmen to act as the ceremonial head of the local government. Likewise, most of the towns are governed by a town council, but in some cases operations are conducted by a town manager.

Taxation and finance. Rhode Island has a sales tax, which exempts food and prescription drugs. In 1971, after many defeats in the General Assembly, the state adopted a personal income tax. Lotteries were widely used in colonial times and after the Revolution to raise capital for civic improvements; they later were prohibited but were reestablished in 1974. A large share of the state's income comes from its tax on pari-mutuel betting at two horse-racing tracks, Narragansett and Lincoln Downs.

Welfare. Early in its history, Rhode Island acted to stamp out slavery by limiting to a maximum of 10 years the period in which anyone could be held a slave. During the Revolution the General Assembly acted to raise a black regiment by decreeing that any slave who enlisted would be granted his freedom. Even in the 18th century there was a strong emancipation movement in the state, drawing much of its support from such men as Moses Brown and other prominent Quakers. In 1866 the General Assembly passed a law prohibiting the exclusion of any person from the public schools because of race or colour, thus closing separate schools maintained in Bristol, Newport, and Providence and admitting blacks to Providence High School.

> Early traditions of toleration

The state maintains elaborate facilities to care for the sick and indigent, from children's centres to institutions for the elderly.

There are jails in cities and towns throughout the state, but most persons awaiting trial or sentenced to prison terms are sent to the Adult Correctional Institutions (ACI) at Howard. The ACI in recent years has adopted a work-release program to rehabilitate prisoners. Rhode Island has a force of more than 300 officers and policemen who operate out of seven barracks located throughout the state.

Education. In 1970 a Board of Regents was created and charged with responsibility over all public education, from elementary schools through the state-operated colleges and the university. A number of private preparatory schools, both sectarian and nonsectarian, send graduates to many of the major colleges and universities, especially in the East. Rhode Island is strong in its institutions of higher education. Brown University in Providence, founded in 1764 as Rhode Island College, is one of the major Eastern universities that make up the so-called Ivy League. It is noted for its library facilities, especially the John Carter Brown Library of early Americana. The Rhode Island School of Design (founded 1877) is widely known, primarily for its training in the visual and graphic arts. The University of Rhode Island, in Kingston, is a land-grant institution dating from 1892. Catholic colleges include Providence College (1917) and Salve Regina College (1947) in Newport. Rhode Island College, mainly for teacher training, dates from 1854.

> Higher education

Cultural life. Library facilities are plentiful throughout the state. The Redwood Library, in Newport, and the Providence Athenaeum, both proprietary institutions housed in architecturally important buildings, have roots going back to the mid-18th century. The public libraries of Providence and Westerly have important holdings, the former having special collections on whaling, printing, slavery, and Irish literature. The Rhode Island Historical Society, in Providence, has more than 1,000,000 manuscripts and is especially strong in its holdings of the state's newspapers. The society also operates John Brown House, a magnificent merchant's mansion in Providence; built in 1786, the house is furnished with masterpieces of the Newport school of cabinetmakers and with other 18th-century antiques.

The Museum of Art of the Rhode Island School of Design is especially strong in Greek and Roman sculpture and antiquities, Postimpressionist French paintings, American painting, and British watercolours. The School of Design also has a fine art library.

In both Providence and Newport, preservation societies have been active in restoring the surviving colonial homes.

The Preservation Society of Newport County operates as museums several mansions that were formerly the summer homes of millionaires. The Newport Historical Society museum, with its fine collections; Touro Synagogue, a magnificent example of colonial architecture; Old Colony House; Redwood Library; Hunter House; the restored colonial homes of the Point section; and the National Lawn Tennis Hall of Fame and Tennis Museum in the Newport Casino building combine to give Newport an extraordinary and varied cultural heritage.

The Rhode Island Philharmonic Orchestra, the Rhode Island Civic Chorale and Orchestra, the Westerly Community Chorus, the Barrington Boys Choir, and numerous smaller groups and organizations are among the state's musical resources. It is visited regularly by the Boston Symphony Orchestra, and it has an annual chamber music series, as well as several series featuring renowned soloists. The State Ballet of Rhode Island performs regularly throughout the state. Many of the restored houses in Newport were the setting for the Newport Jazz Festival, a world-famous event begun with annual summertime jazz concerts in 1954 and joined in the 1960s by folk-music presentations. The festival was moved to New York City in 1972 (and renamed the Kool Jazz Festival in 1981).

> Music festivals

The Trinity Square Repertory Company, with its own home in Providence, is renowned for producing works by new playwrights, as well as for staging novel productions of classic works. In 1968 it became the first regional theatre in the United States to be invited to perform at the Edinburgh International Festival of Music and Drama in Scotland.

Many of the recreational activities of the people of Rhode Island are centred on the state's water. For many years the waters off Newport have been the site of the yacht races for the America's Cup. An annual tuna tournament is held in Rhode Island and Block Island sounds. Newport Casino, one of the early centres of tournament tennis, has an annual grass-court tournament of national importance.

HISTORY

Colonial period. In the state's official name—The State of Rhode Island and Providence Plantations—lies a clue to its founding. The first settlement was made by the minister Roger Williams and a few followers at Providence, near the head of Narragansett Bay, in 1636. They were either under edict of banishment from Massachusetts Bay Colony—Williams for advocating freedom of conscience in religion—or were in trouble with the authorities there. In 1638 a group of prominent Bostonians, in similar difficulties, purchased the island of Aquidneck, now Rhode Island, from Indians and settled Portsmouth. Factional strife split this settlement, and William Coddington and his adherents moved to the southern end of the island, where they founded Newport, leaving Anne Hutchinson and her followers in Portsmouth. In 1643 Samuel Gorton took a dissident group south of the boundaries of Providence Plantations and settled Warwick.

Williams went to England in 1643 and returned the following year with a royal patent for the colony, but the four towns could not agree on a form of government until 1647, when a loose confederacy was established. The colony was never accepted into membership in the United Colonies of New England—comprising Plymouth, Massachusetts, Connecticut, and New Haven—and it was constantly threatened with a takeover by one or another of these governments. Coddington, by going to England and having himself made ruler for life of the island towns, split the colony between the mainland and the island towns. Williams and John Clarke, the latter representing island elements unhappy about Coddington's commission, sailed for England in 1651, succeeded in getting the commission rescinded, and in 1654 set up a reunited government. Clarke remained in England and, in 1663, won a royal charter that was to be the basis of colonial and state government for 180 years.

Although the colony never officially joined the other New England colonies in King Philip's War (1675–76), it suffered greatly. All mainland settlements were burned, including, in the spring of 1676, many houses in Providence. Most of the mainland settlers took refuge on Rhode Island, which was not attacked. The Great Swamp Fight, the battle in which the major portion of the power of the Narragansett Indians was broken, took place in December 1675, a few miles west of the present village of Kingston.

Early commerce with the West Indies

Rhode Island almost from the beginning had commerce with the West Indies, selling horses, barrel staves, and salt fish. Eventually, some of its merchants tried the triangular trade: taking rum to the African coast, where it was traded for slaves, carrying the slaves to the West Indies, where they were traded for molasses, and carrying the molasses to Rhode Island, where it was distilled into rum. The passage of the Sugar Act by Parliament in 1764 seriously affected this trade, and the colony, never overly anxious to obey unpopular laws, began to indulge in considerable smuggling of sugar and molasses. In 1772 the British customs vessel "Gaspee," patrolling Narragansett Bay, ran aground off Namquit (now Gaspee) Point while pursuing a suspected smuggler; that night it was burned by a group of townsmen from Providence. This has been widely regarded as the first act of outright violence against the British crown in the period leading up to the American Revolution.

Traumas of revolution and independence. During the war Newport was occupied by the British. In 1778 a land force under Gen. John Sullivan and the French fleet commanded by the Comte d'Estaing cooperated in an operation designed to dislodge them. Before the French troops could be landed, however, a British fleet appeared in the bay; d'Estaing halted the landing and set out in pursuit. Two days later, before the ships had actually engaged, they were dispersed by a storm. The American ground forces, lacking French assistance, were forced to retreat from the island. At Butts Hill they fought a strong rearguard action that became known as the Battle of Rhode Island and in which a battalion of freed slaves distinguished itself. A Rhode Islander, Gen. Nathanael Greene, distinguished himself as Washington's second in command and as commander of a brilliant campaign in the South.

After the war Rhode Island was reluctant to ratify the Constitution until the Bill of Rights was proposed in the form of 10 amendments. The state's largely agricultural population was opposed to joining the Union, while the merchants of Providence and Newport worked hard for ratification. When threats of commercial isolation from the other states were raised, Rhode Island accepted the document in May 1790, but it did so by a margin of only two votes.

Newport, preeminent before the war, lost much of its economic power during the British occupation, and Providence, led by such merchants as the four Brown brothers, John, Joseph, Nicholas, and Moses, assumed the leadership.

Conflicts over suffrage and equal representation

In 1842 a movement for widening the franchise, which had been limited under the 1663 charter to freeholders and their eldest sons, resulted in a civic conflict known as Dorr's Rebellion. Led by Thomas Wilson Dorr, the son of an aristocratic family, the faction favouring universal suffrage held a convention in 1841 and adopted a constitution embodying this principle. At an election held under this constitution, Dorr was elected governor in 1842, but the election was not accepted as legal by the legislature or the state Supreme Court. When his forces were repulsed in an attempt to seize the arsenal in Providence, Dorr fled the state. Upon his return, he was tried on a charge of high treason, convicted, and sentenced to life imprisonment; he served only one year, however, and was released in 1845. By that time the state had adopted a revised constitution considerably broadening the basis of the franchise, but it was not until the mid-20th century that full rights to vote in all elections were extended to all citizens at the age of 21 (later 18).

In the years after the Civil War the Republican Party, led by such political bosses as Gen. Charles R. Brayton, ruled the state completely, mainly because the cities, which were Democratic, were not represented in either chamber of the General Assembly in proportion to their population. Providence, by far the largest city, had one senator, as did a small town with only several hundred people.

Providence's representation has grown to comprise 11 senators in the state government, while often several small towns are grouped together with a single senator to represent them. Since the 1930s the Democratic Party has controlled the legislature, although Republicans have been elected governor on several occasions, and Dwight D. Eisenhower and Richard M. Nixon, among the Republican presidential candidates, were able to carry Rhode Island.

(B.F.S.)

Vermont

Vermont is one of the six New England states in the northeastern corner of the nation. Its 9,609 square miles (24,887 square kilometres) has relatively few inhabitants, and its capital, Montpelier, is one of the least populous of any of the U.S. state capitals. On the south, Vermont borders Massachusetts; on the west, New York; and on the north, Quebec, Canada. From the Canadian to the Massachusetts border, the Connecticut River separates Vermont from New Hampshire on the east. The river is entirely within New Hampshire.

Heritage of the past

In many ways Vermont is a vigorous survivor of an earlier, simpler time in the United States. Millions of people visit the state each year, and many thousands of out-of-state residents maintain second homes in Vermont. These people primarily seek the beauty and tranquillity of Vermont's mountains and narrow valleys and the sense of the nation's past that pervades the entire state. The steeples of white wooden churches rising above small, mountain-bound towns with trim village greens; the herds of dairy cattle on sloping mountain pastures; and the red-gold leaves of tree-lined autumnal lanes are aspects of scenic Vermont that, in painting and photography, have become symbols of the rural United States.

Many people left their birthplaces in Vermont to join the movement westward, and many of the nation's foremost creative personalities, in turn, have sought the spiritual refuge offered by the state. Vermont has never stood in the mainstream of the nation's history, but its people and land have poured into their country a strength and a sense of continuity that joins the achievements of the nation's past with the purposes of its present.

PHYSICAL AND HUMAN GEOGRAPHY

The land. The land of Vermont does not have great variety, but in place of this it substitutes an intensity and pervasiveness of those features it does possess.

Relief. The Green Mountains that cover most of the state are a northeastward extension of the Appalachian Mountains that run from Canada into northern Alabama. They provide Vermont with a north–south backbone that ranges from 20 to 36 miles (32 to 58 kilometres) in width. Thirty-one mountains in the state rise to more than 3,500 feet (1,100 metres), and only 15 percent of the state's terrain is level land with fertile soil and high productive capability. Vermont's average altitude is about 1,000 feet above sea level. Mt. Mansfield, at 4,393 feet (1,339 metres), is its highest point; and Lake Champlain, at 95 feet (29 metres), is its lowest. On the Vermont–Massachusetts border, the northern end of the Hoosac Range enters the state, and the Taconic Range rises along the southwestern side. North of the Taconic Range are the Red Sandrock Hills, which extend along Lake Champlain to St. Albans.

Drainage. These ranges are broken by only a few river valleys, such as the Winooski, Lamoille, and Missisquoi, all flowing westward into Lake Champlain. Part of the Missisquoi turns north through Canada before returning to Vermont. Lake Champlain's waters empty northward into the Richelieu River and flow 80 miles into the St. Lawrence. The longest river entirely within the state is Otter Creek, which rises in southwestern Vermont and flows northward 90 miles into Lake Champlain. Several small streams, the largest of which is the White River, flow from the central highlands into the Connecticut River. The western portion of Lake Champlain is in New York; and 75 percent of Lake Memphremagog, the second largest lake associated with Vermont, lies in Canada. The largest of the 400 lakes entirely in Vermont is eight square miles (21 square kilometres) in area.

Climate. Snowfall in Vermont usually averages between 70 and 80 inches (1,800 and 2,000 millimetres) each winter in the valleys, and up to 110 inches in the mountains. Rainfall varies from 34 inches in the eastern and western sections to 40 inches in the mountains. Winter temperatures can drop to −30° F (−34° C) and lower, but in the summer they rarely rise above 90° F (32° C). Warm summer days often turn cool after nightfall. The annual growing season is only about 120 days—somewhat longer in the low-lying Champlain Valley—because frost usually comes in September and may strike as late as the beginning of June. The short growing season and rocky soil make dairying the predominant form of commercial farming. In the late 1970s about one-half of all Vermont farms were dairy farms, and the state had more cows per capita than any other state except Wisconsin.

Plant and animal life. A century ago many of Vermont's hilltops had been cleared as pastures and open fields, but most of the state is now forested. As farmers abandoned the hillsides, the open spaces quickly filled with trees. Pine, spruce, fir, and hemlock are common; and maple, birch, and elm are found among the deciduous trees. The state tree is the sugar maple, which reflects Vermont's prominence in maple sugar and syrup production. The wooded areas, with their small brooks and springs, produce an amazing variety of ferns and wildflowers; in the spring and summer they are filled with the many species of birds common to the Northeast.

Vermont has a huge deer population and deer hunting is popular. Bear are still seen, but wild members of the cat family are rare. Small animals abound in Vermont, and fishing in the lakes and streams continues despite warnings that many fish are contaminated by mercury.

Settlement patterns. Most Vermonters live in valley cities and towns. Burlington, in the Champlain Valley, is Vermont's largest city, followed by Rutland, in the Otter Valley, Bennington, in the Walloomsac Valley, and Brattleboro, on the Connecticut River. The Green Mountains were long a barrier between eastern and western Vermont, and judgeships and political candidates often were chosen with an eastern and western sectionalism in mind. Although regional division is now a minor factor, some observers detect it emerging between southern and northern Vermont, presumably a reflection of the south's influx of newcomers and resort developments. Others sense a dichotomy involving small towns and large towns, which revolves around such public issues as state constitutional reforms, welfare aid, and educational innovations. Three isolated northeastern counties have for some time been known as the "Northeast Kingdom." Pragmatically, however, the major sense of regionalism is derived from large towns and their shopping facilities, newspapers and broadcasting media, and related services, all of which form a centre for surrounding rural areas.

The people. Because so many Vermonters are descended from early Americans of Protestant background and English heritage, the people of the state are almost prototypical Yankees. There is scarcely a town in Vermont that does not have a white-frame Protestant church on its village green or main street. Virtually every Protestant sect is represented in Vermont, with a heavy concentration of Presbyterians in the Caledonia County area of northeastern Vermont. The name Caledonia, the Roman designation for northern Britain, was part of the heritage brought by the Scottish immigrants who first settled the region in the 1770s.

In 1848, when railroads were first built in Vermont, a large number of Irish immigrants were hired as labourers. Many of their descendants live today in Rutland, Burlington, St. Albans, and other large towns. During the 1900s French Canadians from Quebec Province settled in the state, many of them in the woollen-mill town of Winooski, and others on farms along the northern border. Immigrants from northern Italy carried with them centuries of quarrying and stone-carving tradition to Barre and other granite-producing areas. They have given Barre a character quite different from what the visitor expects to find in a Vermont city. Other quarry workers from Spain settled in the Barre-Montpelier area. Many Welshmen worked in the slate mines of western Vermont because they were familiar with this type of mining in their native land. The library of the Vermont Historical Society in Montpelier contains a journal written in Welsh that was kept by a Vermont soldier who fought in the Civil War. Immigrants from Poland sought work in Brattleboro, Springfield, and other manufacturing towns. The slight need for industrial labour, and the rural character of the state, have attracted few blacks from the nation's South, and they number less than one-half of 1 percent of the population. The Roman Catholic diocese of Burlington includes all of Vermont, and in the late 20th century Roman Catholics made up about one-third of Vermont's total population.

Vermonters continue their long-standing pattern of leaving the state in order to find employment elsewhere. This tiny state has produced many leaders of U.S. business and political life. Frederick Billings, for example, built the Northern Pacific Railway; Joseph Smith and Brigham Young led the Mormon Church; and Moses Hazeltine Sherman was the realtor who developed Hollywood, California. Presidents Chester A. Arthur and Calvin Coolidge were born, respectively, in Fairfield and Plymouth, and both parents of President Rutherford B. Hayes were Vermonters who migrated to Ohio. The Taft family, famous in U.S. statesmanship, traces its Ohio origins to Vermonter Alphonso Taft, who left Townshend and settled in Cincinnati.

The economy. Farming has declined as family farms have been combined into larger units, and an increasing number of farmers have been unable to modernize their equipment and expand their herds. Labour is not generally well organized in the state, and the cost of many services is relatively low.

Industry. Vermont's approximately 1,000 manufacturing plants also reflect national industrial trends. Machine-tool plants in Springfield tend to expand and retract along with the national economy. The St. Albans area in Franklin County has especially suffered from the decline of the railroad industry, and in 1980 Franklin and Orleans counties had the state's highest rates of unemployment. Textile mills were once major employers in many cities, such as Winooski, but many of these have closed or moved to the South. Some computer industries have moved into Vermont. Other Vermont firms have become subsidiaries of national firms.

Many Vermont industries are small companies that provide specialized products. Fishing rods from Manchester have been known among sports enthusiasts since 1855. Wood and paper products are natural for a state so heavily timbered, and about one-third of Vermont's manufacturing plants make bowls, hockey sticks, furniture, and paper of different kinds. Printing is among the major industries.

Mining. Extractive industries contribute significantly to Vermont's economy. Quarries in Barre are among the largest granite pits in the world; and marble from Proctor is used for constructing commercial and public buildings—outstanding examples include the U.S. Supreme Court building in Washington, D.C., and the United Nations headquarters in New York City. Asbestos is mined in the north central section, and slate quarries operate along the Vermont–New York border.

Tourism. Vacation resorts, motels and hotels, and related tourist services employ many thousands of Vermonters. Massive skiing facilities at Stowe and the Mad River Valley are among the many Vermont winter resorts that attract people from throughout the Northeast. During the summer visitors search through antique shops, study exhibits in the many museums, attend musical and dramatic performances, or simply drive through the state and take photographs.

Governmental participation. The state's department of development and community affairs searches constantly for new industry, while an industrial park authority offers site guidelines. The travel-information office of the former is active in promoting tourism, and its *Vermont Life* magazine depicts the state's scenic resources.

Transportation. Passenger service ceased on Vermont's

(margin notes)

Rainfall and temperature

Regionalism

Ethnic and religious groups

Famous emigrants

Attractions for visitors

railroads in 1966 but was resumed on a limited basis by Amtrak in 1971. Airline service is also limited. The major transportation arteries are north–south routes in the Connecticut River Valley and the lowland valley south of Lake Champlain. Elsewhere, roads are often winding, narrow, and hilly, following the contours of the land they cross. None of these factors is conducive to industrial expansion, and transportation remains a major problem.

Administrative and social conditions. *Government.* On July 8, 1777, Vermont adopted a constitution, the first in the United States to prohibit slavery. It was revised in 1786, and in 1793 the present constitution was adopted. The amending process is long and awkward, and amendments may be considered only once every ten years. Voters are required to take a "freeman's oath," a holdover from colonial America, and to be "of a quiet and peaceable behavior."

The governor of Vermont is elected for a two-year term in November of even-numbered years. Incumbent governors may run for reelection as often as they like. An unwritten two-term limitation was broken in 1966, however, when Philip H. Hoff ran for, and was elected to, a third consecutive term. Members of the General Assembly also serve two-year terms; the House of Representatives and the Senate ordinarily sit from January to April of each year. The House has 150 members, and the Senate 30. Prior to reapportionment in 1965, the 246-member House consisted of one representative from each of the state's 238 towns and eight cities, regardless of their size. Vermont has only one member of the U.S. House of Representatives.

The judicial system in Vermont is headed by the Supreme Court. Beneath it there is a county court in each of the 14 counties, 14 municipal courts, justices of the peace in the towns, and probate courts in 19 districts. The Supreme Court has five justices who, together with justices of the county courts, are elected by the General Assembly. Municipal judges are appointed by the governor, and all other judges, including two assistant judges in each county, are elected by the people.

Vermont is town-meeting country. Every year on the first Tuesday in March, voters throughout the state meet in their town halls or community buildings to debate the town budget and other topics, and to elect local officials for the coming year. Because most communities are small and the state is compact, Vermonters have fairly direct access to elected officials, as well as ample opportunities to voice their opinions publicly on dominant issues.

Repub-
lican
tradition
Vermont has been one of the most Republican states in the Union, but during the late 20th century a balance between the two major U.S. parties began to develop in state politics.

Welfare. There is a state mental hospital at Waterbury and a state prison at Windsor. The state also maintains facilities for the mentally retarded and for juvenile offenders. In 1969 the state assumed responsibility for administering welfare programs, which formerly had been supervised by an "overseer of the poor" in each town.

Education. Vermont strongly supports its schools. Locally elected boards govern all primary and secondary education, while the state provides for much of the funding, teacher training and certification, and for various special programs in such areas as vocational training, arts and crafts, and rehabilitation.

Higher
education
The state system of higher education includes the University of Vermont (chartered in 1791) in Burlington and a number of liberal arts colleges, vocational schools, and other colleges. In addition, there are several outstanding private colleges and junior colleges. The school of languages and the writers' workshops at Middlebury College (1800) in Middlebury and Bread Loaf are known internationally. Bennington College (1932), a women's college, is famous for its fine arts programs and for the major figures in all fields of the arts that regularly serve on its faculty. Marlboro College (1947) is noted for its work in the performing arts and for its summer music festivals.

Cultural life. Vermont enjoys a vigorous cultural life despite its rural and small-town character. Many artists and scholars have followed such famous literary figures as novelist Sinclair Lewis and poet Robert Frost in maintaining vacation homes in the state. Painters find inspiration in the Vermont landscape, and sculptors adapt old materials and forms from rural barns and antique shops to contemporary uses. Among the major galleries in Vermont are the Robert Hull Fleming Museum at the University of Vermont, the Southern Vermont Art Center in Manchester, the Miller Art Center in Springfield, the Chaffee Art Gallery in Rutland, the Wood Art Gallery in Montpelier, and the Bundy Art Gallery in Waitsfield.

Practitioners of various folk arts are numerous, and the state operates an arts-and-crafts service to aid in marketing. The Vermont Council on the Arts and the Vermont Historical Society often sponsor demonstrations by artists and craftsmen. Vermont has a rich heritage of folk music. In warm weather Vermont is vibrant with music and drama, including the annual Marlboro Music Festival. The Craftsbury Chamber Players attract large audiences. Summer theatre is popular in Stowe, Winooski Park, Weston, Dorset, and elsewhere in the state. The Vermont State Symphony Orchestra was the first in the nation to receive a legislative appropriation. The University of Vermont sponsors cultural events in Burlington and other communities, and lectures, films, and concerts are offered frequently by Vermont's other colleges and universities.

Vermont is proud of the way it preserves its heritage. The Shelburne Museum is called "The Museum of the American Spirit" because its historic buildings on 45 acres (18 hectares) contain a wealth of early artifacts and furnishings. The Bennington Museum contains the first "Stars and Stripes," a collection of the primitive-style paintings of Anna Mary Robertson ("Grandma") Moses, and specimens produced by the large Bennington pottery industry. In Montpelier the Vermont Historical Society has created a museum inside a reconstructed Victorian landmark on the statehouse green. The Fairbanks Museum in St. Johnsbury is famous for its natural history displays. Vermont has more than 50 local historical societies and statewide groups, such as the Vermont Archaeological Society and the Green Mountain Folklore Society.

Vermont has more than 100 covered bridges, most of which were constructed before 1912 and are protected by state law. The 1975 state legislature created a state division for historic preservation, which maintains about 50 buildings, including the Bennington Battle Monument, the Old Constitution House at Windsor, and the birthplace and family homestead of Calvin Coolidge at Plymouth. The State House in Montpelier is considered the state's most important historic site.

HISTORY

Exploration and settlement. The first inhabitants of Vermont were Indian tribes that hunted wild animals and travelled on the waterways and footpaths of the region. In 1609 the French explorer Samuel de Champlain discovered a lake there to which he gave his name. The first permanent European settlement was established by the French in 1666 on Isle La Motte, an island in northern Lake Champlain. The name Vermont, derived from the French *vert* and *mont* ("green mountains"), was applied to the region because of the thick coniferous growth that kept its mountains green year-round. During the late 17th and early 18th centuries, Vermont served as a route for French and Indian incursions from Canada into Massachusetts, including raids on Deerfield in 1675 and 1704.

In 1724 the Dutch established a community in Pownal, and the first English-speaking settlers erected Fort Dummer on the Connecticut River near present-day Brattleboro. When the British won the French and Indian War (1754–63), the land was opened to settlement. At the time the Revolution began in 1775, about 20,000 people were living in Vermont. Many Vermont towns bear the names of the Connecticut and Massachusetts towns from which the early settlers came.

Revolution and statehood. Although the region was explored long before the landing of the Pilgrims and was settled before the American Revolution, it began its early development not as a chartered royal colony but as a territory, the possession of which was disputed by New Hampshire and New York. In the decade before the Revolution, disputes—frequently armed conflicts—arose when land grants by New Hampshire conflicted with similar grants issued by New York. Many early settlers joined units of the Green Mountain Boys, led by Ethan Allen, and repulsed the "Yorkers" who tried to control Vermont. Later, when the American Revolution began, the same Green Mountain Boys also asserted their independence from England. Their successful assault on Fort Ticonderoga, on the New York side of Lake Champlain in May 1775, has been called the first offensive action of the Revolution. In 1777 the Vermonters created an independent republic—first as New Connecticut, then as Vermont—and they remained independent until they joined the Union on March 4, 1791, thus becoming the 14th state.

Growth in the early 19th century

Vermont grew from about 85,500 inhabitants in 1790 to about 218,000 in 1810; but by the 1830s, Vermonters had departed in large numbers for the expanding cities and the more fertile lands to the south and west. The opening of the Erie Canal from Albany, New York, to Lake Erie in 1825, and later additional improvements in transportation hastened this emigration. More than 39,000 Vermonters fought in the Civil War. Vermont became the site of the only Civil War action north of Pennsylvania when, on October 19, 1864, a band of Confederates raided St. Albans, robbing the banks and escaping back into Canada.

Post-Civil War period and after. Many veterans left Vermont after the war because the state provided inadequate natural power for industrialization and urbanization or because greater opportunities for individual advance-

ment were available elsewhere. The rural character of the state was thus assured.

After the Civil War, too, the attention of Vermonters returned to domestic affairs. In 1870 the governor's term was increased from one to two years and legislative sessions became biennial. Ninety years later the legislature held an unprecedented adjourned session. A state court reorganization in 1906 relieved the supreme court justices from riding circuit to preside over the 14 county courts, by providing for six superior judges to perform this service. During the late 1880s the expansion in activities of state government increased. The state Board of Health was organized in 1886, and the office of state highway commissioner was created in 1897. State administration was centralized in Montpelier in 1917, a departmental organization was created in 1923, numerous separate agencies were added during the following three and one-half decades, and in 1960 a general reorganization was ordered by the legislature; this last was highlighted by creation of a Department of Administration. Central purchasing dates from 1912, a budget system was developed during the period 1917 to 1923, and a personnel system following World War II. After World War II, the state carried out a comprehensive program of road construction and park development.

In presidential campaigns the state has been Federalist, 1792–1800; Democratic-Republican, 1804–20; Adams-Republican, 1824–28; Anti-Masonic, 1832; Whig, 1836–1852; and Republican from 1856 except in 1964 when it voted Democratic. (C.T.Mo./Ed.)

MIDDLE ATLANTIC REGION

The Middle Atlantic region—including New York, New Jersey, Pennsylvania, Maryland, Delaware, and the District of Columbia—has much in common with New England: it has a considerable amount of poor land, concentration of population in metropolitan centres, and more emphasis on a skilled labour force as a base for industrial prosperity than on raw materials. It also has several advantages over New England: proximity to coal, cement rock, and slate; easier access to the interior of the continent; and larger areas of good farmland with a somewhat longer growing season. The eastern focus of U.S. business developed here; and, in the latter part of the 20th century, the region accounted for nearly one-fourth of all U.S. income.

The high degree of development of this region arose primarily from its position as a gateway to the midcontinent. Geographically this seems paradoxical, for the Appalachian ridges, running parallel to the coast, cut off the coastal plain from the interior. Gaps in the mountains, however, were cut by rivers flowing transverse to the grain of the country, and these rivers terminate in estuaries offering commodious harbours. New York City, with the best of these harbours, is connected inland up the Hudson, navigable by many ocean-going ships as far as Albany. West of Albany, the glacier-broadened Mohawk Valley provided a convenient site for the New York State Barge Canal, successor to the Erie Canal, which connects with the Great Lakes. Philadelphia, more fortunate than New York City in its immediate agricultural hinterland, had to lay out a more difficult trans-Appalachian route up the Susquehanna tributaries and across the Allegheny front to the navigable headwaters of the Ohio River. Baltimore found a similarly difficult route up the Potomac Valley.

Agriculturally, the Middle Atlantic region possesses more level or gently rolling land than New England. The Atlantic coastal plain offers broad areas of sandy soil, suitable, when fertilized, for vegetables. The red soils of the Piedmont lend themselves to dairying and poultry raising and, in the more favoured spots, to corn, wheat, and tobacco. The interior valleys specialize in dairying and fruits. Most of these areas are not naturally fertile; they are passable farmlands made profitable by their proximity to metropolitan markets.

Mega-lopolis

The chain of cities extending from Boston to Washington, D.C., has been called Megalopolis, or the Atlantic

metropolitan belt. Industrial centres, commercial centres, and residential suburbs here merge into one another. The focus of this metropolitan belt is the New York metropolis. One-fifth of all U.S. import tonnage enters through New York, and a good percentage of U.S. manufactures originate there. New York is a leader in such diverse fields as banking, finance, education, fashion, the theatre, publishing, and clothing manufacture, to name only a few. Other cities in the Middle Atlantic region specialize in somewhat heavier industries—for example, steel manufacturing at Bethlehem and Morrisville, Pennsylvania. Baltimore and Philadelphia, while priding themselve on their financial and cultural activities, are more heavily industrialized than New York. Washington, of course, is almost exclusively a governmental centre.

Although the interior contains almost empty lands comparable to the resort areas of New England, there are also scattered small industrial cities. Special note should be made of those along the New York State Barge Canal: Albany, Schenectady, Utica, Syracuse, and Rochester, all of which produce a wide assortment of manufactures. If the region as a whole can be characterized, it is as a closely knit network of towns subdivided by strips of semiwilderness. (O.P.S./Ed.)

Delaware

The first of the original 13 U.S. states to ratify the federal Constitution, Delaware occupies a small niche in the Boston–Washington, D.C., urban corridor along the Middle Atlantic Seaboard. With 2,057 square miles (5,328 square kilometres) it is the second smallest state in the nation (after Rhode Island), and it is one of the most densely populated states. Most of its people live in the north around Wilmington, where its industry is concentrated and where the major coastal highways and railways pass through from Pennsylvania and New Jersey on the north and east into Maryland on the south and west. The rest of the state comprises the northeastern corner of the Delmarva Peninsula, which it shares with Maryland and Virginia.

Overview of the state

Historically, geographically, and economically, Delaware has its closest ties with Pennsylvania, particularly Philadelphia, where the Delaware River and other transportation arteries direct its commerce. The state's three counties—New Castle, Kent, and Sussex—had been established by 1680, and, except for periods during the Revolution and the Civil War, its history has been placid. Stability and conservatism became characteristics of Delaware, especially in the southern areas, which until 1964 had maintained a grip on political life vastly out of proportion to their population. As a result, old institutions were tenaciously preserved.

The manufacturing complex in the north makes Delaware one of the most industrialized states, especially notable for chemical research. The state is often depicted as being dominated by corporations, especially by the vast du Pont industrial empire, but the industrial wealth of the Wilmington area was balanced by the political overrepresentation of the agricultural downstate region until the mid-1960s. All factions have united to perpetuate liberal incorporation laws that encourage many U.S. businesses to make Delaware their nominal home state.

PHYSICAL AND HUMAN GEOGRAPHY

Geographical regions and drainage

The land. *Relief.* With the exception of Florida, Delaware, located mainly within the Atlantic Coastal Plain, is the lowest lying state in the nation. A long sand beach forms the state's ocean front, stretching from the Maryland line, at Fenwick Island, to Cape Henlopen, at the mouth of Delaware Bay. Only one major break, Indian River Inlet, occurs along the 23-mile (37-kilometre) length of that beach. Much of the beach is a low bar between the ocean and a series of lagoons or shallow bays; but at Bethany Beach, near the southern boundary, and again at Rehoboth, near the northern end of the beach, the mainland reaches directly to the ocean.

The shoreline of Delaware Bay is often marshy. The mouths of tributary streams like the Murderkill, the Mispillion, and the St. Jones are so shallow that no good harbours exist except at Lewes, just inside Cape Henlopen, where an artificial harbour protects shipping from Atlantic storms. Farther north, on the banks of the Delaware River, spots of high, dry land appear, as at Port Penn, New Castle, and Edge Moor; but the state's main port, Wilmington, lies on the Christina River, a tributary of the Delaware.

Most of Delaware is drained by streams that run eastward to the Delaware River, Delaware Bay, and the Atlantic Ocean, but the Nanticoke River and its tributaries in southwestern Delaware flow into Chesapeake Bay. So does the Pocomoke River, which drains the Cypress Swamp, or so-called Burnt Swamp, in the extreme south of Delaware athwart the Maryland line.

Most of the coastal plain terrain is fertile and level, seldom more than 60 feet (18 metres) above sea level, but it becomes increasingly sandy to the south. Abundant woodlands, streams, and freshwater ponds interrupt the monotony of the landscape. Occasionally, as at Odessa, villages appear suddenly at the side of the road, with no more warning than the sight of a church steeple.

Near its northern edge the plain is intersected by a great deep ditch, the Chesapeake and Delaware Canal, which has been deepened and straightened for ocean shipping. It shortens the water route between Philadelphia and Baltimore by several hundred miles and also brings Baltimore closer to the ocean than via Chesapeake Bay. The canal is popularly considered to be the boundary between agricultural downstate Delaware and the northern industrial region. Though the land on either side of it is strikingly similar, many Delawareans are convinced that even the weather changes at the canal.

Several high bridges over the canal, as well as the giant twin bridges crossing the Delaware River north of New Castle and the refinery stacks at Delaware City, serve as the major landmarks on the horizon below the hillier northwest corner of the state. There, north and west of a 14-mile line between Wilmington and Newark, lie the rolling hills of a section of the Piedmont extending south from Pennsylvania. The significance of this area belies its size—less than one-fifteenth of the state's total area—for within it and at its edge dwells most of Delaware's population. The highest point in the state, Elbright Road in New Castle County, is only 442 feet (135 metres) above sea level. Probably the most peculiar features are Iron and Chestnut hills, which protrude into the plain southwest of Newark and are scarred by open pits where iron ore once was mined.

The centre of Wilmington lies on hills sloping downward toward the intersection of the Christina and its major tributary, the Brandywine. Here, navigable water brought shipping close to falls that provided power for manufacturing. The railroads and highways, which followed this fall line along the East Coast, have kept Wilmington on major transportation routes between Philadelphia and Baltimore and have promoted the tendency for the urbanization of open land between Wilmington and other cities.

Climate. The climate of Delaware is like that of the rest of the Middle Atlantic area. August, which has the second hottest temperatures after July, is also the rainiest month, with an average precipitation of about $5\frac{1}{2}$ inches (140 millimetres), whereas February has the least precipitation, an average of almost three inches. The yearly average precipitation is nearly 45 inches (1,140 millimetres).

The people. As is characteristic of the Middle Atlantic states, the colonial population of Delaware was quite varied. Swedes (and the Finns who came with them), Netherlanders, and African slaves had settled in Delaware before the English, mainly in present-day New Castle County in the north. The English settlers came not only from overseas but also from Pennsylvania and Maryland. Some of the settlers from Pennsylvania were Quaker artisans and merchants; the settlers from Maryland were often planters who brought slaves with them. With the English came some Welsh settlers and, after 1715, large numbers of Irish, particularly the Presbyterians of Scottish descent known as Scots-Irish. Downstate Delaware was mainly settled by the English and by slaves.

After the Revolution a small group of French came to New Castle and Wilmington from the West Indies, and a few, including the progenitors of the du Pont family, came from France. In the mid-19th century there was a large immigration of Roman Catholic Irish and Germans, and at the end of the century Italians, Poles, and Jews came in large numbers, accompanied by smaller groups of Ukrainians, Russians, Scandinavians, and Greeks. These newcomers settled mainly in Wilmington.

Demography. Though federal laws reduced the flow of immigrants after World War I, Delaware experienced its largest population growth in the middle of the 20th century. From 1950 to 1960 its population grew by about 40 percent, but the rate declined thereafter. Many of the newcomers were highly skilled scientists or technicians. Wilmington also received a large influx of blacks, many of them unskilled.

Process of suburbanization

The suburbs of Wilmington, largely unincorporated, received not only the people fleeing Wilmington but also most of the white newcomers to Delaware after 1945. By the late 20th century, more than half of the state's population lived outside the city of Wilmington but within commuting distance of it. This suburban band includes the second largest city, Newark. Thus, suburbia has become the seat of Delaware's population, political power, and wealth. Suburban areas generally were populated by whites but with a few black enclaves. The descendants of the later immigrant groups have left the city as hastily as have the Anglo-Saxon Protestants.

Interesting ethnic groups in rural Delaware include Polish potato growers in Kent, who came from Long Island; Italian mushroom growers at Hockessin; a colony of Finns that originated at Iron Hill after World War I; an Amish settlement near Dover; and the historic groups of mixed-bloods, called Moors and Nanticokes, at Cheswold, in Kent County, and beside Indian River Bay, in Sussex County.

The economy. Delaware's prosperity depends upon its favourable location: four of the 10 largest cities in the United States lie within 150 miles (240 kilometres).

Agriculture. Though the number of farmers has continued to decline, agriculture remains important. More than half of the farmers' cash income comes from poultry raising, centred in Sussex County. Soybeans are of continuing importance, and other major agricultural products include

Agriculture and manufacturing

corn, milk, and vegetables. The coastal and inland waters produce fish, clams, and crabs. The only mining is of gravel and sand.

Industry. The major economic enterprise in Delaware is manufacturing, especially the chemical industry. Wilmington boasts of being the chemical capital of the world because it is the centre of administration and research of several chemical companies; du Pont, Hercules, and ICI Americas (formerly Atlas) are the largest. Chief chemical products are pigments, nylon, and petrochemicals. Delaware also has automobile-assembly plants, an oil refinery, a synthetic rubber plant, packaging plants, textile mills, and various food-processing plants.

Taxation. In the public sector, because of Delaware's small size, many things are done by the state that elsewhere would be left to local government. Consequently, state taxes and indebtedness are relatively high, whereas local equivalents are low. The largest source of state income is the tax on personal and corporate incomes. There is a state inheritance tax, which frequently produces a windfall when a very wealthy citizen dies.

The second most important source of state revenue is the corporation franchise tax. Delaware has made a business of incorporating companies, many of which operate primarily in other states, since early in the 20th century. It offers them favourable laws that are kept up to date to reflect changing business conditions, a convenient location, very moderate taxation, stable institutions, and a judicial system with experience in corporate litigation.

There is no general sales tax in Delaware and no state property tax. Real estate taxes are, however, the chief support of county and municipal governments. Though the schools are supported chiefly by the state, school districts must raise part of the money for new buildings by property and other taxes, after approval by a referendum. They may also, again with voter approval, raise money to supplement the state appropriation for school operations, including salaries.

Transportation. The chief flow of highway traffic in Delaware is between Wilmington and its suburbs and the interstate traffic crossing northern Delaware between New York or Philadelphia and Baltimore or Washington. Slightly less important is the traffic up and down the state on the du Pont Highway. The state maintains all roads and bridges as well as through streets in municipalities. A joint Delaware–New Jersey agency operates both the twin bridges across the Delaware River near New Castle and a ferry between Lewes and Cape May.

Delaware lies on the railroad passenger line between Philadelphia and Baltimore. Freight service is also available to the southern state line and in northern Delaware. Local bus transportation in the Wilmington area is provided by a public authority. Wilmington has a marine terminal and an airport.

Administrative and social conditions. *Government.* The constitution of Delaware was adopted in 1897 but has been amended many times. Amendments require a two-thirds vote in two successive legislatures, with an election intervening. The governor, who has no veto on amendments, serves a four-year term and may be reelected only once. Traditionally, the legislature has been strong and the governor relatively weak, but adoption of the cabinet form of government in 1970 centralized and strengthened executive authority. The bicameral legislature is known as the General Assembly.

An unusual feature of Delaware's judicial system is the retention of the Court of Chancery, which handles equity cases involving civil rights and litigation concerning Delaware corporations. Most other states have merged their chancery into their law courts. The highest court is the Supreme Court, which hears appeals from the Chancery Court and the Superior Court. At the lowest level in the state judiciary are the magistrate courts, presided over by justices of the peace, who seldom are lawyers. All Delaware judges are appointed by the governor.

Weak county governments have traditionally been the rule in Delaware. Each was headed by an elected levy court that set the tax rate and appropriated funds. The levy courts of New Castle and Sussex, however, have been replaced by stronger elected councils, and New Castle also elects a county executive who appoints the chief administrative officers. Unique to Delaware is the county subdivision known as a hundred, an ancient English governmental unit that has survived nowhere else in the United States. It no longer has a governmental function and is retained purely as a geographical name.

Democrats and Republicans have been fairly evenly matched in Delaware, although the Democrats have the larger number of registered voters. Many voters decline to list party preference, and numerous swing votes may go to either side. Primaries had little significance until 1978, when they were first used for all offices.

After the Civil War, Delaware Democrats used their control of such offices as assessor and tax collector to discourage blacks from qualifying as voters, but Republicans actively sought the black vote and, with its aid, won control of the state early in the 20th century. In 1932 the Democrats abandoned their all-white tradition. At first they won black votes only for the national ticket, but gradually, during the next two decades, Delaware's blacks, like those in other Northern states, realigned themselves with the Democratic Party. Thereafter, only an exceptionally popular Republican was able to win black support. Bipartisan black support was largely responsible for passage of a fair-housing law.

The black voter

Welfare. Delaware maintained racial segregation by both custom and law until the 1950s, when court decisions began to strike down old laws separating the races, as well as acts of discrimination in housing and public accommodations. Integration was accomplished fairly smoothly in many schools, including the University of Delaware and Delaware State College, the latter integrating whites into a formerly all-black student body. In 1977 the 3rd Circuit Court of Appeals ordered the 11 New Castle school districts consolidated into one in order to implement desegregation plans. Federal programs to assist the poor home buyer helped blacks move into vacated housing; some of these blacks earlier had been dispossessed by urban-renewal projects. Even with such programs and the end of legal discrimination, social pressure and economic realities have served to maintain some degree of segregation in education and housing. In Wilmington school integration and fair-housing laws have had the effect of accelerating the number of whites leaving the city.

The state, meanwhile, has been called upon to provide an increasing number of services for its citizens. The demands for expenditures, especially in education and welfare, have been brought on partly by population growth and immigration of young families with children, and partly by recognition of long-ignored needs. Kindergartens, schools for the handicapped, and mental-health clinics have been established. Delaware ranked in the upper half of the states in per capita expenditures for public welfare.

Social services and special schools

Education. The University of Delaware grew from 1,500 students in 1952 to about 20,000 in the late 20th century. Because the small population would make the establishment of a medical school a heavy expense, the state has arrangements with Jefferson Medical College of Philadelphia to save places in each class for Delaware students. Similar arrangements are made for veterinary students and in fields like law and dentistry in which no training is offered in Delaware's public institutions. The state government, not smaller units, assumes the major responsibility for public education.

Cultural life. Two major museums are located in the outskirts of Wilmington. The Henry Francis du Pont Winterthur Museum is noted for its collection of American decorative arts, which are displayed in authentic period rooms. The Hagley Museum portrays the development of American manufacturing through preservations of the early mills and other structures of the du Pont company, as well as by indoor exhibits. Other interesting museums include the Delaware Museum of Natural History, Greenville; the Delaware State Museum, Dover; and the Old Town Hall, Wilmington.

A number of historic houses in the state are permanently open to the public, including the John Dickinson Mansion, near Dover; the Parson Thorne Mansion, in

Historic buildings, houses, and colonial capitol

Milford; and several houses in Odessa and New Castle. Several blocks in New Castle surrounding the colonial capitol, known as the Old Court House, remind visitors of the restorations of colonial Williamsburg in Virginia—except that in New Castle very few buildings had to be restored. Immanuel Episcopal Church, on the Green, was begun in 1703; its graveyard contains numerous interesting stones. The Presbyterian Church nearby dates from 1707. No buildings survive from the Dutch period. Old Swedes Church and Hendrickson House in Wilmington were built in 1698 for a Swedish Lutheran congregation, but it is now Episcopalian. The Swedes brought a tradition of log construction to the New World, but none of their work remains except, perhaps, portions of a few small log structures.

The state's foremost research library is that of the University of Delaware. The Wilmington Institute Free Library is the largest unit in the consolidated New Castle County library system. The Delaware State Library Commission serves the lower counties; and most towns also support a library of their own. Among the specialized libraries, the Eleutherian Mills Historical Library, featuring business and industrial history, and the library division of the Winterthur Museum, specializing in the decorative arts and crafts, are internationally known.

Wilmington long has been the centre of a distinguished group of illustrators, many of them pupils, either directly or indirectly, of Howard Pyle, whose work is displayed at the Delaware Art Museum. N.C. Wyeth, a pupil of Pyle, made his home just across the Pennsylvania line at Chadds Ford, which members of his family have made famous as the home of the Brandywine school, a group of mainly genre and narrative painters.

Wilmington has a legitimate theatre, the Playhouse, as well as the Grand Opera House, restored as a state centre for the performing arts. The small village of Arden is remarkable for its theatrical traditions, both amateur and professional, which include annual productions of Gilbert and Sullivan operettas and, until recently, of Shakespeare by the townspeople.

Delaware's ocean beaches are popular not only with Delawareans but also with people from neighbouring areas, especially Washington, D.C. Rehoboth and Indian River bays are boating, fishing, and clamming centres. State parks, such as Lum's Pond, are also used for recreation. The week-long Delaware State Fair is held annually in Harrington. Pari-mutuel betting lures crowds to racetracks in Stanton, Dover, and Brandywine Hundred.

HISTORY

The colony. The Dutch who established the first European settlement in Delaware at Lewes in 1631 were killed by Indians, and it was not until 1638 that a permanent settlement was planted—by Swedes at Ft. Christina, now Wilmington; they reputedly erected America's first log cabins in this colony of New Sweden. The Dutch from New Amsterdam (New York) conquered the Swedes in 1655, and the English seized the colony from the Dutch in 1664. Thereafter, except for a brief Dutch reconquest in 1673, Delaware was administered as part of New York until 1682, when the Duke of York, acting as proprietor, ceded it to William Penn, who wanted it so that his colony of Pennsylvania could have access to the ocean. Though he tried to unite the Delaware counties with Pennsylvania, both sides resented union. In 1704 he allowed Delaware an assembly of its own. Pennsylvania and Delaware shared a royal governor until the Revolution. Only in 1776 did the name Delaware—deriving from Sir Thomas West, 12th baron De La Warr, a governor of Virginia—become official, though it had been applied to the bay in 1610 and gradually thereafter to the adjoining land.

Revolution and statehood. During the Revolution, Delaware was invaded by a British army en route to Philadelphia and was constantly menaced by British ships. The event best remembered, however, is the spectacular ride (July 1–2, 1776) of Caesar Rodney from his home to Philadelphia to break a tie in the Delaware delegation and cast Delaware's vote for independence. The proudest boast of Delaware is that its speedy ratification of the Constitution, on December 7, 1787, gave Delaware its right to be called "the first state."

As national political parties arose, Delaware became a Federalist state, adhering to the party of Alexander Hamilton and John Adams well into the 1820s. In the next period Delaware became as fervently Whig as it had been Federalist. *19th-century political sentiments*

Civil War and aftermath. The advent of the Civil War did not seriously tempt Delaware to secession. Nominally, Delaware had been slave territory since its days as a Dutch colony, but the number of slaves had declined drastically, mainly through voluntary manumissions (grants of freedom), from 8,900 in 1790 to 1,800 in 1860. A more important consideration was Delaware's economic bond with Pennsylvania and the North, strengthened by the river trade and the new railroad network. Though Unionist in sentiment, Delaware never voted for Lincoln, and the Reconstruction that followed the Civil War drove many voters to the Democratic Party in sympathy with the occupied South. By the end of the 19th century, however, economic realities had regained importance, and Delaware became firmly Republican and remained such until well into the Great Depression of the 1930s.

For over a century, underrepresentation in the legislature was a standing complaint in Wilmington and New Castle County. At first the three counties were about equal in population and had equal membership in the unicameral colonial assembly and the bicameral legislature of the national period. With the increasing industrialization of the Wilmington area, New Castle County overtook the others in terms of population by 1820 and has lengthened its lead ever since. The amended constitution of 1853 provided for proportional representation in the lower house, but this constitution was rejected by the voters. By 1890 New Castle had 58 percent of the state's population—more than the other two counties combined. The constitution of 1897 gave additional representation to the city of Wilmington, but even at the time the city's population was more than 60,000, compared with less than 40,000 for each of the county units. The urban north, populous, wealthy and traditionally liberal, could still be outvoted in the legislature by the rural and traditionally conservative south.

It was not until 1964 that the legislature, under pressure from the U.S. Supreme Court, enacted a sweeping reapportionment, giving suitable representation to Wilmington and its suburbs, with a provision for revision every 10 years. The legislature met in January 1965 with New Castle County having two-thirds of the membership of both houses. In 1967 the plan was ruled unconstitutional by a federal court because of some inequalities in districting. A new reapportionment plan, prepared by computers, was approved by the legislature in January 1968.

Economic growth. Wilmington, meanwhile, had become a manufacturing city so populous that by 1920 it contained not only half of the state's population but also at least a similar proportion of its wealth and economic energy. Diversity characterized the products of Wilmington factories, but in the 20th century the city became renowned as an administrative centre for the nation's chemical industry. Primarily, this meant E.I. du Pont de Nemours & Company and two other powder makers, Hercules Inc. and Atlas Chemical Industries, Inc., all of which transferred their major energies to basic chemicals after World War I.   (J.A.Mu./Ed.)

District of Columbia

The District of Columbia is a U.S. federal district coterminous with the city of Washington, the capital of the United States. It currently lies wholly on the northeast bank of the Potomac River at the head of tide and navigation, 40 miles (64 kilometres) southwest of Baltimore, 135 miles (217 kilometres) southwest of Philadelphia, and 226 miles (364 kilometres) southwest of New York City. Its area is 67 square miles (174 square kilometres).

The climate of the district is characterized by frequent periods of high humidity, occasional periods of oppressive heat in summer, and moderately mild winters. The mean winter temperature (December, January, and February) is 35° F (1.5° C), and the mean summer temperature (June, July, and August) is 75° F (24° C). Extremes range, however, from a maximum of more than 105° F (40° C) to a minimum of below −15° F (−9.4° C).

Consti-
tutional
foundation
The United States was the first nation in the world to plan a capital exclusively for its seat of government. The site of the District of Columbia was authorized by the U.S. Constitution, which empowered Congress (Article I, section 8) "To exercise exclusive Legislation in all Cases whatsoever, over such District (not exceeding ten Miles square) as may, by Cession of Particular States, and the Acceptance of Congress, become the Seat of the Government of the United States, . . ." Congress on July 12, 1790, passed a bill for the creation of a national capital; and on January 24, 1791, Pres. George Washington sent a message to Congress stating that he had selected a site and directed commissioners "to survey and limit a part of the territory of the 10 miles square on both sides of the river Potomac," accepting territories from both Maryland and Virginia, including the town of Alexandria. Major Pierre Charles L'Enfant, a young French engineer who had served in the American Revolution, was commissioned to prepare a plan for the city. The cornerstone of the executive mansion, which later came to be called the White House, was laid on October 12, 1792. The cornerstone of the north wing of the Capitol was laid on September 18, 1793. In June 1800, Pres. John Adams and the staff of the federal government moved to the unfinished city from Philadelphia.

Initially laid out as a 10-mile square on both banks of the Potomac, the District of Columbia in 1846 lost the portion originally ceded by Virginia, including the city of Alexandria and what is now the county of Arlington, which were restored to Virginia. Both Alexandria and Georgetown had campaigned, for economic reasons, for separation from the federal enclave, but only Alexandria succeeded. Ever since 1846 the District of Columbia has consisted only of the former Maryland territory on the northeast bank of the river. Nevertheless, major federal buildings and landmarks associated with Washington were subsequently established on the Virginia side, including Arlington National Cemetery (1864) and the Pentagon (1942), headquarters of the U.S. Department of Defense.

For more detailed treatment of the city, see WASHINGTON, D.C. (Ed.)

Maryland

One of the original 13 states of the United States, Maryland lies at the centre of the Eastern seaboard, astride the great industrial–population complex that stretches from Maine to Virginia. Its small size—10,577 square miles (27,394 square kilometres), about 6 percent of which is water excluding Chesapeake Bay—belies the great diversity of its landscapes and of the ways of life that they foster: from the low-lying and water-oriented Eastern Shore and Chesapeake Bay area, through the metropolitan hurly-burly of Baltimore, its largest city, to the forested Appalachian foothills and mountains of its western reaches.

General
character
of the state
Maryland was named in honour of the wife of King Charles I by a grateful Cecil Calvert, Lord Baltimore, who in 1632 was granted charter for the land as a haven in which his fellow Roman Catholics might escape the restrictions placed on them in England. A deep sense of history still clings to many parts of the state, most notably in the quiet charm of Annapolis, its capital since 1694, and in the white-domed, pillared statehouse, built in 1772 and today the nation's oldest statehouse in continuous use. There, a 40-block area forms the city's Colonial Historic District, the largest in the United States. The narrow, crooked streets of Annapolis, the houses abutting directly on the brickwork sidewalks, the graceful tree-covered green about the statehouse, and the myriad masts of boats at dock or anchor in the harbour more reflect an earlier America than a state with a modern industrial economy.

Mason and
Dixon line
Geography, too, has provided Maryland a role in U.S. history, as a pivot between the North and the South. Its northern border with Pennsylvania is the famous Mason and Dixon Line, drawn in the 1760s to settle disputes between the Penn and Calvert families and traditionally regarded as the boundary between the North and the South. To the south much of the boundary with Virginia is formed by the Potomac River, a symbolic barrier during the Civil War, a contest in which the sentiments and the soil of Maryland were torn apart. On the north bank of the Potomac lies the District of Columbia, coterminous with the city of Washington, a small enclave ceded by Maryland in 1791 for the site of the national capital. East of the Chesapeake, the Eastern Shore shares the Delmarva Peninsula with Delaware on the north and Virginia on the south. In the mountainous west Maryland's panhandle, which is joined to the rest of the state by a narrow waist, forms an interlocking handclasp with the eastern panhandle of West Virginia.

PHYSICAL AND HUMAN GEOGRAPHY

The land. *Relief.* The Atlantic Coastal Plain covers about one-half of Maryland's land area, yielding to the Piedmont plateau at a fall line running from the tip of the District of Columbia through Baltimore and to near the northeastern corner of the state. The Catoctin ridgeline in the west forms the gateway to the Appalachians.

To the south, the Coastal Plain is sandy; to the north, it is loamy and fertile. Its water edges, called salt marshes, or wetlands, exasperate mapmakers as erosion periodically fills in a swamp or deletes an entire island; Blakistone, for example, is about one-tenth its 1634 size. The Chesapeake's 23 estuarial tributaries provide the state with some 3,200 miles (5,150 kilometres) of shoreline—subject to frequent change. The most important of nature-made revisions was an irruption of the ocean, during a storm in 1933, through Fenwick Island into Sinepuxent Bay, just below Ocean City. The lower portion of this barrier sand reef is now a national seashore and state park known as Assateague Island, and the inlet has become a boon to Ocean City's resort fishing fleet.

The Piedmont plateau has good farming soil except for belts of clay that are mined for brick kilns; from the beginning, the exteriors of Maryland buildings have glowed with salmon-coloured brick made from the state's clay. To the west and parallel to the fall line, the low Parr's Ridge forms a barrier between the Potomac and Chesapeake Bay.

Maryland's share of the Appalachian Mountains comprises a series of forested barriers, with many of the intervening valleys still uncleared. Backbone Mountain, hugging the West Virginia line, is the highest point in Maryland, at 3,360 feet (1,024 metres).

Climate. Maryland has two climates. It is continental in the west, with temperature records from −40° F (−40° C) to more than 100° F (38° C). In the east a humid subtropical climate is dependent on the Azores High, a pressure area that moderates the weather but does not prevent ice formation almost every winter on Chesapeake Bay's northern tributaries, summer calms as high as 107° F (42° C), and nearly 100 percent humidity. Ordinarily, rains are enough to make reservoirs overflow and to enable Baltimore and Washington, D.C., to draw all the needed soft water for drinking. Storms sweep in from the west and south, except in late summer, when the fringes of passing hurricanes often drench Maryland from the east.

Settlement patterns. The most salient feature of Maryland's topography is Chesapeake Bay, which serves the Port of Baltimore. The bay also divides the Eastern Shore from what was once called Maryland Main and adds picturesqueness to the Maine-to-Florida Inland Waterway; on a summer weekend as many as 100,000 sail and power boats may be seen on the water. But the bay has drawbacks. Swimmers shun its brackish, murky water after the late-summer onset of billions of small, stinging jellyfish; while the cross-bay bridges are often filled to capacity with the crush of summer weekenders going to and coming from the ocean beaches.

Chesa-
peake Bay

Dredging is necessary to maintain the 42-foot (13-metre) ship channel to Baltimore and to the Chesapeake and Delaware Canal. The bay also must be protected against the threat of pollution by the cities and industries in its drainage area. The bay once was lined with oysters, but silt and pollutants have pushed the diminished survivors into various tributary rivers. Nonetheless, the bay, which was called by the Baltimore sage H.L. Mencken a "great big outdoor protein factory," still affords a living to hundreds of watermen.

Sectionalism within Maryland is dictated by terrain. The Eastern Shore farmer concentrates on chickens, corn (maize), and soybeans. A mercantile appendage of Wilmington and Philadelphia until the bay was bridged, the nine-county Shore has become a vacation and retirement spot for the affluent, who appreciate the privacy of its flat, wooded, little-posted estate areas, serpentined with creeks, guts, necks, and inlets.

Southern Maryland's five counties have built a way of life around state government, tobacco-growing, and military installations. Prince George's County in suburban Washington has become Maryland's most populous county. A nuclear-power project at Calvert Cliffs attracted attention to the marine fossils of the Miocene Epoch, where the bay has exposed dense layers of shark teeth, whale vertebrae, mollusk shells, and other ocean-floor debris from possibly 15,000,000 years ago. These fossils are deemed the world's finest accessible deposit from that period.

Central Maryland comprises the city of Baltimore and five counties. Four of the counties contain most of Baltimore's suburbs, the fifth is Montgomery, on Washington, D.C.'s northwestern edge. By 1980 only about one-sixth of Marylanders lived outside Standard Metropolitan Statistical Areas (SMSA)—and central Maryland was one long, contiguous metropolitan area.

The four counties of western Maryland owe much to road, railroad, and canal builders. The barging of coal and grain ceased in 1924, but the creation of the Chesapeake and Ohio Canal National Historical Park in 1971 assured a stream of excursionists. Interstate and national roads carry city dwellers to Garrett County, where mountainside ski runs complement water sports on Deep Creek Lake, the largest man-made body of water in the state.

The people. The white population, at first all from the British Isles, began to vary when German-speaking farmers and artisans moved from Pennsylvania into western Maryland during the 1700s. The process accelerated after 1848 as Germans and German Jews fled military conscription, and then Russian Jews, Poles, Czechs, Italians, Greeks, and others arrived at Baltimore, which was a major 19th-century immigration centre, and later fanned out into the countryside. This ethnic diversity was one of the first characteristics that set Maryland apart from the regions below the Potomac River. Immediately after the Civil War, this diversity of the state was to some extent countered by an influx of Southerners, who despaired of life in a defeated and devastated homeland.

Maryland's Indian population had been killed off or pushed westward by about 1700. All that remains from their centuries of occupancy are the campsite artifacts, still being unearthed by professional and amateur archaeologists, and place-names, corrupted by uncomprehending whites, such as Chesapeake, Patapsco, Potomac, Wicomico, Patuxent, Piscataway, Susquehanna, and many others.

African slaves were at work in Maryland under the first Calverts. The consciences of many Marylanders, particularly members of the Society of Friends (Quakers), were uneasy; and from 1783 the importation of kidnapped Africans was under prohibitive state tax. While Maryland did not formally outlaw slavery until 1864, it protected the liberty of more free blacks than any other state as slavery neared its end. After the Civil War blacks found Maryland somewhat more congenial than the states of the Confederacy, in which, by 1900, systematic lifetime disfranchisement of blacks was under way. A corresponding effort in Maryland, led by the Democratic Party and coming to a head in 1910, was beaten in referendum by Republicans, with the aid of James Cardinal Gibbons and other leading citizens. Yet it took a U.S. Supreme Court decision in 1934 to force the University of Maryland to admit a black into its School of Law; and it was 1970 before Marylanders first sent a black representative to Congress. The latter reflects in part the changing popu-

The ethnic mix *(margin note)*

lation of Baltimore, which by the late 20th century was more than half black.

The heaviest concentrations of population are centred around Washington, D.C., and Baltimore. Although the rural stretch between the two cities—only 40 miles apart—has been diminishing, the growth outward from the cities has been uneven, and thus a fusion into a common, uninterrupted cityscape has not occurred. To the north and east of Baltimore the transition from farm to suburb in Baltimore and Harford counties suggests ultimate juncture with the Philadelphia–Wilmington sprawl; but Cecil County, at the head of Chesapeake Bay, remains steadfastly rural.

Baltimore is the largest city in the state, but it continues to lose people to the suburbs. Calculations for the next largest cities are impeded by the tendency of municipalities not to incorporate; thus, boundary lines are drawn arbitrarily by census takers.

The economy. *Industry and agriculture.* The major industries are primary metals, electrical equipment, transportation equipment, food and kindred products, and printing and publishing. Most of the establishments are branches of out-of-state corporations; but wages for production workers are slightly above the national average. Coal mining, however, has fallen to a low ebb.

Service industries bulk large in the economy, but agriculture probably directly supports about 30,000 people, including all family members, and farm income, the largest proportion from livestock, has increased. Maryland has one category of nationwide preeminence: oysters. The state's oyster haul rather consistently has led all others. Other saltwater staples include other shellfish, as well as perch, flounder, and other finfish.

The state has taken an increasing interest in the well-being of the private sector, particularly through its Department of Economic and Community Development. The agency encourages outside firms to locate in Maryland, promotes tourism, and keeps a close watch on the economy of the state.

Transportation. Maryland offers the traveller from the north three trunk highways into Baltimore and four highways south to Washington. It is possible to swing around Baltimore and Washington, D.C., on beltways or to avoid them altogether by Eastern Shore routes. The Harbor Tunnel Thruway and Francis Scott Key Bridge provide routes across Baltimore Harbor.

Amtrak provides passenger rail service to Baltimore, and residents of Montgomery and Prince George's counties commute to Washington, D.C., on the Metro subway. Baltimore–Washington International Airport is augmented by more than 20 public airports throughout the state. For freight shipments, the Port of Baltimore has excellent facilities and is one of the nation's busiest ports. The port, supervised by a state agency, is especially adapted to bulk commodities, container shipments, and foreign-made automobiles.

Administrative and social conditions. *Government.* In spite of a provision for statewide voting every 20 years on whether to summon a constitutional convention, repeated attempts to scrap the 1867 document, with its unnecessary detail, obsolete concerns, and silence on points of modern interest, have been failures. The document has been amended more than 100 times.

The form of state government in Maryland is like that of most other U.S. states. The governor, who serves for four years, may be reelected to an immediately succeeding term only once. A 1969–72 reorganization of the state government brought together in 12 departments several hundred agencies, boards, and commissions that previously had lacked coherent direction.

Members of the General Assembly serve four years and may be reelected indefinitely. Reorganization in the 1960s ended rural domination of the legislature and passed power to the counties adjoining Baltimore and Washington, D.C. The General Assembly consists of the Senate, with 47 members, and the House of Delegates, with 141 members.

Below the seven-member Court of Appeals, the highest judicial body, is an intermediate Court of Special Appeals and a series of circuit courts, known in Baltimore as the

The Baltimore–Washington, D.C., corridor *(margin note)*

The labour force and sources of income *(margin note)*

Executive, legislature, and judiciary *(margin note)*

Supreme Bench. Judges are appointed by the governor and must run against their record and anyone filing in opposition in the election following appointment. Appeals judges are elected to 10-year terms, and circuit judges to 15-year terms.

To avoid the greater costs that would be entailed by incorporation as governmental bodies, many of Maryland's most populous areas remain unofficial entities, their services more efficiently and economically provided on a countywide basis. As a result, the basic agency for local administration—aside from the city of Baltimore, which is a separate entity—is a board of county commissioners, who are elected to four-year terms. The county commissioners' power is largely executive, and most local legislation requires an act of the state legislature.

A constitutional amendment allows home rule for counties, under special charter; in 1948 Montgomery County, adjoining the District of Columbia, adopted home rule, and other counties have since followed suit. A charter county is governed by a county executive and county council, both elected to four-year terms; the council is empowered to enact all local laws.

In the 20th century, although free of the intimidation, poll tax, and other evils practiced in some places in the South, many Maryland elections have been machine dominated. The larger group of voters consistently has registered as Democrats, and the Democratic Party usually, but not always, wins. Exceptions have occurred when the Democrats split internally, when a nominee's platform was outrageous, or when a Republican presidential candidate carried the local candidates. A Republican can occasionally rely on the western counties, one or two southern enclaves, the Eastern Shore, and some affluent parts of suburban Maryland. Baltimore, with its party-boss tradition, is a Democratic stronghold, and college-educated and consciously ethnic voters are dependably Democratic. The black vote, long staunchly Republican, switched parties during the New Deal of the 1930s.

The General Assembly remains heavily Democratic, as it has been for decades. Thus, Democratic primary elections were often more important than the general election. When the nation's axis of balance was North–South, numerous presidential nominating conventions assembled in Baltimore, but none has been held there since 1912. In 1970 Marylanders chose their first Jewish governor and black congressman.

Finance. Through its revenues, which are largely derived from income taxes and federal aid, the state has assumed functions and responsibilities that are no longer within the capacity of the local government. It pays all full-time judges, the governor appoints the police commissioner of Baltimore, the construction of all school buildings is approved by a state committee, and Baltimore's airport is jointly operated by the city and the state. The state presents annual subsidies to Baltimore's leading orchestra, art museum, and resident theatre. In many instances, as population and industry moved outward, as old structures were demolished and property-tax assessments and yield dipped, municipalities took the initiative in this transfer of support and direction to the state. Maryland has not been a national leader, however, in the movements to abolish racial discrimination in schools, to increase job opportunities, or to provide better housing.

Education. Control of public education in Maryland is vested in a state board of education and county school boards. All positions are appointive, except in 10 counties where board members are elected to office. State supervision and the support of county public school systems began in 1870; but not until 1951 were 12 years of schooling uniformly required in all counties of the state. The state supports local systems, particularly as regards library services, vocational and rehabilitational instruction, and utilization of federal aid.

During the 1960s the five state teachers colleges were expanded into liberal arts colleges, and Morgan State College in Baltimore added a graduate school. There are two-year community colleges located in Baltimore and in 16 other locations. Crowning the state's system of higher education is the University of Maryland, with its main campus in College Park and branches located in Baltimore, Catonsville, and Princess Anne. The university's origins date from the College of Medicine of Maryland (opened in 1807) and Maryland Agricultural College (1856). The several graduate and undergraduate schools of the University of Maryland were consolidated in 1920, and in enrollment it has become one of the nation's largest universities.

Maryland has more than 20 private institutions of higher learning. The most prominent of these are Johns Hopkins (founded 1876), with several campuses and a world famous medical school; St. John's College (1784) in Annapolis, noted for its emphasis on the great books of the Western world; and Goucher College (1885), a school for women, in Towson.

Health and welfare. The Department of Health and Mental Hygiene, in addition to supervising county services, operates several hospitals for tuberculosis, rehabilitation, and the mentally handicapped. The department is also the centre for state efforts to prevent or reduce pollution. Its environmental-health section monitors the state's water supply and sewage, air quality, and solid-waste disposal. The department also has responsibilities in the area of drug abuse.

The Social Services Administration is in charge of state welfare activities. Direct aid to families with dependent children comprises its largest outlay, followed by general public assistance and foster care.

Cultural life. Maryland has its full share of such nationwide phenomena as institutional uniformity, ebbing respect for local and regional distinctiveness, and transitoriness of residence. In addition, the setting contains sizable quantities of decay, particularly in many residential neighbourhoods; the garish commercialization of streets and highways; the urban waste spaces where torn-down buildings have not been replaced; and always the degradation of the slums—some of them rural.

At the same time, however, the high proportion of Marylanders who are long-time residents (some represent many generations) retain an unusual number of distinctive interests and activities. Echoes of landed gentry of England and of early Maryland are stirred by riding to hounds in pursuit of the fox and taking part in the Grand National Steeplechase and Maryland Hunt Cup races, by breeding Chesapeake Bay retrievers, by jousting on horseback with a spear at rings dangling from a crossbar, and even by appraising the girls making their debuts at cotillions. The outdoors looms large in the life of Marylanders. Popular activities in the state include sailing and crabbing on the bay, trolling for ocean marlin, shooting wild geese in the marshes of the Shore, playing the game of lacrosse (derived from an Indian sport), or hiking the 38-mile (61-kilometre) stretch of the Appalachian Trail across Maryland in a single day.

Sailboat and sports-car racing provide activity for both the participants and the spectators, while the horse racing at Pimlico, notably the Preakness Stakes which is run in the spring; Baltimore's baseball and football teams; and Washington's ice hockey and basketball teams, based in Prince George's County, have audiences that extend beyond Maryland's borders. The gastronomy of Marylanders tends to be centred on terrapin soup, steamed crabs, padded oysters, fish and crab cakes, and beaten biscuits, often washed down with Maryland rye and beer. In almost a different world are the communities of watermen located on various islands of Chesapeake Bay, in which their isolation has worked to preserve their distinct attitudes and ways of life.

Among Marylanders who have made major contributions to artistic and intellectual traditions are the critic H.L. Mencken, the black abolitionist-statesman Frederick Douglass, the poet and short-story writer Edgar Allan Poe, the naturalist Rachel Carson, and the antislavery activist Harriet Tubman.

Baltimore is the centre of much of the state's activity in the arts. It is the home of the Baltimore Symphony Orchestra and of several professional theatres, including the Center Stage Theatre and numerous suburban dinner theatres. The Museum of Art and Walters Art Gallery are supplemented by similar galleries elsewhere, holding

Margin notes:

State assumption of local financing

Distinctive cultural remnants

Pervasiveness of history

in their collections both the arts and the artifacts of the past, as well as by annual art fairs and festivals in several locations.

Virtually all of the towns, cities, and rural areas in Maryland are marked by historical relics. The state and the many county and local historical societies and museums offer only parts of the picture. Walking tours are needed to visit the innumerable private homes from the 17th and 18th centuries; the many old canal locks; the National Road in Garrett County that carried many of the early trans-Appalachian homesteaders westward; and the stone markers of the Mason and Dixon Line set at five-mile intervals. Historic festivals and tours are as numerous as those devoted to the products of the bay or to sporting or artistic events.

THE HISTORY OF MARYLAND

The area's earliest human occupation is accepted as having been by roving hunters, *c.* 8000 BC, as the ice sheet made its final retreat. The records of this pre-Archaic, fluted-blade culture, which left only the points of its weapons, remain imprecise. Later, the numerous Eastern Archaic and then Woodlands Indian populations practiced agriculture and left waterside middens as evidence of the shellfish that they consumed. During the early European settlement the tribes were Algonkian in language and politics, but they were under heavy pressure from the Iroquois to the north. The English promise of support in these wars greatly smoothed relations in the early colonial years.

The colony. Leonard Calvert, the younger brother of Lord Baltimore, landed the founding expedition on St. Clement's (now Blakistone) Island in the lower Potomac in March 1634. The first settlement and capital was St. Mary's City. Aware of the mistakes made by Virginia's first colonists, Maryland's settlers, rather than hunt for gold, made peace with the local Indians and established farms and trading posts, at first on the shores and islands of the lower Chesapeake. The field hands included indentured labourers working off the terms of their passage and, after about 1639, African slaves. The most important crop was tobacco. Roads and towns were few, and contact with the English-model manor houses was largely waterborne.

Religious toleration in the colony

The religious latitude stipulated by the Calvert family was formalized by the General Assembly in 1649 in an Act Concerning Religion, later famous as the Act of Religious Toleration. It granted freedom of worship, though only within the bounds of trinitarian Christianity. Commercial disputes with Anglican Virginia and boundary quarrels with Quaker Pennsylvania and Delaware did not affect this tolerance. Puritan ascendancy in England (1648–60) caused only brief turmoil, and during an interval of crown rule (1692–1715) in Maryland the Church of England was established formally. Maryland, nonetheless, remained a haven for dissidents from sectarian rigidity in other colonies.

As the population centre shifted to the north and west, the capital was moved to Annapolis, and in 1729, Baltimore was founded. Maryland's dominant "country party" early resisted British efforts to make the colonies bear more of the costs of government. Repudiation of the Stamp Act occurred in Frederick County in 1765; and in 1774, the year after the Boston Tea Party, a ship loaded with tea was burned at an Annapolis dock.

Marylanders took an active part in the war, from the siege of Boston to the surrender at Yorktown. The Continental Congress, often on the move to avoid British troops, spent a winter in Baltimore. At the close of the war it convened in Annapolis, where it accepted George Washington's resignation from the army and ratified the Treaty of Paris (1783), which acknowledged the independence of the colonies.

Postwar problems included the disposition of confiscated Loyalist property, the struggle for paper money, and debtor relief. Maryland's controversy with Virginia over the use of the Potomac and lower Chesapeake Bay resulting in the Compact of 1785 was a step leading toward the Constitutional Convention. Such was also the Annapolis Convention of 1786, at which, however, Maryland was not represented. Luther Martin distinguished himself as a

representative of Maryland at the Philadelphia Convention of 1787. Maryland ratified the Constitution on April 28, 1788, and became the seventh state to do so. It also ceded territory and advanced money for public buildings to help form the District of Columbia (1791).

The state. When harassment on the high seas and other factors brought on the War of 1812, Baltimore clippers, sailing as privateers, dealt more than equal punishment to British skippers. In 1814 the British troops who had burned the principal government buildings in Washington, D.C., were repulsed in their attempts to inflict similar punishment on Baltimore. Francis Scott Key, a Georgetown lawyer and an eyewitness of the futile bombardment of Ft. McHenry in Baltimore harbour, wrote the four eight-line stanzas that, set to music, became the national anthem, the "Star-Spangled Banner."

With peace, Maryland and the nation became occupied with "internal improvements" in transport and communication. The National Pike, the first road to cross the Appalachians, was completed in 1818 and was followed by the first U.S. passenger railroad, the Baltimore & Ohio, and two important canals, the Chesapeake and Ohio from Washington to Cumberland, and, across the top of the Delmarva Peninsula, the Chesapeake and Delaware. The nation's first intercity telegraph line was constructed between Washington, D.C., and Baltimore. In 1845 the U.S. Naval Academy was founded on the Severn River in Annapolis.

Impact of the Civil War

The Civil War, however, arrested Maryland's progress. Landed gentry and residents of the Eastern Shore supported the secessionists, while workingmen and western Marylanders stood for the Union; a third faction favoured neutrality. Federal troops occupied Baltimore and Annapolis, and martial law was imposed in this border state. The constitution of 1864 abolished slavery and removed power from the rural aristocracy. Meanwhile, three major invasions by Confederate armies in successive summers resulted in qualified defeat at Antietam, full defeat at Gettysburg, in Pennsylvania, and dissipation of a threat to Washington, D.C., in 1864. The more cautious constitution of 1867 remains in force, though it has been amended almost beyond recognition.

Since 1865. After the Civil War Maryland prospered. The state was first an important entrepôt for raw materials from and consumer goods to the South and Midwest and then a growing centre of industry that rarely was controlled from within the state. Excesses that had won Baltimore the epithet "mob town" gradually were quieted. For many decades, until the mid-1900s, Marylanders consistently voted for Democratic candidates. Increasingly, however, the character of Maryland began to change because of its proximity to the seat of national government. The state became a major centre for federal installations, both military and civilian, during World Wars I and II and afterward. But most important was the radically different face of the Maryland suburbs of Washington, D.C., which reflected change not only in the greater numbers of people but also in their unusually high educational and economic status. (Ja.H.B.)

New Jersey

Although it is a major social, economic, and political force in its own right, New Jersey often is looked upon as a stepchild among the heavily industrialized and populated Eastern Seaboard states of the United States. Only four states in the nation have a smaller area than its 7,836 square miles (20,295 square kilometres), and only a few states have a larger population. As a geographical entity and as a human collective, New Jersey, nonetheless, suffers from a lack of identity among U.S. states. For some 600,000 of its citizens who commute to New York, on the north and northeast, and to Pennsylvania, on the west, New Jersey is a vast "bedroom state." For its transportation system, one of the busiest and most extensive in the world, it is primarily a funnel for goods and people moving between New York City and points north and Philadelphia, Delaware, and points south. For hundreds of thousands of visitors it offers long stretches of fine beaches along the Atlantic Ocean on the east and south; the resort of Atlantic City may be better known than the state itself.

Above all, New Jersey is rife with contradiction and anomaly. Its people fiercely fight off the attempts of state government to end home rule by powerful municipal administrations, which have contributed heavily to the almost uniform depression and decay of its cities. Whereas it has produced some of the most able and respected U.S. governors in the 20th century, its politics have been astonishingly corrupt, and it has achieved notoriety as a major haven for organized crime. It is a wealthy state but is beset with fiscal problems.

New Jersey is called the Garden State because of its many prosperous truck farms, yet it is among the most urbanized and crowded of states. The urban glut of its northeast contrasts sharply, however, with the rugged hills of the northwest and the enormous stretches of pine forest and rolling, lush horse country. It is one of the most important industrial centres in the nation, but it has paid the price in environmental pollution, in dirt and noise, and in congested roads and slums. In sum, New Jersey is a curious amalgam of the urban and rural, the poor and wealthy, the progressive and backward, the parochial and cosmopolitan.

PHYSICAL AND HUMAN GEOGRAPHY

The land. *Relief.* New Jersey comprises four distinct physical regions—the rugged hill country of the northwest, where the Appalachian Mountains slice across the state; the rolling horse country just below the hills; the central plain of the northeast, where the major cities and suburban towns lie; and the coastal plain of the south. In the thinly populated northwest the soil is heavy and contains much limestone and sandstone. The highest elevation, at High Point, is 1,803 feet (550 metres) above sea level. Southward, the hills become lower and gentler, and the soil contains considerable granite; this gives way to soil dominated by shale. The central plain is a mixture of loam and marl, while the coastal plain is composed mainly of sands and loam. The most striking features of the state are its beaches, the hills of the northwest, and the marshy meadowlands of the northeast.

Drainage. Lakes and ponds cover about 315 square miles of the state's surface. New Jersey's major river, which it shares with Pennsylvania, is the Delaware. The Hudson River separates the state from New York. Other major rivers are the Passaic and the Hackensack, both in the northeast, and the Raritan, which runs west to east and is generally regarded as the boundary between North and Central Jersey. Hopatcong Lake in Sussex and Morris counties is the state's largest.

Climate. The climate is moderate, although there is a marked difference in temperatures between the northwest and the southeast. In the north the average temperature is 50° F (10° C)—in winter, 28° F (−2° C), and in summer, 70° F (21° C). In the south the annual average is 55° F (13° C)—in winter, 35° F (2° C), and in summer, 71° F (22° C). Rainfall averages 46 inches (1,170 millimetres) a year—36 inches in South Jersey and 50 inches in North Jersey.

Plant and animal life. Virtually all of the plant life that is common to the northeastern United States can be found in New Jersey, and in the marshes and Pine Barrens of south New Jersey many rare plant species grow, including some insect-ingesting plants. The Barrens are dominated, however, by many varieties of pine and white cedar. Oak, elm, birch, ash, sweetgum, maple, walnut, and chestnut trees are to be found in river valleys. Plants common to the state include wild azalea, rhododendron, honeysuckle, mountain laurel, wintergreen, and cardinal flower.

The Hackensack Meadows and the Great Swamp in Morris County are dominated by grasses. Whereas the ecology of the Swamp is sound, centuries of dumping, filling, and dredging have destroyed much of the plant and animal life of the Meadows. Plume grass is the main plant in the Meadows, but it is of negligible value to fowl or fish. The increasing suburban development of New Jersey has encroached on wildlife habitats, although bears and wildcats can still be found in the Barrens and mountains. Deer are

plentiful, as are opossums and muskrats. There are rabbits, squirrels, chipmunks, woodchucks, and many varieties of snakes. All of the birds common to the Northeast are found in New Jersey, as are many migratory varieties.

Settlement patterns. The most distinctive of New Jersey's regions is its long shore, which stretches for 125 miles (200 kilometres). Much of it is composed of long and narrow sandbars separated from the mainland by bays and inlets that form part of the Intracoastal Waterway, an interconnected water highway that stretches to Florida. Cape May, at the southern tip of the state, was the first U.S. summer resort, and both that community and Long Branch in Monmouth County were known as the playgrounds of presidents during the 19th century. The quality of the Shore ranges from the urban garishness of Asbury Park to the opulence of Deal and Mantoloking. In such resorts as Wildwood and Atlantic City, the nightlife plies its revels until dawn, whereas such other towns as Avalon, Ocean City, and Beach Haven are basically family resorts. The Jersey Shore at its best can be found in its two state parks, Sandy Hook in the north and Island Beach in the south. The dunes there are still topped with coarse but fragile grass, and the osprey still build their nests. The marshes teem with wildlife, and the trees are bent and twisted by wind and salt spray.

Five northeastern counties in the New York metropolitan area—Essex, Hudson, Passaic, Bergen, and Union—contain about two-fifths of New Jersey's population. Four of the six largest cities in the state—Newark, Jersey City, Paterson, and Elizabeth—are located there. The Newark–Hudson County–Elizabeth complex appears to many travellers as one endless industrial city: dingy, smelly, but throbbing with commercial life.

Beyond the cities lie the suburbs. Most are pleasant and prosperous, but some are old and show signs of urban blight. Industrial construction in suburban communities has increased tremendously, but many suburban towns, especially in Bergen County, remain bedroom communities of New York City and of the New Jersey cities. Newark's population doubles every day as the work force pours in. New Jersey remains dominated, however, by the two giant cities just beyond its borders. Hundreds of thousands of New Jerseyites cross the Hudson to New York by rapid-transit trains, by suburban rail, or by bus and automobile on the average weekday. North Jerseyites watch New York television, root for New York athletic teams, and patronize New York theatres and restaurants. The same situation exists in Camden, Burlington, Gloucester, and Mercer counties, where residents cross the Delaware to jobs in Philadelphia and its environs.

For all of this, however, New Jerseyites have an antipathy for these two big cities. Many citizens of the Garden State grew up in New York City or Philadelphia, and, although they retain a lively interest in events there, they profess a profound gladness at being out of the cities, with their crime and financial and housing problems. This attitude is shared by those who never lived in the cities but who grew up in their shadows.

Just below Trenton, the state capital, begins South Jersey, comprising most of eight counties. It includes roughly one-half of the state's area but only about one-fourth of the population. Although the climate is drier than in the north, the loamy soil is well suited to vegetable farming, and most of the land not covered by forest or marsh is farmed. Less than 1 percent of the state's population is engaged in farming, but farm income per acre is among the highest in the nation. Pinelands National Reserve, covering about 1,700 square miles (4,400 square kilometres), was established in 1978; it was the country's first national reserve, in which the federal government provides funds for the purchase of a core of undeveloped land while state and local authorities are responsible for resource evaluation and economic planning in surrounding developed areas.

Central Jersey, all of five counties and part of three, is largely a plain, but hilly areas occur in Hunterdon and Somerset counties. Middlesex and Mercer counties, especially the former, are heavily industrialized. Princeton University is located in Mercer County and the borough

Contradictory nature of the state

The diverse physical regions

The Jersey shore

The metropolitan area

Suburban communities

South Jersey

Central Jersey

of Princeton, which combines the charm of the campus with a rich colonial past to create one of the nation's loveliest towns. Rutgers, the state university, is in nearby New Brunswick. Hunterdon and Somerset counties are a pleasant mixture of farm and woodland.

The four counties of northwestern New Jersey take in a mixture of small town, affluent suburb, and rugged countryside, although two major cities, Passaic and Paterson, are located in Passaic County. The area contains numerous dairy farms and parks and recreation areas.

The Meadow-lands Although relatively small, the New Jersey Meadowlands loom large in importance. Stretching from Perth Amboy to Hackensack, they cover some 19,000 acres (8,000 hectares), much of which is undeveloped. The lack of development results from disputes between the state and private interests over ownership and from the many problems of construction in a marshy area. The value of the Meadowlands is immense, however, because of its location in the centre of the world's busiest metropolitan area. By the late 1960s, New Jersey had put together the machinery to develop this area through the New Jersey Meadowlands Commission. In 1976 the Meadowlands Sports Complex began operations with the opening of a racetrack. In 1977 the Giants (football) Stadium was completed, and the Brendan Byrne Arena opened in 1981.

The people. New Jersey's population has come to reflect the immigration patterns of the 19th and 20th centuries: Germans and Slavs, Russian and European Jews, Irish and Italians. New Jersey was a prime destination for the waves of blacks that left the South during and after World War II. The state has a sizable Puerto Rican population, and many Cubans who left their country after Castro's revolution settled in North Jersey, mainly in Hudson County.

Italian-Americans are the state's largest ethnic group. They are the predominant white bloc in the cities, although the cities also contain sizable Polish, Hungarian, and other eastern European groups. Italian-Americans and blacks dominate the political and cultural life of the cities—a situation that often has brought the two groups into competition and conflict.

The most striking demographic trend in New Jersey, as in the nation as a whole, is the movement of the white population away from the cities and the concurrent proportional growth of the urban black population. The flight of the white middle class from the cities has been accompanied by an emigration of industry and commerce. Old, outmoded factories are left behind for sleek new buildings out of town, and huge suburban shopping centres have replaced the downtown department stores. This shift means more jobs in the suburbs, and the jobs create a commensurate demand for housing. The cities bordering these areas have become increasingly black, a situation that is potentially explosive because of the continuing decay of the cities and the poor quality of housing and services the cities can supply.

The economy. Alexander Hamilton's attempt in 1791 to build the nation's first industrial town at Paterson was a failure. He had the right idea, however, for New Jersey was destined to become an industrial giant. In 1979 the state ranked eighth nationally in value added by manufacturing.

Leader-ship in scientific research *Industry.* One of New Jersey's largest and most prestigious industries is research. New Jersey has the highest number of engineers and scientists per capita in the nation. Although it is not reflected in the manufacturing statistics, a close correlation exists between research and heavy industry. The great inventor, Thomas Edison, was a New Jerseyite, and he established the nation's first research laboratory in Menlo Park in 1876. There he created the electric light, the phonograph, and all manner of electrical gadgets, as well as pioneering the technology of the motion-picture industry. Edison's primitive laboratory has been succeeded by the David Sarnoff Research Center, the Bell Telephone and Western Electric laboratories, the Institute for Advanced Study at Princeton, the James Forrestal Research Center, and many more modern centres dotting the landscape of Central Jersey. New Jersey's major industry is chemicals. The next largest is electric and electronic equipment manufacturing. New Jersey also holds high national ranking in the production of clothing,

food, toys, sporting goods, and stone, glass, and clay products. The state is not noted for its mineral deposits, but South Jersey provided much of the iron for the shot and cannon used during the Revolution. New Jersey's mines are major suppliers of ilmenite, magnesium compounds, and zinc, as well as clays, sand, and gravel.

The spread of industry and housing is costing New Jersey much of its farmland, the most valuable per acre in the nation. The resort industry is a big factor in New Jersey's economy, especially in the south, where a bad year at the Shore hurts the economic well-being of the entire region. In 1976 residents of New Jersey approved a constitutional amendment to permit gambling casinos at Atlantic City, which, with its huge Convention Hall and fine hotels, does a thriving winter convention business. Casinos are taxed, and tax monies go to senior citizens and the disabled.

The State Division of Economic Development, along with the major utilities and business organizations, conducts an effective program of selling New Jersey to industry. The state has attracted many industries, especially corporate headquarters from New York City, largely through its greater space, better transportation, and favourable tax rates.

Transportation. Since colonial days, when New Jersey's toll roads linking Philadelphia and New York City were a major industry, transportation has been the lifeblood of New Jersey's economy. The role of transportation in New Jersey can best be appreciated in the Newark area. There, 12 lanes of the New Jersey Turnpike, one of the busiest in the world, converge with the main line of the Penn Central Railroad, Newark Airport, Port Newark, and Port Elizabeth to provide a steady stream of goods and people. It is perhaps the busiest transportation centre in the world. The economy of northern New Jersey is bound tightly to that of New York City, and the commercial traffic between the two states is the nation's heaviest.

Port Authority of New York and New Jersey In 1921 the states of New York and New Jersey formed the Port of New York Authority, now called the Port Authority of New York and New Jersey—a bistate commission empowered to finance and operate transportation facilities in the New York metropolitan area. The Port Authority, as it is known, is a public corporation operating Newark and Teterboro airports in New Jersey and La Guardia and Kennedy in New York, as well as the Lincoln and Holland tunnels, three bridges, huge piers, bus and rail lines, truck terminals, and the two giant towers of the World Trade Center rising above Lower Manhattan.

A similar but much smaller transit complex exists in the Camden area, linking the South Jersey area with Philadelphia. There is a deepwater port at Camden on the Delaware and high-speed transit to Philadelphia. In addition to the turnpike, which runs 132 miles (211 kilometres) the length of the state from the George Washington Bridge in the north to the Delaware Memorial Bridge in the south, the Garden State Parkway stretches 152 miles (243 kilometres) north to south, and the Atlantic City Expressway runs 44 miles (70 kilometres) to connect Atlantic City with the Camden area. Even before World War II, New Jersey had one of the finest road networks in the nation.

Eleven railroads cross the state. New Jersey also has more airports per square mile than any other state. The largest and busiest field is Newark International Airport.

In 1971 the Port Authority agreed to build a new rail line joining suburban Union County with Penn Station in Newark and with Newark Airport. In 1979 the publicly owned New Jersey Transit Corporation was created by legislation. The corporation has the power to acquire private rail and bus companies or to contract with them for their operation.

Administrative and social conditions. *Government.* New Jersey governors serve terms of four years, and they are permitted reelection to a second term. No other state official runs on a statewide basis, so the governor has no rivals in the executive branch. He appoints, with the advice and consent of the Senate, virtually all top state officers and members of state boards, authorities, and judiciary, and he has the authority to supersede county prosecutors. By virtue of his broad executive and administrative powers, the vast patronage at his disposal, and his unequalled access to the press, radio, and television, the governor of New Jersey is as strong a chief executive as there is in the nation. A two-thirds majority of both legislative houses is necessary to override his veto. The governor can be checked and occasionally defeated by a rebellious legislature or political leaders, but, in the final analysis, New Jersey governors seldom lose wars, only battles. In 1966 the New Jersey legislature abandoned the election of legislators to represent entire counties and adopted the "one-man, one-vote" principle. Since 1973 voters in each of 40 districts have chosen one senator and two General Assembly members. Assemblymen are elected every two years, while senators run for one two-year term and two four-year terms each decade.

Local government

New Jersey's 21 counties are administered by boards of freeholders elected on a countywide basis. The boards vary in size from three to nine members, depending on the size of the county. In addition to these elected officials, the various levels of local government are supplemented by service commissions, boards, and authorities, many of which enjoy wide independence and even autonomy. Attempts to merge municipalities, reduce the number of school districts by consolidation, or strengthen county government have failed because of the fear of compromising local power and prerogatives.

In national elections New Jersey is a "swing" state. It tends to lean Republican, but the Democrats frequently control the state legislature.

Although there have been signs that civic bossism is declining, New Jersey's political system was long dominated by powerful county leaders who drew their power from the patronage and contracts that they dispensed through control of the municipal courthouse or city hall. The most notorious of these bosses was Frank Hague, who operated as the absolute ruler of Jersey City and Hudson County from 1917 to 1947. For three decades Hague dominated the Democratic Party and heavily influenced the Republicans. His philosophy of government was best summed up in his famous reply to critics: "I am the law in Jersey City."

Welfare and education. Most of the services rendered the citizens of New Jersey come from the state, although most of the major counties maintain institutions of one kind or another, and much funding comes through federal agencies. The state has a shortage of hospitals, prisons, and various other institutions, although much has been done to correct the situation since the 1960s.

Higher education

New Jersey's reputation for shirking its responsibilities to higher education is improving. There was no state university at all until 1945, when New Jersey took over full responsibility for Rutgers University, now composed of three separate campuses and a wide variety of colleges and programs. The process of converting the six state colleges from strictly teacher-preparation institutes to full-fledged liberal arts schools was begun in the late 1960s. Princeton University is one of the nation's most prestigious private institutions.

Cultural life. New Jersey has never been noted as a cultural giant because the vast majority of its citizens are well served by such attractions as the New York theatre or the Philadelphia Orchestra. New Jersey helped correct its reputation as a cultural backwater with the opening, in 1968 in Monmouth County, of a beautiful amphitheatre at the Garden State Arts Center, home of the New Jersey Symphony Orchestra. The facility has proved to be an extraordinary success, and its programming of music, drama, and dance has been exceptionally well received.

There are several summer theatres in New Jersey, most of them located near vacation areas. The McCarter Theater, on the Princeton University campus, is open all year and offers high-quality plays and musical presentations.

New Jersey has more than 100 nationally listed museums, many of them operated in conjunction with historic sites or buildings. The New Jersey State Museum, which includes a planetarium, is located in the state capitol complex in Trenton. The Rutgers University Art Gallery, the Newark Museum, and the Princeton University Art Museum are among other well-known museums.

Historic sites

New Jersey's rich traditions are manifested in such historic homes and sites as the Ford Mansion, Washington's winter headquarters in Morristown, where he wrote his farewell address to the Continental Army; Morven, the official governor's residence in Princeton; the restored colonial villages of Batsto and Allaire; and the Camden home of poet Walt Whitman. These and other historic sites attract thousands of tourists each year.

HISTORY

The colony. Before the Europeans came, the Delaware (or Lenni Lenape) Indians spent the summer at the shore feasting on fish and collecting the shells they made into wampum. This is what the Florentine explorer Giovanni da Verrazano found in 1524, when he became the first European to reach New Jersey. Almost a century passed before colonization began with the arrival in 1609 of the English navigator Henry Hudson, who sent a party to explore Newark Bay. The first settlers were English, Scots-Irish, Swedes, and Dutch. The colony was brought under English rule in 1664, although for the next five years the Dutch disputed that claim. In 1676 the province was divided into East and West Jersey, the former going to Sir George Carteret and the latter to a group of Quakers. The division continued until 1702, when all of the province reverted to the crown.

Unlike other colonists, who suffered from the harshness of English rule, the early New Jerseyites were of such an independent and misanthropic nature that it was the royal governors who did much of the suffering. Until 1738 New Jersey and New York were ruled by a single governor. When Lewis Morris took office as the first governor of New Jersey alone, one member of the Assembly advised his colleagues on how governors should be treated: "Let us keep the doges poore and wee'll make them do as we please."

Revolution and after. Typically, considerable division of sentiment occurred within the state over the American Revolution, and Tory activity was heavy. The most significant battle of the conflict was fought in New Jersey on December 26, 1776. Gen. George Washington and his hungry, ragged troops crossed the Delaware River from Pennsylvania in longboats, surprised the garrison of German mercenaries in Trenton, and captured the city. A week later, Washington won another vital battle at Princeton, routing the British forces under Col. Charles Mawhood. The victories breathed new life into the Revolution, and an army of colonials near despair was transformed into an effective fighting force.   (J.Ke./J.McL.)

Delegates from the state attended both the Annapolis Convention in 1786 and the Constitutional Convention at Philadelphia in 1787. At the latter, New Jersey leadership sponsored the small states' position (New Jersey Plan) in opposition to the Virginia or larger states' Plan. The New Jersey Plan left its imprint in the provision of the federal Constitution for equal representation for large and small states in the national senate and for the supremacy of federal law. On December 18, 1787, New Jersey became the third state to ratify the federal Constitution.

The New Jersey Plan

The 19th century. On August 22, 1787, John Fitch demonstrated on the Delaware River one of the first successful steamboats, and 31 years later the Vail works near Morristown built the machinery for the "Savannah," the first steamboat to cross the Atlantic. In 1794, under the auspices of Alexander Hamilton's Society for Establishing Useful Manufactures, chartered by the legislature in 1791, a calico-printing factory inaugurated at the Great Falls of the Passaic the first factory town in the United States, now Paterson. In 1806 a covered wooden bridge crossed the Delaware at Trenton. This material progress was interrupted by the War of 1812, which in the beginning was very unpopular, especially among the Quakers. After the war the construction of the Morris (1824–38) and the Delaware and Raritan (1826–38) canals and the completion of New Jersey's first railway, the Camden and Amboy (1834), provided facilities for a widespread industrial development.

Agitation for democratic reform culminated in a constitutional convention at Trenton (May 14–June 27, 1844), which drafted a new frame of government by which New Jersey abolished property qualifications for suffrage, modified the basis of representation in the assembly, separated the legislative, executive, and judicial powers, and provided for the direct election of the governor.

A bitter railway war followed the Civil War. The Pennsylvania Railroad was charged with virtually monopolizing the route between New York City and Philadelphia as a result of a 999-year lease through which it had gained control of the properties of companies previously granted monopolistic privileges. In 1873 the state opened the route to other railroads. This same period was marked by great cultural, scientific, and industrial development.

Modern times. With no limit fixed either to capitalization or to bonded indebtedness and with a policy of encouraging the holding-company structure, coupled with a tax rate lower for large than for small corporations, New Jersey by 1904 had chartered three of the seven largest trusts and had "mothered" 150 of the 298 next largest business organizations in the United States. A growing concern over the effects of industrialism led to direct primaries (1907, 1911), a new ballot form (1911), the election of Woodrow Wilson as governor (1911–13), and the passage in 1913 to the "Seven Sisters" acts for eliminating the power of trusts to create monopoly, limit production, fix prices, and restrain trade. New laws limited public service franchises to 20 years, subject to municipal referendum.

An intensely industrial state, New Jersey produced great quantities of war matériel during World War II. Important embarkation points for soldiers going to the European theatre of war were at Ft. Dix and Camp Kilmer. The U.S. Signal Corps had its headquarters during the war at Ft. Monmouth.

A constitutional convention, delegates to which had been popularly elected in 1947, assembled in New Brunswick and prepared a new constitution which the voters approved and which on January 1, 1948, replaced the 103-year-old constitution. For the first time in more than 100 years the electorate, beginning in November 1949, could reelect a governor, and for the first time in 40 years the Republicans held the governorship for two successive terms. Legislative sessions in 1948–51 enacted the basic measures for putting into effect the structural changes required under the new constitution.

In 1964, after the U.S. Supreme Court adopted the "one-man, one-vote" doctrine with regard to the composition of state legislatures, the New Jersey Supreme Court struck down those portions of the state constitution of 1947 that applied to legislative apportionment and ordered the legislature to effect adequate reapportionment. After some efforts were made to avoid drastic reapportionment, an interim solution to run through 1967 was allowed, and the state Senate was expanded to 29 members from the long-established 21. In 1966 a nonpartisan state constitutional convention was called and drafted sweeping revisions that were overwhelmingly adopted by the electorate in the November election. They took effect with the legislators elected in November 1967.   (Ed.)

New York

One of the 13 original U.S. states, New York was until the 1960s the nation's leading state in nearly all population, cultural, and economic indexes. Its displacement by California about the middle of the 1960s was caused by the enormous growth rate that has persisted on the West Coast of the United States, rather than by a large decline by New York. It remains the second most populous state in the nation. New York's gross economic product exceeds that of all but a handful of nations throughout the world.

This great population and economic base is situated across a region of substantial contrast—from the Atlantic Ocean shores of Long Island and the skyscrapers of Manhattan through the rivers, mountains, and lakes of Upstate New York to the plains of the Great Lakes. With canals, railroads, and highways, New York is a principal gateway to the west for the Middle Atlantic and New England states and a continuing point of union for much of the nation. The cities of the state—from New York City through Albany (the state capital), Utica, and Syracuse to Rochester and Buffalo on the Great Lakes—and their

An overview of the state

suburbs contain more than four-fifths of all New Yorkers.

New York's central role in the development of the nation was a slowly maturing phenomenon, and both the New England and Southern colonies had a great deal more to do with the movement toward revolution and with stabilizing the new nation during its early decades. Once it got under way, however, New York's growth attained a breakneck pace. The state—and New York City, in particular—remains the centre of much of the nation's economy and finance, as well as of many formative impulses in U.S. arts and culture. The overwhelming presence of New York City actually has tended to divide the state socially and politically, causing long-standing problems for both the city and state, but the influence and image of the state is a major element of national political life.

The 49,576 square miles (128,401 square kilometres) of New York are bounded, from west to north, by Lake Erie, the Canadian province of Ontario, Lake Ontario, and Quebec province; on the east by the New England states of Vermont, Massachusetts, and Connecticut; on the southeast by the Atlantic Ocean and New Jersey; and on the south by Pennsylvania.

PHYSICAL AND HUMAN GEOGRAPHY

The land. Although New York state and New York City are synonymous to many people, the state has a wide range of geographical and climatic conditions. During at least a part of the Ice Age, most of New York was covered by glaciers; the only exceptions were southern Long Island, all of Staten Island, and the far southeastern corner of the state.

Relief. The movement of the glaciers left New York with nine distinct geological regions and, within these, 28 subregions. Each has its own landform, with distinctive geological structures and patterns of erosion. In the northeast the Adirondack upland is characterized by the highest and most rugged mountains in the state, reaching 5,344 feet (1,629 metres) in Mt. Marcy and 5,114 feet (1,559 metres) in Algonquin Peak of Mt. McIntyre. With the exception of some forestry activities, the region has small economic value other than for recreation. A large part of it has been designated as a wilderness preserve by the state.

The St. Lawrence Lowlands extend northeastward from Lake Ontario to the ocean along the boundary with Canada. Within this area are three physiographic divisions: the St. Lawrence marine plain, a flat to gently rolling strip along the St. Lawrence River; the St. Lawrence hills south of the plain; and, farther south, the Champlain Plain Lake.

Another region, the Hudson-Mohawk Lowland, follows the Hudson River from New York City to Albany and then turns west along the Mohawk River. The Hudson Valley portion, between the Catskill Mountains on the west and the Taconic Range on the east, is from 10 to 20 miles (15 to 30 kilometres) wide; the Mohawk Valley portion is 10 to 30 miles wide. These routes provided easy access from New York City and the New England area into the hinterland of New York and formed the natural paths for the canal, railroad, and highway eras that followed. Cutting natural pathways through the mountains of central and western New York, these rivers became the state's major avenues of commerce, serving first as the basis of the Erie Canal and later as the route of the New York Central Railroad and of the New York State (Thomas E. Dewey) Thruway.

To the east of the Hudson River lies the New England Upland, extending eastward into Massachusetts and Connecticut and southward across the Lower Hudson Valley into Pennsylvania.

Two small regions complete the geographic picture in southeastern New York. The Atlantic Coastal Plain, which extends from Massachusetts to Florida, takes in Long Island and Staten Island. A small finger of the eastern Piedmont region juts up from New Jersey for some distance along the west bank of the Hudson.

The Appalachian Highlands, the largest region in New York, comprises about one-half of the state, extending westward from the Hudson Valley to the state's southern and western boundaries. The Catskill Mountains, the peaks of which reach 2,000 to 4,000 feet; the Finger

The routes of settlement and commerce

The Appalachian Highlands

Lakes hills area; and the Delaware Basin are located in this region. The Catskills, with their mountains and lakes, are primarily a recreation area. The Finger Lakes area also provides many opportunities for summer and winter sports, and its valleys provide excellent grasslands for dairying. The Delaware Basin, drained by the Delaware River, is a mixed-farming area.

A plateau-like region known as the Erie-Ontario Lowlands lies to the north of the Appalachian Upland and west of the Mohawk Valley and extends along the southern shores of the Great Lakes. It is composed of lake plains bordering the Great Lakes that extend between five and 30 miles inland from the lakes. Because of the moderating influence of the lakes on the weather, the region has become an important fruit-growing area. Between the lake lowlands and the western reaches of the Adirondacks and north of Oneida Lake lies the Tug Hill Upland, which is one of the least settled parts of the state because of its poor soil and drainage and its severe climatic conditions.

Drainage. Among New York's special geographical features are its two major shorelines: 127 miles (203 kilometres) bordering the Atlantic, and 371 miles (594 kilometres) on Lakes Erie and Ontario. In addition, the state has some 8,000 lakes and nine major rivers. The Hudson and Mohawk rivers have played the most important roles in the state's history, but the Genesee and Oswego, flowing northward into Lake Ontario, also have been important. The Delaware, Susquehanna, and Allegheny drain the southern and western portions of the state and provide a large part of New York City's water supply. The East River connects Long Island Sound with New York Bay and separates Long Island and Manhattan. The most dramatic of the waterfalls that dot the state is Niagara Falls, a source of much hydroelectric power as well as one of the major scenic attractions of the Northeast.

Climate. New York's climate was a great disappointment to the early Dutch settlers. Since Manhattan was actually Mediterranean in latitude, it was rather bewildering to them to find that "it freezes and snows severely in winter." If Manhattan was uncomfortably cold and wet in the winter months, the rest of the state must have been an even greater disappointment.

The mean monthly temperature ranges from a high of 54° F (12° C) in New York City's Central Park to a low of 40° F (4° C) at Lake Placid in the Adirondacks. Average August temperatures range from 73° F (23° C) in New York City to 62° F (17° C) at Indian Lake in the Adirondacks; in February, from 33° F (0.5° C) on Long Island to 14° F (−10° C) at Stillwater Reservoir in the Adirondacks. These figures represent the extremes, but there are substantial differences in climate between New York City and Upstate Albany, Buffalo, Rochester, and Syracuse. A tendency to cloudiness across the state results in few completely clear days. New York City has about 100 such days each year, Syracuse and Buffalo 72, Binghamton 68, and Albany 73.

The growing season also varies substantially: Long Island has the longest, with 200 days, while in the extreme north central region the season is only 85 days long. Rainfall and melted snow produce a range of precipitation from 32 to 45 inches (810 to 1,140 millimetres) a year, with the coastal plain receiving the greatest amount of precipitation, while the Erie-Ontario Lowlands receives the least. Nearly all parts of the state, however, receive sufficient rainfall for adequate crop growing, with the occasional exception being parts of the Erie-Ontario Lowlands. The region around Buffalo receives an unusual amount of snow since it is on the eastern shore of Lake Erie.

Settlement patterns. The cultural and social distinctions among various parts of New York state have diminished. Upstate cities, for example, are nearly as ethnically varied as New York City. Certain cultural and social characteristics brought by early settlers remain visible and, to some degree, still influence life-styles. During the Colonial period and for a number of years after the American Revolution, New England was a major source of immigrants; and there are traces of the New England influence, particularly in the architecture and small-town planning of the northern shore of Long Island and in northern

Westchester County. The Dutch influence around Albany remains in little more than place-names and street names, plus some preserved or rehabilitated Dutch architecture. German and Scottish settlers have left their mark in the Schoharie Valley and parts of the Hudson and Mohawk valleys (German), in Orange and Ulster counties, and in the Cherry Valley area (Scots).

The basic distinction between Upstate and Downstate is normally related to political differences—Upstate, conservative; Downstate, liberal. These political differences are matched by and interact with social differences. Downstate is divided between New York City and the suburbs, and, within the city, differences among the boroughs are important. Although Manhattan has many low-income residents, it is the centre for sophisticated life-styles and liberal politics, the home of the "limousine liberals." The outer boroughs are characterized by relatively stable ethnic neighbourhoods and "communities in transition," more conservative in social attitude but oriented toward the Democratic Party. The suburbs are dominated by white middle- and high-income families living in detached houses, though the income spread in the suburbs has increased, and the inner suburbs are beginning to resemble the city's outer boroughs.

The rural Upstate areas must be distinguished from the Upstate cities and their suburbs. Rural New York remains conservative both politically and socially. The city regions vary from relatively sophisticated Rochester, with its heavy concentration of white-collar technical and managerial employees, to the more conservative Syracuse-central New York area. Buffalo, with its emphasis on heavy industry, has a large blue-collar population.

The people. Since the Colonial period much of New York's growth has resulted from immigration, both from other states and from abroad. Before the American Revolution, the Dutch, English, Scots, and Germans were the primary settlers; they were followed in the first half of the 19th century by New Englanders spreading across developing parts of Upstate and into Westchester and northern Long Island. The influx of European immigrants came first from the northern and central parts of the Continent and later from the southern countries.

In the late 20th century many New Yorkers either were foreign born or had one or both parents born abroad. The nations of origin of this stock are Italy, the Soviet Union, Poland, Germany, Ireland, the United Kingdom, and Canada, while some 1,000,000 people are from a great diversity of other countries.

Related to the concentration of foreign origin is the state's religious composition. About one-third of the population is Roman Catholic, while more than 12 percent is Jewish.

The growth of the nonwhite portion of the population in the 20th century is of particular importance. The first large-scale influx of blacks from the Southern states occurred during World War I, but it was small compared to the migration that occurred during and after World War II. In 1940 only 4.4 percent of the population was nonwhite, but by late 20th century the proportion had increased to more than 20 percent. The nonwhite population is concentrated in the state's metropolitan areas and, within those areas, in the central cities.

Another immigrant group that has had a significant impact on the economy and culture of New York since World War II is the Puerto Ricans. Several hundred thousand reside in the state, mostly in New York City. After a heavy immigration of Puerto Ricans during the 1950s and early 1960s, the growing economic strength of Puerto Rico caused a considerable reduction, with those entering the state being largely offset by those returning to Puerto Rico.

In the 20th century there has been considerable internal migration. This shifting, far from being random, represents a sorting out of the population, with higher and middle-income whites moving to the suburbs, leaving low-income groups and blacks within the central cities. Many economic activities, particularly manufacturing and headquarters of corporations, also have moved to the suburbs. This movement of people and economic activity resulted in the urban crisis that has become familiar across the

Diversity of ethnic, national, and regional influences

Patterns of immigration

The nonwhites

United States: the increasing needs of the cities to combat crime and other symptoms of the poverty concentrated within them, while their social and economic resources to do so are being removed. Although the economic strength of the metropolitan areas is growing, the cities are increasingly unable to participate in the prosperity and seem likely to slip still further behind.

The economy. New York's economy is somewhat similar to those of the other Northeastern states. The economies of other states—in the South, the Midwest, and the Far West—are growing more rapidly than the Northeast, but this more mature region still has great economic strength. New York has a complex network of nearly every form of transportation. Its resources of electrical power for domestic and commercial use are enormous, including conventional coal- and oil-burning plants, hydroelectricity from the Niagara region, and a growing nuclear source.

Industry. New York is represented in every economic category designated by the federal Bureau of the Census. In comparison with the rest of the United States, New York's economy has a disproportionately large share of the country's activity in the fields of wholesale-retail trade, finance-insurance-real estate, transportation-communications-public utilities services, manufacturing, construction, and government. It is, however, underrepresented in farming, and mining.

In spite of these strengths, New York, like the rest of the nation, has a declining proportion of its population engaged in manufacturing. In 1947 more than one-third of its employed population were in manufacturing, while by the late 20th century the figure had shrunk to less than one-fifth. The growth sectors of the economy are nonmanufacturing industries.

There is some economic specialization within different parts of the state. Services and finance-insurance-real estate activities are more concentrated in the New York City metropolitan area than in Upstate. Buffalo is strong in heavy industry, while Rochester dominates the manufacture of photographic and optical equipment and is primarily responsible for the state's strong position in instrument production.

Syracuse ranks high in the state in the production of primary metals, machinery, and paper and allied products, as well as in educational employment. The Utica-Rome area specializes in machinery and transportation equipment, while the Albany-Troy-Schenectady area is strong in the production of paper and allied products. Albany, as the state capital, leads in government employment. The smallest of the state's metropolitan areas, Binghamton, is the original site of the International Business Machine Corporation (IBM) and therefore has a concentration of employment in the computer and business-machine field.

Agriculture. Dairying is by far the most important source of farm income, providing about one-half of the total. Other important sources of farm income are poultry and eggs, livestock products, fruit, vegetables, and field crops. The state raises a variety of horticultural specialties including nursery products, crops grown under glass, and flower bulbs and seed and competes with Vermont in the production of maple sugar. The fruit and vegetable farms supply the large food-processing industry with such products as apples, cherries, peaches, currants, strawberries, tomatoes, peas, beans, sweet corn, and cabbage.

Management of the economy. The state plays both regulatory and promotional roles in the economy. The Public Service Commission controls the rates charged by the public utilities, and the Division of Housing and Community Renewal encourages the production of housing and other community facilities. The Department of Commerce aids in attracting new economic activity to the state, providing information and assistance to industries seeking to locate there, giving some financial support to local communities interested in developing industrial parks, and offering other incentives to encourage the location of more industries within such areas.

New York tends to have somewhat lower unemployment rates during downturns in the national economy than does the rest of the nation, but it also recovers less rapidly. This behaviour results in large measure from the state's

economic mix and its heavy dependence on nonmanufacturing activities.

New York has one of the most highly unionized work forces of any state. Unionization has grown rapidly in the service sector among such government employees as teachers, sanitation workers, police, and firemen. The nature of labour-management relations varies considerably from industry to industry, with workers in construction and the garment and apparel industries wielding great power. Nearly every session of the state legislature devotes attention to the field of labour relations, particularly public-sector employee relations, in which no satisfactory means of settling disputes has emerged. Simple "no-strike" statutes do not work, and the arbitration devices used thus far remain unsatisfactory to both workers and management.

Transportation. Underlying the economic activity of New York state is its transportation system. A great part of New York's economic advantages is a product of its location on important natural transportation routes and facilities that connect urban centres within and without the state.

The Erie Canal, opened in 1825, tied New York City and its port to Buffalo and the westward-expanding nation. The main railroad system followed the route of the canal, with feeder lines that jutted north and south into the remainder of the state. After World War II, the limited-access Thomas E. Dewey Thruway stretched from New York to the Pennsylvania state line, passing through Albany, Utica, Syracuse, Rochester, and Buffalo. The basic paths of these main transportation routes are not substantially different from those that were used by the state's original settlers.

With the completion in 1918 of the New York State Barge Canal System, which incorporated the old Erie Canal, New York had the country's most extensive inland-waterway system. Although this system is an important means for moving bulk goods—particularly petroleum products, which provide nearly half the tonnage—the annual tonnage carried on the system has dropped considerably.

The railways first challenged the supremacy of the canal as a carrier of goods. Beginning in the mid-19th century with the establishment of the New York Central Railroad, a system was built that tied New York's major cities to Chicago, Boston, Montreal, and other urban centres. Although declining in the number of passengers carried, the railroads remain important handlers of freight. Much of this freight originates at the Port of New York, the largest port in the United States, which in 1979 handled about one-tenth of all the nation's imports. Nearly one-half of all passengers to and from the United States pass through this port.

Central to the highway system are the limited-access highways. The Thruway connects at Albany to the Northway, which extends northward to Canada. In central New York a major highway runs from the Pennsylvania state line to Canada, passing through Binghamton, Syracuse, and Watertown. At Syracuse this route intersects with the Thruway, causing the city to remain a transportation hub and accounting, in large part, for its economic viability. Another limited-access expressway extends across the southern tier of the state. On Long Island a set of east-west highways ties the island to New York City, New England, and Upstate New York.

The New York metropolitan area, with its combination of subways, buses, and railroads, has the most complex commuter system in the nation. The nearly 800-mile-(1,280-kilometre-) long New York transit system provides intra-city passenger transport. Commuter railroads serve suburban Long Island, New Jersey, Connecticut, and Westchester County. Many of these transportation networks were brought under the control of a single agency, the Metropolitan Transportation Authority, in 1968.

The three largest airports in the New York City metropolitan area are John F. Kennedy International, La Guardia, and Newark (New Jersey).

Administrative and social conditions *Government.* New York's constitution prescribes the distribution of powers among the branches of state government as well as the

Marginal notes:

Economic strengths and weaknesses

The state's role in the economy

Waterways and railways

Highways

The constitutional framework

system of local government throughout the state. As in some other states, however, the document is excessively detailed and includes provisions that most constitutional scholars consider more appropriately treated in legislative statutes than in a constitution. Because of the detail, articles tend to become outdated rapidly and require fairly frequent conventions for constitutional revision. Since the first convention in 1777, eight others have been held at roughly 20- to 25-year intervals; the last such convention was held in 1967. The constitution requires that the question of holding a convention be placed before the voters of the state every 20 years.

The first constitution established a bicameral legislature and provided for the first popularly elected governor in the United States, but it restricted the suffrage to male property holders. Veto power over legislation was vested in a Council of Revision, comprising the governor and justices of the Supreme Court, while the appointment of nearly all state and local officials lay with the Council of Appointment, comprising the governor and four senators. These councils represented an effort to avoid the autocratic rule that New Yorkers had experienced at the hands of the colonial governors appointed by the British crown. The convention of 1821 abolished the bodies, extended the franchise, and introduced a formal bill of rights.

The convention of 1846, influenced heavily by the populist spirit of Jacksonian democracy, imposed financial limitations on the legislature, which often had extended state credit to private ventures in such areas as railroad and canal building. Many state offices, including the judiciary, were made elective.

The constitution of 1894 is still the basis for New York state law, but it has been amended more than 190 times. Its provisions include a merit civil-service system, limitations on disposal of the state's forest preserve, a commitment to public education, and the first constitutional definition of state-local relations.

Conventions have produced documents that were rejected by the voters or sets of amendments that reflected the spirit of the times. If not accepted, such amendments often were introduced into law through legislation. The conventions of 1938 and 1967 were concerned primarily with social issues—of welfare, labour, and other rights during the Depression years, aid to parochial schools, and the solution of urban social and economic crises. Whereas the voters accepted most of the 1938 amendments, they soundly rejected the 1967 document.

Emerging from the various constitutional revisions and amendments is a state government characterized by a strong governorship based on power over appointments and budget. The governor normally has the upper hand in contests with the legislature.

The governor is somewhat restricted in authority, however, by a number of independently appointed or elected officials. The Board of Regents, for example, which presides over the education establishment of the state, is appointed by the legislature. An independently elected comptroller acts as auditor for both state and local governments.

Legislative and para-legislative committees

The legislature comprises a senate of 60 members and an assembly of 150. Each house has standing committees concerned with issues of public policy. Several committees composed of both senators and assembly members study specific policy issues and make recommendations to the legislature. The state also uses numerous nonlegislative commissions—appointed by the governor, by the legislature, or by both—to investigate such problems as education-aid formulas, state–local relations, the judicial process, welfare administration, and basic governmental organization.

New York is divided into 11 judicial districts. Each district has several elected judges, and together they form the Supreme Court. Four judicial departments act as appeal divisions from the supreme and inferior courts. The highest court is the Court of Appeals. The governor appoints the judges to the appellate departments from those elected to the Supreme Court, while those serving on the Court of Appeals are elected for 14-year terms. At the state level, the Court of Claims hears cases against the state. There is a variety of local courts, including county courts, family and surrogate courts, and the court system of New York City.

Much legislative debate revolves around the allocation of state aid to local jurisdictions. The constitution has contained a home-rule provision since 1896, but court interpretations of the provision, which gives the state the power to act in any matter in which there is a state concern, have tended to weaken the home-rule concept and continue Albany's domination of local governments. Moreover, the increasing interdependence of the state and its parts caused by metropolitanization and industrialization inevitably has reduced the autonomy of local jurisdictions.

The state is covered by county jurisdictions, which are divided into towns. Urban areas may be incorporated as either cities or villages. When it incorporates as a city, a town's jurisdiction is eliminated, but villages remain a part of the town in which they are located, and residents pay town as well as village taxes.

Unlike those states in which either town or county government is weak, New York has strong jurisdictions of both types. This situation often leads to considerable overlapping in the provision of governmental services outside of the cities. Special districts include port and bridge, health, and fire districts, as well as regional market authorities. Port Authority of New York and New Jersey is one of the largest special districts, operating bridges, harbours, and related facilities throughout the New York City metropolitan area, including those in northern New Jersey.

The decision of the U.S. Supreme Court in 1965 requiring legislative districts to be roughly equal in population brought new life into New York's county government, since town supervisors were no longer able to have dual responsibility as county supervisors as well. Many counties, including the most urban outside New York City, have opted for single-executive systems.

Cities and villages generally are governed by a mayor and a council; only a few cities, the largest of these being Rochester, use the city–manager plan. Some of the larger cities have a second legislative body, often called the Board of Estimate. In New York City, the mayor, the president of the City Council, the comptroller, and the five borough presidents serve on this body. In other cities membership usually includes the mayor, the president of the city council, and one or more high-ranking fiscal officers.

State financial aid to local governments

The state–local governing system of New York places heavy responsibilities on local governments, and more than one-half of the state budget consists of aid to local government. Most of the aid is for public schools; other categories include welfare, health, highways, and housing and urban renewal.

Only if the federal government assumed a much larger share in financing welfare could the local governments in New York become concerned primarily with providing traditional municipal services. Such changes would go far toward solving the severe financial pressures of the state's major cities.

To finance such services, New York's relatively healthy economic base provides the source of one of the highest per capita taxation systems in the United States. State impositions include income, sales, business, and excise taxes; local revenues are derived mainly from property and sales taxes. New York City is the sole local jurisdiction imposing an income tax. The broad state base plus the widespread use of local sales taxes allows New York to rely less on local property taxes than do other large or heavily populated states such as California, Massachusetts, and New Jersey.

Political life. The political struggles between Upstate and New York City cannot be reduced entirely to a matter of Democratic–Republican hostility. New York City's politics was once characterized by strong Democratic (Tammany) leaders of the city's five boroughs, especially the boroughs of Manhattan and Bronx, but the leaders of these organizations often had as much difficulty dealing with Democratic governors in Albany as with Republican ones. The Republican Party, generally controlling the state legislature, if not the governorship, remained strongly conservative until its traditional leadership was threatened

The four
major
political
parties
in state
politics

around 1900 by Theodore Roosevelt and Charles Evans Hughes. Although the Democrats and Republicans have strong statewide party organizations, New York is one of the few states in which third and fourth parties have thrived and often played important roles in elections. The Liberal Party in New York City has at times endorsed Republican candidates and in 1969 slated and won reelection for Mayor John Lindsay after he had been rejected by his former Republican sponsors. The splinter movement was originally confined to New York City, but during the 1960s the statewide Conservative Party was established, and its candidate was elected to the U.S. Senate in 1970.

Since 1920 the governorship has been about equally divided between the Democratic and Republican parties. In contrast, both houses of the state legislature have been almost consistently Republican since 1940. Political behaviour is characterized by generally effective party discipline in the legislature and strong leadership by the governor. The most bitter clashes have been between the two strongest political figures in the state, the governor and the mayor of New York City. Even when those holding these offices have been of the same political party, the conflicting necessities of the state and of the metropolis, usually financial, have brought the two into strident confrontation.

Education. New York spends more money per pupil for public education than any other state except California. This public school system, with compulsory schooling between the ages of seven and 16, had its beginnings in the colonial period. Schools were established by churches with government support as early as 1638 in New Amsterdam. It was not until 1791, however, that the state's first public school was established. Some state support was granted in 1795 to elementary schools, and in 1812 a permanent system of public schools was established. Parent-paid fees provided a part of the support, however, until all elementary schools became free in 1867. Public secondary schools came even later. During the 1850s a few cities established such schools, and, during the second half of the 19th century, they spread across the state.

The University of the State of New York, one of the most comprehensive educational organizations in the world, was established in 1784 and its governance placed under a Board of Regents. From 1812 to 1904 the educational system in New York was administered by two departments. In 1904, however, the state legislature placed all educational activities under the direction of the Board of Regents. The board selects the state commissioner of education, approves the establishment of new colleges, licenses entry into the professions, approves new degree programs, and advises the legislature on all educational issues. Standardized exams used in all secondary schools are called regents' exams. Scores on these exams provide a measure for determining school performance and form the basis for the awarding of a wide range of scholarships.

The Board
of Regents

In 1948 the several public institutions of higher education, primarily teachers colleges and two-year agricultural and technical institutions, plus newly established institutions, were incorporated into the State University of New York, an institution distinct from the University of the State of New York but a part of that larger entity. Until the creation of the state university, private institutions dominated higher education. Although private institutions in New York enroll a higher proportion of college students than in most states, the state system has been the most rapidly growing public institution of higher education in the nation since its founding.

The state university system comprises four general types of institution. Major university centres are located at Stony Brook, Albany, Binghamton, and Buffalo. The teachers colleges and several campuses have become general colleges concentrating on undergraduate education but providing some graduate training. Two-year state institutions and community colleges are supported in about equal parts by the state, the county, and student fees. City University of New York is supported by the state and by New York City and provides a great variety of programs, ranging from two-year community colleges to graduate instruction.

Operating alongside this dual public system are more

than 200 private institutions of higher education ranging in size from a few hundred students to more than 45,000 at New York University. This group includes some of the best known universities in the nation. Columbia University, founded in 1754 as King's College, is known for the high quality of its graduate instruction and for the national influence of its teachers' college. Cornell, the base for the agriculture, home-economics, veterinary-medicine, and industrial- and labour-relations units of the State University, is a member of the Ivy League, as is Columbia. Fordham is perhaps the best known of the state's many Roman Catholic colleges and universities. The University of Rochester, known for its pioneering role in music and the natural sciences, and Syracuse University, home of the Maxwell Graduate School, the first university unit established for training students for public service, are also well-known private institutions. Other high-ranked institutions include Colgate, Hamilton, Union, St. Lawrence, Bard, Skidmore, Barnard, and Vassar.

Private colleges and universities

Educational issues dominate much of the public debate in the state: public support of parochial schools, state aid to elementary and secondary schools, establishment of tuition at City University of New York, the relation between the state and city universities, and public support for private higher education.

Cultural life. Much of the style and tone of life in the United States is set in New York City, which remains the artistic, cultural, and economic capital of the nation. The fashion industry is headquartered in its garment district; the main live theatre in the nation is located on and off Broadway; and many television programs originate in New York, where the three major networks have their home offices. The city's museums particularly the Metropolitan Museum of Art, the Museum of Modern Art, and the American Museum of Natural History—set the pace for similar institutions across the land, and more and more motion pictures are being filmed on its streets.

Many major publishing houses, too, have their headquarters in New York, as do a large number of national magazines. Serving their needs and those of the central offices of many of the country's largest corporations are banks, public-relations and advertising firms, management consultants, and legal firms. Because of this concentration of business and culture, New York City maintains a leading national position in many aspects of U.S. life.

Cultural and related activities are not confined to New York City. Many art museums are located in the state's large and small cities. Among them, the Albright-Knox Art Gallery, in Buffalo, has outstanding collections of contemporary paintings and sculptures. In Rochester are the Memorial Art Gallery of the University of Rochester; the Rochester Museum and Science Center; and the International Museum of Photography at the George Eastman House which is devoted to the history of photography. The Everson Museum of Art of Syracuse and Onondaga County is considered an outstanding example of modern architecture, while the city's Canal Museum is the only museum in the nation devoted to canal history. Outstanding symphony orchestras include those of Buffalo and Rochester, while the Eastman School of Music at Rochester is internationally known. Fine architecture is located across the state, and the performing arts are actively pursued by professional and amateur groups. The cultural and artistic life of the state's many college and university towns often is centred on these institutions, notably in departments of art, music, and theatre.

Regional
museums
and
institutions

Numerous artistic and cultural activities are presented throughout the year. The Saratoga Performing Arts Center in Saratoga Springs is the summer home of the Philadelphia Orchestra and the New York City Ballet. Theatrical performances also are held at this modern cultural centre. The Chautauqua Institution, located on Chautauqua Lake in southwestern New York, was founded in 1874 as a training school for Sunday-school teachers. The name Chautauqua has since been adopted to include a wide range of cultural and educational activities, including concerts, opera, drama, and lectures. Other music and art festivals are the Adirondack Chamber Music Festival at

Festivals
and
museums

Schroon Lake, the Signal Hill Festival of Music and Dance at Lake Placid, and the Lake George Opera Festival at Glens Falls.

Cooperstown, founded by the father of James Fenimore Cooper (who used the central New York area as the locale for many of his novels) and known as the village of museums, has six museums, the best known of which is the National Baseball Hall of Fame. At the Angel Moroni Monument on the Hill Cumorah near Palmyra, an annual pageant depicts the founding of the Mormon Church. South of Palmyra are the Greyton H. Taylor Wine Museum in Hammondsport and the Corning Glass Center in Corning. Historic homes, forts, and battlefields dot the state. More than one-third of all the battles of the American Revolution were fought in New York, including the decisive Battle of Saratoga.

New York was the first state in the Union to establish a program for continuing financial support of the arts. The Council of the Arts, which administers the program, funds organizations in the fields of the performing arts, visual arts, film and media, and special programs.

The variety of New York's geography provides not only areas of great beauty but also vast opportunities for recreation, relaxation, and a study of the past. With the cool summers of the Adirondacks, the snowy slopes of the Catskills, the beaches of ocean and lakes, and an almost unlimited repertory of water sports, New York has a broad recreational base.

HISTORY

Two major groupings of Indian tribes were living in the New York region when Europeans first arrived: the Mohegan (Mohican) and Munsee tribes of the Algonkian family near the Atlantic coast and, farther inland, the five tribes of the Iroquois—Mohawk, Oneida, Onondaga, Cayuga, and Seneca—which formed the League of Five Nations about 1570. This confederacy of Indian tribes, with its advanced social and governmental institutions, reached the height of its power around 1700. When these tribes later aligned themselves with the British against the French and the Algonkians, it is probable that they provided the balance of power that was needed for the British to emerge victors in the nearly 150 years of struggle between the two European powers in North America.

Settlement and colonial period. New York was settled originally as a colony of the Netherlands following Henry Hudson's exploration in 1609 of the river later named for him. In 1624 the Dutch established Fort Orange at present-day Albany as the first permanent European settlement in New York. One year later, a similar colony, New Amsterdam, was established at the foot of Manhattan Island. To legalize the settlement, Peter Minuit, the Dutch governor, paid the Indians 60 Dutch guilders—about $24—in the form of merchandise. Although the Dutch established several settlements along the Hudson, their interest was more in trade than in permanent agricultural development. Thus, while the trading posts prospered and aided the general expansion of the empire of the Netherlands, no deep roots of permanent colonization were planted in New York. The likely explanation for this lies in the general economic prosperity and social stability of the homeland. The Dutch citizens had no strong economic motivations to move overseas, nor were there sufficient religious quarrels at this time to promote any such movement. When an English fleet sailed into New York harbour in 1664, Peter Stuyvesant, the governor, surrendered without a fight. Although controversy ensued for several years, the colony was clearly in English hands by 1669. Under the English it was renamed New York after the Duke of York.

Despite this change in ownership and sovereignty, however, the colony was not able to develop rapidly. Like the Dutch, the English crown granted large tracts of land to private individuals. This system of landownership was not very attractive to settlers such as the farmer-colonists who had settled the New England area, and agricultural development, particularly in the areas along the Hudson Valley, remained slight.

The European war between France and England had its

Slowness of growth in colonial period

counterpart in North America. The French, firmly established along the St. Lawrence and in Quebec, made a number of forays into northern and central New York. The relatively strong Five Nations federation of the Iroquois aligned itself with the English in New York and New England because of earlier aid given by the French to the rival Algonkians. This warfare discouraged settlement beyond Albany. The military situation was brought to a conclusion by the Treaty of Paris in 1763, which confirmed English dominance of the New York region. A gradual but steady movement of settlers from New England was the beginning of New York's population explosion. The New Englanders moved across the borders of Connecticut and Massachusetts, some remaining on the east bank of the Hudson, others passing through Albany to the interior.

In 1698 the colony's population was about 18,000, two-thirds of it in and around New York City. By the eve of the American Revolution, however, the numbers had grown to 163,000, and the concentration was nearly exactly reversed; but New York still ranked only seventh among the American colonies. The cosmopolitan and heterogeneous character of its population was already well established. Dutch culture remained quite strong in New York City and in Albany, while most of the settlements in the interior had a flavour and dialect of the New England Yankee, with the addition of several German communities. This emerging pattern of cultural heterogeneity was to have a considerable influence on the politics of the state, as were the waves of immigration from Europe that followed the war and continued well into the 20th century.

Revolution, statehood, and growth. New York contains many of the battlegrounds of the American Revolution. The war in New York took on many of the characteristics of a civil war, since the state probably had a higher proportion of residents who were loyal to the crown than did any other state.

Following the war a part of the state's political leadership aligned itself with like-minded leaders from other colonies to urge establishment of a strong central government for the new nation rather than the loose confederation that was then in power. New York delegates participated vigorously in the Constitutional Convention, one of the leaders of which was New Yorker Alexander Hamilton. Despite the role played by Hamilton and by other New York delegates in drafting the document, the politics of ratification within the state legislature were intense and bitter, and New York was the 11th state to endorse the U.S. Constitution.

The American Revolution and the War of 1812 temporarily interrupted New York's expansion to the westward, but, thereafter, the movement began in earnest. Turnpikes spread westward from Albany and from other locations up and down the Hudson River, and settlers moved across the state. The opening of the Erie Canal in 1825 confirmed New York's position as the gateway to the west from the Atlantic Coast. The railroads followed in quick order and tended to follow the pattern of trade that had earlier been established by the turnpikes and the canal.

Improvements in transportation and the movement westward

According to the census of 1800 New York state had become the second largest state in the Union, trailing only Virginia, and 10 years later it had surpassed all other states. Its leadership was not only in population, size, and growth but also in the areas of manufacturing, trade, and transportation—and in the increasing heterogeneity of its population.

Growth and change also were reflected in the political and governmental history of the state. The original state constitution restricted the suffrage to property holders and established a governing system that was dominated by large property holders and leading commercial interests. The change in population composition, as well as shifting political attitudes in the nation, soon caused New York to move in a more democratic direction. During the 1830s a vigorous campaign was launched against the system of landownership in the Hudson Valley, with renters eventually being given the opportunity to own the land they tilled. The constitutional convention of 1846 confirmed these democratic moves by expanding the suffrage and restricting the power of both legislature and governor.

Emergence of political divisions. New York continued to grow in virtually every dimension, but its political development became centred on the increasing chasm of interest and affection between New York City and Upstate. The issue of "home rule," the demands of the city for total powers of self-government against claims that the city is the creature of the state, has remained central to the conflict.

During the 1780s an organization, eventually to be known as Tammany Hall, was formed in the city to combat attempts by propertied Revolutionary leaders to limit the franchise in the state. Largely middle class in membership, it did not extend its democratic principles to the lower classes or to the immigrants. By the mid-19th century, however, through workers' and equal-rights parties, Irish politicians came to dominate the Tammany organization and the office of mayor, culminating in the control of the Democratic machine after 1868 by William "Boss" Tweed.

Well into the 20th century, the name Tammany was an international byword for municipal corruption at the highest levels. City-state antagonism was fuelled by Democratic domination in the city and Republican domination of the areas Upstate and, in most years, of the statehouse and the legislature as well. Investigations of Tammany Hall and city politics in general were highlighted by those of the Seabury Commission (1931–32), which brought about the resignation of Mayor James J. Walker and led to the reform administration of Mayor Fiorello H. La Guardia (1933–45) and the efforts of subsequent mayors to tread the line between the power of Tammany Hall in municipal elections and an image of political incorruptibility.

Much of Tammany Hall's power was based on its social services to the waves of immigrants that inundated New York City until changes in immigration laws slowed the tide during the 1920s. When the state and federal governments began to take over such services as social security, workmen's compensation, unemployment, welfare, and health benefits, notably during the Depression of the 1930s, Tammany's hold began slowly to erode. The state and city have remained in difficult confrontation though ironically, home rule and increased state financial assistance have become joint demands. Attention remains on the need for the state to provide a growing proportion of services.   (A.K.Ca.)

Pennsylvania

An overview of the state

One of the original 13 American colonies, the Commonwealth of Pennsylvania, as it styles itself, is the fourth most populous state in the nation. Since its founding in 1681, its geographical position has made it the Keystone State, integrating first the older colonies of the Northeast and the South and later the states of the East and the developing territories and states of the Middle West. The role remains in evidence, with the state polarized by two great metropolitan areas: Philadelphia lies athwart the vast population belt stretching along the seaboard from Maine to Virginia, and Pittsburgh is the beginning of the booming industrial belt reaching westward across the Great Lakes plains to Chicago and Milwaukee. Its capital, Harrisburg, nestles in the foothills of the Appalachian Mountains.

The 45,333 square miles (117,412 square kilometres) of Pennsylvania are bounded on the north by Lake Erie and New York; on the east by New York and New Jersey; on the south by Delaware, Maryland, and West Virginia; and on the west by the Panhandle of West Virginia and by Ohio. Although it is classified as a Middle Atlantic state, it does not touch the Atlantic Ocean at any point. Water, nonetheless, has been nearly as crucial in the state's growth as has the wealth of its earth. The boundary with New Jersey is formed by the Delaware River, on which Philadelphia is the major element in the Pennsylvania–New Jersey–Delaware harbour complex known as Ameriport, one of the world's busiest shipping centres. In the northwest, a small panhandle bumps out to separate Ohio and New York, to form a 40-mile (64-

kilometre) waterfront on Lake Erie and to give the state access to the iron-ore barges and other commerce of the Great Lakes. Located at the point where the Allegheny and Monongahela rivers meet to form the Ohio River, Pittsburgh has become one of the nation's busiest inland river ports.

PHYSICAL AND HUMAN GEOGRAPHY

The land. *Relief.* The mountains and rivers that dominate Pennsylvania's natural landscape have had a major influence in determining its use by man. The man-made boundaries that made it nearly rectangular in shape are totally decimated by the Allegheny section of the Appalachian Mountain system. Running across the state from southwest to northeast, it leaves only a triangle of Piedmont and Coastal Plain in the southeast, with Philadelphia and environs at its extreme point. The Allegheny Front and Mountains form an up-and-down diagonal spine across the centre of the state, while to the north and west a rugged plateau region falls almost at the lakefront into the Lake Erie Lowland.

Surface features

In the eastern part of the state, the Delaware is fed mainly by the Lehigh and Schuylkill. The Susquehanna, draining the largest section of the state, is a wide, shallow stream that meanders finally into Maryland and Chesapeake Bay. The Ohio system in the west has several tributaries within the state during its 980-mile course by way of the Mississippi into the Gulf of Mexico. Minor systems lead into Lake Erie in the northwest and the Potomac from the southwest.

From southeast to northwest, Pennsylvania takes in parts of seven physiographic regions. Inland from the fertile Coastal Plains around Philadelphia, the Piedmont is an area of rich limestone soils and prosperous farms that are the mainstay of the state's agriculture. The Reading Prong, part of the New England Upland, is a small tongue of a ridge in the northeast. In the south central region, the northernmost finger of the Blue Ridge extends into the state, its topography having played a large part in the Battle of Gettysburg during the American Civil War.

The Appalachian Ridge and Valley region, running southwestward across the state, to the west of the Piedmont, comprises a series of parallel ridges and valleys, including the long and wide Lehigh, Lebanon, and Cumberland valleys, which were important in America's early westward movement. From this rises the geologically newer Appalachian Plateau, whose rough-and-tumble aspect of small valleys and broken, ragged ridge lines covers more than one-half of the state, from the southwestern and western borders to the Delaware in the northeast and on into New York. Plateaus up to 2,000 feet high cover northern Pennsylvania, including Mt. Davis, at 3,213 feet (979 metres), the state's highest point. The home of the major coal-mining operations, its landscape is dotted with mines and mining towns. The sandstone soils of the mountains and plateaus are poor agriculturally. In the northwestern bump lie the Lake Erie Lowlands, a flat area of gravelly but fertile soils that once lay at lake or ocean bottom and now is a producer of grapes, wine, and potatoes.

Climate. The climate is far less variable across the state than is the landscape. Pennsylvania has a continental climate that is characterized by wide fluctuations in seasonal temperatures, with prevailing winds from the west. The frost-free period lasts the longest in the southwest, the Ohio Valley, and the Erie Lowlands. Higher areas have from three to five months a year without frost. Coupled with some 42 inches (1,067 millimetres) of rain annually, this provides adequately for the cultivation of temperate-zone crops and vegetation. In the north, average temperature ranges from about 22° F (−6° C) in January to about 68° F (20° C) in July. In the southeast and western portions of the state, averages are several degrees higher.

Plant and animal life. Pennsylvania marks the transition zone between the northern and southern forests of North America. More than one-half of the state remains wooded, although only small areas are virgin forest. Hickory, locust, maple, cherry, beech, black walnut, elm, chestnut, poplar, ash, sycamore, willow, linden, white and yellow pine, and other conifers are all common in various parts of the state. The southeast has some trees common to the Mississippi Valley.

Pennsylvania's abundant wildlife makes it a leading state for hunting. Unprotected predatory species include red and gray foxes, wildcats, and weasels. Most large animals gradually have been eliminated by man. Species once common—*e.g.,* the black bear and the Canada lynx—are now rare, although skunks and raccoons, pheasants and other game birds, and, in some areas, deer are still found in abundance. More than 150 species of fish, including trout, bass, chub, pickerel, and white carp, are found in the streams.

Settlement patterns. The Pennsylvania landscape under human settlement is as varied as its physical geography. Although nearly all the land is forested or under cultivation, Pennsylvania is considered an urban, industrial state. Urban areas in the state, however, comprise widely separated enclaves.

The rural areas of Pennsylvania, especially the farmlands, lie mostly in the southeastern counties. In the southwest and in the Susquehanna River Valley, pasturelands dot the landscape. Generally, several small villages, each consisting of a general store, a church, a gasoline station, and a few houses, are located within a short distance of a larger town that serves the surrounding farms. In the mining regions, the town structure was once completely dependent on the mines. By the 1980s, company ownership of stores and miners' homes was no longer the prevalent pattern in these towns. Many miners owned their own homes and shopped at national and regional chain stores.

For the most part, the urban centres of Pennsylvania developed along with specific industries. Reading is known as a textile and hosiery town, Hershey as a chocolate town, Pittsburgh and Bethlehem as steel producers, Erie as a Great Lakes port, and the Wilkes-Barre and Scranton areas as centres of the coal industry. In each case, the city extends its influence into the surrounding areas as a supplier of goods and as the determiner of artistic and cultural life.

The people. *Ethnic distribution.* Four major Indian groups with tribal settlements occupied Pennsylvania at the time of the European incursion. These included the Delaware, or Lenni Lenape, in the Delaware River Basin; the Susquehanna along the Susquehanna River in Pennsylvania and Maryland; the Shawnee along the Susquehanna and near the present site of Easton; and various segments of the Five Nations of the Iroquois. With their bitter and bloody struggle to retain their land, the Indians were a very powerful force in the early history of Pennsylvania, but all were gradually pushed to the north or west as European settlers prospered. Fewer than 9,200 Indians remain today in scattered locations.

Although the Swedes and the Dutch arrived in Pennsylvania first, the English Quakers were by far the most important of the early groups that settled along the Delaware River. With a secure hold on the region, the Quakers quickly turned the Delaware counties—especially Penn's three original counties, Philadelphia, Chester, and Bucks—into a thriving commercial region.

Penn's policies of toleration and his experiments in democratic forms of government encouraged other groups to settle in Pennsylvania in large blocs. Germans from the Rhineland settled in numbers in the inland counties of Lancaster, Lehigh, Berks, and Northampton. By the time of the American Revolution, the Pennsylvania Dutch, as they had become known, constituted fully one-third of the colony's population. They turned their land into one of the richest and most productive farming areas in the world and made their customs, cooking, and artwork famous.

Small subgroups of the German community are important components of Pennsylvania's population in their own right. Largely religious, they include the Amish, the Mennonites, the Moravians, the Schwenkfelders, and the Dunkers. The Amish have attracted special attention because of their old-fashioned dress and educational methods and their preference for living apart and farming without modern machinery.

The third major ethnic group to settle in Pennsylvania were the Scots-Irish. Pressing west past the areas of English

and German settlement, this group settled along the western frontier during the middle of the 18th century. Along with the true Scots, with whom they intermingled, the Scots-Irish composed about one-fourth of the entire population of the colony at the outbreak of the Revolution. In addition to the three main groups listed above, there were small numbers of French Protestants, or Huguenots; Welsh; Cornish; and Irish; and, of course, the Dutch and the Swedes. Through the early years of the 20th century, immigration to Pennsylvania continued to be largely German and Irish.

Until the 1860s, there was open land on the western frontier of the state. During this period the religious character of the commonwealth changed: the Quakers and the Pennsylvania Dutch lost numerical strength to predominantly Roman Catholic immigrants, and Presbyterianism and Methodism gained footholds in the west. During the 20th century, the most important European immigrants to enter the state have been of southern and eastern European origin, particularly Italians and Slavic peoples, who provided manpower for the state's burgeoning industry and manufacturing. During and after World War II, in response to the needs of the economy, black Americans from the rural South began to settle in Pennsylvania in increasing numbers. For the most part, the newly arrived black Americans, like the earlier Italians and Slavs, have tended to settle in urban, industrial areas.

Although Pennsylvania is a melting pot of many ethnic groups, the Quakers and the Pennsylvania Dutch continue to play roles in the culture and tradition of the state out of proportion to their actual numbers.

Demography. The greatest population density is found in Philadelphia and Allegheny counties, the latter including Pittsburgh. In 1790, when the first federal census was taken, 89.8 percent of the population was classified as rural. The turning point came in 1900, when for the first time the urban population, at 54.7 percent, outstripped the rural.

The economy. With fertile farmland, more than 17,-000,000 acres (7,000,000 hectares) of commercial forest land, seemingly inexhaustible supplies of coal, many navigable waterways, and an economically strategic location on the Eastern Seaboard, Pennsylvania has always been one of the most prosperous states in the nation. As the exploitation of its primary wealth—soils, minerals, and forests—proceeded during the 18th and 19th centuries, Pennsylvania held a place that was second only to New York in wealth and population.

Pennsylvania still produces more steel than any other state, and its manufacturing industries are as diversified as those of any state in the Union. In the 20th century, however, the changing nature of modern industry, the use of fuels other than coal, and the growth of the rest of the country have left the Keystone State in fifth place in wealth (as measured in terms of gross personal income) and fourth in population. It is surpassed in manufacturing employment only by New York and California and in value added by manufacturing only by New York, California, Ohio, Illinois, and Michigan. Technological changes have left their mark on the economy, and pockets of poverty and unemployment remain.

Mining. More than $1,000,000,000 worth of products come from Pennsylvania's mines, quarries, and wells each year. The largest share is from coal, in the production of which Pennsylvania ranks fourth among the states. Nearly 80 percent of the soft-coal resources remain. Oil is a minor resource in the west, but oil piped from Louisiana, Oklahoma, and Texas and brought by tanker from Venezuela and the Middle East is processed in the huge refineries lining the Delaware. The state ranks fifteenth nationally, however, in production of natural gas. Small deposits of iron ore have been discovered, along with limestone, silver and gold, copper, cobalt, and zinc. Salt beds recently were discovered in the west.

Industry. Pennsylvania's first ironworks, for the production of wrought iron, was built in Berks County in 1716. The eastern region long was the centre of production, especially after large-scale exploitation of its anthracite fields began. The Pittsburgh area became increasingly important

Rural and urban Pennsylvania

Beginnings of ethnic diversification

An economic overview

as bituminous coal and coke replaced anthracite and as the Great Lakes became the route for barges from the rich iron-ore beds around Lake Superior. In total steel production, the Pittsburgh area is second only to the complex of mills at the southern tip of Lake Michigan.

Pennsylvania has always been known for the variety of its manufactures. In addition to steel, Pennsylvania leads the nation in the production of clay refractories, truck trailers, and inorganic pigments. On the basis of the value of the manufactured products and the number of employees, the leading industries are metal and metal products and textiles. Other major industries include electrical and non-electrical machinery, food and kindred products, chemicals and allied products, and transportation equipment. Industry is unevenly distributed, its greatest concentration being in Philadelphia, Allegheny, and Montgomery counties.

The retail-sales industry is also important. John Wanamaker opened the nation's first department store in Philadelphia in the 1870s. Frank Woolworth opened his first successful five-and-ten-cent store in Lancaster in the same period. Other famous Pennsylvanians in the history of retailing are R.H. Kress, S.S. Kresge, G.C. Murphy, Newberry, and W.T. Grant, all of whom founded chains bearing their names.

Agriculture. Pennsylvania still has a sizable farm population. About one-third of the state is under cultivation in more than 59,000 farms. The greatest farm acreage remains in Lancaster, York, and Berks counties in the southeast, which have the state's richest soils. Dairy products account for almost 50 percent of agricultural income, with milk the main product, followed by eggs and dairy cattle. Pennsylvania is also the leading American producer of mushrooms and cigar-leaf tobacco. It is the second largest national producer of ice cream and frozen dairy products and ranks among the top five states in the production of milk, eggs, sour cherries, apples, and grapes.

Management of the economy. In 1956 the Pennsylvania Industrial Development Authority was set up to assist in the redevelopment of areas plagued by chronic unemployment. The greater part of the available funds is lent to "growth" industries. Two development corporations, the Pennsylvania Development Credit Corporation and the Southeastern Pennsylvania Economic Development Corporation, provide funds for equipment or working capital to business in the Philadelphia area.

Pennsylvania's Department of Environmental Resources is engaged in the protection and restoration of more than 2,000,000 acres (809,000 hectares) of forests under its control. The department's Bureau of Soil and Water Conservation plays an advisory role for farmers and city dwellers.

Transportation. Pennsylvania's three major ports—Philadelphia, Pittsburgh, and Erie—are supplemented by others along the Delaware, the Susquehanna, and the channellized Inland Waterway System, which includes the Allegheny and the Monongahela as well as the Ohio. The greatest percentage of Philadelphia's imports is petroleum, but it has facilities for handling ores, coal, molasses, and general cargo as well. Part of Erie's facilities have been converted to the building of ore carriers for Great Lakes service.

Pennsylvania's highway system, one of the largest in the nation, includes the Pennsylvania Turnpike, a four-lane toll road joining New Jersey and Ohio that was a model for the nation in modern superhighway construction. It is paralleled to the north by Interstate 80, also a superhighway spanning the state.

More than 7,200 miles (11,500 kilometres) of rail lines link the state's industrial communities. These rail lines serve as important economic links for the Middle Atlantic region. Philadelphia and Pittsburgh have major commercial airports, though many other Pennsylvania cities are served by scheduled flights.

Administrative and social conditions. *Government.* Under the constitution of 1968, the executive branch of state government comprises the governor and lieutenant governor, the attorney general, the auditor general, and the members of the Cabinet. The governor is elected for a four-year term and can succeed himself for one additional term. Other elected officials include the lieutenant governor, the auditor general, and the state treasurer. The governor appoints the attorney general and the secretary of education, subject to Senate approval. Among the main powers of the governor are his rights to return bills for reconsideration and to veto portions of appropriation bills. The General Assembly is made up of a Senate and a House of Representatives. Senators are elected for four-year terms and representatives for two-year terms.

A unified judicial system comprises the Supreme Court, Superior Court, Commonwealth Court, and courts of common pleas, community courts, municipal and traffic courts in Philadelphia, and justices of the peace and such other courts as may be established by the General Assembly. The seven justices of the Supreme Court and judges of the Superior Court are elected for 10-year terms; justices of the peace and of the municipal and traffic courts of Philadelphia are elected for six-year terms.

Under the constitution, local government is provided for by the General Assembly, which classifies cities, counties, boroughs, school districts, townships, and special authorities by population. All Assembly provisions must be uniform throughout each class, and no legislation may be directed toward one locality. As the only first-class city, however, Philadelphia becomes the target of legislation aimed at this class. It, with Pittsburgh and Scranton, second-class cities, has a strong-mayor government. Smaller cities have several governmental forms, while boroughs have elected councils and weak mayors.

Pennsylvania has two classes of townships and five classes of school districts. Local authorities are special units that were set up in 1933 to circumvent constitutional restrictions preventing local units from incurring debt. The cities, boroughs, and townships, as all-purpose governmental units, carry out all usual public service. A constitutional amendment in 1968 allowed all local governments to opt for home rule.

Between the Civil War and the 1920s, state government was, with a few breaks, in the hands of a succession of Republican administrations that made the statehouse a seat of "boss rule." A similar dynasty persisted in Philadelphia until the late 1940s. During the late 20th century the membership of the General Assembly was usually about evenly divided between Republicans and Democrats. Pennsylvania generally exhibits the characteristic American pattern of rural conservatism and urban liberalism, although locally such labels may bear no necessary relation to particular parties.

Social divisions. The social and economic divisions in Pennsylvania are wide, from the affluence of Philadelphia's suburban Main Line and Pittsburgh's Oakland section to the black and Puerto Rican ghettos ringing the central city, from the lush and prosperous farms of Lancaster County to the pathetic ghost towns of Appalachia. Philadelphia and other large cities face all the grave problems of contemporary cities: the blighting of human life and of the physical environment, inadequate finances, high unemployment, social instability, racial hostility, and a struggling educational system. The day of the isolated farm or mining community is over, but unemployment in mining regions is chronic. The federal Appalachian Regional Commission, established in 1965, is attempting to encourage economic redevelopment throughout the 13 states involved.

Education. Consolidation of public school districts in recent decades has reduced their number. Districts provide physical facilities, teachers, and textbooks and levy taxes and issue bonds. The state Department of Education oversees statewide standards for teacher certification and curricula and apportions money to local school districts.

Pennsylvania is the home of more than 100 colleges and universities in addition to a state system of two-year community colleges. Pennsylvania State University, in University Park, is the publicly supported land-grant institution; it has 21 branch campuses throughout the state. The University of Pennsylvania, in Philadelphia, was originally a charity school at its founding in 1740 but was transformed by Benjamin Franklin and others into an academy. In 1765 it opened the first medical school in North America. Today, among its most notable divisions are the Whar-

Major farm products and crops

Functions of the executive, legislature, and judiciary

Institutions of higher learning

ton School of Finance and Commerce and the University Museum, a leading sponsor of archaeological expeditions and research throughout the world. Though privately endowed, it receives considerable state aid.

State aid is given also to Temple University (1884), in Philadelphia, whose programs are geared heavily to the urban setting, and to the University of Pittsburgh (1787). Philadelphia is still a major centre of medical education, while in Pittsburgh the Carnegie-Mellon University, formed in 1967 by the merger of the Carnegie Institute of Technology (1900) and the Mellon Institute (1913), makes that city a centre of scientific studies. Other schools with major reputations include Bryn Mawr College, for women (1880); Haverford College (1833) and Swarthmore College (1864), both Quaker schools; and Villanova University (1842), a Roman Catholic institution—all in the Philadelphia vicinity. Dating from the 18th century are Dickinson College (1773), in Carlisle; Franklin and Marshall College (1787), in Lancaster; and Washington and Jefferson College (1787), in Washington.

Health and welfare. More than one-half of Pennsylvania's budget is allotted to education, welfare, and highways. Hospitals and centres throughout the state deal with problems of chronic illness, old age, mental retardation, and the like, and local governments are assisted in welfare payments in a broad range of categories. Urban-renewal programs also receive state and federal funding.

Cultural life. In colonial times, Philadelphia was the focus of the nation's intellectual, cultural, and political life. As Pennsylvania grew and prospered, Pittsburgh and other, smaller cities also became centres of the arts.

Two of the nation's major symphony orchestras are located in Pennsylvania. The Philadelphia Orchestra, under such conductors as Leopold Stokowski and Eugene Ormandy, has become world famous, as has the Pittsburgh Symphony Orchestra, under such conductors as Victor Herbert, Fritz Reiner, and William Steinberg. Philadelphia's Academy of Music provides a home and concert hall for its orchestra, and the world-famous Curtis Institute of Music, founded in 1924, is one of the world's leading conservatories. In addition, many community orchestras perform throughout the state. Noted all over the world is the religious music of the Moravians. At their cultural centre, Bethlehem, the Bach Choir's Bach Festival attracts music lovers every May from many states.

The visual arts: painting and sculpture

Philadelphia is the home of one of the world's finest art museums, the Philadelphia Museum of Art, and of the Rodin Museum. The Pennsylvania Academy of the Fine Arts offers a base for teaching and study as well as for display. The Carnegie Institute's museum and library in Pittsburgh also houses many famous paintings. Among famous artists whose homes were in Pennsylvania are Charles Willson Peale and his two sons Raphaelle and Rembrandt, Benjamin West, Mary Cassatt, Thomas Eakins, and the Wyeths, N.C. and his son Andrew. The Calder family of Philadelphia is famous in sculpture. Alexander Milne Calder's giant statue of William Penn stands atop City Hall, and his grandson, Alexander Calder, gained renown for his free-form mobile sculptures.

Philadelphia long vied with New York as the theatrical capital of the young nation, though today it is basically a tryout town for shows on their way to Broadway. Summer theatres have proliferated across the state, especially in the many resort areas. Temple and Carnegie-Mellon universities offer major programs in theatre. The Pennsylvania Ballet offers entertainment both within and outside the state. Among well-known writers of the 20th century with Pennsylvania origins are Pearl S. Buck, Rachel Carson, James Michener, Christopher Morley, John O'Hara, Mary Roberts Rinehart, and John Updike.

In addition to its art museums, Pennsylvania enjoys many other museums, both general and specialized. The Franklin Institute in Philadelphia is a museum of applied science. The William Penn Memorial Museum and Archives Building in Harrisburg, the Pennsylvania Farm Museum of Landis Valley near Lancaster, the Annie S. Kemerer Museum in Bethlehem, and the Mercer Museum of the Bucks County Historical Society (crafts and craftsmen's tools) in Doylestown house fine collections. There

are also small museums in Allentown, Reading, Scranton, and Greensburg and historical society museums in Lancaster, York, Reading, Wilkes-Barre, and West Chester, to mention a few. The Pennsylvania Historical Commission, established in 1913 and known since 1945 as the Pennsylvania Historical and Museum Commission, is active in conservation of the state's historical heritage; the Philadelphia Historical Commission oversees that city's many historic shrines.

Pennsylvania has retained strong elements of folk culture among its diverse ethnic groups. The "plain people"—the Amish, the Mennonites, and other small sects—have kept their old customs and dress and often resist the use of machinery. In Lancaster County, where the Amish still farm with horses and oxen, their wagons are a familiar sight. The folk art and the cooking of the Pennsylvania Dutch are famous, and their brightly painted hex signs adorn their large barns. At Czestochowa, in Bucks County, the largest Polish church in America is evidence of the area's Polish population.

Communications. Public figures such as Benjamin Franklin were responsible for the emergence of newspapers, magazines, and libraries in the colony. Later, the Lippincott and the Curtis publishing families became giants in the publishing world, the Lippincotts as book publishers and the Curtis family as publishers, until very recently, of such magazines as *The Saturday Evening Post, Ladies Home Journal,* and *Country Gentleman.* The *Farm Journal,* a Philadelphia publication, is one of the nation's largest farm magazines. Several other major publishers are also headquartered there.

Historic eminence in publishing

All of Pennsylvania's cities and larger towns have newspapers, either daily or weekly, and many ethnic newspapers are published throughout the state. The major cities have their own television stations, and most local communities have their own radio stations. Station KDKA, the first commercial broadcasting station in the world, opened in Pittsburgh in 1920.

In the age of television and rapid transportation, the various cultural elements in Pennsylvania see the same movies and television programs, read the same newspapers, and share in a wider national culture.

HISTORY

Swedes were the first European settlers in the area that was to become Pennsylvania. Travelling up the Delaware from a settlement at the present site of Wilmington, Delaware, Gov. Johan Printz of the colony of New Sweden established his capital on Tinicum Island in 1643, within the boundaries of modern Pennsylvania. Other Europeans, principally the Dutch, established trading posts within Pennsylvania as early as 1647, although the Swedes remained at Tinicum until 1655. In that year, rivalry and fighting between the Dutch and the Swedes led Peter Stuyvesant, governor of New Netherland, to seize New Sweden. Dutch control of the region ended in 1664, when the English seized all of New Netherland in the name of the Duke of York.

Swedish and Dutch settlements

The Quaker colony. In March 1681 King Charles II of England signed a charter giving the region to William Penn in payment of a debt of £16,000 that was owed by the King to Penn's father, Adm. Sir William Penn. The charter, which was officially proclaimed on April 2, 1681, named the territory for Admiral Penn and included also the term *sylvania* ("woodlands"), as the younger Penn requested.

William Penn intended that the colony should provide a haven of religious tolerance for his fellow Quakers. While still in England, he drew up the first of his "frames of government" and dispatched his cousin, William Markham, to establish claim to the land and also to establish the boundaries of what became the city of Philadelphia. Penn arrived in 1682 and called a General Assembly to discuss the first Frame of Government and to adopt the Great Law, which guaranteed freedom of conscience in the colony. Under Penn's influence, fair treatment was accorded the Indians, who responded with friendship in return. When Penn returned to England in 1684, the new Quaker province had a firmly established government based on religious tolerance and government by popular will.

Colonial growth. The century that followed was a period of great expansion and of turmoil for Pennsylvania. Its interior included land that was claimed by the French, and as time went on, the Indians became increasingly hostile to the expansion of settlements to the west and north. Much of the fighting during the French and Indian War (1754–63) took place in Pennsylvania. Here the young George Washington began his journey into the Ohio Valley to warn the French to leave; later, it was in Pennsylvania that the English general Edward Braddock suffered defeat at the hands of the French forces and their Indian allies.

For many Pennsylvanians, the period following these conflicts marked growing dissatisfaction with British rule. Official limitations on westward expansion, especially as established by proclamation in 1763, were imposed to pacify the Indians, but Pennsylvanians nonetheless pressed westward over the Alleghenies. Outposts such as Ft. Pitt (Fort-Duquesne under the French and now Pittsburgh) became settlements vital to the growing flow of trade from the opening lands to the west.

By the eve of the American Revolution, Pennsylvania had become a keystone state geographically and a centre of military, economic, and political activity. The first (1774) and second (1775–76) continental congresses met in Philadelphia, the Declaration of Independence was signed there, and after the war the city became the capital of the short-lived confederation and of the fledgling United States government.

Early years as a state. In 1790 a new state constitution was adopted that replaced the unicameral legislature of the Revolutionary period with a bicameral one and a fairly strong governor. In the period of the next 70 years, farm equipment was mechanized, roads were improved and extended, canals were built, and railroads spanned the state, all combining with the economic strength of the thrifty Philadelphians to make Pennsylvania a major commercial power. Beginning in 1820, important mining companies were formed to exploit Pennsylvania's deposits of hard and soft coal, and in 1859 Edwin L. Drake drilled the nation's first successful oil well at Titusville. During this same period the state became a leading producer of textiles, ships, lumber, tobacco, and, most important, iron and steel.

The Civil War and its effects The Pennsylvania Emancipation Act of 1781 had pledged the gradual abolition of slavery in the state. Once the Civil War broke out, Pennsylvania became once again a centre of military and political activity. The southern boundary of Pennsylvania, ratified in 1769, was the Mason and Dixon Line. It became the dividing line between the slave and the free states during the Civil War. At Gettysburg the Union Army won one of the most decisive victories of the war against a Confederate force led by Gen. Robert E. Lee.
(C.L.T.)

Emergence of the modern state. Politically the state was dominated after the Civil War by a remarkable dynasty of "bosses," founded by Simon Cameron and continued by his son James Donald Cameron and by Matthew Stanley Quay and Boies Penrose until the latter's death in 1921. Under their astute management the Republican Party generally ruled Pennsylvania, although reform movements occasionally interrupted their control, as when the Democrat Robert E. Pattison was elected governor in 1882 and 1890. During and after the Civil War, there was tremendous expansion in the iron and steel industry, in coal mining, and other industries, that transformed Pennsylvania from a predominantly agricultural state to an industrial giant. The demand for labour in the growing industrial economy brought a new wave of immigration from 1865 to 1914, and Poles, Italians, Czechs, Hungarians, Russians, and others supplemented the earlier population groups. As the state grew industrially, a labour movement developed and gave rise to the American Federation of Labor and the Congress of Industrial Organizations, both of which began in Pennsylvania.

Progress was made in extending the services of government. Insurance and banking departments were created in 1873 and 1891 as regulatory agencies. During the administration of Gov. Samuel W. Pennypacker (1903–07), a number of new departments were created, including forestry, health, and highways, and a state police force was organized. In 1915 a Department of Labor and Industry was established. Under Gov. William C. Sproul (1919–23) the public school system was reorganized, an extensive program of highway building was undertaken, and a Department of Welfare was created.

After the death of Penrose, the progressives in the Republican Party gained more influence; Gifford Pinchot was elected governor in 1922 and 1930. During his first term (1923–27) the administrative code was enacted to consolidate departments and centralize control, thus increasing the governor's power. This was amended and made still more complete under the conservative Gov. John S. Fisher (1927–31). The New Deal and division in the Republican Party brought victory to the Democrats in 1934 for the third time since the Civil War, and they elected George H. Earle as governor and one United States senator. The Republicans regained the governorship in 1938 by electing Arthur H. James, and then elected three governors in succession, Edward Martin, James H. Duff, and John S. Fine. The Democratic Party, however, did not revert to its former weak position and often won the governorship thereafter.

During the Great Depression the state undertook a program of building construction at health, penal, military, and educational institutions through the General State Authority, approved in 1937. The first section of the Pennsylvania Turnpike from Carlisle to Pittsburgh was begun in 1938. After World War II, the state resumed its extensive construction of public works and highways. Notable progress was made in a conservation program that began with soil conservation, reforestation, and clearing rivers of silt and pollution and went forward with major efforts to preserve historic and scenic areas and to provide "open space" near cities.
(Ed.)

THE SOUTH

The South and the Deep South The South is an extensive region covering approximately the southeastern quarter of the continental United States. There is no clear line of demarcation between it and the body of states to the north and the west, but it is generally considered to include the states of West Virginia, Virginia, North Carolina, South Carolina, Georgia, Florida, Kentucky, Tennessee, Alabama, Mississippi, Arkansas, and Louisiana. (The so-called Deep South embraces Georgia, Alabama, Mississippi, and Louisiana and frequently South Carolina.) Sometimes the South is also presumed to include parts of the states of Texas, Oklahoma, Missouri, Maryland, and Delaware. Since the end of the colonial period the South has formed a major section of the United States, substantially distinct from other sections in agriculture, economic and social structure, and political attitudes.

The land. In its physical geography, the South does not possess any natural unity. In fact, it includes a number of quite diverse geographical districts. Along the coast, from Maryland to the Rio Grande, there is a low coastal plain, marked by a series of alluvial rivers flowing eastward to the Atlantic or southward to the Gulf of Mexico. On the Atlantic shore, this coastal plain rises gradually to the "fall line," where the streams cease to be navigable. There begins an area known as the Piedmont, where the land is rolling or hilly, erosion has taken place, and reddish-yellow clay soils predominate in contrast to the sandy or alluvial soils of the coast. At its western edge, the Piedmont rises into the Appalachian Mountain system, the southern part of which extends from Maryland to northern Georgia and Alabama. The easternmost part of this system consists of the Blue Ridge Mountains, behind which lies the main Appalachian ridge. Beyond the Appalachian ridge

Site of battles and Revolutionary ferment

is the high and mountainous country of the Cumberland Plateau. This mountainous terrain dominates the western parts of Maryland, Virginia, North Carolina, the northern part of Georgia, the eastern parts of Tennessee and Kentucky, and most of West Virginia.

Just as the Appalachian Mountain system is the key to the geography of the eastern or Atlantic coastal part of the South, so the Mississippi River Valley is the key to the western or Gulf coastal part. Although portions of Alabama, Mississippi, Louisiana, and Texas drain directly into the Gulf of Mexico, other parts of these states and all of Kentucky, Tennessee, Missouri, and Arkansas drain into the Mississippi. On its west bank, such major rivers as the Missouri, the White, the Arkansas, the Ouachita, and the Red flow eastward through fertile alluvial valleys directly into the Mississippi. On the eastern side of the valley, the principal southern rivers are the Cumberland and the Tennessee, but instead of flowing westward from the Appalachian ridge into the Mississippi, these streams traverse great semicircular arcs, first swinging southward and then northward across Tennessee and Kentucky into the Ohio River and thence into the Mississippi. Their courses run through rich limestone valleys that give great and distinctive beauty to the Nashville Basin in Tennessee and the bluegrass region of Kentucky.

In terms of climate and soil, the South shows features of uniformity somewhat more than it does in geography. Almost the entire region lies in the same latitudes as North Africa, and the climate is, in general, mild to hot. In the summers, temperatures rise, day after day, above 90° F (32° C) in the shade. But the maximum heat is less significant than the long growing season—a period of 200 to 290 frost-free days during which slow-growing crops such as cotton, rice, and sugarcane may be brought to maturity. There is also abundant rainfall, averaging 40 to 50 inches (1,000 to 1,300 millimetres) per annum in the upper South and 50 to 60 inches in the Gulf Coast region.

Because of the warmth of the region, it was not glaciated during the Ice Age, and this lack of glaciation gives a distinctive quality to the soil. Except in the limestone basins of Kentucky and Tennessee, in the Black Belt across parts of central Georgia, Alabama, and Mississippi, and in the river valleys with their rich alluvial deposit, the soil is predominantly of coarse texture and of mediocre fertility, with high proportions of clay in the Piedmont region, with its "red hills," and of sand in the coastal districts. Soil exhaustion has occurred widely in these areas, both because of their natural lack of fertility and because of the soil-depleting effects of the cotton and tobacco cultures. As a result, the South regularly consumes a large portion of the nation's output of commercial fertilizer. Also, erosion has occurred very widely in the Piedmont area because of the torrential rains, coupled with the exposure of the soil in plowed hills and furrows that are used in the row cropping of cotton and tobacco. This erosion had been so severe that by 1930 the South had suffered a total loss of fertility in 22,500,000 acres (9,100,000 hectares) of its land—an area larger than the entire state of South Carolina.

Soil erosion

The people. The geographical variety has produced a diversity rather than a uniformity of Southern folk—a diversity ranging from the isolated mountaineers of Appalachian valleys to the semi-amphibious bayou dwellers of southern Louisiana and including the "red necks" of the southern hill country, the poor whites of the piney woods, the cattle-herding plainsmen of Texas, the blacks who form more than 80 percent of the population of some areas along the Mississippi, and the cotton-planting farmers, both great and small, who, more than any others, have constituted a "Southern" type.

In terms of the origins of its population, the South presents a pattern that is unlike that of the rest of the country but that, again, shows lack of uniformity within the region itself. The contrast with the non-South lies in the fact that the South received only a small proportion of the immigrants who came to the United States after 1800, and hence it has a relatively small number of people of southern, central, and eastern European antecedents. Most of the population is descended from the settlers who arrived during the colonial period. In the 17th century, English settlers established themselves in the coastal areas of Virginia, Maryland, and the Carolinas. In the 18th century, a heavy influx of Scots-Irish (Presbyterians of lowland Scotland who had migrated first to northern Ireland and then to America) and German settlers moved southward from Pennsylvania into the southern Piedmont. During the same century, the French settled in Louisiana, where their language, religion, and culture are still in evidence, and at Mobile, in southern Alabama. The Spanish at the same time occupied Florida but did not settle in sufficient force to leave an important Hispanic tradition. The most extensive influx of the 18th century was the involuntary immigration of blacks brought as chattel slaves directly or indirectly from the west coast of Africa. This importation had begun as early as 1619 but did not attain large numbers until after 1700. By the year 1790, however, blacks formed more than one-third of the population in the states of Maryland, Virginia, South Carolina, and Georgia; and in the late 20th century they continued to form more than 20 percent of the population in Virginia, North Carolina, South Carolina, Georgia, Alabama, Mississippi, Louisiana, and Arkansas.

The early plantation economy. The one feature above all others that made the South historically a distinctive and somewhat homogeneous region is the fact that, for more than three centuries, it relied almost wholly upon an agricultural economy centred upon staple crops that were cultivated for sale on the world market. Even as late as 1948, the South still derived twice as much of its income from agriculture (16 percent) as did the non-South (8 percent). The first of these crops was tobacco, first cultivated in Virginia about 1612, just five years after the founding of the colony. Tobacco culture spread into Maryland and northern North Carolina, and for nearly 200 years it provided the chief export product of North America. Meanwhile, rice about 1698 and indigo about 1744 took hold in the Carolinas and quickly grew to dominate the economy of the coastal part of that colony. The culture of sugarcane was successfully launched in French Louisiana in 1794, and it also expanded to become the chief economic activity of the region. But none of these crops rivalled cotton, which created Southern wealth, shaped Southern institutions, and, as "king cotton," grew to symbolize the whole South at the height of its power.

"King Cotton"

The long-fibred, or black-seed, cotton was profitably cultivated on the coastal islands of Georgia and the Carolinas before the American Revolution, but the only strain that would grow in most areas on the mainland was the short-fibred, green-seed plant. The latter seemed commercially worthless because the lint clung so firmly to the seed that the separation of the fibres was impracticable. This situation was suddenly changed in 1793, however, when Eli Whitney, a Connecticut Yankee teaching school in Georgia, invented a device, known as a cotton gin, to separate the fibres. Whitney's gin made it possible for the South to supply cotton for a world textile market in which the new technology of mechanical spinning and weaving had created an insatiable demand for raw material. The production of Southern cotton doubled every decade between 1800 and 1861, until it reached 4,400,000 bales in 1861. As this growth took place, the staple-crop economy spread into the Gulf Coast region, and within a single generation the South expanded from the Oconee River in Georgia to the banks of the Brazos in Texas.

The staple-crop economy of tobacco, rice, indigo (declining sharply after the American Revolution), sugarcane, and cotton shaped the character of the South. Since production on a big scale was profitable, large agricultural units known as plantations grew up. Although vast numbers of small, owner-cultivated farms remained, the plantation became a dominant factor. Because the crops were used for commercial purposes rather than for subsistence (such as prevailed in the backwoods), it paid the proprietor to employ labour and thus increase production. The slow-maturing crops needed attention most of the year and thus required a permanent labour force. Because the agricultural tasks were simple enough to be performed by unskilled labour working in gangs, owners resorted to the use of black slaves. Thus the one-crop system, the planta-

Plantation slavery

tion unit, and the presence of a biracial population, with the blacks in a subordinate position, were all developed in the South early in the 18th century, and their grip was tightened by the overpowering rise of the cotton economy. By 1850 there were 3,204,000 slaves in the South, and it was estimated that 1,815,000 of these were connected with the cultivation of cotton.

Ultimately, the complex of staple crops, plantations, and black-slave cultivators gave to the South qualities that made it a distinctive region and set it in an adverse sectional relationship to other parts of the United States. But until the 19th century, the sectional alignment was far from clear-cut. Historians now reject a once-prevalent interpretation that explained the differences between North and South in terms of the dissimilarities between Puritans in colonial New England and cavaliers in colonial Virginia. The British colonists who settled the two regions were not so sharply differentiated as the tradition has claimed. Moreover, in the colonial South the plantation economy and slavery were rather narrowly confined to limited areas around Chesapeake Bay and in the coastal district of the Carolinas and Georgia. The democratic, Presbyterian, Scots-Irish who populated the vast back country of the Piedmont did not share in this regime. They practiced a subsistence economy, cultivated grain crops, had no use for slaves, and were frequently at odds with the aristocratic, Anglican planters. These subsistence farmers of the interior seemed to have more in common with the similarly circumstanced settlers in the interior of Massachusetts and the backwoods of Pennsylvania than either group had with the grandees of the coastal districts—whether merchant princes in Boston or planter-aristocrats in Charleston, South Carolina, and along the James River. Correspondingly, the latter groups showed a greater affinity with one another than with their neighbours to the west. The antagonism between the coastal and the interior districts was chronic and repeatedly manifested itself in incidents of friction such as Shay's Rebellion in Massachusetts and the uprising of the Regulators in the Carolinas. At the time of the American Revolution this east-west division seemed likely to remain the primary line of sectional cleavage.

At that time, the divisions between North and South still remained somewhat tenuous. The leaders of both sections agreed in regarding slavery as an evil. At the same time, both sections practiced it, and it was sanctioned by law in every state. The actual concentration of slaves was overwhelmingly in the South; 94 percent of all slaves in 1790 were held south of Pennsylvania. But many districts in the South had almost no slaves, and slavery was widely regarded as a localized and declining institution.

Between 1775 and 1830, however, both North and South experienced transformations that heightened their dissimilarities and generated deep antagonisms between them. The Northern transformation came as the region slowly began to industrialize. This process committed it politically to the idea of economic self-sufficiency within a national market protected by tariff walls, where agricultural areas and manufacturing areas would complement one another by producing to meet each other's needs and serving as markets for each other's products. Industrialization generated rapid economic change in the North, and this gave sanction to the idea of progress and to the idea of a free society in which the individual can alter his occupation and status to meet changing conditions. Moreover, the use of machines freed the worker from many brute tasks and, by increasing productivity, raised the standard of living. Both of these developments tended to enhance the dignity of the worker.

Meanwhile, in the South the advent of the cotton economy made it possible to convert the whole region to staple-crop agriculture, as had never been possible with tobacco, rice, and sugar. Cotton would grow almost everywhere in the South, and it was more flexible than other staple crops in lending itself to production on any scale, large or small. The cotton economy moved quickly into the up-country, thus obliterating the former divisions between the coastal and the Piedmont areas. By carrying the plantation and slavery with it, it increased the value of slaves and reinvigorated the declining slave system.

Economically, the South looked to the British textile industry for its market, and it therefore opposed the growing economic nationalism of the North and West. Socially, the plantation system discounted the commercial values of thrift, prudence, enterprise, and progress; it exalted qualities of magnanimity, command, manly prowess, and physical courage; and it adopted a cult of chivalry, with a code duello, to enshrine these virtues. The Southern social philosophy, holding to a country-gentry ideal, presented a sharp contrast with that of the North, for it stressed the conservative values of status in a fixed social order rather than of freedom, of stability rather than of progress, and of a way of life rather than accumulation of wealth. Such an emphasis was almost inevitable in a region where one-third of the population occupied a position of fixed legal subordination and was forbidden any measure of self-improvement or even aspiration.

The slavery controversy. The growing divergence between North and South, as well as the dissimilarities in their values, found a focus in the question of slavery. In the North the anti-slavery sentiment of the Revolutionary era continued to grow. Between 1777 and 1804, every state north of Maryland either abolished slavery outright or provided for gradual Abolition. The early anti-slavery movement was moderate in tone and sought to bring about emancipation gradually by persuading slaveowners to free their slaves voluntarily. But about 1830 it entered a new and more militant phase in which immediate Abolition was demanded and slaveowners were denounced in most abusive terms. The militant Abolitionists were always a minority, and historians disagree as to the extent to which the North became "abolitionized," but it is clear that anti-slavery sentiment became very widespread. The immense popularity of Harriet Beecher Stowe's *Uncle Tom's Cabin* (1852) and the election to the presidency of Abraham Lincoln, who had said that "if slavery is not wrong, then nothing is wrong," serve as indexes to this feeling.

While the North passed from mild opposition to strong condemnation of slavery, the South passed from mild opposition to an unqualified defense of the "peculiar institution." Various Southern spokesmen defended slavery on the ground that it was sanctioned by the Bible, that the economic exploitation of wage earners was worse than the exploitation of slaves, that the black was biologically inferior, and that in a well-ordered society it was better for one class to be set apart for the menial duties. Belief that slavery was a positive good became a test of Southern orthodoxy.

With all the cultural dissimilarities and economic conflicts of interest between North and South converted into a dispute on the slavery question, sectional antagonisms were chronically acute between 1830 and 1860 and erupted into war in 1861. The states of the lower South took Abraham Lincoln's election in 1860 as a signal to act. Seven of them (South Carolina, Georgia, Florida, Alabama, Mississippi, Louisiana, Texas) adopted ordinances of secession and proceeded (1861) to form a new union, the Confederate States of America. Lincoln denied the legality of their act and sought to maintain the authority of the Union. As a result, fighting began at Ft. Sumter, in Charleston Harbour (April 1861). Soon thereafter, four other states (Virginia, North Carolina, Tennessee, Arkansas) also seceded and joined the Confederacy. For four years, the United States and the Confederate states fought each other fiercely in the American Civil War.

Southerners in the heat of secession and war believed that the "Southland" or "Dixie," as they now called it, had achieved a full and separate nationality, not only in the political but also in the cultural sense. Historians since then, with an eye to features of cultural distinctiveness, have also recognized an important degree of "Southern nationalism." It is a serious question, however, whether Southern separatism resulted primarily from deep cultural differentiation or whether it was the reaction of a group who were still an integral part of the American people but who had been psychologically (rather than culturally) alienated from their fellow Americans by a long period of minority status, conflicting interests, and defensive rationalization of slavery. The readiness with which the South returned to the Union after the war suggests the latter.

Antebellum mores

The Confederacy

The South after the Civil War. At any event, the South lost the war, and this loss settled two questions. First, it killed the idea of state sovereignty and secession. Second, it ended the institution of slavery. But there were other problems that the war did not solve and that continued to make for Southern distinctiveness for another century. For one thing, the South continued to rely on a one-crop economy, and it continued to cultivate this crop with the labour of blacks, who discovered that, as long as a person went on making his living by hoeing cotton, the transition from slavery to freedom did not altogether revolutionize his life. For another, the South continued to insist upon the inferiority and the subordination of blacks. Slavery had been partly an economic system for the ownership of labour and partly a social system of racial control; and, though emancipation ended the one, it did not end the other.

During the so-called Reconstruction Era (1865–77), the victorious Republican Party made more or less earnest efforts to assure the blacks' equality, but those who wanted the party to help the blacks were probably never as numerous as those who wanted the blacks to help the party. After the latter perceived that the party might fare better without the help of blacks, the crusade for equality was generally abandoned, and the South was left to work out its own arrangements. As a consequence, the institution of slavery was replaced by three institutions: the economic system of sharecropping, the political system of one-party politics, and the social system of segregation, supported both by law and by custom.

Sharecropping. The system of sharecropping, or tenancy, resulted from need for a new link between the soil and the cultivator. The former slaves lacked funds to buy land; the landowners lacked funds to pay wages. Hence, an agreement was made that the landlord would furnish the land, the freedman the labour, and that each would receive a share of the proceeds for his contribution. The cultivator, however, necessarily received the necessities of life on credit during the annual periods between harvests, and the cotton economy was so unprofitable that the tenant's share seldom left a decent surplus after his debts had been settled. Thus Southern tenant farmers were chronically in debt; their indebtedness limited freedom to move or change occupation; and they had a lower standard of living than any other large group in the U.S. population. Moreover, the chronic overproduction of cotton, with its attendant low prices, forced more and more small landowning farmers into tenancy. Between 1880 and 1930 the proportion of Southern farms operated by the tenants increased from 36 to 55 percent. During the last 30 years of this span, white tenants increased by 400,000 and black tenants by 147,000, so that what had begun as an arrangement for the freedmen became more and more a biracial institution.

One-party system. The one-party system was an arrangement to neutralize the political power of the blacks, who had legally been enfranchised by the 15th Amendment to the U.S. Constitution (1870). After a brief period of Southern support for Populism in the 1890s, Southerners conducted their political activity solely within the Democratic Party. Contending that the Democratic Party was a private and not a public instrumentality, they excluded blacks from participation in the primary elections in which party nominees for office were chosen. Moreover, between 1890 and 1910, most Southern states placed in their constitutions literacy and property qualifications from which large groups of whites, at least in some states, were exempted by clauses allowing them to qualify if their forebears had voted before 1860 ("grandfather clauses"). By these devices, by inequitable enforcement procedures, and by a relatively costly poll tax that most blacks found difficult to pay, blacks were effectively excluded from political life. At the same time, the white "solid South" remained Democratic: 11 states from Virginia to Texas elected only four Republican governors between 1876 and 1960. Because of this concentration in one party, Southerners gained a disproportionate share of committee chairmanships and tended to dominate the U.S. Congress during Democratic administrations. After the 1964 pres-

Democratic Party dominance (margin note)

idential election, when the Republican nominee carried five Southern states, there began the demise of one-party rule in the South.

Segregation. The third of the institutions succeeding to slavery was legalized segregation. The practice of segregation, it may be noted, was far older than the segregation laws, and it extended far beyond the South. Throughout the United States, blacks were generally denied access to places of public resort. They were excluded from trade unions, forced to live in segregated residential areas, prohibited from marrying whites, and prevented from mingling freely with the rest of the population. In most areas, this was done informally or by extralegal devices such as restrictive housing covenants, but in the South it was done by law. Among Southern segregation laws, the statutes requiring segregated education were important. Laws requiring blacks to use segregated railroad facilities were upheld as constitutional by the Supreme Court in the case of *Plessy* v. *Ferguson* (1896).

The "New South." Until 1932 the South remained an impoverished and undiversified region. The growth of a textile industry in the Carolinas and the movement to develop a "New South" after the Civil War had not seriously qualified the region's commitment to cotton, to agriculture, and to a rural way of life. The blacks remained a kind of peasantry, and the income of the South stood at only $372 per capita in 1929, while income outside the South was $797 per capita. But after 1933 the South experienced an economic revolution, resulting partly from the New Deal and the collapse of cotton tenancy and partly from rapid economic diversification and industrialization.

During the Great Depression that began in 1929, cotton prices sank to a point that bankrupted the cotton economy. The plight of the sharecropper was desperate, and cultivation continued only because of the lack of alternatives. When this situation was at its nadir, the government stepped in with two devices that exercised an effect more revolutionary than was intended. Agricultural benefit payments for taking acreage out of production led landlords to curtail sharecropping operations. Partly because of this and partly because of the nationwide shift of population to the cities, the number of tenant farms in the South declined from 1,791,000 in 1930 to 366,000 in 1959, while the number of Southern nonwhite tenants declined from 600,900 to 123,000. The second New Deal device was the system of unemployment relief, which drew blacks temporarily to Southern towns where relief payments were issued. During and after World War II, however, there was heavy black migration to Northern industrial centres. By 1960 the proportion of blacks who lived in the South was only 60 percent, whereas in 1920 it had been 85 percent. By 1960 the average black was no longer a rural-dwelling, sharecropping, cotton cultivator but was a city-dwelling, wage-earning industrial worker.

With World War II and its aftermath, industrial developments and diversification revolutionized the economy within the South. Military installations were heavily concentrated in the South during the war, and after the war several new industries enjoyed spectacular growth. In 1948 the value of cotton produced was $2,189,000,000, but this amount was surpassed both by the value of livestock ($3,072,000,000) and of textiles ($2,832,000,000) and was rivalled by the value of chemical products ($1,082,000,-000), lumber products ($889,000,000), petroleum products ($642,000,000), and paper products ($539,000,000), all of which had increased by more than 247 percent in the preceding eight years. Cotton was no longer king.

Industrialization (margin note)

As a result of this economic change, the percentage of workers in the South employed in agriculture declined sharply. Also, the proportion of Southerners living in cities rose from 15 percent in 1900 to more than 55 percent in 1960 (compared with a national increase from 39 to 70 percent). But perhaps the most drastic change of all was reflected in the greater increase of per capita income in the South. While such income was rising from about $700 to $2,600 for the United States as a whole between 1929 and 1964, it rose from about $350 to more than $1,900 for the Southern states.

At the middle of the 20th century, the steady growth

of industrialism, urbanization, and wealth were constantly diminishing those factors of poverty, agrarianism, and ruralism that had operated to preserve the South's historical traditions and its distinctive identity. But although the distinctive elements in the Southern region had been much reduced, the Southern adherence to a biracial system remained strong enough to assert itself with powerful force when challenged in 1954.

From about 1905 (when a protest was framed by black leaders at Niagara, New York), there had been a rising demand in liberal circles for the elimination of discriminatory practices toward blacks, and after about 1927 (when the white primary was ruled invalid), the U.S. Supreme Court began to interpret the guarantees of the 14th Amendment as prohibiting various forms of discrimination. For many years it did not question the legality of segregation in cases where facilities were "separate and equal," but in 1954 in the case of *Brown* v. *Board of Education*, it reversed the *Plessy* v. *Ferguson* decision and declared that segregation in publicly supported schools was unconstitutional.

Sectional antagonisms flared again as the Southern states denounced "judicial usurpation" and invoked the principle of local self-government, while liberals criticized the South for racial prejudice and for the defiance of federal authority. Eleven states (Virginia, North Carolina, South Carolina, Georgia, Florida, Alabama, Mississippi, Louisiana, Texas, Arkansas, and Tennessee) adopted laws to avoid, directly or indirectly, the integration of the schools, and "citizens' councils" were organized to resist it. In the border states, where resistance was not so strong, desegregation achieved several relatively quick and easy triumphs, as in Washington, Baltimore, St. Louis, and notably Louisville. But in the lower South, resistance was determined, federal court orders were resisted, and some states adopted policies of "massive resistance." By the mid-1960s partly because of continued Southern segregation and partly because of generalized race discrimination throughout the country, black unrest had become intense, and mass demonstrations took place on a wide scale. A century after the South had made its supreme assertion of a separate identity and after many decades of steady decline in the significance of the differentials that distinguish the South, the historical heritage of the South's biracial system was dying. The less tangible aspects of old Southernism—its emphasis upon the virtues of the agrarian way of life, its conservative concept of the social order, its ideal of social standards set by the leaders rather than by the masses—were so much overshadowed that it is difficult to estimate the extent to which these features, by themselves, would have continued to make the South a significant and distinctive entity.   (D.M.Po.)

Alabama

One of the Southern states of the United States, Alabama comprises 51,609 square miles (133,667 square kilometres) forming a roughly rectangular shape, elongated in a north to south direction. Tennessee is the bordering state to the north, Georgia to the east, and Mississippi to the west. A westward coastal extension of northern Florida blocks Alabama's access to the waters of the Gulf of Mexico except in the southwestern corner of the state, where Mobile Bay is located.

The ambience of the Deep South adds vivid character to the local landscape; it has permeated the history of the region; and it touches, inescapably, much of the contemporary way of life in the state. It has also molded the images—and indeed the stereotypes—that the name of the state conjures up in the minds of outsiders.

In northeastern Alabama the broken terrain and fine scenery of the southern fringe of the Appalachians are often reminiscent of areas farther north, yet, in a southwesterly progression, past the belching smokestacks of the modern industrial city of Birmingham, the Alabamian landscapes acquire a marked Southern appearance. The band of prairie lowland known as the Black Belt or Cotton Belt has rich soils that cradled a rural, cotton-producing way of life central to the state's development. Further south the historic houses, iron grills, and slave-made brickwork

of old Mobile, the striking ranks of azaleas blossoming in the Gulf breezes, and the swaying, moss-draped oaks of the coastal fringe add an almost tropical note to the state.

The landscape of Alabama has been the scene of many of the major crises in the settlement of the continent and in the development of the modern nation. It was a battleground for European powers vying for the lands of the New World, for the savage fights between the white settlers and the Indians, for the internecine struggles of North and South during the Civil War, and for the forces of economic and social change that have extensively altered many aspects of the Deep South in the years since World War II. Although Alabama continues to trail near the bottom of the states in many significant social rankings, there has been improvement in race relations, particularly in the area of school desegregation and in the election of blacks to political offices. The state's economy has also shown marked improvement. Yet Alabamians and outsiders alike tend to agree that the state's Deep South heritage remains complex and often troubled in the state.

PHYSICAL AND HUMAN GEOGRAPHY

The land.   *Relief.* Although the average elevation of Alabama is about 500 feet (150 metres) above sea level, this represents a gradation from 2,407 feet (734 metres) atop Cheaha Mountain in the northeast down across the Black Belt to the flat, low, southern Gulf Coast counties. Within this gradation, several relief regions may be distinguished.

The southern extremities of the Appalachians, entering Alabama from the northeast, cover almost half the state. In the far north the Cumberland Plateau region, segmented by river action, thrusts south across the state line. Altitudes rise to 1,800 feet in the more rugged eastern portions. The Great Appalachian Valley forms another marked division to the east. A small triangular portion of the Piedmont Plateau juts across from Georgia at an altitude averaging 1,000 feet.

The character of the state changes markedly as the rugged, forest-clad hills and ridges of the Appalachian extremities give way to the lower country of the Coastal Plain. The plain has a number of subdivisions: in the north lie the rolling Fall Line Hills, while farther south the pine and hardwood belts add irregularity to the flat landscapes. Arcing into the heart of the lowlands of Alabama, the Black Belt has been distinctive from its association with the cotton production that long dominated its rich soils. The 53 miles (85 kilometres) of coastline have occasional swamps and bayous, backed by timber growth on sandy soils and fronted by stretches of white-sand beaches.

Climate. The Alabama climate is temperate, with an average annual temperature of about 63° F (17° C), mellowed by altitude to some 60° F (16° C) in the northern counties, and reaching 67° F (19° C) in the southern counties, although summer heat is often cooled somewhat by the winds blowing in from the Gulf. Occasionally on a hot summer day the temperature may rise to 100° F (38° C), while snow may occasionally fall in the northern counties, and frosts are periodic. The average summer temperature is 79° F (26° C); the winter average is 46° F (8° C).

Rainfall is fairly well distributed throughout the year, with a yearly average of 53 inches (1,350 millimetres) and a concentration on the coast. Droughts are infrequent. These favourable conditions have given the state a long growing season, ranging from 200 days in the north to 300 days in the south.

Soils. There are four main soil zones found in Alabama. In the far north, the Tennessee Valley contains the dark loams and red clays that add vivid dashes of colour to the landscape when exposed. Farther south lie the varied soils of a mineral belt, and these are succeeded by the rich limestone and marl soils of the Black Belt. Along the coast of Alabama there are sandy loams and deep porous sands.

Drainage. The Cumberland Plateau region drains to the northwest through the Tennessee River and the often deep valleys of its tributaries, while the rest of the state is drained southward through broader, lazier valleys. The Coosa and the Tallapoosa rivers join north of Montgomery to form the Alabama, which unites with the Tombigbee, draining the state's western portion. Their waters then

Marginal notes:
Southern resistance

Physical and social diversity

The Black Belt

part again and are discharged into Mobile Bay through the Mobile and Tensaw rivers.

Plant and animal life. The warm climate of Alabama has nurtured a rich plant cover, including more than 125 tree varieties. Most of the thick forests are in the north and northeast. Pine trees predominate, while the stately oaks are found statewide, lending grace to the streets of the older towns and cities. Sweet gum and black walnut are also common, while the colourful red cedar is most abundant in the Tennessee Valley and the Black Belt, with the stately black cypress clustering around rivers and ponds. There are many varieties of shrubs and grasses, and bamboo, large canes, and mistletoe are widespread. Muscadines, scuppernongs, and blackberries also flourish. Long clumps of Spanish moss, swaying from the coastal oaks in the Gulf breezes, have added much to the traditional image of the state.

Bird life, too, is rich. Bluebirds, cardinals, blue jays, mockingbirds, doves, woodpeckers, owls, hawks, yellowhammers, and an occasional eagle add flashes of colour to the scenery. Other wildlife includes rabbits, squirrels, opossums, foxes, wildcats, raccoons, muskrats, an occasional deer, and even a few bears. Reptiles include poisonous rattlers, water moccasins, and corals as well as some nonpoisonous types, such as black snakes. Alligators still exist in some of the swamps and bayous of the coastal regions.

Settlement patterns. By 1980 less than two-fifths of the population of Alabama was classified as rural, and the proportion was declining still further as rural residents sought homes in the state's cities or, in many cases, migrated to regions of the North. Eight counties had a population loss during the 1970s. Much of the loss was from the old cotton region of the Black Belt, but general farm consolidation has raised farm size and income and driven many from the land.

For poor white—and especially for black—rural dwellers in Alabama, the rural way of life has nevertheless nurtured a rich oral tradition and culture, often under difficult conditions. The sleepy rural communities and the scattered homes of often direly impoverished sharecroppers and farm tenants nevertheless continue to give a stark aspect to life in the country, while the old mansions of the former plantations, where not fallen into decay, add their own stately note. Some of the isolated upland communities near Tennessee also continue to suffer from poverty and depopulation in spite of the boost that was given by the regional planning of the Tennessee Valley Authority in the 1930s.

By 1960, for the first time, more than half Alabama's population was concentrated in 10 counties, and the dominance of the urban areas has since continued. The sprawling industrial city of Birmingham and its metropolitan area continue to dominate the state, with its increasingly diversified steel-based regional economy employing about one-fourth of the state's workers and producing about one-fourth of all its manufactures. The most developed region in the state is roughly contained in a rectangle bounded by a line linking Birmingham, Tuscaloosa, Anniston, and Gadsden. Outliers of similar development lie around Huntsville in the north; Muscle Shoals in the northwest; Mobile in the southwest; and in a cluster around the capital, Montgomery.

The people. Three-fourths of the state's population is white. The white population is significant for its deep roots in the state: the number of foreign born is very small, and most whites are descendants of 19th-century settlers who came from adjoining regions to the east and north. Black Alabamians have equally deep roots in the state, dating to the days of chattel slavery and the African slave trade. Religious affiliations in the state are predominantly Protestant, with the various church groups in the black community having played an unusually prominent social role since the days when other outlets for such activity were denied.

The birth rate in Alabama, especially in the areas of rural poverty, was somewhat above the national average for many years, but with the depopulation of rural areas and the expansion of the urban economy, the ratio was nearer the national average. One notable result of the exodus of younger people from the state, when considered in conjunction with an influx of retired persons, has been an increase in the numbers of old persons in Alabama.

The economy. Among the 50 states, the relative status of Alabama may be indicated by its per capita income: it has ranked very close to the bottom of the economic scale for a number of years. This low status results, in part, from the depressed state of agriculture, which employs about 10 percent of the population: rural poverty thus drags down the state average, concealing more promising developments and the much stronger economic base that exists in the urban areas.

Agriculture. The Alabamian rural economy presents many facets that challenge the traditional view of a dependency on cotton. Although cotton still remains of local importance, it suffered a heavy blow with the onset of the boll weevil blight in 1915, and acreage continued to decline while mechanization and consolidation increased the average farm size. A more important process was the diversification of agricultural production, which brought a great increase in the acreage devoted to forestry, while cotton fields were given over to pasture for dairy and beef cattle. In the north, notably in the Tennessee Valley area and the old Black Belt cotton region, the gross income from cattle is much more important than that from cotton, making up more than half of the total agricultural sales. The principal crops are cotton lint, peanuts (groundnuts), soybeans, and corn (maize). Farm income, except in the case of the poorer tenants and sharecroppers, continues to rise, and the average value of a farm rose from $13,000 in 1949 to 10 times the figure by 1979.

Industry. Industrial development in Alabama has long been based heavily on the iron and steel industry of Birmingham, the development of which was facilitated by the presence of accessible deposits of iron ore, coal, and limestone. Other minerals of note include the state's well-known white marble. Oil production in commercial quantities dates from 1944, and there are a number of important wells in the coastal regions. World War II defense industries gave an important impetus to the industrial economy of the state. Although iron and steel production continues to be important to Alabama's economy, the growing chemicals and plastics industries have reduced the reliance on primary metals. Since 1960 the George C. Marshall Space Flight Center at Huntsville, producing Saturn booster rockets, has been a major contributor to the state's economy.

Management of the economy. In spite of a very low per capita income that ranks 46th among the states, Alabama spends a high percentage of its total revenue on education, health and hospitals, welfare, highways, and natural resources. Federal funds support programs affecting agriculture, public education, a wide range of health and welfare projects, conservation, urban development and public works, and highway construction. The federal government maintains the Air University in Montgomery, Craig Air Force Base near Selma, the George C. Marshall Space Flight Center, and the Redstone Arsenal at Huntsville, as well as several veterans hospitals and a part of the Tennessee Valley Authority operations.

Transportation. Together, the six major rivers of Alabama provide about 1,300 miles (2,100 kilometres) of navigable waterways, while Mobile Bay has been deepened by a ship channel. Mobile has undergone a spectacular development as a modernized port and ranks among the top dozen seaports of the nation. Although railroad transportation, as elsewhere in the United States, has suffered a relative decline in Alabama, bus, truck, and airline traffic has increased in the state.

Administrative and social conditions. *Government.* Alabama is governed by a bicameral legislature and a governor and cabinet. The legislature consists of 35 senators and 105 representatives who meet annually in regular sessions and are elected for four-year terms. The constitution, a complex and, some have claimed, outdated and often inadequate document, dates from 1901. Various poll tax and other tax provisions aimed at restricting black-voter registration have been declared illegal by the U.S. Supreme Court, and voter registration among blacks has made slow

Margin notes:

Rural traditions

Diversification in agriculture

State and local government

but significant progress since the 1960s. The chief administrative officers of the state, ranging from the governor to the state Board of Education, are all elected for four-year terms. The state Supreme Court of nine elected members is the highest judicial body.

At the county level the chief elected officials in Alabama are the various county commissioners, judges of probate, tax assessors and collectors, and boards of education. In the municipalities of the state there is no uniform system of government: the mayor–council form is most common, but some cities have a commission, and some employ a city manager.

The Democratic Party of Alabama has long been in firm control of the state government, although by the late 20th century there were some signs of a slightly increased Republican showing. Numerous black political organizations have helped increase black voting and participation in the political process.

Education. Alabama has 14 state-supported four-year colleges, many junior colleges and trade schools, and about two dozen private colleges and universities. Black enrollment is higher in the private colleges than in the public system. Most of the black students in the state are enrolled in institutions specifically established for blacks, although an increasing number are attending formerly all-white colleges.

Health and welfare. In rural areas and among non-whites, educational and economic status and opportunities are lower and fewer, and health and medical resources and services are less available. Welfare payments in Alabama rank low by national standards and, it has been claimed, have helped to swell the numbers leaving the state. Penal institutions include several prisons and camps for youthful offenders. Controversy over conditions in these institutions has occasionally erupted, and some measure of reform has been introduced.

Cultural life. There is a clear separation in Alabama between the cultural life of the state, as evidenced by many fine libraries and museums, and a rich vein of folklore and tradition in the rural areas, notably among blacks. Storytelling, in particular, has attracted the attention of folklore specialists, while the deeply felt compositions of rural blues singers have been an important element in the development of modern American popular music, including jazz.

Folk culture

The books of the state library system are distributed through city, county, and regional libraries, the latter using bookmobiles. Special library collections include those at the University of Alabama Medical Center in Birmingham; at the George C. Marshall Space Flight Center in Huntsville; and the well-known Booker T. Washington Collection of black-history material at Tuskegee Institute. The Alabama Department of Archives and History was the first such department established in the United States. Leading museums and art galleries are found in Birmingham, Montgomery, and Mobile; the George Washington Carver Museum at Tuskegee Institute is also well known.

Many historic sites in Alabama are supervised by the state: they include the Mound State Monument in Hale County and Ft. Morgan, standing at the entrance to Mobile Bay. The state also maintains a fine range of parks and public lakes.

Among the state's many weekly and daily newspapers, the *Birmingham News* has the largest circulation. Newspapers published by blacks include the semiweekly *Birmingham World.* Alabama was the first state to establish (1953) a statewide educational television network, which is operated under the guidance of the Alabama Educational Television Commission.

HISTORY

The Indians. The earliest and longest established inhabitants of the present-day state of Alabama were Indians. Visible traces of their occupancy, which spanned almost 10,000 years, may be seen in the great mounds which snake across the landscape near the river valleys. Many place names in the state also indicate an Indian origin. The principal Indian groups at the time of the initial European exploration of the region were the Chickasaw,

in the northwest; the Cherokees, in the northeastern uplands; the Upper Creeks, or Muskogees, in the centre and southeast; and the Choctaws of the southwest. Tribal boundaries, given the migratory nature of their life, were often uncertain.

European rivalry, settlement, and growth. The first known European explorers were of Spanish descent and arrived at Mobile Bay in 1519. In subsequent decades others penetrated inland, discovering several of Alabama's rivers. The main thrust of exploration, however, came from the northwest, when the explorer Hernando de Soto, with an army of more than 500 men, entered the interior from the valley of the Tennessee River in 1540. His expedition, which extensively criss-crossed the area, was important because of his discovery of the Mississippi River, the knowledge he gained of a wide band of southern Indian cultures, and his role in opening up the whole region to European settlement. A battle with the ill-equipped warriors of the Indian chief Tuscaloosa, on October 18, 1540, however, resulted in a slaughter that took the lives of at least several thousand of the Indian peoples: it has been described as the bloodiest single encounter between whites and Indians in what was to become the United States. In 1559 a Spanish fort was established in Mobile Bay.

The de Soto expedition

The ensuing 250 years were characterized by struggles among the French, British, and Spanish for control of the region, often in shifting alliances with the Indians of the area. The French founded a community at Ft. Louis in 1702, the first permanent European settlement in Alabama. The British had also made a number of trips to the region from the Carolinas, but the French settlements—part of a string of forts arcing down from Canada and designed to contain the British—were more numerous. Port Dauphin, also founded in 1702, on Dauphin Island, received the arrival of the first Africans when a slave ship arrived there in 1719.

The Treaty of Paris, in 1763, gave Mobile to Britain and established that country's supremacy in the area. In 1783 American control was recognized, although the Spanish maintained a foothold in the south of the state until the United States, claiming the area as part of the Louisiana Purchase, established authority throughout the state in 1813. Washington County, in the southwest, was established as early as 1800, but the Alabama Territory was created only in 1817, and Alabama was granted statehood in 1819. Gen. Andrew Jackson, meanwhile, had inflicted a decisive defeat on the Creeks at the Battle of Horseshoe Bend in 1814, and earlier the Chickasaw Indians had ceded their northern lands in 1805, followed a few months later by the Choctaw and Cherokees. The influx of population following these actions and the introduction of the cotton gin caused a rapid removal of the Indians to the west. Some of their descendants live in Oklahoma, while only a few hundred Creeks remain in the southern part of Alabama.

The antebellum period. By 1820 Alabama's population was slightly over 125,000, including about 500 free blacks. By 1830 there were 300,000 residents, 38 percent of them slaves, and cotton grown on the plantations of the so-called Black Belt was the principal money crop. The Southern way of life had begun to flourish. Until the Civil War, domestic politics centred around the removal of the Indians, difficulties concerning the banking system, and, with ominously increasing frequency, the questions of slavery and of state and federal rights. By 1860 the population was close to 1,000,000: nearly half were black, and all but 5 percent of the state's population was rural. The University of Alabama (chartered 1820, opened 1831) and other educational institutions were flourishing, including (under an 1852 act) the beginnings of a public school system. The antebellum period was also the time when the first railroad, the first canal, the first textile mill, and the first factory for manufacturing gin-milling machinery were built. By 1850 the mining of coal and iron and the manufacture of steel were becoming big business in the state.

The Civil War and its aftermath. From 1860 to about 1900, the history of Alabama falls into three distinct periods: the Civil War, Reconstruction, and the reaction to

Reconstruction. In 1861 Alabama seceded from the Union and joined the Confederate States of America, which was founded in Montgomery, its first capital. The state legislature conscripted soldiers and appropriated several million dollars for military operations and for the support of the families of soldiers. Some 35,000 of the 122,000 Alabamians who served in the war died. In 1867, following the collapse of the Confederacy and the refusal of the state legislature to ratify the 14th Amendment to the U.S. Constitution, Alabama was placed under military rule; a year later, however, the state was readmitted to the Union.

Reconstruction and after

From 1868 to 1874 the state was in political turmoil. To many whites the Reconstruction period was a "tragic era"; to many blacks it was a period of opportunity and hope. The *Huntsville Advocate* asserted that "This is a white man's government and a white man's state," and the Ku Klux Klan gained considerable influence. There was struggle for political power among whites who had supported the Confederacy, whites known as scalawags who were willing to cooperate with the carpetbaggers, whites who had been loyal or sympathetic to the Union, and blacks. The blacks demanded free schools; most whites insisted that separate schools for whites and blacks were most appropriate. Although blacks participated in the constitutional conventions and in the state legislatures, their political power was not as strong as that of blacks in South Carolina, Mississippi, or Louisiana. In 1874 the white Democrats of Alabama, most of whom had been supporters of the Confederacy, regained control of the state political machinery; blacks were rendered almost powerless until the civil rights movement of the 1960s. Throughout this period, however, some blacks worked diligently to stimulate political activity, to enlighten and influence fellow white citizens, and to influence the state and federal governments to guarantee their political and social rights.

In 1875 a state constitutional convention was held, and a new constitution ratified. In 1876 federal troops were removed from Alabama, and political efforts began to centre around the aim of restricting the participation of blacks in government. By 1901, when another state constitution was ratified, there were virtually no blacks in the government, and a tide of social and political reaction was in full flood. The economy, meanwhile, had recovered somewhat from the devastation of the war and its aftermath, and heavy industry was beginning to flourish in the state. Economic activity generally remained at a low level, however, and depressed agricultural conditions fanned a populist revolt in the small farms in the 1890s. Educationally, life began to develop again in Alabama, with the reopening of old institutions and with the founding of Tuskegee Institute as a major centre of black education in 1881.

The 20th century. By 1900 the state was largely rural in character, and the black population began a slow decline, which reduced their numbers to less than one-third of the total population by mid-century. Patterns of racial segregation under the Jim Crow system were rigidly enforced within and without the law. The onset of the boll weevil in 1915 wrought havoc to the one-crop cotton economy of the Black Belt, forcing a diversification of the rural economy. An exodus of rural dwellers, mostly poor and black, began, both to Alabama's cities and to the North, where cheap foreign labour supplies had dried up during World War I. Rural society began a slow decline, arrested in part by the activities of the Tennessee Valley Authority in the northern areas in the 1930s and by a cooperative agricultural extension service.

Defense industries boosted the urban economy in the World War II years, and the contributions of the federal government became evident in support of agriculture and the provision of such services as road building, education, and welfare. Segregation, nevertheless, continued to give rigidity to the social framework of Alabama and effectively excluded the black population from social and economic power.

Following the 1954 U.S. Supreme Court decision that compulsory racial segregation in public education was unconstitutional and the 1957 Civil Rights Act, which weakened the black voter registration restrictions, black Alabamians and their white allies, many of whom came from outside of the state, were given the encouragement and tools they needed to work to improve race relations. Further aid stemmed from the civil rights acts of 1960 and 1964 and from other legislation.

Progress was nevertheless slow and bitter: the state acquired international significance as the site of such landmark civil rights actions as the bus boycott of 1955–56 in Montgomery; the "freedom riders" of 1961; the use of federal troops to enforce desegregation laws in 1963, a year in which four small Birmingham black children were killed by a bomb that destroyed their Sunday School; and the "Freedom March" from Selma to Montgomery in 1965.

As a result of these activities, black citizens have acquired access to better public services, broader educational opportunities, improved economic opportunities, and freer political participation. By the late 20th century the percentage of blacks registered to vote had increased fivefold. Blacks have been elected in small but increasing numbers to elective state and local government positions. By 1979 there were 16 black U.S. and state legislators and 131 city and county officers. Positions have also been won in clerical and sales and in supervisory and managerial positions in commerce. A number of educational and professional bodies as well as many schools have achieved a good measure of desegregation, though the churches of the state have not. Progress has been slow but, nevertheless, significant. (C.G.G.)

The gains of the civil rights movement

Arkansas

Ever since Arkansas was admitted as the 25th member of the United States in 1836, its people have maintained a remarkable homogeneity, and today most of them are native to the state. Striking cultural contrasts exist within Arkansas, however, with the long-isolated mountain people who eked out subsistence livings in the north and west counterposed to the people to the east and south who created a Southern environment in which cotton growing and sharecropping long were the dominant modes of economic life. Between the two regions lies Little Rock, the capital and the urban and economic centre of the state. Its location and increasingly cosmopolitan character are symbolic of Arkansas's growing unification and urbanization.

Arkansans no longer feel complacent about the state's relative poverty and lack of development. Although Arkansas remains among the lowest ranking states in per capita income and other economic indicators, the overall economy in recent years has gained faster than that of the national average, and the population has increased, reversing a long decline. Programs have been developed to increase these upward trends and to continue the process of equalizing the educational, economic, and social opportunities of the state's citizens.

Arkansas's 53,104 square miles (137,539 square kilometres) make it 27th in area among the states, but, except for Hawaii, it is the smallest state west of the Mississippi River. Its neighbours are Missouri to the north, Tennessee and Mississippi to the east, Louisiana to the south, Texas to the southwest, and Oklahoma to the west. Arkansas has the high Ozark and Ouachita Mountains in the north and west and a heavy tracery of rivers that cut through its rich agricultural lands. Nearly all of the rivers flow from northwest to southeast and empty directly into the Mississippi, which forms the entire eastern boundary.

PHYSICAL AND HUMAN GEOGRAPHY

The land. *Relief.* A line drawn from the southwestern corner to the northeastern corner of the state approximates the division between the highlands lying west and north and the lowlands lying south and east. The highlands are divided by the Arkansas River Valley into the Ouachita Province on the south and the Ozark Plateau on the north. The lowlands include the Mississippi Alluvial Plain in the east and the West Gulf Coastal Plain in the south and extreme southwest. The highlands are covered with the dense pine and hardwood forests of the Ouachita and Ozark national forests.

The Ozark Plateau is broken by broad, flat-topped ridges

Mountains and plains of Arkansas

and steep valleys with fast-flowing streams. The more rugged southern edge, known as the Boston Mountains, contains the highest elevations. Excellent farmland, producing a wide variety of crops, lies in the northern part. The Arkansas River Valley contains the highest point in the state, Mt. Magazine, at 2,753 feet (839 metres) above sea level. The western section has extensive coal and natural-gas deposits. Several peaks in the Ouachita Province reach 2,500 feet. The mountains are eroded, exposing faulted rock, and the ridges extend west and east. The famous Hot Springs National Park is in this area.

The West Gulf Coastal Plain has gentle hills suitable for livestock grazing and general farming. Much of this area consists of pine and white-oak forests, which sustain extensive lumbering industries. Petroleum and natural-gas deposits have been developed in the region around Smackover and El Dorado. The Mississippi Alluvial Plain, much of which was once a vast swamp, is now well-drained and protected against flooding. It contains the state's richest and most fertile farmland. Rice and soybeans have replaced cotton as the major crops. A long, narrow chain of hills, called Crowley's Ridge, runs north and south through the centre of the plain.

Climate. The climate generally is mild in winter and hot in summer. Normal high–low temperatures in Little Rock in January are 51° and 31° F (11° and −1° C); in July temperature extremes are 93° and 71° F (34° and 22° C). The normal annual precipitation of 48 inches (1,200 millimetres) is distributed about equally during the year, though summers tend to be drier than the other seasons.

Plant and animal life. A great variation in soils and elevations in Arkansas supports a large number of plant species. There are more than 200 species of trees, of which the pine, oak, hickory, maple, gum, ash, cypress, and elm are most important. In fall and spring the woodlands are colourful with dogwood, flowering fruit trees, redbud, and innumerable wild flowers.

Arkansas is situated on the Mississippi flyway; migratory water birds and some 300 native species attract hunters to the rice fields and reservoirs of eastern Arkansas. Deer, quail, opossums, turkeys, squirrels, and rabbits are among the more abundant game animals. Bobcats and wolves are not uncommon in the hill country. The lakes and streams of the state offer an abundance of fish—including crappie, bass, drum, catfish, buffalo, gar, and trout.

Settlement patterns. The inhabitants of the Ozarks and Ouachitas once lived in rural isolation, which bred an independence of spirit and a suspicion of strangers. They lived off the land: hunting and fishing were essential to supplement the limited produce of their farms. Since a plantation economy was impracticable in the uplands, few slaves were brought into the region. In eastern Arkansas the plantation economy produced a vast gulf between the sharecroppers and tenants on one end of the social scale and the managers and landlords on the other. The owners of small farms or businesses constituted another class. The croppers lived a bare and meagre existence. Handicapped by lack of economic resources and education, they accomplished remarkable results through the Southern Farm Tenants Union, which they organized in eastern Arkansas in the 1930s; this organization influenced the national farm policy of presidents from Franklin D. Roosevelt onward.

Although changes in the economy of both regions were evident earlier, the rate of change since World War II has been dramatic. The Ozarks are no longer isolated. A network of paved highways brings tourists to enjoy the region's scenic beauty and varied recreational activities. Numerous "retirement villages" attract visitors and buyers from across the country. The tourist industry remains the economic mainstay, though small industrial plants have taken advantage of the climate and the ample labour supply.

Mechanization of farming in eastern Arkansas and the shift from cotton farming to rice and soybeans has virtually eliminated the sharecropper—though not the rural poor. As the pace of mechanization increased, so did the exodus of the former tenant farmers to cities in the North and East. Farming is increasingly a corporate venture rather than a family business. Eastern Arkansas is still, however,

more Southern in character than the mountainous region. Many of the rural shacks are gone and the towns have grown, but mile after mile of cultivated fields are broken only by small woodlands and pastures. There and in central Arkansas reside the majority of the state's blacks, many of whom still work the land as their ancestors did.

Little Rock, the major port on the Arkansas River, lies among the easternmost foothills of the Ouachita Mountains. A marketing centre and the site of an increasing number of manufacturing facilities, the city has completed or undertaken several urban renewal projects in its downtown area, including the construction of a pedestrian mall, the renovation of historic buildings, and the expansion of convention facilities. At the western boundary of the state lies Fort Smith, the second largest city on the Arkansas River. It is the most industrialized city in the state and serves as a regional business and service centre for northwestern Arkansas and northeastern Oklahoma. The economy of Pine Bluff, some 50 miles (80 kilometres) downriver from Little Rock, depends primarily on the surrounding agricultural area. Texarkana, contiguous with the Texas city of the same name, is an important regional rail centre.

The people. Prior to the Civil War, Arkansas's population came largely from Kentucky and Tennessee, a part of the westward movement of Scottish, Scots-Irish, and English stock from Virginia and the Carolinas since early colonial times. The black population in 1860 was about 110,000, or 25 percent of the total; by the late 20th century there were more than 350,000 blacks living in Arkansas, making up a decreasing percentage of the total population. A few counties in eastern Arkansas are more than 50 percent black. The heaviest concentration of population is in the fertile eastern alluvial plain, in the river valleys, and on the plateaus in the northwest.

The largest religious denominations are the Baptist, Methodist, Presbyterian, Church of Christ, and Roman Catholic. The general religious atmosphere is one of conservative fundamentalism, and Arkansas is considered to be a part of the "Bible Belt." This fundamentalism underlies many characteristic attitudes of Arkansans. A state law that forbids teaching of the theory of human evolution has never been repealed, though U.S. Supreme Court decisions have rendered it unconstitutional. The sale of alcoholic beverages is subject to local option; many counties and cities prohibit their sale or permit it only in private clubs and certain other establishments in major cities. The right-to-work amendment to the state constitution in 1944, which prohibits compulsory union membership, was sponsored by the Christian Association, among others. Harding College in Searcy is the site of an annual Freedom Forum, which advocates a blend of religious fundamentalism, extreme patriotism, and free-enterprise capitalism.

The economy. Cotton is no longer king in Arkansas, and the state is no longer primarily agricultural. Industrialization and urbanization are major factors in Arkansas's recent record of economic progress. Labour unions are strong in transportation, utilities, construction, and heavy industry, but most of the state's labour force is unorganized. In both political and economic policymaking, labour is less influential than business.

Resources. Oil fields in southern Arkansas yield natural gas and bromide salts. Coal of a nearly smokeless quality, as well as natural gas, are found in the Arkansas River Valley. There are extensive deposits of lignite in southern Arkansas. Bauxite, obtained by strip-mining near Little Rock, accounts for more than 90 percent of the nation's domestic supply. Magnet Cove, near Hot Springs, contains more than 40 different minerals in one small valley; barite and titanium are the most important. Arkansas whetstones made from novaculite are regarded as among the finest in the world. Near Murfreesboro, in southwestern Arkansas, is the only diamond mine in the nation, now operated only as a tourist attraction. Almost one-half of Arkansas is covered with forests, including extensive stands of pine and white oak.

Hydroelectric power is produced at dams erected by the U.S. Army Corps of Engineers and by private companies.

Contrast of cultures

Mineral wealth

Two nuclear stations have been constructed near Dardanelle, and coal-fired stations have also been built.

Agriculture and industry.   As recently as 1960 cotton was still the major source of agricultural income, but it has been replaced by soybeans, poultry, and rice. Commercial fish farming has begun to take advantage of the extensive rice paddies of eastern Arkansas. Farms have followed the national trend of increasing in size while decreasing in number.

Manufacturing chiefly involves the production of consumer goods. Major industries include food processing and the manufacture of clothing, furniture, electrical and nonelectrical machinery, electronic equipment, and scientific instruments.

Tourism.   Arkansas devotes considerable effort to attract out-of-state vacationers, who annually contribute millions of dollars to its economy. State and national agencies stock lakes and streams with fish, and the state's preserves and conservation practices assure ample game in hunting seasons. The largest single attraction in Arkansas is Hot Springs National Park, which offers both outdoor recreation and luxury hotels throughout the year. Blanchard Springs Caverns, under development by the National Park Service, has become another major tourist attraction in the state.

State finances.   Although state revenues have been increasing, mounting needs for additional funds led to tax increases in 1971, the first since 1957. The state attempts to generate additional revenue by raising per capita incomes through increasing employment opportunities and developing the human resources to their maximum.

Transportation.   Five major railroads provide freight service within Arkansas, as well as to major cities in the central United States. Airline service is provided by national carriers from a growing number of airports to any point in the nation. By interstate expressways more than half of the nation's population is within a two-day driving radius of Arkansas. The McClellan-Kerr Arkansas River Navigation System for navigation and flood control is the largest civil works project ever undertaken by the U.S. Army Corps of Engineers. The project provides access to more than one-half of the nation's navigable inland waterways. Annual freight tonnage along it has exceeded estimates, and significant industrial growth has been attributed to the project.

Administrative and social conditions.   *Government.* Adopted in 1874, Arkansas's constitution has been amended more than 60 times. The governor, who is elected to a two-year term, has the authority to summon the legislature into special session and to veto acts, though a veto may be overridden by a simple majority vote in each legislative house. The Senate has 35 members with four-year terms; the House of Representatives, 100 members with two-year terms. The judicial branch includes the Supreme Court of seven popularly elected members who serve eight-year terms, circuit court districts, and chancery districts. Where established, municipal courts have jurisdiction throughout the county.

Elected officials of the 75 counties include judge (chief executive), clerk, treasurer, sheriff-collector, surveyor, and coroner. Elected justices of the peace make up a Quorum Court, which serves as an advisory body to the judge and exercises some legislative functions. There are numerous local improvement districts and school districts. Although a number of incorporated cities have a city-manager form of government, the traditional mayor–council form is most common.

The Democratic Party has dominated political activity since Reconstruction, with the exception of Republican Winthrop Rockefeller's terms as governor from 1967 to 1971. Unless a candidate receives a majority of votes cast in a preferential primary, a runoff is required. Permanent voter registration replaced the poll tax in 1965.

Social divisions.   The wages of Arkansas's workers are among the lowest in the nation, and living costs approximate those of the south-central region. Blacks live at distinctly lower economic and social levels despite improvements during the late 20th century.

Public-school desegregation is the primary target of civil

rights movements in Arkansas. Attempts to alter discrimination in housing and employment have been less dramatic. The demonstration against school integration in Little Rock in 1957 was a momentary setback; school integration has proceeded with little difficulty in most areas. Opposition has been strongest in eastern and southern Arkansas, where blacks make up a large percentage of some communities. Many private schools have been established to circumvent integration.

Legalized discrimination through Jim Crow laws, which enforced racial segregation, no longer exists. Blacks seek election to the state and local legislatures in increasing numbers. A major problem of the black Arkansans, like that of blacks nationwide, is an economic one: to obtain and hold the better-paying jobs that require both education and skill.

Education.   The public school system functions under the state's department of education and district school boards. Specialized institutions include schools for the deaf and the blind. Two colonies for retarded children have attracted nationwide acclaim.

The University of Arkansas comprises the main campus at Fayetteville and universities at Little Rock, Pine Bluff, and Monticello. The graduate schools of health sciences, technology, and social work are located in Little Rock. Five other universities and several two-year institutions are supported by the state. Several of these were developed from institutions for the agricultural and mechanical sciences and for teacher training.

Health and welfare.   Problems of malaria, pellagra, and pinworm that once plagued the region have been virtually wiped out by widespread efforts of state and local health authorities. The state health department and welfare commission administer many programs funded in part by the federal government. Emigration of young people over the past two or three decades has aggravated health and welfare programs, especially in declining rural areas. Welfare payments are among the lowest in the nation. The mild climate and attractive scenery has fostered the establishment of retirement villages in the Ozarks.

Cultural life.   The people of eastern Arkansas are typically Southern in their speech and customs, and a leisurely pace prevails. Central Arkansas also reflects its Southern heritage, but the speech and manners of its people have been influenced by immigrants from other parts of the country. The rural areas of the Ouachitas and Ozarks have retained to the fullest degree an unchanged culture.

The several symphony orchestras and community theatres and the civic ballet in Little Rock are not of professional quality. Most colleges and universities offer training and performance in the arts. A four-state opera workshop is held each summer in the Ozarks. Arkansas's richest contributions are in the folk arts of the Ozarks. A major folk art centre in Mountain View has been designed to provide a showcase for local and visiting performers in dance and music; to preserve traditional skills in ceramics, jewelry, wood carving, hooked rugs, and basketry; and to offer instruction in the native folk arts. Other aspects of folk culture include the gospel singing of rural areas. Black spirituals and "soul music" flourished in Arkansas long before they became popular nationwide.

The University of Arkansas has a fine collection of archaeological and mineral artifacts. A collection of colonial glassware is featured in the Museum of Science and History, housed in the old federal arsenal in Little Rock. Historic sites include Arkansas Post, the first European settlement in French Louisiana; Washington, the Confederate state capital during the Civil War; and the Territorial Restoration and First State Capitol in Little Rock.

Communications.   Little Rock has the oldest newspaper west of the Mississippi, the *Arkansas Gazette,* founded in 1819; like the *Arkansas Democrat,* it serves the entire state. Central Arkansas is served by radio and television affiliates of the major networks. The state has numerous commercial radio stations, and all major urban centres are able to receive one or more television stations.

HISTORY

Exploration and settlement.   Arkansas's early inhabitants included bluff-dwelling Indians, whose farming and

---

Margin notes:

The Arkansas River Project

Political life

Status of race relations

Folk arts and culture

hunting culture flourished *c.* AD 500. Later mound-building cultures left sepulchral mounds and other remains along the Mississippi.

Spanish and French explorers travelled the trans-Mississippi regions in the 16th and 17th centuries, and the Frenchman Henri de Tonty founded the Arkansas Post on the Lower Arkansas River in 1686. The first permanent white settlement in what is now Arkansas, it served as a fur-trading centre and a way station for travellers between the Gulf of Mexico and the Great Lakes.

Following the Louisiana Purchase by the United States in 1803, Arkansas lay within the territories of Louisiana until 1812 and of Missouri until 1819, when it became a separate territory. Its northern boundary, latitude 36°30′ N, was the famous line of the Missouri Compromise in 1820 that later separated the slave and free states in the newly opening West.

Statehood and Civil War. By the time of statehood in 1836, all land titles of the Quapaw, Osage, Caddo, Cherokee, and Choctaw Indians had been withdrawn by the U.S. Congress, and the tribes were forced westward into the Indian Territory, the future Oklahoma. Violence broke out intermittently along the state's western border until the late 19th century, when the frontier atmosphere disappeared with the white settlement of the Indian Territory.

Although a slave state, Arkansas did not secede from the Union until May 1861—five months after South Carolina did so. Arkansas took this action only after the Confederate capture of Ft. Sumter and President Lincoln's call for volunteers. Union sentiment was strong in northern Arkansas; about 6,000 Arkansans joined the Federal forces. About 58,000, however, fought for the Confederacy. Little Rock fell to Federal troops in 1863, and for a decade the state was a legislative battleground between secessionist supporters and the imposed Republican government. Arkansas was readmitted to the Union in 1868, but internal strife approached open warfare. In 1874 the state returned to the fold of the Democratic Party, and remained there until Winthrop Rockefeller, a Republican, was elected governor in 1966.

War and reconstruction: conflicting sentiments

The war's chief long-range effects on Arkansas, as on most of the other former Confederate States, were a crop-lien sharecropping system, a race problem of formidable and new dimensions, a one-party (Democratic) political system, and widespread poverty. Economic development in Arkansas was severely handicapped by the collapse of state credit following repudiation in 1885 of bonded indebtedness, including interest of nearly $14,000,000.

Recent decades. Until World War II, Arkansas experienced slow economic development, remained predominantly rural, and was tied to a single cash crop—cotton. The Depression of the 1930s was worsened by years of drought that turned many farm families into itinerant labourers. In 1957 federal troops entered Little Rock to maintain order after the state militia had been ordered to prevent the desegregation of one of the city's high schools; the confrontation focussed international attention on the state. In the late 20th century the state's efforts to improve its economic status and diversify its economy were at last succeeding.   (B.A.D.)

Florida

The geographical location of Florida has been the key factor in a long and colourful development, and it helps explain the striking contemporary character of the state. The greater part of Florida lies on a peninsula that protrudes southeastward from the North American continent, separating the waters of the Atlantic Ocean from those of the Gulf of Mexico and pointing toward Cuba and the Caribbean Sea beyond. The nearest foreign territory is the Bahamian island of Bimini, some 50 miles (80 kilometres) to the east of the state's tip. With the exception of Hawaii, Florida is the southernmost state of the United States, with its northernmost point lying 100 miles farther south than California's southern border. The Florida Keys, a crescent of islands that forms the state's southernmost portion, lie within 1,700 miles (2,700 kilometres) of the Equator. Florida lies at the same latitude as Egypt. Its size, 58,560

square miles (151,670 square kilometres), is comparable to that of England and Wales combined.

The state lies close to both the geographical and the population centres of the landmass of the Western Hemisphere, and its position not only commands one entrance to the Gulf of Mexico but also lies along a strategic crossroads between North and South America and historic routes to the European and Mediterranean worlds. Florida played a prominent role in the struggles of the European powers to control the New World, and it is fitting that St. Augustine, founded in 1565 on its northeastern coast, is the oldest European settlement within what were to become the boundaries of the continental United States.

Strategic position

Although agriculture and manufacturing continue to be important in Florida, the climate and scenery of the "Sunshine State" have attracted enormous numbers of visitors, and tourism is now a mainstay of a well-diversified economy.

PHYSICAL AND HUMAN GEOGRAPHY

The land. *Relief.* Florida is a geologically young, low-lying plain, mostly less than 100 feet (30 metres) above sea level. The highest point is in Walton County, a mere 345 feet (105 metres) above sea level. Sedimentary deposits of sand and limestone cover most of the state, with areas of peat and muck marking locations where freshwater bodies once stood. The contemporary topography has been largely molded by running water, waves, ocean currents, winds, changes in sea level, and the wearing away of limestone rocks by solution. These forces have produced enough variation in the state's surface to permit classification into seven basic physiographic regions: the coastal lowlands, the Lake Okeechobee–Everglades Basin, the Kissimmee lowlands, the Marianna lowlands, the central highlands, the Tallahassee hills, and the western highlands, though these scientific divisions are scarcely apparent to the naked eye.

Soils and plant life. The soils and vegetation are closely related to the basic physiographic regions. In general, Florida's soils consist of sand, sandy loam, claylike marl, peat, and muck, but more than 300 soil types have been mapped. There is a great variety of trees, with more than 300 species having been identified; about half of the state is covered by forests. The dominant trees include pines, oaks, cypresses, palms, and mangroves. Many tropical trees thrive in southern Florida, while beech, red maple, sweet gum, tulip, magnolia, and hickory are common in the north. Almost half of the species of trees found in the United States grow in Florida. More than 3,500 other plants have been identified, including many plants imported into the state.

Six broad soil–vegetation regions may be described. (1) The flatwood lowland soils form the largest soil region in Florida, which corresponds roughly to the coastal lowlands. The terrain there is level and underlaid by a hardpan that impedes drainage and encourages flooding; slash and longleaf pine, oak, sabal palm, and grass are typical vegetation. (2) Organic soils are found in many parts of Florida, particularly in the Lake Okeechobee–Everglades Basin—probably the largest area of neutral organic soils in the tropics—where saw grass, cypress, sabal palm, myrtle, willow, elderberry, and gum are important vegetation. In this soggy environment submergence often prevents the oxidation, decay, and shrinkage of peat and muck, but when the soils are drained they deteriorate rapidly. (3) Southern limestone soils occur in the Kissimmee Valley, the Big Cypress Swamp, and the Miami–Homestead area. Pines and oaks grow in some areas, but grasses, along with saw palmettos and sabal palms, predominate in the Kissimmee Valley. The cypress, bay, and gumbo-limbo—a tall tree with a brown, brightly lacquered trunk—are typical of the extreme southern areas of this region. (4) Northern upland soils, ranging from overdrained sands to well-drained loams, occur in the region stretching across the north of the state and support hardwoods, loblolly pine, and longleaf pine. (5) Northern slope soils, usually considered a distinct region, lie immediately to the south, with slash and longleaf pine, oak, and saw palmetto. (6) Central upland soils—with a vegetation similar to that found in northern slope soils—are located in the higher

The organic-soil complex

ridge area of central Florida, westward to the Apalachicola River. There are a number of other distinctive zones of soils and vegetation: dunes fringe the magnificent beaches of the state, while lush, dank mangrove swamps, along with tropical hardwoods and sand pine and oak, are found in the Ocala National Forest.

Drainage. The flat Florida landscape is covered by a latticework of some 1,700 named streams (mostly in the north and northwest) and about 30,000 named lakes (mostly in the central region). The state also contains 17 of the 75 first-magnitude artesian springs in the nation, most of them located in the central region. There are some 39 drainage basins, with the Lake Okeechobee–Everglades Basin (17,000 square miles [44,000 square kilometres]) being the largest. Lake Okeechobee (700 square miles [1,800 square kilometres]) is the third largest freshwater lake entirely in the United States (after Lake Michigan and Iliawna Lake in Alaska). This vast water network is fed by the state's porous limestone substructure, which stores large quantities of water.

Animal life. Florida's rich and distinctive tropical and subtropical environment is inhabited by a huge and varied wildlife population; the rarer forms, such as alligators and crocodiles, are fully protected. Approximately 100 species of mammals are found in the state, including deer, puma, bobcat, boar, black bear, armadillo, otter, mink, and gray fox; bats and other smaller animals are also numerous. Manatees (sea cows) are found along the coast and in warm inland waters, and several species of porpoises and dolphins lend their own distinctive charm to the clear coastal waters.

Huge and varied wildlife population

More than 400 species and subspecies of birds have been identified; land birds include the turkey, quail, dove, eagle, hawk, owl, and most smaller birds common to the southeastern states, while such coastal birds as the gull, brown pelican, sandpiper, osprey, and cormorant are also numerous. Freshwater and marsh birds include the gallinule (marsh hen), duck, goose, coot, egret, heron, ibis (stork), and flamingo. There are vast natural rookeries in the Everglades, and numerous wildlife refuges are maintained for the protection of migratory birds.

The alligator is the king of Florida reptiles, its role as a builder of water holes being vital to southern Florida's ecology, while the crocodile still inhabits part of the Everglades National Park. The 40 species of snakes in the state include the nation's four poisonous types: the coral, rattlesnake, moccasin, and copperhead (the latter restricted to limited areas of northern Florida). Turtles, tortoises, lizards, and frogs are also abundant.

Florida's 4,000,000 acres (1,600,000 hectares) of water (of which some 2,800,000 acres are inland) contain more than 700 species of fish and shellfish. Common saltwater varieties are bluefish, pompano, flounder, mackerel, mullet, trout, redfish, snapper, grouper, snook, sailfish, tarpon, shad, weakfish, bonefish, marlin, and shark. Others include crawfish, oysters, stone and blue crabs, clams, and shrimp. The largemouth black bass is the state's foremost freshwater species, while others include bream (bluegill), sunfish, speckled perch, and catfish.

Climate. Climatically, Florida is divided into two regions. The tropical zone lies generally south of a west–east line drawn from Bradenton along the south shore of Lake Okeechobee to Vero Beach, while to the north of this line the state is subtropical. Summers are uniform throughout Florida. Freezing weather of short duration (but often crippling to agriculture) can occur as far south as Miami, but the Keys have never had frost.

Rainfall is heaviest in summer, with drier weather prevailing in the winter months. The average annual rainfall ranges from 40 inches (1,000 millimetres) in Key West to 62 inches in West Palm Beach. Snow falls occasionally in the northern areas and has been reported as far south as Fort Myers. Hurricanes occur about once a year on the average. These storms may cause great damage, though Florida is no more vulnerable to hurricanes than are the other Gulf states or, indeed, the entire Atlantic coast as far north as Boston. The hurricane season is from June to November, though September is the month during which they are most likely to occur.

Hurricanes

Average annual temperatures show little variation, ranging from 68° F (20° C) in Tallahassee in the north to 77° F (25° C) at Key West in the south. Corresponding monthly averages range from the middle 40s F in the north to the middle 50s F in the south in January, and are in the lower 80s F in August.

Settlement patterns. Northern and southern Florida are often distinguished as separate regions. Northern Florida is generally a colder, historically older, rural and hilly area, oriented toward field agriculture and forestry. Southern Florida is a warmer, flat, urban area, the more recently settled region of the state, with an economy based on tourism, citrus fruits, vegetables, and livestock. A refinement would add central Florida, with its lake region and citrus belt. A more scientific classification might identify the east coast, the west coast, central Florida, the Keys, the Everglades, and the panhandle. More popular regional names are the Gold Coast (the Miami–West Palm Beach metropolitan sprawl), the Sun Coast (the Tampa Bay area), and the Big Bend (centring on Tallahassee). Lesser known designations include the Silver or Platinum Coast (a term applied to the lower southwest), the Island or Mangrove Coast (the extreme southwest), Suwanneeland (the Suwannee River basin), Miracle Strip (the upper northwestern coast), Florida's Crown (the northernmost part of the peninsula), the Surf Coast (the mideast coast), and the Tropi-Coast (Miami–West Palm Beach).

To a stranger entering the state from the north, the Florida landscape may appear quite empty and devoid of human imprint. It is, in fact, being used, but the use is of a type unfamiliar to many visitors. More than half of Florida is covered by commercial, national, and state forests, state and federal parks, lakes, beaches, and military reservations. Less than two-fifths of the state is farmland, and about one-third of this is in either pasture or timber. Only about one-twentieth of Florida's total land is used for harvested crops. Field crops account for half the harvested total, citrus fruit for about one-third, and vegetables for the remainder.

The effect on the landscape is striking: farmsteads are generally common in northern Florida, where field crops are important, but even there timber covers thousands of acres. Citrus groves occupy much of central Florida and the east coast, while along the west coast and north and south of the citrus belt spread vast expanses of cattle land. Around Lake Okeechobee, the cultivation of sugarcane and vegetables has produced the modern equivalent of plantation agriculture. The small, private farm has little place in these systems, having been superseded by mechanization and the use of migratory labour. The social conditions of migrant workers, which have occasionally given rise to national concern, remain one of the negative aspects of a generally affluent state. The rise of what has been termed corporate agriculture has thus led to an inevitable increase in farm size and a corresponding reduction in farm numbers.

Corporate agriculture

Even the small town seems to be disappearing, as more and more people find it relatively easy to commute from urban and suburban centres. The great majority of the people live in urban areas, and only a tiny percentage live on farms. The densest concentration is along the extensive Miami–Fort Lauderdale–West Palm Beach–Boca Raton urban complex in the southeast. This area appeared to many observers to be duplicating the less desirable aspects of the great urban belts burgeoning in other parts of the nation. On the west coast, the Tampa Bay–St. Petersburg metropolitan area contained another concentration of population. Further north, the Orlando–Cape Canaveral–Daytona Beach triangle is central Florida's dominant urban area; Jacksonville is the major centre of the upper east coast and southeastern Georgia; and Pensacola dominates the western panhandle and part of Alabama. Lesser metropolitan areas—including Tallahassee, Gainesville, and Fort Myers—are hubs of local influence.

The people. *Indians.* Ancient Indian groups entered Florida from the north as early as 10,000 years ago, but farming did not appear much before 500 BC, and some southern Indian groups remained hunters, fishers, and gatherers until their extinction. Indians continued to arrive

Contacts
with
Central
America

in small numbers after 500 BC, and contacts with Cuba, the Bahamas, and, possibly, the Yucatán reflected Florida's unique situation. By 1750 virtually all of these peoples had been destroyed by disease, slavers, and wars, the responsibility for their extinction largely resting with English and Creek raiders from Georgia. The latter, accompanied by a few runaway black slaves and renegade whites, were collectively called Cimarrones. The name Seminole evolved from *cimarrón* (Spanish for "wild, unruly, runaway"). There were approximately 5,000 Seminoles in Florida when it came under formal U.S. jurisdiction in 1821. Within 25 years this population had declined to about 150, at which time most of the remaining Seminoles were removed to the territory of Oklahoma. By the late 20th century about 1,000 of the descendants of those who had remained were living in three reservations in southern Florida.

Early Europeans. The first Spanish settlement in 1559 was abandoned in 1561, but San Augustín (St. Augustine), founded in 1565 after the destruction of the French settlement there, became the first permanent European settlement in the United States. For the next 250 years Florida was little more than a wilderness in terms of any permanent European settlement, though its importance as a historical pawn was considerable. A large population of European origin did not develop until the United States established effective civil control in 1822, and the great increases of the late 19th and 20th centuries owed much to economic factors.

Blacks. It is not known when the first blacks arrived in Florida, but it is known that some accompanied the first Spanish expeditions. A few runaway slaves came with the Seminoles, but it was only with U.S. rule that the black population began to increase. By 1830 there were as many blacks (about 11,000) as whites. The subsequent increase of the black population coincided with the development and spread of the Southern plantation system. The Civil War overthrew the slave system, but the agricultural patterns remained, and not until the end of the 19th century did an influx of new settlers cause the white population to increase faster than that of the blacks. The black percentage of the total population continued to decline in the 20th century, though large percentages are still found in the old plantation belt (north central Florida) and in the Everglades truck-farming region.

Other groups. Cubans came to Key West after 1868 when, as a result of revolutionary turmoil in Cuba, Vicente Martínez Ybor moved his cigar factories there from Havana. Labour troubles and a disastrous fire encouraged Ybor to move again in 1886, this time to Tampa, and again many Cubans followed the factories. A similar influx occurred after the Cuban revolution of the early 1960s, when more than 350,000 Cubans fled their homeland. A third of these settled in Florida (mostly in the Miami area) during the decade. Still another wave of Cubans arrived in Florida in 1980, and about 80,000 were integrated (albeit uneasily) into the Cuban community around Miami.

Immigrants from northern Spain came to Tampa at about the time of World War I, drawn largely by the expanding cigar industry and the prospect of living in a Spanish-speaking community. Italians also came in large numbers.

Tarpon Springs was settled about 1880, and by 1905 Greek immigrants, drawing on the traditions of their homeland, had established the nation's major sponge industry. Greek is still widely spoken, and the city is a centre for the Greek Orthodox religion. Other ethnic contributions lending character to the overall population of the state range from a Jewish community at Miami–Miami Beach to a Slovak settlement at Masaryktown.

Demography. The continued migration of older, retired people into the state has given Florida the nation's oldest population. The northwestern counties continue to grow more slowly than the southern urban areas. Those areas heavily dependent on military and space programs continue to be directly affected by federal budgetary decisions that influence such activities. Key West, for example, a Navy-oriented city, suffered a population loss of more than 35 percent between 1960 and 1980. Cutbacks in the space program created one of Florida's highest unemployment rates in the Cape Canaveral area.

The economy. Florida experienced virtually no economic development before 1821, when the United States took formal possession. The 60 years that followed were dominated by small-farm and plantation agriculture; the supplying of naval stores and the production of beef and hides, pork, salt, tobacco, and cotton were the main activities. The 1880s, by contrast, marked the beginning of a new era in Florida. In 1881, phosphate—the state's most important mineral—was discovered in the Peace River Valley, while in that same year Hamilton Disston, a Philadelphia industrialist, bought 4,000,000 acres in the Everglades for 25 cents an acre. This key action freed the state from its post-Civil War debt and opened the way for the development of much of the peninsula. In the west a railroad reached Pensacola in 1883, and in the following year another reached as far as Tampa; the line was financed by a Northern capitalist, Henry B. Plant. On the east coast his counterpart, Henry M. Flagler, was building a rail and hotel empire that soon extended past Miami to Key West. Agricultural development, settlement, industry, and tourism all followed the rails. The 1890 population of the state was double that of 1870, and the total passed 500,000 by the turn of the century and continued its spectacular growth thereafter.

Role of
Northern
capital

Resources. Directly or indirectly, Florida's tropical and subtropical climate affects almost every aspect of the local economy, and it can be quite justifiably considered the state's chief resource. Together with land and water—both of which have a rich potential for economic development—climate forms the basis of the state's wealth. The water resources, important to fishermen and tourists alike, include not only 4,424 square miles (11,460 square kilometres) of fresh inland water but also an even larger area of adjacent saltwater. In the United States only Alaska has a tidal shoreline whose length exceeds that of Florida, which totals 8,426 miles (13,480 kilometres: Gulf Coast, 5,095 miles; Atlantic coast, 3,331 miles). On land, forestry activities are supported by the half of the state (mostly in the north) that is wooded, and livestock raising is supported by the state's large grasslands (mostly in the central and southern areas).

Florida also yields several important minerals. Phosphate, the principal mineral, is used in fertilizer and livestock feed and by the chemical industry. Phosphate is found in the west central portion of the state, whose production accounts for some three-fourths of the national total. Titanium (used in paint and jet engines), zircon (used in foundries, gas engines, and atomic reactors), and such other important heavy minerals as thorium and cerium are mined near Jacksonville, Starke, and Vero Beach and in west central Florida. Petroleum is produced in the northwest and the southwest. Kaolin is mined in Putnam County; Fuller's earth comes from the Tallahassee region; and clay, sand, and gravel are mined in numerous locations, with pure silica sand being extracted mostly in areas around the 100-foot (30-metre) contour line. Limestone, from the northern portion of the peninsula, is used as building stone and road-surfacing material and in cement, concrete, and fertilizer; peat, used as a soil conditioner, is dug in many areas. The versatility of the marine resources of Florida is indicated by a plant at Port St. Joe on the Gulf Coast for the recovery of magnesium from seawater.

Tourism. Approximately 30,000,000 tourists visit Florida annually. Tourism has become the largest income-producing activity in the state and has developed into a year-round business.

Industry. Manufacturing, on a value-added basis, is second only to tourism. Production is well diversified, with food processing leading in value.

Government, trade, and services are big businesses, as are finance, construction, and transportation and communication.

Agriculture. Florida produces about three-fourths of the nation's citrus fruit, and the state is second only to California in vegetable production. Although Florida has millions of cattle, it is perhaps better known for the thoroughbred horses raised near Ocala. Other important products are fish and forest products.

Agricultural specialties

Management of the economy. Labour-management relationships in Florida tend to follow the national pattern. Manufacturing, mining, communication, and transportation tend to be unionized; services are less so, while the professions and agriculture are generally nonunion. The cooperative movement is especially strong in citrus growing and commercial fishing. The Florida Citrus Mutual works closely with growers and the state in research, production, processing, marketing, and regulation, while several fishing cooperatives exist, primarily to help market the catch.

The state government cooperates closely with the private sector of the economy; it is instrumental in inspection, licensing, regulation, and research and education, but the state rarely competes with private business.

Transportation.   Florida's transportation system is comprehensive, covering the entire state except for certain isolated areas in the Everglades. In general, highway arteries run across the north of the state, from Jacksonville to Pensacola; down the east coast, from Jacksonville to Miami; diagonally across the state, from Jacksonville to Tampa–St. Petersburg on the west coast, bisecting the state from Tampa–St. Petersburg to Daytona Beach; and through the southwestern portion, linking Tampa–St. Petersburg to Miami. Rail and air traffic also follow these patterns. Although there is no direct Miami–Tampa railroad, there is a heavily travelled air route between the two cities.

The most heavily travelled throughways are the interstate and state turnpike systems that connect all major cities. There are several airports with regularly scheduled flights, augmented by numerous private airfields; the international terminals at Tampa and Miami are among the most modern in the world. An extensive rail network provides adequate passenger and freight service to most areas. An integrated system for domestic and foreign shipping is provided by eight major deepwater ports and several lesser ports and harbours, while more than 1,000 miles (1,600 kilometres) of navigable channel are maintained by the federal government.

Cape Canaveral

Florida has a moonport, the John F. Kennedy Space Center at Cape Canaveral, which occupies 88,000 acres (35,600 hectares). This is not only a major Florida industry but has also become a prime tourist attraction.

Administrative and social conditions.   *Government.* The government of Florida operates under the revised constitution of 1968, with the executive department headed by the governor and six cabinet officers (secretary of state, attorney general, treasurer and commissioner of insurance, comptroller, commissioner of education, and commissioner of agriculture). The governor and the cabinet, who serve four-year terms (with a consecutive limit of two), control the other executive departments. The legislature is composed of the Senate of 40 members and the House of Representatives of 120 members. Senators serve four-year terms and House members serve two-year terms.

Judiciary powers are exercised through courts established by the constitution: the Supreme Court, four district courts of appeal, 20 circuit courts, and county courts. Appellate judges are initially appointed by the governor; other judges are elected to office on a nonpartisan ballot.

Political trends

Although Florida has become a two-party state in some respects, Democrats ordinarily outnumber Republicans in the legislature. Florida Democrats also hold an overwhelming majority in the U.S. Congress, and the top-level state executive offices are conventionally held by Democrats.

Taxation.   Florida has no state income tax on individuals but does tax corporate income. Approximately half of the state's tax revenue comes from sales and use taxes and taxes on gasoline, alcoholic beverages, and cigarettes. The remainder is derived from a wide range of other taxes, including those on pari-mutuel betting, principally on horse racing, dog racing, and jai alai.

Health and welfare.   Socially, Florida regards itself as a progressive state, and a major proportion of the state's financial resources certainly go into those areas that serve the public, with education, welfare, health, and hospitals receiving about two-thirds of the total appropriations. The state supports the public school system to the extent that no child is deprived of a minimum standard of education, while the counties are expected to supplement this mini-

mum. Virtually the entire population of the state is within commuting distance of a state-supported college or university, part of an extensive system of higher education.

In total personal income, Florida ranks among the top 10 states nationwide. There are no serious labour shortages in Florida except in a few highly skilled and professional occupations and, at certain times, in service occupations. Unemployment in Florida usually runs below the national average, and the diversified economy of the state has not been as subject to labour fluctuations as in many other areas where one industry dominates the economy. The cost of living in Florida is generally below the national urban average, and in some areas, such as clothing, it is considerably below the average—another small but significant benefit accruing from the favourable climate.

Employment and living costs

Cultural life.   Florida is well endowed with a variety of cultural activities and institutions, a situation stemming partly from the importance of tourism and partly from the increasing leisure time available to the growing number of retired residents. The state itself maintains more than 800 parks and recreation areas, many of historic or natural interest; counties and municipalities support another 1,300 parks, as well as almost 600 indoor centres. The Everglades National Park contains 1,400,500 acres (566,800 hectares) in the heart of a unique natural region. Florida's rich history is preserved in such places as St. Augustine, the nation's oldest town, portions of which have been restored, while its famous fort, Castillo de San Marcos, has been made a national monument.

Sarasota is a centre for both art and theatre. The John and Mable Ringling Museum of Art possesses an internationally famous collection, and the city—once the winter quarters of the famous Ringling Circus—also contains a circus museum and hall of fame. The Florida State Museum, located in Gainesville, is but one among the numerous noncommercial cultural attractions in Florida. The Gasparilla Pirate Invasion, a festival comparable to the Mardi Gras celebrations in New Orleans, is held in Tampa in February, and the state fair is held there in March.

Sports are well represented in the state, with the Orange Bowl in Miami, the Gator Bowl in Jacksonville, and Tampa Stadium attracting major university and professional events. The climate of Florida allows it to host a number of outdoor events, including major golf tournaments and internationally known auto races at Daytona Beach and Sebring. Horse racing is also important.

Commercial attractions seem almost countless; many are educational and contribute not only to the cultural well-being of the state but also to state tax revenues. Walt Disney World, near Orlando, has been called the largest single tourist attraction in the country; the facility's Experimental Prototype Community of Tomorrow is a permanent international showcase.

In addition to other cultural offerings, Florida's universities and educational television stations offer broad programs in continuing and adult education and similar ventures, on a scale larger than in most other U.S. states.

HISTORY

Exploration and settlement.   The early history of Europeans in Florida reflects the conflicts of the Spanish, French, and English crowns for empire and wealth. Juan Ponce de León's quest for the Fountain of Youth brought him to the peninsula in 1513 and 1521. Because he landed on the peninsula during the Easter season (Spanish Pascua Florida: Season of Flowers) and because of the vegetation he found there, Ponce de León named the area Florida. An unsuccessful settlement by another Spanish explorer in 1528 led to Indian captivity for Alvar Núñez Cabeza de Vaca and three companions, who spent eight years wandering throughout the South and Southwest. Hernando de Soto landed in 1539 and led a devastating expedition throughout the western coastal area, but he did not establish any settlements. A colony of Protestant Huguenots established on the St. Johns River was wiped out in 1565 by Spaniards, who boasted of slaughtering the French, not for their nationality but for their religion. This Spanish expedition, under Pedro Menéndez de Avilés, founded St. Augustine near the decimated settlement.

Spanish dominion

Shifting alliances and allegiances. During the following centuries there were frequent raids by English seafarers, including Sir Francis Drake in 1586, and clashes with French colonizers along the northern coasts of the Gulf of Mexico and with English settlers in the Carolina and Georgia colonies. Shifting alliances among the three powers reflected the vicissitudes of European politics, and St. Augustine and the English ports of Savannah and Charleston to the north of Florida were besieged at various times throughout the first half of the 18th century.   (R.H.Fu.)

England received Florida in return for Havana in 1763 and replaced its military government with civilian officials.

The provinces of East Florida and West Florida were now formed, and a period of prosperity began. Immigration began; and Andrew Turnbull, and Englishman, brought over a band of about 1,500 Minorcans (1767), whom he engaged in the cultivation of indigo at New Smyrna. Roads were laid out, some of which yet remain; in the last three years of British occupation the government spent liberal sums on the two provinces. Consequently, the people of Florida were for the most part loyal to Great Britain during the American Revolution. Several plans were made to invade South Carolina and Georgia, but none matured until 1778, when an expedition was organized which cooperated with British forces from New York in the siege of Savannah, Georgia. In the following year, Spain having declared war against Great Britain, Bernardo de Gálvez, the Spanish governor at New Orleans, seized most of the English forts in West Florida and in 1781 captured Pensacola.

By the Treaty of Paris in 1783 Florida reverted to Spain and, no religious liberty being promised, many of the British inhabitants left East and West Florida. A dispute with the United States concerning the northern boundary was settled by the treaty of 1795, the line 31° N being established.

Acquisition by the United States. The westward expansion of the United States made it highly desirable to have American ports on the Gulf of Mexico; consequently, the acquisition of West Florida, as well as of New Orleans, was one of the aims of the negotiations that resulted in the purchase of Louisiana in 1803. After the cession of Louisiana to the United States, the people of West Florida feared that that province would be seized by Napoleon. They, therefore, through a convention at Buhler's Plains (July 17, 1810), formulated plans for a more effective government. When it was found that the Spanish governor did not accept these plans in good faith, another convention was held on September 26, declaring West Florida to be an independent state, organizing a government, and petitioning for admission to the union. On October 27, Pres. James Madison, acting on a theory of Robert R. Livingston that West Florida was ceded by Spain to France in 1800 along with Louisiana and was therefore included by France in the sale of Louisiana to the United States in 1803, declared West Florida to be under U.S. jurisdiction. Two years later the U.S. Congress annexed the portion of West Florida between the Pearl and Mississippi rivers to Louisiana (hence the so-called Florida parishes of Louisiana) and that between the Pearl and the Perdido to the Mississippi territory.

In the meantime, war between Great Britain and the United States was imminent. The U.S. government asked the Spanish authorities of East Florida to permit an American occupation of the country in order that it might not be seized by Great Britain and made a base of military operations. When the request was refused, American forces seized Fernandina in the spring of 1812, an action that was repudiated by the U.S. government after protest from Spain, although it was authorized in official instructions. About the same time an attempt to organize a government at St. Mary's was made by U.S. sympathizers; and a petty civil war began between the Americans, who called themselves "patriots," and the Indians, who were encouraged by the Spanish. In 1814 British troops landed at Pensacola to begin operations against the United States. In retaliation Gen. Andrew Jackson captured the place but, in a few days, withdrew to New Orleans. The British then built a fort on the Apalachicola River and from there directed expeditions of Indians and runaway

Florida in the War of 1812

blacks against the American settlements. These expeditions continued long after peace was concluded in 1814. In 1818 General Jackson, believing that the Spanish were aiding the Seminole Indians and inciting them to attack the Americans, again captured Pensacola. By the Treaty of 1819 Spain formally ceded East and West Florida to the United States; the treaty was ratified in 1821, when the United States took formal possession; civil government was established in 1822.

The new territory and statehood. Indian affairs became the most serious problem of the new territory of Florida. Immediately after the cession of Florida to the United States, pressure was brought to bear upon Congress and the president to have the Seminole Indians removed and the country thrown open to settlement. The Indians, who had been allowed to occupy their lands in peace by the Spaniards, could not understand why they should be forced to move to new lands west of the Mississippi; but they consented, by the Treaty of Ft. Moultrie in 1823, to live within certain limits. Conflicts followed, however, as the population increased, and a new demand was made to have the Indians removed. By treaties made in 1832 and 1833, the Indian chiefs agreed to exchange their Florida lands for equal territory in the western part of the United States. But a strong sentiment against removal suddenly developed, and the efforts of the United States to enforce the treaty brought on the Second Seminole War (1835–42), which resulted in the removal of all but a few hundred Seminoles whose descendants continue to live in southern Florida. In 1845 Florida became a state of the United States.

The Civil War and Reconstruction. On January 10, 1861, an ordinance of secession was adopted by a state convention, and Florida became one of the Confederate States of America. The important coast towns were readily captured by Union forces—Fernandina, Pensacola, and St. Augustine in 1862 and Jacksonville in 1863; but an invasion of the interior in 1864 failed, the Union forces being repulsed in a battle at Olustee on February 20, 1864. After the war the state was briefly under military rule. But a new constitution was framed and ratified, and Florida passed from a quasi-military to a full civil government on July 4, 1868.

Before the American Civil War Jacksonville, St. Augustine, and even Tampa had attracted tourists and invalids seeking respite from the colder winters of the northern states, but tourism became a profitable business enterprise only in the 1880s. Among later visitors were several northern capitalists who recognized possibilities for further development in Florida: Hamilton Disston, who bought 4,000,000 acres of land in central Florida in 1881; Henry B. Plant, who bought several short-line railroads and built them into the Atlantic Coast Line system through central Florida to the west coast; and Henry M. Flagler, who built the Florida East Coast Line into Miami and over the seas into Key West. The railroads brought not only winter visitors, but settlers who grew winter truck crops, planted citrus groves, and mined phosphate. The population of the state doubled between 1870 and 1890; by 1900 there were more than 500,000 residents and in each succeeding 20 years the population almost doubled.

Tourism and development

The 20th century. The history of the state in the 20th century was that of rapid expansion and is quickly told in an amazing rise in population. In 1968 Jacksonville inaugurated a consolidated city-county type of government, making it the largest city in area in the United States. Many new industries located or relocated in the state, a number of them providing products and services associated with the missile centre at Cape Canaveral. Tourism became Florida's most important source of commercial revenue in the 20th century. Agriculture remained an important part of the economy, but citrus crops and cattle raising replaced field crops as the chief agricultural products. The growth of metropolitan and urban areas brought a decided shift of population and changed Florida's character from that of a rural state to that of a distinctly urban state. As in other states this resulted in a political fight on the part of the urban areas to secure better apportionment of representation in the state legislature.

The basis of Florida's government was laid in the constitution of 1885, to which, down through the years, about 100 amendments were ratified. In addition, a composite of amendments was adopted during the special session of the legislature in 1968 and ratified by the people in the November 5, 1968, general election. There are a number of important constitutional prohibitions and tax exemptions, including prohibition against an income tax and inheritance tax and exemptions that relate to homesteads.

(Ed.)

Georgia

The largest of the American states east of the Mississippi River, Georgia was founded in 1732, at which time its boundaries were even larger—including much of the present-day states of Alabama and Mississippi. It was by many years the youngest of the 13 former English colonies whose rebellion created the United States. Its landscape presents numerous contrasts, with more soil types than any other state as it sweeps from the Appalachian Mountains in the north (on the borders of Tennessee and North Carolina) to the marshes of the Atlantic Coast on the southeast and the Okefenokee Swamp (which it shares with Florida) on the south. The Savannah and Chattahoochee rivers describe much of Georgia's eastern and western boundaries with South Carolina and Alabama, respectively.

Georgia has an area of 58,876 square miles (152,488 square kilometres). For most of the 19th century the state was the capital of the cotton empire of the South, but poultry products now account for many times the income from cotton. Although industry has far outstripped agriculture in economic importance, almost two-thirds of the industrial workers remain in farm- or forestry-related jobs.

Pre-eminence of Atlanta

Atlanta, the capital, has long been the economic and cultural centre of the Southeast. Its name evokes the largely romantic legends of the pre-Civil War South, of the traditions of Southern gentility, and of white-columned mansions along Peachtree Street, its best known thoroughfare. The history of the state is marked by events of the Civil War: the many major battles fought there; the Confederate prison at Andersonville, in which nearly 13,000 Union prisoners died; and the burning of Atlanta and the devastating "march to the sea" by Union forces under Gen. William Tecumseh Sherman.

Although Atlanta has become very much a nationally oriented city, attracting major corporations as well as citizens from all parts of the United States, race and politics remain inextricably bound together throughout the state. Many forms of discrimination occur, as they do in most parts of the United States, though many Georgians see their state as being in the midst of a slow but definite transition, both socially and politically.

PHYSICAL AND HUMAN GEOGRAPHY

The land. *Relief.* The southernmost portions of the Blue Ridge Mountains cover northeastern and north central Georgia. In the northwest a limestone valley-and-ridge area predominates above Rome and the Coosa River. The higher elevations extend southward about 75 miles (120 kilometres), with peaks such as Kennesaw and Stone mountains near Atlanta rising starkly from the floor of the upper Piedmont. The highest point in the state, Brasstown Bald in the Blue Ridge, reaches to a height of 4,784 feet (1,458 metres) above sea level. Below the mountains the Piedmont extends to the Fall Line of the rivers—the east-to-west line of Augusta, Milledgeville, Macon, and Columbus. Along the fall region, which is nearly 100 miles wide, sandy hills reach in a narrow, irregular belt from Augusta to Columbus. Below these hills the rolling terrain of the coastal plain levels out to the flatlands near the coast, the "pine barrens" of the early days.

Surface features

Soils. From the coast to the Fall Line, sand and sandy loam predominate, gray near the coast and increasingly red with higher elevations. In the Piedmont and Appalachian regions these traits continue, with an increasing amount of clay in the soils. Land in northern Georgia is referred to as "red land" or "gray land." In the limestone valleys and uplands in the northwest, the soils are of loam, silt, and clay and may be brown as well as gray or red.

Drainage. About half the streams of the state flow into the Atlantic Ocean, and most of the rest travel through Alabama and Florida into the Gulf of Mexico. A few streams in northern Georgia flow into the Tennessee River and then via the Ohio and Mississippi into the Gulf. The river basins have not contributed significantly to the regional divisions, which have been defined more by elevations and soils. The inland waters of Georgia consist of 20 artificial lakes, about 70,000 small ponds created largely by the federal Soil Conservation Service, and natural lakes in the southwest near Florida. These have fostered widespread water recreation.

Climate. Maritime tropical air masses dominate the climate in summer, but in other seasons continental polar air masses are not uncommon. The average January temperature in Atlanta is 39° F (4° C); in August it is 79° F (26° C). Farther south, January temperatures average 10° F (6° C) higher, but in August the difference is only about 3° F (2° C). In northern Georgia rain usually averages about 50 inches (1,270 millimetres) annually. The east central areas are drier, with about 44 inches. Precipitation is more evenly distributed throughout the seasons in northern Georgia, whereas the southern and coastal areas have more summer rains.

Plant and animal life. Because of mountains-to-the-sea topography of the southeastern states, Georgia has a wide range of natural vegetation. It ranges from maple and hemlock and birch and beech near Blairsville in the north to the cyprus, tupelo, and red gum of the stream swamps below the Fall Line and to the marsh grass of the coast and islands. Throughout most of the Appalachians, chestnut, oak, and yellow poplar are dominant. Much of this area is national forest. The region that extends from the Tennessee border to the Fall Line has mostly oak and pine, except for an area of pines in the west. Below the Fall Line and outside of the swamps are the pines—longleaf, loblolly, and slash. Exploitation of these trees for pulpwood is a leading economic activity. Much of the land, which had at one time been cleared of trees for agriculture, has gone back to trees, scrub, and grasses.

Variety of natural life

Georgia's wildlife is profuse. There are alligators in the south; bear, with a hunting season in counties near the Okefenokee Swamp; deer, with restricted hunting in most counties; grouse; opossum; quail; rabbit; raccoon; squirrel; sea turtles, with no hunting allowed; and turkey, with quite restricted hunting. In general, wildlife is in a period of transition. Deer have been seen in suburban counties, and bears on golf courses in Atlanta; but solid stands of pine and unbroken pasture are not ideal for wildlife. There is extensive stocking of game birds and fish. The major fish of southern Georgia, except snook and bonefish, are in waters off the coast, and all major fresh-water game fish of the United States are found in Georgia's streams and lakes.

Settlement patterns. Migrations and historical change have tended to blur the traditional regions of Georgia. In an earlier time the coastal mainland and the sea islands were distinct, being separated from the middle part of Georgia by the pine barrens of the lower coastal plain. Rice and sea island cotton were major crops of this area. There was usually a summer exodus of plantation families to the southern highlands and to the North: a Savannah family, for example, might well know more people in Boston, New York City, or Philadelphia than they did in Augusta, Macon, or Columbus. The coastal region and the sea islands still support the unique culture of blacks, who are known as Gullah in South Carolina and as Geechee in Georgia.

Early subsistence farmers, who were known as "crackers," tilled the land in the thinly populated pine barrens just above the coastal area. There the soil is sandy and poorly drained, and the farms and plantations existed amid near-frontier conditions throughout much of the 19th century.

Beyond the pine barrens to the north and west, a prosperous cotton culture flourished for a period of more than a century. The classic period of cotton plantations and farms before the Civil War was brief in several counties. The white-columned houses generally were built in the county seats, or "courthouse towns," whereas the majority of the rural homes could be termed no more than substantial farmhouses. The mountainous area of northern Georgia was an area of small subsistence farms and few slaves.

Blacks were long identified with the commercial agriculture, which produced rice and sea island cotton on the coast and upland cotton in middle Georgia. Some modern historians use the term "black belt" as a demographic description of middle Georgia, where slavery predominated, though its origin stemmed from the dark soils of Alabama.

Plantations were cultivated by supervised group labour before the Civil War. After the war a family-plot system, called sharecropping or tenant-farming, replaced the larger labour groups and reduced immediate supervision. There were two basic arrangements in the sharecrop system with some variations: in middle Georgia the division-by-halves system gave the landowner control of the farm's management and the sale of the crops that were raised. The more independent landowner of northern Georgia, if he did not own a small farm himself, rented by thirds and fourths and had more control.

Rural Georgia was settled in a pattern of separate farms without villages or unified communities. Area names suggested such centres, but these generally were derived from the names of creeks, mountains, and militia districts. Schools, churches, and stores often drew neighbours in different directions, producing a highly diffused rural community life. Urban settlements originally served political and commercial purposes as county seats and cotton markets. The Fall Line cities became railroad points, and later they and some courthouse towns in the upper Piedmont had cotton mills.

Elsewhere the country general store and small local cotton gins declined as the larger towns gradually absorbed the slight commerce and industry. Later, better roads enabled people to travel from these smaller locales to the larger towns and cities. Today shopping centres, neon-lighted restaurants, and service stations are scattered throughout both the rural and urban areas in much of the state.

The people. In 1752, the year Georgia came under direct rule of the British government, it had only about 5,000 inhabitants, many of them English, Jewish or black. Salzburgers from Austria lived at New Ebenezer and Savannah, Scottish Highlanders at Darien, and New England Congregationalists at Sunbury and Midway. Settlement was concentrated on the coast and up the Savannah River to the Augusta area. Irish, German, and other massive immigrations into the United States during the 19th century affected Georgia little, and by 1910 only about 15,000 foreign-born whites resided in the state.

Churches play a significant role in the various subcultures of Georgia. The early movement for racial integration affected the churches even more profoundly than other institutions.

Georgia lost more people than it gained through migration in each decade from 1870 to 1960, but the total population increased steadily because of high birth rates. More whites than blacks left until 1910, generally moving to other Southern states to the west; after 1910 the black exodus was greater, generally to the cities of the North. The boll-weevil plague of the 1920s devastated the cotton economy and caused massive departures of both races. The white emigration loss almost stopped in the 1950s; thereafter there was a net migration gain of both whites and blacks.

Mechanized and chemically controlled agriculture, along with abandonment of cultivated farmlands to pastures and pine forests, were major causes of black migrations. Perhaps even more important, however, were blacks' hopes that elsewhere they would find fewer ingrained patterns of discrimination.

The economy. Georgia's rapid industrialization since 1940 caused a shift in the meaning of such words as "farm" and "industry," and "agribusiness" has become a term in wide use. More people work in industry than on farms, but a great majority of industrial jobs depend on farm or forest products. Income from poultry is regarded as farm income despite the fact that chickens are raised in

factory-like structures; feed prices are quoted for 150-ton lots, and financing is done by complex base-and-incentive arrangements—all indicating an extensive and highly developed agribusiness.

More conventional industries, such as automobile assembly, exploit the nearness of Atlanta to southeastern markets. Several decades of prosperity have also increased commerce, and a large number of New York City stores have branch stores in Atlanta.

Resources. Georgia is one of the nation's major producers of building stone and crushed stone. A white clay known as kaolin is taken from vast pits in middle Georgia, processed, and then shipped in tank cars for use in such products as ceramics and paper. Phosphate deposits in the southern part of the state are largely unexploited, but this region's ample reserves of artesian-well water are proving useful for agricultural irrigation.

Georgia's virgin timberlands have been cut over, but the state ranks first in the nation in growth of timber. Taxation of the state's timber-growing lands is an internal political issue, with growth rates versus tax rates a crucial argument. Lumber, plywood, and paper are major products; but Georgia is especially known for its large production of naval stores—tars and resins—from its pine forests.

Georgia lies to the south of the states that benefit from the many hydroelectric dams of the Tennessee Valley Authority, and water power contributes only about 8 percent of its electrical energy. Coastal waters provide working grounds for a small number of Georgia fishermen, with shrimp being the main catch, though there are commercial sturgeon fisheries on the Coosa and Oosanaula rivers around Rome in the northwestern part of Georgia.

Industry. Cotton textile production has occupied a major sector of Georgia's economy since the late 19th century. The continuation of this specialization in textiles is shown in the great number of rug and carpet mills in northern Georgia. The concentration of looming and weaving skills there make the state one of the major textile producers in the nation. Manufactured items include airplanes, automobiles, mobile homes, chemicals, and processed foods.

Agriculture. With the continuing consolidation of farms into fewer but larger units and the advent of a pervasive agribusiness, Georgia has followed nationwide trends in agriculture. Much of the poultry industry is conducted by large companies that parcel out their work to small farmers—many of whom would otherwise be unemployed—and supply them with modern poultry-raising facilities. Cattle and swine raising are important, especially in the southern part of the state. Cotton is still one of the major crops, although its value is far below the peak years of the early 20th century. Georgia is the leading state in peanut (groundnut) production and ranks high in tobacco. Peaches have become especially identified with Georgia, and pecans and watermelons are grown nearly everywhere in the state.

Management of the economy. The federal government affects Georgia's economy through direct purchases from industry, but even more through payrolls at the several major military installations throughout the state. It produces some hydroelectric power and regulates its sale, much of it to rural electric cooperatives.

The state government, on the other hand, functions in the economic sphere largely to promote further industrial development or financial investment in the state, which continues to rely to a large extent on outside money. Atlanta is the financial centre of the Southeast and the headquarters of the Sixth District of the Federal Reserve Bank. Nearly 60 percent of state taxes are levied on sales, with most of the rest on personal and corporate incomes. Local governments in Georgia rely mainly on general property taxes.

Less than 15 percent of Georgia's workers belong to unions, a figure below the national average. Unions are strongest in construction, the textile trades, and the steel, automotive, aircraft, and other machine industries. Racial tensions exist within unions, but blacks have traditionally been employed in such building trades as carpentry, painting, and masonry. Unionization is hampered by a solidly entrenched "right-to-work" law, which prohibits compul-

Margin notes:

Land divisions and town growth

Patterns of migration

Quarrying and forestry

Worker and employer organizations

sory union membership in any trade or industry, and by the rural origins of many of the union members, which prevent them from achieving a rapid acclimatization to more modern industrial procedures.

Employer groups in the state vary from broad-based organizations which are striving for a good general business climate to one-industry groups with hard-line lobbies at both the state and federal levels. Agribusiness presses hard for exports to European countries, while the cotton-fabrics industry strives just as determinedly against foreign imports.

Transportation. Water transportation determined the location of Georgia's earliest cities. Milledgeville was briefly the centre of an emerging road system for the settled counties in eastern Georgia and for the old military and post road running through Indian territories to Alabama. Atlanta, originally called Terminus on the early railroad survey maps, had a near-optimum location for all but water transport, thus making it a hub of railroad transportation for the Southeast. With the advent of highways and then of air traffic, the city maintained its focal position.

Petroleum, natural gas, and butane pipelines come into the state from the Southwest. More than a dozen cities in the state have commercial air service. A rapid transit system began operating in the Atlanta area in 1979.

Navigation on 500 miles (800 kilometres) of inland waterways has been revived, and a state port authority has created barge service at Augusta, Columbus, Bainbridge, Savannah, and Brunswick for the distribution of chemical, wood, and mineral products.

Administrative and social conditions. *Government.* The structure of state government tends to sever governmental from political processes and thereby prevents a strong executive. The executive branch, however, accounts for more than 90 percent of the state's expenditures.

The Georgia legislature consists of the 56-member Senate and the 180-member House; districts in 1971 replaced counties as units of representation. The basic units of the judiciary are a court of ordinary for probate and guardianships and a superior, or circuit, court of general trial in each county, with auxiliary county and municipal courts. The Court of Appeals and the Supreme Court hear appeals from lower jurisdictions. There are no uniform procedures for supervision or coordination of the superior courts.

County, regional, and municipal government

Georgia has many levels of local government, including 158 counties, 530 municipalities, and more than 385 special districts. Counties remain viable units, often performing municipal-type services. Independently and through multicounty cooperative districts, they operate forestry units, airports, hospitals, and libraries. The counties and the municipalities are organized into 19 area planning and development commissions, which deal with health, housing, criminal justice, and industrial development.

An increasing number of Georgia's cities have strong executives. Relations between cities and their suburbs, in which race continues to be significant, remain largely unsolved.

Georgia politics has been in flux since the 1950s. Voting patterns have changed, and distinctions among local, state, and national politics have increased. Republican or third-party presidential candidates carried the state in the 1964, 1968, and 1972 elections. Pres. Jimmy Carter, a Democrat who had been governor of Georgia in 1971–75, won the state's presidential vote in 1976 and 1980. Local politics and the "courthouse rings" (local elites) remain almost universally Democratic; and Democrats, while remaining shy of identification with the more liberal national party, continue to win the state house offices. Republicans, however, have won seats in Congress.

The political idiom has changed as well. Explicit racial demagoguery is no longer in evidence. Campaigns are long, and, with only occasional captive audiences, gubernatorial candidates are forced to stump and shake hands with the voters throughout the state in a way that was once unnecessary.

Black voting and civil rights

Black precincts in Atlanta and Macon that were 80 to 90 percent Republican in 1956 are now Democratic by that margin or more. Whites in rural and less affluent urban areas may vote for candidates on racial issues, whereas rural elites and affluent suburbanites tend to vote for either party depending on the local, state, or national nature of the contest and the commitments of the candidates.

The civil rights movement in Georgia has been characterized by legal action, many nonviolent and a few violent confrontations, selective buying campaigns, voter registration, and education. The movement has touched life in rural Georgia only a very little. In cities and in settings of high visibility—airports, stores, restaurants, and schools—blacks are seen in dramatically different circumstances from that of earlier decades.

Education. The public high schools have developed largely since 1912. Since 1945 the ages for compulsory attendance have been from seven to 16 years. Since 1964 state support of public schools has been for a period of nine months per year. The racial integration of public schools increased private-school enrollments dramatically.

Public institutions of higher learning, under a unified board of regents, are headed by the University of Georgia (chartered 1785; opened 1801) in Athens and the Georgia Institute of Technology (1885) and Georgia State University (1913), both located in Atlanta. Other state colleges and new junior colleges are increasing the crisis of private colleges in the state. The four undergraduate colleges and the graduate and professional schools of Atlanta University Center, all located on a single campus, and Paine College in Augusta provide higher education primarily for blacks.

Health and welfare. Georgia has a modern mental health program. Regional hospitals for evaluation, emergency, and short-term treatment have been established throughout the state to serve communities within a 50-mile radius. In addition, there are approximately 60 community health-care centres for outpatient treatment. A number of general hospitals have been built through federal programs.

Georgia has imaginative programs in family and children's services. There are state and regional youth-development centres, and no child is committed to a jail. The state aids colleges in training welfare workers, whose activities are supplemented by a widespread volunteer program.

Cultural life. Atlanta is the artistic centre of the Southeast. Its memorial centre, which was completed in 1968, includes a major museum and a school of the visual arts, with performing facilities for its symphony orchestra and a professional resident theatre, both of which have premiered new works. Atlanta also has cooperative galleries run by painters and sculptors, and an active group of filmmakers.

Elsewhere in the state, there are regional ballet companies, and community theatres perform in more than 30 localities. In addition to instruction in theatre, dance, the visual arts, and music in many colleges, Georgia Institute of Technology has a school of architecture, and the University of Georgia offers courses in landscape architecture. About a dozen public museums and numerous college galleries exhibit art, and Atlanta University has a notable Afro-American collection.

Georgia is rich in traditional arts and crafts, especially in the mountainous north. The craft of tufted fabrics was a major factor in attracting the carpet industry that developed around Dalton. Other handcraft workers find sales opportunities through country fairs in Hiawassee and nearby Gatlinburg, Tennessee, at the Plum Nelly Clothesline in Rising Fawn-Trenton, and at many other art festivals across the state. A mountain arts cooperative has a store in Tallulah Falls, and craft shops are attached to several art galleries. A bulletin of the state's agriculture department gives free advertising for crafts, and a quarterly publication describes many of the old craft techniques.

Folk music

Traditional music is sung by folk groups on the sea islands and in the mountains. Country music conventions are held in northern Georgia—with some tension between purists and users of electronic equipment. The ancient sacred harp songs of the northwest, heard in what is known as "fa-so-la" singing, have been collected, and throughout the area many prayers and sermons are delivered in singsong.

Though generally conservative, the press in Georgia has

tended to support the more liberal statewide candidates in recent decades. *The Atlanta Constitution* long has been recognized as one of the nation's outstanding newspapers.

Settlement. Georgia was granted a charter as a colony by George II in 1732, long after the large English migrations of the 17th century. The prime mover in obtaining the charter was the English general and philanthropist James Edward Oglethorpe, who sought to found a colony where the poor of England could get a new start. He and other trustees encouraged the settlers to produce wines, silks, and spices, and thus relieve England of a dependency on foreign sources. The colony also would serve as a bulwark against the Spanish and French in the lands beyond the Carolinas.

The first settlement in Georgia was made at Savannah in 1733. Some colonists paid their way; the colony's trustees paid the expenses of others. Oglethorpe directed the affairs of the colony, primarily its military operations. Government was informal, the economy was not generally successful, and military frustration was frequent; the trustees surrendered all power in the colony to the British government in 1752, a year before their charter was to expire.

Revolution and growth. With the pre-Revolutionary thrust of westward migration, substantial settlement of Georgia began, first in a thin band along the west side of the Savannah River. Georgia's response to the revolutionary tensions of the 1770s was confused, and the war period was chaotic. After the Revolution, settlement expanded rapidly, especially westward from Augusta through the future "cotton counties" of middle Georgia. Speculations in public lands, acquisitions of Indian lands, and the removal of the Creeks and Cherokees from the state paralleled the development of a largely commercial agriculture and a transportation system. The Indian removal itself provided a poignant and traumatic chapter in the state's history. Alabama and Mississippi were already settled by whites, and the Indians' move beyond the Mississippi River was a long one. It left in its wake what came to be known as the Cherokee Trail of Tears. (G.He.)

The slavery controversy and the Civil War. The activity of Georgia in the slavery controversy was important. Popular opinion at first opposed the Compromise of 1850, and some politicians demanded immediate secession from the Union. Others contended that the compromise was a great victory for the South and, in a campaign on this issue, secured the election of such delegates to the state convention (at Milledgeville) of 1850 that that body adopted a series of conciliatory resolutions, since known as the Georgia Platform. The approval in other states of the Georgia Platform caused a reaction in the South against secession.

margin note: The Georgia Platform

The Kansas question and the attitude of the North toward the decision in the Dred Scott Case, however, began arousing the South. Following the election of Pres. Abraham Lincoln, the state's leaders were initially divided over the question of secession; but a state convention overwhelmingly voted 208 to 89 for secession on January 19, 1861.

Toward the close of 1861, Federal warships blockaded Georgia's ports, and early in 1862 Federal forces captured Tybee Island, Ft. Pulaski, St. Marys, Brunswick, and St. Simons Island. In 1863 northwest Georgia was involved in the Chattanooga campaign. In the following spring Georgia was invaded from Tennessee by a Federal army under Gen. William T. Sherman. The resistance of Gen. Joseph E. Johnston and Gen. J.B. Hood proved ineffectual, and on September 2 Atlanta was taken. On November 15 Sherman burned Atlanta and began his famous march to the sea, taking Savannah late in December. In the spring of 1865, Gen. J.H. Wilson, with a body of cavalry, entered the state from Alabama, seized Columbus and West Point on April 16, and on May 10 captured Jefferson Davis, president of the Confederacy, near Irwinville.

Reconstruction. A provisional government established by Pres. Andrew Johnson incurred the suspicion and ill will of Congress; and Georgia was placed under military government, as part of the 3rd Military District, by the Reconstruction Act of March 2, 1867.

Under the auspices of the military authorities, a convention met in Atlanta on December 9, 1867, and by March 1868 had revised the constitution to meet the requirements of the Reconstruction acts. The constitution was duly adopted by popular vote, and elections were held for a governor and legislature. In September 1868, however, the Democrats in the state legislature, being assisted by some of the white Republicans, expelled the 27 black members and seated their defeated white contestants. In retaliation Congress excluded the state's representatives on a technicality. The U.S. Department of War then concluded that the state was still subject to military authority and placed Gen. A.H. Terry in command. With his aid and that of congressional requirements that all members of the legislature must take the test oath of nonsupport to any pretended government—*i.e.,* the Confederacy—and that none be excluded on account of colour, a Republican majority was secured for both houses, and the 15th Amendment was ratified. On July 15, 1870, Georgia was finally readmitted to the Union.

Reconstruction in Georgia was comparatively moderate, largely because a number of conservatives supported the Reconstruction policy of Congress. The election of 1870 gave the Democrats a majority in the legislature. After that the control of the Democrats was complete. Georgia, however, did not frame its home-rule constitution until 1877, when the threat of further military intervention had ended.

Post-Reconstruction. The history of Georgia since Reconstruction has been one of nominal social and economic progress, with the state firmly Democratic in politics until 1964. The 18-year interval following 1872 was dominated by the Bourbon triumvirate of Joseph E. Brown, Alfred H. Colquitt, and John B. Gordon, who stood for low taxes and limited public services and who maintained a close liaison between business and political interests. The leasing of convicts to private concerns (peonage) was the most criticized of their policies. The Independent movement, later backed by the Farmers Alliance, challenged Bourbon control throughout most of the period, but by 1892 the Populist threat, with its greater appeal to rural voters, became more serious. All factions sought the black vote, and political corruption was widespread. The waning of Populism at the beginning of the 20th century was accompanied by the adoption of several new measures. Virtual disfranchisement of blacks was effected by registration requirements in 1908 ("grandfather" laws, which placed restrictions on registration that were difficult for blacks to meet but not for white registrants), and the convict-lease system was abolished. A state-wide prohibition law of 1907 proved unpopular, and this issue remained prominent until adoption of the 18th Amendment to the U.S. Constitution in 1919 brought national prohibition. Laws seeking to protect labour in the state's growing industries and reforms in educational policy, with additional appropriations for public schools, were other notable measures adopted in the first part of the 20th century.

margin note: Bourbon rule

County-unit system and apportionment. The Neill Act of 1917 placed Georgia's primary elections under legal control, establishing the county-unit system for determining winners in such elections. In 1920 a constitutional amendment fixed the number of first-class counties at eight and the number in the second classification at 30, while those remaining were in the third class. First-class counties were the most populous, and each had three representatives in the legislature and cast six unit votes. The second group of 30 counties had two representatives each and was entitled to four unit votes. The remaining 122 counties were the least populous, and each had one representative and cast two unit votes. Thus first-class counties had a total of 48 votes; second-class, 120 votes; and third-class, 244 votes; the total of all votes being 412. Subsequently the number of counties was reduced to 159 and the total of county-unit votes to 410. Because nomination in the Democratic primary in Georgia was tantamount to election, county-unit voting, together with the three-class system of representation, placed political control in the hands of the smaller counties dominated by rural voters. This inequality of representation led in 1962 to a suit in the federal courts, the result of which was the voiding of the county-unit system. A short time later the court ordered that one of the two legislative branches be apportioned on a population basis. Subsequently the 54 senate seats were reapportioned, with 23 going to the urban areas. In 1964 the court ruled that both houses be apportioned on a population basis and rejected as invalid a new constitution framed by the existing legislature. In 1964 the U.S. Supreme Court ruled that the Georgia apportionment for the U.S. House of Representatives was unfair to urban voters and that congressional districts must be established on the basis of "equal representation for equal numbers of people." Congressional districts were reapportioned in 1965, as was the Georgia house of representatives. The plans were accepted as interim measures, but a federal court ordered both houses and districts reapportioned again. A new plan was drawn up in 1967 and, with minor amendments ordered by the court, went into effect in 1968.

Issues of integration. Meanwhile, during these years, rural-dominated Georgia was ruled by a succession of governors who were frequently open in their advocacy of white supremacy and conservatism—including Richard B. Russell, Eugene Talmadge, and Eurith D. Rivers. Resolving the racial problem was thus slow.

A federal court decision in 1945 ordered the Democratic (white) primary in Georgia open to black voters, causing the registration of blacks to increase more than 700 percent by the end of the following year and providing new impetus to the white-supremacy issue. A reregistration act in 1949, containing literacy, character, and citizenship tests and aimed at minimizing the black vote, proved unsatisfactory and was repealed after one year. In 1950 (and again in 1952) a proposed amendment extending the county-unit system to general elections was defeated. In the meantime a sweeping 3 percent sales-tax levy enacted by the Herman E. Talmadge administration, most of which went for educational purposes, resulted in a rapid upgrading of black schools. What promised to prove the most serious issue since Reconstruction was provided in May 1954, when the U.S. Supreme Court announced its unanimous decision that racial segregation in public schools was unconstitutional.

In November, an amendment was ratified enabling the state to abolish public education by granting subsidies to private schools. Marvin Griffin campaigned for governor on the Talmadge position of continued segregation and was elected. In 1955 the legislature passed a standby private-school law to go into effect if the court ordered a specific school to desegregate.

The administration of Gov. Ernest Vandiver, who succeeded Griffin, abandoned the previous policy of "massive resistance" and in effect placed under local option the closing of public schools to prevent integration. The Board of Regents was given similar power to close public colleges. Early in 1961 two black students were admitted with police protection to the University of Georgia under a federal court order. In the next several years a number of public and private colleges were integrated with little fanfare and little resistance. In the meantime the Atlanta school board, under court mandate, on August 30, 1961, enrolled nine black students in four previously all-white high schools. Lester G. Maddox, who was elected governor by the legislature in January 1967, continued the fight against school integration. Maddox was legally unable to succeed himself as governor, and in 1970 Jimmy Carter, a Democrat, was elected. In 1964, when Democratic Pres. Lyndon B. Johnson supported the Civil Rights Act, Georgia voted for a Republican presidential candidate for the first time in its history. In 1968 the state gave its presidential vote to George C. Wallace. Thereafter, however, black participation in government improved radically, lending a liberalizing influence. (Ed.)

Kentucky

The Commonwealth of Kentucky is a south central state of the United States. Long the home of various Indian tribes, Kentucky was settled by Daniel Boone and other frontiersmen in 1769. By 1792, when it was admitted as the 15th state of the Union—the first west of the Appalachian Mountains—Kentucky had drawn nearly 75,000 settlers.

Rivers define Kentucky's boundaries except on the south, where it shares a border with Tennessee along a nearly straight line of about 425 miles (685 kilometres), and on its mountainous southeastern border with Virginia. The Tug and Big Sandy rivers separate it from West Virginia on the east and northeast. From the point where the Big Sandy empties into the Ohio River, the pyramid-shaped northern boundary cuts a jagged line across the country, following the Ohio and meeting the states of Ohio, Indiana, and Illinois to the north. Where the Ohio flows into the Mississippi, the short western edge of the state is separated by the Mississippi from Missouri. These boundaries encompass 40,395 square miles (104,623 square kilometres). The capital, Frankfort, lies between the two major cities, Louisville, which lies on the Ohio River, and Lexington.

Kentucky brings to mind images of coal mines, of the bourbon whiskey that was developed there, of white-suited colonels and their ladies sipping mint juleps on summertime verandas, of mountaineers and moonshiners, of horse breeding and the Kentucky Derby. In actuality, Kentucky has a curious mixture of poverty and wealth, ugliness and beauty. In the late 20th century, several hundred lives were lost in Kentucky's coal mines, and strip-mining has continued to leave countless hillsides to erode after denuding them of their forest cover. Yet the seemingly endless landscape of white-railed horse pens and paddocks, characteristic of the rolling Bluegrass region around Lexington, symbolizes an unhurried and genteel way of life that looks more to Kentucky's ties with the pre-Civil War South than to its position in the industrial frenzy of the nation. Kentucky has always existed in the middle: as a state looking back and ahead, as a crossroads for westward expansion, and as a split personality during the Civil War. It was the birthplace both of Abraham Lincoln, 16th president of the United States, and of Jefferson Davis, president of the Confederate States during that strife.

PHYSICAL AND HUMAN GEOGRAPHY

The land. *Relief.* Kentucky has six major physiographic regions: Mountain, Knobs, Bluegrass, Pennyrile, Western Coal Field, and Purchase.

More than 10,000 square miles (26,000 square kilometres) of the easternmost part of Kentucky lie in the Mountain region, a sloping plateau of the Cumberland and Pine mountain ranges. It is a scenic land of narrow valleys, steep pinnacles, and transverse ridges. The state reaches its highest point at Big Black Mountain, 4,150 feet (1,265 metres) in altitude. An area of deep gorges, natural rock arches, and small valley farms, eastern Kentucky is drained by three major rivers and their tributaries: the Big Sandy, Cumberland, and Kentucky rivers. Natural passages through these mazes of mountains are sometimes provided by winding gaps, such as historic Cumberland Gap, or water gaps, which include the picturesque Breaks of Sandy. The great eastern coalfields of Kentucky lie in the mountains and, though the region has been a major coal-producing area throughout the 20th century, there are billions of tons of coal still buried in the eastern hills. Mining has created the state's paradox of wealth and poverty, and the dilemma of whether to exploit natural resources or preserve the ecology.

A long, narrow region shaped like an irregular horseshoe with both ends touching the Ohio River, the Knobs embraces the Bluegrass country on its inner side, the Mountain area on the east, and the Pennyrile on the west. Its landscape is one of cone-shaped or rounded hills and ancient escarpments. The weathered shale soil is not rich and is easily eroded, making it better adapted to forest growth than to cultivation. Canebrakes grew along some of the lower ground before European settlement and attracted large herds of buffalo and deer. A major portion of the Daniel Boone National Forest lies in the eastern Knobs.

There is a folk saying that when east Kentuckians die they want to go to Lexington, the capital of the Bluegrass. The Bluegrass lies at Kentucky's geographic and legendary heart. Its 8,000 square miles are encircled by the Knobs

Court-ordered reapportionment

Location and size

Physical diversity

and the Ohio River. The region was named for the long-stemmed grass that flourishes there. The underlying limestones are rich in phosphates and have created pasturage for some of the world's most famous horse farms.

The 7,800 square miles of the Pennyrile (or Pennyroyal) touch every other region except the Bluegrass. On the east it joins the Mountains; to the north its irregular boundaries are the Knobs, the Ohio River, and the Western Coal Field; in the west it joins the Purchase; and on the south it is bounded by Tennessee. Its unusual name derives from the local pronunciation of pennyroyal, a plant of the mint family that is abundant in the area. The Pennyrile encompasses wooded rocky hillsides, small stock farms, cliffs, and an area once known as the Barrens—a condition caused by the Indians' continuous burning off of forest cover to make grasslands for the buffalo. Above all, it is a region of caves. Abundant waters, both surface and underground, and the limestones deposited during the Mississippian Period of geologic history (more than 300,000,000 years ago), have combined to create the area known as the Land of Ten Thousand Sinks and such famous subterranean passages as Mammoth Cave. The vast underworld cavern includes three rivers, two lakes, and a sea, and it covers more than 150 miles (240 kilometres) on five distinct levels. Its temperature remains constant at 54° F (12° C) throughout the year. Many other caves underlie the Pennyrile.

Surrounded by the Pennyrile and the Ohio River and crossed by the Green River, the Western Coal Field's 4,680 square miles (12,120 square kilometres) comprise less than half the area of the eastern coal beds and only a little more than half of that of the Bluegrass. The region has a number of coal deposits throughout its extent, however, and it is fertile on some of its rolling uplands and river bottom lands. Hence it is both a mining and farming area.

Bounded by the Tennessee, Mississippi, and Ohio rivers, the Purchase, also called Jackson Purchase, encompasses only 2,569 square miles (6,654 square kilometres) in the southwestern corner of the state. It was purchased in 1818 from the Chickasaw Indians, and Andrew Jackson, later the seventh president of the United States, was one of the signers of the treaty. The Purchase is the lowest topographic area of Kentucky, but it is not uniformly flat. Wide floodplains are broken by low hills that may have been sandbars in ancient oceans. Bluffs, swamps, and lagoons form part of the terrain, and soft rocks of the region erode rapidly, altering the landscape. The area is one of the most fertile sections of Kentucky and is widely known both for crops and for its fine stands of poplar, hickory, and oak.

Climate. Kentucky enjoys a temperate climate, plentiful rainfall, and distinctive soils, which combine to create variety in vegetation, animal life, and landscape. The state's mean annual temperature is between 55° and 60° F (13° and 16° C). The growing season lasts from 176 to 197 days a year. Mean annual rainfall for the entire state is about 45 inches (1,140 millimetres), evenly distributed throughout the year. The greatest differences occur between the southern areas, which average as much as 48 inches annually, and the northeast, which may receive only 40 inches. Prevailing winds are from the south and southwest, although winter's chill frequently arrives on north and northwest winds.

Plant and animal life. Kentucky was part of the great hardwood forest region covering the nation from the Allegheny Mountains to the western prairies. Three-fourths of the state was once covered with magnificent stands of yellow poplar, oak, chestnut, sycamore, and walnut. By the close of the 19th century, however, all but a fraction of these virgin forests had been felled. Trees, shrubs, and plants of many kinds still flourish in all parts of the state, ranging from the native hardwoods and pines on the eastern slopes to the picturesque bald cypresses in the western river marshes, and the maples, beeches, and magnolia found throughout the state. Rhododendron, laurel, dogwood, redbud, and trillium are prominent among the dozens of flowering plants that can be found in the Kentucky mountains.

Birds and animals of Kentucky include those native to the Deep South as well as those of southern Canada. Of the numerous hoofed animals that once roamed Kentucky—bison, elk, moose, and deer—only deer remain. Wolves, beavers, and panthers have likewise disappeared. Among the many small animals found in the state are rabbits, squirrels, foxes, raccoons, opossums, woodchucks, and—in the numerous caves—bats and rodents. The northwestern corner of Kentucky, where the Green River flows into the Ohio, is the site of one of the world's great migratory bird routes. More than 200 species of birds frequent this area, while close to 300 species have been found in the state as a whole. The marshes of the southwestern Kentucky–Tennessee border provide breeding places for such waterfowl as the American egret, great blue heron, and double-crested cormorant. A few wild turkeys remain as a reminder of pioneer days. The swift mountain streams, wide rivers, and man-made lakes of Kentucky provide habitats for more than 100 species of fish. The muskellunge, the largest member of the pike family, and commonly considered a Great Lakes fish, is found especially in the Barren and Green rivers.

Soils. The landscape of Kentucky is as diverse as the life it supports, extending from the wrinkled outcroppings of early Paleozoic rocks to the 2,300-mile (3,680-kilometre) shoreline of Kentucky Lake. Rich alluvial deposits lie along the rivers, while the rest of the state's soil derives from the long and gradual breakdown and decay of underlying rock.

The people. Early settlers of Kentucky, who were predominantly English and Scots-Irish, came from North Carolina, Virginia, Maryland, and Pennsylvania. The migrations of Daniel Boone reflected those of many of his fellow countrymen. He moved from Pennsylvania, where he was born, down the Great Valley of Virginia into North Carolina, where he lived until he led new settlers through Cumberland Gap to Kentucky. Despite the horrors of backwoods warfare during and following the Revolution, the migration into the Bluegrass country continued. In addition to the Cumberland Gap route, the Mississippi brought early French émigrés from New Orleans, particularly to the Louisville area, while during the mid-19th century the Ohio River carried many German settlers and other migrants, via Pittsburgh, from New England and the Middle Atlantic states. There was also a large black population in Kentucky, though the proportion decreased after 1833. Just prior to the Civil War, the Underground Railroad flourished in Kentucky to help transport escaped slaves to free soil, and there was considerable black emigration during and after the war. By the late 20th century only a small percentage of Kentucky's population was black.

From the beginning, Kentucky has been a strongly rural state of small towns and crossroads. Only Louisville and Lexington have big populations. Part of the urban population lives in small cities such as Lexington, Covington, Paducah, and Frankfort. Since World War II many of the younger people have left rural counties for cities both within and outside the state, creating severe economic, educational, and cultural problems.

Distinctive traditions of life have attracted Kentucky historians and sociologists. There is no such thing, it is claimed, as a halfway Kentuckian. Politics occupies a central position in the lives of most residents, with political speeches and barbecues having a special Kentucky flavour. The pace of living for most Kentuckians remains more leisurely than in many other areas of the country, even in the urban areas. Strong family ties and personal relations dominate major aspects of individual and community life. The popular image of the Bluegrass Kentuckian includes leisurely colonels and fast horses, cold mint juleps and a hot game-meat stew called burgoo, while the mountaineer Kentuckian might be idealized as a dulcimer-strumming weaver of old English rhymes and homespun wisdom. Each is rooted, to some degree, in fact and, though Kentuckians are losing many of their distinctive traits, part of the colour and flavour of individualism remains.

The economy. *Agriculture.* In the first half of the 19th century, Kentucky was a leading producer of the nation's

Cave
region

Bird life

Principal
crops

hemp, corn (maize), hogs, oats, rye, tobacco, wheat, and beef. Demands of Kentucky hemp growers brought adoption of the protective-tariff system in the United States. When sailing vessels were replaced by steamships, however, the need for hemp rope declined. Farm products have remained basic to the state's economy; after years of declining, the amount of farm acreage increased slightly during the late 1970s. Tobacco, corn, hay, and soybeans are major crops. Lexington is the heart of the light burley tobacco country, while the extreme western and southwestern parts of the state, known as the Black Patch, produce dark tobacco. Louisville, once the nation's largest tobacco market, has extensive cigarette factories. Corn and hay are essential to livestock production. Though cattle, sheep, and hogs are important, the state ranks first nationally in the breeding of Thoroughbred horses, both as saddle horses and as racehorses. About one-half of the thoroughbred saddle horses in the nation are bred in Kentucky. Production of bluegrass and orchard-grass seed is also important.

Mining and industry. Kentucky ranks second only to West Virginia in coal production. The high death toll in underground mines and the ecological disasters of stripmining have brought national attention to the state's coal industry and its problems. Petroleum, natural gas, asphalt, and iron ores are also among Kentucky's resources. Despite rapid depletion of the forests, lumbering and allied furniture and woodworking industries remain important. Manufactured products include whiskey, which has been produced in Louisville since 1783, textiles, foods, paints and varnishes, machinery, and iron and steel products.

Labour. A strong labour union tradition exists in the Ohio River towns, and the United Mine Workers of America is influential in the coal region. Early struggles between the UMWA and coal operators in eastern Kentucky gave rise to tragic violence. The name of Bloody Harlan commemorates that county's labour wars during the 1920s and 1930s, highlighting working and living conditions that became popularly identified with those of the state as a whole. Numerous ballads recount the history of conflict and death surrounding work in the coal mines.

Transportation. The first road engineers in Kentucky were the buffalo, whose traces to and from salt licks provided roadbeds for the earliest settlers. But, when Daniel Boone and his party hacked a passage through Cumberland Gap in 1775, Kentucky's transportation system was born. The Ohio and Mississippi rivers, bordering Kentucky for more than 700 miles (1,120 kilometres), and the various tributaries of the Ohio provided Kentucky with one of the most extensive systems of navigable waterways in the nation. The waterways supported a colourful era of flatboats, rafts, and steamboats in the 19th century. Along the trails and toll roads, livestock drovers, stagecoach drivers, and hardy horsemen found travel difficult, and rough terrain hampered road building in mountainous areas. Railroads were slow to develop in Kentucky, but in 1859 the first train began to run between Louisville and Nashville, Tennessee.

Highway construction has diminished the isolation of the eastern area. The Mountain Parkway in the east, the Kentucky Turnpike from Louisville south, and the Western Kentucky Parkway are among the scenic highways making each area of the state accessible. Several cities have airline service.

Administrative and social conditions. *Government.* The state government is comprised of the executive, legislative, and judicial branches. The governor is elected for four years and may not seek a second term. The General Assembly includes a Senate of 38 members, half to be chosen every two years for four-year terms, and a House of Representatives of 100 members, who are elected for two-year terms. All tax bills must originate in the House, which has sole power of impeachment. There are several levels in the state judiciary, from the Court of Appeals to local police courts. All judges are elected by popular vote. The major units of local government are the county and the municipality. All county officers are elected to four-year terms. Municipalities are divided into six classes according to population. In 1970 Area Development Dis-

tricts were created by the state to provide more local participation in community-planning decisions. Each of the 15 multicounty districts is governed by a board of directors, which consists of county judges, a mayor from each county, and citizens.

During World War I four military training camps were established in Kentucky. The most famous, Fort Knox, home of the gold bullion depository of the United States since 1936, contains billions of dollars in gold bricks. During World War II Bowman Field and Camps Breckinridge and Campbell were national training sites for the air force.

Education. A long struggle was required to establish and support a public school system in Kentucky. In 1838 the legislature passed a law establishing the first public school system, but efforts at implementation found only scattered support, and during the Civil War the movement received a setback. A state school fund, distributed on a per-pupil basis, provided the sole support of public schools until 1908, when the legislature established each county as a unit of taxation to provide educational funds. Gradually, improvements were made: school laws were codified in 1934, the Council of Higher Education was formed, and in 1954 a base salary for teachers was set in public schools. Increases in appropriations to the program were made possible by a state sales tax. The one-room, one-teacher schools that long characterized many of Kentucky's educational districts have disappeared, and the consolidation of schools has changed the way of life in many remote areas. School attendance of children aged seven to 16 is required. Kentucky adjusted to school-desegregation requirements with varying degrees of speed and success, and Louisville was the first major Southern city to integrate its schools.

Transylvania University (chartered in 1780 as a college), the oldest institution of higher learning west of the Allegheny Mountains, was moved to Lexington in 1788. It had the first library, football team, medical school, and law school in the West. Its enrollment of less than 1,000 students during the early 1980s contrasted sharply with that of the University of Kentucky (1865), also in Lexington, with almost 40,000 students. The University of Louisville, founded by the city council in 1798, is the oldest public college in the state. Other state and community colleges are located in various sections of Kentucky, as are a number of vocational schools. There are numerous private colleges at both the two- and four-year level. Among the most distinctive is Berea College, founded in 1853 to serve youths with small financial resources. Many leaders from the mountain communities were educated there.

Health and welfare. A state board of health was first established in 1878, and the state Department for Human Resources now includes numerous divisions and bureaus that handle such areas as preventive medicine, medical inspection and licensing, medical care for the needy, chronic disease control, sanitation in water supply and sewage, public assistance, and child welfare programs. Despite federal aid granted for the construction of hospitals and other health centres, much improvement in the state's public medical facilities is needed.

Cultural life. One of the more colourful aspects of the social and cultural life of Kentucky is that of the Kentucky Thoroughbred. Lexington is the centre of the world of horse breeding, and its boosters point out that, though they may race the horses at New York or California tracks, they breed, rear, and train them in the rolling Kentucky countryside. There are more than 300 horse-breeding farms around the city; many are open to visitors. At Louisville's Churchill Downs, one of the most colourful traditions of the sports world takes place, as it has since 1875, on the first Saturday of each May, when the Kentucky Derby is run.

Louisville is the centre of much of the cultural life of the state. It has an outstanding symphony orchestra, known for its performances and recordings of contemporary music; a ballet group; the J.B. Speed Art Museum; an active little theatre; and the Kentucky Opera Association. Kentucky continues to make a special contribution to the national culture with its folk arts, especially in the rural areas. Haunting ballads from Elizabethan days

(margin notes)

Mine labour and strife

Governmental branches

Folk arts

and mournful songs relating recent tragedies or desertions combine to create a distinctive musical life among mountain people. Crafts handed down through generations still produce handsome homespun cloth, hand-carved furniture, patchwork quilts, and sturdy pottery. Surrounded by a mechanized, standardized world, Kentucky folksongs and handicrafts preserve a link with earlier days. Among the nationally recognized writers identified with Kentucky are Robert Penn Warren and Irvin S. Cobb.

An extensive system of state parks, from Kenlake in the west to Jenny Wiley in the east, provides ample recreation for Kentuckians and tourists. In addition to providing attractive lodge and camping accommodations and a variety of sports facilities, the parks capitalize on local features of landscape or history. Restoration projects, exhibits, and outdoor pageants recreate specific episodes of pioneer days, the Civil War, and the life of Lincoln and other famous residents. Unique natural wonders, such as Mammoth Cave, are preserved and often made a focal point for the parks.

HISTORY

Exploration and settlement. Before the arrival of Europeans, the Kentucky region was a hunting ground and battlefield for such Indian tribes as the Shawnee from the north and the Cherokee from the south. Even earlier agricultural and hunting peoples left burial mounds and other traces. French and Spanish explorers must have seen Kentucky from the rivers of the Mississippi basin, and traders entered the region from the eastern colonies during the early 18th century. During the 1750s and 1760s Indian resistance and rough terrain hindered successful exploration of the region. In 1769, however, Daniel Boone penetrated to the central plateau region, or Bluegrass country.

Settlement was rapid during the 1770s, though the prophecies of an angry Cherokee chieftain, Dragging-Canoe—that Boone and other whites would find Kentucky "a dark and bloody land"—were in large part fulfilled. British officers spurred the Indians during the Revolution, notably in raids on Boonesboro in 1777 and 1778 and at a bloody ambush at Blue Licks in 1782, and settlers encountered numerous other sieges, scalpings, and skirmishes. Following the war immigrants poured down the rivers and travelled the Wilderness Road from Cumberland Gap. The settlers founded towns and before long began to call for separation of the judicial district of Kentucky from Virginia. Statehood conventions at Danville in the 1780s were somewhat ruffled by the "Spanish Conspiracy" of James Wilkinson and others to ally the region with Spain, but they led ultimately to admission into the Union on June 1, 1792, and to the organization of state government, which took place in a Lexington tavern.

Statehood and crises. Events leading to a second state constitution in 1800 revealed an internal division that has continued to characterize Kentucky. Farmers, who floated their grain, hides, and other products on flatboats down the Mississippi to Spanish-held New Orleans, allied themselves with other antislavery forces to oppose slaveholders and businessmen. The federal Alien and Sedition Acts of 1798, passed in an attempt to control criticism of the government, were vigorously opposed. One of the leading spokesmen for the opposition was the young politician Henry Clay, who was to stamp his personality on the state and national scenes as the "great compromiser."

Kentucky took a lead in the War of 1812, much of which was fought in the adjacent Northwest Territory against combined British and Indian forces. Following the war a land boom, with attendant speculation and inflation, and the chartering of 40 independent banks that flooded the state with paper money led to financial disaster during the national economic panic of 1819. Fierce controversy over relief to debtors split Clay's Whigs and Andrew Jackson's Democrats. Signs of progress from 1820 to 1850, however, included the building of a canal at Louisville, the chartering of railroads, and increased manufacturing. The slavery question was uppermost, however, until the Civil War. The few large slaveholders were located mainly in the plantation agriculture of the Bluegrass and Pennyrile sections, but by 1833, when the legislature forbade importation of slaves for resale, the state was already one-quarter black. Until the Civil War, proslavery forces maintained an iron control of government and prevented any constitutional change that endangered their property.

Civil War and its aftermath. During the war Kentucky was a state divided. Officially, it had sought to avoid war by continuing Clay's tradition of compromise. Some 90,000 soldiers fought for the Union armies and about 40,000 for the Confederacy, though after the war popular sentiment became strongly pro-South. Following the defeat of the Confederate general Braxton Bragg at Perryville, in 1862, the only action in the state consisted of widespread guerrilla warfare.

The opening of new rail lines into the eastern coal country and the introduction of a tobacco economy stirred the state in the last decades of the 19th century. The Ku Klux Klan evoked fears and hatred, but the freed blacks were given the vote and settled as tenant farmers or urban workers. As elsewhere, however, blacks were not to become first-class citizens. Lexington and the Ohio River cities—Louisville, Owensboro, Paducah, and Covington—grew rapidly. (W.D.)

Kentucky was not to escape the panics and agrarian turmoil of the latter half of the 19th century. Agrarian forces undertook to dominate the state government with near disastrous results in the 1880s. There continued, nevertheless, a bitter fight between the corporations and the farmers. In 1899 the railroads, textbook companies, and bankers joined with the Gold Democrats, who had seceded from the Democratic Party, to support the gold standard and Republicans against the farmer-Greenbackers in a bitter gubernatorial campaign. Republican William S. Taylor seemed to have won, but the election was disputed, and the legislative committee on contests decided in favour of the Democratic candidate, William Goebel. Goebel, shot by an assassin on January 27, 1900, died after being sworn into office, and Lieut. Gov. J.C.W. Beckham filled out the term and was reelected in 1903.

Delegates to a fourth constitutional convention had drafted the present constitution in 1891, but Kentucky was not to see peace within its borders for a long time to come. Mountain feuds raged in the east, some of them caused by friction of a state divided in the Civil War. At the same time, farmers in western Kentucky were frustrated by the repeated failures of tobacco prices to pay cost of production, and from 1903 to 1910 they carried on the so-called Night-Riders war against the big companies and farmers who refused to cooperate in controlling the production and marketing of tobacco. Farmers' barns were burned or their crops destroyed, and armed bands invaded market towns to burn warehouses of the "Tobacco Trust."

In a more constructive manner an able cluster of writers and newspapermen were able to bring distinction to their state. Henry Watterson, editor of the *Louisville Courier-Journal* from 1868 to 1918, made that paper nationally famous. James Lane Allen, John Fox, Jr., Annie Fellows Johnston, Alice Hegan Rice, Madison Cawein, Irvin Cobb, and Eleanor Mercein Kelly produced books and poetry of more than local importance. Alben Barkley (1877–1956) of Paducah served as vice-president of the United States and as majority leader of the U.S. Senate.

The modern period. World War I ushered in an era of change. Although the eastern coal fields were opened much earlier, this period saw marked expansion of the industry. Between 1918 and 1945 this industry grew rapidly. Its history, however, was marred by strikes called by the United Mine Workers. The eastern fields were again torn by labour strife in the years 1957—59. Mechanization gradually reduced the human factor in coal production. In both the western and eastern coal fields from 1940 the practice of strip mining was accelerated and stirred bitter public criticism. In 1966 the General Assembly passed a strict stip-mine law to ensure restoration of the natural contour of the land and its reforestation.

The Great Depression of the 1930s, followed by the impact of World War II, went far to bring major changes in Kentucky's social and economic conditions. The construction of better roads, the generation of cheap electrical current, and the improvement of educational facilities

Indian raids and immigration

revolutionized Kentucky life. After 1920 major changes occurred in the population base, with more than half of the state's 120 counties losing people to the industrial northwest and the rising urban centres. (Ed.)

Louisiana

With parts of its land lying farther south than any portion of the continental United States except for southern Texas and the Florida peninsula, and with New Orleans, its largest city, lying on the same parallel as Cairo, Delhi, and Shanghai, Louisiana owes much of its complex personality to its geographical position.

The state commands a once strategically vital region where the waters of the great Mississippi–Missouri River System, draining the continental interior of North America, flow out into the warm, northward-curving crescent of the Gulf of Mexico. It is not surprising that the flags of seven nations have flown over its territories since 1682, when the explorer Robert Cavelier, sieur de La Salle, placed a wooden cross in the ground and claimed the territory for France's Louis XIV. The consequent varieties of cultural heritage run like bright threads through many of the aspects—social, political, and artistic—of life in the state.

The subtropical climate of the state has provided the magnificent, brooding scenery of the coastal bayous, and the lush, dank vegetation of its shores conceals a rich mineral wealth in the form of oil. The fertile soil covering much of the terrain made Louisiana the richest agricultural portion of the Union by 1860, with sugarcane and cotton plantations flourishing. A lumbering boom occurred at the turn of the 20th century, and Louisiana underwent rapid industrialization after World War II. Mineral output is great, and the state ranks among the nation's leaders in petroleum production.

But progress has not been without its tragic and turbulent aspects: bitter territorial disputes and violent internal struggles for political power impeded the social and economic development of the state and crippled many of its political institutions. The wealth of the plantations was *Turbulent* accumulated through the extensive use of slaves, whose *heritage* descendants comprise almost one-third of Louisiana's population and whose culture has contributed much to the social fabric of the state. Racism and racial conflict have marred the development of the state from the Civil War period, through Reconstruction and the ensuing reaction, marked by the activities of the Ku Klux Klan, down to the civil rights conflicts of the 1960s and beyond. Louisiana's Deep South heritage is a complex one.

The state is delineated from its neighbours, Texas, Arkansas, and Mississippi, by four natural and three man-made boundaries. The 48,523 square miles (125,674 square kilometres) of Louisiana include some 3,000 square miles of inland waters.

PHYSICAL AND HUMAN GEOGRAPHY

The land. *Relief.* Louisiana shares the general physiographic characteristics common to the Gulf Coast states of the southern United States, with the vital exception of the Mississippi River, which flows through the state and extends its delta far into the Gulf of Mexico. The changing course of this great North American river has created the huge Atchafalaya Basin and has dumped tons of sediment along the coast. It has been estimated that the beachless coastline of Louisiana is eroding at a rate of about 16 square miles per year as the system of levees, or embankments, constructed by the federal government keeps the Mississippi in a central channel.

Three types of natural regions are found in Louisiana: lowlands, terraces, and hills. The lowlands consist of the coastal marshes and the Mississippi flood plain with its natural levees and moderate relief. Similarly, the Red River Valley has a low elevation relief but with many raft lakes, built up by impounding water from a number of log jams, and red soils in association with its alluvial plain. The terraces include much of the so-called Florida Parishes above and to the northeast of the Mississippi, as well as the prairies of southwestern Louisiana. Upland

hills are found on either side of the Red River Valley and in the northern portion of the Florida Parishes; the state's highest elevation, in northwestern Louisiana, is 535 feet (163 metres) above sea level.

Soils. The soils of Louisiana have been one of the state's priceless resources; nearly one-third of the total land area is covered by the rich alluvium deposited by the overflowing of its rivers and bayous. Muck and peat soils are found within the coastal marshes, while the bottoms hold rich alluvial soils: the lighter and coarser bottom soils of the Mississippi and Red River valleys and older alluvium and loessial, or windblown, soils. Within the uplands, or hills, there are more mature soils that do not sustain such a high degree of fertility.

Climate. Louisiana's climate is subtropical, a natural result of its location on the Gulf of Mexico. As it also lies at the mouth of the vast Mississippi–Missouri River Valley, halfway between the Atlantic and the Pacific oceans, the state is also affected by continental weather patterns. Hot, humid summers, tempered by frequent afternoon thunder showers, alternate with mild winters. Louisiana is subject to tropical storms, and the hurricane season extends for six months, from June through November. *Subtrop-* Average annual temperatures range from 64° F (18° C) *ical charac-* in the extreme north of the state to 71° F (21° C) at the *teristics* mouth of the Mississippi River. The highest monthly average is 83° F (28° C) in August, and the lowest is 46° F (8° C) in January. Summer averages do not extend above the low 80s Fahrenheit, and it is the humidity, rather than the heat, that is one of the more marked characteristics of the state's subtropical climate. The frost season begins between November 1 in northern Louisiana and December 14 in the extreme southeast. The average growing season ranges from 220 to 320 days, and the average precipitation from almost 48 inches (1,220 millimetres) near Shreveport to more than 64 inches between New Orleans and Baton Rouge.

Plant and animal life. Natural vegetation in Louisiana is found in three major divisions: the first consists of forest, upland pines and hardwoods, bottomland hardwoods, and bald cypress; the second of prairie, or dry grassland; and the third of marshland, or wet grassland. In the southern half of the state, along a zone running westward from Baton Rouge, the live oak with its characteristic drapings of Spanish moss predominates, providing a memorable element in the state's landscape. The magnolia, whose blossom is the state flower, grows throughout the state.

Muskrats and other fur-bearing rodents, together with alligators, have been trapped in the marshes of southern Louisiana. There is a great variety of birds, native and migrant, but the once-frequent brown pelican (the state bird), the ivory-billed woodpecker, and the wild turkey are nearly extinct. The grey squirrel, deer, and dove are plentiful. Fish, shrimp, crayfish, crab, and oyster are a source of food and of income in the coastal and swamp areas.

Settlement patterns. Northern Louisiana forms a natural region including the northeastern Louisiana Delta, the Red River Valley, and the northern Louisiana hills. Southern Louisiana, composed of the parish of Avoyelles and all the parishes that lie beneath the 31st parallel, has three major subregions: (1) the Florida Parishes, (2) southwestern Louisiana—which contains many Anglo-Saxon Protestants but also has an important French minority— and (3) in between, a region variously known as the Cajun, or the river and bayou country, or the sugar bowl.

The earliest settlements in the river and bayou parishes were "line" villages, where farmsteads were built at the river front of a long and narrow lot, with the stream serving as a highway. The line village pattern contrasted with the irregular pattern stemming from the ancient land division system of metes and bounds used by the Anglo- *Variety* Saxons of the Florida Parishes. Where the natural levee *of land* was wide enough, plantations were established. During *divisions* the pre-Civil War period people came to the uplands of northern Louisiana from the eastern states and settled in isolated farmsteads among the pine woods. Southwestern Louisiana was developed after 1880, and the prairies of the region were converted into rice fields. The form of settlement there resembled the geometrical pattern—based on a grid system of land division—found throughout the interior of the United States.

The people. If a diversity of landscapes and forms of settlement characterizes the state, its peoples and its cultures also represent many Louisianas. The earliest European settlers were French or Spanish, and only later were the Floridas region and the northern part of the state settled by *les Américains.* Each area of settlement managed to preserve a cultural heritage strongly marked by adherence to either the Roman Catholic or Protestant faith. The Louisiana French, particularly the descendants of the Acadians, came to dominate much of southern Louisiana; many of those who have arrived to live among them have been assimilated to the Cajun way of life. The French language is heard in many parishes, and throughout southern Louisiana one may hear English spoken with a French accent. In addition, there are several cultural islands in both regions of the state. These are made up of Italian, Spanish (*Isleños*), Hungarians, Germans, and Dalmatian-Slavonian communities. There are, as well, several racially mixed settlements.

The peoples of Louisiana exhibit a greater variety than those in other Deep South states not only because of the patterns of historical settlement but also because of the migration to and through New Orleans from Europe, Latin America, and Cuba. The number of foreign-born residents of Louisiana, however, has declined; now more than three-fourths of the population is composed of native-born Louisianians. The vast majority of foreign-born residents are found within the urbanized parishes of the state, especially New Orleans.

From the earliest days of the state, blacks have played an important role; and in the late 20th century they still constituted almost a third of the population. Historically, the black population was concentrated in areas containing the plantations sustained by their labour. During the early 20th century a large out-migration occurred, supplemented, after World War II, by a black migration to the state's urban areas. Although Louisiana's black population has been denied many of the traditional avenues leading to social and economic power, their culture has nevertheless contributed to the life and character of the state and of New Orleans, Louisiana's major city.

The black contribution

In the late 20th century, southern Louisiana contained almost three-fourths of the state's population, and almost one-half of the people in Louisiana lived in the three most populated parishes. A predominantly urban population was achieved for the first time in 1950.

The economy. Louisiana has shared the general condition afflicting Southern states: economic underdevelopment. Prior to 1941 nearly one-third of the labour force was employed in the primary, raw-material-oriented industries while only one-fifth worked in the secondary sector of mining, building, and manufacturing. Such an imbalance had the effect of depressing total personal income per capita, which, until 1930, was but slightly more than half of the national figure.

World War II hastened the industrial growth of Louisiana to the extent that the numbers of the labour force engaged in manufacturing increased considerably. The most important development has been the establishment of a chemical industry, based on the resources of oil, sulfur, salt, and water that are to be found in the area. An investment boom occurred from 1947 to 1957 when the first big move to offshore petroleum production was made. Though the trend subsequently fluctuated, industrial expansion is expected to continue as the state's program of offering inducement to industrial investment is maintained.

Resources. Petroleum resources are found in all areas of the state, but the main oil fields have been developed between Shreveport and Monroe and throughout most of southern Louisiana. Drilling has been moved out into the Gulf. Natural gas resources have also been utilized. Oil in Louisiana is often found in association with the more than 100 known salt domes, blister-like intrusions in the bedrock, and sulfur lies in the caprock overlying the salt. Conservation efforts have capitalized on the resources of soil and climate, and there is, as a result, extensive "tree farming." The natural gas resources of the state have been an important source of industrial power and the abundant mineral fuels that are available have been used to develop electrical power. Louisiana also has a prime asset in its water resources.

Industry and agriculture. Petroleum, chemical products, and food processing are the leading manufactured items. Cotton is no longer king in the agricultural domain: it was first in cash farm receipts in 1960, but within 20 years soybeans had become the leading agricultural product, with beef cattle ranked second. Other farm products include rice, dairy products, and poultry and eggs. The state has become much less dependent upon farming. The port of New Orleans is ranked second in the nation in volume of seaborne freight, while Baton Rouge, farther up the Mississippi River at the head of deep-channel navigation, is important for shipping of petroleum and chemical products, including aluminum, and grain.

The decline of cotton

Trade unions. The labour movement has failed to gain a strong foothold in the state, though union leaders have become effective lobbyists in the state legislature.

Transportation. Louisiana's waterways have always been an important means of transportation. The state's 4,800–7,500 miles (7,680–12,000 kilometres) of navigable waterways include the intracoastal canal. It is Louisiana's only east–west waterway and canal system and runs some 400 miles from Mississippi Sound to the Sabine River, providing the important ports of Baton Rouge, New Orleans, and Lake Charles with access to the Mississippi River.

Railroads became common after the 1830s, initially as feeders to the steamboat traffic, with the Clinton and Port Hudson line being the first railroad in the state. Railroading reached its peak in the early 20th century in connection with a feverish lumbering boom, and there are more than 3,000 miles of track in Louisiana. The state also has several thousand miles of highway. Louisiana has some 75 airports, and New Orleans International Airport, a leading continental link, is a major point of connection with Latin America.

Pipelines are used to carry crude oil to refineries or natural gas to provide energy for homes and industries in state and distant markets. Many miles of electric power lines crisscross the state.

Administrative and social conditions. *Government.* A state constitution that was adopted in 1921 was the 10th in 108 years. It managed to remain in force for more than 50 years, a period during which the state underwent more fundamental change than had occurred in all the preceding 109 years of statehood.

The earliest document (1812) secured the political power of the planters and business classes and gave great appointive powers to the governor: the antebellum documents of 1845 and 1852 extended the suffrage and made every government office, including the judiciary, elective. Representation, based on population, continued legislative domination by the planter masters. The constitution of 1861, which substituted the phrase "Confederate States" for "United States," and its successors of 1864 and 1868, which extended the suffrage to all males, black as well as white, may be called the Civil War documents. The constitution of 1879, marking the end of the Reconstruction period, sought to restrict the action of the legislature and granted executive powers rivalling those of 1812, while the constitution of 1898 disenfranchised the black citizens of the state. The constitutions of 1913 and 1921 were written by delegates of conventions called to grapple with the problems of the 20th century: in many respects, they failed, primarily because of the shadows of the past that hung over them. A new state constitution was established in 1974.

The governor of Louisiana remains the state's most powerful official, not only from the weight of tradition (and personal performance) but also because of the extent of patronage among the more than 250 executive agencies in the state.

Local self-government in Louisiana followed the Virginia system of county government. The parish (county), together with the municipality and special district, are the units of local government. There are 64 parishes with land areas and population that vary from the 197 square miles

The parish system

(510 square kilometres) in Orleans Parish to the 1,441 square miles (3,732 square kilometres) in Cameron Parish. The name of the parish governing board, "the police jury," is not found anywhere else.

There are more than 300 incorporated municipalities in Louisiana, described as state units, which exercise narrowly construed powers. The charter of incorporation detailed by law outlines three classes of municipalities based upon population: city (5,000); town (1,000–4,999); and village (150–999).

Special districts established by the legislature provide for the administration of new or expanding functions of local government.

The closed primary system is used in the nomination of congressmen, state legislators, and all state, district, and parish officers. Usually a runoff is necessary, since nomination requires a majority of the votes cast. Democratic nomination has been tantamount to victory but the Republicans have made the general election important again.

Social divisions. Although many whites continue to indicate a determination to maintain the ways of a segregated society, the traditional barriers are nevertheless coming down. At polling booths, in schools, on public conveyances, in stores and plants, and even at some churches, desegregation of the races is taking place, although it has come about not so much from voluntary choice on the part of the white power structure as from the insistence of federal laws. The civil rights movement has been active in Louisiana, where the National Association for the Advancement of Colored People has, perhaps, been the most effective among various organizations working for the establishment of black rights. Since the 1950s communities have established varieties of biracial human relations councils. Their activities were supplemented during the 1960s by federal monies from the Office of Economic Opportunity, which sustained various organizations designed for community advancement. Through efforts beginning in New Orleans during the 1940s and extending to southern Louisiana rural parishes and other urban areas during the 1950s, hundreds of thousands of blacks have become registered voters.

Justice. Louisiana's legal system is distinguished from that of the other 49 states in that it is based not on common law but on civil law, which is code, or written, law. The state draws upon its colonial inheritance, whereby the adopted code was based upon the Code Napoléon of France and further influenced by Spanish laws, each of which, in turn, had a common source in Roman law. The civil law consists of broad principles drafted by authorities in various fields of law. In Louisiana the law is enacted in the constitution, which vests authority to make law in the legislature, whereas the functions of the courts are limited to the application of the law to given sets of facts. Courts are not bound by previous decisions. The law governs all personal and property rights and has been extended to civil and criminal procedures.

Code Napoléon

Education. Public elementary and secondary education is administered by an elected state board of education and the state Department of Education, whose superintendent is also elected. The schools are locally administered by 64 parish school boards and three independent city school boards. The state board also administers nine colleges and universities, while the Louisiana State University system, with five campuses, two medical centres, and widespread agricultural activities, is administered by its own 15-member board of supervisors.

Health and welfare. The legislature has established programs to provide a system of economic security and social welfare for various categories of citizens, including persons 65 years of age and over. The state gives aid and welfare to mothers and children, care and treatment of crippled children and aid to the needy blind. Various state departments provide some aspects of welfare aid, but by far the most important is the Department of Public Welfare.

The so-called Charity Hospital system, supported and administered by the state, is fairly unusual among the 50 states. The system maintains several general hospitals, as well as hospitals for the mentally ill and for the treatment of tuberculosis. The Charity Hospital of Louisiana in New Orleans has received some public support since 1811.

The Louisiana Department of Health provides services to Louisiana citizens through a central office in New Orleans and local units in 62 parishes.

Penal and correctional institutions operated by the state are administered under the general authority of the Louisiana Board of Institutions. The penal system has often suffered from an excess of political interference.

Cultural life. The extensive power of the Roman Catholic Church in southern Louisiana and the domination of Baptists in northern Louisiana and among the black population remain important influences on social and cultural life. New Orleans and many smaller communities have been able to support the arts and philanthropic institutions. The Creoles (descendants of French or Spanish settlers) developed a distinctive architecture, art, and cuisine centred on New Orleans. Planters emulated the Creoles, and, thus, the people of the alluvial parishes of northern Louisiana are more cosmopolitan in outlook than are the people of the uplands.

In folk culture and the arts Louisiana more than holds its own. This is especially evident in the realm of music, whether it be in black folk songs, including the celebrated rural blues; the Cajun bands at *fais-dodos,* country dances held in southern Louisiana; the community hymn singings of northern Louisiana; the jazz that New Orleans migrants took to Chicago and elsewhere; or the renaissance in dixieland music played by bands at New Orleans' Preservation Hall.

Musical traditions

New Orleans, with its opera, theatre, and painters, was a major cultural centre during the 19th century. Its French Quarter attracted such artists as John J. Audubon, the great wildlife painter, and George Catlin, noted for his portrayals of the American West, together with writers such as Walt Whitman, Sherwood Anderson, and William Faulkner. Since the 1930s other cities, notably Shreveport, Monroe, Baton Rouge, and Lafayette, have evolved their own museums and galleries, orchestras, choruses, and little theatres.

Tourism has developed as an important industry using the appeal, to some, of the antebellum past and the attraction of Creole cuisine, an exquisite blend of French, Spanish, black, and Indian dishes. A series of parades and balls culminating in the main celebration of Mardi Gras (Shrove Tuesday) has become a national attraction in New Orleans. Many parks and gardens are set aside for public use and display, and the state is advertised as a "sportsman's paradise" for hunting and fishing.

The literate Creole culture provided the state with a long press tradition, the first newspaper, *Le Moniteur de la Louisiane,* appearing in 1794. Eight others were published in New Orleans at the turn of the 19th century, and the rural parishes likewise published their own papers. The leading newspapers are concentrated in the urban parishes.

HISTORY

Early settlement. At least 16,000 years before European exploration, Indians occupied the region that was to become Louisiana. At least seven archaeological sites have been excavated, notably the so-called Poverty Point sites (dated at approximately 700 BC), and the Marksville site (dated AD 100 to 550). Most Louisiana Indians lived in hunting and gathering camps in the uplands and coastal prairies, though there were farming villages in the rich, low-lying areas known as bottoms. It is estimated that there were 15,000 Indians in the area when settlement by Europeans began during the 1700s. By 1980 only about one-fifth as many Indians remained. Their heritage is present in the many place-names that lend colour to the state's map.

While the Spanish were the first Europeans to discover the area, it was the French who colonized it. Serious colonization by France began in 1699, when Pierre Le Moyne, sieur d'Iberville, and his brother Jean-Baptiste Le Moyne, sieur de Bienville, explored the area and struggled to found permanent colonies. The city of New Orleans was established by Bienville in 1718. Royal charters covering the area had been granted, first to Antoine Crozat, in 1712, and then, in 1717, to the Scottish businessman,

Initial colonization

John Law, whose Company of the West failed in 1720. When Louisiana became a French crown colony in 1731, its population had grown from fewer than 1,000 to nearly 8,000, including slaves. In addition to the French settlers, many thousands of Germans arrived, settling on the river just above New Orleans on what became known as the German Coast. Colonization was significantly increased during the 1760s with the arrival of the French-speaking Acadians, who had been expelled from Nova Scotia by the British.

In 1762 Louisiana and New Orleans were ceded to Spain by a secret treaty that was to establish nearly four decades of Spanish rule and influence in the area. In 1779 the Spanish wrested Baton Rouge from the British and took all West Florida, which then extended from the peninsula westwards across the Gulf Coast to the Mississippi River. In 1800 the Spanish re-ceded Louisiana to France, and in 1803 the United States concluded the Louisiana Purchase.

The 19th century. Louisiana was subsequently divided into the Territory of Orleans, which consisted essentially of the state within its present boundaries, and the Territory of Louisiana, which included all the vast area drained by the Mississippi and Missouri rivers. In 1810 the Territory of Orleans consisted of 77,000 people, and statehood proposals were beginning to be heard. When, in 1812, the territory petitioned to enter the Union, the eastern region, now called the Florida Parishes—where the people had rebelled against the Spanish and established the Republic of West Florida—was included.

There was an economic boom during the 1830s, generated by slave labour toiling on the flourishing sugarcane and cotton plantations, and sets of natural cleavages emerged in the political affairs of the state as French–American, and later planter–farmer, interests clashed in the political process. While the yeoman farmer held the suffrage, representation rested in the hands of a plantation aristocracy that overcame one-man, one-vote principles by counting slaves in the determination of district units. Under this circumstance, and with the breakdown of the two-party system during the 1850s, sentiment in the state was divided on the issue of secession from the Union. The prosecession group prevailed in the convention of 1861, even though later research would make it appear that a majority of the citizens wanted to stay in the Union.

Separation was short lived in southern Louisiana, for by May 1, 1862, New Orleans was occupied by Union forces. Following the end of the war, Louisiana was readmitted into the Union in 1868, and a severe Reconstruction period began. Political conflict occurred between the federal Republicans who were located in New Orleans and the former Confederates from the rural parishes. After 1876 the Democrats contested with the Republicans as the freed black citizen, whose vote represented the balance of power in the state, became the pawn in the electoral struggle. A number of clashes occurred between the factions, the most noted of which was September 14, 1874, in New Orleans, when the White League briefly wrested control of the city from the Republican police. In 1876 the Democrats claimed that Gen. Francis T. Nicholls was elected governor, but the Republicans claimed that S.B. Packard had won. Their claims were intertwined with the choice of presidential electors for that year in the famous Hayes-Tilden dispute. The Republicans manipulated the state returning board and sent two sets of election returns to Congress, and the Democrats sent their returns. The electoral commission accepted the Republican electors, just as it did those in dispute from South Carolina, Florida, and Oregon. Both Nicholls and Packard took the oath as governor in January 1877 and set up rival governments, which continued until President Rutherford B. Hayes, elected as a part of a bargain, ordered the withdrawal of federal troops from the capital on April 20, 1877, and the white Democratic Party was left in control.

The plantation economy continued to prevail as the farmer class, white and black alike, was squeezed from farm ownership and forced into sharecropping or tenancy. Subsequent agrarian protests that emerged during the 1880s and 1890s produced the Populist (People's) Party and what seemed at the time to be a chance to

The Civil War and its aftermath

overthrow the state's planter–merchant–lawyer rule. By the early 20th century, however, Louisiana was under a restrictive rule, as the elite was able to defeat the reform movement of the farmers in the gubernatorial election of 1896 and to enact the constitution of 1898. As a result, nearly all blacks were legally denied the right to exercise the franchise, while many of Louisiana's whites lost the will to do so.

The 20th century. Extensive lumbering operations attracted large corporations to Louisiana for three decades following 1890, and the simultaneous discovery of oil and gas reserves helped to increase industrial development. While these trends may have laid the foundations for the eventual development of the Louisiana economy, the political leadership of the state was not ready to take advantage of these developments in terms of increased tax revenues and services to the people. Louisiana, therefore, continued to be a backward, segregated, and primarily agrarian society.

Part of the rise of the demagogic and populist Huey P. Long to the governorship during the late 1920s may well be attributed to the seriously arrested socioeconomic development of the state. With the support of the rural areas and the emerging working class, Long substituted a realism for the romance perpetuated by the conservative leadership. Under his administration welfare benefits and educational services were extended, and bridges, roads, and hospitals were constructed, not on the pay-as-you-go basis of the past but through the floating of bonded indebtedness. Since the rise of Longism and its perpetuation under Huey's brother, Earl K. Long (governor in 1948 and 1956), no political administration has seen fit to turn back the series of public benefits financed by increased taxation.

During and after World War II Louisiana underwent further economic development until, by 1960, industrial plants had begun to line the Mississippi between Baton Rouge and New Orleans. Such developments did not ordain more moderate politics, however, and, beginning in 1960, national policies began to take up where the state had lacked impetus, demanding school desegregation and the reenfranchising of black citizens. Conflicts over race and religion broke the bridge the Longs had built between northern and southern Louisiana, and during the late 20th century many state–federal conflicts occurred in local efforts to satisfy federal mandates.   (P.H.H./Ed.)

Civil rights in the 1960s

Mississippi

Originally part of America's Old Southwest, Mississippi became the 20th state of the Union in 1817. Its name has long been symbolic of many of the characteristics attributed, correctly or incorrectly, to the Deep South. Since the 1960s the state has been engaged in efforts to alter economic and social patterns of the past and present. Through the inevitable confrontation of the forces of tradition and change, Mississippians had become conscious of their image as portrayed on the national scene.

General character of the state

For decades an unusually large dependent population and a predominantly agricultural economy helped to keep Mississippi's per capita income low and to create inadequate standards of living for many families. At least half of all Mississippians live in rural areas—but not necessarily on farms—and the state continues to rank low in many economic indexes, including a per capita income that was well below the national average. In 1965 industrial income surpassed agricultural income for the first time in the state's history.

Throughout most of its 47,716 square miles (123,584 square kilometres)—from Tennessee on the north to Louisiana and the Gulf of Mexico on the south, from Alabama on the east to Louisiana and Arkansas on the west—much of Mississippi's soil is rich and deep, and its low-lying landscape is laced with many rivers. Almost inevitably it became an agricultural state. The long dominance of a rural, unhurried way of life has contributed much to the problems of present-day Mississippi, just as it earlier had helped to enhance the state. This way of life has also left a sense of history among some Mississippians, whose ancestors created a culture of gentility that is still evident in the many historic mansions located in such old towns as Columbus, Biloxi, Natchez, and Holly Springs.

PHYSICAL AND HUMAN GEOGRAPHY

The land. Mississippi is a low-lying state, its highest point (in the northeast) reaching only 806 feet (246 metres) above sea level. Its major soil areas encompass hills, plains, prairies, river lowlands, and pine woods. The traditional regions are related generally to physiographic regions. Discernible differences exist, however, in life-styles, political persuasions, economic characteristics, and general cultural variations.

The Delta *Relief.* In the northwest the great fertile crescent called the Delta is the old floodplain of the Yazoo and Mississippi rivers, comprising 4,000,000 acres (1,600,000 hectares) of black alluvial soil many feet deep. Once subject to disastrous floods, the land is now protected by levee and reservoir systems. Though the Delta was only sparsely settled in antebellum days, it has become a region of highly mechanized farming.

East of the Delta looms a high wall of loess bluffs, marking the beginning of the highlands, or hills. A brown loam belt of varying width extends from Tennessee to Louisiana. Most of southern Mississippi, from the brown loam belt to Alabama, lies in the high and rolling Piney Woods. Though settled early, the area did not prosper until the early 20th century, when the great virgin pine forests were exploited and heavily decimated. It has since become a prosperous area based on diverse forest industries, cattle, and some specialty farming.

The coastal area, sometimes called the Coastal Meadows, or Terrace, borders the Gulf of Mexico. The soil is sandy and not well suited to crops, but its location, climate, and industrialization have made the region important.

Along the northern edge of the Piney Woods lies the narrow Central Prairie, separated from the Black Prairie by a section of hills and woods. The two prairies, with fertile black soil that is excellent for many types of agriculture, were once the site of cotton plantations. East of the Black Prairie, in the extreme northeast, are the Tennessee Hills. Arching between Tennessee and Alabama, these hills form the only area in Mississippi in which the terrain and people are reminiscent of the southeastern mountains.

West of the Black Prairie another highland area, the Pontotoc Ridge, ranges south from the Tennessee border. This great ridge, averaging 400 to 600 feet (120–180 metres) above sea level, is one of the state's most distinctive topographic features. Its fertile, sandy loam is excellent for orchards. A low-lying region called Flatwoods skirts the western edges of the Pontotoc Ridge and the Black Prairie. Its heavy clay soils drain poorly, and the area has never developed a prosperous economy. The North Central Hills range through northern and central Mississippi and eastward to Alabama. Their red clay soil, though not fertile, supports small farms. Before scientific farming methods were widely adopted, erosion ruined thousands of acres in these hills.

Drainage. Mississippi has many rivers, creeks, bayous, and other drainage. The state has five principal river systems, in addition to some important smaller ones. Except for a small area in the northeast that drains into the Tennessee River, these streams empty into the Gulf, either directly or through the Mississippi and other rivers.

Climate. Mississippi's location endows it with a very favourable climatic range. The growing season is long (virtually year-round on the coast), rainfall is abundant, and extreme temperatures are unusual. Summers are warm, with temperatures sometimes exceeding 95° F (35° C). Autumn's bright, crisp days have the least rain and are usually the most agreeable of the year. January temperatures average from 42° F (6° C) to 50° F (10° C). Snowfall is rare but does occur. Supplies of water are abundant, and rainfall is usually adequate for replacement. The state's annual average is more than 50 inches (1,270 millimetres), varying by region. The coastal area is subject to hurricanes from June to October.

Plant and animal life. The mild climate, long growing season, and abundant rainfall provide Mississippi with a remarkable variety of plant and animal life. Live oaks and palms vary the landscape of the southern counties, and fruit trees and hardwoods thrive in the north. The magnolia and pecan trees are favourites throughout the state. More than half the land area is in forests, and both natural and cultivated floral displays are diverse and abundant.

Opening land to farming and heavy hunting reduced the once-abundant wildlife to near extinction. The wolf and panther (cougar) are gone, the bobcat is rare, and the bear even rarer. Yet deer are once more abundant and wild turkeys have increased. The state has a great variety of resident and migratory birds. Some game fish can be taken throughout the year, with catfish, bream, bass, and perch the leading freshwater species. The Gulf is rich in shrimp, oysters, and fish, which are the mainstays of extensive commercial fishery.

Settlement patterns. Almost every Mississippian knows and uses such regional designations as the Delta and the Hills; South Mississippi and the Coast; the Prairie or the Black Belt; and North Mississippi and the Northeast. The landscape of Mississippi is mainly one of forests, fields, and towns. Cities and factories take a lesser place. Cotton is king no more, and soils unsuited to row crops may support tree farms, pastures, or orchards. The two Standard Metropolitan Statistical Areas are Jackson, with about 320,000 residents, and coastal Biloxi–Gulfport, with nearly 192,000.

Geographers may speak of the Yazoo Basin, but to the people of the state it is the Delta. The Deltans pay homage to aristocratic plantation traditions, tend to be politically conservative, and usually display more solidarity than most other regions in the state. The leading families are patrons of the arts and letters and tend to be well-read and travelled. The Hill people, however, do not defer to the Deltans, many of whose families originally came from the Hills.

Regional distinctions

What historians call the Piney Woods, covering most of the state south of Jackson, the people call South Mississippi. Its population and prosperity have grown in the 20th century, and change seems to come easier there than in most other regions. Farmers are rapidly being replaced by workers in commerce and industry.

The coastal area is atypical of the state as a whole. More Catholic and Mediterranean than upstate, it blends French, Spanish, Latin-American, Dalmatian, and British heritages in the most heterogeneous of Mississippi's regions.

The Prairie region has some of the ways and style of both the Delta and the Hills. Its lands, however, are more productive than the Hills, its people are more expansive, and some traditions from the antebellum era remain. Northeast Mississippi developed as an area of small family farms and few plantations, and it has the lowest nonwhite population in the state.

The people. The white population of Mississippi is remarkably homogeneous. More than 98 percent native-born of native stock, whites are predominantly of British, Irish, and northern European ancestry. The black population of the state is almost entirely native-born.

Until about 1940 blacks were in the majority, but by the late 20th century, largely because of a very high rate of out-migration, blacks made up only a third of the population. A few thousand Indians (mostly Choctaw) live on or near a reservation. Other groups are represented, but in very small numbers.

Various Protestant denominations dominate Mississippi's religious life, most notably Baptists and United Methodists. The Catholic population is mainly concentrated in the urban centres and the southernmost areas, especially the coastal counties. The Jewish community is almost entirely urban.

Mississippi has no great extremes of population concentration, nor are there extensive uninhabited areas in the state. Since 1950 there has been a slow but steady loss of farm population and a decline of smaller towns, and most of the centres of over 10,000 inhabitants have had significant growth.

Mississippians, who inherited the frontier tradition of "moving on," have become as mobile as most other Americans. Frequent movement by sharecroppers and tenant farmers from one farmstead to another was commonplace

Patterns of migration

before 1920, at about which time the economic focus (and the locus of emigration) shifted to the cities and towns. About three-fourths of the white emigrants moved to one of the other Southern states, whereas the same proportion of black emigrants left the South entirely. The net loss by emigration has largely offset Mississippi's high rate of natural increase. Significant population growth in Mississippi would require that the state retain more of its young people.

The economy. In many economic indexes Mississippi ranks low in its region and in the nation. There has been some improvement in employment, wages, and personal income; but the proportionate national and regional growth has been even greater, and the relative economic disadvantage continues. Nearly 95 percent of personal income is derived from eight sources. Manufacturing is the largest single source. The other main sources are the federal government, property, farms, state and local governments, wholesale and retail trade, operation of nonfarm commercial enterprises, and personal and business services.

Resources. Mineral fuels account for more than four-fifths of the value of all minerals. In 1979 Mississippi ranked ninth and 12th, respectively, in petroleum and natural-gas production among the states. Important non-metallic minerals include sand and gravel, clays, and magnesia. Iron has been mined intermittently since 1887. Aluminum ores are low in quality, and they have been little exploited.

About half of the land area is in commercial forests that produce lumber, paper pulp, naval stores, and other forest products. Seafoods from Gulf waters are processed in coastal plants.

Electrical power produced within the state is from steam-generating plants. Hydroelectric power is brought into Mississippi from Tennessee Valley Authority dams or through interconnections with power companies in other states. Two private companies, numerous rural cooperatives, and several municipal generating systems are in operation. Several large transmission facilities bring gas into and through the state.

Management of the economy. State agencies administer regulatory functions in the area of utilities, transportation, oil, gas, insurance, and pollution. The Agricultural and Industrial Board seeks new businesses and aids in expanding existing ones by such means as loans used to train and recruit workers. It is aided by the Mississippi Research and Development Center through research in economic development. The several economic-development districts promote activities in their constituent counties. Private enterprise also advertises the state's advantages.

Labour-union membership Labour-union membership is relatively small, although widely dispersed. Most large employers have a union membership, though Mississippi has a "right-to-work" law that prohibits compulsory union membership.

Transportation. The declining fortunes of rail transportation and the existence of obsolete segments of the state's highway system have created problems in transportation. The heaviest volume of traffic is along the Gulf Coast, where it merges into the flow from the numerous upstate north–south and east–west patterns. The 200-mile (320-kilometre) Natchez Trace Parkway, which extends from Natchez to Nashville, Tennessee, and is part of the National Park Service, is protected from commercialization and truck traffic. Peaceful and bucolic, it preserves the natural surroundings and encompasses many sites of historic and other interest.

Commercial transportation, in addition to highway trucking, is very diversified. Of the railways in the state, half are entirely intrastate. Scheduled airlines serve Mississippi, and 10 airports are certified for commercial service. Several interstate bus companies maintain service through the state, and almost all major cities and towns are served by one or more bus lines. Gulfport and Pascagoula can accommodate oceangoing ships, and low-draft oceangoing vessels can travel up the Mississippi to Natchez, Vicksburg, and Greenville. Barge traffic moves on the Mississippi, Pearl, and Yazoo rivers. The Gulf Intracoastal Waterway passes just off the coast across the Mississippi Sound.

Administrative and social conditions. *Government.* The state government has executive, legislative, and judicial branches, but it differs from some states in that most heads of executive departments are elected rather than appointed. The bicameral legislature, which meets in limited annual sessions, comprises a 122-member House of Representatives and a 52-member Senate.

Persons elected to statewide offices serve four-year terms, and the governor and treasurer cannot immediately succeed themselves. In addition to commanding the National Guard, the governor may call upon the state highway patrol in times of civil disorder.

Executive, legislature, and judiciary

Justice of the peace courts have original jurisdiction in misdemeanors and may have concurrent jurisdiction with county or circuit courts where fines, sentences, and judgments do not exceed prescribed limits. Chancery courts have jurisdiction over matters of equity, probate, juvenile delinquency (where county courts do not exist), divorce, and mental competence. Circuit courts are the main trial courts for major suits, criminal cases, and appeals from justice and county courts. The Supreme Court is the court of appeal; its nine justices are elected, from three judicial districts, for staggered terms of eight years.

Each county is governed by a board of supervisors. The sheriff formerly functioned also as the tax collector and was compensated on a fee basis. Municipalities may be incorporated as villages, towns, or cities, though no new villages may be chartered. Governments of these units are of the mayor–council type with aldermen, the commission type with three commissioners (including the mayor), or the city-manager type, in which the manager is appointed by the council.

State and county officials are elected in the November general election. Under a system adopted by the legislature, all candidates must stand in a preferential primary in October. If no person receives a majority, the two candidates with the highest number of votes are placed on the ballot in the November election.

From the end of Reconstruction until the late 1940s, Mississippi was a one-party state, in which the Democrats usually won. Disaffection with the national party broke the pattern in following decades, when, except for 1952 and 1956, states'-rights candidates and other conservative presidential candidates received the state's electoral ballots. For offices below the national level there is considerable emphasis on personality and political philosophy on local issues.

In effect, Mississippi now has two Democratic parties. The traditional state party structure is conservative and has official recognition in the state. The Loyalist Democratic Party, allied with the more liberal national party, symbolizes the growing importance of black voters. An increasing impact has been felt from drives to register black voters, court decisions banning literacy and other tests, and redistricting under court order. Beginning in the 1960s blacks won election to an increasing number of municipal and county posts throughout Mississippi.

Race and politics

Finances. Sales taxes are the state's major source of revenue, followed by personal and corporate income taxes and gasoline taxes. Local governments derive their greatest income from property taxes. Considerable amounts of federal monies are provided through numerous federal and state agencies.

Social services. Education, health, welfare, and other measurements of the quality of life in Mississippi necessarily must be considered in the perspective of the state's long history of segregation. Though segregation was by no means limited to the South, let alone Mississippi, the nearly equal numbers of whites and blacks in the state intensified the actions and reactions on both sides and made the state a national scapegoat in the eyes of some and a symbol of the problem in the eyes of others.

Education. The educational attainment of blacks has continued to lag far behind that of whites, and the overall educational attainment in Mississippi continues to be among the lowest in the country.

The years of confusion and emotion since the reversal of the "separate but equal" doctrine in 1954 have drastically altered the Mississippi schools. The year-by-year changes brought on by integration have produced a condition of flux. With the implementation of court-ordered school desegregation in 1970, many white children were withdrawn from the public school system and were enrolled in private schools. The very low per pupil expenditure by the state is largely the result of low tax bases and the high proportion of school-age children in the population. In terms of money spent for instruction, as distinct from buildings and utilities, the state ranks much higher than the comparative national figures indicate.

Despite its problems, Mississippi has a distinguished history in education. In 1884 it established the first U.S. state-supported institution granting diplomas to women. The University of Mississippi, in Oxford, was chartered in 1844 and opened in 1848. In addition, the state supports 16 junior colleges, nine four-year colleges, eight universities, a medical centre, the Gulf Coast Research Laboratory, and the Mississippi Sea Grant Consortium.

Health and welfare. Almost all counties have some form of relief or welfare programs, many of which involve federal funds. In addition, welfare services include aid to the blind and disabled, the elderly, and dependent children. Health programs are administered by several state agencies, including the Board of Health, which dates from 1877. Historically, the state has been in the vanguard of various public health services. The causes of pellagra were discovered in 1915, through experiments at the state penal farm. A model mosquito-control program eradicated yellow fever, and the state tuberculosis sanitarium became recognized nationally. Pioneer work has continued in Mississippi in the education of blind and deaf children.

Cultural life. Before the Civil War the "Planter Society" and those who identified with it had a highly developed sense of gentility. The life-style to which they aspired made patronage of the arts obligatory. They built Georgian mansions and furnished them with art objects and fine furniture; their children were tutored in the social graces and the arts; and hospitality became an art in itself. The rural gentry, however, was only a part of the total society. The small landowner and slave alike fashioned simple, sturdy furniture, made their own oxbows and spinning wheels, and patiently crafted musical instruments. When they rested, they heard folk songs, ballads, or African lullabies. Their literature was myth, legend, and tall tale, and their dances were traditional or improvised.

The cultural milieu

From these varied sources came the present-day cultural and artistic heritage of Mississippians. In the 20th century, technology, mobility, and mass communication have created an adherence to a homogenized national culture. A freshening sense of history is evident, however, in the efforts to preserve historic landmarks and in the intensity of the collectors of the artifacts and furnishings of the past—of folk songs, implements and utensils, furniture, and manuscripts.

Mississippi has been a vital part of the flowering of Southern literature during the 20th century. The mythical county of Yoknapatawpha and the generations of its people were created by William Faulkner in a celebrated series of novels. The works of this Nobel Prize-winning Mississippian are often ranked among the highest attainments in American literature. Other natives of international literary renown include novelist Eudora Welty, novelist-critic Stark Young, and playwright Tennessee Williams.

In music, both white and black folk traditions are found: in English and Scottish ballads, and in blues, spirituals, and sacred harp singing (religious hymns or songs sung to the accompaniment of a harp). The state has several symphony orchestras, an opera guild in Jackson, and extensive musical activities at several colleges. The theatrical tradition dates from 1800, when a Natchez audience saw the first dramatic production to be presented west of the Alleghenies. Today some 20 community theatres and 30 colleges and universities offer dramatic fare, in addition to a semiprofessional company in Jackson. (J.N.B./Ed.)

HISTORY

The Indians. The principal Indian tribes living in Mississippi when the white men came were the Chickasaws, the Choctaws, and the Natchez. The Chickasaws lived in the northern part of the state, the Natchez in the south-western portion, and the Choctaws in the remainder. It has been estimated that there were 20,000 or 30,000 Indians living within the present boundaries of Mississippi. At first the white men were most interested in trade and in converting the Indians to Christianity, but later they became interested in settling the area for permanent homes, which brought on conflict.

Exploration and settlement. In the first half of the 16th century the Spanish began the exploration of Mississippi. The most important expedition was led by Hernando de Soto in 1540. He entered Mississippi near the present site of Columbus and spent the winter near Pontotoc. The failure of succeeding expeditions to find any precious metals, however, caused the Spanish to lose interest in the area.

More than 100 years later, French explorers came down the Mississippi River from their colony in Canada. Finally, a successful French colonizing expedition led by Pierre le Moyne, sieur d'Iberville, arrived off the coast of Mississippi in 1699. After the exploration of the lower reaches of the Mississippi River and the coastline, Le Moyne decided to settle on Biloxi Bay. There the colonists built a fort and named it Ft. Maurepas. In 1702 Ft. Louis, on Mobile Bay, was established, and 10 years later Mobile was founded. Soon other settlements were begun near the mouth of the Pascagoula River. The oldest house now standing in Mississippi, called Old Spanish Fort, dates from this period. Ft. Rosalie, now Natchez, was established in 1716.

Earliest settlements

When the English won the French and Indian War (1754–63), the French were forced to cede all of their territorial claims east of the Mississippi River, except New Orleans, to England. The British colony of West Florida included the lands west of the Apalachicola River and those south of the 31st parallel, but later the northern boundary was extended to 32° 28'. Pensacola was the capital but Mobile the principal settlement. Ft. Rosalie, renamed Ft. Panmure, was not important until a new wave of immigrants came into the area in the 1770s to escape the unrest on the eastern seaboard. West Florida prospered under British rule, but it was occupied by the Spanish during the American Revolution. When the British signed the treaty of peace with the 13 colonies in 1783, the southern boundary was fixed at 31° though Spain did not recognize this boundary. The area was in dispute until the Treaty of San Lorenzo between the United States and Spain was signed in 1795. (Ed.)

Statehood. The original Mississippi Territory created by the U.S. Congress in 1798 was a strip of land extending about 100 miles (160 kilometres) north to south and from the Mississippi River to the Chattahoochee on the Georgia border. The territory was increased in 1804 and 1812 to reach from Tennessee to the Gulf. In 1817 the western part achieved statehood as Mississippi (the eastern part became the state of Alabama in 1819). Natchez, the first territorial capital, was replaced in 1802 by nearby Washington, which in turn was replaced by Jackson in 1822.

The 1820s and 1830s were marked by the decline of the Jeffersonian Republicans, the ascendancy of the Jacksonian Democrats, and the removal of the Indians to Oklahoma. They were the days of steamboats, land speculation, and the growth of a plantation-based cotton economy, with its concomitant slave population. Slave owning, however, was not common among the small landowners, who became more numerous than the large planters but had little influence on public affairs for many years.

Civil War and Reconstruction. The period between 1850 and 1860 was marked by an intensive discussion of the slavery question. The Whigs and the Democrats united in support of slavery and its extension into the territories. In 1859 the Democratic state convention adopted a resolution favouring immediate secession if a Republican were elected to the presidency. After Lincoln's election Mississippi took immediate steps to withdraw from the Union. A convention that met in Jackson on January 7, 1861, passed two days later an ordinance of secession by a vote of 84 to 15. Mississippi was the second state to pass such an ordinance, and it joined other Southern states to form the Confederate States of America. The legislature took immediate steps to prepare for defense, and Earl Van Dorn became commander of the Mississippi troops.

Jefferson Davis, one of Mississippi's most distinguished citizens, became the president of the Confederacy.

Many battles and skirmishes of the American Civil War were fought on Mississippi soil, but the most important campaign was the fight for Vicksburg, which involved many months of planning and three campaigns. Gen. Ulysses S. Grant led the third campaign, which culminated in the siege and capture of the city (July 4, 1863). Federal troops, under the command of Gen. B.H. Grierson, moved across the state from Tennessee to Baton Rouge, Louisiana. During this raid the Federals burned public buildings, destroyed factories, and wrecked railroads. Other Federal troops, under the command of Gen. William Tecumseh Sherman, moved across Mississippi from Vicksburg to Meridian destroying property and confiscating livestock and provisions. The war ended in Mississippi when Gen. Richard Taylor surrendered his command on May 4, 1865.

Many historians consider the Reconstruction period that followed to be as bad as the war itself. Political control passed to a group comprising Radical Republican carpetbaggers, black freedmen, and scalawag whites. The excesses and abuses of Reconstruction ended by 1876, but the seeds of new problems had been planted. Controversy over the sharecropping system, ideas of "white supremacy," one-party (Democratic) rule, and economic policies would plague the state for 100 years.

The aftermath. Mississippians hoped to find economic salvation in the coming of industry and the railroads, but the hope was only partially realized. Emancipation had made the former slaves free to go where they wished, but most remained and eventually were absorbed into the tenant-farming system. The continued economic interdependence of the two races kept intact many of the customs and social systems that had developed before the war. The constitution of 1890 effectively disfranchised most of the black population.

Hardening of rural dominance and social traditions

World War I hastened the end of Mississippi's physical and psychological isolation, and most of the bitterness remaining from the Civil War was lost in a surge of patriotism. Between the wars the state was affected by the agricultural depression of the 1920s, the devastating 1927 flood, the Great Depression of the 1930s, the coming of farm-production controls, and the beginnings of new industrialization. After World War II government farm programs and mechanization on a broad scale created another agricultural revolution.

Civil rights movement. After World War II a series of events developed that may be characterized as a revolution in race relations. Many long-accepted practices, customary throughout much of the South, received their first major jolt in 1954 with the U.S. Supreme Court decision declaring racially segregated schools to be unconstitutional. The decision was followed by years of increasing protest against other aspects of segregation and by large-scale registration of black voters. Within the black community leaders emerged who sometimes were aided by whites, often from outside the state.

Tensions between tradition and change

Many white Mississippians felt the entire fabric of their lives threatened by demands for massive and immediate change. They reacted strongly to what they believed was the duress imposed upon them by outside government forces and private reform groups alike. Pressures, publicity, and recrimination were accompanied by bitter words, confrontations, name-calling, sit-ins and boycotts by blacks, and even acts of violence. Among these were the murder of civil rights workers and the bombing of black churches. These acts of militance made international headlines. Yet through the slow process of historical change the people of the state adjusted to many new laws and to new interpretations of long-standing laws. By the late 20th century much had changed, and a more tranquil atmosphere existed. Many observers found Mississippi's schools to be among the most integrated in the nation, and blacks were elected to a number of local offices.

In politics, disaffection developed between the state and national Democratic parties. Traditionally Democratic, Mississippians broke the trend and voted for other presidential candidates who appeared to be more conservative or more favourably disposed toward the region. There have been some indications that increasing urbanization of the state, economic changes, and the growing role of blacks might move the state toward a more conventional two-party system. (J.N.B./Ed.)

North Carolina

General character of the state

One of the 13 original states of the United States, North Carolina lies on the Atlantic coast midway between New York and Florida. It is the leading industrial state of the South Atlantic states. More than one-half of the state's inhabitants live outside urban communities, giving it one of the largest rural populations in the nation.

North Carolina's beginnings are tied closely to the earliest attempts at English colonization of the New World. Roanoke Island in the northeast, a part of the heavily indented and island-fringed coast, was the site of the famous Lost Colony that vanished sometime after the original landing in 1587. This eastern region retains much of the flavour of colonial life, while the higher Piedmont region centred around the capital, Raleigh, has become the state's hub of industry and population. The mountains of the west remain the focus of a lively folk culture and the home of the largest group of North American Indians east of the Mississippi River.

Bounded on the north by Virginia, on the east by the Atlantic Ocean, on the south by South Carolina and Georgia, and on the west by Tennessee, North Carolina has an area of 52,586 square miles (136,197 square kilometres). Its 3,788 square miles of inland water, the fifth largest such area of any state, are concentrated both in the extensive marshlands of the coastal tidewater and in the lakes of the Piedmont and Appalachian regions. These three physical regions are related to major diversities in life-styles among the people of the state, creating three distinct cultures within the state's boundaries.

PHYSICAL AND HUMAN GEOGRAPHY

The land. *Relief.* The physical, biological, and human characteristics of North Carolina's Coastal Plain (or Tidewater), Piedmont, and Appalachian Mountain regions are quite different. As the land reaches westward from sea level, it rises gradually to the Fall Line, a zone some 30 miles (48 kilometres) in width that separates the Coastal Plain from the Piedmont. In the latter, the topography becomes irregular and rises about five feet (1.5 metres) a mile to the base of the Appalachians, a distance of about 140 miles. The mountains, many over 6,000 feet, have a worn, rounded appearance, reflecting a geological origin older than the rugged peaks of the American West. Mt. Mitchell, rising to 6,684 feet (2,037 metres), is the highest peak east of the Mississippi.

Climate. North Carolina's climate ranges from medium continental conditions in the mountain region, though summers are cooler and rainfall heavier, to the subtropical conditions of the state's southeastern corner. The growing season ranges from 275 days along the coast to 175 days in the mountains. Average annual temperatures range from 66° F (19° C) in the eastern region, to 60° F (16° C) in the central, and 55° F (13° C) in the mountains. July and August are the wettest months, and October and November are the driest. Annual rainfall varies from 46 to 54 inches (1,170 to 1,370 millimetres) on the coast, 44 to 50 inches in the Piedmont, and 40 to 80 inches in the mountains. Severe storms are rare and heavy snow infrequent. Hurricanes occasionally occur along the coast, and there have been tornadoes inland.

Plant and animal life. Soil and vegetation vary greatly throughout the state because of the geographical and climatic differences of the three main regions. Trees that once covered the landscape as dense forests have been cut and burned and now cover only slightly more than 50 percent of the state. Erosion and leaching of the soils necessitates large amounts of lime to neutralize acidity and fertilizers to replace the leached nutrients.

A greater variety of plant life is found in North Carolina than in any other state in eastern North America. There are many species of hardwood trees. Subarctic spruce and balsam fir are found in the mountains, and the subtropical palmetto and the carnivorous Venus's-flytrap grow in the southern coastal area.

The common fauna of North America, including rabbits, squirrels, raccoons, opossums, deer, and also bears and wildcats, are found within the state. The commonest birds are the cardinal, wren, mockingbird, chickadee, and many varieties of woodpecker and warbler. Inland-water fish such as bluegills, crappies, bass, and sunfish are common. Brook and rainbow trout are found in the mountains.

Settlement patterns. Comprising some 45 percent of the state, the Coastal Plain consists of a gently rolling, well-drained interior and a swampy tidewater area close to the coastline. The latter region was the first to be explored and settled. A long chain of islands, the Outer Banks, extends from Virginia to South Carolina, generally covered with sand dunes from a few feet to more than 100 feet (30 metres) in height. Three capes—Cape Hatteras, Cape Lookout, and Cape Fear—jut into the ocean in an area known as the "Graveyard of the Atlantic," a reference to the many ships that have gone down in the dangerous waters. The entire area averages less than 20 feet above sea level. Only small craft navigation is possible because of silting and shallow sounds and estuaries. The Intercoastal Waterway threads its way between the Outer Banks and the mainland on its way from New Jersey to the Gulf of Mexico. The inner Coastal Plain extends from 120 to 140 miles (190–225 kilometres) westward to the Piedmont.

Eastern North Carolina has been the citadel of the state's history since Raleigh's dream of colonization came to so mysterious an end. Close to Roanoke Island are the sand dunes of Kitty Hawk, where in 1903 Wilbur and Orville Wright ushered in the age of powered flight. Legends tell of pirate treasure buried beneath the dunes of the Outer Banks. Rusting smokestacks, masts, and boilers protrude from offshore waters, testimony to the more than 2,000 ships that have gone down. Nearby Nags Head got its name, according to tradition, because unscrupulous settlers tied lanterns to their horses' necks and drove them along the coast to lure unsuspecting seamen to the reefs. On Ocracoke Island, so named by Blackbeard, visitors are astonished at the Elizabethan speech of the residents, for whom "high tide" is "hoigh toide."

Further south in New Bern, the state's second oldest town, named by its Swiss settlers, is Tryon Palace, a restored palace and garden that has been called the most beautiful building in the colonial Americas. Along the southern coast, fishermen set out to battle large deepwater fish of the Gulf Stream, and in Edenton memories survive of the colonial ladies who held one of the first tea parties to protest duties imposed by the British. Morehead City and Wilmington are the state's two deepwater ports, both significant in world trade, while major military installations in the area add to the state's economic life.

Containing about 38 percent of the state's area, the North Carolina Piedmont is a region of rolling, forested hills. The prominent ridges and hills of the eastern Piedmont may be the remains of an ancient mountain chain that paralleled the Appalachians, from which spurs extend into the western Piedmont. The area is well drained by rivers flowing into the Coastal Plain or South Carolina. Dams on the Catawba and Yadkin rivers are important sources of hydroelectric power.

This region is a prime symbol of the "New South," in which modern industry has largely replaced the traditional agriculture. A concentration of industry occurs in a sweeping crescent westward and southward from Raleigh to below Charlotte, the state's largest city. Such cities as Durham, Greensboro, and Winston-Salem have made North Carolina the capital of the nation's tobacco industry. The colleges and universities that have been so influential in the state's history are centred in this region.

In spite of industry the many antebellum homes in these cities maintain an aura of serenity, and cotton and tobacco fields are still found close to the city limits. The many lakes and the upper reaches of the rivers provide quiet havens for fishing and camping, and in many small towns amply stocked general stores still serve the rural populations. Under the city streets of Charlotte—described

(margin: Coastal Plain)

(margin: Piedmont Plateau)

by Lord Cornwallis, the English general of Revolutionary fame, as "a piddlin little place"—are traces of early mines, which once produced many tons of gold.

The mountain region comprises a highly desiccated intermontane plateau bounded by two ranges of the southern Appalachians. On the east are the Blue Ridge Mountains, which rise steeply from the Piedmont to peaks of 3,000 to 4,000 feet with several to 6,000 feet (1,830 metres) or more. In the far west the Unaka Mountains contain the Great Smoky Mountains that roll westward into Tennessee. This region is divided into several cross ridges and a number of smaller plateaus and basins. One of the chief ridges is made up of the Black Mountain group. A total of 43 peaks rise above 6,000 feet (1,830 metres) and 82 above 5,000 feet in western North Carolina.

In North Carolina's mountains, ways of life change slowly. Many communities, relatively isolated since the early history of the state, have become self-sufficient. Wood carving, basketry, needlework, rug and bedspread making, and ceramics are among the many cottage industries whose crafts have been passed down through the generations. The serenity is beginning to be broken, however, both in the mountains and in the resort centre of Asheville. Winter and summer sports have become popular on the slopes, and the Pisgah National Forest is among the areas that attract a growing number of tourists and campers. One of the world's largest satellite-tracking stations is located at Rosman.

The people. Archaeologists have found traces of human habitation in the state that date back some 16,000 years. It is estimated that when the first European explorers arrived there were between 35,000 and 50,000 Indians in the region. In the late 1830s the last group of Indians, the Cherokee, were forcibly removed to lands west of the Mississippi, recorded in history as the "Trail of Tears" (1838–39). In the late 20th century about 65,000 Indians lived in the state, the largest group east of the Mississippi and the fifth largest in the nation.

Settlers came into North Carolina in the 1650s from the English colony at Jamestown, Virginia. Others came from Philadelphia and down through Virginia on the great wagon road from Pennsylvania through the Great Appalachian Valley into the Piedmont. Many came by ship from Europe, all yearning for a plot of land and for freedom from rigid class and religious restrictions. The early North Carolinians were a heterogeneous group, representing a variety of religious faiths, nationalities, and economic and social classes. The Anglican Church was established by law in the early 18th century, but there were also Presbyterians, Quakers, Moravians, Lutherans, Reformed, Baptists, Methodists, and a small number of Jews. Nationalities represented included English, Scottish, Irish, Welsh, French and German.

Blacks were an important part of the early North Carolina population; the labour-demanding crops of rice, indigo, tobacco, and cotton accounted for the spread of slavery in the state, especially after the perfection of the cotton gin. Today blacks account for less than one-quarter of the population.

North Carolina's population is more rural than urban, despite the large industrial employment. Many industrial plants are located in small towns, and workers tend to commute long distances and live in rural areas. Rapid urbanization and the persistence of extremely rural areas accentuate the demographic contrasts in the state. Traditional patterns of subsistence farming and small farms are giving way to consolidated farms; there also has been a marked decrease in the number of tenants and sharecroppers.

The economy. North Carolina's economy depends on manufacturing and agriculture, but tourism is gaining in importance.

Industry and agriculture. North Carolina is endowed with numerous resources that are of great value to manufacturers. The state has one of the nation's largest phosphate reserves; other important minerals include kaolin, mica, feldspar, granite, copper, limestone, marble, marl, olivine, talc, sand, gravel, and shale. Forestry and fishing are other important sources of income. About 10 percent

(margin: Mountain region)

(margin: Traditional cultures of the isolated communities)

(margin: Ethnic and religious backgrounds of early settlers)

of the labour force is employed in the metalworking, electronic, chemical, paper and paper products, plastics, and food-processing industries.

The principal crops are tobacco, corn (maize), soybeans, and peanuts (groundnuts). Farm income tends to be greatest in the central and southern counties of the Coastal Plain, with Duplin County leading the state and ranking among the top 100 agricultural counties in the nation. Forest products are used for furniture and as a source of pulp for paper. An active reforestation program has resulted in a growth of forest reserves.

Tourism has a diversified base, including the attractions of both ocean and mountains as well as the memorials to the state's past.

Transportation. Geographically the state is one day's trucking time to New York City or to the rapidly expanding Florida market. Several airlines, operating out of a dozen airports, serve the state.

Marine traffic

North Carolina has two Atlantic gateways to world markets. Modern ports are found at Wilmington and Morehead City, both of which are equipped to handle any type of cargo. In addition, 20 feeder ports are equipped to handle barges and small ships.

There are more than 3,600 miles (5,760 kilometres) of railroad track in the state.

Administrative and social conditions. *Government.* The structure of the government of North Carolina is based on constitutions of 1776 and 1868. There have since been numerous amendments.

Administration of the state is supervised by elected executives, including the governor, lieutenant governor, and the heads of numerous state agencies, all of whom serve four-year terms. The governor has great appointive powers but no veto over legislation—the only governor in the nation who lacks this power. All state fiscal and management agencies are consolidated in one department, the Department of Administration. The General Assembly consists of the 50-member Senate and the 120-member House of Representatives. Both senators and representatives are elected for two-year terms.

The court system has 30 district courts that deal with less serious civil and criminal cases. The superior courts, one for each judicial district, handle the more serious criminal and civil cases. Superior court judges are elected in general elections for a term of eight years. There are eight special superior court judges appointed by the governor for four-year terms. Above the superior courts are the Court of Appeals and the Supreme Court. The latter is the highest state court; it has seven justices elected for eight-year terms. The Court of Appeals was set up in 1967 to help relieve the state's Supreme Court by hearing the less important cases. It has nine judges, all elected for eight-year terms.

North Carolina is divided into 100 counties. County governments act for the state in providing education, health, and welfare services. Locally elected officials include county commissioners, the sheriff, the register of deeds, the clerk of the superior court, and the school board. There may be other elected officials in counties with large populations. Town and city governments also provide local services. There has been legislation to reduce redundancy of town and county governments and services. A constitutional amendment in 1972 discouraged the incorporation of new towns, and in 1973 the General Assembly empowered counties to provide such services as water and sewer facilities, fire protection, and waste disposal in newly created service districts.

Education. The public school system, supported by the state since 1933, has improved steadily, though it is still below national levels. Other problems include a relatively low salary scale for teachers, an expenditure per pupil that is below the national average, and racial integration that is far from complete.

Institutions of higher education

In higher education, however, North Carolina has a number of institutions of national standing. The public university system is headed by the University of North Carolina, with its main campus in Chapel Hill; opened in 1795, it is one of the oldest state universities in the nation. Other campuses are located in Greensboro, Asheville, Charlotte,

and Wilmington. The state also has 15 state universities, 17 community colleges, and 40 technical institutes. These facilities make it the sixth largest state university system in the nation. Among the dozens of private institutions around the state, most of them supported by various Protestant denominations, Duke University (established 1924; formerly Trinity College) in Durham is noted for its undergraduate and postgraduate programs.

Health and welfare services. State-funded hospitals cover a number of specialized areas such as children's orthopedics, alcoholism, retardation and mental illness, cerebral palsy, and tuberculosis. An effective public health program has been in operation since 1877, and each county has a local health department. State aid is provided also to the aged or disabled, to families with dependent children, and to various counselling and other social service programs. The state's social expenditures, however, remain far below the national average.

In spite of continuing disparities between white and black living conditions, blacks have made impressive gains during the 20th century in the arts, sports, business, education, and politics. In the early 1970s Chapel Hill had a black mayor and Charlotte had a black mayor *pro tem.* The Democratic party in the state depends heavily on the black vote, with Democratic affiliation running nearly twice as high among blacks as among whites. The major areas of polarization remain in educational and religious institutions.

Cultural life. An arts council was established in 1964 to assist in bringing the highest obtainable quality in the arts to the greatest number of people in the state and also to expand the role of the arts. The council sponsors numerous projects, including tours and dance workshops.

The North Carolina Museum of Art was the first in the country to be established by a state and to be supported mainly by state funds. The museum sends out travelling exhibits to schools, libraries, and civic clubs, and to other museums throughout the state. The North Carolina State Art Society donates funds for purchasing additional works of art.

The North Carolina Symphony has the distinction of being the first state symphony in the country. The orchestra tours the state from October through April. More than half of the performances are free matinees for children. The North Carolina Symphony Society, through membership drives, raises enough money to sponsor local adult and children's concerts and to stimulate interest in music.

It is in the field of the folk arts and of historical pageantry that North Carolina excels. The many cottage industries of the western mountains combine with those of the coastal communities to offer some of the richest folk culture in the United States. Outdoor pageants are held all summer long in Manteo on Roanoke Island, where the drama *The Lost Colony* revives the colonizing escapades of Sir Walter Raleigh in the court of Elizabeth I and on the soil of Roanoke itself; in Boone, where *The Horn of the West* recreates such characters as Daniel Boone; and in Cherokee, where *Unto These Hills* is played by the descendants of the Cherokee Indians upon whose history the saga is based. A major force in the cultural life is the Carolina Playmakers. The group was founded in 1918 at the University of North Carolina by Frederick Koch, an advocate of folk drama who had a strong influence on numerous playwrights and movements in U.S. theatre.

Historical dramas

HISTORY

Discovery and colonization. The first Europeans to explore the coast of North Carolina were the French led by Giovanni de Verrazano in 1524. Two years later, Lucas Vazquez de Ayllón led a Spanish expedition from Santo Domingo and planted a colony of more than 500 people near the mouth of the "Rio Jordan," probably the Cape Fear. In 1540 Hernando de Soto's expedition from Florida penetrated the mountains of North Carolina before turning west and discovering the Mississippi River. Neither the French nor Spanish made further efforts to colonize this region.

It was the English who permanently colonized and held the area. Receiving from Queen Elizabeth I a patent for colonization in the New World, Sir Walter Raleigh in April 1584 sent Philip Amadas (or Amidas) and Arthur Barlowe to find a suitable site for a colony bordering Florida, then a Spanish posession. Amadas and Barlowe returned in September with a glowing account of the coast of North Carolina; and on April 19, 1585, a colony of 108 men under Ralph Lane left Plymouth in a fleet of seven small vessels commanded by Sir Richard Grenville. The colony was established at the north end of Roanoke Island on August 17, and about a week later Grenville returned to England for supplies. Threatened with famine and by hostile Indians, the entire colony left for England on June 19, 1586, on Sir Francis Drake's fleet. A few days after their departure Grenville arrived with supplies and more colonists, 15 of whom remained when he left. Greatly disappointed at the return of the first colony, Raleigh dispatched another company of 121 persons under John White, with instructions to move the plantation to the shores of Chesapeake Bay. The company arrived at Roanoke Island on July 22, 1587, and were forced to remain there by the sailors who refused to carry them farther. Of the 15 persons left by Grenville not one was found alive. White's granddaughter, Virginia Dare (born August 18, 1587), was the first English child born in America.

White returned to England for supplies and was detained there until 1590. He found upon his return no trace of the colony, only the word "Croatoan" carved on a tree; hence the colony was thought to have gone to friendly Indians of that name. The fate of the "Lost Colony" is still a mystery.

Thereafter, the region remained Indian territory for decades. A grant by King Charles I in 1629 for the lands south of Virginia brought the term Carolina into being, but no permanent settlement was made until farmers from Virginia moved into the Albemarle Sound area in the 1650s. This resulted in a grant from Charles II in 1663 that created Carolina, but for years the settlers resisted the ineffective government imposed by the proprietors in England. Between 1712 and 1729 the separate province of "North Carolina" was ruled by a deputy dispatched from Charleston, which had become the centre of proprietary government. Boundaries between North and South Carolina were agreed upon in 1735 but not surveyed until 1815.

Difficulties of settlement and government

North Carolina's growth was hampered by restrictions on shipping imposed by Virginia on its already significant tobacco crop; by economic and religious quarrels with absentee proprietors that led to rebellions in 1677 and 1708; by war with the Tuscarora Indians (1711–13); and by coastal piracy involving Edward Teach (Blackbeard) and others. Unlike other colonies, which had grown up around coastal towns that represented the first settlements, North Carolina had no town until Bath was settled by French Huguenots from Virginia after 1700. By 1729, when the colony came under royal rule, several other communities had been founded.

The decades of royal rule saw a turnabout in the colony's fortunes. The population rose rapidly, settlement spread across the Piedmont, and the wealth and quality of life expanded toward that of the other colonies. A large slave population maintained an agricultural economy based on tobacco and rice, and on naval stores from the region's extensive pine forests. Prior to the American Revolution, the beginnings of an intense east–west hostility had grown into several insurrections, but joint antipathy to British rule united North Carolinians and forced the flight of the royal governor in 1775.

Statehood. The Revolution in North Carolina comprised not only a miniature civil war involving the many Tories in the new state but also the suppression of Cherokee uprisings in the west. Much of the state's energy went to resolving the conflicting interests of the eastern counties and those of the west until constitutional reforms in 1835 broke the dominance of the east. A period of great economic and social progress, first under the Whigs and after 1850 under the Democrats, was slowed by the furor over slavery and was ended by the U.S. Civil War.

(Pe.S.G.)

Civil War and after. The northeastern part of the state was captured by Federal troops in 1862 and held throughout the war. The battles of Ft. Hatteras, Plymouth, Ft. Fisher (the "Gibraltar of America"), and Bentonville, Gen. William T. Sherman's invasion in March 1865, and Gen. Joseph Johnston's surrender to Sherman near Durham on April 26, 1865, were the most notable events of the war in North Carolina. Wilmington remained the most important blockade-running port in the Confederacy until the fall of Ft. Fisher in January 1865. The war bled North Carolina white and left it with a depressing heritage of defeat.

Reconstruction was a difficult experience in North Carolina. Carpetbaggers, freed blacks, and native whites known as scalawags were in control of affairs. The Republican Party, organized in the state in 1867, took the lead in writing and adopting the constitution of 1868—a very liberal document—and captured control of the state government. Gov. W.W. Holden (elected 1868) was so unpopular and tyrannical that he was impeached, convicted, and removed from office by the legislature in 1871. Under his successor, Tod R. Caldwell, there was some improvement in the condition of affairs, and in 1875 a constitutional convention at Raleigh, with the Democrats slightly in the majority, amended the constitution, their work being ratified by popular vote at the state election later in the year. The native white element completely regained possession of the state with the reelection of Zebulon B. Vance as governor in 1876.

Late 19th century. For the next 20 years the Democratic Party gave the state respectable, cheap government; but, under control of the conservative element, the "Bourbon Democrats," it neglected the great mass of farmers, catered to railroads and other business interests, and sought to perpetuate itself in power by appeals to party loyalty and race prejudice rather than by meeting the social, educational, and political needs of the state. Cotton, tobacco, and furniture manufactures grew rapidly after 1880. Business prospered, but agriculture was in a sad plight, as it was throughout the nation generally. Finally, the organized farmers of the state formed the Populist (People's) Party, which in 1894 fused with the Republicans and carried the state; two years later, Daniel Russell, a Republican, was elected governor. The race question dominated the elections of 1898 and 1900, when the Democrats again came into power, and in 1900 a constitutional amendment (the literacy test and the so-called "grandfather clause") virtually disfranchising blacks was adopted.

Populist revolt

The 20th century. Decades of significant economic and social developments followed, being succeeded by the Great Depression of the 1930s, which brought widespread hardship and severe curtailment of education and other public services. The state government relieved the counties by assuming substantially the cost of highways in 1931 and of public schools in 1933. By 1940 the state began to enjoy another period of progress. Meanwhile, statewide prohibition, in effect since 1908, was superseded in 1933 by a system of state-supervised county liquor stores.

In the 1940s the national defense program and World War II affected North Carolina. Some of the country's largest military installations were located in the state: Ft. Bragg and Camps Lejeune, Butner, Davis, Mackall, and Cherry Point. Almost $2,000,000,000 was spent in the state by the armed forces for manufactured war supplies, not including subcontracted materials, and North Carolina delivered more textile goods to the Army than did any other state.

The state established a pension and retirement system for teachers and other state employees in the 1940s, provided a nine months' term and a 12th grade for public schools, and launched a vast medical care program providing for a four-year medical school and hospital at the state university and hospitals throughout the state. Legislative appropriations were made to the North Carolina Art Society and to the North Carolina Symphony Society, the first instances of state financial aid to art and music. The State Art Museum at Raleigh came to be considered the most outstanding art collection in the South. Many bond issues for construction of public school buildings were later voted.

Rapid industrialization, accompanied by urbanization, made manufacturing the chief source of the state's wealth and gave it preeminence in the nation in tobacco, cotton textiles, and wooden furniture. Industrial expansion and diversification after 1950 were almost phenomenal.

In national politics North Carolina went Republican for the first time since Reconstruction when it voted for Herbert Hoover in 1928, but in 1932 the state returned to the ranks of the Democratic "solid South." Beginning in the 1960s, the Republicans again won significant gains, suggesting the development of a two-party state.   (Ed.)

South Carolina

One of the original 13 states of the United States, South Carolina lies on the southern Atlantic Seaboard of the nation. The state, roughly triangular in shape, has an area of 31,055 square miles (80,432 square kilometres). It is bounded by North Carolina on the north and northeast, the Atlantic Ocean along its southeastern leg, and Georgia along the southwestern leg, where the boundary is formed entirely by the Savannah River. Columbia is its largest city and the capital.

South Carolina generally is regarded as a state of the Deep South, a designation suggesting the traditions that have distinguished it since its early years in the 17th century. The coastal enclave from around Charleston south to Savannah, Georgia, produced an aristocratic culture that remains unique, even in the Deep South. The dominant agricultural economy and the institution of slavery upon which this culture was based were shattered by the Civil War and its aftermath. For a century and more, South Carolina, like its neighbouring states to the west, was beset by political and social turmoil that was intensified beginning in the 1950s by the nationwide civil rights movement, which eventually changed many of the state's institutionalized ways of life.

South Carolina has closed much of the gap separating it from the mainstreams of U.S. life. The majority, however, of the more than 3,000,000 residents, nearly one-third of whom are black, remain proud of the historical accomplishments of the state and strive to conserve the finer elements of their traditions. Charleston is well known for its antebellum atmosphere and architecture, characteristic of the special heritage and history that pervades many parts of the state.

PHYSICAL AND HUMAN GEOGRAPHY

The land. *Relief.* South Carolina includes parts of two large natural regions, the Coastal Plain and the Appalachian Highlands, with elevations ranging from sea level to about 3,560 feet (1,085 metres).

The Coastal Plain encompasses about two-thirds of the state's area and extends from the Atlantic Ocean to the Piedmont, about 120–150 miles (190–240 kilometres) inland. The region is comprised of loosely consolidated or unconsolidated marine sediments. It may be divided further into the outer Coastal Plain, less than 100 feet (30 metres) above sea level, and the inner Coastal Plain, which rises gradually toward the Piedmont, reaching elevations of nearly 300 feet. The outer Coastal Plain has the longest history of human settlement in the state and is known locally as the Low Country. From the border of North Carolina to Garden City Beach, the coast is a smooth, unbroken crescent beach. Midway along this stretch of coast is Myrtle Beach, a favourite tourist attraction. Southwest of Garden City Beach and continuing into Georgia, the coast is broken by numerous islands. These islands are the Sea Islands, where the excellent long-staple cotton was grown until ravaged by the boll weevil. The islands are climatically the most tropical part of South Carolina; some islands, such as Hilton Head, rarely have freezing temperatures. There is much tidal and freshwater marsh. Huge pines, gums, live oaks, cypresses, and magnolias are draped with Spanish moss. Alligators and every poisonous snake that is known in the United States live in these swamps. Deer, wild hog, and wild turkey are among the game animals that are hunted on the Coastal Plain.

Separating the Coastal Plain and the Piedmont is a strip of land as much as 10 miles (16 kilometres) wide that geographers call the fall zone. The area is easily recognized by the rapids in the streams, which have a gradient sufficiently strong to permit hydroelectric production.

The state has no large natural lakes, although on the Coastal Plain there are hundreds of small, shallow, egg-shaped depressions, many of which are filled with water. Geomorphologists cannot explain these curious natural features, known as Carolina Bays.

Although the Piedmont is frequently referred to as a plateau, the description is misleading, for it is really an erosional plain, or peneplain. Numerous monadnocks (protuberances of resistant rock) are evidence of a surface that was once much higher. Comprising about one-third of the state, the Piedmont is known locally as the Up Country, and, economically and politically, it has always differed greatly from the Low Country. Everywhere on the Piedmont, rivers have cut valleys, leaving a surface rolling to steeply sloping. Most of the highways, cities, towns, railroads, and farm fields are on the flat, broad tops of the hills and ridges of the Piedmont.

A rugged mountainous portion of the Blue Ridge Mountains lies in a small northwestern part of the state. Elevations in this area are 1,000 to 2,000 feet higher than those of the highest portions of the Piedmont. Sassafras Mountain, the highest point in the state (3,560 feet), is on a crest in this region.

Climate. South Carolina generally has a mild climate. Summers are long, hot, and humid; winters are short, cool, and drier. Average January temperatures range from 45° to 51° F (7° to 11° C). Mean July temperatures range from 79° to 82° F (26° to 28° C). Most of the state receives about 48 inches (1,220 millimetres) of rain per year, but the mountains may receive as much as 70 inches. Average snowfall amounts vary from a trace along the coast to seven inches in the mountains. The growing season varies from 200 days in the mountains, to about 260 days in the southern, lower portions, and 300 days or more on some of the Sea Islands.

The people. English and Irish settlers were the first people to arrive in South Carolina directly from Europe. A group of Dutch from New York moved to South Carolina in 1671, and 45 French Protestants from England arrived there in 1680. After 1685 large numbers landed directly from France following the revocation of the Edict of Nantes and the persecution of the Protestant Huguenots. Negotiations were begun in 1682 to bring in Scots, and during the 18th century many Germans arrived. Placenames in the state reflect the national origins of those early arrivals. By the late 20th century, however, South Carolina had the lowest proportion, 0.5 percent, of foreign-born residents of any state in the nation. The majority of South Carolinians are of English-speaking ancestry, since immigrants from central and southern Europe largely bypassed the state.

Five blacks were among the 148 people who arrived in 1670 to establish the first permanent settlement, and by 1708 there were more blacks than whites in the colony. The first U.S. census, in 1790, reported that 43.7 percent of the population was black; in 1880 the figure was 60.7 percent. By the late 20th century, however, the percentage of blacks had declined to about 30.

South Carolina's population is almost one-half rural, unlike the nation as a whole, although the rural–urban mixture is changing in favour of the cities. Since World War II urbanization has proceeded rapidly. There was, until the early 1970s, a steady out-migration to other states— mainly North Carolina, New York, and Pennsylvania.

Distribution of population remains uneven. Large areas of the outer Coastal Plain are only sparsely populated, and a substantial portion of the state is unpopulated. The three main belts of dense population are along the coast, with centres of population at Beaufort, Charleston, Georgetown, and the Conway–Myrtle Beach district; along the fall zone, with concentrations at North Augusta, Aiken, Columbia, West Columbia, Cayce, Camden, and Cheraw–Bennettsville; and the area around Greenwood, Anderson, Greenville, and Spartanburg, in the upper portion of the Piedmont.

The economy. *Agriculture and forestry.* Contrary to its image, South Carolina is not primarily an agricultural

Location and general character

The subtropical Sea Islands

The ethnic mix

Rural and urban settlement

Farm products

state. Farms constitute less than half the total land area of the state, and only one-sixth of the farmland is used for crops. Soybeans, tobacco, corn (maize), and peaches are the principal crops, while poultry and eggs, cattle and calves, and dairy products are the principal sources of income from livestock.

About two-thirds of South Carolina is woodland. Dense hardwood forests are a principal source of supply for the state's furniture industry. The outlook for industries dependent upon large high-quality timber is bleak, but for those industries able to shift their use to smaller, lower quality timber, the outlook is much brighter, since the supply and growth of small softwoods and hardwoods has been increasing.

Industry. From a modest beginning in 1820, the textile industry has grown to be the overwhelming giant of South Carolina's manufacturing industry. Textile manufacturing employs more than one-third of all manufacturing employees in the state.

Chemicals and allied products, wearing apparel, and paper and allied products are other products of major industries.

The 200,000-acre (81,000-hectare) Savannah River Plant in southwestern South Carolina, operated by the federal government, is one of the largest nuclear plants in the nation. The main purpose of the plant is to manufacture plutonium for use in nuclear weapons, but it also produces heavy water and irradiates cobalt for use in treating cancer.

Transportation. Among South Carolina's prime assets is the vast network of rail lines and highways that crisscross the state. The combined facilities of the state's railroad companies provide accessible supplies of raw materials and the means of reaching markets.

The air-transportation network comprises several commercial airlines serving eight cities and several score public and private airports.

Port facilities

Steamship lines with regular service operate out of Charleston, which has expansive harbour facilities. Georgetown, Port Royal, and Beaufort are the only other South Carolina ports with facilities for handling oceangoing freighters. Along the coast of South Carolina is the Atlantic Intracoastal Waterway, providing storm-free passage for pleasure boats, as well as for commercial vessels, moving between Miami and New York City.

Administrative and social conditions. *Government.* Governmental authority in South Carolina derives from the constitution of 1895. The highest executive authority of the state is the governor, who is elected for four years and cannot seek a second term. The lieutenant governor is president of the Senate; in the event the governor's office becomes vacant, the lieutenant governor takes that position. The secretary of state, comptroller general, attorney general, treasurer, adjutant and inspector general, superintendent of education, and commissioner of agriculture are also elected for four-year terms. The General Assembly has the power to increase the duties of all these executive officers and to establish new departments when necessary for carrying on government business. Some departments thus established include health, agriculture, education, and highways.

Legislative power is vested in the General Assembly, composed of the Senate and the House of Representatives. The Senate is composed of 46 members apportioned among 16 districts according to population; members serve four-year terms. The 124 members of the House are elected for two years.

The power of the judicial department is vested in a Supreme Court consisting of a chief justice and four associate justices elected by the General Assembly for a term of 10 years. The term of one justice expires every two years so that there are always experienced justices serving. The Circuit Court is comprised of the Court of Common Pleas, which has civil jurisdiction, and the Court of General Sessions, which deals with criminal cases only. For these courts there is a judge, elected by the General Assembly, and a solicitor, elected by the people, in each of the 16 judicial circuits into which the state is divided.

The unit of local government is the county, which is divided into townships, largely for tax-assessment pur-

poses. Counties are administered by commissions that are appointed by the governor upon recommendation of the county legislative delegation. With the exception of the auditor and treasurer, who are appointed by the governor with Senate confirmation, county officers are elected.

Since there is no legislative body on the county level, the state legislature is oppressed with a mass of local legislation. In practice, the county delegation to the state legislature governs the county and forms in effect a county legislature.

A two-party system has gradually evolved in the state. In 1970, for the first time, Republicans held a primary election to choose candidates for national and state offices. Efforts by concerned South Carolina citizens, as well as efforts from outside the state, have resulted in a large increase in registered black voters and black legislators. Although the state remains basically conservative, continued immigration is diluting the degree of conservatism.

Education. The average age of South Carolina's population is relatively low, and the high percentage of its population in public schools has contributed to major problems in public education. By every statistical measure of educational attainment, South Carolina ranks near the bottom of all the states. With one of the lowest literacy rates of any state, and with an alarming school dropout rate, South Carolina faces a monumental task in raising the educational level of its citizens to equal the national average.

Educational efforts

The state supports nine institutions of higher education. The largest institution is the University of South Carolina in Columbia, chartered as South Carolina College in 1801 and opened for instruction in 1805. Clemson University, a land-grant college incorporated in 1896, has a main campus in Clemson and regional centres. Winthrop College at Rock Hill (1886) was long known as the South Carolina College for Women but is now coeducational. One of the few state-supported military colleges, The Citadel, is located in Charleston, as is The Medical University of South Carolina. South Carolina State College, for years a black college, was chartered in 1896; it is now integrated. The College of Charleston, the oldest publicly supported institution in the United States, chartered in 1770, officially became a part of the state-supported system of colleges and universities in 1971. There are numerous private institutions supported by major Protestant denominations throughout South Carolina.

Health and welfare. Although the cities and larger towns have excellent medical and health facilities, some of the rural counties are woefully lacking in such services. Most of the state's health problems are concentrated in areas of rural poverty. Malnutrition and parasitic infestations, such as hookworm, continue to be problems in some areas; respiratory ailments and other contagious diseases have declined as a result of educational programs and free inoculations at county medical clinics.

Cultural life. South Carolina's antebellum society was said to have been based on the plantation, slavery, and romanticism. Interest in education—most early families sent their sons to England or the Continent for their university education if they could afford to do so—and the arts and the love of entertainment and gracious living began early. Wealthy families hired tutors to educate their children or sent them to private schools. Musical societies, such as the St. Cecilia Society in Charleston, ultimately became the organizations that sponsored elaborate debutante balls for introducing the daughters of member families to society.

It is thought that the first play produced in the United States was performed in Charleston. The Dock Street Theatre, built in 1736, was rebuilt in 1927 and is used regularly by the Footlight Players. Columbia, Greenville, and other cities have theatre groups of professional calibre. Columbia's Town Theatre claims the distinction of being the oldest continuously performing theatre group in the United States.

The prolific novelist William Gilmore Simms was a major antebellum literary figure and the head of a group that founded *The Southern Review* in 1828 and otherwise maintained Charleston's status as the cultural centre of the South. Other notable literary figures include DuBose

Heyward, who wrote the novel *Porgy* (published in 1927) upon which George Gershwin based his opera *Porgy and Bess,* although the latter was not seen in Charleston until 1970, when a local cast performed it as a part of South Carolina's tricentennial celebration. Jasper Johns, whose paintings were selected for hanging in the art pavilions at the Seattle World's Fair (1962), Expo 67 in Montreal (1967), and in Ōsaka, Japan, for Expo 70 (1970), is probably South Carolina's best known painter. The Columbia Philharmonic Orchestra has developed into an orchestra of stature.

The annual Spoleto Festival, U.S.A.—an American version of the music festival in Spoleto, Italy—is held in Charleston and features hundreds of actors, singers, dancers, musicians, and other artists in more than 100 events. Both festivals were created by Gian Carlo Menotti.

Early American architecture Charleston is noted for its splendid, well-preserved examples of late 18th- and early 19th-century architecture in both domestic and public buildings. Beaufort, Georgetown, and Columbia also provide examples of Early American architectural designs. Local historical societies have been successful in obtaining and restoring old houses of historic architectural interest and in preserving public buildings of equal interest for future generations.

HISTORY

Exploration and colonization. The first Europeans to visit the South Carolina coast were a party of Spaniards from Santo Domingo (Hispaniola) in 1521. The first settlement, most probably at Winyah Bay, was made by Spaniards under Lucas Vazquez de Ayllón in 1526, but after a few months it was abandoned. The Spaniards again, settling in 1566, maintained a fort on Parris Island for about 20 years. In the meantime (1562) French Protestants under Jean Ribault made an unsuccessful attempt to establish a colony on Parris Island. In 1629 Charles I granted to his attorney general, Sir Robert Heath, all the territory lying between the 31st and 36th parallels and extending through from sea to sea, but no settlement was made; and in 1663 the same territory was granted to Edward Hyde, 1st earl of Clarendon, and seven other favourites of Charles II. A second charter in 1665 extended the limits to 29° and 36°30'. The proprietors were to legislate for the province "by and with the advice, assent and approbation of the freemen."

The first permanent English settlement was made in April 1670 at Albemarle Point on the west bank of the Ashley River, but as the situation proved unfavourable the government and most of the people moved over in 1680 to the point between the Ashley and Cooper rivers, the site of the present city of Charleston. The area of settlement was gradually extended along the coast in both directions but did not penetrate far into the interior until after 1730. There were many English from Barbados and French Protestants, both of whom strongly influenced the history of the province.

South Carolina's political history during the colonial era is the story of a struggle between popular and prerogative interests, between the people and the lords proprietor, then, later, between the people and the crown. By 1693 the popularly elected assembly gained the right to initiate legislation, but reactionary rule by the proprietors during the early 1700s and the imposed establishment of the Church of England were among the factors leading to the overthrow of proprietory rule in 1719.

Under crown rule from 1729, the Carolinas prospered as an outpost of the empire in which the European wars of the 18th century could be fought and from which a healthy trade in pelts, rice, and indigo could be expected. Charleston became the commercial centre of the Southern coast, and its citizens evolved a social structure that stressed a refinement and cultural attainment rare even in such older cities as Boston, New York City, and Philadelphia.

The demand of the assembly for the right to control finances was perhaps a primary factor that led the Carolinians into revolutionary league with the other colonials. In September of 1775 the royal governor fled the colony. After a British fleet captured Charleston in 1780, there were more engagements in the region than there were in any other part of the country, although most of the conflicts were small.

Statehood, Civil War, and aftermath. Well before the Revolution, a fundamental rivalry had developed between the older seaboard settlements and those inland, the latter comprising tough frontier people whose numbers increased dramatically after statehood. By 1808 the interior, or Up Country, had four-fifths of the population, but the coastal region, or Low Country, had four-fifths of the wealth. Among several political compromises that helped to maintain internal harmony was the establishment by the General Assembly in 1786 of Columbia, in the interior, as the capital.

The unity of white South Carolinians was achieved largely by the antislavery agitation and other external threats. In 1832 a federal tariff that was harmful to Southern commerce led the state to attempt nullification of the law within its boundaries; the chief spokesman for the South was the South Carolina senator John C. Calhoun; and from 1847 to 1852 its secession from the Union was blocked only by the nonsupport of the other Southern states. The state's act of secession in December 1860 and the engagement with federal troops at Ft. Sumter in Charleston harbour in April 1861 led the nation into the Civil War. Nullification and secession

During the war nearly one-fourth of South Carolina's army of 63,000 soldiers was killed, and Columbia was burned in 1865. But the humiliation of the Reconstruction years, filled with rule by corruption and bribery, left an even greater scar on the people of the state. By retaliatory fraud and the intimidation of blacks, white South Carolinians regained state rule in 1876.

In 1878–80, under the leadership of M.W. Gary (1831–81), the old conflict between upcountry and low country became a fight mainly between the poorer masses and the propertied classes.

The triumph of the former under Benjamin R. Tillman (governor, 1890–94; U.S. senator, 1895–1918), a blatant racist and prominent farmers' movement leader, was facilitated by acute agricultural distress. In the subsequent general election, Col. A.C. Haskell, a conservative representing the Bourbon class who had ruled the state since 1876, bolted the party and campaigned against Tillman, making his appeals to both conservatives and blacks. His efforts failed and served only to embitter feelings among the whites. The farmers', or more broadly "reform," movement was marked by the establishment of Clemson Agricultural College (1889), the chartering of Winthrop College for Women (1886), the dispensary system of state liquor monopoly (later abandoned because of corruption), and the work of the constitutional convention of 1895 disfranchising so far as possible all blacks.

State politics after 1890 presented a strange combination of rancorous personal politics, mass conservatism, and dislike for "aristocratic" influence. Class feeling was strongly manifested in the campaigns of Coleman L. Blease (governor, 1911–15).

Agriculture and banking suffered severely in the deflation of 1920–21, and all business still more from 1929 to 1937. North and South Carolina were the only states voting against the repeal of national prohibition in 1933. Extensive violent strikes in 1935–36 reinforced a conservative reaction. Pres. Franklin D. Roosevelt's attempt to have the ultra-conservative senator E.D. Smith defeated resulted in Smith's overwhelming reelection in 1938, although the state supported Roosevelt's general policies.

From 1876 almost the entire white population was Democratic, partly from historical reasons and partly because of the conviction that union was necessary for the maintenance of white supremacy. In 1948 the state bolted the Democratic Party, casting its eight electoral votes for Gov. J. Strom Thurmond of the States' Rights Democratic Party. Thereafter, the state gave its strongest support since Reconstruction to Republican presidential candidates, and in 1964 and 1968 cast its electoral votes for Barry Goldwater and for Richard M. Nixon.

Thurmond, having became a U.S. senator, became a nationally recognized spokesman for Southern conservatives who opposed the civil rights movements.

In spite of South Carolina's forceful reaction against this movement and occasional outbreaks of violence, since the early 1970s the state has generally complied with federal laws against racial discrimination.

As in other parts of the South, the state began an industrial revolution in the 1940s, to a large extent attributable to expansion and building related to World War II. This trend in South Carolina was accelerated following the war and was officially encouraged by the State Development Board (established 1945). Changing the character of the state has been the growing diversification of its industry. Considerable growth occurred after 1939 in clothing, furniture, meat packing, and the chemical and paper and pulp industries. The U.S. Atomic Energy Commission also established its huge Savannah River plant in the state. Accompanying the 20th century industrial revolution was a relative decline of the agriculture that once dominated the state's economy. (D.O.B./Ed.)

Tennessee

Although Tennessee is classified as an east south-central state of the United States, it is best described as a state of the upper South in its traditions. It joined the Union in 1796 as the 16th member, and, with the disappearance of the Old Southwest in the early 1800s, it became a part of the Old South both in spirit and in way of life. Such native sons as the frontiersman-legislator Davy Crockett and the soldier-president Andrew Jackson symbolized the state's contribution of a populist political and social philosophy that in the early part of the 19th century broke the hold that an educated Eastern Seaboard gentry had maintained on the federal government during the first four decades of the nation's history. Unlike the Deep South, in which huge plantations were the symbol of the cotton empire, Tennessee developed largely as an agglomeration of smaller farms, but most of its people enthusiastically followed the Confederacy into secession and the Civil War.

Populist politics and symbols

In the 20th century, however, Tennessee has adapted somewhat more readily than most of its neighbouring states to national rather than regional patterns of life. From the very beginning, a geography that divided it into three distinct regions tended to soften its Southern cast. Eastern Tennessee has long been distinguished by its Northern attitudes, and the two-party political system has returned to full flower. Although the state has been beset by many conflicts involving civil rights since the 1950s, leaders of both whites and blacks remain hopeful that further accommodations that are acceptable to both races can be effected.

Four of the state's major cities and their surrounding counties have attained metropolitan size, reflecting Tennessee's growth in population, industry, and urbanization at a generally more rapid pace than that of its neighbours. Knoxville, the site of the University of Tennessee, and Chattanooga, where in 1863 Confederate and Union soldiers clashed in the famous "Battle Above the Clouds" on Lookout Mountain, are the major centres of east Tennessee. Nashville, the state capital and the cultural centre of middle Tennessee, is perhaps best known as the national capital of country-and-western music. Memphis is the hub of western Tennessee, and its history includes its major role in the Mississippi River steamboat traffic and its prominent and colourful position in the development of jazz.

The geography of Tennessee, an area of 42,244 square miles (109,411 square kilometres), is unique. Its extreme breadth of 432 miles (695 kilometres), stretches from the Appalachian Mountain boundary with North Carolina in the east to the Mississippi River borders with Missouri and Arkansas in the west. Its narrow width, only 112 miles (179 kilometres), separates its northern neighbours, Kentucky and Virginia, from Georgia, Alabama, and Mississippi on the south.

PHYSICAL AND HUMAN GEOGRAPHY

The land. *Relief.* Eastern Tennessee comprises beautiful rugged mountains and broad valleys that give way to the rolling hills and wide basins of middle Tennessee. West-ern Tennessee, however, is a relatively undulating plain broken by deep gullies.

The state is divided into six natural regions. In the extreme eastern part of the state lie the Unaka Mountains—a section of which is popularly known as the Great Smoky Mountains—with 16 peaks that rise above 6,000 feet (1,830 metres); the tallest of them, Clingmans Dome, rises to 6,643 feet (2,025 metres). The Great Appalachian Valley, varying from 30 to 60 miles (48–96 kilometres) in width, includes a series of low ridges that rise 800 feet or more above the intervening valleys. The Cumberland Plateau has a generally flat, slightly undulating surface, but it has been cut by deep and sometimes wide river valleys. The Interior Low Plateau in middle Tennessee, the largest of the regions, is dominated by the Nashville Basin and the Highland Rim. About 60 miles wide and running roughly north to south across the state, the basin floor is a slightly rolling terrain punctuated by small hills known as knobs. To the west, the Eastern Gulf Coastal Plain undulates only slightly and is laced with meandering, low-banked streams. In the extreme west, the plain ends in the Mississippi Alluvial Plain, a narrow strip of swamp and floodplain alongside the river.

Peaks, plateaus, and plains

Drainage and soils. The land drains directly into three major rivers. The Tennessee River, which flows southward in the east and northward in the west, drains the east, the southern part of the middle region, and a major part of the west. The Cumberland River, dipping into the state from the north, drains the upper middle region, while the Mississippi River directly drains a small portion of the west. The damming of the Tennessee and, to a lesser extent, of the Cumberland has created an impressive chain of slack-water lakes, sometimes known as the Great Lakes of the South, many of which lie in Tennessee. The valleys and upland basins of Tennessee have moderately fertile soil of limestone origins, and the streams have created rich alluvial lands along their beds. The soils of the ridges and the plateau, however, are thin, stony, and moderately acid, while the coastal plain has a sandy, thin soil that does not support agriculture. Approximately one-third of the soils of the state are unfit for any kind of cultivation.

Climate. Tennessee has a moderate climate featuring cool, but not cold, winters and warm, but not hot, summers. The drop in elevation causes temperatures to rise significantly from east to west. Mountain summers in the east are like those of more northerly states. The growing season ranges from 160 days in the east to 260 days in the southwest. The state receives ample precipitation, about 50 inches (1,270 millimetres) a year, rather evenly distributed over the seasons and regions.

Plant and animal life. Due to the state's central position in the eastern half of the United States and its diverse elevations, many plants, animals, and fish identified more with the extreme Northern and Southern parts of the nation are found in the state. About one-half of Tennessee is forested, and there are more than 200 species of trees, of which 59 are commercially valuable. Such trees as locust, poplar, maple, oak, elm, beech, pine, spruce, walnut, hickory, and sycamore are found throughout the state.

Settlement patterns. The late settlement of the western portion of Tennessee, long an Indian reserve, and the obvious geographical separations of the state have created a strong sectionalism within Tennessee. The Civil War further accentuated the differences, with most of the people in the eastern part remaining Union and loyal, whereas the western and middle areas of the state became a Confederate stronghold in ideology. The east thereby formed a traditional tie to the Republican Party, while the other regions became more aligned with the Southern wing of the Democratic Party. The east became known as a fortress for "mountain culture"—small farms and underemployed mountaineers, poor but proud and independent—whereas middle Tennessee, particularly in the Nashville Basin, allied itself closely with the New South of the late 19th and early 20th centuries, a South that adopted much of the modern technological life but clung to the romanticism of the Old South in its popular lore. The west emphasized the Jacksonian democracy of entrepreneurial yeomen and vigorous Democratic politics for its white majority. Although

Sectionalism and sentiment

there are superhighways and airlines spanning Tennessee, each region exerts its own influence upon the politics and thinking of the state. Memphis and surrounding Shelby County, radically different from agricultural western Tennessee, is becoming another distinct section.

Small farms and small towns still characterize much of the landscape of Tennessee. The metropolitan areas of the four major cities—Memphis, Nashville, Knoxville, and Chattanooga—with their varied industrial bases, spreading suburbs, and urban opportunities and problems, are similar to metropolitan areas across the nation. Tennessee's traditional rural character, although deeply embedded, is being eroded.

The people. Uniformity and homogeneity once aptly described Tennessee's white population, for it was relatively untouched by the waves of immigration into the United States. From its beginnings, Tennessee literature and folklore has stressed the Anglo-Saxon tradition celebrated by frontiersmen like Davy Crockett and Andrew Jackson, by such modern heroes as World War I army sergeant Alvin York, and by the entertainers at Nashville's country-and-western-music mecca known as the "Grand Ole Opry." The state's white population is primarily Protestant—about three-fourths of the church members belong to the Southern Baptist and United Methodist churches—and they are characterized by a fundamentalist American approach to such values as patriotism, honesty, courage, work, duty, and personal morality.

Segrega-
tion

Yet from the very beginning, uniformity and homogeneity pertained only in part. Slavery had entrapped more than 280,000 blacks by 1860, some 26 percent of the population. Black and white Tennesseans, although touching each other in many ways, generally have lived apart and isolated from one another. In their separate institutions—the church, the lodge, the schools, and other public places—blacks developed an important subculture within the general culture. Since the 1950s, after decades of protest and the slow accumulation of power, many leaders of black Tennesseans have organized and have worked for an integrated Tennessee: in schools, in factories, and in public places. Their demands for a fair and equal society have reverberated across the state. The turns and twists of this civil rights movement have had a profound impact on the people of Tennessee, creating strains in the social and political life of whites and blacks alike as the legal structure of segregation and some of its customs have been broken. Although clashes of culture and power are likely to continue, a countertrend of black and white accommodation and understanding can also be found at work.

The trend of greater emigration than immigration was broken during the 1960s, when Tennessee became the only east south-central state to have a greater inflow than outflow of people. In the same decade, urbanization continued, and a slight movement of population from east to west could be detected. Blacks continued to migrate to the cities in large numbers: by the late 20th century more than four-fifths of the black population lived in the four metropolitan areas.

The economy. Tennessee's agricultural resources have been slim: almost 70 percent of the land is regarded as unfit or poor for cultivation, and less than 2 percent can be classified as good. Until the state's agonizing shift from agriculture to manufacturing began during the 1940s, these weak resources were reflected in high underemployment, low income, low educational levels, substandard housing, and deficient health facilities. The shift to a manufacturing economy has improved Tennessee's position in national rankings only slightly, since the nation as a whole has boomed even more. Tennessee became a manufacturing state more quickly and more extensively than any other east south-central state, however, and its per capita personal income, more than 80 percent of the national average, is the second highest among the states of this area. Tennessee ranks among the top 15 states in value added by manufacture and in manufacturing employment.

Industry
and
standards
of living

Industry and agriculture. Manufacturing has become the largest employer in Tennessee. The industrial growth reflects in part the state government's aggressive policy, over several decades, of enticing industry from other states.

The major industries in value added by manufacture are chemicals, food processing, electrical machinery, apparel, and textiles. Agriculture produces less than 5 percent of personal income. The state has moderate coal and stone deposits and leads the nation in zinc production.

The creation of the Tennessee Valley Authority (TVA) in 1933 greatly enhanced the transition to industry in Tennessee as well as in neighbouring states affected by it. The growing stock of electricity from the authority's dams, steam plants, and nuclear stations, which made the TVA the nation's largest producer of electricity, attracted such major industries as the Oak Ridge nuclear plant and the works of the Aluminum Company of America. It brought major changes also in rural life throughout much of the South, providing the first electrification to many areas. The TVA is regarded as a major U.S. achievement in regional economic development, upgrading the land, industry, and overall standards of living.

Transportation. During the last half of the 19th century, railroads were built through the valleys and across the ridges of Tennessee, but the peak mileage of 1920 has declined to less than 3,100 miles (4,960 kilometres) of track. Major airline service to the metropolitan cities and the increasing use of barge tows along the Cumberland and Tennessee rivers supplement the transportation network. The cities of Tennessee are congested with traffic, however, because of their lack of modern mass transit systems.

Administrative and social conditions. *Government.* The constitution of 1870 differed little from the original document formulated in 1796. It reflects the needs and points of view of an earlier United States and remained unaltered until, beginning in 1953, a series of amendments were passed that have helped to modernize state government.

Among the changes effected were clauses that liberalized the complicated amendment procedure, increased the terms of the governor and state senators from two to four years (with the provision that the governor cannot seek a second term), increased the pay of state legislators, provided for annual rather than biennial meetings of the state legislature, abolished the poll tax, and increased the power of cities to govern themselves independently of the state.

The structure of the executive, legislative, and judicial branches of government in Tennessee resembles closely that of many other states. The governor is the only popularly elected executive official. The speaker of the state Senate serves as lieutenant governor. Other executive officers, as specified by the state constitution, are elected by the legislature, while the attorney general is appointed by the Supreme Court. Executives of major departments and important state commissions are appointed by the governor. The bicameral General Assembly comprises the 33-member Senate and the 99-member House of Representatives. It can override a governor's veto by a simple majority. The legislature is not considered a full-time occupation, for its members receive only token remuneration.

The judicial system consists of a complex of inferior courts—chancery courts, circuit courts, and criminal courts—that try various types of cases. The Supreme Court and the lower Court of Appeals have their judges apportioned among the three traditional sections of the state.

Local government reflects the national pattern. In some counties a county court made up of elected trustees collects taxes and maintains most county services. Education and safety forces, however, are administered by an elected or appointed school board and the sheriff. In several counties the county court is composed of an elected county judge together with justices of the peace elected by districts. City government includes city manager–council, mayor–council, and commissioners–council forms.

Tennessee has under way a major experiment in local government. In 1962 Nashville and Davidson County began consolidation into a single governmental unit called Metropolitan Government, or "Metro." Metro has solved some of the old problems, left others untouched, and created some new ones of its own. Because this type of extended-area government frequently has been suggested as a step toward possible improvements in urban crises, urban planners across the country have been studying Metro closely.

Experi-
mentation
in local
govern-
ment

Tennessee never had the multifactional, one-party politics that characterized many other Southern states. The Democratic domination was leavened always by the possibility of successful challenges from the Republicans, whose strength remained steady in eastern Tennessee. The result was a Democratic Party usually made up of two factions, not always ideologically differentiated, that fought in the primary elections and then united for the general election. Though still a minority, Republicans today dramatically have increased their representation in state and local government.

Education and welfare. Tennessee's social needs are many and its wealth is slim. Tennessee's annual budget is financed principally by a general sales tax, license and privilege taxes, and corporation income taxes; it was one of only a few states without a general income tax. Tennessee's lower living costs are balanced by average weekly and hourly wage rates well below the national average. The state's population generally ranks very low in educational attainments. Its expenditures for public schools make it among the lowest ranked states in the nation, and its per capita expenditure for institutions of higher education ranks among the lowest third. Tennessee's expenditures on public welfare also rank in the lowest third of the states. Federal and state activity to solve the state's economic and social problems during the late 20th century has been almost revolutionary in comparison to previous decades, but Tennessee, hampered by its Appalachian poverty, its low-wage industry, and its depressed western Tennessee agriculture, has not been a national leader in these trends.

Cultural life. Tennessee has had a national image as the "hillbilly state." The mountaineer—a person of drawling speech dressed in blue-denim overalls, operating an illegal whiskey still—became a figure of national mythology. The image actually was nurtured and sustained by a remarkable institution, the "Grand Ole Opry," founded in Nashville in 1925. This radio broadcast of country-and-western music made Nashville the capital city of country America. Nashville has become a leading centre for the production and distribution of phonograph records, particularly the country-and-western variety, but it is also the seat of Vanderbilt University, founded in 1873, one of the most highly regarded universities in the South.

Learning, communications, and the arts

Tennessee is in many ways a cultural carbon copy of the nation. It has more than 75 institutions of higher education, both public and private. More than 300 libraries and branches provide books and learning materials for Tennesseans. All four major cities have active professional symphonic orchestras, and each city supports several art galleries. Museums, such as the American Museum of Science and Energy at Oak Ridge, help to create an important educational environment. Nashville has major publishing houses for the Baptist and Methodist churches. Graceful antebellum architecture dots the landscape, in startling contrast to examples of strikingly modern architecture. The TVA dams and steam- and nuclear-power plants, symbols of industrial Tennessee, modify considerably the "hillbilly" image. In short, Tennesseans participate fully in the major cultural and social movements of their times.   (J.A.Ho.)

HISTORY

Exploration and settlement. Southeastern Tennessee was the home of the Cherokee Indians when white men first entered the area. Believed to have orginally been one of the tribes of the Iroquois, the Cherokees were probably the most civilized of all North American Indians. Many of them were in Georgia and South Carolina, but the strongest towns and villages of the Cherokee nation, including the capital (Chota), were situated along the river valleys of the Great Smoky Mountains. The Creeks, Shawnees, and Chickasaws also hunted in Middle Tennessee. The western portion of the state, between the Tennessee and Mississippi rivers, was claimed by the Chickasaws.

The first white man known to have visited Tennessee was the Spanish explorer Hernando de Soto, who in 1540 briefly entered the southeastern portion of the state. Père Marquette, the French missionary and explorer, in his voyage down the Mississippi in 1673, camped on the western border of the state and eight years later René Robert Cavelier, sieur de la Salle, and his companions built Ft. Prud'homme in 1682 upon a Chickasaw bluff, near the present site of Memphis.

A party of Virginians led by Thomas Walker in 1750 reached the Cumberland River and Cumberland Mountains and named them in honour of the royal duke, and other explorations and brief settlements followed. The first permanent white settler in Tennessee was William Bean, who in 1768 built a cabin along the Watauga River in the northeastern portion of the state. Within the next decade hundreds of additional settlers arrived in the area. In 1780 a settlement was established at Nashborough (renamed Nashville three years later).

At this time Tennessee was a part of North Carolina. After the American Revolution the legislature of North Carolina offered in 1784 to cede its western territory to the general government. The Watauga settlers, indignant at this transfer without their consent, held three successive conventions and eventually, early in 1785, established the new state of Franklin, electing a governor and filling a number of offices. Both Congress and North Carolina refused to recognize the new state, and by 1788 it had withered and ceased to exist. In 1789 North Carolina formally ceded the territory to the U.S. government, and on June 1, 1796, Tennessee was admitted to the union.

The state of Franklin

Democrats and Whigs. Andrew Jackson was the dominant figure in Tennessee politics during the first two quarters of the 19th century. The state's first representative in Congress and one of its first superior court judges, Jackson's career had gone into virtual eclipse until his well-earned fame in the War of 1812 revived it. His nomination for president in 1824 ushered in a period during which he literally dictated his party's policies, but his attempt to dictate the election of Martin Van Buren as his presidential successor in 1836 brought about a revolt against him in his own state. Sen. Hugh Lawson White received Tennessee's electoral votes that year and his followers became the leaders of the newly formed Whig Party. During the next 20 years that party carried every presidential election in Tennessee, including even that of 1844, when a native son, James K. Polk, was the Democratic candidate for president.

The American Civil War. When the Whig Party split nationally on the slavery issue, Tennessee became nominally Democratic. Proslavery sentiment was strong in middle and west Tennessee, but less strong in east Tennessee; loyalty to the Union, however, was strong in all sections of the state. The lack of a strong secessionist sentiment among the people of the state helped prevent the adoption of extreme measures when the representatives of nine Southern states met in Nashville in 1850 to consider the sectional issues confronting the country. In 1860 Tennesseans again demonstrated their loyalty by voting for the Constitutional Union Party's candidates, John Bell and Edward Everett, in the presidential elections. As late as February 9, 1861, voters defeated a proposal to hold a convention for the consideration of seceding from the Union.

This pro-Union sentiment changed almost overnight when Pres. Abraham Lincoln called on Tennessee to provide troops to help put down the Southern rebellion. On May 7, 1861, the state entered into a "military league" with the Confederacy, and on June 8 the people of middle and west Tennessee voted overwhelmingly to sever their ties with the Union; by an equally overwhelming majority east Tennessee voted to remain in the Union. Thus, when Gov. Isham G. Harris proclaimed that Tennessee had declared its independence of the Union, Andrew Johnson of east Tennessee refused to resign his seat in the U.S. Senate and was upheld in that action by the people of his section. East Tennessee remained Unionist throughout the Civil War and has been strongly Republican in its politics ever since.

Next to Virginia, the state was the chief battleground during the Civil War, and the battle names of Fort Donelson, Shiloh, Stones River (Murfreesboro), Chattanooga, and Nashville were long remembered.

Civil War battlefields

Reconstruction and after. Tennessee was the first of the

Confederate states to be readmitted to the Union (July 24, 1866) after ratifying the 13th and 14th amendments to the U.S. constitution. Tennessee freed its slaves by an amendment to the state Constitution ratified by a vote of the people on February 22, 1865, but suffrage was not conferred upon blacks until two years later (February 25, 1867). The state escaped "carpetbag" government, but the native whites in control, under the leadership of William G. Brownlow, exhibited almost every phase of the harsh Reconstruction policy. In reaction, the Ku Klux Klan, originating in 1865 at Pulaski, Tennessee, spread over the state and the entire South, and in 1869 nine counties in the middle and western section were placed under martial law because of the Klan's activities against the Loyal (or Union) League, an organization supporting the Union and the blacks.

A constitutional convention met in January 1870 and revised the old constitution, which was ratified by the people in May. In 1873 a school law was passed that provided for state and county superintendents, separate schools for white and black children, and a state tax to aid in paying the expenses of these schools.

The 20th century. In the new century, Tennessee became a major industrial state, largely as a result of the Tennessee Valley Authority. This giant network of dams to improve navigation, control floods, and produce electric power on the Tennessee River and its tributaries began with the construction of Wilson Dam at Muscle Shoals, Alabama, in 1916. This dam, intended originally for the production of nitrates and left unfinished at the end of the war, became the focus of the controversy in the 1920s between private power interests and those who advocated governmental development of the hydroelectric potential of the Tennessee River. The dedication of Sen. George W. Norris of Nebraska to the development of public power facilities that could be used as a "yardstick" against which to measure the rates of private power companies reached fruition in 1933 when the TVA was created as a part of Pres. Franklin D. Roosevelt's New Deal program. The subsequent building of dams that provided cheap electric power and the later development of giant steam plants that provided additional power both for industry and for atomic power installations in Tennessee and Kentucky did much to improve Tennessee's economy.

Except for the years 1881–83, 1911–15, and 1921–23, the Democratic Party had controlled the executive office since 1870. In 1920 and again in 1928 the state gave its electoral votes to the Republican presidential candidate. Tennessee returned to the Democratic fold in 1932, but in the post-World War II era, the Republican Party frequently won the state's electoral votes. The first Republican elected to the U.S. Senate from Tennessee by popular vote was Howard H. Baker, Jr., in 1966. The trend toward Republicanism became even more apparent in the 1970 elections when William Brock defeated Democrat Albert Gore in his bid for a fourth term in the U.S. Senate and Republican Winfield Dunn captured the governorship.

(Ed.)

Virginia

Virginia, the "Old Dominion," has one of the longest continuous histories among the American states, dating from the settlement of Jamestown in 1607. It was named for Elizabeth I, the "virgin queen," and under its original charter was granted most of the unexplored lands west of the Atlantic seaboard settlements, to the Mississippi River and beyond. The contributions of such Virginians as George Washington, Thomas Jefferson, and James Madison were crucial in the formation of the American nation, and in the early decades of the republic the state was known as the birthplace of presidents.

Although Virginia gave its support—including the leadership of Robert E. Lee and other generals—to the Confederacy during the Civil War, it has developed in the 20th century into something of a bridge state between the North and the South. Its northern counties reflect, in the composition of their large populations, the cosmopolitan character of the national capital, Washington, D.C.,

The Jamestown settlement

which lies across the Potomac River to the north. Other areas of the state tend to retain the tinge of conservatism developed over centuries of agricultural life and through aristocratic traditions that, in early America, made the term "a Virginia gentleman" synonymous with gentility and cultural refinement.

History and nature combine to make Virginia a leading tourist and vacation centre. Within its borders lie some of the nation's most important historical monuments. They include colonial reconstructions, such as those at Williamsburg; the elegant homes of Washington, Jefferson, and other noted Virginians; and many of the battlefields of the War of Independence and the Civil War. Although it is becoming increasingly an industrialized and urbanized state—with all that such a change implies in terms of modern problems—three-fifths of Virginia's land remains under forest cover as it descends from the high mountains and the wide valleys in the west to the sandy beaches of the Atlantic shore. Virginia has an area of 40,817 square miles (105,716 square kilometres).

PHYSICAL AND HUMAN GEOGRAPHY

The land. *Relief.* Western Virginia comprises three physiographically defined mountain provinces shared with the neighbouring states of West Virginia, Kentucky, Tennessee, and North Carolina. From west to east, they are the Appalachian Plateau, the Ridge and Valley province, and the Blue Ridge. The state's highest point, Mount Rogers, at 5,729 feet (1,746 metres) above sea level, lies in the Blue Ridge area. The Piedmont province of middle Virginia is a region of lower rolling hills, reaching from the Blue Ridge to the fall line, the place where rivers descend, often in rapids, from higher and geologically older regions onto the flatter coastal plains. The Coastal Plain province (also known as the Tidewater) lies low between the fall line and the Atlantic coast, deeply interlaced by its tidal rivers and split into three peninsulas—the Northern Neck and the Middle and Virginia peninsulas—all west of Chesapeake Bay. East of the Chesapeake and separated from the rest of the state is the Eastern Shore, the southern tip of the Delmarva Peninsula, which Virginia shares with Delaware and with Maryland's Eastern Shore. The Coastal Plain also contains the area south of the James River, including the Norfolk region and the 750-square-mile (1,950-square-kilometre) Dismal Swamp, which extends south into North Carolina.

Drainage and soils. The six major drainage systems that empty into the Atlantic include the Potomac, which receives the waters of the north-flowing Shenandoah River at Harpers Ferry, in West Virginia, and becomes the state's border with Maryland on its way to the Chesapeake. The Rappahannock, York, and James rivers indent the coast to form the main peninsulas. Two other systems pass into North Carolina, while in the extreme southwest corner of the state two major systems flow eventually into the Gulf of Mexico. The soils of Virginia are generally fertile. In the Coastal Plain, the tidal lowlands are usually covered with loam, a mixed soil rich in organic materials. To the west, sandy loams and clays predominate. In the Piedmont, clay and limestone soils dominate, and, in the valley areas west of the Blue Ridge, limestone soils are found.

Climate. The state's climate, generally mild and equable, varies according to elevation and proximity to Chesapeake Bay and the Atlantic. In southeast Virginia and the Eastern Shore, winter temperatures rarely go below 15° F (−9° C) or in summer above 100° F (38° C). These temperatures allow growing seasons of up to eight months, or three months longer than those in the mountains of far western Virginia. Elsewhere in the Coastal Plain and Piedmont, continental weather gradually overcomes the eastern marine influence to produce colder winters. In the mountains, winter temperatures of 0° F (−18° C) may occur, but cool nights in summer follow daytime highs that usually stay below 90° F (32° C). Throughout the state, rainfall averages from about 32 to about 48 inches (813 to 1,219 millimetres). Snowfall averages from a few inches in the southeastern part of the state to about 30 inches in the mountains.

Plant and animal life. Of the state's large forest cover,

Mountain heights and seascapes

the Coastal Plain and Piedmont areas have mainly pine and some hardwood. Cover other than trees includes marsh grass in the Tidewater section, and broom sedge, crabgrass, wire grass, and cultivated crops elsewhere. The mountainous areas, which at the highest levels are similar to New England in cover, contain tracts of various coniferous species and hardwoods such as hickory and walnut. Bluegrass and field crops generally cover nearby valleys. Wildflower plants and berry bushes abound, the types depending on climate and soils.

At the time of European settlement of the Great Valley of Virginia (*c.* 1730), large herds of native bison abounded along the banks of the Shenandoah. As elsewhere on the American frontier, the vast bison populations were destroyed. A few elk, originally imported from Wyoming, have joined the small number of black bears in the mountains. Other common wild animals are rabbits, chipmunks, squirrels, opossums, muskrats, woodchucks, foxes, and deer. Less common are otter, beavers, mink, and wildcats. The main game birds are doves, quail, ducks, and geese; a few wild turkeys and woodcocks may be found. Scavengers include coastal sea gulls and the ubiquitous turkey buzzard. Predatory birds include a number of hawks, owls, and the scarce golden and bald eagles. There are numerous songbirds, including the cardinal, the state bird. Game fish and panfish abound in inland waters and offshore. Chesapeake Bay is the world's richest marine-life estuary, noted for finfish, blue crabs, oysters, and clams. Poisonous reptiles include rattlesnakes, copperheads, and water moccasins.

The people. About 80 percent of Virginia's people are of European descent. Approximately one-fifth are black, serving as a reminder of the important role that African slaves played in the development of the state. Few of the residents are foreign-born, but other ethnic groups are represented, especially in the northern counties located around Washington, D.C.

Most of eastern Virginia was first settled by the English, their speech denoting their origins mainly in the midland and southern counties of England, and especially in and around London. During the 1700s the Welsh, together with French Huguenot Protestants, were prominent among the immigrants, and a large number of people of Scots-Irish and German descent moved south from Pennsylvania into the Shenandoah Valley. Their speech patterns enriched those of the English and Huguenots who came over the mountains from the east. People of Scots-Irish and English ancestry still predominate, notably in western and southwestern counties. Over the centuries, differences in speech developed as a result of both burgeoning class structure and isolation. Folk speech was largely localized, the more "cultured" or mainstream patterns attaining a wider regional usage. Virginia's main speech patterns are Southern, but increasing population mobility has somewhat diffused the local patterns and introduced others from different parts of the United States.

Blacks were first brought to Jamestown in 1619 as indentured servants. Legalized slavery was not introduced for several decades. Black slaves were the foundation of the plantation agriculture that began in the Tidewater and spread into the Piedmont. At the start of the Civil War, about half the state's population was black, a proportion that has dropped drastically since then, despite the doubling of the total number of blacks.

In the 20th century greatest growth has occurred in the urban corridor, an area that stretches south from Washington, D.C., through Arlington and Alexandria to Richmond, the state capital, and bends southeast to Norfolk. This area is often classified as an extension of the great population mass, or megalopolis, arcing across the northeastern United States from Boston to Washington, D.C. Major metropolitan areas—aside from the densely populated northern counties, Richmond, and the Norfolk–Portsmouth region—include those around Roanoke and Lynchburg, with a number of emerging metropolitan areas in the south, west of the Blue Ridge, and around Charlottesville.

The increase in agricultural mechanization and productivity, with an attendant decrease in acreage and number of farms, has sent both blacks and whites to the cities for livelihood. Richmond is more than one-half black; rural Charles City County, lying in the urban corridor, is more than three-fourths nonwhite. The counties west of the Blue Ridge have mainly small, family-run farms, and the black population is small in comparison with the Piedmont and Tidewater regions.

Throughout Virginia, race relations have been less violent than in many other parts of the nation, North or South. Despite some defiance of federal school-desegregation orders, a general atmosphere of mutual interest and moderation has, in the view of many Virginians, developed over the years during which black and white citizens have worked together.

Bruton Parish Church in Williamsburg, still active, was the court church in the colonial capital. The Anglican Church, which was disestablished during the Revolution, became the Episcopal Church, retaining only one-third of the population adhering to a denomination. Dissenters, primarily Presbyterians, Quakers, Baptists, and Methodists, made up the balance. Virginia continues its basically Protestant tradition, although there is a sizable number of Roman Catholics. The largest denominations are the Baptists, United Methodists, Roman Catholics, Presbyterians, and Episcopalians.

The economy. Virginia has developed a resilient economy far beyond its original agricultural base. Its many advantages include its proximity to Washington, D.C., and the consequent establishment of much research and development work and many military installations. Its historical heritage and natural beauty offer much in the way of recreation; its excellent port facilities are among the most active in the nation. The personal income of Virginians is slightly less than the national average.

The fastest growing segments of Virginia's economy are services, retail trade, transportation, and public utilities. Virginia's unemployment rate is less than the national average, although there are pockets of unemployment in the southwest and among the black population.

The federal government is Virginia's largest employer. The great concentration of military facilities covers some 450 square miles (1,165 square kilometres). These facilities are led in importance by the Pentagon, the administrative centre of the federal Department of Defense, in Arlington. Numerous army installations feature training, engineering, supply, and transportation centres throughout the state: all have considerable impact on local economic conditions. Naval activities are concentrated around the Norfolk Naval Base situated on the waters of Hampton Roads. The Marine Corps installation at Quantico is a major development and education base. The U.S. Air Force, the National Aeronautics and Space Administration (NASA), and the Coast Guard also have facilities in the state.

Industry. Manufacturing is the second largest employer, accounting for about one-fifth of the work force. Chemicals and allied products head the list, followed by other nondurable goods, such as food, tobacco products, textiles, and apparel. The manufacture of durable goods is headed by transportation equipment, centred on the huge and efficient Newport News Shipbuilding and Dry Dock Company. Other important durables included furniture, electrical equipment, and wood products.

Third and fourth positions in employment are the wholesale and retail trades and services, the latter including most members of Virginia's substantial travel industry. These sectors are followed by transportation and public utilities, construction, finance, insurance, and real estate. A few thousand persons are engaged in fishing and forestry.

Agriculture and mining. Truck farms dot the Eastern Shore and Norfolk areas, and other farms are spread throughout the state. Products include a standard array of milks and cheeses, grains and feed, and vegetables. Tobacco is a feature of the southern Piedmont, and the state's apples and peaches are famous, especially those from the huge orchards around Winchester in the horse-breeding country of northwestern Virginia. Rockingham County in the Shenandoah Valley has one of the nation's major turkey-raising industries. The major forest product is pine timber. The main commercial minerals are coal

Mammals and birds

Patterns of immigration

Military establishments

from the southwest, and stone, clay, cement, sand, and gravel. Products from fisheries include menhaden, oysters, and crabs.

Management of the economy. The role of the state government in the economy is considerable in terms of its revenues and expenditures, of its services and promotion, and of its controls and enforcement of regulations through a host of agencies. Most management of the economy, however, rests in the private sector, with due regard to governmental regulations, public needs, and employee and stockholder pressures. The major coalition of business is the state Chamber of Commerce, with counterparts in local chambers. Trade associations abound in the state, from the Virginia Travel Association to the Virginia Turkey Association.

Following the pattern of Southern states, Virginia has a right-to-work law that forbids the all-union, or closed, shop. As a result, only a small percentage of Virginia's nonagricultural labour force is unionized.

Transportation. Although there are pipeline and water transportation facilities and the port of Hampton Roads is second only to the port of New York City in foreign trade tonnage, Virginia's major transportation facilities are roads, railroads, and airports. Most traffic is north–south, adding to Virginia's status as a "bridge" state. Among the many scenic routes through national parks is the Colonial National Historical Parkway, connecting Jamestown, Williamsburg, and Yorktown. The Blue Ridge Parkway and Skyline Drive, which are connected at Rockfish Gap, provide spectacular views from the Blue Ridge Mountains. Also striking is the 23-mile- (37-kilometre-) long Chesapeake Bay Bridge–Tunnel linking Cape Charles on the Eastern Shore with the vacation centre of Virginia Beach, east of Norfolk. Comprising a trestled roadway raised above the mouth of the bay and two tunnels (under the main shipping channels) permitting ship passage, it is the nation's largest structure of its kind.

A network of about 100 commercial airports, including Dulles International and Washington National, makes air transportation available for commercial passenger and freight traffic, and also for private flying. Railways in the state have more than 3,300 miles (5,280 kilometres) of track. The most important rail cargo is coal, which is hauled from the mines of the Appalachian Mountains in Kentucky, West Virginia, and Virginia, to Hampton Roads for water transport.

Administrative and social conditions. *Government.* The official name of the state is the Commonwealth of Virginia. The first Virginia constitution, of 1776, was revised for the seventh time in 1971. In it the state retains the basic powers first delineated separately in the third constitution (1851), which enumerated the organization of the executive, legislative, and judicial branches. The only elected administrative officials are the governor, the lieutenant governor, and the attorney general. The legislature, known as the General Assembly, includes a senate and a house of delegates, which meet annually in Richmond. State and local government is structurally simple and intended to be responsive to citizens' needs and complaints. The 95 counties are governed by elected boards of supervisors. Below them are about 190 towns within the counties and some 40 chartered cities separate from county administration and governed by elected councils employing city managers.

The Democratic Party thoroughly dominated state politics from its revival in 1883 until the Republicans elected their first governor in a century, in 1969, and six of the 10 state representatives, in 1970. In 1972 a Republican U.S. senator and seven Republican representatives were elected. The General Assembly, however, has remained substantially Democratic, and the electorate continued to show moderately conservative tendencies.

The Virginia judicial system, in contrast with that of many other states, is relatively uncomplicated. With three levels of courts, it avoids numerous special courts and levels at which cases may be originated or appeals made.

The seven judges of the Virginia Supreme Court, the highest state judicial body, are elected to staggered 12-year terms by the General Assembly. The primary work of this court is to receive appeals from lower court rulings. The second level includes more than 30 circuit courts. Judges of these courts are elected to eight-year terms by the General Assembly. The third level consists primarily of county, municipal, juvenile, and domestic-relations courts. Towns may also have police courts, while each county and city has one or more justices of the peace, although these lack trial jurisdiction.

Counties and cities have a commonwealth's attorney, whose main job is criminal prosecution. Two judicial conferences annually discuss improvements in justice, and the Judicial Council conducts continuing studies of the judicial system. Practitioners of law in Virginia belong to the Virginia State Bar, an official agency of the state Supreme Court. The Virginia Board of Bar Examiners grants licenses to practitioners. Law enforcement is largely the responsibility of local police departments and county sheriffs. The main job of the Department of State Police is patrolling highways.

Education. The public schools, which date as an institution from 1846, have accelerated improvements in facilities and curricula since the 1960s, and the state has moved closer to the national average in terms of years of education completed. The state Board of Education supervises public primary and secondary education, and the State Council of Higher Education coordinates higher public education. In higher education Virginia has a strong public community-college system, with branches throughout the state. Its four-year public and private colleges and universities are numerous. The best known are the College of William and Mary in Williamsburg, founded in 1693 and the second oldest college in the nation, and the University of Virginia in Charlottesville, founded in 1819 largely as the creation of Thomas Jefferson, both in its organization and in the design of its buildings and grounds. Virginia Polytechnic Institute and State University is one of Virginia's land-grant institutions. Public urban universities have developed. A large percentage of the private colleges were founded by religious denominations.

Health and welfare. Private and public facilities in Virginia share in providing health care. Hospital and surgical insurance cover more than 2,500,000 Virginians under the age of 65. Various state departments supervise the state's health programs. Public services involved directly or indirectly include water and sewage, immunization, and care for crippled children and the mentally ill. Welfare and public assistance are administered in conjunction with local welfare boards and superintendents.

Cultural life. Many of Virginia's settlers and leaders were immigrants from the educated, often aristocratic, classes in England. They set the tradition of a strong cultural life that appears somewhat contradictory when considered against the state's long agricultural background.

The arts are an active concern of the state government, as well as of private patrons. The Virginia Museum of Fine Arts in Richmond was the first state museum of the arts when it was established in 1936. The museum also sponsors an active program in the performing arts. Using local arts groups as affiliates and travelling galleries called Artmobiles, its influence is statewide. In addition to the Virginia Museum there is a state Commission of the Arts and Humanities.

The Barter Theatre was privately established in 1932 in the tiny southwestern town of Abingdon; its charge for admission is produce, handicrafts, or whatever the prospective viewer can afford. In 1946 it received a state subsidy and since then has performed year-round in schools and community centres throughout the state. Dozens of art galleries are located throughout Virginia. There are several ballet companies, orchestras, civic choruses, and opera and theatre companies, as well as numerous festivals of the arts.

Millions of visitors annually are attracted to Virginia's historical sites. In the forefront of these is Colonial Williamsburg and its 88 reconstructed 18th- and 19th-century buildings, representing expert research. Striking examples of colonial architecture are found at such preserved homes as that of George Washington at Mount Vernon and that of Thomas Jefferson at Charlottesville.

Scenic routes

Higher education

Battlefield monuments in the state include Manassas, or Bull Run, near Washington, D.C., and Appomattox Courthouse, the site of General Lee's surrender in 1865. There are more than 100 historical societies and museums in the state and several scholarly and popular historical journals with national readership.

HISTORY

Settlement and colonial period. The purposes of the Virginia Company that landed at present-day Jamestown in May 1607 were not only to colonize but also to Christianize, to open new areas for trade, and to guard against further Spanish inroads. Hunger, poor shelter, Indian hostility, and rampant disease plagued the early years, but while the colony tottered constantly on the brink of dissolution, a tobacco industry was begun by John Rolfe and a representative assembly was convened. In 1624 the company's charter was revoked and Britain's first royal colony established. In the following years new settlements were made and local administrative systems were devised.

The governorship of Sir William Berkeley—begun in 1642, interrupted by Puritan rule from 1652 to 1660, and ending in 1677—marked the solidification of the colony. The many anti-Puritan cavaliers who fled to Virginia after 1649 added an important element to the population, much of which consisted of indentured white and black servants. A rebellion in 1676, led by Nathaniel Bacon, though short-lived, led to Berkeley's recall and signalled a growing restlessness for more self-government among the colonists. This sentiment became increasingly strong during the century that followed, during which time England attempted to govern fairly but did not allow the inhabitants of its American colonies the full rights of Englishmen at home.

This was a period of expansion as well as of internal strengthening. Settlers from the Tidewater region spilled over into the Piedmont, across the Blue Ridge, and, by the 1740s, into the Ohio country beyond, there running afoul of French ambitions for that region. For decades the popularly elected House of Burgesses led the way in opposing royal prerogatives in the colony, and, following England's prohibition of westward expansion in 1763, a concerted drive to rationalize rebellion began. On the eve of the Revolution, Virginia had more than 120,000 residents, many of them persons of considerable sophistication and learning, and a stable—if narrowly based—economy.

Independence and statehood. Virginians were among the leaders of the American Revolution and of the events leading to it, including the calling of the first Continental Congress in 1774. Thomas Jefferson was the primary author of the Declaration of Independence, while George Washington assumed command of the armies. It was at Yorktown that the British armies were forced to surrender to combined American and French forces on October 19, 1781, virtually ending hostilities and leading to acknowledgement of the colonies' independence in the Treaty of Paris of 1783.

National leadership during the Revolution

The state continued its national leadership in the following decades, furnishing four of America's first five presidents and, especially through Jefferson and James Madison, much of the intellectual ferment out of which the basic political institutions of the young nation gradually were shaped. The state had abolished the African slave trade in 1778, but slavery itself continued as the basis for the state's agricultural economy. Nat Turner's slave insurrection in Southampton County (1831) raised tensions.

(C.L.Q.)

Civil War and Reconstruction. In 1861 Virginia seceded from the Union. Richmond became the capital of the Confederacy, and Virginia was the chief battleground throughout the war that followed. In 1863 the state lost one-third of its territory to form West Virginia. In 1867 Congress placed the South under military rule, Virginia being Military District No. 1, with Gen. John M. Schofield in command; it was not readmitted as a state of the Union until 1870.

Virginia escaped much of the punishment that Reconstruction inflicted on other states, but it had lost thousands of its young men and had been devastated by invading armies, its banks had been closed, its currency turned into worthless paper, its labour force demoralized, and its territory occupied by its former enemy. In April 1871 it also had a prewar debt, made for internal improvements, amounting to over \$45,000,000, more than one-third of which was interest accrued during the war and Reconstruction.

Strife over the state debt was the prominent feature of political life during the 1870s and '80s. When the pre-Reconstruction leaders regained control of the government, they provided for payment of the entire debt, designating one-third as West Virginia's share, for the payment of which Virginia assumed responsibility. The bankrupt state could not meet its obligations to its citizens and pay interest to its creditors, however, and the new system of public schools, organized in 1870, suffered accordingly. Then in 1882 a group known as the Readjusters, claiming that the debt and interest needed pruning and with aid of the Republicans, seized control of the government and "readjusted" the debt, both principal and interest. Not until 1891–92 was a satisfactory compromise settlement reached with the creditors, and later West Virginia paid its share. The Democratic Party was revived in 1883. Virginia adopted a new constitution in 1902.

The 20th century. In 1926 Harry F. Byrd became governor of Virginia and within four years had revolutionized the governmental machinery. During the first 60 days of his administration, the General Assembly instituted a remarkable group of reforms through statutes or constitutional amendment. It revised the tax system; reformed the fee system; initiated constitutional amendments that greatly shortened the ballot, concentrating authority in the governor's hands; and encouraged industries to settle in the state. The years after World War I found the state's prosperity increasing as agriculture was diversified, manufacturing grew in importance in the economy, and the tourist business became a major enterprise.

Reforms of 1926

The Great Depression of the 1930s was less severe in Virginia than in many other states. In the period before U.S. entry into World War II, Virginia was the first to set up a state defense system. The war brought tens of thousands of soldiers into its military camps. The Hampton Roads area had a great boom with the expansion of the Norfolk naval base and the shipbuilding activities in Newport News. Employment continued at a high rate after the war, with continued growth in the nonagricultural sector, including government, and agricultural production became more diversified.

In presidential elections the state voted for the Republican candidate in 1928, for the first time since 1872. In 1948 the plurality of voters supported the Democratic candidate, Harry S. Truman, while the majority was split between the Republicans and Dixiecrats; and in subsequent elections the majorities were usually Republican.

In the state, political leadership continued to be exercised by former governor Byrd, who became U.S. senator by appointment in 1933 and by election in 1934, remaining in office until his retirement in 1965. Before Byrd's death in 1966 his organization—"a loose organization of friends who believe in sound government," as he described it, and one that insisted on integrity and frugality in government and a "strong love for tradition and the Virginia way of life"—was rapidly becoming more sensitive to the political, social, and economic needs and rights of all the people.

A revised constitution, effective July 1, 1971, did not change the fundamental structure of the state. It deleted outmoded and nonfundamental sections and added provisions responding to the requirements of modern conditions, such as an updated fiscal policy, annual legislative sessions, conservation and environment.

Following the U.S. Supreme Court's order in 1954 to desegregate public educational facilities, the schools of Prince Edward County gained nationwide attention by closing their doors from 1959 to 1964. Despite such events and a few sporadic outbreaks, Virginia was able to avoid much of the racial strife afflicting North and South alike and moved carefully to implement civil rights laws. (Ed.)

West Virginia

West Virginia justifies in every way its nickname, the Mountain State. With an average altitude of 1,500 feet (457 metres) above sea level, it is the highest of any U.S. state east of the Mississippi River. It is a region tied economically and socially to the mountain spines that span its length and breadth and to the rivers that enclose it on many sides. The settlers of northwestern Virginia who, in 1861, defied the state's secession convention, choosing instead to remain within the Union and to form a new state, acted much in the tradition suggested by the motto of West Virginia, *"Montani semper liberi"* ("Mountaineers always freemen").

The state's image

In comparison with the national standards and averages of the United States, West Virginia is poor in personal incomes and in overall economic development. For decades the rich coal beds underlying most of the 55 counties made West Virginia the leading producer of soft coal in North America, but they also tied much of the state's energies and population to the grinding life of the mines. The gnarled terrain locked West Virginians into their small communities in the narrow valleys and posed both literal and symbolic obstacles to people from the outside world. From 1940 to 1970 large numbers of the state's population left West Virginia for places offering greater employment opportunities. The early 1970s, however, marked a turning point in out-migration and the beginning of a return. West Virginians have become determined to develop a more modern social and economic climate in their state.

PHYSICAL AND HUMAN GEOGRAPHY

The land. *Relief.* The maximum elevation in West Virginia is 4,860 feet (1,481 metres) at Spruce Knob in the east. The lowest land is 247 feet (75 metres) at Harpers Ferry, located on a steep tongue of land rising above the confluence of the Shenandoah and Potomac rivers. The land is rugged, ranging from hilly to mountainous, and there are no extensive expanses of level land. The state's two panhandles, one knifing northward between Pennsylvania and Ohio, the other eastward between Maryland and Virginia, provide West Virginia's alternate nickname, the Panhandle State.

Mountain regions

All of West Virginia is a part of the Appalachian Mountain system. It is commonly subdivided, however, into two major physiographic regions: the geologically older Allegheny Plateau and the newer Appalachian, or Great Valley, region. These are separated by the Allegheny Front, dividing the waters that flow to the Atlantic Ocean from those flowing to the Gulf of Mexico. The Allegheny Plateau covers the western two-thirds of the state and coincides with the Ohio River drainage basin. It is a region severely dissected by streams into a maze of hills and valleys, and, in places, the original plateau surface shows as the uniform top levels of the remaining ranges. The northeastern portion of the Allegheny Plateau near the Pennsylvania border, with the highest mountains of the state, is sometimes referred to as the Allegheny Mountains. More than 40 of these mountains stand in excess of 4,000 feet (1,220 metres), creating a great deal of precipitation and making the area the wettest in the state and the source of many of its rivers. The eastern edge of the state and the eastern panhandle comprise the second region. This geological province takes in most of the Potomac River basin and is famous for its northeast–southwest folded mountain alignment, part of the chain reaching from Canada to central Alabama. The northern end of the Blue Ridge Mountains forms a minor region in the easternmost end of the panhandle.

Drainage and soils. The pattern of drainage east of the Allegheny Front features a short, trellised drainage system flowing toward the northeast and ultimately draining into the Potomac. The western portions drain across an inclined plane by a longer system that flows generally northwest into the Ohio River. A very small area drains into the eastward-bound James River system of Virginia.

Drainage over West Virginia's rugged surface has created some of the most productive and level alluvial soils on the larger river floodplains. The weathered limestone soils

of the east are suited for pasture and orchards. The acid, sandstone-derived soils of most of West Virginia produce a variety of agricultural activities depending upon combinations of depth, slope, and fertility. Some of the clay soils along the Ohio River are excellent bases for the ceramics industry.

Climate. The state has distinct seasons of about equal length. It has a humid continental climate except for a marine modification in the lower panhandle. Mean annual temperatures reflecting latitude and altitude range from about 56° F (13° C) in the south to 52° F (11° C) in the north and 48° F (9° C) in the most mountainous regions. January is the coldest month, with a statewide average of 33° F (1° C), and July is warmest with a 73° F (23° C) average. The growing season averages 160 days but ranges from 120 to 180 days. Mean annual precipitation varies from more than 60 inches (1,520 millimetres) in the mountainous areas to 35 inches in the eastern panhandle. Snowfall, which makes up some 8 percent of the total precipitation, varies from a seasonal average of less than 20 inches in the southwest to more than 64 inches in the northern mountains.

Plant and animal life. Forests cover about 75 percent of the state. Accessible virgin forests were harvested by the turn of the 20th century, but excellent successional forests are now established except in agricultural and urban concentrations. The plateau forests consist of hardwoods of red and white oak, yellow poplar, sugar and red maple, hickory, beech, basswood, black cherry, and yellow birch. Softwoods of loblolly pine, shortleaf and white pine, spruce, and hemlock cover the high mountain slopes, deep gorges, and other scattered areas. The eastern section is predominantly an oak and pine woodland. Other species such as the sycamore, locust, chestnut, elm, and dogwood are common.

Rabbits, squirrels, gray foxes, opossums, skunks, raccoon, and groundhogs are common in West Virginia. The larger white-tailed deer found in abundance by the settlers is numerically increasing in the remote and protected areas, and black bears are found in the isolated high country. Mountain streams feature trout, bass, pike, and muskellunge, while the improving water quality of the larger rivers accommodates increasing numbers of perch, bluegills, catfish, and other species.

Settlement patterns. Broad, level ridge tops and valley bottoms are commonly cleared for agriculture and living. The field patterns are usually linear, in conformity with the landscape. Rural dwellings are distributed as ribbons of settlement along the highways or near other transportation systems. Many rural dwellers commute to urban areas for employment because of the decline in agriculture and the mechanization of mining.

Urban and rural patterns

West Virginia has a number of cities with populations of more than 20,000. Of these, Huntington, Wheeling, Parkersburg, and Weirton are situated on the Ohio River, where water and rail transport and room for expansion have permitted growth. Most urban development and industrial growth extends along other streams, as in the Kanawha and Monongahela valleys. The larger cities, with their industrial concentrations, their political importance, and the cultural centres in their colleges and universities, dominate the state's activities. County seats of government in the rural regions exert considerable influence over the areas they serve.

The people. The first pioneer settlement in what became West Virginia was by Germans along the Potomac River at Shepherdstown. Later German settlements were too scattered to establish patterns within the area. The 1790 census reported 55,873 inhabitants, of whom about 15,000 were of German descent. In the early 1800s many orders of the Virginia government relating to the frontier occupants were printed in both German and English. English descendants dominated the settlement of the Greenbrier, New, Kanawha, and Monongahela valleys, while Scots-Irish tended to settle in the less accessible areas. Americans of African descent shared in this early heritage, although the number of slaves in western Virginia was limited since the rugged topography curtailed extensive agriculture. Only two counties, Jefferson and Kanawha, ever had more than 2,000 slaves, and in one-third of the counties slaves constituted less than 1 percent of the population. After the Civil War the development of railroads, mining, and industry attracted many blacks from the South as well as numerous labourers from southern Europe. The contrasting cultural influence of these more recent immigrants is especially apparent in the industrial northern panhandle and in the towns dominated by coal mining.

The Quaker and Presbyterian denominations were established by the 1730s, with Baptists entering Berkeley County in the eastern panhandle in 1743. A Methodist circuit was established in Berkeley and Jefferson counties in 1778. Leading denominations in West Virginia are Methodist, Baptist, and Presbyterian. Roman Catholic and Lutheran adherents were prevalent in the early years of West Virginia, but they were limited primarily to the German settlements. Expansion of these faiths, particularly of Roman Catholicism, occurred with the immigration of Irish and German labourers.

A number of major factors caused the large migration out of the state during the 1950s and 1960s. After 1950 mine mechanization and declining coal use contributed to a decreasing demand for labour. Rugged land and limited farm size hampered mechanization of agriculture, and the competitive advantage shifted to states with more level and expansive land. Foreign competition in the glass and ceramics industry also reduced economic opportunity. Some industries neglected to make progressive changes or could not create space for expansion, and the increasingly obsolete facilities hampered competition.

During the 1970s resurgence of coal as a major energy resource and progressive government efforts to improve social and economic conditions in the region reversed the migration flow. The chemical, steel, and glass industries were modernized, and new high-technology industries were established in the Ohio and Kanawha valleys. These factors brought about migration within the state from poorer agricultural and mining regions to the urban areas, where better employment and educational opportunities exist. The greatest population increases occurred in counties adjacent to the Charleston metropolitan area, in the Eastern Panhandle, and in several of the coal-producing counties of southern and central West Virginia.

The economy. Although West Virginia has traditionally been very poor relative to other states, there has been considerable economic progress in recent years because of greater state-planning, emphasis on manufacturing, increased demand for the state's coal and minerals, and stabilization of the labour force in the bituminous coal industry. Increased tourism and associated activities have also added substantially to the economic gains.

Mining and energy. West Virginia has an abundance and variety of natural resources. The vital mineral is bituminous coal. The John E. Amos thermoelectric plant, completed in 1973 on the Kanawha River, is one of the largest in the world. West Virginia ranks among the leading states in thermal electric production. Natural gas dominates the state's west central portion. Petroleum is extracted in the northern two-thirds of the gas-producing areas. The eastern quarter of the state has unlimited amounts of limestone. Some 2,400 square miles (6,215 square kilometres) of northwestern West Virginia is underlain by rock-salt beds averaging 100 feet (30 metres) in thickness, and 27 southwestern counties have brine salt deposits.

The natural resources development has influenced industrial location and greatly affected the economy of certain areas. Industrial cities of the Ohio, Kanawha, and Monongahela valleys are dependent on local coal, limestone, clay, salt, glass sands, oil, and gas, as well as on the ready availability of water. Belatedly, government at every level is developing a concern for environmental quality and resource conservation.

Management of the economy. West Virginia's leaders have made progress in eliminating many of the economic handicaps to industrial growth. In 1961 the West Virginia Industrial Development Authority was created to provide financing not otherwise available to new and expanding businesses and industries. The legislature in 1963 approved issuance by counties or municipalities of tax-exempt industrial development bonds for the financing of new or expanding industries. Regional, county, and city planning agencies have inaugurated development programs supplemented by banks, utility companies, railroad companies, and others in the private sector. Existing industry was given new incentive by the enactment of a tax credit for industrial expansion in 1969. The attraction of new industry and the expansion of old have since been spectacular.

New and expanding industries

Transportation. The larger cities and the state's perimeters are well served by transportation facilities. The mountainous interior, with its narrow, winding roads, and the smaller communities are not. The rugged terrain of West Virginia limited early transportation and contributed to isolation and slow economic growth. It is still a formidable obstacle, but phenomenal progress has been made. The major river systems of the western plateau provide 450 miles (725 kilometres) of navigable waterway. Huntington, located at the confluence of the Ohio and Guyandotte rivers, is the state's largest port. Commercial airlines serve the major cities, but many runways are relatively short, and expansion of facilities will require costly investments. Despite this problem, the aviation industry continues to update airport facilities and expand services. Three rail companies with a strong east–west orientation provide haulage over the 3,500 miles of line.

Administrative and social conditions. *Government.* West Virginia's present constitution dates from 1872, but it has been amended frequently. The governor is assisted by an elected secretary of state, auditor, treasurer, attorney general, and agriculture commissioner, in addition to a superintendent of schools appointed by the state board of education. The legislature consists of the Senate and the House of Delegates. Two senators are elected from each of the 17 senatorial districts; their four-year terms are so arranged that one of them must stand for reelection every two years. The House of Delegates is composed of 100 members, each serving a two-year term. Fifteen of the smaller counties have been grouped into seven districts with nine delegates. Of the remaining counties represented on the basis of population, 11 have one delegate, while Kanawha County has 13. The legislature meets annually for 60 days, but the governor is empowered to convene special sessions. At the top of the judiciary division is the Supreme Court of Appeals, consisting of five judges elected to 12-year terms. The 31 circuit courts try most of the major cases, but 14 special courts relieve them of some burdens. Many municipalities establish police courts or justice-of-the-peace court systems to adjudicate cases at the local level.

The Department of Public Safety provides law enforcement at the state level and maintains bureaus of criminal identification, motor-vehicle inspection, and accident prevention. County law enforcement is handled by a sheriff, constables, and a prosecuting attorney working with county and municipal police. Under the state constitution, each county is governed by three commissioners elected for six years. Other elected county officials are sheriff, prosecuting attorney, assessor, members of the board of education, and surveyor. Some towns have a mayor–council form of government, others a council–manager form. All officials except the city manager are elected.

County and municipal government

Education. The public school system, directed by the state board of education, is under a county-unit plan allowing local supervision under county boards. Racial integration in West Virginia's schools was achieved largely without turmoil. The state-controlled system of higher education includes the University of West Virginia at Morgantown and Marshall University at Huntington. There are, in addition, junior colleges, several teacher-training and specialized technical institutions, and a number of private and sectarian colleges. The Bureau of Vocational, Technical and Adult Education provides an important educational supplement with courses in agriculture, home economics, practical nursing, and technical, industrial, and distributive skills. The National Radio Astronomy Observatory at Green Bank is a unique educational and research facility. A national centre for the reception and study of radio waves that come from space, it is open to all users and has undergone expansion.

Health and welfare. The State Department of Health has responsibility ranging from collecting statistics on various diseases and health-control matters to overseeing all matters relating to public health and medical facilities. County and municipal boards of health assist at the local level. The state also oversees public assistance programs in such areas as child welfare, distribution of commodities and food stamps, and matters regarding old age, blindness, dependent children, disability, and general relief. There are four hospitals for the mentally ill and numerous programs for mentally handicapped children.

Cultural life. The early isolation of West Virginia resulted in the development and transmittal of strong, self-reliant local heritage relatively unaffected by circumstances from beyond the hills. Musical instruments, ballads, and handicrafts of earlier generations are still in evidence. Numerous fairs, craft centres, and collectors have assured a permanence of this cultural past. The making and playing of dulcimers, old-time fiddle contests, ballad singing, Elizabethan speech patterns, patchwork quilting, furniture caning, primitive drawing, and a host of other arts, crafts, and other remnants from the past persist in the rural regions.

In addition to the folk arts and crafts, the Huntington Galleries and the Sunrise Foundation at Charleston have excellent cultural facilities. In local art exhibitions picturesque landscapes and townscapes of the state are shown in a majority of works, but often they indicate awareness of advanced artistic styles. The universities are cultural centres as well, fostering work in the visual arts, theatre, dance, and music.

A thriving tourist and recreation industry has developed around West Virginia's cultural heritage as well as around its various historical and natural resources. Harpers Ferry, for decades almost a ghost town, has been designated a national historical site. More than 1,100,000 acres (445,-000 hectares) of West Virginia are publicly owned and devoted to conservation or recreation. There are more than 35 state parks, including Pipestem State Park, in which an amphitheatre, a country store, and a craft centre are typical of installations to promote the state's heritage and to encourage the tourist industry. The resort at White Sulphur Springs is world famous.

HISTORY

Some 14,000 years ago Indian hunters entered the Ohio and Kanawha valleys in the west in pursuit of mammoths. Around 9000 BC the Archaic People, with a small-game hunting, fishing, and gathering culture, occupied the area. Their successors, the Adena, or Mound Builders (*c.* 500 BC to *c.* AD 100), created numerous earthworks still visible in the Moundsville and Charleston areas. The Adena were absorbed by the Fort Ancient people, who dominated the territory until they were wiped out by the Iroquois League around 1650. Except for scattered villages the area that was to become West Virginia remained Indian hunting grounds and battlegrounds when Europeans arrived in the 1700s.

Colonial period and Virginia's dominion. The second charter of Virginia in 1609 provided for colonization of that state's western frontiers. Exploration and trade were further encouraged by Gov. William Berkeley after 1660. The Blue Ridge was reached in 1670, and, in 1671 another expedition encountered the first west-flowing stream, the New River, in southwestern Virginia. The expedition descended the river to Peter's Falls on the future Virginia–West Virginia border and claimed for England all the land drained by the New River and its tributaries. Subsequent Trans-Allegheny frontier settlement was handicapped by such factors as mountain barriers, Indian resistance, conflicting English and French claims in the Ohio Valley, disputed land titles, and a royal proclamation of 1763 prohibiting occupancy.

Despite these obstacles, the population increased, and discontent with the government east of the mountains became endemic. The Vandalia Colony, proposed in 1769, and the "fourteenth state" movement for the establishment of a Westsylvania in 1776, indicate an early interest in a separate government for the Trans-Allegheny country. Dissatisfaction among the pioneers in that region mounted in the cultural, social, economic, and political realms. The frontier residents, who came from many areas, were distinctly different from the aristocratic eastern settlers. Furthermore, topographic differences rendered slavery economically unsound, and cultural heritage made it undesirable. Voting representation and taxation, however, decidedly favoured eastern Virginia.

Separatist sentiment

Civil War and statehood. The advent of the American Civil War fuelled new desires for a politically separate western area. At the Virginia secession convention of April 1861 a majority of the western delegates opposed secession. In subsequent meetings at Wheeling (May 1861), dominated by the western delegates, the ordinance of secession was declared an illegal attempt to overthrow the federal government. The second Wheeling convention (June) pronounced the Richmond government void, established a restored Government of Virginia, and provided for the election of new state officers. The restored governor, Francis H. Pierpont, secured federal recognition and maintained civil jurisdiction over the region until Congress consented to the admission of West Virginia to the Union as the 35th state on June 20, 1863. A condition of entry was the gradual emancipation of slaves in the region. The capital was permanently established at Charleston in 1885.

The Wheeling conventions

Civil War engagements were few in the state, although the war itself was in part precipitated by the seizure of the federal armory at Harpers Ferry in 1859 by a small band of men under the antislavery zeal of John Brown. Brown was captured by federal troops and subsequently was tried and hanged in Charles Town, but his exploits enflamed tensions between the nation's proslavery and antislavery factions. To the abolitionists of the North he became a martyr. During the Civil War nearly 32,000 soldiers enlisted in the Union army, and about 9,000 served the Confederacy, although some authorities maintain the latter figure to be low.

The modern period. West Virginia's industrial emergence, encouraged by railroad expansion, began in the 1870s. Its natural resources of timber, coal, salt, oil, and gas substantially contributed to the establishment of the modern industrial system of the United States. The labour troubles that flared in mining areas between 1912 and 1921 required the intervention of the National Guard (twice) and the U.S. Army (four times) to quell violence, but the right to organize labour unions, which was granted by national statutes in 1933 and 1935, brought a measure of peace to the state. Neither national political party has dominated the state for long periods, although the Democrats have tended to outnumber Republicans and usually had more than twice the number of registered voters. (S.E.C.)

MIDDLE WEST

The Middle West, also frequently called the Midwest, is the northern portion of the central United States and is usually defined to include the states of Ohio, Indiana, Illinois, Missouri, Michigan, Wisconsin, Iowa, Minnesota, Kansas, Nebraska, North Dakota, and South Dakota. Missouri and all or most of the western tier of states are sometimes excluded—Missouri being sometimes classified in the South, and North and South Dakota, Nebraska, and Kansas being separately designated as the "Plains states." The term Middle West came into general use with the settlement of the Far West.

Identification of the Middle West as a region or section rests on geographical, historical, economic, and other grounds. The region exhibits great diversity in climate, soil, and resources. Although it has no large deposits of oil or precious metals, it does possess a vast extent of rich farming land, an excellent river and lake system, extensive forest lands principally in the lake states, and enormous deposits of base metals and minerals, notably iron, limestone, and coal.

Settlement patterns. Settlement north of the Ohio River, which marks the southeastern boundary of the Middle West, began slowly. The few land seekers who crossed the Appalachians before the American Revolution settled mostly in Kentucky and Tennessee. During the Revolution, states with no claim to western lands insisted that those lands should become the common possession of the United States. By 1783 enough states had agreed to cede their western lands north of the Ohio to the national government so that the creation of a public domain was assured. Kentucky and Tennessee, as extensions of Virginia and North Carolina, were settled under regulations of their parent states, but the region north of the Ohio River was occupied under rules laid down by Congress. In 1785 Congress adopted a land ordinance providing that Indian title be extinguished and the lands surveyed before being offered for sale. The survey system provided that the land be laid out in rectangular townships, six miles (9.6 kilometres) square. Each township was to be divided into 36 sections of 640 acres (259 hectares); these in turn could be subdivided into halves, quarters, etc. The land was to be sold at auction at a minimum price of a dollar an acre, with alternating townships offered in their entirety, intervening ones in lots of 640 acres. One section in each township was to be reserved for the benefit of the common schools. Congress sought to assure compact settlement and wide distribution of the land.

Seven tiers of townships lying immediately west of the Pennsylvania border were designated for survey and sale, but bureaucratic deliberateness and Indian hostility prevented prompt action. Meanwhile, numerous land speculators sought large grants west of the surveyed land. The most energetic of these, the Ohio Company, organized by New Englanders, arranged a large purchase on the Muskingum River. Congress, at the insistence of the company, adopted a plan of government for the territory in the famous Northwest Ordinance of 1787. This ordinance prohibited slavery, guaranteed trial by jury and other civil rights, and provided for the later formation of states. Under the first stage of government, known as the district, the government was controlled by officers appointed by the central government. When the adult male population reached 5,000, a second or territorial stage, which permitted an elective legislature, could be entered. When the total population reached 60,000, the territory was eligible to draft a constitution and enter the Union on a basis of equality with the other states. Three to five states were to be erected in the Northwest Territory. Although often hailed as a great liberal document, the ordinance in the district stage allowed settlers fewer political rights than the English colonists had before the Revolution. The saving feature of the plan consisted of permitting the territory to grow to statehood.

For a decade after 1783 Indian hostility discouraged immigration. A small settlement at Marietta, in what later became Ohio, and a few scattered along the river as far south as Cincinnati marked the beginning of white occupation. After two disastrous attempts had been made to quell the Indians, troops under Gen. Anthony Wayne decisively defeated them at Fallen Timbers near the rapids of the Maumee in 1794, and the next year the Treaty of Greenville brought peace to most of what became Ohio. By 1800 the rush of people to the Middle West was beginning in earnest. Thereafter the spread and direction of settlement is roughly charted in the dates of admission of the states: Ohio entered the Union in 1803; Indiana in 1816; Illinois, 1818; Missouri, 1821; Michigan, 1837; Iowa, 1846; Wisconsin, 1848; Minnesota, 1858; Kansas, 1861; Nebraska, 1867; North Dakota and South Dakota, 1889.

In 1796 Congress, in revising the Land Law of 1785, raised the minimum price an acre to $2.00. Four years later it reduced to 320 acres the minimum amount that could be purchased and allowed four years to complete payment. In 1800 the Northwest Territory had a popula-

tion of 51,000 compared with about 2,600,000 each in the northeastern states and the South. By 1840 the population of these two sections had doubled; that of the Middle West had increased almost 60-fold to 3,300,000. By 1870 population of all three sections was roughly equal—a condition that would continue for many decades.

Unlike the region south of the Ohio River, which drew settlers largely from the older southern states, the Ohio Valley was attractive to immigrants both from the older states and from Europe. Germans, Irish, Scandinavians, and others joined the push into the region, contributing to the heterogeneity of the population.

With relatively little waste land in the region, productive farms soon blanketed the area. With growing markets in the South, the East, and Europe, the great problem was to find ways to reach these markets with the farm produce. Bulky commodities such as corn and wheat could be marketed locally or down river as grain or flour. Corn could also be sent to market as pork, beef, or whiskey. In the first decade of the 19th century, farmers in the Scioto Valley fattened cattle on corn and drove them across the mountains to eastern markets, thus initiating a business that would continue until railroads made such long drives unprofitable. Hogs were sometimes driven but more often were slaughtered locally and the meat processed and barrelled for river shipment.

In the second decade of the century steamboats came into extensive use on the rivers. Agricultural and related commerce of the interior further increased with completion of the Erie Canal in 1825. The success of this canal and the need for more transportation induced the states of Ohio, Indiana, Illinois, and Wisconsin to launch ambitious canal building projects all aimed at connecting the Great Lakes with the Ohio or Mississippi rivers. By the 1850s railroads had begun to capture the carrying trade of the upper Mississippi Valley, and during this decade New York displaced New Orleans as the great ocean port of the Middle West. The superintendent of the eighth census, in reviewing the grain trade of the United States up to 1860, declared it to be "one of the chief marvels of modern commercial history . . . . the leading agency in the opening up of seven-eighths of our settled territory." Without the great European demand for American foodstuffs, he declared, "Capitalists could not have been encouraged to construct our immense canals, and lines of railroads, nor to have built our fleets of grain-carrying vessels to traverse the lakes and seas."

The richly productive farms also called into existence innumerable rural villages to serve their immediate needs, as well as cities, many located along the waterways, to supply machinery and to collect, process, and market the vast flood of meat and grain. Cincinnati became known to the world in the 1820s as Porkopolis. Later Carl Sandburg heralded Chicago as "Hog Butcher for the World" and "Stacker of Wheat." Slaughtering and meat processing plants, flour mills, breweries, distilleries, and a host of other industries emerged. Chronic labour shortage, rich soil, large fields, and growing markets combined to encourage both invention and the widespread use of farm machinery. Before 1860 the McCormick brothers, for example, moved to Chicago and Jerome I. Case, manufacturer of threshing machines, located in Racine, Wisconsin. Others established themselves in this area. By 1860 approximately half the farm implements produced in the United States were being manufactured in the Middle West. Similarly, machine shops provided equipment for the lumber camps and the burgeoning sawmills of the lake states. They continued to supply the industry when it moved to the Pacific Northwest. Even after the rest of the nation was settled, the Middle West did not lose its primacy. In the late 20th century, seven of the leading agricultural states were in the Middle West. Of the leading manufacturing states, three (Illinois, Michigan, and Ohio) were in the Middle West.

The Middle West is the region of checkerboard patterns on the land. The air traveller going west knows when he reaches Ohio because for the first time he sees farms that still retain the rectangularity imposed by the first surveys. The square townships spread westward to the great plains and beyond. The survey township tended to become the

*The
Northwest
Ordinance*

*Steamboats
and
railroads*

basis for the smallest unit of civil government. Elections were held, taxes levied, and roads laid out and built in relation to township and section lines. (V.Ca./Ed.)

The regions. *The Corn Belt.* From the air this region in the centre of the Middle West appears in sharp contrast to the partly wooded, much dissected regions to the east and southeast. The relatively flat to rolling landscape made it possible to lay out fields, farms, and roads in close accord with the rectangular land survey. A lime-rich veneer of glacial deposits, commonly several hundred feet thick, covers almost the entire region. This fertile soil and the hot, humid summers, ideal for growing corn, form the bases for Corn-Belt agriculture.

Corn is usually grown on about half of the land, but only in the cash-grain areas near large markets is it sold as grain. The prevailing system is to feed the corn to cattle, hogs, and poultry and to obtain cash from the sale of milk, eggs, and, especially, meat. Some of the cattle are shipped in lean from western grasslands for fattening. The manure remains on the farm to maintain the fertility of the already rich soil. Lime, chemical fertilizers, and weed killers are also added, and these with the use of hybrid seeds have greatly improved per-acre yields.

Crop rotation is normally practiced and wheat, oats, alfalfa, hay, and especially soybeans are widely cultivated. Most farmers raise vegetables, fruit, and fodder for home consumption and frequently have small surpluses for the market.

The typical Corn-Belt farm is a big, well-operated business. The farm outbuildings are spacious and the machinery is elaborate. Probably nowhere in the world is so much land efficiently tilled with so little labour. The mechanization of the Corn Belt has caused a decline in the rural population, and surplus farm labourers have moved into adjacent towns and cities to find jobs in industry, especially in factories producing farm tools and consumer goods. East of central Iowa, industrial income surpasses farm income in most counties.

Chief cities The large cities of the region—Kansas City, Missouri, Des Moines, Iowa, Indianapolis, Indiana, and Omaha, Nebraska, especially—owe their initial development to the packing and marketing of Corn-Belt produce. They have, however, attracted diverse industrial and commercial activities.

The lower-lakes region. North of the Corn Belt, dairy products and hay push corn into a secondary place. More significant, however, is the network of transportation routes around the Great Lakes, the greatest freshwater navigation system in the world. Buffalo, at the eastern end of the region, was and still is important as a transshipment point from lake steamer to canal barge and to ocean freighters via the St. Lawrence Seaway.

Cleveland is noted as the financial centre for the Lake Erie area. Its industry is diversified with emphasis on hardware, machine tools, chemicals, and electrical equipment. The many smaller cities along or near the lake shore have local specialties, for example, steel in Lorain and rubber goods in Akron, Ohio.

Detroit was a commercial centre long before it became the automobile capital of the world. Its rise to that position was partly an accident of history, but Detroit was not without natural advantages for the automotive industry. In 1900 Michigan had lumber and associated furniture, wagon, and carriage industries. As steel bodies became important, Detroit was at first convenient to lower-lakes steel centres and later used lake-borne ores and coal to produce its own steel. Finally Detroit could draw on a large number of smaller industrial cities in the lower-lakes region to supply batteries, tires, automobile parts, and accessories.

Chicago, located nearly at the southern end of Lake Michigan, became the terminus of the eastern railroads and the starting point of those going to the West. Meats and grains from an arc of farmlands extending at least 1,000 miles (1,600 kilometres) to the west were brought there for processing and shipping, and the city was the logical place for the wholesale and mail-order businesses serving the same area. Because raw materials could be brought in easily by rail and lake steamer, and from the south by

canal and pipeline, it was the best place to manufacture many of the goods sold by Chicago merchants. Chicago manufactures goods ranging from bacon to watches to steel girders; it surpasses even the New York area in the variety of its industries, although New York City holds preeminence in finance, commerce, and cultural activities.

The upper-lakes region. The northern half of the Great Lakes area is a region of rigorous winters and pleasant summers. There the glaciers scraped away much of the soil and blocked the drainage, forming numerous lakes and extensive swamps. The cool, damp climate is conducive neither to the formation of fertile soil nor to the growth of most crops. Only in the southern portion is the land really suitable for fodder crops and dairying; northward it is limited to pine trees, potatoes, and rye. Immigrants from Northern Europe found conditions on the upper lakes similar to those of their homeland, and the population is largely of Scandinavian origin.

Wisconsin and southern Minnesota are ideal dairying areas. Clover and timothy hay, corn for silage, and other fodder crops flourish. Large silos for fodder storage and huge barns for the comfort of the cattle enable the herds to survive the long winters. Milk is marketed in the lower-lakes region, but there is also a huge surplus that is converted into butter, cheese, and evaporated and powdered milk. Some of the surplus cream is shipped as far as New York by tank car.

Dairying regions

Farther north, the original pine, birch, and maple forests have been cut over and are regrowing slowly into second-growth forests providing pulpwood for paper mills and wilderness pleasing to summer fishermen and winter hunters. Unless they contain minerals, these northern lands are for the most part abandoned. The major mineral, hematite iron ore, is approaching exhaustion, and several companies are using low-grade ore (taconite) that must be concentrated before it can be used in blast furnaces.

The largest cities, Minneapolis and St. Paul, Minnesota, first developed with the nearby dairying and lumber area and the Wheat Belt to the west, now have diverse industries including electronics and machinery. Duluth's economy is mainly based on iron ore and on the city's services as a Great Lakes port.

The Wheat Belt. The dark soils of the flattish Wheat Belt are extremely fertile, and in years when the rainfall is good a bumper crop can be produced at low cost. This type of farming, however, is hardly for the poor man. To survive, the farmer must have a sufficient reserve to carry him through drought, hail, infestations of locusts, wheat rusts, and the many other threats to his crop. He must also have enough capital to buy expensive machinery and the square mile or more of land required to operate it efficiently.

The risk of farming in the Wheat Belt is so great that throughout its history political groups have arisen to assist the farmer who meets with disaster—disaster that often affects whole counties or even whole states. Besides the natural hazards, the price of wheat is uncertain, and even a bumper crop may be unprofitable. In an attempt to level out the ups and downs of Wheat-Belt agriculture, some steps have been taken toward diversification. Cattle, both beef and dairy, are common throughout the region. Oats, barley, rye, flax, and potatoes help to vary the crops and, when used in rotation with wheat, assist in maintaining soil fertility.

Throughout the entire region settlement is sparse and towns are small and far apart. The rectangular-field pattern of the Corn Belt is universal, but there is little need for the big cities and prosperous industrial towns that lend variety to the Corn-Belt economy. Except in a few peripheral cities, population is stagnant or declining as farms grow larger and machinery more efficient. "Suitcase farming," tillage by farmers who live elsewhere, is a rapidly developing practice in many counties.

A distinction should be made between the northern and southern parts of the Wheat-Belt region. In the south, winter wheat is planted in the fall, dies down under the winter snow, grows rapidly in the spring, and is ready for harvest in early summer. In the north, spring wheat is planted in the spring, grows all summer, and is harvested in late summer or early fall. Both wheats are hard and well suited for the manufacture of bread flour.

(O.P.S./Ed.)

Politics. In politics the Middle West was tied initially more closely to the South than to the northeastern states and tended to support the Democratic party. As that party came to be the voice of the southern slave owners in the *Republican* 1840s, Middle Westerners, unhappy with both Whigs and *Party roots* Democrats, helped create the new Republican Party and contributed heavily to the Republican presidential victory in 1860. The region supported the Union with men and material during the Civil War and for decades thereafter held the Democratic Party responsible for the war. The Republican Party ruled supreme in most of the Middle Western states much of the time from 1865 until the Great Depression of the 1930s.

But the region was not without political ferment. Even before the Civil War there were rural protests against railroad rates. Immediately after the war a host of splinter parties, some within the Republican Party, appeared, dedicated to bringing railroads, grain elevators, and sometimes banks and corporations under state regulation. When, in the late *The* 1860s, Oliver H. Kelley and associates formed the Pa- *Grange* trons of Husbandry, also called the Grange, the protesters found a focus and a vehicle for united action. Grangers captured the state governments and wrote regulatory laws in most of the Middle Western states in the early 1870s, and the U.S. Supreme Court upheld the right of states to regulate. The Middle West also contributed support to the Greenback Movement and in the 1890s provided leaders and support for the Populist Party. This party offered a comprehensive list of reforms which, although rejected by the voters in 1892 and 1896, found its way in succeeding years into the platforms of the major parties and later into the law of the land.

In the 20th century the region continued to furnish reformers, conspicuous among whom were Robert M. La Follette of Wisconsin, Albert B. Cummins of Iowa, and George W. Norris of Nebraska, all nominal Republicans. Nor had agrarian protest ended. In 1916 the Nonpartisan League arose in North Dakota, protesting against the familiar monsters—railroads, grain elevators, and banks. During the Great Depression, the Middle West was the land of the farm holiday and milk strikes. The sit-down strike was introduced in the United States, and the industrial union the CIO (Congress of Industrial Organizations) was born in the Middle West in the same years. During and after World War I, the region came to be known as the isolationist Middle West.

Although often described as the most materialistic part of the country, intent upon work and moneymaking, the Middle West also made substantial contributions to the literature, art, and architecture of the nation; and the influence of men such as Twain, Hemingway, Frank Lloyd Wright, and many others transcends national boundaries.

The Middle West, whatever else it is, is a region of material abundance, variety and practical unorthodoxy.

(V.Ca./Ed.)

Illinois

An east north-central state of the United States admitted as the 21st member of the Union in 1818, Illinois is a state that long has been profoundly divided within itself. The growth of Chicago in the 19th century into a great world centre of population, industry, transportation, and finance created the first and most basic division that was to have deep social, economic, and political consequences for the *Overview* state and its people. Illinois continues to be essentially two *of the state* states, with a majority of Illinoisans living in the Chicago metropolitan area and maintaining a minimum of common interests and sympathies with people "Downstate." A downstater visiting Chicago for sight-seeing or shopping travels in and out of the city by train or expressway, rarely seeing deeply into the city and the problems behind its swift-paced, modern facade. A Chicagoan seeking relaxation is most likely to drive to Wisconsin or Michigan, thus never developing a feeling for "the other Illinois."

The divisions go even deeper, with large pockets of poverty existing in a state that is one of the most affluent in the nation by many economic indexes. Illinois's divisions, however, are far more social than economic. Internal distrust is probably the most serious symptom: distrust between races, between the nationality groups, and between urban and rural populations. To compound difficulties, Illinois is both a Northern and a Southern state in attitudes. It encompasses 56,400 square miles (146,075 square kilometres) and stretches 400 miles (644 kilometres) from Wisconsin in the north to the area known as "Little Egypt," which lies farther south than Richmond, Virginia. These divisions among the people of Illinois manifest themselves at the administrative and legislative levels of the state and are carried over into organizations, institutions, and political parties.

These problems, not unique to Illinois, perhaps became magnified through the state's critical role in the economic and political life of the nation. Rich in coal and oil reserves and ideally located for the acquisition of raw materials and distribution of finished goods, Illinois ranked second among states in exports in the late 1970s, and was third in agricultural income and fourth in manufacturing. Chicago, America's third largest city, has one of the busiest railroad systems in the country; its O'Hare International Airport is the world's most heavily trafficked, and Illinois highways and waterways are thick with commercial traffic. Politically, Illinois has continued to be a "swing state," its votes often mirroring fluctuating social tensions that underlie the growing, but unevenly distributed, economic prosperity.

PHYSICAL AND HUMAN GEOGRAPHY

The land. *Relief.* Illinois is drained by more than 500 streams emptying into either the Mississippi or the St. Lawrence River systems, the latter through Lake Michigan. The state is bounded on the north by Wisconsin, on the northeast by Lake Michigan, on the east by Indiana, on the southeast by Kentucky, and on the west by Missouri and Iowa.

Flat prairies cover much of Illinois, with irregular plains in the western, northern, and southern sections. The southernmost part of the state is in many ways out of character with the rest of Illinois. Shawnee National Forest, the only federal forest or park area in Illinois, covers a great part of this region. Southern Illinois consists of open hills, gently sloping with crests, which have Ozarkian or Appalachian characteristics. Gently rolling hills in the northwest include the state's highest point, 1,241 feet (378 metres) above sea level. The statewide average elevation is about 600 feet. Most of the 368 lakes of 40 acres (16 hectares) or more are man-made. Water lies under all *Water con-* of Illinois in natural underground reservoirs. Except for *sumption* Chicago and the lakefront communities, which draw their *and* water from Lake Michigan, most of northern Illinois's *resources* public water is pumped from underground wells. Some of these regions face a dwindling water supply; around Joliet, the water table has been lowered more than 700 feet in the past 100 years.

The deep black soil of much of northern and central Illinois has unusual richness, and its quality for agriculture is among the finest in the world. The soils of the southern third of the state are far less suited for farming.

Climate. As is true in most temperate zones, Illinois experiences typically cold, snowy winters and hot summers although extremes are somewhat ameliorated around Lake Michigan. Mean winter temperatures are about 22° F (−6° C) in the north, and 37° F (3° C) in the south; summer equivalents are 70° F (21° C) and 77° F (25° C). Mean annual precipitation in the north ranges from 32 to 48 inches (810 to 1,220 millimetres) and in the south from 48 to 64 inches. The growing season varies from 210 days in the south to 160 days in northernmost counties.

Plant and animal life. Illinois vegetation is traditionally separated into the Fayette prairie of northern and central Illinois and the oak-hickory forest of the western and southern regions. Before white settlers moved in, oak-hickory forests prevailed also in the north. The settlers' needs for fuel and construction material and the lumbering industry stripped most of the trees, leaving only 10 percent of the forests in northern and central Illinois. Some 4,000,000 acres of forests remain in the west and south, more than 700,000 of them in the Shawnee National Forest. The state's great length—the equivalent of from New England to Virginia—gives it an unusual variety of northern and southern plant life. Both northern and southern wild flowers grow in Illinois, as well as a great variety of trees such as white pine, tamarack, walnut, cypress, and tupelo gum.

Before 1800 wildlife in abundance roamed the prairies and forests, but the bison, bear, wolf, mountain lion, and elk have disappeared entirely. Wild deer became extinct in 1910, but in 1933 the Department of Conservation placed small herds that resulted in a growing deer population. Game birds such as quail and pheasant are still in abundance, as are waterfowl during spring and fall migration. Pollution has nearly wiped out many fish that once were plentiful, but bullheads, carp, and catfish still abound.

Settlement patterns. Aside from the aforementioned distinction between the Chicago area and Downstate derived from population patterns, Illinois can be separated into three broad regions that differ markedly in their economic and social characteristics. A highly urbanized band—with extensive farming areas in between—reaches across the state in the north from Chicago to the Rock Island–Moline complex on the Mississippi and includes Kankakee, Joliet, and Rockford. Most of the farmland, although decidedly rural, has easy access to a sizable urban centre. The region is characterized by heavy industry around Chicago and the other large centres with a sprawl of large suburban developments of shopping centres, single-family dwellings, and apartment-house complexes.

Economic and social regions

The central third of the state includes such cities as Springfield, Bloomington, Peoria, Champaign, Danville, Galesburg, Quincy, and Decatur. The economic base of the region is its highly developed agriculture. Some cities (such as Peoria) support such large industries as farm machinery and construction equipment; others are centred on institutions—the state government complex in Springfield and the University of Illinois in Champaign–Urbana. The focus of communications and transportation is scattered among four or five metropolitan areas. The character of the people tends to remain rural or small-town, with a highly developed sense of tradition and history. The 1970 census showed a large influx of people into the Bloomington–Normal area, the home of two large universities, and the area's population continued to increase from 1970 to 1980, although at a slower rate. The more rural counties, however, have experienced only slight population increases, if any.

St. Louis, Missouri, tends to dominate southern Illinois. East St. Louis, Belleville, Alton, and Granite City are medium-sized cities, but they are located in only two counties, leaving the rest rural. Since it was the region of Illinois that was settled earliest, most of its communities have longer historical traditions than do their northern neighbours. The unique features of southern Illinois are its coal mines, oil wells, and the Shawnee National Forest, which covers parts of 10 counties. The region is Southern-mountain in character, and the pace of living is slightly slower because of fewer cities and a depressed economy. The rapidly growing Southern Illinois University in Carbondale has provided considerable economic and cultural stimulation to the region.

The people. After most of the French had left Illinois following the French and Indian War, English settlers and colonists of Anglo-Saxon stock from Virginia, Tennessee, and Kentucky moved in. New Englanders and New Yorkers arrived by way of the Great Lakes or the National Road. When the United States experienced the great waves of European immigrants beginning in the 1840s, large numbers of Germans and Irish went to northern Illinois; and from the 1880s until World War I, immigrants streamed in from such countries as Poland, Hungary, Italy, Norway, Sweden, Austria, and Russia. In 1910 Germans ranked first in number among the foreign-born, Austrians and Hungarians ranked second, about 200,000 each, followed by Russians, Scandinavians, Irish, and Italians. Among the immigrants were the Jews. Culturally an urban-oriented group, they settled heavily on Chicago's south and west sides.

The great ethnic mix

Recent immigrants have tended to come from origins different and more diverse than in the 19th century. In Chicago, particularly, it is common to hear Greek, Persian, Polish, Spanish, and Czech spoken. Small, stable communities of Japanese, Chinese, Filipino, Puerto Rican, and Mexican peoples also make Chicago their home.

Blacks have lived in Illinois since the first slaves were imported in 1719, but their numbers remained low until the Civil War. By 1870 the blacks numbered 28,000, and by 1910 migrant blacks had settled in the southern counties and totalled 110,000. With World War I, a steady flow of blacks began to the major industrial centres, and by the late 20th century blacks in Illinois made up about 13 percent of the state's population, almost all of them in Chicago. In addition, whites from poverty-stricken Appalachia, American Indians, and Puerto Ricans searching for higher paying employment opportunities have joined the migration to Chicago.

The religious diversity in Illinois is reflected in the different origins of the people themselves. In the early 1800s Methodist circuit riders nourished tiny congregations throughout downstate Illinois, and the Methodists remain strong today in the small towns. The Irish, some of the Germans, and later the southern and eastern Europeans brought the Roman Catholic faith to the larger cities, and the Roman Catholic archdiocese of Chicago continues to be the nation's largest in membership. Also serving the city are scores of Eastern Orthodox and Protestant churches and Jewish synagogues.

Illinois has population characteristics similar to those of the nation as a whole: cities continue to lose whites to suburban areas, while both the number and percentage of blacks within city limits have increased. The flight of young people from rural areas and small towns, however, has slowed.

The economy. The diversified nature of its economy—strength in manufacturing, agriculture, finance, mining, transportation, government, and services—makes Illinois a microcosm of the national economic scene as a whole. This diversity generally provides greater stability at times when other states with more narrowly based industries suffer—as, for example, when military contracts are cut, with a resulting increase in unemployment.

Industry. Illinois has the second highest number of factories producing fabricated metals in the nation, and the third highest number of electrical machinery and printing and publishing establishments. It ranks fourth as a centre for establishments producing nonelectrical machinery, which accounts for a large share of its foreign exports. Illinois is a major automotive centre as well. Some 250 industrial parks are scattered throughout the state, the greatest concentration being in the Chicago metropolitan area.

Resources. The 40 or more coal seams in Illinois are relatively thin, but the underground mines in the south have among the highest production per man-day in the country. Peak petroleum production was reached in 1940 and has declined since; nevertheless, output remains fairly high. Illinois also leads in mining of lead, zinc, limestone, and silica sand used in the glass and steel industries.

The resources of coal and oil contribute heavily to the production of electrical power, although atomic-energy stations are beginning to assume increasing shares of the state's industrial and consumer needs. The Argonne National Laboratory, near Lemont, is a major research and development installation of the U.S. Department of Energy, and the Dresden Nuclear Power Station, near Joliet, produces electricity for eight companies in and around Chicago. A facility located in Zion on Lake Michigan began commercial operation in 1973.

Developments in nuclear power

Agriculture. Illinois's greatest natural resource, however, is its rich, black soil. Farms cover more than 80 percent of the state's area. For years Illinois has been the nation's major soybean producer, and from year to year it trades places with Iowa for first-place rank in corn. Illinois is also noted for pork products, grains, dairy products, and meat animals. In spite of a growing national trend toward large corporate-farm operations, family-owned farms account for the greatest percentage of farms in Illinois.

Finance. In 1980 Illinois ranked second only to Texas in number of independent banks, attributable to the state's prohibition against branch banking. This issue long has produced complex political battles in Springfield, with frequent charges and occasional exposures of political graft connected with it. Observers see opposition to change coming primarily from small banks downstate that fear elimination by the huge Chicago banks and from the currency exchanges that operate with high service charges, especially in inner-city areas that cannot support an independent banking institution.

In addition to its banking strength, Illinois is a major insurance centre, headquartering the two largest automobile insurers in the world. Chicago is the seat of the seventh district of the Federal Reserve Bank as well as of the Midwest Stock Exchange and the Chicago Board of Trade. Although well below the New York and American exchanges in volume, the Midwest Stock Exchange experiences considerable trading. The Board of Trade is the nation's oldest and largest commodity market, dealing in contracts for grains, soybeans and their products, silver, plywood and lumber, livestock, and dairy products.

Management of the economy. The state and private business organizations give considerable attention to expanding Illinois's balanced economy. The Illinois Department of Business and Economic Development has an office in Brussels to stimulate the importation into Europe of Illinois products. The department also aggressively seeks to attract new industries to Illinois and to provide advice to communities that wish to do the same. This department and the Department of Labor also provide data on economic trends, wages, local taxes, and marketing. The state offers services relating to the development of business enterprises by blacks and other ethnic minorities and disseminates information to private enterprises that wish to benefit from new technological developments. Private organizations, local and regional in nature, traditionally have played a significant part in attracting industry, in the development or rehabilitation of downtown areas, and in technological advancement.

Strong union-political ties

Trade unions are strong in Illinois, both politically and economically, but neither they nor the employer groups are strong enough to impose their will on the other. Mediation in labour-management disputes by politicians is a frequent occurrence, notably in Chicago, where union ties to political parties and leaders are accepted facts of life.

In recent years Illinois has found itself more and more deeply involved with the dual needs of maintaining its economic stability and of improving the environment. Politicians found themselves involved with the demands of the public and of conservationists, the uncertainty of federal pollution (and related) standards, and the self-defenses of industry. The increasing pollution of Lake Michigan, of the skies of the industrial centres, and of streams throughout the state by industry, by public utilities, and by municipalities themselves posed one of the most perplexing questions for the state's economic future.

Transportation. Illinois is recognized as the transportation centre of the United States. Few comparable areas are served by so many different means of transportation. Before the Amtrak (federal) passenger train merger in 1971, 30 passenger railroads and 37 industrial lines served the state. Chicago remains the country's rail capital, and the state's more than 11,000 miles (17,600 kilometres) of track rank it second highest in the nation. Eight commuter railroads continue to serve the Chicago area, carrying an average of 250,000 passengers every weekday.

Railways, waterways, and airways

Water transportation became more efficient when Lake Michigan was connected to the Mississippi River in 1848 by means of the Illinois and Michigan Canal, linking the Chicago and Illinois rivers. With other later canals, barge traffic linking Chicago, the Mississippi, and Gulf Coast ports has become extensive. The St. Lawrence Seaway stimulated the commercial expansion of the Port of Chicago. Harbours for oceangoing freighters have been developed at Navy Pier near the downtown area and at Calumet Harbor in South Chicago.

Chicago has two major airports, O'Hare International and Midway, and a third on the lakefront, Meigs Field, which serves small planes.

Administrative and social conditions. *Government.* The first state constitution was adopted in 1818, a second in 1848, and in 1870 a third that was to remain in effect for 100 years.

The constitution adopted by the people in December 1970 added new concepts to the Illinois Bill of Rights: no discrimination on the basis of race, creed, colour, national ancestry, or sex in employment or the sale or rental of property; no discrimination on the basis of sex; no discrimination against the physically or mentally handicapped; and the promotion of individual dignity.

Major provisions of the 1970 constitution

Throughout the new document were examples of modernization in the structure and tone. A new article proclaimed a public policy of maintaining a healthful environment, to be enforced by state law; it provides that "Each person has the right to a healthful environment. Each person may enforce this right against any party, governmental or private, through appropriate legal proceedings . . . ."

The larger cities and counties were granted powers to tax, to license, and to incur debt without prior authorization of the state legislature. The governor was granted powers to reorganize state government, and his veto power was augmented by the authority to reduce appropriations and to object to certain portions of legislation without having to veto the entire act. The election of the judiciary was retained, as was the unique electoral framework of the House of Representatives, under which each district sent three representatives to Springfield, with the district's minority party virtually assured of one seat. In 1980 a referendum abolished this system in favour of single-member districts. Voters rejected separate constitutional proposals to abolish the death penalty and reduce the voting age to 18, though the latter issue was resolved by an amendment to the federal constitution in 1971.

Illinois recognizes three levels of local government—county, township, and municipality—plus innumerable special districts. Counties are classed as township and nontownship, with Cook County, containing Chicago and most of its major suburbs, in a class by itself. All counties elect a number of administrative officials. The 85 township counties are governed by boards of commissioners elected from districts, the 16 nontownship counties by three-member boards elected at large, and Cook County by a 15-member board, 10 from Chicago and five from the suburbs.

Townships act primarily as road-maintenance and general-assistance units. The annual town meeting, a gathering of all qualified voters, is still a feature of local government remaining from earlier centuries. Municipal government usually is of the mayor-council type, though other forms are permitted; villages utilize a president-trustee system.

Overall, Illinois has more than 6,300 units of local government, resulting in a crazy-quilt of overlapping administrative, educational, park, fire, sanitary, sewage, drainage, and other special districts. Most were formed to circumvent restrictions in the old constitution but have become self-perpetuating. Patterns of taxation are similarly chaotic. In addition to the usual taxes on personal and business income, cigarettes, liquor, and retail sales, Illinois formerly imposed a personal-property tax, which drew public and official complaints because of its uneven enforcement, few residents of Chicago even being billed for it. Real-estate taxes contribute the major local support for schools and other services, though the state supplies "no-strings-attached" grants to municipalities and counties from income-tax revenues.

The chaos of taxation

With the proliferation of districts and officials, elections and referendums are held frequently throughout Illinois. Although widespread support has been voiced for adoption of the Missouri Plan, under which judicial candidates and incumbent judges at all levels are reviewed by qualified nonpartisan boards and then appointed, the partisan election of judges continues. Judges at all levels run for reelection on their record, the voter designating "yes" or "no" on retention. Until three-member districts were abolished by the voters in 1980, Illinois had a unique system for electing state representatives; a voter could cast 3 votes for 1 candidate, 1½ for each of 2, or 1 vote for each of 3.

Social divisions. Since World War II the profound social divisions within Illinois probably have been based most strongly on the issue of race. Chicago with its one-third or more black population, its heavy concentration of many white ethnic groups staunchly maintaining their identities as they move into the middle class, and its almost hereditary political control by an alliance of white ethnic, union, and business leaders, inevitably has been the focus. The appeals of Chicago to the state for funds to remedy its problems in education, housing, transportation, and welfare produced years of acrimonious debate in the legislature and between Chicago's city hall and the statehouse. Observers have seen this continuing contention as stemming both from a great lack of understanding of urban problems by downstate and urban legislators and from a basic unwillingness of the city administration to enforce laws designated to ameliorate and ultimately eliminate the effects of racial segregation and unequal opportunity.

Divisiveness of ethnic groups and geographic regions

Instances of violence and heated confrontations have not been limited to the Chicago area, however, and such southern Illinois cities as East St. Louis and Cairo have undergone prolonged sieges with overt racial overtones. In addition, sporadic student and other minority-group outbreaks have occurred, the best known of which were between police and youthful demonstrators during the 1968 Democratic National Convention in Chicago.

Health and welfare. Health and welfare assistance and services are provided by both state and local government, most of which receive funds from diverse federal agencies, although representatives of the low-income groups most requiring the services have been in frequent conflict with local officials over the question of who is to administer the funds and the programs.

Chicago's public housing is primarily a municipal or county responsibility, often with federal aid. Both the Model Cities Program, public housing funded entirely by the federal government, and the Chicago Housing Authority (CHA) have met with strong opposition to proposals to locate public housing in predominantly white neighbourhoods. Welfare assistance to poor families, dependent children, and other groups has met resistance in the legislature in Springfield, whereas independent attempts to establish free neighbourhood medical clinics in low-income black and Spanish-speaking areas of the city has encountered hostility from city administrators.

Thus, whereas medical facilities throughout most of Illinois are among the finest in the nation, and Chicago is a major centre for medical and psychiatric services and training, many Illinoisans continued to be served inadequately. And despite the fact that per capita income in Illinois is the highest of any state in the Midwest and among the highest in the nation, the increasing burdens of public assistance seemed far from solution or even agreement on goals. Illinois, in the social sphere as in the economic, might well be seen as a microcosm of the American nation as it approached the final decades of the 20th century.

Education. In the field of education as well, Illinois displays a startling juxtaposition of wealth and poverty. In many academic subjects the University of Chicago (founded 1891) is respected as among the finest institutions of higher learning in the nation, yet it is situated like an island on the south side amid one of the most deteriorated of the city's ghetto sections. Northwestern University (1851), in nearby Evanston, has a distinguished faculty in several areas, as do the Illinois Institute of Technology, in Chicago, and Southern Illinois University, in Carbondale and Edwardsville. In addition to the last-named institution, the state system includes four state universities as well as the University of Illinois, with campuses at Champaign–Urbana and Chicago, and two state colleges. Numerous sectarian and nonaffiliated private colleges are scattered throughout the state along with numerous community and junior colleges.

Institutions of higher learning

The Illinois Office of Education was created in 1975 after the new Illinois Constitution directed that responsibilities for public elementary and secondary education be transferred from an elected superintendent to a state Board of Education. The board consists of 17 members appointed by the governor with the consent of the state Senate. The Chicago system, as operated by the city's board, has been continuously controversial. Most schools in the system adhere to neighbourhood housing patterns, and critics long have charged deliberate gerrymandering of districts to keep racial integration minimal. The issue of funding of Chicago schools long has been among the most bitter points of city–state contention.

Cultural life. In spite of its reputation of being a brash industrial and commercial city, Chicago long has been one of the major centres of the arts in the United States. By 1900 Chicago architects were designing commercial and private buildings that became models for schools of modern architecture throughout the world. In the 1910s and 1920s it was a major centre for literary leaders, and today the holdings of its public and private institutional libraries are enormous. Its Art Institute, Museum of Science and Industry, Field Museum of Natural History, and other civic landmarks have collections and research facilities among the most complete in the world. Although it is no longer a major centre of the performing arts—before Hollywood was discovered about 1910, it was the centre of the American film industry—its downtown, suburban, and experimental theatres offer a broad spectrum of standard and avant-garde works. Dance is widely available, and its symphony orchestra is among the five major American musical organizations.

Communities outside the Chicago area have thriving artistic lives as well, often revolving around the theatre, music, art, or various science departments of the many colleges and universities in Illinois or around community theatre or musical organizations. Belleville boasts the second-oldest symphony orchestra in the nation, founded in 1867. The Eagle's Nest Art Colony, founded in Oregon in 1898 by the sculptor Lorado Taft, included many well-known Illinois artists; it was acquired by Northern Illinois University in 1950. The Illinois Arts Council was created by the state in 1965 as the primary agency to fund statewide or local programs in the several arts, including free street programs in the cities. It is supported by the state; the National Endowment for the Arts, a federal agency; and private donors.

Aside from Chicago's great number of historic memorabilia, recreational facilities, and tourist attractions, much of Illinois's full repertory remains relatively unknown, even to Illinoisans. Among old cities of interest on the Mississippi are Galena, which preserves the home of Pres. Ulysses S. Grant, and Nauvoo, founded in 1839 by the Mormons and their point of departure in 1846 on the trek that took them to Utah. New Salem, near Springfield, is a preservation of the community of log cabins in which Abraham Lincoln spent much of his young manhood. Throughout much of central Illinois the Lincoln Trail joins many places associated with the president, including his home in Springfield and the sites of his famous debates with Sen. Stephen A. Douglas. The Spoon River Trail in north central Illinois leads through the country made famous by the poet Edgar Lee Masters. Major scenic areas include the Mississippi Palisades State Park and Apple River Canyon State Park in the northwest, Starved Rock State Park in north central Illinois, and the forests of the south. The Chicago suburb of Oak Park, home of the pioneer modern architect Frank Lloyd Wright, contains many of the best examples of his early work.

Among Illinois's finest recreational offerings are the sandy beaches of Lake Michigan, from Chicago to the Wisconsin border, and the forest preserves that bring rustic retreats close to the state's urban areas. Although Illinois has virtually no wilderness areas, many camping sites are located throughout the state, and boating and fishing are avidly pursued on the state's many lakes and streams.

Newspapers and the broadcast media

About 80 daily and 700 weekly newspapers are published throughout Illinois. The largest of these papers, the *Chicago Tribune,* became a nationally recognized symbol of the political and social conservatism of the Midwest under the long reign of publisher Robert R. McCormick, and it continues to have wide distribution throughout the Midwest. Its point of view is offset somewhat by the more moderate-to-liberal *Chicago Sun-Times,* the second largest daily in Chicago. The *Chicago Daily Defender,* with a circulation of more than 17,000, is published primarily for the black community. Southern Illinois is influenced also by newspapers and broadcasts from St. Louis.

Chicago is the third largest publishing centre in the nation, exceeded only by New York City and San Francisco. Much of its publishing is specialized in the areas of education, encyclopaedias, medicine, and business.

HISTORY

Archaeologists have found evidence dating from around 8000 BC of a paleo-Indian culture in southern Illinois. The Mississippian people, whose religious centre was Cahokia in southwestern Illinois, constituted probably the largest pre-Columbian (around AD 1300) community north of Mexico in the Mississippi River Valley floodplain. Indian tribes in Illinois were all of the Algonkian stock. In the north, the Kickapoo, Sac, and Fox roamed; the Potawatomie, Ottawa, and Ojibwa (Chippewa) dominated the Lake Michigan area; the Kaskaska, Illinois, and Peoria stalked the central prairies; and the Cahokia and Tamaroa roamed the south.

Settlement. The first Europeans to visit Illinois were the French explorers Louis Jolliet and Jacques Marquette, in 1673, when they explored the Mississippi and Illinois rivers. Near present-day Peoria, Lasalle established the first French foothold, Ft. Crèvecoeur, and built Ft.-Saint-Louis near Ottawa. After the French and Indian War in the 1760s, France ceded to Britain its claim to lands east of the Mississippi. The following years were uneasy—British policy was unfavourable to the area's economic development, Indians resented the British, and settlements were without civil government. By 1773 the number of settlers had declined to about 1,000 plus a few hundred slaves.

In 1778 the American capture of Kaskaskia, the British seat of government, made Illinois a county of Virginia. The first settlement on the site of Chicago was made in 1779 by the black pioneer Jean Baptiste Point Sable (or Pointe du Sable). On July 4, 1800, the Northwest Territory was divided, and the Illinois country was made a part of Indiana Territory; Illinois Territory was formed March 1, 1809, by dividing Indiana Territory. Illinois was admitted as the 21st state on December 3, 1818.

Early years of statehood. At the time of statehood, two-thirds of the population lived along the eastern and western edges of southern Illinois, primarily engaged in the fur trade. By 1830 the population had risen to nearly 160,000. The final conflict with the Indians was the Black Hawk War in 1832.

Southern and central Illinois remained the more heavily settled areas of the state during the early 19th century. In 1848 the Illinois and Michigan Canal was completed, linking points on the Illinois River on opposite sides of the Mississippi–Lake Michigan watersheds. With rail expansion many towns became prosperous. The National Road, leading westward from Maryland and terminating at Vandalia, brought many settlers to Illinois.

Slavery as a constitutional issue

The Illinois Constitution of 1818 gave blacks the status of indentured servants, and slavery would have been legalized except for fear that such a move would prevent admission. In 1824 Illinois voters rejected a proposal for a constitutional convention whose implicit if unstated purpose was to legalize slavery. Following the heavy influx of Yankees into northern Illinois during the 1830s and 1840s, which offset the southern attitudes, abolitionist sentiment translated itself into the Constitution of 1848, which abolished slavery and forbade the importing of slaves.

When the Civil War broke out, northern Illinois remained loyal to the Union and to the Illinoisan in the White House, Abraham Lincoln. A movement to ally southern Illinois with the Confederacy failed. Some 250,000 Illinoisans fought for the Union; among them was its most able general and future president, Ulysses S. Grant.

Economic and social maturation. Chicago's great fire of 1871 proved only a temporary deterrent in its progress toward becoming an industrial colossus among American cities. Its mills, railyards, and slaughterhouses were filled with workers recruited from the waves of Irish, Poles, Bohemians, and other Europeans who joined the many freed black immigrants who came to Illinois beginning in the 1860s. Until well into the 20th century, Illinois was a main focus of the American labour movement. Two events in Chicago, the Haymarket Square Riot of 1886 and the Pullman strike of 1894, became landmarks in the militant rise of the unions.

At the same time, Illinois was becoming a pioneer in social legislation, with a state board of health created in 1877; a compulsory school-attendance law in 1883; a "sweatshop act" providing for factory inspections and restrictions on child labour; and an eight-hour-day, 48-hour-week work limit for children, both enacted in 1893. The World's Columbian Exposition of 1893, missing by one year the 400th anniversary of Columbus' landing in the New World, was America's first international exhibition of the nation's vast technological and scientific strides during the 19th century.

The 20th century. During the decades up to and including the 1920s and 1930s, the name Chicago became an international byword for bootleg liquor, gangsterism, and syndicate crime. Downstate Illinois at the same time was gaining its share of notoriety as a region of violence. Williamson County first gained the epithet "Bloody Williamson" for a feud, beginning in 1868, among five families of Tennessee and Kentucky origin. A dispute over a card game in a tavern near Carbondale grew into an eight-year vendetta fought by ambush or nighttime murder in barnyards, bars, and country stores. This violent tradition continued into the 1920s with the antiblack crusades of the Ku Klux Klan, the coal strikes, and the wars among the Shelton, Birger, and other bootleg gangs.

"Bloody Williamson" County

Amid the violence and the scandals that periodically rocked both state and municipal governments in Illinois, the state underwent tremendous growth economically and culturally. A reorganization of state government in 1917 brought more than 100 independent agencies and commissions under the governor and became a managerial model for many other states. Chicago became America's second largest city in the 1880s, and in 1933–34 its Century of Progress Exposition drew attention again to further industrial achievement. In 1942 the world's first controlled atomic chain reaction was set off at the University of Chicago, ushering in the atomic age.

Since the Civil War Illinois has had intense competition between the Republican and Democratic parties. This factor and its large electoral vote make it a major battleground in presidential elections. The three distinguishable political regions are Chicago, which is heavily Democratic; Chicago's suburban metropolitan area and the rich farmlands of north and central Illinois, which are strongly Republican; and southern Illinois, which may swing one way or the other. In recent years both parties have had almost equal strength statewide.

The two parties are highly organized, from precinct to state levels. During the state's history both parties have been so frequently the target of corruption and fraud that Illinois politics has gained a checkered reputation on a nationwide scale. From 1955 until his death in 1976, Mayor Richard J. Daley of Chicago built up enormous statewide—and nationwide—power in the Democratic Party, largely through his administrative control of all city, and, effectively, Cook County departments and their patronage. If the governor is Republican, he almost always leads the party, but is ordinarily unable to command the huge bloc vote possible in Chicago.   (R.T.L./J.M.Ca.)

Indiana

Indiana, though officially classified as an east-north central state of the United States, is perhaps the most Southern in character of all Northern states. This is in large degree a reflection of the heavy early settlement of the region by immigrants from the Southern hills, who carried with them the institution of slavery and a hearty distrust of the federal government. Indiana's 36,291 square miles (93,993 square kilometres) make it, except for Hawaii, the smallest

An over-
view of
the state

state west of the Appalachian Mountains. The capital has been at Indianapolis since 1825, nine years after Indiana was admitted as the 19th state of the Union.

Indiana is basically a manufacturing state, and its northern half lies in the mainstream of the great industrial belt stretching from Pennsylvania and New York state westward to Illinois. Many of its people, nevertheless, continue to cherish an image derived from 19th-century America: largely white, dedicated to the Protestant ethic of sobriety and hard work, oriented to the small town and medium-sized city, and, especially, interested in maintaining the prerogatives of local self-determination. It is not by coincidence that Indiana's federal aid is one of the lowest per capita of any American state or that the Indianan's nickname, "the Hoosier," remains a symbol in the nation's lore for a kind of homespun wisdom, wit, and folksiness that harkens back to what is popularly regarded as a less hurried and sophisticated period of history.

Indiana is, as its motto states, "in the center of things." Its borders face Lake Michigan and the state of Michigan on the north, Ohio on the east, Kentucky on the south, and Illinois on the west, making it an integral part of the Midwest. The northwestern cities form an industrial, economic, and social continuum with neighbouring Chicago. Their heavy black populations and black political power aspirations contrast strikingly with life in the cities and towns on the Ohio River. The state is at once Northern and black, Southern and white-dominated, with all the problems attendant on both circumstances. Though generally considered a conservative and Republican stronghold, Indiana has voted into both state and national office an almost equal number of liberals and Democrats.

PHYSICAL AND HUMAN GEOGRAPHY

The land. *Relief.* Indiana forms part of the east central lowlands that slope downward from the Appalachians to the Mississippi. Approximately five-sixths of its surface was modified by glacial action, leaving a vast quantity of excellent soil material and extensive deposits of sand gravel. The more eroded southern part of the state gives way to the central plain, an extremely fertile agricultural belt with large farms, and then to the flat and heavily glaciated northern regions. The highest elevation is along the Ohio border, at 1,257 feet (383 metres) above sea level, while its low point, 320 feet (98 metres), is where the Wabash enters the Ohio. About 90 percent of the land lies between 500 and 1,000 feet, and Indianapolis, in the centre of the state, has an elevation of 793 feet (242 metres).

Natural
environ-
ment

The general slope and drainage pattern is toward the southwest, though an almost imperceptible groundswell in the northeast forms a St. Lawrence–Mississippi water divide. The Wabash, the Ohio, and the east and west forks of the White River follow this slope, forming part of the Mississippi Basin. In the north, the St. Joseph River meanders into Lake Michigan, while in the east the Maumee flows northeastward into Lake Erie. The northern half of the state is dotted with many small lakes, including several of the state's largest. Forest cover totalled 3,943,000 acres (1,596,000 hectares) in 1977, of which 97 percent was commercially owned. Among the dramatic features of the landscape are the sand dunes along Lake Michigan, most of which have been removed from the public domain by industry and private homes. This situation was remedied somewhat with the dedication in 1972 of Indiana Dunes National Lakeshore. The most scenic part of the state is the south-central region around Brown County, an area popular with tourists, and Indiana University.

Climate. Indiana has four distinct seasons and a temperate climate, usually escaping extremes of cold and heat. The mean temperature in January ranges from about 35° F (2° C) in Evansville on the Ohio River to 25° F (−4° C) in South Bend in the north. In July ranges are from about 78° F (26° C) to 73° F (23° C) in corresponding regions, and precipitation varies from 44 inches (1,120 millimetres) in the south central region to 35 inches (890 millimetres) in the north. Snow may fall over a six-month period and averages more than 20 inches annually, with the cities along the north central border often reporting

more than 100 inches. Fall is perhaps the most delightful season, with colours provided by maples, oaks, tulips, and a wide variety of other trees, whereas the spring is generally erratic and unstable. Year-round weather systems moving over Lake Michigan tend to afflict the north central regions with extremes of rain or snow, and, in the spring and early summer, Indiana is part of the belt of states called Tornado Alley as a result of air currents from the Gulf of Mexico.

Plant and animal life. Indiana is typical of east north central America in its variety of trees, birds, and small game animals, and like its neighbours it has through the years thinned out the numbers of many of these, including the great variety of life once common to the sand dunes. The steady growth of agriculture, cities, and industry and the consequent varied forms of pollution have taken a steady toll of natural life. Pollution of both air and water is particularly severe along the southern tip of Lake Michigan.

Settlement patterns. The three major regions of Indiana, which generally follow physiographic divisions, are: the flat northern region of industry and truck gardening; the fertile central plains; and the large southern region, less fertile but forested, which is the site of caves and limestone quarries.

The nighttime skies of northwestern Indiana are alive with the belching volcanoes of its steel furnaces, and during the daytime such cities as Gary and Hammond are darkened by clouds of smoke and airborne industrial wastes. Because of this dramatically apparent air pollution, the contamination of inland and lake waters, and the steady encroachment of industry upon the dunes and other lakefront areas since the early years of the 20th century, the area has become a major national target of conservationists. Southward to the Wabash Valley are rich farmlands, obtained largely by draining and deforesting marshes. To the east, South Bend is an important manufacturing city and a noted educational centre. The northeastern part of the state is more forested and pastoral, although Elkhart and Fort Wayne are major industrial cities.

Indianapolis, a city designed after Versailles, France, and Washington, D.C., dominates the central plains. It is a strongly conservative city and a national symbol of superpatriotism; its growth has occurred largely through immigration from rural areas and annexation. A railway and highway hub, Indianapolis also serves the surrounding farming belt as packer and distributor, and it is a major industrial city as well.

The advent of industry and railroads ended southern Indiana's early dominance, which was based on the river traffic of the Ohio and Wabash. The region's major city, Evansville, also serves adjacent areas of Kentucky and Illinois, and between it and Terre Haute to the north lie most of the state's oil and coal deposits. Many handsome examples of pre-Civil War architecture are found in the river towns. An old buffalo trace used by pioneers moving from Kentucky to the western prairies leads from New Albany, across the Ohio from Louisville, Kentucky, to the Wabash at Vincennes. Southward from Bloomington is a vast limestone belt underlain by numerous caves, which makes the state a major limestone producer. Brown County remains largely a backwoods area where log cabins abound on hillside farms.

The people. The people of Indiana are predominantly white, native-born Americans of native-born parents, most of whom trace their ancestry ultimately to England, Scotland, Ireland, and Germany. Notable exceptions occur in Indianapolis and such areas as South Bend and northwestern Lake County, which have black populations of more than 70 percent in Gary and about 30 percent in East Chicago. Citizens of Polish descent form the largest ethnic group in South Bend; and, along with Hungarian, Belgian, Italian, and Mexican groups, they are numerous throughout the north. The Amish people constitute a small group located in the northeast, in and around Middlebury, Nappanee, and Goshen. They conduct a model farm at Amish Acres in Nappanee. Mennonites, who also live in this area, have established a college in Goshen. The state's overall lack of ethnic and linguistic mix—common on the

White
Protestant
domina-
tion

East and West coasts and in most large cities—helps to account for the continuing strength of Hoosier localism.

Almost one-third of the people of Indiana are Protestant, a figure considerably above the national average. Roman Catholics, who make up 15 percent of the population, are concentrated largely in the urban areas with large continental and Irish ethnic groups, particularly South Bend. Jews, comprising a very small percentage of the state's population, live almost exclusively in urban centres.

About one-half of the state's residents live in the more than 60 cities with populations over 10,000. More than one-fifth of the people are concentrated in the Indianapolis Standard Metropolitan Statistical Area, and another fair percentage are in the Gary–Hammond–East Chicago complex. The national pattern of deserting the central city for the suburbs has generally occurred throughout the state, with South Bend, for example, losing population while its surrounding county grew. Of the counties losing population, most were located in the south.

The economy. During the 1960s *Fortune* magazine found Indiana the state most preferred by companies planning to build or relocate industrial facilities. Other studies have suggested the availability of labour and essential materials to be major advantages, as well as the state's location within 800 miles (1,280 kilometres) of 40 of the nation's 50 largest consumer and industrial markets and its high rank in interstate-highway mileage. The legislature passed laws in 1965 providing financial incentive for industrial expansion, and the two areas consistently receiving the most federal grants in the state are highways and agriculture. Heavy industrialization, however, has made the state's economy particularly vulnerable to recession.

The American Railway Union, America's first industrial (as distinct from craft) union, was founded in Terre Haute in 1893 by Eugene Debs, five-time Socialist candidate for president. The following year it was heavily involved in the Pullman Strike that brought the intervention of federal troops and Debs's imprisonment. Since that time Indiana has had its share of labour strife, especially in the steel industry, but, in general, the state Chamber of Commerce and the unions tend to work with the state government to help maintain an atmosphere attractive to industry.

Resources. Indiana is a major producer of U.S. building stone, quarried in the Bedford–Bloomington region. Bituminous coal from the southwest is the state's leading commodity for heating and generating electrical power. Natural gas must be brought in by pipelines, though during the 1880s Indiana's "Gas Belt" was the world's largest. Few attempts were made to conserve the gas, however, and by 1898 the supply was virtually exhausted. The Indiana and Michigan Electric Company's nuclear generating station in southwestern Michigan began operation in 1975.

Industry. Since the 1850s manufacturing gradually has become the dominant source of income for the state, with the steel industry a major component. Features of interest include production of musical instruments, of which Indiana is a major manufacturer, and Fort Wayne's diamond-tool industry, producing a large proportion of the world's supply. Overall, Indiana ranks among the nation's top 10 states in manufacturing.

Agriculture. Along with forestry and fisheries, agriculture employs about 3 percent of the labour force. Technological changes have resulted in startling increases in output per acre, per animal, and per worker, despite drops in total farm acreage and number of farms. Indiana ranks near the top nationally in cash receipts from farm marketing. Major crops include corn (maize), soybeans, and wheat, with tomatoes the principal vegetable crop. Hogs continue to be the most numerous livestock, with cattle, sheep, and poultry of increasing importance.

Transportation. Signs on the Indiana Toll Road proclaim the state to be the "Main Street of the Midwest," perhaps a fair estimate of its position in interstate transportation, whether by highway, waterway, air, or rail. Indianapolis is served by more major highways than any other American city, some of the nation's largest moving companies have their headquarters there.

Responsibility for road construction and maintenance rests with city, county, state, and federal governments.

County and state highway departments are subject to a widely deplored spoils, or patronage, system under which changes in administration bring on political dismissal and employment, resulting in instability in management. Nonetheless, Indiana ranks high nationally in road mileage per square mile of area, and almost all of its rural roads are paved. Though quantity may sometimes surpass quality of highway mileage, virtually all intrastate passengers and much commercial produce travel by road. Indiana has about 5,300 miles (8,500 kilometres) of mainline railroad track and about 2,800 miles of other trackage. All lines running east from Chicago and St. Louis pass through Indiana. As in other states, however, the Amtrak system that went into operation in 1971 has sharply reduced passenger service. Commercial air service is available in major Indiana cities, and there are more than 300 public and private airports in the state.

The Ohio River, linking Indiana with the Mississippi River system, carries more low-cost freight than does the Panama Canal. The Port of Indiana Harbour, on Lake Michigan about 10 miles (16 kilometres) east of Gary, created artificially and opened in 1970, connects Indiana with world commerce by way of the St. Lawrence Seaway.

Administrative and social conditions. *Government.* Indiana's executive, legislative, and judicial structures are similar to those of other states, but they show some marked differences. The governor is elected for a four-year period and can serve no more than two consecutive terms. As a result, gubernatorial influence on the General Assembly is generally weak during the second half of an administration. The governor has veto power over legislation, but the veto can be overridden by a simple majority of the two houses. The governor's authority is wielded largely through statutory power to appoint and remove heads of nearly all departments, commissions, and governing boards of institutions. Several thousand jobs are subject to the spoils system.

The bicameral General Assembly includes 50 senators, serving four-year terms, and 100 representatives, serving for two years. They may be reelected, but there is often a high turnover. In 1970 the voters approved annual sessions for the two bodies. The state constitution requires that the legislature reapportion itself according to population every six years. This law was ignored, however, from 1923 to 1963, during which time the rural areas exerted an influence far out of proportion to their declining population. Under pressure from the U.S. Supreme Court, the state eventually achieved a reapportionment based on the "one man, one vote" principle in 1965.

The Indiana constitution provided for the establishment of a Supreme Court, circuit courts, and other courts as the General Assembly deemed necessary. The Supreme Court is composed of five judges appointed by the governor and a judicial nominating commission after a rigorous screening procedure. A new judge serves for a period of two years and then, if retained, for a term of 10 years. The Court of Appeals consists of three regional divisions with three appellate judges each. Decisions are expected to be two to one, but cases are not referred automatically to the Supreme Court if there is a lack of consensus.

The four principal types of local government are the county, township, town, and civil city. There are also school towns, townships, and cities concerned with the operation of the school system; these may be independent or may overlap other political units. Townships, greatly reduced in importance, function primarily in the area of welfare. The county, town, and city have many areas of overlapping activity. Boards of county commissioners have executive and legislative powers, while county councils are concerned almost exclusively with fiscal affairs. City voters elect a mayor and common council.

Indiana is a two-party state, the Republicans having a slight advantage since the last quarter of the 19th century, especially in control of the governor's office and the General Assembly and in presidential voting. Voting trends show about one-third of the counties to be Republican, one-third Democratic, and one-third doubtful. In 1967 Gary and Cleveland, Ohio, became the first major U.S. cities to elect black mayors.

Margin notes: Sources of economic strength · The highway system · The General Assembly · Overlapping of governmental units

At the national level, the state can claim one president, Benjamin Harrison, the grandson of William Henry Harrison, and four vice presidents. In 1940 the Indiana native son Wendell L. Willkie was the Republican candidate for president.

Finances. Indiana's state and local governments rely largely on personal and corporate income taxes, retail sales taxes, and taxes on such items as motor fuels, tobacco products, and alcoholic beverages. Until the late 1970s, however, Hoosiers paid a lower per-capita state tax than the average U.S. citizen, and they continue to pay property taxes that are well below the national median. In keeping with its traditional distrust of the federal government, the state accepts only a minimal amount of federal aid. In addition, Indiana's revenue from corporate taxes is significantly below the national average. To ease local property taxes, legislation in 1967 provided for disbursement to local governments of 8 percent of revenues from income and sales taxes.

Welfare. Hoosiers take their politics seriously and do not take well to the idea of supporting public welfare programs. Indiana is among the more prosperous states in the nation, but like many other states it fails to apply its wealth to public programs. For example, not until the 1970s did the average weekly unemployment benefit in Indiana exceed the national average.

In comparison with its neighbouring states, Indiana ranks lowest in per-capita allotments for public welfare. Approximately 70 percent of Indiana's public assistance funding comes from federal and state funds; few other states in the nation finance so large a proportion of their assistance programs from local levels. Partially for this reason, Indiana is well below the national average in the number of recipients of general assistance per 1,000 population. Distrust of federal programs has tended to militate against making maximum use of aid that could be available, thus necessitating continued taxes at the state and local level that are a greater burden on the aged, on those with fixed incomes, and on the working and lower middle classes. The problem that the state confronts in financing public welfare programs is as much ideological as it is financial.

Despite federal and state prohibitions, slavery continued to exist well into the first half of the 19th century. In 1831 blacks entering the state had to deposit $500 bonds as surety that they would not become burdens on the state, but the total exclusion of blacks in the constitution of 1851 was the high point of such sentiment.

Racial integration

Despite annulment of that provision, blacks continued to be the victims of vigilante and other less-open methods of repression; by the early 1900s the Ku Klux Klan was flourishing and for some years all but controlled state government. Only in 1943 were teams from black schools allowed to participate in the annual state high school basketball tournament. The "Jim Crow" ward of Indianapolis Marion County General Hospital was not abolished until 1949, and hospitals moved only gradually after that to admit black doctors to their staffs. All forms of segregation were officially declared illegal in 1949, and since the 1950s the state has slowly emerged as one of the most effective enforcers of civil rights legislation in the nation, although there are persisting pockets of school and housing segregation in some cities, such as Gary and East Chicago.

Education. The state's educational system is headed by a board of education and a superintendent of public instruction. Indiana ranks in the lower half of the states in per-pupil outlay. The state's elementary and secondary educational systems are good, but they are not considered to be innovative or outstanding.

In the realm of higher education, on the other hand, Indiana has made notable achievements. The three leading universities of the state are Indiana, in Bloomington; Purdue, in West Lafayette; and Notre Dame, in South Bend. Indiana University, founded in 1820, has become noted for its work in several fields, including English, foreign languages, biology, medicine, and law, and its university press rates among the nation's finest, especially in the arts. More than a dozen of its departments were rated among the nation's best in a study by the American Council on Education. The university's School of Music has become

internationally known; among its performance series are works staged annually by the Opera Theater. Purdue, organized in 1869 as a land-grant college, is one of the nation's leading engineering and agricultural schools.

Notre Dame, dating from 1842, is widely regarded as the leading Roman Catholic university of the United States. Its faculty in a dozen graduate programs has become recognized at the national level, helping to overcome its image as an institution devoted solely to athletics. Notre Dame, originally a men's school, in 1972 began enrolling women from St. Mary's College, also located in South Bend.

Cultural life. The fine arts flourish in most of Indiana's major cities and even in some of the smaller towns. The Indianapolis Symphony has a respected place among the nation's fine orchestras, and the city also boasts the Indianapolis Museum of Art and the Civic Theater, the nation's oldest continuously operating theatrical organization. South Bend and Fort Wayne also have symphony orchestras, and one of the best known art colonies in the United States is located in Nashville, in the heart of Brown County.

Indiana has made a special contribution to the popular arts in the United States, with the prototypical Hoosier poet James Whitcomb Riley, novelists Booth Tarkington and Lew Wallace, satirist George Ade, and the World War II chronicler of the foot soldier, Ernie Pyle. Some of the country's most popular songs have been written by such Hoosiers as Hoagy Carmichael ("Star Dust"), Cole Porter ("Begin the Beguine"), J. Russel Robinson ("Margie"), Albert von Tilzer ("Take Me Out to the Ball Game," "In the Evening by the Moonlight"), and Paul Dresser ("On the Banks of the Wabash," "My Gal Sal"), brother of the novelist Theodore Dreiser. Among the most notable of Indiana comedians have been Herb Shriner and Red Skelton.

The popular arts

Sports and recreation. Almost every citizen seems to participate in "Hoosier Hysteria," the state's annual high school basketball tournament. Notre Dame, well known for its football talent, vies annually with Purdue and Indiana to provide Hoosiers with exceptional intercollegiate athletics. Indiana University has also become a mecca for basketball and for some of the world's greatest swimmers. At the professional level, Indianapolis is internationally known for the "Indy 500," the world's most spectacular auto race, which is held annually on Memorial Day. The first race was held in 1911, while the city was still an automobile-manufacturing centre. The entire month of May has become devoted to the race, with such attendant events as a major professional golf meet. Indianapolis is also the site of the annual U.S. Clay Court Championships, which attract top international tennis players.

Hoosiers fond of the outdoor world can find haven in walking or camping in its many state parks. Though they were among the leading state parks in the nation in the early part of the century, they have become badly in need of remodelling, expanding, and refurbishing.

HISTORY

Exploration. Archaeologists have discovered remains of the earliest known inhabitants at Angel Mounds, an archaeological site on the Ohio River near Evansville. Early historical records show that Algonkin (Algonquin) Indians organized tribes of the area into the Miami Confederation, which fought to protect the lands from the unfriendly Iroquois. Other important Indian tribes were the Potawatomi and the Delaware. In the 17th century the French made treaties with the Iroquois allowing them to trade with the Miami Confederation.

In 1679 Robert Cavelier, sieur de La Salle, travelled by boat from Michigan down the St. Joseph River. To the south, traders from the Carolinas and from Pennsylvania settled on the Ohio and the Wabash river shores, threatening the French traders, to whom the region was a means of connecting Canada and Louisiana. To protect the route to the Mississippi, the French built Fort-Miami (1704); Fort-Ouiatanon (1719), near present-day Lafayette; and Fort-Vincennes (1732), one of the first permanent white settlements west of the Appalachians.

In 1763 the area, part of what came to be known as the

Northwest Territory, was ceded to England, which forbade further white settlement. The prohibition was largely ignored, and in 1774 Parliament annexed the lands to Quebec. During the American Revolution, Virginia, Connecticut, and Massachusetts made claims on the land, and in 1779 George Rogers Clark secured the area for the rebelling colonies by leading his troops on a surprise march from Kaskaskia to Vincennes.

Territorial period. The Northwest Territory was ceded to the United States by the Treaty of Paris ending the Revolution in 1783, and the following year the first U.S. settlement was established at Clarkville, in the southern part of the state. Warfare between the Indians and the westward-moving whites continued until 1794, when Gen. Anthony Wayne defeated the Indians in a battle near Fallen Timbers, near the present-day Ohio–Indiana line, and the Indians were forced to make land concessions. Increasing numbers of white immigrants from Southern states entered the area after 1800, leading to renewed Indian resistance, and in 1811 the last major encounter, the Battle of Tippecanoe, was fought near Lafayette, with Gen. William Henry Harrison the victor. Between 1820 and 1840 the major Indian tribes abandoned the area. The Ordinance of 1787 creating the Northwest Territory prohibited slavery, but it did not abolish slavery already in existence, and in 1800 the territory had at least 175 slaves. With the end of Indian resistance came rapid settlement and in 1816 statehood. The territorial capital, Corydon, became the first state capital.

Indian warfare

Statehood. The patterns of rural life and local autonomy were established in the first half of the 19th century as settlement progressed from south to north. The utopian community of New Harmony, on the Wabash River in the southwest, was settled by George Rapp in 1815 and taken over by Robert Owen in 1825. In 1801 the first college was founded in Vincennes, and in 1820 Indiana University was chartered. A single-car, horse-drawn railroad arrived in Shelbyville in 1834. The new constitution of 1851, which remains the framework of state government, made it nearly impossible for the state to go into debt, reinforced the powers of local government, and created a tax-supported public-school system. Article XIII of the constitution prohibited the entrance of blacks into the state, but this was struck down by the U.S. Supreme Court, in 1866, as being in conflict with the federal Civil Rights Act of that year.

The period from 1850 to 1900 was one of agricultural and then industrial growth. The Civil War gave impetus to industrialization, and the northern part of the state emerged as a major sector in its own right. With the founding of the steel-making city of Gary in 1906, midway between the iron ore of Minnesota's Mesabi Range and the coal of southern Indiana and Illinois, and with the subsequent development of automobile manufacturing in South Bend, Indiana moved from an agricultural to an industrial base. The isolation, independence, and spirit of Jeffersonian and Jacksonian democracy that underlay the constitution of 1851, however, continued to leave their mark upon the state. The document was written when towns and villages were days rather than minutes and hours apart. It was not until 1970 that annual rather than biennial meetings of the legislature were approved. Other features of the constitution remain impediments to effective management of 20th-century social and political problems, and the ideology of localism is still deeply ingrained. (W.V.D'A.)

Development of rural–industrial dichotomy

Iowa

Iowa is one of the north-central states of the United States, forming a bridge between the forests of the east and the grasslands of the high prairie plains that lie to the west. The state's gently rolling landscape rises slowly as it extends westward from the Mississippi River, which forms its entire eastern border. The state is bounded on the north by Minnesota, on the east by Wisconsin and Illinois, on the south by Missouri, and on the west by Nebraska and South Dakota. Its area is 56,290 square miles (145,790 square kilometres). Des Moines has been the capital since 1857, 11 years after Iowa was admitted as the 29th state of the Union.

The popular image of Iowa—one of corn (maize) and hogs, flat prairies, and conservative people—is not altogether incorrect, but it masks both a subtle variety and the fact that Iowa and its people are very much in a middle position—economically and politically as well as geographically. With 94 percent of its land cultivable—third highest among the states—Iowa became, in the 20th century, a major breadbasket of the United States and of the world, ranking with the much larger states of California and Texas in combined agricultural output. In addition, a large part of its industry is directly related to the field of agriculture, and the population is about equally divided between its rural and urban areas. Iowans are strongly Republican in most years, but they exhibit a lively independence when they feel that the times dictate a different tack. Although Iowa has not shared the full benefits that have accrued from economic and demographic expansion, neither has it been crushed by the periodic economic downswings that have afflicted some of the other regions of the nation.

PHYSICAL AND HUMAN GEOGRAPHY

The land. Iowa's terrain and rich soils are the products of the continental ice sheets that covered the state during the Pleistocene Epoch, between 2,500,000 and 10,000 years ago. All four of the major glacial stages are represented by drift deposits or glacial debris in some portion of the state. The first, or Nebraskan, ice sheet covered the entire state but was in turn covered by the younger Kansan drift, except in the northeastern portion near the Mississippi River. These two drifts filled the preglacial stream valleys, and little evidence of them remains.

Glaciation

The Illinoian ice sheet covered a small area of southeastern and extreme eastern Iowa, and in so doing it diverted the Mississippi and created a temporary valley along its western front that can still be seen. Some 20,000 to 25,000 years ago, the Wisconsin ice sheet moved southward in a lobe that ended at about the site of the present city of Des Moines. Accompanying the last two stages of glaciation were extensive deposits of windblown silt, or loess, which in the western portion of Iowa were derived from the glaciation of the Great Plains that had taken place farther west. As the ice sheets retreated, tremendous quantities of drift carried by the melting waters were deposited in the valleys. These various deposits form the basis of the Iowa landscape and make up the parent materials of the present soils.

Relief and soils. The most varied relief anywhere in Iowa is in the northeastern part of the state, which was covered by Nebraskan ice but escaped Kansan glaciation. The region has been studied intensively by geologists because it retains so much of the character of the preglacial land. There tributaries of the Mississippi cut deeply into the underlying bedrock. The Mississippi bluffs stand 300 to 400 feet (90 to 120 metres) above the valley, and the network of tributaries creates a scenic and hilly landscape.

Surface features

Most of the state is underlaid by Kansan drift, which has been eroded for at least a few hundred thousand years by a network of streams that is extremely dense for a glaciated region. Lakes or swamps that were left by the ice have long since been drained by natural erosion, and the result is a rolling landscape of great uniformity throughout most of the state. Near the Missouri River Valley on the western border, the loess was piled 80 to 100 feet over the underlying drift surface, producing a line of bluffs 100 to 200 feet high. The highest point above sea level (1,675 feet [511 metres]) is in the northwest. The broad, flat uplands—which form the popular image of Iowa—are found mainly in the Des Moines lobe, a gently sloping, poorly drained drift plain that covers 12,300 square miles (32,000 square kilometres) in the central and north central portions of the state. Most of Iowa's lakes are in the northwestern part of this lobe.

Most of the soils of Iowa, formed under prairie vegetation, are thick, dark in colour, and rich in organic matter and minerals. Only in the rough northeast and along the dissected river valleys of the south and southeastern portions of the state are there lighter coloured and less fertile forest soils.

Climate. Iowa's climate reflects the state's position deep in the interior of the continent. Winters are cold, with January temperatures averaging about 15° F (−9° C) in the northwestern section and 25° F (−4° C) in the southeast. Snowfall is relatively light when compared with the amount received in states to the east and north. Summers are warm and more humid, with daytime temperatures throughout the state averaging 75° F (24° C) in July but varying from region to region. Maritime tropical air masses from the Gulf of Mexico bring frequent thunderstorms, with precipitation in June four times that of the winter months. Precipitation ranges from less than 28 inches (700 millimetres) in the northwest to more than 34 inches in the southeast.

Plant and animal life. Countless species of wildflowers cover the prairies, and, though most of Iowa's virgin timber was cut long ago, almost 1,500,000 acres (600,000 hectares) are still forested. The only evergreen is the red cedar, which was once found in profusion along the Cedar River. The state's streams are well stocked with dozens of species of fish, and trapping of muskrat and raccoon for furs is still widespread. The ring-necked pheasant—imported early in the 1900s—and quail are the major game birds, replacing the nearly extinct wild turkey. Small animals and a wide variety of other birds are also found.

Settlement patterns. Although Iowa is not a featureless plain, the relative homogeneity of physical characteristics has led geographers and other social scientists to use the state as an example of large-scale uniformity. Quarter sections of 160 acres (65 hectares) formed the basis of much of the original settlement pattern. Consequently, farmsteads and the smaller towns generally are evenly spaced in the form of a grid, and most of the roads in the state follow a north–south or east–west line. Farmhouses amid the square or rectangular patterns usually have a row of trees serving as a windbreak, as well as providing shade from the bleakly pervasive midcontinental sunlight. The largest city, Des Moines, is sited approximately in the middle of the state, above the widening of the Des Moines River known as Lake Red Rock. The other large cities are on the Missouri and Mississippi rivers at the western and eastern boundaries, or on the Cedar River in the east.

The people. Iowa was settled largely by immigration from states lying directly to the east of it and from northwestern Europe. Until 1850 the southern third of Iowa received many settlers from the border states of the South, particularly Kentucky; but the influx from Ohio, Indiana, and Illinois and the New England and Middle Atlantic states was more important in the northern area. Settlers from Europe took on greater significance after 1850. The single most numerous group came from Germany, but Britain and Ireland were well represented. In the later years of the century, many Scandinavians settled throughout the western and central parts of the state. By 1915 there were few foreign-born people in southern Iowa, except Austro-Hungarians and Italians in the coalfields and Dutch near Pella. The larger of Iowa's cities, particularly those on the Mississippi, attracted a variety of groups.

Several ethnic and religious groups—a good example is the Czech population of Cedar Rapids—are still present in Iowa. Among several experiments in communal living, the only survivors of the first years of pioneer hardship are the Amana colonies, a religious group originally from Germany that migrated to Iowa from Buffalo, New York, in 1855. This group changed to a corporate form in 1932 and has been quite successful in maintaining its integrity while modifying its economy to fit the changing times. The strong religious and social traditions of the Amish group living south of Iowa City and near Independence have come into conflict with modern society over state education laws. Mormons fled through Iowa on their way to Utah to escape further persecution in Illinois and New York, and one large group remained behind at Lamoni, in southern Iowa. Quakers were important in the Springdale–West Branch area east of Iowa City in the mid-19th century. This area was an important link in the Underground Railroad, which helped slaves escape from the South be-

Sources of immigrants (margin note)

fore the Civil War. John Brown often visited there, and Pres. Herbert Hoover was born there of Quaker parents. West Branch is the site of the Hoover Presidential Library.

The only notable immigration into Iowa during the 20th century has been that of blacks to the larger urban centres. More than 10 percent of the populations of Des Moines and Waterloo are nonwhite. Despite state and national civil rights laws, blacks generally live in the decaying urban areas, and in the 1960s there were numerous cases of racial confrontation. Most Indians moved westward after federal land purchases in the 19th century, but some, unhappy with life on the plains, returned to purchase a small reservation near Tama.

Most of Iowa's population is Protestant, because major immigration was from northwestern Europe. Roman Catholics are strong in the northeast, in the Dubuque area, and in the larger cities. In its outlook southern Iowa is more Fundamentalist; this had such social ramifications as the prohibition of liquor by the drink until 1963. The political strength of the more conservative rural areas was weakened considerably by reapportionment of the legislature in the 1960s.

Iowa's population is evenly distributed, a factor that, together with the relative uniformity of the state's physical conditions, has made Iowa an excellent location for the testing of geographic and economic theories. Among the several cities are Des Moines, Cedar Rapids, Davenport, Sioux City, Waterloo, and Council Bluffs. Most of the remainder of the population lives in scattered, evenly spaced small towns or in dispersed farmsteads.

Population distribution (margin note)

The economy. The popular image of Iowa as basically an agricultural state is—unlike many such popular images—entirely correct.

Industry. Iowa is located on the western fringe of the American manufacturing belt, and, although its manufacturing and trade exceed farming in income, much of the former is devoted to food processing or to the manufacture of agricultural machinery. In only a few instances does Iowa contribute significantly to the national economy in areas not related to agriculture. The production of electronic materials in Cedar Rapids, household appliances in Newton, refrigeration equipment in Amana, tires in Des Moines, writing instruments in Fort Madison, and rolled aluminum in Bettendorf are a few exceptions. Exploitation of mineral resources, except for portland cement and gypsum, plays a relatively minor role in the state's economy.

Agriculturally based economy (margin note)

Agriculture. The agricultural position of Iowa on the national scene is based on the feeding and selling of animals. During the late 20th century Iowa ranked second in the nation in total value of all livestock, first in hogs, and second in cattle and calves. Iowa also ranked high in corn for feed, soybeans, oats, and hay.

Management of the economy. The state attempts to aid industrial development and improve the general economic situation in Iowa in a number of ways, including the establishment of trade missions and the Industrial Development Commission. Corporate income taxes contribute a very small part to revenues. The government's debt is low, and the overall labour picture is relatively bright. Unemployment rates and work stoppages tend to lag behind national trends.

Transportation. In the 1920s Iowa developed an extensive rural road system designed to serve the relatively low population density. It now has an excellent system of surfaced roads. There are approximately 5,800 miles (9,280 kilometres) of first- and second-class railroad track. The amount of railroad track in active use, however, has decreased over the years, and many Iowa towns have lost all railroad service. The state also has more than 240 public airports. Inland waterway traffic is important along the Mississippi River, and a nine-foot- (2.7-metre-) deep channel runs up the Missouri to Sioux City.

Administrative and social conditions. *Government.* Iowa's constitution at the time of admission in 1846 proved to be unsuitable, and a second version was drafted and ratified in 1857. This remains the fundamental law of Iowa, though it has been amended numerous times. The constitution provides for a separation of governmental powers into executive, legislative, and judicial components.

In the executive branch the governor, lieutenant governor, secretary of state, auditor, treasurer, secretary of agriculture, and attorney general are elected for four-year terms. A number of commissions, boards, and departmental executives are appointed by the governor, though most employees of the state departments are under a civil-service system. The Iowa Civil Rights Commission investigates charges, holds hearings, and gives decisions on complaints of discriminatory practices in public accommodations, housing, employment, and education.

The bicameral General Assembly meets every year; longer sessions are held in odd-numbered years, when major budget items are decided. The House of Representatives has 100 members elected for two-year terms, while the Senate has 50 members elected for four-year terms. Both bodies are reapportioned every 10 years to ensure compliance with the "one man, one vote" decision of the U.S. Supreme Court.

The state judiciary is headed by the Supreme Court, which has considerable jurisdiction over the lower courts. The nine members of this body elect their own chief justice. Justices are appointed by the governor, are subject to a confirming popular vote one year later, and after an eight-year term may declare their candidacy for another term. There are 13 judicial districts in the state, with the number of judges varying according to population and case load. Most larger cities have municipal courts; the others have police and mayor's courts. Justices of the peace are elected in those townships that lack municipal courts.

Local authority is vested in each county's board of supervisors, under which serve the elected auditor, sheriff, recorder, treasurer, clerk of district court, and county attorney. The county government collects municipal, school, county, and state taxes; manages welfare; and operates the road system in cooperation with the State Highway Commission. Municipalities, deriving their authority from the General Assembly, have only those powers that have been specifically granted to them. This was an issue of considerable contention when the legislature was controlled by rural forces, but after reapportionment in the 1960s the urban–rural discord was much reduced. Most of the smaller incorporated towns have a mayor–council form of government, whereas most of the larger cities have a council–manager or commission administration.

Republican voting record

Iowa's political tradition has been more or less Republican. Between 1848 and 1968, only seven Democrats represented Iowa in the U.S. Senate. The Democrats failed to elect a candidate to the governorship until the Depression of the 1930s. Disquiet over farm prices, however, has elicited a substantial Democratic vote on several occasions.

Welfare. Iowa ranks above the median for the United States in family income, but this is largely due to the significant fraction that is derived from agriculture. The cost of living is generally less than that in metropolitan centres of the East and far West but above that of the South and Southwest.

Welfare is managed on the county level, as are many health services, though federal and state funds support these activities. Health facilities are generally adequate in the larger cities, and especially in the University of Iowa medical centre in Iowa City, but rural areas suffer from a lack of doctors and hospitals. Intensive efforts have been taken to rectify this situation. Hospitals are being upgraded, often with federal support. Most methods to lure doctors into rural practice have proved relatively unsuccessful: about two-thirds of the doctors trained in Iowa medical schools establish their practices in other states.

Education. For many years Iowa's rate of literacy has been the nation's highest. Its first public school was opened in 1830, and its system of tax-supported schools dates from 1834. Iowa ranks above more than half of the other states in per-pupil expenditure, with financing from local property taxes and state and federal supplements. The University of Iowa (founded 1847), in Iowa City, is especially noted for the programs in fine arts, and Iowa State University (1858), in Ames, has shown national and international leadership in the basic sciences, agriculture, veterinary medicine, and related fields. There are also a great number of other public and private institutions

of higher learning; nearly all of the latter have religious affiliations.

Cultural life. A widely dispersed population with relatively small urban centres makes it difficult for Iowans to support many of the cultural amenities that exist in large urban settings. Travelling shows, including theatre and dance, symphonies, and guest artists visit many places in the state each year. The major cultural centres are the large state and smaller private universities and colleges. The fine arts are notably supported at the University of Iowa, where the regional painter Grant Wood (1892–1942) did much of his work and where the Writer's Workshop enjoys a national esteem. Art museums of significance are found in Iowa City and Des Moines. Such towns as Cherokee and Decorah have museums emphasizing the area's presettlement character or the early European settlers, while Davenport, Des Moines, Cedar Rapids, Sioux City, Dubuque, and Fort Dodge have museums or art galleries.

In a region generally lacking large urban centres, sporting events furnish much of the cultural life. The University of Iowa has long been one of the national leaders in basketball and football attendance. In every college town in the state, football weekends form the centre of the autumn social season. High school basketball and wrestling tournaments evoke great community enthusiasm near the end of the long, cold winters. Outdoor sports of all types are extremely popular, with hunting, fishing, boating, and camping especially prevalent.

Folk traditions are maintained in the Amana colonies (Oktoberfest); in the Dutch community of Pella, with its annual tulip festival; among the Czechs of Cedar Rapids; and in other localities.

HISTORY

From territory to statehood. The first Europeans to reach Iowa were probably the French explorers Louis Jolliet and Jacques Marquette in 1673. Permanent settlement, however, did not take place until the early 1830s, though Spanish land grants were occupied in the late 1700s, principally to exploit the lead-mining potential around the site of Dubuque. In the interim, both pioneers and Indians moved through the area exploring or hunting. The combined French and Indian history can be seen in geographical names throughout the state: for example, Des Moines, Dubuque, and Le Mars; Ottumwa, Keokuk, and Onawa.

The area that includes the modern state of Iowa was included in the Louisiana Purchase from France in 1803, and during the War of 1812 a U.S. garrison was driven from Ft. Madison on the Mississippi River. Following the purchase of eastern Iowa from the Sauk and Fox Indians in the 1830s, U.S. settlers rapidly moved in to till the land. The Territory of Iowa was established in 1838, with a population of 23,242. In 1846 Iowa was admitted to the Union as part of a compromise that was reached between the slaveholding South and the free North. By 1860 there were nearly 675,000 people in the state, and with the construction of railroads the frontier was pushed further westward. The population of Iowa more than tripled during the 1850s, and the Spirit Lake Massacre in 1857 marked the final instance of Indian hostility in the state. The years immediately prior to the Civil War were Iowa's frontier days, however, with lawlessness, vigilantes, and lynchings accompanying the unsteady beginnings of a settled society.

Rapid settlement

Iowa was deeply involved on both sides of the issues that led to the Civil War, to which the state contributed more troops in proportion to its population than any other state. No battles were actually fought in Iowa, though a Confederate guerrilla raid from Missouri occurred in 1864.

Economic stabilization. The coming to an end of the Civil War, railroad expansion, and the removal of the Indian threat opened the prairie to settlement by massive waves of immigrants from states to the east and also from northwestern Europe. By 1900 claims to the land had filled the state, and the population showed a slight decline in the decade that followed. The wide use of barbed wire permitted diversified agriculture, and the draining of wetlands began the development of an efficient agricultural production that often threatened the financial stability of the state with too plentiful a harvest. Corn was the basis of Iowa's agriculture from the beginning, nearly all the crop being fed to livestock in order to fatten them for market.

World War I created short-term demands for maximum production and high prices, and since then the state has been plagued with recurring agricultural surpluses, low prices, and high land values. The various economic panics and depressions of the 19th and 20th centuries were only temporary impediments to this pattern of growth. In the past century Iowa politicians have appeared most prominently on the national scene when farm crises have been major issues.

The last significant case of exploitation of natural resources occurred in the coalfields of southern Iowa, beginning in the mid-19th century and reaching its peak in the first two decades of the 20th century. Most of the coal was quickly exhausted, however, and the miners moved on, leaving behind decaying towns and a deteriorating landscape.

After World War I population growth of Iowa slowed considerably. Attempts were made to entice industry into the state to diversify the economy, as animal feeding had diversified agriculture half a century before. Such attempts were not entirely successful, and there is a growing feeling that lack of population growth may be a blessing in disguise—that Iowa can escape many of the problems of environmental pollution and severe economic rises and falls by not encouraging large-scale urban and industrial growth.   (N.E.S.)

Kansas

Lying amid the westward-rising landscapes of the Great Plains of the North American continent, Kansas in 1861 became the 34th state of the United States. In that year the capital was located in Topeka by popular vote, outpolling nearby Lawrence by some 2,700 ballots. The state's 82,264 square miles (213,063 square kilometres) are bounded by Nebraska on the north, Missouri on the east, Oklahoma on the south, and Colorado on the west. The state's name was derived from that of the Kansa, or Kaw, Indians.

Whatever the Kansas slogan, "Midway U.S.A.," lacks in inspiration, it makes up for in aptness. The geographical centre of the 48 coterminous states of the nation is marked by a limestone shaft and a flag located in a pasture near Lebanon, Kansas, close to the Nebraska border. Some 40 miles (65 kilometres) to the south is the magnetic, or geodetic, centre of the terrestrial mass of North America.

Kansans live in what was once looked upon as the agricultural heartland of the nation. After 1952, however, industry contributed more to the economy than the vast wheat fields and cattle ranches of the plains. Wichita, the state's largest city, is known locally as the "Air Capital of the World" because it produces more small aircraft than any other city.

PHYSICAL AND HUMAN GEOGRAPHY

The land. *Relief.* Kansas has been erroneously characterized as a featureless plain, but its topography, while rarely spectacular, is varied. The land rises slowly but steadily from 700 feet (213 metres) above sea level in the southeast to 4,039 feet (1,231 metres) near the Colorado border. The far western section consists of high plains with few natural trees and appears to be flat and endless. Actually these seemingly flat plains are creased with shallow gullies, called draws, the product of millennia of erosion. In this part of Kansas are some of the state's most spectacular geological formations. Castle Rock, south of Quinter, consists of chalk spires rising high above the level plains. Monument Rocks, a few miles to the west, resemble sphinxes. Near Jetmore is Horse Thief Canyon, a miniature of the Grand Canyon.

Millions of years ago, much of Kansas was the floor of an inland sea. The land was built up by the deposit of soil and vegetable matter from streams feeding the sea. This residual soil is some of the most fertile in the world, and in it prehistoric fossils of great importance have been found.

Under irrigation, southwestern Kansas in recent years has produced truck crops and sugar beets. Northeastern Kansas, once covered by the glacier that crept over most of the northern United States, is hilly and timbered, with many creeks and springs. The southeast, lying near the foothills of the Ozark Mountains, is rough and covered in parts with scrub oak. In south central Kansas, near Medicine Lodge, are the Gypsum Hills, which resemble the mesas of the Southwest and are named for the gypsum found in them. In east central Kansas, the Flint Hills stretch from north to south; gentle, rolling, largely treeless, and covered with bluestem grass, they provide one of the world's best natural grazing regions. The principal rivers are the Kansas and the Arkansas. Tributaries of the Kansas are the Blue, the Republican, the Solomon, the Saline, and the Smoky Hill, all in northern Kansas. The Arkansas flows into the state from Colorado and winds through southwestern and south central Kansas, continuing through Oklahoma and Arkansas to the Mississippi. Tributaries of the Arkansas are the Cimarron, the Verdigris, Neosho (Grand), and the Marais des Cygnes.

Climate. The climate of Kansas is temperate but continental, with great extremes between summer and winter temperatures but few long periods of extreme hot or cold. The annual average temperature is 55° F (13° C). The growing season ranges from mid-April to mid-September. Normal annual rainfall ranges from less than 20 inches (500 millimetres) in the west to more than 40 inches in the southeast.

Plant and animal life. Buffalo grass is native in the west and central areas of the state, bluestem around the Flint Hills, and bluegrass in the east. Wild flowers of many kinds are to be found in all parts of the state, and sunflowers grow in profusion (Kansas is popularly known as the Sunflower State). The cottonwood grows throughout Kansas, while in the northeast there are many oak, walnut, and maple trees, as well as cedar and elm. Western Kansas abounds in quail, prairie chicken, and pheasant. Deer, once almost extinct, were protected by law for many years and have multiplied to the degree that hunting is again allowed in season. The buffalo that once proliferated across the plains are to be found only in parks and zoos.

Settlement patterns. Most western Kansas farms or ranches are large, covering not less than one section (a square mile, or 640 acres [259 hectares]) of land, though a farmer's holdings may not always be contiguous. Eastern Kansas began with small farms, some of no more than 40 acres; but these have grown in size. A Kansas law forbids other than family corporations for farming purposes. Most of the small towns are modern and well-kept, with paved streets and full utilities. Many of the small cities, especially in the west, present unexpected cultural and commercial resources, perhaps because they often lie far apart and draw from large trade territories. In the east the cities are older, closer together, and generally less progressive, though most of them are attractive, with broad, well-shaded residential streets and adequate downtown shopping facilities.

Wichita, the largest city, is characterized by the state's largest buildings, biggest industries, and most venturesome businesses. In Topeka, where state government once was the largest industry, more people now are employed in services. Kansas City, Kansas, merges with its larger neighbour, Kansas City, Missouri, and contains a significant part of the industrial complex of that region. Leavenworth, the state's oldest city, is built around institutions, including an army post at Ft. Leavenworth, a federal prison, a state penitentiary, and a veterans' hospital. Lawrence, home of the state's largest university, depends heavily on the school for its economy, though the city has been working aggressively and successfully for industry since the 1960s. Most of the other cities depend primarily on farm trade and agriculturally related business.

Kansas suffered during most of its history from two kinds of regionalism: one that pits rural against city dwellers; the other, the east against the west. The two are related in some ways, for none of the state's principal cities is in the western half of the state. More thinly populated than the east, western Kansas has always feared and fought eastern domination, while the east often has ignored the west.

Loca-
tion and
general
character

Rural and
urban life

Wichita, one of Kansas' three metropolitan areas, contains approximately one-seventh of the state's population. The Kansas City–Topeka area of northeastern Kansas, containing two metropolitan areas, is less populous but still is the centre of much industry. Rivalry has existed between these two urban areas, but it is diminishing gradually as the cities gain more representation in the state legislature. People from the rural areas, mostly farmers, ranchers, and owners of small businesses, as well as residents from the smaller towns, have tended to distrust the cities, often bringing about an impasse in the state legislature.

The people. Kansas' early settlers were principally antislavery New Englanders of Anglo-Saxon stock. After the Civil War and with the building of the railroads, many central Europeans were attracted by the promise of jobs laying track and of free land when the jobs were finished. Small communities populated by citizens of predominantly Russian, Bohemian, German, or Scandinavian ancestry still dot the state. The original languages have largely disappeared, though here and there church services are still conducted in German or Swedish, and a few communities hold festivals each year at which the old folkways, foods, and languages are featured. During World War II there was an influx of servicemen and aircraft workers, many of whom remained. The state is largely Protestant, though there are some small Roman Catholic communities. Virtually every sect is represented in the state, including such rare ones as the Amish, Dunkard Brethren, Mennonite, and Eastern Orthodox.

Because of insufficient employment opportunities, Kansas loses a considerable number of its young people to other states, but this loss is almost balanced by in-migration. The birth rate, however, produces a slight natural increase in population in most years. The most conspicuous demographic trend is from the farms to the cities. As further technological advances in farming are made and individual landholdings increase in size, this trend undoubtedly will continue.

The economy. *Agriculture and industry.* Both agriculture and manufacturing contribute significantly to Kansas' economy—the former contributing many of the raw materials for the latter. The production of its farms and ranches places Kansas first among the U.S. states in wheat and first in sorghum grains. It also ranks high in wild hay, beef, and hogs. Some 4,300 manufacturing and processing plants produce everything from airplanes to zinc castings. Wichita is the world's largest producer of camping gear; it also manufactures heating and air-conditioning equipment, snowmobiles, and a variety of other products. In addition to ranking first in the world in production of small private aircraft, Wichita also is an important manufacturing centre for military aircraft. Other plants in the state turn out baby foods, pet foods, prefabricated houses, mobile homes, greeting cards, tires, paint, and dishwashers. Grain milling, though not as important as it once was, still is a major industry, and the meat-packing and processing industry is growing.

Kansas has large mineral resources, a good labour force, a healthy retail trade, ample electrical power, plenty of water, and a central location. Kansas is among the 20 top mineral-producing states. It is rich in oil and gas, helium, portland cement, stone, clay and clay products, sand, salt, gravel, zinc, bituminous coal, and lead. There is an almost unlimited supply of chalk. Many plants produce gasoline, oil, grease, and paving materials from the oil pumped from Kansas wells.

Despite large oil production, Kansas has imposed only a small severance tax (laid at the time of severance, or extraction from the ground) on oil or gas for the purposes of conservation and pollution prevention. It has a tax rate on manufacturing plants that compares favourably with that of other states. Most Kansas cities issue revenue bonds to encourage new industry. The state has a right-to-work law that forbids compulsory unionism.

Two long-established army posts have contributed significantly to the state's economy. Ft. Leavenworth, with its renowned Command and General Staff College, dates from 1827. The fort was a major outpost in the early Indian wars and during the Civil War and has offered the

most sophisticated training to field-grade officers for many years. Ft. Riley, near Junction City, was established in 1853 and was also an Indian outpost. In the 20th century it has been an important infantry training centre. During World War II air force bases were established in Topeka and Wichita.

Transportation. Kansas has an excellent system of railroads for east–west transport but, except in the east, has less adequate north–south lines. The same may be said of its highways, with the best ones generally carrying east–west traffic. An exception is the state's single toll road, the Kansas Turnpike, which runs southwesterly from Kansas City to the Oklahoma line south of Wichita. Although Kansas has more than 200 airports and is served by eight airlines, the only major airport with transcontinental service is in Wichita.

Administrative and social conditions. *Government.* Kansans elect a governor, lieutenant governor, attorney general, and secretary of state, while other state officers are appointed. Its legislature comprises 125 representatives and 40 senators, the former elected for two-year terms, the latter for four-year terms. The legislature holds a session in odd-numbered years and meets for a briefer period in even-numbered years. Each of the 105 counties elects three commissioners, a county attorney, a treasurer, and several other officers. Judges of the 29 judicial districts are elected, but the seven justices of the Supreme Court are appointed by the governor, subject to senate approval, from a panel presented by a Supreme Court nominating commission. The justices must subject themselves to the approval of the voters, but none has ever received a vote of "no confidence." If that were to happen, the justice would be replaced by appointment.

The first legislative council in the United States was inaugurated in Kansas in the 1930s. It was an interim body designed to work between legislative sessions at analyzing and drafting laws. Several other states later adopted legislative councils. The 1969 legislature provided for prefiling of bills between sessions, a change that persuaded the legislature that the council was no longer necessary. It was replaced in the 1971 session by the Legislative Coordinating Council, made up of the leadership of both houses.

In 1933 Kansas enacted a "cash basis law," which requires that no state money be expended until it has been raised and appropriated by the legislature. Bonds have been issued only for capital improvements, such as college dormitories and highways, in which case they are retired by user fees.

Kansas once was known as the most Republican state in the nation, but it now has a sizable Democratic minority, a growing independent vote, and small Conservative and Prohibition parties. The first legislature, in 1861, gave women the right to vote in school elections. In 1887, women's suffrage was extended to city and bond elections, and in that year the world's first woman mayor was elected in Argonia. The state constitution of 1861 granted women equal rights to own property and to have control of children. Universal suffrage was granted in Kansas in 1912.

The Farmers' Alliance and the Populist Party both had their origin in Kansas, and for a few years in the 1890s they played an important part in the politics of the Midwest. Kansas pioneered the direct primary, and a Kansas senator introduced the resolution in the U.S. Congress that put direct election of U.S. senators into the federal Constitution.

Kansas was the first state to adopt the constitutional prohibition of alcoholic beverages. The prohibitory amendment was added to the state constitution in 1880 and was not repealed until 1948. Liquor is sold only in package stores operated by licensed individuals under strict state control. Drinkers have little difficulty slaking their thirst, however, in a multitude of "private clubs" that operate under state license.

Education. A landmark civil rights case of the 20th century, *Brown* v. *Board of Education*, originated in Topeka in 1951, when the clergyman father of a nine-year-old black girl led her to the door of an all-white school. She was denied enrollment, and the decision that was handed down by the U.S. Supreme Court in 1954—basically stat-

---

Margin notes:

Migrations past and present

Innovations in government and law

ing that segregated, even "separate but equal," education is inherently unequal and must be eliminated with all due speed—became the basis for most of the civil rights decisions that have been applied to schools since that time.

In the mid-1960s Kansas abolished its office of state superintendent of public instruction and substituted the Department of Education headed by a commissioner and an elected state board of education. More than 400,000 pupils attend public schools in the some 300 school districts throughout the state. A number of two-year junior colleges are operated by the communities in which they are located.

Universities and colleges

Kansas has six state universities. Fort Hays State University, Kansas State University of Pittsburg, and Emporia Kansas State University offer liberal arts degrees but specialize in training teachers. The University of Kansas is located in Lawrence, Kansas State University in Manhattan, and Wichita State University in Wichita. Kansas State, recognized as having one of the country's leading agricultural colleges, was the first land-grant college in the United States. The state's medical school is part of the University of Kansas College of Health Sciences and Hospital, with its campus at Kansas City. In 1971 the School of Medicine established a second campus at Wichita to expand its clinical teaching facilities. There are two law schools, one at the University of Kansas, the other at Washburn University of Topeka, a municipal school. In addition, there are 17 private four-year colleges in Kansas, all church-affiliated and all offering liberal arts degrees.

Health and welfare. The State Board of Health, consisting of appointive members, supervises the activities of one of Kansas' largest administrative departments, including doctors, dentists, sanitary engineers, hospital administrators, and veterinarians. Kansas operates three mental hospitals; they have been rated among the best in the nation and work in close conjunction with the renowned Menninger Foundation of Topeka. The health education division supplies information films on preventable diseases and distributes an equal number of pamphlets on subjects related to health. The board of health also has divisions of geriatrics and chronic diseases, hospital facilities, and services in public health nursing, nutrition, maternal and child health, mental hygiene, sanitation, and tuberculosis control.

Since 1862 Kansas has had some form of public assistance for the needy. The state welfare department, which is overseen by an appointed board, offers both financial assistance and special education to those requiring it. Special divisions care for crippled children, dependent children, the aged, and the blind. Vocational and rehabilitational services also are provided for the handicapped. There are schools for the mentally retarded at Parsons and at Winfield, and a children's home has operated at Atchison since 1855. There is a Kansas treatment centre for mentally disturbed children at Topeka and a reform school for girls at Beloit.

The state has a fair-housing law and a civil rights commission that hears grievances and attempts to mediate them.

Cultural life. The citizens of Kansas resent the suggestion that they live in a cultural desert, but the assertion is at least partially true. Most of the larger cities have amateur theatre groups, while Topeka and Wichita support symphony orchestras. The numerous colleges and universities in the state provide a concentration of art and music in many small communities that otherwise would have no comparable activities. In the sparsely populated areas of western Kansas, however, a large number of the small communities have few cultural institutions except a public library. Wichita, however, has two art galleries and a cultural and civic centre with two theatres, an exhibition hall, and a convention hall. Civic music series are sponsored in most of the larger cities of Kansas, but most professional road companies appear in theatrical productions only in Wichita. The extreme eastern areas of Kansas mainly rely upon Kansas City, Missouri, for cultural attractions. In the mid-1960s the Kansas Cultural Arts Commission was formed; funded by the state, it seeks to encourage the development of the arts, often providing seed money for communities or organizations that have

the desire to develop cultural events. The University of Kansas has an outstanding museum of natural history and an art museum.

In addition to an art gallery, the small community of Lindsborg has a biennial folk festival, the Svensk Hyllnings Fest, which honours the Swedish pioneers who settled the town. It features Swedish costumes, traditional food, folk dances, and displays of the arts and crafts of local artisans. Wilson has a Czech festival each year. Examples of bizarre sculpture are found in Lucas, where a self-taught artist, working in wet concrete, sculpted his own idea of the Garden of Eden and other biblical stories.

Traditional commemorations

HISTORY

Indians, explorers, and settlers. Archaeological exploration has uncovered evidence of Indian cultures that existed in Kansas for many centuries before the Europeans settled on the land. From about 1200 to 1500 there had been a thriving agricultural society in the area of the Republican and Blue rivers.

The first known European explorers were Spaniards under Francisco Vázquez de Coronado, who in 1541 rode northward from Mexico seeking the gold of the legendary Seven Cities of Cíbola. Juan de Padilla, a priest with the expedition, founded the first mission in the territory, possibly north of present-day Wichita. The territory was claimed for France in 1682 by Robert Cavelier, sieur de La Salle. During the 18th century French fur traders had a flourishing exchange with the Indians in what is now the northeastern part of the state.

The region passed to the United States as a part of the Louisiana Purchase in 1803. The explorer Zebulon Montgomery Pike passed through Kansas in 1806 and described it as the "Great American Desert"—a false image that still persists, to the dismay of the state's boosters. Kansas was thoroughly explored during the following decades, but westward-bound settlers and miners passed through it without staying.

From 1830 to 1854 Kansas was in an area designated as Indian Territory, actually an area in which to relocate Indian tribes who occupied lands wanted by whites. The Kansas–Nebraska Act of 1854, however, created two territories and opened both to settlement. It also provided that residents could determine whether their future states would be free or slave. The rush began, and Kansas became a major breeding ground for the U.S. Civil War as North and South each attempted to send the most settlers into the new territory. Most early settlement was near the eastern border, and free staters were harassed constantly by "Border Ruffians" from Missouri. One notable incident was the sacking of Lawrence by Southern guerrillas in 1856. The abolitionist John Brown, with his sons and a few other men, retaliated by dragging five of their proslavery neighbours from their homes and killing them. Proslavery forces attempting to avenge this massacre were captured by Brown, who became a hero to the Northern sympathizers. Hundreds of such incidents won the territory the name "Bleeding Kansas."

Statehood. Kansas entered the Union as a free state in 1861. Before and after the Civil War, sporadic fighting occurred between the settlers and the Indians. In 1867 a peace treaty was signed in which the Indians agreed to sell their land; in return, the United States agreed to build homes for them in what is now Oklahoma and to provide money, food, and clothing. The U.S. Congress did not honour the treaty, and when the Indians returned they found their land occupied by white settlers. Further sporadic battles continued until the last Indian raid, in 1878.

Early settlers in wooded eastern Kansas lived in log cabins, but in the west they had only dugouts or houses made of buffalo-grass sod. The unpredictable weather, the recurring Indian raids, the droughts and dust storms, and the grasshopper invasions discouraged many early settlers. One of the heroes of this era was William Mathewson, known as the original Buffalo Bill, who hunted buffalo for the settlers all of one winter without pay, providing meat by the wagonloads. The coming of the railroads in the late 1860s and the 1870s made first one village and then another into boisterous cow towns. Texas cattlemen drove herds northward to Caldwell, Wichita, Dodge City, Ellsworth, Newton, and Abilene to reach the railhead. Although this development brought prosperity to Kansas and created a persistent image, the cow-town era lasted less than a decade.

The most important event in Kansas' agricultural history may have been the arrival of the Mennonites in 1874, who brought with them trunks full of hand-selected grains of Turkey Red wheat. This excellent strain provided the basis of the abundant crops that became an important part of the Kansas economy. Many of the Mennonites' descendants remain as prosperous farmers.

By about 1890 most of the land was occupied, and Kansans settled into a peaceful life dominated by agriculture. World War I produced a great demand for food, and more and more virgin prairie was plowed and put Expansion into production, which led to temporary prosperity but of contributed directly to the terrible dust storms that devastated the state in the 1930s. World War II contributed to Kansas' growing eminence in aircraft and brought many people from Oklahoma and Arkansas to work in Wichita's aircraft plants. (C.G.P.)

Michigan

Since its admission in 1837 as the 26th state of the Union and the fourth to be carved from the Northwest Territory, Michigan has become a mainspring in the economic life of the United States; the name of its largest city, Detroit, has become a byword throughout the world for the U.S. automotive industry. The state also has retained its prominence in agriculture, and, because of its many inland lakes, its borders on four of the five Great Lakes, and its many wilderness tracts, Michigan has evolved into one of the nation's leading tourist regions.

Michigan is the only one of the 49 continental states to be split into two large land segments: the sparsely populated but mineral-rich Upper Peninsula, which slices east-The Upper ward from northern Wisconsin between Lakes Superior and Lower and Michigan, and the mitten-shaped Lower Peninsula, peninsulas which reaches northward from Indiana and Ohio. The two landmasses have been joined since 1957 by "Big Mac," the five-mile (eight-kilometre) Mackinac Bridge across the Straits of Mackinac, which separate Lake Michigan to the west from Lake Huron to the east. Between Lake Huron and Lake Erie, in the southeast, the Lower Peninsula is separated from the Canadian province of Ontario by Lake St. Clair and the St. Clair and Detroit rivers. The state's name is derived from an Ojibwa (Chippewa) Indian word meaning, approximately, "large lake." Though its 58,216 square miles (150,779 square kilometres) rank the state only 23rd nationally in size, the inclusion of Great Lakes waters over which it has jurisdiction raises the figure to 96,791 square miles (250,689 square kilometres), placing it 11th.

More than 70 percent of the state's residents live in urban areas, with a heavy concentration in the industrialized centres of the Lower Peninsula. This factor, together with a broad array of ethnic and national stocks among the people and a high number of lesser skilled workers attracted to Michigan by the union-dominated labour scene, has created in many cities the typical marks of economic progress and poverty existing side by side, with a sometimes tenuous social stability. The state government, in the capital of Lansing, coordinates a vast network of programs attempting to reduce these contrasts, and it has provided a system of public higher education that is among the most diversified and renowned in the nation.

PHYSICAL AND HUMAN GEOGRAPHY

The land. *Relief.* The mildly rolling country appealed to the early agricultural settlers. Even the elevations are not high. The highest point in the Lower Peninsula, near Cadillac, rises only about 1,200 feet (370 metres). Elevations rise to 2,000 feet only in the western Upper Peninsula.

Several physical features of Michigan are unusually appealing to lovers of scenic beauty. The sand dunes on the Lake Michigan shore are used annually by thousands

of vacationers, and approximately 3,000 state and local parks throughout the state, containing nearly 4,000,000 acres (1,619,000 hectares) of wooded land, include varied landscapes that have helped Michigan to become a major tourist attraction of the Midwest.

Drainage. Michigan's rivers, the majority of them in the southern portions of the Lower Peninsula, drain vast interior areas. Most of them are rather shallow and narrow. Their navigability and the ease of bridging them were factors that encouraged settlement. Several of the rivers, especially in the Upper Peninsula, have sufficient falls to serve as a basis for water power.

Michigan's 11,000 inland lakes range from a few acres in size to the 19,000 acres (7,700 hectares) of Houghton Lake in the north central part of the Lower Peninsula. The shores of many lakes are ringed with summer cottages, as are the shores of the Great Lakes in many places. Two of the scenic recreational areas in the state include the Pictured Rocks National Lakeshore on Lake Superior and the Sleeping Bear Dunes National Lakeshore on Lake Michigan.

About 500 islands dot the lakes and rivers. Belle Isle, a public recreation centre, and Grosse Ile, largely residential, are well-known features of the Detroit River. Mackinac Island is a resort on which motor vehicles are prohibited. Isle Royale, a virgin wilderness of nearly 850 square miles, is a national park in northern Lake Superior.

Climate. The Great Lakes cool the hot winds of summer and warm the cold winds of winter, giving Michigan a milder climate than some other north central states. Though the Upper Peninsula is cooler, the temperature ranges in the far northern and far southern cities do not differ excessively. Northern Sault Ste. Marie has an average maximum temperature of about 50° F (10° C) and an average minimum of 30° F (−1° C). In Detroit, in the southeast, the maximum temperature averages about 58° F (14° C), and the minimum averages 42° F (6° C). The greatest amount of moisture is received in southern Michigan, and the state's average is about 33 inches (838 millimetres). The central portion of the state has less precipitation than does the Upper Peninsula, and the coastal strip along Lake Michigan receives an unusually large snowfall from westerly storm fronts moving across the lake. The growing season ranges from approximately three months in the Upper Peninsula to as long as six months in the more southerly portions of the Lower Peninsula.

Plant and animal life. Animals native to the area are numerous. Whitefish in abundance swim in the Great Lakes, and many of Michigan's streams contain various edible trout. The Conservation Department operates hatcheries and encourages tourism around the inland lakes, where carp and bass abound. The beaver was sought eagerly by early traders, and other fur-bearing mammals were also found in large numbers. Deer, as well as quail and ducks, remain numerous in many counties. Some 80 out of 83 Michigan counties were once heavily wooded, with genuine prairies or clearings found only in southwestern Michigan. Hardwood timbers included the hickory, ash, oak, and hemlock, though the white and Norway pine were the most common timber in the north.

Settlement patterns. Many of Michigan's people think Geo-of their state as divided into the Upper and Lower Penin-graphical sula, but the two physiographic divisions, the Superior divisions Upland and the Central Lowland, follow this plan only in part. The Upland comprises only the rugged western region of the Upper Peninsula, where the abundance of copper and iron ores has made the area economically dependent on the mining industries. Calumet, Hancock, Houghton, and Marquette are among the better known cities of the area. Agriculture is of little significance, but tourist and recreational potentialities offer some possibilities for diversifying the economy.

Geographical as well as historical forces unite the eastern counties of the Upper Peninsula and the Lower Peninsula north of a Bay City–Muskegon corridor to create the area popularly known as "northern Michigan." There the white-pine forests were ruthlessly exploited. Some agriculture is successful, for even the sandy soil, with adequate moisture, can produce an abundant yield of potatoes and grain. Fruit-growing in the region near Traverse City has succeeded because Lake Michigan's influence prevents early killing frosts. The towns serve as regional centres for tourists and farmers and often as headquarters for governmental services. Many of the larger communities have attracted small-scale manufacturing. Thriving cities include Sault Ste. Marie, Petoskey, Ludington, Manistee, and Cadillac.

South of the Bay City–Muskegon corridor a fertile clay soil and a longer growing season permit a wider variety of crops, especially grains. The southern agricultural counties, resembling those of northern Ohio and Indiana, produce much of the state's agricultural wealth. The region also contains the great industrial concentrations, and large cities are numerous. As in Detroit, the sixth largest city of the United States, the automotive industry played an important role in the growth of Flint and Lansing. Grand Rapids attained prominence through its furniture industry, and Battle Creek is known nationally for its cereals. The majority of the cities, however, have more widely diversified industries than their reputations might suggest.

The people. The diverse backgrounds of Michigan's people, in nationality, religion, and ethnic stock, has been important in shaping the state's character. The percentage of foreign-born and first-generation citizens is small, however, even in Detroit.

Germans, the most numerous of the early non-English-speaking immigrants, settled in both rural and urban areas. Detroit had a large German community by the mid-1830s, as did several rural counties by 1850. The large Irish population remained basically urban, although Irish farmers were found in southern Michigan and by 1860 in the Upper Peninsula. Other groups left an impact, though their numbers were not large. Dutch influences are still observable in western counties around Holland, where Dutch settlers pioneered successfully in 1847. Finns have been important in the economic and cultural life of the Upper Peninsula. Early Polish immigrants settled in rural areas until the 1890s, when a large number of Poles concentrated in Detroit. The city's present-day population includes many people of Polish ancestry.

The most significant population phenomenon of the 20th century has been the growth of the black population from fewer than 16,000 in 1900 to well over over 1,000,000 in the late 20th century. More than 60 percent live in Detroit, which had become nearly two-thirds black by the late 20th century. Many blacks have moved to suburbs that have had long-established black neighbourhoods and substantial black populations. They also have moved into older neighbourhoods where the prices of homes are not exceptionally high. The trend has been similar to that in the central city, where blacks continue to replace whites. The majority of the newer Detroit suburbs, however, have very small black populations, since the price of housing is generally more than what many blacks can afford.

Michigan's religious history differs somewhat from that of many of the other Midwestern states. Since the first European settlers in Detroit were Roman Catholic, many immigrants of that faith were attracted to the city even before the large Irish, Italian, and Polish immigrations of the 19th century. Detroit was made a diocese in 1833 and an archdiocese in 1937. Other dioceses were established at Marquette, Grand Rapids, Lansing, Saginaw, Gaylord, and Kalamazoo. Of the Protestant denominations, Lutheranism has had many German and Scandinavian adherents, while Methodism has been important in both rural and urban Michigan. The Baptist Church has a large membership throughout the state. The first Dutch settlers were members of the Christian Reformed Church, which was opposed to the state church of the Dutch. The Michigan group was highly independent and conservative in its doctrine and social mores. Altogether, Michigan has almost 200 Protestant denominations, some with only small memberships. The first Jewish immigrants to come to Michigan were of German background. In 1851 Detroit Jews founded a synagogue. Synagogues throughout the state reflect all shades of Jewish theological persuasion.

The economy. *Resources.* With new methods of iron-ore processing, Michigan's huge mineral reserves should be exploitable through the end of the 20th century. Some deposits of gypsum for cement have not been touched, and the continuing search for petroleum and natural gas may yield rich new fields.

Agriculture. The fertile soils will probably continue to make Michigan a major agricultural state. The future of Michigan's agriculture is, however, dependent in part on prices. Many farmers work part-time in industry or for the government, supplementing their income and providing an important factor in the economy of many rural communities.

Industry. Many reasons have been advanced for the rise of the automotive industry in Detroit. The city long had been noted for the manufacture of carriages, wagons, bicycles, and marine engines. The large number of skilled and semiskilled labourers was another important factor. Other cities, however, offered inducements equal to those of Detroit, and in fact, during the pioneering phase of the industry, Detroit had a number of rivals.

Unquestionably, personalities played a major role in making Detroit the world's automotive centre. The industry began with Ransom E. Olds of Lansing, whose father manufactured gasoline engines. Subcontractors found themselves pioneers in this new and profitable industry. Olds's success by 1901 focussed the attention of automotive people on Detroit. Henry Ford brought even greater fame. Organizing the Ford Motor Company in 1903, he was by 1908 confining production to the standard, low-priced Model T. He emphasized ease of repair, garage service, and the utility of his product. In that same year W.C. Durant of Flint recognized that the automobile would be purchased by persons who desired transportation rather than by faddist motorists. He hoped through the formation of a company with large-scale capital to speed up technological advances and thus capture a large portion of the untapped middle-class market. The General Motors Corporation stands as a testimony to his thinking. The successful Michigan manufacturers succeeded because their models were designed for a national market, whereas many companies had models that could not be operated in mountainous country.

The industry paid high wages, and many automotive workers became members of the middle class. Because of the high wages there was little interest in unionism until the Great Depression of the 1930s.

Michigan's tourist industry, which ranks as the state's second largest industry, is dependent largely upon water resources threatened by pollution.

Management of the economy. The state government encourages a climate that is favourable to economic expansion. Many sections of the government maintain research divisions that offer assistance to various segments of the economy. The Department of Agriculture administers a division of animal health, a division of marketing, and a division of soil conservation. The state tax structure has been evaluated as one that makes an attempt to avoid discrimination against the private sector of the economy. For the labour sector Michigan has had a workers' compensation law since 1912. Extensive programs of social legislation, including unemployment compensation, were undertaken in Michigan before World War II and have since been broadened.

Transportation. The first railroad in Michigan, the Erie and Kalamazoo, was completed between Toledo and Adrian in 1836, and by 1870 the state had more than 1,600 miles of rail. The peak of 9,000 miles in 1910 was reduced to about 4,000 (6,400 kilometres) in the late 20th century.

In contrast, the gains in motor-vehicle ownership have been staggering. State and local governments have combined to give Michigan a modern system of state highways, county roads, and city streets. The interstate express system has been built largely with federal assistance.

Air passenger service in Michigan began in 1926 with flights scheduled between Detroit and Grand Rapids. Detroit Metropolitan Wayne County Airport services millions of airline passengers annually, and there are some 20 other major airports throughout the state and several small commuter air lines. Much of the air freight of metropolitan

Marginal notes:

The growing black population

Natural resources

Air services in Detroit

Detroit is handled at the Willow Run Airport, a facility constructed as a bomber site during World War II.

The waterways, the sole basis of travel for the first pioneers, still carry tremendous tonnage, with many of the state's exports shipped from Detroit's harbour. Ores and other bulk materials destined for the interstate trade are generally sent by water.

Administrative and social conditions. *Government.* Michigan has more than 2,600 local governmental units, including counties, municipalities, townships, school districts, and such special districts as park authorities. The basis of this complex system is the new constitution of Michigan, ratified by the voters in 1963. The new document included a number of innovations designed to streamline the government and to make it more responsive to the problems of a modern industrial and urban society. Amendments may be submitted to the electorate by the legislature or by initiative petitions, but all amendments must be approved by a referendum of the voters.

Executive power is vested in the governor, who serves for four years. This official is nominated by a primary election, but the lieutenant governor is chosen by party convention. The governor appoints a large number of administrative commissions that are responsible to the executive and to several advisory commissions. The majority of the important governmental services are combined under departments responsible to the governor. A few of these bodies, such as the State Highway Commission, must be bipartisan.

The legislative branch comprises the Senate of 38 members elected for four-year terms and the House of Representatives of 110 members elected for two-year terms. The legislative districts are redefined by a special bipartisan commission after each federal census. The highest court is a seven-member state supreme court. The state also has a court of appeals, a circuit court, a probate court, and courts of limited jurisdiction that are specified by the legislature.

Local government

The organization of units of local government in Michigan is very flexible. Though the majority of counties are governed by a board of supervisors, the home-rule privilege allows larger counties to entrust management to county commissioners. Extensive privileges of home rule are authorized for the cities as well. School districts are classified by population and enjoy differing privileges of government.

The precinct is the primary unit in the structure of political party organization, and the precinct delegates carry considerable importance in the annual party conventions. These conventions nominate the candidates for lieutenant governor, attorney general, and the members of the boards that govern the state system of higher education and the Board of Education. They also nominate justices of the Supreme Court, but these nominees do not bear a partisan label on the ballot. The state party conventions also select delegates to the national presidential conventions.

A new interest in politics has resulted from the civil rights movement and from the formation of coalitions among college students. The civil rights groups have been responsible for a new awareness of politics on the part of black voters. Blacks have been nominated for major state and local offices by both parties; the first black mayor of Detroit was elected in 1973. Unions have been very active in Michigan politics, and the UAW has endorsed candidates at the municipal, state, and national levels.

Finance. The personal and corporate income tax is the major source of general revenue, though receipts from the sales tax play a major role in assuring the financial structure of the state. Gasoline and vehicle taxes are reserved exclusively for highways.

Welfare. Michigan devotes a major portion of its annual budget to social programs. A mental institution in Kalamazoo that received patients as early as 1859 was a forerunner of a number of other institutions caring for the needy. Since 1936 many of the state welfare services have followed a federal formula in transmitting aid to units of local government. Payments to recipients of old-age assistance, for example, and aid to dependent children, the blind, and the disabled have required special personnel at the state level, though disbursal of most funds is done locally.

Education. Education is one of Michigan's major governmental services. Many of the legislature's major appropriation bills are for support of the numerous public institutions of higher learning and the many community colleges. Large sums, however, are returned to the local districts to enable public elementary and secondary schools to maintain a high standard. Many of these schools, both in the inner-city areas and in the suburbs, are under frequent study for the identification of problems, and experiments in improved methods of instruction are often conducted by educators and psychologists from the state's universities.

Higher education

The greatest of the monuments to Michigan's cultural heritage, combining the traditional and the popular, are its some 90 colleges and universities, both public and private. In 1817 Judge Augustus Woodward, one of the major figures in the state's early history, conceived of the idea of a "Catholepistemiad," an academy of universal knowledge. This was achieved in some measure in 1841, when the University of Michigan opened its doors in Ann Arbor. During the 20th century it has come to be widely regarded as one of the nation's, and perhaps the world's, finest universities, with programs on both the undergraduate and graduate levels. In 1852 a teacher-training institution began instruction at Ypsilanti, and in 1857 Michigan Agricultural College, now Michigan State University, was formally established in East Lansing. The latter shares much of the wide regard of its rival in Ann Arbor, having moved far beyond its early identification with agriculture in many areas of research and scholarship.

Several teacher-training institutions became state universities during the 20th century, as did the Michigan Technological University at Houghton. In 1956 the state acquired Wayne University, a Detroit municipal university, founded in 1868. Wayne State University, as it was renamed, has fostered much educational experimentation, and in the 1960s its campus and physical plant were landmarks in U.S. educational architecture through the designs of the Japanese-American architect Minoru Yamasaki.

Michigan is also the home of widely recognized specialized schools. In 1927 the School of Music was founded in Interlochen, the forerunner of the National Music Camp that now offers instruction in music, dramatics, and related arts. The Cranbrook and Kingswood schools, in Bloomfield Hills, designed by Eliel Saarinen, pioneered advanced art courses for students of high-school age.

Cultural life. Detroit dominated the cultural life of early Michigan. Many of its citizens had the leisure and wealth that allowed them to devote time to cultural pursuits, and the multifacetted backgrounds of its population gave it a cosmopolitan atmosphere. The state's first travelling theatrical companies performed in Detroit, and an opera house was erected there before the Civil War. In 1819 the Young Men's Society was organized by Lewis Cass, who led many early civic endeavours, to promote debates, lectures, and general intellectual life.

The cultural milieu

The pioneer farmers, however, had little time for cultural pursuits. Many respected only the more elementary aspects of cultural life that might have utilitarian value—the community dance that eased the strains of plowing or harvesting, the county fairs that provided a ritual summation of the year's achievements. Thus Michigan's culture, perhaps like that of the nation as a whole, tended to become broadly based on popular life, having many of the aspects of "mass culture." In the major parks the city of Detroit promoted band concerts and, later, symphony concerts to bring other types of music to thousands. The Detroit Institute of Arts, maintained municipally, has always emphasized exhibits that appeal to a broad public.

With the emphasis upon popular culture, Michigan increasingly is commemorating its past. The Michigan Historical Commission has designated sites of historic importance, such as the location of battles and the first home of the Ford Motor Company. Many cities emphasize Homecoming Day, usually the anniversary date of the incorporation of the community. Local folk festivals have been given a greater emphasis. Holland's Tulip Festival,

Folk and regional festivals

held each May, has become an event of more than local importance. The annual Bavarian Festival, in Frankenmuth, appeals to others besides those of German background. Traverse City sponsors a popular Cherry Festival, and the Lake Huron cities commemorate the lumbering era with their highly publicized Paul Bunyan Days. Many ethnic groups in Detroit and other cities sponsor folk festivals that recall their cultural ties to Europe. The Afro-American Museum in Detroit is a continuing reminder to the black population of its distinguished heritage extending far back into the pre-American centuries.

The Detroit Institute of Arts, which can be traced to a private museum established in 1889, holds one of the nation's major collections. In 1969 it was the recipient of the Robert. Hudson Tannahill collection, which included Picassos, van Goghs, Cézannes, Renoirs, and Degas, as well as works by Rouault, Modigliani, Rousseau, Manet, Chardin, and Corot. The institute also has noted Baroque, African, and German Impressionist collections. The Muskegon Museum of Art, founded in 1911 by a wealthy philanthropist, the Kalamazoo Institute of Arts, and the Grand Rapids Art Museum are among other art museums that have won recognition. Lansing is the home of the Michigan Historical Museum, famous for its military and Indian collections, while many county museums commemorate local history.

The state library was founded in 1828. A state library board was created in 1936, but major public libraries are found only in the larger cities. Among the outstanding special libraries are the William L. Clements Library at the University of Michigan, a depository for records pertaining to the American Revolution, and the Burton Historical Collection of the Detroit Public Library, specializing in local history and genealogy.

HISTORY

In the 17th century the Indian population of what is present-day Michigan was estimated at between 12,000 and 15,000. The majority of these Indians, including the Ottawa, Ojibwa, Miami, and Potawatomi, belonged to the Algonkian linguistic group or family. A lesser number, located primarily in southeastern Michigan, were Hurons and Wendats (Wyandots). The Ottawa and Ojibwa, hav-

French heritage

ing been conditioned extensively by their Great Lakes environment, were of great assistance to the French in the development and expansion of the fur trade. The Ottawa, with their primitive commercial interests, had developed a type of canoe that was highly serviceable in the Great Lakes area. The Miami and Potawatomi Indians were identified more with the culture of the woods. The Hurons were the most advanced in their agricultural practices. All of the Indians of the Michigan area lived in small communities and were lacking in the concept of territorial boundaries.

Settlement. Étienne Brulé, the first European to visit the area (1622), was the forerunner of numerous explorers, missionaries, and fur traders who paved the way for French control over Michigan. The oldest community in Michigan is Sault Ste. Marie, founded in 1668 at a site where in 1641 missionaries held services for 2,000 Ojibwas. In 1701 Antoine de la Mothe Cadillac established Detroit as a fur-trading centre and administrative post; it soon became the leading French community in the entire Great Lakes area.

In 1760 the French garrisons were surrendered to an English force, and in 1763, by the Treaty of Paris, England acquired jurisdiction over Canada and the French empire east of the Mississippi River except for New Orleans. Under English rule Michigan remained a part of Canada, and a handful of English-speaking traders helped to give Detroit and other communities a more English character. During the American Revolution Detroit was a major supply centre for British troops who raided the Kentucky country until 1779, when the British general Henry Hamilton was captured.

U.S. territory. Although Michigan had been awarded to the United States in 1783, the British refused to leave Detroit and other major military posts until 1796. In 1787 it was made a part of the newly created Northwest Territory. Indian opposition to U.S. rule in the area was ended

by the victory of Anthony Wayne at the Battle of Fallen Timbers, near present-day Toledo, Ohio. After 1796 the Americanizing of the regions was accomplished within a few years. Detroit became the capital of the Michigan Territory, which was separated in 1805 from Indiana. Although the first governor, William Hull, surrendered Detroit to the British early in the War of 1812, American rule was restored late in 1813 by the victory of Commodore Oliver Hazard Perry at the Battle of Lake Erie.

Process of Americanization

The real growth of Michigan Territory began soon after the war. The personality of the new governor, Lewis Cass, and the encouragement that he gave to settlement helped to promote its growth. New modes of transportation were even more significant. In 1818 steamship navigation linked Detroit and Buffalo, New York, inaugurating a new era in lake transportation. Cass's crude highway chain from Detroit to Chicago, Saginaw, and Port Huron helped to establish the patterns of settlement in the interior. Completion of the Erie Canal in 1825 made Detroit a leading distribution point for settlers seeking new homes in the Great Lakes area.

Statehood and growth. Michigan was anxious for statehood in order that it might undertake a more ambitious program of internal improvements. The first constitution was drafted in 1835, but admission to statehood was delayed until 1837 by the Toledo War, a boundary dispute with Ohio. In return for relinquishing its claims to the mouth of the Maumee River, at Toledo, Michigan was awarded the western half of the Upper Peninsula as well as the eastern portion, which was historically part of the territory.

The state grew rapidly through the 1840s and 1850s. Thousands of prospective agricultural settlers, including many foreign-born, established new homes in the state. Detroit and other leading cities profited, and in the 1840s the rich iron and copper resources of the Upper Peninsula became known. Tension over the slavery issue resulted in the formation of the present-day Republican Party at Jackson in July 1854. The new party captured the Michigan delegation to the U.S. Congress and immediately made impressive nationwide gains.

Throughout the U.S. Civil War, Michigan made major contributions to the Union cause, losing some 14,000 of its 90,000 men who served. A black regiment from Michigan included enlistees from many states and from Ontario. The Republican Party become dominant after the war, and in the 1890s Hazen Pingree implemented progressive legislation as the mayor of Detroit and subsequently as governor.

The 20th century. Before 1900 all of Michigan's 83 counties had been settled. Agriculture, lumbering, mining, and manufacturing created a stirring economic tempo. Throughout the 20th century the economy has been modified greatly and often dominated by the automotive industry, which has contributed further to the rapid growth of Detroit, Flint, and other cities. During World War I, industrial production at all levels was intensified. The emergence of new problems connected with this urban–industrial growth was recognized by features of the new constitution approved in 1908.

Increasing economic tempo

The 1920s were characterized by more economic expansion and a new urban sophistication, as both state and nation continued to lose their rural character and values, and urban crime rates began to rise. The Great Depression was unusually severe in Michigan, the industrial products of which were not among the necessities of life. Unemployment and deflation were far above the national averages: early in 1933, one-third of Detroit's labour force was unemployed.

In 1932 Michigan departed from the Republican fold, and thereafter it became one of the doubtful, or swing, states. Organized labour became a powerful political and economic factor during the 1930s. In 1937 the United Automobile Workers (UAW) became the bargaining agent for production workers at General Motors Corporation, and by the outbreak of World War II it was the dominant union in all automotive plants. During the war Detroit became known as the "Arsenal of Democracy," and industrial production continued at a peak afterward to restock the nation with new cars and other war-depleted consumer goods.

In Detroit the inner-city population reached its peak during the early 1950s. An influx of blacks to war plants in the area created social tensions that brought on a major race riot in 1943, and in 1967 another major racial disturbance resulted largely in burning and looting. Other cities had less severe disorders in following years. Large-scale layoffs in the auto industry during the late 20th century particularly affected Detroit's black population.   (S.Gl.)

Minnesota

Near the heart of North America, Minnesota lies at the headwaters of the Mississippi River, which flows southward to the Gulf of Mexico; the Great Lakes, which drain eastward to the Atlantic Ocean; and the Red and Rainy rivers, which flow northward into Hudson Bay. The state's 84,068 square miles (217,735 square kilometres) are bounded on the north by the Canadian provinces of Manitoba and Ontario, on the east by Lake Superior and Wisconsin, on the south by Iowa, and on the west by North and South Dakota. With a small extension on the northern boundary, Minnesota is the most northerly of the 48 coterminous U.S. states. The state is dominated by a single large metropolitan area, the Twin Cities of Minneapolis and St. Paul (the capital) and their suburbs, where about one-half of all Minnesotans live.

Minnesota is a land of rugged winters, innumerable lakes, and iron mines. The variation from cold winters to warm summers and the nearly 5,000 square miles of inland water—more than that of any other coterminous state except Texas—serve as pacemakers for the way of life in Minnesota. About one in four Minnesotans has some Scandinavian blood, but Germans comprise the largest ethnic stock in the state. Flour milling, which was symbolic of the state's economic dominion over the vast grain belt to the west and northwest, reached its peak in 1920, when Minneapolis was the world's leading producer of flour; since then, however, milling has declined into a relatively unimportant role in the economy of the state. At one time Minnesota's Mesabi Range produced more than one-half of all the iron ore in the world, but the high-grade ores in the range have been almost completely depleted.

PHYSICAL AND HUMAN GEOGRAPHY

The land.   *Relief.* Although it straddles three continental watersheds, Minnesota's elevations range only from 600 feet (180 metres) above sea level, at Lake Superior, to 2,300 feet (700 metres), at Eagle Mountain. Most of Minnesota was at one time covered with glaciers, and the surface of the land was shaped by the movement and the melting of those glaciers. Among the major remnants of these glaciers are the many thousands of lakes, some 15,300 of which are more than 10 acres (four hectares) in area. The greatest glacial moraine development in Minnesota stretches from Albert Lea, in the south, northward to the Twin Cities area; then westward and northward through Willmar, Glenwood, Alexandria, and Detroit Lakes; eastward to Park Rapids and Leech Lake; and south to Mille Lacs Lake. The greatest of the lake plains is that of Lake Agassiz, which existed in glacial times along the Minnesota–North Dakota border and is now known as the Red River Valley. In northeastern Minnesota there are many areas of bare rock, stream valleys, and deep, clear lakes that were scoured by glaciers from the landscape. Extreme southeastern Minnesota was the only unglaciated part of the state. There, streams have cut their way through layers of limestone for thousands of years, and steep, rocky bluffs rise to heights of 500 feet or more above the valleys.

Climate.   The surprisingly great variations of temperature and growing season that occur not only seasonally but also from one part of the state to another reflect the fact that the state stretches from the edge of the sub-Arctic forest to the heart of the Corn Belt. The northeastern part of the state lies in the moist northern Great Lakes storm belt, while the western border lies at the edge of the semiarid Great Plains.

In July average daily maximum temperatures range from

85° F (29° C) in southern Minnesota to 80° F (27° C) in the northwest to 70° F (21° C) along the shore of Lake Superior; minimums in the same areas are, respectively, 60° F (16° C), 55° F (13° C), and 50° F (10° C). Average daily January highs range from 25° F (−4° C) in the south to 15° F (−9° C) in the north; minimums are from 5° F (−15° C) to −5° F (−21° C). The average frost-free periods range from less than 90 days in parts of the north to more than 160 days in parts of the south. The average annual precipitation ranges from more than 30 inches (750 millimetres) in the southeast and the extreme northeast to less than 20 inches in the northwest. Average seasonal snowfall ranges from less than 40 inches in the western part of the state to more than 70 inches in the extreme northeastern tip. Most parts of Minnesota have continuous snow cover for at least 90 days, from about mid-December to mid-March.

Soils.   The most fertile soils in Minnesota are to be found in the grassland regions of the south and west, where they are rich in organic matter and high in soluble mineral plant food. Soils that have formed beneath the coniferous forest in northeastern Minnesota are light coloured, acidic, and low in organic matter, while those formed in the hardwood areas are intermediate in colour and natural fertility.

Plant and animal life.   Minnesota stands astride one of the major physical geographic boundaries in the world, the sharp transition from forest to prairie in the heart of North America. The natural vegetation of Minnesota may be divided into three general categories: needle-leaf forests, hardwood forests, and tallgrass prairie. The needle-leaf forests originally occupied the northeastern third of the state and included pine, spruce, and fir, with tamarack in the bog areas. A belt of hardwoods extends from southeastern Minnesota to the Canadian border, passing through the Twin Cities and lying immediately to the south and west of the coniferous forest. The hardwood forest is known as the big woods and averages some 40 to 80 miles in width. It consists primarily of oak, maple, and basswood. South and west of the hardwood forests lies the tallgrass prairie.

Belts of forest and prairie

Mammals include black bears, moose, deer, lynx, wolves, coyotes, wildcats, porcupines, foxes, squirrels, hares, rabbits, muskrats, opossums, minks, weasels, skunks, raccoons, and woodchucks. The last native woodland caribou in conterminous United States disappeared from Isle Royale between 1927 and 1929. Among the game birds are quail, grouse, ducks, geese, coots, brant, woodcocks, snipe, and plover, as well as imported Chinese ring-necked pheasants. Of songbirds the favourites are the robin, thrush, bobolink, oriole, chickadee, meadow lark, catbird, bluebird, wren, and warbler. Among fish, whitefish, walleyes, lake trout, perch, herring, sunfish, bass, smelts, sturgeons, pike, chub, suckers, mullets, sheepshead, and carp abound in the lakes. Speckled, brown, and rainbow trout thrive in many of the streams.

Settlement patterns.   During a century of white occupancy, virtually all of the prairies were cultivated. The coniferous forestlands, mostly cut by 1920, have become covered again by aspen, birch, and jack pine, while much of the big woods has been cleared for crops and pasture. Minnesota reached its peak in cultivated farmland in 1945. Since then the agricultural frontier has retreated, and farms have been abandoned in the less fertile areas in north central and northeastern Minnesota. The big woods area has become primarily a dairying area. Within 100 miles (160 kilometres) or so of the Twin Cities, dairying has intensified, but beyond that—and particularly in west central and northwestern Minnesota—dairying has declined in importance. The prairie areas of southern and southwestern Minnesota have a characteristically Corn Belt crop and livestock agriculture.

The people.   The New England Yankees who first settled Minnesota were businessmen and lumbermen who helped establish the institutions and many of the traditions that remain important in Minnesota. The first major immigrant groups in the latter half of the 19th century were German, Swedish, and Norwegian; they were primarily farmers and tradesmen.

The
ethnic
blend

The German settlers dominated the push up the Mississippi, continuing into the central and south central parts of the state. Norwegian settlers moved westward across the southern tier of counties, forming the major ethnic group in west central Minnesota and the Red River Valley. The major area of Swedish settlement is in five or six counties immediately north of the Twin Cities area. Substantial numbers of Finns live in northeastern Minnesota, Poles in central Minnesota, Bohemians south of the Twin Cities area, French and French Canadians just north of the Twin Cities and in northwestern Minnesota, Dutch and Flemish in parts of southwestern Minnesota, Icelanders in northwestern Minnesota, and Danes and Swiss in scattered pockets.

These ethnic groups influenced the distribution of religious denominations throughout the state. Central and south central Minnesota are heavily Roman Catholic, reflecting the German, Polish, and Bohemian populations. German ethnicity is also manifest in the Lutheran Church—Missouri Synod membership throughout the state. The American Lutheran Church has many members in southern and western Minnesota, reflecting the Norwegian population. Swedish communities are predominantly followers of the Lutheran Church in America. Many of these ethnic clusters have retained a high degree of purity in the rural areas. They have been sources of population movement to urban areas, but they have attracted few inmigrants to alter the original stock.

The larger and growing urban areas—the Twin Cities area, in particular—have been built from many different ethnic groups and have become major areas of cultural contact and variety. These urban centres also have attracted populations not found in significant numbers in the rural areas: Ukrainians, Irish, Italians, Greeks, Jews, blacks, and Spanish-Americans. The Indian population, numbering about 35,000 is primarily Ojibwa; of that number, about one-half live in urban Twin Cities neighbourhoods. Slightly more than 1 percent of the population is black, about 90 percent of whom live in the Twin Cities area.

The economy. The economic growth of early Minnesota was related closely to the exploitation of the primary natural resources: agriculture, minerals, and timber. These activities, in turn, stimulated the growth of such ancillary activities as railroads, processing of natural resources, and services. During the late 1960s and early 1970s activities based on natural resources, as well as railroads and associated manufacturing, began to decline. By the late 20th century, however, the business of agriculture was still Minnesota's largest industry; one in three employed persons worked in agriculture or related industries.

Mining. By 1951 Minnesota was producing 82 percent of the nation's iron ore, and, as the high-grade ores have been depleted, the seemingly unlimited reserves of low-grade ore, or taconite, have been developed. During the late 20th century Minnesota was producing more than two-thirds of the nation's iron ore, mostly low-grade processed ores. Related activities include sand and gravel, granite, and limestone quarrying.

Industry. Although fewer than one in five workers is employed in manufacturing, the growth rate of manufacturing in Minnesota exceeds the national rate. The Twin Cities area dominates the state in manufacturing and accounts for more than one-half of the state's employment, but growth has been greater outside the metropolitan area. The service and government sectors have grown steadily. The effect of these changes is an employment growth in Minnesota above the national rate.

Minnesota is a net exporter of agricultural commodities such as meat, dairy, and grain products, as well as iron ores and goods tied to natural resources, including pulp and paper and primary metals. It is a net importer of most manufactured goods not tied to natural resources—with such exceptions as electrical machinery and instruments. No coal, oil, or natural gas is produced in Minnesota, and the geologic formations are such that the discovery of such minerals is highly unlikely.

Probably no region in the country is so dominated by one urban centre as is the upper Midwest by the Twin Cities in wholesaling, finance, and cultural activities. This multistate region includes western Wisconsin, Minnesota, northern Iowa, North and South Dakota, and eastern Montana. No urban area in the region approaches the Twin Cities area in population. The continued growth of the Twin Cities area has been partly a result of its regional dominance and partly a result of the diversified economic base that contributes to its economic stability. At the same time the Twin Cities area in many ways is becoming more closely tied economically to other major urban centres in the nation and the world.

Multistate
domination
by Twin
Cities

Transportation. The movement of people and goods in Minnesota and the upper Midwest is centred on the Twin Cities area. Regional and transcontinental rail and highway systems radiate outward from the Twin Cities, tying the towns and hamlets into one interdependent network. Independent of this major transportation network is the rail system of northeastern Minnesota, which brings iron ore and taconite products for transshipment by boat at the Lake Superior ports of Duluth and Superior. Wheat from the Dakotas and Montana also has been an important product transshipped from rail to boat at Duluth. Since the opening of the Great Lakes waterway to ocean vessels in 1959, products of the upper Midwest are carried directly to locations throughout the world.

River transportation was the first important mode for the movement of both people and goods in many parts of the state. Barges on the Mississippi carry bulk products to and from the major inland ports at St. Paul and Minneapolis. Carried upstream are such bulk products as coal, oil, and salt; grain, sand, and gravel are transported downstream.

The Twin Cities area, also the air hub of the upper Midwest, is served by several commercial airlines. The Minneapolis–St. Paul International Airport is supplemented by a satellite network of eight additional airports. Several other communities in Minnesota are served by smaller airports.

Administrative and social conditions. *Government.* Minnesota has two constitutions. The constitution of 1974 was a restructuring and rewording of the original constitution of 1858. Despite the change, the two documents are similar, and the original document retains final authority in constitutional disputes. Minnesota's constitutional law provides for an executive branch consisting of a governor, a lieutenant governor, a secretary of state, an auditor, a treasurer, and an attorney general, all of whom are elected for four-year terms. The heads of the 20 executive departments are appointed by the governor.

Executive,
legislature,
and
judiciary

The Minnesota legislature convenes in odd-numbered years for 120 legislative days. The House of Representatives comprises 134 members elected for two-year terms; the Senate has 67 members elected for four-year terms. Two political organizations compete for seats in the legislature: the Democratic-Farmer-Labor Party, and the Independent-Republican Party.

The judicial branch comprises the Supreme Court, district courts, probate court, county courts, municipal courts, and justices of the peace. Nine justices—a chief justice and eight associates—constitute the Supreme Court; each is elected for a six-year term.

The state's 87 counties range in size from 155 square miles of land area to 6,092 square miles and in population from more than 3,000 to about 1,000,000 people. Counties and municipalities provide many of the local governmental services, but townships assume some authority for planning and zoning and for maintenance of public works, parks, and hospitals. The number of school districts has been declining steadily through consolidation, especially in rural areas. Special districts, much fewer in number than in many states, provide for sewers, conservation, water supply, fire protection, parks, airports, and mosquito control.

Finances. One of the most difficult problems facing Minnesota is meeting the increasing cost of government and increasing the sources of revenue that support government. Traditionally, Minnesotans have been willing to tax themselves at a high rate to obtain needed public services, but inequities have existed in the abilities of local governments to provide those services. Several important legislative acts have been based on an equalization concept. In 1967 a bill establishing a metropolitan council in the Twin Cities metropolitan area was passed, and in 1969 the concept of regional cooperation was extended to 10 other multicounty areas of the state. These other regions are gradually becoming established on a voluntary basis. In 1971 a revenue-sharing bill required that 40 percent of the property-tax revenue from newly located industries within the Twin Cities metropolitan area be returned to the area and redistributed to municipalities and school districts. Another tax bill passed in 1971 stipulated that state funds rather than local property taxes were to pay the major costs of operating local school districts.

The Twin Cities Metropolitan Council, the members of which are appointed by the governor, is responsible for the development of certain area-wide services that local government is unable to provide, including sewage and water systems, transportation, and major land uses. It plays a coordinating and regulatory role among the more than 350 local governmental jurisdictions within the Twin Cities area.

Social issues. Among Minnesota's most significant characteristics is its political environment and high degree of citizen involvement in public affairs. These traditions were established by the early settlers from New England, who brought their town-meeting form of government to this new frontier. That foundation was reinforced by the Scandinavian and German immigrants, with their ambition and high regard for education. Government has always been accepted as the legitimate means for public decision making in Minnesota, and business has played an important role as a strong participant in public decisions.

The traditions of citizen involvement can be seen in the many neighbourhood and community organizations and ad hoc issue-related groups in the state and in the relatively large number of Minnesotans of national political prominence. Minnesota has been a leader in such national movements as those to guarantee the rights of women, homosexuals, and American Indians. The average Minnesotan is usually well informed about public issues. As a result the political parties usually have focussed their attention on the visible public issues, thus maintaining a political system in which neither major party has been dominant over an extended period.

Education. The University of Minnesota was established in 1851, with its main campus in Minneapolis. Together with the smaller St. Paul campus, the Twin Cities campus has the largest daytime enrollment of full-time students in the country—more than 50,000 students during the early 1980s. Smaller branches of the university are located in Duluth and Morris, with four-year programs, and in Crookston and Waseca, with two-year programs.

To the six four-year Minnesota state colleges in smaller cities across the state, the legislature in 1971 added a seventh in the Twin Cities metropolitan area. This "college without a campus" utilizes diverse physical facilities throughout the area, bringing higher education to the neighbourhoods. In addition, the state operates large systems of junior colleges and of post-secondary vocational–technical schools. Twenty-five private four-year colleges and eight private junior colleges supplement the public system.

Health and welfare. The Twin Cities and Rochester serve as national health care centres. The Mayo Clinic in Rochester, famous for its comprehensive approach to health care, has served patients from around the world since the late 19th century. The University of Minnesota Hospitals complex in the Twin Cities area has been a pioneer in medical research, while numerous hospitals across the state provide an effective network of medical care.

Several studies have ranked Minnesota high among the states in the quality of health and welfare services. The reports have praised the state's high standard of general medical services, its extensive children's health and welfare programs, and the support given to assistance programs for the elderly.

Cultural life. Cultural life in Minnesota is highly diversified and seasonal. Many activities are outdoor oriented; they include swimming, boating, canoeing, camping, hunting, fishing, and winter sports. Minnesota ranks fourth among the states in the number of fishing-license holders, and it has more boats per capita than any state except Michigan. A high proportion of Minnesotans own second homes on one of the state's many lakes and streams, which are easily accessible to the urban centres. Voyageurs National Park, authorized by Congress in 1971, is located along the Canadian border.

Whereas "outstate" Minnesota—beyond the Twin Cities area—serves as the outdoor playground for the state, the Twin Cities area serves as the centre of cultural institutions. The best known musical organization is the Minnesota Orchestra, which was formed in 1903 as the Minneapolis Symphony Orchestra and has been acclaimed as among the finest symphony orchestras in the nation. Other important musical organizations include the St. Paul Chamber Orchestra, the Schubert Club, the Minneapolis Civic Orchestra, the Center Opera Company, and the Duluth Symphony. Colleges and universities throughout the state make substantial contributions to the arts within their communities and regions.

The Twin Cities area has nearly a dozen resident professional theatres. The best known is the Tyrone Guthrie Theatre Company, formed in 1963. The Children's Theatre Company is nationally recognized as one of the finest of its kind. The Minnesota Dance Theatre and the Northern Theatre Ballet Company are resident dance companies in the Twin Cities.

The Minneapolis Institute of Arts, the Walker Art Center, and the Minnesota Museum of Art are among the most important art museums in the state. Other major museums that serve the Twin Cities area include the St. Paul Arts and Science Center, the Bell Museum of Natural History, the Minnesota Historical Society, the American Swedish Institute, the Natural History Museum and Planetarium of the Minneapolis Public Library, the University of Minnesota Landscape Arboretum, and the Como Zoo and Conservatory.

HISTORY

Until the middle of the 19th century, two major Indian tribes occupied what is now Minnesota: the Ojibwa (Chippewa) in the north and east and the Sioux in the south and west. Between the time of European exploration and statehood, the Ojibwa occupied the forested areas of the state and pushed the Sioux southward and southwestward onto the prairie. Indians of tribes from as far away as the Appalachians and the Rocky Mountains met in a sacred place of peace in southwestern Minnesota to quarry a hard red rock that was used for making peace pipes; today this area is preserved as the Pipestone National Monument.

European settlement. Investigation of the Kensington Stone, found in west central Minnesota in 1898 and bearing inscriptions allegedly made by Norsemen who penetrated the continent in the 14th century, has proved it to be a forgery. The earliest verifiable Europeans in the area were 17th-century French explorers who were searching for a Northwest Passage. The first white settlement was made where the French fur traders known as voyageurs had to leave Lake Superior to make a nine-mile (15-kilometre) portage around the falls and rapids of the Pigeon River, the longest portage in their transcontinental water route.

The first permanent U.S. settlement was at Fort Snelling, a military outpost that was established in 1819 overlooking the Mississippi and Minnesota rivers; the site of this first settlement has been restored as a state park. Immigration into the region was slow during the first half of the 19th century, but, once the value of the vast forestlands of northern and central Minnesota was realized, lumbermen from New England, seeking to exploit the pine, balsam, and spruce forests that covered nearly 40 percent of the land, led a large wave of permanent settlers. An additional quarter of the state was covered with noncommercial hardwood.

Territory and state. Minnesota became a territory in 1849, its boundaries at that time reaching as far west as the Upper Missouri River, but most of its approximately 4,000 white settlers were located in the Fort Snelling–St.

Citizen involvement in politics

Prevalence of outdoor life

Diversity of Indian tribes

Paul area in the eastern part of the territory. The lumber industry developed rapidly, and major sawmills were soon built at Stillwater, on the St. Croix River, and at the Falls of St. Anthony, on the Mississippi River, the major source of waterpower in central North America. The two villages at the falls were merged in 1872, with the village of St. Anthony on the east bank being absorbed into the larger and more aggressive city of Minneapolis on the west bank.

Minnesota became a state in 1858, its boundaries being cut back from the Missouri to the Red River. The most rapid period of settlement in Minnesota was during the 1880s, when homesteaders—many of whom were recruited from Germany, Sweden, and Norway—rushed into western and southwestern Minnesota. In the same period, lumbering was at its peak and flour milling, using power provided by the St. Anthony falls, was becoming important. Both Minneapolis, as the lumber, milling, and retail centre, and its neighbouring city of St. Paul, as the transportation, wholesaling, finance, and government centre, tripled in population during the 1880s. The rivalry between the two cities became particularly intense after the census of 1880, when Minneapolis surpassed St. Paul in population.

Commercial iron-ore production began in Minnesota in 1884 at Soudan, on the Vermillion Range. After the huge iron reserves of the Mesabi Range were discovered at Mountain Iron in 1890, large-scale production began, and the population along the Mesabi Range and in the Lake Superior port cities of Duluth and Superior grew rapidly during the next two decades. Most of the valuable pine, balsam, and spruce in central and northeastern Minnesota had been cut before 1900, after which time the lumbering industry declined rapidly in importance. Wood products, however, remained important in northern and northeastern Minnesota.

The 20th century. The mechanization of agriculture and changes in transportation technology had significant effects in Minnesota. The former allowed greater productivity for farm workers, resulting in increased farm size and a decline in farm population. New modes of transportation improved the accessibility of all parts of the state, thus accelerating urbanization and extending the commutation zones for many miles around the growing urban areas. These two factors have had a particularly important impact on the density and location of population and the economic activity in the state in the 20th century. The impact was apparent after World War I, with the great popularity of the automobile, but was repressed during the Depression and World War II. From 1945 to 1970 the impact of these factors was particularly dramatic; urban areas grew while rural areas thinned out. Since 1970 the urban population has increased only slightly, suggesting that the rural-to-urban trend may have peaked.

(N.C.G./Ed.)

Missouri

Near the centre of the conterminous United States, Missouri is the meeting place of the timberlands of the East and the prairies of the West, of the cotton fields of the South and the cornfields of the North. It has represented the political and social sentiments of a border state since its admission as the 24th member of the Union in 1821. The question of its admission as a slave or free state produced in Congress the Missouri Compromise (1820), which regulated the spread of slavery in the western territories.

Missouri was the westernmost state of the nation until the admission of Texas in 1845, and for decades it served as the eastern terminus of the Santa Fe and Oregon trails, over which tens of thousands of explorers and settlers plunged deeper into the frontier. For the West, St. Louis, Missouri's largest city, long was its closest contact with the more settled society and the culture of the East, and for the East the state had a reputation as the chief gateway to the West.

The Missouri River cuts across the state from Kansas City in the west, through Jefferson City (the state capital) in the centre, to just above St. Louis in the east, where the river joins the Mississippi. With the exception of Tennessee, Missouri has more neighbouring states than any other U.S. state. To the north lies Iowa; across the Mississippi River to the east, Illinois, Kentucky, and Tennessee; to the south, Arkansas; and to the west, Oklahoma, Kansas, and Nebraska. The area of Missouri is 69,686 square miles (180,486 square kilometres). Slightly more than half of Missouri's population lives in the two major cities, St. Louis and Kansas City, and their surrounding counties, and about 15 percent live in smaller urban areas.

Among its neighbouring states, Missouri ranks second only to Illinois in the degree of urbanization and the amount of industrial and economic activity, though it maintains a vigorous and diversified agriculture. The rugged Ozark Plateau is a scenic beauty, and many lively folk traditions persist among its communities. Missouri retains numerous conservative characteristics of the rural life that predominated prior to the 1930s. In Missouri, as in the Southern states, the Democratic Party does not necessarily represent more liberal political philosophies than the Republicans, and the latter have made inroads into the traditional Democratic orientation. Continuing low tax bases prevent the elaboration of social services, a problem felt most acutely in the two major cities, which have had an increasing loss of wealth to the suburbs, coincident with greatly expanding needs of the cities.

Comparisons with neighbouring states

PHYSICAL AND HUMAN GEOGRAPHY

The land. *Relief.* North of the Missouri River, Missouri's landscape is characterized by gently rolling hills; open, fertile plains; and well-watered prairie country. South of the Missouri, except in the extreme southeastern corner of the state and along the western boundary, the land is rough and hilly, with some deep, narrow valleys and clear, swift streams. It is a region abounding with caves and extraordinarily large natural springs. Much of the land is 1,000 to 1,400 feet (300 to 425 metres) above sea level. Near the western border, however, the elevation rarely exceeds 700 to 800 feet, and southeastern Missouri is a part of the alluvial plain of the Mississippi, less than 500 feet.

Drainage and soils. Drainage and soil conditions permit farming in all of Missouri's counties, although the Ozark Plateau only supports subsistence farming because of the region's thin soil. Northern Missouri is generally well drained, much of it covered by rich soils. The alluvial soils in the bottom lands along the many rivers and streams, which some soil experts believe to be the most extensive in the nation, also add to the farming potentiality. Except for the rivers that flow southeasterly into the Mississippi, many through Arkansas, the Missouri drains most of the state.

Missouri's many lakes have been created by damming rivers and streams. The Lake of the Ozarks is a large artificial lake, with an area of 65,000 acres (26,000 hectares) and a shoreline of 1,672 miles (2,690 kilometres). Most have been built primarily to furnish hydroelectric power and to prevent flooding, but they provide Missouri with excellent recreational resources. Many natural springs, some of them among the largest in the world, have a daily flow in excess of 1,000,000 gallons (4,000,000 litres) each.

Climate. Missouri is susceptible to the influences of cold Canadian air; of warm, moist air from the Gulf of Mexico; and of drier air from the southwest. Though winds are variable throughout the year, summer winds generally blow from the south and southwest, whereas winter winds come from the north and northwest. Rainfall, usually sufficient for crops, varies from around 35 inches (890 millimetres) in the north and northwest to 45 or more inches in the extreme southeast. About one-third of it falls in April, May, and June. Heavy snows are unusual, most snow occurring in February and March. While Missouri does not have as many tornadoes as Oklahoma and Kansas, it does lie in "Tornado Alley," the zone of maximum occurrence, and has an average of 27 tornadoes annually. Maximum January temperatures range from about 35° F (2° C) in the north and northwest to 48° F (9° C) in the southeast. The extreme northwest usually has cooler summers than the southeast, but summer temperatures well above 100° F (38° C) may occur in any part of the state.

Plant and animal life. Originally, about two-thirds of Missouri was forested, and the remainder was covered with prairie grasses. The river bluffs and canyons of the Ozark Plateau have a wide variety of unusual plants. Fameflower, royal catchfly, Trelease's larkspur, coneflower, gayfeather, and fringed poppy mallow are limited in their normal distribution to the Ozark Ridge. Trelease's larkspur and the coneflower are found only in Missouri. Elk, deer, bison, and bear once were plentiful, as were such smaller animals as beaver, otter, and mink. After settlement and the development of agriculture, most of the larger animals, with the exception of deer, disappeared, and animals with valuable fur were trapped until extinction.

Settlement patterns. Missouri's regions reflect the ethnic, religious, and political persuasions of the residents.
The "Bootheel," the Ozarks, and other regions
The "Bootheel" in the extreme southeast was settled by planters from the South and was appended to Missouri at the time of statehood through the great influence of one planter; it is the centre of Missouri's cotton culture, which has declined due to cotton disease and is being replaced primarily by the cultivation of soybeans. The Ozark Mountains area, whose rugged terrain is unsuited to extensive agriculture, has been among the poorer regions of Missouri, but it constitutes one of the great tourist attractions of the state. "Little Dixie" is a block of counties that lies generally north of the Missouri River and extends westward along its banks to the middle of the state. It was initially settled by persons sympathetic to the South, to slavery, and to Democratic politics. Some of the finest examples of antebellum residences are found there. South of Little Dixie, on the bluffs and uplands south of the Missouri River and west of St. Louis, is a concentration of German settlements, known traditionally as the "Missouri Rhineland." In the western part of the state, north and east of the Missouri River, is "Mormon Country." There, followers of Joseph Smith settled around 1831, first at Independence and subsequently in other counties, until they were driven out by hostile neighbours. In the centre of the state, around Boonville, Franklin, and Columbia, is the "Boone's Lick Country," where the frontiersman Daniel Boone and his sons moved from Kentucky to make salt.

Human settlement has altered Missouri's landscape significantly. Only one-third of the state remains forested, mostly on the hills and slopes of the Ozarks. Nearly all of the prairie land has been brought under cultivation. The damming of streams has produced numerous lakes and reservoirs, and in the southeast, drainage systems have converted former swamps into one of the state's richest agricultural regions. Agriculture in the state traditionally has been characterized by family-owned farms, but, as elsewhere in the nation, the number of farms has been decreasing, while acreage and productivity per farm have increased. Urbanization also has reduced the amount of land available for agriculture. Although urban settlements are scattered throughout the state, Kansas City and St. Louis are Missouri's important centres of commerce and manufacturing and the nuclei of large metropolitan areas that extend into Kansas on the west and Illinois on the east.

The people.
Patterns of immigration
After the early French settlers, immigration came largely from states to the east and northeast, as well as from the South, with the implantation of its type of economy and society in the Bootheel and in Little Dixie. The first immigrants from abroad—particularly Germans, Irish, and English—came in great numbers after 1820. By 1860 large groups of Germans had settled in Missouri, mainly in St. Louis and immediately to the west, while many Irish had settled in the city. Between 1860 and 1870 the immigration from Ohio, Illinois, and Indiana exceeded that from the upper South, while an increasing number of immigrants from Germany arrived, most of them settling in urban centres. Subsequently, St. Louis and Kansas City attracted sizable communities of Italians and Greeks as well as Poles and Jews.

Missouri has been affected by the northward migration of many blacks from the rural South. From 1940 to 1960 the white population increased by 11 percent, whereas the nonwhite population increased 62 percent. By the late 20th century blacks made up 10 percent of the state's total population, largely concentrated in St. Louis and Kansas City.

It is not unusual that a crossroad state should exhibit great religious diversity. The Roman Catholic Church, which was dominant until the Louisiana Purchase, remains powerful, particularly in the St. Louis and Kansas City areas. After 1803 the chief Protestant denominations as well as many smaller sects were established. Jewish communities have flourishing congregations in the larger cities.

Missouri's population has grown modestly, but people continue to leave the state, a pattern more characteristic of heavily rural or economically less developed states. The exodus of young Missourians is expected to continue and may further increase the proportion of older people in the state. A simultaneous rise in conservatism and need for social services could result from such changes.

The economy. Although agriculture has remained important as an income-producing activity, manufacturing has forged ahead since World War II. Missouri has become the commercial and industrial leader among all its adjacent states, except Illinois. In some types of manufacture, particularly in the production of aerospace and transportation equipment—including automobile assembly—Missouri ranks among the leading states in the nation. Kansas City and St. Louis have always been important trading and commercial centres for large regions reaching into neighbouring states. They rank among the foremost grain and cattle markets of the nation.

Industry and agriculture. The state's variety of resources includes lead and iron ore, limestone, timber, animal hides, vegetable fibres, and hydroelectric power. Its chief sources of personal income are, in order, manufacturing, wholesale and retail trade, and services. Manufacturing is led by the production of aerospace and transportation equipment, followed by the processing of food and kindred products and the production of chemicals. Farm-related products and automotive sales are the leading sources of revenue for wholesale and retail trade, while business demands predominate the services sector.

Minerals
Mineral-rich Missouri leads the nation in lead production, and continuing discoveries of lead, as well as iron ores, assure that it will maintain its position. About two-thirds of the forest stand lies in the Ozarks, and since the 1950s industry has made increasing use of these resources. The acreage of many marginal farms in the Ozarks is being given over to tourism, one benefit of which is their return to forest.

Finance and planning. Missouri ranks among the top dozen states of the nation in commercial and savings and loan bank assets. Federal reserve banks are located in St. Louis and in Kansas City, and the regional offices of the Internal Revenue Service in Kansas City serve much of the Midwest.

Workers in Missouri generally have enjoyed the benefits of an expanding economy, and per capita income has kept pace with national averages. Unions have had great influence in increasing the salary levels of teachers and clerical workers across the state, as well as those of workers in the trades and crafts. In spite of favourable comparisons with other states in income and revenue, Missouri has consistently ranked near the bottom in terms of state tax revenue. As a result it has suffered from a lack of sufficient tax revenue to meet the critical needs and services that modern governmental agencies are expected to provide.

The state Department of Consumer Affairs, Regulation and Licensing includes several divisions and commissions that have had a significant influence upon the state's economic development. Local chambers of commerce and private financial groups also have stimulated the state's economic growth.

Transportation. The most remote towns and villages are not far from modern highways, the major flows of traffic within the state are from east to west along the Missouri Valley and southward along the Mississippi. Missouri has more than 30,000 miles (48,000 kilometres) of state-controlled highways and is served by seven interstate highways. Its 6,000 miles of railroads are linked with most of the nation's major trunk lines. St. Louis, Kansas City, and Jefferson City are served by Amtrak passenger service.

The Mississippi and Missouri rivers, providing 1,000 miles of navigable waterways within the state, connect water-borne traffic with New Orleans. St. Louis and Kansas City are served by several airlines.

Administrative and social conditions. *Government.* Missouri is governed under its fourth constitution, ratified in 1945, but the basic structure of government has remained constant since the first constitution of 1820. Governors are elected for four-year terms and may succeed themselves. They have the power of "item veto," by which they may strike individual provisions from any appropriation bill, except those for public school support or payments on the public debt. The governor thus exercises enormous control over fiscal affairs. In the General Assembly each senator represents equivalent population units, whereas each county has one representative, regardless of its population. During the early 1960s voters in 42 rural counties had nearly 10 times as many representatives as citizens living in St. Louis, St. Louis County, and Kansas City and surrounding Jackson County. Redistricting was completed in 1971 to meet the 1965 order of the U.S. Supreme Court for equality of representation.

The judicial system is similar to that of most states, with a Supreme Court as the highest tribunal. Below it are three courts of appeals and 42 circuit courts. An unusual feature of Missouri's judicial system is a method of selecting judges by merit, known as the Missouri Court Plan. It virtually eliminates partisan political considerations and has been adopted by several states. Under the plan the governor fills a vacancy in the court by appointing one of a three-member panel selected by a nonpartisan judicial commission. When the appointee's term is about to expire, his name must appear on the next election ballot to be voted on. To remain a judge, a person must first be appointed and then elected.

The city and the county are the most important units of local government. The state has 114 counties plus the city of St. Louis, which is independent of surrounding St. Louis County. Counties are administered by a county court consisting of three elected judges, who have no judicial authority but are responsible for administering county affairs. Counties with a population of more than 85,000 are permitted to adopt their own charters. Missouri was the first state in the nation to permit cities to adopt their own governing charters and there are now more than 20 cities across the state with home-rule charters.

Missouri tends to lean Democratic, but voters have elected Republican governors and returned Republican majorities to the General Assembly on a number of occasions. Both parties contain factions espousing liberal and conservative approaches to social and economic questions. The Democratic Party is somewhat stronger in the two large metropolitan centres.

Social issues. In spite of its high degree of urbanization and its relatively high economic ranking, Missouri retains a strong conservative bent that is especially evident in its handling of social issues.

Missouri retained discrimination against blacks long after World War II. In 1957, however, the General Assembly established the Commission on Human Rights; and in 1961 it enacted the Fair Employment Practices Act, which made discrimination on racial or religious grounds unlawful in firms employing 50 people or more. Four years later it passed a public accommodations law, forbidding any business offering goods or services to the general public from practicing discrimination based on "race, color, creed, sex or ancestry."

In 1972 the Fair Housing Practices Law was enacted, which prohibits discrimination in the purchase, sale, or rental of any dwelling in the state. While some discrimination still exists, particularly in housing, Missourians generally have shown a willingness to conform to these laws. Blacks have become increasingly conscious of their rights; in major cities there have been numerous confrontations and occasional riots. Kansas City was the scene of a serious disturbance in April 1968, but racial disturbances did not reach the magnitude of similar outbreaks in other large cities.

Education. Since 1945 many small school districts have been consolidated into fewer large ones, and school enrollments and revenues have declined significantly since the early 1970s. Missouri has lagged behind other states in support of public education. After 1954 schools were usually desegregated rather smoothly.

Higher education has expanded both in the public and private institutions. The University of Missouri has campuses in Kansas City, St. Louis, and Rolla, in addition to the main and oldest campus in Columbia. There are also seven state colleges plus Lincoln University, founded originally for blacks but now enrolling whites. Among the more than 20 private institutions are Washington University and Jesuit-run St. Louis University, both in St. Louis. Financial support of higher education consistently has been inadequate.

Health and welfare. The state Department of Social Services and the Department of Mental Health, both established in 1974, provide services for the ill and the indigent. In cooperation with federal agencies, St. Louis and Kansas City have undertaken massive urban-renewal programs to help relieve the problems of inner-city blight and congestion.

Though costs of living have risen, especially in the larger population centres, per capita income also has risen. Pockets of poverty exist in depressed rural areas and in city slums, but Missouri generally has not had the severe poverty of states with more heavy industrialization or a greater amount of subsistence farming. The disparities between rich and poor are greatest in and around St. Louis and Kansas City. Missouri has six Standard Metropolitan Statistical Areas: St. Louis, Kansas City, Springfield, Joplin, St. Joseph, and Columbia. Because those of St. Louis and Kansas City cut across state lines, their problems of metropolitan government and management are compounded.

Cultural life. Diversity characterizes Missouri's cultural milieu, from the centres of fine art, music, and theatre along the St. Louis–Kansas City axis to the folk culture and native crafts of the Ozarks.

The state has furthered cultural opportunities through the Missouri State Library, established in 1946, and the Missouri State Council on the Arts, created in 1965, the second such body in the nation established with legislative support. The state library has been responsible for the rapid growth of county and regional libraries. The larger cities have their own library systems. The council on the arts has stimulated communities to expand their cultural resources.

From the state's beginnings, the arts have flourished in Missouri. In painting, George Caleb Bingham and Thomas Hart Benton have been preeminent. If expatriate poet T.S. Eliot, a St. Louis native, is disqualified, Samuel Langhorne Clemens, known as Mark Twain, remains Missouri's most distinguished literary figure, both for his world-renowned works and for his immortalization of mid-19th-century life in Hannibal and along the Mississippi. There are schools of art and design in St. Louis and Kansas City, and music flourishes in both. St. Louis' Gateway Arch, designed by Eero Saarinen, is a spectacular example of the diverse architectural styles in evidence throughout the state.

The Ozarks abound in folk traditions, tales, and ballads. The growth of tourism there has generated a revival of culture and native crafts. The Ozark Ridge was settled primarily by pioneers from the southern Appalachians, who brought with them traditional songs and ballads, some of which were brought over from England and Scotland in the 17th century. Native crafts once practiced out of necessity by the pioneers have begun to flourish again in response to the interest of tourists and also because of recognition of the intrinsic merit of the objects made. Weaving, basketmaking, and pottery are among some of the most important crafts, and their development is encouraged through the Missouri Federation of Arts and Crafts.

Besides its universities and colleges, Missouri has outstanding cultural institutions, among them the St. Louis Symphony Orchestra, the second oldest U.S. civic orchestra and one of the major musical ensembles in the nation. In Kansas City, the William Rockhill Nelson Gallery of

Conservatism in social issues

Folk traditions and crafts

Art–Atkins Museum of Fine Arts owns one of the finest collections of Oriental art in the Western Hemisphere, and the Linda Hall Library of science and technology has an outstanding scientific collection. Independence is the home of the Harry S. Truman Library and Museum. Fulton, where the British leader Winston Churchill made his famous "Iron Curtain" speech, has a collection of Churchilliana in the St. Mary Aldermanbury Church, whose stones were reassembled there after its destruction in the World War II bombings of London.

Kansas City and St. Louis are the homes of major-league baseball and football teams, along with other professional sports. Increased leisure time and mobility have stimulated an enormous interest in recreation, and Missouri has developed a superb system of state parks and historic shrines and memorials that are attractive to residents and visitors alike. Numerous man-made lakes afford fishing and water skiing, while the clear, cool rivers of the Ozark Plateau offer pleasure to canoeists, fishermen, and campers.

The Missouri Press Association, established in 1867, has had an important effect upon the development of the press in the United States. It was responsible for establishing the world's first school of journalism at the University of Missouri and for founding the Missouri State Historical Society, with the largest membership in the nation. In addition to numerous local newspapers and journals, Missouri publishes newspapers of national distinction, including the *St. Louis Post-Dispatch,* made famous by Joseph Pulitzer, and the *Kansas City Star* and *Kansas City Times.*

HISTORY

Before the coming of European explorers, and for long thereafter, the land that was to become Missouri was the home of a diverse group of Indian tribes whose mounds and other remains dot the state. One of the tribes was called the Missouris.

Exploration and settlement.   The recorded history of the region dates from the settlement of some French lead miners and hunters from Kaskaskia in the Illinois country at Ste. Genevieve, on the western bank of the Mississippi around 1735. At some distance from its original site, Ste. Genevieve remains the oldest continuously inhabited white settlement in Missouri. Some 30 years later, Pierre Laclede, a French fur trader from New Orleans, founded St. Louis. At the time of the Louisiana Purchase in 1803, most of the 10,000 residents of the region were French settlers from the Illinois country, but some Americans had come from Kentucky and Tennessee, which, with Virginia, were the major immediate sources of settlers in following decades.

Statehood and controversy.   The "pull of the West" solidified Missouri's position as a land of passage after it achieved statehood as a slave state in 1821. Migrants bound for Texas outfitted in Missouri, and later, thousands of people poured through Saint Joseph, Independence, Westport Landing, and the City of Kansas (Kansas City) headed for Oregon or searching for gold in California.

(E.J.W.)

Well-to-do Southerners moving west for cheap land chose Missouri in preference to the Northwest Territory, where slavery was forbidden. Slave labour also had been used extensively in French lead mining. At the outbreak of the American Civil War there were 144,000 slaves and 29,000 masters in a total Missouri population of 1,182,000. The traditional Southern institution came under question by later arrivals from the North and by the German immigrants who began to arrive in the 1830s. To a certain extent free labour was discouraged by slave competition, but the growing Abolition Movement was based on moral rather than economic grounds, while defense of slavery was involved in the emotional issue of states' rights.

The controversy mounted after statehood was granted under the Missouri Compromise. Thomas Hart Benton (U.S. senator from 1821 to 1851) as early as 1828 sought backing for gradual emancipation allied with an educational program. Elijah P. Lovejoy in 1837 was forced to leave St. Louis by a mob that pillaged the print shop from which his Abolitionist *The Observer* was issued; five weeks later he was killed across the river, in Alton, Illinois. The

Abolition-ism and violence (marginal note, left)

difficulties experienced by the Mormons in Independence and later in Daviess and Caldwell counties (1831–39) were based partly on the fact that the Mormons, mostly Northerners and Easterners, were Abolitionists, while their neighbours, many from Southern states, were not. The legislature in 1847 established penalties for teaching any black to read or write and forbade any free black to enter the state. Benton's opposition to slavery ended his 30 years in the Senate in 1851.

The Dred Scott Case, originating in St. Louis in 1846 and calling into question the constitutionality of the Missouri Compromise limitation on slavery, sharpened the issues. Annexation of Texas, war with Mexico, and the Kansas-Nebraska Act of 1854 found Missouri officially on the slavery side. The Kansas-Nebraska Act, leaving the question of free soil or slavery to residents of the territories, led to persistent border troubles between Missouri and Kansas, in which peaceful citizens suffered. Emancipation was advocated by the Free-Soil movement in 1856, led by Francis P. Blair, Jr., and B. Gratz Brown.

Civil War and Reconstruction.   After the presidential election of 1860, when the question of secession was submitted to the people in February 1861, they elected a convention that voted 80 to 1 against immediate secession. But there was a very strong sentiment for compromise or even neutrality. The governor, Claiborne F. Jackson, indignantly repudiated Pres. Abraham Lincoln's call for troops and intrigued to gain possession of the U.S. arsenal at St. Louis and to put the state on a war footing. Nathaniel Lyon and the Federal troops, with Blair's support, broke up an encampment of state militia at Camp Jackson, St. Louis, and began open hostilities by driving the governor out of Jefferson City. In August, Lyon was defeated and killed by state and Confederate forces at Wilson's creek near Springfield, but next spring these forces were driven into Arkansas and defeated.

Meanwhile the convention reassembled in 1861, ousted Governor Jackson and the legislature, and elected Hamilton R. Gamble provisional governor. Until his death in 1864 he maintained, with Lincoln's support, a loyal state government accepted by the majority of Missourians, in the face of lack of funds and the impatience of Federal military authorities. In 1861 a minority of the fugitive legislature adopted an ordinance of secession, and Missouri was admitted to the Confederacy. The Unionist convention, after refusing Lincoln's plan of emancipation with compensation in 1863, enacted a plan of gradual emancipation. It is also provided an oath of loyalty for officials and voters. Records show that 109,111 men were mustered into the Federal service while perhaps 50,000 served in the Confederate armies. In the election of 1864 the more radical elements swept the state, and in 1865 a new convention abolished slavery immediately and without compensation. It also drew up a new constitution that included an extremely rigorous test oath, covering in great detail all sympathy or indirect aid to the Confederacy, and imposed not only on voters but on professional men also. Although the latter sections were declared unconstitutional by the U.S. Supreme Court, the wholesale disenfranchisements and the rigid registration laws maintained the radicals in control until 1870. In that year Carl Schurz led a revolt of the more liberal Republicans and, with the support of the reorganized Democratic Party, elected B. Gratz Brown governor, repealing the test oaths. In 1872 the Democrats secured control of the state government and retained it until 1908.

Radical Recon-struction (marginal note, right)

Economic, political and industrial progress.   Missouri emerged from this Reconstruction period with a heavy debt, state and local, incurred in loans to the railroads and in war expenditures. Railways, however, were extended, valuable zinc and lead deposits were discovered in southwest Missouri, and after 1880 the development of the southwestern portion of the United States led to the rapid growth of Kansas City. Though hard hit in the panic of 1893, Missouri's economic and especially its industrial development after 1900 was steady. William J. Bryan and free silver swept the state in 1896 and 1900. Theodore Roosevelt, who endorsed many of the Populist ideals and appealed to the younger generation, carried Missouri in

1904, and Folk, the reform Democratic candidate, was elected governor. Between 1908 and 1928 Missouri was a doubtful state politically, voting alternately Republican and Democratic. From 1932 through 1948 Missouri voted consistently Democratic but thereafter was again a two-party state.

Major historical developments in the 20th century have included the farming and adoption in 1945 of a new state constitution, including the nonpartisan plan for electing judges that came to be known as the "Missouri Plan" (installed by referendum in 1940 and followed by several other states); the general trend toward increasing urban population and declining rural population; the successful integration of public and parochial schools; the development of public health and welfare programs; and economic developments marked by increasing farm mechanization and expanding industrial and mineral production.   (Ed.)

Nebraska

One of the west-central states of the United States, Nebraska, during its early history in the first half of the 19th century, was primarily a water and land route to the rich trapping country to the north and west. With the development of railroads after the Civil War and the consequent immigrations, however, the excellent soils of Nebraska were broken by the plow, and its grasslands gave rise to a range cattle industry. As a result, the state has been, almost since its admission to the Union in 1867 as the 37th state, a major producer of food commodities for the nation.

Rivers were important to Nebraska's geography and settlement. The Missouri River, a major highway to the trans-Mississippi West in the early 19th century, forms the eastern boundary with Iowa and Missouri and about a fourth of the northern boundary with South Dakota. The name Nebraska is derived from an Indian word meaning "flat water," a reference to the Platte River, which served as a magnet for urban clusters as it crossed the state. The river is formed by the confluence of the North and South Platte rivers, both of which rise in Colorado on the southwest, although the North Platte swings northward through Wyoming, on the west, before entering Nebraska. The southern boundary with Kansas was established when the two territories were created by the Kansas–Nebraska Act in 1854, legislation that heightened the sectional hostilities that exploded into the Civil War. A majority of Nebraskans today live close to the Missouri and Platte, leaving much of the state's 77,227 square miles (200,017 square kilometres) lightly populated.

Agriculture is basic to Nebraska's economy, but only one-seventh of its labour force is employed directly in farming or ranching. Economic conditions have had a direct bearing on the state's political life, including a brief period of protest through the agrarian-oriented Populist Party during the 1890s. Although Nebraska traditionally has been considered a Republican stronghold, changes that have taken place within the state have allowed Democrats to make several inroads.

PHYSICAL AND HUMAN GEOGRAPHY

The land. *Relief.* Nebraska comprises parts of two physiographic regions, the till plains of the Central Lowland (in the eastern third) and the Great Plains.

The elevation rises from a minimum of 840 feet (256 metres) above sea level in the southeast to a maximum of 5,426 feet (1,654 metres) near the Colorado–Wyoming boundaries. Much of the land is gently rolling prairie, although the river valleys, much of south central Nebraska, and a large portion of the panhandle district are flatlands. The Sand Hills country of north central and northwestern Nebraska is a vast, treeless, grass-covered region that comprises almost one-fourth of the area of the state.

Soils. All of Nebraska's six basic soils are excellent for agriculture. The prairie soils of the southeast are outstanding for the production of corn (maize), while the rich humus soils of central and northeastern Nebraska are, given adequate moisture, highly suitable for general farming. South of the Platte and west of the prairie-soil area,

the soil is best suited to small-grain production. Winter wheat adapts to the soil and marginal precipitation of western Nebraska. The unique wind-deposited soil of the Sand Hills, because of limited precipitation and the danger of erosion, is suited solely to cattle grazing. With many small lakes and luxuriant grasses, the Sand Hills area is a superb rangeland. The alluvial soils of the Missouri and Platte river valleys and the valleys of smaller streams are outstanding for raising corn and other crops.

Drainage. Nebraska lies within the Missouri River drainage system; the Platte, the major Nebraska tributary, joins the Missouri south of Omaha. Although the Platte is shallow and unnavigable, its water is vital to the state's irrigation. The Elkhorn River enters the Platte west of Omaha, while the Loup River, formed by three tributaries flowing out of the Sand Hills, also discharges into the Platte. The Republican and Big Blue rivers flow through southern Nebraska, emptying into the Missouri in Kansas via the Kansas (Kaw) River. The Niobrara, a swift-moving stream that rises in the high country just east of the Wyoming border, flows across extreme northern Nebraska. The state also has a vast supply of underground water that has made possible the extensive development of well irrigation.

Climate. Hot winds from the southwest often push summer temperatures in Nebraska above 90° F (32° C) and sometimes above 100° F (38° C). Average July temperatures range from 73° F (23° C) in the panhandle to 78° F (26° C) in the southeast. In the winter northwestern winds often bring in Arctic high-pressure masses from Canada, and temperatures commonly fall well below 0° F (−18° C). Low-pressure systems, moving out of the southwestern states, sometimes bring great blizzards to the state and pose a danger to travellers and stock raisers. Average January temperatures vary from 24° F (−4° C) in the panhandle to about 13° F (−11° C) in the northeast. The average growing season is 168 days in the southeast and 133 days in the panhandle. The average annual precipitation varies from 33 inches (840 millimetres) in the southeast to less than 16 inches in the extreme west. Since a minimum of 20 inches is usually considered necessary for normal crop production, approximately one-half of Nebraska may be considered semiarid. Irrigation is used extensively in eastern and central Nebraska, whereas the practice is essential to certain types of agriculture in the western part of the state.

Plant and animal life. A wide variety of grasses originally covered Nebraska's prairies, and the slopes of the river valleys were well covered with deciduous trees. Cottonwood, elm, and some oak and walnut are found along the bluffs of eastern Nebraska, while conifers grow in the Wild Cat and Pine Ridge highlands and the Niobrara Valley. The Nebraska National Forest in west central Nebraska resulted from a human effort to bring trees to the barren plains. Until their near-extermination at the hands of Europeans, bison roamed widely over the Nebraska plains. Some of these animals remain in their natural habitat on the Fort Niobrara National Wildlife Refuge, near Valentine. Antelope and deer are also native to the state, as are prairie dogs, coyotes, jackrabbits, skunks, and squirrels. Migratory birds and pheasants are common.

Settlement patterns. After the specifications of the Ordinance of 1785, the land was surveyed into townships, six miles (10 kilometres) square and containing 36 sections; the section, comprising 640 acres (259 hectares), was the basic unit of land. Nebraska has retained this orderly grid-like survey system, which has its roots in New England. Most of the towns and villages were located close to rivers, streams, and timber. A number of them developed as railroad terminals, but changing patterns of transportation brought about growth for some communities and stagnation or oblivion for many others.

Economics, geography, and politics created certain sectional distinctions within Nebraska. The placement of the capital of Nebraska Territory at Omaha so enraged the people south of the Platte that they sought annexation to Kansas. The animus against Omaha did not die, and in 1867 the state capital was moved to Lincoln, south of the Platte. The polarity between Omaha and "out-state"

Margin notes:

An overview of the state

Drainage to the Missouri River

has continued, with the life-style of Omaha reflecting the boisterousness of urban commercialism, a contrast to the more sedate and university-oriented atmosphere of Lincoln and the generally conservative image of the smaller communities to the west.

Diversity of life-styles

The people. In addition to the Americans who came to Nebraska, large numbers of Europeans settled in the state during the late 19th century. From 1866 to 1879 the Nebraska State Board of Immigration employed an agent in Europe to recruit settlers. The Burlington and Union Pacific railroads made much greater efforts than did the state government in this direction. The largest immigrant group was the Germans, who in 1890 numbered 72,000; immigrants from the Scandinavian countries (particularly Sweden), Bohemia and the British Isles, also made important contributions to the settlement of Nebraska.

As a result of the European influx, Nebraska was not molded in the traditional Anglo-American form that had characterized much of the nation's earlier development. Large numbers of Roman Catholics from Bohemia, Germany, and Ireland and Lutherans from Germany and Scandinavia gave diversity to the religious life of Nebraska. Nebraska has had a number of German-language newspapers, although the linguistic identity of the Germans and other non-English-speaking groups has gradually faded away.

The black community

Blacks came to Nebraska early in the history of the state. Most settled in Omaha, which by 1900 had a black population of more than 3,400, a figure that by the late 20th century had increased more than tenfold. Blacks were concentrated in Omaha's near North Side, an area that increasingly became characterized by the social and economic problems common to the ghettos of other large cities. This core of the black community has declined markedly in population, however, as many blacks have moved to adjacent neighbourhoods; the white population in these areas has also declined. A number of racial disturbances have occurred in Omaha, emphasizing the need for improved economic opportunities and better police–community relations.

The most striking trend in Nebraska's demography—one that is neither new nor unique to the state—has been the steady decline of the population of the rural areas and the marked growth of the cities and their suburbs. Urban growth has been stimulated by the mechanization of agriculture, which brought about the working of more land by fewer persons, decreases in the number of farms, and increases in average farm sizes. Similarly, most small towns, reliant upon the local farm trade, have continued to lose population, a condition undoubtedly hastened by a modern highway system that has enlarged the trade areas of the cities. Although employment opportunities have been diminishing in rural Nebraska, there has been an increase in the number of work opportunities in manufacturing. The exodus from the farms and small towns is expected to continue, and Nebraska's urban areas may absorb many of the Nebraskans who move.

The economy. Wholesale and retail trade, government, manufacturing, transportation, utilities, and farming are the major sources of income.

Agriculture. Although farm income has the slowest growth rate among the major components of Nebraska's economy, the state remains a leading agricultural producer. The principal crops are corn, sorghum, soybeans, hay, and wheat. Nebraska ranks high among the states in the production of corn for grain and in wheat, sorghum, and sugar beets, as well as in the number of cattle, hogs, and pigs.

Farm production

Industry. Food processing is the most important industrial activity of the state in terms of value added by manufacture. Other leading industrial activities are machinery, chemicals and allied products, printing and publishing, primary- and fabricated-metal industries, and transportation equipment.

Crude petroleum accounts for almost one-half of the value of the state's mineral extraction. Nebraska also produces some natural gas and gas products, as well as significant amounts of cement, lime, pumice, sand, gravel, stone, and clay. Additional quantities of natural gas, how-

ever, are imported to serve the commercial, industrial, and residential needs of the state. All electrical utilities are publicly owned, and consumer rates are among the lowest in the nation.

Nebraska, and Omaha in particular, is known as a major centre of the U.S. insurance industry.

Management of the economy. In addition to local property taxes, Nebraska has state and local sales taxes, a state income tax based upon the federal income tax, and a gasoline tax, which is an important source of revenue. The state generally has been conservative in labour matters and ranks low nationally in percentage of unionized nonagricultural workers. Nebraska has a right-to-work law that forbids compulsory union membership.

Nebraska's economic development is heavily dependent upon private investment from outside its borders. The state Department of Economic Development was established in 1967 to bring new industry to Nebraska. As the problems of urban life in the major economic and industrial centres of the nation have become more acute, the incentive for decentralization may work to the benefit of Nebraska.

Transportation. Nebraska is located on some of the most important arteries linking the East and West. Within the state traffic in the east tends to flow toward Omaha, Lincoln, and Sioux City, Iowa, and toward the cities in the Platte Valley. Much of western Iowa lies within the trading area of metropolitan Omaha. A large portion of the traffic in western Nebraska is oriented toward Denver, Colorado.

Nebraska has a good network of modern highways. The most important route is Interstate Highway 80, which carries heavy traffic east–west across the state. The state is served by five railroads. Omaha is an important port for commercial barge traffic on the Missouri. Air carriers serving Nebraska include both major national lines and those that provide "feeder" service to the smaller communities of the state.

Administrative and social conditions. *Government.* Nebraska functions under a frequently amended constitution dating from 1875. Since 1937 it has had a one-house legislature whose members are elected without political-party affiliation—the only such legislative body in the nation. The 49 members of the legislature, or "Unicameral," are popularly elected for four-year terms following primary and runoff elections in their districts, which are equally proportioned by population. Unicameral meets for sessions of 90 legislative days in odd-numbered years and 60 days in even-numbered years.

The unicameral, nonpartisan legislature

The nonpartisan feature of the legislature has many critics, who charge that the lack of political parties in the Unicameral results in a lack of leadership in that body. Nebraska's Unicameral, however, ranks high among the 50 state legislatures in procedural standards. In addition, although the majority of legislators generally are Republican in political inclination, the system allows the electoral campaigns to be fought on the basis of local issues rather than party loyalties. Omaha's black community long has had representation in Unicameral.

The governor, the chief executive officer, is elected for four years on a partisan ballot and is limited to two consecutive terms. The governor is responsible for the operation of 17 administrative departments and is an ex officio member of various boards and commissions. As the state's chief fiscal officer, the governor must present a detailed budget to the state legislature, which needs an affirmative three-fifths vote to appropriate more funds than recommended by the governor or to override a gubernatorial veto. Other elected state officers also run on partisan ballots.

Nebraska's court system, reorganized in 1972, comprises the Supreme Court, with seven justices, and 21 district courts, with almost 50 judges. In addition, there are a number of conciliation courts, county and municipal courts, and juvenile courts, as well as a workman's compensation court. Nebraska has adopted the Missouri Plan, originated in that state in an attempt to create a nonpolitical judiciary. Judicial nominating commissions, chosen by the governor and the Nebraska Bar Association,

The nonpartisan judicial system

compose lists of nominees to fill vacancies on the bench. The governor then appoints one of the nominees to fill a particular position. Nebraska also has a merit system under which the electorate determines whether judges will be retained in office.

County government is vested in boards of supervisors or commissioners of from three to seven members, who like other county officials are elected on partisan ballots. The city manager and mayor–council forms of government are used in Nebraska's cities, and governmental authority in villages is vested in elective boards of trustees.

Nebraska Territory was the creation of a Democratic administration in Washington, D.C., and Democrats dominated Nebraska politics until the Civil War. The 30 years after 1860 were marked by Republican preeminence in Nebraska, but the political ferment during and after the 1890s brought an end to one-party rule. Although a slight majority of Nebraska's voters are registered Republicans, Democrats often are elected to office.

Social issues. The social and economic problems of Nebraska, although manageable, are pressing. Better housing, improved educational and employment opportunities, and an upgrading of police–community relations are fundamental necessities in Omaha's black community. An active civil rights movement has pressed for these improvements. In certain rural counties as well, the level of income is far below state and national averages. Wage levels in Nebraska are slightly below the national average, yet inflation and unemployment have been less pronounced than in many other parts of the country.

Health and welfare. Nebraska's programs of public assistance include medical aid and financial assistance for dependent children, the aged, the blind, and other disabled persons. Federal funding provides more than half of Nebraska's public-assistance expenditures, slightly above the national average. Although federal, state, and county welfare funding has steadily increased, the average monthly public-assistance payments in Nebraska are below the national average. Nebraska also has participated in various antipoverty operations of the federal government.

The state maintains a system of mental hospitals and other specialized health, correctional, and care facilities, but expanded medical facilities are needed in some rural areas. Omaha ranks as a medical centre of national significance.

Education. Since 1968 state aid for education to local governments has increased more than tenfold, and the number of school districts has been cut drastically in order to make more efficient use of educational facilities and programs.

There are more than 30 institutions of higher education in Nebraska; about one-half are private schools, and the rest are state operated four-year institutions and junior colleges. The University of Nebraska (established in 1869) is the largest educational institution in the state and is composed of three semi-autonomous campuses, the main campus in Lincoln and two campuses, including the medical school, in Omaha. Graduate-degree programs are offered at the University of Nebraska and Creighton University (Omaha), both of which offer programs in medicine, law, and dentistry, and at state colleges in Chadron, Kearney, and Wayne.

Cultural life. In less than two generations, Nebraska was converted from a wilderness inhabited by a small number of native Indians to a settled commonwealth of more than 1,000,000 residents. This conquest was an important achievement of the 19th century, and it is natural that the cultural contributions of Nebraska, like those of other Western states, are centred on this frontier experience.

Such Nebraska novelists as Willa Cather, Mari Sandoz, and Bess Streeter Aldrich were among those who wrote perceptively of life on the plains and won national audiences. The relationship of the pioneers to a capricious natural environment, the life-styles and interaction of settlers of diverse social and ethnic backgrounds, and the plight of the Indians were among the important themes of these writers. The poet John G. Neihardt wrote feelingly of plains Indian life; he also re-created the adventures of the explorers of the 19th-century West. In the early 1970s

Margin note (left): Higher education

his narrative *Black Elk Speaks* achieved national recognition some 40 years after it had originally been published.

The Nebraska State Historical Society, organized in 1878, continues to make important contributions to an understanding of life in Nebraska and the West. In 1960 the University of Nebraska Press launched the paperback Bison Series, reprints of early and modern works on the American West, including histories, collections of lore from Indian and white settlers, and other important documents, many of which had been out of print.

Increased urbanization and affluence have promoted continued artistic expression in Nebraska. The Joslyn Art Museum in Omaha and the Sheldon Memorial Art Gallery in Lincoln contain the state's major collections in the visual arts. Omaha and Lincoln also have a number of theatrical groups and symphony orchestras. Various folk observances, such as the Czech Festival at Wilber, are periodic reminders of the diverse origins of the people of Nebraska. Ogallala, a roaring cow town during the 1870s and 1880s, relives its colourful past with its "Front Street" festivities held each summer. Each October, the Knights of Ak-Sar-Ben (Nebraska spelled in reverse), an Omaha civic organization founded in 1895, crown a king and queen of Quivira. This elaborate event commemorates the search through the plains in 1541 of the Spanish explorer Francisco Vázquez de Coronado for the legendary Seven Golden Cities of Cibola in the Kingdom of Quivira. The University of Nebraska football team has attained national prominence, and few subjects hold the attention of Nebraskans as do the fortunes of the "Cornhuskers." The benefits derived from the citizens' enthusiasm for football are important in several areas of the state's economy.

Margin note (right): Folk and historical festivals

HISTORY

Various prehistoric peoples inhabited Nebraska as early as 8000 BC. In the 19th century semisedentary Indian tribes, most notably the Ponca, Omaha, Oto, and Pawnee, lived in eastern and central Nebraska. The west was the domain of the nomadic Brulé and Oglala Sioux, but other tribes, such as the Arapaho, Comanche, and Cheyenne, also roved the area.

Exploration and settlement. The region that was to become Nebraska was included in the Louisiana Purchase, the vast tract of the midcontinent acquired from France in 1803. The French had lost interest in the trans-Mississippi West after less than three years of rule, and the Spanish before them had done little to develop the territory.

In 1804 the Lewis and Clark Expedition visited the Nebraska shore of the Missouri River and conducted the first systematic exploration of the area. Shortly thereafter, a vigorous fur trade developed along the Missouri, but Nebraska was primarily a highway to richer fur-trapping areas to the north and west. During the 1840s the Platte Valley became another highway, as thousands of settlers moved westward over the Oregon, Mormon, and California trails.

Much interest soon developed in Nebraska and in the Platte Valley as a potential railroad route to the Pacific. Frontier land speculators in western Missouri and Iowa anticipated great financial gains if the Nebraska country, part of the large Indian domain between the Missouri River and the Rocky Mountains, were opened for settlement. With the adoption of the Kansas–Nebraska Act in 1854, the federal government extended political organization to the trans-Missouri region. As originally established, the Nebraska Territory comprised 351,558 square miles, but by 1863 the organization of the Colorado, Dakota, and Idaho (including the states of Montana and Wyoming) territories had reduced Nebraska almost to its present dimensions.

Much of the economy of the early Nebraska settlements along the Missouri River was based on land speculation. Agriculture began to develop within a few years, however, and some river towns became important transfer points for freight and passengers going west. The completion of the Union Pacific Railroad in 1869 and the railroad construction that followed contributed to the development of the state.

Statehood. After Nebraska's admission to the Union,

Margin note (right): Roles of speculators and railroads

in 1867, and despite a depression and grasshopper plague, the population increased from about 120,000 to more than 1,000,000 by 1890. The Indian resistance on the frontier was broken during these years, and settlement extended westward into the panhandle of the state. During the 1880s Omaha first became an important industrial and meat-packing centre, and Lincoln became prominent as the state capital and as the seat of the University of Nebraska.

In the 1890s Nebraska's farmers, afflicted with poor crop prices, high transportation costs, and depression, ex-

In the 1890s Nebraska's farmers, afflicted with poor crop prices, high transportation costs, and depression, expressed their protest through the Populist Party. Although the Populist movement was short-lived, it invigorated the political life of the state. Prosperity returned by 1900 and continued for two decades. Through the 1920s Nebraska's agriculture again was beset with mediocre marketing conditions, and, with the advent of the Great Depression of the 1930s, the state's economy deteriorated, a condition that was alleviated by massive federal assistance. By World War II the economy had recovered, and since then Nebraska has had steady, though unspectacular, economic growth.
(H.A.D.)

Marginal note (left): Impact of economic cycles

North Dakota

Officially classed as one of the seven west north-central states of the United States, North Dakota is a land of clear skies, seemingly endless grain farms, and vast cattle ranches. North Dakota is even more rural, more agricultural, and more sparsely populated than the other states of the region; it also has less manufacturing. Its terrain rises through three regions from east to west, incorporating parts of the two major physiographic provinces that separate the Appalachian and the Rocky Mountain systems.

The state has an area of 70,665 square miles (183,022 square kilometres). The largest city is Fargo, and Bismarck is the centrally located capital.

Among the last regions of the American frontier to be settled, the area that became the state of North Dakota in 1889 experienced comparatively little of the fighting, lawlessness, and gold-rush excitement that give other frontier areas a colourful or lurid history. Instead, the region developed first as the home of hunting and farming Indian peoples, later as a trading area for white fur traders and for steamboats working the upper Missouri from St. Louis, and then as a rich farming land for white settlers. The cool, subhumid climate of its location made it ideal for spring wheat and for cattle ranching. The area subsequently developed a way of life dependent on outside centres of population, industry, and economic power. With adaptation to the environment, however, the people of North Dakota also developed constructive reactions to the circumstances that made their state dependent.

PHYSICAL AND HUMAN GEOGRAPHY

The land. *Relief.* North Dakota has parts of two major physiographic provinces. The eastern half belongs to the Central Lowland, which stretches westward from the Appalachians, while the western half is part of the Great Plains, which extend to the Rocky Mountains. The state is like three broad steps rising westward: the Red River Valley lies 800 to 1,000 feet (250 to 300 metres) above sea level, the Drift Prairie from 1,300 to 1,600 feet, and the Missouri Plateau from 1,800 to 2,500 feet. The highest point in the state is White Butte, at 3,506 feet (1,069 metres). The Central Lowland portion comprises the Red River Valley, a flat, glacial lake bed extending from 10 to 40 miles (16 to 64 kilometres) on either side of the Red River of the North, and the Drift Prairie, a rolling country covered with glacial drift. On the west, the Missouri Escarpment separates the Drift Prairie from the Great Plains. The North Dakota portion of the Great Plains is known as the Missouri Plateau. East and north of the Missouri River, it is covered with a thick layer of glacial drift. The Altamont Moraine in this area, which is one of the principal flyways for migrating wildfowl, has numerous potholes, lakes, and sloughs. Like the Drift Prairie, this region has a young drainage system, because there are few rivers in areas once covered by the great ice sheets.

About two-fifths of the state is drained by the systems of

Marginal note (left): River systems

the Red and Souris rivers, whose waters flow eventually into Hudson Bay. The Missouri Plateau and the James River system form a part of the drainage of the Missouri, which drains almost two-fifths of the state and flows into the Mississippi and thence into the Gulf of Mexico. West of the Missouri River the landscape has been shaped by running water that has carried away as much as 1,000 feet of sedimentary deposits. In some places, especially along the Little Missouri River, it has carved spectacular cliffs, buttes, and valleys that form a landscape known as the North Dakota Badlands.

Climate. North Dakota's location at the centre of the North American continent gives the state a continental climate: hot summers and cold winters, warm days and cool nights in summer, low humidity and low precipitation, and much wind and sunshine. The western part of the state has lower humidity, lower precipitation, and milder winters than the eastern half. For the state as a whole, the average precipitation is about 17 inches (430 millimetres). The southwestern counties, the warmest, have an annual mean temperature of about 42° F (6° C); the northeastern counties, the coldest, about 38° F (3° C). The growing season in North Dakota ranges from 134 days at Williston, in the northwest, to 104 days at Langdon, in the northeast.

Plant and animal life. Before settlement, 95 percent of the state was covered by grass, for low precipitation, drought, and grass fires inhibited tree growth. Long-lived perennial grasses begin to grow early in the spring, produce seed quickly, and go into a dormant state in drought. They protect the soil from erosion and provide food for grazing animals. The heavy grass cover of the Red River Valley and the Drift Prairie formed black soils, while the lighter grass cover of the Missouri Plateau formed lighter, thinner, dark-brown soils. The North Dakota grassland was a natural habitat for great herds of buffalo and antelope. Belts of timber and brush along the rivers provided homes for animals such as white-tailed deer, elk, and bear. The remaining small buffalo herds are protected in parks.

Settlement patterns. The regions are reflected to some degree in the character of the people. The inhabitants of the Missouri Plateau tend to be more Western in their manners and dress, whereas those of the Red River Valley are more influenced by Eastern life-styles. The Drift Prairie is a transition zone in this respect, as it is in climate and in plant and animal life.

North Dakota is a land of large farms and ranches; its vast, open country has few fences. There is beauty in the great fields and pastures, the big sky, the endless view of flat or rolling prairie with the black earth of the plowed land, the green blanket of a new crop, or the yellow cover of ripened grain. The clean, dry air and the bright sun give a wholesome look to the land of North Dakota, but the large holdings, which averaged more than 1,000 acres (400 hectares), make the countryside seem lonely and almost uninhabited.

Marginal note (right): The typical landscape of North Dakota

With the loss of farm population, many small towns have also disappeared, while in others businesses and houses stand empty. The larger cities and towns provide a sharp contrast, with their new stores, public buildings, and housing developments and their air of vigour and prosperity. The sparsity of population affects not only the state's economy but also the character of the people, who tend to be friendly, spontaneously helpful, and straightforward. Distances create isolation, but the rise of electronic media keep North Dakotans well informed.

The people. When white traders reached what was to become North Dakota, several Indian peoples lived in the region: Mandans, Hidatsas, and Arikaras along the Missouri River, Chippewas and Crees in the northeast, Assiniboins in the north, Yanktonai and Wahpeton Dakotas in the southeast, and Teton Dakotas and Crows in the west. The fur trade brought the French, Scots, English, Canadians, and Americans, and, by 1800 the Métis, of mixed white and Indian ancestry, were an established element in the population.

The earliest white settlers included many Norwegians, Canadians, and Germans who had earlier migrated to Russia. By 1890 the foreign-born constituted about 43 percent of the population, a higher percentage than in any other state; and in the census of 1920, when settlement had been completed, only 32 percent of the white population was of native-born American parentage. By the late 20th century, however, less than a quarter of the population was foreign-born.

There is still much poverty, ill health, and alcoholism among the Indians in North Dakota. Many, however, have success as farmers, ranchers, professionals, politicians, and athletes.

Most North Dakotans have religious affiliations. Almost one-half are Lutherans, more than one-third are Roman Catholics, and most of the remainder are United Methodists, Presbyterians, and members of the United Church of Christ.

The economy. North Dakota's cool, subhumid climate and its location far from the nation's markets have helped to shape its economy. Among the west north central group of states to which it belongs, North Dakota has the lowest farm income, the smallest cities, the lowest average rainfall and temperature, the shortest growing season, and the least manufacturing.

Major
crops *Agriculture.* The state produces large numbers of beef cattle and ranks first in the nation in the production of barley and flaxseed; it also produces wheat, rye, and oats. It also sends dairy products, sugar beets, and potatoes to outside markets, from which it buys automobiles and trucks, farm machinery and equipment, automotive fuels, and lumber and building materials, as well as clothing, television sets, and other consumer goods. Manufacturing accounts for less than 10 percent of the state's income, and its lignite, the largest supply of solid fuel in the United States, has come to play a minor role in its economic life. Wheat is the most important source of farm income.

Although agricultural production largely pays for the things the state buys in outside markets, it employs only about one-fifth of the labour force. Farming's economic disadvantages contrast sharply with its rapid increase in efficiency since World War II, brought about by increased mechanization and the decline in number but increase in size of farms.

Industry. The discovery of oil at Tioga in 1951 has since made North Dakota one of the largest producers of crude petroleum in the nation. In the 1950s and 1960s the economy was stimulated by substantial investment of federal and state government funds in Garrison Dam, in highway construction, in rural electrification, and in air bases and missile installations. Federal expenditures continue to be of importance in the state.

Transportation. Intrastate and interstate traffic moves primarily over east–west and southeast–northwest routes in North Dakota and secondarily over north–south routes. Fargo is the main centre for intrastate traffic; interstate traffic moves between it and other trading centres in North Dakota and Minneapolis–St. Paul, the nearest metropolis, and the Pacific Northwest. North Dakota's transportation network includes more than 5,000 miles (8,000 kilometres) of rail lines; almost 13,000 miles of hard-surfaced and more than 59,000 miles of gravelled highways; and airlines that provide scheduled service to a number of cities..

Administrative and social conditions. *Government.* To many observers, North Dakota suffers from too much government. The state government consists of a governor who is elected for a four-year term, nine elected heads of executive departments, a bicameral legislature of 50 senators and 100 representatives, and several levels of state courts. In addition, it has almost 150 departments, boards, and agencies, as well as two state-owned industries. By 1978 more than 53,000 people, including teachers, were employed by state and local governments. In 1981 North Dakota ranked 31st in property taxes per capita and 32nd in all taxes per capita.

Extensive-
ness of
govern-
mental
machinery

Voting trends usually favour Republican candidates, but many voters in North Dakota are independent.

Education. Nearly half of North Dakota's high school graduates go to college. Many high schools, however, remain too small to provide adequate programs, since enrollments range from as few as 18 to almost 3,000.

Higher education has been greatly expanded. More than one-half of the students are enrolled in the two univer-

sities, the University of North Dakota, in Grand Forks (founded in 1883), and North Dakota State University, in Fargo (1890), both of which offer a full range of undergraduate and graduate work.

Health and welfare. North Dakotans receive excellent medical care despite the state's low population density. Although some towns of less than 1,000 population have a doctor, medical practice is concentrated in the four larger cities—Fargo, Bismarck, Grand Forks, and Minot—often in group practice in well-equipped clinics. Few people live more than a two-hour drive from one of the centres. The state has 60 general hospitals, a rehabilitation centre, five regional mental-health centres, and a state hospital for the mentally ill. The state health department and smaller health districts provide public health services. Colleges of medicine and nursing at the University of North Dakota train health personnel.

Economic assistance and social services are provided by the state public-welfare board, county welfare boards, and private welfare agencies, especially denominational groups. The state welfare board gives aid to aged, blind, and disabled persons and to dependent children; it also provides eight regional social-service centres. County welfare boards administer general assistance and medical aid for the aged. Welfare assistance for the able-bodied is a minor expenditure. More than two-thirds of the funds paid to or for welfare recipients are from federal sources, while most of the remainder is from the state. Most of the money for dependent children, the second most expensive program, goes to families broken by divorce, separation, or desertion; the program provides payments that are higher than the national average.

Cultural life. The traditional North Dakota spirit of self-reliance and voluntary cooperation, except where internal or external pressures have dictated institutionalization, is reflected in the cultural life of the state. Without a large metropolitan centre, the cities and towns with universities or colleges provide the main cultural leadership. Symphony orchestras have headquarters in Fargo, Minot, and Grand Forks, though they make appearances throughout the state. The North Dakota Ballet is located in Grand Forks, where in 1971 the University of North Dakota established the state's first College of Fine Arts. Most of the community art associations, public concert associations, and community theatre groups are also located in college or university towns. A summer School of Fine Arts is held at the International Peace Garden, a large park located on the border between North Dakota and Manitoba near the Turtle Mountain area.

Inter-
locking
educational
and
cultural
activities

There is some federal-assistance funding for arts projects in the state, but most other funds for the arts, apart from those expended by educational institutions, have had to come from public subscription. In 1971, however, a small state appropriation made to the North Dakota Council on the Arts and Humanities, the agency through which federal funds for the arts are dispensed, was considered the beginning of a long-term state commitment to the arts.

Among the weakest aspects of North Dakota's cultural life is library service. Because the larger part of the population lives in the country or in small villages, about one-half of the people have virtually no contact with library facilities. The libraries of towns with populations of 5,000 or more vary widely in their adequacy. Civic leaders have sought to meet the needs of the rural population with county and regional libraries and with bookmobiles.

Indigenous folk traditions continue within the state among the Dakota, or Sioux, peoples of Fort Totten and Standing Rock Indian Reservation, among the Plains Ojibwa (locally called Chippewa) people of the Turtle Mountain Reservation and area, and among the people of the Three Tribes—the Arikaras, the Hidatsas, and the Mandans—of Fort Berthold. Traditional music and dances, together with beadwork and other crafts, attract many art lovers to the state. The durable and attractive pottery of the Three Tribes is particularly sought after.

Indian arts
and other
ethnic
activity

Scandinavian cultural traditions remain vigorous. Although none of the 50 Norwegian-language newspapers published between 1878 and 1955 survives, Norwegian language and literature are taught at the University of

North Dakota and in several elementary schools. The Sons of Norway have more than 9,700 members in the state. Norwegian costumes, customs, and cookery are observed on many occasions but especially on Norwegian Independence Day, May 17. North Dakotans of Icelandic, Czech, and German ancestry also retain some ethnic customs, and in many families the ancestral languages are still spoken.

The individualistic character of North Dakotans is reflected in their sports and pastimes, which include fishing, hunting, and trapping. Snowmobiling is increasing, and ice skating, skiing, and ice hockey remain popular winter sports.

HISTORY

The recorded history of North Dakota falls into three periods: the period of Indian trade, from about 1738 to 1871; the period of white settlement, from 1871 to 1915; and the period of adaptation, since 1915.

Explorers and traders. Although European goods were traded among the Indian peoples before his arrival, the first known white visitor to North Dakota was Pierre Gaultier de Varennes, sieur de La Vérendrye, a native of Canada who visited a cluster of earthen-lodge villages near present-day Bismarck in 1738. Traders from Hudson Bay and Montreal began to come to the area on a regular basis in the 1790s. The best known visitors of the early years were Meriwether Lewis and William Clark, whose expedition made winter camp in 1804–05 near present-day Stanton.

In the 1820s and 1830s American traders made the upper Missouri country a hinterland to St. Louis. They brought in guns, kettles, blankets, and axes, as well as liquor and disease. The white man's goods made the Indians dependent on the traders, his liquor demoralized them, and his diseases killed them. In 1837 smallpox, carried up the Missouri by passengers aboard a steamboat of the American Fur Company, reduced the Mandan population from about 1,800 to 125 in a few months. Indian hostility grew when steamboat traffic increased after the discovery of gold in Montana in 1862 and when the U.S. Army built forts along the rivers. In 1876 Lieut. Col. George A. Custer and the 7th Cavalry set out from Ft. Abraham Lincoln, south of present-day Mandan, for their fateful encounter with the Sioux and Cheyenne on the Little Bighorn River in Montana.

Pioneering and statehood. The fur trade declined in the 1860s, and white settlement began in earnest in 1871, when railroads reached the Red River from St. Paul and Duluth, Minnesota. A flood of pioneers acquired land under the Homestead Act and turned to wheat farming. During the period known as the Dakota Boom (from 1878 to 1886), the many giant farms publicized the new country, and North Dakota wheat made Minneapolis, Minnesota, the milling centre of the nation in the 1880s. The Northern Pacific and Great Northern railroads vied with one another to reach the richest grain centres. Dependence on wheat unified the farmers and strengthened the populist revolt against eastern monopolistic practices. The Dakota Territory was divided in 1889, and both North and South Dakota were admitted to the Union on November 2, 1889.

The modern state. Revolt against outside exploitation reached a climax soon after the period of pioneer settlement ended in 1915. Controlling the state government after the 1918 election, the Nonpartisan League enacted a socialistic program that included a state-owned bank and a flour mill and grain elevator. The league soon lost political control, but the North Dakota Farmers Union (founded in 1927) launched a strong cooperative movement to control the selling of grain and the purchase of farm supplies. Such radical farm movements made many North Dakotans oppose American intervention in both world wars, because they identified participation with war profits for Wall Street.

Since 1915 North Dakota's history has been marked by continuing adaptations to the cool, subhumid grassland environment, the most important of these being the increasing mechanization of agriculture, the enlargement of farms, the loss of rural population, and the widespread use

Populist strength

of the automobile. After World War II came rural electrification, soil conservation, and highway construction. In the 1950s North Dakota became an oil-producing state, and in the 1960s air bases, missile sites, and antiballistic-missile installations were built there. National and international trends have thus become an important influence on the affairs of the state.　　　　　　(E.B.R./B.O'K.)

Ohio

The first state to be carved from the Northwest Territory when it became the 17th member of the Union in 1803, Ohio, in the 20th century, reflects the urbanized, industrialized, and ethnically mixed United States that developed from an earlier agrarian period. The pattern of its life is so representative of the nation as a whole that it is often used to test attitudes, ideas, and programs in education, politics, and industry. Significantly, Ohio has supplied by birth or residence one-fifth of the presidents—William H. Harrison, Ulysses S. Grant, Rutherford B. Hayes, James A. Garfield, Benjamin Harrison, William McKinley, William H. Taft, and Warren G. Harding.

Overview of the state

The state's accessibility has been perhaps the key factor in its growth. Its location between the populous states of the Eastern Seaboard and the growing Midwest and its lack of natural barriers to movement made it a corridor for east–west travel, whether by riverboat down the Ohio River, by packet across Lake Erie, or by wagon, railroad, or automobile and truck across its land. With Pennsylvania on the east, West Virginia and Kentucky on the southeast and south, Indiana on the west, Michigan on the northwest, and Lake Erie on the north, Ohio lies in the heart of the nation's most industrialized area, close to major resources of raw material and labour and to the markets of the East, Midwest, and South.

Ohio's area of 41,222 square miles (106,764 square kilometres), excluding 3,457 square miles in Lake Erie, ranks only 35th in size among the states; it is the smallest state, after Hawaii and Indiana, west of the Appalachian Mountains. The state ranks near the top, however, in population. The state capital, after being located in Chillicothe and Zanesville during the early years of statehood, was finally established in newly founded and centrally located Columbus in 1816.

PHYSICAL AND HUMAN GEOGRAPHY

The land. The topography, river systems and groundwater, and soils in most of Ohio are the products of glacial activity. These factors have strongly influenced the patterns of human settlement and land use.

Relief. Three large physiographic provinces extend into Ohio. The Allegheny Plateau reaches westward from Pennsylvania and West Virginia into the counties along Ohio's eastern border, from near Lake Erie to the Ohio River. The northeast is only partially glaciated, while the unglaciated terrain in the southeast has made it the only region in the state that has shown a decline in population and economic power for decades. Throughout the plateau the land is dissected by rivers winding among steep hills, and many elevations reach 1,400 feet (425 metres).

The Lake Plains stretch along Lake Erie to the northwestern counties and the Michigan border and then extend irregularly to the south. These level to slightly rolling lands were once under water, and the swampiness of the northwest, around Toledo, posed obstacles to settlement before drainage made it more arable. The Central Plains, which extend westward beyond the Mississippi, include parts of western and southwestern Ohio and provide a deep soil. Curiously, the state's highest and lowest points are found there: the highest point, at 1,550 feet (472 metres), is located near Bellefontaine; the lowest, at 425 feet (130 metres), lies at the confluence of the Miami and Ohio rivers, near Cincinnati.

Drainage. The principal water sources are the rain-fed streams, lakes, and reservoirs. Floods, once prevalent, are controlled by numerous state and federal dams and other conservation measures throughout the state. Groundwater is used widely for public supplies, though the major industrial and population centres have limited resources.

Huge stores of these waters are buried in preglacial valleys in central and south central Ohio; cities, which require millions of gallons daily for industrial use alone, have contemplated the use of these sources.

Lake Erie, with an average depth of only 62 feet (18.9 metres), is the shallowest of the Great Lakes. It is also the most tempestuous, with frontal storms often roaring across it from Canada, and the most liable to shoreline erosion, harbour silting, and filling of its bed. Its shallowness, coupled with the concentration of population and industrial plants in its watersheds, led to severe pollution. Programs in various areas have begun to deal with the problems of the lake, which continues to be the principal source of water for many lakeside cities. By the late 20th century attempts to abate pollution in Lake Erie began to show signs of success. Fish returned to previously uninhabitable waters, and there were sizable reductions in pollutant discharges into the lake.

A low watershed separates the 30 percent of Ohio drained by the Maumee, Cuyahoga, and other rivers into Lake Erie from the 70 percent drained by the Miami, Scioto, Muskingum, and others into the Ohio–Mississippi system. The Ohio, no part of which is under state jurisdiction, is canalized and channelled for its entire length, as is the Muskingum from Zanesville to Marietta. Of the 110 lakes in Ohio, most have been built for industrial, supply, recreational, and other purposes.

Soils. Most of Ohio's soils are well suited to agriculture. The Great Plains soils are mainly rich glacial limestone, but the Lake Plains are the most productive. The sandstone soils of central and northeastern Ohio are best adapted to pasturelands, while the thin and heavily eroded hilly areas of the southeast support little productive farming. State and federal conservation and reforestation programs have been undertaken in the area.

Climate. Temperatures in Ohio are similar to those across the north central and eastern United States, with summer highs and winter lows seldom reaching 100° F (38° C) and −20° F (−29° C), respectively. The state is open to cold, dry fronts from Canada and to warm, moist fronts from the Gulf of Mexico. The frequent meeting of such fronts causes much of the state's precipitation, which totals about 38 inches (965 millimetres) annually, including an average annual snowfall of about 28 inches, which is about one-seventh of the total precipitation.

Plant and animal life. The great hardwood forests that covered 95 percent of Ohio prior to European settlement have been reduced to less than 20 percent. The forests in the glaciated areas have less forest but better stands of timber, which include oak, ash, maple, walnut, basswood, hickory, and beech. Both wild and domestic flowers abound, though the clover, wild rye, and bluegrass of early Ohio are gone.

Of the 350 bird species found in Ohio, at least 180 are native. Among the 170 fish species are bass, trout, and perch, while the 60 or more species of wild animals include deer, opossum, fox, skunk, groundhog, and rabbit.

The people. The urban areas of Ohio first exceeded the rural in population in 1910, and by the late 20th century the urban population made up about 75 percent of all Ohioans. Counties surrounding major cities contained more than a third of the population. Ohio's large cities, however, are following the national pattern of losing population to surrounding suburban areas. The growth of Columbus proper is largely attributable to municipal annexation of the suburbs.

The people who laid the foundations of Ohio, most of them of English ancestry, came from the older seaboard states. The first permanent white settlement in Ohio and the Northwest Territory was at Marietta in 1788 by a company of New Englanders who had fought in the Revolution. In the same year a group from New Jersey established a settlement near Cincinnati, and in the next few years other villages sprang up. In the south, particularly in the Virginia Military District between the Scioto and Miami rivers, many of the settlers came from Virginia and Kentucky. In 1796 the Western Reserve in northern Ohio was first settled, mainly by New Englanders from Connecticut.

Pioneers from other European nations arrived in Ohio prior to 1830. Germans and Swiss came from Pennsylvania to the east central area. Many settlers of Ulster Protestant background came from the Middle Atlantic and Southern states. After 1830 settlers came directly from Germany and Ireland. Many Irish came from the Erie Canal to work on the Ohio canals and stayed on, and when the railroads were built, the Irish and German workers remained as permanent settlers. Germans who drained the Black Swamp country of the northwest stayed on to develop the farmlands around such centres as New Bremen, New Bavaria, and Minster.

After 1830 immigrants from southern Ireland settled in such cities as Cleveland, Defiance, and Cincinnati, where by 1850 they were second in number to the Germans among foreign-born residents. In the 1830s Columbus also became an important centre of German population, as did Lancaster, where immigrants from Württemberg joined the Pennsylvania Germans who had founded the city.

In northeastern Ohio such towns as Massillon, Alliance, and Canton were established at an early date by Pennsylvania Germans, as was Steubenville, farther east. German settlers also were attracted to the rolling surface and fertile soil of Wayne County, which became one of the top agricultural counties in the nation. German-speaking Moravian missionaries came to Christianize the Indians in the early 1760s under the leadership of John Heckewelder, David Zeisberger, and Frederick Post. In 1817 Joseph Bimeler founded an experimental communistic settlement in Zoar that lasted until 1898. The Swiss settled around Dover and Sugar Creek in Tuscarawas County, as well as in Monroe County. This general area is sometimes referred to as the "Little Switzerland of Ohio." In Holmes County, Amish immigrants from Germany and Switzerland established settlements that still remain. There are now more Mennonites in Ohio than in Switzerland.

The Welsh arrived in the early 19th century to develop the mineral resources in Jackson County, and for a long period Welsh was the only language that was spoken there. The Eisteddfod, a festival of Welsh bards, and other elements of Welsh culture and music flourished. The language persisted to the third generation in many communities, with old Welsh songs passed on from one generation to the next.

In 1850 the principal racial stock was Scots-Irish, although the Germans and the English also were important elements. In 1870 nearly 14 percent of Ohio's population and 40 percent of Cleveland's were foreign-born. The New England character of northern Ohio's beginnings was changing. Each new group established its own newspapers, clubs, social life, and churches.

Increasing numbers of immigrants from eastern and southern Europe came to Ohio after 1880. By 1920 large numbers of Italians, Poles, Hungarians, Russians, and other groups had come to Cleveland, Toledo, Youngstown, Akron, Dayton, Middleton, and other industrial communities. No other Ohio city, however, acquired such a polyglot population as did Cleveland. Cleveland's foreign-born population was supplemented between 1880 and 1890 by new arrivals from Austria, The Netherlands, Russia, Hungary, Portugal, Greece, China, Japan, Turkey, and Mexico. The city's culture eventually was enriched by more than 48 groups with different languages and backgrounds. There were many new Roman Catholic and Eastern Orthodox churches, as well as synagogues. The Greeks brought their coffeehouses, and the Slovenes and Poles brought their social halls. Through the action of the "melting pot" character of Ohio, the descendants of these ethnic groups have firmly established themselves in the social, economic, and political life of the state.

The changing ethnic character of the state is shown as well in the growth of the black population. In 1843, when the Wendat Indians left Ohio for new lands west of the Mississippi, the black population of Ohio was about 25,000. By 1870 it had risen to more than 62,000, most of which was in southern Ohio, where Wilberforce University, one of the first permanent black educational institutions, was established. By the late 20th century the black population had risen to more than 1,000,000, most of it in the cities.

Sidenotes:

Lake Erie and the river systems

The northern European stock

The diversity of Cleveland's population

The economy. A good physical location, a rich store of natural resources, productive soils, and ample transportation facilities made Ohio one of the first great industrial states in the nation. More than half of the nation's population is within 500 miles (800 kilometres) of its borders; and coal, iron, water, salt, limestone, ferroalloys, chemicals, clays, and plastics are close at hand. About two-thirds of the raw materials processed in Ohio's factories come from its mineral, agricultural, and forest resources. Although more than one-fourth of its labour force is employed in manufacturing, its continuing activity in agriculture and mineral production provides economic balance and diversity.

Agriculture. In 1850 Ohio ranked first among the states in agricultural production, and it has continued to rank near the top. Although its farming acreage and the number of farms and farmers have decreased, more than 60 percent of Ohio is still farmland. Ohio farms have become larger, supplying more food with less work through the application of science and technology. In 1900 the farm was an almost self-sustaining unit, providing its own food, fertilizers, and fuel; it still requires, however, machinery, motor power, electricity, and tractors, as well as a substantial investment of money and skill. Ohio is a leading state in the production of corn (maize), oats, and hay, and it maintains large marketing inventories of fruit, feed, and vegetables, as well as livestock and poultry.

Mining. Ohio's mineral resources include stones and clays for manufacturing and construction and such mineral fuels as coal, petroleum, and natural gas for heat, power, and transportation. The value of Ohio's mineral production has reached new highs. Coal production accounts for the highest return, followed by industrial minerals, oil, and gas.

Coal was discovered in Ohio as early as 1808. It was adapted for use with iron and limestone in the pioneer iron-making enterprises that sprang up in the eastern and southwestern parts of the state. Later, the discovery of deposits of iron ore in the upper Midwest gave rise to important iron and steel centres in northern Ohio. Usable coal supplies are found in 32 eastern and southeastern counties. Almost three-fourths of the coal is produced by strip mining, which has left a scarred landscape, polluted water supplies, and a generally damaged environment. Although Ohio has laws regulating strip mining and requiring restoration, the results have not been satisfactory. Citizen groups have led the battle for stronger safeguards.

Limestone is used in many construction and manufacturing processes. Ohio is first among the states in sandstone production, accounting for about two-thirds of the nation's building sandstone, and it is fourth in sand and gravel production. The abundance and quality of surface clays, plastic fireclays, shales, and some gypsum and peat have made Ohio a leader in the manufacture of ceramic products. The majority of its extensive salt production comes from large rock-salt mines, with the remainder from brine. Important industrial consumers of salt in Ohio are the soda-ash and chlorine industries. Geologists estimate that the state's salt deposits could supply the nation's need for centuries to come.

Petroleum and natural gas production

Ohio has been a producer of oil and natural gas since 1860, but by 1900 billions of barrels of crude oil had been removed, and production in the state declined. In the early 1960s, however, new oil and gas deposits were discovered, and the industry was revived.

Other natural resources of importance to Ohio's economy are its forest products and water supplies. Climate and soil are conducive to the production of fine hardwood. Ohio is a leading state in the industrial use of water, with countless industries depending on the groundwater supply.

Industry. Ohio's manufacturing is its most important economic activity and represents the largest single segment of the state's employment. Nonelectrical machinery, fabricated metal products, and transportation equipment are the most important manufacturing enterprises in terms of employment. In spite of increased activity in other parts of the nation, the manufacturing belt that stretches from the Northeast through Ohio still constitutes the chief industrial strength of the country. Ohio is a national leader in all industrial classes, particularly in such diversified manufactures as rubber products and porcelain, electrical machinery and apparatus, pumps and plumbing equipment, and steam shovels.

Economic regions. Governmental planners have identified eight regions throughout Ohio that have distinctive economic characteristics in terms of their human and physical resources, landforms, transportation, communications, and other attributes.

The Maumee Valley region, comprising 10 counties in the northwest, is primarily agricultural, though it lies in the path of industrial expansion from east and west. Corn and wheat, as well as hogs and dairy and poultry products, are important. Its largest city, Lima, has a growing manufacturing base.

Economic diversity

The Lake Plains region, comprising 10 counties on the southwestern shores of Lake Erie, also has flat, fertile plains with highly productive soils. Toledo, the major city, is an important centre in the Great Lakes industrial belt and the leading coal-handling port in the United States. It supplies glass and transportation equipment to nearby Detroit and processes the farm products of the region.

The Lakeshore and Uplands region comprises 16 counties in the north and northeast. This area, approximately one-fifth of the state's land, contains Ohio's largest industrial concentration and holds more than two-fifths of its population. Cleveland is the industrial, financial, and cultural centre. Akron is a centre of the rubber industry, a trucking centre, and a large cereal producer. Youngstown, in the nation's "Ruhr Valley," is a major metal producer and fabricator, and Canton specializes in roller bearings, bank vaults, and vacuum cleaners.

The Miami Valley region, in southwestern Ohio, centres on Cincinnati and Dayton. Cincinnati leads the world in the manufacture of machine tools, soaps and detergents, and playing cards. Dayton is the world's largest producer of cash registers and magazines and the nation's largest producer of putty and plastics; it is the home, as well, of Wright-Patterson Air Force Base, a major flight-testing and research centre.

The Sandusky Valley region, comprising seven counties, is basically agricultural, though the small cities of Marion, Galion, and Bucyrus have some manufacturing.

The Scioto Valley region of rolling plains in central Ohio has a diversified economic base. Columbus, its central city, is the home of the state government and of numerous educational institutions, including Ohio State University. About two-fifths of the working force is employed in government, education, finance, and other service occupations.

The sparse populations of the Tuscarawas Valley region of eastern Ohio, and of the Ohio Valley region in the southern and southeastern portions of the state, are predominantly rural. Terrain limits agricultural productivity in both regions. In the southwestern part of the region, wheat, corn, tobacco, and hogs are the principal products. Mining and lumbering provide the largest proportion of income in the southeastern region. Stone, clay, glass, chemicals, and metal fabrication are major industries.

Transportation. Ohio's chief transportation system in the first years of statehood, as in the territorial period, was its water routes. Lake Erie and the Ohio River provided east–west passage for Indian traders, pioneers, and settlers, and many rivers provided access to the interior. Shortly after statehood, the development of land transportation facilities was begun, and in 1811 the federal government began to build a major portion of the National Road running from Cumberland, Maryland, to Vandalia, Illinois. In the same year the first steamboats appeared on the Ohio River, and in the 1820s the era of canal building began and lasted for some 30 years. The first railroad was constructed in 1832, and in the 1850s the first great east–west rail lines were constructed across Ohio as the shortest and easiest route to the Western cities and prairies and beyond.

Ohio's transportation facilities play a major role in moving passengers and goods from east to west and from north to south, by highway, railroad, river, lake, and air. The shipping to and from its lake ports is worldwide, and the Ohio River carries 30 percent more tonnage than the Panama Canal. The railroad mileage is the nation's sixth largest, though Cleveland and other major cities lost most interstate passenger service when the semipublic Amtrak system went into operation in 1971. The pioneer experiments of Dayton's Wright brothers, Orville and Wilbur, led to the first successful aircraft flight, at Kitty Hawk, North Carolina, in 1903, and Ohio is now both a testing and a commercial aviation centre. Ohio has many research and development facilities, a number of which are administered by Ohio State University.

Administrative and social conditions. *Government.* Ohio's government, which is more extensive than that of many small nations, is a multibillion-dollar enterprise. The state and local governments are similar to those in other states.

Executive, legislature, and judiciary

The executive branch, which is headed by the governor and other elected officials, includes the heads of 22 agencies who serve as an executive cabinet. The General Assembly comprises the Senate and the House of Representatives. It has broad powers in policy formulation and monetary appropriation. The judiciary, which interprets and applies the law in cases before it, comprises the Supreme Court, 10 courts of appeals, courts of common pleas and of probate in each of the 88 counties, and such other lower courts as the legislature may establish. All judges are elected for six-year terms.

Each county exists as a quasi-municipal corporation, an arm of the state government but without general authority of self-government in the legislative field. Various optional forms are available, and the increasing social and economic problems of the multicounty metropolitan areas may lead to newer forms. Most larger cities operate under home-rule charters that permit them to choose the form most suitable to their needs. The mayor–council type is most common, though Cincinnati operates under a city-manager–council plan. The township, Ohio's oldest form of government, remains an important government unit, though the number is diminishing as they are annexed into municipalities or as newly incorporated villages assume their functions.

State laws carefully prescribe the rules for forming and running political parties, conducting elections, and balloting. The two-party system has prevailed generally, but Ohio has produced such minor-party leaders as Norman Thomas, many times a presidential candidate on the Socialist Party ticket; Victoria Claflin Woodhull, the first woman to run for president, with the Equal Rights Party; and such leaders of fringe political groups as Jacob Coxey, who led the march of "Coxey's Army" from Massillon, Ohio, to Washington, D.C., in 1894 to demand various economic reforms.

Since its inception the Republican Party has been slightly more successful than the Democratic in statewide elections. In national politics the parties are evenly matched, and Ohio has become a centre of national electioneering. William Howard Taft served as president and as chief justice of the U.S. Supreme Court. Although political dynasties are rare in Ohio political life, Taft's father had been secretary of war and attorney general under Pres. Ulysses S. Grant and was later U.S. minister to Russia and Austria-Hungary. His son, Robert A. Taft, served in the U.S. Senate from 1939 to 1953, and his grandson, Robert A. Taft, Jr., served in the U.S. Senate from 1971 to 1976.

Major expenditures of state government are for education, health, welfare, and highways. A number of executive agencies administer the programs in these areas, often in conjunction with federal agencies.

Higher education

Education. Ohio often has been called a "land of schools and colleges," and it ranks among the top 10 states in the number of accredited colleges. Ohio University was established by Ohio's first legislature in 1804 as the first state institution of higher education west of the Alleghenies. In 1809 Miami University became the second state university. Both these institutions conduct important programs of work, have large enrollments, and maintain numerous branches. Ohio State University, founded in 1870, is one of the largest state-assisted universities. A land-grant college and a major graduate and professional centre, it

also has one of the largest undergraduate enrollments in the nation. It maintains several regional campuses and a graduate program at Dayton. Many of Ohio's small independent colleges have made distinguished contributions to the state and have pioneered in education in various ways. Oberlin College, founded in 1833, became the first coeducational college in the United States and one of the first to admit blacks. Antioch College, founded in 1852, is one of the nation's oldest experimental liberal arts colleges. Like some other Ohio institutions, it has implemented innovative programs for advancing minority students. The University of Cincinnati, established as Cincinnati College in 1819, is the nation's oldest municipal university.

Welfare and social services. The aged and poor, the blind and disabled, and crippled and dependent children are among the groups that benefit from the welfare activities of several state agencies. Other state bodies oversee programs in the prevention and cure of illnesses. A youth commission operates diagnostic and training centres, youth corps, and schools. State activities with labour and industry include programs in employment and unemployment services, industrial safety, and worker's compensation.

The development and use of natural resources fall under the jurisdiction of the Department of Natural Resources, which handles forestry, reclamation, parks, wildlife, and similar environmental concerns. The responsibilities of the Department of Agriculture include economic and health problems of farm life and the regulation of foods through food-and-drug laws. Organized research is carried out at Ohio State University and at the Ohio Agricultural Experiment Station in Wooster. A department of urban affairs cooperates with local and regional bodies and coordinates state programs that deal with community problems.

Cultural life. Early settlers of Ohio put the stamp of their former homes—New England, the Middle Atlantic states, Kentucky, and Virginia—on several sections of the state. Because of its location at the crossroads of the nation and its ever-changing society, Ohio never developed a distinctive state culture.

There has never been a clearly identifiable Ohio school in any of the arts, though there has been great activity in all of them. Such diverse Ohio writers as William Dean Howells, Ambrose Bierce, Paul Laurence Dunbar, Brand Whitlock, Charles F. Browne ("Artemus Ward"), David R. Locke ("Petroleum V. Nasby"), Sherwood Anderson, Louis Bromfield, and James Thurber drew upon their Ohio background. None of them, however, attempted to develop a distinctive regional character in his work.

When the log-cabin phase of early Ohio ended, most of the settlers followed the building styles that they had known in their former homes. In the Virginia Military District, where Southern influence was marked, the red-brick and stone houses were built in the Southern Federal architectural style. In the Western Reserve and the Marietta area, the New England influence was manifested in the austere lines of the colonial style and the modified Georgian style. Later developments tended to follow the fashions of American architecture in general, most of them revivals of earlier European modes such as Greek, Gothic, and Romanesque. In line with international trends, the present emphasis is on simplicity in design and on function.

The thousands of musical organizations in Ohio range from symphony orchestras to local choral societies. The symphony orchestra of Cleveland is among the finest in the world, and that of Cincinnati (which was considered the musical centre of the inland United States in the early days) is also renowned. The Blossom Music Center, located between Cleveland and Akron, is the site of a summer festival. Programs in music, theatre, dance, and the visual arts abound in Ohio's colleges and universities. With community theatres and arts centres, they serve as the cultural centres for many cities and towns. The Cleveland Playhouse (1915–16) and the Karamu House (1915), an organization that attempts to bridge black and white cultures, also in Cleveland, have long had a national reputation. The Cincinnati Playhouse in the Park (1960), noted for its experimentation, has become one of the nation's major regional professional theatres. The Cincinnati Opera is one of the major regional companies

The performing arts: music and the theatre

in the United States. The Ohio Arts Council, which was established in 1965 by the state legislature, aids communities and arts organizations in stimulating greater interest as well as participation.

Ohio has several hundred public libraries in addition to college and university facilities containing more than 20,500,000 volumes and about 140 specialized libraries in many fields. The Ohio State Library, in Columbus, serves the entire state. Bookmobile service is a feature of rural areas.

Reflecting Old World origins are the Welsh Eisteddfod festivities in Cleveland, Steubenville, Lima, Columbus, and Jackson, and a German Saengerfest (Song Festival). More than 40 other nationality groups—including Hungarians, Bohemians, Swiss, Scandinavians, and Irish—present folk music and dances at festivals throughout the state. Other gatherings, in addition to the annual state and county fairs, include the Apple Festival in Jackson, the "River Days" Festival in Portsmouth, the Ohio Hills Folk Festival in Quaker City, and the Pumpkin Show in Circleville.

Sites of public interest. Ohio has more than 200 museums of art, science, and history. The Cleveland Museum of Art ranks among the foremost art galleries in the nation, and those in Cincinnati, Toledo, Youngstown, and Columbus also hold major art collections. In addition, many historical sites are maintained by state and local societies, including Indian mounds, old forts and battle sites, reconstructions of early settlements, and graves, homesteads, and similar memorials to Ohio's presidents and other leading citizens.

Recreational facilities include more than 184,000 acres (74,500 hectares) of state park facilities for water sports, hiking and camping, or picnicking—in addition to numerous municipal recreational areas. The Cuyahoga Valley National Recreation Area lies between Cleveland and Akron. Public gardens, zoos, caves and caverns, and privately run amusement parks add to Ohio's recreational repertory.

A top-ranking state in scientific personnel, Ohio has a large number of laboratories maintained by specialized institutes, industries, educational institutions, and national and state agencies. Reflecting industrial concentrations, Akron is the world centre for rubber research, and Cleveland is well known for research in lighting. Battelle Memorial Institute, in Columbus, is one of the largest private research organizations in the world. Glass, steel, soap, and electronics are among the many other products undergoing constant testing and evaluation. A number of federal centres are devoted to aviation medicine, aeronautics and space, atomic energy, agriculture, and forestry.

HISTORY

Prehistory and settlement. Remains of ancient civilizations dating from 5,000 to 7,000 years ago have been found in Ohio. Among later cultures, the Hopewell culture, which disappeared about AD 400, represented the highest prehistoric development. Their burial mounds contained exquisitely crafted artifacts. The earliest European explorers in the 18th century found the region occupied largely by Miami, Shawnee, Wendat (Wyandot), and Delaware Indians, as well as a host of smaller tribes.

Indian cultures

The region between the Appalachians and the Mississippi River was an almost constant cause of dispute between France and Great Britain until 1763. Ordinances of 1785 and 1787 by the new U.S. government set the pattern for settlement and for government, though the Virginia Military District in southern Ohio and the Western Reserve (*i.e.,* of the state of Connecticut in 1786) in northern Ohio were set aside for veterans of the Revolution.

Statehood. After Ohio attained statehood in 1803, the foundations for social and economic diversification were laid. Threats of Indian warfare were halted, and in 1813 the naval battle on Lake Erie played a major role in the War of 1812. Despite several economic panics, a program of internal improvements created a network of land, water, and rail transportation. By 1850 Ohio was the third most populous state in the nation, with nearly 2,000,000 residents, and the leader in diversified agriculture, but it was still an essentially rural, agricultural state.

Economic growth. The basis of Ohio's industrial structure was built between 1850 and 1880, when the value of its manufacturing grew to more than twice that of agriculture. A major stimulus was provided by the U.S. Civil War (1861–65), in which Ohio supported the North, though there was strong antiwar sentiment in the state. After the war the growth continued, notably in the northeast and around Lake Erie. This growth led to considerable economic and social dislocation. After 1900 considerable attention was given to municipal reforms in Cleveland, Toledo, and other cities and to statewide programs of social legislation that attempted to alleviate problems caused by industrialization. In 1920 two Ohioans, Warren G. Harding and James M. Cox, faced one another for the presidency, and Ohio has continued to play a pivotal role in national political life.

Ohio reflected the racial strife that was widespread in the United States in the summer of 1966, when disorders in the predominantly black Hough district of Cleveland took four lives. In 1968 Carl B. Stokes became the first black mayor of a U.S. city as large as Cleveland, though in 1967 and 1968, respectively, Springfield and Dayton also came under the administration of black mayors. The state became the focus of national attention in May 1970 when four students were killed by national guardsmen, who had been called out as a result of demonstrations at Kent State University, near Akron.

In the late 1970s Cleveland had severe economic problems, and the city had to default on its debts in 1978. Although these difficulties were resolved, the subsequent national recession and federal reductions in aid hampered the economy of Cleveland and the state. (F.R.A.)

South Dakota

South Dakota is one of the plains states of the United States. It is bounded on the north by North Dakota, on the east by Minnesota and Iowa, on the south by Nebraska, and on the west by Wyoming and Montana. The state comprises 77,047 square miles (199,551 square kilometres), which are split into the two nearly equal segments of "east-river region" and "west-river region" by the broad Upper Missouri River Basin. Pierre, at the centre of the state, is among the smallest of state capitals, with less than 2 percent of the state's residents. The state's name is derived from the Dakota (Sioux) Indians who roamed the plains before the arrival of Europeans.

South Dakota is one of the few states still predominantly rural in population. This condition reflects, in part, the 19th-century settlement of the land by immigrants from northern and central Europe who bypassed the more developed states to the east to pioneer the frontier. It recalls also the rapid influx of prospectors in the 1870s and 1880s after the discovery of gold in the Black Hills, in the southwestern part of the Dakota Territory. The town of Deadwood became a symbol of the flamboyant era of the bonanza seekers and a part of Western lore. Although South Dakota is the nation's second largest gold producer—its Homestake Mine is one of the largest in the Western Hemisphere—the economy of the state is more closely tied to its agriculture and to the millions of tourists who visit the exotic, vividly eroded Badlands and other points of interest in the state.

Frontier heritage

PHYSICAL AND HUMAN GEOGRAPHY

The land. *Relief.* Although it is divided into three distinct regions, South Dakota, save at isolated places, does not have marked variations in its physical environment.

Eastern South Dakota and some river valleys in the west near the Missouri lie within the glaciated physiographic province known as the Prairie Plains. The western half, except for the Black Hills in the southwestern corner, has the rolling topography of the unglaciated Great Plains, characterized by high buttes, rough canyons, and wide expanses of nearly level tablelands. It includes the Badlands, which extend along the White and Cheyenne rivers for more than 100 miles (160 kilometres). This eroded landscape has been a rich source of fossilized prehistoric animals.

The Black Hills—two-thirds of which lie in South

Dakota, with the remainder in Wyoming—are a dome-shaped uplift rising 3,500 feet (1,100 metres) above the surrounding plain. Harney Peak, 7,242 feet (2,207 metres) above sea level, is the highest point in North America east of the Rocky Mountains.

Drainage. The Missouri River drains most of the state except for the Minnesota Valley lowland, which is drained by Big Stone Lake and Lake Traverse in the northeastern corner. In the east-river area the principal tributaries of the Missouri—the Big Sioux, Vermillion, and James—flow southward into valleys formed by glaciation. The main rivers of the west-river region—the Grand, Moreau, Cheyenne, Bad, and White—flow eastward.

Climate. The climate is characterized by extremes in temperature, persistent winds of moderate velocity, low precipitation, and relatively low humidity. The skies are generally clear. Cyclonic storms occur frequently in the east-river section during the summer. The mean annual temperature for the state is about 45° F (7° C). A weather station at east central Huron reports average lows of 2° F (−17° C) and highs of 25° F (−4° C) in January, as well as average lows of 61° F (16° C) and highs of 90° F (32° C) in July. Extreme temperatures recorded are −34° F (−37° C) and 110° F (43° C). The average number of frost-free days ranges from 160 in the southeast to 110 in the Black Hills.

The average annual precipitation for the state is 19 inches (480 millimetres), but it ranges from about 24 inches along the eastern border to 14 inches or less in the northwestern corner. In the centre of the state, the transitional zone from the Prairie Plains to the Great Plains, precipitation drops from 20 inches to 18 inches. About three-fourths of the rain falls during the growing season, and snowfall ranges from about 22 to 60 inches. The Black Hills region receives more moisture, especially in winter, than the surrounding plains.

Soils. The soil types to be found in South Dakota vary. The chernozem, or black, soils, formed mostly from glacial drift and well adapted for wheat and corn (maize), cover the east-river area. Within the Great Plains province are the chestnut and Pierre, or gumbo, soils, distinguished by their heavy, sticky texture. They are well adapted to grassland regions.

Plant and animal life. At the time of settlement the east-river region was a prairie grassland with a thick matte of tall grasses growing to a height of three feet or more. These tall grasses have a deep root system, adapted to subhumid conditions. The shortgrass species, comprising chiefly the grama, buffalo, and western wheatgrasses, are endemic to the Great Plains. They are drought resistant and have a shallow root system and the capacity to mature quickly. Aside from its forest, the ecology of the Black Hills is much like that of the Great Plains.

The wooded areas lie mostly in the Black Hills and along the buttes in the northwestern part of the state. Most wooded acreage is incorporated into the Black Hills National Forest and the Custer National Forest. The western yellow, or ponderosa, pine is the chief commercial tree.

Custer State Park in the Black Hills maintains a herd of more than 1,000 bison. Other Black Hills species include antelope, deer, elk, beaver, bobcat, and porcupine. Coyotes, jackrabbits, and prairie dogs are plentiful in other sections. The state has nearly 300 species of birds. Bald and golden eagles are found in diminishing numbers along the Missouri Valley and in the Badlands. The Missouri is an important route for the north–south migration of waterfowl, mostly ducks and Canadian geese. For many years South Dakota has been a hunter's paradise because of its plentiful supply of ring-necked pheasants, a game bird introduced into the state early in the 20th century.

Settlement patterns. Early in South Dakota's history, the west-river region was distinguished from the farming settlements of the east-river area by the large Indian population, the open-range cattle industry, the physiographic characteristics of the Great Plains, and the Black Hills mining economy. There is still a strong distinction between the two sections, and it forms the basis for differing views in the legislative halls.

Except for the Black Hills region, the west-river area has

only about two persons per square mile, a sharp contrast with the northeastern and southeastern regions, in which the density is generally four times greater. Only about one-fifth of the rural residents in the state live in the west-river region. Some 12 percent of the state's area consists of tribal and individually owned Indian land. Most of it is located in the west-river section in the remaining portions of the old Great Dakota Reservation created in 1868.

The east-river section is divided into two areas approximately north and south of a line running eastward from Pierre. General farming prevails in the northern part, with the main reliance on wheat and other small-grain crops. The southern part represents a more diversified farming economy, with feed grains and livestock production as its specialties.

The people. *Ethnic distribution.* The earliest settlers generally came from the Upper Mississippi Valley, many of them with a New England background. Immigrants arriving directly from the northern and central countries of Europe also played an important part in the colonizing process. In 1890 one-third of the white residents were foreign-born. Although today only about one-sixth of the residents are foreign-born, nearly half the population are only two or three generations removed from Europe. The Americanization process generally had run its course by the end of World War I, but Old World customs and speech still prevail in many communities.

Those of Scandinavian descent—Danes, Norwegians, and Swedes—make up about a third of the foreign stock. The Norwegians, located mostly in the east-river region, exert an especially strong influence. Compact Danish and Swedish communities are found in the southeastern part of the state.

Persons of German descent make up about a sixth of the population. They include German-Russians, who are heavily concentrated near Yankton in the southeast and in three north central counties. The Bohemians, or Czechs, generally live in the south central counties. Other important ethnic groups are the Dutch, the Finns, and the Welsh.

The descendants of the original Dakota Indians form a major segment of the population. The old tribal system has largely disappeared, but about three-fourths live in reservation areas scratching out a living by farming and stock raising. The Teton Dakota live mainly in the west central part of the state between the Black Hills and the Missouri; the Yankton Dakota, on the Yankton Reservation; and the Sissetons, on the Sisseton Reservation in the northeastern corner of the state.

Low living standards in reservation areas have led to a substantial migration of young Indians to nearby communities. The resulting racial tension amid charges of social and economic discrimination led, in 1963, to a civil rights law that prohibited exclusion of any person from a public place because of race, colour, religion, or national origin. In 1980 the U.S. Supreme Court ordered the federal government to pay the Dakota Indians of South Dakota $205,000,000 in compensation for the illegal seizure in 1877 of the Black Hills.

Religions. Immigrant groups established about half of the state's churches. Their religious institutions not only promoted social solidarity but also played an important part in the acculturation process. In 1890 there were 12 religious sects in the state, the Roman Catholics being most numerous and the Lutherans a close second; by the late 20th century, however, Lutherans outnumbered Roman Catholics. Other leading organizations are the Methodist, United Church of Christ, Presbyterian, Episcopal, and Baptist churches.

The German-Russian groups include Mennonites and members of the Hutterian Brethren. Although the Hutterites, in some of their religious beliefs, are related closely to the Mennonites, they practice a form of religious communism, living in colonies and holding all goods and property in common, in accordance with a strict interpretation of early Christian teachings. There are more than 50 Hutterite communities, many of them in the James River Valley; in 1955 a state law prohibited the expansion of colonies or the formation of additional communities. The Hutterites have circumvented this law by changing

Virgin prairie grasslands

West-river and east-river areas

Immigrant pioneers

Mennonite and Hutterite sects

their legal status from that of a church to a corporation.

Some parts of the Indian community still adhere to ancient Indian faiths. The majority, however, profess Christianity, most of them identifying themselves as Roman Catholics and Episcopalians.

The economy.   *Agriculture.* Cash income from livestock and livestock products is generally about three times that from crops. The state ranks high in the production of rye and flaxseed as well as spring wheat. It also ranks among the top 10 states in corn and alfalfa-seed production. In many years it produces half the nation's supply of Kentucky bluegrass seed. Normally, 150,000 acres (60,-700 hectares) are under irrigation, mostly in the west-river region.

Industry. The major industrial groups are food products, industrial machinery, and lumber and wood products. Meat processing is the largest single industry, representing about one-fourth of the value added by manufacturing in the state.

Leading mining products are gold, cement, stone, and sand and gravel. The yearly output of gold is produced by the Homestake Mine. Large lignite beds containing low-grade uranium deposits await development.

Electri-
fication

The multipurpose Big Bend, Fort Randall, Gavins Point, and Oahe dams have made South Dakota a major producer of hydroelectric power. Seven small hydroelectric plants, all but one located in the Black Hills, are privately owned. Only a small portion of the total production of electric energy is generated by coal or gas. More than 96 percent of South Dakota's farms are electrified; most of them are served by rural electric cooperatives.

Unions. Organized labour has not found a congenial climate in South Dakota, and there have been few major disturbances. A "right-to-work" amendment was adopted in 1946, making it illegal to require union membership as a condition of employment. It was followed by legislation that placed restrictions on boycotts and picketing. About half of the union membership lives in Sioux Falls.

Transportation. South Dakota has a network of roads totalling more than 83,000 miles (133,000 kilometres). The state trunk system of nearly 9,000 miles carries the bulk of the highway traffic. The Missouri River, not bridged until 1924, can be crossed at 10 different points, including the crests of the four dams. Passenger bus and motor freight lines have kept pace with highway improvements.

As motorized transportation has increased, rail services have declined. About 3,000 miles (4,800 kilometres) of railroads remain in operation, but passenger trains have been discontinued, and many small-town freight depots have been abandoned. With the aid of federal funds, air transportation has increased steadily since World War II. There are more than 70 public and almost 80 private airports, and several commercial airlines operate from nine certified terminals.

Administrative and social conditions.   *Government.* The state constitution was adopted in 1889 and has been amended more than 80 times to reflect changing conditions and attitudes about the basic law.

In addition to the governor and lieutenant governor, four administrative officials are chosen by the electorate, all for four-year terms. The superintendent of public instruction is appointed by the governor. The legislature comprises the Senate of 35 members and the House of Representatives of 70 members. In 1951 the Legislative Research Council was created to provide continuity between the annual sessions. The judicial system comprises the Supreme Court, consisting of five judges elected for eight-year terms; the Circuit Court, consisting of 36 judges operating within eight judicial districts; and a local system of 19 county-court districts and a municipal court in each of the three largest cities. All judges are chosen by nonpartisan ballot. There are also provisions for justices of the peace in rural areas and police magistrates in the smaller cities and towns. The machinery for law enforcement includes the state's attorney and sheriff at the county level and the office of attorney general at the state capitol. Special enforcement agencies include a state highway patrol and a force of game wardens. There are correctional and penal institutions at Plankinton and Sioux Falls.

Law
enforce-
ment

The state has more than 3,500 units of government below the state level. These units include 66 counties, more than 310 incorporated towns and cities, and 1,050 organized township governments. There are also more than 100 special districts, most of them concerned with soil conservation and drainage.

The state constitution forbids deficit spending. The major sources of income for the state government are a sales tax, revenue from licenses and other fees, and federal aid, which accounts for more than one-fourth of the income. The general property tax is reserved for local governments. Most of the state's expenditures are for highways, education, and welfare.

A primary election is held in June during even-numbered years, followed by general elections in November. Special elections often decide local issues. The Republicans have been the dominant party since early settlement.

Education. The public school system is administered by local and county boards but is subject to policies formulated by the Department of Education. Since 1943 direct legislative appropriations for the support of the common schools have supplemented the general property tax and revenues from the common school lands. School district reorganization remained on a voluntary basis until 1968.

Among the state-supported institutions of higher learning are the University of South Dakota in Vermillion (founded 1882) and in Springfield; South Dakota State University in Brookings (1883); South Dakota School of Mines and Technology in Rapid City (1885); and a number of teachers colleges. The oldest of the several private colleges and junior colleges continuously established in the state is Yankton College (1881).

Health and welfare services. The Department of Health is responsible for programs dealing with communicable diseases and sanitation, as well as with the inspection and licensing of hospitals and nursing homes and the collection of vital statistics. There are some 70 licensed hospitals in the state. The elderly are served by more than 140 nursing homes and extended-care facilities.

The welfare needs of the state are the responsibility of the Department of Public Welfare. Nearly two-thirds of funds for public assistance are received from federal grants. Greater welfare and delinquency problems prevail among the Indian population because of cultural differences and the unfavourable economic conditions. Institutions maintained by the state include a school for the blind at Aberdeen, a school for the deaf at Sioux Falls, a centre for the mentally handicapped at Redfield, a mental hospital at Yankton, and a veterans' home at Hot Springs.

Cultural life. The early settlers were not oblivious to cultural refinements. They attended musical and dramatic performances by travelling artists in local opera houses, and they heard national lectures sponsored by lyceum bureaus. Schoolhouses were centres of community social life, and local reading circles and library associations developed into modern libraries. South Dakota has more than 100 municipal libraries. Eighteen libraries are maintained by state and private institutions, including the library of the South Dakota State Historical Society in Pierre. A travelling library system, operated under the Free Library Commission, was established in 1913.

The dramatic arts manifest their appeal at community and summer theatres and the departments of dramatic art on college and university campuses. Notable among the summer theatres is the Black Hills Playhouse, which has operated in Custer State Park since 1946. More spectacular is the Black Hills Passion Play, which has been presented during the summer at Spearfish since 1939. The musical arts are represented by seven symphony orchestras.

In the graphic arts two native-born artists, Harvey Dunn and Oscar Howe, gained wide recognition. Harvey Dunn, reared on a pioneer Dakota homestead and one of the nation's leading illustrators, became well known for his paintings of pioneer life. Oscar Howe, a Yanktonai Dakota, has made use of the motifs and symbolism of his Indian heritage. Another outstanding artist to identify himself with the state was Gutzon Borglum, whose stone carvings of four U.S. presidents on Mt. Rushmore in the Black Hills are a major tourist attraction.

Native
artists

In literature many native writers have dealt with the South Dakota scene. Among them were the writer of frontier stories Hamlin Garland, who launched his career in the state, and Norwegian-born Ole Edvart Rölvaag, who spent his early immigrant life near Sioux Falls, the locale portrayed in his *Giants in the Earth* (1927). The *South Dakota Review*, a literary quarterly published by the University of South Dakota since 1963, affords an outlet for regional as well as local talent.

HISTORY

Settlement and gold rush. A lead plate, discovered at Ft. Pierre in 1913, records the presence of French explorers during 1742–43. Twenty years later Spain acquired sovereignty over the region, and its rule led to U.S. ownership in 1803. Trappers and fur traders were virtually the only Europeans in the area until 1856, when Ft. Randall was built on the Missouri River. The permanent settlements of Vermillion and Yankton were established in 1859. The Dakota Territory was created in 1861, but for several years settlement was confined to the southeast between the Big Sioux and Missouri rivers.

The discovery of gold in the Black Hills in 1874 attracted settlers to the western part of the territory, which had been closed to white entry under an earlier treaty with the Teton Dakota tribes. In the year following the Battle of the Little Bighorn in Montana, in 1876, the Indians were forced to accept a reduction of their reservation and to cede the Black Hills. Despite the major attention that Deadwood commanded, Rapid City emerged as the main gateway city to the region. Freight and stage lines connected the mining population with the east until railroads were constructed across the Indian country in 1905.

Statehood and homesteading. The gold rush was followed by a flood of settlers into the east-river region, swelling its population from about 80,000 to 325,000 between 1878 and 1887. This rapid expansion led to calls for division of the territory at the 46th parallel and separate statehood for the southern half. In the north, and in Congress, a single state was favoured. The southern section held constitutional conventions in 1883 and 1885; at the latter the state of Dakota was established. Dual statehood based on a division below the 46th parallel received congressional approval in 1889, and South Dakota was admitted as the 40th state in the Union.

The Black Hills agreement with the Dakota Indians opened up not only the mining region but also the contiguous grazing lands, and by an agreement in 1889 additional Indian lands became available in the west-river region. Cattlemen remained in control until the early 1900s, when homesteaders broke up the range and received for settlement an additional 4,000,000 acres (1,619,000 hectares) of Indian land. Severe droughts during 1910 and 1911 brought the land rush to a halt, but in the next decade the semiarid west-river region increased in population from about 44,000 to 138,000. Further droughts, onslaughts of grasshoppers, and dust storms from increasingly eroded soils seriously depressed the farm economy of the state during the 1930s.

Conservatism and progressivism. South Dakota's political history is similar to that of its neighbouring states. During the 1890s the appeal of the Populist Movement led it temporarily and briefly away from the Republican Party. A four-year fusion administration, however, produced only the nation's first initiative and referendum law. At the turn of the 20th century the state was influenced

Political traditions

by the wave of progressivism. An insurgent, progressive wing dominated the Republican Party in 1906 and enacted legislation that called for direct primary elections and railroad regulation. From 1917 to 1919 the state adopted a still more radical program, which established a rural credits plan, a system of state hail insurance, a state coal mine, and a cement plant. Of these state-operated enterprises, only the cement plant at Rapid City remains in operation. Since the 1920s the voters have shown a more conservative bent. A major exception to this conservatism was the state's support of liberal Democrat George McGovern, who was the only Democrat elected to Congress from South Dakota between 1936 and 1970. McGovern,

however, failed to carry South Dakota in his 1972 presidential bid.   (H.S.Sc.)

Wisconsin

One of the north-central states of the United States, Wisconsin became the 30th member of the Union in 1848. It is situated between Lake Michigan to the east and the Upper Mississippi River on the west. On the north it touches the western portion of Lake Superior and the Upper Peninsula of Michigan. Minnesota and Iowa lie to the west and southwest respectively; on the south is Illinois.

The economy of Wisconsin is diversified with individual elements spread generally throughout the state, though its three major facets had specific regions of concentration. Its southeastern industrial belt, extending across the state line along Lake Michigan from the Chicago area to and beyond Milwaukee, the state's largest city, is the primary factor in making Wisconsin the 11th-largest manufacturing state in the nation. The generally undulating landscape of the southern two-thirds of the state supports an agricultural life that makes it the major milk and cheese producer in America, a distinction the state long has fought to protect. The sparsely settled, northern evergreen-hardwood forest and lake country hosts much of the tourist and recreational activity of the upper Middle West, though other facilities, particularly in the south, are heavily used by residents of the Chicago area.

An overview of the state

The area of Wisconsin is 56,154 square miles (145,438 square kilometres), a territory slightly larger than England. The name given to the frontier territory in 1836 was an anglicized version of a French rendering of an Indian name said to mean "our homeland." Madison has been capital of the territory and state since 1837 and home campus of the University of Wisconsin since 1848.

PHYSICAL AND HUMAN GEOGRAPHY

The land. *Relief.* Wisconsin comprises five physical regions. The Northern Highland is a broad upland underlain by granitic bedrock. The Lake Superior Lowland is a narrow plain to which the surface of the Northern Highland drops abruptly. The upland slopes gently southward to the Central Plain, a crescent-shaped region on a sandstone bed that stretches across the centre of the state. In the southwest rises the picturesque Western Upland, a region etched into ridges and valleys by streams that have cut into the limestones and sandstones. The Southeastern Ridges and Lowlands are formed by three broad, parallel limestone ridges running north–south and separated by wide and shallow lowlands. There are thick glacial deposits throughout the state, except the southwest, whose irregular surface may in places consist of rough, boulder-strewn moraines; marshy wetlands; lakes, occurring in clusters or singly; or, more commonly, broad expanses of undulating topography. Northern Wisconsin, like neighbouring Minnesota, has one of the three or four greatest concentrations of lakes in the world. Wisconsin is one of the few states in which essentially all drainage is outflowing.

The five physical regions

Unusual surface features include the Apostle Islands in Lake Superior; the rocky Door Peninsula between Lake Michigan and Green Bay; the broad gorges of the Mississippi and lower Wisconsin rivers, cut 300 to 500 feet (90 to 150 metres) below the general surface; ancient mountain remnants such as the Baraboo Range, Rib Mountain, and the Gogebic Range; the irregular glacial "kettle moraine" west of Milwaukee; the narrow river gorge known as the Wisconsin Dells; sandy beaches of Lakes Michigan and Superior; and wild rivers such as the Wolf and the Brule.

Climate. Wisconsin has long, cold winters and warm but relatively short summers. Average temperatures in January range from 10° F (−12° C) in the north to 22° F (−6° C) in the southeast; in July, from 66° F (19° C) in the north to 72° F (22° C) in the southwest. The Great Lakes ameliorate both summer and winter temperatures along their margins. The length of the growing season diminishes westward and northward, from about six months in the southeast—where the best soils are found—to about three months in parts of the Northern Highland.

Annual rainfall averages about 30 inches (760 millimetres), the bulk of it occurring between May and October. Snowfall varies from about 30 inches in the south, with an 85-day cover, to 50 or 60 inches in the north, with a 140-day cover along Lake Superior. Streams and lakes in the state may be frozen from December to mid-April or later.

Plant and animal life. Forests, covering about 45 percent of the state, are most heavily concentrated in the Northern Highland and Central Plain. Trees are second-growth hardwoods—*e.g.,* maple, birch, oak, aspen, elm, basswood, and ash—and evergreen—white, red, and jack pine, hemlock, balsam fir, white and black spruce, white cedar, and tamarack. Much of the pine acreage is plantation growth.

White-tailed deer, foxes, cottontail rabbits, skunks, woodchucks, squirrels, chipmunks, and gophers are common in all areas. Black bear, coyotes, a few wolves, porcupines, beaver, eagles, and ruffed grouse live in the north. Pheasants are stocked in southern farming areas. Waterfowl are abundant, and migratory Canada geese by the thousands visit refuges twice annually. There are approximately 174 kinds of fish, including various trout species, bass, walleye, northern pike, muskellunge, and sturgeon.

Settlement patterns. The varied physical landscape of Wisconsin has contributed to a great diversity in human usage and patterns of settlement.

Among the more interesting regions is Door County, a long peninsula in Lake Michigan with miles of rocky shoreline and sandy beaches. A noted vacation land, it is forested but interspersed with summer cottages, stone fences, orchards, and small communities with summer theatres and arts-and-craft shops. Northern Wisconsin is a sparsely settled, heavily forested area whose hundreds of lakes and clear streams make it the epitome of the "north woods" for hunters, fishermen, and campers. Indian enclaves include Menomonee County, in which Indians hold their land as a group, and several reservations. The unglaciated "Driftless Area" in the southwest is scenic hill and valley country with steep, wooded slopes and bare rock exposures, rural pastoral scenes, old lead and zinc mines, and various European ethnic communities. The Sand Country of south central Wisconsin is a thinly settled region in which many mesa-like bluffs rise clifflike from the flat landscape. Sandy and marshy, it is covered with scrub oak and jack pine and produces cranberries and vegetables.

Rural agricultural settlement consists of dispersed farmsteads. Field shapes and road patterns give a checkerboard appearance to the land and reflect the township and range survey system from which they are derived, except where rough surfaces, wet lands, or contour farming patterns break the regularity. The traditional red dairy barn (considerably larger than the farm house) dominates the farmstead along with its milk house and cylindrical silos. The rectangularity of the open countryside moves into the small towns in which rectangular lots, each with its dwelling, line the crisscross streets oriented in cardinal directions.

Towns of less than 1,000 people dot the entire state, but most of the larger cities are in roughly the southeastern part of the state.

Milwaukee, with its satellite cities, is one of the country's major manufacturing centres, specializing in machinery, electrical equipment, and beer. It is a seaport and a cultural and educational centre. Madison, scenically located between lakes Mendota and Monona, is the capital and the location of the main campus of the University of Wisconsin.

Racine and Kenosha, on Lake Michigan south of Milwaukee, are small ports and between them produce tractors, automobiles, and metal goods. Green Bay is a lake port at the mouth of the Fox River and a paper centre. As the home of the Green Bay Packers, it is the sole survivor among major-league franchises of the small Middle Western cities that gave birth to professional football. Appleton is the largest city of a major paper-manufacturing area on the Fox River where it leaves Lake Winnebago. Oshkosh, on the western shore of Lake Winnebago, is a woodworking centre. La Crosse, a Mississippi river port, manufactures varied products.

The people. Wisconsin's population is predominantly of Northern European origin. German immigrants were most numerous, followed by Poles, Scandinavians (primarily Norwegians), and British. Persons of German ancestry are widely distributed today but more concentrated toward the east and in Milwaukee. Poles are numerous but live mainly in Milwaukee and the Stevens Point area. Norwegians are more numerous toward the west and south, with Swedes more toward more the north and northwest. By the late 20th century few persons were of foreign birth, and the majority have become a blend of different national ancestries. The black population lives in the southeastern lakeshore cities, with more than four-fifths in Milwaukee, where blacks make up about a quarter of the population. The only other cities with appreciable black populations are Racine, Madison, and Beloit, though blacks live in all of the 72 counties. About 29,000 American Indians remain, many of them in Menomonee County and the city of Milwaukee.

From the Depression of the 1930s to the late 1960s, northern Wisconsin generally lost population, but since that time the downward trend has reversed. Much of the Western Upland and the Central Plain show continuing decreases but at a slower rate. Although the southeast continues to increase in population, the rate of increase in that area has slowed.

Thus, although the majority of the population lives in the southeast and that area continues to increase in numbers faster than the rest of the state, it is increasing at a slower rate than formerly. The historic flow of migration from the north and the west to the southeast appears to be ebbing. Another migratory trend of nationwide dimensions is the continued movement from the urban centres to the suburban areas.

The economy. Wisconsin's economy ranks well on national scales, behind other, more populous, eastern north-central states such as Illinois, Michigan, and Ohio but in most respects ahead of the western north central states across the Mississippi. The major markets for its products, the sources of most of its energy supplies, and a high proportion of its raw materials lie outside the state, creating inward and outward flows that keep the state in close harmony with the nation's overall economy. It ranks among the top one-fourth of the states in farm income and value added by manufacture.

Resources. Small amounts of iron are mined in Wisconsin, but nonmetallic minerals such as sand and gravel, building and monumental stone, and agricultural lime are more important to the state's economy. Although 75 percent of the forests are hardwoods, paper pulp is the major timber product. In commercial fishery, most of it in Lake Michigan, the prized lake trout and whitefish show signs of responding to restoration measures after depletion by sea lamprey. Sport fish and wildlife figure in the economy through the expenditures made in quest of them, and the tourist and recreation industry is one of the most important elements in Wisconsin's economy. Almost three-fourths of the hydroelectric potentiality has been developed—mainly on the Wisconsin, Mississippi, and Chippewa–Flambeau rivers—but about 65 percent of the power is produced in coal-burning plants.

Industry and agriculture. The major producers of income in Wisconsin are manufacturing and processing, wholesale and retail trade, services (covering much of tourism), government, and construction. Manufacturing is concerned mainly with the production of metal goods and with the processing of agricultural and forest products. Agriculture is largely dairy farming. About four-fifths of farm incomes is derived from livestock and livestock products, more than one-half from dairy products alone. Wisconsin produces almost one-fifth of the nation's milk and almost two-fifths of its cheese. Dairy interests formerly so dominated the legislature that until 1967 the sale of coloured margarine was prohibited in the state. Among the features of Wisconsin highways and communities are stores specializing in cheeses of all kinds, wide varieties of wurst (sausage), and similar products, many of them manufactured locally. In addition, Wisconsin is one of the major beer-producing—and consuming—states

(Margin notes:)

Door County and the "north woods"

Principal cities

Migratory trends

Manufacturing and agriculture

in the nation, in some way a reflection of its strong German heritage.

Management of the economy. In addition to federal agencies and cooperatives, the economy of Wisconsin is influenced strongly by state agencies that are concerned with such areas as industry, labour, and human relations; agriculture; revenue; banking; and securities.

The Bureau of Vacation and Travel Services promotes tourism through information centres in Chicago, Milwaukee, and Minneapolis, through advertising in periodicals, and through the issuance of films, brochures, and other materials.

Labour unions are strong throughout the state, enrolling teachers, firemen, police, and civil-service employees as well as the industrial trades. Major employer organizations include the Wisconsin Association of Manufacturers and Commerce and the Building Trades Employers Association. The Wisconsin Employment Relations Commission, with roots dating to the Progressive era, serves as a mediator between labour and management.

In general the state's economic policy has been directed toward creating additional jobs; upgrading of the labour force through vocational and technical education; aiding small businesses, especially minority enterprises; and adding maximum value to raw materials before shipment out of state. Governmental programs to improve the economic self-sufficiency of persons living on the lower rungs of the economic ladder have not been as successful as was hoped, though poverty in general has been reduced sharply.

Transportation. Transportation route patterns concentrate toward the southeast, with Milwaukee and Chicago as the focal points, reflecting the greater population density and industrial concentration of that area. Intercity as well as intracity bus service is widespread. Of communities with more than 500 inhabitants, more than 90 percent are reached by natural-gas pipelines. Wisconsin ports handle more than one-fourth of the domestic freight tonnage on the Great Lakes; the largest are Superior, Milwaukee, and Green Bay. Railroad and automobile ferries cross Lake Michigan from four ports. Madison and Milwaukee are served by large commercial airlines and, along with smaller cities, by regional or commuter lines.

Administrative and social conditions. *Government.* The first Wisconsin constitution of 1848, as amended, is still the basic law. Amendments are passed by both houses of two successive legislatures and approved by referendum. Constitutional officers, since 1970 elected for four-year terms, are the governor, lieutenant governor, attorney general, secretaries of state and treasury, and superintendent of public instruction. The legislature comprises the Senate of 33 members elected for four-year terms and the Assembly of 99 members serving two-year terms of office.

The Supreme Court, primarily an appellate court, consists of seven judges elected statewide for ten-year terms. The state also has a Court of Appeals and a circuit court of original jurisdiction.

Units of local government include counties, towns, cities, and villages. Counties, which are agents both of the state and the locality, are governed by elected boards of supervisors. Within a county, all areas not part of a municipality are organized into towns, which usually coincide in boundary with the six-mile-square government townships. At annual town meetings, qualified voters make policy decisions that are carried out by a three-member town board.

Nonpartisan office elections are held in the spring, partisan ones in the fall; both are preceded by primaries. Chosen in nonpartisan elections are judges, the state superintendent of public instruction, school-board members, county supervisors, and city, village, and town officers. All other local, state, and national officers are chosen on a partisan basis. Primaries are open; that is, a person may vote in the primary of any one party regardless of accustomed party affiliation or of how the voter plans to vote in the general election. Wisconsin political leaders who have gained national prominence embrace all reaches of the ideological spectrum, from the Progressive traditions of the La Follettes to the controversial conservative senator Joseph McCarthy.

There are two systems of party organization, statutory and voluntary. The actual party power is in the latter, which consists of dues-paying members. Each voluntary party holds a state convention and develops a party platform, which is officially adopted at the statutory party platform convention.

Social issues. State government in Wisconsin is deeply involved in many aspects of the social milieu, often in cooperation with federal agencies and programs. Although per capita personal income is below the national average, Wisconsin had a lower percentage of poverty than all but three states in 1975, indicating less of a spread between high and low incomes than is true of most areas. The percentage of poor is twice as great in rural areas, but they number about as many as the urban poor, who cluster mainly in the inner cities. High percentages of blacks, migrant workers, and Indians live in poverty.

Education. Overall responsibility for elementary and secondary education lies with the Department of Public Instruction, with local boards of education overseeing local districts.

The major system of public higher education is the University of Wisconsin System, which in 1974 incorporated the Wisconsin State Universities System to create 13 four-year, degree-granting campuses, 14 two-year (Center System) campuses, and the University Extension system. In addition there is a vocational, technical and adult education system and a few remaining two-year county teachers' colleges. Among the major private degree-granting institutions are Marquette (Milwaukee; founded 1857) and Lawrence (Appleton; 1847) universities and Beloit (Beloit; 1846), Carroll (Waukesha; 1846), Ripon (Ripon; 1850), and St. Norbert (West De Pere; 1893) colleges. The school of architecture located on the grounds of Taliesen East, the home of Frank Lloyd Wright in Spring Green, is a mecca for both students and experienced architects.

Health and welfare. Within the Department of Health and Social Services is a division operating correctional institutions that include prisons, a reformatory, schools or camps, and state farms. Other divisions coordinate programs for the aged, administer child-welfare programs, and supervise county administration of welfare funds. The Divisions of Health and of Mental Hygiene are also active.

Cultural life. The settlers of Wisconsin represented extreme diversity in ethnic background, ranging from New Englanders and Southerners to an across-the-board selection of almost every European nationality. Those of like origin tended to settle in enclaves, each retaining much of its transplanted cultural heritage, and gave the state a wide variety in arts and art forms. As the population became more homogenized in statewide and nationwide terms, these unique modes of expression remained in large part, producing both a rich diversity and a widespread appreciation of the arts in general among the populace.

The University of Wisconsin has reflected and enhanced the statewide interest in the arts. It was the first university in the country to sponsor an artist in residence. It supports the Fine Arts Quartet in Milwaukee and the Pro Arte String Quartet in Madison, a group with a long and esteemed international reputation. Through University Extension it has over the years sponsored and worked with artists' groups, writers' groups, and theatrical and dance groups throughout the state. In summer it operates music clinics for high school students from throughout the country. The Elvehjem Art Center (1970) is both an instructional and display museum.

In 1957 the Extension was instrumental also in bringing into being the Wisconsin Arts Foundation and Council, which later became an official state committee known as the Wisconsin Arts Council. In 1973 the government created the Arts Board, an agency designed to administer aid to groups and individuals in the arts. By the late 1970s about $250,000 per year in state funds were being appropriated for artistic and cultural activities.

Milwaukee is a major arts centre. Each year the United Performing Arts Fund raises about $2,500,000 earmarked for the support of performing groups. The Milwaukee Art Museum, an institution established by the merger of the Layton Art Gallery and the Milwaukee Art Institute, has, with the gift of the Bradley Collection, become one of the world's outstanding collections of 20th-century art. Many smaller cities also have art museums.

Ethnic festivals

Many of the national groups continue to hold annual festivals. The William Tell Pageant by the Swiss in New Glarus features the production of Schiller's play *Wilhelm Tell*. Norwegians hold the Syttende Mai festival in Stoughton, and perform the Song of Norway at the Little Norway Museum in Blue Mounds. The Fyr Fest is held on Washington Island by persons of Icelandic origin. Numerous arts-and-crafts fairs are held in centres throughout the state.

Among the many historical sites and museums in the state is the Circus World Museum in Baraboo, which collects and displays artifacts and other materials from circuses around the world. Many of its wagons and other paraphernalia are used in Milwaukee's annual circus parade.

(Ro.W.F.)

HISTORY

Early settlement. Wisconsin was visited by a French explorer, Jean Nicolet, in 1634 and was under French control until 1763, when it was acquired by the British. It was subsequently ceded to the United States by the Treaty of Paris in 1783, which ended the American Revolution.

After the war a new era began for the region between Lake Michigan and the Mississippi River. In 1816 military garrisons were established at Ft. Howard (Green Bay) and Ft. Crawford (Prairie du Chien) and, in 1828, after a brief Winnebago Indian uprising, at Ft. Winnebago near Portage. Beginning in 1818 civil government was administered from the Michigan territorial capital at Detroit. A part of the old Northwest Territory, the Wisconsin region had been nominally attached to Indiana from 1800 to 1809, to Illinois from 1809 to 1818, and thereafter to Michigan until 1836. The governor of Michigan promptly established counties west of Lake Michigan, appointed local officials, and, in 1820, made a long canoe voyage of inspection.

A law in 1816 excluded foreigners from the fur trade and enabled the American Fur Company to rise to wealth and power. Exploitation of another of Wisconsin's natural resources, the lead deposits, brought a flood of miners into the southwestern area, reaching an estimated 2,500 by 1830. The influx was briefly halted by the Black Hawk War in 1832, but the war broke the Indian power in Wisconsin.

Black Hawk War

Wisconsin Territory and statehood. In 1836 Wisconsin became a separate territory, with its western boundary at the Missouri River until 1838. The vigorous and populous mining area assumed control in organizing the territory. Henry Dodge, hero of the Black Hawk War, received the appointment as governor. On May 29, 1848, Wisconsin was admitted to the Union with its present boundaries. Nelson Dewey of Cassville was elected the first governor.

The first years of statehood were at a time of great social, economic, and political activity. The population reached 305,000 by 1850; of these, over 36 percent were foreign born, with Germans predominating. The temperance crusade, the nativist, or Know-Nothing, movement, and anti-slavery agitation sweeping the North found strong support in Wisconsin. Wheat became the first commercial crop, and in 1860 Wisconsin produced the greatest wheat crop in its history. Lumbering ranked next to agriculture in importance, the industry spreading rapidly up the river valleys and along the eastern lakeshore. Water power sites became flour mill and sawmill cities; Mississippi River and Lake Michigan harbours became flourishing commercial ports.

Strongly Democratic at the time of admission, Wisconsin gradually shifted its political faith. In passing on the case of an escaped black slave the state Supreme Court declared the Fugitive Slave Law unconstitutional and void in Wisconsin. A protest meeting at Ripon in March 1854 proposed that a new party be formed, to be called the Republican Party. A state organization was effected that July and in 1856 a Republican governor took office. Wisconsin helped elect the Republican Abraham Lincoln in 1860 and supported his administration during the Civil War.

In the business boom that followed the war, railroads expanded rapidly, and small lines were consolidated into a few powerful companies. The postwar years saw the enormous expansion of the lumber business, which reached a peak in the decade 1890–1900. The uncontrolled power of the railroads and the fall of farm prices in the panic of 1873 turned numbers of voters to a political coalition that elected a Democratic governor in 1873 and enacted the Potter Law, pioneer legislation to regulate railway rates, which was soon repealed. With diminishing returns from wheat crops, farmers began to turn to diversified farming and dairying.

The Wisconsin Idea. The decade of the 1890s saw a four-year reversal of the long Republican rule. The Democratic vote was largely a protest against national measures, accentuated in Wisconsin by the Bennett Law, providing for the enforcement of the teaching of English in all public and parochial schools, which many foreign-born citizens regarded as a move to outlaw parochial schools. Dissension was brewing within the Republican Party, dominated by lumber barons and railroad magnates. Against their rule Robert M. La Follette led a reformist revolt and won the governorship in 1900. Through a close working relationship with social scientists at the University of Wisconsin, known as the "Wisconsin Idea" and based on a willingness to experiment in meeting changing needs, the Progressive faction instituted a number of reforms: equitable taxation of railroads, the direct primary and civil service, and in later years a stringent corrupt practices act, workmen's compensation, state income tax and industrial commission, and other pioneer social and economic measures. After 1905 La Follette continued his reform crusade in the U.S. Senate, where he served as a leader of the progressive wing of the Republican Party until his death in 1925. La Follette's long term in office was remarkable in view of his open opposition to the declaration of war against Germany in 1916 and to the League of Nations.

The "Wisconsin Idea"

Pattern of modern development. The census of 1930 revealed that Wisconsin had become predominantly urban. By this time the pattern of modern development had been set. Wisconsin was an industrial state, with manufacturing concentrated on the Lake Michigan shore and in river basin areas. Industrialization brought problems connected with metropolitan life and demands of a labour population for recognition. Farms and farmers decreased in number, but farm production rose with the advance of scientific agriculture. The dairy cow still symbolized Wisconsin's pride.

In politics Wisconsin maintained its liberal traditions but spread its party votes. Two La Follette sons held the offices of governor and U.S. senator for six years and 21 years, respectively; each was succeeded by a conservative Republican. In 1934 the progressive wing formally set up a separate party but united with the regular Republicans in 1946. Joseph McCarthy, a conservative Republican, served in the U.S. Senate from 1947 until his death in 1957. In recent years, control of the legislature's lower house and state offices has seesawed between parties; and, although the state's U.S. congressmen have usually approached an even political division, the Republicans have predominated.

(Ed.)

THE SOUTHWEST

The "Southwest" is a term that has long been in use in the United States to denote a geographic area, and its meaning has changed over the years as the nation has expanded. After the War of 1812, the Southwest generally meant Missouri, Arkansas, and Louisiana. After Texas was annexed, it too was included. In the wake of the war with Mexico, the Southwest embraced most, but not all, of the territory acquired under the Treaty of Guadalupe Hidalgo (1848). California's littoral and great interior valleys were so different in physiography and development that the term never settled easily upon them. Rather, the Southwest came to mean, by and large, the 1,000-mile (1,600-

kilometre) stretch of arid land from Texas and Oklahoma, through New Mexico and Arizona, to the deserts athwart the lower Colorado River. It could include the contiguous parts of Colorado, Utah, and Nevada as suited the convenience of the person using the term.

Early explorers found a diverse and difficult topography. The high, dry plains of Texas, sliced in the north by such unexpected abysses as Palo Duro Canyon, rose imperceptibly to the Pecos Valley of New Mexico, a dividing line that the myriads of buffalo farther east seldom crossed. Beyond the Pecos and embracing its headwaters were the southern spurs of the Rocky Mountains, cool with evergreens. West of the Rockies came vast horizontal strata of highly coloured sandstone; in places these beds formed broad peneplains whose dry monotony was broken by occasional mesas or buttes. Where the beds were higher they were cut by spectacular gorges, four of which—Zion, Bryce, and the Canyonlands in southern Utah and the Grand Canyon in Arizona, all on the Colorado River— became national parks. Westward beyond a forested uplift that cut across Arizona from northwest to southeast, lay the true deserts marked by prickly plant growths and parallel chains of north-south mountains, gaunt and almost devoid of vegetation.

Colorado River gorges

The common denominator of the land was aridity. Although the highest peaks of New Mexico and Arizona caught 30 inches (750 millimetres) of rain or more a year, the annual average was less than half that amount; indeed, the western deserts might receive only 2 inches (50 millimetres) or less. Except for the snow on the mountains, the bulk of this scanty precipitation came during violent thunderstorms; the flash floods that they produced did much to give the region its scarred and angular topography.

High temperatures and rapid evaporation intensified the dryness. Precipitation that would support dry farming in the Dakotas or Nebraska proved, generally speaking, inadequate in the Southwest: crops could be grown there only with irrigation. Yet the region's two principal rivers, the Colorado and the Rio Grande (both of which rise outside the area), as well as the smaller streams of the local mountains, could be tapped at only a handful of widely scattered spots. This overwhelming geographic fact turned some of the prehistoric Indians into sedentary agriculturalists, determined the shape of the Spanish occupation, and ultimately led the American inhabitants to an alliterative folk description of their economy as one of "copper, cattle, cotton, and climate."

Despite oversimplification, there is much to justify this summation. Geologic evidence even suggested that aridity might have had some bearing on the Southwest's huge deposits of low-grade copper ore, the so-called porphyry coppers. Mexicans were working the richer streaks of the long-productive ore body at Santa Rita, New Mexico, before 1800; other veins were opened in southeastern Arizona following the Civil War. The great development, however, came after 1910, when the handling of enormous tonnages by power shovels in open-pit mines lifted Arizona to first place among the copper-producing states. Compared with this outpouring of copper, the Southwest's brief stampedes for gold and silver and later for oil and uranium achieved little more than regional significance.

The dryness of the land enforced a pastoral agricultural economy that began in 1598, when Juan de Oñate established in the Rio Grande Valley of New Mexico the first permanent colonies of the western United States. Because of the difficulty of supervision, cattle were not popular with the first settlers. Horses, however, multiplied rapidly and were soon spread among the Indians by barter and theft. Sheep ranches grew to enormous size (in the early 1800s New Mexico's governor, Bartolomé Baca, owned 2,000,000 head), and social cleavage was largely between those who owned sheep and those who herded them. The Pueblo Indians took readily to the animals and learned to weave wool just as they were already weaving a native cotton. The Navaho learned the craft from the Pueblo, developed their famous blankets, and as late as World War II accounted for half the sheep raised in Arizona.

During the period of Spanish ascendancy, the sheep were

Earliest permanent settlement

driven to market among the silver mines of Mexico. In the 1850s the California goldfields offered an outlet for those owners willing to brave the long trek across mountains and desert to the coast. After the Civil War the demand of the new Southwestern Indian reservations and army posts for beef lured herds of longhorns west from Texas. When the Apaches of the mountains were brought under control, permanent establishments took root in New Mexico and Arizona, sometimes in violent conflict with rival sheep ranches. High profits made overgrazing of the public domain a more serious threat to the economy of the Southwest than the Indians ever were. Only federal control, exerted through an increasing number of agencies, was able to check the trend and start restoring the ranges.

Other federal intervention came in the management of water resources. Irrigation had been practiced before AD 1000 by the Pueblo Indians in New Mexico and central Arizona. The Spanish added a few *acequias*, or "ditches," of their own, often as part of the huge land grants belatedly made by the Mexican government in the hope of establishing agricultural communities as buffers against the encroaching Americans. In their turn these Americans, individually and through cooperatives, struggled to increase the paltry stream diversions; but measures commensurate with the problems were not possible until the Reclamation Act of 1902 made available the resources of the national government.

The Reclamation Service's first successful large-scale project in the nation was Theodore Roosevelt Dam near Phoenix, completed in 1911. The largest project in the Southwest was Hoover Dam on the Colorado River, completed in 1936 (though the Glen Canyon Dam, upriver from Hoover, completed in 1964, closely approached it in size). But the water proved expensive and led to intensive cultivation of high-income crops: alfalfa, citrus, and long-staple cotton. It also led, in the case of streams crossing state boundaries, to complex legal disputes, the bitterest of which concerned the diversion of the Colorado River water far from its natural channels. Various state compacts were entered into by the claimants, but sectional jealousies militated against a satisfactory solution. After World War II the water shortage was made even more critical when developments associated with aviation and nuclear energy brought an unprecedented influx of industry and population into all of the Southwest's urban areas.

Though the crisp climate and scenic landscapes were a curse to agriculture, they were a boon to businesses catering to tourists and health-seekers. These visitors, it was shortly discovered, had a lively interest in the once-despised cultures of the Indians and Spanish-Americans. The heavily beamed, flat-roofed Indian pueblo, as modified by the Spanish, became the inspiration for the region's new architecture. Indian dances, Spanish fiestas, and cowtown rodeos, catching hold first as tourist attractions, became the year's social and economic high points for scores of communities. Although the showier forms of this evolving culture were not truly typical of any of its founding strains, they fixed themselves, in the popular mind at least, as an even more distinctive feature of the American Southwest than the ancient angular topography and dazzling sunlight. (D.S.La./Ed.)

Revival of native cultures

Slightly to the east, in Texas and Oklahoma, another kind of prosperity developed. This was oil country, and oases of prosperity resulted from local oil booms.

Along the Gulf Coast a flourishing industrial region developed around Houston and the nearby ports of Galveston, Corpus Christi, Port Arthur, and Beaumont, Texas. Houston and Galveston first developed as exporters of cotton, grain, and oil. Subsequently the wealth of local petroleum, natural gas, salt, sulfur, and minerals from the sea made the chemical industries so predominant that the region is sometimes called the petrochemical belt. Other industries include packing, transportation, and construction.

Inland, the cities of central Texas are found close to the belt of limey soil known as the black waxy prairie. Cotton is still important, but livestock raising and general farming are now more common. Toward the west the country changes from farmland to mediocre grazing land; and the threat of drought, prevalent throughout Texas, becomes more serious, as in the rest of the Southwest. Irrigation and dry farming support considerable cotton.

The cities vary widely in character. Dallas, an eastern city in appearance, is the financial capital not only of Texas but of the entire Southwest as well. Neighbouring Fort Worth is a trade centre for the ranches, dryland farms, and oil fields to the west. Austin, nestled against the Balcones escarpment, is the state capital and the site of the University of Texas. San Antonio, most Mexican of large Texas cities, is noted for stockyards and meat packing. All of these cities have some manufacturing, but the greatest industrial development has occurred between Dallas and Fort Worth, where instrument, electronic, aircraft, and automobile-assembly plants have sprung up.

To the north, in Oklahoma, wheat fields border cotton fields. Oil refining is the outstanding industry, but cities such as Tulsa and Oklahoma City add meat packing, flour milling, textiles, and light mechanical and electronic industries. (V.Ca./Ed.)

Arizona

A classic symbol of America's Old West, Arizona is rich in legends of the Indian leaders Geronimo and Cochise and of towns such as Tombstone, where feuding between the Earps and Clantons erupted into the West's most famous shoot-out, the gunfight at the O.K. Corral. Comprising an area of 113,909 square miles (295,023 square kilometres), Arizona today, with its modern cities, sprawling suburban developments, and transportation arteries, shows quite a different face. Nevertheless, in its broad expanses of sparsely settled country, its extraordinarily coloured rock walls and mountains rising above dramatic desert plains, and its adobe pueblo buildings and baroque Spanish missions, much of the natural and human landscape that characterized its frontier days has been preserved.

The state is part of the rapidly growing southern rim of the Sun Belt. Its early ties with Mexico, however, have continued both in trade and tourism and in the problem of illegal movements across the border. Since World War II Arizona has become less of a corridor to California and more of a destination for new residents. Many people are attracted by the state's climate, scenery, and life-style, as well as by the economic opportunities available.

Internal contradictions | Arizona is a deceptive state, even beyond the most obvious contrasts between its sophisticated urban life and its open ranges with cattle roaming across roadways. It has long been touted as one of the healthiest areas of the country; yet for its poor, including nearly 150,000 Indians, the rate of infant mortality and of such diseases as tuberculosis and diphtheria is well above the national average. Industries and automobiles and other phenomena of modern living have clouded the once clear skies of the state, especially around Tucson and Phoenix, the capital and largest city in the Mountain States. Irrigated vegetable and cotton farms spread greenery from one horizon to another in parts of the state, but water supplies have become a major problem. Thousands of people have migrated to Arizona, but population growth has destroyed some of the state's attractive qualities. Although many newcomers anticipate a land of personal fulfillment, the state's divorce and crime rates are among the highest in the country. The many opportunities offered by a booming economy are also accompanied by an extremely high bankruptcy rate and by unsatisfactory job opportunities for many. Arizona is attempting to build a modern industrial society in a dry land and to conserve as much as possible a landscape and quality of life that could so easily be sacrificed in the process.

PHYSICAL AND HUMAN GEOGRAPHY

The land. Next to climate, the beauty and variety of Arizona's landscape constitute its greatest natural attraction. The terrain's broad, sloping plains provide a foreground for seemingly ever-present mountains, cliffs, and hills. The charm of its relief is enhanced by the widespread exposure of colourful rocks. The brilliant sunlight illuminates vegetative cover that ranges from green-carpeted pine and fir forests to shrub and cactus deserts, all augmented by brief bursts of colour from spectacular seasonal displays of wild flowers.

Relief. To Arizona's two major physiographic divisions, the Colorado Plateau and the Basin and Range Province, local authorities add the Transition. The northeastern two-fifths of Arizona is part of the scenic Colorado Plateau. Far less rugged than adjacent portions in Utah, these tablelands in Arizona consist mainly of plains interrupted by step-like escarpments. Although labelled mesas and plateaus, their ruggedness and inaccessibility has been exaggerated. The incomparable Grand Canyon of the Colorado River provides the major exception to what has proven to be an area easily traversed. Forest-clad volcanic mountains atop the plateaus provide the state's highest points, Humphreys Peak, 12,633 feet (3,851 metres), in the San Francisco Mountains, and Baldy Peak, 11,590 feet (3,533 metres), in the White Mountains. | Land forms

More than 200 miles (320 kilometres) of the southern border of the Plateau is marked by a series of giant escarpments known collectively as the Mogollon Rim. West and south of the rim, a number of streams follow narrow canyons or broad valleys south through the Transition region and into the Basin and Range Province. The Transition region bordering the plateaus comprises separated plateau blocks, rugged peaks, and isolated rolling uplands.

The Basin and Range region of the southern and western third of the state, containing the bulk of the population but none of the large canyons and mesas for which Arizona is famous, consists largely of broad, open-ended basins or valleys of gentle slope. Isolated mountains rise like islands in the desert plain.

Contrary to desert stereotypes, sand dunes cover less than 1 percent of the state, and stony desert surfaces are seldom visible. The younger soils of river floodplains provide the more desirable soils for agriculture. Only the Colorado River and several dozen small headwater streams in the well-watered White Mountain–Mogollon Rim–Transition areas have year-round flows. Old records indicate that such major rivers as the Gila, Verde, San Pedro, and Santa Cruz once had stretches of permanent water with fish, beaver, and otter.

Climate. About half of Arizona is semiarid, one-third is arid, and the remainder is humid. The Basin and Range region has the arid and semiarid subtropical climate that attracts most winter visitors and new residents. Receiving more than 80 percent of the possible sunshine, January days have a mean maximum temperature of 65° F (18° C) in Phoenix. Occasional light frosts occur at most locations during a four-month period, and light rains punctuate the winter months, interrupting exceedingly dry springs and mildly dry falls. Summer daily maximum readings average 104° F (40° C) in Phoenix, and night temperatures drop to an average of 78° F (26° C).

Moisture-laden air from the Gulf of Mexico appears in July, bringing more than two months of irregular but sometimes heavy thundershowers that are locally referred to as the "summer monsoon." Phoenix and Tucson receive more than one inch (25 millimetres) of rain in July. Winter rains come from the Pacific.

The Colorado Plateau has cool to cold winters and a semiarid climate. Near mile-high elevations and direct exposure to polar air masses can produce January mean highs and lows as divergent as the 46° F (8° C) and 19° F (−7° C) in Winslow. Summer temperatures on the plateau are generally 10° cooler than those of Phoenix. Most of the region receives from 10 to 15 inches (250–375 millimetres) of rain, with a winter maximum along the western borders.

Because of the great amount of relief, climatic conditions within the Transition vary widely over small areas. Despite its desert image, 17 percent of Arizona falls into the humid class, much of it lying in the Transition and adjacent high southern edge of the Plateau.

Plant and animal life. Considering the variety in relief and climate, it is not surprising to find similar diversity in the vegetation. About 10 percent of Arizona is forested, 25 percent woodland, 25 percent grass, and 40 percent desert shrub. Elevations above 6,000 to 7,000 feet (1,830–2,130 metres) host forests of ponderosa pine, topped in

Variety
of natural
life

the highest areas by Douglas and other firs, spruces, and aspen. Below the forests, piñon pine dominates the plateau woodlands, and evergreen oak or chaparral the Basin and Range. Plains grasses cover about one-third of the plateau, and Sonoran or desert grass carpets the higher elevations of the basins. Mesquite trees are invading many former grasslands in the south. Foothills in the Tucson–Phoenix area carry giant saguaro cacti of the Sonoran Desert, matched in areas of the northwest Basin and Range by dramatic stands of Joshua trees. Shrubs dominate the lowest portions of all areas: big sagebrush and saltbush in the plateau, creosote bush in the Basin and Range.

Animal life is even more varied, with representatives of the Rocky Mountain, Great Plains, and Mexican ecological communities. Important larger animals are black bear, deer, desert bighorn sheep, antelope, and wapiti, or elk. The tropical coati, a raccoon-like mammal, has spread northward into Arizona, while the javelina ("wild pig") is a favourite game animal in the south. Among the several cats, the bobcat and the mountain lion are most prized. Coyotes, skunks, and porcupines abound, as do cottontails and jackrabbits, and there are several varieties of foxes. Lying along a major flyway, the state's southern border area is rich in birds, which attract thousands of watchers. Game birds include turkeys and a variety of quails and doves. Among native fish are the Arizona trout and the Colorado squawfish. Poisonous animals include the rattlesnake, scorpion, and Gila monster.

Settlement patterns. Despite Arizona's romantic image as a land of picturesque ghost towns and mining camps, isolated ranches, primitive Indian reservations, and bucolic cotton and citrus farms, more than five-sixths of its population is concentrated in urban settlements of more than 2,500 residents. The Phoenix and Tucson metropolitan areas together account for more than two-thirds of the state's population. The unincorporated status of mining centres with populations of up to 6,000 and of new towns comprising retirement and resort communities of from 2,000 to 30,000 people further obscures the degree of urbanization of the Arizona population. Hundreds of "subdivisions," which consist only of street names, lot numbers, and a few dwellings, are located throughout the state.

Rural and
ranching
life

Approximately 30,000 people live on the more than 5,000 recognized farm and ranch units. The typical ranch house and headquarters stands at the mouth of a canyon or some other source of dependable water. The irrigated lands of the central and southern regions contrast with the surrounding desert, presenting a flat, green, tree-studded landscape that often resembles cultivated plains of the Midwest and South. Rectangular fields planted in rows of cotton, sometimes paralleled by concrete-lined irrigation ditches with earthen banks, give regularity and linearity to the landscape.

Most towns and cities have low population density, the result of large lots and considerable vacant land within built-up areas. Residential building during the 20th century adhered almost exclusively to styles popular in the West, producing relatively uniform neighbourhoods of bungalow, Spanish revival, and ranch-style houses. Smaller towns contain mostly wood-frame dwellings and brick commercial buildings, and buildings of adobe can be seen in older areas in southern Arizona. Prescott, the first capital of Arizona, reflects its founding by Northerners in its red-brick buildings, central courthouse square, and dwellings more typical of the eastern United States.

Dominance of the Phoenix trading area, which extends over much of the state, began with its selection as the permanent location for the state capital, its central location, and the extensive agricultural economy that developed after the completion of Roosevelt Dam and Reservoir on the Salt River in 1911. Tucson, the early centre of Mexican and Anglo settlement, continues as the wholesale, retail, and entertainment centre of southern Arizona. It maintains well-developed commercial and medical ties with Sonora and northern Sinaloa states in Mexico.

The people. Arizonans traditionally identify themselves as Anglo, Mexican, Indian, black, and Chinese. The numerically dominant Anglos in the cities have a variety of

European backgrounds, but few are foreign born, and ethnic identification is less important than association with a prior home state. Traces of the heavy Texas contribution to the rural population can be detected in speech, attitudes, and customs.

Most of the Arizonans of Hispanic heritage are Mexican. Relations between Mexicans and Anglos in Arizona generally have had a history of cordiality that has been absent in other border states. Mexicans live in a variety of neighbourhoods and, especially in southern Arizona, often participate fully in business, political, and social life. Many prominent families in southern Arizona are Mexican. Intermarriage is common, especially in border cities such as Nogales. Mexican food, building styles, home furnishings, clothing, social customs, and music have been incorporated into the Arizona life-style. Barrios, where the Spanish language and Mexican culture dominate, continue to reflect historic, economic, or voluntary forces. Mexican organizations designed to help individuals, to preserve Mexican culture, and to guard against discriminatory practices vary greatly in their militancy.

The
Mexican
influence

Arizona has long been associated with the American Indian, for many of the final, dramatic conflicts between frontiersman and native occurred in the state. Few native Arizona Indian tribes experienced the tragic annihilation or displacement that occurred elsewhere, and more Indians now live in Arizona and comprise a higher percentage of the total population than in any other state. The Indians group themselves into some 15 tribes on 17 reservations, which range in size from the 85-acre (34-hectare) Tonto Apache reserve to the almost 9,000,000-acre reserve of the Navajo. The latter tribe, numbering more than 92,000 in Arizona, presses vigorously to direct the development of its land and people, and the tribal government assumes partial or complete responsibility in many areas of social and economic life.

Among the remaining tribes, the best known are the once-militant Apache and the highly talented Hopi people, each of whom also pursues aggressive development programs similar to those of the Navajo. Less well-known are the Papago and Pima tribes, historic allies of the frontiersman. The peaceful Papago may well be the nation's poorest people. The larger tribes, however, are increasingly active in managing all aspects of reservation life.

For Arizona's black residents, constituting 3 percent of the total population, housing remains largely segregated, but Arizona schools desegregated voluntarily in the early 1940s.

The economy. As Arizona's population grew, its economy shifted from a frontier stage emphasizing industries oriented toward natural resources to industries associated with more advanced economies.

Industry and tourism. Manufacturing has become the most important basic industry; notable are the electrical, communications, aeronautical, and aluminum industries. The great increase in manufacturing employment since World War II has given Arizona one of the most dynamic economies in the nation.

Tourist expenditures account in part for the high per capita employment and volume of retail sales. Manufacturing and tourism both depend upon natural resources in an essentially nonconsuming fashion. Manufacturers find a large, talented labour pool attracted by the state's climate and scenery. Tourism reflects even more directly the attraction of the warm winters and the physical features of the landscape. Natural and human features of historic, scientific, and recreational value have been protected and developed by the government, probably to a greater extent in Arizona than in any other state. There are more than 50 government-administered areas, including state and tribal parks and national parks, monuments, memorials, forests, recreation areas, historic sites, and game and wildlife refuges.

Management of the economy. The magnitude of the federal government's role in the Arizona economy is evident also in its numerous military facilities. The total personal income of federal military and civilian employees exceeds that of all occupations except services, manufacturing, and retail trade. These expeditures reflect in part

Presence
of the
federal
government

the federal government's ownership of nearly 45 percent of Arizona's land and another 27 percent under the jurisdiction of the Bureau of Indian Affairs. Only about 18 percent of Arizona is private land, but there is no shortage of acreage for urban settlement. Although the economic effects of large public holdings remain controversial, the positive contribution of public lands to the aesthetic quality of the landscape is unquestioned.

Agriculture. Farming has continued to thrive in Arizona in spite of the state's water problems. Agricultural employment, however, has declined. Cotton, followed by grain, hay, and produce, is the leading cash crop. Arizona produces a large percentage of the nation's long-staple (Pima) cotton. Compared to cotton, grain and hay take up larger amounts of acreage and more water, but their economic returns are lower. Citrus growing has continued to increase in the Yuma area. Except for several thousand acres on northern Indian reservations, all crops are irrigated, and some deliver yields more than twice the national average. The average size of farms in Arizona is larger than that in any other state.

The grazing of livestock occupies 30 times more land than crop raising, but its cash value generally has declined relative to crop farming. Feeder lots near agricultural areas, though less romantic than the open range, hold about half of the approximately 1,000,000 cattle within the state.

Agriculture uses almost 90 percent of the water in Arizona. Groundwater remained private property until 1958. A series of court decisions in the 1960s and 1970s restricted the transfer of water between basins, and in 1977 a state bill was passed that formulated comprehensive water regulations. Rights to the scarce water have been complicated further by suits filed by Arizona Indian tribes to recover water claims.

Mining and forestry. Copper remains Arizona's most distinctive contribution to the national economy, accounting for about two-thirds of the nation's total annual production. The highly efficient open-pit operations employ a relatively small labour force. Interest in small-scale mining greatly exceeds the actual production. Petroleum from the Four Corners area of the Navajo Reservation is modest; coal from the Black Mesa area of the Hopi Reservation is used in generating stations.

The lumber and pulp-paper industry deserves notice because it clearly contradicts two widely held illusions about Arizona: that the state is all desert and that a shortage of water has deterred industrialization. Most of the ponderosa pine comes from the Mogollon Rim–White Mountain area.

Transportation. Arizona's transcontinental routes carry more people and goods through the state than into it. The east–west interstate highway traversing the relatively level Colorado Plateau in the north provides the nation's major highway and railway link between the Midwest and southern California. A historically older but less used route through the valleys and basins of the south is followed by the Southern Pacific Railroad and an interstate highway. Interstate highways also serve the north–south route connecting Flagstaff, Phoenix, Tucson, and Nogales. The large amount of gentle relief and the small amount of rainfall make unpaved roads serviceable for remote areas, except immediately following a rain. Owners of four-wheel-drive vehicles and motorcycles explore the backcountry on weekends—to the increasing concern of cattlemen and environmentalists. Both Phoenix and Tucson have direct air flights to major cities in the United States and to Mexico.

Administrative and social conditions. *Government.* The constitution of Arizona reflects the strength of the Progressive movement at the time of the constitutional convention in 1910. It provides for maximum citizen participation through initiative and referendum on legislation and recall of all elected officials including judges. It also features a broad dispersal of executive power: the governor's office shares administrative authority with numerous other elective offices. A reorganization of the state government in 1972 strengthened the power of the governor and streamlined the executive branch. The secretary of state, who succeeds to the governorship in case of a vacancy, holds the second most highly contested elective office in the state.

The legislature comprises the 60-member House of Representatives and the 30-member Senate. The massive growth of Phoenix and Tucson, combined with reapportionment, has given urbanized Maricopa and Pima counties three-fourths of the seats in both houses.

A constitutional amendment in 1960 restructured the judicial branch into the Supreme Court, the Court of Appeals, Superior Court, and local justice and other courts; there are no special courts. Judges of the Supreme Court and the Court of Appeals are appointed by the governor from nominees chosen by a commission. Other judges are appointed or elected.

The 14 counties, acting as agents of the state, constitute the basic unit of local government. Elected county supervisors are relatively free of legislative direction other than imposed restraints upon taxation and budgeting. There are no township governments. State law prescribes the type of town government available for settlements under 3,000 population and the city form to be used by larger communities, but metropolitan centres have considerably more freedom in organization and operation.

Arizona has changed from a traditional one-party state dominated by the Democrats to a two-party system. Republican strength is centred in the Phoenix area, but the party also receives support from rural, conservative "Pinto" Democrats. Liberal Democratic factions continue to receive support in mining communities, among traditionally Democratic Mexican-Americans, and from segments of the metropolitan populations, especially in Tucson. In several rural southern counties, Democrats run unopposed for local offices.

Social issues. Because wages and income vary greatly between the extremes of manufacturing and the part-time seasonal work in agriculture and services, average figures are misleading. The large number of employees in high-paying electronic and military-related industries push the average wage in manufacturing to the national level. The large underemployed Indian, Mexican, and black population, however, coupled with the inflow of newcomers, keeps wages depressed in many fields. Contrary to popular opinion, the cost of living in Phoenix and Tucson is above the average of the 25 largest cities in the country.

Health and welfare. Public opinion consistently ranks Arizona among the healthiest areas in the nation, if not the world, although actual data are not adequate to support the belief. Among some groups, infant mortality and several diseases occur at high rates, and San Joaquin Valley fever (primary coccidioidomycosis) is common. Evidence indicates that the low humidity and mild winters have a therapeutic or arresting effect on some forms of pulmonary and arthritic health problems, but it has not been demonstrated scientifically that the general native-born population or young immigrants can expect to be healthier than residents elsewhere in the United States.

The state Department of Health Services controls a variety of administrative, aid, and inspection services, including institutions for children and mental patients in Phoenix; counties maintain public hospitals. Private medical care in the metropolitan areas is excellent, but for the state as a whole, the number of physicians and dentists is at about the national level. Despite its attractiveness to the ill and the aged, Arizona has no more than its per capita share of the nation's hospitals and nursing homes. The College of Medicine at the University of Arizona and university-affiliated nursing programs work toward expanding the supply of medical personnel.

A generally modern approach to public welfare by the legislature has been coupled with financial restraints that limit the effectiveness of the programs. The Department of Economic Security works mainly through county agencies with a variety of programs for children and for the aged, blind, and disabled.

Education. Public education has struggled to meet the rapid increase in students accompanying the population boom. Children must attend school between the ages of 8 and 16, or until graduation from the eighth grade. Elementary, secondary, and consolidated districts operate

[margin note left] Historic and contemporary routes

[margin note right] Arizona as a health mecca

with the assistance of county and state superintendents and an appointed state Board of Education. State support for local districts has been increasing, accompanied by tighter controls over maximum annual budget increases. Public school districts have begun to supplement and replace some reservation schools operated by churches and the federal Bureau of Indian Affairs.

Like most states in the Rocky Mountains, Arizona's higher education is dominated by large public universities. The Arizona Board of Regents assumes responsibility for the University of Arizona (founded 1885) in Tucson, Arizona State University (1885) in Tempe, and Northern Arizona University (1899) in Flagstaff. To meet the need for higher education throughout the state, a community college system, under state and local control, has been established. In addition, there are private two- and four-year colleges in the state.

Cultural life. Although traditionally a centre for Indian folk arts and crafts, Arizona had no early circles of painters and writers comparable to those of neighbouring New Mexico. Interest in painting, crafts, drama, music, and publishing, however, has increased with population growth. Architecture and the graphic arts have been particularly influenced by Southwestern regional themes. Writers of fiction and nonfiction alike have focussed their attention upon Arizona's 19th-century frontier era. Among the best known earlier writers of popular fiction were Zane Grey and Harold Bell Wright, both of whom employed local settings and lived and worked in the state during periods of their careers. Later contributions of note were made by Oliver La Farge, Will Comfort, and Ross Santee.

Indian arts and crafts   Contemporary Indian arts and crafts, executed within the dynamic traditions of the tribes but with considerable individual creativity, receive enthusiastic support from tribal organizations and the general public. The Hopi and Navajo have among them outstanding painters, silver and jewelry craftsmen, weavers, basketmakers, and potters; and Papago women produce a variety of handsome baskets.

No city dominates as an art centre, although Scottsdale, Tucson, Sedona, and Tubac have colonies of working artists. Outstanding collections, mainly paintings, can be viewed in the Phoenix Art Museum and the Museum of Art at the University of Arizona in Tucson. The Arizona State Museum at the University of Arizona in Tucson, the Heard Museum in Phoenix, and the Museum of Northern Arizona in Flagstaff feature archaeological and traditional collections of Indian arts and crafts. The Arizona–Sonoran Desert Museum in Tucson has received worldwide attention as a living museum dedicated to the natural world of the Sonoran Desert.

Mexican music can be heard in Arizona, particularly in the south. Symphony orchestras, theatres, ballets, and opera are well supported in Phoenix and Tucson. In spite of its relatively small size, Tucson's history of support for the arts has been outstanding.

More than any other art form, architecture embodies the conflict between the regional traditions of the Southwest and modern international trends. Perhaps the best known modern structure is Frank Lloyd Wright's auditorium at Arizona State University. Among the many structures in the Spanish style, the Heard Museum is outstanding, and the Nogales Public Library synthesizes the Spanish Southwestern and contemporary styles. Probably the most photographed and beloved building in all of Arizona is the San Xavier del Bac Mission, the "White Dove of the Desert," located near Tucson, completed by the Franciscans in 1797.

The University of Arizona's library is the largest in the state. In addition to other college and university libraries, there are several specialized collections. County and state regional systems supply library services throughout the state.

The state's leading book publisher, the University of Arizona Press, releases a variety of scholarly and popular titles, most with a Southwestern focus. The state's most widely known publishing venture, *Arizona Highways,* brings varied features of Arizona to a worldwide audience.

A variety of sports and recreational activities provide diversified entertainment and leisure. Varied desert and forest terrains and many man-made lakes attract thousands of hunters, fishermen, campers, hikers, and amateur prospectors and historians to the open country throughout the year. Rodeos revive the Old West in all of the cities and on the larger Indian reservations.

HISTORY

Early settlements. Humans lived throughout the area from at least 25,000 BC; the earliest cultures were those of the Hohokam (after about 300 BC) and Anasazi (after about AD 100). The nomadic Apache and Navajo Indians arrived only a few centuries before the Spanish. These Europeans arrived in large numbers after the collapse of the Anasazi and Hohokam civilizations. Cliff dwellings of the Anasazi and remnants of the elaborate Hohokam irrigation systems dot the northern and central sections of present-day Arizona. The dryness has helped preserve artifacts and, occasionally, bodies.

Aboriginal civilizations

Spanish and Mexican territory. Francisco Vázquez de Coronado and other Spanish explorers of the 16th and 17th centuries unsuccessfully sought precious metals in Arizona. European settlement began in the late 17th century but extended only as far north as Tucson, founded in 1776. After Mexico achieved independence from Spain in 1821, Apache resistance gradually eliminated the settlements, except for Tucson.

U.S. territory and state. After the Mexican War, Arizona was ceded as part of New Mexico to the United States in 1848, and the Gadsden Purchase, an area south of the Gila River, was added in 1853. California gold brought adventurers and miners into the area in the 1850s, but the U.S. Civil War and troop withdrawal delayed settlement and allowed the Apache continued sway. In the 1870s and 1880s ranches and towns finally spread into former Indian lands, although a few lawless whites and Indians kept the bloody frontier tradition alive.

Arizona became the 48th state on February 14, 1912, and the Salt River project, completed in 1911, began to deliver water to an area that has become the state's agricultural heartland. Since World War I cotton has joined copper and cattle as one of the state's major industries. During the 1920s motels, dude ranches, and resorts were built to accommodate increasing numbers of tourists and winter visitors. Military bases expanded during World War II, and the first large-scale manufacturing began in Phoenix and Tucson, creating a population boom that has continued. In 1963 the U.S. Supreme Court affirmed Arizona's right to 2,800,000 acre-feet (3,500,000,000 cubic metres) of water annually from the Colorado River and to all of the Gila River's flow; in 1968 the U.S. Congress authorized the Central Arizona Project, to provide water to the Phoenix and Tucson areas.   (M.E.H.)

New Mexico

A state of the U.S. Southwest, New Mexico is part of the "Old West" of cattle drives, cowboys, and clashes between pioneers and Apache Indians. In the vast flatness of its Great Plains and the rough, weather-scored peaks of its mountain ranges, it still retains much of its frontier flavour. Severe tensions and increasingly frequent confrontations between its Spanish-American, Indian, and "Anglo" (English-speaking) populations are a continuing reminder of the bitter antagonisms that characterized its long history and were still unresolved when it became the 47th state in the Union in 1912.

Frontier flavour

The 121,666 square miles (315,113 square kilometres) of New Mexico make it the fifth largest of the U.S. states; it has only 221 square miles of water. Rectangular in shape except for a small panhandle in the southwestern corner, New Mexico is bounded on the north by Colorado, on the east by Oklahoma and Texas, on the south by Texas and the Mexican state of Chihuahua, and on the west by Arizona, which was part of the Territory of New Mexico from 1850 to 1863. At its northwestern corner it joins Arizona, Utah, and Colorado in the only four-way meeting of states in the nation.

Despite the traditionally agrarian nature of the state, augmented by successful irrigation methods, New Mexico has become highly urbanized. Large numbers live in Albuquerque and surrounding Bernalillo County. The capital, Santa Fe, is a much smaller city, but its founding in 1610 preceded that of Albuquerque by 96 years, and it is the oldest continuously used seat of government in North America. It was also the southwestern terminus of the Santa Fe Trail, a wagon trail that was a major commercial and migration route from Missouri to the Southwest from 1821 to 1880, when the last section of the railroad was completed.

PHYSICAL AND HUMAN GEOGRAPHY

The land. *Relief.* New Mexico has some of the flattest land in the world and also some of the most rugged mountains. Some portions have pine forests, rich meadows, and fish-laden mountain streams, while other areas are devoid of streams, and even cacti struggle to survive. The eastern third of the state is an extension of the Great Plains. The central third is the southern extension of the Rocky Mountains, the ranges interspersed with valleys and running in a north–south direction. The western third is a high plateau, but it also contains many plains and short mountain ranges.

Surface features

The average elevation ranges from 5,000 to 8,000 feet (1,500 to 2,500 metres) above sea level in the northwest to less than 4,000 feet in the southeast, with 85 percent of the state more than 4,000 feet above sea level. The highest mountain peaks, Wheeler Peak (13,161 feet [4,011 metres]) and South Truchas Peak (13,102 feet [3,993 metres]), are in the Sangre de Cristo range in the north central part of the state. The numerous valleys between the ranges are indispensable to agriculture and grazing. Unique volcanic formations abound as reminders of past lava flows. The caverns near Carlsbad are among the most spectacular natural rock formations in the world.

Drainage. Five major river systems—the Rio Grande, Pecos, Canadian, San Juan, and Gila—drain the state. The Rio Grande, which has played an influential role in New Mexico's history, virtually bisects the state. Agriculture in its floodplain has been significant since prehistoric times; European settlers initially lived exclusively in its valleys and those of its tributaries. The Pecos, east of the Rio Grande and approximately parallel to it, was also a popular route for explorers. The Canadian River, rising in the Sangre de Cristo Range and flowing east across the arid plains, was a useful avenue for explorers despite its deep canyons. The San Juan and Gila rivers lie west of the Continental Divide, in the northwest and southwest respectively. All but the Gila, which is not dammed in New Mexico, provide water for irrigation, recreation, and flood control.

Climate. Although New Mexico's average annual temperature is 53° F (12° C), extremes range from 116° F (47° C) to −50° F (−46° C). Variations are caused more by altitude than latitude, with temperatures falling by 5° F with every 1,000-foot increase (2.8° per 300 metres) in elevation. Nighttime temperatures tend to fall sharply. The average annual rainfall is 15 inches (375 millimetres), though precipitation tends to increase with elevation. About 40 inches of rain falls in the higher mountains, whereas lower areas may get no more than eight to 10 inches. Generally, precipitation is greatest in the eastern third of the state and least in the western third.

Zones of vegetation

Plant and animal life. New Mexico has six vegetation zones, which are determined mainly by altitude. The Lower Sonoran zone, in the southern sections of the Rio Grande and Pecos valleys and in the state's southwestern corner, usually occurs at altitudes below 4,500 feet. It includes nearly 20,000 square miles (52,000 square kilometres) of New Mexico's best grazing area and irrigated farmland. The Upper Sonoran, comprising about three-fourths of the state and including most of the plains, foothills, and valleys above 4,500 feet, is a region of prairie grasses, low piñon pines, and juniper shrubs. At higher altitudes, better stands reflect the more abundant rainfall. The Transition zone, covering some 19,000 square miles, is identified chiefly by the ponderosa pine. The Canadian zone, covering 4,000 square miles at elevations of 8,500 to 9,000 feet, contains blue spruce and Douglas fir. The Hudsonian and Arctic-Alpine zones, above 9,500 feet, are too small in area and too sparsely covered to be of great importance.

The diversity of natural vegetation and elevation affect the wildlife, and the inaccessibility of much of New Mexico has helped preserve its abundance. Mule deer, brown bear, bighorn sheep, mink, muskrat beaver, fox, mountain lion, and bobcat live in the mountain and forest areas above 7,000 feet, while at lower elevations antelope, coyote, and jackrabbit are found. Barbary sheep from North Africa have been introduced into several mountain areas. Many species of trout are common in the mountain streams, and warm-water fish abound in lower streams. Approximately 300 species of birds can be found year-round, including various game birds. Rattlesnakes and black widow spiders are common.

Settlement patterns. The first Spanish settlements were in the central Rio Grande Valley and its tributaries. The Spanish-speaking inhabitants are still concentrated in the north central portion of the state. The eastern third of the state is frequently referred to as "Little Texas" or the "East Side." It is an extension of the Great Plains of western Texas and was originally settled as a cattle frontier expanding westward from Texas after the Civil War. It continues to attract Protestant Anglos from Texas as ranchers, farmers, or oil-field workers, and they are often at odds with the Spanish-American Roman Catholics of Albuquerque and Santa Fe. The southwestern corner of the state, settled by Anglo miners after the coming of the railroads, also has little in common with the central area. The northwest corner received Mormon settlers from Colorado, but the greatest growth of this area resulted from oil and natural-gas discoveries after World War II.

Spanish villages

Early settlers remained along streams because of the scarcity of water elsewhere. In a typical community adobe houses opened onto a plaza from which four streets ran outward, and the entire enclave was enclosed by a wall for defense. Nearby were small agricultural plots and orchards owned by individuals. Just beyond, in a great circle, was the ejido—land for communal grazing, recreation, or firewood. Despite fear of Indian attack, ranches away from settlements often were established. At the time of the American conquest, New Mexico was a self-sufficient agrarian community, with most people residing in small villages.

After the Civil War vast cattle ranches appeared on the East Side, their size limited only by the availability of water. The coming of the railroads in 1879 brought several waves of Anglo farmers, but frequent droughts ruined many who tried to till the soil as they had in their more humid homelands. Dry farming—tilling that uses drought-resistant crops or otherwise conserves soil moisture—saved many who remained, but today irrigated farming is the most important form of agriculture.

The people. The people of New Mexico are primarily Anglos, Spanish-Americans, or Indians. The original Spanish settlers intermarried with the Indians, and their descendants are designated as Spanish-Americans or Hispanics rather than Mexican-Americans, as elsewhere in the Southwest. Spanish-Americans were in the majority until the 1940s, and by the late 20th century still made up about 40 percent of the population. After World War II an influx of Anglos accompanied a widespread desertion of small agricultural villages by their Spanish-speaking residents, who moved to urban centres in the state or to California. Many such villages became ghost towns.

Indian population

The large Navajo reservation extends over the northwestern corner into Arizona, and nearby Gallup is famous as "the Indian capital of America." There are also reservations for the Utes, and for the Jicarilla and Mescalero Apaches; Pueblo Indians live on 1,581,000 acres (640,000 hectares) of scattered land grants. The Indians preserve many of their ancient ways, tending flocks of sheep and producing handicraft items. But dissatisfaction with their low income, inadequate housing, poor health standards, and lack of educational opportunity has led to a growing militancy and an increasing exodus from their reservations or pueblos to urban centres.

New Mexico, traditionally rural, has joined the national

trend toward urbanization. Since 1920 its rate of population growth has exceeded that of the United States as a whole. A growth rate of nearly 40 percent during the 1950s was largely the result of a proliferation of federal expenditures in the state for defense and research and of the discovery of oil and other minerals. The reduction of federal outlays and the levelling off of mining booms, however, caused the growth rate to drop. Urbanization has involved a number of factors: the movement of Spanish-Americans away from their rural homes, the consolidation of farms, and the increasing inclination of many farmers to abandon their isolation for the larger towns and commute to their fields and flocks.

The economy. New Mexico's economy is similar to that of the developing nations of the world in that it is largely at the mercy of forces over which it has little control. Relying heavily on the export of raw materials and on federal expenditures for programs of no certain permanence, it is subject to shifting demands from outside the state. Overall, government spending accounts for nearly one-fourth of the state's economy. New Mexico is a comparatively poor state.

Agriculture. Under Spain and Mexico the people who lived in what is now New Mexico were self-sufficient, growing beans, corn (maize), cotton, and squash on the alluvial plain of the Rio Grande. Sheep thrived in the arid land and remained important until the 20th century. The Anglos brought cattle raising from Texas, and the sale of beef now accounts for more than one-half of the marketing receipts from agricultural products. Cotton is the leading cash crop, and hay ranks second. Wheat and sorghum are raised on the dry farms of the eastern part of the state, but the irregularity of rainfall makes this type of agriculture hazardous. Two-fifths of the total cropland is irrigated; such lands furnish the overwhelming share of the crop dollar.

Mining. The mining industry, which contributes 10 percent of the state's income, brought many settlers and attracted outside capital in territorial days. Gold and silver mining began in the 19th century, reached its peak in 1915, and has since declined. Copper mining remains important; coal mining, which declined with the increased use of other fuels, expanded in the 1960s as the result of improved technology. The share of coal in generating electricity in the state increased from less than 2 percent in 1960 to more than 65 percent in the late 20th century. New Mexico produces about 85 percent of the nation's potash and, since the discovery of uranium deposits in 1950, it has led the nation in uranium production. Iron, lead, zinc, manganese, and molybdenum are also mined, but oil and natural gas account for about 60 percent of the state's mineral income. Natural gas is mainly produced in the southeastern corner and in the San Juan Basin in the northwest.

Industry. Manufacturing in New Mexico was originally limited to the production of consumer goods, but it has increased rapidly since World War II and now accounts for 7 percent of the state's income. Food processing, petroleum refining, smelting, railroad maintenance, and the manufacture of construction materials are leading industrial activities. Atomic research is carried on at the Los Alamos National Laboratory, with testing taking place at Sandia Military Base, in Albuquerque, or at the White Sands Missile Range, near Alamogordo. An offshoot of this is the private manufacturing of such products as ordnance, electronic equipment, and precision instruments. Because of the limited development of industry, unions are not widespread and are confined largely to the mining, smelting, and petroleum industries.

Recreation and tourism. The distinctive Indian and Hispanic cultures continue to draw large numbers of visitors. State and national parks and monuments, historic sites, hunting and fishing, skiing, and Indian ceremonials are major attractions.

Transportation. Geographic isolation was a basic cause of New Mexico's slow economic development. In the Spanish and Mexican periods, it took about six months to travel the distance between Mexico City and Santa Fe. The Santa Fe Trail route was much shorter and faster,

and American consumer goods helped prepare the way for conquest. This isolation ended when the railroads reached Albuquerque and Santa Fe in 1880. Today an extensive rail network unites the state. Highways link New Mexico's major population centres; three of these highways are part of the federal interstate system. Mountainous terrain makes road construction expensive, but secondary roads are adequate. Air transportation provides a vital link with other parts of the nation.

Administrative and social conditions. *Government.* In most instances the state's constitution can be amended by a majority vote of the legislature and by a majority vote of the electorate. A public referendum on major issues is permitted, but public initiative on legislative matters is not. Nomination to office is by closed primary.

The governor has the usual powers of pardon, reprieve, and veto, but this executive has more authority than those of most states. The governor appoints most of the state boards, departments, agencies, and commissions, and consequently is the virtual master of patronage and the political organization. Like the lieutenant governor and other executive officials, the governor is elected for one four-year term. Officials are ineligible for state elective positions for four years thereafter, but the lieutenant governor may run for governor.

A legislature composed of 42 members of the Senate, elected to four-year terms, and 70 members of the House, elected to two-year terms, meets for a 60-day session in odd-numbered years and a 30-day session in even-numbered years. Heading the judiciary are five Supreme Court justices elected for eight years, with overlapping terms. Judges of the 11 judicial districts are elected for six years and serve ex officio as judges of juvenile courts.

Each of New Mexico's 32 counties is administered by three commissioners elected for terms of two years. Other county elective officers are assessor, clerk, sheriff, surveyor, treasurer, and probate judge. In the territorial era citizens usually favoured Republicans, but since statehood Democrats have tended to dominate.

Education. A public school system was established in 1891, and, since statehood, education has improved tremendously. In 1968 the educational attainment of the Anglo adult population averaged 12.1 years—compared, however, to only 8.1 years for Spanish-Americans. Most improvements in education have been in the urban centres, however, and many rural and small-town schools remain substandard. Because Hispanics are dominant in these areas, education is poorer for their children. Legalized segregation for the Hispanic minorities in the eastern third of the state ended in the 1950s, but *de facto* segregation remains, primarily on the elementary level.

The state's largest institution of higher education is the University of New Mexico, in Albuquerque, established in 1889. Other state-supported institutions include New Mexico State University (1888), in University Park; Eastern New Mexico University (1934), in Portales; New Mexico Highlands University (1893), in Las Vegas; Western New Mexico University (1893), in Silver City; and New Mexico Institute of Mining and Technology (1889), in Socorro. Northern New Mexico State School at El Rito, originally established in 1909 to train Spanish-speaking teachers, is today a resident high school. In addition, the state universities have established branch campuses, while some cities have organized junior colleges. There are also several private colleges.

Health and welfare. The state's department of health, created in 1919, administers an extensive social-service program, often in collaboration with federal agencies. New Mexico has about 60 hospitals, including the Carrie Tingley Crippled Children's Hospital, but medical services in rural areas are generally inadequate. The Emergency Health Communication network links emergency vehicles, including helicopters, with medical facilities throughout the state. Other state institutions include a penitentiary, an industrial school for boys, a girls' welfare home, schools for the blind and the deaf, a development centre for mentally retarded children, and eight special state-supported schools.

Social issues. The greatest social problem that New

Major crops

Colleges and universities

Mexico faces is the cultural clash between Spanish-Americans, once dominant in the state, and the now-dominant Anglos. Distrust, hostility, prejudice, and discrimination exist between the two groups. Efforts in 1967 of an Hispanic group, the Alianza de los Pueblos Libres (Alliance of Free City-States), to regain lost land was a result of the frustration growing out of their declining social, educational, and economic status, for which demands for land grants became a symbol. Hispanics have legal equality, but in practical matters they are second-class citizens in their homeland. Their income averages little more than half that of Anglos, their education is less adequate, and they are under-represented in the professions. The percentage of Spanish-Americans living in substandard housing is higher than for other groups. Desertion of native villages for urban centres creates problems of social and economic adjustment that will take years to resolve.

Cultural life. Writers and architects have been influenced by New Mexico's Indian and Spanish heritages, which in turn are influenced by Anglo culture. The appearance of cowboys and miners, and the conflicts of the frontier territory in the 19th century, have also been dominant cultural themes. Painters have been concerned especially with the unique landscape, since no other area of the United States presents such a variety of scenery or so many modes of life existing side by side. New Mexico's cities have attracted artists in all fields from many parts of the nation and of the world. Taos was the first to have an important art community, but it is now rivalled by Santa Fe and Albuquerque. The state institutions of higher education, through their libraries and their departments of art, music, dance, and theatre, have played a key role in the dissemination of cultural knowledge. This has been accomplished directly and through the training of public-school teachers. The success of the Santa Fe Opera Association, organized in 1956, reflects the growth of musical appreciation. The company performs in an outdoor theatre in the Sangre de Cristo Mountains near the city, presenting a repertory that has won the group worldwide acclaim.

The historical atmosphere of New Mexico and its fusion of three cultures is represented by its unique architecture. Indian pueblo buildings were modified by Spanish settlers when they built Santa Fe, and many of these original structures have been restored. The statehouse, most public buildings, and many private ones have recently been constructed in the modified Spanish mission style.

Local Indians produce beautiful pottery of high quality. Each village has its own design to identify the work of its people. Navajo blankets are famous the world over. Many Indians make buttons, beads, pins, rings, necklaces, earrings, and belts, mainly for sale to the growing number of tourists. The United States Indian Arts and Crafts Board has attempted to preserve the authenticity of Indian jewelry by establishing standards in handworked silver. Individual pueblos preserve native dances by performing at numerous fiestas, the most important being the Inter-Tribal Ceremonial, which draws thousands of visitors to Gallup every summer.

Spanish folk art has been preserved largely by the Penitentes, a religious group within the Roman Catholic Church. In rural areas medieval Spanish music and art has been preserved.

The Museum of New Mexico, housed in the Palace of the Governors in Santa Fe, helps preserve archaeological sites, mementos, and folk arts of the past. The state archives also contain important relics. The Wheelwright Museum of the American Indian is in Santa Fe. In Taos is the Kit Carson Memorial Foundation, a history and art museum housed in the Kit Carson home.

HISTORY

New Mexico's first inhabitants were various groups of Indians, who farmed and hunted on the land for at least 10,000 years before white explorers appeared. The more peaceful agriculturists included the later groups, whose pueblo ruins dot the state. These groups had well-developed irrigation systems by the time the more aggres-

sive and nomadic Navajo and Apache arrived from the north, probably in the 15th century.

Spanish and Mexican rule. Reports of the fabled seven cities of gold brought the first European explorers into New Mexico in 1540, led by the Spanish adventurer Francisco Coronado. The journey was fruitless, and they returned to Mexico. After several decades of desultory exploration by soldiers and friars, Juan de Oñate was given contracts for colonization in 1595 and made the first permanent white settlements during the following years, founding Santa Fe in 1610.

For the next century missionary work predominated, but attempts to eradicate Indian religion and culture brought on an uprising and massacre in 1680 that cleared out the Europeans for many years. By 1700 the Spanish had reasserted themselves, and for the next century there was considerable settlement. Albuquerque, founded in 1706, was the focal point in the south, and Santa Fe was the centre of the north. When New Mexico became a part of the Republic of Mexico, founded in 1821, it already had begun to trade with the United States over the Santa Fe Trail, and this trade led to still another allegiance 25 years later.

Territory and state. During the Mexican War, which began in 1846, New Mexico was taken by the Army of the West under Gen. Stephen Kearny. All residents were granted amnesty and citizenship in return for an oath of allegiance to the United States. The Territory of New Mexico was established by Congress in 1850. During the Civil War an invading Confederate force was driven out by the Colorado Volunteers.

The Navajo tribes were quelled and in 1868 were given a large reservation; but the Apaches, settled on two reservations in 1880, continued their struggles until 1886. The burgeoning cattle industry was the main development of these decades, and the territory often was bloodied by battles between cattlemen and sheepmen, large landowners and homesteaders. The legendary Billy the Kid and his lawman-nemesis, Pat Garrett, were products of this struggle. Apache leaders Geronimo, Cochise, and Victorio, though mainly active in Arizona, made forays into southwestern New Mexico. The Atchison, Topeka and Santa Fe Railway, which reached Albuquerque in 1880, brought new immigration, and farming grew rapidly with development of new irrigation methods and resources.

Following admission as a state on January 6, 1912, New Mexico retained its agricultural bases until World War II, when atomic research opened a new era in the state. Its best known scientific installation is at Los Alamos, centre of the project that created the first atomic bomb in 1945. The development of mineral resources has also helped the economy and income of the state.   (W.A.B.)

Oklahoma

In its land and its people, Oklahoma is a state of contrast and of the unexpected. The terrain varies from the rolling, timbered hills of the east, where the state borders Missouri and Arkansas, to the treeless high plains that extend into Texas and New Mexico to the west. Oklahoma's east central region is dominated by the lowlands of the Arkansas River, sweeping in from Colorado and Kansas on the north, and its tributaries and by the Red River, which forms nearly all of its southern border with Texas. Once basically agricultural—and the dust-bowl locale of John Steinbeck's famous novel *The Grapes of Wrath*—Oklahoma now has hundreds of lakes and a diversified economy.

The word Oklahoma is derived from two Choctaw Indian words: *okla,* "people," and *humma,* "red." During the 19th century the future state was a symbol of one of the least glorious chapters in U.S. history, becoming known as Indian Territory, the dumping ground for Indian tribes displaced by white settlers' ever-increasing hunger for land. Since its admission in 1907 as the 46th state of the Union, however, Oklahoma has achieved an integration of its Indian citizens into modern economic and social life that probably is unmatched by any other state. There is no reservation in the usual sense for the Indian population.

Status of Spanish-Americans

Indian arts

Colonial period

Indian Territory

Though numbers of "blanket Indians" may possess no more than their bedrolls, others have risen to positions of distinction. Many share with their fellow Oklahomans the great wealth that oil resources have brought to the state.

Oklahoma covers an area of 69,919 square miles (181,-089 square kilometres). The customs of the Deep South are reflected in the habits and attitudes of southern Oklahoma—"Little Dixie"—where cotton production, but not loyalty to the Democratic Party, has declined. The wheat growers in the north, however, show their largely Kansan origins by their dedication to Republican politics.

PHYSICAL AND HUMAN GEOGRAPHY

The land. Lying in a transitional zone in topography, climate, and other features, both east to west and north to south, Oklahoma comprises a jumble of environments.

Relief. Three of the nation's large physical regions extend into or across the state. The Interior Highlands is in the east; the Coastal Plain, extending through Texas to the Gulf of Mexico, is in the south; and the Interior Plains, including the Central Lowland and Great Plains, cover the remainder. Ten subregions lie within Oklahoma. Three are mountainous and in the south—the Ouachita, Arbuckle, and Wichita mountains—and are characterized by rough topography and thin soils. They have lumbering, grazing, some farming, and mining as their principal economic activities. The northeastern Ozark Plateau, most of which lies in Missouri and Arkansas, has rough terrain and small fields devoted primarily to growing fruits and vegetables. Once important as a lead and zinc producer, the plateau has a Cherokee heritage and beautiful rivers that make it a major recreation and tourist attraction.

The Sandstone Hills, a wide band stretching through the east central portion between the Red River and the Kansas border, is poor in agriculture and timber but important for its oil, gas, and coal deposits. The region is sprinkled with deserted or dying oil-boom towns, with Tulsa a prosperous exception. The sparsely populated Gypsum Hills section of western Oklahoma is devoted largely to grazing and farming, with large wheat acreages in the north and smaller cotton farms in the south.

The remaining four areas are flat to rolling and are agricultural. The Red River Plains, once the area of the best farmlands in the state, has been depleted by cotton. Its agriculture has been diversified by the addition of peanuts (groundnuts), melons, and vegetables grown on medium-sized plots. Its population is relatively dense, with many small towns serving as trade centres. The Prairie Plains region in the northeast is marked by grazing in its rougher portions and vegetable farms in the river valleys. Oil and gas fields are common, as is strip-mining for coal. It contains a number of middle-sized towns, some of which have small manufacturing plants. The Red Beds region is the largest, running through the middle of the state. The greatest population density is located there, as are most of the larger towns. Oil provides much of the income. Although cotton rules in the south and wheat in the north, corn (maize), watermelons, sorghum, alfalfa, vegetables, and livestock are common. The High Plains region of the northwest and the Panhandle offers a marked contrast. With the highest elevation and the least moisture, the eastern portion is dominated by wheat, and the western by grazing.

Oklahoma's drainage pattern, consisting of the Arkansas and Red rivers and their tributaries, slopes from an elevation of 5,000 feet (1,500 metres) in the northwest to 500 feet in the southeast.

Climate. Rainfall varies from more than 50 inches (1,270 millimetres) annually in the Ouachitas to less than 15 inches in the western Panhandle. Wheat and sorghum predominate in the drier western sections, whereas corn, vegetables, and berries grow in the damper east. Virtually all of the 10 regions have enough water for grass; hence, ranching is common.

Oklahoma has a southern humid belt merging with a colder northern continental one and humid eastern and dry western zones that cut through the state. The result is normally pleasant weather and an average annual temperature of about 60° F (15.5° C), increasing from northwest

Moisture and ecology

to southeast. No region is free from wind; and, as the collision point for warm and cold air masses, with sudden rises and falls in temperature, the state has heavy thunderstorms, blizzards, and tornadoes.

Plant and animal life. Oklahoma is a transitional area for plant and animal life. More than 130 species of trees are native: the eastern forests of maple, sweet gum, hickory, oak, and pine change into the cottonwood, elm, hackberry, and blackjack and post oaks of the grasslands. The arid-zone plants are chiefly mesquite, sage, and cacti. There are deer, elks, antelope, rabbits, coyotes, wolves, foxes, prairie dogs, and American bison. Native fish include bass, perch, catfish, and buffalo, and virtually every bird common to the land between the Mississippi and the Rockies is found. Horned toads, lizards, many varieties of nonpoisonous snakes, and rattlesnakes and cottonmouth moccasins are native.

Settlement patterns. The outlines of roads and farms generally produce a pattern of unusual symmetry in the landscape, revealing the original survey divisions into townships, sections, and quarter sections. Small squares predominate where small-scale farming is common and very large ones where wheat and ranching prevail. As elsewhere in the nation, however, the trend has been toward urbanization. The Red Beds in the centre of the state grew most rapidly, and three of the state's four largest cities are found there, the exception being Tulsa.

Oklahoma City, the capital, is near the centre of the state and in area comprises one of the larger metropolitan areas in the nation. Banking, insurance, manufacturing, trade and transportation, state and federal installations, and educational facilities have made it the commercial and industrial heart of the state. Tinker Field, a U.S. Air Force base and the state's major employer, is located in nearby Midwest City. Tulsa, a former Creek Indian village in the Sandstone Hills region, grew slowly until the discovery of oil nearby. Refineries and facilities for manufacturing and distributing oil-field supplies have made it the logical headquarters for many oil companies, and it has many other financial and industrial functions. Lawton is a centre for the Ft. Sill army reservation, the Wichita wildlife recreational centre, and the rural population of the area. Norman, seat of the University of Oklahoma and site of the major state mental hospital, is also a "bedroom" city for Oklahoma City and Midwest City commuters.

The people. Most of Oklahoma's Indians live in the former Indian Territory in the eastern part of the state. The Plains tribes remain in western Oklahoma. Some Indians live on tribal landholdings that are informally called reservations. Most blacks in the state are descended from slaves of the Five Civilized Tribes, although some migrated from the South after 1865, and others came during the land runs. The majority live in urban centres or in the southern and eastern parts of the state, and several towns have entirely black populations.

Ethnic and religious groups

A wide variety of other racial and ethnic strains have contributed to Oklahoma's population. The original French claimants left their names and bloodlines, usually in conjunction with Indian families, and a mining boom in the 1870s brought Europeans into the Choctaw Nation. Descendants of these Italian, Slavic, Greek, Welsh, Polish, and Russian miners still live in Little Dixie. The land rushes brought homesteaders from China, Japan, Mexico, England, France, and Canada, and the spread of wheat farming attracted German Mennonites and Czechs to the northwest. German was the language of instruction in some public schools as late as World War I. By the 1970s, however, nearly all of Oklahoma's residents reflected a typically Midwestern American culture.

The state's religious sects bear out this trend toward uniformity. Of the Protestant majority, the Southern Baptists and the United Methodists predominate, and the resulting conservatism has placed Oklahoma in the Bible Belt. (This fundamentalism was a primary cause for Oklahoma's retention of the prohibition of liquor sales until 1959.) Other leading denominations include the Disciples of Christ, Presbyterians, Congregationalists, and Episcopalians. Roman Catholics and Greek Orthodox are represented throughout the state, but Jewish synagogues are limited to the cities. Most Indians have adopted some form of European religion, although the Native American Church—in which use of the drug peyote is a part of the worship—is recognized by state charter. The Sun and Ghost dances of the western tribes reflect more primitive religious practices as well as reactions to whites.

Though most Oklahomans have kept their religious ties, they have changed their places of residence. In 1890 less than 4 percent of the population lived in towns; but by 1950 50 percent were urban, half of them living in the metropolitan areas of Oklahoma City, Tulsa, and Lawton.

The economy. *Agriculture.* Traditionally, agriculture has furnished an important part of Oklahoma's income, though Oklahoma's more than 85,000 farms, which are slightly larger than the nation's average in size, have slightly less value per acre. In line with national trends, the averages will likely remain the same, but the number of units will probably continue to decline. In commercial agriculture, livestock ranks first, followed by grain, dairy products, cotton, and other field crops and general produce.

Industry. Oklahoma remains somewhat of an economic satellite of the industrial North and East, furnishing food, raw materials, and fuels. Despite great efforts to diversify, the state still has far to go. Fewer than a quarter of its workers are in manufacturing, lower than the national average. Wholesale and retail trade employed the greatest number of people, followed by manufacturing, services, transportation and public utilities, finance, health services, insurance and real estate, construction, and mining. Union membership has not kept pace with the increases in nonagricultural employment.

Oklahoma ranks high nationally in the value of mineral production, which includes petroleum, natural gas, natural-gas liquids, and stone. Timber is also important; commercially exploitable timber is divided almost equally between softwoods and hardwoods. In 1970 the first major commercial effort was made to establish a pulp and paper industry.

Transportation. Oklahoma's transportation facilities partially account for its favourable record in attracting new industry. Tulsa and Oklahoma City act as the major collection and distribution points. The state has about 110,000 miles of roads and highways. Railroads operate about 4,700 miles (7,520 kilometres) of track within the state. Several airlines provide direct flights for passengers and freight to most cities. Intricate networks of pipelines move the petroleum products, with the newest addition to transportation a barge system linking Tulsa to the Gulf of Mexico by way of locks and dams on the Arkansas River.

Administrative and social conditions. *Government.* Oklahoma's political identity began with the establishment of autonomous tribal governments in the 1820s. Indian Territory consisted of five republics, or nations, with fixed boundaries, written constitutions, courts, and other governmental apparatus similar to those of the Eastern states. The major difference was that in each republic all land was held jointly, or in severalty, by the individual tribes. The first major threat to these governments came when, as former allies of the South, they were placed under military rule during the Reconstruction period. The treaties of 1866 committed the tribes to eventual union under a single government, but this had not been accomplished when Congress, in its haste to open the unassigned lands, admitted whites in 1889 without making any provision for government.

In this interval the U.S. Congress steadily encroached on Indian sovereignty by the extension of federal law and the demand that landholding practices be brought into conformity with U.S. custom. On May 2, 1890, the Oklahoma Organic Act established a territorial government and provided that all reservations in the western Indian Territory, when opened for non-Indian settlement, would be annexed automatically to the new Oklahoma Territory. The last step came when the remaining tribal lands in eastern Oklahoma were distributed among the tribes. It was originally agreed that tribal governments would cease in 1906, but they continue in a limited form.

That same year the Oklahoma Enabling Act set the formula for statehood: the two territories—Oklahoma in the west, Indian in the east—would unite and draw up a single constitution. The resulting document reflected the influence of the progressives and reformers who dominated U.S. politics. It became inordinately long in an effort to protect against corporations, bosses, and future redefinitions of intent by judicial interpretation. The general structure is common to other states, but Oklahomans strengthened the legislature by limiting the governor's appointive powers and ability to succeed himself, the latter prohibition removed in 1970, and making the judiciary elective. Also unusual was the right of initiating legislation by popular initiative and referendum. The governor is elected for four years, whereas the 48 senators serve similar but staggered terms, and the 101 house members serve two years. Each of the original 75 counties, later increased by two, has at least one representative. Constitutional provision was also made for township and city governments, though the former was abolished in 1913. This constitution, often amended, is still in force.

Eight of nine territorial governors were Republicans, but after statehood Oklahomans favoured the Democrats. Even when the state supports Republican presidential nominees, normally that party can hope for but one or two congressional seats, and it was not until 1962 that it won the governorship. Nevertheless, Oklahomans have a history of giving strong support to third parties; in 1914 the Socialists received 53,703 votes, and in 1968 the Southern states' rights candidate, George Wallace, received more than 20 percent of the total vote.

A major governmental change was the revision of the state's court system in 1967, which abolished justices of the peace and established selection of major judgeships according to what has become known as the "Missouri Plan." Under this plan judges are nominated by a joint commission chosen by the governor and the state bar association rather than by the political parties. The state Supreme Court has exclusive appellate jurisdiction in civil cases, while the Court of Criminal Appeals has exclusive appellate jurisdiction in criminal cases. The Court of Appeal, with a judge elected from each congressional district, hears only cases assigned to it by the Supreme Court, and there is no appeal from its decisions to other state courts. Lower courts include 24 district courts, with judges elected on nonpartisan ballots. In 1966 county attorneys were replaced by 27 district attorneys.

Social issues. One of Oklahoma's major sociopolitical issues since statehood has involved civil rights. Although its black population is small, as a border state Oklahoma was one of the first to feel the demand for equal education. All public education was segregated, and blacks who wanted advanced or professional degrees were furnished tuition for out-of-state institutions until 1948, when the U.S. Supreme Court ruled that a black must be admitted to the University of Oklahoma Law School. In 1949 all graduate work and in 1955 all higher education was opened to any qualified applicant. Economic, social, and public school integration moved forward with a minimum of violence.

Education. Supervision of public schools is under elected state and county superintendents, and higher education is coordinated by the regents for higher education, appointed by the governor. The state university system is often regarded as overextended in relation to the state's needs and resources. Exceptions are the University of Oklahoma (founded 1890) in Norman, and Oklahoma State University (1890) in Stillwater. Both have a large number of graduate departments ranked above average in achievement. Private institutions enroll only about one-fifth of the college population.

Health and welfare. The Commission of Charities and Correction has general charge of mental hospitals in Norman, Vinita, and Fort Supply, the state penitentiary in McAlester, and the reformatory in Granite. The majority of other similar institutions are under the Department of Institutions, Social and Rehabilitative Services. In spite of a generally conservative attitude toward federal intervention in local social questions, most federal welfare programs operate in Oklahoma. In addition, more than 100 recognized agencies or groups within the state have

Margin notes:

Manufacturing and labour organization

Civil rights progress

resulted from minority initiative by Indians, blacks, and Hispanics.

For financial support of its functions, Oklahoma relies basically on taxes on gasoline, income, and sales. The sales tax is earmarked for welfare, and property taxes are used largely for the support of county, municipal, and school needs. A major check on spending since 1939 has been Oklahoma's "budget balancing" amendment, by which the legislature is forbidden to appropriate more money than in the previous year plus estimated additional revenues.

Cultural life. Oklahoma is a blend of the old and new. Cowboys and Indians may be seen at the national finals of the Rodeo Association or at the American Indian Exposition. As host of the annual exposition and the site of Indian City U.S.A., the National Hall of Fame for Famous Indians, and the Southern Plains Indian Museum, Anadarko is a major tourist attraction. Among the features are full-sized reproductions of the homes of various tribes, pictures and busts of their leaders, and extensive displays of their artifacts. The National Cowboy Hall of Fame and Western Heritage Center, at Oklahoma City, is noted for its Western art and its exhibits of cowboy paraphernalia. The Will Rogers Memorial museum at Claremore stresses exhibits depicting early Oklahoma and Rogers' career as a cowboy and entertainer.

Oklahoma's best known graphic artists are Indian, and Indian works as well as those of European masters are represented in many museums. Oil as a symbol of Oklahoma has placed derricks on the capitol grounds and made the state influential on the international petroleum landscape, but those that it has enriched have contributed much to the artistic scene. The Thomas Gilcrease Institute of American History and Art and the Philbrook Art Center, both in Tulsa, and the Woolaroc Museum, in Bartlesville, originally reflected individual tastes, but they have joined other art museums (notably the Oklahoma City Art Center) in offering wide-ranging displays.

The performing arts

Symphony orchestras are supported in Oklahoma City, Tulsa, Lawton, Enid, and Norman. A public school music program culminates each spring in the Tri-State Music Festival. Several ballerinas of international fame are of Oklahoman Indian descent, the most noted of whom are Rosella Hightower and the sisters Maria and Marjorie Tallchief. Theatres have been sources of entertainment since frontier days. Universities and civic groups continue to provide a wide variety of dramatic experiences and professional training. Several towns feature annual folk plays or pageants, while Tulsa boasts an opera company with a regional reputation. The 7,000-member Tulsa Little Theater has given nearly 50 years of uninterrupted productions, and the Oklahoma City Mummers have constructed a large building and become a resident professional company. The state is unusually active in literature, with numerous writers' clubs, poetry societies, and folklore groups.

HISTORY

Early habitation and European exploration. Of the newer states, Oklahoma is one of the oldest in terms of human occupation. The abundant game of its plains attracted hunters of the Clovis and Folsom cultures 15,000 to 10,000 years ago. Others followed, producing between AD 500 and 1300 a golden age of exquisite pottery, textiles, sculpture, and metalware. Evidence indicates a widespread system of trade and communication. This high culture apparently fell before the onslaught of primitive peoples from the western plains, and until the expedition of Francisco Vázquez de Coronado in 1541 the region's population included representatives of at least three major Indian language groups.

Coronado claimed the area for Spain, but it became little more than a highway for wide-ranging Spanish explorers. In 1714 Juchereau de Saint Denis visited Oklahoma, and subsequent Frenchmen established a fur trade with the Indians. France and Spain struggled for control until 1763, leaving only the natives to contest Spanish authority until the return of the French flag in 1800. Three years later, through the Louisiana Purchase, Oklahoma was acquired by the United States.

American dominion. As one of the purchase's most attractive parts—because of trade opportunities—the area might well have become one of its first states; but it was, in fact, the last. Because of hostile Indians, Spanish intrigue, the mislabelling of its treeless plains as the American Desert, and the pressure for removal of the Indians from the settled East, the U.S. Congress in 1828 reserved Oklahoma for Indians and required all whites to withdraw. By 1880 more than 60 tribes had joined the local ones in Indian Territory. Some were sedentary, peaceful, agricultural, and semicivilized; others were migratory, belligerent, and barbaric. Indian sovereignty remained unchallenged until early in the U.S. Civil War, when unhappiness with the federal government caused leaders of the Five Civilized Tribes—the Cherokee, Choctaw, Chickasaw, Creek, and Seminole—who had come from Southern states and some of whom owned plantations and held slaves, to sign treaties annexing Indian Territory to the Confederate States of America.

The Indian Territory

Not only did Indian land become a battleground during the war but defeat also brought other losses. The Reconstruction treaties required, among other things, land cessions to the former slaves, the resettlement of additional outside tribes, and railroad rights-of-way. Although a scheme to colonize free blacks in Oklahoma never materialized, the weakness of the Indian governments encouraged both blacks and whites from adjoining states to trespass. Thus, the territory again became a dumping ground for Indians and an even greater cultural hodgepodge of red, white, and black people.

White settlement and statehood. Railroads seeking revenue and whites seeking property, both inside and outside the territory, coveted the Indians' land. By 1879 organized bands, the Boomers, were moving in despite federal law. Although most were ejected, pressure continued until Congress opened some 2,000,000 acres (800,000 hectares) of western Indian Territory, bringing on the famous land run beginning at noon on April 22, 1889. Known as Oklahoma Territory, the new area came to include, through further land runs, about half of the former Indian domain. Then its settlers, many called Sooners for entering the area before official permission, sought union of the two territories in statehood. The remaining Indian Territory was dissolved by assignment of lands to the various tribes, and the Indians joined in approving the constitution of the proposed state in 1907.

The drought years of the 1930s blighted many rural areas of Oklahoma, driving thousands of farmers into long migrations in search of some form of livelihood. The economic boom of World War II allowed the economy to diversify. The major event of the 20th century probably was the exploitation of the state's vast petroleum reserves.

(J.S.E.)

Texas

The vastness and diversity of Texas, the largest of the 48 coterminous states of the United States, are evident in nearly all aspects of the state's physical character, of its history, and of the economic and social life of its people. As a classic example, January temperatures in the Rio Grande Valley have been known to register well over 90° F (32° C), while at the same time, nearly halfway to Canada, blizzards were blocking highways in the Panhandle section of the state. The image of the state was that of a raw and lawless frontier when, in 1845, it surrendered its status as an independent republic to become the 28th state of the United States. This picture has altered drastically in order to incorporate Texas' present-day combinations of agricultural wealth with high national rankings in industry and finance, of huge urban centres that foster a cosmopolitan cultural life with seemingly unending stretches of high prairie and range devoted to cattle and cotton.

Image and heritage of Texas

Texas, with the fourth longest seacoast among the coterminous states and a large shipping industry to match, occupies the south central segment of the nation. Its 267,338 square miles (692,402 square kilometres) make it larger than any nation in Europe with the exception of the Soviet Union. Water delineates many of its borders:

the Rio Grande carves a shallow channel that separates Texas from Mexico on the southwest; the Gulf of Mexico laps its crescent-shaped coast on the southeast; the Sabine River forms most of the eastern boundary with Louisiana, where by land it is bounded by Arkansas as well; and the wriggling course of the Red River on the north makes up two-thirds of the state's boundary with Oklahoma. The Panhandle section juts northward, forming a counterpart in the western part of Oklahoma, and New Mexico lies to the west.

Like other former states of the Confederacy, Texas has been struggling in the past few decades to right inequities in education, economic opportunity, and housing that have mitigated in particular against the personal advancement of Mexican-Americans—or Chicanos or Hispanics, as many prefer to call themselves—and of blacks. The economic expansion since World War II has spread its benefits unequally, widening the gap between the affluent and the marginal-income families. The concept that those who fail simply have not exerted the necessary will power or zeal for work long helped to keep Texas among the lowest ranking states in welfare and other social services, and the notion is fading only reluctantly. The Republican Party in Texas has gained unusual strength for a former Confederate state, perhaps through a recognition that its more conservative stance on the national level may provide a more appropriate voice for many Texans than does the national Democratic Party. Recognition has come, also, that much of the economic growth of the state has come primarily from the exploitation of its natural resources, an avenue that cannot continue to offer ever-increasing rates of expansion.

PHYSICAL AND HUMAN GEOGRAPHY

The land. *Relief.* Far from being merely wide, arid plains that are filled with cattle and cowboys, Texas comprises a series of gigantic steps, from the fertile and densely populated Coastal Plains in the southeast to the high plains and mountains in the west and northwest.

Stretching inland from the Gulf Coast, the Coastal Plains range from sea level to about 300 feet (90 metres). These flat, low prairies extend inland to form a fertile crescent, varying in width from 50 to 200 miles (80 to 320 kilometres), that is well adapted to farming and cattle raising. Near the coast much land is marshy, almost swamp, except where drained by manmade devices.

Agriculture on the coast

The western anchor of the Coastal Plains is the Rio Grande Valley, where a heavy investment in citrus farming has been frequently damaged by rare but disastrous freezes. It now features diversified farming, with vegetables intermingled with citrus. The low coastal lands between Port Lavaca and Port Arthur are ideal for rice cultivation. Inland from Houston the flatlands provide grazing for fine-breed cattle. Forests of pine and cypress grow extensively from Beaumont to the Red River and spill into Louisiana and Arkansas, making lumbering and paper mills important industries.

Access to water transportation, reservoirs of natural gas and oil, and availability of raw materials have made the coastal area the centre of industry in Texas. It is also the most densely populated part of the state. Houston, Texas' largest city and one of the fastest growing cities in the United States (with a population of 1,594,000 in 1980), is a focal point; while Fort Worth, Dallas, Waco, Austin, and San Antonio form a line at the inner edges of the Coastal Plains. Corpus Christi, Galveston, and the Beaumont-Port Arthur-Orange complex augment Houston's port, one of the nation's largest.

The Coastal Plains, encompassing about one-third of the state's land area, break abruptly at the Balcones Escarpment, where in the distant geological past the surface of the earth cracked and slipped. Northwest of the fault, the land rears up into the Texas Hill Country and then into the tablelands of the Edwards Plateau to the south and the North Central Plains to the north. These last two regions generally are considered extensions of the Great Plains. The entire region varies from about 750 to 2,500 feet (230–760 metres) above sea level. Farming and cattle raising constitute the basic economy. The Hill Country

mixes orchard crops with ranching, small industries, summer camps, and tourism.

At the western edge of the North Central Plains lies the Cap Rock Escarpment, an outcropping of rock that stretches to the north and south for about 200 miles. Protruding above the plains like a huge barricade, it is starkly visible in some places in cliffs that rise from 200 to 300 feet. Beyond that escarpment lies the third big step of Texas: the High Plains country and, to the south, the Trans-Pecos region.

From the High Plains country emerged many of the legends of Texas weather and of the Texas cowboy. In this region lies the flat, dry area known as the Staked Plains (Llano Estacado). According to legend, as the Coronado expedition moved westward, it laid down stakes to serve as guides for the return trip, and even Indian tribes hesitated to venture across these lands. On these plains, sandstorms can obstruct vision in midday, filter tiny bullets of sand into the best-built homes, and scour the paint from exposed automobiles. Many wide, flat riverbeds remain dry most of the year, but they can become sluiceways for flash floods. Through the northern portal, beyond Amarillo, "blue northers" sweep out of the Rocky Mountains with a frenzy of freezing wind, ice, and snow. In the 19th century such famous ranches as the XIT, the Yellow Horse, and the Matador spread their cattle over these ranges.

The Staked Plains

The North Plains subdivision, which is centred around Amarillo, depends economically on grain farming, ranching, oil, and small industries. The South Plains subdivision, with Lubbock as the principal city, has large underground water reservoirs that allow large-scale irrigated cotton farming.

The state's most rugged terrain lies to the west of the Pecos River. Trailing down from the Rockies, the Guadalupe Mountains lead into mountains of the Big Bend country, a name that is derived from a loop of the Rio Grande. The highest peak in Texas is Guadalupe Peak, which rises 8,749 feet (2,667 metres) above sea level. Big Bend National Park preserves the native ruggedness of the region.

Climate. Generalizations about Texas weather on a statewide basis are almost meaningless. The Gulf Coast area around Houston has an average annual temperature of about 70° F (21° C) and rainfall of 45 inches (1,145 millimetres), whereas the Panhandle averages about 60° F (16° C) and less than 19 inches of rain. The driest region is the Trans-Pecos country, and the wettest is the northeast. Southern areas have freezing weather only rarely. In Brownsville, the southernmost city, no measurable snow has fallen in the 20th century, but the northwestern corner averages 23 inches annually.

The people. Texas has long been a huge reservoir for diverse streams of races, and cultures. For the bands of prehistoric hunters, for the waves of Indian tribes, for the Spanish and Mexicans pushing northward, for the Anglo-Americans from the North and East, and for colonizers who came to Texas direct from Europe, there was more than enough room for settlement and opportunity for their influence on the institutions of the state. Some churches still conduct services in Swedish, Czech, or Spanish; throughout the south and west, Spanish remains the family language of many people.

Diverse ethnic stock

During the 19th century there were streams of migration into Texas. Between 1821 and 1836 an estimated 38,000 settlers, on promises of 4,000 acres per family for small fees, trekked from the United States into the territory. In the 30 years before the Civil War came shiploads of Germans, Poles, Czechs, Swedes, Norwegians, and Irish, suffering many hardships but establishing footholds in the frontier land. By 1850, about 33,000 Germans, one-fifth of the state's population, had settled there.

Land ownership—difficult to acquire in Europe—provided an impelling motive for many immigrants. Many families fled Europe to seek personal and religious freedom in Texas. These included many believers in suffrage, human rights, and education. Turning generally to farming, they were frugal, hardworking, and civic-minded, with a large reservoir of fortitude. Church-oriented, they brought with them a stern dedication to the Roman Catholic or Protestant faiths.

During the post-Civil War years numerous families moved from devastated Southern plantations to farms and ranches of the Southwest. From the North Central states came communities of farming families with Swedish, Polish, and Irish backgrounds seeking relief from the tight economy. Others came from Europe, including Belgians, Danes, and Greeks, to become city dwellers, craftsmen, and keepers of small shops.

About 40,000 Indians live in Texas, but this figure fails to account for the many families in the state who have some Indian ancestry. Most of the present-day Indians are city dwellers, but two tribes remain cohesive units. The Alabama-Coushatta Indians occupy one of the two reservations in the state, in east Texas. About 500 Tigua live on a reservation in El Paso.

Up to 20 percent of Texans probably are of Mexican-American descent. Many of the communities along the U.S. side of the southwestern border are almost totally Mexican-American, and larger cities such as Brownsville, Laredo, Corpus Christi, El Paso, and San Antonio carry the mark of Spain and Mexico in their architecture, names, and language. With the urbanization of the state and the decrease in the demand for agricultural workers, large Hispanic populations have converged on the major metropolitan centres that lie farther from the border.

In spite of improved conditions during the years that followed World War II, Hispanics remain at the bottom of all the state's ethnic groups in terms of education, income, and political power. Overcoming these deficiencies has become an increasingly strong goal of the Hispanics. School systems that once barred the use of Spanish and seemed in many ways to belittle the home life and cultural patterns of Hispanics have begun to adopt new approaches. Community control by Anglo minorities has been challenged with considerable success by voter-registration drives and balloting. Occasional violence has erupted, and charges have been made that law-enforcement officers show favouritism for Anglos, but Hispanics have gained control of some political offices.

The Civil War brought freedom for thousands of black slaves within the state. In recent decades the black population has clustered in the central parts of the larger cities, and more than 40 percent of blacks are concentrated in the urban areas of Dallas and Houston. The civil rights movements and the actions of federal courts have given blacks greater access to the ballot. Black candidates have been elected to school boards, to city councils, and to the state legislature. In many ways, however, the position of blacks in Texas resembles their position nationwide. Moving from rural communities and clustering in the central city, while whites move to suburbs in which mere lip service is paid to the open-housing principle, blacks are often faced with subtle discrimination in education and employment.

The economy. Cotton, cattle, and oil—all based on land resources—dominated the successive stages in Texas' economic development until the mid-20th century, and they have continued to undergird the state's basic wealth. Retailing and wholesaling, banking and insurance, and construction have been among the activities reflecting the general affluence, urbanization, and diversification of the state's economy.

Numerous national corporate headquarters have moved to Texas, and petroleum companies have explored for new sources of energy to continue their leadership in providing fuel for the nation. The National Aeronautics and Space Administration (NASA), headquartered in Houston, is among many federal air installations in Texas. In addition, tourism has become a major business, and Dallas has attracted attention as a fashion centre—generally a low-wage industry, however, for most employees. Texas also has become preeminent in its oceanographic investigations into uses of the continental shelf and in the relatively unpublicized areas of medicine and surgery.

Agriculture. The fertile lands of east Texas attracted cotton farmers before the Civil War, and, following that struggle, cotton became the state's major crop. As mechanized farming developed, cotton production shifted to the High Plains country of west Texas, where irrigation and

fertilizer fostered bountiful crops and maintained Texas' national leadership in cotton production. Occasional crop failures due to drought led to crop diversification. In total value of farm crops, Texas consistently has ranked from second to fourth among the states during the past few decades and has been a leading producer of grain sorghums, peanuts (groundnuts), and grapefruit.

All of the mohair that is produced in the United States comes from the Angora goats of Texas. The state leads all others in the raising of beef cattle and sheep. The vast cattle empires of the 19th century have tended to shift to coastal areas during the 20th century, reversing the path of cotton.

The average farm size has more than doubled since 1940, absentee ownership has increased, and farmers have encountered increasing difficulty in surviving.

Mining. New uses for oil were being developed when in 1901 the Spindletop gusher blew in near Beaumont. Today, Texas leads all other states in oil production and is second in natural-gas production. It also ranks first in oil-refining capacity. Oil deposits have been found under more than two-thirds of the state's area, though many finds seem too light for commercial development. More than 50 percent of the nation's sulfur comes from large primary deposits and as a by-product of oil and gas refining.

Industry. Manufacturing began naturally with the processing of local raw materials: cotton gins and cotton-seed mills, meat-packing plants, flour mills, and fruit- and vegetable-canning plants. The production of machinery, excluding electric machinery, is the largest manufacturing employer and ranks second in value added by manufacture.

Oil refining is a major processor of raw materials, though the manufacture of oil-field equipment has proved profitable. The Gulf Coast area is the centre for the petrochemical industrial complexes. A large percentage of the basic petrochemicals that are produced in the United States come from plants ranging from Beaumont to Corpus Christi.

Reflecting a maturing economy, manufacturing has moved toward the fabrication of finished consumer products. In this category the growth of the electronics industry has been outstanding. Other finished goods manufactured in quantity include air conditioners, furniture, boats, household appliances, machinery, leather goods, and clothing.

Transportation. The vastness of Texas and its contrasts in terrain posed great difficulties for transportation yet greatly stimulated its development. The desire to develop inland areas was one factor leading to the establishment of Austin as the capital. In 1852 the legislature granted public lands to railroads for each mile of track constructed, and in 1883 it authorized a county road tax for farm-to-market dirt roads. By 1900 railroads crisscrossed the state, and dirt roads straggled between most communities.

The state has more than 70,000 miles (112,000 kilometres) of highways, and counties and cities maintain more than 164,000 miles of other public roads.

As in other states, the actual mileage of mainline railroads has diminished, and passenger transportation has been discontinued over most lines. Operating freight revenues, however, have increased tremendously over recent decades.

Texas was a pioneer in the development of the airplane. In or near San Antonio were the first army flying schools, established at Ft. Sam Houston in 1910; Kelly Field, which became a training camp for pilots in 1917; and Randolph Field, which by 1931 was serving as "the West Point of the Air." The need for air power in World War II brought air training to more than 40 military bases in Texas. Focal centres for civil air travel are Dallas–Fort Worth, Houston, and San Antonio. The Dallas–Fort Worth airport is one of the nation's largest and busiest. Houston's intercontinental airport encompasses 7,300 acres (2,955 hectares) and provides a computer-run train that is used to carry passengers from the terminals to the flight gates.

The discovery of oil and gas necessitated the cheaper avenue of water transportation to markets in the East and North. Federal aid permitted harbour improvements

Situation of Hispanics

Mineral wealth

at Galveston, Sabine Pass (opening water routes to Port Arthur and Beaumont), Aransas Pass, and Corpus Christi. The opening of a 50-mile (80-kilometre) channel has made Houston an international port, the third largest in the nation in tonnage moved. In the 1930s an inter-coastal canal was completed from New Orleans to Sabine Pass and from Galveston to Corpus Christi, and in 1946 the Gulf Intracoastal Canal was opened from Brownsville to Florida. Continuous dredging operations have opened lanes of ocean commerce to many smaller ports. Galveston, oldest among the major ports, is the headquarters port for extensive commercial fishing enterprises.

Administrative and social conditions. *Government.* The constitution of 1876 outlines the prevailing structure of Texas government. The governor, elected for a four-year term, may initiate legislation, call special legislative sessions, veto bills, and appoint boards and commissions. The governor's power is limited, however, because numerous officials and executive boards are elected rather than appointed. The bicameral legislature comprises the Senate of 31 members who serve for four years and the House of Representatives, with 150 members elected for two years. The top court for civil matters is the Supreme Court, with a chief justice and eight associate justices elected for six-year terms. The highest court for criminal matters is the Court of Criminal Appeals, with nine justices elected for six-year terms. There are 14 courts of civil appeal and more than 240 state district courts, with judges elected for four-year terms. Lower courts comprise county courts, justice of peace courts, and municipal courts.

Texas comprises 254 counties ranging in size from Brewster County, with 6,204 square miles—equal to the combined areas of Connecticut and Rhode Island—to Rockwall County, with 147 square miles. Within constitutional limitations the legislature may create new counties. Each county is administered by a commissioners' court, which is an administrative rather than a trial body. Cities with a population of more than 5,000 may adopt their own home-rule charters.

Local government and taxation

The more critical problems of local government inevitably involve finances. The traditional source of local financing has been the property tax, but the movement of workers to suburbs and a hodgepodge of governmental agencies with taxing power has complicated the scene.

Traditionally, the Democratic Party has dominated elections since the Reconstruction period. Except on rare occasions the Democratic primary, pitting the many splinters of the party against one another, has determined the eventual winners of state offices. Within the one party the political philosophies of candidates have ranged from extreme liberalism to extreme conservatism. Certain contrary trends have emerged, however. The influx of new businesses and industries has brought many Republicans into Texas. The conviction that a two-party system would allow elections based on issues rather than personalities has led some Democrats into the Republican camp, and strong support of civil rights by the national Democratic Party has caused widespread defections by conservative Democrats. In addition, many influential Texas liberals have begun subtly to lend influence to Republicans, whom they consider more liberal than the old-time Democratic leaders.

Emergence of two-party political life

Political campaigning also has changed. It was possible once for W. Lee "Pappy" O'Daniel, a little-known flour salesman, to burst upon the electorate in the late 1930s with a whirlwind of country music and a slogan of "pass the biscuits, Pappy!" and emerge as governor. The public-relations expert, however, has replaced the entertainer. Old-fashioned oratory has yielded to a soft-voiced message, loaded with sincerity, speaking personally and intimately from the television set.

Politics also is becoming more organized. Both Hispanics and blacks have discovered the power of the ballot to elect city officials, to influence state decisions, and to move upward in the power structure. The increasing tempo of party rivalry and the efforts of the minorities to gain power may stimulate a citizenry that often is apathetic at election time.

Education. Efforts to meet, understand, and solve educational problems arising from the multitudinous social, economic, and other changes since World War II have brought mixed results. Some schools have library self-study in buildings designed to accommodate innovation and to place the educational emphasis upon individual growth rather than grade classification. Conversely, there are also formal classrooms in which Hispanic children are forbidden to utter a word in their family language and where dogmatic instruction is regarded as the bridge to wisdom. In general, local school systems, despite minimum standards established by the state, vary greatly in accordance with local financial resources, prevailing adult educational levels, and demands for equal education for all segments of the population.

Public lands have been used to support education from the years of the Texas Republic. The Texas Congress in 1839 set aside lands in each county to support schools and a university. The constitution of 1876 affirmed the endowment of 52,000,000 acres (21,000,000 hectares) for public schools and another 2,000,000 acres for a state university and agricultural college.

Following the Supreme Court's rejection of the separate but equal principle in 1954, public school systems prepared to integrate, but the legislature in 1957 made it illegal for school boards to abolish segregation without approval by local election. Nevertheless, the federal Civil Rights Act of 1964 and the threat of withholding federal funds from schools that did not integrate adequately conquered resistance in most areas. One of the major obstacles to school integration has resulted from discrimination in housing. In addition, black youths from segregated schools find it difficult to gain admission to better colleges or to survive academically if admitted. These problems are by no means peculiar to Texas, of course, nor to the South, but pervade all urban centres in the nation.

Some Mexican-American families have been Texans since the Spanish and Mexican regimes. Many are scholars of distinction or wealthy leaders in professions, but the majority are not. In an effort to break the barriers of language and culture, schools in heavily Mexican-American areas long forbade the use of any language but English in the classroom and pursued curricula oriented toward Anglo social institutions. During the past few decades, however, increased recognition of the Hispanic cultural heritage has made the use of the family language an expression of ethnic pride.

In spite of these bright spots, a far greater proportion of Mexican-Americans and blacks than Anglos remain outside the educational structure, fail to reach high school, or receive an inadequate education.

The University of Texas system enrolls nearly 100,000 students, more than half of them on the main campus in Austin. The state has about 150 colleges and universities, including nearly 25 public senior institutions and 50 public junior colleges. The University of Texas has one of the country's leading graduate schools. Rice University, a private institution in Houston, long has been recognized for the scholarly excellence of its faculty and its high academic standards.

Texas has more than 35 private or church-supported colleges and universities. Baylor University, in Waco, founded in 1845, is the only remaining university of the five established during the republic.

Health and welfare. Programs for the mentally ill and mentally retarded have been slow to develop in Texas, but public concern has made itself felt in the legislature. There are nine mental health hospitals within the state. For aged senile patients there are two geriatric centres, and there is also a neuropsychiatric institute. Increasing attention has been given to outpatient clinic services. Nine state centres care for the mentally retarded.

In medical education, research, and preventive medicine the state ranks among the nation's leaders. The University of Texas Southwestern Medical School, in Dallas, is typical of these vigorous programs. It has developed a Life Sciences Center that emphasizes prevention, cure, and control by combining medicine with the social sciences.

Cultural life. The sense of the past has traditionally been strong in born and bred Texans. The emphasis long was based upon the heroics of living in a frontier land, upon individuals and their deeds, but an increasing ap-

Appreciation of cultural diversity

preciation of the diverse cultures that have enriched the life of Texas has helped to preserve and strengthen those customs. Throughout the state regional historical associations quietly search out and help to restore striking examples of 19th-century homes. San Antonio has recreated the early-18th-century Mexican-Spanish flavour in both restoration and in public shopping and walking areas in the heart of the city. Fredericksburg, with its historic German background, preserves many 19th-century customs and continues to cling to German as a family tongue. Even a metropolitan city like Houston has found space adjacent to its downtown area for restored historic homes. Brownsville vividly dramatizes the marriage of Mexican and Anglo cultures with an annual Washington's birthday parade and fete. Particularly evident are influences from Mexican culture, from the deep-rooted impact of the cattle country, and from the newer yet vibrant life fashioned by oil booms, wildcatting, refineries, and pipelines.

Art, music, and literature occupy significant places in the lives of many communities in Texas. The Amon Carter Museum of Western Art in Fort Worth, dedicated to "the visual documentation of the culture of western North America," houses many paintings and bronzes of Western artists and maintains a microfilm collection of Western newspapers published before 1900. With the Fort Worth Art Center, the William Edrington Scott Theatre, the Kimbell Art Museum, and the Fort Worth Children's Theater, the Amon Carter Museum provides a cultural centre for study and appreciation of the arts.

The Civic Center nestles in 150 acres (61 hectares) amid the tall buildings of downtown Houston. It serves as the home for the Houston Symphony Orchestra and the Grand Opera Association. The world-famous Alley Theater has moved into quarters nearby. Dallas has developed diverse centres for cultural activities. The Margo Jones Theatre was opened in the 1960s, and the Dallas Theater Center provides an outlet for cultural and educational groups. The Dallas Symphony Orchestra is among the better known classical ensembles in the nation. Cultural interests, however, are not restricted to large metropolitan areas. Odessa, for example, supports the unique Museum of the Presidents, showing extensive memorabilia of the U.S. presidents, as well as an accurate replica of London's Globe Theatre, in which a summer program of Shakespearean and other Elizabethan plays is produced. Colleges and universities in the state are active in all areas of the arts.

Water has added new dimensions to popular recreation. In 1913 there were only eight major lakes or reservoirs in Texas, but by the late 20th century there were more than 160, many built to store water against periodic droughts. Several national parks and some 70 state parks dot the state, many of them providing fishing, swimming, camping, and picnicking facilities. An increasing tourist trade has turned sports fishing into a major recreation along the Gulf Coast.

Other dimensions of entertainment—for tourists and Texans alike—include Six Flags over Texas, a Westernized amusement park halfway between Dallas and Fort Worth, and, near the Dallas suburb of Mesquite, a reservation into which motorists can drive, as on an African safari, and watch apparently free-roaming elephants, giraffes, and other African wildlife. In Houston the well-publicized Astrodome has become a centre of professional sports, rodeos, bullfights (with no killing), circuses, and other spectaculars.

Book publishing, though not a big business within the state, has gained a strong foothold. The University of Texas Press has gained national acclaim through its scholarly and historical works, and the Southern Methodist University Press likewise has established discriminating standards. Several commercial publishing companies concentrate on books and monographs related to the history of the Southwest.

The university libraries, art galleries, and special collections contain remarkable treasures. The Armstrong Browning Library at Baylor houses more than 5,000 books and manuscripts by and about Robert and Elizabeth Barrett Browning. At the University of Texas in Austin, the new Presidential Library, dedicated in 1971 and operated as a branch of the Library of Congress, houses millions of documents on public affairs since the mid-1930s, related to the public career of former president Lyndon B. Johnson. Also available at the university are a Latin-American collection, the Michener Collection of Art, and a number of other special collections.

HISTORY

The forerunners of the west Texas Indians lived in camps whose remains indicate that they were made perhaps as much as 37,000 years ago. Possessing only crude spears and flint-pointed darts, these hunters survived primarily on wild game. In the more fertile areas of east Texas, some of the tribes established permanent villages and well-managed farms and evolved political and religious systems. Forming a loose federation in order to preserve peace and to provide for mutual protection, they came to be known as the Caddo confederacies. By 1528, when the first Europeans set foot on Texas soil, the area was sparsely settled, but the culture and habitation of the Indians exerted measurable influence on the later history of the region.

Settlement. By the 1730s the Spanish had sent more than 30 expeditions into Texas. San Antonio, which by 1718 housed a military post and one or more missions, had become the administrative centre. Missions, with military support, were established in Nacogdoches in east Texas, Goliad in the south, and near El Paso in the far west. The French poked their way briefly into Texas. The explorations of Robert Cavelier, sieur de La Salle, and his colony at Matagorda Bay were the bases of French claims to east Texas.

Anglo-American colonization gained impetus when the United States purchased the Louisiana Territory from France in 1803 and claimed title to lands as far west as the Rio Grande. By 1819, however, the United States had accepted the Sabine River as the western boundary of the Louisiana Territory. Moses Austin secured permission from the Spanish government to colonize 300 families on a grant of 200,000 acres (81,000 hectares). When Mexico became an independent country in 1821, his son, Stephen F. Austin, received Mexican approval of the grant. He led his first band of settlers to a site named San Felipe de Austin near the Gulf Coast. By 1832 Austin's several colonies had about 8,000 inhabitants. Other impresarios with similar grants brought the territory's Anglo-American population to about 20,000.

Spanish-Anglo confrontations

Revolution and the republic. Unrest throughout Mexico, including Texas, resulted in a coup by Antonio López de Santa Anna, who assumed the presidency in 1833. Texans, hopeful for relief from restrictive governmental measures, supported Santa Anna. Austin expected a friendly hearing about these grievances but instead was imprisoned in Mexico City for encouraging insurrection. He was freed in 1835 and returned home to find that skirmishes had already developed between the colonists and Mexican troops and that Santa Anna was preparing to send reinforcements. Texans formed a provisional government in 1835, and in 1836 issued a declaration of independence at Washington-on-the-Brazos. David G. Burnet was chosen provisional president of the new Republic of Texas, Sam Houston was appointed to be its military commander, and Austin became commissioner to the United States with the mission of securing strategic aid and enlisting volunteers.

The famous siege of the Alamo in San Antonio lasted from February 23 to March 6, 1836. The strategic objective of the stand was to delay Mexican forces and thereby permit military organization of the Texas settlers. As the battle climaxed with a massive attack over the walls, the defenders (about 187) were all killed. Among the dead were the famous frontiersmen Jim Bowie and Davy Crockett. On April 21, Sam Houston led a surprise attack on the Mexican troops at San Jacinto, and he succeeded in capturing Santa Anna and in securing victory for the Texans.

The Texan revolution was not simply a fight between the Anglo-American settlers and Mexican troops; it was a revolution of all the people who were living in Texas against what many of them regarded as tyrannical rule from a distant source. Many of the leaders in the revolution and many of the armed settlers who took part were Mexicans.

The Republic of Texas was officially established with Sam Houston as president and Stephen Austin as secretary of state. Cities already had been named in their honour: Houston was the capital until 1839, when Austin was approved as the permanent capital.

The republic led a difficult 10-year life. Financing proved critical, and efforts to secure loans from foreign countries were unsuccessful. Protection against raids from Mexico and occasional attacks by Indians required a mobile armed force. Before the revolution certain commissioned officers in the colonies had been called Rangers. During the republic a squad of armed men, the famous Texas Rangers, was maintained to ride long distances quickly to repel or punish raiding forces.   (DeW.C.R.)

Annexation and statehood.   Throughout the life of the republic there were varying movements for annexation to the United States. Andrew Jackson schemed with his friend Sam Houston to get the land of the United States, and gradually Texas became one of the great political issues of the time. Opposing Pres. John Tyler's hope of taking Texas into the nation, Daniel Webster resigned as secretary of state. The issue was not so much Texas as slavery: Texas would be another slave state. Sam Houston hurried toward his goal of annexation by pretending to deal with Great Britain. The British, though they had no wish to acquire Texas, opposed annexation by the United States and at one time thought of using force to prevent it. The U.S. Congress, fearing Britain's motives, narrowly approved annexation on December 29, 1845.

Under the annexation agreement Texas assumed responsibility for its debts and retained ownership of its public domain, which was expended for various purposes, including the building of a state capitol, but primarily in allocation of 32,153,878 acres in grants to railroads and 42,549,400 acres to public schools. The original claim of Texas was to 172,687,000 acres, including the three-league coastal area handed down from Spanish and Mexican sovereignty, but the U.S. Supreme Court decided against Texas ownership of this coastal area of more than 2,000,000 acres in its decision in the Tidelands Case of 1950.

Annexation by the United States, together with the secondary issue over the ownership of the area between the Rio Grande and the Nueces River, precipitated the Mexican War (April 1846–September 1847). U.S. forces under Gen. Winfield Scott and Gen. Zachary Taylor invaded Mexico after several skirmishes in the Rio Grande Valley and terminated the war by the capture of Mexico City on September 14, 1847. By the Treaty of Guadalupe-Hidalgo (February 2, 1848) the Mexican claim to Texas was relinquished, along with cession of large area west of the Louisiana Purchase.

Within this newly ceded territory, Texas claimed the area as far west as the upper Rio Grande and, in addition, portions of present Colorado, Wyoming, Kansas, and Oklahoma. As a part of the compromise of 1850, Texas relinquished its claim in return for $10,000,000, $2,000,000 of which was apportioned to Texas schools, thereby establishing the permanent school fund.

Civil War and aftermath
Overwhelmingly a slave state, Texas seceded January 28, 1861. The U.S. Civil War brought intense disruption to the state. Gov. Sam Houston strongly opposed secession, and, after refusing to take the oath of allegiance to the Confederacy, he was removed from office. During the war Texans had to defend themselves from Indian attacks, from Mexican encroachments, and from Federal gunboats and invading Union soldiers. Federal forces ultimately gained control of much of the Gulf Coast but were unable to move far inland.

Texans sought immediate readmission to the Union by electing a Unionist governor in 1866 and adopting a constitution renouncing the right of secession and slavery. Under the "radical" plan of Reconstruction evolved in Congress, however, military law was declared in 1867 and Gen. P.H. Sheridan was placed in command of the Texas-Louisiana military district. The radical Unionist element took over. A new constitution was readmitted to the Union, but it remained under radical rule until the defeat of Edmund J. Davis by Richard Coke for governor in December 1873. This ended the carpetbag rule, and in 1876 the present constitution was adopted.

The modern period.   During the last three decades of the 19th century there were rapid developments in population and economy of Texas. The state was readmitted to the Union under a new constitution in 1869. By 1874 the Comanches had been forced onto a reservation in present-day Oklahoma. Under waves of immigration from the North and South as well as from Europe, towns were established, farming spread throughout the central areas of the state, and the cattle industry began to thrive on the plains of west Texas. Railroad building and increased shipping fashioned new links with the rest of the world. Manufacturing, forced into life by the isolation of Civil War years, continued to grow. By 1900 the population had grown to more than 3,000,000.

In 1901 the oil well that blew in at Spindletop redirected the entire economy of the state. By the second half of the 20th century Texas was the nation's major petroleum producer, but already the state had begun to diversify its economic base. During the same period population increased more than fourfold, creating several metropolises, and the state system of education became one of the nation's largest.

The great governor of modern Texas history was James Stephen Hogg, a Progressive, who was elected in 1890 on a platform promising regulation of corporations, especially of railroads, which he had disciplined earlier as attorney general. The most important reform of his two terms was the creation of the Texas Railroad Commission. The commission later became the most influential state regulatory body in the U.S. when control of oil production was added to its powers. A large man in character and physique, Hogg's altruistic influence was effective for nearly 20 years. Three other but very different political figures abused and for long periods influenced the state during the first half of the 20th century: James E. Ferguson, impeached as governor in 1917; his wife, Miriam A. Ferguson, afterward twice governor; and W. Lee O'Daniel, twice governor and twice U.S. senator. The flamboyance and rural demagoguery of this trio gave an additional dimension to the state's reputation for eccentricity. Texas' first Republican senator since Reconstruction, John G. Tower, won a special election in 1961 to fill the vacancy caused by the resignation of Lyndon B. Johnson, who was elected vice-president of the U.S. in 1960. The Republicans, gaining popularity in the South and Southwest, selected Dallas as the site of their party's 1984 presidential convention.   (Ed.)

Texas Railroad Commission

MOUNTAIN REGION

The mass of plains, plateaus, mountains, canyons, deserts, salt lakes, forests, scrublands, prairies, and irrigated valleys known as the mountain region is as varied as would be expected for a region occupying almost one-fifth of the United States. Yet its development is limited to a few tourist, mining, and irrigation centres, and the whole huge area supports less than 3 percent of the population of the United States. The mountain region of the Great Plains and the High West is centred in the states of Colorado, Wyoming, Montana, Idaho, Utah, and Nevada; but it may be considered to contain portions of the bordering states of North and South Dakota, Nebraska, Kansas, Oklahoma, Texas, New Mexico, Arizona, California, Oregon, and Washington.

The American West begins with the Great Plains. In the regions of the Middle West to the east, settlement is fairly continuous; to the west settlement is scattered. While the more densely populated areas are taking on a resemblance to the older parts of the country, and the West of the movies and television is largely a thing of the past, many parts of the West lack water, minerals, or any other basis for settlement.

Water resources

The flat or gently rolling plains of the Wheat Belt of the Middle West pass without a conspicuous break into the pasture lands of the Great Plains. Water supply on the Plains is uncertain. Much of the available water originates in the Rockies towering to the west. Some of it flows from the mountains through long braided streams such as the Arkansas, the Platte, and the Yellowstone and is used to irrigate narrow strips of intensively cultivated land yielding sugar beets, melons, grain, and fodder crops. In other cases, water from the Rockies flows underground and is brought to the surface through wells.

A relatively small percentage of the Great Plains is cultivated by dry farming—a laborious method of conserving rainfall so that a grain crop can be raised on the dry margin of cultivation. For the most part, however, the land is pasture that supports a few cattle or sheep per square mile and even fewer men. The small towns are widely spaced along the east-west railways and highways and except for agricultural and mineral production there is little business activity.

The rocks underlying the Plains are sedimentary, and there are few ore deposits. The minerals include low- or middle-grade coal mined for local consumption and some building stone. Petroleum has brought prosperity to a few areas in the Wyoming Basin and western Montana. Some of the ores from the Rockies are smelted on the Plains—for example, at Great Falls, Montana, and Pueblo, Colorado.

Such cities as there are on the plains are generally located close to the Rocky Mountains. Denver, Colorado, the largest, orginally a supply centre for mining camps, still manufactures mining machinery. In addition, it has the leading stockyard in the West and the leading sheep market in the country and is also the principal financial and wholesale centre for both the Rockies and the Plains.

The Rockies themselves are high, sharp-edged mountains divided into numerous discontinuous ranges. On the slopes the grasslands of the adjacent plains blend gradually into open pine forest until at the timberline the forest gives way to alpine pastures overshadowed by snow-capped peaks. The Rockies are rich in minerals—gold, silver, lead, tungsten, and molybdenum in the Colorado Rockies; copper, silver, and gold around Butte, Montana; and silver, lead, zinc, and copper in the Coeur d'Alene district of Idaho.

Mineral wealth

The Cascade-Sierra Nevada ranges make up the western wall of the highlands. The fir-covered Cascades are volcanic mountains whose conical, snow-capped peaks rise abruptly from the surrounding plateau. The wooded Sierra Nevada is a huge block of rock tilted up toward the east where its snow-covered crest overlooks the Great Basin. Neither of these ranges is as rich in minerals as the Rockies.

Between the western wall and the Rockies are two huge plateaus and two immense areas of basins and ranges that in a few places contain rich mineral deposits (for example, Bingham, Utah). In the north the volcanic Columbia Plateau contains much fertile soil suitable for wheat farming and some arid areas that, when irrigated, support prosperous orchards. In contrast is the almost barren Colorado Plateau, whose major industry is tourism (Grand Canyon). Between these two plateaus is the vast Great Basin, an area of inland drainage subdivided into flattish arid basins by abrupt north-south trending ranges. The land is barren or poor pasture except in the few places where irrigation is possible.

As would be expected in an arid and semiarid area, the outstanding commercial centres were located at oases. Salt Lake City, Utah, for instance, was founded where a river drops onto the eastern edge of the Great Basin. Few sections of the High West can support cities, and there is little prospect for its intensive development.   (V.Ca./Ed.)

Colorado

Colorado is classified as one of the Mountain States of the United States, although only about one-half of its approximately 104,247 square miles (269,998 square kilo-

metres) lies in the Rocky Mountains. It borders Wyoming and Nebraska on the north, Nebraska and Kansas on the east, Oklahoma and New Mexico on the south, and Utah on the west.

Like the geological past that is revealed on its surface, Colorado's human history is written in the names of its cities, towns, mountain ranges, and passes. Indian and Spanish names alternate with those of American frontiersmen, and many ghost towns are mute reminders of the thousands of prospectors who streamed into the territory in the mid-19th century to pursue their dreams of gold bonanzas. The vast cattle ranges and agricultural acreage fed by huge irrigation projects are more characteristic of modern Colorado, however, as are the diversified industries and the educational and research facilities in its urban centres.

PHYSICAL AND HUMAN GEOGRAPHY

The land. *Relief.* Colorado's natural landscape is too varied to be encompassed within a single profile. The land ranges from the flat, grass-covered high plains, through the rolling, hilly Colorado Piedmont paralleling the Rocky Mountain front, to the high and numerous mountain ranges and plateaus that make up the southern Rocky Mountains and the Colorado Plateau. Within these areas the state rises from about 3,500 feet (1,100 metres) in the east to more than 14,000 feet in the Rockies.

Lack of water is the dominant characteristic of Colorado's eastern high plains region. The average annual precipitation of 16 inches (410 millimetres) is erratic. Approximately 70 percent of it falls during summer, and hail is frequent. The Arkansas and South Platte are the major rivers, but both rise in the mountains to the west. Many other rivers are dry during much of the year, and the land is flat. Underlain by layered rocks, sandstones, shales, and limestones covered by a short grass vegetation, the natural environment is inhabited by prairie dogs, jackrabbits, coyotes, rattlesnakes, antelope, and such birds as the meadowlark and lark bunting. The climate, flatness, and layered rocks have produced very fertile soils that lack only moisture. Nearly all of the high plains are covered by brown soils, which support a strong mat of buffalo and grama grass, a valued resource for cattle grazing.

The barren stretches

About 50 miles (80 kilometres) wide and 275 miles long, the Colorado Piedmont is a picturesque, hilly to mountainous landscape sandwiched between the high plains and the southern Rocky Mountains. It encompasses all of the large urban complexes, the major transport arteries, most of the industry, a majority of the major colleges and universities, and four-fifths of the state's people. The layered rocks have been uptilted and dissected into prominent stream divides and deep valleys by the major rivers and numerous smaller streams that debouch onto the piedmont from the mountains. Terrain, ground cover, and climatic conditions provide suitable habitats for rabbits, waterfowl, pheasants, coyotes, deer, raccoon, and, on the arid foothills and unirrigated uplands, rattlesnakes. Many species of birds prevail, of which the meadowlark, crow, dove, and western magpie are most numerous. The climate and land of the Colorado Piedmont are strong attractions for tourists, homeseekers, and farmers. Multicoloured ridges, or hogbacks, and parallel, or strike, valleys make fine homesites. The major cities and the wealthy farm areas lie where the streams have broadened the valleys. Among the attractive features of the landscape is the high, grotesque, and multicoloured agglomeration of sandstones northwest of Colorado Springs known as the Garden of the Gods. In the foothills southwest of Denver is one of the world's largest and most beautiful outdoor amphitheatres, Red Rocks Park. Since 1880, more than 400 reservoirs have been built in the piedmont to store water for irrigation. These sites are meccas for water sports, hunting, and house building.

The more habitable climes

The western half of Colorado is the huge mountain upthrust, comprising most of the southern Rocky Mountains. High plateaus, mesas, and mountain ranges alternate with broad, intervening valleys and deep, narrow canyons. This mountain land provides water for six states and Mexico. Snow and rain, almost equally divided, fall copiously on the mountains in amounts ranging from 20 to 50 inches

The mountainous west

(500–1,250 millimetres) annually. The drainage pattern from the Rockies is oriented by the mountains themselves, which form the Continental Divide, the main watershed of the continent.

The mountainous half of Colorado comprises a great number of individual mountain ranges. In the north and northwest the Front, Medicine Bow, Park, and Rabbit Ears ranges are major uplifts, and Rocky Mountain National Park (established 1915) is a major attraction. The western and southwestern extremity of the state comprises the tilted and acutely uplifted layered rock of the Colorado Plateau. The Grand Mesa and the White River Plateau, both above 10,000 feet (3,000 metres), are major attractions. The region also contains several national monuments and parks, some of them primarily scenic, others the remnants of Indian settlements.

The San Juan Mountains, a large, heavily ice-dissected volcanic plateau above 13,000 feet, rise in the southwest. The Sangre de Cristo Range is a prominent linear range in the south central region of the state. At the western base of this range are some of the largest sand dunes in the interior of the North American continent, an area of 61 square miles set aside in 1932 as the Great Sand Dunes National Monument.

The Sawatch, Colorado's highest range and the central core of the Colorado Rockies, consists of Mt. Elbert—at 14,433 feet (4,399 metres) the highest point in the state—and many other elevations above 14,000 feet. The Colorado Rockies contain a significant share of the U.S. public domain in the form of 12 national forests, which total almost 13,800,000 acres (5,585,000 hectares) of land. There are 53 peaks more than 14,000 feet in elevation and 831 peaks between 11,000 and 14,000 feet.

Climate. Summer temperatures on the high plains average 75° F (24° C) for July and August, with extremes above 100° F (38° C). In the summer daily temperatures may vary as much as 40° to 50° F (22° to 28° C), although the general variation is about 25° F (14° C). Winters are dry, cold, windy, and generally harsh. The high plains form a playground for the wind, and, though snowfall is light, the winter blizzard becomes a dread element for both humans and animals. Average winter nighttime low temperatures range from 10° to 30° F (−12° to −1° C), with daily highs from 40° to 60° F (4° to 16° C). From October through February the precipitation, usually snow, rarely exceeds two inches.

There is less precipitation annually than on the high plains, though about 70 percent of it falls in summer also, mostly in thunderstorms. July temperatures in Denver, the state capital, average 73° F (23° C); and January temperatures, 29° F (−2° C). Short hot and cold spells of above 90° F (32° C) and below 10° F (−12° C) are not uncommon. The chinook wind—a very dry, descending airstream from the high mountains that is warmed by compression as it descends—often raises temperatures 30° to 40° F (16° to 22° C) in less than an hour, melts the snow cover, and can produce violent winds that have been recorded in excess of 100 miles per hour (160 kilometres per hour). The soils of the Colorado Piedmont are alluvial, or water transported.

Plant and animal life. Ecologically, there are six life zones from the high plains to the high mountain peaks. In the foothills zone, from 5,500 to 7,000 feet, oak, mountain mahogany, juniper, and piñon pine are the dominant vegetation. Higher zones, from 7,000 to 12,000 feet, feature a coniferous forest in which the ponderosa pine, Douglas fir, and blue and Engelmann spruce are dominant, interspersed with some deciduous, broad-leaved species. The alpine tundra zone, from 12,000 to 14,000 feet, has sparse vegetation, mainly mosses and sedges.

Most species of the animal kingdom have no permanent habitat in the Colorado Rockies. They move to high elevations where food and cover are plentiful during summer and return to the warmer lower elevations during winter. Deer, elk, and mountain sheep are the most common game animals. Among the furbearers, the coyote, wildcat, badger, marten, muskrat, and beaver are prevalent.

The people. The first Colorado territorial census, in 1860, showed a population of 34,277, 86 percent of it ru-

ral. This pattern continued until 1910, when 50.3 percent of the nearly 800,000 inhabitants were urban. After 1950 the urban percentage rose sharply, reaching more than 80 percent of the population in the late 20th century. The number of blacks is small, but a few hundred thousand Coloradans are of predominantly Mexican descent. As in most of the nation, minority groups are hampered by inadequacies in education, housing, and economic opportunity. The conditions of seasonal migratory labour have been of increasing concern at all levels of government. An overall consideration of Colorado's population, like that of its physical environment, is most meaningful in a regional context.

The demography of Colorado's high plains is much affected by the region's rigorous physical geography: its dryness, bareness, wind, and capricious precipitation. The seven high-plains counties comprise 14 percent of Colorado's land area but have a dwindling population, the density of which rarely exceeds five persons per square mile. The towns of the high plains, all located on highways and railroads, serve vast rural hinterlands where livestock raising is important and where wheat and sorghum are major products. Limon, Burlington, Cheyenne Wells, and Yuma, each with fewer than 4,000 people, are the largest towns.

Ready availability of water, a climate conducive to outdoor work and recreation, and proximity to the mountain front are mainly responsible for the large population growth of the Colorado Piedmont. The 22 counties occupy 35 percent of the land area, and more than 70 percent of the state's people live in the metropolitan areas of Denver–Boulder, Colorado Springs, and Pueblo.

In population density and distribution Colorado's mountain counties mirror the rigours of the environment. Terrain, isolation, severe winters, and separation from the piedmont counties by the mountainous Continental Divide are major limiting factors. The 34 mountain counties occupy 51 percent of the state's land area, but some counties have fewer than two people per square mile. Unlike the high plains, however, the population is increasing slowly. The rural population is settled mainly in restricted mountain valleys, where ranching and irrigation farming support the family unit.

The economy. Location, soil, minerals, water, space for expansion, and physical beauty are positive resources in Colorado's growth. Among the Rocky Mountain states Colorado accounts for two-fifths of the population but about one-half of all manufacturing employment.

Industry. Major industries include printing and publishing, machinery production, food and food products, metal production, lumber and wood products, and military ordnance and accessories.

Agriculture. From the outset, agriculture has been the most basic asset of Colorado's economy. Colorado was the first state to abrogate the riparian doctrine of water use, based on English common law, which gave prior water rights to owners of adjoining lands. It evolved instead a totally new concept for use of water resources based on the rights of the larger public. This Colorado doctrine has been adopted and adapted by most of the 17 Western states. The state ranks high among the U.S. states in the amount of land under irrigation. Corn (maize), wheat, hay, and sugar beets are the major crops.

Animals and animal products are significant aspects of the agricultural economy. Colorado is an important cattle producer and also raises large numbers of hogs and lambs. Weld, Morgan, Larimer, and Boulder counties are the national centre for the production of cattle fattened in feedlots rather than on the open range. A spectacular sight of the piedmont landscape is the acres of fat cattle feeding on corn, alfalfa (lucerne), and sugar beets near Greeley. There is much corporate farming, and generally it is highly mechanized.

Tourism. Although manufacturing, agriculture, and summer tourism are the mainstays of Colorado's economy, winter sports have grown at an almost alarming rate. Transport, housing, and lift facilities are inadequate for the annual ski invasion.

Mining. Although it is by no means the leader that it was in the mining bonanzas of a century ago, the

Population statistics

Cattle production

minerals industry continues to make substantial contributions to the economy. Among the principal minerals are coal, petroleum, molybdenum, and sand and gravel. Northwestern Colorado has some of the largest and most valuable coal deposits in the United States, but the industry is relatively dormant because of decreasing national demands. Petroleum and gas reserves, are mostly in the form of oil shales.

Power.   Basic to all aspects of Colorado's life and economy are the state's power resources. Power generation is based on coal, hydropower, petroleum, and natural gas. Consumption is immense, and demands are difficult to meet. About two-fifths of the total capacity and production is privately owned.

Transportation.   Colorado ranks first among the Mountain States in road mileage, with more than 82,000 miles (131,000 kilometres) of highways and rural roads. There is no set road pattern, although main highways tend to be east–west, circumvent high mountain masses, and follow valleys and canyons to their heads in the 32 mountain passes over the Continental Divide. The highest of the passes, at 12,183 feet (3,713 metres), is Trail Ridge Road in Rocky Mountain National Park. Seventeen other passes exceed 10,000 feet in elevation. Several portions of the Interstate Highway System run through the state and radiate to neighbouring states in all directions. There are twin vehicular tunnels under the Continental Divide.

Denver's Stapleton International Airport is a major centre in the nation's air-traffic pattern. It is served by several major airlines, and carriers also link Denver with other Colorado cities and with neighbouring states. Several large air-freight depots adjoin Stapleton Airport. Railroad lines in Colorado are mainly bulk-freight carriers using multilevel railcars and flatcars for containerized freight. There are more than 3,450 miles (5,520 kilometres) of track, which connect the major urban areas in the state.

Administrative and social conditions.   *Government.*   In 1875 a convention drew up the constitution for the prospective state, and in 1876 Colorado was admitted to the Union as the 38th state. From its admission 100 years after the signing of the Declaration of Independence, it became known as the Centennial State.

The executive branch of government has six offices: governor, lieutenant governor, secretary of state, attorney general, treasurer, and auditor. All offices were created by the Colorado constitution, and the elected officials serve four-year terms. Numerous commissions, boards, and examiners are appointed to discharge the executive functions of state government. At the county level, the constitution provides for several kinds of officers.

The Colorado General Assembly, which meets annually, comprises a Senate of 35 members elected to four-year terms and a house of representatives of 65 members elected to two-year terms. The Legislative Council, created by statute in 1953, is a 13-member fact-finding agency of the General Assembly, and the Joint Budget Committee, established in 1959, is the permanent agency for fiscal and budgetary review. Under the Administrative Organization Act of 1968, the Commission on Uniform State Laws was created; and the Commission on Interstate Cooperation dates from 1937.

The Colorado judiciary is composed of courts at various levels. The highest is the state Supreme Court, with seven justices. Below it are district courts, which encompass one or more counties, and a county court in each county. In addition, such special bodies as juvenile and probate courts are set forth in the constitution, as are the municipal courts, which provide the grass-roots core of the judicial system.

Political balance

Since World War II each state political campaign has involved the issue of extension of federal activities, with Democrats generally committed to extension, and Republicans opposed. Since the 1920s each of the two parties has won control of the legislature in about one-half of the elections, indicating a fairly even balance within the state.

Welfare and health.   Colorado's per capita income is higher than the national average, and its expenditure on public assistance is also higher. The requisite age of old-age pensioners is 65, and they must have resided in Col-

orado in five of the previous nine years. Average monthly benefits for retired workers are lower than the national average, but benefits for disabled workers and Medicare payments are higher.

Education.   The people of the Colorado Territory, despite being on the edge of the frontier, were concerned with education, and they created the University of Colorado in 1861. The school did not open until 1877, but publicly supported primary education began in 1862, with secondary schools opening in the following decade. The great population increases since the end of World War II have produced severe problems in funding, in instructional space, and in busing to achieve improved instructional programs. Curriculum and instructional revision has been undertaken in all areas, although foreign languages and mathematics have been particularly stressed.

In addition to the University of Colorado, at Boulder, the University of Denver (1864), the Colorado School of Mines, at Golden (1869), and Colorado State University, at Fort Collins (1870), were founded before statehood. By 1979 Colorado had 41 colleges, junior colleges, and universities, 23 of them publicly supported. Of special note is the U.S. Air Force Academy, authorized by Congress in 1954. In 1958 it moved into its campus near Colorado Springs.

Cultural life.   Red Rocks Park, a large natural amphitheatre in the foothills west of Denver, is Colorado's best known theatre; it hosts frequent musical events. The Central City Opera House, dating from 1878, has a summer season of opera and drama. Summer fare is available as well at Elitch Gardens Theatre, opened in Denver in 1890, and at festivals in Aspen and Boulder. The Fine Arts Center in Colorado Springs is a regional art centre. In 1971 additions to the Denver Art Museum were completed to house collections of Renaissance and Peruvian paintings.

Libraries have an important function in Colorado's cultural milieu. There has been a continuing trend to organize regional libraries to provide adequate service to every community. The Bibliographical Center for Research, Rocky Mountain region, is one of three such centres in the United States and has a catalogue of 5,000,000 cards. The Colorado State Library is responsible for furnishing all Colorado institutions with research, reference, and general reading services.

Because of its location and altitude, Colorado has three important observatories. The High Altitude Laboratory, with high-altitude-research facilities at Mount Evans, and the Chamberlain Observatory are operated by the University of Denver. The National Center for Atmospheric Research is a cooperative project of more than 30 U.S. universities, sponsored by the National Science Foundation. It has ties also to the Department of Astrophysics and Atmospheric Physics of the University of Colorado.

The State Historical Society maintains nine historic properties. These include the Colorado State Museum in Denver, several houses and forts dating from the early days of the state, and the Ute Indian Museum in Montrose and the El Pueblo Museum in Pueblo. On the western and southwestern plateaus, the Black Canyon (established 1933), Colorado (1911), and Dinosaur (1915) national monuments are preserved as scenic attractions. Because of their cultural and historic value, Mesa Verde National Park (1906) and Hovenweep (1923) and Yucca House (1919) national monuments in the southwest—all relics of former Indian civilizations—are preserved for public use and for archaeological study and exploration.

HISTORY

The earliest inhabitants.   The influence of Indian culture on Colorado's development and culture has been strong. Not only have Indian place-names enriched the English vocabulary, but also Indian folktales, music, and dances have been assimilated into American culture. Of more practical value, Indian food and artwork has made valuable and unique contributions to the Colorado economy. The cliff dwellings in Mesa Verde National Park are among the physical remains of early Indian communities.

The Plains Indians, mainly Arapaho and Cheyenne, helped the explorers, traders, and trappers to find their

Indian and Spanish heritages

way across the plains. The Indians knew the streams, the natural routes, the sources of fresh water and firewood, the areas of natural protection, and the feeding grounds of the buffalo. The Great Basin Indians, mainly the Utes, made similar contributions to knowledge of the Rocky Mountains.

The Indians, however, were displaced by Spanish explorers from Mexico in search of cities of gold and silver. Fearing attacks by the United States, they strengthened the Spanish frontier in the 1840s with huge land grants reaching as far north as the Arkansas River. On these grants were established the first permanent white settlements in Colorado and, in 1851, the first recorded irrigation. The Spanish language is imprinted on Colorado geography. The state was named from the Spanish *colorado* ("red," or "ruddy"). Twenty large streams in Colorado are called *ríos,* and numerous cities, villages, and mountain ranges and peaks have such Spanish names as the Sangre de Cristo (Blood of Christ) Mountains.

The U.S. territory. Immediately after the purchase of the Louisiana Territory by the United States in 1804, American exploration began. Dispatched to map, to explore, and to record scientific data about the new land were Zebulon Pike in 1806, Stephen Long in 1820, and John C. Frémont in 1842. As knowledge of the area spread, fur traders and trappers followed. Permanently stamped on the land are the names of such frontier scouts as Kit Carson and Jim Bridger. Ft. Bent and Ft. St. Vrain served as collection points for furs, places for food and supplies, and shelter and protection from Indians.

The Colorado gold rush

In 1859 gold was discovered. A sudden great influx of people took place to the cry of "Pikes Peak or bust," and the bustling gold-dust towns of Central City, Black Hawk, Gold Hill, and Cripple Creek made mining history. The first gold was panned from the stream beds, after which came the search for the mother lode in the mountains.

In these frontier mining districts civil and criminal codes were drawn up, and penalties for crimes were established. Of the thousands of seekers for gold, only a few found their bonanza. By 1890 the mountains were empty except for a few permanent mining towns.

Contemporaneous with the mining rushes was Colorado's period of territorial government. In 1861 congressional legislation provided for administrative officials to be appointed by the president. Seven governors were appointed in 15 years, and none served a full four-year term, a fact suggesting the social instability of the Colorado Territory. In 1875 a constitution was drawn up and ratified by the territorial assembly, and on August 1, 1876, Colorado became a member of the Union.

Economic and social growth. It was not possible to bring enough food by wagon train to feed the thousands of miners in Colorado. Shortages of food during the gold rush led enterprising pioneers to initiate a new and significant component to the regional economy. Water was taken from the streams and put onto the land in what has been called the single most significant event in Colorado history. There evolved an entirely new social code and economy and a western water law. The industries and inhabitants of cities and towns came to depend upon irrigation agriculture. Sugar factories, which extracted the juice from the sugar beet, sprang up across the landscape.

By 1881 the buffalo herds on Colorado's high plains had been massacred, and the buffalo were replaced by cattle and sheep. From its mountain valleys, plains, and feed lots, Colorado became a major producer of meat. Automobiles, railroads, and a tunnel through the mountainous backbone united the mountains and high plateaus of western Colorado with the flat eastern half of the state, and the flow of resources set the pace for industrial development. In 1892 the Colorado Fuel and Iron Company, based on local deposits of iron ore and coal, was established in Pueblo, and it became a major steel producer. By 1930, 16 sugar factories were in operation. During World War II the need for metals, especially molybdenum, led to new industry. In the 20th century Colorado became a tourist state because of its climate, majestic scenery, and national parks and monuments. Since 1955 it has been not only the leading ski area in the United States but also a base for sophisticated scientific research and development.

(M.J.Lo.)

Idaho

Idaho is one of the Mountain States; but, along with Oregon, Washington, and the northwestern counties of Montana, Idaho is often also classified as part of the Pacific Northwest region, a region unified by the Continental Divide as an eastern boundary and by the Columbia River drainage basin, which covers virtually the entire area.

With 83,557 square miles (216,412 square kilometres), including 880 square miles of inland water, Idaho has twice the combined area of the six New England states. Its boundaries are both geographical and historical in derivation. The boundary with the Canadian province of British Columbia on the north follows the 49th parallel of latitude, while the southern border with Utah and Nevada follows the 42nd parallel—a line that was established between the United States and Spain in 1819. The state's eastern border with Wyoming follows the Continental Divide and incorporates a small slice of Yellowstone National Park before twisting northwestward atop the Beaverhead Mountains and the Bitterroot Range of the Rockies bordering Montana. On the west, Idaho's border with Washington and Oregon is a 480-mile (770-kilometre) straight stretch except between Weiser and Lewiston, where Hells Canyon of the Snake River serves as a natural boundary.

Geographical and historical borders

Idaho appropriately is shaped much like a logger's boot, thereby accidentally reflecting the state's rugged forest and mountain terrain in which logging and mining play major roles. The residents of Idaho enjoy some of the largest unspoiled natural areas in the United States, including about 2,500,000 acres (1,012,000 hectares) of wilderness and primitive land in which roads and vehicles are seldom to be found. Since its development in 1936 Sun Valley has become an internationally known area for winter sports. The state also has large supplies of underground water. Artesian wells are used to heat some homes and buildings in Boise, the capital, whose name (French *boisé,* "wooded") reflects its settlement as an oasis for explorers who were crossing the desolate Snake River Plains. A frontier character is still evident in the individualism of voting that makes the crossing of party lines, especially to support liberal issues and candidates, a frequent occurrence in an otherwise fairly conservative climate.

PHYSICAL AND HUMAN GEOGRAPHY

The land. Diversity of the natural environment is the most common characteristic of Idaho's landscape, creating a sectionalism that is reflected in its community life, politics, economy, and cultural development, as well as in the varieties of its soils and animal and plant life. Altitude is often a more important factor in controlling Idaho's climate than is latitude. The northern areas of the state are lower in elevation on the average than are much of the central and southern areas. Prevailing westerly winds from the Pacific Ocean blanket most of the state, especially the northern and southwestern regions. A drier, colder, continental climate is more noticeable in the southeastern counties, but Idaho has a milder climate than most of the states located in the same latitudes east of the Continental Divide.

Relief. The controlling physiographic features of Idaho are the Northern Rocky Mountains and the drainage patterns that they produce. These mountains dominate the characteristics of the state's rivers, landscapes, vegetation, animal life, and climate. The geographical regions of the Northern Rockies are the Lost Rivers, Sawtooth, Seven Devils, Bitterroot, and Cut Over. These regions cover most of the state that lies to the north of the Snake River Plains, with the exception of the Palouse and Camas Prairie region in the northwest. The other regions are the Caribou, a part of the Middle Rockies in the southeast, the Owyhee Plateau in the southwest, and the Basin and Range region following the Snake through the south.

Mountain ranges and rivers

From these geographical regions flow 10 major rivers. The Kootenai and St. Joe flow into the Columbia drainage area. The Clearwater, Salmon, Weiser, Payette, Boise, and Wood flow into the Snake River drainage area, which joins the Columbia in eastern Washington. The Bear River flows into Utah's Great Salt Lake, and the five Lost rivers disappear into the earth on the northern edge of the Snake River Plains.

The Snake River, next to the Northern Rocky Mountains, is the major natural feature of the state. It rises in the southeastern part of the state, with tributaries in Yellowstone National Park, and flows from east to west through "sagebrush Idaho." With huge reclamation projects, the valley contains the greatest amount of Idaho's irrigated land, and three-fourths of Idahoans depend upon it for support. The course of the Snake includes Hells Canyon, North America's deepest (7,900 feet [2,400 metres]) gorge, and 212-foot- (65-metre-) high Shoshone Falls, while its valley is a geologically complex sequence of lakes, lava beds, and desertscape symbolized by the barren craters and cones of the Craters of the Moon National Monument.

Idaho has 81 distinct mountain ranges and more than 2,000 lakes, with water its greatest single resource. A major portion of the industry, agriculture, and population follows the Snake, which furnishes an abundance of water for one of the nation's largest irrigated areas and developed hydroelectric-power sources.

The topography and climate provide a haven for big-game animals, game birds, fur animals, and migratory birds, and the rivers and lakes yield plentiful fish.

Climate. Average rainfall in the northern part of the state is 20 inches (510 millimetres) annually, and 12 inches in the southern portion, but most of it falls outside the growing season. The average mean temperature ranges from 52° F (11.1° C) at Lewiston, at 1,413 feet in elevation, to 41° F (5° C) at Montpelier, at 6,000 feet. The average for the middle Snake is 55° F (12.8° C). The growing season varies between 120 and 300 days.

Settlement patterns. Many influential factors—religion, agriculture, transportation, topography, industry, cultural ties, and sectional pride—have contributed to Idaho's diverse regional characteristics. For many years writers and politicians consistently referred to the division of Idaho as northern Idaho—the 10 northern counties—and southern Idaho—the rest of the state. Studies of voting behaviour, however, indicate that four sections with distinct voting patterns have emerged: the 10 northern counties and three separate areas in the south, roughly the southwestern, the south central, and the southeastern sections. A more realistic regionalism has developed around trading and marketing centres, sometimes crossing the state boundaries. It consists of the following areas: Lewiston and Spokane, Washington, in the north; Boise, Twin Falls, Pocatello, and Idaho Falls in the south; and the Logan–Ogden–Salt Lake City axis in northern Utah.

With the exceptions of mining and lumbering settlements, most of the settlements in southern Idaho tend to follow the course of the Snake River. In a narrow strip running from Pocatello northeast, agriculture is the economic base except in Pocatello itself, where manufacturing predominates. Agriculture continues its dominance to the west as far as the Boise Valley, where the state's largest population is located. Agriculture, service industries, and public employment are the most important factors in this area's economy. The Palouse and Camas Prairie are primarily agricultural, while Nez Perce County (Lewiston) is industrial and service oriented. Mining, lumbering, and agriculture are important throughout the north, while rural villages centre around a community life that includes churches, schools, commercial trading, banking, and service businesses to support the region's population. The only city in the state with more than 50,000 residents is Boise.

The people. The rural counties of Idaho continue to lose people to the cities, although farms and ranches continue to get larger. With few exceptions, even the villages continue to lose population to the cities. Most of the immigration comes from the Western, North Central, and Southern states, whereas the bulk of emigration goes to the West. The population is more than 95 percent white, with only about 3,000 blacks and 40,000 members of other

races, including Indians. Almost one-third of the European stock comes from the United Kingdom, Germany, Norway, Sweden, and Denmark, some by way of Canada. There are about 400,000 church members in the state and about half of them are Mormons. The next largest denominational groups are Roman Catholic, Methodist, Presbyterian, Church of the Nazarene, Lutheran, Episcopalian, Church of Christ, and Baptist. The proximity to Mormon headquarters in Salt Lake City has resulted in strong religious ties to Utah, and the populations of some of the cities in the southeastern part of the state are 95 percent Mormon.

The economy. In its economic development, Idaho occupies a position between the highly developed and the underdeveloped states. Industrial expansion has been a feature of the 20th century, replacing traditional dependence on agriculture, lumbering, and mining, and by the late 20th century the state had emerged among the top dozen states in tourist income. Government furnishes the second largest portion of Idaho's income. Labour, except in agriculture and small business, is heavily organized.

Agriculture. Huge herds of beef cattle and sheep graze not only in the prairie regions but also among the plateaus of the mountain regions. Of the farm crops, potatoes have become almost synonymous with Idaho, though wheat and other grains, sugar beets, peas, beans, and alfalfa seed are important sources of farm income. More than one-third of the state's area is in forests, and about 1,800,000,000 board feet (4,250,000 cubic metres) of lumber are cut from commercial timber lands each year.

Mining. Although the discovery of gold and the subsequent gold rush created Idaho's mining industry, gold is no longer important to the state's economy. Idaho, however, ranks among the three leading states in silver, lead, and zinc production. Phosphate mining and processing is important in the southeast.

Hydroelectric power, much of it provided by power stations on the Snake River, is the main source of energy for both business and private users in Idaho. Natural gas and oil have been used increasingly, while waste wood products have declined in importance. The Idaho National Engineering Laboratory near Arco, operated primarily as a research and testing site for nuclear reactors by the federal government, also is used for energy production.

Industry. Value added by, and personal income from, manufacturing exceeds the contributions of agriculture to the economy. Much of it is related to the processing of foods and forest and mining products, however, indicating how dependent the economy remains on primary products.

Transportation. The primitive area in central Idaho and the mountains have made transportation difficult. Idaho has more than 65,000 miles (104,000 kilometres) of roads, but only one major highway connects southern and northern Idaho. Almost all interstate highways that pass through the state run from east to west. Three transcontinental railroads cross the Panhandle, and one railroad serves the southern portion. Geographical conditions influence air travel as well, with many small airfields providing service to remote areas. These airfields are used largely by private and contract fliers. Scheduled airlines serve a number of commercial airports. Idaho has a water route to the ocean, from Lewiston by way of the Snake and Columbia rivers. Due to slack water that permits oceangoing barges to dock at Lewiston, the city is an important industrial and shipping centre.

Administrative and social conditions. *Government.* Typical of states admitted to the Union after the Civil War, Idaho has a constitution establishing the usual separation of executive, legislative, and judicial powers but limiting the governor's strength. The constitution is detailed and includes many provisions that rightly belong in the statutes, and it has been amended more than 90 times.

The only change in the government between 1890 and 1914 was the creation of numerous service and regulatory commissions and boards largely independent of the governor. Administrative reorganization after World War I consolidated these agencies in an effort to make them democratically responsive. The Depression of the

Executive, legislature, and judiciary

Sectional characteristics

1930s brought on dozens of new commissions and boards, however, and the growth has continued. In 1974 the state government was again reorganized. The executive branch consists of six elected officers, independent of the governor, and 19 departments, under which more than 100 boards, commissions, councils, and committees are placed. The legislature meets annually and comprises 35 senators and 70 representatives. Justice is administered by the Supreme Court and seven district courts, and county magistrate's courts. The district courts may originate cases and hear appeals. Civil and criminal cases generally are tried within a short time. This factor may result from the state's relatively low rates of crime against persons or property, which may reflect inadequate reporting or low rates of apprehension.

Voter independence

Few voters in the nation are as independent as those of Idaho, and party cohesiveness is difficult to maintain. National, state, and local officials elected at one time often show a startling diversity of party and ideological stances. This independence usually is issue oriented in state and national elections and personality oriented in local elections.

In 1892 the Populist Party dominated the state, and in 1918 members of the Nonpartisan League successfully filed as candidates for all major state posts on the Democratic Party ticket and, with one exception, were nominated. Aside from these events, the two major parties have dominated Idaho's political life. The voters have chosen Republican candidates slightly more than half the time, but the crossover vote, usually issue oriented, can swing the outcome of any statewide election. The major crossover vote has historically been a liberal vote, which, when added to either party's normal support, swings an election. The pre-primary party convention has been replaced by open primaries.

Finances. Of Idaho's more than 1,700 units of government, less than one-half have taxing power, and state debt is limited constitutionally to $2,000,000. The difficulty of achieving an equitable base for a sound system of public finance is further increased by federal and state ownership of about 70 percent of Idaho's land area. The state's major revenue comes from personal and corporate income taxes and a sales tax, most of which is returned to public school districts. The state controls virtually no businesses or utilities except liquor sales, and among conditions made favourable to business development is the state's stance as a service rather than as a regulatory agency.

Sources of state revenue

Education. Indian mission schools were supplemented by classes for whites when settlement began during the 1860s, and by the time of statehood the land-grant university had been chartered. The state Department of Education, dating from 1912, supervises appropriated funds, teacher certification, and related functions. The junior college system, begun on a district basis in 1939, became a state function in 1965. The publicly supported University of Idaho (created in 1889 at Moscow), Idaho State University (1901, in Pocatello), and Boise State College (1932), as well as the private College of Idaho (1891, in Caldwell), offer advanced degrees. The University of Idaho is both a college of agriculture and the state's major educational institution, offering bachelor's and advanced degrees in areas that are related to the state's economy—engineering, mining, forestry, and wildlife-and-range science—and in other areas of business, education, and arts and letters.

Welfare. The electorate of Idaho is generally conservative on economic matters, but the allocations in the social and educational areas are liberal and are endorsed by both parties. In addition, notable achievements have been based on a sense of social ethics, including a superior civil rights law.

Living standards are relatively high because labour contracts follow national patterns, and living costs are below those of many states. Nearly one-fifth of the state tax revenues goes into public health and public assistance programs.

Cultural life.   The opera houses in the mining camps, with various types of musical shows and serious drama, were Idaho's first "culture." The missionaries and the churches set the patterns of cultural development for a long period. The University of Idaho has taken a leading role in developing programs in music, art, architecture, creative writing, and theatre. Students who return to small towns—many as teachers, farmers, or foresters—are, in many instances, the only college-educated people in the community, with the exception of the local attorney and physician. Such other institutions of higher learning as Ricks College, Northwest Nazarene College, College of Idaho, Lewis-Clark Normal School (now Lewis-Clark State College), Boise State University, and Idaho State University have developed strong fine arts programs. Although public education leans toward practical subjects and university education toward agriculture, mining, engineering, and forestry, the fine arts are still a major feature of educational curricula.

Although a young state in terms of culture, Idaho has contributed artists with wide reputations, including Vardis Fisher, a novelist whose writing decried dogma and tyranny; and Carol Ryrie Brink, who wrote books for adults and children. Ernest Hemingway wrote many of his books while living in Idaho, which he enjoyed for its wilderness aspects.

All of the colleges and universities have symphony orchestras, choral groups, and theatre programs, and a number of cities—including Boise, Pocatello, and Lewiston—have orchestras. The University of Idaho and the cities of Coeur d'Alene, Lewiston, McCall, and Caldwell have summer theatres. The Idaho Commission on the Arts and Humanities has sponsored and promoted the development of art exhibits, lectures, literature, films, theatres, and music throughout the state.

HISTORY

The original inhabitants.   Before the 1840s, when the buffalo herds disappeared and the wagon trains of settlers who were bound for California began to arrive, Indians had lived in the Idaho region for at least 10,000 years. The internal political structures of the five linguistic and cultural groups were weak, as were the ties between them. In the north were the Kutenai, the linguistically identical Salish (Kalispel), the Coeur d'Alene, and the Nez Percé. Northern Paiute lived in the west central region, while the western Shoshoni and the northern Shoshoni occupied most of the southern lands. Most of these groups lived in small villages, consisting largely of family groups that moved according to the fishing, hunting, and wild-plant gathering seasons. The tribes still live in approximately the same areas, some on the several reservations that are located within the state.

Indian groups

Settlement.   When the Lewis and Clark Expedition reached Idaho on their journey of exploration in 1805, there were about 8,000 Indians living in the region. A trading post was erected on Pend Oreille Lake in the north in 1809, and fur traders were followed by missionaries of all persuasions. Gold seekers by the thousands poured through the area on their way to California in 1848, but many returned eastward after gold was discovered in northern Idaho in 1860. The settlers who followed wanted land and political stability, which had hitherto been uncertain; and slowly agriculture acquired economic dominance.

Territorial period.   What is now the state of Idaho was originally in Oregon country, claimed in turn by Spain, Russia, Great Britain, and the United States, the last two settling, by treaty in 1846, on the 49th parallel as the northern U.S. border. Oregon Territory (created in 1848) included initially the present state of Idaho, as well as what is now Oregon, Washington, and part of Montana. Idaho was then split between the new Oregon and Washington territories from 1853 to 1859. It then was entirely in Washington until 1863, when it was organized separately as the Idaho Territory and included present-day Montana (until 1864) and the greater part of Wyoming (until 1868).

From a population of fewer than 17,000 in 1863, the territory expanded to nearly 90,000 at the time of statehood in 1890. Many of these new arrivals were Confederate refugees who, in the years following the Civil War, often dominated the legislature and opposed the Republican governors that were appointed by the federal

Frontier days

government. Political strife and vigilante committees were important elements in frontier life during the territorial decades. Among some of the other events and trends that coloured the state's political and social life were the religious conflicts between the polygamous Mormons (Church of Jesus Christ of Latter-day Saints) and other sects; a strong sectionalism that divided various regions of the territory; a pioneer democracy that emphasized the rights and achievements of the individual; the completion of railroads, which fostered economic and population growth; the beginning of lead and silver mining in the mountains; and the creation of the University of Idaho in 1889 by the last territorial legislature that was convened prior to statehood.

Statehood. Labour protests that often erupted into violence were features of the 1890s era in Idaho. Through his unsuccessful prosecution in 1907 of William D. Haywood, an organizer of the Industrial Workers of the World (IWW), Sen. William Borah became Idaho's major national figure until his death in 1940. During the 20th century Idaho has been engaged in developing its agriculture, forestry, and industry, while maintaining the more satisfying aspects of modern life at the doorstep of a natural wilderness.

(B.A.M./Ed.)

Montana

Although its name is derived from the Spanish *montaña* ("mountain," or "mountainous region"), Montana has an average elevation of only 3,400 feet (1,040 metres), the lowest among the Rocky Mountain states. The mountains sweep down from the Canadian province of British Columbia into the western third of the state, into Idaho on Montana's western and southwestern border, and southward into Wyoming. The eastern two-thirds of the state, however, is a gently rolling landscape, with millions of grazing cattle and sheep, and with only scattered evidences of human habitation. It forms a part of the northern Great Plains, shared with the provinces of Alberta and Saskatchewan to the north, North and South Dakota to the east, and northeastern Wyoming.

Only three states—Alaska, Texas, and California—have an area larger than Montana's 147,138 square miles (381,-086 square kilometres), which is larger than that of Japan; and only two states—Alaska and Wyoming—have a lower *Sparse settlement* population density. The residents are relatively far from the markets for their cattle, grain, lumber, metals, and petroleum, as well as from the nation's manufacturing and supply centres. Nature is omnipresent, and the state is strongly oriented toward the out-of-doors, toward summer and winter sports, toward hunting and fishing, and toward the long-distance trip for socializing and entertainment or as a cure for the frequent prairie- or mountain-born restlessness, cabin fever.

In spite of its northern location, Montana is very much a Western state, with high-heeled cowboy boots more fashionable than shoes and cattle rustling not merely a memory from the past. The main street of the capital, Helena, is Last Chance Gulch, the city's original name and a reminder of the prospectors who invaded the hills in the 1860s to pan for gold. By 1889, when Montana became the 41st state of the Union, the cattle drive was an institution, and the state had begun to emerge as the copper-mining capital of the nation.

PHYSICAL AND HUMAN GEOGRAPHY

The land. The heavily forested western third of Montana includes the tumbled, rugged Rocky Mountains and the Continental Divide, contrasting with the generally treeless, gently rolling eastern portion, which is broken by buttes, tree-bordered streams, and small, isolated mountain ranges.

Relief. The eastern three-fifths of the state is in the Great Plains and is characterized by vast stretches of range land and dry-farming areas sharply cut by many small streams leading to the larger rivers. Near the centre of the state distinctive isolated mountains, known as mountains of the plains, rise abruptly. These mountains cause sufficient precipitation to promote the growth of grass and

trees and provide irrigation water for adjacent communities. The alternating ranges and valleys of the Rocky Mountains occupy the western two-fifths of the state. The Continental Divide follows the boundary line between Montana and Idaho west and northwest of Yellowstone National Park to Ravalli County; it turns eastward through Deer Lodge and Silver Bow counties, then northward to Lewis and Clark County, and from there extends northnorthwest to Glacier National Park and Canada.

The area west of the Continental Divide is made up of fertile valleys of rare beauty. The Bitterroot Valley merges into the broad Missoula Valley, and to the north Flathead Lake and its adjacent timber and ranch lands are bounded on the east by the majestic Mission Range. To the east of the Bitterroot Valley the high mountain valleys of Flint Creek and Deer Lodge lie at the headwaters of the Clark Fork of the Columbia River. The Clark Fork rises near Butte and is joined by the Little and Big Blackfoot rivers from the east, the Bitterroot from the south, and the Flathead from the north. The Kootenai River has carved a beautiful valley in the extreme northwest corner of the state. Here, near Troy, is the lowest point in the state, 1,800 feet (549 metres) above sea level.

Crossing the Continental Divide just south of the Canadian border is Glacier National Park. It was created in 1910 and contains 1,013,129 acres (410,013 hectares) of towering mountains and long, narrow mountain lakes. The Glacier watershed drains into the Pacific and Atlantic oceans and Hudson Bay. Nearly all of Yellowstone National Park lies in Wyoming, but the park has three entrances from Montana. Just north of Yellowstone Park lie the Absaroka and Snowy ranges, and to the east the Beartooth Range contains Granite Peak (12,799 feet [3,901 metres]), the highest point in the state. The Great Plains slope from about 4,000 feet above the sea at the foothills of the mountains to 2,000 feet in northeastern Montana. Several isolated mountain groups such as the Highwoods, Bear Paws, Little Rockies, and Sweet Grass hills modify the character of the plains in mid Montana.

Drainage. The state is unusual in that its waters contribute to three major drainage systems. On the west side of the divide, streams flow into the Clark Fork and Kootenai rivers and then, through the Columbia River, into the Pacific Ocean. East of the divide, the Madison, Jefferson, and Gallatin rivers meet at Three Forks to form the mighty Missouri, which, with its major tributary, the Yellowstone, finally joins the Mississippi. From parts of Glacier National Park, in the northwest, streams drain northward into Hudson Bay by way of the Belly and St. Mary rivers. Cruise boats ply the upper Missouri, notably in the spectacular trip through the Gates of the Mountains, above Helena.

Richness of water resources

Most of the natural lakes are in the Rockies, and some of the most beautiful are in Glacier National Park. Flathead Lake, with a surface area of 197 square miles (510 square kilometres), is the largest in the state. A new lake was formed in 1959, when an earthquake toppled a mountain into the Madison River northwest of West Yellowstone; the resulting body of water is known as Quake Lake, or Earthquake Lake. Some large man-made lakes are reservoirs that are backed up behind multipurpose government dams. Major dams are Fort Peck on the Missouri River near Glasgow; Canyon Ferry on the Missouri near Helena; Hungry Horse on the South Fork of the Flathead near Columbia Falls; Yellowtail in the Bighorn River Canyon, creating Bighorn Lake, which extends into Wyoming; and Libby Dam on the Kootenai, producing Koocanusa Lake, part of which lies in British Columbia.

Climate. Montanans tend to be defensive about their climate, and they do not react gratefully to expressions of sympathy from New Yorkers, New Englanders, or North Dakotans. The state was called "the icebox of the nation" before Alaska achieved statehood. A temperature of −70° F (−57° C) was registered at Rogers Pass on January 20, 1954, but the cities of Duluth, Minneapolis, and St. Paul, in Minnesota, have lower average temperatures. In July, the warmest month, Montana's average is about 65° F (18° C); in January, the coldest, about 15° F (−9° C). Humidity is generally low, and the same aridity that requires dryland farmers to be ingenious about conserving moisture makes both summer and winter more comfortable than thermometer readings suggest.

Average precipitation is low—about 18 inches (460 millimetres) in the west and 13 inches in the east—resulting from the position of the Rocky Mountains and the state's interior location on the continent. The Rockies sometimes warm part of the east and north by creating a chinook wind, which melts snow rapidly and gives quick relief from cold. Destructive hailstorms sometimes occur in July and August, damaging unharvested grain.

Soils and plant life. Montana's soils differ widely. Eastern, prairie soils are mature, underlaid by lime deposits, and productive when enough moisture is available. Many mountain soils are immature and thin because erosion has carried the richer decomposed materials into the valleys. Because of the grasslands east of the Rockies, Montana is one of the great range states. Only Texas outranks it in the number of cattle raised on native grasses; Texas and Wyoming exceed it in range-raised sheep. About one-fourth of the state is classified as forest land, and about one-third of this is also suitable for grazing. In general, where there are mountains, there are forests. Most of the trees, and all those cut for timber, are softwood conifers. There are no hardwood forests in Montana.

Animal life. Large game animals abound, mainly in the mountains. They include moose, elk, mule and white-tailed deer, grizzly and black bears, bighorn sheep, and mountain goats. Herds of pronghorn antelope run free on the prairie. A few bison, once abundant beyond counting, were saved from extinction, and a herd of between 300 and 400 is maintained on the National Bison Range, near Moiese. A herd belonging to the Crow Indians, which had to be destroyed because of undulant fever, is being rebuilt. There is some trapping of mink, beaver, and muskrat for their fur. Predators include mountain lions, bobcats, and coyotes.

Game birds are abundant, including grouse, ducks, pheasant, partridge, and geese. About 500 trumpeter swans, once almost extinct, live in the area of Yellowstone, Hebgen, and Red Rock lakes, forming the largest colony of these birds in the conterminous United States. Kokanee and silver salmon, whitefish, and several kinds of trout predominate as attractions for recreational fishermen.

Settlement patterns. Air travellers can fly over Montana's prairie for miles without seeing a town, a road, or a railroad track. This is grazing country for cattle and sheep. In dryland-farming areas the fields are big; and, where wind blows the soil, green swaths of growing grain alternate with brown swaths of fallow ground, on which last year's stubble catches and holds such rain and snow as fall. In the mountains, forests are dark on steep slopes and in deep canyons, with occasional scars of logging roads and patches of timber burned in forest fires.

The main urban settlements developed from mining camps; from trading centres for farmers, stockmen, and forest workers; and from early railroad division points. With improved roads and plentiful automobiles, rural communities have lost stores, banks, and other businesses. Billings, the largest city, boomed when it became the business centre for the state's oil industry. Hydroelectric power was responsible for the growth of Great Falls, the second largest city.

The people. In the early years of the 20th century, many families from northern Europe settled on homesteads to farm on the eastern prairie, and immigrants from across Europe came to work in the mines. Their descendants have been well assimilated. Place-names such as Belgrade, Glasgow, Havre, Harlem, and Malta do not indicate the national origin of the settlers but were bestowed by railroad officials when the towns were established. If there is a social status in the state, it is conferred less by wealth than by descent from pioneers.

Several Indian tribes, usually on the move in search of game, lived in Montana when the first explorers arrived. Indians now constitute the state's only large racial minority group, with almost 80 percent of some 47,000 nonwhites by 1980. About three-quarters of Montana's Indians live on seven reservations: Blackfeet, Crow, Northern Cheyenne,

Rocky Boy's (Ojibwa [Chippewa] and Cree Indians), Fort Peck (Dakota and Assiniboin), Flathead (Flathead, Kutenai, and Pend d'Oreille), and Fort Belknap (Assiniboin and Atsina, or Gros Ventre). Most of the reservations are poor in natural resources except for grazing land, much of it leased to non-Indians. The reservations are partially self-governing through tribal organizations, and the federal Bureau of Indian Affairs is the principal agency overseeing Indian activities. Employment opportunities on the reservations are few, and most Indians find it difficult to tear themselves away from strong family ties to work among strangers. Life is even harder for the landless Indians, who came to the state after the reservations were established and do not have a legal right to live on them. About half of the almost 2,000 blacks live in the Great Falls area.

About half the people in Montana are affiliated with an organized religious group, with slightly more than half of them Roman Catholics. Through vigorous missionary activity the Mormon Church, centred in nearby Salt Lake City, Utah, has been increasing its membership for several years.

The economy. Montana specializes in industries that, nationally, are growing slowly if at all. Some tax concessions are offered to new businesses. Tourism is an important if only seasonal source of employment in the state. Trade unions are strongest and most active in communities where one or two major employers predominate: in Butte, Anaconda, and Great Falls.

Agriculture. The state's largest single source of income is agriculture, with livestock (cattle, sheep, and hogs) accounting for about one-half of cash income, and crops the remainder. The state raises barley, wheat, sugar beets, and oats. Following a nationwide trend, the number of farms has been diminishing, while the average size of individual farms has increased.

Mining. Copper is the leading metal, representing nearly half of the state's metal production. Gold, the basis of pioneer settlement in the 1860s, is now only a by-product of copper mining, along with silver and lead. Among other mineral resources are phosphates, used in manufacturing fertilizers and elemental phosphorus; vermiculite; bentonite; sand and gravel; and gypsum. Montana has enormous reserves of coal that could be exploited by both underground and surface-mining methods. Although visible coal deposits in southern Montana were noted by a military expedition in 1876, these resources have scarcely been touched. Coal has gained importance as a fuel to produce electrical power. Legislation adopted in 1971 required mine operators to restore the surface of the mined land for other uses, such as grazing. Montana imposes a 30 percent severance tax on coal mined in the state and has attempted to enact legislation to tax hard-rock mining. Petroleum was discovered in commercial quantities at Elk Basin in 1915. The Elk Basin, Kevin-Sunburst, and Cut Bank fields led in production for several years. The great Williston Basin was developed in 1951, but the Bell Creek field in Powder River County has been the most productive.

Forestry. Lumbering and forest-products manufacture are vital to western Montana. Of the more than 14,000,-000 acres (5,700,000 hectares) of commercial forest land, more than two-thirds is owned by the federal and state governments. The forestry industry includes the manufacture of plywood and of pulp and paper products. About half of Montana's forest products are sold to states in the Midwest.

Transportation. Railroad passenger service in Montana has decreased since the 1960s. In-city bus lines operate only in Butte, Anaconda, and Billings.

By the late 20th century the state had more than 1,000 miles (1,600 kilometres) of interstate highways. There were more than 6,000 miles of primary highways and less than 5,000 miles of secondary roads. Several major airlines and air-taxi lines serve the state, and many small planes are privately owned.

Administrative and social conditions. *Government.* The only copy of Montana's first proposed state constitution was mislaid on the way to the printer in St. Louis, Missouri, in 1866, and its contents remain a subject of histori-

Prevalence of wildlife

Indian reservations

Exploitation of natural resources

The political process

cal curiosity. A second attempt to achieve statehood failed in 1884; but Pres. Grover Cleveland signed an enabling act in 1889, and the third constitutional convention produced a constitution of 21 articles. As the state grew and the needs of the population changed, so many amendments were added that in 1970 voters called for a constitutional convention. The new constitution was adopted by the electorate in 1972.

Allegiance is so evenly divided between the Republican and Democratic parties that election patterns are not predictable. Ticket splitting is common. The governor and the lieutenant governor, formerly elected separately, now are elected on one ticket. The state has an open primary; voters need not declare party affiliation, and registration is permanent unless a voter misses a general election.

The executive branch was reorganized so that in 1973 some 160 state boards and agencies were consolidated into 19 cabinet-style departments, with virtually all appointments directly controlled by the governor.

The two-house legislature, which under the state's 1972 constitution meets in odd-numbered years, is composed of 50 senators and 100 representatives.

Judges are elected without party designation. The highest court is the five-member Supreme Court. The state is divided into 19 judicial districts, in which 29 district judges serve. On the lowest level are justices of the peace, who serve organized townships, and police judges, whose authority is limited to cases involving municipal ordinances.

Income from taxation on personal property, the most important source of tax revenue, varies widely from county to county because of differences in valuation by county assessors.

The county is the highest level of local government. Its powers and duties are defined and limited by state statutes. Three elected commissioners are the chief administrators, though a full-time manager may be employed instead. Government in low-population counties is especially expensive and burdensome. Municipal governments, like those of counties, have no inherent powers but derive all their authority from the state. They can, however, enact local ordinances, whereas counties cannot.

Municipalities have police forces, whereas organized townships have elected constables whose major duty is to serve legal papers. Each county has an elected sheriff, who appoints deputies and has jurisdiction outside towns and cities. Because cattle rustling is a continuing problem, some sheriffs and deputies act as brand inspectors to prevent the sale of stolen livestock.

Health, education, and welfare. Montanans pay various penalties for the wide-open spaces they enjoy. An increasing number of communities have no physician, dentist, or hospital. Although rural schools continue to consolidate and introduce bus transportation, many children attend small and not always adequate one- or two-teacher country schools. School districts are corporate bodies headed by a county superintendent of schools and governed by elected school boards.

The state's system of higher education, chartered in 1893, includes universities at Missoula and Bozeman and four-year colleges at Billings, Butte, Havre, and Dillon. There are church-affiliated private colleges in Great Falls, Helena, and Billings; junior colleges in Miles City, Glendive, and Kalispell; and public postsecondary vocational–technical schools in Great Falls, Billings, Missoula, Helena, and Butte.

Montana's welfare program is state supervised and administered by county departments of public welfare. Because of sparse population and few private social-service agencies, costs are relatively high. Welfare departments are caught between pressures from the public to curb programs and from organized low-income groups to provide wider services. There are special problems on Indian reservations, where winter allowances are provided to help recipients of public assistance meet clothing and fuel costs in the cold months. Tuberculosis, once endemic among Indians, is now under control.

Cultural life. Most artistic activity centres in the cities with colleges and universities, several of which sponsor visits by lecturers and professional artists of various kinds

in addition to presenting the work of faculty members and students. Several cities have symphony orchestras that include some professional musicians.

The Montana Institute of the Arts, founded in 1948, is a grass-roots organization that ties together the scattered, often isolated practitioners of various arts and crafts through publications, an annual festival, and travelling exhibits. The Montana Arts Council, a state agency affiliated with the National Endowment for the Arts, funds dozens of local cultural organizations, primarily for music, drama, dance, literature, and the visual arts. Among other activities, it provides short poet-in-residence programs for children in the public schools of small communities. In addition to dramatic performances by students in various colleges, there are summer theatres in more than a half dozen communities; and the Montana Repertory Theater, based in Missoula, tours both inside and outside the state.

State cultivation of the arts

Several Indian tribes hold traditional dance ceremonies at which outsiders are welcome. Crow Indians and whites cooperate in an annual reenactment of the Battle of the Little Bighorn on the Crow Indian Reservation. Rodeos abound, as do games on horseback known as *o-mok-sees* and square-dance groups. In Red Lodge an annual nineday Festival of Nations, originated to ease tensions among several European ethnic groups of coal miners, has become a proud tradition.

The Montana Historical Society maintains a fine museum, art gallery, and specialized library in Helena. The Trigg-Russell Memorial Gallery in Great Falls, specializing in the works of the cowboy artist Charles Marion Russell, is the property of the city. Billings has the Yellowstone County Fine Arts Center, operated in a former city jail, and the Yellowstone County Museum. The excellent, small Museum of the Plains Indians is in Browning, the agency town for the Blackfeet tribe. Many communities nurture art galleries and small museums of local historical interest.

HISTORY

Settlement. The first Europeans known to have set foot in Montana were the members of the Lewis and Clark Expedition in 1805–06, though French fur traders were in the area as early as the 1740s. Other trappers and traders followed, setting up forts to trade with the Indians. The only early trading post to become a permanent town was Fort Benton, which was established in 1846 and became an important port on the Missouri River and head of navigation for steamboats from St. Louis. Jesuit missionaries followed the fur traders. Father Pierre-Jean de Smet, a Belgian, established St. Mary's Mission near present-day Stevensville in 1841, and Father Anthony Ravalli, an Italian, joined him in 1845.

Miners and adventurers flocked in after rich placer gold deposits were discovered at Bannack in 1862 and Alder Gulch in 1863. A secretly organized gang of holdup men and murderers, known as road agents and led by Sheriff Henry Plummer, was identified late in 1863. The hastily formed Committee of Vigilance destroyed the gang by hanging more than two dozen road agents in a few weeks in 1864. Montana Territory, formerly part of Idaho Territory, was established in that year, with Bannack its first capital and Virginia City, on Alder Gulch, its second. Farmers settled in the Bitterroot, Deer Lodge, and Gallatin valleys to raise grain and vegetables.

Gold miners and vigilantes

Large-scale cattle and sheep raising began with the first big herd of cattle being driven overland from Texas in 1866. The vast grasslands of central Montana were ideal for cattle, but in the severe winter of 1886–87, some owners lost 90 percent of their herds to freezing and starvation. Since that time, stock growers have raised hay for winterfeed.

As pressure from settlers increased, the native Indians fought to protect the hunting grounds that provided the necessities of life for their people. Dakota (Sioux) and Cheyenne won their last major victory in June 1876, at the Battle of the Little Bighorn, also known as the Custer Massacre. A band of Nez Percé under Chief Joseph won a battle in the Big Hole Basin the following year and fled toward Canada, only to be met and defeated by U.S.

troops a few miles south of the "Medicine Line," the international boundary.

The growth of population in the territory led to a demand for independent political status. The region had been under various administrations during the preceding half century. The area east of the mountains had been included in the Louisiana Purchase of 1803 and its subsequent government. The western section had been a part of the Oregon country following the treaty with Great Britain establishing the boundary at the 49th parallel in 1846. The Territory of Idaho, created in 1863, included the Montana area, but access to the capital at Lewiston was difficult. The rise of a large band of thieving road agents caused the organization of the Vigilantes of Montana, an extragovernmental law enforcement agency. To provide more adequate government services for the area, the Territory of Montana was created May 26, 1864, with Sidney Edgerton as the first governor. The first territorial legislature met at Bannack, but the following year the capital was moved to Virginia City and, in 1875, to Helena. Montana entered the Union on November 8, 1889, with Joseph K. Toole as the first governor.

Growth of the state.   As gold mining declined in importance, world demand for copper increased, and the immense ore deposits at Butte, known as "the richest hill on earth," attracted outside capital. From 1895 to 1905 the so-called copper kings—William A. Clark, Marcus Daly, and Frederick Augustus Heinze—fought for control of the mines and of the state government, which became notoriously corrupt.

After 1909 homesteaders poured into the plains country to claim farms of 320 acres (130 hectares). During the "county-busting era," from 1910 to 1925, the number of counties doubled from 28 to the present 56, most of the new ones lying in the grain-growing part of the state in the east and north. The expected population growth did not materialize, however, for, after a few years of bumper wheat crops and high prices, a cycle of drought years brought financial disaster. Hundreds of mortgages were foreclosed and more than 200 banks closed permanently between 1920 and 1926. Thousands of settlers sought livelihoods elsewhere; since then, farming methods more suitable for the semiarid prairie land in the state have been developed.

Economic booms and busts

Thus, Montana was already depressed when the nationwide depression began in 1929. Droughts continued, many mines closed, and markets for forest products were few. The federal government undertook several big irrigation and soil-conservation projects. Fort Peck Dam, a multipurpose project on the Missouri River, was completed in 1940. During World War II both mining and agriculture returned to their boom levels of earlier years.

Petroleum production, which had begun on a small scale in 1915, was expanded in 1951 with major discoveries in the Williston Basin in the northeast. A very rich field at Bell Creek near Broadus was opened in 1967. In July 1980 a 20-week labour strike, the longest in the U.S. copper industry since 1968, occurred. In September of the same year a copper smelter in Anaconda and a refinery at Great Falls were closed down, resulting in the loss of 1,500 jobs.

(D.M.J./Ed.)

Nevada

Location and general character

Located in a mountainous region that includes vast semiarid grasslands and sandy alkali deserts, Nevada is a part of the Old West that in 1864 became the 36th state of the United States. Its name was derived from the Spanish *nevada* ("snow clad"), a reference to the high mountain scenery of the Sierra Nevadas that are located on the state's southwestern border with California. Other neighbouring states sharing many of the geographical features that make Nevada the nation's most arid state are Oregon and Idaho to the north, Utah to the east, and Arizona to the southeast. After Alaska, Wyoming, and Montana, Nevada is the most sparsely populated state in the nation. Carson City is the state capital.

Nevada appears far removed from the days when Virginia City was a fabled frontier town, thriving on the rich silver mines of the Comstock Lode. Many frontier qualities persist, though subtly transformed into a sophisticated urban environment. The prospector digging against odds to find a bonanza has been replaced by the fortune seekers in the gambling casinos of Las Vegas and Reno, and the erstwhile "saloon diversions" have evolved into lavish nightclub entertainment.

While the great majority of Nevadans live in the two main cities—more than one-half of them in the Las Vegas metropolitan area and almost one-fourth in that of Reno—the vast undeveloped lands of the state provide a largely unknown resource for the future. Combined with the major scientific activity related to the federal government's atomic-research facilities, the modern cities and desert reaches make Nevada a fascinating and unique phenomenon among U.S. states.

PHYSICAL AND HUMAN GEOGRAPHY

The land.   *Relief.*   Most of Nevada lies within the Basin and Range Province, or Great Basin, where the topography is characterized by rugged mountains, flat valleys with occasional buttes and mesas, and sandy desert regions. More than 30 north–south mountain ranges cross the state; the highest elevations are Boundary Peak, at 13,-140 feet (4,005 metres) and Wheeler Peak, at 13,061 feet (3,981 metres). The southern area of the state is within the Mojave Desert, and the lowest elevation, 470 feet (143 metres), is in the Colorado River Canyon.

Drainage.   The state's rivers depend for the most part on the melting of winter snows and on spring rainfall. Almost all of the rivers drain into lakes that have no outlets or into shallow sinks that in summer evaporate into alkaline mud flats. The Humboldt, the largest of Nevada's rivers, provides the state's only major east–west drainage system. The Truckee, Carson, and Walker rivers, which rise in the Sierra Nevadas, serve extensive irrigation and reclamation projects in their areas. The Muddy and Virgin rivers in southern Nevada are related to the Colorado River system.

Several lakes provide scenic and recreational attractions. Lake Tahoe on the California–Nevada border is particularly notable for its clarity, depth, and scenic beauty. Pyramid, Walker, and Winnemucca lakes are remnants of an ancient sea. In relation to its area, however, Nevada has comparatively little surface water. The increasing demands of urbanism, industry, and agriculture are exhausting both underground and surface resources, and scarcity of water is an increasing concern. The impounded waters of Lake Mead, extending for 117 miles (188 kilometres) behind Hoover Dam, provide significant relief for the southeastern area.

Scarcity of water

Climate.   The high Sierras along the western boundary often cause clouds of Pacific origin to drop their moisture before reaching Nevada, thus producing a semiarid climate. The driest regions are in the southeast and near Carson Sink, where annual rainfall seldom exceeds four inches (100 millimetres). The northeast has as little as eight inches of precipitation, whereas that of the northwestern mountains often reaches 24 inches. Temperatures vary as widely. In the north July temperatures average 70° F (21° C), and in the south 86° F (30° C). In January the averages range from 24° F (−4° C) in the north to 40° F (4° C) in the south. The northern and eastern areas have long, cold winters and short but relatively hot summers, whereas in southern Nevada the summers are long and exceedingly hot, and the winters brief and mild. Regional differences are pointed up by variations in the growing season: Las Vegas has 239 days, Reno 155, and Elko only 103.

Plant and animal life.   Despite aridity and rugged terrain, Nevada shows considerable variety in vegetation. In the lower desert areas, mesquite, creosote, greasewood, yucca, and more than 30 varieties of cacti abound, while sagebrush and Joshua trees flourish at the higher elevations. Throughout the state, particularly during the period after the spring rains, more than 2,000 varieties of wild flowers have been identified. Mountain forests contain pine, fir, and spruce as well as juniper and mountain mahogany. The piñon pine is characteristic in the high mountain regions, and the rare bristlecone pine—one of the oldest living species of trees—is native to the To-yaibe Range.

The animal population of Nevada includes those species that are best adapted to temperature extremes and to lack of moisture. Among the larger animals are bighorn sheep, several varieties of deer, and the pronghorn antelope. Rabbit and other rodents are found in abundance; the desert harbours such reptiles as geckos, horned toads, tortoises, and sidewinder rattlesnakes; and predators such as the coyote and bobcat are common. The permanent bird population of the state is somewhat limited, but there are seasonal visitations by a great variety of migratory birds. Game birds that can be found in the state include sage grouse, pheasants, and quails; and Nevada's rivers and lakes contain large quantities of bass, trout, crappy, and catfish.

The people. The great majority of Nevadans are of European ancestry, about 95 percent of whom were born in the United States. An estimated 5,000 to 10,000 persons trace their ancestry to Basques recruited as sheepherders from their ancient Pyrenean homeland. Mexican-Americans are concentrated in the southeast. Descendants of the Paiute, Shoshoni, and Washoe Indians live on several reservations. Blacks, mostly in the Las Vegas and Reno areas, make up a very small percentage of the state's population.

The two predominant religious groups are Mormons, who migrated westward from neighbouring Utah and who comprise almost 10 percent of the total population, and Roman Catholics, with about 20 percent of the population. Other Protestant denominations and a Jewish minority account for the remainder of Nevada's religious adherents.

Contemporary demography. From the 1950s through the 1970s Nevada's population grew by about 70 percent, and Nevada rose from 47th to 43rd in population among the 50 states. In spite of a birthrate slightly above, and a death rate slightly below, the national averages, this growth was largely the result of a steady immigration of people from other states. The impact of this immigration has been felt most strongly in Las Vegas and surrounding Clark County and in Reno and surrounding Washoe County. In the late 20th century most Nevadans were urban and engaged in the booming and diversifying economies of those two metropolitan areas.

Immigration and urbanization

The economy. Although the traditional bases of Nevada's economic life, mining and agriculture, remain important, they are far overshadowed by manufacturing, government, and tourist-related services.

Mining. One of the richest mineral regions of the nation extends eastward from California across Nevada and into Arizona. Nevada is an important mineral producer; the value of its production accounted for about one-third of the total value of goods produced in the late 1970s. Copper production, which had been the largest component of mineral production, dropped dramatically in the late 1970s, however, when the three leading copper producers shut down operations. Gold has replaced copper as the most commercially valuable of the state's minerals, and the annual output is among the highest in the nation. Nevada is also the leading producer of mercury, and the McDermitt Mine in Humboldt County is the largest single source of mercury in the United States. Nevada ranked first in barite production in 1979, with output nearly doubling after 1976. Although silver production dropped in the late 1970s, new mines were scheduled to begin operation in the 1980s. Other important minerals include sand and gravel, gypsum, crushed stone, tungsten, and manganese. Petroleum was discovered in Nye County in 1954.

Continuity of the traditional economy

Agriculture. Nevada's agriculture is largely dependent upon irrigation. Even in the river valleys, farmers and ranchers pump additional underground water for their crops and livestock. About 850,000 acres (340,000 hectares) are classified as croplands, compared with about 9,000,000 acres used for pasture and rangeland. In the past several decades farms and ranches have increased in acreage while declining in number.

Farms are devoted mainly to forage crops or truck farming, though southeastern farms also produce cotton. Livestock ranching, however, is the primary source of agricultural income. The large cattle and sheep ranches are chiefly in Elko, Humboldt, and Lander counties, where many ranchers graze their herds for part of the year on leased public lands. Most of the cattle are shipped to California or the Midwest for fattening and marketing. Dairy and poultry farms have become important in western and southeastern Nevada, where horse ranches also have been developed.

Approximately 12,000,000 acres (4,900,000 hectares), or about 17 percent of Nevada's total acreage, is devoted to forests and woodlands. More than 5,000,000 acres have been designated as national forests, and private holdings support only a small-scale lumber industry. Aside from lumber production, the forests are of importance for the conservation of water and wildlife and in providing recreational opportunities.

Industry. Manufacturing has expanded and diversified, and most of the larger enterprises are located in Clark or Washoe counties. The leading product groups are stone, clay, and glass products; printing and publishing; food and food by-products; and chemicals. The largest industrial complex is located in Henderson, where major factories process titanium ore and produce industrial chemicals.

More than one-half of the electricity is generated by coal, about one-fourth by natural gas, and about one-eighth by hydroelectric plants. Coal and natural gas are used in power plants in southern Nevada. Hoover and Davis dams are major power sources, supplemented by imports of hydroelectric power from California.

About 87 percent of Nevada's land is owned by the federal government. Following establishment of the Nevada Test Site by the federal government in the 1950s, a complex of research and development enterprises, mainly in the aerospace, civil-defense research, biomedical environmental protection, and electronics fields, developed in the Las Vegas area. By the late 20th century they rivalled similar industries in California and in the Boston and Washington, D.C., areas. The test site itself is a major centre for underground nuclear detonation and for 15 years, until 1972, for nuclear rocket development. Thousands of military personnel are stationed also at Nellis Air Force Base and Fallon Naval Air Station.

Tourism. Tourism and its related activities bring millions of visitors, contribute more income than mining, agriculture, and manufacturing combined, and employ about one-third of the work force. Although millions of people visit Lake Mead and other recreational and scenic areas, the tourist industry centres on several attractions that are unique to Nevada among the U.S. states.

The 24-hour-a-day gaming casinos bordering the "Strip" in Las Vegas are the most publicized aspect of the legalized-gambling industry. Most such activities are conducted within the law and have contributed to the state's treasury, but there also have been intermittent investigations into the involvement of underworld crime syndicates in Nevada gambling. Important adjuncts to the casinos are the luxury hotels and nightclubs that have made Las Vegas—and, to a lesser extent, Reno and Lake Tahoe—a major centre of live entertainment in the nation.

Legalized gambling and related lures

In addition, Nevada law has long permitted divorces after only brief residence and marriages without waiting periods. Nevada's divorce law attracts thousands of people annually from throughout the country, while the ease of marriage is taken advantage of mainly by people from neighbouring states. The existence of legal prostitution is a unique circumstance in the sparsely populated rural counties of central Nevada.

Unions. Union organization has had a substantial resurgence. Entertainers and restaurant workers have built large, influential unions that parallel those of the teamsters, operating engineers, plumbers, carpenters, and sheet-metal workers.

Transportation. Its vast size makes Nevada heavily dependent upon air transportation. The state is served by several national airlines. There are more than 100 airports and airfields, and both Las Vegas and Reno have been designated as international ports of entry.

Three major railroads cross the state, while short lines serve as feeders where truck competition has not caused their discontinuance. Nevada's public roads include primary and secondary highways as well as municipal and rural roads. Two of the nine federal highways are part of the interstate system. Several national bus lines and trucking lines serve the state.

The three major transportation and trade centres of the state are Reno, the principal distributive centre for northwestern Nevada and northeastern California; Elko and Ely, in northeastern Nevada; and Las Vegas, the commercial centre for southern Nevada and nearby areas of Utah and Arizona. Warehousing and trucking industries flourish because of Nevada's strategic geographical location and the "free port" tax exemption for goods continuing in transit.

Administrative and social conditions. *Government.* Nevada is governed under its original constitution, adopted in 1864 but since amended in many respects. The chief officials, including the governor, lieutenant governor, attorney general, secretary of state, controller, and treasurer, are elected to four-year terms. In addition to the usual departments and agencies supervising areas of public concern, the state Equal Rights Commission oversees areas of discrimination of various kinds, while the Gaming Control Board oversees operations of the gambling industry.

Nevada's bicameral legislature comprises the Senate of 20 members elected for four-year terms and the Assembly of 40 members elected for two-year terms. It convenes in January of odd-numbered years.

The highest judicial body is the Supreme Court, composed of a chief justice and four associate justices. There are also district courts, subdivided into departments on a population basis. Cities and townships have courts staffed by municipal judges and justices of the peace. All judicial offices are subject to nonpartisan elections.

Local government comprises 16 counties, 16 cities and towns, and 55 townships. Since Nevada traditionally has been rural oriented, the county remains the primary unit of local administration. Each county has a public administrator, board of commissioners, district attorney, sheriff, and other officials. Cities and towns are incorporated under charters granted by the legislature, most of them with a mayor–council form of government.

Finance. Nevada's fiscal policies have been markedly conservative. The constitution rigidly limits both taxation and indebtedness. The bonding capacity cannot exceed 1 percent of the total assessed valuation of real property in the state, and there is a maximum tax rate on real estate. Even more unusual is the absence of state taxation upon inheritances and all types of income.

State taxation, however, provides about 60 percent of governmental income, with most of the balance coming from federal grants and subventions. A selective sales tax is the chief source of state revenue, of which the amusement tax is the largest component. The general sales tax is the next largest source of revenue. Principal expenditures are for education, health and welfare, and highways.

Education. The public school system is controlled by an elected Board of Education, which delegates administrative responsibilities to an appointive superintendent of public instruction. Local school districts, coextensive with the counties, receive supplementary funding from the state. School attendance is compulsory for those between the ages of seven and 17.

The University of Nevada originally was established at Elko in 1874 under the provisions of the Morrill Land-Grant College Act; 12 years later it was moved to Reno. In 1951 an extension branch was established in Las Vegas, which since has become the autonomous University of Nevada, Las Vegas. Northern Nevada Community College is within the university system, and the 1971 legislature established similar two-year colleges—Western Nevada Community College and Clark County Community College—for the western and southern regions. To supplement campus instruction, the Desert Research Institute and the Agricultural Experiment Stations provide statewide research services.

Health and welfare. Nevada's social welfare programs and its custodial institutions are administered by the Department of Human Resources. Old-age and welfare allotments are given to those qualified on the basis of need,

Executive, legislative and judicial branches of government

Institutions of higher education

and public assistance is available for the blind and other handicapped individuals. Support payments are provided for dependent children, and state orphanages are located near Carson City and Las Vegas. The state mental hospital is in Sparks, and a mental-health facility exists in Las Vegas. Penal and rehabilitation institutions include the state prison in Carson City, a girls' training centre at Caliente, and an industrial school for boys at Elko.

Health care, housing, and public safety are responsibilities of local government or private enterprise.

Cultural life. Nevadans traditionally have mingled rural conservatism and the individualism of the Old West. During its first century the population was relatively small and dispersed, and cultural values remained those of an agrarian society. With the establishment of sophisticated resort industries and increases in population, however, Las Vegas and Reno developed marked metropolitan characteristics. Not only has the economy diversified but cultural activities also have burgeoned. Recognizing this trend, the 1967 legislature established the Nevada State Council on the Arts to coordinate and stimulate cultural activities.

Both major cities have well-established programs in the performing arts. The universities sponsor lectures, concerts, and theatrical productions, while the tourist industry regularly features some of the most famous entertainers in show business. Both Reno and Las Vegas support symphony orchestras and have commercial and public art galleries. Varied handicrafts are promoted by artists' and craftsmen's organizations. Traditional Indian arts and crafts have been revived on reservations and in urban colonies.

Nevada's frontier heritage is commemorated by annual pageants and festivals, which provide natives with both sentimental nostalgia and additional commercial opportunities. Perhaps the best known is Helldorado Week, held in Las Vegas each May, for which the townspeople wear Western garb and stage a series of rodeos and parades. A unique ethnic event is the Basque Festival in Elko, and the Reno Rodeo is an outstanding Fourth of July celebration. The entire state observes its anniversary, Admission Day, on October 31, highlighted by a picturesque parade and costume ball in Carson City.

Old West festivals

Nevada has several museums and more than 40 libraries. The Nevada State Museum, located in the old federal mint building in Carson City, emphasizes the mining industry and mineral collections. Anthropological artifacts are featured at the Lost City Museum in Overton, at the University Museum in Las Vegas, and at the Southern Nevada Museum in Henderson. The Mackay School of Mines Museum, on the Reno campus of the state university, is oriented to metallurgical, mineralogical, and geological specimens. The Nevada Historical Society, also in Reno, has pioneer mementos, the most complete holding of Nevada newspapers, and a sizable historical reference library. The library of the University of Nevada, Reno, has the largest collection of books in the state, while the Nevada State Library in Carson City is notable for its excellent collection of legal works.

State and federal governments maintain four historic monuments, 16 state parks, and several developed recreational areas. The Valley of Fire State Park, near Overton, is widely known for its brilliantly coloured rock formations, Indian pictographs, and petrified forest. Mormon Station Historic State Monument, in Genoa, includes the site of the first permanent settlement in Nevada, and Cathedral Gorge, near Caliente, displays red and gold rocks that resemble church spires. The famed Death Valley area lies on the border between Nevada and California, and Lehman Caves National Monument, near Baker, has underground pools and unique limestone formations.

HISTORY

Anthropological evidence indicates that prehistoric Indian settlements existed in Nevada more than 20,000 years ago. Cave-dwelling tribespeople left picture writings on rocks in southern Nevada, and Basket Makers and Pueblo Indians also flourished there. Explorers of the early 1800s found Mohave, Paiute, Shoshoni, and Washoe Indians at various locations within Nevada.

Explorers and settlers. Missionaries and fur traders were in the vanguard of the exploration of the Nevada area. The missionary travels of Francisco Garcés from New Mexico to California in 1775–76 were imitated by other Spanish Franciscans. In 1825 Hudson's Bay Company trappers explored the northern and central region, and two years later Jedediah Smith led a party of Americans into the Las Vegas Valley and across the Great Basin. By 1830 the Old Spanish Trail was bringing traders to the area from Santa Fe and Los Angeles, and in 1843 and 1845 John C. Frémont's military explorations publicized the Great Basin and the Sierra Nevada region. During the 1840s American pioneers followed the Humboldt Valley–Donner Pass route to the Pacific Coast, and the Forty-Niner Gold Rush greatly expanded migration through Nevada to California.

Nevada, which came under U.S. sovereignty through the Mexican Cession of 1848, was a part of California until it was incorporated into the newly organized Utah Territory in 1850. In 1849 a settlement was made at Genoa (then Mormon Station) in Carson Valley, but the population
Discovery of mineral wealth remained sparse until the discovery of the Comstock Lode in 1859. From that time on Nevada ceased to be merely a highway for gold seekers on the way to California. Thereupon Virginia City became the most famous of all the Western mining camps, and the rapid influx of prospectors and settlers resulted in the organization of Nevada Territory in 1861.

Simultaneously, the U.S. Civil War gave strategic importance to the new territory. President Lincoln realized that Nevada's mineral wealth could help the Union, and he also needed a Northern state to support the proposed antislavery amendments to the Constitution. Although Nevada Territory had only about one-fifth of the 127,381 persons required for statehood, Nevadans were encouraged to seek admission to the Union. Congress accepted the proposed state constitution and voted for statehood in 1864.

Mining and cattle-ranching decades. Throughout its early decades Nevada's economy was dependent on mining and ranching. The rich Comstock mines reached a maximum annual output of $36,000,000 in silver in 1878. During the 1870s, however, the federal government limited the role of silver in the monetary system, causing a decline in silver prices, the closing of many Nevada mines, and the decay of once thriving communities into ghost towns.

As mining declined, cattle ranching became a major industry. But beef prices were unpredictable, high railroad rates were burdensome, and severe winters often killed thousands of cattle. In the late 1880s many cattle ranchers were forced into bankruptcy. Depressed in mining and ranching, the state's population dropped from 62,000 in 1880 to 47,000 in 1890.

Prosperity returned to Nevada only after the beginning of the 20th century, when rich silver ores were discovered near Tonopah and major copper deposits around Ely and when a major gold strike occurred at Goldfield. Thousands of miners answered the lure of these bonanzas, and the railroads built extensive branch lines to bring in equipment to the mining areas and haul out the ore. Accessible railroads and reduced rates also encouraged cattle ranchers to renew large-scale production. Irrigation of fertile river valleys produced sizable hay crops. Thus assured of winter feed, ranchers further expanded their herds in the upland regions. World War I demands for Nevada's beef and metals kept the boom going, but the failing markets of the 1920s brought the return of depression.

During its first three decades as a state, Nevada was strongly oriented to Republican control. Reflecting the lax standards in national politics, the state was often manipulated by corrupt politicians. Mine owners and ranchers frequently subsidized government officials, and there were accusations that rich men in the state had bought seats in the U.S. Senate. Monetary issues became of paramount importance in the 1890s, and the Free Silver Party swept four consecutive state elections. By 1900, however, the traditional two-party system was again in control, and since then Nevada has voted consistently in line with national trends.

Creation of a modern economy. During the Great Depression of the 1930s, when agriculture and mining were in acute distress, Nevada began its transition to a modern economy. After the legalization of gambling in 1931 and
Advent of the resort and scientific communities the reduction to six weeks of the residence requirement for divorce, Nevada became a marriage, divorce, and resort centre. The principal resort areas are Las Vegas, Reno, and Lake Tahoe. Las Vegas attracts most of its tourists from the Los Angeles area, and it is famous for its resort hotels and gambling casinos. Reno draws many pleasure seekers from the San Francisco Bay area. The gambling tax is second only to the sales tax in revenue from taxation for the state. Nevada's liberal divorce laws attract people from all parts of the country; because of the no-waiting period for marriages, however, many more weddings than divorces are performed in the state.

Construction of Hoover Dam on the Colorado River substantially aided the economy of southern Nevada, and its cheap hydroelectric power opened the way for manufacturing. The importation of hydroelectric power from Bonneville Dam on the Columbia River and piped-in natural gas also has brought industrial development in the northwestern region.

In the 1950s the establishment of the Nevada Test Site by the federal government expanded employment opportunities and stimulated the development of technical industries within the state. Overshadowing the new industrialization, and fundamentally responsible for the current prosperity, is the diversification and expansion of the tourist trade to include not only the gaming and entertainment facilities of the Reno and Las Vegas areas but also the scenic and recreational opportunities statewide.   (R.J.Z.)

Utah

A Rocky Mountain state of the United States, Utah became the 45th member of the Union in 1896 after decades of failing to attain statehood. In its earlier history Utah represents a unique episode in the settlement of the United States, a story of a religious group that trekked and was driven across three-quarters of the continent in search of a "promised land." The state capital, Salt Lake City,
Overview of the state is the world headquarters of the Church of Jesus Christ of Latter-day Saints, commonly known as the Mormon Church, and the spiritual home of adherents throughout the world. With Mormons making up some 70 percent of the state's population, the beliefs and traditions of the Mormon Church continue to exert profound influences on many facets of the state's life and institutions.

From the very beginning of settlement in 1847, the Mormon pioneers set about wresting a green land from the deserts, gradually supplementing their crops with the products of industry and the earth. The economy of present-day Utah is based on manufacturing, tourism, and services, in addition to agriculture and mining. Although the state is generally conservative in political ideology, the two major parties are relatively well balanced.

Mountains, high plateaus, and deserts form most of Utah's landscape, which displays many of the most spectacular geological phenomena on the North American continent. The state's 84,916 square miles (219,931 square kilometres) lie in the heart of the West, with Idaho to the north, Wyoming to the northeast, Colorado to the east, Arizona to the south, and Nevada to the west. At its "Four Corners," in the southeast, Utah meets Colorado, New Mexico, and Arizona at right angles, the only such meeting of states in the nation.

PHYSICAL AND HUMAN GEOGRAPHY

The land. *Relief.* The Colorado Plateau comprises slightly more than half of Utah. Relatively high in elevation, this region is cut by brilliantly coloured canyons. Utah's growing tourist industry relies upon the attraction of the region's fiery, intricately sculptured natural bridges, arches, and other masterpieces of erosion.

The western third of the state is part of the Basin and
Desert and mountain landscapes Range Province, or Great Basin, a broad, flat, desert-like area with occasional mountain peaks. Great Salt Lake lies in the northeastern part of the region; to the southwest is

the Great Salt Lake Desert, covering some 4,000 square miles, which include the Bonneville Salt Flats, famous for land speed racing. During the Pleistocene Epoch, from 10,000 to 2,500,000 years ago, the region's huge Lake Bonneville covered an area as large as Lake Michigan. Great Salt Lake and saline Sevier Dry Lake are the remnants of evaporation.

The Middle Rockies in the northeast comprise the Uinta Mountains, the only major mountain range in the United States running in an east–west direction, and the Wasatch Range. Along the latter run a series of valleys and plateaus known as the Wasatch Front. The Wasatch Range area and the red deserts of the east and gray deserts of the west make up more than 90 percent of Utah.

Altitudes range from 13,528 feet (4,123 metres) at Kings Peak in the Uintas to about 2,000 feet in the southwestern corner of the state. The Oquirrh and Deep Creek ranges of the Great Basin are important for their deposits of copper, gold, lead, and zinc.

Climate. Utah's geographical location in relation to the mountain systems of the West, which divert much of the precipitation, makes it basically an arid state. Anomalous southwestern Utah, which has a warm, almost semitropical climate, is referred to as Utah's "Dixie." The southern part of the Colorado Plateau has cool, dry winters and wet summers, with frequent thunderstorms. Northern Utah is affected by air masses from the North Pacific and continental polar air; it receives most of its precipitation in the cool season.

The state has four distinct seasons. Average temperatures in July range from 65° to 80° F (18° to 27° C). In winter the average temperature is slightly below freezing except in "Dixie." Daily temperatures vary widely: when Salt Lake City has July highs of 90° F (32° C) or above, the nights are 55° to 65° F (13° to 18° C). Relatively low humidity prevails; average precipitation is 12 inches (300 millimetres) a year, varying from less than five inches annually over the Great Salt Lake Desert to 50 inches in the Wasatch Mountains. The average annual snowfall is 54 inches, ranging from none in the southwestern valleys to more than 10 feet (three metres) at ski resorts. The average growing season is 128 days.

Soils. The desert soil that covers most of the state lacks many organic materials but contains adequate lime. Lack of adequate drainage in the Great Basin has damaged surrounding soils with saline materials and alkali salts. The richest soils are in the old Lake Bonneville area, along the delta deposits of the Wasatch Front. Most farming is done in these alluvial soils. Mountain soils provide a rich habitat for conifers and other trees.

Drainage. Utah contributes to three major drainage areas—the Colorado and Columbia rivers and the Great Basin. The Colorado and its tributary, the Green, drain eastern Utah. The Upper Colorado River Storage Project includes several dams and many lakes in that area. Great Basin rivers include the Bear, Weber, Provo, Jordan, and Sevier, all of which are landlocked. All the river systems are important for their irrigation and power potential.

Plant and animal life. Utah's 4,000 plant species represent six climatic zones, from the semitropical Lower Sonoran in the southwestern Virgin Valley to the Arctic on mountain peaks. In the south are found creosote bush, mesquite, cactus, yucca, and Joshua tree; the alkaline deserts are the habitat of shad scale, saltbush, and greasewood. Juniper and sagebrush grow in the foothills and mountain valleys, as do piñon pine, cedar, and native grasses for grazing. In the mountains grow pines, firs, aspen, and blue spruce. Timber covers about 16,000,000 acres (6,500,000 hectares), but only about one-fourth of the forestland is commercially valuable.

The mule deer is the most common of Utah's large animals since elk, bison, timber wolves, and grizzly bears have largely disappeared. Coyotes, bobcats, and lynxes are hunted. Game birds include grouse, quail, and pheasants; golden eagles, hawks, owls, and magpies are numerous. Great Salt Lake bird refuges are the home of sea gulls, blue herons, and white pelicans. Several species of game fish are native, while others have been introduced. Reptiles and amphibians, both poisonous and nonpoisonous, are native.

Settlement patterns. In Utah's 29 counties, about two-thirds of the land is federally owned, and 7 percent is owned by the state. About 4 percent of federal land is reserved for Indian use.

The Wasatch Front, extending north–south from Ogden to Provo and also including Salt Lake City, is the main area of urban and industrial development. Salt Lake City is the political, cultural, and religious capital of Utah. Historically a trade centre, it continues to be a hub for industry, commerce, and interstate transportation.

The front has not only the largest part of the population but also the best farmland in the state. Although tens of thousands of acres of cropland have been urbanized since 1958 and an urban trend continues, a rural society is still observable. Rural settlements typically have a "Mormon village" flavour, with a readily recognizable Mormon chapel or tabernacle within the town, wide streets, and a cultivated area surrounding the town itself.

Irrigation was among the first Mormon pioneer efforts in 1847, and since then irrigation and water conservation have become increasingly important. The irrigation complex in Utah comprises a vast number of diversion dams, multipurpose dams, storage reservoirs, canals and ditches, pipelines, and flowing wells, exclusive of the large Glen Canyon and Flaming Gorge dams. State boards and departments regulate water use, while the division of health maintains quality water standards under the Water Pollution Control Act of 1953.

A state air-conservation program was begun in 1967, with special attention to the Wasatch Front. Other programs of federal, state, or joint jurisdiction include watershed management and conservation, protection of wildlife resources, conservation of oil and gas reserves, and reclamation.

The people. The population is about 95 percent white, mainly of northern European ancestry. The remainder are Indians, Orientals, blacks, and other minorities.

The population of San Juan County is about one-half Indian, containing almost 30 percent of Utah's Indians. The Navajo, famous for their wool blankets, silverwork, and turquoise jewelry, reside primarily in the Four Corners region. About 1,800 Utes live on the Uintah and Ouray Indian Reservation. Having received a large settlement from the federal government for their lands, they have built new homes with modern conveniences. Annually sponsored events include the Bear Dance in the spring, the Sun Dance in July, and the Uinta Basin Industrial Fair in August or September. About 200 Southern Paiutes, among the most depressed of the tribes, live on six small reservations in southern Utah. Except for Indians, nearly 80 percent of the minority racial population lives in the three Wasatch Front counties of Salt Lake, Davis, and Weber.

One minority group included within the white statistics is that of about 60,000 Mexicans. Increasing attention is being paid to the problems of educating and acculturating this group, many of whom are low-income workers in agriculture, mining, manufacturing, and services.

The economy. From 1847 to 1868 the Mormons, with a high degree of mutual cooperation, built a self-sufficient economy based on agriculture, handicrafts, and small industry. From 1869 to 1896 this cooperative economy was supplemented by a non-Mormon enclave devoted to mining and trading. After statehood the exportable resources of the state were exploited to an increasing extent by outside corporations and enterprisers, and the agriculture of the state turned toward such commercial crops as sugar beets, wool, and range cattle. The depressions of 1921 and 1933 were severe, but federal programs and the welfare program of the Mormon Church helped the state to recover. During World War II several defense plants and air bases were built, and Utah had a uranium boom, followed in the late 1950s by the erection of several large plants to build rocket engines for missiles.

The state's economy emerged in the late 20th century with strong diversification. The large agricultural and mining sectors were supplemented by light and heavy manufacturing, finance, transportation, and tourism. Salt Lake City is a regional centre of finance and trade, and many large enterprises have offices there. Utah workers, in the Mormon tradition, have the reputation of being

Margin notes:

Irrigation, pollution control, and conservation

Traditional Indian cultural activities

Characteristic flora

industrious and well disciplined, and productivity is high. With its many summer and winter recreational facilities, Utah is well above average as a desirable place to work.

Mineral reserves and sources of income

Mining. A fair percentage of the nation's new copper is produced annually in Utah, accounting for about one-fifth of the value of the state's mineral production. Utah is the world's foremost producer of beryllium, and it ranks among the top five states in the nation as a producer of gold, silver, lead, uranium, and molybdenum. Salt was once the only mineral extracted in quantity from the Great Salt Lake, but sophisticated chemical industries now operate on the shores of the lake, using its brines to produce potassium sulfate and sodium sulfate for industrial use throughout the world.

Utah is a major producer of coal west of the Mississippi, but petroleum has replaced coal as the leading mineral fuel. Utah is the only state producing Gilsonite, a source of road oil, paving binder, and asphalt tile. In addition to steam plants, Utah has many hydroelectric plants.

Industry. State and federal government employment has increased at a faster rate than any other sector of the economy. The state remains below average, however, in the proportion of personal income derived from manufacturing. Printing and publishing, food processing, transportation equipment, nonelectrical machinery, petroleum refining, and fabricated-metal products are the major manufacturing sectors.

Agriculture. Following the national trend, farm employment and farm size in Utah have declined since 1960, but productivity has increased. Almost three-fourths of Utah's farm income comes from livestock products, the remainder from field crops, fruit, and canning crops.

Transportation. Utah's transportation industry, with easy access to all national markets, is the basis for the state's development as a major distribution centre for the West. More than 1,600 miles (2,600 kilometres) of rails cover the state. Road traffic is expanding rapidly; several interstate highways supplement the state system. In addition to the major airport serving Salt Lake City, there are excellent feeder line facilities in Ogden, Logan, Provo, Cedar City, and St. George.

Administrative and social conditions. *Government.* Utah's constitution, dating from 1896, guarantees basic personal freedoms consistent with the federal Bill of Rights, prohibits sectarian control of public schools, forbids "polygamous or plural marriages," and grants equal civil, political, and religious rights, including suffrage, to all citizens. Voting requirements follow national patterns, though for elections affecting tax levies a voter must have paid a property tax the previous year.

Constitutional framework of the government

The governor is aided by a secretary of state, auditor, treasurer, and attorney general, while much of the administration of routine state affairs is done through more than 50 state agencies. Each of these officials serves a four-year term.

The governor has the right to veto any bill, but that decision may be overruled through repassage of that bill by a two-thirds majority of each house of the legislature. Any bill passed by the legislature and not acted upon by the governor within five days while the legislature is in session automatically becomes law. The governor, secretary of state, and the attorney general together form the State Board of Examiners, which reviews all official state transactions.

Legislative power is vested in the Senate and House of Representatives, as well as in the voters, who have the power to initiate legislation and to hold a referendum on all laws not passed by a two-thirds majority of both houses. After reapportionment in 1972 the legislature comprised 29 senators serving four-year terms and 75 representatives serving two-year terms.

The legislature meets annually, with regular 60-day sessions in odd-numbered years and 20-day budget sessions in even-numbered years. Special sessions may be held subject to call by the governor. Four full-time councils provide interim work on investigation and research of specific legislative and state problems; advice on budgetary matters and appropriation requests, with legal counselling and legislative accuracy; and legislative administration. In

1971 the legislature was rated by a nonpartisan committee reviewing all state legislatures as 15th in overall effectiveness, fifth in accountability to the citizenry, and eighth in being informed.

The highest judicial authority is the state Supreme Court, composed of five justices elected to 10-year terms, one every two years. Judges of the seven district courts are elected for six-year terms. The state also has circuit courts and justices of the peace. A juvenile court system has its own districts and judges.

The constitution requires that each county have a county-commission form of government comprising three commissioners and several other elected officials to carry out administrative, judicial, law enforcement, financial, and health, education, and welfare functions.

Forms of municipal government vary according to population. Cities with populations of more than 90,000—Salt Lake City alone—elect a mayor and four commissioners. Cities between 15,000 and 90,000 elect a mayor and two commissioners, while smaller cities elect a mayor and five council members. Incorporated towns are governed by a president and four trustees. Any city commission or town council has the power to appoint a city manager.

Although Utah is referred to frequently as a Republican state, in actuality no party can claim dominance. Elected officials from both parties work well together and show a reasonable degree of harmony. This has been true since the early 1890s, when the normally homogeneous Mormon populace was divided into political parties by church leaders to comply with federal requirements for statehood; a remarkably even division was achieved for the 1896 election by volunteers for each party.

Finance. Utah's broadly based tax structure appears to distribute the costs of government without discrimination against, or hardship to, any segment of the economy. The rate structures for the various taxes are generally competitive with those of neighbouring states. The corporate-income-tax rate is lower than that of any other Western state. Legislation providing for a phaseout of the state's inventory tax and a liberal free-port tax law granting tax exemptions on goods warehoused and processed in Utah are incentives to commerce.

Health and welfare. Although minorities are not politically important in Utah, the state, county, and local governments have developed programs to improve the economic and social status of Indians, Mexican-Americans, blacks, and other minority groups.

Health, welfare, and housing services are administered by the Department of Social Services. County health services are supervised and coordinated by the state Board of Health, which also works with school boards for child health care. Outstanding hospital systems are administered by the Mormon, Roman Catholic, and Episcopal churches.

Health, welfare, and housing

The state administers a substantial welfare program, including comprehensive old-age assistance, unemployment insurance, workers' compensation, and other social benefits. Efforts have been made to improve and upgrade outdated labour and hazardous-occupation laws. A division of low-income housing was created within the Department of Community Affairs in 1971 to facilitate better planning and coordination in that area. The Mormon Church also has an extensive welfare program.

Education. More than one-half of Utah's governmental expenditure is for education. Utah has the highest proportion of its population in public schools, the highest proportion of high school graduates, and the highest median level of school years completed of any state in the nation.

The school districts can levy local taxes to support public education; these taxes pay for almost one-half of educational expenses, with the remainder paid by the state. General public school regulations are administered by the state Board of Education, while elected local boards exercise more specific control. The U.S. Department of the Interior maintains the Intermountain Indian School in Brigham City, a secondary school for Navajo Indians of Utah and neighbouring states.

The largest of Utah's state universities is the University of Utah, in Salt Lake City. It was founded in 1850 as the University of Deseret and has a reputation for outstanding

| Higher education | graduate and professional schools of medicine, law, and pharmacology. Utah State University, in Logan, founded in 1888 as a land-grant school, has achieved national status in the fields of agriculture, forestry, education, engineering science, and the fine arts. Brigham Young University, in Provo, is owned and operated by the Mormon Church. It is the largest of Utah's universities and has a campus that is among the most beautiful in the Western states. It ranks in the nation's top three institutions of higher learning in the number of Indian students.

Weber State College (1889), in Ogden, is a four-year school with rapidly expanding programs and facilities. Technical schools are located in Salt Lake City and Provo, while Westminster College (1875), in Salt Lake City, is operated by three Protestant denominations.

Cultural life. More than two-thirds of the population are Mormons, and the church has a strong influence on the state's cultural life and traditions. The church is divided into "stakes," consisting of six to 10 local congregations, or "wards," of about 500 members each. Each stake has a "tabernacle," or stake centre, with one or more chapels and recreational and cultural facilities. Each ward, or occasionally two or three wards together, owns a chapel with a centre for collective worship, classrooms, a basketball court, and a dance hall. Mormon culture emphasizes closely knit family life, widespread interest in family genealogy, no consumption of alcoholic beverages or tobacco, a relatively small amount of "night life," and participation in sports and personal development programs. Other denominations also are active in cultural areas. Particularly notable is the annual St. Marks Arts Festival, which includes music, dancing, poetry reading, drama, and other creative arts.

The large number of Indians gives a unique flavour to Utah life. About 4,000 Indian children are taken into Mormon homes during the school year, putting Indian pupils into nearly every elementary-school classroom. They are active in sports, public speaking, and school government, and almost every block has a family with an Indian foster child. In the summer these children return to their families.

Sports and outdoor life. Salt Lake City has professional basketball, hockey, and baseball teams, and auto racing on the Bonneville Salt Flats has gained international importance. The Mormon Church sponsors competitive team sports involving thousands of players and one of the largest basketball, softball, and golf tournaments in the nation.

Utah's nine national forests and other undeveloped areas offer great tracts of land for hunting, fishing, camping, hiking, skiing, and snowmobiling. Other natural attractions include the national parks (Arches, Bryce Canyon, Capitol Reef, Zion, and Canyonlands); the national monuments (Cedar Breaks, Dinosaur, Natural Bridges, Timpanogos Cave, Rainbow Bridge, and Hovenweep); the national recreation areas (Flaming Gorge and Glen Canyon); and the Golden Spike National Historic Site. There are 43 state parks, including the Pioneer Monument State Park at Salt Lake City.

Historical institutions and celebrations. The Utah State Historical Society has an outstanding collection of manuscripts, publications, and photographs. It publishes the *Utah Historical Quarterly,* monographs, and full-volume diaries. The Daughters of Utah Pioneers and their counterpart, the National Society of the Sons of Utah Pioneers, with about 1,000 branches throughout the nation, maintain monuments, preserve old landmarks, mark historical sites, collect relics and histories, keep a library of historical matter, and secure unprinted manuscripts, photographs, maps, and data to clarify the truth about Utah pioneers. Their 38-room museum depicts pioneer implements and way of life. *The Western Historical Quarterly,* the official publication of the Western History Association, is published by Utah State University.

Park City and Pioneer Village in Salt Lake City are Old West towns using the original buildings and furnishings. Every county holds a fair in the autumn, highlighted by displays and competitions, concessions, and often a rodeo.

On July 24 almost all communities hold Pioneer Day, commemorating the entrance of the Mormon pioneers into the Salt Lake Valley. It includes parades, fireworks, |

(left margin labels: "Impact of Mormonism on the cultural milieu")

rodeos, orations, and colourful reminders of Utah's early settlers.

The arts. The Division of Fine Arts is a department of the state government whose purpose is to promote all branches of the fine arts and to cooperate with the federal government in these matters. It sponsors the Utah Governor's Conference on the Arts, and it allocates funds advanced to the state by federal agencies to finance cultural activities.

The most famous buildings in Utah are the many-spired Mormon Temple and the turtleback Mormon Tabernacle, both in Salt Lake City. The latter was built in the 1860s without nails, holds up to 10,000 people, and has rare acoustical qualities to enrich the sounds of its world-famous organ with 10,700 pipes. Mormon temples in St. George, Manti, Provo, Ogden, and Logan reflect architectural magnificence. Homes reflect the usual sequence of styles in American domestic architecture.

| | Among the performing arts, music is emphasized. The Mormon Tabernacle Choir, consisting of 375 members with trained but nonprofessional voices, presents a national weekly radio and television broadcast. The choir gives concerts in the United States and abroad and records with a major company. The Utah Symphony Orchestra and the Salt Lake Oratorio Society are other major ensembles. Annual tourist-oriented performances include the Mormon musicals *Promised Valley,* presented for 50 performances in July and August, and *All Faces West,* presented in Ogden in July. The major universities have symphonies and choral groups performing in winter, as well as summer festivals and concerts. | Music, dance, and theatre |

Among the many dance companies in Utah are Salt Lake City's Ballet West, which is ranked among the best in the nation, and the Repertory Dance Theatre, which features modern dance. The University of Utah Children's Dance Theatre has performed on the East and West coasts as well as in Utah schools. The Brigham Young University folk-dance troupes have toured the United States and most parts of the world.

Utah gained an early start in drama with the opening of the Salt Lake Theater in 1862. A replica has been constructed on the University of Utah campus, and performances are held there regularly. The Mormon Church emphasizes folk drama in its youth organization; more than 2,000 wards produce at least one play a year, many of them written locally. These culminate biennially in a large drama festival in Salt Lake City. An annual event that has gained national fame and reputation is the Utah Shakespearean Festival, held since 1960 in Cedar City. Brigham Young University Motion Picture Productions centres on topics of interest to the Mormon Church.

HISTORY

| | **Prehistory and white exploration.** As early as 10,000 BC, small, mobile groups of hunters and gatherers lived in caves by the great inland sea, prehistoric Lake Bonneville. This desert culture was replaced about AD 400 by the more advanced Pueblo, or Anasazi, culture, which came into Utah from the Southwest and Mexico. These Indians constructed superb communal cliff dwellings and raised corn (maize), squash, and beans. They left Utah about 1250, perhaps because of an extended drought. | Early inhabitants and cultures |

When white explorers and settlers came to Utah in the 18th and 19th centuries they encountered Shoshoni Indians—the Southern Paiute, Gosiute, and Ute (from whom the state takes its name)—practicing a desert culture like that of the earliest period. Some of them raised corn and pumpkins by a simple system of irrigation. Ute Indians in eastern Utah lived in a region of higher rainfall and had a better way of life. Having acquired horses from Plains Indians, their nomadic life centred around the buffalo.

Two Franciscan fathers, Francisco Atanasio Domínguez and Silvestre Vélez de Escalante, explored Utah in 1776, and soon afterward Utah was visited by occasional Spanish trading parties. Fur trappers and overland immigrants to California and Oregon were in the region in the 1820s and 1830s. The first four of some 16 annual rendezvous between trappers and buyers were held in Utah from 1825 to 1828, indicating the early importance of the area to the fur trade. The "mountain men" who explored and established trading posts included James Bridger, who first visited the Great Salt Lake in 1824, and Jedediah Smith, who first traversed the state from north to south and west to east in 1826–27. Explorers sent by the government included John C. Frémont, who led scientific expeditions to northern Utah in 1843 and the western Great Salt Lake area in 1845.

Mormon settlement and territorial growth. The period of settlement and territorial status is notable for the ending of the long quest (1845–47) for a Mormon homeland, wresting a civilization from an arid environment, the contest for sovereignty between Utah and the United States, and the conflict with indigenous Indians over the use of the land. The Mormon Church was founded in Fayette, New York, in 1830 and from the beginning had gathered its members together in religious, social, and economic cooperation. In Kirtland, Ohio; Jackson County, Missouri; and Nauvoo, Illinois, the Mormons had grown rapidly, but wary neighbours eventually forced their removal from each such gathering place. From Nauvoo, which the Mormons had built up from Mississippi River swampland into a prosperous community, some 16,000 Mormons escaped violent mobs in 1846 by fleeing across Iowa to Council Bluffs. When wagonloads of Mormon pioneers under the leadership of Brigham Young first entered the valley of the Great Salt Lake in 1847, they were determined to transform the arid valley land into a green and wholesome "Kingdom of God." They succeeded.

From Salt Lake City settlers were directed to colonize in all directions until they had developed a prosperous and stable economy and political structure in a territory that was originally 210,000 square miles in area, stretching from the Rockies to the Sierra Nevada and from the Columbia River in Oregon to the Gila in Arizona. Immigrant converts continued to stream into Utah from Europe and the eastern United States; they were organized into colonizing parties based on allocations of skills and leadership abilities and sent out to build the territory. By 1860 more than 150 self-sustaining communities with a total of 40,000 residents had been established, producing crops by means of water from mountain streams carried through canals to the alluvial valley lands. Utah's place in the national scene was symbolized by the driving of the golden spike at Promontory in 1869, uniting the eastward- and westward-reaching lines of the nation's first transcontinental railroad.

Conflict with the Indians was held to a minimum because of the Mormon view that it was cheaper to feed them than to fight them. As the presence of the colonizers became more and more ubiquitous, however, some local Indians began to raid the settlements to obtain food. The Utes were eventually placed on a reservation in the Uinta Basin, the Southern Paiutes and Shoshoni on smaller reservations, and later the lands south of the San Juan River were incorporated into a Navajo reservation.

Mormons federal conflicts

The propensity of the Mormons to establish their own political and social system and the incompetency of federal territorial officials led to an era of conflict with the federal government. In 1857 Pres. James Buchanan, believing the Mormons to be in a state of open rebellion, ordered some 2,500 soldiers to Utah to replace Young, who had served as governor during the early years. This episode is referred to as the Utah War, although no clashes occurred. With the outbreak of the U.S. Civil War in 1861, a new camp was established east of Salt Lake City under the command of Col. Patrick Connor. Connor openly supported his troops in prospecting for minerals and sought to "solve the Mormon problem" by initiating a miners' rush to Utah. A substantial enclave of non-Mormon miners, freighters, bankers, and businessmen was the result, and there were three decades of Mormon–non-Mormon conflict until Utah attained statehood in 1896.

Before and after statehood. The Mormon settlers applied for statehood in 1849 under the name Deseret, a word from the sacred *Book of Mormon* meaning "honeybee" and signifying industry. This bid was rejected, as were the efforts of five subsequent constitutional conventions between 1856 and 1887. Before the U.S. Congress

and the national administration would assent to statehood for Utah, Mormon leaders were required to discontinue the church's involvement in politics through its People's Party, withdraw from an economic policy in which Mormons dealt primarily with each other, and discontinue the practice of polygamy.

After its acceptance into the union in 1896, Utah moved rapidly into the larger social, political, and economic mainstreams of the nation. The political structure changed from theocracy to a conventional democracy: non-Mormons were elected to important positions, including the office of governor. The Mormon Church has been officially neutral in politics since the early 1900s, and the influence of economic blocs—manufacturing and mining corporations, public utilities, stockmen, educators, and labour—has become far more important. The initial equal political division among Republicans and Democrats in the early 1890s is still reflected in the contemporary political balance, though the state has tended to be Republican since World War II.   (L.J.A.)

Wyoming

In the 20th century the "mountain men" of Wyoming, who guided pioneering parties across the Oregon Trail and opened the pathway for the first transcontinental railroads, have been replaced by the outfitters, guides, and dude ranchers who cater to the state's large tourist industry and by the rangers who oversee such geologically spectacular national parks as Yellowstone and Grand Teton. A landscape of frontier ranges, over which cattlemen and sheepherders engaged in open warfare until well after Wyoming became the 44th U.S. state in 1890, has given way to one of modern Western towns and small cities away from the mainstream of contemporary urban development. The state ranks low in its contribution to the national economy, largely because of its identical ranking in manufacturing and farm value; yet it is an important producer of raw materials and a major supplier of cattle and other livestock.

Wyoming's area of 97,914 square miles (253,596 square kilometres) has a sparse population, but the majority live in the state's small urban areas, which are separated by great stretches of arid high prairies, mountains, or desert. The older settlements, following the original rail lines across the southern part of the state, include Cheyenne, the capital, and Laramie, where the University of Wyoming, the state's only four-year institution of higher learning, has its main campus. Neighbouring states are Montana on the north and northwest, South Dakota and Nebraska on the east, Colorado on the south, Utah on the southwest, and Idaho on the west. Although Wyoming is classified as a Mountain State, a large percentage of its territory lies in the high western plateaus of the Great Plains, anticipating the great upward thrust of the Rocky Mountains.

PHYSICAL AND HUMAN GEOGRAPHY

The land. *Relief.* Wyoming is mostly a land of vast vistas ending in a mountainous horizon. Its average elevation of 6,700 feet (2,040 metres) above sea level is second only to that of Colorado. Elevations range from 3,125 feet (952 metres), where the Belle Fourche River leaves the northeastern corner of the state, to 13,804 feet (4,207 metres) at the top of Gannett Peak in the Wind River Range.

The eastern quarter of the state, except for the low Black Hills, which extend into South Dakota, lies within the Great Plains. Elsewhere, more than a dozen mountain ranges, most of which follow a north–south axis, are separated by basins that appear on the surface as plains or valleys. The Teton Mountains, culminating in the 13,747-foot (4,190-metre) Grand Teton, the Big Horn Mountains rising to 13,165 feet (4,013 metres) at Cloud Peak, and the Wind River Range are among the most spectacular ranges. Notable plains include the Big Horn Basin, Jackson Hole, Star Valley, and the Wind River Basin in the northwest; the Green River Basin, Great Divide Basin, and Washakie Basin in the southwest; and the Laramie Plains between the Laramie and Medicine Bow mountains in the southeast. Earthquakes are common along Wyoming's western

Mountains, basins, springs, rivers, and gorges

boundary, particularly in the Yellowstone Park region, the site of numerous hot springs and geysers. Hot springs are also found near Thermopolis in the Big Horn Basin and in Saratoga, between the Medicine Bow and Sierra Madre mountains.

Drainage. The Continental Divide extends along the crest of the Sierra Madre, splits into two lines around the Great Divide Basin, follows the crest line of the Wind River Range, crosses the Togwotee Pass near the 9,600-foot (2,926-metre) elevation level, and continues northwestward through the Washakie Mountains and Yellowstone National Park. Consequently, 76 percent of Wyoming's drainage is carried down the Missouri–Mississippi system to the Gulf of Mexico, while most of the remainder flows either into the Pacific Ocean by way of the Snake–Columbia river system and Green–Colorado river system or into the Great Salt Lake through the Bear River. Great canyons such as the Flaming Gorge on the Green River and those named after the North Platte, Wind, Bighorn, and Laramie rivers are features of interest and importance, since many are used as recreational areas and for hydroelectric power facilities. Yellowstone Lake in Yellowstone National Park is the state's largest body of water, but many lakes are associated with mountain ranges, and numerous lakes have been created by dams.

Soils. Except in the mountains, where the earth is primarily acidic and of generally low quality, Wyoming's soils range in fertility from good to excellent. They lack only adequate water for optimal productivity. The richest soils lie in the Great Plains areas. Desert soils are found in the eastern Big Horn Basin and a large part of the Green River drainage region and the nearby Great Divide Basin.

Plant and animal life. Grasses, sages, and other desert or semidesert shrubs cover about 80 percent of Wyoming, while trees, largely conifers, are found in the mountains and along stream banks. The ponderosa pine is most numerous in the east, while the lodgepole pine, Douglas fir, and Engelmann spruce are most common in the west. Such deciduous species as the aspen and cottonwood are indigenous to some lower slopes and to streams in the south and east.

The deer and the antelope are the most widespread of the large animals. Both are found in all parts of the state, but antelope tend to roam the plains, while the deer prefer wooded areas. There are elk (wapiti) herds in several higher mountain ranges, but the largest numbers are in the national parks and the Jackson Hole area. Moose, less numerous than elk, are confined to the northwestern part of the state and the Bighorn Mountains. Black and brown bears still live in most mountains, but the grizzly bear is rarely found outside Yellowstone. The only region with bighorn sheep is an area of mountain ledges and crags running from the Wind River Range through the Absaroka Range to the Montana border.

Climate. Semidesert conditions occur in all parts of Wyoming, while true deserts exist throughout much of the Big Horn Basin and in and near the Great Divide Basin. Mountains invariably terminate in tundra, barren rock at the crest lines, and glaciers, of which there are 90 in the Wind River Range alone. Precipitation varies from approximately five inches (125 millimetres) in desert areas to 40 inches in some of the highest mountain regions. Snowfall exceeds 30 inches annually almost everywhere and surpasses 200 inches in several mountainous regions. Warm-season thunderstorms are common throughout the state, reaching an average of 60 a year in the southeast, where they bring on several hailstorms each year along the Laramie Mountains just west of Cheyenne. Temperatures have varied in Wyoming from −60° F (−51° C) to 114° F (46° C). Average temperatures in January range from 9° F (−13° C) to 28° F (−2° C); in July it varies from 75° F (24° C) to 52° F (11° C). Humidity, except during May and June, tends to be low everywhere throughout the year. Windy conditions that prevail during afternoons offer a contrast with the calm of early-morning hours.

Settlement patterns. Except in Yellowstone National Park and some steep mountain ranges in the northwest, Wyoming was surveyed under the township and section system. Evidence of this design in the landscape, how-

ever, as exemplified by township- or section-line roads, fence lines, or a pattern of fields is not nearly as common as in the Midwest. Many roads, paved or unpaved, cross open-range land. Both farmsteads and ranchsteads are usually found inside artificially planted windbreaks of shrubs and trees. Their seemingly haphazard pattern is seldom without direct reference to the presence of water. Urban settlements must also consider water supply, but their actual placement was dictated originally by the rail lines or mineral discoveries. These settlements are typical of small-town America: shaded avenues; buildings seldom more than six stories high; small, nonfamily businesses; great dependence upon the automobile for transportation; faith in the educative processes as manifested in public schools; and little air pollution.

The people. Almost 90 percent of all non-Indian Wyomingites trace their ancestry to European countries. Nationality enclaves, whose descendants often occupy original sites, include Mexicans in the Cheyenne and the Rock Springs area, Scandinavian groups around Laramie and Rawlins, Italians in the Rock Springs regions, and Germans in the Sheridan area. Cheyenne has always had the majority of the state's approximately 3,400 blacks. Most of Wyoming's nearly 8,000 Indians live, as they have for more than 100 years, on the Wind River Reservation, which was partially opened for white settlement during the first years of the 20th century.

Religion and settlement

Religion was a factor in the settlement of several western border areas and of the Big Horn Basin. In the last three decades of the 19th century the Mormons established colonies from their Salt Lake City base at such sites as the Bear River Valley, Star Valley (Salt River), Jackson Hole, and in the Big Horn Basin around such communities as Lovell, Cody, and Basin. The Roman Catholic Church always has been strongest in the southern counties, while Protestant groups have been most prominent in the northern counties. There is, however, a mixture of all religions throughout the state.

Since about 1935 most of the larger communities have been gaining population, whereas a few areas, such as the east central border region, have lost as much as 60 percent. Significant petroleum discoveries made since mid-century in the region west and southwest of the Black Hills and some uranium and soda-ash finds in other areas have reversed the trend. The American westward movement remains as much a phenomenon as it was earlier: immigrants to Wyoming still come largely from adjacent states to the east or south, such as Nebraska and Colorado, whereas Wyomingites tend to continue westward toward California and Oregon. The outflow of people from Wyoming has, in some years, almost exceeded the combined inflow and natural increase from births over deaths.

Patterns of migration

The economy. The basic income of the state is derived from mining and quarrying, agriculture, tourism, manufacturing, and the forest industries. Much of the economy is in the hands of outside investors, especially in the mining industry. Trade unions often hold strong bargaining positions because of the scarcity of competitive personnel, but the state has a right-to-work law prohibiting compulsory union membership. In general, state government officials at every level have made considerable effort to promote industrial and tourist activity of all types.

Mining. Before 1920 coal was Wyoming's most valuable mineral, but by the late 20th century it ranked second in importance. About 40 percent of the state lies above huge seams of coal. Wyoming ranks among the top five states in coal production and reserves. Petroleum has succeeded coal as the leading mineral. The value of oil and natural gas has averaged three times that of all other minerals combined. Throughout a large portion of central Wyoming the mining of uranium clays has, since 1950, made the state one of the largest producers of basic radioactive materials in the nation. Since 1951 the state also has produced much of the nation's trona for soda ash and bentonite clay for oil-well drilling and other uses. With iron-ore mines at Atlantic City and Sunrise, Wyoming is one of the largest iron producers west of the Mississippi River. Important quantities of gypsum, phosphate, and stone and other clay products also are mined.

Coal and oil

Flora and fauna of desert and mountain

Because of its enormous resources of oil, natural gas, coal, and uranium and the hydroelectric development of its great rivers, Wyoming is a major exporter of electricity by means of a large system of transmission lines. These same resources supply the raw materials that produce power in other states.

Agriculture. There is an abundance of good soil nearly everywhere in the state outside of the mountains, but low temperatures during the growing season, insufficient precipitation, and lack of irrigation water limit cropping to 34,000,000 acres (13,800,000 hectares) of farmland, of which about 5 percent is under irrigation. Livestock grazing occupies at least 24,000,000 acres of grassland. Summer grazing occurs on additional lands within or near the state's 10 national forests. These forested areas are located almost exclusively in mountainous regions and constitute the basis of a large timbering industry.

Transportation. The original east–west transcontinental railroad route is still Wyoming's primary corridor, comprising also a major interstate highway, oil and gas pipelines, and other basic communications facilities. The second major corridor extends in a jagged diagonal direction through the centre of the state from the southeast to the northwest corners, connecting the cities of Cheyenne and Casper with the Big Horn Basin. This corridor has the better airline routes, but it carries considerably less traffic. There are no water routes or ports in the state, nor is there a single city with a public transportation system such as a bus line, streetcar line, or motor railway. Railroads remain the major carrier of general freight into, out of, and within the state. For intrastate travel, most persons use automobiles, intercity bus lines, or airlines.

Administrative and social conditions. *Government.* Wyoming's constitution, amended more than 45 times since statehood, provides for a governor but no lieutenant governor. It also specifies a bicameral legislature composed of the House of Representatives and the Senate. The 62 representatives and 30 senators meet for a 40-day session in January of odd-numbered years and a 20-day session in even-numbered years, but may be called into special session at any time by the governor. Internal dissension necessitated federal court reapportionment of the Senate in 1965, resulting in a sharp decline in rural representation.

In addition to the federal judiciary, Wyoming maintains a three-level state court system. The five-justice Supreme Court primarily hears appeals from lower courts. The district courts, each with one or more judges, have original jurisdiction as general trial courts of both civil and criminal cases. They also take appeals from the justice of the peace, municipal, and police courts, which take minor civil and criminal cases. Judges of the Supreme Court, district courts, and justices of the peace are elected on a nonpartisan basis; municipal and police-court judges are appointed by the local mayor.

Local government

At the local level there are 23 counties and numerous cities, towns, school districts, and special districts—irrigation, fire, and the like. The number of counties has not changed since 1922, when the last one was formed. The number of special districts has been increasing quite rapidly; but the number of school districts has been decreasing. In 20 of the 23 counties, the seat of government is the largest town or city in the county. Municipal government takes the mayor–council form in all cities except Laramie, Casper, and Sheridan, which use the council–manager form.

Nonpartisan politics at the municipal level are an important feature of Wyoming government. At most other levels the policies and politics of the Republican and Democratic parties are major aspects of the campaign and election periods. Since statehood the Republican Party has most often won elections for the governorship and for the U.S. Senate and House, as well as control of the state legislature, but Democrats have been well represented. The southern tier of Wyoming counties tends to vote for Democrat candidates, while the northern counties almost inevitably support Republicans. Elections generally turn out a much greater percentage of the registered voters than the nation as a whole.

Perhaps because its people need to feel less isolated, Wyoming always has welcomed armed forces. F.E. Warren Air Force Base, located on the western edge of Cheyenne, is the centre of a widely dispersed network of underground silos containing intercontinental ballistic missiles. Smaller military detachments are located throughout the state.

Education, health, and law enforcement

Education and welfare. In addition to the University of Wyoming, there are seven two-year community colleges and 400 schools for primary and secondary education. The state Department of Health and Social Services conducts a full range of welfare services. Towns with fewer than 1,000 residents often are unable to obtain trained medical and dental personnel, but there are no shortages in the larger towns and cities.

Crime rates are below the national average. Most law enforcement is carried out at the local level through county sheriffs, town marshals, municipal police, county prosecuting attorneys, and county coroners. Wages paid to the state's workers are slightly below the national average, although per capita income is far higher than the state's economic ranking would suggest.

Cultural life. In the tradition of the Western frontier, the people of Wyoming have not neglected social organization at either the local or statewide levels. Special-interest groups such as those associated with athletics (including the University of Wyoming football team), education, religion, card playing, racing, politics, the professions, trade, service or social clubs, ranching, and travel are well organized. The annual Wyoming State Fair is held in Douglas in late August. Every county has its own fair—usually combined with a rodeo, Cheyenne's Frontier Days at the end of July being notable. Many towns or their Chambers of Commerce sponsor festivals, special events, and anniversary celebrations for tourists and residents during the summer. The annual Green River Rendezvous in Pinedale or the All-American Indian Days in Sheridan are popular state festivities. Museums and collections of guns or other relics are found in a number of places. Although distances between neighbouring towns often are great, Wyomingites are confirmed travellers.

Fairs and rodeos

Perhaps because it has different and spectacular scenery and a Western life-style, Wyoming attracts a wide range of entertainers. Concerts, music festivals, and theatres have enthusiastic audiences. The Jackson Hole country in the shadow of the spectacular Teton Mountains has a colony of artists and writers, and one of its ski areas is the site of world championship races. The Grand Teton and Yellowstone national parks are visited each year by millions of tourists. Near Fort Washakie on the Wind River Indian Reservation, tribal celebrations in the late spring recall the Indian customs, culture, and ancestral traditions.

The University of Wyoming, which has extension facilities elsewhere, is the centre of cultural change in the state. Cheyenne is the home of the Cheyenne Symphony Orchestra and the Cheyenne Choral Society, while Casper has the Casper Civic Symphony and the Casper Troopers Drum and Bugle Corps. The Whitney Gallery of Western Art and the Buffalo Bill Museum are located in Cody. Every county has at least one library, and some have several branches. The University of Wyoming's library is the state's largest.

HISTORY

The early days. Humans have lived in Wyoming for at least 9,000 years and probably much longer. The numbers of early Indians probably never reached 15,000 at any one time, for they were forced to live a largely nomadic existence dependent on hunting and gathering. Such tribes as the Crow, Ute, Bannock, Blackfoot, Cheyenne, Comanche, Kiowa, and various Dakota (Sioux) groups lived throughout the region at one time or another, but when the Indians were consigned to the Wind River Indian Reservation in 1869, only the Shoshoni and Arapaho, totalling 1,800, were numerous enough from among the strictly indigenous tribes to warrant inclusion.

The original Indian population

There are legends of Spanish explorers visiting the region, and the French explorer Pierre Gaultier de Varennes, sieur de La Vérendrye, may have crossed it in 1743. The first known white intruder was John Colter, a member of the

Lewis and Clark Expedition, who left the group, wandered for months, and returned to white settlements in 1807 with tales of the natural wonders of the Yellowstone region.

For a period of about 15 years after 1824 an annual trading rendezvous was held near the headwaters of the Wind, Bighorn, Snake, Green, or Sweetwater rivers in the area of west central Wyoming. When pioneers in large numbers began to head for Oregon, Great Salt Lake, and California, Wyoming "mountain men" guided them over the South Pass and established the famous Oregon Trail. Still later, the relatively easy Wyoming passages enabled large-scale crossing along the Overland Trail, by means of Pony Express (1860), and along the earliest telegraph routes (1861). From 1867 to 1869 they prepared the way for the transcontinental Union Pacific Railway route, during which period the major southern settlements were founded.

The territory.   The railroad brought white settlers and their towns, mines, farms, livestock, and other accoutrements of America's European-derived civilization. To protect these incursions from continuing Indian retaliation, the Territory of Wyoming was created in 1868. The name, a corruption of a name meaning "large plateau between the mountains," had been given by the Delaware Indians to a valley in northeastern Pennsylvania; its application to the new territory was the notion of persons unknown. The Indian menace confined settlement largely to the southern strip until 1876, when, following the overpowering of Lieut. Col. George Custer's troops at the Little Bighorn, further army campaigns opened the north to white exploitation. During the following decades vast cattle ranges were opened, initially through the large cattle drives by cowboys and wranglers from the overstocked prairies of Texas. When Wyoming became a state in 1890, it contained fewer than 63,000 residents, below the number required for statehood.

Since statehood.   Beginning with coal in 1867 and continuing with oil and gas on a major basis in 1912, bentonite during the 1930s, trona (soda ash) in 1948, and uranium oxides during the late 1950s, mining has assumed great importance as an economic activity. Cattle and sheep raising, together with dry farming after 1905, has continued to contribute heavily. The establishment of Yellowstone National Park in 1872 and the Eaton Brothers' dude ranch west of Sheridan in 1904—both the first of a kind—and of Grand Teton National Park in 1929, helped tourism grow to major significance. Wyoming has been nicknamed the "Equality State." The first territorial legislature, in 1869, granted voting rights to women as well as men, a principle incorporated into the constitution of 1889. In 1925 Nellie Tayloe Ross became the first woman governor in the United States.   (R.H.Br.)

First national park

PACIFIC COAST

The Pacific Coast of the United States possesses two unifying geological and geographic properties—the Pacific Ocean, which constitutes a natural western border, and the coastal mountain ranges that form the western shoreline of the United States. The physiographic interior consists of a diverse assortment of valleys, plateaus, river systems, and mountains, each of which possesses a distinctive geologic history. For this reason, as well as for historical and sociological reasons, it is difficult to establish firm inland boundaries for the region. The most commonly accepted definition of the Pacific Coast is largely a political one; it defines the region as comprising the states of California, Oregon, Washington, and Alaska. Hawaii is frequently included statistically in the "Pacific" states of the United States, even though, as a group of Polynesian volcanic and coral islands more than 2,000 miles (3,200 kilometres) from the U.S. Pacific Coast, it has little in common geologically or sociologically with the mainland states.

Before white men reached North America, the Pacific Coast was inhabited by native peoples belonging several culture areas and language families. The California Indians possessed a very simple culture pattern and spoke a great variety of languages, whereas the dominantly Salishan- and Nadene-speaking Indians of the Pacific Northwest, as well as the Eskimo-Aleut groups of the Bering Sea area, had distinctive and relatively highly developed cultures. Intruding upon both of these major segments were the Indians of the Columbia Plateau whose culture was profoundly influenced by the northern desert and northwest coastal tribes.

The Spaniards were the first to explore the Pacific Coast. Following Balboa's discovery of the Pacific Ocean in 1513, the Spaniards intensified their search for a sea passage to the East Indies; their voyages along the Pacific Coast led to the discovery of California by Juan Rodríguez Cabrillo in 1542. During the ensuing century and a quarter Mexican-based voyages carried these seafaring Spaniards steadily northward. By the time of the American Revolution the Spaniards had already gained familiarity with the California coast, cruised in Alaskan waters, established a base of sorts in Nootka Sound on Vancouver Island, and used the coastal waters for part of the famed Manila-Acapulco galleon trade. Except for the unplanned "visit" of Francis Drake to the vicinity of San Francisco Bay in 1579 and his assertion of an English claim to New Albion (the name given the region by this English navigator), the Spanish hold on California remained unchallenged for three centuries.

This enviable position was in large measure due to Spain's role as a colonizer. During the period 1769—1823, Spain established many missions and ranchos in California's fertile and semihumid south-coastal valleys. Under Spain's (after 1822, Mexico's) suzerainty Alta (Upper) California became a somewhat self-sustained pastoral community. A sunny climate, a generally inviting countryside, trade possibilities, and an appealingly simple life offered irresistible attractions to foreigners. During the first half of the 19th century a Spanish and Christianized Indian population of about 16,000 inhabitants became hosts to more than 3,000 foreign settlers, mostly Americans. The presence of Americans in California, and U.S. official desire to acquire West Coast ports were among the significant factors bringing on the war with Mexico in 1846–48. By the terms of the Treaty of Guadalupe Hidalgo (February 2, 1848) at the end of the war, California was included in the Mexican territory ceded to the United States. The discovery of gold in California on January 24, 1848, led the next year to the famous gold rush of the "Forty-niners." In 1850 California was admitted to the Union as the 31st state, and the decades that followed witnessed a rapid population growth, far-reaching agricultural developments (involving reclamation of arid areas), the discovery and exploitation of rich petroleum resources, and industrial and commercial expansion. In 1964 it became the most populous state according to official U.S. Census Bureau estimates.

The northern portion of the Pacific Coast, called the Pacific Northwest, has had a somewhat different history from that of California. It was Vitus Bering, the Russian-sponsored explorer, who in 1728 became the first to navigate the strait named in his honour. This initial Muscovite interest led to the formation in 1799 of the Russian-American Company, which established trading posts in parts of Alaska. In 1867 Russia sold Alaska to the United States, and in 1958 Alaska became the 49th state in the Union.

Russian exploration

North of California lay the Oregon country, a region roughly as large as Alaska and possessing strikingly varied physical features, soil, and climate. The humid Willamette-Puget Sound trough dominates the region west of the Cascade Mountains; an elevated arid plateau spreads over the region east of the Cascades; and binding together the major portions of the Oregon country is the mighty Columbia River.

During the last quarter of the 18th century ships of British and American registry carried on extensive maritime explorations along the Oregon coast and concurrently devel-

oped there a thriving sea otter fur trade. The discovery of
Oregon's rich fur resources led, after the turn of the century, to an accelerated British and American competition
in the establishment of inland trading operations. British
companies—first the Northwest Company and then the
Hudson's Bay Company—gained control of the region
north of the Columbia River; American traders, missionaries, and pioneer settlers dominated the region south of the
river. Following the relinquishment of territorial claims by
Russia and Spain, it remained for Great Britain and the
United States to resolve their overlapping claims to the
Oregon country. After a period of agreed upon "joint occupation," the 49th parallel was established in 1846 as a permanent boundary line to Puget Sound (but not including
Vancouver Island). The territory north of this line went to
Great Britain; the territory south of it to the United States.

American public interest in this Pacific Coast region dur-
"Oregon ing the mid-1840s has been referred to as "Oregon fever."
fever" What had begun as a small American overland migration
to Oregon in 1841 (by way of the Oregon Trail) gained
momentum, and after the boundary settlement the tide of
migration grew steadily. In 1848 Oregon was made a U.S.
territory; and as settlement spread, new states were formed
from it. Oregon was admitted to the Union in 1859, and
Washington in 1889.

Situations peculiar to the Pacific Coast have given this
geographically and historically diversified region at least
some measure of cohesiveness. Until the admission of
Hawaii as a state in 1959, the Pacific Coast represented
the western borderland area of the United States. As such
the people and the press of this region displayed over the
years a degree of regional self-consciousness. For example, the Pacific Coast population felt that it was relatively
isolated from the rest of the nation. This feeling was
early manifested by Pacific Coast efforts to bring about a
union of eastern and western lines of transportation and
communication, an enhancement of maritime trade, and
adequate Pacific Coast military defenses. Because of this
feeling of isolation, innumerable regional business and professional groups have emerged on the Pacific Coast over
the years and are still active. Some of these organizations,
however, exist simply as branches of nationally organized
bodies. Quite apart from this feeling of isolation, which
has diminished by high-speed means of communication
and travel, the Pacific Coast has been obliged to cope
with many problems of a peculiarly western nature. For
example, Oriental immigration has been largely a Pacific
Coast issue. Another issue peculiar to this region has been
the heavy dependence of West Coast business enterprises
upon eastern capital investment. For reasons traditionally associated with the most westerly segments of U.S.
settlements, the people of the Pacific Coast are generally
credited with being youthful, exuberant, and optimistic in
spirit; casual or "western" in dress; progressive in business
management; eager to promote population growth and
business booms; and, by virtue of location, more conscious than their fellow citizens in the East and Middle
West of America's destiny in the Pacific Ocean area.

(O.O.W./Ed.)

Alaska

When it became the 49th state of the United States in
1959, Alaska increased the nation's area by nearly 20
percent. The new area included vast stretches of unexplored land and untapped resources. But when Secretary
of State William H. Seward negotiated its purchase from
Russia in 1867, it was known as "Seward's Folly." Since
its acquisition, its settlement and exploitation have been
hindered by its distance from the rest of the nation, the
climate and terrain, and the slowness of communications.
Many problems still stand in the way of immigration and
economic development, and Alaska continues to be the
country's last frontier. More than two-fifths of the inhabitants reported in the 1980 census lived in and around the
city and borough of Anchorage. The capital is Juneau, 573
miles (922 kilometres) to the southeast in the Panhandle
region. A new capital site at Willow, however, was chosen
by referendum in late 1976.

Itself a landmass of subcontinental proportions, Alaska
lies at the extreme northwest of the North American   Area and
continent and is the largest peninsula in the Western   bounda-
Hemisphere. Its 586,412 square miles (1,518,800 square   ries
kilometres) include some 15,000 square miles of fjords
and inlets, and its three faces to the sea have about 34,-
000 miles (54,400 kilometres) of indented tidal coastline
and 6,600 total miles of coast fronting the open sea. The
marine borders are the Arctic Ocean on the north and
northwest, Bering Strait and Sea on the west, and the
Pacific Ocean and Gulf of Alaska on the south. The land
boundaries on the east cut across some 1,150 miles of
high mountains to separate the state from the Canadian
Yukon Territory and province of British Columbia. Rimming the state on the south is one of the Earth's most
active earthquake belts, associated on the mainland with
zones of volcanic activity. In the Alaska Range north of
Anchorage, Mt. McKinley, at 20,320 feet (6,194 metres),
is the highest peak in North America.

In the late 20th century the problem of development versus preservation was symbolized by commercial and ecological uses of land, by the Alaskan Highway gas-pipeline
project, by native Alaskans' land claims, by noncommercial whaling by native peoples, and by related issues. The
conflicts between conservationists and petroleum companies over the Trans-Alaska Pipeline from the oil-rich
North Slope on the Arctic Ocean to Valdez in the south
and beyond appear to have been only another incident in
the century-long effort to find a balance between conservation and development in this enormous land.

PHYSICAL AND HUMAN GEOGRAPHY

The land. The immense area of Alaska has a great
variety of physical characteristics. Nearly one-third of the
state lies within the Arctic Circle and has permanent frost
and treeless tundra. The southern coast and the Panhandle at sea level are fully temperate regions. In these latter
and in the adjoining Canadian areas, however, lies the   Physio-
world's largest expanse of glacial ice outside Greenland   graphic
and Antarctica. Off the extreme western end of the Seward diversity
Peninsula, Little Diomede Island, part of Alaska, lies in
the Bering Strait only 2.5 miles (four kilometres) from
Soviet-owned Big Diomede; both nations have shown a
tacit tolerance of unintentional airspace violations, which
are common in bad weather.

Relief. Alaska is composed of nine distinct environmental regions.

Much of the mainland Panhandle region, a narrow strip
of land 25 to 50 miles wide lying west and south of
the St. Elias Mountains, is composed of the Boundary
Ranges. There are several large ice fields, and the peaks
include Mt. St. Elias, from whose summit the Alaska–
Yukon border swings due north. The western extension
of this mountain chain is the Chugach Range, a giant arc
at the northernmost edge of the Gulf of Alaska. Many
remote valleys and high ridges are still unexplored, and
the relief and glaciation inhibit exploitation. The coast is
characterized by frequent and intense oceanic storm systems that have produced dense rain forests on the coastal
mountain flanks. In the valleys rivers produce devastating
annual floods.

The region of the south coastal archipelago and the Gulf
of Alaska islands includes the Alexander Archipelago in
the Panhandle region, with 11,000 islands, plus Kodiak
Island and its satellites south of Cook Inlet. These islands,
extensions of the southern region, are lower, less rugged,
and less glaciated. All receive extraordinarily heavy rain
and are affected by encircling waters warmed by the
Kuroshio Current.

The Aleutian region includes the narrow Alaska Peninsula and the 1,100-mile-long Aleutian chain that separates
the North Pacific from the Bering Sea. The chain includes
14 large islands, 55 significant but smaller ones, and
thousands of islets. The largest are Unimak, Unalaska,
and Umnak; these three also have the largest permanent
populations. On the occasionally clear summer days, active volcanoes and such glacier-covered peaks as symmet-   Shishaldin
rical Shishaldin Volcano (9,372 feet [2,857 metres]) on   Volcano
Unimak can be seen. Such magnificent views represent

the Aleutians at their scenic best. Usually, however, the weather is wet and stormy, the winds cutting, and the fog all-pervading.

A curving interior cordillera, the broad Alaska Range region connects the Aleutian Range across the southern third of mainland Alaska to the Wrangell Mountains, which abut against the vast complex of the St. Elias Mountains. The Wrangell Mountains have large active volcanoes and high valley glaciers. The flanks of this subarctic range are largely tundra-covered.

The low-lying interior-basin region between the Alaska Range in the north and the Chugach–Wrangell–St. Elias mountains to the south enjoys a relatively temperate climate. The lower valleys contain good farmlands, such as the fertile Matanuska area, and it is there that most of the people of Alaska live.

The central plains and tablelands constitute a vast region west and north of the Alaska Range; they reach as far north as the Brooks Range. The area is rolling and dissected by numerous streams tributary to the Yukon River. The plains extend from the Canadian border to Norton Sound and the Yukon Delta on the Bering Sea. It is characterized by river flats and truncated upland tablelands. A region with abundant game, it is an important nesting ground for waterfowl, including great numbers of migrating birds.

A major mountain chain north of the central plains and extending from the sea nearly to the Yukon border, the Brooks Range gradually slopes northward to a narrow linear coastal plain bordering the Arctic Ocean and westward to lower hills north of Kotzebue Sound. There are a few high Arctic glaciers, and the area is semiarid. The lower flanks and valleys are tundra-covered, with permafrost features.

The coastal lowland north of the Brooks Range, sometimes called the North Slope, is the home of great herds of caribou. The environment is truly polar, with the seacoast frozen eight months a year and the ground permanently frozen except for a thin zone of summer melting. It is treeless, though in summer grasses and Arctic-alpine flowers abound. A large navy petroleum reserve is located there, and the Prudhoe Bay oil fields are found in the east.

The islands of the Bering Sea represent a small but unique Arctic maritime environment, typified by St. Lawrence, Nunivak, and St. Matthew islands and the Pribilof group. These tundra-covered islands are surrounded by sea ice in winter and serve as protected refuges for the world's largest herds of fur-bearing seal and sea otter, as well as sea lion and walrus. A large herd of domesticated reindeer is tended by Eskimos on Nunivak Island.

Climates. The wide-ranging geographical provinces and the great physiographic relief, extending from sea level to more than 20,000 feet, provide Alaska with much climatic diversity. Summers are mild, and midwinter along the coast is often clear and dry. It is thought likely that an approximately 90-year cycle of climatic change may bring another cold interval toward the end of the 1900s. Five general climatic zones may be delineated, excluding the great mountain ranges.

Temperature and rainfall

Southern coastal and southeastern Alaska, the Gulf of Alaska islands, and the Aleutians have average temperature ranges in the summer of 40° to 60° F (4° to 16° C) and in the winter of 40° to 20° F (4° to −7° C). Rainfall varies locally from 60 to 160 inches (1,525 to 4,065 millimetres), and the Panhandle and southern islands are covered with Sitka spruce and other evergreens. The Cordova-Valdez region has the state's highest precipitation, 200 inches or more. At Valdez 200 inches of snow is not uncommon. Precipitation is less in the Aleutians, but even there about 250 rainy days occur annually.

The interior basin ranges from 45° to 75° F (7° to 24° C) in summer and 20° to −10° F (−7° to −23° C) in winter. The region is drier than the coast and only slightly colder in winter, with Anchorage receiving about 25 inches of precipitation annually. The pleasant conditions and proximity to the sea have made the area the centre of the state's population.

The islands and coast of the Bering Sea have summer temperatures of 40° to 60° F (4° to 16° C) and winter temperatures of 20° to −10° F (−7° to −23° C). Temper-

ing influences of the Pacific dissipate north of the Pribilof Islands, and Arctic sea ice often reaches this area.

The central plains and uplands range from 45° to 75° F (7° to 24° C) in the summer and −10° to −30° F (−23° to −34° C) in the winter. Average rainfall is 10 to 20 inches, though less than 10 inches is common.

The ameliorating effects of the Arctic Ocean keep temperatures of the North Slope—35° to 55° F (2° to 13° C) in the summer, −5° to −20° F (−21° to −29° C) in the winter—less severe than those of the interior plains. About five inches of precipitation nonetheless remain on the ground as snow about eight months a year. The 24-hour sunlight of summer can produce strong buildups of radiant energy, sending temperatures to 90° F (32° C).

The people. English, Russian, Spanish, and French place-names reflect early European exploration, but equally as prominent are dozens of names carried down from the pre-Western era. The name Alaska itself is derived from the Aleut *alaska* and the Eskimo *ālakshak,* both meaning "mainland."

Long before Bering's voyages the Tlingit Indians lived in the southern and southeastern coastal area; the Aleuts on the Aleutian Islands and the Alaska Peninsula; and the Eskimos on the Bering shore and the Arctic Ocean coast. The interior natives were the Tinneh Indians, whose language was Athabascan, that of the Plains Indians of the interior continent to the south. The Indian groups are presumably descendants of the earliest immigrants from Asia, perhaps more than 15,000 years ago, with the Alaskan Indians reflecting the migratory wave that reached as far as the southern extremity of South America. Eskimos and Aleuts appear to be much later immigrants, having arrived perhaps 3,000 to 8,000 years ago. Rather than going south, they remained in the islands and coastal regions of the far north. All groups are involved in the debates over public land grants.

Native population and cultures

The wave of youthful immigrants attracted from the "South 48" beginning in the 1960s suggested a faith in the burgeoning opportunities in a still-frontier environment. The discovery of oil fields and the emergence of Alaska as an international air crossroads added impetus to the influx of the 1940s and 1950s, a period of new settlement and expansion that raised the population from 70,000 to 226,-000. Prior immigration—the first wave of which occurred in the decade before World War I as an aftermath of the gold rush—was a response to Alaska's initial concentration on its mineral, fish, and timber resources. Of the current population about one-sixth are Eskimos, Aleuts, and Indians. The remaining citizenry include about 80,000 military personnel and their families, and a melting pot of mixed American, Russian, Japanese, Chinese, Filipino, and other nationalities.

In addition to the large percentage of Alaskans living in the southern interior basins around Anchorage, most of the remainder live in the Panhandle region, where Juneau is the major city and the administrative centre of the state, and in the interior plains around Fairbanks. Tiny pockets of people are scattered in small villages, the most sparsely occupied being the Arctic plains, the Bering shores, and the Aleutians. Only slightly more than 20 percent of the white population was born in Alaska. Many frontier conditions persist: a male-to-female ratio of 5 to 1 in 1910 was reduced by the late 20th century to near equality, but bars are frequently as numerous as churches.

Population distribution

The economy. The Alaskan economy is conditioned strongly by the state's frontier stage of development, but its formerly inadequate tax base for state and municipal growth ended with the development of the North Slope oil fields. High costs of labour and transportation still tend to discourage outside investment, however. The development of the state's natural resources has assisted markedly in the transition from a federal military to a private, self-supporting economic base.

Government. From 1940 to 1960 the federal government invested nearly $2,000,000,000 in the development of military bases in Alaska. Nothing else in Alaska's history has produced such long-term results, bringing thousands of residents into the territory and creating jobs and a vast array of transportation and communications facilities extending to remote corners of the state. The defense installations continue to add much to Alaska's economy.

Agriculture. More than 3,000,000 acres (1,200,000 hectares) of tillable land are available for farming, but much clearing has yet to be done. Most acreage is near Anchorage and on the Kenai Peninsula, though there is some near Fairbanks, and stock ranching is practiced on Kodiak and Unimak islands. As a result, most foods must be imported, tremendously increasing the cost of living. Closure of the Homestead Act, ending settlement of the native land claims issue, has further curtailed development of new land. In spite of a short growing season, the long hours of summer sunlight are adapted to the successful production of wheat, oats, rye, barley, potatoes, and hay, and all cool-climate vegetables.

Fishing. Fishing has been Alaska's most constant source of revenue. Fish are found mostly in waters off the southern coasts, salmon being the main product. The centre of the world's salmon-packing industry is at Ketchikan, and it flourishes also on Kodiak Island and at Bristol Bay ports in the southern Bering Sea. Fleets also bring in quantities of halibut, herring, sablefish, Dungeness crab, king crab, and shrimp. A serious threat to fish conservation and a source of continuing international friction in the North Pacific has been the unregulated incursion of Soviet and Japanese fishing vessels into Alaskan waters.

Forestry. Most of Alaska's timber resources are in the Tongass and Chugach national forests, in the Panhandle and on the southern coast, respectively. Pulp is an important industry in Ketchikan and Sitka.

Furs. Pribilof sealskins represent more than half of the state's annual fur production. Other furs, largely from controlled farms, are processed as well. A new industry in the 1960s was the production of reindeer hides from a herd on Nunivak Island that was managed by the Alaska Native Association.

Hydroelectric power. Alaska's immense waterpower reserve is virtually untapped. The largest project is at Eklutna, near Anchorage. A hydroelectric development near Juneau delivers power to the Panhandle area. In many communities diesel and coal plants produce much of the required municipal power.

Mining. Petroleum was first extracted and refined between 1917 and 1933, but the development of the Kenai oil field in 1961 made the petroleum and natural-gas industry Alaska's most important mineral production. Oil seeps were known as early as the 1880s in the North Slope region, which by the late 20th century had become a field of major economic importance to both the state and the nation. By the late 20th century Alaska ranked second only to Texas in oil production.

Alaska's gold production declined drastically from the 1940s through the 1960s because of rising labour and transportation costs. By the late 20th century only a few small operations still remained. Copper mining as a major industry ended with the closing of the Kennecott Mine in 1938, although a few new prospects elsewhere show promise. Coal has remained an important industry. An important activity is the extraction of sand, gravel, and clay to serve the construction industry.

Since 1880 many hard-rock ore minerals have been mined in Alaska, gold, copper, and silver accounting for 95 percent of this amount. Prospecting continues, with modern scientific technology and aerial exploration. The areas of maximum mineral potential lie in the Panhandle, the Chugach and Alaska ranges, and the Seward Peninsula.

Tourism. Alaska has had an upsurge of tourism. Travellers can now cover large areas by airplane and road. The influx is partly the result of the 500-passenger, 100-car ferries that operate as the Alaska Marine Highway. One ferry system connects Kodiak with mainland Seward and the Alaska Railroad; another links Cordova and Valdez.

Transportation. High costs of transportation continue to sap Alaska's economic development, largely because the major transportation links, both internal and external, are by air, which provides the fastest way to cross Alaska's great distances and formidable terrain. Two dozen airlines serve Alaska, with daily service from the "South 48" and Canada, Europe, Hawaii, and Japan. Nearly 400 airfields,

seaplane bases, and emergency strips are in use throughout the state, and few villages are without service at least by bush pilots. More than 10,000 miles of roads, most of them surfaced, are in use. The Alcan Highway and its Haines cutoff connect Alaska's internal road network to the outside and provide relatively easy access for tourists. Some road construction was so severely damaged by the 1964 earthquake that it was abandoned. In 1969 a 356-mile (570-kilometre) haul road from Fairbanks to Prudhoe Bay was completed. It connects with the existing highway system to provide a winter-only overland route from the ice-free southern ports to the Arctic Ocean.

The government-owned Alaska Railroad runs for about 500 miles (800 kilometres), linking Seward, Anchorage, and Fairbanks. The privately owned White Pass and Yukon route, a narrow-gauge railroad, links Skagway and Whitehorse. Ocean shipping connects Seattle, Vancouver, and the trans-Canada railhead of Prince Rupert to towns in the Panhandle an ' westward to Cordova, Valdez, Seward, and Kodiak. Ocean vessels also run during the ice-free midsummer months to Nome and Barrow and to the oil regions of the Arctic coast. A natural-gas pipeline, which was completed in 1961, runs between the Kenai gas fields and Anchorage. The Trans-Alaska Pipeline delivers North Slope oil to Valdez.

In the mid-1950s the Alaska Communication Cable was installed between Seattle and Alaska. Radio telephones connect all interior communities.

Administrative and social conditions. *Government.* The state constitution was adopted in 1956. The governor and secretary of state are the only executive officers and are elected by the same vote. The 40-member House of Representatives and 20-member Senate are elected for terms of two and four years, respectively. The Supreme Court has a chief justice and four associate justices. There are four district courts. A single federal district court, replacing the territorial courts, sits alternately in Juneau, Anchorage, Fairbanks, and Nome.

Public financing is through various personal income and business taxes. As a part of the Act of Admission, Congress granted Alaska certain revenues from the sale of furs and of federal lands.

State and borough governments have difficulty in providing the usual range of services because of the limited extent of the economy and a high unemployment rate. The vast area and the difficult terrain increase these problems.

Activities on behalf of the native population have turned largely on the U.S. Bureau of Indian Affairs (BIA), which assists Alaska's natives in achieving economic and social self-sufficiency. Despite a number of helpful programs, most of Alaska's natives have remained at the bottom of the economic and social ladder—suffering from unemployment, low income, and poverty. The native peoples were educated first by missionary groups, though by the time of statehood the BIA had assumed most of the responsibility for education. Funds are provided for vocational training and the development of job opportunities and for welfare, social work, and medical and health needs. The BIA also assists natives in organizing their villages under federal and state laws. Some oil revenues from native lands have been applied in self-help programs. Settlement of the native land claims in 1971 may improve their economic plight.

Education. Education is compulsory through the eighth grade or until age 16 and is administered by a state board and a commissioner of education. There are several federal schools on military bases. The University of Alaska, founded in 1917 and located at College, near Fairbanks, is the only state university, but there are community colleges in Anchorage, Juneau–Douglas, Kenai–Ketchikan, Palmer, and Sitka. Alaska Pacific University in Anchorage, Inupiat University in Barrow, Alaska Bible College in Glennallen, and Sheldon Jackson Junior College in Sitka, a two-year college for native peoples, are the only other institutions of higher learning.

Welfare and health. The elderly, dependent children, and the blind are aided by the state, and a special fund benefits sick and disabled fishermen. The state also operates a psychiatric hospital, a tuberculosis sanatorium, a youth camp, and a prison.

Transportation networks

Native welfare

Medical and health clinics and hospitals available to the general public are provided by municipal and borough governments or private agencies, or are run as church-operated facilities. Health standards have been raised markedly since 1950 through visits by U.S. Public Health Service nurses and doctors to the remote villages. The large number of airfields, the radio communications network, and the extensive use of bush pilots operating through the state make it possible for most persons, even in the remote villages, to reach medical facilities when there is serious need.

Cultural life. Alaska's past, including the arts and crafts of its native peoples, figures heavily in Alaskan culture. Juneau is the site of the state's historical library and state museum. The university has a large museum, as do other communities, including Sitka, Haines, Valdez, and Skagway. Eminent Alaskan artists have included both whites and Eskimos. Native ivory and wood carvings are well known, and the nearly lost art of totem carving has been revived in part through private and public stimulus.

Wildlife refuges and ranges abound throughout Alaska, with more than 19,000,000 acres (7,700,000 hectares) managed by the U.S. Fish and Wildlife Service. The federal Bureau of Land Management also holds about 25,000,000 acres for waterpower development.

National wilderness preserves One national park, one national historical park, and two national monuments constitute another 7,500,000 acres. Denali (formerly Mt. McKinley) National Park was established in 1917; it has a diverse abundance of wildlife, including brown and grizzly bears, caribou, and moose. Katmai National Monument (1918), on the Alaska Peninsula, includes the Valley of Ten Thousand Smokes, an area of active volcanoes that in 1912 produced one of the world's most violent eruptions. Glacier Bay National Monument (1925) features magnificent fjords, as well as glaciers that are retreating slowly. Sitka National Historical Park (1910), with a large totem pole collection, commemorates the stand of the Tlingits against early Russian settlers. The Tongass and Chugach national forests in the southeast and south central regions, respectively, are also federal public land reserves. The U.S. Department of the Interior has continued to study the need for withdrawing further regions from public domain into reserves. In 1980 a presidential bill allotted more than 104,000,000 acres from federal holdings to national parks, wildlife refuges, and wilderness areas.

The sporting industry, including guide and outfitter services and boat charters, continues to be a colourful activity. Alaska provides the nation's only significant Arctic wilderness, and much research is done in glacier, mountain, tundra, and polar oceanography fields by federal, state, and private agencies. These projects, too, bring income to the state. The University of Alaska carries out extensive research on Arctic problems through its Geophysical Institute, Institute of Marine Science, Institute of Arctic Biology, and other groups. At Barrow the U.S. Naval Arctic Research Laboratory opened in the 1940s to conduct Arctic research, including sea-ice and oceanographic studies. Since 1946 an international glaciological and environmental research and field-sciences training program has been conducted on the Juneau Icefield.

HISTORY

Explorations. As early as 1700, native peoples of Siberia had reported the existence of a huge piece of land lying **Russian pioneering** due east. An expedition appointed by the Russian tsar and led by a Danish mariner, Vitus Bering, in 1728 determined that the new land was not linked to the Russian mainland, but because of fog it failed to locate North America. On Bering's second voyage, in 1741, the spectacular peak of Mt. St. Elias (18,008 feet [5,489 metres]) was sighted, and men were sent ashore. Sea-otter furs taken back to Russia opened a rich fur commerce between Europe, Asia, and the North American Pacific Coast during the ensuing century.

Early settlement. The first European settlement was established in 1784 by Russians at Three Saints Bay, near present-day Kodiak. It served as Alaska's capital until 1806, when the Russian-American Company, organized

in 1799 under charter from the emperor Paul I, moved its headquarters to richer sea-otter grounds in the Alexander Archipelago at Sitka. The company governed Alaska until its purchase by the United States in 1867. Alaska's first governor (then termed chief manager), Aleksandr Baranov, was an aggressive administrator whose severe treatment of the native Indians and Eskimos led in 1802 to a massacre at Sitka.

A period of bitter competition among Russian, British, and American fur traders was resolved in 1824 when Russia granted equal trade rights for all. The near extinction of the sea otter and the political consequences of the Crimean War (1853–56) were factors in Russia's willingness to sell Alaska to the United States. The Russian minister made a formal proposal in 1867, and, after much public opposition, the purchase was approved by the U.S. Congress, and the U.S. flag was flown at Sitka on October 18, 1867.

Political growth. As a U.S. possession, Alaska was governed by military commanders for the War Department until 1877. During these years there was little internal development, but a salmon cannery built in 1878 was the beginning of what became the largest salmon industry in the world. In 1884 Congress established Alaska as a judicial land district, federal district courts were established, and a school system was initiated.

In 1906 the first representative to Congress, a nonvoting delegate, was elected, and in 1912 Congress established **Establishment of the territory** the Territory of Alaska, with an elected territorial legislature. Alaskans voted in favour of statehood in 1946 and adopted a constitution in 1955. Congressional approval of the Alaska statehood bill in 1958 was followed by formal entry into the Union on January 3, 1959.

Mining booms. Other significant events in Alaska's history included early gold discoveries on the Stikine River in 1861, at Juneau in 1880, and on Fortymile Creek in 1886, and later the stampede to the Atlin and Klondike placer goldfields of adjoining British Columbia and Yukon Territory in 1897–1900. Gold discoveries followed at Nome in 1898 and at Fairbanks in 1903. The gold rush made Americans aware of the economic potential of this previously neglected land. The great hard-rock mines in the Panhandle were developed, and in 1898 copper was discovered at McCarthy. Gold dredging in the Tanana River Valley was begun in 1903 and continued until 1967.

Economic growth. A dispute between the United States and Canada over the precise boundary between British Columbia and the Alaska Panhandle was decided by an Alaska Boundary Tribunal in 1903. The U.S. view that the border should lie along the crest of the Boundary Ranges was accepted. Between 1898 and 1900 a narrow-gauge railroad was built across the precipitous White Pass to link Skagway and Whitehorse in the Yukon, and shortly afterward the Cordova-to-McCarthy line was laid up the Copper River. Another milestone was the 538-mile Alaska Railroad connecting Seward with Anchorage and Fairbanks in 1923. In 1935 the government encouraged a farming program in the Matanuska Valley near Anchorage, and dairy herds and crop farming became established there and in the Tanana and Homer regions.

In 1942, during World War II, Japanese forces invaded Agattu, Attu, and Kiska islands and bombed Dutch Harbor on Unalaska. This aggression prompted the construction of large airfields as well as the Alaskan, or Alcan, Highway linking Dawson Creek, British Columbia, and Fairbanks with more than 1,500 miles (2,400 kilometres) of road. Both proved later to be of immense value in the commercial development of the state. A devastating earthquake on March 27, 1964, affected the northwestern Panhandle and the Cook Inlet areas, destroying parts of Anchorage; a tsunami wave that followed wiped out Valdez; the coast sank 32 feet (9.75 metres) at Kodiak and Seward, while a 16-foot rise destroyed the harbour at Cordova.

Oil discoveries in the Kenai Peninsula and offshore drilling in Cook Inlet in the 1950s created an industry that by the 1970s ranked first in the state's mineral production. **Discovery of oil** In the early 1960s a pulp industry began to utilize the forest resources of the Panhandle. Major paper-pulp mills were constructed at Ketchikan and Sitka, largely to serve the Japanese market. The discoveries in 1968 of petroleum on lands fronting the Arctic Ocean gave promise of relief for Alaska's economic lag, but problems of transportation across the state and to the "South 48" held up exploitation of the finds. In 1969 a group of petroleum companies paid the state nearly $1,000,000,000 in oil-land revenues, but the proposed pipeline across the eastern Brooks Range, interior plains, and southern ranges to Valdez created heated controversies among industry, government, and conservationists. In November 1973 a bill passed Congress and was signed, making possible construction of the pipeline, which began in the following year. The completed 48-inch (122-centimetre) pipeline, 789 miles (1,262 kilometres) long, came into operation on June 20, 1977.   (M.M.M.)

California

During the 1960s immigration to California was so great that it was described as giving a westward tilt to the United States. California surpassed New York as the most populous state in the nation, and its personal income is one of the highest in the world. The fluid nature of its social, economic, and political life, so much affected by the influx of people from other states, gives California the aura of a laboratory for testing new modes of living.

Californians make up the most urban population in the nation, centred mainly along the coast, with more than a third of the population in the Los Angeles and San Francisco metropolitan areas. As in most of the nation's larger states, the capital, Sacramento, is not a major population or economic centre.

California has an area of 158,693 square miles (411,013 square kilometres), exceeded only by Alaska and Texas. The state is bounded on the north by Oregon, on the east by Nevada and Arizona, on the south by the Mexican state of Baja ("lower") California, and on the west by the Pacific Ocean.

The state's physical contrasts

Since its admission to the Union in 1850 as the 31st state, California has been recognized as a land of stunning physical contrasts: from the rainy northern coast to the parched Colorado Desert of the south. The Sierra Nevada exceeds the Rocky Mountains in height. Within 85 miles (137 kilometres) of each other lie Mt. Whitney and Death Valley, respectively 14,494 and 282 feet (4,418 and 86 metres) above and below sea level, the highest and lowest points in the 48 coterminous states. Despite its urbanization, California is also the principal agricultural state of the nation, though only about 15 percent of its area is urban or cultivated. Almost half of its land is federally owned, with national parks and monuments in every part of the state devoted to irreplaceable forest, desert, mountain, and other natural resources.

PHYSICAL AND HUMAN GEOGRAPHY

The land. California offers startling contrasts of landscape and examples of physical diversity.

Coast ranges. The long coastline is mountainous, most dramatically in the Santa Lucia Range south of San Francisco, where the homes of Big Sur perch on cliffs 800 feet above the sea. Hills of lesser height flank entrances to the coast's three major natural harbours, at San Diego, San Francisco, and Eureka. Coastal mountains, made up of many indistinct chains, are from 20 to 40 miles in width and from 2,000 to 8,000 feet in height.

The mountains of California

Sierra Nevada. The eastern portions of the state, particularly in the south and extreme northeast, are occupied by sparsely settled desert, high in the north and low and increasingly hot in the south. The majestic Sierra Nevada rises to the west of this desert, extending for 430 miles. The eastern escarpment is sheer, dropping 10,000 feet within 10 miles near Owens Lake. On the west the range slopes to the Central Valley, comprising the San Joaquin and Sacramento valleys, in gradually declining foothills. From the wall that rises near volcanic Lassen Peak in the north, the Sierra Nevada extends south for 430 miles to the fringes of Los Angeles. It is 50 to 80 miles in width and 27,000 square miles in area. Aside from Mt. Whitney, 10 other peaks exceed 14,000 feet in altitude. East–west passes are few and high, some at more than 9,000 feet.

The largest lake of the Sierra Nevada and one of the loveliest in the United States is Lake Tahoe, astride the California–Nevada border at 6,229 feet (1,899 metres). A mountain-ringed Alpine lake almost 200 square miles in area, it ranks 11th in the world in average depth: the 1,200-foot line runs near shore, and the maximum depth exceeds 1,600 feet (488 metres). Elsewhere in the Sierra lie hundreds of smaller lakes, some above the timberline in regions of tumbled granite and smooth-walled canyons. There are three national parks in these highlands: Kings Canyon, Sequoia, and Yosemite—the latter rising from the purplish foothills of the Mother Lode gold country through ice-carved valleys of the Merced and Tuolumne rivers, with their waterfalls and granite domes.

Central Valley. In a north–south arc through the centre of California, the Central Valley runs for 450 miles (720 kilometres), forming a deep trough between the Coast Ranges to its west and the Sierra Nevada to its east. The valley constitutes the state's agricultural heartland. Its single opening is the delta through which the Sacramento and San Joaquin rivers drain into San Francisco Bay. The valley is sealed off at the northeast by the Cascade Range and at the northwest by the Klamath Mountains. This far north the terrain is rugged and sparsely populated, heavily timbered and wet on its coastal side and drier and barren in the higher northeast. In the south the Central Valley is closed off by the transverse ranges, notably the Tehachapi Mountains, which are regarded as a dividing wall between southern and central California.

Coastal settlement and forests. Southern California's dense settlement lies along a coastal plateau and in valleys ranging from 40 to 60 miles inland. North of the Tehachapis, where the Coast Ranges move closer to the shore, population becomes sparser along the coast. The populous coastal area around San Francisco Bay gives way to the less developed northern coast, where lumbering and fishing villages lie beside creeks and rivers flowing from the Coast Ranges. This is the area of coastal redwood forests and Redwood National Park. These trees, among the tallest in the world, may reach 300 feet (90 metres) in height, 15 to 35 feet in diameter, and 4,000 years in age. Before European settlement the redwoods covered an estimated 1,500,000 acres (607,000 hectares) of California. Most redwood forests have been cut, but 109,000 acres of redwoods are protected in state and national parks.

The redwood forests

Deserts. Temperature contrasts in the deserts are great. The Colorado Desert of southeastern California has summer temperatures of up to 130° F (54° C), almost the highest temperatures recorded on Earth, with annual rainfall averaging 3 to 4 inches (75–100 millimetres). More than 4,000 square miles of this desert lie below sea level. The 300-square-mile (775-square-kilometre) inland Salton Sea, below sea level, was created in 1905–07 when the Colorado River broke out of its channels. Northward, in the higher Mojave Desert, temperatures are somewhat less oppressive. Still relatively untouched by development, this area of more than 25,000 square miles reaches from the Tehachapi and Sierra Nevada to the Colorado River. It has some mining, several military reservations, and aviation test facilities. Farther north, the eastern desert lies from 2,000 to 7,400 feet above sea level, with temperatures ranging from 75° F (24° C) to −25° F (−32° C). It remains sparsely populated.

Climate. The climate is very different from that of the Atlantic Coast, and indeed very different from that of any part of the country save that bordering California. The climate of the entire Pacific Coast is milder and more uniform in temperature than that of the states in corresponding latitudes east of the mountains. A mean annual temperature as low as that of Halifax, Nova Scotia (latitude 44° 39′ N), is not found at any Pacific Coast point south of Sitka, Alaska (latitude 57° N), while the mean at San Diego is 6° to 7° F (4° to 4.5° C) less than that at Vicksburg, Mississippi, and Charleston, South Carolina, in roughly the same latitude. Moreover, the means of winter and summer are much nearer the yearly mean in California than in the East. This condition is not so marked as one goes inward from the coast; yet everywhere, save in the high mountains, the winters are comparatively mild.

Division of the year into two seasons—a wet one and a dry one—marks this portion of the Pacific Coast in the most decided manner, being truly characteristic neither of Baja California (Lower California) nor of the greater part of Oregon, though more so of Nevada and Arizona. And except on the coast the dryness of the air and the consequent rapidity of evaporation greatly lessen the disagreeableness of summer heat.

Summer temperatures in its low-lying southern desert compare with the highest of Africa's Sahara, and winter temperatures atop the Sierra Nevada are Arctic. Rainfall ranges from extremes of 174 inches (4,420 millimetres) in the northwest to traces in the southeastern desert, but moderate temperatures and rainfall prevail along the coast. The average annual temperature is about 65° F (18° C) in Los Angeles and 57° F (14° C) in San Francisco. Annual precipitation averages about 14 inches in Los Angeles and 21 inches in San Francisco.

The moderate climate has been a major factor in the concentration of settlement along the coast, where cool ocean breezes hold off heat, and temperatures seldom exceed 90° F (32° C) or drop to freezing. Low humidity usually prevails. Climate changes rapidly with the altitude extremes of California, and the coastal cities are only hours away from mountain skiing or desert sports.

Drainage and water resources. Water is chronically scarce in southern California and the desert regions, but excesses of rain and snowmelt cause winter flooding along the rivers of the northern coast. More than 70 inches of rain falls at Crescent City, near the Oregon border, about 370 miles north of San Francisco; and the village of Honeydew, in the redwoods of Humboldt County, has received as much as 174 inches in a year. Southern California, in contrast, has 60 percent of the state's population and about 2 percent of its water, with an average annual rainfall of 15 inches, entirely in the winter months. Complex systems of dams and aqueducts move water from north to south, but not without citizen protests. The Colorado River Aqueduct moves water from the river, at the Arizona border, across the southern California desert and mountains to serve 119 communities. The California State Water Project, launched in 1960, is the largest water-transfer system ever undertaken. It is designed to deliver water daily from the Feather River to communities as far south as the Mexican border.

The people. *Ethnic distribution.* The Indians and the Spanish settlers of the 18th and 19th centuries are of only vestigial importance in contemporary California. Spanish influence is evident in architecture and place-names. The many Californians with Spanish surnames reflect largely the 20th-century immigration from Mexico—to escape that nation's revolution (1910–17) or to find agricultural jobs. Indians are increasing in number. Of the Indian population of about 200,000, some 12,500 lived on 78 reservations totalling more than 450,000 acres.

The first settlers from the United States were mostly Mid-western farmers of Anglo-Saxon descent. With the Gold Rush a more cosmopolitan mix appeared. Ships sailed into San Francisco from the Atlantic Seaboard, Europe, and the Orient. In 1850 more than half of the Californians were in their 20s, typically male and single. Only a few hundred Chinese lived in the state in 1850, but two years later one resident out of 10 was Chinese; most performed menial labour. Irish labourers came with the railroad-construction boom during the 1860s. The Irish, French, and Italians tended to settle in San Francisco. As Los Angeles began to grow at the end of the 19th century, it lured Mexicans, Russians, and Japanese, but primarily an additional influx of Anglo-Saxons from the Midwest.

Discrimination grew strong, especially against Orientals. An alien land law intended to discourage ownership of land by Orientals was not ruled unconstitutional until 1952. At one time the testimony of Chinese in courts was declared void. Separate schools for Orientals were authorized by law until 1936, and not until 1943 was the Chinese Exclusion Act repealed by Congress. As discrimination against the Chinese flared, Japanese were encouraged to immigrate, and in 1900 alone more than 12,000 entered California. Prospering as farmers, they came to control more than

10 percent of the farmland by 1920, while comprising only 2 percent of the population. Los Angeles became the centre of the nation's Japanese community, while San Francisco's Chinatown became the nation's largest Chinese settlement.

Discrimination against the Japanese smoldered until World War II, when about 93,000 Japanese-Americans lived in the state. Some 60 percent were American-born citizens known as Nisei; most of the others were Issei, older adults who had immigrated before Congress halted their influx in 1924. Never eligible for naturalization, the Issei were classed as enemy aliens. During 1942 almost all of California's Japanese-Americans, both Nisei and Issei, were moved from their farms and homes to isolated inland camps and held under guard until 1945. At the end of the war they found their property sold for taxes or storage fees and their enclaves overrun. After years of litigation about 26,000 claimants were reimbursed for their losses at about one-third of the claimed valuation. About 85 percent of the Japanese-Americans had been farmers, but with their land gone they became gardeners or went into businesses and professions.

The third generation of Japanese-Americans, the Sansei, plays a prominent role in southern California. The Japanese-American community of Los Angeles is estimated to be in excess of 150,000. More than a third of the Chinese in the country live in California, predominantly in San Francisco. With a stream of refugees from Hong Kong and Taiwan, the population of San Francisco's Chinatown surged dramatically in recent years.

Few blacks settled in California until World War II, but between 1940 and 1980 the black population in San Francisco rose from about 5,000 to about 86,000 and in Los Angeles from 64,000 to more than 900,000. California has had among the largest gains of any state in black population, with those leaving the Southern states attracted to such cities as Los Angeles and Oakland despite high unemployment rates there.

More than half the nation's Mexican-Americans, or Chicanos, live in California. Chicano communities have experienced frequent confrontations with police and other officials, especially in Los Angeles, in protests against discrimination and unemployment. None has reached the proportion, however, of the black riots that levelled much of Los Angeles' Watts area in 1965.

Religion. Both traditional churchgoing and an interest in flamboyant mystical or evangelical sects declined steadily in California in the years following World War II. About one-third of Californians list church affiliations, a proportion far below the national average. Judaism is strongest in the Fairfax and Beverly Hills areas of the Los Angeles Basin, Roman Catholicism in San Francisco, and fundamentalist Protestant sects in those parts of southern California inhabited by migrants from the South and Southwest. Many of the conventional faiths in California resort to unconventional techniques, advertising worship services in newspapers, offering free bus service, and employing public relations counsellors.

Los Angeles is notorious for its exotic cults. Aimee Semple McPherson, whose Angelus Temple boasted 35,000 members, is the best remembered of such evangelists; she died in 1944 after an overdose of sedatives. Faith healers still are popular. Scientology, calling itself "the common people's science of life betterment," thrived in southern California under the leadership of a former film writer, L. Ron Hubbard. Zen Buddhism enjoyed popularity in San Francisco during the 1950s, with English-born Alan Watts serving as its Occidental interpreter to a following that included the "Beat Generation" of that era, forerunner of the hippies.

Demography. Native-born Americans remained the dominant factor in California's growth phenomenon in the mid-20th century. Many workers who flooded the defense industries during World War II remained as residents, along with hundreds of thousands who first visited the state as servicemen. About three-fifths of the population is concentrated south of the Tehachapi Mountains in about one-fourth of the state's area, with the greatest concentration in the small coastal area.

Long-distance transportation of water

Present-day migratory patterns

By 1970, however, net immigration was showing annual declines, and the state's growth began to level off. Later migration took place from the crowded cities of California to rural areas and cities of the Rocky Mountain states. Demographers predict continued population increases for California, which is likely to maintain its rank as the nation's most populous state, but these predictions have been scaled down from earlier years.

Economic overview

The economy. In economic terms California is more aptly compared with nations than with states. Its total personal income is surpassed only by that of the United States as a whole and of a few other industrialized nations.

Since the Gold Rush, Californians have shown considerable mastery of the state's resources, and their innovative society has created its own economic momentum. Industry has triumphed over remoteness; lacking iron and coal deposits, it has developed light industry. Financiers have been imaginative in seeking and employing capital, and many of the nation's largest banks and corporations are California-based, the latter principally involved in aerospace, electronics, computers, and oil and gas. California supplanted New York in 1965 as the leading state in the export of manufactured goods. The state is dominant in aerospace, agriculture, wine making, and the film and television industries. Despite soaring taxes, the California climate and its social freedoms continue to attract high-income immigration and technologically oriented industry.

Agriculture. The foundation of California wealth lies in agriculture. Its fields and orchards yield more than 200 agricultural products of astonishing diversity from more than 7,800,000 acres of irrigated farmland. Its major cash products are cattle, milk and cream, cotton, and grapes. California produces about one-third of the nation's canned and frozen vegetables and fruits. About half of the farm output comes from the Central Valley, which is irrigated through a labyrinth of dams, canals, and power and pumping plants.

The state's agricultural supremacy dates from 1947, when its farm output first exceeded that of any other state. Due to the growing season of nine to 10 months, Fresno, Imperial, Kern, and Tulare counties rank among the top five counties in the nation in value of farm produce. Most farms are huge, and more than two-thirds of farm income is earned by less than 15 percent of the farms. Many large landholdings have derived from federal land grants to railroads, notably the Southern Pacific, which in 1919 was the state's largest landowner. Such farms have tended to become agricultural assembly lines with absentee owners, high mechanization and productivity, and persistent labour strife. Most farms specialize in one or two crops: almonds grow north of Sacramento; cotton and forage crops, figs, and grapes near Fresno; and in the wet delta, asparagus, tomatoes, rice, safflower, and sugar beets. Such specialization has been enhanced by agricultural research at the University of California at Davis; this institution also counsels the California wine industry in its production of 80 percent of the wine consumed in the United States. The citrus industry, almost destroyed in the 1940s by a virus, ranks second to that of Florida in production of oranges.

Premium wine grapes grow in the picturesque Napa and Sonoma valleys north of San Francisco and in adjacent areas. The Imperial Valley in the Colorado Desert in the extreme south, though smaller in area than the Central Valley, has about 500,000 irrigated acres (202,000 hectares) of farmland. Other major farming areas include the Coachella Valley near Palm Springs, where dates and grapefruit grow, and the Salinas Valley and Monterey Bay region.

The farm-labour pool is made up of low-income labourers, including the many migrants and Mexican nationals crossing the border in harvest seasons. Long abused, migrant labourers organized in the late 1960s under the leadership of César Chavez and began lengthy strikes that drew nationwide support in the form of consumer boycotts. Thereafter, however, Chavez' United Farm Workers lost much of its membership to the Teamster Union.

Mining. Petroleum production grew rapidly after 1895, with oil strikes in the Los Angeles–Long Beach area. Cal-

Farming as big business

ifornia led all states in petroleum production from 1900 to 1936. Reserves now, however, are being depleted at a rapid rate, and fuel and natural gas were being imported. Petroleum continues, however, to exceed the total of all other minerals in value of production. Gold mining is now insignificant. Other production includes natural gas, cement, sand and gravel, borate, soda, and salt.

Fisheries and forestry. California is also important for commercial fish products. Largely ocean fish, the yield included albacore and bluefin tuna, mackerel, sole, squid, sardine, and salmon. Ownership of commercial forest land is almost equally divided between public agencies and private interests, with a total of almost 17,000,000 acres in use.

Industry. The aircraft plants and shipyards were supplemented after World War II by branch plants of many Eastern and Midwestern industries. Federal research-and-development funds allocated to California organizations also contributed to the dynamic postwar economy. Despite mercurial rises and declines responding to the shifting population, construction became a major industry.

All federal military services have major facilities in California, significantly affecting both the social and economic life of the state. San Diego, Long Beach, and San Francisco have home-port naval bases. Recruit training is the major role of naval and marine corps bases in San Diego, and infantry training takes place at Fort Ord near Monterey. Camp Pendleton, a marine base, encompasses the last large undeveloped area along the southern California coast. Air force activity centres around the Vandenberg base on the central coast and six other air commands, including the remote and esoteric test facilities on the Mojave Desert.

Film industry. The industry for which California has traditionally been most popularly known is that of movies and television, centred in and around Hollywood. The pioneers of the motion-picture industry found southern California extremely well suited to their needs of maximum sunshine, mild temperatures, varied terrain, and a labour market. In 1908 one of the first "story" moving pictures, *The Count of Monte Cristo,* begun in Chicago by William N. Selig, was finished in the Hollywood area by Francis Boggs.

The 1920s, '30s, and '40s saw Hollywood as the centre of a movie industry with a worldwide market. Real estate boomed, and riches were extravagantly displayed. The studios were ill prepared, however, for the revolution that they faced as a result of competition with television beginning after World War II. Grown soft from the ready demand for any product, they found that millions were staying home to see anything on television in preference to going out to the motion-picture house. At about the same time, a series of court decisions judged the major producing companies to be trusts in restraint of trade. Although new techniques such as wide screen, richer colour, new lenses, and stereophonic sound were introduced, serious losses were suffered by the industry. Major studios began to sell their film backlogs and to sell or lease their facilities to television concerns. Some studios, such as Universal, became mammoth television producers. The presence of thousands of technically skilled artisans in the Hollywood area, as well as vast amounts of equipment, made it unlikely that the entertainment industry would ever be completely uprooted.

Transportation. Transportation, primarily by automobile and airplane, is in part both the cause and the product of the restless mobility of Californians, who move their residences more often than the average American and travel considerably more both for business and pleasure. California has the greatest concentration of motor vehicles on Earth and the most extensive system of multilane divided freeways. The BART (Bay Area Rapid Transit) system, completed in the early 1970s, provides ample transportation for residents in the San Francisco Bay area.

The freeway system is so extensive that one can drive on arterials from San Diego almost 500 miles northward through Los Angeles and the Central Valley without encountering any traffic signals or stop signs. Freeway construction has continued despite growing public opposition

The freeway system

based on ugliness, pollution, and usurpation of private and community property rights. The rise of the freeway system after World War II coincided in Los Angeles with the demise of a 1,200-mile (1,920-kilometre) interurban rail system that had once been the longest such system in the nation. The lack of a conventional urban core in Los Angeles, along with low population densities, dims the prospects for any rapid-transit system.

Transport of goods in California is predominantly by trucks, and agricultural and trucking lobbies have joined those of the automobile clubs, freeway builders, and the oil industry to perpetuate freeway development. The intricate canals and waterways of the Sacramento River Delta carry some waterborne freight traffic, and there is some coastal freight traffic.

Air commuting has increased phenomenally. The air corridor connecting San Francisco, Los Angeles, and San Diego has a greater volume than that linking Washington, D.C., New York City, and Boston. Air-traffic congestion has grown critical, but not yet so dire as that of the ground traffic around airports.

Administrative and social conditions. *Government.* California is governed under a constitution framed in 1878–79, its detail reflecting the disillusionment of the period with rampant graft. Before a series of deletions began in 1966, it had grown longer than any governmental constitution except those of Louisiana and India. Reform has often been undertaken in California through constitutional amendment. Those instituted by Gov. Hiram Johnson in 1911 included provisions for voter initiative of and referendum on legislation, recall of elected officials, the direct primary, women's suffrage, and a unique system that allowed candidates to run in primaries of opposing political parties. Since 1962 constitutional revision may be made by voters without calling a convention.

State executive officers are elected for four-year terms, with members of more than 50 boards and commissions being appointed by the governor. The legislature comprises the Senate, with 40 members, and the General Assembly, with 80 members. Reapportionment in the mid-1960s gave legislative dominance to populous southern California at the expense of rural areas.

The judicial system has five levels, including the seven-member Supreme Court, district courts of appeal, and superior, municipal, and justice courts. Superior courts are the major trial courts, whereas the more numerous municipal districts hear lesser matters.

Local government is conducted through almost 4,000 agencies, including 58 counties and a few hundred incorporated cities. Under the constitution counties and cities may establish charters or accept general-law provisions and statutory laws. Cities operate under variations of mayor–council–manager control. Los Angeles and San Francisco operate under mayor–council, while San Diego and San Jose employ city managers, who assume a large share of administrative duty.

Volunteer party organizations often have usurped roles ordinarily fulfilled by the Democratic and Republican party structure. The parties are forbidden to endorse any candidate prior to the primary, but unofficial organizations do so and are often better funded and organized than the party structure. To overcome this party ineffectiveness, candidates turn to professional campaign managers to enhance their public images.

Attempts at machine politics have proven ineffectual because of voter mobility, lack of party entrenchment, and the prime role of civil service in bestowing jobs. The vastness of the state and the political cleavages between the liberal north and the conservative south make it difficult for one party to sweep statewide offices, even with majority registration. Before abolition of cross-filing in 1959, candidates of one party sometimes avoided facing general elections by sweeping the primary elections of both parties. Traditional party alignments seem less significant to many Californians, and crossovers are common despite heavy Democratic pluralities in registration.

Finances. In 1978 voters approved Proposition 13, which mandated a 57 percent reduction in property taxes. Property taxes continue to provide the chief source of local revenue, however. Rising income, sales, and gasoline taxes support state expenditures dominated by highway building, education, and welfare costs.

Education. California is oriented toward tax-supported public education. The two-year junior or community college was introduced in California in 1907, and there are now about 100 such colleges. Nineteen four-year state colleges and the nine-campus University of California system complete the public higher-education structure. The University Extension system exists in locations throughout the state. Less than 10 percent of California schoolchildren and a slightly higher percentage of college-age students attend private schools.

A landmark in California higher education was achieved in 1960 with a master plan that attempted to avoid overlapping roles in the complex system of public colleges and universities. In general the top one-third of high school graduates is eligible to enroll at one of the 14 university campuses, which retain supervision over doctoral degrees. Four-year state colleges also draw from among the top one-third of high school graduates. High school graduates from the lower two-thirds of their classes attend two-year colleges and often are able to transfer at the end of that period to one of the four-year campuses.

University of California campuses have been developed at Berkeley, Los Angeles, Davis, Riverside, Santa Barbara, San Francisco, Irvine, Santa Cruz, and San Diego. The campuses at Santa Cruz and San Diego were established on variations of the Oxford University system of numerous small independent colleges sharing limited central facilities or services. The original campus at Berkeley was founded in 1868 and has remained one of the most prestigious academic communities in the nation.

Health and welfare. California long has been considered a liberal state in the extent of its health and welfare statutes. Its mental health programs have been expanded. State funds are dispersed through four major systems: aid to families with dependent children, aid to the totally disabled, aid to the blind, and old-age security.

Cultural life. It is too soon to speak of any cultural tradition rooted in California. As a state it has harboured—and given birth to—a notable procession of creative people in all the arts, yet much of their work cannot be associated with the region.

California's culture has not yet taken form. It is marked by widespread public involvement with the arts and enthusiasm for cultural trappings as symbols of achievement, often in the form of lavish expenditures to erect galleries, museums, and concert halls. There is an antipathy toward traditional culture among some segments of the population.

Early writers associated with California came from outside the state: Bret Harte, born in New York; Mark Twain, in Missouri; Joaquin Miller, in Indiana; and Ambrose Bierce, in Ohio. But the San Francisco of the Gold Rush days provided an eager audience for their writing, as it did for theatre and music. There followed a line of writers who came as close to establishing a regional tradition as have artists in any medium. Jack London, chronicler of men amidst frontier violence, was born in San Francisco. Frank Norris and Upton Sinclair, who opposed the social ills of their times in a foreshadowing of the later work of John Steinbeck and, to a lesser degree, of William Saroyan, were California-born but left the state in the 1940s. The naturalist John Muir, the progenitor of a school of environmental writers that became prominent in the 1960s and 1970s, extolled the state's natural wonders. Robinson Jeffers, who lived in California from 1914 until his death in 1962, was the state's most renowned poet. An influx of literary figures as screenwriters into Hollywood in the 1930s and 1940s established little in the way of regional cultural tradition, and the California milieu became instead a favourite target of satire in such novels as Nathanael West's *The Day of the Locust* and Evelyn Waugh's *The Loved One,* and in works by F. Scott Fitzgerald, Budd Schulberg, Raymond Chandler, and Ross Macdonald.

San Francisco has produced such painters as David Park, Elmer Bischoff, and Richard Diebenkorn. Los Angeles seems more successful as a marketplace for art, with a thriving colony of galleries along La Cienega Boulevard comparable to Manhattan's Madison Avenue. The numerous wealthy art collectors in southern California are prominent in funding the Los Angeles County Museum of Art, which opened in 1965. The Music Center of Los Angeles County is a concert and theatre complex that was constructed during the 1960s by private contributions.

The California Arts Commission was given the task in 1963 of establishing "the paramount position of this state in the nation and in the world as a cultural center." Its contribution was hobbled by a low budget, however, and it has been limited largely to inventorying the arts in California and to providing token sponsorships. Tax-supported state institutions, most prominently the University of California and its extension program, are active in presenting dance recitals, plays and films, concerts, and lectures. The Theater Group of the University of California at Los Angeles is one of the most innovative in the nation. Experimental theatre in San Francisco has bloomed from time to time, especially with the Actor's Workshop between 1952 and 1965, after which the company moved to New York City. An often distinguished mixture of light and avant-garde theatre is offered throughout the year at several theatres, including the community-sponsored Old Globe Theater in San Diego. Amateur theatrical groups are everywhere, as are community orchestras, chamber-music societies, and weekend artists. Carmel, Big Sur, and Sausalito have harboured communities of workers in diverse arts. The symphony orchestras of San Francisco and Los Angeles have achieved international recognition, as has the San Francisco Opera Company. San Diego supports a fine symphony orchestra, opera, and ballet company through voluntary donations to a combined-arts council.

Hollywood still is responsible for the bulk of the national movie and television output, and as such it remains an international symbol of glamour. An increasing number of national magazines and periodicals emanate from editorial offices that are located in California. Metropolitan California newspapers have decreased in number, but their total circulation has grown, led by the *Los Angeles Times,* with the largest number of readers in the state.

HISTORY

Exploration.   Modern California derives from the discovery of gold at Sutter's Mill in 1848, just nine days before Mexico signed the Treaty of Guadalupe Hidalgo, ceding to the United States a vast area of the Southwest that included all of present-day California. The region had received little attention from Europeans for more than three centuries after its first sighting in 1542 by the Spanish navigator Juan Rodríguez Cabrillo. The merchant Sebastián Vizcaíno sailed the southern California coast in 1602, naming San Diego, Santa Catalina Island, Santa Barbara, and Monterey Bay. Despite these early explorations, California was left to its Indian population—estimated at 130,000 when Spanish explorers reached California in 1542.

Settlement.   Pressure for settlement came from missionaries anxious to convert the Indians and from the intrusion of Russian and British traders, primarily in search of sea-otter pelts. In 1769 the Spanish viceroy dispatched land and sea expeditions from Baja California, and the Franciscan friar Junípero Serra established the first mission at San Diego. Gaspar de Portolá set up a military outpost in 1770 at Monterey. Colonization began after 1773 with the opening of an overland supply route across the southwestern deserts.

The 21 missions established by Serra and his successors were the strongest factors in developing California. While attempting to Christianize the Indians, the padres taught them farming and crafts. With the labour of the Indians, the padres irrigated vast ranches and traded hides, tallow, wine, brandy, olive oil, grain, and leatherwork for the manufactured goods brought by Yankee trading vessels around Cape Horn.

U.S. colonization and acquisition.   Secularization of the missions was sought by Spanish–Mexican settlers known as Californios when Mexico became independent of Spain

in 1821. Between 1833 and 1840 the mission ranches were parcelled out to political favourites by the Mexican government. The padres withdrew, and the Indians, decimated by European diseases and driven off the mission lands, were cruelly exploited and diminished. In 1841 the first wagon train of settlers left Missouri for California. The colony grew slowly, but in 1846 the Northwest became a part of the United States, and settlers at Sonoma proclaimed an independent California republic. In May the United States declared war on Mexico, and in July the U.S. flag was raised at Monterey. Only minor skirmishes occurred before the Californios surrendered to troops under John C. Frémont near Los Angeles in January 1847. Within a year the form of the present-day United States was nearly cast.

The Gold Rush.   Early in 1848 James Wilson Marshall, a carpenter from New Jersey, picked up nuggets of gold from the American River at the site of a sawmill he was building near Coloma. By August the hillsides above the river were strewn with the tents and wood huts of the first 4,000 miners. From the East, prospectors sailed around Cape Horn or risked disease in hiking across the Isthmus of Panama. The hardiest took the 2,000-mile overland route, where cholera proved a greater killer than Indians. About 40,000 came to San Francisco by sea in 1849. Some 6,000 wagons, carrying about 40,000 more, moved west that year over the California Trail. Few of the prospectors struck it rich. The work was hard, prices were high, and living conditions were primitive. The wiser emigrants became farmers and storekeepers.

Gold hastened statehood in 1850 (as a part of the Compromise of 1850); and, though the Gold Rush peaked in 1852, the momentum of settlement did not subside. Nearly $2,000,000,000 in gold was taken from the earth before mining became almost totally dormant.

The Civil War and after.   The slavery question was not settled for California in the Compromise of 1850. Until the American Civil War the division between the Whig and Democratic parties, whose organization in California preceded statehood, was based essentially on slavery. The followers of Sen. William M. Gwin, one of the first two U.S. senators to represent the state, hoped to divide California into two states and hand the southern over to slavery; on the eve of the Civil War they considered the scheme of a Pacific Coast Republic. The state remained loyal to the North, however, when war came. The later 1850s have been characterized as a period of "moral, political and financial night." National politics were put first—to the complete neglect of needed reform of excessive taxation, financial extravagance, ignorant legislation, and corruption.

In state gubernatorial elections after the Civil War, the Democrats won in 1867, 1875, 1882, 1886, and 1894; the Republicans were successful in all the other contests. Features of political life and of legislation after 1876 were a strong labour agitation, the struggle for the exclusion of the Chinese, the struggle for the control of hydraulic mining, irrigation, and the advancement of the fruit interests through state aid. Labour conditions were peculiar in the decade following 1870. Mining, war times, and the building of the Central Pacific Railroad (later the Southern Pacific) had up to then inflated prices and prosperity. Then there came a slump. The dismissal by the Central Pacific lines (principally in 1869–70) of about 15,000 Chinese, who flocked to San Francisco, augmented discontent and the reaction from flush times. Labour unions became strong and demonstrative. This is called the "sand-lots agitation" from the favourite meeting place (in San Francisco) of the agitators.

The outcome of these years was the constitution of 1879, and the exclusion of Chinese by national law. Congress reenacted exclusion legislation in 1902. All authorities agree that the Chinese in early years were often abused in the mining country and their rights most unjustly neglected by the law and its officers. The exclusion had much to do with making the huge single-crop ranches unprofitable and with leading to their replacement by small farms and varied crops.

In 1906–07 there was throughout the state a remarkable

Establishment of the Spanish missions

anti-Japanese agitation, centring in San Francisco and affecting international relations and national politics. The Japanese question was brought to an acute situation in 1913 by the Webb Alien Land Law, which prevented Japanese from holding real estate. The question was then taken up diplomatically between the United States and Japan; and Japan, in a "Gentlemen's Agreement," agreed to the exclusion of further immigration of its citizens.

The 20th century. The period 1910–25 was one of reform, designed largely to secure greater popular control of government. The state's subsequent history broadly paralleled that of the nation as a whole.

The Great Depression of the 1930s, although generally less pronounced than in most other states, created great social unrest, accentuated by the influx of migrant labourers, chiefly from the Dust Bowl area of the Great Plains. A result was the rise of various radical socioeconomic nostrums—such as the "end poverty in California" (EPIC) plan, a comprehensive social welfare scheme presented by Upton Sinclair, and various old-age pension plans—and the rapid growth of the Democratic Party, long of minor importance in the state. Except for four years (1939–43), California was led by Republican governors during the first half of the 20th century, including among others Earl Warren, who resigned the governorship in 1953 to become chief justice of the United States, the first Californian to hold that office.

In 1958, however, a Democratic victory installed Edmund Brown as governor. With the Republican defeat, which reflected a national trend, Democrats not only won gubernatorial and U.S. senatorial races but for the first time in the 20th century received a majority of seats in both houses of the state legislature. In 1959 the Democrats ended the California system of cross-filing, whereby a candidate could file for both parties in primary elections— a system that had most often been of profit to the Republicans. Governor Brown was reelected in 1962. In the 1966 elections, Republicans made a comeback, carrying into the governor's office Ronald Reagan, a former actor who in 1981 became president of the United States. From the 1960s on, the state seesawed between the Democrats and Republicans.

Meanwhile, the economy and population advanced. The tide of immigration first moved toward southern California around 1900, spurred by citrus, oil, and some wariness of San Francisco after the earthquake and fire of 1906. Land booms came and went. Agriculture in inland valleys and industry in the cities boomed. During World War II aircraft plants and shipyards expanded, and in the 1950s research and educational facilities burgeoned as the movement of people to the West Coast came to include an unusual share of scientists and academicians. The state has nearly doubled in population every 20 years since 1860. San Francisco remains the financial and corporate centre, while the southern one-third of the state exceeds the rest in population.   (N.Mo./Ed.)

Hawaii

A group of volcanic islands in the central Pacific Ocean, Hawaii was characterized by Mark Twain as "the loveliest fleet of islands that lies anchored in any ocean." It became, in 1959, the 50th state of the United States.

Hawaii is economically vigorous, with diversified agriculture and manufacturing; strategically important to the global defense system of the United States; a Pacific Basin transportation and cultural centre, often called "the Crossroads of the Pacific"; and a major tourist mecca. Hawaiian activities of national and international importance include research and development in oceanography, geophysics, astronautics, satellite communications, and biomedicine.

The capital city of Honolulu, on the island of Oahu, is 2,397 miles (3,857 kilometres) from San Francisco to the east, and 5,293 miles from Manila, in the Philippines, to the west.

PHYSICAL AND HUMAN GEOGRAPHY

The land. *Relief.* The land area of the state of Hawaii actually consists of the tops of a chain of submerged vol-

canic mountains that form eight major islands and 124 small islets, stretching in a 1,500-mile crescent from Kure Island in the west to the island of Hawaii in the east, with a combined land area of 6,425 square miles (16,641 square kilometres). With the exception of Midway, a U.S. naval reservation near the western end of the archipelago, the leeward coral atolls and central lava islets, forming a total of only 3¼ square miles, are in the Hawaiian Islands National Wildlife Refuge. The eight major islands at the eastern end of the chain are, from west to east, Niihau, Kauai, Oahu, Molokai, Lanai, Kahoolawe, Maui, and Hawaii. The volcanic activity that molded the island landscapes has since become dormant, with the exception of the volcanoes of Mauna Loa and Kilauea on the easternmost and largest island, Hawaii, where spectacular eruptions and lava flows take place from time to time. The highest Hawaiian mountains are Mauna Kea and Mauna Loa, reaching 13,796 feet (4,205 metres) and 13,677 feet (4,169 metres) above sea level, respectively.

Islands comprising Hawaii

There is little erosion in the geologically young areas, where the terrain is comparatively domelike and the volcanic craters are clearly defined. In the contrasting older areas, during the glacial age the mountains were shaped and eroded by ice and by the action of sea, rain, and wind. Their aspects thus include sharp and craggy silhouettes; abrupt, literally grooved cliffs pocked with caves; deep valleys; smoothed saddle areas; and coastal plains. The powerful Pacific surf, churning and crashing against the fringing coral shelves and the lava shorelines, has carried minute shells onto the shore and reduced coral and large shells to sand, creating the state's famous expanses of beach.

Volcanic ash, gravel, rotted vegetation, crumbling lava, and windblown sand and dust all help to make up the alluvial, residual, and organic soils found in various depths and densities in valley floors, the regions between mountain ranges, and along the shores. Oxidation of iron causes a ubiquitous bright-red soil and rock strata. The iron content is, however, insufficient for smelting, and there are no coal or oil deposits.

Soils and drainage patterns

Because the topography is generally abruptly descending or sloping, there are few surface collecting basins or lakes. Excess rainfall seeps through porous mountain areas to collect in subterranean chambers and layers retained by less permeable lava and ash beds, or it is prevented by underlying salt water from seeping to the sea. The resultant artesian water supply is tapped for use in irrigation and also for human consumption.

Where rainwater has converged in high mountain pockets and then plunged for great distances, it has dug deep pools at the foot of the falls, overflowed, and cut streams downward in its pursuit to the sea. Some streams and small rivers meander and wind through wide valleys to lowlands and debouch concisely into the ocean or disperse themselves into swampland.

Climate. Although Hawaii lies in the earth's tropical zone, its climate is temperate. The Pacific anticyclone, a large atmospheric eddy located to the northeast of Hawaii, is the generator of prevailing trade winds from the northeast, which are cooled by their journey over the ocean. The ocean is, in effect, a natural air-conditioner for the islands.

The average temperature in Honolulu is 72° F (22° C) in the coolest month and 78° F (26° C) in the warmest, with extremes from 57° F (14° C) to 88° F (31° C) having been recorded there. The average water temperatures off Waikiki Beach, near Honolulu, range from 75° F (24° C) in late February to 79° F (26° C) in late September. Mountainous regions are considerably cooler, especially during the winter months, when there can be frost; temperatures as low as 14° F (−10° C) have been recorded on the summit of Haleakala, on Maui, and winter snows frequently blanket the crests of Mauna Kea and Mauna Loa, on the island of Hawaii.

Rainfall variations throughout the state are dramatic. Mt. Waialeale, on the island of Kauai, is the wettest spot in the world, with an annual average rainfall of 460 inches (11,684 millimetres) over a 32-year period, the highest ever recorded in the world. The driest area in the islands

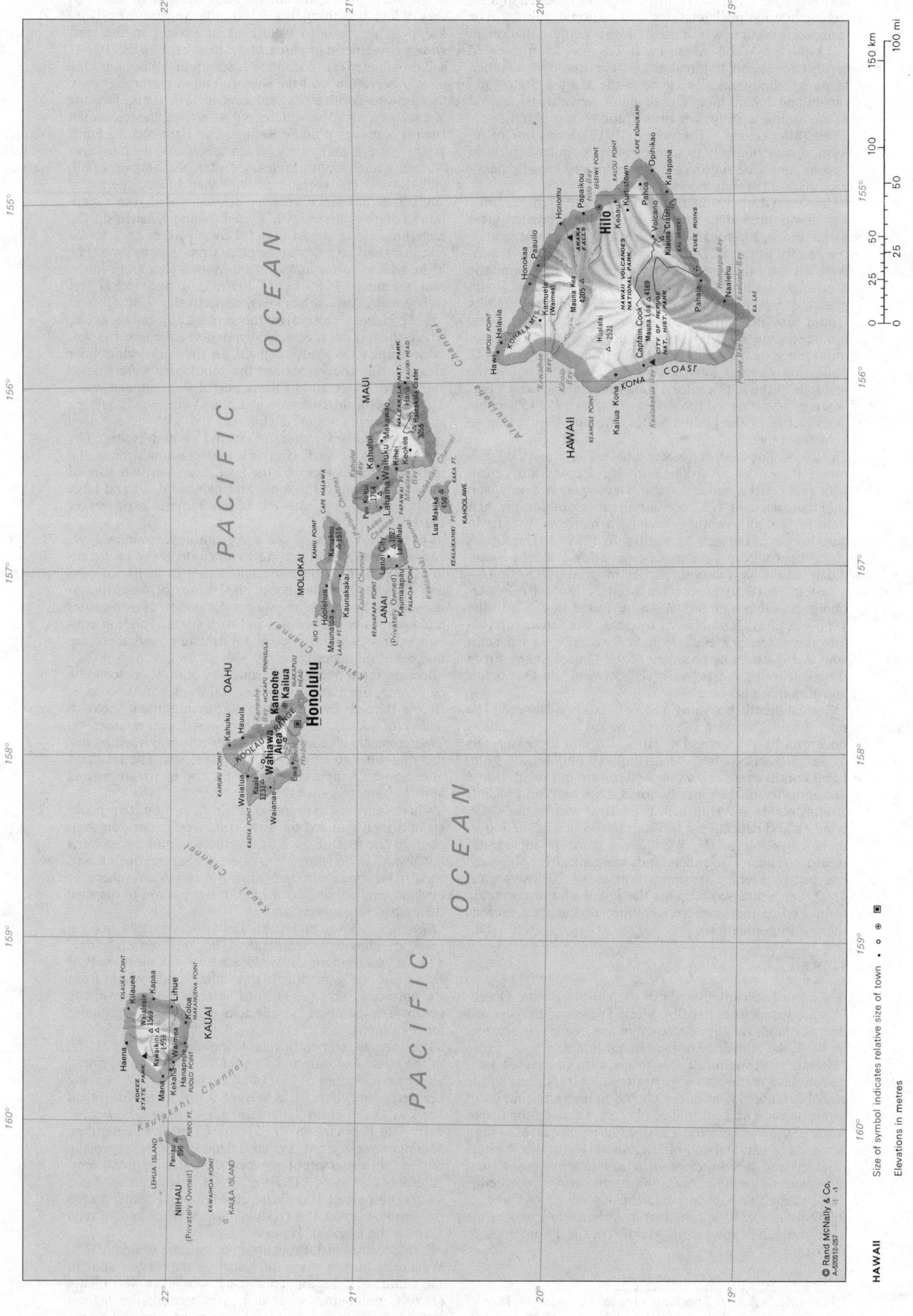

HAWAII

Size of symbol indicates relative size of town

Elevations in metres

is at Puako, on the island of Hawaii, where the average annual rainfall is only 9½ inches (240 millimetres). The average yearly rainfall in Honolulu is 24 inches, and, in Hilo, it is 134 inches.

As moisture-laden air is carried over the islands, most frequently by the trade winds, it is apt to condense, form cap clouds, and dissipate against the shores and mountains of the windward coasts, which are therefore more lush in foliage than the leeward coasts.

Plant and animal life. The seeds of endemic plant species were carried to Hawaii by birds, riding winds, or moving in currents and tides, bringing about extensive forestation, shrubbery, and grasslands, where soil and precipitation were favourable. Since the first Polynesian settlement, a tremendous variety of food and ornamental plant life from many parts of the world has been introduced. Food plants grown commercially or in backyards for home consumption include sugarcane, pineapples, papayas, bananas, mangoes, guavas, lichee, coconuts, avocados, breadfruit, macadamia nuts, limes, passion fruit, taros, and tamarinds. Nearly all varieties of common garden vegetables are raised in the islands, and flowers abound all year.

The effects of isolation on natural life
Endemic birds, long isolated from others of their kind, have taken on certain characteristics of their own. These include the nene (Hawaiian goose), the Hawaiian stilt, and a variety of small forest birds. Some species have become extremely rare, but as the result of an increased environmental awareness, great strides have been taken to preclude their extinction. Seabirds nest in profusion on the western islands of the archipelago and to a far lesser extent among the major eastern islands. There has been considerable importation of birdlife. Quantities of mynas, sparrows, cardinals, and doves live in the trees in both urban and country areas. Every fall the small golden plover make an awe-inspiring, nonstop 3,000-mile (4,800-kilometre) flight from Alaska to Hawaii, where they spend the winter, together with ducks from Alaska, Canada, and the northwestern United States.

Most forms of common domestic animals and poultry are raised on farms and beef ranches, and a large percentage of Hawaiian households keep dogs and cats as pets. The wild-animal life includes mongooses, rats, frogs, toads, and, in the more remote regions of some of the ranches, deer, sheep, pigs, and goats. The Hawaiian insect population is multitudinous, and marine life abounds in Hawaiian waters.

Settlement patterns. Agricultural and fishing activities bring about extensive and scattered rural settlement, ranging from tiny fishing villages far off the main roads, scant clusters of small houses in isolated valleys, solitary farm and ranch houses, to large coastal and upland villages and plantation and ranch towns.

The older houses in the smaller villages are largely single-family, raised, frame structures, with corrugated-iron roofs. Plants of native origin skirt the foundations of houses, and the yards are informally planted with fruit and flower trees. In all but the very small villages, there are a school, markets, post office, firehouse, and at least one church. The day's activities traditionally begin early and end early, following the sun. The life-style of the rural people is simpler and less sophisticated than that of the urban populations, who are exposed to constant and varied activity, and the country dwellers tend to retain more of the speech patterns and customs of their distinctive ethnic backgrounds.

Village and urban life
During the 1950s and 1960s there was a building boom in Hawaii of such magnitude that the configuration of entire towns was altered. The most graphic example of this was in the city of Honolulu, where construction of 20- and 30-story buildings gave the city, once sprawling and low, a thrusting, multilevelled skyline. On Oahu, erstwhile vacation or agricultural towns have become expansive residential areas for commuters to Honolulu and Pearl Harbor.

Urban settlement once consisted almost entirely of single-family dwellings, individual business houses and shops, small markets, and three- or four-story hotels. With the increase of residents and tourists since 1950, however,

Hawaiian towns and cities are building more and more high-rise apartment houses, hotels, and business establishments, with the traditional individual shopkeepers becoming absorbed into the complexes of shopping centres and supermarkets.

The concept of the planned city later gained momentum and has been developed in areas that were previously open spaces or given over to agriculture. Throughout the state there are large hotels and resort complexes, creating communities that are not without colour in themselves.

Construction is still thriving, and the physical aspect of Hawaii, as influenced by human settlement, continues to undergo considerable change.

The people. Most anthropologists believe that the original settlement of Hawaii was by Polynesians who migrated northeast from the Marquesas Islands perhaps as early as AD 400, to be followed by a second wave of immigration that sailed from Tahiti during the 9th or 10th century. Once they had established themselves in Hawaii, the Hawaiians had no further need to obtain supplies from their old homeland and underwent centuries of isolation. Although there are still rather close resemblances in linguistics, physical characteristics, and general customs and life-styles between the Hawaiians and their Polynesian relatives, a degree of racial individuality evolved.

The original Hawaiians were a brown-skinned people of large stature, highly skilled in fishing and farming, who adhered to an extremely rigid and strict system of laws that was set down by their chiefs and their priests. They worshipped and feared a group of gods not unlike, in character and power, the ancient Greek deities of Mount Olympus.

The first recorded contact between the Hawaiians and Europeans took place in 1778, when Capt. James Cook came upon the islands. During the ensuing four decades the influence of further European and U.S. explorers, adventurers, trappers, and whalers stopping for fresh supplies at Hawaiian islands was to have a profound effect.

Impact of the cultural mix
Contact with people of different cultures, and with a belief in only one god rather than fear of swift punishment from vengeful gods, eventually brought about a spiritual revolution among the Hawaiians. In a series of defiant acts led by members of the royal family, the basic beliefs of the Hawaiian religion were undermined, the priests were overthrown, and by 1820—the year when the first group of Christian missionaries arrived from the United States—Hawaiians were experiencing something of a religious void. Loss of faith in the old gods, intense interest and curiosity about the ways of the people of the United States and Europe, avid interest in learning to read and write, and a desire for spiritual identity brought about a swift adoption of Christianity on the part of the Hawaiians. By the mid-19th century the Hawaiian kingdom was largely a Christian nation.

It has been estimated that the population of the Hawaiian Islands at the time of Captain Cook's discovery was approximately 300,000. Virtually disease free, this population had no natural immunity to the diseases introduced from both West and East and fell easy prey to venereal disease, cholera, measles, bubonic plague, and leprosy, all of which contributed to the decimation of the native peoples.

In 1853 the population of the Hawaiian kingdom consisted of 70,036 native Hawaiians, 983 part-Hawaiians, 1,687 Caucasians from Europe and the United States, 364 Chinese, five Filipinos, and 62 people of other racial extractions, making a total of 73,137 people.

The racial and religious makeup of Hawaii has undergone some quite dramatic change since that time. Thousands of settlers from the Pacific Basin—primarily from China, Japan, Korea, and the Philippines—as well as immigrants from Europe and from the U.S. mainland carried their own customs, languages, and religions into the Hawaiian way of life. The descendants of these later settlers now far outnumber the descendants of the original Hawaiians. There is also a continuous influx and outflow of military and naval personnel and their dependents, connected closely to the continuing U.S. presence in the Pacific.

The majority of the state's residents live on the island of Oahu, with almost two-fifths in Honolulu proper and another two-fifths in outlying districts. Because there are vast areas of Oahu devoted to agriculture and forest reserves, the majority of the population actually resides in high-density clusters. There are no legally incorporated towns or cities in the state.

Linguistically, Hawaii is English speaking. Although Hawaiian, formerly a major means of communication, is all but extinct, it remains in place-names and street names and in songs, and the local residents liberally sprinkle their speech with words and phrases from the traditional language. A pidgin English, differing from standard English in both word usage and inflection, is spoken throughout the state in varying degrees of richness, while some of the older immigrants from Japan and China continue to speak their native tongues. As Filipinos continue to move to Hawaii, their language, too, is frequently heard in the state.

The economy.   Hawaii ranks relatively low among the states in terms of personal income, farm products sold, value of manufacturing shipments, retail sales, and bank deposits.

A major economic problem in Hawaii is the high cost of living due in large part to Hawaii's insularity and dependency on imports. Transportation costs are included in the purchase prices of nearly all consumer goods. As the population increases, housing is difficult to acquire, and when acquired, by purchase or lease, it is disproportionately expensive when compared with housing costs in many of the mainland states. Building materials, most of which are imported, are expensive. Residential land is limited and highly priced, since much of the property throughout the islands, notably on Oahu, is owned by corporations and trusts. Efforts have been made through legislation to remedy this situation. Carefully planned housing, located in communities in which, in addition to high-rise, high-density dwellings, the single-family home gives way to cluster housing around recreational areas, has become one solution to the shortages and expense associated with urban housing.

Since Hawaii has no important mineral deposits, its only natural resources are its temperate climate, water supply, soil, vegetation, and surrounding ocean and rock, gravel, sand, and earth quarried for use in construction and landscaping. Electric power is supplied throughout the state by a small number of power companies operating oil-powered steam and diesel generators. Several military installations and some private institutions generate their own power, and a small amount of hydroelectric power is generated on the islands of Hawaii and Kauai.

Tourism.   Tourism is Hawaii's largest industry. Expansion has been particularly rapid since World War II, and the growth has resulted in part from continued improvements in transportation and the stimulus provided by the state government and local businesses. The majority of visitors come from the U.S. mainland, Canada, Australia, and countries of the Far East and South Pacific. More than 60 percent of the hotel units are on Oahu, chiefly in Waikiki and the adjacent Ala Moana area. Visitors have access to a wide range of recreational and cultural facilities, such as golf courses, tennis courts, parks, surfing sites, beaches, restaurants, theatres, musical attractions, and sporting events. Tourism has stimulated the state's economy and has helped Hawaii to become the centre of the international market of the Pacific Basin. Capital investment by U.S. mainland and foreign companies has increased tremendously.

Agriculture.   Although the second largest source of income in Hawaii is the federal government, primarily through defense expenditures, agriculture remains the basis of the local economy. Hawaii is the largest sugarcane-producing state in the nation. Sugarcane and pineapple plantations maintain high yields through the use of sophisticated irrigation systems and planting and harvesting machinery. There has been a slow but steady growth of diversified agriculture, including grain sorghum, corn (maize), flowers, and nursery products. Livestock, poultry, and dairy production, together with some lumbering and commercial fishing, are other important sources of income. Approximately half of the commercial fish catch is aku (skipjack tuna).

Industry.   Hawaii has several hundred companies engaged in diversified manufacturing. Heavy-manufacturing plants, using raw materials for the most part imported from the U.S. mainland, include an oil refinery that produces a variety of petroleum products and chemical compounds, a steel mill manufacturing reinforcing bars, two cement plants, a concrete-pipe plant, and an aluminum-extrusion plant. Heavy manufacturing activity is confined mainly to the island of Oahu. Most building lumber is imported from the mainland. Some 80 garment manufacturers, largely situated in Honolulu, produce printed fabrics and apparel bright with colours and designs inspired by the local flora and marketed locally, nationally, and abroad.

A wide variety of Hawaii-grown foodstuffs are bottled, canned, jarred, or packaged in the state, sold in local grocery stores, and exported to the mainland. These include Oriental and Hawaiian food specialties, such as tropical fruit juices, jams and jellies, candies, coffee, macadamia nuts, and various alcoholic beverages.

Trade.   Exports to foreign countries are largely in the form of sugar, canned pineapple, garments, flowers, and canned fish. Major foreign imports are fuel, vehicles, food, and clothing.

Management of the economy.   More than half of the land in the state is owned by private individuals or corporations, although the state itself, holding more than one-third of the land, is the largest single landowner. State and county governments hire a larger number of employees at a higher wage scale than do most other states. Hawaii is the regional headquarters of the federal government, which owns 7 percent of the land.

State taxes are collected under a centralized tax system. The chief sources of the state's revenue are a general excise tax, corporate income taxes, and real property tax.

Major Hawaiian industries are unionized, as are many of the service and construction industries. The largest union in the state, and one with a turbulent history, is the International Longshoremen's and Warehousemen's Union.

Transportation.   Ocean-surface transportation is Hawaii's lifeline. Consumer goods and raw materials are brought to Hawaii, and Hawaiian goods are exported in freighters, tankers, container ships, and barge "sea trains." Gigantic high-speed cranes load and unload the containers.

Honolulu Harbor, with its extensive docks, warehouses, and storage sheds, is the centre of Hawaiian shipping. A large percentage of the cargo ships ply between Hawaii and California ports, a few between Hawaii and the East Coast of the United States via the Panama Canal, and others from western Pacific ports. Around-the-world passenger ships carry visitors through Honolulu, as do passenger liners from the West Coast of the United States. Tug-pulled barges and small freighters transport goods from Honolulu to the outer islands, returning with agricultural crops and livestock. There is no interisland steamer service.

The majority of voyagers to and from Hawaii travel by air, as do nearly all interisland passengers. The Honolulu International Airport, on Oahu; General Lyman Field at Hilo, on Hawaii; and the Kahului Airport, on Maui, are the state's major civilian airports capable of serving large-jet traffic. There are several smaller airports among the islands and a number of small private airfields. Military authorities maintain a number of airports throughout the state.

Throughout the state there are more than 4,000 miles (6,400 kilometres) of roads, most of them following the lowland contours, circling the islands along or near the shorelines, and only crossing islands between mountain ranges. In addition, there are many spectacular mountain roads zigzagging down cliff faces. On Oahu two tunnels bring traffic from the heads of two valleys behind Honolulu through the Koolau Mountain Range and out into the windward, or northeastern, side of the island. Hawaiian roads range from narrow country tracks to an eight-lane freeway, which crosses the city of Honolulu.

Administrative and social conditions.   *Government.* Hawaii is governed by a state constitution that was originally adopted in 1950; it was amended in 1959, at the time of admission to statehood, and further amended at the constitutional convention of 1968. The governor and lieutenant governor, elected for concurrent terms of four years, must be members of the same political party. The only other elected members in the 17 departments of the executive branch are the members of the Board of Education. Hawaii's bicameral legislature consists of the Senate, with 25 elected representatives from eight senatorial districts, serving four-year terms, and the House of Representatives, consisting of 51 members elected from 27 districts for two-year terms. The state judicial system consists of the Supreme Court, four circuit courts, and 27 district courts, as well as a family court, a land court, and a tax appeal court.

Hawaii's governmental structure is unique among the states in that it is limited to two levels of government: the state and the four counties, each with a mayor and a council. There are no municipal governments.

Primary elections are held in October and general elections in November. Party competition is intense in Hawaiian politics. During the first half of the century, the Republican Party remained dominant, but party success at the polls began to seesaw somewhat after this, and the Democratic Party has captured a majority of House, Senate, and council seats on several occasions.

Military. Hawaii holds a strategic position in the defense system of the United States. Pearl Harbor, a vast shipyard for the repair and overhaul of U.S. fleet units, is the home port for many U.S. naval ships. It serves as a training base for submarine and antisubmarine warfare forces. The headquarters of the commander in chief, Pacific, and of the Fleet Marine Force, Pacific, are at Camp H.M. Smith. The major army, Marine Corps, and air force bases are Schofield Barracks, Ft. Shafter, Ft. De Russy, Hickam and Wheeler air force bases, and the Kaneohe Marine Corps Air Station. In addition to these, there are military installations, camps, and airfields of varying sizes throughout the state. More than 100,000 U.S. military personnel and their dependents are stationed in or have their home port in Hawaii, and their presence has an important influence on the local economy and social life.

Social issues. Hawaii has a unique reputation as a place in which the population, stemming from many different roots, has created a harmonious society; a degree of social division takes place, following the patterns of ethnical and cultural backgrounds, but the groups tend to appreciate and enjoy the variations of other such groups. As in other parts of the United States, poverty and wealth coexist, sometimes in startling contrast.

Education. Hawaii's school system provides educational facilities from nursery school through the Ph.D. level. Hawaii college-level institutions include the University of Hawaii, five smaller private colleges, and a state-established system of six two-year community colleges. Private business, technical, and specialized schools provide even further educational facilities and opportunities.

A unique educational institution is the Center for Cultural and Technical Interchange Between East and West, commonly referred to as the East-West Center. A project of the federal government, it is housed at the Manoa campus of the University of Hawaii and annually provides specialized and advanced academic programs and technological training to students from the United States and from countries in Asia and the Pacific.

Health and welfare. A state department of health maintains hospitals, health centres, clinics, care centres, and nursing services. The Hawaiian Homes Commission controls the transfer of land use to qualified persons of Hawaiian racial origin for homesteading.

Cultural life. Hawaii's cultural milieu, the result of overlay after overlay of varied cultural groups, is rich in its admixture. The force of the original culture remains highly evident in the islands, although the Hawaiian race has become diminished and diluted over the years through death and intermarriage.

Vestiges of U.S. culture in the New England tradition remain, as do the traditional cultures of the early Asian and Filipino immigrants. With the advent of fifth-, sixth-, and seventh-generation descendants of Asian and Caucasian immigrants and the massive influx of Americans from all parts of the country, the cultural overlays have melded to form a uniquely Hawaiian culture.

Interest in the arts is high, and many distinguished artists, photographers, and theatrical and musical performers have been native residents. Appreciation of classical, modern, and experimental art forms is manifest in attendance figures at galleries, concerts, legitimate-theatre performances, and museums. Many ethnic groups preserve the traditions of their ancestors or combine or modify music and dance forms.

An assortment of cultural and scientific institutions in Hawaii provides a wide variety of opportunity for the appreciation and understanding of the fine arts, history, traditions, and sciences. The Bernice P. Bishop Museum, founded in 1889 in Honolulu, is a research centre and museum dedicated to the study, preservation, and display of the history, sciences, and cultures of the Pacific and its people. The Honolulu Academy of Arts, often called the most beautiful museum in the world, houses a splendid collection of Western art, including works by the late 19th- and early 20th-century masters of modern art: Monet, van Gogh, Matisse, Gauguin, and Picasso. Its collection of Oriental art is also one of the finest in the Western world. The University of Hawaii's art, music, and drama departments contribute to the expanding cultural life of Hawaii, while the state has several legitimate-theatre organizations, professional and amateur. The Honolulu Symphony Orchestra performs concerts in Honolulu and on the other major islands. Its home is the Honolulu International Center, a municipal theatre–concert-hall–arena complex, where touring opera companies and ballet troupes and musical artists of international renown also perform. Honolulu's Chamber Music Society gives a concert series each year. The active art, music, and drama departments in Hawaiian schools and colleges and the innumerable students receiving private instruction in the arts also contribute toward the maintenance and growth of Hawaii's cultural life.

HISTORY

The first inhabitants of Hawaii probably reached the islands by canoe about AD 400, and for nine centuries such contacts continued with other parts of Polynesia, notably Tahiti. Powerful classes of chiefs and priests emerged and established themselves, as did internecine conflicts, similar to the feudal struggles in Europe, with complicated land rights contributing to the disputes. The early Hawaiians lacked a written language, and their culture was entirely oral and rich in myth, legend, and practical knowledge, especially of animals and plant life. The material life of the islands was hampered by the lack of metal, pottery, or beasts of burden, but there was great skill in the use of wood, shell, stone, and bone, and the huge double and outrigger canoes were technical marvels. Navigational methods were well developed, and there was an elaborate calendar. Athletic contests encouraged warrior skills.

European discovery. Capt. James Cook, the English explorer and navigator, is regarded as having made the first European discovery of Hawaii, first landing at Waimea, Kauai Island, on January 20, 1778. Upon his return in the following year, he was killed during an affray with a number of Hawaiians at Kealakekua Bay.

The initial discovery by Cook was followed by a period of intermittent contact with the West during which the remarkable Kamehameha I, using European military technology and weapons, emerged as an outstanding Hawaiian leader, seizing and consolidating control over most of the island group. For 85 years thereafter, monarchs ruled over the Hawaiian kingdom. In the early 19th century the U.S. whaling fleet took up the practice of wintering in Hawaii, and the islands were visited with mounting frequency by explorers, traders, and adventurers. Capt. George Vancouver introduced livestock to the island in 1792. In 1820 the first of 15 companies of New England missionaries arrived. By the middle of the century there were frame houses, horsedrawn vehicles, schools, churches, taverns, and mercantile establishments. A written language had been introduced, and European and U.S. skills and religious beliefs—Protestant and Roman Catholic—had been imported. Hawaiian culture was irrevocably changed.

Establishment of U.S. dominance. Political manoeu-

Margin notes:

Executive, legislative, and judiciary

Higher education

Uniqueness of Hawaii's cultural heritage

The performing arts

The early Hawaiians

vring between U.S., British, and French consuls and naval forces brought about uncertainty in the governmental situation. The foundations of constitutional government were nevertheless laid down with the promulgation, by Kamehameha III, of the Declaration of Rights (June 7, 1839), the Edict of Toleration (June 17, 1839), and a written constitution (October 8, 1840). These progressive steps—made under missionary influence—were followed by formal avowals of Hawaiian independence by the United States, Great Britain, and France. The ambitions of these powers continued unabated, however, with a succession of overt and covert diplomatic moves, culminating in the signing of a reciprocity treaty with the United States in 1875. Hawaiian kings continued to attempt to preserve their peoples' culture and society, but the turbulent second half of the 19th century was marked by the joint annexation resolution of Congress in 1898, the final stamp of U.S. domination. This status was confirmed by the establishment of a territory on June 14, 1900.

The period until 1940 was distinguished by a rapid growth in population, the development of a modern economy based on the production of sugar and pineapples for consumption on the U.S. mainland, and the growth of transport and military links. Movements for statehood, based in part on Hawaii's obligation to pay U.S. taxes without having corresponding legislative representation, began to emerge. The Japanese attack on Pearl Harbor, on December 7, 1941, precipitated not only Hawaii but the United States as a whole into World War II, and the islands were beset by an upsurge of military activity and a sometimes controversial curtailment of civil liberties. The post-1945 period was marked by further economic consolidation and a long constitutional path to statehood, a status finally achieved on March 18, 1959.   (J.P.M.S.)

Oregon

An overview of the state

Admitted to the Union as the 33rd state in 1859, Oregon comprises a region of startling physical diversity, from the moist rain forests, mountains, and fertile valleys of its western third to the naturally arid and climatically harsh eastern deserts. Mountains, plateaus, plains, and valleys of different geological ages and materials are arrayed in countless combinations, including such natural wonders as the Columbia River Gorge, Oregon Caves National Monument, Crater Lake National Park, the majestic snow-covered peaks of the Cascade Range, and the "moon country" of central Oregon.

Historically, Oregon comprised all of the U.S. Pacific Northwest, a region that includes the states of Oregon, Washington, and Idaho, and a small portion of Montana west of the Rocky Mountains. To the north of the state's 96,981 square miles (251,181 square kilometres) of land and inland water lies Washington, from which Oregon receives the waters of the Columbia River; to the east, Idaho, much of its border formed by the winding Snake River and its Hells Canyon, the deepest gorge on the North American continent; to the south, Nevada and California, with which Oregon shares its mountain and desert systems; and, to the west, the Pacific Ocean, which produces the moderate climate of Oregon's western lands.

The forested mountains of western and northeastern Oregon have supplied the traditional core of the state's economy. Its many forest-product plants produce more than one-fourth of the nation's softwood lumber, more than one-half of its soft plywood, and large quantities of hardboard, pulp, and paper. In addition, the multipurpose development of the Columbia River System provides huge quantities of electricity, water for irrigation and industry, shipping channels, and water for recreation. The heartland of Oregon, however, is the Willamette Valley, containing the major cities of Portland, Eugene, and Salem (the capital) and a rich and diversified agriculture.

PHYSICAL AND HUMAN GEOGRAPHY

The land. The great diversity of landforms and climates in Oregon is reflected in the different patterns of human settlement and varying bases of economic activity that can be seen throughout the state.

Relief. Oregon has nine major landform regions: the Coast Range, the Klamath Mountains, the Willamette Valley, the Cascade Range, the North Central Oregon Plateau, the Blue–Wallowa Mountains, the High Lava Plains, the Basin and Range Province, and the Malheur–Owyhee Upland.

The forest-blanketed Coast Range, which borders the Pacific Ocean from the Coquille River northward, is the lowest of Oregon's main mountain systems. Its elevations are usually below 2,000 feet, but Marys Peak, southwest of Corvallis, reaches 4,097 feet (1,249 metres), the highest point in the range.

Elevations

The Klamath Mountains, which extend from California, lie south of the Coast Range and west of the Cascades. Of ancient resistant rocks, they have had a complicated geologic history. They are higher and more rugged than the Coast Range and lack the north–south orientation. The Rogue River, bisecting the area, provides the major drainage. Thick forests grow on these mountains, which also contain the state's richest mineral deposits.

The Willamette Valley is essentially an alluvial plain produced by burying stream-modified lowland with enormous quantities of sediments brought down by tributary streams from the bordering mountains. The low, hilly areas in the central and northern portions are composed of resistant rocks. This valley contains the prime land of the state, and its soils support intensive agriculture.

The Cascade Range in Oregon forms a broad lava plateau. The wider western section is deeply eroded by numerous streams fed by heavy precipitation. The eastern section, less dissected, is crowned with a chain of volcanic peaks. Mt. Hood, reaching 11,239 feet (3,428 metres) above sea level is the highest peak in Oregon, and Mt. Jefferson, rising to 10,499 feet (3,200 metres), is the second highest. The western slopes of the Cascades are mantled with Douglas fir forests; on the upper slopes western hemlock and true firs become dominant. The forests of the drier east side are largely of ponderosa pine.

In the North Central Oregon Plateau, a portion of the Columbia River Basin, streams are entrenched and provide some bold relief. The areas lying between the streams are broad, little-dissected, smoothly rolling surfaces that provide the land for Oregon's large wheat ranches.

The Blue–Wallowa Mountains comprise two separate highland masses in the northeastern part of the state. The name Blue Mountains refers to the eroded plateaus and ranges extending westward from the agriculturally important La Grande and Baker valleys. Basins and valleys, headquarters for large cattle ranches, are scattered through the Blue Mountains. The Wallowa Mountains, east of the La Grande and Baker valleys and near the Idaho border, contain the highest elevations in northeastern Oregon. They were heavily glaciated and display some of the most spectacular scenery to be found in the western United States.

The area of the flat High Lava Plains, or High Desert, is located south of the Blue Mountains and eastward from the Cascade Range. The smoothness of the surface is broken by cinder cones, buttes, and craters, and other features include immaturity of erosion and localized interior drainage. Low precipitation, short and erratic growing seasons, and the absence of soil in many places result in an arid landscape of skimpy vegetation, with the details of the surface features commonly visible.

The Basin and Range Province to the south, which merges with the High Lava Plains, is a geologically young, high lava plain interrupted by mountains and fault troughs. Small volcanoes are numerous in the western portion, where an extensive sheet of pumice greatly modifies surface runoff, vegetation, and land use. Irrigation agriculture is practiced in the Upper Klamath Lake area, and hay is grown with irrigation in a number of other basins and valleys, but most of this region is used by range livestock.

The Malheur–Owyhee Upland of southeastern Oregon is generally a high, warped plateau. It contains older lava and has been more eroded than the High Lava Plains. The major drainage system, the Owyhee River, has incised several notable canyons in an area locally called the "Rimrock Country." Along the Snake River in the east central portion of the state there is highly productive irrigation agriculture, but most of this region is livestock-grazing country.

Climate. Oregon's climates range from equable, mild, marine conditions on the coast to continental conditions of dryness and extreme temperature in the interior. Location with respect to the ocean, prevailing wind and storm paths, and topography and elevation are the principal controls. Six climatic areas can be recognized.

The narrow coastal area and the bordering mountain slopes are marine influenced. Temperatures are mild and equable: July temperatures average 55° to 60° F (13° to 16° C), January temperatures about 40° F (4° C). Summers are relatively dry, but receive only half of the possible sunshine; other seasons are cloudy and wet. Annual precipitation ranges from 60 to 120 inches (1,500 to 3,000 millimetres) or more.

The lowlands of the Willamette, Umpqua, and Middle Rogue rivers are warmer in summer, slightly cooler in winter, and have less precipitation than the coast. July averages 67° to 72° F (19° to 22° C), with 65 to 70 percent of the possible sunshine; January averages about 40° F (4° C). The rainy season extends from October through April, with precipitation averaging 35 to 40 inches, except in the Middle Rogue Valley, where 20 to 25 inches are common.

The Cascade Range has copious winter precipitation, including phenomenal snow depth, and short, dry, sunny summers. Above 3,000 feet, January average temperatures are below 32° F (0° C). Snow begins to fall in October and remains through April, with large patches persisting until July. The higher peaks support snowfields and small glaciers throughout the year. July average temperatures range from 50° to 60° F (10° to 16° C) depending on elevation.

The North Central Oregon Plateau, stretching from northern Wasco County through northern Umatilla County, is sufficiently elevated and exposed to receive 10 to 20 inches of precipitation annually. Distribution is fairly even, but the majority of the rainy days occur in winter. Summers are sunny, with July temperatures averaging 70° to 75° F (21° to 24° C). The brisk winters have considerable sunny weather, and January temperatures average 31° to 33° F (−1° to 1° C). The plateau area of central and southeastern Oregon has climatic characteristics similar to the north central plateau except for somewhat less precipitation and lower temperatures at higher elevations.

The Blue–Wallowa Mountains have a climate that varies with location. The intermontane basins and valleys are similar to the north central plateau, with colder winters, while the higher, exposed elevations receive comparatively heavy precipitation, much of it in the form of snow during winter.

Plant and animal life. The semiarid plateau has a covering of western juniper, sage, and salt grasses. Forests cover 30,000,000 acres (12,141,000 hectares) in the mountain and coastal areas. On the eastern slopes of the Cascades occur great stands of ponderosa pine in association with ground coverings of bitter brush, green manzanita, and herbaceous plants. The western slopes of the Cascade, Klamath, and Coast ranges are heavily forested with stands of Douglas fir. Mature forests of Douglas fir have thick understories of vine maple, dogwood, huckleberry, and other plants and admit intrusions of other tree growths such as hemlock, spruce, cedar, and varieties of pine and fir. Immature or second growth stands of Douglas fir crowd out both undercover and intrusions. In cleared areas of the damp coastal region are found alder and noncommercial deciduous growth. In the alpine zones of the mountains, larch, mountain hemlock, and alpine firs occur in association, and mountain mahogany is found in the Blue Mountains.

Oregon's animal life is related to its climatic zones. Deer and elk flourish in less populated parts; antelope are found in the eastern high plateau, and bear and fox in the mountain foothills. The lakes are breeding grounds for waterfowl and resting places for many different kinds of migratory birds.

Settlement patterns. At least five major patterns of land use emerge from the tangle of Oregon's natural land-scapes and climates. The forested mountains—the Coast Range, the Cascades, the Klamath, and the Blue–Wallowas—show relatively little evidence of human habitation or modification except for the harvest pattern of clear-cutting in the Douglas fir region, the logging and forest-management roads, and scattered roadside homesites at lower elevations. Most loggers—few in number because of technological efficiency—live in the valley towns.

The western valleys, dominated by the Willamette, are Oregon's main centres of population, industry, and transportation. Most persons live close to well-populated centres. The nearly 1,300 small sawmills that in 1947 were located in valley towns or up tributary valleys into the forested mountains had, by the late 20th century, dwindled to about 30 large, integrated operations.

In the rolling, sparsely populated wheat country of north central Oregon, ranches commonly exceed 1,500 acres (600 hectares) in the eastern portion and double that size to the west, where wheat-fallow rotation is practiced. In regions of natural erosion alternate bands of crop and fallow occur. Farmsteads are widely separated, and owners often live in towns.

The growth of natural feed in open range country is relatively poor, and cattle scatter over enormous areas; seldom do more than a few cluster. Appurtenances of the area include fences and occasional watering places with metal tanks. Ranchsteads are few and located at great distances from one another, and ranchers travel in four-wheel-drive pickup trucks.

Most of the eastern Oregon towns, except Pendleton, lie in the area of irrigated agriculture, on the eastern slopes of the Cascades or near the Idaho border. Farming is highly mechanized.

The people. Oregonians are predominantly U.S.-born, with less than 4 percent foreign-born, mainly older persons who emigrated from the Scandinavian countries, Finland, and Canada. Roman Catholics form the largest single religious denomination in Oregon, but more than three-quarters of the church members are of the Protestant faiths. Methodists, Baptists, Presbyterians, Disciples of Christ, and Lutherans are the major Protestant groups.

The people are unevenly distributed, the great majority living west of the crest of the Cascade Range in the Willamette Valley. Approximately two-thirds of all Oregonians live in the three Standard Metropolitan Statistical Areas of the state, Portland, Eugene, and Salem. Portland, near the confluence of the Willamette and Columbia rivers and the largest city in the state, is a leading West Coast port and the major commercial, industrial, service, and cultural centre of the state. Eugene and Salem, the second and third largest cities, respectively, are important for trade and processing. Salem, the state capital, is among the nation's leading food-processing centres. The major cities outside the Willamette Valley are Medford, in the Rogue Valley; Klamath Falls, in south central Oregon; and Pendleton, in the north central plateau.

The economy. Traditionally, Oregon has had a resource-oriented economy, strongly dependent upon its forests and farms. In recent years diversification has occurred as various new industries have been established and trade and service activities have grown.

Industry. Forest-products manufacturing ranks as Oregon's leading industry. About one-half the land area of the state is forested. Public agencies control about 60 percent of Oregon's commercial forest, and private owners the remaining 40 percent. Another 5,600,000 additional acres of forest are reserved for recreation and watershed use.

The forest industry began as a producer of lumber: since 1938 Oregon has been the leading state in softwood lumber. In recent years the products have been changing radically, and by late 20th century only 40 percent of the forest income was from lumber. More than one-third of the logs harvested went into plywood, which accounts for about one-third of the value of forest products. Pulp and paper plants and hardboard and particle-board plants contribute most of the remainder.

The development of sources of electricity, the availability of natural gas via pipeline, abundant water, and the growth of population are the assets upon which new in-

(marginal notes:)
Climatic variation

Man's uses of the land

Rural and urban Oregon

Forestry as the economic base

dustries have been based. The metals-related group of industries—including primary metals, fabricated metals, electrical and other machinery, and transportation equipment—has been the pacesetter. The greatest concentration of metals-related industries is in the Portland metropolitan area, but an aluminum smelter is located at The Dalles, and Albany has metal-processing plants.

Agriculture and fishing. The agricultural land base of Oregon includes both cropland and pastures and rangeland. Livestock products contribute more than one-third of the total commodity value, led by cattle and calves; dairy and poultry products are also significant. Wheat is the leading crop, with vegetables and fruits as other major crops.

Chinook, silver, chum, pink salmon, and shellfish are the most valuable fishery products. Other fish include flounder, tuna, ocean perch, and rockfish.

Mining. In mining, sand and gravel make up the bulk of the value. Quarrying occurs in every county, but the greatest quantities are taken near the growing urban areas. The only nickel mine in the nation is located near Riddle. Studies have shown that the state likely has additional extractable reserves.

Transportation. Oregon had almost 44,000 miles (71,-000 kilometres) of highways and roads under the jurisdiction of the state, the federal government, and counties and municipalities. In addition, some 80,000 miles of forest development roads, national park roads, and military and Indian reservation roads are controlled by federal agencies and various local governments. About 5,000 miles of railroads provide north–south and east–west routes. The largest airport is Portland International Airport; other significant commercial airfields are at Eugene, Medford, Pendleton, Klamath Falls, and Redmond.

Waterways and shipping

Throughout the state's history water transportation has been important to Oregon. Six of the port districts are located on the Columbia above the head of deep navigation, where barge traffic is composed principally of grain and petroleum downstream and cement and structural steel upstream. Portland, open to oceangoing vessels, is by far the most important port. The other districts stretch along the Oregon coast and up the Columbia on the deep-draft channel. Astoria, Newport, and Coos Bay, in addition to Portland, have regular shipments to and from foreign countries.

Administrative and social conditions. *Government.* Oregon has been in the vanguard of several innovative movements in American government collectively known as the "Oregon System." In 1902 the concepts of initiative and referendum were introduced, by which voters are able to initiate and vote upon statutes or constitutional revisions; these were supplemented in 1908 by the system of recall, under which the removal of elected officials can be initiated by the voters. The state was also one of the earliest to impose a state income tax, which it did in 1923.

The "Oregon System": initiative, referendum, and recall

State government in Oregon follows the pattern of most states, though the governor probably has more power than in many. Limited to two four-year terms within any 12-year period, the governor supervises the state budget, agency heads, boards, and commissions, and coordinates their activities, initiates future planning, and is the focus of federal–state interaction. The governor may also veto individual items in appropriation bills.

Legislative power is shared by the people of Oregon, through the system of initiative and referendum, and their elected legislators. The legislature comprises the Senate, with 30 members serving for four-year terms, and the House of Representatives, with 60 members serving for two-year terms.

The court system is headed by the seven-justice Supreme Court, which has general administrative authority over all other courts. The justices, elected for six-year terms, elect one of their members as chief justice.

Oregon gives its towns and cities home rule; *i.e.,* the right to choose their own form of government. Most cities with populations of more than 5,000 have the council–manager form of government, whereas smaller cities usually are governed by a city council and a mayor. Portland is governed by four commissioners and a mayor.

In 1958 home rule was extended to counties. In most counties a county judge and two commissioners or a board of three commissioners exercise the powers of government. These officials usually are elected for terms of three years.

Finances. Oregon's biennial budget consists of segments supported by General Fund and Other Fund revenues. The General Fund is derived from personal and corporate income taxes; excise, inheritance, and insurance taxes; and liquor sales. Other Fund revenue comes from federal grants, use taxes, trust funds, licenses, and the sale of services and commodities.

Health, education, public welfare, corrective institutions, legislative and judicial functions, and general government administrative functions are supported out of the General Fund. Activities substantially supported by the Other Fund include transportation programs, employee-protection programs, regulatory activities such as public utilities, banking, and corporations, and some natural resources functions. In 1971 the legislature passed a far-reaching program intended to deal with the growing problem of air and water pollution.

Republicans have dominated Oregon's politics through much of the state's history, although with post-World War II industrial and population growth, Democrats have come to outnumber Republicans in registration. An unusual number of Oregonians have made their mark in the U.S. Congress by their independent stances, perhaps a reflection of frontier attitudes.

Social issues. Although crime and related problems have increased, Oregon has been far less beleagured than many other states by issues related to such social ills as deteriorating inner cities and inadequate tax bases to pay for rising costs in education, welfare, and health care. Racial problems have been few, and only Portland, since World War II, has had a significant black community.

Education. French Prairie, modern Wheatland, was the site of Oregon's first school, in 1834; 15 years later the first free public school system was created by the territorial legislature. In 1951 the legislature established a board of education, appointed by the governor, and an elected superintendent of public instruction.

Opportunities for education after high school are provided by 13 community colleges, a state system of higher education comprised of three universities, three regional colleges, two specialized schools, and some 20 independent colleges. The community colleges (operating under state law and guidelines established by the state's board of education) are administered by lay boards, locally tax supported and especially responsive to local needs in their curricula.

Reed College in Portland is a private liberal arts institution with a relatively short (founded 1911) but notable history. A high proportion of its graduates take advanced degrees elsewhere. Willamette University (1842) in Salem and Lewis and Clark College (1867) in Portland both offer similar liberal arts curricula.

Cultural life. As a relatively young region of the United States, and one in which the imprints of humans are scarcely visible over vast stretches of land, Oregon has not developed a cultural identity equivalent to those of the longer settled or more heavily populated regions. Its people, however, no less in the sparsely settled areas of the east than in the Willamette Valley centres, take full part in the increasingly homogeneous character of American life. Portland has three large auditoriums and a coliseum. Theatrical and musical groups are found in all of the cities and larger towns, and the Oregon Shakespearean Festival in Ashland draws thousands of viewers each summer to its productions. University and college communities have public offerings in the arts and other cultural activities.

The cultural milieu

In addition to sporting events, both spectator and participatory, Oregon has a number of attractions related to its history and its location. These include the Pendleton Round-Up, which attracts participants from across the West and spectators from around the Northwest. Albany's World Championship Timber Carnival, which takes place each July 4, features logger events, carnivals, and a parade. Portland's Rose Festival in early June is perhaps the best known of the state's communal celebrations.

The Multnomah County Library, in Portland, was the first to serve the public on a large scale; it began membership service in 1864 and free service in 1902. The Oregon State Library in Salem maintains a general reference service and loan collection for use by the public either directly or through local libraries.

The Oregon Historical Center in Portland and the Horner Museum at Oregon State University own large collections of items of pioneer days in the Oregon Country. The Oregon Museum of Science and Industry in Portland features demonstrations of science at work in Oregon industries. The Portland Art Museum features Northwest Indian art and pre-Columbian Mexican art in its collection. The Murray Warner Collection of Oriental Art at the University of Oregon has one of the largest Asian collections in the United States.

HISTORY

The Indian cultures of Oregon

When the first Europeans arrived in the Oregon Country—a region vaguely defined at the time but roughly comparable to the present Pacific Northwest—about 125 Indian tribes with a population estimated at 100,000 to 180,000 lived in and around the area. In what became the state of Oregon, the leading tribes were the salmon-eating Chinook along the lower Columbia River; the Tillamook, Yamel, Molala, Clackamus, and Multnomah in the northwest; the Santiam and Coos in the southwest; the Cayuse, Northern Paiute, Umatilla, Nez Percé, and Bannock in the dry lands east of the Cascade Range and in the Blue–Wallowa Mountains; and the Klamath and Modoc in the south central area. Their mode of life resulted in a relatively small population: they had no form of agriculture and no domesticated animals, other than the dog; they depended entirely upon the natural fauna and flora of the land and water; and they utilized crude implements for gathering, hunting, and fishing. The tribes along the Columbia River, known as the Canoe Indians, fashioned excellent canoes from logs.

The explorers. The first Europeans to see the Oregon coast were Spanish sailors searching for a northwest passage to facilitate trade with the Orient. In 1579 the English buccaneer Francis Drake, in quest of Spanish loot and a northwest passage in his "Golden Hind," anchored in an inlet north of the Golden Gate and with a brass plate "took possession" of the country for Queen Elizabeth I. Until the third quarter of the 18th century, when the Spanish renewed exploration along the coast, the Oregon Country remained unexplored. In 1778 the English sea captain James Cook visited Oregon. His men bought beaver and other skins, which they sold for huge profits in China.

In 1787 Boston merchants sent two ships to the Oregon Country under Captains Robert Gray and John Kendrick. On his second voyage Gray entered the harbour that bears his name (in Washington), and in May 1792 he sailed over the bar of the Columbia River and named it after his ship, the "Columbia." This was the first U.S. claim to the Pacific Northwest by right of discovery.

The Northwest was also approached by land. Two English fur companies, the Hudson's Bay Company and the North West Company, raced across the continent to open routes to the Pacific; the Americans were not far behind. Meriwether Lewis and William Clark reached the mouth of the Columbia in 1805, strengthening the U.S. claim to the region.

John Jacob Astor, at the head of the Pacific Fur Company, began white settlement of the Oregon Country with the establishment of a trading post at Astoria in 1811. In 1824 the Hudson's Bay Company established Ft. Vancouver, and Dr. John McLoughlin was appointed to head this company's far-flung operations. For the next 22 years he was the dominating figure in the region.

Permanent settlement. Beginning in 1830, thousands of people from the Middle West migrated to the Pacific Northwest. Missionaries played a role in settlement. In 1834 the Methodists, headed by Jason Lee, established the first permanent settlement in the Willamette Valley. The migrations that carved the deep wagon wheel ruts still visible in the Oregon Trail began in the early 1840s. These settlers pressed for a practical answer to the unde-

termined ownership of the Oregon Country. After 1838 U.S. claims and rights to the region were constantly before Congress. Settlers in the Willamette Valley made known their desire to become part of the United States. In 1843 representatives met at Champoeg to organize a provisional government; a set of laws patterned after those of Iowa was accepted. By 1844 the British government had concluded that the Columbia River boundary line would have to be abandoned, and the Hudson's Bay Company moved its chief Northwest depot to Ft. Victoria. In spite of the "Fifty-four Forty or Fight" slogan of the presidential campaign of 1844, the 49th parallel was accepted by both nations as the boundary, and the Oregon Country was added to the United States in 1846.

Disputes over ownership

The influx of population led to political agitation, and in 1853 the Washington Territory was given independent status; the Idaho Territory gained similar status in 1863.

Statehood and growth. By 1883, following several conflicts with whites, most of the Indians of Oregon were on reservations. The same year a railroad linking Oregon with the rest of the nation was begun, which vastly improved the opportunity for economic growth. Agriculture and forestry were especially stimulated, and by the turn of the 20th century two-thirds of the people of Oregon lived in rural areas. During the 20th century, however, the cities have grown rapidly, and by the late 20th century more than two-thirds of the people were living in urban areas. Since 1940 there has been substantial diversification of the economy and a significant increase in the number of people emigrating to Oregon from other states.

(R.M.Hi./Ed.)

Washington

Admitted in 1889 as the 42nd member state of the United States, Washington lies at the northwestern corner of the country. It is bounded by the Canadian province of British Columbia on the north, by Idaho on the east, by Oregon on the south, and by the Pacific Ocean on the west. Its location in relation to Canada and the Pacific, its role as the point of departure and supply for growing Alaska, and its considerable foreign commerce give the state an unusually outward-looking posture. Washington cities have "sister cities" in Japan; the state regularly sends trade missions to countries of the Pacific; the value of its exports is the highest per capita in the nation; and professional and trade associations commonly include members from Canadian provinces.

Although Washington, with 68,192 square miles (176,-616 square kilometres), is smaller in area than its fellow states of the Pacific Northwest, Oregon and Idaho, it is the largest in population. The majority of the population live in the metropolitan areas of Seattle–Everett, Tacoma, the state capital of Olympia, and Bremerton, all of which are located along the shores of Puget Sound.

Washington shares with Oregon the many anomalies of terrain and climate produced in large part by the high Cascade Range. This range divides the state roughly into a western one-third that is heavily influenced by the Pacific and has some of the highest rainfalls in the United States and an eastern two-thirds that contains large desert areas in the rain shadow of the Cascades. Western Washington has industries that use the forests and sea, as well as substantial manufacturing, while eastern Washington is largely agricultural, growing wheat and raising livestock and having vast irrigation projects that bring moisture to the soils, fruit, and vegetables.

PHYSICAL AND HUMAN GEOGRAPHY

The land. *Relief.* Washington has seven distinct geographical regions. In the northwest the Olympic Peninsula, bordering the Pacific south of the Strait of Juan de Fuca, is marked by the wild Olympic Mountains reaching 7,954 feet (2,424 metres). Rainfall in the region is extreme, varying from more than 140 inches (3,560 millimetres) a year along the coast to only 16 inches in the northeast. Densely wooded rain forests extend along the western slopes.

To the south, another region, the Willapa Hills, runs along the coast from Grays Harbor to the Columbia River.

Diversities of terrain and climate

The land in this region is more open and gentle, with good deepwater harbours for the seafood and wood-product industries of the area. Rainfall is heavy, averaging 75 inches.

The Puget Sound Lowland region, between the Olympics and Willapas on the west and the Cascade Mountains on the east, stretches from Canada to Oregon. Its mild climate, relatively flat terrain, and excellent harbours have brought dense population and the major share of the state's manufacturing.

The Cascade Mountains region, east of the Puget Sound region, has peaks ranging from 4,000 feet in the south to 8,000 feet in the north. The chain contains several spectacular peaks of volcanic origin ranging from 10,000 feet to the 14,410-foot (4,392-metre) Mt. Rainier, the fifth highest peak in the coterminous United States.

The Columbia Basin region covers most of central Washington between the Cascade Mountains and the Idaho border and between the Okanogan Mountains to the north and the Blue Mountains to the south. This great plateau lies at about 1,000 to 2,500 feet above sea level. The Columbia and its largest tributary, the Snake, dominate this fertile agricultural area. The tremendous volume of their flow and the sharp drops through their courses give the region almost one-third of the nation's actual and potential hydroelectric power.

The Okanogan Highlands region in the northeast is an extension of the Rockies. Although less rugged than the Cascade and Olympic mountains, they range from 4,000 to 8,000 feet in height and contain most of the minerals and metals mined in the state.

The Blue Mountain region of the southeast is a relatively unsettled area, though river valleys foster agriculture and the mountains provide summer pasture for livestock.

Climate. Both western and eastern Washington display considerable geographical diversity, and despite the rain shadow of the Cascades the climates of both parts are dominated by the Pacific. Although not as mild as the western part, the eastern part generally is protected by the Rockies from cold Canadian Arctic air. Thus Washington has a climate milder than that of any other state at the same latitudes. Seattle, on the west, has an average January temperature of 40° F (4° C) and a July temperature of 63° F (17° C), while Spokane, on the east, registers 28° F (−2° C) and 69° F (21° C).

Plant and animal life. With about 23,000,000 acres (9,308,000 hectares) of forest, much of it still virgin timber, Washington ranks among the leading states in total forest area. Big game animals include bears, elks, and several species of deer. The wide variety of small fur-bearing animals includes beavers, mink, muskrat, rabbits, and bobcats. Game birds include wild ducks and geese, pheasant, mountain partridge, grouse, and several varieties of quail. Freshwater fishing includes that for rainbow, cutthroat, and steelhead trout, while the saltwater variety provides rich hauls of salmon and halibut in particular, as well as mackerel, herring, sole, and cod. Crabs, oysters, and clams abound in coastal waters.

Fisheries

Settlement patterns. Because Washington is a comparatively new section of the country, its pattern of settlement is still closely related to the pattern of its physical resources and regions: a sparsely populated, rural, and agriculturally oriented east and a heavily populated west oriented to manufacturing and commerce.

About four-fifths of the people live in metropolitan areas, all of which, except Spokane in the northeast, lie in the Puget Sound Lowland.

More than 50 percent of the population lives in the Seattle area and in the Tacoma area only 25 miles (40 kilometres) to the south. The harbour cities of Puget Sound and of the Pacific Coast were originally shipping points for wood products and fish and, to a lesser extent, transshipment points for trade with Alaska and the Orient. As settlement increased, they also became important fabricating and processing centres for products of the sea, soil, and forest, for transportation equipment and aluminum, and for oil refining. Spokane, with about 8 percent of the population, is the main commercial and service centre of eastern Washington.

Most of the people living outside the Puget Sound region

are engaged in forest-related industries and agriculture. On the western side many smaller towns are lumbering centres or fishing ports. In eastern Washington smaller cities and towns feature grain elevators and food-processing plants and provide services for the surrounding agricultural regions. The low rainfall and desert sections in the centre of the state respond well to irrigation. Fruits, vegetables, hops, potatoes, sugar beets, and hay are grown intensively. Farms tend to be less than 100 acres (40 hectares) in size, although many orchards run substantially larger. In the dry-farming areas farther east, the rainfall is adequate for large yields of wheat, peas, and barley. Where the rainfall is so low as to require that lands be left fallow in alternate years, the wheat farms are generally more than twice as large as those in areas with sufficient rainfall for an annual crop rotation. In the coastal and Puget Sound regions, the cool, humid climate encourages dairy farming. The separate croplands allocated to such specialized crops as cranberries and blueberries, as well as to truck farming, tend to be less than 100 acres.

The people. The early settlers, from the 1830s through the 1850s, came primarily from the Midwest along the Oregon Trail. Growth was slow until the 1880s, when railroads began to link Puget Sound and the Columbia River to the East and to California, ending the frontier era of the Pacific Northwest. The population of Washington grew fivefold from 1881 to 1890, to almost 360,000—and by 1920 it reached almost 1,360,000.

Migrants to the state continued to pour in, particularly from the Middle West, and, until restrictive national quotas on foreign immigration of the 1920s, large numbers of foreign-born people entered the state, especially from Canada and the Scandinavian countries. The Japanese came late; by 1930 they numbered about 18,000 and during World War II, whether citizens or not, they were moved from the coastal areas to relocation camps in inland regions. After the war only a few received back their homes and property, and many chose to live elsewhere.

The making of the ethnic mix

Washington has a relatively small percentage of blacks. It ranks among the top 10 states, however, in numbers of Indians, Chinese, Japanese, and Filipinos.

For decades the general western movement of the nation's population dominated Washington's growth. This situation changed during the 1950s, however, when for the first time, and by a wide margin, natural increase became a greater factor in population growth than immigration. Immigration has regained some of its former importance, but it remains below natural increase as a growth factor.

The economy. *Resources.* Among Washington's important natural resources is the water in its rapidly flowing rivers. It leads all states in hydroelectric generation, with more than one-fifth of the national total. Its forests contain nearly 4 percent of the national commercial forest area. Its coastal location and harbours provide other valuable resources.

Interaction of geography and economy

Industry. With the exception of its leading industry, aircraft and aircraft parts, the state's most important manufactures are based on its natural resources. They include lumber and wood products, processed food, primary metal industries, paper and allied products, and nonelectrical machinery.

Government is unusually important. Only 55 percent of the land is in private hands. Most irrigated land is served by federal projects, and almost all of the state's electric power is generated by the government. In the late 1970s the government employed more than one-fifth of nonagricultural workers, well above the national level.

In 1973 the U.S. Navy began construction of one of the largest projects in military history: the Trident Nuclear Submarine Base in Kitsap County, Washington. Military projects such as the Trident base have been common in the Puget Sound region, and, although they have been partially responsible for rising personal incomes and, at times, high employment, Washington's unusual dependency on military contracts and the aerospace, construction, and wood-products industries has resulted in an extremely vulnerable economy.

Agriculture. Among relatively large agricultural crops is wheat, in which Washington regularly ranks third or fourth in the nation in value of crop production. It supplies one-fourth of all fresh apples and ranks among the top states in potato harvesting. It is a leading producer of a number of vegetables, including sweet corn, green peas, and beans for canning and freezing.

Transportation. Waterways have played a vital role throughout Washington's history. Puget Sound, with its excellent year-round harbours, offers access to world ocean routes. With the completion of a series of dams, the Columbia River system, an inland waterway of great importance historically, will allow heavy barge traffic from the ocean to Wenatchee on the Columbia and to Clarkston on the Snake at the Idaho border.

The highway system covers about 84,000 miles (135,000 kilometres). About 5,300 miles of railway crisscross the state. Air links with other sections of the country and abroad are extensive, in addition to considerable local commercial air traffic. The Seattle–Tacoma Airport ranks among the top airports nationally in passenger travel between countries.

Administrative and social conditions. *Government.* Washington's constitution of 1889, reflecting the distrust of government that was characteristic of the time, contained many restrictions on state power. One reflection of this was the creation of a divided executive. Unlike the federal executive branch, to which only the president and vice president are elected, the state has eight separately elected officials. The most important is the governor.

Divided executive branch

The legislature comprises the Senate of 49 members and the House of 99 members, elected, respectively, for four- and two-year terms. Important limitations on legislative powers include the earmarking of certain funds to specific purposes—*e.g.,* the gasoline tax to highways. Because the constitution prohibits a state income tax, Washington depends on more than one-half of its tax revenues from a general sales tax, which accounts for about 30 percent of the state's total income. Initiative and referendum on legislation and recall of elected officials give the voters a check on the legislature. Unique among the states is Washington's expansion of the governor's power of "item veto" to include all legislation, except referendums and initiatives, to the extent of eliminating single words.

The courts are divided into four levels. Courts of limited jurisdiction—justice, municipal, and police—are local and hear traffic cases, minor criminal and civil cases, and small-claims actions. Superior courts are general trial courts, having original jurisdiction in major criminal cases (felonies) and in civil cases not delegated to the limited courts. The Supreme Court and the appellate courts are almost solely courts of review, ruling on whether the law was properly applied in a particular case. All judges, except for some classes of appointed municipal and police judges, are elected on nonpartisan ballots. Grand juries, created by a superior court, are used mainly to investigate political corruption, though their legal powers are considerably broader.

Washington's 39 counties are classified according to population by the legislature, which sets up uniform rules of operation for each class. The governing body in almost all counties is the board of county commissioners, whose three members act as both the chief executive officers and the legislative body for the county. The Optional Municipal Code was adopted in 1969, substantially expanding the powers of cities choosing to come under it. Cities with populations of 10,000 or more can adopt a home-rule charter if such a referendum is approved by the electorate, while municipalities of 300 to 10,000 are granted optional, noncharter home rule by statute.

Elections and political parties are regulated by state law. The unique feature of the nomination process in Washington is the "blanket primary," which replaced the closed primary in 1935, permitting citizens to vote for any candidate without disclosing their party membership. This law reflects a characteristic independence among the state's voters. Split voting has been reported by three-fourths of the voters in both primaries and final elections. This tendency to look at the candidate and not the party has tended to benefit incumbents. The defeat of an incumbent, particularly for Congress, is relatively unusual.

Openness of electoral processes

Since 1940, Washington has been a two-party state, though from the turn of the 20th century until 1932 it was almost exclusively Republican. Since the early 1940s two-party competition has become well established.

Education. The first territorial legislature provided for a school system with a permanent school fund, and the constitution acknowledged the state's duty to educate all children. Direct state support for elementary and secondary education was begun by "The Barefoot School Boy Law" in 1895, which provided $6 per student from state funds.

The State Board of Education sets general requirements and standards for courses of study, and the state Superintendent of Public Instruction administers them. The state is divided into more than 300 school districts, each electing a board of directors to administer school affairs.

Higher education is predominantly a state function in Washington. The oldest and largest institution is the University of Washington in Seattle, founded in 1861. Washington State University, in Pullman, was founded in 1890 as the state's land-grant institution. Three state colleges were established in the 1890s and a fourth in 1971. An extensive system of community colleges was combined into a state system in 1967.

Higher education

Welfare and health. In 1936, in response to the federal Social Security Act of 1935, the state assumed major responsibility for governmental welfare. The Department of Public Assistance administers many programs, mainly involving money grants, nursing-home care, and general medical care. Since the mid-1960s about one-half the budget has come from federal grants, and Washington has regularly ranked among the top 15 states in per capita expenditure on public welfare. The basic economic and social condition of the Indians of Washington runs from relatively good among some tribes of coastal Indians to poor among some river and inland tribes. Innovative projects are under way to stimulate tribal interest in their historical and cultural patterns and in economic improvement.

Cultural life. Culturally, as a relatively new state, Washington retains a Western and pioneer flavour. There is great interest in the history of the state, in the cultural pattern of the original Indians, and in the archaeological explorations, carried on extensively by Washington State University scientists. The unique interdisciplinary approach to prehistory has resulted in spectacular discoveries illustrated by two totally different archaeological sites. Marmes Rockshelter, in the desertic centre of eastern Washington, has yielded a 10,000-year-long sequence of tools left by hunters and gatherers and the earliest well-documented human skeletal remains in the Western Hemisphere. The Ozette site on the Olympic Coast has produced perfectly preserved clothing, basketry, and harpoons of people who fished and hunted seals and whales in prehistoric times. Thus the ecological diversity of the state has resulted in an equally diverse cultural heritage from earliest known human times.

Popular cultural events are often related to historical and economic patterns. There are Indian festivals, rodeos (especially in eastern Washington), and apple-blossom, timber, and flower festivals. A major event is the annual Seattle Seafair, featuring parades, boat racing, and water carnivals. Water sports in general abound in the Puget Sound region, whereas the large areas of relative wilderness in the Olympic Peninsula, the Cascades, and elsewhere allow many kinds of outdoor recreation and sports.

Opportunities for outdoor life

Accompanying this outdoor interest is a substantial and growing one in the fine arts. The Seattle Symphony has become well known; the Seattle Repertory Theater has drawn national attention; the Seattle Opera Association's annual presentation of Richard Wagner's *Der Ring des Nibelungen* has become internationally acclaimed; and the School of Drama at the University of Washington, one of the earliest such schools at an institution of higher learning, was a modern pioneer in the use of arena staging. Governmental support of the arts is given by the State Arts Commission and by the governor's Festival of the Arts, which honours outstanding artists and authors.

Among the approximately 25 major art galleries and museums, the Seattle Art Museum has extensive collections of Oriental art and work by Pacific Northwest artists. The

Thomas Burke Memorial Washington State Museum on the University of Washington's Seattle campus has an important collection relating to Pacific Northwest Indians. Also of interest are the Museum of History and Industry and the Pacific Science Center, both in Seattle. Among important historical museums is the Washington State Historical Society Museum in Tacoma.

The first library in the state, the Washington State Library in Olympia, traces its financial aid by the Congress to part of the Territorial Act of 1853. Rapid development of the public library system occurred in the first decade of the 20th century, when the Carnegie Foundation provided building funds. More than 250 libraries serve the state. Libraries of note include the two state university libraries and the Seattle Public Library.

HISTORY

The early frontier. The early history of the Northwest is intertwined with efforts to find the fabled Northwest Passage, the development of the fur trade with the Orient, and the attempts of Catholic and Protestant missionaries to convert the Indians. Spaniards had sailed along the coast earlier, but the rich sea-otter skins secured from the Indians on one of the voyages of Capt. James Cook in 1778 and resold in the Orient marked the start of real exploration and of the maritime fur trade. George Vancouver, sent by Britain in 1792, tried to find the Northwest Passage and to map the coast. Robert Gray was the first trader from the United States; his explorations resulted in the discovery of the Columbia River in 1792. By 1812, the United States almost completely dominated the fur trade. The British Hudson's Bay Company, however, maintained areas of dominance into the 1840s.

Missionaries were generally welcomed by the Indians, though often not so much for Christian salvation as for the knowledge and material advantages the whites could bring. Among the most famous missions were those of the medical missionary Marcus Whitman and the Rev. Henry Spalding, established in 1836 in southeastern Washington, and the Catholic missions established by Pierre-Jean DeSmet in northeastern Washington.

The Protestant missionaries felt that white civilization was necessary for the Indian and thus encouraged white settlement. With the opening of the Oregon Trail the first large group, about 1,000 people, reached the Northwest in 1843. These and others following first went mainly into the Willamette Valley of what became Oregon, and later into the area north of the Columbia River (in present-day Washington), then still dominated by the Hudson's Bay Company. The Indians were initially receptive but the settlers' inconsistent dealings with the Indians led to such conflicts as the Cayuse War (1848–50), the

Explorers, trappers, missionaries, and settlers

Yakima War (1855–58), and the Nez Percé War (1877).

Territory and state. Until the 1840s citizens of both the United States and Britain by agreement could settle and trade in what was still known as the Oregon Country. In 1846 the two countries agreed on the present boundary between the United States and Canada, and in 1848 Congress established the Oregon Territory including all of the present-day states of Oregon, Washington, and Idaho and parts of Wyoming and Montana. This enormous area, with its sparse population and poor communications, was difficult to govern from the territorial capital in the Willamette Valley. As the population around Puget Sound grew, agitation arose to form a separate territory of the area north and west of the Columbia. In 1853 Congress created Washington Territory, extending it east of the Columbia River to the crest of the Rockies, including parts of present-day Idaho and Montana.

Different rates of population growth and difficulties of communication continued to cause problems, and various movements called for the creation of a separate territory in eastern Washington and even the creation of an independent Pacific Republic. In the 1870s and 1880s the extension of the telegraph and the railroads to the Northwest strengthened the feeling of unity with the United States, and attention turned to seeking statehood, which was granted in 1889.

Gold discoveries in the interior in the 1850s made Walla Walla the centre of eastern Washington for a time, but these were merely a prelude to Washington's role in provisioning the gold miners who set out for the Alaskan strikes of the late 1890s. The gold stimulated the trade of cities on Puget Sound, and the new prosperity was celebrated at the Alaska-Yukon Exposition in 1909. The site of the exposition and some of the buildings became part of the University of Washington.

Perhaps the major development in the state through the first half of the 20th century was the Columbia Basin and related projects designed for purposes of hydroelectric power generation, irrigation, flood control, navigation improvement and stream-flow regulation, and recreation. The first navigation improvement project on the river was authorized in 1911. Construction of Bonneville and Grand Coulee dams in the Columbia Basin project began in 1933; Bonneville was completed in 1937, and the main structure of the Grand Coulee in 1941. Irrigation on the project began in 1948, and irrigation with water from behind Grand Coulee Dam began in 1952. The power plant at Grand Coulee was completed in 1951.

Washington's prosperity and its growing role in the commerce of the Pacific were among the features celebrated in the Seattle World's Fair of 1962, named "Century 21 Exposition." (E.Cl./Ed.)

TERRITORIES

The so-called United States Outlying Territories consist of about 2,360 islands, islets, atolls, and cays (small low islands). They reach almost halfway around the world from east to west and are spread over nearly half the distance between the North and South poles. Their total area (excluding disputed islands in the Pacific Ocean) amounts to 4,692 square miles (12,152 square kilometres), or a little less than the size of Connecticut.

Scattered through the Caribbean Sea and the Pacific Ocean, the outlying territories consist of areas that have U.S. sovereignty or are otherwise under U.S. jurisdiction or administration. These far-flung locations are most extensive in the Pacific, where they penetrate the Eastern Hemisphere and extend south of the Equator into the Southern Hemisphere.

The term United States may be interpreted in two ways. In a narrow sense it identifies the 50 states and the District of Columbia. The U.S. Board on Geographic Names approves this usage and further defines the term continental United States as comprising the 49 states and the District of Columbia located on the North American continent. A third approved term, conterminous United States, refers

to 48 states and the District of Columbia and excludes both Hawaii and Alaska. In a broad sense the term United States can encompass territory beyond that of these definitions. In most instances the inhabitants of the outlying areas are U.S. citizens or nationals, thus giving some validity to the broader concept of national territory.

The various outlying territories break down into two major regional categories, those associated with the Caribbean and those lying in the Pacific. The groupings for the two regions may be listed as follows:

(1) *Caribbean:* Commonwealth of Puerto Rico; Navassa Island; Quita Sueño Bank, Roncador Cay, and Serrana Bank; Swan Islands; Serranilla Bank; and Virgin Islands of the United States.

(2) *Pacific:* American Samoa; Guam; Howland, Baker, and Jarvis Islands; islands under U.S. administration; Johnston and Sand Islands; Kingman Reef; Midway Islands; Palmyra Island; Trust Territory of the Pacific Islands; and Wake Island.

(Both Colombia and Honduras claim Quita Sueño Bank and Roncador Cay. In addition, Colombia has claimed Serrana Bank; the United States recognized Colombian

Territorial regions

sovereignty in 1981 but other nations disputed the claim.)

The relatively small land surface of the territories is equal to only 0.13 percent of that within the 50 states.

Physical and human geography

THE LANDS

Locations. In the Caribbean area the outlying territories are extended in a wide arc, extending through the western segment of the Caribbean to Puerto Rico and to the Virgin Islands at the eastern extremity of the Greater Antilles. By far the largest, and most important, unit is Puerto Rico, making up well over half of the total area of all United States Outlying Territories and accounting for nearly 90 percent of the total population. In striking contrast, Quita Sueño Bank, Roncador Cay, and Serrana Bank must be measured in acres rather than square miles and are uninhabited. They represent formations that are largely underwater, with only a few small surfaces emerging above the high water level to form true islands.

In the Pacific the outlying territories are far more scattered, though they tend to be concentrated in the Southwest Pacific region. The area of all the islands totals 1,021 square miles (2,644 square kilometres); the area of those directly under undisputed U.S. sovereignty amounts to only 295 square miles. Among the latter, Guam is the largest with an area of 212 square miles (549 square kilometres), followed by American Samoa with 77 square miles (199 square kilometres). Population of the Pacific islands is unimpressive in size, totalling only about 288,-000; about half of these live in the Trust Territory of the Pacific Islands. The Trust Territory of the Pacific Islands is widely scattered, encompassing more than 2,000 islands, of which 96 have residents. Though occupying only 726 square miles of land surface, the islands extend over an oceanic area of 3,000,000 square miles, nearly as large as the 48 conterminous states.

In both the Caribbean and Pacific, many of the United States Outlying Territories lie near or among territories of other countries and in some instances within actual sight of them. The Virgin Islands of the United States make up only the western part of an archipelagic cluster, the remainder forming the British Virgin Islands. In the Pacific the United Kingdom, France, New Zealand, and Australia also have widely scattered island realms, while Japan's offshore islands extend as far as 1,500 miles (2,400 kilometres) east of continental Asia.

Geographic relief. The United States Outlying Territories are all insular. The islands, regardless of size, tend either to be volcanic and to have a rough topography, or to be formed of coral and to be low-lying. Cerro de Punta Mountain in Puerto Rico, rising to an elevation of 4,389 feet (1,338 metres), represents one extreme of altitude, while many atolls lie only feet, if not inches, above the sea. Despite some rugged relief on the volcanic islands, some of the islands have coastal plains, streams, valleys, and rolling hill lands that permit extensive agricultural development.

Climates. Only the Midway Islands lie outside the tropics, but even these are subtropical. Throughout the entire area the climate is consistently warm but seldom excessively hot because of the moderating influence of the sea. Rainfall, however, varies enormously from place to place.

Hurricanes and typhoons

Exposed windward slopes may receive great amounts while leeward slopes or flat areas may obtain relatively little. Climatic hazards usually take the form of hurricanes in the Caribbean and typhoons in the Pacific. Puerto Rico has had several destructive hurricanes in the 20th century, and every year storm warnings constitute reminders of the potential danger. In the Pacific there is the added menace of tsunamis, which from time to time may sweep over an entire island and leave destruction in their wake.

Vegetative growth closely follows the climatic pattern, being primarily dependent upon rainfall. In Puerto Rico a mountain known as El Yunque stands in an equatorial rain forest with dripping, luxuriant foliage, while at the other extreme some of the low-lying islands have desert-like characteristics. Because a high sun means high evaporation, 30–40 inches (750–1,000 millimetres) of rainfall produces less growth than it would in a cooler climate.

THE PEOPLES

Demography. Populations in the major outlying territories have been growing at comparable or more rapid rates than on the U.S. mainland. From 1970 to 1980, for example, the increase in Puerto Rico was 485,000 inhabitants, or 17.9 percent. On the three organized unincorporated territories of Samoa, Guam, and the Virgin Islands, population increase was greater, being 18.9 percent, 24.7 percent, and 54.6 percent, respectively. The small islands, including those in the Caroline, Mariana, and Marshall groups, generally do not have the economic advantages associated with major installations, nor are their economies substantially developed; their populations consequently inch upward in defiance of the limitations imposed by the local means of subsistence.

Ethnic distribution. The racial characteristics throughout the outlying territories vary with location. Puerto Ricans are frequently of Spanish ancestry, while in the Virgin Islands the majority of local inhabitants are descended from African slaves who worked on the Danish sugar plantations. Pacific islanders stem from the peoples associated with specific island groups before the coming of the Europeans. The Chamorro of Guam and the Polynesians of American Samoa in many ways live as they did before U.S. rule. With only a few exceptions the inhabitants of the Trust Territory of the Pacific Islands are Micronesians, though within this broad category they belong to different ethnic groups, including the Palauan, Trukese, and Marshallese. On all islands U.S. citizens from the mainland are present as administrators or as technical personnel. Others represent U.S. organizations or are members of the armed forces.

Linguistic patterns follow ethnic lines to a marked degree, although the English language has made great inroads on other tongues. Spanish is in wide local use in Puerto Rico. The English spoken by blacks in the Virgin Islands is of a dialect peculiar to the eastern West Indies, which Americans from the mainland often find difficult to understand. On the Pacific islands each ethnic group continues to use its own language or dialect. In the Trust Territory of the Pacific Islands, for example, nine major languages are in use, though Japanese is widely spoken and English is official. In all instances English holds an important position in the educational system.

Religions. Traditional religious practices have largely disappeared. Roman Catholicism, traceable to early Spanish influence, prevails in Puerto Rico and Guam. In the Virgin Islands the Roman Catholic, Protestant, and Jewish faiths are represented. Missionary groups throughout the Pacific have succeeded in converting the majority of the islanders to Christianity.

THE ECONOMIES

The United States must necessarily spend large sums to sustain the economies of these territorial entities in order to support their growing populations. Such assistance is provided by preferential legislation, subsidy, or direct aid. Natural resources that permit vigorous economic development are lacking. None of the islands has substantial mineral deposits, while commercial agriculture is limited to a few crops, particularly sugarcane and coconuts, which in general do not yield revenue commensurate with the number of people employed in their production. A principal source of income for local inhabitants is often provided by tourism or by the servicing of government offices and installations, military and civilian. More than 2,000,000 tourists visit Puerto Rico each year, and in the Virgin Islands the tourist industry constitutes the primary economic activity. Development of tourism in many of the Pacific territories, however, is secondary to development of agriculture and manufacturing. Transportation is well developed in all the populated islands.

ADMINISTRATIVE CONDITIONS

Status of the territories. The statuses of the various outlying territories are by no means uniform. Those in which the United States has residual sovereignty include the Commonwealth of Puerto Rico and the organized unincorporated territories of the Virgin Islands of the United

Variations in status

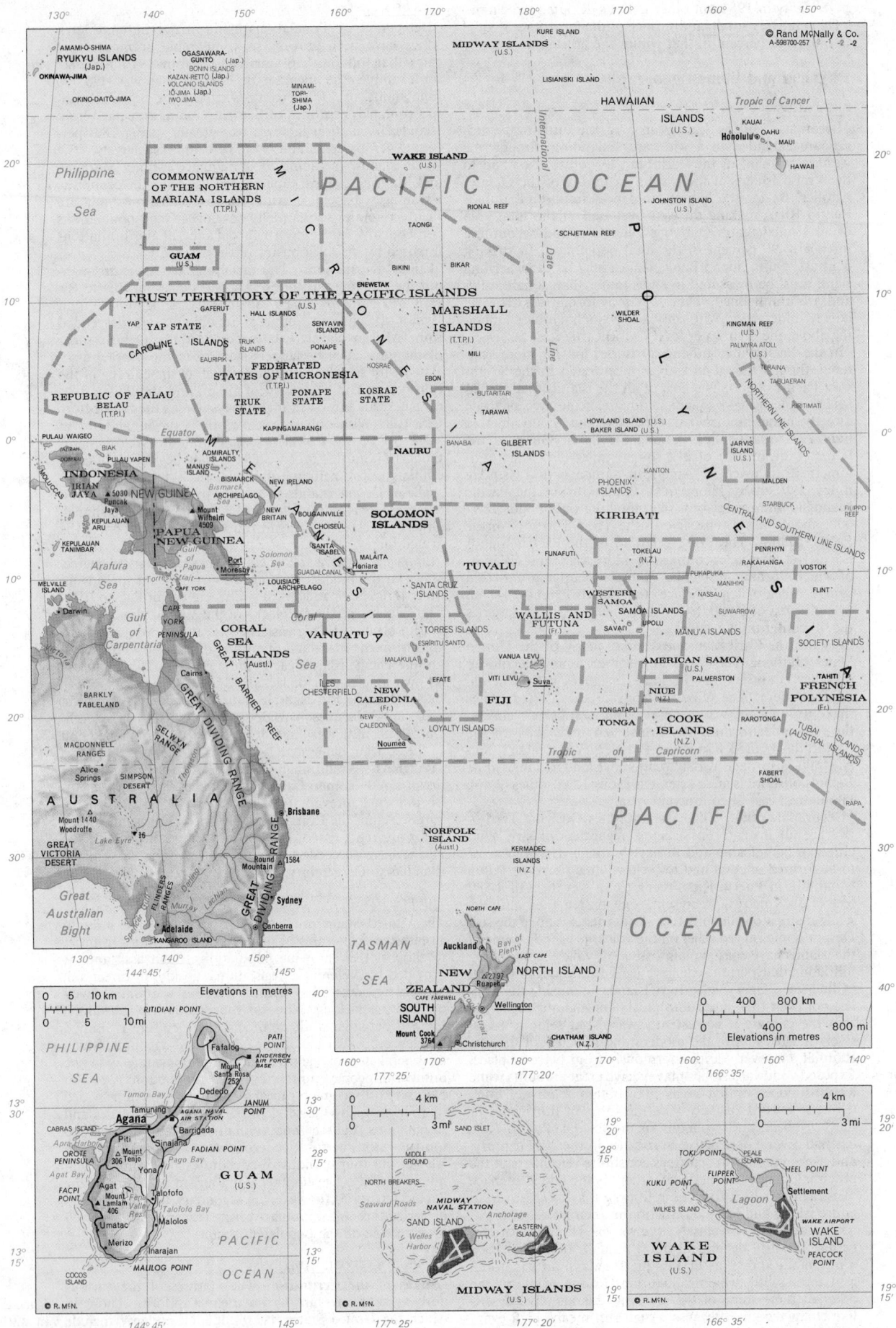

© Rand McNally & Co.
A-598700-257

AMAMI-Ō-SHIMA
RYUKYU ISLANDS (Jap.)
OKINAWA-JIMA
OKINO-DAITŌ-JIMA

OGASAWARA-GUNTO (Jap.)
BONIN ISLANDS
KAZAN-RETTŌ (Jap.)
VOLCANO ISLANDS
IŌ-JIMA (Jap.) (IWO JIMA)
MINAMI-TORI-SHIMA (Jap.)

KURE ISLAND
MIDWAY ISLANDS (U.S.)
LISIANSKI ISLAND

HAWAIIAN
ISLANDS (U.S.)
KAUAI
Honolulu OAHU MAUI
HAWAII

Tropic of Cancer

Philippine Sea

COMMONWEALTH OF THE NORTHERN MARIANA ISLANDS (T.T.P.I.)

WAKE ISLAND (U.S.)

PACIFIC OCEAN

RIONAL REEF
TAONGI
SCHJETMAN REEF

JOHNSTON ISLAND (U.S.)

GUAM (U.S.)

TRUST TERRITORY OF THE PACIFIC ISLANDS (U.S.)

BIKINI BIKAR
ENEWETAK

MARSHALL ISLANDS (T.T.P.I.)

WILDER SHOAL

KINGMAN REEF (U.S.)
PALMYRA ATOLL (U.S.)
TERAINA
TABUAERAN

YAP YAP STATE
CAROLINE ISLANDS
GAFERUT
HALL ISLANDS
SENYAVIN ISLANDS
TRUK ISLANDS
PONAPE
KOSRAE
MILI

FEDERATED STATES OF MICRONESIA (T.T.P.I.)

EAURIPIK
REPUBLIC OF PALAU BELAU (T.T.P.I.)
TRUK STATE
PONAPE STATE
KOSRAE STATE
EBON
BUTARITARI
TARAWA

KIRITIMATI

HOWLAND ISLAND (U.S.)
BAKER ISLAND (U.S.)

JARVIS ISLAND (U.S.)

NORTHERN LINE ISLANDS

Equator

KAPINGAMARANGI

NAURU
BANABA
GILBERT ISLANDS

PHOENIX ISLANDS

KANTON

MALDEN

STARBUCK

CENTRAL AND SOUTHERN LINE ISLANDS

FILIPPO REEF

PULAU WAIGEO
BIAK PULAU YAPEN
ADMIRALTY ISLANDS
MANUS ISLAND
NEW IRELAND
BISMARCK ARCHIPELAGO

INDONESIA
IRIAN JAYA
NEW GUINEA
Puncak Jaya 5030

NEW BRITAIN
BOUGAINVILLE
CHOISEUL

SOLOMON ISLANDS

KIRIBATI

KEPULAUAN ARU
Mount Wilhelm 4509
PAPUA NEW GUINEA
SANTA ISABEL
MALAITA
Honiara

VOSTOK

KEPULAUAN TANIMBAR
Gulf of Papua
Port Moresby
Solomon Sea
GUADALCANAL

TUVALU
FUNAFUTI
TOKELAU (N.Z.)
PENRHYN
RAKAHANGA
FLINT

Arafura Sea
Torres Strait
CAPE YORK
LOUISIADE ARCHIPELAGO
SANTA CRUZ ISLANDS
PUKAPUKA
MANIHIKI

MELVILLE ISLAND
CAPE YORK PENINSULA
Coral Sea
CORAL SEA ISLANDS (Austl.)

WESTERN SAMOA
SAVAI'I
SAMOA ISLANDS
UPOLU
NASSAU
SUWARROW

Darwin
Gulf of Carpentaria
Cairns
GREAT BARRIER REEF
VANUATU
TORRES ISLANDS
ESPIRITU SANTO
MALAKULA
EFATE

AMERICAN SAMOA (U.S.)
MANU'A ISLANDS
PALMERSTON

SOCIETY ISLANDS

BARKLY TABLELAND
ÎLES CHESTERFIELD
NEW CALEDONIA (Fr.)
VANUA LEVU
VITI LEVU
Suva
FIJI

NIUE (N.Z.)

TAHITI
FRENCH POLYNESIA (Fr.)

MACDONNELL RANGES
Alice Springs
SIMPSON DESERT
SELWYN RANGE

NEW CALEDONIA
LOYALTY ISLANDS
Nouméa

TONGATAPU
TONGA

COOK ISLANDS (N.Z.)
RAROTONGA

TUBAI (AUSTRAL ISLANDS)

Tropic of Capricorn

AUSTRALIA
GREAT VICTORIA DESERT
Mount Woodroffe 1440
Lake Eyre
GREAT DIVIDING RANGE
Mount 1584 Round Mountain
Brisbane

FABERT SHOAL

PACIFIC

RAPA

GREAT DIVIDING RANGE
FLINDERS RANGES
Murray
Sydney
Canberra

NORFOLK ISLAND (Austl.)

KERMADEC ISLANDS (N.Z.)

OCEAN

Great Australian Bight
Adelaide
KANGAROO ISLAND

TASMAN SEA
NORTH CAPE
Auckland
Bay of Plenty
EAST CAPE
NEW ZEALAND
NORTH ISLAND
Ruapehu
SOUTH ISLAND
Wellington
CAPE FAREWELL
Mount Cook 3764
Christchurch
CHATHAM ISLAND (N.Z.)

0 400 800 km
0 400 800 mi
Elevations in metres

U.S. Outlying Territories inset (Guam):

Elevations in metres
0 5 10 km
0 5 10 mi

RITIDIAN POINT
PHILIPPINE SEA
Fafalog
PATI POINT
Mount Santa Rosa 252
ANDERSEN AIR FORCE BASE
Tumon Bay
Tamuning
Dededo
JANUM POINT
AGANA NAVAL AIR STATION
Agana
Barrigada
CABRAS ISLAND
Piti
Sinajana
FADIAN POINT
Apra Harbor
OROTE PENINSULA
Mount Tenjo 306
Yona
Pago Bay
Agat Bay
Agat
Mount Lamlam 406
Fena Valley Res.
Talofofo
Talofofo Bay
FACPI POINT
Umatac
Malolos
GUAM (U.S.)
Merizo
Inarajan
PACIFIC OCEAN
COCOS ISLAND
MALILOG POINT

Midway Islands inset:

0 4 km
0 3 mi
SAND ISLET
MIDDLE GROUND
NORTH BREAKERS
Seaward Roads
MIDWAY NAVAL STATION
SAND ISLAND
Anchorage
EASTERN ISLAND
Welles Harbor
MIDWAY ISLANDS (U.S.)

Wake Island inset:

0 4 km
0 3 mi
TOKI POINT
PEALE ISLAND
HEEL POINT
KUKU POINT
FLIPPER POINT
Settlement
Lagoon
WILKES ISLAND
WAKE AIRPORT
WAKE ISLAND
WAKE ISLAND (U.S.)
PEACOCK POINT

U.S. OUTLYING TERRITORIES IN THE PACIFIC OCEAN

States, American Samoa, and Guam. Before they became states in 1959, Alaska and Hawaii each had the status of incorporated territories—that is, areas that the U.S. Congress had "incorporated" into the United States by making the Constitution applicable to them. In addition, a number of smaller islands, including the Swan Islands, Navassa Island, Midway Islands, and Wake Island, are unincorporated territories. In all cases these small islands are uninhabited or have only a few residents, thus making an organized governmental structure impractical.

Beyond these fragments of sovereign territory belonging to the United States, several others are included as outlying territories by virtue of other types of jurisdiction or for purposes of administrative control. Until 1977 the Canal Zone was under U.S. jurisdiction according to the provisions of a 1903 treaty with Panama; but the Panama Canal Treaty of 1977 (effective October 1, 1979) abolished the Canal Zone, made Panama sovereign over the area, and permitted the United States only limited rights over the operation and defense of the Panama Canal itself.

The Trust Territory of the Pacific Islands, consisting of the Caroline, Mariana (except Guam), and Marshall islands, in 1947 was placed under the international trusteeship system established by the Charter of the United Nations.

In the western Caribbean, several low-lying islands and banks have special jurisdictional association with the United States. The United States maintains control under an arrangement whereby the claims of these countries are not prejudiced.

The Bonin, Volcano, and Daito island groups and Marcus Island were formerly under U.S. administration. These islands, located some hundreds of miles south and southeast of Tokyo, were returned to Japan in 1968; the southern Ryukyu Islands, also formerly under U.S. administration, were returned to Japanese jurisdiction in 1972.

The outlying territories of the United States are no longer considered to be colonies, nor are those with significant populations generally referred to as possessions. The decline of colonialism throughout the world has brought about this change in terminology. In each instance the status accorded the populated United States Outlying Territories permits a degree of autonomy commensurate with the capacity of the inhabitants to assume responsibilities of self-government. Puerto Rico, its rank as a commonwealth interpreted as a "free associated state," is in some ways similar to an independent country. It is sometimes considered "semi-independent" or "quasi-independent," being free to govern itself but conforming to U.S. policies in matters of postage, currency, customs, and in international relations and defense. Organized unincorporated territories have limited self-government, though within their borders the Constitution has not been expressly and fully extended.

Degrees of autonomy

Government. Each of the United States Outlying Territories has a civil government closely associated with, or under the direct control of, some federal agency in Washington, D.C. An exception is Puerto Rico, but even in this instance the commonwealth maintains an office in the U.S. capital. The remainder of the islands stand in relationship to one or another of the U.S. executive departments and thus have U.S. cabinet members as chief officials. The U.S. Departments of the Interior and of the Navy have the greatest responsibilities, while the U.S. Department of State is responsible for all affairs pertaining to islands in dispute.

Four of the outlying territories have governors and legislatures. In Puerto Rico elections are held for the governorship and for the Senate and House of Representatives. American Samoa, Guam, and the Virgin Islands have appointed governors, but the local inhabitants are endeavouring to effect legislation for elected governorships. In anticipation of official dissolution of the Trust Territory of the Pacific Islands, the following distinct governmental units were created: the Commonwealth of the Northern Mariana Islands (1978), in association with the United States; the Federated States of Micronesia (1979), comprised of Kosrae, Ponape, Truk, and Yap states; the Republic of the Marshall Islands (1979); and the Republic of Palau (Belau; 1981). The trust territory continued in force, however, awaiting its formal dissolution by the United Nations.

Canton and Enderbury atolls were jointly administered by the United States and the United Kingdom from 1939 until 1979, when the United States relinquished its claim and the atolls came under the administration of Kiribati (the former Gilbert Islands). The Central and Southern Line Islands, which also had been claimed by both the United States and the United Kingdom, became a part of Kiribati in 1980.

History

All the United States Outlying Territories were officially acquired or claimed between 1856 and the end of World War II. Each acquisition was made in conjunction with some advantage thought to accrue to the country, whether economic, political, or strategic. The first insular possessions came under the U.S. flag through an Act of Congress (Guano Act of 1856) in order to secure rich deposits of natural fertilizer made up of bird droppings that had accumulated. As a result of the Treaty of Paris of 1898 that ended the Spanish–American War, Puerto Rico and Guam became U.S. possessions, as also did the Philippines, which remained a U.S. commonwealth until 1946, when it became independent. In 1917 the United States purchased the Virgin Islands from Denmark as a measure of protection against German submarines. From a strategic viewpoint, the Canal Zone was for most of the 20th century a centre of U.S. interest in the Caribbean, with Puerto Rico and the Virgin Islands serving as sentinels to guard its approaches. Following World War II it proved expedient to maintain control over the Caroline, Mariana, and Marshall islands, which made up the Trust Territory of the Pacific Islands. The island of Guam, though geographically a part of the Marianas, was excluded from the trusteeship. The southern Ryukyu Islands, including Okinawa, were under U.S. administration (1945–72) and the United States maintains military installations there.

Throughout the western Pacific the various outlying areas—outposts over America's western horizon—have served as stepping stones in the development of transportation patterns across the world's widest ocean. Midway and Wake, for example, made air transportation history as stops along Pan American's early transpacific routes. Others—such as Kwajalein, Saipan, and Eniwetok (now Enewetak)—were battlegrounds during World War II. After the war, nuclear tests were conducted on Bikini and Enewetak. (G.E.P./Ed.)

Margin note: Acquisition as the aftermath of wars

BIBLIOGRAPHY

Physical and human geography. *The land:* Although no treatment of the contemporary American landscape has yet appeared that is comprehensive and adequate for both town and countryside, several items do provide useful introductions to the topic. DAVID LOWENTHAL, "The American Scene," *Georgrl. Rev.,* 58:61–88 (1968), skillfully sets forth several basic themes apparent in the visual landscape and the attitude of Americans toward it. A serviceable description of many landscape features and a manual for their improvement is available in CHRISTOPHER TUNNARD and BORIS PUSHKAREV, *Man-Made America: Chaos or Control?,* new ed. (1981); while a more pessimistic assessment of the situation is given in IAN NAIRN, *The American Landscape: A Critical View* (1965). Rural land use is treated in terms of both historical development and modern physical pattern in FRANCIS J. MARSCHNER, *Land Use and Its Patterns in the United States* (1959). The historical geography of open-country and village settlement in the early Atlantic Seaboard is discussed in GLENN T. TREWARTHA, "Types of Rural Settlement in Colonial America," *Geogrl. Rev.,* 36:569–596 (1946); and the same area and topic, along with much else, is dealt with in HENRY GLASSIE, *Pattern in the Material Folk Culture of the Eastern United States* (1975). These works are also valuable in the study of traditional regions. For a concise but substantial survey of the townscapes of the nation and their evolution, see CHRISTOPHER TUNNARD and HENRY HOPE REED, *American Skyline* (1955). JOHN W. REPS, *The Making of Urban America: A History of City Planning in the United States* (1965), is a masterly account in word and map of the development of urban street patterns and related matters. Two exemplary presentations of the geography and history of specific metropolitan areas may be found in JEAN GOTTMANN,

Megalopolis: The Urbanized Northeastern Seaboard of the United States (1961); and HAROLD M. MAYER and RICHARD C. WADE, *Chicago: Growth of a Metropolis* (1969). The only general discussion of the traditional regions of the country and related subjects is WILBUR ZELINSKY, *The Cultural Geography of the United States* (1973). Of the several general texts covering the human geography of the continent, perhaps the most stimulating and informative is J. WREFORD WATSON, *North America, Its Countries and Regions* (1967). Two atlases that are indispensable for the serious study of any aspect of the American human or physical scene are CHARLES O. PAULLIN and JOHN K. WRIGHT, *Atlas of the Historical Geography of the United States* (1932, reprinted 1975); and the UNITED STATES GEOLOGICAL SURVEY, *The National Atlas of the United States of America* (1970). Although several sections of the country lack adequate monographic treatment, there are commendable volumes for a few areas, notably: RUPERT B. VANCE, *Human Geography of the South: A Study in Regional Resources and Human Adequacy,* 2nd ed. (1968); HANS KURATH (ed.), *Linguistic Atlas of New England,* 3 vol. (1939–43); D.W. MEINIG, *Imperial Texas: An Interpretive Essay in Cultural Geography* (1969), and *Southwest: Three Peoples in Geographical Change, 1600–1900* (1971).

CHARLES B. HUNT, *Physiography of the United States* (1967), is solid and well illustrated, though geology receives disproportionate attention. An excellent brief summary comprises the first three chapters of J. WREFORD WATSON's lucid and authoritative *North America, Its Countries and Regions* (1967), which includes a useful bibliography. (*Landforms and geology*): A standard work on American landforms is W.D. THORNBURY, *Regional Geomorphology of the United States* (1965), superbly illustrated with maps, diagrams, and air photos, an excellent bibliography, and balanced discussions of controversial questions. NEVIN FENNEMAN, *Physiography of Western United States* (1931), and *Physiography of Eastern United States* (1938), are exhaustive and still standard reference. An authoritative treatment of American tectonics is PHILIP B. KING, *The Evolution of North America,* rev. ed. (1977). The effects of Pleistocene glaciation are exhaustively analyzed in a collection of scholarly essays, H.E. WRIGHT, JR. and D.G. FREY (eds.). *The Quaternary of the United States* (1965). (*Maps of landforms*): Overwhelmingly the best depiction of American landforms is ERWIN RAISZ, *Landforms of the United States,* 6th rev. ed. (1957). The UNITED STATES GEOLOGICAL SURVEY, *Tectonic Map of the United States Exclusive of Alaska and Hawaii* (1962), is invaluable. Essential for understanding Northeastern landscapes are the *Glacial Map of the United States East of the Rocky Mountains* (1959), showing the main deposits of continental ice, and *Pleistocene Eolian Deposits of the United States, Alaska, and Parts of Canada* (1952), which maps the location of glacially-derived loess and sand; both are published by the GEOLOGICAL SOCIETY OF AMERICA. For small areas, excellent large topographic maps and air photos are available for most of the country from the United States Geological Survey. (*Mineral resources*): Basic data on mineral deposits, production, exports, and imports are collected by the UNITED STATES BUREAU OF MINES and published annually in the *Minerals Yearbook.* (*Climate*): U.S. climate and its role in human affairs is intelligently treated in the classic *Yearbook of Agriculture: Climate and Man,* by the UNITED STATES DEPARTMENT OF AGRICULTURE (1941, reprinted 1975), which contains numerous maps and statistical data. Excellent atlases of American climate include C.W. THORNTHWAITE, *Atlas of Climatic Types in the United States 1900–1939* (1941), including detailed maps that show the annual variations over 40 years; STEPHEN S. VISHER, *Climatic Atlas of the United States* (1954), with more than 1,000 maps showing every aspect of American weather and climate; and the UNITED STATES DEPARTMENT OF COMMERCE, ENVIRONMENTAL DATA SERVICE, *Climatic Atlas of the United States* (1968), a careful and authoritative assemblage of maps and selected statistics in paperback. (*Vegetation and animal life*): HENRY A. GLEASON and ARTHUR CRONQUIST, *The Natural Geography of Plants* (1964), is a highly readable and beautifully illustrated introduction to plant ecology and geography, with heavy emphasis on North America. An authoritative regional treatment of U.S. plant and animal ecology is VICTOR E. SHELFORD, *The Ecology of North America* (1963). Environmental impact and economic constraints are considered by DENNIS C. PIRAGES and PAUL R. EHRLICH, *Ark II: Social Response to Environmental Imperatives* (1974). Perhaps the most honoured treatment of American forests is E. LUCY BRAUN, *Deciduous Forests of Eastern North America* (1950). An excellent medium-scale map of U.S. vegetation patterns is A.W. KUCHLER's authoritative "Natural Vegetation," in E.B. ESPENSHADE (ed.), *Goode's World Atlas,* 13th ed. (1970). (*Soils*): C.F. MARBUT, "Soils of the United States," part 3 of the *Atlas of American Agriculture* (1935), remains an authoritative description of American soil geography. *Soils and Men* (1938), and *Soil* (1957), contain a wide variety of useful information. All three works are issued by the UNITED STATES DEPARTMENT OF AGRICULTURE.

The people: The *Statistical Abstract of the United Staes,* published annually by the BUREAU OF THE CENSUS, is the standard summary of statistics on the social, political, and economic organization of the United States. The Census Bureau also published *Historical Statistics of the United States,* Bicentennial ed., 2 vol. (1975), which contains similar data from colonial times to 1970. For interpretation of demographic data, see EDWARD G. STOCKWELL, *Population and People* (1968); and RICHARD M. SCAMMON and BEN J. WATTENBERG, *The Real Majority* (1970); for analysis of national values and their historical development, D.W. BROGAN, *The American Character* (1944); and SEYMOUR MARTIN LIPSET, *The First New Nation: The United States in Historical and Comparative Perspective* (1963, reissued 1979); for contemporary attitudes, and opinions, ALBERT H. CANTRIL and CHARLES W. ROLL, JR., *Hopes and Fears of the American People* (1971); for history of the era of mass immigration, 1860–1920, OSCAR HANDLIN, *The Uprooted,* 2nd enl. ed. (1973); and for an examination of contemporary American minority groups, NATHAN GLAZER and DANIEL P. MOYNIHAN, *Beyond the Melting Pot: The Negroes, Puerto Ricans, Jews, Italians, and Irish of New York City,* 2nd ed. (1970); STEPHAN THERNSTORM (ed.), *Harvard Encyclopedia of American Ethnic Groups* (1980); FRANK D. BEAN and W. PARKER FRISBIE (eds.), *The Demography of Racial and Ethnic Groups* (1978).

The economy: General surveys of the U.S. economy include SHEPHARD B. CLOUGH and THEODORE F. MARBURY, *The Economic Basis of American Civilization* (1969); EDWARD F. DENISON, *The Sources of Economic Growth in the United States and the Alternatives Before Us* (1962); CHARLES H. HESSION, *The Dynamics of the American Economy* (1956); UNITED STATES ECONOMIC DEVELOPMENT ADMINISTRATION, *Regional Economic Development in the United States* (1967); and EMMA WOYTINSKY, *Profile of the U.S. Economy: A Survey of Growth and Change* (1967). Trends in production and employment are analyzed in CLOPPER ALMON et al., *Nineteen Eighty Five Interindustry Forecasts of the American Economy* (1974); EDITORS OF FORTUNE, *Markets of the Seventies: The Unwinding U.S. Economy* (1968); NATIONAL INDUSTRIAL CONFERENCE BOARD, *The Consumer of the Seventies* (1969); UNITED STATES BUREAU OF LABOR STATISTICS, *Patterns of U.S. Economic Growth: 1980 Projections of Final Demand, Inter-industry Relationships, Output, Productivity, and Employment* (1970); and the UNITED STATES NATIONAL GOALS RESEARCH STAFF, *Toward Balanced Growth: Quantity with Quality* (1970). Issues of economic policy are treated in GEORGE L. BACH, *Making Monetary and Fiscal Policy* (1971); COMMITTEE FOR ECONOMIC DEVELOPMENT, *Fiscal and Monetary Policies for Steady Economic Growth* (1969); WALTER W. HELLER, *New Dimensions of Political Economy* (1966); ARTHUR M. OKUN, *The Political Economy of Prosperity* (1970); MELVILLE J. ULMER, *The Welfare States, U.S.A.: An Exploration in and Beyond the New Economics* (1969); and the PRESIDENT'S TASK FORCE ON ECONOMIC GROWTH, *Policies for American Economic Progress in the Seventies* (1970). Various points of view are in NEIL W. CHAMBERLAIN (ed.), *Contemporary Economic Issues,* rev. ed. (1973); and WALTER W. HELLER (ed.), *Perspectives on Economic Growth* (1968). WILFRED OWEN, EZRA BROWN, and the EDITORS OF LIFE, *Wheels* (1967), a book on the technological development of transport throughout history and on proposed scientific innovations to help solve future problems. WILFRED OWEN, *The Metropolitan Transportation Problem,* rev. ed. (1966), an analysis of the transportation problems and traffic congestion of American cities concluding that solutions lie to a major degree in the design of the city and urban region; GEORGE M. SMERK (ed.), *Readings in Urban Transportation* (1968), a varied collection of essays by widely known authors in the field. ROBERT FERBER, *Social Experimentation and Economic Policy* (1982), a review of contemporary social experimentation in economics.

Administrative and social conditions: The contemporary political and social milieus are analyzed in an avalanche of publications expressing every conceivable philosophy of government and social management; few have yet been able to achieve the necessary distance, in time or sentiment, for unaffected analysis of the structure or functioning of U.S. government, politics, or social dynamics. A few, however, can provide a valuable beginning. In government and politics, the *United States Government Organization Manual* (annual), offers a broad overview of the federal structure; while the *Congressional Record* and the *Congressional Quarterly* provide closer views of the public record of the federal legislature. Other basic books on government include *The Book of the States,* published yearly by THE COUNCIL OF STATE GOVERNMENTS; AARON WILDAVSKY and NELSON W. POLSBY (eds.), *American Governmental Institutions* (1968); PETER WOLL, *American Gov-*

ernment: Readings and Cases, 6th ed. (1978); and ROBERT A. GOLDWIN (ed.), *A Nation of States* (1963). Among the more penetrating insights into the complexities of politics are JOSEPH R. FISZMAN (ed.), *The American Political Arena,* 2nd ed. (1966); FRED I. GREENSTEIN, *The American Party System and the American People,* 2nd ed. (1970); the series by THEODORE WHITE begun with *The Making of the President, 1960* (1961) and continued to cover subsequent presidential elections; RICHARD M. SCAMMON and BEN J. WATTENBERG, *The Real Majority: How the Silent Center of the American Electorate Chooses Its President* (1970), based on studies of voting behaviour in 1968; and SHIRLEY CHISHOLM, *Unbought and Unbossed* (1970). The U.S. military is studied in terms of its politics in ADAM YARMOLINSKY, *The Military Establishment* (1971). The political and social structures are bridged in C. WRIGHT MILLS, *Power Elite* (1956); while other studies probing special areas of politicosocial concern include BARBARA and JOHN EHRENREICH, *American Health Empire: Power, Profits, and Politics* (1970); MICHAEL HARRINGTON, *The Other America,* rev. ed. (1969), a study of poverty in the United States; JANE JACOBS, *The Death and Life of Great American Cities* (1961), an inquiry into the structuring and destruction of the city; HARRY M. CAUDILL, *Night Comes to the Cumberlands: Biography of a Depressed Area* (1963), a historical survey of the development of poverty in the southern Appalachians; and ROBERT C. COLES on rural poor and effects of their migrations to the city. For social statistics see the *Statistical Abstracts of the United States* (annual). NEIL R. PIERCE and JERRY HAGSTROM, *The Bank of America* (1983), an insightful look at persistent social differences among various regions of the country.

Cultural life: A good approach to the study of cultural life and institutions in the United States is through MARSHALL MCCLUHAN, *Understanding Media: The Extensions of Man* (1964). Although McLuhan's works have been highly controversial, no writer has done more to stimulate awareness of the role of media in modern culture. A broad introduction to the "counterculture" is THEODORE ROSZAK, *The Making of a Counter Culture: Reflections on the Technocratic Society and Its Youthful Opposition* (1969). Information about minority cultures and movements must be found primarily in their polemical writings. Interesting discussions of all phases of contemporary literature, including nonfiction journalism, and the theatre, as well as poetry and fiction, appear in ELIZABETH JANEWAY (ed.), *The Writer's World* (1969); and ROBERT E. SPILLER (ed.), *Literary History of the United States: History,* 4th rev. ed. (1974). A useful survey of Pop art is LUCY R. LIPPARD *et al.,* *Pop Art* (1966); while BARBARA ROSE, *American Art Since 1900,* rev. ed. (1975), carries the discussion of American art into the early 1970s. Two books by MICHAEL KIRBY cover multimedia experiments: *Happenings* (1965), and *The Art of Time: Essays on the Avante-Garde* (1969). Rock music is explored in CARL BELZ, *The Story of Rock,* 2nd ed. (1972). A valuable study of the television industry is LES BROWN, *Television: The Business Behind the Box* (1971); while a more historical treatment of radio and television is ERIK BARNOUW, *A History of Broadcasting in the United States,* 3 vol. (1966–70). WALTER TERRY, *The Dance in America,* rev. ed. (1971), documents the development of distinctly American forms of ballet and modern dance. LOUIS GIANNETTI, *Masters of the American Cinema* (1981), describes major American film producers and their works. The magazine *Saturday Review* (biweekly), provides a broad suvey of social and cultural aspects of American life. PETER CLELAK, *America's Quest for the Ideal Self: Dissent and Fulfillment in America, 1960–1980* (1983), a contention that the activisms of the 1960s and 1970s shared a common motivation.

History. *Colonial development to 1763:* CHARLES M. ANDREWS, *The Colonial Period of American History,* 4 vol. (1934–38, reprinted 1964), the starting point for any study of colonial America; LAWRENCE H. GIPSON, *The British Empire Before the American Revolution,* 15 vol. (1936–70), the culmination of the "British Imperial school" of interpretation; CLARENCE VER STEEG, *The Formative Years, 1607–1763* (1964), the best one-volume synthesis of the colonial period written to date; DANIEL J. BOORSTIN, *The Americans: The Colonial Experience* (1958), a brilliant, but perhaps overstated interpretation of American cultural and intellectual development during the colonial period; CURTIS NETTELS, *The Roots of American Civilization,* 2nd ed. (1963), one of several competent textbook histories of the colonial period. (*Settlement*): PERRY MILLER, *The New England Mind* (1939) and *The New England Mind: From Colony to Province* (1953), together these comprise perhaps the finest work of intellectual history ever written by an American historian; EDMUND MORGAN, *The Puritan Dilemma: The Story of John Winthrop* (1958), an accurate, readable account of the early years of the Massachusetts Bay settlement; WESLEY F. CRAVEN, *The Southern Colonies in the Seventeenth Century, 1607–1689* (1949), a competent survey of the early development of the

Southern colonies; GARY NASH, *Quakers and Politics: Pennsylvania 1681–1726* (1968), account of the founding of Pennsylvania; JOHN POMFRET, *The Province of West New Jersey, 1609–1702* (1956) and *The Province of East New Jersey, 1609–1702* (1962), standard accounts; LAWRENCE LEDER, *Robert Livingston, 1654–1728 and the Politics of Colonial New York* (1961). NEAL SALISBURY, *Manitou and Providence: Indians, Europeans, and the Making of New England, 1500–1643*, vol. 1 (1982), an ethnohistory of New England Indians and the early contacts with European culture. (*Imperial organization*): CHARLES M. ANDREWS (*op. cit.*); GEORGE L. BEER, *The Old Colonial System, 1660–1754*, 2 vol. (1912, reprinted 1958), an old, but still reliable history of British colonial policy; LEONARD W. LABAREE, *Royal Government in America* (1930), still the classic work on the subject of the royal governors of America. (*The growth of provincial power*): CARL BRIDENBAUGH, *Myths and Realities: Societies of the Colonial South* (1952), a persuasive argument that the colonial South consisted of not one, but three separate sections; CHARLES SYDNOR, *Gentlemen Freeholders: Political Practices in Washington's Virginia* (1952), still the most reliable account of political behaviour in 18th-century Virginia; JACK P. GREENE, *The Quest for Power: The Lower Houses of Assembly in the Southern Royal Colonies, 1689–1776* (1963), details the process by which provincial leaders acquired power at the expense of royal officials; VIOLA BARNES, *The Dominion of New England: A Study in British Colonial Policy* (1923), still the standard work on the subject; RAY A. BILLINGTON, *Westward Expansion*, 3rd ed. (1967), the best general survey of the movement of Americans westward; LEWIS C. GRAY and E.K. THOMPSON, *History of Agriculture in the Southern United States to 1860*, 2 vol. (1933, reprinted 1969), indispensable source for an understanding of Southern economic life during the colonial period; WILLIAM B. WEEDEN, *Economic and Social History of New England, 1620–1789*, 2nd vol. (1890, reprinted 1963); FREDERICK B. TOLLES, *Meeting House and Counting House: The Quaker Merchants of Colonial Philadelphia* (1948), a good survey of economic and social life in colonial Philadelphia; LAWRENCE HARPER, *The English Navigation Laws* (1939, reprinted 1964), an important source on the effect of British legislation on the colonial economy. (*Cultural and religious development*): DANIEL J. BOORSTIN (*op. cit.*); LOUIS B. WRIGHT, *The Cultural Life of the American Colonies, 1607–1763* (1957), a general survey of American cultural achievement in the colonial period; VERNON L. PARRINGTON, *Main Currents in American Thought*, 3 vol. (1927–30; reprinted in 1 vol., 1958), a provocative, if often polemical interpretation of the development of liberal America; WILLIAM W. SWEET, *Religion in Colonial America* (1942), one of the standard surveys of religious development in colonial America; ALAN HEIMERT, *Religion and the American Mind: From the Great Awakening to the Revolution* (1966), an important new contribution to our understanding of the Great Awakening. DAVID W. GALENSON, *White Servitude in Colonial America: An Economic Analysis* (1983), a demographic study of indentured servants between 1607 and 1776. (*America, England, and the wider world*): LAWRENCE H. GIPSON (*op. cit.*); FRANCIS PARKMAN, *A Half-Century of Conflict*, 5th ed., 2 vol. (1893; reprinted 1965); HOWARD PECKHAM, *The Colonial Wars, 1689–1762* (1964), an excellent overview of the balance of power struggles in America; MAX SAVELLE, "The American Balance of Power and European Diplomacy, 1713–78," in RICHARD B. MORRIS (ed.), *The Era of the American Revolution* (1939), an important interpretation of the place of the American continent in the balance of power struggles of Europe.

From 1763 to 1815: The classical work on the coming of the Revolution is LAWRENCE H. GIPSON (*op. cit*); Gipson's one-volume summary, *The Coming of the Revolution, 1763–1775* (1954), is less valuable. Far better is MERRILL JENSEN, *The Founding of a Nation* (1968); for a good brief treatment see EDMUND S. MORGAN, *The Birth of the Republic, 1763–1789* (1956). A provocative and controversial view is CHARLES H. MCILWAINE, *The American Revolution: A Constitutional Interpretation* (1923, reprinted 1958). American arguments are set forth in RANDLOPH G. ADAMS, *The Political Ideas of the American Revolution*, 3rd ed. (1958). An excellent account of the development of American ideology, suffering only by inattention to the importance of Bolingbroke and his circle in shaping thinking of American radicals, is BERNARD BAILYN, *Ideological Origins of the American Revolution* (1967). PHYLLIS R. BLAKELY and JOHN N. GRANT (eds.), *Eleven Exiles* (1982), an account of 11 loyalists and their social and political ideas. On British politics during the period, the indispensable work is LOUIS NAMIER, *England in the Age of the American Revolution*, 2nd ed. (1961). CARL BECKER, *The Declaration of Independence* (1922, reprinted 1942), is a masterpiece of historical literature, though it and Becker's other works on the Revolution are no longer highly regarded. On the Confederation and Constitution, Jensen's *Articles of Confederation* (1940) is extremely valuable, his *New Nation . . . 1781–*

1789 (1950) is less so. E. JAMES FERGUSON, *The Power of the Purse* (1961), is excellent on the crucial matter of public finance in the wartime and postwar years. ALLAN NEVINS, *The American States During and After the Revolution, 1775–1789* (1924), is a standard work but contains many inaccuracies and other shortcomings. CHARLES A. BEARD, *An Economic Interpretation of the Constitution of the United States* (1913), was for decades the most influential work on the making of the Constitution, but the consensus of historians is that his work was effectively disproved by ROBERT E. BROWN, *Charles Beard and the Constitution* (1956); and FORREST MCDONALD, *We the People* (1958). McDonald's own interpretation of the event, followed in the present account, is *E Pluribus Unum: The Formation of the American Republic, 1776–1790* (1965). On the 1790s the best one-volume narrative is JOHN C. MILLER, *The Federalist Era, 1789–1801* (1960). For a provocative essay from the Republican point of view, see JOSEPH CHARLES, *Origins of the American Party System* (1956). Adams' presidency is covered—adequately, if one discounts the bias against both Hamilton and Jefferson—by STEPHEN KURTZ, *The Presidency of John Adams* (1957); and MANNING J. DAUER, *The Adams Federalists* (1953). More useful than either, perhaps, is CHARLES PAGE SMITH, *John Adams*, 2 vol. (1962). On politics in general, see WILLIAM N. CHAMBERS, *Political Parties in a New Nation: The American Experience, 1776–1809* (1963). On the years after 1800 the classical work, still towering over everything written since, is HENRY ADAMS, *The History of the United States of America During the Presidencies of Thomas Jefferson and James Madison, 1801–1817,* 9 vol. (1889–91). Also useful are JULIUS PRATT, *The Expansionists of 1812* (1925); and ROGER H. BROWN, *The Republic in Peril: 1812* (1964).

From 1816 to 1850: (*The era of mixed feelings*): GEORGE DANGERFIELD's two books, *The Era of Good Feelings* (1952) and *The Awakening of American Nationalism, 1815–1828* (1965), are highly readable and comprehensive works, particularly useful on foreign affairs. SHAW LIVERMORE, JR., *The Twilight of Federalism: The Disintegration of the Federalist Party, 1815–1830* (1962), is a detailed study of what became of the Federalist Party after the War of 1812.

Books, the topics of which are clearly stated by their titles, are MURRAY N. ROTHBARD, *The Panic of 1819* (1962); DEXTER PERKINS, *The Monroe Doctrine, 1823–1826* (1927, reprinted 1966); F. LEE BENNS, *The American Struggle for the British West Indies Carrying Trade, 1815–1830* (1923); GLOVER MOORE, *The Missouri Controversy, 1819–1821* (1953); and BRAY HAMMOND, *Banks and Politics in America: From the Revolution to the Civil War* (1957). (*The transportation revolution and the beginnings of industrialism*): GEORGE R. TAYLOR, *The Transportation Revolution, 1815–1860* (1951), is a survey of other than agricultural economic developments during the entire period. Also useful as surveys are DOUGLASS C. NORTH, *The Economic Growth of the United States, 1790–1860* (1961); and STUART BRUCHEY, *The Roots of Economic Growth, 1607–1861* (1965). An example of the "new economic history," with its stress on econometric interpretations of quantitative data is PETER TEMIN, *The Jacksonian Economy* (1969). (*Social developments*): Many European visitors wrote accounts of America. Among the most valuable are ALEXIS DE TOCQUEVILLE, *De la démocratie en Amérique*, 3rd ed., 2 vol. (1838; Eng. trans., *Democracy in America*, 2 vol., 1898, reprinted 1964); FRANCIS TROLLOPE, *Domestic Manners of the Americans*, 2 vol. (1832, reprinted 1969); HARRIET HARTINEAU, *Society in America*, 3 vol. (1837); and MICHEL CHEVALIER, *Lettres sur l'Amérique du Nord*, 3rd ed., 2 vol. (1838; Eng. trans., *Society, Manners, and Politics in the United States*, 1839, reprinted 1969). Useful scholarly studies are FREDERICK JACKSON TURNER, *The Frontier in American History* (1920, reprinted 1962); CARL R. FISH, *The Rise of the Common man, 1830–1850* (1937); ROBERT RIEGEL, *Young America,* (1949); and EDWARD PESSEN, *Jacksonian America: Society, Personality, and Politics* (1969). For discussions of immigration and immigrant life during the era, see OSCAR HANDLIN, *Boston's Immigrants, 1790–1865* (1941); MARCUS LEE HANSEN, *The Atlantic Migration, 1607–1860* (1940); and ROBERT ERNST, *Immigrant Life in New York City, 1825–1863* (1949). LEON LITWACK, *North of Slavery, The Negro in the Free States, 1790–1860* (1961), is comprehensive. Modern studies of urban developments are RICHARD C. WADE, *The Urban Frontier: The Rise of Western Cities, 1790–1830* (1959); D. CLAYTON JAMES, *Antebellum Natchez* (1968); ROBERT A. DAHL, *Who Governs? Democracy and Power in an American City* (1961); and JEFFREY G. WILLIAMSON and JOSEPH A. SWANSON, "The Growth of Cities in the American Northeast, 1820–1870," *Explorations in Entrepreneurial History*, 2nd Series, vol. 4, pp. 3–101 (1966). EDWARD PESSEN, "The Egalitarian Myth and the American Social Reality: Wealth, Mobility, and Equality in the 'Era of the Common Man,' " *American Historical Review*, 76:989–1034 (1971), a detailed, factual refutation of the thesis that antebellum America was egalitarian. Making a similar point are DOUGLAS T. MILLER, *Jacksonian Aristocracy: Class and Democracy in New York, 1830–1860* (1967); and GARY B. NASH, "The Philadelphia Bench and Bar, 1800–1861," *Comparative Studies in Society and History,* 7:203–220 (1965). (*Jacksonian democracy*): Comprehensive studies whose interpretations are diametrically opposed are ARTHUR M. SCHLESINGER, JR., *The Age of Jackson* (1945), which sees the Jacksonian movement as radical and dedicated to the interests of have-nots; and EDWARD PESSEN (*op. cit.*), which disagrees. GLYNDON G. VAN DEUSEN, *The Jacksonian Era, 1828–1848* (1959), is a brief survey of national politics. JOHN W. WARD, *Andrew Jackson, Symbol for an Age* (1955), is an interpretation of Jackson's popular appeal; and MARVIN MEYERS, *The Jacksonian Persuasion* (1957), discerns tensions and ambivalence in the movement's political beliefs. For the "new politics" of the era, see RICHARD P. MCCORMICK, *The Second American Party System: Party Formation in the Jacksonian Era* (1966); CHILTON WILLIAMSON, *American Suffrage: From Property to Democracy, 1760–1860* (1960); ROBERT V. REMINI, *Martin Van Buren and the Making of the Democratic Party* (1959) and *The Election of Andrew Jackson* (1963); SIDNEY H. ARONSON, *Status and Kinship in the Higher Civil Service* (1964); and LEONARD D. WHITE, *The Jacksonians: A Study in Administrative History, 1829–1861* (1954). For national issues see ROBERT V. REMINI, *Andrew Jackson and the Bank War* (1967); JOEL H. SILBEY, *The Shrine of Party: Congressional Voting Behavior, 1841–1852* (1967); and an old but still important study, ARTHUR C. COLE, *The Whig Party in the South* (1914, reprinted 1962). A useful collection of newer viewpoints is EDWARD PESSEN, *New Perspectives on Jacksonian Parties and Politics* (1969). ALFRED A. CAVE, *Jacksonian Democracy and the Historians* (1964), contains summaries of the various interpretations of Jacksonian Democracy. (*An age of reform*): The most comprehensive single treatment of reforms is ALICE FELT TYLER, *Freedom's Ferment: Phases of American Social History to 1860* (1944), a book more descriptive than analytical. LOUIS FILLER, *The Crusade Against Slavery, 1830–1860* (1960), covers its subject thoroughly. Useful collections are edited by MARTIN DUBERMAN, *The Antislavery Vanguard: New Essays on the Abolitionists* (1965); RICHARD O. CURRY, *The Abolitionists: Reformers or Fanatics?* (1965); GEORGE F. WHICHER, *The Transcendentalist Revolt Against Materialism* (1949; rev. by GAIL KENNEDY, *The Transcendentalist Revolt*, 1968); and DAVID BRION DAVIS, *Ante-Bellum Reform* (1967). Studies that explore the connection between religious enthusiasm and reform are WHITNEY R. CROSS, *The Burned-Over District: The Social and Intellectual History of Enthusiastic Religion in Western New York, 1800–1850* (1950); DAVID M. LUDLUM, *Social Ferment in Vermont, 1791–1850* (1939); JOHN HUMPHREY NOYES, *A History of American Socialisms* (1870, reprinted 1961); HENRY STEELE COMMAGER, *Theodore Parker* (1936, reprinted 1960); CLIFFORD S. GRIFFIN, *Their Brothers' Keepers: Moral Stewardship in the United States, 1800–1865* (1960); and TIMOTHY L. SMITH, *Revivalism and Social Reform in Mid-Nineteenth-Century America* (1957). (*Expansionism and political crisis at midcentury*): Valuable discussions of the ideology of expansionism are conducted by ALBERT K. WEINBERG, *Manifest Destiny: A Study of the Nationalist Expansionism in American History* (1935, reprinted 1958); FREDERICK MERK, *Manifest Destiny and Mission in American History* (1963); and NORMAN A. GRAEBNER, *Empire in the Pacific: A Study in American Continental Expansion* (1955). Useful studies of the process of expansionism include RAY A. BILLINGTON, *The Far Western Frontier, 1830–1860* (1956); FRANCIS PARKMAN's classic, *The California and Oregon Trail* (1849, reprinted 1964); BERNARD DEVOTO, *Across the Wide Missouri* (1947) and *The Year of Decision, 1846* (1943); FREDERICK MERK, *The Oregon Question: Essays in Anglo-American Diplomacy and Politics* (1967); WILLIAM C. BINKLEY, *The Texas Revolution* (1952); ALLEN NEVINS, *Fremont, Pathmaker of the West,* new ed. (1955); A.H. BILL, *Rehearsal for Conflict: The War with Mexico, 1846–1848* (1947); and OTIS A. SINGLETARY, *The Mexican War* (1960). For the poltical conflicts stemming from expansionism and the war with Mexico, informed coverage is provided by HOLMAN HAMILTON, *Prologue to Conflict: The Crisis and Compromise of 1850* (1964); and ERIC FONER, *Free Soil, Free Labor, Free Men: The Ideology of the Republican Party Before the Civil War* (1970).

From 1850 to 1877: The best general synthesis of modern scholarship, covering the entire era, is J.G. RANDALL and DAVID DONALD, *The Civil War and Reconstruction,* 2nd ed. rev. (1969), which contains an extensive annotated bibliography. Though outdated at many points, JAMES FORD RHODES, *History of the United States from the Compromise of 1850 . . . to 1877,* 8 vol. (1893–1906; abridged ed., 1966), gives sweeping coverage. More recent scholarly interpretations are incorporated in ALLAN NEVIN, *Ordeal of the Union,* 2 vol. (1947); *The Emergence*

of Lincoln, 2 vol. (1950); and *The War for the Union,* 4 vol. (1959–71), which cover the period from 1848 to 1865. CLEMENT EATON, *A History of the Old South,* 2nd ed. (1966), is the best general history of the region. ULRICH B. PHILLIPS, *American Negro Slavery* (1918, reprinted 1966), depicts the peculiar institution as essentially kindly, while KENNETH M. STAMPP, *The Peculiar Institution* (1956), sharply criticizes it from an abolitionist point of view. AVERY CRAVEN, *The Coming of the Civil War,* 2nd ed. (1957), is a provocative work, which stresses the possibility that the war could have been averted. The most perceptive account of the political conflicts of the late 1850s in ROY F. NICHOLS, *The Disruption of American Democracy* (1948). THOMAS J. PRESSLY, *Americans Interpret Their Civil War* (1954), offers a thorough review of the literature on the causes of the conflict. BRUCE CATTON, *The Centennial History of the Civil War,* 3 vol. (1961–65), is an eloquent and moving treatment, which stresses military developments. The best accounts of Lincoln's presidency are CARL SANDBURG, *Abraham Lincoln: The War Years,* 4 vol. (1939); and J.G. RANDALL and RICHARD N. CURRENT, *Lincoln the President,* 4 vol. (1945–55). Two comprehensive general histories of the South at war are CLEMENT EATON, *A History of the Southern Confederacy* (1954); and CHARLES P. ROLAND, *The Confederacy* (1960). HUDSON STRODE, *Jefferson Davis,* 3 vol. (1955–64), is the most ambitious account of the Confederate President. Three excellent syntheses of recent scholarship on the Reconstruction period are REMBERT W. PATRICK, *The Reconstruction of the Nation* (1967); JOHN HOPE FRANKLIN, *Reconstruction: After the Civil War* (1961); and KENNETH M. STAMPP, *The Era of Reconstruction, 1865–1877* (1965). JEAN H. BAKER, *Affairs of Party* (1983), a discussion of the strong partisan attachments of ordinary citizens in the mid-19th century; WILLIAM E. NELSON, *The Roots of American Bureaucracy: 1830–1900* (1982), a history of the growth of the federal bureaucracy. Though old, W.E.B. DU BOIS, *Black Reconstruction* (1935, reprinted 1956), remains an invaluable account of the part played by blacks. The best account of Grant as President is WILLIAM BEST HESSELTINE, *Ulysses S. Grant, Politician* (1935, reprinted 1957), which, however, should be supplemented with ALLAN NEVINS, *Hamilton Fish: The Inner History of the Grant Administration,* rev. ed. 2 vol. (1957). DAVID DONALD, *Charles Sumner and the Rights of Man* (1970), offers a full account of one of Grant's principal critics. PAUL L. HAWORTH, *The Hayes–Tilden Disputed Presidential Election of 1876,* new ed. (1927, reprinted 1966), is the standard account of the political compromises that ended Reconstruction, but C. VANN WOODWARD, *Reunion and Reaction* (1951), tells more about behind-the-scenes political and economic negotiations. The definitive account of the South in the post-Reconstruction era is C. VANN WOODWARD, *Origins of the New South, 1877–1913* (1951). MICHAEL WAYNE, *The Reshaping of Plantation Society: The Natchez District, 1860–1880* (1983), a valuable case study of the reemergence of plantation society.

The late 19th century: (*The West*): The one comprehensive study of the several "frontiers" of the period is HAROLD E. BRIGGS, *Frontiers of the Northwest* (1940). WALTER PRESCOTT WEBB, *The Great Plains* (1931, reprinted 1957), is a scholarly classic by a man who knew and loved the Plains. Important works dealing with special aspects of the post-Civil War West include RODMAN W. PAUL, *Mining Frontiers of the Far West 1848–1880* (1963); E.S. OSGOOD, *The Day of the Cattleman* (1929); J.B. FRANTZ and J.E. CHOATE, *The American Cowboy: The Myth and Reality* (1955); and ROBERT E. RIEGEL, *The Story of the Western Railroads* (1926). HENRY E. FRITZ in *The Movement for Indian Assimilation 1860–1890* (1963), traces the development of Indian policy after the Civil War. Two excellent studies of the occupation of the Plains by the farmers are FRED A. SHANNON, *The Farmer's Last Frontier: Agriculture 1860–1897* (1945, reprinted 1968); and GILBERT C. FITE, *The Farmer's Frontier, 1865–1900* (1966). EVERETT DICK presents a scholarly and interesting treatment of phases of frontier life unique to the Plains in *The Sod-House Frontier, 1854–1890* (1937, reprinted 1954). (*Industrial development*): Among many accounts of the development of industry after the Civil War, see EDWARD C. KIRKLAND, *Industry Comes of Age: Business, Labor, and Public Policy, 1860–1897* (1961). SAMUEL P. HAYS in *The Response to Industrialism, 1885–1914* (1957), offers a perceptive appraisal of the impact of industry upon many aspects of American life. Among many biographies of individual industrialists, two are noteworthy: ALLAN NEVINS, *John D. Rockefeller,* 2 vol. (1940, reprinted 1969), which is generally sympathetic with its subject; and JOSEPH WALL, *Andrew Carnegie* (1970), which is scholarly and unusually well balanced. The best brief summary of the role of the trade unions during the period is NORMAN J. WARE, *The Labor Movement in the United States, 1860–1895* (1929, reprinted 1964). (*Politics*): The literature dealing with the politics of the period is extensive, both in monographs and biographies. One contemporary study that is still invaluable for an understanding of the politics of the time is JAMES BRYCE, *The American Commonwealth*, 2 vol. (1888; new rev. ed., 1931–33), by a distinguished British scholar and public servant. LEONARD D. WHITE, *The Republican Era, 1869–1901* (1958), presents a careful and useful analysis of political and administrative policies of the period. Two valuable books that cover all or part of the period are H. WAYNE MORGAN, *From Hayes to McKinley* (1969); and HAROLD U. FAULKNER, *Politics, Reform and Expansion, 1890–1900* (1959). Books dealing with major parties include H.S. MERRILL, *Bourbon Democracy of the Middle West, 1865–1896* (1953); and ROBERT D. MARCUS, *Grand Old Party: Political Structure in the Gilded Age, 1880–1896* (1971). The standard study of Populism, regarded by some as too sympathetic with the Populists, is JOHN D. HICKS, *The Populist Revolt* (1931, reprinted 1961). DAVID F. TRASK, *The War with Spain* (1981), an excellent, one-volume account. Two works dealing with major political issues of the period are GABRIEL KOLKO, *Railroads and Regulation, 1877–1916* (1965), which attributes much of the support for regulation to railroad management rather than to reform groups; and H.B. THORELLI, *Federal Antitrust Policy* (1954). Among the numerous biographies of political leaders of the time, a few of the most important are HARRY BARNARD, *Rutherford B. Hayes, and His America* (1954); ALLAN NEVINS, *Grover Cleveland: A Study in Courage* (1932); H.J. SIEVERS, *Benjamin Harrison: Hoosier Statesman* (1959); LOUIS W. KOENIG, *Bryan: A Political Biography of William Jennings Bryan* (1971); MARGARET LEECH, *In the Days of McKinley* (1959); and HERBERT CROLY, *Marcus Alonzo Hanna: His Life and Work* (1912, reprinted 1965), which is still the only satisfactory biography of the man who was the chief architect of Republican policy at the end of the century.

Imperialism, Progressivism, and America's rise to power in the world, 1869–1920: ERNEST R. MAY, *Imperial Democracy* (1961) and *American Imperialism* (1968); WALTER LAFEBER, *The New Empire: An Interpretation of American Expansion, 1860–1898* (1963); WILLIAM APPLEMAN WILLIAMS, *The Roots of the Modern American Empire* (1969); and JULIUS W. PRATT, *Expansionists of 1898* (1936, reprinted 1964), present varying interpretations of imperialism. FRANK FREIDEL, *The Splendid Little War* (1958), is the best account of the Spanish-American War, while JULIUS W. PRATT, *America's Colonial Experiment* (1950), is nearly definitive on the administration of the American overseas empire. A. WHITNEY GRISWOLD, *The Far Eastern Policy of the United States* (1938, reprinted 1962), remains the standard work on this subject, but for the Open Door policy and relations with China, see also TYLER DENNETT, *John Hay* (1933) and *Roosevelt and the Russo-Japanese War* (1925); and CHARLES VEVIER, *The United States and China, 1906–1913* (1955). The story of American penetration and domination of the Caribbean is well recounted in SAMUEL F. BEMIS, *The Latin American Policy of the United States* (1943, reprinted 1967); DEXTER PERKINS, *The Monroe Doctrine, 1867–1907* (1937, reprinted 1966); and, most authoritatively, DANA G. MUNRO, *Intervention and Dollar Diplomacy in the Caribbean, 1900–1921* (1964). The best introduction to the United States during the progressive era is ROBERT H. WIEBE, *The Search for Order, 1877–1920* (1967). Still the standard work on Populism and its continuing contributions is JOHN D. HICKS, *The Populist Revolt* (1931). For the contributions of intellectuals to progressivism, see HENRY S. COMMAGER, *The American Mind* (1950): for the muckrakers, LOUIS FILLER, *Crusaders for American Liberalism*, new ed. (1964); for the social workers, ROBERT H. BREMNER, *From the Depths: The Discovery of Poverty in the United States* (1956); and ALLEN F. DAVIS, *Spearheads for Reform* (1967); and for the Social Gospel, CHARLES H. HOPKINS, *The Rise of the Social Gospel in American Protestantism, 1865–1915* (1940); HENRY F. MAY, *Protestant Churches and Industrial America* (1949); and AARON I. ABELL, *American Catholicism and Social Action* (1960). Excellent examples of the growing literature on urban and state progressivism are JAMES B. CROOKS, *Politics and Progress: The Rise of Urban Progressivism in Baltimore, 1895 to 1911* (1968); ZANE L. MILLER, *Boss Cox's Cincinnati* (1968); HOYT L. WARNER, *Progressivism in Ohio, 1897–1917* (1964); and SPENCER C. OLIN, JR., *California's Prodigal Sons: Hiram Johnson and the Progressives, 1911–1917* (1968). FRANK TARIELLO, *The Reconstruction of American Political Ideology: 1865–1917* (1982), a deprecation of progressivism's values. The best surveys of American national politics from Roosevelt through Wilson are GEORGE E. MOWRY, *The Era of Theodore Roosevelt, 1900–1912* (1958); and ARTHUR S. LINK, *Woodrow Wilson and the Progressive Era, 1910–1917* (1954). Biographical studies are particularly important for this period. Some of the best are WILLIAM H. HARBAUGH, *Power and Responsibility: The Life and Times of Theodore Roosevelt* (1961); HOWARD K. BEALE, *Theodore Roosevelt and the Rise of America to World Power* (1962); HENRY F. PRINGLE, *The Life and Times of William Howard Taft*, 2 vol. (1939, reprinted 1964); and ARTHUR S. LINK, *Wilson*, 5 vol. (1947–65), which concentrates on Wilson's public career from 1910 to 1917 and gives as much attention to foreign affairs as to domestic politics. The last three volumes of Link's *Wilson* contain the most definitive account of the struggle for neutrality and American entrance into World War I, but see also ERNEST R. MAY, *The World War and American Isolation, 1914–1917* (1959); and CHARLES SEYMOUR (ed.), *The Intimate Papers of Colonel House*, 4 vol. (1926–28, reprinted 1971). American mobilization is well covered by BERNARD M. BARUCH, *American Industry in the War* (1941); and DANIEL R. BEAVER, *Newton D. Baker and the American War Effort, 1917–1919* (1966). For special aspects, see SEWARD W. LIVERMORE, *Politics Is Adjourned: Woodrow Wilson and the War Congress, 1916–1918* (1966); ZECHARIAH CHAFEE, JR., *Free Speech in the United States* (1941); and HORACE C. PETERSON and GILBERT C. FITE, *Opponents of War, 1917–1918* (1957). On Wilson and the Russian Revolution, see GEORGE F. KENNAN's magisterial *Russia Leaves the War* (1956) and *The Decision to Intervene* (1958), published together as *Soviet-American Relations, 1917–1920* (1967); and the more compact monograph, BETTY M. UNTERBERGER, *America's Siberian Expedition, 1918–20* (1956). ARNO J. MAYER, *Political Origins of the New Diplomacy, 1917–1918* (1959), is a brilliant account of the development of Wilson's peace program in its worldwide context. Still the best studies on Wilsonian and American participation in the Paris Peace Conference are PAUL BIRDSALL, *Versailles Twenty Years After* (1941); and RAY STANNARD BAKER, *Woodrow Wilson and World Settlement*, 3 vol. (1922); but see also THOMAS A. BAILEY, *Woodrow Wilson and the Lost Peace* (1944); ARNO J. MAYER, *The Politics and Diplomacy of Peacemaking* (1967); and N. GORDON LEVIN, JR., *Woodrow Wilson and World Politics: America's Response to War and Revolution* (1968). The fight over the treaty is amply covered by THOMAS A. BAILEY, *Woodrow Wilson and the Great Betrayal* (1945); DENNA F. FLEMING, *The United States and the League of Nations, 1918–1920* (1932); JOHN A. GARRATY, *Henry Cabot Lodge* (1953); and RALPH STONE, *The Irreconcilables: The Fight Against the League of Nations* (1970). Nearly definitive is WESLEY M. BAGBY, *The Road to Normalcy: The Presidential Campaign and Election of 1920* (1962).

From 1920 to 1945: FRANK FREIDEL, *America in the Twentieth Century*, 3rd ed. (1970), a textbook, provides a good survey of the period. A comprehensive political review of the twenties is JOHN D. HICKS, *Republican Ascendancy, 1921–1933* (1960); while WILLIAM E. LEUCHTENBURG, *The Perils of Prosperity, 1914–32* (1958), is a lively and enterprising short account. A second volume by Leuchtenburg provides a balanced examination of the New Deal: *Franklin D. Roosevelt and the New Deal, 1932–1940* (1963). Three vividly written and richly detailed volumes by ARTHUR M. SCHLESINGER, JR., *The Age of Roosevelt* (1957–60), cover the New Deal through the 1936 election. See also FRANK FREIDEL, *Franklin D. Roosevelt*, 3 vol. (1952–56), covering down to the 1932 election. Companion volumes providing the standard economic view for this period are GEORGE H. SOULE, *Prosperity Decade: from War to Depression, 1917–1929* (1947); and BROADUS MITCHELL, *Depression Decade: From New Era Through New Deal, 1929–1941* (1947). FREDERICK L. ALLEN's two engaging contemporary studies of the social history of this era are *Only Yesterday: An Informal History of the Nineteen-twenties* (1931, reprinted 1957) and *Since Yesterday* (1940); while ARTHUR A. EKIRCH, *Ideologies and Utopias: The Impact of the New Deal on American Thought* (1969), offers a fine study of the intellectual milieu. Two solid summaries of diplomatic developments are FOSTER R. DULLES, *America's Rise to World Power, 1848–1954* (1955); and SELIG ADLER, *The Uncertain Giant, 1921–1941: American Foreign Policy Between the Wars* (1965). Roosevelt's wartime years are accurately portrayed in JAMES MacGREGOR BURNS, *Roosevelt: The Soldier of Freedom, 1940–1945* (1970); while A. RUSSELL BUCHANAN emphasizes military and administrative matters in *The United States and World War II*, 2 vol. (1964). GEOFFREY PERRETT, *America in the Twenties* (1982), an overview of political, social, and cultural aspects. ROBERT S. MCELVAINE (ed.), *Down and Out in the Great Depression* (1983), a collection of letters sent to Roosevelt during the Depression.

From 1945 to the present: The diplomatic history of the period after 1945 has attracted broad attention and interpretation. Among these, especially valuable are surveys of American foreign policy by WALTER LAFEBER, *America, Russia, and the Cold War, 1945–1966* (1967); and JOHN SPANIER, *American Foreign Policy Since World War II*, 2nd rev. ed. (1965). The difficulty of adjustment to world responsibility in foreign affairs is emphasized by HERBERT AGAR in *The Price of Power: America Since 1945* (1957); and by JOYCE and GABRIEL KOLKO in their *The Limits of Power: The World and United States Foreign Policy, 1945–1954* (1972). Important insights on presidential elections in the sixties can be gained from THEODORE H. WHITE, *The Making of the President,* 3 vol. (1960–68). Among the valuable works on individual presidents are CABELL PHILLIPS, *The Truman Presidency* (1966) BARTON J. BERNSTEIN and A.J. MATUSOW (eds.), *The Truman Administration* (1966); and ROBERT J. DONAVAN, *Eisenhower: The Inside Story* (1956). Two authors close to the Kennedy administration produced court studies of his presidential years that are important because of their inside knowledge of events. ARTHUR M. SCHLESINGER, JR., *A Thousand Days: John F. Kennedy in the White House* (1965); and THEODORE C. SORENSEN, *Kennedy* (1965). The Johnson years are examined in detail in ERIC F. GOLDMAN, *The Tragedy of Lyndon Johnson* (1969). Several studies of American society deserve mention. ERIC F. GOLDMAN, *The Crucial Decade* (1959), catches the tone of the immediate postwar years, 1945–55; while JOHN KENNETH GALBRAITH, *The Affluent Society,* 2nd ed. rev. (1969), emphasized the wealth and complacency of America in the '50s. WILLIAM O'NEILL, *Coming Apart: An Informal History of America in the 1960's* (1971), is a lively study of the quality of American life under the impact of changing social values. RONALD BERMAN writes of *America in the Sixties: An Intellectual History* (1968). WALT W. ROSTOW, *Politics and the Stages of Growth* (1971), offers an insightful commentary on national and international economic forces. JAMES GILBERT, *Another Chance: Postwar America, 1945–1968* (1982), a concise history; JAMES BENNETT and MANUEL H. JOHNSON, *The Political Economy of Federal Government Growth: 1959–1978* (1980), a comprehensive introduction to the study of U.S. bureaucratic growth.

New England. *Connecticut:* Connecticut: A Guide to Its Roads, Lore, and People (1938), one of the "American Guide Series" describing all parts of the state; CHARLES M. ANDREWS, *The Colonial Period of American History: The Settlements,* vol. 2 (1934, reprinted 1964), the most authoritative account of early Connecticut history; JOHN W. BARBER, *Connecticut Historical Collections* (1836), a town-by-town description by an investigator who travelled and knew the state personally in the 1830s; CONNECTICUT DEPARTMENT OF COMMERCE, *Connecticut Market Data* (annual), statistics on population and economy, and *Your Connecticut Guide* (annual), a comprehensive guide to tourist attractions in the state; *The Physical Geography of Connecticut* (1963), one of a valuable series including other economic, political, and social areas; CONNECTICUT, SECRETARY OF THE STATE, *State Register and Manual* (annual), compendium of facts about Connecticut state and local governments; FLORENCE S.M. CROFUT, *Guide to the History and the Historic Sites of Connecticut,* 2 vol. (1937), the definitive work on this topic; JOHN W. DE FOREST, *History of the Indians of Connecticut from the Earliest Known Period to 1850* (1851, reprinted 1970), the basic reference on Connecticut's Indians; JOSEPH B. HOYT, *The Connecticut Story* (1961), a children's history, well illustrated and with geographical insights; ARTHUR H. HUGHES and MORSE S. ALLEN, *Connecticut Place Names* (1976), an exhaustive list of place-names that includes a wealth of information on the history of the state; LEAGUE OF WOMEN VOTERS OF CONNECTICUT, *Connecticut in Focus* (1974, revised periodically), a description of Connecticut government; ODELL SHEPARD, *Connecticut, Past and Present* (1939), well-written essays about the appearance as well as the history of Connecticut; CHARD POWERS SMITH, *The Housatonic, Puritan River* (1946), a work on one of the most important rivers of New England; WAYNE R. SWONSON, *Lawmaking in Connecticut* (1978), a good survey and analysis of the General Assembly; ALBERT E. VAN DUSEN, *Connecticut* (1961), a history of Connecticut that is weighted on political developments but is rather weak on geographical and economic aspects of the state; LAWRENCE F. WILLARD and A.V. SIZER, *Pictorial Connecticut* (1962), a collection of excellent photographs by an able photographer, with descriptive text.

Maine: An authoritative general history of Maine is LOUIS C. HATCH (ed.), *Maine: A History,* 5 vol. (1919; reprinted with a new introduction and bibliography by WILLIAM B. JORDAN, JR., 1973). RONALD F. BANKS (comp.), *A History of Maine: A Collection of Readings on the History of Maine, 1600–1970* (1969), provides a good sampling of contemporaneous sources. DORRIS A. ISAACSON (ed.), *Maine: A Guide Down-East,* 2nd ed. (1970), is a valuable introduction to contemporary Maine, with travel suggestions and bibliography. STANLEY B. ATTWOOD, *The Length and Breadth of Maine* (1946; reprinted 1973), is the authoritative work on Maine's geography and natural resources. The MAINE DEPARTMENT OF ECONOMIC DEVELOPMENT, *Maine Pocket Data Book: An Economic Analysis* (annual), is a useful collection of economic facts and analysis. The *Maine Register* (annual), is filled with facts and figures on elections, state government, organizations, and businesses. The MAINE STATE PLANNING OFFICE, *The Economy of Maine: An Overall Assessment* (1979), and *Governor's Report on the Maine Economy* (1981), provide studies of Maine's economy during the late 1970s and early 1980s. ISABELLE P.

CONGDON, *Indian Tribes of Maine* (1961), is a good, brief account of Maine's Indians. PHILIP T. COOLIDGE, *History of the Maine Woods* (1963), is a social and economic history of a dominant part of Maine life. Among the books that give a flavour of Maine's folklore and cultural heritage are: ROBERT P. TRISTRAM COFFIN, *Lost Paradise: A Boyhood on a Maine Coast Farm* (1934; reprinted 1971); E.F. WILDER and G.A. MELLON (eds.), *Maine and Its Role in American Art, 1740–1963* (1963); FANNIE HARDY ECKSTROM and M.W. SMYTH (comps.), *Minstrelsy of Maine: Folk-Songs and Ballads of the Woods and the Coast* (1927; reprinted 1971); JOHN GOULD, *This Trifling Distinction: Reminiscences from Down East* (1978); SARAH ORNE JEWETT, *The Country of the Pointed Firs* (1896; reprinted with other stories, 1956 and 1979); and W. STORRS LEE (comp.), *Maine: A Literary Chronicle* (1968).

Massachusetts: The history of Massachusetts merges somewhat with that of England, and the early literature is extensive. Both William Bradford and John Winthrop, early colonial governors, wrote journals. The Adams family has been called "the writingest family" in American history, and their papers make up more than 80 volumes, without touching the 20th century. For a study of Puritan thought, the works of Perry Miller are authoritative. The intellectual history from the early Puritans through the Transcendentalists is thoroughly documented. Modern political history is less well covered, but it has become increasingly subject to scholarly scrutiny. A history of Harvard University is central to an understanding of the commonwealth. The following merely touches the surface of a vast literature. WRITERS' PROGRAM, *Massachusetts: A Guide to Its Places and People,* new ed. (1971); VAN WYCK BROOKS, *The Flowering of New England, 1815–1865* (1936, reprinted 1981), and *New England: Indian Summer, 1865–1915* (1940); CLEVELAND AMORY, *The Proper Bostonians* (1947). A.B. HART (ed.), *Commonwealth History of Massachusetts: Colony, Province and State,* 5 vol. (1927–30, reissued 1966); CHARLES M. ANDREWS, *The Fathers of New England: A Chronicle of the Puritan Commonwealths* (1920), and *The Colonial Period of American History,* 4 vol. (1934–38); SAMUEL ELIOT MORISON, HENRY STEELE COMMAGER, and WILLIAM E. LEUCHTENBURG, *The Growth of the American Republic,* 6th ed., 2 vol. (1969); SAMUEL ELIOT MORISON, *The Maritime History of Massachusetts, 1783–1860* (1921, reissued 1979), and *Builders of the Bay Colony* (1930, reprinted 1981); OSCAR HANDLIN, *Boston's Immigrants, 1790–1880,* rev. ed. (1959); RICHARD D. BROWN, *Massachusetts* (1978).

Periodicals include *Proceedings and Collections* of the MASSACHUSETTS HISTORICAL SOCIETY, Boston; the *Proceedings* of the AMERICAN ANTIQUARIAN SOCIETY, Worcester; publications of the Essex Institute, Salem; publications of the Colonial Society of Massachusetts; and the *New England Quarterly.* COMMITTEE FOR A NEW ENGLAND BIBLIOGRAPHY, *Massachusetts: A Bibliography of Its History* (1976), is an extensive work. B.K. EMERSON, *Geology of Massachusetts and Rhode Island* (1917); HENRY F. HOWE, *Salt Rivers of the Massachusetts Shore* (1951); WALTER MUIR WHITEHILL, *Boston: A Topographical History* (1959); ARTHUR B. TOURTELLOT, *The Charles* (1941); WALTER R. HARD, *The Connecticut* (1947). OSCAR and MARY F. HANDLIN, *Commonwealth: A Study of the Role of Government in the American Economy: Massachusetts, 1774–1861,* rev. ed. (1969); L.A. FROTHINGHAM, *A Brief History of the Constitution and Government of Massachusetts* (1925).

New Hampshire: J.D. SQUIRES, *The Granite State of the United States,* 4 vol. (1956), a comprehensive history of the state, and *The Story of New Hampshire* (1964); *New Hampshire Register* (annual), a collection of facts on New Hampshire's government and economy. F.A. BURT, *The Story of Mount Washington* (1960), a vivid account of the state's highest mountain; C.E. CLARK, *The Eastern Frontier: The Settlement of Northern New England 1610–1763* (1970), an admirable review of the frontier era; DAVID E. VAN DEVENTER, *The Emergence of Provincial New Hampshire, 1623–1741* (1976), a study of the socioeconomic development of colonial New Hampshire; M. CLEVELAND, *New Hampshire Fights the Civil War* (1969), a definitive work on the topic; D.B. COLE, *Jacksonian Democracy in New Hampshire, 1800–1851* (1970), an excellent analysis; J.W. GOLDTHWAIT, *The Geology of New Hampshire* (1925), readable and helpful; W.R. HARD, *The Connecticut* (1947), and R.P. HOLDEN, *The Merrimack* (1958), two fine surveys of these river valleys; C.B. KINNEY, *Church and State: The Struggle for Separation in New Hampshire, 1630–1900* (1955), a complete review of the intricate subject; M. MELCHER, *The Shaker Adventure* (1941), an excellent work on this theme; W.G. SALTONSTALL, *Ports of Piscataqua* (1941), an admirable survey of maritime New Hampshire; E.C. TEAGUE, *Mount Washington Railway Company* (1970), a history of the oldest mountain cog railway in the world; M. WADE, *The French Canadians, 1760–1945* (1955), a comprehensive survey of an important ethnic minority in New Hampshire; H.F. WILSON, *The Hill Country* of Northern New England: Its Social and Economic History, 1790–1930 (1936, reprinted 1967), a classic work.

Rhode Island: The biennial Rhode Island Manual contains extensive factual data on governmental officials, committees, etc.; while the annual Journal-Bulletin Rhode-Island Almanac contains recent election results, economic data, and much miscellaneous information not easily obtainable elsewhere. The FEDERAL WRITERS' PROJECT, Rhode Island (1937, reissued 1973), is excellent for its factual material on the state's various communities. EDWARD FIELD (ed.), State of Rhode Island and Providence Plantations at the End of the Century: A History, 3 vol. (1902), though old, remains the most complete history for the period covered; HOWARD M. CHAPIN, Documentary History of Rhode Island, 2 vol. (1916), is indispensable for the earliest years of settlement; WILLIAM G. MCLOUGHLIN, Rhode Island (1978), is a shorter, interpretive history of the state. SAMUEL H. BROCKUNIER, The Irrepressible Democrat, Roger Williams (1940), is the best biography of Williams; while PERRY MILLER, Roger Williams: His Contribution to the American Tradition (1953), is the most important reassessment of Williams' position as a liberal thinker. JAMES B. HEDGES, The Browns of Providence Plantations, 2 vol. (1952–68), is a classic study of Rhode Island's most influential family. ANTOINETTE F. DOWNING and VINCENT J. SCULLY, JR., The Architectural Heritage of Newport, Rhode Island, 1640–1915, 2nd ed. rev. (1967), contains detailed studies of the architectural developments from colonial days to the "summer palaces" of the millionaires. Publications of the Rhode Island Historical Society, especially the quarterly Rhode Island History, are valuable for recent developments.

Vermont: Probably the best one-volume portrait of Vermont and its people is RALPH NADING HILL, Contrary Country: A Chronicle of Vermont, 2nd ed. (1961). CHARLES JELLISON, Ethan Allen: Frontier Rebel (1969), provides excellent coverage of Vermont's development to 1789. Also useful are DAVID LUDLUM, Social Ferment in Vermont, 1791–1850 (1939, reprinted 1966); and HAROLD WILSON, The Hill Country of Northern New England: Its Social and Economic History, 1790–1930 (1936, reprinted 1967). Ethnic tensions between Yankees and newcomers is treated in ELIN ANDERSON's study of Burlington, Vermont, entitled We Americans: A Study of Cleavage in an American City (1937, reissued 1967). The exodus from Vermont is ably covered in Migration From Vermont by LEWIS STILWELL (1948). Population statistics for 1980, with some past figures, are available in Vermont: 1980 Census of Population (1981), by the U.S. DEPARTMENT OF COMMERCE, BUREAU OF THE CENSUS. The best book about public affairs in Vermont is Vermont State Government and Administration by ANDREW and EDITH NUQUIST (1966). The files of Vermont History, the quarterly magazine of the VERMONT HISTORICAL SOCIETY (continuing its Collections and Proceedings, first published in 1846), are valuable for historical interpretations; and the files of Vermont Life (since 1946), a magazine published quarterly by the VERMONT DEPARTMENT OF DEVELOPMENT AND COMMUNITY AFFAIRS, are helpful in giving an up-to-date depiction of folkways and other aspects of life in the Green Mountains. The Vermont Legislative Directory and State Manual, published biennially by the SECRETARY OF STATE, contains basic information about the state and biographical summaries of state officials and other prominent citizens. Also valuable is the Vermont Yearbook, published annually by the NATIONAL SURVEY OF CHESTER, VERMONT. Biennial reports of state agencies, and brochures and other literature from the Vermont Department of Development and Community Affairs, Montpelier, Vermont, explain current trends. MARCUS GILMAN, Bibliography of Vermont (1897), is valuable for the period it covers; HAROLD A. MEEKS, The Geographic Regions of Vermont: A Study in Maps (1975), is a study of physical, economic, and cultural characteristics of the state.

Middle Atlantic region. Delaware: ALFRED D. CHANDLER, JR., and STEPHEN SALSBURY, Pierre S. du Pont and the Making of the Modern Corporation (1971), a serious, thorough study; PAUL DOLAN and JAMES R. SOLES, Government of Delaware (1976), the best book on its subject; FEDERAL WRITERS' PROJECT, Delaware: A Guide to the First State, new and rev. ed. by JEANNETTE ECKMAN (1955), very useful, though old; HAROLD B. HANCOCK, Delaware During the Civil War, A Political History (1961), Liberty and Independence: The Delaware State During the American Revolution (1976), and The Loyalists of Revolutionary Delaware (1977), accounts of critical periods; CAROL E. HOFFECKER, Wilmington, Delaware: Portrait of an Industrial City, 1830–1910 (1974), Delaware—A Bicentennial History (1977), valuable interpretative works, and Readings in Delaware History (1973); JOHN A. MUNROE, Federalist Delaware, 1775–1815 (1954), a monograph, and Colonial Delaware (1978) and History of Delaware (1979), narrative accounts; H. CLAY REED and MARION BJÖRNSON REED, A Bibliography of Delaware Through 1960 (1966), and its supplement by the REFERENCE DEPARTMENT, HUGH M. MORRIS LIBRARY, UNIVERSITY OF DELAWARE,

Bibliography of Delaware, 1960–1974 (1976); C.A. WESLAGER, Delaware's Forgotten Folk: The Story of the Moors & Nanticokes (1943), a study of mixed-blood groups, The Delaware Indians, A History (1972), and The English on the Delaware, 1610–1682 (1967).

Maryland: Books on all aspects of Maryland are legion. Historical works include M.L. RADOFF (ed.), The Old Line State, 3 vol. (1957, reprinted 1971); M.L. CALLCOTT, The Negro in Maryland Politics, 1870–1912 (1969); C.B. CLARK, The Eastern Shore of Maryland and Virginia, 3 vol. (1950); M. MITCHELL, Annapolis Visit (1969); MARYLAND DEPARTMENT OF STATE PLANNING, Maryland Historical Atlas (1973); M.P. ANDREWS, History of Maryland (1929, reprinted 1965); S.H. OLSON, Baltimore, the Building of an American City (1980); W.T. RUSSELL, Maryland, the Land of Sanctuary: A History of Religious Toleration, 1634–1776 (1907); RAPHAEL SEMMES, Captains and Mariners of Early Maryland (1937); and J.M. WRIGHT, The Free Negro in Maryland, 1634–1860 (1921, reprinted 1971). JOHN BARTH's novel, The Sot-Weed Factor (1960), is an uproarious but atmospheric tale of the 17th-century Maryland colony.

Maryland's landscape comes alive in such works as the FEDERAL WRITERS' PROJECT, Maryland (1940); H. FOOTNER, Rivers of the Eastern Shore: Seventeen Maryland Rivers (1944); M.V. BREWINGTON, Chesapeake Bay: A Pictorial Maritime History, 2nd ed. (1956); A.A. BODINE, Chesapeake Bay and Tidewater, 3rd rev. and enl. ed. (1968), and The Face of Maryland, 3rd ed. (1970); and DEREK THOMPSON et al., Atlas of Maryland (1977).

People and institutions are covered in G. BYRON, The Lord's Oysters (1957, reprinted 1977); G. WOLFE, I Drove Mules on the C and O Canal (1969); K. SCARBOROUGH, The Homes of the Cavaliers (1930); H.C. FORMAN, Maryland Architecture: A Short History from 1634 Through the Civil War (1968); and G.G. CAREY, Maryland Folklore and Folklife (1970) and Faraway Time and Place (1971).

New Jersey: J. VOLNEY LEWIS, The Geology of New Jersey, rev. and rewritten by HENRY B. KÜMMEL (1940), covers the geography and geology of the state in detail, as does PETER E. WOLFE, The Geology and Landscapes of New Jersey (1977). LARRY R. GERLACH, Prologue to Independence (1976), gives an excellent account of New Jersey's role in the revolutionary movement. FRANCIS B. LEE, New Jersey As a Colony and State, 4 vol. (1902); IRVING STODDARD KULL (ed.), New Jersey: A History, 6 vol. (1930–32); and WILLIAM STARR MYERS (ed.), The Story of New Jersey, 5 vol. (1945), are thorough and detailed works. A good study of the state's ethnic background is JOHN E. BRUSH, The Population of New Jersey, 2nd ed. (1958). See also HERSCHEL LEE SCHENECK, Indians of New Jersey (1951). ADELAIDE ROSALIA HASSE, Index of Economic Material in Documents of the States of the United States, New Jersey, 1789–1904 (1914, reprinted 1965), is a prime source for information on New Jersey's industrial economy during the 19th century. HOMER HOYT, An Economic Survey of the State of New Jersey (1950); and JOHN T. CUNNINGHAM, Made in New Jersey (1954), are also useful. For a picture of the state's economy, the DEPARTMENT OF LABOR AND INDUSTRY, Facets of New Jersey, a periodically dated series of pamphlets, is a good and concise account. STATE ECONOMIC POLICY COUNCIL and OFFICE OF ECONOMIC POLICY, New Jersey Profile, updated and revised periodically, gives basic economic facts and trends. The FEDERAL WRITERS' PROJECT, New Jersey: A Guide to Its Present and Past, new and rev. ed. by LIDA NEWBERRY (ed.) (1977), contains an excellent section on the arts. LOLITA L.W. FLOCKHART, Art and Artists in New Jersey (1938), also contains valuable information. The LEAGUE OF WOMEN VOTERS OF NEW JERSEY, HELEN M. KUSHNER (ed.), New Jersey Spotlight on Government, 3rd ed. (1978), is a comprehensive, one-volume study of the state government. Fitzgerald's Legislative Manual (annual), contains a wealth of biographical information on governmental leaders plus election returns, the organization of state departments, lists and memberships of agencies, authorities and commissions, the text of the state constitution, and many other important pieces of information. The New Jersey Tercentenary Commission in 1964 published a 26-volume New Jersey Historical Series covering a wide variety of topics. DUANE LOCKHARD, The New Jersey Governor: A Study in Political Power (1964), part of the series, is an especially readable and analytical source of information on modern government.

New York: Many state agencies publish annual reports in several areas, but the 16 volumes of the NEW YORK TEMPORARY STATE COMMISSION ON THE CONSTITUTIONAL CONVENTION, Reports (1967), are especially valuable. Other general works include the New York Red Book (biennial); the FEDERAL WRITERS' PROJECT, New York: A Guide to the Empire State (1940); R.J. RAYBACK, Richards Atlas of New York State (1959); and JOHN H. THOMPSON (ed.), Geography of New York State (1966; paperback edition and supplement, 1977). Historical works include D.M. ELLIS et al., A History of New York State, rev. ed. (1967), containing a large annotated bibliography, *New York: The Empire State,* 5th ed. (1979), and *New York: State & City* (1979), including bibliographic references and index. A host of books cover special aspects of the state's history, among them OSCAR HANDLIN, *Al Smith and His America* (1958); WILLIAM RITCHIE, *The Archaeology of New York State,* rev. ed. (1969, corrected printing 1980), which is lavishly illustrated; H.W. HERTZBERG, *The Great Tree and the Longhouse: The Culture of the Iroquois* (1966), one of many works on New York's Indians; LIONEL D. WYLD, *Low Bridge! Folklore and the Erie Canal* (1962); and CARL L. CARMER, *The Tavern Lamps Are Burning: Literary Journeys Through Six Regions and Four Centuries of New York State* (1964); and H.W. THOMPSON, *Body, Boots and Britches* (1940, reprinted 1979), among many works on folklore and related topics. For state government, see L.K. CALDWELL, *The Government and Administration of New York* (1954); and ROBERT RIENOW, *Our State and Local Government,* rev. ed. (1965).

Pennsylvania: The best current source material about Pennsylvania may be found in the many publications issued by the state in Harrisburg; these are available at little or no charge. The *Pennsylvania Manual* (biennial) has outlines of the history of the state, its government, and its economic development. This manual, a direct offspring of THOMAS JEFFERSON, *A Manual of Parliamentary Practice* (1801), provides invaluable and voluminous reference material. The *Pennsylvania Statistical Abstract* (annual) is also rich in detail, with graphs and maps to illustrate the statistical tables, as is E. WILLARD MILLER, *Socioeconomic Patterns of Pennsylvania: An Atlas* (1975). For the history of Pennsylvania, one of the most interesting and detailed one-volume studies is SYLVESTER K. STEVENS, *Pennsylvania: Birthplace of a Nation* (1964). Other works of Stevens include *Pennsylvania: The Keystone State,* 2 vol. (1956); *Pennsylvania: Titan of Industry,* 3 vol. (1948), with more detailed economic history; *Portrait of Pennsylvania* (1970), a small volume of photographs with a lively text; and a paperback, *Pennsylvania History in Outline,* 4th ed. (1976). A more detailed work on Pennsylvania's geography is RAYMOND E. and MARION MURPHY, *Pennsylvania: A Regional Geography* (1937). Pennsylvania's rivers are featured in three volumes of the "Rivers of America" series: RICHARD E. BANTA, *The Ohio* (1949); FREDERICK WAY, *The Allegheny* (1942); and RICHARD P. BISSELL, *The Monongahela* (1952). Newer books describing travel in Pennsylvania include JAMES and M. CAWLEY, *Along the Old York Road* (1965); GOTTLIEB MITTELBERGER, *Journey to Pennsylvania* (1960); and ERWIN L. PETERSON, *Penn's Woods West* (1958). Pennsylvania's agriculture is discussed in STEVENSON W. FLETCHER, *Pennsylvania Agriculture and Country Life,* vol. 1, 1640–1840 (1950, reissued 1971), and vol. 2, 1840–1940 (1955). On government, an authoritative small handbook is the second edition of *A Citizen's Guide to Pennsylvania Local Government,* published by the commonwealth in 1975. On the people of Pennsylvania there are many interesting studies, among them: SOLON J. and ELIZABETH H. BUCK, *The Planting of Civilization in Western Pennsylvania* (1939); JOHN A. HOSTETTLER, *Amish Society,* 3rd ed. (1980); FREDRIC KLEES, *The Pennsylvania Dutch* (1950); WILLIAM I. SCHREIBER, *Our Amish Neighbors* (1978); the studies of Quakers and Quakerism by FREDERICK B. TOLLES, including *Quakers and the Atlantic Culture* (1960, reprinted 1980); and PAUL A.W. WALLACE, *Indians in Pennsylvania* (1961).

The South. *Alabama:* JESSE M. RICHARDSON (ed.), *Alabama Encyclopedia and Book of Facts,* vol. 1 (1965), a volume of comprehensive data on a variety of topics including an excellent chronology; WRITERS' PROJECT, *Alabama: A Guide to the Deep South,* rev. ed. by ALYCE BILLINGS (ed.) (1975), a semipopular historical account of the political, economic, educational, and cultural life within the state; ALABAMA PLANNING DIVISION, *Alabama State Plan* (1978), a discursive and statistical report on the housing, education, health, and transport sectors and on the natural resources of the state, discussing historical trends and future goals; NEAL G. LINEBACK and CHARLES T. TRAYLOR, *Atlas of Alabama* (1973). LILLIAN ESTELLE WORLEY, *Alabama's People* (1945), a historical description; THOMAS PERKINS ABERNATHY, *The Formative Period in Alabama, 1815–1828,* 2nd ed. (1965), the story of Alabama as a part of the Mississippi Territory; CHARLES SHEPARD DAVIS, *The Cotton Kingdom in Alabama* (1939, reprinted 1974), an economic report on the relations among slavery, economics, and the law; WALTER LYNWOOD FLEMING, *Civil War and Reconstruction in Alabama* (1949), an account of the factors leading to the secession of Alabama from the Union in 1861 and of conditions during the Civil War and Reconstruction; ALLEN JOHNSTON GOING, *Bourbon Democracy in Alabama, 1874–1890* (1951, reprinted 1972), an analysis and interpretation of the period; CHARLES GRAYSON SUMMERSELL, *Alabama History for Schools,* 5th ed. (1975), a well-organized and well-written history of Alabama for upper elementary and secondary school children; ELLEN LLOYD TROVER (ed.), *Chronology and Documentary Handbook of the State of Alabama* (1972); VIRGINIA VAN DER VEER

HAMILTON, *Alabama* (1977), a concise interpretative history. CARL CARMER, *Stars Fell on Alabama* (1934), a report of selected observations and experiences while travelling in the Alabama Black Belt, Red Hills, Conjure Country, Mobile, and the Bayou Country over a six-year period; CLARENCE CASON, *90° in the Shade* (1935, reprinted 1970), observations on the South—a psychograph of Southern people in their physical setting. JOHN EGERTON, "Alabama: Six Years After 'The Stand'," *State Universities and Black Americans,* pp. 24–34 (1969), an account of the policy and practice of admitting black students and employing black teachers at the University of Alabama; RAY JENKINS, "Majority Rule in the Black Belt: Greene County, Alabama," *New South,* 24:60–67 (1969), a journalistic account of the political action of blacks who were successful in winning most of the elective offices in the county government in 1969.

Arkansas: ARKANSAS HISTORICAL ASSOCIATION, *Arkansas Historical Quarterly* (1942–   ); JOHN GOULD FLETCHER, *Arkansas* (1947), one of the best single volumes about the state; LEAGUE OF WOMEN VOTERS OF ARKANSAS, *Government in Arkansas—'76* (1976), a comprehensive treatise; MARGARET ROSS, *Arkansas Gazette: The Early Years, 1819–1866* (1969), an excellent account of an old and respected newspaper; ORVILLE W. TAYLOR, *Negro Slavery in Arkansas* (1958); GEORGE H. THOMPSON, *Arkansas and Reconstruction: The Influence of Geography, Economics and Personality* (1976); ELLEN LLOYD TROVER (ed.), *Chronology And Documentary Handbook of the State of Arkansas* (1972); UNIVERSITY OF ARKANSAS, *Arkansas Business and Economic Review;* a quarterly publication containing economic data. Folklore about Arkansas may be found in several of the volumes compiled by VANCE RANDOLPH, including *Pissing in the Snow and Other Ozark Folktales* (1976).

Florida: A. MORRIS, *The Florida Handbook* (biennial), the best source for general information, containing statistics, personality sketches, history, geography, and detailed material on the state government; *Florida Trend* (monthly), Florida's foremost magazine of business and finance with information on many other subjects, providing one of the most reliable sources of current information about Florida; F. COWLES *et al., What to Look For in Florida, and What to Look Out For,* 3rd ed. (1974), a book about living in Florida, with information on prices, housing, real estate, employment, business, taxes, and government; R. WOOD and E.F. FERNALD, *The New Florida Atlas: Patterns of the Sunshine State* (1974), an updated version of the comprehensive *Atlas of Florida* by E.J. RAISZ and J.R. DUNKLE (1964); R.B. MARCUS and E.F. FERNALD, *Florida: A Geographical Approach* (1975), a geography of Florida, containing information on history, geology, water resources, vegetation, soils, agriculture, minerals, industry, tourism, and climate; O.C. BRYAN, *Soils of Florida and Their Crop Adaptation,* rev. ed. (1962); J.T. BRADLEY, *Climates of the States: Florida,* National Oceanic and Atmospheric Administration, rev. ed. (1972); FLORIDA DEPARTMENT OF TOURISM, *International Guide to Tourism* (1977); and DEL MARTH and MARTHA J. MARTH (eds.), *The Florida Almanac* (revised frequently), an enormous compendium of information, both statistical and discursive, on the state. C.W. TEBEAU, *A History of Florida,* rev. ed. (1980), the best history available; FEDERAL WRITERS' PROJECT, *Florida: A Guide to the Southernmost State* (1939, reprinted 1973); and D.B. MCKAY (ed.), *Pioneer Florida,* 3 vol. (1959).

Georgia: ELLIS MERTON COULTER, *Georgia: A Short History,* rev. ed. (1960), one of the best one-volume histories of the state for the general reader; KENNETH COLEMAN, *Colonial Georgia* (1976), an account of the period from the founding of the colony to the Revolutionary War, and *The American Revolution in Georgia, 1763–1789* (1958), a study of Georgia through three decades of crisis; HORACE MONTGOMERY, *Cracker Parties* (1950), a study of politics in antebellum Georgia; NUMAN V. BARTLEY, *From Thurmond to Wallace: Political Tendencies in Georgia, 1948–1968* (1970), an excellent study, especially of voting; HENRY T. MALONE, *Cherokees of the Old South: A People in Transition* (1956), a study of Georgia's best known Indians; T. CONN BRYAN, *Confederate Georgia* (1953), a thorough and scholarly study of Georgia during the Civil War; ALAN CONWAY, *The Reconstruction of Georgia* (1966), a study of the social and economic aspects of Reconstruction, written by a Welsh scholar; JOHN DITTMER, *Black Georgia in the Progressive Era, 1900–1920* (1977), an examination of race relations in early 20th-century Georgia; JAMES C. BONNER, *A History of Georgia Agriculture, 1732–1860* (1964); and WILLARD RANGE, *A Century of Georgia Agriculture, 1850–1950* (1954), valuable as a complementary scholarly studies.

Kentucky: THOMAS D. CLARK, *Kentucky: Land of Contrast* (1968), a lively and readable history and evocation of the state, and *The Kentucky,* rev. ed. (1969), an interesting discussion of Kentucky's chief river and its history; LEWIS COLLINS, *History of Kentucky,* rev. and enlarged by RICHARD H. COLLINS (1874, reprinted 1979), an early, valuable history of the state; GEORGE MORGAN CHINN, *Kentucky Settlement and Statehood, 1750–1800* (1975); and HAMBLETON TAPP and JAMES C. KLOTTER, *Kentucky: Decades of Discord, 1865–1900* (1977), two volumes of a projected four-volume study published by the Kentucky Historical Society; JOSEPH O. VAN HOOK, *The Kentucky Story*, 4th ed. (1974), a general text; MOSES E. LIGON, *A History of Public Education in Kentucky* (1942); WILMA DYKEMAN and JAMES STOKELY, *The Border States* (1968), an account of Kentucky, past and present, and its four neighbouring states; HARRY M. CAUDILL, *Night Comes to the Cumberlands* (1963), the authoritative work on strip-mining in Kentucky's mountains; FEDERAL WRITERS' PROJECT, *Kentucky: A Guide to the Bluegrass State* (1939, reissued 1973), an excellent book on all aspects of Kentucky life; HARRIETTE SIMPSON ARNOW, *Flowering of the Cumberland* (1963), and *Seedtime on the Cumberland* (1960), thorough, detailed studies of the development of the Cumberland River country; JOHN FETTERMAN, *Stinking Creek* (1967), an excellent, factual account of life in one mountain community of Kentucky; ALLAN W. ECKERT, *The Frontiersmen* (1967), recreation of life on America's frontiers, covering much of the history of early Kentucky; P.P. KARAN and COTTON MATHER (eds.), *Atlas of Kentucky* (1977), a thematic atlas.

Louisiana: T.R. BEARD (ed.), *The Louisiana Economy* (1969), a comprehensive review of economic processes in the state; THE UNIVERSITY OF NEW ORLEANS' DIVISION OF BUSINESS AND ECONOMIC RESEARCH and THE LOUISIANA STATE PLANNING OFFICE, *Statistical Abstract of Louisiana* (annual, 1965–), a useful and comprehensive summary of the census and other materials, updated with estimates; H. CARTER (ed.), *The Past as Prelude: New Orleans 1718–1968* (1968), a wide canvas of the city's place in the state's history; E.A. DAVIS, *Louisiana: The Pelican State*, 4th ed. (1975), a standard history of the state, and (ed.), *The Rivers and Bayous of Louisiana* (1968); N. GRAY, *A Short History of Louisiana* (1960), with attention given to the black community's role; GLENN R. CONRAD (ed.), *The Cajuns* (1978), essays on Acadian history and culture; R. HEBERLE, *The Labor Force in Louisiana* (1948), the only standard account of the topic, based on 1940 census data, providing a benchmark from which to study the state's industrial development; P.H. HOWARD, *Political Tendencies in Louisiana*, rev. ed. (1971), a comprehensive historical and sociological account of political structure and voting behaviour; F.B. KNIFFEN, *Louisiana: Its Land and People* (1968), exhaustive treatment from the standpoint of cultural geography; HARRY HANSEN (ed.), *Louisiana: A Guide to the State*, new and rev. ed. (1971), an indispensable survey of life in Louisiana; *Louisiana Almanac* (annual), a useful general almanac; LOUISIANA LEGISLATIVE COUNCIL, *The History and Government of Louisiana* (1964), a brief narrative account of state history and extensive treatment of the organization and administration of state government; JOE GRAY TAYLOR, *Louisiana* (1976), an interpretive, introductory history; R.W. SHUGG, *Origins of Class Struggle in Louisiana* (1968), a classic treatment of the political process from 1812 to the 1880s; T.L. SMITH and H.L. HITT, *The People of Louisiana* (1952), the standard demographic analysis, unfortunately outdated.

Mississippi: Of historical interest is WILLIAM BARNEY, *The Secessionist Impulse: Alabama and Mississippi in 1860* (1974). HODDING CARTER, *Lower Mississippi* (1942), is an interesting study by a major journalist. The classic definition of the Delta appears in DAVID COHN's autobiographical *Where I Was Born and Raised* (1948, reissued 1967), containing his earlier *God Shakes Creation* (1935). ARTHUR H. DE ROSIER, JR., *Removal of the Choctaw Indians* (1970), is a scholarly contribution. HORACE S. FAULKERSON, *Random Recollections of Early Days in Mississippi* (1885), contains stories from a time when vices and virtues were exaggerated. WILLIAM L. GILES, "Agricultural Revolution in the Delta," *Journal of Mississippi History*, 31:79–88 (1969), is essential for an understanding of contemporary plantation agriculture. RICHARD AUBREY MCLEMORE (ed.), *A History of Mississippi*, 2 vol. (1973), a detailed scholarly account, includes a geography and prehistory of the state. LOUISE H. MOREHEAD, *Old Spanish Trail Along the Mississippi Gulf Coast* (1955), provides colourful material, as does W.A. PERCY, *Lanterns on the Levee* (1941, reissued 1974). WILLIE MORRIS, *North Toward Home* (1967), is the autobiography of the former editor of *Harper's* magazine; and his *Yazoo: Integration in a Deep-Southern Town* (1971), continues his brilliant reportage. JOHN RAY SKATES, *Mississippi* (1979), is a concise interpretive history by a native. Research and opinion includes MISSISSIPPI STATE COLLEGE, AGRICULTURAL EXPERIMENT STATION, *Mississippi's Counties: Some Social and Economic Aspects*, ed. by WILLIAM A. STACEY, TOMMY W. ROGERS, and CARLTON R. SOLLIE, 3rd ed. (1966); VERNON L. WHARTON, *The Negro in Mississippi, 1865–1890* (1947, reissued 1965); and JAMES W. SILVER, *Mississippi: The Closed Society*, new enl. ed. (1966), an unfriendly account by a noted scholar. Also recommended is the *Atlas of Mississippi*,

ed. by RALPH D. CROSS, ROBERT W. WALES, and CHARLES T. TAYLOR (1974).

North Carolina: H.T. LEFLER and A.R. NEWSOME, *North Carolina: The History of a Southern State*, 3rd ed. (1973); H.T. LEFLER, *A Guide to the Study and Reading of North Carolina History*, 3rd ed. rev. (1969). Plantations and slavery are examined in JEFFREY CROW, *The Black Experience in Revolutionary North Carolina* (1976); and in GUION G. JOHNSON, *Ante-Bellum North Carolina: A Social History* (1937). R.E. LONSDALE, *Atlas of North Carolina* (1967), includes maps of the state showing points of local and historical interest. Also noteworthy is *North Carolina Atlas: Portrait of a Changing Southern State*, ed. by JAMES W. CLAY, DOUGLAS M. ORR, and ALFRED W. STUART (1975). NORTH CAROLINA CROP REPORTING SERVICE, *North Carolina Agricultural Statistics* (annual), a report on crops, fruits, vegetables, nuts, livestock, and prices paid and received in 100 counties; EMPLOYMENT SECURITY COMMISSION OF NORTH CAROLINA, *General Economic Summary of North Carolina*; *Biennial Report* of the NORTH CAROLINA BOARD OF HIGHER EDUCATION; *North Carolina Manual*, issued biennially by the Secretary of State, gives names, departments, and duties of various governmental agencies and officials; NORTH CAROLINA WILDLIFE RESOURCES COMMISSION, *Wildlife in North Carolina* (monthly).

South Carolina: DAVID DUNCAN WALLACE, *The History of South Carolina*, 4 vol. (1934), and *South Carolina: A Short History, 1520–1948* (1951, reprinted 1969); ERNEST MCPHERSON LANDER, *A History of South Carolina, 1865–1960* (1970); and ROBERT I. VEXLER and WILLIAM F. SWINDLER, *Chronology and Documentary Handbook of the State of South Carolina* (1978), are standard accounts of South Carolina's history. NELL S. GRAYDON, *Tales of Columbia* (1964), is a collection of materials dating from the antebellum period. DORIS E. HARLESS, *South Carolina: An Economic Profile* (1964), provides a summary view of South Carolina's economy in 1963 but also includes historical data. GEORGE C. ROGERS, JR., *Charleston in the Age of the Pinckneys* (1969), is a history of Charleston during its greatest years. GEORGE C. ROGERS, JR., *Evolution of a Federalist: William Loughton Smith of Charleston (1758–1812)* (1962), shows the relationship between the changing economic fortunes and political interests of South Carolinians. BEN ROBERTSON, *Red Hills and Cotton, An Up Country Memory* (1942, reprinted 1960), consists of reminiscences by a well-known journalist of Up Country life in the first half of the 20th century. JULIAN J. PETTY, *20th Century Changes in South Carolina Population* (1962), is an exhaustive treatment of population changes and their importance. J. DOUGLAS CONKLIN, *Selected South Carolina Economic Data* (1964), is an analysis of South Carolina's economic growth and development.

Tennessee: A good history of the state is STANLEY FOLMSBEE, ROBERT CORLEW, and ENOCH MITCHELL, *Tennessee: A Short History* (1969). The extensive bibliography on pp. 579–613 directs the reader to the richness of Tennessee's history. JOHN BALLENGER KNOX, *The People of Tennessee: A Study of Population Trends* (1949), examines the demography of Tennessee from the 1790s through the 1940s. For information about the contemporary state, see the occasional publications of the Tennessee State Planning Commission, whose studies are directly concerned with the demography, economic and human resources, and social structure of the state, as well as leading problems of government; TENNESSEE, SECRETARY OF STATE, *Tennessee Blue Book* (biennial); and TENNESSEE, CENTER FOR BUSINESS AND ECONOMIC RESEARCH, *Tennessee Statistical Abstract*, 5th ed. (1980). Information on publications may be obtained from the State Library and Archives, Nashville. For the basic physical geography of the state, see HAROLD C. AMICK and L.H. ROLLINS, *The Geography of Tennessee* (1937). A good interpretative work on Tennessee politics in the 20th century may be found in V.O. KEY, JR., *Southern Politics in State and Nation*, pp. 59–81 (1949). See also NORMAN PARKS, "Tennessee Politics Since Kefauver and Reece: A Generalist View," *Journal of Politics*, 28:144–168 (1966). HUGH DAVIS GRAHAM, *Crisis in Print: Desegregation and the Press in Tennessee* (1967), gives good insight into racial conflict in the state. See also HARRY HOLLOWAY, *The Politics of the Southern Negro: From Exclusion to Big City Organization*, pp. 65–90, 272–309 (1969), on race relations in the state.

Virginia: JEAN GOTTMAN, *Virginia in Our Century* (1969), a comprehensive analysis through 1968; RICHARD L. MORTON, *Colonial Virginia*, 2 vol. (1960), an excellent account of a single American colony; EDMUND S. MORGAN, *American Slavery—American Freedom: The Ordeal of Colonial Virginia* (1975), analyzes the social basis of early Virginian political thought; PARKE ROUSE, JR., *Virginia: The English Heritage in America*, new ed. (1976), Virginia's changes prior to the Civil War and a short epilogue that gives a contemporary assessment of the state. See also E.G. SWEM (comp.), *Virginia Historical Index*, 2 vol. (1934–36); VIRGINIUS DABNEY, *Virginia, The New Do-*

minion (1971); and publications of the Virginia State Library and of the Virginia Historical Society. A.E. DICK HOWARD *et al., Virginia's Urban Corridor* (1970), a thorough, if unwieldly, description of the political and social profile of a rapidly growing region in Virginia; HANS KURATH, *A World Geography of the Eastern United States* (1949), discusses forms of speech in Virginia. VIRGINIA DIVISION OF INDUSTRIAL DEVELOPMENT, *The Virginia Economy* (annual), a monograph containing a good analysis of Virginia's economy for each year; OFFICE OF THE COMPTROLLER, COMMONWEALTH OF VIRGINIA, *Revenues and Expenditures for Fiscal Years Ending June 30* (annual), a report with informative charts and explanatory materials concerning Virginia's finance. INSTITUTE OF GOVERNMENT, UNIVERSITY OF VIRGINIA, *The University of Virginia Newsletter* (monthly), covers a number of timely topics on Virginia's government; VIRGINIA STATE CHAMBER OF COMMERCE, *Virginia's Government*, rev. ed. (1974), a straightforward description of how Virginia's government operates in all its phases. J. HARVIE WILKINSON III, *Harry Byrd and The Changing Face of Virginia Politics, 1945–1966* (1968); and A.W. MOGER, *Virginia: Bourbonism to Byrd, 1870–1925* (1968), are two excellent works. ARTHUR KYLE DAVIS, *Folk-Songs of Virginia* (1949, reissued 1965), a collection citing 984 separate folk songs and 3,179 versions or variants of them known in Virginia; VIRGINIA CULTURAL DEVELOPMENT STUDY COMMISSION, *The Forms of Culture* (1967).

West Virginia: C.H. AMBLER, *West Virginia: The Mountain State,* 2nd ed. (1958), historic coverage from early exploration to present-day conditions; S. CLAGG, *West Virginia Fact Bank* (1970), a collection of facts relative to history, geography, economics, politics, sociology, and other areas of the social sciences (special emphasis is placed on techniques for converting the data to maps); E. COMETTI and F.P. SUMMERS (eds.), *The Thirty-Fifth State: A Documentary History of West Virginia* (1966), a look at the history of West Virginia by examination of the documents of the people making the history; P. CONLEY (ed.), *The West Virginia Encyclopedia* (1929), a classic, but dated, general reference—excellent for history and for conditions that are relatively changeless; E.L. CORE, *Vegetation of West Virginia* (1966), a brief survey of West Virginia vegetation as to the combinations of species in communities and their relative abundance; C.J. DAVIS *et al., West Virginia State and Local Government* (1963), basic information on West Virginia state and local government with brief background information and a critical analysis of procedures; R.E. JANSSEN, *Earth Science: A Handbook on the Geology of West Virginia* (1964), a study of the principles of geology and earth science in the state; *West Virginia Blue Book* (annual), a comprehensive collection of statistics, political organization of the state, and the names of officials; O.K. RICE, *The Allegheny Frontier: West Virginia Beginnings, 1730–1830* (1970), a thorough investigation of social, economic, and political affairs in pioneer West Virginia from 1730 to 1830; L.M. SIZER, *Population Change in West Virginia with Emphasis 1940–1960* (1968), an excellent analysis of the sociological aspects of population in West Virginia; WEST VIRGINIA'S GOVERNOR'S OFFICE OF ECONOMIC AND COMMUNITY DEVELOPMENT, *West Virginia Economic Profile* (1980), a collection of data treating the socioeconomic factors in the state's industrial development.

Middle West. *Illinois:* RONALD E. NELSON (ed.), *Illinois: Land and Life in the Prairie State* (1978), a good general geography; JOHN CLAYTON, *The Illinois Fact Book and Historical Almanac, 1673–1968* (1970), a comprehensive compilation of political, geographical, and historical information about Illinois—includes data on primitive man in Illinois, local government, all municipalities and their populations from the year of incorporation to 1960, maps, and a short Illinois Who's Who; ILLINOIS SESQUICENTENNIAL COMMISSION, *Illinois Guide and Gazetteer* (1969), an interesting guide that describes many cities and towns, provides several excellent motor tours throughout the state, and includes an extensive description of the cultural aspects of Chicago emphasizing the architectural heritage of the city; BAKER BROWNELL, *The Other Illinois* (1958), a historical, colourful portrait of southern Illinois from the early 18th century to the present, with interesting details of a culture of a relatively obscure region; DAVID KENNEY, *Basic Illinois Government: A Systematic Explanation*, rev. ed. (1974), a scholarly, comprehensive review of Illinois government and political parties from the state's inception (particularly good in the detailed history of politics in Illinois), including an extensive bibliography and informative maps; L.E. AHLSWEDE, *Township Government Today* (1968), a short study on township government in Illinois, explaining the importance of the annual town meeting and the future of township government; ILLINOIS, SECRETARY OF STATE, *Illinois Blue Book* (biennial), a compilation of information on the functions of Illinois state government, including portraits and biographies of state officials.

Indiana: JACOB PIATT DUNN, *Indiana and Indianans*, 5 vol.

(1919), one of the earliest documented studies of Indiana; HUBERT H. HAWKINS (comp.), *Indiana's Road to Statehood* (1964), a publication authorized by the Indiana Sesquicentennial Commission consisting of a selection of documents relating to the transition from territory to state; JAMES B. KESSLER (ed.), *Empirical Studies of Indiana Politics* (1970), a series of articles dealing with political behaviour in Indiana; IRVING LEIBOWITZ, *My Indiana* (1964), a highly readable view of the political and social events in Indiana, written by a journalist; THEODORE DREISER, *A Hoosier Holiday* (1916; reprinted 1974), an account by the native-son novelist; JULIA HENDERSON LEVERING, *Historic Indiana*, rev. ed. (1916), an interesting and detailed sociocultural history of Indiana, including a bibliography; CLIFTON J. PHILLIPS, *Indiana in Transition: The Emergence of an Industrial Commonwealth, 1880–1920* (1968), part of a five volume series discussing most of the significant political, economic, and social changes involved in Indiana's transition from a primarily rural-agricultural society to a predominantly urban-industrial commonwealth; MORTON M. ROSENBERG and DENNIS W. MCCLURG, *The Politics of Pro-Slavery Sentiment in Indiana, 1816–1861* (1968), a well-documented monograph on the immigration pattern in Indiana in relation to the rise and decline of proslavery sentiment; DAVE O. THOMPSON and WILLIAM L. MADIGAN, *One Hundred and Fifty Years of Indiana Agriculture* (1966), a description of the lives and activities of the pioneers, settlers, builders, experimenters, and agricultural scientists of early Indiana; EMMA LOU THORNBROUGH, *Since Emancipation: A Short History of Indiana Negroes 1863–1963* (1963), an historical survey, which includes a summary of trends and developments and a bibliography.

Iowa: CYRENUS COLE, *Iowa Through the Years* (1940), a highly readable account of the history of Iowa, largely politically oriented; FEDERAL WRITERS' PROGRAM, *Iowa: A Guide to the Hawkeye State* (1949, reprinted 1973), one of the WPA series of state guides, still quite useful and the only comprehensive guide to the background of many localities in the state; PHILIP FRANKLAND and STEPHEN AIROLA, *Atlas of Selected Iowa Services* (1978); *Iowa Official Register* (biennial), voting records, political history, administrative structure of the state, and capsule summaries of history and other related facts; MARSHALL MCKUSICK, *Men of Ancient Iowa* (1964), on archaeology and historical Indians, their culture, movements, and artifacts; H.L. NELSON, *A Geography of Iowa* (1967), a nontechnical survey of the agriculture, physical resource base, manufacturing, commerce, and cities of Iowa; ROBERT V. RUHE, *Quaternary Landscapes in Iowa* (1969), a discussion of the effects of the Pleistocene Epoch on the landscape of Iowa, together with consideration of the development of the land surface and soils since the Pleistocene.

Kansas: Sources of general information about the state are *The Kansas Directory* (biennial), containing a brief history, statistics, and information about state government, officials, and points of interest; and THE UNIVERSITY OF KANSAS, *Kansas Statistical Abstract* (annual). LOUISE BARRY, *The Beginning of the West: Annals of the Kansas Gateway to the American West, 1540–1854* (1972), is an excellent account of the earliest history to its opening for settlement. WILLIAM E. UNRAU, *The Kansa Indians: A History of the Wind People, 1673–1873* (1971), is a good account of the tribe from which Kansas got its name. One of the best histories of the turbulent days from the opening of the Kansas Territory to the U.S. Civil War is ERIC CORDER, *Prelude to Civil War: Kansas–Missouri, 1854–61* (1970). The colourful history of the trail that brought thousands of people to and through Kansas is outlined, with suggestions for additional reading, in JACK D. RITTENHOUSE, *The Santa Fe Trail: A Historical Bibliography* (1971). The story of the cattle trails and legendary cow towns is well recounted in ROBERT R. DYKSTRA, *The Cattle Towns* (1968). One of the most difficult periods in modern Kansas history, the drought and dust-bowl days, is admirably covered in FRANCIS W. SCHRUBEN, *Kansas in Turmoil, 1930–1936* (1969). One of the most readable brief histories of the state from its earliest days to recent times is BLISS ISELY and WALTER M. RICHARDS, *The Kansas Story* (1961). Another that contains both history, good illustrations, and information about the geography and geology of the state is MOSE J. WHITSON and BARNEY SLAWSON, *Kansas: Its Geography, History and Government* (1968). A good account of the present condition and habits of Indians in Kansas is RUTH LANDES, *Prairie Potawatomi: Tradition and Ritual in the Twentieth Century* (1970). WILLIAM F. ZORNOW, *Kansas: A History of the Jayhawk State* (1957), is among the best of the modern overviews of the entire development of Kansas from earliest times to the recent era. For an interesting picture of the legends, early customs, hardships, and adventures of the pioneers, SAMUEL J. SACKETT and WILLIAM E. KOCH, *Kansas Folklore* (1961), is recommended.

Michigan: Good general histories include: BRUCE CATTON, *Michigan* (1976); WILLIS F. DUNBAR, *Michigan: A History of the*

Wolverine State, rev. ed. (1979); and MILO M. QUAIFE and SIDNEY GLAZER, *Michigan: From Primitive Wilderness to Industrial Commonwealth* (1948, reissued 1980). More specialized studies of state history are: FLOYD RUSSELL DAIN, *Education in the Wilderness* (1968); WILLIS F. DUNBAR, *All Aboard: A History of Railroading in Michigan* (1969); GEORGE N. FULLER, *Economic and Social Beginnings of Michigan: A Study of the Settlement of the Lower Peninsula During the Territorial Period, 1805–1837* (1916); CALVIN GOODRICH, *The First Michigan Frontier* (1940); and ANGUS MURDOCH, *Boom Copper* (1943), a history of the mining counties. Interesting studies of the Michiganders include: RICHARD M. DORSON (ed.), *Negro Folktales in Michigan* (reprinted 1974); W. VERNON KINIETZ, *The Indians of the Western Great Lakes, 1615–1760* (reissued 1965); and C. WARREN VANDERHILL, *Settling the Great Lakes Frontier: Immigration to Michigan, 1837–1924* (1970).

Minnesota: THEODORE C. BLEGEN, *Minnesota: A History of the State,* 2nd ed. (1975), an authoritative history; JOHN R. BORCHERT and DONALD D. CARROLL, *Minnesota Settlement and Land Use, 1985* (1971), geographic patterns of population and major land use, with projections; JOHN R. BORCHERT and DONALD P. YEAGER, *Atlas of Minnesota Resources and Settlement,* rev. ed. (1969), maps of social, economic, and demographic conditions; KENNETH CARLEY, *The Sioux Uprising of 1862,* rev. ed. (1976), a readable, accurate account with illustrations and maps; HELEN B. CLAPESATTLE, *The Doctors Mayo,* 2nd ed. (1954), a history of the Mayo Clinic; HIRAM M. DRACHE, *The Challenge of the Prairie: Life and Times of Red River Pioneers* (1970), a look at family, social, religious, and economic life in the Red River Valley area; JOHN FISCHER, "The Minnesota Experiment: How To Make a Big City Fit To Live In," *Harper's,* 238:12–32 (1969), on the political environment that led to the Twin Cities Metropolitan Council; WILLIAM W. FOLWELL, *A History of Minnesota,* rev. ed., 4 vols. (1956–69), the most authoritative, comprehensive history; JUNE D. HOLMQUIST (ed.), *They Chose Minnesota,* a survey of the more than 60 ethnic groups that settled in the state from 1850 to 1980; MERRILL E. JARCHOW, *The Earth Brought Forth* (1949), an authoritative account of the pioneers of Minnesota agriculture; LUCILE M. KANE, *The Waterfall That Built a City: The Falls of St. Anthony in Minneapolis* (1966), a lively history of Minneapolis; MINNESOTA, SECRETARY OF STATE, *The Legislative Manual of the State of Minnesota* (biennial), a reference book on state government; G. THEODORE MITAU, *Politics in Minnesota,* 2nd ed. (1970), an insightful discussion of parties, issues, leaders, the legislative process, and the political environment; ROBIN PANLENER (ed.), *Minnesota Guidebook to State Agency Services, 1980–81* (biennial), published by the state government; GEORGE M. SCHWARTZ and G.A. THIEL, *Minnesota's Rocks and Waters,* rev. ed. (1963), a popular description and interpretation of Minnesota landscape, with suggested field trips.

Missouri: CARL H. CHAPMAN, *The Archaeology of Missouri,* 2 vol. (1975–80), a study and characterization of local prehistoric cultures from the earliest occupation to around AD 1450; LOUIS HOUCK, *A History of Missouri from the Earliest Explorations and Settlements Until the Admission of the State into the Union,* 3 vol. (1908; reprinted 1971), the definitive history of Missouri to statehood; DUANE MEYER, *The Heritage of Missouri: A History,* rev. ed. (1970), perhaps the best one-volume history of Missouri; WILLIAM E. PARRISH (ed.), *A History of Missouri* (1971–   ), a comprehensive historical survey, projected to be five volumes; MILTON D. RAFFERTY, *Historical Atlas of Missouri* (1981), an atlas with historical emphasis; NOEL P. GIST (ed.), *Missouri: Its Resources, People and Institutions* (1950), essays and studies on every aspect of Missouri's development—perhaps the most useful single volume for the interested reader; FRANCES LEA MCCURDY, *Stump, Bar, and Pulpit: Speechmaking on the Missouri Frontier* (1969), a delightful study of speeches and speech-makers in early Missouri, with excellent bibliographical references; STATE AND REGIONAL FISCAL STUDIES UNIT, UNIVERSITY OF MISSOURI, *Statistical Abstract for Missouri* (biennial), a compilation of economic and demographic statistics; MILTON D. RAFFERTY, RUSSELL L. GERLACH, and DENNIS J. HREBEC, *Atlas of Missouri* (1970), a useful atlas emphasizing economics and political and demographic resources, divisions, and concentrations; MACKINLAY KANTOR, *Missouri Bittersweet* (1969), delightful recollections of a trip through Missouri by a distinguished novelist.

Nebraska: JAMES C. OLSON, *History of Nebraska,* 2nd ed. (1966), is an excellent general historical work, including a useful bibliography. The NEBRASKA STATE HISTORICAL SOCIETY, *Proceedings and Collections,* 25 vol., and *Nebraska History,* a quarterly magazine, are essential to an understanding of the history of the state. The NEBRASKA LEGISLATIVE COUNCIL, *Nebraska Blue Book and Historical Register* (published biennially since 1915), is a useful compendium of information on the state's government. The NEBRASKA DEPARTMENT OF ECONOMIC DEVELOPMENT, *Nebraska Statistical Handbook* (biennial), has valuable information on economic and other aspects of Nebraska life.

North Dakota: Two books serve as an introduction to the literature on North Dakota. The FEDERAL WRITERS' PROJECT, *North Dakota: A Guide to the Northern Prairie State,* 2nd ed. (1950, reissued 1968), is a survey of all aspects of North Dakota life. Ten tours cover every part of the state and give short histories of every community. ELWYN B. ROBINSON, *History of North Dakota* (1966), is generally judged the definitive account; it covers all aspects of the state's history from the earliest times to about 1960, with more emphasis given to the trends of the 20th century. Both volumes have extensive annotated bibliographies and picture sections. Three books deal with the flora and fauna of the state: JOHN E. WEAVER and F.W. ALBERTSON, *Grasslands of the Great Plains: Their Nature and Use* (1956); ORIN ALVA STEVENS, *Handbook of North Dakota Plants* (1950), a scientific work; and VERNON BAILEY, *A Biological Survey of North Dakota,* published by the U.S. Department of Agriculture, Biological Survey Bureau (1926). Indian life in the early history of North Dakota is in ALFRED W. BOWERS, *Mandan Social and Ceremonial Organization* (1950). Much detail on the Indians and Métis at Pembina appears in the letters of missionaries found in *Documents Relating to Northwest Missions, 1815–1827,* ed. by GRACE LEE NUTE (1942). Two scholarly works throw some light on the Indians as they deal with related subjects: WILLIAM E. LASS, *A History of Steamboating on the Upper Missouri River* (1962); and JOHN E. SUNDER, *The Fur Trade on the Upper Missouri, 1840–1865* (1965). The conditions of tribes on the Missouri River in 1867–69 are detailed in the diary of an army officer: *Military Life in Dakota: The Journal of Philippe Régis de Trobriand,* trans. and ed. from the French original by LUCILLE M. KANE (1951). An outstanding volume on the Indians' Ghost Dance is ROBERT M. UTLEY, *The Last Days of the Sioux Nation* (1963). A volume that carries the story from the fur trade through the settlement period is VERA KELSEY, *Red River Runs North!* (1951). A broad picture of farming and farm life developments is STANLEY NORMAN MURRAY, *The Valley Comes of Age: A History of Agriculture in the Valley of the Red River of the North, 1812–1920* (1967). An intimate picture of the farming frontier is in AAGOT RAAEN, *Grass of the Earth: Immigrant Life in the Dakota Country* (1950). There are other books on social and cultural life. The story of the German-Russians is well told in ADOLPH SCHOCK, *In Quest of Free Land* (1964); while a vivid picture of farm life in the 1930s is found in *The Bones of Plenty: A Novel* (1962), and *Reapers of the Dust: A Prairie Chronicle* (1964), both by LOIS PHILLIPS HUDSON. An excellent study of early 20th-century North Dakota political history is ROBERT L. MORLAN, *Political Prairie Fire: The Nonpartisan League, 1915–1922* (1955).

Ohio: CARL WITTKE (ed.), *The History of the State of Ohio,* 6 vol. (1941–44, reprinted 1968), is the best work on this subject. EUGENE H. ROSEBOOM and FRANCIS P. WEISENBURGER, *A History of Ohio,* 2nd ed. (1967), an authoritative one-volume account, contains a valuable annotated bibliography on Ohio. *Ohio History* (quarterly), presents articles on a variety of Ohio historical subjects. Highly readable accounts of various aspects of Ohio history may be found in HARLAN HATCHER, *The Buckeye Country,* rev. ed. (1947), and *The Western Reserve: The Story of New Connecticut in Ohio* (1949); GEORGE W. KNEPPER, *An Ohio Portrait* (1976); DAVID A. GERBER, *Black Ohio and the Color Line, 1860–1915* (1976); and WALTER HAVIGHURST, *The Heartland: Ohio, Indiana, Illinois* (1962), and *Ohio* (1976). Ohio's economic geography and governmental processes are examined at length in ALFRED J. WRIGHT, *Economic Geography of Ohio,* 2nd ed. (1957), and in FRANCIS R. AUMANN and HARVEY WALKER, *The Government and Administration of Ohio* (1956). Data on Ohio's economy, vital statistics, housing, education, science, religion, and welfare may be obtained from a number of publications prepared by the ECONOMIC RESEARCH DIVISION OF THE DEVELOPMENT DEPARTMENT OF THE STATE OF OHIO, such as *Ohio Manufacturing* (1965); *Ohio's Economic Regions* (1964); *Ohio Population* (1968); *Ohio Economic Outlook* (1969); and the *Statistical Abstract of Ohio,* 2nd ed. (1969). *The Ohio Almanac,* 9th ed. (1980), is a comprehensive source that provides statistics, local profiles, and biographical sketches, as well as historical and geographical information.

South Dakota: E.P. ROTHROCK, *A Geology of South Dakota* (1943), a description of the land surface; LYLE M. BENDER, *The Rural Economy of South Dakota* (1956), an analysis and survey by a farm management specialist; SOUTH DAKOTA STATE GEOLOGICAL SURVEY, *Mineral and Water Resources of South Dakota* (1964), descriptive and historical compilation. HERBERT S. SCHELL, *History of South Dakota,* 3rd rev. ed. (1975), a standard account; DOANE ROBINSON, *History of South Dakota,* 2 vol. (1904), a general account; GEORGE W. KINGSBURY, *History of Dakota Territory,* 2 vol. (1915, reprinted 1980), a detailed work; HOWARD R. LAMAR, *Dakota Terri-*

tory, 1861–1889: A Study of Frontier Politics (1956), a well-researched study concerned with an interpretation of political behaviour; HAROLD E. BRIGGS, *Frontiers of the Northwest: A History of the Upper Missouri Valley* (1950), various aspects of early South Dakota history; J. LEONARD JANNEWEIN and JANE BOORMAN (eds.), *Dakota Panorama* (1961), a publication of the Dakota Territory Centennial Commission, covering various topics, with a bibliography of more than 1,000 titles dealing with the state; FEDERAL WRITERS' PROJECT, *South Dakota: A Guide to the State,* rev. ed. (1952, reprinted 1974), a good descriptive account for the general reader; ROBERT I. VEXLER and WILLIAM F. SWINDLER (eds.), *Chronology and Documentary Handbook of the State of South Dakota* (1979), a useful compilation of dates and sources for the state's history.

Wisconsin: The most widely informative work is the *Wisconsin Blue Book,* published biennially by the Legislative Reference Bureau; it contains basic material on state government and statistics of many kinds. Each issue includes scholarly feature articles on various aspects of the state, among the most valuable of which are EDGAR G. DOUDNA, "Wisconsin—the Thirtieth Star" (1948); and JAMES R. DONAGHUE, "The Local Government in Wisconsin" (1979). The State's geography is covered in C.W. COLLINS, *An Atlas of Wisconsin,* 2nd ed. (1972), an inclusive compilation of maps, graphs, and statistical data; R.W. FINLEY, *Geography of Wisconsin: A Content Outline* (1976), a broad picture of the physical and human geography in outline form; and A.H. ROBINSON and J.B. CULVER, *The Atlas of Wisconsin* (1974). WILLIAM FLETCHER THOMPSON (ed.), *The History of Wisconsin* (1973–), is projected to be a comprehensive six-volume work upon completion; W.F. RANEY, *Wisconsin: A Story of Progress* (1940, reissued 1963), an excellent single-volume history, may be supplemented by ROBERT C. NESBIT (comp.), *Wisconsin Since 1940: A Selection of Sources* (1966). The periodical *Transactions of the Wisconsin Academy of Sciences, Arts, and Letters* contains scholarly articles on the state, notably GUY-HAROLD SMITH, "The Settlement and Distribution of Population in Wisconsin," 24:53–108 (1929). Among many valuable publications by the state is the *Wisconsin Employment and Economic Indicators.* Informative compilations by the League of Women Voters include *Local Government in Wisconsin* (1966), and *Know Your State—Wisconsin* (1973).

The Southwest. *Arizona:* UNIVERSITY OF ARIZONA FACULTY, *Arizona: Its People and Resources,* rev. 2nd ed. (1972), the most comprehensive source available; DONALD W. MEINIG, *Southwest: Three Peoples in Geographic Change, 1600–1700* (1971), a description of the finest American example of how humans settle and organize an area through a period of time; ROGER DUNBIER, *The Sonoran Desert* (1968), an account of human use of natural setting of southern Arizona and the Sonora; PEGGY LARSON, *The Deserts of the Southwest* (1977), a publication that includes information for personal exploration; MELVIN E. HECHT and RICHARD W. REEVES, *The Arizona Atlas* (1981), with more than 100 maps, the story of where the people live, how they live, and how they have changed the landscape; WILLIAM CROFT BARNES, *Arizona Place Names,* rev. ed. by BYRD H. GRANGER (1960), an excellent travelling companion as well as an armchair introduction to Arizona's places; WRITER'S PROGRAM, *Arizona, the Grand Canyon State: A State Guide,* 4th ed. rev. by JOSEPH MILLER (1966); ODIE B. FAULK, *Arizona: A Short History* (1970), a well-written, factual account; JAY J. WAGONER, *Early Arizona: Prehistory to Civil War* (1975), and *Arizona Territory, 1863–1912: A Political History* (1970), two of the most authoritative histories; EDITORS OF SUNSET BOOKS AND SUNSET MAGAZINE, *Arizona* (1962), and *Southwest Indian Country* (1970), brief guides; CHARLES H. LOWE, *Arizona's Natural Environment* (1964), a concise, authoritative, well-illustrated account of the natural habitats; WILLIAM D. SELLERS and RICHARD H. HILL (eds.), *Arizona Climate, 1931–1972,* rev., 2nd ed. (1974), a description and analysis of the climate, with data for hundreds of locations; MAURICE M. KELSO, WILLIAM E. MARTIN, and LAWRENCE E. MACK, *Water Supplies and Economic Growth in an Arid Environment: An Arizona Case Study* (1973), a sensitive and sensible analysis by economists, written in laymen's language; BRUCE B MASON and HEINZ R. HINK, *Constitutional Government in Arizona,* 4th rev. ed. (1972), an evaluation as well as description; EDWARD H. SPICER and RAYMOND H. THOMPSON (eds.), *Plural Society in the Southwest* (1975), selected papers on the complex ethnic mix; CLARA LEE TANNER, *Indian Arts and Crafts* (1976), a beautifully illustrated and intelligent discussion of an increasingly popular subject; *Arizona Highways* (monthly), excellent photographs accompanied by sometimes lyrical, sometimes solid text; JOSEPH WOOD KRUTCH, *The Desert Year* (1952), and *The Voice of the Desert* (1955, reprinted 1969), perhaps the finest literary reflections on southern Arizona; MALCOLM L. COMEAUX, *Arizona: A Geography* (1981), a systematic geographic study of the patterns of human activities and their effects on the landscape.

New Mexico: VERNON BAILEY, *Life Zones and Crop Zones of New Mexico* (1913), a basic reference on this area, and *Mammals of New Mexico* (1931; reprinted under title *Mammals of the Southwestern United States,* 1971), a standard source; H.H. BANCROFT, *Arizona and New Mexico, 1530–1888* (1888, reprinted 1962), though dated in many areas, still a basic source, especially for its bibliography; W.A. BECK, *New Mexico: A History of Four Centuries* (1962), a single-volume text, and, with YNEZ D. HAASE, *Historical Atlas of New Mexico* (1969), maps and text dealing with all phases of history and geography; T.C. DONNELLY, *The Government of New Mexico* (1947), a basic text long used in the teaching of the state's government; NANCIE L. GONZALEZ, *The Spanish Americans of New Mexico: A Heritage of Pride,* rev. and enl. ed. (1969), a sociological study containing valuable statistics; B.L. GORDON *et al., Regions of New Mexico* (1961), a brief geographical study; L. GREBLER, J.W. MOORE, and R.C. GUZMAN, *The Mexican-American People: The Nation's Second Largest Minority* (1970), a massive study suffering from sociological jargon; J.E. HOLMES, *Politics in New Mexico* (1967), a complete analysis of the political environment since 1900; R.W. LARSON, *New Mexico's Quest for Statehood, 1846–1912* (1968); WRITERS PROGRAM, *New Mexico: A Guide to the Colorful State,* rev. ed. by JOSEPH MILLER (1953, reprinted 1974), one of the superb American guide series; F.D. REEVE, *History of New Mexico,* 3 vol. (1961), the most complete work, with an excellent volume of biographies of the state's luminaries; MARC SIMMONS, *New Mexico* (1977), an introductory history; A.M. SMITH, *New Mexico Indians* (1966), an analysis of the economic, educational, and social problems of the state's Indians, with a summary of each tribe.

Oklahoma: The best single volume covering the history, politics, economics, and social conditions is A.M. GIBSON, *Oklahoma: A History of Five Centuries,* 2nd ed. (1981). For biographical sketches as well as general history, see GASTON LITTON, *History of Oklahoma,* 4 vol. (1957). A concise, interpretive history is H. WAYNE MORGAN and ANNE HODGES MORGAN, *Oklahoma* (1977). An updating of an older WPA guide that is strong in local descriptions is WRITER'S PROGRAM, *Oklahoma: A Guide to the Sooner State,* ed. by RUTH KENT (1957). An excellent source for geography is J.W. MORRIS and E.C. MCREYNOLDS, *Historical Atlas of Oklahoma,* 2nd rev. ed. (1976). M.H. WRIGHT, *A Guide to the Indian Tribes of Oklahoma* (1951), is essential to understanding the Indian history of the state. IRVIN HURST, *The Forty-Sixth Star: A History of Oklahoma's Constitutional Convention and Early Statehood* (1957), is excellent for its descriptions of Oklahoma's founders. A brief description of Oklahoma's judicial system is given in MARTINDALE-HUBBEL, "Oklahoma Court Calendar," *Law Directory 1969* (1968). A brief description of the organization and history of higher education is given in the OKLAHOMA STATE REGENTS FOR HIGHER EDUCATION, *The Oklahoma State System of Higher Education* (1971). A comprehensive single reference source for statistical data is the *Statistical Abstract of Oklahoma* (revised periodically). Coverage of the oil industry and of ranching is found in C.C. RISTER, *Oil: Titan of the Southwest* (1949); and E.E. DALE, *The Range Cattle Industry: Ranching on the Great Plains from 1865 to 1925* (1930, reprinted 1969).

Texas: A valuable volume of facts about various aspects of Texas life and industry is *The Texas Almanac,* published every two years. The *Handbook of Texas,* ed. by WALTER PRESCOTT WEBB, 2 vol. (1952), and *Supplement,* ed. by ELDON STEPHEN BRANDA (1976), provides encyclopaedic information about individuals, ranches, Indians, colonizations, education, government, and other glimpses into Texas development. The comprehensive *Texas: A Guide to the Lone Star State,* rev. ed., ed. by HARRY HANSEN (1969), is particularly helpful in its guide to the large and middle-sized cities of the state. CLIFTON MCCLESKEY, *The Government and Politics of Texas,* 6th ed. (1978), is an authoritative book on Texas government, emphasizing the social and economic contexts. Lively glimpses of 20th-century Texas, written with attention to human interest and colour, include STANLEY WALKER, *Texas* (1962); and GEORGE M. FUERMANN, *Reluctant Empire* (1957). Each author examines the people and their doings with the eyes of an interpretative reporter. The student of the West, seeking authentic information on frontier days, will find information in such books as J. FRANK DOBIE, *The Mustangs* (1952), which recaptures the smells, sounds, and sights of the Western plains and the wild horses that once lived there. WALTER PRESCOTT WEBB, *The Texas Rangers: A Century of Frontier Defense,* rev. ed. (1965), is an excellent book about the subject. W.W. NEWCOMB, JR., *The Indians of Texas from Prehistoric to Modern Times* (1961), is a scholarly and lucid report. FRED B. GIPSON, *Cowhand: The Story of a Working Cowboy* (1953), is a day-by-day real-life story that has the movement and feeling of fiction. R. HENDERSON SHUFFLER *et al., From Many Texans: A Gathering of Cultures* (1970), relating colourful stories of the mixture of cultures in the Southwest; and CURTIS and GRACE BISHOP, with C.I. MARTIN, *Trails to Texas* (1965), recreating the cattle decades, are written for young people but appeal to adults as well. The INSTITUTE OF TEXAN CULTURES in San Antonio produces a series of monographs depicting the various ethnic or immigrant streams of life that have flowed into the Southwest, including *The Indian Texans* and *The Norwegian Texans* (both 1970). THOMAS R. PLAUT, *Net Migration into Texas and its Regions: Trends and Patterns* (1979), provides an introduction to the phenomenal growth of Texas in the 1970s.

Mountain region. *Colorado:* CARL UBBELOHDE, *A Colorado History,* 5th ed. (1982), concise history articulating major developments since territorial days; L.R. HAFEN (ed.), *Colorado and Its People,* 4 vol. (1948), discussion of its history from simple cultures to industrial society, transportation, culture and the arts, with biographical sketches; MARSHALL SPRAGUE, *Colorado* (1976), a readable one-volume history; M.E. GARNSEY, *America's New Frontier, the Mountain West* (1950), comprehensive book dealing with the economic and geographic development of the Rocky Mountain states; T.K. KELLEY, *Living in Colorado* (1964), geographic analysis of how the resources of Colorado are used with the land, and how they affect population growth and distribution; M.S. WOLLE, *Stampede to Timberline,* 2nd ed. (1974), analysis of the miners' surge into the mountains, with drawings of ghost towns and descriptions of life in mining camps; *Colorado Magazine* (quarterly), a historical journal that portrays Colorado's history in its special and general aspects. FRANCIS RAMALEY, *Colorado Plant Life* (1927), classic book dealing with plants as they are affected by environmental changes; T.D.A. COCKERELL, *Zoology of Colorado* (1927), full account of the animal life ranging from its genesis to description, and to geographic distribution; PUBLIC LAND LAW REVIEW COMMISSION, *One Third of the Nation's Land* (1970), description of the entire life ladder in Colorado, from mammals to birds, fishes, mollusks, insects, crustaceans, and protozoans; M.J. LOEFFLER, *The Population Syndromes on the Colorado Piedmont* (1965), analysis of the population geography of the Piedmont corridor.

Idaho: MERRILL D. BEAL and MERLE W. WELLS, *History of Idaho,* 3 vol. (1960), the most complete history of Idaho; JAMES H. HAWLEY, *History of Idaho,* 4 vol. (1920), a detailed account of Idaho politics from 1890 to 1919, written by a former governor; BOYD A. MARTIN, RAY C. JOLLY, and GLENN W. NICHOLS (eds.), *State and Local Government in Idaho: A Reader* (1970), thorough coverage of state and local government; *Idaho Blue Book* (annual), an expanded report on the secretary of state, including some history, election returns, and the names of all public officers of state and local governments; *The Idaho Almanac: Territorial Centennial Edition, 1863–1963* (n.d.), a special edition providing encyclopaedic coverage for these 100 years; ROBERT I. VEXLER, *Chronology and Documentary Handbook of Idaho* (1978), a concise reference of basic data on the state; M.S. GHAZANFAR, *Idaho Statistical Abstract,* 3rd ed. (1980), a ready reference to state statistics.

Montana: *The Montana Almanac 1959–60* (latest edition) is the best source of general information, though somewhat dated. ROBERT L. TAYLOR, EDIE J. MILTON, and CHARLES F. GRITZNER, *Montana In Maps* (1974), is a state atlas that shows the distribution of various commodities and physical features. M.G. BURLINGAME and K. ROSS TOOLE, *A History of Montana,* 3 vol. (1957); N.P. LANGFORD, *Vigilante Days and Ways* (various editions); T.J. DIMSDALE, *The Vigilantes of Montana* (various editions); C.B. GLASSCOCK, *The War of the Copper Kings* (1954); MICHAEL P. MALONE and RICHARD B. ROEDER (eds.), *Montana: A History of Two Centuries* (1976), and *Montana's Past: Selected Essays,* 2nd ed. (1973); K. ROSS TOOLE, *Twentieth-century Montana: A State of Extremes* (1972). *Montana Economic Study,* part 1, "The Montana Economy," Summary, Bureau of Business and Economic Research, University of Montana (October 1970); "Some Views from Indian Country," special issue of *Montana Business Quarterly,* vol. 8, no. 4 (Autumn 1970).

Nevada: The FEDERAL WRITERS' PROJECT, *Nevada: A Guide to the Silver State* (1940), provides a thorough but dated overview of the state. For a comprehensive bibliography, see RUSSELL R. ELLIOTT and H.J. POULTON, *Writings on Nevada: A Selected Bibliography* (1963). An excellent historical survey is JAMES W. HULSE, *The Nevada Adventure,* 5th ed. (1981); and still useful are JAMES G. SCRUGHAM (ed.), *Nevada: A Narrative of the Conquest of a Frontier Land,* 3 vol. (1935); and RICHARD G. LILLARD, *Desert Challenge: An Interpretation of Nevada* (1942, reprinted 1979). For special topics, see ELEANORE BUSHNELL, with DON W. DRIGGS, *The Nevada Constitution: Origin and Growth,* 5th ed. (1980); JOHN A. BRENNAN, *Silver and the First New Deal* (1969); RUSSELL R. ELLIOTT, *Nevada's Twentieth-Century Mining Boom* (1966); MARY ELLEN GLASS, *Silver and Politics in Nevada* (1970); NEVADA, SECRETARY OF STATE, *Political History of Nevada,* 7th ed. (1979); ELIOT LORD, *Comstock Mining and Miners* (1883); STANLEY W. PAHER, *Nevada Ghost*

Towns and Mining Camps (1970); and WILLIAM WRIGHT, *The Big Bonanza* (1947).

Utah: Available introductions to Utah and its people include the Federal Writers' Project, *Utah: A Guide to the State* (1954); DONALD W. MEINIG, "The Mormon Culture Region," *Ann. Assoc. Am. Geogr.,* 55:191–220 (1965); and WALLACE STEGNER, *Mormon Country* (1942, reprinted 1968). A rich source of information on the land, the people, and the institutions is DEAN C. GREER *et al., Atlas of Utah* (1981). The geological history is told in J. STEWART WILLIAMS, *Geological Studies in Utah* (1948); and WILLIAM L. STOKES and EDGAR B. HEYLMUN, *Outline of the Geologic History and Stratigraphy of Utah* (1958). JESSE D. JENNINGS, "Early Man in Utah," *Utah Historical Quarterly,* 28:3–27 (1960), takes up prehistoric Indian cultures. The best history is S. GEORGE ELLSWORTH, *Utah's Heritage,* rev. ed. (1977). A good introduction is EVERETT L. COOLEY, *Utah: A Students' Guide to Localized History* (1968). Surveys to 1900 that also describe social and economic developments include NELS ANDERSON, *Desert Saints: The Mormon Frontier in Utah* (1966); and LEONARD J. ARRINGTON, *Great Basin Kingdom: An Economic History of the Latter-day Saints, 1830–1900* (1958, paperback 1966). General histories include MILTON R. HUNTER, *Utah in Her Western Setting,* 2nd ed. (1943); and GUSTIVE O. LARSON, *An Outline History of Utah and the Mormons,* 3rd ed. (1965). A good survey of the literature on the Mormons is WILLIAM MULDER and A.R. MORTENSEN (eds.), *Among the Mormons: Historic Accounts by Contemporary Observers* (1958, reissued 1973). The most complete history is BRIGHAM H. ROBERTS, *A Comprehensive History of the Church of Jesus Christ of Latter-day Saints: Century I,* 6 vol. (1930, reprinted 1970). One-volume histories include RAY B. WEST, JR., *Kingdom of the Saints: The Story of Brigham Young and the Mormons* (1957); and THOMAS F. O'DEA, *The Mormons* (1957), the latter by a non-Mormon. A monograph on the conflict between Mormons and non-Mormons is GUSTIVE O. LARSON, *The "Americanization" of Utah for Statehood* (1971). Utah folklore is given charming treatment in AUSTIN and ALTA FIFE, *Saints of Sage and Saddle: Folklore Among the Mormons* (1956, reprinted 1980). Utah economic activity is described in MERIN B. BRINKERHOFF and PHILLIP R. KUNZ, *Utah in Numbers: Comparisons, Trends, and Descriptions* (1969), and in the publications of the BUREAU OF ECONOMIC AND BUSINESS RESEARCH of the University of Utah, such as *Utah Statistical Abstract,* 8th ed. (1979). Utah politics is treated in the UTAH FOUNDATION, *State and Local Government in Utah* (annual); FRANK H. JONAS (ed.), *Politics in the American West* (1969); and JEDON EMENHISER, *Rocky Mountain Urban Politics* (1971). Among treatments of Utah culture and its history are JAMES L. HASELTINE, *100 Years of Utah Painting* (1966); and UTAH STATE INSTITUTE OF FINE ARTS, *Report on the Fine Arts in Utah* (1968). There also are articles on culture in the *Utah Historical Quarterly.*

Wyoming: Basic sources of statistical material may be obtained from the more important biennial reports, statistical summaries, and other publications of the numerous agencies of the Wyoming state government. Additional sources include: DWIGHT M. BLOOD and CLYNN PHILLIPS, *Outdoor Recreation in Wyoming* (Wyoming Recreation Commission, 1969); ORRIN H. and LORRAINE BONNEY, *Guide to the Wyoming Mountains and Wilderness Areas,* 3rd rev. ed. (1977); ROBERT H. BROWN, *Wyoming Occupance Atlas* (1970), and *Wyoming: A Geography* (1980); WRITERS' PROGRAM, *Wyoming: A Guide to Its History, Highways and People* (1941, reprinted 1966); LEWIS L. GOULD, *Wyoming: A Political History, 1868–1896* (1968); TAFT A. LARSON, *History of Wyoming,* 2nd ed. rev. (1978), and *Wyoming: A Bicentennial History* (1977); JOHN B. RICHARD, *Government and Politics of Wyoming,* 2nd ed. (1969); MAE URBANEK, *Wyoming Wonderland* (1963), *Wyoming Place Names,* 3rd ed. rev. (1974), and with JERRY URBANEK, *Know Wyoming: A Guide to Its Literature* (1969).

Pacific Coast. *Alaska:* H.H. BANCROFT, *History of Alaska, 1730–1885* (1890, reprinted 1959), definitive narrative historical accounts of early explorations; JUDY BRADY, "Native Land Claims," *Institute of Social, Economic and Government Research,* vol. 4 (1967), a review of the land freeze of 1967 with a map of the disputed areas; *The Alaska Survey and Report* (annual), an all-inclusive book on Alaska; *Alaska Blue Book* (biennial), brief information about the government and the constitution; *Alaska Almanac* (annual), short reference about Alaska; Federal-State Landuse Planning Commission for Alaska, *Resources of Alaska: A Regional Summary,* rev. ed. (1975), contains narrative, statistical, and cartographic resource information, and an overview of the Alaskan environment; S.C. CARRIGHAR, *Icebound Summer* (1953), and *Moonlight at Midday* (1958), books on Alaskan living and the nature of the land and its people; R.A. COOLEY, *Alaska: A Challenge in Conservation* (1966), overview of the status and future of land development and use and the need for a conservation ethic; GREGG ERICKSON, "Alaska's Petroleum Leasing Policy," *Institute of Social, Economic and Government Research,* vol. 7 (1970), discussion of petroleum policies and pertinent legislation and administration; W.E. GARRETT, "Alaska's Marine Highway," *Nat. Geog. Mag.,* 127:776–819 (1965); J.L. GIDDINGS, *Ancient Men of the Arctic* (1967), archaeology of Alaska and the Arctic; ERNEST GRUENING, *The State of Alaska* (1954), authoritative text on the political and economic scene in Alaska in the decade before statehood; C.C. HULLEY, *Alaska: Past and Present,* 3rd. ed. (1970), general history from the Russian days to the 1960s; E.L. KEITHAHN, *Monuments in Cedar* (1963), professional account of Tlingit cultural heritage and Indian art of the Alaskan Panhandle; M.M. MILLER, "Alaska's Mighty Rivers of Ice," *Nat. Geog. Mag.,* 131:194–217 (1967), survey of Alaska's spectacular glacier coast and explanation of the intriguing pattern of glacier variation in historic time; GEORGE W. ROGERS, "Alaska's Economy in the 1960's," *Institute of Social, Economic and Government Research,* vol. 7 (1970), a review of Alaska's economic picture; U.S. DEPT. OF THE INTERIOR, *Mid-Century Alaska* (1957), and *Natural Resources of Alaska* (1967).

California: For general points of view on California, see NEIL MORGAN, *The California Syndrome* (1969), and *The Pacific States,* rev. ed. (1970). Older but invaluable are CAREY MCWILLIAMS, *Southern California: An Island on the Land* (1946, reissued 1973), and *California: The Great Exception* (1949, reprinted 1976). Early California histories by H.H. BANCROFT and T. HITTELL are excellent. Bancroft's voluminous works include: *History of California, 1542–1890,* 7 vol. (1884–90); *California Pastoral, 1769–1848* (1888); *California Inter Pocula, 1848–56* (1888); and *Popular Tribunals,* 2 vol. (1887). Hittell's is *History of California,* 4 vol. (1885–97). Other California histories include: J.W. CAUGHEY, *California: A Remarkable State's History,* 3rd ed. (1970); WALTON BEAN, *California: An Interpretive History,* 2nd ed. (1973); ANDREW F. ROLLE, *California: A History,* 3rd ed. (1978); and ROBERT GLASS CLELAND, *From Wilderness to Empire: A History of California,* ed. by GLENN S. DUMKE (1959). An outstanding regional overview is EARL POMEROY, *The Pacific Slope* (1965). Of detailed value but variable accuracy is the FEDERAL WRITERS' PROJECT, *California: A Guide to the Golden State,* rev. ed. (1939, reprinted 1974). More accurate guidebooks are *Northern California,* 3rd ed. (1970), and *Southern California,* 3rd ed. (1970), published by SUNSET BOOKS; and ANDREW HEPBURN, *Complete Guide to Northern California,* and *Complete Guide to Southern California* (both 1962). For geography and landscape, see DAVID W. LANTIS, RODNEY STEINER, and ARTHUR E. KARINEN, *California: Land of Contrast* 3rd ed. (1977). Among JOHN MUIR's many important works on California is *The Mountains of California* (1898, reprinted 1975). MICHAEL W. DONLEY et al., *Atlas of California* (1979), provides a wealth of geographic, demographic, and economic data; WILLIAM L. KAHRL, *The California Water Atlas* (1979), is a comprehensive account of the state's extensive water resources. Among the best books on San Francisco's earthquake is WILLIAM BRONSON, *The Earth Shook, The Sky Burned* (1959). FRANCIS P. FARQUHAR combines history and geography in *History of the Sierra Nevada* (1965). A photographic study of Yosemite is ANSEL ADAMS, *Yosemite and the Range of Light* (1979). A still-outstanding work on immigration to California is MARY R. COOLIDGE, *Chinese Immigration* (1909, reprinted 1969). The problems of the Japanese in California are addressed in ROGER DANIELS, *The Politics of Prejudice: The Anti-Japanese Movement in California and the Struggle for Japanese Exclusion,* 2nd ed. (1977). Important works are BERNARD DEVOTO, *The Course of Empire* (1952), *Across the Wide Missouri* (1947), and *The Year of Decision: 1846* (1942). A large bibliography of Gold Rush history may be found in JOHN WALTON CAUGHEY, *Gold Is the Cornerstone* (1948, reissued under the title *The California Gold Rush,* 1975). A notable primary source is *The Gold Mines of California:* Two Guidebooks (1849, reprinted 1974). A good guidebook is *Gold Rush Country* (1967). The Watts riots of 1965 are analyzed in *The Los Angeles Riots: A Socio-Psychological Study,* ed. by NATHAN COHEN (1970). An early economic history of California is that by ROBERT G. CLELAND and OSGOOD HARDY, *March of Industry* (1929). Economic affairs are discussed in NEIL MORGAN, *Westward Tilt* (1963). For railroad history, see OSCAR LEWIS, *The Big Four* (1938, reprinted 1981); on labour, see IRA B. CROSS, *A History of the Labor Movement in California* (1935, reprinted 1974). An excellent book about California politics is GLADWIN HILL, *Dancing Bear: An Inside Look at California Politics* (1968). An overview of California politics is found in GEORGE E. MOWRY, *The California Progressives 1900–1920* (1951); and FRANK H. JONAS, *Western Politics* (1961). A fine novel of California politics is EUGENE BURDICK, *The Ninth Wave* (1956).

Hawaii: Since Captain Cook penned his journal at the time of his discovery of Hawaii for the Western world, the islands have been the source material and inspiration for hundreds of writers from many nations; the complete bibliography is vast. An understanding of the insular nature of the state, its geographical reference to the Pacific, and its topography and active volcanoes are basic to an understanding of Hawaii and its history. HAROLD THORNTON STEARNS, *Road Guide to Points of Geologic Interest in the Hawaiian Islands,* 2nd ed. (1978), is especially valuable for its descriptions of points of interest along the roadside, maps, statistical tables, and a glossary of volcanic terms. See also GORDON A. MACDONALD and DOUGLASS HOPWOOD HUBBARD, *Volcanoes of the National Parks in Hawaii,* 3rd ed. rev. (1965); STATE OF HAWAII, *Data Book, A Statistical Abstract* (annual); and DEPT. OF GEOGRAPHY, UNIVERSITY OF HAWAII, *Atlas of Hawaii* (1973). PETER H. BUCK, *Vikings of the Sunrise* (1938, reprinted 1959), covers Polynesian migration in the Pacific by a noted anthropologist. Fact, legend, and myth brought to the written word are a mine of information, passed by memorization through generations, about the early Hawaiians. MARTHA W. BECKWITH, *Hawaiian Mythology* (1940; reissued with a new introduction by KATHERINE LUOMALA, 1970), is valuable. Personal journals from the late 18th and early 19th centuries form a major source of information regarding life in Hawaii. Outstanding are ARCHIBALD CAMPBELL, *A Voyage Around the World, From 1806 to 1812* (1816, reprinted 1969), one of the best accounts of life in Hawaii before any significant settlement by non-Hawaiians; and LAURA FISH JUDD, *Honolulu: Sketches of Life in the Hawaiian Islands from 1828–1861* (1880, reprinted 1966), an excellent documentary by the wife of a U.S. medical missionary. Good histories include ALAN GAVAN DAWS, *Shoal of Time: A History of the Hawaiian Islands* (1968), one of the best single-volume histories of Hawaii; ANDREW W. LIND, *An Island Community* (1938, reprinted 1968), an excellent study of the racial migrations of Hawaii and subsequent race relations; RUTH M. TABRAH, *Hawaii* (1980), an introductory work that includes social history; and RALPH S. KUYKENDALL and A. GROVE DAY, *Hawaii: A History, from Polynesian Kingdom to American State,* rev. ed. (1961, reissued 1976), another good history of the period covered. Descriptions of flora and fauna include LORRAINE E. KUCK and RICHARD C. TONGG, *Hawaiian Flowers and Flowering Trees* (1958); MARIE C. NEAL, *In Gardens of Hawaii,* new and rev. ed. (1965), the latter containing a plant guide as well as legends; and GEORGE CAMPBELL MUNRO, *Birds of Hawaii,* rev. ed. (1970), a well-illustrated guide to Hawaiian birds. THE AMERICAN INSTITUTE OF ARCHITECTS, HAWAII CHAPTER, *A Guide to Architecture in Honolulu, 1957* (1957), illustrated; and RUTH L. HAUSMAN, *Hawaii: Music in Its History* (1968), are two good books on the arts. JEAN SCOTT MACKELLAR, *Hawaii Goes Fishing* (1956, reprinted 1968), is a very readable book about different methods of fishing; THOMAS EDWARD BLAKE, *Hawaiian Surfboard* (1935, reprinted 1961), includes stories of surfing and instructions; BEN R. FINNEY and JAMES D. HOUSTON, *Surfing, the Sport of Hawaiian Kings* (1966), a history and guide; JOHN MELVILLE KELLY, *Surf and Sea* (1965), a good complete guide, including an explanation of the tides and currents that create waves; and H. ARTHUR and M.C. KLEIN, *Surf's Up! An Anthology on Surfing* (1966), are all recommended books on sports in Hawaii.

Oregon: EWART M. BALDWIN, *The Geology of Oregon,* 3rd ed. (1981), a handy summary reference; CHARLES W. BOOTH, *The Northwestern United States* (1971), a description and analysis of the geographical character of the region; PHIL F. BROGAN, *East of the Cascades* (1964), a popularization of central Oregon's geology; SAMUEL N. DICKEN, *Pioneer Trails of the Oregon Coast* (1971), a regional geography; RICHARD M. HIGHSMITH and A. JON KIMERLING (eds.), *Atlas of the Pacific Northwest,* 6th ed. (1979), a regularly revised sourcebook of maps of the Pacific Northwest; EDWIN R. JACKMAN and R.A. LONG, *The Oregon Desert* (1964), a definitive work on the Oregon ranch country; WILLIAM G. LOY, STUART ALLAN, and CLYDE P. PATTON, *Atlas of Oregon* (1976), a comprehensive reference book on Oregon; GORDON B. DODDS, *Oregon* (1977), an introductory history; RICHARD L. NEUBERGER, *The Lewis and Clark Expedition* (1951), an outstanding historical contribution; *The Oregon Blue Book* (biennial), regularly revised information on all aspects of Oregon's political organization, population, settlement, and economy.

Washington: Two excellent general histories are MARY W. AVERY, *Washington: A History of the Evergreen State* (1965); and DOROTHY O. JOHANSEN, *Empire of the Columbia: A History of the Pacific Northwest,* 2nd ed. (1967). CHARLES W. BOOTH, *The Northwestern United States* (1971), is a summary regional history emphasizing geographical factors. RICHARD M. HIGHSMITH and A. JON KIMERLING (eds.), *Atlas of the Pacific Northwest,* 6th ed. (1979), is authoritative on the geography of the area and on land use. The role of the federal government in the economic development of the Northwest is related in CHARLES MCKINLEY, *Uncle Sam in the Pacific Northwest: Federal Management of Natural Resources in the Columbia River Valley* (1952); and the development of public power and the controversies surrounding it are outlined in GEORGE SUNDBORG, *Hail Columbia: The Thirty-Year Struggle for Grand Coulee Dam* (1954). The best general description of all aspects of state and local government and administration is MARY W. AVERY, *Government of Washington State*, rev. ed. (1973). Two fascinating political accounts are DANIEL M. OGDEN and HUGH A. BONE, *Washington Politics* (1960); and Bone's essay, "Washington State: Free Style Politics," in FRANK H. JONAS (ed.), *Politics in the American West* (1969). Useful for the flavour of the state's cultural and artistic development are such publications as the FEDERAL WRITERS' PROGRAM, *New Washington: A Guide to the Evergreen State,* rev. ed. (1950); the files of the weekly Northwest news magazine, *Argus;* and various brochures and pamphlets available from the state government.

Territories: UNITED STATES DEPARTMENT OF STATE, OFFICE OF THE GEOGRAPHER, *United States and Outlying Areas* (1965), documents the official status of all United States Outlying Territories. For current information, see *Statesman's Year Book* (annual); *Statistical Abstract of the United States* (annual); and the *Hammond Almanac* (annual). A general overview of Puerto Rico is found in KAL WAGENHEIM, *Puerto Rico: A Profile,* 2nd ed. (1975); RAFAEL PICÓ, *The Geography of Puerto Rico* (1974; orginally published in Spanish, 1969), covers physical, economic, and social aspects. LOUIS CRIPPS SAMOILOFF, *Puerto Rico: The Case for Independence* (1974); and BYRON WILLIAMS,

Puerto Rico: Commonwealth, State or Nation? (1972), analyze relations between Puerto Rico and the United States; GORDON K. LEWIS, *Puerto Rico: Freedom and Power in the Caribbean* (1963, reprinted 1974), examines Puerto Rican life and U.S. contribution to politics. PUERTO RICO UNIVERSITY. SOCIAL SCIENCE RESEARCH CENTER, *Bibliografía puertorriqueña de ciencias sociales,* 2 vol. (1977———), is a bibliography on social and economic conditions, politics, and government covering the period 1931–60; social conditions are dealt with in KENT EARNHARDT, *Development Planning and Population Policy in Puerto Rico: From Historical Evolution Towards a Plan for Population Stabilization* (1982); RUBÉN DEL ROSARIO, ESTHER MELÓN DE DÍAZ, and EDGAR MARTÍNEZ MASDEU, *Breve enciclopedia de la cultura puertorriqueña* (1976), is a volume of illustrated articles. KENNETH R. FARR, *Historical Dictionary of Puerto Rico and the U.S. Virgin Islands* (1973), includes data on persons, events, historically significant places, and geographical and political subdivisions. PEARL VARLACK and NORWELL HARRIGAN, *The Virgins: A Descriptive and Historical Profile* (1977), includes a bibliography. ROBERT D. CRAIG and FRANK P. KING (eds.), *Historical Dictionary of Oceania* (1981), gives comprehensive coverage of anthropological backgrounds, culture, exploration, economy, politics, and decolonization; NAPOLEONE A. TUITELELEAPAGA, *Samoa: Yesterday, Today and Tomorrow* (1980), is an overview of history, social life, and customs; FREDERICK K. SUTTER, *Samoa* (1971), is a photographic essay on Western Samoa.

Uruguay

U ruguay (officially known as the República Oriental del Uruguay and locally still called the Banda Oriental, the "eastern shore" of the Uruguay River) is the smallest independent state in South America. With an area of 68,536 square miles (177,508 square kilometres), it is bounded by Brazil to the north and east, by the Atlantic Ocean to the southeast, and by the Río de la Plata to the south, while to the west the Uruguay River separates it from Argentina. The capital and largest city is Montevideo.

While throughout most of the 20th century Uruguay was known for its political stability and advanced social legislation, by the latter half of the century mounting economic difficulties and social unrest had thrown a pall of uncertainty over its political future. The activity of the Tupamaros, an urban guerrilla movement named after Tupac Amaru (an 18th-century Inca who rebelled against Spanish rule) that was harassing the government in a variety of ways, seemed to many to symbolize the new and violent element that had entered Uruguay's political life. (Ed.)

The article is divided into the following sections:

Physical and human geography

THE LAND

Relief and drainage. The eastern and southern half of Uruguay is a low hilly land, with a subsoil of weathered ancient schist (a crystalline rock) and granite, through which protrude low ridges of less weathered rocks. In central and north central Uruguay a basement of ancient schist is overlain by nearly horizontal layers of rock dating from the Permian Period (from 280,000,000 to 225,000,000 years ago) that form a low plateau. The northwestern portion is occupied by a southward extension of the Paraná Plateau of southern Brazil. This plateau is formed of horizontal beds of Triassic red sandstone (from 225,000,000 to 190,000,000 years old) of continental origin, in places faulted and capped by sheets of Triassic basalt. The plains of Uruguay are covered with deposits of sand and clay of the Pleistocene Epoch (2,500,000 to 10,000 years old) and with alluvial beds.

The northeastern part of the country consists of low rolling hills, a southward extension of the Brazilian highlands. The coastline is fringed with tidal lakes and sand dunes; the banks of the two rivers are low, unbroken stretches of level land. The northwestern section of the republic presents greater variety of relief, with occasional ridges and low plateaus, alternating with broad valleys, a southward extension of southern Brazil. None of the hills and plateaus of Uruguay exceeds 2,000 feet (610 metres) in elevation.

There are no large rivers entirely within Uruguayan territory. Río Negro, the largest stream, is navigable only in its lower part. The Uruguay River, along the border, is navigable for steamers of 14-foot (4.3-metre) draft from its mouth to Paysandú and above that point for smaller vessels to the falls at Salto, 200 miles (320 kilometres) in all. No other streams are navigable except for vessels of light draft. The Santa Lucía, Queguay Grande, and Cebollatí are the other principal watercourses.

The rivers

Climate. Uruguay has a truly temperate climate, the average temperature for the summer months of January and February being about 71° F (22° C) and that of the coldest month, July, being 50° F (10° C). Frost is almost unknown along the coast. The weather of both summer and winter varies from day to day, a result of the passing of storm centres associated with cyclones (large-scale wind and pressure systems characterized by low pressure at the centre and circular wind motion). Brusque wind

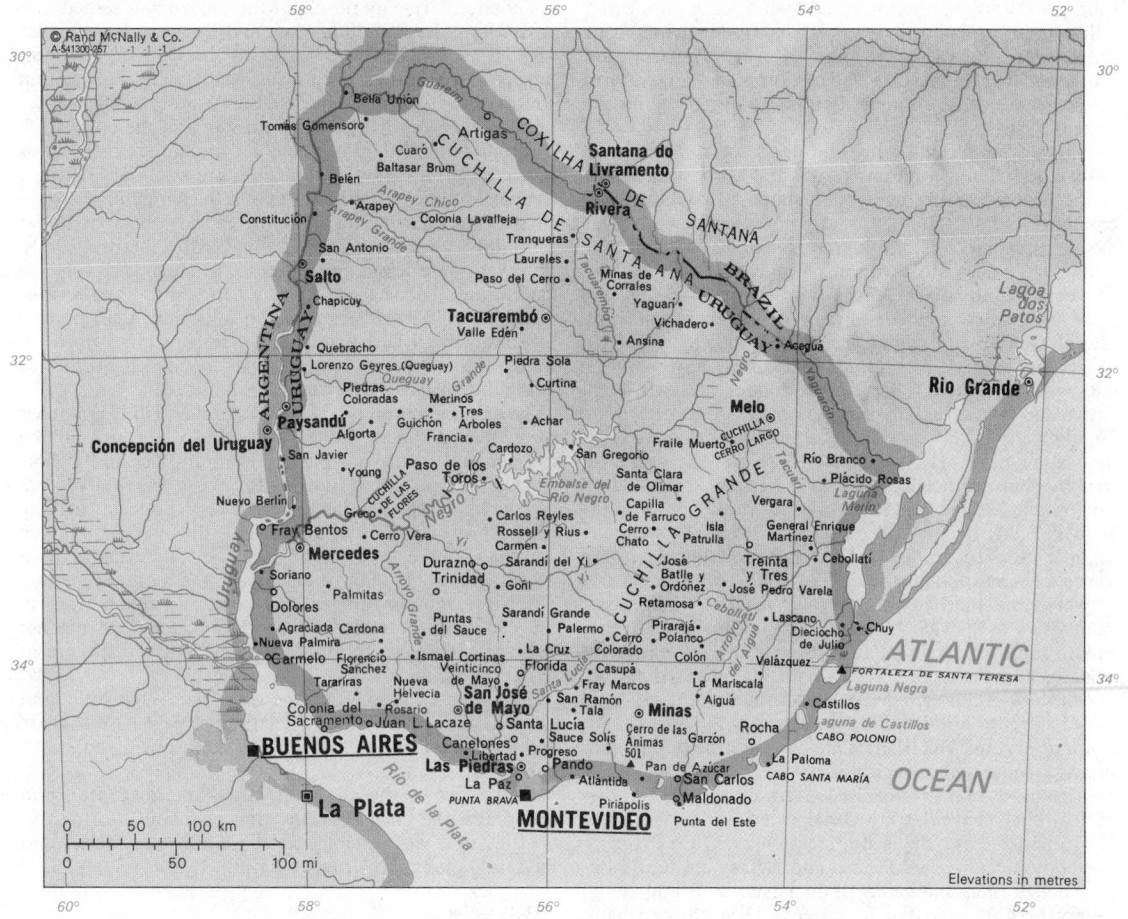

© Rand McNally & Co.
A-541300-257

Elevations in metres

MAP INDEX

Cities and towns

Acegúa..........31·52s 54·12w
Achar..........32·25s 56·10w
Agraciada......33·48s 58·15w
Aiguá..........34·12s 54·45w
Algorta........32·25s 57·23w
Ansina.........31·54s 55·28w
Arapey.........30·58s 57·32w
Artigas........30·24s 56·28w
Atlántida......34·46s 55·45w
Baltasar Brum...30·44s 57·19w
Belén..........30·47s 57·47w
Bella Unión....30·15s 57·35w
Canelones......34·32s 56·17w
Capilla de
  Farruco.......32·53s 55·25w
Cardona........33·53s 57·23w
Cardozo........32·38s 56·21w
Carlos Reyles...33·03s 56·29w
Carmelo........34·00s 58·17w
Carmen.........33·15s 56·01w
Castillos......34·12s 53·50w
Casupá.........34·07s 55·39w
Cebollatí......33·16s 53·47w
Cerro Chato....33·06s 55·08w
Cerro Colorado..33·52s 55·33w
Cerro Vera.....33·11s 57·28w
Chapicuy.......31·39s 57·54w
Chuy...........33·41s 53·27w
Colón..........33·53s 54·43w
Colonia (del
  Sacramento)...34·28s 57·51w
Colonia Lavalleja..31·06s 57·01w
Constitución...31·05s 57·50w
Cuaró..........30·37s 56·54w
Curtina........32·09s 56·07w
Dieciocho de
  Julio.........33·41s 53·33w
Dolores........33·33s 58·13w
Durazno........33·22s 56·31w
Florencio
  Sánchez.......33·53s 57·24w
Florida........34·06s 56·13w
Fraile Muerto..32·31s 54·32w
Francia........32·33s 56·37w
Fray Bentos....33·08s 58·18w
Fray Marcos....34·11s 55·44w
Garzón.........34·36s 54·33w
General Enrique
  Martínez......33·12s 53·48w

Goñi...........33·31s 56·24w
Greco..........32·48s 57·03w
Guichón........32·21s 57·12w
Isla Patrulla..32·59s 54·35w
Ismael Cortinas..33·58s 57·06w
José Batille y
  Ordóñez.......33·28s 55·07w
José Pedro
  Varela........33·27s 54·32w
Juan L. Lacaze..34·26s 57·27w
La Cruz........33·56s 56·15w
La Mariscala....34·03s 54·47w
La Paloma......34·40s 54·10w
La Paz.........34·46s 56·15w
Lascano........33·40s 54·12w
Las Piedras....34·44s 56·13w
Laureles.......31·22s 55·51w
Lavalleja, see
  Minas
Libertad.......34·38s 56·39w
Lorenzo Geyres
  (Queguay).....32·05s 57·55w
Maldonado......34·54s 54·57w
Melo...........32·22s 54·11w
Mercedes.......33·16s 58·01w
Merinos........32·24s 56·54w
Minas..........34·23s 55·14w
Minas de
  Corrales......31·35s 55·28w
Montevideo.....34·53s 56·11w
Nueva Helvecia..34·19s 57·13w
Nueva Palmira..33·53s 58·25w
Nuevo Berlín...32·59s 58·03w
Palermo........33·48s 55·59w
Palmitas.......33·31s 57·49w
Pan de Azúcar..34·48s 55·14w
Pando..........34·43s 55·57w
Paso del Cerro..31·29s 55·50w
Paso de los
  Toros.........32·49s 56·31w
Paysandú.......32·19s 58·05w
Piedras
  Coloradas.....32·23s 57·36w
Piedra Sola....32·04s 56·21w
Pirarajá.......33·44s 54·45w
Piriápolis.....34·54s 55·17w
Plácido Rosas..32·45s 53·44w
Polanco........33·54s 55·09w
Progreso.......34·40s 56·13w
Punta del Este..34·58s 54·57w
Puntas del
  Sauce.........33·51s 57·01w

Quebracho......31·57s 57·53w
Queguay, see
  Lorenzo Geyres
Retamosa.......33·35s 54·44w
Río Branco.....32·34s 53·25w
Rivera.........30·54s 55·31w
Rocha..........34·29s 54·20w
Rosario........34·19s 57·21w
Rossell y Rius..33·11s 55·42w
Salto..........31·23s 57·58w
San Antonio....31·22s 57·48w
San Carlos.....34·48s 54·55w
San Gregorio...32·37s 55·50w
San Javier.....32·41s 58·08w
San José (de
  Mayo).........34·20s 56·42w
San Ramón......34·18s 55·58w
Santa Clara de
  Olimar........32·55s 54·58w
Santa Lucía....34·27s 56·24w
Sarandí del Yi..33·21s 55·38w
Sarandí Grande..33·44s 56·20w
Sauce..........34·39s 56·04w
Solís..........34·36s 55·29w
Soriano........33·24s 58·19w
Tacuarembó.....31·44s 55·59w
Tala...........34·21s 55·46w
Tarariras......34·17s 57·37w
Tomás
  Gomensoro.....30·26s 57·26w
Tranqueras.....31·12s 55·45w
Treinta y Tres..33·14s 54·23w
Tres Árboles...32·24s 56·43w
Trinidad.......33·32s 56·54w
Valle Edén.....31·50s 56·09w
Veinticinco de
  Mayo..........34·12s 56·22w
Velázquez......34·02s 54·17w
Vergara........32·56s 53·57w
Vichadero......31·48s 54·43w
Yaguarí........31·31s 54·58w
Young..........32·41s 57·38w

Physical features
and points of interest

Aigúa, Arroyo
  del, *river*......33·38s 54·23w
Ánimas, Cerro de
  las, *mountain*...34·46s 55·19w
Arapey Chico,
  river..........30·57s 57·30w

Arapey Grande,
  river..........30·55s 57·49w
Atlantic Ocean...34·00s 52·00w
Brava, Punta,
  point..........34·56s 56·10w
Castillos, Laguna
  de, *lake*.......34·20s 53·54w
Cebollatí, *river*...33·09s 53·38w
Cerro Largo,
  Cuchilla, *hills*..32·44s 54·03w
Flores, Cuchilla
  de las, *hills*...32·51s 57·09w
Fortaleza de
  Santa Teresa,
  national park...33·59s 53·32w
Grande, Arroyo,
  river..........33·08s 57·09w
Grande, Cuchilla,
  ridge..........33·15s 55·07w
Guareim, *river*...30·12s 57·36w
Merin, Laguna,
  lagoon.........33·10s 53·25w
Negra, Laguna,
  lake...........34·03s 53·40w
Negro, *river*.....33·24s 58·22w
Plata, Río de la,
  estuary........34·45s 57·30w
Polonio, Cabo,
  cape...........34·24s 53·46w
Queguay Grande,
  river..........32·09s 58·09w
Río Negro,
  Embalse del,
  reservoir......32·45s 56·00w
Santa Ana,
  Cuchilla de,
  hills..........30·50s 55·35w
Santa Lucía,
  river..........34·48s 56·22w
Santa María,
  Cabo, *cape*.....34·40s 54·10w
Tacuarembó,
  river..........32·25s 55·29w
Tacuarí, *river*...32·46s 53·18w
Uruguay, *river*...34·12s 58·18w
Yaguarón, *river*..32·39s 53·12w

shifts are common, a hot northerly wind sometimes being followed immediately by the chill pampero (wind from the pampas—the vast grassy plains of Argentina) from the southwest, which brings a sudden drop in temperature. These changes give a middle latitude character to the climate of Uruguay.

There are no decided rainy and dry seasons. Maximum rainfall occurs in the autumn (April and May), rather than in the winter months, as is often supposed. Winter rains are most frequent but autumn rains are heaviest. The mean annual precipitation is greater than 40 inches (1,000 millimetres), decreasing with distance from the sea but everywhere well distributed throughout the year. In summer there are frequent thunderstorms. Fogs are common from May to October but seldom last all day on land.

Plant and animal life. Uruguay is mostly covered with tall, rich prairie grass. There are more trees, however, both native and introduced, than on the pampas, but these are found chiefly in narrow ribbons along the bottomlands of the watercourses. The principal species are the ombú (a scrubby plant with capacity to survive in dry areas), alder, aloe, poplar, acacia, willow, and eucalyptus. The *montes,* by which are understood plantations as well as native thickets, produce, among other useful wood, the algarrobo (carob tree) and the quebracho (a tree the wood and bark of which are used in tanning and dyeing). Indigenous palms grow in the valleys of the Sierra de San José Ignacio and, to some extent, in the departments of Lavalleja, Maldonado, and Paysandú. The myrtle, rosemary, mimosa, and the scarlet-flowered ceibo are common.

The valleys within the hills are fragrant with verbena and aromatic shrubs. The prairies are gay with the scarlet and white verbenas and other brilliant wild flowers.

As in most of the inhabited parts of the world, the wild animals have largely disappeared. Even the rhea (the American ostrich) is now seldom seen, except in a semidomesticated state. Pumas and jaguars are found on the wooded islets and banks of the larger rivers and along the northern frontier. The fox, deer, wildcat, the capybara (or water hog), and a few small rodents nearly complete the list of native quadrupeds. A small armadillo, the mulita, is the living representative of the extinct giants, mylodon and megatherium, the fossils of which are found over the pampa.

Birdlife　There are a few specimens of the vulture, a native crow (lean, tall, and ruffed), and many partridges and quails. Parakeets are plentiful in the *montes,* and the lagoons swarm with waterfowl. The most esteemed is the *pato real,* a large duck. A characteristic sight on the prairies is that of the tiny burrowing owl sitting on top of every little eminence. Large flocks of the lapwing terutero are common; they have the habit of warning other game of the approach of danger. Of birds of bright plumage, the hummingbird and cardinal—the scarlet, the yellow, and the white—are the most attractive. White herons are frequently seen in swampy lands. The scorpion is rare, but large and venomous spiders are common.

The principal reptiles are a lizard, a tortoise, the *víbora de la cruz* (a dangerous viper, so called from marks like a cross on its head), and the rattlesnake in the department of Maldonado in the southeast and the stony lands of the Minas region nearby. The caiman (alligator) is not uncommon along the upper waters of the Uruguay River. Seals are found on small islands off the southeast coast, particularly on the Isla de Lobos.

Settlement patterns. Uruguay is one of the most coherent states in Latin America. When the country became independent in 1828, its national territory was used almost exclusively for the grazing of herds of scrubby cattle on the unfenced range, and there were few permanent settlements outside of Montevideo and Colonia del Sacramento and the villages along the Uruguay River. The grazing lands along the eastern shore of the Uruguay River constituted a kind of no-man's-land between the Portuguese in Brazil and the Spaniards in Argentina.

After independence, Uruguay received a small influx of immigrants, chiefly from Italy and Spain. This was during a time when Argentina was torn by civil strife and settlement on the pampas was not yet attractive. The newcom-

ers entered Uruguay through Montevideo and settled in a zone along the Río de la Plata and Uruguay River. After 1852 the European immigrants to the Plata region went largely to Argentina. As a result, the agricultural zone in southern Uruguay remained static, because, unlike the situation in Argentina, livestock grazing and the cultivation of crops remained in separate geographic areas. Even as late as 1940, there was a notably sharp boundary between the pastoral region to the north and the agricultural region to the south, as at the town of Florida, only 50 miles (80 kilometres) north of the capital. After the mid-1940s, however, there was a great increase in the area devoted to agriculture. The sharp boundary between the two regions disappeared. Crops became more important than pasture as far north as Durazno, more than 100 miles north of Montevideo, and the crop zone also extended northward along the Uruguay River as far as Salto.

The grazing of animals in the pastoral region is no longer　Cattle
on unfenced range. Barbed wire is used throughout the　raising
interior to separate one pasture from another and to border the highways and animal driveways. Planted pasture grasses have replaced the native grasses, and the carrying capacity is high—about one animal unit per acre. There are many large ranches, or estancias, some larger than 25,000 acres (10,000 hectares), in the pastoral region. Sheep are more significant than cattle in the northwest, especially on the relatively dry, low plateaus on diabase and red sandstone. South of the Río Negro cattle are of major importance.

The agricultural zone, on the other hand, has little land devoted to pasture. The chief crop is wheat, but there are also important areas of maize, flax (for linseed), oats, barley, and grapes.

Montevideo is the country's largest urban centre, and it contains the chief concentration of manufacturing. Industries were also established at Fray Bentos, Salto, and Paysandú along the Uruguay River.　(P.E.J.)

THE PEOPLE

The people of Uruguay are predominantly white, most of them descendants of 19th- and 20th-century immigrants from Spain, Italy, and other European countries. The Indian population is almost completely extinct, and only a very small proportion of Uruguayans exhibit any noticeable Indian physical characteristics. There are few blacks or mulattoes.

Comprehensive statistical data on religious affiliations of Uruguayans are lacking, but less satisfactory sources of information are sufficient to indicate that the large majority profess the Roman Catholic faith. Spanish is the official language and the one used in the home by an overwhelming majority of the families. In the sections along the Brazilian border, however, the language in daily use includes a large admixture of Portuguese words and phrases.

The city of Montevideo contains about half of the nation's people, with many thousands more residing nearby in the adjacent department of Canelones. The remainder of the inhabitants are concentrated in those departments that front upon the Río de la Plata, namely, Colonia, San José, and Maldonado (the chief town of which is Punta del Este), and among those adjacent to the Uruguay River, especially Soriano, Salto, and Paysandú. In addition to Montevideo, the most important cities are Salto, Paysandú, Punta del Este, Rivera, Las Piedras, Melo, Mercedes, and Minas.　(Ed.)

THE ECONOMY

The foundation of Uruguay's economy is said to have been laid in 1603, when a far-seeing governor of Paraguay, Hernando Arias de Saavedra, having observed the fertility of the empty southern pastures, shipped about 100 head of cattle and 100 horses downstream from Asunción. The animals were landed on the Uruguayan riverbank, where they were left to run wild. Later in the century, the herds were so abundant that they attracted gauchos, who crossed the Río de la Plata from Buenos Aires and began a trade in hides. The gauchos were nomads, with no desire to settle, but, gradually, merchants from Buenos Aires established themselves on the Uruguayan side of the estuary. As more

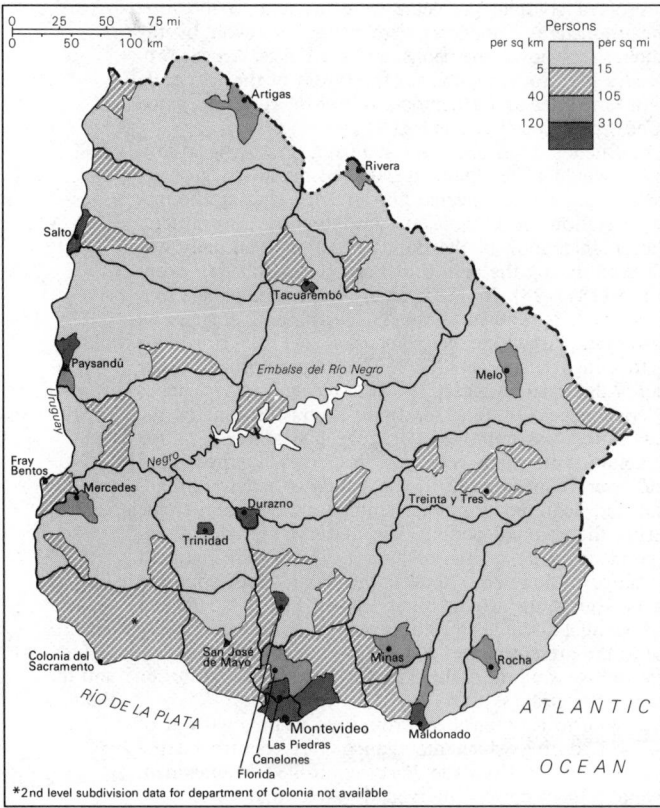

Population density of Uruguay.

*2nd level subdivision data for department of Colonia not available

electric installations were formerly dependent on imported coal or oil; but hydroelectric plants, built primarily along the Río Negro, by the early 1980s were providing about two-thirds of the country's electricity.

The processing of food and other products of the land is the basic form of industry. The subsidized wool-combing industry has added to the country's exports. Consumer goods manufactured locally (mainly around Montevideo) include textiles, tires and other rubber goods, shoes, and household appliances.

Trade. Wool, meat, and by-products are the major exports. Hides and skins are the other principal export items. The chief markets are the United Kingdom, Italy, West Germany, Brazil, the Soviet Union, The Netherlands, and the United States. The main imports are raw materials for industry, vehicles, machinery, and fuels. The chief suppliers of these imports are the United States, Brazil, West Germany, Argentina, Nigeria, Japan, and the United Kingdom. Despite import controls, the balance of trade is usually unfavourable. Uruguay was a founder-member of LAFTA (Latin American Free Trade Association), set up at Montevideo in 1960.

Finance. The functions of a central bank are exercised by the state-owned Banco Central, formed in 1967. Another state bank, the Banco de la República, regulates many aspects of foreign trade and is the country's largest commercial banking organization.

Transportation. In the late 20th century Uruguay possessed about 2,000 miles (3,200 kilometres) of railway and more than 8,000 miles of paved or surfaced highways, both systems radiating from Montevideo. The resultant competition has mainly favoured road transport, and international loans have been obtained to improve the highways, particularly those providing links with Brazil. About 1,000 miles of the country's inland waters are navigable. Local shipping handles only a small proportion of the country's foreign trade. There is a hydrofoil service from Montevideo to Buenos Aires. The main airport is at Balneario Carrasco, 13 miles from Montevideo; a state airline, Primeras Líneas Uruguayas de Navegación Aérea (PLUNA), provides services within Uruguay and to neighbouring countries.

In the late 20th century the state telephone service had a few hundred thousand subscribers (most residing in Montevideo). Broadcasting services, including many television channels, are operated by state and private companies. Several cable companies provide foreign communication links; an international telex service was inaugurated in mid-1964.

Telephone and broadcasting services

(I.C.Cn./G.Pe./C.P.D.)

ADMINISTRATIVE AND SOCIAL CONDITIONS

Government. The military government that took power in 1973 suspended the provisions of the 1966 constitution. The 1966 constitution had restored the presidential system of government and repudiated a *colegiado* (plural-executive) system previously in use. According to the constitution, the president is chief of state and commander of the armed forces. The legislative branch consists of a Senate and a Chamber of Deputies, whose members are elected for four years by universal suffrage, the political parties having proportional representation.

The 1966 constitution

Uruguay consists of 19 departments, each, according to the constitution, governed by a departmental council, which exercise executive functions, and by a legislative assembly; both the councils and the assemblies are elected by popular vote. Under military rule, the departments were administered by appointees of the central government.

Two of the three principal traditional political parties are the Colorado Party (which traditionally has had an urban base), and the Blanco Party (supported by the landowners). The third party, the Frente Amplio (Broad Front), representing a coalition of Christian Democrats, Socialists, Communists, and dissident members of the two other parties, was outlawed by the military regime. The activities of the radical-revolutionary Tupamaros guerrilla movement, which operates outside the parliamentary system, were often cited as justification for the military takeover of the government.

Structure of the economy

cattlemen arrived, boundaries had to be fixed, and thus there came into existence the great estancias that are still characteristic of the country.

The relatively high standard of living enjoyed in and around Montevideo is closely related to the earnings from pastoral and agricultural exports; prosperity is somewhat precarious because these primary products are subject to sudden fluctuations in world demand and prices. To reduce the nation's dependence on external trade, successive governments have encouraged the development of domestic industry by means of protective tariffs, import controls, exemptions of machinery from import duties, and preferential exchange rates. But, as there are no local sources of petroleum, coal, or iron and little heavy industry, Uruguay is obliged to import most of its fuel, industrial raw materials, vehicles, and industrial machinery. These essential supplies are paid for primarily with the produce of the ranches and farms and the income derived from tourists. Uruguay is noted among Latin American countries for its highly developed social services, but these were placing an excessive burden on the country's resources.

Agriculture. Pastoral farming is Uruguay's most important economic activity. Wool and beef are its chief products and the source of about one-fourth of its total earnings from foreign trade. All available land is in use for grazing or agriculture, and production can be increased only by improved techniques. Government policy has generally sought to achieve national self-sufficiency in wheat. This has sometimes led to overproduction of this cereal and to a partial neglect of livestock farming. Other crops include corn (maize), linseed, sunflower seed, oats, barley, rice, sugarcane, and sugar beets. Fruits grown are oranges, lemons, peaches, grapes (sufficient for the local wine industry), pears, and apples.

Industry. The state operates a large number of public corporations. It controls electricity and the refining of imported petroleum; it manufactures alcohol and cement; it directs a meat-packing plant and the processing of fish; and it controls the railways (purchased from their British owners at the end of World War II), several banking institutions, and insurance.

The public corporations

Since the low, rolling countryside of Uruguay is not generally suited to hydroelectric development, most of the

Justice. A Supreme Court of five judges is elected for a 10-year term by the General Assembly (*i.e.,* the two houses of the legislature). The courts were controlled by the executive branch of government following the military coup. The death penalty has been abolished since 1907.

The armed forces. The army is composed of volunteers enlisting for one or two years and comprises regiments of cavalry, engineers, infantry, artillery, and tanks. There is a small navy and air force. A reserve force is trained every year under a compulsory military training law.

Education. Uruguay has long been renowned for its progress in education, after reforms instituted in the late 19th century that established a system of free, compulsory, coeducational, and secular education. This progress was reflected in the high literacy rate.

Higher education

The Universidad de la República (founded in 1849) has 10 faculties, including a distinguished medical school that draws students from many South American countries. There is also a privately supported Instituto de Estudios Superiores (Institute of Higher Studies) devoted to scientific research. Vocational training is given by the Universidad del Trabajo del Uruguay, which organizes and controls a number of industrial and night schools.

Health and welfare. Since the early years of the 20th century, Uruguay has played a leading role in the development of social security. The country's comprehensive program includes extensive provisions for unemployment insurance, compensation for injuries to workmen, family allowances, and aid to the aged and indigent. With respect to problems of health and sanitation, Uruguay is among the most fortunately situated of the Latin-American countries. Long a South American pioneer in international cooperation, Uruguay participates in the technical assistance programs of the United States, the Organization of American States, and the United Nations.

CULTURAL LIFE

Uruguay falls within the same cultural context as other Spanish-speaking American states. Interest in literature and the arts has flourished. There has been traditionally a thriving press, both in Montevideo and the provinces; censorship was virtually nonexistent prior to 1973. Recreational facilities are provided by the sandy beaches on the coast, as well as by the wildlife resources of the interior; both have served as tourist attractions. Football is the principal sport, but basketball and horse racing are also popular.

(G.I.B./Ed.)

History

COLONIAL PERIOD

The area was explored by Juan Diaz de Solís, who sailed into the Río de la Plata in 1516; other early explorers were Ferdinand Magellan and Sebastian Cabot. Little was done with the land since there was no mineral wealth and the local Charrúa Indians were fierce nomads. The latter were eventually pacified by Jesuit and Franciscan missionaries. The Banda Oriental del Uruguay (the east bank of the Uruguay River), as it was called, became a tremendous unfenced pasture where wild cattle practically roamed freely and where bands of cattle skinners made periodic forays. In 1680 the Portuguese moved down from Brazil and established Novo Colonia do Sacramento on the Río de la Plata opposite Buenos Aires. In order to counteract Portuguese influence, the Spanish set up San Felipe de Montevideo in 1726 as a garrison town and drove the Portuguese back. This exemplified the colonial period, which was marked by a prolonged struggle between the Spaniards of Argentina and the Portuguese of Brazil. In 1776 the country became part of the Spanish Viceroyalty of Río de la Plata, capital of which was Buenos Aires.

(T.L.S.)

THE STRUGGLE FOR NATIONAL IDENTITY (1811–90)

Montevideo was the site of a Spanish naval installation; in 1811 an armed insurrection led by the rural spokesman José Artigas broke out in its hinterland, the Banda Oriental del Uruguay. Spanish authority was challenged, and

Artigas' revolt

unresolved colonial problems were brought to the fore. The *estancieros* (ranchers) were joined in revolt by the gauchos (cowboys), the peons, and the slaves. Artigas proposed a plan for a republican federation of the Río de la Plata territories and a democratization of rural life based on advanced social principles.

The Buenos Aires oligarchy, realizing how Artigas' proposals would affect them, decided to crush his growing power; their forces defeated him in 1816, ending the first manifestation of Uruguayan autonomous government. The emancipation of the Banda Oriental eventually was achieved during the period of Portuguese-Brazilian occupation (1817–28). In 1825, Juan Antonio Lavalleja and his supporters (known as the "33 *orientales*") formed an army with Argentine help and defeated the Brazilians at Ituzaingó (February 20, 1827). A preliminary peace pact with Brazil (August 27, 1828) recognized Uruguay's independence. On July 18, 1830, a constitution for the new nation was approved. Uruguay had scarcely 74,000 inhabitants; its main economic resources, livestock and land, were concentrated in the hands of a few families who had acquired economic empires in the countryside during the colonial period. The first two decades of independence were a time of testing. There were frequent uprisings in the interior, and, in the urban areas, opposing factions grew up around their leaders Fructuoso Rivera and Manuel Oribe. The colours used by each faction gave rise to the present names of Uruguay's main political parties: red, or Colorado, for Rivera's group, and white, or Blanco, for Oribe's.

The Colorados and the Blancos

Antagonism between these groups led to the civil war of 1839–51, during which the Blanco Party controlled the interior and the Colorado Party controlled Montevideo. Several foreign powers intervened—Argentina on the side of the Blancos, England and France on the side of the Colorados.

The period ended without losers or victors, and the failure to achieve national unity opened a whole new era of turbulence and uprisings, frequently involving the country in Brazilian and Argentine affairs. This led to Uruguay's participation with Brazil and Argentina in war against Paraguay (1865–70). Successive attempts at political coexistence and internal order, indispensible to Uruguay's modernization and entrance into world economics, were frustrated. Internally the caudillos (personalist leaders) struggled for power with liberal parliamentarians known as *principistas* or "doctors." In the 1870s, control of the government passed into the hands of the military.

During the administration of Col. Lorenzo Latorre (1876–80), power was more firmly centralized: pacification of the rural areas permitted advances in stock breeding and ended the power of the caudillos. Capitalist development and internal stability continued under the governments of Gen. Máximo Santos and Gen. Máximo Tajes (1880–90).

THE PROSPERITY OF THE EXPORT ECONOMY (1890–1954)

By the time civilian rule was restored under Julio Herrera y Obes in the 1890s, the rural economic structure had adapted itself to the demands of external markets. Wool and dried (or jerked) beef exports rose greatly. The population, as a result of immigration from Mediterranean Europe, more than doubled during the last quarter of the 19th century, rising from 450,000 people in 1875 to about 1,000,000 in 1900. The adoption of new fiscal policies and the development of transportation and communication facilities (railroads and telegraphs) stimulated foreign loans and investment, usually of British origin.

At the beginning of the 20th century, the country was again torn by a factional dispute, based on the Blanco (or Nationalist) Party's demands for greater participation in government affairs. After a Blanco uprising and the assassination of the Colorado president, Juan Idiarte Borda, in 1897, tension between the two parties reached a climax in 1904. At this time, a year after being elected president, the Colorado leader, José Batlle y Ordóñez, was confronted by a Blanco revolt headed by Aparicio Saravia. After eight months of bloody fighting and the death of Saravia, the conflict was ended by the Peace of Aceguá. This agreement was followed by a reorganization of the political parties and marked the beginning of a long period of internal peace and orderly government for Uruguay.

From 1904 until his death in 1929, José Batlle y Ordóñez dominated the political scene. Twice president of the republic (1903–07; 1911–15), he designed reform programs that became the objectives of the modern Uruguayan state.

Administrative reforms included the creation of a Supreme Court of Justice, greater municipal autonomy, and the creation of more public services. Social reforms included the removal of public education from the control of the Roman Catholic Church, the extension of free education on the secondary and university levels, a reform of the university system, extension of the right of divorce to women, and, finally, separation of church and state in 1917.

Advanced labour legislation that was passed (the right to strike, an eight-hour workday, obligatory accident insurance) emphasized the role of the state as mediator between management and labour.

Batlle's policies discouraged foreign intervention in Uruguay's economic affairs. While North American penetration pushed on the frozen meat industry, he promoted a strong policy of nationalism, by means of several government monopolies, assuring state control of areas usually dominated by private or foreign capital (mainly British, toward which Batlle showed an open disaffection).

During World War I, the agriculturally based economy flourished with the export boom. At the same time, domestic production and consumption of manufactured goods increased, in reaction to protective tariffs in other countries and the spiralling cost of imported goods. This economic expansion was accompanied by political reform. President Batlle, fearing the power of the presidency, proposed its abolition and the substitution of a nine-member executive council. A plebiscite defeated the idea (1916), but it was partially retained in the constitution of 1917 that, while retaining the presidency, provided for the creation of a National Council of Administration made up of nine elected members. This constitutional reform, combined with the extension of suffrage rights in 1924, gave new impulse to representative government in Uruguay.

At the same time the economy entered a bad period. Exports declined with the reorganization of European markets following the war. U.S. capital was used to finance road construction, in competition with the British railway system, and U.S. business investments heralded the shift from British to U.S. economic domination. The New York stock market crash of 1929 caused a further decline in exports and a price decrease for Uruguayan goods. Complicating the situation were the Ottawa Agreements (1932), which greatly limited the accessibility of Río de la Plata meats to British markets. An austerity program was instituted to improve the economic situation. In 1933, however, Pres. Gabriel Terra, of the Colorado Party, proclaimed himself dictator. The constitution of 1917 was invalidated and full power was restored to the president; this situation lasted until mid-1938, when Gen. Alfredo Baldomir was elected president.

With the beginning of World War II, President Baldomir kept Uruguay neutral. Many Uruguayans sympathized with the Allies, but the leader of the Blanco Party, Luis Alberto de Herrera, campaigned for strict neutrality and sought to prevent the installation of North American naval bases in the country. Other leading Blancos had definite Nazi-Fascist sympathies. Nevertheless, Uruguay, along with most of the other Latin American republics, declared war on the Axis powers in 1945.

At the beginning of 1942 President Baldomir dissolved the Congress and prepared a new constitution. His support came not only from his own Colorado Party but also from the independent Blancos (members of the Blanco Party who, in 1933, had separated from it because of their opposition to the ideology of Herrera). The takeover of the government by Juan José Amézaga in 1943 marked a return to democratic liberalism. Once again, a war aided the Uruguayan economy. As had happened during World War I, the value of livestock products rose disproportionately, a lucrative European market opened up, and imports declined tremendously. Small industries prospered, filling the gap created by the import decline. The standard of living rose. Internal consumer markets grew, unemployment dropped, educational opportunities opened up, and labour legislation bettered the existing social security system.

Tomás Berreta, a disciple of Batlle y Ordóñez, was elected president in 1946, but his sudden death left the government in the hands of Batlle's nephew, the urban caudillo Luis Batlle Berres. The government readopted the principles of the 1917 constitution, and after reaching an agreement with the Blanco Party, created, in the constitution of 1951, the National Council of Government, which replaced the presidential office with a nine-member council.

Uruguay became a haven for exiles from Argentina who opposed Juan Perón, that country's president from 1946 to 1955. They used the Uruguayan press and radio networks to win support for their cause, with the tacit approval of the Uruguayan government. An opposition campaign and anti-Peronist committees, based in Montevideo, found support in the liberal temper of the country. Uruguay's relations with Argentina deteriorated, reaching their lowest point just before Perón's overthrow in 1955.

DEVELOPMENTS SINCE 1954

The Korean War precipitated a brief economic boom that ended in 1954. Uruguay then entered a period of economic stagnation, followed by a period of recession aggravated by the lowering of world prices on its chief exports (wools, meat, leather products) as well as by the rising price of manufactured goods. The economic deterioration resulted in labour riots, demonstrations, and general discontent among the populace.

The 1958 elections reflected this discontent. For the first time in 93 years, the Colorado Party was defeated, and the Nationalists (Blancos), promising an improvement in the economy, came to power under Martin R. Echegoyen. The change of government came at a time of tremendous inflation. In 1959, a monetary reform law was passed, providing for successive devaluations of the currency. Tension and discontent rose among all sectors of the population.

In the same year (1959), Herrera, former leader of the Blanco Party, died, and divisions within the party deepened. The Blanco government was unable to deal effectively with the crisis. Its free enterprise orientation allowed economic elite groups to import luxury items at a time when official government policy limited imports to essential consumer goods.

The second Blanco administration (1963–66) was characterized by an even sharper disintegration of the traditional political parties, resulting in the proliferation of groups and subgroups under personalist leaders. Inflation was not halted. A 1965 bank failure staggered the monetary economy. Furthermore, the cost of living rose, affecting those income groups (mainly urban) that were least able to afford it. The inflation and production slump continued into the 1970s. (J.A.O.)

Economic crisis incubated the Tupamaro urban guerrilla movement, the widespread terrorist activities of which brought on a military coup in 1973. The military governed first through the previously elected Colorado Party president Juan María Bordaberry Arocena (1972–76) and then replaced him in 1976 with Aparicio Méndez, who was succeeded in 1981 by Gen. Gregorio Conrado Álvarez Armelino. Authoritarianism earned Uruguay the reputation of having the highest ratio of political prisoners to population in the world. The government turned to free market economics, but economic recovery was impeded by the need to import all the country's oil and by the unwillingness of the Common Market countries of Europe to import meat, a principal Uruguayan export. (M.I.V.)

BIBLIOGRAPHY

Physical and human geography: Three general introductions to the country—its geography, history, economy, and culture—are RUSSELL H. FITZGIBBON, *Uruguay: Portrait of a Democracy* (1954); GEORGE PENDLE, *Uruguay,* 3rd ed. (1963); and JORGE CHEBATAROFF, *Geografía de la República Oriental del Uruguay* (1979). See also D.C. REDDING, "The Economic Decline of Uruguay," *Inter-American Economic Affairs,* 20:55–72 (1967), a careful report on how the Uruguayan economy has been overloaded by the measures of a welfare state; and RONALD H. MCDONALD, "Electoral Politics and Uruguayan Political Decay," *ibid.*, 26:25–45 (1972), presents the argument that one of the more democratic societies of Latin America was undermined by an organized minority. Other works of interest concerning government and the economy include CARLOS M. RAMA, *Ensayo de sociología Uruguaya* (1957) and *Las clases sociales en el Uruguay* (1960); JOHN STREET, *Artigas and the Emancipation of Uruguay* (1959); PHILIP B. TAYLOR, JR., *Government and Politics of Uruguay* (1962); MILTON I. VANGER, *José Batlle y Ordóñez of Uruguay: The Creator of His Times, 1902–1907* (1963); and MARVIN ALISKY, *Uruguay: A Contemporary Survey* (1969), a descriptive account of the economy.

History: EDUARDO ACEVEDO, *Anales históricos del Uruguay*, 2nd ed. (1933–36), a detailed description of political, economic, and administrative events covering the period 1830–1930; J.P. BARRAN and B. NAHUM, *Historia rural del Uruguay moderno, 1851–1914*, 7 vol. (1967–78), the major history of rural Uruguay, with provocative interpretations; EDITIONES DE LA BANDA ORIENTAL, *Historia Uruguaya*, 6 vol. (1975), series by six different authors covering Uruguayan history from discovery to 1929; S.G. HANSON, *Utopia in Uruguay* (1938), an

analysis of different economic sectors affected by Batlle's reforms, covering the era 1911–30; EDY KAUFMAN, *Uruguay in Transition: From Civilian to Military Rule* (1979), a political science analysis of the 1973 military coup and its aftermath; G. LINDAHL, *Uruguay's New Path* (Eng. trans. 1962), a review of programs, finances, and economic structures from 1919 to 1933; GEORGE PENDLE, *Uruguay*, 3rd ed. (1963), a survey of contemporary Uruguay, with particular emphasis on the birth and evolution of the welfare state; J.E. PIVEL DEVOTO and A. RANIERI DE PIVEL DEVOTO, *Historia de la República Oriental del Uruguay, 1830–1930* (1945), a didactic synthesis tracing the political processes that accompanied the formation of an independent Uruguay; JOHN STREET, *Artigas and the Emancipation of Uruguay* (1959), a concise, documented study explaining the significance of the role of Artigas; M.I. VANGER, *José Batlle y Ordóñez of Uruguay: The Creator of His Times, 1902–1907* (1963) and *The Model Country: José Batlle y Ordóñez of Uruguay, 1907–1915* (1980), studies of the presidencies of Batlle and of the history of that era; MARTIN WEINSTEIN, *Uruguay: The Politics of Failure* (1975), a flawed attempt to explain the collapse of Uruguayan democracy. ALBERTO ZUM FELDE, *Proceso histórico del Uruguay*, 4th ed. (1963), an interpretive essay based on now outdated sociological data but still valuable.

Velázquez

The most important Spanish painter of the 17th century, Diego Velázquez is universally acknowledged as one of the world's greatest artists. The naturalistic style in which he was trained provided a language for the expression of his remarkable power of observation in portraying both the living model and still life. Stimulated by the study of 16th-century Venetian painting, he developed from a master of faithful likeness and characterization into the creator of masterpieces of visual impression unique in his time. With brilliant diversity of brushstrokes and subtle harmonies of colour, he achieved effects of form and texture, space, light, and atmosphere, that make him the chief forerunner of 19th-century French Impressionism.

The principal source of information about Velázquez' early career is the treatise *Arte de la pintura* ("The Art of Painting"), published in 1649 by his master and father-in-law Francisco Pacheco, who is more important as a biographer and theoretician than as a painter. The first complete biography of Velázquez appeared in the third volume (*El Parnaso español;* "The Spanish Parnassus") of *El Museo pictórico y escala óptica* ("The Pictorial Museum and Optical Scale"), published in 1724 by the court painter and art scholar Antonio Palomino. This was based on biographical notes made by Velázquez' pupil Juan de Alfaro, who was Palomino's patron. The number of personal documents is very small, and official documentation relating to his paintings is relatively rare. Since he seldom signed or dated his works, their identification and chronology has often to be based on stylistic evidence alone. Though many copies of his portaits were evidently made in his studio by assistants, his own production was not large and his surviving autograph works number fewer than 150. He is known to have worked slowly, and during his later years much of his time was occupied by his duties as a court official in Madrid.

Seville. Born in Seville, Diego Rodríguez de Silva Velázquez was baptized on June 6, 1599. According to Palomino, his first master was the Sevillian painter Francisco Herrera the Elder (*c.* 1576–1656). In 1611 he was formally apprenticed to Francisco Pacheco, whose daughter he married in 1618. "After five years of education and training," Pacheco writes, "I married him to my daughter, moved by his virtue, integrity, and good parts and by the expectations of his disposition and great talent." Although Pacheco was himself a mediocre Mannerist painter, it was through his teaching that Velázquez developed his early naturalistic style. "He worked from life," writes Pacheco, "making numerous studies of his model in various poses and thereby he gained certainty in his portraiture." He

was not more than 20 when he painted the "Water Seller of Seville" (*c.* 1619; Wellington Museum, London), in which the control of the composition, colour, and light, the naturalness of the figures and their poses, and realistic still life already reveal his keen eye and prodigious facility with the brush. The strong modelling and sharp contrasts of light and shade of Velázquez' early illusionistic style closely resemble the technique of dramatic lighting called tenebrism, which was one of the innovations of the Italian painter Caravaggio (1573–1610). Velázquez' early subjects were mostly religious or genre (scenes of daily life). He popularized a new type of composition in Spanish painting, the *bodegón,* a kitchen scene with prominent still life, such as the "Old Woman Frying Eggs." Sometimes the *bodegones* had religious scenes in the background, as in "Christ in the House of Martha and Mary." The "Adora-

First paintings

By courtesy of the Museo del Prado, Madrid

"Las Meninas" (with a self-portrait of the artist at the left and reflections of Philip IV and Queen Mariana in the mirror at the back of the room and the Infanta Margarita with her *meninas,* or maids of honour, in the foreground), oil on canvas by Diego Velázquez, *c.* 1656. In the Prado, Madrid, 3.18 × 2.76 m.

tion of the Magi" is one of the few Sevillian paintings of Velázquez that have remained in Spain.

Court painter in Madrid. In 1622, a year after Philip IV came to the throne, Velázquez visited Madrid for the first time, in the hope of obtaining royal patronage. He painted a portait of the poet Luis de Góngora (1622; Museum of Fine Arts, Boston), but there was no opportunity of portraying the King or Queen. In the following year he was recalled to Madrid by the prime minister, Count Olivares, a fellow Sevillian and a future patron. Soon after his arrival he painted a portrait of Philip IV that won him immediate success. He was appointed court painter with a promise that no one else should portray the King. Pacheco describes an equestrian portrait of Philip (lost) painted soon afterward, "all taken from life, even the landscape"; the portrait was exhibited publicly "to the admiration of all the Court and the envy of members of the profession." The envy of fellow artists, who accused Velázquez of only being able to paint heads, is said to have been the occasion of the King ordering him to paint a historical subject, the "Expulsion of the Moriscos" (lost), in competition with other court painters. Velázquez was awarded the prize and the appointment in 1627 of gentleman usher to the King. Though he continued to paint other subjects, as court painter he was chiefly occupied in portraying members of the royal family and their entourage, and he painted numerous portraits of Philip IV during the course of his life. "The liberality and affability with which he is treated by such a great monarch is unbelievable," writes Pacheco. "He has a workshop in his gallery and His Majesty has a key to it and a chair in order to watch him painting at leisure, nearly every day."

Velázquez' position at the court gave him access to the royal collections, rich in paintings by the Venetian Renaissance master Titian (c. 1490–1576), who was to have more influence than any other artist on the development of his style. The full-length portraits of Philip IV (c. 1626; Prado) and his brother the Infante Don Carlos (c. 1626; Prado) are in the tradition of Spanish royal portraits established by Titian and are to some extent influenced by his style. In these portraits the detailed description and tenebrism of Velázquez' Sevillian paintings have been modified; only the faces and hands are accentuated and the dark figures stand out against a light background. In his later court portraits, Velázquez was to adopt something of the more elaborate decor and richer colouring of the Flemish Baroque master Peter Paul Rubens (1577–1640), whom he met during the latter's second visit to the Spanish court in 1628. Pacheco tells how Rubens praised Velázquez' works very highly because of their simplicity. Velázquez' painting of Bacchus, known as "Los Borrachos" ("The Topers" or "The Triumph of Bacchus") seems to have been inspired by Titian and Rubens, but his realistic approach to the subject is characteristically Spanish and one that Velázquez was to preserve throughout his life.

First Italian journey. Velázquez' visit, with Rubens, to see the famous paintings in the royal monastery of the Escorial near Madrid is said by Palomino to have aroused his desire to go to Italy. Having obtained leave and two years' salary from the King and money and letters of recommendation from Olivares, he sailed from Barcelona to Genoa in August 1629. In letters from Italian ambassadors in Madrid he is referred to as a young portrait painter, favourite of the King and Olivares, who was going to Italy to study and to improve his painting. The visit did in fact have an important effect on his artistic evolution. He stopped in Venice, where Palomino says he made drawings after Tintoretto (1518–94), the master of late 16th-century Venetian painting, and then hurried on to Rome. Pacheco relates that he was given rooms in the Vatican palace, which he found very isolated. Having obtained permission to return to the Vatican to make drawings after Michelangelo's "Last Judgment" and the paintings of Raphael, he moved to the Villa Medici, which was "high and airy" and had "antique sculptures to copy." An attack of fever obliged him later to move nearer to the Spanish ambassador. After a year in Rome he returned to Spain, stopping on the way in Naples; he arrived back in Madrid early in 1631.

None of Velázquez' Italian drawings appear to have survived. Of the few paintings that he made in Italy, a "famous portrait of himself" painted in Rome, mentioned by Pacheco, is possibly the "self-portrait" known only in replicas (Uffizi, Florence; Museo Provincial de Bellas Artes de San Carlos, Valencia). The chief works of his Italian visit are the two "celebrated pictures" painted in Rome, which Palomino records he took back to Spain and offered to the King: "Joseph's Bloody Coat Brought to Jacob" and "The Forge of Vulcan." These two monumental figure compositions are far removed from the limited realism in which he had been trained. As a result of his Italian studies, particularly of Venetian painting, his development in the treatment of space, perspective, light, and colour and his broader technique mark the beginning of a new phase in his lifelong pursuit of the truthful rendering of visual appearance.

Middle years. After his return from Italy, Velázquez entered upon the most productive period of his career. He took up again his chief office of portrait painter and was occasionally called on to represent mythological subjects for the decoration of the royal apartments. From now on his religious works are rare and individual. The devotional quality of his early Sevillian paintings finds moving expression in the "Christ on the Cross," a composition of monumental simplicity and naturalness. In "The Coronation of the Virgin" the solemnity and dignity of the holy persons are set off by their voluminous, colourful robes in a composition of exceptional splendour specially fitting for a painting of the Queen of Heaven made to adorn the oratory of the Queen of Spain.

For the decoration of the throne room of the new Buen Retiro palace, completed in 1635, Velázquez painted a series of royal equestrian portraits (Prado), following a tradition that goes back in Spain to Titian's portrait of "Charles V at Mühlberg" (1548; Prado) and was continued by Rubens. Velázquez' equestrian groups have a balance and poise closer to Titian's than to Rubens' Baroque compositions, and after his return from Italy, he achieved a three-dimensional effect without detailed drawing or strong contrasts of light and shade but with a broad technique of brushwork and natural outdoor lighting. "The Surrender of Breda," Velázquez' famous contribution to the series of military triumphs painted for the same throne room, is his only surviving historical subject. Though the elaborate composition was based on a pictorial formula of Rubens, he creates a vivid impression of actuality and of human drama by means of accurate topographical details and the lifelike portraiture of the principal figures.

Though Velázquez frequently followed traditional compositions, particularly for his royal portraits, it was from no lack of ability to compose or invent. With his portraits of Philip IV (c. 1635; Prado), the Infante Fernando (c. 1632–35; Prado), and Prince Baltasar Carlos as huntsman, painted for the King's new hunting lodge, the Torre de la Parada, he created a new type of informal royal portrait. For the same place he painted hunting scenes of which "Philip IV Hunting Wild Boar" (National Gallery, London) is possibly an example, and some classical subjects, including probably the portraitlike figures of "Aesop" and "Menippus" (1639–40; Prado). The portraits of court dwarfs (Prado), painted during the next few years, display the same impartial and discerning eye as those of royal and noble sitters, while the character of the dwarfs' deformities is revealed through their awkward, unconventional poses, their individual expressions, and by the exceptionally free and bold brushwork. The "Lady with a Fan," one of the few informal portraits of women, is, on the other hand, remarkable for the subtle and delicate painting and for the sensitive portrayal of personal charm.

Second Italian journey. At the beginning of 1649 Velázquez left Spain on a second visit to Italy. This time he was on official business as gentleman of the bedchamber. He was given a carriage for pictures, possibly gifts from Philip IV to Pope Innocent X. The chief purpose of the journey was to buy paintings and antiques for the King for the decoration of new apartments in the royal palace and also to engage fresco painters to decorate the ceilings of the apartments and to reintroduce fresco painting into Spain.

Influence of Titian and Rubens

Equestrian portraits

Once again, Velázquez found fresh inspiration in Italy, particularly from Titian. First he went to Venice, where he bought paintings by Titian, Tintoretto, and Veronese. He then went on to Modena, where he saw the famous ducal collection, which included his own portrait of the Duke of Modena, painted in Madrid in 1638. According to Palomino, he also stopped in many other cities, including Bologna, where he contracted fresco painters to work in Madrid. Palomino recounts that on reaching Rome Velázquez was befriended by eminent prelates and artists, including the great French painter Nicolas Poussin (1594–1665) and Gian Lorenzo Bernini (1598–1680), the leading Italian sculptor of the Baroque style. He gives a list of the antiques selected by Velázquez, from which it seems that he followed the tradition of great collectors since the 16th century: rather than inferior originals he chose casts of the most famous statues in Rome. "Without neglecting his other business he also did many paintings," in addition to the portrait of Innocent X. Palomino relates that before portraying the Pope, as an exercise in painting a head from life, Velázquez made the portrait of his mulatto assistant, Juan de Pareja. This is an exceptional unofficial portrait, unusually boldly painted, which creates a powerful effect of familiar and living likeness. When sold in 1970 the sum of $5,544,000 was paid for this picture—at the time the highest price paid for a work of art at auction.

The portrait of Innocent X
For the portrait of Innocent X, one of his most important official works, Velázquez followed a tradition for papal portraits created by Raphael in the likeness of "Julius II" (c. 1511–12; National Gallery, London) and later used by Titian in portraying "Paul III and His Grandsons Ottavio and Cardinal Alessandro Farnese" (1546; Museo e Gallerie Nazionali di Capodimonte, Naples). The powerful head, the brilliant combinations of crimson of the curtain, chair, and the cope are painted with fluent technique and almost imperceptible brush strokes that go far beyond the late manner of Titian and announce the last stage in Velázquez' development in the direction of Impressionism. This portrait, which has long been Velázquez' most famous painting outside Spain, was copied innumerable times and won him immediate and lasting renown in Italy. In 1650 he was made a member of the Accademia di San Luca (Academy of St. Luke) and of the Congregazione dei Virtuosi al Pantheon, Rome's two most prestigious organizations of artists. The portrait earned for him the Pope's support for his application for membership of the most exclusive Spanish military order, though the difficulties arising from the fact that he was not of noble birth were so great that he did not receive the habit of the Order of Santiago until 1659.

The two small views of the Villa Medici, where Velázquez stayed during his first visit to Rome, must, for stylistic reasons, have been painted during his second visit. They are unique examples of pure landscape in his surviving work and among those of his achievements that foreshadow 19th-century Impressionism. The so-called "Rokeby Venus" was also probably painted in Italy and is one of the few representations of the female nude in Spanish painting before the 19th century. The theme of the toilet of Venus, the rich colouring and warm flesh tones, are inspired mainly by Titian and other Venetian painters. But Velázquez has characteristically made no attempt to disguise or idealize his model, and his superbly painted Venus is exceptional for his time as a lifelike portrayal of a living nude woman.

Last years. Velázquez returned to Madrid in the summer of 1651 with some of his purchases and was warmly welcomed by the King who, in the following year, appointed him chamberlain of the palace, an office that entailed the arrangement of the royal apartments and of the King's journeys. During his absence Philip had remarried, and the young queen Mariana of Austria with her children provided new subjects for him to portray. For his portraits of the Queen (1652–53; Prado) and of the King's oldest daughter, the Infanta María Teresa (1652/53; Kunsthistorisches Museum, Vienna), he used similar compositional formulas, and numerous studio replicas of them were made. The royal ladies appear as doll-like figures with their enormous coiffures and farthingale hoops.

Late portraits

The effect of form, texture, and ornament is achieved in Velázquez' late manner without any definition of detail, in a free, "sketchy" technique. The portraits of the young infanta Margarita (1659; Kunsthistorisches Museum, Vienna) and Prince Felipe Próspero, similar in composition and manner, are among the most colourful of his works, and he most sensitively reveals the child-like character of his sitters behind the facade of royal dignity. Velázquez' late bust portraits of Philip IV (c. 1654; Prado and c. 1656; National Gallery, London), of which many studio versions exist, are very different in character and are exceptional as royal portraits for their informal appearance. These last close-up views of the sad and aging monarch are among the most intimate of all Velázquez' royal characterizations.

In addition to his many official portraits, Velázquez painted during his last years two of his most original figure compositions and greatest masterpieces. "Las Hilanderas," a genre scene in a tapestry factory, is at the same time an illustration of the ancient Greek fable of the spinning contest between Pallas Athena and Arachne. Here, the mythological subject—like the religious scene in some of the early *bodegones*—is in the background. But in this late work there is no barrier between the world of myth and reality; they are united in an ingenious composition by formal and aerial perspective. In "Las Meninas" ("The Maids of Honour") also known as "The Royal Family," he has created the effect of a momentary glance at a casual scene in the artist's studio while he is painting the King and Queen—whose reflection only is seen in the mirror in the background—in the presence of the Infanta Margarita with her *meninas* and other attendants. In this complex composition, the nearly life-size figures are painted in more or less detail according to their relation to the central figure of the Infanta and to the source of light, creating a remarkable illusion of reality never surpassed by Velázquez or any other artist of his age.

Velázquez' last activity was to accompany the King and court to the French border, in the spring of 1660, to arrange the decoration of the Spanish pavilion for the marriage of the Infanta María Teresa with Louis XIV. Shortly after his return to Madrid, he fell ill and died on August 6, 1660. Velázquez left few pupils or immediate followers. His European fame dates from the beginning of the 19th century. Many of his early Sevillian paintings were acquired then by foreign (chiefly English) collectors. Most of his later official works were incorporated in the Prado Museum, in Madrid.

MAJOR WORKS
"Old Woman Frying Eggs" (1618; National Gallery of Scotland, Edinburgh); "Christ in the House of Martha and Mary" (c. 1618; National Gallery, London); "Water Seller of Seville" (c. 1619; Wellington Museum, London); "Adoration of the Magi" (1619; Prado); "Los Borrachos" ("The Topers") or "The Triumph of Bacchus" (c. 1628–29; Prado); "The Forge of Vulcan" (1630; Prado); "Joseph's Bloody Coat Brought to Jacob" (1630; El Escorial); "Christ on the Cross" (c. 1631; Prado); "Equestrian Portrait of Philip IV" (c. 1634–35; Prado); "Equestrian Portrait of Prince Baltasar Carlos" (c. 1634–35; Prado); "Equestrian Portrait of Olivares" (c. 1634–35; Prado); "The Surrender of Breda" (1634–35; Prado); "Prince Baltasar Carlos as Huntsman" (1635–36; Prado); "Duke of Modena" (1638; Galleria e Museo Estense, Modena); "Lady with a Fan" (c. 1635–40; Wallace Collection, London); "The Coronation of the Virgin" (c. 1641–42; Prado); "Philip IV at Fraga" (1644; Frick Collection, New York); "Mars" (c. 1645–48; Prado); "Portrait of Juan de Pareja" (1649–50; Metropolitan Museum of Art, New York); "Portrait of Pope Innocent X" (1650; Galleria Doria-Pamphili, Rome); "Views of the Villa Medici, Rome" (c. 1650; Prado); "The Toilet of Venus," known as "The Rokeby Venus" (c. 1651; National Gallery, London); "Queen Mariana of Austria" (1652–53; Prado); "The Infanta Margarita in a Pink Dress" (1653–54; Kunsthistorisches Museum, Vienna); "Las Hilanderas" ("The Spinners") or "The Fable of Arachne" (c. 1655; Prado); "Las Meninas" ("The Maids of Honour") (1656; Prado); "Mercury and Argus" (c. 1659; Prado); "Prince Felipe Próspero" (1659; Kunsthistorisches Museum, Vienna).

BIBLIOGRAPHY. CARL JUSTI, *Diego Velazquez und sein Jahrhundert,* 2 vol. (1888; 2nd rev. ed, 1903; Eng. trans., *Diego Velazquez and His Times,* 1889; Spanish ed., 1953), a classic monograph, though out-of-date, still the most important and comprehensive study of the subject; MADLYN M. KAHR, *Velázquez: The Art of Painting* (1976), for the general reader;

MAURICE SÉRULLAZ, *Velázquez* (1981), an overview; AUGUST L. MAYER, *Velázquez: A Catalogue Raisonné of the Pictures and Drawings* (1936), a well-illustrated catalog of works by and related to Velázquez; ENRIQUE LAFUENTE, *Velazquez: Complete Edition* (1943), an introductory essay followed by a critical catalog, fully illustrated, of all the paintings and drawings considered by the author to be by Velázquez; ELIZABETH DU G. TRAPIER, *Velázquez* (1948), a well-documented study of the artist's life and work that includes most of the information brought to light since the publication of Justi's book, with a comprehensive bibliography, *Varia velazqueña: homenaje a Velázquez en el III centenario de su muerte, 1660–1960*, 2 vol. (1960), and *Velázquez: homenaje en el tercer centenario de su muerte* (1960), two volumes containing transcriptions of all known source material, biographical and documentary, relating to Velázquez; JOSÉ LÓPEZ-REY, *Velázquez: A Catalogue Raisonné of His Oeuvre, with an Introductory Study* (1963), a revised and enlarged edition of Mayer's *Catalogue,* amended in the light of new discoveries and of the author's own views on attribution and dating—a comprehensive and fully illustrated corpus of the artist's work; JOSÉ ORTEGA Y GASSET, *Velazquez, Goya and the Dehumanization of Art* (1972), essays on art, including discussion of Velázquez; JUAN A. GAYA NUÑO, *Bibliografía crítica y antológica de Velázquez* (1963, reissued 1973), a comprehensive critical bibliography of Velázquez, with analytical indexes, a work of major importance for the study of the artist.

Venezuela

Venezuela, known as the "Gateway to South America," is a republic located at the northern extremity of the South American continent. It is bounded by the Caribbean Sea and the Atlantic Ocean to the north, Guyana to the east, Brazil to the south, and Colombia to the southwest and west. Venezuela also possesses some islands in the Caribbean, of which the largest is the offshore Margarita Island, and the most northerly is Aves Island, about 250 miles (402 kilometres) north of Margarita. Venezuela also claims an additional 58,000 square miles (150,000 square kilometres) of territory now located in northwestern Guyana.

Venezuela is the sixth largest country in South America. According to tradition, the name Venezuela, or "Little Venice," was given to the country by Amerigo Vespucci, who, on seeing the native Indian houses built over the water on stilts, was reminded of the Italian city of Venice. Venezuela's north coast on the Caribbean was the first part of South America to be explored and settled by Europeans. The present-day composition of the country's population is the result of many centuries of mixing of whites, blacks, and aboriginals. Spanish is the official language and Roman Catholicism the main religion of the country. Venezuela is a federal republic with a democratic and representative form of government. Caracas is the national capital.

Until the 20th century, Venezuela was a poor, backward, and feudal agricultural nation. The discovery of oil in the vicinity of Lago de Maracaibo in 1917, however, transformed the economy and brought prosperity. By the late 20th century Venezuela had become one of the world's largest oil-producing nations. Because of the wealth of its oil reserves, it has been able to initiate land reform, to improve its agriculture, and to promote industrial development.

The article is divided into the following sections:

Physical and human geography

THE LAND

Relief. The physical relief of Venezuela varies from the level topography of the plains to the peaks of the Andes heights, and the rugged mass of the Guiana Highlands. Three broad geographical divisions may be observed—the coastal mountain region (which reaches heights of about 16,500 feet, or 5,000 metres, above sea level); the plains (about 1,000 feet above sea level); and the forest region (about 8,200 feet above sea level).

Within these three broad divisions, seven physiographical provinces can be distinguished—the islands and coastal plains; the Lago de Maracaibo Basin; the coastal mountain system; the valleys and hills of the states of Falcón, Lara, and Yaracuy within the northwestern part of the country; the Andes mountain range (Cordillera of the Andes); the Llanos; and the Guiana (Guaiana, Guayana) continental block (in Spanish, Macizo de Guayana).

The islands and the coastal plains (covering 18 percent of Venezuela) are located in the north and northeast of the country, from the Caribbean Sea to the northern mountain range (Cordillera de la Costa). Within this region are two important basins—the Unare Basin and the Orinoco Delta—and the main ports of La Guaira, Puerto Cabello, and Puerto la Cruz. Of the chain of islands, the principal one is Margarita Island.

The Maracaibo Basin, which contains a shallow, freshwater lake with an area of about 5,000 square miles, consists of sedimentary rocks. It contains the most important oil wells in Venezuela and the port of Maracaibo.

The coastal mountain system is located between the narrow coastal belt to the north and the plains of the interior to the south; though it represents only 3 percent of the national territory, it contains the greatest concentration of population. It is formed by two parallel mountain ranges—the coastal range and the interior range. The highest points are the peak of Naiguatá (9,069 feet [2,765 metres]) in the central sector of the coastal range and the Turimiquire (8,104 feet [2,470 metres]) in the eastern sector of the coastal range. The interior range reaches its maximum height at Platillón (6,323 feet [1,931 metres]).

Three important cities are located in the valleys of this region—Caracas, the capital; Valencia; and Maracay.

The valleys and hills of the states of Falcón, Lara, and Yaracuy have altitudes of from 1,600 to 5,500 feet. This region forms a transitional zone between the coastal mountain range and the Andes mountains and comprises about 3 percent of the country's territory. The only desert of Venezuela—the city of Coro's sand dunes—is found in this region.

The Venezuelan Andes

The Andes range, the highest mountain system in the country, forms the northernmost prolongation of the South American Andes. In Colombia, immediately to the west of Venezuela, it divides into two branches. One—the Sierra de Perijá—runs roughly south to north along the Colombia–Venezuela border; the other—the Cordillera de Mérida—runs generally northeastward toward the Caribbean Sea. The two branches enclose the Lago de Maracaibo Basin. The highest point is Pico Bolívar (16,423 feet [5,007 metres]). The Andes ranges comprise approximately 6 percent of the national territory and form another of the more densely populated regions, containing such important cities as Mérida, San Cristóbal, Valera, La Grita, and Tovar.

The Llanos, or plains, is a region with an almost level relief, occupying approximately a third of the country's territory. From the Atlantic Ocean at the mouths of the Orinoco River, the plains extend for about 800 miles up to the Andean foothills, varying in width from 60 miles in the east to 250 miles in the west.

South of the Orinoco and bordering Brazil and Colombia is the Guiana Highlands, a mountainous mass that is one of the largest granite blocks in the world. It is the most extensive natural region of Venezuela and occupies about 45 percent of its total area. It is also the least known and the most sparsely inhabited. Its granitic base is covered with stratified alluvium, in which erosion has carved different types of relief. In places are found gigantic mounds or masses, known as *tepuis*—some as high as 6,000 feet—which have resisted erosion. To the southeast of the Guiana Highlands and encircled by *tepuis* lies a region known as La Gran Sabana (the Great Plain). Located in this area is the Auyan-Tepui mound, 8,400 feet high, as well as Angel Falls, the highest waterfall in the world—3,212 feet (979 metres) high. The Guiana Highlands is an excellent mining region, abounding in deposits of iron ore, gold, and diamonds; it also possesses a considerable hydroelectric potential, as well as vast forest resources.

Drainage. The Venezuelan drainage network consists almost entirely of two great watersheds—one emptying into the Atlantic Ocean (82 percent), the other into the Caribbean Sea (17.5 percent). The remaining 0.5 percent constitutes the small endoreic basin (a drainage basin having no outlet) of Lake Valencia, located in the central section of the coastal range.

Atlantic and Caribbean watersheds

The great Orinoco River drains a 366,000-square-mile basin and runs 1,337 miles from its source close to the Brazilian border until it empties into the Atlantic Ocean through a number of distributaries, or *caños*, which form a delta. In the upper Orinoco region the waters are tumultuous and rapid and flow in an east–west direction as far as the village of San Fernando de Atabapo; some of the river waters are diverted to the Amazon River through the Casiquiare channel and the Río Guainía. In its middle course the Orinoco runs slowly and follows a northern direction, until it is joined on the left bank by the waters of the Río Apure. The lower Orinoco flows due east.

Among the main tributaries of the Orinoco River is the Río Caroní, which flows at a rate of 200,000 cubic feet per second. It has great hydroelectrical potential because of its numerous falls; in the Necuima area, the Guri Dam forms a lake with an area eight times greater than that of Lake Valencia. Other tributary rivers are the Caura, Aro, Ventuari, and Meta.

The rivers of the Caribbean watershed flow from the northern slopes of the Andean and coastal ranges. In it is found the basin of Lago de Maracaibo (18,000 square miles), which receives the waters of the Cordillera de Mérida and Sierra de Perijá ranges. Also into the Caribbean watershed flow the waters of minor coastal basins, the

rivers of which have dry beds during the several low-rainfall winter months of the year.

The Lake Valencia basin, only about 140 square miles in extent, is steadily shrinking as the result of a continuing combined process of sedimentation and evaporation. Scientific farming and ever growing industry have given the basin great economic value.

Soils. Venezuelan soils are mainly laterites (red soils with a high content of iron oxides and aluminum hydroxide). The most valuable for cultivation are in the valleys of the state of Aragua, in the cocoa-growing area of the Río Tuy basin, and in the sugarcane-growing area of the Turbio, Tocuyo, Aroa, and Yaracuy river basins. Of lesser value but also of agricultural importance are the soils found in the lowlands of the western plains and south of Lago de Maracaibo. Other soils are typical of the vast flooded plains of the lowlands. Limestone soils are found in the mountains of the state of Falcón and in the Andes. Swampy plains are found around Lake Valencia and in the Orinoco Delta.

Areas of most valuable soils

(I.S. de S.)

Climate. The climate throughout Venezuela is tropical, with the seasons marked more by differences in rainfall than in temperature. The year is divided into two seasons, the rainy and the dry (locally known as winter and summer), the rains occurring mostly from April to October or November, and the dry season most marked from November through March or April. The wet and dry seasons regulate agricultural activities, affect travel and transportation, and determine vacation periods.

Rainfall varies much from district to district. The northeast trade winds blow across the coastal areas without leaving much precipitation, in places less than 20 inches (508 millimetres) per year. La Guaira, for example, receives an average of only 11 inches. Areas lying behind topographic barriers also get little rain, while windward slopes are generally well watered. In some areas enough rain falls to support lush jungle growth, in others true selva (rain forest). The Llanos suffer severely from drought from about January to April and then suffer equally from an overabundance of precipitation, with the flooding of whole countrysides from June to October.

Temperature differences, on the other hand, are slight throughout the year. The average annual temperature at Caracas, for example, is 70° F (21° C), and no month averages more than 72° F (22° C) or less than 64° F (18° C). Altitude, however, affects temperatures in marked fashion. For example, Maracaibo, at sea level, averages just above 82° F (28° C) for the year, while Mérida at 5,383 feet (1,641 metres) averages just above 64° F (18° C). On some of the higher mountain peaks, temperatures are low enough to maintain permanent snow. Whatever the average temperature, there is little difference from month to month; the day-to-night variation is markedly greater, however.

Plant life. About two-fifths of Venezuela is covered with forests of some kind. A little less than half is still in wild grass, though much of this is used for at least occasional grazing. Less than 5 percent, most in the valleys of the Andes and of the coastal ranges, is under permanent cultivation. The vast Llanos, most of the lofty tablelands of the Guiana Highlands, and numerous smaller areas in the Andean *páramos* (high, bleak plateaus) have little in the way of trees. In the better watered places, the grass is compact and tall; in drier areas, such as high Andean districts and parts of the Guiana tablelands, it is sparse and hard. Rain forest covers an area found in the lower Orinoco Basin and Delta, in the far southern Orinoco drainage basin bordering on Colombia and Brazil, and in smaller extensions about the windward lower and middle slopes of the northern highlands.

Forests and grasslands

Most of the plant life of Venezuela is tropical and non-deciduous, retaining its foliage throughout the year, or shedding it little by little, never becoming entirely leafless. Even in the arid regions where the vegetation is sparse and the foliage scant, there is little change from season to season.

Both indigenous and introduced plants cover a wide range because of the differences in altitude. The true tropical vegetation, whether moist or dry, extends to an altitude of about 1,500 feet, above which it gives way (except in the moister districts) to semitropical growth. This zone, marked by tree ferns and orchids, reaches up to about 5,000 feet. From this point to about 7,000 to 8,000 feet, there is a transition into a mountain type; above 8,000 or 9,000 feet, the characteristic *páramo* vegetation begins, with plants of an alpine character dominating.

The principal plants of economic value are coffee, cacao, sisal, and bananas. Corn (maize), beans, rice, potatoes, sugarcane, cotton, tobacco, sweet potatoes, oranges, lemons, coconut palms, papayas, avocados, mangos, guavas, and cassava are commonly grown for local consumption.

Animal life. The animal life of Venezuela is similar to that of the neighbouring regions of Colombia, Brazil, and the Guianas. The open Llanos of the Orinoco form something of a neutral district between the great forested regions on the east, south, and west. Among the indigenous animals are seven species of the cat family, including the puma, the jaguar, and the ocelot; the wild dog; representatives of the marten family, including two species of otter and one of the skunk; and two species of bear. There are six species of monkeys corresponding to those of the Guiana Highlands and the Amazon Valley; the sloth and anteater; and more than 10 known genera of rodents. The tapir (a large, hoofed quadruped resembling a swine) is found in the forests of the Orinoco. There are two species of the peccary (resembling the pig); two species of deer; and three species of opossum. On the coast and in the Orinoco are found aquatic mammals, such as the manatee (which is herbivorous and gregarious and has two flippers and a spoon-shaped tail) and the dolphin.

Among reptiles there are crocodiles; lizards; caimans (crocodilians related to alligators); several species of turtles; and many snakes, including the striped rattlesnake and the bushmaster. Nonvenomous snakes include the boa constrictor and the anaconda. Amphibians include tree frogs, toads, and salamanders.

Bird life is represented chiefly by migratory species. In the *garzeros* ("heron rendezvous") are to be found nearly every kind of crane, heron, stork, and ibis. Ducks, including a small one called the *güirirí* in imitation of its cry, and birds of prey are numerous. The *guácharos,* or oilbirds, live in caves, especially in Caripe, and are caught for the oil extracted from them. The bellbird is common in the forests of the Orinoco.

There are almost 100 families of insects. Locusts are common in the interior, though seldom constituting a plague. Mollusks, including the pearl oyster, are common on the coasts and in the freshwater streams and lakes.

Domestic animals include about 10,000,000 cattle, mostly in the great herds that pasture on the Llanos. There are about 1,500,000 goats, 300,000 sheep, and more than 2,000,000 swine. Oxen and horses and a few mules are used as draft animals on some farms, and farmyard poultry is common.

(R.E.Cr./E.P.Ha.)

Settlement patterns. *Regions.* The six traditional regions of Venezuela can be clearly differentiated, even though the development of communications has tended to reduce differences; they are the central, western, Zulian, Andean, plains, and eastern regions.

The central region is composed of the Federal District and of the states of Miranda, Aragua, and Carabobo, situated along the northern Atlantic coast. A high proportion of the population of the region is urban; the principal urban concentration occurs around Caracas. The region contains the greater part of the nation's industry and commerce and its principal ports and airports.

The states of Falcón, Lara, and Yaracuy comprise the western region. Its population is about equally divided between urban and rural inhabitants. Agriculture is the principal economic activity, although industrialization is becoming important.

The Zulian region, including Lago de Maracaibo, is a major oil-producing area. Commercial and agricultural activities are stimulated by industrial development.

The Andean region consists of the mountainous states of Táchira, Mérida, and Trujillo. It is predominantly rural, and its economy is based on the cultivation of small farms and on some industrial and commercial activity.

The plains region occupies the states of Cojedes, Guárico, Portuguesa, Barinas, and Apure. The people inhabiting this area are largely engaged in agriculture and cattle raising. The plainsman ("llanero") is reputedly frank yet shrewd, with a sense of humour. This region has developed a folklore of its own.

The eastern region consists of the states of Anzoátegui, Sucre, Nueva Esparta, Monagas, and Bolívar, as well as the Delta Amacuro and the Amazonas territories. Its population is about equally divided between urban and rural elements. Agriculture and fishing engage the greatest part of the active population, although the petroleum industry and mining are also important.

Rural settlement. The rural landscape is characterized by the division of land into small farms (*minifundios*) and large estates (*latifundios*). The estates are mainly engaged in extensive cattle raising and the commercial cultivation of such crops as sugarcane and sesame. The small farms are predominantly subsistence units on which corn and legumes are cultivated. A mixture of Spanish, African, and Indian traditions is conserved, so that the rural areas form a repository of national folklore. Diet is directly related to local agricultural products; there is a preference for cereals and legumes. The characteristic house, called a *rancho,* has adobe (sun-dried brick) or mud walls, a thatched or sheet-metal roof, dirt floors, and minimum hygienic and service facilities. The type of clothing worn is related to environmental conditions; the cool *liquiliqui* (cotton or linen man's suit) is worn by plainsmen and the thick *ruana* (woollen poncho, or cape) by inhabitants of the Andes.

Urban settlement. Cities are often specialized in function. Ciudad Guayana, for example, is industrial; Barquisimeto is commercial; and Mérida is a university town. Caracas, as the capital city, is cosmopolitan and more diversified. The daily rhythm of life in the cities is based on a five-day work week and an eight-hour work day. In housing, a contrast exists between Spanish traditional architecture and the boldest lines of modern design. Styles of dress are largely Western, and diet is related to level of income. In the low-income group the diet is based on beans, corn, rice and plantain, while in the medium- and high-income groups it contains a higher nutritional value, including animal proteins and vitamins from vegetables and fruit.

Rural settlement patterns

THE PEOPLE

The official language of the country is Spanish; it is enriched by numerous local idioms and colloquialisms. English is used in business, and Italian is spoken by most

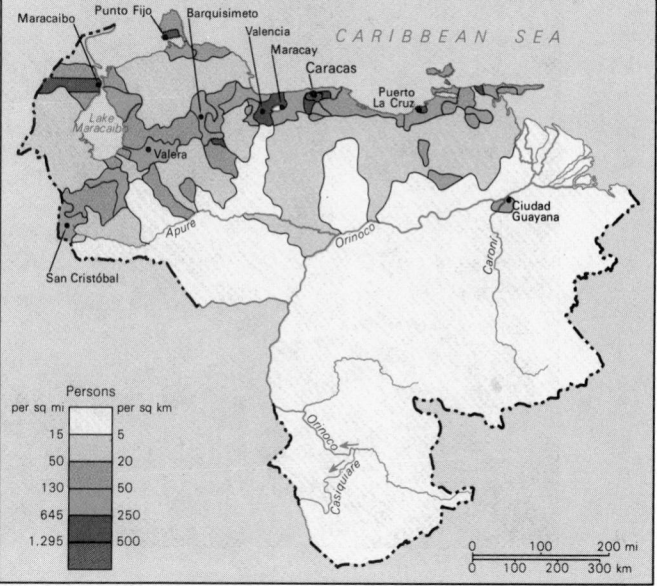

Population density of Venezuela.

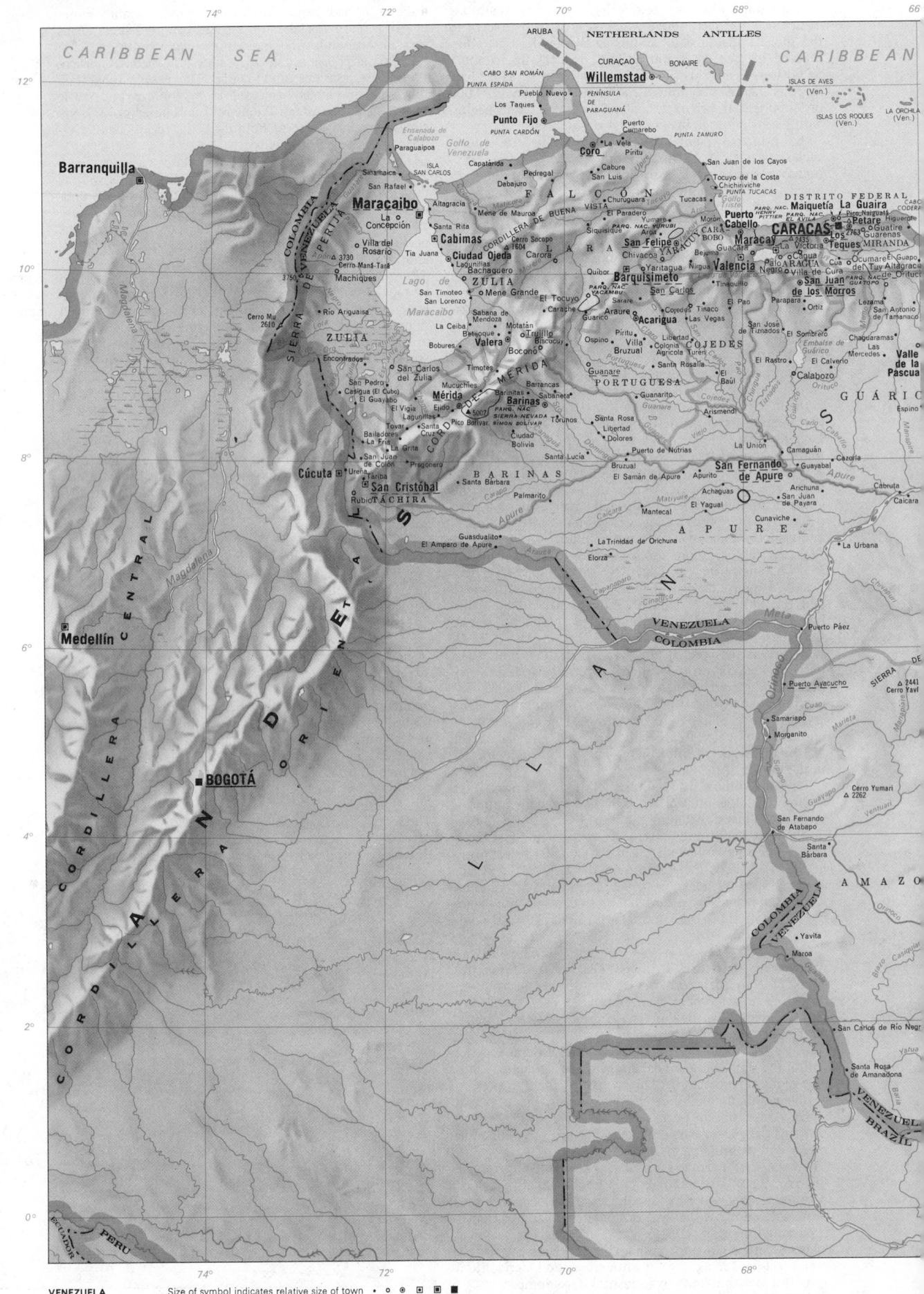

SEA

LA BLANQUILLA
(Ven.)
ISLAS LOS HERMANOS
(Ven.)

GRENADA
(U.K.)

A LA TORTUGA
(Ven.)

NUEVA
ESPARTA
ISLA DE
MARGARITA
Juangriego
La Asunción
Porlamar
ISLAS LOS TESTIGOS

TOBAGO

Boca del Pozo
PUNTA DE PIEDRAS
Punta de Piedras
ISLA CUBAGUA
ISLA COCHE
Río
Caribe

PUNTA PEÑAS

TRINIDAD

Port of Spain AND

Macuro

1254△

Yoco

Irapa

Güiria

Yaguaraparo

TRINIDAD   TOBAGO

Carúpano
Araya PEN. DE ARAYA
PUNTA DE ARENAS
Golfo de Cariaco
Cumaná

Casanay

El Pilar

Cariaco
San Antonio
del Golfo
Cumanacoa

Gulf of Paria

Puerto la Cruz
Barcelona
Guanta
Pozuelos

Caripe

△2596 Cerro Caripito
Cerro Caripito
Turimiquire

SUCRE

Puerto Piritu
Clarines
Bergantin
Aragua de Maturin

Valle de
Guanape

Quiriquire

Pedernales

San Mateo
Onoto
Aragua de
Barcelona

Caicara de Maturin
Punta
de Mata

Jusepin

Maturín

San José
Guaribe

MONAGAS

DELTA   DEL

Tucupita

Anaco

Santa Ana de Barcelona
Cantaura

Uracoa

ORINOCO
Coporito

Bahía
Tobe
Jube

ISLA IDUBUROJO

Zaraza

El Tigre
San Tomé
San José
de Guanipa

Temblador

Boca
Grande

El Socorro

Santa María
de Ipire
Pariaguán
Santo
Tomás

Barrancas
DELTA AMACURO

CORCORO ISLAND

Sacupana

ANZOÁTEGUI

Curiapo

Las
Bonitas

Soledad
Ciudad Guayana

Mapire

Moitaco

El Pao
Upata

Ciudad
Bolívar

El Palmar

Maripa
Cerro Mato
△1883

802△
Cerro Bolívar

El Manteco

Guasipati
El Callao

Ciudad
Piar

El Perú
Tumeremo

G U I A N A

La Paragua

El
Dorado

B O L Í V A R

H I G H

Canaima

SALTO ANGEL
ANGEL FALLS

GUAMPÍ

Cerro Guaiquinima
△2100

SIERRA
DE
GUAMPÍ

△2500
Auyán-Tepuí

LA GRAN

GUYANA

VENEZUELA

Luepa

Georgetown

El Oso

PARQUE NACIONAL
CANAIMA
SABANA

Mount Roraima
2772

L A N D S

Arabelo

Santa Elena de Uairén

PAKARAIMA MOUNTAINS

△ Cerro Marahuaca
2579
△Cerro Duida
2400
Esmeralda

S I E R R A   P A R I M A

BRAZIL
GUYANA

SURINAM (Neth.)
GUYANA

SIERRA DE
CURUPIRA

Pico Tamacuarí
2340

1800

Equator

Negro

© Rand McNally & Co.
A-541400-257   -1- -1- -1-

0	50	100		200		300 km

0		50		100		200 mi

ATLANTIC

OCEAN

immigrants. In the Indian regions of the east, south, and west, more than 25 different languages are spoken, most of which belong to the three linguistic families, Cariban, Arawak, and Chibcha. There are also some Indian languages of unknown origin spoken by isolated groups.

For the past four centuries, Venezuela has acted as an ethnic melting pot. The dominant ethnic type is the mestizo (a person of mixed ancestry). The white population results from immigration from Europe during the 20th century, largely from Italy and Spain. One percent are unassimilated Indians. The various Indian tribes live in isolated regions of the Lago de Maracaibo Basin, in the Orinoco River Basin, and in the delta of Amacuro.

Composition of the population

The overwhelming majority of the population is Roman Catholic. The largest minority religion is Protestantism; and Judaism, Islām, and Orthodox Christianity are also practiced. Indigenous Indian religions are characterized by a prevailing fear of evil spirits. The national constitution guarantees freedom of religion.

THE ECONOMY

The increasing participation of Venezuela in the world economy since the 1920s has been directly related to the production of petroleum. Its exports of petroleum have penetrated U.S., European, and Latin American markets; increased imports, on the other hand, have included agricultural equipment, industrial machinery, and consumer goods. During the 1960s Venezuela began to reduce dependence on imported goods by encouraging local manufactures, in addition to further expanding its petrochemical and steel industries and developing its hydroelectric potential.

Venezuela is a member of the Latin American Free Trade Association (LAFTA) and joined the Andean Subregional Agreement (Andean Pact) in 1979; the purpose of the latter agreement is to economically integrate the Andean countries as a step toward integration of Latin America as a whole.

Resources. The country's most important mineral resource is petroleum. The largest and richest deposit is in the Lago de Maracaibo Basin. The two other main deposits of oil and natural gas are located north of the Orinoco River in the states of Monagas, Guárico, and Anzoátegui and in the western Llanos in the states of Portuguesa and Barinas.

Petroleum resources

Iron ore, which is 60 percent pure, is found in the Guiana region. Large deposits of bauxite were discovered in Bolívar State along the Orinoco River in the late 1970s. Gold, as well as both industrial and gem diamonds, is also mined in the Guiana area. Lowgrade bituminous and lignite coal is found in the Andean foothills, and salt deposits are located in the Araya Peninsula. There are also scattered deposits of limestone.

Various minerals exist in less extensive deposits. These include manganese, nickel, vanadium (a metallic element found combined in minerals and used to form alloys), chrome, lead, zinc, copper, phosphate, and asbestos.

The grasslands of the extensive plains provide grazing for cattle. Of the nearly 30,000,000 acres of total forest reserves, about 85 percent is in Guiana; the greater part of the remaining reserves are in the western plains. The commercial timber includes cabinet woods such as mahogany. Fish are found in abundance in the country's rivers and lakes, as well as in the coastal waters.

Apart from oil, the nation's rivers constitute the most important power resource. The greatest hydroelectric potential is held by the Orinoco River and its tributary, the Caroní. The Río Santo Domingo, which flows through the states of Mérida and Barinas, is the second most important power resource. There are also hydroelectric potentialities in the Uribante and Caparo rivers in the Andes.

Hydroelectric resources

Agriculture. Agriculture contributes only a small percentage of the gross national product (GNP) and provides work for about one-sixth of the economically active population. The principal agricultural products are meat (beef, pork, fowl, goat, mutton), milk, corn, potatoes, cassava (manioc), plantain and bananas, eggs, coffee, sugarcane, rice, and sesame.

About 80 percent of agricultural output is produced on

large landholdings, with the remaining 20 percent on small farms. Agrarian legislation, adopted in 1960, assures the small farmer of his property rights and guarantees him technical assistance, credit, and a market for his produce. In addition, under the land-reform measures, many rural families had been settled in rural communities, or *asentamientos,* which are agricultural units of houses equipped with basic services; the units are grouped on seven to 25 acres of land given to peasant families.

The national government owns 80 percent of the nation's forests; the rest is held privately. The forestry industry is, however, little developed. Despite its potential, fishing is also an undeveloped, mostly local, activity. A small portion of the annual catch, mainly sardines and shellfish, is canned for export.

Mining. The exploitation of Venezuela's vast oil reserves is the principal source of the nation's income. Oil production has permitted the increase of public spending, the strengthening of the country's import capacity, the creation of basic industries, and the development of agriculture. Gross foreign investment in Venezuela was concentrated in the oil industry prior to nationalization in 1976; most such investment is now directed toward the manufacturing industries and more than one-half is made by U.S. interests.

The Venezuelan Petroleum Corporation is a state-owned organization that produces, refines, and distributes petroleum products in competition with Venezuelan and foreign private industry. Before the 1960s, all oil was refined outside the country; natural gas, obtained in the process of oil exploitation, was wasted. Since then, however, domestic oil refineries have been established. Natural gas became subject to a law that limits its exploitation and gave Venezuela the rights for its industrialization. The gas is now distributed by pipeline to be used as fuel, as a raw material in the petrochemical industry, and for the manufacture of liquid gas.

Venezuela is an important producer of iron ore. Reserves at Cerro Bolívar and El Pao are mined by U.S. companies under government concessions. The Venezuelan government also operates iron mines in the Guiana Highlands.

Limestone is quarried extensively to provide the raw material for the domestic cement industry. The government has entered the coal-mining industry through controlling shares in private companies. Exploitation of salt is a government monopoly. Most gold is mined by the government; output has, however, decreased since the 1950s, and in the late 20th century most gold was imported for jewelry, coinage, and dental work.

Industry. Manufacturing industries were originally concentrated in the Caracas area. Since the 1960s, however, the government has striven to promote the establishment of industrial centres in several different locations. Ciudad Guayana, on the lower Orinoco River, is the major centre for processing the mineral wealth of the Guiana region.

Dispersal of industrial centres

Morón, on the coast 106 miles west of Caracas, is the centre of the petrochemical industry; among its manufactures are fertilizers, caustic soda, explosives, insecticides, and organic chemicals. Manufacturing in Maracaibo is concerned with the processing of foodstuffs, the remodelling and rebuilding of heavy machinery, and the production of paper articles, pharmaceuticals, and electrical equipment.

The Guri Dam, a major source of hydroelectric energy in South America, is located in Venezuela on the lower Río Caroní where it flows down from the Guiana Highlands to join the Orinoco.

Finance. Financial services are provided by the Central Bank, which issues the national currency, as well as by a number of private banks. There are also banks with mixed capital, such as the Workers' Bank (Banco de Los Trabajadores); and state banks such as the Labourer's Bank (Banco Obrero). The construction of housing for the middle- and lower-income groups is financed by the Labourer's Bank. The National Agrarian Bank (Banco Agrario Nacional) deals with agricultural loans. Mortgage banks make long-term loans on urban real estate. The Venezuelan Development Corporation (Corporación Venezolana de Fomento), a government institution, promotes industrial development by means of long-term loans.

Insurance companies occupy a secondary position in the financing of economic activities. Venezuela has two stock exchanges, but the volume of their transactions is moderate. The financial market, favoured by a marked stability of its prices and by the absence of obstacles to money exchange, is mainly supplied by internal savings.

Management of the economy. The public sector plays a major role because of governmental participation in the oil and iron-ore industries. Revenues from those industries finance other economic or social activities of the government. The building industry, for example, depends largely on public works including the construction of highways, roads, airports, and buildings. About 60 percent of the fiscal income is derived from taxes on the oil industry. Oil revenues take the form of taxes on oil production, and a large tax on profits. Other governmental revenue is obtained from a graduated income tax and from other sources such as customs.

The role of government

Organized labour includes individual trade unions as well as the powerful Confederation of Venezuelan Workers (Confederación de Trabajadores de Venezuela). Employers' organizations are grouped together in the Federation of Chambers of Commerce and Production.

Foreign capital and technology have played an important role in promoting the expansion of manufacturing. To a lesser extent, joint participation by foreign and Venezuelan capital has been used to develop certain enterprises such as the manufacture of stoves and the assembly of automobiles.

Transportation. The nation's transportation system is well developed, especially in the northern and northwestern regions. Domestic travel depends largely on the road network. Industrial transportation needs are served by coastal shipping routes as well as by inland waterways. Air services provide access to regions without other means of communication.

There are three trunk roads—a section of the Pan-American Highway that runs southwestward from Caracas to Cúcuta, Colombia; the Western Highway that runs along the Andes foothills from Valencia to San Cristóbal; and the Llanos Highway that extends eastward from Caracas to San Tomé. There are several branch and feeder roads.

Railways, both for passenger and freight transport, are relatively unimportant. One public line built as part of a previous nationwide railway plan runs northeastward from Barquisimeto in Lara state to Puerto Cabello on the coast and to Caracas. Private railways serve the iron and steel industry, running from mines in the Guiana region to Ciudad Guayana on the Orinoco River.

Almost all of the nation's foreign commerce is carried by sea. There are a number of ports, of which several are used by international shipping; many small ports serve fishing or coastal trade purposes. General cargo is handled at eight ports run by the government—La Guaira, Maracaibo, Puerto Cabello, Guanta, Puerto Sucre, Carúpano, Las Piedras, and Ciudad Bolívar.

Inland waterways are in use principally around Lago de Maracaibo or the Orinoco River. A dredged channel between the Golfo de Venezuela and Lago de Maracaibo allows sea-going vessels to dock at the ports of Maracaibo, Bobures, and La Salina. A dredged channel through the Orinoco Delta permits sea-going vessels also to sail upriver to Ciudad Guayana. The upper Orinoco and the Apure rivers are used as waterways because of a lack of connecting roads.

Transoceanic air routes use Venezuelan international airports as a stopover, as do flights between North and South America. There are three national airline companies, one of which operates international air services.

ADMINISTRATIVE AND SOCIAL CONDITIONS

Government. The Venezuelan constitution is based on principles of republican, democratic, and representative government. Its federal form of government is exercised through its executive, legislative, and judicial branches, none of which may prevail over the others.

Executive power is exercised by a directly elected president who is the head of state and of the armed forces. A council of ministers, whose members individually act as secretaries of state, constitutes the principal auxiliary for carrying out executive functions. Legislative power is invested in a two-chamber congress consisting of the Senate and the Chamber of Deputies. The Senate is composed of two elected representatives from each of the 20 states and from the Federal District. The number of deputies is in proportion to the number of inhabitants in each state.

In addition to the 20 states and the Federal District, there are two federal territories, and 10 islands in the Caribbean are organized as federal dependencies. The states are officially autonomous units, each headed by a governor who is appointed by the president. The state legislative assemblies are composed of two elected representatives from each administrative district and are empowered to approve or reject the governor's annual report. The basic political-administrative unit of the Venezuelan state is the municipality, which is composed of a municipal council that functions in the capital of each district. They are locally autonomous units that operate within the state and national framework.

Elections are held at five-year intervals. The president of the republic and the senators, deputies, and state and municipal councils are elected for five-year terms by universal suffrage, with direct and secret voting. The elections are contested by political parties, the existence of which is guaranteed by the constitution.

The administration of justice is national in character; there are no autonomous state courts. The highest judicial body is the Supreme Court of Justice, the members of which are appointed by the Congress. It hears cases of a civil, criminal, or political-administrative nature. The judges and members of the lower courts of ordinary or special jurisdiction are appointed by the Judiciary Council, which is composed of seven members, five of whom are appointed by the Congress and two by the president. All decisions in first-instance courts may be appealed to a higher court, but there is no appeal from decisions of the Supreme Court. Each municipality has its own police force. The Ministry of Justice is responsible for the prison system as well as for the auxiliary police.

Education. During the late 20th century, educational services were greatly expanded throughout the nation. Primary education is free and compulsory. Private schools play a significant role at the primary and secondary levels. Higher education, free to competent students, is provided by a number of public and private universities and teachers' colleges and one polytechnic institute.

Health and welfare. The government is engaged in expanding health and welfare services. To improve health conditions, sanitary facilities are being constructed, hospitals and rural medical centres are being built, and more doctors and nurses are being trained. Medical assistance is both public (free) and private. Public medical assistance is given by the Ministry of Health in public hospitals and other centres. The Instituto Venezolano de los Seguros Sociales offers medical and economic assistance to urban workers and employees. The aged and the physically handicapped are aided by the Patronato Nacional de Ancianos e Inválidos.

Although the majority of the people have satisfactory housing, hundreds of thousands must live in shacks on the periphery of urban areas, principally around Caracas. Conditions in rural areas are often worse. The high rate of population growth increases the problem. Both public and private sectors are attempting to alleviate the situation. The Ministry of Housing and the Workers' Bank is responsible for providing additional housing for the lower- and middle-income groups. Private building firms and mortgage banks also provide financing for housing of middle-income groups.

A well-organized trade-union movement has successfully promoted legislation affecting working conditions. In consequence, almost all management and labour relationships are governed by collective wage contracts; periodically renewed, they provide for adjustments to maintain a balance between wages and the cost of living. Venezuela is one of the few countries in the world to have generally kept inflation under control. Such inflationary tendencies

as do exist spring from conditions abroad, particularly in the United States, with which Venezuela maintains close relations.

CULTURAL LIFE

The fine arts in Venezuela have been influenced by the most recent trends in Europe, the United States, Mexico, and Brazil. At the same time, Venezuelans have themselves made important contributions to the plastic arts, and exhibitions by Venezuelan artists are shown in Europe and the United States. Jesús Soto is an outstanding producer of "kinetic art," which contains moving parts. Some Venezuelan authors have also achieved international fame. The most outstanding writers are the novelist Rómulo Gallegos and the novelist and essayist Arturo Uslar Pietri.

Venezuelans are traditionally known for their musical abilities. Different regions of the country each produce distinctive musical expressions. Since the 1920s the government has sponsored one of the most outstanding symphony orchestras in Latin America. The government also sponsors an Institute of Culture and Fine Arts (INCIBA), which promotes the publication of books and arranges for the free distribution of some of them, directly or indirectly subsidizes magazines of cultural value, sponsors exhibitions, and maintains various museums, academies, and cultural centres, as well as the Biblioteca Nacional (National Library) in Caracas.

Among the numerous artistic or learned societies are the Asociación Venezolana Amigos del Arte Colonial (Venezuelan Association of the Friends of Colonial Art), the Sociedad Amigos del Museo de Bellas Artes (Society of the Friends of the Museum of Fine Arts), and the Asociación Nacional de Escritores Venezolanos (Venezuelan Writers' Association). International cultural institutes include the British Council and the Centro Venezolano-Americano (Venezuelan-American Centre). There are numerous specialized, university, and government libraries throughout the country.

The museums in Caracas include the Museo de Bellas Artes de Caracas (Fine Arts Museum), the Museo Bolivariano (Bolívar Museum), the Museo Arte Colonial (Museum of Colonial Art), and the Museo de Ciencias Naturales (Natural Science Museum). The Museo "Talavera" in Ciudad Bolívar contains exhibits of pre-Columbian and colonial artifacts. The Museo "Urdaneta" Histórico Militar (Museum of Military History) is located in Maracaibo. For statistical data, see the "Britannica World Data" section in the current *Britannica Book of the Year.*

History

The oldest inhabitants of Venezuela were primitive food-gathering Indians who arrived in the Late Paleolithic Era. There followed, successively, invasions by other food-gathering groups, by community-dwelling Arawaks, and by warlike, cannibalistic Caribs. The most advanced Venezuelan Indians were the farming tribes of the Andes; nomadic hunting and fishing groups roamed Lake Maracaibo, the Llanos, and the coast.

THE COLONIAL ERA

Christopher Columbus arrived in what is now Venezuela in 1498, during his third voyage to the New World. The first quarter-century of European contact was limited to the northeast coast and confined to slave hunting and pearl fishing; the first permanent Spanish settlement, Cumaná, was not made until 1523. In the second quarter of the 16th century, the centre of activity shifted to the northwest region, where the Welser banking house of Augsburg purchased exploration and colonization rights; German attempts to find precious metals and to occupy the area failed, however, and Spain repossessed the area in 1546.

In the latter half of the 16th century, Spanish agriculturalists, using Indian slave labour, began effective colonization. Caracas was founded in 1567, and by 1600 more than 20 settlements dotted the Venezuelan Andes and the Caribbean coast. During the 17th and 18th centuries, the Llanos and Maracaibo regions were gradually taken over by various Roman Catholic missionary orders.

The colonial economy was based on agriculture and stock raising. Maize, beans, and beef were the domestic consumption staples; sugar, cacao, tobacco, and hides were the principal exports. Spain's European rivals, the French and English in the 16th century and the Dutch in the 17th century, succeeded in taking over most of Venezuela's commerce until the early 18th century, when Spain established a monopoly trading company. The interests of the latter, however, proved contrary to those of Venezuelan producers, who forced dissolution of the company during the 1780s.

Venezuelan society during the colonial era was headed by agents of the Spanish crown. Royal bureaucrats monopolized the top governing posts, and Spanish clergymen dominated the high church offices. Creoles (native-born whites), however, owned the colony's wealth, principally land, and used it to hold the coloured races in bondage: mestizos (persons of mixed ancestry) were generally without property, social status, or political influence; Indians performed forced labour on interior farms or were segregated on marginal lands; Negroes were slaves on the coastal plantations. In theory, Venezuela was governed by the Spanish crown through the Audiencia of Santo Domingo in the 16th and 17th centuries and through the Viceroy of New Granada (at Bogotá) from its incorporation in 1717. In practice, however, the Venezuelans exercised a great deal of local autonomy throughout the colonial era.

THE INDEPENDENCE MOVEMENT

A group of Venezuelan Creoles boldly proclaimed their country an independent republic in 1797. Although their effort failed, it constituted the first forewarning of the revolutionary movements that were soon to inflame all of Latin America.

In 1806 Francisco Miranda—who had earlier fought under George Washington against the British; served as a general in the French Revolution, and fought with the French against Prussia and Russia—tried unsuccessfully to land on the Venezuelan coast with a group of mercenaries whom he had recruited in New York. He was recalled to his country four years later, set up a revolutionary junta, had a constitution drafted, and established an independent nation with himself as dictator. In the ensuing war with royalist forces, however, he surrendered to the Spaniards, who sent him first to Puerto Rico and later to Spain, where he died in prison in 1816.

Simón Bolívar   Early in 1813, the revolutionary junta appointed Simón Bolívar commander of the Venezuelan forces. Born in Caracas in 1783 of a wealthy family of Creole landowners, Bolívar had tasted freedom during his student years in France and England and had long been a leader in the independence movement. He suffered many reverses in his war against the Spanish forces but was helped by the new Republic of Haiti and by a foreign legion of British and Irish soldiers. The Republic of Gran Colombia, with its capital at Bogotá, was proclaimed December 17, 1819, but the fighting was not yet over. On June 24, 1821, Bolívar defeated the royalist army in the Battle of Carabobo, and the last of the royalist forces surrendered at Puerto Cabello October 9, 1823. In 1824 Bolívar marched south to liberate Peru, and the following year he freed Bolivia from Spanish rule.

During his absence, regional rivalries broke out in Gran Colombia, and even his great prestige was not enough to hold the country together after his return. Venezuela broke away in 1829, and Ecuador soon after. Bolívar died in Santa Marta, Colombia, in 1830, penniless, disillusioned, and almost alone. Today he is honoured everywhere as the principal architect and hero of Venezuelan and Latin-American independence.

THE CAUDILLOS (1830–1935)

After the destruction of the colonial system, Venezuela passed through an era of government-by-force that lasted well over a century, until the death of Juan Vicente Gómez in 1935. Backed by their personal armies, much on the order of the later Chinese warlords, a series of caudillos (leaders) assumed power, which they exercised for their personal benefit rather than for that of the nation.

Páez and the Conservatives.   The first of the military dictators was Gen. José Antonio Páez, who gave the country better government than it would see again for nearly a century. Bolívar had left Páez in charge of the armed forces of Venezuela, and he was soon in full control of the country. He led the separation movement from Gran Colombia in 1829 and in 1830 convoked a constitutional convention to draw up a separate constitution for Venezuela. He dominated Venezuelan politics throughout the period 1830–48; he was president from 1831 to 1835 and was elected to another four-year term in 1839. He established law and order by subduing ambitious provincial caudillos. Páez ruled in cooperation with the large landholders and leading merchants of the Conservative Party. The constitution that they enacted in 1830 reflected their social and political philosophy—a centralist state, property qualifications for voting, death penalty for political crimes, freedom of contracts, and continuance of slavery. The church lost its tax immunity and its educational monopoly, and the army was shorn of its autonomy; thus, state supremacy was achieved. Stability thus assured, reconstruction of the war-torn economy began. Government finances were put in order, the nation's credit was firmly established abroad, and amortization of the national debt was begun. Construction of new roads promoted interior commerce and the export of coffee and cacao.

In contrast to the troubled times that preceded and followed it, the 1830–48 period of Conservative Party domination was an era of political stability, economic progress, and responsible administration. An opposition movement began to develop in 1840, however, when Antonio Leocadio Guzmán, the leading spokesman for dissident merchants and professional men, founded the Liberal Party. Guzmán's new liberal newspaper, *El Venezolano,* demanded abolition of slavery, extension of voting rights, and protection for the debtor classes. Declining demands in the world market for Venezuela's agricultural commodities during the 1840s produced economic difficulties, which in turn contributed to the increasing opposition to the Conservative oligarchy.

The Monagas and the civil wars.   The growing political crisis was brought to a head in 1848 by Gen. José Tadeo Monagas. Although elected president as a Conservative in 1846, he soon gravitated toward the Liberals. He intimidated the Conservative congress and appointed Liberal Party ministers. When Páez rebelled in 1848, Monagas defeated him and forced him into exile.

The decade 1848–58 was one of dictatorial rule by José Tadeo Monagas and his brother, Gen. José Gregorio Monagas, who alternated as president during the period. Liberal Party laws were passed abolishing slavery, extending suffrage, outlawing capital punishment, and limiting interest rates, but they were not implemented. Integrity in government waned; heavy deficit financing ruined the nation's credit; the economy began to stagnate and decay. In 1857 the Monagas brothers attempted to impose a new constitution extending the presidential term from four years to six and removing all restrictions on reelection. The Liberal leaders thereupon joined the Conservative opposition, and in March 1858 they brought the Monagas dynasty to an end. This first successful rebellion in Venezuela's national history set off five years of revolutionary turmoil between the Liberals and Conservatives. The issues in these so-called Federalist Wars were, on the Liberal side, federalism, democracy, and social reform and, on the Conservative side, centralism and preservation of the political and social status quo. The conflicts were extremely bloody, and control of the central government changed hands several times. General Páez returned in 1861 to restore Conservative hegemony for two years, but in 1863 final victory went to the Liberals, led by the generals Juan Falcón and Antonio Guzmán Blanco.

A new constitution enacted in 1864 incorporated the federalist principles of the victors. Local freedoms quickly disappeared, however, at the hands of provincial caudillos. As president in 1864–68, Falcón appeared content to allow subordinates, many of them irresponsible, to rule at both the state and national levels. Liberal mismanagement and increasing political chaos provided an opportunity for the

The Conservative oligarchy, 1830–48

Liberalism and federalism, 1848–70

Conservatives, now led by José Tadeo Monagas, to return to power in 1868. But this merely opened the floodgates of civil war. General Guzmán Blanco rallied the Liberals to his cause, overthrew the Conservatives, and assumed power in 1870.

The reigns of Guzmán Blanco and Crespo. Guzmán Blanco's triumphal entry into Caracas in April 1870 halted the political chaos and economic stagnation that had plagued the nation since 1858. The new president took the field himself and pacified the country in less than two years; he thereupon launched a broad program of reform and development.

A new constitution in 1872 proclaimed representative government, universal suffrage, and direct election of the president. Economic reforms, such as restoration of the nation's credit by means of new bond issues, liberal concessions to foreign investors, and an ambitious communications and transportation development program, gave further evidence of Guzmán Blanco's apparent devotion to Liberal Party principles. He ordered establishment of a nationwide system of public primary education and liberal state support for secondary and higher education. He not only abolished ecclesiastical privileges, cut off state subsidies to the Roman Catholic Church, proclaimed religious liberty, and legalized civil marriage but he also confiscated church properties, exiled the archbishop, and closed the convents.

Guzmán Blanco was the popular choice for president in the 1873 election. He departed for Europe in 1877, leaving a puppet successor in charge; but when the opposition rebelled, he returned to crush it and resumed the presidency in 1878. The following year he left Gen. Joaquín Crespo in charge. Guzmán Blanco returned from Europe in 1886 to serve a final two years in the face of growing popular opposition to his policies.

Unquestionably, Guzmán Blanco's regime had both positive and negative results for the nation. His admirers point to his political and military genius and to his administrative, economic, educational, and religious reforms. His detractors emphasize his tyrannical ruling methods, his financial chicanery, his monumental vanity, his superficial educational reforms, and his unwarranted attacks upon the church. For four years after the end of his regime, Venezuela floundered in new political chaos as various civilian political groups tried unsuccessfully to establish responsible representative government. In October 1892 Crespo seized power. His six-year rule was troubled by continued political turmoil, growing economic difficulties, and the nation's first serious diplomatic problem—concerning a dispute with Great Britain over the boundary between eastern Venezuela and western British Guiana. This jungled "no man's land," in which gold was discovered in 1877, had been the object of alternating claims and counterclaims between Venezuela and Great Britain for more than half a century. Great Britain repeatedly refused Venezuela's requests to refer the matter to arbitration, and in 1887 Venezuela suspended diplomatic relations. President Crespo appealed to the United States, and, in 1895, U.S. president Grover Cleveland pressured Britain to arbitrate. An international tribunal handed down a decision in 1899 that failed to satisfy Venezuela's demands.

The Andinos. The turn of the century was a turning point in Venezuelan history. In 1899 Gen. Cipriano Castro, a caudillo from the Andean state of Táchira, descended with his provincial army upon Caracas and seized the presidency. For the next 59 years, except for an interlude in 1945–48, five successive military strongmen from Táchira, known as Andinos, controlled the nation. Castro ruled from 1899 to 1909. His regime was characterized by administrative tyranny, financial irresponsibility, almost constant domestic revolt, and frequent foreign intervention. The most serious internal uprising occurred in eastern Venezuela in 1902–03. This and subsequent revolts were put down by Gen. Juan Vicente Gómez. Castro's cavalier treatment of foreign businessmen and diplomats and his refusal to pay for foreign properties damaged in domestic insurrections resulted in a British-German-Italian blockade of the Venezuelan coast in 1902–03 and a Dutch attack upon Venezuela's navy in 1908. Ill health forced

Castro's departure for Europe for medical attention in 1908, whereupon Gómez usurped the presidential powers and did not relinquish them until his death 27 years later.

Gómez was an effective dictator. By manipulating elections, abolishing all organized political activity, and monopolizing appointive powers, he was able to establish a completely subservient legislative and judicial structure. He muzzled the press and stifled the opposition with an elaborate spy service, and he used arbitrary arrests, exiles, long imprisonments, and assassinations to insure his control. Efficient police and army organizations, modernized and professionalized by Gómez, maintained his power through unrestricted use of force.

Political order and liberal concessions attracted foreign petroleum investors. Dutch and British petroleum interests—the Royal Dutch–Shell combine—entered Venezuela just before World War I; immediately after the war, Standard Oil interests from the United States arrived to compete with the British and Dutch. By 1928 Venezuela had become the world's leading exporter of oil and was second only to the United States in oil production. The oil industry brought the nation such benefits as high-paying jobs, subsidies to agriculture, expanded government revenues, and increased domestic and foreign trade. Continued high levels of petroleum exports in the 1930s saved the economy from collapse during the world depression.

The extraordinary income from oil provided the wherewithal for economic progress. Networks of roads, railroads, and port facilities were constructed; many new public buildings were erected; the entire foreign debt was paid off; the large domestic debt was drastically reduced. Yet the oil prosperity was unevenly distributed; most Venezuelans continued to live in abject poverty, and their health, housing, and education needs were ignored by the state. Meanwhile, Gómez and the top bureaucrats and army officers enriched themselves; the dictator became the nation's largest landholder, biggest stock raiser, and wealthiest citizen; and he remained master of the political and economic system until his death, from natural causes, in 1935.

VENEZUELA SINCE 1935

Eleazar López Conteras, who had been war minister under Gómez, succeeded him and served as president until 1941. López restored civil liberties, sanctioned political activity, and permitted labour to organize during 1936; but he restored the dictatorship in 1937, when the opposition became too threatening. In 1938 he inaugurated a three-year development plan that included construction of public schools and hospitals and support for agriculture and private industry.

Isaías Medina Angarita, a fellow Táchira general, was president in 1941–45; he continued this development program and also restored political liberties. A World War II transportation squeeze resulted in a sharp decline in petroleum revenues during 1941 and 1942, and President Medina revised upward—under a 1943 oil law—the nation's share in the profits of the petroleum industry. As the transportation shortage eased and new concessions were granted, a petroleum boom stimulated an upsurge in the whole economy during 1944 and 1945.

In October 1945, at the height of the wartime prosperity, the Medina administration was suddenly overthrown. This revolution was the most fundamental in the nation's history; it marked the assumption of power, for the first time, by a political party (Acción Democrática) that had the support of a majority of the Venezuelan people. Party leader Rómulo Betancourt headed a civilian–military junta that ruled the nation for 28 months. On July 5, 1947, a new constitution reflecting the labour-leftist philosophy of the party was adopted, and in December 1947 novelist Rómulo Gallegos was elected to the presidency.

Acción Democrática promptly launched a sweeping program of reform: a fifty-fifty tax decree assured the nation of at least half the profits of the petroleum industry; labour was encouraged to organize and to bargain hard for its rights; broad government support was granted for health, housing, and education and for agricultural and industrial development. These democratic reforms provoked strong

Castro and Gómez, 1899–1935

Prosperity, reform, and military rule, 1935–58

opposition from conservative forces that culminated in a November 1948 military coup. The new ruling junta was headed by Lt. Col. Carlos Delgado Chalbaud and Maj. Marcos Pérez Jiménez; two years later the former was assassinated, and the latter became Venezuela's new strongman.

Thus, from 1951 to 1957 the nation was again controlled by a Táchira military dictator. Pérez Jiménez outlawed political activity, crushed the labour movement, closed down the universities, and muzzled the press. Acción Democrática's nationwide reform programs were abandoned in favour of modernizing Caracas and enriching the dictator and his army associates. Finally, popular opposition grew so great that the navy and air force joined to overthrow Pérez Jiménez in January 1958. A civilian–military junta ran the country for one year, after which Rómulo Betancourt was elected president.

Democracy and economic nationalism, 1959 to the present

The second Betancourt administration (1959–64) was considerably more moderate than the first. This time, Acción Democrática, in contrast to its earlier exclusivism, cooperated with the next largest party, the middle-of-the-road Christian Democrats, and set up a coalition government. This government launched programs designed to modernize agriculture, develop domestic industry, improve the nation's health, and eliminate illiteracy. In 1960 it passed an agrarian reform law intended to provide farms for all rural families. In 1962 it inaugurated a national steel industry, the Siderúrgica del Orinoco, to process part of the vast iron-ore deposits exploited by U.S. companies under concessions granted in 1950.

Despite broad developmental progress, the Betancourt administration was troubled by political unrest and economic crisis. The armed forces launched several unsuccessful coups, and civilian elements on both the right and left resisted the moderate reform programs. To complicate matters, a sharp depression occurred in 1960–63. In foreign affairs, Venezuela severed diplomatic relations with the Dominican Republic in 1960 (after Dominican agents attempted to assassinate Betancourt) and broke relations with Cuba in 1961 (following repeated Cuban attempts to aid the Venezuelan Communists).

The 1963 presidential elections, held in an atmosphere of great political tension, were narrowly won by the Acción Democrática candidate Raúl Leoni. The Christian Democrats thereupon withdrew from the governing coalition, but they were replaced by the labour-leftist Unión Republicana Democrática. The oil and iron-ore industries began to boom once more, and a new petrochemical industry was launched. Although the return of prosperity accelerated the development and reform programs begun in the early 1960s, growing popular impatience and dissatisfaction strengthened the opposition Christian Democrats, whose presidential candidate, Rafael Caldera, won the 1968 elections.

Caldera's inauguration in 1969 marked the first time in Venezuela's history that an incumbent government peacefully surrendered power to an opposition electoral victor. The political ideology and domestic programs of the Christian Democrats were scarcely distinguishable from those of Acción Democrática, but Caldera was more flexible in his foreign policy. He improved relations with Cuba, the Soviet Union, and the Latin-American military dictatorships. In the early 1970s, rising economic nationalism resulted in Venezuelan majority ownership of foreign banks, state control of the natural-gas industry, and a moratorium on the granting of oil concessions.

Pres. Carlos Andrés Pérez Rodriguez, the Acción Democrática victor in the 1973 elections, nationalized the iron-ore industry in 1975 and the petroleum industry in 1976. Following the Arab–Israeli War of 1973, Venezuela, as a founding member of the Organization of Petroleum Exporting Countries (OPEC), more than quadrupled the price of its oil. The result was a spending orgy that attracted a wave of South American immigrants, increased food and luxury imports, produced growing waste and corruption, and created a privileged economic elite while doing little to alleviate the poverty of the masses. In an attempt to reduce the domestic inflationary effects of increased oil revenues, Venezuela set up a Latin-American development fund to

Oil wealth

assist the country's less fortunate neighbours. Popular dissatisfaction with government management of the new oil wealth resulted in another Christian Democratic presidential victory in 1978 by Luis Herrera Campins. He in turn, however, came under attack from both conservatives and labour unions for failing to cure the economic troubles or to stem bureaucratic inefficiency. In the 1983 elections, Acción Democrática was again returned to power and the new president, Jaime Lusinchi, announced austerity measures to cope with Venezuela's serious economic problems. For current political history, see the annual issues of the *Britannica Book of the Year.* (E.Li./Ed.)

BIBLIOGRAPHY

Physical and human geography: VENEZUELA, DIRECCIÓN DE CARTOGRAFÍA, *Atlas de Venezuela,* 2nd ed. (1979); PABLO VILA, *Geography of Venezuela* (1969; trans. of selected chapters from *Geografía de Venezuela,* 1960–), studies the Venezuelan physical, cultural, and geographical landscapes; ARTURO USLAR PIETRI, *La tierra Venezolana,* 3rd ed. (1980), conveys literary and graphic impressions of several cities and regions of the country; HOWARD I. BLUTSTEIN *et al., Area Handbook for Venezuela* (1977), is a concise introduction to many physical, social, and political facts about Venezuela. DANIEL H. LEVINE, *Religion and Politics in Latin America: The Catholic Church in Venezuela and Colombia* (1981), examines the social roles of bishops, clergy, lay organizations, and other elements of the church, and his *Conflict and Political Change in Venezuela* (1973) studies the development of Venezuelan democracy. LORING ALLEN, *Venezuelan Economic Development: A Politico-Economic Analysis* (1977), is a general reference work with facts about important economic institutions and activities; BANCO CENTRAL DE VENEZUELA, *Informe económico* (annual), is a wide analysis of the development of every sector of the Venezuelan economy, and *Memoria* (annual) presents an overall view of the evolution of the national economy and compares it with the world economy; MINISTERIO DE AGRICULTURA Y CRIA, *Anuario estadístico agropecuario* (annual), is a summary of the statistics on agriculture; JOSÉ ANTONIO MAYOBRE, *Las inversiones extranjeras en Venezuela,* 2nd ed. (1972), investigates the amount of foreign investment in the country. U.S. OFFICE OF EDUCATION, *The Educational System of Venezuela* (1975), is a booklet providing basic information on the history and the state of public education in the mid-1970s.

History: JOHN V. LOMBARDI, *Venezuela: The Search for Order, the Dream of Progress* (1982), is a concise history supplemented by a chronology and a fine bibliographic essay; EDWIN LIEUWEN, *Venezuela,* 2nd ed. (1965), has long been a standard survey of the history, society, economy, and political system; FRANCISCO GONZÁLEZ GUINÁN, *Historia contemporánea de Venezuela,* 15 vol. (1954), contains an encyclopaedic treatment of the 19th century; JOSÉ LUIS SALCEDO BASTARDO, *Historia fundamental de Venezuela,* 8th ed. (1979), is a thorough, standard history; J.M. SISO MARTÍNEZ, *Historia de Venezuela,* 5th ed. (1956), is an excellent one-volume history in Spanish; DONNA K. and G.A. RUDOLPH, *Historical Dictionary of Venezuela* (1971), provides succinct information on major events and persons through 1969; MARIANO PICÓN-SALAS *et al., Venezuela independiente, 1810–1960* (1962), includes fine essays on the evolution of society, culture, the economy, and political system; JOHN LYNCH, *The Spanish-American Revolution, 1808– 1826* (1973), presents a unified history of the continental independence movement; BENJAMÍN A. FRANKEL, *Venezuela y los Estados Unidos, 1810–1888* (1977), is a fine account of 19th-century diplomatic relations; GERHARD MASUR, *Simón Bolívar,* rev. ed. (1969), is a major English-language biography; ROBERT L. GILMORE, *Caudillism and Militarism in Venezuela, 1810–1910* (1964), discusses the evolution from military personalism to military professionalism; WINFIELD J. BURGGRAAFF, *Civil-Military Relations in Venezuela, 1935–1959* (1967), is an account of the 20th-century role of the military; JOHN D. MARTZ and DAVID J. MYERS (eds.), *Venezuela: The Democratic Experience* (1977), is a systematic history of Venezuelan politics and economy since 1958, with an excellent treatment of the political system; JOHN D. MARTZ, *Acción Democrática: Evolution of a Modern Political Party in Venezuela* (1966), is a sympathetic history and analysis of the period 1941–64; DONALD L. HERMAN, *Christian Democracy in Venezuela* (1980), is a comprehensive study of another major political party; EDWIN LIEUWEN, *Petroleum in Venezuela: A History* (1954, reprinted 1967), is a detailed history of the industry from 1907 to 1950; RÓMULO BETANCOURT, *Venezuela: Oil and Politics* (1979; trans. of his *Venezuela: política y petróleo,* 2nd ed., 1967), is a democratic reformer's view of 20th-century politics and economics; FRANKLIN TUGWELL, *The Politics of Oil in Venezuela* (1975), studies relations between government and the petroleum companies from 1959 to 1973.

(I.S. de S./E.Li./Ed.)

Venice

A city that is uniquely wedded to the sea, Venice (Italian Venezia) is a major seaport of northern Italy, the capital of the province of Venezia and the region of Veneto, and the former centre of a maritime republic whose economic and political power was felt throughout the Mediterranean world for more than 1,000 years. Although other cities are built on islands, are also laced with canals, and are rich in art and architecture, although other cities have been world powers, there is only one Venice. Perhaps no other city of the West has so long and so strongly appealed to the romantic imagination: for the gondolas and gondoliers of its canals, for the multitude of great canvases upon which its faces have been recorded over the centuries, for the vast expanses of buildings and monuments that make it virtually a living museum of the past, and for the pervasive general atmosphere that seems to set it apart not only from all other cities of the world but also from the contemporary world itself.

Venice lost a bit of its island character and some of its insular mentality in 1846, when a causeway nearly two miles (three kilometres) in length brought the railway across 222 arches from the mainland—even more in 1932 when a parallel causeway brought the automobile. Each link was long and stoutly resisted by persons who would leave the city unchanged, and they succeeded in forcing wheeled vehicles to be garaged at the landward edge of the island. Similar battles continue between traditionalists and modernists, but the most urgent problems of present-day Venice are environmental. In addition to damage wrought by an increasing frequency of high tides and flooding, the islands themselves have been found to be sinking into the lagoon at a much faster rate than in previous centuries. And, as in other cities in which many monuments and art treasures stand exposed, air pollution already has virtually defaced many priceless examples of stonework from the Venetian past.

This article is divided into the following sections:

Physical and human geography

THE LANDSCAPE

Site. Historic Venice—*La serenissima* ("the most serene city"), as it styled itself—lies almost in the centre of a crescent-shaped lagoon that stretches from northeast to southwest for about 32 miles (51 kilometres). This body of water varies in width from five to nine miles (eight to 14 kilometres) and is separated from the Adriatic Sea by a barrier of narrow islands and peninsulas. The city's historic centre is built upon an archipelago of islets and mudbanks about two miles long and one mile across. The limits of the modern city, embracing the whole 90-mile perimeter of the lagoon, include 10 principal islands aside from those of the mother city and the two industrial boroughs of Mestre and Marghera on the mainland, all of which were incorporated into the city in 1927.

Waterways and walkways. Venice's 180 canals—28 miles (45 kilomeres) of them, with an average width of 12 feet (3.7 metres)—follow the original watercourses among the 118 original islands. The Grand Canal (Canale Grande) flowing around two opulent curves through the city, is the main stream through the isles. Its name, Rivo Alto, given to the little archipelago before it was called Venice, persists today in the name Rialto. About two miles long, the Grand Canal has a mean depth of nine feet; it is 228 feet (69 metres) wide at its broadest point and is never narrower than 120 feet (37 metres). It is bordered by 200 palaces built from the 12th to the 18th century, 10 churches, and one maritime gasoline station. It encounters 46 side canals in its course, "the finest street in the world," according to 15th-century chronicler Philippe de Commynes.

The Grand Canal and its bridges

Until the 19th century, a single bridge crossed this majestic avenue, the Rialto Bridge (Ponte di Rialto). The present high, single-arched bridge crowded with tiny shops was built (*c.* 1590) to the plans of Antonio da Ponte, who won the design competition against Michelangelo and other major artists of the day. It is the fifth bridge on this site, and the first not built of wood. Two other bridges—flat, ugly, cast-iron structures erected by occupying Austrians in 1854—were replaced in 1932 to accommodate newer, larger water-buses. The railroad station bridge was rebuilt in stone, while the Ponte dell' Accademia, rather Japanese in appearance, with steps going over a high arch, was constructed of tarred wood. Other wooden bridges, so temporary as to be ephemeral, appear for the day of a religious festival and then vanish until the following year.

Of all the permanent bridges of Venice, of which there are some 400, the Bridge of Sighs (Ponte dei Sospiri) is perhaps the most celebrated. This short, covered passageway, high over the little canal between the Doges' Palace (Palazzo Ducale) and the Republic's prison, is wreathed in romantic legend based on injustices perpetrated long before the Baroque stone bridge was constructed in 1600.

In 1881 a French company introduced steam-powered water-buses on the Grand Canal; they are still called *vaporetti* ("little steamers"), though diesel-powered for decades. Since then the number of gondolas has declined from 10,000 to less than 400. The gondolier is now also obliged to compete with the motor-launch taxis. The word gondola, the origin of which is still disputed, was apparently first recorded in the 11th century. The craft evolved its form by adapting to function, and by the 17th century it had become the long, sleek, keelless boat operated today. Built in tiny boatyards in Venice, gondolas are constructed of several different woods—the forked rowlocks are always carved from a single block of walnut—and are immensely strong. The boat is deliberately lopsided, one side curving outward much more than the other to facilitate handling and to counter the weight of the oarsman standing on the stern. Since 1562, in obedience to sumptuary laws seeking to suppress ostentation in civil dress and decoration, all gondolas have been painted black. The gleaming *ferro* remained to decorate the upcurving prow: it has six metal prongs facing forward and one pointing astern, the whole topped by a curved halberd-like blade. The significance of this symbol—if it ever had any—has been lost.

There are almost as many different kinds of water-

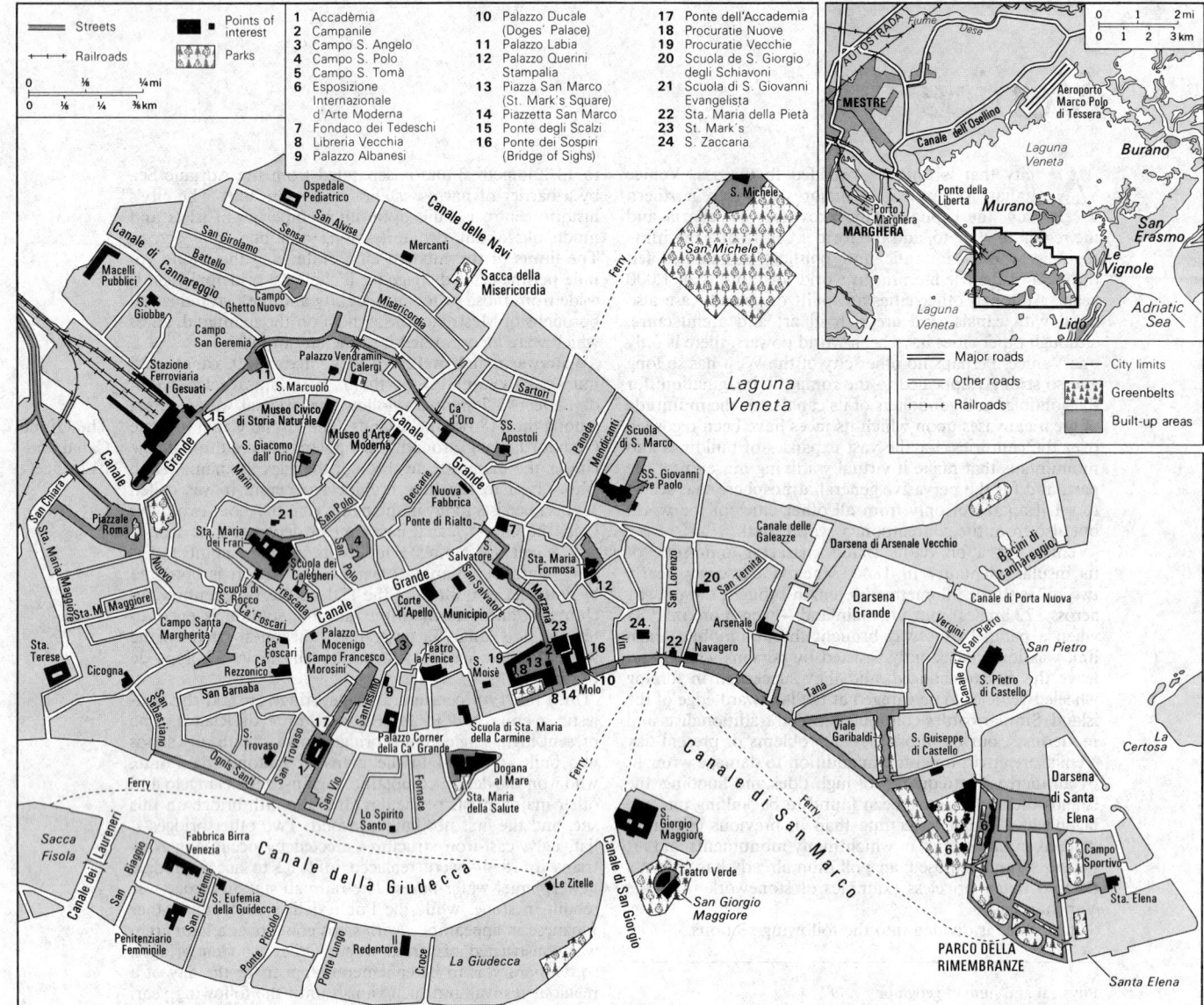

Legend (Points of interest):

Streets	Points of interest	Parks
Railroads		

1 Accadèmia
2 Campanile
3 Campo S. Angelo
4 Campo S. Polo
5 Campo S. Tomà
6 Esposizione Internazionale d'Arte Moderna
7 Fondaco dei Tedeschi
8 Libreria Vecchia
9 Palazzo Albanesi
10 Palazzo Ducale (Doges' Palace)
11 Palazzo Labia
12 Palazzo Querini Stampalia
13 Piazza San Marco (St. Mark's Square)
14 Piazzetta San Marco
15 Ponte degli Scalzi
16 Ponte dei Sospiri (Bridge of Sighs)
17 Ponte dell'Accademia
18 Procuratie Nuove
19 Procuratie Vecchie
20 Scuola de S. Giorgio degli Schiavoni
21 Scuola di S. Giovanni Evangelista
22 Sta. Maria della Pietà
23 St. Mark's
24 S. Zaccaria

Venice and (inset) its metropolitan area.

craft in Venice as there are surface vehicles in a mainland city, from the dainty little *sandolo,* rowed standing with crossed oars, to giant ocean liners. Blue ambulance motorboats, red fireboats, gray garbage scows, bright-coloured soft-drink barges, police speedboats, tall-masted fishing vessels, black-tasselled funeral gondolas, a car ferry for the swimming beaches of the Lido (where automobiles are allowed), railroad cars on heavy lighters, warships from the local naval station, pilot boats, tugs, customs cutters, work-a-day rowboats, and barges pass amid the water-buses, the gondolas, the taxis, and an endless variety of commercial and pleasure craft.

"Streets full of water. Please advise," read the cable to New York City from humorist Robert Benchley on his

Footpaths and neighbourhoods arrival. There are in fact some 3,000 solid streets—or at least passageways—in Venice. A quayside walk is a *riva* or, if very wide, a *fondamenta; rio terro* indicates a filled-in canal; *piscina,* a filled-in pond; *ruga,* a shopping street; *calle,* a lane; *salizzada,* a paved alley; and *ramo,* a branch alley (the Ramo Salizzada Zusto is two and a half feet [76 centimetres] wide). The word *campo* indicates where original settlements had a field (now a paved square), and there are smaller open spaces called *campiello* and *campazzo.* The *campi,* with trees, cafés, shops, and a church, have remained the nuclei of the neighbourhoods that were once separate villages. In the 12th century the settlements were compacted into six *sestieri,* or wards. House numbers do

not run by street but by district, going up streets, through alleys, and over canals.

Layout and architecture. In the eccentric dialect of Venice, street and other names are not always pronounced as they are written. The word for house, *casa,* becomes *ca'.* Not only are pronunciation and speech rhythms local but often the vocabulary is local as well.

Architecture, also, has a Venetian accent. Succeeding styles were accepted slowly over the centuries, adapted rather than adopted. Each of the extremely varied architectural elements of the cityscape—Italian, Arabic, Byzantine, Gothic, Renaissance, Mannerist, and Baroque—has been artfully hyphenated (*e.g.,* Veneto-Byzantine). Other factors contribute to the harmony of the architectural ensemble: the repeated motif of street, bridge, and canal; and the unique optical effects of the lagoon's light and water, which seem to render solid stone translucent, the buildings appearing as insubstantial as their reflections in the water and the whole washed in coloured light reflected, refracted, and repeated between sea and sky.

St. Mark's, the Piazza, and environs. The uncommon harmonies of Venetian stone, air, water, and time are fully orchestrated in St. Mark's Square (Piazza San Marco), one of the most famous squares in the world. This marble salon, 574 feet long and 260 feet wide (175 by 79 metres), was for centuries the social and political centre of *La serenissima.* Arcaded on three sides and spiked with the 324-foot (99-metre) Campanile, its eastern end is closed

Gondolas on the Grand Canal, Venice. In
the centre is Sta. Maria della Salute.

Carl Frank

by the Cathedral (Basilica) of St. Mark and the Doges'
Palace—the church golden, the palace pink, and
both grandiose constructions seeming to float airily against the
sky. It is, as it was contrived to be, a stunning display of
the pride, wealth, and power of *La serenissima*.

The water entrance to the Piazza is built where the Grand
Canal meets the broad Basin of St. Mark. The steps and
the quay are called the Molo, and from there inland, between the Old Library (Libreria Vecchia) and the Doges'
Palace, the patterned pavement of the Piazzetta (Little
Square) leads past the Campanile into the main piazza.
The Molo is marked off from the Piazzetta by two granite
columns brought from the eastern Mediterranean in the
12th century. Atop the gray column a 4th-century Levan-
tine basilisk with agate eyes has been transformed into St.
Mark's lion, and on the red column is a Hellenistic statue
of a man standing on a crocodile, disguised as the Greek
St. Theodore triumphing over a dragon. (Theodore was
the city's patron before Venetian agents stole the body of
St. Mark from Alexandria in 829.)

The Doges' Palace was first built in 814, and its chapel,
St. Mark's, was built 16 years later. Both were burned in
the 976 uprising against Doge Pietro Candido IV and immediately rebuilt. The palace was damaged in subsequent
fires (accidental), and its present style was determined in
an early 14th-century rebuilding. In the following century
the palace was extended and altered. The ground-floor
gallery of Gothic arches carries a balustrade from which
sprout marble stalks, whose fretted fronds support the
roseate bulk of the building. The interior was decorated to
overawe representatives of other states with its opulence.
The "Golden Stair" leads up to ornate chambers decorated
by many of Venice's great artists.

The Cathedral of St. Mark—called the Basilica, although
not basilical in form—was completed in 1073 as a replacement for the earlier church. The five portals are
surmounted by five arches, above which shine five domes.
The undulating roofline of the façade is garnished with

*Adorn-
ment of
the Doges'
Palace and
St. Mark's*

statuary and golden Gothic turrets. The arches are faced
with mosaics glowing against a golden background, the
facets of each fragment angled to catch the light. Over
the main portal prance four magnificent horses, Greek
in origin, transported from the Roman Forum to Constantinople, then taken by the Venetians, who lost them
to Napoleon, whose successors returned them from Paris.

Over the centuries, both the inside and the outside of
the church were enriched with the loot of conquest until St. Mark's became a veritable museum of Venetian
acquisitiveness. The interior is Oriental and mysterious,
with gold, ivory, fine marbles, and mosaics luminous in
the gloom. St. Mark's became the cathedral only in 1807,
replacing S. Pietro di Castello, which occupies its own
little island at the seaward tip of the city. The see is administered by a patriarch, one of the two Roman Catholic
patriarchs in Europe.

The cathedral's clock and its bells are in two separate
buildings some distance from the church. The 15th-century
clock tower, the timepiece marked with the signs of the
zodiac, is noted for its two Moors, mechanical figures that
strike the bell with mallets to mark the hours. On the opposite side of the Piazza is the red-brick Campanile, begun
under Doge Pietro Tribuno (died 912) but remade to its
familiar form early in the 16th century. So commanding,
so enduring that it was called "The Landlord," the tower
shocked Venetians by collapsing in 1902. On the day of
the fall the city council ordered it to be rebuilt "as it was,
where it was," a work accomplished by 1912.

The arcaded Procuratie Vecchie on the north side of the
Piazza was built early in the 16th century, the Procuratie
Nuove on the south side, a century later. The similarly designed Nuova Fabbrica was constructed in 1810 by order
of Napoleon, after a church was razed to open the construction site. The ground floors of these buildings contain
luxury shops and some world-known cafés. The upper
floors of the newer parts house the Museo Civico Correr,
a civic display of local costumes, pottery, and works of
art. Among the paintings is the Carpaccio fragment "Two
Venetian Women," which the 19th-century critic John
Ruskin considered the "best picture in the world." The
Museo del Risorgimento, dealing with Venice's history
after the fall of the republic, is there.

Around the corner, facing the Piazzetta, is the richly
sculptured Libreria Vecchia, and at its end toward the
canal, the Zecca (mint) where *zecchini* (literally, sequins)
were coined. Both are mid-16th-century works of Jacopo
Sansovino. Fleeing to Venice from the sack of Rome by
Spain, he contributed a strictly classical style of building
to the Venetian scene. He designed the Loggetta at the
foot of the Campanile, contributed sculptures to the Doges' Palace and St. Mark's, and designed parts of three
churches as well as the Palazzo Corner della Ca'Grande
on the Grand Canal and the cloister of S. Salvatore, now,
respectively, police headquarters and the telephone exchange. His Piazzetta buildings contain the Museo Archeologico and the Biblioteca Nazionale Marciana, the main
city library, which maintains an exposition of illuminated
manuscripts and 15th-century fine Venetian printing from
the presses of Johannes de Spira, Nicolas Jenson, and
Aldus Manutius.

The Piazza is still the centre of Venice, seemingly never
empty, even in the snowy pre-dawn hours of winter. In
summer the café tables push out like breakwaters into the
tides of tourists, while guides declaim, bands play, photographers immortalize, and the pigeons gluttonize. The
pampered pigeons are among the many enemies of Venetian art, tons of their droppings having accumulated on
roof beams of palaces. When Niccoló Bambini's "Moses
and the Eternal Father," a ceiling painting in S. Moisè
church, was taken down for restoration in 1967, more
than 1,000 pounds of guano were found on its back.

In the Piazza, as everywhere else in Venice, the symbolic
lion of *La serenissima* is to be seen in all shapes, sizes, and
materials, from gold to plastic, with and without wings.
The main entrance to the Doges' Palace alone has 75 of
them. There are still some *bocca de leone*, the stone lion
letter boxes into whose mouths were dropped denunciations addressed to the Council of Ten. One of the more

*The lion
symbol of
La serenis-
sima*

curious is the scrawny white marble beast from Piraeus among the several in front of the Arsenale. Its shoulder and rump are marked with runes graved by Norse mercenaries serving Byzantium in the 11th century.

The Arsenale, the ghetto, and the Rialto.   The Arsenale, founded in the 12th century, was one of the first assembly-line factories ever conceived. Enclosed by two miles of walls and employing 16,000 workers at its 16th-century peak, it delivered a new galley every day for 100 days in the war against the Turks. "Arsenal," from the Arabic, is one of the many words Venice has given to the Western world. Another is "ghetto," probably from *gettare,* "to cast in metal." In 1516, all Venetian Jews were forcibly concentrated around the Campo Ghetto Nuovo, where the iron foundries had been grouped on a small island in the northwestern corner of town. Lack of space obliged the ghetto residents to build exceptionally high, and many of their bleak tenements still stand. Napoleon ended the residence restrictions in 1797.

From under the arch of the Piazza clock tower, a long, elegant shopping street, the Marzaria, makes its way to the Rialto. John Evelyn, the English diarist, admired the richness of its shops in 1645. The Rialto was the spot from which Europe's business affairs were dominated during the three centuries that Venice was the financial and commercial link between East and West. The earliest state bank, the Banco Giro, was established there in the 12th century, close to the Venetian offices of navigation, commerce, and shipping. It was mentioned as a gathering place of merchants and moneylenders in Shakespeare's play *The Merchant of Venice (c.* 1596). A few banks remain in the neighbourhood, but the vast old Fondaco dei Tedeschi, where the German merchants lived and traded (and for which they hired Titian and Giorgione to do the frescoes), long has been Venice's central post office. The old Turkish trading enclave, farther along the Grand Canal, now houses the Museum of Natural History. The commerce that throbs along the Rialto these days is purely local in scope: fish, meat, cheese, poultry, vegetables, and fruit glow in stalls, and Venetian shoppers carry on their tradition of buying just enough for one meal.

Palaces and museums.   There are more than 450 palaces and old houses of artistic and historic merit in Venice. The typical old house, designed for one family, was built on pilings or on stone fill over which planking was laid. Foundations of rough stone blocks, faced with dressed stone, rose a little more than four feet (1.2 metres) above water level, where the brick walls, also often faced with stone, began. Before 1800, damp-proof courses were not laid, and old brick walls are saturated with moisture. The entrance was directly off the canal—the back door usually led into a courtyard and garden—and the lowest floor served as a storeroom for merchandise. The first floor, the *mezzanino,* was reserved for offices, the floor above that, the *piano signorile,* for the master's residence. Upper floors housed other members of the household: the higher the floor, the lower the station. On the roof, among the distinctively shaped chimney pots, was the *altana,* a small platform on which the ladies rested to sun-bleach their hair.

Today only a very few such houses remain in the hands of the original families. Most of the grand residences have been cut up into apartments, some have become office buildings, some are shops dealing in antiques or Venetian glass. The best known hotels on the Grand Canal are ancient palaces. The International Centre of Arts and Costume, the prefecture, the Court of Appeal, the Town Hall in the Palazzo Loredan, and the municipal pawn shop are installed in historic palaces. Radiotelevisione Italiana moved into the renovated Palazzo Labia in 1970, leaving the 16th-century Palazzo Véndramin-Calergi, in which German composer Richard Wagner died, entirely to the Municipal Casino. The Ca' Rezzònico, in which English poet Robert Browning died, now houses the civic museum of 18th-century art. The 16th-century Palazzo Querini-Stampalía is a public picture gallery and library, and the Baroque Palazzo Pesaro (1710) houses two museums: Oriental art on the top floor and modern art in the lower stories. One of the most famous of the hundreds of

palaces is the Venetian Gothic Ca' d'Oro (Golden House; 1420–c. 1440), which in its pristine glory was rather garishly painted red and blue in the places that were not gilded. It was restored and given to the state in 1922 along with an art collection that includes Mantegna's "S. Sebastiano" and Francesco Guardi's endlessly copied view of the Piazzetta.

Venice's principal museum of art is the Accademia on the Grand Canal, occupying the former convent, church, and *scuola* of Sta. Maria della Caritá. The collection spans Venetian painting beginning with 14th-century primitives Paolo and Lorenzo Veneziano. Among the others are Giovanni Bellini, the first recognized genius among Venetian artists, and his brother Gentile, Giorgione, Vittore Carpaccio, Cima da Conegliano, Titian, Giovanni Battista Tiepolo, Lorenzo Lotto, Giovanni Battista Piazzetta, Rosalba Carriera, Canaletto, and Francesco Guardi. One of the major canvases is the vast "Feast in the House of Levi," by Paolo Veronese, originally painted as "Last Supper." The Inquisition demanded changes in the picture, but only the title was changed.

Religious buildings.   Some of the Accademia's treasures come from churches and *scuole,* some of which no longer exist. The *scuole* were confraternity guilds, and two of them still function as charitable institutions in their original buildings: the Scuola di S. Giorgio degli Schiavoni (Slavs) still boasts its Carpaccio works in a 16th-century structure restored by Italian public subscription in 1971; while the Scuola Grande di S. Rocco (1515–60), restored by funds from the United States, maintains all of its original decorations, the most noted of which are by Tintoretto. The Scuola dei Calégheri in the Campo San Tomá is now an upholstery shop, the Baroque S. Teodoro is a motion-picture theatre, and the Greek confraternity, S. Niccolò, is a museum of Byzantine painting. The 15th-century Scuola di S. Giovanni Evangelista long ago lost its Carpaccio and Bellini pictures to the Accademia, but it preserves what is said to be a fragment of the True Cross. The early 16th-century Scuola degli Albanesi (Albanians) still stands, but bereft of its Carpaccios. The 17th-century Scuola dei Carmini retains its Tiepolo ceiling. Now the municipal hospital, the Scuola di S. Marco guards intact its astonishing *trompe l'oeil* facade, its grand assembly rooms, and its ornate chapter chamber.

Near the hospital stands the huge pink-brick Gothic church of SS. Giovanni e Paolo (S. Zanipòlo in Venetian dialect), begun for the Dominicans in 1430. Its Titian and Bellini altarpieces were lost in a fire in 1867. Remaining are a Bellini polytych and, in the Chapel of the Rosary, a Veronese ceiling originally in the Umilitá church. S. Zanipòlo is the burial place of 46 doges.

On the other side of the Grand Canal is another friars' church, this one Franciscan, Sta. Maria dei Frari, usually called simply the Frari. It dates from the mid-13th century but was rebuilt in Gothic style in the 15th century. Built on approximately the same plan as the Dominican church, it is a more restrained and lofty building. Titian is buried in the Frari, with his "Assumption" (1516–18) on the high altar and his "Pesaro Madonna" (1519–26) near the tomb of the Pesaro doge. On the sacristy altar is Bellini's triptych "Madonna and Child with Saints" (1488), a serene expression of Venetian 14th-century tradition. A wooden "St. John the Baptist" (1450) by Donatello shows how far ahead of his contemporaries the Florentine was.

Directly across the Basin of St. Mark from the Piazzetta, on a little island, is one of the prizes of Venice, the church of S. Giorgio Maggiore and its court of attendant buildings. There have been churches on that site since the 8th century, and this one, by the Mannerist architect Andrea Palladio, was begun *c.* 1565. The campanile, essential to the composition in balancing the mass of the church, is newer than the other structures, having been rebuilt after a collapse in 1791. On nearby La Giudecca island are two more Palladio churches: the small, simple church known as Le Zitelle (the Virgins) and the grand Il Redentore (the Redemption; 1577–92). On the mainland around Vicenza, Palladio built country villas that directly influenced English country houses and North American colonial architecture.

Closer to the Doges' Palace, Sta. Maria della Salute (1631–56), another state-built votive church, sits at the entrance to the Grand Canal, just behind the golden-globed Dogana al Mare customhouse. Viewed from atop a campanile or from a boat in the lagoon, it dominates the scene even more than S. Giorgio Maggiore to its south or the Doges' Palace to its north. The church is massive, the drum of its cupola sustained by giant Baroque scrolls and its towers tipped with domes. The architect was Baldassare Longhena. Among the church's works of art are Tintoretto's "Marriage at Cana," and three paintings of Old Testament subjects by Titian.

Music. As the commercial importance of Venice waned, its eminence as a centre for music waxed. Claudio Monteverdi, a chief pioneer of the opera form, wrote the first opera ever performed in Venice, *Proserpina rapita.* His masses and psalms were sung at St. Mark's, where he was choirmaster. In the 18th century, four *ospedali,* orphanages attached to churches, were conservatories of music famed for their choral singing. Antonio Vivaldi, a Venetian native, was music master at the *ospedale* of Sta. Maria della Pietá from 1703 to 1741. The 19th century marked a flowering of opera in the city. At the Teatro la Fenice, a 1792 building reconstructed with minor changes after a fire in 1836, Rossini's *Tancredi* (1813) was first performed, followed by his *Semiramide* (1823). Verdi's *Ernani* (1844), *Rigoletto* (1851), and *La traviata* (1853) had their premieres in the theatre. In 1951 Igor Stravinsky's opera *The Rake's Progress* was first performed in La Fenice. The pink-and-gilt theatre, with its 18th-century banqueting rooms, still presents a season of opera each winter, but citizens of Venice are few among the audience.

Environmental threats to the city. In addition to normal decay—of 170 campaniles standing, few are perpendicular—Venice is threatened by floods at the times of *acqua alta* ("high water"), by subsidence of the city itself, and by air pollution. In the 1950s it became apparent that the deterioration of the city's art treasures and buildings had suddenly accelerated. Simultaneously, residents began to quit the historic island centre, more than 40,000 leaving for modern homes on the mainland or the barrier coast between 1958 and 1968. Following disastrous floods in 1966, the United Nations Educational, Scientific, and Cultural Organization (UNESCO) began the mobilization of international forces, including subscriptions from various nations, to save historic Venice.

Flooding. Acqua alta occurs when a number of lunar, meteorological, and hydrographic factors coincide to bring a spring tide in on top of lagoon waters that already have reached abnormally high level. Among the contributing factors, according to one theory, is a vast underground movement of the Italian peninsula that is tilting the southwestern coast upward and the northeastern coast downward. It is also possible that the narrow Adriatic Sea is subject several times a year to seiches, surges of liquid such as those made by soup in a nudged tureen.

The frequency of flooding has increased remarkably: on 58 occasions between 1867 and 1967 floods of at least three feet above normal occurred, but 30 of these were in the last decade of that period. Since the bad floods of the 1960s the Italian government, working with international experts, has devised alert systems to give 12 hours' warning of *acqua alta* and has proposed a movable barrier to control water flow at the openings through which the sea passes in and out of the lagoon.

Subsidence. It has become evident as well that Venice is sinking almost three times as fast as it did in earlier centuries—at a current rate of 12 inches (300 millimetres) per century as against the former rate of four and one-half inches—while the level of the sea is rising almost four inches per century. This subsidence is partially caused by the sheer weight of the city on the 1,600 feet (490 metres) of alluvial silt and clay overlying the solid strata under the floor of the lagoon. Another more significant cause is the emptying of mountain-fed underground water deposits at an increasing rate by electric pumping, especially by industry. Once the elastic liquids have been drained, the pockets tend to be crushed flat, and the earth above sinks. Water extraction is now strictly controlled by law.

Causes of flooding and sinking of the islands

It is expected that all deep wells will be closed after the construction of aqueducts to bring water from the hills.

Air pollution. The chief destructive agent in Venetian air is sulfuric acid, produced in great quantity by domestic and industrial smoke, as well as by natural decay of vegetation on the lagoon's intertidal flats. In 1969 it was discovered that one of the ancient traditional crafts, glassmaking, yields large amounts of sulfuric acid, and the glass furnaces on the island of Murano discharge directly into the wind that sweeps the city. Stone monuments are host to microorganisms that generate sulfuric acid, which in turn eats the stone. Eventually, only gas and electricity will be allowed for domestic heating, and industrial smoke will be filtered.

THE ECONOMY

Industry and tourism. Traditional crafts—predominantly glass, lace, and textiles—employ a large number of Venetians. Between 20 and 30 percent of the work force is connected with port activities, but the port of Marghera, a borough of Venice created on fill on the mainland in 1917, now handles a greater capacity than that of the old town. Tourism is also a major industry, employing about one-third of the working population, but most of this traffic is concentrated into three summer months.

Transportation. Ships connect Venice with other Mediterranean ports and with all continents. Rail communication with central Europe is made through the Brenner and Camporosso (Tarvisio) passes, and a line to Yugoslavia goes around the north end of the Adriatic via Trieste. A causeway built across the lagoon beside the railway connects Venice with the road network of the mainland. The city is also served by the Marco Polo Airport, which is linked to the centre of Venice by a direct motorboat service for passengers and luggage.

ADMINISTRATIVE CONDITIONS

Venice is governed by an elected municipal council and appointed regional administrators. The decisions of these bodies, however, can be superseded by the national government in matters subject to ministerial authority—which in Venice seem to be endless—including fine arts, historical sites and monuments, navigable waterways, international commerce, military and naval installations, aviation, public housing, health, education, and museums, among others. In addition, many Venetian industries either receive government aid or are owned (in whole or in part) by agencies of the government.

All of the suggested schemes for the salvation and the reinvigoration of Venice must have the legal approval and the technical resources of the municipal government. The enormous sums required are also derived from the national government as well, since they surpass any amounts obtainable by the municipality.

CULTURAL LIFE

Venice has always been famous for its festivals. Under the republic the chief festival, called La Sensa because it took place on Ascension Day, was Venice's symbolic marriage to the sea over which it had dominion. Other traditional festivals are still celebrated, such as the Biennale d'Arte (an international art review and exhibition), the international drama festival, the international festival of contemporary music, the international film festival, and the international speedboat competition.

Festivals

The best known of the traditional festivals is the Festa del Redentore (Feast of the Redeemer), held on the night of Saturday to Sunday in the third week of July. In the early evening thousands of boats decorated with branches and Chinese lanterns gather on the Giudecca Canal while a large crowd on shore watches the fireworks. When the first light of dawn appears the boats make for the Lido, where they await the sunrise. Later in the morning a great religious procession crosses a temporary bridge of boats from St. Mark's to the church of Il Redentore on La Giudecca, which was built in 1577–92 in thanksgiving for the end of a plague.

A church built in thanksgiving after a later plague is the centre of the Festa della Salute, celebrated on November

21, when a bridge of boats conducts pilgrims across the Grand Canal to Sta. Maria della Salute.

The Fresco Notturno takes place by night along the Grand Canal in the last two weeks of August. Hundreds of festooned and illuminated gondolas proceed past exquisitely lit palaces and landing stages in the wake of a float on which a choral and orchestral concert is performed.

The best known of the Venetian regattas is the Regata Storica, which has taken place along the Grand Canal in September for seven centuries. It opens with a magnificent procession of gondolas and also of the historical Venetian eight-oared boats (*bissoni*) with persons in historical costume on board. A contest then takes place among several small racing gondolas, each rowed by the best known oarsmen, one at each end. (B.E.)

History

THE EARLY PERIOD

Origin of the city. Unique among the chief cities of Italy, Venice came into existence after the fall of the Roman Empire in the West. The Lombard invasion of northern Italy in AD 568 caused inhabitants of Altino and Aquileia at the northern end of the Adriatic to take refuge in the lagoons, where only a few fishermen and salt workers lived without fixed abodes. The first islands to be occupied were Torcello, in the Venetian lagoon north of Burano, and Grado near Aquileia in the Marano lagoon. When the Exarchate of Ravenna was created *c*. 584 the region formed part of it. Oderzo, the last remaining mainland city of the Byzantines, fell to the Lombards in 641, and political authority was transferred to an unnamed island later called Cittanova Eracliana in the Venetian lagoon. The Veneto-Byzantine area was then restricted to the lagoons and isolated politically, though not for trading purposes, from the other Byzantine possessions in Italy.

The first elected doge (duke) was Orso, chosen in an anti-Byzantine military declaration in 727, but he was succeeded by Byzantine officials until *c*. 751, when the Exarchate of Ravenna came to an end. There followed decades of internal political strife among various settlements vying for supremacy and between pro- and anti-Byzantine factions; also involved were attempts by church authorities to acquire temporal influence. Finally the doge Obelerio and his brother Beato formed an alliance with the Franks of Italy and brought Venice under the subjection of the young king Pepin (died 810) in order to free themselves from Byzantine overlordship.

Pro-Byzantine reaction to this event under the doges of the Parteciaco family led to the transfer of the seat of government to the Rialto group of islands, by then the natural centre for the exiles of the factional fighting. The move both centralized political activity and assured territorial and political independence. These were accompanied by a parallel development of the social and economic life of the lagoon islands, particularly the Rialto itself. Though a Franco-Byzantine treaty of 814 guaranteed to Venice political and juridical independence from the rule of the Western Empire, it did not confirm any effective dependence on the Byzantine Empire, and by 840–841 the doge was negotiating international agreements in his own name without involving the Byzantine authorities. This freedom from Byzantine control was never sanctioned by any diplomatic or juridical document, but it became hallowed by custom and by centuries of uncontested power. The unusual legal and political position of a small duchy situated in territorial isolation between two great empires contributed greatly to its function as a trading middleman.

A succession of serious internal crises concerning the office of doge, from the time of the Parteciaco to that of the Badoer, Candiano, and Orseolo families, did not halt the rapid development of trade. Increase in private wealth led to the gradual achievement of internal stability by creating a broader ruling class that was capable of putting a limit to the power of the doge. Gradually a national consciousness developed, of which the first signs reflected in the daily life of the citizens were the reforms of Doge Orso Parteciaco I in the late 9th century. The national church, ruled by the patriarch of Grado, was reorganized

Acendancy of the Rialto islands

by the institution of five new bishoprics. From the time of Giovanni Parteciaco's successor (887) the doge was chosen by popular election, though without destroying the monarchic system or the custom of co-regency, which assured the continuity of power. Finally the group of Rialto islands was solemnly transformed into the city of Venice (*civitas Venetiarum*).

Creation of Venice

The new order. The final collapse of family faction rule under the Orseolo regime led to a change in the system of government, inaugurated by Doge Domenico Flabanico (1032–42). He restored to the people the sovereign right (obscured during civil strife) to elect the doge, but the term *populus* was in practice restricted to the residents of the Rialto and, more narrowly, to the group of nobles who regularly frequented the doge's palace. The executive organ was the ducal curia (*dux* and *judices*), and the legislative assembly was summoned to approve the doge's acts. A new church was built for St. Mark, symbol of the Venetian spirit, under Doge Domenico Contarini (1043–70), an energetic defender of Grado's metropolitan rights and of the religious independence of the duchy.

GROWTH OF TRADE AND POWER

In external affairs Contarini and his successors remained neutral (despite the complaints of Pope Gregory VII) in the conflict between papacy and empire, while safeguarding Venetian economic interests in the Adriatic when the conflict began to be reflected on the Dalmatian coast. But the greatest danger to Venetian interests was the 11th-century Norman expansion under Robert Guiscard, which threatened to cut Venetian communications to the south. The successful action taken against the Normans by Doge Domenico Selvo and his successor Vitale Falier was intended more to assure Venetian freedom on the sea than to aid the Byzantine Empire, and it made clear that Venice's control of trade routes in the Mediterranean must rest on a firmer basis than mere usage. In gratitude for Venetian aid against the Normans, the Byzantine emperor Alexius I Comnenus granted Venice unrestricted trade throughout the Byzantine Empire, with no customs dues, a privilege that marked the beginning of Venetian activity in the East (1082). The Adriatic, however, was not yet under control, as the Dalmatian ports were threatened by the Hungarians and Slavs, with whom it was difficult to come to agreement. Zadar (Zara), the most important of these ports because it controlled the northern Adriatic, changed hands frequently until it finally became Venetian in 1409.

Toward the end of the 11th century the Crusades centred the newly awakened trading interests of the West on the Mediterranean. At first, however, Venice was concerned chiefly to gain control only of the European trading ports of the Byzantine Empire, leaving to private interests the trading opportunities with Syria and Asia Minor. As the 12th century progressed, the two other Italian merchant republics, Genoa and Pisa, came into conflict in the new trading area that had been opened up. The Venetians, who were the first to win trade concessions from the Byzantine Empire, also aroused the hatred of the Byzantines by their arrogance and highhandedness and by the conflict of interests continually rekindled by day-to-day contacts in the same market. Thus when the Byzantines and the Venetians should have been cooperating at sea against a revival of Norman expansion in Corfu (1143–44), they let slip the fruits of victory and vented on each other the fury of mutual hatred. In 1169 the Byzantine emperor Manuel I Comnenus made a trade agreement with the Genoese and in 1170 with the Pisans. In 1171 he tried to free himself from Venetian competition by arresting every Venetian in the empire and confiscating his goods.

Competition from Genoa and Pisa

The commune. All this time the expansion of Venice abroad and along the borders of the lagoon in the communes of Padua, Treviso, and Ferrara, as well as in the patriarchate of Aquileia, not only enriched its patrimony but also created an awareness of its own political power. Between 1140 and 1160 the most revolutionary change in Venice's political structure took place: the doge lost his monarchic character, becoming a mere official (though he still assumed resounding titles), and the commune took over the powers, functions, and prerogatives of the state.

All political and administrative matters were placed in the hands of the Maius Consilium (Great Council) of 45 members, which had evolved from a lesser body called the Consilium Sapientium (Council of the Wise). A Minor Council of six members exercised executive powers alongside the doge, and magistrates were granted administrative and judicial functions. This systematic reorganization of the state was necessitated by the exigencies of social development, the need for economic expansion corresponding to the scale of political needs and to the needs of the national communities formed on the Dalmatian coast.

Trade conflicts. The hatred between the Byzantines and the Venetians reached its culminating point when The Fourth Crusade the doge Enrico Dandolo diverted the Fourth Crusade to sack Constantinople in 1204. This reaction of the Western world in defense of its own interests brought great territorial gains on the Continent to those who took part in it, but Venice preferred to assure for itself the dominion of the seas by acquiring the title of "lord of the fourth part and a half" (*Dominus quartae partis et dimidiae*) of the Byzantine Empire. The republic thus took possession of an extensive island patrimony from the Aegean to Crete and the lookout posts of Modon and Coron (modern Methóni and Koróni, Greece), and dominated the whole eastern Mediterranean, reaffirming an economic supremacy that quickly aroused the covetousness of the Genoese and the Pisans. The tremendous conflict between Venice and Genoa (the Pisans played a minor role) lasted for the better part of two centuries. Early attempts at cooperation were wrecked by the pressure of events, especially in Syria, where the Genoese had prior rights. Defeated at Acre (1258), the Genoese by the Treaty of Nymphaeum (1261) with the Byzantine Empire (then based at Nicaea) engineered the downfall of the Latin Empire of Constantinople set up by the Venetians in 1204. The Venetians, however, not only retained their island possessions but also recovered their trading privileges in Constantinople after a Genoese–Byzantine conflict had broken out. Syria had by then fallen to the Muslims, and the rivalry between Venice and Genoa was played out in Constantinople, dragging on in a long war of privateering on the seas.

The patriciate. Meanwhile at home the Venetian state was being built up. In 1242 the civil statutes of Jacopo Tiepolo regulated civil and economic relations, and maritime statutes had been established in 1239. From the Popular Assembly to the Great Council the scope of the commune was progressively enlarged. The elective members of the Great Council were raised from 45 to 60 and then to 100 by an increase in the ex officio members (the total of magisterial office holders). The Council of 40 (first mentioned in 1223) received powers of jurisdiction, and the Consiglio dei Rogati (60 members; founded mid-13th century), invested with the control of economic affairs, in time assumed all legislative functions and the honorific title of Senate. National, political, and economic interests abroad were protected wherever Venetian influence existed by obtaining trade concessions and reorganizing the national organs of jurisdiction in the colonial centres (from Constantinople to Tyre and Acre) or abroad (from Zadar to Ragusa, Crete, and Euboea).

In the 11th and 12th centuries the Michiel and Falier families had tried in vain to perpetuate the ducal power, and restrictive electoral systems designed to prevent the formation of committed family factions had been introduced. In the 13th century similar attempts by the Ziani and Tiepolo families also failed, and the governing class strengthened its organization by translating into law the order already hallowed by custom. In 1268 an interlocking process of choice by lot and voting alternately among the members of the Great Council was introduced in order to select 41 persons who then, by a majority of not less than 25 votes, agreed on the next doge.

Between 1290 and 1300 new laws restricted the right to take part in the government to families traditionally performing magistrate's duties. The patrician class was not created by the "closing of the Great Council" (*serrata del Maggior Consiglio*) achieved by these laws, but it received

its legal status from them. Henceforward anyone claiming personal power had to act outside the patrician order and rely on the people; and the people were linked so closely to the patricians by economic needs that he would never find sufficient support. Thus the conspiracy of Marin Bocconio failed (1299), as did those of Bajamonte Tiepolo and the Querini brothers (1310) and later of Marin Falier (1354).

The special conditions of Venetian society created a governing class very different from that of the other Italian communes or of the continental states. To counter any attempts at sole personal rule, the Council of Ten was Council established (1310) to police the patrician order and defend of Ten the existing regime.

Struggle for naval supremacy. This consolidated internal regime aroused the jealousy of those who felt offended by the arrogance of Venice. By the beginning of the 14th century it was swept into struggles on the mainland of Italy and became involved in Adriatic and Mediterranean problems. Thus Venice took an active part in a war with Ferrara to safeguard the vital trade route of the Po, disputed by the Holy See, and when the Scaligers came to power in Verona the republic made alliance with the Carraresi of Padua, with the Florentines, and with the Visconti of Milan, who feared the rise of a strong territorial lordship in the heart of northern Italy. Deviating from its strictly maritime policy, Venice established sovereignty over Treviso, thereby assuring itself of its own food supply but also providing itself with a land frontier to be defended.

Meanwhile, the antagonism and rivalry with Genoa were rekindled. On Genoa's side was the King of Hungary, the Patriarch of Aquileia, and the Visconti of Milan, while Venice had the support of the Carraresi and the distant king of Aragon. The conflict, chiefly carried on in Dalmatia, was made more difficult for all by the spread of the Black Death (1348), by the economic and financial crisis caused by the prolongation of the war itself, and by the inanity of operations, which quickly disillusioned and dismantled the ill-assorted coalitions. The alternation of victories and defeats brought no conclusion to either side, but both exhausted their energies and resources. At last a second anti-Venetian coalition brought the war almost into Venice itself: at Pula and at Chioggia Venice first was defeated and then won the victory (1380–81). The Peace of Turin (1381) eliminated Genoese political influence from the Mediterranean and the East, leaving the Venetian government as arbiter of the sea routes.

THE ZENITH AND DECLINE OF VENICE

The Venetian victory over Genoa took place under the threat of Turkish advance in the East. The Venetians had to negotiate a state of neutrality with the Turks and find another base to compensate for the smaller yield now to be expected from the East. So they turned to the Italian mainland to rid themselves of the nuisance of neighbouring lordships and later to defend and exploit the rich land Territorial that they had acquired, whose yield was no less important than overseas trade for the national economy. The restlessness of the Carraresi, Scaligers, Aquileiesi, and Visconti encouraged intervention, at first through subsidies to support one party against another and later by dissolution of the realm of Gian Galeazzo Visconti (1402). For a time Venetian territorial rule went no further than the Rivers Mincio and Livenza, but beyond the Livenza lay the politically and economically important principality of the patriarch of Aquileia through which passed the main routes to Germany and to Istria. Because the patriarch could not guarantee peace and order, Venice incorporated the principality in the Venetian domains (1420).

Venetian territory now covered roughly the areas of the modern regions of Veneto and Friuli-Venezia Giulia, together with the Istrian Peninsula; and the doge Tommaso Mocenigo claimed that his city had reached its political and economic zenith. It had a solid base in Italy that could largely compensate for its losses in the East, and it should not expect indefinite progress—in fact, efforts to enlarge its conquests might be dangerous, and it was better to preserve, not to risk, its accumulated wealth. This warning was not heeded, however, by Mocenigo's successors.

The doge Francesco Foscari risked a further policy of conquest in mainland Italy, dismembering the realm of Filippo Maria Visconti while the Turks encroached upon the Byzantine Empire in the East. Foscari carried out his first Lombard conquests in the territory of Brescia in 1426, just as Thessalonica fell to the Turks, and held the River Adda (1432–54) while the Turks took Constantinople (1453). Greed for territorial conquest involved Venetian policy in the tangled web of Italian balances of power and in the conflicts between the great powers of Europe on a scale out of proportion to Venetian forces and aims. The Peace of Lodi (1454) did not ease the situation in Italy, which was threatened by foreign intervention. It was followed by the formation of the Italian League for the restoration of political balance among the Italian states, which produced a merely ephemeral accord.

Turkish expansion in the eastern Mediterranean after the fall of Constantinople involved Venice in war: Euboea (Negroponte) fell in 1470 to the Turks, with whom the Venetians finally made peace in 1479. But Venice was soon involved in another war, this time with Ferrara (1481), in which it conquered the Pulesine (1484). This merely increased the opposition of the other Italian states to Venetian territorial expansion.

Europe against Venice. This internal discord made Italy a prey to invading foreigners, Spanish, French, and German. By 1508 these powers, together with the Pope, the Hungarians, the Savoyards, and the Ferrarese, united to form the League of Cambrai against the Venetians, who were defeated at the Battle of Agnadello. Venice was saved from the worst results of this event by internal discords within the League of Cambrai, but Venetian territories on the mainland were diminished, and at the same time the consequences of the economic crisis could no longer be avoided. Not only was the Eastern market lost but the discovery of new lands to the West and new trade routes to the East released Europe from dependence on the Venetian market. Venice ceased to be a Mediterranean power; it became a European power but without the advantages of the Atlantic states, now open to the New World.

Venetian policy in the 16th century was dictated by the need to keep intact its political, economic, and territorial heritage against the advance of the Turks on the one side and the pressure of the great Western European powers on the other. This need supplied the reason for Venice's intervention in the Italian crisis of the emperor Charles V and in its struggle against the Turks, from the defeat of Préveza in 1538 to the victory of Lepanto and the loss of Cyprus in 1571; and for its tenacious resistance to ecclesiastical pressure from the pope. So Venice declined into economic stagnation, embittered by a constitutional conflict between the Consiglio dei Rogati and the Council of Ten for control of the public finances. As the great Venetian statesman and historian Paolo Paruta (1540–98) pointed out, Venetian peace and neutrality meant defending the immediate interests of the nation but ceasing to take part in problems in which it was not directly concerned. Thus the spirit of political and religious conservatism grew increasingly tenacious in Venice.

The political crisis caused by the papal interdict of Venice in 1606 was not concerned with heresy or reform but with temporal prerogatives of the papacy. Paolo Sarpi, the energetic defender of Doge Leonardo Donà's policy, which had provoked the Roman Curia, never contested the legitimacy of papal power, but in the temporal sphere he denied that it carried any prerogatives superior to the sovereign rights of the state.

After a long campaign (1645–69) Crete, Venice's last possession in the eastern Mediterranean, fell to the Turks—the Venetians being allowed to retain merely a few strongholds. This blow to Venetian morale was mitigated, however, by the preservation of Dalmatia, and the government, after allying itself with Austria, attempted to reestablish itself in the eastern Mediterranean by liberating the Morea (Peloponnese) from the Turks. There the brilliant campaign of Francesco Morosini in 1684–88 assured Venice of this

new Greek territory, which was finally handed over by the Treaty of Carlowitz (Sremski Karlovci; 1699). The conquest, however, proved a burden of great and unprofitable expense, and by the Treaty of Passarowitz (Požerevac; 1718) the Morea returned to the Turks. Thus ended Venetian activity in the eastern and southern Mediterranean, save for an unsuccessful attempt on Algerian and Tunisian pirates under Angelo Emo (1769).

The end of the Venetian Republic. The last period of the Venetian republic was spent in neutrality, estranged from the fervour of new ideas germinating in other nations. Venetian life had crystallized into a system from which escape was not possible. The plans of Angelo Querini, Giorgio Pisani, and Carlo Contarini, the supposed reformers of the 18th century, did not go beyond the mentality of the noble class that for three centuries had controlled the government and that existed to uphold ancestral tradition or to satisfy personal ambition.

The end of the republic came after the outbreak of the French Revolution. Napoleon, determined to destroy the Venetian oligarchy, claimed as a pretext that Venice was hostile to him and a menace to his line of retreat during his Austrian campaign of 1797. The Peace of Leoben left Venice without an ally. The government offered no resistance, and Ludovico Manin, the last doge, was deposed on May 12, 1797. A provisional democratic municipality was set up in place of the republican government, but later in the same year Venice was handed over to Austria.

Between 1798 and 1814 Venice was passed back and forth between Austria and France until finally assigned to the latter. In the Revolution of 1848 a provisional republican government was set up by Daniele Manin but it fell the following year. The defeat of Austria by the Prussians in 1866 led to the incorporation of Venice into Italy. Its subsequent growth was attendant upon its role in the commercial life of Italy and upon exploitation of its inherent physical and aesthetic attributes, which for centuries have attracted visitors from around the world. (R.Ce.)

BIBLIOGRAPHY

General works: G. LORENZETTI, *Venezia e il suo estuario*, 2nd ed. (1956; Eng. trans., *Venice and Its Lagoon*, 1961), a complete historical, architectural, and artistic guide; JAMES MORRIS, *Venice* (1960), an excellent account of the city; HUGH HONOUR, *The Companion Guide to Venice* (1965).

The arts: The following are major studies: JOHN RUSKIN, *The Stones of Venice* (1851–53, reprinted 1964; abridged ed., 1981); BERNHARD BERENSON, *The Venetian Painters of the Renaissance* (1897); MICHAEL LEVEY, *Painting in XVIII Century Venice* (1959); ROBERTO LONGHI, *Viatico per cinque secoli di pittura veneziana* (1946); GIUSEPPE MAZZOTTI, *Le Ville Venete* (1954), a complete catalog of villas on the Venetian mainland; ADRIAN D. STOKES, *Venice* (1945), an aesthetic study; S.T. WORSTHORNE, *Venetian Opera in the Seventeenth Century* (1954); JOHN MCANDREW, *Venetian Architecture of the Early Renaissance* (1980), on the buildings existing around 1500.

History: EDWARD HUTTON, *Venice and Venetia*, 4th ed. (1954), a popular, mainly historical account; ROBERTO CESSI, *Storia della repubblica di Venezia* (1944), a history by Venice's foremost historian; W. CAREW HAZLITT, *The Venetian Republic: Its Rise, Its Growth and Its Fall*, 4th ed., 2 vol. (1915), the fullest history in English; D.S. CHAMBERS, *The Imperial Age of Venice, 1380–1580* (1970); MAURICE ROWDON, *The Fall of Venice* (U.S. title, *The Silver Age of Venice;* 1970), are readable period histories, the latter of Venice in the 18th century; JOHN J. NORWICH, *A History of Venice* (1982; U.K. title, 2 vols.), a general history covering the period from the city's beginnings to 1797.

Other works: The chapters on Venice in GIACOMO GIROLAMO CASANOVA's 18th-century autobiography *Histoire de ma vie,* new ed. (1960–62; Eng. trans. by WILLART R. TRASK, 1966–), are a vivid portrayal of contemporary manners; H.R.F. BROWN, *Venetian Studies* (1887), *Life on the Lagoons* (1884), and other studies are the work of an appreciative foreigner; as is W.D. HOWELLS, *Venetian Life* (1866; rev. ed., 1907); DANIELE VARE's recapitulatory essays in *Ghosts of the Rialto* (1956), have charm, while FREDERICK ROLFE's novel *The Desire and Pursuit of the Whole* (1934, reissued 1953), is the unusual story of an English expatriate in the city; F.C. LANE, *Venetian Ships and Shipbuilders* (1934), is historical.

League of Cambrai

Loss of Crete

Victoria and the Victorian Age

Queen of the United Kingdom of Great Britain and Ireland from 1837, Victoria in 1876 also became empress of India.

Lineage and early life. The only child of Edward, duke of Kent, fourth son of King George III, Victoria was born at Kensington Palace, London, on May 24, 1819. On the death in 1817 of Princess Charlotte, daughter of the Prince Regent (later George IV), there was no surviving legitimate offspring of George III's 15 children. In 1818, therefore, three of his sons, the dukes of Clarence, Kent, and Cambridge, married to provide for the succession. The Duke of Kent's wife was Princess Mary Louisa Victoria of Saxe-Coburg-Gotha. The Duke of Kent died when his daughter (who was christened Alexandrina Victoria) was eight months old; accordingly, on George IV's accession (1820) she became third in the line of succession to the throne after the Duke of York (died 1827) and the Duke of Clarence (subsequently William IV), whose own children died in infancy.

Victoria, by her own account, "was brought up very simply," principally at Kensington Palace, where her closest companions, other than her homely and impoverished mother, were her half-sister, Féodore, and her governess, Louise (afterward the Baroness) Lehzen, a native of Coburg. Her mother's nearest adviser was her brother, Victoria's uncle Leopold. Until he became the first king of the Belgians in 1831, Leopold lived at Claremont, near Esher, Surrey, where Victoria visited him. From her father's family she was virtually isolated, growing up to

EB Inc.

Queen Victoria.

regard herself as a Coburg rather than as a member of the house of Hanover. Her mother's morbid fear of Victoria's uncle, the duke of Cumberland, and after the death of George IV (1830), her pretentiousness on her daughter's behalf, led to an estrangement from Victoria herself and to friction between the Duchess and William IV. Early in life Victoria learned caution in her friendships; she also revealed a liking for her own way; nor did her retentive memory allow her to forgive readily. She was small, carried herself well, showed too much gum when she smiled, and retained a delightful silvery voice all her days.

The legend (upon which the Queen herself was to cast some doubt) ran that she was unaware until she was 12 years of age that she would one day succeed to the throne. "I will be good" she is reported to have responded when she heard the news. Not long afterward she began the detailed and highly characteristic journal that she kept throughout her life.

If in Great Britain at mid-20th century the crown is at the centre of society and but rarely concerned with political decisions, at Victoria's accession in 1837 it was almost the reverse. Society in the conventional sense revolved not so much around the court as around the great houses whose owners ("the fashionables" as she called them) might still look down upon, or at least look askance at, the palace. Politics, however, still revolved around the throne. As recently as 1834 the ministry of Lord Melbourne had been dismissed by William IV, and prime ministers such as Sir Robert Peel who had served their political apprenticeship before the Reform Bill of 1832 were still likely to hold that "the confidence of the crown" was a political necessity to an administration. The political role of the crown when Victoria came to wear it was by no means clear; nor was the permanence of the throne itself. When she died and her son Edward VII moved from Marlborough House to Buckingham Palace the change was one of social rather than of political focus; there was no doubt about the monarchy's continuance. That was the measure of her reign.

Accession to the throne. In the early hours of June 20, 1837, Victoria received a call from the Archbishop of Canterbury and the Lord Chamberlain and learned of William IV's death. Later that morning the Privy Council was impressed by the graceful assurance of the new queen's demeanour. The accession of a young woman was romantically popular; moreover, because of the existence in Hanover of the so-called Salic law, which prevented succession by a woman, the crowns of Great Britain and Hanover became separated, the latter passing to William IV's eldest surviving brother, Ernest, the unpopular duke of Cumberland.

The new queen, who had never before had a room to herself, exiled her mother to a distant set of apartments when they moved into Buckingham Palace. Sir John Conroy, her mother's over-familiar majordomo, was pensioned off; only Louise Lehzen, of whom she was still in awe, remained close to the Queen. Even her beloved uncle Leopold was politely warned off discussions of English politics. "Alone" at last, she enjoyed her new-found freedom. "Victoria," wrote her cousin, Prince Albert of Saxe-Coburg-Gotha, who later married her,

is said to be incredibly stubborn and her extreme obstinacy to be constantly at war with her good nature; she delights in Court ceremonies, etiquette and trivial formalities . . . She is said not to take the slightest pleasure in nature and to enjoy sitting up at night and sleeping late into the day.

It was, in retrospect, "the least sensible and satisfactory time in her whole life"; but at the time it was exciting and enjoyable, the more so because of her romantic friendship with Lord Melbourne, the prime minister.

Together with the threat of Cumberland as heir apparent, two episodes in 1839, revealing that if she had too little in her head she had perhaps too little in her heart also, may explain why "those who had her welfare most at heart were anxious," as she wrote long afterward, "to secure for her without delay a husband's guidance and support." Lady Flora Hastings, a maid of honour with Tory connections, was forced by Victoria to undergo a medical examination for suspected pregnancy. The gossip, when it was discovered that the Queen had been mistaken, became the more damaging when later in the year Lady

Political role of the crown

Flora died of a disease that was not diagnosed by the examining physician. The enthusiasm of the populace over the coronation (June 28, 1838) swiftly dissipated.

Between the two phases of the Hastings case "the bedchamber crisis" intervened. Lord Melbourne had proved a delightful and devoted mentor to the young Queen; but, by surrounding the Queen with Whig ladies, he had allowed her to become a Whig partisan. When he resigned in May 1839, Sir Robert Peel, the Conservative leader, stipulated that the Whig ladies of the bedchamber should be removed. The Queen imperiously refused, not without Melbourne's encouragement. "The Queen of England will not submit to such trickery," she said. Peel therefore declined to take office, which Melbourne rather weakly resumed. "I was very young then," wrote the Queen long afterward, "and perhaps I should act differently if it was all to be done again."

Marriage to Albert

Albert arrived at Windsor on October 10, 1839, on a visit to the English court. For a short time the Queen wrestled with her desire for continued and enjoyable independence until on October 15, 1839, she proposed to him. Her letters became ecstatic; his were more circumspect. They were married on February 10, 1840, the Queen dressed entirely in articles of British manufacture.

The "Albertine Monarchy." At first the Queen was insistent that her husband should have no share in the government of the country. Within six months, on Melbourne's repeated suggestion, the Prince was allowed to start seeing the dispatches, then to be present when the Queen saw her ministers. The concession became a routine, and during her first pregnancy the Prince received a "key to the secret boxes." Quickly, too, she learned from her husband to dislike London and to abandon late parties. His was, in some ways, the stronger personality. It was the "Prince who insisted on spotless character, the Queen not caring a straw about it," the Duke of Wellington told the diarist Charles Greville—the Prince was "extremely strait-laced and a great stickler for morality whereas she was rather the other way." Royal dinner parties became a conspicuous model of decorum.

Blissfully happy herself, the Queen settled down to have children while the Prince busied himself with the administration of the royal properties. The "mere amusement" of the gossipy days with Melbourne was past. Later, she recorded talking them over with her husband, and discussing her "unbounded affection and admiration for Lord Melbourne which I said to Albert I hardly knew from what it arose excepting the fact that I clung to someone and having very warm feelings. Albert thinks I worked myself up to what really became rather foolish."

It is convenient to summarize here the growth of the royal family. Victoria, the princess royal (the "Vicky" of the *Letters*), was born in 1840; in 1858 she married the Crown Prince of Prussia and later became the mother of the emperor William II. The Prince of Wales (later Edward VII) was born in 1841. Then followed Princess Alice, afterward grand duchess of Hesse, 1843; Prince Alfred, afterward duke of Edinburgh and duke of Saxe-Coburg-Gotha, 1844; Princess Helena (Princess Christian of Schleswig-Holstein), 1846; Princess Louise (duchess of Argyll), 1848; Prince Arthur (duke of Connaught), 1850; Prince Leopold (duke of Albany), 1853; Princess Beatrice (Princess Henry of Battenberg), 1857. The Queen's first grandchild was born in 1859, her first great-grandchild in 1879. There were 37 great-grandchildren alive at her death.

Relations with Peel

The Prince came into his own to negotiate with Peel a compromise on the bedchamber question after the Melbourne government had been defeated in the general election of 1841. The Queen's first interview with Peel went well, eased by Melbourne's advice to his successor:

The Queen is not conceited—she is aware there are many things she cannot understand and she likes to have them explained to her elementarily—not at length and in detail but shortly and clearly.

If, as Lady Lyon once noted, "there was 'a vein of iron' which ran through the Queen's extraordinary character," her personal happiness as wife and mother evoked a less willful humility. Peel's very real distress when in the summer of 1842 an attempt was made to assassinate the

Queen—together with the affinity between the Prince and the new prime minister—soon converted the "cold odd man" of the Queen's earlier comment into "a great statesman, a man who thinks but little of party and never of himself." Lord Aberdeen, the foreign secretary, also became a great favourite. "We felt so safe with them both," she told King Leopold. It was under Albert's influence that she came to adopt what she later called "the obvious but up to that time much neglected doctrine that it is the paramount duty of a constitutional monarch to maintain a position of neutrality towards the leaders of party on both sides." At the election of 1841 the Queen had subscribed, through Louise Lehzen, £15,000 to the Whig cause.

By the autumn of 1842 Lehzen had left for Germany forever and the Prince could reorganize the palace. He became effectively the Queen's private secretary—according to himself, "her permanent minister"—using his own staff, George Anson and Gen. Charles Grey, for the purpose. In 1842 Victoria had made her first railway journey. Railway travel made an important contribution to the Queen's contentment, for it enabled her to spend much of the year in the Isle of Wight and in Scotland, ministers taking turn in "doing service" (as Lord Palmerston was to call it), by residing in attendance. An estate at Osborne in the Isle of Wight was purchased on Peel's advice, and the residence—"our island home"—was built between 1845 and 1851 out of the Queen's savings from her income once the Prince had got her properties into shape. She had already paid off her father's debts.

The lease of the original Balmoral House near Ballater was taken in 1848 after three previous visits to Scotland. In 1852 the estate was bought, and in 1855 a great castle in "Scotch baronial" was almost completed. At Balmoral she was happiest. There it was possible to form a new establishment without the difficulties that the Prince had encountered in organizing the palace or Windsor Castle. In Scotland, moreover, he did not have to face the unpopularity so frequently his experience in England. At Balmoral the royal pair and their family were able to live "with the greatest simplicity and ease," wrote Greville. The Queen soon came to hold the Highlanders in more esteem than she held any other of her subjects. She liked the simpler life of the Highlands, as her published journal was to reveal: she came to make the most of the thin stream of Scottish blood in her veins; also, so long as the sermons were short enough, to prefer the Scottish form of service. "You know," she was to tell Gladstone, "I am not much of an Episcopalian"; and she developed a comfort in the consolations of the Rev. Norman Macleod, as also a delight in the plain speech of John Brown, the Highland servant who stalked with Albert.

The political circumstances within which the monarchy operated in the Prince's lifetime are peculiarly worth remarking. After the repeal of the Corn Laws (1846) there was a period, not ending until the election of 1868, when politics tended to consist of a series of temporary alliances between splinter groups and no single group could guarantee its extended control over the House of Commons: the golden age of the private member, a condition rendering active political intervention by the crown not only possible but sometimes even necessary. There was a role for the cabinet maker, especially in helping to compose coalitions. Its significance must not, however, be overemphasized; although Victoria probably would not have admitted it, the Queen's role albeit "substantial," was always "secondary."

Foreign affairs

The tradition also persisted that the sovereign had a special part to play in foreign affairs and could conduct them alone with a secretary of state. Victoria and Albert had relatives throughout Europe and were to have more. Moreover, they visited and were visited by other monarchs: the tsar Nicholas I and Louis-Philippe, for example, and later Napoleon III. Albert was determined that this personal intelligence should not be disregarded and that the Queen should never become (as his own mentor the Baron Stockmar had indicated) "a mandarin figure which has to nod its head in assent or shake it in denial as its Minister pleases." The result was a clash with Lord Palmerston, the foreign secretary, who could look back on a career of high office beginning before the royal couple was born. The Prince distrusted Palmerston's character, disapproved of his methods, thought his policy shallow, and prompted by Stockmar, disagreed with his concept of the constitution.

In the ensuing contest Victoria, as Albert's disciple, outran her lord and master in her vehemence and in 1850 thought

> it right in order to avoid any mistakes for the future, shortly explain what it is she expects from her foreign secretary. She requires: (1) that he will distinctly state what he proposes in a given case in order that the Queen may know as distinctly to what she has given her royal sanction; (2) having once given her sanction to a measure, that it be not arbitrarily altered or modified by the minister.

Palmerston's habits did not change and when without consultation he expressed his approval of the coup d'état of Louis Napoleon (later Napoleon III) in 1851, the prime minister, Lord John Russell, at once dismissed him using the occasion to make public the Queen's memorandum just quoted. Within a few months Palmerston was back in office, however, as home secretary. On the eve of the Crimean War (1854–56) the royal pair encountered a wave of unpopularity, and Albert was suspected, without any foundation, of trying to influence the government in favour of the Russian cause. There was, however, a marked revival of royalist sentiment as the war wore on. The Queen personally superintended the committees of ladies who organized relief for the wounded and eagerly seconded the efforts of Florence Nightingale: she visited crippled soldiers in the hospitals and instituted the Victoria Cross for gallantry.

(margin: Crimean War)

The importance of the Albert period lay in the training the Queen received: in orderly ways of business, in hard work (which she certainly never learned from Melbourne), in the expectation of royal intervention in ministry making at home, and in the establishment of a private (because royal) intelligence service abroad. The English monarchy had changed. "In place of a definite but brittle prerogative it had acquired an undefinable but potent influence." (From G.M. Young, *Victorian England*, 2nd ed., Oxford University Press, London, 1953.)

Widowhood. With Albert, the Queen had played a "substantial" (if "secondary") part in choosing and putting into office the earl of Aberdeen's ministry when the earl of Derby resigned in December 1852. The habit died hard, for after the nervous breakdown—the "two dreadful first years of loneliness"—following the Prince Consort's death (December 14, 1861), she sought, on her recovery, to behave as he would have ordained. Her testing point was, then, her "dear one's" point of view; and this she had known at a particular and thereafter not necessarily relevant period in English political life. Her training and his influence were ill suited to the "swing of the pendulum" politics that better party organization and a wider electorate enjoined after the Reform Bill of 1867. She was a widow at 42 with nine children when Albert died. And since she blamed her son and heir for his death—the Prince Consort had come back ill from Cambridge, where he had gone to see the Prince of Wales regarding an indiscretion the Prince had committed in Ireland—she did not hesitate to vent her loneliness upon him. "It quite irritates me to see him in the room," she startled Lord Clarendon by saying. The breach was never really healed, and as time went on the Queen was clearly envious of the popularity of the Prince and Princess of Wales. She liked to be, but she took little trouble to see that she was, popular.

(margin: Balmoral and Osborne)

To Balmoral (to which telegraphic communication with London was established in the 1860s) and to Osborne, for four months in the year, she came to retreat in turn, giving the impression to shrewd observers like Walter Bagehot (whose *English Constitution* was published in 1867) that she was "a retired widow"; and, although his division between the dignified or "theatrical" and the efficient or "business" parts of the constitution, came to grow truer in her case, her *Letters* (which Bagehot of course could not then read) reveal that, so far as she was concerned, she was determined to remain, as Albert had taught her, very much one of the efficient parts of the constitution. From the point of view of the populace, however, who required a more splendid court, she carried into effect all too few of the "theatrical" aspects of her task. She had been an adoring wife and, if Albert had left her prejudices less narrow, he had not, of course, been able to alter her temperament. "My nature is too passionate," she told an old friend, "my emotions are too fervent; he guided and protected me, he comforted and encouraged me." Not only was Albert gone but the advisers of earlier days were dead too—Melbourne, Peel, Wellington, and Aberdeen—and Stockmar had retired in Coburg. "Uncle Leopold" died not long afterward. And the old men who survived, she had never liked: Palmerston, Derby, or Russell, to whom there soon came a black-edged reproach from Osborne warning him not to take up Palmerston's habit of sending off drafts "without the Queen's having first seen them" (January 14, 1862). Moreover, there were to be changes, because of retirement, in the next few years, in the household, and one of them was of some moment. "Good, excellent General Grey," who had been Albert's secretary, stoutly resisted her attempt to make herself a recluse. He urged ministers to press her to appear in public. He realized what an infliction it was to ministers that she stayed so long at Balmoral and Osborne nursing her grief; he advised "a strong—even a *peremptory* tone." Grey had been prepared to lose his temper with her—and survive. After his death (1870) nobody dared to do so, except John Brown. Henry (later Sir Henry) Ponsonby, Grey's successor, was too young to try. No longer restrained, her *Letters* became more forcefully characteristic, and, as Lady Ponsonby told Sir Henry, "When she is disagreed with, even slightly, she thinks nothing too bad to say of the culprit."

It was despite, yet because of, Albert that she succumbed to Benjamin Disraeli. Albert had thought him insufficiently a gentleman and remembered his bitter attacks on Peel over the repeal of the Corn Laws in 1846; the Prince on the other hand had approved of Disraeli's political rival, William Ewart Gladstone. Yet Disraeli was able to enter into the Queen's grief, flatter her, restore her self-confidence, and make the lonely crown an easier burden. Behind all his calculated attack on her affections there was a bond of mutual loneliness, a note of mystery (which she had already found of interest in Napoleon III), and, besides, the return to good gossip. Moreover, Disraeli told the Queen in 1868 that it would be "his delight and duty, to render the transaction of affairs as easy to your Majesty, as possible." Since the Queen was only too ready to consider herself overworked, this approach was especially successful. Gladstone, on the other hand, would never acknowledge that she was, as she put it, "dead beat," perhaps because he never was himself; whereas Disraeli tired easily. The contrast between Disraeli's gay, often malicious, gossipy letters and Gladstone's 40 sides of foolscap is obvious. And there was no Albert to give her a neat precis. Moreover, Gladstone held the throne as an institution in such awe that it affected his relations with its essentially feminine occupant. His "feeling" for the crown, said Lady Ponsonby, was "always snubbed." There was fairly early a lack of personal understanding between the Queen and Gladstone, which was fostered by Disraeli. Dean Gerald Wellesley, her favourite cleric, warned Gladstone in 1868, before he took office, that

(margin: Disraeli)

> everything depends upon your manner of approaching the Queen. Her nervous susceptibility has much increased since you had to do with her before and you cannot show too much regard, gentleness, I might even say tenderness, towards Her.

Gladstone took the advice to heart, and although they might differ on a particular issue, such as the disestablishment of the Irish Church in 1869, it did not prevent the Queen's active cooperation. In that particular issue, her intervention with the bishops was decisive in averting clashes between the two Houses of Parliament. Friction began in 1871 when Gladstone, alarmed at the wave of republican feeling, tried to persuade the Queen to reappear in public and postpone her departure to Balmoral. She threatened abdication, and Disraeli made matters worse for Gladstone by defending the Queen's seclusion in a speech savouring of what Gladstone called his "usual flunkeyism." When Gladstone subsequently appeared at Balmoral he noted "the repellent power which she so well knows how to use has been put in action towards me . . . I have felt myself on a new and different footing with her."

Over the problem of Ireland, their paths separated ever more widely. Whereas "to pacify Ireland" had become the "mission" of Gladstone's life, the Queen (like the majority of her subjects) had little understanding of, or sympathy for, Irish grievances. She disliked disorder and regarded the suggestion of Irish Home Rule as sheer disloyalty. The proposal of an Irish "Balmoral" was repugnant to her, especially when it was suggested that the Prince of Wales might go in her place. To avoid the Irish Sea, she claimed to be a bad sailor; yet she was willing in her later years to cross the English Channel almost every year. In all, she made but four visits to Ireland, the last in 1900 being provoked by her appreciation of the gallantry of the Irish regiments in the South African War.

Gladstone's defeat in 1874 The news of Gladstone's defeat in 1874 delighted the Queen. "What an important turn the elections have taken," she wrote.

> It shows that the country is not *Radical*. What a triumph, too, Mr. Disraeli has obtained and what a good sign this large Conservative majority is of the state of the country, which really required (as formerly) a strong Conservative party!

If, years before, Melbourne, almost despite himself, had made her a good little Whig, and if Albert had left her, in general, a Peelite, temperamental and subsequently doctrinal differences with Gladstone helped make it easy for Disraeli to turn Victoria into a stout supporter of the Conservative Party. And he took an artist's pleasure in doing so (as his *Letters to Lady Bradford and Lady Chesterfield* [the Marquess of Zetland, ed. 2 vol., 1929] make quite evident).

By 1878 Lady Ponsonby could write to her husband:

> I *do* think Dizzy has worked the idea of personal government to its logical conclusion and the seed was sown by Stockmar and the Prince. While they lived, the current of public opinion, especially among the Ministers, kept the thing between bounds, but they established the superstition in the Queen's mind about her own prerogative, and we who know her, know also perfectly how that superstition, devoid as it is of even a shadow of real political value, can be worked by an unscrupulous Minister to his own advantage.

Lady Ponsonby went on to hint at a future clash with Gladstone. When in September 1879 a dissolution of Parliament seemed imminent, the Queen wrote to the Marchioness of Ely (who was, after the Duchess of Argyll, perhaps her most intimate friend):

> Dear Janie,—I wish it were possible for Sir H. Ponsonby *to get at some* of the *Opposition,* and to point *out* the *extreme danger* of binding themselves by foolish, violent declarations about their policy beforehand. I hope and trust the Government will be able to go on after the Election, as change is so disagreeable and so bad for the country; but if it should *not,* I wish the *principal* people of the Opposition should *know* there *are certain* things which *I never can* consent to.
>
> 1. Any lowering of the position of this country by letting Russia have her way in the East, or by letting down our Empire in India and in the Colonies. This *was* done under Mr. Gladstone, quite *contrary* to Lord Palmerston's *policy,* which, whatever faults he had, *was always* for *keeping up England,* which of late years had *quite* gone down, so that we were *despised abroad.*
>
> 2. That I would never give way about the *Scotch Church,* which is the real and true stronghold of Protestantism.
>
> *These* are points which I *never* could *allow* to be *trifled with,* and I could have *no* confidence in any men who attempted this. Our position in India, and in the Colonies, *must* be *upheld.* I wish to *trust my* Government whoever it is, but they should be *well aware* beforehand I never could if they intended to *try* and *undo* what has been done.
>
> In the same way I never COULD take Mr. Gladstone or Mr. Lowe as my Minister again, for I never could have the slightest *particle* of confidence in Mr. Gladstone *after* his violent, mischievous, and dangerous conduct for the last three years, nor could I take the *latter* after the very offensive language he used three years ago against *me.*
>
> Sir H. Ponsonby has so many Whig friends that he might easily *get* these things *known.* In former days *much* good was done by Baron Stockmar and Mr. Anson paving the way *for* future arrangements and *preventing* complications at the moment, like Sir R. Peel's failure in '39 about the Ladies. Ever yours affectionately, V.R. and I. I never *could* take Sir C. Dilke as a *Minister.*

Conservative defeat in 1880 After the blow fell with the Conservative Party's defeat in 1880, Victoria sent for Lord Hartington.

> Mr. Gladstone *she* could have nothing to do with, for she considers his whole conduct since '76 to have been one series of violent, passionate invective against and abuse of Lord Beaconsfield, and that *he caused* the Russian war.

Nevertheless, as Hartington pointed out, it was Gladstone whom she had to have. She made no secret of her hostility, she hoped he would retire, and she remained in correspondence with Lord Beaconsfield (as Disraeli had become). Gladstone, indeed, said that he himself "would never be surprised to see her turn the Government out, after the manner of her uncles." Over the abandonment of Kandahar in Afghanistan, in 1881, for example, Ponsonby had never seen her so angry: "The Queen has never before been treated," she told him, "with such want of respect and consideration in the forty three and a half years she has worn her thorny crown. . . ." Over the third Reform Bill of 1884 she was able to mediate usefully to bring about a compromise between the views of the two Houses, and it would seem that it was the Marquess of Salisbury who caused most difficulties before the bill was passed; nevertheless she blamed Gladstone, "The Lords," she said,

> are *not* in disharmony with the people, but unfortunately Mr. Gladstone's government leans so much to the extreme Radical side, instead of to the sound and moderate portion of his following, that measures are presented to the House of Lords which the Conservatives and moderate Liberals do not feel they can with safety agree to. No one is more truly Liberal in her heart than the Queen, but she has always strongly deprecated the great tendency of the present Government to encourage instead of checking the stream of destructive democracy which has become so alarming. This it is that, she must say justly, alarms the House of Lords and all moderate people. And to threaten the House of Lords that they will bring destruction on themselves is, in fact, to threaten the Monarchy itself. Another Sovereign but herself must acquiesce in any alteration of the House of Lords. She will not be a Sovereign of a Democratic Monarchy.

Victoria's firm rule Of the three great rights (to be consulted, to encourage, and to warn) that Walter Bagehot had awarded the crown in his *English Constitution,* Victoria had come to make partisan use. Nothing escaped her "drill eye." She insisted on consultation, whoever was in power—and over the most trivial detail. As time went on, she came to encourage the Conservatives and to warn the Liberals. The considered view of the Radical Joseph Chamberlain, not notably a friend of royalty, is of interest: "The Queen does interfere constantly," he wrote,

> more, however, when Liberal Ministers are in power than when she has a Conservative Cabinet, because the Conservatives on the whole do what she likes, as she is a Conservative; whereas the Liberals are continually doing the things she does not like. But it is very doubtful how far her interference is unconstitutional, and it would be quite impossible to prove it. . . . The Queen is a woman of great ability . . . she writes to the Prime Minister about everything she does not like, which when he is a Liberal means almost everything that he says or does . . . she insists that administrative acts should not be done without delay for the purpose of consulting with regard to them persons whose opinions she knows will be unfavourable . . . her action to my mind is strictly speaking constitutional . . . it would be difficult to maintain that with her immense experience the Queen is not justified in asking for time in order that men of distinction should be consulted upon various acts.

Her warnings in 1884 about the dangerous delay in sending help to Gen. C.G. Gordon, who was besieged in Khartoum, passed unheeded, and when he was killed in January 1885 she sent her reproof (February 5, 1885) in an unciphered telegram.

The lengthening experience of the Queen, laid up in the most retentive and faithful memory, was making her an excellent person to talk things over with; if she had mastered the nervous horror of London which drove her to Balmoral or Osborne, and had kept her Ministers under the charm at Buckingham Palace, her influence would have grown with her experience. . . . On three occasions after the Prince's death she intervened with decisive effect: in checking the hysterical fussiness with which Palmerston and Russell were behaving over Schleswig-Holstein under the grim contemptuous eyes of Bismarck; in promoting the passage of the Reform Bill of

1867; in releasing the deadlock of the Houses over Reform and Redistribution in 1884. But Disraeli had made her a partisan: the hoarded experience which might have been freely at the disposal of all her Ministers was reserved for such favourites as Salisbury and Rosebery, and the influence was dissipated in reprimands and injunctions, often shrewd, always vigorous, but sometimes petulant and sometimes petty.... Now that her relations with her ministers are known with some degree of intimacy, it is permissible to say that if she never overstepped the limits of her admitted powers, she did not always behave well within them: she did her duty but often with a reluctance and temper which in a more critical age might have been even dangerously resented. (From G.M. Young, *op. cit.*)

She never acclimatized herself to the effects of the new electorate on party organization. No longer was the monarchy normally necessary as cabinet maker—but she still had an obscure desire to have a coalition and she had been brooding, since 1880, over getting "the moderate men of both parties," as she called them, into a coalition together as an anti-Radical bloc. Irish Home Rule provided her with a solution.

In 1885 Ponsonby explained to Sir William Harcourt that "her idea was that 'extremes' [meaning Gladstone and Lord Randolph Churchill] should be got rid of, that Hartington should be Prime Minister and Salisbury Foreign Secretary under him, the whole of the rest of the Cabinet being Liberal and Whig." She had already sounded the Duke of Argyll in the matter and she pressed George Joachim (afterward Viscount) Goschen to act as go-between. "Out of this," she said, "might grow a Coalition in time." In this she was right, and in the Salisbury administration (1895–1902), with which her long reign ended, she was eventually to find not only the sort of ministry with which she felt comfortable but one which lent a last ray of colour to her closing years by its alliance, through Joseph Chamberlain, with the mounting imperialism that she had so greatly enjoyed in Disraeli's day when he had made her empress of India (1876). Before that, however, she was to have two more rounds of bickering with Gladstone and the short-lived administration of Lord Rosebery, whom she herself chose unadvised in 1894 as her prime minister.

Last years. Victoria absorbed a great deal of the time of her ministers, especially Gladstone's, but after 1868 it may be doubted whether, save in rare instances, in the long run it made a great deal of effective difference, politically. She may have postponed an occasional evil day; she certainly hampered an occasional career. And sometimes that "continuous political experience," which Bagehot remarked as a long-lived monarch's greatest asset, was invaluable: in stopping "red tapings," as the Queen called them, or in breaking a logjam. Meanwhile—"a comparatively late growth"—she had gained the affection of her subjects. Lord Salisbury observed in the House of Lords (January 25, 1901) after her death that:

She had an extraordinary knowledge of what her people would think—extraordinary, because it could not come from any personal intercourse. I have said for years that I have always felt that when I knew what the Queen thought, I knew pretty certainly what views her subjects would take, and especially the middle class of her subjects.

Bagehot had emphasized the fact that the court stood aloof from the rest of the London world and had "but slender relations with the more amusing part of it." The court was, then, unfashionable. But the Queen, as the Jubilees of 1887 and 1897 showed, was popular. Gone were the days when pamphlets were circulated asking what she did with her money. More and more fully with advancing years, she was able to satisfy the imagination of the middle class—and the poorer class—of her subjects.

Character and personality

Many of the movements of the day passed the aged Queen by, many irritated her, but the stupendous hard work that Albert had taught her went on—the meticulous examination of the boxes, the regular signature of the papers. "Wiggings" (as her scoldings of family and ministers were familiarly called) grew more infrequent. When in 1896 the Prince of Wales wanted her to give the Kaiser (William II) a "good snubbing," she replied, "Those sharp answers and remarks only irritate and do harm and in Sovereigns and Princes should be most carefully guarded against. William's faults come from impetuousness (as

well as conceit); and calmness and firmness are the most powerful weapons in such cases." She had mellowed. She had come into calmer, if very lonely, waters. Those who were nearest to her came completely under her spell; yet all from the Prince of Wales down stood in considerable awe. A breach of the rules could still make a fearsome change in the kindly, managing great-grandmother, in black silk dress and white cap. The eyes began to protrude, the mouth to go down at the corners. Those who suffered her displeasure never forgot it, nor did she. Yielding to nobody else's comfort and keeping every anniversary, she lived in overheated rooms surrounded by mementos, photographs, miniatures, busts, and souvenirs at the end of drafty corridors down which one tiptoed past Indian attendants to the presence. Nobody knocked; a gentle scratching on the door was all that she permitted. Every night at Windsor, Albert's clothes were laid out on the bed, every morning fresh water was put in the basin in his room. She slept with a photograph—over her head—taken of his head and shoulders as he lay dead.

Queen Victoria had fought a long rear guard action against the growth of "democratic monarchy"; yet, in some ways, she had done more than anyone else to create it. She had made the monarchy respectable and had thereby guaranteed its continuance—not as a political power but as a political institution. Her long reign had woven a legend, and as her political power ebbed away her political value grew. It lay, perhaps, more in what the electorate thought of her, indeed felt about her, than in what she ever was or certainly ever believed herself to be. Paradoxically enough, her principal contribution to the British monarchy and her political importance lay in regard to those "dignified" functions that she was accused of neglecting rather than to the "business" functions that, perhaps sometimes, she did not neglect enough.

Death

The Queen died at Osborne on January 22, 1901, after a short and painless illness. "We all feel a bit motherless today" wrote Henry James, "mysterious little Victoria is dead and fat vulgar Edward is King." She was buried beside Prince Albert in the mausoleum at Frogmore near Windsor. "She had lived long enough. The idol of her people, she had come to press on the springs of government with something of the weight of an idol, and in the innermost circle of public life the prevailing sentiment was relief." (From G.M. Young, *op. cit.*) Her essential achievement was simple. By the length of her reign, the longest in English history, she had restored both dignity and popularity to a tarnished crown: an achievement of character, as well as of longevity. Historians may differ in their assessment of her political acumen, her political importance, or her role as a constitutional monarch. None will question her high sense of duty or the transparent honesty, the massive simplicity, of her royal character. (E.T.W.)

BIBLIOGRAPHY. The most important authority for the Queen's life is *The Letters of Queen Victoria* in three series: *1837–61,* 3 vol., ed. by A.C. BENSON and VISCOUNT ESHER (1907); *1862–85,* 3 vol., ed. by G.E. BUCKLE (1926–28); and *1886–1901,* 3 vol., ed. by G.E. BUCKLE (1930–32). *Further Letters of Queen Victoria* (1938, reprinted 1976), was edited by HECTOR BOLITHO, who also consolidated his own several studies of the Queen and her family in *The Reign of Queen Victoria* (1948). Correspondence between the Queen and her eldest daughter was edited by ROGER FULFORD: *Dearest Child* (1964, reissued 1977), covering the years 1858–61, *Dearest Mama* (1968), covering 1861–64, *Your Dear Letter* (1972), covering 1865–71, *Darling Child* (1976), covering 1871–78, and *Beloved Mama* (1981), covering 1878–85. Her correspondence with Gladstone, *The Queen and Mr. Gladstone,* 2 vol. (1933, reissued 1969), was edited, with commentary, by PHILIP GUEDALLA; and with Palmerston (1837–65), *Regina v. Palmerston* (1962), by B. CONNELL. *Leaves from the Journal of Our Life in the Highlands from 1848 to 1861* (1868, reprinted 1969) and *More Leaves ... 1862–82* (1884), both ed. by SIR ARTHUR HELPS, were published in the Queen's lifetime and played their part in securing the eventual public affection. CECIL BLANCHE WOODHAM-SMITH, *Queen Victoria* (1972), is an account of her childhood and marriage. For the early days of the reign, see *Victoria, Albert, and Mrs. Stevenson,* ed. by EDWARD BOYKIN (1957); and LORD DAVID CECIL, *Lord M* (1954). LYTTON STRACHEY's well-known *Queen Victoria* (1921, reissued 1978) was written before the second and third series of her *Letters* had been published. FRANK

HARDIE, *The Political Influence of Queen Victoria, 1861–1901,* 2nd ed. (1963), took a somewhat different view from that expressed here. An excellent modern life is that of ELIZABETH, COUNTESS OF LONGFORD, *Victoria R.I.* (1964; abridged ed. 1973). Later sources include MARINA WARNER, *Queen Victoria's Sketchbook* (1979), a narrative text accompanying a collection of the Queen's artistic works; DAVID DUFF (ed.), *Queen Victoria's Highland Journals,* new rev. ed. (1980), well-illustrated

selections from journals published during Victoria's lifetime; JEFFREY L. LANT, *Insubstantial Pageant: Ceremony and Confusion at Queen Victoria's Court* (1980), a study of royal ritual in Victorian times; see also TYLER WHITTLE, *Victoria and Albert at Home* (1980); JONATHAN ROUTH, *The Secret Life of Queen Victoria* (1980); ALISON PLOWDEN, *The Young Victoria* (1981); and DOROTHY MARSHALL, *The Life and Times of Victoria* (1982).

Vienna

The capital city of Austria, Vienna (German Wien; Czech Vídeň; Hungarian Bécs) is situated in the northeastern corner of the country on the Danube River, at the point where the Alps give way to the broad Pannonian Basin of eastern Europe. For more than 2,000 years it has been one of the great gateways between East and West, at times the bride of history, at times the victim. From 1558 to 1806, Vienna was the seat of the Holy Roman Empire and until 1918 it served as the capital of the Austro-Hungarian Empire. Since the end of World War I, this imperial city of palaces and royal parks has been the capital of a small, mountainous, middle-European republic: in an aptly descriptive phrase attributed to the British statesman Winston Churchill, it is like an elephant in a backyard.

Vienna is the least spoiled of the great, old western European capitals. Many of the urban prospects remain basically those contrived centuries ago by royal gardeners and architects. The city skyline is still dominated by the spire of St. Stephen's Cathedral (1433) and by the giant Ferris wheel (1873) in the Prater. It is still possible to live in Vienna at almost the same pace and with nearly the same grace as in the days when Adolf Hitler was a very minor employee at the Academy of Fine Arts. The same music is being played in the same concert halls, the same sourish local wines (*Heuriger*) are being served in the local taverns (*Heurigen*) in the postcard villages on the outskirts of town, and the same mountains of whipped cream are being served at Sacher's and Demel's tea rooms. Provincials and children are seen in the streets dressed in Alpine suits with forest-green trim.

Vienna has avoided many of the gravest problems afflicting other Western cities. It has no financial crises and has never borrowed money to meet deficits. No serious social unrest exists among the predominantly Roman Catholic Viennese, and no one group is economically underprivileged. Crime rates are low. No serious decay has occurred in the well-inhabited central core, and there is no shortage of housing, schools, parks, and public recreational facilities, or cultural resources. A modern subway brings people rapidly into the centre of town. Hospital and library systems are expanding, and since 1888 the Viennese have been provided with social-security and health-insurance coverage.

This article is divided into the following sections:

Physical and human geography

THE LANDSCAPE

Layout and architecture. With an area of 160 square miles (415 square kilometres), Vienna crosses the Danube on one side and climbs into the Wiener Wald (Vienna Woods) on the other, where it includes the 1,778-foot (542-metre) Hermannskogel. The Wiener Wald slope descends to the river by four roughly semicircular terraces, with the city centre sited on the second lowest terrace. A channelized branch of the Danube, the Donau Kanal (Danube Canal), winds through the populous part of the city. Only two of the city's 23 districts are on the far side of the Danube. The powerful Danube, whose average width is 902 feet (275 metres), was transformed in the 1970s by the construction of a flood-control bypass canal immediately parallel to the main stream. Separating the two bodies of water is an island 13 miles long and 750 feet wide (21 kilometres by 230 metres). Fashioned from former floodlands and equipped as an all-sports park, the island adds to the city's already generous recreational space.

The Lobau, another wooded section along the river, has long been, like the Wiener Wald, a protected greenbelt area. Since the 1970s the open spaces on the far side of the Danube have been exploited for building, and even outlying housing and industrial developments are within two or three miles of the old city walls. The walls were erected with six fortified gates and 19 towers in the 13th century, and until the end of the 17th century, almost no Viennese lived outside.

Located in the centre of the city is St. Stephen's Cathedral (Stephanskirche), one of the chief Gothic buildings in Europe. It incorporates remnants of the original Romanesque edifice, probably built between 1137 and 1147, which was destroyed by fire. Reconstruction of the cathedral began in the early 14th century. The Romanesque west front, with its Portal of the Giants (Riesentor), and the two Towers of the Pagans (Heidentürme) were preserved, and from 1304 to 1450 the Gothic structure rose slowly behind them. The southern tower, 446 feet (136 metres) high, was finished in 1433. The northern tower, never completed, was topped off with a Renaissance dome in 1587. This zigzag pattern of glazed, coloured tiles on the massive, almost hunchbacked roof is said to represent the prayer rug of the East. The cathedral was again burned in World War II but was later reconstructed. The 20-ton Pummering bell, made from captured Turkish cannons in 1711, was recast and rehung with much ceremony.

St. Stephen's Cathedral

Other Gothic churches include the Church of St. Augustin (Augustinerkirche), the Church of St. Mary-on-the-Bank (Sankt Maria am Gestade), and the Church of the Friars Minor (Minoritenkirche), all dating from the 14th century. St. Rupert's Church (Ruprechtskirche), dating from the 13th century with parts from the 11th century, is Vienna's oldest church and is believed to have been originally built in 740. St. Peter's Church (Peterskirche), standing on the site of a church allegedly founded by Charlemagne in 792, was built chiefly by Johann Lucas von Hildebrandt in 1702–33. Other fine examples of Baroque art are the richly frescoed university church (1627–31) and the Capuchin Monastery Church (Kapuzinerkirche; 1632), which contains the crypt of the imperial

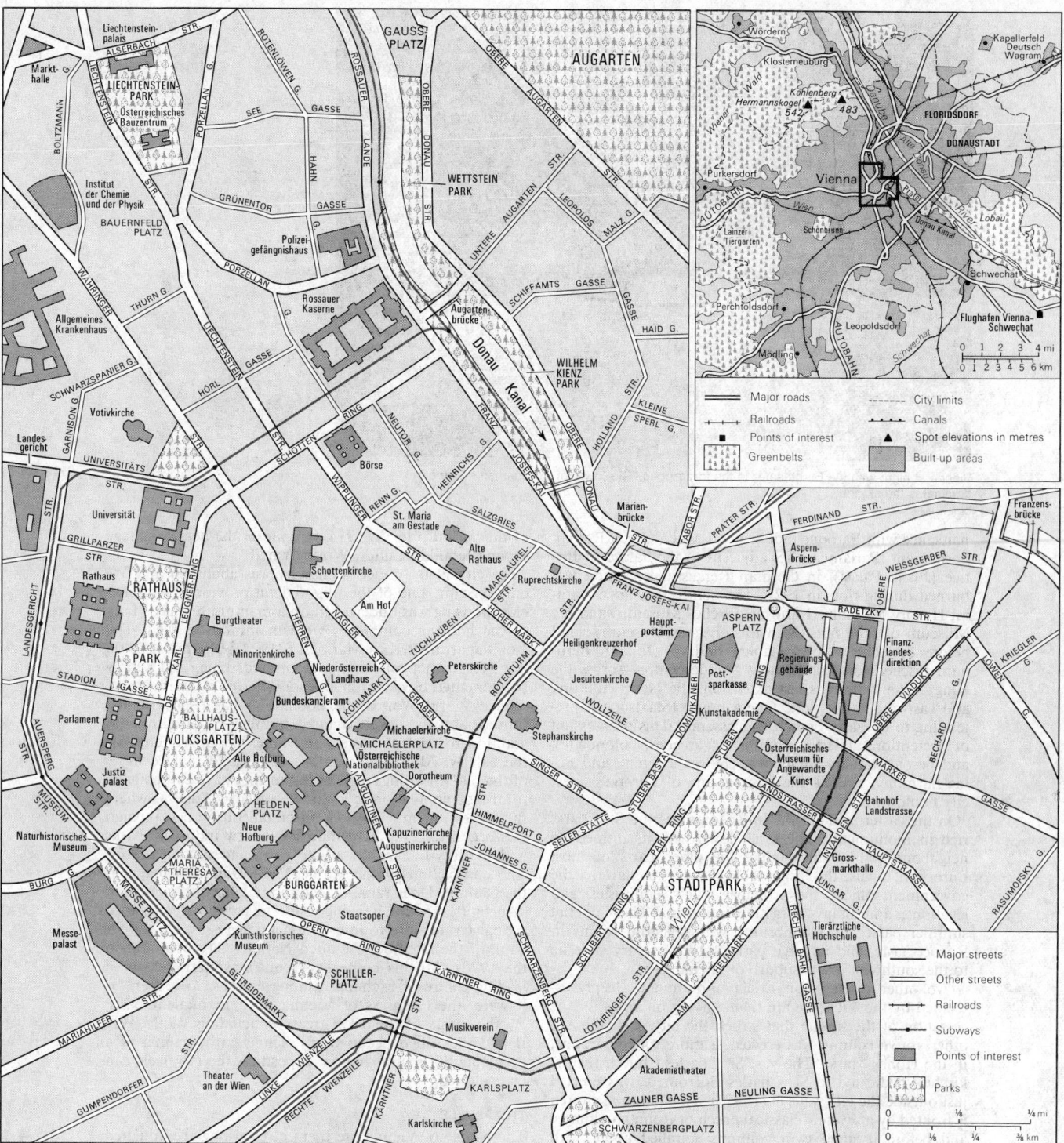

Central Vienna and (inset) the municipal area.

family. The Church of the Scots (Schottenkirche), founded in 1155, together with a monastery of Scottish and Irish monks, was rebuilt in late Italian Renaissance style in 1638–48. Most of the noteworthy secular buildings, such as the Harach and Kinsky palaces and the Winter Palace of Prince Rugene of Savoy, are Baroque.

A circular road surrounding the central city is called the Ringstrasse. It is lined with important buildings, monuments, and parks. The vast complex of the imperial palace, the Hofburg, adjoins the Ring. It consists of a number of buildings of various periods and styles, enclosing several courtyards, the oldest part dating from the 13th, the latest from the end of the 19th century. It abounds in magnificently appointed private and state apartments and also houses the imperial treasury of the Holy Roman and Austrian empires; the Austrian National

Library (Österreichische Nationalbibliothek); the Albertina and several other museums; and the Winter (or Spanish) Riding School. The state apartments of the Hofburg wing adjoining the Ballhausplatz are now the offices of the president of Austria.

Other important buildings along the Ring include a Neoclassic-Renaissance Stock Exchange (Börse) and the pseudo-Gothic Votive Church (Votivkirche), Francis Joseph's thanksgiving for an escape from assassination in 1853. Nearby is the neo-Italian Renaissance University of Vienna (Universität), the second-oldest German-language university; it was founded in 1365, but its original buildings have disappeared. Another landmark is the City Hall (Rathaus) in neo-Flemish Gothic, with Renaissance touches, that faces—across its park and the Ring—the national theatre (Burgtheater), in neo-High-Italian Re-

The Rathaus and Burgtheater

Vienna at night with the Burgtheater in the foreground. The tower of St. Stephen's Cathedral dominates the skyline.
Camera Press—Publix

naissance with Baroque indulgences. A neo-Greco-Roman Parliament (Parlament) lies adjacent to the Palace of Justice (Justiz Palast), in German Renaissance, which was burned during riots in 1927. The neo-Renaissance Natural History Museum (Naturhistorisches Museum) and the Museum of Fine Arts (Kunsthistorisches Museum) stand before the former royal stables, built by Johann Bernhard Fischer von Erlach, now a trade centre. Across the Ring is the Hofburg's last extension, the Neue Hofburg, and eastward is the State Opera house (Staatsoper), pretending to be Early French Renaissance. This progression of pretentions, pilasters, pinnacles, arcades, colonnades, and heroic statuary somehow achieves a serene and noble harmony; overall, the Ring is one of Europe's finest city boulevards.

On the eastern side of the inner town lies the Stadtpark, rich in monuments. The inner town with its immediate neighbourhood is still, unlike the older parts of most European towns, the fashionable quarter, containing the government offices, the principal hotels, embassies, and legations, and many attractive buildings. The imperial summer palace of Schönbrunn, with splendid rooms in Rococo taste, and its large park of 18th-century style lie to the southwest in the suburb of Hietzing.

Two other Fischer von Erlach monuments deeply esteemed by the Viennese are thanksgiving offerings for the cessation of the plague that struck the city in 1713. Another votive column was erected, a more sober Baroque, in the Hoher Markt. The vast St. Charles Church (Karlskirche), dedicated to St. Charles Borromeo, was erected just outside the city walls (1716–39). This Baroque church is fronted by a severely classical porch of Roman columns, and before it stand twin columns spiralled about with scenes from the saint's life.

Several streets away from the church is the Theater an der Wien (1788), in which Mozart conducted the first performance of *The Magic Flute,* and three Beethoven symphonies had their first public hearing. All the celebrated operetta composers of the 19th century presented works on its boards. In 1962 the municipality bought the dilapidated house, restored it, and operates it.

The Belvedere palace

The Belvedere is really two palaces at either end of a terraced garden, built by Hildebrandt for the warrior-poet Prince Eugene of Savoy. The Lower Belvedere (1714–16) was a summer-garden palace, whereas the Upper (1721–22) was designed as a place in which to give entertainments. The Lower houses the museums of Austrian Baroque art and of Austrian medieval art. The Upper was arranged in 1954 as a gallery of Austrian art of the 19th and 20th centuries.

The town as a whole has preserved its general character of the period prior to 1914, in spite of the heavy damage of, and rebuilding after, World War II.

The city plan.   Once monarchy was abolished and Vienna became one of the nine federal provinces, working-class housing was undertaken on a mammoth scale. Many of the housing complexes were mammoth as well. The 1,600-apartment Karl Marx Hof (1927–30), almost 3,900 feet (1,190 metres) long, presents red, blue, and yellow battlemented blocks of pugnacious 1920s "modern."

Since World War II the population has risen and the municipality has built a large number of dwellings, in addition to student hostels and hotel-like apartments for the elderly. Although there is still need to replace more of the older housing, the city authorities have campaigned to attract population from other parts of Austria, where the wages are much lower. Simultaneously, a campaign was begun to bring light industry to new industrial parks and to duty-free zones at the river and at the airport. The completion of the Rhine–Main–Danube canal and the Danube–Oder canal helped to revitalize the river port.

Ancient grandeur is being made to pay dividends, with six palaces for hire to international congresses. On the far bank of the Danube, a United Nations City was built in the 1970s. All this bespeaks Vienna's aspiration to be a leading centre of exchange among nations, to reopen, as it were, the Congress of Vienna on a permanent basis. By the terms of the 1955 treaty concluding World War II and the Allied occupation, Vienna is the capital of a permanently neutral nation, a position the city feels can be exploited.

THE PEOPLE

The people of Vienna are themselves a long-accumulated experience. They are the product of cross-fertilization between mountain and plain, a blend in which the impulsive Balkan strain is checked by the measured Teutonic. Viennese attitudes and traditions are equally hybrid, bred of centuries of intermingling peoples and beliefs. A strong tendency toward pomposity is balanced by an irrepressible urge for self-mockery. Two very Viennese words are *Wichtigmacher* ("important-maker") and *Besserwisser* ("better-knower"). A revealing, oft-repeated comment on the return of prosperity in the 1960s was "The postwar German economic miracle was the result of sound planning, hard work and determination, but in Austria the miracle was really a miracle."

The citizen's very real civic pride does not impede his game of outsmarting the tax collector. Though the average resident regularly attends the opera, concert, and theatre, he is early to bed: performances let out by 10:00 PM, and street lights are dimmed after midnight, but some

Characteristic way of life

cafes remain open until 2:00 AM. The Viennese continue to speak a special language, Wienerisch, with its special intonations and accent. The emperor and his court spoke either French or Wienerisch, eschewing the Hochdeutsch, or High German, of Prussia.

Although they love their city and are prideful of its monuments, the Viennese are not awed by them. One finds restaurants, taverns, and wineshops burrowed into imposing official buildings, and shops often line the street floor. The two surviving religious cloisters in the inner city have shops in their hidden garden courtyards, including wineshops, and one adds a tavern and a café as well.

Cafes, at least the palatial, plush, and cut-glass 19th-century temples, are dying out. A few remain, with their racks of newspapers from the capitals of Europe and their waiters refilling the glass of water that always accompanies the cup of coffee. The conservative Viennese has accepted the espresso bar as once he accepted the horseless carriage and the actor talking out of an electronic box.

THE ECONOMY

Government on all levels is a major employer in Vienna. The Austrian state theatre alone employs several thousand people in the operation of the Vienna State Opera house, the Volksoper, the Burgtheater, and the Akademietheater. Tourism is a growing economic factor as well. The base of the economy, however, remains trade and industry. Vienna produces almost a third of the gross national product, including most of the Austrian-made electrical appliances, nearly half of the paper and clothing, and a large portion of the machine tools.

ADMINISTRATIVE AND SOCIAL CONDITIONS

Government. The mayor is also deputy of the province of Vienna. The municipal upper house (Town Senate) is simultaneously the provincial government, while the lower house sits in separate sessions as the provincial legislature. The affairs of the 23 municipal districts are handled by appointed magistrates for each district under elected chairmen and representatives. Vienna sends 12 members to the Bundesrat, the upper house of the federal legislature.

Socialist administration

Conservative as the Viennese may be, they have elected a socialist government at every free municipal election since 1918. The government not only runs the city but also operates many business enterprises. Among these are low-cost restaurants, a major publishing house, an insurance company, motion-picture theatres, and the third largest savings bank in the country. Every infant born in Vienna receives a free layette from the municipal government and a savings bankbook with a free opening deposit. The city rents out all trash cans in town and regularly carts them off for a free cleansing at what may be the world's only automatic garbage-can-washing station.

Eminence of medical services

Health. Viennese hospitals and medical training have been held in high esteem since early in the 18th century. The admonition *"Wenn Sie schon unbedingt krank werden müssen, dann werden Sie es in Wien"* ("If you really must fall sick, then do it in Vienna") long contained not only humour but also practical advice. A new General Hospital (Allgemeines Krankenhaus) attached to the University Medical School was opened in 1971. The chronic ailments of old age are cared for in geriatric institutions rather than hospitals. There are many general and specialized hospitals.

CULTURAL LIFE

Operas, concerts, and theatres are well attended. The Vienna Boys' Choir sings every Sunday morning at the Castle chapel (Burgkapelle). The concerts of the Vienna Philharmonic Orchestra are usually on Saturday afternoons and Sunday mornings, because in the evening it is employed as the State Opera orchestra. Music has remained a Viennese passion throughout the centuries, and for long the city was the music capital of the world. One generation of composers alone included Haydn, Mozart, Beethoven, and Schubert. A century later the Viennese music generation included Brahms, Anton Bruckner, Hugo Wolf, and Gustav Mahler. Leaders of the following generation were Arnold Schoenberg and his pupils Alban Berg and Anton

von Webern. There was also the dynasty of Strausses and the gay, compelling company of operetta composers including Franz von Suppé and Franz Lehár.

Museums

The museum-goer in Vienna has an agony of choice among 16 state museums, 12 city museums, and special exhibition halls in such places as the National Library. There are some little-known collections, such as the Hofburg's Esperanto Museum, and others celebrated the world over, such as the palace's treasure room with the regalia of the Holy Roman Empire and the House of Habsburg. The Albertina, at the far end of the palace, has one of the world's largest hoards of graphic art, including some renowned Albrecht Dürer and Rembrandt engravings. The Museum of Fine Arts houses the superb Habsburg collection of old masters, especially rich in Flemish and Dutch painting. Vienna has preserved as museums three houses in which Beethoven lived and worked, and it has assembled collections in former residences of Mozart, Haydn, and Schubert. In 1971 the Sigmund Freud museum was opened in the apartment that had served as his home and office for nearly 50 years.

History

THE ANCIENT CITY AND MEDIEVAL GROWTH

The river site between mountain and plain has been inhabited since the Neolithic Period. The Celtic fortified town, Vindobona, was annexed by the Romans in the 1st century BC, and its population grew to 15,000 or 20,000 by about the 3rd century AD. The Romans were swept away in the turmoil of the 5th century, but enough of Vindobona remained to serve as the nucleus of the medieval city, which followed the original layout. Removal of bombing rubble after World War II revealed Roman ruins under the Hoher Markt, the centre of medieval and modern Vienna.

Ancient structures

In 881 the name Wenia appeared for the first time in the Salzburg Annals. In 1147, 10 years after Vienna won its charter as a city, St. Stephen's Cathedral, a possessively loved landmark, was begun. The city already had another major church, St. Ruprecht's (8th century), whose Romanesque fabric was brutally modernized by Gothic builders. According to ill-founded legend, there was yet another, St. Peter's, established in 792 by Charlemagne, but in fact it was started later than St. Stephen's and has been totally rebuilt many times.

The dukes of Babenberg made Vienna their capital in 1156, enhancing an already flourishing trade. In 1221 it was granted a trade monopoly as a staging point for the Crusades and, later, to help support the Teutonic Knights, an order whose chapter house and chapel (14th century) are still open near the cathedral. The city was swept by fire in 1258 but swiftly recovered. In 1276 the first of the Habsburg rulers was installed; the last was to depart only in 1918, and the city remains physically a Habsburg seat to this day.

Construction of the city walls in the 13th century was paid for by revenue from an innovation in the Crusade-staging monopoly: Richard I the Lion-Hearted of England was held for ransom as he paused in Vienna on his way home from the Holy Land. The pope so disapproved of this departure from knightly norms that he threatened to excommunicate Duke Leopold VI if the money were not paid back.

An astute policy of territorial acquisition through marriage made the Habsburg seat one of the great capitals of the world by the 16th century. The effort of the Thirty Years' War (1618–48) interrupted the surge of construction that had begun in the previous century, during which major sections had been added to the Hofburg. The Estates of the province of Niederösterreich (Lower Austria) built their meeting chambers on the Herrengasse in 1515 in Gothic, but with a Renaissance portal in the courtyard. The Renaissance facade of the Palffy Palace, across the Josefsplatz from the Hofburg, dates from 1575. The city walls, which had been extended and strengthened in the 15th century, were further rebuilt in the 16th.

EVOLUTION OF THE MODERN CITY

Baroque Vienna. In 1679 plague struck the city, taking a fearful toll of life during the year it lasted. In 1683

Turkish
siege and
its relics

another scourge struck Vienna: the Turks, having failed in a siege of the city in 1529, advanced with an army of about 300,000 men. The Emperor and a good part of the population fled. The city walls were manned by 24,000 defenders, many of them townspeople rallied by Burgomaster Liebenberg, to whom a grateful populace erected a memorial obelisk 200 years later. For two months the Turks camped before the walls, firing their cannon into the city. Suddenly on the high ground of the Kahlenberg in the Wiener Wald, which unaccountably had been left unoccupied by the gifted Grand Vizier Kara Mustafa, there appeared the Polish army and a multinational force gathered by the Duke of Lorraine, 80,000 in all. Caught between two fires, the Turks retreated. The Holy Roman Emperor gained new glory as the buckler of Christianity against the sword of Islām, and his capital gained prestige as well.

The prizes taken from the Turks—ornate tents, horsetail battle streamers, and jewelled scimitars—can still be seen in the Army Museum. Among the baggage were sacks of green beans that were, on the advice of an Austrian spy, roasted and brewed. The resulting concoction, coffee, began an addiction that still grips the Viennese populace. Plans were drawn up for an outer circle of city defenses, and in 1704–06 the Linienwall was built in a large semicircle around the old wall. In the late 19th century this was razed and made into the Gürtel (girdle), an outerbelt boulevard.

The Muslim threat over, Vienna indulged in an orgy of Baroque building that lasted for 70 years. Venerable monuments were given Baroque decoration and sometimes rebuilt entirely in the new mode of Vienna Gloriosa. The Old Town Hall (Alte Rathaus), which had been rebuilt several times since the 13th century, got a Baroque facade; 12th-century St. Peter's was rebuilt; the 14th-century Hofburg parish church was Baroqued (de-Baroqued in 1784), as was the palace chapel; the 13th-century Minoritenkirche was also made Baroque (an "improvement" removed a century later); and the richly Baroque Jesuit church (1627–31) of the university was further decorated. This refashioning passion concluded only in 1781, when St. Michael's, across from the Hofburg, was rebuilt as Baroque but retained its tower from 1340.

Though the first Baroque palaces in the city centre—Lobkowitz, Starhemberg, Harrach, and Mollard-Clary—are from the late 17th century and designed by Italian architects, the still-clear image of Baroque Vienna was shaped by three native sons, Johann Lucas von Hildebrandt, Johann Bernhard Fischer von Erlach, and his son Josef Emanuel. Both Hildebrandt and the elder Fischer von Erlach designed the Reich Chancery in the royal palace. The Fischers von Erlach created several other portions of the palace, notably the father's National Library (Nationalbibliothek) (1723–26) and the son's Winter (or Spanish) Riding School (1729–35), where pure white Lippizaner horses continue to perform movements of 17th-century dressage, refinements of battle training that survive nowhere else in the world.

In 1691 Prince Liechtenstein had the daring to build his summer palace beyond the city walls. It was the first of the "garden palaces," in what would later become the suburbs and that are now well within the city, creating oases of grace and calm. The most celebrated of the garden palaces are the Belvedere, by Hildebrandt, and Schönbrunn, by the elder Fischer von Erlach. The latter was planned as a residence to rival France's palace of Versailles. By 1696 only a much-reduced main building was complete, and succeeding architects changed and enlarged until only the entrance facade remained of Fischer von Erlach's work. Finally there were 1,500 rooms, a hilltop folly, a palm house, formal gardens, a Rococo theatre, a collection of royal carriages and sleighs, and a zoo that has made the word Schönbrunn synonymous with "zoo" to Viennese infants.

The
Schön-
brunn

The harmony of the whole is due more to colour ("Maria Theresa yellow") than to design, but there is the tint of history as well. There the empress Maria Theresa's 16 children were raised, including the four blonde archduchesses who spoke of their idyllic childhood while reigning over foreign lands. The palace was twice the headquarters of Napoleon and the site of the gilded exile of his pallid son, King of Rome and Duke of Reichstadt. Emperor Francis Joseph was born and died there, and there, on November 11, 1918, Charles I signed the Habsburg abdication.

The Schönbrunn grounds were opened to the public in the late 18th century by Emperor Joseph II, who also offered the Viennese free access to his gardens at Augarten Palace on the far side of the Donau Kanal and to his hunting preserve, the Prater, by the Danube. He also founded the Imperial and Royal Inquiry and Pawnbroking Office at the former Dorothea Convent, whence its current name, "Dorotheum," or sometimes, "Aunt Dorothy." Another of this monarch's gifts to the people of Vienna was the still-functioning General Hospital.

Between 1792 and 1815, Austria was spasmodically at war with France. Napoleon twice occupied Vienna, in 1806 and again in 1809. In 1804 Beethoven's Eroica Symphony, dedicated to Napoleon, was performed in the Lobkowitz Palace. The composer later effaced the dedication with such vehemence that he tore the title page. The palace is now the Institut Français (French Cultural Institute).

In 1806 Napoleon constrained Francis II to divest himself of the title of Holy Roman emperor. Then, as was his wont in occupied capitals, he began rearranging Vienna. He affixed imperial eagles to the Schönbrunn gateway and ordered a wall of the Minoritenkirche to be covered with a mosaic copy of Leonardo da Vinci's Last Supper; both additions remain. He ordained the demolition of the city wall gate at the Hofburg and had a stretch of the wall itself flattened. In 1823 this section of levelled rampart was made into the Volksgarten, the first public park in Vienna, other than the royal parks. This implanted the notion that the walls might come down with great benefit to the city. After Napoleon was removed to Elba, the yearlong Congress of Vienna (1814–15) convened to decide the future of Europe. The meetings of the Congress were held in the Hildebrandt-designed Privy Court Chancery (Bundes-Kanzler Amt 1716–21) across the Ballhausplatz from the Hofburg.

The
period of
Napoleon
and the
Congress
of Vienna

When an elderly diplomat was asked "Comment marche le Congrès?" ("How is the Congress going?"), he replied "Le Congrès ne marche pas, il danse" ("It doesn't march, it dances"). Dance it did, in the Winter Riding School, in the reception halls of the Hofburg, in the ballrooms of the Schönbrunn, in all the palaces of Vienna. Music was everywhere, and Beethoven conducted one of the gala concerts. The decisions made by the many crowned heads and their renowned diplomats are not often recalled in Vienna now outside history classes, but the froth of music, splendour, and coquetry on which the decision makers were wafted is a cherished memory.

The most Viennese of dances, the waltz, derived from Tirolean folk dances, was well established by 1820. The years that followed are called the Vormärz ("before March") in Austria, the year 1848 being understood. This time is also known as the Biedermeier (roughly, "good citizen Meier") period and produced a fulsome, good-hearted domestic architecture and decoration that corresponds in spirit as well as date to Early Victorian and Louis-Philippe in England and France. The age of great music continued—Beethoven died in 1827, Schubert in 1828—and the great age of Viennese operetta flourished. Then came the mighty social and political upheaval of March 1848. The 18-year-old Francis Joseph I had just mounted the throne. Vienna was in an uproar, and the freedom-seeking Hungarians were subdued only by a crushing Russian intervention.

Vienna of the Ring. The Habsburgs prevailed and the capital continued to grow, both inside and outside the walls. By mid-19th century, despite the number of churches, palaces, convents, and government buildings in the inner city, there were 65,000 inhabitants within the walls. The rest of the 440,000 Viennese lived between the inner and outer walls or crammed into the Leopoldstadt, on the far side of the Donau Kanal.

In 1857 Francis Joseph I decreed the razing of the walls. In their place around the old city, the Ringstrasse thoroughfare was created. Buildings in "Ring architecture," though not on the Ringstrasse, also rose during this period. An example is the 1869 Musikvereinsgebäude (concert hall), the home of the Vienna Philharmonic Orchestra, and the gilt-encrusted, crystal-chandeliered main hall is famed for its splendid acoustics.

While the Ring buildings and parks were under construction—the last major structure was completed in 1913—Vienna was a vast building site. To accommodate the immigrants from the eastern reaches of the empire, *Zinskasernen* ("rent barracks") were jammed into the eastern outskirts. Lightless, airless, and comfortless warrens, they were unfortunately solidly built, and they have not yet all been replaced.

Emergence of modern architectureNew commercial buildings rose in the inner city and new housing in what had been the between-walls suburbs. About three-quarters of what had existed before was replaced. By the late years of the 19th century, architects and artists revolted against the Ring styles and found support from the municipality and even the national administration. The church for the new (1874) central cemetery was a large, domed structure in curvilinear Art Nouveau style. The stations for the overhead-underground metropolitan railway were designed by Otto Wagner, who also did the Post Office Savings Bank (Post Sparkasse, 1904–12), an aluminum-pillared building. Wagner was one of the founders of the Sezessionist school of art that produced painting, sculpture, furniture, and pottery according to the motto carved on the lintel of their 1898 headquarters building: "To each time, its own art: to that art its own freedom." With Sezession, Schoenberg, and Sigmund Freud, Francis Joseph's Vienna helped shape the 20th century.

BIBLIOGRAPHY

General: CHRISTA ESTERHAZY, *Vienna* (1966), a short but informative account from the "Cities of the World" series; JOSEPH WECHSBERG, *Sounds of Vienna* (1968; U.S. title, *Vienna My Vienna,* 1968), an illustrated book that conveys the character of the city; MARTIN HURLIMANN, *Wien: Biographie einer Stadt* (1968; Eng. trans., *Vienna,* 1970), includes a popular historical account, with many illustrations; DOROTHY MCGUIGAN, *Vienna Today . . . A Complete Guide,* 10th rev. ed. (1960). WALTER B. GOLDSTEIN, *1000 Jahre Wien und die Habsburger: Eine Europäische Legende* (1981), is a historical overview of the city and the House of Habsburg; HANS PEMMER and NINI LACKNER, *Der Prater: Von den Anfängen bis zur Gegenwart,* 2nd rev. ed. by GÜNTER DÜRIEGL and LUDWIG SACKMAUER (1974), describes one of the greatest parks in Europe; ROBERT MESSNER, *Der Alsergrund im Vormärz* (1970), is a historico-topographical survey of suburbs and environs of Vienna; social conditions and social aspects of city life are discussed in ERICH BODZENTA *et al., Wo sind Grossstädter daheim?* (1981); LEOPOLD REDL and HANS WÖSENDORFER, *Die Donauinsel. Ein Beispiel politischer Planung in Wien* (1980), analyzes economic conditions and municipal government.

The past: MARCEL BRION, *La Vie quotidienne à Vienne à l'époque de Mozart et de Schubert* (1960; Eng. trans., *Daily Life in the Vienna of Mozart and Schubert,* 1961), a detailed account of Vienna's golden age. Other sources on the history of the city include PETER CSENDES, *Geschichte Wiens* (1981); WIENER STADT- UND LANDESARCHIV, LUDWIG BOLTZMANN INSTITUT FÜR STADTGESCHICHTSFORSCHUNG, *Historische Atlas von Wien* (1981); JOHN W. BOYER, *Political Radicalism in Late Imperial Vienna: Origins of the Christian Social Movement, 1848–1897* (1981); FREDERIC MORTON, *A Nervous Splendor: Vienna, 1888–1889* (1979); CARL E. SCHORSKE, *Fin-de-Siècle Vienna: Politics and Culture* (1979).

Musical: EGON GARTENBERG, *Vienna: Its Musical Heritage* (1968), emphasizes Vienna's influence on music. Cultural and social life of Vienna is presented in the lavishly illustrated WILLIAM M. JOHNSTON, *Vienna, Vienna: The Golden Age, 1815–1914* (1981); see also KAREN MONSON, *Alma Mahler, Muse to Genius* (1983).

Chiefly photographic: MARIA NEUSSER-HROMATKA, *Beautiful Vienna* (1959), with explanatory notes by author; ANTON MACKU, *Vienna* (1957), with historical introduction and commentary by the author. Later illustrated descriptions include INGE MORATH *et al., Bilder aus Wien* (1981); ANNA GIUBERTONI, CLAUDIO MAGRIS, and TONI NICOLINI, *Austria* (1981); GÜNTER DÜRIEGL, *Wien auf alten Photographies* (1981); RUPERT FEUCHTMÜLLER, *Die Herrengasse* (1982).

(B.E./Ed.)

Virgil

Virgil was regarded by the Romans as their greatest poet, an estimation that subsequent generations have upheld; his fame rests chiefly upon his national epic poem, the *Aeneid,* which tells the story of Rome's legendary founder and proclaims the Roman mission to civilize the world under divine guidance. His reputation as a poet endures not only for the music and diction of his verse and for his skill in constructing an intricate work on the grand scale but because he embodied in his poetry aspects of experience and behaviour of permanent significance.

Publius Vergilius Maro (the spelling Virgil has become traditional in English, although the form Vergil also is current) was born of peasant stock at Andes, near Mantua, in Italy on October 15, 70 BC. His love of the Italian countryside and of the people who cultivated it colours all his poetry. He was educated at Cremona, at Milan, and finally at Rome, acquiring a thorough knowledge of Greek and Roman authors, especially of the poets, and receiving a detailed training in rhetoric and philosophy. It is known that one of his teachers was the Epicurean Siro, and the Epicurean philosophy is substantially reflected in his early poetry but gradually gives way to attitudes more akin to Stoicism.

Political background. During Virgil's youth, as the Roman Republic neared its end, the political and military situation in Italy was confused and often calamitous. The civil war between Marius and Sulla had been succeeded by conflict between Pompey and Julius Caesar for supreme power. When Virgil was 20, Caesar with his armies swooped south from Gaul, crossed the Rubicon,

Virgil (centre) holding a scroll with a quotation from the *Aeneid,* with the epic Muse (left) and the tragic Muse (right), Roman mosaic, 2nd–3rd century AD. In the Musée Le Bardo, Tunis.
By courtesy of the Musee Le Bardo, Tunis

and began the series of civil wars that were not to end until Augustus' victory at Actium in 31 BC. Hatred and fear of civil war is powerfully expressed by both Virgil and his contemporary Horace. The key to a proper understanding of the Augustan Age and its poets lies, indeed, in a proper understanding of the turmoil that had preceded the Augustan peace.

Personal life

Virgil's life was devoted entirely to his poetry and to studies connected with it; his health was never robust, and he played no part in military or political life. It is said that he spoke once in the lawcourts without distinction and that his shy and retiring nature caused him to give up any ideas he might have had of taking part in the world of affairs. He never married, and the first half of his life was that of a scholar and near recluse. But, as his poetry won him fame, he gradually won the friendship of many important men in the Roman world. Gradually, also, he became a Roman as well as a provincial. (The area in which he had spent his youth, the area around the River Po known as the province of Cisalpine Gaul, was not finally incorporated into Italy until 42 BC. Thus Virgil came, as it were, to Rome from the outside. The enthusiasm of a provincial for Rome is seen in the first eclogue, one of his earliest poems, in which the shepherd Tityrus tells of his recent visit to the capital and his amazement at its splendours.)

Literary career. Some of Virgil's earliest poetry may have survived in a collection of poems attributed to him and known as the *Appendix Vergiliana,* but it is unlikely that many of these are genuine. His earliest certain work is the *Eclogues,* a collection of ten pastoral poems composed between 42–37 BC. Some of them are escapist, literary excursions to the idyllic pastoral world of Arcadia based on the Greek poet Theocritus (flourished *c.* 280 BC) but more unreal and stylized. They convey in liquid song the idealized situations of an imaginary world in which shepherds sing in the sunshine of their simple joys and mute their sorrows (whether for unhappy love or untimely death) in a formalized pathos. But some bring the pastoral mode into touch with the real world, either directly or by means of allegory, and thus gave a new direction to the genre. The fifth eclogue, on the death of Daphnis, king of shepherds, clearly has some relationship with the recent death of Julius Caesar; the tenth brings Gallus, a fellow poet who also held high office as a statesman, into the pastoral world; the first and ninth are lamentations over the expulsion of shepherds from their farms. (It was widely believed in antiquity that these poems expressed allegorically Virgil's own loss of his family farm when the veteran soldiers of Antony and Octavian—later the emperor Augustus—were resettled after the Battle of Philippi in 42 BC. It was thought that he subsequently recovered his property through the intervention of his powerful friends. However that may be, it is certain that the poems are based on Virgil's own experience, whether in connection with his own farm or with those of his friends; and they express, with a poignant pathos that has come to be regarded as specially Virgilian, the sorrow of the dispossessed.)

But one eclogue in particular stands out as having relevance to the contemporary situation, and this is the fourth (sometimes called the Messianic, because it was later regarded as prophetic of Christianity). It is an elevated poem, prophesying in sonorous and mystic terms the birth of a child who will bring back the Golden Age, banish sin, and restore peace. It was clearly written at a time when the clouds of civil war seemed to be lifting; it can be dated firmly to 41–40 BC, and it seems most likely that Virgil refers to an expected child of the triumvir Antony and his wife Octavia, sister of Octavian. But, though a specific occasion may be allocated to the poem, it goes beyond the particular and, in symbolic terms, presents a vision of world harmony, which was, to some extent, destined to be realized under Augustus.

One of the most disastrous effects of the civil wars— and one of which Virgil, as a countryman, would be most intensely aware—was the depopulation of rural Italy. The farmers had been obliged to go to the war, and their farms fell into neglect and ruin as a result. The *Georgics,* composed between 36 and 29 BC (the final period of the civil wars), is a superb plea for the restoration of the traditional agricultural life of Italy. In form it is didactic, but, as Seneca later said, it was written "not to instruct farmers but to delight readers." The practical instruction (about plowing, growing trees, tending cattle, and keeping bees) is presented with vivid insight into nature, and it is interspersed with highly wrought poetical digressions on

Composition of the *Georgics*

such topics as the beauty of the Italian countryside (Book II. line 136 ff.) and the joy of the farmer when all is gathered in (II.458 ff.).

The *Georgics* is dedicated (at the beginning of each book) to Maecenas, one of the chief of Augustus' ministers, who was also the leading patron of the arts. By this time Virgil was a member of what might be called the court circle, and his desire to see his beloved Italy restored to its former glories coincided with the national requirement of resettling the land and diminishing the pressure on the cities. It would be wrong to think of Virgil as writing political propaganda; but equally it would be wrong to regard his poetry as unconnected with the major currents of political and social needs of the time. Virgil was personally committed to the same ideals as the government.

In the year 31 BC, when Virgil was 38, Augustus (still known as Octavian) won the final battle of the civil wars at Actium against the forces of Antony and Cleopatra and from that time dates the Augustan Age. Virgil, like many of his contemporaries, felt a great sense of relief that the senseless civil strife was at last over and was deeply grateful to the man who had made it possible. Augustus was anxious to preserve the traditions of the republic and its constitutional forms, but he was in fact sole ruler of the Roman world. He used his power to establish a period of peace and stability and endeavoured to reawaken in the Romans a sense of national pride and a new enthusiasm for their ancestral religion and their traditional moral values, those of bravery, parsimony, duty, responsibility, and family devotion. Virgil, too, as a countryman at heart, felt a deep attachment to the simple virtues and religious traditions of the Italian people. All his life he had been preparing himself to write an epic poem (regarded then as the highest form of poetic achievement), and he now set out to embody his ideal Rome in the *Aeneid,* the story of the foundation of the first settlement in Italy, from which Rome was to spring, by an exiled Trojan prince after the destruction of Troy by the Greeks in the 12th century BC. The theme he chose gave him two great advantages: one was that its date and subject was very close to that of Homer's *Iliad* and *Odyssey,* so that he could remodel episodes and characters from his great Greek predecessor; and the other was that it could be brought into relationship with his contemporary Augustan world by presenting Aeneas as the prototype of the Roman way of life (the last of the Trojans and the first of the Romans). Moreover, by the use of prophecies and visions and devices such as the description of the pictures on Aeneas' shield or of the origins of contemporary customs and institutions, it could foreshadow the real events of Roman history. The poem, then, operates on a double time scale; it is heroic and yet Augustan.

The enthusiasm that Virgil felt for the reborn Rome promised by Augustus' regime is often reflected in the poem. The sonorous and awe-inspiring prophecy by Jupiter (I.257 ff.), giving a picture of Rome's divinely inspired destiny, has a moving patriotic impact: "To these I set no bounds in space or time—I have given them rule without end" (278–279); and again, under Augustus, "Then shall the harsh generations be softened, and wars shall be laid aside" (291). The speech ends with a memorable image depicting the personified figure of Frenzy in chains, gnashing its bloodstained teeth in vain. At the end of the sixth book, Aeneas visits the underworld, and there pass before his eyes the figures of heroes from Roman history, waiting to be born. The ghost of his father (Anchises) describes them to him and ends by defining the Roman mission as one concerned with government and civilization (compared with the Greek achievement in art and literature and theoretical science). "Rule the people with your sway, spare the conquered, and war down the proud": this is the vision of Rome's destiny that the emperor Augustus and the poet Virgil had before them—that Rome was divinely appointed first to conquer the world in war and then to spread civilization and the rule of law among the peoples. As Horace told the Romans in one of his odes, "Because you are servants of the gods, you are masters on earth."

The vision of Rome that the *Aeneid* expresses is a noble one, but the real greatness of the poem is due to Virgil's

Virgil's attachment to simple virtues and traditions

awareness of the private, as well as the public, aspects of human life. The *Aeneid* is no panegyric; it sets the achievements and aspirations of the giant organization of Roman governmental rule in tension with the frustrated hopes and sufferings of individuals. The most memorable figure in the poem—and, it has been said, the only character to be created by a Roman poet that has passed into world literature—is Dido, Queen of Carthage, opponent of the Roman way of life. In a mere panegyric of Rome, she could have been presented in such a way that Aeneas' rejection of her would have been a victory to applaud; but, in fact, in the fourth book she wins so much sympathy that the reader wonders whether Rome should be bought at this price. Again, Turnus, who opposes Aeneas when he lands in Italy, resists the invader who has come to steal his bride. It is clear that Turnus is a less civilized character than Aeneas—but in his defeat Virgil allows him to win much sympathy. These are two examples of the tension against Roman optimism; in many other ways, too, Virgil throughout the poem explores the problems of suffering and the pathos of the human situation. Yet in the end, Aeneas endures and continues to his goal; his devotion to duty (*pietas*) prevails, and the Roman reader would feel that this should be. "So great a task it was to found the Roman nation" (I.33).

The *Aeneid* occupied Virgil for 11 years and, at his death, had not yet received its final revision. In 19 BC, planning to spend a further three years on his poem, he set out for Greece—doubtless to obtain local colour for the revision of those parts of the *Aeneid* set in Greek waters. On the voyage he caught a fever and returned to Italy but died soon after arrival at Brundisium. Whether the *Aeneid* would have undergone major changes cannot be guessed: the story goes that Virgil's dying wish was for his poem to be burned, but that this request was countermanded by the order of Augustus. As it stands, the poem is a major monument both to the national achievements and ideals of the Augustan Age of Rome and to the sensitive and lonely voice of the poet who knew the "tears in things" as well as the glory.

Influence and reputation. Virgil's poetry immediately became famous in Rome and was admired by the Romans for two main reasons—first, because he was regarded as their own national poet, spokesman of their ideals and achievements; second, because he seemed to have reached the ultimate of perfection in his art (his structure, diction, metre). For the latter reason, his poems were used as school textbooks, and the 1st-century Roman critic and teacher Quintilian recommended that the educational curriculum should be based on Virgil's works. A few years after his death, Virgil was being imitated and echoed by the younger poet Ovid, and this process continued throughout the Silver Age. The study of Virgil in the schools has lasted as long as Latin has been studied. By the 4th century a new reason for admiration was gaining ground: the store of wisdom and knowledge discovered by scholars in Virgil's poems—for which he was saluted not only as a poet but as a repository of information. This aspect figures largely in the writings of the writer and philosopher Macrobius (flourished *c.* AD 400), those of Virgil's commentator Servius of the late 4th and early 5th century, and of many later writers. Allegorical interpretations began to gain ground and, under Christian influence, became especially widespread throughout the Middle Ages. The two main bases for Christian allegorization were the fourth eclogue, believed to be a prophecy of the birth of Christ, and the near-Christian values expressed in the *Aeneid,* especially in its hero, a man devoted to his divine mission. The culmination of this view is Virgil's place of honour in Dante's *Divine Comedy* as the poet's guide through Hell and Purgatory up to the very gates of Paradise.

Virgil's influence on English literature has been enormous. He is Spenser's constant inspiration for the fanciful beauty of *The Faerie Queene.* The *Aeneid* is the model for Milton's *Paradise Lost* not only in epic structure and machinery but also in style and diction. In the English Augustan age, John Dryden and countless others held that Virgil's poetry had reached the ultimate perfection of form and ethical content. There was some reaction against him in the Romantic period, but the Victorians, such as Matthew Arnold and Alfred, Lord Tennyson, rediscovered in full measure that sensitivity and pathos that the Romantics had complained he lacked.

MAJOR WORKS

Eclogae (42–37 BC; *Eclogues*), comprising 10 poems also known as the *Bucolica; Georgica* (36–29 BC; *Georgics*), comprising 4 books of poems on farming and rural life in Italy; *Aeneis* (30–19 BC; *Aeneid*), an epic poem in 12 books.

There are many English translations of Virgil's works including verse translations by Gavin Douglas (1553), John Dryden (1697), C. Day Lewis (1940–63), and Rolfe Humphries (1951). Among prose translations are those by J.W. Mackail (2nd ed. rev., 1908–14), H.R. Fairclough ("Loeb Series," 1934–35); and W.F. Jackson Knight (1956). There is a French translation of all the works in the "Budé Series" (1926–56).

BIBLIOGRAPHY. Detailed bibliographical information about Virgil may be found in the lists in *L'Année philologique* (annual). In English there are bibliographical surveys by G.E. DUCKWORTH, *Classical World,* vol. 51 (1957–58) and vol. 57 (1963–64), reissued as *Recent Work on Vergil,* 2 vol. (1964); the summaries in *Vergilius* (annual), the journal of the Vergilian Society (U.S.); the reviews of important modern works in the *Proceedings of the Virgil Society* (annual), the journal of the Virgil Society (U.K.); and the survey by R.D. WILLIAMS, *Virgil* (1967).

Texts: The best texts of Virgil's work (including discussion of the manuscripts) are those of R.A.B. MYNORS, "Oxford Classical Texts" (1969), replacing Hirtzel's 1900 edition; R. SABBADINI (1930; reprinted with minor alterations by L. CASTIGLIONI, 1945–52); E. DE SAINT-DENIS (*Eclogues,* 1942; *Georgics,* 1956); and GOELZER-DURAND-BELLESSORT, *Aeneid,* 2 vol. (1925–36), in the "Budé Series."

Commentaries: The commentaries by SERVIUS have been edited by GEORG THILO and HERMANN HAGEN, *Servii Grammatici qvi fervntvr in Vergilii carmina commentarii,* 3 vol. (1881–1902); and by EDWARD K. RAND *et al.* (*Aeneid,* books 1 and 2, 1946; books 3 to 5, 1965); JAMES HENRY, *Aeneidea,* 4 vol. (1873–92, reprinted 1972); CONINGTON-NETTLESHIP-HAVERFIELD, 3 vol. (1858–98); THOMAS E. PAGE, *The Aeneid of Virgil* (1894–1900); and R.D. WILLIAMS, *The Aeneid of Virgil,* 2 vol. (1972–73).

Biography and criticism: For such biographical facts as are known about Virgil, see the introduction to JOHN W. MACKAIL, *Aeneid* (1930); and W.F. JACKSON KNIGHT, *Roman Vergil,* rev. ed. (1966, reissued 1971). GILBERT A. HIGHET, *Poets in a Landscape* (1957, reprinted 1979), gives a popular and readable account. The ancient sources are collected in *Vitae Vergilianae Antiquae* (1954, reissued 1966). An excellent critical evaluation of Virgil's *Aeneid* is W.A. CAMPS, *An Introduction to Virgil's Aeneid* (1969). Other important works are T.R. GLOVER, *Virgil,* 7th ed. (1942, reissued 1969); C.M. BOWRA, *From Virgil to Milton* (1945, reissued 1967); BROOKS OTIS, *Virgil: A Study in Civilised Poetry* (1963); KENNETH QUINN, *Virgil's Aeneid: A Critical Description* (1968); D.R. DUDLEY (ed.), *Virgil* (1969); and J. WILLIAM HUNT, *Forms of Glory* (1973), an introductory study of the *Aeneid.* On the *Eclogues,* HERBERT J. ROSE, *The Eclogues of Vergil* (1942); and WILLIAM BERG, *Early Virgil* (1974); on the *Georgics,* L.P. WILKINSON, *The Georgics of Virgil* (1969, reissued 1978); MICHAEL C.J. PUTNAM, *Virgil's Poem of the Earth* (1979); and GARY B. MILES, *Virgil's Georgics: A New Interpretation* (1980). On Virgil's influence, see G.A. HIGHET, *The Classical Tradition* (1949, reissued 1967); R.R. BOLGAR, *The Classical Heritage and Its Beneficiaries* (1954, reissued 1973); D. COMPARETTI, *Vergil in the Middle Ages* (1895); J.H. WHITFIELD, "Virgil into Dante"; and R.D. WILLIAMS, "Changing Attitudes to Virgil," chapters 4 and 5 in D.R. DUDLEY (cited above). (R.D.W./Ed.)

Viruses

Viruses are a unique group of infectious agents that are characterized by their small size, simple composition, and the need to grow in an animal, plant, or bacterial cell. In general, viruses are much smaller than bacteria, ranging in size from about 20 to 400 nanometres (nm) in diameter (1 nanometre = 10^{-9} metre). They are composed of a core of nucleic acid, a coat of protein, and, in some cases, lipid (fatty) and carbohydrate material. Viruses vary in their detailed morphology (form and structure) and in their specificity for different types of host cells.

Some viruses are known to cause diseases in animals, man, and plants. Cancer is one of the many diseases in humans suspected of having a viral origin. Besides being of great interest from a medical and agricultural point of view, viruses are useful to the researcher in investigating the mechanisms of normal cell function.

This article is divided into the following sections:

HISTORICAL BACKGROUND

Identification of viral diseases. Viral diseases have been known to man for many years. Historic accounts of a smallpox-like disease are found in Chinese literature of the 10th century BC. Yellow fever, another viral disease, has been known for centuries in tropical Africa. Since the 18th century, the virus that causes cowpox has been used in vaccines to prevent smallpox; the French chemist Louis Pasteur developed an attenuated (weakened) rabies virus for therapeutic use in 1884. Viral diseases of plants have been known for several hundred years; one in particular, tulip break virus, has been cultivated since the 16th century because of its use in producing an ornamental variegation in the tulip bloom. A tobacco disease characterized by mottled or "mosaic" lesions on the leaves was shown in 1898–99 to be transmitted by a submicroscopic agent (*i.e.,* virus) in the tobacco sap of infected plants. Because this and similar agents could not be removed by the finest of filters—those that could separate bacteria from other materials—such biological entities were called filterable agents. In 1911 it was found that such a filterable agent, or virus, could produce malignant tumours in chickens. This finding was the prelude to the eventual discovery of many types of tumour-producing viruses in both animals and plants. (For a discussion of viral diseases, see below

Pathogenesis of viral disease. See also the *Macropædia* articles INFECTIOUS DISEASES; DISEASE.)

Development of modern virology. It was not until the independent discovery of viruses that infect bacteria (bacteriophages, or phages) by two bacteriologists, Frederick William Twort in 1915 and Felix d'Hérelle in 1917, that modern virology began. These workers convincingly demonstrated the particulate nature of viruses and developed the simple but elegant and useful assay technique still used for determining the total number of infectious viral particles in a culture. The technique involves the mixing of a small number of viruses (about 100) with a large excess of sensitive bacterial cells (about 1,000,000) in a culture medium of melted agar and allowing the agar mixture to cool and solidify; a virus particle diffuses through the agar until it encounters a bacterial cell, which it then infects. After 20 to 30 minutes, the infected cell bursts, releasing 50 to 100 progeny that infect other bacteria nearby. Meanwhile, the bacteria remote from a virus particle continue to grow, forming an opaque "lawn" of confluent bacteria. Against this background "lawn," areas of viral growth are seen as clear, round plaques that are devoid of bacteria. The number of plaques represent the number of infectious viruses in the mixture.

The ease of experimentation with bacterial viruses (phages) attracted many scientists in the 1940s and 1950s interested in problems related to the chemistry of heredity. These scientists have been responsible for much of the recent progress in molecular biology. Today, there is hardly an area of biology that has not felt the impact of discoveries related to bacteriophages.

MORPHOLOGY AND CHEMISTRY OF VIRUSES

Detailed study of various types of viruses reveals a remarkable variation in size, shape, and composition. Some viruses have a core of deoxyribonucleic acid (DNA); others have a core of ribonucleic acid (RNA). Depending on the type of virus, the nucleic acid component may be composed of either one strand or two strands. All viruses have a coat of protein, called the capsid, around the nucleic acid core. Some viruses also contain one or more proteins associated with the core. The function of these proteins, called internal proteins, has not yet been established with certainty. Some viruses that infect animal cells have additional structural components, such as a lipid-containing membranous envelope surrounding the virus. The presence of this membrane usually renders the virus susceptible to inactivation by agents that dissolve lipids, such as ether and chloroform. Only one bacterial virus is known to contain some lipid material that appears in an envelope-like structure surrounding the particle. Thus, the complete virus particle, which is called a virion, is composed of a nucleic acid core, capsid proteins, and, in some cases, internal proteins and an outer envelope.

Classification of viruses. At present, no generally accepted, satisfactory scheme for the classification of viruses exists. Classification usually means grouping related organisms together. In the case of viruses, however, it is not clear what criteria should be used to define relatedness. Morphology, chemical composition, host cell type, and physiological characteristics are not satisfactory criteria for classification purposes. Moreover, there is little to suggest evolutionary relationships among viruses. Yet certain viruses, such as the bacteriophages T2, T4, and T6, are clearly genetically related because the structures of their DNAs have significant similarities.

A meaningful classification scheme based on the genetic relatedness of many viruses may eventually result from recent studies concerning the degree of similarity between the DNA of one virus and that of another. In the meantime, lacking a suitable classification system, the

Assay technique

Names of viruses

nomenclature of animal and plant viruses has generally been derived from the name of the disease produced by the virus—*e.g.,* poliovirus, measles virus. Bacterial viruses (bacteriophages), on the other hand, have been designated by laboratory code names related to the order in which they were isolated or to certain growth characteristics, such as phages T1, T3, T7, lambda, MS2 (*m*ale-*s*pecific 2), φX174, and fd. Although this way of naming viruses may be convenient for the virologist, it does not help to systematize knowledge about them.

A classification system that does seem useful is one that has been proposed by André Michael Lwoff, a French microbiologist and virologist. Lwoff's system is based on the structure and composition of the virions: viruses are divided into DNA- and RNA-containing types; capsid (coat protein) symmetry and structure are additional major classification features. This system results in the grouping of known related viruses, such as T3 and T7 bacteriophages, and also the placing in the same group of such seemingly unrelated viruses as poliovirus and tomato bushy-stunt virus. Although the last two viruses are morphologically and chemically very similar, their hosts are quite different—*i.e.,* mammals and plants, respectively.

Shape and structure. The gross morphology of viruses can be studied with the electron microscope (Figure 1).

By courtesy of (top right) I. Brunovskis and H. Zweernik

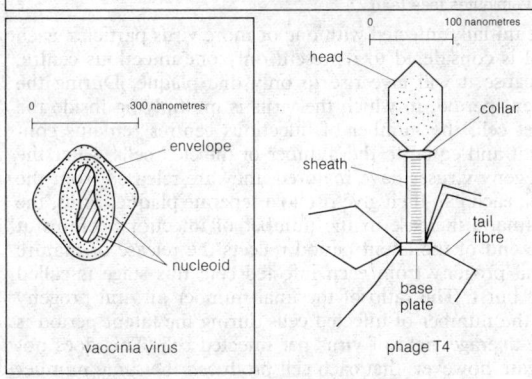

Figure 1: *The morphology of several types of virus.* (A) Bacteriophage T7 (the scale marker indicates 100 nanometres). (B) Vaccinia virus (cowpox). (C) Bacteriophage T4.

Some viruses appear as long, rodlike filaments, such as tobacco mosaic virus (TMV) and bacteriophage fd. Others, such as poliovirus and bacteriophage φX174, are small spherical structures. Larger bacteriophages, such as T4, have a "head" that is roughly hexagonal in shape and a complicated "tail" structure. Viruses with envelopes are usually large (about 200 to 400 nm in diameter) and show evidence of surface structure. Some have a structurally distinct core called the nucleoid body. Detailed study of the filamentous phage fd shows that it is composed of about 1,920 protein molecules called B-protein with a molecular weight of 5,170 amu (atomic mass units; 1 amu = 1.66×10^{-24} gram) and one molecule of another protein called A-protein with a molecular weight of 70,000 amu. The molecules of B-protein are arranged around a core consisting of one single-stranded DNA molecule with a molecular weight of 2,000,000 amu. The single molecule of A-protein is believed to be located at one end of the phage and may serve to attach the virus to its host.

The protein structure of the small spherical phage φX174 has been shown to be icosahedral (20-sided) in shape, with

a "spike" structure at each of its 12 vertexes consisting of proteins that are different from those of the coat. The shape of many animal viruses, such as the influenza virus, on the other hand, is less well defined; they occur in a variety of shapes, from spherical to ovoid. This plasticity may result from the fact that the nucleoprotein core is enclosed within a flexible lipid-containing, membranous-like envelope. Yet other enveloped viruses, such as the one that causes encephalitis, appear spherical.

Nucleic acid core. *Number and size of molecules.* The study of the structure of the nucleic acid component of viruses has attracted much attention. The first problem to be considered by investigators was the number and size of the nucleic acid molecules in each virion. In general, the core of most viruses contains only one molecule of either DNA or RNA. In a few cases, however, the RNA core seems to consist of multiple pieces of RNA that are not chemically linked to each other.

The problem of determining the number of nucleic acid molecules in a viral core was initially approached by comparing the number of radioactive phosphorus (^{32}P) atoms in an intact virus (bacteriophage T2) with the number of ^{32}P atoms in a DNA molecule that had been extracted from the same virus preparation. Because the number of ^{32}P atoms in the virus was found to be the same as that in the extracted DNA molecule, it was concluded that there is only one DNA molecule in each virus particle. The specific activity (number of ^{32}P atoms per amu of nucleic acid), which can be obtained from the total extracted DNA, can be combined with the number of ^{32}P atoms per virus to calculate the size of the DNA molecule in the virus. *(margin note: Radioactive analysis)*

Because phosphorus is found only in the nucleic acid component, the ratio of nucleic acid to protein can be determined by chemically analyzing the phosphorus and nitrogen content of a virus. This information, together with the total size of the virus, allows an independent calculation of the size of the nucleic acid molecule in a virion. These results agree remarkably well with those obtained from the radioactivity method described above. The problem of determining the size of nucleic acid molecules is a difficult one, because the usual techniques of macromolecular (large-molecule) chemistry are difficult to apply directly to these large molecules.

Identification of the nucleic acid. The type of nucleic acid (DNA or RNA) in the core of a virus has been determined in several ways. Direct chemical analysis of the nucleic acid for the sugar component of nucleic acids (ribose or deoxyribose) is used if large quantities of virus are available. Enzymes (biological catalysts) that specifically break down either DNA or RNA sometimes are used but may give incorrect results; *e.g.,* one virus with a double-stranded form of RNA is resistant to the degradative action of the enzyme ribonuclease, which is effective only with single-stranded RNA. Hence the lack of action of ribonuclease could lead to the erroneous conclusion that the nucleic acid is DNA. Another method for determining the type of viral nucleic acid is by measuring its buoyant density when spun in a centrifuge with a salt solution such as cesium chloride; DNA and RNA each have characteristic density ranges.

Labelling with specific radioactive precursors (compounds used in the formation of other substances) has also been used to determine if the core of a virus contains RNA or DNA. The compound uracil, for example, is usually found only in RNA, whereas the compound thymine is a component of DNA. There are, however, exceptions, such as the bacteriophage PBS-2, in which the DNA contains uracil instead of thymine.

Identification of "strandedness." In addition to size and type, the shape of the nucleic acid in a virus is also important. Some viral DNAS and RNAS consist of a single-stranded molecule; others consist of a double-stranded molecule. In general, viruses whose cores contain single-stranded DNA are small; those that contain double-stranded DNA vary from small to large. On the other hand, viruses whose cores contain double-stranded RNA are large; those that contain single-stranded RNA range from very small to very large. *(margin note: "Stranded-ness" and size)*

The "strandedness" of a viral nucleic acid can be determined by an analysis of several of its physical and chemical properties; for example, in certain kinds of solutions double-stranded nucleic acid melts at temperatures between 70° and 90° C (160° and 190° F). At the melting temperature, a sharp change occurs in certain properties of the DNA; these changes indicate that the two strands have separated into a single-stranded nucleic acid. Such melting transitions do not occur in nucleic acids that are initially single stranded.

In addition, an analysis of the component subunits (nucleotides) or bases of the nucleic acid can help determine if the molecule is single or double stranded. The amount of guanine in double-stranded nucleic acid molecules must equal the amount of cytosine, and the amount of adenine must equal the amount of thymine (or uracil in RNA). This condition is imposed by the base pairing that is necessary in a double-stranded nucleic acid structure (see GENETICS AND HEREDITY).

Double-stranded nucleic acids also react with such compounds as the dye acridine orange so that molecules of the dye are inserted between adjacent base pairs (guanine-cytosine and adenine-thymine). Because single-stranded nucleic acid does not have such an arrangement of base pairs, the reaction with the dye molecules does not occur.

Electron-microscopic studies of viral nucleic acid molecules have shown that they are either linear or circular. The small, single-stranded DNAs from the bacteriophages φX174 and fd exist in the virion as closed loops. The double-stranded DNA from polyoma virus, SV-40, and phage PM-2 is a closed structure that appears tangled upon itself as a result of extra twists in the helical (spiral) configuration of the DNA molecule. The molecule can be converted to a "relaxed" (untangled) circular form by cutting one strand. It is believed that the circular form of the DNA is important in the synthesis of progeny viral DNA during the process of viral multiplication.

VIRAL GROWTH AND DEVELOPMENT

Because the processes of viral multiplication have been extensively studied, many details of viral growth and development are now known. As pointed out above, viruses must inhabit a host cell in order to grow and multiply. Their growth cycle begins with their attachment (adsorption) to a susceptible cell. The nucleic acid component and, in some cases, the protein components of the virus then enter the host cell, after which intracellular viral development proceeds under the direction of the viral genome (its collection of genes). Specific steps in viral development include replication (duplication) of its nucleic acid, which creates numerous progeny viral genomes, and virus-directed protein synthesis to produce the protein components necessary for the assemblage of complete virions, which are finally discharged from the cell. A change in the structure of the virus may give rise to viral strains that can infect a wider variety of host cells than can the parental strain. These altered particles are said to have an extended host range.

Summary of growth cycle

Viral adsorption. Adsorption of a bacteriophage to a host cell requires the interaction of a specific viral structure with a specific site on the surface of the host bacterial cell. If the virus does not have the appropriate structure, it cannot adsorb to certain cells. Similarly, the phage cannot adsorb to certain cells. Similarly, the phage cannot adsorb if the host cell lacks the appropriate site, in which case the cell is resistant to infection by that particular virus. The phages fd, R17, and Qβ, for example, adsorb to a structure on the bacterium *Escherichia coli* that is called the F-pilus. Because this structure is present only on certain *E. coli* (*i.e.*, those of the "male mating type), the phages can infect only "male" *E. coli*.

In addition to the necessity for appropriate structures on the virus and its host, other factors can influence viral adsorption—notably physiological conditions during the infective process. Bacteriophage T4, for example, requires the presence of the amino acid tryptophan for successful infection; the presence or absence of salt may also affect viral adsorption. The attachment of T4 is mediated by its "tail," which frequently is composed of several components, such as tail fibres, a base plate, and a tube-and-sheath arrangement through which the nucleic acid core passes from the virus "head" into the host cell (Figure 1). Although the mechanism by which phages "inject" their nucleic acid into the host cell is not yet fully understood, it is known that the protein head and tail remain outside the cell; the nucleic acid molecule enters the cell and initiates the process of infection.

Growth of bacterial viruses. Bacteriophage growth can be studied by simultaneously infecting most of the cells in a culture. If the titre (concentration) of infectious units is determined at various times after infection, a period occurs during which the number of so-called infectious centres remains constant; following this, a rapid and usually large increase occurs in the number of such centres (see Figure 2). This may be interpreted as follows. Although all cells

Infectious centres

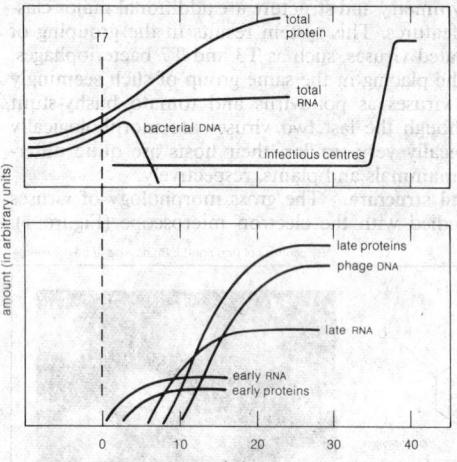

Figure 2: Times course of an infection of *Escherichia coli* with a bacteriophage, such as T7. Dissolution of the culture, with the production of a phage burst, occurred at 35 minutes (see text).

are initially infected with one or more virus particles, each cell is considered to represent only one infectious centre, because it will give rise to only one plaque. During the latent period, in which the virus is multiplying inside the host cell, the number of infectious centres remains constant and equal to the number of infected cells. After the progeny viruses have matured, they are released from the cell; each can then give rise to a separate plaque. Thus, the dramatic increase in the number of infectious centres at the end of the latent period reflects the release of mature viral progeny from each infected cell; this stage is called the burst. The ratio of the final number of viral progeny to the number of infected cells during the latent period is the average yield of virus per infected cell. This does not mean, however, that each cell produced the same number of progeny. To determine the size of the progeny burst from each infected cell, a somewhat different experimental method is used.

In the so-called single-burst experiment, the infected cells are diluted during the latent period into numerous small test tubes, so that the chances are small (because of the highly diluted culture) that any one tube will contain more than one infected cell. The infected cells are then allowed to complete the infectious cycle and burst, after which the total number of viral progeny in each tube is determined by the plaque-assay method (see above *Development of modern virology*). The single-burst experiment provides an estimate of the variation in burst size from cell to cell in a population of infected cells. Results from experiments with phages of *E. coli* show that single bursts can vary by a factor of eight or ten, indicating the variability of intracellular multiplication of the virus.

RNA synthesis. After viral nucleic acid has been injected into the sensitive host cell, an orderly sequence of biochemical steps ensues, during which the viral genes direct the various processes involved in viral multiplication and in the eventual assembly of mature progeny viruses. The first event after injection of the nucleic acid is probably the specific association of the viral genome with some component of the host cell, perhaps a membrane-bound

Messen-
ger RNA

site. This part of the infectious process is not yet well understood.

Subsequently, certain genes in the viral genome direct the production of a phage-specific nucleic acid that is called messenger RNA, or mRNA. The mRNA molecules, which serve as the template for protein synthesis during the latent period of viral multiplication, can be divided into two general classes, early and late RNAs. These classes were originally defined according to the time of protein synthesis during the course of an infection. The terminology has now been modified, so that the early RNA refers to that class of viral RNA molecules whose production is initiated by the chemical machinery that is already present in the host cell prior to its infection by the virus. In general, the production of the late class of RNA molecules requires the functioning of at least one protein that is coded by the virus. In some viruses, the late class may be further divided into subclasses on the basis of the same principles—an early protein is needed for synthesis of late class A RNA, and a late class A protein is needed for synthesis of late class B RNA.

Because it is a model for the general problem of how certain genetic control mechanisms function, the mechanism by which the switch from early to late RNA synthesis is mediated has been the subject of intense study. In the case of bacteriophage, the early RNA is copied (transcribed) from the viral DNA genome by an enzyme in the host cell, RNA polymerase. The activation of late RNA synthesis is accomplished in one of several ways, each of which is characteristic of a particular virus. In the case of phage T7 of *E. coli,* for example, one protein synthesized by the early RNA is a new phage-specific RNA polymerase, which is able to copy only the late genes of the phage into late RNA. In the case of phage T4, one protein synthesized by the early RNA seems to result in the modification of the RNA polymerase of the host in such a way that it will copy a subclass of the late genes. One or more of these late proteins is responsible for directing the modified host RNA polymerase to copy the remaining late genes. The exact mechanism of this second switch in RNA synthesis is not yet known.

Protein synthesis. As implied in the above discussion of the classes of RNA molecules produced after viral infection, the various phage-specified proteins can be grouped into the same classes, because the proteins are the direct product of the translation of the early and late RNAs. (Translation is the formation of a protein under the direction of a specific mRNA molecule.) In general, the early proteins are enzymes that function to replicate the viral DNA, inactivate the host cell, and activate late genes, which are generally responsible for producing proteins that comprise the structure of the mature viral particle; *e.g,* head and tail components. The early proteins (enzymes) made by phage T4 include DNA polymerase and enzymes that break down the host DNA to nucleotide subunits that are utilized by the virus in forming its own nucleic acid.

Assembly of the viral particle. Also well studied has been the replication of the nucleic acid of the injected viral genome, which functions as a template for the synthesis of multiple copies of progeny molecules. These progeny genomes are packaged in the coat and other structural proteins and then released from the cell as mature infectious virus particles.

The assembly of a virus particle seems to be a stepwise process. In the case of phage T4 at least, it starts with the aggregation of the phage head proteins into a regular array to form a structure that is filled with the newly synthesized DNA. The various tail structure components then attach to the DNA-containing head. Because some of the assembly steps seem to be spontaneous—*i.e.,* they occur without any enzymatic involvement—it would appear that the shape of the protein molecules relative to the sites at which they bind to other protein molecules must in some way specify the very well-ordered morphology of the virus particle. Other assembly steps, however, require the action of a specific enzyme to direct the specific interaction necessary for assembling parts of the T4 particle. In the case of the tobacco mosaic virus (TMV), the assembly of the virus can proceed in the test tube without the action of additional enzymes. The RNA molecule in TMV serves as a core along which the TMV coat protein molecules aggregate in a very specific and well-ordered way to form an infectious particle.

Although the release of the virus from the infected cell is not well understood, it seems to depend on the rupture of the host cell wall by a combination of processes. The structure of the cell wall can be weakened by enzymes, such as lysozyme, produced by the virus; metabolic alterations in the infected cell have also been implicated in the disruption of the cell membrane.

Release of
progeny

Other replication mechanisms. For the most part, replication of the small, single-stranded DNA phages is similar to the general procedures described above for double-stranded phages, with the following exceptions: only the early class of RNAs and proteins occur; because the injected DNA genome is single stranded, it is replicated in a rather specialized and complicated manner; and, in the case of the filamentous phages (fd, fl, M-13), the progeny viruses are released from the infected cell without lysis (dissolution) and killing of the host.

Another exception to the general mechanism for viral replication is found in those viruses in which single-stranded RNA is already present as the genetic material. Because these viruses utilize their genome directly, as messenger RNA, they do not have to use host enzymes, nor do the host cells have enzymes capable of replicating the RNA genome. Instead, its replication is accomplished by a viral enzyme, RNA replicase. This enzyme first transcribes the single stand of RNA into a double-stranded RNA molecule; it then copies this molecule to generate a large number of single-stranded RNA molecules. Because RNA phage genomes are easy to prepare, relatively small, and synthesize only three proteins, they have been extensively used as a model system for studying the structure and function of messenger RNA molecules.

Growth of animal viruses. Viruses that infect animal cells differ in two general aspects from the bacteriophage systems described above. The entry and exit of the virus is more complicated, and, in a number of instances, the virus carries some proteins with key enzymatic functions into the cell in the process of infection. Animal viruses do not possess the elaborate tail structure typical of many bacteriophages. Instead, they seem to enter the cell by adsorption to specific sites on the membrane of susceptible cells and then undergo a series of poorly understood steps that result in the penetration of all or part of the virus particle into the cell. It has been suggested that the interaction of the cell membrane receptor site with the capsid proteins or the membranous envelope of the virus causes a rearrangement of the virus structure that enables it to inject its nucleic acid core into the host cell. In the case of some viruses—*e.g., vaccinia* (the cowpox virus)—an "uncoating" process takes place inside the host cell; during this process, the lipid portion of the virus is stripped off, presumably by enzymes already present in the cell. The second stage of the uncoating process requires the synthesis of a new protein under the direction of either the entering viral particle or a host protein.

It has been demonstrated that many animal virus particles already contain enzymes as part of their complement of protein. One such enzyme is an RNA polymerase that, when tested in pure form in the test tube, is active in copying the viral DNA. Another such enzyme utilizes an RNA template to synthesize a complementary DNA strand; this enzyme may be involved in the process of cell transformation by tumour-producing viruses.

Experimentally induced viral infections. Thus far, only infection by intact viral particles has been considered. Under certain conditions, however, it is possible to initiate infection experimentally with only the nucleic acid portion of the virus; frequently the viral coat serves no other function than to protect the virus as it is transported from one intracellular environment to another. Some bacteria, such as *Bacillus subtilis,* for example, will take up DNA when grown in certain media. Other bacteria, such as the rod-shaped *E. coli,* can be converted to spheroplasts (globular-shaped bodies) by treatment with the enzyme lysozyme, which digests away part of the cell wall. The spheroplasts will then take up and be infected by viral nucleic acid from the surrounding medium. The RNA of tobacco mosaic virus can be introduced into plant cells by rubbing a leaf with some abrasive material.

Trans-
fection

To initiate a successful infection using only viral nucleic acid—a process that is sometimes called transfection—requires the presence of all the genetic information of the viral genome, either in the form of an intact genome or as several fragments that together contain all the information in the entire genome. The infectivity of small viral genomes is much higher than that of large nucleic acid ones because a small molecule has less chance of being degraded or destroyed by random breakage than does a very large one.

TYPES OF INFECTIOUS PROCESSES

Lysogeny.   Because the pattern of viral growth and development described above involves the disintegration or dissolution of cells (lysis), it is called the lytic type of infection. Some viruses, however, do not replicate and then lyse the host cell with the release of many progeny. Instead, in what is known as the lysogenic, or temperate, type of infection, the infecting viral genome forms a stable association with the chromosome of the host cell and then replicates in concert with that chromosome. Such a virus is called a provirus or prophage. In lysogeny, no progeny viruses are produced, and the infecting virus seems to disappear unless the cells (lysogens) harbouring the latent viral genome undergo certain treatment, such as exposure to ultraviolet light. The viral genome is then "induced": viral multiplication and maturation take place, with the subsequent lysis of the cell and the production of many viral particles. Thus, when an apparently normal cell can be induced to produce viruses, it can be concluded that the viral genome exists inside the cell.

Detailed genetic and biochemical studies of the lambda bacteriophage have revealed the mechanism of lysogeny. These temperate viruses have a special set of early genes that control the lysogenic response. The first gene expressed is one that synthesizes a protein called the repressor, the function of which is to block the expression of all other viral genes. Such an infection would be futile were it not for the fact that, before enough repressor can be made, a few more viral genes are activated. If these genes, which direct the integration of the viral genome into the host DNA, act quickly enough, the lambda genome will be integrated before the concentration of the repressor protein becomes great enough to block further viral expression. Thus, the continued synthesis of repressor keeps the viral genes in a quiescent state, and they will be replicated only when the host DNA replicates. If, however, integration of the viral genome does not occur in time, viral genes are activated that replicate the viral DNA, block the synthesis of the repressor, and make structural proteins of the phage. In this case, the phage undergoes the lytic cycle of infection.

Induction of the prophage involves destruction of the activity of the repressor molecule in the lysogenized cell. This may be done by ultraviolet irradiation or, if the virus synthesizes a repressor that is thermosensitive, by heating the lysogen. After destruction of the repressor, viral genes that catalyze the removal of the viral genome from that of the host are activated. This is followed by synthesis of the DNA replication enzymes and the structural proteins needed for producing a burst of progeny virus.

This mechanism also explains why the lysogenized cell is resistant to infection by another lambda phage (super-infection immunity). Because of the high concentration of repressor protein in the lysogen, a superinfecting phage is immediately repressed, even before it has a chance to express any of its genes. Because it is not integrated and cannot activate its own replication mechanism, the superinfecting phage is eventually diluted out of the cell population as the lysogen continues to grow and divide.

Super-
infection
immunity

Figure 3 illustrates the mechanism of integration during lysogeny of the lambda phage. Following infection of a host *E. coli* cell, the linear viral DNA becomes a circular structure, after which an enzyme synthesized by a viral gene promotes a recombination (crossover) event between the circular DNA and the host DNA at specific sites on both

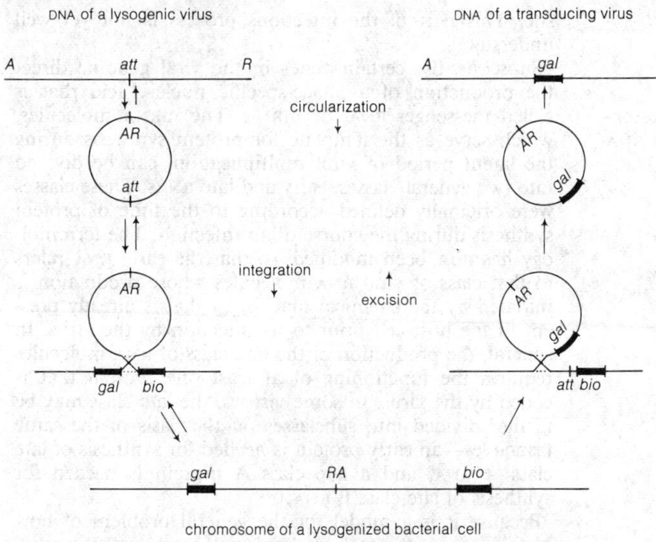

Figure 3: *Mechanisms of lysogeny and special transduction.*
A and *R* represent the terminal genes of the viral genome; *att* is the specific attachment site on the viral DNA and the host DNA; *gal* and *bio* represent the host genes on either side of the host *att* site (see text).

DNAs. This results in the insertion of the lambda genome into the *E. coli* chromosome at a specific site called the lambda attachment site. Different lysogenic phages have specific attachment sites on the host DNA.

Transduction.   Closely related to the phenomenon of lysogeny is that of transduction. In this process, some genes from one host cell are incorporated into the virus particle and carried to another host cell when the virus initiates another cycle of infection. If the lytic type of infection does not ensue, these cellular genes have a chance of being incorporated into the chromosome of the infected cell by a genetic recombination event. In this way the virus serves as the mediator of exchanges of genetic material between two host cells.

General transduction.   There are two types of transduction, one of which is called general transduction because it involves the transduction of any of the genes of the host cell. This results from the integration of random fragments of the host DNA into phage particles during the late stage of virus multiplication. Thus, with a certain low probability, the viral particle that is released from the infected cell contains, instead of the viral genome, a piece of host DNA that is injected by the particle into a phage-sensitive cell. Once inside the cell, this foreign DNA can be incorporated into the host genome. If, for example, the lysogenic, general transducing phage P1 is grown on *E. coli* that has the ability to ferment the sugar galactose and also to make the amino acid tryptophan, a few viral particles in the burst of viral progeny will contain the gene for galactose fermentation (*gal* [+]), a few will contain the gene for tryptophan synthesis (*trp* [+]), and most will contain the P1 phage genome. If this stock of phage is then used to infect another strain of *E. coli* that is unable to ferment galactose (*gal* [-]) and cannot synthesize its own tryptophan (*trp* [-]), the cells that are infected with the *gal* [+] particle will frequently incorporate this characteristic and become permanently *gal* [+]. Likewise, cells infected with the *trp* [+] transducing particles frequently become permanently able to synthesize tryptophan. These genetically stable changes are passed on to all of the progeny cells of the original cell.

There are two ways by which a cell can acquire both the *gal* [+] and *trp* [+] genetic markers: either the cell is simultaneously infected by two separate particles, each carrying an individual *gal* [+] or *trp* [+] marker, or one particle carries both markers.

It is known that the size of the transducing fragment of host DNA is limited by the size of the P1 phage head; this means that genetic markers must be located near each other on the DNA genome of the host. Geneticists have measured the frequency with which two markers are acquired in studies involving the linear organization of genes on the host DNA (*i.e.,* its genetic map). In the case cited above, the *gal* $^+$ and *trp* $^+$ genes are not acquired by one particle; hence it can be concluded that they are not very close together on the DNA genome of the host. Transduction can also be used to construct genetically new bacterial strains—mutant genes (those containing new genetic characteristics) of one cell can be incorporated into particles that are put into another cell, which may already have mutant genes of its own. In this way, the genetic potential of the cell can be manipulated.

Special transduction. The second type of transduction is called special transduction; it is characterized by the fact that only a few specific genetic markers can be transduced. Bacteriophage lambda is a specialized transducing phage, a property that results from the integration of the viral genome into the host DNA during lysogeny. As mentioned above, the integration site in the host DNA is specific; for lambda phage, it is located between the host genes for galactose fermentation and for synthesis of the compound biotin, a component of certain enzymes. Occasionally, when the lambda prophage is induced to form progeny, the exact reversal of the step by which the genome was integrated into that of the host does not take place. Instead, removal of the lambda DNA occurs in such a way as to include a little of the host DNA that is to the left or right of the attached lambda genome (Figure 3). Thus, if the excision includes host DNA to the left, the viral particle that emerges from the cell has the *gal* $^+$ genes as well as most of the lambda DNA; if, however, the excision includes DNA to the right of the lambda, the particle has some of the genes for biotin (*bio* $^+$) synthesis. Hence, in the lysate (product) of an induced lambda lysogen, there are some particles that can transduce for *gal* $^+$ and some that can transduce for *bio* $^+$. Because a piece of DNA that includes the normal lambda genome as well as both the *gal* $^+$ and *bio* $^+$ genes would be too large to fit into a lambda phage particle, *gal* $^+$ and *bio* $^+$ cannot occur on the same lambda genome under these conditions. This mechanism also explains why transduction by lambda is highly selective for only a few genetic markers.

Viral conversions. When certain phages are present as prophage in a lysogen, the host cell acquires new properties that are seemingly unrelated to the virus infection. Such cases are called virus-mediated conversions. One well-studied example is the conversion by phage epsilon[15] of certain strains of *Salmonella* bacteria from one antigenic class to another (antigens are substances that stimulate the formation of antibodies when introduced into an animal). The cell wall of *Salmonella,* one strain of which causes typhoid fever, contains a polysaccharide, a carbohydrate whose molecular structure determines the antigenic class to which the strain belongs. A *Salmonella* strain may have an antigen designated as class 10 on its surface, but after lysogenization it will exhibit the antigenic properties characteristic of a class 15 antigen. As long as the prophage epsilon[15] is present, the cell has class 15 antigen; but, when the prophage is lost, the cell reverts to class 10 antigen. The mechanism of this conversion resides in the phage-induced repression of the synthesis of the host enzymes involved in polysaccharide biosynthesis. Another conversion phenomenon occurs when certain phages lysogenize the bacterium *Corynebacterium diphtheriae.* The normal cell is non-disease-causing and does not produce toxin; upon lysogenization by toxogenic phage, however, the bacterium is converted to a disease-causing state and produces diphtheria toxin.

Conversion phenomena in bacteria have many features in common with the events associated with the transformation of animal cells by tumour-producing viruses. As described below (see *Cultivation of viruses*), the presence of a provirus in certain animal cells grown in culture causes an alteration in the antigenic properties of the cell and also the loss of some specific surface properties of the cell.

VIRAL GENETICS

The study of the genetic structure of the *E. coli* phages T7, T4, φX174, and lambda has illuminated key problems dealing with genetic recombination, nucleic acid replication, control of gene expression, protein synthesis, and assembly processes for macromolecular structures. Viruses have been particularly useful genetic tools because viral genomes are small, relative to those of cells, and because large quantities of virus can be easily prepared in the laboratory. It was the ease of assay and the quantitative nature of plaque-counting methods that quickly led to a detailed analysis of the genetic structure of several different viruses. Then, what had originally seemed a drawback in phage genetics became a great help—phages are haploid; that is, unlike most organisms, which are diploid, each phage has only one copy of its genome instead of two. This means, however, that lethal mutations (those changes in the characteristics of a gene that are fatal to the organism) are lost because the virus does not survive. This situation is different from that in diploid organisms, in which one chromosome compensates for the effect of a lethal gene that may be present in its twin.

Phage mutations. *Plaque-type mutants.* The mutations used in the early work on phage genetics are known as plaque-type mutants; these form a plaque with a distinctive appearance; for example, one useful plaque-type mutant is the rapid lysis or *r* mutants of phage T4. This mutant forms large, clear plaques that can be distinguished from the small plaques made by normal (wild-type) T4. Two classes of these *r* mutants, called *r*IIA and *r*IIB, have been used extensively in analyzing mutation and the recombination between mutants of T4.

Conditional lethal mutations. It was the discovery of phage mutations called conditional lethal mutations that resulted in striking progress in viral genetics. They are lethal under one set of experimental conditions but viable under other conditions. This means that the virus can be grown and genetically manipulated under favourable (permissive) conditions, after which the mutation is identified by failure of the virus to grow under nonpermissive conditions. One useful type of conditional lethal mutation is a temperature-sensitive mutant phage that will grow normally at 30° C (86° F) but fails to grow at 42° C (108° F). Wild-type phage, on the other hand, grows well at both temperatures. The explanation for this temperature-sensitive behaviour is that, as a result of a mutation in a gene that directs the synthesis of an essential protein, one amino acid in some portion of the protein molecule is replaced by a different amino acid, a substitution that renders the protein less stable and nonfunctional at a high temperature. In principle, such mutations could be found in every viral gene that directs the synthesis of an essential protein.

Another class of conditional lethal mutations found in phages are those called suppressor-sensitive (sus) mutations. These are mutant viruses that cannot grow in one strain of host cell but can grow in another strain if the host has in its own genome a suppressor mutation. In this case, the mutation can suppress the effect of another mutation in the viral genome. The best studied type of sus mutation is known as the amber mutation. In phages with an amber mutation, the DNA has been altered in such a way that one of its genes cannot direct the synthesis of the protein for which it is responsible. In a permissive host that carries the suppressor mutation, however, the genetic defect in the phage is compensated for by the effect of the suppressor mutation; protein synthesis thus is not blocked in the cell of that host.

Quantitative studies also are being carried out on the genetics of conditional lethal mutations of animal viruses, and evidence for the existence of other types of virus mutants has been obtained from epidemiological observations (studies related to the incidence, distribution, and control of a disease) on strains of certain viruses. It is known, for example, that repeated epidemics of influenza seem to result from infection by mutant strains of a virus to which a given population has not yet been exposed. Such continuing spontaneous mutations provide a variability that is of selective advantage to viruses that infect hosts capable of rapidly developing a resistance to the infection.

Genetic mapping. After a large number of different mutant phages have been isolated, a genetic map can be constructed. The distance between any two mutations can be estimated experimentally by measuring the recombination frequency between them. This means that, if two different mutant phages infect the same cell, there is a certain probability that breakage and rejoining of the two DNA molecules or their progeny in that cell will produce an intact molecule with both mutations on one strand, while another strand does not have either mutation. In other words, the latter is like a wild-type phage. The wild-type molecule (recombinant) will then make phage that grows under conditions that are nonpermissive for the mutant parent phage. Because the probability of such an exchange is more or less constant per unit length of DNA, the frequency of occurrence of wild-type recombinants reflects the distance along the DNA molecule between the two mutations.

From mapping data based on recombination frequencies, several interesting discoveries have been made. In the case of phage T4, it has been found that the genetic map is circular; that is, markers order themselves linearly as follows: a–b–c; b–c–d; c–d–a; and d–a–b. Because physical studies indicate that the DNA molecule of phage T4 is linear, the former result was at first puzzling. It has been shown, however, that this seeming paradox derives from the fact that, in a collection of T4 phages, there is not just one sequence of genes along the DNA molecule; rather, in a collection of DNA molecules, the sequence is permuted (changed in order of arrangement). The presence of redundant genes at each end of the molecule suggests that the mature T4 DNA is cut sequentially from a long precursor molecule, with tandemly repeating segments to generate the permuted gene sequence—e.g., abcd . . . wxyza; bcd . . . wxyzab; cd . . . wxyzabc; d . . . . Subsequent studies on the mode of replication of T4 DNA have confirmed the essential features of this model.

The rII mutants of T4 are conditional lethal mutants that fail to grow in host strains that contain the lambda prophage. Although the mechanism of this restriction is not clear, genetic analysis of rII mutants has provided fundamental information for understanding the nature of the processes of mutation and recombination. One advantage of the rII system in the T4 phage is its very high sensitivity: a single recombinant in 1,000,000,000 mutant phages can be detected; this permits "fine structure" mapping of mutations that are very close and, hence, very infrequent. It was also through a study of rII mutations that experimental evidence was first obtained indicating how the nucleotides in DNA direct the synthesis of a protein (see GENETICS AND HEREDITY: Genes and development: The genetic code).

In addition to the mapping of viral genomes by genetic recombination between mutant phages, another technique called heteroduplex mapping has shown great promise for certain cases. This method utilizes electron microscopy to observe directly the DNA molecule of the virus. If two viruses are to be compared, complementary strands of the DNA in each are separated and the right strand of one virus is annealed (joined) to the left strand of the other virus. In regions of the DNA where the genes are identical, the two DNAs will form a double strand of DNA: in those regions where the genes are different, however, the noncomplementary DNAs will not anneal and will reveal themselves under the electron microscope as single-stranded regions. Because many phages are now known that contain deletions or additions of viral or host genes—for example, gal+ lambda DNA—this method can be combined with conventional genetic mapping to correlate the physical map seen in the electron microscope with the genetic map.

Heteroduplex mapping

CULTIVATION OF VIRUSES

Whether in research or in the large-scale production of viruses for vaccine, the virologist is usually faced with similar problems—having the appropriate host cell in a state so that it is susceptible to the virus; having an adequate stock of pure virus to initiate the infection; having a suitable assay system; and having a suitable system to purify and concentrate the progeny viruses so that they remain viable.

In the case of bacterial viruses, a pure viral stock usually can be obtained from one plaque and inoculated into a rapidly growing bacterial culture. The culture eventually lyses after several rounds of infection, each of which involves a successively larger number of cells in the culture. After lysis, the phage can be collected either by centrifugation or by various precipitation methods; it is then further purified by centrifugation techniques.

A plant virus such as TMV is cultivated by mechanical inoculation of the virus into the leaves of healthy tobacco plants. After several days the leaves are harvested and ground up in a blender to form an extract. The liquid part of the extract contains the virus, which is purified. The assay of a plant virus is more laborious and less quantitative than is the plaque assay of bacterial viruses. Direct determination of infectivity is accomplished by mechanically inoculating leaves with a measured amount of virus preparation. The titre (concentration) is then estimated by the number of lesions that appear on the leaves. This assay is inefficient, however; other methods include direct chemical measurement of the virus and counting the virus particles by means of an electron microscope.

The methods for cultivating animal viruses are more highly specialized and vary according to the individual virus being grown. Many animal viruses can be grown in a manner similar to that used to cultivate bacteriophage. Cells in tissue culture are inoculated with a virus, and, after a certain latent period, the virus progeny are released into the medium, from which the virus can be recovered and purified. Because most animal viruses have stringent host requirements, many different types of cells are used. Some viruses must be grown in or isolated from infected tissues or organs of living animals. Hepatitis virus, for example, has not yet been successfully cultivated in a cell culture, but it can be isolated from and grown in humans and chimpanzees.

Prior to the development of in vitro tissue culture methods (outside the body, in an artificial environment), many animal viruses were cultivated in the laboratory in tissues of the chick embryo. The chick embryo also has served as an assay tool for some animal viruses. The number of lesions made in one of the embryonic membranes can be used to estimate virus titre. Newer assay methods, however, usually involve some type of plaque assay analogous to the system used for bacteriophage, or the hemagglutination assay for certain viruses. This latter technique is based on the fact that some viruses can alter the surface of an infected cell; affected red blood cells, for example, will attach themselves to the surface of such cells. Microscopic analysis of infected cells in the presence of red blood cells permits an estimate of the number of virus particles present.

Use of chick embryo in assays

PATHOGENESIS OF VIRAL DISEASES

Viral infection can result in a broad spectrum of effects that range from inapparent infection to acute disease or the induction of cancer. The course of the infection depends on several factors: the route of infection, the virulence of the virus, the susceptibility of the host cells, the effect of the virus on the functions of the host cells, and the host response to the infection.

Viral mutants with reduced virulence are known as attenuated strains; such mutants have less severe effects on the host cells than does the parental strain. Attenuated strains, however, which are often used in vaccines, frequently have normal virulence in cells from another host species.

Effects of viral infection.   Susceptible cells can respond in four general ways to viral infection: inapparent effect, in which the virus becomes an endosymbiont (lives dormantly in the host cell); cytopathic effect, in which the cell dies; hyperplastic effect, in which the cells are stimulated to divide prior to cell death, followed by cell death; and cell transformation, in which the cells are stimulated to divide, take on abnormal growth patterns, and become cancerous. The cytopathic effect (CPE) results in lysis of the infected cells or death of the cells without lysis because of their inability to reproduce. This type of effect is commonly observed in cultures of cells infected with poliovirus, herpes virus (cold sores), and influenza virus. After infection, the processes of the host involved in DNA, RNA, and protein synthesis are inhibited; this is probably the main cause of the CPE. Sometimes cells are stimulated to divide several times before their death. This occurs in pox-virus infection of a membrane in the chick embryo. The resulting pock lesions are the product of hyperplastic proliferation, followed by cell death. Both the CPE and hyperplastic responses to animal viruses can be observed as morphological alterations in the structure of the infected cells. (Inapparent infection and cell transformation are discussed below.)

Differences in the susceptibility of cells are usually related to differences in the ability of the viruses to adsorb to the cells. The required cell surface receptors may or may not be present, depending on the culture conditions and the state of growth of the cells. Differences can also be found in the receptor activity of cells in vivo (inside the body). Moreover, many viruses are much more virulent toward embryonic or newborn animals than toward adults; these differences relate both to the receptors on the cells and to changes in the intracellular rate of viral multiplication.

Immunological reactions. Host responses to viral infection include immunological reactions, production of compounds known as interferons, and nonspecific responses. The existence of neutralizing antibodies (substances in the body that counteract infections) in the serum of an infected animal greatly influences the outcome of the infection. Viruses are frequently very good antigens (substances that stimulate the production of antibodies): about seven to 14 days after the animal has been exposed to a given virus, it produces antibodies that confer varying degrees of resistance to subsequent infection by the same virus. The increase in specific antibodies in the serum can be used as a diagnostic tool to identify the virus responsible for a given illness.

Prophylactic immunizations with many viruses have been successful in controlling viral infections. Inoculation of susceptible animals with an attenuated strain of a virus or with viruses that have been inactivated with chemicals or radiation allows exposure of the animal to the antigenic component of the virus without significant risk of infection. The host can then produce antibodies that will protect against subsequent infection. Such immunization, which is called active immunity, is now routine for measles, poliovirus, smallpox, and yellow fever virus. In the case of smallpox, the vaccinia virus (cowpox) is used as an attenuated strain. This procedure, called vaccination, was introduced into common use by Edward Jenner in 1796 in England, although immunization with virulent smallpox virus had been practiced much earlier (see also IMMUNITY).

Active immunity

Production of interferon. Interferons are proteins produced by cells infected with animal viruses; they are able to inhibit the intracellular multiplication of viruses in other cells. Interferons seem to be cell specific rather than virus specific; thus, chick cells infected with influenza virus will produce interferon that inhibits the growth of influenza as well as other viruses in the cells. Although the efficiency of chick interferon in blocking virus multiplication in mouse cells is very low, occasionally there is some cross-species effectiveness—monkey kidney interferon, for example, is effective in human cells as well as in monkey cells. Interferon can be assayed by the reduced number of plaques formed by a given dose of test virus on cells that are susceptible to the particular interferon.

Because interferon is produced by the infected cells, viruses that cause a rapid cytopathic effect are usually poor inducers of interferon; viruses that multiply slowly, however, result in a high level of interferon synthesis. The mechanism of interferon induction is not clear; experiments indicate that double-stranded RNAs are efficient inducers of interferon. Even synthetic double-standed RNAs function well in this respect. It seems likely, therefore, that interferon is one cellular response to the presence of a foreign nucleic acid, whether viral or synthetic in origin. Interferon's mechanism of action appears related to its ability to block the translation of the viral messenger RNA into a protein essential for viral multiplication. This blockage is specific for viral messenger RNA; normal cells show little or no effect of interferon treatment. The interferon itself is not the blocking agent, however; apparently it activates a cellular gene that is directly responsible for inhibiting the virus from expressing itself in its normal mode.

Nonspecific responses. Nonspecific factors that influence the host response to viral infection include regulatory substances (hormones) and temperature. Hormones from the adrenal cortex (the surface layer of the adrenal gland, which is located at the top of the kidney), such as cortisone, can greatly increase the susceptibility of many animals to viruses that infect the nervous system and often aggravate infections with herpes virus and chickenpox virus. Certain viruses that show optimal growth at 37° C (99° F) are inhibited at higher temperatures; others are inactivated at temperatures only slightly higher than 37° C (normal human body temperature). It may be, therefore, that the febrile (fever) response inhibits the virus and contributes to the recovery of the animal from viral disease.

Fever

Infectious patterns. *Localized infections.* There are three patterns of infection by animal viruses: localized, disseminated, and inapparent. In localized infection, viral growth and development are confined to the area where the virus enters the body. The virus may spread, however, by local infection of adjacent cells, as in a plaque in tissue culture; in some cases it may be spread mechanically or carried in secretions. The wart virus, for example, is a typical local infection in which the virus is found only in the vicinity of the lesion but may be spread to adjacent areas by activity such as scratching.

Disseminated infections. Disseminated infections develop stepwise from the site of viral entry and eventually spread to many distant locations in the body. In the stage called the primary viremia, the virus usually multiplies first in the cells and lymph nodes near the site of entry. (Lymph nodes are glandlike bodies located along the paths of lymph vessels; they filter and remove foreign substances from lymph, a colourless fluid that bathes tissues and flows through the body in its own system of channels and ducts.) The progeny viruses are distributed throughout the body by the bloodstream and the lymphatic circulation, establishing viral infections in other organs, in which viral multiplication again takes place. The virus is further disseminated (secondary viremia) to the target organ or tissue, in which it multiplies to produce its characteristic pathological effect and is recognizable as a clinical disease. The time between primary infection and the production of symptoms in the target organs is called the incubation period. An animal frequently transmits the virus during the incubation period, and overt disease does not appear until after the virus is widely distributed and has multiplied extensively. Diseases that follow this pattern of infection include measles, poliomyelitis, and mumps, in which the target organs are the skin, the central nervous system, and the salivary glands, respectively.

Inapparent infections. Inapparent viral infections are of two types: those that normally produce overt symptoms and those that produce changes that do not manifest themselves until many years after the initial infection. The attenuated strains of virus, such as those used in vaccines, usually result in apparent infections. If the host has some level of immunity to the virus, however, these infections are often transient and inapparent as well. In such inapparent infections, the virus is soon eliminated from the animal.

In latent infections, on the other hand, the virus persists in a quiescent state in the host. Herpes simplex virus, which produces cold sore lesions on the lips and mouth, exists in such a latent form and periodically becomes activated to give rise to acute episodes. The activation of the herpes virus seems to be caused by physiological changes in the host organism such as fever, exposure to intense sunlight, psychological stress, and menstruation. Other viruses, called slow viruses, have such a long incubation period that the infection is inapparent for many years; slow viruses are responsible for neurological diseases such as kuru, which occurs in the Fore people in New Guinea. Some tumour-producing viruses also have a very long latent period; for example, if infant mice are infected with mammary tumour virus transmitted in the milk from the mother, the effect of the virus does not become evident until the animals reach old age, at which time they develop cancer of the mammary gland.

Treatment and control of viral diseases. There are three general approaches to the control of virus diseases: supportive treatment of the symptoms such as treating dehydration with fluid therapy, specific treatment directed at the viral infection, and epidemiological control of the spread of the virus between individuals. Supportive treatment of the infected organism varies with the particular viral disease and is considered in INFECTIOUS DISEASES.

Specific treatment. Specific treatment of a given viral infection with antibodies has been successful in many instances. Passive immunization, which is a short-term immunity to a specific disease, can be achieved by injecting the antibody fraction (gamma globulins) from the serum of an animal that has already been exposed to the virus and therefore has produced antibodies to it. This approach is useful if applied soon after infection by or exposure to a virus, before it is widely disseminated in the body. Treatment with gamma globulins is effective in tempering or preventing the infection by such viruses as hepatitis, mumps, and measles. Active immunization, which produces long-term immunity by infection with inactivated or attenuated virus so that the organism develops its own antibodies, is also useful.

Although therapy with drugs and chemicals (chemotherapy) has been very successful in treating bacterial infections, the chemotherapy of viral infections is not yet well developed. This is because, in order to grow and multiply, viruses utilize many of the host cell functions. Inhibiting any of the steps in viral development, therefore, means inhibiting the functions of the host cell. There are, however, two chemical substances that are effective in combatting certain viral infections. One is a compound that, because it specifically inhibits the multiplication of pox viruses, is used in treating people who have been exposed to smallpox. When used as a preventive measure, this drug has proved quite effective; when given to individuals who already have the symptoms of smallpox, it is ineffective because symptoms appear only after extensive multiplication and dissemination of the virus. Another drug, which is useful in treating herpes simplex infection of the cornea (the transparent part of the coat of the eyeball that covers the lens and iris), inhibits the DNA synthesis of the virus. Because in this disease the drug is applied directly to the infected corneal cells, toxicity of the drug to the rest of the organism is eliminated.

Promising results have been shown by recent attempts to treat infected cells with synthetic double-stranded RNA to induce the production of interferon, which inhibits viral multiplication. Some of the synthetic interferon inducers are toxic to the host, however, and this problem has thus far limited the utility of this type of therapy.

Epidemiological control. Probably the most successful virus control measures are those that are epidemiological in nature. Because viruses are frequently spread by contact, insect carriers (vectors), or such contaminated materials as food or biological substances, interruption of the transmission process can sometimes eliminate a virus from certain populations. Insect-borne diseases of animals and plants are frequently controlled by measures directed at reducing the insect population. The yellow fever virus, for example, is carried from one human to another by a species of mosquito; adequate protection of humans from this mosquito together with a reduction in the insect population have resulted in satisfactory control of the disease. Likewise, smallpox has been essentially eradicated from such countries as the United States and Great Britain by a program of vaccination and strict immigration rules. Some viruses, however, exist in various hosts as inapparent infections and serve as a reservoir of infection in the cycle of transmission by insects or other vector species.

Tumour-producing viruses. The first indication that tumours can be produced by viral infection was obtained in 1908 by two investigators who were able to transmit leukemia from one chicken to another. As mentioned at the beginning of this article, it was found in 1911 that a solid tumour could also be transmitted between chickens. Despite such evidence, biologists for many years were hesitant to admit that viruses could cause cancer; now, however, the evidence is incontrovertible. Tumours

of many kinds can be produced in nearly all types of experimental animals by viral infection. Although proof that viruses cause human cancer is not yet available, many viruslike particles with the morphology of tumour-producing viruses have been isolated from human tumour tissue. It is difficult to prove viral carcinogenicity in humans because moral considerations place limitations on the design of experiments that could adequately test this hypothesis. Results of comparative biological studies, however, indicate that this is true.

It should be emphasized that although cancer is, in many cases, of viral origin and hence infective, this does not mean that it is especially contagious. The available evidence does not support the idea that oncogenic (tumour-producing) viruses are readily transmitted between individual animals.

Cells in culture respond to tumour-producing viruses either cytopathically (*i.e.,* by dying) or by transformation. Transformation involves changes in the morphology and surface properties of the cells; in addition, they divide rapidly and do not show normal growth inhibition (contact inhibition) in crowded culture conditions. Because such transformed cells will cause a tumour when injected into an animal, it is believed that transformation of cells in culture is analogous to viral-tumour production in an animal.

In many cases in which the infecting virus cannot be recovered from the transformed cell, it has been shown that the virus exists as a provirus; *i.e.,* it is integrated into the chromosome of the host cell. This phenomenon seems to be similar to the lysogeny of bacteria by lysogenic bacteriophage. Moreover, several of the genes of the oncogenic provirus continue to be expressed, which results in the maintenance of the transformed or malignant state. In this respect, the transformation of animal cells by oncogenic viruses resembles the phenomenon of conversion by lysogenic bacteriophage. And, just as bacterial prophage can be induced by various treatments, evidence indicates that oncogenic viruses can exist in a latent form and can be induced to multiply and infect other cells, thereby producing tumours. X-rays, for example, can induce the production of mouse leukemia, which is then transmissible by a virus obtained from the leukemic cells. Many chemical carcinogens are suspected of producing cancers by activating a latent virus. The mechanisms by which the oncogenic viruses alter the cellular biochemistry and cause a malignancy have not yet been established with certainty. (See CANCER.)

ORIGIN AND EVOLUTION OF VIRUSES

Because many strains of certain bacteriophages have been developed under controlled conditions and can be compared, much is known about their evolution, at least in the laboratory environment. With respect to the origin of viruses, however, there is only speculation thus far.

The relationship of viruses to their host cells indicates that the same mechanisms are used by both entities to achieve common ends. Both the virus and host, for example, use the same genetic system to synthesize proteins. Moreover, proteins synthesized by the virus are fundamentally the same as those of its host. It is not correct, however, to conclude that viruses are "little cells"; rather, the virus is an independent genetic system capable of transferring itself from one cell to another.

Since the discovery of lysogeny, it has been suggested that viruses represent sets of cellular genes that have gained the additional capacity to replicate autonomously and to coat their nucleic acid with protein. Some evidence that such events may take place comes from the finding of so-called cryptic prophage, in which a few genes of phage lambda are integrated into the genome of a bacterial cell. That these genes were ever functional in the bacterial cell, however, is conjecturable. There are, on the other hand, several bacterial strains that contain independent genetic elements called plasmids. Plasmids are pieces of DNA that may be integrated into the host DNA or that may replicate independently in the cell. Some plasmids, however, consist of genes that direct the host cell to transfer specific genetic material to another cell lacking the material. In this

Passive immunity

Cell transformation

Plasmids

respect, the plasmid can function similarly to viruses; this suggests that viruses may have originated as a fragment of cellular nucleic acid that has evolved a certain amount of independence from the host cell.

Conversely, it may be argued that viruses originated from more complicated parasitic organisms. By successive loss of function, the virus could have become more and more dependent on the host cell. In fact, the finding of cryptic prophage and defective viruses that can grow only in the presence of other "helper" viruses suggests such loss of function. This hypothesis suffers, however, from the lack of any known intermediate levels of organization between viruses and known intracellular parasites.

It is possible that both processes are occurring. Although one difficulty with the hypotheses of the cellular origin of viruses is that it does not explain how viruses with an RNA genome could have evolved, the discovery of enzymes that copy RNA into DNA has provided a plausible explanation for a possible evolutionary leap from a cellular DNA genome to a viral RNA. It is also possible that a virus may have originated by evolution from an independent set of host genes to produce a sort of parasitic genetic system, which, in turn, has undergone evolutionary modification involving both the loss and the acquisition of certain functions.

BIBLIOGRAPHY. B.D. DAVIS et al., Microbiology (1967), a college-level text treating both animal and bacterial viruses; S.E. LURIA and J.E. DARNELL, JR., General Virology, 2nd ed. (1967), a comprehensive textbook on virology; F.M. BURNET and W.M. STANLEY (eds.), The Viruses, 3 vol. (1959), a collection of specialized articles; K. MARAMOROSCH and H. KAPROWSKI (eds.), Methods in Virology, 4 vol. (1967–68), covers the technology of virology; G.S. STENT, Molecular Biology of Bacterial Viruses (1963), an elementary introduction; W. HAYES, The Genetics of Bacteria and Their Viruses, 2nd ed. (1968), an advanced monograph; S.S. COHEN, Virus-Induced Enzymes (1968), an advanced account of the biochemistry of viral infection; J. CAIRNS, G.S. STENT, and J.D. WATSON (eds.), Phage and the Origins of Molecular Biology (1966), historical accounts of developments in bacterial virology; C.K. MATHEWS, Bacteriophage Biochemistry (1971), a comprehensive account of the biochemistry of phage infection. CAROL ERON, The Virus That Ate Cannibals (1981), is a popularly written account of research on viruses and the diseases caused by them; DAVID LOCKE, Virus Diseases: A Layman's Handbook (1978).

(W.C.S.)

Volcanism

Volcanism is the discharge of magma, rock fragments, gases, and water vapour at the surface of the Earth. It takes various forms. In some cases, rock debris is ejected violently from the central vent of a conical landform. In others, molten-rock material pours out from fissures that occur along a fracture or a series of fractures extending several kilometres in length. In still other instances, groundwater heated by magma buried within the Earth is spouted forth from a geyser or as steam from a vent known as a fumarole. This article treats all such manifestations of volcanism and the processes that produce them. It also delineates the types of materials ejected during volcanic eruptions and the structures that result from the explosive and effusive activity. For specifics about volcanic events on the seafloor, see OCEANS: *The ocean basins.* Further information on the formation and occurrence of volcanoes will be found in PLATE TECTONICS. (Ed.)

This article is divided into the following sections:

General considerations

AREAS OF ACTIVE VOLCANISM

About 800 volcanoes are known to have been active during historic time and many thousands more were active at some time during Late Tertiary and Quaternary time. Perhaps two-thirds of these volcanoes are associated with active arcs; most of the remainder are related to the world-wide rift system, which includes the mid-ocean ridges and continental rifts such as that of East Africa. A few, such as Hawaii and Mt. Cameroun in Africa, are not clearly related to either the rifts or the arcs. In Hawaii, as in some other mid-oceanic island chains, volcanism has progressed regularly along the arc. The oldest islands of the Hawaii group are to the northwest and the youngest, still active islands, are those to the southeast. The basic character of the volcanic rocks, and the lack of a deep trench, deep-focus earthquakes, and a large gravity anomaly clearly indicate that the Hawaiian Islands differ markedly from the typical arc and should not be so designated (see also OCEANS: *Oceanic trenches and island arcs*).

Most of the arc-associated volcanoes are found in the so-called circle of fire that rings the Pacific, and their pattern, in general, is that of the arcs because they make up the inner or volcanic arc. If only recently active volcanoes are considered, however, there are some differences in detail in correlation between the arcs and the volcanoes. In the Aleutians there is no modern volcanic activity at the westernmost segment of the arc, but there is substantial activity near the middle of the arc, which continues to the east, through the Alaskan peninsula and the Valley of Ten Thousand Smokes. Along the Canadian west coast, which is not a proper island arc, there is no active volcano. The Cascades in Washington and Oregon are active volcanoes, composed of andesite (a volcanic rock intermediate in composition between basalt and silica-rich varieties), not associated with an arc that is active at present, but it appears that the tectonic pattern has changed recently in this area and that this volcanic activity is a remnant of a former arc. There is considerable volcanism in Mexico along an east–west trend and also along the west coast of Central America where it is associated with the Middle America Trench. Volcanic activity occurs at a number of sites along the western coast of South America, but this belt ends just south of 40° S.

The North Island of New Zealand is the southern extremity of the volcanic activity of the Tonga-Kermadec Arc. The belt continues to the north and west and includes volcanoes in the New Hebrides and Solomon Islands and in New Guinea. West of New Guinea, the belt of activity bifurcates; one belt passes through the Philippines, Taiwan, and Japan and continues up the Kurile Arc into Kamchatka, where this trend ceases abruptly at about the point where the Aleutian trend intersects the Kamchatka Peninsula. A spur south from Japan through the Bonin Islands is very active. The other belt from New Guinea passes westward through the highly active East Indian arc

The circle
of fire

that includes the famous Krakatoa and terminates at Barren Island west of Burma.

Although the geologic information and the seismicity indicate continuation of the tectonic belt through the Himalayas, no active volcanism is found in this segment of the belt. Just south of the Caspian Sea active volcanism is again found and the belt continues through Mt. Ararat into Greece. In the Alpine belt activity is limited, but the famous volcanoes of Italy and Sicily are prominent. The Pacific "circle of fire" makes two forays into the Atlantic, one ringing the Caribbean, and one, the Scotia Sea. In both cases modern volcanism is largely confined to the easternmost portions of these arcs.   (J.E.O.)

HISTORIC VOLCANIC ERUPTIONS

Volcanic eruptions in inhabited areas have been the causes of disastrous loss of life and property. Data collected from the year 1500 to 1914 suggest that volcanic eruptions may have caused the loss of about 190,000 human lives. It should be noted, however, that associated sea waves, mud slides, and other catastrophic events that accompany eruptions often cause additional fatalities.

During explosive eruptions of the volcano Laki (Iceland) in 1783, ashes that fell on the surrounding region caused famine and epidemics that led to the death of 10,000 people. In 1792 the volcano Unzen-dake (Japan), after explosive activity, produced a series of mud streams (lahars) that enveloped villages situated on its slopes, claiming 10,452 lives.

Tambora and Krakatoa

An eruption of Tambora (Indonesia) that took place in 1815 produced a rain of rock fragments and ashes in which 12,000 people lost their lives; the devastation that followed brought famine, and 80,000 people fell victim in the neighbouring islands of Sumbawa and Lombok. In 1883 the volcano Krakatoa in the Malaysian islands exploded with extreme violence; a resulting sea wave submerged the coastal regions of the neighbouring islands of Java and Sumatra and 36,000 people lost their lives.

In 1902, during the eruption of Mt. Pelée, Martinique, a glowing cloud burst out with terrific force and rolled down the side of the mountain. It swept over the town of Saint-Pierre with the force of a hurricane, killing 29,000 of its inhabitants. After 18 years of absolute calm, the volcano Kelud (Java) suddenly renewed its activity with a violent explosion. The water of the crater lake that had accumulated during dormancy—about 38,000,000 cubic metres, or 50,000,000 cubic yards—mixed with volcanic ash and flowed down the volcano slopes. The ensuing mudflow killed about 5,100 people.

Such fateful events clearly show the need for direct observation of volcanic activity in populated areas and for basic research in the study of volcanic evolution. Not every eruptive event constitutes a grave danger at the outset, but it may evolve to a very violent stage. Research in the forecasting of these ultimate eruptions is therefore extremely important.

Types of volcanism

Although they are an aspect of volcanic activity, catastrophic eruptions represent only one part of the field and are generally of limited duration. A second and more common aspect of volcanic activity consists of manifestations of more modest proportions, which are less spectacular but are of great significance in the interpretation of eruptive phenomena.

HOT SPRINGS, GEYSERS, AND FUMAROLES

Among these less violent manifestations are hot springs that are common in all volcanic areas, even where the volcanoes are no longer active. They represent the final stage of heat loss by igneous (crystalline rock) masses beneath the Earth's surface, which continue to give off high-temperature vapours and gases while slowly cooling down. This gaseous phase is composed primarily of overheated steam that loses a part of its heat while coming up to the surface and expands and is transformed into water, forming hot-water springs.

Geysers and fumaroles are both manifestations of hot springs. Geysers (Icelandic *geysir,* from *geysa,* "to rush forth," or *gjósa,* "to gush") are spouting hot springs that throw forth intermittent jets of water and steam. Many hot springs that are not geysers may exhibit periodicity: some show periods of agitation or of violent boiling, and some alternately discharge water and gas. A sharp distinction between geysers and other hot springs cannot always be drawn.

Fumaroles are steam vents (Latin *fumus,* "smoke"); the "smoke" is water vapour, the dominant constituent, but acid gases, such as carbon dioxide and hydrogen sulfide, characteristically occur. Fumaroles that yield hot vapour and sulfurous gases are called solfataras (Italian *zolfo,* "sulfur"). The temperature of fumaroles varies widely and in any one fumarole is subject to great variations over time. In the famous Valley of Ten Thousand Smokes, which was formed by the tremendous eruption of the volcano Katmai, Alaska, in 1912, temperatures up to 645° C (1,193° F) were measured. In the dying volcano La Solfatara (or Forum Vulcani) at Pozzuoli, Italy, known from antiquity, the temperature of the steam oscillates between 100° and 165° C (212° and 329° F).

Solfataras

With this group are included the paint pots, porridge pots (Figure 1), and mud volcanoes, all of which are hot

By courtesy of T.F.W. Barth

Figure 1: Porridge pots in the Solfatara Crater, Pozzuoli, Italy.

springs of limited water supply and acid reaction. Their immediately adjacent surface rocks are undergoing active chemical attack from magmatic steam and acid gases to provide the porridge, whereas the iron content of the rocks provides the paint. Another related form, the Mofettes (German *Muff,* "musty smell"), are vents that issue carbon dioxide, some methane and other hydrocarbons, nitrogen, and oxygen at low temperature. Mofettes mark the very last stage of volcanic activity.

Physical and chemical characteristics of hot springs. Hot springs are fed by ordinary groundwater heated by magmatic steam. The development of various types of hot springs, including fumaroles, acid or alkaline springs, geysers, and tepid pools, is therefore dependent on the groundwater conditions at the locality. Such factors as topography, porosity and other rock properties, and local meteorologic conditions, particularly rainfall, are all important. The development of hot springs requires a source of local volcanic heat.

Water composition. The waters of hot springs fall

roughly into three groups: (1) waters carrying calcium carbonate in solution, (2) siliceous acid waters, and (3) siliceous alkaline waters. The acid springs are of low volume and contain hydrochloric or sulfuric acid.

Calcium carbonate (or bicarbonate) lends the water special properties that are easily observed, particularly the ability to precipitate large quantities of travertine, or hard tufa (sedimentary rocks formed by precipitation from springwaters), consisting predominantly of the mineral calcite but also of aragonite, on the surface. Huge terraces of exquisite beauty may develop from this process. In Yellowstone National Park the Mammoth Hot Springs (Figure 2) provide an outstanding example. A unique

Figure 2: Mammoth Hot Springs terraces, Yellowstone National Park, Wyoming.

scenic aspect is the deposit form of cones and basins; the high terraces were deposited along a steep slope by small rushing streams of springwater and now resemble the successive billows of a frozen cataract. In order for this type of springwater to develop, the source water must pass through limestone or other calcite-bearing rocks. In volcanic regions that are underlain by limestone or dolomite, as in Italy and Greece, extensive deposits of travertine are common.

Siliceous water types and their evolution Siliceous types of springwater form an evolutionary series from acid to alkaline and throw much light on the chemical reactions taking place underground. There is no doubt that steam prevails among the gases given off by a magma. But, in addition, acid gases, such as carbon dioxide and hydrogen sulfide, characteristically occur. If oxygen is available, then sulfur dioxide forms, and the waters carrying the emanations will be highly acid. On the pH scale, a measure of the hydrogen-ion content, which ranges from 1 (extremely acid) to 14 (extremely alkaline), a pH of 7 is neutral, but these waters typically exhibit a pH of 4.

In the early evolutionary stages, hydrogen sulfide in acid solution will effectively precipitate silver, mercury, lead, bismuth, copper, cadmium, arsenic, antimony, and tin supplied by the magma. The acid solutions attack the rock minerals and mix with large quantities of groundwater; thus, they become neutral or alkaline, the pH value increasing from 4 to perhaps 10. The resulting alkaline waters then remove silica in colloidal solution (a very fine grained suspension). Thus, the general relation produced is one of increasing pH values with increasing distance from the mother magma to the place of eruption of a particular spring.

Many elements are precipitated as the solutions become alkaline. Iron and aluminum are the commonest of these elements; they are present only in springwater more acid than that with a pH of about 5. Calcium and magnesium are present in waters with a pH of about 7. Sodium and potassium are not affected by acidity, but sodium is always present in great excess over potassium. Except where

there is a surplus of calcium carbonate, the issuing waters thus contain silica in great relative excess over all other rock constituents except sodium. The relative contents of the spring gases also evolve. Hydrogen and hydrogen sulfide in acid waters gradually diminish; they are still less abundant in neutral waters and are completely absent in alkaline waters.

Incrustations and deposits. High-temperature deposits from vapours around acid fumaroles and hot-gas vents are dominantly sal ammoniac. Sulfate-bearing incrustations and efflorescences (mainly of ammonia, magnesium, iron, and aluminum) occur in deposits of somewhat lower temperature, and large amounts of native sulfur and gypsum are deposited around acid hot springs at the boiling temperature. Minor amounts of other sulfates and of pyrite, limonite, and opal also occur.

Siliceous sinter (a variety of opal) is the deposit typically formed by alkaline hot springs. In some areas it comprises extensive deposits of domes, terraces, or flats. The most distinguished example was the great "White Terrace" beside Lake Rotomahana, in New Zealand, which was destroyed in a volcanic eruption in 1886. Alkaline springs are almost always deep and are often distinguished by the brilliant, bluish colouring of the water, which contrasts beautifully with their white sinter deposits. The sinter is white or grayish, scaly to massive, and sometimes porous, filamentous, or cauliflower-like. Chemical analyses show 80–90 percent silica and about 10 percent water; the remainder is mostly aluminum, iron, and small amounts of magnesium, calcium, and sodium. **Siliceous sinter deposits**

Rather unusual and related to travertine deposits are small globules of mercury and cinnabar (a mercury sulfide mineral) deposited as coatings on calcareous tufa of some boiling springs in Idaho and California.

Another special occurrence is a salt crust on Lake Magadi, Kenya, which is a natural evaporation pan, fed by four copious hot springs (aggregate flow is about 2,840 litres, or 750 gallons, per second). This crust yields 72,700,000 kilograms (80,000 tons) of soda ash and 36,400,000 kilograms (40,000 tons) of salt annually, but the inflow of sodium salts far exceeds the rate of exploitation. Mineral-spring brines are worked at many places in the world.

Hot springs and fumaroles in Larderello, Italy, also have been the subject of considerable attention. Boric acid, ammonium sulfate, and carbon dioxide are recovered.

Discharge and thermal energy. Large amounts of hot groundwater emerge in alkaline hot-spring areas, whereas acid hot springs, solfataras, and fumaroles characteristically occur in drier areas and have a much smaller discharge. Indeed, observations indicate that acid waters make up 1 or 2 percent of the total hot-water discharge in Iceland and in Yellowstone National Park, although the acid-hot-spring areas are more extensive than those of the alkaline springs.

Because of the great porosity of rocks in Iceland, much hot water runs off as overland flow and subsurface discharge to be lost to the sea (Figure 3). Drilling has

Figure 3: Deildartunguhver River, north of Reykjavik, Iceland.

raised the yield considerably; the surface discharge in low-temperature areas of Iceland amounts to 1,135 litres (300 gallons) per second, but the additional discharge from drill holes is 1,515 litres (400 gallons) per second. The surface discharge in Yellowstone National Park is 3,030 litres (800 gallons) per second, and the total discharge in all of Japan is 16,650 litres (4,400 gallons) per second.

A conspicuous example of the copious water supply of alkaline springs can be seen at Deildartunguhver, 48 kilometres (30 miles) north of Reykjavík, Iceland. Cascades of boiling water belch forth from several rents and fissures in a steep wall of hardened boulder clay of red, blue, and yellow colours; they meet to form a steaming river, the largest "boiling river" in the world, yielding approximately 245 litres (65 gallons) per second. The temperature at the place of issue is approximately 99° C (210° F); at the confluence with Reykjadalsá, about 130 yards downstream, the temperature is 82° C (180° F).

Utilization of thermal energy Although a tremendous amount of heat is released at the surface by the activity of hot springs, the utilization of this energy has been relatively slight.

Thermal energy is used only for home heating, greenhouses, and the drying of such substances as seaweed and diatomaceous earth. Leaky underground chambers and other technical difficulties have restricted the use of the mechanical energy (pressure) of fumaroles and geysers. Only at Larderello, southwest of Florence, have larger energy projects been developed. In 1904 the first generating station operated on natural pressurized steam was installed. Subsequently, a great number of additional borings were made, and the energy output increased from 3,000 kilowatt-hours in 1916 to 2,694,000,000 kilowatt-hours in 1968. This was approximately 2.6 percent of the total energy consumption of Italy in 1968.

Some electricity is generated from wells in the geyser region of Sonoma County, California, and the utilization of hot springs also has been accomplished in New Zealand.

Geysers and geyser activity. There are three major areas of geyser action in the world: Yellowstone National Park contains at least 200 geysers, or about 10 percent of the total number of hot springs in the park; Iceland has about 30 active geysers, or less than 1 percent of the total number of hot springs; and New Zealand has fewer geysers than Iceland but is famous for having had the greatest one in the world, the Waimangu Geyser, which played daily to heights above 300 metres (1,000 feet) between 1902 and 1905.

True geyser action, one of the rarest phenomena in nature, is one of the most beautiful and conspicuous to behold. Geysir, in Iceland, is the most famous geyser in the world. It was known to science centuries before Waimangu, in New Zealand, had been heard of or before the performances of Old Faithful, in Yellowstone National Park, had been seen by Western men. The behaviour of Geysir had attracted tourists as well as learned men, and the notes and descriptions of this geyser from the 17th century to the present are legion.

The magnitudes of geyser eruption range from insignificant (throwing the water a few centimetres high) to those of famous fountains that playfully attain heights of many hundred feet. Each geyser has its individual performance pattern; some are regular and rhythmical, whereas some are unpredictable. This is because no two geyser edifices and water paths are alike, and the precise causes of eruption cannot always be followed in detail.

Discharge and temperature of geysers Some geysers have negligible discharge, but the larger geysers disperse an amount of water that is many times greater than the volume of their accessible tubes during eruption. One or more storage basins of considerable size are therefore necessary to account for the volume of the visible eruptions. This fact was ascertained for many geysers of Yellowstone National Park and for the Geysir, in Iceland, which in a single 24-hour period (including numerous eruptions) may eject an amount of water equal to at least 100 days' normal or customary discharge.

Most geysers erupt close to the boiling point, 100° C (212° F) at sea level, and some also will boil between eruptions; others will cool considerably. In the upper part of a geyser vent, the temperature often increases with depth, whereas in the lower part it is constant or decreases. This is a general pattern for all hot springs. Many geysers exhibit very irregular temperature—depth curves, but one important point should be emphasized: boiling temperatures are attained only in the uppermost parts of a geyser system; at greater depths the temperature recedes from the boiling point for that depth.

In Yellowstone National Park, the changing behaviour of geysers is well-known. Contrary to common belief, most geysers do not erupt with regularity, nor are they constant in the intensity of water jets or the heights attained. Even Old Faithful (Figure 4)—which in all tourist brochures during the 1920s and '30s was said to erupt at intervals of precisely one hour and five minutes—when under continuous observation was actually shown to erupt at intervals varying between 30 and 90 minutes. The highest measured eruption, originating in Beehive Geyser, was 67 metres (220 feet). It is possible that the great Excelsior Geyser, active in the 1890s, may have attained greater heights.

Crater Hills Geyser differs in pattern from most geysers: an eruption lasts for about 30 minutes, followed by a quiet interval of only two minutes. In most geysers the eruption period is shorter than the quiet period. There is no discharge, even during an eruption (all water falls back into the basin), and this is another unique characteristic. The eruption starts when the water level in the basin is low, whereas most geysers erupt only when the basin is full. And, finally, the maximum temperature during eruptions in August 1947 was 73° C (163° F); most geysers erupt when their water temperature is close to the boiling point.

Geyser eruptions have been compared to volcanic eruptions. The dimensions are usually different, but, when a geyser throws steam and water 300 metres (1,000 feet) into the air, it approaches the activity of a small volcano. The peculiar volcano Siretoko-Iô-Zan, in Japan, acts in some ways as if it were a tremendous irregular geyser. After a dormancy of 46 years, it sustained a continuous eruption for several months in 1936, during which it successively developed the following stages: (1) liquid-sulfur eruptions, (2) explosive emissions of hot water and steam, and (3) intermittent gushing of boiling water and steam.

Seawater geysers and nagawakis A geyser spouting seawater, situated at the southwestern tip of Iceland, probably first erupted in 1906 and was said to be an active geyser at flood tide, quiet at ebb. In 1927 it was a true geyser with a regular period of 15 minutes, and the splashes were between three and six metres (ten to 20 feet) high. But in July 1928 the spring underwent a

UPI

Figure 4: Old Faithful Geyser, Yellowstone National Park, Wyoming.

Figure 5: (Top left) Eruption of Mt. Etna in 1964. After a period of quiescence the volcano erupted from the main crater, beginning with a violent explosive phase. In a few hours, the volcanic activity, becoming essentially effusive, resulted in a lava stream outflow from a large gap in the crater rim. (Top right) Explosive activity at the northeast crater of Mt. Etna as seen from the central crater. During such a stage, belonging to the "permanent activity" of the volcano, volcanic gases and fragments of molten lava are rhythmically emitted. (Bottom left) Effusive phase of the "permanent activity" of Mt. Etna in 1970, with the lava stream flowing from a small dome-shaped edifice at the base of the northeast crater. (Bottom right) Spectacular columnar jointing, Giant's Causeway, Northern Ireland. Fracturing results from thermal contraction during the cooling of a lava mass.

By courtesy of Letterio Villari, Instituto Internazionale di Vulcanologia, Catania, Italy.

marked change. The period became irregular and, on the average, somewhat longer; after 20 to 25 minutes the water jets became lower. Eventually, the geyser action ceased, and in 1937 the spring became an incessantly boiling pot.

A real geyser, manifestly spouting seawater, is certainly one of the rarest phenomena of the natural world. The former geyser at Atami, Japan, situated 1,000 metres (3,300 feet) from the sea at an altitude of 18 metres (60 feet), is the best example. In many respects it was a peculiar spring. It dispersed diluted seawater, and in 1906 it threw small water jets 0.5 metre (1.6 feet) high, at regular intervals of about five hours. The rhythmic activity was broken by irregularly occurring eruptions, called *nagawaki,* that would go on for 12 hours, discharging large amounts of water and vapour.

Fumaroles. The intimate connection between fumaroles and simple hot springs is obvious in areas in which there exists a strong contrast between dry and wet seasons. During the dry season, hot springs are transformed into fumaroles, which in turn, during the wet seasons, become hot springs again. Growler Spring, in Yellowstone National Park, is a good example: its temperature is at a boiling point appropriate to its elevation (93° C or 199° F), but after long-continued dry weather it becomes a fumarole with a temperature of 103° C (217° F). Such seasonal variations indicate that hot-spring waters are derived from groundwater that is heated by magmatic gases and that hot springs are essentially "drowned fumaroles." Recent studies of water chemistry support this view and indicate that all thermal waters are essentially of meteoric (atmospheric) origin. This includes high-temperature fumarolic steam that contains such magmatic matter as sulfates, borates, and arsenates that are not present in the rock through which the water has passed.

The steam emitted by solfataras and fumaroles is usually regular rather than intermittent and is never violent. Under particularly favourable conditions, it can reach pressures above 25 atmospheres (one atmosphere equals 14.66 pounds per square inch) and temperatures over 230° C (450° F).   (T.F.W.B./L.C.V./Ed.)

VOLCANIC ERUPTIONS

Ejection of fragments. When the opening of a volcano vent is very narrow, the escape of steam is impeded and the emissions occur at intervals of several minutes. Their speed is such that they merge to form clouds at a certain height above the crater. The emissions may be accompanied by a violent roaring or hissing sound that is impressive.

Open-vent steam emission is generally observed in volcanoes that produce a relatively fluid lava, such as Etna and Vesuvius (see Figure 5). In this type of volcano, steam emission can gradually be transformed into the ejection of scoriaceous (highly vesicular) lava fragments. This happens when the magma ascends the vent to a level at which the steam can act upon it and hurl lava fragments from the volcanic orifice. The still-glowing shreds of magma cool down during their flight through the air, and their contained gases escape and give the fragments an extremely vesicular appearance.

Types of fragments. Gas-rich magmas, rapidly expanding, may produce pumice—a highly inflated foam with bubbles enclosed by thin glass walls—as well as glass shards formed by shattering of bubble walls (Figure 6). Glassy particles include mafic (iron-magnesium) as well as silicic varieties, but silicic glass is most common (see MINERALS AND ROCKS: *Igneous rocks*).

In its greatest expanded state, the porosity values of silicic pumice may attain 90 percent or more; density values are less than water. Vesicles, ranging in size from less than .003 millimetre (.0001 inch) to cavities larger than 10 centimetres (4 inches), are typically distorted by

Importance of steam emission

Figure 6: Photomicrograph of silicic glass shards formed from broken bubbles. White zones within some shards are microvesicular frothy areas (magnified 60 ×).
By courtesy of R.V. Fisher

Varieties of pumice and scoria

impinging bubbles, but because viscosity values of silicic magma increase very rapidly as it cools, cavities are rarely connected (Figure 7).

The shapes of vesicles in some varieties of pumice are roughly circular, whereas in others they are tubular and impart a strong fibrous structure to the pumice. During an initial gas-rich eruptive phase, rapid expansion and extrusion may produce pumice characterized by roughly circular vesicles, but, with a progressive loss of volatile gases, vesicles may be drawn out into tubular shapes during flowage up the vent. Thus, within pumice accumulations produced by different eruptive phases, a progressive loss of volatiles for each phase may be recorded: basal layers containing relatively high amounts of nonfibrous pumice will be succeeded upward by layers containing abundant fibrous pumice. This has been noted for each of 10 eruptive cycles in New Zealand that produced a relatively thick accumulation of pumice layers (the Younger Taupo Pumice).

Scoria, another highly vesicular rock, commonly develops in the early gas-rich phases of basaltic eruptions. Unlike silicic pumice, vesicles in such mafic varieties (Figure 8) are usually undistorted spheres. Those that touch

readily coalesce with smooth openings into one another. The striking differences between mafic and silicic pumice illustrate the effects of viscosity on bubble growth, gas migration, and pumice structures.

A less common form of mafic pumice is reticulite ("thread lace scoria"), a highly unusual rock that attains maximum porosity values between 98 and 99 percent. It consists of an open three-dimensional framework of triangular glass rods connected in regular, somewhat rounded, polygons. Unlike silicic pumice, it quickly sinks in water because the voids are interconnected. The rods occupy quickly chilled bubble junctions that solidified after the bubbles broke and surface tension drew the fluid into each junction. Glassy outer surfaces of reticulite samples have the appearance of partially melted cotton candy; they probably formed as breaking bubbles ran together during breakdown of the foam from the surface. Reticulite is an almost perfect natural replica of a Kelvin minimum area tetrakaidecahedron, which is the best model for a foam with a stable configuration. The tetrakaidecahedron is defined as a body that can be filled with neighbours of the same shape and size in such a way as to fill all available space.

The most common variety of glass shard forms during rapid vesiculation and gaseous disruption or mechanical abrasion of silicic pumice. As governed by structures of the original bubbly foam, they occur in curved plates, pieces with angular prongs where two or more bubbles once joined, or small fragments of microvesicular pumice. Mafic glass shards are produced from finely divided basalt spray formed during fire-fountaining from mechanical abrasion of mafic pumice or from steam explosions as ascending basalt contacts water. Steam explosions caused by basalt flows entering water also produce typical mafic shards.

The ejection of ashes is a form of activity that is similar to the ejection of scoriae. It generally is a persistent activity and is characteristic of the state of a volcano for long periods of time. The ejection of ashes usually is caused by an obstruction in the vent as a result of sliding or collapse of the inner wall of the crater, or when the vent is partially or totally blocked. The magnitude of individual bursts depends on the resistance of the material blocking the vent and, consequently, on the pressure attained by the underlying gases before their escape.

These blocked-vent eruptions are in most cases associated with highly viscous magma, but they also occur in volcanoes with more fluid magma. They are undoubtedly the most common type of eruption and vary greatly according to the nature, viscosity, and quantity of magma emitted. Eruptions of this kind are always somewhat dangerous because they rapidly evolve toward explosive stages of extreme violence. The eruption of Santa Maria in Guatemala, for example, began on October 24, 1902, and ended two days later. Loose material was thrown up to a height of 10,000 metres (33,000 feet) and was deposited over an area with a radius of approximately 14 kilometres (nine miles). The volume of the emitted material was estimated to be 5,500 cubic metres (194,000 cubic feet).

When the gas pressure reaches very high values, the material emitted will be of greater dimensions, and volcanic bombs and blocks will be ejected, together with ashes and sand. Bombs solidify from clots of fresh lava during ejection and flight, their final shapes determined by flight velocity, viscosity, and initial size. Fresh lava may be shaped by frictional air resistance into oval-shaped spindle bombs: some have twisted ends caused by in-flight differential rotation between a rigid exterior and fluid centre. Highly fluid basalt may eject large filaments that freeze as ribbon bombs; spheroidal globs may be flattened into cowdung or pancake bombs. Partially solidified outer surfaces may crack from internal expansion of vesicles and produce bread-crust bombs. A deposit known as an agglutinate forms by accumulations of liquid or slightly tacky bombs that stick together upon impact. Blocks vary widely in shape and composition, depending upon type of rock beneath the volcano. Broken angular shapes are common, but vents may penetrate and eject water-worn gravels, as at Menan Buttes, Idaho.

Bombs and blocks

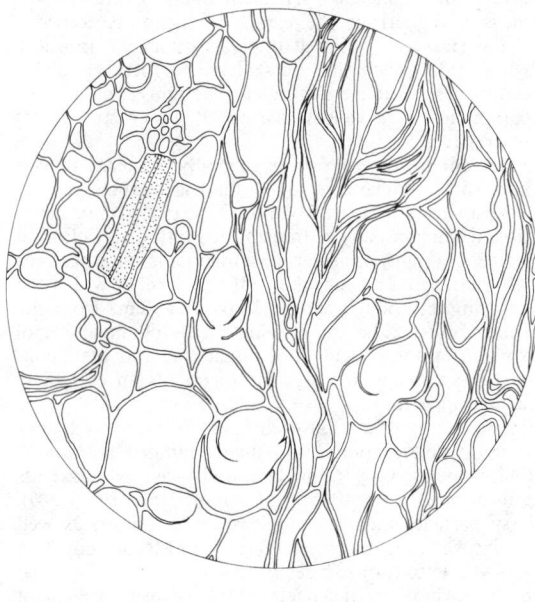

0	0.2 millimetre

Figure 7: Vesicular structure of silicic pumice as seen under microscope.

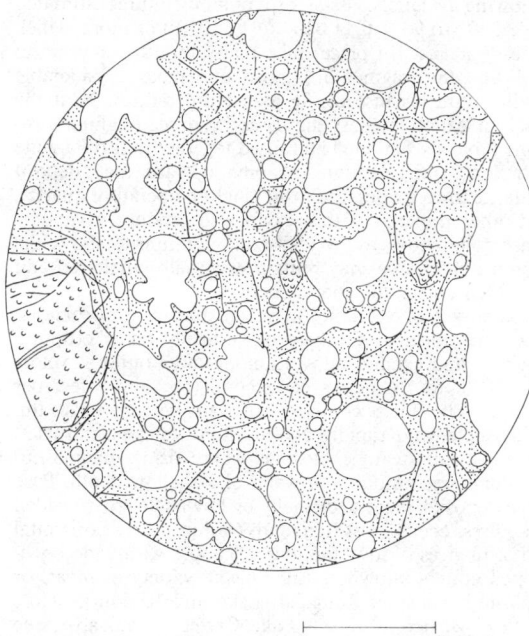

Figure 8: Vesicular structure of mafic pumice as seen under a microscope.

Ashes, pumice, scoriae, and bombs are formed by lava that is emitted while still in its molten state. These ejecta are therefore of magmatic origin, whereas volcanic sands and blocks are fragments of varying size that erupted in a solid state. All fragmentary material, whether emitted in a molten or solid state, is called pyroclastic, meaning fragments formed by fire. The average size of an individual fragment is eight to 10 centimetres (three to four inches), whereas, in exceptional cases, a diameter of 50 centimetres (20 inches) may be attained. The deposits formed by such pyroclastic material are called tephra if in a loose state, and tuff if secondarily compacted.

Dispersal of ejecta. The distribution patterns and geometry of tephra deposits depend largely upon wind directions at various altitudes and upon magmatic factors that determine the volume of ejected debris, the size, shape, and density of individual fragments, and the altitude attained by the particles. Fragments with the highest settling velocities tend to accumulate nearest the source; those of progressively lower settling velocities are carried increasingly farther away, although progressive changes are not regular in detail.

According to the kinetic energy imparted to the ejected debris, a size limit exists above which fragments follow ballistic trajectories and below which they are suspended by turbulence in the eruption cloud. As turbulent energy within the cloud progressively decreases, the maximum size at which particles can be suspended become less, and increasingly smaller particles drop back to Earth unless they are small enough for turbulent suspension by atmospheric wind. Strong winds, however, modify the paths of all but the largest particles; ballistic paths may become elongate downwind, and eruption clouds are pushed en masse in the same direction.

The ground pattern of tephra deposits reflects wind velocity and direction. At any given moment in time, however, velocities and directions may differ at different altitudes, and can change during the course of eruption. Above about 9,000 metres (29,500 feet) frictional interaction with the ground is negligible and winds are regular, but irregularities and variations are more pronounced nearer the surface. Thus, tephra may be dispersed in different directions at different altitudes, providing that ejecta is delivered to that height, as determined by eruption energy. An example is the 1919 eruption of Kelud, Java: ash below 3,200 metres (10,500 feet) was carried eastward; above 3,200 metres it was carried to the west (Figure 9). If winds are undirectional, the largest volume of tephra is distributed in an elongate, symmetrical, oval pattern,

(margin: Aerial dispersal)

with an axis of maximum thickness coinciding with the geometric axis. Thickness tends to decrease downwind exponentially. Decrease in fragment sizes tends to follow the same patterns. If low-level winds distribute the bulkier coarse-grained ejecta in directions different than high-level winds (which spread the fine-grained ejecta and therefore determine the outer limits of distribution), the two axes will not coincide. This also may happen if inclined and strongly directed eruptions, like that at Bezmianny, Kamchatka, in 1956, carry most of the coarsest ejecta at an angle to wind directions.

Size-distribution parameters, such as median size and sorting within a single ejecta blanket, commonly show progressive lateral variations. Such variations are rarely completely systematic because of pulsations in eruptive energy (controlling fragment sizes and their ejected height), shifting wind directions, irregularities of turbulent cell energy in the eruption cloud, associated rainfall, and topographic irregularities.

Subject to the many variables, median diameters of particles from samples from a single ash fall layer tend to decrease exponentially with distance, as shown by tephra from the 1947 eruption of Hekla, Iceland. The slope of the median diameter–distance curve depends upon a combination of eruption energy, wind strength, and particle settling velocity. Plots of data compiled from several different volcanoes, therefore, show wide variations in median grain sizes at a given distance. Points on the high side of the curve, for example, which include Mount Mazama (Crater Lake) samples, reflect higher energy variables (eruption and wind) and lower particle settling velocities (such as abundant pumice) than do points on the low side of the curve (Figure 10).

Because the settling velocity of a particle is in part a function of its composition, lateral size changes in a layer should produce lateral chemical changes as well. This is borne out by ash layers from eruptions of Krakatoa (1883), Kelud, Java (1919), and Quizapú, Chile (1932). The process, known as eolian differentiation, begins in the magma, where the interstitial fluid becomes increasingly more silicic as crystallizing minerals continue to abstract heavier components from the melt. Violent eruption may separate the crystals from the fluid component, which may cool quickly to form glass shards. Shards will settle more slowly than compact crystals of the same size and therefore can be carried farther. As the shard component increases downwind, the chemical composition of the resulting deposit begins to approach that of the interstitial pre-eruption liquid. Toward the source, the layer becomes less silicic. Indeed, because silicic components are carried farther downwind and are relatively depleted, the bulk composition of the deposit near the source can be more mafic than the original magma. The composition of the original magma is approximated by determining the composition of juvenile bombs within the deposits (Table).

Subaerial (on the ground surface—beneath the air, literally) pyroclastic flows are composed of ejecta that travel with hurricane forces along the ground. Dispersal patterns are controlled in large measure by topography, depending upon the surface relief and the size of the flow. Glowing avalanches are hot pyroclastic flows from summit eruptions or from fissures. Those associated with summit eruptions may originate by laterally directed explosions immediately before or during the rise of a volcanic dome (Pelée, 1902), by the rapid fallback of abundant debris from the margin of vertical eruption columns (La Soufrière, St. Vincent,

(margin: Subaerial flow)

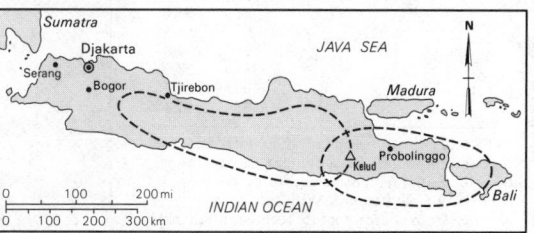

Figure 9: Distribution of ash fall deposits in Java following the eruption of Kelud in 1919.

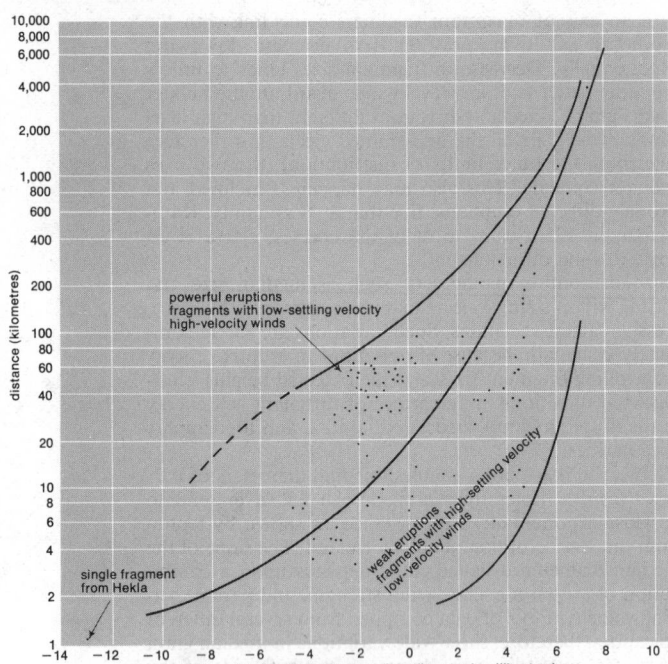

Figure 10: Relation of median size of ash particles to distance from source.

From R.V. Fisher, *Journal of Geophysical Research* (1964)

1902), or by vertical low-pressure eruptions from craters (Krakatoa, 1883). Fissure eruptions occur from the low-pressure upwelling of effervescing magma (Valley of Ten Thousand Smokes, 1912). The world's largest deposits, however, are of Quaternary age (the last 2,500,000 years) or older and have vented from fissures associated with subsidence structures, either calderas or volcanic-tectonic depressions.

Glowing avalanches are derived mainly from silicic to intermediate magmas: their deposits may be termed ignimbrite. Many geologists, however, prefer the term ash-flow for the process of flowage, and ash-flow tuff for the deposits. Glowing avalanches produced from summit eruptions are comparatively small in lateral extent and volume. Their deposits are usually unconsolidated mixtures of lithic (rock), crystal (mineral), or vitric (glass) particles in various proportions that form the matrix within a chaotic mixture of blocks, bombs, and lapilli of pumice, or accessory debris.

Variations in Silica Content of Tephra With Distance From Source, Two Examples*

| eruption | SiO₂ content of original magma (percent)† | SiO₂ content at varying distances | |
		distance (km)	SiO₂ content (percent)
Quizapú, Chile		230	67.5
(1932)	63.8	780	70.2
	64.6	1,120	69.8
		downwind	
Kelud, Java	57.6	36	54.3
(1919)		36	55.0
		54	57.0
		166	60.0
		upwind	
		5	56.1
		9	54.5
		9	54.8
		36	58.0
		36	58.7
		360	60.8

*The table illustrates eolian differentiation. Nearest the source, silica content may be lower than the initial magma as shown by samples from 1919 Kelud tephra. With increasing distance from source, tephra becomes relatively more silicic. †Determined by composition of bombs.

Glowing avalanches issue forth at temperatures estimated to be 550° to 900° C (1,020° to 1,650° F) or more. Thick deposits at rest (in place) take many months or years to cool, and the fragmental deposit undergoes considerable modification because of the high temperatures. Near the base, for example, glass shards and pumice fragments become typically flattened and fused together to form a zone of welded tuff. Vapours escaping upward may deposit hematite (iron oxide), tridymite (high-temperature quartz), and other minerals within cavities to produce a vapour-phase zone above the welded zone. Ignimbrite above the vapour-phase zone may remain essentially unaltered and unwelded during the cooling period.

Base surges of volcanic origin are turbulent pyroclastic flows that form at the base of vertically rising eruption columns and expand outward along the ground at velocities of 20 to 50 metres per second (65 to 165 feet per second). The flows, composed of water vapour or steam, solid ejecta, and rapidly cooling fluid volcanic particles, develop from steam explosions where rising magma encounters large amounts of water at a shallow depth. Base surge deposits, identified chiefly by low-angle cross-bedded structures, occur most frequently within nearly horizontal rim sequences of low-standing volcanoes with wide bowl-shaped craters known as tuff rings, a variety of maar, or explosion, volcano. Zuni Salt Lake and Kilbourne Hole in New Mexico, and Salt Lake Crater, Oahu, are three outstanding examples of tuff rings with well-exposed cross-bedded deposits. **Base surge flow**

Eruptions on land have contributed large volumes of silicic and intermediate ash to the sea. Depending upon the volume, settling rates, and bottom currents, the fragments are variously mixed with nonvolcanic particles. Considerable mixing by marine organisms may occur in some layers. Undisturbed layers commonly have sharp bottom contacts and diffuse upper contacts, and grade upward according to decreasing particle-settling rates. The slow rate at which pumice fragments become waterlogged inhibits their sinking; they eventually settle on top of the smaller crystals and shards unless ocean currents carry them away. The distribution of submarine ash deposits, despite reduced settling rates in water and the consequent increase in the influence of water currents, is controlled in large measure (before deposition in the sea) by the direction of high-level winds, as indicated by the 1815 Tambora ash found on the sea floor north and east of Java. Lack of systematic thickening of 1912 Novarupta (Katmai) ash in the Gulf of Alaska, however, suggests that the ash was redistributed by bottom currents. Both factors probably are operative. **Sub-aqueous deposits**

(L.C.V./R.V.F./Ed.)

Effusion of lava. Slow effusive activity is typical of fluid-lava volcanoes, being a stage in their persistent activity that can occur in the summit (terminal effusion) or on the slopes (lateral effusion). The main characteristics of these slow effusions are high temperature, extreme fluidity, and a remarkably low gas content. This low gas content is not an inherent property of the magma but is caused by the escape of gases while the magmatic masses are in the vent prior to eruption. This is particularly true when a lava lake is formed at the summit of the vent. The surface of a lava lake is further heated by the combustion of the gases escaping from the magma; on contact with the atmosphere, this produces clearly visible flames. As a direct consequence of this heating, the surface viscosity decreases and thus facilitates the additional escape of gases.

Lateral effusions are caused by the infiltration of magma across the volcanic edifice and its surface emergence on the slopes of the mountain. It creates a radial fracture from the central vent through which the lava can pour out at lower and lower points along the slope. When the outflow ceases through lack of supply, the lower parts of the fracture cool down and the lava solidifies to obstruct them. The magma then begins to climb rapidly up the vent until it finds a new way out in the upper, open parts of the fissure. In such way, the fissure is gradually healed from the lower part to its top, and the magma level once more reaches the upper parts of the vent and reestablishes the initial conditions of persistent activity.

Solid pro-
trusions
and glow-
ing clouds

Eruptive phenomena leading to the extrusion of dome-shaped masses and solid protrusions in viscous magma volcanoes are similar to terminal effusions. The viscosity and relatively low lava temperature of volcanoes that extrude domes and solid protrusions prevent the vent from remaining open during periods of inactivity. With every new eruption, the vent must be cleared, and so there is absolutely no form of preliminary activity. When the magmatic mass reaches the vent, it accumulates to form a great dome. The growth of an edifice of this kind is very slow and not continuous, and, in fact, its development is often interrupted by explosive phases that partially destroy it, after which the growth continues with the reconstruction of the parts blown away by the explosion.

If the magmatic mass is extremely viscous, columns of previously solidified lava may be thrown up through the vent. These are called solid protrusions and are also extruded very slowly and with interruptions. The so-called aiguille of Mt. Pelée in Martinique is a famous example; the height attained is about 350 metres (1,150 feet). Slow extrusion phenomena are generally accompanied by frequent and sometimes catastrophic explosions. Following on these explosions, masses are formed by suspensions of solid and partially fused material in high-temperature gas. This suspension is so heavy that it cannot be thrown up to a great height, and so it roars down the volcano slopes, eliminating everything in its path within a few seconds. In most cases, the explosion freeing these suspensions or glowing clouds occurs at the base of the dome or solid protrusion present; thus the cloud emerges laterally.

Volcanic structure and form

Volcanoes can be subdivided into central and fissure types and, with regard to mode of eruptive mechanism, may be monogenetic or polygenetic. Central, monogenetic-lava volcanoes are rarely found as independent structures. They appear more frequently at the foot of more complex volcanoes, as essential elements of the main edifice. Fissure volcanoes emit lava through fractures in the Earth and can cause gigantic lava floods over extensive surface areas.

Explosive fissure volcanoes are less common than effusive ones, but examples are known; the 1886 eruption of Tarawera (New Zealand) along a 14.5-kilometre (nine-mile) fracture produced much pyroclastic material.

Polygenetic lava volcanoes are much more common than monogenetic ones. They are particularly associated with high-temperature, fluid magmas because these do not tend to solidify within the vent and block it. The lava flows emitted tend to pile up, and this leads to the formation of shield volcanoes.

SHIELD VOLCANOES AND STRATOVOLCANOES

The sides of shield volcanoes exhibit angles of slope between three and eight degrees, and their summits usually contain a steep-walled crater with a flat base. This particular crater form is called a pit crater and is characteristic of shield volcanoes.

Hawaiian
and
Icelandic
volcanoes

Shield volcanoes are subdivided according to their size and structure into Icelandic and Hawaiian types. The small, Icelandic shield volcanoes are formed by terminal lava effusions and have an average height of between 100 and 1,000 metres (330 to 3,300 feet) and a base diameter about 20 times that height. The diameters of the summit craters range from 100 to 2,000 metres (330 to 6,600 feet). Skjaldbreidh and Kollótadyngja are examples of this type.

Hawaiian-type shield volcanoes, in contrast, are of gigantic proportions and represent the largest volcanic formations on the Earth, apart from the big basaltic plateaus (Figure 11). Mauna Loa, including its underwater part, is about 10,000 metres (33,000 feet) in height and has a base diameter of about 400 kilometres (250 miles). The Hawaiian shield volcanoes differ from the Icelandic ones because of their greater size, and also because their average angle of slope is not more than six degrees and their summit is a vast plateau.

All shield volcanoes are formed almost totally of basalts (calcium–magnesium-rich rocks) and olivine basalts. In Hawaiian shield volcanoes, other extrusive rocks—such

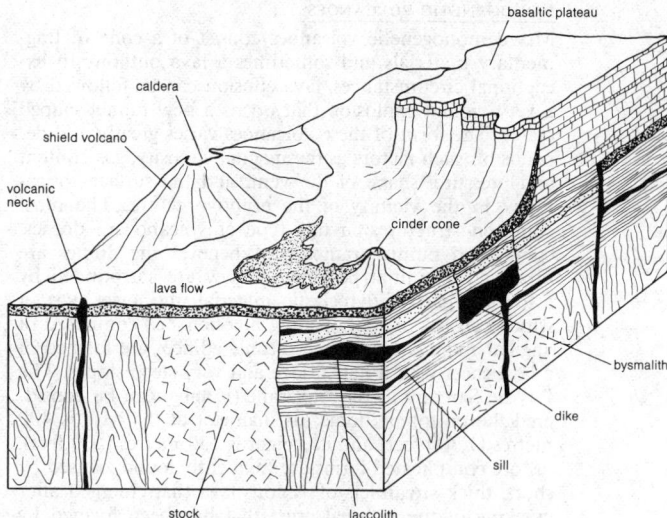

Figure 11: Block diagram showing common volcanic and plutonic structures.

as tephrites, trachytes, and phonolites—are found in only subordinate quantities, derived from basaltic magma by local processes of differentiation (chemical segregation within a magma). The primary magma of the shield volcanoes in the Pacific has the composition of an olivine-rich basalt.

So-called stratovolcanoes include all volcanic edifices that consist of lava flows that alternate with pyroclastic deposits. The name has often been criticized because shield volcanoes and pyroclastic ones are also stratified edifices, but the term is firmly entrenched in the literature to indicate mixed polygenetic volcanoes.

The simplest form of stratovolcano is a cone with a crater at its summit, where most of the eruptions take place. Radial fissures often open through the slopes and lateral eruptions also may occur. Cinder cones frequently formed along these radial fractures contribute to the development of the main edifice. The summit craters of stratovolcanoes undergo frequent variation because of the alternation of explosive and effusive activity. In fact, strong explosive eruptions widen and deepen the crater, whereas slow lava effusion often causes it to become totally filled in.

The internal structure of small stratovolcanoes is normally very simple. Lava flows and pyroclastic materials are regularly deposited on the mountain slopes in such a way that the upper slopes are predominantly formed of lava flows, whereas the fragmentary materials accumulate at the foot of the cone. The internal structure of large stratovolcanoes is complicated by the presence of numerous radial dikes (crosscutting layers of solidified magma) that spread out along the volcanic layers. Further complications are produced by large collapsed zones in summit areas, caused by explosive eruptions that empty the whole vent and sometimes the upper part of the magma chamber. These crater-form depressions are called calderas, and other volcanoes often develop within them, forming multiple volcanic complexes.

A particular type of stratovolcano is the mixed volcanic ridge resulting from the concentration of several single edifices along one fissure; these often fuse together to form one ridge with several craters. A good example of this kind is the volcano Hekla in Iceland.

Compo-
sition of
strato-
volcanoes

Stratovolcanoes are generally formed of rocks containing less than 55 percent silica, such as basalt, andesite, and tephrite. Most of the magmas of this composition form stratovolcanoes in which lava predominates; the more viscous ones yield edifices rich in fragmentary material. Acid magmas, in which the silica content exceeds about 58 percent, yield rocks such as latite, trachyte, phonolite, dacite, and rhyolite. These do not generally form stratovolcanoes but mixed monogenetic volcanoes, because reopening of the vent is practically impossible: it always remains blocked after eruption of an acid magma and can be reopened only by a highly explosive eruption.

MONOGENETIC VOLCANOES

Mixed monogenetic volcanoes consist of a cone of fragmentary materials and sometimes a lava outflow. In exceptional circumstances, lava effusion can be followed by a very violent explosion that opens a new funnel-shaped crater. The form of these volcanoes varies greatly and depends on such factors as the magma viscosity, gas content and pressure, shape of the vent, and the surface topography in the vicinity of the eruptive centre. The most common structures in this type of volcano are domes, cones, and pumice ramparts. Whenever the domes are produced by initial perforation, they are surrounded by a low rampart of pyroclastic material, the lower part of which consists of vent-opening breccia (rock composed of angular fragments). These volcanic edifices are formed of a lava sheet with a flat surface and very steep slopes. The Puy de Sarcouy in the Auvergne (France) can be considered the prototype dome; its diameter at the base is 400 metres (1,300 feet) and its height is 150 metres (500 feet).

More complicated forms are frequently found, caused by short, thick streamlets of viscous lava that emerged after cracking of the external crust that had been formed by cooling. The domes have ribs and outgrowths produced by lateral lava effusions. If a lava effusion occurs at the base of the edifice, it can cause the complete emptying of the dome and the collapse of its summit as internal support is removed. In that case, there is a summit crater with subvertical walls. A similar morphology can be caused by a retreat of the magma in the vent.

Monogenetic volcanoes formed only of pyroclastic material are known to be the product of a single, viscous magma, explosive eruption. They never attain the size of stratovolcanoes but are found in groups in which the individual edifices are partially overlapping. The oldest edifices are often partly destroyed by successive eruptions or become covered over by them. The most common forms are cones and pumice ramparts. Often they are gradually transformed; those farthest from the centre of origin become sheets of pumice and ashes that can sometimes extend for tens of kilometres in the direction the wind was blowing during the eruption.

COMPOSITE VOLCANOES

In the course of time, all magmas undergo variations in chemical composition, essentially because of the gravitational settling out or separation of the crystals that are being formed, and also because of the different temperatures and pressures that prevail through time. Every variation in the magma causes a corresponding variation in the eruptive mechanisms and, therefore, in the form and structure of the volcano. Because the normal evolution of a volcano tends toward increasingly more explosive phases, a systematic classification of volcanoes could be set forth according to their evolution. There is, however, no clear-cut distinction between one group and another, because all transitional phases are represented in nature.

Normal, recurrent, and inverse volcanic activity

Normal composite volcanoes are characterized by a continuous magmatic evolution toward increasing acidity. Their type of structure varies from lava volcano to stratovolcano and then to pyroclastic volcano. A typical sequence occurs when an olivine–basalt shield volcano is subject to a series of more recent andesitic flows and, superimposed on them, little cones of pyroclastic material and sometimes domes. In the opinion of some authorities, West Maui and Waianae in Hawaii are of this type.

Another fairly common sequence in normal composite volcanoes is a basaltic shield volcano covered by an andesitic stratovolcano, the older base of which is mainly formed of lava flows. Etna is an example of this type.

Also resulting from normal evolution are those edifices with a stratovolcano rich in andesitic lava as a base but that are formed almost exclusively of pyroclastic material toward the top, sometimes with dacitic or rhyodacitic (dacite and rhyodacite are volcanic rocks that are relatively rich in quartz) domes. Volcanoes of this type are very frequent in Indonesia (*e.g.*, Merapi, Semeru, Batur), Japan, Kamchatka, the Aleutian Islands, and the Lesser Antilles (Mt. Pelée).

Recurrent composite volcanoes have, as the name suggests, a recurrence of the emitted products and a repetition of the form of activity and structures of the previous stages. A typical recurrence sequence is an andesitic stratovolcano in which a summit caldera has been produced by a highly explosive dacitic or rhyolitic eruption and inside of which a new stratovolcano has been formed. An example of this is Krakatoa, in which the subsequent volcano Anak Krakatoa has been formed in the caldera.

Hekla in Iceland represents a clear case of recurrence of emitted products, even if it is not equally typical in its morphology and structure. The eruptions of this volcano consist of an initial explosive phase producing rhyolitic ashes, followed by ejection of ashes, scoriae, and basaltic effusions, practically without interruption. The repetition of such eruptions leads to the formation of a rhyolitic and basaltic series without intermediate rock types. The products of every individual eruption can be easily distinguished because they are marked at the base by a layer of white rhyolitic ashes.

Inverse composite volcanoes form a numerically small group that consist of volcanic products and structures that are exactly the opposite of normal types. One of the best examples is Stromboli, where the lava has undergone a general evolutionary trend from andesite to basalt. This series is precisely the inverse of that due to normal magmatic differentiation. Vesuvius also has undergone an inverted development with respect to its products and to its eruptive phenomena. It has passed from fairly acid magmas to basic magmas and from explosive activity to a mixed one but with predominantly effusive phases (see Figure 12).

Highly explosive eruptions can instantly empty the whole vent of a volcano and sometimes the upper part of the magma chamber as well. In this case, the central, unsupported part of the volcano collapses and colossal collapse craters, called calderas, are formed. Various types of caldera can be distinguished, according to their form and the mechanisms by which they originate. Summit craters, even very large ones, are called summit calderas, but most calderas are usually much bigger, and the collapse from which they originate essentially covers the entire volcanic edifice. Calderas that formed as a result of a particularly violent, single-explosive eruption are generally circular or elliptical in shape. Their form also depends on the depth at which the explosion occurred, the shape of the magma chamber, and the preexistent fractures and other rock structures that can be reactivated as a result of the collapse.

Formation of calderas

Many calderas owe their formation not to a single eruption but to a series of eruptions that occurred during long intervals of time. Here, the calderas are polygenetic and result from the occurrence of a group of individual, smaller calderic structures with intersecting rims.

In some cases, the magma ascending a volcanic vent that is blocked by a compact lava column has difficulty in breaking the plug and manages more easily to make a new vent parallel to the old one. The vent axis is then shifted and the new eruptive orifice is near, but not coinciding with, the old crater. Under these conditions, the newly formed caldera is eccentric to the axis of the volcanic edifice and its rim obliquely cuts the old cone.

SUBMARINE VOLCANOES

Seamounts, also called guyots, are among the best known submarine volcanic structures. They are basically truncated cones of very regular form and consist of slightly cemented volcanic material.

The phenomena of submarine eruptions are not very different from those of subaerial ones, except for the shape and the deposits of materials produced. The differences increase with depth, to the seabed where the eruptions take place. At a depth of more than 2,000 metres (6,600 feet), prevailing pressure prevents the formation of steam. As a consequence, eruptions are not violent and the ocean floors tend to be covered by lava flows.

When the eruptions do not take place in deep water, the material ejected by the explosions can penetrate the water above it. The water that comes into contact with the lava fragments and high-temperature gases is abruptly heated and transformed into steam, the expansion of which helps

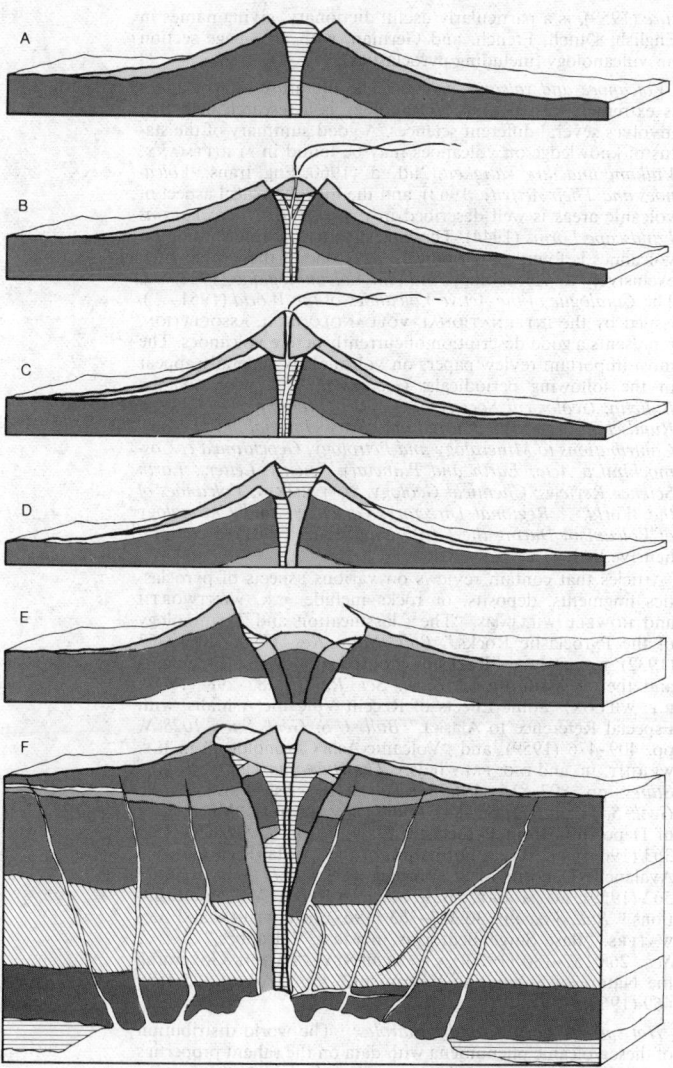

Figure 12: Development of Vesuvius since prehistoric times.
(A) Wide summit crater after last prehistoric eruption; (B)
subsequent buildup of central cone; (C) formation of a single
cone 3,000 metres high (8th century BC); (D) great eruptions
and crater filling (8th century BC); (E) broad summit caldera
after eruption that destroyed Pompeii and Herculaneum (AD
79); and (F) present cone of Vesuvius.

From A. Rittman, *Volcanoes and Their Activity* (1962); John Wiley & Sons, Inc.

produce spectacular steam columns containing glassy lava
fragments.

Sometimes a pyroclastic cone emerges from the sea, forming a short-lived island that is soon afterward destroyed
by the action of the waves. This occurred during the
eruption of the island of Surtsey (1963–64) in the North
Atlantic, when two new, smaller islands were formed in
the immediate vicinity and disappeared within a few days.
Whenever there are numerous repetitive eruptions within
short intervals of time, the volcanic activity may overcome the destructive action of marine erosion and form a
permanent volcanic island. The island of Anak Krakatoa
in the Sunda Strait and Falcon Island in the Tonga group
have originated in this way.

The form and structure of eruptive products in the oceans
differ from those on land because of the abrupt cooling
effect on contact with the seawater. This lava chilling
leads to the formation of a thin, glassy crust on eruptive
material. The crust is rapidly fragmented because of thermal contraction upon cooling and the pressure applied
by the lava within that is still in a fluid condition. The
material resulting from such fragmenting action is called
hyaloclastite (palagonite tuff) because it is composed of
minute glassy fragments that have been altered by contact
with seawater.

Hyaloclastic products can also be formed as a result of
explosive activity in shallow water. Such a process was

**Effects
of rapid
cooling by
seawater**

observed during the eruption of the island of Capelin-
hos in 1957, from which it was possible to discern that
the fragmentation occurs not only because of the violent
expansion of the gaseous phase in the magma, but also
because of the abrupt cooling of the lava fragments.

Basaltic and tephritic submarine flows are further characterized by the presence of rounded-lava forms called
pillow lavas. There are two theories concerning their origin. The first involves ejection of still-fluid lava from the
cooling contraction cracks of the glassy crust and assumes
formation of rounded protuberances that can be detached
from the tubular feed pipes and accumulate at the edges
of the flow itself. The second theory holds that the pillows
are formed only when lava flows down slopes of a certain
gradient; the masses that become detached from its surface
and its front by reason of gravity are thought to take on
immediately the spherical shape of pillows.

Submarine eruptions in the island arcs that ring the Pacific are generally produced by very viscous magmas that
form short and powerful flows of lava blocks or domes.
Contact with seawater causes a glassy crust to be formed
on these products and, because of cooling tensions, a
structure consisting of numerous small concentric cracks
is characteristic. This is called perlitic structure and the
glassy volcanic rock in which it occurs is a perlite.

The origin of volcanoes

Magma consists of a molten-silicate mass within the Earth,
of varying composition and with a temperature of between
800° and 1,500° C (1,500° and 2,700° F). There are several theories about the origin of magmas and the forms
of energy responsible for their motion. Two hypotheses
are widely accepted. According to the first, all magmatic
masses have a common origin from the Earth's mantle
beneath the crust. This assumes that the upper mantle is
in a molten state and that the various types of magma that
emerge during volcanism are formed by differentiation of
this single, primary magma. The second hypothesis is that
of bimodality, which presupposes two primary magmas:
one from the upper mantle and the second derived from
the total or partial fusion of the Earth's crust in areas
where the crust is downbuckled and melted. The actual
origin of magma is arguable (see further MINERALS AND
ROCKS: *Igneous rocks*), but of principal concern here is the
upward migration of magma, which leads to volcanism.

Magmas can be classified in two large groups on the
basis of their upward penetration of the Earth's crust.
The first is of basaltic composition, is very hot and fluid,
and has a specific gravity higher than that of the average
rocks of the Earth's crust. Under these conditions, the
magma is absolutely unable to reach the Earth's surface
unless it can make use of wide, open fissures that allow
it to penetrate. The opening of a fissure causes a drop
in pressure and an immediate decrease of viscosity. Thus
magma becomes very fluid and can easily penetrate the
fissure, where its gaseous content is discharged. The decrease in pressure in an open fissure permits a volume
increase of the ascending magma and, hence, a decrease
in its specific gravity. When this becomes less than that
of the surrounding rocks, an additional thrust is provided,
facilitating its ascent.

Geological observations made in eroded and exposed sections of the Earth's crust confirm the theory that fissures
filled by magma expand in their lower part. In this way,
wedge-shaped magmatic basins are formed having their
thinnest part facing the surface; this is the basic form of a
magmatic chamber and smaller ones or offshoots can be
formed from them.

The simplest case is the lateral intrusion of magma along
bedding planes or surfaces of discontinuity of any kind.
The most important intrusions occur at the discordance
between the crystalline basement rocks and the overlying
cover of sedimentary rocks. Pressure upon and within the
magma makes it act as a wedge; not being able to raise
the sedimentary cover because of its great weight, the
magma finds a way out by forcing down the crystalline
rocks. An inversion of position thus takes place between
the crystalline basement and the magma, and to achieve

**Upward
migration
and
penetra-
tion of
magma**

this, a far smaller energy is needed than that required to raise the sedimentary cover.

The crystalline basement is often subdivided into blocks, bordered by faults (fractures along which earth movements occur), which gives the whole a mosaic-like aspect. In these cases, the intrusion of magma that causes the movement of one of the blocks leads to the formation of parallelepiped-shaped chamber often of considerable thickness. The formation of large magma chambers is nearly always confined to surfaces of discontinuity between the crystalline basement and sedimentary mantle.

Small magma chambers that branch off from large ones seldom feed long-lived volcanoes; they do so only when they can be fed continuously from larger chambers. Often, the connection with the main chamber is only by a small pipe that may become rapidly filled in, thereby interrupting the flow of magma and making the small chamber autonomous, after which it is soon exhausted.

Magmatic energy content

The energy content of magma can be equated to the quantity of heat given off during cooling and the total steam pressure developing during the cooling process. This pressure is proportional to the original gas content. The life of a magmatic chamber and of the volcanoes it feeds depends on the degree of heat, but the quantity and pressure of the volatile components are the result of the potential eruptive energy. A very hot fluid magma will therefore have great total potential energy, but its eruptive energy will be very limited. During cooling and crystallization, the total energy decreases, whereas the eruptive energy increases. In particular, the eruptive energy can attain very high values as a result of differentiation processes that lead to the formation of small quantities of magmas deriving from that source.

Viscous and relatively cold magmas (of about 800° C [1,500° F]), generally of rhyolitic or dacitic composition (acid magmas), have a total energy content lower than that of basaltic magma, but their gas content, and thus their eruptive energy, is much greater. They may be compared to a basaltic-magma differential, but their potential eruptive energy is decidedly higher. Rhyolitic and dacitic magmas are furthermore characterized by a lower specific gravity than that of the surrounding rocks, so they always have a strong ascending thrust within the Earth's crust. Furthermore, they have the ability to make their own path to the surface, thereby creating tensions in the overlying rocks.

The decrease in pressure during the ascent is, as in the case of basaltic magmas, responsible for the formation of a gaseous phase, but the higher viscosity prevents the release of the gases and this causes a progressive increase in their tension. Instead of foaming, the magma expands until the gas pressure overcomes the viscosity resistance. Once it reaches that point, the gases expand violently and free the eruptive energy they had accumulated. The highly explosive eruptions resulting from this lead to the formation of pumice and glowing cloud.   (L.C.V.)

BIBLIOGRAPHY

General works: A. HOLMES, *Principles of Physical Geology,* rev. ed. (1965), an elementary text on physical geology that includes thorough discussions of island arcs, volcanism, and earth tectonics; A.A.G. SCHIEFERDECKER (ed.), *Geological Nomenclature* (1959), is a particularly useful dictionary, giving names in English, Dutch, French, and German, with a 58-page section on vulcanology (including pyroclastics).

Volcanoes and volcanic debris: The literature on volcanoes is extremely vast because volcanology is a research field that involves several different sciences. A good summary of the status of knowledge on volcanoes may be found in A. RITTMANN, *Vulkane und ihre Tätigkeit,* 2nd ed. (1960; Eng. trans., *Volcanoes and Their Activity,* 1962); and the morphological aspect of volcanic areas is well described in C.A. COTTON, *Volcanoes as Landscape Forms* (1944). The largest source of information on volcanoes is found in periodicals; only one of these is devoted exclusively to volcanology: *Bulletin Volcanologique* (1933–   ). The *Catalogue of the Active Volcanoes of the World* (1951–   ), issued by the INTERNATIONAL VOLCANOLOGICAL ASSOCIATION, represents a good description of currently active volcanoes. The most important review papers on volcanology generally appear in the following periodicals: *Geological Society of America Bulletin; Geological Society of America Memoirs; Geologische Rundschau; American Journal of Science; Journal of Petrology; Contributions to Mineralogy and Petrology; Geochimica et Cosmochimica Acta; Earth and Planetary Science Letters; Earth Science Reviews; Chemical Geology.* TOM SIMKIN, *Volcanoes of the World: A Regional Directory, Gazetteer, and Chronology of Volcanism During the Last 10,000 Years* (1981), a comprehensive listing.

Articles that contain reviews on various aspects of pyroclastics fragments, deposits, or rocks include: C.K. WENTWORTH and HOWELL WILLIAMS, "The Classification and Terminology of the Pyroclastic Rocks," *Bull. Natn. Res. Coun.,* 89:19–53 (1932); R.V. FISHER, "Rocks Composed of Volcanic Fragments and their Classification," *Earth Sci. Rev.,* 1:287–298 (1966); R.E. WILCOX, "Some Effects of Recent Volcanic Ashfalls, with Especial Reference to Alaska," *Bull. U.S. Geol. Surv. 1028-N,* pp. 409–476 (1959), and "Volcanic-Ash Chronology," in H.E. WRIGHT, JR. and D.G. FREY (eds.), *The Quaternary of the United States,* pp. 807–816 (1965); R.L. SMITH, "Ash Flows," *Bull. Geol. Soc. Am.,* 71:795–841 (1960); R.V. FISHER, "Mechanism of Deposition from Pyroclastic Flows," *Am. J. Sci.,* 264:350–363 (1966); R.L. HAY, "Formation of the Crystal-Rich Glowing Avalanche Deposits of St. Vincent, B.W.I.," *J. Geol.,* 67:540–562 (1959); J.G. MOORE, "Base Surge in Recent Volcanic Eruptions," *Bull. Volcan.,* 30:337–363 (1967); R.V. FISHER and A.C. WATERS, "Base Surge Bedforms in Maar Volcanoes," *Am. J. Sci.,* 268:157–180 (1970); A.R. MCBIRNEY, "Factors Governing the Nature of Submarine Volcanism," *Bull. Volcan.,* 25:455–469 (1963).

Hot springs, geysers, and fumaroles: The world distribution of these volcanic phenomena with data on the salient properties and mode of occurrence has been compiled in an impressive publication by G.A. WARING, "Thermal Springs of the United States and Other Countries of the World," *Prof. Pap. U.S. Geol. Surv. 492,* rev. by R.R. BLANKENSHIP and R. BENTALL (1965). The U.S. DEPARTMENT OF COMMERCE, NATIONAL OCEANIC AND ATMOSPHERIC ADMINISTRATION has published a *Thermal Springs List for the United States* (1980). A summary report on thermal waters of the world was edited by G. KACURA, *Mineral and Thermal Waters of the World,* 2 vol. (1968), the proceedings of the 2nd Symposium of the 23rd International Geological Congress; and E.T. ALLEN and A.L. DAY published a most illuminating study in *Hot Springs of the Yellowstone National Park* (1935). There is a similar monograph on the springs of Iceland in T.F.W. BARTH, *Volcanic Geology, Hot Springs and Geysers of Iceland* (1950, reissued 1979); and an interesting account of the Valley of Ten Thousand Smokes was provided by E.G. ZIES, "The Fumarolic Incrustations in the Valley of Ten Thousand Smokes," *Tech. Pap. Natn. Geog. Soc.,* Katmai series, vol. 1, no. 3 (1924).

Voltaire

Voltaire, one of the greatest French authors, though only a few of his works are still read, is held in worldwide repute as a courageous crusader against tyranny, bigotry, and cruelty. He embodies characteristic qualities of the French mind—a critical capacity, wit, and satire. His whole work vigorously propagates an ideal of progress to which men of all nations have remained responsive. His long life spans the last years of classicism and the eve of the revolutionary era; during this age of transition his works and activities influenced the direction taken by European civilization.

Voltaire, portrait by an unknown artist after a portrait by Nicolas de Largillière, 1718. In the Château de Versailles.

Heritage and youth. Voltaire's background was middle class. According to his birth certificate he was born François-Marie Arouet in Paris on November 21, 1694, but the hypothesis that his birth was kept secret cannot be dismissed, for he stated on several occasions that in fact it took place on February 20, 1694. He believed that he was the son of an officer named Rochebrune, who was also a songwriter. He had no love for either his putative father, François Arouet, a onetime notary who later became receiver in the Cour des Comptes (audit office), or his elder brother Armand. Almost nothing is known about his mother of whom he hardly said anything. Having lost her when he was seven, he seems to have become an early rebel against family authority. He attached himself to his godfather, the Abbé de Châteauneuf, a freethinker and epicurean who presented the boy to the famous courtesan Ninon de Lenclos when she was in her 84th year. But it is doubtless that he owed his positive outlook and his sense of reality to his bourgeois origins.

He attended the Jesuit college of Louis-le-Grand in Paris, where he learned to love literature, the theatre, and social life. While he appreciated the classical taste the college instilled in him, the religious instruction of the fathers served only to arouse his skepticism and mockery. He witnessed the last sad years of Louis XIV and was never to forget the distress and the military disasters of 1709 nor the horrors of religious persecution. He retained, however, a degree of admiration for the sovereign, and he remained convinced that the enlightened kings are the indispensable agents of progress.

He decided against the study of law after he left college. Employed as secretary at the French embassy in The Hague, he became infatuated with the daughter of an adventurer. Fearing scandal, the French ambassador sent him back to Paris. Despite his father's wishes, he wanted to devote himself wholly to literature, and he frequented the Temple, then the centre of free-thinking society. After the death of Louis XIV, under the morally relaxed Regency, Voltaire became the wit of Parisian society, and his epigrams were widely quoted. But when he dared to mock the dissolute regent, the Duc d'Orléans, he was banished from Paris and then imprisoned in the Bastille for nearly a year (1717). Behind his gay facade, he was fundamentally serious and set himself to learn the accepted literary forms. In 1718, after the success of *Oedipe,* the first of his tragedies, he was acclaimed as the successor of the great classical dramatist Jean Racine and thenceforward adopted the name of Voltaire. The origin of this pen name remains doubtful. It is not certain that it is the anagram of Arouet le jeune (*i.e.,* the younger). Above all he desired to be the Virgil that France had never known. He worked at an epic poem whose hero was Henry IV, the king beloved by the French people for having put an end to the wars of religion. This *Henriade* is spoiled by its pedantic imitation of Virgil's *Aeneid,* but his contemporaries saw only the generous ideal of tolerance that inspired the poem. These literary triumphs earned him a pension from the regent and the warm approval of the young queen, Marie. He thus began his career of court poet.

Early drama and poetry

United with other thinkers of his day—literary men and scientists—in the belief in the efficacy of reason, Voltaire was a Philosophe, as the 18th century termed it. In the salons he professed an aggressive Deism, which scandalized the devout. He became interested in England, the country that tolerated freedom of thought; he visited the Tory leader Viscount Bolingbroke, exiled in France—a politician, an orator, and a philosopher whom Voltaire admired to the point of comparing him to Cicero. On Bolingbroke's advice he learned English in order to read the philosophical works of John Locke. His intellectual development was furthered by an accident: as the result of a quarrel with a member of one of the leading French families, the Chevalier de Rohan, who had made fun of his adopted name, he was beaten up, taken to the Bastille, and then conducted to Calais on May 5, 1726, from where he set out for London. His destiny was now exile and opposition.

Exile to England. During a stay that lasted more than two years he succeeded in learning the English language; he wrote his notebooks in English and to the end of his life he was able to speak and write it fluently. He met such English men of letters as Alexander Pope, Jonathan Swift, and William Congreve, the philosopher George Berkeley, and Samuel Clarke, the theologian. He was presented at court, and he dedicated his *Henriade* to Queen Caroline. Though at first he was patronized by Bolingbroke, who had returned from exile, it appears that he quarrelled with the Tory leader and turned to Sir Robert Walpole and the liberal Whigs. He admired the liberalism of English institutions, though he was shocked by the partisan violence. He envied English intrepidity in the discussion of religious and philosophic questions and was particularly interested in the Quakers. He was convinced that it was because of their personal liberty that the English, notably Sir Isaac Newton and John Locke, were in the forefront of scientific thought. He believed that this nation of merchants and sailors owed its victories over Louis XIV to its economic advantages. He concluded that even in literature France had something to learn from England; his experience of Shakespearean theatre was overwhelming, and, however much he was shocked by the "barbarism" of the productions, he was struck by the energy of the characters and the dramatic force of the plots.

Meetings with English men of letters

Return to France. He returned to France at the end of 1728 or the beginning of 1729 and decided to present England as a model to his compatriots. His social position was consolidated. By judicious speculation he began to build up the vast fortune that guaranteed his independence. He attempted to revive tragedy by discreetly imitating Shakespeare. *Brutus,* begun in London and accompanied by a *Discours à milord Bolingbroke,* was scarcely a success in 1730; *La Mort de César* was played only in a college (1735); in *Eriphyle* (1732), the apparition of a ghost, as in *Hamlet,* was booed by the audience. *Zaïre,* however, was a resounding success. The play, in which the sultan Orosmane, deceived by an ambiguous letter, stabs his prisoner, the devoted Christian-born Zaïre, in a fit of jealousy, captivated the public with its exotic subject.

At the same time Voltaire had turned to a new literary genre: history. In London he had made the acquaintance of Fabrice, a former companion of the Swedish king Charles XII. The interest he felt for the extraordinary character of this great soldier impelled him to write his life, *Histoire de Charles XII* (1731), a carefully documented historical narrative that reads like a novel. Philosophic ideas began to impose themselves as he wrote: the King of Sweden's exploits brought desolation, whereas his rival Peter the Great brought Russia into being, bequeathing a vast, civilized empire. Great men are not warmongers; they further civilization—a conclusion that tallied with the example of England. It was this line of thought that Voltaire brought to fruition, after prolonged meditation, in a work of incisive brevity: the *Lettres philosophiques* (1734). These fictitious letters are primarily a demonstration of the benign effects of religious toleration. They contrast the wise Empiricist psychology of Locke with the conjectural lucubrations of René Descartes. A philosopher worthy of the name, such as Newton, disdains empty, a priori speculations; he observes the facts and reasons from them. After elucidating the English political system, its commerce, its literature, and the Shakespeare almost unknown to France, Voltaire concludes with an attack on the French mathematician and religious philosopher Pascal: the purpose of life is not to reach heaven through penitence but to assure happiness to all men by progress in the sciences and the arts, a fulfillment for which their nature is destined. This small, brilliant book is a landmark in the history of thought: not only does it embody the philosophy of the 18th century, but it also defines the essential direction of the modern mind.

Life with Mme du Châtelet. Scandal followed publication of this work that spoke out so frankly against the religious and political establishment. When a warrant of arrest was issued in May of 1734, Voltaire took refuge in the château of Mme du Châtelet at Cirey in Champagne and thus began his liaison with this young, remarkably intelligent woman. He lived with her in the château he had renovated at his own expense. This period of retreat was interrupted only by a journey to the Low Countries in December 1736—an exile of a few weeks became advisable after the circulation of a short, daringly epicurean poem called "Le Mondain."

The life these two lived together was both luxurious and studious. After *Adélaïde du Guesclin* (1734), a play about a national tragedy, he brought *Alzire* to the stage in 1736 with great success. The action of *Alzire*—in Lima, Peru, at the time of the Spanish conquest—brings out the moral superiority of a humanitarian civilization over methods of brute force. Despite the conventional portrayal of "noble savages," the tragedy kept its place in the repertory of the Comédie-Française for almost a century. Mme du Châtelet was passionately drawn to the sciences and metaphysics and influenced Voltaire's work in that direction. A "gallery" or laboratory of the physical sciences was installed at the château, and they composed a memorandum on the nature of fire for a meeting of the Académie des Sciences. While Mme du Châtelet was learning English in order to translate Newton and *The Fable of the Bees* of Bernard de Mandeville, Voltaire popularized, in his *Éléments de la philosophie de Newton* (1738), those discoveries of English science that were familiar only to a few advanced minds in France, such as the astronomer and mathematician Pierre-Louis de Maupertuis. At the same time, he continued to pursue his historical studies. He began *Le Siècle*

Interest in history [marginal note]

Interest in science and metaphysics [marginal note]

de Louis XIV, sketched out a universal history of kings, wars, civilization and manners that became the *Essai sur les moeurs,* and plunged into biblical exegesis. Mme du Châtelet herself wrote an *Examen,* highly critical of the two Testaments. It was at Cirey that Voltaire, rounding out his scientific knowledge, acquired the encyclopaedic culture that was one of the outstanding facets of his genius.

Because of a lawsuit, he followed Mme du Châtelet to Brussels in May 1739, and thereafter they were constantly on the move between Belgium, Cirey, and Paris. Voltaire corresponded with the crown prince of Prussia, who, rebelling against his father's rigid system of military training and education, had taken refuge in French culture. When the prince acceded to the throne as Frederick II (the Great), Voltaire visited his disciple first at Cleves (Kleve, West Germany), then at Berlin. When the War of the Austrian Succession broke out, Voltaire was sent to Berlin (1742–43) on a secret mission to rally the King of Prussia—who was proving himself a faithless ally—to the assistance of the French Army. Such services—as well as his introduction of his friends the brothers d'Argenson, who became ministers of war and foreign affairs, respectively, to the protection of Mme de Pompadour, the mistress of Louis XV—brought him into favour again at Versailles. After his poem celebrating the victory of Fontenoy (1745), he was appointed historiographer, gentleman of the king's chamber, and academician. His tragedy *Mérope,* about the mythical Greek queen, won public acclaim on the first night (1743). The performance of *Mahomet,* in which Voltaire presented the founder of Islām as an imposter, was forbidden, however, after its successful production in 1742. He amassed a vast fortune through the manipulations of Joseph Pâris Duverney, the financier in charge of military supplies, who was favoured by Mme de Pompadour. In this ambience of well-being, he began a liaison with his niece Mme Denis, a charming widow, without breaking off his relationship with Mme du Châtelet.

Yet he was not spared disappointments. Louis XV disliked him, and the pious Catholic faction at court remained acutely hostile. He was guilty of indiscretions. When Mme du Châtelet lost large sums at the Queen's gaming table, he said to her in English: "You are playing with cardsharpers"; the phrase was understood, and he was forced to go into hiding at the country mansion as the guest of the Duchesse du Maine in 1747. Ill and exhausted by his restless existence, he at last discovered the literary form that ideally fitted his lively and disillusioned temper: he wrote his first *contes* (stories). *Micromégas* (1752) measures the littleness of man in the cosmic scale; *Vision de Babouc* (1748) and *Memnon* (1749) dispute the philosophic optimism of Gottfried Wilhelm Leibniz and Alexander Pope. *Zadig* (1747) is a kind of allegorical autobiography: like Voltaire, the Babylonian sage Zadig suffers persecution, is pursued by ill fortune, and ends by doubting the tender care of Providence for human beings.

The great crisis of his life was drawing near. In 1748 at Commercy, where he had joined the court of Stanisław (the former king of Poland), he detected the love affair of Mme du Châtelet and the poet Saint-Lambert, a slightly ludicrous passion that ended tragically. On September 10, 1749, he witnessed the death in childbirth of this uncommonly intelligent woman who for 15 years had been his guide and counsellor. He returned in despair to the house in Paris where they had lived together; he rose in the night and wandered in the darkness, calling her name.

Death of Mme du Châtelet [marginal note]

Later travels. The failure of some of his plays aggravated his sense of defeat. He had attempted the *comédie larmoyante,* or "sentimental comedy," that was then fashionable: after *L'Enfant prodigue* (1736), a variation of the prodigal son theme, he adapted William Wycherley's satiric Restoration drama *The Plain-Dealer* to his purpose, entitling it *La Prude;* he based *Nanine* (1749) on a situation taken from Samuel Richardson's novel *Pamela,* but all without success. The court spectacles he directed gave him a taste for scenic effects, and he contrived a sumptuous decor, as well as the apparition of a ghost, for *Sémiramis* (1748), but his public was not captivated. His enemies compared him with Prosper Jolyot, sieur de Crébillon, who was pre-eminent among French writers of tragedy at this time. Though Voltaire used the same subjects as his rival (*Oreste, Sémiramis*), the Parisian audience preferred the plays of Crébillon. Exasperated and disappointed, he yielded to the pressing invitation of Frederick II and set out for Berlin on June 28, 1750.

At the moment of his departure a new literary generation, reacting against the ideas and tastes to which he remained faithful, was coming to the fore in France. Disseminators of the philosophical ideas of the time, such as Denis Diderot, Baron d'Holbach, and their friends, were protagonists of a thoroughgoing Materialism and regarded Voltaire's Deism as too timid. Others had rediscovered with Jean-Jacques Rousseau the poetry of Christianity. All in fact preferred the charm of sentiment and passion to the enlightenment of reason. As the years passed, Voltaire became increasingly more isolated in his glory.

At first he was enchanted by his sojourn in Berlin and Potsdam, but soon difficulties arose. After a lawsuit with a moneylender, and quarrels with prominent noblemen, he started a controversy with Maupertuis (the president of Frederick's academy of science, the Berlin Academy) on scientific matters. In a pamphlet entitled "Diatribe du docteur Akakia" (1752), he covered him with ridicule. The King, enraged, consigned "Akakia" to the flames and gave its author a thorough dressing down. Voltaire left Prussia on March 26, 1753, leaving Frederick exasperated and determined to punish him. On the journey he was held under house arrest at an inn at Frankfurt, by order of the Prussian resident. Louis XV forbade him to approach Paris. Not knowing where to turn, he stayed at Colmar for more than a year. At length he found asylum at Geneva, where he purchased a house called Les Délices, at the same time securing winter quarters at Lausanne.

Major historical studies

He now completed his two major historical studies. *Le Siècle de Louis XIV* (1751), a book on the century of Louis XIV, had been prepared after an exhaustive 20-year interrogation of the survivors of *le grand siècle.* Voltaire was particularly concerned to establish the truth by collecting evidence from as many witnesses as possible, evidence that he submitted to exacting criticism. His desire was to write the nation's history by means of an examination of its arts and sciences and of its social life, but military events and politics still occupy a large place in his survey. The *Essai sur les moeurs,* the study on customs and morals that he had begun in 1740 (first complete edition, 1756), traced the course of world history since the end of the Roman Empire and gave an important place to the Eastern and Far Eastern countries. Voltaire's object was to show humanity slowly developing beyond barbarism. He supplemented these two works with one on Russian history during the reign of Peter the Great, *Histoire de l'empire de Russie sous Pierre le Grand* (1759–63), the *Philosophie de l'histoire* (1765), and the *Précis du siècle de Louis XV* (1768).

At Geneva, he had at first been welcomed and honoured as the champion of tolerance. But soon he made those around him feel uneasy. At Les Délices his presentation of plays was stopped, in accordance with the law of the republic of Geneva, which forbade both public and private theatre performances. Then there was his mock-heroic poem "La Pucelle" (1755), a most improper presentation of Joan of Arc (*La Pucelle d'Orléans),* which the booksellers printed in spite of his protests.

Attracted by his volatile intelligence, Calvinist pastors as well as women and young people thronged to his salon. Yet he soon provoked the hostility of important Swiss intellectuals. The storm broke in November 1757, when volume seven of Diderot's *Encyclopédie* was published. Voltaire had inspired the article on Geneva that his fellow philosopher Jean d'Alembert had written after a visit to Les Délices; not only was the city of Calvin asked to build a theatre within its walls but also certain of its pastors were praised for their doubts of Christ's divinity. The scandal sparked a quick response: the *Encyclopédie* was forced to interrupt publication, and Rousseau attacked the rational philosophy of the Philosophes in general in a polemical treatise on the question of the morality of theatrical performances, *Lettre à d'Alembert sur les spectacles* (1758). Rousseau's view that drama might well be

abolished marked a final break between the two writers.

Voltaire no longer felt safe in Geneva, and he longed to retire from these quarrels. In 1758 he wrote what was to be his most famous work, *Candide.* In this philosophical fantasy, the youth Candide, disciple of Doctor Pangloss (himself a disciple of the philosophical optimism of Leibniz), saw and suffered such misfortune that he was unable to believe that this was "the best of all possible worlds." Having retired with his companions to the shores of the Propontis, he discovered that the secret of happiness was "to cultivate one's garden," a practical philosophy excluding excessive idealism and nebulous metaphysics. Voltaire's own garden became Ferney, a property he bought at the end of 1758, together with Tourney in France, on the Swiss border. By crossing the frontier he could thus safeguard himself against police incursion from either country.

Candide

Achievements at Ferney. At Ferney, Voltaire entered on one of the most active periods of his life. Both patriarch and lord of the manor, he developed a modern estate, sharing in the movement of agricultural reform in which the aristocracy was interested at the time. He could not be true to himself, however, without stirring up village feuds and went before the magistrates on a question of tithes, as well as about the beating of one of his workmen. He renovated the church and had *Deo erexit Voltaire* ("Voltaire erected this to God") carved on the facade. At Easter Communion, 1762, he delivered a sermon on stealing and drunkenness and repeated this sacrilegious offense in the following year, flouting the prohibition by the bishop of Annecy, in whose jurisdiction Ferney lay. He meddled in Genevan politics, taking the side of the workers (or *natifs,* those without civil rights), and installed a stocking factory and watchworks on his estate in order to help them. He called for the liberation of serfs in the Jura, but without success, though he did succeed in suppressing the customs barrier on the road between Gex in the Jura and Geneva, the natural outlet for the produce of Gex. Such generous interventions in local politics earned him enormous popularity. In 1777 he received a popular acclamation from the people of Ferney. In 1815 the Congress of Vienna halted the annexation of Ferney to Switzerland in his honour.

His fame was now worldwide. "Innkeeper of Europe"—as he was called—he welcomed such literary figures as James Boswell, Giovanni Casanova, Edward Gibbon, the Prince de Ligne, and the fashionable philosophers of Paris. He kept up an enormous correspondence—with the Philosophes, with his actresses and actors, and with those high in court circles, such as the Duc de Richelieu (grandnephew of the Cardinal de Richelieu), the Duc de Choiseul, and Mme du Barry, Louis XV's favourite. He renewed his correspondence with Frederick II and exchanged letters with Catherine II of Russia.

There was scarcely a subject of importance on which he did not speak. In his political ideas, he was basically a liberal, though he also admired the authority of those kings who imposed progressive measures on their people. On the question of fossils, he entered into foolhardy controversy with the famous French naturalist Comte de Buffon. On the other hand, he declared himself a partisan of the Italian scientist Abbé Lazzaro Spallanzani against the hypothesis of spontaneous generation, according to which microscopic organisms are generated spontaneously in organic substances. He busied himself with political economy and revived his interest in metaphysics by absorbing the ideas of 17th-century philosophers Benedict de Spinoza and Nicolas Malebranche.

Scientific, political, and religious controversies

His main interest at this time, however, was his opposition to *l'infâme,* a word he used to designate the church, especially when it was identified with intolerance. For mankind's future he envisaged a simple theism, reinforcing the civil power of the state. He believed this end was being achieved when, about 1770, the courts of Paris, Vienna, and Madrid came into conflict with the pope; but this was to misjudge the solidarity of ecclesiastical institutions and the people's loyalty to the traditional faith. Voltaire's beliefs prompted a prodigious number of polemical writings. He multiplied his personal attacks, often stooping to low cunning; in his sentimental comedy *L'Écossaise* (1760), he mimicked the eminent critic Élie Fréron, who had attacked him in reviews, by portraying his adversary as a rascally journalist who intervenes in a quarrel between two Scottish families. He directed *Le Sentiment des Citoyens* (1764) against Rousseau. In this anonymous pamphlet, which supposedly expressed the opinion of the Genevese, Voltaire, who was well informed, revealed to the public that Rousseau had abandoned his children. As author he used all kinds of pseudonyms: Rabbi Akib, Pastor Bourn, Lord Bolingbroke, M. Mamaki "interpreter of Oriental languages to the king of England," Clocpitre, Cubstorf, Jean Plokof—a nonstop performance of puppets. As a part-time scholar he constructed a personal *Encyclopédie*, the *Dictionnaire philosophique* (1764), enlarged after 1770 by *Questions sur l'Encyclopédie*. Among the mass of writings of this period are: *Le Blanc et le noir* ("The White and the Black"), a philosophical tale in which Oriental fantasy contrasts with the realism of *Jeannot et Colin; Princesse de Babylone,* a panorama of European philosophies in the fairyland of *The Thousand and One Nights;* and *Le Taureau blanc,* a biblical tale.

Again and again Voltaire returned to his chosen themes: the establishment of religious tolerance, the growth of material prosperity, respect for the rights of man by the abolition of torture and useless punishments. These principles were brought into play when he intervened in some of the notorious public scandals of these years. For instance, when the Protestant Jean Calas, a merchant of Toulouse accused of having murdered his son in order to prevent his conversion to the Roman Catholic Church, was broken on the wheel while protesting his innocence (March 10, 1762), Voltaire, livid with anger, took up the case and by his vigorous intervention obtained the vindication of the unfortunate Calas and the indemnification of the family. But he was less successful in a dramatic affair concerning the 19-year-old Chevalier de La Barre, who was beheaded for having insulted a religious procession and damaging a crucifix (July 1, 1766). Public opinion was distressed by such barbarity, but it was Voltaire who protested actively, suggesting that the Philosophes should leave French territory and settle in the town of Cleves offered them by Frederick II. Although he failed to obtain even a review of this scandalous trial, he was able to reverse other judicial errors.

By such means he retained leadership of the philosophic movement. On the other hand, as a writer, he wanted to halt a development he deplored—that which led to Romanticism. He tried to save theatrical tragedy by making concessions to a public that adored scenes of violence and exoticism. For instance, in *JL'Orphelin de la Chine* (1755), Lekain (Henri-Louis Cain), who played the part of Genghis Khan, was clad in a sensational Mongol costume. Lekain, whom Voltaire considered the greatest tragedian of his time, also played the title role of *Tancrède,* which was produced with a sumptuous decor (1760) and which proved to be Voltaire's last triumph. Subsequent tragedies, arid and ill-constructed and overweighted with philosophic propaganda, were either booed off the stage or not produced at all. He became alarmed at the increasing influence of Shakespeare; when he gave a home to a grandniece of the great 17th-century classical dramatist Pierre Corneille and on her behalf published an annotated edition of the famous tragic author, he inserted, after *Cinna,* a translation of *Julius Caesar,* convinced that such a confrontation would demonstrate the superiority of the French dramatist. He was infuriated by the Shakespearean translations of Pierre Le Tourneur in 1776, which stimulated French appreciation of this more robust, nonclassical dramatist, and dispatched an abusive *Lettre à l'Académie.* He never ceased to acknowledge a degree of genius in Shakespeare, yet spoke of him as "a drunken savage." He returned to a strict classicism in his last plays, but in vain, for the audacities of his own previous tragedies, timid as they were, had paved the way for Romantic drama.

It was the theatre that brought him back to Paris in 1778. Wishing to direct the rehearsals of *Irène,* he made his triumphal return·to the city he had not seen for 28 years on February 10. More than 300 persons called on him the day after his arrival. On March 30 he went to the

Late dramatic works

Académie amid acclamations, and, when *Irène* was played before a delirious audience, he was crowned in his box. His health was profoundly impaired by all this excitement. On May 18 he was stricken with uremia. He suffered much pain on his deathbed—about which absurd legends were quickly fabricated; on May 30 he died, peacefully it seems. His nephew, the Abbé Mignot, had his body, clothed just as it was, swiftly transported to the Abbey of Scellières, where he was given Christian burial by the local clergy; the prohibition of such burial arrived after the ceremony. His remains were transferred to the Panthéon during the Revolution in July 1791.

Assessment. Voltaire's name has always evoked vivid reactions. Toward the end of his life he was attacked by the followers of Rousseau, and after 1800 he was held responsible for the Revolution. But the excesses of clerical reactionaries under the Restoration and the Second Empire rallied the middle and working classes to his memory. At the end of the 19th century, though conservative critics remained hostile, scientific research into his life and works was given impetus by Gustave Lanson. Voltaire himself did not hope that all his vast quantity of writings would be remembered by posterity. His epic poems and lyrical verse are virtually dead, as are his plays. But his *contes* are continually republished, and his letters are regarded as one of the great monuments of French literature. He bequeathed a lesson to humanity, which has lost nothing of its value. He taught men to think clearly; his was a mind at once precise and generous. "He is the necessary philosopher," wrote Lanson, "in a world of bureaucrats, engineers, and producers."

(R.H.Po.)

MAJOR WORKS

STORIES: *Les Voyages du baron de Gangan* (1739; an earlier version of *Micromégas,* 1752); *Zadig* (1747; Eng. trans. by J. Butt, 1964); *Vision de Babouc* (1748); *Candide* (1759; Eng. trans. by J. Spencer, 1966, and by Robert M. Adams, 1966); *Le Blanc et le noir* (1764; *The Two Genies,* 1895); *Jeannot et Colin* (1764); *La Princesse de Babylone* (1768; Eng. trans. 1969); *Le Taureau blanc* (1774; Eng. trans. 1774—attributed to Jeremy Bentham).

HISTORY: *Histoire de Charles XII* (1731; Eng. trans. by C. Messiter, 1860); *Le Siècle de Louis XIV* (1751; Eng. trans. by J.H. Brumfitt, 1966); *Histoire de l'empire de Russie sous Pierre le Grand* (1759–63; Eng. trans. 1763); *Précis du siècle de Louis XV* (1768; Eng. trans. 1774, 2 vol.).

PHILOSOPHY: *Lettres philosophiques* (1734); *Éléments de la philosophie de Newton* (1738; Eng. trans. 1738); *Essai sur les moeurs* (1756; Eng. trans. by Nugent, 1759); *Dictionnaire philosophique* (1764; Eng. trans. by H.I. Woolf, 1945); *Philosophie de l'histoire* (1765; Eng. trans. 1965).

PLAYS: *Zaïre* (1732; Eng. trans. by A. Wallace, 1854); *Alzire* (1736; *Tragedy of Alzira,* trans. by A. Hill, 1817); *Mérope* (1743; Eng. trans. by A. Hill, 1803).

OTHER WORKS: *La Henriade* (1728; Eng. trans. by R.G. Macgregor, 1854), an epic poem; *Voltaire's Correspondence,* ed. by Theodore Besterman (including translations into English such as *The Love Letters of Voltaire to His Niece,* 1958; and *Select Letters of Voltaire,* 1963).

BIBLIOGRAPHY. MARY MARGARET BARR, *Century of Voltaire Study: A Bibliography of Writings on Voltaire, 1825–1925* (1929, reissued 1972); and *Quarante années d'études voltairiennes . . . 1926–1965* (1968). Beginning in 1955, *Studies on Voltaire and the Eighteenth Century* (several books a year) was issued by the Institut et Musée Voltaire (and later by the Voltaire Foundation).

Editions: Les Oeuvres complètes is an edition begun in 1968, directed first by THEODORE BESTERMAN, then by GILES BARBER, with introductions and notes in English and French. Among the volumes published are 51 volumes of Voltaire's complete correspondence and related documents.

Biography: GUSTAVE DESNOIRESTERRES, *Voltaire et la société au XVIII⁰ siècle,* 2nd ed., 8 vol. (1871–76), an anecdotal work that was the basis for most later Voltaire biography—outdated now because of the numerous documents discovered since its publication; THEODORE BESTERMAN, *Voltaire,* 3rd ed. (1976), an excellent, thorough biography; IRA O. WADE, *The Intellectual Development of Voltaire* (1969), a scholarly biography; A. OWEN ALDRIDGE, *Voltaire and the Century of Light* (1975), a thorough examination of the life and works; JEAN ORIEUX, *Voltaire* (1979; originally published in French, 1966), a detailed biographical account by a French historian; PEYTON E. RICHTER and ILONA RICARDO, *Voltaire* (1980), an introductory life for the general reader; and HAYDN MASON, *Voltaire* (1981), a scholarly study of Voltaire's life, that places particular emphasis on the philosopher's later years.

Critical studies: DAVID D. BIEN, *The Calas Affair: Persecution, Toleration, and Heresy in Eighteenth-Century Toulouse* (1960, reprinted 1979), an original work in which the author shows how the economic and social crisis after the Seven Years' War revived the religious passions against the Calvinist minority in Toulouse; J.H. BRUMFITT, *Voltaire, Historian* (1958; reprinted with a new preface, 1970), a study of the principal features of Voltaire's historical works and an analysis of the theories behind them; PETER GAY, *Voltaire's Politics: The Poet as Realist* (1959, reprinted 1965), a work that deals with Voltaire's politics in relation to England, France, Prussia, Russia, and Geneva and relates his ideas for social reform directly to experiences in 18th-century Europe; RENÉ H. POMEAU, *La Religion de Voltaire,* rev. ed. (1969, reissued 1974), an examination of the religious problems of Voltaire within the intellectual background of the 18th century (concluding that Voltaire was indeed a deist); JEAN SAREIL (ed.), *Voltaire et la critique* (1966), a collection of critical essays, both in English and French, from the 18th century to the mid-1960s, devoted to Voltaire as poet, historian, philosopher, storyteller, and propagandist; VIRGIL W. TOPAZIO, *Voltaire: A Critical Study of His Major Works* (1967), a lucid analysis of the thought and work of Voltaire the storyteller, historian, playwright, and philosopher; JACQUES VAN DEN HEUVEL, *Voltaire dans ses contes, de "Micromégas" à "L'Ingénu,"* 2nd ed. (1970), a new interpretation of these stories showing how Voltaire, in his *contes,* gives utterance to his inner conflicts and aims at resolving them.

The Technology of War

T he technology of war encompasses the whole range of weapons, equipment, structures, and vehicles with which man has armed himself. The objects are found on land and sea and in the air, in such forms as guns, tanks and artillery, ships, airplanes, and missiles. The objects may be offensive or defensive. A club, a spear, or an automatic rifle is an "arm" that a man uses offensively to extend his reach, hoping to strike effectively from a greater distance or with greater force. A shield, a suit of armour, or a fort is something that he uses defensively to ward off blows directed against him. This article is about these objects of war, of objects used in combat between human beings; wars and armed forces are treated in the article WAR, THE THEORY AND CONDUCT OF.

The article is divided into the following sections:

Weapons and delivery systems

Weapons are of two general types: shock weapons and missile weapons. Shock weapons are held in the hands; missile weapons are thrown with either muscle power or by a delivery system of some sort. This article traces the development of both types. As weaponry developed, weapons took distinctive forms, such as artillery, small arms, and rocketry. In addition, specialized types appeared, associated with land, naval, and aerial warfare. By mid-20th century, weapons, weapons carriers, and weapons delivery systems had immense variety, complexity, and sophistication.

PRIMITIVE AND ANCIENT WEAPONS

Primitive men doubtless fought with their hands, feet, and teeth. Not as well endowed by nature as many other animals, they did not dominate their rivals until after they began to use weapons. By the middle Pleistocene Epoch, roughly 250,000 years ago, men were already fashioning and carrying crude arms, which they used in combat with beasts and other men.

Shock weapons. Primitive man probably used pieces of wood and stone as clubs in critical situations long before he began to carry them about with him. A club found in driftwood might be improved in various ways. So could pieces of stone, which were eventually sharpened by chipping or abrasive rubbing.

No great arms-making skill was needed to fit a sharp piece of stone into a wooden handle, although a man so armed had an advantage over an even more powerful rival who had only a club. Seasoned saplings, with points hardened and sharpened in fire, could be used for thrusting. Hard, sharp pieces of natural rock were reshaped into blades to cut and pierce. A stone knife, mounted at the end of a wooden shaft with the centrelines coinciding, was also an effective spear.

These early inventions were probably made countless times in different places; once made within a group, the advantages must have been obvious. Spears and stone axes could be used to strike an antagonist before he reached grappling range. Blows delivered with shafted weapons were more powerful because of leverage and the use of both hands.

Information about Stone Age crafted weapons is scanty because the wooden portion did not survive. Since axes became unwieldy as handle length increased, and spears with stone heads could not be effective if shafts were too long, trial and error undoubtedly led to compromises that produced maximum efficiency.

The quest for effective weapons led, after many millennia, to the replacing of stone with metal in most weapons. This change occurred slowly and at different dates in

different areas. Stone weapons were still being made and used in the 20th century in remote places, but bronze was employed in the Middle East 5,500 years ago. This alloy of copper and tin, roughly in proportions of about ten to one, was superior because it could be formed into weapons that were lighter, sharper, and more durable than similar pieces of stone.

Even more important, bronze, iron, and, later, steel could be fashioned into long, relatively slender blades that were effective for both cutting and thrusting. Metal knives were useful both in peace and in war.

Men discovered independently in several parts of the world the value of a long knife that could be used with speed and efficiency. Swords came about early in most bronze cultures; iron blades were even better. Metal sword blades or parts of blades survive in many different shapes, lengths, widths, and thicknesses. As a group, swords have been the most widely made and used of all shock small arms. They often developed in company with other weapons, however, such as spears and axes.

Missile weapons. Primitive men undoubtedly threw stones at their enemies long before they carried any form of weapon about with them. Missiles have been thrown back at men by some apes, although the lower primates never carry them around. A missile offered two advantages: it could wound at a distance, and it could overtake even a fleet-footed animal.

Any shock arm can be thrown, even a sword, but special throwing spears, or javelins, were probably the most effective early missiles. One or more of these could be carried, in addition to a shock weapon, when dangerous targets were to be engaged. In early times ranges were probably not great, but a salvo of javelins could inflict fatal wounds on even the largest animals and destroy the cohesion of a disciplined group of human adversaries. Stone points of several sizes that appear to have been suitable only for throwing spears have been found throughout the world, but javelins with metal heads were more efficient.

The act of throwing a javelin requires space, training, and unusual physical ability for maximum performance. Before men evolved metal weapons, they invented what is now referred to as a delivery system to convert their muscular energy into missile flight. Bows and arrows came into being far back in prehistory and in widely separated places. Arrows could be shot farther with bows than could even the lightest of javelins be thrown. Men using bows needed less space, and their effectiveness as archers did not fall off as rapidly with increasing age. Penetration by these early missiles was limited, but men and animals could be incapacitated even by arrows with stone heads. Bronze arrowheads and improvements in bow construction made archers even more formidable.

Another missile-delivery system well known to the an-

Development of metal weapons

cients was the sling. David used one to kill Goliath almost 3,000 years ago. The Roman slingers propelled round or elongated lead pellets not unlike musket balls and appear to have achieved relatively high velocity, range, and accuracy, perhaps greater than those of the archers of their day. The principle of the sling is simple. A projectile is held in a pouch between two leather straps and whirled by the slinger around his body or head so as to attain high speed. One strap is then released so that the pebble or lead pellet can continue in a straight line until acted upon by gravity and friction with the air, as if it were a modern bullet. The problem is control and accuracy. A variation of the sling principle for throwing a stone consists of a single leather strap that can be attached to a missile, whirled around the head and the whole assembly projected at a target by releasing the strap.

A third major pregunpowder missile-delivery system was the crossbow. In this weapon, muscular energy is stored from the time that the weapon is stressed and set, or cocked. The power is released when the trigger is pulled. Crossbows have had different shapes; arrows, often called bolts or quarrels, have also varied. Efficiency depends upon the bow itself and on the way the weapon is designed to be cocked. In a crossbow of the simplest type, the operator grasps the string attached to the ends of his bow with both hands, holding the entire mechanism stationary—either against the ground with his feet or against his chest—and then pulls the string back behind a short projection attached to the trigger. A projectile set in position in front of the string is driven forward when the string is released. The extent to which hand-held crossbows were actually used in classical times is in doubt, but the principle was definitely known.

In the Middle Ages, levers and other mechanical contrivances were used to increase the amount of energy stored in crossbows during the cocking procedure. Arrow energy was increased considerably, although the increased weapon weight impeded mobility. Crossbowmen were superior to most conventional bow-armed archers in accuracy and range, although their rate of fire was lower. They also did not need prolonged training or unusual physical strength to achieve combat efficiency.

On the other hand, a new conventional bow appeared in Europe during the Middle Ages that was more effective in battle than any crossbow. This delivery system, complete with arrows, is known as the English longbow, although it probably originated in Wales in the 12th century. Arrows fired from these bows—which were as tall as a man—when drawn by strong men accustomed to their use had larger range and were more lethal than arrows from common bows. Furthermore, the archers were more mobile and fired faster than crossbowmen.

Brief mention should be made of other early missile-delivery systems. Blowguns with poisoned arrows are still in use. Boomerangs and javelins, thrown with the assistance of a holder called a throwing stick, were being used in combat well into the 20th century. War hammers and throwing axes have both been employed effectively in the past.

Missile-throwing engines. The idea of throwing heavy missiles by means of engines is old. According to the Bible (II Chron., 26:15) Uzziah, who reigned in the 8th century BC, "made in Jerusalem engines . . . to shoot arrows and great stones." The simplest mechanism for doing this would have been a giant crossbow on a carriage. Energy built up slowly by several men, using various simple mechanical contrivances, could be suddenly released to project a heavy missile.

It would appear, however, that these early engines did not often use the resiliency of a long homogeneous bow. Energy was more easily stored in coils of animal sinews or ropes into which short levers fitted. These military engines were of several types; names for the same machine sometimes changed. They were in intermittent use for more than 2,000 years. Despite much scholarly research many unanswered questions remain, but a few details can be mentioned.

Ballistae were the giant crossbow type of engines in which the bow arms were generally levers held in vertical torsion

Principle of the sling

Ballistae and catapults

coils, one on either side of the projectile. Catapults used a single torsion-powered arm that rose from the horizontal to the vertical to discharge a projectile held either in a cavity in the end of the arm or in a sling attached to it. Engines of the catapult type are also referred to as mangonels and onagers.

Energy could also be stored in a single springy arm mounted rigidly in a vertical position without relying on torsion. When the top of this arm was pulled back toward the horizontal, it could be used to cast stones or to impart forward velocity to arrows with strong heavy butts struck by the arm at the end of its free return. This latter type of engine is now sometimes referred to as a springal and is surely of ancient origin but was probably never really effective.

The trebuchet is an engine that came into general use in the Middle Ages. In the trebuchet, gravity is harnessed to do the work. A tapered beam is pivoted near the heavy end, to which a great weight is attached. When the slender end is pulled down slowly the weight attached to the opposite end is raised, with the consequent storing of energy. Upon release by a trigger mechanism, the weight falls and jerks up sharply the long slender arm. A projectile in a scooped-out pocket at the end of this arm could be thrown considerable distances.

All these missile engines could be built in various sizes. The largest could throw heavy projectiles hundreds of yards, but accuracy was limited. Philip II and Alexander the Great of Macedon made some that were light enough to be carried in pieces on pack animals, assembled quickly, and used effectively in the field.

All the ancient engines were used primarily for discharging projectiles, but they could also be employed to deliver flaming mixtures and putrid animals or dead bodies, with the intention of causing disease. Burning sulfur and oils of various types might ignite buildings inside besieged cities.

Siege weapons and methods. Archaeologists and travellers have discovered evidence of astonishing military engineering projects used centuries ago in connection with siege operations, especially in desert environments. If a place to be taken was important enough and the besiegers sufficiently powerful and skillful, it could be totally surrounded by a wall. Enormous mounds were sometimes erected to equal or even exceed the height of the walls of the place besieged. Mining to cause the defensive walls to collapse was also effective, especially when the walls themselves were erected without proper foundations. Tunnels were sometimes driven under the defenses so that men could enter the enemy town or fortress.

There were also battering rams of various types. One consisted of a roofed shed with a heavy metal-headed wooden beam suspended from the roof. The shed protected scores of men as they swung the beam horizontally against a gate or a wall. Sometimes the whole was mounted on wheels; in other cases the shed was moved by means of rollers. Movable towers were also rolled close to walls so that attackers could be on a level with, or even above, the garrison. A drawbridge could be let down from a tower of this sort to enable a storming party to cross over to the wall under attack. Boring devices may have been employed to get through walls of poor construction.

Early weapons carriers on land. As long as a man had to carry his weapons, their size and total weight were limited by his own strength. For millennia, the only improvement with respect to land warfare was to employ domesticated animals. Donkeys, small horses, and other animals pulled wheeled chariots at least as early as 2,000 BC. A man or men riding in these chariots could discharge missiles and also use shock weapons. In addition, the vehicle and the team of animals exerted shock. British war chariots used against the Romans had sword blades extending out from their axles.

Men rode domesticated animals from an early date, but cavalry appears not to have been used in war until around 1000 BC. A strong horse or camel permitted the use of heavier weapons. Even more imposing, several different armies over many centuries employed elephants. These powerful beasts could carry a miniature fort on their backs, complete with projectiles and simple delivery systems. In

Battering rams and movable towers

motion, the war elephants were themselves extremely effective shock weapons. Charging elephants were successful not only because of the damage done by the men they carried and by their tusks, feet, and bodies but also because of the fear they inspired—their psychological shock. Where several were used together the total effect was far greater than that from the same number when scattered.

Early naval arms. The earliest naval combat undoubtedly involved the same shock and missile arms used on land, with the vessels operating close together. Eventually it was found that a vessel itself could be used as a weapon for ramming, or perhaps shearing off, the oars of an antagonist. Special fighting vessels were developed with this in mind. Early in classical history relatively long, slender, oared galleys were used in this manner. They could destroy by shock with their powerful beaks and were extremely nimble.

A full ship's complement aboard a trireme (a large galley) of the Peloponnesian War (5th century BC) appears to have consisted of slightly more than 200, of whom perhaps 180 were sailors who rowed. The others were armour-protected soldiers who fought with shock and missile arms. These men with their expensive weapons were more important than their number indicates. Without them, a ship could have been captured easily at night or when the vessels were in confined spaces and could not manoeuvre.

In Roman times, men-of-war began to carry missile engines that threw projectiles and combustibles. Still later, perhaps at the siege of Constantinople in AD 673, Greek Fire came into being. This mysterious composition burned fiercely and could not be put out with water. It may have been a mixture of sulfur, oil, resin, and one or more sodium or phosphorus compounds.

Weapons systems and tactics. Early in the evolution of war men found that the effectiveness of a group acting together was greater than the sum of individual capabilities. Discipline, organization, and control by a competent leader all aided combat efficiency.

Further, military capability is often increased when a unified group of men is not uniformly armed. The earliest division of fighting labour was probably between lightly armed and mobile missile men (javelin throwers, archers, or slingers) and the heavier infantry of the line, who fought mostly with shock weapons. The light troops, or auxiliaries, could sometimes damage the main force of the enemy with missiles from a distance and protect their own heavy infantry from similar attacks. Cavalry could also be used in various ways. A skillful commander could combine units of men armed in different ways to produce an integrated fighting system more effective than the sum of its parts.

The Macedonians. One of the early effective weapons systems was evolved by Philip II in Macedon and used by his son Alexander the Great. The Macedonians had light troops to injure and disrupt from a distance; heavy cavalry, with both mobility and shock power; and, finally, heavy infantry, partly armoured and equipped with long pikes.

The Romans. Greek commanders after Alexander tended to make their armies too complicated; they even had war elephants. A younger, simpler people from the West, the Romans, defeated them with a different weapons system. Cavalry, archers, and slingers were sometimes attached to Roman legions (divisions of 5,000–10,000 infantry) but as auxiliaries of no great significance. The Roman legions were effective mainly because of their ten subordinate units, or cohorts, of medium armed infantry. Each man carried a heavy, short-range javelin that could penetrate the enemy armour used at that time. He also had a short sword, along with a large curved shield, a helmet, and some body armour. This combination of missile and shock weapons for a single soldier was not new, but the integrated mobility that came from Roman organization, discipline, and training was an innovation. The javelins (pila) could defeat Macedonian infantry phalanxes. The Roman short swords, combined with armour, gave great offensive effectiveness.

Because of their armour the legions were nearly impervious to light missile attack, and could defeat cavalry by using their pila as pikes. These units also developed an internal strength based on efficient logistics, fortified camps, regular pay, and strenuous training. While a single Roman soldier may or may not have been superior in strength, courage, and weapons skill to one of his enemies, a legion could defeat a large number of less thoroughly organized enemies. Its weapons system of combined missile and shock arms maintained the western Roman Empire for 500 years.

The Eastern (Byzantine) Empire survived for almost 1,000 years, in part because of a development in its cavalry weapons systems. In Byzantine mounted units, the same horsemen used bows and arrows as well as lances, swords, and battle-axes. The cavalry of Belisarius (early 6th century AD) could discharge arrows from bows while mounted but stationary. When this onslaught had disorganized the enemy, the mounted archers charged.

Medieval Europe. During the early Middle Ages in the West, organization and weapons systems declined. In the later Middle Ages, a combination of developments, including the breeding of heavy horses and the production of hardened iron armour and tempered steel offensive weapons, brought a revolution in warfare. The new military system was based on feudal castles as well as armoured cavalry and permitted relatively small groups of knights to control large regions. Weapons, both offensive and defensive, became extremely costly.

At the dawn of the 14th century in Europe, battles were usually won by heavily armoured horsemen who could ride in rough formations over almost any number of foot soldiers. As has often happened in military history, an effective offensive-weapons system produced an equally efficient way of defeating it—in this case, two ways. One of these depended upon the already mentioned English longbow. This delivery system was often ineffective against the armoured horsemen themselves but was effective against their horses because the horses' armour was never complete.

Another way of defeating armoured cavalry was with a hedge of pikes sufficiently protected by crossbowmen and other light troops to prevent enemy archers from doing fatal damage. The Swiss introduced an unusual weapon called a glaive or halberd, a pole arm that was used, ax fashion, against armour and was effective because of its weight, the keenness of its long cutting blade, and the leverage obtained because of its long shaft.

By the 14th century a commander who relied on soldiers of a single type was likely to be defeated. In the open field, armoured cavalry could still destroy many types of adversaries but not an army that had real longbow strength or squares of resolute pikemen. But both of these types of infantry were, in turn, vulnerable. A fully effective weapons system had to balance the weaknesses of some weapons with the strengths of others. There was no single totally effective weapon at this time, not even for infantry alone.

Non-European nations. War outside Europe evolved in much the same manner as in the areas discussed. There was an intermittent but significant interchange of weapons and tactics between Europe and Asia, especially in the many and varied campaigns in which a conqueror from one area overran the other. Alexander and the Romans on one hand, and Attila and Genghis Khan on the other, penetrated deeply and left military legacies. The Saracens and Arabs came from the southeast into Europe; the Crusaders went in the opposite direction. Cavalry was particularly effective in the heartland of Asia because of the distance involved, but solid infantry, with a combination of shock and missile weapons, was also important.

Primitive weapons survived in areas cut off from the mainstream of history, especially in America, southern Africa, and the world's islands. Stone Age arms continued to be used in these areas, including some made of wood hardened in the fire, into modern times.   (J.We./Ed.)

DEVELOPMENT OF ARTILLERY

Gunpowder, or black powder, was employed in China centuries before artillery was practical. The Arabs and the Tartars used military rockets in Europe during the 13th century AD. With the introduction of gunpowder

Ramming and shearing by boats

Composition of Roman legions

Defense against armoured horsemen

into Europe, the whole conception of long-range weapons changed. Gunpowder set in motion a process of development that over the centuries produced more and more massive bombardments. As has remained the case throughout history, the older weapons continued to be employed after the introduction of the new. The "engines of war" operated concurrently with guns using explosives for several decades.

Considering the lack of communications in the 14th century and the revolutionary nature of the invention, it is remarkable how quickly gunpowder was adapted to military purposes. It is quite certain that it was not introduced into Europe before the first decade of the 14th century, although it, or some similar explosive, seems to have existed in China before then. Doubts exist as to when guns were first employed in battle. Some historians give credit for making the first gun to a German monk, Berthold Schwarz. Claims for the first use of guns in battle have been made for the siege of Metz (1324) and at Cividale in Italy (1331). There is little doubt that after 1325 cannon existed all over western Europe and were certainly used by the English under Edward III at Crécy (1346).

First use of guns in battle

The probable inefficiency of these early guns would account for the continuance for a considerable time of some of the older weapons, particularly the longbow used by English archers.

The missiles for these early guns were originally in the form of a spear, somewhat like a harpoon; later, shaped stones, and later still, iron balls were employed. The guns themselves were mostly made of cast bronze or brass. These materials were followed by wrought-iron guns, but it was not until the 15th century that cast iron was used.

Gunnery in the 16th and 17th centuries. One of the difficulties of early gunnery was the erratic behaviour of gunpowder, the ingredients of which did not readily mix and which tended to deteriorate after mixing, particularly when transported. This made it unpredictable in use. Early in the 15th century, however, a new process, known as "corning," was invented; this improved method of mixing went a long way toward producing a standardized powder.

Nevertheless, the progress made in the development of artillery during the next 300 years, although steady, was far from sensational. As with some new weapons in modern times, guns did not at first fulfill the expectations of their proponents. This was not altogether the result of the extremely crude structure of the first types; the high efficiency of some of the older weapons, the paucity of communications, and the general conservatism of the times contributed. As a result, as late as the reign of King Henry VIII of England (1509–47), 200 years after the introduction of gunpowder, weapons of the old "engines of war" type were still in use.

During the 15th century a number of very large guns, known as bombards, were manufactured in widely different countries. Edinburgh Castle's famous "Mons Meg" weighed some five tons (4,540 kilograms) and was said to throw a 19.5-inch (49.5-centimetre) iron ball nearly a mile; a 13-ton bombard, "Dulle Griete" of Ghent, had a 25-inch calibre and threw a 700-pound (318-kilogram) missile; an even larger weapon was the "Tsar Cannon" of Moscow, which had a 36-inch bore and weighed some 40 tons. Details are lacking of the formidable pieces known to have been used by the Turks when they captured Constantinople in 1453. All of the above were smoothbore weapons. It is said that rifling (*i.e.,* grooving the inside of the gun barrel to impart spin to the projectile) was attempted in the 15th century and again in the 17th, but with little success.

It must be appreciated that these heavy and cumbersome weapons, using ammunition difficult to produce and handle, were of little value except as part of the armament of a fortress or for siege operations planned well in advance.

During the 15th century a good deal of experimental work took place with a view to producing guns sufficiently mobile to accompany field armies and take part in encounter battles. Early attempts by mounting guns on sledges drawn by oxen proved unsatisfactory. Under Charles VIII of France (1483–98) guns were mounted on wheeled vehicles drawn by especially trained horses.

Efforts to produce mobile weapons

About the same time trunnions were introduced—a pair of wooden devices forming a cradle to balance the gun on the carriage, by which the muzzle could be elevated or lowered for range adjustment, and through which some of the shock of discharge was transferred to the carriage. These measures succeeded in producing weapons that could keep pace with marching infantry on reasonably good roads over flat country. The Italians also produced field guns, and an Italian condottiere, Bartolomeo Colleoni (died 1475), introduced a special form of tactics for field artillery in which the guns fired from the rear through gaps left by the infantry.

There is evidence that the 15th century also saw the introduction of what has become known as "case shot," in which, instead of a single missile, a large number of round bullet-sized shots were fired, which scattered widely like the pellets of a shotgun, for use at short ranges.

The 16th century did not mark any revolutionary step forward in artillery techniques but rather an improvement on existing types of guns and their better classification and organization.

Hitherto standardization had been unknown, but in 1544 Charles V of Spain decided on seven different types of cannon for use in his armies. These included a 40-pounder (firing projectiles weighing 40 pounds, or 18 kilograms), a 34-pounder, two types of 12-pounder, two 6-pounders, and a 3-pounder. In France in 1550 Henry II standardized with six types, the heaviest a 33-pounder (drawn by 21 horses) and the lightest a 2-pounder (drawn by 2 horses). Later (in 1584) a 12-pounder and a 24-pounder were added. In the German states, standardization, although attempted, did not progress to the same extent. In the period 1550–1600 there were said to be 11 different types of gun, from a 1-pounder to a 94-pounder, which with variations in each type brought the total to around 40.

Weapon standardization

In England, Henry VIII took a personal interest in the provision of guns, but in the absence of a home industry was forced to rely on overseas products. By employing a Fleming, Hans Poppenruyter, he acquired some 150 guns of varying calibres, including the celebrated bombards known as the "Twelve Apostles." About 1515 he imported a number of foreign armourers and established schools of instruction for English craftsmen. Largely because of Henry's encouragement, two crude types of shell were introduced, which can be recognized as the forerunners of the explosive shell and the incendiary missile of modern times.

Perhaps the most important development of the 16th century was the beginning, in Italy, of the science of ballistics, which in time was to promote gunnery from an empirical rule-of-thumb operation to one of scientific precision.

By the first half of the 17th century artillery was taken seriously. In an attempt to improve mobility, Gustavus II Adolphus of Sweden introduced the "leather gun" in 1626. By making the external casing of the barrel of leather, and the bore of copper tubes, he reduced the weight of the gun to 90 pounds (40 kilograms), with a corresponding reduction in the weight of the carriage. Its mobility was excellent, but it generated excessive heat and was dangerous to operate. In 1631 it was discarded in favour of a less mobile but safer weapon.

Although the organization and standardization of the artillery of most countries became less haphazard than in the previous century, ammunition supply remained a problem, and there appears to have been no arrangement for the supply of spare parts for either guns or carriages.

Siege warfare, and operations in mountainous country, demanded a weapon with a high trajectory. This requirement was met by the mortar, sometimes called a bombard or howitzer, which could lob a missile into a fortress or castle or over a small hill. These were smoothbore weapons with very short barrels; the length of the barrel was sometimes no more than its calibre.

Not long after the introduction of artillery its potential in sea warfare was recognized. As early as 1509 a Venetian fleet, equipped with guns adapted to the galleys of the time, rowed up the Po to within a few miles of the capital of the Duke of Ferrara. The guns of the Venetians, however, proved no match for the Duke's land artillery, and the Venetian fleet was destroyed. In addition to greatly increasing the prestige of artillery, this action gave birth to a principle that lasted for more than 400 years; namely, that, unless in overwhelming strength, naval guns are always at a disadvantage against shorebased artillery.

Defeat of the Armada

The progress of naval gunnery, and the differing doctrines for its employment during the Middle Ages, is well illustrated by the series of actions in the English Channel in July and August 1588 between the Spanish Armada and the English fleet. In these engagements the Spanish fleet relied on large ships equipped with heavy but comparatively short-range guns (average weight of shot 17 pounds). The English, on the other hand, relied on much smaller but more mobile ships with light guns (average weight of shot 7.5 pounds) with a longer range than those of the Spaniards. The English tactics paid a good dividend as they were mostly able to keep out of range of their enemy's big guns while inflicting damage with their own weapons. Moreover, the heavy guns of the Spaniards soon ran out of ammunition. The extent to which guns had come to play an active part in naval warfare by the end of the 16th century is demonstrated by the number judged to have been available to the two sides; namely, Spain 1,124 (44 percent heavy, short-range and 56 percent lighter, medium-range); England 1,972 (5 percent heavy, short-range and 95 percent light, long-range).

18th-century improvements. In the nearly 400 years from the introduction of gunpowder until the end of the 17th century there had been a considerable increase in the range of guns, and this in turn had produced changes in the tactical handling of artillery. There had also been a steady increase in the number of pieces available. Apart from this, however, little progress had been made in the guns or their projectiles. Gunnery remained haphazard, uninfluenced by ballistics and other sciences still in the experimental stage.

This slow pace quickened during the 18th century. In France measures were introduced for the better classification of guns, and in 1776 the organization of the French artillery was greatly simplified by a reduction in the number of calibres and improvements in the design, and particularly the uniformity, of ammunition. It was not until their Revolutionary Wars, however, that the French introduced horse artillery—guns light and mobile enough to accompany cavalry in the field.

The Seven Years' War in Europe (1756–63) found Prussia in the process of making a series of artillery experiments, as was Austria, particularly with the more precise weighing and measuring of ammunition with a view to achieving uniformity of flight.

Perhaps the greatest progress was made in Great Britain, where Benjamin Robins published his *New Principles of Gunnery* in 1742. This work exposed the fallacy of many of the old theories and methods and, for the first time, brought science into the field of practical gunnery. Robins' invention of the ballistic pendulum enabled the velocity of missiles to be judged accurately at any stage of their flight. The year 1784 marked the invention by Henry Shrapnel,

Invention of shrapnel

a British officer, of the form of ammunition that bears his name—an antipersonnel projectile timed to burst in the air toward the end of its flight and discharge a large number of small, bulletlike balls over a wide area. Shrapnel remained a major artillery missile until World War I.

An important 18th-century advance was the introduction of limbers, vehicles towed behind the gun carriage for the carriage of ammunition, tools, and spare parts and for carrying some members of the gun team. In most European armies artillery was divided into three main categories: horse, for use with cavalry; field, for use with infantry; garrison, for coast defense and other static roles.

Despite the increasing attention devoted to artillery and its increased prestige as a battle-winning factor, the number of guns deployed was still, by modern standards, modest. In one of the greatest battles of the 18th century, Blenheim (1704), the French and Bavarians had approximately 120 guns and the British and their Allies under Marlborough about 60. During the whole of Marlborough's campaign in Europe the average proportion of guns to infantry in his Allied army was about nine guns to 10,000 men.

19th-century advances. The 19th century saw remarkable developments in every aspect of gunnery: the pieces, the projectiles, and the propellants.

There were three main reasons for this rapid progress. The first was the influence of Napoleon, whose sensational victories, in many people's view, were the result of his use of artillery. This was probably an exaggeration, but it undoubtedly added to the prestige of the arm. Napoleon introduced the method of using massed artillery at what he judged was the vital point of battle; he also raised the status of his artillery men by making them a *corps d'élite*. Second, the advance of science made possible improvements in both guns and ammunition. Third, the number of wars—the Napoleonic Wars ending in 1815, the Crimean War (1853–56), the American Civil War (1861–65), the Franco-Prussian War (1870–71), and many colonial wars in Africa and Asia—provided an incentive to produce better guns. The better organization of armed forces, including the general staff system initiated by Prussia, promoted greater and more efficient use of artillery.

As a result of scientific progress and war experience, several improvements came about. Rifled gun barrels were introduced. These imparted spin to the missile, resulting in greater accuracy, less deflection by wind, and a heavier and shaped missile in place of the mostly round balls previously used.

Introduction of rifled barrels

Improved powder to propel the heavier ammunition was made available by the researches of Capt. (later Gen.) Thomas J. Rodman (U.S. Army); but this in turn (in the 1860s) was superseded by the introduction of guncotton by Baron General von Lenk of the Austrian Army. This explosive had the advantage of being smokeless. It was, however, dangerous in storage until a French chemist, Paul Vieille, in 1887 produced a process that made it safe.

The provision of guns sufficiently robust to withstand the increased charges that had become available posed a serious problem. Various attempts to solve this problem were made in France, in the United States, and in Britain. The answer came in 1851, when Alfred Krupp of Germany displayed in London an all-steel gun drilled out of a single block of cast metal. This weapon was only a sixpounder, but within 10 years Krupp was producing guns of cast steel of more than eight-inch bore.

Toward the end of the century two problems were solved that had defied the efforts of inventors; namely, a satisfactory breech-loading mechanism and a satisfactory recoil system. Breech loading was achieved in the 1860s and 1870s almost simultaneously in a number of countries—France, Germany, Spain, and the United States. About the same time, the recoil problem was overcome by the introduction of a system for absorbing the shock of discharge and leaving the gun in approximately the same position after firing as before (see Figure 1).

Consideration was also given to other types of artillery. In the second half of the century pack guns were introduced; these were light weapons broken down into convenient loads for carriage on packhorses or mules, for use in mountain warfare. These were employed extensively by the British on the northwest frontier of India and survived in World War II when they were used in Italy and other mountainous theatres. Attention was also given to guns of larger calibre than had hitherto accompanied field armies, with the use of railroad transport. One of the surprises of the early weeks of World War I was the German deployment of heavy guns of Austrian manufacture to bombard the forts around Liège.

Introduction of pack guns

The 19th century saw a radical change in artillery tactics. In the Napoleonic Wars the short range of guns made it necessary to site them well forward. The increasing range of artillery gradually made this unnecessary; it became the custom to deploy the guns well in rear of the infantry to shoot over their heads.

Finally, there was a brief revival of interest in rockets, with which British warships were equipped during the Napoleonic Wars. The development of artillery temporarily put an end to rocketry as a military weapon.

World War I gunnery. When in August 1914 World War I began, conventional artillery and the techniques for its employment had approached their zenith. Improve-

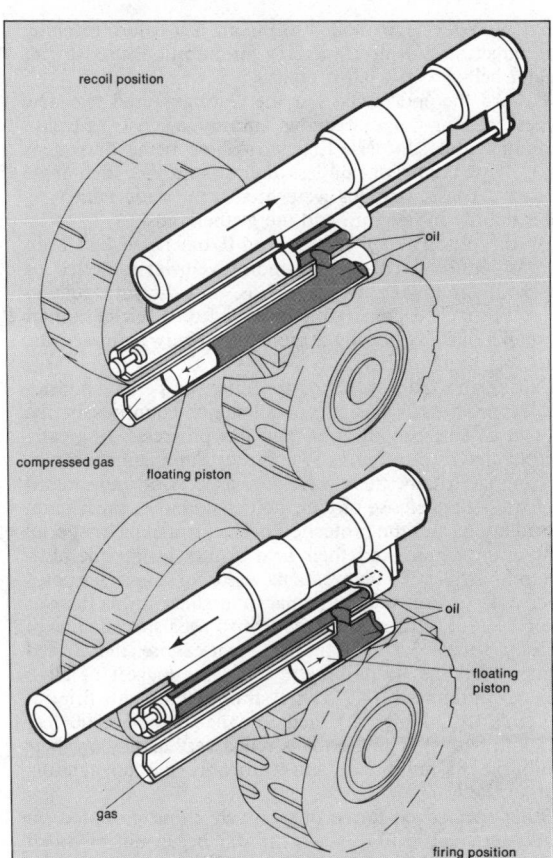

Figure 1: Simple recoil system used on field gun. When the gun is fired, oil is forced into the cylinders, compressing the gas and absorbing the recoil.

Adapted from I.V. Hogg, *The Guns 1939–45* (Copyright © by Ian V. Hogg); Ballantine Books, Inc./A Division of Random House, Inc.

ments made during the war did not touch fundamentals. Heavier types of gun were developed, and quantities of both guns and ammunition startled the military world, but basically the artillery pattern remained quite similar to that in the Franco-Prussian War of 1870–71. Light (or field) artillery, plus a few heavier guns, formed part of divisional artillery in all major armies, with more of the heavy pieces under higher direction. As the war progressed it became common practice for all light artillery plus a few medium guns to remain with divisions, most of the medium artillery (including counterbattery pieces) under corps control, and heavy, superheavy, and antiaircraft under army headquarters control.

In the opening stages of the war the artillery of a British division comprised three brigades each of three batteries of 18-pounder guns, and one brigade of three batteries of 4.5-inch (11.4-centimetre) howitzers and one heavy battery of 60-pounder (5-inch) guns. The divisions of other major belligerents were equipped on much the same lines with only minor differences. French batteries were four-gun; British, six-gun. The French medium and heavy pieces within the division were 4.8-inch guns and 5.9-inch howitzers; the Germans employed 5.9-inch and 8-inch howitzers.

Light guns of World War I
Practically all the light guns in service in 1914 stood the test of war. Special mention, however, must be made of the French 75-millimetre (2.9-inch) guns, first brought into use in 1897, that not only remained the French Army's chief artillery weapon throughout the war but also was the main equipment for the American divisions during the latter stages.

To understand the vastly increased ammunition requirements of World War I it is necessary to understand the change in the pattern of fighting. The armies of the great powers had been equipped in peace in the belief that the next war would be a short one and the fighting open and fluid in character. These conditions required highly mobile light artillery firing mainly antipersonnel projectiles

(*i.e.*, shrapnel). By the end of 1914 the opposing armies on the Western Front had settled down to siege warfare—continuous lines of trenches with deep dugouts and concrete machine-gun emplacements, protected by barbed wire. This setting required a higher percentage of heavy guns and high-explosive shells, and a vastly greater number of all types of guns and projectiles, if either side was to carry out a successful offensive. On the Eastern Front the same trend toward trench warfare was present but in a less marked degree than in France and Belgium.

In the continental countries of Europe, with their large **Production** conscript armies, the problem was difficult but not desper- **of artillery** ate. They had a good proportion of heavy guns, and their industries had been geared in peace to the production of large quantities of guns and ammunition. In Britain, with its small volunteer army and original Expeditionary Force of no more than six infantry and one cavalry division, the position was very different. It was necessary to create the industries for war production at the same time as the nation expanded its army to many times its peace strength. The United States was to experience similar difficulties when it entered the war in April 1917.

Some idea of the immense increases in artillery as the war progressed can be seen in statistics: In August 1914 the first six divisions of the British Expeditionary Force (BEF) in France had a total of about 486 guns, all but about 24 being light fieldpieces. By May 1915 the total of guns with the BEF had risen to 700 18-pounders; 200 15-pounders; 125 13-pounders; 80 4.7-inch guns; 28 60-pounders; 50 5-inch howitzers; 130 4.5-inch howitzers; 40 6-inch howitzers; and 12 9.2-inch howitzers, for a total of 1,365. At the Armistice in November 1918 the total of all types was 6,437.

On the opening day of the Battle of the Somme, July 1, 1916, the number of heavy guns on the 18-mile (29-kilometre) front of the British attack was 455, or one heavy gun every 57 yards (52 metres). In addition there was the whole of the light artillery of some 19 divisions (about 72 per division).

By the Battle of Messines (Mesen) in 1917 the number of guns supporting the attack was 2,266. Of these 756 were heavy pieces—one to every 20 yards. The preliminary bombardment began on May 21, and the attack was made on June 7. Altogether 3,500,000 shells were fired at an estimated cost of £17,500,000.

In the attack on the Saint-Mihiel salient by United States troops in September 1918, on a front of about 12 miles, the attacking divisions were supported by 3,010 guns of all calibres, or one every seven yards.

In addition to the greatly increased size of guns, there **Technical** were several areas of technical improvement. The first was **improve-** range. All light artillery achieved ranges of at least 10,000 **ments** yards (9,000 metres), and the German 21-centimetre gun, **in guns** known as "Big Bertha" and used for shelling Paris in 1918, attained a range of 76 miles (122 kilometres). Night firing became a matter of normal routine, and defensive fire or counterpreparation, usually a static barrage or line of bursting shells, was introduced. Later, the creeping barrage, a line of fire that moved forward slowly, and behind which the infantry advanced, became normal practice in attack. Finally, artillery communications were greatly improved by field telephones and radio, and the location of targets by means of aircraft and captive balloons.

The greatly increased use of aircraft brought into use special guns, firing shrapnel, for anti-aircraft purposes. In the absence of adequate fire-control methods, which came later, these weapons were not very effective in World War I.

Along with the developments in guns came improvements in ammunition and increases in the variety of shells. Except with a few heavy guns and howitzers, in which the propelling charge remained separate, all artillery projectiles used in World War I were self-contained, with propelling charge, bursting charge, shrapnel (if any) all in one piece, commonly called a "shell." Many different types of shell were used in addition to the shrapnel and high explosive of 1914. Smoke and gas shells were used by most armies.

Conditions of trench warfare on the main battlefronts,

and technical improvements, resulted in changes in artillery tactics. Guns had to be more dispersed and concealed and protected by earthworks and sandbags and their crews by deep dugouts. With the introduction of defensive fire and creeping barrages, guns had to be deployed differently and more attention devoted in defense to counterpreparation, to counterbattery fire and fire to disperse enemy troops during the process of concentration and forming up for attack.

In some of the secondary theatres, such as the Middle East, the new trends did not apply, and artillery was used more in the manner prescribed in peace for mobile warfare.

The introduction of tanks by the Allies on the Western Front in 1916 eased the role of their artillery, as two of the main tasks of the latter, crushing and making gaps in the wire and silencing machine-gun posts, were carried out increasingly by tanks. The reverse was the case for the Germans, who, until they produced their own tanks in the closing months of the war, had to deploy a proportion of their light artillery in an antitank role.

Trench warfare increased the importance of high-angle fire, leading to a revival of the use of mortars. Mostly small and of smooth bore, these were easy to produce. They were, however, very different in design from those of an earlier age. The Germans were the first to use these weapons extensively in World War I, but they were quickly followed by the British, whose three-inch (7.6-centimetre) Stokes mortar was the archetype of several produced later. In comparison with its small bore it had a relatively long (three feet, or one metre) barrel. The missiles were dropped down the barrel from the muzzle end, the fall of each round on the base of the barrel exploding the propellant charge. This enabled a high rate of fire for a short period; as many as six rounds could be in the air at one time.

During the early decades of the 19th century, naval gunnery had lagged behind land-based artillery in design of guns and gunnery technique. By the beginning of the 20th century this gap had been closed. It was realized in all major countries that the formidable battleships of the times made ideal platforms for modern guns. By the beginning of World War I, naval guns of up to 13.5-inch (34.3-centimetre) calibre existed, firing shells at ranges exceeding 10,000 yards (9,100 metres). The fire of these weapons was controlled by what was known as "director fire," a device that calculated movement of target, movement of own ship, effect of wind and temperature, and even effect of wear-and-tear of gun barrels.

World War I also saw major developments in the employment, particularly by the Germans, of torpedoes fired from submarines, and occasionally from destroyers.

World War II gunnery.   Except in anti-aircraft guns the interwar period saw little advance in artillery pieces or their projectiles; some advance was made in gunnery technique, and aids such as radar were introduced.

As a generalization it can be said that artillery and naval gunnery played a less important part than they did in 1914–18. The tank had partly relieved the gun of its destructive role of crushing wire and earthworks, and tactical bomber aircraft often relieved it of its bombardment role. At sea, aircraft played an increasingly important role, and in some naval operations—particularly in the Pacific in the latter stages of the war—the decision was reached by aircraft action before the opposing fleets had come within gun range or sight of each other.

Even on the Russian front the density of artillery did not reach the heights of World War I. In some of the bigger battles the concentration of guns was considerable, but it was never equal to the vast arrays of 1916–18 with their huge expenditure of ammunition. The demand was for light, mobile guns and a consequent reduction in the heavier types. There were, however, a greater variety of artillery weapons, particularly in the field of anti-aircraft and antitank guns.

Except for two new types, few important changes were made in ammunition. The two exceptions were proximity-fuzed ammunition, an American product used by American and British forces, which, by means of a small

electronic device, exploded in the air just before reaching the target; and armour-piercing ammunition, used by all major belligerents against tanks.

Toward the end of the war the Germans used two new types of long-range weapons, mostly against Antwerp, London, and southern England—these being known as V-1, flying bombs or pilotless aircraft, and V-2, high-angle rockets. These weapons were fired from static launching sites mainly in Belgium and the Netherlands.

By the outbreak of World War II the horse had been almost entirely replaced by motor vehicles (wheeled or tracked) for towing artillery. This, and the introduction of self-propelled guns (guns mounted on vehicles similar to tanks but less heavily armoured), greatly increased the mobility of all artillery.

During the latter years of the interwar period, considerable progress was made in all major countries in the design of anti-aircraft guns, and this progress was greatly accelerated during World War II. For European countries, including Britain, there were two aspects of anti-aircraft defense—the defense of their homeland cities, towns, and installations and the protection of their warships by special anti-aircraft guns and their field armies by mobile anti-aircraft artillery. The weapons used for these purposes increased in size, velocity, range, and efficiency as the war progressed. For these roles the British used special guns of mostly 3-inch, 3.7-inch, and 4.5-inch calibre; the United States used the 90-millimetre and—the biggest of all—the 120-millimetre (4.7-inch) "stratosphere" gun firing a 50-pound (23-kilogram) shell to a height of 50,000 feet (15 kilometres). The Germans relied very largely on their multirole 88-millimetre gun—probably the outstanding gun of the war.

Other specialized forms of gun were those mounted on tanks, of small calibre when the war began but of much greater size and range by 1945.

Mortars, as an adjunct to artillery and mostly in support of infantry, were employed extensively by all countries in a variety of calibres. The Soviet Army used several heavy types, including one of 240 millimetres (9.4 inches). The Germans developed a variety of types and tended to replace guns with mortars, particularly among their airborne troops.

Although the basic artillery weapons did not greatly change in World War II, great advances were made in the technique and methods of operating guns and gunlike weapons. The technique known to artillerymen as "survey" (employing map grid coordinates), enabled selected targets to be located in relation to the guns with great accuracy. This made the old method of actually firing trial shots at selected targets (known as ranging by registration) unnecessary, which in turn greatly increased the chances of surprise in offensive operations. The invention of radar enabled moving objects to be located, and their movements followed, long before human senses could detect them, and in the case of aircraft it was possible to distinguish friend from foe. This was of special assistance to anti-aircraft gunners. In addition, there were marked increases in the efficiency of radio communication.

These inventions, together with increased ranges and mobility, improved the flexibility of artillery. Whereas in World War I gunfire was largely confined to the particular sector behind which the guns were deployed, it now became possible to concentrate the artillery of one, or even more, divisions on a single small target area in a matter of minutes. It was common practice for a single battalion performing some special task, or in difficulties, to receive the support of the whole divisional artillery, without the necessity of redeploying the guns.

The heavier types of artillery, now much more mobile than in previous wars, tended to be concentrated under higher command but ready at short notice to proceed to any part of the battle area where they might be required. Typically a unit of this kind attached to an army or army group headquarters contained proportions of heavy, medium, and anti-aircraft guns and howitzers.

Modern artillery and gunlike weapons.   The explosion of two nuclear bombs on Japanese cities in August 1945 changed the whole conception of war in almost a flash.

Battle-ships as gun platforms

Improved anti-aircraft guns

Improvements in gun operation

It was clear that any nation, or group of nations, with a monopoly of this weapon could impose its will on those not in possession of it. By the 1960s this situation had changed, with the two giants—the United States and the Soviet Union—reaching near parity in nuclear weapons and thereby creating a deterrent to nuclear war. Meanwhile, wars had taken place in many parts of the world— in Korea, Vietnam, and the Middle East on a large scale, and in many other places on a smaller scale—with conventional weapons. Conventional artillery and gunlike weapons, although overshadowed by the publicity given to the nuclear types, have thus remained in widespread use and have undergone considerable development either as new weapons or in improved versions of World War II types.

To a certain degree the advent of the well-organized and well-trained guerrilla fighter has contributed to the decline in the usefulness of conventional artillery. Even the lightest traditional artillery pieces are too heavy for the guerrilla fighter, and in close country he usually offers a target too small and too difficult for the regular gunners to locate. For both types of fighter the light and inconspicuous mortar is often a better weapon. Thus although traditional surface-to-surface artillery still plays a part in modern war and will continue to do so into the foreseeable future, many of its roles are better suited to the new weapons. This is even truer in the surface-to-air dimension, where the guided missile has very largely superseded the antiaircraft guns of the two World Wars.

Influence of guerrilla fighting

Gun design and manufacture. The process by which sophisticated war material, including guns, is produced involves a number of stages, of which the following is a simplification:

1. General staff specification. This states the military requirement in some detail—weight, calibre, range, type of projectile, etc.
2. Drawing-board design.
3. Manufacture of prototypes.
4. Trial of prototypes with troops under varying conditions of terrain and climate.
5. Mass production (if trials prove satisfactory).
6. Issue to troops.

In most Western countries the production of a high proportion of artillery weapons is carried out by private firms, under close government supervision and sometimes with the government as a major shareholder. In the Communist countries all arms production is, of course, carried out in nationally owned factories. Some countries, of which Sweden is a notable example, make arms for export as well as for their own defense forces. Indeed, the export trade in arms is almost universal, partly to help allies and partly to reduce the cost by producing in economic quantities.

The number of private firms making guns and other war material is too numerous to list; some, such as Krupp in Germany and Vickers in Britain, have been designing and manufacturing guns and other war equipment for generations and have become household names.

Special problems in gun production

The production of arms, and gunlike weapons in particular, involves problems that are not usually encountered in most other manufacturing industries. In addition to being meticulously accurate, a gun must be simple to operate and maintain; it must be robust against rough treatment and severe weather conditions, but light enough to ensure maximum mobility.

But perhaps the most important factor is the quality of the material of which the gun is made. Armed forces continually demand longer and longer ranges and, in most categories of gun, ever-greater velocity, in order to reduce the missile's time of flight between the gun and a moving target. These improvements nearly always result in an increase in the propelling charge, which in turn makes it necessary to ensure that the metal of which the firing mechanism is made can withstand the additional shock of discharge. Because of the rough treatment to which war material is subjected, a good margin of safety must be allowed.

In practice under modern conditions the design and planning of a weapon is, almost invariably, entrusted to a team of experts who combine the necessary skills required for the project. The most important of these skills in the case of a gun, or gunlike weapon, are metallurgy and ballistics. Metallurgy is the science and technology of metals. Ballistics is the branch of applied physics concerned with the propulsion, flight, and effect on the target of missiles of all kinds (see MECHANICS: *Ballistics*).

Although these two skills are the most important, there are many others, including the production and operation of computers to analyze and store data, and, in the case of weapons for which training with live ammunition is difficult or impossible, the production of simulators for training purposes.

It is apparent that the problems connected with rockets— in which the propulsion charge is contained within the missile—are more difficult and exacting than with a shell from a conventional gun. If a guiding device is added to the rocket the problem becomes even more complicated.

Projectiles. Until the time of the Napoleonic Wars the missile was comparatively simple compared with the gun itself. Today it is highly complex, and in some cases it far exceeds the launcher in intricacy of design and manufacture.

For the purpose of this article the term projectiles includes all missiles fired from guns or gunlike weapons.

There are two main classes of projectile—shells and rockets. A shell is a missile propelled entirely by an explosive charge fired within the launching agency (*i.e.,* the gun, howitzer, or mortar) and not repeated during flight. The characteristic of a rocket is that the propelling mechanism is contained within the missile itself and continues to operate during flight. This characteristic gives rockets much longer ranges than shells.

Each of these two groups of projectile is subdivided into many different kinds. Shells are high-explosive shrapnel (rarely used today), antitank, anti-aircraft, canister or case shot (still used occasionally in mid-20th century), chemical, smoke, nuclear, etc. Rockets include intercontinental ballistic missiles, medium-range and submarine-launched; and many types of short-range, or tactical, rockets.

There are also a few varieties of projectile that do not fall conveniently within the two above definitions, among them torpedoes and recoilless rifle ammunition.

In nontechnical language a shell consists of two parts— one containing the propelling charge and the other a bursting charge. A rocket contains an additional mechanism for boosting its propulsion during flight.

The explosives used in shells are of two kinds, the propellant charge and the bursting charge.

The ideal propellant charge should be smokeless and flashless to avoid detection and should have no tendency to absorb moisture. An explosive with all these qualities has been difficult to obtain; the one in most common use is known as "smokeless powder."

The requirement for the bursting charge is an explosive with great shattering effect that at the same time can withstand the shock of the propellant charge without exploding.

During the first half of the 20th century the most common fillers for high-explosive shells were TNT (trinitrotoluene) and amatol. The TNT was particularly satisfactory, but ordnance scientists continued to seek improvements. Among those produced were that called cyclonite by the United States and RDX by the British, which, with some special processing, was used extensively in World War II; haleite, named after a U.S. chemist; PETN (pentaerythritol tetranitrate); and pentolite, half TNT and half PETN, used for antitank shells.

Nuclear weapons have, of course, completely eclipsed in destructive effect all other explosives. As early as 1953 the United States demonstrated a 280-millimetre atomic shell with a diameter of about 11 inches and a range of about 20 miles (32 kilometres). The tactical atomic shell, with limited and manageable effect, for battlefield use, is now a part of the armament of several major armies, although its use is restricted by the deterrent effect of nuclear weapons in general.

Range-finding, guidance, and related systems. The object of gunnery is to propel a missile onto a selected target—enemy personnel or material objects such as buildings, earthworks, equipment, or industrial centres. The

Early
range-
finding
procedure

main technical consideration is the determination of the distance and direction from gun to target, the technique known as range-finding.

Until the second half of the 19th century, range-finding was done by direct and quite simple methods. The range was either estimated or established by means of an optical instrument known as a range finder; the sighting equipment of the gun was then adjusted to the range and aligned on the target, and the missile was sent on its way. Certain adjustments had, of course, to be made for wind, the known error of particular guns, and other factors. After the first one or two rounds, corrections were made. The technique was much the same in naval gunnery as on land. The essential was for the gunner to see his target. If it was hidden by a hill, woods, or buildings, shooting was little more than guesswork. Except at close range, firing by night or in fog was impracticable and shooting at moving targets at long range very difficult.

The position is quite different today. Modern science and technology not only offer a variety of methods of range-finding but also provide missiles that can be guided to the target during flight or are attracted to it in the latter part of their flight.

In World War I improved maps and aerial photographs often made possible reasonably accurate shooting at unseen static targets. The lack of reliable air-to-ground radio communication made spotting from the air ineffective, however. The system known as registration ensured great accuracy in the conditions of trench warfare. By this means one gun could, by firing trial shots, ascertain the range of a number of prominent landmarks in a given area. From this information other targets could be judged with considerable accuracy, and other guns in the vicinity of the registering guns could make use of the same data. The drawback of this system was its slowness and forfeiture of surprise. Field telephones facilitated the employment of forward observing officers, and observers in captive balloons were used, but both were in danger from enemy fire.

During the interwar years (1918–39) three factors increased the efficiency of gunnery. First, the rapid development of air-to-ground radio, improving spotting from aircraft; second, the system known as "survey," enabling certain points in the target area to be plotted in relation to the gun positions; and, finally, improved line and wireless communications that, combined with survey methods, made it possible to concentrate quickly the fire of many guns on a single target.

All these methods for increasing the accuracy, speed in action, and general effectiveness of artillery fire were further developed in World War II, whose most important innovation, introduced late in the war, was the proximity fuze, which caused the charge to explode when the projectile reached the vicinity of the target. Since 1945 science has provided the gunner with many new devices, enabling targets to be engaged at vastly longer ranges and with much greater accuracy than formerly. Nevertheless, operations in the Middle East and Asia show that in the absence of sophisticated equipment, or in conditions in which it is impracticable to use it, the methods developed and employed so successfully in World War II are still practiced extensively.

The increased range of traditional artillery and gunlike weapons, and the introduction of rockets of much greater ranges, accentuated the difficulties connected with the identification and selection of targets and the methods of directing projectiles onto them. To a very great extent these problems have been solved by a series of new inventions and by the adaptation of older ones to new purposes. There has also arisen a classification of the types of target best suited to the increased variety of weapons. These are:

1. Strategic targets, long-range targets outside the operational area that can be engaged by weapons in the intercontinental ballistic missile (ICBM) class.

2. Battlefield rear-area or interdiction targets, up to a range of some 500 miles (800 kilometres) behind the battle area, such as centres of rail and road communications, areas of known troop concentrations, airfields, military depots, and other installations.

3. Battlefield support targets, engaged by traditional artillery types that include mortars and also some antitank guided missiles of post-World War II design.

In the case of (1) and (2) the question of "extreme" accuracy does not arise; the target is an area, not a point. The longer the range and more powerful the projectile the less important its accuracy. A strategic rocket with a nuclear warhead, fired at a range of 5,000 miles, may be a mile or more off the centre of the target and still have a shattering effect. There is no difficulty in calculating the exact range of targets for these weapons: the distance from any prominent place on earth to another is known, or easily obtainable by well-established methods, and the necessary data can be recorded in advance. Some doubt must exist, however, as to the accuracy of the missiles themselves, which, because of their power, complexity, and high cost, cannot be as readily tested as less sophisticated types. Their reliability must be assessed largely by the scientist's opinion and will depend largely on the accuracy of calculations relating to factors other than range and direction.

Accuracy
of the
strategic
rocket

Similarly, weapons used against targets classified under (2) above, with ranges between about 85 and 500 miles (135 and 800 kilometres), such as the United States Sergeant and Pershing missiles, present little problem as regards range-finding. With modern computing equipment, it is now routine practice to integrate quickly all the factors—range, wind and other atmospheric conditions, error of the weapon—to direct the missile onto what are mostly area targets.

Battlefield targets present a different problem: a high proportion demand pinpoint accuracy. An enemy tank, machine-gun position, or occupied building requires a direct hit or a very near miss. If the target can be seen, the range is quickly obtainable by established methods in the case of traditional guns and howitzers, or the target may be engaged by one of the wire-controlled guided missiles such as Swingfire (Britain), Dragon (U.S.), or Snapper (U.S.S.R.).

In addition to wire-controlled guided missiles, systems based on radar are employed to locate unseen targets at longer ranges and direct the missile toward them. "Homing" devices within missiles also exist; these attract the missiles to the target when they get within close range.

Carriages and mobility systems.   Until World War I the problem of conveying artillery pieces to the battlefield quickly remained difficult. The march of armies was frequently delayed and operations postponed because of the slow forward movement of guns and ammunition. Horses, mules, oxen, and even camels and elephants were used to haul cumbersome pieces along unmetalled roads, or as pack animals for mountain artillery and other light guns capable of being broken down into pack loads.

During the 19th century the mobility of artillery appreciably increased, but mobility remained a problem and continued so until World War I. Such progress as was made was the result of the improved design of the mount or carriage on which the piece was fixed and which in reality became part of the gun itself. Teams of horses were able to move light pieces and, if the terrain was favourable, bring them into action at a gallop. But even in the early stages of World War I the movement of heavier artillery pieces was a slow and difficult matter.

By World War II the developments in mechanical vehicles in general, and tracked vehicles in particular, together with increases in the number of hard-surfaced roads, revolutionized the movement of all artillery. With modifications, and minor improvements, the position is much the same today. Guns and howitzers rely on two main systems for movement: mechanical towing vehicles, which usually also carry the ammunition and crew; and as self-propelled weapons—that is, mounted on the vehicle that propels them. Sometimes, but not always, the gun team and ammunition are also carried on the vehicle. The vehicle may be wheeled or tracked, the modern tendency favouring the latter. The earliest example of the self-propelled gun was one mounted on a tank, although its main purpose was, and still is, to protect the tank against enemy tanks while it carries out its assault role. In contrast, self-propelled guns perform the normal supporting role of artillery; the vehicles on which they are mounted are designed to enable

Systems
for gun
movement

them to perform this role and are less heavily armoured than tanks.

Although self-propelled guns are becoming increasingly popular, and have many obvious advantages, they also have a higher silhouette and are consequently more difficult to conceal in action. Also, a mechanical breakdown immobilizes a self-propelled gun, not necessarily the case with a towed gun, whose vehicle can usually be replaced.

The strategic movement of artillery has been greatly facilitated by the use of modern aircraft. All but the heaviest pieces, including some self-propelled weapons, can be transported by air, and artillery is now part of the equipment of all modern airborne forces. Helicopters are capable of carrying light guns.

Despite modern mechanization there are occasions in mountain and jungle country when the only means of providing artillery support is with mountain artillery, broken down into light pack loads for horses or mules. Indian troops on India's northeast frontier are equipped in this manner, as are other armies likely to be involved in difficult terrain.

Essential as it is for modern armies to take advantage of mechanical progress, the advent of large numbers of mechanical vehicles, of which towed and self-propelled artillery and its supporting administrative vehicles form a considerable part, provides major staff problems. In large-scale operations, columns of mechanical vehicles many miles long are normal. All vehicles travelling in such columns must be capable of moving at approximately the same speed. A distance of 100 miles (160 kilometres) or more in a day is not uncommon, and at the end all personnel must be fed, vehicles replenished with fuel, and running repairs carried out. Staff work of a very high order is required if movements of this kind are to run smoothly. Failure in this respect caused considerable confusion in the German forces when Hitler's troops moved into Austria in March 1938; the lesson was noted by the general staffs of all the nations that went to war 18 months later, when the technique of modern road movement had been greatly improved.

Contemporary types of artillery. There are some gunlike weapons that were first developed for the close support of infantry and therefore classed as infantry weapons. In recent years, however, circumstances have arisen that leave the validity of this classification in doubt. These circumstances are partly technical and partly the result of changes in the pattern of warfare since 1945. The weapons concerned fall into two categories: recoilless rifles and mortars.

Recoilless rifles. At a very early stage in World War II it became apparent that a short-range, light, manhandled and one-man or two-man operated, antitank weapon was required. The British began the war with the Boys .55-inch (14-millimetre) antitank rifle, a weapon of the elephant-gun type. It was effective against lightly armoured vehicles but made little impression on German battle tanks. The first truly recoilless rifles were produced in the United States, first as a 57-millimetre bore weapon, later in 75-millimetre and 105-millimetre (2.24-, 2.95-, and 4.13-inch) versions.

Today, one of the most notable weapons of this kind is the 84-millimetre (3.31-inch) infantry antitank gun that is in common use in a number of NATO countries. In Sweden, where it originated, it is known as the Carl Gustav. It is shoulder-controlled and capable of destroying any known tank at a range of 500 metres (1,600 feet). Its weight is 36 pounds (16 kilograms), and it can be carried and operated by one man; a second man is required to carry the ammunition and act as loader.

Guerrilla fighters in the Middle East and Asian theatres of war have used Soviet or Chinese weapons of this kind in recent years. The Israeli Army is equipped with 106-millimetre recoilless rifles mounted on jeeps.

Mortars. During the trench warfare of World War I, greatly improved mortars came into use, with much longer ranges, greater accuracy, and very much greater rates of fire. Improved methods of transporting these weapons and their ammunition resulted in their increased use in open warfare in World War II.

Conditions since 1945 have increased still further the usefulness and popularity of mortars and also have improved their performance. In the fluid conditions of European warfare, modern mortars often provide more mobile and less vulnerable weapons than guns or howitzers. In mountain and jungle country their high-angle fire enables them to reach targets inaccessible to other supporting weapons, and their light weight and inconspicuousness enable them to be brought into action quickly in difficult terrain. They are easily transportable by air, and they provide useful and early close support for troops carrying out an opposed landing from the sea. In some cases they can be fired from a vehicle. Moreover, they are inexpensive to manufacture, simple to operate, and robust and easy to maintain. With these advantages it is not surprising that sophisticated armies, particularly that of the Soviet Union and other Warsaw Treaty countries, should turn to mortars as an alternative to some of their light artillery. In the Soviet Army a considerable proportion of the divisional artillery has been replaced by mortars.

The types of mortar in service in the various armies and guerrilla forces throughout the world are legion. All are improved models of the original Stokes mortar invented by the British in World War I. Typical of modern mortars is the United States's 81-millimetre mortar.

Light and medium artillery. The classification of "light" and "medium" artillery is basically the same everywhere, varying only slightly in detail from country to country.

Today, surface-to-surface guns and howitzers, classified as light, form the bulk of the artillery of a division or similar mixed force, such as a brigade group, combat group, or army task force. The improvement in the mobility of artillery pieces, by reason of tracked towing vehicles and the introduction of self-propelled guns, has, however, made it possible for weapons classified as medium to be added to the establishment of divisions and similar mixed forces in greater numbers than formerly.

The position today is that both light and medium artillery are usually available to support the close combat arms (armour and infantry) at very short notice. Additional medium artillery is normally retained under higher control as corps or army artillery, but readily available as a reinforcement in the combat area. Not all countries use the terms light and medium (*e.g.,* the British term for light normally is "field"). As a general rule, however, it can be said that pieces of a calibre up to about 105 millimetres (4.1 inches) are classified as light and those over 105 millimetres, but not more than about 155 millimetres (6.1 inches), as medium. All major armies have guns in these categories. Soviet medium artillery includes truck-mounted multibarrelled rocket launchers.

Some light and medium artillery pieces rely for movement on a towing vehicle, others are self-propelled.

There are a few categories of specialized artillery that come within the light classification; *i.e.,* artillery used solely in an antitank role, mountain artillery pieces that can be broken down into loads for pack animals or light aircraft, and artillery pieces especially designed for the use of airborne troops and conveyance by air.

The function of light artillery is to support combat troops in attack and defense, including antitank defense. That of medium artillery is the same, with the additional roles of counterbattery fire and bombardment of troop concentrations, installations, and communications in the immediate rear of the combat area.

Recently improved techniques and changes in the pattern of warfare have resulted in an increasing tendency to substitute mortars for light artillery as the close support of infantry.

Heavy artillery. Until the end of World War II the term heavy artillery applied to pieces of large calibre that were too immobile to accompany and support the leading troops in fluid operations. Heavy guns were reserved for static operations, such as those on the Western Front in 1914–18; for siege operations; and as fixed armaments in fortresses and coastal-defense installations. Since 1945, however, the term has been given a wider implication and may now be taken to include the various types of long-range strategic rockets.

The pattern of World War I, combined with the limited range and weight of shells of light artillery, gave rise to demands by all belligerent armies for heavy and extraheavy

Problems of movement

Advantages of mortars

Decline of
heavy
artillery

artillery. Since 1918 there has been a progressive decline in this demand, for a variety of reasons, including the development of bomber aircraft and rockets to take on bombardment roles and improvements in towing vehicles and self-propulsion that have made many heavy pieces classifiable as light from the point of view of mobility. In the 1960s it was found that the armed helicopter was often able to perform the harassing role that heavy artillery alone could carry out in the past.

The defense of ports and fortresses by conventional guns, known variously as fortress, coastal, and garrison artillery, has now been almost entirely discontinued by the leading powers. Gone too are the cumbersome heavy guns and howitzers that took days to move a few miles and could only fire a few shots per hour. There are, however, a number of guns, howitzers, and rockets of large bore, and firing projectiles of considerable weight, that still form part of the equipment of the armies of both West and East. The conventional artillery pieces are either self-propelled or have mobile towing vehicles; the rocket launchers have been made reasonably mobile by similar means or have been given sufficient range to compensate for lack of mobility.

Anti-aircraft artillery. In modern military parlance the term anti-aircraft artillery covers a wide variety of weapons, all products of the 20th century and mostly of post-World War II origin. They range from rockets with a ceiling of over 100,000 feet (30 kilometres) down to highly mobile weapons for dealing with aircraft flying at treetop level.

Innova-
tions in
anti-
aircraft
defense

Two developments since 1945 have changed the basic pattern of anti-aircraft defense. These are the increased height at which modern aircraft can fly and the development of intercontinental ballistic missiles (ICBM's).

These two innovations have resulted in the production of the surface-to-air guided missile for dealing with aircraft at the higher altitudes, and the search for a practical antimissile missile.

It appears likely that in the foreseeable future the rocket missile will entirely replace aircraft as a means of long-range bombardment, and in consequence there will be an acceleration in the development of antimissile missiles. A foreseeable trend is the development of two distinct types of antimissile/anti-aircraft weapons: one to intercept and destroy long-range missiles, the other to deal with enemy aircraft in the operational or battle area.

There are many factors that make it impossible to classify or describe these weapons with precision. In addition to the secrecy that shrouds operational characteristics, new types are being produced at bewildering speed.

The most powerful and sophisticated weapons are deployed in the strategic-air-defense forces of the two major powers: the joint U.S.-Canadian North American Air Defense Command (NORAD) and the Soviet Union's Air Defense Command (PVO-Strany). These two organizations exist to defend their countries' homelands against attack by aircraft and to give warning and, to a limited degree, protection against attack by ballistic missiles.

Among the antimissile missiles are the Nike-Zeus (U.S.) and the Galosh (U.S.S.R.). A difficulty in the development of this type of weapon is the immense cost and the fact that, in order to be effective against a saturation (all-out) attack, they must be deployed thickly on the ground.

Air artillery. These weapons include two distinct classes, air-to-surface and air-to-air, the latter being in reality antiaircraft weapons.

The projectiles usually associated with aircraft are the small-calibre machine gun for air-to-air and air-to-surface use, and the bomb for air-to-surface. During and after World War II a series of rockets was developed for use by normal aircraft and helicopters.

The short-range air-to-surface rocket is still in service, in both winged aircraft and helicopters, for harassing convoys of vehicles, troop concentrations, and other targets. The longer range, or "stand-off," type is in service for use with or without a nuclear warhead. Its purpose is to attack heavily defended targets from outside the zone of enemy defensive fire.

Rockets and guided missiles. The technique of guiding projectiles to a target is so closely associated with rockets as to make it convenient to consider them together.

From a technical gunnery point of view a rocket is a missile that is propelled by a rearward flow of hot gases generated in the rocket itself during flight, as distinct from the propellant charge of a conventional gun or howitzer shell, which ceases to operate after the initial explosion within the launching weapon.

A guided missile is one capable of receiving postlaunching guidance during flight. There are three main methods of guidance. Wire control is used for short-range surface-to-surface weapons within sight of the firer, a thin wire being trailed out to connect the missile and the operator. By this means the firer, who can see the missile in flight, directs it onto the target. Radio guidance can be used for longer range missiles. Finally, "homing" devices based on heat sensing attract the missile to the target.

Tech-
niques of
missile
guidance

The classification of rockets and guided missiles is complicated by a number of factors. The design, technique for use, and even the existence of some is highly secret; some are strategic weapons with ranges of thousands of miles; some with shorter ranges are for battlefield use; most can use either nuclear or conventional warheads, but a few are confined to one or the other; and their organization and method of employment vary from country to country. (For information on specific rockets and missiles, see section below on rockets and missiles.)   (C.N.B./Ed.)

Naval guns and torpedoes. Although the main armament of the modern warship is the guided missile, guns are still needed in ships for shore bombardment in support of land forces, for close-range air defense, and for such peacetime duties as fishery protection. Apart from the 16-inch guns in the U.S. battleships recently recalled from the reserve ("mothball") fleet, the largest gun afloat today is the eight-inch (203-millimetre) with which some U.S. cruisers are armed, a calibre considered to be the minimum for effective shore bombardment. But the high rate of fire necessary for anti-aircraft defense cannot be attained with a calibre greater than 5-inch (127-millimetre); the majority of modern ships are armed either with such guns or with 4.5-inch (115-millimetre) or 3-inch (76-millimetre) types. The essential function of target acquisition is assured by new types of stabilized radar, protected against electronic countermeasures and capable of detecting low-flying aircraft. Tracking is done by radar assisted by computers. A fire-control system widely employed is the N.V. Hollandse Signaalapparaten of The Netherlands; another offering a wide choice of missiles and guns is Contraves Sea Hunter 4 of Switzerland. The efficiency of the modern gun as measured by the firepower-to-weight ratio is twice the level of World War II, and crew requirements have been greatly reduced. The Italian Oto Melara three-inch (76-millimetre) gun has a rate of fire of 90 rounds per minute, weighs 6.3 tons, and has a crew of three. It features fully automatic loading to ensure instant readiness, and reaction time is less than 10 seconds.

The torpedo, still a very effective antiship weapon, is today mainly used against submarines. The diameter varies from 22 inches (559 millimetres) to 12.75 inches (324 millimetres). As mentioned, various means are employed for airlifting torpedoes to the vicinity of their targets. Propulsion systems used include compressed air, electric cells, solid propellant, and liquid monopropellant. Guidance is active acoustic, passive acoustic, wire, or terminal acoustic, or a combination. In active acoustic a sonar transmitter in the head seeks out the target and homes the torpedo on to it; in passive acoustic a listening device in the head picks up the propeller noise of the target and homes the torpedo on to it; in terminal acoustic the torpedo follows a preset path to the target area and on reaching it circles or zigzags to and fro, the charge being triggered by an acoustic proximity fuse when the target comes within range. Guidance by means of a wire is also employed. This system enables the controlling ship to direct the torpedo towards the target. The torpedoes are launched directly from ships and submarines, by rockets, aircraft, and helicopters (see below *Naval ships and craft*).   (Ed.)

Propulsion
systems

DEVELOPMENT OF SMALL ARMS

Military small arms are the weapons of infantry soldiers and other troops, including sea and air forces. They include firearms, usually issued in companies and platoons and operated by individuals or by small crews. For details on propellants and explosive charges, see below *Ammunition*.

Developments from the 14th to the 19th centuries. Shock and missile arms of various types had reached a considerable state of efficiency long before explosives were practical for military use. Small military firearms were used in Europe during the 14th century.

Hand cannon. As soon as artillery became effective, inventors began a crude process of miniaturization. Early hand cannons were small enough to be handled by one man but required him to direct his attention towards two different objectives. The weapon had to be aimed with one hand and fired with the other; both operations required part of the soldier's vision. These weapons were fired by inserting a hand-held, red-hot wire into the powder charge through a touchhole on top of the rear of the barrel. Hitting a moving target was difficult at best.

Firing by red-hot wire

An early improvement was to make the weapon larger and to employ a crew of two to handle it: one man aimed while the other fired on command. Firearms of this sort, however, were heavy and usually required a support. Neither type of hand cannon was militarily effective. Two other early improvements helped. A slow-burning match, consisting of a soft cord that had been soaked in nitre and dilute alcohol and then dried, was substituted for the red-hot wire about 1400. The touchhole was moved from the centre of the barrel to the side, and a small pan for priming powder was added.

Matchlock weapons. The first great small-arms invention appears to have been made about 1425. A length of glowing match was secured in the end of an S-shaped lever, or "serpentine," which pivoted on a pin. When the firer pressed on one end of this serpentine, the other carried the glowing end of the match precisely to the priming powder in the pan. A soldier could concentrate on his target and know that positive firing depended only on his pressing the lever.

With a matchlock weapon, individual enemies could be hit even while moving. The new firearms were accepted almost immediately. They were improved by making the lock itself (*i.e.,* the mechanism for igniting the charge) more compact, by enclosing it within the weapon, and by having the serpentine operate by trigger pressure against a spring. A cover for the pan holding the priming powder was introduced, and a fence was installed behind the touchhole and pan in order to shield the face and eyes of the firer from the flash of the priming powder. The match was improved; loading was made more convenient. A few matchlock handguns or pistols were also used, but this form of ignition was found to be unsuitable for horsemen.

For more than a century from around 1425 to 1550 matchlock shoulder weapons in widely varying sizes and shapes were used more or less haphazardly in battle. A curved stock to reduce recoil and facilitate aiming was probably introduced about 1500. A Spanish general produced a semi-standardized weapon and introduced tactics that for the first time made infantry firearms truly effective in battle. Spanish infantry in formation began to use matchlock *mosquetes* ("muskets") that were capable of sending bullets through the best armour that could be worn by a mobile soldier. These weapons weighed as much as 25 pounds (11 kilograms) and usually required a forked staff as a rest to enable a man of normal strength to fire them accurately from the shoulder. They were slow and clumsy to load, so that pikemen had to be included in infantry battalions to protect musketeers from enemy cavalry. Almost overnight, however, firepower from muskets became the dominant force in war.

Musket and pike infantry

The matchlock musket and pike were virtually the only armaments of infantry from about 1550 to 1675. The muskets became smaller as more powerful gunpowder was created; fully armoured soldiers almost disappeared from European battlefields toward the end of the 16th century. Armour-piercing capability was no longer required so that lighter weapons used without rests were normal.

Pikemen gradually became less effective and decreased in numbers until another major small-arms invention

eliminated them. The long muskets of the 17th century could be converted into tolerable short pikes by mounting knives in or around their muzzles. This improvement began modestly in the French infantry around the middle of the 17th century. The name bayonet probably originated in the town or district of Bayonne in southwest France. Plug bayonets, which fitted into the muzzles of muskets, were used first. Ring and socket bayonets, which attached to the barrel without obstructing the bore, became common early in the 18th century; sword or knife bayonets, which could be used for a variety of purposes, appeared soon thereafter and are still in use.

Firelock muskets. All matchlock muskets required a long piece of match secured in the small vise at the end of the serpentine before the weapons could be fired. In a rainstorm, the match could not be ignited or kept alight. Surprise was nearly impossible for soldiers armed with matchlock muskets because of the smell, glow, and noise of the matches themselves. There was always the danger that a matchlock-armed infantryman would accidentally set off his own or a companion's ammunition.

Two other forms of firearms ignition were known for at least a century before the end of the military matchlock era. Both were called firelocks in most records that survive, though they are now known as wheel locks and flintlocks. They have several advantages over matchlocks. Both can be loaded and primed at leisure and then fired with only a moment of notice. They were not, however, as satisfactory as matchlock muskets in sureness of fire or in the number of rounds that could be fired in a given time on a fine day without cleaning. Both were considerably more expensive and more likely to need repairs.

The wheel lock may have been invented by Johann Kiefuss at Nürnberg, Germany, about 1515. It was never widely employed by infantry. A military wheel lock musket of the earliest successful type is similar to a matchlock, save in its method of ignition. The lock itself is more complicated, bulkier, and composed essentially of a serrated wheel wound under spring tension and a piece of iron pyrites held against it in a doghead vise (not shown). When the trigger (see Figure 2) is pressed a stream of sparks is directed, cigarette-lighter fashion, into the priming powder in the pan. A well-made device of this type, properly adjusted, wound, and dry, would almost surely fire if the weapon itself was properly loaded. Since this lock could be waterproof-covered and the trigger pulled without disturbing the covering, it could deliver one shot even in a rainstorm. On the other hand, it was slow to load and more complicated. Military wheel-lock weapons

Use of serrated wheel

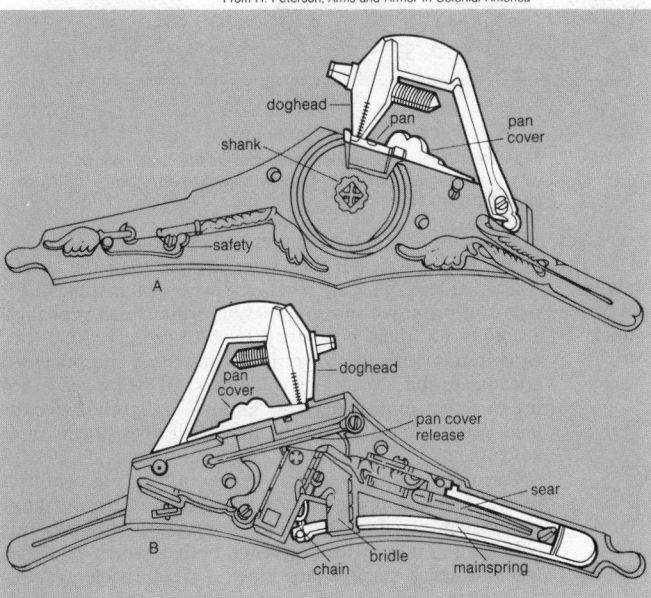

From H. Peterson, *Arms and Armor in Colonial America*

Figure 2: Typical wheel-lock mechanism of the mid-16th century. Phantom view: (A) right side (outer), (B) left side (inner).

were found to be appropriate for cavalry because they could be carried, loaded and ready to fire, in holsters for hours or even days. Long, heavy pistols of this type had a considerable influence on tactics in north Europe.

Flintlock muskets are believed to be not so old as the wheel-lock types but were known by the middle of the 16th century, about a hundred years before they made their appearance in quantity in infantry units. A flintlock musket is similar to a wheel lock except that ignition comes from a blow of flint against steel, with the sparks directed into the priming powder in the pan. This lock was an adaptation of the tinderbox concept used for starting fires.

In the several different types of flintlocks that were produced, the flint was always held in a small vise, called a cock, which described an arc around its pivot to strike the steel (generally called the frizzen) a glancing blow (see Figure 3). A spring inside the lock, similar to that used in most wheel locks, was connected through a tumbler to the cock. The sear, a small piece of metal attached to the trigger, either engaged the tumbler inside the lock, as shown, or protruded through the lock plate to make direct contact with the cock. Locks of the latter sort persisted in Spain and Spanish America until the end of the flintlock era.

From H. Peterson, *Arms and Armor in Colonial America*

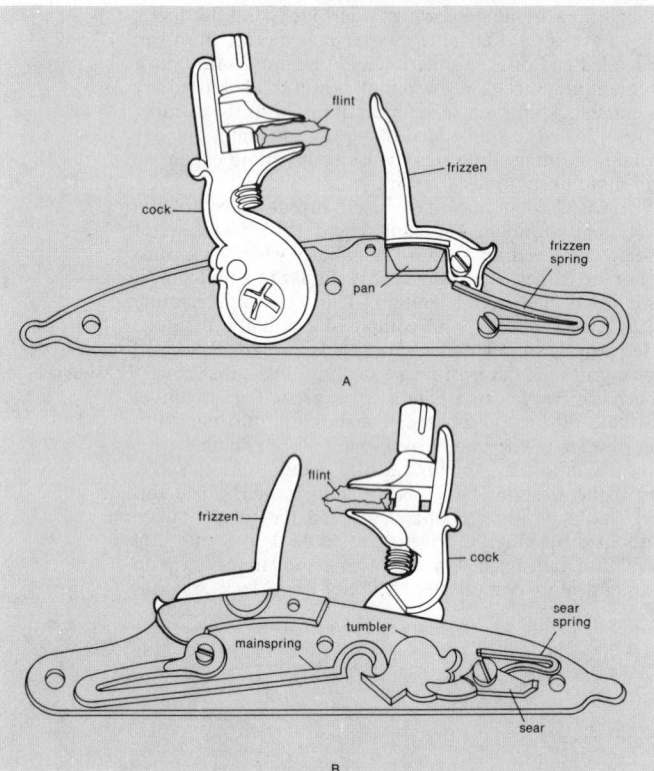

Figure 3: Typical flintlock mechanism, *c.* middle 17th century, with sear in safety position. Phantom view: (A) right side (outer), (B) left side (inner).

Advantages and disadvantages of the flintlock

Flintlocks were not as surefire as either the matchlock or the wheel lock, but they were cheaper than the latter, contained fewer delicate parts, and were not as difficult to repair in primitive surroundings, a virtue which probably accounts for their popularity in 17th-century America. In common with the wheel locks they have the priceless advantage, for use in the wilderness, of being ready to fire one shot immediately. A flintlock is slightly faster to load than a matchlock, if the flint itself does not require adjustment.

Percussion ignition systems. Early in the 19th century, several persons appear to have discovered a firearms ignition system based on the explosive property of potassium chlorate and fulminate of mercury, both of which detonate when struck a small, sharp blow. A Scottish clergyman, Alexander John Forsyth, is credited with this invention in 1805. In the early Forsyth weapons, a small pill of detonating explosive was usually placed below a plunger at the entrance to the touchhole. A hammer, similar to

the flintlock cock, struck the plunger when the trigger was pulled. Small tubes containing detonating substances were also used.

The percussion cap was invented about 1815, possibly by Joshua Shaw of Philadelphia. A truncated cone of metal—copper was best—contained a small amount of fulminate of mercury inside its crown, protected by foil and shellac. This cap was shaped to fit tightly over a steel nipple rigidly set in the gun barrel or an extension thereto. When the cap was detonated, a jet of flame passed down an open channel in the nipple into the powder charge. The rest of the lock was similar to that used in flintlock weapons, with a hammer substituted for the cock.

Percussion military muskets were possible before 1820; the advantages of the new system over the flintlocks were obvious both in regard to speed and sureness of fire. The percussion systems were simpler, cheaper, and did not require the special personal attention to small pieces of flint that was necessary for all flintlocks. The new form of ignition was not used regularly in any army, however, until the middle of the 19th century, probably because in Europe and to some extent in America most armies were oversupplied with flintlock muskets following the Napoleonic Wars; there was also the fear that units that relied entirely on the new caps might not always get a supply when needed.

Flintlock weapons predominated in the U.S. and Mexican armies that fought in 1846 and 1848, but many percussion arms were used in the British, French, Russian, and some other national forces which fought in the Crimea in 1854–56. By the American Civil War of 1861–65, flintlock weapons were obsolete. Percussion forms of ignition have been used in most firearms since that time.

Breech-loading weapons. Another major 19th-century advance in military small arms was breech-loading. Breech-loading weapons (*i.e.,* weapons loaded at the rear of the bore) were not new, and in fact the fieldpieces employed at the Battle of Crécy in 1346 were probably breechloaders. A few breech-loading flintlock rifles were used briefly by a small corps in the British Army during the American Revolution. Breechloaders, both rifles and smoothbores, were made and issued in small numbers to special American units between 1819 and the middle of the century. Percussion ingition, however, greatly simplified breechloading and made it practical for general military use. Literally dozens of new military breechloaders were invented and used in small numbers between 1820 and 1865. One group required that the projectile and the propellant, perhaps wrapped in paper, be introduced at the breech but fired by means of a separate percussion cap on a nipple outside the barrel as if it were a normal percussion muzzle-loader. Among the best known of these were the American Sharps and the British Westley Richards. Both are sometimes referred to as cap-and-ball breechloaders.

Another group of breechloaders used paper- or cloth-wrapped cartridges but included inside them a percussion primer. The German Dreyse military rifle, by far the best known of this type, was widely used in the Prussian and allied armies for many years. In the Dreyse paper cartridge, the percussion cap is located in the base of the bullet. A long, slender firing pin pierces the cartridge from the rear, goes entirely through the propellant powder, and strikes the primer. This system worked fairly well as far as sureness of fire went but allowed gas to escape at the breech in the user's face. Dreyse weapons required considerable maintenance and fouled badly with continued firing. The needlelike firing pins had to be replaced frequently. The early French Chassepot rifle also used an internally primed cartridge similar to the Dreyse, but with the primer in a disk to the rear.

There were many percussion systems that combined unburnable cartridge cases with separate percussion caps, but none was militarily important. The American Burnside carbine may have been the best. It used copper or brass cartridges that contained the propellant and the bullet, but it required a musket cap to be placed on a nipple in the breechlock.

Rim- and centre-fire cartridges. The first cartridge containing propellant, bullet, and primer to be successfully

Breech-loaders at Crécy

employed in war was the U.S. Spencer rimfire, in the American Civil War. A ring of fulminate of mercury was deposited all around the entire base of a thin copper cartridge. Force from an external hammer crushed the case rim in one spot and fired the round. Tens of thousands of Spencer carbines and millions of rimfire cartridges for them were used by the U.S. cavalry during the Civil War.

Rimfire cartridges were not satisfactory for infantry use, however, because they had to be made of a metal that would be light and soft enough to crush easily and positively. A powerful cartridge such as was thought necessary for infantrymen would create too much pressure and repture the rimfire cases. Spencer infantry rifles were unsatisfactory. There were also entirely self-contained pinfire cartridges, fired by means of a small rod that crushed a fulminate cap inside the base, but these were used mostly in pistols.

The concept of centre-fire ammunition, with the percussion cap positioned in the centre of the base of a strong cartridge case, was known before the middle of the 19th century, but practical copper and brass cases of this type were not issued until after 1865. Within a decade they had replaced all other types for military use. A soldier could load his weapon from the breech, fire it, and quickly remove the cartridge case. The closure at the breech was complete; most of the fouling went out in the discarded case. The weapon could be fred many times without cleaning, although accuracy fell off with bore fouling.

Few changes in ammunition Centre-fire metallic cartridges of drawn brass, containing propellant, bullet, and primer, are still essentially the same after more than a century. Bullets are longer, but smaller in diameter; new priming compositions have been introduced from time to time, but fulminate of mercury is still the most positive. Propellant powders are more powerful and burn cleaner and practically without smoke. In aggregate, however, ammunition changes over the past century have been limited.

The early rifles and their disadvantages. A projectile that spins about its long axis in flight is more accurate than one that moves unpredictably; the feathers in arrows and fins on crossbow bolts were sometimes placed at an angle to the shaft to cause the missile to revolve in flight. Spiral or rifling grooves on the inside of a barrel can cause bullets to spin in the same manner. These were first used as early as the 16th century. Some early rifles, however, have straight grooves, perhaps to inhibit spin or reduce fouling.

Rifled small arms, which make their bullets spin, have been used for accurate shooting at game and targets for some 400 years. Even today, a single bullet carefully loaded into a rifled wheel-lock weapon more than 300 years old will shoot with precision to about 150 yards (140 metres). Every shot can be placed on a man-sized target at this range, an achievement that is virtually impossible with a smoothbore musket at 75 yards (70 metres).

Early problems with rifled barrels Efforts were made to take advantage of this increase in accuracy of rifled arms in military weapons, but they were not practical because of loading difficulties. In order to spin accurately in flight, a bullet has to fit tightly into the rifling of the barrel, either with direct lead-to-iron contact, or by means of a patch of cloth or leather between the two. Loading a spherical lead ball of the proper size tightly into a clean bore is not difficult. As the bore becomes dirty from repeated firing, however, the loading operation becomes progressively more difficult. For this reason, early rifle-armed military units were not a success. Daniel Morgan's famous battalion of Pennsylvania and Maryland riflemen of the American Revolution were re-equipped with smoothbore muskets before the end of the war, because these weapons were more satisfactory for use in battle.

A special loading procedure was used in British rifle units during the Napoleonic Wars, so that the Baker military flintlock rifle could be loaded with patched balls for accurate shooting when the weapon was clean and then with bare balls smoothbore-fashion thereafter. The early rounds were accurate, but those fired later were inferior to bullets from regular Brown Bess muskets—smoothbore shoulder weapons used in the British and other services

for about 150 years. Several other flintlock and percussion rifles employing essentially the same system with spherical lead bullets were used around the world, but with limited success. A small increase in accuracy was offset by loading problems. The obvious solution—breech-loading, so that the balls did not have to be forced down clogged bores—encountered another problem: sealing the breech was almost impossible before metallic cartridges. Modern test-firing of such weapons as Ferguson and Hall flintlock breech-loading rifles casts serious doubt on their military efficacy.

The Minié and contemporary systems. Beginning about 1830, a number of men in different countries began to experiment with ways to load a rifle easily from the muzzle and have the bullets take and hold the rifling on the way out. A number of workable systems were invented. Perhaps the simplest arrangement was to abandon spherical bullets in favour of a formed projectile of some sort to fit special riflings. Elongated cylindrical projectiles with two or four ribs cast into them to fit the wide, deep rifling grooves in their barrels showed promise. Another system was to make the inside of the bore in the shape of a regular polygon with rounded corners, and a twist. Whitworth rifles, used briefly in the British army and in the Confederacy during the American Civil War, had hexagonal bores and bullets with a relatively quick twist.

Years before the Whitworth system was developed several French officers conducted experiments in which they deformed spherical and elongated projectiles in the breech of their rifles so that the bullets actually filled the grooves in the rifling before they were fired. Accuracy was poor, however, because the deformed bullets had poor ballistic shapes.

The principle of Minié rifling In 1849 a French captain, Claude-Étienne Minié, developed a better rifling concept. Minié used a cylindrical projctile with a rounded point and a hollow base into which a conical plug was fitted. The bullet's diameter was such that it slid freely down the bore. On being fired, however, the conical plug in the hollow base was driven forward to expand the lead bullet into the rifling grooves. This muzzle-loading Minié system was an immediate success. It did not even require the plug; powder gases alone sufficed to expand the lead bullet. Minié bullets were superior to almost all others not only in accuracy, but also in range. Spherical bullets lost velocity because they were light in proportion to their cross-sectional area. The elongated bullets of the Minié and other similar systems were stable in flight even out to 1,000 yards (900 metres).

Muzzle-loading percussion rifles designed to fire Minié bullets were introduced into several armies in the 1850s and were of extreme importance tactically. Infantry armed with them could be effective with fire up to five times the maximum range of the old muskets, with little or no sacrifice in speed of loading. The old balance between infantry and cavalry was at once upset in favour of the infantry: horsemen received five times as many bullets before they were close enough to use their sabres or lances, essentially their only effective weapons when mounted. The old infantry–artillery balance was also upset. Gunners and their pieces could at one time approach infantry to within 200 yards (180 metres) and fire multiple-projectile charges known as grapeshot and canister, the only really lethal ammunition of that era. The Minié rifles kept enemy artillery so far back, however, that the pieces were nearly useless. They could only reach enemy infantry with solid projectiles or the ineffective shell of that era, which burst into only a few fragments. Grapeshot and canister

Breech-loading small arms. The Minié system, in spite of its great advantages over its predecessors, was shortlived. The breech-loading, metallic-cartridge firearms made all muzzle-loaders obsolete soon after 1865. A bullet loaded at the breech did not need to be expanded at the moment of firing in order for the grooves in the bore to grip it tightly. The early rimfire cartridges were not powerful enough for infantry rifles, but centre-fire cartridge rifles, introduced as early as 1866, were fully equal to the muzzle-loading Minié types.

Most armies changed from muzzle-loaders to breechloaders without adopting entirely new weapons. In several cases,

Minié-type muzzle-loaders were converted to breechloaders by cutting off the rear of the barrel, threading it, and screwing it into a new single-shot action. The British calibre .577 Snider was of this type. (Calibre is a measure of bore diameter; in British and United States firearms, it is expressed as a decimal fraction of an inch.) In the American Allin-Springfield, the conversion was made in this manner, but the old barrel was reduced to calibre .50 by the insertion of a liner. Similar new single-shot, metallic-cartridge, military breechloaders were developed in France by Antoine-Alphonse Chassepot, in Germany by Paul von Mauser, and in the United States by the Remington Arms Company, among others.

Repeating rifles. During the 1880s, new breech-loading rifles gained another dimension by becoming repeaters. Mauser, Chassepot, and others added tubular magazines under the barrels of their rifles. Spencer rifles and carbines had a magazine in the buttstock which contained seven cartridges that were fed by means of a trigger-guard operating lever into the chamber in succession. None of these early repeating systems, however, was entirely satisfactory for military service. Mauser, the Austrian Ferdinand Ritter von Mannlicher, Remington Arms Company, and others gradually developed more practical box magazines which by the late 19th century were almost universal. The basic bolt action Mauser rifle of this sort, first made for Belgium in 1889, was adopted by armies throughout the world with small changes and modifications until it became the most popular type. The U.S. Model 1903 Springfield and the Japanese Arisakas, used in both world wars, are remarkably similar.

The early infantry breechloaders fired bullets similar in diameter and shape to those used by the Minié muzzle-loaders, about 0.5 inch (1.27 centimetre) in diameter. These weapons used essentially the same propellant, black powder, that had been employed for centuries, but in a more efficient manner. Cartridge and bullet diameters were soon reduced slightly, usually to about calibre .45 (11 millimetres).

Nitrocellulose, or guncotton, was invented in 1846 but was not utilized successfully for propellants until smokeless powder (nitrocellulose or nitroglycerin-nitrocellulose) was first used for military purposes by the French about 1885. This powder is much more powerful because it burns more completely; rifle projectiles could be made longer and thinner and be given more energy by a smaller charge because their lighter weight and better shape gave them higher velocities. Bore diameters dropped again to about calibre .30 (eight millimetres), with increases in both range and accuracy.

First use of smokeless powder

These smokeless-powder rifles generally fired jacketed lead bullets that weighed half an ounce or less, travelled at a velocity of between 2,000 and 2,800 feet (600–850 metres) per second leaving the muzzle, and were reasonably accurate up to 1,000 yards (900 metres) under ideal conditions. Their high muzzle energies gave them lethal power at as much as 3,000 yards (2,700 metres). Cartridges were usually made of drawn brass; the lead bullets were normally encased in a harder jacket that contained copper or nickel or both. In emergencies, both cartridge cases and the bullet jackets could be made of soft iron.

The new bolt action had a number of variations. The Mauser, Dreyse, and Chassepot rifles, along with the American Green, were all bolt-action breechloaders, in which the bolt itself turned. In all early bolt actions one or more projections, frequently called lugs, revolved from open space into recesses in the receiver, the rear portion of the weapon. The bolt handle itself often acted as a locking lug, the only one in some early types. In the Mauser actions of 1889 and later, however, locking lugs were at the front end of the bolt, which is still the most common position.

In another type of bolt-action military rifle, the bolt itself does not turn at all, but simply slides backward and forward for extraction, ejection, and reloading. Locking is accomplished when the lugs are thrust out into recesses at the end of each forward stroke. When all goes well and ammunition is clean, straight-pull rifles can probably fire faster than turning bolt types. The Austrian, Swiss, and some other armies found them satisfactory; the Canadian Ross straight-pull rifle was not reliable for combat in World War I.

Military pistols. The early hand cannon and wheellock pistols for cavalry were succeeded by flintlock and percussion muzzle-loading handguns and single-shot, metallic-cartridge pistols. All functioned similarly to contemporary shoulder weapons but were far less useful. Mechanical repeating pistols existed toward the end of the 19th century but were too complicated and expensive for general issue. In fact, pistols have rarely been effective in military combat, because of inherent range and accuracy disadvantages in comparison with shoulder weapons. They are essentially personal-defense weapons that may be more important psychologically than for their ability to harm an enemy in battle.

From an early date, however, officers and others in military service wanted repeating handguns. Flintlock revolvers and even mechanical flintlock repeaters were made. So-called pepperbox percussion revolvers, essentially several separate small pistols revolving around a central pivot, saw some service. Heavy and bulky for their power, they were not really practical.

Toward the middle of the 19th century, several inventors separately perfected repeating pistols in which a cylinder could be loaded from the front with five, six, or more rounds with a percussion cap on each chamber. The pistol could then be operated to fire all chambers in succession when the hammer was cocked by hand and the trigger pulled. These cap-and-ball revolvers were popular because several moderately powerful shots could be fired before reloading, and the weapon was of reasonable bulk and weight. They were widely issued in some armies for cavalry service, and when satisfactory metallic cartridges were available, revolvers became even more attractive. All handguns continued, however, to have inherent disadvantages in accuracy and range.

Cylinder repeating pistol

Early machine guns. The desire to fire a number of projectiles from a single weapon in a brief time was first satisfied by the simple expedient of charging a weapon with more than one bullet. The results were not very effective, because all projectiles from a single discharge followed roughly the same path, and the propelling charges gave reduced velocity under the heavier weight of projectiles. A similar idea was to load more than one charge into a single barrel and fire them successively through different touchholes. Military weapons of this type survive from an early date, but test firing has not shown them to be satisfactory. Volley shoulder weapons were also tried from time to time; they generally involved a number of barrels loaded separately, but fired together. Dispersion, obtained by making the barrels not quite parallel, was rarely uniform.

The middle years of the 19th century brought dozens of inventions involving larger military weapons that would fire several projctiles either together or serially. The percussion system of ignition helped in regard to these. A number of volley field pieces were designed and made, especially in the United States and France. Less effective than howitzers loaded with grapeshot and canister, they took longer to load because of their many barrels and were more expensive to produce.

Even the concept of the modern machine gun, a number of serial discharges from a single barrel, is of ancient origin. A small revolving cannon that required a manually applied match to fire was patented in England as early as 1718; examples of it survive in museums. Even after percussion ignition was well established, mechanical repeaters not using mass-produced metallic cartridges were not really satisfactory for military use. But as soon as centre-fire rifle cartridges of satisfactory quality were produced in large numbers, there were dozens of inventions, many of which were produced and tested. The best known were the U.S. Gatling gun and the French mitrailleuse, both developed in part before metallic cartridges were common, but both requiring mass-produced centrefire ammunition to be militarily effective.

Gatling guns had several barrels mounted around a central stem and revolved by means of a hand crank. After a barrel fired a round, it went through successive unlocking, extracting, ejecting, reloading, and relocking. In the most successful Gatling guns, magazines held 400 cartridges, but, by means of a feed device, stacks of rounds could be fed to give continuous fire for long periods. Gatling weapons were made to take a variety of ammunition, up to a full inch (2.5 centimetres) in bullet diameter. Though practical, they never saw extended service in a major war. A few were used by United States forces in Cuba in 1898 and in minor military operations around the world. Gatling guns operated best with ammunition loaded with fulminate of mercury primers and black powder propellants, a combination in which ignition was sure and quick. They were often unsatisfactory with the early smokeless powder propellants because a cartridge that did not go off precisely when its primer was struck—a hangfire—would damage the mechanism.

The French mitrailleuse was also a multibarrelled, serially fired weapon. It used a loading plate that contained a cartridge for each of its 25 barrels. The barrels and the loading plate remained fixed, but a mechanism (operated by a crank) struck individual firing pins in succession. The mitrailleuse issued in the French Army fired standard Chassepot rifle ammunition. The weapon weighed more than 2,000 pounds (900 kilograms). The French forces in the Franco-Prussian War of 1870–71 endeavoured to use them in a manner similar to artillery, but they were no match for Prussian, steel, breech-loading cannon made by Krupp, firing explosive shell. For a time the failure of the mitrailleuse discouraged machine-gun development. Several more manually operated types were made and tried out. Some were put into service in small numbers in various armies and navies, generally chambered for artillery ammunition of small size.

World War I guns. *Maxim guns.* The first successful automatic machine gun was invented by Hiram Stevens Maxim, an American working in Europe. Beginning about 1884, he produced a number of weapons in which operation was based on recoil energy. In all Maxim guns, the force that opened and closed the action, feeding successive rounds to the chamber and ejecting spent cartridges, came from the cartridge itself as it was fired. The bullet's recoil energy was employed to unlock the bolt (or breechblock) from the barrel, to eject the fired case from the gun, and to store sufficient energy in a main spring to push the bolt forward, pick up a fresh round, load the chamber, and lock the piece. If the trigger was held back, the weapon fired again and continued to fire until it had expended all the rounds in the magazine. Both barrel and action recoiled a short distance to the rear locked together; then the action continued back alone after unlocking. An early feature of Maxim automatic machine guns was a positive control of the rate of fire, from one round in ten seconds, or even slower, to about 13 rounds per second, depending on ammunition. This variable fire control feature, however, was not retained.

Maxim weapons were ideal for firing the new smokeless-powder rifle cartridges. Until the cartridge went off there was no power to operate the weapon; though delayed firing was almost certain to damage a Gatling gun, it did no harm in a Maxim weapon, because the cycle did not begin until the cartridge actually fired. Since it operated by the power of the cartridges, it could be made lighter than the mechanical types. Its light weight made it satisfactory for use by special infantry elements. Since the effectiveness of combat infantry depended on firepower from rifles, weapons delivering several hundred bullets per minute with accuracy considerably increased the combat potential of foot soldiers.

Maxim guns were first used by the British in a colonial war in 1895 and were employed on a much larger scale in the Russo-Japanese War (1904–05). The Russians used Maxim water-cooled machine guns manufactured in Great Britain. The Japanese used the French Hotchkiss (see below). The Maxim guns sold to most European nations were chambered for the national rifle cartridge. The Russian Model 1910 weighed about 160 pounds (70 kilograms), including mount, water-cooling apparatus, and a steel shield for the gunner. The German Model 1908 with sled mount weighed 100 pounds (45 kilograms). On the

eve of World War I, armies differed radically in how to place machine guns in their organizations. In the German infantry, some companies were equipped with machine guns but British rifle battalions—each of which consisted of several companies—had no weapons of this type; they were used throughout the war by Great Britain in a separate machine-gun corps.

Machine guns of the heavy Maxim type were deadly throughout World War I, from 1914 to 1918. Their defensive fire so limited the offensive power of enemy infantry that the entire Western Front, from the Swiss border to the English Channel, became one vast siege operation. A few of these weapons sometimes caused thousands of casualties. On the other hand, because of their bulk and weight, they were only marginally useful for offensive operation by the infantry.

Other machine guns of World War I. Not all the heavy machine guns of World War I were of the watercooled Maxim type in which recoil pushed both the barrel and the action to the rear for a short distance before unlocking. Gas operation was also employed. A piston located in a cylinder below the barrel was driven to the rear by gas from the barrel through a port to unlock the action and sent the bolt back to extract, eject, and compress the main spring; a new round was picked up, moved into the chamber, and fired on the forward stroke. The best known gas-operated heavy machine gun was the French Hotchkiss. It was air-cooled, but the barrel itself was heavy and provided with metal fins to increase heat radiation. The breech remained open at the end of each burst, a feature possible with any machine gun and used by many of them. Two machine guns of this type are said to have fired 75,000 rounds each in the defense of Verdun, and remained serviceable.

The Austrian Schwarzlose Model 1907/1912 operated on a third principle often called "blowback." In this, the action and barrel are never locked rigidly together; the barrel does not move, nor is there a gas cylinder and piston. To prevent too early opening of the action and case rupture, the block is heavy and the main spring strong. There is usually also a linkage of parts not quite on centre to delay the actual opening. Finally, the barrel is shorter than standard. The Schwarzlose, which was water-cooled and in the Maxim class in weight, was a delayed blowback. The weapon was entirely satisfactory in combat.

Light machine guns and automatic rifles. Heavy machine guns of the Maxim and Hotchkiss types were satisfactory for defensive roles but were not really portable. A number of lighter machine guns that could be carried by one man without great inconvenience began to be used in 1915 and later. These include the British Lewis gun (invented in America but manufactured and improved in Great Britain), the French Chauchat, several German weapons, and the U.S. Browning automatic rifle known as the BAR. All these were light enough to be carried and fired by one man. They could be fired rifle-fashion but were also capable of delivering from a prone position, with bipod, full automatic fire almost as effective as that from the heavy machine guns, restoring some of the offensive power of foot soldiers.

Most, but not all, of these light weapons were gas-operated. Almost all were air-cooled. Generally, a light machine-gunner had an assistant to help him carry ammunition. Toward the end of World War I, one light machine gun was issued per squad or section of six to 10 men in most armies. These light machine guns usually fired from magazines rather than belts of ammunition because they were more convenient and more easily transported. The guns weighed as little as 15 pounds (7 kilograms), giving rise to the idea that a similar infantry rifle could be constructed that would operate semi-automatically. Several such automatic rifles were issued in small numbers by 1918, but none was a military success. Recoil-operated weapons were prohibitively expensive at that time, and the gas-operated types needed too much cleaning to remain reliable. The principle causes of malfunctions in all weapons of this type are the accumulation of powder residue in the gas system and the breakage of small parts.

Automatic pistols and submachine guns. The anticipated

Use of
recoil
energy in
Maxim
guns

The
Hotchkiss
gun at
Verdun

success of the automatic machine guns late in the 19th century led to dozens of different so-called automatic pistols, actually semi-automatic; when the trigger is pulled, the cartridge in the chamber is fired producing power to extract and eject the empty case, load another round, and cock the weapon. There is no mechanical problem in making a pistol fully automatic (*i.e.,* causing it to fire continuously until the trigger is released or the weapon is empty), but only the first bullet will be target effective, the rest going high.

The early automatic or self-loading pistols operated by means of recoiling or blowback action. There have been no successful gas-operated military pistols. If the cartridge power is high, recoil operation is preferable. The best known military pistols of this class used in World War I were the German Lugers and Mausers and the U.S. Model 1911. Similar pistols used in other armies included the British Webley, the Austrian Steyr, and the Italian Glisenti. In all of these, the barrel and action move a short distance to the rear before unlocking.

Simple blowback-operated pistols were also widely used, firing relatively weaker cartridges. These have less than half the muzzle energy of the more powerful pistol ammunition. Accuracy and range are both limited compared with that of a shoulder weapon. Early in the history of self-loading pistols, however, the more powerful types were often equipped with a detachable stock that functioned as a holster when the weapon was not in use. Probably the most widely issued weapon of this sort was a special long-barrelled German Luger with a 32-shot drum magazine. It was normally carried as a secondary arm by machine-gunners; it fired only one shot per trigger pull.

This Luger and other similar arms confirmed the belief that a shoulder small arm that fired pistol ammunition could be militarily effective. The result was the submachine gun. The first successful weapon of this type was developed by a German, Louis Schmeisser, who at first used the 32-shot Luger magazines and the nine millimetre Parabellum or Luger cartridge. The Model 1918 Schmeisser was of rifle weight and conformation, but with a barrel only 7.9 inches (20 centimetres) long. It was blowback operated, easily possible with this cartridge and barrel length, because of the relatively heavy bolt and main spring, and was moderately effective in the few months it was used before the end of World War I.

Other fully automatic shoulder weapons firing pistol ammunition in World War I included the Italian Villar Perosa and the Pedersen device, but neither was of much combat importance. The Villar Perosa was used mostly in dual mounts for missions better accomplished by light machine guns. The Pedersen device allowed the standard U.S. Springfield to deliver fully automatic fire with a special, powerful, calibre .30 pistol-type cartridge, but the rifle could be converted back to fire rifle ammunition quickly if the soldier had not lost his bolt. Pedersen devices were in France before the Armistice in 1918; training results with them were encouraging, but they saw no combat service. All were scrapped soon after the war ended, although the cartridge was used later in French semi-automatic pistols and submachine guns.

Infantry support weapons. The widespread use of water-cooled machine guns in field fortifications and other innovations in World War I encouraged the introduction of new weapons into rifle companies. A small, light cannon firing a low-velocity explosive shell about 37 millimetres (1.5 inches) in diameter gave units of this size a means of destroying enemy machine-gun nests, although weapons of this type were not totally successful. The advent of tanks led to the development of infantry antitank weapons. The Germans produced a single-shot Mauser rifle of about calibre .51 (13 millimetres) capable of penetrating the armour of most 1918 tanks. It gave trouble because of its excessive weight and recoil but was reasonably effective.

The conditions of trench warfare also led to the reintroduction, after about 150 years, of hand grenades. Heavier bombs were projected in a number of ways, but simple muzzle-loading mortars were by far the most common. These trench mortars of about three-inch bore continued in the infantry inventories of the major armies after the war was over but were soon known simply as mortars.

Guns of World War II and the postwar era. Research and development in small arms as in the other weapons was virtually suspended in most countries at the end of World War I, partly because of peace, partly because of the vast stocks on hand. With the rise of Hitler in Germany in the 1930s, militarism and military production began to revive.

Rifles and assault rifles. To improve on the bolt-action, box-magazine rifles of 1914–18, every nation having an arms industry sought to produce a semi-automatic or self-loading weapon that would load the next round in the chamber without the necessity of pulling back the bolt. The Soviet army was equipped in part with Tokarev semi-automatic rifles, but in 1941 these were abandoned after a few months of combat. The Germans produced only a small quantity of semi-automatic rifles (FG-42s) chambered for their full power 7.92-millimetre round. The United States armies of 1942 and later were supplied, however, with an ever-increasing flow of the U.S. M1 Garand semi-automatic rifles. The Japanese produced a copy of the Garand, but poor material and execution made it unsatisfactory.

In addition, many fully automatic weapons of infantry weight (eight to ten pounds) were designed. The search for a satisfactory light machine gun before and during World War I led to experimental production of self-loading arms in the rifle-weight class. Several different principles worked well in sporting arms, including both short and long recoil, gas operation, and various forms of delayed blowback operation. The submachine gun, though not used in quantity during World War I, became extremely popular in the next 20 years. These weapons will be discussed below, but their use in the German Army led to what may be called a new infantry weapon, the assault rifle.

The Germans used a number of good submachine guns early in World War II, but all were chambered for the nine-millimetre Luger, which lacked both range and power. The German FG-42, firing a full-power rifle round, recoiled too much for burst-fire accuracy even in a prone position. A round was developed in 1943, the 7.92 Kurz (short), which fired a bullet intermediate in power between the 7.92-millimetre Mauser rifle and the Luger pistol. The German assault rifle finally developed to fire this round is usually called the MP-44. Bursts from it were as accurate as from most submachine guns, but effective out to at least 1,000 feet (300 metres).

After World War II the Soviets adopted the German assault rifle in their AK-47 (Kalashnikov Model 1947). This assault rifle (see Figure 4) was more powerful than a submachine gun and more stable in burst fire than weapons chambered for full-power rifle rounds. Later they were equipped with detachable box magazines to facilitate reloading. A Soviet carbine, the SKS or Simonov, had to be recalled because of loading troubles when ammunition was transferred from long clips into an integral box magazine. Both the MP-44 and the AK-47 were gas-operated with cylinders and pistons above the barrel, fired both fully and semi-automatically, and weighed about 12 pounds (five kilograms) loaded with detachable 30-round box magazines. Both fired from closed bolts but differed from each other in minor respects.

Communist armies, including the Chinese, adopted the AK-47 and an associated family of small arms firing the same cartridge. Other armies, however, had little success at first with the assault-rifle concept. In the early 1950s, the United States was unwilling to give up full-power rifle ammunition. The North Atlantic Treaty Organization (NATO) armies adopted a new common round, the 7.62-millimetre

From W. Smith, Small Arms of the World

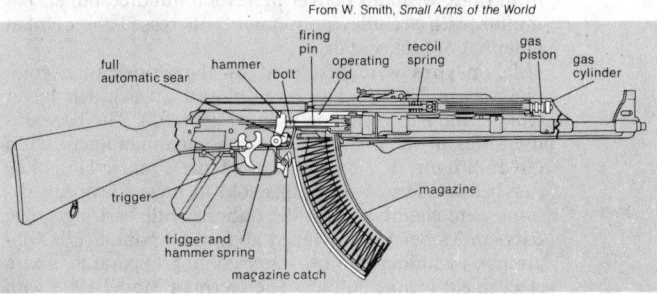

Figure 4: Soviet AK-47 assault rifle.

Pistols of World War I

Combination stock and holster

The NATO common round

(0.3-inch) NATO, in 1952, which is shorter and lighter than most old rifle cartridges but is still of full rifle power. Several new rifles, chambered for this round, have been introduced into various Western armies. The best known are the Belgian FN, the German G3, the U.S. M14, the Japanese Model 1962, and the Italian Beretta.

In the early 1970s, however, the U.S. Armed Forces were changing from the World War II M1 and the more recent M14 to a new weapon, once called the AR-15 but now known as the M16, which fires a 5.56-millimetre (0.22-inch) round. The M16 is a true assault rifle, capable of delivering bursts with reasonable accuracy. Its great advantage is lightness of both weapon and ammunition; roughly twice as many rounds can be carried for the same total load, weapon and ammunition combined. But the M16 has a much shorter effective range than the full-power rifles, perhaps 350 yards (320 metres) compared with about 1,000 yards (900 metres). The Soviet 7.62 intermediate-power cartridge is heavier than the 5.56 but probably has more effective range. U.S. allies in Southeast Asia have many M16 rifles and some other weapons firing the same cartridge, and the British Army also has used them.

Most military rifles of the late 20th century were gas-operated; that is, the power for the unloading-reloading cycle came from the propellant gases in the barrel before the bullet left the muzzle. In such a rifle a port in the barrel, usually closer to the muzzle than the breech, is uncovered when the bullet passes; gas enters, forcing a piston to the rear, and compressing a main spring, an operation similar to the early gas-operated machine gun. Both full and intermediate power cartridges can be handled equally well in light gas-operated actions. In assault rifles, the operating cylinder is frequently above, rather than below, the barrel in order to provide for an "in line" stock. Assault rifles generally fire from a closed breech.

Pistols and submachine guns. Pistols have never been satisfactory for military use because of their lack of accuracy and power. In the 20th century, many major nations have endeavoured to abandon military pistols entirely, but none has succeeded. Some soldiers cannot perform their major duties encumbered by any form of shoulder weapon, yet need something for personal defense. In guerrilla war situations, all war personnel need some kind of weapon, but often the need is for something convenient to carry, especially into and out of vehicles (for example, see Figure 5).

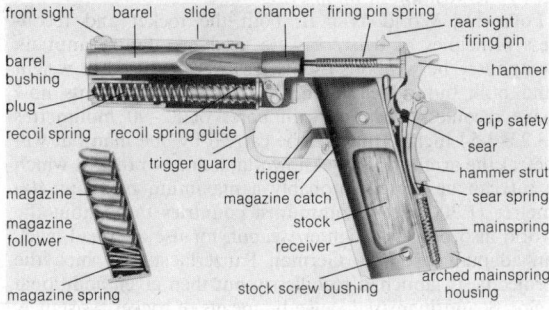

Figure 5: Colt semi-automatic pistol, calibre .45.

Submachine guns, which developed astonishingly after 1918, have distinct advantages. They are shorter than rifles but are much more accurate and have greater magazine capacity than pistols. Submachine guns lack rifle or even assault-rifle power and range, but they can fire reasonably accurate bursts, an enormous psychological advantage.

Hugo Schmeisser of Germany (son of Louis Schmeisser mentioned above), who produced the best submachine gun of World War I, developed a new model in 1928, which took long, straight magazines, extending out to the left side. This widely copied weapon was blowback-operated. An infantry soldier equipped with a weapon of this sort was thought to be more effective in some combat situations, especially in towns, than if he had a rifle. During the Spanish Civil War of 1936–39, rifles and submachine guns were issued in about equal numbers in some infantry units. The riflemen took care of long-range targets, and the submachine gunners gave close-in firepower.

Both the German and Soviet armies issued submachine guns widely in infantry units during World War II. The Germans used mainly Schmeisser types. The Soviets had two submachine guns: the first, known as the PPsh, often used a 71-round drum magazine that gave trouble and fired too fast for accuracy (900 rounds per minute); the second, the PPS, was an outstanding success because it was simple, slow firing, and light. The 7.62 Soviet pistol and submachine gun cartridge had greater range than the German nine-millimetre Parabellum because of its smaller diameter bullets, which had higher velocity. A spare magazine loaded with 35 rounds weighed only 1.5 pounds (0.7 kilogram). Many Soviet infantrymen used the PPS in their final successful offensives against the Germans late in 1944 and in 1945.

The first submachine gun issued in the United States armed forces was the well-designed Thompson Model 1928, the "tommy gun" of the American underworld and motion pictures. The early Thompsons were satisfactory, but complicated and expensive, and needed careful cleaning and maintenance. They were not at first straight blowbacks but used a locking system that was not necessary. They were employed in small quantities by American troops in Caribbean actions and by the Western Allies early in World War I. A wartime redesign changed them into the U.S. M1 submachine gun, in which they did become blowbacks. The M1 was replaced by the M3, which fired more slowly and reliably and could be produced for a fifth of the man-machine hours.

The U.S. during World War II had another weapon midway between the rifles and pistols in power, the semi-automatic M1 carbine, which fired a special calibre .30 cartridge. Toward the end of the war, this weapon was issued with a switch to allow fully automatic fire, but results were not satisfactory—the weapon was too light for the rate of fire.

Other individual weapons. Bayonets and knives continue to be carried in most modern infantry units. A few Japanese officers used swords during World War II. Grenades are still widely issued, although their effectiveness when hand thrown is subject to question. Special skill, strength, and coordination are required for range and accuracy in combat. Shotguns have high efficiency when range is short, but they are ineffective beyond about 75 yards (70 metres) and their ammunition is heavy.

The outstanding new individual small arm since World War II is the U.S. M79 grenade launcher, a light, single-shot, shoulder-fired rifle with a large (40-millimetre, or 1.6-inch) bore designed to project small bombs at the remarkably low velocity of 250 feet per second (fps; 76 metres per second). These little shells weigh slightly less than six ounces (186 grams), but their segmented wire and powerful explosive give them about the same killing power as World War I hand grenades. Maximum range is said to be 400 metres (about 435 yards).

The concept of discharging bombs from a small arm has also been incorporated into a 2.5-pound (1.1-kilogram) attachment for an infantryman's rifle. These were used in combat in small numbers in Vietnam with mixed results. The combination of a rifle and grenade launcher is versatile, but clumsy and heavy. Supplies of ammunition for both are difficult to carry in rough terrain during poor weather.

Machine guns. The heavy, water-cooled machine guns of World War I were widely used during World War II and later, but lighter, air-cooled weapons began to take their place during the 1930s. The most important were the several different models known collectively as the German MG-34, all recoil-operated. Their greatest virtue lay in their effectiveness both as light machine guns fired from bipods and as substitutes for the old heavy machine guns when mounted on tripods for sustained fire. A shift in terms occurred between the wars. In 1918 a heavy machine gun was typically a water-cooled Maxim, firing rifle cartridges. In 1939 the same weapon was considered to be medium; the term heavy now referred to machine guns firing cartridges of several times rifle power.

The MG-34s and the similar MG-42s were reliable and satisfactory in both light and medium roles, especially models with barrels that could be changed quickly. Even with their tripods, they were lighter and more portable than the

"Tommy gun"

The MG-34

weapons they replaced. These dual-purpose machine guns used belts for holding their ammunition, but short lengths could be carried in containers like magazines.

Light machine guns

The light machine guns of World War II, usually issued with bipod mounts only, were normally magazine-fed. There is a difference in tactical value between belt-fed and magazine-fed types in regard to firepower. If a weapon fires from a magazine, it is out of action between the time one magazine is exhausted and another is installed. Belt-fed weapons can be in action continuously for short periods at least, because one belt can be attached to another while the first is being fired. Belt-fed weapons, on the other hand, are usually longer, heavier, and more troublesome when carried in thick jungle than those that use magazines.

The best-known light machine guns of World War II were the Soviet Degtyarev (DP and DPM), the British Bren, and the already mentioned U.S. BAR. There are different models of each of these, but all are gas-operated and magazine-fed, and weigh from slightly over 20 pounds (nine kilograms) to more than 30 (14 kilograms) loaded. They fire slowly enough to deliver accurate bursts from their bipods, 350–600 rounds per minute. In general, lighter weapons must be fired more slowly to achieve accuracy.

Heavy machine guns

The new heavy machine guns were designed partly to overcome the insufficient power of rifle ammunition for some tactical missions, especially for attacking armoured vehicles. Even before World War I, fully automatic weapons were used with ammunition more powerful than rifle cartridges, but smaller than that for conventional artillery. Such ammunition was not necessary for infantry missions, however, until foot soldiers encountered armoured vehicles. During the 1930s, many higher powered weapons were manufactured and tested. Several were actually adopted, although only two had outstanding success. The U.S. calibre .50 Browning is still widely used throughout the non-Communist world. The cartridge delivers bullets of various weights and types at high muzzle velocities, roughly five to seven times the energy of full, rifle power ammunition. The weapon is essentially the Model 1917 calibre .30 weapon, increased in size. It is recoil-operated and was at first water-

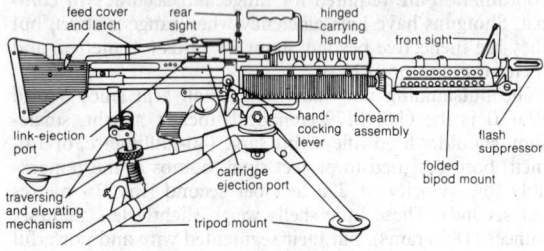

Figure 6: Components of a typical machine gun (U.S. M60).

cooled, but this refinement was found to be unnecessary for most ground missions. Firing rate is about 450 rounds per minute; the air-cooled M2 weapon with tripod and 500 rounds joined with disintegrating links weighs about 300 pounds (135 kilograms). The Soviet 12.7-millimetre weapon, the DShK, is similar and is almost as widely used in the Communist armies, but is gas-operated. The two bullets are almost identical in diameter, and the cartridge cases and ballistics are similar.

Since 1945, several super-heavy machine guns (above calibre .50) have been developed in several countries, mostly for aircraft and antiaircraft use. The Soviets introduced a 14.5-millimetre weapon into their ground forces especially for use in armoured vehicles. It is recoil-operated and belt-fed and has a barrel that can be changed quickly. Armoured personnel carriers also often carry small automatic cannon, up to even 30 millimetres, but these cannot be considered small arms.

At the other end of the modern machine-gun spectrum, there are weapons firing assault-rifle ammunition of intermediate power. In the early 1970s the Communist nations, their allies, and their weapons customers were using a machine gun chambered for the 7.62 intermediate round. A successful light machine gun firing the same cartridge used in rifles offers advantages at the platoon level, but lack of effective range may more than counterbalance them.

Additional platoon and company support weapons. During World War I, small mortars came to be associated with infantry instead of artillery. Weapons with bores of two to three inches (50 to 75 millimetres) in diameter were issued throughout World War II in most infantry platoons or companies and continue to be used by them to deliver high-angle fire like artillery. Accuracy and range depend, of course, on size, stabilization, mounting, and sighting equipment as well as the skill of the crew. A good crew with the latest in equipment can deliver effective fire out to 4,000 metres (13,000 feet). Larger mortars are usually classified as artillery.

Infantry antitank weapons became extremely important early in World War II. The Germans had a single-shot rifle that delivered an extremely high-velocity 7.92-millimetre rifle bullet with a hardened core that could penetrate the armour of tanks of the 1939–41 era. The British had a calibre .55 "shoulder" rifle similar to the German Mauser of World War I, save that the British weapon had a recoil-absorbing device incorporated in the stock. Tank armour soon became too strong and thick, however, for either of these. Kinetic-energy projectiles (*i.e.*, those that penetrate because of their own weight and velocity) that could defeat tank armour after 1943 required a delivery system too heavy for infantry companies.

On the other hand, a discovery made before World War II led to a highly effective means of attacking armour with light weapons firing low-velocity projectiles. A hollow cone of high explosive, with its open end toward the target, was detonated several inches from the armour to be penetrated. A jet of white-hot gas and molten steel was projected forward and penetrated several inches of the best armour plate. These "shaped-charge" projectiles could be delivered even by means of fin-stabilized rifle grenades discharged from the muzzle of an individual soldier's weapon, though they were more effective in larger sizes. Two new types of infantry-support weapons were introduced to launch larger projectiles: the bazooka, from which a rocket was launched out of an open tube; and a recoilless device such as the German Panzerfaust. The Panzerfaust was held in the hands of a soldier; the thrust is generated as in artillery, but with an exact balance between the energy of the projectile moving forward and gases from the propellant moving to the rear. These weapons resembled rocket launchers but were better in both accuracy and range. The backblast, however, gave away the position of the firer.

Following World War II, both the rocket and recoilless principles of delivery were used in infantry antitank weapons. The weapons themselves were reduced in weight and bulk but increased in effectiveness. Rifle units now have recoilless weapons with bores of 82–90 millimetres (3.23–3.54 inches) that can be carried by one man but will defeat the armour of any known tank at any range at which a hit can be scored, probably a maximum of about 400 metres (1,300 feet). Communist countries throughout the world also possess a lighter weapon for use at squad level, an adaptation of the German Panzerfaust, in which the projectile is launched recoillessly but then given additional velocity and increased range by means of rocket assistance. It is known officially as the RPG-7 antitank weapon but is often called a grenade launcher. In the early 1970s, the United States and her allies used a light 66-millimetre non-reloadable rocket launcher known as the LAW (light antitank weapon) weighing less than four pounds but with a shaped charge capable of destroying any enemy tank it can hit in a vital spot.

(J.We./Ed.)

Shaped charges

DEVELOPMENT OF AMMUNITION

In modern military usage "ammunition" is a generic term that includes a great variety of missiles and other devices designed and constructed to inflict damage upon enemy personnel or materiel by action of an explosive, pyrotechnic, or chemical agent. The term includes, but is not limited to, such items as projectiles, propellants, cartridges, bombs, rockets, torpedoes, grenades, explosive mines, and guided missiles. The term ammunition is commonly used in a more restrictive sense, however, to designate only that which is intended for firing in guns. Ammunition for guns is divided broadly into small-arms ammunition—pistols, rifles, shotguns, and machine guns—and artillery ammunition, intended for firing in cannon.

Ammunition size is usually expressed in terms of calibre, which is approximately the diameter of the projectile, given either in inches or in millimetres. A complete round of ammunition includes all of the components necessary for one firing of the gun. The components (see Figure 7) normally include a projectile, a charge of propellant, and a primer that ignites the propellant. Other components such as a cartridge case, fuze, and bursting charge are frequently included. If the components of a complete round are assembled into a single unit, the round is called a cartridge.

A   fuze
B   booster
C   shell
D   ogive
E   bourrelet
F   bursting charge
G   rotating band
H   crimp
J   base cover
K   cartridge case
L   propelling charge
M   primer

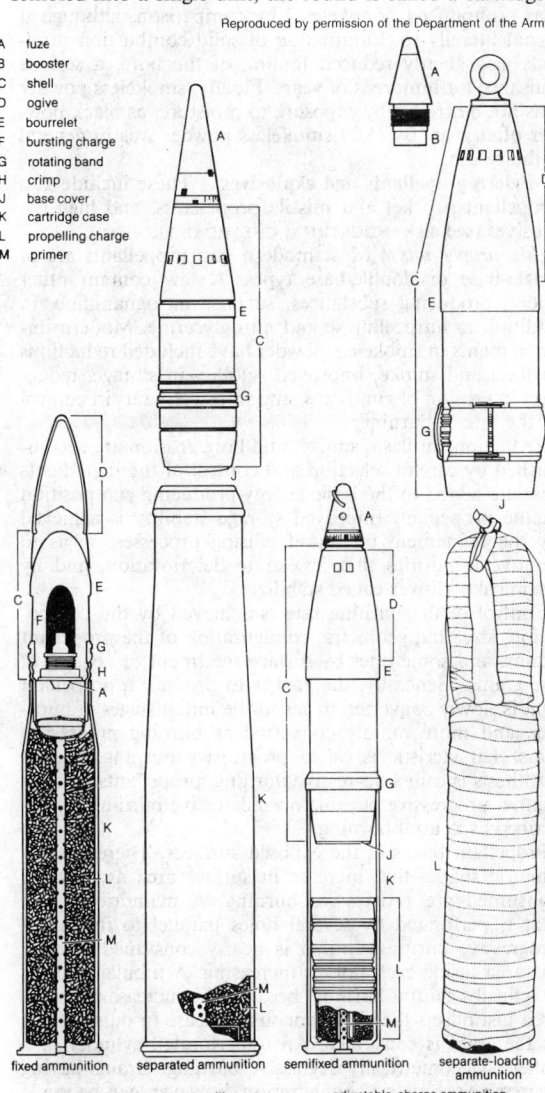

fixed ammunition   separated ammunition   semifixed ammunition   separate-loading ammunition

nonadjustable-charge ammunition   adjustable-charge ammunition

Figure 7: Terms used to identify the principal parts of typical kinds of artillery ammunition.

Rockets and guided missiles are sometimes classified as artillery ammunition, although they are not ordinarily launched from cannon. A rocket is a self-propelled missile that cannot be controlled after launching. A guided missile is also self-propelled, but it can be controlled during flights, either by internal means or remotely.

Early firearms projectiles. An illustrated manuscript executed in 1326 contains one of the earliest drawings of a gun and ammunition. The manuscript depicts a primitive cannon in the act of being fired; the projectile emerging from the muzzle resembles a large crossbow quarrel. Balls of stone, lead, bronze, or iron were also used during the 14th century. The smaller firearms usually fired metal balls, but the larger guns fired balls of stone; these were lighter than solid metal balls and therefore better suited to the uncertain strength of the primitive cannon. Large mortars were sometimes loaded with numerous medium-sized stones, which were fired on high trajectories to fall among the enemy. Wadding or softwood plugs were sometimes employed to reduce the escape of propellant gases around the loosely fitting projectiles in the gun barrel. For incendiary purposes, iron balls were heated red-hot in a fire before loading. In that case, moist clay was sometimes packed atop the wadding to prevent premature firing of the powder charge by the red-hot ball.

Explosive projectiles were in use by the 16th century, perhaps even earlier. First used only in mortars, these were hollow cast-iron balls, filled with gunpowder, called bombs. A crude fuze was employed, consisting of a short tube, filled with a slow-burning powder, driven into a hole through the wall of the bomb.

Other early artillery projectiles, developed for special purposes, included the carcass, canister, grapeshot, chain shot, and bar shot. The carcass was a thin-walled shell containing incendiary material. Rounds of canister and grapeshot consisted of numerous small missiles, usually iron or lead balls, held together in various ways for simultaneous loading into the gun but designed to separate upon leaving the muzzle. Because they dispersed widely upon leaving the gun, the projectiles were especially effective at short range against massed troops. Bar shot and chain shot consisted of two heavy projectiles joined by a bar or a chain. Whirling in their trajectories, they were especially effective in cutting the spars and rigging of sailing vessels.

Projectiles for small arms did not change significantly in form or material from their earliest use until the 19th century. Lead balls, fired either singly or several at a time (as in a shotgun), were almost universally the ammunition of small arms for more than 400 years.

Developments during the 18th and 19th centuries. Advances in the physical sciences and in technology during the 18th and 19th centuries enabled the ordnance (military supplies) engineer to put into practice many ideas that had been conceived earlier but that had remained impractical. Weapon and ammunition developments were closely interrelated, each affecting the other. The breech-loading gun and the rifled bore were the most important weapon developments, while percussion ignition, projectiles for rifled guns, and smokeless powder were the most significant innovations in ammunition.

Ammunition for rifled guns. Rifling is the term applied to a system of helical grooves cut into the interior surface of a gun bore. The raised portions of the rifled bore that remain between the grooves are called lands. The function of rifling is to impart spin to the projectile in its passage along the bore. Though the date of the original invention of rifling cannot be determined precisely, it was in limited use at least as early as the 15th century. A rational explanation of the benefits of rifling was not put forth until 1747, however, when the English mathematician and engineer Benjamin Robins published a treatise on the subject. Systematic development of rifled guns began in the mid-18th century.

Rifling improves the accuracy of a round ball by imparting uniform spin. A greater benefit, however, is that rifling can impart the kind of stability manifest in a spinning top or a gyroscope to elongated projectiles, thus enabling such projectiles to maintain a point-forward attitude in flight. Elongated projectiles are aerodynamically much superior to round balls of the same weight and thus sustain their velocities better in flight. The introduction of rifling made possible the change from round lead balls to the now familiar bullet form of projectile, which is called cylindro-conoidal, or, sometimes, cylindro-ogival.

Experiments with cylindroconoidal bullet forms began about 1825. Difficulties were experienced at first because the bullet was required to fit tightly in the barrel, and it was excessively difficult to load a tight-fitting bullet in a muzzle-loading arm. The most successful solution to this problem in small arms was a soft lead bullet having a cavity in the base. The bullet was made small enough for convenient loading; the gas pressure upon firing expanded the hollow base to fit tightly in the grooves and lands of the barrel. The best known projectile of the hollow-base type was the Minié bullet. Cylindroconoidal bullets were widely used in small arms by the mid-19th century.

Grape-
shot

The
Minié
bullet

The solution represented by the soft-lead Minié bullet in small arms could not be practically applied to projectiles for muzzle-loading artillery. Though many ingenious attempts were made to solve the problems of using cylindroconoidal projectiles in muzzle-loading cannon, none was entirely satisfactory. Artillerymen continued to fire shperical projectiles from smoothbore cannon for about 50 years after the practice was abandoned in small arms, or almost until the end of the 19th century.

Percussion ignition. The development of practical percussion-ignition is generally credited to Alexander Forsyth, a Scottish clergyman, whose avocational interests included both chemistry and firearms. Forsyth's priority in this invention is not unchallenged, because other men were achieving some degree of success, independently, at about the same time. Forsyth's percussion gunlock, patented in 1807, employed a small charge of chemical explosive (mercury fulminate or potassium chlorate) for ignition, which detonated upon being struck a sharp blow by the hammer of the gun. Such materials, originally called detonating powders, were not new in 1807. Forsyth's contribution was in the application of the material to guns.

For convenience in handling, and for protection from the elements, detonating powder was soon encapsulated in paper, foil, or thin metal for use in gunlocks. The percussion system was much more reliable than the flintlock. Trials were conducted in England during 1834, in which 6,000 rounds were fired in flintlock muskets and 6,000 in percussion guns. The weapons were loaded and fired at a rate of about three rounds per minute. The average frequency of misfires in the flintlocks was one per six or seven rounds, whereas the average frequency for the percussion arms was only one misfire per 166 rounds.

Ammunition for breech-loading guns. The development of strong and practical breech-loading cannon immediately solved the problems that had formerly thwarted efforts to use cylindroconoidal projectiles in artillery. A projectile soon emerged that had a band of soft metal encircling it at the rear, slightly larger in diameter than the body of the projectile. The rifling lands were removed from the gun bore adjacent to the breech to accommodate the banded rear part of the projectile and the powder charge seated behind it. The band on the projectile is called a rotating band or, sometimes, a driving band. When the gun is fired the band is engraved by the rifling lands, imparting spin to the projectile and sealing the bore against escape of the propellant gases. This design has not been superseded; it is still used in modern artillery ammunition.

In the case of small arms, the development of practical breech-loading weapons and self-contained cartridges proceeded together. The self-contained cartridge consists of a tube (the cartridge case) having the bullet affixed at the front end and the cap or primer at the rear, with the propellant contained in the tube between. Thus, all components for a complete round are contained in one convenient assembly for handling and loading into the gun. The cartridge case also solved the problem of breech sealing (called obturation), which had been the most formidable obstacle to the development of practical breech-loading small arms.

Muzzle-loading rifles were obsolescent for military use by the end of the American Civil War in 1865. A great variety of breech-loading sporting arms and ammunition also appeared, especially in the United States, during the period 1865 to 1900.

Smokeless powder. The first smokeless powder successfully used in guns was invented in 1864. Moderately successful in sporting ammunition for shotguns, it burned too rapidly for rifles or cannon. The first successful smokeless powders for military use appeared between 1880 and 1890. There were two types, called single-base and double-base. Both were produced from guncotton, a form of nitrocellulose first described in 1846. Guncotton was not itself suitable as a propellant because it burned much too rapidly. Single-base powder, consisting almost entirely of nitrocellulose, was first prepared in France about 1884. Double-base powder, containing both nitrocellulose and nitroglycerine, was invented about 1888. Both types of powder were prepared by plasticizing guncotton with suit-

The self-contained cartridge

able solvents, rolling it into thin sheets, and cutting the sheets into small squares called granules or grains, which were then dried. The thickness and size of the grains controlled the rate of burning. Other types of double-base and single-base propellants soon appeared.

Smokeless powder has several important advantages over black powder. It produces about three times as much energy as black powder for the same weight of charge. The products of combustion are substantially all gaseous, whereas the combustion of black powder produces approximately 40 percent gaseous and 60 percent solid products. It was the solid products that produced much of the smoke upon firing black powder, and the new powder was pronounced "smokeless" by comparison, although it is not literally so. Elimination of solid combustion products also greatly reduced fouling of the bore, a serious nuisance for hundreds of years. Finally, smokeless powder was not destroyed by exposure to moisture, as black powder often was. By 1900 smokeless powder was in general military use.

Modern propellants and explosives. These include gun propellants, rocket and missile propellants, and high explosives (see also INDUSTRIES, CHEMICAL PROCESS).

Gun propellants. Most modern gun propellants are of single-base or double-base types. A few contain other energy-producing substances, such as nitroguanidine, in addition to nitrocellulose and nitroglycerine. Modern improvements in smokeless powder have included reductions in flash and smoke, improved stability in storage, reduction in erosion of gun bores, and improvements in control of the rate of burning.

Improvements in smokeless powder

Reductions in flash, smoke, and bore erosion are accomplished by careful selection and control of the ingredients that are added to the basic energy-producing composition of the propellant. Improved storage stability is achieved by the refinement of manufacturing processes, so as to remove impurities that accelerate deterioration, and by chemical additives called stabilizers.

Control of the burning rate is achieved by the composition, size, and geometric configuration of the propellant grains, and sometimes by surface treatment or coating of the grains. Generally, the goal is to produce a propellant that is slowly converted to gas in the initial stages of burning, and more rapidly converted as burning progresses. This characteristic is called progressive burning, and its antithesis is called degressive burning; propellants that are neither progressive burning nor degressive burning are described as neutral burning.

Propellant burns at the exposed surfaces. Therefore, geometric shapes that increase in surface area as they are consumed are progressive burning. A cylindrical grain that is perforated by several holes parallel to its axis is progressive burning until it is nearly consumed because the area inside each hole is increasing. A tubular grain is practically neutral burning, because the increase in inside area just offsets the simultaneous decrease in outside area as the grain is consumed. An unperforated cylinder or a sphere is geometrically degressive burning. Grains having degressive geometric configuration, however, can be made to burn progressively by impregnating the exposed surface with a substance called a deterrent coating, or moderant, which retards the burning rate of the basic material. Deterrent coatings are commonly used on modern small-arms propellants.

Rocket and missile propellants. Modern rocket and missile propellants are solid or liquid. Solid propellants are characterized, according to their composition, as double-base, cast perchlorate, and composite. Double-base rocket propellants are similar in composition to double-base gun propellants. Cast perchlorate propellants use mixtures of various perchlorates as oxidizers, with materials such as asphalt oil or polysulfide rubber as the fuels that are oxidized. Composite propellants usually contain ammonium picrate, potassium nitrate, or sodium nitrate, and a plastic binder.

Liquid propellants may be classified as monopropellants, bipropellants, or multipropellants. A monopropellant is a single liquid, containing both an oxidizer and a fuel, which is ignited by some external means in a manner similar to the ignition of solid propellants. Bipropellants consist of a liquid oxidizing agent and a liquid fuel that are kept separate and mixed only at the time of combustion. The ignition of bipropellants or multipropellants may occur spontaneously upon mixing, a phenomenon called hypergolic ignition. Liquid monopropellants are generally rather sensitive and unstable; for this reason bipropellants or multipropellants are usually preferred. Nitromethane is an example of a liquid monopropellant. One simple and effective bipropellant consists of liquid oxygen and liquid hydrogen, but there are literally thousands of other feasible combinations for bipropellants and multipropellants. German experimenters during World War II tested several thousand different combinations in developing propellants for their long-range rockets.

High explosives. High explosives differ from propellants (classified as low explosives) in respect to the rapidity with which they decompose. Whereas propellants are decomposed by burning, high explosives are decomposed by a phenomenon called detonation, which proceeds roughly 100,000 times as rapidly as the burning of a gun propellant.

High explosives are classified, according to their sensitivity, as primary or secondary. Primary high explosives are relatively sensitive to detonation by shock, heat, or friction, but are generally inferior in strength and brisance (shattering effect) to secondary explosives. Because their detonation is easily initiated, primary explosives are used in small quantities to detonate the more powerful but less sensitive secondary explosives. Such an arrangement, in which a series of progressively less sensitive explosives are detonated in sequence, is called an explosive train. Some commonly used primary explosives are mercury fulminate, lead azide, and lead styphnate. A few examples of secondary explosives are TNT (trinitrotoluene), tetryl, and RDX (cyclo-trimethylene trinitramine, or cyclonite), but these and other substances are combined in various ways to make a great variety of secondary explosives that are used in modern ammunition.

Modern projectiles. Modern projectiles are divided into two general classes, according to whether they are intended to accomplish their purposes by kinetic or chemical energy. Kinetic-energy projectiles produce their effects on the target solely by virtue of their mass and striking velocity. Chemical-energy projectiles achieve their effects primarily by the explosion of a bursting charge, which is a chemical reaction.

Projectiles are also classified as spin-stabilized or fin-stabilized. Spin-stabilized projectiles remain point-forward in flight by virtue of gyroscopic action and must be fired from rifled guns. Fin-stabilized projectiles have arrow-like stability and may be fired from smooth-bore guns. Fin-stabilized projectiles can be designed to encounter less air resistance and thus retain more of their velocity in flight, but spin-stabilized projectiles usually fly more accurately along the desired trajectory.

Armour-piercing projectiles. Kinetic-energy armour-piercing projectiles depend upon a penetrator of hardened steel or of a harder material such as tungsten carbide. If the penetrator is the solid body of the projectile, it is called a full-calibre penetrator. When the penetrator takes the form of a hard core in the projectile, it is called a subcalibre penetrator.

Modern chemical-energy armour-piercing projectiles usually depend upon a shaped charge, a high explosive formed around a thin-walled metal cone, usually of copper. The open end of the cone faces the target and is covered by a hollow ballistic cap, or windshield. The cap enhances the flight characteristics of the projectile and also provides a predetermined optimum space, or stand-off distance, between the target and the explosive charge at the instant of detonation. The fuze and detonator are situated at the rear of the charge, behind the apex of the cone. Upon impact of the shell, the detonation begins at the rear of the charge, and the conical liner begins to collapse. The progressive collapse of the cone, starting at the apex, is accompanied by formation of a jet, along its central axis, moving at very high velocity. It is this high-velocity jet that achieves the remarkable penetration obtained with a shaped charge.

General-purpose and anti-personnel projectiles. The effectiveness of a general-purpose high-explosive shell depends in part upon the number, size, and velocities of fragments or submissiles that are produced upon detonation of the bursting charge. A small number of low-velocity submissiles is generally less effective than a large number of high-velocity submissiles. In an ordinary high-explosive shell, the fragments of the shell body are the submissiles. The number, size, and velocities of fragments are controlled by proper selection of the explosive used, by the metallurgical properties of the shell body, and by the mechanical design of the shell.

Another approach to improving the effectiveness of submissiles is to preform them and arrange for their projection and dispersal by the bursting charge. This approach was taken during the 19th century by a British officer, Henry Shrapnel, who encased musket balls inside the shell, from which they were propelled by a charge of black powder. A great improvement was the use of small steel darts, called fléchettes, expelled at high velocities by the bursting charge; a modern 90-millimetre (3.54-inch) projectile of this type contains more than 4,000 fléchettes.

Fléchettes have also been used to increase the effectiveness of canister projectiles, which do not contain a fuze or a bursting charge but are designed to burst open immediately upon leaving the muzzle of the gun, thus releasing the submissiles. A modern canister for a 152-millimetre (six-inch) gun used by the United States contains approximately 10,000 fléchettes and has an effective range of 400 metres (1,300 feet). Though the use of fléchettes in small-arms ammunition has been explored in several countries, no such ammunition is yet in common use.

Nuclear artillery projectiles. The modern development of nuclear artillery ammunition is of profound potential importance, because the effects of nuclear bursting charges are enormously greater than those of chemical-energy explosives.

The first nuclear bombs developed were very large; minimum size was fundamentally limited by the physical processes of nuclear fission, upon which their functioning depended. Fundamental improvements were required to develop nuclear munitions small enough to be fired from guns. In 1953 development of the first artillery weapon having a nuclear capability was announced. Calibre was 280 millimetres (11 inches), and the gun weighed approximately 85 tons (77,000 kilograms), not including the two motorized transporters that were required to move it. Subsequently, nuclear artillery of smaller calibres was developed; the U.S. Army reported an eight-inch (203-millimetre) projectile in 1956 and a six-inch (152-millimetre) projectile in 1963. Details of such nuclear projectiles have not yet been publicly disclosed by any nation.

Fuzes. Fuzes must be safe against inadvertent firing and reliable in action when initiated. The two basic conditions of a fuze are unarmed and armed. Unarmed fuzes are substantially incapable of functioning and are therefore safe to transport, handle, and affix to the munition for which they are intended. Armed fuzes are prepared to function, upon receiving the proper stimulus. Arming is accomplished in various ways, appropriate to the type of munition involved. Bomb fuzes may be armed by aerodynamic forces or by changes in barometric pressure. Fuzes for gun-launched projectiles may be armed by forces generated during firing, such as by linear acceleration (called setback), or spin. Fuzes for emplaced munitions, such as mines, may be manually armed. Combinations of these techniques are often used.

Missile fuzes are required to be safe, not only before launching but until they are sufficiently far along the trajectory so that a premature functioning would not endanger the launching weapon or its crew. The interval between launching and arming is called arming delay.

Fuzes can be classified according to the means by which stimulus for functioning is effected. The categories on this basis are impact, time, proximity, command, and combination fuzes. Impact fuzes, initiated by contact of the munition with a target, are sometimes called contact fuzes. They are categorized as superquick, nondelay, or delay, according to the interval of time between initiation

[Marginal notes:]
Liquid oxygen and hydrogen propellants

Stabilization of projectiles

Fléchettes

and functioning. Time fuzes initiate functioning at some predetermined interval after the munition has been fired, dropped, or emplaced. The time interval is adjustable and may be controlled by a pyrotechnic train, mechanical clockwork, electrical circuitry, or other means. Proximity fuzes, also called influence, or VT, fuzes, function when an internal sensing mechanism detects that the target is close enough for effective functioning. The sensing element is generally a small radio unit that transmits signals and receives reflections from the target. Command fuzes, designed to receive a radio or wire-line signal sent from some remote point, are useful for emplaced munitions, such as mines or demolition charges, and for some types of guided missiles. Combination fuzes employ the functioning principles of two or more other types. Time fuzes, for example, may be designed so as to function upon impact if they strike a target before the set time has elapsed. Anti-aircraft shells may be fuzed to burst aloft (self-destruct) in the event they miss the target, so as to avoid the hazards of a burst upon ground impact in friendly territory.

Complete rounds. These include artillery ammunition and military and nonmilitary small-arms ammunition.

Artillery ammunition. In separate-loading artillery ammunition (Figure 7), a complete round consists of three components: the fuzed projectile, the propellant charge (in several combustible cloth bags), and the primer. In fixed rounds, all the components are securely joined together by a cartridge case. In semifixed ammunition, the projectile is not securely joined to the cartridge case, an arrangement that allows for field adjustment of the propellant charge. After the charge has been adjusted, the projectile is loosely inserted into the cartridge case and loaded in the weapon in the same manner as a fixed round. Separated ammunition consists of a primed cartridge case containing the propellant charge and sealed by a closing plug, and a projectile separately handled and separately loaded into the gun. Though brass was almost invariably used for cartridge cases before World War II, it has since been largely superseded by steel. A recent innovation is a combustible cartridge case, entirely consumed upon firing.

Complete rounds are further classified according to the type of projectile employed, such as high-explosive, or armour-piercing. There are also special-purpose types, including blank rounds and dummy rounds, used for saluting, ceremonies, manoeuvres, drills, instruction, or displays.

Recoilless ammunition

A special type of complete round is made for recoilless guns. The cartridge cases for recoilless ammunition are so designed, often by a pattern of perforations in the cartridge wall, that propellant gas rapidly escapes from them on firing. The gun chamber containing the case is also vented, allowing gas to escape into a peripheral space around the case, from whence it is directed rearward, where it finally escapes through a venturi nozzle (containing a constricted part to control the rate of gas flow) in the breech. The rearward escape of gas through the venturi is carefully regulated to ensure that the resulting forces of reaction are equal to the recoil forces caused by propulsion of the projectile and the gases expelled at the muzzle. The gun is thus acted upon simultaneously by two opposite impulses of equal magnitude, the sum of which is zero, and the gun is not disturbed by the forces of firing.

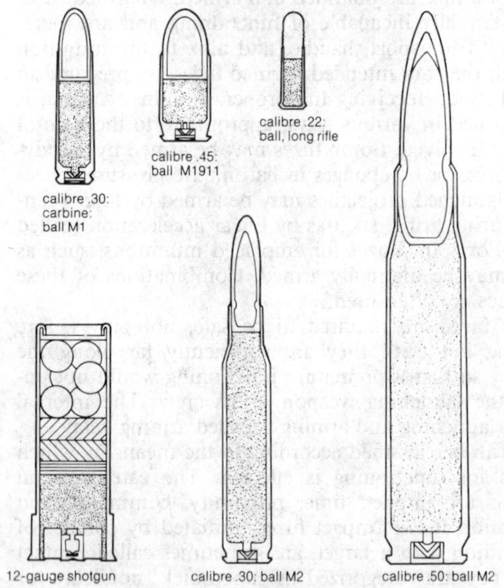

Small-arms ammunition. Small-arms ammunition is always of the fixed type; complete rounds (see Figure 8) are usually called cartridges. In calibres larger than 0.60 inch (15 millimetres), the projectiles are similar to artillery projectiles, and the nomenclature of the ammunition is generally the same. In calibres of 0.60 inch or less, small-arms projectiles are usually called bullets.

Cartridge cases for small-arms ammunition are most commonly made of brass, although steel is also widely used. Though lighter materials, such as aluminum and plastics, have received consideration, they have not yet found significant use in military ammunition. Caseless cartridges, employing a type of molded propellant charge, have also been investigated experimentally.

The most common type of military small-arms ammunition is called general-purpose in England, and ball in the United States. The term ball is historical nomenclature, having originated when the lead ball was the common form of small-arms projectile. The bullet of modern ball ammunition usually consists of a lead-alloy core, encased in an envelope or jacket of harder metal. Jackets are usually made of a copper alloy, or of mild steel coated with a copper alloy. Cores of ball ammunition are occasionally made of mild steel instead of lead alloy.

Special-purpose ammunition for small arms includes armour-piercing, tracer, incendiary, and various dual-purpose or multi-purpose types that combine different characteristics, such as armour-piercing-incendiary-tracer (API-T). Other special-purpose ammunition includes blank, dummy, grenade, and spotting cartridges.

Armour-piercing bullets have cores of hardened steel or are made of harder materials, such as tungsten carbide. Tracer bullets have a column of pyrotechnic composition in the base that is ignited by the flame of the propellant; this provides a visible pyrotechnic display during the bullet's flight. Incendiary bullets, intended to ignite flammable materials such as gasoline, contain a charge of chemical incendiary agent. Spotting bullets contain chemical agents that produce a visible flash, or a puff of smoke, upon impact. They are used principally to adjust the fire of larger guns so arranged that the trajectory coincides approximately with that of the spotting bullet. Blank cartridges contain no projectile, and are used for manoeuvres and training. Grenade cartridges contain no projectile, but contain a special propellant charge for launching rifle grenades, which are affixed separately to the muzzle of the rifle in preparation for firing. Dummy cartridges contain no explosive components and are used for instruction, display, and similar purposes.

Incendiary bullets

A significant 20th-century improvement in small-arms ammunition was the development of primer compositions to replace the old mixtures containing potassium chlorate, of which a decomposition product was potassium chloride, a corrosive substance.   (W.C.Da./Ed.)

DEVELOPMENT OF ROCKETS AND MISSILE SYSTEMS

Rocket is the generic term used broadly to describe a variety of jet-propelled missiles, research vehicles, thrust devices, fireworks, and space-launch vehicles. Forward motion results from reaction to the rearward ejection of matter, usually hot gases, at high velocity. The propulsive jet of gases usually consists of the combustion products of solid or liquid propellants. Stored, high-pressure cold gas, heated hydrogen gas, or ions can also be used.

Rocket propulsion is a unique member of the family of jet-propulsion engines that includes turbojet, pulse-jet, and ramjet systems. The rocket engine is different, however, in that the elements of the propulsive jet (fuel and oxidizer) are self-contained within the vehicle. The thrust produced is independent of the medium through which the vehicle

Reproduced by permission of the Department of the Army

calibre .30: carbine: ball M1

calibre .45: ball M1911

calibre .22: ball, long rifle

12-gauge shotgun   calibre .30: ball M2   calibre .50: ball M2

Figure 8: Types of small-arms cartridges.

travels. Other kinds of jet-propulsion engines carry only their fuel and depend on the oxygen content of the air for burning. Thus these varieties of jet engines are called air breathing and are limited to operation within the Earth's atmosphere. The upper limit of travel for air-breathing jet engines is about 90,000 feet (27 kilometres). A rocket engine is necessary for flight beyond the atmosphere into the immense reaches of space.

A guided missile is broadly any military missile that is capable of being guided or directed to a target after having been launched. Modern guided missiles are powered by some type of jet propulsion, usually rocket propulsion. There are numerous kinds of guidance systems as well as range and functions of such missiles. Accuracy is of prime importance. Explosive warheads may be high explosive or nuclear.

Rocket power has been used in crude form for hundreds of years for military purposes, signalling, and fireworks displays. During the first half of the 19th century, several European armies had rocket brigades, but interest waned with improvement in accuracy and range of artillery. Guided missiles had their origin during World War I but were not then developed to operational use. During World War II, however, rocket power and guided missiles were extensively developed, primarily by Germany. Since then, most technologically capable nations have developed rocket-propelled guided missiles for military purposes and for space research.

Early history. There is no reliable early history of the "invention" of rockets. Most historians of rocketry trace the development of rockets to China, a land noted in ancient times for its fireworks displays. In 1232, when the Mongols laid siege to the city of K'ai-feng, capital of Honan Province, the Chinese defenders used weapons that were described as "arrows of flying fire." There is no explicit statement that these arrows were rockets, but some students have concluded that they were because the record does not mention bows or other means of shooting the arrows. In the same battle, it is reported, the defenders dropped from the walls of the city a kind of bomb described as "heaven-shaking thunder." From these meagre references some students have concluded that by 1232 the Chinese had discovered black powder (gunpowder) and had learned to use it to make explosive bombs as well as propulsive charges for rockets. Drawings made in military documents much later show powder rockets tied to arrows and spears. The propulsive jet evidently added to the range of these weapons and acted as an incendiary agent against targets.

In the same century rockets appeared in Europe. There is indication that their first use was by the Mongols in the Battle of Legnica in 1241. The Arabs are reported to have used rockets on the Iberian Peninsula in 1249; and in 1288 Valencia was attacked by rockets. In Italy, rockets are said to have been used by the Paduans (1379) and by the Venetians (1380).

Nature of early rockets

There are no details of construction of these rockets, but it is presumed that they were quite crude. The tubular rocket cases were probably many layers of tightly wrapped paper, coated with shellac. The propulsive charge was basically a mixture of finely ground carbon (charcoal), saltpetre (potassium nitrate), and sulfur. The English scientist Roger Bacon wrote formulas for black powder about 1248 in his *Epistola*. In Germany, a contemporary of Bacon, Albertus Magnus, described powder charge formulas for rockets in his book *De mirabilibus mundi*. The first firearms appeared about 1325; they utilized a closed tube and black powder (now referred to as gunpowder) to propel a ball, somewhat erratically, over varying distances. Military engineers then began to invent and refine designs for guns and rockets on a parallel basis.

The French historian Jean Froissart suggested that firing rockets from tubes would give them better direction. An Italian writer conceived a number of novel weapons based on rocket propulsion, including a rocket-driven car, designed to breach walls or gates, and a naval torpedo, designed to skim across water and ram its spiked nose into ships. Many other ideas were suggested in print, such as rockets with parachutes and underwater explosive rockets.

The extent to which many of these designs were reduced to working models or weapons is not known. By this time rockets were used also for signalling and, especially by pirates, for setting fire to the tarred rigging of sailing ships. They had many names, such as flying fire or wild fire. There is reason to believe that some of these devices were hurled or catapulted incendiaries rather than actual rockets, particularly in night attacks.

Of considerable interest are the historical origins of rocket designs that were to be employed many years later: the staged (or step) rocket, the clustered rocket, and the winged rocket. These designs evolved both from applications and requirements of fireworks and their adoption by ordnance masters. The earliest records of these concepts are contained in a manuscript by Conrad Haas, an artillery officer and chief of the arsenal at Sibiu, Romania, in the 16th century. In 1590 a German fireworks expert published a small illustrated book reproducing Haas's designs. A Polish artillery expert published essentially the same designs (see Figure 9) in a book translated into French, German, English, and Dutch, but practically no use was made of these concepts for clustered, winged, and step rockets for several hundreds of years, except perhaps in fireworks displays.

By courtesy of M. Subotowicz (Poland)

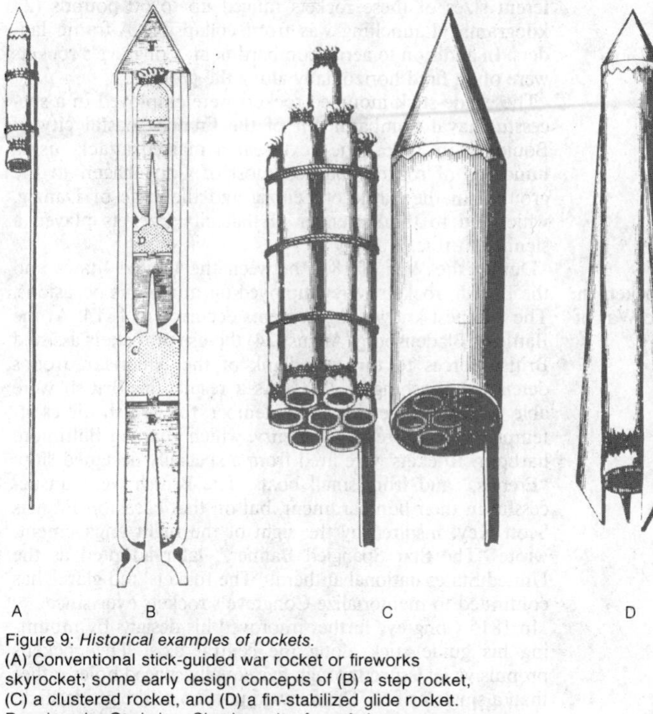

Figure 9: *Historical examples of rockets.*
(A) Conventional stick-guided war rocket or fireworks skyrocket; some early design concepts of (B) a step rocket, (C) a clustered rocket, and (D) a fin-stabilized glide rocket. Drawings by Casimirus Siemienowicz from *Artis magnae artillerae, pars prima*, 1650.

By 1668 military rockets had increased in size and performance. In that year, a German colonel designed a rocket weighing 132 pounds (60 kilograms); it was constructed of wood and wrapped in glue-soaked sailcloth. It carried a gunpowder charge weighing 16 pounds (7.3 kilograms). Nevertheless, the use of rockets seems to have waned, and for the next 100 years their employment in military campaigns appears to have been sporadic.

A revival commenced late in the 18th century in India. There Hyder Ali, prince of Mysore, developed war rockets with an important change: the use of metal cylinders to contain the combustion powder. Although the hammered soft iron he used was crude, the bursting strength of the container of black powder was much higher. Thus a greater internal pressure was possible, with a resultant greater thrust of the propulsive jet. The rocket body was lashed with leather thongs to a long bamboo stick. Range was perhaps up to three-quarters of a mile (more than a kilometre). Although individually these rockets were not accurate, dispersion error became less important when large numbers were fired rapidly in mass attacks. They were particularly effective against cavalry and were hurled

Hyder Ali's metal-clad rockets

into the air, after lighting, or skimmed along the hard dry ground. Hyder Ali's son, Tippu Sultan, continued to develop and expand the use of rocket weapons, reportedly increasing the number of rocket troops from 1,200 to a corps of 5,000. In battles at Seringapatam in 1792 and 1799 these rockets were used with considerable effect against the British.

19th-century developments. The news of the successful use of rockets spread through Europe. In England, William Congreve began to experiment privately. The fact that his father, of the same name, was comptroller of the Royal Arsenal at Woolwich undoubtedly facilitated his efforts.

Several important improvements in rockets were made by Congreve. First, he experimented with a number of black-powder formulas and set down standard specifications of composition. He also standardized construction details and used improved production techniques. Also, his designs made it possible to choose either an explosive (ball charge) or incendiary warhead. The explosive warhead was separately ignited and could be timed by trimming the fuse length before launching. Thus, air bursts of the warheads were feasible at different ranges.

Congreve's metal rocket bodies were equipped on one side with two or three thin metal loops into which a long guided stick was inserted and crimped firm. Weights of eight different sizes of these rockets ranged up to 60 pounds (27 kilograms). Launching was from collapsible A-frame ladders. In addition to aerial bombardment, Congreve's rockets were often fired horizontally along the ground.

These side-stick-mounted rockets were employed in a successful naval bombardment of the French coastal city of Boulogne in 1806. The next year a massed attack, using hundreds of rockets, burned most of Copenhagen to the ground. In the Battle of Leipzig and the siege of Danzig, which led to the surrender of that city, rockets played a significant role.

Rockets in the War of 1812During the War of 1812 between the United States and the British, rockets were employed on numerous occasions. The two best known engagements occurred in 1814. At the Battle of Bladensburg (August 24) the use of rockets assisted British forces to turn the flank of the American troops defending Washington, D.C. As a result, the British were able to capture the city. In September, the British forces attempted to capture Ft. McHenry, which guarded Baltimore harbour. Rockets were fired from a specially designed ship, "Erebus," and from small boats. The British were unsuccessful in their bombardment, but on that occasion Francis Scott Key, inspired by the sight of the night engagement, wrote "The Star Spangled Banner," later adopted as the United States national anthem. "The rockets' red glare" has continued to memorialize Congreve's rockets ever since.

In 1815 Congreve further improved his designs by mounting his guide stick along the central axis. The rocket's propulsive jet issued through five equally spaced holes rather than a single orifice. The forward portion of the guide stick, which screwed into the rocket, was sheathed with brass to prevent burning. The centre-stick-mounted rockets were significantly more accurate. Also, their design permitted launching from thin copper tubes.

Maximum ranges of Congreve rockets were from one-half mile to two miles, depending upon size. They were competitive in performance and cost with the ponderous 10-inch mortar and were vastly more mobile.

Congreve wrote a brief but classic work, *The Details of the Rocket System* (1814), detailing the deployment and use of his rockets. Recognizing the importance of massed fire for maximum effect, he recommended the simultaneous firing of 50 rockets at a time, and never less than 20. Volleys could be fired as rapidly as every 30 seconds.

The use of Congreve rockets spread rapidly through Europe. Rockets based on Congreve designs were developed in France, Denmark, Spain, Italy, Switzerland, Sweden, Austria, and Russia. One interesting rocket design of the Swedish Rocket Corps was a stickless, delta-winged glide missile that was fired from a hand-held launcher.

The next significant development in rocketry occurred about the middle of the 19th century. William Hale, a British engineer, invented a method of successfully eliminating the deadweight of the flight-stabilizing guide stick.

By designing jet vents at an angle, he was able to spin the rocket. He developed various designs, including curved vanes that were acted upon by the rocket jet. These rockets, stabilized by means of spin, represented a major improvement in performance and ease of handling.

Manufacturing techniques and materials had improved, too. The use of improved steel and rivetted rocket bodies permitted pressures as high as 23,000 pounds per square inch.

Decline in use of rocketsEven the new rockets, however, could not compete with the greatly improved artillery with rifled bores. The rocket corps of most European armies were dissolved, though rockets were still used in swampy or mountainous areas that were difficult for the much heavier mortars and guns. The Austrian Rocket Corps, using Hale rockets, won a number of engagements in mountainous terrain in Hungary and Italy. Other successful uses were by the Dutch colonial services in Celebes and by Russia in a number of engagements in the Turkistan War.

Hale sold his patent rights to the United States in time for some 2,000 rockets to be made for the Mexican War, 1846–48. Although some were fired, they were not particularly successful. The U.S. Ordnance Manual of 1862 lists 16-pound (7.3-kilogram) Hale rockets with a range of 1.25 miles (two kilometres).

Rockets were used in a limited way in the American Civil War (1861–65), but reports are fragmentary, and apparently they were not decisive.

During the 19th century two important peacetime applications of the war rocket developed: the lifesaving rocket and the whaling rocket.

In the era of sailing ships many lives were lost in the grounding and breakup of ships a short distance offshore, particularly during storms. The idea of using a rocket to carry from ship to shore or shore to ship a light line, which then could haul a heavier lifesaving line to aid passengers and crew to reach shore, was developed first by Henry Trengrouse of Cornwall, in England. In 1807, after watching the loss of 100 crewmen in a shipwreck near the coast, he built a series of line-carrying rockets. The first lives were saved by a line-carrying rocket in 1832. John Dennett modified a small Congreve rocket and in that year was able to save 19 persons from the "Bainbridge" aground on Atherfield Rocks. By mid-century numerous other designs had appeared (see Figure 10).

Lifesaving rockets spread to maritime nations and to the United States. Records kept of their use in Great Britain alone list at least 15,000 lives saved between 1871 and 1962.

As steam and diesel power replaced sails, the need for lifesaving rockets declined. In the late 1960s, however, The Netherlands still maintained coastal stations from which special trucks could rush line-throwing rockets to the nearest point on shore to aid a grounded ship.

Rocket-propelled harpoonsRocket propulsion was first applied to whaling harpoons in 1821. The most successful concept was that of Capt.

By courtesy of Mitchell R. Sharp

Figure 10: Rescue operation using lifesaving rocket, from a drawing of the 1870s. The light line carried to the ship by the rocket (centre foreground) has been replaced by a heavier line, and a breeches-buoy transfer is in operation.

Thomas W. Roys, of the United States, whose design of a rocket harpoon carried an explosive warhead. The harpoon was fired through a tube launcher from a small boat. If the aim, burning time of the rocket, speed of flight, and distance travelled were correct, the explosive bomb killed the whale quickly and affixed a toggle and rope in the carcass. These devices enjoyed only a brief lifetime, however.

Both the United States Army and the British Navy conducted experiments with rocket-propelled torpedoes in the period 1860–80, and several ingenious devices were designed. Nevertheless, none of this work led to a real weapon. One of the fundamental problems of the rocket torpedo, as pointed out by William Hale, was that as the powder in the rocket motor was consumed, the torpedo grew lighter, making it difficult to hold the torpedo at constant level below the surface.

Meanwhile, there were individual enthusiasts and inventors in nearly every country. Largely unknown, and sometimes considered a dangerous nuisance, they achieved varied success and recognition. In the early 19th century Claude Ruggieri, a prominent Italian fireworks maker, staged a number of shots in Paris in which rats and mice were sent aloft by rockets and returned by parachute. It is reported that Ruggieri even planned to send up a small boy, using a rocket cluster, but the police intervened.

In 1881 a Russian explosives maker, Nikolay Ivanovich Kibalchich, imprisoned for his part in an assassination attempt on Tsar Alexander II, conceived a rocket airplane that functioned by successive explosions of compressed powder candles. Kibalchich was executed and his writings remained in prison archives until the Revolution in 1917.

A few years later a German inventor, Herman Ganswindt, conceived of an intermittent-firing propulsion system similar to that of Kibalchich but employing steel cartridges loaded with dynamite. Ganswindt went further. He wanted to give his vehicle sufficient speed to attain escape velocity; i.e., to leave the Earth. Apparently, Ganswindt was the first to connect rocket propulsion with space flight. But in Russia in 1895 a young mathematics teacher published his first article on space travel. Konstantin Eduardovich Tsiolkovsky was among the first to grasp the importance of exhaust velocity and the reason that rockets had been limited by black-powder formulas. He saw that by using liquid propellants (*e.g.*, liquefied hydrogen and oxygen) much greater efficiencies would result. Tsiolkovsky made important contributions to the theory of space vehicle design, including the concept of a closed biological cycle, utilizing plant life to produce oxygen on long voyages. The fact that he wrote in Russian, combined with his retiring nature, left him scarcely known abroad for many years.

Importance of exhaust velocity

Developments in the 20th century to World War II. In Sweden, about the turn of the century, Wilhelm Unge invented a device described as an "aerial torpedo." Based upon the stickless Hale rocket, it incorporated a number of design improvements. One of these was a rocket motor nozzle that caused the gas flow to converge and then diverge. Another was the use of smokeless powder based on nitroglycerin. Unge believed that his aerial torpedoes would be valuable as surface-to-air weapons against dirigibles. Velocity and range were increased, and about 1909 the Krupp armament firm of Germany purchased the patents and a number of rockets for further experimentation.

In the United States, meanwhile, Robert Hutchings Goddard was conducting theoretical and experimental research on rocket motors at Worcester, Massachusetts. Utilizing a steel motor with a tapered nozzle, he achieved greatly improved thrust and efficiency. Another of Goddard's concepts was a high-altitude research rocket whose motor was fired in pulses. Somewhat similar to the pulsed-momentum principle suggested by Kibalchich and Ganswindt, the impulses were to have derived from charges of solid fuel injected into the combustion chamber in rapid succession. In 1916 Goddard approached the Smithsonian Institution for financial support. It was forthcoming in a few months.

During World War I Goddard developed a number of designs of small military rockets to be launched from a lightweight hand launcher. By switching from black powder to double-base powder (40 percent nitroglycerin, 60 percent nitrocellulose), a far more potent propulsion charge was obtained. These rockets were proving successful under tests by the United States Army when the Armistice was signed; they became the forerunners of the bazooka of World War II. Goddard's main interest, however, was in utilizing the new potential of rockets to reach high altitudes. His notebooks ultimately revealed such imaginative concepts as a circumlunar rocket to carry a camera to photograph the far side of the Moon, ion and nuclear rocket propulsion, and manned and unmanned interplanetary exploration.

Backed by the Smithsonian Institution, Goddard switched from solid to liquid propellants and launched the first liquid-propellant rocket (liquid oxygen and gasoline) on March 16, 1926 (see Figure 11). It reached an altitude of only 41 feet (12 metres) and landed only 184 feet (56 metres) away, but the significance was as great as the few feet flown by the Wright brothers at Kitty Hawk.

By courtesy of Mrs. Robert H. Goddard

Figure 11: R.H. Goddard, U.S. rocket pioneer, with the liquid-propellant rocket he designed and launched in 1926.

Picking up the pieces, Goddard modified the motor nozzle length, increased the throat diameter, strengthened the launching stand, and flew the apparatus again on April 3. No public report of this success was made.

Later, supported by Clark University and Guggenheim Foundation funds, Goddard developed further research rockets in Roswell, New Mexico. Although he never achieved the results he knew were possible, Goddard was a brilliant inventor. His later designs utilized both turbine-driven pumps and gyroscopic stabilizers. Vanes were used to deflect the rocket exhaust to correct deviations from the planned flight path.

In his paper "A Method of Reaching Extreme Altitudes" Goddard discussed the possibility of a rocket reaching the Moon with a payload of flash powder to signal its arrival to astronomers. The significance of this work, like that of Tsiolkovsky's, was that the suggestions were made not by an exuberant inventor or enthusiast but by a thoughtful scientist with a sound academic background.

World War I actually saw little use of rocket weapons, despite successful French incendiary antiballoon rockets and a German trench-war technique by which a grappling hook was thrown over enemy barbed wire by a rocket with a line attached. Many researchers besides Goddard used the wartime interest in rockets to push experimentation, the most noteworthy being Elmer Sperry and his son, Lawrence, in the United States. The Sperrys worked on a concept of an "aerial torpedo," a pilotless airplane, carrying an explosive charge, that would utilize gyroscopic, automatic control to fly to a preselected target. Numerous flight attempts were made in 1917, some successful. Because of interest in early military use, the U.S. Army Signal Corps organized a separate program under C.F. Kettering in Ohio late in 1918.

Seventy-five aircraft were ordered built just before World War I ended.

The Kettering design used a gyroscope for lateral control to a preset direction and an aneroid barometer for pitch (fore and aft) control to maintain a preset altitude. A high angle of dihedral (upward tilt) in the biplane wings provided stability about the roll axis. The aircraft was rail-launched. Distance to target was determined by the number of revolutions of a propeller. When the predetermined number of revolutions had occurred, the wings of the airplane were dropped off and the aircraft carrying the bomb load dropped on the target.

The limited time available to attack the formidable design problems of these systems doomed the programs, and they never became operational.

In Britain, even earlier, A.M. Low conceived of a similar project, but two tests made in 1917 had little success. Following World War I the British continued a small development program of radio-controlled seaplanes, with known flights being made in 1927 and 1930. In the United States the Sperry automatic control system was utilized in work from 1920 to 1926.

In 1923 an obscure German mathematics teacher, Hermann Oberth, published *Die Rakete zu den Planetenräumen* ("The Rocket into Interplanetary Space"). In this thin pamphlet was set forth, with a grasp remarkable for his time, the potentialities of rockets to achieve great velocity and to provide the means for manned space exploration. In *Wege zur Raumschiffahrt* ("Way to Space Travel"), in 1929, Oberth not only set forth design concepts for immense interplanetary space vehicles utilizing clustered liquid-propellant motors but also included a chapter on electric propulsion and the ion rocket (see below *Electrical propulsion systems*) predating actual development work on electrostatic propulsion by 30 years.

The decade that followed was an exciting one. Germans such as Walter Hohmann and the Austrians Baron Guido von Pirquet and Hermann Noordung published technical studies on rocket power and space vehicles. In France, the famous aviator and test pilot Robert Esnault-Pelterie lectured and wrote on high-altitude rockets and interplanetary flight. It was Esnault-Pelterie who first used the term astronautics. In 1929 Esnault-Pelterie and the French banker André Hirsch established an annual astronautics award for the experimenter who had done most to further space flight. In the Soviet Union, researchers were interpreting and expanding Tsiolkovsky's work. In the period 1927–33 rocket and space flight societies were formed in Germany, Austria, the Soviet Union, the United States, and Great Britain. These groups provided a meeting place for discussion and experimentation, and their journals became a means of disseminating information.

As World War II approached, minor and varied experimental and research activities on rockets and guided missiles were underway in a number of countries. But in Germany, under great secrecy, there was concentrated effort. In the Soviet Union, experimental sounding rockets were built by enthusiasts in Moscow and Leningrad. Minor financial support was given by the government. Liquid-propellant motors were designed and tested, and in 1936 a sounding rocket altitude of more than three miles was reported. Other research was conducted on an engine for a rocket-powered airplane designed by S.P. Korolev, who later became the leading Soviet space vehicle designer.

In the United States, Goddard was at Roswell, working with a small crew of technicians, making many improvements in his sounding rocket design. There he constructed and launched 31 rockets, reaching 2,000 feet (600 metres) altitude in 1930 and 7,500 feet (2,300 metres) in 1935. Goddard was a brilliant innovator. He worked under self-imposed secrecy, and few details of his work were known until after World War II.

Elsewhere in the United States, the American Rocket Society conducted a number of rocket engine and flight tests in the vicinity of New York City. At the California Institute of Technology, under Theodore von Kármán, a number of graduate students started a program of rocket research and development in 1936. Backed by Guggenheim Foundation funds, detailed scientific studies of solid and liquid-propellant rocket technology were made, and with military support solid-propellant formulations were developed. Rockets also were studied for the purpose of assisting the takeoff of heavily loaded aircraft.

In France, Esnault-Pelterie and others were receiving some military support on small liquid- and solid-propellant rocket motors. Across the Channel in Great Britain, amateur rocket enthusiasts were prevented from experimentation by stiff laws relating to explosives. Military rocket research was confined to utilizing smokeless cordite powder.

But in Germany, successful flights as high as one mile with gasoline–oxygen-powered rockets were made in 1931–32 by the German Rocket Society. Funds for such amateur activities were scarce, and the society sought support from the German Army. The work of Wernher von Braun, a member of the society, attracted the attention of Capt. Walter R. Dornberger. Von Braun became the technical leader of a small group developing liquid-propellant rockets for the German Army. By 1937 the Dornberger–Braun team, expanded to hundreds of scientists, engineers, and technicians, moved its operations from Kummersdorf to Peenemünde, a deserted area on the Baltic coast. Here the technology for a long-range ballistic missile was developed and tested (see below *Surface-to-surface*).

Two other prewar German activities deserve mention. One was the rocket engine design and development work of the Austrian Eugen Sänger. A brilliant engineer, Sänger had built and tested rocket motors at the University of Vienna. The German Air Force invited Sänger to build a rocket research establishment at Trauen near Hannover.

The other development was the work of Hellmuth Walter, who developed hydrogen peroxide rocket motors. An experimental Heinkel aircraft powered by such an engine made a successful flight in February 1937.

Developments in World War II and the postwar era. World War II saw the expenditure of immense resources and talent for the development of rocket-propelled weapons. Except in the case of Germany, the greater part of the effort was in development of unguided rockets. As German resistance collapsed in 1945, the Allies avidly sought details of rocket and guided missile development. Particularly sought were the key personnel, who had years of experience in the design, development, and testing of missile system components: propulsion, airframe, guidance, and warheads. More than 100 specialists, headed by the foremost expert, Wernher von Braun, surrendered to the U.S. Army and moved to the United States in 1945.

The four major categories of military rockets and guided missiles are: surface-to-surface, surface-to-air, air-to-surface and air-to-air. Free flight, or unguided, military rockets are included in appropriate surface- or air-launch categories. Submarine- (underwater-) launch missiles are included in the surface-to-surface launch category. In the following summation, the developments relating to each of the four categories are taken up in turn.

Surface-to-surface. Germany used widely a battlefield rocket, the Nebelwerfer, of 15-centimetre (about six-inch) and 21-centimetre calibre, from six-barrelled launchers. The 15-centimetre rocket was about 40 inches (100 centimetres) long, weighed about 80 pounds (36 kilograms), could be fired at the rate of one per second, and carried a high-explosive warhead. Maximum range was more than 6,000 yards (5.5 kilometres).

Other German developments included the Panzerfaust and Panzerschreck, hand-held tube-launched rockets. One other noteworthy rocket was the Rheinbote, a four-stage, solid-propellant rocket. It weighed nearly two tons, was about 40 feet (12 metres) long, and had an impressive range—135 miles (220 kilometres). The payload of 88 pounds (40 kilograms) of high explosive, however, could not compete with other weapons such as aircraft bombardment and the V-2. The Rheinbote was significant, nevertheless, in that practical recognition was made of the value of the step principle suggested by Haas almost 400 years before.

In Great Britain, a five-inch (13-centimetre) rocket with a 30-pound (13.6-kilogram) explosive warhead was developed. Its range was two to three miles (three to five kilometres). These rockets, fired from specially equipped naval vessels, were used in heavy coastal bombardment prior to landings in the Mediterranean. Firing rates were 800–1,000 in less than 45 seconds from each ship.

The United States did not commence active development of rockets until mid-1940. At that time, the National Defense Research Committee (NDRC) authorized a program under the direction of C.N. Hickman, who had worked with Goddard on the tests of hand-launched rockets at Aberdeen in 1918. Hickman supervised the development of a refined design, known as the bazooka. About 20 inches (50 centimetres) long and weighing 3.5 pounds (1.6 kilograms), the rocket was fired from a shoulder launcher that weighed 14.5 pounds (6.6 kilograms). The bazooka was used extensively against tanks. Its maximum range was short (600 yards, or 550 metres) and it travelled slowly, but it carried a potent shaped-charge warhead.

Another United States Army development was the Calliope, a 60-tube launching projector for 4.5-inch (11.4-centimetre) rockets mounted on a Sherman tank. The launcher was mounted on the tank's gun turret, and both azimuth (horizontal direction) and elevation were controllable. Rockets were fired in rapid succession (ripple-fired) to keep the rockets from interfering with one another as they would in salvo firing. Other launchers were developed for trucks and jeeps.

Close liaison was established between the U.S. committee and similar research groups in Great Britain. Advantage was taken of earlier rocket developments by the British. In this cooperative effort the United States developed an antisubmarine rocket-propelled weapon, known as Mousetrap, based upon a similar British design, Hedgehog.

Other conventional rockets developed in the United States included a 4.5-inch barrage rocket with a range of 1,100 yards (1,000 metres) and a five-inch rocket of longer range. The latter was used extensively in the Pacific theatre of war from launching barges against shore installations, particularly just before landing operations. The firing rate of these flat-bottom boats was 500 per minute. Other rockets were used for smoke laying and demolition. Because the United States had great industrial capacity, unhampered by air raids, and urgent needs for its own forces as well as for its Allies, its production of solid-propellant rockets increased to a high rate by the end of the war. The United States produced more than 4,000,000 of the 4.5-inch rockets and 15,000,000 of the smaller bazooka rockets during the war.

Soviet barrage rockets

As far as is known, Soviet rocket development activity during World War II was limited. Extensive use was made of barrage, ripple-fired rockets. Both A-frame and truck-mounted launchers were used. The Soviets mass-produced a 5.1-inch rocket known as Katyusha. From 16 to 48 Katyushas were fired from a boxlike launcher known as the Stalin Organ, mounted on a gun carriage.

After World War II, the impetus of advanced rocket designs of free-flight rockets continued at a much slower pace. By 1950 the United States Army had begun development of the Honest John rocket; it became operational in 1955. The Honest John is 24.8 feet (7.6 metres) long, about 30 inches (75 centimetres) in diameter, and weighs 4,700 pounds (2,100 kilograms). It has a range of about 23 miles (37 kilometres) and can be equipped with either a high-explosive or nuclear warhead. The rocket is both spin-stabilized and fin stabilized. After it leaves the launcher, small rocket motors located forward of the head of the sustainer engine (but arranged tangentially to it) fire and impart a slow spin to the rocket. The four large stabilizing fins at the aft end of the rocket are set at a slight angle to maintain the spin.

A smaller version, Little John, was developed especially for use with airborne infantry divisions. Unlike the larger rocket, Little John is spin stabilized by the launching rail as it is fired; the spin is maintained by slightly offset fins.

Following World War II the Soviet Union produced its Frog series of large, solid-propellant, ballistic free-flight rockets. (In the absence of public designation of Soviet missiles, the code names [*e.g.*, Frog] used by the North Atlantic Treaty Organization are used in this article.) The Frog 1 missile, in service since about 1957, is a single-stage spin-stabilized rocket 31 feet (9.4 metres) long with a body diameter of about two feet (0.6 metre), a bulbous nose, and six fins with a span of three feet three inches (one metre). The gases exhaust through a cluster of seven nozzles. The

missile is carried on a tracked armoured vehicle and is believed to be capable of delivering either a conventional or a nuclear warhead a distance of about 15 miles (24 kilometres). The latest version is the Frog 7, displayed in 1965. This appears to be a much cleaner design, cylindrical in shape, with four small fins and a main nozzle ringed by 12 small nozzles. It is rail-launched and carried by a wheeled transporter erector.

Between the end of World War II and 1960 the development of smaller solid-propellant rockets spread to other countries, primarily because of the effectiveness of such weapons. Thus by the 1960s all major powers were developing and producing antitank and battlefield-support rockets.

In Germany, as mentioned above, the army was developing a long-range ballistic missile at Peenemünde. The A-4 (popularly known as the V-2, for Vergeltungswaffen Zwei, "Vengeance Weapon Two") was a remarkable engineering achievement (see Figure 12).

Camera Press

Figure 12: German V-2, nearly 47 feet long, a 13.5-ton missile with a 200-mile range. First fired in 1944, it carried a conventional warhead weighing one ton.

The V-2 rocket was nearly 47 feet (14 metres) long, had a cylindrical diameter of 5.5 feet (1.7 metres), and weighed about 13.5 tons at takeoff, including the one-ton (910 kilogram) warhead. Propellants were liquid oxygen and a 75 percent ethyl alcohol–water mixture. Approximately 8,400 pounds of alcohol and 10,800 pounds of oxygen were burned at a rate of 300 pounds (135 kilograms) per second. The rocket motor produced a 55,000-pound thrust for about one minute, after which the engine was shut off. Propellant supply was by turbopump. Yaw and pitch control was accomplished by two pairs of graphite carbon vanes in the rocket exhaust. Ignition of the alcohol–liquid oxygen propellants was effected by a pyrotechnic pinwheel inserted in the motor. Maximum range was about 200 miles (320 kilometres).

The first operational V-2 was fired against Paris on September 6, 1944. Two days later, the first of more than 1,000 missiles was fired against London. The missile travelled on a ballistic arc trajectory, reaching a maximum speed of more than one mile (1.6 kilometres) per second and an altitude of 60 to 70 miles (96 to 112 kilometres). Since it approached the target faster than the speed of sound, there was no warning of its approach. By the end of the war about 4,000 of these missiles had been launched from

V-2 fired against London

mobile bases against Allied targets. During February and March 1945, only weeks before the war in Europe ended, an average of 60 missiles was launched weekly.

Although the V-2 did not become a decisive weapon, it was a landmark achievement in rocketry. Large rocket motor developments after World War II, in both the United States and the Soviet Union, drew heavily upon V-2 engine design.

The only other relatively long range, surface-to-surface guided missile to see action in World War II was the V-1, or "buzz-bomb," a development of the German Air Force. The V-1 has been called, from an engineering point of view, an aerial counterpart of the naval torpedo. The analogy is striking in several ways. Once the V-1 was launched, its course could not be corrected, being determined by a preset guidance system. An accelerometer, a sensitive instrument for detecting accelerations, sensed deviation to the left and right of the programmed flight path and sent correcting signals to the control surface actuators. The missile's altitude was sensed and maintained in a similar manner by a barometer, and range was determined by the number of revolutions turned by a small propeller in the nose of the missile. When the requisite number of revolutions, corresponding to a linear range, had been made, a signal was sent to the aerodynamic control surface actuators to cause the V-1 to dive vertically onto the target. The average range was 150 miles. Launching ramps and a hydrogen peroxide-powered catapult boosted the V-1 to flying speed.

Pulse-jet engine in the V-1

The V-1 used a unique pulse-jet engine that found later employment in early post-World War II Soviet and U.S. missiles. Air enters a diffuser through a series of spring-loaded flapper valves that open as the air passes through them and then close when the air is in the combustion chamber. At this point in the firing cycle, kerosene from a gas-pressurized tank is sprayed into the chamber and ignited by a spark plug. As the chamber pressure of the burning gas rises, the flapper valves close and the exhaust gases are forced through the nozzle of the motor. The V-1 warhead was a 2,200-pound (1,000-kilogram) charge of high explosive set off by an impact fuze.

A final but significant weapon under development by the Germans during World War II, and one that spurred investigation in Great Britain, France, the Soviet Union, the United States, and Switzerland, was the X-7 antitank missile. Although this missile was not developed in time for combat, its technology set the pattern for practically all antitank guided missiles developed during the next 20 years. The X-7 was a solid-propellant winged rocket with a shaped-charge warhead and a range of about half a mile. This missile was to have been guided in flight by means of signals sent over two wires connected to control surfaces located on the wings, similar to the X-4 air-to-air missile (see below). The operator visually followed the missile in flight and sent guidance correction signals by manual control.

When World War II came to a close in August 1945, development and production of rockets was a massive enterprise in the United States and Great Britain. Despite a few ingenious uses of rocket power, however, the major effort was along conventional lines, adapting technical improvements to existing weapons. Nowhere else was there the depth of appreciation and scope of plans for tactical guided missiles or long-range ballistic rockets that there was in Germany. Recognition of the potential of rocket power by the Allied powers came too late in the war to enable them to catch up with German developments.

Appreciation of the potential importance of German technical efforts was indicated by the speed with which technical intelligence teams followed close behind frontline troops as they moved across Germany. These teams obtained masses of technical data, design drawings, and missiles. They also interrogated key scientists and missile engineers. The top planning and technical staff of Peenemünde, headed by Dornberger and von Braun, fled south in the last few days of the war in order to surrender to U.S. troops. The Soviet troops that captured Peenemünde found mostly wreckage and had orders to destroy what was left. Soviet forces, however, took many German technicians to the Soviet Union. Thus, the U.S., France, Great Britain, and the Soviet Union all had the benefit of information on rockets and guided missiles captured in Germany. In general, early postwar

development of rockets followed most of the lines suggested by German work. Rockets were used to propel all types of guided missiles, competing successfully in these missions with air-breathing jet engines.

The United States obtained not only the services of top German rocket experts but also, from the underground V-2 factory at Niedersachswerfen, enough V-2 components for about 100 complete vehicles. About 70 V-2s were fired during the period 1946–51 at White Sands (New Mexico) Proving Ground. These firings provided much experience in the handling and launching of large rockets.

V-2 firings in the U.S.

The long-range ballistic missile was not a major development in the United States until 1954. Until that time air-breathing subsonic missile developments such as the Snark and Navaho were counted upon by military planners to supplement and supersede long-range, strategic-bomber aircraft. These vehicles were essentially unmanned, turbojet- or ramjet-engine-powered, high-speed aircraft equipped with warheads. The Corporal (75-mile, or 120-kilometre, range), with a mobile launcher, developed by the U.S. Army, was operational by this time as a battlefield support weapon.

By the 1960s the Pershing missile (400-mile, or 640-kilometre, range) replaced the Corporal. Capable of carrying either a conventional or nuclear warhead, Pershing is deployed in Europe.

Numerous wire-guided antitank rockets presently operational have been built by the United States, Great Britain, France, and many other countries.

In 1954 two developments put the intercontinental ballistic missile (ICBM) in a new light. One of these developments was the thermonuclear bomb, with destructive power measured in megatons (millions of tons of TNT equivalent). The other was the miniaturization and refinement of inertial guidance systems, so that they became sufficiently accurate to place the warhead of the ICBM close to a target 5,000 miles (8,000 kilometres) or more away.

The first ICBM authorized in the United States was the Atlas, followed later by the Titan. The Atlas was a one and one-half-stage vehicle. Whereas a two-stage vehicle drops both first-stage rocket engine and tankage, the one and one-half-stage vehicle drops only the rocket engine, and the second stage continues to use the original tankage. The first Atlas was fired full range from the Cape Canaveral (now Cape Kennedy, Florida) missile range in November 1958. The Titan I ICBM was a conventional two-stage vehicle. First successful tests of the Titan were made in 1959. Both the Atlas and Titan burned liquid oxygen and hydrocarbon fuel (similar to kerosene).

A major logistic problem in ballistic missiles using cryogenic (extreme low-temperature) propellants such as liquid oxygen is the necessity for fuelling just prior to launching. This weakness, which means delay in defensive, retaliatory fire, can be eliminated by the use of solid propellants or storable noncryogenic propellants. A later version of Titan, Titan II, used a higher performance propellant combination of nitrogen tetroxide and hydrazine-based fuel. This propellant combination permits the missile to stand ready, fully loaded for firing.

Development of solid propellants to a level of performance near that of liquids achieved such progress by 1958 that a solid-fuelled ICBM, the Minuteman, was authorized.

For greater defense against attack, the Minuteman was designed to be launched from a 90-foot (27-metre) underground concrete silo. Minuteman I was first launched in 1961. Consisting of three stages, the missile was 54 feet (16 metres) long. In September 1964, 650 Minuteman I missiles were in place and an improved Minuteman II was in development. By 1971 a further improved Minuteman III was test launched. A recent version is nearly 60 feet long and has the capability of carrying MIRV warheads (see below *Warheads*). Range is over 7,000 miles.

In 1947 the United States Navy demonstrated that a V-2 could be launched from the deck of a ship at sea. The problems associated with the production and storage of liquid propellants aboard ships soon turned the navy toward a quest for a solid-propellant IRBM; the result was the two-stage Polaris, first tested in 1958 and fired underwater in 1960.

Launching of Polaris missiles is accomplished by com-

The
Polaris
missile

pressed air. The first-stage rocket motor fires only after the missile is in the air, above the surface. Sixteen Polaris missiles are carried in two parallel rows of eight on each of the nuclear-powered United States fleet ballistic missile submarines. In 1971 a program to replace Polaris missiles with the longer, wider diameter Poseidon missile (see Figure 13) was begun. The Poseidon, like Minuteman III, is capable of carrying MIRV warheads.

By courtesy of the U.S. Navy

Figure 13: U.S. Poseidon missile being launched from a nuclear-powered submarine.

Another submarine-launched missile is the antisubmarine Subroc. Launched submerged, the missile breaks the surface and is rocket-propelled on a ballistic trajectory toward an enemy submarine. Re-entering the water, the missile assumes the role of a homing torpedo.

Ten years after World War II, the United States Air Force and Army each undertook the development of an IRBM. The air force Thor and the army Jupiter used the same liquid-propellant engine, and each had a range of 1,600 miles (2,600 kilometres).

Great Britain commenced development of the Blue Streak IRBM but cancelled it in 1960. France, after a late start, began development of a three-stage, solid-propellant, 2,000-mile-range ballistic missile, but progress has been slow. The technology has been used also for the French space launch vehicle, Diamant.

Developments in IRBM and ICBM design in the Soviet Union paralleled United States efforts in the years immediately following World War II. The Soviets fired several captured V-2 missiles from the rocket proving ground at Kapustin Yar in 1946 and 1947.

Early Soviet surface-to-surface guided-missile developments borrowed heavily from German technology, but later Soviet weapons were original designs. The Scud A is a liquid-fuelled, single-stage missile that appears to derive from the German Wasserfall surface-to-air missile. This missile and its successor, the Scud B, are both believed to have a range of about 50 to 100 miles and probably are guided by radio commands.

The first Soviet IRBM's were the Shyster (700-mile range), Sandal (1,200-mile range), and Skean (2,000-mile range), all single-stage vehicles. The Shyster is basically a stretched and uprated version of the German V-2 rocket and is fuelled by liquid oxygen and kerosene. The Sandal and Skean are powered by storable propellants and appear to be essentially original Soviet designs. The Sandal was the missile deployed to Cuba in 1962 and withdrawn after crisis negotiations.

The
Soviet
Scud
missiles

Soviet tactical and medium-range missiles are highly mobile, mounted on cross-country vehicles that allow them to advance with combat troops. They can be concealed in wooded country, making detection by aircraft and satellites more difficult. Scud is an example. Two variants of this storable-liquid-propellant missile are known. Scud A travels on a tracked vehicle of the type used for the unguided

missile Frog, while the larger Scud B is carried on a fully enclosed cross-country vehicle of the type first shown in November 1965. Each is placed on a simple launch platform at the rear of the vehicle by a tubular cradle that elevates into a vertical position. It is believed that guidance is achieved by a preset inertial system acting upon steerable tail fins.

Scapegoat is carried by a tracked transporter-erector, the full weapon system being designated Scamp in NATO nomenclature. The 35-foot (10.7-metre) missile appears to be the top two stages of Savage, the Soviet silo-based solid-propellant ICBM.

Scrooge, also mobile on a heavy tracked transporter, is concealed within a cylinder 62 feet (19 metres) long. This launch tube is raised vertically behind the vehicle, and the missile is fired directly from it.

Weapons of this type can be moved effectively along the entire frontier of the Soviet Union, providing coverage of western Europe, the Middle East, and Southeast Asia. Scrooge has been reported deployed as far east as the Chinese border near Buir Nuur in Mongolia. Estimated range is 3,000 to 3,500 miles.

The first Soviet ICBM, the SS–6 ("Sapwood"), has been a dual-purpose vehicle used originally as an ICBM and later (as the "A" series) as the basic booster for much of the Soviet space program. It was displayed publicly for the first time at the 1967 Paris Air Show, where it was placarded as the booster for the Vostok spacecraft, but it has probably been in use since the late 1950s. The vehicle is parallel staged, with a central sustainer core to which are attached four large, tapered boosters. The sustainer and boosters are powered by clusters of thrust chambers, all of which ignite upon launching; midway in the powered flight the four-booster tank and engine combinations are detached while the sustainer continues burning. The propellants are liquid oxygen and a hydrocarbon, and the engines develop a total sea-level thrst of about 1,000,000 pounds.

In 1964 and 1965 the Soviets displayed the Sasin and Scrag, both tandem, liquid-propellant, long-range rockets. Scrag, which has three stages that are separated by interstage trusses, was described as being from the same family as the launch vehicles that placed Soviet cosmonauts into orbit. It does not appear, however, to have become operational as an ICBM.

The premier Soviet missiles in this class are the SS 11, SS 13 Savage, and SS 9 Scarp. The SS 11 is reported to employ storable liquid propellants, but by 1971 it had not been publicly displayed by the Soviet authorities. Savage, solid-fuelled, follows the format of the U.S. Minuteman ICBM but is somewhat larger. The liquid-fuelled Scarp is much larger, on the lines of the U.S. Titan ICBM. The first stage has six fixed-thrust chambers and four swivel-mounted vernier rocket motors, small auxiliaries used for trajectory correction. It can be used both as a conventional ICBM launched across the Northern Hemisphere or as a fractional orbit bombardment system (FOBS) weapon.

In the FOBS application the Scarp could be launched almost to orbital velocity to attack the United States over the Southern Hemisphere, thus avoiding the Ballistic Missile Early Warning System (BMEWS) radar stations in Britain, Greenland, and Alaska.

By the spring of 1970 the number of SS 11 and SS 13 ICBM's deployed were stated by the U.S. secretary of defense to be around 800. Also deployed were about 220 SS 9s, each capable of carrying a warhead of some 25 megatons yield.

In 1962 the Soviets displayed a 48-foot- (14.6-metre-) long missile, Sark, describing it as a submarine-launched missile, although its very heavy construction and large size made it seem unsuitable for operational use in submarines. Two years later the smaller Serb was displayed and also credited with a submarine application. The 33-foot- (10-metre-) long missile is similar in configuration to the U.S. Polaris. It has two solid-fuelled stages with a range of less than 1,000 miles. A submarine-launched ballistic missile that has recently become operational is Sawfly. First displayed in 1967, the two-stage missile is 42 feet (13 metres) long and about five feet nine inches (1.75 metres) in diameter. The four first-stage nozzles are gimbal-mounted, permitting the stages to be moved freely so that their direction (thrust vector) can

The Soviet
Sawfly

be controlled. Range is reported to be around 1,300 miles (2,100 kilometres).

The most advanced Soviet nuclear-powered submarine in the early 1970s was the Y-class, which has 16 launch tubes for missiles of the Sawfly family.

Regardless of the country of origin, all IRBM's and ICBM's are equipped with either nuclear or thermonuclear warheads, because (1) it is economically impractical to use such an expensive missile to deliver a relatively small amount of high explosive; and (2) the unavoidable inaccuracies in range and direction make essential the far-reaching effects of a nuclear explosion.

Surface-to-air. The major purpose of the class of surface-to-air weapons is to intercept and destroy enemy aircraft, particularly at altitudes beyond the effective capability of conventional anti-aircraft artillery. During World War II high-altitude bombing above this range necessitated the development of rocket-powered weapons.

In Great Britain, initial effort was aimed at achieving the equivalent destructive power of the three-inch (7.5-centimetre) and later the 3.7-inch anti-aircraft gun. Single, double, and then multiple launchers were produced.

Two important innovations were developed by the British in connection with the three-inch rocket. Both devices were directed against German dive bombers. One was a rocket-propelled aerial-defense system. A parachute and wire device was rocketed aloft, trailing a wire that unwound at high speed from a bobbin on the ground. Altitudes as high as 20,000 feet (6,100 metres) were attained. Several versions of this were used, quite successfully, from ships. The other device was a type of proximity fuze utilizing a photoelectric cell and thermionic amplifier. A change in light intensity on the photocell caused by light reflected from a nearby airplane (projected on the cell by means of a lens) triggered the explosive shell.

The only significant anti-aircraft rocket development by the Germans was the Taifun. A slender, six-foot liquid-propellant rocket of simple concept, the Taifun was intended for altitudes of 50,000 feet (15,250 metres). The design embodied coaxial tankage of nitric acid and a mixture of organic fuels. This weapon, though planned for mass production, never became operational.

During World War II Germany made efforts to produce effective surface-to-air missiles. Three of those under development were subsonic (less than the speed of sound): the Schmetterling and Enzian resembled stubby midwing aircraft, and the Rheintochter had cruciform wings. All used solid-propellant boosters, or takeoff rockets, and sustainer motors, except that there was a liquid-propellant version of the Rheintochter. Altitude capability was about 50,000 feet.

Wasserfall
supersonic
missile

The Wasserfall was a superior weapon designed to operate at supersonic (greater than the speed of sound) speeds. A single-stage missile weighing 7,800 pounds (3,550 kilograms) at takeoff, this weapon was powered by a 17,000-pound-thrust motor and reached a velocity of 2,500 feet (760 metres) per second. Maximum altitude was 60,000 feet (18,300 metres), and the weight of the warhead was 330 pounds (150 kilograms). Propellants were nitric acid and an organic liquid, vinyl isobutyl ether. All of these weapons would have been effective against enemy aircraft flying at 15,000 to 30,000 feet. Although none became operational, their development reached a point of experimentation that proved that missiles could be guided by radar beams.

Two anti-aircraft missiles were designed in the United States in the latter days of the war: the Lark and the Little Joe. The former was a 14-foot- (4.3-metre-) long liquid-propellant weapon with semi-active radar homing. Weighing 1,200 pounds (545 kilograms), it was accelerated to operational speed by two solid-propellant jato (jet-assisted-takeoff) units. It could deliver a 100-pound (45-kilogram) warhead to a range of 38 miles (60 kilometres). The Little Joe was an 11-foot- (3.4-metre-) long solid-propellant missile with a range of 2.5 miles (4 kilometres). Its payload was a 100-pound warhead designed to counter Japanese kamikaze attacks on U.S. Navy ships. Neither weapon became operational.

Following World War II the major nations continued the development and refinement of anti-aircraft guided missiles. In the United States the navy initiated a research pro-

gram the purpose of which was to develop a ramjet engine suitable for use in a high-performance anti-aircraft missile. Ultimately the Talos missile resulted. Thirty-three feet (10 metres) long, this ship-launched missile has a slant range of about 75 miles (120 kilometres). Other U.S. Navy surface-to-air missiles are the Terrier, Tartar, and Sea Sparrow. The Standard missile is replacing Terrier and also has a surface-to-surface capability.

The United States Army concentrated its efforts in the field of anti-aircraft weapons on the Nike group of missiles. The first of these was the Nike Ajax, which was first test-fired in 1951 and which remained deployed with the army until 1961. The missile was 21 feet (six metres) long and weighed 2,455 pounds (1,115 kilograms). With a range of 25 miles (40 kilometres), it had a liquid-propellant engine and a velocity of 1,500 miles (2,400 kilometres) per hour.

An advanced version of the Ajax was conceived in 1953, known first as Nike B, later as Nike Hercules. The Hercules was 41 feet (12.5 metres) long and weighed 10,000 pounds (4,550 kilograms). It had a solid-propellant motor, could carry both nuclear and high-explosive warheads, and had a range of 85 miles (135 kilometres). Both the Nike Ajax and the Nike Hercules employed radar-command guidance.

Out of the early experience in the Nike program also grew the possibility for an antimissile missile. The U.S. version was the safeguard antiballistic missile (ABM) system. Safeguard consisted of two missiles, the 55-foot (16.8-metre) Spartan for high-altitude missile interceptions and the 27-foot (8.2-metre) Sprint for low-altitude operations. Both were designed to carry nuclear warheads.

Safeguard
anti-
ballistic
missile
system

The U.S. Air Force Bomarc is ramjet powered and capable of interception at ranges as great as 400 miles (640 kilometres). Solid-propellant boosters are used on ramjet-powered missiles to bring the engine up to operational speed of flight.

Other significant current U.S. surface-to-air missiles include the Hawk, capable of intercepting low-flying aircraft, as is the shoulder-launched Redeye. Both have homing devices.

The Soviet Union has shown numerous surface-to-air missiles: Guild, Guideline, Goa, Griffon, Gainful, Ganef, and Galosh. Of these, Guideline has been widely deployed in the Soviet Union, in Warsaw Pact countries, and in certain Middle East countries, as well as in Cuba, Indonesia, and Vietnam. It was used in Vietnam against U.S. aircraft with limited success.

In Egypt, during the Six-Day War of 1967, an advanced version of Guideline was used against the Israeli Air Force. The weapon, similar in many respects to the U.S. Nike Ajax, has a solid-fuel booster and a liquid-propellant (nitric acid–kerosene) sustainer. Later versions are reported to have a slant range of about 28 miles (45 kilometres), an altitude ceiling above 60,000 feet (18,300 metres), and a maximum speed of mach 3.5 (3.5 times the speed of sound).

Goa, first displayed in 1964, is a low-to-medium-altitude weapon mounted on a twin launcher. Used on ships of the Soviet Navy, it has also been developed as a field weapon and appeared in Egypt in 1970.

Guild was an early surface-to-air missile. Solid-fuelled, it was about 39 feet (12 metres) long and appeared in Moscow parades mounted on an articulated trailer behind a truck.

Another low-level weapon is Gainful, first displayed in 1967. Three of the 19.5-foot-long solid-fuel missiles are carried on a tracked vehicle for the defense of Soviet units in the field.

As a surface-to-air weapon, Ganef is unique among Soviet missiles in its use of a ramjet for main propulsion. Four small, strap-on, solid-fuel boosters provide initial velocity. Two missiles are carried on a tracked vehicle, and the system depends on command guidance.

Griffon, a long-range anti-aircraft missile, is also stated to have an antimissile capability.

The more definitive antimissile missile is Galosh, a cone-shaped weapon first shown in 1964 within a tubular container measuring 67 by nine feet (20.4 by 2.7 metres). The first stage has four rocket nozzles. Launching is from fixed emplacements under radar command. First sites were being established on the perimeter of Moscow in 1967.

Air-to-surface. In World War II, Great Britain, Germany, the Soviet Union, Japan, and the United States all developed airborne rockets for use against surface as well as aerial targets. These were almost invariably fin stabilized because of the effective aerodynamic forces when launched at speeds of 250 miles (400 kilometres) per hour and more. Tube launchers were used at first, but later straight-rail or zero-length launchers, located under the wings of the airplane, were employed.

One of the most successful of the German rockets was the two-inch- (five-centimetre-) diameter R4M. The tail fins remained folded until launch, facilitating close loading arrangements.

The U.S. achieved great success with a 4.5-inch (11.4-centimetre) rocket, three or four of which were carried under each wing of Allied fighter planes. These rockets were highly effective against motor columns, tanks, troop and supply trains, fuel and ammunition depots, airfields, and barges.

Whereas British and German aircraft rockets were fin stabilized, the U.S. designs were spin stabilized, resulting in greater accuracy. The largest such rocket was the Tiny Tim. Slightly over 10 feet (three metres) long, it carried 150 pounds (68 kilograms) of TNT. The solid-propellant motor developed 30,000 pounds of thrust for one second. More than 7,000,000 aircraft rockets were produced in the U.S. during 1940–45.

Glide bombs

A variation on the airborne rocket was the addition of a rocket motor and fins to conventional bombs. This had the effect of flattening the ballistic trajectory, extending the range, and increasing the velocity at impact, useful against concrete bunkers and strengthened (hardened) targets. These weapons were called glide bombs, and the Japanese had 224-pound and 815-pound (102-kilogram and 370-kilogram) versions. The Soviet Union employed 56-pound and 220-pound versions, launched from the Stormovik fighter aircraft.

Among the first air-to-surface guided missiles developed by the Germans was the radio-controlled, armour-piercing Fritz-X, which sank the Italian battleship "Roma" after its surrender to the Allies in 1944. Another was the Hs 293 winged bomb. More than 11 feet (3.3 metres) long and weighing about 2,300 pounds (1,045 kilograms), this radio-controlled weapon destroyed a number of merchant ships in Allied convoys. Although these early versions of glide bombs required optical tracking (and, therefore, clear weather), plans were under way for television viewing of the target by the weapon and radar spotting for nighttime and foul-weather use. The U.S. developed a controlled glide bomb called the Bat, similar to the Hs 293.

The Hs 293 was a radio-guided bomb with a rocket engine using hydrogen peroxide as a propellant. This chemical was decomposed into steam by the use of aqueous potassium permanganate as a catalyst. A crew of three, a pilot, an observer, and a bombardier, were necessary to launch and direct the Hs 293 to its target. The observer's duty was to set the gyroscope that established a reference plane for the missile, and the bombardier piloted the bomb by remote control after its release from the aircraft. It was especially adaptable to targets at sea and found its greatest use there, sinking many merchant ships.

The Bat

The United States Bat had a much greater range—up to 20 miles (32 kilometres). In guidance it was in advance of the Hs 293, since it employed an active radar homing device. The Bat was a glide bomb, however, having no propulsion system. It weighed 1,000 pounds (455 kilograms) and was 12 feet (3.7 metres) long, with a wing span of ten feet. Developed primarily as a weapon for use against ships, the Bat was to be released from an airplane at an altitude of three to five miles. The bomb's velocity of 300 miles per hour was considerably slower than the 470-mile-per-hour Hs 293. Built in considerable numbers before the end of the war, the Bat was not actually used until April 1945, when it was credited with sinking a Japanese destroyer at the maximum range of 20 miles.

After 1945 the U.S. Air Force explored more complex versions of the air-to-surface missile. One of these was the Rascal, a liquid-propellant missile with inertial guidance and a range of 100 miles (160 kilometres). By the mid-1950s development turned to achieving longer ranges. This effort was aided by the advent of lighter weight nuclear warheads.

Two of the weapons developed, the United States Hound Dog and the British Blue Steel, had ranges of about 500 miles. The U.S. Skybolt missile, cancelled in 1963, was to have had a range of 1,000 miles. The cause of the cancellation was essentially the difficulty in guidance from an aerial launch; development was stopped in favour of alternative weapons, such as the fixed-base ICBM.

By the early 1970s the United States had seven operational air-to-surface missiles. Systems utilizing a basic missile, with modification for either air or surface launch, such as the Standard missile, were gaining favour.

The Soviet Union has displayed a variety of air-to-surface missiles on bomber aircraft that have been given the NATO designations Kangaroo, Kennel, Kipper, Kitchen, and Kelt. The first three have turbojet propulsion; the last two appear to have liquid-propellant rocket engines.

The largest of these missiles is the 50-foot- (15-metre-) long, swept-wing Kangaroo carried by the Tu-20 aircraft. Its range probably exceeds 300 miles.

Kennel, another aircraft-launched missile, is carried by the Tu-16 Badger aircraft. Powered by a turbojet, it is about 28 feet (8.5 metres) long with a wing span of about 16 feet. Its role is antishipping. A variant, Kelt, is rocket-powered with an enlarged radome.

Kipper, another antishipping missile, is also launched by the Tu-16. Turbojet-powered, it has a range of about 120 miles.

Kitchen, a more advanced Soviet air-to-surface cruise missile, is powered by a liquid-fuelled rocket engine and carried by the Tu-22. Range is probably about 200 miles.

The complexity and expense of air-to-surface missiles is great. Particularly difficult is the guidance problem. At extreme ranges, programmed and command systems generally are not feasible, and it is necessary to rely on such delicate and exacting systems as inertial guidance.

Air-to-air. As might be suspected, aircraft-launched rockets can be used against aerial as well as ground targets, provided that the aerial targets are propeller-driven aircraft with a speed of 400 knots (740 kilometres per hour) or less. Near the end of the war the German Me 262 jet fighter carried 48 such rockets. On one sortie, six Me 262s shot down 14 B-17 bombers during a daylight raid, without the loss of one fighter aircraft.

Rockets launched by Me 262 aircraft

After World War II the United States fitted many aircraft with 2.75-inch (6.9-centimetre) Mighty Mouse and Aeromite folding-fin rockets. Firing could be singly or in clusters. Another postwar development by the U.S. was a version of the army's five-inch, spin-stabilized rocket loaded by belt and fired from within the wing of the navy Skyraider aircraft.

Other countries fitted airborne rockets to aircraft for air-to-air weapons, notably Sweden (Gerda, three inches, 15.5 pounds), Italy (2.4 inches, 7.9 pounds), and Switzerland (3.15 inches, 22 pounds).

As in the case of other guided missiles, Germany led in the development of the air-to-air category, although, similarly, the weapon, called the X-4, never reached operational use. An ingenious design, the X-4 was 6.5 feet (two metres) long, 8.6 inches (21.8 centimetres) in diameter, and weighed 132 pounds (60 kilograms). It had two sets of cruciform wings and fins. Two opposing wings carried pyrotechnic guide flares, and the other two carried streamlined bobbins, which trailed as much as four miles of fine copper wire. Along these wires travelled corrective directional signals that automatically imparted drag to the rear fins while the vehicle, travelling almost 600 miles (950 kilometres) per hour, spun slowly. The X-4 was powered by a rocket motor using nitric acid–hydrocarbon fuel and carried a 44-pound (20-kilogram) warhead.

After World War II the first U.S. air-to-air guided missile was the Firebird. It was 10 feet (three metres) long and had a solid-propellant booster and a liquid-propellant sustainer motor. It was aimed initially by radar from the launching aircraft, and it homed on the target, guided by an onboard radar system. First test-launched in 1947, the Firebird was considered obsolete three years later. It was replaced by more sophisticated supersonic missiles, such as the Sparrow, Falcon, and Sidewinder.

By the 1970s air-to-air missiles had become increasingly so-

Increased
range of
air-to-air
missiles

phisticated. Although short-ranged (two miles) missiles such
as Sidewinder 1A were still in operational use, supersonic
aircraft required longer range missiles. Ranges have grown
to 10 to 12 miles (16 to 19 kilometres), and the Phoenix
and Falcon (AIM-47A) have ranges as great as 100 miles.

The Soviets have displayed five air-to-air missiles, NATO-
coded as Alkali, Anab, Ash, Atoll, and Awl. Atoll, which
resembles the U.S. Sidewinder, is widely used by the Soviet
Union and by Warsaw Pact countries. It has also been
exported to Afghanistan, Egypt, Cuba, Finland, India, Indonesia, Iraq, and Syria.

Anab, in both infrared and semi-active radar homing versions, arms a number of all-weather interceptors. The much
larger Ash, again with alternative infrared and radar homing versions, is carried by the Tupolev Tu-28 Fiddler long-
range interceptor.

The earlier Alkali missile arms the all-weather MiG-17
and MiG-19 aircraft.

Drones and decoys. A drone is basically a pilotless aircraft, usually under radio-command guidance and widely
employed as a target for anti-aircraft weapons. Powered by
propeller or by turbojet, ramjet, or rocket engines, a large
number of these manoeuvrable vehicles have been developed, with operating velocities as high as four times the
speed of sound. Recovery, if the drone is not destroyed,
is effected by controlled landing or by parachute. Another
Drones in
reconnais-
sance
application for drones is military reconnaissance. Equipped
with photographic or television cameras, the drone may be
shifted from radio control to programmed inertial guidance
and flown over targets at a relatively low speed and low
altitude under operationally hazardous conditions.

Other applications of drones are electronic communications, surveillance, antisubmarine warfare (detection equipment and depth charges are carried by a drone helicopter),
and even the rescue of downed airmen at sea.

An example of a drone target vehicle is the United States
Army Roadrunner. This 25-foot (7.6-metre), swept-wing,
unmanned aircraft is powered by a ramjet engine. Boosted
to flight velocity by a solid-propellant rocket, the Roadrunner can fly 30–40 minutes at speeds as great as mach 1.5. It
flies at low altitude and is used to train personnel to operate
Hawk surface-to-air missiles and to evaluate performance
of other defense missiles.

A decoy is a device designed to simulate by electromagnetic radiation an aircraft or ballistic-missile warhead. The
purpose is to divert defensive anti-aircraft or antimissile
fire. Thus a relatively small decoy can be made to appear,
by electromagnetic techniques, as large as a bomber on
radar screens. Or it can emit infrared and other radiation to
simulate a re-entering ICBM warhead. For military reasons,
details of such devices are not released to the general public.

Guidance and control. Most free-flight rockets require
stabilization of some sort to minimize flight-path deflection
caused by wind, nonuniformity of rocket structure, rocket-
jet misalignment, and other factors.

In the case of some barrage-type rockets launched by the
thousands, dispersion errors may be accepted because of the
overlapping explosive effect in the target area. Aircraft rockets are often stabilized by fixed fins located at the rear of
the rocket. Folding fins that open by inertia after firing are
also used. Short-range bazooka rockets and ballistic rockets
of five- to 10-mile (eight- to 16-kilometre) range are usually
Methods of
stabili-
zation
fin stabilized. Spin stabilization is used on some rockets.
In these designs, the rocket nozzle is replaced by a series
of smaller nozzles, canted at an angle to impart torque as
well as thrust.

A unique method of wire control, based upon the German air-to-air X-4 rocket, has been used. This technique
is utilized in some antitank rockets of about one-mile (1.6-
kilometre) range. Fine wire is trailed from a pair of bobbins
on the fins of the rocket, and command signals are given
by the operator observing its flight through a telescope.

If a rocket is designed to operate at high altitudes, as in
the case of sounding rockets, satellite launchers, and ballistic missiles of ranges greater than 100 miles, aerodynamic
forces are no longer available for control because of the low
density of the air. One technique, employed first by Goddard, is to place carbon or molybdenum deflection vanes
within the rocket exhaust. Usually two pairs are employed

for corrections about all three axes; one pair for pitch,
the other for yaw and, in opposition, for roll. In flight,
deviations from flight path are sensed by gyros within an
automatic control (autopilot) system, and corrective signals
are sent to motors that operate the vanes. This deflection
system may be used also to program the tilt from vertical
launch to ballistic flight path. Radio command also may be
used to initiate the file program.

A modification of the jet vane method is the "jetevator," a
ring-shaped deflector mounted at the nozzle periphery that
rotates slightly into the edge of the rocket jet as required.
Gimbal mounting of the engine, permitting the motor to
swivel a few degrees in any direction, is widely used for
flight-path control. This system was developed for the U.S.
Viking and has been used successfully on IRBM's and ICBM's.

Injection of high-pressure gas in the rocket nozzle to create
a local shock wave and differential pressure is a further technique of jet deflection in use. This technique is known as
thrust vector control (TVC). Magnetohydrodynamic (MHD)
deflection of a rocket jet is another possible flight-control
concept; since a rocket jet may be highly ionized, it is
conceivable that a magnetic field may induce deflection of
the exhaust gases without physical contact.

Roll control (*i.e.,* rotation about the long axis) is sometimes required, particularly on larger ballistic missiles. Small
jets mounted transversely on the side of the missile are
commonly used for this purpose.

Details of guidance systems in modern missiles are, of
course, secret, particularly frequencies of operation, since
electronic "jamming" or confusion by deliberate transmission of spurious signals by the enemy may be possible. Pulse-
coded directional signals have been used to avoid jamming.
Some missiles carry their own small radar systems and are
launched when the missile is electrically "locked-on" to the
target. A ship may utilize its large radar to track the target
aircraft or vessel and continuously compute the range and
bearing of the target while sending flight-correction signals
to the missile in flight. Some air-to-surface missiles use
television guidance, maintaining the image on the scanning
screen in the same relative position after launching.

Sometimes the target may emit a signal that a missile can
sense and track. Some missiles can lock on to the exhaust
jet of an enemy aircraft, others on enemy radar transmitting systems.

The Snark was an early United States postwar intercontinental guided missile that utilized stellar navigation,
comparing the position of stars and correcting an on-board
inertial guidance platform. Powered by turbojet engines,
this missile became operational in 1958 but was superseded
by the Atlas ICBM. Long-range ballistic missiles have a flight
time of about 30 minutes. The guidance system for these Inertial
guidance
in ICBMS
missiles is invariably inertial, using gyros and accelerometers
to sense variations in velocity in each of the three axes: roll,
pitch, and yaw. Having sensed a variation, the system gives
correction to the flight controls to place the missile back on
the programmed trajectory. Travelling along a preplanned
launch path, the final-stage rocket engine is shut down at
the precise moment when required velocity (about 15,000
miles, or 24,000 kilometres, per hour) and direction are
achieved. The warhead and final stage continue to travel
upward and follow a ballistic trajectory to the target.

Warheads. Rocket and missile warheads are conveniently
divided into three categories: (1) high-explosive, (2) nuclear,
or atomic, and (3) special-purpose. The first of these is
generally employed on short-range tactical weapons. While
it is possible to design such warheads to produce damage
by either concussion (blast) or fragmentation, most depend
upon some form of fragmentation. The efficiency of high-
explosive warheads is a function of the size, number, weight,
and velocity of the fragments produced, and the reliability
of the warhead is largely a function of its fuzing system. The
spray pattern of the fragments is also important and is established by the geometry of the high-explosive charge and
the arrangement of the fragments upon it. Nonfragmenting
high-explosive warheads for antitank weapons usually incorporate the shaped charge principle to achieve maximum
penetration by concentrating the blast at one point. Nuclear
warheads are used primarily, but not exclusively, on the
IRBM's and ICBM's, since it would be uneconomical and

inefficient to use high-explosive heads on these long-range missiles. Typical of such missiles are the U.S. Titan, Minuteman, and Polaris. Very long range air-to-surface missiles (particularly the so-called standoff bombs), some air-to-air missiles, as well as certain short-range tactical or battlefield rockets and missiles also may employ nuclear warheads. The nuclear warheads may be either fission or fusion types; in the latter case they are called, popularly, H-bombs. The power of nuclear warheads is indicated by comparing the release of energy of a certain weapon to an equivalent weight of TNT. Thus a 10-kiloton warhead or bomb has the same explosive force as 10,000 tons of TNT, a five-megaton device has the force of 5,000,000 tons of TNT.

Because of the development of antiballistic missiles and tracking radar that can locate and identify an incoming warhead, several further refinements of warhead systems should be noted. One concept is a rocket-powered re-entry vehicle that would cause the warhead to change course to a target. By the mid-1960s, as a result of the development of antiballistic missile (ABM) sites around Moscow and other cities, the United States pressed the development of MIRV— multiple independently targeted re-entry vehicles. This system embodies a multiheaded ICBM, one that has three separately targeted nuclear warheads sent on their independent ways after the main propulsion stages of the ICBM have shut down. Installation of MIRV warheads on Minuteman III ICBM's is reported to have commenced in May 1971. U.S. Navy Poseidon fleet ballistic missiles are also scheduled to carry MIRV warheads. (F.C.D.III/Ed.)

Marginal note: Development of MIRV

DEVELOPMENT OF NUCLEAR WEAPONS

Nuclear weapons derive their enormous explosive force from either the fission or fusion of atomic nuclei. Their significance may best be appreciated by the coining of the words kiloton (1,000 tons) and megaton (1,000,000 tons) of TNT equivalent to describe their blast effect. For example, the first nuclear fission bomb, the one dropped on Hiroshima, Japan, in 1945, released energy equalling 20,000 tons (20 kilotons) of chemical explosive from less than 100 pounds (45 kilograms) of uranium. Fusion, or thermonuclear, bombs (H-bombs) have given yields ranging up to 60 megatons. The first nuclear weapons were bombs delivered by aircraft; warheads for ballistic missiles, however, have come to be by far the most important nuclear weapons. There are also smaller tactical, or battlefield, nuclear weapons that include artillery projectiles, howitzer shells, and demolition munitions.

The basic principle of nuclear fission weapons involves the assembly of a sufficient amount of the uranium isotope uranium-235 or of the plutonium isotope plutonium-239 to "go supercritical"—that is, for neutrons (which cause fission and are in turn released during fission) to be produced at a faster rate than they can escape from the assembly. There are two ways in which a subcritical assembly of fissionable material can be rendered supercritical and made to explode. The subcritical assembly may consist of two parts, each of which is too small to have a positive multiplication rate; the two parts can be shot together by a gun-type device. Alternatively, a spherical subcritical assembly surrounded by a shell of chemical high explosive may be compressed into a supercritical one by detonating the explosive.

The basic principle of the thermonuclear, or fusion, weapon is to produce ignition conditions in a thermonuclear fuel, such as deuterium, an isotope of hydrogen with double the weight of normal hydrogen, or lithium deuteride. The Sun may be considered a thermonuclear device; its main fuel is deuterium, which it consumes in its core at temperatures of 10,000,000° to 20,000,000° C (18,000,000° to 36,000,000° F). To achieve comparable temperatures in a weapon, a fission device is used.

Fission weapons. Following the discovery of artificial radioactivity in the 1930s, the Italian physicist Enrico Fermi performed a series of experiments in which he exposed many elements to low-velocity neutrons. He obtained more than 400 new radioactive substances, but nearly all were isotopes of the exposed elements—that is, the same elements chemically but with a different atomic mass. When he exposed thorium and uranium, however, he encountered a striking exception: chemically different radioactive products resulted, indicating that new elements had been formed, rather than merely isotopes of the original elements. Fermi concluded that he had produced elements beyond uranium (element 92), then the last element in the periodic table; he called them transuranic elements and named two of them ausenium (element 93) and hesperium (element 94). During the autumn of 1938, however, when Fermi was receiving the Nobel Prize for his work, Otto Hahn and Fritz Strassmann of Germany discovered that one of the "new" elements was actually barium (element 56).

Marginal note: The mystery of uranium fission

The Danish scientist Niels Bohr visited the United States in January 1939 and carried with him the explanation given by the Austrian refugee scientist Lise Meitner and her nephew Otto Frisch. A new process explained Hahn's surprising data. Low-velocity neutrons caused the uranium nucleus to fission, or break apart, into two smaller pieces; the combined atomic numbers of the two pieces— for example, barium and krypton—equalled that of the uranium nucleus. Much energy was released in the process. This news set off experiments at many laboratories. Bohr worked with John Wheeler at Princeton; they postulated that the uranium isotope uranium-235 was the one undergoing fission; the other isotope, uranium-238, merely absorbed the neutrons. It was discovered that neutrons were produced during the fission process; on the average, each fissioning atom produced more than two neutrons. If the proper amount of material were assembled, these free neutrons might create a chain reaction. Under special conditions, a very fast chain reaction might produce a very large release of energy; in short, a weapon of fantastic power might be feasible.

Development of the fission bomb. The possibility that such a weapon might first be developed by Nazi Germany alarmed many scientists and was drawn to the attention of Pres. Franklin D. Roosevelt by Albert Einstein, then living in the United States. The President appointed an Advisory Committee on Uranium; it reported that a chain reaction in uranium was possible, though unproved. Chain-reaction experiments with carbon and uranium were started in New York City at Columbia University, and in March 1940 it was confirmed that the isotope uranium-235 was responsible for low-velocity neutron fission in uranium. The Advisory Committee on Uranium increased its support of the Columbia experiments and arranged for a study of possible methods for separating the uranium-235 isotope from the much more abundant uranium-238. (Normal uranium contains approximately 0.7 percent uranium-235, most of the remainder being uranium-238.) The centrifuge process, in which the heavier isotope is spun to the outside, as in a cream separator, at first seemed the most useful, but at Columbia a rival process was proposed. In that process, gaseous uranium hexafluoride is diffused through barriers, or filters; more molecules containing the lighter isotope, uranium-235, would pass through the filter than those containing the heavier isotope, slightly enriching the mixture on the far side. A sequence of several thousand stages would be needed to enrich the mixture to 90 percent uranium-235; the total barrier area would be many acres.

During the summer of 1940, Edwin McMillan and Philip Abelson of the University of California at Berkeley discovered element 93, named neptunium; they inferred that this element would decay into element 94. The Bohr and Wheeler fission theory suggested that one of the isotopes, mass number 239, of this new element might also fission under low-velocity neutron bombardment. The cyclotron at the University of California at Berkeley was put to work to make enough element 94 for experiments; by mid-1941, element 94 had been firmly identified and named plutonium, and its fission characteristics had been established. Low-velocity neutrons did cause it to undergo fission, and at a rate much higher than that of uranium-235. The Berkeley group, under Ernest Lawrence, was also considering producing large quantities of uranium-235 by turning one of their cyclotrons into a super mass spectrograph. A mass spectrograph employs a magnetic field to bend a current of uranium ions; the heavier ions

Marginal note: Discovery of neptunium and plutonium

(uranium-238) bend at a larger radius than the lighter ions (uranium-235), allowing the two separated currents to be collected in separate receivers.

In the spring of 1941 a review committee reported that a nuclear explosive probably could not be available before 1945; a chain reaction in natural uranium was probably 18 months off; it would take at least an additional year to produce enough plutonium for a bomb; it would take three to five years to separate enough uranium-235. Further, it was held that all of these estimates were optimistic. In late June 1941 President Roosevelt established the Office of Scientific Research and Development under the direction of the United States scientist Vannevar Bush; a British committee simultaneously recommended pushing their uranium-235 bomb project at maximum speed.

In the fall of 1941 the Columbia chain-reaction experiment with natural uranium and carbon yielded negative results. A review committee concluded that boron impurities might be poisoning it by absorbing neutrons. It was decided to transfer all such work to the University of Chicago and repeat the experiment there with high-purity carbon. At Berkeley, the cyclotron, converted into a mass spectrograph (now called a calutron), was exceeding expectations in separating uranium-235, and it was enlarged to a 10-calutron system with a total ion current of one ampere, capable of producing a tenth of an ounce (about three grams) of uranium-235 per day.

The U.S. entry into World War II in December 1941 was decisive in providing funds for a massive research and production effort for obtaining fissionable materials. In May 1942 the momentous decision was made to proceed simultaneously on all promising production methods. Bush decided that the army should be brought into the production plant construction activities. The Corps of Engineers opened an office in New York City and named it the Manhattan Engineer District Office. After considerable argument over priorities, a workable arrangement was achieved with the formation of a three-man policy board chaired by Bush and the appointment of Gen. Leslie Groves as head of the Manhattan Engineer District. Groves arranged contracts for a gaseous diffusion separation plant, a plutonium production facility, and a calutron pilot plant, which might be expanded later. The day before the success of Fermi's chain-reaction experiment on December 2, 1942, Groves signed the construction contract for the production reactors. Many problems were still unsolved: the diffusion barrier had not yet been demonstrated as practical. Berkeley had been successful with its empirically designed calutron, but the Oak Ridge pilot plant contractors were understandably uneasy about the rough specifications available for the massive separation of uranium-235, which was designated the Y-12 effort. Plutonium chemistry was almost unknown; in fact, it was not known whether or not plutonium gave off neutrons during fission, or, if so, how many.

Meantime, as part of the reorganization in June 1942, J. Robert Oppenheimer became the director of Project Y, the group that was to design the actual weapon. The effort was spread over several locations; in the fall, Groves and Oppenheimer chose the former Los Alamos Ranch School, some 90 miles (140 kilometres) north of Albuquerque, New Mexico, as the site for the Los Alamos Scientific Laboratory. By July two essential and encouraging pieces of experimental data had been obtained—plutonium did give off neutrons in fission, more than uranium-235; and the neutrons were emitted in a short time compared to that needed to bring the weapon materials into a supercritical assembly. The theorists contributed one discouraging note: their estimate of the critical mass for uranium-235 had risen over threefold, to something between 50 and 100 pounds (23 and 45 kilograms).

The emphasis during the summer and fall of 1943 was on the gun method of assembly: the projectile, a subcritical piece of uranium-235 (or plutonium-239), would be placed in a gun barrel and fired into the target, another subcritical piece of uranium-235. After the mass was joined (now supercritical), a neutron source would be used to start the chain reaction. A problem developed with the plutonium gun. In manufacturing plutonium-239 from uranium-238

in a reactor, some of the plutonium-239 absorbs a neutron and becomes plutonium-240. This material undergoes spontaneous fission, producing neutrons. Some neutrons will always be present in a plutonium assembly and cause it to begin multiplying as soon as it goes critical, before it reaches supercriticality; it will then explode prematurely and produce comparatively little energy. The gun designers tried to beat this problem by achieving higher projectile speeds, but they lost out in the end to a better idea—the implosion method.

In April 1943 a Project Y physicist, Seth Neddermeyer, proposed to assemble a supercritical mass from many directions, instead of just two as in the gun. In particular, a number of shaped charges placed on the surface of a sphere would fire many subcritical pieces into one common ball at the centre of the sphere. John von Neumann, a U.S. mathematician who had had experience in shaped-charge, armour-piercing work, supported the implosion method enthusiastically and pointed out that the greater speed of assembly might solve the plutonium-240 problem. U.S. physicist Edward Teller suggested that the converging material might also become compressed, offering the possibility that less material would be needed. By late 1943 the implosion method was being given an increasingly higher priority; by July 1944 it had become clear that the plutonium gun could not be built. The only way to use plutonium in a weapon was by the implosion method.

By 1944 the Manhattan Project was spending money at a rate of over $1,000,000,000 per year. The situation was likened to a nightmarish horse race; no one could say which of the horses (the calutron plant, the diffusion plant, or the plutonium reactors) was likely to win or whether any of them would even finish the race. In July 1944 the first Y-12 calutrons had been running for three months but were operating at less than 50 percent efficiency; the main problem was in recovering the large amounts of material that reached neither the uranium-235 nor uranium-238 boxes and, thus, had to be rerun through the system. The diffusion plant was far from completion, the production of satisfactory barriers remaining the major problem. The first reactor at Hanford, Washington, had been turned on in September, but it had promptly turned itself off. Solving this problem, which proved to be caused by absorption of neutrons by one of the fission products, took several months. These delays meant almost certainly that the war in Europe would be over before the weapon could be ready. The ultimate target was slowly changing from Germany to Japan.

In April 1945, two weeks after he had become president, Harry Truman was briefed on the status of the project: the uranium-235 gun design had been frozen, but sufficient uranium-235 would not be accumulated until around August 1. Enough plutonium-239 would be available for an implosion assembly to be tested in early July; a second would be ready in August. Several B-29s had been modified to carry the weapons; support construction was under way at Tinian, in the Mariana Islands, 1,500 miles south of Japan.

The test of the plutonium weapon was named "Trinity"; it was fired before dawn on July 16, 1945. The theorists' predictions of the energy release ranged from the equivalent of 1,000 tons of TNT to an optimistic 5,000 tons. Instead the test produced an energy, or yield, equivalent to 20,000 tons of TNT.

A single B-29 bomber flew over Hiroshima, Japan, on August 6, 1945, at 8:15 in the morning, local time. The untested uranium-235 gun assembly was air burst 2,000 feet (600 metres) above the city to eliminate local fallout. Two-thirds of the city area was destroyed. The second weapon, a duplicate of the plutonium-239 implosion assembly tested in "Trinity," was to be dropped on Kokura on August 11; a third was being prepared in the U.S. for possible use in late August or early September. To avoid bad weather, the schedule was moved up two days to August 9. The B-29 spent 45 minutes over Kokura without sighting its aim point; it then proceeded to the secondary target of Nagasaki. About 50 percent of that city's area was destroyed.

Fission weapon programs outside the United States. Sci-

Implosion technique

The bombing of Hiroshima

Move toward actual production

entists in several countries performed experiments in connection with nuclear reactors and fission weapons during World War II, but no country other than the U.S. carried its projects as far as separating uranium-235 or manufacturing plutonium-239. In Paris, Jean-Frédéric Joliot-Curie and two colleagues had measured the number of neutrons emitted during fission and concluded that a chain reaction was possible. Another French scientist introduced the concept of critical mass and calculated that a sphere of several tons of pure uranium might produce a self-sustaining reaction. During the fall of France in June 1940, Joliot-Curie's two colleagues reached England with the world's entire supply of heavy water (400 pounds, or 180 kilograms) and continued their chain-reaction experiments at Cambridge.

The British weapon project started informally, as in the U.S., among university physicists. In April 1940 a short paper by Professors Frisch and Rudolf Peierls, expanding on the idea of critical mass, estimated that a super weapon could be built using several pounds of pure uranium-235 and that this amount of material might be obtainable from a chain of diffusion tubes. A group known as the MAUD Committee was set up in the Ministry of Aircraft Production. This committee's feasibility report, in July 1941, caused the U.S. to propose a joint production effort, but the British were cool toward the proposal. A year later, when the British wished to merge the two projects, the U.S. had lost interest in a joint effort. A number of British scientists did join the weapon design effort at Los Alamos. By 1943 the British project was abandoned, and the U.K. did not explode its first fission device, fueled with plutonium-239, until 1952.

In the Soviet Union the news of Joliot-Curie's experiments had excited great interest. Igor Kurchatov and others at Leningrad started studies on nuclear reactors and, by late 1940, felt ready to approach the government for the necessary funds to build one. The German attack in July 1941 focussed most physicists' attention on more immediate problems. One of Kurchatov's students observed the gradual disappearance of articles on fission physics from the U.S. journals; in May 1942 he wrote an impassioned plea to several outstanding Soviet physicists and the State Defense Committee that the chain reaction experiments should continue, that nuclear weapons should not be abandoned. A government review committee, including leading Soviet scientists, recommended that the work be continued with Kurchatov in charge.

A Uranium Institute with a few dozen physicists was established in Moscow; studies were started on nuclear reactors, on the separation of the uranium isotopes by barrier diffusion, and on the ballistic problems of gun assembly. Uranium metal and carbon of sufficient purity, however, did not become available until after World War II. The Soviet government then expanded the effort and set a national goal of highest priority to produce a nuclear weapon. The first Soviet chain-reaction experiment went critical on Christmas 1946; the first nuclear weapon was tested on August 29, 1949. The time between the two events, two and a half years, was the same as that between Fermi's successful experiment in Chicago and the "Trinity" test at Alamogordo.

In Germany the War Office also received an enthusiastic letter, in April 1939, advocating nuclear weapon development. By the time the war had started, Germany had a special office for the military application of nuclear fission; chain-reaction experiments with uranium and carbon were being planned, and ways of separating the uranium isotopes were under study. Some measurements on carbon, later shown to be in error, led the physicist Werner Heisenberg to recommend that heavy water be used, instead, for the moderator. This dependence on scarce heavy water was a major reason why the German experiments never reached a successful conclusion. The isotope separation studies were oriented toward low enrichments (about 1 percent uranium-235) for the chain reaction experiments; they never got past the laboratory apparatus stage, and several times these prototypes were destroyed in bombing attacks. As for the fission weapon itself, it was a rather distant goal, and practically nothing but "back-of-the-envelope" studies were done on it.

The French and Chinese nuclear weapon projects were postwar efforts. Some French scientists had worked in exile during the war in Britain and Canada and returned to work for the Commissariat à l'Energie Atomique. This French effort, however, was aimed at energy production; not until 1954 was a section for military applications formed. The first French plutonium production reactor went on line in 1956; the first nuclear weapon was tested in 1960.

The Chinese program started in 1958 with a slightly enriched uranium reactor, which was part of a technical aid program provided by the Soviet Union. When that aid program was stopped a year or two later, foreign intelligence experts estimated it would be the early 1970s before China could produce enough plutonium to test a weapon. China's first test bomb (1964), however, contained no plutonium at all—it used uranium greatly enriched in uranium-235. China continued to move rapidly. Its second test bomb was dropped from an airplane; its fourth was delivered by a missile. Its sixth test was a multimegaton thermonuclear device. India exploded a nuclear device in 1974, and there were rumours that several other countries (such as Israel, South Africa, and Pakistan) had completed all the necessary research, development, and production of materials and lacked only the final credential, a proof test, to be considered nuclear powers.

Thermonuclear weapons. *The United States project.* The U.S. Super project started from a conversation early in 1942 between Fermi and Teller. Fermi suggested that the explosion of a fission weapon could be used to start something similar to the reactions in the Sun. Teller undertook to analyze the thermonuclear processes in some detail and presented his work several months later to a summer study group of theoretical physicists in Berkeley. They concluded that a weapon based on the thermonuclear fusion of deuterium was indeed possible. Oppenheimer made a special trip east to arrange for experimental studies, and as the news leaked to physicists at Berkeley and Chicago, several volunteered for the new laboratory at Los Alamos.

The Super project's first and most obvious requirement, however, was a working fission weapon. It was suggested that the addition of tritium (an isotope of hydrogen with three times the normal weight) could lower the required ignition temperature, because the reaction rate of a deuterium–tritium mixture was many times larger than the rate for pure deuterium. Tritium, then, seemed to be a necessity. Groves made arrangements for a pilot plant operation to manufacture tritium from lithium in the experimental reactor at Oak Ridge (tritium is produced when a neutron is captured by the lithium-6 isotope of lithium). The net effect of a review in 1944, however, was to delay further work on the Super until after the war.

Even after the war, the Super continued to be a low-priority program, behind testing and stockpiling fission weapons. The test of the Soviet Union's first fission weapon on August 29, 1949, provoked a vigorous debate among United States scientists and political and military leaders. The Atomic Energy Commission was divided; the majority recommended against the development of the Super at that time. The General Advisory Committee had concluded that the theoretical studies were incomplete, that success might require large amounts of tritium, but that an imaginative and concerted attack on the problem had a better than even chance of producing a fusion weapon within five years. They observed that such a superweapon could not be confined to military targets and hoped that its development could be avoided.

The Joint Chiefs of Staff also made a study but did not recommend a high-priority program to build a Super, although it did urge a speedy determination of feasibility and some prudent plans for long lead-time production items. The Joint Committee on Atomic Energy of the U.S. Congress was strongly in favour of the Super. On January 31, 1950, President Truman made his decision that work on the Super would proceed.

The production facilities for thermonuclear materials were pushed steadily. By the end of 1950, a pilot plant

Soviet
nuclear
beginnings

German
difficulties

for the production of heavy water was completed, and a Savannah River (South Carolina) site was selected for building up to six dual reactors capable of producing either tritium or plutonium. The Super theoretical studies went less smoothly.

The development of thermonuclear weapons, which came to be known as hydrogen bombs, or H-bombs, because their energy comes from "burning" the deuterium isotope of hydrogen, was intimately associated with electronic computers. The calculations needed in early 1950, however, were larger than any existing computer could handle. Drastically simplified calculations, suitable for available computers, showed that Super appeared to be marginal because much more tritium would be required than previously believed.

In the spring of 1951, a new approach was mapped, and a Pacific test of thermonuclear principles proved successful. By fall Los Alamos had gone on a six-day work week to ensure that the first device test would be completed before the end of 1952. On the morning of November 1, 1952, the test was successful, obliterating a small island and leaving a wave-washed crater more than a mile in diameter.

Deployment of nuclear weapons. The main role played by nuclear weapons has been a strategic one—to support a country's doctrine of deterrence. In the U.S. this doctrine has ranged from so-called massive retaliation in the 1950s to mutual deterrence in the late 20th century. Most new nuclear powers have chosen the long-range heavy bomber as their first nuclear weapon carrier. Early carriers were simply modified versions of existing aircraft; later planes were specifically designed for the long ranges, high speeds, and other characteristics thought necessary.

Several developments, such as reliable guidance systems, were needed before the intercontinental ballistic missile (ICBM) became militarily attractive. As missile design improved, with solid propellants replacing the operationally awkward liquid propellants and with guidance that reduced the warhead yield requirement, great progress was also made in producing higher thermonuclear yields per pound of warhead weight, as well as in reducing the overall size. The fleet ballistic missile system of the U.S. Navy, started in 1956, saw the first Polaris submarine, the nuclear-powered "George Washington," become operational on November 15, 1960. The sixth Polaris submarine conducted an operational test, including the detonation of the warhead, near Christmas Island in May 1962. The Minuteman missile system of the U.S. Air Force, started in 1958, saw its first squadron become operational in early 1963. In the 1970s new versions of the Polaris and Minuteman were deployed, capable of carrying multiple, independently targeted re-entry vehicles (MIRV).

The Soviet Union deployed its nuclear weapons in a pattern similar to that of the U.S., except for the early postwar years when it built a large, intermediate-range ballistic missile (IRBM) force, targeted for western Europe. For many years, the Soviet ICBM force lagged behind the U.S.; strategic parity with the U.S. for ICBM's was attained in 1969. At that time, the U.S. estimated the Soviet ICBM threat at about 300 SS–9s, capable of carrying 25 megatons each, and 700 SS–11s, a Minuteman-like missile using a storable liquid propellant. In the early 1970s, the Soviet Union also had a number of Polaris-like submarines.

The United Kingdom and France have selected a submarine-launched ballistic-missile system as their main nuclear deterrent force. Both nations had deployed Polaris-like submarines. In addition, France was emplacing IRBM's in silos in Haute-Provence. (W.J.F./Ed.)

DEVELOPMENT OF NONBALLISTIC WEAPONS

In addition to nuclear weapons and guided missiles, science and engineering have brought a number of other weapon innovations.

Chemical warfare. Chemical agents, especially those that burn personnel and start secondary fires, are of ancient origin. Stenches, mainly from sulfur compounds, and smoke were also used in ancient times. These early chemicals were dwarfed in World War I when on April 22, 1915, the Germans released many cylinders of chlorine to be driven by the wind toward British and French lines in the Ypres salient. This gas created thousands of casualties, more than the users had thought possible. Both sides then used poison gases of several types, the agents themselves becoming more deadly and the techniques of handling them more efficient. Though many more gas casualties were inflicted, the introduction of gas masks prevented the first success from being repeated.

Gases and other toxic chemicals are extremely unpopular in world opinion. They are difficult to use effectively, especially against the armed forces of an industrialized nation capable of providing defensive devices quickly. Only two nations are believed to have used deadly gas between 1918 and 1970, Italy against Ethiopia (1935–36) and Japan against China (1937–42).

In World War II both the Germans and the Western Allies stockpiled chemical warfare agents of advanced types and had delivery systems ready, but they were never employed, probably because of the fear of retaliation. By 1943, for example, Germany had a new series of nerve gases believed vastly more toxic than earlier agents, but German cities were by that time being attacked successfully from the air.

Several varieties of tear gases have been used by the U.S. and other nations for special purposes in low-level combat and riot control. Another type, one of the so-called sneeze gases, was considered by the United States for use in Vietnam. A number of American volunteers allowed themselves to be gassed; they were immobilized for about 12 hours with no fatalities or serious aftereffects. Medical officers reported, however, that its use might be dangerous, especially in areas where tuberculosis was widespread, and the agent was not used.

The use of chemicals that burn is as old as war. In modern times, however, the Germans introduced flamethrowers in World War I. In World War II, American scientists developed a means of thickening gasoline with the aluminum soap of naphthenic and palmitic acids into a sticky syrup that carries further from projectors and burns more slowly but at higher temperature. This mixture, known as napalm, can also be used in aircraft or missile-delivered warheads against military or civilian targets. A small, high-explosive charge scatters the flaming liquid, which sticks to what it hits until burned out.

White phosphorus is used as a shell and grenade filler in combination with a small high-explosive charge. It is both an incendiary and the best known producer of vivid white smoke. Small bits of it burn even more intensely than napalm when they strike personnel. Incendiary attacks from the air, using small thermite bombs, were also extremely effective in starting relatively small fires, which were often fed with combustibles also delivered by bombers.

Chemicals also have been used as poisons but never very effectively.

Biological warfare. The use of biological agents as weapons has always had an even more adverse world opinion than chemical warfare. So far as is known, no nation has used germs intentionally and successfully against the personnel of another in the 20th century, although the Germans infected the horses of Romanian cavalry with glanders in 1914.

Although a culture of germs could be delivered in various ways deep inside an enemy's country, such germs would have to be of a type already in existence; damage done would thus depend on public health facilities and services. Germ warfare would probably be more difficult to use successfully than many alarmists indicate.

Biological weapons that attack domesticated animals, or even basic food plants, might be more effective than those that cause human illness and death. Such agents might be introduced surreptitiously, but positive data is lacking.

Defoliation is possible, but at considerable cost. It has been used mostly against jungle but could be employed against food crops. If useful at all, it is limited to small conflicts of the guerrilla type.

Psychological warfare. There have been many examples of psychological war throughout history. Messages delivered in various ways to the enemy, and even to neutrals, may be considered weapons. Ancient military noisemakers, special headdresses to make soldiers seem taller, and the painting of the human body to inspire dread—all were psychological devices. Threats delivered by one nation to another over the radio or by other means fall into the same category. All of these are seldom as effective as the men who use them hope.

On the other hand, certain forms of overt propaganda directed at enemies, or potential enemies, have in the 20th century become undeniably useful in achieving military and political objectives. Messages that are credible, simple, and properly timed are weapons, sometimes powerful weapons. Imaginative leaders of nations and armies have realized for thousands of years the military value of introducing schism into the ranks of their enemies. Units fight poorly when they become doubtful of their objectives or their leaders. In the 20th century, political movements have achieved many successes through a combination of military and psychological warfare.

Psychological warfare delivery systems are more difficult to analyze and control than those that convey material projectiles, although printed matter is, in fact, similar to projectiles and can be delivered in roughly similar ways; *e.g.,* the dropping of leaflets from the air. Radio and, to some extent, television are also now important, but both are subject to jamming.

Teaching, although not a new technique, has been used in a more scientific way since World War I. Since class and guerrilla warfare are fought mostly in the minds of the people, teaching, in the form of direct communication, has become a weapon. Statements repeated often enough are believed. Prophecies can become self-fulfilling.

In conflicts of the insurgency type, there appears to be no satisfactory substitute for personal contact, although printed leaflets with graphics, or graphics alone, are useful. In literate countries newspapers and magazines may be employed, but volume is usually limited. Handmade posters and similar material can be valuable for influencing local populations.

Use of printed propaganda

The government can use all these and more, but anything identified with propaganda is often self-defeating. Delivery systems work best where the people who receive the messages are reasonably free. The use of radio broadcasts, prepared government messages, and loudspeakers operating from low-flying aircraft, used by the U.S. and South Vietnamese forces during the Vietnam War, proved virtually useless because the guerrillas were normally able to prevent people from listening. Government arguments that do get through are easily countered.

Economic warfare. For millennia, nations have striven to injure their enemies by seizing their food and raw materials in transit, damaging their agriculture, and carrying off or destroying means of production and labour. In the 20th century, economic warfare has been magnified and refined. Economists help select bombing targets. Other specialists have guided wartime trade policies to prevent strategic losses and to deprive the enemy. When neutral trade is involved, possibilities are sometimes extremely complicated.

Another form of economic warfare is in the area of cost effectiveness. Combat statistics, intelligence data, availability of spare parts, and other factors are reduced to computer-digestible form, and decisions made. The technique is as yet by no means foolproof. (J.We.)

Protective installations and equipment

FORTIFICATIONS

Fortifications are military positions that have been strengthened against attack. Fortification is the military art or science of strengthening such positions. Permanent fortifications include elaborate forts and troop shelters; they are usually constructed of masonry and are most often erected in times of peace or upon threat of war. Field fortifications are constructed when in contact with an enemy or when contact is imminent. They consist of entrenched positions for personnel and crew-served weapons; cleared fields of fire; and obstacles such as explosive mines, barbed-wire entanglements, felled trees, and antitank ditches. Both field and permanent fortifications often take advantage of natural obstacles, such as canals

and rivers, and they are usually camouflaged or otherwise concealed.

Both field and permanent fortifications assist the defender to obtain the greatest advantage from his own strength and weapons while preventing the enemy from using his resources to best advantage. When supported by covering fire, for example, fortifications may force the enemy to deploy prematurely into open and less controllable formations. Fortifications may also be used to deny easier invasion routes and channel enemy operations into less advantageous paths.

Before the advent of the most modern weapons, almost all important cities and trade centres were defended by permanent fortifications, either a high wall encircling the city, a series of forts on the periphery, a walled and moated citadel within the heart of the city, or a combination or variations of the three. Fortifications also might be established at strategic points along likely routes of invasion. Throughout history coastal fortifications have been constructed to guard seaports against naval attack or to counter amphibious assault.

Some fortifications may be considered semipermanent, such as the extensive trench systems employed in World War I or the forts and base camps used in more recent times in Southeast Asia, Korea, and the Middle East. These were usually entrenched fighting positions and troop shelters reinforced by log or timber revetments and earth-filled burlap or plastic bags.

Neither fortifications nor the obstacles contributing to them are of optimum value unless actively defended by troops and guns. Antitank obstacles, for example, may be covered over by bulldozers or destroyed by demolition charges. Since no fortifications, however stoutly constructed, can be considered impregnable, an integral part of the defense is the sally or sortie, whereby troops rush out from the fortifications to engage the enemy in close combat, or the counterattack, whereby reserve forces seek to destroy or eject any troops who may have penetrated the defenses.

Importance of adequate defense

Before the invention of gunpowder led to the creation of artillery firing powerful explosive projectiles, permanent fortifications might hold up an attacker for months and even years. Sometimes starvation or the threat of starvation was all that finally induced defenders to surrender.

The effect of even fairly primitive artillery was dramatically demonstrated at Constantinople in AD 1453 when a besieging Turkish force in 55 days breached defenses that had earlier withstood sieges as long as five years. Improvements in design and construction retained considerable advantage for fortifications through ensuing years, despite improved artillery. In the two world wars, some permanent fortifications held up well against the most powerful bombardment.

Yet, in no case have fortifications proven impervious to modern weapons, and against atomic weapons permanent fortifications as known throughout history may well be a thing of the past. Although all types of fortifications have continued even in recent years to be of some value, certainly in part because nuclear weapons have not been employed, most fortifications designed to counteract the vast new explosive power of the nuclear age are constructed deep underground, not as conventional fighting positions but as protection for headquarters staffs, command and control systems, and antiballistic missiles.

Ancient fortifications. Both field and permanent fortifications played an important role in warfare in the ancient world, but permanent fortifications were particularly effective against the limited power of ancient offensive weapons. Even the lengthy siege aimed at starving the defenders was not always effective, for the defenders were often able to supply themselves better than the besieging army could live off a hostile land. Sometimes a ruse or subterfuge, as in the legend of the Trojan Horse, was more effective than any weapon.

Early civilized tribes of Africa fought from behind a parapet filled with alternate layers of stone, earth, and logs. Sometime later came walls made of mud, sun-dried brick, or masonry and towers constructed at intervals along the wall to serve as sentry posts or as defensive bastions from which archers could cover the approaches between towers.

The first fortresses. As early as 7000 BC the city of Jericho was protected by a wall 21 feet high encompassing an area of 10 acres and by an outer moat 15 feet wide and nine feet deep (seven by five by three metres) hewn through solid rock. In ancient Egypt and Assyria walls as thick as 30 feet (nine metres) and as high as 120 feet (37 metres) were constructed, frequently with a ditch in front to keep attackers at a distance. To counter such defenses, attacking forces developed devices such as scaling ladders, battering rams, torsion-activated catapults for throwing heavy missiles, tension-activated ballistae for shooting large spears, and movable towers from which to overlook the walls and rain incendiary arrows into the fortress. The defenders reinforced their bastions with similar engines of war, firing them from atop or behind the walls. The attackers sometimes resorted to mining, digging tunnels beneath the defenses, then setting fire to the timber that shored up the tunnels, causing the earth above to collapse.

One of the most renowned of the ancient fortresses was the city of Tyre, built on an island half a mile from shore. Only after a seven-month siege did one of history's great captains, Alexander the Great, succeed in breaching the defenses. The Tyrians defeated Alexander's first efforts to build a mole 200 feet (60 metres) wide from the mainland to the walls, but after gaining mastery of the sea around the fortress, Alexander built a fleet of barges armed with war engines and anchored them at strategic points along the defensive works. From the barges he mounted his successful assault.

Siege of Rhodes

Another famous siege was the unsuccessful Macedonian attack on the city of Rhodes, undertaken some years after Alexander's death. So large was one of the towers used in the attack that 3,400 men were required to move it up to the walls. Another 1,000 men were needed to wield a battering ram 180 feet (55 metres) long. Despite such impressive efforts by the attackers, Rhodes held out for six years until finally relieved by allied forces that drove off the Macedonians.

The fortresses and towers and assault devices of early Greece and Rome remain a wonder to modern engineers accustomed to steam-, hydraulic-, and diesel-operated machinery. The Romans, for example, constructed huge siege towers, one of which Caesar mentions as being 150 feet (46 metres) high. The lower stories housed the battering ram, which had either a pointed head for breaching or a ramlike head for battering. Archers in the upper stories shot arrows to drive the defenders from their ramparts. From the top of the tower, a hinged bridge might be lowered to serve a storming party. To guard the attackers against enemy missiles, the Romans used mantelets, which were great wicker or wooden shields, sometimes mounted on wheels. In some cases the attackers might approach the fortress under the protection of wooden galleries.

Protective walls. Massive, elongated walls were also a feature of early permanent fortifications. The Great Wall of China, built by the emperor Shih Huang Ti in the 3rd century BC to discourage incursions by nomadic tribes, was 1,500 miles (2,400 kilometres) long, generally 25 feet (eight metres) wide at the base and 17 feet (five metres) at the top, with an average height of about 30 feet (nine metres). When the frontiers of the Roman Empire rested in northwestern Europe and Africa, the Romans built a number of continuous walls, including an important German defense some 250 to 300 miles long (400 to 480 kilometres) from the Rhine near Neuwied to the Danube near Ratisbon, and Hadrian's Wall in Britain, 73 miles long (117 kilometres) from the Solway Firth to a point on the North Sea coast just north of Newcastle-on-Tyne. The Limes was for half its length an earthen mound with a ditch and for the other half a rough stone wall four feet (1.2 metres) thick. Hadrian's Wall was originally built of earth but later strengthened by a masonry wall eight feet (2.4 metres) thick and 16 feet (4.8 metres) high. None of the walls was defended along its entire length. Sentry posts, watchtowers, or roving patrols gave notice of enemy incursions, whereupon reserves operating from camps spaced at intervals either along the wall or several

miles behind it moved to eliminate them. Remarkably preserved vestiges of these walls, including the Great Wall of China, remain to this day.

Early field fortifications. The main purpose of early field fortifications, particularly among the Greeks, was to secure an advantage by standing on higher ground so that the enemy was forced to attack uphill. The solid mass formation of the Macedonian phalanx was particularly effective on the defense when supplemented by natural or man-made obstacles. The Romans were especially adept at field fortifications, preparing fortified camps at the close of each day's march. Roman camps normally were square or rectangular, though they could vary with the details of terrain. The troops usually required three to four hours to dig a ditch around the periphery, erect a rampart of palisade from timbers carried by each man, lay out streets, and pitch tents. In hostile territory as much as half of each legion might mount guard or engage the enemy while the remainder worked. During extended campaigns the Romans strengthened the camps with towers and outlying redoubts, or small forts, and used the camps as a base for offensive forays into the surrounding territory.

Roman fortified camps

In the campaign in Gaul against the insurgent Arverni chieftain, Vercingetorix, the Romans under Julius Caesar performed a formidable engineering feat in surrounding a large number of Gauls in the fortified town of Alesia near the present French city of Dijon. With about 55,000 men, Caesar built two separate walls of "contravallation"— facing the town—and "circumvallation"—facing outward, the latter 14 miles (23 kilometres) in circumference. While holding Vercingetorix at bay with these fortifications, Caesar defeated three attempts by a Gallic relief army to break through to the besieged force. Facing starvation, Vercingetorix at last surrendered.

Among the Teutonic barbarians, the Goths developed their own version of the fortified camp. When travelling, the Goths moved in a large convoy of wagons, which they assembled at night in a circle, or laager, providing an effective fort both for defense and as a base for forage and plunder. The methods later used by the wagon trains of American pioneers against the Indians of the western plains were similar, as were procedures adopted by armoured divisions in World War II.

The Middle Ages. With the decline of the Roman Empire and the rise of feudalism, the importance of field fortifications diminished. The mounted knight depended for protection in the field on his heavy armour, while the art of permanent fortifications centred on the medieval castle. The castle built of heavy stone on high ground came early to the mainland of Europe (11th century) but was slower to develop in Britain, where simple ditches and wooden palisades continued longer. William the Conqueror used wooden forts to consolidate his conquest of England.

The medieval castle. The continental castles were typified by the Normans' motte-and-bailey castles. The motte was a mound surrounded by a ditch and surmounted by a wall and a single large tower, the keep or donjon. The bailey was a forecourt protected by another ditch and wall, its purpose originally being to protect the domestic animals. Entrance to the castle was by way of a retractable drawbridge. The concept of the castle was one of almost totally passive defense, for however difficult it was for the attacker to reach and assault the defenses, located as they were on virtually inaccessible terrain, it was almost as difficult for the defender to debouch rapidly to harass the attacker. Although a new weapon was introduced, the trebuchet, or mangonel, a missile-hurling machine propelled by counterweight rather than tension or torsion, starvation continued to constitute the principal offensive weapon in sieges.

Motte-and-bailey castles

As a result of the Crusades (AD 1095–1291), fortifications in western Europe underwent something of a revolution. The crusaders' encounter with powerful walled Byzantine cities and fortresses with double or triple concentric lines of turreted walls led to a strengthening of castle and city defense. The most impressive single example was the Chateau Gaillard, built by Richard the Lionhearted in Normandy, which actually improved on the eastern prototypes, although the castle's siege and capture by Philip

II (1203–04) proved that an attacker willing to devote sufficient resources and time to the effort might overcome even the most powerful defenses. Yet long campaigns in this era were the exception, since feudal levies could be called to service for only a few weeks each year and mercenary armies were too expensive to maintain indefinitely.

Castles continued to be built well into the 14th century and, growing increasingly elaborate, constituted some of the most efficient fortifications of any age. The later versions were protected by a series of concentric powerful curtain walls fronted by a moat, often a lake. Gate houses were three or four stories tall, surmounted by twin towers. Machicolations (overhanging parapets), portcullises, and loopholes strengthened the defenses. Sometimes the central bailey was large enough to include a town. An example of the later castles is the Bastille in Paris (1370–83).

Mongol field fortifications. Both the art of siegecraft and that of field fortifications were rejuvenated by the Asian Mongols in both their eastern and western conquests (1190–1400). The Mongols employed mammoth siege trains with missile engines and other equipment carried on wagons and pack animals. The main body of Mongol warriors often went on to further conquest while leaving reduction of the fortress to a subordinate force. In field operations the Mongols consistently followed a tactic of defending their centre by entrenchment, employing the troops thus released for strengthening flank operations on the wings of the defended position.

The age of firearms. Although gunpowder weapons appeared at least as early as the mid-14th century, they were at first inaccurate and generally ineffective cannon consisting of small metal pots or tubes. Only after the opening of the 15th century did most European armies and the Turks possess artillery weapons that posed a genuine threat to the existing medieval fortifications. When Henry V's cannon in 1415 began the second half of the Hundred Years' War by battering down the walls of Harfleur, the era of impregnable fortifications can be said to have passed.

Siege warfare. The early gunpowder weapons, tubes of cast or wrought iron, were used almost exclusively for siege operations. Known as bombards, they were moved about on ox-drawn sledges and had to be emplaced on mounds of earth or log platforms. Projectiles were either iron or stone and had no explosive content. They were nevertheless effective, as in the siege of Constantinople in 1453 when Turkish bombards battered down walls that had stood for centuries. The Turkish cannon included 70 heavy pieces, one a 19-ton behemoth firing stone balls up to 1,500 pounds (680 kilograms) in weight for a distance in excess of a mile (1.6 kilometres).

By the mid-15th century so effective was the artillery of Charles VII of France—the best on the Continent—that the French were able to reduce all of the castles of Normandy in one year. Partly because artillery was not yet adaptable to emplacement atop or within fortifications to provide counterbattery fire, but mainly because of the increased power of the cannon, artillery by the close of the century had rendered medieval fortifications obsolete. The use of gunpowder in mining further increased the vulnerability of the castles.

Not until the closing decade of the 15th century, when the French introduced a relatively light cast-bronze cannon on two-wheeled carriages pulled by horses, was artillery to figure prominently in field operations and thus to become an important element in field fortifications. Nevertheless, as early as the Hussite Wars (1419–36) in Bohemia, the Hussite leader, John Ziska, in creating a defense called the *wagenburg,* an adaptation of the laager tactic of the Goths, effectively employed bombards in the intervals between his wagons.

Yet despite these developments, field fortifications were seldom used during the early years of the age of gunpowder. Since cannons were still relatively inaccurate and firearms cumbersome and of short range, most armies in the field relied on the strength of men en masse to repel attack. Important in the defense were bodies of disciplined, heavily armoured pikemen who stood in a variety of close formations, their pikes planted firmly on the ground and slanted toward the attacker. Pikemen of the Swiss army

gained a reputation for solid defense unequalled since the days of the Macedonian phalanx.

The strengthening of permanent fortifications. By the 16th century the revolution in permanent fortifications occasioned by gunpowder was in full swing, as even the most massive medieval fortifications had become vulnerable to heavy siege guns. Some of the greatest figures of the Renaissance contributed to new developments in permanent defenses: Leonardo da Vinci, Michelangelo, and Niccolo Machiavelli, among others. The German artist, Albrecht Dürer, wrote extensively on the theory of fortification.

As new fortifications were constructed, the walls tended to be broad and low, sometimes even sunk below ground level, in order to keep the portion exposed to artillery fire to a minimum. Triangular bastions extended outward from the walls so that defending artillery might sweep all approaches. The usual fort had five or six bastions, leading to the name of star fortress. The main wall was known as the enceinte; the top of it, the parapet; the area behind the parapet, the terreplein. An escarp or forward face of the wall led down to a wide ditch, beyond which stood the counterscarp, a low outwork defended by light artillery and small arms. Earth excavated from the ditch was spread in front of the counterscarp to create a gradually sloping terrace, or glacis, which added to the strength of the counterscarp and absorbed many of the projectiles fired from artillery pieces of limited range and elevation (see Figure 14).

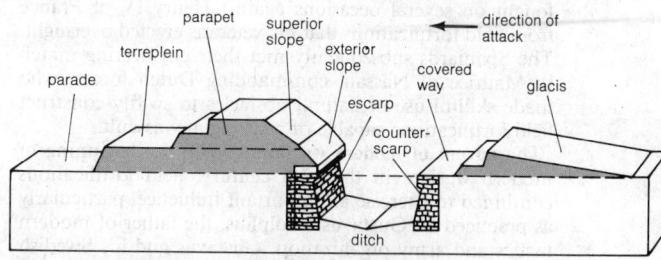

Figure 14: Cross-section of the main wall of a fortress.

As military engineers continued to search for increased defensive strength, the star fortress was replaced by the tenaille trace (see Figure 15A) in which the flanks of the bastions were placed back-to-back between the faces. Yet a certain amount of the ditch still could not be reached by fire from the bastions. This led to development of the bastioned trace (see Figure 15B), its flanks directly opposite each other and linked by curtain walls. In succeeding decades, fortifications employed varied geometric patterns with a wealth of gates, sally ports, redans, coverings and other refinements. Each part of the fortification became

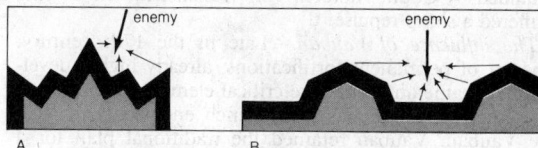

Figure 15: (A) Tenaille trace and (B) bastioned trace.

a separate fort that could be self-sustaining with its own garrison while providing mutual support to the remainder of the units in the system.

These fortresses were constructed either as outposts or citadels in the defense of cities or as barriers along strategic routes. Border towns such as Metz and Verdun in France and Liège, Namur, and Charleroi in Belgium became critically important. Nations sought to control the approaches to their territory while retaining a base or springboard from which to counterattack or to launch a retaliatory invasion. Since the more powerful cannon now became a part of naval armament, port cities had to be protected with fortifications guarding against assault from the sea.

Modification of siege operations. The new methods of fortification having outstripped gunnery developments, long, difficult sieges again ensued. Such old devices as mantelets, galleries, and siege towers were of no use in the face of gunpowder, and even mining was of limited use because the range of artillery dictated that tunnels had

Effect of artillery

Improved fortress designs

to be so long that fresh air could not reach the diggers. The besiegers resorted to digging approach entrenchments. Covered by artillery fire, troops dug trenches in the direction of the fortification's outer works, then threw up earthen walls as protection for their own artillery. The guns were brought up under cover of darkness, and the process was repeated until the attackers were close enough to overwhelm the counterscarp defenders. The process again had to be repeated against the main walls.

Sieges grew longer and more costly. In 1522 the Ottoman Turks besieged Rhodes, the eastern Mediterranean stronghold of the Knights Hospitallers of St. John (a military order formed during the Crusades). Rhodes was one of the earliest of the new bastion fortresses. Although the defenders were greatly outnumbered and cut off from resupply and although the Turks at one point penetrated into the city, so appalled was the Turkish commander at his losses that he withdrew and offered honourable terms for a treaty.

The difficulty of siege operations against the new permanent fortifications and the increased effectiveness of small arms rejuvenated the art of field fortifications. The first to combine the new power of small arms with field works was Gonzalo de Córdoba of Spain. He discerned that a few arquebusiers might utilize entrenchments to cover extensive frontages, thus enabling smaller forces to contain and then outmanoeuvre larger forces. Alexander of Parma (16th-century Spanish commander in the Low Countries) fought on several occasions against Henry IV of France from field fortifications that his veterans erected overnight. The Spaniards subsequently met their engineering match in Maurice of Nassau, commanding Dutch forces, who made skillful use of natural obstacles to swiftly construct field fortifications capable of resisting any assault.

The advent of modern warfare. With the beginning of modern warfare in the 17th century, field fortifications continued to exercise an important influence, particularly as practiced by Gustavus Adolphus, the father of modern tactics and army organization. Gustavus and his Swedish troops constructed outposts defended by redoubts and protected their forts with palisades and entanglements. In the manner of the Romans, the Swedes dug in each night and built a wall around their camp. On the banks of the Elbe, Gustavus' troops, fighting from field fortifications backed by cannons firing at point-blank range, twice repulsed assaults by the army of the Holy Roman Empire under Johann Tserclaes, Graf von Tilly. On the other hand, field fortifications of his enemy led to one of Gustavus' more serious defeats: at Nuremberg Gustavus grew impatient for battle and ordered his forces from their entrenchments to attack the imperial army, now commanded by Count Albrecht von Wallenstein; the Swedes suffered a sharp repulse.

The influence of Vauban. Late in the 17th century, the art of permanent fortifications, already highly developed, became an even more critical element of warfare as the result of the genius of a French engineer, Sébastien de Vauban. Vauban retained the traditional plan for a fortress—inner enclosure, rampart, moat, and outer rampart—but he extended the outworks as far as possible in order to compel the enemy to begin his siege operations at a distance. He also insured that every defensive face was flanked and supported by the works behind and beside it, in the process creating a vast polygon replete with great bastions at every angle interspersed with smaller ones in between, each of which was close enough to the next to provide supporting small-arms fire.

Vauban's new siege technique

Vauban also was a master of siegecraft. Before his time, the usual method was to approach the walls with zigzag trenches, then, with artillery brought forward, to assault from the head of the trench. Since the defenders could concentrate their fire against the head of the trench, this was a costly process. Vauban instead instituted a system of parallel trenches (see Figure 16). Some 600 yards (550 metres) from the fortress—the approximate maximum range of contemporary artillery—his engineers dug a trench parallel to the periphery of the fortress to serve as protection for the infantry while a preliminary artillery duel raged. Thereupon the engineers dug a series of zigzag

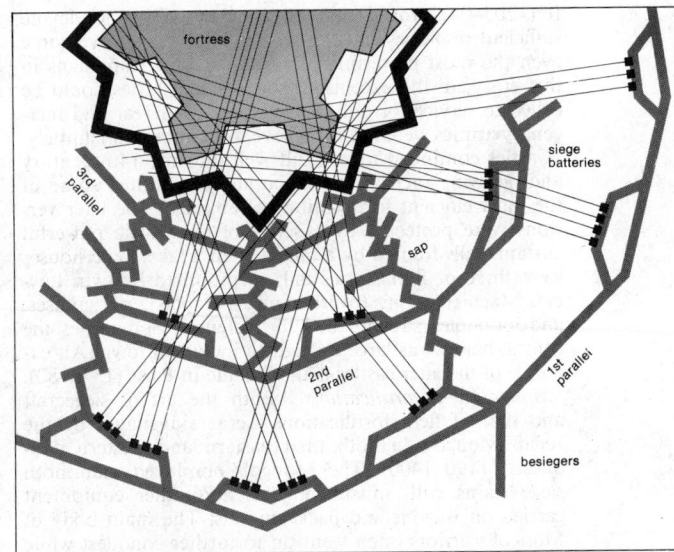

Figure 16: Attack upon a fortress using the Vauban system.

trenches (called saps), culminating in a second parallel about halfway to the wall and within musket range; this served as forward cover for infantry and artillery. The engineers—who gradually acquired the name sappers after the name of the trenches—then dug slowly ahead under cover of wheeled shields called gabions. They dug a final third parallel near the glacis. From that point, with breaching batteries brought forward, the infantry could assault at a number of points simultaneously. Vauban's methods of fortification and siege remained standard until the later 19th century, although such 18th-century commanders as the Duke of Marlborough and Frederick the Great of Prussia came to deplore siege warfare and to circumvent it by disciplined marches designed to manoeuvre the enemy away from the permanent forts and by expert battlefield tactics.

In North America, in the meantime, the frontier fort surrounded by a log palisade had been an integral part of warfare as Europeans pushed their settlements westward. In North America, too, in the Revolutionary War, American soldiers demonstrated again the value of field fortifications: the hasty entrenchment, the waist-high parapet, the cover of a tree or stone hedge. Within a generation American troops under Andrew Jackson at the Battle of New Orleans made effective use of cotton bales to defend their position against advancing British troops.

American improvisations

In the Napoleonic period the outstanding example of field fortifications was the Torres Vedras line, erected by the Duke of Wellington 25 miles (40 kilometres) north of Lisbon (1810): three lines of mutually supporting batteries and redoubts running for 30 miles through a range of low hills between the Tagus River and the sea. The rapid movements of the Napoleonic Wars generally discouraged elaborate defensive works, though Russian field fortifications played a central role in the bitterly fought battle of Borodino (1812).

Increased use of entrenchment. In the American Civil War, field fortifications emerged as an essential of warfare with both armies employing entrenchments to an extent never before seen. Troops learned to fortify newly won positions immediately, employing spades and axes carried in their packs, first digging rifle pits, then expanding them into trenches. Early in the war, Gen. Robert E. Lee adopted the frontier rifleman's breastwork composed of two logs on the parapet of the entrenchment, and many of Lee's victories were the result of his ability to use hasty entrenchments as a base for aggressive employment of fire and manoeuvre. In two notable sieges, that of Vicksburg, Mississippi, in the west, and Petersburg, Virginia, in the east, trench warfare was the accepted method of siege. In the Vicksburg siege, which lasted for almost a year, Union troops tunnelled under the defenses and placed a powder charge timed to explode after they had pulled back. In the Cold Harbor, Virginia, campaign, when Gen. Ulysses S.

Grant sent his troops against Confederate earthworks, he lost 14,000 men in 13 days. Field mines and booby traps were used extensively, and trench mortars were developed to lob shells into opposing trenches.

The defense of Washington

At the start of the war, the United States had few permanent fortifications except on the coast, such as Fort Sumter in Charleston harbour where the first shot was fired, but the Confederate threat to Washington prompted early construction of a defense system around the capital. It included 68 separate forts, a number of blockhouses, and 20 miles (32 kilometres) of connecting trenches. Although never put to a test, the fortifications had a considerable indirect influence on the campaigns in nearby Virginia; in the summer of 1864 they contained Confederate General Jubal Early's threat to Washington.

World War I. The lesson learned in the American Civil War was for a time lost on European commanders. Even the bitter experiences of appalling losses in the Crimean, Franco-German, and Boer wars failed to lessen an ardour for the theory of the offensive that was so fervent as to leave little concern for defensive tactics in the field. Few took notice of the immense casualties the Turks inflicted from behind field fortifications in the Russo-Turkish War of 1877–78, and even though the Russo-Japanese War soon after the turn of the century underscored the lethal power of the machine gun and breech-loading rifled artillery, most European commanders saw the increased firepower as more a boon to the offensive than to the defensive.

The permanent fort. Most defensive thinking was reserved for the permanent fort, which was designed to canalize enemy advance and to afford time for national mobilization. The leading fortification engineer of the time was Henri Brialmont, who was considered a Belgian Vauban. He placed his forts, built of concrete, at an average distance of four miles from a city, as with 12 forts at Liège, and at intervals of approximately 2½ miles (four kilometres). At Antwerp his defense system was even more dense. He protected the big guns of his forts with turrets of steel and developed disappearing cupolas. Some forts were pentagonal, others triangular, with much of the construction underground. In building defenses along the frontier facing Germany, French engineers emulated Brialmont, with particularly strong clusters of fortresses at Verdun and Belfort. So monstrous were the forts of the time that they were known as "land battleships."

By marching through Belgium with a strong right wing (the Schlieffen plan), the Germans circumvented the powerful French fortresses. Passing between the forts at Liège, which Brialmont had intended to be connected with trenches, they took Liège in only three days, then systematically reduced the forts. Namur, also heavily fortified, resisted the powerful German guns for only four days. The concrete of the Belgian fortifications crumbled under the pounding, but the French forts at Verdun, of more recent and sturdier construction, later absorbed tremendous punishment and served as focal points for some of the war's bloodiest fighting.

The trench systems. Despite German success against the Belgian forts, the fallacy of the belief that the new firepower favoured the offensive was soon convincingly demonstrated. Once the French had checked the German right wing at the Marne River, the fighting degenerated into what was in effect a massive siege. For 600 miles (960 kilometres), from Switzerland to the North Sea, the landscape was soon scarred with opposing systems of zigzag, timber-revetted, sandbag-reinforced trenches, fronted by tangles of barbed wire sometimes more than 150 feet (45 metres) deep and featured here and there by covered dugouts providing shelter for troops and horses and by observation posts in log bunkers or concrete turrets. The trench systems consisted of several lines in depth, so that if the first line was penetrated, the assailants were little better off. Rail and motor transport could rush fresh reserves forward to seal off a gap faster than the attackers could continue forward. Out beyond the trenches and the barbed wire was a muddy, virtually impassable desert called no-man's-land, where artillery fire soon eliminated habitation and vegetation alike. The fighting involved masses of men, masses of artillery, and masses of casualties. Toxic gases—asphyxiating, lachrymatory and vesicant—were introduced in a vain effort to break the dominance of the defense, which was so overpowering that for more than two years the opposing lines varied less than 10 miles (16 kilometres) in either direction.

The Hindenburg Line

During the winter of 1916–17, the Germans prepared a reserve trench system, the Hindenburg Line, containing deep dugouts where the men could take cover against artillery fire and machine guns emplaced in concrete shelters called pillboxes. Approximately two miles (3.2 kilometres) behind the forward line was a second position, almost as strong. The Hindenburg Line resisted all Allied assaults in 1917, including a vast British mining operation under the Messines Ridge in Belgium that literally blew up the ridge, inflicting 17,000 casualties at one blow; the advance failed to carry beyond the ridge.

In northern Italy the fighting assumed much the same complexion. Only on the Eastern Front did the vast distances dictate a more open form of warfare but one equally expensive in casualties.

World War II. *The Maginot Line and the West Wall.* In the interval between world wars, several European countries built elaborate permanent fortifications. The largest was the French Maginot Line, named after a minister of defense, a system of mammoth, self-contained forts stretching from Switzerland to the vicinity of the Belgian frontier near Montmédy. The reinforced concrete of the forts was thicker than any heretofore used, the disappearing guns bigger and more heavily armoured. Ditches, embedded steel beams, and minefields guarded against tank attack. A large part of the works were completely underground. Outposts were connected to the main forts by concrete tunnels. But since French and British military leaders were convinced that if war came again with Germany, the Allies would fight in Belgium, the French failed to extend the line to the sea, relying instead on an outmoded system of unconnected fortresses left over from before World War I. It was this weakness that the Germans subsequently exploited in executing a modified version of the Schlieffen plan, cutting in behind the permanent defenses and defeating France without having to come to grips with the Maginot Line.

The Germans confronted that portion of the Maginot Line facing the Saar River with fortifications of their own, the West Wall. Later extended northward to the Dutch frontier and southward along the Rhine to Switzerland, the West Wall was not a thin line of big forts but a deep band, a mile to five miles (eight kilometres) thick, of more than 3,000 small, mutually supporting pillboxes, observation posts, and troop shelters. For passive antitank defense the line depended upon natural obstacles, such as rivers and lakes, and upon "dragon's teeth," five rows of pyramid-shaped reinforced concrete projections.

The Germans did not rely on the West Wall to halt an attack but merely to delay it until counterattacks by mobile reserves could eliminate any penetration. The value of their concept remains undetermined; the line was not attacked until late 1944, after the German armies had incurred severe defeats and lacked adequate reserves. The West Wall nevertheless forced Allied troops into costly attacks to eliminate it.

Other fort series. Elsewhere in World War II many fortifications similar to these two basic types were built. The Italians constructed a series of new fortifications and modernized existing World War I defenses along the country's mountainous northern and northeastern frontiers; the Finns maintained a World War I defense facing the Soviet Union: the Mannerheim Line (named after a Finnish marshal and statesman); the Soviets built the Stalin Line facing Poland; the Czechoslovaks constructed what became known as the Little Maginot Line to oppose Germany; the Greeks built the Metaxas Line facing Bulgaria; and the Belgians erected a series of elaborate forts along the Albert Canal. German capture of the most elaborate and allegedly impregnable of the Belgian forts, Eben Emael, in a matter of hours in the first two days of the campaign against France and the Low Countries in 1940 startled the world. Arriving silently by night in gliders, troops landed atop the fort and began systematically

The capture of Eben Emael

to destroy turrets and casemates. Soon after daylight they were joined by 300 men arriving by parachute. Around noon of May 11 the 1,000-man garrison surrendered.

Despite at least comparable surprise and the same so-called blitzkrieg methods, the Germans required more time to penetrate the more dispersed forts of the Stalin Line in the U.S.S.R. The delay gained two months of invaluable time for the Soviet troops, without which they might well have been unable to stop the Germans at the gates of Moscow.

The other notable Soviet use of permanent fortifications was at Leningrad, where, with a combination of old Baltic forts, field fortifications, water barriers, and ruined buildings, they held out for 900 days—from September 1941 until January 1944—when they finally were relieved. The ordeal of Leningrad constituted one of history's more notable sieges, a defense sustained by incredible fortitude and such exigent methods as a seasonal supply line across the frozen surface of Lake Ladoga. In the historic defense of another city, Stalingrad, the Soviet army made notable use of a new material for field fortifications: rubble of a city's buildings.

In Asia and the Pacific, the most renowned permanent defenses, those of the British at Singapore, revealed an unexpected weakness. Singapore's guns faced the sea, while the Japanese approached the city from the landward side, crossed the narrow channel separating Singapore island from the mainland, and forced a British capitulation. Another famed Far East fortification, the American bastion of Corregidor in Manila Bay, held out for less than a month.

German channel defenses.   The Germans employed Fritz Todt, the engineer who had designed the West Wall, and thousands of impressed labourers to construct permanent fortifications along the Belgian and French coasts facing the English Channel: the Atlantic Wall. The line consisted primarily of pillboxes and gun emplacements embedded in cliffsides or placed on the waterfronts of seaside resorts and ports. Included were massive blockhouses with disappearing guns, newsreels of which the Germans sent out through neutral sources in an effort to awe their adversaries, but the numbers of big blockhouses actually were few. Behind the line, in likely landing spots for gliders and parachutists, the Germans emplaced slanted poles, which the troops called *Rommelsspargel* (Rommel's asparagus), after their commander Field Marshal Erwin Rommel. Embedded in the sand of the beaches below the high-tide mark were numerous obstacles, varying in shape and depth, some topped with mines. Barbed wire and antitank and antipersonnel mines interlaced the whole. On the French southwestern and southern coasts similar, though less formidable, defenses were erected.

The Allies first tested the German fortifications in August of 1942 at the resort town of Dieppe in a raid by a 6,100-man force, primarily Canadians. The result was nearly catastrophic: all but 1,650 of the 5,000 who got ashore were lost.

Despite the example of Dieppe, when the Allies landed in force on the Cotentin Peninsula of Normandy on D-Day—June 6, 1944—they found the defenses far less formidable than they had anticipated. This was attributable to a number of reasons. The Germans had constructed the strongest defenses in the Pas-de-Calais region facing the narrowest part of the English Channel and had stationed their most battleworthy troops there; demands of other fighting fronts had siphoned many of the best German troops from France; the Germans lacked air and naval support; Allied airpower was so strong that movement of German reserves was seriously impeded; landings of Allied airborne troops behind the beaches spread confusion in German ranks; and the Germans were deluded into believing the invasion was a diversion, that a second and larger invasion was to follow in the Pas-de-Calais. Only at one of the two American beaches, given the code name Omaha, was the success of the landing ever in doubt, partly because of rough seas, partly because of the chance presence of an elite German division, and partly because of the presence of high bluffs. Paradoxically, the Allies had less difficulty with the highly publicized beach defenses than they had later with field fortifications based

Beach defenses in Normandy

on the Norman hedgerows, earthen embankments several feet thick and five feet (1.5 metres) high that local farmers through the centuries have erected around thousands of irregularly shaped little fields to fence their cattle and protect their crops from strong ocean winds.

Field fortifications.   Field fortifications were even more extensively employed in World War II than in either the American Civil War or World War I, but they were in general less of the semipermanent trench type than of the individual or two-man position, called a slit trench, rifle pit, or foxhole. There were exceptions: great masses of humanity poured from the threatened cities of the Soviet Union, such as Leningrad, Moscow, and Stalingrad, to dig miles of zig-zag trenches not unlike those on the western front in World War I. In beleaguered footholds, such as the Bataan Peninsula and the Allied beachhead at Anzio in Italy, foxholes and other positions often were connected by communications trenches. The German Todt organization built a series of formidable field positions in the craggy mountainous terrain of Italy, oftentimes hewing them with explosives from solid rock. From the Gustav Line (so named from the symbol for *G* in the German military's phonetic alphabet) behind the Garigliano and Rapido rivers, anchored on the forbidding slopes of Monte Cassino, the Germans held the Allies at bay throughout the entire winter of 1943–44. Some of the defensive positions consisted of prefabricated steel turrets or cupolas placed over excavations. Through the winter of 1944–45 the Germans in northern Italy held a similar position called the Gothic Line, located in the precipitous northern Apennines below Florence.

On the Pacific islands the Japanese proved to be pertinacious masters of defense from field fortifications. Rapidly growing jungle foliage afforded ideal concealment for natural caves and log emplacements, so that Allied troops often incurred severe losses even in locating the Japanese positions. Artillery, mortars, and naval gunfire were helpful in reducing them, but more often than not final reduction was the province of little groups of infantrymen fighting with individual weapons and portable flame throwers. When the Japanese elected to defend the invasion beaches, as on Tarawa, casualties among both attackers and defenders were enormous; indeed, Tarawa was one of the bloodiest division-sized actions of the war. Even when the Japanese chose to forego beach defense, as on Okinawa, they subsequently employed field fortifications and natural obstacles with tremendous skill to prolong the campaign. The final battle, and one of the largest of the war in the Pacific, the conquest of Okinawa, required almost three months of intensive fighting. The last defenders resisted from caves on a coral promontory at the southern end of the island, their defense culminating in a mass suicide that included the commanders. More than 100,000 Japanese died on Okinawa. Another of the more tenacious Japanese defenses was conducted amid the volcanic ash and coral caves of the tiny island of Iwo Jima, later used as a way station for big American planes bombing the Japanese home islands.

The defense of Okinawa

As caves were readily adaptable by the Japanese for defense on Pacific islands, so towns and cities of masonry construction in North Africa and Europe in many cases provided steadfast fighting positions. If cities were defended, the fighting almost always was slow and costly, as in Stalingrad on the eastern front and Aachen in the west. Even when bombing and shelling demolished many of the buildings, the defenders often fought even more tenaciously from the rubble. When some Allied commanders proposed bombing the historic Benedictine abbey atop Monte Cassino in Italy on the theory that the Germans were using it for observation and for troop shelter, others objected not only for cultural considerations but in the belief that the Germans could fight better from rubble than from the intact edifice. It was an anomaly that some earlier permanent fortifications, such as the forts around Metz dating from the mid-19th century and the medieval citadel of Jülich on the Roer River required prolonged and costly attacks to subdue them, for all the power of 20th-century weapons.

Except where sturdy buildings were available—or following a breakthrough resulting in pursuit operations in which enemy riposte was unlikely—combat troops of any army seldom paused for even brief periods without digging hasty field fortifications, either slit trenches or foxholes; and if the possibility of aerial bombardment existed, even troops performing rear-echelon duties had to have some form of protection at hand. In a hasty defensive position, a line of outposts or listening posts was usually established several hundred yards forward of the main line of resistance, while telephone or radio provided ready support from mortars and artillery to the rear. For more prolonged pauses, mines, booby traps, and trip flares were emplaced; barbed wire was strung; foxholes were covered with logs; and trees were felled to blockade roads. In forests, such as the jungles of the Pacific and Southeast Asia or the evergreen forests of northwestern Europe, overhead cover for foxholes was essential to guard against tree bursts of artillery shells, which rained deadly fragments upon the forest floor. A convenient, readily emplaced form of barbed wire was the "concertina," a coil of wire three feet (one metre) in diameter, which could be stretched out in the manner of a concertina to create an effective delaying obstacle.

The foxhole. The foxhole, or variation thereof, constituted the basic field fortification of World War II. It was dug usually with an entrenching tool carried by the individual soldier and was two to five feet (0.6 to 1.5 metres) in diameter, depending upon whether it was to be occupied by one man, two, or three, and at least four feet (1.2 metres) deep. Sometimes it had a firing step and a drainage pit. If concealment was vital, the earth taken from the hole was carted away or dispersed beneath foliage; otherwise it might be used to create a small parapet. Holes for crew-served weapons, such as machine guns and mortars, were appreciably larger. In severe winter weather the troops might use small explosive charges to break through the frozen top crust of earth and enable them to dig. The foxhole—particularly if covered—afforded effective protection against almost any shelling except a direct hit and if dug in firm ground, was effective against the grinding action of tank treads.

The nuclear age. At the close of World War II most military theorists considered that permanent fortifications of the type previously employed were economically impracticable in view of their vulnerability to the incredible power of nuclear explosives and the methods, such as vertical envelopment from the air, that might be employed to reduce them. Field fortifications were another matter, since these are less costly and impose at least some delay on an enemy advance. The foxhole was expected to continue to be the mainstay of field fortifications but with even greater dispersion, both laterally and in depth, than in World War II.

As events developed through and past mid-century, neither strategic nor tactical nuclear weapons were employed, although the threat of their use was often present. Consequently, field fortifications not unlike those of World War II, but with local adjustments, were used.

The Korean War. Fought with weapons and methods little changed from World War II, the Korean War (1950–53) produced little new in fortifications. There were few permanent fortifications on the Korean peninsula, and the foxhole, barbed wire, mines, and other familiar devices comprised the field fortifications. The Chinese Communists often elected to defend the reverse slope of a hill or mountain, keeping only outposts on the forward slope and thus achieving a measure of protection for the bulk of the defenders from direct fire. In later stages of the war, as the fighting sometimes evolved into position warfare in some ways similar to that of World War I, both sides constructed extensive field fortifications across the entire breadth of the peninsula. Aside from sandbag-reinforced and covered foxholes, these included squad huts or bunkers made of heavy timber and covered with earth or sandbags, timber-revetted firing positions for crew-served weapons, and extensive communications trenches. During the long period of truce negotiations, the lines were constantly improved, and in the years of uneasy truce following the armistice, they took on many of the characteristics of permanent

fortifications. A special feature was a tall wire fence across the peninsula running through the so-called demilitarized zone and protected by minefields. Constant roving patrols of each side watched for infiltrators.

The war in Vietnam. In the guerrilla warfare waged in Southeast Asia during the French Indochina War (1945–54) and the Vietnam War, a number of unusual types of field fortifications were employed, yet their origins could be traced to other eras. The *agroville,* for example, a consolidated and fortified hamlet designed to protect the population from guerrilla incursions, in many ways resembled the fortified towns of ancient or medieval times. Similar methods were used by the British in defeating an insurgency in Malaya and by the Filipinos in countering the Huk rebellion in the Philippines. Triangular-shaped forts with walls of dried mud, usually occupied by local militia, and camps in remote regions manned by tribesmen with the help of U.S. Army Special Forces advisers looked much like the primitive forts of ancient times. Both U.S. and South Vietnamese forces constructed fortified base camps with exterior walls of earth topped by occasional sentry towers, in some ways resembling the semipermanent camps set up by Roman legions. The French defensive position at Dien Bien Phu, capture of which precipitated the end of the French Indochina War, had many of the characteristics of field fortifications in other eras: sandbagged and timber-revetted bunkers and firing positions, communications trenches, triangular-shaped bastions, outposts, and redoubts.

The *agroville*

Both U.S. and South Vietnamese forces made extensive use of fire support bases, which were semipermanent entrenchments and bunkers protecting artillery batteries. Along the demilitarized zone separating North and South Vietnam, some bases had concrete emplacements and bunkers. Some of the bases served both for defense against enemy attack and as bases for patrols. The North Vietnamese and the Viet Cong insurgents established base camps in remote areas protected by log bunkers covered with earth and cleverly camouflaged. A good number of the facilities were housed in labyrinthian underground tunnels or in natural caves. The Viet Cong laced the countryside with countless booby traps of various types.

To provide a measure of protection for helicopters and other aircraft from random mortar and rocket attacks, the Americans built earth or concrete revetments several feet thick and four to five feet high on aircraft parking aprons alongside runways. Chemical defoliants were used to clear fields of fire around bases, destroy food crops in Viet Cong controlled areas, and eliminate concealed ambush positions along roads and waterways. To prevent the enemy from reoccupying base camps in jungle areas, special bulldozers called "Rome plows" levelled hundreds of acres of forest.

Other modern fortifications. Meanwhile, in the Arab-Israeli confrontations, semipermanent forts similar to the French position at Dien Bien Phu were built along the frontiers. Often Israeli farms and settlements had to be protected with field fortifications against incursions by Palestinian guerrillas.

An unusual fortification was the Berlin Wall constructed by the Communist East German government through the heart of Berlin, not to keep intruders out but to prevent citizens from fleeing to West Germany. Long lines of barbed wire protected by minefields and sentry posts ran along the western boundaries of East Germany, Czechoslovakia, and Hungary for the same purpose.

The Berlin Wall

No nation has in recent years constructed permanent linear fortifications such as those used in World War II. The pillboxes of the West Wall have been demolished or abandoned, and though most of the elaborate forts of the Maginot Line still exist, their utility in future conflicts is problematical, though they might provide some protection to troops and supplies against nuclear explosions.

Most permanent fortifications of the nuclear age have been designed as headquarters sites or command and control installations or are in some way related to antiaircraft and antimissile defense. A joint U.S.-Canadian project, the North American Air Defense Command (Norad), includes a series of radar posts across northern Canada and

Alaska to provide early warning of the approach of hostile bombers or missiles. The system and the aircraft and missiles supporting it are controlled from a vast underground complex embedded in rock of Cheyenne Mountain near Colorado Springs, Colo. Giant Spartan and Minuteman missiles are housed underground in "silos" with thick concrete walls. Soviet SS-9 ballistic missiles presumably are similarly protected.   (W.H.B./C.B.MacD.)

BODY ARMOUR

Body armour refers to any body covering designed for protection in combat. From very early times, armour for the fighting man and his horse was improved steadily to counteract improvements in weapons and, to some extent, tactics. For the greater part of its history only excavated fragments survive; the main evidence is found in art, where its interpretation is often difficult and subject to argument. Development was at first slow, but in Europe, between the 13th and 17th century, improvement of blade-making techniques and the introduction of more efficient missile weapons helped accelerate the development of plate armour. In the 16th and 17th centuries, improved firearms forced armourers to increase the thickness and, therefore, the weight of their product, until finally plate armour was largely abandoned in favour of increased mobility. However, armour never entirely disappeared among European cavalry, surviving in the form of a hat lining or helmet, a cuirass for the body, and high boots, until modern times. Elsewhere it survived until the introduction of firearms.

The large number of head wounds caused by overhead shell bursts during World War I led to the adoption of steel helmets by all combatant nations. Renewed interest in experiments with various types of body armour began at the time of the American Civil War, and such armour was used on a limited scale by both sides in both world wars. Continuing experiments now aim at development of body armour that is bulletproof yet sufficiently light and flexible for the infantryman to wear in action.

Types of armour materials.   Armour falls into three main groups, depending on its construction: leather or fabric, sometimes of several thicknesses, sometimes reinforced by quilting with some material such as cotton; mail, consisting of interlocking iron or steel rings; and rigid armour of metal, whalebone, ivory, horn, bark, wood, plastic, or *cuir-bouilli* (leather hardened by boiling in wax). The last group can be further divided according to the methods of connecting the pieces: (1) small overlapping plates attached outside a leather or fabric garment (scale) or attached inside the garment (brigandine); (2) lamellar, which consists of small overlapping plates held together by laces; (3) small plates held together by mail or let into mail garments; (4) large plates, usually of metal, linked by loosely closed rivets and by internal leathers to allow the wearer maximum freedom of movement.

Leather armour.   Armour of hide is probably the oldest of all types, and in its simplest form is indistinguishable from ordinary clothing. Coats made of five to seven layers of rhinoceros skin were worn in China in the 11th century BC, and an apparently similar armour of ox hide was used by the Mongols in the 13th century AD. North American Indians, such as the Shoshoni, wore jackets of several layers of hide glued or sewn together and also had leather horse armour. The jaguar skin jackets of Aztec chiefs seem to have been part of their regalia and not defensive. Coats made of stout buff leather were first worn under European plate armour in the 16th century. The leather sleeves and skirts, retained after plate arms were abandoned, were sufficiently sturdy to deflect a sword cut, and buff leather was used for the cuffs of cavalry gauntlets until the 19th century. Leather has also been used widely as a base for other defenses, such as the boars' tusk helmets of Mycenae and a much later jacket covered with modern coins found in Alaska.

Fabric armour.   Early evidence of fabric armour is rare since fabric rarely survives on archaeological sites. A fragment consisting of 14 layers of linen was found in a Mycenaean grave of the 16th century BC, and there are

Cuir-bouilli

Figure 17: (Left) "Coat of a Thousand Nails," reinforced with steel plates, from Rājput, India, 18th–19th century. In the Wallace Collection, London. (Centre) Mail shirt, from Sinigaglia, near Bologna, Italy, first half of the 14th century. In the Royal Scottish Museum, Edinburgh. (Right) Japanese armour, the cuirass and shoulder guards of lamellar construction, c. 1800. In the Armouries, Tower of London.

occasional literary references throughout antiquity. The Assyrians of Xerxes are said to have had linen armour, and the Greek heavy infantry of the 5th–4th centuries BC wore a linen cuirass in preference to bronze, probably to increase their mobility. Throughout the Middle Ages quilted coats (aketons) were worn either alone or under mail or plate to prevent chafing. Silk quilted armour was experimentally introduced in England in the 17th century. In northern India quilted coats, sometimes with helmets and trousers to match, were worn until the 19th century and were usually velvet covered and studded with small gilt nails, with some steel plates let into their surface (see Figure 17, left). Quilted coats and helmets were also worn in China and Korea. The short jackets, with or without sleeves, illustrated in Central American art, may be the quilted armour reported by the conquistadores. Horse armour of quilting has been used in many areas, from England in the 13th century to Nigeria in the 20th. Particularly elaborate rope armours made from coir, a coarse fibre obtained from coconut husks, were worn until the 19th century in the Gilbert and Ellice Islands. Fabric armour is used today in, for example, the U.S. Navy's four-pound, synthetic-felt combined life jacket and armoured vest.

Mail. The place and date of the origin of mail is at present unknown, but pieces have been found on a site near Kiev dating from the 5th century BC. Surviving examples are of iron or steel wire, occasionally with brass rings around the edges or, in Oriental mail, forming an all-over pattern. Mail is flexible and relatively impervious to slashing strokes when worn over quilting, although a thrusting weapon can

The mail shirt

force the rings apart in spite of their rivetted closure. In the form of a simple shirt, mail was worn throughout the Roman Empire and beyond most of its frontiers (see Figure 17, centre). It formed the main armour of western Europe until the 14th century, with leg harnesses of mail appearing in the 11th century, mail hoods added during the 11th–13th century, and long sleeves ending in mail gloves added during the later period of its use. The mail shirt and aketon were worn in India and Persia until the 19th century, and in the Sudan and Nigeria until modern times. After the development of complete plate armour in Europe, mail gussets were laced to the arming clothes to close the gaps in the plates. A curtain of mail was often attached to the lower edge of the conical helmet, acting as a throat and neck protection, on the 14th-century European basnet and also on many Oriental helmets, particularly Indo-Persian. Sleeves of mail were used by light troops in the 16th century, and mail shoulder straps were adopted by light cavalry in the 19th century. The Japanese used mail to a limited extent from the 14th century AD, but the Japanese rings were arranged in a variety of ways, producing a more open construction than found in Europe.

Scale armour. Although usually of metal, scale armour has been made of horn, bone, and leather and from the scales of such naturally armoured animals as the pangolin. The small plates usually have a curved or pointed lower edge overlapping a joint in the next row. The area of distribution of scale armour differs slightly from that of lamellar. Scales have been found on an Egyptian site of the 17th century BC. It is found throughout the Middle East; in the classical Greek area including southern Russia; in the Roman Empire; and in all of Europe, particularly in the 10th–12th centuries AD, but occasionally as parts of an armour until the 15th century; and in eastern Europe in the 17th century. It was worn in India and China until the early 19th century and was readopted at that time by European heavy cavalry for use as shoulder defenses.

Brigandine. The origin of brigandine is at present unknown. Although studs are shown on a garment represented in art, there is no proof of the presence of plates within the garment. Brigandine apparently was in use in the 8th century AD in China and later in Korea; in both places it was worn until the 19th century. From the 18th century some Chinese brigandines are purely ceremonial, made with rivets but without plates. A number of cuirasses made up of many plates originally rivetted to a cloth cover have been excavated on European sites of the 14th century, and apparently similar garments occur in European paintings from about 1240. These remained the most common

form of body armour until about 1400, after about 1360 usually with a one-piece breastplate also under the cover. Short brigandine coats remained popular for European light troops until about 1600, particularly in a less costly version—the jack—with its plates simply tied in. Brigandine construction was also used for other parts of the armour, including gauntlets and thigh defenses. Fifteenth-century Persian and later Mughal miniatures show what are probably brigandine coats.

The construction of most modern bulletproof jackets is based on the principle of the brigandine or jack. Small overlapping plates of alloy steel line a waistcoat and a groin protection. The plates are not rivetted but are contained in pockets within a vest of synthetic fibre or snapped into a plastic framework. Metal is now being replaced by such synthetics as fibreglass or boron carbide, making the garment less cumbersome and more bullet resistant.

Bulletproof jackets

Lamellar armour. Lamellar armour consists of strips made up of numerous narrow plates with their long axes vertical, each overlapping its neighbour. The strips usually overlap upward. This armour is more flexible than scale and cheaper to manufacture than mail. Although illustrated in Egyptian paintings of the 15th century BC, lamellar probably originated in Persia and was carried to western Europe by the Avars and to the Far East by other nomads. It was usually made up into a shirt, sometimes with capelike sleeves or, in the East, with a separate bolero to which the sleeves were attached. Lamellar was worn in Persia until the 16th century, during its later use with plate forearm and shin defenses. The construction reached China and Korea by the 1st century AD, passing to Japan in the 5th century and achieving its greatest elaboration in the colourfully laced and lacquered armours of the Japanese Heian period (794–1185). Lamellar remained in use in Japan (see Figure 17, right) until armour was abolished in 1867 and was still employed in Tibet, for man and horse, early in the present century. Although it is illustrated in Mughal miniatures, no actual example of lamellar has been found south of the Himalayas. The simple cuirasses of wooden slats and rods laced together worn by North American Indians before the introduction of firearms probably derive from the bone and ivory lamellar armours of Siberia and Alaska.

Plate and mail armour. Small plates linked by mail or let into mail garments first appeared in Persia and Turkey in the 15th century AD in the form of hoops around the body with smaller overlapping plates in the arms and skirts. Sixteenth-century Russian and Turkish armours of that construction had a large circular breastplate let into the mail and narrow vertical rows of small plates at the back. Full armours of this type, including helmets and trousers, were used in northern India in the 17th–19th centuries. Horse armours, and even elephant armours, were made in the same way. Similar armour worn by the Moros of the Philippines, made with brass mail and plates of either brass or horn, probably derived from contacts with the Arabs, although their helmets were based on European models.

Ancient and medieval armour. A complete bronze armour, consisting of a cuirass, a deep skirt of overlapping hoops, broad shoulder defenses, and short greaves to protect the lower leg, was found in a Mycenaean grave of about 1450 BC. As the disappearance of the war chariot necessitated lighter equipment, Greek armourers of the 7th–5th centuries BC produced a combination worn by the Greek foot soldier: cuirass, long greaves sprung onto the shins, and a deep helmet—all of bronze. The large, round shield of bull's hide, sometimes faced with bronze, had both a handgrip and a forearm brace. Later bronze cuirasses, modelled closely on the muscles of the torso, extended down over the stomach, a type also worn by Roman commanders, and possibly at Byzantium, and revived for parade use in the Renaissance.

The corselet of the Roman legionary, worn between the end of the 1st century AD and the beginning of the 3rd century, consisted of a cylindrical cuirass made up of some seven horizontal hoops of steel, with openings at the front and back, where they were laced together. The cuirass was buckled or hooked to a throat piece flanked by several half-hoops protecting the shoulder. The individual plates were

Roman steel armour

linked internally by articulating leathers, as on all later plate armour, allowing free movement.

Apart from helmets, armour of large plates was probably unknown in western Europe during the Dark Ages, but in the late 12th century references occur to the cuirie, a leather body armour reinforced with plates. During the 13th and 14th centuries the entire body and limbs were gradually enclosed in plate, although the body armour itself, until 1400, was usually of brigandine, sometimes having a steel breastplate fixed over it. The complete steel body armour, with no cover and consisting of breast, back, and a hooped skirt opening down the side, appeared about 1400. The design of the armour was perfected during the 15th and 16th centuries, with added reinforcement, and adapted for a variety of combats. By the 16th century a good-quality armour would normally have had a number of pieces of exchange to adapt it for use in the field or tournament, mounted or on foot (see Figure 18). Wealthy nobles and

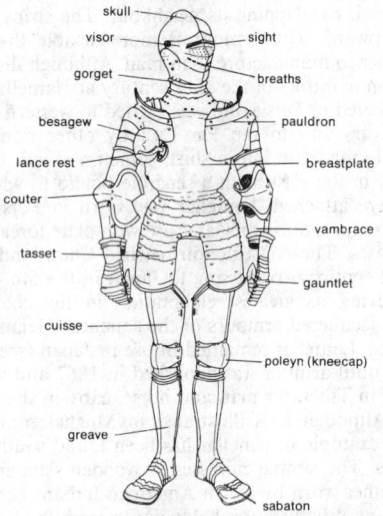

Figure 18: Complete armour, South German, about 1510.

princes had great series of armours, decorated to match, for use in a variety of combinations. The major European manufacturing centres were in iron-producing areas—Milan, Brescia, Innsbruck, Augsburg, Nürnberg, and Landshut. Besides finely etched and gilded armours for the aristocracy, large numbers of uniform armours were turned out to equip the specialized regiments that developed during the 16th century. Most courts employed a small group of armourers to supply armour for their own immediate needs and to be presented as diplomatic gifts. Although full armour still appears in portraits of commanders in the 18th century, all but the cuirass and helmet had actually been discarded by about 1650.

Plate armour, consisting of forearm defenses and four large plates around the thorax, was worn in Persia and India until the 19th century, usually over a mail shirt. There was an increasing use of plate in Japan, sometimes disguised as lamellar, from the 15th century.

The head, the most vulnerable area, has been protected by plate since early times. The basic form of most helmets is a conical or hemispherical bowl, sometimes extended downward to protect the base of the skull, as shown in Sumerian monuments of about 3000 BC. This type, with or without a neck guard, cheek or ear pieces, with or without a mail or scale curtain to protect the throat and neck, is found in almost all periods and areas. The bowl was sometimes made up of several plates rivetted or laced together, a form carried to extremes in Japan, where a bowl sometimes consisted of as many as 62 segments. Occasionally, as in Persia, Turkey, and Russia in the 16th century, the helmet reached an acute apex. In Turkey, in the 15th century, a peak was added over the eyes with a movable nasal or nosepiece. The prestige of the Turkish armies made this form widely popular in Europe until about 1650. The movable nasal was also adopted in Persia and India. The European helm of the 13th–14th centuries developed from the uniting of the

neck guard with a nasal that had gradually spread to cover all of the face but the eyes. The helm never completely ousted the basic bowl forms, which from about 1300 were often fitted with a movable visor. Close helmets, made by hinging or pivoting plates to the bowl, completely enclosing the head and turning with it, appeared in western Europe about 1410, remaining in use until about 1650. Light troops continued to wear openfaced helmets, usually peaked or brimmed, until the late 17th century. From the second half of the 15th century the bowl of European helmets was strengthened by a fore and aft comb, increasing in height until about 1600.   (A.V.B.N.)

The visored helm

Modern armour.   Toward the end of the 17th century, armour increased in weight in order to remain effective against musket fire. At the same time, however, new strategy and tactics called for greater infantry mobility, and armour fell into general disuse and was not widely used again until World War I.

The increased use of high-explosive artillery shells in World War I resulted in a high proportion of wounds caused by shell fragments. Steel helmets were designed and, after the first year of war, were worn by all troops. Torso armour of both fibre and steel was issued to troops for special purposes but was generally too heavy for full acceptance. In World War II, casualties from shell fragments rose to 80 percent; and, with 70 percent of all wounds affecting the torso, it became highly desirable to produce a suitable body armour. Armour for bomber crews and ground troops was developed of steel, aluminum, and resin-bonded fibre-glass plates, as well as of heavy nylon cloth.

The flak vests developed for fliers and the anti-fragment vests used by soldiers and marines during World War II and in the Korean War contained plates made of either manganese steel or a bonded fibreglass called Doron. By 1951 some armies and navies were using semiflexible vests made of basket-weave nylon and plates. These vests gave adequate protection against fragments from bursting mortar, artillery, or anti-aircraft shells but would not stop an armour-piercing bullet, although titanium plates introduced in 1967 gave improved protection against smaller fragments and fléchettes.

In the Vietnam War, low-flying aircraft and hovering helicopters made tempting targets for small-arms ground fire, and better protection for pilots and aircrew was suddenly needed. The principle of compound armour was again called upon in designing armoured vests, using hard-faced, tough-backed composites that could shatter the armour-piercing bullet on impact and then absorb the fragments. The two types developed in the early 1960s were dual-hardness steel and ceramic-plastic composites.

The dual-hardness composite-steel armour gave about 50 percent greater ballistic protection than an equal weight of aluminum armour and showed a greater capacity to absorb multiple hits than the ceramic armours. It consisted of a very hard front face, bonded metallurgically to a tougher crack-preventing rear face. The plates were then usually roll-bonded to the specified thickness, fabricated, and then hardened by quenching and tempering.

Heavy personal armour could be intolerable for some applications, such as a navy pilot in a small high-performance jet, a sailor on river patrol, or a marine in combat. The ceramic-plastic composite armour was designed to provide lightweight protection for such men against armour-piercing projectiles.   (Ed.)

ARMOURED VEHICLES

Tanks are the principal type of tracked military armoured vehicle. Essentially mobile platforms for direct-fire weapons, they make the weapons mounted in them more effective by virtue of their cross-country mobility and the protection that they provide for their crews. Tank weapons have ranged from a single machine gun of small calibre to present-day combinations of one or more machine guns with a large gun of 75- to 152-millimetre (2.95- to 6-inch) calibre. A few experimental tanks have been armed with even larger guns, and some tanks are now supplied with guided missiles.

Other major tracked armoured vehicles include: personnel carriers, originally conceived only for transporting infantrymen into battle, but since also used for fighting, although they are less powerfully armed than tanks; self-propelled guns, which are sometimes unarmoured and wheeled; armoured cars, which often resemble the lighter reconnaissance types of tanks but run on wheels; and other specialized vehicles, including armoured recovery vehicles, bridgelayers, and armoured bulldozers, all of which are principally intended to assist tanks, and amphibious armoured vehicles that are used for assault landing operations.

Earliest developments. Ideas for armoured fighting vehicles may be traced as far back as the 2nd millennium BC, when horse-drawn war chariots were used in the Middle East by the Egyptians, Hittites, and others as mobile platforms for fighting with bows and arrows. Other concepts, including protection of armoured vehicles, can be traced back through wheeled siege towers and battering rams in the Middle Ages to similar devices used by the Assyrians in the 9th century BC. More recent forms of the protected vehicle idea may be found in battle cars proposed in 1335 by Guido da Vigevano, by Leonardo da Vinci in 1484, and by others down to J. Cowan, who secured a patent in England in 1855 for a wheeled, armoured vehicle based on the steam tractor.

It was only at the beginning of this century, however, that armoured vehicles began to take practical form. By then, the essential mechanical elements had been developed. In particular, the traction engine and the motor car became available for military application. The first self-propelled armoured vehicle was produced in 1900 in England when John Fowler & Company armoured one of their steam traction engines for hauling supplies in the South African War of 1899–1902. The first use of the motor car as a gun carrier was in 1899, in England, when a Maxim machine gun was mounted on a powered four-wheeled vehicle with a bicycle seat and handle bar steering (quadricycle). The inevitable next step was a vehicle that was both armed and armoured. Such a vehicle was constructed and exhibited in London in 1902. In the latter part of 1899 a machine-gun-armed motor car was built in the United States and in 1902 a partially armoured machine-gun car was exhibited in Paris by the Société Charron, Girardot et Voigt, which two years later developed a fully armoured car with a turret. By 1904 a turreted armoured car was also built in Austria by the Austro-Daimler Company.

To complete the evolution of the basic elements of the modern armoured vehicle, it remained only to adopt tracks as an alternative to wheels, and this became inevitable with the appearance of the tracked agricultural tractor. There was no incentive for this development, however, until after the outbreak of World War I.

Proposals for tracked armoured vehicles failed to arouse the interest of military authorities. Suggestions for an armoured tracked gun made in 1903 in France and five years later in Britain were both denied consideration. Similarly, a design for a tracked armoured vehicle put forward in 1911 was rejected, in turn, by both the Austro-Hungarian and German general staffs, and in 1912 the British War Office turned down still another design.

World War I. The outbreak of World War I in 1914 radically changed the situation. Its opening stages of mobile warfare accelerated the development of armoured cars, numbers of which were quickly improvised in Belgium, France, and Britain. Trench warfare, which ended the usefulness of armoured cars, brought forth new proposals for tracked armoured vehicles. Most of these resulted from attempts to make armoured cars capable of moving off the roads, over broken ground, and through barbed wire. The first tracked armoured vehicle was improvised in July 1915, in Britain, by mounting an armoured car body on a Killen-Strait tractor. The vehicle was constructed by the Armoured Car Division of the Royal Naval Air Service, whose ideas, backed by the First Lord of the Admiralty, Winston S. Churchill, resulted in the formation of an Admiralty Landships Committee. A series of experiments by this committee led in September 1915 to the construction of the first tank, called "Little Willie." A second model, or "Big Willie," quickly followed; it was designed to cross wide trenches. "Big Willie" was accepted by the British Army, which ordered 100 tanks of this type in February 1916.

Simultaneously but independently, tanks were also being developed in France. Like the very first British tank, the first French tank (the Schneider) amounted to an armoured box on a tractor chassis; 400 were ordered in February 1916. But French tanks were not used until April 1917, whereas British tanks were first sent into action on September 15, 1916. Only 49 were available and their success was limited. On November 20, 1917, however, 474 British tanks were concentrated at Cambrai and achieved a spectacular breakthrough. These tanks, however, were too slow (four miles [6.4 kilometres] per hour) and had too short a range (20–40 miles [32–64 kilometres]) to exploit the breakthrough. In consequence, demand grew for a lighter, faster type of tank, and in 1918 the 14-ton (12,700-kilogram) Medium A appeared with a speed of eight miles per hour and a range of 80 miles. After 1918, however, the most widely used tank was the French Renault F.T., a light and slow 6-ton vehicle designed for close infantry support (see Figure 19, right).

When World War I ended in 1918, France had produced 3,870 tanks, and Britain 2,636. Most French tanks survived into the postwar period; these were the Renault F.T., much more serviceable than their heavier British counterparts. Moreover, the Renault F.T. fitted well with

First self-propelled armoured vehicle

First tracked armoured vehicle

By courtesy of the Imperial War Museum, London; photographs, Camera Press

Figure 19: *Tanks of World War I.*
(Left) British Mark I tank with anti-bomb roof and "tail," 1916. (Right) French Renault F.T. light tank, 1918.

traditional ideas about the primacy of the infantry; the French Army adopted the doctrine that tanks are a mere auxiliary to infantry. France's lead was followed in most other countries; the U.S. and Italy both assigned tanks to infantry support and copied the Renault F.T. The U.S. copy was the M1917 light tank, and the Italian the Fiat 3000. The only other country to produce tanks by the end of the war was Germany, which built about 20.

Interwar developments. The Renault F.T. remained the most numerous tank in the world into the early '30s. Aware of the need for more powerful vehicles, if only for leading infantry assaults, the French Army took the lead in developing well-armed tanks. The original 1918 French Schneider and St. Chamond tanks already had 75-millimetre (2.95-inch) guns while the heavier British tanks were at best armed with 57-mm (2.24-inch) guns. After the war the French built 10 68-ton (61,700-kilogram) 2C tanks with the first turret-mounted 75-mm guns and continued to develop 75-mm-gun tanks, notably the 30-ton Char *B* of 1936.

In the meantime, Britain took the lead, technically and tactically, in developing the mobility of tanks. Even before World War I had ended, work had started on the Medium D with a maximum speed of 20 mph (32 kilometres per hour). The British Army ordered 160 of the new Vickers Medium tanks between 1923 and 1928. They were virtually the only tanks the British Army had until the early '30s and the only tanks to be produced in quantity anywhere in the world during the mid-'20s. Capable of 20 mph, the Vickers Mediums stimulated the Royal Tank Corps to develop mobile tactics. Various experiments during the '20s and early '30s resulted in general adoption of two separate categories of tanks. Mobile tanks were intended for the role performed earlier by horse cavalry. Slower but more heavily armoured tanks provided infantry support.

Before this division into mobile and slow tanks had crystallized, several different designs were tried. The British Independent tank of 1925 with five turrets started a trend toward many turrets among heavy tanks. Another trend Tankettes setter was a small turretless tankette originated in Britain by Maj. G. le Q. Martel and J. Carden in the mid-'20s, and a slightly heavier, turreted two-man light tank. The number of light tanks and tankettes grew rapidly after 1929, as several countries started to produce armoured vehicles. The Soviet Union was by far the most important producer; on a much smaller scale Poland, Czechoslovakia, and Japan entered the field in 1930–31. Concurrently, tank production started up again in France and Italy. As tank production grew and spread among nations, the value of tankettes and light tanks armed only with machine guns decreased and heavier models armed with 37- to 47-mm (1.46- to 1.85-inch) guns for fighting other tanks began to displace them. An early example was the Vickers-Armstrongs 6-ton model of 1930, copied on a large scale in the Soviet Union (as the T-26). The most successful example was the BT, also built in large numbers in the Soviet Union. Fastest tank of its day, the BT was based on the designs evolved in the U.S. by J.W. Christie, who in 1928 built an experimental model capable of 42.5 mph (68 kilometres per hour). Christie's vehicles could run on wheels after the removal of tracks, and, far more significant, had road wheels independently suspended. This feature enabled them to move over broken ground faster than tanks with the usual arrangement of wheels.

Although they were relatively well armed and mobile, tanks of the T-26 and BT type were underarmoured (plates 10 to 15 millimetres [0.4 to 0.6 inch] thick) and were not, therefore, suitable for close infantry support. This was clearly demonstrated in 1937 during the Civil War in Spain where T-26 and BT tanks were used by the Communist forces. Even before this time, it had become clear that tanks that moved at the slow pace of the infantry and were therefore exposed to the full effect of anti-tank guns had to be thickly armoured. This realization led, in the mid-'30s, to such infantry tanks as the French R-35 with 40-mm and the British A.11 with up to 60-mm (2.4-inch) armour.

Apart from being lightly armoured, the Soviet BT, the equivalent British cruiser tanks, and the German Pz. III also required support from more heavily armed tanks if they were to engage in fighting of any intensity. The need for more powerful 75-mm (2.95-inch) gun tanks was clearly recognized in Germany, leading to 1934 design of the Pz. IV. The problem was realized less clearly in the Soviet Union, even though the T-28 and T-35 multiturret tanks with 76-mm guns were first built there in 1932–33. But the Russians recognized more quickly than others the need for the next step, which was to replace all the light-medium tanks armed with 37- to 47-mm (1.46- to 1.85-inch) guns by medium tanks armed with 75- or 76-mm guns. Thus, in 1939, while the Germans were still developing the Pz. III from a 37-mm to a 50-mm (1.97-inch) gun version, the Russians were already concentrating on the T-34 medium tank with a 76-mm gun.

In Britain even 40-mm (1.57-inch) gun tanks were scarce on the eve of World War II, and all but 80 of the 1,148 British tanks produced between 1930 and 1939 were still armed only with machine guns. Italy was even worse off, with only 70 M/11 tanks with 37-mm guns while the rest of its total of 1,500 were L/3 tankettes. Except for a few experimental models, the U.S. had only about 300 machine-gun-armed light tanks. Most of the 2,000 tanks produced in Japan were equally lightly armed. By comparison, France had a more powerful tank force—2,677 modern tanks, of which, however, only 172 were the Char *B,* armed with 75-mm guns. The largest force was the U.S.S.R.'s, which, as a result of a massive production program started 1930–31, had about 20,000 tanks by 1939, considerably more than the rest of the world put together.

World War II. The most effective tank force proved to be the German, composed in 1939 of 3,195 vehicles, including 211 Pz. IV's. What made the German tanks so formidable was that instead of being divided between various infantry and cavalry tank units they were all concentrated in the panzer divisions. The successes of the panzer   German divisions during the first two years of World War II led   panzer the major armies to reorganize most of their tanks into   divisions similar formations; this resulted in a dramatic increase in production, as shown in the following table:

Tank Production During World War II

year	country				
	Germany	Britain	U.S.	U.S.S.R.	Japan
1939	249	969	...	...	462
1940	1,460	1,399	331	2,794	1,023
1941	3,256	4,841	4,052	6,590	1,024
1942	4,278	8,611	24,997	24,668	1,165
1943	5,966	7,476	29,497	20,000	776
1944	9,161	...	17,565	17,000	342

The campaigns of 1940 and 1941 in which armoured forces played such an important role also intensified development of tanks and other armoured vehicles. The German Pz. IV and Soviet T-34 were rearmed in 1942 with longer barrelled, higher velocity guns; soon afterward, these began to be displaced by more powerfully armed tanks. In 1943 the Germans introduced the Panther medium tank with a long 75-mm gun having a muzzle velocity of 3,070 feet per second (ft/sec; 936 metres per second) compared with 1,260 ft/sec for the original Pz. IV and 2,460 ft/sec for its 1942 version (see Figure 20, left). The 43-ton Panther weighed almost twice as much as its predecessor and was correspondingly better armoured. Germany also introduced the still more powerful Tiger tank, armed with an 88-mm (3.46-inch) gun. Its final version (Tiger II), at 68 tons, was to be the heaviest tank used during World War II. To oppose it, the Russians brought out the JS, or Stalin, heavy tank that appeared in 1944 armed with a 122-mm (4.8-inch) gun. Its muzzle velocity was lower than that of the German 88-mm guns, however, and it weighed only 46 tons (41,700 kilograms). At about the same time the T-34 was rearmed with an 85-mm gun.

In contrast to the breakthrough role of the earlier heavy tanks, the Tiger and JS tanks functioned chiefly to support basic medium tanks by destroying enemy tanks at long range. German and Soviet armies also developed other heavy vehicles for this purpose, such as the 128-mm-gun

Figure 20: *Tanks of World War II.*
(Left) German Pz. IV (foreground) and Pz. III (background) tanks, 1942. (Right) U.S. Army M26
Pershing tank with 90-millimetre gun (foreground) and M4 Sherman tank with 76-millimetre
gun.

By courtesy of (right) the U.S. Army; photograph, (left) Ullstein

Jagdtiger and the 122-mm-gun ISU, which, in effect, were turretless tanks. In addition, all armies developed lightly armoured self-propelled antitank guns and the U.S. Army developed a specialized category of tank destroyers, which resembled self-propelled guns in being relatively lightly armoured but, like tanks, had rotating turrets.

Turretless tank

The turretless tank type of vehicle originated with the Sturmgeschutz or assault gun introduced in 1940 by the German Army for infantry support but subsequently transformed into more versatile vehicles particularly suited for destroying enemy tanks. No such vehicles were produced in Britain or the U.S. To the end of World War II, however, the British Army retained a specialized category of infantry tanks, such as the Churchill, and of cruiser tanks, such as the Crusader and Cromwell. The former were well armoured, and the latter were fast, but none was well armed compared to German and Soviet tanks. As a result, during 1943 and 1944, British armoured divisions were mostly equipped with U.S.-built M4 Sherman medium tanks (see Figure 20, right). The M4 was preceded by the mechanically similar M3 medium, also armed with a medium-velocity 75-mm gun, but mounted in the hull instead of the turret, because this could be put into production more quickly when tanks were urgently required in 1940 and 1941. Production of the M4 began in 1942 (it replaced the stopgap M3); eventually 49,234 were built, making it the principal tank of U.S. and other allied armoured forces. Successful when first introduced, it was, by 1944, no longer adequately armed and should have been replaced by a new medium tank. Several factors kept it in production, including a contemporary obsession with numbers inspired by the usual overestimates of enemy strength. Furthermore, the U.S. Army, like the British, believed the fallacious doctrine that armoured divisions should confine themselves to exploitation of infantry breakthroughs and did not, therefore, need powerfully armed tanks. Only toward the end of the war did the U.S. Army introduce a few M26 Pershing heavy tanks with a 90-mm (3.54-inch) gun comparable to that of the original German Tiger. Similarly, the British Army introduced the prototypes of the Centurion tank with a 76-mm gun comparable to that of the German Panther. Otherwise, U.S. and British tanks were well behind the German and Soviet tanks in their gun power.

Tanks in the nuclear age

Modern tank design. After World War II it was generally recognized that all tanks must be well-armed to fight enemy tanks. This finally ended the division of tanks into undergunned categories of specialized infantry and cavalry tanks, which the British Army retained longer than any other. Still not fully recognized were the advantages of concentrating tanks in fully mechanized formations; the British and U.S. armies continued to divide tanks between the armoured divisions and the less mobile infantry divisions. After World War II, tanks also suffered from one of the periodic waves of pessimism about their future. New antitank weapons, such as rocket launchers and recoilless rifles, and the mistaken belief that the value

of tanks lay primarily in their armour protection caused this attitude. The Soviet Army, however, maintained large armoured forces; the threat they posed to western Europe as the Cold War became more intense, together with the havoc created by Soviet-built T-34/85 tanks during the invasion of South Korea in 1950, provided a new impetus to development.

Development of tactical nuclear weapons in the mid-'50s changed the situation again. These new weapons dictated employment of mobile forces capable of dispersed operation in small self-contained units that could make up for the low troop density on the battlefield by their mobility and weapon power and that could better evade destruction by keeping the situation fluid. Nuclear weapons consequently encouraged the use of armoured forces because of their cross-country mobility and relatively high ratio of weapon to manpower. Moreover, tanks and other armoured vehicles, by virtue of the protection that they provide against blast and radioactivity, can operate fairly close to nuclear explosions and can cross areas that have been subjected to nuclear strikes without undue risk to their crews. Armoured units survive enemy nuclear weapons better and can better exploit the devastating effects of nuclear strikes. Thus tanks and other armoured vehicles have become even more important with the advent of tactical nuclear weapons.

The British Centurion. The most significant feature of tank development since World War II has been the emphasis placed on armament. Progress in this field is best illustrated by the British Centurion, which started in 1945 with a 76-mm gun but in 1948 was rearmed with an 83.4-mm (3.28-inch), 20-pounder gun firing newly developed, tungsten-carbide-cored, armour-piercing ammunition with a muzzle velocity of 4,800 ft/sec (1,465 metres per second). As a result, the 83.4-mm gun could penetrate armour almost twice as thick as that which the most powerful 88-mm gun of the German Tiger penetrated. In 1959 the Centurion was again upgunned, this time with a 105-mm (4.13-inch) weapon.

As a result of its outstanding performance the Centurion was adopted not only by Britain and major Commonwealth countries but also by Sweden, Switzerland, and later Israel; it was also delivered under the U.S. military aid program during the 1950s to The Netherlands and Denmark, the total exported from Britain amounting to more than 2,500. In the meantime the British Army had developed an even more powerful tank, the Conqueror, which was armed with a 120-mm (4.72-inch) gun firing armour-piercing ammunition, introduced in 1954 as a heavy gun tank to support the Centurions. Unfortunately its thick armour gave the Conqueror a weight of 65 tons (59,000 kilograms) in contrast to the Centurion's 50 tons; when the Centurions were rearmed with the longer ranged 105-mm guns, the Conqueror was withdrawn from service (1958).

Adoption of the British Centurion

Soviet tanks. At about the same time the Soviet Army also began to withdraw some of its heavy tanks, the JS-3,

Figure 21: *Tanks and armoured vehicles since World War II.*
(Top) U.S. Army M132 armoured personnel carriers, mounted with flame throwers. (Left)
Soviet T-62 tanks armed with 115-millimetre guns. (Right) British Chieftain tank with
120-millimetre gun.

By courtesy of (top) the U.S. Army, (right) Central Office of Information, London, Crown copyright reserved; photograph, (left) Tass—Sovfoto

and later the T-10, both armed with 122-mm guns. The basic Soviet tank for many years after World War II was the T-34/85, of which 11,778 had been produced in 1944. It was finally replaced by the T-54, which evolved from the T-34/85 through the T-44 but had a 100-mm (3.94-inch) gun in a much better profiled turret, a crew of four instead of five, a transversely mounted engine, and other improvements.

Introduced about 1953, the T-54 became during the late '50s the standard tank of the Communist bloc, manufactured not only in the U.S.S.R. but also in Poland and Czechoslovakia. A copy of the T-54 was also produced in China, which exported some to Pakistan in 1966 while the U.S.S.R. supplied more than 2,000 to Egypt, Syria, Iraq, and Algeria after 1955 and exported some to Finland, Afghanistan, and Cuba. In 1963, however, the T-54 and its improved version, the T-55, began to be replaced in the Soviet Army by the current T-62 (see Figure 21, left). The T-62, externally similar to the T-54, has a much more powerful, high-velocity 115-mm (4.53-inch) gun; it represents concentration on a single type of battle tank as well-armed as contemporary technology will allow.

U.S. tanks. At first the U.S. Army also subscribed to a policy of developing heavy as well as medium tanks. Formulated in 1946, this policy led to the design of the 90-mm- (3.54-inch-) gun T42 medium and the 120-mm- (4.72-inch-) gun T43 heavy tanks. Designated as the M103, a few T43s were built, between 1951 and 1954, mainly for the U.S. Marine Corps. Meanwhile the T42 was supplanted in 1948 by the M46 medium tank. This was basically the earlier M26 heavy tank with a new 810 horsepower air-cooled engine and cross-drive transmission. After the conflict in Korea in 1950, the turret of the T42, which for the first time incorporated a stereoscopic range finder, was mounted on the hull of the M46 to produce the M47 medium. This, in turn, was succeeded in 1952 by the M48, which was similar to the M47 except for a ballistically superior turret and hull and a four-man instead of five-man crew.

The M48 became virtually the only battle tank of the U.S. Army during the late '50s, while the M46 and M47 tanks were transferred to the French and Italian armies. More M47 tanks were later supplied to Belgium, West Germany, Greece, Spain, Turkey, and several other countries, followed still later by deliveries of the M48, which was being replaced in the U.S. Army by the 47-ton M60. The M60 was essentially the M48 with an air-cooled diesel in place of the gasoline engine and a British-designed 105-mm (4.13-inch) gun instead of the 90-mm gun of the earlier American tanks.

The 105-mm British tank gun was also adopted for the Swiss Pz. 61, the first tank ever produced in Switzerland. One of its characteristics is its relatively light weight of 36.5 tons (33,100 kilograms). However, an even lighter tank, the 34.5-ton Type 61, was produced in Japan, the first after the demilitarization of 1945; it was armed with the same 90-mm gun as the U.S. M48.

France and Germany. After World War II the French Army started developing a single battle tank, the AMX-50, armed at first with a 100-mm (3.94-inch) gun and then a 120-mm gun. After building a number of prototypes, however, the French concluded that the disadvantages of such heavy, 50-ton (45,400-kilogram) tanks outweighed their advantages and developed instead a lighter battle tank, the AMX-30. This 36-ton tank is armed with a French-designed 105-mm gun, which fires an unusual type of armour-piercing projectile with a shaped charge mounted in ball bearings to prevent spinning and thereby retain its performance. The AMX-30, first produced in 1966, was originally designed to a specification agreed to in 1957 by France, Germany, and Italy. Italy subsequently withdrew from the agreement, however, and adopted the U.S. M60, some of which have since been built in Italy. France and Germany, on the other hand, adopted their own alternative designs, the German being the Leopard. The first prototypes of the Leopard were built in 1961, the first tanks built in Germany since 1945. The first of 1,845 Leopards ordered by the German Army were built in 1965; subsequently Leopards were ordered by the Belgian, Norwegian, and Dutch armies to replace their earlier U.S. or British tanks. The Leopard is armed with a British 105-mm tank gun and in spite of being four tons heavier than the AMX-30 it has the same high power-to-weight ratio of 20 horsepower per ton due to its 830-hp diesel.

Chieftain. A tank having the same main armament and general characteristics as the Leopard was developed at about the same time in Britain by the Vickers Company but for the Indian and not the British Army. Called the Vijayanta, production began in 1966 in India, where no tank had been built before. But in contrast to the Leopard, as well as the AMX-30, Pz. 61, and the U.S. M47, M48, and M60, the Vickers Vijayanta does not have an optical range finder. Instead it has a 0.5-inch (13-mm) ranging machine gun, in addition to the usual rifle-calibre coaxial machine gun. The ranging-machine-gun system was originally introduced on the upgunned 105-mm Centurions and adopted in the later British Chieftain. The Chieftain (Figure 21, right), which first came into service in 1966, is armed with a high-velocity 120-mm (4.72-inch) gun and weighs 51 tons (46,300 kilograms). In the early '70s it was the most heavily armed and armoured battle tank in service anywhere in the world. It also embodies several novel features, including a supine position for the driver to lower the height of the hull, a two-stroke, opposed-piston diesel engine and, recently, a laser range finder.

Sweden's S-tank. The most original design is, however, the Swedish S-tank, developed since 1956 and adopted by the Swedish Army in 1964. This turretless vehicle has its 105-mm (4.13-inch) gun fixed to the hull so that the gun can only be elevated by altering the pitch of the hull. This is accomplished by means of an adjustable hydropneumatic suspension. To turn the gun in a different direction, the crew must turn the entire tank. Elimination of the turret and the fixed gun mounting considerably reduced the silhouette of the S-tank and facilitated installation of a loading mechanism, which made it possible to reduce the size of the crew from four to three. The consequent reduction in tank size has kept the weight down to 36.5 tons (33,100 kilograms) without sacrificing armour.

The S-tank also has an original engine installation consisting of a diesel and a gas turbine coupled to a common output shaft. All other battle tanks since the U.S. M48 and the British Centurion and an increasing number of lighter armoured vehicles are powered by diesel, rather than gasoline engines, because of their greater overall efficiency and range.

MBT-70. Another significant departure from general practice is represented by the U.S. M60A1E1 and M60A1E2 tanks, which have a 152-mm (5.98-inch) gun-launcher. The gun-launcher fires Shillelagh guided missiles as well as conventional projectiles but its barrel is too short to fire high-velocity armour-piercing shots; this reduces its flexibility in attacking enemy tanks. This shortcoming has been corrected in a more recent version of the 152-mm gun-launcher, which can fire armour-piercing ammunition as well as high explosive shells and missiles and which was mounted in the MBT-70. Development of the MBT-70 was started by the U.S. and Germany in 1963; in addition to the 152-mm gun-launcher it incorporated several advanced features, including a 1,475 hp diesel, which gave a power-to-weight ratio of almost 30 hp per ton, and an adjustable hydropneumatic suspension instead of the customary torsion-bar suspension. The MBT-70 was also provided with an automatic loader, which reduced its crew to three men. For the first time the crew was concentrated

in the turret, which became an environmental control capsule protecting from radiological, chemical, and biological effects. Location of the driver in the turret alongside instead of below other crew members reduced the height of the MBT-70. This necessitated, however, a counter-rotating cupola for the driver to keep him pointed forward irrespective of the rotation of the turret, thus complicating the driving controls. All the sophistication incorporated in the MBT-70 made it very expensive. Production cost per tank was estimated in 1969 at $750,000 to $850,000, compared with $200,000 to $250,000 for the M60, Leopard, and Chieftain. As a result, Germany withdrew from its joint development in 1970 and the U.S. Army in 1972 abandoned its more austere XM803 version.

The most controversial feature of the MBT-70/XM803 was its gun-launcher. Its Shillelagh missiles gave it an advantage over enemy tanks at long ranges where tank guns are rather inaccurate, but they were highly questionable on cost-effectiveness grounds at the usual tank combat ranges of less than 2,000 metres (2,200 yards), since one missile costs about $3,000, or the equivalent of 20 armour-piercing rounds. The gun-launcher is also a compromise between the requirements of gun and missile systems; it necessitates an overlarge gun to accommodate the large diameter missile and at the same time it prevents the missiles being launched without the vehicle exposing itself. Consequently, at an early stage the Germans wanted to rearm the MBT-70 with a 120-mm (4.72-inch) gun and favoured the development of special vehicles to fire missiles only. These are exemplified by the Jagdpanzer Rakete, a tank destroyer armed with SS-11 or HOT missiles.

Airborne and amphibious vehicles. In 1941, the U.S. Army commenced development of the T9, the first air-transportable light tank. The first tanks actually flown into battle, however, were British Tetrarchs, a few of which were landed by glider in Normandy on D-Day in 1944. After 1946, the French Army built the AMX-13, a 14.3-ton (13,000-kilogram) air-transportable vehicle (75-mm [2.95-inch] gun), used chiefly as a tank destroyer and reconnaissance vehicle. Less successful was the M41 76-mm-gun light tank, constructed in 1950 by the U.S. Army. At 22.8 tons (20,700 kilograms), this vehicle proved too heavy for contemporary transport aircraft. The latest U.S. light tank is the M551 Sheridan, equipped with a 152-mm (5.98-inch) gun-launcher.

The Sheridan was designed to meet two military needs, that of reconnaissance for a highly mobile vehicle, and that of airborne operations for a light but effective self-propelled weapon. Usually these two requirements have been met by separate vehicles. Thus the Soviet Army has the ASU-85, an 85-mm (3.35-inch) turretless assault gun, for its airborne forces, and the PT-76 amphibious light tank for its reconnaissance units. The development of amphibious tanks dates back to the Medium D of 1919. Though all amphibious tanks have sacrificed armament for light weight and have been bulky to achieve sufficient buoyancy, the overall mobility of tanks such as the PT-76 made them effective reconnaissance vehicles.

Since the middle of World War II many other tanks have been made amphibious by collapsible flotation screens, which, when erected, allow even relatively heavy tanks to float. This method was first used with M4 medium tanks during the D-Day landings in Normandy in 1944. More recently, flotation screens have been permanently installed on the S-tank, the Vickers Vijayanta, the M551 Sheridan, and the Scorpion light reconnaissance tank introduced in 1969 by the British Army.

An alternative method to crossing rivers is "submerged fording," first tried in 1940 with the British A.9 cruiser and the German Pz. III and IV. Since World War II, provision for submerged fording has been built into several tanks including the Soviet T-54 and T-62 and the Leopard and the AMX-30.

An entirely different problem is posed by amphibious landings from the open seas; to solve it the U.S. Marine Corps developed the Landing Vehicle Tracked, or LVT. Originally built in 1941 as an unarmoured cargo carrier, the LVT quickly acquired armour. Two types evolved: an armoured amphibious personnel and cargo carrier, and

The
German
Leopard

Crew
protection

Landing
Vehicle
Tracked

a turreted amphibious gun-vehicle for close fire support during landing operations. Altogether 18,620 LVTS were built during World War II; these played a prominent role in the Pacific campaigns from Guadalcanal onward. After World War II, LVTS were successfully used in Korea, notably for the 1950 Inchon landing. Two new models were built between 1951 and 1957: a 39-ton (35,400-kilogram) LVTP5 amphibious carrier, capable of carrying as many as 37 men, and an LVTH6 armed with a turret-mounted 105-mm howitzer. Both are still in service but a new LVTPX12 was developed during the late '60s to replace them. It incorporates several improvements, the most important being a boatlike hull with a stern instead of bow loading ramp and two water-jet propulsion units that greatly improve its performance in comparison with that of the earlier LVTS (propelled in water as well as on land by means of their tracks). At the same time the LVTPX12 has retained the seagoing qualities of the earlier LVTS, which could negotiate rough seas and Pacific surf in contrast to other amphibious vehicles intended primarily for crossing inland water obstacles. The use of water jet propulsion units in the LVTPX12, however, has been preceded by their use in several amphibious reconnaissance vehicles, including the Soviet PT-76.

Self-propelled guns. Development of self-propelled guns has also continued since World War II, except for self-propelled antitank guns. These became largely superfluous when it was recognized that all tanks needed to be sufficiently well armed to fight enemy tanks. Turretless assault guns, much favoured during World War II by the German and Soviet armies, have also largely disappeared except for a few specialized models such as the Soviet ASU-85 and the 90-mm-gun Jagdpanzer Kanone of the German Army. The general trend among the remaining self-propelled guns has been either toward lightly but completely armoured models with guns mounted in turrets with all-round traverse, like most tanks, or toward partially armoured models that are essentially tracked chassis with guns mounted on top. Examples of completely armoured guns are the 155-mm (6.1-inch) M109 self-propelled howitzer used by the U.S. and several west European armies, and the British 105-mm (4.13-inch) Abbot self-propelled gun. Partially armoured models include the U.S.-built M107 175-mm (6.89-inch) gun, the M110 8-inch howitzer, and the French 155-mm howitzer on the AMX-13 chassis. Though the Soviet Army has not produced either type of self-propelled gun, continuing to rely on tractor-towed guns, it has developed several armoured self-propelled launchers for its tactical missiles that make use of PT-76 and IS tank chassis.

Armoured personnel carriers. Since World War II armoured personnel carriers have become the next most important armoured vehicle after battle tanks. Though a few experimental models were built in Britain at the end of World War I, development of armoured carriers did not really begin until they were adopted for the panzer division infantry at the beginning of World War II. Germany's example was quickly followed by the U.S. which, by the end of the war, had produced 41,000 carriers. Both the German and U.S. carriers of World War II were of the half-track type and provided only light protection; nevertheless, they represented a major advance on the earlier method of transporting infantry into battle in unarmoured trucks. Moreover, the panzer grenadiers used them effectively as combat vehicles and fought from them on the move, thus greatly increasing the mobility of the infantry on the battlefield.

After World War II the U.S. Army led in developing fully tracked carriers with all-round protection (see Figure 21, top). The first postwar carrier was the M44 armoured utility vehicle of 1945. Though unduly large, this vehicle demonstrated the advantages of its type. Next came the M75, first built in 1948. Essentially a scaled-down M44 with a similar box body, it carried 12 instead of 27 men. Adopted in 1953, the M75 became the first tracked armoured personnel carrier used in quantity. The war in Korea, in which a few M75s successfully carried infantry under fire, added impetus to armoured personnel carrier development. When the 1955 tactical nuclear weapons

The M75 in Korea

tests in Nevada demonstrated that armoured carriers permitted infantry to operate relatively close to nuclear explosions, armoured carriers were demanded for infantry as well as armoured divisions.

By 1955 the M59 began to replace the M75. Though similar, the newer M59 was less expensive and able to swim across calm inland waters. In 1960 the M59 was supplanted by the current M113, lower and considerably lighter due partly to the contemporary development of aluminum armour. The M113 was in fact the first aluminum-armoured vehicle to be put into large-scale production. Since its appearance an increasing number of the lighter vehicles have been built using aluminum armour, including the M109 155-mm self-propelled howitzer, M551 Sheridan, LVTPX12, Scorpion, and the Fox armoured car. Battle tanks, however, have continued to use steel armour, which is more effective against large-calibre armour-piercing projectiles and does not have to be as thick as equivalent aluminum armour.

Aluminum armour

As well as being lighter, the M113 was also less expensive than its predecessors, costing only $22,000, a significant factor in its large-scale adoption, first by the U.S. Army and then by several other armies. By 1970 about 40,000 M113 carriers had been produced, making the type the most numerous armoured vehicle outside the Soviet bloc. M113 carriers were used on a large scale in the war in Vietnam, often as combat vehicles, though they were not designed for the role and were at a disadvantage in spite of the addition of roof-mounted machine guns with shields. The shortcomings of the M113 stem from the original U.S. Army doctrine that infantry must dismount from carriers to close with the enemy. As a result the M113 and the earlier U.S. carriers were designed as transport rather than fighting vehicles.

The first attempt to produce a tracked armoured carrier from which the infantry could fight on the move was made by the French Army. The AMX-VTT production began in 1958; from within, its occupants could fire their own hand weapons and a machine gun mounted in a turret. A further step forward was taken when the German Army ordered the HS-30 carrier for its panzer grenadiers. This offered better protection and had a turret with a 20-mm (0.79-inch) automatic cannon, which enabled it to fight other light armoured vehicles.

By the mid-'60s the need to replace the original type of carrier by what came to be known as the mechanized infantry combat vehicle, or MICV, was generally recognized and the U.S. Army developed its first vehicle of this type. The experimental XM701 had a 20-mm gun turret and provision for its occupants to fire their own weapons from within. A basically similar vehicle, the Marder, was adopted by the German Army.

Like the British, the Soviet Army originally relied mainly on wheeled armoured carriers. The early BTR-152s were little more than armoured six-wheeled trucks but the more recent BTR-60P is a much more advanced amphibious vehicle with eight-wheel drive and a water jet-propulsion unit. The first Soviet tracked carrier, the BTR-50P, introduced around 1955, was little more than the PT-76 tank without its turret; but in 1967 the Soviet Army revealed a much more advanced tracked amphibious armoured personnel carrier or mechanized infantry combat vehicle. This has a turret with a medium-calibre gun and a machine gun and is also fitted with antitank guided missiles. In consequence it represents a versatile fighting unit, which, in some circumstances, could rival tanks as the basic armoured vehicle. (R.M.O.)

Naval ships and craft

The first craft fitted purposely to make war were undoubtedly conversions of the dugouts, inflatable bladders, papyrus rafts, or hide boats used in everyday transport. It is probable that the conversion at first consisted simply of a concentration of weapons in the hands of a raiding party. In time conversions added offensive and defensive powers to the craft itself.

As vessels became more seaworthy and more numerous, warships designed as such developed both as marauders and as defenses against marauders. In succeeding millennia the warship went through many changes, some with revolutionary impact upon civilization. Though many ships are designed for a warlike purpose, the practice of converting peaceful ships to wartime uses has also survived. Any major war demands far more fighting ships than a nation can economically maintain during peace, and, even in World Wars I and II, merchant ships as large as passenger liners were converted into cruisers. The first craft designed and built especially for combat may have sailed in the fleets of Crete and Egypt 5,000 years ago. The word craft, it may be noted, has come increasingly to be applied to smaller vessels, with the term ship reserved for larger ones.

THE ANCIENT WORLD

First warships

Near East. *Egypt.* The first recorded appearance of warships is on the Nile, where Egypt's history has centered since antiquity. Built of bundles of reeds lashed together to form a narrow, sharp-ended hull and coated with pitch, these were hardly suited for tempestuous seas; by 3000 BC larger wooden seagoing versions of the reed craft sailed for distant cruising, trade, and conquest.

Hieroglyphics recount the dispatch of 40 armed ships to Byblos on the Phoenician coast about 2900 BC to buy cedarwood (from the famous cedars of Lebanon) to build ships. These vessels had both oars and sails, being fitted with a bipod (inverted V) mast and a single, large, square sail. The whole mast could be lowered when under oars. Large Egyptian ships had over 20 oars to a side, with two or more steering oars. The war galley was built to the same pattern but was of stouter construction; modifications that could be easily incorporated in a merchant hull under construction included elevated decks fore and aft for archers and spearmen; in later Egyptian warships, a wider sail that could be furled; in the 12th century BC, planks fitted to the gunwales to protect the rowers, and a small fighting top high on the mast to accommodate several archers; and on some galleys a projecting ram, well above the waterline, which may have been designed to crash through the gunwale of a foe, ride up on deck, and swamp or capsize him.

Crete. By about 2000 BC Crete had evolved into a naval power exercising effective control of the sea in the eastern Mediterranean. Little record exists of Minoan seapower, yet these maritime people are known to have had an organized navy that cooperated with Egypt in suppressing piracy. They may also have been the first to build a warship designed as such from the keel up, rather than as a modification of a merchant ship. Sometime before their sudden and mysterious overthrow by the Mycenaeans from the Greek mainland in the 15th century BC, the Minoans began to differentiate between war craft and merchantmen and between the rowing galley and sailing vessel.

Sometime in this 2nd millennium BC, the commodious merchantman evolved as a beamy "round ship" powered by sails and emphasizing cargo capacity at the expense of speed. Fast fighting craft developed both as predator on and protector of maritime trade and coastal cities. This "long ship" was narrower, faster, and more agile than the tubby cargo ship. She hoisted her sails for cruising but depended on oars when in action.

The Cretan warship

The Cretan warship had a single mast and a single bank of oars. The sharply pointed or "beaked" bows suggest an emphasis on the tactical use of the ram. Relatively little else is known about the fighting craft, but the lack of defensive walls around Cretan cities may testify to the navy's effectiveness.

Phoenicia. Beginning about 1100 BC, the Phoenicians dominated the eastern Mediterranean for about three centuries and sailed beyond the Pillars of Hercules into the Atlantic. Information about Phoenician ships is fragmentary and somewhat inconclusive, though they appear to have been built primarily for trading, with a capacity to fight effectively if necessary. What little is known about their vessels comes from highly stereotyped representations.

These indicate that the Phoenician trading ships were galleys, mounting a single pole mast with a square sail and with steering oars to port and starboard. The war galleys show a Cretan influence: low in the bow, high in the stern, and with a heavy pointed ram at or below the waterline. Both these and the trading galleys are depicted as two-banked. The rowers of the upper bank may have sat on thwarts mounted on sponsons—*i.e.,* long platforms projecting outward above the waterline. This would have meant a narrow underwater hull with a high length to beam ratio, resulting in a slender and graceful vessel. Oars could be carried in a staggered, two-bank arrangement, allowing more oars to be mounted in a ship of a given length and increasing power and momentum.

Because the ram was the principal weapon, both the finer lines and greater rowing power were important in providing more speed for the decisive shock of battle. Coins of Sidon and Assyrian sculptures show the staggered-bank oar arrangement that the Phoenicians probably introduced.

Greece. Unlike the Egyptians, for whom wood was scarce and costly, the Aegean peoples had an abundance of timber for shipbuilding. Their earliest warships may have been large dugouts, perhaps 65 feet (20 metres) long, fitted with outriggers (timber frames built out from either side of the hull) for stability.

Tactically, they and their successors for centuries were used more to carry attack personnel than as fighting vessels. No mention is made in the *Iliad,* for instance, of sea warfare. Even the pirates of the time were sea raiders seeking their booty ashore, like the later Vikings, rather than in sea actions. The so-called long pentaconter, mentioned by Herodotus, was employed in exploring, raiding, and communicating with outlying colonies. Light and fast, with 25 oars to a side, it even more than the "round-built" merchant ship, played an important role in the early spread of Grecian influence throughout the Mediterranean. As the Greek maritime city-states sped the growth of commerce and thus the need for protection at sea, there evolved a galley built primarily for fighting. The first galleys, called uniremes (Latin *remus,* "oar"), mounted their oars in a single bank and were undecked or only partially decked. They were fast and graceful with high, curving stem and stern. In Homeric times some carried an *embolon*—a beak or ram—that became standard in succeeding centuries.

Biremes and triremes. The bireme, probably adopted from the Phoenicians, followed and became the leading warship of the 8th century BC. Greek biremes were probably about 80 feet (24 metres) long with a maximum beam around 10 feet (three metres). Within two or three generations the first triremes (ships with three banks of oars) appeared. This type gradually took over as the primary warship, particularly after the great sea victory of Salamis (480 BC).

The first triremes

Like its predecessors, the trireme mounted a single mast with a broad, rectangular sail that could be furled. The mast was lowered and stowed when rowing into the wind or in battle. Built on an entirely different system from the Egyptians—with keel, frames, and planking—these were truly seagoing warships.

The arrangement of oars has fed a scholarly controversy for generations. Two principal theories survive. One holds that there were, in fact, banks of benches for oarsmen—two for the bireme, three for the trireme—and that oarsmen of upper rows sat on thwarts slightly forward of the corresponding rower below. The other school argues that the thwarts ran at an angle obliquely from the galley's centre line. For a trireme, two oarsmen sat alongside each other on an upper thwart extending outward into a sponson with their oars projecting through ports in the sponson itself. The third oarsman in the group sat on a lower thwart with his oar projecting through a port in the hull.

After Salamis, the trireme continued as the backbone of the Greek fleet, with the ram continuing as the primary weapon. Its keel, like those of its predecessors, formed the principal-strength member, running the length of the ship and curving upward at each end. The ram, usually shod in bronze, formed a forward prolongation that gained effectiveness from the heavy keel back of it. Additional longitudinal strength came from a storming bridge—*i.e.,* a gangway along the centre line from bow to stern along which the crew raced to board when a foe was rammed. Gradually, with ships becoming steadily heavier, boarding assumed greater importance and the ram lost some of its importance. Many war galleys also had full spar decks instead of the centre-line gangway.

A trireme of the 5th century BC may have had a length of 125 feet, a beam of 20 feet, and draft of three feet (about 38 by six by one metres). Her great length required extra longitudinal strength, which was provided by wales (belts) around the outside of the hull. Manned by about 200 officers, seamen, and oarsmen (perhaps 85 on a side), with a small band of heavily armed *epibatai* (marines), she could reach seven knots under oars and was a formidable foe.

Rowers in the ancient world, into early Roman times, were free crewmen rather than slaves. The captain of a Greek trireme was usually a wealthy man, a political appointee, who could afford to fit out and operate the warship for a year. The navigator was an experienced seaman.

With only scant room for provisions, such warships could not remain long at sea. A voyage usually consisted of short hops from island to island or headland to headland. Even the largest triremes put into shore and beached, stern first, for the night, resuming the passage in the morning, weather permitting. Light construction and little endurance made short distances between bases essential and frequent refits imperative.

Early Greek naval battle tactics were rudimentary. The basic tactical disposition was simply two opposing battle lines of galleys drawn up on line abreast, each trying to overwhelm the other by ramming and boarding. By the 5th century BC, however, skilled fleet commanders dared to essay the manoeuvre of "breaking through the line," or turning the foe's flank. Breaking through the enemy's battle line consisted of a sudden thrust at the centre of the opposing fleet. Piercing it, the attackers would then wheel to right and left behind the gap to take the rest of the line in the rear. For success, the manoeuvre required speed, surprise, and great coordination that only much training could achieve.

Later developments. Athens employed quadriremes (four-bank rating) by the middle of the 4th century BC, with quinqueremes appearing soon thereafter. In the late 4th and early 3rd century BC an arms race developed in the eastern Mediterranean, producing even larger multi-banked ships. Macedonia's rulers built 18-banked craft requiring crews of 1,800 men. Ptolemaic Egypt capped them with 20's and 30's. Ptolemy III even laid down a 40 (tesseraconter) with a design length of over 400 feet (122 metres) and calling for a crew of 4,000 rowers. The vessel was never actually used. The multiplicity of "banks," once a puzzle to historians, signifies the number of rowers on each oar rather than an almost unimaginable piling up of banks. While representations of biremes and triremes with staggered oars exist, nothing portrays any further superimposition of oars. The ratings were of "man-power" propulsion banks, similar to modern horsepower ratings.

This same arms race brought other changes of significance. Until the late 4th century BC, manoeuvre, marines, and the ram constituted a warship's offensive strength. Archers provided close-in fire, though perhaps not to the same extent as in the early Egyptian navy, in which the bow was favoured. Demetrius I Poliorcetes of Macedonia is credited with introducing heavy missile weapons on ships, at the end of the century, starting a trend that still has not ended.

Demetrius' ships mounted crossbow-like catapults for hurling heavy darts, and stone-throwing machines of the type the Romans later called ballistae. From this time on large warships carried these weapons enabling them to engage a foe at "standoff" ranges, though ramming and boarding also continued. Temporary wooden turrets—forecastles and sterncastles—were similarly fitted to provide elevated platforms for archers and slingers.

Following the fragmentation of the brief empire of Alexander the Great, sea power developed elsewhere. The city-state of Rhodes built a small but competent fleet to protect its vital shipping. Rhodian warships were reported to have made use, in at least one action, of firepots suspended on spars projecting from their bows, anticipating Greek fire by several centuries.

Meanwhile to the west, Carthage, a state with ancient maritime origins, rose to prominence on the north coast of Africa, and by about 300 BC had become the foremost Mediterranean naval power. Carthage's navy consisted probably of the same ram-galley types developed by its ancestral Phoenicians and by the Greeks.

Rome. Coincidentally, across the sea to the north the city-state of Rome expanded to include most of the southern Italian peninsula with its extensive seacoast and maritime heritage. Rome's growth southward collided with Carthage's ambitions in Sicily, leading to the First Punic War, which began in 264 BC. Unlike their seafaring opponents, the Romans were not a naval power. When in the fourth year of the war Carthage sent a fleet against Sicily, Rome realized her fatal disadvantage and moved to remedy it. The Greek city-states she had conquered had long seagoing experience. Employing their shipbuilders and learning also from the foe, Rome built a fleet of triremes and quinqueremes, the latter patterned after a Carthaginian warship that ran aground in Roman territory early in the war. While galleys were being built, oarsmen trained on dummy rowing benches ashore (an early ancestor of the training devices of modern navies). The first Roman battle fleet with effective crews soon put to sea.

Not content with copying the enemy's tactics, the Romans took land warfare to sea and forced the Carthaginians to fight on Roman terms. Each Roman galley had fitted in the bow a hinged gangplank with a grappling spike or hook (the *corvus*) in the forward end, thus providing a boarding ramp. They added to the crews many more marines than warships usually carried.

The Phoenicians and Greeks had emphasized ramming, with boarding as a secondary tactic. A Roman captain rammed and then dropped the gangplank. Ram and *corvus* locked the galleys together, and the Roman marines boarded, overwhelming the opponent. The Roman fleet had extraordinary success in the great naval battle of Mylae off northeast Sicily, destroying or capturing 44 ships and 10,000 men.

After other victories, and some defeats, by the end of the First Punic War, 241 BC, Rome had become the leading sea-power. A generation later, in 218 BC, Rome again engaged in war with Carthage. The genius of Hannibal almost overwhelmed Rome and probably would have had Carthage put forth major effort at sea and supported him in Italy. When the war ended in 201 BC, Carthage surrendered its navy and was never again to become a maritime power.

At the end of the Second Punic War Rome began a long effort to subdue the pirates of the eastern Mediterranean. After several generations of intermittent operations, in 67 BC Pompey was given a three-year commission to finish the task. The Mediterranean was divided into "naval districts"; regular patrols were established; the sea was systematically cleared and held. This operation helped convince Roman rulers of the need for a standing fleet.

As the Roman navy evolved, so did its warships. Though pictorial evidence is ambiguous, it seems clear that the gangplank and *corvus* disappeared as the Romans gained experience in sea warfare. Later Roman warships appear to have been conventional fully decked ram-galleys mounting one or two wooden turrets (probably dismountable) for archers. To the single mast with rectangular sail was added a bowsprit carrying a small sail, the artemon. Falces, or long spars tipped with blades, were used by Julius Caesar's fleet against the sailing vessels of the Veneti of northwest Gaul to cut their rigging and immobilize them. Catapults and ballistae served as "artillery," and it was under their fire that Caesar's legions landed in England.

Early Roman warships were all large; to escort merchantmen and combat pirates Rome found need for a lighter type, the liburnian. Probably developed by the pirates themselves, this was originally a light, fast unireme; the Romans added a second bank of oars. In the Battle of Actium, 31 BC, Octavian's (later Augustus') skilled fleet commander, Agrippa, used his liburnians to good effect.

The Byzantine Empire. Although polyremes continued to be built after Actium, the liburnian became the predominant Roman man-of-war. With the break-up of the western Roman Empire, naval organization and activ-

[margin note: Evolution of naval tactics]

[margin note: Roman techniques]

[margin note: The light liburnian]

ity in the west decayed. In the eastern Roman Empire, however, the need for sea power was well appreciated. During the 11 centuries that the Roman Empire centred on Constantinople, the Byzantine rulers maintained a highly organized fleet. Their original type of warship was the liburnian, called in Greek the *dromōn*, or runner, a word that, like liburnian, eventually came to denote any warship; it was built in several different sizes; the heavier designed to bear the weight of battle; the lighter single-bank dromons serving as cruisers and scouts.

Throughout the eastern Roman Empire's existence warships changed little except in rig and armament. An average large dromon measured up to 150 feet (45 metres) in length, with 100 oars and one or two fighting towers for marines. Other than some widening of the stern and its superstructure to provide more accommodation aft, the hull differed little from the Roman type. At some point early in the Christian Era, the lateen sail, three-cornered and suspended from an angled yard, probably adopted from the Arabs, came into general use. Eastern warships had two or three masts. In a departure from classical customs, these were left in place in battle. Contemporary pictures show rams above the waterline. Oars may have projected directly from the ship's side rather than from an overhanging sponson.

Missile-launching weapons grew in size, some hurling projectiles as large as 1,000 pounds (450 kilograms) up to 750 yards (685 metres). Greek fire, a combustible material for setting fire to enemy ships, was invented in the 7th century or earlier. The various compounds passing under the name used a blend of some of the following: pitch, oil, charcoal, sulfur, phosphorus, and salt. The pitch was inflammable resin, the oil, usually crude petroleum or naphtha, the salt probably crude nitrate of potash. As its composition improved, tubes shaped into the mouths of savage monsters were placed in the bows of war galleys and the flaming terror, which water merely spread, was hurled on the enemy. At close quarters marines also used a type of hand projector. In later tubes the charge was placed in a brass cup resembling a beer stein and inserted in the breech end of the tube. Significantly, the first guns (except handguns) followed the same practice.

Greek fire was an important factor in terrifying and repelling the Muslim fleet in sieges of Constantinople from the early 8th century on.

EARLY WAR VESSELS OF NORTHERN EUROPE

The earliest northern warships of which record exists were the sailing ships used against Julius Caesar by the Veneti of Gaul. During the Roman period, ships in European waters were of the Roman pattern—war galleys (mounting mast and sail but basically rowing vessels) and merchant ships. Like their Greek predecessors, the latter were slow, beamy sailing ships designed for cargo capacity rather than speed and manoeuvre. Like warships, the merchantmen mounted one mast with a single rectangular sail. They also hoisted two triangular topsails spread between the yard and masthead, as well as the artemon. Large Roman merchantmen were over 175 feet (53 metres) long, with a beam of perhaps 50 feet (15 metres).

Viking vessels. In addition to dugouts, early Scandinavian craft are believed to have included craft built of hides stretched over wood frames. These proved suitably strong and seaworthy for coastal operations. By the beginning of the Viking period, about AD 800, the early craft had evolved into the well-known Viking ship, a sturdy, double-ended, clinker-built (*i.e.,* with overlapping planks) galley put together with iron nails and caulked with tarred rope. It had a mast and square sail, which was lowered in battle; high bow and stern, with removable dragon heads; and a single side rudder on the starboard (steer-board) quarter. This method of construction had existed for about five centuries, though a keel providing strength for distant open-water operations and a rudder actually attached to the hull first appear in a recovered boat dating around AD 600; the mast and sail seem to have come into use later.

Viking vessels were essentially large open boats. Like the Homeric Greeks, the Vikings at first made no distinction between war and cargo ships, the same vessel serving either purpose as the occasion demanded. Later, however, they built larger ships specifically designed for war. By AD 1000 they sailed three categories of these: those with fewer than 20 thwarts (40 rowers); those with up to 30; and the "great ships" with more than 30, which might be considered the battleship of the time. Expensive and unhandy, though formidable in battle, the great ship was never numerous. The middle group, manoeuvrable and fast, proved most valuable.

These long ships played an important role in exploration (reaching Greenland and America before Columbus), in the consolidation of kingdoms in Scandinavia, and in far-ranging raids and conquests. It was in them that the Norsemen early invaded the British Isles and established themselves in Normandy, whence their descendants under William I the Conqueror crossed the Channel to win England in 1066.

English warships. English war vessels reflect developments that were going on elsewhere in western Europe. Early English warships resembled their Viking counterparts. Rather than being built specifically for fighting, most were called into national service only in time of emergency, though King Alfred built ships "full twice as long" as previous British craft, swifter and higher in the water, to battle the Danes at sea.

To about the end of the 13th century, the typical ship in northern waters remained a clinker-built, single-masted, square-rigged descendant of the long ship. In this century, and even more in the 14th, changes began that would bring an end to the long dominance of the oar in battle. Around AD 1200 came one of the great steps in the history of sail: the introduction, probably in The Netherlands, of the stern rudder. This rudder, along with the deep-draft hull, the bowsprit and, in time, additional masts, transformed the long ship into the true sailing ship that could beat into the wind as well as sail with it.

Thus the beamier round ship also became the warship. Fleets of this period, and indeed through the 16th century, were owned for the most part by feudal lords, merchants, and port cities, though some were royal ships. In time of peace the king's, as well as private, vessels were used as merchantmen and manned by civilian crews. When a need arose, the king mustered his own ships, called on vassals for theirs, and hired whatever others he needed. Temporary wooden castles added at bow and stern provided bulwarked platforms for archers and slingers. A complement of men-at-arms embarked, in addition to the ship's seamen. Tactics were usually simple and straightforward, opposing fleets closing and attempting to beat down each other's archers before grappling and boarding. At war's end, off came the castles, and the ships went back to trading.

Warships of feudal lords

THE AGE OF GUN AND SAIL

The trading vessel that could be promptly adapted to war did not, however, fulfill the need of a nation for a navy. The coming of gunpowder and the period of world exploration brought changes that were to cause the sailing man-of-war to become increasingly distinct from the merchantman.

Until the 15th century, northern ships probably continued to have single masts, though in the Mediterranean a two-mast rig carrying lateen (fore-and-aft) sails had existed for some time. Then change came rapidly in the north, spurred on by Henry V's construction of large and strongly built warships for his cross-Channel French campaigns. The remains of one of these, "Grâce Dieu," reflected the clinker-built construction of the Viking long ship, but had a keel to beam ratio of about 2½:1 and now carried a second mast. The removable castles had become permanent parts of the ship, mounting many small guns.

Some historians believe that "Grâce Dieu" carried a third mast. At any rate, in a few decades ships had three and, by the end of the century, large vessels mounted four masts carrying eight or more sails. A three-master carried a large sail on each mast and in addition a main topsail and the spritsail under the bowsprit—the rig, in fact, of "Santa Maria" in 1492. Ships, no longer dependent on fair winds, could and did range the world.

Gun-armed warships. Employment of guns afloat, bringing a slow but progressive revolution in warship construction and naval tactics, had its first small beginnings by the 14th century. One of the compositions of Greek fire, given by Marcus Graecus in AD 846, was one part live sulfur, two of charcoal of willow, and six of saltpetre (potassium nitrate) ground into fine powder in a mortar and mixed. This recipe is a forerunner of black powder, the basic gun propellant until the late 1800s.

Gradually, saltpetre's properties became more widely known. In the 13th century, Mediterranean Muslims made hand grenades and fired small balls from hand tubes or lance heads. The first gun used at sea, undoubtedly a hand weapon, was probably in a Mediterranean galley in the 13th or early 14th century. It played a minor role. In fact, in the numerous sea battles of the Greeks, Genoese, Moors, Turks, and Venetians during this period there is no mention of guns. But by the middle of the 14th century, the English, French, Spanish, and other navies mounted guns. Most were relatively small "mankillers" located in the castles fore and aft. Later, heavier guns were added. The Mediterranean galleys of Turkey and Spain at first simply shackled a heavy gun on the forecastle to fire forward, supplementing the ram.

First guns used at sea

European guns were originally built up of wrought-iron bars welded together to form a tube, then banded with a thick iron hoop. Initially, they were breechloaders with an open trough at the rear of the barrel through which the ball was loaded and a cylindrical chamber filled with powder inserted and wedged tight. Inherently weak and low-powered, they were replaced in the British navy after 1500 by brass muzzle-loaders, cast in one piece with bores drilled out. Some of these attained great size for their day; by the mid-16th century even some 60-pounders (firing 60-pound [27-kilogram] solid shot) were mounted in the largest ships. In this century also, increasing knowledge of iron metallurgy led to the production of large cast-iron cannon that slowly replaced the bigger brass guns in ships, though brass remained predominant for the lighter calibre well into the 19th century.

Henry VII of England created the first true oceangoing battle fleet. The "king's ships" carried many guns, but most of the impressively large numbers were small breechloaders. Following him, Henry VIII initiated gunports in English warships, a development that was to have a far-reaching effect on man-of-war design and, indeed, on world history. Neither stability nor structural strength favoured heavy guns in the high castles. Henry's introduction of gunports (perhaps following an earlier use across the Channel), at first low in the waist of the ship and afterward along the full broadside, made possible the true heavy-gun warship. The cutting of gunports in the hull must also have been a factor in causing the northern nations to shift from clinker-built ships to caravels with flush-fitting planks, a change that took place in the early 1500s.

The armament of an English man-of-war of the early 16th century consisted of four or five short-barrelled cannon, or curtals, a similar number of demicannon, and culverins. The average cannon, a short-range gun, hurled an iron ball of about 50 pounds (23 kilograms), and the demicannon one of 32 pounds (14.5 kilograms). The culverin, a longer and stronger gun, fired a smaller shot over a longer range and was likely to be more accurate at other than point-blank range. Supplementing these standoff "ship killers" were the smaller demiculverin, saker (quarter culverin), falcon (half saker), falconet, robinet, in descending size of ball fired, down to several ounces.

A great warship of the 16th century mounted a total of large and small pieces approximating the numbers mounted in battleships of World War II. Henry VIII's best known warship, "Henry Grâce à Dieu," had 186 guns for her original complement in 1514, mostly small, but a number of iron "great guns."

As the 17th century advanced, guns and powder improved and classification became standardized. The long gun (culverin type) ran 18 to 25 calibres (bore diameters) in length; the short cannon, 15 calibres. Gun carriages had heavy wooden sides called brackets, with sockets for the gun trunnions, joined by similar flat timbers called transoms, supported on wooden trucks and hauled out after recoil by heavy tackle.

Galleasses, galleons, and great gun battles. The coming of mighty men-of-war, like "Henry Grâce à Dieu," did not mean the immediate end of oared warships. In fact, some types of galleys and oared gunboats continued to serve well into the 19th century. Venice had galleys when conquered by Napoleon. Throughout the 18th century Russia and Sweden employed galleys and, later, oared gunboats. Indeed, Russian oared gunboats were built in 1854 and engaged in action that year. The United States employed "row galleys" or oar-driven gunboats in the War of 1812 and the Mexican War (1846–48).

Survival of oared warships

Galleasses at Lepanto. The climactic action of the age of oar was Lepanto, fought off Greece in 1571, in which a combined European fleet defeated the Turkish fleet in an action that differed little from traditional galley warfare with two exceptions. First, galleys now carried guns, perhaps five heavy and medium guns forward to supplement the shock effect of the ram and more small breechloaders complementing bows, lances, and swords.

Second, the European line of battle included six Venetian galleasses, a compromise type developed in the transition from oar to sail. These huge vessels, which depended on sail as well as oar, bristled with guns, including heavy ones in broadside. Although cumbersome to manoeuvre, their concentrated fire contributed importantly to victory.

Galleasses outside the Mediterranean differed somewhat from Venice's in that they were basically full-rigged sailing ships carrying broadsides of heavy guns and a bank of auxiliary oars for mobility. The hybrid existed only in small numbers and soon passed out of fashion to the north.

The galleon and the Spanish Armada. The "great ships" of Henry VII and Henry VIII were carracks: starting basically with the lines of beamy, seaworthy merchant ships, designers had added stronger timbers, masts, sailpower, broadside guns, and forecastles and aftercastles, with the forecastle triangular and overhanging. In the galleon, the successor to the carrack, the general principles of design of sailing men-of-war were established and ruled, without fundamental change, for three centuries. The galleon retained certain of the characteristics of the galley, such as its slender shape; it had a greater length to beam ratio than the carrack, standardizing in England for a time at about three to one but later increasing to considerably greater ratios. The triangular, overhanging forecastle of the carrack gave way to the long raised beak of the galley projecting beyond the stem and with a square-ended forecastle set back under the foremast. Like carracks, the larger galleons might carry a single mizzenmast or two relatively small masts, the second being called the bonaventure.

In the longer, leaner galleon, the number of heavy guns was increased until they ran the full length of the broadside in one or two tiers (and later three). This advance in firepower was incorporated in "Henry Grâce à Dieu" during its rebuilding in 1536, though it remained a carrack.

The galleon came into favour in the north during the following decades, leading to the first ships of the line. The far-ranging experience of mariners and improved construction techniques led to great fighting ships that were both lower in the water and more seaworthy than their predecessors. They also carried comparatively large batteries of heavy guns, affecting the design of ships. The sides now sloped inward from the lowest gun deck up to the weather deck. This tumble home helped concentrate the weight of the big broadside guns toward the ship's centre line, improving stability. Sir Francis Drake's flagship, "Revenge," for example, displaced only 500 tons, yet she mounted a broadside of 34 guns ranging from 32-pounders to nine-pounders, plus smaller guns.

Heavy gun batteries

By that time it had become normal for northern warships to mount powerful broadsides of 28 or more ship-smashing guns, a much heavier armament, in proportion to their size, than their predecessors. For their handy, manoeuvrable ships, the British had also concentrated on the long-range-culverin type, and by the time of the Armada most of their principal ships carried these in broadsides. Thus they were designed for off-fighting, permitting the English fleet to get the most out of its superior manoeuvring qualities. These early ships of the line began the true reign of the big gun at sea, maintained until World War II when the carrier and submarine became more formidable. Today the rocket missile (ballistic and guided) has taken the gun's leading role, except in amphibious warfare.

When the Spanish Armada arrived in 1588, the British sought and fought a sea battle with ship-killing guns, rather than the conventional fleet engagement of the past that concentrated on killing men, ramming, and boarding. With superior ability and long-range culverins, they punished the invading fleet outside the effective range of the heavy but shorter range cannon the Spanish favoured. This historic running battle of July 1588 closed one era and opened a greater one of big-gun sailing navies.

Ship of the line. The late Elizabethan galleon that began the true fighting ship of this type reached its culmination in England's "Prince Royal" of 1610 and the larger "Sovereign of the Seas," along with similar great ships in other European navies. These two English ships mounted broadside guns on three decks, "Sovereign of the Seas," most formidable ship afloat of its time, carrying 100 guns. This was the standard minimum armament for a first-rater long into the future.

In this mobile fortress of approximately 1,500 tons there was some reduction of height and the bonaventure mizzen disappeared, leaving the standard three masts that capital ships thereafter carried.

Soon ships began to be standardized into different categories. James I organized his ships into four ranks, and, by the mid-17th century, six rates existed as a general concept, though not yet a system. The number of guns carried determined rate, with a first-rater mounting 100 and a sixth-rater 18. An important improvement came in the standardization of batteries in the higher rates so that guns on the same deck were of the same weight and calibre rather than mixed, as originally in "Sovereign of the Seas." Near the end of the century, guns began to be described by their weight and calibre, with the 32-pounder long gun favoured as the standard lower deck weapon for British warships, though three-deckers might carry 42-pounders in the lowest tier.

Rates were periodically revised. By the middle of the 18th century, while the rate concept continued for some official purposes, ships were generally known by the number of guns they were rated to carry—*e.g.,* "Victory," 108. Similar developments took place in other navies. The French seemed to emphasize scientific shipbuilding more than the British, hence class for class their warships were often more efficient. The Dutch and Spanish also built excellent warships, the former favouring shallower draft vessels.

Tactical use of guns. The frequent hard-fought sea battles of the 17th century between fleets closely matched in size and skill, particularly in the Anglo-Dutch wars, led to the column formation of heavy warships called line ahead. In 1653 the British Admiralty prescribed the line ahead as the principal combat formation, with the intention of enabling the commander to control the fleet and bring the entire force into action at the same time.

Two schools of British Navy thought existed as to the tactics of engaging the enemy. The formalists urged aligning the full line of battle from van to rear parallel with the foe before bearing down in a concerted manoeuvre that would engage all of the ships at the same time. The second school believed in prompt attack, closing the enemy quickly after a formal approach had brought the fleets near enough together, whether or not in exact alignment. They held that speed of onslaught more than compensated for lack of a completely concerted attack.

Both schools believed in fighting at close quarters where the fire of even the smallest guns could be effective. This shift from the tactics against the Spanish Armada did not do away with the long gun, but in time led to the introduction of larger bore, shorter range guns like the cannon of the early period. The change in viewpoint may have been strengthened in the world wars of the 18th century by the tendency of the French and Spanish to concentrate on damaging upperworks and rigging. They fired on the uproll, while the British, concentrating on the hull, fired on the downroll to smash the ship.

A large ball has greater crushing effect, but factors like those of recoil, weight, and metallurgy considerations required a short-bore gun. Late in the 18th century, the Scottish firm of Carron Company Ironworks brought out "The Smasher" of eight-inch (20-centimetre) bore, firing a close-fitting 68-pound (31-kilogram) ball with only 5½ pounds (2½ kilograms) of powder. Carronades, as they came to be called, had a short bore. They gave ships massive close-range firepower without the weight and recoil problems of similar long guns. They could not replace the long gun and were valuable only because navies, in a sense, continued the tactics of the Romans—smashing with heavy artillery and boarding.

Ship design changes. Warships gradually improved in design through the 17th and 18th centuries. New types of sails, providing more canvas and more versatile combinations for varying weather conditions, such as staysails and the jib sail, came into use in the 17th century. Soon thereafter the steering wheel replaced the old whip staff, or tiller.

The adoption of line-ahead tactics made it necessary to standardize the battle line, which had consisted of ships of widely varying strength. Now only the more powerful warships were considered suitable "to lie in the line of battle." Hence the origin by the 1700s of the term line-of-battle ship, or the ship of the line, and, in the second half of the 19th century, the derived term battleship—ships that could hit the hardest and endure the most punishment.

Some first-raters were built to carry as many as 136 guns, but the biggest ships were often cumbersome, hence relatively few were built. The handier 74-gun third-rater proved particularly successful, combining sufficient hitting power with better speed and manoeuvrability. Most of the ships of the line of the late 18th and early 19th centuries were 74s. One of these might be approximately 175 feet (50 metres) long with two full gun decks, the lower mounting the heaviest guns, by the Napoleonic Wars usually 32-pounders. The upper gun deck customarily carried 24-pounders, while the forecastle and quarterdeck mounted lighter guns or carronades. The bigger ships were similar but had three covered gun decks instead of two. Viscount Nelson's "Victory," built in 1765 and preserved in dry dock as she was at Trafalgar in 1805, is a classic example of this powerful type.

Frigates and other types. Ships of the line, first to fourth rates, had strong fast frigates as consorts. This ancestor of the modern cruiser evolved during the mid-18th century for scouting, patrol, and escort, as well as for attacking enemy merchantmen. The frigate carried its main battery on a single gun deck with other guns on forecastle and quarterdeck. Like the ship of the line, they varied in size and armament, ranging from about 24 guns in early small frigates to as many as 56 in some of the last. Two classic examples, still preserved, are the United States Navy's "Constitution," of 44 guns, and "Constellation," of 38.

Smaller vessels aided frigates in their blockade, escort, commerce raiding, and other duties. The single-masted cutter served as scout and coastal patrol craft. Brig and schooner-rigged types, generally called sloops of war, by the time of the American Revolution grew into the three-masted, square-rigged "ship sloop." Called a corvette on the Continent, the fast ship sloop complemented frigates on the fringes of the fleet. Smaller sloops, schooners, brigs, and luggers were widely used for special service. Fleets also needed ordnance and supply ships and other auxiliaries; these were usually merchantmen taken into service in war emergency. Converted merchantmen, such as John Paul Jones's "Bonhomme Richard," often played combat roles. Fleets also had various special types, such as fire ships and bomb ketches. The latter, with two large mortars hurling bombs of about 200 pounds, were developed by France in the late 1600s, and were used with devastating effect against Barbary pirate ports.

THE AGE OF STEAM AND IRON

As the Industrial Revolution unfolded in the 19th century, the age of wood and sail gave way to that of steam and iron. Phenomenal changes took place in nearly every aspect of warship design, operation, and tactics. These

Anglo-Dutch formations

The 74-gun third-rater

changes ended the reign of the majestic ship of the line by the mid-1800s, but another half century elapsed before it was clear what form her replacement as the backbone of fleets would take. The changes may be summarized under two headings: propulsion and ship construction and armament.

Propulsion. Steam for propulsion of vessels was tried with varying success in several countries during the late 18th century. Engines and supporting machinery were at first not adequate for this fundamental advance in ship capability, but useful steam craft appeared in the early 1800s, suitable for operation on inland and coastal waterways. The earliest steam warship was "Demologos" of the U.S. Navy (renamed "Fulton" after her designer). Built in the War of 1812, this well-gunned, double-hulled, low-powered ship cruised briefly in the New York Harbor area before the war ended and later was destroyed by an accidental fire.

First steam warship

The earliest steam warships in action were small paddle wheelers used by British and American navies against weak foes. USS "Sea Gull," a New York Harbor steam tug, operated against pirates in the West Indies during the 1820s.

As engines gradually improved, navies experimented with them in standard warships, first as auxiliaries to sail, which was then essential for endurance. The paddle-wheels were particularly vulnerable to enemy fire. In 1843, through the drive of Capt. Robert Field Stockton of the U.S. Navy and the inventive skill of John Ericsson, a Swede whom Stockton brought to America, the United States launched the world's first screw-driven steam man-of-war, USS "Princeton," a large 10-gun sloop.

The screw propeller was an old idea going back to Archimedes, but, with Stockton's assistance, Ericsson made it effective for large warships, as Sir Francis Pettit Smith was doing at about the same time in England for large merchantmen. By the mid-1840s, boilers, engines, and machinery had improved to the point that thereafter practically all of the new warships had steam propulsion. The French Navy's "Napoléon" was a particularly successful application of steam to a great ship of the line. The U.S. Navy's experience in the Mexican War of the 1840s and the allied experience in the Crimean War of the 1850s demonstrated the outstanding advantages of steam warships for restricted-waters operations, as well as in adverse winds and tides.

Among the advances of this period were two other milestones. In 1834 Samuel Hall of England patented a type of steam condenser that made it possible to use fresh instead of corrosive salt water for boilers. In 1824 James Peter Allaire of the United States invented the compound-expansion steam engine, in which the steam was used in a second cylinder at a lower pressure after it had done its work in the first. Eventually it was made practical by progress in metallurgy and engineering; in 1854 John Elder, shipbuilder on the Clyde, installed a successful two-stage engine in the merchant steamer "Brandon." The higher efficiency was of great importance for ocean-keeping navies.

Ship construction and armament to the American Civil War. The change from wood to iron and armour that followed the introduction of steam propulsion came slowly, in considerable part because the new material required new techniques and experience in shipbuilding. By mid-century a handful of iron ships had appeared in various navies; the general use of iron for warships, however, awaited realization of the full value of the shell gun, the resulting development of armour, the employment of armoured batteries in the Crimean War, and the recognition of the significance of the battle between "Monitor" and "Virginia," better known as "Merrimack."

Slow change from wood to iron

Guns. "Princeton" not only set the course for propeller warships but exemplified the rapid development of armament that with steam and other factors brought navies increasing capabilities against each other and in operations against land defenses. She mounted 12-inch (30-centimetre) shell guns, which still had many unsolved manufacturing problems; in a gala demonstration for Pres. John Tyler one of the guns blew up, killing the Secretary of the Navy and several others.

Basic changes in armament that would advance rapidly throughout the 19th and 20th centuries had begun in the 18th century. In the British Navy steps to make possible heavier long-range guns began with the introduction of strong springs to take up the first shock of recoil, aided by inclined-plane wedges behind the trucks. Flintlocks pulled by a lanyard, instead of a match, fired the guns. Sights also improved. In the early 1800s navies began to employ mercury fulminate in caps to initiate firing. Efficient percussion locks came into use within a few years.

Smooth-bore guns were still inaccurate, and successful efforts were made to bring back the rifling, as well as breech-loading, of early guns, thus increasing speed and accuracy of fire. In the 1840s, Italian and Austrian inventors brought out sliding-wedge breechblocks. Later the French developed an interrupted screw system, originally an American invention. A British firm produced a rifled breech-loading gun that the British Navy used until 1864, when a number of accidents brought a temporary reversion to muzzle-loaders. But defects were eventually remedied, and breech-loading brought phenomenal increases in naval rates of fire.

French 6.5-inch (16.5-centimetre) cast-iron rifles in the Crimean War demonstrated superiority in range, destructive power, and accuracy. Along with the advent of armour, they helped impress all of the navies with the need for rifling. Slower burning powder was badly needed. Black powder was gradually improved during 600 years of use in firearms, but it still retained its primary defect, too rapid burning. This required keeping the charge down (and therefore the range) to prevent the bursting of even the best guns. Just before the American Civil War the U.S. Army developed large, perforated, dense grains of black powder that were a start toward the controlled burning ultimately achieved with smokeless powder.

Shell guns in warships' main batteries were preceded by bombs fired from mortars, small-shell guns, and solid hot shot heated to cherry red. A principal architect in bringing big-shell guns to sea was Henri-Joseph Paixhans, a general of French artillery. The first large-shell guns from Paixhans' design, chambered howitzers firing a 62½-pound (28½-kilogram) shell (thicker walled than bombs to penetrate before exploding) was tested in 1824 against a moored frigate with remarkable accuracy and incendiary effect.

Big-shell guns at sea

The new guns began to come into use afloat in the 1830s, a French squadron firing them in bombardment of Vera Cruz, Mexico. The U.S. Navy began installation, including 16 eight-inch-shell guns in the three-decker "Pennsylvania," along with 104 32-pounder solid-shot guns. The British made similar installations. There was good reason for navies to proceed cautiously. Powder charges had to be limited, so shell guns had shorter range, and shell was less accurate than shot. Improvements in metallurgy, gun construction, and fire control, along with the manoeuvrability of steam warships, at last were beginning to lead to an important extension of range that the big gun had promised from the beginning.

In 1853 the dramatic destruction of a weaker Turkish squadron by a Russian fleet in the harbour of Sinope of Turkey's Black Sea coast attracted world attention and increased interest in shell guns. England, the United States, and others built big-steam frigates (as they were misleadingly called) with large-shell guns. Their great striking power and manoeuvrability under steam made them the capital ships of the day, superseding the ship of the line for a brief time before the ironclads took over.

Larger guns, increased powder charges, and greater tube pressures were made possible by the replacement of cast iron by built-up wrought-iron guns (later, cast steel and, eventually, forged steel). Hoops were shrunk on over the powder chamber and breech end of the tube to give the strength required for the greater pressures.

Armour. The use of larger guns with more penetrating power and explosive shells made armour imperative. Among early experiments were floating armoured batteries built for the Crimean War. These flat-bottomed vessels could carry large-shell guns close inshore. Heavy wrought-iron plates over a thick wooden backing gave them outstanding protection. In October 1855 in a hard-fought duel, French floating batteries silenced a Russian fort at Kinburn, at the mouth of the Dnepr (Dnieper) River and forced its surrender, suffering little damage themselves from Russian shellfire and solid shot.

Other developments followed swiftly. The British soon built the first iron-hull floating batteries. The French followed with "Gloire," the first seagoing armoured warship, protected throughout her entire length by a wrought-iron belt of 4.3- to 4.7-inch (10.9- to 11.9-centimetre) armour backed by 26 inches (66 centimetres) of wood. Displacing 5,617 tons, she mounted 36 large-shell guns and could steam at 13.5 knots (one knot equals 1.15 miles per hour or 1.85 kilometres per hour); a three-masted sailing rig supplemented the engines. "Gloire" was the first of a series of ironclads laid down by Napoleon III; 13 similar ships soon followed, then two-decker armoured rams.

Great Britain countered with "Warrior," the first iron-hull, seagoing, armoured man-of-war. Much larger than "Gloire," she displaced 9,210 tons, mounted 28 seven-inch- (17.8-centimetre-) shell guns, had slightly lighter armour, carried sails, and was one knot faster. These first ironclads were commissioned on the eve of the American Civil War, in which ironclads were destined to take a decisive part. The war itself produced several spectacular developments, including pioneer submarines, the first aircraft carriers (to handle balloons for observation), and the torpedo boat, one of several means the Confederates explored in trying to break the blockade. These little craft had weak steam engines and mounted a torpedo lashed to a spar projecting from the bow. Called Davids, they frightened the blockaders and might have sunk a wooden warship; but the one successful attack struck the armoured "New Ironsides." The explosion caused considerable damage, requiring shipyard repairs, but did not lift the blockade. The David was a weak but definite forerunner of the torpedo boat and then the versatile destroyer.

The ironclads
Ironclad warships were crucial, perhaps decisive in the North's victory. Partial ironclads appeared early on the western rivers, and, under Flag Officer Foote, spearheaded Ulysses Grant's victories in 1862. River and coastal ironclads (ultimately, mostly monitors) dominated the war against the South in attacks from the sea and in decisive support of land operations from the Mississippi system to the Chesapeake Bay and James River. Most memorable of the combats was the duel between "Monitor" and "Virginia" ("Merrimack"). When the Federal forces lost Norfolk Naval Shipyard, Portsmouth, Virginia, April 1861, they burned several warships, including the heavy steam frigate "Merrimack." The Confederates raised "Merrimack," installed a ram and slanting casemates made from railroad track over thick wooden backing, as had been done in "Gloire," and renamed her "Virginia." Mounting 10 guns, including four rifles, "Virginia," with yard workmen still on board finishing up, sailed on March 8, 1862, for her trial run. Defying concentrated fire of ship and shore batteries, she sank two of the wooden blockading fleet before retiring with the ebbing tide. In this dramatic moment Ericsson's "Monitor" arrived from New York during the middle of the night. Displacing fewer than 1,000 tons, less than a third of "Virginia," "Monitor" had a boxlike iron hull supporting an iron-plated wooden raft on which revolved the turret. The 172-foot- (52-metre-) long vessel had little freeboard except for the thickly armoured rotating turret that mounted two 11-inch (28-centimetre) smoothbores. (Although new on warships, the revolving turret was an old idea; a turreted warship was built in England at about the same time.)

"Monitor" had many deficiencies. Not really a seagoing warship, she had nearly sunk on her voyage down from New York and did sink on her next sea voyage. Yet she proved the equal of her rival in their duel on March 9. The battle ended in a draw with neither ship seriously injured, but repercussions swept the world.

On April 4, scarcely more time than required for a ship to cross the Atlantic, Great Britain ordered the 131-gun ship of the line, "Royal Sovereign," to be cut down, armoured, and fitted with turrets. Only three and a half weeks later she laid down "Prince Albert," the Royal Navy's first iron-hull turret ship, mounting four turrets.

The Union Navy ordered 66 coastal and river monitors, low freeboard ships not suitable for high-seas action and most not for long voyages. Many were not completed in time for war service. The North also laid down four double-turreted Kalamazoo-class monitors to carry 15-inch (38-centimetre) guns that would have been seagoing battleships; these, however, were not completed by the war's end and were scrapped.

Coastal and river monitors

Besides "Virginia," the Confederates began a number of other ironclads from Richmond south on the east coast and on the inland rivers. Several of these rendered valuable service and probably lengthened the war. But most had to be destroyed before completion; David Glasgow Farragut's decisive fleet dash into New Orleans, Louisiana, forestalled completion of two powerful ironclads that might have stopped him. Out of a combination of characteristics of the "Monitor" and "Virginia" types evolved the battleship that was next to rule the sea.

Underwater. The South developed innovative subsurface weapons, including mines (called torpedoes) that were detonated by contact or electrically, and a submarine armed with a torpedo attached to a spar. (For a detailed description, see the section on submarines below.)

Warship development to the end of the century. The later 19th century continued to be a time of great flux in warship design. European nations tried numerous arrangements of guns and armour, such as centre-line turrets, a central armoured citadel with large guns on turntables at each corner, lightly armoured big guns topsides in barbettes (open-top breastworks), torpedoes in even the largest vessels, and substitution of high speed for armour.

For a time even the ancient ram was revived. When the Austrians won the Battle of Lissa from the Italians in 1866 by ramming, its value for the future seemed confirmed. Hence for years most large ships carried rams, which proved to be more dangerous to friend than foe when ships were sunk in peacetime collisions.

Ships. The trend toward the centre-line-turret, all-big-gun battleship finally became clear. In it were combined the seagoing hull, armour, and habitability of "Virginia," "Gloire," and "Warrior" with the turret and massive big guns of "Monitor."

HMS "Monarch," 8,300 tons, mounting four 12-inch (30.5-centimetre) guns in two turrets, commissioned in 1869, was perhaps the first true seagoing turret warship. HMS "Devastation," 9,330 tons, four 12-inch guns in two turrets, and massively armoured, completed four years later without sail, was a next step toward the ultimate 20th-century battleship, a ship with an armoured citadel around the propulsion plant, powder magazines, and handling rooms. Rising out of it, protecting big guns and crews, were barbettes and turrets. The main battery shrank to a few powerful guns, but these took the place of many in broadside because of their great size and ability to fire through a wide arc of bearings. The change was vividly illustrated by the "new navy" the United States began building in the 1880s, consisting not of improved monitors but of powerful seagoing capital ships with mixed-calibre main batteries. In 1891 the United States laid down "Indiana," "Massachusetts," and "Oregon." Displacing 11,700 tons, these sister vessels had 18-inch (46-centimetre) belt armour, a speed of 15 knots, and mounted four 13-inch (33-centimetre) guns in two turrets. They also mounted eight eight-inch (20-centimetre) guns in four turrets, smaller guns for defense against torpedo boats, and six torpedo tubes. The plan was, as in other navies, to employ the heavy guns against enemy machinery and magazines while the faster firing eight-inch guns attacked his superstructure.

The armoured cruiser was developed in this period as a large, fast vessel armed with intermediate-calibre guns and protected by armoured deck and medium-weight belt armour. Designed for commerce protection and raiding, as well as to cooperate with the battle line in fleet action, it was considered powerful enough and sufficiently protected to fight any ship capable of catching it and able to outrun battleships. Some even held it should become the principal warship.

Armoured cruisers

Less heavily armoured was the protected cruiser, the engines and magazines of which were shielded by an armoured deck, but which lacked an armour belt. Unprotected cruisers had little or no armour, carried fairly light guns, and were designed primarily for scouting, patrolling, and raiding.

In this period there were fundamental advances in underwater weapons. An Austrian naval captain and a Scottish engineer produced an underwater projectile driven by compressed air to strike the unprotected hull below the waterline. At first slow, inaccurate, and of short range, it was progressively improved. Advances included stabilizing devices, more powerful warheads (initially of dynamite), and, very importantly, alcohol-burning steam-turbine power instead of compressed air.

Carrying this new self-propelled weapon, the torpedo boat had great potential, particularly under conditions of low visibility. Small, unseaworthy, and useful only in restricted waters with the then short range, slow torpedoes, the new boats did not immediately live up to expectations; nevertheless, as craft and torpedo improved, they were soon regarded as a major menace. Torpedo-defense batteries of rapid-firing small guns joined the main batteries of larger warships. Heavy ships added searchlights and torpedo nets. The threat also brought a new type of warship. The torpedo-boat destroyer first appeared in Great Britain in 1893. It was essentially a larger torpedo boat, mounting quick-firing guns, as well as torpedoes, of high speed, and capable of operating on the open sea. It was intended to accompany a battle line at sea, screen it from torpedo boats, and attack the enemy line with torpedoes. HMS "Havock," of 240 tons, was the first of the new type.

General improvements in technology. Engines for all of the types of warships steadily improved. Stronger metals made possible higher steam pressures and weight reduction. With higher pressures the two-stage compound engine added a third and even a fourth stage; then as the century ended, the steam turbine appeared to provide a marked increase in the speed of ships.

Early armour had been of wrought iron backed by wood. To increase resistance against ever more powerful rifled guns, compound armour of steel backed with iron was devised to combine steel's surface hardness with iron's resiliency. The firm Schneider & Cie in France invented an oil-tempering process to produce a homogeneous steel plate that had good resiliency and greater resistance than compound armour. The later addition of nickel further improved its resistance.

Steel-armour-piercing shells came into use in the late 1880s, again threatening the armoured ship. An American engineer, Hayward Augustus Harvey, perfected a face-hardening process, applying carbon to the face of the steel plate at very high temperatures for an extended period and tempering. Harvey nickel-steel armour superseded earlier types. Then, in 1894, the Krupp firm of Germany devised hot-gas tempering, based on Harvey's process, that in turn became standard with world navies. Later, the addition of chromium to nickel steel was found to be a further improvement.

The impact of developments in guns and powder exceeded even that of warship design in their effect upon navies. In the two decades after the American Civil War the main difficulties with breech mechanisms were resolved. Better guns, along with breech-loading, made possible both longer ranges and higher rates of fire.

New powders were equally important. About 1880 brown or cocoa powder appeared, employing incompletely charred wood. It burned slower than black powder, hence with a given maximum pressure the sustained pressure was much greater. To take advantage of this for longer-range firing, large gun calibres jumped to 30–35 times bore diameter.

Several nations began to achieve success with smokeless powder of nitrated cellulose and usually some nitroglycerin. Calibres of guns again advanced. With greater striking power available, armour-piercing projectiles became more formidable. These were originally solid shot designed simply to punch through armour plate. In the 1890s, better steel and fuses made it possible to add an explosive charge. The resulting semi-armour-piercing shells became highly destructive, and in time all of the armour-piercing projectiles carried explosive charges.

In 1881 the British Admiralty advertised for an anti-

Development of turbines

torpedo-boat gun to fire cased ammunition at a rate of 12 shots per minute. Benjamin Berkeley Hotchkiss, an American ordnance engineer with a factory in Paris, produced a series of one-, three-, and six-pounder rapid-fire guns that eventually went into nearly all of the navies, though he got his first order from the United States Navy. The rate of fire vastly increased for small guns. For larger ones, loading times also improved; in 1884 the average time to load a 12-inch gun was about four minutes. By World War I it had shrunk to about 20 seconds.

Other technical developments in these decades that had great impact on naval craft were the appearance of the internal-combustion engine and the electric motor, which at last made possible an effective submarine. Experiments in wireless telegraphy foreshadowed control of the operation of ships out of sight of the fleet commander.

Increases in rate of fire

TOWARD WORLD WAR I

The dreadnought battleship. By the 1890s the capital ship had evolved into what is known historically as pre-Dreadnought, characterized by its mixed main battery. Studies reinforced by battle experience in the Spanish-American (1898) and Russo-Japanese (1904–05) wars indicated that fire from large guns at longer ranges was more effective than mixed-battery fire closer in. Only big-gun shells had sufficient impact to do serious damage to well-armoured ships. Improved gunsights, new spotting techniques, and developing range finders made long ranges practicable.

Both the United States and Great Britain designed all-big-gun, centre-line-turret battleships, but the British "Dreadnought," completed in 1906, was the first to be commissioned. Equipped with 10 12-inch (30-centimetre) guns, turbine drive, 21-knot speed, she gave her name as a generic term to a new type. Other navies promptly sought to match and excel her.

Battle cruisers, essentially a further development of the armoured cruiser but with battleship guns, were designed to run down and destroy hostile cruisers and to protect friendly shipping. The battle cruiser was several knots faster than contemporary battleships, speed being achieved by reducing armour. Germany's battle cruisers had slightly less speed but better protection than their British equivalents, both in armour and compartmentation. German crews were intensively trained in damage control.

As the naval race speeded up, progressively more powerful ships appeared. All of the navies quickly adopted turbine propulsion. The United States went to oil fuel even for its capital ships. With oil supply more of a problem, European nations nevertheless followed suit because of oil's superior efficiency. Newer battleships that could hit more and more accurately at ever increasing ranges rapidly made older ships obsolete. Guns increased in size and striking power with intensive research going into propellants, shell design, and detonating explosives. Improvements in range-finding and fire-control equipment rapidly extended the effective battle range. Director firing (control of several or all of a battery from a single station) made for better coordination of fire, as well as more precise spotting and salvo shooting. World War I speeded up these developments, especially in range keepers and other fire-control equipment that made possible rapid and accurate calculation of target course and speed. The complex elements of the fire-control problem were so well-handled that early hitting became possible, sometimes on the first salvo—no mean feat when the target is many miles away racing through the sea.

This extension in range was a factor in the adoption of larger guns. Because accuracy, range, and the destructive power of guns all increase with calibre, given the same initial velocity and accuracy of fire control, it is evident that as soon as range-finding and spotting can determine the fall of shot beyond the effective range of existing guns, a larger calibre is demanded. "New York" and "Texas" of the United States Navy, commissioned in early 1914, mounted 14-inch (35.5-centimetre) guns. Great Britain's Queen Elizabeth class, joining the fleet in 1915–16, mounted 15-inch (38-centimetre) guns and sped through the water at 25 knots, virtually outmoding the

Steady increase in gun calibre

battle cruiser. The United States' Colorado class mounted 16-inch (41-centimetre) batteries.

The battleship saw little combat in World War I as compared to the heavy service of its ship-of-the line predecessor and the role it was destined to play in World War II. Yet World War I was in many ways the zenith of the battleship's influence. Despite submarines, aircraft, and destroyers, the outcome of the war still hinged upon control of the sea by the battleship. Had superiority in battleships passed to Germany, Great Britain would have been lost, and the Allies would have lost the war. The one moment when this might have happened was the one large-scale clash of battleships, the Battle of Jutland. Fought in May 1916 in mist, fog, and darkness, the combat revealed the strengths and weaknesses of the battleships and battle cruisers; superb seamanship on both sides demonstrated that miles-long battle lines lost in the mist could be effectively controlled. Three British battle cruisers were lost. Several German battleships, thanks to watertight subdivision and efficient damage-control systems, survived despite more hits. But the British advantage in numbers of battleships was decisive. Germany turned to the submarine as a means of countering the Allied blockade.

Cruisers and destroyers. On the eve of World War I, Britain had 145 cruisers in commission or building, almost as many as the other major naval powers combined; Germany had 57, the United States 32. Cruisers of the first part of the 20th century did not show the phenomenal changes in size and power of the battleship. They benefited from the same advances in propulsion, gunnery, and materials that made all of the warships more effective. Cruisers had only a modest speed advantage over battleships until the Omaha class of the United States Navy, designed late in World War I and built afterward. Small tube boilers and superheated steam gave them a speed of 35 knots, about a 50 percent increase over other United States cruisers.

Destroyers experienced radical development. HMS "Havock" that started the type in 1893 soon had an outstanding successor. HMS "Viper," powered by improved turbines, on trials in 1899, achieved the then unprecedented speed of 34 knots. The destroyer grew in size, power, habitability, and functions into World War I, when the submarine gave it enormous importance. In August 1914 Britain had nearly 300 destroyers, Germany about half as many, the United States about 50. When Germany adopted unrestricted submarine warfare in February 1917, Great Britain felt an acute shortage of destroyers. Shipping losses soon forced diversion of destroyers from fleet duty to convoy protection and antisubmarine warfare.

When the United States entered the conflict it brought 67 destroyers in commission, with a few on the ways, and began a massive naval shipbuilding effort primarily in destroyers and smaller antisubmarine vessels and the host of merchant ships needed to sustain the vast overseas logistic flow into France and Britain. Most of the 247 United States destroyers laid down were completed after the Armistice; but these 35-knot ships of 1,200 tons, or more, a generation later played an important role in World War II. The U.S. and other Allied destroyers of 1917–18, equipped with hydrophones and depth charges, as well as guns and torpedoes, overcame the submarine threat and had a large share in the safe convoy of 2,000,000 American troops to Europe without loss of a single soldier.

Submarines. The last half of the 19th century brought the many technical advances that made possible undersea craft. Paradoxically, most of the development was carried out in France, Great Britain, and the U.S., though the craft were to be used primarily by these nations' adversary, Germany, in World War I.

Germany started building undersea craft later than other countries. In 1914 it had 38 in commission when war broke out—fewer than Britain, France, Russia, or the United States, counting those nearing completion. Despite the number in existence, since the submarine was unproven in war, its true potential was not generally appreciated.

The submarine of World War I (and indeed of World War II) was still essentially a surface ship that could dive for brief periods. It could maintain moderate submerged speed for only a few hours until its batteries became exhausted, forcing it to surface to recharge with the engines. At night, and at other times whenever possible, the submarine cruised on the surface, rigged for quick diving, depending on its low profile to escape detection before it sighted the foe—an advantage that the airplane negated. Submarines would often make the first part of approach on a target surfaced at high speed to get in position to attack. Thus systematic ship and aircraft patrol severely restricted the U-boat's capabilities in the patrolled area. Of the 372 submarines the Germans had or commissioned during the war, over half were lost.

Mines. Like most modern naval weapons, mines have long ancestry, including British and United States efforts in the 17th and 18th centuries. In the 19th century, the Confederates employed mines (called torpedoes) with considerable success in the American Civil War. Their versions included contact mines and percussion or electrically detonated mines fired from shore when the ship was in the right position. This controlled type sank USS "Cairo" on the Yazoo River in 1862, the first destruction of a warship by a mine in combat.

When Robert Whitehead's self-propelled underwater device appeared, it took the name torpedo whereas the term mine reverted to the underwater weapon that lies and waits (or drifts with the current) for its target.

During the latter part of the 19th century the Herzhorn, an improved method of firing contact mines that began to make this one of the most effective weapons in war, appeared. The horn, or tube, protruding from the mine contains a glass tube of acid. When struck by a ship, the glass breaks and releases the acid to form the electrolyte of a small battery that generates enough of an electrical charge to fire a detonator, which in turn sets off the mine.

Early moored mines were laid with a preselected length of mooring cable to suspend them at proper depth below the surface. Later mines of this type were fitted with automatic devices that paid out the cable from a reel in the anchor (or sinker) to position the mine.

Mines were used in the Spanish-American War without result, but in the Russo-Japanese War both sides employed them effectively, destroying three battleships, five cruisers, and eight other warships. During World War I the belligerents laid nearly 250,000 mines. Submarines joined surface ships as minelayers. During the last year of the war, mines began to be employed in large numbers against submarines. Allied minefields sank 44 U-boats, more than were sunk by any other means.

Naval aviation. The airplane had just begun to go to sea on the eve of World War I. In Chesapeake Bay in November 1910, the scout cruiser USS "Birmingham" launched the first airplane ever to take off from a ship. Two months later in San Francisco Bay, January 18, 1911, a plane was landed on an improvised flight deck built over a turret of the armoured cruiser USS "Pennsylvania." The next year the United States Navy bought its first plane, as did the British. Within a few years, larger warships were able to launch planes underway—thus navies were acquiring far-seeing "eyes of the fleet" greatly surpassing the scout cruiser and its frigate ancestor.

In 1914 the British Admiralty converted Channel steamers to carry seaplanes and converted a tanker hull for use as a seaplane carrier for ten planes. "Ark Royal" served in the Dardanelles campaign and in the North Sea in 1918, flying her planes against Zeppelin bases.

The British modified a number of other ships to take planes, including fighters with wheel landing gear that could be launched but could not land on board. A passenger liner was completed as HMS "Argus," the world's first true flush-deck carrier that could launch and land planes on a flight deck extending from bow to stern. But although scores of aircraft went to sea in warships during the war, most naval planes of this period, both sea and land types, operated from shore bases, principally against submarines. Nevertheless, navies put a substantial effort into pioneering air warfare. The United States Navy developed a flying bomb, a pilotless, remote-controlled airplane, an ancestor of the guided missile, and giant seaplanes for distant over-

The first carriers

The World War I submarine

water cruising. In 1919 one of them, NC-4, completed the world's first crossing of the Atlantic by plane, arriving in Lisbon via the Azores on May 27.

Naval planes employed bombs against ships and shore bases. The Royal Navy also added torpedoes starting early in the war, and, by 1915, had seaplanes specially built for torpedo attack. In August of that year, operating from a seaplane tender, they sank two Turkish auxiliaries in the Dardanelles.

To counter the airplane, significant changes were made in warship armament. Early in the century, navies had standardized on two gun sizes for battleships—the centreline-turret main battery providing concentrated massive fire on most bearings and a secondary broadside battery of smaller calibre guns with the typical naval characteristics of high initial velocity, low trajectory, and short time of flight to combat high-speed targets—*i.e.,* destroyers and torpedo boats. The appearance of aircraft, smaller and even faster, demanded rapid-fire, high-angle guns and new fire control. Capital ships again used many types of guns on board with a third battery in U.S. battleships of 3″/.50 calibre anti-aircraft guns. These and 0.30-calibre machine guns were a beginning of intensive developments in air defense.

TOWARD WORLD WAR II

Naval limitations treaties. The end of World War I found Great Britain, France, and Japan building or planning large, new capital ships, and the United States continued a major construction program that would have given it the world's leading navy. To end what was turning into an arms race among former allies, the Washington naval treaty of 1922, and later London naval treaty of 1930, prescribed limits for navies of signatory powers (5:5:3 for the United States, Great Britain, and Japan). Battleships could not be armed with guns larger than 16 inches (41 centimetres; Britain had designed the battle cruiser "Furious" with 18-inch [46-centimetre] guns during the war, and a race for new super guns was feared), could not exceed 35,000 tons standard displacement, and could only be replaced when 20 years old. Any man-of-war over 10,-000 tons was designated a capital ship, thus fixing this as the top limit for cruisers.

Change in warships continued to accelerate, affecting every field of naval warfare, including aircraft and missiles, communications, the revolutionary introduction of radar, anti-aircraft gunnery, propulsion plants and other elements of surface ships, submarines, torpedoes, and mines.

Battleships. Battleship construction, halted for several years, began again in the late 1930s as the disarmament treaties expired. All of the major navies laid down battleships of superior size and quality to the earlier generation. The largest were two Japanese vessels, "Musashi" and "Yamato." Displacing 70,000 tons, mounting 18.1-inch (46-centimetre) guns, with armour capable of withstanding projectiles of equal calibre, these two giants were never surpassed in battleship construction. Four turbine engines gave each a speed of 27 knots, with fuel capacity for a cruising radius of 7,200 miles (11,600 kilometres) at 16 knots. Improvement in engineering plants, including higher steam pressures, added markedly to the speed and radius of the new capital ships; the United States Iowa class had a speed of 33 knots. All of the new battleships bristled with anti-aircraft guns.

In World War II, the new U.S. battleships served primarily with fast, carrier, task forces, protecting carriers from surface attack and providing anti-aircraft protection. They were also frequently used for bombardment of shore targets and occasionally fought surface action in traditional manner, as at Guadalcanal in 1942. Late in the war, United States battleships bombarded the coast of Japan. The newest ships survived hits by torpedoes, gunfire, and Japanese suicide planes (kamikaze) and continued to operate until they could be sent to port for repair.

Great Britain, Germany, and Japan lost new battleships to air attack, in which torpedoes from carrier-based aircraft were the primary weapon, or to a combination of air and submarine or, in the case of "Bismarck," to surface-ship gunfire and torpedoes. Had any of these battleships

been given reasonable air protection, it would have survived. Even old United States battleships went through campaigns from Tarawa to North Africa, Normandy, and Okinawa without loss, though a number were hit.

At Pearl Harbor (December 7, 1941) several old battleships suffered fearfully in the peacetime surprise attack. This was inevitable for any ship not in a condition of maximum gun and watertight-door-closure readiness, employed at times of possible enemy contact and relaxed at other times for the sake of rest and habitability. Yet all but two were repaired—some quickly—and served valuably in amphibious assaults in both oceans.

Naval aviation. After World War I several nations built aircraft carriers, a new type of capital ship that Great Britain had pioneered during the war by converting warships and merchantmen. HMS "Hermes," laid down January 1918, was the first ship begun as an aircraft carrier. After its launch in 1919 the Japanese laid down the second carrier, "Hosho," and pushed it to completion ahead of "Hermes." The fundamental techniques of takeoff and landing were worked out on the "Hosho" and on British and United States ships in the early 1920s. A characteristic feature, the "island," or bridge for navigation and command, was added, though the Japanese continued to operate a few flush-deck carriers for several years. Following the limitations set by the Washington naval treaty of 1922, Japan, the United States, Great Britain, and France all converted capital ships into large carriers, most of which saw service in World War II.

Seaplane tenders were employed for patrol-plane operations. Battleships and cruisers were outfitted with aircraft for scouting and spotting. Techniques for these functions as well as torpedo-attack, dive-bombing, and fighter operations were refined into doctrine.

Among carrier planes in various navies, the United States SBD was probably the best dive bomber flying at the time of Pearl Harbor. The United States Navy's F4F was a rugged and dependable fighter. The lighter, faster Japanese "Zero" could outmanoeuvre it; but, in combat, American pilots had a much higher rate of success, in considerable part because of armour, self-sealing fuel tanks, and heavier gunfire. Improved types of all of the planes were developed during the war.

Carriers played a dominant role in every aspect of the war at sea. The Pacific conflict began with the Japanese carrier strike against Pearl Harbor and ended with American and British carriers operating with impunity against the Japanese homeland. In between, the Battle of the Coral Sea, May 1942, was the first in history in which opposing fleets fought without ever coming in sight of each other. A month later off Midway atoll, carriers again played the decisive role.

The Battle of Midway reinforced a conviction already clear, especially from British operations in the Mediterranean with and without air support, that control of the sea now also meant control of the air over the sea. For the rest of the war this axiom ruled with increasing force. In the autumn of 1942 the Solomon Islands campaign underlined the importance of both aircraft and submarines in fleet operations, emphasized that modern sea power is a trident of air, surface, and undersea forces.

The powerful United States task forces of the war's later stages were composed of three or four task groups that included three to four carriers, six to seven battleships and cruisers, and 13 to 14 destroyers. Improved fighters, guided by the carriers' combat-information centres, radar plots, and fighter direction, provided the basic air defense. Supported by aircraft, destroyers gave antisubmarine protection and set up an outer screen of anti-aircraft fire. Battleships and cruisers ensured protection from surface foes and massive anti-aircraft support closer in to the carriers. The introduction of radar fire control and the proximity fuze, which exploded the projectile in the vicinity of the target, for the 5-inch (13-centimetre) anti-aircraft batteries, made it almost impossible for enemy planes to penetrate the defense.

The phenomenon of radar had been observed in the 1920s. By the late 1930s, prototype sets with huge antennas were operating. A plane or ship as well as land

Arms limitations

Importance of air protection

Dominant role of attack aircraft carriers

Use of radar

reflected the transmitted beams, bouncing an echo back to the antenna on the ship's mast and thence to the receiving-set screen. Reaching ranges up to 200 miles (320 kilometres), radar became invaluable for observation and control of a carrier's own planes and for detection and tracking of hostile planes. It also became a principal factor in antisubmarine warfare (especially for aircraft), for surface-ship formation-keeping and manoeuvring, and for navigation. Radar added markedly to the effectiveness of gunfire, especially anti-aircraft, because at any range it could give distance measurements accurate to within a few yards.

Navies needed carriers for duties that did not require the high speed and complex fighting capability of the first-line, capital-ship attack carrier. A simpler type sufficed for the demands of convoy escort, antisubmarine duties, and amphibious assault. Conversions from merchant-ship hulls initially provided the ships that carried out these duties, thus continuing the time-honoured practice of using merchantmen as warships. Later these escort carriers, as they came to be called, were laid down as such. Most ranged around 8,000 tons, though some displaced over 11,000 tons, similar to the light attack carriers. They had a speed of 18 or 19 knots, carried 28–30 aircraft, and mounted one or two 5-inch guns, plus numerous smaller anti-aircraft batteries.

Seaplane tenders also served with the fleets. The largest could transport seaplanes. Any cove or inlet not controlled by the enemy could serve as an advanced seaplane base immediately upon the arrival of the tender. Seaplanes carried out valuable search, reconnaissance, patrol, and surveillance duties. Naval land-based patrol planes served similar functions; as their ranges increased they began to supplant the slower seaplane but did not do so completely until long after World War II.

Antisubmarine measures. Most major nations built submarines between the wars. The Soviet Union commissioned a very large fleet. Germany began the war with only 57, of which 49 were available for service, whereas the Soviet Union had 235. Germany was also very slow in building up production, losing more submarines than it commissioned in the first 15 months of the war—thus giving Britain time to develop defenses. The new submarines were larger, faster, could dive deeper, and had longer endurance than their World War I predecessors, and carried more powerful torpedoes. The fall of the Low Countries and France in May 1940, providing long, open coastline for submarine and air bases close to British shipping routes, enabled the handful of U-boats to become very effective, but although Germany belatedly put tremendous effort into building submarines, massive antisubmarine measures defeated them.

In addition to large numbers of escort vessels, there were improved weapons. Sonar gear became more efficient. New explosives increased the destructive effect of depth charges. The British produced the hedgehog, a multiple, mortar-like device, mounted forward, that threw a pattern of 24 contact depth charges ahead of the ship while sonar operators could still detect the target on their equipment. This eliminated the blank period unavoidable in a depth-charge attack astern. Patrol aircraft and radar also contributed; the range of patrol planes steadily expanded to permit covering more and more of the convoy ocean routes where submarines might surface to recharge batteries. The extension of range together with the installation of radar on ships and planes made possible night detection and often surprise of the surfaced submarine.

The escort carriers provided air search and attack close to the convoy, forcing U-boats to remain submerged and making it harder for them to get into position for attack. Ultimately, when patrol planes gained endurance to accompany a convoy over much of its route, the escort carriers operated independently in areas of known submarine concentration, making all of the parts of the ocean near shipping routes unsafe for submarines.

Late in the war, when surfacing even at night to recharge batteries had become very hazardous, the Germans adopted the snorkel, a Dutch invention. This air-intake-and-exhaust funnel permitted running the engines while submerged, to recharge batteries without surfacing, and presented a very small radar target.

Mines. Both Great Britain and Germany devised magnetic mines in World War I. Germany continued development, and early in the Battle of Britain small minecraft, submarines, and airplanes laid magnetic bottom mines, detonated by changes in the magnetic field caused by the passage of the iron hull of a ship. The mines caused serious loss and dislocation until one was recovered and suitable minesweeping gear devised. A supplementary countermeasure was degaussing, passing an electrical current through a cable strung horizontally around the ship, thus setting up a magnetic field to counter the mine or the magnetic torpedo-firing mechanism.

In the following years, navies brought out a wide variety of firing mechanisms for mines that included a combination of various influence types, such as the acoustic and, near the end, the almost unsweepable pressure type, actuated by a change in pressure caused by a ship's passage.

Surface vessels, aircraft, and submarines on both sides laid mines in every theatre. British air-laid mines caused many losses and severely hampered Axis operations from the Baltic Sea to the Mediterranean. The Allies lost numerous warships and 1.4 million tons of merchant shipping to mines.

In the Pacific, United States carrier planes, submarines, and surface vessels laid mines, but the largest effort was by the United States Air Force, laying naval mines. In the spring and summer of 1945, B-29s, operating from the Mariana Islands, laid over 12,000 influence-type mines in Japan's home waters, sinking about a half-million tons of Japan's merchant marine.

Cruisers and destroyers. Powerful new warships of these types appeared in all of the major navies in the 1930s. Two cruiser classifications came into common use: "heavy," armed with 8-inch (20-centimetre) guns, and "light," with 6-inch (15-centimetre) guns. Both mounted 5-inch double purpose batteries, and in the war added 40-millimetre and 20-millimetre (1.6- and 0.8-inch). The United States also built anti-aircraft cruisers with 5-inch guns as the main battery. Several other nations also built anti-aircraft cruisers. Cased ammunition and automatic loading systems increased the rate of fire of all of the naval anti-aircraft. Radar, developed for gun directors, greatly improved accuracy, making possible automatic tracking of targets and precise firing in fog and darkness. Another anti-aircraft improvement was the influence or proximity fuze, a tiny electronic device that detonated the projectile at a predetermined distance from the target to produce maximum damage.

Because the disarmament treaties did not limit them, most nations built a series of new destroyers of increasing capabilities. In 1939 the British Navy had over 100 of modern construction. These and older destroyers satisfied only a beginning of Great Britain's needs, despite the small number of German submarines. Beginning in 1941 the British produced convoy-escort ships called sloops and corvettes, smaller, slower, and less complex than destroyers. The United States commissioned over 400 fast destroyers between 1939 and 1945, and, starting in 1942, turned out a stream of nearly twice that many smaller and slower destroyer escorts that were effective both for convoy escort and in hunter-killer task groups.

The Japanese also improved their destroyers, notably in the areas of night optics and torpedoes. They inflicted severe losses on the United States and Allies in cruisers and on the United States in destroyers. The large United States building program soon changed the balance in destroyers as in other ships.

Service ships. Logistic ships, indispensable for World War II fleet operations, included tenders with spare parts and repair shops to act as mother ships for destroyers, submarines, tankers, supply ships, ammunition ships, netlayer-tenders, and various other types. Minesweepers were indispensable, both for attack and defense.

In operational handling of service and logistics ships, the United States Navy pioneered two developments widely copied since: first, the establishment of floating advanced bases, capable of taking care of the whole fleet's needs

Margin notes:

Improved anti-submarine measures

New destroyer types

and including floating dry docks, floating cranes, repair barges and ships, barges for degaussing (demagnetizing), and storage and issue of ammunition and supplies; and second, underway replenishment, which made it possible for task forces to remain at sea for months at a time without returning to port. Fuel for ships and planes far outweighs in tonnage any other logistic requirement of warships, followed, in combat operations, by munitions, food, and other supplies.

Amphibians. Although the failure of the Dardanelles campaign in World War I had somewhat discredited amphibious operations, both the United States and Japanese navies practiced such operations between the two wars. The Japanese opened their offensive in 1941–42 with successful amphibious assaults against Wake Island, the Philippines, Indonesia, and several other points. After Midway, the United States launched its first amphibious assault, against Guadalcanal, in August 1942, an operation that involved several new types of landing craft as well as all classes of ship, from battleship to converted merchantman. A long series of amphibious assaults followed in both Pacific and European waters, with increasing refinements of landing and support craft. The final amphibious operation of the war, against Okinawa in 1945, involved about 1,500 vessels. An advance force of battleships, destroyers, minesweepers, landing craft, and other auxiliaries entered the area a week before the main assault, sweeping mines, clearing obstructions, and establishing a repair-logistic anchorage in a nearby island group, simultaneously carrying out an intensive bombardment of the landing area. In the assault, large merchantmen types, converted or built for assault, participated. They carried numbers of landing craft with bow ramps, some for troops, some for vehicles and troops. Some landing craft were armed with guns, mortars, or rockets. Amphibious tractors and trucks also waded ashore. The highly complex operation, with its great variety of ships and craft effectively coordinated, significantly illustrated the growing ability of sea-based power to outweigh that ashore.

Amphibious assaults

WARSHIPS IN THE NUCLEAR AGE

The generation since World War II has seen the continuation of swift change in warships that has characterized the past century and a half. Among developments that may be termed epochal are nuclear propulsion, ballistic missiles with atomic warheads, guided missiles, and space satellites for naval operations. Many other advances have taken place; carrier jet planes fly at two to three times the speed of sound, and submarines extend their operations to thousands of feet below the surface.

Attack carriers. After World War II, the rapid development of jet aircraft required longer and stronger carrier decks. The angled deck and the steam catapult were developed by the British and quickly adopted by the United States to handle increasingly larger and faster planes.

Of the new carriers, the most powerful was "Enterprise," which displaced 89,600 tons with an overall length of 1,123 feet (342 metres) and extreme width of flight deck of 257 feet (78 metres). She carried over 70 of the new, large planes and her powerful reactors thrust her through the water at speeds much above 30 knots. Her greater manoeuvrability and endurance at high speed, without delays for refueling (except for planes), gave her outstanding advantages over other carriers.

The "Enterprise"

The modern carrier task force roughly follows the pattern of World War II, with one to three carriers accompanied by cruiser and destroyer types as available. Ships and equipment are far more sophisticated. Topsides bristle with electronic gear, radars, communication antennas, and missile guidance and countermeasure equipment. Anti-aircraft armament consists of guided missiles, supplemented by a few rapid-fire, medium-calibre guns. The numerous small-calibre mounts of World War II have disappeared; future air attack is anticipated as coming from long-range missiles.

Several navies today employ antisubmarine carriers. Most are World War II types built by Great Britain or the United States, though France and the United Kingdom completed a handful during and after the Korean War. In general, all of these carry a mixture of helicopters and fixed-wing planes. Both carriers and aircraft have extensive electronic gear. Weapons include depth charges and homing torpedoes.

An important supplement may be the helicopter mated to destroyer types. Great Britain, Canada, and the United States participated with other NATO allies in development and test of suitable helicopters and equipment to handle and house helicopters on the rapidly pitching and rolling decks of smaller ships. Canada, for example, has solved most of the problems met even in heavy seas.

Amphibious carriers. As successful helicopters evolved, the U.S. Marines modified amphibious assault techniques to include vertical envelopment, landing by air to the rear of hostile beach defenses. The United States Navy converted some World War II carriers into helicopter carriers for amphibious assault, and their success led to the construction of "Iwo Jima," commissioned in 1961 as the first ship designed and constructed for helicopters. She and six sister ships can each carry a marine battalion landing team, with guns, vehicles, and equipment, and a helicopter squadron to lift them to the beach. As vertical-and-short-takeoff-and-landing planes go into service, this type may also take on functions of the escort carriers. Displacing 18,000 tons, full load, this type transports about 2,000 troops and helicopters to take them to the beach.

Carriers of the Soviet Union. The first carrier built for the Soviet Navy was a helicopter carrier; in 1967 "Moskva" was commissioned, followed by a sister ship, "Leningrad." "Moskva" and "Leningrad" combine a carrier deck for helicopters (situated aft) with the guided missile armament of a cruiser forward. At 18,000 to 19,000 tons, full load, they are suitable for antisubmarine or amphibious operations. Their appearance coincided with intensive work in the Soviet Union on vertical-and-short-takeoff-and-landing planes. The Soviet Union now flies at least three types of short-takeoff fighters with maximum speeds ranging from 2 to 2.8 times the speed of sound. Experimental models of vertical-takeoff planes are also being tested, in subsonic versions that represent important progress toward supersonic successors. A carrier, probably to handle these, was under construction in the mid 1970s.

Soviet helicopter carriers

Cruisers. Construction of this class with guns as its main armament appears to have ended. Except for the nuclear-powered, missile-armed "Long Beach," the United States has only a handful of cruisers in commission, laid down in World War II and converted to carry guided missiles. In the 1950s the Soviet Union built 14 gun-armed light cruisers (19,000 tons displacement) but thereafter changed to smaller types mounting antiship or anti-aircraft missiles for the main battery and also fitted with strong antisubmarine capability. The largest of these are the 6,000-ton Kynda class, carrying two, surface-to-surface, quadruple, Shaddock missile mounts and the newer 7,000-ton Krestas, with two twin Shaddock launchers and considerably increased missile capability. Navies in the 1970s built surface warships not so much to fight one another as to combat submarines, aircraft, and guided missiles.

The United States Navy's "Long Beach" was the first surface warship in the world to steam under atomic energy and remains the only cruiser so propelled. She can race through the water indefinitely at speeds probably exceeding 35 knots. Her armament consists of guided missiles, two-5 inch guns, and antisubmarine weapons.

First nuclear-powered surface warship

Superdestroyers. While gun cruisers pass from the scene, destroyers have grown larger until some are, in fact, small cruisers. The United States calls her largest types frigates, a term most other navies tend to reserve for smaller escort or antisubmarine types.

The United States Belknap class, laid down in the early 1960s and the latest United States Navy operational non-nuclear type, displaces nearly 8,000 tons full load. Armament includes five- and three-inch guns and a twin missile launcher for anti-aircraft and antisubmarine missiles. Development of the antisubmarine missile concept, as in an improved United States version and in the Australian Ikara missile, provides for sending target information from the firing ship's sonar or helicopter sonar into the automatic fire-control data-computing system that controls the missile throughout its flight to keep it directed on the target regardless of manoeuvres.

The United States has also built the only destroyers with nuclear power. The first, "Bainbridge," of 8,500 tons displacement, was commissioned in 1962. "Truxtun" was commissioned in 1967.

Destroyers. The large frigates that merge the destroyer type with the small cruiser merely continue a process underway from the first torpedo-boat destroyer. Tasks multiplied for this high-speed, versatile vessel, whose appearance in the fleet coincided with the birth and swift growth of submarines and aircraft, and combatting these hazards became principal duties. The phenomenal growth in effectiveness of these two foes through nuclear power for submarines and jet engines for aircraft has coincided with a similar increase in the destroyer's powers to combat them.

Instead of many guns, destroyers bristle with an array of sensors and are packed with electronic gear for swift detection, identification, and computation of firing data. Magazines hold supersonic, homing, guided missiles—as well as projectiles for the minimum number of guns that must remain in the armament. The complex warship carrying all of this must also have high speed, excellent sea-keeping ability, and long endurance. Lightweight materials such as fibreglass and aluminum and the use of solid-state devices and other miniaturization steps have compensated for only part of the additions. The result is that the size of destroyers had to increase.

The newest in most fleets now range in displacement up to 5,000 tons. Soviet destroyers built in the 1960s displace 4,000 to 4,600 tons, as do most of those of the United States. Destroyers of France and The Netherlands on the ways displace about 1,000 tons more. The United States has begun to build the Spruance class, displacing more than 7,000 tons, driven by gas-turbine engines and carrying two helicopters.

United States terminology, distinguishing destroyer leaders (frigates) from conventional destroyers, largely implies only more command functions. Otherwise, the two have essentially the same armament, speed, and employment in fleet-escort duties. The United Kingdom and many other nations call both large types destroyers and assign frigate classification to the slower, usually smaller, and lighter gunned ocean escort, sometimes called the junior destroyer. Destroyer escorts have also grown and have acquired characteristics in many cases close to those of destroyers. In the 1950s a number of nations built escort types of under 2,000 tons displacement. Yet the rapid advance in submarine performance, especially under nuclear propulsion, has caused these types to experience marked growth. This has been necessary to accommodate helicopters, the more complex sensors (radar and sonar; hull-mounted and variable-depth), weapons, and associated equipment more complex than ever before. At the end of the 1960s and in the 1970s, many displaced 4,000 tons or more. Canada, notably successful in building destroyer escorts of just under 3,000 tons, particularly in helicopter operations, now builds in the 4,000-ton range to accommodate advanced weapon systems. Great Britain has under construction gas-turbine patrol frigates estimated to displace under 3,000 tons and to run at a top speed of 40 knots. If successful in handling the most effective antisubmarine weapon systems, this type could bring marked improvement to surface-ship antisubmarine operations.

Patrol boats and other small ships. Corvettes, fast patrol ships, and other small types serve in various fleets for coastal and limited-radius deep-sea operations. These vessels may range in size from France's new corvette types of about 1,300 tons, and the Soviet Union's 1,200-ton Mirkas, to Japan's 500-ton submarine chasers. Several nations have also built small, fast, torpedo, gun, or missile boats, most of which do not have antisubmarine capability. Great Britain has two 114-ton fast patrol boats with over 50 knots maximum speed. The Soviet Union has 125 or more 35- to 40-knot surface-to-surface-missile boats displacing 100 or 200 tons according to class. One of these on loan to Egypt sank the Israeli destroyer "Elath"

with Styx missiles at a range of 13–14 miles (21–22 kilometres) in 1967.

The Asheville 240-ton class of gunboats was commissioned in the late 1960s, with diesel and gas-turbine propulsion that gives top speed of over 40 knots. The United States also has two small 60-ton hydrofoil gunboats and two larger experimental vessels (one of 310 tons) in the 40–50 knot speed range, which may be forerunners of fast escort ships of the future.

Amphibians, minecraft, and auxiliaries. *Amphibians.* The United States has set the pace in amphibious developments since World War II. The Soviet Union has made much progress in amphibious buildup, including its new helicopter carriers and improved versions of old British-American landing vessels such as her 15-knot Alligator LST (tank landing ship). The United States, however, has brought out a whole family of new or vastly improved types—generally faster, larger, and far more effective. Examples are:

The World War II LST, of which the United States built 1,041, displaced about 4,000 tons full load and transported about 150 troops with equipment at 10–11 knots. The current, fourth-generation Newport class displaces over 8,000 tons, transports amphibious craft, tanks, and other combat vehicles, along with up to 500 men, to a hostile shore at over 20 knots. Instead of simply beaching, like her predecessor, she has an extendable ramp supported by huge projecting derrick extensions on each side of the bow. As the ship grounds, the ramp shoots forward hydraulically 112 feet (34 metres). While vehicles and troops land over the ramp, amphibious tractors in the tank deck move out the stern gates.

Besides the helicopter assault carriers earlier described, becoming operational in the middle 1970s was another completely new, giant type of amphibious assault ship displacing 40,000 tons and combining the functions of several types of landing ships. By carrying a balanced load of troops, combat vehicles, and cargo for a full battalion landing team, this vessel maintains their tactical integrity together. With a large dock well, under a flight deck extending the full length of the ship, it can land the team by helicopter and landing craft. Vertical-and-short-takeoff-and-landing planes will in time give it much of the necessary capability of close air support that World War II escort carriers provided.

Two other important ships are notable. The LSD (dock landing ship) that proved so useful in World War II has been improved in speed and troop-carrying capacity.

The LPD (amphibious transport dock) was developed from the LSD but provides more versatility. "Nashville," representative of the latest, displaces 17,000 tons and cruises at better than 20 knots.

Riverine warfare has close affinity to conventional amphibious operations. Since VE Day the Soviet Union has built numerous small ships and craft to maintain strong river and coastal forces. The powerful Soviet Danube River flotilla alone has about 100 craft including 120-ton armoured gunboats, large landing craft, fast artillery boats, assault boats, and hydrofoils. Missile patrol boats and smaller vessels of the deep-sea fleet can also participate in river operations.

As a result of the Vietnam War, the United States developed several new types of river craft, including 50-foot (15-metre) Swifts, adapted from oil-drilling support craft; river patrol boats developed from fibre glass yacht-design hulls, with Styrofoam flotation gear to keep them afloat even when shot-riddled; monitors converted from medium landing craft, heavily armoured and armed with a 105-millimetre (4.13-inch) howitzer, 81-millimetre (3.19-inch) mortar, or 40-millimetre (1.57-inch) machine gun in the turret, along with machine guns; and assault-support boats, multipurpose craft, well armoured, heavily gunned, and capable of 15-knot speed, about twice that of the other armoured craft.

Minecraft. Like other weapons, mines of each decade are progressively more sophisticated. Acoustic, magnetic, and pressure-firing devices become harder to sweep. Nuclear mines have introduced the ultimate in explosive power. The Soviet Navy has the largest minelaying force,

Growth of destroyer escorts

Capabilities of newest amphibious vessels

including fast surface minelayers with four launch tracks and below-deck capacity for 400 mines. Mine racks can be installed in any ship, naval or merchant. Most submarines can serve as minelayers, as can aircraft.

Since the Korean War, the United States has maintained a strong mine-warfare capability by development of mines and minecraft, including wooden-hull, nonmagnetic vessels for sweeping some of the advanced firing mechanisms in modern mines.

Auxiliaries. Many different types of ships and craft must serve to meet the everyday requirements of a fleet in normal operations. When crisis comes, the need mounts and is met in the initial stage by ships in reserve and by conversion of commercial vessels. Of notable potential value in this connection are the Soviet Union's new merchantmen, ocean-fishing and hydrographic ships, most of which are, in concept and design, fleet auxiliaries.

In addition, the Soviet navy has constructed a series of destroyer, submarine, and other tenders, oilers, ammunition and other special-purpose ships, emphasizing at-sea logistic replenishment and service.

Of the United States Navy's approximately 100 types of ships, a good number are auxiliaries—tenders, tankers, refrigerator ships, ammunition ships, net, survey, oceanographic research, salvage, degaussing, and other types of essential and usually unsung ships. In key combat-type auxiliaries the United States has made significant progress during the last two decades, especially in design.

(E.McN.E./R.L.Sc./J.C.Re./Ed.)

DEVELOPMENT OF SUBMARINES

A submarine is a naval vessel capable of operation underwater. Submarines first became a major factor in naval warfare during World War I (1914–18), when Germany employed them as commerce destroyers; they played a similar role on a larger scale in World War II (1939–45), in both the Atlantic (by Germany) and the Pacific (by the United States). In the 1960s the nuclear-powered submarine, capable of remaining underwater for months at a time and of firing long-range nuclear missiles without surfacing, had come to be regarded by most military strategists as the most important of all strategic weapons. Nuclear submarines armed with torpedoes as well as anti-ship and antisubmarine missiles were in the 1970s considered a key element of naval warfare.

For centuries man has attempted to descend into the depths for scientific observation, for salvage, to reap the animal and mineral riches of the oceans, and for the purpose of attacking enemy ships in time of war. Herodotus, Aristotle, and Pliny the Elder all mentioned attempts to build diving bells or other such devices. A 13th-century French manuscript, *La Vrai Histoire d'Alexandre,* described a fictitious underwater venture by Alexander the Great (356–323 BC) in a glass barrel. Among the many inventions associated with the genius of Leonardo da Vinci was a device for underwater exploration.

The first submarines. The first serious discussion of a "submarine"—a craft designed to be navigated underwater—appeared in 1578 from the pen of William Bourne, a British mathematician and writer on naval subjects. Bourne published *Inventions or Devises,* in which the "18th Devise" was a completely enclosed boat that could be submerged and rowed underwater. It consisted of a wooden frame covered with waterproof leather; it was to be submerged by reducing its volume by contracting the sides through the use of hand vises. Bourne did not actually construct his boat, and Cornelis Drebbel (or Cornelius van Drebel), a Dutch inventor, is usually credited with building the first submarine. Between 1620 and 1624 he successfully manoeuvred his craft at depths of from 12 to 15 feet (four to five metres) beneath the surface during repeated trials in the Thames River, England. King James I is said to have gone aboard the craft for a short ride. Drebbel's submarine resembled that proposed by Bourne in that its outer hull consisted of greased leather over a wooden frame; oars extended through the sides and, sealed with tight-fitting leather flaps, provided a means of propulsion both on the surface and underwater. Drebbel's

first craft was followed by two larger ones built on the same principle.

A number of submarine boats were conceived in the early years of the 18th century. By 1727 no fewer than 14 types had been patented in England alone. An unidentified inventor, whose work was described in the *Gentleman's Magazine* of 1747, proposed an ingenious method of submerging and returning to the surface: his submarine design had goatskin bags attached to the hull with each skin connected to an aperture in the bottom of the craft. He planned to submerge the vessel by filling the skins with water and to surface by forcing the water out of the skins with a "twisting rod." This arrangement was a forerunner of the modern submarine ballast tank.

The submarine was first used as an offensive weapon in naval warfare during the U.S. Revolution (1775–83). The "Turtle," a one-man craft invented by David Bushnell, a student at Yale, was built of wood in the shape of a walnut standing on end. Submerged, the craft was powered by propellers cranked by the operator (Figure 22). The plan

Fishing and hydrographic ships

Bushnell's "Turtle"

By courtesy of the U.S. Navy

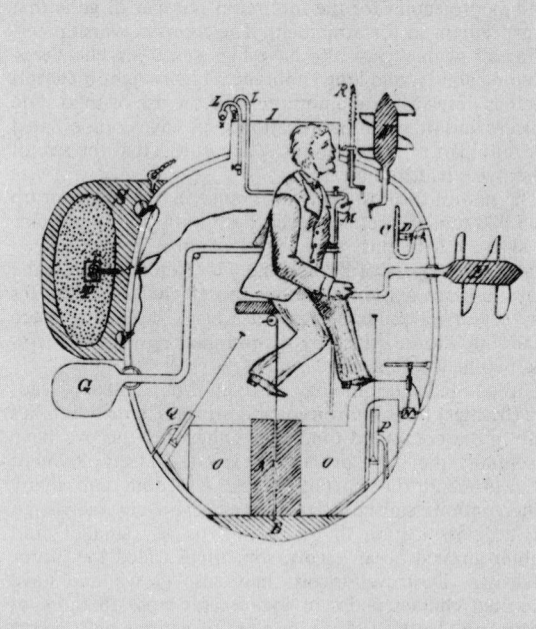

Figure 22: Bushnell's submarine torpedo boat, 1776. Drawing of a cutaway view made by Lieut. Comdr. F.M. Barber in 1885 from a description left by Bushnell.

was to have the "Turtle" make an underwater approach to a British warship, attach a charge of gunpowder by a screw device operated from within the craft, and leave before the charge was exploded by a time fuse. Piloted by Ezra Lee, an army sergeant from Lyme, Conn., the "Turtle" made a night attack on HMS "Eagle" in New York harbour. After repeated failures to force the screw through the copper sheathing on the warship's hull, Lee gave up, released the charge, and withdrew safely. The powder exploded without damaging the "Eagle," which shifted to a berth farther out in the harbour.

Robert Fulton, famed U.S. inventor and artist, experimented with submarines several years before his steamboat "Clermont" steamed up the Hudson River. In 1800, while in France, Fulton built the submarine "Nautilus" under a grant from Napoleon Bonaparte. Completed in May 1801, this craft was made of copper sheets over iron ribs. A collapsing mast and sail were provided for surface propulsion, and a hand-turned propeller drove the boat when submerged. A precursor of a conning tower fitted with a glass-covered porthole permitted observation from within the craft. The "Nautilus" submerged by taking water into ballast tanks, and a horizontal "rudder"—a forerunner of the diving plane—helped keep the craft at the desired depth. The submarine contained enough air to keep four men alive and two candles burning for three hours underwater; later a tank of compressed air was added.

The "Nautilus" was intended to attach an explosive

charge to the hull of an enemy ship in much the same manner as the "Turtle." Fulton experimentally sank an old schooner moored at Brest but, setting out to destroy British warships, was unable to overtake those he sighted. France's interest in Fulton's submarine waned, and he left for England, offering his invention to his former enemy. In 1805 the "Nautilus" sank the brig "Dorothy" in a test, but the Royal Navy would not back his efforts. Fulton then came to the United States and succeeded in obtaining congressional backing for a more ambitious undersea craft. This new submarine was to carry 100 men and be powered by a steam engine. Fulton died before the craft was actually finished, however, and the submarine, named "Mute," was left to rot, eventually sinking at its moorings.

During the War of 1812 between the United States and England, David Bushnell built another submarine, which attacked HMS "Ramillies" at anchor off New London, Conn. This time the craft's operator succeeded in boring a hole in the ship's copper sheathing, but the screw broke loose as the explosive was being attached to the ship's hull. The attempt failed, but again the submarine escaped.

The next U.S. attempt at submarine warfare came during the Civil War (1861–65) when the Confederate States resorted to "unconventional" methods to overcome the Union Navy's superior strength, exerted in a blockade of Southern ports. In 1862 Horace L. Hunley of Mobile, Alabama, financed the building of a Confederate submarine named "Pioneer," a craft that was 34 ft (10 m) long and was driven by a hand-cranked propeller operated by three men. It probably was scuttled to prevent its capture when Union forces occupied New Orleans (although some records say the "Pioneer" was lost with all hands during a dive while en route to attack Union ships).

The second submarine developed by the same builders was a remarkably advanced concept: a 25-ft (7.5 m) iron boat intended to be propelled by a battery and electric motors. Not surprisingly, no suitable motors could be found, so a four-man-cranked propeller was again adopted. The submarine sank without loss of life in heavy seas off Mobile Bay while seeking to attack the enemy.

Confeder-ate submarines   The third submarine of the Confederacy was the "H.L. Hunley," a modified iron boiler lengthened to between 36 and 40 ft (11 and 12 m). Ballast tanks and a system of weights submerged the craft; it could travel at a speed of four miles an hour, powered by eight men cranking its propeller. Its armament consisted of a "torpedo," filled with 90 pounds (41 kilograms) of gunpowder, towed behind the submarine at the end of a 200-foot (60-metre) line. The "Hunley" was to dive under an enemy warship and drag the torpedo against its hull. After a successful test against a barge, the "Hunley" was moved by railroad to Charleston, South Carolina. There the vessel suffered a number of disasters, sinking three times and drowning a number of crewmen including Hunley himself. Manned for a fourth time, the "Hunley" was fitted with a "torpedo" on the end of a long spar and made several successful dives. On the night of February 17, 1864, the submarine attacked the Union warship "Housatonic" in Charleston harbour. The torpedo's detonation exploded the warship's magazines: the "Housatonic" sank in shallow water with the loss of five men, but the "Hunley" also was destroyed and her crew killed.

One of the more intrepid submarine inventors of the same period was Wilhelm Bauer, a noncommissioned officer of Bavarian artillery, who built two boats, "Le Plongeur-Marin" (1851) and "Le Diable-Marin" (1855). The first boat sank in Kiel harbour on February 1, 1851, but Bauer and his two assistants escaped successfully from a depth of 60 ft (18 m) after the craft had been on the bottom for five hours. His second craft, built for the Russian government, was successful and reportedly made 134 dives before being lost at sea. In September 1856, during the coronation of Tsar Alexander II, Bauer submerged his submarine in Kronstadt harbour with several musicians on board. An underwater rendition of the Russian national anthem was clearly heard by persons inside ships in the harbour.

Advent of the machine-powered submarines. A major limitation of these early submarines was their lack of a suitable means of propulsion. In 1880 an English clergy-man, the Rev. George W. Garrett, successfully operated a submarine with steam from a coal-fired boiler that featured a retractable smokestack. The fire had to be extinguished before the craft would submerge (or it would exhaust the air in the submarine), but enough steam remained in the boilers for travelling several miles underwater.

Similarly, Swedish gun designer Torsten Nordenfelt constructed a steam-powered submarine driven by twin propellers. His craft could be submerged by vertical propellers to a depth of 50 ft (15 m) and was fitted with one of the first practical torpedo tubes. Several nations built submarines to Nordenfelt's design.

In an effort to overcome the problems of propulsion, two French naval officers built the 146-ft (45-m) submarine "Le Plongeur" in 1864, powered by an 80-horsepower (hp) compressed-air engine, but the craft quickly exhausted its air tanks whenever it got underway. Development of the electric motor finally made electric propulsion practicable. The submarine "Nautilus," built in 1886 by two Englishmen, was an all-electric craft. This "Nautilus" was propelled on the surface at a speed of six knots by two 50-hp electric motors operated from a 100-cell storage battery. But the battery had to be recharged and overhauled at short intervals, and the craft was never able to travel more than 80 miles (130 km) without a battery recharge. In France, Gustave Zédé launched the "Gymnote" in 1888; it, too, was propelled by an electric motor and was extremely manoeuvrable but tended to go out of control when it dived.

The end of the 19th century was a period of intensive submarine development, and Zédé collaborated in a number of designs sponsored by the French Navy. A most successful French undersea craft of the period was the "Narval," designed by Maxime Laubeuf, a marine engineer in the Navy (Figure 23). Launched in 1899, the "Narval" was   The French "Narval"

By courtesy of Henri Le Masson

Figure 23: French "Narval" submarine, c. 1905.

a double-hulled craft, 111½ ft (34 m) long, propelled on the surface by a steam engine and by electric motors when submerged. The ballast tanks were located between the double hulls, a concept still in use today. The "Narval" made a large number of successful dives. To demonstrate her capabilities, the "Narval" once cruised for 48 hours in the English Channel during a simulated combat mission, then forced the narrow and carefully watched entrance of the roadstead at Brest and fired her four externally carried torpedoes at targets. French progress in submarines was marked by the four Sirène class steam-driven undersea craft completed in 1900–01 and the "Aigrette," completed in 1905, the first diesel-driven submarine of any navy.

Similarly, there were submarine successes in the United States by rival inventors John P. Holland (an Irish immigrant) and Simon Lake. Holland launched his first undersea craft in 1875. This one and its successors were significant in combining water ballast with horizontal rudders for diving. In 1895, in competition with Nordenfelt, Holland received an order from the U.S. Navy for a submarine. This was to be the "Plunger," propelled by steam on the surface and by electricity when submerged. The craft underwent many design changes and finally was abandoned before completion. Holland returned the funds advanced by the navy and built his next submarine (his sixth) at his own expense. This was the "Holland," a 53¼-ft (16-m) craft launched in 1897 and accepted by the navy in 1900.

For underwater propulsion the "Holland" had an electric motor and was propelled on the surface by a gasoline engine. The submarine's armament consisted of a bow torpedo tube, for which three torpedoes were carried, and two dynamite guns. The guns, one pointing forward and one aft, were built into the hull and aimed by pointing the submarine directly at or away from the target. With its nine-man crew the "Holland" was a successful boat and was modified many times to test different arrangements of propellers, diving planes, rudders, and other equipment.

Holland's chief competitor, Simon Lake, built his first submarine, the "Argonaut I," in 1894, powered by a gasoline engine and electric motor. This and Lake's other early boats were fitted with wheels for the submarine to roll over the ocean floor. He envisioned submarines sending out divers to cut cables, destroy enemy mines, and telephone enemy ship movements back to the submarine; in peacetime, such submarine-diver operations could be used for sea-floor mineral mining. In 1898 the "Argonaut I" sailed from Norfolk, Virginia, to New York under its own power, predating the cruises of the French "Narval" and marking the first time an undersea craft operated extensively in the open sea. Lake's second submarine was the "Protector," launched in 1901. After the U.S. Navy rejected this craft, Lake offered the "Protector" to Russia and Japan. Tsarist Russia bought the vessel and five more like it. Simultaneously, Japan bought several Holland boats, but neither side used them during the Russo-Japanese conflict (1904–05).

Of the major naval powers at the turn of the century, only Britain remained indifferent toward submarines. Finally, in 1901, the Royal Navy ordered five of the Holland-design undersea craft. Germany completed its first submarine, the *Unterseeboot* No. 1, in 1905. This craft was 139 ft (42 m) long, powered on the surface by a heavy oil engine and by an electric motor submerged, and was armed with one torpedo tube. Thus, the stage was set for the 20th-century submarine, a craft propelled on the surface by diesel engines and underwater by electric motors, submerging by diving planes and taking on water ballast, and armed with torpedoes for sinking enemy ships. The quarters inside these early craft were cramped, generally wet, and stank from diesel oil.

World War I. By the eve of World War I all of the major navies included submarines in their fleets, but these craft were relatively small, were considered of questionable military value, and generally were intended for coastal operations. The most significant exception to the concept of coastal activity was the German Deutschland class of merchant U-boats, each 315 ft (95 m) long with two large cargo compartments. These submarines could carry 700 tons of cargo at 12- to 13-knot speeds on the surface and at seven knots submerged. Manned by a crew of 8 officers and 21 enlisted men under the command of Capt. Paul Koenig, a veteran merchant-ship skipper, the "Deutschland" herself made two successful cargo trips between Germany and the United States in 1916 despite a British naval blockade. The "Deutschland" became the "U-155" when fitted with torpedo tubes and deck guns and with seven similar submarines served in a combat role during the latter stages of the war. In comparison, the "standard" submarine of World War I measured slightly over 200 ft (60 m) in length and displaced less than 1,000 tons on the surface.

The prewar submarines generally had been armed with self-propelled torpedoes for attacking enemy ships. During the war submarines also were fitted with deck guns. This permitted them to approach enemy merchant ships on the surface and signal them to stop for searching (an early war policy) and later to sink small or unarmed ships that did not warrant expenditure of torpedoes. Most warbuilt submarines had one and sometimes two guns of about three- or four-inch calibre (diameter of the projectile); however, several later German submarines carried 5.9-inch (15-centimetre) guns (including the Deutschland class in military configuration).

Late in the war the British completed the first of three M class submarines, each armed with a 12-inch (30-centimetre) gun (in addition to four torpedo tubes and an anti-aircraft gun). These submarine monitors were intended to steam off an enemy coast with their decks submerged and only the muzzle of the 12-inch gun and a sighting periscope protruding through the water. Capable of firing far inland, these giant submarines were 296 ft (90 m) long, displaced 1,650 tons on the surface, and had diesel-electric propulsion that could drive them at 14 knots on the surface and 8 knots submerged.

Another armament variation was the submarine modified to lay mines during covert missions off an enemy's harbours. The Germans constructed several specialized submarines with vertical mine tubes through their hulls; some U-boats carried 48 mines in addition to their torpedoes.

Also noteworthy was the development, during the war, of the concept of an antisubmarine submarine. British submarines sank 17 German U-boats during the conflict; the early submarine-versus-submarine successes led to British development of the R class submarine intended specifically for this role. These were relatively small craft, 163 ft (50 m) long and displacing 410 tons on the surface, with only one propeller (most contemporary submarines had two). Diesel engines could drive them at nine knots on the surface, but once submerged, large batteries permitted their electric motors to drive them at the high speed of 15 knots for two hours. Thus, they were both manoeuvrable and fast. Advanced underwater listening equipment (asdic/sonar) was installed, and six forward torpedo tubes made them potent weapons. Although these submarines appeared too late to have any actual effect on the war, they pioneered a new concept in the development of the submarine. ^{Anti-submarine submarines}

All World War I-era submarines were propelled by diesels on the surface and by electric motors submerged, except for the British Swordfish and K class. These submarines, intended to operate as scouts for surface warships, required the high speeds then available only from steam turbines. The Swordfish was of conventional size, but the K boats were 340 ft (100 m) long and displaced 1,780 tons on the surface; the steam plant of the K boats propelled them at 23½ knots on the surface, while electric motors gave them a 10-knot submerged speed, a common underwater speed for submarines until after World War II.

Interest in submarines continued high within the world's navies during the period between World Wars I and II. A particularly attractive notion was that of developing large, heavily gunned submarines for commerce raiding. The British "X-1," completed in 1925, was a long-range submarine with four 5.2-inch (13-centimetre) guns in twin, armoured turrets, in addition to six torpedo tubes. The French "Surcouf," completed in 1934, mounted two eight-inch (20-centimetre) guns in a single turret, in addition to ten torpedo tubes, and also had a small hangar to accommodate a seaplane. The aircraft was to be used to search for merchant ship victims. The seaplane–submarine team also was investigated by the Royal Navy, which removed the 12-inch (30-centimetre) gun from the submarine monitor "M-2"—the 12-inch gun being unsuitable for use against surface ships—and fitted her to carry a seaplane. The U.S. Navy similarly fitted the submarine "S-1" with a hangar and small seaplane, while the Japanese Navy modified a number of submarines to operate small seaplanes. ^{Commerce raiding}

During this period the U.S. Navy built its first large, long-range submarine, the "Argonaut." Completed in 1928, she was 381 ft (116 m) long, displaced 2,710 tons on the surface, was armed with two six-inch guns and four forward torpedo tubes, and could carry 60 mines. The "Argonaut," the largest non-nuclear submarine ever built by the U.S. Navy, led to the highly successful Gato and Balao classes used in World War II.

During the 1930s the rejuvenated Soviet shipyards began producing large numbers of submarines, primarily coastal craft, in an attempt to make the U.S.S.R. a sea power without major expenditures for surface warships. But though the Soviet program achieved quantity, their ships were unsuitable for operations against the German Navy, their crews were poorly trained, and Soviet bases were blocked by ice much of the time.

World War II. World War II (1939–45) saw extensive submarine campaigns on all of the world's oceans. In the Atlantic the principal German U-boat was the VII type, a relatively small but effective craft when properly employed. The Type VIIC variant was 220¼ ft (67 m) long, displaced 769 tons on the surface, and was powered by diesel-electric machinery at a speed of 17 knots on the surface and 7½ knots submerged. Armament consisted of one 3.5-inch (nine-centimetre) deck gun, various anti-aircraft guns, and five torpedo tubes, four forward and one aft. Either 14 torpedoes or 14 tube-launched mines were carried. Manned by a crew of 44, these submarines had a surface endurance of 6,500 miles (10,400 kilometres) at 12 knots, but, when they were submerged, their batteries would remain active a little less than a day at four knots.

Three German designs warrant special mention: The VIIF design was an elongated boat 254¾ ft (78 m) long intended to replenish other U-boats at sea with torpedoes—25 spares were carried, above a normal complement of 14—and fuel oil—199 tons carried, compared with 114 tons in Type VII submarine. The ultimate diesel-electric submarine evolved in the war was the German Type XXI, a 250-ft (75-m), 1,600-ton craft that could attain 17½ knots submerged for more than an hour, could travel at six knots underwater for two days, or could "creep" at slower speeds for four days. These submarines were fitted with *schnorchel* devices (see below) that made it unnecessary for them to surface fully to recharge their batteries after operating submerged. The Type XXI had an operating depth of 850 ft (260 m), more than twice what was then normal, and was armed with four 33-millimetre (1.3-inch) guns and six forward torpedo tubes (23 torpedoes carried). Existing Allied antisubmarine forces would have had serious trouble coping with these craft had the war continued past the spring of 1945.

A final German war design of particular interest was the Walter turbine propulsion plant. The need for oxygen for combustion had previously prevented the use of steam turbines or diesels while the submarine was submerged, and air was at a premium. Hellmuth Walter, a German scientist, developed a turbine propulsion system using oxygen generated by hydrogen peroxide to operate the turbine while submerged. A simplified submarine, the "V-80," built in 1940 and propelled by a Walter turbine system, could attain speeds of more than 26 knots submerged for a short period of time. After many delays, the first Walter-propelled Type XVII combat submarines were completed and could reach 25 knots underwater for brief periods, and a submerged run of 20 knots for 5½ hours was achieved on trials. But these submarines, like the Type XXI, were not ready for full-scale operations when the war ended.

A notable German submarine development of World War II was the *schnorchel* device (anglicized by the U.S. Navy to "snorkel"). Its invention is credited to a Dutch officer, Lt. Jan J. Wichers, who in 1933 advanced the idea of a breathing tube to supply fresh air to a submarine while running submerged. (Robert Fulton had a similar device in his "Nautilus" of 1801.) The Netherlands Navy began using snorkels in 1936, and some fell into German hands in 1940. With the advent of radar to detect surfaced submarines, the Germans fitted hundreds of U-boats with snorkels to permit operation of diesels at periscope depth to recharge batteries for underwater propulsion with less of a possibility of detection by Allied radar-equipped ships and aircraft.

Japanese submarines — In the Pacific War the Japanese employed a large number of submarines of various sizes and types, including submarine-carried aircraft, midget submarines, and "human torpedoes" carried by larger submarines. Two Japanese designs are of special interest. The Japanese I-201 class was a high-speed submarine 259⅙ ft (79 m) long, displacing 1,291 tons, that had diesel propulsion for 15 knots on the surface; while underwater, large batteries and electric motors could drive the vessel at a speed of 19 knots for almost one hour. Each boat had two 25-millimetre (one-inch) guns and four forward torpedo tubes and carried ten torpedoes. The Japanese, who constructed one-man submarines, also built the largest conventionally powered undersea craft ever built, the I-400 class. These submarines were intended as underwater aircraft carriers

and had a hangar that could accommodate three floatplanes and parts for a fourth. The I-400 submarines were 400¼ ft (122 m) long and displaced 5,700 tons, about the size of a light cruiser. The aircraft were housed in a hangar 12 ft (3.7 m) in diameter and 102 ft (31 m) long and launched by a catapult built into the deck. Each submarine was armed with a 140-millimetre (5.5-inch) deck gun plus seven 25-millimetre (one-inch) anti-aircraft guns, eight torpedo tubes, and 20 torpedoes. (They were never actually used for their intended purpose, which was to launch planes against the Panama Canal, but were employed as cargo submarines to supply bypassed island garrisons in the Pacific.)

The highly successful U.S. submarine campaign in the Pacific war was waged mainly with the Gato and Balao class submarines. These were approximately 311½ ft (94.9 m) long, displaced 1,525 tons, and had diesel-electric machinery for 20-knot surface and 9-knot underwater speeds. The principal difference between the two designs was the 300-ft (90-m) operating depth for the Gato class and 400-ft (120-m) depth for the Balao boats. Manned by 65 to 70, these submarines had one or two five-inch (13-centimetre) deck guns plus smaller anti-aircraft weapons, 10 torpedo tubes (six forward, four aft), and carried 24 torpedoes.

After the war the Allies were quick to adopt advanced German submarine technology. The British built two peroxide turbine-propelled experimental submarines, the "Explorer" and "Excalibur," but this concept lost favour because of the unstable properties of hydrogen peroxide and because of American success with nuclear propulsion. The U.S.S.R. began building a modification of the Type XXI submarine. Some 235 of these W class submarines were completed between 1950 and 1958, more submarines than built by all of the world's other navies combined between 1945 and 1970. (In that period Soviet shipyards produced a total of 560 new submarines.)

In the postwar period the U.S. Navy studied German technology and converted 52 war-built submarines to the Guppy configuration (an acronym for Greater Underwater Propulsive Power with the "y" added for phonetics). These submarines had their deck guns removed and streamlined conning towers fitted; larger batteries and a snorkel were installed; four torpedoes and, in some craft, one of the four diesel engines were removed. The result was an underwater speed of 15 knots and increased underwater endurance. During the postwar years the U.S. Navy built 21 diesel-powered submarines, several of which were highly specialized craft for antisubmarine warfare, guided-missile launching, underwater research, training, and radar picket operations in support of surface ships. Several war-built submarines were converted to these roles and also were used for the transport of Marine reconnaissance troops and frogmen.

Nuclear propulsion. The first efforts to develop a submarine nuclear power plant were made at the U.S. Naval Research Laboratory in Washington, D.C., under the direction of Ross Gunn, beginning in the spring of 1939. A report submitted that summer by Gunn noted that such a power plant would not require oxygen to operate, "a tremendous military advantage [which] would enormously increase the range and military effectiveness of a submarine." All work on nuclear propulsion was halted, however, as efforts in this field were devoted toward the atomic bomb development. After the war Gunn and Philip Abelson of the Carnegie Institution resumed work on a nuclear power plant, resulting in a report in the spring of 1946 calling for a nuclear submarine. The U.S. Navy took no action in this regard until Capt. Hyman G. Rickover, appointed to head the navy's cooperation in a nuclear project at the Oak Ridge, Tennessee, research centre, became a crusader for this type of submarine propulsion. Subsequently, a land-based prototype submarine power plant was constructed, followed by installation of a duplicate plant in the USS "Nautilus."

The USS "Nautilus" — The "Nautilus" got underway on January 17, 1955. Resembling a conventional submarine in appearance, it is 320 ft (98 m) long, displaces 3,530 tons, and has six forward torpedo tubes. Her top speed of 20 knots, both surface and submerged, was good but not spectacular compared with her diesel-electric contemporaries. But her underwater range at high speed is virtually unlimited. Measured in terms of "years" rather than miles, this endurance made her a revolutionary ship, in fact the first true submarine. All of her predecessors had been merely surface craft capable of brief operation under water.

Seven additional nuclear submarines were built to conventional hull designs, including one for launching guided missiles and one for radar picket missions. The navy then combined the advanced "tear drop" hull design of the research submarine Albacore with a nuclear propulsion plant to produce the Skipjack class of very fast submarines, capable of underwater speeds estimated at over 30 knots. This design has been incorporated in the subsequent Thresher and Sturgeon classes. These later nuclear submarines, however, have their large bows devoted entirely to detection equipment (sonar) and have their four torpedo tubes amidships, angled out with two on each side (a concept tested by the Germans in World War II). This places their sonar at the most advantageous position, as far forward as possible and away from the ship's machinery and propeller noises. The Sturgeon class submarines are 292 ft (89 m) long and displace 3,860 tons; however, they probably are slower than the earlier Skipjack class because they have the same propulsion machinery but larger hulls.

Almost all U.S. nuclear submarines are primarily intended to detect and attack enemy submarines, except for those armed with strategic Polaris or Poseidon missiles. Beginning with the "George Washington," the U.S. Navy completed 41 Polaris-armed submarines between 1960 and 1967. Of these, 31 are Lafayette class submarines that are to be converted to fire the improved Poseidon missile. The Lafayette class submarines, each carrying 16 missiles plus four torpedo tubes, are 425 ft (130 m) long and displace 6,650 tons. The only larger nuclear submarine is the "Triton" completed in 1959; she is a radar picket craft 447½ ft (136 m) long and displacing 5,940 tons. The "Triton" also was the first submarine propelled by two nuclear reactors; the Soviet Yankee class missile submarines also may have two reactors, according to some U.S. Navy estimates, but all other nuclear submarines have only one.

Soviet nuclear submarines

The U.S.S.R., maintaining the largest and newest submarine fleet in the post-World War II era, reached a maximum strength of almost 500 diesel-electric submarines in the early 1960s. The first Soviet nuclear submarine, designated November class, was completed in 1959 or 1960 and was 360 ft (110 m) long and displaced about 3,500 tons. The November class submarines generally are credited with a surface speed of about 25 knots and a submerged speed of 25 to 30 knots, with some of the later November submarines possibly exceeding 30 knots submerged. Armament consists of six bow torpedo tubes.

During the 1960s the U.S.S.R. produced large numbers of diesel-electric and nuclear submarines for three distinct missions: attack or torpedo-armed submarines to attack surface ships and other submarines; cruise missile-armed submarines to attack enemy surface warships, especially aircraft carriers; and ballistic-missile submarines armed with long-range strategic missiles. By 1971 the U.S. and Soviet navies each had built some 90 nuclear-powered undersea craft and had a rate of production of just over four atomic submarines per year for the United States and 12 to 14 per year for the Soviet Union. (Soviet production of two new classes of nuclear submarines of exceptional size and performance was reported in the late 1970s.)

The first British nuclear submarine was the "Dreadnought," completed in 1963, a torpedo-armed submarine of advanced design and fitted with an American propulsion system. Subsequent British nuclear submarines, attack and ballistic-missile types, have British-designed and fabricated machinery. The first French nuclear submarine was to have been the hull designated "Q-244" begun in 1958; however, the project was cancelled, and the hull was subsequently completed as the diesel-electric missile trials submarine "Gymnote." Subsequently the French built four nuclear-powered, ballistic-missile submarines, the first being "Le Redoutable," completed in 1969. During the 1960s the Soviet, British, and French navies continued constructing advanced diesel-electric submarines. In many

roles the diesel-electric submarine can perform equally to a nuclear craft, especially when very quiet operation for limited periods is required. Also significant is the higher cost of nuclear propulsion; the European nations can sell conventional submarines to lesser navies that cannot afford nuclear craft.

The overall superiority of nuclear-propelled submarines cannot be questioned. Only this form makes possible the relatively invulnerable ballistic-missile submarines that can cruise the oceans for months without surfacing or extending an air-intake tube to the surface. Nuclear submarine performance can be measured by such exploits as: "Nautilus" (U.S.), making the first submerged polar transit from Point Barrow, Alaska, to the Greenland Sea, travelling 1,830 miles (2,945 km) under the polar ice pack (August 1–5, 1958); "Skate" (U.S.; Figure 24), a similar polar-icepack voyage (August 9–20, 1958), travelling 2,405 mi (3,870 km) and surfacing 40 mi (64 km) from the North Pole; "Seawolf" (U.S.), remaining submerged for 60 con-

Submerged polar transits

AP/Wide World Photos

Figure 24: USS "Skate," a nuclear-powered submarine, arriving in Portland, Dorset.

secutive days and travelling 13,761 mi (22,146 km; August 5–October 6, 1958); "Triton" (U.S.), circumnavigating the world submerged, following roughly the route taken by Magellan (1519–1592), and travelling 36,014 mi (57,946 km) February 24–May 10, 1960); "Leninsky Komsomol" (U.S.S.R.), reportedly operating under the polar ice pack and surfacing near the North Pole in 1962; a November class submarine (U.S.S.R.), remaining submerged for almost 50 consecutive days while steaming about 25,000 mi (40,000 km). None of these feats is considered possible with conventionally propelled submarines.

Like their conventional sisters, nuclear submarines have encountered difficulties in the hostile depths. To the list of submarines sunk accidentally in both peace and war, by 1971 three nuclear submarines had been added: the USS "Thresher," off New England, with 129 lives lost, April 10, 1963; USS "Scorpion," off the Azores, with 99 lives lost, May 1968; and a Soviet November class, in the eastern Atlantic, April 12, 1970 (no loss of life).

Modern structure and uses. *Construction features.* To operate underwater a submarine has a strengthened steel pressure hull that provides protection from water pressure to the crew, machinery, and certain equipment. A double-hull technique is generally used, with the space between the inner (pressure) hull and outer hull providing room for water ballast and fuel tanks. This double-hull feature also provides additional protection for the pressure hull from nearby detonations of antisubmarine weapons. Until recently, above the hull and extending the length of the submarine there was a nonwatertight, free-flooding superstructure that formed the main deck for use when the submarine was surfaced. Modern high-speed submarines, both diesel-electric and nuclear, do not have the superstructure deck, as it interferes with optimum underwater shape. Also, nuclear-powered submarines do not have the normal double-hull configuration because they require only small amounts of diesel fuel for their auxiliary machinery; hence, these fuel tanks and water-ballast tanks are fitted within the pressure hull and a partial double hull.

Above the submarine's hull is a conning tower or sail structure. In older submarines this was a watertight conning tower that served as the command centre during combat. On post-World War II submarines there is a streamlined "sail" structure that does not contain a watertight compartment. The conning tower and sail structure both house the retracting periscopes, radar and radio antennas, and snorkel tubes and provide a platform or bridge for the navigating officers and lookouts when the submarine is on the surface.

Normally, the submarine submerges by flooding the water-ballast tanks to attain a neutral buoyancy and then diving by forward motion coupled with the use of small diving planes, somewhat like rotating wings. Most submarines have stern diving planes and a second pair installed on their sail structure or at the bow. To surface, the submarine uses the diving planes and forward motion, supplemented by expulsion of water from the ballast tanks with compressed air. The compressed air can be produced within the submarine and stored in tanks or "bottles" until required. The submarine is kept in a state of neutral buoyancy with water-trim tanks that are partially flooded to compensate for changes in the submarine's volume caused by increasing pressure as the craft goes deeper and by the effects of changing water temperature and salinity or by weight changes from firing torpedoes or missiles.

Control room The control room in a modern submarine is carefully designed to achieve the maximum efficiency during operations, with centralized command positions from which the submarine and its weapons can be directed. The modern submarine relies more on its sonar than on the periscope for detecting and attacking an enemy; in addition, the modern submarine has a complex inertial-navigation system that provides information on its position independent of any outside sources except gravity and earth rotation. These data are periodically checked by a special star-tracking periscope device or radio navigation antenna that is projected above the water for very brief periods. The actual control of the submarine is achieved by aircraft-line controls, with one or two men sitting in "pilot" chairs and manoeuvring the craft. Some undersea craft have analog "pictures" of a simulated roadway, presented to the "pilots" on a television-like screen, in addition to the conventional dials and pointers that indicate course, speed, and depth with numbers.

The modern submarine is a relatively comfortable craft, dry inside and fully air-conditioned, the latter feature for both crew habitability and for the great amount of sophisticated electronic equipment that requires carefully maintained humidity and temperature conditions. Modern, especially designed electric kitchens provide food that is traditionally considered of high quality. The crew sleeping or dining spaces also are used for motion pictures and as game rooms. The officers have their own sleeping area and wardroom.

Oceangoing submarines can remain at sea for two or three months, carrying all provisions required by the crew during that period. Diesel-electric submarines periodically raise a snorkel device to draw in air for the diesel engines and crew and to carry away exhaust gases. Nuclear-powered submarines need not draw in air for their engines and can manufacture oxygen for the crew from the surrounding seawater to supplement oxygen carried in tanks.

Two-way communication with submerged submarines is difficult because radio waves cannot be produced underwater. Thus, the modern submarine cannot send radio messages while fully submerged but must raise an antenna mast up into the air to communicate by radio. The submarine can receive radio transmissions while submerged, however, through built-in antennas or by trailing a wire antenna through the water.

Sensors. The prime sensors of a submarine are sonars, periscopes, and radars. Submarines employ both passive sonar (sound detection and ranging), which listens for the noises generated by another submarine or a surface ship, and active sonar, which sends out an acoustic pulse that is reflected upon hitting another submarine or ship. The submarine uses sonar for detection of an enemy, for sea-floor and under-ice navigation, and for directing torpedoes.

The periscope is the "eye" of the submarine. Early submarines had small glass portholes for direct observation. This required the submarine to be partially surfaced. In 1854 E-H. Marié-Davy of France designed a submarine sight tube containing two mirrors, one above the other, held at a 45° angle and facing in opposite directions. The mirror-tube provided some degree of sight from a submerged submarine but was faulty at best, and in 1872 prisms were substituted for mirrors.

The periscope

Subsequently, the prism periscope was improved and made to telescope, so that it could be housed within the submarine's hull when not in use and extended above the submarine for reconnaissance. Modern periscopes are about 40 ft (12 m) long and taper to about one inch in diameter at the top to reduce detection from the surface. Special features permit considerable magnification, night reconnaissance, photography through periscopes, sextant use for celestial navigation while submerged, and viewing of the air around the submarine as well as the surface.

Radar (radio detection and ranging) was fitted to most U.S., British, and German submarines during World War II, initially to detect aircraft while the submarine was operating at periscope depth or on the surface. Subsequently, surface-search radar was provided, and during the latter part of the war radar-approach attacks against surface ships were common. Submarine radars are now used primarily for navigation in coastal waters. The antenna is mounted on a retractable mast and is withdrawn into the sail structure when not in use.

Propulsion. Shortly after the beginning of the 20th century, most submarines were fitted with diesel engines for surface propulsion and to recharge the batteries needed for electric-motor submerged propulsion. (The steam-turbine and peroxide-turbine variants are discussed above.) Engines burning diesel oil had a significant advantage over gasoline motors for surface propulsion because of the highly volatile properties of gasoline, and advantages over steam propulsion because of the high temperatures generated by the boilers necessary for steam turbines before the advent of nuclear propulsion.

Once submerged, the diesel engines are shut down, and electric motors are started, turning the same propeller shafts. The electric motors, drawing their energy from storage batteries, require no combustion and can be used without regard for the submarine's air supply. Electric motors have the additional advantage of being quiet, an important factor in submarine operations.

The submarine nuclear power plant consists of an atomic reactor that generates enormous amounts of heat through nuclear fission (see also ENERGY CONVERSION). The reactor is controlled by inserting and withdrawing control rods that penetrate the reactor core. When the rods are completely inserted the reaction ceases, and when they are completely withdrawn the reaction is at its maximum. The heat is carried by the primary coolant (pressurized water) to a steam generator, where the heat is transferred to a secondary water system that creates steam to drive the submarine's turbines. The primary coolant water is radioactive from passing near the radioactive core and thus cannot be used directly with the turbine. On most nuclear submarines reduction gears are used between the turbines and the propeller shaft; however, a few incorporate turbo-electric drive (notably the USS "Tullibee" and USS "SSN-685"). Here the steam turbine drives an electric generator, which in turn drives the electric motors coupled to the propeller shaft.

The nuclear power plant

Nuclear-powered submarines are "refuelled" by replacement of the uranium core in their nuclear reactor. The "Nautilus" steamed 62,562 mi (100,681 km) on her first nuclear core, which was replaced in 1957; 91,324 mi (146,968 km) on her second core, which was replaced in 1959; and approximately 150,000 mi (240,000 km) on her third core, replaced in 1964. The cores now being installed in U.S. nuclear submarines will have an endurance of approximately 400,000 mi (640,000 km).

All nuclear-powered submarines are fitted with auxiliary diesel-electric machinery (and snorkel) for use in the event of a main machinery casualty and to generate power when the main machinery is shut down while in port.

Weapons. The primary weapon of the submarine traditionally has been the self-propelled torpedo. Modern submarines are fitted with internal torpedo-launching tubes 21 inches (53 centimetres) in diameter and about 21 ft (6.4 m) long. The tubes are horizontal in the bow or amidships, with some submarines also having stern tubes. The tubes are loaded from within the submarines and normally are loaded with reloads kept within the submarine when the craft goes to sea. Each tube has doors at both ends so that the inner door can be opened when the outer door is closed and vice versa, permitting firing and reloading without water entering the submarine. The tubes are fired electrically or mechanically by hand.

Most torpedoes today are intended for use against other submarines; they either home on their target acoustically with self-contained sonar or are guided by electronic commands passed to them through a threadlike wire paid out behind the torpedo as it travels away from the launching submarine. Another submarine-to-submarine weapon is the U.S. Navy's submarine rocket (Subroc). Fired from a torpedo tube while the craft is submerged, Subroc streaks to the surface, leaves the water, and, propelled by a rocket, travels through the air on a ballistic trajectory. The weapon re-enters the water an estimated 25 to 30 mi (40 to 48 km) from the launching submarine, and a nuclear warhead detonates.

During World War II, the German Navy experimented with small guided missiles and large ballistic missiles launched from submarines and submarine-towed containers, respectively. After the war, the U.S. and Soviet navies developed guided cruise missiles, jet- or rocket-propelled vehicles with stub wings that resembled pilotless aircraft. These were carried in watertight hangars on the submarine deck and fired after the submarine surfaced. The U.S. Navy operated the Regulus I missile with a 500-mi (800-km) range from several submarines between 1958 and 1964 and developed but did not use the Regulus II missile with a range of 1,000 mi (1,600 km). The Soviets developed similar missiles and now use the Shaddock missile with a maximum range of 450 mi (720 km) from a number of conventional and nuclear submarines. These missiles, which have a variable flight path, are considered the most potent threat to surface warships. (Some newer Soviet submarine-launched cruise missiles may be capable of underwater launching.)

Submarine-launched ballistic missiles are strategic weapons intended for use against cities and other fixed land targets. They cannot be effectively used against ships. The Soviet Navy began deploying conventional submarines with short-range ballistic missiles in the late 1950s, while the first U.S. Navy strategic missile submarine, the "George Washington," was first deployed in 1960; it carried 16 Polaris A-1 missiles, each with a nuclear warhead and a range of 1,380 mi (2,220 km). These and subsequent ballistic missiles can be fired when the submarine is submerged. Subsequent U.S. Polaris submarines were fitted with the A-2 missile with a range of 1,725 mi (2,775 km) and then the A-3 missile with a 2,875-mi (4,625-km) range. Some A-3 missiles also have three-vehicle warheads that can "shotgun" three nuclear bombs at the target. In 1970 the U.S. Navy began to rearm most Polaris submarines with the Poseidon missile, which has about the range of the A-3 missile but which carries 10 small warheads that can be aimed at individual targets. (A new class of large submarines that will carry the new Trident missile was scheduled for completion by 1981.) Similarly, British strategic missile submarines are armed with the Polaris A-3 missile, French submarines with the MSBS missile with a range of 1,900 mi (3,000 km), and Soviet submarines with the 1,300–1,500-mi (2,000–2,400 km) SS-N-6 missile. (A longer range, 2,700–3,000-mi submarine missile, developed by the Soviets, was scheduled for deployment during the 1970s.) All of these strategic submarines carry 16 missiles in addition to torpedoes. The Soviet Navy also operates a number of smaller nuclear and conventional submarines that fire three strategic missiles with lesser range. (N.C.P.)

The Polaris missile

FUTURE DEVELOPMENTS IN NAVAL SHIPS AND CRAFT

Though the future of navies is unclear, it is possible to speculate on the basis of current trends.

Manned-satellite space stations may come into use to perform or monitor naval missions. Unmanned satellites for communications, navigation, mapping, reconnaissance, weather information, and perhaps even antisubmarine warfare will increase in value.

Advances in vertical- and short-takeoff-and-landing planes will cause a proliferation in numbers and kinds of warships carrying high-performance supersonic planes. As a consequence, super aircraft carriers may have reached the maximum in size. Medium-to-small carriers will take over a number of the many functions of this indispensable type of warship. The Soviet Union, China, and other nations will begin or continue light-carrier programs. Helicopter programs in many navies are part of the increasingly widespread employment of aircraft from ships. Although slow, helicopters serve admirably for antisubmarine warfare, reconnaissance, enemy-missile warning, and midrange guidance of friendly missiles.

The principal menaces to ships will continue to be undersea weapons and long-range missiles from ships and planes. Antimissile systems and weapons will grow in complexity, speed of reaction, and effectiveness. Among these the gun may make a surprising comeback. With very high rates of fire, automatic operation, rocket-assisted projectiles, and, possibly, in-flight guidance, the shell from guns may supersede many, more expensive, guided missiles.

Hydrofoils and air-cushion or surface-effect war vessels will make striking advances in size and usefulness. They have particular promise for operations through submarine waters.

Nuclear-propulsion plants will become smaller and cheaper, though remaining costly for initial installation. More surface ships will enjoy their advantages. In non-nuclear plants, the trend will be toward the use of the gas turbine.

Automation, solid-state electronics, miniaturization, module replacement, and other steps will permit reduction in size of crews. These steps will also make possible small, fast warships to fill the gap left by the growth in size of destroyer types. Many navies have already built small, swift gunboats; a more versatile type, displacing between 1,000 and 2,000 tons, is likely to be an important development.

Trend toward smaller craft

Antiballistic-missile ships will appear, capable of intercepting hostile missiles over the ocean. Ballistic missiles will probably go into some surface ships.

Submarines will run faster, quieter, deeper, and be armed with larger, longer-range missiles. Measures to combat them will include super-quiet attack submarines, helicopters on small ships, other airborne efforts, distant-detection devices, and advanced weapons. (Ed.)

Military aircraft

In addition to fighters, bombers, and reconnaissance craft, aircraft used for military purposes include numerous specialized types, such as trainers, communications aircraft, transports, and carrier-based aircraft. Lighter-than-air balloons and airships, used extensively up to the end of World War II, have since been discarded. Unpowered gliders, employed for the transport of airborne troops in World War II, have also disappeared from the inventory of modern air forces.

EARLY HISTORY

The concept of military aviation is almost as old as human interest in flying. Drawings of the legendary Persian king Keykāvūs show his clutching a bow and arrows as he travels through the air on a throne to which four eagles are harnessed. When the first practical aircraft were produced, in the form of hot-air and hydrogen balloons, in 1783, they were adopted quickly for nonoffensive military duties. In 1793 the French Convention authorized formation of a company of "Aérostiers" for military observation from tethered balloons, an operation that came into being on April 2, 1794. Two months later, the first military reconnaissance from such a balloon was made before the city of Maubeuge. Until the "Aérostiers" were disbanded in 1799, their reports contributed to the success of French armies in many battles and sieges. Similar reconnaissance balloons were used later by other armies, notably by both armies during the American Civil War and by the British in Africa from 1884 to 1901. Large man-lifting kites were evaluated by the British Army in the first decade of the 20th century but were soon abandoned.

Napoleon studied the possibility of using large balloons as troop transports for an invasion of England, and in 1849 the Austrians launched primitive unmanned "flying bombs" against Venice. Consisting of small, hot-air balloons made of paper, and each carrying a 30-pound (14-kilogram) bomb fitted with a time-fuse, these caused little damage and few casualties.

True military aviation began with perfection of the navigable airship and airplane. The brothers Wilbur and Orville Wright, who made the first powered, sustained, and controlled flights in an airplane on December 17, 1903, believed such an aircraft would be useful mainly for military reconnaissance. They considered that it might even make wars impossible by exposing every movement of opposing armies. When they received the first contract for a military airplane in February 1908, it called for an aircraft capable of carrying two persons at a speed of at least 40 miles per hour (64 kilometres per hour) for a distance of 125 miles (200 kilometres). This first machine, an improved version of their 1903 design, crashed during demonstration flights at Ft. Myer, Virginia, on September 17. A replacement was delivered nine months later as "Airplane No. 1, Heavier-than-air Division, United States aerial fleet."

Subsequently, the U.S. lost the initiative in military aviation. Between 1908 and 1913 it allocated only $430,000 for further buildup of its "aerial fleet." In the same period, France and Germany each spent an estimated $22,000,000 on military and naval aviation, Russia about $12,000,000, and even Belgium spent $2,000,000. The most formidable aircraft of the era were the huge metal-framed airships designed and built in Germany by Graf Ferdinand von Zeppelin. Typical was the L.3, which served with the German Navy at the outbreak of World War I. This craft had a length of 490 feet (150 metres), gas capacity of 795,000 cubic feet (22,500 cubic metres), and three 210-horsepower Maybach engines, which gave it a speed of 47 miles per hour (about 76 kilometres per hour) and a ceiling of 6,000 feet (1,800 metres). It could carry five 110-pound (50-kilogram) high-explosive bombs and 20 6½-pound (three-kilogram) incendiary bombs at a time when most military airplanes were without any form of weapons, being intended only for reconnaissance.

Experiments with airplane armament were made spasmodically after 1910, when August Euler took out a German patent on a machine gun installation. In 1911 a French Nieuport two-seater was fitted with a machine gun, while in England Maj. Robert Brooke-Popham of the Air Battalion, Royal Engineers, armed his Blériot monoplane in the same way. He was promptly ordered to remove the gun.

A new low-recoil machine gun, developed by Col. Isaac Newton Lewis in the U.S., was tested on a Wright Model B biplane. In trials at College Park, Maryland, on June 2, 1912, the gun was fired in the air, and a request was made to the U.S. Army Ordnance Department for 10 more guns. The request was refused; Colonel Lewis left for Europe and, in January 1913, formed a company named Armes Automatiques Lewis, at Liège, Belgium, and began manufacture of what was to become a standard aerial weapon, the Lewis gun.

Bombing techniques were evolved simultaneously, with the U.S. again pointing the way. Dummy bombs were dropped on a target in the form of a ship by Glenn Curtiss on June 30, 1910. This test was followed by the dropping of a real bomb and the devising of the first bombsight. In England the Royal Flying Corps (RFC) fitted some of its aircraft with bomb carriers, which consisted of a kind of pipe rack beside the observer's cockpit in which small bombs were retained by a pin. The pin was pulled out over the target by tugging on a string. It was primitive but it worked, and, as the Naval Wing of the RFC became more ambitious, attempts were made, successfully, to drop torpedoes from Short and Sopwith seaplanes, following a little-known earlier air launch of such a weapon in Italy.

This practice suggested a great future for torpedo aircraft, and ships to carry them were already being developed. In 1910–11 a Curtiss biplane had been flown from and onto wooden platforms erected over the decks of two cruisers anchored in Hampton Roads, Virginia, and at San Francisco, California, respectively. In May 1912 a pilot of the Naval Wing, RFC, flew a Short S.27 biplane from HMS "Hibernia" while the ship was steaming at 10½ knots. One further step toward the aircraft carrier of the future came in the following year. The old cruiser "Hermes" was fitted with a short deck from which seaplanes took off on wheeled trolleys that were fitted under their floats and dropped away as the machines became airborne.

Thus, by 1914, fighter, bomber, reconnaissance, and carrier-based aircraft all were evolving. Some had been used in action. The first use of an airplane in war was on October 23, 1911, during the Italo-Turkish War, when an Italian pilot made a one-hour reconnaissance flight over enemy positions between Tripoli and al-ʾAzīzīyah, in North Africa, on a Blériot XI monoplane. This flight was followed nine days later by the first bombing raid, when a pilot dropped four heavy grenades on ʾAyn Zārah and the oasis of Tājūrā. Psychological warfare was tried next, on January 10, 1912, when propaganda leaflets were showered from the air, suggesting that the local Arabs abandon the Turks and surrender. The first reconnaissance photographs of enemy positions were taken on February 24–25, and on April 19 motion pictures were made of an enemy encampment from the military airship P.3.

Other nations were quick to follow the Italian example. When the first Balkan War began in 1912, the Bulgarians dropped finned canisters of explosive by hand on Turkish-held Adrianople from the rear seat of Blériot monoplanes.

WORLD WAR I

At the outbreak of war in August 1914, Germany had the largest air force and probably the best, as many of its 260 aircraft were powered by the highly efficient Mercedes liquid-cooled engines that had made possible a series of altitude and duration records. The RFC had 63 airplanes; its former Naval Wing, now the Royal Naval Air Service (RNAS), had 39 landplanes, 52 seaplanes, and 7 airships. The French Air Force, although smaller than that of its enemy with 156 airplanes, had behind it the world's leading aircraft industry. For the first two years of the war, this industry supplied equipment to the British and other allied forces, as well as to the French Air Force. Every engine in the 73 airplanes taken to France and Belgium by the RFC and RNAS in August 1914 was of French manufacture, and 22 of the airplanes were wholly French. Not until April 1918 did the British air services cease to fly airplanes built in France.

Zeppelins. At the start of the war the German Navy had one Zeppelin airship, and the Army six, plus three converted commercial Zeppelins and three smaller airships. The army made the mistake of sending its Zeppelins over heavily defended areas in daylight, and three were shot down before the end of the first month of the war. Thereafter the German Navy achieved outstanding successes in the North Sea with such aircraft by keeping constant watch on allied shipping movements from the Zeppelins, each of which was reckoned to be worth five or six cruisers. Naval airships also spearheaded German air attacks on Britain. In 51 raids between January 19, 1915, and August 5, 1918, they dropped 5,806 bombs totalling 196.5 tons; 557 people were killed and 1,358 injured. The raids caused sizeable damage, had a considerable effect on British civilian morale, hampered war production, and kept twelve RFC squadrons with 110 airplanes and 2,200 personnel and a large force of anti-aircraft guns and searchlights manned by 12,000 personnel engaged on home defense.

Finest of the Zeppelins was LZ-70, commanded by Fregattenkapitän Peter Strasser, who led the naval airship service throughout its entire period of wartime successes and ultimate defeat. The LZ-70 was 740 feet (225 metres) long, able to fly above 16,000 feet (4,900 metres), and had a range of 7,500 miles (12,000 kilometres), which enabled Strasser to plan an air raid on New York by three such craft. Before this could be attempted, the LZ-70 was shot down, and the big rigid (metal-framed) airship was never again employed as a combat aircraft. Smaller, nonrigid airships were used throughout World War I by the British for antisubmarine patrol, convoy escort, and coastal reconnaissance. This type was revived by the U.S. Navy during World War II and was notably successful in protecting convoys against submarine attack.

Unpowered, captive balloons also were used in large numbers in both world wars. Most were of the elongated Drachen type, with stabilizing tail fins. All of the opposing armies used them for observation in World War I, and the crews were among the first to be provided with parachutes for use if the balloons were punctured or set on fire by enemy action. By World War II, such craft had become so vulnerable that they could be used only in unmanned form as anti-aircraft barrage balloons. Over Britain, by making enemy bombers fly high, they reduced the average number of shells required to destroy an airplane from 20,000 to under 3,000 by February 1941. Later, they brought down 232 German V-1 pilotless "flying bombs" over England, when the missiles flew into their cables; but there is no military service today that continues to use lighter-than-air balloons or airships of any kind.

Reconnaissance aircraft. When World War I began, few military leaders believed that heavier-than-air flying machines were useful for anything but reconnaissance (*i.e.,* "aerial cavalry" to keep track of enemy troop movements). So, while the German Zeppelins began raiding cities in Belgium and France from the first days of the war, reconnaissance airplanes began the task that was to remain of primary importance throughout the war. They soon proved their worth. If the German armies that had advanced to the River Marne had not been held, the war might have ended in a few weeks. That they were held was due in no small measure to the complete and accurate information on enemy dispositions furnished by aerial reconnaissance.

Aerial photography

Techniques slowly improved. Photography was added to visual observation by the RFC on September 15, 1914, when photographs were taken of German positions during the battle of the Aisne. Developed and printed on the ground, they were forerunners of a huge photographic map of the entire western front, in thousands of sections, that was kept constantly up-to-date as an essential aid to tactical and strategic combat planning in the latter stages of the war. Radio was also coming into use at this time as a means of passing messages between reconnaissance aircraft and the ground.

Development of fighters. One of the key tasks undertaken by air forces was artillery spotting. This action involved circling endlessly over the battlefield, spotting where the shells from friendly artillery were falling, and correcting the aim of the gunners to ensure economy of effort. The value of this activity, plus that of photoreconnaissance, persuaded the military leaders of both sides that the time had come to deny freedom of movement to enemy air forces. From the start of the war, some reconnaissance crews had carried revolvers or rifles. A few lucky shots had forced opponents down. One RFC pilot even persuaded his opponent to surrender by performing such hazardous manoeuvres immediately above the German aircraft that the pilot was happy to land. Clearly, however, the real answer was to fit a machine gun to aircraft that would have the specific task of fighting other aircraft.

The Vickers company of Britain had pioneered such an airplane in 1913, when they displayed their E.F.B.1 (Experimental Fighting Biplane No. 1), named the "Destroyer," in a London air show. Although typical of its time in general layout, with a pusher engine aft of its crew, it was unique in carrying in its nose a belt-fed Vickers-Maxim machine gun with a field of fire of 60 degrees up

and down and left and right. From it was evolved the F.B.5 "Gunbus," which began reaching RFC squadrons in France in February 1915. Its top speed was only 70 miles (110 kilometres) per hour, and the new 100 horsepower Gnome Monosoupape engine was so unreliable at first that one pilot logged 22 forced landings in 30 flights. Nevertheless, the "Gunbus" proved the potential of the fighting airplane.

The "Gunbus"

It was realized from the start that greater success depended on higher speed. The fastest airplanes of the time were single seaters with a tractor engine (*i.e.,* with the propeller at the nose). The difficulty was to devise a method of firing a machine gun forward from such an airplane without shooting away its own propeller. Some British Bristol Bullets and French Nieuports overcame the problem by having a Lewis gun mounted centrally above the top wing, firing above the propeller. The main drawback of this arrangement was the difficulty of changing the Lewis's 47-round drums of ammunition. An alternative idea was to mount the gun at an angle on the side of the fuselage, so that it fired outward past the propeller. This arrangement called for exceptional skill on the part of the pilot, as the airplane had to be flown crabwise when making an attack.

A far superior idea was the interrupter or gun-synchronizing gear, which enabled bullets to pass between the blades of a spinning propeller. This device had been invented before the war by several people, but the designs were pigeonholed and forgotten. Franz Schneider, chief designer of a German company, came nearest to success. He patented his synchronizing gear on July 15, 1913, and fitted it in due course to a prototype two-seat monoplane. While on its way to the front for combat testing in 1915, however, this aircraft was lost and no replacement was built.

Only in France did the prewar concepts lead to modest success in combat. A machine gun and an interrupter gear had been fitted to a Morane-Saulnier monoplane. This arrangement worked quite well, except that some bullets tended to "hang fire" and hit the propeller. To avoid damage, a steel plate was attached to each propeller blade to deflect bullets that would otherwise have hit it. In the spring of 1915, the prewar French sporting pilot Roland Garros fitted similar deflector plates and a machine gun to a Morane-Saulnier type N monoplane and shot down three German aircraft on April 1, 13, and 18. On the 19th, Garros himself force landed with engine trouble and was taken prisoner. With the secret of the "mystery Morane" revealed, the German authorities ordered their leading manufacturer, Anthony Fokker, to fit deflector plates and guns to his "scouts." Instead, his designers evolved a practical interrupter gear and this device, embodied in the Fokker Eindecker (monoplane) series of single-seat scouts (see Figure 25), gave the German Air Force complete superiority over the Western Front.

Fokker Eindecker

By courtesy of John W.R. Taylor

Figure 25: Fokker Eindecker, German fighter plane of World War I.

The operation that became known as the "Fokker Scourge" lasted from October 1915 until May 1916. The British and French air forces were almost shot from the sky by the Fokker Eindeckers, whose synchronized machine guns more than offset low performance (top speed of the E.I was only 82 miles [130 kilometres] per hour). The British B.E.2c reconnaissance biplanes suffered in particular because their designers had concentrated on giving them inherent stability for optimum observation capability, so that they lacked the manoeuvrability to elude attacking Fokkers. The observer had a machine gun but was so surrounded by struts and wires in the forward cockpit that he could seldom fire it effectively.

The airplanes that ended the Fokkers' period of mastery were new versions of the French Nieuport, with a gun above the top wing, and the British D.H.2 and F.E.2b "pusher" fighters with a nose-mounted gun. These latter machines represented the limit of usefulness of the "pusher" configuration. By mid-1916, the British and French air forces had efficient interrupter gears of their own, and thereafter both sides virtually standardized on tractor biplanes and triplanes with one or two forward-firing synchronized machine guns, an arrangement that was to remain the normal single-seat fighter armament until the mid-1930s. The allied interrupter gears were of original design.

Sopwith Camel

Many variations of armament were tried experimentally. After standard Sopwith Camel fighters had achieved a reputation as deadly trench-strafers, one aircraft of this type was fitted with two fixed guns, pointing downward through the floor of the fuselage, so that it could rake enemy troops with fire while flying fast and level above their trenches. As early as 1911, Louis Blériot had tested on the ground a gun that fired through the hollow propeller-shaft. The idea was revived by Hispano-Suiza in the form of the *moteur-canon* of 1917. A 37-millimetre (1.45-inch) Puteaux single-shot shell-firing gun, mounted between the cylinder blocks of a 220-horsepower Hispano engine and firing through the propeller shaft, was used successfully by the French fighter aces Georges Guynemer and René Fonck, but the low muzzle velocity, excessive vibration, and high standard of marksmanship demanded by the *moteur-canon* prevented wider acceptance in World War I. Other large-calibre guns were tried in both fixed and flexible (manually aimed) installations. Large firework-type rockets, carried on the wing struts, and upward-firing machine guns were used on a limited scale, mainly against airships and observation balloons. Canisters of steel darts, known as *fléchettes,* were showered without much success on troops on the ground and airships in flight.

Only two variations of the standard two-gun tractor single-seat fighter formula met with enduring success. The first was the evolution of the fighter-bomber, with small bombs added to fixed guns for ground-attack duties. A typical example was the installation of racks for four 25-pound (11-kilogram) bombs under the centre fuselage of some Camels. Second was the two-seat fighter, pioneered by another Sopwith design, the 1½-Strutter. In addition to a flexible gun in the rear cockpit, this plane had a fixed forward-firing gun fitted with synchronizing gear. Unaware for a time of the existence of the latter, German pilots made frontal attacks on 1½-Strutters—a hitherto safe direction from which to approach a two-seater—only to be met by fire from the front gun. The two-seat formula was continued even more successfully by the later Bristol Fighter, which became one of the most formidable combat types of 1917–18.

Development of bombing aircraft. The main task of all fighters was to attack enemy reconnaissance and bombing aircraft. The early development of the bomber owed much to Comdr. Charles Rumney Samson, RNAS. Impatient at being limited to a passive reconnaissance role after he had been sent to Belgium with 10 aircraft at the outbreak of war, he decided to initiate a strategic bombing offensive with Zeppelins as the primary target. The first air raid into German territory, with four aircraft, on September 22, 1914, was ineffective. The second, made by two single-seat, 80-horsepower Sopwith Tabloids, each carrying a few 20-pound (nine-kilogram) bombs, on October 8, was a spectacular success. One pilot attacked Cologne railway station. Another dropped his bombs on the airship sheds at Düsseldorf, one of which was destroyed, along with the latest Zeppelin, Z.9, inside it.

On November 21, three RNAS pilots attacked the Zeppelin works at Friedrichshafen. Convinced of the potential of strategic bombing, the Admiralty's Air Department com-

Handley Page

missioned Handley Page, Ltd. to develop "a bloody paralyser of an aeroplane." This plane flew on December 18, 1915, as the prototype H.P. O/100, which was to become

the world's first heavy night bomber. Meanwhile, other air forces began building and putting into service strategic day bombers. Among the first were French Voisins. Known as "chicken coops" because of their abundance of struts and wires, these were built in thousands and served throughout the war. The type L, which equipped four artillery observation squadrons in August 1914, had an engine of only 80 horsepower and was used in early 1915 to carry about 130 pounds (59 kilograms) of small bombs that simply lay in the bottom of the cockpit until the time came for the observer to drop them overboard. Later models had various engines, rated at up to 350 horsepower, and were equipped alternatively as attack aircraft, carrying up to 660 pounds (300 kilograms) of bombs, or *canon* types with a 37-millimetre gun mounted in the nose. None flew faster than 84 miles (135 kilometres) per hour; so the Voisins operated mainly under cover of darkness in the last year of the war.

Italy, too, was quick to appreciate the value of heavy and persistent air attacks on enemy targets. Its big three-engined, twin-tailboom Capronis were among the finest bombers of World War I (see Figure 26). Their rear gunners were some of the war's great heroes, for they often

By courtesy of John W.R. Taylor

Figure 26: Italian Caproni bomber of World War I.

stood on open platforms behind the wings as the aircraft flew slowly over the Alps and back in winter during long raids on targets in Austria. Even larger in size were the Russian Ilya Muromets bombers of the tsar's Eskadra Vozdukhnykh Korabley (Squadron of Flying Ships). Designed by Igor Sikorsky, now best remembered as the world's outstanding helicopter pioneer, these biplanes spanned about 100 feet (30 metres) and were descended from his "Russky Vityaz" of May 1913, the world's first successful four-engined airplane. About 80 were built, and they made 400 raids on German targets with the loss of only one plane. The best-known German strategic bombers of World War I were the Gothas, twin-engined "pusher" biplanes, which made several daylight raids on London in formation in the summer of 1917. All large German bombers tended to be called Gothas by the people they attacked. In fact, the raiding forces often included other types. The German Air Force also operated a family of giant four-engined metal bombers known as *Riesenflugzeug,* or R-planes. Most of those used in action were produced by the Staaken and Zeppelin companies. Typical was the Staaken R.VI number R.25, with four 260-horsepower Mercedes engines, which attacked St. Pancras railway station, London, on February 17–18, 1918. The plane spanned 138 feet 5½ inches (42.2 metres), was 72 feet 6 inches (22 metres) in length, and had a take-off weight of 25,269 pounds (11,485 kilograms), which included a crew of seven and a bomb load of up to 4,000 pounds (1,800 kilograms).

The Gotha

The Gothas and R-planes, which were inspired by Sikorsky's Ilya Muromets, took over Germany's strategic bombing offensive when the Zeppelins became too vulnerable to fighter attack. The threat the planes posed, more than the limited destruction they caused, prompted integration of the RFC and RNAS into the Royal Air Force (RAF) in April 1918 and formation of the Independent Force of the RAF in France in that year. Successor to the 41st Wing, which had carried out a nonstop offensive against enemy military centres by day and night in the winter of 1917–18 and the following spring, it was the first independent air force in the world formed specifically for a strategic bombing role. Its four squadrons of Handley Page O/100 and O/400 night bombers, single squadron of F.E.2b night bombers, and four squadrons of D.H.4, D.H.9, and D.H.9A day bombers dropped 550 tons (500,-000 kilograms) of bombs in the last five months of the war, 390 tons by night. About 40 percent of the total fell on German aerodromes, with such effect that not a single allied airplane was destroyed by enemy bombing during that period.

The achievements of the Independent Force influenced the entire future development of strategic bomber forces. No less important was the example of the D.H.4, which was fast enough to elude most enemy fighters in daylight, thus pioneering a formula that was to produce many years later the British Mosquito of World War II and postwar jet-powered aircraft that relied on speed, rather than guns, for their defense.

Development of naval aviation. Equally significant progress was made in naval flying in World War I, notably by the RNAS. Two distinct categories of combat aircraft emerged. One was the long-range overwater reconnaissance and antisubmarine airplane, operated from coastal bases; the other was the ship-borne airplane, which followed the pattern of land-based air forces by evolving from reconnaissance craft to, eventually, a range of offensive and defensive combat types.

Most efficient of the coastal-based airplanes were large twin-engined flying boats. These had their beginnings in the Curtiss "America," which was being prepared for an attempted transatlantic flight just before World War I. One of the two designated crew members was an Englishman, John Porte, who rejoined the RNAS at the outbreak of war and persuaded the Admiralty to order a number of flying boats similar to the "America." They were followed successively by larger Curtiss machines of the same general design and then by the "F" flying boats, evolved from them under Porte's leadership at Felixstowe, England. Despite their bulk, these aircraft were sufficiently fast and manoeuvrable to engage enemy airplanes and Zeppelins in combat. The flying boats also pioneered the technique of searching for submarines in a methodical pattern by flying strictly controlled courses shaped like a huge spider web over a patrol area in the North Sea. It took a surfaced submarine ten hours to cross the area, and a single flying boat could search a quarter of the "web" in five hours. The first positive success of a flying boat was logged on May 20, 1917, when a Curtiss "Large America" bombed and sank the submarine U.C.36.

Carrier-based air power also advanced rapidly under the stress of war. In early 1916 the first landplanes (Sopwith Pups) were being flown off the 200-foot (61-metre) decks of primitive carriers that had been converted from merchant ships. The planes still had to alight on the sea and be hauled back on board by crane at the end of a flight until, on August 2, 1917, a pilot landed a Pup on the takeoff deck of HMS "Furious" while the ship was under way. The concept of the true aircraft carrier had been born, and the "Furious" was soon fitted with a rear landing deck in addition to the foredeck.

Much more research and development were required before the modern carrier was perfected. For example, the Pups and 1½-Strutters based on the "Furious" had skid landing gear fitted with hooks that engaged ropes extending fore and aft along the landing deck to bring them to a halt. This primitive device, coupled with the unpredictable air currents flowing around the superstructure of the midship, caused many landing accidents. Nevertheless, it was now possible to plan more formidable naval aircraft, and in October 1918 a squadron of Sopwith Cuckoos, each able to carry an 18-inch (46-centimetre) torpedo, was embarked in HMS "Argus." The war ended before it could go into action; but the RNAS had already used torpedoes

Curtiss "America" (margin note)

Torpedo aircraft (margin note)

dropped from Short seaplanes to sink enemy ships in the Mediterranean, and the Cuckoo, with its modest top speed of 103 miles (165 kilometres) per hour and endurance of four hours, heralded the eventual demise of the battleship in the face of air-power dominance at sea.

Alternative concepts, such as towing aircraft behind fast warships on lighters from which they could take off when within range of air or surface targets, were soon abandoned. The only adjunct to the carrier that persisted was the idea of carrying one or two defensive fighters or reconnaissance aircraft on board cruisers and battleships. During World War I, such aircraft were stowed on and took off from wooden platforms built over gun turrets, which were turned into the wind for takeoff. After the war, the turret-platforms were replaced by catapults, enabling heavier, faster airplanes to be launched.

Air transport and training. Military air transport did not emerge on any scale in 1914–18, the most notable operations being those in which food and supplies were dropped over a brief period to troops cut off or besieged by enemy forces. The first such operation was mounted in April 1916, when the British dropped bags of food and other supplies to troops under siege at Kūt al-Imāra (al-Kūt), Mesopotamia. No proper equipment was available for the task, and the bags were simply slung on each side of the aircraft's fuselages or on the landing gear.

The training airplanes of 1914–18 were mainly older types, no longer good enough for combat duty, plus small numbers of operational fighters, bombers, and reconnaissance aircraft. The whole concept of training pilots for military duty, however, was changed by Maj. Robert Smith-Barry, RFC, at the School of Special Flying, Gosport, England. Instead of training his pupils on slow, sedate Farmans, he standardized on the Avro 504J, with the 100-horsepower Gnome Monosoupape engine. Pupil, not instructor, sat in the rear (pilot's) seat, though dual controls were fitted. And the whole essence of instruction was "not to prevent flyers from getting into difficulties or dangers, but to show them how to get out of such situations satisfactorily and, having done so, to make them go and repeat the process alone." For the first time, military pilots flew into action as complete masters of their airplanes, and the sort of flying pioneered at Gosport was adopted eventually at training schools throughout the world.

INTERWAR DEVELOPMENTS

In the 21 years between the end of World War I and the start of World War II, the military airplane underwent a complete transformation. The best fighter of 1918 was probably the German Fokker D.7. Most airplanes of the period were all wood, with fabric covering. The D.7 differed in having a sturdy steel-tube fuselage structure. It was a biplane and, when powered by a 160-horsepower Mercedes engine, had a top speed of 117 miles (187 kilometres) per hour. Armament was two machine guns. The British Supermarine Spitfire of 20 years later was an all-metal monoplane, with a 1,030-horsepower Rolls-Royce Merlin engine, maximum speed of 355 miles (570 kilometres) per hour and armament of eight machine guns. Its landing gear was retractable; its pilot sat in an enclosed cockpit, could breathe oxygen at high altitudes, and was in constant contact with his base and other pilots by radio. Even then engineers and scientists were evolving a revolutionary new kind of aeroengine and electronic equipment that would enable pilots to shoot down aircraft they could not see.

The transition took place, understandably, from 1934 to 1939. During World War I France had built 67,982 aircraft, Britain 55,093, Germany 47,637, and Italy about 20,000. Of these, a total of more than 57,000 remained in service with the French, British, and German air forces as the war ended. The United States had relied mainly on its allies for aircraft used in action in France but had produced 15,000 airplanes during the 21 months of its participation in the war and was at last creating a sound aircraft industry.

With so many airplanes available and the war over, no government was willing to spend large sums of money on new military aircraft, and the industry faced a reces-

Fokker D.7 (margin note)

sion in the early 1920s. As an economy measure, which could be tolerated in areas where no air or anti-aircraft opposition was to be expected, there was a concentration on general-purpose aircraft when new types were ordered to replace the 1918 veterans. Typical were the big British twin-engined Vickers Vernons, which could be used for bombing as well as for their intended task of transporting troops or casualties. Equally versatile were the Westland Wapitis, which finally replaced D.H.9As (but used many 9A components) and which were designed for both reconnaissance and light bombing.

Other nations with colonial commitments, such as France and Italy, evolved similar general-purpose types; but the most significant technical advance in the 1920s was the switch to metal structure, still fabric covered, to provide the strength needed to cope with various climates throughout the world and steadily improving engine performance.

Design improvements. When the more drastic changes came, they resulted from research born of competition in sport flying rather than from military requirements. For the international seaplane contests for the coveted Schneider Trophy and for the national Pulitzer races in the 1920s, the Curtiss company produced a remarkable series of high-speed biplanes for the U.S. Army and Navy. Far cleaner in design and more streamlined than any of their predecessors or contemporaries in these events, the CR, R2C, R3C aircraft were built around closely cowled Curtiss liquid-cooled engines developing up to 610 horsepower in the R3C-2. Piloted by Lt. James Doolittle, an R3C-2 won the 1925 Schneider Trophy contest with a speed of 232.5 miles (374 kilometres) per hour, compared with the winning speed of 145.62 miles (234 kilometres) per hour achieved in 1922 before the Curtiss seaplanes took part in the event.

During a visit to the U.S., the British manufacturer C.R. (later Sir Richard) Fairey was so impressed by the standard of streamlining offered by the Curtiss D-12 engine that he acquired license rights to build it. Fairey installed this engine in his Fox two-seater, which advanced the speed of RAF day bombers by 50 miles (80 kilometres) per hour. The Fox was, in fact, faster than any single-seat fighter then in service and had a great influence on military design in Europe. Many of the outstanding fighters and bombers that followed it into service had closely cowled liquid-cooled engines in the tradition of the D-12. The U.S., home of the Curtiss engine, favoured the air-cooled radial engine, offsetting its less streamlined shape by careful cowling design and by the weight saving and reduced vulnerability in combat offered by absence of a cooling system.

In the year that Doolittle won the Schneider Trophy contest, an even more revolutionary design had appeared briefly on the scene. Designed by R.J. Mitchell of Supermarine, the S.4 seaplane was a wooden cantilever monoplane that set an unprecedented standard of streamlining. It crashed because of wing flutter before it could display its full potential in the contest, but from it evolved a series of aircraft that won the contest three times. The Supermarine S.6B, which achieved the last victory, in 1931, gave Britain permanent possession of the trophy; raised the world speed record above 400 miles (640 kilometres) per hour; and inspired Mitchell to design the Spitfire fighter (see Figure 27).

The S.5, winner of the trophy in 1927, had come at the period when aircraft were switching from wooden to metal construction. Its wings were wire braced for added strength, but no such external bracing was needed when the Spitfire prototype was built and flown nine years later, on March 5, 1936. Earlier military aircraft had utilized a metal basic structure still covered largely with fabric. The Spitfire was typical of the new high-speed designs of the mid-1930s in having metal covering as well as metal structure, with the skin helping to bear the stress loads and so permitting a reduction in the weight of interior structure. Like the slightly earlier Hawker Hurricane, which was to be its partner in the Battle of Britain in 1940, the Spitfire also had the then-revolutionary armament of eight 0.303-inch (7.7-millimetre) Browning machine guns, mounted in the wings outboard of the propeller so that no interrupter gear was needed.

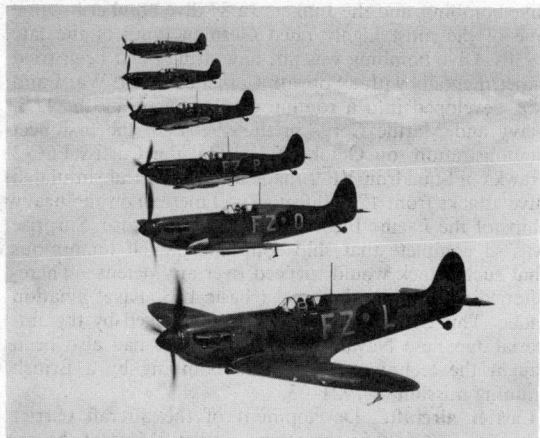

Figure 27: Supermarine Spitfires, British fighter planes of World War II.
By courtesy of John W.R. Taylor

Bombers. Bombers evolved in parallel with fighters, changing to high-strength metal construction in the late 1920s and to monoplane design, which brought higher speeds, in the early 1930s. In 1921–23, the fiery leader of the U.S. Army Air Service, Gen. William ("Billy") Mitchell, had used formations of Martin MB-2 twin-engined bombers to sink several old German and U.S. battleships at sea. Although the ships were stationary and defenseless, the exercises left no doubt of the dominant part that air power would play in future warfare at sea. Mitchell claimed that they proved the obsolescence of large naval craft and pressed the point so strongly that he was eventually court-martialled and suspended from duty, only to be honoured more than 20 years later, after his death, when the truth of his claims had been borne out by events.

The lessons taught by Mitchell's bombing experiments, added to the achievements of World War I bombers, helped to maintain an interest in strategic attack in the interwar years, even during the period when military appropriations were at their lowest. Thus, in 1931, the Boeing Aircraft Company used experience gained with its Monomail transport to produce the B-9 bomber. Predating such fighters as the Spitfire, the B-9 was the progenitor of all modern combat aircraft, with its all-metal cantilever monoplane design, semiretractable undercarriage and variable-pitch propellers—*i.e.*, propellers whose blade angle could be varied. Two 600 horsepower engines gave it a speed of 188 miles (300 kilometres) per hour, representing a 50 percent improvement over the big Keystone biplanes then in service, without any reduction in bomb load.

Within months of its first flight, the B-9 was overshadowed completely by the Martin B-10 of 1932, which brought the biggest single advance in bomber design since the Handley Page O/400. To the innovations of the B-9 it added enclosed cockpits and an internal weapons bay for its 2,260-pound (1,030-kilometre) bomb load. Maximum speed went up to 213 miles (340 kilometres) per hour, making the B-10 faster than the fighters of its day. Following its success, the U.S. Army ordered prototypes of two gigantic bombers, the four-engined 72-ton Douglas XB-19 and the Boeing XB-15. Neither type went into production, but Boeing built in 1935 a smaller four-engined machine known as the Model 299 that became the prototype of the B-17 Flying Fortress. The concept of this famous bomber was to make possible penetration to any target in daylight by fitting sufficient defensive armament to battle past fighter opposition. It led to development of one of the great combat aircraft of World War II, although combat experience was to prove that formations of day bombers could never protect themselves adequately by their own concentrated cross fire without a fighter escort.

Unlike the U.S. Army Air Corps and the RAF, the reformed German Air Force and the Soviet Air Force continued to regard the close support of troops as their primary duty. Even heavy bombers had to be capable of

Curtiss liquid-cooled engines (margin)

Spitfire (margin)

Flying Fortress (margin)

dive bombing, and the Junkers Ju 87 dive bomber became one of the most highly rated German types of the late 1930s. Dive bombing was not new. It had first been tried experimentally with a Sopwith Camel in World War I and was developed into a routine combat tactic by the U.S. Navy and Marine Corps in the 1920s. In the first fleet demonstration, on October 22, 1926, the Curtiss F6C-2 Hawks of Squadron VF-2 made almost vertical simulated dive attacks from 12,000 feet (3,650 metres) on the heavy ships of the Pacific Fleet as they left San Pedro. Surprise was so complete that ship commanders felt unanimous that such attack would succeed over any defense. Thereafter, dive bombing became a basic U.S. naval aviation tactic. This development was not overlooked by the Imperial Japanese Naval Air Service, which had also been taught the technique of torpedo bombing by a British training mission in 1921–23.

Carrier aircraft. Development of the aircraft carrier progressed rapidly in the interwar years. Most of the essential features had been perfected by the early 1930s, when ship-based aircraft had arrester hooks for picking up cables strung transversely across the deck to bring them to a halt, and folding wings that enabled them to be taken by elevator to below-deck servicing hangars. Because of the additional equipment that naval aircraft had to carry and the strengthened structure necessary for deck landing, they tended to be inferior in performance to land-based types. As radio and navigation equipment became more extensive and important, the Royal Navy also began to favour a crew of two, even for fighters, which imposed further penalties on performance. The Royal Navy also retained a biplane configuration for its Swordfish and Albacore torpedo-bombers into World War II, when all other combat types were monoplanes, believing that the resulting slow-flying capability and manoeuvrability offered the best possibility of penetrating between a screen of escort ships and the capital ships that would be the prime target of an attack.

Other developments. All categories of aircraft benefitted from the technical progress made in the interwar years by engine, equipment, and instrument manufacturers. Superchargers, to boost engine power at high altitudes, were in common use in the 1930s. With crew members now seated in enclosed cockpits and provided with oxygen systems, fighters could maintain full effectiveness at an altitude of 15,000–20,000 feet (4,570–6,100 metres). Combat pilots were taught blind flying for safety and improved operational readiness at night or in bad weather; and first-line aircraft were fitted with blind-flying instrument panels as standard equipment. Variable-pitch propellers, for optimum performance at both takeoff and in cruising flight, had been introduced on German Messerschmitt Bf 109 fighters during the Spanish Civil War; they were being produced for RAF Hurricanes and Spitfires in 1939–40. The Bf 109 had also pioneered the use of heavy-calibre cannon armament to ensure the greatest possible destruction against metal-skinned aircraft in the short periods during which the target could be kept in the gun sight at rapidly increasing combat speeds. British fighters were being adapted to take 20-millimetre (0.79-inch) guns by the time World War II began.

Armour plating behind the pilot's seat and bullet-proof windshields were becoming standard on fighters by 1939. Gun turrets for bomber defense had been pioneered by Machines Motrices in France, and a license-built version of their turret appeared on the British Boulton Paul Overstrand bomber in 1934. This international collaboration and the independent work of the Frazer-Nash Company in the U.K. led to the installation of hydraulically operated multigun turrets on such later RAF fighters as the Defiant and all the aircraft that were used in the wartime British bomber offensive. The U.S. Army Air Force claimed that its highly secret Norden bombsight provided such accuracy that "a bomb could be placed in a pickle barrel from 20,000 ft." Perhaps most important of all, the pilots of RAF Fighter Command were trained to be guided toward their targets by ground radar operators, eliminating the need for wasteful and wearying standing patrols.

Norden bombsight

WORLD WAR II

Bombers. The early air fighting in 1939–40 pointed quickly to the need for further technical improvements. RAF Wellington bombers when intercepted in daylight proved particularly susceptible to fire when their fuel tanks were ruptured. This weakness led to universal adoption of self-sealing fuel tanks on combat aircraft and caused the RAF Bomber Command to switch largely to night operations for the duration of the war. Operational analysis revealed that its heavy and costly operations had achieved only limited effect by the autumn of 1941. Only one aircraft in three was dropping its bombs within five miles of its designated target; over the heavily defended Ruhr this accuracy average fell to one aircraft in ten. This knowledge lent urgency to the development of radio and radar navigation aids, culminating in such equipment as the H2S radar, carried entirely on board the bombers, which could produce maplike pictures of the terrain beneath the aircraft through clouds and in all weather so that identification of targets was always possible. Such equipment, allied to the availability of a new generation of four-engined bombers (the Stirling, Halifax, and Lancaster) and everlarger bombs, eventually swamped the German defenses by night. Bomber losses were kept to within acceptable limits by their heavy defensive armament, which totalled ten machine-guns in four turrets on the Lancasters. This effectiveness continued even after the German fighters began carrying radar to aid interception.

At the outbreak of war, bombs normally ranged in weight up to 500 and 1,000 pounds (227 and 454 kilograms). The Lancaster was designed to carry bombs of up to 4,000 pounds; it was adapted progressively to accommodate weapons weighing 8,000, 12,000, and finally 22,000 pounds, the largest bombs dropped in World War II.

Another successful RAF bomber was the all-wood Mosquito, designed to avoid the use of metals that were scarce in wartime, and fast enough with a speed of 415 miles (665 kilometres) per hour in its Mk.XVI version to need no defensive armament. Although small in size, with a crew of two, Mosquitoes had sufficient range to attack Berlin and could carry a 4,000 pound bomb. Variants served as radar-equipped night fighters, as close-support fighter-bombers, and as reconnaissance aircraft.

Day bombers made parallel progress in World War II, notably with the U.S. Army Air Force. As the war continued, the B-17 Flying Fortress and its partner, the four-engined B-24 Liberator (see Figure 28), acquired progressively heavier armament, until the B-17G had no fewer than 13 50-calibre (0.50-inch [13-millimetre]) guns in chin, nose, dorsal, centre-fuselage, ventral, waist, and tail positions. These bombers also were fitted with turbo-supercharged engines that enabled them to fly at or above a height of 30,000 feet (9,100 metres). Even so, losses were high until such escort fighters as the P-51 *B* Mustang were

By courtesy of the U.S. Air Force; photograph, from the Air Force Museum, Wright-Patterson Air Force Base, Ohio

Figure 28: U.S. Consolidated Vultee B-24 Liberator bombers attacking oil refineries at Ploesti, Romania, May 31, 1944.

produced with sufficient range to accompany the bombers throughout their longest raids.

Germany's Ju 87 dive bomber (see Figure 29) achieved considerable success in the early stages of the war in Europe but proved vulnerable when matched against the more numerous modern fighters of the RAF in the summer of 1940. Short-range attack in daylight was undertaken mainly by conventional twin-engined bombers with heavy defensive armament from that time, although the fighter-bomber gradually assumed greater importance.

UPI

Figure 29: German Junkers Ju 87 dive bomber.

Fighter-bombers and fighters. Among the first types to demonstrate the effectiveness of a small, high-speed strike aircraft flying at ground level was the Soviet Ilyushin IL-2 Stormovik. Heavily armoured for protection against ground fire and defended by a gunner in the rear of the two-seat cabin, the IL-2 could fly at up to 280 miles (450 kilometres) per hour and was able to attack ground targets with cannon, bombs, and rockets. It was the first close-support type to employ rockets in vast quantities and had a great influence on the adoption of such weapons by other allied air forces. In 1944, the RAF evolved the "cab rank" tactic. Under radio control from the ground, rocket-firing Typhoon fighter-bombers were directed into a line of aircraft one after another (line astern) to attack German armoured columns. This method played a major part in the Normandy campaign.

Another major development in fighter tactics dates from the autumn of 1940, when RAF Blenheims went into action against German night bombers, using on-board radar to locate their targets. Satisfactory results from such attacks came only with the introduction of faster Beaufighter and Mosquito night fighters. The radar itself evolved rapidly from an early version using a number of separate widely spaced aerials to a type that could be wholly enclosed in a small nose "thimble" radome. Interception armament was normally a mix of machine guns and 20-millimetre cannon, with four guns of each type in the Mosquito fighter.

Rockets and missiles. A major advance came with the addition of small unguided air-to-air rockets on German fighters. These rockets proved highly effective but were never used on a large enough scale to affect the course of the war in the air. Similarly, the air-to-air and surface-to-air guided missiles under development in Germany were not perfected in time to play any significant part in the war. Air-to-surface missiles did demonstrate their effectiveness on a number of occasions, notably as anti-shipping weapons. One of their most spectacular early successes occurred when the Italian battleship "Roma" was sunk by direct hits with Fritz X radio-controlled glide bombs launched from Dornier Do 217K-2 bombers on September 9, 1943. Later, Azon radio-controlled bombs dropped by U.S. Liberator squadrons in Southeast Asia proved particularly valuable for pinpoint attacks on Japanese-held bridges.

In general, the German guided missiles were too late to play any major part in World War II, although they had great influence on later military strategy and tactics. Unguided or semiguided V-1 flying bombs and V-2 rockets were used in considerable numbers against London and other targets in 1944–45, each carrying a heavy explosive warhead. Allied to the atomic bomb, which, dropped on two cities in Japan in August 1945, brought World War II to an end, the V-2 foreshadowed the intercontinental ballistic missiles of the postwar era.

Naval aircraft. At sea, air power fulfilled its promise of making the big capital ships obsolete, notably during operations in the Pacific. At Pearl Harbor, on December 7, 1941, Japanese carrier-based dive bombers and torpedo-carrying aircraft struck a heavy blow at the U.S. Pacific Fleet. In later battles, such as the Coral Sea and Midway, U.S. carrier-based aircraft employed similar tactics to inflict crippling blows on Japanese naval forces at sea. Such battles were the first that could be won decisively by one of the fleets engaged without the two surface forces ever coming within sight of each other.

A few of the more successful carrier-based aircraft of World War II, such as the British Swordfish biplane, seemed thoroughly obsolete by comparison with their land-based counterparts. In contrast, naval fighters progressed rapidly to the stage where they were as good as—in some cases better than—contemporary air force types. The performance of the Japanese Mitsubishi A6M, known to the Allies as the "Zero," far overshadowed that of Allied fighters opposing it in the early stages of the war in the Pacific.

Of the 10,937 "Zeroes" built, many were used for kamikaze (suicide) attacks on Allied ships in 1944–45, side-by-side with other combat types and smaller numbers of specially designed suicide aircraft. A peculiarly Japanese tactic, kamikaze operations entailed diving bomb-laden aircraft into targets at sea and were highly effective in terms of both ships sunk and lowering of Allied morale. The 1,228 Japanese naval aircraft expended in kamikaze attacks sank 34 ships and damaged 288 others. Off Okinawa, they inflicted more casualties in the U.S. fleets than were lost as a result of Japanese army action against the invading troops in the long battle ashore.

As the war progressed, maritime aircraft used a variation of the interceptor's search radar to find enemy surface vessels and submarines at sea. Standard attack weapons were bombs, rockets, depth charges, and air-dropped mines; but some aircraft were fitted with large guns, such as the 57-millimetre (2.24-inch) six-pounder Molins gun in the Mosquito XVIII and the Army 75-millimetre (2.95-inch) gun carried by the B-25G and H versions of the North American Mitchell. Flying boats were used on a large scale for maritime patrol and antisubmarine duties; but the steady improvement in range of land-based aircraft, coupled with the construction of concrete runways for large landplanes all over the world, initiated the gradual postwar disappearance of combat flying boats from the air forces of most countries except the Soviet Union and Japan.

Reconnaissance aircraft. Reconnaissance proved as vital as it had been in World War I. It was impossible to plan a major bombing offensive without thorough and up-to-date coverage of the target area beforehand. It was equally important to discover after each attack precisely how much damage had been done. Sometimes routine sorties brought surprising results, as when a Spitfire photographic sortie revealed that the Germans were using defensive radar in western France in November 1940, at a time when the RAF believed it had a monopoly of such equipment. Later, a chance reconnaissance photograph taken over Peenemünde enabled a sharp-eyed woman photo-interpreter to suggest that the enemy had a flying bomb almost ready for service—a discovery that precipitated a heavy raid on this German rocket research centre.

Many different types of aircraft were used for reconnaissance, but the most successful were probably the high-speed fighters, stripped of armament and all other disposable items to save weight and to increase performance, which raced low to the target areas, took their photos in a few quick passes, and then escaped homeward at maximum speed. High-flying aircraft also took photographs on motion-picture film that could be made up into mosaic maps of vast areas, pointing the way to postwar progress in aerial surveys for map making.

Air transport. Equally significant for postwar civilian operations were the major advances in air transportation made during the war. Mass drops of parachute troops had been pioneered by the Soviet Union in the 1930s, but the German Air Force first used the technique operationally, notably during the invasion of Crete. More than 15,000 of the 22,000 soldiers who captured the island in May 1941 went by air, in 700 transport aircraft and 80 gliders. The price they paid was so high that the Germans never again mounted a major airborne operation, but airborne and parachute troops played a leading role in many subsequent allied assaults. The troop-carrying glider was one of the developments of World War II that had no continuing place in postwar air forces; but the transport airplane was only at the beginning of its useful life. The main transports used in the war were the Douglas DC-3 (C-47) on the allied side and the Junkers Ju 52 on the German side. Their capability was best shown in Burma, where a British Army of 300,000 men was supplied entirely from the air by 23 squadrons of aircraft in the last year of the war against Japan. Their success was such that designers all over the world began work on specialized military freighters with nose- and tail-loading features, roller conveyors in the floor, and other ideas that would speed turnaround on the ground and facilitate the air-dropping of supplies and equipment in flight. None of these airplanes was ready in time to play a significant part in the war but, again, they pointed the way to postwar progress in both military and commercial air freighting.

Jet and rocket propulsion. No wartime development was more significant than the appearance of the first jet-propelled airplanes. Frank Whittle had run the first turbojet, in England, on April 12, 1937, but it was the German
Heinkel
He 178
Heinkel He 178 that, on August 27, 1939, became the first jet-propelled airplane to fly. Both nations pressed on as rapidly as possible to perfect jet fighters during the war, and the RAF's Gloster Meteor and German Messerschmitt Me 262 were both operational by the summer of 1944. They and the other jet aircraft evolved during the war years played only a small part in the fighting; but their high speed and operating ceiling left little doubt that the days of the piston-engined combat airplane were numbered, and in 1945 a Meteor raised the world air speed record in one jump from 469 to 606 miles (755 to 975 kilometres) per hour.

It is also worth noting that Germany had used operationally a small tailless rocket-powered interceptor, the Me 163, which had a speed of 596 miles (959 kilometres) per hour. High fuel consumption gave it a powered endurance of only 2½ minutes after its climb to operating height, and several pilots were killed when remaining propellants mixed and exploded during landing. Although Me 163s achieved some success in attacks on allied bomber formations, they remain the only rocket-powered airplanes ever to have achieved operational status.

THE SUPERSONIC AGE

Two years after the end of World War II, on October 14, 1947, Maj. Charles Yeager of the U.S. Air Force became the first person to fly faster than the speed of sound. He made his supersonic flight in a Bell X-1 rocket-powered research airplane, launched in the air from the bombbay of a B-29 Superfortress of the kind that had dropped the atomic bombs on Japan. Six months later, on April 26, 1948, the prototype North American XP-86 Sabre jet fighter also flew at supersonic speed in a shallow dive during its development tests, and military aviation entered the supersonic age.

Supersonic fighters. German wartime research had shown that the use of swept-back wings eased the shockwave problems associated with flying at very high speeds. The Sabre had swept-back wings; so did the Soviet MiG-15 fighter that flew a few weeks after the prototype XP-86, on December 30, 1947. These two aircraft set the pattern for most fighters that followed, although some have adopted

a delta-wing layout, while others, notably the F-104 Starfighter, have benefitted from subsequent aerodynamic knowledge to revert to unswept wings. All use a gyro-stabilized gunsight of the type developed during World War II, and their instrumentation and equipment have become steadily more sophisticated. The latest all-weather fighters, in particular, are semi-automatic. After takeoff, they can be flown automatically on preset courses by linking their automatic pilot with a computer-controlled flight system. Radar equipment can search for, locate, interrogate, and "lock on" to an enemy airplane, fly the fighter toward it by controlling the flight system, fire the armament automatically at the optimum moment, and then break away for the return to base. Self-contained inertial navigation and Doppler-radar systems, allied to other navigation aids, offer high standards of navigational accuracy (see also NAVIGATION). Head-up displays enable the pilot to see all vital information in pictorial form projected on his windscreen without the need to glance down at his instruments during critical periods of flight or landing.

Guided weapons, mostly of the self-homing type, have become standard interceptor armament but are supplemented by heavy-calibre guns and unguided rockets for close-range combat. Support of ground forces remains a major fighter duty, with the weapons of World War II supplemented by air-to-surface missiles and tactical nuclear weapons. Napalm incendiary tanks, utilized in the last years of World War II, have remained a primary fighter weapon in postwar campaigns. A few fighters capable of flying at three times the speed of sound (Mach 3) have appeared, notably the experimental Lockheed YF-12A in the U.S. and the MiG-23 in the Soviet Union. These have to be built of special heat-resistant metals, but almost all other aircraft in service in 1970 continued to have aluminum alloy basic structures that limit maximum speed to about Mach 2.5.

Supersonic bombers. Interceptors have been supplemented rather than replaced by ground-launched missiles; the same is true of bombers. For more than 20 postwar years the jet-propelled heavy bombers of the U.S., U.K., and the U.S.S.R. maintained the deterrent policy of peace through the mutual fear of atomic attack. This role has been taken over largely by intercontinental thermonuclear missiles based in the U.S. and U.S.S.R. and on board submarines (see in section on rockets and missile systems above). Nevertheless, both the U.S. and U.S.S.R. retain forces of long-range bombers armed with nuclear missiles and other weapons. These aircraft have more extensive versions of the automatic navigation systems carried by fighters and can also make use of electronic countermeasures (ECM) devices to jam enemy search and fighter/missile-control radar, decoys that give the same signal as a bomber on enemy radar screens, missiles that home on the emissions from defense radar, and automatic landing systems for safe touchdown in fog or bad weather.

Other recent military aircraft. Close-support aircraft include such airplanes as the General Dynamics F-111, which is in the class of a light bomber and has a "swing-wing"; i.e., a wing whose geometry can be varied in flight to combine high operational speed with the ability to land and take off comparatively slowly. This development reflects the need for combat aircraft to be as independent as possible of fixed bases in a nuclear age. Most first-line combat types are designed to operate from comparatively short, unprepared strips, and this requirement has led to development of a number of STOL (short takeoff and landing) and VTOL (vertical takeoff and landing) aircraft. Typical of the former is the Swedish Saab-37 Viggen, which uses a tandem-wing layout to combine a Mach 2 performance with the ability to operate from especially prepared sections of highway. The first true VTOL type in service in the 1970s was the Hawker Siddeley Harrier (see Figure 30), which uses a single vectored-thrust turbo-fan, with rotating exhaust nozzles, for both vertical take-off and forward propulsion.
F-111
bomber

Maritime patrol aircraft, powered increasingly by turbofan engines offering high speed with lower fuel consumption, carry highly complex equipment to detect and track

Figure 30: Hawker Siddeley Harrier VTOL fighter plane.
By courtesy of Hawker Siddeley Aviation, Ltd.

modern deep-diving, nuclear-powered submarines. This equipment includes radar, magnetic anomaly detection (MAD) gear in a tail "sting" to search out metallic objects underwater, sonobuoys that are dropped into the water to listen for and pinpoint submarines, a device that can detect traces of smoke or fumes emitted by a ship or submerged submarine, and a searchlight, as well as a variety of attack weapons and ECM equipment. Reconnaissance aircraft also carry ECM devices and rely heavily on electronic and infrared sensors to supplement their film cameras. Their tasks are to locate and photograph targets, using radar and conventional photographic techniques, and to probe enemy electronic defense systems to discover and evaluate the types of radio and radar equipment that are in use. They do this by offshore patrols, just outside territorial limits and, more rarely, by overflights. The best-known type used for overflights since the war was the Lockheed U-2, which could supplement its long endurance at very high altitude by shutting down its engine and gliding for a time. Successor to the U-2 is the Lockheed SR-71, which can cruise at above Mach 3 at 80,000 feet (24,400 metres) for very long periods. At the other extreme are small pilotless "drones," which can be launched either in the air or from the ground, for reconnaissance flights over enemy territory or in a battle area, carrying photographic, radar, or television sensors. In peacetime, however, most work of this kind is performed by reconnaisance satellites.

Carrier-based aircraft differ little from their land-based counterparts; in some cases, such as the American McDonnell F-4 Phantom II, the same basic types serve both afloat and ashore. The early warning aircraft, a specialized carrier type, has a large radar to detect aircraft or ships approaching the fleet over which it circles. Some airplanes in this category, such as the U.S. Grumman E-2 Hawkeye, can also control interceptor fighters defending the fleet; and this kind of AWACS (airborne warning and control system) airplane has appeared in land-based air forces to detect low-flying enemy raiders and direct interceptors toward them. The first aircraft of this type was a Soviet conversion of the Tu-114 turboprop transport, known to North Atlantic Treaty Organization forces as "Moss."

Modern air forces make use of many other types of aircraft. Transports are often similar in design to commercial designs, ranging from small STOL liaison machines to such huge transports as the USAF Galaxy, largest airplane in the world, with a payload of 265,000 pounds (120,000 kilograms). Training aircraft are mostly jets, although a few piston-engined aircraft are sometimes used for the most elementary stages of flying instruction. Flying tankers, usually converted from transports or bombers, are used to refuel combat types in flight and so increase their range or endurance.

Helicopters. The helicopter first made its impact during the Korean War (1950–53), when it proved its ability to put down men, guns, and supplies in otherwise inaccessible places. By evacuating casualties speedily, it reduced the death rate to the lowest figure in military history. To these basic duties, the military helicopter has since added the retrieval of damaged aircraft in its flying crane role,

antisubmarine search and attack from platforms on virtually any kind of ship, and even close support of ground forces in its "gunship" form, with armament of guns, rockets, grenade throwers, and missiles. No aircraft illustrates better the all-important "go-anywhere" versatility of modern military aviation. (J.W.R.T.)

Warning and detection systems

Because military tactics from time immemorial have stressed the value of surprise, through timing, location of attack, route, and weight and character of arms, defenders have sought to construct warning systems to cope with all these tactics. Many types of warning systems exist. Longterm, or political, warning systems employ diplomatic, political, technological, and economic indicators to forecast hostilities. The defender may react by strengthening his defenses, by negotiating treaties or concessions, or by taking other action. Political warning, equivocal and incapable of disclosing fully an attacker's intention, often results in an unevaluated and neglected situation.

Medium-term, or strategic, warning, usually involving a time span of a few days or weeks, is a notification or judgment that enemy-initiated hostilities may be imminent. Short-term, or tactical, warning, often hours or minutes in advance, is a notification that the enemy has initiated hostilities.

Warning and detecting are separate functions. The sensors or detection devices perceive either the attack, the possibilities of an attack, the nearness of the enemy, his location, his size, his activities, his weapon capability, or some changes in his political, economic, technical, or military posture.

Warning systems include detection devices but also imply the judgments, decisions, and actions that follow receipt of the sensor's information. Warning encompasses communications, analysis of information, decisions, and appropriate actions. Visual observation still remains important, supplemented by telescopes, cameras, heat-sensing devices, low-light-level devices, radar, acoustic, seismic, chemical, and nuclear detection devices. The product, or output, of these sensors is complicated and voluminous and requires computers to condense and summarize the data for the decision maker. Often, the most expensive portion and weakest link of the warning system is not the sensor but the communication and evaluation systems. Technology of all types is required in modern warning systems.

HISTORY

History abounds with examples of successful military surprises; examples of effective warning are difficult to find. Military training emphasized the value of surprise, stratagem, and deception, but the value of warning was long neglected. Flank and rear guards, to protect marching columns, patrols and scouts to locate the enemy, and sentries to guard camps, were of course used in war from earliest times. Animals were sometimes employed to detect the approach of an enemy; dogs and horses were especially favoured, though, according to the ancient historian Livy, the Romans used geese to detect the night attack of the Gauls on Rome in the 4th century BC. High ground, favourable for observation, was often supplemented by watchtowers, such as those placed along the Great Wall of China and on Hadrian's Wall in Britain.

An important technological advance with strong detection potential was the balloon. First used in warfare by the French in the late 18th century, primarily for offensive reconnaissance on the battlefield, its defensive possibilities were revealed in the American Civil War; in May 1863, a balloon of the army of the Potomac detected the movement of Lee's Army from its camp across the Rappahannock to commence the Gettysburg Campaign. Aerial photography had already been pioneered by the French and used in the War of Italian Independence (1859).

A balloon observer in the Spanish-American War of 1898 is credited with discovering an alternate route up San Juan Hill during the battle there. A few other successes are ascribed to such observation before the balloon was supplemented by the far more valuable airplane in World

Lockheed U-2

Balloon reconnaissance and aerial photography

War I. Nevertheless, the balloon never fulfilled its potential as a warning device.

In sea warfare, warning and detection were equally neglected. As far back as the Minoan civilization of Crete, patrol ships were used, but mainly for offensive purposes. In later centuries, raised quarterdecks and lookout posts atop sailing masts were provided, but the beginnings of serious maritime detection technology did not come until the advent of the submarine.

The first observation airplanes

Binoculars, telescopes, the telegraph, and telephone were well established military equipment by 1914; the airplane, first used by the Italians in the Italo-Turkish War of 1911, showed its potential as an observation device at the Battle of the Marne. Radio communications provided the means to make air observations immediately available. Aerial combat became inevitable as each side tried to deny the other its aerial reconnaissance.

Searchlights, first used in the Russo-Japanese War (1904), saw large-scale use in World War I to detect dirigibles and aircraft in night bombardment missions. Flares were used to illuminate the battlefield between trenches to detect raiding parties. Acoustic devices, using directional horns to detect and locate enemy aircraft, were also used with limited success.

Despite the novelties of World War I, World War II produced far more technological innovation. Radar made obsolete the slow and inaccurate older listening devices. Radio communications made great strides, particularly in the very high frequency region. The combination of radar and interference-free very high frequency communications was pivotal in permitting the Royal Air Force to resist Hitler's aerial attack and win the Battle of Britain.

Notwithstanding radar sophistication, ground spotters played an important role in filling the gaps between radar coverage. Their messages, forwarded to a plotting centre, were assembled to trace the progress of intruders (tracking).

The advent of nuclear weapons (1945), especially when later coupled to the speed and range of intercontinental missiles, gave new dimensions to the value of surprise for the attacker. Long-term warning was suddenly of paramount importance. Not only did all forms of unequivocal warning become indispensable but the warning had to be made credible to an aggressor; that is, an assurance had to be given that the retaliatory weapons would not all be destroyed by a first strike. Bomber aircraft were kept in the air to avoid destruction on the ground and attempts made to provide a degree of protection for the civilian population through shelters.

Practically all aspects of science and technology have been introduced into today's warfare and warning systems: airplanes, helicopters, submarines, earth satellites, television, lasers, and magnetic, acoustic, seismic, infrared, nuclear, and chemical detectors.

ELECTROMAGNETIC SENSORS

Modern detector technology. *The visible region.* Binoculars and telescopes have changed very little. Where vibration and motion create interference, gyroscopically stabilized optics are used in surface vehicles, ships, and aircraft.

The straight scope

Newer in character are the image intensifiers used for nighttime detection (see Figure 31). These devices receive the moonlight or starlight reflected from targets on a sensitive screen, amplify the image electronically, and present it at much higher light level on a small cathode-ray tube similar to that used in a television receiver. Typical of these devices is the starlight scope, resembling an oversized telescopic sight, with which riflemen can aim at night at 1,000–1,300 feet (300–400 metres) range. Artillery, tanks, helicopters, and aircraft use similar, larger devices having longer range. In aircraft, the direct-viewing device is replaced by a cathode-ray tube in the instrument panel; this version is called low-light-level television.

Ordinary searchlights can often be used at night even in combat situations; but to avoid drawing fire, invisible light, in the ultraviolet or near infrared, can be used with appropriate viewing devices. Conventional photography, used in aerial reconnaissance and essential to long-term warning, must have high resolution despite operation in

Figure 31: The night observation device, which provides a high degree of night vision capability to detect, locate, and identify the enemy. Using image intensification techniques, the low-light-level illumination of the night sky (*i.e.,* moonlight) reflected from the object and its background form a clearly defined image to the observer.
By courtesy of the United States Army

an unfavourable temperature and vibration environment. To cover wide areas, panoramic cameras, scanning from side to side, record high-quality images. Frame cameras also are used, especially for mapping. At night, droppable flares or flashing lights on aircraft are used.

Infrared. Infrared sensors on the ground, or in aircraft or spacecraft, can detect such hot spots as motor-vehicle engines, hot jet engines, missile exhausts, even campfires. They have good location accuracy and high sensitivity to signals, without registering such false targets as sun reflections.

Infrared imaging detectors also are used. In the very near infrared region, specially sensitized photographic film forms camouflage-revealing images. More important are the detectors used in the far infrared region; objects at room temperature radiate sufficient energy for detection at ranges of several miles. Infrared imagery can have longer range than image intensifiers and can operate without starlight. When the humidity is high, the effective range is reduced.

The sniperscope, an early device that used infrared illumination and an infrared view, has been largely replaced by the image intensifier and by laser illuminators.

Radar. Radar is used by ground forces for many purposes: in portable sizes, for infiltration detection; in intermediate sizes, for mortar and artillery shell tracking; and in large sizes, for early warning, search, and control of air-defense weapons (interceptors and surface-to-air missiles).

Radar is used in fighter aircraft for finding enemy aircraft and controlling air-to-air missiles, rockets, and guns. It is used in bombers to find surface targets, fixed or moving, and to navigate and avoid obstacles. It is used in large aircraft as an airborne warning and control system, searching the skies over great distances for enemy aircraft, tracking them, and controlling interceptors. It also is used to search the seas for surface vessels or surfaced submarines. Radar also can be used in spacecraft to locate patterns of activity.

In all applications of radar, clutter in the form of reflections from surface objects or the terrain, or the disturbed sea, competes with reflection from the targets and must be cancelled by appropriate circuitry. Side-looking radars are used to obtain higher resolution than conventional radar, improving the ability to recognize surface targets.

Conventional radar operates at microwave and ultrahigh frequencies that propagate in straight lines like light rays; consequently, they cannot ordinarily detect objects below the earth's horizon. Because high-frequency waves reflect from the ionosphere, over-the-horizon radars have been built to operate in this region.

Over-the-horizon radar

Radio sensors. Radio receivers can be used to detect and locate enemy radio. Enemy radars can be similarly located and warning information derived. Messages can be intercepted. This form of warning has been combatted by radio silence and by spoofing, the transmission of signals intended to deceive this form of warning. In 1967 the Israelis transmitted voluminous radio messages from empty airfields to hide the fact that aircraft had been moved to other locations.

Radio direction finders can be used to locate nuclear bursts, because the explosion generates a large amount of energy in the radio frequency region.

Acoustic techniques. While electromagnetic waves do not propagate well under water, acoustic waves do and can be used to detect submerged submarines. These detection systems, called sonar, may intercept propeller or other noise generated by the submarine, may send out sounds, and receive echoes from the submarine hull. Sonar devices can be operated aboard surface ships, aboard submarines, on floating "sonobuoys," or suspended by cables from helicopters and dunked in the ocean.

Sonar systems are limited in range by attenuation (weakening) of the sound energy in propagating through the water, bending caused by temperature differences in water layers, and by extraneous noises, including reflections from the sea bottom.

Acoustic receivers also are used on land in sensors deployed near trails to detect the presence of personnel or vehicles along roads. The sounds are sent by radio to listening posts. Acoustic sensors also are used in monitoring nuclear explosions.

Seismic detectors. Seismic detectors (see Figure 32)— as well as underground acoustic detectors called Geophones—are used in sensors for infiltration and vehicle detection. Both types must be used, since either alone can yield false detections caused by the movement of animals.

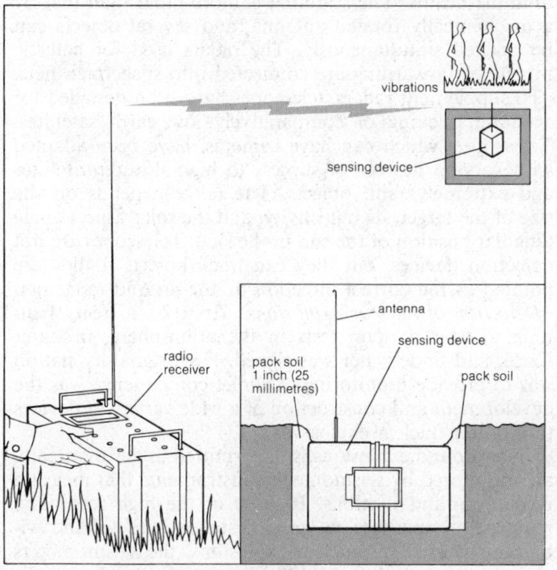

Figure 32: *Distant sensing and identification.*
The acoustic sensing device is buried in the ground as shown. It detects movement of people and vehicles by sensing vibrations they cause in the earth and transmits a code to a special radio receiver.

Magnetic detectors. Sensitive magnetic detectors (magnetometers), flown in aircraft over the sea, are used to detect submarines because the large metallic mass of the submarine hull disturbs the earth's magnetic field. Buried on land, magnetometers are used to detect the passage of vehicles.

Nuclear detectors. Underground nuclear explosions are detected by sensitive seismometers. To increase the sensitivity and reject natural earth tremors, seismometers are often used in large arrays, extending for hundreds of miles.

For atmospheric or space explosions, radio-pulse receivers, light flash and acoustic detectors are used, as well as devices to measure the fallout products. Aircraft and rockets can be used to collect radioactive debris, while high-altitude satellites carry detectors for gamma rays and other emissions.

Chemical sensors. Concealed chemical sensors, sensi-

tive to minute amounts of body products, are capable of detecting personnel from short distances.

Future developments. Certain trends can be seen in sensor development for future warning systems. Infrared detectors of higher sensitivity and resolution are being developed. Higher powered and smaller lasers will aid night warning systems. These and other lines of research, centred on lighter weight and more efficient optics and on obtaining more efficient detectors, should result in much cheaper systems with resolution approaching visual sensors. Perhaps most important are improvements in the resolution and brightness of the display—the chief limitation of most night viewing systems.

Photography has already reached an advanced state of technology, yet improvements in resolution are actively pursued. Lightweight optics, more sensitive and fine-grained film, film that can be developed quickly by heat, and better compensation for the motion of the aircraft are some of the areas where successful results will improve photography.

Developments in large ground radars centre around the phased array radar having electronically steered beams. The beams must be computer controlled. Moving target discrimination and Doppler processing are built out of digital circuitry as used in digital computers. This permits sensitive discrimination and rapid response.

The advent of the transistor and solid-state devices is making possible small radars for infantrymen and tank operators. The miniature components and high reliability of these devices makes possible extremely complex and sophisticated circuitry.

Airborne radar is in its early stages of development. Side-looking Doppler-processing radar has already yielded high resolution, but not quite as good as conventional photography. Developments in progress indicate that soon images comparable to photographic images will be obtained from airborne radar. Imperfections now common in radar imagery should be removed as a result of present research.

A great deal of effort in several countries has reduced the vulnerability of radars to electronic countermeasures; at the same time, however, similar improvements in electronic jamming and deception have taken place. All indications are that such electronic warfare will grow.

Nuclear propulsion enables submarines to remain submerged and escape detection by radar. This, added to its increased speed, makes the nuclear submarine a formidable threat. To combat this, sonar sensors for detection of submarines are now being formed into arrays. This increases the sensitivity and rejects extraneous noise, especially important in regions of turbulence.

The search for more sensitive systems of detection will clearly go on. Measurement of the temperature change in the water in which a submarine lies, and the magnetic anomaly observable when it is under the water, are two directions in which study is being pursued. A range of such measurements may become possible. Testing of laser beams for underwater recognition capability has been proceeding for some time. The problem is extremely difficult, water being a medium quite different from air, and much work will be needed to overcome the obstacles.

The subject is closely linked with the study of undersea conditions generally; that is, oceanography. American efforts dwarf those of any other Western nation, though France, a pioneer in undersea exploration, is active. Underwater acoustic navigation enables ships to be used for missile or satellite tracking. Underwater communication over very long distances is essential for the control of nuclear submarines, to make the most of their almost unlimited radius of operation.

WARNING SYSTEMS

Modern systems. *Air defense systems.* Radar and Identification Friend or Foe (IFF) equipment comprises the forward elements of complex systems that have appeared throughout the world. Examples include semi-automatic ground environment (SAGE), augmented by a mobile backup system called BUIC in the United States, NATO air defense ground environment (NADGE) in Europe, a similar system in Japan, and various land-mobile, airborne, and

[Margin notes]
Sonar systems

Underwater laser beams

ship command and control systems. Little information concerning the Soviet systems is available, but they are known to be extensive, automated, and capable (see also MEASUREMENT AND OBSERVATION: *Radar*).

Air-defense systems require computers and communication nets to process the radar data. Position reports from the radars are formed into tracks of each detected aircraft. Height-finding radars add the third dimension. The IFF information, together with known flight plans, is correlated; clutter, false returns from clouds, and any electronic countermeasures are rejected. Decisions are made on whether to counter the attack with interceptors or surface-to-air missiles. The counterattack is controlled by guiding a missile or directing an intercept.

To avoid excessive centralization of equipment that would make the system vulnerable to nuclear attack, the computers and communication facilities are widely dispersed and supplemented by mobile facilities.

In addition to large conventional radars, small distributed radars (called gap fillers) are used to detect low-flying aircraft penetrating gaps in large radar coverage. Over-the-horizon radars and airborne warning and control systems are even more promising. The latter consist of large radar and computation, display, and control systems, housed in large aircraft. First introduced for naval defense, they have become potentially effective over land with new developments in clutter rejection circuitry.

Large aircraft with powerful radars connected to sophisticated computer and display equipment can survive a nuclear attack and have a low-altitude surveillance capability. Their use, delayed because of problems caused by interference from land clutter, is growing.

The DEW line

A unique air-defense system is the U.S.–Canadian Distant Early Warning system stretching across the northern portion of North America. The radars are used strictly for early warning; no control of missiles or interceptors is provided. Elaborate communications to control centres to the south are part of the system.

Air-defense systems disseminate the warning to the civil population by sirens and radio alerts. Extensive communication nets are built for this service. Air-defense systems also select and assign the defensive weapons to particular threats. If interceptors are used, a control centre is assigned to transmit control information by digitally encoded radio messages.

If surface-to-air missiles are used, the target is designated to the missile control system, which has its own target-tracking and missile-control radar. Practically all surface-to-air missile systems have some autonomous capability of warning and target acquisition. Examples of these systems are the American Nike Hercules and Hawk, the British Thunderbird, Bloodhound, and Rapier, the French-German Roland, and the Italian Indigo. In sea warfare, such missiles as the U.S. Terrier and Talos, the British Sea Dart, and the French Masurca have autonomous radar capability.

At sea, air defense also uses large radars on ships, but more use is made of airborne radar and control systems. The weight and size of long-range radars restricts their installation to the larger ships; airborne radar over the ocean does not have severe land clutter to contend with, making it simpler than overland systems; the horizon limits are at a greater range; and the aircraft can patrol a large area. As in land defenses, extensive computer and display complexes, and communications between the ships, are used. In the U.S. Navy, the Airborne Tactical Data System, consisting of airborne radar, computers, memory and data links, is connected with the Naval Tactical Data System, located in fleet headquarters, which processes, organizes, and displays information of the overall picture of the tactical situation.

Ballistic missile warning. In the second half of the 20th century, warning against ballistic missiles with nuclear warheads has taken precedence over all other warning systems. Large ground radars, operating in the vhf or uhf region, are used. The radars both search the skies and track objects detected. Computers calculate the trajectory to determine if the target is a missile or an earth-orbiting object. Depending upon the trajectory, the number of ob-

jects, and other criteria, alerts, tentative warnings, or all-out warning signals are transmitted to command centres.

Surface-based radars have one serious flaw: they can detect the missile only after it appears above the earth's horizon. For earlier warning, over-the-horizon radars or satellite-borne infrared detectors can be used.

There are two types of over-the-horizon radars, operating in the high-frequency region, which can reflect from the ionosphere, to furnish missile warning. One system, called forward scatter, transmits from one location and receives the signal several thousand miles away on the other side of the launch point. The back-scatter system receives the signal from the same location as the transmitter, as is done in conventional radar. Both systems detect variations in the received signal due to fluctuations in the ionosphere caused by the missile's exhaust plume as it traverses the ionosphere.

Ballistic missile defense. Ballistic missile defense systems have their own warning and acquisition radar systems. These large radars are more sophisticated than the warning radars because they must form accurate tracks for the engagement radars. Decoy objects and lightweight metallic reflectors called chaff must be identified and rejected. To do this, the radars must be able to measure the velocity of all the objects, since lightweight objects decelerate more rapidly than heavy objects due to atmospheric drag and friction.

Space surveillance. Closely allied to warning systems are space-object detection and tracking systems. It is likely that only the U.S. and the Soviets have developed and operate these systems. A variety of very large radars are used, although the newer installations are phased-array radars that have stationary antennas with electronically steerable multiple beams. The scanning is more rapid than that by a mechanically rotated antenna, and several objects can be tracked simultaneously. The radars used for ballistic missile early warning are connected into spacetrack nets.

Tracking by telescope

To supplement radars, telescopes have been designed for accurate tracking of comparatively low earth satellites. Telescopes, which can have cameras, have been adapted with varying degrees of success to high-altitude satellites and extremely faint objects. The range depends on the size of the target, its reflectivity, and the solar aspect angle (angular position of the sun in the sky). Telescopes are not detection devices, but they can track objects if they are pointed in the correct direction by the ground radar net.

Detection of nuclear explosions. In 1963 a treaty banning nuclear weapon tests in the atmosphere, in outer space, and underwater was signed. Each signatory nation was to provide monitoring. A direct consequence was the development and construction of a wide variety of devices to monitor nuclear explosions.

Underground explosions, still permitted under the treaty, are monitored by seismometers, instruments that measure minute ground motions. Because of the high sensitivity required to measure at great distances the ground vibrations caused by nuclear explosions, the seismometers record many extraneous motions from natural sources; these are called noise. To reduce noise, a large number of seismometers arranged in arrays is used to reinforce the desired signal and exclude unwanted signals. Elaborate data processing, with the help of recorders and computers, further refines the output. Despite these measures, there is a limit to the sensitivity of underground and underwater systems, so that very small nuclear explosions at great distance from the receiving sites may not be detected or may be wrongly identified as a small earthquake.

Sensing an explosion in space

Detection of explosions in the atmosphere and in space depends upon measuring the products of an explosion. Acoustic sensors are used to measure the sound waves created by the blast, aircraft and rockets to collect possibly radioactive debris samples, flash detectors to detect the light flash as well as the radio pulse generated by the explosion, and a number of radio-detection techniques to measure the considerable disturbance of the ionosphere. None of the techniques is adequate by itself, since each is disturbed by various background signals. Analyzed together, however, they yield positive results.

To detect explosions in space, high-altitude satellites are

used. They carry detectors of X-ray emissions, gamma rays, and neutrons, all of which are generated by a nuclear explosion. They can be detected because there is essentially no atmosphere in space to absorb the emissions.

Infiltration and base defense systems. The growth of insurgency warfare has made necessary the development of a variety of sensors to detect vehicles and personnel in the jungle along trails or on roads. Acoustic, seismic, magnetic, infrared, radar, and Doppler radar (radars that detect movement by shift in frequency of received signal) are the sensors.

The sensors are connected to processing centres where the progress of an infiltrating column or truck convoy can be monitored. This process eliminates many false detections due to random noise or animals. Because the sensors are widespread and the processing quite sophisticated, the systems have become known as the instrumented battlefield or electronic barrier.

Aerial reconnaissance. Aerial reconnaissance has grown in importance; it now encompasses all phases of warning. Visual observation from aerial platforms furnishes short-term information and warning. Direct receiving and image-recording infrared equipment in night reconnaissance, high resolution radar in bad weather, and conventional photography all contribute to medium and long-term warning by observing tactical preparations or discerning new military capabilities.

Manned aircraft are used more frequently than other platforms for these sensors. Unmanned aircraft, however, flying at low and high altitudes; helicopters, including small unmanned helicopters; and space vehicles are all used for various reconnaissance missions.

Photography from rockets was undertaken first in 1906. A model for military reconnaissance was built in 1912, but by this time photography from airplanes had been shown to be feasible. After the launching of the first Soviet satellite, Sputnik 1, in 1957, the potential of observations from space vehicles became obvious and various applications were developed.

Detection from a satellite

Satellite platforms can carry a variety of sensors. Cameras in space can collect images on photographic film, infrared images, or television-type signals. Radars can be carried aloft for operation at night or through clouds that could otherwise obscure the images. Infrared sensors can be used to detect missile or space warnings. Sensors to detect nuclear explosions can also be used to monitor possible violations of the nuclear test treaty.

To be useful, the sensors must have high resolution. The large distances involved make this difficult. Cameras must have telescopic optics and must be quite large and heavy. As the ability to lift larger weights to orbital altitudes increases, the capabilities of the sensors will improve. Infrared sensors also need heavy equipment to provide high enough utility. Radar sensors are limited not only in resolution (generally much poorer than optical sensors) but by electrical power limitations, since quite powerful radar transmitters are necessary.

Photographic resolution of about one second of arc is achievable today. At 200 miles (320 kilometres) altitude, this would be equivalent to a resolution of ten feet (three metres); that is, an object ten feet in diameter could be clearly distinguished. Vibration and high speed reduce this resolution considerably.

Antisubmarine system. The limited range of both active (echo-ranging) and passive (listening) sonar makes necessary the use of many sensors in submarine detection. To guard a shore, a line of sensors can be set on the ocean floor. In the broad ocean area, however, the sensors on ships and submarines leave vast spaces uncovered. To fill these gaps, sonobuoys, floating buoys with sonar sensors and radio transmitters, are used. The signals from the sonobuoys are received by patrolling aircraft; these then track the submarines.

Naval vessels use helicopters for submarine detection and warning. Each carries a sonar sensor at the end of a cable, lowering it into the water to detect submarines. Such sensors are called dunked sonar sensors.

Future developments. Research and development on air-defense systems have reached a plateau, as the growth of the missile threat has diverted emphasis. An exception is air defense in the sea because the threat of aircraft attack on naval vessels remains high. Air-defense systems for military forces also receive priority, especially air-to-surface missiles. The trend in air-defense systems is to use the newer phased-array radar as budgets permit. Better, more secure identification systems are being introduced. More capable and smaller computers are gradually being substituted.

Based upon research efforts, ballistic missile warning systems are tending to greater use of satellite systems, rather than surface radar. Earlier and more certain warning can be provided by these platforms.

The ability to rendezvous in space has been demonstrated, and experiments are continuing at a measured pace. This portends the possibility of space intercept unless treaties outlaw this mode of warfare before it starts.

Space intercept

Space tracking will become more difficult as more spacecraft are launched and space debris (unused or inoperative objects) accumulates.

Aerial reconnaissance will continue to improve, with the most promising capability being the use of the laser. As boosters get larger, enabling larger payloads to be carried, larger sensors could be carried aloft, thus providing better resolution, eventually competing with that obtainable from airborne platforms.   (Ha.D.)

Military communication

Military communication, or signalling, has long played an important role in warfare. It provides the means for transmitting information from reconnaissance and other units in contact with the enemy and the means for exercising command by transmitting the orders and instructions of commanders to their subordinates. It comprises all means of transmitting messages, orders, and reports, both in the field and at sea and between headquarters and distant installations or ships.

EARLY DEVELOPMENT

Messengers have been employed in war since ancient times and still constitute a valuable means of communication. Alexander, Hannibal, and Caesar each developed an elaborate system of relays by which messages were carried from one messenger post to another by mounted messengers travelling at top speed. They were thus able to maintain contact with their homelands during their far-flung campaigns and to transmit messages with surprising speed. Genghis Khan at the close of the 12th century not only emulated his military predecessors by establishing an extensive system of messenger posts from Europe to his Mongol capital but also utilized homing pigeons as messengers. As he advanced upon his conquests he established pigeon relay posts across Asia and much of eastern Europe. He was thus able to utilize these messengers to transmit instructions to his capital for the governing of his distant dominions. Before the end of the 18th century European armies used the visual telegraph system devised by Claude Chappe, employing semaphore towers or poles with movable arms. The Prussian Army in 1833 assigned such visual telegraph duties to engineer troops.

Genghis Khan's homing pigeons

At the same time that these elementary methods of signal communication were being evolved on land, a comparable development was going on at sea. Early signalling between naval vessels was by prearranged messages transmitted by flags, lights, or the movement of a sail. Codes were developed in the 16th century that were based upon the number and position of signal flags or lights or on the number of cannon shots. In the 17th century, the British admiral Sir William Penn and others developed regular codes for naval communication; and toward the close of the 18th century, Adm. Richard Kempenfelt developed a plan of flag signalling similar to that now in use. Later Sir Home Popham increased the effectiveness of ship-to-ship communication by improved methods of flag signalling.

ADVENT OF ELECTRICAL SIGNALLING

Despite the early pioneering efforts on land and sea the real development of signal communication in war did

Figure 33: International alphabet flags used for signal communications between ships.

not come until after invention of the electric telegraph by Samuel F.B. Morse. In his successful demonstration of electric communication between Washington, D.C., and Baltimore in 1844, he provided a completely new means of rapid signal communication. The development of the Morse Code of dots and dashes used with key and sounder was soon used to augment the various means of visual signalling. Vice-Adm. Philip Colomb's flash signalling, adopted in the British Navy in 1867, was an adaptation of the Morse Code to lights. The first application of the telegraph in time of war was made by the British in the Crimean War in 1854, but its capabilities were not well understood, and it was not widely used. Three years later, in the Indian Mutiny, the newly established telegraph, which was controlled by the British, was a deciding factor.

In the U.S. Civil War (1861–65) wide use was made of the electric telegraph. In addition to its employment in spanning long distances under the civilian-manned military telegraph organization, mobile field service was provided in the Union Army by wagon trains equipped with insulated wire and lightweight poles for the rapid laying of telegraph lines. Immediately before and during the Civil War visual signalling also received added impetus through development of a system, applying the Morse Code of dots and dashes, that spelled out messages by flags by day and lights or torches by night. Another development for light signalling placed a movable shutter, controlled by a key, in front of a strong light. An operator, opening and closing the shutter, could produce short and long flashes to spell out messages in Morse Code.

Simultaneously, the Prussian and French armies also organized mobile telegraph trains. During the short, decisive Prussian campaign against Austria in 1866, field telegraph enabled Count Helmuth von Moltke, the Prussian commander, to exercise command over his distant armies. Soon afterward the British organized their first field telegraph trains in the Royal Engineers.

Another instrument was added to the techniques for visual signalling through the development of the heliograph. It employed two adjustable mirrors so arranged that a beam of light from the sun could be reflected in any direction. The beam was interrupted by a key-operated shutter that permitted the formation of the dots and dashes of the Morse Code. Where climatic conditions were favourable this instrument found much use, notably by the British Army in India and the United States Army in the southwestern United States. Because consistency and regularity of sunshine were important, the heliograph was never widely adopted throughout the armies of continental Europe.

The invention of the telephone in 1876 was not followed immediately by its adoption and adaptation for military use. This was probably due to the fact that the compelling stimulation of war was not present and to the fact that the development of long-distance telephone communication was not achieved for many years. The telephone was used by the U.S. Army in the Spanish-American War, by the British in the South African (Boer) War, and by the Japanese in the Russo-Japanese War. This military use was not extensive, and it made little material contribution

Telegraph in the U.S. Civil War

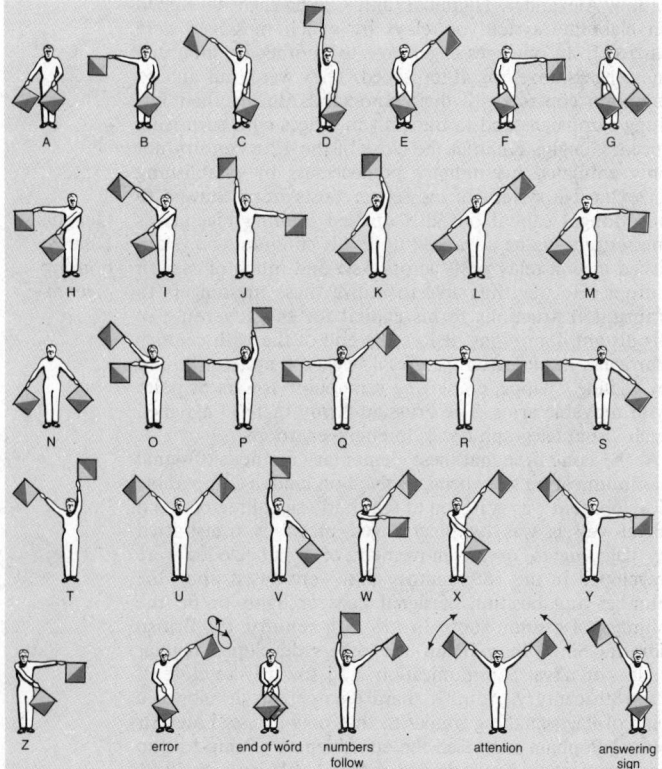

Figure 34: Semaphore flag signals.
The numbers from one to nine are the same as the first nine letters of the alphabet and are sent after the "numbers follow" signal. Zero is the same as the letter J.

to the development of voice telephony. Between the start of the 20th century and the outbreak of World War I, military adaptation of the telephone did take place, but its period of major growth had not yet arrived.

Near the close of the 19th century, a new means of military signal communication made its appearance—the wireless telegraph, or radio. The major powers throughout the world were quick to see the wonderful possibilities of this new agency for military and naval signalling. Its development was rapid and continuous; and, by 1914, it was adopted and in extensive use by all the armies and navies of the world. It soon became apparent that wireless telegraphy was not an unmixed blessing to armies and navies, because it lacked secrecy and messages could be heard by the enemy as well as by friendly forces. This led to the development of extensive and complicated codes and ciphers as necessary adjuncts to military signalling. The struggle between the cryptographer and the crypt-analyst expanded greatly with the adoption of radio and continued to be a major factor affecting its military use.

International numeral pennants

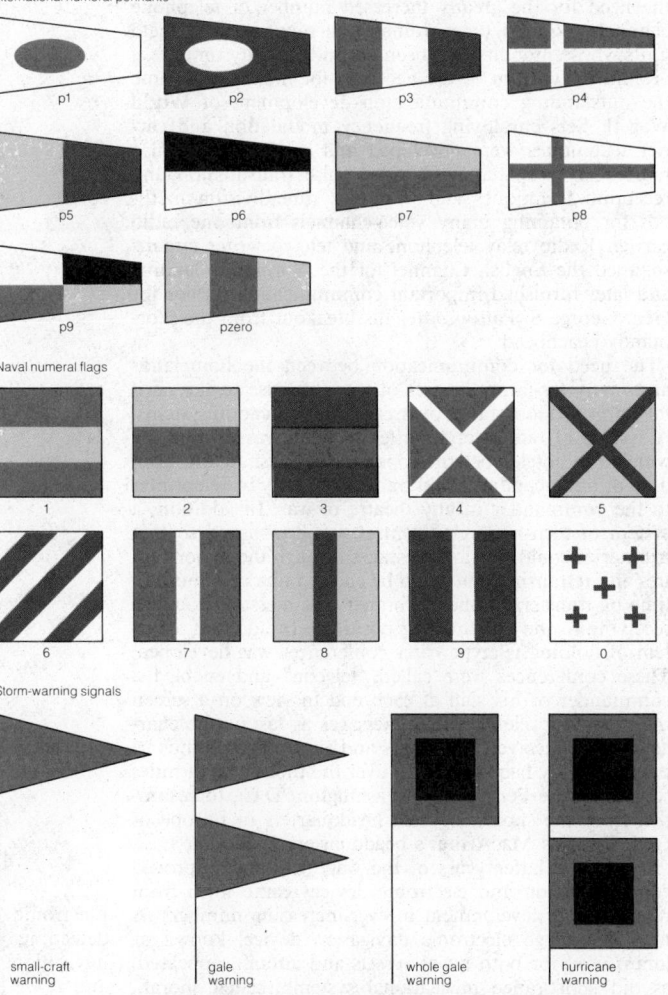

Naval numeral flags

Storm-warning signals

small-craft warning | gale warning | whole gale warning | hurricane warning

Figure 35: (Top) International numeral pennants used for numbers in a call sign. (Centre) Naval numeral flags used for numbers in a flag-hoist message. (Bottom) Storm-warning signals raised by the National Weather Service along the coasts of the United States and Puerto Rico and along the shores of the Great Lakes.

FROM WORLD WAR I TO 1940

The onset of World War I found the opposing armies equipped to a varying degree with modern means of signal communication but with little appreciation of the enormous load that signal systems must carry to maintain control of the huge forces that were set in motion. The organization and efficiency of the armies varied greatly. At one end of the scale was Great Britain, with a small but highly developed signal service; and at the other end stood Russia, with a signal service inferior to that of the

American Union Army at the close of the Civil War. The fact that commanders could not control, coordinate, and direct huge modern armies without efficient signal communication quickly became apparent to both the Allies and the Central Powers. The Germans, despite years of concentration on the Schlieffen Plan, failed to provide adequately for communication between higher headquarters and the rapidly marching armies of the right wing driving through Belgium and northern France. This resulted in a lack of coordination between these armies, which caused a miscarriage of the plan, a forced halt in the German advance, and the subsequent withdrawal north of the Marne. On the Allied side, the debacle of the Russian forces in East Prussia—a crushing defeat at the hands of Gen. Paul von Hindenburg in the Battle of Tannenberg—was largely due to an almost total lack of signal communication.

As the war progressed there was a growing appreciation of the need for improved electrical communications of much greater capacity for the larger units and of the need within regiments for electrical communications, which had heretofore been regarded as unessential and impractical. Field telephones and switchboards were soon developed, and those already in existence were improved. An intricate system of telephone lines involving thousands of miles of wire soon appeared on each side. Pole lines with many crossarms and circuits came into being in the rear of the opposing armies, and buried cables and wires laid in trenches were installed in the elaborate trench systems leading to the forwardmost outposts. The main arteries running from the rear to the forward trenches were crossed by lateral cable routes roughly parallel to the front.

Thus there grew an immense gridwork of deep buried cables, particularly on the German side and in the British sectors of the Allied side with underground junction boxes and test points every few hundred yards. The French used deep buried cable to some extent but generally preferred to string their telephone lines on wooden supports set against the walls of deep open trenches. Thus electrical communication in the form of the telephone and telegraph gradually extended to the smaller units until front-line platoons were frequently kept in touch with their company headquarters through these mediums.

Despite efforts to protect the wire lines, they were frequently cut at critical times as the result of the intense artillery fires. This led all the belligerents to develop and use radio (wireless) as an alternate means of communication. Prewar radio sets were too heavy and bulky to be taken into the trenches, and they also required large and highly visible aerials. Radio engineers of the belligerent nations soon developed smaller and more portable sets powered by storage batteries and using low, inconspicuous aerials. Although radio equipment came to be issued to the headquarters of all units, including battalions, the ease of enemy interception, the requirements for cryptographing or encoding messages, and the inherent unreliability of these early systems caused them to be regarded as strictly auxiliary to the wire system and reserved for emergency use when the wire lines were cut. Visual signalling returned to the battlefield in World War I with the use of electric signal lamps. Pyrotechnics, rockets, Very pistols, and flares had a wide use for transmitting prearranged signals. Messenger service came to be highly developed, and motorcycle, bicycle, and automotive messenger service was employed. Homing pigeons were extensively used as one-way messengers from front to rear and acquitted themselves extremely well. Dogs also were used as messengers and, in the German Army, reached a high degree of efficiency.

A new element in warfare, the airplane, introduced in World War I, immediately posed a problem in communication. During most of the war, communication between ground and air was difficult and elementary. To make his reports the pilot had to land or drop messages, and he received instructions while in the air from strips of white and black cloth called "panels" laid out in an open field according to prearranged designs. Extensive efforts were made to use radiotelegraph and radiotelephone between the airplanes and ground headquarters. The closing stages of the war saw many planes equipped with radio, but the

The telephone in World War I

Radio-equipped aircraft

service was never satisfactory or reliable and had little influence on military operations.

During World War I, wireless telegraph communication was extensively employed by the navies of the world and had a major influence on the character of naval warfare. High-powered shore and ship stations made possible wireless communication over long distances.

One of the war lessons learned in most of the major nations was the compelling need for scientific research and development of equipment and techniques for military purposes. Although the amount of funds devoted to military development during the period from World War I to World War II was relatively small, the modest expenditures served to establish a bond between industry, science, and the armed forces of the major nations.

Of great importance in postwar radio communication was the pioneering by the amateurs and by industry and science in the use of very high frequencies. These developments opened up to the armed services the possibilities of portable short-range equipment for mobile and portable tactical use by armies, navies, and air forces. Military work in these fields was carried out actively in Germany, Great Britain, and the United States. As early as 1938 Germany had completed the design and manufacture of a complete line of portable and mobile radio equipment for its Army and Air Force.

Between World Wars I and II the printing telegraph, commonly known as the teleprinter or teletypewriter machine, came into civilian use and was incorporated in military wire-communication systems, but military networks were not extensive. Before World War II military radioteleprinter circuits were nonexistent.

FM radio

Another major communication advance that had its origin and early growth during the period between World Wars I and II was frequency-modulated (FM) radio. Developed during the late 1920s and early 1930s by Edwin H. Armstrong, an inventor and a major in the United States Army Signal Corps during World War I, this new method of modulation offered heretofore unattainable reduction of the effect of ignition and other noises encountered in vehicular radio applications. It was first adapted for military use by the U.S. Army, which, prior to World War II, had under development tank, vehicular, and man-pack frequency-modulated radio transmitters and receivers.

On the eve of World War II, all nations employed generally similar methods for military signalling. The messenger systems included foot, mounted, motorcycle, automobile, airplane, homing pigeon, and the messenger dog. Visual agencies included flags, lights, panels for signalling airplanes, and pyrotechnics. The electrical agencies embraced wire systems providing telephone and telegraph service, including the printing telegraph. Both radiotelephony and radiotelegraphy were in wide use, but radiotelephony had not as yet proved reliable and satisfactory for tactical military communication. The navies of the world entered World War II with highly developed radio-communication systems, both telegraph and telephone, and with development under way of many electronic navigational aids. Blinker-light signalling was still employed. The use of telephone systems and loud-speaking voice amplifiers on naval vessels had also come into common use. Air forces employed wire and radio communication to link up their bases and landing fields and had developed airborne long-range, medium-range, and short-range radio equipment for air-to-ground and air-to-air communication.

WORLD WAR II AND AFTER

In the communication and electronic field, World War II was in one sense similar to World War I; the most extravagant prewar estimates of military, naval, and air communication requirements soon proved to represent only a fraction of the actual demand. Requirements for all kinds of communication equipment and for improved quality and quantity of communications pyramided beyond the immediate capabilities of industry. Expansion of manufacturing facilities became vital, and the expansion of research and development activities in the communications-electronics field was unprecedented. The early German blitzkrieg, with tank and armoured formations, placed a

new order of importance on reliable radio communication.

The development of the air, infantry, artillery, and armoured team created new requirements for split-second communication by radio between all members. Portable radio sets were provided as far down in the military echelons as the platoon. In every tank there was installed at least one radio and in some command tanks as many as three. In the field of wire communications multiconductor cables were provided; they could be rapidly reeled out and on them as many as four conversations could take place simultaneously through the use of carrier telephony. The Germans were the first to bring forth this type of military long-range cable, and their example was promptly followed by both the British and the U.S. forces. High-powered mobile radio sets became common at division and regimental level. With these sets telegraph communication could be conducted at distances of more than 100 miles (160 kilometres) with vehicles in normal motion on the road. Major telephone switchboards of much greater capacity were needed. These were developed, manufactured, and issued for use at all tactical headquarters to satisfy the need for the greatly increased number of telephone channels required to coordinate the movements of field units whose mobility had been expanded many times.

Mobile communications

Radio relay, born of the necessity for mobility, became the outstanding communication development of World War II. Sets employing frequency modulation and carrier techniques were developed and used, as were also radio relay sets that used radar pulse transmission and reception techniques and multiplex time-division methods for obtaining many voice-channels from one radio carrier. Radio relay telephone and teletypewriter circuits spanned the English Channel for the Normandy landing and later furnished important communication service for Gen. George S. Patton, after his breakout from the Normandy beachhead.

The need for communication between the homelands and many far-flung theatres of war gave rise to the need for improved long-range overseas communication systems. A system of radioteletypewriter relaying was devised, by which a radioteletypewriter operator in Washington, London, or other capitals could transmit directly by teleprinter to the commander in any theatre of war. In addition, a system of torn-tape relay centres was established so that tributaries could forward messages through the major centres and retransmission could be effected in a minimum of time by transferring the perforated tape message from the receiving to the transmitting positions. In addition a system of holding teletypewriter conferences was developed. These conferences were called "telecon" and enabled a commander or his staff at each end to view on a screen the incoming teletypewriter messages as fast as the characters were received. Questions and answers could thus be passed rapidly back and forth over the thousands of miles separating the Pentagon in Washington, D.C., for example, from the supreme Allied headquarters in Europe or Gen. Douglas MacArthur's headquarters in the Far East.

During the latter years of the war, new and improved communication and electronic devices came forth from research and development in ever-increasing numbers. A new long-range electronic navigation device, known as loran, used for both naval vessels and aircraft, appeared, as did short-range navigational systems, called shoran. Combinations of radar and communications for the landing of aircraft in zero visibility were perfected. One such system was the GCA or ground-controlled approach system. Combinations of radio direction-finding, radar, and communications systems were developed and used for ground control of intercept aircraft—the system called GCI (ground-controlled intercept). Radio-controlled guidance of falling bombs was brought forth to enable the operator in the bomber to direct the bomb to the target. Electronic countermeasures made their appearance in the form of jamming transmitters to jam radio-communication channels and radar, navigation, and other radio aids to military operation.

Electronic detection, navigation, and guidance

The military services learned well from their wartime experiences the importance of scientific research and development in all fields, including communications electronics. Advances were made toward increasing the communication capacity of wire and radio relay systems and toward improving electronic aids for navigation. Measures to provide more comprehensive and more reliable communication and electronic equipment continued to be stressed in the armies, navies, and air forces of the major powers.

After mid-century, accordingly, military efforts in all the many facets of signal communication continued to intensify almost as extravagantly as during World War II. Two major additions in the U.S. Army were television and "electronic brain" equipment. The latter, in many forms of digital and analogue computers and of such data-processing devices as punch-card machines, were applied increasingly to personnel record handling and to depot and supply operations interconnected over wide areas by signal-communication networks.

Television systems proved valuable as training aids in military schools, where mass instruction, especially in manual techniques, was needed and where instructors were few. Such systems enabled a single instructor to teach many small classes simultaneously, each grouped before a receiver where they could watch demonstrations closely. Two-way communication systems permitted the instructor to call and question any student in any classroom and, inversely, enabled any student to put questions to the instructor. Portable television equipment in the field proved valuable for sending back to headquarters, by antenna radiation or coaxial cable, a picture of any scene of operations such as a river crossing. Equally valuable was a television camera in the hands of a forward scout or in a reconnaissance aircraft, whether piloted or remotely controlled, to scan enemy territory.

Thus signal communication, combining in itself the powers of photography, television, radar, and other instruments using the electromagnetic radiation spectrum, moved into such new areas of military communications electronics as battle area surveillance and electronic warfare devices to interfere with, or jam, enemy transmitters. In the U.S. Army, battle area surveillance activity radically augmented conventional reconnaissance methods. An electronically controlled target acquisition system, to discover enemy troops or transport on the ground or in the air, was being developed using optical, sonic, photographic, infrared, and radar equipment. The aggregate of information gathered by these devices over a wide enemy front can be electronically assembled and displayed in the headquarters where the combat commander can quickly estimate the situation and make tactical decisions.

Military signal communications in the late 20th century employed a new technology that enabled it to attain very great ranges, coupled with high-quality service. This was communications by satellite relay.   (G.I.Bk./G.R.T.)

BIBLIOGRAPHY. JAC WELLER, *Weapons and Tactics* (1966), is a general history of war technology from the Battle of Hastings to World War II. Two other general works are EDWIN TUNIS, *Weapons: A Pictorial History* (1954); and R.M. OGORKIEWICZ, *Armoured Forces* (1970). For ancient history, see YIGDEL YADIN, *The Art of Warfare in Biblical Lands* (1963); and SIR RALPH PAYNE-GALLWEY, *A Summary of the History, Construction and Effects in Warfare of the Projectile-Throwing Engines of the Ancients* (1907). For detailed information on the Middle Ages, see C.W.C. OMAN, *A History of the Art of War in the Middle Ages* (1898; 2 vol., 1924). GEORGE S. PATTON, JR., *War As I Knew It* (1947), covers World Wars I and II. J.F.C. FULLER, *Decisive Battles of the Western World and Their Influence upon History,* 3 vol. (1954–56), discusses the history of armament to WW II. DWIGHT D. EISENHOWER, *Crusade in Europe* (1948), describes World War II from the allied point of view. See also G.M. BARNES, *Weapons of World War II* (1947). For information on the Korean conflict, see LYNN MONTROSS and NICHOLAS A. CANZONA, *U.S. Marine Operations in Korea, 1950–1953,* 4 vol. (1954–58).

Artillery: H.W.L. HIME, *Origin of Artillery* (1915), a standard historical work; CHARLES OMAN, *History of the Art of War in the Middle Ages* (1924), useful for background information; A. MANUCY, *Artillery Through the Ages* (1949), a comprehensive history of artillery; B.P. HUGHES, *British Smooth-Bore Artillery: The Muzzle Loading Artillery of the 18th and 19th Centuries* (1969), a well-illustrated and comprehensive work. *Brassey's Annual: Defense and the Armed Forces 1970,* ch. 17–19 (1970), provides

an up-to-date description of developments in the sea, land and air equipment (including gunnery) of all major countries; INSTITUTE FOR STRATEGIC STUDIES, *The Military Balance* (annual), contains reliable data concerning the latest guns and gunlike weapons of all major countries. B.B. SCHOFIELD, *The Royal Navy Today* (1960), background information, and "Developments in Maritime Forces," *Brassey's Annual* (1965–70), a yearly annual progress survey; W.T. GUNSTON, "Developments in Aircraft and Missiles," *Brassey's Annual* (1968–70); W.D. O'NEILL III, "Gun Systems? for Air Defense?" *Proc. U.S. Nav. Inst.,* 97:44–55 (1971).

Small arms: An entire literature composed of hundreds of authors and thousands of volumes and articles has grown up in this field since weapons of all types began to be studied exhaustively in the 19th century. The following books are especially recommended: JOHN G.W. DILLIN, *The Kentucky Rifle* (1946); WILLIAM B. EDWARDS, *The Story of Colt's Revolver: The Biography of Col. Samuel Colt* (1953); T.F. FREMANTLE, *The Book of the Rifle* (1901); CLAUD E. FULLER (comp.), *Springfield Muzzle-Loading Shoulder Arms* (1930); IAN GLENDINNING, *British Pistols and Guns, 1640–1840* (1951); ALDEN HATCH, *Remington Arms in American History* (1956); THOMAS J. HAYES, *Elements of Ordnance: A Textbook for Use of Cadets of the United States Military Academy* (1938); G.S. HUTCHISON, *Machine Guns: Their History and Tactical Employment, Being Also a History of the Machine Gun Corps, 1916–1922* (1938); MELVIN M. JOHNSON, JR., and CHARLES T. HAVEN, *Automatic Weapons of the World* (1945); BERKELEY R. LEWIS, *Small Arms and Ammunition in the United States Service* (1956); W. KEITH NEAL, *Spanish Guns and Pistols* (1955); THOMAS B. NELSON, *The World's Submachine Guns (Machine Pistols),* vol. 1 (1963); H. OMMUNDSEN and ERNEST H. ROBINSON, *Rifles and Ammunition and Rifle Shooting* (1915); HAROLD L. PETERSON, *Arms and Armor in Colonial America, 1526–1783* (1956); W.H.B. and JOSEPH E. SMITH, *The Book of Rifles,* 3rd ed. (1963); Great Britain, WAR OFFICE, *Textbook of Small Arms* (1929).

Ammunition: For general information, see C.S. CUMMINGS, *Everyday Ballistics* (1950); and E.D. LOWRY, *Interior Ballistics: How a Gun Converts Chemical Energy into Projectile Motion* (1968). T.J. HAYES, *Elements of Ordnance* (1938), contains professional-level material on small arms, artillery, and weapons.

Rockets and missiles: K. GATLAND, *Missiles and Rockets* (1975); R. PRETTY (ed.), *Jane's Pocket Book of Missiles,* new ed. (1978); and M.J.H. TAYLOR, *Missiles of the World,* 3rd ed. (1980), provide worldwide coverage of rockets and missiles. M.S. KNAACK, *Encyclopedia of U.S. Air Force Aircraft and Missile Systems* (1978–), published by the U.S. Office of Air Force History, is still in progress. W. LEY, *Rockets, Missiles, and Men in Space* (1968); and W. VON BRAUN and F.I. ORDWAY III, *History of Rockets and Space Travel,* 3rd ed. (1975), are standard histories. Also by Von Braun and Ordway is *The Rocket's Red Glare* (1976), a nontechnical, narrative history. D. BAKER, *The Rocket* (1978), is a more technical, topical account. E.C. GODDARD and G.E. PENDRAY (eds.), *The Papers of Robert H. Goddard* (1970), includes his research reports to the Smithsonian Institution. W. DORNBERGER, *V2, der Schussins ins Weltall* (1952; Eng. trans., V-2, 1954); and E. KLEE and O. MERK, *Damals in Peenemünde* (1963; Eng. trans., *The Birth of the Missile,* 1965), tell the story of rocket development at Peenemünde. J.E. BURCHARD, *Rockets, Guns and Targets* (1948), contains accounts of U.S. rocket development during World War II. J.L. CHAPMAN, *Atlas: The Story of a Missile* (1960); J. BAAR and W.E. HOWARD, *Polaris!* (1960); and E.G. SCHWIEBERT, *A History of the U.S. Air Force Ballistic Missiles* (1964), are accounts of postwar ballistic missile developments. M.W. ROSEN, *Viking Rocket Story* (1955), relates the development of this significant postwar sounding rocket. K.W. GATLAND, *Spacecraft and Boosters* (1964), provides details of postwar developments in the United States and Soviet Union; M. STOIKO, *Soviet Rocketry* (1970), chronicles Soviet rocket development. For current technical information, see publications of the American Institute of Aeronautics and Astronautics, New York City.

Nuclear weapons: R.G. HEWLETT and O.E. ANDERSON, *A History of the United States Atomic Energy Commission,* vol. 1, *The New World 1936/1946* (1962); R.G. HEWLETT and F. DUNCAN, *ibid.,* vol. 2, *Atomic Shield 1947/1952* (1969); M.M. GOWING, *Britain and Atomic Energy, 1939–1945,* vol. 1, *An Official History of the U.K. Atomic Energy Project* (1964); D.J.C. IRVING, *The German Atomic Bomb* (1967), a history of the German Atomic Energy Project (1939–46), based on 400 German documents captured by the U.S. Alsos mission; I.N. GOLOVIN, *I.V. Kurchatov: A Socialist-Realist Biography of the Soviet Nuclear Scientist* (1968; orig. pub. in Russian, 1967), a biography of the U.S.S.R. physicist who headed the Soviet Union's fission weapon project.

Fortifications: R.E. and T.N. DUPUY, *The Encyclopedia of*

Military History: From 3500 B.C. to the Present (1970), is the most recent work to provide considerable material on the subject, and is amply indexed. Other works by distinguished historians on fortifications from ancient times to the present include: MONTGOMERY, VISCOUNT OF ALAMEIN, *A History of Warfare* (1968); C.B. FALLS, *The Art of War: From the Age of Napoleon to the Present Day* (1961); LYNN MONTROSS, *War Through the Ages,* 3rd rev. and enl. ed. (1960); THEODORE ROPP, *War in the Modern World* (1959); and J.F.C. FULLER, *A Military History of the Western World,* 3 vol. (1954–56). Less recent but nevertheless commendable works also covering fortifications are: U.S. MILITARY ACADEMY, DEPT. OF MILITARY ART AND ENGINEERING, *Notes on Permanent Land Fortifications* (1944); QUINCY WRIGHT, *A Study of War,* 2 vol. (1942); O.L. SPAULDING, H. NICKERSON, and J.W. WRIGHT, *Warfare: A Study of Military Methods from the Earliest Times* (1925); W.A. MITCHELL, *Outlines of the World's Military History* (1931); B.H. LIDDELL HART, *The Decisive Wars of History* (1929); R.G. ALBION, *Introduction to Military History* (1929); and E.M. LLOYD, *Review of the History of Infantry* (1908). Another work particularly helpful for the period covered is C.B. FALLS, *A Hundred Years of War, 1850–1950* (1962). Greater detail on fortifications in World War II may be found in the official history series, U.S. DEPT OF THE ARMY, OFFICE OF MILITARY HISTORY, *United States Army in World War II* (1947–); *Australia in the War of 1939–1945* (1952–); and most notably in the campaign volumes of J.R.M. BUTLER (ed.), *United Kingdom Military Series* (1952–) in *History of the Second World War* (1949–). For a treatment of Korean fortifications, see R.E. APPLEMAN, *South to the Naktong, North to the Yalu* (1961). Literature on the French Indochina War and the American experience in Vietnam is extensive; but see in particular, B.B. FALL, *Hell in a Very Small Place: The Siege of Dien Bien Phu* (1966).

Body armour: A.M. SNODGRASS, *Arms and Armour of the Greeks* (1967); H.R. ROBINSON, *Oriental Armour* (1967); and C. BLAIR, *European Armour, circa 1066 to circa 1700* (1958), are three completely reliable works basic for the study of this subject. Extensive bibliographies are included in G.C. STONE, *A Glossary of the Construction, Decoration and Use of Arms and Armor in All Countries and in All Times* (1934); SIR GUY LAKING, *A Record of European Armour and Arms Through Seven Centuries,* 5 vol. (1920); and SIR JAMES MANN, *Wallace Collection Catalogue of European Arms and Armour,* part 3 (1944) and vol. 2 (1962). P. COUISSIN, *Les Armes romaines* (1926), although now somewhat dated, has not been replaced as the major study of Roman armour. Other interesting works are B. DEAN, *Helmets and Body Armor in Modern Warfare* (1920), on the modern period up to and including World War I; and W. HOUGH, "Primitive American Armor," *Annual Report of the Board of Regents of the Smithsonian Institution,* part 2, pp. 631–680 (1893–95), the only writer to deal with the armour of the American Indians.

Armoured vehicles: P. CHAMBERLAIN and C. ELLIS, *British and American Tanks of World War II* (1969), an extensive collection of photographs and descriptions of British and U.S. tanks built during WW II; A. DUVIGNAC, *Histoire de l'armée motorisée* (1948), an account of the development of French tanks and other military vehicles from early attempts to 1937–38; J.F.C. FULLER, *Tanks in the Great War, 1914–1918* (1920), a contemporary account of the development and employment of British tanks and tank units during WW I, with some discussion of French and U.S. tanks; O.H. HACKER *et al., Heigls Taschenbuch der Tanks,* 2 vol. (1935), a classic work, although inaccurate on a number of points, containing a fully illustrated catalogue of armoured vehicles of all countries to 1934–35; R.J. ICKS, *Tanks and Armored Vehicles* (1945), an account of developments to 1943–44, similar in principle to Hacker *et al.,* but less extensive. R.M. OGORKIEWICZ, *Design and Development of Fighting Vehicles* (1968), the only book in English treating the more technical aspects of the design and development of armoured vehicles, and *Armoured Forces* (1970), a comprehensive account of the development of armoured forces, their organization, and the different types of vehicles employed to 1956–57, with revisions to 1969; F.M. VON SENGER UND ETTERLIN, *German Tanks of World War II* (Eng. trans. 1969), an extensive collection of illustrations and descriptions of German armoured vehicles, 1926–45, and *Taschenbuch der Panzer* (1969), an illustrated catalogue of armoured vehicles used throughout the world, 1960–70; B.T. WHITE, *British Tanks and Fighting Vehicles 1914–1945* (1970), photographs and descriptions of British armoured vehicles, and *Tanks and Other Armoured Fighting Vehicles 1900–1918* (1970), descriptions of the earliest armoured vehicles.

Naval ships and craft: Useful general works on the strategic and tactical use of modern naval forces include SAMUEL ELIOT MORISON, *History of United States Naval Operations in World War II,* 15 vol. (1947–62); STEPHEN W. ROSKILL, *The War at Sea, 1939–1945,* 3 vol. in 4 (1954–61), which have no peer in covering the strategy, tactics, logistics, and types of naval vessels prior to and during World War II; Roskill's *Strategy of Sea Power* (1962); and the *United States Naval Institute Proceedings* (monthly) and its annual *Naval Review.* These give a useful look at the naval thinking of the World War II period and since. SIR HERBERT W. RICHMOND, *Sea Power in The Modern World* (1934), is valuable background for study of the pre-World War II period. PHILIP COWBURN, *The Warship in History* (1965); RICHARD A. HOUGH, *Fighting Ships* (1969); and DONALD G. MACINTYRE and B.W. BATHE, *Man-of-War* (1969), discuss and illustrate the general evolution of the warship from early to modern times. HANSON W. BALDWIN, *Strategy for Tomorrow* (1970), on the U.S. Navy; and E.M. ELLER, *Soviet Sea Challenge* (1971), cover the development of the two current leading navies and strategy. The origin and growth of the gun-armed warship are traced in DOUGLAS G. BROWNE, *The Floating Bulwark: The Story of the Fighting Ship, 1514–1942* (1963); and FREDERICK L. ROBERTSON, *The Evolution of Naval Armament* (1921), which devotes as much attention to ships as to weapons. MICHAEL A. LEWIS, *The Navy of Britain* (1948), while focussing on the Royal Navy, provides a lucid discussion not only of the development of ships and weapons but also of tactics of war at sea from the Middle Ages to World War II. E.H.H. ARCHIBALD, *The Wooden Fighting Ship in the Royal Navy, A.D. 897–1860* (1970); and HOWARD I. CHAPELLE, *History of the American Sailing Navy: The Ships and Their Development* (1949), concentrate on the age of the wooden sailing warship. WILLIAM HOVGAARD, *Modern History of Warships* (1920); and the SOCIETY OF NAVAL ARCHITECTS AND MARINE ENGINEERS, *Historical Transactions, 1893–1943* (1945), provide concise summaries of developments in ships, armament, and machinery since the introduction of steam propulsion and armour. The multivolume *Dictionary of American Naval Fighting Ships* (1959–), contains not only concise histories of ships, with profuse illustrations, but also numerous appendixes on various types. Evolutionary treatments of major modern warship types include: OSCAR PARKES, *British Battleships* (1950), invaluable also to the study of foreign battleship development; SIR ARTHUR HEZLET, *Aircraft and Sea Power* (1970) and *The Submarine and Sea Power* (1967); and NORMAN POLMAR, *Aircraft Carriers* (1969). Four general descriptive handbooks of the world's warships are *Les Flottes de combat* (Paris, 1908–); *Jane's Fighting Ships* (London, 1898–); *Taschenbuch der Kriegsflotten* (Munich, 1900–); and *Weyer's Warships of the World* (United States, 1968–). These internationally known annuals give general descriptive and illustrative coverage to the navies of this century. More recent volumes also include information on naval aircraft. *Jane's Weapon Systems* (1969–), a new annual, includes descriptions and illustrations of naval guns, missiles, fire control systems, and the like. Eight editions of JAMES C. FAHEY, *The Ships and Aircraft of the U.S. Fleet* (1939–65 and 9th ed. by SAMUEL L. MORISON and JOHN S. ROWE, 1971), contain photographs and much tabulated information on the United States Navy's matériel.

Submarines: W.R. ANDERSON, *Nautilus 90 North* (1959), and J. CALVERT, *Surface at the Pole* (1960), popular accounts of nuclear submarine operations, by the commanding officers of the "Nautilus" and the "Skate"; E. ROSSLER, *U-Boottyp XXI* (1966), a description of one of the most successful submarine designs of World War II (in German); W. FRANK, *The Sea Wolves* (1955), a discussion of the political, material, and operational aspects of German submarines in World War II; M. HASHIMOTO, *Sunk!* (1954), an account of Japanese submarines and their activities during World War II; A.R. HEZLET, *The Submarine and Sea Power* (1967), a comprehensive look at submarines and their influence on warfare by a leading British naval strategist; W.J. HOLMES, *Undersea Victory* (1966), an excellent study of U.S. submarine operations in the Pacific during World War II; *Jane's Fighting Ships* (annual), dimensions and characteristics of most of the world's submarines; W.S. JAMESON, *The Most Formidable Thing* (1965), a British naval officer's analysis of submarine development and operations during World War I; P.K. KEMP, *H.M. Submarines* (1952), an official treatment of British submarine operations; H. LE MASSON, *Du Nautilus (1800) au Redoutable* (1969), the story of submarine development in France, written by a leading warship authority. H.T. LENTON, *German Submarines,* 2 vol. (1965), detailed dimensions and particulars of German U-boats of the World War II era; F.W. LIPSCOMB, *The British Submarine* (1954), British submarine development and operations; S. LAKE, *Submarine* (1938), an interesting autobiography of a pioneer designer providing considerable insight into early approaches to submarine development; R.K. MORRIS, *John P. Holland* (1966), a biography of a pioneer submarine designer, with considerable data on the politics of early submarine development; N. POLMAR, *Atomic Submarines* (1963), a detailed description of nuclear-powered submarine development from the late 1930s to the loss of the submarine "Thresher," and *Death of the Thresher* (1964); D.A. THOMAS,

Submarine Victory (1961), a description of the contribution of British submarines to the Allied triumph in World War II.

Military aircraft: WALTER RALEIGH and H.A. JONES, *The War in the Air,* 7 vol. (1922–37), is the classic history of air fighting in World War I, centred on the British air services. Similar works treating World War II are DENIS RICHARDS and HILARY ST. GEORGE SAUNDERS, *Royal Air Force, 1939–45,* rev. ed., 3 vol. (1974–75); and W.F. CRAVEN and J.L. CATE (eds.), *The Army Air Forces in World War II,* 7 vol. (1948–58, reprinted 1979). A detailed history of the Royal Air Force is recorded by JOHN W.R. TAYLOR and P.J.R. MOYES, *Pictorial History of the R.A.F.,* 3 vol. (1968–70). Books describing and illustrating military aeroplanes from 1909 are JOHN W.R. TAYLOR (ed.), *Combat Aircraft*

of the World (1969), and *Jane's All the World's Aircraft* (annual). Aircraft used by individual services are treated by F. GORDON SWANBOROUGH and PETER M. BOWERS, *United States Military Aircraft Since 1909,* rev. ed. (1971), *United States Navy Aircraft since 1911,* 2nd ed. (1976); M.S. KNAACK, *Encyclopedia of U.S. Air Force Aircraft and Missile Systems* (1978–   ) published by U.S. Office of Air Force History, OWEN THETFORD, *Aircraft of the Royal Air Force Since 1918,* 7th ed. (1979); *British Naval Aircraft Since 1912,* 4th rev. ed. (1978); PETER GRAY and OWEN THETFORD, *German Aircraft of the First World War,* 2nd ed. (1970); RÉNÉ J. FRANCILLON, *Japanese Aircraft of the Pacific War,* new ed. (1979); and BILL SWEETMAN, *The Presidio Concise Guide to Soviet Military Aircraft* (1981).

The Theory and Conduct of War

War in the popular sense is a conflict among political groups involving hostilities of considerable duration and magnitude. In the usage of social science certain qualifications are added. Sociologists usually apply the term to such conflicts only if they are initiated and conducted in accordance with socially recognized forms. They treat war as an institution recognized in custom or in law. Military writers usually confine the term to hostilities in which the contending groups are sufficiently equal in power to render the outcome uncertain for a time. Armed conflicts of powerful states with primitive peoples are usually called pacifications, military expeditions or explorations; with small states, they are called interventions or reprisals; and with internal groups, rebellions or insurrections. Such incidents, if the resistance is sufficiently strong or protracted, may achieve a magnitude which entitles them to the name "war."

The article is divided into the following sections:

THE INSTITUTION OF WAR

Theory of war

In all ages war has been an important topic of analysis. In the latter part of the 20th century, in the aftermath of two world wars and in the shadow of nuclear, biological, and chemical holocaust, more is written on the subject than ever before. Endeavours to understand the nature of war, to formulate some theory of its causes, conduct, and prevention, are of great importance, for theory shapes human expectations and determines human behaviour. The various schools of theorists are generally aware of the profound influence they can exercise upon life, and their writings usually include a strong normative element, for, when widely accepted, their ideas can assume the characteristics of self-fulfilling prophecies.

The analysis of war may be divided into several categories. Philosophical, political, economic, technological, legal, sociological, and psychological approaches are frequently distinguished. These distinctions indicate the varying focusses of interest and the different analytical categories employed by the theoretician, but most of the actual theories are mixed because war is an extremely complex social phenomenon that cannot be explained by any single factor or through any single approach.

EVOLUTION OF THEORIES OF WAR

Reflecting changes in the international system, theories of war have passed through several phases in the course of the past three centuries. After the ending of the wars of religion, about the middle of the 17th century, wars were fought for the interests of individual sovereigns and were limited both in their objectives and in their scope. The art of manoeuvre became decisive, and analysis of war was couched accordingly in terms of strategies. The situation changed fundamentally with the outbreak of the French Revolution, which increased the size of forces from small professional to large conscript armies and broadened the objectives of war to the ideals of the Revolution, ideals that appealed to the masses who were subject to conscription. In the relative order of post-Napoleonic Europe the mainstream of theory returned to the idea of war as a rational, limited instrument of national policy. This approach was best articulated by the Prussian military theorist Carl von Clausewitz in his famous classic *Vom Kriege* (1832–37; *On War*, 1873).

World War I, which was "total" in character because it resulted in the mobilization of entire populations and economies for a prolonged period of time, did not fit into the Clausewitzian pattern of limited conflict, and it led to a renewal of other theories. These no longer regarded war as a rational instrument of state policy. The theorists held that war, in its modern, total form, if still conceived as a national state instrument, should be undertaken only if the most vital interests of the state, touching upon its very survival, are concerned. Otherwise, warfare serves broad ideologies and not the more narrowly defined interests of a sovereign or a nation. Like the religious wars of the 17th century, war becomes part of "grand designs," such as the rising of the proletariat in Communist eschatology or the Nazi doctrine of a master race. Some theoreticians, however, have gone even further, denying war any rational character whatsoever. To them war is a calamity and a social disaster, whether it is afflicted by one nation upon another or conceived of as afflicting humanity as a whole. The idea is not new—in the aftermath of the Napoleonic Wars it was articulated, for example, by Tolstoy in the concluding chapter of *War and Peace*. It has in the second half of the 20th century gained new currency in peace research, a contemporary form of theorizing that combines analysis of the origins of warfare with a strong normative element aiming at its prevention. Peace research concentrates on two areas: the analysis of the international system and the empirical study of the phenomenon of war.

World War II and the subsequent evolution of weapons of mass destruction made the task of understanding the nature of war even more urgent. On the one hand, war has become an intractable social phenomenon, the elimination of which seems to be an essential precondition for the survival of mankind. On the other hand, the use of war as an instrument of policy is calculated in an unprecedented manner by the nuclear superpowers, the United States and the Soviet Union. War also remains a stark but rational instrumentality in certain more limited conflicts, such as those between Israel and the Arab nations and India and Pakistan. Thinking about war is, consequently, becoming increasingly more differentiated because it has to answer questions relating to very different types of conflict.

Clausewitz cogently defines war as a rational instrument of foreign policy: "an act of violence intended to compel our opponent to fulfil our will." Modern definitions of war, such as "armed conflict between political units," generally disregard the narrow, legalistic definitions characteristic of the 19th century, which limited the concept to formally declared war between states. Such a definition includes civil wars but at the same time excludes such phenomena as riots, banditry, or piracy (see below *Law of war*). Finally, war is generally understood to embrace only armed conflicts on a fairly large scale, usually excluding conflicts in which fewer than 50,000 combatants are involved.

Definitions of war

THE INCIDENCE AND SEVERITY OF WAR

Knowledge of primitive, preliterate warfare is limited. The function of warfare in prehistory probably differed somewhat from that among animals: instead of aiming primarily at the preservation of the species and secondarily at the preservation of the individual, primitive warfare seemed to have functioned mainly to preserve the social group by increasing its solidarity. It seems also to have served the purpose of satisfying certain psychic needs of the individual. It was conducted with very primitive weapons, and its conduct was frequently ritualized, which decreased the damage done. Its incidence varied; some tribes clearly were (and are) more peace loving than others.

With the evolution of the literate civilizations came an increase in the incidence and severity of wars. The establishment of the first cities was followed by the establishment of the first professional armies, which gradually increased in size, both absolutely and in relation to the total population. The techniques of war became more sophisticated; and whereas wars became more geographically widespread, they also became more concentrated in time, giving rise to a clear distinction between war and peace. Wars were fought mainly for territory, to secure domination, or to ward it off.

The technological inventions of the 15th and 16th centuries, especially the development of explosives, and, later, improvements in metalworking, greatly improved weapons techniques. The incidence of wars seemed to be cyclical, reaching a peak about every 50 years. Their average duration fluctuated, although in the 20th century it grew to the exceptional average length of four years. Armies steadily increased in size: the mercenary forces of the 16th century seldom surpassed 20,000–30,000; the 17th-century nationalized armies doubled and during the next century trebled in size. Napoleon, who led armies of 200,000 into battle, at one time mobilized about 1,000,000, about 5 percent of the total population of France. In the relatively peaceful remainder of the 19th century, western European armies, which absorbed an average of five per thousand of the population, grew in step with the population. Military expenditures came to average one-third of general state expenditure. It is difficult to determine with any degree of precision an index of the intensity, in terms of loss of life and material damage, of wars; but such losses seem to have reached a peak in relative terms during the religious wars of the 17th century, declined gradually in the subsequent centuries, but climbed to unprecedented heights in the 20th century (see below *Economics of war*).

World expenditures on defense

The upward trend in the human and economic costs of warfare has continued since 1945. In 1980, it was estimated, the world spent $541,000,000,000, or 4.6 percent of its gross national product, on defense, compared to a similar 4.6 percent on education and 3.2 percent on health. In the relatively peaceful year of 1980, defense establishments involved a total approaching 24,700,000 men under arms. A nuclear war would, of course, be of a very much greater magnitude than any previous war. The ground blast of a relatively small one-megaton bomb hitting a city of 1,000,000 would leave almost one-half of the population injured and one-quarter of the accommodations usable. It should be borne in mind, however, that recovery and reconstruction after the two world wars were unexpectedly rapid, and it has been convincingly argued that recovery after a sizable nuclear exchange could also be unexpectedly rapid.

MODERN THEORIES

Contemporary theories of war divide roughly into two major schools. One attributes war to certain innate biological and psychological factors or drives, the other attributes it to certain social relations and institutions. Both schools include optimists and pessimists concerning the preventability of war.

Ethological approaches. Theories centring upon man's innate drives are developed by ethologists (students of animal behaviour, especially as it relates to human behaviour), who draw analogies from animal behaviour, and also by psychologists and psychoanalysts.

Ethologists start with the persuasive argument that study of animal warfare may contribute toward an understanding of war as employed by man. The behaviour of monkeys and apes in captivity and of young children, for example, shows some basic similarities. In both cases it is possible to observe that aggressive behaviour leading to a fight usually arises from several drives: rivalry for possession, the intrusion of a stranger, or frustration of an activity. The major conflict situations leading to aggression among animals, especially those concerning access of males to females and control of a territory for feeding and breeding, are usually associated with patterns of dominance.

Relevance of animal warfare

The analogies of animal to human behaviour drawn by many ethologists, however, are severely questioned by their more restrained colleagues as well as by many social scientists. The term aggression, for example, is imprecisely and inconsistently used, often referring merely to the largely symbolic behaviour of animals involving such signals as grimaces.

Observed animal behaviour can be regarded as a possible important source of inspiration for hypotheses, but these must then be checked through the study of actual human behaviour. As this has not yet been adequately done, the hypotheses advanced have little foundation and are merely interesting ideas to be investigated. Further, human behaviour is not fixed to the extent that animal behaviour is, partly because man evolves different patterns of behaviour in response to environmental factors, such as geography, climate, and contact with other social groups. The variety of these behaviour patterns is such that they can be used on both sides of an argument concerning, for example, whether or not men have an innate tendency to be aggressive.

Two particularly interesting subjects studied by ethologists are the effects of overcrowding on animals and animal behaviour regarding territory. The study of overcrowding is incomplete, and the findings that normal behaviour patterns tend to break down in such conditions and that aggressive behaviour often becomes prominent are subject to the qualification that animal and human reactions to overcrowding may be different. Ethologists have also advanced plausible hypotheses concerning biological means of population control through reduced fertility that occurs when animal populations increase beyond the capacity of their environment. Whether such biological control mechanisms operate in human society, however, is a subject for further investigation.

Findings concerning the "territorial imperative" in animals—that is, the demarcation and defense against intrusion of a fixed area for feeding and breeding—are even more subject to qualification when an analogy is drawn from them to human behaviour. The analogy between an animal territory and a territorial state is obviously extremely tenuous. In nature the territories of members of a species differ in extent but seem to be generally provided with equivalent resources, and use of force in their defense is rarely necessary, as the customary menacing signals generally lead to the withdrawal of potential rivals. This scarcely compares with the sometimes catastrophic defense of the territory of a national state.

Psychological approaches. One school of theorists has postulated that the major causes of war can be explained in terms of man's psychological nature. Such psychological approaches range from very general, often merely intuitive assertions regarding human nature, to complex analyses utilizing the concepts and techniques of modern psychology. The former category includes a wide range of ethical and philosophical teaching and insights, including the works of such figures as St. Augustine and the 17th-century Dutch philosopher Spinoza.

Modern writers utilizing psychological approaches emphasize the significance of psychological maladjustments or complexes and of the false, stereotyped images assertedly held by decision makers of other countries and their leaders. Some psychologists posit an innate aggressiveness in man. Others concentrate upon public opinion and its influence, particularly in times of tension; others stress the importance of decision makers and the need for their careful selection and training. Most believe that an improved social adjustment of individuals would decrease

The role of maladjustments

frustration, insecurity, and fear and would reduce the likelihood of war. All of them believe in the importance of research and education. Still, the limitations of such approaches derive from their very generality. Also, whether the psychological premises are optimistic or pessimistic about the nature of man, one cannot ignore the impact upon human behaviour of social and political institutions that give man the opportunities to exercise his good or evil propensities and to impose restraints upon him.

The state as a cause of war. Whereas psychological explanations of war contain much that seems to be valid, they are insufficient because man behaves differently in different social contexts. Hence many thinkers have sought their explanations in these contexts, focussing either on the internal organization of states or upon the international system within which these operate.

The most voluminous and influential theories attributing war to the nature of the state fall into two broad streams, which can be loosely called liberal and Socialist.

Liberal analyses. The early or classical liberals of the 18th and 19th centuries distinguished three basic elements in their analysis—individuals, society, and the state—and regarded the state as the outcome of the interaction of the former two. They assumed that society is self-regulating and that the socioeconomic system is able to run smoothly with little interference from the government. Economy, decentralization, and freedom from governmental control were the classical liberal's main concerns, as shown particularly clearly in the writings of John Stuart Mill. They accepted the necessity of maintaining defense but postulated the existence of a basic harmony of interests among states, which would minimize the incidence of wars. Economic cooperation based upon an international division of labour and upon free trade would be in the interests of everybody—commerce would be the great panacea, the rational substitute for war.

> The concept of a self-regulating world society

In explanation of wars that did occur, however, liberals emphasized a variety of factors. First, they focussed on autocratic governments, which were presumed to wage war against the wishes of peacefully inclined people. It thus became a major tenet of liberal political philosophy that war could be eliminated by introducing universal suffrage because the people would surely vote out of office any belligerently inclined government. From the early American pamphleteer Thomas Paine onward, a major school of liberals supported republicanism and stressed the peaceful impact of public opinion. Although they could not agree about actual policies, they stressed certain general ideas concerning relations between states, paralleling their laissez-faire ideas of the internal organization of the state with ideas of a minimum amount of international organization, use of force strictly limited to repelling aggression, the importance of public opinion and of democratically elected governments, and rational resolution of conflicts and disputes. Later in the course of the 19th century, however, and especially after World War I, liberals began to accept the conclusion that an unregulated international society did not automatically tend toward peace and advocated international organization as a corrective.

Socialist analyses. Whereas liberals concentrated upon political structures, regarding them as of primary importance in determining the propensity of states to engage in war, Socialists turned to the socioeconomic system of states as the primary factor. Early in the 20th century the two streams did, to some extent, converge, as evidenced by the fact that the English radical liberal John Hobson explained wars in terms later adopted by Lenin.

> Marx's analysis of the causes of war

Karl Marx attributed war not to the behaviour of states but to the class structure of society. To him wars occurred not as an often voluntary instrument of state policy but as the result of a clash of social forces. To Marx the state was merely a political superstructure; the primary, determining factor lies in the capitalist mode of production that leads to the development of two antagonistic classes: the bourgeoisie and the proletariat. The bourgeoisie controls governmental machinery in its own interests. In its international relations, the capitalist state engages in wars because it is driven by the dynamism of its system—the constantly growing need for raw materials, markets, and

supplies of cheap labour. The only way to avoid war is to remove its basic cause, by replacing capitalism with Socialism, thus abolishing both class struggle and states. The Marxist doctrine, however, gave no clear guidance about the interim period before the millennium is reached; and the international solidarity of the proletariat proved a myth when war broke out in 1914, facing the European Social Democratic parties with the problem of adopting an attitude to the outbreak of the war. The Second International of working-class parties had repeatedly passed resolutions urging the working classes to bring pressure upon their respective governments to prevent war, but, once war had broken out, each individual party chose to regard it as defensive for its own state and to participate in the war effort. This was explained by Lenin as being due to a split in the organization of the proletariat that could be overcome only through the activity of a rigidly organized revolutionary vanguard.

Socialists in the West turned increasingly, although in varying degrees, to revisionist interpretations of Marxism and returned to their attempts to revise the socioeconomic structures of their respective states through evolutionary constitutional processes, seeing this as the only possible means of preventing wars. In the Soviet Union the Socialist theory of war changed as the new Communist regime responded to changes in circumstances. Soviet theoreticians have distinguished three major types of war: between capitalist states, between capitalist and Socialist states, and colonial wars of liberation. The internecine wars among capitalist states are supposed to arise from capitalist competition and imperialist rivalries, such as those that led to the two world wars. They are desirable, for they weaken the capitalist camp. A war between capitalist and Socialist states is one that clearly expresses the basic principle of class struggle, and is, therefore, one for which the Socialist states must prepare. Finally, wars of colonial liberation can be expected between subjugated people and their colonial masters.

The weakness of the theory is that the two major expected types of war, the intracapitalist and the capitalist–Socialist, have not materialized as frequently as Soviet theoreticians predicted. Further, the theory failed to analyze adequately the situation in the Soviet Union and in the Socialist camp. For even in Communist countries, nationalism seems to have proved to be more powerful than Socialism—"national liberation" movements have appeared and have had to be forcibly subdued in the Soviet Union, despite its Communist regime. War between Socialist states is not unthinkable, as the doctrine indicates—only the colossal preponderance of Soviet forces prevented a full-scale war in 1956 against Hungary and in 1968 against Czechoslovakia. And the possibility of a war between the Soviet Union and the People's Republic of China is considered seriously in both countries. Finally, the theory does not provide for wars of liberation against Socialist states, such as was conducted in Afghanistan after the Soviet invasion of 1979.

Nationalism as a cause of war. Many theories claim or imply that wars result ultimately from the allegiance of men to nations and from the intimate connection between the nation and a state. This link between the nation and the state is firmly established by the doctrine of national self-determination, which has become in the eyes of many the major basis of the legitimacy of states and the major factor in their establishment and breakup. It was the principle on which the political boundaries of eastern Europe and the Balkans were arranged after World War I and has been the principal slogan of the anticolonial movement of the 20th century, finding expression in Chapter I, article 1, of the Charter of the United Nations in the objective of "self-determination of peoples," as well as in the more specific provisions of Chapters XI and XII. It is this intimate link between nationalism and statehood that renders them both so dangerous. The rulers of a state are ultimately governed in their behaviour by what is loosely summed up as the "national interest," which occasionally clashes directly with the national interests of other states.

> Influence of the idea of national self-determination

The ideal of the nation-state is never fully achieved. In no historical case does one find all members of a particular nation gathered within one state's boundaries. Conversely, many states contain national minorities. This lack of full correlation has frequently given rise to dangerous tensions that can ultimately lead to war. A government inspired by nationalism may conduct a policy aiming at the assimilation of national minorities, as was the general tendency of central and eastern European governments in the interwar period; it may also attempt to re-unite the members of the nation living outside its boundaries, as Adolf Hitler did. National groups that are not in control of a state may feel dissatisfied with its regime and claim self-determination in a separate state, as demonstrated in the attempt to carve Biafra out of Nigeria and the separation of Bangladesh from Pakistan.

There is no rational basis for deciding on the extent to which the self-determination principle should be applied in allowing national minorities to break away. As a rule, the majority group violently opposes the breakaway movement. Violent conflicts can ensue and, through foreign involvement, turn into international wars. No suitable method has been found for divorcing nationalism from the state and for meeting national demands through adequate social and cultural provisions within a larger unit. Such an attempt in the Austro-Hungarian Empire before its dissolution in World War I failed. Whether the U.S.S.R. will be permanently successful in containing its large proportion of national minorities remains to be seen.

Nationalism not only induces wars but, through the intensity of its influence, makes compromise and acceptance of defeat more difficult. It thus tends to prolong the duration and to increase the intensity of wars. Possibly, however, this is the characteristic only of new, immature nationalisms, for nationalism has ceased to be a major cause of conflict and war among the nations of western Europe.

Nationalism is but one form of ideology: in all ages men seem to develop beliefs and try to proselytize others. Even within particular ideological groups schisms result in conflicts as violent as those between totally opposed creeds, and heretics are often regarded as more dangerous and hostile than opponents. As long as individual states can identify themselves with explosive differences in beliefs, the probability of a war between states is increased, and its intensity is likely to be greater.

The role of special-interest groups.   Whereas some theories of war regard the state as an undifferentiated whole and generalize about its behaviour, other theorists are more sociologically oriented and focus on the roles played within the state by various special-interest groups.

A distinction is made by these theorists between the great mass of people and those groupings directly involved with, or that have influence upon, government. The people, about whose attitudes adequate knowledge is lacking, are generally assumed to be taken up with their daily lives and to be in favour of peace. The influential groups, who are directly involved in external affairs and, hence, in wars, are the main subject of analysis. Warlike governments dragging peace-loving people into international conflict is a recurrent theme both of liberal and Socialist analyses of war. Some writers have gone to the length of postulating a continuous conspiracy of the rulers against the ruled that can be traced to prehistoric times, when priests and warriors combined in the first state structures. Most writers, however, narrow the field and seek an answer to the question of why some governments are more prone to engage in war than others; and they generally find the answer in the influence of important interest groups that pursue particular and selfish ends.

The chief and most obvious of such groups is the military. Military prowess was a major qualification for political leadership in primitive societies; the search for military glory as well as for the spoils of victory seems to have been one of the major motivations for war. Once the military function became differentiated and separated from civilian ones a tension between the two became one of the most important issues of politics. The plausible view has generally been held that the military strive for war, in which they attain greater resources and can satisfy their status seeking and sometimes, also, an aspiration for

Role of the military in the decisions to wage war

direct and full political power. In peacetime, the military are obviously less important, are denied resources, and are less likely to influence or attain political power directly. At the same time, a second, although usually subsidiary, consideration of the military as a causal agent in war holds that an officer corps is directly responsible for any fighting and is thus more aware of its potential dangers for its members and for the state as well. Although intent on keeping the state in a high state of preparedness, the military may be more cautious than civilians about engaging in war. On the other hand, it is often held that increased military preparedness may result in increased tensions and thus indirectly lead to the outbreak of war.

Closely allied are theories about groups that profit from wars economically—capitalists and the financiers, especially those involved in industries catering to war. All of these play a central part as the villains of the piece in Socialist and the liberal theories of war, and even those not subscribing to such theories do not deny the importance of military-industrial complexes in countries in which large sectors of the economy specialize in war supplies. But, although industrialists in all of the technologically advanced systems are undoubtedly influential in determining such factors as the level of armaments to be maintained, it is difficult to assume that their influence is or could be decisive when actual questions concerning war or peace are being decided by politicians.

Finally, some scientists and technologists constitute a new, much smaller, but important group with special interests in war. To some extent one can generalize about them, although the group is heterogeneous, embracing as it does nuclear scientists, space researchers, biologists and geneticists, chemists, and engineers. If they are involved in defense work, they all share the interest of the military in securing more resources for their research: without their military applications, for example, neither nuclear nor space research would have gone ahead nearly as fast as it has. War, however, does not enhance the status and standing of scientists; on the contrary, they come under the close control of the military. They also usually have peaceful alternatives to military research, although these may not be very satisfactory or ample. Consequently, although modern war technology depends heavily upon scientists, and although many of them are employed by governments in work directly or indirectly concerned with this technology, scientists as a group are far from being wedded to war. On the contrary, many of them are deeply concerned with the mass destruction made possible by science and participate in international pacifist movements.

The idea of a scientific lobby

THE CONTROL OF WAR

The international environment within which states and the men within them operate is regarded by many theorists as the major factor determining the occurrence and the nature of wars. War remains possible as long as individual states seek to ensure self-preservation and to promote their individual interests and rely on—in the absence of a reliable international agency to control the actions of other states—their own efforts. It is no accident that reforms of the international system figure prominently in many prescriptions for the prevention of war. Whereas the reform of human propensities or of the state is bound to be a long, drawn-out affair, if it is at all possible, relatively straightforward partial reforms of the international system may produce significant restraints upon resorting to war; a thorough reform could make war impossible.

Some theorists, being more optimistic about the nature of states, concentrate upon the removal of the fear and suspicion of other states, which is characteristic of the present as well as of all historical political systems; others, being less optimistic, think mainly in terms of possible controls and restraints upon the behaviour of states. The underlying reasoning of both parties is generally similar. If individual states in competitive situations are governed by a short-term conception of their interests, acute conflicts between them will occur and will show a strong tendency to escalate. Thus, one state erects a tariff barrier to protect its industry against the competition of a trade partner, and the partner retaliates, the retaliatory interaction being repeated until the two countries find themselves in a trade war. Armaments races show a similar tendency to escalate, particularly so in an age of rapid technological change. The economic and the scientific efforts necessary to avoid falling behind rivals in the invention and development of rapidly improving weapons of mass destruction have already reached unprecedented heights.

And yet, neither trade wars nor arms races necessarily end in violent conflict; there seem to be operating some restraining and inhibiting factors that prevent an automatic escalation. Much of the theory of war concerns itself with the identification, improvement, and development of these restraining factors.

Conflict resolution through diplomacy. The outcome of starkly competitive behaviour leading to wars is clearly against the interests of states, and it is rational for them to seek more desirable outcomes. If competitive behaviour is dangerous, theorists seek for alternative methods of cooperative behaviour that would not jeopardize the interests of the state through exposing it to the possibly less cooperative behaviour of others. Some theorists concentrate upon improving the rationality of the decision making of individual states through a better understanding of the international environment; through eliminating misperceptions and irrational fears; through making clear the full possible costs of engaging in war and the full destructiveness of an all-out war, possible in our age.

The relative paucity of wars and their limited nature throughout the century following the Napoleonic Wars (1815–1914) have stirred great theoretical interest in the nature of the balance-of-power system of that period—that is, in the process by which the power of competing groups of states tended toward equilibrium. Contributing to the successful operation of the balance-of-power system of the 19th century were relatively slow technological change, great diversionary opportunities for industrial and colonial expansion, and the ideological and cultural homogeneity of Europe. Pursuit of a balance of power is a way of conducting foreign policy that is perhaps less prone to war than other types of policy because, instead of indiscriminately increasing their power, states increase it only moderately, so as not to provoke others; and instead of joining the strongest, they join the weaker side in order to ensure balance. States in a balance-of-power system must, however, be ready to abide by constraints upon their behaviour in order to ensure stability of the system.

The application to international relations of a branch of mathematics—game theory—that analyzes the strategy of conflict situations has provided a new tool of analysis. In state interaction, as in any game situation, one side's strategy generally depends upon that side's expectations of the other side's strategy. If all sides in a game are to maximize their chances of a satisfactory outcome, it is necessary that some rational rules of behaviour be conceptualized and agreed upon, and this idea of a set of rational rules can be applied to competing states in the international system. Game theorists distinguish antagonistic situations called zero-sum games in which one state's gain can be only at the expense of another state because the "payoff" is fixed. Even then a mutually acceptable distribution of gains can be rationally reached on the basis of the "minimax" principle—the party in a position of advantage satisfies itself with the minimum acceptable gain because it realizes that the other party, in a position of disadvantage, would yield on the basis of its possible minimum loss but would violently oppose a distribution even more to its detriment. In other situations called non-zero-sum games, the payoff is not constant but can be increased by a cooperative approach; the gain of one participant is not at the cost of another. The contestants, however, have to agree about the distribution of the gain, which is the product of their cooperation.

The theory of games is the foundation of theories of bargaining that analyze the behaviour of individual states in interaction. Diplomacy based upon such theories is less likely to lead to war. Policy makers pursuing such strategies will conduct conflicts of the zero-sum type so that war is avoided. More than that, with some skill, such situations can be transformed into the non-zero-sum type

by introducing additional benefits accruing from cooperation in other interactions and also, more generally, by eliminating the likelihood of war and, consequently, by reducing the costs of preparing for one.

Regional organization. Because wars within states have been eliminated through the establishment of suitable political structures, such as central governments that hold a monopoly of coercive power, many theories concentrate upon the establishment of parallel structures within the international context. Regional integration (cooperation in economic, social, and political affairs, as, for example, within the European Economic Community) and the establishment of security communities, such as the North Atlantic Treaty Organization, have made much greater advances than attempts at the reform of the entire, global international system. Because conflicts among neighbours tend to be frequent, regional integration is an important advance toward reducing the incidence of war. Even if it were to become generally successful, however, regional integration would simply shift the problem of war to a different level: there would be fewer possibilities of war because intraregional conflicts would be contained, but interregional conflicts could still give rise to wars of much greater scope and severity. The phenomenon of war must, therefore, be analyzed at the universal level.

International law. Some of the most influential thinking about war and the international system has come from specialists in international law. All of them postulate that there exists an international society of states that accepts the binding force of some norms of international behaviour. These norms are referred to as international law, although they differ fundamentally from municipal law because no sovereign exists who can enforce them. Most international lawyers realistically accept that international law (*q.v.*) is, consequently, among rather than above states. It is, according to legal doctrine, binding on states, but unenforceable.

International law concerns itself largely with two aspects of war: its legality and its regulation. As far as the legality of war is concerned, there has arisen in the 20th century a general consensus among states, expressed in several international treaties, including the Covenant of the League of Nations, the Kellogg–Briand Pact of 1928, and the Charter of the United Nations, that resort to armed force, except in certain circumstances, such as self-defense, is illegal. Such a legalistic approach to the prevention of war, however, remains futile in the absence of a means of enforcement. The enforcement provisions of the Covenant of the League of Nations and those of the United Nations Charter, which entail the application of military and economic sanctions, have never been applied successfully, due to political disagreement among the major powers. This underlines the fact that legal norms, to be effective, must reflect an underlying political reality.

The United Nations. The United Nations is charged with the maintenance of international peace and security. The several approaches to peace outlined in its Charter and developed in its practice are based upon and clearly reflect the cumulative development of the relevant theories of war.

Drawing heavily upon the experience of the League of Nations, the Charter develops three interrelated approaches: first, pacific settlement of disputes, which would leave nations with nothing to fight about; second, collective security, which would confront aggressors with too much to fight against; and third, disarmament, which would deprive them of anything substantial with which to fight.

Peaceful settlement of disputes. Pacific settlement of disputes is based upon the assumption that war is primarily a technique for settling disputes, although it can, of course, also serve other purposes, such as allaying fears and expressing dislike. Further assumptions are that war frequently comes about because of the unawareness of decision makers of the possibility of settling disputes peacefully to the mutual advantage of both sides—an unawareness due to mere ignorance, pride, lack of imagination, or selfish and cynical leadership. It is thus possible that international organizations can contribute to the prevention of wars by devising and institutionalizing alternative, peaceful techniques for the settlement of disputes and by persuading the states to use them. The scope of this approach is limited, for states are notoriously reluctant to abide by impartial findings on matters they regard as being of vital importance. Hence, what the procedures really offer is a means of slowing down the progression of a dispute toward war, giving reason a chance to prevail.

Collective security. Collective security is an approach to peace involving an agreement by which states agree to take collective action against any state defined as an aggressor. Leaving aside the problems of settling disputes or enforcing law or satisfying justice, it concentrates upon forestalling violence by bringing to bear an overwhelmingly superior international force against any aggressor. Although collective security, in somewhat different forms, played a prominent part in the League of Nations Covenant and is embodied in the United Nations Charter, it has completely failed in both cases. Failing an international government capable of ultimately determining the issues, nations have not managed to agree on an unequivocal definition of aggression, have not in practice accepted the principle that aggression must be acted against independently of the identity of the perpetrator, and, therefore, have not established the international collective security force envisaged in the Charter.

Disarmament. Disarmament and limitation of armaments are based upon the theory that states are inclined to strive for predominance in arms over any potential rivals, and that this leads to arms races that tend to end in war. The major besetting sin of this theory is that it often tends to confuse cause with effect. Although arms races develop momentum of their own, they are themselves the result of political tensions leading to war. In short, it is the tensions that cause war, not the arms race. To hold otherwise is to mistake a symptom for a cause. Hence, reducing the levels of armaments does not necessarily reduce these tensions. Furthermore, it is the instability of strategic balances, rather than their level, that leads to war; agreements about disarmament or limitation of armaments may easily disturb the existing precarious balance and, therefore, be actually conducive to war. Although numerous disarmament negotiations have been conducted in the interwar and the postwar periods, they have been spectacularly unsuccessful.

New United Nations approaches to the maintenance of peace

As these major approaches to peace envisaged in its Charter have not proved very fruitful, the United Nations has developed two new procedures aiming at the limitation of wars. First, "preventive diplomacy," largely comprising the diplomatic initiatives of the secretary general and the stationing of peace-keeping forces, has served to contain local conflicts and to prevent escalation, especially the involvement of the superpowers. Second, although the General Assembly's recommendations have no legal binding force, they have become increasingly influential, for by the mid-1970s the assembly was becoming an important agency for what has been called the collective legitimization of state policies. Resort to war becomes most costly when a state is faced with the prospects of a collective condemnation. This new restraint upon war does not, however, act upon conflicts that the assembly may favourably regard as wars of colonial liberation. Nor could the assembly's disapproval be relied upon to deter states from waging war in pursuit of an interest they deemed to be truly vital.

Both the shortcomings and the limited practicability of all the approaches to the elimination of war through the reform of the international system have driven many thinkers to accept the idea that war can only be abolished by a full-scale world government. No midway solution between the relative anarchy of independent, individual states and a world government with the full paraphernalia of legislative powers and of an overwhelming military force would provide a sufficiently stable international framework for the nations to feel that wars would not break out and thus stop them from behaviour that is often conducive to wars. In an age faced with the danger of a war escalating into a general extermination of mankind, the central importance of preserving peace is obvious and is generally accepted. But here the thinkers divide. Some press on from this analysis to the logical conclusion that mankind must, and, therefore, will establish a world gov-

ernment, and they advance ideas how best to proceed in this direction. Others regard the world government as completely utopian, no matter how logical and desirable it may be. Yet, in terms of actual policies, the adherents of the two schools do not necessarily divide. Whether they do or do not believe that world government is attainable, they do agree that the complex phenomenon of war represents a potential calamity of such a magnitude that all theorists must endeavour to understand it and to apply their understanding to the prevention and mitigation of war with all the means at their disposal.   (J.Fr./Ed.)

Law of war

The laws of war are those portions of international law that deal with the inception of war, the conduct of war, and the termination of war. They regulate the relations between states at war and the relations of those states with neutral powers, and they apply whether the war is declared or undeclared. Related to the laws of war are a special category of normative offenses called "war crimes."

Although the international law of war, like international law generally, is concerned primarily with relations between states—in this case their warlike relations—it also prescribes rights and duties for individuals involved in war.

Since World War II, it has become increasingly necessary to regulate internal war because of the effects such war may have on international relations. Major powers often involve themselves in the civil wars of smaller countries but mask their participation in order to avoid direct confrontation with other major powers.

In the past, the regulation of internal war has been left almost entirely to the individual state concerned, except when rebel forces were recognized as belligerents, in which case the international laws of war became operative. By the mid-20th century, however, the concern of nations regarding internal war had been embodied in Article 3 of each of the Geneva Conventions (1949), which prescribes regulations for war inside nations.

DEVELOPMENT OF LAWS OF WAR

History. In early history, war appears to have been a matter of almost unrelieved barbarity. Practically no restraints were observed in methods of war; there was little discrimination between combatant and noncombatant; and torture, slavery, death, and confiscation of property awaited the conquered forces and population.

Yet, identifiable features of the present law can be traced back to ancient times in diverse parts of the world. As a rule, however, the mitigating features of law represented only an ideal, and so the law was actually applied only during wars between kindred peoples or like civilizations.

Such were the conditions that persisted through ancient times into the Middle Ages, until, prompted by religion and ideas of chivalry on one hand and by the increase of rationalist and humanist sentiment on the other, a substantial body of law had come into being by the late Middle Ages. Such laws governed certain aspects of war, at least among fellow religionists. Most noteworthy of these early laws, perhaps, was the insistence that prisoners, if they were Christians captured by Christians, could no longer be enslaved.

Nevertheless, neither the law of war of the ancients, nor the law of war of medieval times in Europe can be described as genuinely international law. The ancients merely applied their own law to limited aspects of warfare, and the medieval law of war was really only a professional code for soldiers. It applied mainly to relations between gentlemen-soldiers with relatively little regard for either the humble soldier or for civilians, who suffered grievously in war.

The first law of really international character came into existence only with the emergence of a community of fully independent states, which did not occur until the beginning of the modern era in western Europe. The existence of such an international community set the stage for what is, perhaps, the best known exposition of that law in the epochal work of Hugo Grotius, *On the Law of War and Peace* (*De Jure Belli ac Pacis*), published in 1625.

Grotius: the first international formulations

Grotius' book, as its title proclaims, was in the main devoted to the law of war, and, indeed, war was the chief preoccupation of the writers in international law who preceded and succeeded him, until the present century.

Along with the growth of the destructive power of weapons, the middle of the 19th century saw great strides in the mitigation of warfare. In 1856, the Declaration of Paris on maritime law abolished privateering. In 1863, during the American Civil War, President Lincoln issued his General Orders, No. 100 (*Instructions for the Government of Armies in the Field*), prepared by Francis Lieber, which greatly influenced subsequent developments in the law of war. At much the same time, on the initiative of Henri Dunant, of Geneva, Switzerland, the first of the great Geneva Conventions was concluded in 1864, to protect the wounded in war. Then, following an abortive international conference on the law of war at Brussels in 1874, two great conferences were held at The Hague in 1899 and 1907, which codified in various conventions much of the existing law of war and neutrality, and added new material, besides. These Hague Conventions, together with the Geneva Conventions, provide most of the definitive law of war as it exists today.

The 1907 conference was followed by a London conference, resulting in the treaty known as the Declaration of London of 1909, which codified aspects of naval warfare. This treaty was never ratified, however, and has therefore never come into formal legal effect.

The Geneva Convention, which was adapted to maritime warfare at the Hague Conference of 1899 and again at the conference of 1907, was revised in its general part in 1906, and again in 1929, when a Geneva Convention on prisoners of war was added. The convention was revised still again in 1949, when the four existing Geneva Conventions came into being. These relate respectively to the wounded and sick of armed forces in the field, to the wounded, sick, and shipwrecked of armed forces at sea, to prisoners of war, and to civilians in war.

From 1868 on, a series of treaties banned the use of particular weapons in war. The Geneva Protocol on Gas Warfare of 1925 prohibited the use of asphyxiating, poisonous, or other gases and of bacteriological methods of warfare. Currently, efforts are being made to strengthen the prohibitions against biological and gas warfare.

Closely related to the law of war, a Convention on Genocide was adopted in 1948 by the United Nations General Assembly, and in 1954, a special convention was signed at The Hague for the protection of cultural property in war.

With man's penetration into space an accomplished fact, the 1960s saw the beginning of international efforts to prevent space from becoming an area for warfare. In 1967, a treaty was concluded to prohibit the stationing of nuclear weapons in outer space and to bar the use of the moon and other celestial bodies for other than peaceful purposes. Attempts to control nuclear weapons also resulted in the 1963 treaty to prohibit their testing in the atmosphere, outer space, or underwater, and in the 1968 treaty to prevent spread of nuclear weapons among states. In addition, a treaty concluded in 1971 prohibits stationing of nuclear weapons on ocean floors.

Sources of the laws of war. The customs of war developed out of mutual forebearance in regard to practices of war. Gradually, they gained legal effect, the breach of which was punishable. Such customs are one important source of the laws of war.

Another source consists of treaties, especially those that have been acceded to by many parties, thus indicating general acceptance. Much pre-existing customary law has been incorporated in such treaties.

Other sources are the same as those for international law in general, which include "the testimony of those who are skilled in [the law of nations]," as Grotius stated it in *On the Law of War and Peace;* the decisions of the world's great courts, international and national, which exercise a persuasive influence, but have no binding effect as such; and the general principles common to the legal systems of the world.

The exercise of all force by one state against another is legally governed today by the United Nations Charter, whose principles have been accepted by practically all of the states in the world. Basically, the use of force is limited by the charter to self-defense as set out in Article 51, which provides that a state has ". . . the inherent right of individual or collective self-defense if an armed attack occurs against [it]," a right that continues until the United Nations Security Council takes the necessary action to secure peace.

But the words of the article have been the subject of much controversy among international lawyers. Some maintain that self-defense is limited to the case of actual armed attack; others hold that, in addition, states also retain the broader right of self-defense that international law gave them before the Charter came into effect, including preventive action against an imminent attack.

To a degree, the problem hinges on the elucidation of what constitutes "armed attack," which all agree does give the right of self-defense. A simplistic interpretation of armed attack would assert that such occurs only with the firing of the first shot and that until then the defender is barred from responding. Such an interpretation appears to ignore or misunderstand the very nature of armed attack, in which shooting may be only the last stage in an entire process. In fact, an attacker with sufficient strength may accomplish his objective without really firing his weapons, as happened in the Nazi German invasions of Austria (1938) and Czechoslovakia (1939) and in the Soviet Russian invasions of Hungary (1956) and Czechoslovakia (1968). It would seem to be more reasonable, therefore, to define armed attack as one in which the attackers carry arms, even though they do not fire them. *(Defining an armed attack)*

As for the moment when armed attack may be considered to have begun, such can only be a matter for factual assessment. Logic would place it at the point at which a military process or manoeuvre undertaken by the attackers must inevitably result in engagement. If the intended victim has to wait until the enemy's war machine has attained full momentum before responding with force, his right of self-defense is gravely diminished. This is peculiarly relevant in regard to defense against nuclear missile attack, when so little time is available.

Although the United Nations Charter appears to limit the right of a state to use force for self-defense only, the question must still be raised whether a state may exercise the other traditional forms of self-help, involving a use of force short of war against other states, for the redress of injury. Such traditional measures include reprisals and intervention.

Intervention in this context means forcible interference by one state in the affairs of another. Current legal opinion tends to be doubtful about any purported right of intervention, in face of the United Nations Charter, but the question is much debated and is the subject of conflicting views. Most opinion agrees that no state may forcibly intervene in the affairs of another state so as to deny the other state its right to determine freely its own form of national existence.

Reprisals in peacetime are actions, often forcible, that are illegal under international law, but to which a state has recourse as a means of obtaining justice from a state that has wronged it. Most interpretations of the United Nations Charter would exclude any right to resort to forcible reprisals, but any such prohibition has to be based on the assumption that the United Nations will ensure justice to the injured state, without any need of self-help. In practice, it has been found that the United Nations, in particular the Security Council, has not always been able to act effectively in securing justice. As a result, states, great and small, have continued to resort to forcible reprisals, thus giving such actions a certain degree of recognition, in spite of the terms of the Charter. *(Illegality of reprisals in peacetime)*

JUSTICE AND LEGALITY IN THE INITIATION OF WAR

At the outbreak of World War I in 1914, under international law each sovereign state was the sole judge of its motives or justification for engaging in war. Since that time, however, developments in the law have served to make legal justification obligatory. The notion that wars may be just or unjust goes back to ancient times, when *(Just and unjust wars)* the question was essentially a theological matter. In ancient Greece and Rome, for example, a just war (*bellum justum*) meant not one that was just in nature, but one that complied with the formalities demanded by law and religion for engaging in war. The modern concept, in contrast, is legal and secular.

In the later Roman Empire, the idea of the just war was reinterpreted in a Christian context. The early Christian Church had been firmly opposed to war and participation in war, but when Christianity became dominant in the Roman Empire, writers such as St. Augustine (354–430) introduced the doctrine of the just war to defend the continued use of war on the part of the Empire. Both the early doctrine and the modern doctrine of the just war developed, at least in the ideal sense, as a means of strengthening international morality and in the context of a search for universal peace. The doctrine of a just war persisted in the Christian world for many centuries, most notably in the writings of St. Thomas Aquinas, and still has a certain influence.

Nevertheless, in medieval times, the term "just war" applied to the authority for levying the war, rather than to the substance of the cause or complaint. If levied on the authority of an independent prince, the war was considered just, since there was no higher authority to judge the cause, and battle settled the issue.

Although writers into the modern era continued to discuss just and unjust war, from the 18th century to World War I the view prevailed that each nation was the judge of its own cause in war.

Following the war of 1914–18, the Covenant of the League of Nations advanced the viewpoint that a war of aggression was a matter of grave international delinquency. Then, in 1928, the Treaty for the Renunciation of War, also known as the Pact of Paris and the Kellogg–Briand Pact, solemnly condemned recourse to war and 63 states renounced war as an instrument of national policy, although the terms of the pact did allow for self-defense and collective action under the League Covenant. This treaty later greatly influenced the judgment on crimes against peace of the International Military Tribunal that tried the major German war criminals at Nürnberg (Nuremberg) after World War II.

Role of the Nürnberg Tribunal

That tribunal's judgment in 1946 synthesized several diffuse elements of the law on illegal war that the preceding three decades had produced, including treaties, state customs, and practices, in a comprehensive statement of responsibility that could be applied judicially against individual offenders. The court thus provided a cutting edge for what hitherto had been largely legal abstractions that were difficult to apply.

Time has confirmed the validity of the judgment, which is now deeply rooted in international law. It has been followed in enactments and courts throughout the world, in peace treaties, in the United Nations, and in the International Law Commission's draft code of offenses against the peace and security of mankind, which was prepared in 1954.

The Charter of the United Nations, 1945, has further strengthened the condemnation of aggression and, like the League of Nations Covenant before it, has in effect limited any resort to war to justifiable self-defense—which will be discussed later—or to United Nations action to enforce international security.

Although the terms just war and legal war have often been used interchangeably, the Communist doctrine of the just war appears to maintain that even illegal wars may be justified, provided their ends are regarded as commendable. Some wars that advanced the cause of Communism have thus been labelled as just, even though waged in alleged violation of international law and the United Nations Charter. The Communist invasions of Hungary in 1956 and of Czechoslovakia in 1968 provide examples. Some "wars of national liberation," including those waged by non-Communists, have been thus justified. If these views are considered in a legal and historical context, the Communist doctrine of the just war bears a strong resemblance to the holy wars, the crusades and jihad, of past centuries.

STANDARDS IN THE CONDUCT OF WAR

The idea that law can regulate war is sometimes alleged to involve a contradiction, since war itself is a resort to force for the settlement of disputes and appears to exclude the application of law. Basically, such an argument implies that in war all civilized considerations are abandoned. In fact, war is a political act, usually undertaken only when it appears that all other alternatives have failed.

Certainly war offers obvious opportunities for the basest behaviour, but essentially it is a regulated exercise of violence for particular political ends; since it is a political act, it cannot be allowed to injure irretrievably the functioning of human society and must provide for subsequent reconciliation between the warring parties. Law in war balances the advantages of maintaining a rational humanity against military necessities. It therefore allows for the application of all necessary force to compel the enemy to submit but attempts to restrain excesses in the use of force. The application of law is, in this sense, entirely compatible with the nature of war.

Neither is the relationship between the belligerents exclusively one of violent confrontation. Even during war there is a need for many nonhostile contacts between enemies. Flags of truce, armistices, safe-conducts, and other such contacts are possible only on the basis of legal regulation and scrupulous good faith by both sides.

The universal character of the laws of war is such that even if one side or the other regards itself as the victim of aggression, both it and its opponent are still bound to conduct their hostilities in accordance with recognized conventions and laws of war.

Enforcing the law

The means for the enforcement of the laws of war include reprisals, the judicial punishment of war crimes, and the pressure of world opinion. The right to compensation for breaches of the law of war, to be discussed later, may also be considered a sanction. The taking of hostages to ensure enforcement, or for any other purpose, is now regarded as obsolete. Reprisals, themselves, are actually illegal acts of war in response to illegal actions on the other side, but their purpose is to warn the enemy to conform to the law. Ultimately, the primary responsibility for trying and punishing war criminals, whether soldiers or civilians, devolves on their own state. Otherwise, since there is no world government, each sovereign state, belligerent or neutral, has the right and duty to enforce the laws of war.

The area of combat. The arena in which war may be conducted comprises in general the territories and territorial waters of the belligerent states, the high seas, and the air space above these areas. It may, however, extend to neutral territory if the neutral power fails to prevent enemy troops from operating there. The exclusion of outer space has been discussed.

Military objectives belonging to the enemy may be attacked wherever they are located. These include fortifications, military encampments, depots of war material, warships, war planes, and war factories.

Some places and objects may not be attacked, unless they are used for hostile military purposes. These include hospitals, hospital ships, medical aircraft and various kinds of educational, cultural, and religious property. Their protection from attack is usually indicated by various signs, including the Red Cross.

In general, the destruction or seizure of any property in war can be justified only by military necessity. Pillage is always strictly forbidden.

Neutral states. A neutral state is one that does not participate in a war between other states. It is required to maintain strict impartiality toward both sides in the war. It has been questioned, however, whether a member of the United Nations can maintain neutrality in instances in which that organization takes enforcement action against a delinquent state, since the Charter requires members to support such action (Articles 2 [5] and 25).

Nevertheless, the practice of member states in regard to such actions has shown that it is possible for them to adopt a stance of virtual neutrality. It may also be noted that the effective operation of the Geneva Conventions of 1949 is at least partly predicated on the existence of neutral powers.

Neutral
persons'
rights
in war

The term nonbelligerent indicates a qualified or limited neutrality, which international law does not recognize except, perhaps, in relation to a United Nations enforcement action.

It is clear that the most vital right of a neutral is that his territory not be violated by the belligerents. Correspondingly, his duty is to do what he can to ensure against such violation.

In contrast to neutral states, neutral persons may furnish belligerents money and war material, but not warships or operational military aircraft. Neutral states and neutral individuals alike are entitled to express their opinions regarding the hostilities, and, in fact, such expression has often proved valuable in restraining breaches of the laws of war by belligerents.

The methods of destruction. International law limits the methods and weapons that belligerents may use against an enemy. With respect to methods, the law particularly forbids the use of treachery, for instance, using the (white) flag of truce or Red Cross as a cover for hostilities. Also forbidden is a declaration that no quarter (mercy) will be given to enemy troops who are captured or surrender. Torture is also prohibited. Espionage is permissible, but spies may be punished as a means of discouraging such activity.

As for weapons, all arms, projectiles, or material calculated to cause unnecessary suffering and unnecessary death are forbidden. Poison and poisoned weapons are prohibited. Most opinion also agrees on forbidding dumdum bullets (designed to expand or flatten easily in the human body), suffocating and poisonous gases, bacteriological warfare, and radiological weapons.

The
legality of
nuclear
weapons

Regarding nuclear weapons, the preponderance of legal opinion has condemned the effects of nuclear radiation from these weapons as being "akin to those inflicted by the use of poison or poisoned weapons. . . . Thus, in principle, the use of such weapons is illegal" (International Law Association, *Report of the Fiftieth Conference held at Brussels* 1962, pp. 219, 222).

Most legal opinion does not regard the use of fire weapons such as flamethrowers and napalm and incendiary bombs as illegal.

Distinguishing between combatants and noncombatants. One of the most essential principles of civilized warfare involves the distinction between the peaceful civilian and the military and the prohibition of deliberate attack on the former. If this distinction is obliterated, warfare must inevitably degenerate into barbarity. Yet, the practice of air bombardment in World War II eroded this principle. At least some of the responsibility must be laid on the influential writings of an Italian general, Giulio Douhet, who, between the two world wars, advocated air bombardment of civilian centres as a means of breaking the enemy's will to resist and, therefore, as a key to victory.

Following World War II, some leading international legal opinion attempted to convert this practice into legal principle, by denying the distinction between combatants and noncombatants as a recognized principle of war. Those who hold this opinion have accordingly refused to condemn the indiscriminate effects of nuclear weapons. The advocates of such a position would limit the law of war to a simple humanitarian code. Others have argued to the contrary that if civilians were to be considered fair targets, it is difficult to see how such immunities as those granted to prisoners of war and the wounded could last.

In fact, the principle of the distinction between combatant and noncombatant is fundamental to the operation of the whole law of war and, since World War II, has been embodied in the Geneva Conventions of 1949.

Distinguishing between military and civilian. The military are, in law, distinguished from civilians by four obligatory characteristics. They are under the control of a commander; their clothing shows that they are of the military; they carry their arms openly; and they obey the laws and customs of war. Only the military may engage in combat, though civilians may defend themselves from unlawful attack. While peaceful civilians may not be deliberately attacked, they are, of course, subject to the incidental risks of war.

The role of the guerrilla often blurs the distinction between the military and civilians. Yet, for the protection of both the soldier and the innocent civilian it is essential to maintain the dividing line between the two. The Geneva Conventions of 1949, therefore, ruled that resistance fighters must comply with the four conditions stated above if they wish to be recognized as combatants. Otherwise, they are liable to trial and punishment as illegal combatants. The inhabitants of an invaded territory who rise up spontaneously to protect it are, however, lawful combatants provided only that they carry their arms openly and obey the laws and customs of war.

Problems
posed by
guerrilla
war

United Nations forces engaged in an enforcement action must observe the customary rules of war and, in spite of controversy, there appears to be no valid legal reason why they should not also be bound by the Geneva Conventions of 1949 and other treaties regulating the conduct of war.

Prisoners of war. The treatment of wounded and sick of the enemy's armed forces and of prisoners of war is governed by the principle that those who have lost the capacity to wage war and have ceased to be combatants must be protected from further attack. The wounded, sick, and shipwrecked must, according to law, be respected, protected, and given humane treatment and care. Protection is also extended to those whose duty it is to care for them, as well as to chaplains. The dead are also to be respected and honorably interred.

Prisoners of war must be humanely treated and protected, particularly from violence, intimidation, insults, and public curiosity. They are not to be detained for purposes of punishment but merely to be prevented from taking any further part in the war. If they offer violence, or attempt to escape, they may in the last resort be fired on. Most of their rights and duties are contained in the third Geneva Convention of 1949, which must be made available in their own language for the information of prisoners in every prisoner-of-war camp.

When active hostilities in the war cease, prisoners of war must be released and repatriated without delay. It would appear, however, that they may refuse repatriation on political or ideological grounds.

War at sea. The most definitive rules of warfare are those relating to war on land, largely because an authoritative code on land warfare was adopted in the fourth Hague Convention of 1907. No comparable codes exist in regard to sea and air warfare.

The Declaration of London, 1909, which attempted to codify aspects of the law of naval warfare, particularly in regard to blockade, contraband and prize, was, as has been noted, never brought into legal effect, and whatever persuasive influence it may have had was dissipated in World Wars I and II. The rules applicable to naval warfare are, therefore, derived from customary rules, the principles of land warfare, the Geneva Conventions, various Hague Conventions of 1907 that regulate particular aspects of naval war, and the London Protocol on submarine warfare of 1936, relating to the use of submarines against merchant vessels.

Sources of
the rules of
naval
warfare

In practice, the belligerents waged near total war at sea in both world wars, even going so far as to sink without warning neutral shipping in various so-called operational zones. Since the belligerents justified such practices as reprisals, however, they appear to have implicitly recognized the continuing validity of the pre-existing laws of sea warfare. These laws forbid firing on unresisting enemy merchant ships (and obviously on neutral shipping), prohibit attack without warning on enemy merchant ships, or sinking them unless some assurance can be given for the safety of the passengers and crew. They also protect neutral commerce with the enemy in nonmilitary goods.

The rather chaotic state of much of the law of sea warfare was recognized by the Nürnberg Tribunal, when it abstained from punishing the German Admirals Karl Dönitz and Erich Raeder for violations in conducting submarine warfare against merchant shipping. On the other hand, the war crimes courts did punish such inhumane actions as firing on the survivors of sunken vessels.

War by aircraft. The regulation of air warfare is in an even less satisfactory state than that of naval war. An attempt was made to set up an authoritative code for this type of war after World War I when an international commission of jurists drafted the Hague Rules of Aerial Warfare (1923). Although never adopted as a legal instrument, they constitute the chief guide to the legal conduct of air warfare and, as such, exercise a strong persuasive influence.

Otherwise, the conduct of air warfare is governed by applicable rules of land and sea warfare, by the Geneva Conventions, and by those customary rules that have developed in regard to this particular sphere of war, such as the prohibition against attacks on enemy airmen bailing out from disabled planes.

The illegality of indiscriminate and terroristic air attack on civilian centres was discussed earlier. Yet, in view of the practices of both sides during the war and the uncertainty concerning the law of air warfare, no charges concerning this or any other illegality in air war were brought in the war crimes trials after World War II and no rulings on air warfare were made by those courts.

CONVENTIONS ON THE TERMINATION OF WAR

A peace treaty is the most desirable way to end a war, because it provides the opportunity to settle all differences outstanding between the parties. War may, however, be terminated without formal agreement merely by both sides ceasing hostilities and tacitly ending the war. In effect, the parties agree to let the situation as it exists at the close of hostilities govern their future relationship, even though to do so may leave many issues in doubt.

Claims for compensation are usually dealt with in the peace treaty. The same document also often provides for the payment of indemnities or reparations. While such payments may compensate a state for its losses in the war, they are sometimes levied as spoils of victory or as a means of punishment.

War may also be ended by the subjugation of one side, the annexation of its territory, and its extinction as an independent state. Unlike annexation, mere occupation of territory during war does not cause the legal title to pass to the occupying power. The occupant exercises only temporary rulership, subject to numerous safeguards laid down by the law of war for the protection of the inhabitants.

The actual hostilities in war are often brought to an end by means of a general armistice, which suspends the fighting until peace is achieved.

Legal status of territory acquired through conquest The question arises whether any of the three methods of ending war can legalize the acquisition of territory by a victorious power. Certainly in regard to aggressive war it is clear that the aggressor cannot be allowed to obtain legal title to the fruits of his aggression, even if he succeeds in imposing a peace treaty on his victim. In 1932, the United States set forth this principle in what has become known as the Stimson Doctrine. At that time, U.S. Secretary of State Henry Stimson warned China and Japan that his government "does not intend to recognize any situation, treaty or agreement" brought about by means of aggression. Since then, this viewpoint has been generally accepted by the community of nations.

On the other hand, to hold that an aggressor state must be entitled to recover territory lost in a war of aggression, is to safeguard the aggressor against risk. Neither the terms of the United Nations Charter nor general international law lend themselves to such a proposition.   (M.Gre.)

THE DEFINITION AND PUNISHMENT OF WAR CRIMES

The term war crimes has never been successfully defined, but after World War II three categories of offenses against the law of nations came to be recognized as such: (1) crimes against peace, which involve planning, preparing for, initiating, or waging a war of aggression or a war in violation of international treaties, agreements, or assurances or participating in a common plan or conspiracy for the accomplishment of any of the foregoing; (2) war crimes (also called conventional war crimes), which involve violations of the laws or customs of war, such as murder, ill treatment, or deportation of the civilian population of occupied territory, murder or ill treatment of prisoners of war or persons on the seas, killing of hostages, plunder of public or private property, wanton destruction of cities, towns, or villages, or devastation not justified by military necessity; (3) crimes against humanity, which include murder, extermination, enslavement, deportation, and other inhumane acts committed against any civilian population, either before or during a war, or persecutions on political, racial, or religious grounds in execution of or in connection with any other war crime.

Early instances of war crimes Trials of individuals for specific violations of the laws or customs of war (the so-called conventional war crimes) have a long history. Thus, the Scottish national hero Sir William Wallace is reported to have been tried in England in 1305 for the wartime murder of civilians; he allegedly spared "neither age nor sex, monk nor nun." The *Instructions for the Government of Armies in the Field,* issued in 1863, specified that prisoners of war remained answerable for offenses committed prior to capture against the captor's army or its people. When the American Civil War ended, in 1865, Henry Wirz, a former Confederate officer, was tried and convicted by a federal military tribunal and was executed for murdering and conspiring to ill treat federal prisoners of war confined at the Andersonville (Georgia) prisoner-of-war camp, which Wirz had commanded; and several other persons (including at least one civilian) were also tried for offenses of the same general nature. The treaty of peace that ended the South African War in 1902 specifically provided that certain acts contrary to the usages of war that had been committed by Boers would be tried by British courts-martial.

World War I. Early in 1919 a Commission on the Responsibility of the Authors of the War and on Enforcement of Penalties was created by the preliminary peace conference to inquire into "the responsibilities relating to the war." In its report, the commission recommended war-crimes trials before national courts (of the victors) and, when appropriate, before a high tribunal that would be inter-Allied in composition. The report contemplated trials for violations of the laws or customs of war (of which it listed 32 categories) and for crimes against humanity. Failure to take the necessary action to prevent or end violations of the laws or customs of war would itself constitute a war crime. The commission recommended that "special measures" be taken to deal with those responsible for instigating the war and for violating the neutrality of Belgium and Luxembourg. The United States representatives on the commission dissented from the portions of the report that referred to crimes against humanity, to the conclusion that heads of state should be liable to criminal prosecution, and to the conclusion that special measures should be adopted to deal with those responsible for the war. The Japanese representatives made a reservation to the conclusion under which heads of state would be held criminally responsible for political acts; and they did not concur in the provision making failure to act to prevent or end violations of the laws or customs of war an affirmative offense.

The Treaty of Versailles of 1919 called for the trial of the former German kaiser, William II, by a specially constituted international tribunal. The treaty also contained German recognition of the right of the Allies to bring to trial before national or international military tribunals persons accused of having committed acts in violation of the laws or customs of war, and an undertaking by the German government to hand such persons over to the Allies for trial. The treaty contained no provision for trials for the offense of crimes against humanity, and only indirectly (in the charges against the former kaiser) was there provision for a trial for the offense of crimes against peace. Because The Netherlands, where the Kaiser had taken refuge, refused the Allied request for extradition, he was never tried. And, because of German resistance to the surrender of persons accused of war crimes, the Allies ultimately agreed to permit the cases to be tried by the supreme court of Leipzig. This method of attempting to punish persons accused of war crimes proved ineffective. The great majority of those tried were acquitted, despite strong evidence of guilt; those convicted received what were generally agreed to be grossly inadequate sentences (and, in several instances, were quickly permitted to escape from prison); and all were treated as heroes by the German press and public.

World War II. Beginning early in World War II, various announcements were made concerning the intention of the Allies to mete out punishment to those guilty of war crimes. On October 25, 1941, while the United States was still neutral, Pres. Franklin D. Roosevelt called attention to the atrocities being committed by the Nazis in occupied countries. On that same day Prime Minister Winston Churchill associated the British government with the Roosevelt statement and made retribution for these crimes one of the major purposes of the war. In November 1941 and January 1942 Soviet Foreign Minister V.M. Molotov circulated diplomatic notes specifying in detail a number of Nazi violations of the laws and customs of war. On January 13, 1942, the St. James Declaration was signed by the governments in exile of nine European countries that were then occupied by the Nazis. These nations, too, made the punishment of war crimes a principal war aim. During the course of the war there were other pronouncements on this subject, the most important of which were the Moscow Declaration of November 1, 1943, and the Potsdam Declaration of July 26, 1945. In the Moscow Declaration, the United States, Great Britain, and the U.S.S.R. stated that at the time of the granting of any armistice to Germany those German officers and men and members of the Nazi Party responsible for atrocities, massacres, and executions in occupied areas would be sent back to the countries in which their acts had been committed for trial and punishment "according to the laws of these liberated countries and of the Free Governments which will be erected therein" and that those "major criminals" whose offenses had no particular geographical location would be punished by a joint decision of the Allied governments. The Potsdam Declaration with respect to Japan, made by the United States, Great Britain, and China, and later adhered to by the U.S.S.R., stated that "stern justice shall be meted out to all war criminals including those who have visited cruelties upon our prisoners."

Plans for the trial of Nazi leaders

During October 1943, representatives of 17 of the Allied nations, including all the major powers except the U.S.S.R., met in London and established the United Nations War Crimes Commission. Among the functions assigned to the commission were the formulation and implementation of the general measures necessary to ensure the detection, apprehension, trial, and punishment of persons accused of war crimes. A Far Eastern subcommission was subsequently established and performed similar functions in Chungking, Szechwan Province, China. On August 8, 1945, at the conclusion of the war, representatives of the United States, the United Kingdom, the U.S.S.R., and the provisional government of France signed the London Agreement, which included a charter for an international military tribunal for the trial of the major Axis war criminals whose offenses had no particular geographical location. Nineteen other governments later adhered to this agreement. After listing the three categories of crimes falling within the jurisdiction of the tribunal (set forth above) for which there was to be individual responsibility, the charter specified that the official position of a defendant as head of state or as a responsible government official would not be considered as a ground for either freeing him from responsibility or mitigating his punishment; that the fact that a defendant had acted pursuant to the order of his government or a superior would not free him from responsibility but might be considered in mitigation of punishment; and that the tribunal might declare any group or organization to have been criminal in character, and, if it did so, any national, military, or occupation courts of any signatory state could thereafter bring individuals to trial for membership therein, and the criminal nature of the group or organization could not be questioned. In order to ensure fair trials for the accused, it was provided that a defendant would be entitled, at a reasonable time before trial, to receive a copy of the indictment, including full particulars of the charge on which he was to be tried; the right to give any explanation relevant to the charge made against him; the right to a preliminary examination in or translated into his own language; the right to conduct his own defense or to have the assistance of counsel; and the right to cross-examine prosecution witnesses and to present evidence in support of his defense.

The Nürnberg tribunal. The first session of the tribunal, which consisted of a member and an alternate appointed by each of the four original signatory countries, took place in Berlin on October 18, 1945, under the presidency of the Soviet member, Gen. I.T. Nikitchenko. At that time an indictment was lodged against 24 former Nazi leaders, charging them with numerous crimes against peace, conventional war crimes, crimes against humanity, and conspiracy and charging a number of groups and organizations (such as the Gestapo, the Nazi secret police) with being criminal in nature. All subsequent sessions of the tribunal, beginning on November 20, 1945, were held in Nürnberg, Germany, under the presidency of the British member, Lord Justice Geoffrey Lawrence (later Baron Trevethin and Oaksey). The other members of the tribunal were Francis Biddle of the United States and Henri Donnedieu de Vabres of France. The chief prosecutors consisted of Justice Robert H. Jackson for the United States, Sir Hartley (later Lord) Shawcross for the United Kingdom, François de Menthon and Auguste Champetier de Ribes for France, and Gen. R.A. Rudenko for the U.S.S.R. During the course of the trial one of the defendants, Robert Ley, committed suicide; and the tribunal decided that another defendant, Gustav Krupp von Bohlen und Halbach, could not then be tried because of his physical and mental condition.

After a trial that was conducted in four languages (English, French, Russian, and German) and that lasted more than 10 months (216 actual trial days), the reading of the judgment of the tribunal with regard to the remaining 22 individual defendants and the seven groups and organizations named in the indictment was concluded on October 1, 1946. Three of the individual defendants were acquitted; 12 were sentenced to death by hanging; three were sentenced to life imprisonment; and four were sentenced to imprisonment for terms ranging from 10 to 20 years. The decision of the tribunal was unanimous, except that General Nikitchenko dissented from the acquittal of the three defendants, from the refusal of the tribunal to sentence the defendant Rudolf Hess to death (he was sentenced to life imprisonment), and from the decision not to declare the *Reich* cabinet and the general staff and high command of the German armed forces to be criminal organizations. In his report to Pres. Harry S. Truman, Justice Jackson said:

One of the chief obstacles to this trial was the lack of a beaten path. A judgment such as has been rendered shifts the power of the precedent to the support of these rules of law.

Trial of Japanese war leaders. On January 19, 1946, U.S. General of the Army Douglas MacArthur, supreme commander for the Allied powers in Japan, issued a charter for the International Military Tribunal for the Far East for the trial of major war criminals in that area. Although this charter, as amended, closely followed that drafted at London to govern the trial of the Nazi leaders, it differed in a number of respects. The tribunal was to consist of from six to 11 members who would be nominated by the nine Allied signatories to the instrument of surrender of Japan and, in addition, by India and the Philippines. The official position held by a defendant at the time of the alleged offense, as well as the fact that he had acted pursuant to the orders of his government or a superior, could be considered in mitigation of punishment. Instead of having a chief prosecutor from each country, there was to be one chief of counsel appointed by the supreme commander for the Allied powers; the other nations that had been at war with Japan could each appoint an associate counsel; the trial was to be conducted only in English and Japanese. The tribunal ultimately consisted of the representatives of 11 nations (Australia, Canada, China, France, India, The Netherlands, New Zealand, the Philippines, the U.S.S.R., the United Kingdom, and the United States). The trial began in Tokyo on May 3, 1946, under the presidency of Sir William Flood Webb of Australia and with Joseph B. Keenan of the United States as chief of counsel. It ended more than two years later with the reading of the judgment on November 4–12, 1948. The 28 defendants were

Composition of the tribunal

charged with various crimes against peace, murder, other conventional war crimes, and crimes against humanity. Two of the defendants died during the course of the trial, and one was declared unfit to stand trial. Of the 25 defendants against whom sentences were adjudged, seven were sentenced to be executed by hanging, 16 to life imprisonment, and two to lesser terms of imprisonment. Sir William Webb and Judge Delfin Jaranilla of the Philippines filed separate concurring opinions. Judges Henri Bernard of France and B.V.A. Röling of The Netherlands dissented in part from the majority opinion, while Judge R.M. Pal of India dissented generally.

Other World War II trials. The London Agreement of 1945 had contemplated a series of trials to be conducted by the international military tribunal. After the Nürnberg trial, however, Justice Jackson recommended against such proceedings because he felt that, inasmuch as most of the remaining defendants could be charged with single and specific crimes, the most expeditious and least costly method of trial would be for each occupying power in Germany to conduct trials within its own zone. His recommendation was ultimately followed. In the United States zone of occupation, 12 other trials of major war criminals were held at Nürnberg under international authority. These trials, called the Subsequent Proceedings, had as their legal basis Control Council Law No. 10, promulgated on December 20, 1945, by the zone commanders of the four powers occupying Germany. Each trial involved a number of former Nazi officials from a particular field (the Ministries case, the Justice case, the Medical case, the High Command case, etc.). In addition, thousands of Germans and Japanese were tried by various national courts, either military or civilian, for conventional war crimes of all types. It has been estimated that well over 2,000 separate trials took place (including approximately 950 conducted by the United States, 650 by Great Britain, and 275 by Australia) involving many times that number of defendants. These statistics do not include trials conducted by the Soviet Union and the eastern European countries, for which not even approximations are available. Included in the trials conducted by U.S. military commissions were those of generals Yamashita Tomoyuki and Homma Masaharu in Manila in 1945. These former Japanese commanders unsuccessfully attempted to secure the intervention of the U.S. Supreme Court to prevent the imposition of their death sentences.

Criticism of the trials. From the very outset the post-World War II program for the punishment of war criminals was vigorously attacked and vigorously defended on both political and legal grounds. One of the legal arguments most frequently advanced against the program was that war-crimes trials punished acts that had not been criminal when they were committed. This ex post facto argument was directed primarily at crimes against peace and at some of the crimes against humanity.

The Nürnberg Tribunal, however, held that, long before the Nazi or other aggressions of World War II, a series of international declarations, acts, and treaties, culminating in the Kellogg–Briand Pact (Pact of Paris) of 1928, ratified by Germany and nearly all other states, had established a rule of customary international law that made aggressive war illegal and the initiation or waging of such a war, with knowledge of its character and freedom of choice, an individual crime. Many of the crimes against humanity and the majority, if not all, of the conventional war crimes (murder, rape, pillage, etc.) are offenses under the criminal law of every civilized nation. In regard to these offenses, criticism was directed at the fact that the vanquished were being tried in the courts of the victors, in which, it was claimed, they could not receive fair and objective treatment. This particular criticism was heard less and less frequently as time went on; and, in the great majority of cases, war-crimes courts demonstrated their objectivity and fairness. Much criticism was also directed at the courts that tried these cases, because they refused to entertain such defenses as the one that an act had been committed as a matter of military necessity or as the result of the receipt of orders from a superior. The dispute as to the validity of the latter defense occurred repeatedly,

despite the fact that at the Leipzig trials after World War I the German court had itself recognized that it was not a valid defense and that it could be advanced only in mitigation of punishment. The principle is now well embedded in the law, and it is contained in the instructions on the law of land warfare issued by both the United States and Great Britain for the guidance of their military forces. As one of the so-called Nürnberg Principles, it is also strongly supported by the Soviet Union and a number of other countries. In addition, it has been included as an established principle in several of the United Nations resolutions and conventions discussed below.

Despite the criticisms, it would appear that trials for war crimes are now so much a part of the law of war that they may be expected after any conflict that ends with one side victorious and the other defeated. The passage of time, however, resulted in a lessening of the antagonism felt toward persons who were convicted of war crimes after World War II and who were sentenced to imprisonment. Both the peace treaty with Japan and the Bonn agreements that terminated the occupation of the Federal Republic of Germany contained provisions that resulted in advancing the dates of release of all but a handful of such persons.

Later developments. Each of the four Geneva Conventions of August 12, 1949, for the protection of war victims (wounded and sick, wounded and sick at sea, prisoners of war, and civilians), to which more than 125 countries are parties, contains a "grave breaches" provision that makes punishable a number of specific offenses committed against persons protected by that particular convention. Unfortunately, the enactment of laws implementing these provisions and the actual trials of offenders have been left to the individual countries.

During the hostilities in Korea, the United Nations Command had identified and held for trial for violations of the law of war a large number of North Koreans who were prisoners of war. Because of the provisions of the armistice that ended hostilities, all the prisoners of war so identified and held were repatriated without trial or punishment.

Some years after the end of World War II, the Federal Republic of Germany began a program of prosecutions of individuals who had been guilty of criminal conduct under the guise of official Nazi activities. This was referred to by many as a war-crimes program, which it was not. The crimes for which prosecutions were instituted were, for the most part, committed by German nationals against other German nationals in German territory. Such offenses are not war crimes and are punished under the local laws of the country concerned. The misunderstanding arose because many of the offenses prosecuted fell within the category of "crimes against humanity"—specifically, what has come to be known as genocide, the elimination of an entire race—and because the newspapers usually refer to these prosecutions as war-crimes trials. With respect to this program, it is interesting to note that in 1965, when German law would have automatically outlawed further prosecutions, public opinion in West Germany was sufficiently strong to bring about the extension until 1969 of the time within which cases could be prosecuted; and in the latter year the right to prosecute was extended for an additional 10 years. In 1979 the statute of limitations for murder was eliminated entirely.

In 1960 Adolf Eichmann, one of the leaders in the Nazi program for the extermination of the Jews of Europe (the Nazi "final solution of the Jewish problem"), was located by Israeli agents in Argentina and taken to Israel, where he was tried as a war criminal. He was convicted and sentenced to death. The conviction was affirmed by the Supreme Court of Israel in 1962, and he was executed.

The General Assembly of the United Nations exhibited an early and continuous interest in the field of war crimes. In 1946 it adopted a resolution affirming that genocide was an international crime, and in 1948 it approved and called upon its members to ratify the Convention on the Prevention and Punishment of the Crime of Genocide, to which more than 75 countries are parties. In 1947, when establishing the International Law Commission, the General Assembly requested that body to formulate a set of principles based upon the charter and judgment of the

Post-war prosecutions in Germany

Action in the United Nations

Nürnberg court and to draft a code of offenses against the peace and security of mankind. In its 1950 report the commission presented to the General Assembly a set of principles so formulated; and in its 1951 report it submitted to the General Assembly a Draft Code of Offenses Against the Peace and Security of Mankind. On a number of occasions the General Assembly has called upon states generally to arrest and extradite war criminals who have not been tried for their offenses. In 1968 it approved the Convention on Non-Applicability of Statutory Limitations to War Crimes and Crimes Against Humanity. A number of countries, including the United States, will probably refrain from ratifying this convention, because there have been injected into it references to economic and political rights and apartheid (racial segregation, especially as practiced in the Republic of South Africa). In 1970 the General Assembly requested the secretary general of the United Nations to continue the study of war crimes and crimes against humanity.

The question has arisen of whether or not the law governing the conduct of hostilities is applicable in all conflicts, including national conflicts denominated as civil wars, guerrilla wars, or wars of national liberation. If it is applicable, then, of course, its violation is a war crime. Each of the 1949 Geneva Conventions contains an article that is stated to be applicable "in the case of armed conflict not of an international character." This article requires the humane treatment of noncombatants, persons taken prisoner of war, and the sick and the wounded and specifically prohibits violence to life or person, the taking of hostages, outrages upon personal dignity, and the passing of sentence or the carrying out of an execution without the judgment of a regularly constituted court entered after a fair and properly safeguarded trial. The binding effect of these provisions, especially as regards antigovernment (rebel) forces, is hotly disputed. Although it is argued by many, including the United States and the Soviet Union, that the international law of war, including the foregoing provisions, is applicable in national conflicts, others deny this. During the Algerian War of Independence, numerous charges of violations of the law of war were made, with apparent justification, by both sides. Ultimately, France agreed, as had been contended by the Algerians, that the 1949 Geneva Convention provisions were applicable. It is not believed, however, that any trials were conducted by either side in that conflict.

War crimes in Vietnam

Numerous allegations have been made of the commission of war crimes in Vietnam during the long civil war there. The South Vietnamese were accused of shooting prisoners of war and of ejecting them from helicopters in flight. The Viet Cong, or rebel forces, by their own admission executed American prisoners of war without trial as reprisal for the execution by South Vietnamese authorities of convicted Viet Cong terrorists. The United States charged the North Vietnamese with numerous violations of the grave-breaches provisions of the 1949 Prisoners of War Convention. And the North Vietnamese contended at one point that all captured Americans were war criminals. In 1966 the North Vietnamese indicated that they contemplated conducting a series of war-crimes trials of captured American pilots; but they were apparently dissuaded from this course by adverse worldwide reaction. Under the aegis of Bertrand Russell, the United States was "tried" for war crimes in Vietnam by a self-constituted tribunal that sat in Stockholm. That this was a juridical farce was demonstrated by the fact that the offer of a Swedish attorney to represent the United States was rejected by the "court."

Publicity concerning an incident at the hamlet of My Lai 4, in which more than 100 South Vietnamese men, women, and children were shot and killed by American soldiers during a "search and destroy" mission conducted in March 1968, once again focussed public attention on the problem of war crimes, particularly with respect to the defense of "superior orders." A number of individuals had charges preferred against them as a result of this incident. Some of the accused were tried and acquitted, and one, an officer, was found guilty of premeditated murder and sentenced to life imprisonment at hard labour.

There have been numerous charges of the commission of war crimes by Israel in the territories occupied as a result of the Six-Day War of 1967. The International Committee of the Red Cross has found a number of violations of the provisions of the 1949 Convention for the Protection of Civilian Persons in Time of War, but many of these are technical violations that cannot be considered as attaining the status of war crimes. A United Nations committee that investigated the charges during 1970 found practically all of them to have occurred. Israel, however, challenged the validity of the report, because the committee was composed of the representatives of three countries that had, in every instance, supported the Arab position in the Middle East. Several neutral countries had apparently refused invitations to serve on the committee. The committee was, for this and other reasons, not permitted to visit the occupied territories. This situation illustrates the difficulty of attempting to reach conclusions about war crimes while a state of war still exists.   (H.S.L.)

Economics of war

The economics of war and defense are concerned with the economic effects of military expenditure, the management of economics in wartime, and, more recently, with the management of peacetime military budgets and the economic administration of armed forces.

Although war and armed forces are great consumers of resources, economists have not traditionally paid much attention to them. To most economists of the 19th and 20th centuries, war has appeared as an aberration from the normal acquisitive behaviour that has been viewed as the proper concern of economics. Certainly war brings to the fore many emotional forces and unquantifiable goals that greatly complicate analysis, and it is, thus, not surprising that only in recent decades have economists turned much attention to the economic foundations of military power, to the internal management of armed forces, and to the theory of strategy itself.

This intrusion of economists into spheres hitherto largely the preserve of the professional man-at-arms owes much to the vastly increased scale on which warfare is waged and armed forces are maintained in the latter part of the 20th century. The outstanding characteristic of military history in the last two or three centuries has been the steady expansion of force and the soaring rise in the resources that war can consume and destroy.

The military system of an age reflects, and in turn influences, the social and economic structure of its time. In feudal societies military service was thus linked with the tenure of land, and the rise of money economies saw a transition to professional, mercenary forces. During the modern period, which saw the consolidation of the centralized, bureaucratic state in the decades of continuous European warfare from about 1685 to 1714, a need arose to maintain large and more lavishly equipped armies. This stimulated the elaboration of administrative machinery to raise taxes and to feed, equip, and pay the forces in the field. Substantial standing armies necessitated arsenals and attention to logistics. The efforts of the state to meet these requirements increased its capacity to conduct policy in other spheres. In particular, the state developed a more coherent diplomacy directed to the conscious pursuit of the "national interest." The armed forces thus became the instrument of a more consistent statecraft rather than participants in what has been described as the "general melee" of 17th-century warfare.

Maintaining even the modest armed forces of the 18th century was, however, a great strain on the state and its revenues, so that armies could only campaign for limited periods, over limited range, and at favourable seasons. The religious passions of the 17th century expended, states fought for limited purposes for which their hired armies felt little personal enthusiasm. War, both in its purposes and its effects, was much isolated from the general public.

Several revolutionary developments transformed this state of affairs and ultimately produced the kind of warfare experienced in the 20th century. The U.S. War of Independence and, even more, the conflicts following the French Revolution made war an almost popular affair in whose

The rise of modern warfare

outcome even the common man could perceive a stake. There emerged the concepts of universal military service, of the nation in arms, and of the mass army. Simultaneously, the Industrial Revolution of the late 18th and early 19th centuries made vastly more effective weapons available, and, through the technique of mass production (which itself owed much to the military market), arms became available in vastly greater quantities. No less important were the developments in transport—railway and steamship—that transformed logistics. Armies could now move great distances and still be supplied. As the technological revolution gained pace, the telegraph, the radio, and electronics carried both weapons and communications to new levels. With increasing velocity modern military equipment expanded in power and variety, but at rapidly increasing cost.

Physical characteristics offer a better notion of the scale of expansion than do financial data. In the late 17th century there was rarely one artillery piece for 1,000 armed men. By 1709 there were usually two or three. In 1916 the French massed 2,000 guns on 10 kilometres of front; at Stalingrad in 1942–43 the Russians assembled 4,000 guns on four kilometres. In 1660 the British Royal Navy had only five ships over 1,000 tons; many modern ships exceed 80,000 tons. At the Battle of Trafalgar in 1805, Nelson's flagship was 46 years old; navies of today usually reckon 20 years as the maximum life for a warship.

The size of armed forces has also increased immensely. In the 18th century the average size of a large field army was 47,000. In the U.S. Civil War (1861–65), the federal army reached a maximum size of 622,000. In World War I, over 63,000,000 men were mobilized and at least 8,500,000 killed. The German armies alone exceeded 11,000,000. In World War II the total number mobilized was about 107,000,000; the U.S.S.R. mobilized 22,000,000 and the United States 16,000,000.

PROBLEMS OF ECONOMIC MOBILIZATION

In the years before 1914, technological and administrative evolution convinced an overwhelming majority of military men that the initial stages of a new great European war would be decisive. This belief placed a premium on the rapid mobilization and quick deployment of the largest and best equipped forces. The emphasis was consequently on large forces in being and on speedily available reserves. This need could be met only by conscription, especially as the spread of modern industry had bid up the price of labour. The need to place the greatest possible force on the line at the outset also encouraged the formation of a network of standing alliances. There was also a continuing search for some advantage in equipment, a contest well exemplified in the Anglo-German naval race, which affords one of the best early illustrations of an arms race driven forward by the pace of innovation even in the absence of trial by battle.

All of this was maintained only at steadily increasing expenditure, accompanied by active propaganda to justify the burden. The expenditure of Germany on armed forces rose from £10,800,000 in 1870 to £28,800,000 in 1880, and to £110,800,000 in 1914. Over the same period Austria-Hungary increased spending from £8,200,000 to £13,200,000 to £36,400,000. The British bill, inflated by the wage costs of an all-volunteer system, rose from £23,400,000 to £25,200,000 to £76,800,000 in 1914. At a rough estimate, these expenditures constituted, in 1914, 4.6 percent of the German gross national product (GNP), 6.1 percent of the Austro-Hungarian, and 3.4 percent of the British.

The first war economies

World War I. But World War I belied most expectations. The anticipated quick, decisive victories did not materialize. The war became a war of mobilization in a different sense—not the rapid deployment of forces in being, but the steady application of industrial resources to produce and sustain an increasingly mechanized military capacity. The equal pace of mobilization on both sides and the temporary ascendancy of defensive tactical weaponry kept the military situation in equilibrium. The strategy of the war increasingly became one of attrition, an explicitly economic conception of exhausting the enemy's reserves of men and productive capacity, best exemplified perhaps in the Allied blockade and German U-boat warfare. The nation-in-arms assumed a new dimension. Not merely the men mobilized but the whole population became part of the war effort. Governments found themselves compelled to take positive action to keep men out of the firing line, so that they could serve production at home.

Neither military men nor economists had given any significant thought to the problems of mobilizing economies on this scale. The degree to which material demands outran expectations is well illustrated by the French writer Raymond Aron's citation of French requirements for 75-millimetre ammunition. The General Staff had anticipated a daily consumption of 13,600 rounds. By mid-September 1914, they requested 50,000 a day, a rate they received in March 1915. But in January 1915 they had already asked for 80,000. By the time this was supplied, in September 1915, the demand was 150,000, or ten times the prewar estimate. By the time demand and supply were in equilibrium in 1917, it had become necessary to employ 1,600,000 French workers in producing munitions instead of the expected labour force of 50,000. Such examples could be multiplied indefinitely. The British Army, for instance, had 100 motor trucks in 1914; by 1918 it had 60,000.

Not unnaturally governments were slow to recognize that they faced an unprecedented challenge. Even after they belatedly realized that the war might be a long one, they took time to appreciate that they needed new methods to mobilize their economic resources. Initially they all assumed that, as in the past, the forces of supply and demand in the market would meet military needs. The armed forces, often competing with each other, placed increased contracts according to their established procedures and waited for industry to respond.

In all the belligerent countries the response was inadequate. The physical capacity to make armaments on the scale required was lacking, and resources could not have been switched to military production by any method at a speed fast enough to satisfy the swelling demand from the front. Leaving the process to the laissez-faire competition of the services with each other and with the demands of the civilian economy was certainly ineffectual. The demands of the military distorted demand in national and international markets and, by increasing economic activity, stimulated the competing demand of the civilian sector. With military mobilization and increased industrial activity, manpower became particularly scarce, despite the relatively widespread underemployment of 1914 and the gradual mobilization of women in some countries.

The inevitable inflationary process released by such excessive demand was made more acute by the particular methods used to finance the war effort. Governments used too much borrowing and too little taxation to pay for the current war effort, and the form of borrowing chosen—from banks rather than individuals—greatly increased the money supply. This, even more than the shortage of goods, accounted for rapidly rising prices and distortions of demand. A great deal was admittedly raised from taxes, at least on the Allies' side, on which there was a democratic tradition of paying for wars by increased taxation. British direct taxes thus rose from £94,000,000 in 1913–14 to £504,000,000 in 1917–18 and to £721,000,000 in 1919–20. Direct taxes rose from 57 percent of total revenue in 1914 to 80 percent in 1917–18. Taxes, nevertheless, accounted for little over a third of government expenditure, and the paper-money supply in Britain rose from £57,000,000 in 1913 to £459,000,000 in 1919. By 1920 the purchasing power of the pound sterling had fallen to a third of that in 1913. Germany, which did not even have an income tax in 1914, and had a tradition of paying for wars by indemnity extracted from its defeated foes, made even more use of inflationary finance.

Government intervention in the economy

A general dearth of military supplies, acute shortages of goods for the civilian sector, and widespread confusion led governments into interventionist economic policies of an unprecedented kind. The allocation of resources and goods came to be determined less by the free-market price mechanism, more by administrative determinations. Intervention usually began in order to deal with a shortage in a particular commodity. This, however, almost inevitably had repercussions elsewhere in the economy, calling in turn for further intervention. As a result of this piece-meal approach, the elaborate systems of planning that had emerged by the end of the war were not what a comprehensive strategy from the beginning might have dictated.

British experience was typical in many respects. From the outbreak of war the government took over control of the railways, shipping, gold reserves, and a few strategic materials. By the spring of 1915 it was clear that the system was not producing the requisite munitions and a "shell scandal" led to the creation of a Ministry of Munitions under the dynamic leadership of David Lloyd George. The emergence of a single key figure to dominate mobilization was typical, paralleled, for instance, by the emergence of Walther Rathenau, and later of Gen. Erich Ludendorff, in Germany, and of Bernard Baruch in the United States.

After 1915 controls spread steadily throughout the British economy, from military materials to related areas of the civilian economy. The methods of control ranged from direct governmental management of industries to requisitioning, licensing, government monopoly of purchasing of special commodities, price fixing, and the direction of civilian labour.

The management of labour in Britain proved to be an especially delicate matter. It was only with difficulty that the unions were persuaded to surrender many restrictive practices and to suspend the practice of striking. This agreement was achieved by promises of a favourable official policy toward unions after the war and by the imposition of an excess-profits tax on industry. To offset absolute shortages and the socially discriminatory effects of inflation, direct rationing of food and other consumer goods was instituted. The results of all this were substantial, and by the end of the war 5,700,000 men had been released to the armed services from the economy with virtually no reduction in overall output. Almost half the national income was in government hands by the end of the war.

American experience was not dissimilar. There was much initial confusion, but the United States profited considerably from the fact that Allied orders for munitions had already stimulated some adjustment of U.S. industry, and that the mobilization along the Mexican border after the Mexican Revolution of 1911 had taught the United States Army some needed logistical lessons. A Council of National Defense had been set up in August 1916, bringing together the secretaries of war, navy, interior, agriculture, commerce, and labour. Under this council was an Advisory Commission consisting of seven members. A few months after the U.S. declaration of war in April 1917, the council established a War Industries Board, which became the central coordinating body for the conversion of industry to war needs.

The full results of all this activity were never to be realized, for the U.S. effort was directed toward a peak of production in 1919 and 1920, which were assumed to be the years of victory. The U.S. expeditionary forces thus fought largely with British and French equipment. But had the war not ended, a great flood of U.S. war matériel would almost certainly have been forthcoming in 1919.

The mobilization of the German economy took a different course, a course that was to exercise considerable influence on the outcome not only of World War I but of World War II also. Germany had shared, in particularly acute form, the expectation that the war would be short. As already remarked, moreover, Germany expected its vanquished foes to pay for the war. A new and autocratic state, Germany had no tradition of common financial sacrifice in war, as did Britain, France, and the United States. A high degree of aristocratic and bourgeois privilege hindered any attempt at systematic and equitable central direction. Thus, although the Prussian ministry of war established a Raw Materials Department as early as 1914 and achieved great success in finding alternative supplies of war material, it was not until 1916 that the idea of systematically involving the whole society in the war effort took hold.

General Ludendorff's conception of "national service" was implemented as an unyielding sacrifice of the civil-ian sector to the battlefront. Germany was to become a vast munitions factory. The almost feudal mixture of competing forces—the generals, the emperor's court, the civilian government of the chancellor, the industrialists, the workers, and the political parties—continued to impede cooperation. No adequate measures were taken to see that workers did not suffer disproportionately or to ensure that sacrifice could be seen to be equitably distributed. Nor were skilled workers retained from the front. Munitions and troops were thus produced at the price of the depletion of the civilian sector. In other words, the German leaders failed to see beyond "war production" to the conception of a "war economy" capable of operating for a prolonged period.

The greatest error of the German war leaders was in removing labour from agriculture without compensating by increased mechanization or use of fertilizer. This, rather than the Allied blockade, was why food shortage broke the back of a nation that had been more than 80 percent self-sufficient in foodstuffs before the war. By 1918 the German people had only 64 percent of the cereals, 18 percent of the meat, and 12 percent of the fats that they had consumed in 1913. This was a major cause of the German collapse in 1918.

During the interwar years many practices introduced during the war were retained, at least in principle. Governments maintained standby machinery for the implementation of economic mobilization and the kind of economic warfare that had evolved around blockades, embargoes, and blacklists. Some stockpiling of strategic materials took place, and in some cases "shadow" factories were built to provide spare capacity for specialized military production. Financial lessons had also been absorbed, so that when war came again greater efforts were made to extract resources from the economy by noninflationary methods. These efforts met with noticeable but limited success. According to one estimate, the proportion of war expenditure met from taxation in World War I was, for the United States, 37 percent, and, for Britain, somewhat over 30 percent (as compared with only 12 percent in Germany). For World War II the proportions were: United States, 44 percent, and Britain, 50 percent.

World War II. When World War II broke out, much of the familiar machinery of control was reinstituted in the democracies, though the mobilization of production lagged during the early months. The defeats of 1940 launched the British into a crash program of aircraft and munitions production. The same period saw the inception of lend-lease in the United States, a procedure by which the president was authorized to transfer defense articles up to value of $1,300,000,000 to any nation whose security was vital to the United States, and to have manufactured similar articles for the same purpose up to an initial value of $7,000,000,000; a sum soon raised to $13,000,000,000.

The lend-lease program served to give U.S. war industry a flying start, though little of the new capacity was in production at the time of U.S. entry into the war at the close of 1941. The United States government instituted controls reminiscent of the previous war, and, once again, there emerged a single man as central arbiter of priorities under the president. This time the man was James Byrnes, who, as director of the Office of War Mobilization, earned the informal title of assistant president.

The most striking feature of economic mobilization in World War II was the degree to which the American economy outstripped all others. Aided in rapid expansion by the very depressed level of economic activity in 1940, and hence the large amount of unemployed capacity, U.S. industry added a net 7,000,000 workers to its strength while contributing over 3,000,000 to the armed forces. Altogether the United States was responsible for 40 percent of total world munitions production and for 55 percent of war expenditure, while simultaneously doubling national income during the war years and expanding civilian consumption by 50 percent. By the end of the war, lend-lease supplies to allies were running at $15,000,000,000 a year.

Germany also remembered lessons from World War I, but because its experience had been different, it drew different and probably fatal conclusions. While Britain and the United States had moved some way toward strengthening the political framework of consultation and consent that experience suggests is the firmest basis for a war effort of common sacrifice, Germany had acquired a dictatorial government that nevertheless lacked the comprehensive apparatus of terror that gave Stalin his ascendancy and enabled him, by a process the details of which are almost entirely obscure, to conduct a desperate war of national defense. Hitler seems to have had a constant anxiety not to provoke opposition by excessive demands on the workers. Nor, indeed, was he primarily military in his sympathies. Contrary to contemporary impressions, Germany avoided heavy mobilization until well after the democratic war machines were in high gear. Public civil works continued and civilian consumption did not fall below the pre-Depression levels of 1929 until 1942. At the end of the war food supplies were no worse than those of 1918, despite invasion and strategic bombing.

It could be said that Hitler's policy, whether consciously or not, was long directed to keeping war production low. Used to making conquests by mere military demonstration or by quick campaigns conducted with forces immediately available, Hitler even initiated cutbacks in production during the early years of the war. Thus, in September 1940, at the height of the Battle of Britain, aircraft production was cut below the rate of daily combat losses, and soon after the Russian campaign began in 1941, production for the army was cut by nearly a third.

Defeat at Stalingrad and the rise of Allied strategic bombing galvanized Germany into action. German achievements were henceforth remarkable. Arms production at the end of 1944 was two and a half times that of 1942, and this was achieved while dispersing a great deal of industry for defense against bombing and developing a range of synthetics, particularly fuels. Had the effort come earlier, it might well have altered the outcome of the war.

Since 1945: the age of forces-in-being.   World War II ended with the use of the atomic bomb on Japan. Until then the war had been one very much like its forerunner from the economic point of view. The war was a long one, in which victory went to the most prolific producers. The peaks of production were reached by a prolonged mobilization of resources after the war had begun.

In some respects the atomic bomb was seen to be revolutionary from the outset. Its production at a cost of more than $1,000,000,000 was an extreme example of the new levels of military expenditure. But the bomb was scarce and its power far less than the thermonuclear fusion weapons that were to follow and that gave the nuclear age its character. Consequently, postwar planning began on the assumption that another great war would be not unlike that which had just ended. In the Soviet Union no suggestion was tolerated that the course of a new war would not be dictated by the "permanently operating factors" laid down by Stalin in 1942—*i.e.,* the stability of the rear, the morale of the army, the quality and quantity of divisions, and the organizational capacity of the commander. The United States, which possessed the bomb, regarded it as an extension of the armory of strategic bombardment that now constituted a major part, but only a part, of modern warfare. In 1948 George Marshall, then secretary of state and formerly the wartime head of the American military command, declared that "however much any future war starts in the air, as in the past, it will end up in the mud and on the ground."

Postwar military preparation therefore laid a heavy emphasis on maintaining the capacity to mobilize once again should a war break out. Standby controls were established, offices of defense mobilization or their equivalent were set up, and stockpiling was recommenced. Perhaps the most conspicuous single testimony to the belief that a new war would be one of attrition was the heavy emphasis placed on preparing to fight a new Battle of the Atlantic.

Gradually, however, the fuller implications of the new military technology emerged. Toward the end of the Korean War in 1953, atomic weapons were becoming plentiful, the thermonuclear weapon was proving practicable, and the Soviet Union had come into possession of both. Long-range bomber forces were becoming numerous and

Changing conceptions of future war

long-range missiles were under development. It became clear that future wars between great nuclear powers either would have to be deliberately limited or would become destructive to an unprecedented extent. In a total war with the thermonuclear weapons, there would be little chance to carry out postattack mobilization and little left to fight about. Total war thus became a doubtful possibility, both for reasons of high policy—it being difficult to conceive war aims to justify such a catastrophe—and at the level of strategy—a Battle of the Atlantic loses its significance if there are no surviving ports or war economies to service.

For such reasons, the problems of mobilization for sustained struggle after the outbreak of hostilities have lost much of their interest. The offices of mobilization are in decay, and such tasks as defending sea routes no longer receive strategic priority. Instead, military technology has brought a return to expectations akin to those entertained before 1914—that the initial stages of battle will be decisive and that superiority then might win the war. There is, thus, a renewed premium on forces-in-being; and, though any hope of emerging from a major nuclear war with anything remotely resembling traditional conceptions of victory has passed, readiness at least retains its value as an instrument of deterrence.

The adoption of policies of readiness and the continuance of Soviet–American rivalry have resulted in much higher levels of peacetime military expenditure. Additional expenditures have been incurred because of the strategy of maintaining considerable conventional forces to fight possible limited wars. The lesser powers have continued more traditional military policies.

The modern military technology that has brought about these strategic revolutions has a self-sustaining and accelerating dynamic of its own that has pushed up the so-called unit cost of military equipment. Better versions of familiar weapons and many entirely new devices continually appear. Whereas the fighter aircraft of 1939 cost about $25,000, one of the more economical equivalent aircraft of the 1970s has a price of $1,500,000. A modern nuclear submarine can have a cost of over $100,000,000. Much of the added expense arises from the almost entirely new field of electronics. The advanced destroyer of 1937 had some 60 electron tubes aboard, that of 1957 about 4,000, and that of 1961, 29,000.

Ascertaining what national and total world military expenditures are is a more difficult task than it might at first appear. Most countries, even the more secretive, publish an overall figure of annual defense spending, though China under Communist government has been reticent even with this. But merely to accept and compare published figures of this kind would lead to serious errors. In the first place, military budgets are closely related to many secret aspects of national strategy. Consequently, all nations conceal certain special expenditures, and some may publish deliberately deceptive information. Even without deliberate concealment, however, problems arise from great differences in national methods of accounting. Nations differ as to what constitutes military expenses and as to the manner of presenting them. It is particularly significant to recognize that, given its importance as a military power, the Soviet Union has an official defense budget that excludes much of what NATO countries would include as military procurement of "hardware," research and development (much of which is budgeted as "science"), and testing. Many countries, furthermore, because of administrative incompetence, may not have a very clear idea themselves of what their military costs are. Even in a country such as Britain there can be serious controversy as to how to reckon arms exports stimulated by national defense policy when trying to assess the effects of that policy on the balance of payments. Almost without exception, governments publish a great deal of financial information in forms designed to meet standards of public accountability rather than to facilitate economic analysis and international comparison.

International comparisons are also seriously bedevilled by a virtually intractable problem of commensurability. National expenditures are naturally declared in national currencies. These afford a very imperfect basis for compar-

Difficulties of international comparison

ison in a world in which most exchange rates are arbitrarily fixed. There are also special problems affecting prices in the military field. Military power depends on many items and materials for which there is no national market and no free international trade to fix a price. Many countries have no real market and price system at all, prices being merely a device by which administrative decisions about the allocation of resources are implemented. Even in more or less free-market economies, the true significance of military prices is obscured by subsidies, tax policies, and other devices. Armed forces, typically, have the use of land without proper valuation of its alternative uses. In the United States, the armed forces have received nuclear materials without the true cost or anything remotely near it appearing in the military budget. Above all, in nearly all countries, compulsory military service provides the armed forces with manpower at far below its market price. Given the very high proportion of military costs that manpower constitutes, this is a major distortion of true costs. Many of the same and similar problems beset the effort to measure and compare gross national products (GNP's). Thus, estimates that relate military expenditure to gross national product must be viewed with particular caution.

Relatively little effort has been devoted to analyzing these problems in public, and it is doubtful whether much progress has been made by official intelligence organizations. A survey of world defense expenditure, if approached with due caution, nevertheless serves to depict the general pattern of military spending.

The most widely quoted public tabulations of defense expenditure are those of the international Institute for Strategic Studies, based in London. These presentations are normally made simply from the public, official figures in current national currencies, except that a special effort is made to deal with the Soviet Union. In that case the method employed is to accept the more convincing attempts of economists to estimate Soviet GNP, and then to assess the Soviet military budget by estimating what the dollar cost would be of mobilizing the real resources believed to go into the Soviet Union's military effort. A declared Soviet military budget of 17,700,000,000 rubles, for example, would be increased to 23,000,000,000 rubles to take account of assumed military spending concealed elsewhere in the budget. As the price paid by the Soviet government for armaments does not represent the true economic cost of producing them, the latter figure might then be expanded to $39,333,000,000 to permit comparison.

Such large military expenditure obviously represents a considerable consumption of real resources and a heavy burden on many national economies. This burden and the need to raise revenue to pay for it at a time when governmental budgets are also coming to embrace an unprecedented range of welfare programs, have led to concern as to what the economic effect of defense expenditure may be and as to whether substantial reductions could be made. On the other hand, there are doubts as to whether the world could adjust to the elimination of such a large and dynamic area of economic and technological activity without serious dislocation and economic depression.

Consideration of what the economic effects of large-scale disarmament might be, whether optimistic or gloomy, cannot begin by assuming that the whole $540,000,000,-000 estimated total world expenditure (early 1980s) or so could be saved for civilian purposes. Not all military expenditure, for example, is without nonmilitary utility. In many countries, and particularly less developed countries in which the burden of defense looms large in the budget, the armed forces perform many tasks of construction and education. In addition, much research and development for military purposes has important beneficial results for civil society, particularly in the fields of engineering and medicine. It is far from certain that all the manpower and talent engaged in military service, or in service to the military, could readily be redeployed into civilian pursuits. Nor, even if this were theoretically practicable, can it be assumed that the political will and administrative capacity would appear to make the necessary transfers or to sustain the overall level of economic activity if the stimulus of supposed military necessity were removed.

Not even on the most optimistic assumptions about disarmament could all military establishments be abolished. Even the most ambitious schemes envisage some substantial form of an international peace-keeping force. Beyond that, armed forces play important roles in maintaining domestic order. In many countries, particularly the less developed, this is in fact their prime function.

These considerations suggest that there is no realistic hope of transferring more than about half of the total world expenditure on arms to peaceful purposes. Such an estimate assumes more or less complete success in finding productive outlets for the resources freed from military employment. The economic effects of disarmament would, in fact, depend very much upon the arrangements made for the transition to a demilitarized economy. The process would have to be phased over a period of years. The speedy transition from a war to a peace economy after 1945, sometimes cited as a hopeful precedent, is scarcely relevant because of the great volume of pent-up money savings that sustained the level of demand in the economy, and because of the postwar reconstruction work that stimulated activity. After the Korean War the decline of the United States' military budget was accompanied by a noticeable stagnation in the U.S. economy. This, however, must be related to deliberately deflationary policies of the administration of the day.

Economic problems of demilitarization

Much would depend on the energy with which governments devoted themselves to stimulating alternative investment and economic enterprise. In this respect national attitudes to government expenditure and manipulation of the economy would be major determinants of success. Whatever policies of redeployment were adopted, there undoubtedly would be particular problems in geographic regions disproportionately dependent on military activity, and in industries dependent on defense contracts. The vast amount of investment, both human and material, in very sophisticated military technology might be especially difficult to redeploy, and it may be that, in this respect, the military sector of the economy is becoming increasingly less interchangeable with the civilian. The conclusion of most economists seems to be, however, that there is nothing inherently insoluble about the problem of smooth adjustment to a disarmed economy. The problem would be chiefly one for the advanced economies in which most of the military expenditures takes place, and in these the task, though large, would not be out of proportion to the regulatory, countercyclical activity already undertaken by government.

A related and more general question is whether high military expenditures and, perhaps even more, compulsively large programs of research and development have become an indispensable element in economic and technical progress at the rate to which the developed countries have become accustomed. The economic performance of West Germany while disarmed, and the even more spectacular growth of the Japanese economy under similar conditions, can be cited as evidence that a large national defense budget is certainly not a necessity for economic growth. Indeed, the record of these two countries is commonly cited as evidence of the burden military expenditure imposes on a nation's prosperity. But such arguments cannot be conclusive in the presence of so many other variables.

For the sake of completeness, it is also necessary to note one or two other features of the present high level of military expenditure. For nations that station large military forces in foreign countries or that make large imports of weapons and war material, serious balance-of-payments difficulties may arise. Considerations of this kind played a major part in compelling Britain to withdraw from its military presence "East of Suez" and in leading the United States to seek a reduction in its widespread overseas military commitments. The stationing of large British and American forces in Germany has occasioned a continuous drain on foreign exchange for the two countries in the postwar decades. This problem has been partially solved by so-called offset payments by which the West German government has undertaken to buy British or American military goods or medium-term American securities.

Partly for balance-of-payments reasons, partly because of

a desire to preserve an arms industry independent of the United States, and partly because of a belief in the technologically stimulating effects of advanced military research and development, several western European nations have taken a new departure by collaborating in the production of weapons. These efforts frequently entail accepting considerable extra costs incurred as a result of the frictions of cooperation and necessary compromises on weapon design. By 1969 there were under way in Europe five major cooperative aircraft construction projects, seven aero-engine ventures, and four tactical missile projects, together with numerous lesser enterprises. In many of these, political motives were dominant and the longer term economic prospects remained controversial.

International trade in armaments The international trade in armaments also remained buoyant in the 1970s. It is calculated that the world spent in constant 1979 dollars $5,300,000,000,000 on military forces and "hardware" in the decade 1971–80 of which $199,000,000,000 was transferred internationally by way of trade or gift. The bulk of this trade was between the developed countries of the major alliances, but the less developed countries were also heavily engaged. Less developed countries spend some $133,000,000,000 a year on military equipment. The United States sold about $22,800,000,000 worth of arms (1976–80) to less developed countries and transferred more free of charge. For the U.S.S.R. the sale figure was about $32,900,000,000; for Britain, $4,600,000,000; for France, $8,000,000,000. From 1976 to 1980 less developed countries bought, acquired for import, or made under foreign license about 4,400 combat aircraft, 1,800 other aircraft, 2,400 helicopters, 25,000 surface-to-air missiles, 13,400 tanks, 210 warships, and 480 patrol and other defensive craft. A trade of these proportions clearly puts a strain on developing economies, but it will not be easy to arrest. The major problem is the sense of political insecurity felt by the governments of the important countries, whether vis-à-vis domestic or foreign foes. But there are also powerful economic forces to keep the trade alive.

The day of the private arms salesman is largely over; though he exists, he works very much within a framework of government policy and control. But governments themselves have economic as well as politico-strategic reasons to push arms exports. Sales offices have become a feature of ministries of defense. The trade, moreover, is divided among an increasing number of competitors. Nations that are now major suppliers of sophisticated arms include the United States, the Soviet Union, Britain, France, West Germany, China, Italy, Switzerland, Sweden, Czechoslovakia, Israel, The Netherlands, and Canada. Any attempt at control of the arms trade is correspondingly complicated.

MODERN MILITARY BUDGETING

The scale of modern military expenditure, the complexity of military tasks, and the ever-widening variety of equipment available to discharge them have combined to bring about a major evolution in defense management. For the greater part of the present century, the concern of economists with war and the armed forces has been directed toward the issues of the allocation of resources between the military and civil sectors and toward the possible effect of this allocation on the national economy and its growth. In the nuclear age economists have also become concerned with the question of allocation within the armed services—that is, with the size and character of the armed forces and with the choice and design of weapons.

The application of economic analysis to military affairs faces fundamental difficulties. A private firm in a free economy has a clear goal—profit—and can measure success in money terms. The military machine, like many other public activities, has an ultimate goal—national security—that cannot be measured in money or even quantified. Its component parts, the armed forces, make contributions that are difficult to weigh and compare. Analysis may lay out the relative consequences—strategic, financial, and other—of particular courses but cannot decide what to do in the light of the analysis, for that requires political decision derived from the broadest conceptions of national security and welfare. A system of defense management can, therefore, aim only at putting the best conceivable array of evaluated and explicit choices before the appropriate decision-maker in the most comprehensible manner possible.

The prototypes of new methods of analysis were developed in the United States, from where versions have spread to other nations, including Britain, Canada, and West Germany. The system of military budgeting operating in the United States after 1945 was designed to meet the recommendations of the Hoover Commission (1947–48) that military budgets display functions and activities rather than the traditional lists of manpower and purchases authorized. Budgetary presentation was shaped to satisfy legislative requirements for fiscal control, and the accounting categories employed were typified by such breakdowns as "research and development," "procurement," and "construction." There was, consequently, no clear indication of the cost of a particular mission, such as anti-submarine warfare or tactical air support. But the new system helped the U.S. Congress control more effectively the allocation of men and material, the subjects in which it was most interested. Individual services were able to consolidate their central control; and the growing habit of reviewing the budget in terms of the functional categories rather than by service permitted, at least, better comparative assessments than before.

But the system also had disadvantages. It still encouraged the services to stress the value of what they were habitually doing rather than to seek new and better ways of contributing to a cooperative program of national defense. The budget still had one-year perspective, which obscured the long-term implications of current decisions and encouraged the tactic of beginning a program in the hope of being allowed to continue it later, when it became expensive, by arguing that cancellation would waste all the money already spent. Success was still thought of as obtaining a larger budget rather than doing more for a given sum.

Mission-oriented budgets All these disadvantages were clear enough by the late 1950s, and in 1959 U.S. Gen. Maxwell Taylor suggested a "mission-oriented" budget around such concepts as atomic retaliation and air defense. Congress subsequently asked that the budget for fiscal 1961 be based on "functional categories." The idea of the new system in budget and management was to replace intermediate military "inputs" by strategic "outputs" directly describing the policy's intended effects in the international arena.

In the 1960s, under Secretary of Defense Robert McNamara, programming budgeting was set in a five-year program. This program was organized in eight major functional or performance categories, originally: strategic retaliatory forces; continental defense; general purpose forces; lift; reserves; research and development; general support; and military assistance. These categories were subdivided into almost a thousand "program elements," such as "Minuteman" (missiles). The advantages of this system are said to include: displaying programs so as to make clear their long-term implications; revealing the implications of one program for another; and minimizing service parochialism by encouraging the services to conceive new contributions to integrated national security programs.

Such a system can be no better than the accuracy and significance of its data permit. A second aspect of the new management has consequently been to develop a more refined system analysis to determine the characteristics of military systems and to produce a more rigorous cost analysis to attribute all relevant costs to specific systems. This requires close and careful cooperation of cost analysts with system designers, system analysts, and military users.

Long-term programming and cost-benefit analysis are certainly not panaceas. Their widespread adoption outside the military field testifies to their utility, but they are not of universal applicability. The patterns and methods hit upon in the early years of operation have already undergone much modification. What is unlikely to be cast off, however, is the search for explicitness and rationality in making choices that is the characteristic contribution of economists to the new methods of defense management.

(L.W.M.)

THE PRACTICE OF WAR

Military conduct of war

FUNDAMENTALS OF STRATEGY

Definitions of strategy

Strategy, narrowly defined, means "the art of the general" (from the Greek *stratēgos*). In a strictly military sense, the term first gained currency at the end of the 18th century, when warfare was still relatively simple and limited. In its military aspect, the term had to do with stratagems by which a general sought to deceive an enemy, with plans he made for a campaign, and with the way he moved and disposed his forces in war. Often defined as the art of projecting and directing campaigns, military strategy came to pre-empt almost the whole field of generalship, short of the battlefield itself. It also came to include the planning of naval warfare. To tactics (see below) military jargon reserved the art of executing plans and handling forces in battle.

The term strategy has expanded far beyond its original military meaning. As society and warfare have steadily grown more complex, military factors have become more and more inseparable from the nonmilitary in the conduct of war and in programs designed to secure peace. Nations have found it necessary to adjust and correlate political, economic, technological, and psychological factors, along with military elements, in the management of their national policy. The demarcation between strategy as a purely military phenomenon and national strategy of the broader variety became blurred in the 19th century, particularly in wartime. The distinction became even less clear in the 20th century when nations became more interdependent and the line between war and peace less clearly definable. As a result, the appearance of the term grand strategy (or higher strategy), meaning the art of employing all the resources of a nation or coalition of nations to achieve the objects of war (and peace), steadily became more popular in the literature of warfare and statecraft of the 20th century.

This broadened scope of strategy has tended to blur distinctions customarily drawn by earlier writers between strategy and statesmanship and between garden varieties and higher, or "grand," forms of strategy. Though there is still no agreed definition of the precise meaning of the term strategy, few students of the subject any longer accept the earlier narrow definition. Also, few contest that strategy, whether in its narrow or broad sense, will, by the very nature of its shifting bases, continue to be a changing art.

The search for principles. The starting point of all strategic planning and action is national policy. Once the national aims are set forth by the leaders of the state, the commander sets about drawing up his plans. He must take many matters into account; for example, factors of space and time, the state of his own forces, the enemy's capabilities and intentions, and reactions at home and abroad to his projected moves. The strategist deals in many uncertainties and imponderables. Indeed, the art of the strategist is the art of the "calculated risk."

The debate over the principles of strategy

The growing complexity of modern warfare has led some students to take a fresh look at the principles that have traditionally guided military strategists in war. It has long been a favourite occupation of military theorists to seek to distill from the great mass of military experience simple but all-pervasive truths—lists of principles—to guide commanders. Usually they have derived such principles from a study of campaigns of the great captains of history; occasionally outstanding practitioners have set them down on the basis of personal experience. As far back as 500 BC Sun Tzu, a Chinese general, set forth 13 principles. The axioms range from U.S. Civil War Gen. Nathan Bedford Forrest's simple admonition about getting there first with the most men to Napoleon's 115 maxims. The stress varies from list to list. It ranges from the emphasis of the followers and interpreters of the 19th-century theorist Carl von Clausewitz on the belief that the battle is all, and defeat of the enemy's armed forces the correct objective and path to victory, to that of exponents of "the strat-

egy of indirect approach," of victory by indirect methods.

Though there is no complete agreement on the number of principles, most lists include the following: the objective, the offensive, cooperation (unity of command), mass (concentration), economy of force, manoeuvre, surprise, security, and simplicity. The British have added one called "administration"; the Russians, another, translated as "annihilation." Despite debate over their precise number and meaning, the principles of war are widely taught, and most military students accept them as basic concepts.

The individual authors of the lists have almost uniformly claimed the principles to be immutable. They have argued that success in military strategy in the past has been the result of adhering to them and that the advantages of the offensive, the concentration of force, the effort to achieve surprise, the proper movement of forces and their security from attack, sabotage, or subversion are in the province of modern as well as ancient warfare. Some authorities have even argued that since war is not the concern of soldiers only, the "principles" deserve a wider application throughout government—in grand as well as military strategy.

Other authorities have argued that the claim of immutability cannot be accepted literally, that there is little agreement as to what the principles are and mean, that they overlap, that they are fluid and require constant reexamination, that they are not comparable with scientific laws since no two military situations are ever completely alike, that the so-called principles are not really principles at all but merely methods and commonsense procedures adopted by great commanders of the past, and that changes in the conditions of war alter their relative importance.

The debate over principles was renewed with the coming of the atomic era. Some theorists argued that the new weapons had destroyed whatever value the principles once had; others contended that the principles were as valid as ever, even more so. To some extent this was a debate over semantics. Defenders pointed out that each age must make its own applications of the "fundamental truths" of strategy. Opponents argued that there can be no set rules for the art; the so-called principles must by no means be interpreted as pat formulas for victory to be followed blindly and rigidly; the only sound guide in war and strategy is flexibility.

Relation between strategy and tactics. In the theory of warfare, strategy and tactics have generally been put into separate categories. The two fields have traditionally been defined in terms of different dimensions: strategy dealing with wide spaces, long periods of time, and large movements of forces, tactics dealing with the opposite. Strategy is usually understood to be the prelude to the battlefield, and tactics the action on the battlefield itself. As a result, much of the literature and theory of strategy has in the past been preoccupied with the proper approach to the battlefield, the leading of troops up to the time of contact with the enemy. This situation explains the attention to strategic manoeuvre—aimed at putting one's army into the most favourable position to engage the enemy and compelling the enemy to engage at a disadvantage and depriving him of freedom of movement. Indeed, early writers on strategy dealt heavily in the so-called "geometrical strategy"—the angles formed by lines of movement and supply of opposing armies.

Strategy viewed as the "prelude" to the battlefield

Despite distinctions in theory, strategy and tactics cannot always be separated in practice. In fact, the language of strategic manoeuvre (for example, "envelopment," "penetration," "encirclement") is also largely the language of tactics. Movement begets action, and action results in new movement. The one merges into the other. Strategy gives tactics its mission and wherewithal and seeks to reap the results. But tactics has also become an important conditioning factor of strategy, and as it changes, so does strategy. Battles and fronts are no longer necessarily restricted in space and time, and the distinction between battles and campaigns is no longer so clearcut, as the tridimensional warfare of World Wars I and II demonstrated. Indeed, in

World War II, theatre commanders were as much concerned with the actual fighting of armed forces in battle as they were with larger strategic decisions—*e.g.,* relations to allies, economic problems, and political questions on the ground. Although in theory strategy continues to occupy a middle ground between national policy and tactics, in practice the line dividing it from the other two fields has become increasingly difficult to draw.

Strategic leadership and war planning. Count Alfred von Schlieffen, the famous German military leader of the period just before World War I, once said: "A man is born, and not made, a strategist." But it is obvious that even a born strategist—if there be such a natural genius—has much to learn. In the past strategic leadership was a relatively simple affair. J.F.C. Fuller, the British student of warfare, pointed out in *The Foundations of the Science of War* (1926) that until relatively recent times the death, capture, or wounding of either of two opposing generals normally decided a conflict, "for the general *was* the plan." He could personally devise the plans and direct his troops. By mid-20th century this was rarely possible. As warfare has become complicated, strategic leadership has become more difficult. The art has taken on many more facets, and systematic training is required to master them. The strategist has retired from the scene of battle, and large, specialized staffs have grown up to help him. Although the responsibility for strategy remains the general's, many of his functions have been delegated to his planning staff. In modern states corporate leadership has become the rule in the management of military strategy, as in the direction of large business enterprises.

"Corporate" leadership in modern strategy

The example of an Alexander the Great completing his advance planning and leaping into battle at the head of his troops would in modern warfare be considered most unusual. Napoleon was wont to make his plans and then retire with his retinue of trusted advisers to survey the battlefield on horseback from the top of a hill. Generals in World War I were often pictured in their offices in large headquarters—usually in a chateau behind the lines, studying a map on the desk and dispatching orders via the telephone and motorcar at hand. In World War II the headquarters staffs of commanders in the theatres of war grew even larger and more elaborate. Tridimensional warfare—land, sea, and air—had enlarged the field of operations far beyond individual battlefields, and usually a high commander reached his decisions in a headquarters far removed from the field of battle and months before the battle itself took place. Far from striking the classic pose of the officer on a well-schooled charger, some of the greatest generals issued their orders from desks and fought their most important battles at conference tables. As strategic planning became a highly organized affair, planning committees and conferences in the capital cities of the warring powers made the blueprints for victory in the global, coalition struggle. In their capital command posts, military leaders kept in touch with the manifold phases of the national government's war effort and dealt with the worldwide problems transcending those of the individual theatres of war. With the aid of new devices for rapid communication, these leaders and their staffs sought to set the patterns of strategy and keep abreast of the movement of armies as the Caesars and Napoleons had done in earlier eras.

Strategic planning as a peacetime function

As war became more total, war planning became an increasingly significant peacetime function of governments. The manufacture of strategic plans has become a highly specialized industry in modern military establishments. At the same time, more and more governmental agencies have been drawn into the business of planning for national security. The plans they produce may vary from a simple design to shift a small task force to a danger spot to an elaborate plan for the conduct of war in its entirety. To be realistic, strategic plans and estimates must constantly be re-examined and brought into harmony.

Against this general background in the nature of the art, it is now possible to sketch the important contributions made in key periods to modern strategic theory and practice. It is important to remember that the art of strategy has changed from age to age, just as has war itself, and that each is the product of its own society and time.

HISTORICAL DEVELOPMENT OF STRATEGY

Though the serious and systematic study of modern strategy may be dated from the 18th century, various authorities have identified strategic precedents going back to earliest times. Students of warfare of primitive ages have associated with primitive tribes and clans a stratagem of surprise from darkness or by ambush, and they have identified a strategy of hunt and pounce, like that of a lion or tiger. The Bible points to the care with which Moses prepared his operations—an early form of advance planning. The ancient world developed a strategy of mass attack by phalanx, legion, or cavalry. Alexander, Hannibal, and Caesar, who combined in their own persons political and military direction of the state, planned their famous campaigns far ahead. They have been singled out as forerunners of the modern art of grand strategy. Writers in modern times have used the campaigns of these great captains to illustrate practically every known "principle of war." But important as their attention to strategic considerations in war and especially to strategic approaches to the battlefield may have been, the foundations of the ancient art of warfare were tactics and battles. To a considerable extent battles—often short and furious—also held the centre of the military stage in the European Middle Ages. Strategy was notably absent in the excursions of the Huns, the Muslims, and the crusaders. Far more important from a strategic viewpoint were the campaigns of Genghis Khan and his general, Sabutai, in the 13th century. Their advance planning and bold strategic manoeuvres in broad sweeps from Mongolia across Asia and Europe showed an appreciation of strategic problems most unusual for their age.

In the transition to modern times two other figures who touched on the field of strategy are often mentioned—Niccolò Machiavelli in the realm of military thought and Gustavus II Adolphus in the field of generalship. Machiavelli's *Art of War* (1520) emphasized the larger aspects of war, particularly the close relationship between the civil and military spheres. A century later, Gustavus, ruler-general of Sweden, intervened in the Thirty Years' War and, manoeuvring skillfully, drove his enemy's armies out of northern Germany.

18th-century warfare. After the death of Gustavus Adolphus in 1632, warfare again settled down to a slower pace and a more stable mold. The 17th and 18th centuries experienced the growth of professional armies loyal to the king. But the great cost of building and maintaining such armies led to a concern for their safety, a hesitation to risk them in bloody encounters, and a preoccupation with defense and fortifications. Strategy during this period was essentially of limited aim and was greatly concerned with the art of siegecraft, for which elaborate rules were prescribed. In Prussia of the mid-18th century, however, circumstances compelled Frederick the Great to try a new and aggressive approach and to break through the accepted military pattern of the day.

Confronted at the outset of the Seven Years' War (1756–63) by a coalition of Austria, France, Russia, Sweden, and Saxony, Frederick found himself virtually surrounded. His task was to devise a strategy to defend his territory and not to dissipate his outnumbered troops. The strategy he evolved did not follow set rules or recipes. Indeed, never was the definition of strategy as a "system of makeshifts"—offered in a later age by the Prussian general Count Helmuth von Moltke—better demonstrated. In his planning Frederick capitalized on two valuable assets—his army, a superior and highly disciplined instrument of war, and a central position. He sought always to keep the initiative, to attack first one enemy and then another, to assemble at decisive points a force superior to that of his foe, and to avoid long, drawn-out wars. Using his central position to concentrate against individual armies of the enemy before they could be reinforced by others, he developed the classical "strategy of interior lines." But even Frederick, the statesman-warrior, could not entirely escape the conditions imposed by the warfare of his times. Indeed, the statesman imposed caution on the warrior. He could not expose his costly armies to the risk of destruction and bloody decision by battle. His battles were not those of

The aggressive, flexible strategies of Frederick the Great

annihilation. In the end his wars were decided by reasons of state, and those wars left his nation exhausted.

The age that immediately followed Frederick chose to imitate his caution rather than his aim. Military theory was characterized by ideas of victory without battle, manoeuvring for position, a system of lines and angles of operation. Geometric concepts and cunning tricks and artifices replaced the aim to destroy enemies. Great emphasis was put on terrain and the occupation of key geographic points. The 18th century, it must be remembered, was the era of enlightenment, and warfare conformed to the spirit of the age. Strategy, like all warfare, became "mathematical" and "scientific." Theorists optimistically maintained that a general who knew mathematics and topography could direct campaigns with geometrical precision and win wars without even fighting. But the new mode of warfare ushered in by the French Revolution and the Napoleonic era was soon to challenge these optimistic assumptions.

Napoleonic warfare. The French Revolutionary and the Napoleonic periods (1789–1815) witnessed great changes in the methods of war—the revolution in society accompanying and reinforcing the one in warfare. When Napoleon, the first great military strategist of the modern Western world, burst upon the European scene, the groundwork for a new age in warfare had already been laid. The French Revolution gave birth (1793) to the "nation in arms," and all Frenchmen became liable for military service. The patriotic citizen-soldier succeeded the mercenary professional. Skirmish tactics, or the loose formation, replaced the straight line; divisional organization came into use, along with light-weight artillery of great range and firing power. When Napoleon came to reap the benefits of these changes, he completely transformed strategy as well as tactics. He applied the same basic principle to the one as to the other—never to divide his forces but to concentrate all his might against the enemy forces at the critical point. His emphasis was on careful preparation, on uniting his forces before the action, on overpowering weight of striking power, on shock attack, on great daring, and on bloody decision by battle. His methods were simple, direct, overpowering—even brutal; his aim was nothing short of the destruction of the enemy forces. Against such power, neat geometric calculations stood little chance and ordinary stratagems were helpless. Again and again he showed his military genius for bringing a mass to bear against the flanks of his enemy, for selection of battle-grounds advantageous to his forces, and for deploying his forces for battle. He gave supreme expression to the idea of victory by battle.

The Napoleonic weaknesses in grand strategy Though as a military leader, operational strategist, and tactician of the battlefield he is regarded by many as unparalleled, in the larger field of national or grand strategy he had shortcomings. Embodying in his own person the leadership of the state and its military affairs, he recognized the value of incorporating political and economic measures, along with military moves, to increase the chances of victory in war. But he could not successfully grasp and cope with the challenge finally put to him by Great Britain and its European allies. British strategy sought to meet the Napoleonic threat to Europe by using naval power to blockade the Continent and by conducting a war of exhaustion on land through peripheral warfare, such as the Duke of Wellington's famous campaign on the Iberian Peninsula. Napoleon's reply to the British naval blockade was the continental system prohibiting British goods from entering. But this helped bring his downfall, since he was needed everywhere—to hold the coast, fight in Spain, Holland, against Austria and Russia. His veteran French forces were dissipated, and he had to rely on impressed nationalities of Europe. Eventually the coalition of his enemies was to use the methods and means of warfare that the French Revolution had introduced and Napoleon had perfected to re-invigorate their own forces and overwhelm him.

Despite his mistakes, Napoleon's pre-eminent place in the history of strategy is secure. His tactics and strategy influenced military leaders for a century. His maxims were widely studied and were said to have been carried in the saddlebag of the famous Confederate general of the U.S.

Civil War, Thomas J. ("Stonewall") Jackson. Students of strategy have long pointed to Napoleon's battles and campaigns for classical illustrations of "principles" of war—of surprise, mobility, concentration of force, and economy of force. Possibly more than that of any other general, his competent practice oriented modern military theory toward the search for underlying principles. Indeed, the art of strategy as evolved by theorists since 1800 may be traced largely to his operations.

Carl von Clausewitz. For this development two great interpreters of Napoleonic strategy, Antoine-Henri Jomini and Carl von Clausewitz, were especially responsible. Clausewitz (1780–1831), a Prussian, was the first great student of strategy and the father of modern strategical study. Trained in systematic study of philosophy in the school of Immanuel Kant, it was natural for him to range widely over the whole field of military knowledge and to reduce Napoleonic warfare to a unified philosophical conception. His famous work, *On War,* written as an outgrowth of his studies of Napoleon's campaigns, remains the best general study of the art of war. He died with his work unfinished, but his writings published after his death became the standard textbooks on war in Prussia and elsewhere. Their influence was felt profoundly in the Franco-Prussian War of 1870, and leading generals of World Wars I and II were brought up on them and on the works of his followers.

The contributions of Clausewitz to strategic thought are many and diverse. To some his work is the Bible of strategy, and, like that great book, susceptible to many conflicting interpretations. His work set forth fully and clearly for the first time the relationship between political and military leadership. He dwelt on decision by battle as the first rule of war, on seeking the destruction of the enemy's forces, and on achieving superiority at the decisive spot. Rejecting the optimism and rationalism of the 18th century, he held that war was not a scientific game but an act of violence. Mathematical and topographical factors, he held, were important in tactics but less so in strategy. "We . . . do not hesitate," he asserted, "to regard as an established truth that in strategy more depends on the number and the magnitude of the victorious combats than on the form of the great lines by which they are connected" (*On War,* vol. 1, bk. 3, ch. xv, p. 223; Routledge & Kegan Paul, Ltd., London, 1940). The key to victory was battle, however bloody. He defined strategy as the employment of battles to gain the end of war. Clausewitz on the relations between political and military strategy

Clausewitz devoted much of his work to showing that war is both a social development and a political act. He went further and said that "War is not merely a political act, but also a real political instrument, a continuation of policy carried out by other means" (Maj. Gen. Sir F. Maurice, *British Strategy,* p. 44; Constable & Co., Ltd., London, 1929). War was therefore not an independent phenomenon unto itself to be handed over to soldiers and sailors. Again and again he asserted that military and political strategy must go hand in hand. "War," he declared, "admittedly has its own grammar, but not its own logic" (*On War*).

Clausewitz' emphasis on the aim of strategy as the destruction of the enemy's forces on the battlefield has had a great influence on subsequent military thinking. His disciples, however, have generally overlooked the fact that he also recognized another strategical form—a strategy of limited aim for limited warfare, of wearing down an opponent. When Clausewitz wrote, warfare was conducted in two dimensions, and it was rarely possible for one nation to impose its will without first destroying the opposing army. But Clausewitz recognized clearly what many of his followers in subsequent generations forgot, that the destruction was only a means to enforce policy and not an end in itself.

Antoine Jomini. In the history of military thought, the French general Antoine-Henri Jomini (1779–1869), one of Napoleon's staff officers and a contemporary of Clausewitz, presents a striking contrast to the Prussian philosopher of war. Lacking the philosophical bent of Clausewitz, Jomini concentrated his thinking on what he regarded as practical issues in war rather than on war as a whole. He became the chief expounder of Napoleonic methods, and out of his studies evolved a theory of strategy. Although he opposed "systems of war" purporting to provide for all contingencies, he nevertheless believed that in the field of strategy certain rules and general principles—eternally true—could and should be formulated "as a compass for the commander-in-chief of an army." To establish these principles, he believed, was the major problem of military science.

Jomini's emphasis on geography

The heart of Jomini's theory lay in the theatre of war and the campaign. But he thought primarily of occupying all or part of the enemy's territory rather than of annihilating his army. This occupation was to be achieved by progressive domination of zones of territory. Jomini emphasized throughout his work the proper choice by the general of decisive manoeuvring lines and their adaptation to geometrical configurations of zones of operation. Campaigns must be carefully planned in advance. The task of strategy is to make preliminary plans—to establish lines of operation and to bring military means into conformity with geographic realities of the chosen zone of operations. He laid down two basic principles: massing troops against fractions of the enemy by rapid movement and striking in the most decisive direction.

Jomini's great contribution to military thought lay in his definition of the place of strategy in warfare. Probably more than any other work, his *Précis de l'art de la guerre* fixed the major fields of modern military art. Subsequent wars were to cast doubt on much of his work, particularly on his conception of geographical campaigns and of the superiority of interior lines of operation. But, like Clausewitz in German strategic thinking, Jomini had an enduring influence on French military thought. His emphasis on planning for operations and on intelligence took root in military staffs and schools throughout Europe, and his work became the textbook for the conduct of the U.S. Civil War.

U.S. Civil War to World War I. Often called the first of the really modern wars, the U.S. Civil War (1861–65) marked a transition to a new era in strategy. It gathered up new phenomena that had begun to influence warfare in the middle of the 19th century and whose fuller consequences were to be felt in the half century that followed. It was a period marked by refinement of the old in strategic theory and practice and by the addition of new strands— by such famous figures as Robert E. Lee, Ulysses S. Grant, and William T. Sherman on the battlefield and Count von Moltke, Count von Schlieffen, Hans Delbrück, and Alfred T. Mahan in the literature of strategy.

Strategies of North and South in the U.S. Civil War.

Modern technology, economy, and manpower in the U.S. Civil War

The Civil War is significant in the history of strategy in a number of ways. The basis of strategy—particularly factors of time and space—began to change. The use of steam power for land and water military transportation received its first major test. Railroads gave strategy a new speed of movement but tended to make strategy stick to straight lines and fixed routes. The Civil War also tested ironclad ships and heavy naval ordnance. The relation among the combat arms was completely upset by the introduction of the long-range infantry rifle. The accuracy of long-range weapons in the hands of defending infantry shattered the effectiveness of the rapidly concentrated attack in which Napoleonic strategy had culminated. But, as so often has been noted in the history of warfare, armaments and weapons are more readily changed than ideas, and Napoleon's principles continued to be maintained, sometimes with disastrous consequences on the battlefield.

Aside from the effect of new inventions, the Civil War revealed the growing importance of the economy and manpower in war. Industry was called on more and more, and conscription was adopted to provide manpower. The war also revealed the impact of systematic West Point training received by the leading generals on both sides. Finally, the Civil War was long studied for classic examples of manoeuvre and of offensive and defensive strategy and for lessons in the relation among policy, strategy, and means of war. Essentially the Civil War demonstrated local or theatre strategy and tactics. Though elements of grand strategy were at hand—political, economic, military, and psychological—the art was still not well understood or

consistently applied. Despite conscription and the partial mobilization of industry and the railroads, there was no well-worked-out grand design correlating the widely scattered forces and the war industries that supported them.

Effects of political objectives on strategy

The strategies of the North and South were rooted in different political objectives. The objective of the North was to prevent the Confederate states from seceding from the Union, that of the South was to attain independence. Because the South was greatly inferior to the North in population and resources, it could not hope to conquer the North. The dual purposes of its strategy were to convince the North that forcing the South to remain in the Union was not worth the cost and to bring about foreign intervention in favour of the South. Gen. Robert E. Lee, the great Southern leader, believed the best way to realize these objectives was to carry the war into the North and to defeat the Northern armies in their own territory. For a time, therefore, his strategy was essentially offensive. But after his defeat at Gettysburg, Pennsylvania, he no longer had the wherewithal to continue the offensive, and at the same time it became obvious that foreign intervention would not be forthcoming. From that time to the end of the war his strategy was defensive, with the object of wearing down the patience, if not the power, of the North.

To achieve its political object, the North, on the other hand, developed another strategy. The Federal design had three main goals: (1) to blockade and isolate the Confederacy, (2) to cut it in two, and (3) to strike at Richmond, Virginia, its capital. The naval blockade, though not completely effective, brought virtual commercial isolation to the South. Partition was gained by capturing Vicksburg on the Mississippi in July 1863 and by severing the east–west railroad connections. The capture of Vicksburg cut the South off from its sources of supplies beyond the Mississippi. Only gradually did the North change its design from that of attacking Richmond to that of striking at the main army of the Confederacy and the remaining sources of supply. Grant's elevation to the supreme command of the armies in March 1864 enabled him to put this concept into effect. The famous march of Gen. William T. Sherman through Georgia to the sea in the fall of 1864 was an outstanding example of strategic manoeuvre and surprise. Leaving his supply line, Sherman feinted against one city and attacked another, finally cutting off Lee's army in Virginia from its war resources in the South. The cooperation of the Federal eastern and western armies in a grand converging movement resulted in the evacuation of Richmond and, finally, in the surrender of Lee's army to Grant at Appomattox Court House in Virginia in April 1865.

The period from the close of the Civil War to the outbreak of World War I saw the further growth of trends already apparent. Space and time factors began to appear in a new light. A nation with a well-developed railway net gained significant advantages in war. The speed of mobilizing and concentrating armies became a basic element in strategic calculations, and the timetable based on it became the heart of staff plans drawn up in anticipation of war. Increased firepower in the machine gun, universal liability of able-bodied males for military service, rapid mobilization of reserve military units, and increased potential of fortifications influenced military planning.

The Prussian-German strategists. Strategic thinking in the half century before World War I showed a remarkable diversity. To the Prussian-German school—Moltke and Schlieffen—the new trends in warfare seemed to reinforce Clausewitz' teachings about battles and the aim of defeating the enemy's armies.

Moltke's emphasis on offense and "ad hoc expedients"

To Field Marshal Count Helmuth von Moltke (1800– 91) belongs the chief credit for molding the Prussian army into a formidable war machine, which defeated the Danes (1864), Austrians (1866), and French (1870–71). Moltke agreed with Clausewitz that battles were the primary means of breaking the will of the enemy. But Moltke did not believe a strategist could follow a rigid set of rules. To him strategy was a system of "ad hoc expedients." It was "the art of action under the pressure of the most difficult conditions." No plan of operations, he believed, could look with any assurance beyond the first encounter with the main enemy forces. The offensive, according to Moltke, is "the straight way to the goal," whereas the defensive is "the long way around." He became famous for his skillful conduct of operations on the outer line leading to encirclement. In addition to exploiting the altered conditions of space and time created by the railroads and improved highways, he capitalized on the possibilities offered by the telegraph for handling armies of great size. Recognizing that the field of operations had become too vast to be surveyed by the eye of the commander, he introduced a new system of delegating power to subordinate commanders. Broad directives took the place of detailed orders. Moltke always fought with superior forces, and his wars, culminating in that against France in 1870–71, are regarded by some authorities as classical models of conception and execution in military strategy.

The Schlieffen plan and "strategy of annihilation"

Field Marshal Count Alfred von Schlieffen (1833–1913), chief of the Prussian general staff before World War I and ablest of Moltke's successors, carried the strong line of strategic reasoning running from Napoleon through Clausewitz and Moltke to its logical conclusion in his conception of a "strategy of annihilation." Like Moltke, he stressed the military side of strategy, the concentration on decisive victory by battle. But, unlike Moltke, he could not count on superior forces and had to prepare for war on two fronts. The basis for German strategy before World War I as developed by him was embodied in the famous Schlieffen plan. The plan was extremely simple. The bulk of the German forces were to attack the nearest opponent, the one in the west (France), and to defeat him in a great battle; meanwhile, in the east (Russia) the Germans would stand on the defensive. Schlieffen proposed to gain the decision in the great battle by means of an enveloping attack—if possible, by a double envelopment. Once the enemy in the west was defeated, the Germans would attack the foe in the east. This was the essence of the plan with which the Germans entered World War I.

Schlieffen's theories were to have wide influence, largely through his book *Cannae*. Analyzing Hannibal's great victory over the Romans in 216 BC, he had developed his theory of the battle of annihilation by means of encirclement and double envelopment. The decisive German campaign against the Russians at Tannenberg, East Prussia, in August 1914 was fought in this mold, and Schlieffen's theories were studied exhaustively in the higher army schools of the United States and Europe after World War I. As Gen. Walter Bedell Smith, chief of staff to Gen. Dwight D. Eisenhower, supreme commander of the Allied Expeditionary Force in World War II, pointed out, General Eisenhower and many of his staff officers, products of these schools, "were imbued with the idea of this type of wide, bold maneuver for decisive results."

Combined political and military strategy. Moltke and Schlieffen thought of war as military action—the speediest decisive defeat of the main opponent. But the closing years of the 19th and early years of the 20th centuries witnessed the emergence of new approaches and different emphases in strategy. Two thinkers looking to past history for light on the problems of their times made signal contributions to strategic theory—one, Alfred Thayer Mahan (1840–1914), an American, in the field of naval strategy, the other, Hans Delbrück (1848–1929), a German, in the area of military strategy. Each recognized an intimate relationship between war and politics in every age, that political and military (or naval) strategy must be in harmony. Each showed an awareness of the growing importance of the economic bases of strategy, of state policy, geographic position, and available means as determinants of the mode of strategy, and of accommodating strategic action to suit the particular times and needs.

Delbrück's "strategy of exhaustion"

Carrying forward a line of thinking already suggested by Clausewitz, Delbrück presented his theory of the "strategy of exhaustion"—of wearing down an opponent by a variety of means. Clausewitz had merely indicated the existence of two methods of conducting war—one aimed at annihilation of the enemy, the other limited warfare. Delbrück expounded on the differences. The sole aim of the strategy of annihilation he identified as the decisive battle. The second type he called variously the "strategy

of exhaustion" and "two-pole strategy." The commander could move between battle and manoeuvre; the political object of war could be obtained by other means than battle—by occupying territory, blockade, destroying crops or commerce. In Delbrück's view, Alexander, Caesar, and Napoleon had been strategists of annihilation; Pericles, Gustavus II Adolphus, and Frederick the Great, equally great generals, exponents of the strategy of exhaustion. Holding that the strategy of exhaustion was just as valid as the strategy of annihilation—each depending on the political aims and means at hand—Delbrück's theories ran counter to the military thinking of his day and brought down a storm of criticism about his head. But he persisted in reminding his age, intent on victory by battle, of other important and forgotten aspects of Clausewitz' teachings.

Mahan's strategy of sea power. While Delbrück was battling his military critics in Germany, a scholarly navy captain and teacher at the Naval War College in Newport, Rhode Island, was quietly breaking ground in pursuing his brilliant researches in military and naval history and strategy. This pioneer was Alfred Thayer Mahan, indefatigable student of the strategy of Napoleon and Jomini. His masterly works, *The Influence of Sea Power upon History, 1660–1783* (published in 1890) and *The Influence of Sea Power upon the French Revolution and Empire, 1793–1812* (published in 1892), marked a revolution in naval thought. While advances in technology were affecting naval architecture and weapons, and steam, armour plate, and rifled guns were coming into vogue, Mahan aimed to bring naval strategic thinking up to date. The books and articles that poured from his pen down to World War I about warfare of the second dimension—the sea—had a profound influence on the theory of warfare and on naval policy and strategy in many countries.

An advocate of a big navy, of overseas bases, of national greatness through sea power, he was the American apostle of "looking outward." Mahan emphasized the significance of commerce in war and of economic warfare through the application of sea power. His researches convinced him that the nation or group of nations that commanded the seas could best draw on the trade, wealth, and economic resources of the world and was the more likely to win wars. Strongly influenced by Jomini's teachings, he looked for fundamental truths and formulated "principles" of naval strategy. Naval strategy and sea power, he recognized, were conditioned by a nation's insular or continental situation. To Mahan, a central position gave the same great advantages on the sea or on land—interior lines. Concentration of force he viewed as a fundamental principle of land and sea warfare. The backbone of fleet strength, in his opinion, was the battleship or capital ship. Under Mahan's tutelage, command of the sea approaches took the place of the twin theories of coastal defense and commerce raiding that hitherto held sway in American naval strategy. His concepts of naval strategy and faith in preponderant naval power and the use of the navy as an instrument of national power were accepted by the U.S. Navy and Pres. Theodore Roosevelt. His doctrines stimulated the trend toward overseas expansion and growth of the navies of the world between 1898 and 1914. The sudden acquisition of an overseas empire in the Spanish-American War of 1898 greatly changed the strategic position and problems of the United States. Its emergence as a world power, beginning in these years, was to have important bearings on the strategic balance of power among the nations of the world, an equilibrium that World War I altered profoundly.

World War I. World War I, the first of the great coalition wars of the 20th century, was an important landmark in the story of the evolution of modern strategy. Never was the phenomenon of cultural lag as applied to warfare more clearly demonstrated. Beginning in the accepted mold of strategic planning popular since 1870, it soon ran head on into countertrends that were altering the very bases of strategic action and that strategic thinking in the intervening years had not yet fully grasped. Despite the experiences in the South African and Russo-Japanese wars with the machine gun as a defensive weapon of tremendous firepower, French and German military leaders at

The failure of mass offensives in 1914

the outbreak of the war continued to put their faith in the offensive. In fact, they were convinced that new weapons and methods of control, the radio and telephone, actually improved the offensive capabilities of their mass armies. The universal underestimation of the effect of modern firearms on the defense had important repercussions on strategy both during and after the war.

The first moves in the war began in 1914 as French and German strategists had planned. In seven days the Germans concentrated over 3,000,000 men on the eastern and western fronts from mobilization points. In approximately the same time the French assembled 1,200,000 men on the western front. Both sides made heavy use of railroad lines to speed assembly of great masses of troops. Both sides were determined to attack. Out of the movements of mass armies came the first battles on the frontiers. As Schlieffen had planned, the Germans catapulted into Belgium, but the enveloping wing was not as strong as Schlieffen, who had died the previous year, had wished. It was compressed into a smaller corridor by the political decision not to violate Dutch neutrality. The anticipated six-week campaign of annihilation against France envisaged by Schlieffen could not be executed. The French attack also soon hit a snag. Though the French Army's right wing reached the Rhine, its centre was endangered by a German pincer movement. Only a hasty retreat and a counteroffensive at the Marne River saved Paris. "Pinwheel strategy"—each side attacking and driving the enemy back—had stalled badly.

Meanwhile, on the eastern front, the German prewar strategy of holding until France had been quickly defeated was compromised by the desire of the Austrian ally to push against the Russians, partners of the French. The German victory at Tannenberg counterbalanced the Austrian defeat at Lemberg (Lvov). The eastern front became stabilized.

By the close of 1914 the war had become a stalemate on both the eastern and western fronts. The conflict had resolved itself into trench warfare from Switzerland to the English Channel. Machine guns and artillery took over the battlefield. The conflict had settled down into a war of position, and strategic mobility was lost. World War I became a classic case of arrested strategy.

The first phase of the war was over by the end of 1914. Prewar plans had failed; the war of movement, of mass offensives, had ceased. The big question thenceforth was how to dig the war out of the trenches. In answering that question important elements of grand strategy came into play. The heavy demands upon industry for munitions of war multiplied, and technology was called upon for new means—the tank and poison gas—of breaking the stalemate. Britain's naval blockade to starve Germany took on added significance. The German countermeasures helped bring the United States into the war in 1917. But the United States was not prepared for war, and the buildup of its forces across the Atlantic was slow. The Germans, seeking in 1918 to forestall the full impact of U.S. might, put their resources into a great offensive that came close to succeeding. When the Americans finally arrived in force, they played a valuable part in military strategy in reducing the salients within the Allied lines. Eventually the German allies were defeated; the German armies reached a point of exhaustion and the homeland a stage of semistarvation. Germany asked for an armistice.

Blend of political, military, economic, and psychological factors

Though much has been written about World War I, the strategic lessons of that conflict for coalition warfare have not been fully comprehended. Never was the dependence of strategy on statecraft more clearly demonstrated. As political circumstances of the war changed, strategy changed. The Central Powers, led by Germany and Austria-Hungary, never had a common plan of campaign or effective unity of command. The Allied side achieved unity only under the pressure of necessity. Along with the military factors, economic and psychological considerations proved important in conducting the war and gaining the victory. Though the aim of annihilating the enemy was paramount with both sides—especially in the opening campaigns—the desire to exhaust him also influenced strategy, and fresh confirmation was given to Moltke's description of strategy as a "system of makeshifts."

Military leaders in World War I had to master three basic factors in strategic calculations: masses of men, technological advances, and wide areas. The movement of huge masses became an art in itself, for armies had taken on unprecedented dimensions. Millions of men were in action. Railroads and motor transport became important not only for concentrations but also for establishing new strategic points on the fronts themselves. The arena of war embraced whole continents. Battles lasted for days and weeks, and the fighting continued even after the great battles were over.

New weapons came into play. Aerial reconnaissance enabled a commander to gain some insight into the enemy's intentions and movements. New means of communication—telephone, radio telegraphy, the automobile, and the airplane—promoted faster execution of orders and unified command over widely scattered forces. The overwhelming firepower of modern weapons checked the effectiveness of the attack, long considered the ideal path to victory. The tank, however, offered fresh possibilities in redressing the balance between the defensive and the offensive. Tactics became more than ever a prelude and conditioning factor of strategy, since without freedom of movement, strategy was only an academic exercise. Tactics came to mark the beginning rather than the conclusion of an operation.

But there were also larger strategic influences at work. If World War I was a war of masses, it was also a war of matériel. War was becoming increasingly total and cut deeper into the life of the nation. Some of the foremost leaders and students of World War I—notably Winston Churchill and Georges Clemenceau—recognized that military strategy had become but a part of a greater national strategy. Symptomatic of this thinking was Clemenceau's widely quoted statement that war was too important a business to be left to soldiers. More than ever strategy and politics would have to be correlated. The increasing totality of modern war would have to be matched by a broader national strategy. But the large impact of the war in the international sphere—the effects of the defeat of Germany, the weakening of England and France, the rise of the Soviet Union on the strategic balance of power in the world—could not yet be foreseen.

Between World Wars I and II. The period between 1918 and 1939 saw strategy once more in process of flux. As an outgrowth of the experience of World War I, strategy came largely to mean defense. In France, particularly, a mentality favouring fixed defenses began to take hold, eventually leading to the building of the concrete fortifications of the Maginot Line, bordering Germany. The belief was strong that field fortifications aided by the machine gun would contain any attack. The huge losses of World War I would thereby be avoided.

The importance of air power and motorization

Countertrends, however, were soon to dispute this prevalent emphasis in strategic thinking. One strong challenge came from the new school of exponents of air power. In World War I the air arm had had its beginnings. The period between the end of World War I and the beginning of World War II saw it come into its own; air forces and air organization expanded greatly. Theorists began to develop the strategy of warfare of the third dimension. Foremost among these was the Italian general Giulio Douhet (1869–1930). He first presented the doctrine that the air arm alone would decide wars of the future. In his view, land and sea forces would no longer be decisive. On the ground, armies could act henceforth only on the defensive, since attack, and with it the decision, could be gained only through the air. Air power could quickly conquer time and space. The air arm could circumvent every kind of ground resistance and nullify fortified positions and obstacles of terrain. It could strike at the enemy's sources of power before his armies could fire a shot. It could strike at his capital, industrial centres, and communications. In short, it could so reduce his ability and willingness to resist that he would surrender. Douhet proposed to expand the air arm as much as possible, keep land and sea forces only as support for war in the air, and gain control of the air by defeating enemy air forces in battles or destroying them in their airfields. He made strategic bombing and the industrial objective—strikes at the opponent's heart—the core of his doctrines.

Douhet's epoch-making ideas found many supporters in other countries. This school of thought generally argued that huge armies would no longer be necessary. The opponent's will could be overcome even if his armed forces remain undefeated. Some of Douhet's adherents went further and demanded the abolition of land and sea forces altogether. In any event, the rise of air power accentuated the need of thinking of strategy as dealing with something more than the movements of armies on land or of ships at sea.

Meanwhile, army leaders began to advocate another solution to break the strategic stalemate of World War I. To overcome the superiority of the defensive, they put their faith in developing a modern cavalry of tanks and armoured, motor-driven vehicles. The best known among the great champions of mechanization and motorization that arose in Great Britain was Maj. Gen. J.F.C. Fuller (1878–1966). These advocates saw in the armoured vehicle, combining firepower, extreme mobility, and armoured protection, the best answer to overcoming defensive forces relying on machine guns. This system was particularly suited to needs of an insular country, protected by a strong air force and navy, and of a relatively small army intended primarily for expeditionary purposes in support of continental allies. But this solution on the ground found support in Germany, Russia, and the United States. In France, Charles de Gaulle bucked the strong tide of opinion and advocated tank warfare to restore a strategy of mobility and the offensive.

In the late 1930s the Germans combined air power and tanks into a new form of assault that also aimed to overthrow defensive superiority. Developing a highly mobile form of warfare for lightning strikes and mechanized attacks, they were to contribute the art of the blitzkrieg—the spearhead of a conquering, offensive strategy that Hitler unleashed in World War II.

The theory of total war

In Germany, too, other influences supporting offensive strategy came to the fore. To overcome strategic stalemate of the World War I variety, the German general Erich Ludendorff contributed his theory of total war. He envisaged total mobilization of a nation's manpower and resources for war. The nation at war would be led by a supreme military commander; strategy would dictate policy. The concept of total war moved geography and economics into prominent positions in Nazi thinking. Even before World War I the British geographer Halford J. Mackinder had posed the potential threat of a heartland power, in control of Eurasia, to sea power—a counter to Mahan's theory of control of the seas. The German geopoliticians after the war took over the "heartlands" concept, and through their teachings the concept of control of Eurasia became imbedded in Nazi statecraft. Their doctrines gave support to the main strands in Hitler's offensive strategy—continental expansion, autarky (national economic self-sufficiency), and *Lebensraum* ("living space").

Before war burst upon Europe in 1939, it was apparent that important changes also were brewing in naval strategy. All major sea powers were producing high-speed battleships, and the aircraft carrier was becoming a significant and integral member of the fleet. In the crucible of World War II, the emerging elements in ground, air, naval, and nonmilitary strategy were to take clearer shape.

World War II. Strategy came into its own in World War II. Global and coalition warfare on an unprecedented scale required global and coalition strategy to match it. The new trends in military, air, and naval strategy were put to the test. At the same time, the worldwide conflict lifted strategy out of the purely military sphere into the field of grand strategy and international relations. The war cut more deeply than ever into every phase of life. It touched all nations, directly or indirectly, all continents and oceans, the air, the land, and the sea. Political, economic, technological, and psychological factors were drawn into the web of the strategy of all-out effort. The strategy for war grown increasingly total was conditioned by massive armed forces, revolutionary scientific and technological advances, tridimensional warfare, and miracles of industrial production and logistics.

World War II began with independent offensive moves of the Axis nations—Germany, Italy, and Japan. Though these nations formed a war coalition, they never formulated a common blueprint of strategy or achieved the degree of cooperation that the Allied coalition did. The Axis war effort nevertheless marked an epoch-making development in strategy. The Axis concept of total war, particularly as developed in Nazi philosophy, revealed more clearly than before that the traditional view of strategy—the art of employing military forces—was too narrow. Diplomacy, propaganda, espionage, geography, economics, technology, and morale all entered into the Nazi concept of strategy. In Nazi strategy, the line between war and peace could no longer be clearly defined. The course of Hitler's campaigns, before and after the outbreak of actual war in 1939, showed that military operations and battles were only the last resort against an enemy, to be applied after all other modes of conquest had failed. Hitler early recognized that armed forces are only one of many means available to grand strategy. Indeed, his greatest victories were the bloodless ones before the war was joined in September 1939, following the invasion of Poland. Thereafter, military strategy perforce came into greater play. Like Caesar and Napoleon, Hitler combined in his own person the two functions of strategy and policy. But his reputation as a military strategist was not to compare with his early triumphs in political warfare.

The Nazi implementation of total war

Hitler gave the art of offensive strategy a new twist. Like Napoleon, he failed to master all the elements of grand strategy. But in developing and correlating an assortment of modern means of breaking an enemy's will, he showed himself to be far ahead of his opponents.

Despite great German blitzkrieg victories on the Continent, successes in the Middle East, and strategic bombardment of England, the winter of 1941 found Germany still without the victory it sought. Though it had tried to avoid a two-front war, by June 1941 it had become embroiled with the U.S.S.R. In December the Japanese struck at Pearl Harbor, and the United States came in to aid England and the U.S.S.R. against the Axis powers. The worldwide strategic contest was then joined in earnest. The Axis nations had the advantage of interior lines; the Allies, other than Russia, had to fight on exterior lines, and their lines of support had to fan out from the factories of Britain and the United States all over the world. Inevitably the Allies turned to the strategic weapon of blockade against the Axis powers, and Germany and Japan turned to submarine warfare to cripple the Allied lifelines.

The story of Allied strategy in World War II is the search for common denominators among three sovereign powers drawn together in a grand alliance by a common bond of danger. From the beginning, the inner web of the Grand Alliance was the close relationship between the United States and Great Britain. The Soviet Union's part in developing and directing the combined strategy of the war was to be relatively small. Compared with the worldwide demands facing the United States and Great Britain, its strategic problem was simple, consisting of war on only one front at a time; it did not enter the conflict with Japan until the closing days of World War II. Thus the Russians took formal part in strategic decisions only at the international conferences at Moscow (October 1943), Tehrān (November 1943), Yalta (February 1945), and Potsdam (July 1945), and even these were called at the initiative of the Western powers. Throughout World War II, the Russians remained outside the combined staff system, developed for the coordination of the western effort in the global war.

The elements of the Grand Alliance

The basic procedures for formulating Allied strategy emerged in 1941 and 1942. In January 1942, Britain and the United States joined to establish the Combined Chiefs of Staff (CCS), the agency for hammering out Allied strategy and for day-to-day conduct of the war. Since the three principal British military officers for army, air, and navy normally had to direct the operations of their services from London, they sent senior representatives to function for them in the Combined Chiefs of Staff. The American members were the U.S. Joint Chiefs of Staff, composed of the president's chief of staff and the senior officers of the army, navy, and army air forces. The CCS was a unique organization in coalition machinery. Decisions were arrived at by common agreement; no votes were taken. The leaders concerted policies and plans, outlined strategies, discussed timing of operations, approved programs of allocations, and measured requirements against resources. Their decisions were, of course, subject to the approval of Pres. Franklin D. Roosevelt and Prime Minister Winston Churchill.

The Prime Minister and the President, who were over and above the CCS system, were responsible for all decisions. Each wore two hats—one political, the other military. As political leaders they sometimes had more in common with each other than with their respective staffs. Advising Churchill at the summit of the British system of intragovernmental planning was a war cabinet with which the chiefs of staff committee sat. Although President Roosevelt could and did draw on the assistance of the war-born U.S. joint staff system, he never established anything remotely resembling the British war cabinet. The differences between the two politico-military systems— one loosely built, the other closely tied—were sometimes strikingly illustrated at the international war conferences.

The full-dress Anglo-American conferences usually came about when planning had reached a point where top-level decisions on important matters of Allied strategy and policy were necessary. The conferences and the CCS system provided the framework for the important decisions in European and Asian strategy. Decisions in the war in the Pacific against Japan were handled somewhat differently. The U.S. Joint Chiefs of Staff, who were early given the responsibility for this war, submitted their decisions on plans and operations against Japan to the conferences. There the combined chiefs usually gave their stamp of approval.

Beneath the top-level machinery, and funnelling into it, was a whole network of specialized combined and joint planning agencies. At the bottom of the hierarchy lay the planning staffs of the individual services in the capitals. Unique among them on the American side was the War Department's Operations Division, which, under the army chief of staff, Gen. George C. Marshall, developed into the "Washington command post" to control the strategic deployment and activities of the army forces scattered all over the world. As the war progressed, the highly organized planning machinery in the capitals was supplemented by the big theatre headquarters staffs. Such theatre commanders as General Eisenhower in the European theatre and Gen. Douglas MacArthur in the southwest Pacific began to play an increasingly important role in strategic decisions. The vast and speedy network of telecommunications circling the globe enabled strategic plans and decisions to be quickly made and executed. Never had the processes and machinery of strategic planning been so highly organized as in World War II.

From the beginning of discussions, the western partners agreed that the first and major object of Anglo-American grand strategy must be the defeat of Germany. Political expediency combined with geography and logistics in arriving at this decision—perhaps the single most important one made by the British and U.S. in World War II. British and Soviet power lay close to Germany. Great Britain offered a base for massing western air power; in the Mediterranean, operations against Germany could soon be undertaken. The Soviet Union and Great Britain could not wait for a decision in the war against Japan. Before the West could come to grips with Japan decisively, U.S. naval striking power would have to be restored, ships built, and advance bases and lines of communications extended across the far Pacific. It followed, therefore, that defeat of Germany should be the first major objective and that in the meantime the Japanese should be contained until the Allies could assemble enough strength to take the offensive in the Pacific.

The divergent approaches of the Allies were most clearly reflected initially in the conflict between U.S. and British strategy against Germany. The 1941–42 period saw the emergence of what may be called the peripheral theory, espoused by Churchill and the British staff, and the theory of mass and concentration, advocated by General Marshall and his staff. The British stood for hitting the German Army at the edges of the Continent; the Americans, for concentration at the decisive point to defeat the main body of the enemy. In the peripheral concept, emphasis would be on swift campaigns of speed and manoeuvre, on probing soft spots, on a war of attrition. The cross-Channel operation would follow as a last blow against a Germany already in process of collapse. The British concept was in accord with its small-scale economy and limited manpower, its experience of heavy losses in World War I, and the prime minister's predilections. The United States early thought of defeating the German Army decisively. This view reflected U.S. optimism, reliance on the industrial machine to produce the necessary wherewithal, and military faith in a large citizen army built and trained for offensive purposes. Both justified their theories and plans as ways of relieving the pressure upon the Russians. The divergent approaches lay behind the debate in 1942 over the notion of an early cross-Channel attack versus the invasion of North Africa—Operation Torch. The British view triumphed, the President overruling the U.S. staff, and November saw the start of Mediterranean operations.

The cross-Channel versus Mediterranean debate of midwar was argued in and out of the big international conferences, though always both sides agreed on the need for strategic bombardment of Germany to pave the way. Finally, the meeting at Tehrān in November 1943, where, for the first time in the war, the President, the Prime Minister, and their staffs met with Marshal Joseph Stalin and his staff, became the decisive conference for strategy. Churchill made eloquent appeals for operations in Italy, the Aegean, and the eastern Mediterranean, even at the expense of a delay in the cross-Channel invasion—Operation Overlord. But Stalin put Soviet weight squarely behind the U.S. concept of strategy. Further operations in the Mediterranean, he insisted, should be limited to the invasion of southern France in support of Overlord. In turn, he promised to launch an all-out offensive on the eastern front.

Stalin's stand put the capstone on Anglo-American European strategy and in a sense fixed western strategy. Germany was to be crushed by a great pincers—the Anglo-American drive on the west and a Soviet drive from the east. General Eisenhower was appointed commander for Overlord, and preparations for the cross-Channel thrust began. The decision at Tehrān marked a subtle but significant change in the relationship of the Allies. Britain was growing relatively weaker, the United States and the Soviet Union stronger.

The final phase of the strategy story—from the summer of 1944 to the surrenders of Germany and Japan—was the period of the payoff. In this period the problems of winning the war began to come up against winning the peace. The curtain began to lift on the divergent national objectives of the Allies—objectives hitherto obscured by the common military danger. The western drive unfolded according to plan. The thrust across France coincided with the invasion from the Mediterranean; the Rhine was crossed, the Ruhr encircled, and the drive across Germany met up with the Russian advance. But to Churchill, warily watching the swift Soviet advance into Poland and the Balkans, the war had become more than ever a contest for great political stakes. As the strategy unrolled in the field, the two approaches to the war boiled down to a question of military versus political manoeuvres.

While the war in the West was drawing to a close, the strategy for defeating Japan had been taking gradual shape. As the war had advanced, Allied strategy in the Pacific shifted from the defensive to the offensive. Though firm, final plans had to await the defeat of Germany, the momentum of advances in the Pacific was so fast that it almost caught up with the European conflict. Island-to-island advance was gradually changed to island hopping. The Battle of Midway in 1942 foreshadowed a new trend in naval strategy, in which opposing fleets did not get within gun range of each other but duelled with their air power and submarines. Submarine warfare, amphibious assaults, task forces built around aircraft carriers, the strengthened American fleet—all speeded the pace in midwar. A twofold approach—along the southwest and central Pacific axes—

Global network of specialized agencies

The divergent British and American concepts of European strategy

The conflict of military and political manoeuvres

took the Allies to the threshold of Japan by the time the European war closed. Before final plans for invasion were put into effect, however, the Japanese surrendered. A multiplicity of factors led to this result—including the threat of invasion, the attrition of Japanese shipping, air bombardment, the entry of the Soviet Union into the war against Japan, and the dropping of two atomic bombs.

In retrospect, the strategy of World War II represented a curious mixture of old and new strands. Never had strategy had so vast a scope, for this was the first really global war. Never in history had two partners pooled their efforts and ideas so closely as had the Americans and British in the Grand Alliance. Once more the scales of war were tipped in favour of the offensive. To the age-old primary aim of seeking the defeat of the enemy's armed forces was added the objective of striking at his industrial heart. Both these aims, for example, were present in the directive given to General Eisenhower for the European campaign. In Pacific strategy, it long remained a question whether invasion and defeat of the enemy forces on their home grounds would even be necessary. Strategic bombardment and sea power gave support for a strategy of attrition and destruction of industrial capacity. But the thesis that the sole aim of strategy was to support air power in order to annihilate the enemy's industrial power was only partially tested. It had been impossible to put all production and manpower into the air strategy. Nor were ground and sea enthusiasts on the basis of World War II experiences disposed to yield the field of strategy completely to the new air arm. Allied military strategy, despite attention to "principles," had been a hybrid product, largely hammered out on the anvil of necessity. Final answers in military strategy to the problems of proper aims and emphases, and of best combinations and permutations, were still not clear.

It was clear, however, that modern war had grown more total than ever and that science, industry, diplomacy, and psychology all had to be harnessed to it. Campaign strategy could no longer be clearly differentiated from national strategy; military strategy—in the sense of disposing armed forces for battle—was overshadowed by grand strategy. Where all this would lead was still not clear at the end of World War II, for hanging over all society was the weapon that threatened to revolutionize all warfare, the atomic bomb. (Ma.M.)

MODERN STRATEGY AND WEAPONS OF MASS DESTRUCTION

The nature and consequences of nuclear weapons. The advent of weapons of mass destruction has given rise to completely novel conditions that have fundamentally affected the concept of warfare and that have exerted a decisive influence on the conduct of policy in peacetime. These novel conditions have been appreciated only gradually, but they have given birth to a new branch of strategy—nuclear strategy—developed over the period from 1945 to 1965.

The atomic bombing of Hiroshima, Japan, in 1945 showed that the atomic explosive had placed at the disposal of belligerents a weapon of a potency out of all proportion to anything hitherto known. With its 20 kilotons of explosive power, the Hiroshima bomb produced a semi-instantaneous explosion of a violence equal to that of a salvo from 4,000,000 World War I field guns. The "small" one-megaton thermonuclear bomb is equivalent to a salvo from 200,000,000 field guns. The effect of this colossal release of energy, capable of destroying everything over a considerable area, is increased by the radioactive fallout produced by low-altitude explosions; this can contaminate large swathes of territory downwind, extending for 30 to 600 miles, depending on the force of the explosion. Recovery from a massive thermonuclear exchange would be affected by both the severity and breadth of destruction, wherein all major urban and industrial centres would at least temporarily cease to function as productive economic units. Among the most devastating results of such an attack would be the elimination of most physicians and medical facilities at a time of unprecedented need.

In itself, however, the atomic explosive, whatever its potency, would have had only limited influence on strategic thinking had not modern technical progress simultane-

ously produced the resources required to transport and "deliver" it under conditions unthinkable in World War II: first the long-range bomber and then the ballistic missile endowed nuclear firepower with an extraordinary range and increasingly instantaneous destructive effect. Intercontinental missiles can strike any target in the world within some tens of minutes, and the orbital bomb can reach its target even faster. And this colossal threat can be actuated by a team consisting of only a few men. It is a development of extraordinary proportions.

These revolutionary characteristics of nuclear weapons have given rise to a phenomenon that is entirely new: there is no longer any relation between power and numbers. Whereas previously the destruction of a city required thousands of aircraft or the guns of a whole army, a single weapon launched by a few individuals is now enough. This overwhelming firepower, moreover, can be endowed with almost total mobility, enabling any point on enemy territory to be struck within an hour. The entire basis of conventional strategy has therefore been upset.

In the face of this spectacular progress the traditional type of armed forces appear impotent. Defense on the frontier does not protect a country against physical destruction or radioactive contamination. The armed forces themselves are extremely vulnerable to nuclear firepower. At first sight, therefore, it may seem that in the atomic age conventional armed forces are no longer capable of fulfilling their role and that they have consequently become useless. So far-reaching a conclusion has not been accepted, however, because it became evident that conventional forces still possessed a role that could not be disregarded. But it is a partial role only; the main role is now played by the nuclear forces, since they alone are capable of counterbalancing the enemy nuclear forces. As a result, the general balance and structure of conventional military forces has had to be fundamentally revised in the light of the tasks allotted to them. Many nonnuclear powers have been forced to ally themselves with the nuclear powers in order to gain their protection. As a result, strategy now has a profound influence on political policy.

As understanding of nuclear strategy increased, it was realized that the traditional concepts of warfare would have to be subjected to very far-reaching revision. Initially it was thought that a general war similar to World War II was possible, with free use being made of atomic firepower. As soon, however, as it became clear that both sides had a large number of nuclear weapons available, it was seen that such a policy was impossible since it would lead to a mutual holocaust, the most obvious result of which would be uncontrollable general chaos. It became clear that general war was the worst form of nuclear warfare and that it could no longer be considered as an instrument of policy.

In view of the need to avoid general war, the main aim of nuclear strategy was radically changed: instead of concentrating on the possible course of a nuclear war, as they had done so far, strategists now had to look for methods of preventing the outbreak of nuclear war. The result was deterrent strategy, which has become the core of nuclear strategy. It will be analyzed in detail below.

Conflicts of interest, which usually lie at the bottom of armed conflict, did continue to exist. But the threat of annihilation made resort to general nuclear war in resolution of these conflicts impossible. Nuclear deterrence seemed likely to impose a sort of status quo on the world almost everywhere. The question thus arose of how to bring about those changes that developments in power relationships, both psychological and material, might render essential. Even more pressing was the question of whether, should tensions become too great, there would be any alternative to all-out nuclear war.

The answers to these basic questions were provided gradually by the march of world events. It became increasingly clear that the extent to which resort to war was deterred by the nuclear threat depended upon the significance of a particular conflict in relation to the interests of the nuclear powers. In geographical areas in which the vital interests of the nuclear powers were at stake—Europe, for example—the degree of deterrence seemed very high; rigidity seemed the order of the day. In geographical ar-

The first truly global war

The power of nuclear and conventional weapons compared

eas in which conflicts of interest proved to be marginal, limited armed conflict remained possible, provided that the nuclear powers were not directly involved against each other. This is the lesson to be drawn from the Korean War, the Arab–Israeli war, and the war in Vietnam and other parts of Indochina. Limited war, therefore, is still possible in peripheral areas in which it can be kept below the nuclear level.

Most of these peripheral conflicts have taken the form of "revolutionary" wars based on some ideology and have seen the use of various types of guerrilla tactics. The continuing war in Indochina showed that guerrilla war constituted an effective method of checkmating superior conventional forces; this form of strategy, therefore, was an imperative for the militarily weaker side provided it could call into play sufficiently potent political motives to inspire the population to take part in resistance. Revolutionary war has proved to be a formidable process, perfectly suited to the narrow margin of liberty of action left by nuclear deterrence.

In sensitive areas such as Europe, on the other hand, conventional military conflict makes sense only if the aggressor judges that his enemy will not have the courage to resort to nuclear war. Very limited and short-lived incidents can perhaps take place without resort to nuclear weapons, but any major aggression is extremely likely to escalate very rapidly, at least to the tactical nuclear weapon level.

The idea of a return to conventional warfare has often been considered as a method of avoiding the mutual nuclear holocaust and therefore of "humanizing" war. But this is probably a false hope, for with modern resources conventional war can be terribly destructive. Acceptance of the possibility of a conventional war also markedly reduces the value of the nuclear deterrent, and, furthermore, no one can be sure that the conflict would not escalate rapidly on to the nuclear level. In short, this is an idea fraught with danger.

The logic of nuclear strategy. From the outset nuclear strategists found themselves facing considerable theoretical difficulties. It very soon became obvious that conventional strategy provided no effective answer to the nuclear problem, for physical protection against the effects of a nuclear weapon can be no more than partial and inadequate. The efficiency with which nuclear weapons can be intercepted is equally inadequate, and preventive destruction of enemy weapons is still an uncertain affair. Yet a very small number of thermonuclear weapons can produce appalling destruction. Under these circumstances it became obvious **The key** very early that genuine protection could be achieved only **role of** by a threat of retaliation on a scale such that the enemy **deterrence** would be deterred from using his weapons. The object, **in nuclear** therefore, is to exert a direct effect on the will of the en- **strategy** emy without having to go through the intermediate stage of a trial of force. In pursuance of this general idea of deterrence, strategists developed a new body of theory that sought to relate the essentially psychological aspects of the deterrence relationship to the offensive and defensive capabilities of the two sides.

If deterrence depends on a threat of retaliation, the threat first must be formidable, posing the necessary degree of destructive capability, accuracy, and power of penetration; and second, must remain formidable after having absorbed the first enemy strike—in other words, possess an adequate survival capability. This postulates a high state of alert, and it requires the ability either to take avoiding action or to achieve physical protection and conceal missiles in underground silos or submarines.

All these capabilities are in fact dependent upon technical factors stemming from the characteristics of the equipment used by the two sides. It follows that the calculation of results likely to be achieved by the first enemy strike and the response thereto depends on the estimated importance attached to all these technical factors, and this must remain a matter of uncertainty. If these technical factors change to any marked extent, the strategic balance between the two sides may change considerably. This is the logical basis for the technological race characteristic of the development of nuclear strategy; it has led to a silent and relentless war involving the expenditure of immense

sums of money. It is clear, therefore, that the stability of deterrence can be increased or made uncertain as a result of technical advances made by either side.

But deterrence depends very much on psychological as **Psycho-** well as technical factors. The estimate of what constitutes **logical** an "unacceptable" level of casualties is the product of sub- **aspects of** jective opinions, which themselves are basically variable; **deterrence** in one case a threat involving some hundreds of thousands of casualties will produce deterrence, in another it may be necessary to raise the threat to several tens of millions of casualties. The threat of retaliation, moreover, becomes real only if supported by an obvious and undoubted determination. The credibility of the enemy's threat is thus crucial to the maintenance of deterrence, for only the certainty that the opposing side has both the power and the will to retaliate can impose that degree of restraint on both parties that is necessary to prevent nuclear war.

In view of the impossibility of an accurate estimate of the psychological factors, nuclear strategy attempts to determine the rationality of the various possible decisions that may have to be taken in a nuclear conflict. This leads to the lines of thought discussed below.

The irrationality of a first-strike strategy. A country contemplating launching a nuclear attack would, logically, aim its missiles at the enemy's nuclear forces (a "counterforce" strike) rather than at its cities. The enemy would thus be rendered incapable of retaliation, but its population and productive resources would remain largely intact. The enemy would be open to invasion by conventional forces, the advance of which would be facilitated by the threat of further nuclear attacks (this time, against the enemy's cities) should resistance be offered. A country that is able to thus disarm its enemy is said to possess a "first-strike capability." A country that is able to launch a retaliatory response, even though its missile sites have been attacked, is said to possess a "second-strike capability."

But counterforce action (a first or second strike against **The diffi-** the enemy's nuclear forces) is extremely difficult: it presup- **culties of** poses excellent and complete information, great accuracy, **defense** and a negligible or very low level of enemy interception. In view of recent developments—including nuclear submarines that are more or less undetectable, missiles in concrete emplacements requiring several weapons to ensure their destruction, and antiballistic missiles able to intercept a certain percentage of the first strike—the effect of a first counterforce strike is fairly uncertain. It must in fact be assumed that the enemy will have a formidable second-strike capability available. First-strike capability has therefore become something very difficult to achieve.

This conclusion is further supported by the growth of nuclear forces. Given the numbers of weapons possessed by the Soviet and American sides, the casualties to be expected from a nuclear exchange might be of the order of 180,000,000 Russians and 120,000,000 Americans. These figures indicate that, if the enemy's retaliatory power is to be brought to an "acceptable" level, it must be possible for counterforce action and interception to reduce these casualties by over 99 percent. Such a reduction in casualties is in fact a technical impossibility.

Because both the United States and the Soviet Union have possessed a second-strike capability since the early 1960s, nuclear strategy proves to be a strategy of threat of retaliation—basically a deterrent strategy. This means that the nuclear weapon is not designed for war, since nuclear war would be a major catastrophe for both sides; its threat, however, is utilized to keep the peace.

Responses to a failure of the deterrent. But insofar as nuclear strategy must deal with decisions to be taken in the event of failure of the deterrent (a major but secondary problem, since the object is to ensure that deterrent strategy succeeds), the strategist is still faced with the problem of how to respond to a variety of possible enemy aggressions. Such enemy initiatives might range from an attack with conventional weapons on a friendly, allied country, to an all-out nuclear attack on the main opposing country. The possible responses to such an enemy action are equally varied, and should be designed to deter the enemy from further hostile action, while at the same time minimizing the risk of escalation.

One response to an enemy aggression would be to destroy the enemy's population centres. For the enemy this constitutes the maximum threat, since it can inflict on him extremely heavy and widespread destruction. On the other hand, his nuclear resources will remain intact and will therefore be capable of retaliating in devastating fashion against this opponent's cities. The concept is, therefore, a dangerous one.

A second possible reaction would be to destroy the enemy's nuclear forces. Such a strategy is difficult because of the existence of missile-carrying submarines, missiles in concrete emplacements, and the possibility of some degree of interception by antiballistic missiles. This being so, such all-out counterforce retaliation can reduce the enemy's destructive capability, but only to a certain extent. The enemy will still be able to produce a counteraction against cities. This idea is therefore less dangerous than the first, but it is still extremely bold.

A further possibility is to resort to limited strategic retaliation as a warning intended to bring pressure on the enemy to bargain. This solution is obviously only applicable to those cases in which the enemy has not initiated the conflict with large-scale use of nuclear weapons. Targets for these warning shots would be certain enemy cities or forces. Destruction of cities would inevitably lead to retaliation in kind and is therefore justified only if the enemy has attacked cities in his first strike. Destruction of some enemy nuclear forces may constitute a more effective warning without involving the same risk of retaliation against cities. Since it is only a limited action, however, the enemy's retaliatory capability remains formidable. In fact, the only object of limited retaliation is to demonstrate to the enemy the will to resort to nuclear weapons, and so lead him to revise his ideas about his opponent's determination. Limited strategic retaliation is a double-edged weapon, for, although it may lead the enemy to negotiate, it may also start a process of escalation fraught with risk. A solution of this nature therefore requires the most detailed consideration.

The use of tactical nuclear weapons It seems that the best and least dangerous solution to a limited attack against a nuclear power or an allied state is to destroy with tactical nuclear weapons the enemy's tactical invading forces. This achieves three objectives at one and the same time: it demonstrates determination to fight and to use nuclear weapons; it stops the enemy invasion; and it restricts destruction to the combat zone. The enemy may reply similarly or retaliate on the strategic level; but also the defeat of his invasion might cause him to look for a compromise without resorting to nuclear escalation. This solution, moreover, does not necessitate use of strategic nuclear forces and can be implemented by tactical nuclear forces alone.

Any employment of tactical nuclear weapons raises some extremely delicate problems; the use of any type of nuclear weapon will rapidly produce dangerous situations; and, there being no precedents, no one can foresee how such a battle would develop. Such dangers and uncertainties are not, however, without value, for they suggest that the threat of employing tactical nuclear weapons does have a considerable deterrent effect in dissuading an enemy, who might be deluding himself that he could keep war on the conventional level, from embarking on an adventure.

To summarize, each of the responses described above is the answer to a different situation:

If the enemy is powerful and initiates hostilities by widespread use of nuclear weapons, the obvious answer is massive retaliation, primarily counterforce but also to some extent against cities. Nuclear resources available to both the United States and the U.S.S.R. are adequate for both purposes.

If the enemy is powerful and initiates hostilities by an invasion, deluding himself that he can keep the war conventional, nuclear retaliation against his tactical forces is the order of the day. In this situation a series of limited strategic nuclear warning shots would be both ineffective and highly dangerous; pressure on the enemy would be minor; defending tactical forces might still be rapidly defeated; and the psychological inhibition against the use of nuclear weapons would have been broken, paving the way for the massive employment of strategic nuclear forces.

Finally, if the enemy is powerful but has initiated hostilities with only a limited use of nuclear weapons, limited nuclear retaliation may be justified. Such a response would also be highly effective against an enemy less powerful on the nuclear level, who might have launched an invasion in the hope of keeping the conflict conventional.

The realization that a wide range of reactions to enemy aggression is possible has thus given rise to the strategy of "flexible response." All-out, massive retaliation is no longer regarded as being the only reply that may be made to a hostile move on the part of the opposing side. The strategy of flexible response, however, to some extent runs counter to the strategy of deterrence in that it proclaims an attitude of moderation—which may to some extent reduce the value of the strategic nuclear threat. This is the basis of European reservations regarding flexible response; Europeans would prefer to risk general war in an attempt to avoid war altogether rather than have Europe become a theatre of operations for limited war.

The strategic posture of the superpowers since 1945. The foregoing analysis attempts to define the principles of nuclear strategy in order to establish the national postures that could be adopted. It is now relevant to examine how the nuclear powers have applied these principles over the last 25 years. As will be shown, these years have been years of discovery; governments on several occasions have found themselves in situations unforeseen by the theorists. The opposing nuclear forces have developed notably and rapidly, more rapidly, it seems, than new theories, which have generally lagged behind events.

The development of the strategic balance between the two superpowers may be divided, for the sake of argument, into three main phases, which will be dealt with in turn.

1945–55. During the first decade after the end of World War II, the United States enjoyed first a real nuclear monopoly and then an overwhelming nuclear superiority. The U.S.S.R., on the other hand, which had never really demobilized its World War II armies, had large-scale conventional forces.

The American response to the Soviet threat to western Europe was comprised of three elements: the economic reconstruction of Europe by means of the Marshall Plan; the conventional rearmament of Europe under the NATO treaty; and the formation of an airborne nuclear striking force to lend substance to the threat of massive retaliation. Because of the limited range of the American bombers of the time, the airborne nuclear deterrent was dependent on the establishment of a complete network of foreign bases. This threefold strategy was successful in removing the threat of the establishment of Communist regimes throughout Europe by means of political coups backed by Soviet armed force.

The only response open to the Soviet Union was a defensive deterrent strategy combined with an indirect strategic offensive in Korea and Indochina. In the nuclear field the U.S.S.R. began by launching a psychological campaign, the so-called Peace Congresses, which were intended to inhibit the Americans in the use of nuclear weapons. During this period the Soviet Union succeeded in constructing a few atomic bombs, in forming an embryonic striking force, and in improving its air defenses with a radar system.

Faced with these initial Soviet steps toward development of a nuclear threat and an air defense system, the United States expanded its striking force and improved its ability to penetrate Soviet defenses by introducing new and faster bombers with a higher ceiling. At this point United States superiority was indisputable, and Secretary of State John Foster Dulles was able to enunciate the principle of "massive retaliation"; that is, of an all-out nuclear response to an enemy attack. The armed forces of Europe, however, had not developed sufficiently, and their role was therefore confined to that of alerting the largely American strategic forces, whose action would be sufficient to put the enemy out of action. American strategic nuclear superiority forced the Soviet Union to accept compromise solutions in Korea and Indochina.

1955–62. During this second phase Soviet nuclear forces developed and the nuclear threat became bilateral. Although the two threats were not equivalent, a sort of

The strategy of flexible response

"Balance of terror"

initial "balance of terror" was reached. The United States, however, still had a certain first-strike capability.

The development of Soviet nuclear power, particularly its acquisition of the thermonuclear weapon, faced the United States with a considerable problem, aggravated by the Soviet launching of an indirect political offensive in the Middle East. The choices open to the United States included the improvement of the deterrent by further reinforcement of offensive capability, especially by means of a missile program; the partial neutralization of the enemy threat by the establishment of a North American air defense system; and the reinforcement of tactical forces in order to avoid a situation in which the only choice open would be massive retaliation or surrender. The debate on these questions opened in 1955 and ended with the following decisions being reached: a vast air defense system was to be constructed covering Europe and the United States; the Strategic Air Command's tactics were to be improved by means of aircraft continually in the air, reduced alert time, and intercontinental bombers based in America; and the European tactical shield was to be reinforced with tactical nuclear weapons to give it a certain resistance capability. The idea was that the enemy threat would thus be reduced, and, in the event of an accident, the resistance of the European-based forces would permit postponement of a decision to launch massive retaliation until aggression could be clearly established.

The 1955 decision produced a certain temporary stability, but it was clearly too conciliatory to ensure the maintenance of deterrence. The Soviet Union, ahead of the United States this time, completed a force of intercontinental missiles. In 1957 the U.S.S.R. put up the first satellite, and its tests proved that it could produce accurate and powerful nuclear explosions; the U.S. air defense system, designed against aircraft, was completely obsolete. At the same time, the Soviet Union equipped its land forces for an offensive tactical nuclear war and was thus in a position to get the better of most of the U.S. defensive dispositions.

The United States nevertheless still had a considerable measure of superiority both in numbers of nuclear weapons and in intelligence resources; these two factors ensured it a fairly effective counterforce offensive capability. Deterrence, therefore, was still operative, but the margin of security was becoming increasingly narrow, as the Cuban crisis was to prove. In 1962 the Soviet Union attempted to bring the United States under threat from medium-range missiles placed in Cuba; the American response was restrained, consisting of a series of pressures including a naval blockade, which forced the Soviet Union to abandon its plan. American nuclear superiority was quite clear. But the danger of nuclear war had been a serious one and showed that other solutions were required.

The acquisition of second-strike capability

Since 1962. During this third phase the United States stepped up its deterrent capability considerably by equipping itself with a practically invulnerable retaliatory force. The United States thus had the advantage of a second-strike capability, tantamount, from the enemy's point of view, to a guarantee of almost total destruction. The Soviets also achieved a second-strike capability, however, and so the situation soon became symmetrical—the phase of mutual deterrence.

The strategy sponsored by Pres. John F. Kennedy was designed to deal with a number of problems. There was first of all a need to reduce the possibility of war by miscalculation; hence the reinforcement of presidential control over nuclear weapons in order to avoid spontaneous escalation. There was next an urgent need to deprive the Soviet Union of all first-strike capability; hence the decision to construct an invulnerable retaliatory force. This was made possible by new technical developments, including atomic (Polaris) submarines and missiles in hardened emplacements (Minuteman). There was, thirdly, a need for a war strategy that would allow a conflict to be restricted to a limited level; hence the decision to strengthen the tactical shield and to abandon the principle of massive retaliation in favour of the flexible response.

The first two aims have been largely achieved. As soon, however, as the Soviet Union had reached a comparable

position, it became clear that the Soviet and American forces neutralized each other and that the credibility of any nuclear initiative had therefore become very small. The absence of such credibility—that is, of a belief that the opposing side might resort to a first strike in response to an indirect or limited aggression—is extremely dangerous, since it makes such actions all the more likely. In an attempt to maintain the credibility of a first strike, both the Soviet Union and the United States have adopted certain psychological postures. The Soviet Union has tried to maintain credibility by making play with an attitude of irrationality. The United States, on the other hand, has tried to recapture some degree of credibility for a first strike by proclaiming a desire not to proceed beyond limited action; that is, it has indicated to the Soviet Union that some degree of first-strike action is still contemplated by the United States. That credibility has in fact been maintained is demonstrated by the fact that an extremely stable situation of mutual deterrence exists between the United States and the Soviet Union in the late 20th century.

Kennedy's third aim was not immediately achieved. Europeans were reluctant to increase their conventional forces since they had no wish for limited war. In a situation of mutual deterrence, limited war could be dangerous, since it held out the possibility of a conventional conflict to which there was no adequate response.

Technological developments continue, however, with important effects on the strategic relations of the superpowers. Both have developed antiballistic missile (ABM) defense systems. The development of the ABM has in turn resulted in efforts to increase penetration capability. This has produced MIRV (multiple independently targeted reentry vehicles), which in effect scatter one's shots and baffle defense.

The high cost of this arms race, together with the fact that the security of none of the participants is improved, and may in fact be reduced—because of the uncertain consequences of new weapons—has led to attempts to limit strategic arms by negotiation. Initial strategic arms limitation talks took place in Helsinki and Vienna in 1970.

Continuous changes are thus taking place in nuclear strategy. Situations have never been lasting and the life of defense systems has been short. So vast an expenditure of resources seems to be an increasingly heavy price to pay for a degree of security that must remain uncertain.

The general trend of development has, in summary, been as follows: initially it was believed that nuclear war was possible, and there was fear of a surprise attack. Very soon the necessity of deterrence was understood, but, when deterrence became mutual, the pursuit of first-strike credibility became concentrated on psychological factors until the threat of a new armaments race made the opening of arms limitation negotiations necessary: nuclear strategy embarked on a phase of diplomacy.

The strategy of the Western Alliance. Within the framework of the two superpowers' bilateral strategy the basic objective of the Western Alliance has been to ensure the defense of Europe by means of a combination of forces located in Europe and in the United States. In the light of developments in bilateral strategy described above, the Alliances' strategy has undergone important changes.

1950–55. In response to the threat of Soviet military and political aggression against western Europe, the western powers signed the North Atlantic Treaty in 1949. The treaty established the North Atlantic Treaty Organization (NATO). Under primarily American direction, the initial objects of the treaty were to give concrete expression to the solidarity between the United States and Europe, thus enabling Europe to benefit from the American deterrent, and to rearm Europe, primarily by means of American credits and equipment. The first rearmament program (the Lisbon program) dealt only with conventional armaments for Europe. Basically, therefore, it visualized the traditional type of defense, known as the "shield"—the "sword" being constituted by the American strategic forces.

The Lisbon program was never completely fulfilled, for French rearmament was delayed by the Indochina war, and German rearmament was slow. U.S. advances in the strategic field, however, enabled the United States to pro-

The formation of NATO

claim the strategy of massive retaliation. Deterrence in Europe was then assured, the task of the "shield" being not to resist an attack but merely to act as a trip wire to set off a massive U.S. nuclear response. In these circumstances, members of the Alliance felt strong enough to extend their protection first to Norway and then to Greece and Turkey. The policy of "containment" of possible Soviet expansion was in force from the North Cape of Norway to the Caucasus.

1955–62. During this second phase the presence of a Soviet nuclear threat—more pressing, it may be noted, for Europe than for the United States—produced a peculiar situation in Europe. The decision to launch massive retaliation became a delicate one because it would result in the virtual annihilation of Europe, which was within easy range of Soviet bombers and missiles. It seemed necessary to establish a complementary deterrent in Europe by endowing the tactical "shield" with an appreciable resistance capability. This was to be accomplished by the provision to Allied forces, for use under certain restricted circumstances, of U.S. tactical nuclear weapons hitherto kept under American control. This strategy came into force in 1957. The result was both to raise the effectiveness of the deterrent and to provide for a possible initial phase of war during which massive retaliation would be held back as a threat; a "nuclear threshold" was thus laid down, above which massive retaliation, in other words general war, would be launched.

This strategy led to the elaboration of techniques for the employment of tactical nuclear weapons in a violent defensive battle with a large number of weapons available. Studies and exercises carried out on these lines showed that such a battle would lead to rapid attrition of the tactical forces on both sides for the sake of very doubtful operational results. From the point of view of the defense this was a disappointing conclusion; on the other hand, it provided a most convincing argument for deterrence, since no aggressor could predict the result of an invasion.

Since 1962. During this third phase the abandonment by the Americans of the principle of massive retaliation and the adoption of the flexible response strategy led to a certain number of difficulties in Alliance strategy.

The first result of the flexible response strategy was to produce some doubts among the European Allies as to what the flexible response might be and as to when the decision to use nuclear weapons would be taken. Lengthy discussions were initiated to try to find a solution to the problem of sharing strategic nuclear responsibilities. Meanwhile, on the U.S. side, attempts were made to form national nuclear forces in Europe and to integrate them under U.S. command. One proposal was to form a multinational force including contingents from the United States, Great Britain, and France and a multilateral force consisting of ships with mixed crews from the other nations of the Alliance. This scheme did no more than conceal unresolved problems; it failed because it was opposed by France, and even more by the Soviet Union, which was afraid of seeing Germany become a nuclear power as a result. A similar British plan was no more successful.

The second effect of the flexible response strategy was, as described above, to throw doubt on the credibility of the U.S. deterrent against Soviet aggression in Europe. Within the Western Alliance this led to a stand by France, which announced that it was determined to adhere to the principle of massive retaliation in order to create uncertainty in the mind of the enemy, which might well find the flexible response reassuring. Following the same line of thought, the Germans proposed to lay a line of nuclear mines along the frontier (the Trettner Line) to demonstrate to the Soviets that Germany was determined to accept colossal destruction rather than allow itself to be invaded. This proposal, which was later taken up by the Turks, was not agreed to by the Americans.

Both Great Britain and France possessed small nuclear forces, and the question arose as to whether these forces were to be integrated into the Alliance under American command or were to remain under strictly national control. The British, who had always worked very closely with the Americans, accepted the principle of integration except

The flexible response strategy

British and French striking forces

for cases in which the "national interest" was involved. France, on the other hand, announced that its "striking force" would remain national and that the French government alone would be responsible for the decision to use it. France did, however, accept the principle that this force would cooperate with the nuclear forces of the United States and Great Britain, but this cooperation was never organized, because of the French withdrawal from NATO. It may be argued that the existence of independent British and French nuclear forces reinforces the credibility of a resort to nuclear war and thus strengthens the mutual deterrence between the Western powers and the Soviet Union.

Soviet strategy. Profound developments have taken place in Soviet strategy since 1945. During the initial postwar phase, when the nuclear cupboard was bare, Soviet strategy made play with the trump card provided by its possession of large-scale conventional forces. These were a considerable threat and, therefore, a deterrent.

During the second phase the Soviets were in possession of the thermonuclear weapon and followed the Americans in forming a striking force. They thus acquired a certain measure of nuclear deterrence, but not until about 1960, with the development of intercontinental weapons, was the Soviet Union in position to exert a noticeable and direct threat against the territory of the United States.

In line with these developments in the nuclear field, Soviet land forces were completely reorganized during the 1950s and 1960s to enable operations to be conducted in a nuclear setting. The threat to Europe was increased by the construction of numerous intermediate range ballistic missiles.

The 1960s saw a prolonged effort not only in the nuclear field but also in the naval. In the space of a few years the U.S.S.R. developed its nuclear and naval forces until it had attained a form of parity with the United States. Having achieved this, and perhaps wearied by the effort, the U.S.S.R. agreed to open negotiations for a limitation of nuclear weapons, both offensive and defensive.

A particular facet of Soviet strategy is that concerned with the strategy of the Warsaw Pact, a 20-year mutual defense treaty between the U.S.S.R. and its east European satellites, established in 1955 in response to Germany's rearmament and admission to NATO. The pact is only one of the components of Soviet overall strategy. Not being nuclear, the forces of the satellite states play only an auxiliary role; the territories of these states, on the other hand, are of major strategic importance since they form a defensive barrier for the U.S.S.R. and provide an assembly area for an offensive.

Role of the Warsaw Pact

Chinese strategy. The acquisition of a nuclear capability by the People's Republic of China and the estrangement between China and the Soviet Union are new factors of major strategic importance. Being a competitor of the U.S.S.R. in the revolutionary field and irredentist as regards certain Soviet territories that were once part of China, China stands in opposition to the U.S.S.R. The Communist world is thus split. The nub of divergence seems to be essentially ideological: the Chinese concept of Marxist revolution differs fundamentally from that of the U.S.S.R.

China has developed a strategy of its own. It has abandoned all efforts to provide itself with modern conventional forces, which are very expensive and which could hardly compete with Soviet conventional forces. China's defense is to be assured by recourse to a people's war conducted by the army and countless militiamen; the enemy will be deterred from invading by the threat of guerrilla warfare, which was so successful against the Japanese and the Chinese Nationalists under Chiang Kai-shek.

But this is an insufficient deterrent, since the U.S.S.R. and the United States have the nuclear resources to destroy China's urban and industrial centres. Mainland China must, therefore, possess a nuclear deterrent force. Accordingly, the Chinese have made a considerable effort to develop a modern nuclear industry, starting from the basis provided for them by the Soviet Union up to 1958. Progress has since been rapid. In 1964 a uranium bomb was exploded, and in 1967 China's first thermonuclear weapon was detonated. A bomb detonated in 1966 was rocket fired. In the 1970s China began developing an arsenal of ICBM's (intercontinental ballistic missiles) and IRBM's (intermediate-range ballistic missiles). The deterrent value of the Chinese nuclear force is thus increasingly formidable.

By the late 20th century, therefore, the bipolar distribution of strategic power between the United States and the U.S.S.R., which had dominated international relations since the close of World War II, changed to a multipolar one. This, together with the likely proliferation of nuclear weapons to smaller countries, changes fundamentally the world strategic balance of power.

Proliferation and its consequences. Proliferation—that is, the acquisition of nuclear weapons by many countries—has been regarded as the main danger of the nuclear age. In a world in which large number of independent nuclear forces existed there would exist a likely possibility that some of them would come under the control of ambitious and irrational governments, or even, in the case of internal revolution, of ill-informed people. Terrorist methods using nuclear weapons might be employed, making it difficult to identify rapidly the aggressor power.

The U.S.S.R., the United States, Great Britain, France, and China in turn acquired a nuclear capability. The development of nuclear energy for peaceful purposes led further to the spread of knowledge of nuclear techniques and to an increase in the production of material capable of being turned into nuclear explosive. Faced with this situation, some international action was obviously necessary in the hope of obtaining an international agreement to put an end to the danger of proliferation. The result was a Treaty Banning the Proliferation of Nuclear Weapons, which became open to signature in 1968.

The treaty calls for a renunciation by the nonnuclear powers of any intention of providing themselves with nuclear weapons; it also provides for control and inspection. After lengthy discussions, the treaty was accepted in principle by the majority of states, although France abstained and China refused to be associated with it.

The main difficulties raised by the treaty are that it ties the hands of the nonnuclear powers but does not include any obligation on the part of the nuclear powers to refrain from giving away nuclear weapons. It therefore sets the seal on an unequal status between nations without, however, mitigating the nuclear arms race between the nuclear powers. The proposed inspection system would also give wide access to any new developments or discoveries that might be made in the peaceful uses of atomic energy. Many countries, therefore, fear that any progress they achieve, which may be of great commercial importance, will be open to exploitation by the inspecting countries. In addition, nuclear explosives, which might be used in various peaceful ways, would remain the monopoly of the nuclear powers.

The nonnuclear states consider that their renunciation of nuclear weapons should be compensated by worthwhile guarantees of security. The nuclear powers, however, were willing to give a guarantee only against nuclear aggression, whereas the nonnuclear states wanted this guarantee to apply to all forms of aggression, whether nuclear or not. In the light of these reservations, agreement on the Non-Proliferation Treaty is only a first and inadequate step. Many states reserved the right to repudiate the treaty, should the situation so require, and the treaty in fact makes explicit provision for this.

The treaty was more in the nature of a concerted action on the part of the United States and the U.S.S.R. to preserve their de facto monopoly in nuclear weapons. The U.S.S.R. had a further object—to prevent West Germany from becoming a nuclear power. Finally, the absence of China detracted greatly from the practical value of the agreement.

Other solutions to the spread of nuclear weapons have been envisaged, in particular the creation of denuclearized zones, already in existence in South America and Africa, in which nuclear weapons are banned by agreement of the countries concerned. In 1958 Poland proposed to denuclearize central Europe, an idea that raised major difficulties

Main provisions of the Non-Proliferation Treaty

of a strategic nature. Such zones are only conceivable in areas in which tensions are no more than minor. If serious tensions develop, denuclearization has small prospect of continuance.

The proliferation problem is likely to become acute when nuclear techniques have become really inexpensive and when the majority of states will be rich enough to acquire nuclear weapons, whether clandestinely or not. This is a truly disturbing prospect, and it is to be hoped that it will cause the nuclear powers to agree among themselves, and with the nonnuclear states, on a vast international security system that will at last guarantee peace.   (A.Be.)

FUNDAMENTALS OF TACTICS

Tactics, the art and science of fighting battles, is concerned with the approach to combat, the disposition of troops, the use made of various arms, and the execution of movements for attack or defense. Carl von Clausewitz defined tactics as "the formation and conduct of single combats in themselves" and strategy as "the combination of single combats with each other.... In other words, strategy forms the plan of the war, maps out the proposed course of the various campaigns which compose the war, and regulates the battles to be fought in each."

No matter how precisely the two terms may be defined, however, there is seldom any fixed line of demarcation. Strategy is frequently limited by the tactical potentialities of the forces involved, and tactics in turn depend on such strategic considerations as the planning and conduct of campaigns. Actually, the two overlap more often than not. In recognition of this fact, the term "grand tactics" gained currency during the Napoleonic era, and 20th-century military commentators have used the phrase "operational strategy" to describe concentrations of such major units as corps and divisions in preparation for battle.

The elements of tactics are dual in character. Attack and defense, cohesion and dispersion, protection and mobility, missile and shock effect, moral and material values—these elements have been changeless throughout the ages, regardless of variations in arms and communications. The barbarian's bow was as effective a missile weapon in its day as the machine gun in its, and elephants were esteemed for shock effect many centuries before the invention of the tank.

Seldom do armies decide arbitrarily on the tactics they will adopt. The swing from one pole to another is nearly always influenced by geographical, climatic, and economic factors. Nomads of the plains become cavalry warriors from necessity rather than choice, just as mountaineers fight on foot. Primitive tribes and nations, unsure of their military skill, were drawn toward the cohesion of the human wall, or phalanx. As such peoples grew in strength and confidence they tended to adopt formations of dispersion, which are better suited to aggressions. Thus the Romans of the early city-state period fought in an eight-rank phalanx, but the Romans of the conquering republic developed that marvellously flexible tactical instrument known as the legion.

One of the most cherished delusions of the ancient world was the belief that a formation had a shock effect in proportion to its depth. But adding ranks to the phalanx did not add to the material might of the attack; it merely contributed to the moral impetus of the attackers. Shock effect is rarely the product of an actual physical impact. The shock is communicated to the soldier's mind rather than his body, and during the cavalry age he was morally defeated by his dread of being trampled, though horses seldom ran down foot soldiers who stood their ground.

Basic tactical principles are few and simple. The complexity and difficulty appear when such principles as surprise, secrecy, deception, security, and the gathering of intelligence are put into actual practice.

So obvious are the tactical advantages to be gained by deception and surprise that they are sought instinctively by primitives. Both principles are combined in that most primitive of tactics, the ambush. Even wild animals know enough to hide while lying in wait to attack. And the ambush has remained one of the most effective tactics of warfare; it was used by both British and German ar-

Relations between tactics and strategy

Factors determining tactics

moured columns in the complicated North African desert campaigns of World War II and by the Viet Cong in Vietnam in the 1960s. Surprise depends simply on the degree of secrecy with which a general masks his intentions and capabilities.

So essential is intelligence to the tactician that a good spy is sometimes worth more to an army than a good general. Reconnaissance patrols, prisoner interrogations, and observation or listening posts also play an important part in arriving at an estimate of an enemy's intentions and capabilities.

Security, like secrecy, has been maintained in all military ages by unremitting vigilance. Although the firepower of missile weapons has often been given the sole credit for the prolonged stalemate in World War I, violation of age-old principles of tactics cannot be overlooked. Several promising Allied offensives met failure because surprise and deception were sacrificed to make possible the tremendous artillery "preparations" that had no decisive effect on an enemy burrowed deep into the earth. Such large quantities of shells were required for these bombardments that the area and extent of the impending offensive were revealed to the enemy by aerial photographs of ammunition dumps.

Tactical formation. Far back in man's past his primitive ancestors perceived that superior numbers did not always make for superior force. A great deal depended on the tactical direction and speed with which this force was applied, and the solution was to group fighting men so that they could give one another the most support while doing the most harm to the enemy. This was the beginning of tactical wisdom.

The line and column

The two basic formations are the line and the column, which differ only by 90° of the compass: a column of men in four files, facing north, has only to execute a "right face" to become a line of four ranks, facing east.

Neither of these formations is useful for all tactical purposes. Although the column is best adapted to marching and manoeuvre, its narrow front and vulnerable flanks are liabilities in combat. The line lacks depth and mobility, but it is more suitable for deployment on the battlefield. Mention should also be made of two other formations which appear less frequently in the chronicles of war— the hollow square and its counterpart, the 360° perimeter. Some stout stands have been made by men facing outward in all directions, but the defect of such formations is that ability to manoeuvre is sacrificed.

Even in the remote past it was evident that forming warriors into a line or column was not enough. Some attention also had to be paid to problems of deploying them so as to make the best of both shock and missile weapons. When men learned to fight on horseback, a cavalry arm came into being. The "eyes" of the primitive army, when used for scouting and reconnaissance, horsemen were also effective for pursuing a broken foe. A crude artillery arm appeared as early as the 8th century BC, when the Old Testament dates engines of war. Not even the tactical ancestor of the tank was lacking. Armoured chariots manned by archers and spearmen led the infantry in battles on the plains of Mesopotamia many centuries before the Christian Era.

The tactics of attack. Descriptions of battles often give the impression that victories are won entirely by physical pressure, as measured by the casualties inflicted. It has been the experience of history, on the contrary, that moral or psychological forces play a much larger part in the outcome than material means. An army's combative spirit is not often broken because the ranks have been so thinned that the survivors are crushed by sheer human tonnage. They are beaten because of their conviction that further resistance is hopeless, and it is the business of the tactician to convince rather than crush his opponents.

The test may be found in the fact that casualties of 30 percent are usually the most an army can endure without losing combative spirit. Yet seven men out of ten are still able to fight, and it may be that they outnumber the entire force of adversaries who accepted battle with a numerical disadvantage. History records instances of losers being routed while still possessing a two-to-one

numerical superiority. They were not crushed; they were simply convinced.

The methods of creating a conviction of defeat may be reduced to a few plans of attack that repeat themselves throughout history. Most simple of all is the plain frontal assault all along the line. Justifiable and even desirable under some circumstances, it is as a rule the resort of unimaginative generalship. As for the direct rear attack, it is so rare as to be associated only with ambush or pursuit.

In an early age it was discovered that armies, like the individuals composing them, dread an attack from the flank or rear. An assault from one side or another is not enough, since an adversary can face in the new direction, whereupon the effort becomes a mere frontal attack. In order to deliver a true flank attack, part of the offensive force must fix the enemy's front, perhaps even defensively, while the assault force swings around to strike simultaneously from the side. If this force can make a wide enough swing to threaten an opponent's rear, the attack becomes a single envelopment. And in instances when the rear is assailed from both sides with concentric thrusts, a double envelopment is the result. Neither a flank attack nor envelopment may be possible when a general secures his flanks with natural obstacles. In that case it is sometimes possible to create two new flanks by rupturing an adversary's front and driving through the gap to strike at his rear. That is the battle of penetration, and it has some distinguished victories to its credit.

Effectiveness of flank and rear attacks

In any event, the effectiveness of the attack is in direct proportion to the conviction of defeat it can instill. As evidence, history is filled with occasions when the casualties of a beaten army were the result rather than the cause of defeat.

Offensive and defensive tactics. The relative merits of the offensive and defensive have been subjects of argument in all military ages. From one century to another each has dominated in turn, the new cycle being brought about by the introduction of new weapons or tactics.

The attacker is usually able to choose the time of the assault and sometimes the place as well. If there are several points where the blow might fall, he has an opportunity to utilize the principles of deception and surprise against an opponent who must prepare as best he can to meet every alternative.

The defender often has the advantage of choosing and fortifying his own ground, but at least temporarily he must concede the initiative to the enemy. In most instances, of course, he expects to regain it by means of a decisive counterattack after exhausting his adversary or placing him in an unfavourable position. Passive defenses are seldom the resort of a general who retains freedom of action, though there are exceptional occasions when the object is to inflict crippling casualties on a rash enemy.

Cordon defenses are put into effect along a frontier on which troops can be thinly dispersed and quickly reinforced by reserves in the event of trouble. The mobile, or elastic, defense is based on the theory that if the enemy makes a penetration his flanks will be open to counterattack. The so-called defensive–offensive action merely implies that the defender has initially planned to launch a counterstroke when he has an opportunity.

Breaking off contact with the enemy is a delicate operation calling for that specialized form of the defense known as a delaying action. The rearguard force holds just long enough to compel the pursuer to deploy, then pulls back to the next prepared position before becoming seriously engaged. In a two-line delaying action the first and second lines retire through each other in turn until the main body of troops is out of danger.

The delaying action

The ideal instrument would be an army equally formidable in offensive and defensive tactics, but there have been few such in military chronicles. Probably the most effective combination throughout history has been the strategic offensive and tactical defensive. Invading armies are often able to choose their ground and await an attack, since the enemy is obliged for the sake of national morale to defend the homeland. No better example of this compulsion could be found than the situation faced by Roman generals after Hannibal's crossing of the Alps into Italy. One after another, they met him in headlong attack, only to go down to crushing defeat. Finally the proud republic was reduced to avoiding battle in order to recuperate.

Until the 19th century, offensive and defensive cycles were of long duration. Improvements in weapons have come so rapidly since the Napoleonic era that the swing from one to another is a matter of only a few years. Generals of all armies were confident at the outbreak of World War I that the offensive power of the arms of 1914 would prevail in a few months. The machine gun had the leading part in turning the conflict into a stalemate, however, and not until the last few months of the war did the tank provide the victors with an offensive weapon capable of breaking the deadlock. Even so, a school of military thought held after the war that the defensive remained powerful enough to curb an aggressor in the next conflict. That illusion was soon dispelled when the German armies of 1940 drove on to a succession of early victories.

HISTORICAL DEVELOPMENT OF MILITARY TACTICS

In fighting the unending war for survival, prehistoric man employed tactics that from the first involved the three elements of firepower, movement, and protection. He employed missile weapons (stones, wooden spears, darts) and hand or side weapons (stone and flint knives and handaxes); he used terrain and flame as protection against both animals and the elements, and he also used fire as a weapon to force beasts from the protection of caves. His first military tactics were decidedly primitive—single encounters won by the strongest opponent. But as walled towns sprang up and armaments improved, as the wheel was invented and the horse domesticated, battle grew more sophisticated. Eventually tribes organized specific armies, trained and disciplined them, and developed metal weapons and armour.

The age of the chariot. Around 1800 BC the Hyksos, migrating south from Asia, introduced the horse-drawn chariot as a tactical weapon in a series of battles that wrested most of present Syria and Israel from the Egyptians. These vehicles were small, usually holding one or two men armed with the bow. The front was protected. In battle, chariots preceded units of foot soldiers, a tactic that thoroughly disrupted the Egyptian formations.

The Egyptians quickly adopted the new tactics. Ahmose I and his successors developed a wider, lighter chariot and also introduced iron wheels with spokes, a notable improvement over the solid wooden wheels. In building a new empire, Thutmose I employed a navy to establish forward supply bases that supported armies spearheaded by chariots and using two types of foot troops: heavy infantrymen, who carried spears and long shields, and light infantrymen, armed with spears, bows, battle-axes, and slings. The light, broad chariots generally carried specially trained bowmen. Thutmose's armies were probably formidable enough, but his continued prosperity seems to have hinged more upon a wise overall strategy, particularly in the political sphere, than upon any special ground tactics which in any event were doomed by the rise of the Assyrians.

The Assyrians. The Assyrians, who later conquered Egypt and by 671 BC dominated the eastern Mediterranean, made war their chief business. Employing weapons made of iron (taken from the Hittites), the Assyrians in open battle relied on both cavalry and heavy chariots backed by archers, spearmen, and shield bearers. They developed a chariot heavier than the Egyptians' and used protective felt coverings for the horses. They deployed both light archers, who often fought as skirmishers without protection, and heavy archers, who alternated with spearmen in the use of shield bearers. They began to use mounted bowmen and swordsmen independently, the first cavalry force. They also relied on terror for tactical purposes and were famed and feared for hard, fast actions.

To take cities, the Assyrians employed catapults and battering rams. The latter grew very sophisticated, at times reaching 20 stories in height and manned by hundreds of soldiers; Josephus speaks of one that was pulled by 300 oxen and manhandled into position by 1,500 soldiers.

The Persians. Assyrian tactics were adopted in part by the Persians who, commencing in about 553 BC, rose to power under Cyrus II. According to Herodotus' chronicle of these early wars, in the decisive Battle of Thymbra in 546 BC, Cyrus' chariots were backed by infantry followed by javelin-equipped soldiers and archers with cavalry on the flanks and in the rear. Cyrus enjoyed a reputation for cunning. Frustrated in his later siege of Babylon, he posted armies "at the point where the Euphrates river enters the city, and another body at the back of the place where it issues forth." He then took a body of troops and diverted the Euphrates by a canal into a marsh; his troops entered the city through the river beds, taking the Babylonians by surprise and winning the city.

Expansion and consolidation continued under Cyrus' successors, most notably Darius I (reigned 522–486 BC) and Xerxes (486–465 BC). Intent on protecting the empire in the east and west, Darius placed more emphasis on archers than on infantry and supported them with heavy chariots. To increase the shock value Darius attached scythes to the blades and wheels. A bit later, three curved blades were fastened to the pole, one straight forward, the others fanning out in front of the horses. These added to the terror of the attack.

Perhaps Darius' major contribution to military science was the reorganization of his ground force into divisions—each, of 10,000 men, organized into 10 battalions, each battalion into 10 companies, and each company into 10 sections. James H. Breasted described this organization as "one of the most remarkable achievements in the history of the ancient Orient, if not of the world." (*The Conquest of Civilization,* 1926.)

The Greco-Macedonian phalanx. The Greek city-states militarily emphasized the infantry phalanx, considered by some theorists to be the germ of all future European military development. Citizen-soldiers fought in an eight-rank phalanx of heavy infantry supported by contingents of light foot. Although Homer's *Iliad* mentions horse and chariots a millennium before the Christian Era, cavalry was not suited to a mountainous peninsula, and the incessant strife of the city-states was usually decided by the clash of opposing hedges of infantry spears.

Greek warfare was distinguished more for brawn and fortitude than for the intellectual brilliance that made for greatness in other aspects of Greek life. Even the double envelopment that won the Battle of Marathon (see Figure 1) for the Greeks in 490 BC seems to have been the product of a fortuitous event rather than generalship. Attacking at a fast pace, before the Persian superiority in cavalry and missile weapons could become effective, the Greek hoplites (heavily armed infantrymen) of both wings hurled back the lightly armed invaders in their path. Meanwhile, their own hard-pressed centre gave ground before the enemy advance until it seemed that defeat was imminent. As it proved, this withdrawal created the opportunity for the heavy infantry of the Greek wings to converge on the flanks and rear of the Persian host. Thus the battle ended

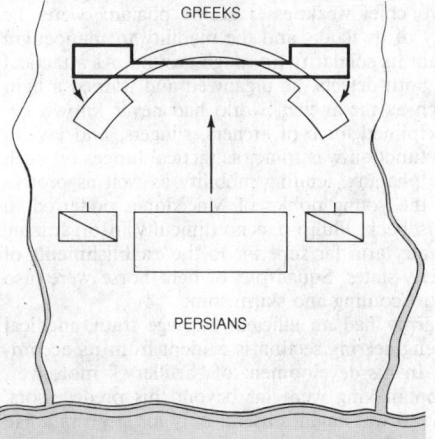

Figure 1: Battle of Marathon (490 BC), showing tactics of concentric attack.

with the demoralization and rout of an army at least twice that of the Greeks.

The Greek cavalry   Defending their homeland against the Persians, the Greeks learned to place increased reliance on cavalry and missile weapons—mercenary horsemen from the plains of Thessaly and bowmen from Crete. The first Greek to distinguish himself as a tactician was Epaminondas in 371 BC. Facing a Spartan army of 10,000 men with a force of 6,000 that included undependable allies, the Theban commander drew up a strange oblique order of battle by advancing his left wing and reinforcing it with his best troops to a depth of 48 ranks (see Figure 2). On the other wing he placed his doubtful allies. The Battle of Leuctra opened with a cavalry clash won by the better-trained Theban horse. Then Epaminondas bore down with the infantry of his heavy left wing on the right of the Spartan phalanx, and the factor of surprise probably had more to do with the outcome than physical shock. At any rate, the Spartan right recoiled in disorder on its own centre, and a phalanx thrown into confusion was little better than a mob. The muscular tactics of Sparta were of no avail to demoralized men too crowded together to use hand weapons, and the Thebans gained a one-sided victory.

Epaminondas was mortally wounded while winning a second battle with his oblique order, and it remained for a barbarian prince to assemble the tactics of the disputatious Greeks into a system capable of conquest. Young Philip II of Macedon (382–336 BC) studied Epaminondas' methods while spending three years in Thebes as a hostage. He returned to his northern kingdom to organize the first army of ancient history to combine effectively such arms as infantry, cavalry, and artillery.

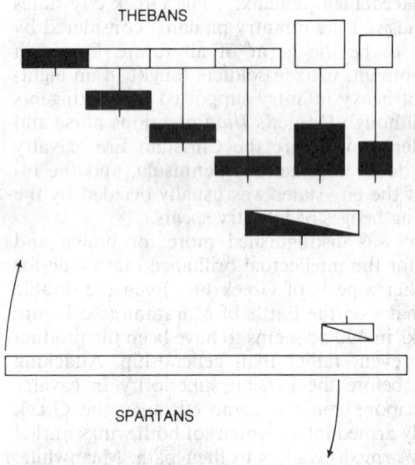

Figure 2: Battle of Leuctra (371 BC), showing tactics of the oblique order.

The new tactical system was built about the phalanx. Philip strengthened the mobile human fortress by doubling the eight-rank formation of the Greeks and arming his warriors with a longer and heavier spear. He perceived that the two chief weaknesses of the phalanx were the vulnerability of its flanks and the inability to manoeuvre or even retain its solidarity on rough ground. As a tactical remedy for both defects, he organized and trained a light infantry such as the ancient world had never known before—a disciplined force of archers, slingers, and javelin men. Their function was to act as tactical hinges on both sides of the phalanx, lending mobility as well as protection. Since the young nobles of Macedonia preferred to fight on horseback, Philip had no difficulty in organizing a heavy cavalry arm far superior to the establishments of the Greek city-states. Squadrons of light horse were also employed for scouting and skirmishing.

That the army had an efficient baggage train, medical corps, and engineering section is evident from its accomplishments. In his development of "artillery," moreover, the Macedonian king went far beyond his predecessors, **Philip's use of the phalanx** who had found war engines useful only for siegecraft. He originated the idea of carrying only the essential parts on the march and depending on his engineers to cut timbers for the framework whenever needed.

On the battlefield the full phalanx of about 8,000 heavily armoured spearmen was doubtless a fearsome spectacle as it advanced with menacing steel points. Several such bodies of troops might be employed as the central bulwark of the battle line, the pivot either of offense or defense. On the wings were the heavy cavalry squadrons trained for shock effect. Between the phalangial centre and cavalry wings, the tactical hinges of light foot supplied the flexibility for manoeuvre.

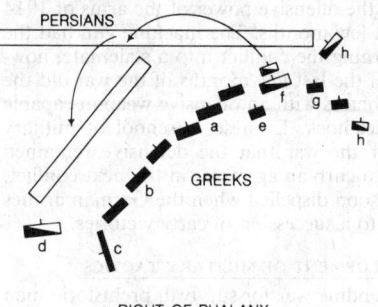

a RIGHT OF PHALANX
b LEFT OF PHALANX
c LIGHT INFANTRY
d CAVALRY
e SHIELD BEARERS
f HEAVY CAVALRY
g LIGHT INFANTRY
h LIGHT CAVALRY

Figure 3: Battle of Arbela, or Gaugamela (331 BC), showing tactics of rear attack.

This was the army that Philip led to the conquest of Greece and his son Alexander (356–323 BC) made the instrument of world conquest. The Greco-Macedonian tactical system met its greatest test on the field of Arbela, or Gaugamela, in 331 BC. Darius III, the Persian monarch, had a numerical advantage of perhaps five to one over Alexander's 7,000 cavalry and 40,000 foot. The action took place near the ruins of ancient Nineveh on a plain suited to the Persian cavalry and chariots (see Figure 3). Despite the odds against him, Alexander rejected the plan of a night attack urged by his nobles. He opened the battle by seizing the initiative with a rapid advance of his right wing, followed in echelon by the rest of the army. The local superiority in numbers enabled him to drive so deeply between the enemy's left and centre as to reach the rear. A more perfect example of the battle of penetration can scarcely be found in the pages of history, for the Persian host was routed while still possessing a great numerical superiority over Alexander's army.

Alexander's campaigns took him as far as modern India and Afghanistan during the six years after his conquest of Persia. Among his most troublesome foes were the Scythian horsemen who preyed upon his flanks and rear, seeking to cut off detachments. That the nomadic riders of the Asian plains could be formidable opponents was convincingly demonstrated in later centuries when no fewer than four Roman armies were lured to their destruction.

The Scythians and Parthians were made natural warriors by a harsh environment. Shunning action at close quarters, fleeing when pressed, then returning to the attack in swirling envelopments, they could discharge arrows while riding at top speed.

Alexander refused to be drawn into extended pursuits by feigned flights. Noting that a lack of discipline among the Scythians made them reckless at times, he trained his light infantry to launch surprise counterattacks and beat the nomads at their own game by cutting off detachments. Once the lightly armed Scythians were at close quarters, they were no match for Alexander's cavalry.

The Roman legion.   The conqueror's death was followed by the rapid crumbling of the great empire he had founded during his lifetime. But while Alexander's former generals disputed for mastery in the east, a young and vigorous war power was rising in the west. Fighting in a simple phalanx of heavy infantry at first, the Romans learned by defeat that the human wall is not suited to battle on rough ground.

The new tactical system that gradually evolved was the

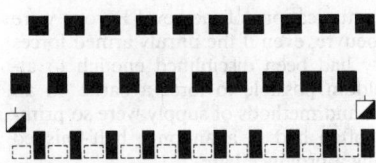

Figure 4: *Legion in battle order.*
First two lines, heavy infantry. Third
line, cavalry and light infantry alternated
with reserves.

Organiza-
tion of the
legion

legion (see Figure 4). Under the republic it consisted of small and supple infantry units known as maniples, each numbering 120 men in 12 files and 10 ranks. In a typical battle order the first two lines, drawn up in chessboard array, were composed of 10 maniples each. An interval equal to a maniple's front of 60 feet separated the units, enabling the second line to merge with the first or the first to fall back into the second. The advantages of mobility could thus be exchanged for those of solidarity, since the two lines combined had a depth of 10 ranks and a front of 1,200 feet.

In the third line 10 units of light foot were alternated with a like number of reserve units, the former numbering 120 men each and the latter 60. The three lines were 250 feet apart, and from front to rear one maniple of each classification formed a cohort. This was the Roman equivalent of a battalion, numbering 420 men. Ten cohorts made up the infantry strength of a legion, but 20 were customarily combined with a small cavalry force and other supporting units into a self-sustaining little army of about 10,000 men.

The two famous Roman infantry weapons were the *pilum* and *gladius*—the first a seven-foot javelin used for both throwing and thrusting and the latter a 20-inch cut-and-thrust sword with a broad, heavy blade. For protection the legionary had a metal helmet, cuirass, and convex shield, but aggressive action was deemed a Roman's best defense. The first line attacked on the double, hurling javelins and diving in with swords before the enemy had time to recover. Then came the maniples of the second line, and only a resolute foe could rally from the two successive shocks.

The Battle of Cannae. When Hannibal descended from the Alps in 218 BC with an army of Iberian, Numidian, and Gallic mercenaries, the Roman Republic paid the penalty of placing too much reliance on heavy infantry and failing to develop a cavalry arm and missile weapons. Two Roman armies, destroyed in the early encounters, were outmanoeuvred and cut to pieces by the Carthaginian horse. Finally, the Romans incurred a disaster that has made the name of Cannae a symbol ever since of the battle of annihilation and double envelopment (see Figure 5).

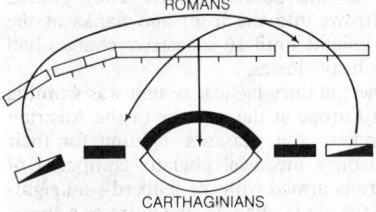

Figure 5: Battle of Cannae (216 BC), showing
tactics of double envelopment.

Tactic of
double
envelop-
ment

Hannibal provoked an action, though much outnumbered by a Roman army of 85,000 men. Adopting a convex formation of his foot in the centre, he gradually withdrew it in a feigned retreat until the Roman infantry rushed in recklessly, raising the victory shout. When the converging legionaries were too crowded together to use their weapons, the Carthaginian closed the trap by assailing the flanks and rear of the Roman infantry with his cavalry after driving the inferior enemy horse from the field. The result was a prolonged slaughter of helpless men that lasted until only about 15,000 scattered fugitives survived Rome's greatest disaster.

Tactics of the cohorts. The patriotic citizen-soldier of the republic's early years was gradually replaced by a professional soldiery serving for pay and donatives. The cohort of an average field strength of 360 men gradually replaced the maniple as the tactical unit of increasingly larger Roman armies. Ten cohorts made up a legion in the operations of Sulla and Caesar. The 3,600 heavy infantry were supported by enough horse and light infantry to bring the numbers up to 6,000 in all.

The maniple survived only as a unit of a cohort of eight or 10 ranks. Four cohorts in the first line and three each in the second and third lines were drawn up in chessboard array, with intervals between units so that one line could merge with another (see Figure 6). Seven legions in three lines, comprising about 25,000 heavy infantry, occupied a mile and a half of front. This was an average of about 11 men to a metre of front, as compared with 28 in Alexander's army.

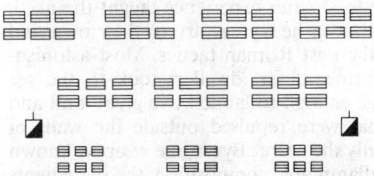

Figure 6: *Legion in battle order.*
Four cohorts in the first line and three each in
the second and third lines with cavalry.

The practical good sense that distinguished Roman tactics was at its best in field fortification. No greater demonstration was ever seen in the ancient world than the 50 miles of works with which Caesar gained the submission of Vercingetorix and 80,000 Gauls at Alesia. The Romans began by surrounding the strong natural defenses with a system of walls and trenches. When Gallic allies marched to the rescue of his opponent, Caesar surrounded his own army with works of circumvallation and beat off all attacks. Finally the relieving army disintegrated and Vercingetorix was starved into surrender.

Roman
fortifica-
tions

The Byzantine tactical system. After the fall of Rome in AD 476, the Eastern or Byzantine Empire managed to survive by means of bribing the most formidable barbarians and inducing them to move on to the occupation of Italy. The respite enabled Constantinople to develop during the reign of Justinian (AD 527–565) a cavalry tactical system that won victories on three continents.

This system was built about the horse archer. The invention of the stirrup had given an impetus to cavalry warfare, and the historian Procopius has described the tactics of the mounted mercenaries whom Belisarius led to conquests in Persia, North Africa, and Italy.

But the horsemen of the present time go into battle wearing corselets and fitted out with greaves which extend up to the knee. From the right side hang their arrows, from the other the sword. And there are some who have a spear also attached to them and, at the shoulders, a sort of small shield without a grip, such as to cover the region of the face and neck. They are expert horsemen, and are able without difficulty to direct their bows to either side while riding at full speed, and to shoot an opponent whether in pursuit or flight. They draw the bowstring along by the forehead about opposite the right ear, thereby charging an arrow with such impetus as to kill whoever stands in the way, shield and corselet alike having no power to check its force. Still, there are those who take into consideration none of these things, who reverence and worship the ancient times, and give no credit to modern improvements. (Procopius, *Works*, trans. by H.B. Dewing [Loeb Classical Library], vol. i, p. 7; Harvard University Press, Cambridge, Mass., 1914.)

Byzantine tactics were eminently practical, the spirit of chivalry being unknown in an empire constantly fighting for existence. Greek in speech as well as tradition, Constantinople reduced war to a science with a series of treatises and manuals. The *Tactica* of Emperor Leo the Wise, written about 900, urged that operations should be varied to take advantage of each foe's peculiar weaknesses. Fraud and feigned flights were suggested without apology. If a foe could be bribed more cheaply than defeated, Eastern Roman emperors deemed it no disgrace to pay tribute.

Since most of Constantinople's foes were mounted, the tactical system placed the emphasis on heavy cavalry,

Realism of
Byzantine
tactics

both archers and lancers. But even though the infantry ranked as a secondary army, it was well trained and combined with mounted troops in proportions suited to tactical demands. Squadrons of light horse were employed for scouting and reconnaissance.

Byzantine armies stood between the West and Asian invaders at a time when the impoverished Europe of the Dark Ages would probably have been overrun. Charles Martel and his Franks had difficulty in repulsing a single large-scale Moorish plunder raid on the field of Tours in 732. Yet Constantinople held its own in an 83-year war with the Saracens when Islām was at the height of its conquering momentum.

At the outset the Muslims were cavalry warriors using much the same tactics as the Parthians and Scythians. They differed from other plains horsemen in their ability to learn from their foes. After experience taught the need, the Saracens organized a heavy cavalry of their own and adopted many of the East Roman tactics. Most astonishing of all, these former desert dwellers took to the sea and built ships large enough to launch two great land and water invasions that were repulsed outside the walls of Constantinople. Only the secret Byzantine weapon known as Greek fire (an inflammable composition, the ingredients of which are unknown) saved the imperial city in 673.

The Franks and Vikings. It was fortunate that Europe was spared a severe test, for as late as the 8th century the Franks could raise only untrained and largely unarmoured men using the most primitive tactics. The low esteem in which the Franks were held by skilled warriors is evident from Leo's *Tactica.* Admitting that the headlong charge of mounted Franks with lance and broadsword could be formidable, he nevertheless advised that one could

> take advantage of their indiscipline and disorder; whether fighting on foot or on horseback, they charge in dense, unwieldy masses, which cannot manoeuvre, because they have neither organisation nor drill.... Hence they readily fall into confusion if suddenly attacked in flank and rear—a thing easy to accomplish, as they are utterly careless and neglect the use of pickets and vedettes and the proper surveying of the countryside. (C.W.C. Oman, *A History of the Art of War in the Middle Ages,* vol. ii, p. 204.)

Charlemagne made an unceasing effort to create a disciplined army of mailed cavalry out of the Frankish host of unarmoured foot, but despite his reforms Europe was long helpless against the plunder raids of the Vikings. Their single-decked ships with curved prows and shield-hung bulwarks were fast and seaworthy, and experience had taught them effective tactics of seizing a beachhead after pushing up such rivers as the Loire and Meuse. The Vikings were formidable fighters with axe and sword, and their forays grew so bold during the last half of the 9th century that they sacked London and laid siege to Paris.

There was not time to summon large armed forces from a distance against these fleet raiders. Each district had to fend for itself, and the feudal system burgeoned as Europeans paid military duty to the local lord upon whom they relied for protection. Cavalry tactics were also given another impetus, for only mailed horsemen could cope with the Vikings. Seldom has the social progress of an age been so largely shaped by tactical factors.

The age of the medieval knight. In 1066, at the Battle of Hastings, the last infantry host of western Europe went down to defeat in England before the descendants of Norsemen who had settled in France and learned to fight on horseback. The mounted and armoured men-at-arms had become virtually the tactical unit of artless battles that had as their first object the seizing of opponents to hold for ransom. Serfs who fought on foot were held in such low esteem that no count was taken of their numbers or losses.

In contrast to the supremacy of the offensive in Asia, the defensive was all-powerful in medieval Europe. Concentric fortification added to the difficulties of besiegers by making it necessary to attack walls within walls as well as outer wards and foreworks, while the crossbow provided the garrison with a means of enfilade fire from rounded keeps. Meanwhile, the gradual transition from chain to plate armour made the mailed knight and his barded charger more invulnerable to the weapons of the day.

The wretched communications of medieval Europe were a deterrent to manoeuvre, even if the unruly armed forces of the 13th century had been disciplined enough to attempt it. It was seldom possible to force a battle on an unwilling opponent, and methods of supply were so primitive that an army often had to abandon a half-finished campaign after eating a province bare.

That the tactical superiority of the knight owed a great deal to his monopoly of the prerogative of bearing arms was demonstrated by despised Flemish burghers at the Battle of Courtrai in 1302. French men-at-arms, putting down a revolt, launched their usual thundering charge only to bog down in disorder upon reaching marshy ground they had not troubled to reconnoitre. The Flemish foot clubbed the knights out of the saddle and dispatched them as they lay helpless in the mud, too burdened with armour to defend themselves.

The Mongols. Except for a few crossbowmen, Europe's armies had no infantry worthy of the name. A similar situation prevailed in Asia, where the Mongols led by Genghis Khan built up a formidable cavalry system. The bow, lance, and scimitar were the weapons of fierce horsemen who used two varieties of bows and three "calibres" of arrows for various tactical purposes. The Great Wall of China, with its 1,500 miles of earth-filled brick or granite, proved to be no serious obstacle to invaders who swept like a pestilence from the Yangtze to the Vistula during the 13th century without incurring a single major defeat. Whether they could have continued to win victories in the mountains and forests of western Europe is open to speculation, for they returned to Asia after defeating the feudal horsemen of Hungary and Poland.

The late Middle Ages in Europe. *Longbow and halberd.* The use of gunpowder in the 14th century made it inevitable that the supremacy of the man of iron in his house of stone could not be long maintained. But the first handguns were not as effective as either the crossbow or English longbow, and it was actually the rise of disciplined forces of yeomen using infantry tactics that restored the balance between the offensive and defensive in medieval Europe.

Although a few weapons using gunpowder were present on the field of Crécy in 1346, the outcome owed more to the discipline and tactics of an English army in which every man received a fixed and regular wage. For it was truly a national army that Edward III led to France, and the French knights would probably have been defeated even if the invaders had been armed with a less effective weapon than the six-foot longbow. Its superiority over the crossbow of the Genoese mercenaries was proved in a preliminary exchange of missiles. Edward had placed his dismounted men-at-arms in the centre as spearmen, and on both projecting wings the lightly armoured archers stood behind ditches and pointed stakes. They poured deadly flights of arrows into the front and flanks of the advancing French knights until 16 successive charges had been repulsed with heavy losses.

Meanwhile, another infantry tactical system was winning victories in central Europe at the expense of the Austrian knights. Swiss burghers and peasants, fighting for their liberties, depended on a medieval phalanx composed of spearmen and warriors armed with the halberd—an eight-foot shaft that had the blade of an ax, the point of a spear, and a hook for pulling a rider out of the saddle.

The Swiss phalanx of the 15th century consisted of three-fifths halberds, one-fifth spears, and one-fifth missile weapons, chiefly crossbows, with handguns slowly gaining in favour. In the interests of mobility the men of the Swiss cantons discarded all armour except the helmet and cuirass. Marching 30 miles a day to meet the enemy, they attacked with a celerity and discipline that were disconcerting to medieval adversaries. If hard-pressed, the Swiss "formed the hedgehog" by facing outward in all directions as men from the rear ranks filled any gap in front.

Early victories of gunpowder. After beating mailed horsemen who had resisted tactical change, the English and Swiss in their turn were defeated because they lagged behind the military progress of the age. It had taken weapons of gunpowder a century and a half to have much

Amphibious warfare of the Vikings

The cavalry of Genghis Khan

The Battle of Crécy

influence on tactics, but at the siege of Orléans in 1428–29 both sides used cannon firing stone balls. The French guns were better served than the mortars and bombards brought by the English, who met defeat at the Battle of Patay after abandoning the siege.

Charles VII of France (1403–61) raised the first standing army of the Middle Ages—9,000 permanent troops, paid and armed by the king. This force gradually won back the French territory conquered by the English in the Hundred Years' War, and at the Battle of Formigny in 1450 the invaders were decisively beaten after making their customary defensive stand with the longbowmen on both wings. Instead of launching their usual charge, the outnumbered French brought up culverins, or medieval fieldpieces, and cut the English archers to pieces with enfilade fire. The Swiss phalanx was granted a longer period of grace, but there was no hope and eventually it too was to pay with defeat for clinging obstinately to outworn tactics.

Of all the early exponents of gunpowder weapons, perhaps the most remarkable was the army of Bohemian peasants commanded by Jan Žižka (c. 1376–1424). Several crusades were proclaimed by Pope Martin V against these dissenting followers of Jan Hus, but the German and Hungarian knights encountered the most advanced tactical system of the new age of gunpowder. Combining the strategic offensive with the tactical defensive, the Hussite military genius drew up a line of "wagonforts"—armoured wagons affording cover to infantry armed with both handguns and crossbows. Between the vehicles were cannon mounted on four-wheeled carts and protected by infantry with pikes. Behind both wings the cavalry waited in readiness to deliver either a counterstroke or lead a pursuit.

The combination of the three arms continued to prevail without a single reverse after the death of the blind leader. More than 50 battles and combats were won by the Hussites in 14 years, but civil war led to the destruction of the armies that had been invincible against the invading knights.

The age of transition. In 1453 it was evident that a new military age had dawned when the Turks breached the walls of Constantinople with a siege train of 70 cannon. After 40 days of bombardment enough towers had been levelled and holes opened in the masonry for a general land and sea assault to succeed.

If weapons of gunpowder could batter down the strongest walls of Europe, it was plain that a defensive based on iron men in stone castles was no longer dominant. By the middle of the 15th century the plate armour panoply had become so heavy that special breeds of horses, the ancestors of Percherons and Belgians, were reared as chargers. Only armour of prohibitive weight could stop a ball from a handgun at close range, and men were beginning to suspect that mobility offered more protection than iron.

Fortification and siegecraft had changed but little in 2,000 years. Down to the 14th century an Assyrian of 700 BC would not have found much to astonish him in the attack and defense of walled strongholds in Europe. But after the fall of Constantinople it was realized that the wall was obsolescent. Works of the future must be low and screened, burrowing into the earth for security. Besiegers must dig their way forward in a maze of parallels and approaches affording shelter from the fire of the besieged.

About this time the ponderous handgun was being superseded by the harquebus, a comparatively portable matchlock that could be fired from the shoulder. Improvements in the manufacture of the wheeled cannon had resulted in slender guns of cast iron or bronze, thus increasing mobility, and the invention of the trunnion permitted the muzzle to be elevated or depressed for more accurate aim.

New firearms such as the harquebus gun and lighter cannon were utilized by brilliant captains in the struggle between France and Spain for control of Italy early in the 16th century. Tactical values changed from one battle to another with bewildering rapidity. On the field of Cerignola in 1503, the French infantry and Swiss mercenary pikemen were mowed down by the fire of Spanish harquebusiers who counterattacked and captured the enemy's entire artillery train. Nine years later, at the Battle

of Ravenna, the Spaniards again used entrenched harquebusiers. But this time the French moved 24 cannon to the enemy's flank and surprised the Spanish infantry with an enfilade fire that decided the battle.

Pike and harquebus. The Spaniards founded a new school of infantry tactics that was to rule the battlefields of Europe for a century and make possible incredibly daring conquests in the New World. Solid columns of infantry were drawn up in groups known as battles. Various combinations of "shot and pike" were used, but usually the harquebusiers were drawn up on the corners of battles 25 ranks deep. After firing at the word of command, each rank withdrew to the rear to reload and gradually moved forward by successive volleys until its turn came again. It was the function of the pikes to protect the harquebusiers while reloading. When the enemy's ranks were broken by firepower, the pikemen evolved from square into line and advanced, shoulder to shoulder, in a massive charge calculated to sweep the field (see Figure 7).

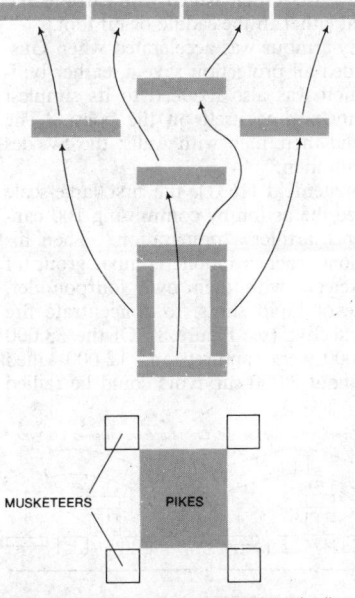

MUSKETEERS   PIKES

Figure 7: Evolution of the square into the line.

The *tercio* of about 3,000 foot was the basic Spanish tactical unit. Consisting of 12 companies of about 250 men each, the fighting strength in 1534 was divided equally between pikemen and harquebusiers. Cavalry was represented in one-twelfth of infantry strength, and artillery by an average of one gun to each 1,000 foot.

The value of tactics and discipline was illustrated during the reign (1519–56) of the emperor Charles V when small bands of Spaniards won amazing victories over hordes in Mexico, Peru, and the islands of the Caribbean. The Indians were not wanting in sacrificial courage, and their advantage in numbers compensated for inferiority in weapons. One Aztec might have been a match for a Spaniard in single combat, but a thousand Aztecs were routed by a hundred Spaniards because they lacked the tenacity instilled by discipline as well as tactical system and precision.

Gustavus Adolphus and the Thirty Years' War. It fell to the Swedish king Gustavus II Adolphus (reigned 1611–32) to institute tactical innovations that earned him the title "father of modern tactics." The Swedish king organized his infantry into brigades, each consisting of two regiments that in turn included two battalions. Each battalion of 1,000 men was divided into eight companies of an average strength of 75 muskets and 60 pikes.

Swedish armourers had developed a lighter musket, and Gustavus is credited with being first to introduce paper cartridges to speed reloading. His six ranks advanced in open order and closed up into three, the first rank kneeling and the other two standing while firing a volley.

The Swedish artillery also benefitted from innovations. Advances in metallurgy having made possible a lighter fieldpiece, Gustavus recalled most of his old ordnance.

These pieces were recast into fourpounders of 3 feet 10 inches (117 centimetres) in length, 400 pounds (181 kilograms) in weight, and 2.6-inch (6.6-centimetre) calibre. Four men or a single horse could handle the new gun on the field, though the fourpounders of other armies weighed half a ton (450 kilograms) or more.

The first artillery cartridge was developed as ammunition—a thin wooden case holding a prepared powder charge wired to the ball. Improvements were also made in the "bomb," or shell—a hollow iron sphere filled with gunpowder and fired with a lighted fuse. Reloading was speeded to such an extent that the Swedish fourpounder could be discharged eight times while the best musketeers fired six volleys. This was the first regimental piece of history, and each Swedish regiment of 1,000 men brought two fourpounders into the field.

It was characteristic of the forthright Swedish king to train his cavalry entirely for shock effect with pistol and sabre. He organized Europe's first regular dragoon corps—a tactical hybrid made up of men armed with carbine and sabre who could fight either in the saddle or on foot.

The decline in body armour was accelerated when Gustavus himself discarded all protection save a leather buff-coat. Field fortification was also reduced to its simplest elements by an army priding itself on the boast, "The Swedes do not defend their men with walls; the Swedes defend their walls with men."

In the Battle of Breitenfeld (1631), the first large-scale test, Gustavus opened the action by committing 100 cannon to a long-distance artillery "preparation." Then his self-sustained battalions, each a mobile combat group of pikemen and musketeers with their own fourpounder, were able, by virtue of rapid shifts, to concentrate fire where it was most effective (see Figure 8). Of the 33,000 opposing troops, 7,000 were captured and 12,000 killed or wounded. Only about 2,000 survivors could be rallied after the pursuit.

From Captain Liddell Hart, *Great Captains Unveiled*, Blackwood

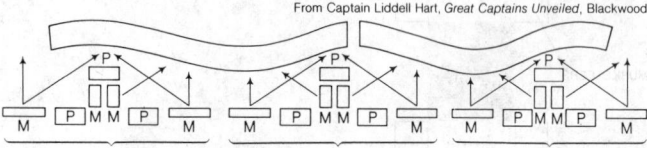

P—PIKEMEN   M—MUSKETEERS

Figure 8: Companies of musketeers and pikemen drawn up in combat formation by Gustavus II Adolphus.

Although Gustavus won another victory in the Battle of Lützen the following year, he paid for it with his life. In two years of campaigning he had overrun Germany, but after his death the army soon degenerated into another of the plundering hosts that made the war one of the most destructive of history.

The age of linear tactics. After the bloody battles of the Thirty Years' War (1618–48) resulted in a prolonged stalemate, the Vicomte de Turenne, commanding mercenaries paid by France, cleared the enemy from Bavaria in a campaign of manoeuvre, compelling the elector Maximilian I to sue for an armistice. Avoiding battle unless he had an overwhelming advantage, the French tactician relied upon caution, precision, and surprise to drive the enemy into ravaged areas while retaining his own sources of supply.

Thus the savage excesses of the war were made to appear futile by tactics that foreshadowed the most moderate era of strife in modern history. The founding father of the new military age was the Marquis de Louvois (1639–91), minister of war at the court of Louis XIV of France. Recognizing that tactics are dependent on supply, he organized a quartermaster general's department and a trained commissariat. As fixed points of manoeuvre, he established magazines at strategic centres for storage of reserves of food, ammunition, and equipment. The French minister also foresaw that two recent improvements in weapons would lead to tactical change. The first was the socket bayonet, which superseded the pike by providing every musketeer with his own means of protection. Equally important was the invention of the flintlock musket, making it possible to dispense with the clumsy lengths of smoldering "match."

Even Gustavus Adolphus had not been able to reduce the depth of his formations to fewer than six ranks. But now that it was no longer necessary to combine pikes with muskets, Louvois perceived that the day of linear warfare had dawned. His famous drillmaster, Gen. Jean Martinet, whose name has lived as a byword, trained the troops of the new French armies to deploy from column into line and advance in three ranks, pausing to fire platoon volleys at the word of command. The effect depended on precision of approach, and the men were trained to move forward in unison, keeping step at a stately cadence of 80 paces a minute.

The French army had no equal in numbers as well as quality when Louis XIV began the aggressions that were to involve him in wars throughout his long reign. But the Battle of Seneffe in 1674 made it plain that grievous losses were to be expected by the best troops when opposing lines traded volleys at 50 paces as a prelude to charging with the bayonet. Only iron discipline could fit men to stand firm and fill the gaps in the ranks, for the death casualties alone in this clash amounted to 17 percent for both armies.

The American Revolution. Many of the tactics of the Napoleonic era had their roots in the American Revolution. It was evident to observers that the American frontier rifle ranked as history's first infantry firearm of precision. Although it took twice as long as a smoothbore musket to reload, it had from two to three times the effective range in addition to an accuracy that was beyond comparison.

Although a majority of the Americans carried smooth-bore muskets, the farmers and villagers of the New World were accustomed to hunting small game at a time when laws against poaching and possessing firearms prevailed in Europe. The greenest American recruits took aim instinctively while European regulars were trained to point the piece in the general direction of the foe and fire at the word of command. Thus at the Battle of Bunker Hill, most of the British shots passed harmlessly over the heads of Americans who inflicted casualties of 45 percent with their limited ammunition by taking "aim at the handsome waistcoats." Because of the broken country, light-infantry tactics flourished in the American Revolution. And since all the armies were small, a two-rank line gained approval as a means of adding to infantry firepower.

French Revolutionary and Napoleonic tactics. The "horde tactics" of the French Revolutionary armies evolved from military poverty. Lacking magazines, the *sans-culottes* gained in mobility by becoming less dependent on bases and lines of communication. Lacking tents, they learned to bivouac in the field, where all units could be more swiftly concentrated. Lacking supply wagons, they learned to march at a more rapid cadence than their opponents. Lacking training for the precision of linear tactics, they gradually developed a more effective attack of their own.

At least two lessons of the American conflict were put into effect—firing at will, as distinguished from volley fire, and taking natural cover on the skirmish line. Upon coming in contact with the enemy, the bolder spirits of a revolutionary army swarmed out to fire from ditches or behind hedges. The platoon volleys of linear tactics were not effective against these elusive French skirmishers, who took to their heels when threatened with a bayonet charge. Fighting of this sort was so interesting and comparatively safe that more and more men participated. Finally, at the Battle of Hondschoote in 1793, French forces concentrated swiftly and almost literally mobbed an Allied rearguard detachment with a wild bayonet attack.

Bonaparte's early victories. It is taking no credit away from Bonaparte's genius for war to point out that he adapted rather than originated his tactics. He was the heir not only of French Revolutionary tactics but also of an army of battle-hardened veterans who had won some notable victories over the Allies. From the old royal army he inherited the system of dispersion and concentration of divisions and brigades.

Bonaparte was not a great battlefield tactician. He was at his best in that hybrid between tactics and strategy known as "grand tactics"—the assembling of units prior to battle for a last-minute concentration by forced marches on the battlefield itself. No longer could an adversary refuse combat, as in the days of linear tactics. Bonaparte forced such an opponent to fight by sending a column around to threaten his line of communications. When the enemy was brought to bay, Bonaparte could summon his own outlying columns as mobile reserves in less time than could the armies trained for linear tactics.

The preliminary swarms of skirmishers, the cannonading by regimental guns firing grapeshot at close ranges, the battlefield concentration, and the attack by bayonet columns of infantry—these were the four stages of Bonaparte's early victories. Some of them were gained by envelopment, some by penetration, and others by plain frontal assault, according to the dictates of his intuition.

Wellington's tactics.   At a time when other generals were imitating Napoleon's methods, the Duke of Wellington defeated French columns with linear tactics and depended on seaborne supplies while outmanoeuvring an enemy living on a country eaten bare. He, too, was an adapter rather than an originator, for the British tactical system was largely the creation of Sir John Moore. In 1803, in training troops to meet an expected Napoleonic invasion, Wellington reduced the standard three ranks to the two-rank line of the American Revolution. He applied another American lesson by organizing three regiments of riflemen for his light division, soon to win fame as the most celebrated unit of British battles in Spain.

Moore was killed in his first peninsular operation, but Wellington applied his tactics so successfully as to become one of history's few unbeaten generals. The French, as Europe's masters, felt obliged to attack. Their opponent profited by being able in every major battle to choose his own ground and draw up his "thin red line" behind a low ridge. This gave him the double advantage of protecting his men from ricochetting cannonballs and compelling the French bayonet columns to advance uphill. A screen of skirmishers from the light division was deployed along the forward slope. Since their rifles outranged French muskets, they were able to harass the enemy columns with aimed fire while the British artillery thinned them with shrapnel. The two-rank line gave the redcoats a wider front for musketry, and Wellington met the main French shock with steady platoon volleys. If the enemy wavered, he ordered a British bayonet counterattack.

Wellington's reliance on directed fire

This was the tactical formula, repeated with few variations, that won victories over Napoleon's marshals for five years in Spain. Wellington proved to be a match for the French in swift concentrations, and on one occasion his light division completed a march of 43 miles in 22 hours. But it was with infantry firepower that he beat opponents who trusted too much in the bayonet, for Napoleon had refused to adopt the rifle and neglected musketry training in spite of his assertion that "the power of infantry lies in its fire."

Half a century of transition.   At Waterloo, Wellington needed only the tactics that had won for him in Spain. But an era came to an end on that June day in 1815, when infantry, cavalry, and artillery were in close contact and could be controlled by the general as easily as a regiment a century later. All this was changed by the widespread adoption of the percussion cap and long bullet, which multiplied the range as well as accuracy of the rifle and made it a universal military weapon. No longer was it possible to place the guns in front of the infantry, as was done sometimes during the Napoleonic era, with the cavalry close behind. No longer was it possible to mass cannon only 500 yards from the enemy, as at Borodino, and blast a bloody path to victory. Thus the old battle order, which had changed but little in essentials since the day of Gustavus Adolphus, was relegated to the past. To command an army as Wellington did at Waterloo was out of the question; to render its separate parts cooperative demanded staff work and not merely a powerful voice.

During the half-century preceding the American Civil War, inventions came so rapidly that soldiers could not keep pace. The revolver and repeating carbine opened up new vistas for the cavalry and rendered obsolete the charge of lancers. Rifled and breechloading fieldpieces worked a revolution in artillery tactics, just as the telegraph, the railroad, and the steamship made it necessary to revise previous ideas of military transport and communication.

Few precedents were available when green armies of citizen-soldiers met in the opening engagements of the U.S. conflict. But if they had more to learn, they also had less to forget than the tradition-ridden soldiers of Europe. And before the four-year struggle ended, the Americans had put into effect many of the tactics that would shape the outcome of World War I.

The U.S. Civil War.   Four million men bore arms in the U.S. conflict. More than 2,000 combats took place, of which 149 were of enough importance to be called battles. Yet these far-flung operations were dominated throughout by the defensive power of the rifle, supported by the ax and the spade.

The railway gun, the land mine, the wire entanglement, the observation balloon, the hand grenade, the field telegraph—these were some of the innovations or revivals of the Civil War. But they were second to the demonstrated ability of the man in the rifle pits to hold his own against three attackers. Since most of the operations occurred in wooded country, soldiers of both sides learned to cut "head logs" with firing slits to give added protection along the parapets of trenches. Generals were taught by experience that marksmen in log-faced earthworks, supported by rifled artillery, could seldom be dislodged except at a ruinous cost in casualties. Gen. Robert E. Lee at Gettysburg and Gen. Ulysses S. Grant at Cold Harbor—the best tacticians of the war—met bloody repulses when they underestimated the firepower of opposing riflemen.

Advantages of defensive tactics

On the other hand, paradoxical as it may seem, the defensive power of the entrenched rifleman enabled Lee to launch successful attacks on opponents with a material advantage. Relying on the proved ability of one rifleman to stand off three adversaries, the Confederate general dared repeatedly to divide his army in the face of a more numerous enemy.

European soldiers professed to see in the Civil War only the incoherent clashes of armed mobs, and in 1870 the French and Prussians made it evident that they had learned nothing from the American precepts. They sent cavalry in suicidal charges against infantry men with breechloading rifles with an effective range of 1,000 yards; they took needless losses from rifled artillery as the penalty of close formations; and they persisted in infantry frontal attacks despite the fact that neither side succeeded in taking a single position by such tactics.

World War I.   *The Battle of the Marne.* It was the tragedy of World War I that the century of comparative European peace since Waterloo seemed to have made romanticists out of the professional soldiers who held in their hands the lives of millions of conscripted citizens. Despite the lessons of the U.S. conflict, confirmed by the machine guns of the Russo-Japanese War, France's generals of 1914 had a mystical faith in the *offensive à l'outrance*—the headlong offensive, compounded of mass, velocity, and morale. They believed that the prewar scale of two machine guns to a battalion was adequate; and as late as 1915 the British commander Sir Douglas (later Earl) Haig asserted that it was "a much overrated weapon" and agreed that the French scale was "more than sufficient." The German generals were more realistic, but they too had complete faith in the offensive and regarded any reference to defensive advantages as bordering on defeatism. Both the French and German tacticians considered a defensive action excusable only when "each man will die in place rather than give ground."

Initial belief in offensive tactics

The Germans, who were better prepared at the outset, seemed to be proving their case as they swept through Belgium and northern France. The French soldiers, uniformed in red breeches for the sake of morale, endured frightful losses. But since the German generals held that "the abandonment of close-rank formations is an evil which should be avoided whenever possible," their troops in turn provided the French artillery with lucrative targets.

In the Battle of the Marne the French stopped the invaders by taking advantage of blundering last-minute revisions in the German envelopment plan. Then began the "race to the sea" that was to result in a continuous front of trenches from the Channel to the Alps. The German losses of the first four months were 747,465 killed and wounded; the French had 854,000 casualties during the same period.

Deadlock on the Western Front. In the spring of 1915 the French and British believed that artillery was the key to the deadlock. But even after a prolonged bombardment by 1,140 pieces of heavy artillery, 53 French infantry divisions were able to advance only 3,000 yards on a 12-mile front. The enemy simply weathered the storm of steel in deep dugouts until the barrage lifted, then manned the machine guns to cut down attackers plodding across no-man's-land under heavy burdens of equipment.

Use of poison gas

The Germans risked the censure of neutral nations in an attempt to win a decision with poison gas in the Neuve Chapelle sector. But the Canadians held out until they could be reinforced, and millions of soldiers were soon carrying gas masks as all armies resorted to chemical warfare. Steel helmets also were generally adopted as protection against shell fragments.

The offensives of 1917. The Western Front was not the only theatre of war, but it was recognized that France would be the area of ultimate decision. In the spring of 1917 it was still thought that by increasing the density of artillery the infantry could make headway behind a rolling barrage timed to the advance. But even a ratio of a gun to six yards of front was not enough, and the German machine guns continued to reap their deadly harvest.

It had been necessary for a civilian, David Lloyd George, to provide the British Army with a realistic scale of machine guns and trench mortars in spite of the reluctance of Haig and Lord Kitchener. Another civilian spoke for the dead of France when Premier Georges Clemenceau remarked that "modern war is too serious a business to entrust to soldiers."

Although Belgian engineers had warned against destroying the drainage system of reclaimed lands, 103,000 tons of shells were fired in the preliminary British bombardments of the third Battle of Ypres, known to the soldiers as Passchendaele. Mustard gas was added to the horrors of the 100-day battle as both armies wallowed in the swamp created by 4,300,000 British shells. Haig's gains were negligible despite 300,000 casualties, and the Germans considered Passchendaele "the supreme martyrdom."

Early use of tanks

One of the few successes of a gloomy year was the British breakthrough at Cambrai on a six-mile front with 381 tanks supported by infantry. Attacking by complete surprise, after a last-minute hurricane barrage, the clanking cavalcade ripped through defenses in depth and took 7,500 prisoners and 120 guns at a low cost in casualties. Adequate infantry forces had not been provided by high-level British generals who envisioned a cavalry exploitation, and the territorial gains of Cambrai were lost to a German counterattack. Even so, the operation had demonstrated that armour was the key to a decision on the Western Front.

The Germans, meanwhile, had developed a key of their own in a new concept of offensive tactics known as "infiltration." It called for the rapid advance of dispersed "storm groups," armed with automatic rifles and light mortars, preceding the main body of infantry. These specialists were to probe for weakness and break through wherever they could find an opening. Their mission was to surprise enemy machine guns and artillery from the flanks and rear while leaving the strong points to be enveloped frontally by following waves of infantry, closely supported by artillery and tactical aircraft. These new tactics of infiltration, carried out by secretly trained troops, promised to create enough demoralization for a penetration as far back as corps command posts and communication centres.

Leaders of both sides realized early in 1918 that it was destined to be the year of decision. All the nations that had participated from the beginning were war-rotted except Great Britain and Germany, and it was a question whether the newly trained U.S. divisions could cross the Atlantic in time to compensate for the defection of Russia, convulsed by revolution.

The mobile warfare of 1918. Infiltration won the first

round. The German spring offensive in Picardy resulted in gains for a few days such as the Western Front had not known since 1914. Within a week a salient had been extended to a maximum depth of 40 miles in the British sector by German columns that threatened to drive to the sea. Then, suddenly, the attack ground to a halt and the front was stabilized once more.

German supply failures

This loss of momentum was no coincidence. What had happened was that the Germans had outrun their supplies, for the rail transportation and horse-drawn artillery of 1918 were not adequate to nourish a rapid advance. Gen. Erich Ludendorff made four bids for a decision, and each time the early gains merely resulted in creating another salient and two more German flanks.

The last effort, on July 15, 1918, was a complete failure. Attacking on the Champagne front, the Germans were trapped in the French elastic defenses planned by Gen. Philippe Pétain. Here, for the first time in the war, land mines were used on a large scale, and the attackers never reached the main French positions.

The riposte came three days later when Americans and French Moroccans counterattacked on July 18 along the right face of the salient created by the German drive to the Marne. Complete surprise was achieved by rushing the assault troops up in trucks under cover of darkness. Without any preliminary bombardment, the infantry advanced at dawn with 352 tanks and penetrated so deeply as to threaten the whole salient when other French and U.S. troops attacked the opposite face. Before the Germans could pull out, they left 30,000 prisoners behind and suffered about the same number of killed and wounded.

The precept of motor transport set at Verdun in 1916 bore further fruit as Entente generals learned that they could gain surprise unfailingly by these tactics. Dispensing with bombardment and bringing the assault forces up in trucks meant that there would be neither ammunition dumps nor troop concentrations to warn the enemy by means of his aerial observation.

The Amiens salient was next to be reduced, as 13 British divisions attacked on August 8 with 450 tanks, while armoured cars manned by automatic riflemen spread confusion in German rear areas. On September 2 another British attack struck the enemy in Flanders, and on the 12th an army composed of new U.S. divisions wiped out the Saint-Mihiel salient.

The end was in sight during October as the British on the left and French in the centre rained blow after blow, striking by surprise when and where such strikes were least expected. These victories stemmed in large measure from the pressure exerted on the enemy as the U.S. troops on the right slugged their way forward in the 46-day Battle of the Meuse-Argonne against an enemy who was using a fourth of his entire strength on a 20-mile front in difficult terrain.

World War II. *The post-World War I reaction.* During the postwar years the reaction of the victorious powers was in the direction of defensive tactics. The casualties inflicted by the machine gun were remembered when the victories of the tanks were forgotten. This tendency went so far as to resemble in some instances the wishful tactical thinking of 1914 in reverse.

The Maginot Line

The French, with traumatic memories of two German invasions in half a century, translated their theories of the all-powerful defensive into the concrete and steel of the Maginot Line—a bristling belt of underground forts and tank traps extending from the Vosges westward to the Ardennes, where it was believed that the hills and woods would turn back armoured columns. The British also had a defensive military philosophy, the main tenet of which was that postwar improvements in weapons added to the risks and perils awaiting a future aggressor.

When the Spanish Civil War served as a rehearsal for Soviet as well as German and Italian tactics, it was belatedly realized that improvements in weapons favoured the offensive to such an extent as to endanger laggards in preparations. Tanks were many times as fast and powerful as those of 1918; motorized artillery, on rubber tires, showed an enormous gain in mobility over horse-drawn, iron-wheeled vehicles; and motor trucks poured from the assembly lines by the thousands to solve the transport and supply problems of a new lightning warfare.

Early German victories. Any doubts as to the effectiveness of German preparations were dispelled during the first two years of World War II as Hitler's armoured columns swept on to victory after victory. The Maginot Line was outflanked by German tanks that broke through in the Ardennes and drove from the Meuse to the Channel in a week, cutting off 335,000 men of the British Expeditionary Force and attached French units. It seemed an authentic miracle when these beleaguered troops were evacuated by sea from Dunkerque (Dunkirk), leaving their heavy arms behind, as the German columns raced on to the occupation of Paris.

Blitzkrieg tactics

From the late summer of 1939 to the autumn of 1941 the Germans never met with a serious reverse in land warfare. Their triumphs were gained with such swiftness, such precision and economy of means that the blitzkrieg, or lightning war, was popularly accepted as a brilliant new tactical system. Actually it was the legitimate offspring of the infiltration tactics of 1918 mated with tank tactics. There was nothing new that could not be explained by the gains of two decades in the offensive powers of such weapons as the tank, motorized artillery, and tactical aircraft. With a few exceptions, such as anti-aircraft guns, defensive weapons had lagged in the armament race while armour and artillery were leaping ahead from the 3 miles per hour of 1918 to the 30 miles per hour of 1938.

The French Army of 1940 was essentially a World War I instrument, patched here and there with tactical changes, just as the Maginot Line was in effect a modernized western front. Despite warnings that the enemy might strike through the gap in the Ardennes between the French and Belgian fortified lines, the French in the Sedan area were unprepared for German "tactics of the space and gap." Only three penetrations on a 12-mile front, each no wider than 2,000 yards, were enough as the starting point of a major breakthrough. Like a flood enlarging holes in a dam, tanks and combat groups in armoured cars poured into the gaps, depending on surprise and speed as well as Stuka dive bombers for flank protection. Their direction of attack was lateral as well as forward, the object being to widen the gaps for following German forces. Within four hours the invaders were overrunning command posts and communications centres in French rear areas too demoralized for effective resistance. The Maginot Line had simply been bypassed and left behind by the torrent of armoured invasion that inundated northern France in a week.

Predictions that Hitler would meet his downfall in the U.S.S.R. were not upheld by military results of the first few months. The Soviet Army seemed doomed to extinction by its very bulk as German armoured envelopments swallowed up prisoners by the division and corps. Political factors influenced tactics when Hitler's doctrines of racial superiority led to cruelties that drove Russian peasants into guerrilla warfare. Effective resistance of this sort, combined with Soviet scorched-earth tactics and a seemingly endless reserve of manpower, enabled the Soviet Army to survive until the German transport bogged down in autumnal mud.

Even so, the tactics of Hitler's armies were so successful during the first two years that a serious defect might easily be overlooked: the apparent lack of preparation for amphibious tactics in a global war. Although the British were desperately short of arms after the Dunkerque evacuation, the Germans had neither the training nor the equipment to land troops across a few miles of water. In Crete they proved their mastery of airborne attack techniques, but a clumsy attempt at an amphibious combat landing ended in disaster.

The war in the Pacific. After the United States and Japan entered the lists as enemies, the war in the Pacific necessarily consisted in large part of amphibious operations. Events showed that the U.S. forces had developed an effective system of amphibious combat tactics. Three continents were opened up to invasion by this system, which won a score of major victories without suffering a single major defeat. In the 1920s the "Orange" plans, adopted by the United States for offensive operations in the event of war with Japan, called for attacks on that nation's shield

U.S. amphibious tactics

of fortified islands in the Pacific. By a directive (1927) of the joint board of the U.S. Army and Navy, the Marine Corps was given the mission of preparing for the conduct of landing operations.

The outer barrier of Japan's island defenses was breached by U.S. ship-to-shore assaults. Months of detailed planning and rehearsal preceded each operation. Supply ships were "combat-loaded" so that tanks, trucks, artillery, fuel, rations, and water would be made available to the landing force in the order needed. Intricate firing plans were drawn up for artillery and rocket bombardments to scorch the target area while armoured landing craft took the assault troops to the beaches under cover of air strikes. The transition from one element to another was the critical moment. Manoeuvre was seldom possible during the controlled chaos of the landings, and repulse meant a disaster that could hardly be retrieved. Once the beachhead was won, special units unloaded cargo ships, established supply dumps, and regulated traffic while the assault troops drove inland with the support of tanks and artillery as soon as they could be landed.

The amphibious offensive had become by 1943 the most decisive tactical system of World War II, not only in the Pacific theatre but also in North Africa and Europe. Neither the Japanese nor the Germans ever found the clue to a successful defense. Landings in Morocco, Algeria, Sicily, and Italy were followed by the climactic operation of June 6, 1944, when 4,100 ships put ashore five divisions complete with tanks and artillery on the beaches of Normandy. Nine days later in the Pacific an equally successful amphibious combat landing on Saipan brought U.S. bombing planes within striking distance of Tokyo and led up to the assaults on Iwo Jima and Okinawa that made Japanese defeat inevitable.

Significance of amphibious warfare in World War II

Wide variety of World War II tactics. So varied were the geographical and climatic conditions that it is difficult to generalize about the tactics of a war in which a score of major campaigns were being waged simultaneously in different parts of the world.

Tank battles on the plains of the U.S.S.R. began with tremendous artillery "preparations" and ended with armoured envelopments in which as many as 20 divisions were surrounded. In such instances the beleaguered forces were sometimes able to form a "hedgehog," or circular formation, and fight their way out of the encirclement with the aid of airborne supplies. In the long run it was a grinding war of attrition in which the Soviet Army gained the upper hand largely as the result of arms and equipment delivered by Britain and the United States in spite of heavy losses suffered by sea convoys.

Armoured columns in the desert warfare of North Africa achieved a mobility that makes their operations instructive to the student of tank tactics. But Gen. Erwin Rommel's defeat was foreordained by the inability of the Germans to mount an amphibious assault on Malta. The campaign in the desert was actually a battle of supply, and while the British held Malta they could provide air escorts for convoys of cargo ships in the Mediterranean.

On all fronts, special units equipped for special tasks were employed to an extent never known before. Infantry was the arm of decision in most operations, but it became standard practice to organize task forces ranging in size from platoons to divisions, reinforced by tanks, artillery, rocket launchers, or such other support weapons as might be indicated for the specific mission.

So potent were the missile weapons of World War II that survival for the individual soldier depended on cover and concealment. Small infantry units took on increasing importance as experience taught that latitude of decision must be left to troops in direct contact with the enemy, since victory often depended on the initiative and intelligence displayed by platoon commanders.

Some of the infantry combat teams became standardized. The British commando units, made up of soldiers, sailors, and marines organized on a permanent basis, conducted raids throughout the war. In Burma, the British developed special penetration groups of infantry to operate behind the enemy's lines, attacking headquarters and supply dumps while being supplied by air.

Techno-
logical in-
novations

All armies made an unceasing effort to gain a decision by the introduction of new weapons and tactics. But the German V-1 jet-propelled bomb came too late to change the outcome, as did the more formidable V-2 rocket. On the Allied side, the 2.36-inch (six-centimetre) rocket launcher and the 57-millimetre and 75-millimetre (1.45- and 1.91-inch) recoilless rifles provided the infantry with weapons that were tank killers under favourable circumstances. The variable-time artillery fuse enabled a shell to be exploded automatically in electronic reaction to waves reflected from the target itself. These tactical innovations seemed trivial, however, after the atomic bomb was dropped on Hiroshima on August 6, 1945.

Thus, at the conclusion of World War II the participants were confronted by the fact that "the bomb" might render obsolete all the tactics of victory. Even the discovery of gunpowder does not represent a comparable turning point in tactical history, for the first handguns were not as deadly as the crossbow. Nor did gunpowder have a rapid evolution, considering that the TNT of the 20th century was only about twice as powerful as the explosives of the Middle Ages. Yet the world of 1945 had to adjust itself overnight to the necessity of revising all military standards of the past.

Tactics in the nuclear age. *War in Korea.* It is one of history's ironies that the first war of the strident new nuclear age should have been waged with tactics reminiscent of the Western Front in 1917. Combat in Korea (1950–53) consisted for the most part of infantry fights with small arms on the platoon and company levels.

Called a "police action" at first, the intervention of 1950 proved during its first year to be the fourth most costly military effort of U.S. history. After a preliminary period of mobility, the United Nations and Chinese Communist forces faced each other in lines of trenches and defenses in depth extending across the peninsula. Neither side attempted to hold its front in force. Bunkers and outposts on the main line of resistance sheltered combat groups whose duty it was to maintain contact with the enemy and warn of a large-scale attack. Patrols ranging in size from an infantry squad to a platoon crept through no-man's-land in the darkness as both sides found the ambush an effective tactic.

The Korean War showed that even in the nuclear age an Asian peasant army using semi-guerrilla tactics can be formidable in mountain terrain suited to its operations. Atomic weapons would not have been effective in such a war, and the Korean experience made it appear unlikely that sound infantry tactics would soon become outdated.

Introduc-
tion of
helicopters
and body
armour

The two great tactical innovations of the war were the combat helicopter and the revival of infantry body armour. Rotary-wing aircraft had been developed too late for an extensive test in World War II, but in Korea the helicopter proved its value immediately in tactical as well as logistical respects. A U.S. brigade commander found it possible to maintain combat control over units 25 miles apart with the use of rotary-wing transportation. When a U.S. squadron of transport helicopters reached the front, it was demonstrated that a battalion of infantry could be lifted in a few hours to the main line of resistance in mountainous country where an all-day march otherwise would have been necessary. On an occasion when an infantry company was surrounded, six helicopters flew in ten tons of ammunition and evacuated casualties, thus enabling the encircled troops to fight their way out of the trap.

The revival of body armour, after a lapse of several centuries, was made possible by 20th-century plastics. Nylon pads and thin slabs of Fiberglas were combined in a sleeveless vest weighing about eight and a half pounds (3.9 kilograms) and allowing freedom of movement. The armour was capable of stopping .45-calibre automatic pistol bullets, submachine gun slugs, and most shell, mortar, or grenade fragments of a velocity less than 1,100 feet (335 metres) per second.

All U.S. combat troops in Korea were equipped with the garment before the war ended. On the basis of U.S. Army and Marine Corps surveys, it was established that body armour prevented from 60 to 70 percent of chest and ab-

dominal wounds, while reducing the severity of 25 to 30 percent of the wounds resulting from penetrations. Aside from humanitarian aspects, this meant that a large proportion of the enemy's most effective antipersonnel weapons were rendered useless. The tactical value of body armour was increased by its contribution to morale. Troops on the defensive had their foxholes and trenches, but the vest-protected men advanced in the open during an attack, when protection was most needed. The result, according to U.S. infantry officers in Korea, was a marked increase in combative spirit.

Later tactical organization: Vietnam. In 1961 a new divisional structure consisting of an "all-purpose" divisional base with three brigade headquarters to which could be attached varying numbers and types of combat manoeuvre battalions was introduced by the U.S. Army. This reorganization provided a division whose size (10,500 to 19,950 men) and equipment could be tailored to each specific mission and to the type of terrain encountered in its accomplishment. Other results of the change were improved balance between nuclear and nonnuclear firepower, greater internal flexibility, and an improved command and control structure.

Still another change in tactical thinking occurred during the war in Vietnam in the 1960s and '70s with the establishment of special forces for carrying on small-unit guerrilla warfare behind enemy lines or cooperating with indigenous populations in antiguerrilla operations. The helicopter again proved its value in Vietnam, where troops and supplies, including heavy equipment, could be speedily transported over impassable jungle areas. A significant new development was the introduction of armed helicopters that played an active role in attacking the enemy. Helicopter flight crews wore a lightweight, flexible "flak jacket" that covered the upper torso. Marine Corps ground troops were not required to wear such protective body armour, because of the heat and humidity, but it was available for those who chose to wear it.   (L.Mo.)

HISTORICAL DEVELOPMENT OF NAVAL TACTICS

Naval tactics may be said to begin when the opposing forces first "sight" each other visually or by means of radar. Tactical manoeuvres are then instituted with the object of employing weapons to the greatest possible advantage, usually by concentrating overwhelming strength on one portion of the enemy fleet, and of preventing the effective employment of the enemy's weapons. Though victory won at sea has generally been the consequence of successful strategic dispositions, tactics have always set the final seal to that victory by sinking, capturing, or putting out of action a substantial proportion of the enemy fleet.

The age of sail. Naval broadside tactics have been determined chiefly by the weapons mounted in fighting ships. Thus the principal weapon of the oar-propelled galley was the ram, and throughout its long period of dominance (chiefly in the Mediterranean) fleets endeavoured to disable enemy ships by ramming and then to capture them by boarding. The arrival of the cannon in the 14th century, and still more the mounting of heavy guns on the broadside of fighting ships in the mid-16th century, rendered the galley obsolescent. The purpose of fleet commanders thenceforth became to manoeuvre under sail so as to bring their full broadsides to bear on the enemy in the most effective manner. Because a sailing ship's hull was least well protected at the bow and stern (especially the stern), and shot fired into it from right ahead or right astern could travel most of the length of the ship and so wreak great havoc, a much-favoured tactical purpose was to achieve a position from which the enemy could be "raked" in that manner. The easiest way of accomplishing this was by "breaking the enemy line." Hence arose the importance attached throughout the era of sail to gaining the windward position or "weather gauge." Though the enemy line could also be broken from the leeward position, it was far easier for the holder of the weather gauge to accomplish such a manoeuvre. Breaking the line also destroyed the enemy fleet's tactical cohesion, so making it possible to overwhelm individual ships by bringing greatly superior strength to bear on each of them in turn.

The
tactics
of
ramming
and
broadside

The regularization of tactical manoeuvres under sail can confidently be ascribed to the issue of the first English *Fighting Instructions* in 1653, which made the line-ahead formation obligatory in battle. In the Anglo-Dutch wars of the 17th century both sides normally engaged in the line-ahead formation, which led to a large number of stubbornly fought battles from which sometimes one and sometimes the other side emerged victorious. With the decline of the United Provinces and the emergence of France as a naval power toward the end of the 17th century, the French school of naval tactics became influential. The principles formulated by Paul Hoste, Sébastien Bigot de Morogues, and others were in general more elastic than the English *Fighting Instructions*, which continued to exert a cramping and restrictive influence, leading to many unsatisfactory actions in the Anglo-French wars of the early 18th century.

Tactical success depends largely on the possession of an efficient system of communication between the admiral and his fleet, and the limitations of the early signal books often produced serious misunderstandings. It was a British admiral, Richard Kempenfelt (1718–82), who initiated a revolution in signalling, and so in the ease and confidence with which tactical manoeuvres could be carried out. This, allied to the genius of Nelson, which refused to be shackled by *Fighting Instructions*, brought the British Navy to its peak of tactical success in the Napoleonic Wars.

Modern naval tactics. The smoothbore gun mounted in wooden sailing ships remained the dominant weapon at sea until the Crimean War (1854–56) showed that the explosive shell had made wooden ships totally obsolete. When steam propulsion began to release warships from their long dependence on the wind, and improvements in gun design made action at much longer ranges possible, a new era of naval tactics opened. The first action between ironclads took place (March 9, 1862) during the U.S. Civil War, which also saw the first use of mines and torpedoes. In the Austro-Italian War there took place the first engagement between squadrons partly composed of ironclads off Vis (Lissa; July 20, 1866), and the success of the Austrian admiral Wilhelm von Tegetthoff in ramming and sinking his adversary's flagship caused a wave of enthusiasm for such tactics. In spite of the fact that the range at which actions could be fought was increasing all the time, some battleships continued to be fitted with rams until well into the 20th century. The first occasion on which the tactics of the era of steam propulsion and the long-range gun were tested on a large scale was in the Battle of Tsushima (May 27–28, 1905), when the Japanese admiral Tōgō Heihachirō, by skillful and resolute handling of his fleet, almost annihilated his Russian adversaries.

In 1906 the launching by the British of the all-big-gun battleship "Dreadnought" ushered in the brief final period of the tactical dominance of the long-range gun. Of the actions fought during World War I, the Battle of Jutland is by far the most interesting tactically. The British commander in chief, Adm. Sir John Jellicoe, gained a position of tactical advantage after he had deployed from his cruising disposition into line of battle; but his centralized and rigid system of tactical control resulted in the sacrifice of that advantage, and the greater part of the German High Seas Fleet, though markedly inferior in strength, escaped in safety to its bases during the night. The battle revealed serious defects in the British armour-piercing shell and in the magazine protection of their capital ships, which resulted in their suffering much the heavier losses.

Submarine warfare

Almost from the beginning of World War I the submarine exerted a profound influence on naval tactics as well as strategy. Together with the mine, submarines made close blockade of enemy bases impossible; they produced the need to screen the heavy ships of the fleet with antisubmarine vessels; and they forced the combatants to expend a very large effort on defending their principal ports and bases against penetration by submarines. In the North Sea the Germans frequently tried to catch the British heavy ships as they were entering or leaving their bases and to draw them over a submarine trap while at sea; but these tactics rarely produced much result because of the slow speed and limited vision of the submerged submarine. By far the greatest influence of the submarine lay in the field of the *guerre de course*, or attack on trade. Almost from the beginning the Germans used submarines against merchant ships, but it was not until February 1917 that they adopted "unrestricted" submarine warfare—torpedoing any merchant ship in the "war zone" around the British Isles on sight. During the "restricted" phase, German submarines made an effort to comply with international law, warning merchant ships and using guns to sink them after they had been abandoned. This led to the arming of Allied merchant ships. In the unrestricted phase the submarines almost invariably used torpedoes, often fired while the submarine was on the surface at night, a procedure that amounted to using the submarine as a torpedo boat. In World War II the Germans carried the tactics employed in World War I a stage further by the introduction of group attacks by 20 or even more submarines operating under the direction of the shore headquarters and in loose tactical coordination with each other. The British Navy, especially in the Mediterranean, and the U.S. Navy in its operations against Japanese merchant shipping ultimately adopted similar tactics.

Influence of air power on navies

The most important naval question left unanswered by the events of World War I was the influence of aircraft on naval strategy and tactics. The conventional view that aircraft were still no more than a valuable auxiliary to the heavy gun prevailed, and all the naval powers continued to build battleships in the period 1918–39. Britain, the United States, and Japan did, however, devote considerable attention to the development of carrier-borne aircraft, and very soon after the outbreak of war in 1939 it became clear that these had indeed replaced the big gun as the dominant weapon. The British aircraft carrier attack on the Italian fleet in Taranto (November 11, 1940), the Japanese attack on Pearl Harbor (December 7, 1941), the Japanese destruction of the British battleship "Prince of Wales" and the battle cruiser "Repulse" off Malaya (December 10, 1941), and many other actions all pointed in the same direction. The development of effective carrier air tactics now became the predominant requirement. The purpose was to gain the first sighting of the enemy and then to launch the air striking forces against the enemy carriers so as to arrive at the most advantageous moment, while fighter aircraft protected their own carriers against the expected counterblow. It was the U.S. Navy that led the field in the development and application of such tactics, and in a whole series of carrier air battles, starting with the Coral Sea and culminating in the Battle of Leyte Gulf (October 1944), a decisive superiority was established. The Japanese adopted "suicide" air attacks in reply, but this proved quite inadequate to stem the victorious progress of the U.S. carrier task forces. With the postwar development of the nuclear submarine it seemed possible that the period of the tactical dominance of the carrier aircraft would prove even shorter than that of the battleship. (S.W.R.)

HISTORICAL DEVELOPMENT OF AIR TACTICS

Peripheral role of air power in World War I. At the beginning of World War I, flying was in its infancy, and the few military aircraft in existence were unarmed and used mainly for reconnaissance. By the time of the Armistice in November 1918, many thousands of aircraft were in use and were employed mostly in direct support of the armies. During the war the British air forces in particular developed the theory of offensive air action against the opposing air force with the object of denying the initiative to the enemy. Today this is known as the achievement of air superiority and is an essential adjunct to army operations.

This offensive policy could not be pursued in its entirety, however, since the German Zeppelin and Gotha bombing attacks on London (both very successful initially) required a large air defense organization to counter them.

There was one important exception to the air support role: in May 1918 the British government formed the Independent Air Force to undertake a sustained bombing offensive against the German munitions industry. Although the force achieved little, it was a portent of things to come and provided an early example of the flexibility of air power.

In all, however, in spite of the large numbers of aircraft in use by the end of the war, they exercised practically no direct influence on the outcome.

World War II. At the outbreak of World War II it was clear that if enemy airfields and aircraft industry could be directly attacked in sufficient strength, the opposing air force would be increasingly thrown on the defensive. Such attacks would be even more successful if they were supplemented by a bombing offensive against the enemy homeland. This was in fact how the indirect defense of the United Kingdom was achieved—by the combined U.S. and British bombing offensive in the later stages of the war. German aircraft production consequently had to be concentrated almost entirely on defensive fighters. The Allies thus had almost complete command of the air for the invasion of the Continent in 1944 and the subsequent advance into Germany.

Tactics of the Battle of Britain, 1940–41
But such an approach was not possible in the years of the war when Britain was unable to attack Germany effectively. In the Battle of Britain in the summer of 1940, and the night bombing attacks that followed, the Luftwaffe threw the Royal Air Force (RAF) on the defensive. The British were equipped with approximately 600 fighters (Hurricanes and Spitfires) with which to oppose the Luftwaffe's 2,700 bombers and fighters. In terms of the quality of aircraft and of the aircrew there was little to choose between the two air forces; the decisive factor was the British radar early warning and fighter control system that had been developed in the years immediately preceding the war. This enabled the British to position their intercepting squadrons according to the scale and direction of the attacks and thus avoid wasteful dispersion of their scarce aircraft and pilots. In the end, the German attacks gradually tapered off, until by the summer of 1941 they had almost ceased. Attacks by German bombers did not present a serious threat for the remainder of the war.

In 1944, however, a new threat was posed by the V-1 pilotless aircraft, which, carrying a load of high explosive, proved a most effective weapon against southeast England. It was countered partly by defensive measures—involving fighters, anti-aircraft guns, and barrage balloons—and by bombing attacks on the launching sites. In August 1944, an even more serious threat developed, one that could not be countered by defensive measures—attacks by V-2 rocket missiles. This threat was quickly eliminated, however, by the bombing of launching sites and the Allied advance into Europe.

Throughout the war the flexibility of the bomber and the ease with which it could be switched from one type of target to another meant that there was always a variety of conflicting opinions on the best way to employ the force. The situation was further complicated by differing views on whether the attack of area targets (entire cities, for example) or precision targets (such as a particular factory) would pay the best dividends.

Tactics of the Allied bombing offensive
The Allied bombing offensive, known as Pointblank, was decided on at the Casablanca Conference in January 1943 and was intended as a strategic preparation for the invasion of the Continent. Its purpose was to bring about a disruption of German military and industrial production and a decline in German morale, which were regarded as essential preliminaries to a successful invasion. A combined (RAF and USAF) bomber offensive was launched, and the system of "round-the-clock" bombing, which gave Germany no respite by day or night, was evolved. This combined offensive forced the Luftwaffe more and more on the defensive, so that by the time of the Allied invasion of Europe in the summer of 1944 almost complete air superiority was held by the Allies over the operational area. Prior to the invasion and at times thereafter, Operation Pointblank took second place to a massive bombing assault in direct support of the invading armies, mainly by attacks on communications.

The British bomber force relied for its protection on the cover of darkness to evade the enemy fighters, and on its own firepower, supplemented by radar countermeasures, to confuse the defense. The USAF bomber force favoured day attacks, but, after heavy initial losses, it became nec-

essary to provide long-range escorting fighters, which, on the more distant raids, operated in relays.

Tactical use of aircraft with ground forces. In the opening months of World War II, culminating in the fall of France in June 1940, the Luftwaffe provided massive support for their army by dive-bombing attacks on the British and French troops and on key points holding up the German advance. The Allied air forces were unable to provide an effective defense, not so much because of faulty tactics or unsuitable aircraft but because they were greatly outnumbered. In the later stages of the war, during the British and Allied campaigns in North Africa, the Allied air forces gradually gained the upper hand.

The technique of tactical air support on a major scale was pioneered by the British Air Marshal Arthur (later Baron) Tedder in North Africa. In this technique the tactical air forces were organized on a highly mobile basis so as to be able to provide reconnaissance, fighter cover, and close support on call for the army as it advanced.

These campaigns had also shown how essential it was for the army to fight under cover of air superiority during a war of movement if the advance was not to be held up. So successful were Tedder's methods that he was appointed deputy supreme commander under General Eisenhower for the invasion of the Continent in 1944. As such he coordinated the operations of the thousands of Allied aircraft that provided direct support for the Allied armies during the original assault and subsequent advance into Germany.

Influence of missile development. The bomber controversy appeared to have been finally settled when the war against Japan concluded with the dropping of atomic bombs on Hiroshima and Nagasaki in 1945. It appeared as if the bomber had become the supreme arbiter in war, and additional emphasis was given to this apparent supremacy by the development of the much more powerful hydrogen bomb, which was first successfully tested by the United States in the Pacific in 1952. But the supremacy of the bomber was short-lived. As first the United States and then the Soviet Union developed long-range nuclear missiles, the role of the bomber was progressively transferred to the missile. By the late 20th century only a small number of heavy bombers remained in service in the U.S. and the U.S.S.R.

Obsolescence of the heavy bomber

Defensive anti-aircraft missiles were also developed and are gradually replacing the fighter. These defensive missiles have also been a factor in the decline of the bomber, since the deep penetration of enemy territory that they provide would almost certainly result in an unacceptably high casualty rate if the explosives were carried by aircraft.

To realize their full potential, however, anti-aircraft missiles require a highly sophisticated control and reporting system, and their use is therefore mainly confined to areas such as western Europe, the United States, and western U.S.S.R., where a static air defense system can be established. In undeveloped countries anti-aircraft missile systems are usually confined to the defense of key points, heavy reliance still being made on the fighter.

The main roles of aircraft, apart from air transport, in a major war are now confined to the provision of reconnaissance and tactical support for the army, and even in these roles aircraft are being gradually replaced by the satellite and missile. While it may still be possible to attain air superiority over the battle area against attacks by enemy aircraft, no effective defense against missiles is yet in sight. Protection can therefore only be provided by direct attack, by missile or aircraft, on the launching sites. In limited war in undeveloped countries, however, the tactical support aircraft should continue to have an important role to play for many years to come. But even in these theatres the missile is supplementing or replacing the aircraft.

Recent air tactics. Two features in particular have been common to nearly all the local wars fought since the ending of World War II. First, there has been little or no air opposition in the operational theatres. In Korea, Malaysia, and Vietnam the air forces of the West have therefore had almost complete command of the air. Second, these wars were strictly limited. Air power was rarely used outside the area of conflict and then only on a small scale against precision targets. Air superiority has not, however, proved a decisive factor in warfare of the counterinsurgency type, although it has conveyed immense advantages.

Air tactics in Vietnam

Counterinsurgency operations by the United States in Vietnam were based on a country-wide air patrol system that enabled troops and tactical air support to be called up at short notice. The troops themselves were moved by a large helicopter and air transport force that enabled them to be rapidly positioned so as to bring the enemy to action. These direct attacks were backed up by air attacks on enemy concentrations, supply dumps, and invasion trails in the rear areas. In addition, defoliants were widely used to deny the enemy cover in the approaches to bases, towns, and villages.

In the brief Middle East war of 1967, both sides had approximately equal air forces, but the Israelis fully appreciated the importance of establishing air superiority to assist their advance. In the opening stages of the campaign the Israelis therefore eliminated the Egyptian Air Force, whose aircraft were caught on the ground and destroyed in dawn attacks on airfields. Thereafter the Israeli Air Force had almost complete command of the air, an advantage that greatly facilitated the rapid defeat of the Egyptian Army.   (W.M.Y.)

INTEGRATION OF LAND, SEA, AND AIR TACTICS

Cooperation between sea and land forces has been a feature of war from very early times, and with the advent of aircraft in the second decade of the 20th century the partnership became threefold. This, and increasingly sophisticated equipment, has made such operations much more complicated. In World War I both the equipment and methods used were crude. This was exemplified in the Dardanelles campaign of 1915, when British troops landed from open boats, without adequate artillery or air support, sometimes against prepared Turkish defenses.

The great powers made little progress in integration between the two wars; but in World War II the subject was given special study by U.S. and British forces, whose operational roles were carried out exclusively overseas. This brought the term combined operations into use to denote any operation of war involving a combined effort by sea, land, and air. The term joint operations was used for operations involving two or more Allies. The first large-scale combined operation in World War II was carried out by the Japanese in December 1941, in their assaults on American, British, and Dutch possessions in the Far East and Pacific. There followed a series of combined and joint operations against Germany and Italy by American and British forces: the landings in French North Africa (Operation Torch, November 1942); later landings in Sicily and Italy; and the greatest single combined operation of all time against the Normandy coast (Operation Overlord, June 1944). American forces also carried out a unique series of combined operations against Japan in the Pacific.

Combined operations in World War II

Although these operations are described correctly as combined operations, they were not carried out by fully integrated forces. The appointment of a supreme commander (as in the Allied invasion of Europe during World War II) for each theatre of operations, aided by a staff and advisers from each of the three services, was, however, the first move toward tactical integration.

After the cessation of hostilities in 1945, developments in integration occurred more slowly than might have been expected and were confined mostly to the integration of command and staffs at higher levels. In its Marine Corps the United States possesses the only permanently integrated fighting force in the world. There is, however, a level below which integration cannot go. The skills and duties of a soldier, sailor, and airman are very different, and they cannot all be acquired by one individual or one combat unit. The trend in most countries has been to integrate fully at the highest administrative level (ministry or department of defense) and to adopt a supreme commander and integrated staff system in large operational commands. War and staff colleges and other educational establishments can be made to cater for personnel of all fighting services. In administrative units—medical, supplies, labour, communications, and so on—the tendency is to integrate as far as possible; but within front-line combat units integration is clearly impracticable.

The secret of tactical success in combined operations lies in integration at command and higher staff levels; in all combat officers having a good understanding of the duties of services other than their own; and in frequent combined training and the integration of educational establishments and logistic services.   (C.N.B./Ed.)

GUERRILLA WARFARE

Guerrilla warfare is a type of warfare characterized by irregular forces fighting small-scale, limited actions, generally in conjunction with a larger political–military strategy, against orthodox military forces. Guerrillas are usually nondescript in dress, unconventional in weapons and equipment, lack formal supply lines, and employ highly unorthodox tactics. In addition to extremely mobile, aggressive operations, these tactics embrace all aspects of psychological warfare, including the use of sabotage and terrorism. Although this type of warfare occurs throughout history, the word guerrilla (the diminutive of Spanish *guerra*, "war") stems from the Duke of Wellington's Iberian campaigns (1809–13), during which Spanish–Portuguese irregulars, or *guerrilleros* (also referred to at the time as partisans and insurgents), helped drive the French from the peninsula. In World War II the word partisan became synonymous with guerrilla; later the word insurgent came into vogue.

Guerrilla warfare is by tradition a weapon of protest employed to rectify real or imagined wrongs levied on a people either by a foreign invader or by the ruling government. As such it may be employed independently or used to complement orthodox military operations, in which case it can be employed either inside enemy territory or in areas that have been seized and occupied by an enemy.

The importance of guerrilla warfare has varied considerably through history. After World War II it came to play a significant role in what has been termed revolutionary or insurgency warfare or what Communists call people's wars and wars of national liberation.

Since World War II, guerrilla warfare has been employed by non-Communist insurgencies in such countries as Indonesia, Cyprus, and Algeria, where it was successful, and by Communist insurgencies in Malaya and the Philippines, where it ultimately failed. In a complementary role, in which the guerrilla force first fights independently and later evolves into an orthodox insurgent army, it has been successfully employed by Communist insurgencies in China, Indochina, and Cuba.

History. Ancient and medieval chronicles offer countless examples of guerrilla actions, usually of an independent type undertaken by peasant bands and normally resulting in little more than temporary embarrassment to the incumbent ruler or temporary harassment to the invader. These chronicles also describe numerous campaigns undertaken by marauding tribes that practiced an offensive style of warfare often marked with definite guerrilla overtones. The genesis of modern guerrilla warfare, however, is found in the American Revolution, during which the colonists, many of them veterans of Indian fighting, formed loosely knit bands of riflemen that practiced highly unorthodox tactics against the formally trained British redcoats. Despite George Washington's later, more standard approach to warfare, vestiges of the guerrilla tendency remained. For example, in 1780–81 one of the former Indian fighters, Francis ("the Swamp Fox") Marion, organized a ragtag group of guerrillas that complemented orthodox warfare in South Carolina by conducting continual, devastating raids in the rear of British Gen. Charles Cornwallis' lines.

A far more important role, however, was played by Spanish–Portuguese guerrillas in Wellington's campaigns in Portugal and Spain. Throughout this long war, effectively commanded guerrilla bands made life miserable for the French armies by completely disrupting their lines of communication—"by blocking the roads, or intercepting couriers and convoys" and even "waging regular war" (Charles Oman, *A History of the Peninsular War*, 6 vol., 1902). Numbering no more in the field than 20,000 and

Guerrilla campaigns of the Napoleonic wars

despite their weakness in the open field, their intestine quarrels, their frequent oppression of the countryside, and their ferocity, they rendered good service . . . by pinning down . . . twice their own numbers of good French troops.

In 1812 Napoleon was to suffer heavily from guerrilla strikes during the long retreat from Moscow. Bands of Russian peasants, working with mounted Cossacks, harassed the French until they had been driven out.

Guerrilla warfare, in both its independent and its complementary roles, has been employed extensively since the time of Napoleon. A striking example of the protest role of guerrilla warfare is the Taiping Rebellion (1850–64) in China. Begun by impoverished peasants and by jobless coolie porters, opium smugglers, and pirates, the unsuccessful rebellion against the Manchu dynasty cost an estimated 20,000,000 lives and, in the opinion of some sinologists, constituted one of the great social upheavals of modern times.

Lesser but nonetheless significant independent guerrilla actions were fought against the British in India and Africa, the French and Spanish in Morocco, the Turks and Austro-Hungarians in the Balkans, and the Americans in the opening of the West. In 1899–1900 the Boxer Rebellion in China constituted a protest action against a foreign invader (in the form of the Western powers whose influence, ironically, had grown as a result of the Taiping Rebellion), as did both the Philippine insurrection (1899–1902), in which the guerrillas ultimately lost to American regulars, and the South African War (1899–1902), in which the Afrikaners quickly abandoned orthodox tactics in favour of highly mobile, irregular operations undertaken by mounted groups called commandos, which the British regulars defeated only with the greatest difficulty.

Equally impressive is the concurrent record of complementary guerrilla operations. The most successful guerrilla leader in the American Civil War was a Confederate cavalry officer, John Mosby. Leading a small band of mounted volunteers, Mosby so disrupted Union operations by his constant, dashing raids in northern Virginia that Union forces were finally forced to devastate the region in order to deprive the guerrilla force of its base. Mexican guerrillas led by Emiliano Zapata and Pancho Villa played a leading role in the Mexican Revolution.

Guerrilla activity in World War I

The static nature of World War I prevented guerrilla warfare on the western front, but subsidiary theatres offered scope for guerrilla activity. In the Middle East a British officer, T.E. Lawrence, led a revolt of Arab tribesmen in a prolonged guerrilla action that claimed the lives of some 35,000 Turkish soldiers and resulted in another 35,000 captured or wounded; the guerrillas finished the war in control of about 100,000 square miles (259,000 square kilometres)—a significant contribution to the British victory in Palestine. In German East Africa (modern Tanzania), a German officer, Lieutenant Colonel Lettow-Vorbeck, led a small force of German regulars supplemented by a few hundred tribesmen in a holding operation against much larger British forces, which could have been used on the western front. Although bereft of supply and physically nearly exhausted, the group had still not surrendered when the war ended.

Guerrilla fighting of a different nature broke out in southern Ireland, which was in rebellion against British rule. Beginning in Dublin on Easter Monday, 1916, the original insurrection did not prove popular and was instantly put down by the British army garrison. But then the military authorities made a major political and psychological error by court-martialling and condemning to death the 15 principals. The easygoing Irish public was horrified, and the result was a guerrilla war characterized by the most brutal terroristic killings and ambushes, which lasted until 1921.

A different type of guerrilla action was fought in Russia, where in 1918 Lenin's Bolsheviks had taken control of the revolution and were fighting White Russian counterrevolutionary forces supported by various of the great powers, including the United States. This support was probably unwise, since the intervention of foreign powers brought a great wave of patriotism to the Russian masses, many peasants joining partisan movements.

During the interwar period the Communist Party in China and its army, after many vicissitudes and under the leadership of Mao Tse-tung, fought the invading Japanese and, after World War II, wrested control of the country from Chiang Kai-shek's Nationalist government. In Spain the Popular Front left-wing government had to rely primarily on guerrilla forces to hold the Nationalist armies while the government built up conventional forces. The war assumed a distinctively ideological character, the Nationalists being supplied with arms and air power primarily by the Fascist governments of Germany and Italy, the Loyalists being supplied by Russia.

Communist guerrilla activity in World War II

Guerrilla warfare in World War II was also marked with strong ideological overtones. Since Communist parties had been operating, usually clandestinely, in most of the invaded countries, their members were ideally suited for guerrilla warfare. In the West, primarily in France and Italy, the Communists either formed their own bands or joined other bands, such as the French and Belgian maquis, covert organizations engaged in espionage, sabotage, and terrorist activities. Communist cadres in the Balkans and the Far East formed guerrilla bands that usually operated independently, sometimes in competition with guerrillas representing the legal governments, as Tito did in Yugoslavia. Although some of these groups spent as much time eliminating indigenous opposition while consolidating their own hold on the country as in fighting the enemy, they nonetheless contributed sufficiently to the war effort to win impressive shipments of arms and equipment from the Western powers—the result of an Allied decision in which the political goal was subordinated to the demands of military strategy. The decision resulted in Communist bands in Yugoslavia, Greece, Burma, Thailand, Indochina, the Philippines, and Indonesia receiving arms from the Allies.

Another important guerrilla action of World War II was fought in the Ukraine. The peasantry, stung by German atrocities, formed into numerous partisan bands. Once these semi-independent bands were organized by the Soviet high command (which never entirely trusted them), they caused widespread and, at times, vital damage to German communications. In the autumn of 1943, in addition to large police and security forces, the German command in the U.S.S.R. was expending 10 percent of its strength—25 field divisions—in fighting the partisans. Although estimates vary, these guerrillas probably killed more than 250,000 German soldiers, while blowing up thousands of trains and trucks and inflicting an inestimable psychological pressure.

In some countries the Communist guerrilla forces formed in World War II facilitated the quick establishment of Communist regimes. In Yugoslavia the takeover of government was simple and direct, while in other cases, such as Czechoslovakia and China, it was complicated and delayed. In Vietnam it succeeded only after nearly three decades. In Malaya and the Philippines it was foiled. Non-Communist insurgencies used guerrilla warfare with considerable success in Cyprus, Kenya, and Algeria. In Latin America the failure of several attempts to emulate the guerrilla campaign that resulted in the overthrow of the Batista regime in Cuba in 1959 led to a concentration on revolutionary activity within the cities, or urban guerrilla warfare, as it came to be termed. The extent to which the intermittent bombings and kidnappings in such countries as Brazil, Argentina, and Guatemala indicate the existence of the discipline, organization, and overall strategy that are the hallmark of guerrilla warfare remains uncertain. But the increasing urbanization of the population does suggest that the cities present the best opportunities for guerrillas to engage in disruption and to engender the lack of confidence in the ability of the government to control the situation that is essential to the success of a guerrilla campaign.

Strategy and tactics. The broad strategy underlying successful guerrilla warfare is that of protracted harassment accomplished by extremely subtle, flexible tactics designed to wear down the enemy while gaining time either to develop sufficient military strength to defeat him in orthodox battle or to subject him to internal and external political and military pressures sufficient to cause him to seek peace. This strategy embodies political, social, economic, and psychological factors to which the military element is often subordinated. It is essentially a strategy for the morally strong and materially weak.

Writings of Sun-tzu

Many of the essential rules of guerrilla tactics are to be found in *The Art of War* (*Ping-ta*) by the Chinese general Sun-tzu (*c.* 350 BC). Sun-tzu instructed his generals in words familiar to successful, latter-day guerrilla leaders: "And therefore I say: Know the enemy, know yourself; your victory will never be endangered. Know the ground, know the weather; your victory will then be total." A successful general "avoids strength and strikes weakness"; the use of tactics based on deception and surprise is the hallmark of a victorious commander (Sun-tzu, *The Art of War,* trans. by S.B. Griffith, 1963).

Sun-tzu's indirect approach was largely ignored in the written commentary on wars of later centuries. Such an approach does appear now and again—Xenophon wrote in the 4th century BC of the importance of psychological factor in warfare, while in the 18th century the French commander Marshal Saxe suggested that it is possible to win a war without fighting battles. Saxe was writing in a time of limited, formal wars, which soon gave way to the total warfare introduced in the Napoleonic era and which was subsequently treated by the Prussian officer-scholar Carl von Clausewitz.

Clausewitz argued that a weaker adversary does not have to destroy the enemy's army in order to gain victory, but rather that he must destroy the other's will to wage war. He argued that partisan warfare could further the wearing process, provided the theatre of operations was large enough, the terrain sufficiently rugged, and the partisans themselves temperamentally suited to this type of fighting. A contemporary, the Cossack Gen. Denis Vasilyevich Davydov, who led a partisan force during Napoleon's retreat from Moscow, later wrote that this type of warfare "is concerned with the entire area which separates the enemy from his operational base." Its objectives are

to cut the communication lines, destroy all units and wagons wanting to join up with him, inflict surprise blows on the enemy left without food and cartridges and at the same time block his retreat. This is the real meaning of partisan war (Otto Heilbrunn, *Warfare in the Enemy's Rear,* 1963).

Tactics of T.E. Lawrence

Nearly a century later T.E. Lawrence offered the world a dramatic demonstration of Davydov's definition. Sent to lead dissident Arab tribes in revolt against the Turks, Lawrence followed a Clausewitzian precept by isolating the Arab political aim, which "was unmistakably geographical, to occupy all Arabic-speaking lands in Asia." Lawrence wrote,

The Turkish army was an accident, not a target. Our true strategic aim was to seek its weakest link, and bear only on that till time made the mass of it fall. The Arab army must impose the longest possible passive defense on the Turks (this being the most materially expensive form of war) by extending its own front to the maximum. Tactically, it must develop a highly mobile, highly equipped type of force, of the smallest size, and use it successively at distributed points of the Turkish line.

By making the Arabs "an influence, a thing invulnerable, intangible, without front or back, drifting about like a gas," Lawrence would gain "five times the mobility of the Turks [thus] the Arabs could be on terms with them with one-fifth their number."

About the time that Lawrence was incorporating these thoughts into an article for the *Encyclopædia Britannica,* Mao Tse-tung was developing a doctrine of peasant warfare in China. Mao was a young, devoted student of revolution as preached by Marx, practiced by Lenin, and qualified by Mao's own considerable experience. Since 1927 he and a band of comrades had been on the run from the Nationalist Generalissimo Chiang Kai-shek. In the Fukien–Kiangsi borderlands, Mao had helped turn peasants and bandit bands into the first crude Chinese Communist army, one that spent the next eight years fighting for its life against Chiang's forces. Mao's experience had led him to defy his Russian teachers by concluding that the Communist revolution in China could come only from the country peasants, not from the urban proletariat. His theory was

tested when pressure from Chiang's armies forced him and his followers to undertake a 6,000-mile (9,656-kilometre) march to the north, to Yen-an, a mountain hideout in Shensi Province.

The rebel leader then began to codify a doctrine of revolutionary warfare. Mao saw two enemies: the Japanese invader and the regular Kuomintang armies headed by Chiang Kai-shek. He looked on a country

half colonial and half feudal; it is a country that is politically, militarily, and economically backward . . . a vast country with great resources and tremendous population, a country in which the terrain is complicated and the facilities for communication are poor. All these factors favor a protracted war; they all favor the application of mobile [that is, orthodox] warfare and guerrilla operations (Mao Tse-tung, *On Guerrilla Warfare,* trans. by S.B. Griffith, 1961).

Mao came to the conclusion that

The concept that guerrilla warfare is an end in itself and that guerrilla activities can be divorced from those of the regular forces is incorrect . . . in sum, while we must promote guerrilla warfare as a necessary strategical auxiliary to orthodox operations, we must neither assign it the primary position in our war strategy nor substitute it for mobile and positional warfare as conducted by orthodox forces.

Mao's view of the role of guerrilla warfare

He borrowed freely from Sun-tzu's thesis of the indirect approach:

Guerrilla strategy must be based primarily on alertness, mobility, and attack. It must be adjusted to the enemy situation, the terrain, and the existing lines of communication, the relative strengths, the weather, and the situation of the people.

It should be used

to exterminate small forces of the enemy; to harass and weaken large forces; to attack enemy lines of communication; to establish bases capable of supporting independent operations in the enemy's rear; to force the enemy to disperse his strength; and to coordinate all these activities with those of the regular armies on distant battle fronts.

To accomplish these goals, Mao demanded tactics based on surprise and deception:

In guerrilla warfare, select the tactic of seeming to come from the east and attacking from the west; avoid the solid, attack the hollow; attack, withdraw; deliver a lightning blow, seek a lightning decision.

As opposed to orthodox warfare, which is frequently static, Mao wanted

constant activity and movement. There is in guerrilla warfare no such thing as a decisive battle; there is nothing comparable to the fixed, passive defense that characterizes orthodox war. In guerrilla warfare, the transformation of a moving situation into a positional defensive situation never arises. The general features of reconnaissance, partial deployment, general deployment, and development of the attack that are usual in mobile warfare are not common in guerrilla war.

Instead of fixed defense, Mao called for

alert shifting . . . when the enemy feels the danger of guerrillas, he will generally send troops out to attack them. The guerrillas must consider the situation and decide at what time and at what place they wish to fight. If they find that they cannot fight, they must immediately shift.

Although the guerrilla will defend his own operational bases, these must be abandoned when necessary.

We must observe the principle, "To gain territory is no cause for joy, and to lose territory is no cause for sorrow."

Such tactics demand

careful planning . . . those who fight without method do not understand the nature of guerrilla action. A plan is necessary regardless of the size of the unit involved; a prudent plan is as necessary in the case of the squad as in the case of the regiment.

As Lawrence put it, "Guerrilla war is far more intellectual than a bayonet charge."

Good planning depends on superior intelligence, of course, and this can be gained only from the people, who, in turn, must withhold such from the enemy:

Many people think it impossible for guerrillas to exist for long in the enemy's rear. Such a belief reveals lack of comprehension of the relationship that should exist between the people and the troops. The former may be likened to water and the latter to the fish who inhabit it. How may it be said that these two cannot exist together? It is only undisciplined troops who make the people their enemies and who, like the fish out of its native element, cannot live.

Mao's basic strength came from the people—from the water that produced, then supported, the fish. From the Yen-an haven, his agents went forth to select suitable base areas for organization and consolidation, a process in which volunteers were trained and indoctrinated as agitators and propagandists, who in turn went forth to the countryside to enlist peasant support.

In Mao's scheme of things, this phase merges into one of limited direct action, mainly sabotage and terrorism designed to eliminate members of the opposition and to gain arms and supplies for the embryo guerrilla force. This expansion phase may last for years, but if it succeeds it merges into a decisive phase: the destruction of the enemy largely with orthodox military forces.

Mao's teachings, though perhaps only partially utilized, nonetheless underlie most of the revolutionary wars fought since World War II. In fact, his doctrine has become a blueprint for the "national wars of liberation" that China and Cuba have promised to foment and support in Asia, Africa, and Central and South America.

Physical and social components of guerrilla warfare. *Motivation.* Fundamental to the revolutionary process is a cause, which unfortunately is not difficult to find in the underdeveloped countries of the world. The cause may assume several guises: to the world it may be presented as liberating a country from the colonial yoke; to the peasant being converted to Communism it may be freedom from serfdom, from oppressive taxation, or from payment of oppressive rents to absentee landlords.

Whether real or artificial, whether inspired by Communism or by virulent nationalism, the political goal is fundamental in motivating people to action. Mao leaves no doubt as to its importance:

Without a political goal, guerrilla warfare must fail, as it must if its political objectives do not coincide with the aspirations of the people and their sympathy, cooperation, and assistance cannot be gained.

Popular support. The guerrillas' affiliation with the people is constantly stressed in revolutionary writings. Guerrillas spring from the people, who in turn support their spawn, not only by furnishing their sons to the cause but also, when called upon, by furnishing money, food, shelter, refuge, transport, medical aid, intelligence—support that they must attempt to deny the enemy. Although Lawrence called for no more than

a friendly population, not actively friendly, but sympathetic to the point of not betraying rebel movements to the enemy,

he also wrote that his rebels

had won a province when the civilians in it had been taught to die for the ideal of freedom: the presence or absence of the enemy was a secondary matter.

Gen. Georgios Grivas, the non-Communist professional soldier who led the Cypriot rebellion, wrote that a guerrilla war stands no chance of success unless it has "the complete and unreserved support of the majority of the country's inhabitants."

Organization. Protracted revolutionary warfare as defined by Mao demands a complicated organization on both the political and the military levels. Mao recommends a clandestine system of parallel hierarchy beginning with the cadre or cellular party structure at the hamlet–village level and proceeding to the top via district, province, and regional command structures.

The tactical organization of guerrilla units varies according to operational demands. Mao called for a guerrilla squad of nine to 11; Grivas employed sabotage groups of four or five. In the Vietnam fighting, the Viet Minh and, later, the Viet Cong ranged from small squads up to battalion and even regimental strengths.

Arms. The guerrilla by necessity employs a wide variety of weapons, some self-manufactured, some captured, and some supplied from outside sources. In the earlier stages of the war, the weapons are usually primitive. Americans in Vietnam frequently encountered homemade rifles, hand grenades, and Claymore mines; trails booby-trapped with *punji* stakes soaked in urine; and shallow pits lined with

nail boards. Nearly every guerrilla war has produced ingenious improvisation, both from necessity and to avoid a cumbersome logistic "tail." Nothing can be simpler to construct and use than a Molotov cocktail or a *plastique* bomb, yet under certain conditions nothing can be more effective.

Terrain. It is axiomatic to Mao and his followers that revolution begins in the country. Once sufficient base and guerrilla areas are established, it is possible to extend operations to include cities and lines of communication susceptible to attack. This rural strategy is influenced by such factors as the political goal, geography, the insurgent strength, and the government's strength.

Such was the combination of these in Russia that the 1917 revolution was decided in the cities and only later successfully defended in the country by orthodox Communist armies employing guerrilla forces in a complementary role. The Irish Rebellion was also fought largely in the cities, and General Grivas opened the semisuccessful Cypriot rebellion with a few combat groups especially trained in terrorist–sabotage tactics. As his strength grew, he resorted to guerrilla warfare across the entire island. On the basis of this and other examples, Grivas later argued that, contrary to Mao's ideas, guerrilla warfare need not be rural based and, further, that it is sometimes possible for guerrilla warfare alone to accomplish the political objective.

Terror. One of the most hideous characteristics of guerrilla warfare is the use of terror: assassination, a hand grenade thrown into a crowd, an indiscriminate bombing—actions familiar to any insurgency.

Terror is used for several reasons: to focus world attention on the rebel cause, to eliminate opposition leaders, to paralyze normal government activity, to intimidate the general populace, and to keep one's own guerrillas from defecting. It is difficult to assess the psychological impact of terrorist tactics on the general population. It would seem that even those sympathetic to the guerrilla cause may be alienated by the indiscriminate use of terrorism. The defending forces, moreover, may reply in kind, so that the population is subject to terror from both sides. The question of political sympathy or loyalty may then become irrelevant, the local populace being ready to cooperate with whichever side is in control at a particular moment.

Sanctuary. Guerrilla forces cannot fight all the time. They must control safe areas to which they can retire, voluntarily or involuntarily, for rest, recuperation, and repair of arms, clothing, and equipment and where recruits can be indoctrinated, trained, and equipped. Such areas traditionally are located in remote, rugged terrain, usually mountains, forests, and jungles; but guerrilla areas may be developed in which whole villages and hamlets serve a sanctuary role. The sea can also provide sanctuary, as it did in the Peninsular War, when the British navy succored the Duke of Wellington's cooperating Portuguese–Spanish guerrillas.

Sanctuary may also be provided by sympathetic neighbouring countries: during the Greek Civil War (1946–49) the Communist guerrillas frequently retreated into Yugoslavia, which offered not only physical sanctuary but also arms and supplies; and it was only after the Yugoslavs closed the border that the guerrillas were finally defeated, though not for that reason alone. Similarly, Ho Chi Minh's guerrillas, in the later stages of the war against France, relied on China for refuge, training, and supply of arms and equipment.

The people offer a final form of sanctuary. At one time during the Cypriot revolt, Grivas was surrounded by a British force for nearly two months but, though spotted, was repeatedly able to escape capture or death. An Algerian rebel leader was able to install himself within 200 yards of the army commandant's headquarters in Algiers, avoiding capture for several months. In South Vietnam, American officials discovered that several thousand supposedly government-controlled, "fortified" hamlets were in fact controlled by Viet Cong guerrillas "who often used them for supply and rest havens" (Staff of the Senate Republican Policy Committee, *The War in Vietnam,* 1967).

Leaders and recruits. The unusual requirements of

Rural- and urban-based guerrilla campaigns

guerrilla warfare call for outstanding leadership at all levels if a guerrilla force is to survive and prosper. The vicissitudes of these wars demand a leader not only endowed with extraordinary intelligence and courage but also buttressed by an almost fanatic belief in himself and his cause. Lenin, Trotsky, Lawrence, Mao, Tito, the Filipino Luis Taruc, the Kenyan Jomo Kenyatta, Ho Chi Minh, Vo Nguyen Giap, the Algerian Ahmed Ben-Bella, Castro, Ernesto "Che" Guevara—these and dozens of their lieutenants at lower levels have all been unusual, unorthodox personalities, generally with civilian backgrounds. But all were able to attract followers, to organize them, and to instill a disciplined zeal matched only in the most elite military organizations.

Selectivity is the key to effective guerrilla recruitment. The guerrilla recruit must be resourceful and enduring and must be committed totally to the cause if he is to withstand the hardships and dangers that guerrilla fighting involves. The strength of a guerrilla movement is thus directly related to the degree to which the objectives of the campaign can evoke a response from youths of military age. Historically, the cause has invariably been a desire for national independence and autonomy, sometimes combined with an ideological commitment to Communism or the overthrow of corrupt and repressive regimes or both. Recruitment to such causes has rarely presented much

Use of conscription

difficulty to guerrilla leaders, although, in those cases in which the conflict has been large-scale and extended over a long period of time, it has been necessary to abandon selectivity and resort to conscription. Such was case in Indochina, where Communist recruiting normally began at the village level, generally by inducing peasant candidates to join one or more front groups and participate, if only indirectly, in the war effort. After exposure to political indoctrination, the candidate joined the village guerrilla cell, after which he might be promoted to the regional and regular forces.

Since it is essential for the guerrilla to win and retain popular support, he is also taught to practice circumspect behaviour when among the people. Communist leaders in China, Cuba, and Vietnam have drawn up lengthy codes of individual behaviour: the Chinese guerrilla, for example, was required to pay a peasant for food, to respect his property, and not to offend propriety by undressing in front of a peasant woman.

It is questionable to what depth party-imposed discipline descends in the average Communist guerrilla. Unquestionably, the hard-core guerrilla practices an almost ascetic association with the people, while approaching his military tasks with dogged determination. But, judging from interrogations of Viet Cong guerrilla prisoners and from the number of Viet Cong defectors, the guerrilla's discipline varies as ideological beliefs ebb and flow in the physical and moral tides of war.

Counterguerrilla warfare. In waging this type of warfare, which calls for location, isolation, and elimination of the entire guerrilla apparatus (political as well as military), orthodox military commanders have employed and continue to employ a wide range of weapons and tactics that, judged by results, are more appropriate to a conventional-warfare situation. Wholesale bombings and mass artillery interdictions of suspected sanctuary areas, division- and corps-strength "sweeping" operations in which only a few guerrillas are captured or killed but whole villages are destroyed, the establishment of defended but isolated chains of military outposts, mass arrests and interrogations—each has failed to achieve triumphs.

Throughout history, nations have impelled insurgencies because of political errors, and military commanders have failed to quell insurgencies because of political ignorance. In Communist revolutionary warfare, especially, the political factor is paramount. If the Communist guerrilla is not supported by the people—if he is not a fish in the sea of humanity—he cannot effectively operate for any length of time. Consequently, the government must win the people's support, both to deprive the guerrilla of this support and to obtain information on which to base tactics of destruction. It is not enough to break up guerrilla bands and kill individual guerrillas. A government can claim victory

only when the subversive organization behind each level of an insurgency has been destroyed and when viable government has been achieved.

Such counterinsurgency campaigns as those conducted in the Philippines and in Malaya prove that the Communist guerrilla ultimately can be defeated (but not necessarily eliminated). The means of defeat, however, lie only in a patient and judicious application of a host of civil and military measures, involving social and economic reform, effective policing, and military security. Although in the course of a counterinsurgency campaign one or another of these factors may assume a temporary supremacy, in the end each must remain integral to an overall political consideration.

Mixed strategy of counter-guerrilla warfare

Indeed, political realism is the first essential in conducting a counterinsurgency: the recognition of weakness as well as strength, of failure as well as success. An insurgency indicates a breakdown of government in that a minority is able to defy law and order while coercing others to offer either active or passive support to the cause. The opening phase of an insurgency, in which subversion is supported by selective terrorism, must be met by specific governmental measures, both covert and overt. Because this phase is generally covert, the government, usually the police, must practice considerable subtlety in a difficult environment in which internal weakness, ineptness, or corruption is at work. If the insurgency is not contained at this level it usually flares into the second, "armed struggle" phase, which brings guerrilla warfare into the open.

In the opening phase of an insurgency, a government is usually on the defensive. In Malaya this was a period in which the government was able to prevent the enemy from taking over and to keep the insurgency from escalating. The general strategy was security, both by maintaining police functions and, militarily, by splitting up (but not attempting to destroy) the larger guerrilla units. These holding operations gave the government time to marshal its forces (not just police and military) in order to fight the second, or offensive, phase, in which the enemy's power was broken, and, finally, the third, or victory, phase, which destroyed the last remnants of guerrilla forces while establishing a stable, independent government.

One veteran of the Malayan campaign ascribes the government's success to certain basic principles, which he holds essential for the conduct of any counterinsurgency: (1) the government must have a clear political aim, ideally "to establish and maintain a free, independent and united country which is politically and economically stable and viable"; (2) in ferreting out, neutralizing, and destroying guerrillas, the government, no matter how tempted, must function in accordance with law and with a carefully developed counterinsurgency plan, which grants priority to defeating the political subversion, not the guerrillas per se; and, (3) finally, in fighting the offensive phase the government must first develop base areas before commencing aggressive tactics (Robert Thompson, *Defeating Communist Insurgency,* 1966).

These principles need not unduly restrict the counterguerrilla efforts. Most authorities agree that emergency regulations, often harsh, must be legally invoked. In Malaya these included compulsory census, an enforceable identity-card system, suspension of habeas corpus (but with carefully publicized safeguards), permission to search private property without a warrant, the death sentence for persons caught with unauthorized weapons, harsh sentences for those aiding the Communists, flexible power of curfew; later extraordinary measures included the right to shoot on sight in prohibited areas, the right to resettle whole villages, and the right to control food distribution with harsh penalties, including death, for those found guilty of aiding the enemy.

Such regulations, or course, are not attractive. If indiscriminately applied, as, unfortunately, is sometimes the case, they will lead to an increasing alienation of the civil population from the government. When properly applied, however, they will greatly aid the police and military forces in their essential mission of providing security to the civil populace, which, in turn, will then feel more free to provide essential information on which to base further counterguerrilla operations.

Holding
and
clearing
operations

The exact nature of such operations must vary in accordance with the enemy's strength and the area concerned. The first priority of government is to re-establish law and order, which, in a rural area, means revitalizing the rural police function. The military effort, the strength of which is dictated by necessity, concentrates on clearing operations, designed to break up and disperse large guerrilla formations, then to keep them deprived of the initiative by small-unit tactics, mainly patrols and ambushes based on valid intelligence. The clearing operation is followed by the holding operation, which is designed to "restore government authority . . . and to establish a firm security framework" (Thompson, *op. cit.*). The holding operation is the period of "winning the hearts and minds" of the people, first by providing security, which will be maintained by strategic hamlets defended by organized hamlet militias working in conjunction with government forces where necessary, and second by providing social reforms (land reform, schools, hospitals, community projects) that will identify the government with the people's best interests. Once won over, the people will deprive the guerrillas of vital support, besides furnishing information necessary for police and military forces to penetrate and destroy the local insurgent organization.

The clearing and holding operations provide the key to successful counterguerrilla warfare. When they have been carefully applied, as in Malaya, they have proved successful; when applied quantitatively, as in Vietnam, they have in large part failed. Even under the most favourable circumstances, most governments lack the necessary civil, police, and military resources to carry out clear and hold operations simultaneously in all areas. For this reason, the military effort may have to extend to secondary operations in lower priority areas. These are designed to keep the guerrilla off balance until the civil effort can be enlarged. Such operations may include large-scale sweep and clear actions, in which large numbers of aircraft and helicopters are used; they may include long-term, deep-penetration operations, in which units are parachuted into guerrilla sanctuaries and supplied by airdrop while establishing and maintaining permanent ambushes, sometimes with the aid of friendly tribes.

Such may be the strength of the insurgency and the weakness of the legal government that outside aid is called for, as happened in Vietnam. Unless limited to supply, technical training, and professional advice, outside aid may well prove a two-edged sword. If the donor government underestimates the dimensions of the conflict, as happened with the United States in the case of Vietnam, it is persuaded to a military intervention that, by escalating to the extent needed for victory, tends to take over the war from the host government, thus widening the gulf between the people and their government and providing the guerrillas with propaganda for the charge of imperialist aggression.

Legal status of guerrillas. For understandable reasons, the orthodox military commander has always placed the guerrilla in an extralegal status. After the British were stung several times by Francis Marion in the Revolutionary War, they complained that he fought neither "like a gentleman" nor like "a Christian." Napoleon's marshals on the Spanish peninsula were driven to violent reprisals against Spanish–Portuguese guerrillas, with the result that for every guerrilla shot a French prisoner paid with his life, a "barbarous system" finally concluded by mutual agreement. The problem arose again in the American Civil War; when Gen. Eleazar A. Paine, the Union commander in western Kentucky, was unduly harassed by guerrillas, he published this proclamation:

> I shall shoot every guerrilla taken in my district, and if your Southern brethren retaliate by shooting a Federal soldier, I will walk out five of your rich bankers, and cotton men, and make you kneel down and shoot them. I will do it, so help me God" (Richard Bennett, *The Black and Tans,* 1959).

Rules
applicable
to
guerrillas

The Brussels international conference of 1874 provided that, in order to be recognized as lawful belligerents, guerrillas must answer to a specific commander, wear a distinctive badge, carry arms openly, and conform in operations to the laws and customs of war. The Hague conferences on the rules of land warfare in 1899 and 1907 adopted this definition with a few modifications, and it is also contained in the Geneva Conventions (1949) on the laws of war.

The Hague ruling has not been complied with, mainly because conformance would nullify the advantages of guerrilla warfare but also because sabotage and terrorist tactics often breed brutal reprisals. The guerrilla has invariably been held fair game for torture or for execution without trial. As in the Peninsular War of the early 19th century, the guerrilla, unable to expect just treatment, has continued to render unjust treatment, a cycle of horror reaching its zenith in the Spanish Civil War, in the partisan actions of World War II, and in Vietnam.   (R.B.A.)

FUNDAMENTALS OF LOGISTICS

Definitions
of logistics

In the conduct of war, the vast area of war-making activity behind the cutting edge of combat has always defied simple definition because of the heterogeneity of the functions and activities involved. Apart from the adjective noncombat, which indicates only what these activities are not, the military vocabulary offers only a few general descriptive terms, such as administration and services or service support, with equivalents in other languages (such as the French *intendance*). All are badly corrupted by loose usage and have lost whatever precise meaning that they may once have possessed; all fall short, even in their broadest connotations, of blanketing the entire area of noncombat activities; and all carry additional, though related, meanings that make them ambiguous.

The word logistics belongs to this group and suffers from the same defects. One of its original meanings, the science of computation (from the Greek *logistikos,* "skilled in calculating"), is now archaic but persists in mathematical terminology in the logistic or logarithmic curve. Some sources trace its military use back to the term *logista,* allegedly an administrative official in Roman and Byzantine armies. But the first systematic effort to define logistics with some precision and to relate it to other elements of war making was made by Antoine-Henri Jomini (1779–1869), the noted French military thinker and writer. In his *Précis de l'art de la guerre* (1838) Jomini defined logistics as "the practical art of moving armies," by which he evidently meant not merely transportation (though movement was the heart of the concept) but the whole range of functions involved in moving and sustaining military forces—planning, administration, supply, billeting and encampments, bridge and road building, even reconnaissance and intelligence insofar as they were related to manoeuvre off the battlefield. In any case, Jomini was less concerned with the precise range of functions embraced by logistics than with the staff function of coordinating them. He stated, as though from common knowledge, that the word was derived from the title of the *major général* (or *maréchal) des logis* in French 18th-century armies, who, like his Prussian counterpart, the *Quartiermeister,* had originally been responsible to army commanders for the administrative arrangements for marches, encampments, and troop quarters (*logis*). As military administration grew more complex, these functionaries became the equivalent of chiefs of staff to the commanders of the day and began to develop the functional staff system that was to evolve into the general or "capital" staffs of the late 19th century.

Logistics
as the staff
coordination of
noncombat
activities

Jomini's discussion of logistics was really an analysis of the functions of the Napoleonic general staff, particularly of the chief of staff, a post that he himself had filled with distinction. He conceived of the staff as the commander's right arm, facilitating his decisions and seeing to their execution; the scope of its activity was therefore functionally unlimited, since it encompassed all matters of concern to the commander. The mobility and gargantuan scale of Napoleonic warfare had left the simple old logistics of marches and encampments far behind. If logistics was the science of general staffs, then, said Jomini, the new logistics had become the science of generals in chief as well, comprising all the functions involved in "the execution of the combinations of strategy and tactics."

Jomini's conception of logistics as staff coordination of all, or virtually all, noncombat activities supporting military operations had some validity at a time when the staff's functions were still relatively simple and when its role was limited, in the main, to coordination. In his day a commander could personally study the intelligence reports and strength returns, plot the enemy's dispositions on the map, and plan his own deployments and manoeuvres. Jomini leaves an engaging picture of Napoleon doing just that—sprawled on the floor of his tent, marking each division's route of march on the map with a pair of dividers.

The evolving state of the art, however, soon undermined the usefulness of Jomini's simple concept. In all countries in the 19th and 20th centuries, staff organization developed a complex subdivision of functions, with a deep line of cleavage between planning (in Jomini's day performed largely by the commander himself) and operational coordination. The translation of the commander's strategic and tactical designs into deployment and manoeuvre plans became a major category of staff activity, supported by the autonomous functions of intelligence (collection and analysis) and the calculation of capabilities for executing plans. The coordination function, in turn, tended to split between specific planned and ongoing routine operations, with subgroups of like activities. In both planning and coordination, as the scope of staff activity expanded beyond what a commander's immediate staff could manage directly, there proliferated descending layers of delegated authority in the staff organization. Most countries developed something like the American differentiation between general and special staffs (the latter being concerned with technical support activities) and, below the staff level, large functional and geographic operating organizations that grouped administrative and service activities in various ways.

In this process of increasing complexity and functional subdivision, the term logistics soon lost its association with staff functions and almost disappeared from the military vocabulary. It does not appear at all in the great military study *On War* (1832–37), by the brilliant Prussian historian Carl von Clausewitz, and it is used only occasionally in later treatises. After the mid-19th century it tended to become the exclusive property of scholars and theorists, usually in the restricted sense of supply, transport, and quartering of troops; and many ordinary dictionaries today define it in this way. But in the 1880s the American naval historian Alfred T. Mahan introduced it into U.S. naval usage, and in the decade or so before World War I the navy's concern with the economic foundations of its expansion began to broaden the connotation, especially in naval circles, to encompass industrial mobilization and the war economy. Reflecting this trend, a U.S. Marine officer, Lieut. Col. Cyrus Thorpe, published his *Pure Logistics* in 1917, arguing that the logical function of logistics, as the third member of the strategy–tactics–logistics trinity, was to provide all the means, human and material, for the conduct of war, including not merely the traditional functions of supply and transportation but also war finance, ship construction, munitions manufacture, and other aspects of war economics.

After World War II the most notable effort to produce a theory of logistics was a project sponsored by the U.S. Navy and headed by a retired rear admiral, Henry E. Eccles, whose *Logistics in the National Defense* appeared in 1959. Expanding Thorpe's trinity of war-making elements to five (strategy, tactics, logistics, intelligence, communications), Eccles and his co-workers developed a conceptual framework that envisaged logistics as the military element in the nation's economy and the economic element in its military operations—that is, as a continuous chain or bridge linking combat forces with their roots in the national economy. Within this framework they developed an elaborate taxonomy of the logistical process and an enlarged vocabulary distinguishing various categories of logistics (consumer, producer, military, civilian, strategic, tactical, and operational). Eccles stressed the intricate interdependence of the various elements of the logistical process, the tendency of logistical costs to rise (the logistic "snowball"), and, echoing Jomini, the essential role of command in logistical planning and operations. Through this analysis ran the theme that, for all the diversity of logistical activities, logistics has an inherent unity deriv-

ing from its central function of sustaining combat forces. Except in occasional staff papers and war college dissertations, however, Eccles' work has had no counterpart in the other services or in other countries, and his overarching conception of logistics has not been widely accepted outside the U.S. Navy.

Components of logistics. For purposes of historical and functional analysis it is useful to distinguish four basic logistical components or elements: supply, transportation, facilities, and personnel services. (Management, or administration, sometimes considered an element or function of logistics, is not included in this analysis because it is common to all organized human activity.) Strictly speaking, all four elements involve the provision of services with appurtenant commodities, which armed forces need in order to live, move, communicate, and fight.

Supply. Supply is the function of providing the material needs of military forces. It may be construed most broadly as a process embracing all stages in the provision and servicing of military material, including those preceding its acquisition by the military—design and development, manufacture, purchase and procurement, storage, distribution, maintenance, repair, salvage, and disposal. (Transportation, an essential link in this chain, is ordinarily analyzed separately and has separate organizational status.) Along with these principal stages go a variety of subsidiary services such as testing, inspection, packing and packaging, warehousing, and veterinary service, as well as parallel administrative functions such as contracting, pricing, scheduling, determination of requirements, allocation and control of raw materials, components, and facilities, stock and inventory control, quality control, conservation, and requisitioning.

The whole process can be conveniently divided into four broad phases: (1) the design–development–production process of creating a finished item of military material; (2) the largely administrative process by which military agencies acquire finished items from producing agencies; (3) the distribution–servicing processes undergone by military material while "in the service"; and (4), dominating the whole, the planning–administrative process of balancing supply and demand—that is, the determination of requirements and assets and the planning of production, procurement, and distribution.

Although the character of military supply has varied with the changing technology and modes of warfare, it has always had the basic aim of providing military forces the material needed to live (food, water, clothing, shelter, medical supplies), to move (vehicles and transport animals, fuel and forage), to communicate (the whole range of communications equipment), and to fight (weapons, defensive armament and materials, other combat equipment, and the expendables of missile power and firepower). In all these categories are items, such as clothing, vehicles, and weapons, that are used repeatedly and therefore need to be replaced only when lost, destroyed, or worn out; and materials, such as food, fuel, and ammunition, that are expended or consumed—that is, used only once—and therefore must be continuously or periodically resupplied. From these characteristics are derived the basic classifications of initial issue, replacement, and resupply. The technical classifications and categories of supply vary among countries and services. The British Army, for example, recognizes two broad classes: (1) supplies, which include all the expendables except ammunition, and (2) stores, which include ammunition and military hardware in general. The U.S. Army in World War II and for many years after used five main classifications: (1) subsistence and forage; (2) equipment and other items issued to organizations and individuals on the basis of regular allowance tables; (3) fuels; (4) equipment and materials of irregular issue such as construction materials; and (5) ammunition. These five classes have been expanded to ten by designating as separate classes certain large categories, such as vehicles, medical material, repair parts, and sales items, which formerly were considered as subclasses.

Historically, food and forage made up most of the bulk and weight of supply until the 20th century, when with mechanization and air power, fuel displaced forage and

Logistics as a combination of economics, supply, and transportation

Logistics as the link between military operations and the national economy

Types of supply: initial issue, replacement, and resupply

The supply of food, forage, and fuel

became the principal factor in all supply. The demand for food and water is unremitting and undeferrable, the one constant of logistics. A man's daily ration makes a small package; the U.S. Army's generous ration in World War II weighed only six pounds (2.7 kilograms), that of the Japanese Army then, and of the North Vietnamese later, much less. But an army of 50,000 may consume in one month as much as 4,000 tons (3.6 million kilograms) of food.

Animals require much more. The standard grain and hay ration in the 19th century was about 25 pounds (11.4 kilograms), and the daily forage of a corps of 10,000 cavalry weighed as much (allowing for remounts) as the food for 60,000 men. Forage requirements tended, moreover, to be self-generating, since the animals needed to transport it also had to be fed. The number of animals accompanying an army varied widely. Napoleon described as an ideal, which he himself failed to attain, a supply train of no more than 500 wagons in an army of 40,000 men; with a corps of 7,000 cavalry, this would amount to about 10,000 animals exclusive of remounts and spare draft animals. Northern armies in the U.S. Civil War, whose transport was probably more lavish than the historical norm, commonly numbered half as many animals as soldiers. A force of 50,000 men might thus require more than 300 tons (272,000 kilograms) of forage daily. This was more than twice the weight of gasoline that an equivalent force of three World War II infantry divisions, using motor vehicles exclusively, needed to operate for the same length of time. In the latter case, moreover, fuel requirements diminished markedly when an army was not moving, whereas the premechanized force had to feed its animals whether moving or not. It was the immense forage requirements of premechanized armies, more than any other single factor, that restricted warfare before the 20th century so generally to seasons and climates when animals could subsist partly on the countryside and made most winter operations, as late as World War I, an affair of short campaigns and long sieges.

The expendables of movement in 20th-century warfare, however, include fuel for rail and water transport as well as for motor vehicles, and also the immense fuel requirements of modern air power. In World War II, without counting requirements for transoceanic shipment (which are statistically difficult to calculate), fuel made up half the total resupply and replacement needs of U.S. forces in Europe. Technologically advanced warfare in the 20th century has, in fact, vastly increased the consumption of fuel both absolutely and relatively to other supply needs. By the early 1970s it was estimated that the continued development of mechanization and air power had almost doubled the fuel requirements of large-scale conventional military operations since World War II. Conversely, food requirements, a nearly constant six to seven pounds for modern Western soldiers, represent a small and diminishing proportion of the total burden.

The supply of ammunition and equipment Before the advent of mechanization, complex weapons, and massive firepower in the late 19th and 20th centuries, equipment replacement and ammunition resupply were a relatively small part of an army's needs. Missile power, before the invention of gunpowder, was limited by the difficulty of bringing large supplies of missiles to the battlefield. In a protracted battle, spent arrows and javelins were gathered up and fired back at their former owners.

For the first five centuries of the gunpowder era the provision of ammunition was not a major logistical problem. Not until the use of field artillery on a large scale in the 18th century, and the development of quick-firing shoulder arms in the 19th, did ammunition begin to constitute a substantial proportion of resupply needs. As late as 1864, in the Atlanta campaign of the U.S. Civil War, the Union Army's average daily ammunition requirements amounted to only one pound (0.45 kilogram) per man, as against three pounds for rations; Confederate forces in that war were reported to expend, on the average, only half a cartridge per man per day.

The great increase in firepower in the 20th century upset the historic ratios. In World War II the average ammunition requirements of Western forces in combat zones were 12 percent of their total supply needs. In the Korean War ammunition expenditures climbed higher, and there is no reason to expect that the trend would be reversed by a conflict on a similar scale today. Material replacement requirements have also mounted, in absolute terms, especially in the lavishly equipped U.S. forces, but as a percentage of the total they are declining.

Transportation. Before the development of steam propulsion, armies depended for mobility on two sources of energy: the muscles of men and animals and the force of the wind. On land they used men and animals to haul and carry; on water they used oar-driven and sail-propelled vessels. Among these various modes the balance of advantage and disadvantage was often delicate. A force moving by water was vulnerable to storm and enemy attack; navigation was an uncertain art; transports were expensive and of limited capacity. Large expeditions could be undertaken only by wealthy states or seafaring peoples, such as the Scandinavians of the 8th and 9th centuries, who combined the roles of mariners and warriors. Seaborne armies were rarely strong enough to overcome a resolute land-based foe.

Land, sea, and air transport

On the other hand, armies have usually been able to move faster by water than by land and with a better chance of avoiding enemy detection. Good roads are rare in military history, and most successful seaborne invasions have caught the defenders by surprise. In the 19th and 20th centuries the revolution in ship design and propulsion made water travel largely independent of wind and weather and permitted the overseas movement and support of larger forces than ever before. After the mid-19th century the technology of road building and, above all, the railroad began to offset the historic advantages of water transportation to some degree. In some countries, notably Europe and the United States, motor vehicles and more road building in the 20th century extended the conquest of rough terrain. The airplane finally freed military movement, for modest forces and limited cargo, from bondage to earth altogether. Yet the costs of mobility on land—in equipment, materials, and energy—remained high, and large military movements were still confined, in the late 20th century, to narrow ribbons of rail and road, which in many parts of the world were still rare or lacking.

On land the soldier himself has been the basic burden carrier of armies. As a matter of simple economy, he represents a large available carrying capacity at no extra cost. His equivalent, in an army of 50,000 in the preindustrial era, would be 1,875 wagons drawn by 11,250 horses or mules, for which additional wagons would be needed to haul forage. A difference of only five pounds (2.3 kilograms) in the soldier's load could add or subtract a requirement for 125 wagons and 750 animals. Since the days of the Roman legion, the soldier has had to carry, on the average, about 55 or 60 pounds (25 or 27 kilograms). The ratio between weapons and other items in the soldier's load has varied widely, but the modern soldier in Western armies has relegated most of his food to vehicle transport while carrying a heavier burden of weapons and ammunition. After World War II some advanced armies made drastic reductions in the combat load.

Human and animal haulers

Before the age of mechanization, the soldier's carrying capacity was often supplemented by additional carriers and haulers, human and animal. Each had its advantages. A team of six horses ate about as much as 30 to 40 men, but the men could carry more on their backs than the horses could haul, and considerably more than the horses could carry. Men could negotiate rougher terrain, and they required less care. On the other hand, when men were used as carriers, their loads had to be distributed in small packages; and men proved less efficient than animals when teamed to haul heavy and bulky loads. The horse and mule, besides, have less strength and stamina, though more agility, than the ox, history's primary beast of burden. Cavalry armies have always commanded attention; but with rare exceptions, such as the 13th-century Mongols, they have been shackled, like infantry, to their slow-moving transport and to their bases. In general, animal transport has been favoured in the Western world, where manpower historically has been scarce, whereas in the Orient, where manpower is plentiful, men have been used even more than animals as military burden carriers. Both modes of transport continue to be used widely in the 20th century, wherever mechanical transport is insufficient, breaks down, or runs out of fuel.

Facilities. Tradition has it that logistics owes its origin as a distinct sphere of military activity to the staff function of arranging for the quartering (*logis*) of troops. This was a routine administrative task, naturally associated with the daily planning of an army's route of march, in the formalized, rather leisurely warfare of the 18th century. Normally it was accomplished by arranging with town or village authorities for quartering the troops in the homes of the citizenry, an ancient and disagreeable custom. Lacking such accommodations, armies on the move slept at night in tents or improvised shelters, or without shelter at all, depending on circumstances; and the extent to which they were willing to dispense with these amenities—like the Mongol armies of the 13th century or the citizen-soldiery of the French Revolution—has often been a large factor in their mobility. The Roman legion on campaign was almost unique in military history in its ability to carry a heavy load of fortification and building materials and to construct a complete fortified camp each night, without reducing its remarkable mobility.

The provision of military facilities, as distinct from fortification, did not become a large and complex sphere of logistical activity until the transformation of warfare in the industrial era. In that transformation the ancient function of providing nightly accommodations or winter quarters for the troops dwindled to relative insignificance in the mushrooming panoply of fixed and temporary installations, serving a multitude of technical purposes, which became part of the military establishments of the major industrial powers. Modern armies, navies, and air forces own and operate factories, arsenals, laboratories, power plants, railroads, shipyards, airports, warehouses, supermarkets, office buildings, hotels, hospitals, homes for the aged, schools, colleges, and most of the other types of structures used by advanced societies in the 20th century—as well as barracks, the original military facility. They are among the world's great landowners. The management of all this improved real estate is one of the largest areas of modern logistical administration.

Personnel services. Services may be defined as activities designed to enable personnel or material to perform more effectively. Usage recognizes no clear distinction between logistical and nonlogistical services, but a somewhat blurred one has grown out of the traditional and opprobrious identification of logistics with noncombat rear-area activities. Thus intelligence and communications personnel and combat engineers in the U.S. Army have long claimed the label of "combat support" as distinct from the "service support" functions of supply, transportation, hospitalization and evacuation, military justice and discipline, custody of prisoners of war, civil affairs, personnel administration and nontactical construction (performed by "construction" engineers). Training of combat troops is hardly ever considered a logistical service, whereas training of service troops sometimes is. Usage does not, however, always equate "service support" with logistics. Personnel administration (recruitment, induction, classification, assignment, records maintenance, career management, separation) is an old, highly institutionalized sector of the military establishment, and personnel administrators tend to reject the logistics label. Personnel services (medical, spiritual, legal, personal, informational, educational, recreational, financial) are more heterogeneous and have varied origins; most definitions of logistics include them.

Most service activities, logistical and nonlogistical, are of recent origin and, as organized specialities, peculiar to the military establishments of advanced nations, reflecting both the complex technology of modern warfare and the institutional complexity of modern society. Over the long haul of military history, the services considered necessary to keep armed forces in fighting trim were generally of a rudimentary character. From the earliest times, however, they posed a serious logistical problem. To armies and their lines of communications they added numbers of

people who did not, as a primary function, belong to the fighting force and who, if not properly organized, might weaken its capacity to fight. Soldiers seldom possessed the technical skills required to perform any but the simplest logistical services; sometimes, as members of a warrior elite, they were prohibited by social prerogative from performing them. A classic feature of armies, consequently, has been its long train of noncombatants, often far outnumbering the fighting men.

Logistical services also added to the baggage of armies a growing burden of specialized equipment, tools, and materials needed for the performance of the services. Services tended to generate more services: service equipment itself had to be serviced, sometimes by additional technicians, and service personnel themselves required services. Logistical services thus meant more people to be fed, clothed, and sheltered, and more people and baggage to be transported. What the British call the "administrative tail" is as old as military history.

Special features of naval logistics. Most of the distinctive features of naval logistics stem from the fact that the basic unit of a naval force is the individual ship, as is the individual soldier in an army and the individual aircraft in an air force. It is the individual ship that moves, fights, and must be supplied; the individual crew member or gun has no separate role (unlike the soldier, who often functions independently of his unit).

The substantial carrying capacity of the warship made it an indispensable element in its own logistical support, particularly in the era before steam power eliminated the problem of covering long distances between ports. For centuries the most critical item of supply was water, which sailing ships found it difficult to carry in sufficient quantities and to keep potable for long ocean voyages. Food was somewhat less of a problem, except for its notoriously poor quality in the days before refrigeration, the sealed container, and sterilization.

During the long reign of the sailing ship, the absence of a fuel requirement was a major factor in the superior mobility of fleets over armies. The shift to steam was, in a sense, a return to the principle of self-contained propulsion earlier embodied in the oar-driven ship (the oarsmen had to be fed, as the ship's engines had to be fuelled). The gain in control was of course an immeasurable improvement for the long haul, but for a time the inordinate amount of space that had to be allocated to carry wood or coal seriously inhibited the usefulness of the early steam warship. Eventually the maritime nations established networks of coaling stations, which became part of the fabric of empire in the late 19th century. The shift to oil a few years before World War I involved a major dislocation in naval logistics and changed the stakes of imperial competition.

For modern navies, of course, the importance of bases goes far beyond the need for periodic replenishment of fuel, although this remains essential. Ships must be repaired, overhauled, and resupplied with ammunition and food; and, an ancient requirement, the crews must be given shore leave. Within limits, these needs can be and are being fulfilled by specialized auxiliary ships either accompanying naval forces at sea or stationed at predetermined rendezvous points. Naval operations in World War II saw a vast proliferation of these auxiliary vessels; in 1945 only 29 percent of the U.S. Navy consisted of purely fighting ships. By using auxiliaries and by rotating ships and personnel, modern fleets can remain at sea almost indefinitely, especially if not engaged in combat. U.S. fleets in the Mediterranean and far Pacific have done so for years, although the feat is less impressive than that of the British Admiral Lord Nelson's fleet, which lay off Toulon, France, continuously, without rotation, for 18 months during the Napoleonic years from 1803 to 1805. With nuclear propulsion, thus far applied only to submarines and a handful of large warships, the basic logistical function of replenishing fuel should eventually disappear. But that day will be long in coming, and the other functions of naval logistics will remain.

The issue of power versus movement. The potential effectiveness of a military force lies in three attributes: fighting power, mobility, and range of movement. Each

Provision of quarters, arsenals, warehouses, hospitals, etc.

The ship as the basic unit for supply and maintenance

The importance of bases and auxiliary supply ships

depends on physical ingredients and logistical services that place a burden on transport and sources of supply. Since logistical capabilities are almost always limited, power, mobility, and range must compete for the available supply, transport, facilities, and services. Over the ages, this competition has usually centred on transport, which for an army in the field almost invariably determined the amount and kind of supplies and the scale of services that could be provided. Three methods have been used, in various combinations, to supply forces in the field, based on the employment of transport and the sources of its supply: self-containment, local supply, and supply from bases.

Self-containment in supply

The idea of complete independence from external sources of supply—the hard-hitting, self-contained "flying column"—has always exerted a powerful fascination but has seldom fully materialized. Self-containment in equipment, services, and ammunition or missiles was common enough before the great expansion of firepower and replacement requirements in the last century. But few military forces have been able to operate for long or move far without frequent resupply of food and forage or fuel.

Self-containment is the least economical of all methods of supply. Accompanying transport is fully employed only at the beginning of the movement, serving thereafter as a rolling warehouse that is progressively depleted as the force moves. Fast-moving self-contained forces thus have typically left a trail of abandoned vehicles and, in earlier times, dead animals. The basic trade-off in self-containment is between the speed permitted by eliminating delays and detours for foraging and the drag of a large supply train. When Hannibal crossed the Alps into northern Italy in 218 BC, he gained the advantage of circumventing the Roman army guarding the easier coastal route; but his rate of movement through the mountain passes was painfully slow, and he lost almost half his entire force to cold, disease, and hostile tribes along the way.

Local supply

Until modern times, supply from local sources (including captured stores) in the regions where armies operated was the commonest method of resupplying food and forage and providing labour and other simple services. In fertile country an army could usually satisfy a large part of its need for the major expendables at low cost in transport and without sacrificing fighting power or range. When efficiently organized to reduce delays and diversions, local supply even permitted a high degree of mobility. Normally, however, an army living off the country tended to straggle and to load itself down with loot. If it moved too slowly or was pinned down by the enemy, it might sweep the region bare and starve. In winter or in deserts and mountains local supply offered meagre fare. And a hostile population, as Napoleon discovered in Russia and Spain, could bring disaster to an army that had to scrounge for its food.

Even when troops could be fed by other means, the animals usually had to shift for themselves, for the burden of transporting forage any considerable distance could be prohibitive. Local supply of forage was in fact almost universal during the centuries before the advent of mechanized transport. Moreover, cattle driven with an army could transform forage into food, a supply technique as ancient as the Bible and still common in the 19th century. Unwieldy and slow moving though it was, the accompanying herd had the great merit of transporting itself and dwindling as it was consumed.

When mechanical transport replaced animals, one of the great continuities of military history was broken. Mechanized armies can operate in winter and desert areas as long as they have fuel; when that is gone, they grind to a halt. Until power can be packaged in capsules or, like forage, gathered along the route of march, the door to both self-containment and local supply is likely to remain closed.

Supply from bases

The alternative to self-containment and local supply is continuous or periodic resupply and replacement from stores prestocked at accessible points. Each of these points, or all together, constitute a supply base, a term also applied to a region from which a force draws its supplies—such as the Nile Delta for the British 8th Army in World War II.

Supply from bases involves three serious disadvantages. First, supply routes to the using force are vulnerable to attack and difficult to defend. Second, an army shackled to its bases lacks flexibility and moves slowly, and its progress is likely to become slower as it moves farther from its base. Finally, the transportation costs of maintaining a flow of supply over substantial distances are heavy and, beyond a point, prohibitive. The reason is twofold; first, because the transport engaged in supplying the force must operate a continuous shuttle—that is, for each day's travel time, two vehicles are needed to deliver a single load—and, second, because additional food and forage or fuel must be provided for the personnel and animals of the supply train. In the era of animal-drawn transport this multiplier factor set practical limits to the operating radius of an army, which the U.S. general William T. Sherman, on the basis of his Civil War experience, fixed at about 100 miles (160 kilometres), or five days' march from its base. The problem can be illustrated by a hypothetical example. A force consuming 100 tons (91,000 kilograms) of supplies per day and operating 150 miles (240 kilometres) from its nearest base would need approximately 2,000 wagons, including spares, to keep it supplied. But because each wagon's team of horses or mules would consume a little more than a full wagonload of forage during the 15-day round trip between base and army, and because the additional wagon's team would need a similar amount, requiring still another wagonload, and so on *ad infinitum,* it can be seen that the in-transit forage requirement at this operating radius would saturate any amount of transport that was provided. (Even at 100 miles' distance, about three times as much transport would be needed to haul forage as to supply the army.)

With modern mechanized transport the theoretical maximum operating radius is so great that other limitations come into play long before it is reached. (The U.S. Army's truck-and-trailer used in World War II, with three to five times the capacity of a Civil War wagon, could travel as far on 100 pounds (45 kilograms) of fuel as the latter could travel on 750 pounds (341 kilograms) of forage.) Nevertheless, the in-transit fuel requirement can add major increments to the basic transport capacity needed to supply a force from distant bases, and under conditions that markedly reduce the speed or increase the fuel consumption of the vehicles, it can become prohibitive. Thus, a force operating 360 miles (580 kilometres) from its base in mountainous country over poor roads might need as many as 3,700 vehicles merely to bring forward its daily supplies, plus another 2,000 to meet the cumulative fuel requirement. Normally a modern army draws its daily supplies from supply points much closer than in this example, but these too must be stocked by vehicles that consume fuel. The bogdown of the U.S. 3rd Army's drive across France in the summer of 1944 for lack of fuel illustrates the problem of supplying a rapidly advancing force from distant bases.

HISTORICAL DEVELOPMENT OF LOGISTICS

Ancient and medieval logistical systems. In ancient history the combination of local supply for food and forage and of self-containment in hardware and services appears often as the logistical basis for operations by forces of moderate size. Some of these operations are familiar to many a schoolboy—the long campaign of Alexander the Great from Macedonia to the Indus, for example, and Hannibal's campaigns in Italy. The larger armies of ancient times—like that of the Persian Xerxes in the invasion of Greece in 480 BC—seem to have been supplied by depots and magazines along their routes of march. The Roman legion combined all three methods of supply in a marvellously flexible system. The legion's ability to march fast and far owed much to superb roads and an efficiently organized supply train, which included mobile repair shops and a service corps of engineers, artificers, armourers, and other technicians. Supplies were requisitioned from local authorities and stored in fortified depots; labour and animals were drafted as required. When necessary, the legion could carry in its train and on the backs of its soldiers up to 30 days' supply of provisions. In the First Punic War, the war against Carthage (264–241 BC), a Roman army marched an average of 16 miles (26 kilometres) a day for four weeks.

One of the most efficient logistical systems ever known was that of the Mongol cavalry armies of the 13th century. It rested mainly on self-containment and local supply, supplemented by bases. In normal movements the Mongol armies divided into several corps and spread widely over the country, accompanied by trains of baggage carts, pack animals, and herds of cattle. Routes and camp sites were carefully selected for accessibility to good grazing and food crops; food and forage were stored in advance along the routes of march. On entering enemy country, the army abandoned its baggage and herds, divided into widely separated columns, and converged upon the unprepared foe at great speed from several directions. In one such approach march a Mongol army covered 180 miles (290 kilometres) in three days. Commissariat, remount, and transport services were carefully organized. The tough and seasoned Mongol warrior could subsist almost indefinitely on dried meat and curds, supplemented by occasional game; when in straits, he might drain a little blood from a vein in his mount's neck. The Mongol pony, bred on the steppe, was equally tough. Every man had a string of ponies; baggage was held to a minimum; equipment was standardized and light.

Logistics of the early modern era. *The revolution in welfare.* In the early 17th century, King Gustavus II Adolphus of Sweden and Prince Maurice of Nassau, the military hero of the Netherlands, restored to European warfare a mobility not seen since the days of the Roman legion, mainly by careful organization of supply. The Swedish armies were based on prestocked magazines, but they also had compact supply trains with well-organized services, a flexible tactical system, and light, standardized artillery. An important feature of Gustavian logistics was a system of orderly requisitioning that contrasted with the indiscriminate looting characteristic of the warfare of the day.

Transport and supply in formalized 18th-century warfare

The formalized warfare of the 18th century was based on an elaborate system of logistics that sacrificed both range and mobility. This was the era of the rolling magazine and of intricate systems of fortified depots and defended lines of communications. The growing size of armies, increasing use of artillery, and greater attention to the creature comforts of a mercenary soldiery all combined to place heavier burdens on transport. The retinues of baggage and servants accompanying higher officers assumed monumental proportions. At the same time, a revulsion against the depredations and inhumanity of the 17th-century religious wars brought curbs on looting and burning. Local supply took the form of regulated requisitioning administered through municipal and provincial authorities under terms often defined by treaty. Since soldiers were expensive, there was a tendency to avoid pitched battles (which, when they occurred, were bloody), and campaigns tended to degenerate into sluggish manoeuvres with the primary aim of threatening or defending bases and lines of communications. War became an appendage of logistics in which, as Frederick the Great of Prussia remarked, "the masterpiece of a successful general is to starve his enemy."

The era of the French Revolution and the Napoleonic domination of Europe (1789–1815) brought back both mobility and range to European military operations, along with an immense increase in the size of armies. Logistics became simpler and in many respects cruder. French armies largely abandoned the rolling magazine, the elaborate depot system, and the orderly requisitioning of the preceding period. Baggage trains were pared down to the essential needs of fighting power and mobility. The soldier was often heavily burdened with weapons, ammunition, and necessities formerly carried by the train; his greatcoat now served as his tent. Even so, he marched faster and farther than his opponents and predecessors. The system leaned heavily on the willingness of the citizen-soldier to do without and to suffer and die for lack of the rudiments of medical care. Napoleon himself avowedly counted on a brief campaign climaxed by a resounding victory to solve most of his logistical problems. The system, such as it was, tended to degenerate. Baggage trains grew larger, and, unable to keep up with the pace of advance, they left the troops dependent on a devastated countryside.

Logistics in the industrial era. Between the mid-19th and the mid-20th centuries the conditions and methods of logistics were transformed by a fundamental change in the tools and modes of making war—perhaps the most fundamental change since the beginning of organized warfare. The revolution had four facets: (1) the mobilization of mass armies; (2) a vast increase in firepower; (3) an economic revolution that provided the means to feed, arm, and transport mass armies; and (4) a revolution in the techniques of management and organization, which enabled nations to mobilize their economic and human resources to operate their military establishments more effectively than ever before.

These interrelated developments did not occur all at once. Armies of unprecedented size had appeared in the later years of the Napoleonic wars. But for almost a century after 1815, the world saw no comparable mobilization of military manpower except in the U.S. Civil War. Meanwhile, the growth of population (in Europe, from 180,000,000 in 1800 to more than 600,000,000 in 1970) was creating a huge reservoir of manpower. By the end of the 19th century most nations were building large standing armies backed by even larger partially trained reserves; in the world wars of the 20th century the major powers mobilized armed forces numbering millions.

The revolution in weapons had started earlier with a series of inventions and technical innovations dating back at least to the late 18th century. By the 1850s and 1860s the rifled percussion musket, rifled and breech-loading artillery, large-calibre ordnance, and steam-propelled armoured warships were all coming into general use. The technological revolution proceeded with gathering momentum thereafter, but it remained for mass armies in the 20th century to realize its full potentiality for destruction.

The new weaponry

By the mid-19th century the Industrial Revolution had already given Great Britain, France, and the United States the capacity to produce munitions, food, transport, and many other items in quantities no commissary or quartermaster had ever dreamed of. In the U.S. Civil War the abundant output of munitions in the North dimly suggested the latent capabilities that might have been realized. But, in general, the wars of the 19th century hardly scratched the surface of the existing war-making potential. The nature of the international rivalries of the period tended to limit war objectives and the mobilization of latent military power, and it may be doubted whether existing managerial knowledge would have been adequate to the task in any case. Only in the crucible of World War I, at the cost of colossal blunders and wasted effort, did nations begin to learn the techniques of "total" war.

Thus the full implications of the revolution in warfare were not revealed until the 20th century. Long before 1914, however, new instruments and techniques of logistics had begun to emerge.

Transportation and communication. The railroad, the steamship, and the telegraph had a profound impact on logistical methods during the last half of the 19th century. After the period of the Crimean War (1854–56), telegraphic communication became an indispensable tool of command, intelligence, and operational coordination, particularly in controlling rail traffic. In the 20th century it yielded to more efficient forms of electronic communication—especially the telephone, radio, radar, television, and telephotography.

Railroads spread rapidly over western and central Europe and the eastern United States between 1850 and 1860. They were used—mainly for troop movements—in the suppression of the central European revolutions of 1848–49, on a considerable scale in the Italian War of 1859, and extensively in the U.S. Civil War, where they also demonstrated their capacity for long hauls of bulky freight in sustaining the forward movement of armies.

Influence of the railroads and the iron steamship

In Europe, from 1859 on, the railroads shaped the war plans of all the general staffs, the central features of which were the rapid mobilization and concentration of troops on a threatened frontier at the outbreak of war. In many countries railroad building was planned with this end in view. Germany's strategic rail network in the centre of Europe enabled it to exploit to the full the advantage of interior lines. In 1870, at the outset of the Franco-Prussian

War, it was able to concentrate 550,000 troops, 150,000 horses, and 6,000 pieces of artillery on the French border in 21 days, and its recognized efficiency in mobilizing influenced the war plans of all the European powers in 1914. In both world wars Germany's railroads enabled it to shift troops rapidly between the Russian and the Western fronts.

In the 19th century, steam propulsion and iron ship construction also introduced new logistical capabilities into warfare—the latter by breaking down earlier limitations on the size of seagoing ships, the former by freeing seaborne transportation from the vagaries of the wind. Steamships moved troops and supplies in support of the overseas operations of the United States in the Mexican War of 1846–48 and on a much larger scale in the transport of British and French armies in the Crimean War of 1854–56; river steamboats played an indispensable logistical role in the U.S. Civil War.

Influence of motor transport   The complement of the railroad was the powered vehicle that could travel on ordinary roads and even unprepared surfaces, within the operating zones of armies, forward of railhead. This was a 20th-century development, a combination of the internal-combustion engine, the pneumatic tire, and the endless track. Motor transport was first used on a large scale in World War I, along with animal-drawn transport, and in World War II it became, next to the railroad, the dominant means of land movement. Another innovation was the pipeline, used to move water in the Palestine campaign of World War I, and extensively in World War II to move oil and gasoline to storage points close to the combat zones. More revolutionary was the development of large-scale air transportation. In World War II, units as large as a division were carried in one movement by air over and behind enemy lines and resupplied by the same means. Cargo aircraft maintained an airlift for more than three years from bases in India across the Himalayas into China; during the last eight months of operation it averaged more than 50,000 tons per month. But the fuel costs of such an operation were exorbitant. Air transportation remained primarily a means of emergency movement when speed was an overriding consideration.

The growth in quantity.   The most conspicuous logistical phenomenon of the great 20th-century wars was the enormous quantity of material used and consumed. One cause was the growth of firepower, which was partly a matter of increased rapidity of fire of individual weapons, partly a higher ratio of weapons to men—both multiplied by the vast numbers of men now mobilized. A U.S. Civil War infantry division of 3,000 to 5,000 men had an artillery complement of up to 24 pieces; its World War II counterpart, numbering about 15,000 men, had 328 artillery pieces, all capable of firing heavier projectiles far more rapidly. A World War II armoured division had an armament of nearly 1,000 pieces of artillery. Twentieth-century infantrymen, moreover, were armed with semiautomatic and automatic weapons instead of the single-shot muzzle-loaders used by most troops in the Civil War.

The increasing consumption of ammunition   The upward curve of firepower was reflected in the immense amounts of ammunition required in large-scale operations. Artillery fire in the Franco-Prussian War (1870–71) and in the Russo-Japanese War (1904–05), for example, showed a marked increase over that in the Civil War. But World War I unleashed a firepower whose existence had hardly been hinted at in the previous conflicts. In the seven-day battle of the Somme in 1916, British artillery fired about 4,000,000 rounds, or roughly 125 times as many as the Union artillery in the three-day Battle of Gettysburg during the U.S. Civil War. In World War II the United States procured only about four times as many small arms as it had in the Civil War, but 43 times as much small-arms ammunition. The Confederacy fought through the four years of the Civil War on something like 5,000 or 6,000 tons of gunpowder; U.S. factories in one average month during World War I turned out almost four times this quantity of smokeless powder. Again, in one year of World War II, 7,000,000 tons of steel went into the manufacture of tanks and trucks for the U.S. Army, 4,000,000 tons into artillery ammunition, 1,000,000 tons into artillery, and 1,500,000 tons into small arms—as

contrasted with less than 1,000,000 tons of pig iron used by the entire economy of the Northern states during one year of the Civil War. To the ammunition expenditures in the world wars of the 20th century were added, moreover, the immense tonnages of explosives used in air bombardment. Yet ammunition and explosives remained a relatively small item among military expendables; the weight of fuel and food was three or four times as great.

With growth in quantity went a parallel growth in the complexity of military equipment. The U.S. Army in World War II used about 60 major types of artillery above .60-calibre, from the 20-millimetre automatic aircraft cannon to the 16-inch (40-centimetre) coast artillery gun. For 20 different calibres of cannon there were about 270 types and sizes of shells. The list of military items procured for U.S. Army ground forces added up to almost 900,000, and each end item contained many separate parts; fire control instruments for some anti-aircraft guns contained as many as 25,000 precision-made parts. To convert and expand a nation's peacetime industry to the production of such an arsenal posed staggering technical problems. Manufacturers of automobiles, refrigerators, soap, soft drinks, bed springs, toys, shirts, and microscopes had to learn how to make guns, gun carriages, recoil mechanisms, and ammunition.   **The increasing complexity of military equipment**

Staged resupply.   Long before mechanization relegated local supply to a minor role in the support of modern armies, growing supply requirements had made armies dependent on more or less continuous resupply from bases. The *Etappen* system of the Prussian Army in 1866 was essentially a modification of the rolling magazine of the 18th century. Behind each army corps trailed a series of supply trains, shuttling continuously between the advancing troops and the nearest magazines in the rear. The magazines were repeatedly moved forward to keep within one or two days' march of the advance and were in turn replenished by a lengthening chain of magazines extending back as far as the railhead. Only a small train accompanied the troops, carrying a basic load of ammunition, rations, and baggage; each soldier carried three days' emergency rations. The system was geared to a steady, slow advance on a rigid schedule and a predetermined route, and the individual soldier was still heavily laden.

Staged, continuous resupply became the basic logistical system for all armies in the industrial era. Sustained reliance on self-containment and local supply virtually disappeared. Accompanying loads were limited mainly to fighting equipment and a small reserve of fuel and ammunition, and soldiers carried a day or two of emergency rations. The administrative tail of magazines and shuttling transport stretching far back to the army's sources of supply became a regular feature of modern land warfare. In World War II, supplies moving to U.S. armies overseas normally passed through seven or eight major stages, besides numerous intervening ones: from a depot in the U.S. to a port of embarkation, to an overseas port, to a rear-area depot and perhaps to an intermediate or advanced depot, to a regulating station, to an army-area supply point, to a division or regimental supply point, and finally to the troops.   **Decreased reliance on self-containment and local supply**

Under this system, even though it was frequently described as a pipeline, supplies never flowed continuously from ultimate source to consumer. Reserves of material were stocked as far forward as was safe and practicable, making possible regular supply of food and fuel, and immediate provision of ammunition, replacement equipment, and services when needed. Before any major operation, large reserves had to be accumulated close behind the front; the build-up of U.S. war matériel in the British Isles preceding the Normandy invasion of 1944 went on continuously over a period of two years and involved the shipment of 16,000,000 tons of cargo across the Atlantic from the United States. In essence, the system strove to convert supply from bases into an approximation of local supply, by moving the bases close to the troops.

Behind the armies, in the continental European theatre in World War II, spread the rear-area administrative zone, a vast complex of depots, traffic regulating points, railway marshalling yards, troop cantonments and rest areas, repair shops, artillery and tank parks, oil and gasoline storage tanks, airfields, and headquarters—through which ran the lines of supply stretching back to ultimate sources. In the Pacific, the administrative zone covered vast reaches of water, and most of the bases were on islands. Communication and movement in this theatre depended largely on shipping, supplemented by aircraft, and one of the major logistical problems was moving forward bases and reserves as the fighting forces advanced. Late in the war, supply ships often sailed all the way from the U.S. West Coast, bypassing intermediate bases, to forward areas where they were held as floating warehouses until their cargoes were exhausted.

The system of staged resupply gave modern armies considerable range of movement and sustained offensive power, but it undermined their mobility. The natural habitat of the system was the creeping or sealed front of World War I. Even then, many offensives on the western front bogged down, after gaining a few miles, through failure of supplies to keep up with the advance. World War II brought back manoeuvre and rapid movement, but mobile forces remained tied to their bases; they could move only as far and as long as their supplies could be carried to them.

Effects of modern logistics on defense
One of the striking lessons of World War II, often obscured by the tactical achievements of air power and mechanized armour, was the great power that modern logistics gave to the defense. In 1943 and 1944 the ratio of superiority enjoyed by Germany's enemies in output of combat munitions was about 2.5 to 1; the whole apparatus of Germany's war economy was subjected to relentless attack from the air and had in addition to make good the enormous losses of matériel resulting from a succession of military defeats. Yet Germany was able, for about two years, to hold its own, primarily because its waning logistical strength could be concentrated on sustaining the firepower of forces that were stationary or were retiring slowly toward their bases, instead of on the immensely expensive effort required to support a rapid forward movement.

Logistical specialization. For many centuries the soldier was a fighting man and nothing else; he depended on civilians to provide the services that enabled him to live, move, and fight. Even the more technical combat and combat-related skills, such as fortification, siegecraft, and the service of artillery, were traditionally civilian. After the mid-19th century, with the rather sudden growth in the technical complexity of warfare, the military profession faced the problem of assimilating a growing number and variety of specialized noncombatant skills. Many of the uniformed logistical services date from this period; examples are the British Army's Transport Corps (later the Royal Army Service Corps), Hospital Corps, and Ordnance Corps. In the U.S. Civil War the Union Army formed a railway construction corps, largely civilian in composition and operation but under military control. A little later, Prussia created a railway section in the great General Staff and a combined military–civilian organization for controlling and operating the railroads in time of war.

Ratios of combat and noncombat personnel
Not until the 20th century, however, did organized military units performing specialized logistical services begin to appear in large numbers in the field. By the end of World War II, what was called "service support" comprised about 45 percent of the total strength of the U.S. Army. Only three out of every 10 soldiers had combat functions, and even within the ranks of a combat division, one man out of four fell into the noncombatant category. Even so, the specialized services that the military profession succeeded in assimilating were only a small fraction of those on which the combat soldier depended. Throughout the vast administrative zones behind combat areas and in the national base, armies of civilian workers and specialists manned depots, arsenals, factories, communications centres, ports, and the other apparatus of a modern society at war. Military establishments employed a growing number of civilian administrators, scientists, management and public relations experts, and other specialists. Within the profession itself, the actual incorporation of specialized skills was limited, in the main, to those directly related (or exposed) to combat, such as the operating and servicing

of military equipment, though even here the profession had no monopoly. Soldiers also served as administrators and supervisors over civilian specialists with whose skills they had only a nodding acquaintance. On the whole, the fighting man at mid-20th century belonged to a shrinking minority in a profession made up largely of administrators and noncombatant specialists.

Logistics in the nuclear age. The dropping of the first atomic bombs in August 1945 seemed to inaugurate a new era in warfare, demanding radical changes in logistical systems and techniques. The bombs did, in truth, give birth to a new line of weaponry of unprecedented destructive power. Within a decade they were followed by the thermonuclear weapon, an even greater quantum leap in destructive force. Development of intercontinental missiles and nuclear-powered, missile-firing submarines a few years later extended the potential range of destruction to targets anywhere on the globe. The 1960s saw dramatic new developments in the offensive capabilities of nuclear weapons and also, for the first time, in defenses against them. But the world moved into the late 20th century without any of the new nuclear weaponry having been used in anger. Throughout the whole period most warfare was limited in scale and made little use of advanced technology. It produced only six highly mobilized war economies: the two Koreas (1950–53), Israel (1956 and 1967), North Vietnam (1965–75), and Biafra (1967–70)—all except Israel previously undeveloped industrially.

The first major conflict in this period, the war in Korea (1950–53), seemed in many ways an extension of World War II. Its principal operations resembled the positional warfare in Italy in 1943–45, and it was fought very largely with World War II weapons, in some cases improved versions, and with stocks of munitions left over from that conflict.

The effects of air superiority on logistics
United Nations forces had an excellent base in nearby Japan, whose factories made a major contribution by rebuilding U.S. World War II material. Both Japan and Pusan, South Korea's major port of entry, were free from Communist air attack throughout the war. Chinese bases north of the Yalu enjoyed a similar immunity from UN air raids. This curious circumstance greatly simplified the supply problem of UN forces, enabling them to funnel through Pusan supply tonnages comparable to those handled by the largest ports in World War II and to concentrate depots and other installations in the Pusan area to a degree that would have been suicidal without complete air superiority.

By World War II standards, the Korean War was a limited conflict (except for the two Korean belligerents, on whose soil it was fought). It involved only a partial, or "creeping," economic mobilization in the United States, the major UN participant, and a modest mobilization of reserve manpower. Yet this was no small war. During the three years that it lasted, about 37,200,000 measurement tons of cargo were poured into the South Korean ports, more than three-fourths of the amount shipped to U.S. Army forces in all the Pacific theatres from December 1941 to August 1945. And the combined UN forces reached a peak strength of almost 1,000,000 men, of whom more than a third consisted of U.S. and other non-Korean contingents. Communist forces were considerably larger.

New modes of land and air transport
New technology. Advances in the technology of supply and movement after 1945 were not commensurate with those in mass-destruction weaponry. On land, internal-combustion vehicles and railroads, with increasing use of diesel fuel in both, remained the basic instrument of large-scale troop and freight movements, despite their growing vulnerability to attack. In the most modern systems, substantial amounts of motor transport were capable of crossing shallow water obstacles. In areas not yet penetrated by rail or metalled roads—areas where much of the warfare of the period occurred—surface movement necessarily reverted to the ancient modes of human and animal porterage, sometimes usefully supplemented by the bicycle. Some exotic types of vehicles capable of negotiating rough and soft terrain off the roads were designed and tested; the "hovercraft," or air cushion vehicle, for instance. But none of these innovations came into

general use. The most promising developments in overland movement were helicopters and vertical-takeoff-and-landing aircraft, along with techniques of rapid airfield construction, which enabled streamlined airmobile forces and their logistical tails to overleap terrain obstacles and greatly reduced their dependence on roads, airfields, and forward bases. Helicopters also permitted the establishment and maintenance of isolated artillery fire bases in enemy territory.

In air movement there was a spectacular growth in the range and payload capacity of transport aircraft. The piston-engine transports of World War II vintage that carried out the Berlin airlift of 1948–49 had a capacity of about four tons (3,640 kilograms) and a maximum range of 1,500 miles (2,400 kilometres). The U.S. C-141 jet transport, which went into service in 1965, had a 45-ton (40,900-kilogram) capacity and a range of 3,000 miles (4,800 kilometres); it could take an average payload of 24 tons from the U.S. West Coast to South Vietnam in 43 hours and evacuate wounded back to the East Coast (10,000 miles) in less than a day. By 1970 these capabilities were dwarfed by the new "global logistics" C-5A, with payloads up to 130 tons and ranges up to 5,500 miles. It is estimated that ten C-5As could have handled the entire Berlin airlift, which employed more than 140 of the then available transports. Very large cargo helicopters were also developed, notably in the Soviet Union, as were new techniques for packaging and air-dropping cargo.

New modes of sea transport

In this period, movement by sea was the only branch of logistics that tapped the huge potential of nuclear propulsion. Its principal application, however, was in submarines, which did not develop a significant logistical function, although nuclear tanker submarines were in prospect. The U.S.S.R. produced a nuclear-powered icebreaker in 1957, and the United States launched the first nuclear-powered merchant ship in 1959. But high initial and operating costs and (in the West) vested mercantile interests barred extensive construction of such vessels; and, except for the supertankers built after the Suez crisis in 1956, large seaborne cargo movement still depended on merchant ships not radically different from those used in World War II. The chief technical improvement in sea lift, embodied in a few special-purpose vessels, was the "roll-on-roll-off" feature, first used in World War II landing craft, which permitted loading and discharge of vehicles without hoisting. Containerization, the stowage of irregularly shaped freight in sealed, reusable containers of uniform size and shape, became widespread in commercial ship operations and significantly affected ship design.

This period saw further development, from World War II models, of large vessels, such as the landing-ship dock and the amphibious-transport dock, capable of discharging landing craft and vehicles offshore or over a beach as well as transporting troops, cargo, and helicopters in amphibious operations. For follow-up operations, improved attack cargo ships were built, such as the British landing-ship logistic, with accommodations for landing craft, helicopters, vehicles and tanks, landing ramps, and heavy-cargo-handling equipment. More revolutionary additions to the technology of amphibious logistics were the American landing vehicle hydrofoil and the BARC, both amphibians with pneumatic-tired wheels for overland movement and, in the latter case, capacity for 100 tons of cargo. Hydrofoil craft, which skimmed at high speeds above the water on submerged inclined planes, had developed a varied family of types by 1970; they, and the hovercraft mentioned earlier, had evident logistical potential for amphibious and other maritime operations.

The effects of new electronic communications and computers

The spectacular developments after World War II in the field of electronic communications lie beyond the scope of this article, but their profound impact on logistical administration should be noted. In advanced logistical systems the combination of advanced electronic communications with the high-speed electronic computer almost wholly replaced the elaborate processes of message transmission, record search, and record keeping formerly involved in supply administration, making the response to supply demand automatic and virtually instantaneous.

Strategic mobility. Because the major military powers did not directly fight each other during the decades after World War II, none of them had to deal with the classic logistical problem of deploying and supporting forces over sea lines of communication exposed to enemy attack. The Soviet Union, for example, was able in 1962 to establish a formidable missile base in Cuba manned by some 25,000 troops without interference by the United States until its offensive purpose was detected. Similarly, the vast deployments of U.S. forces to Korea, Southeast Asia, and elsewhere encountered no opposition.

Yet the problem of strategic mobility was of major concern after 1945 to the handful of nations with far-flung interests and the capacity to project military power far beyond their borders. In the tightly controlled power politics of the period, each major power needed the capability to bring military force quickly to bear (usually mainly for deterrent purposes) to protect its interests in local emergencies at remote points—as Great Britain and France did at Suez in 1956, the United States in Lebanon in 1958 and in the Taiwan Straits in 1959, and Great Britain in the Falkland Islands in 1982. The most effective instruments for such interventions were small, powerful, mobile task forces brought in by air or sea and forward-deployed naval-carrier and amphibious forces. The United States developed strong and versatile intervention capabilities, with major fleets deployed in the far Pacific and the Mediterranean; a worldwide network of bases and alliances; large ground and air forces in Europe, Korea, and Southeast Asia; and, in the 1960s, a mobile strategic reserve of several divisions with long-range sea-lift and airlift capabilities. The U.S.S.R., Great Britain, and France had more limited capabilities, the last two having liquidated most of their overseas military commitments; the U.S.S.R. began in the late 1960s to deploy strong naval and air forces into the eastern Mediterranean and also maintained a naval presence in the Indian Ocean.

Comparisons of naval carriers and land air bases

The logistics of strategic mobility was complex and was decisively affected by the changing technology of movement. During the 1950s the proponents of naval and land-based air power debated the relative costs and effectiveness of naval-carrier forces and fixed air bases as a tool of emergency intervention. Studies seemed to show that the fixed bases were cheaper if all related costs were considered but that the advantage of mobility and flexibility lay with the naval carriers. In the 1970s the growing range and capacities of transport aircraft provided an increasingly effective tool for distant intervention and were a large factor in the reduction of the American and British overseas base systems. On the other hand, the usefulness of the big new transports was limited by the paucity of large airfields with adequate facilities in the less developed areas.

In practice, emergency situations called for using the means available and involved a great deal of improvisation, especially for second-rank powers. In 1961, when the newly independent state of Kuwait requested help against a threatened Iraqi invasion, Great Britain in less than a week brought in a mixed force of about 5,700 troops with two fighter squadrons, a helicopter carrier, and two fleet carriers, mostly from nearby bases—Aden, Bahrain, Kenya, Trucial Oman—but in part from as far away as West Germany, the United Kingdom, and Hong Kong. Although only part of the total movement was by air, it utilized almost half of Great Britain's strategic airlift of 200 transports. All this was accomplished although the only airfield available was the uncompleted civil airport at Kuwait, which lacked modern ground control equipment and was often closed during sandstorms.

Management. Both during and after World War II the United States operated the largest and most advanced logistical system in the world. Its wartime operations stressed speed, volume, and risk-taking more than efficiency and economy. The postwar years, with accelerated technological change, skyrocketing costs for military hardware, and diminished public interest in defense, brought a revulsion against military prodigality, manifested by calls for reduced defense budgets and a growing demand for more efficient management of the military establishment. This demand culminated in a thorough overhaul of the whole system in the 1960s.

One result was the organization of logistical activities in the three military services generally along functional lines by abolishing most of the historic commodity-oriented technical services and bureaus and establishing large logistical commands under functional staff supervision. In each service, however, each major weapon system was centrally managed by a separate project manager during the phases from design through initial distribution; and central inventory control was maintained for large commodity groups. In 1961 a new defense supply agency was established to manage on a wholesale basis the procurement, storage, and distribution of common military supplies and the administration of certain common services.

The most far-reaching managerial reforms of the period were instituted by U.S. defense secretary Robert S. McNamara (1961–68) in the resource allocation process. A new unified defense planning–programming–budgeting system provided for five-year projections of force, manpower, and dollar requirements for all defense activities, classified into eight or nine major programs (such as strategic forces) that cut across the lines of traditional service responsibilities. The system was introduced in other federal departments after 1965, and elements of it were adopted by the British and other governments. In 1966 a program was inaugurated to integrate management accounting at the operating level with the programming–budgeting system. The operating manager of a unit or activity was made accountable for resources and services actually used in performance of his mission, and these expenses were charged directly to program elements in the five-year defense program. At the end of the 1960s a new administration restored some of the initiative in the planning–budgeting–programming cycle to the Joint Chiefs of Staff and the military services.

The reforms of the 1960s exploited the whole range of current managerial methodology. The basic techniques—systems and operations analysis, systems engineering, linear programming, and several others—all stressed precise, scientific, usually quantitative formulations of problems and mathematical approaches to rational decision making. Systems analysis, the technique associated with defense planning and programming, was a method of economic and mathematical analysis useful in dealing with complex problems of choice under conditions of uncertainty. It stressed precise definition of objectives, exploration of alternative solutions with their probable consequences, and weighing of costs against effectiveness in arriving at preferred solutions. The technological foundation of this improved logistical management was the high-speed electronic computer, which was being used chiefly in inventory control; in automated operations at depots, bases, and stations; in transmission and processing of supply data; in personnel administration; and in vast command-and-control networks.

War in Vietnam. One of the most significant developments in logistics after 1945 was the pitting of advanced high-technology systems against highly organized low-technology systems operating on their own ground. The Korean War, already described, and the anticolonial wars in French Indochina and Algeria were the principal conflicts of this kind in the 1950s. The war in Vietnam following large-scale U.S. intervention in 1965 brought into conflict the most effective of both types of systems.

By 1965 the United States already had a modest logistical establishment in South Vietnam, supporting its own air bases and military advisers and the supply of South Vietnamese forces. The growing insecurity of overland communications had forced the Americans to depend more and more on movement by sea between ports and by air to inland bases and outposts. The country lacked most of the facilities on which modern military forces depend. Accordingly, the massive U.S. deployment that began in the spring of 1965, reaching 180,000 men by the end of that year and more than 550,000 in 1969, was accompanied, rather than preceded, by a huge ($4,000,000,000) construction program, carried out partly by army, navy, and air force engineer units and partly by a consortium of engineering contractors. Under this program were built 7 deepwater and several smaller ports, 8 jet air bases with 10,000-foot (3,050-metre) runways, 200 smaller air-

fields, and 200 heliports, besides millions of square feet of covered and refrigerated storage, hundreds of miles of roads, hundreds of bridges, oil pipelines and tanks, and all the other apparatus of a modern logistical infrastructure. Deep-draft shipping brought in all but scarce items of airlifted supplies and came mainly from the U.S. directly, instead of through intermediate bases as in the Korean War.

The soldier in the field received lavish logistical support. By means of helicopter supply, troops in contact with the enemy were often provided with hot meals; most of the wounded were promptly evacuated to hospitals and serious cases were moved by air to base facilities in the Pacific or the United States. Medical evacuation, combined with advances in medicine, helped to raise the ratio of surviving wounded to dead to 6 to 1, in contrast to a World War II ratio of 2.6 to 1. Logistical support of army forces was organized under a single logistical command having a strength of 30,000 and employing 50,000 Vietnamese, U.S., and foreign civilians. Ultimately there were four or five support personnel for every infantryman who bore the brunt of contact fighting with the enemy.

The Communist logistical system in this war centred in the highly mobilized society of North Vietnam. In its integration, efficiency, and resiliency under concentrated and prolonged bombing it rivalled the war economy of Germany in World War II. Its resiliency owed much, however, to the fact that it was a village-centred agricultural society, with modest material needs and a limited industrial base, which produced no steel, very little pig iron, and only one-fifth as much electric power as a single power plant in a small American town.

By late 1967 the Communist war effort in South Vietnam depended heavily on the flow of troops, equipment, and supplies from North Vietnam, supplied principally by the Soviet Union. The troops and most of the supplies moved over the Ho Chi Minh Trail, originally a network of footpaths and dirt roads (often paved after 1967) through Communist-controlled areas in Laos and Cambodia. Supplies also came into South Vietnam by sea and across the northern border and, increasingly after 1967, through the Cambodian port of Kompong Som and overland into the Mekong Delta.

The Ho Chi Minh Trail was a long, slow-moving pipeline, requiring from three to six months in transit by truck, barge, ox cart, bicycle, and foot, but its capacity was ample for the modest demands placed upon it. In mid-1967, U.S. intelligence estimated the total nonfood requirements of all Communist forces in South Vietnam, except in the northernmost provinces, to be as low as 15 tons (13,640 kilograms) per day (about 1.5 ounces, or 47 grams, per man); food was procured locally and in nearby Cambodia and Laos. This austerity reflected the Communist forces' lack of mechanized equipment and heavy weapons and the generally low intensity of combat in 1967. In 1968, when the pace of the war quickened and Communist forces were substantially augmented, estimated nonfood requirements rose to about 120 tons per day. (A single U.S. division required about five times this amount.)

American bombing had little effect on the flow of troops to the south, and the Communist logistical system stood up remarkably well—and ultimately victoriously—under the crushing weight of American air power. Its strength lay primarily in its austerity, but also in efficient organization, lavish use of manpower, availability of sanctuary areas in Laos and Cambodia, and a steady flow of imported supplies.

Trends and prospects. For logisticians the fundamental dilemma posed by the quantum leap in weapons technology after World War II was the absence of any comparable development in logistics—with the possible exception of the electronic computer, which reached an advanced stage of development and military application only in the 1960s. No other technical innovation perfected and applied in this period, in transportation, supply, or administration, had an impact on the conduct of war comparable to that produced in the 19th and early 20th centuries by the railroad, the steamship, the telegraph, the internal-combustion machine, and mass production.

Conversely, nuclear weapons threatened to sweep away every vestige of the logistical system of the industrial era. None of the elaborate apparatus of rear-area administration, lines of communications, or even sources of supply seemed likely to survive the nuclear firepower that could be brought to bear against it. From the 1950s to the 1970s the problem was studied and restudied, and a great deal of hopeful doctrine was developed for logistical operations in a nuclear war. It revolved about such concepts as dispersion, mobility, small targets, duplication, multiplicity, austerity, concealment, and automaticity, and formulated procedures and technologies compatible with these concepts. Yet all of it, by the late 20th century, was still hardly more than a planner's dream. At best it promised to reduce somewhat the inherent vulnerability of the surface-bound installations and transport on which military forces for the foreseeable future were likely to depend. Dispersion and duplication were enemies of economy and efficiency. The net effect could only be to increase the costs of logistical support and diminish the yield of delivered supplies and services.

In any case, nuclear war, whether strategic or tactical, seemed far less likely than a continuation of the confused patterns of limited and conventional war and quasi-war that had filled the decades since the end of World War II. Under these conditions the central problems of logistics would be the historic ones of weight and bulk, which inhibited mobility and range of movement and were the primary causes of vulnerability to the new firepower. The technologies of these decades had accelerated the basic logistical trends of the industrial era: increasing complexity and cost in military hardware, increasing overall weight and volume of material (despite a reverse trend toward reduced numbers in some major items, such as aircraft), and, above all, an enormous increase in expenditures of ammunition and fuel. Logisticians in the 1970s had to face the probability that in another large-scale conventional conflict between advanced powers the new vehicles would consume almost twice as much fuel and the new weapons would expend almost three times as much ammunition as had been consumed and expended in World War II.

Increasing
consump-
tion of
fuel and
ammuni-
tion in
limited
warfare

Some of the new tools of logistics were highly effective in specialized environments, notably the growing family of helicopters used in conjunction with conventional and short-takeoff-and-landing air transports, which permitted a mobility and a range of movement over difficult terrain far beyond the capabilities of surface transport. Whether an airmobile logistical system could survive the firepower likely to be encountered in a conflict with an adversary disputing command of the air was a question to which experience had not yet given an answer. In any case, the system purchased its mobility and range at a fuel cost several times higher than that of the cost involved in surface transport.

How well the "sophisticated" systems, with their growing burden of weight and bulk, would function under a threat to their previously immune supply lines was perhaps the most serious challenge facing modern logisticians. Nuclear propulsion offered a theoretical solution, but there seemed little hope for its early application to large sectors of military movement. Replacement of the existing merchant shipping fleets by nuclear-powered carriers would be a transformation of greater magnitude than the change from sail to steam in the 19th century. A nuclear-powered military sea transport service was a reasonable prospect, though not an early one, and it would not suffice for a major overseas war. More fundamentally, fuel consumption on the sea lanes was not the crux of the problem, and nuclear propulsion offered no solution to the vulnerability of surface vessels to air and submarine attack. The massive fuel consumers were aircraft and ground vehicles, and serious technical obstacles barred the application of nuclear energy to their power plants.

The reckoning, if there was to be one, might be long postponed. Given the existing distribution and equilibriums of power among the advanced nations, on the one hand, and the high cost and slow diffusion of sophisticated military technology to the less-developed two-thirds of the world, on the other, limited warfare seemed likely for a long time

to come to remain at low technical levels. Meanwhile, sophisticated logistical systems were increasingly tangled in their own complexity and absorbed in the endless pursuit of efficient management and in the struggle to control the waste and friction involved in delivering the tools of war to their users.   (R.M.Le./Ed.)

MILITARY ENGINEERING

Military engineering is the oldest of the engineering skills, and military engineers were the first scientific soldiers, out of whose experience the profession of civil engineering came into being. Since then, the arts of military and of civil engineering have developed side by side.

Today the wartime function of military engineers is to apply at all stages engineering knowledge and resources to the furtherance of their commander's plan. Their role can conveniently be divided into three main tasks: (1) combat engineering, or tactical engineer support on the battlefield; (2) strategic support by execution of works and services needed in the communications zones, such as the construction of airfields and depots, the improvement of ports and road and rail communications, and the storage and distribution of fuels; and (3) ancillary support such as the provision and distribution of maps and the disposal of unexploded bombs and warheads.

The military engineers also carry out in peacetime a wide variety of civil works programs. Some are employed on vast projects dealing with coastal engineering and flood control, improving navigational capabilities of major rivers, development of hydroelectric power, water supply, provision of recreational amenities, and pollution control. Military engineers are also employed in providing aid to the civil community, particularly in disaster relief following earthquakes, hurricanes, and severe floods.

Ancient and medieval fortifications. Evidence of the work of the earliest military engineers can be found in many parts of the world; for example, in Europe the hill forts constructed by the men of the late Iron Age, in the Middle East the massive fortresses incorporating the remarkably sophisticated military ideas of the Medes and Persians, and in Africa the high dressed-stone wall fortifications protecting the holy city of Zimbabwe in Zimbabwe, built by the military engineers of a lost civilization. The greatest ancient defensive work ever built by human hands is probably the Great Wall of China, started in the 3rd century BC to defend the 1,000-mile frontier of the Celestial Empire from its barbarian neighbours. Another epic feat of ancient military engineering is known only through the written record of Herodotus, the Greek historian of the Persian wars of the 5th century BC. According to Herodotus, the Persian king Xerxes ordered his engineers to construct a pontoon bridge across the Hellespont (modern Dardanelles), which was accomplished by a mile-long chain of boats, 676 in all, arranged in two parallel rows.

Examples of Roman military engineering works can still be seen throughout Europe and the Near East. Their *castra,* or military garrison towns, were protected by ramparts and ditches and interconnected by straight military roads along which their legions could speedily march to wherever they were needed. Like the Chinese, the Roman military engineers also built walls to protect the limits of their empire, though not of the same size and extent. A famous example is Hadrian's Wall in Britain, 73 miles (117 kilometres) long, from the Solway Firth to the North Sea just north of Newcastle-upon-Tyne, which protected the northern frontier of Roman Britain from the turbulent Picts and Scots. Throughout the long Punic Wars (264–146 BC), when Rome and Carthage struggled for supremacy at sea, harbours and defended naval bases were built, along with a system of watchtowers and forts, to guard against sea raiders. Roman military engineers thus became skilled in the construction of seaward defenses, harbours, and lighthouses and other navigational aids, tasks that remained the military engineer's province for many centuries. Roman engineers also developed a battering ram, slung from a beam mounted on a wheeled platform and provided with overhead cover, to be used against the wall or gate of an enemy fort. They also developed such engines as the giant catapult and the ballista, a large crossbow whose bowstring was drawn back by a windlass. These devices were used to hurl heavy rocks, showers of stones, or firebrands at defended places or at troops in the open. Still another impressive area of achievement by Roman military engineers was bridging; Caesar gives a detailed account of how his soldiers constructed a wooden lashed-trestle bridge over the Rhine, a feat that would tax the ingenuity of a modern military engineer.

The arts of fortifying and of attacking fortified places reached new heights in the centuries following the fall of the Roman Empire, partly as a result of the growth of cities in the later Middle Ages. Medieval engineers, both Arab and European, became proficient at mining operations, by which tunnels were driven under walls of castles or cities and their timbering set fire, causing the masonry overhead to collapse.

Prefabricated forts in 1066

William the Conqueror brought a novel wooden fort, or donjon, from Normandy to England in prefabricated sections to erect on the Hastings beachhead in 1066. As he advanced through the country William built a great number of such temporary forts. The method used was to raise a high mound of earth, called a motte, the top of which was flattened and surrounded by a wooden palisade. Within this palisade a tall wooden tower, or donjon, was built. Timber was used because it lent itself to rapid construction and was readily available locally. Furthermore, the unconsolidated made-up earth of the motte would not have supported the weight of a stone tower. Around the motte an outer defense was provided, called the bailey, consisting of a ditch the soil from which was thrown inward to form a bank that was surmounted by a wooden palisade. These temporary forts were abandoned as castles of permanent construction were built to replace them; the motte and bailey design was retained, however. The donjon, later known as the keep, was often a great tower made of flint, bound together by cement, with walls 20 feet (six metres) thick at the base. The outer defenses of the bailey were equally massive. These castles were an emblem of conquest and became the most effective instruments for enforcing law and order and the most important military and administrative centres in the land. A system of military roads, following the Roman pattern, interconnected them.

Early in the 12th century the crusaders, having captured Jerusalem and retaken the Holy Places, were faced with the problem of defending their conquests with minimum garrisons. Their solution was to build great fortresses, the most impregnable of their day, in strategic locations chosen mostly by French military engineers. As the increasing power of the Muslims gradually forced the knights out of the Holy Land, they withdrew first to Cyprus, then to Rhodes, and finally to Malta. Employing Italian and Spanish engineers, they constructed a series of fortifications on Malta and defenses covering dockyard creeks essential for the maintenance of their ships. In 1565 Süleyman the Magnificent sent a vast naval and military force against Malta. The Turkish forces landed and overran some of the outer defenses of the island, but the remaining works withstood all attacks, and Süleyman's expedition ignominiously withdrew.

Early modern equipment and fortresses. The Renaissance produced a succession of outstanding military engineers and men of remarkable genius, the most famous being Leonardo da Vinci. The age also witnessed rapid development of the cannon and all forms of firearms, a development that brought about a reappraisal of the design of fortifications and the techniques of siege warfare. Leonardo brought his fertile and inventive brain to bear on all facets of military engineering. He carefully analyzed the elementary military engineering tasks of using pick and shovel and basket and barrow for removing excavated soil. He developed the art of casting cannons and was expert in the use of gunpowder, both as a propellant and as a demolition explosive. He designed cranes, earth-moving equipment, and other devices of military value. Leonardo also invented types of assault boats and bridges and several siege devices. A gifted hydraulic engineer, he was a forerunner of the British military engineers who

later built vast irrigation projects in India and of the 20th-century U.S. Army Corps of Engineers, which is responsible for flood control and works connected with the rivers, harbours, and other waterways of the United States.

The frequent campaigns fought in the Low Countries during the 17th century largely involved besieging and defending the great barrier fortresses guarding the frontier between France and The Netherlands. The twin techniques of fortification and siege warfare were exclusively a matter for the military engineer. By midcentury these techniques reached such a state of perfection that they did not change until the latter half of the 19th century, when breech-loading artillery and the high explosive shell called for drastic alterations in the design and construction of defenses.

The outstanding military engineer of this era was Sébastien Le Prestre de Vauban of France (1633–1707). Although he is credited with having said "You do not fortify by systems but by good sense and experience," the design of his fortresses was often rigidly stylized and elaborate. The lines, or traces, of his fortifications, moreover, designed so that direct or flanking fire from both gun and musket could be brought to bear on all approaches, were slavishly copied by succeeding generations of military engineers. Indeed, Vauban's bastion trace became the accepted trace for the fire trench of World War I (see WAR, THE TECHNOLOGY OF: *Fortifications*).

So lasting was Vauban's influence that the French school of military engineering was held to be the leading authority on the profession for many generations, and when the Army Corps of Engineers was constituted in 1779 during the U.S. War of Independence, George Washington turned to France to provide him with military engineer officers.

In the French Revolutionary and Napoleonic Wars (1793–1815), armies grew to unprecedented sizes. Fighting spread from Portugal to Moscow and further afield to the Americas, Egypt, South Africa, and India. In the many campaigns, siege operations were carried out by the traditional Vauban methods. When the French threatened England, vulnerable points on the southern coast of England were defended by hastily erected Martello towers, built on the Norman motte and bailey principle. The outer walls, however, consisted of masonry bastions and the thick-walled stone tower was armed with cannon. The Martello tower construction was later used for coast defense in both Canada and the United States.

The Martello tower

An entirely new system of field defenses was adopted during the construction of the Lines of Torres Vedras by the Duke of Wellington during the Peninsular War in Portugal. Artillery fire could be brought down from a series of mutually supporting redoubts of low silhouette sited in great depth on dominant features and covering all approaches. Fields of fire for the guns were cleared of all obstructions, and streams were dammed to produce inundations to channel enemy lines of approach. Each redoubt was defended by a small close-support garrison of Portuguese militia. Wellington's field army was left available for manoeuvre and counterattack. Though Wellington had less than half as many men as the French, the latter could not risk assaulting these defenses and had to withdraw.

19th-century military engineering. The long period of peace that followed the Napoleonic Wars witnessed another great step forward in the fields of science and engineering and a rapid opening of new territories. The military engineers were quick to study how these technological advances could be put to a military use. In the new territories, they often found themselves the only professional engineers in the land and took personal responsibility for their exploration, mapping, defense, and development.

The U.S. Army Corps of Engineers led the way in exploring much of the American West, breaking trail for the immigrants who followed. They explored, surveyed, and mapped the land, built forts and roads, and later assisted in building the transcontinental railways. They also improved harbours and inland waterways and constructed dams and levees. They were responsible for maintaining coastal defenses. Similarly in Canada, India, Australia, New Zealand, and other countries of the British Empire, the surveys and many of the public buildings and utilities, roads, bridges, railways, telegraphic communication systems, irrigation projects, harbours, and maritime defenses were the work of the British military engineers.

British and French military engineers first used the electric telegraph in the Crimean War (1853–56). Forward headquarters were connected by land line to their respective commanders in chief, who in turn were connected by means of a 340-mile (550-kilometre) submarine cable, laid by the Royal Engineers, to an existing transcontinental line to their governments in London and Paris. A new era in the control of war had dawned; among other political effects, the public at home received prompt news reports from correspondents at the front.

Submarine mining and searchlights. During the U.S. Civil War (1861–65), some 40 ships were sunk or disabled by mines or torpedoes; and interest in this form of warfare was intensified. Engineer submarine mining units were formed to lay electrically controlled mines in time of war to protect naval bases and important commercial ports. The Brennan torpedo, an underwater wire-controlled guided missile with a range of 1,000 yards (900 metres), was also developed. Submarine mining later became a naval responsibility, and the military engineers then developed defense electric lights to illuminate targets by night for coastal batteries. Subsequently they developed anti-aircraft searchlights and sound locators for air defense. Though infrared light and radar made searchlights obsolete in their traditional role, they are still used for battlefield illumination by military engineers.

For many hundred years military engineers used gunpowder and firing accessories obtained from the artillery when they had to carry out demolitions. In the 1860s, however, guncotton with detonating fuse was introduced as a demolition explosive. World War I produced trinitrotoluene (TNT), which was used to fill high-explosive shells and, later, shaped demolition charges that produced a jet of molten metal to penetrate the target. The search for new high explosives during the interwar years produced cyclonite (RDX), which probably represents the limit of what is chemically practicable for a service explosive. In 1942 plastic explosive (PE) was introduced. It made explosives quicker and easier to place and was more resistant to weather and battle hazards. Ammonal, common in World War I, was retained in World War II for mined charges. Pellets of RDX–wax–aluminum and ammonium nitrate and fuel oil slurries have since been used in mined charges with success.

Early military aviation. Early in the 1860s French, British, and U.S. military engineers adapted balloons for a variety of military purposes, mostly intelligence. Subsequently, man-carrying kites were employed for artillery spotting when the wind was too strong for captive balloons. Later, powered airships and airplanes were brought into service. Aerial navigational aids, ground-to-air wireless communication, and aerial photography followed. The pioneering days of military flying were over, and shortly before World War I military engineers of most armies handed over their responsibility for aeronautics to other organizations.

Transportation and movement control. Since the introduction of railways, military engineers have been responsible in theatres of war for the construction and maintenance of the permanent way and bridges of railway systems, the control of the rail movement of troops and military matériel, and the repair of locomotives and rolling stock. They have operated armoured trains and have been responsible for the rail mounting of superheavy guns. Military-operated railways played a constantly growing role in wars of the 19th and 20th centuries as logistical requirements grew.

Road mechanical transport and power tools. To increase mobility and work capacity, steam traction engines, capable of towing a train of trailers, were introduced into the service by military engineers in the 1860s. These were the forerunners of military road mechanical transport. Employed as static machines these traction engines could, by means of certain attachments, be used as cranes or as prime movers to operate a variety of power tools. From this beginning the vehicle-mounted air compressor and its associated pneumatic tools later developed. Many of these pneumatic devices in their turn were replaced by electric power tools driven by lightweight generators. Thus over the years the source of power has become smaller, while the output from individual tools for use in the field has simultaneously increased.

Developments during World War I.   Protracted trench warfare in World War I called upon all of the traditional siegecraft skills of the military engineers. Mining and countermining were carried out on a scale never before attempted. The greatest achievement was the firing in June 1917 by British sappers of over 1,000,000 pounds (450,000 kilograms) of explosive, placed in 16 chambers 100 feet (30 metres) deep, which completely obliterated Messines Ridge in Belgium and inflicted 20,000 German casualties.

Trench tramways and light railways were built for the maintenance of forward troops. Large camouflage projects were carried out to screen gun positions, storage dumps, and troop movements from enemy observation. Forestry and quarrying units were raised and production workshops established, for provision of trench-fortification matériel and pit props and to meet the requirements of the vast construction projects carried out in rear areas.

The scope of military signalling increased enormously and reached such a size and complexity that, when World War I ended, military telecommunication engineers became a separate corps in all armies. New techniques were developed for fixing enemy gun positions. Map making by use of aerial photographs (photogrammetry) developed. Field printing presses were set up to provide vast quantities of maps of the fighting areas, and a grid system was introduced for maps covering the whole theatre of operations (for a full discussion, see MAPPING AND SURVEYING). German, British, and French military engineers also introduced means of using toxic gas and flame throwers, and tanks as weapons of war were developed by the British and French.

In the Middle East, British and Indian engineers carried out several major river-crossing operations in Mesopotamia (Iraq) and operated craft on the Tigris and Euphrates rivers, which were used as the main supply routes for the campaign. In the Sinai Peninsula of Egypt and in Palestine the provision of water for the horse cavalry divisions was a major engineering task. The Royal Engineers piped Nile water from Egypt across the Sinai Desert to Jerusalem.

Defense was the major concern of most European governments during the interwar years. French military engineers designed and constructed the Maginot Line, a most sophisticated and assumed impregnable defensive system protecting France's common frontier with Germany and Luxembourg. The Germans constructed their Siegfried Line covering the same frontiers, and the Czechs built a defensive system to protect their northern frontier. The Russians constructed a looser system covering their long western frontier. For the air defense of Great Britain anti-aircraft batteries and searchlight positions were built to defend towns and service installations, and for passive air defense deep, gas-proof air raid shelters were constructed in large numbers, and attempts were made to camouflage vulnerable points from aerial observation.

Developments during World War II.   Military engineers of World War II faced and mastered problems on a scale and often of a character previously not experienced. Because of the importance of air power, airfields and airstrips had to be built, usually in great haste, frequently under fire. Amphibious operations, involving the landing of troops on a hostile shore, created a host of engineering problems, from underwater demolition of obstacles to rapid construction of open-beach dock facilities, such as the prefabricated mulberry harbour to maintain the Normandy landings in 1944. To meet the logistical needs of huge armies operating in remote regions, enormous base facilities were constructed.

The air battle. The construction and maintenance of forward airfields was a major problem for the engineers of all armies, especially the British and U.S. Allied airfields could never have been built without large quantities of earthmoving machinery mostly of American origin. For

The Brennan torpedo

Photogrammetry in map making

the construction of forward airfields it was often necessary to airlift light items of plant and later to lift sections of heavier items that could be reassembled on the ground. Great advances were made in the science of soil stabilization, and a variety of rapid airfield surfacing materials were developed, the American pierced steel plank being the most successful. For combined operations in the Pacific, floating airfields, consisting of prefabricated sections bolted together, were developed. Methods of piping aviation and other fuel from seagoing tankers, and its storage ashore in tank farms, were brought to a high state of perfection. After the Allied landing in Normandy in 1944, a pipeline was laid on the bed of the English Channel to supply fuel to the Allied forces in northwestern Europe.

Development of floating airfields

Armoured warfare. The most common devices used by World War II military engineers to stop enemy armour were the antitank ditch and the antitank mine. The ditch was only effective in locations where it could not be bypassed and where it could be kept under constant observation and fire. The antitank mine was first widely used during the fighting in the Western Desert of Egypt, where the minefield was the most easily provided obstacle to the movement of armoured forces. Special mine-warfare drills, techniques, and equipment were developed by the British and German military engineers for minelaying, mine location, and breaching minefields. As an adjunct to the antitank mine, antilifting devices, antipersonnel mines, and booby traps were introduced.

Bridging. Most armies at the outbreak of World War II possessed bridging equipment that would carry a tank weighing up to 30 tons. By 1940, however, tanks of 40-ton weight were being built, and it was known that this would soon not be the upper limit. To carry these increased weights, the Bailey Bridge was developed by the Royal Engineers in Britain. Its pin-connected rectangular truss panels made it easy to mass-produce. It also provided great flexibility on span and load capabilities. It could be used as a fixed span bridge or, with pontoons, as a raft or floating bridge. It was simple to construct quickly by day or at night. The equipment was produced in large quantities in Great Britain, the United States, and Italy and was a vital factor in preserving the mobility of Allied armies in all theatres of operations, thus making a substantial contribution to ultimate victory. On the eastern front Soviet engineers developed a type of bridge with a deck just below the surface of the water, making it difficult to spot from the air.

Military roads. One of the most extraordinary feats of military engineering during World War II was the building in 1944 by Allied forces of a supply road from Ledo, India, to the Burma road at a point where the road was still in Chinese hands. This Stilwell, or Ledo road, as it was called, opened in January 1945, was 478 miles (770 kilometres) long, twisting through mountains, swamps, and jungles.

American amphibious operations were the main feature of the war in the Pacific. Amphibious operations in the European theatre culminated in the Normandy landings, the greatest combined operation in military history.

Although the engineering tasks varied in size in these operations, they were basically similar. They included the removal of beach obstacles and the neutralization of beach mines, the construction of beach roadways, the clearance of beach exits and the liquidation of fixed defenses, the construction of roads and administrative areas on the beachhead, and the construction of forward landing grounds and air-dropping zones. Special equipment, including armoured engineer equipment that had to be capable of wading ashore from landing craft, was developed for these tasks.

Great advances were made in air survey due largely to the use of American equipment and calculating machines to speed up survey computations. Methods of map and air chart reproduction also became more sophisticated, and the requirement for military maps for all theatres of operations reached astronomical proportions. All of the camouflage techniques developed during World War I were employed, and, in addition, inflatable dummy tanks, vehicles, and landing craft were produced, mostly in the United States, and used extensively in deception plans.

Despite the many novel tasks imposed by World War II, traditional engineering jobs played a substantial role. Armies on the defensive constructed fortifications and carried out defensive demolitions on a scale never before seen. Outstanding were the German fortifications along the Atlantic coast ("Fortress Europe") as well as the Siegfried Line in Germany. Concrete pillboxes played a major role, in addition to a variety of obstacles, many underwater; mines, both land and underwater, were laid by the millions. These vast works were constructed by the German Todt organization, which also specialized in demolition as German armies slowly retreated through the Soviet Union, Italy, and France.

The Manhattan Project. But the largest task carried out by World War II engineers, and indeed by any military engineering establishment in history, was undoubtedly the Manhattan Project, which produced the atomic bombs dropped on Hiroshima and Nagasaki. Civilian scientists as well as engineers were recruited in large numbers for this mammoth project. Its success made it a model for later large-scale engineering efforts involving many scientists and engineers from different disciplines. In a sense, it brought military engineering full circle; whereas early military engineers were the first all-round scientific soldiers, the modern military engineering project must enlist a team bringing together experts in all branches of engineering and scientific knowledge.

Developments since World War II. In the late 1950s the U.S. Corps of Engineers constructed a network of radar warning systems across Canada and a series of Nike batteries to defend vulnerable points against the possibility of an attack across the polar ice cap by jet aircraft carrying nuclear bombs. In the 1960s they constructed a series of intercontinental ballistic missile bases. Introduction of these intercontinental missiles caused military surveyors to take a closer interest in the shape and size of the world. They developed ways of linking missile bases with far distant targets using geodetic satellites. Modern weapon systems, using advanced tracking, navigation, and locating devices, require mapping information direct from a computer.

The military confrontation of the Cold War and the conflicts in Korea and Vietnam resulted in construction of strategically placed air bases in Europe, the countries bordering the Arctic, Africa, and the Far East. In the varying emergencies military engineers performed not only their traditional combat and support roles but also, in addition, often carried out important peaceful works, such as dams and power stations to assist underdeveloped countries.

Construction of air bases

In the foreseeable future military engineers will probably continue to carry out their present civil-engineering tasks, such as river control. Their skills will be required in disaster areas stricken by earthquake, flood, or hurricane. In confrontations and insurgencies the military engineers will continue to combine traditional combat engineering with civil tasks. They will, of course, be equipped and trained for war in which nuclear weapons may be used. They will also undoubtedly play a part in the exploitation of the seabed and the continued exploration of the moon and deep space.   (J.H.S.L./Ed.)

Modern armed forces

Although modern-day armed forces are as a rule national institutions, the forces of different nations are very similar in structure and function. They all tend to have the same values and norms of behaviour; they also resemble each other in rank system and organization pattern, technology and training programs, and rituals and life-styles.

Common characteristics of armed forces

One reason for this lies in the similarity of their function. In principle, all armed forces are in competition with each other, either in preparation for actual combat or in that modern form of military struggle known as an arms race. The competition extends to more than weapons; personnel and morale are also involved. Continual competition tends to make the armed forces of different countries increasingly alike.

Another reason for their similarity lies in their historical development. During the period following the Middle

Ages, a type of military and naval organization came into being and has since become the standard model. While numerous variants have been developed and many innovations have risen from the technicalities of weapons (the most important of them being air forces), the basic structure of the military has remained essentially unchanged. The model was exported throughout the world by Europeans through their colonial armies and later was adopted by the armed forces of new nations.

Thus the armed forces are not only national instruments but an international type of social institution and may be studied on a comparative basis more readily than other social institutions.

THE MILITARY SYSTEM

The management of violence. The principal purpose of armed forces is, of course, the management and carrying out of violence; their effectiveness depends almost entirely upon their success in doing this. But modern armed forces have become complex and include not only combat groups but various support and service units with tasks that range from planning to transportation and from the improvement of morale to the cultivation of relations with the public.

During the Civil War in the 1860s, about 90 percent of the lower army positions in the United States could be called strictly military, but the proportion diminished to 35 or 40 percent during World War I. A similar trend occurred in the U.S. Navy: whereas in 1800 about 90 percent of a frigate's deckhands, or almost its complete crew, were used for fighting and operating the ship, after 1880, when the steamship came into use, this percentage fell to 55.

Military forces are distinguished from other armed groups such as brigands or bands of rioters by the fact that their functions are usually carried out in the name of a legal authority. There are obvious exceptions to this. Armed revolts and guerrilla warfare represent illegal forms of military activity. If the rebels are successful, however, they are increasingly recognized as legitimate, while their opponents will come to be called counterrevolutionaries and terrorists.

Armed forces differ from police in that their operations are directed against the armed forces of other political communities, usually countries, but here, again, the lines cannot always be sharply drawn. In many states the police have paramilitary units that function together with the army in suppressing rebels and pacifying restive areas. These operations sometimes take on a semimilitary character. On the other hand, in a number of countries with military regimes, the army is not primarily an apparatus to be used against other countries but an internal factor of power employed by politicians and military leaders in the domestic political struggle.

Three criteria of armed forces

In general, however, armed forces are characterized by all three of the foregoing criteria: the collective exercise of violence, in the name of a legal authority, directed against other political societies.

Exceptional role of the military. Practically all countries have armed forces. It is generally, though not universally, held that a modern state must have an army just as it has a post and telegraph service.

In modern times, nevertheless, armies are much less active than they have been in other historical periods when conflicts were more frequent and the military virtues more highly regarded. The military are now used only as a last resort, after other means have failed. War is felt to be a catastrophe for civilization.

The gap between social and military morale has seldom been wider than at present, and this has two far-reaching consequences for the armed forces and their social role. In the first place, they have an exceptional status in comparison with other social organizations, existing in a state of readiness but seldom being used. Their primary task is to keep themselves up-to-date with developments in military technology, strategy, and tactics. From the standpoint of psychology and morale, this means that in time of peace the armed forces are not much more than an enormous training and maintenance system oriented toward events that may not occur for generations. The prestige of military leaders, the morale of their troops, and the financial resources of the military apparatus may be difficult to maintain under these circumstances.

An allied problem arises in the transition from a peacetime army to a wartime army, which may be accompanied by enormous losses. Defense preparations carried out over many years and at great cost may fail completely, as in the classic case of France's Maginot Line in 1940.

A second consequence of the exceptional nature of military action is that the military institution becomes isolated within society. During war the isolation is lessened as civil society adopts and supports the values and aims of the armed forces. When peace returns the military system again becomes a painful symbol of collective violence. Since World War II, however, the role of the military has been less exceptional than it was in previous generations. Because of their use in international politics, the armed forces have become in some respects an essential part of the political order.

The armed forces as a formal organization. For all of the romance, tradition, and ceremony associated with military life, military institutions are rational and artificial constructions, quite consciously designed and developed for their purposes. In this respect they differ from other social organizations such as families or business enterprises. Their artificial character makes possible an extreme formalization and standardization of structure and function. Even early forms of military organization such as ancient and primitive armies have placed an emphasis on habit and routine. In large armed forces this formalizing has led to something that seems at first sight contradictory to the heroic and danger-loving tradition of the military craft: bureaucracy. Large armies were the earliest large social organizations to adopt bureaucratic ways, with their striving for calculability and predictability as norms of human behaviour. This formalizing of behaviour, subsequently adopted in many other large organizations such as government and industrial enterprises, goes further in the armed forces than elsewhere. All behaviour is exactly prescribed and standardized in manuals, from the writing of a letter to the greeting of comrades, from methods of bayonet fighting to the conduct of funeral ceremonies. In time of peace the ritualism and ceremonialism are often given an exaggerated and superfluous emphasis. The justification of such extreme regulation of behaviour lies in the necessity of working under stress and of being able to maintain a functioning organization even if the personnel are suddenly replaced. At the same time, there is a danger that those in command may lose the capacity to be flexible and to innovate. To prevent this, a military elite has to be placed above the managerial-bureaucratic level to control policy.

The military is more than a specialized organization: it contains within it almost all of the functions of civil society, with the difference that in the military the separate, relatively autonomous institutions of civil life are combined into one large institution, a "total institution." A large military camp or base is for thousands of persons at the same time a restaurant, hotel, school, place of work, hospital, transportation system, repair station, and post office. The military establishment as a whole also comprises research institutions, administrative staffs, training grounds, warehouses, and even factories. The military world forms a kind of subsociety, making itself as independent as possible within the total society. In addition to being self-sufficient, it must also be mobile; it has to be able to cross oceans and to populate deserts. This comprehensive character of the armed forces is symbolically accentuated by the soldier's uniform, by the geographic isolation of military installations, and by the norm that members are technically in service 24 hours a day.

The military as a total organization

In recent decades, in some countries, the institutional claims of the military apparatus have been weakened. Relationships have become closer with the surrounding society, enlisted men more often take their furloughs at home, and terms of service have been shortened. The professional soldier of the military academy is less inclined to regard his career as a lifelong commitment, the more so as the military profession itself has come to resemble certain civil professions. But these and other changes have not gone so far as to alter the fundamental characteristics described above.

THE MILITARY BUREAUCRACY

Plural authority.   The structure of power and authority in military organizations resembles that in other large organizations but with marked differences of degree. As in any bureaucracy, the hierarchic principle prevails: the office guarantees the authority of the man who, once appointed, enjoys all the authority connected with his position without regard to his personal characteristics. These offices are mutually related through quite detailed organization charts and managed with the aid of equally minute and elaborate organization manuals. The structuring of authority according to function is accompanied by very pronounced differentiations in rank. "An order is an order" means that any superior can give orders to any subordinate, even if it runs counter to or outside of the functional division of labour. The two sources of authority—function and rank—sometimes conflict with each other, in that men may be forced to choose between obeying regulations and following orders. Although this conflict exists in all large organizations, it is extremely severe in the armed forces. Business organizations usually give precedence to rank. Nonmilitary government organizations generally stick to the regulations. In military bureaucracies, however, rank and regulations are held to be equally important.

Authority in the military environment has, however, a third basis: the attained result. In time of war, particularly, the aims have to be attained at all costs. Consequently it is seldom useful to observe all the rules, and neither is it always best to follow only the formal lines of command. Informal hierarchies arise, determined by their success in action. Success may be rewarded later with citations, promotions, and important assignments.

Success, however, is not always easy to judge. Lower field officers have to take into account the expectations of their subordinates, who tend to measure successful leadership by the extent to which it reduces the casualty rate. Higher commanders have other criteria, such as occupying strategic points or wiping out enemy positions.

Modern peacetime armies tend to be bureaucratic, with an emphasis on regulations. Rank is emphasized by combat units in peacetime but by noncombat sectors only in wartime. The third basis of authority, results attained, becomes the ultimate one under conditions of wartime combat.

The armed forces of different countries vary in the types of authority to which they give most emphasis. Complex modern military forces tend to stress regulations. Less complex ones emphasize rank. For elite formations and for critical operations, a combination of rank and performance will prevail. But the social environment also plays a part. Armed forces that are very strong on rank will try to reduce the influence of the social environment by staffing themselves with volunteers or professionals rather than conscripts, unless they are functioning within a social order that accepts extreme emphasis on rank (as in Prussia). Armies with a citizen tradition (Switzerland, Canada, and Australia) will emphasize the ultimate result of the operations as a first standard for good military leadership.

Ascription and achievement.   The distinction often made between social positions that are acquired and those that are taken without effort (for instance, through right of birth) can be applied to the sources of military authority.

The decline of class differences

In European countries membership in the officer corps was traditionally reserved to sons of the nobility. When commoners became officers, they were made peers. The tradition survives in the expressions "an officer is a gentleman," and *das Portepee adelt* ("the Portepee ennobles"— the *Portepee* is an ornamental tassel on the sabre). The rank and file, on the other hand, were recruited from the lowest and poorest categories of the population. Soldiers and sailors, particularly in the time before national armies and navies, had a very low occupational status.

By the latter part of the 20th century, the ascriptive base of military authority had been greatly diminished. The contemporary national army draws its officers as well as its enlisted men from all strata of society. The profession of officer has tended to become a middle-class occupation, while the social and educational level of the troops has gone up. Class differences still persist: in the United States about half the officers come from white-collar families and a third from blue-collar families, while less than a fifth of the enlisted men come from white-collar backgrounds and over half from blue-collar families. But this is of secondary importance in the authority structure. Other important ascriptive sources of rank authority remain; for example, in racially divided societies in which black people are less frequently admitted to the higher ranks.

The caste system in the armed forces has not disappeared with the decline of class differences. The traditionally great distance between officers and men has become more self-sustaining; it is fixed in social intercourse, ritual, and language. Even in countries in which the social prestige of the officer is relatively low, as in many west European countries, his authority within the rank system has been little affected. Even the noncommissioned officer does not participate in this authority. The caste barrier makes it extremely difficult for noncommissioned officers to achieve promotion to commissioned officer rank. Even promotions on the battlefield are exceptional. It is quite common for very young, inexperienced officers to receive command over much older and experienced noncommissioned officers.

Generalists and specialists.   A more important distinction in contemporary armed forces is that between generalists and specialists.

Specialization had its start at the periphery of the military system. Engineering and artillery were the first to develop special bodies of knowledge requiring formal training. The older sections of the military establishment resisted the idea of academies for officers until well into the 19th century, partly because officers came from the educated classes and partly because of the belief that leaders are born and not made.

The notion that military men should be generalists rather than specialists is still strong, although most officers attend a variety of schools and training courses during their professional careers. The practice of rotating officers among jobs is more prevalent in military than in civilian life. The table compares the lengths of stay of officers at a U.S. air base and of the managers of a very large U.S. business corporation. Almost half of the officers had been stationed for one year or less on their base, while only 2 percent of the business managers had been with their company for

Length of Stay of Officers and Business Executives Within a Single Organization		
length of time in the organization	military installation (percentage)	business firm (percentage)
1 year or less	45.5	2.1
2 years	18.8	2.0
3 years	15.7	3.9
4 years	14.4	4.6
5 years or more	5.6	87.5
Total	100.0	100.1
Number of cases	554*	1,219†

*Two cases were not ascertained.   †21 cases were not ascertained.
Source: Oscar Grusky, "The Effects of Succession; A Comparative Study of Military and Business Organization," in Morris Janowitz, *The New Military; Changing Patterns of Organization* (1964).

such a short period. Nine out of 10 business managers had been at least five years with their company, while only one out of 20 officers had been on their base for that length of time. The same pattern prevails in other armed forces. While there are important differences between an air base and a business firm, the foregoing comparison shows the emphasis placed on mobility of personnel.

The military solution to the problem of specialization was the development of the concept of the military staff. A staff consists of advisers and planners who assist the

The general staff

commander in issuing orders but do not have line or command authority; the commander alone is responsible and cannot delegate his responsibility. A distinction is often made between the general staff that is concerned with such areas as personnel, intelligence, operations and training, or logistics, and other staff groups specialized according to weapons and services. The latter include many more specialists than does the general staff, which is often populated with generalists who happen to be expert in particular problems. Naval staffs are of more recent origin than army staffs and have not acquired the size and importance of the former.

As weapons technology has grown more complex, the staff system has extended downward to lower levels of command. More and more specialists have been attached to line organizations, with the result that the old pyramidal structure of the armed forces has changed to a diamond-shaped structure, particularly in technical and maintenance units. Before World War II, 50 percent of the enlisted men in the U.S. Army and Air Force were in the lowest of the seven grades; after 1945, the percentage was less than 15.

Another result of technological change is a growth in the number of officers and noncommissioned officers who owe their rank to their technical skills rather than to the number of subordinates they command. The growth in size and complexity of the armed forces has produced a continuously expanding military bureaucracy. More and more officers work in offices at great distances from the troops. The moment when a professional soldier gives up active command of troops and takes a desk position in the higher echelons comes earlier and earlier in his career. In the ground forces particularly, the majority of the career officers work in high command and staff positions during wartime, while in many cases the combat forces are led predominantly by reserve officers and noncoms or even by men who have been conscripted.

Commanders and leaders

A distinction may be made between command and leadership—or between executive leadership and operational leadership. The act of commanding has an upward orientation; it is the carrying out of a general plan. The act of leading, on the other hand, points downward toward the people by whom the plan is to be carried out. The commander is essentially a coordinator who has to think in abstract terms while working with the aid of numbers and charts, while the leader must deal directly with people and induce them to act successfully in combat situations. The commander, though shielded from the hazards of battle, is exposed to types of uncertainty quite beyond the personal experiences of the leader. The tensions to which the leader is exposed are those of men in danger, facing immediate physical loss.

At some levels in the organization both roles are equally important. But in most cases the accent falls on one or the other, and, generally speaking, the senior officer acts as commander while the junior fulfills the role of leader. The military leader participates in the life and dangers of his unit as the person responsible for the welfare of his people as well as for the execution of assignments from the top.

The task of the leader is especially aggravated by two circumstances. Modern war has become, much more than the combat of earlier times, a matter of improvisation requiring initiative at the lowest level; there is no longer the blind obedience to orders of earlier times or troop movements directed en masse from the top; the junior officer has to make decisions himself. In the second place, authority in small combat units is no longer simply a matter of the leader dominating his subordinates but requires an ability to deal with and motivate men, to inspire confidence and loyalty.

Leadership is a difficult undertaking for young officers and noncommissioned officers, the more so when their advantages in age, education, and social class are often quite small. Modern military schools accordingly emphasize courses in leadership training.

THE PROFESSIONAL SOLDIER

The military mind. Much has been written about "the military mind," especially by critics of the military's per-

formance. Although some of this is merely captious, one can discern among military men certain characteristic habits of thought. The soldier's occupation tends to lead to a less idealistic and more pessimistic view of man; he comes to be skeptical of words and promises and to place certainty only in power and the means of power. Power is for him the ultimate guarantee of the social and political order. In this respect the military man may not, as a rule, share the optimistic social philosophy of liberalism; his views may differ from those of liberalism in their emphasis on discipline and leadership. He may have less confidence in the development of the individual, seeing man as weak and irrational and in need of organization. His concern with order, however, may not make the soldier a natural supporter of extreme right-wing philosophies. He tends to distrust ideology and romanticism and notions of racial or national superiority.

The soldier's realism and pessimism

The realistic and conservative character of the military mind can be explained in several ways. One reason for it may be the hazardous character of the military enterprise, in which naked power is the main guarantee of success. In a world of international strife, the soldier is forced to see every neighbour as a potential enemy. His enormous responsibilities make him a distrustful and realistic thinker. Because it is difficult to estimate the character and weight of future risks, the soldier will always overestimate them. His desire for ever stronger forces and more potent weapons is perhaps given stimulus by the effect these have on his own prestige and chances of promotion.

A second cause of military conservatism is the soldier's traditional position among the social elite. Although these bonds have weakened in recent decades, the professional soldier tends to identify with the social order whose sword he wields. In many new countries in which rapid social and economic changes offer opportunities for careers, soldiers may side with progressives who aim to accelerate their countries' development. But they will usually reject extreme leftist tendencies, as has been shown, for example, by the military regimes of the Arab countries despite strong support from the Soviet Union.

A third explanation of the soldier's viewpoint is that he tends to have an authoritarian personality. It has been shown that this type of personality is more common in armed forces and police organizations than in other professions, probably because it is selected in the recruiting process. The pattern may change in the future, however, given the gradual change in the style of military leadership and in the general requirements for a military career. It is also notable that there are important differences in attitude and outlook among the various services (the infantry, for example, being more traditional in outlook than the technologically oriented air force).

Military professionalism. The phrase professional soldier has traditionally been applied to soldiers who pursue a lifetime career with the armed forces. In the 19th century, particularly among officers, the professional soldier developed into a technician in the management of violence. Professionals came to form the backbone of all the armed services. But the phrase professional soldier is also used to mean that the career soldier has characteristics in common with those of the doctor, the teacher, the architect, and the engineer. The characteristics of such professionalism include (1) the monopoly of a well-integrated body of knowledge and skill imparted through formal training, (2) the capacity to apply this knowledge and skill according to ethical standards as a socially valued service, and (3) the legal establishment of the profession, including the right to control the admission, selection, and training of new members. While military officers share these characteristics in some degree, the officer as a professional figure almost always finds himself being used as an instrument of power by his government; he is also lodged in a hierarchy of command that prevents him from making independent decisions.

Comparison of the military profession with others

The degree to which the military services have been professionalized varies among countries. In Communist countries the officer is not only a military specialist but also part of the political elite. In some of the new countries, nonprofessional considerations such as ethnic origin, tribal relationship, class background, and political adherence are often the main factors in a military career. There is a parallel here with several European countries of the 19th century, where aristocratic origin and family ties were important; not until the end of that century did the profession of officer in Germany and Great Britain become accessible on the basis of competitive examinations open to the majority of the population.

Crisis of the military profession Since World War II, military professionalism has been confronted with challenges from several directions. Technological change has created a number of new fields of specialization that differ radically from the traditional military skills. These technicians, logisticians, comptrollers, management specialists, and personnel administrators are not trained in the way that combat infantry officers and aircraft pilots are, and they tend to have more in common with their civilian counterparts than with their military colleagues. This means that the professional structure is becoming a congeries of diverse functions without much unity. The development of new weapons, particularly long-range ones, has undermined the old professional norms of military behaviour. The aerial bombardment of civilian populations and some of the methods of counterintelligence units are difficult to square with the traditional code of military conduct.

Another influence at work upon the profession is the politicization of the military through its involvement in the Cold War. The creation of multinational forces such as those of NATO in western Europe and the Warsaw Pact in eastern Europe requires political orientation among their officers; patriotism as the basis of morale tends to be replaced by a common ideology.

Along with this there has been an increase in civilian influence in military affairs, partly because of the new technical personnel referred to above and partly because of the so-called think tanks and strategic research institutes that have sprung up all over the world, manned by civilian experts. Important developments in military- and political-strategic thinking no longer originate with the professional soldier.

The increase in the proportion of noncombat troops in contemporary armed forces has had a subtle effect on the outlook of the officer corps: many officers are inclined to put intellectual standards above fighting spirit or to prefer managerial qualities to traditional military qualities. Some experts have even suggested that the military profession model itself upon civilian service institutions. This is not usually taken to be a viable solution, however, because it is felt that, while it might help to offset the unpopularity of the modern military apparatus by minimizing its destructive and violent aspects, it would at the same time be likely to increase the frustration of many career soldiers. Although some marginal functions of the military can very well be taken over by civilian authorities, the main task of the armed forces remains unique.

Middle-class status **Social position of the professional soldier.** The military profession is a middle-class one. Its status has declined since the 19th century, when in some countries officers belonged to the social elite; today, in the developed countries, career officers are regarded as standing socially below the academic professions and quite often below public school teachers. In many developing countries, on the other hand, officers are highly esteemed because of their superior education and their competence in modern forms of activity; the profession in these countries attracts some of the most capable men. In Communist countries the position of the officer corresponds to what it was in western Europe in the 19th century: aloof from civil society, respected, seldom criticized, and sharing in the prestige of the regime.

The decline in status of the military in Western countries is reflected in the social class from which the majority of officers are drawn. Since World War II, in western Europe, officers have been mainly of middle-class or even lower class origin. In the United States in 1910–20, one-quarter of the general officers were from the upper class, and two-thirds were from the upper middle class; in 1950, only 3 percent came from the upper class, while half came from the lower middle and lower classes.

The change has been greatest in the Communist countries, where the old aristocratic officers corps were eliminated and replaced by officers of very predominantly proletarian origin. In the U.S.S.R. after the 1917 Revolution, many former tsarist officers continued for some time to hold important positions. In the German Democratic Republic, Poland, Czechoslovakia, and other east European countries, however, where the Communists took power after World War II, the transition was so abrupt that nontrained proletarian officers were chosen above others who were thought to be less reliable. According to official data, in 1965 more than 80 percent of the officers in the German Democratic Republic, 60 percent in Czechoslovakia, and about 50 percent in Poland came from the working class. In the developing nations the majority of the officers are usually of the middle and lower middle class.

Many officers come from military families, although it is not clear that this tendency to follow the father's occupation is more pronounced among military men than in civilian professions. The proportion of officers coming from officers' families has ranged in recent decades from 10 to 50 percent, the highest percentages occurring in France, Spain, and Brazil. Prestigious military schools such as West Point, Sandhurst, and Saint-Cyr attract many officers' sons. Twenty-five percent of the 1960 class at West Point was composed of officers' sons.

PATTERNS OF ORGANIZATION

Armies vary greatly in the way they are organized and structured. Many are so loosely organized as to resemble social movements, as did the crusaders, the Teutonic Knights, and many revolutionary armies. Some armies combine mass enthusiasm for an ideal with a high degree of formal organization. Others show considerable egalitarianism—for example, the European mercenary armies of the 16th and 17th centuries, the guilds of the early artillerists, and the soldiers' councils of the 20th-century Russian and Hungarian revolutions. **The military emphasis on organization**

As a rule, however, armed forces are the most strictly organized groups in existence, drawing much of their strength from the thoroughness with which they regulate the behaviour of their members. In this respect the military organization has served as a model for other fields. Many of the early industrial principles of organization, such as standardization, line and staff, and training of personnel, were derived from the military.

Purposes of organization. The main functions of organization are to reduce complexity and to cope with changing reality. The need for organization in the military field is particularly evident, since the degree of uncertainty confronting the soldier is so great.

Military organization has passed through two stages in its development. The first was one of simple organization, in which the emphasis was put on reducing everything to fundamentals. By standardizing actions (drill, routine, ritual), homogenizing elements (weapons, formations), and directing movements from a central point (through a hierarchy), a social machine was constructed that was well integrated internally and capable of absorbing external shocks. This was the system applied in the Roman legions, the European armies of the 16th century, the early naval formations, and many other armed forces before the 19th century. The drawback of the system was its rigidity.

The second stage emphasized flexibility. Military formations were decentralized, and authority was delegated to a larger number of officers who were expected to demonstrate more initiative. The new model had less internal cohesion but was more flexible in response to external challenges. This development has continued up to the present. The decentralization that began at the top and was carried down through the senior commanders to junior officers has now reached the smallest combat units (guerrilla warfare).

In peacetime the armed forces tend to fall back upon the simple system of organization. With the coming of war this structure collapses, and the organization must with great effort be transformed into one capable of responding to the exigencies of wartime. In early times this was done by concentrating the forces in a relatively small area, such as a battlefield or fleet formation, where they could easily be commanded; the early battlefield formations were compact and could readily be integrated as fighting forces. In modern times the task is more complex. Greatly extended formations are now the rule, and they require a network of long-distance communications to handle the continuous flow of information among their subdivisions. This also applies to the interaction between the armed forces as an organization and the social environment: the allocation of resources to the military has become largely a problem of communication; the carrying out of such functions as supply and transportation have become less physical and more mental than in former days.

But more than formal organization and coordination are required to keep modern armed forces in readiness. It is no longer sufficient to allot weapons and functions to military personnel and place them under a leader; the men must also be made to realize the meaning of their task as part of the larger whole.

Organization and operation. In principle, every armed force has three levels of responsibility and control: political, professional, and technical. The political level is generally the uppermost, concerned with overall political and strategic matters. The technical level is at the bottom, where actual operations are carried on. In between is the professional level, in which the majority of officers do their work of management.

The centre of gravity in this organizational pyramid will vary, depending on circumstances. In matters involving nuclear weapons and strategic air operations, political as well as military men participate, and sometimes the head of state himself assumes responsibility. In guerrilla warfare the centre of gravity is very low, with important responsibility borne even below the level of the junior officers. This responsibility encompasses not only combat but also supply and intelligence tasks; the junior commander may even have to exercise political authority in areas in which his unit moves. In conventional warfare the centre of gravity lies in the middle of the organization, with the professional soldier; most of the preparation, planning, and organization, as well as control over the results, is in the hands of those at the managerial level.

Differences in outlook naturally arise among those engaged at different levels of the military operation. Those concerned with problems of nuclear weapons have scientific habits of mind, placing education and rational calculation above arguments from historical experience. Those in charge of special operations and counterinsurgent warfare think in terms of physical courage, group loyalty, and personal leadership. Many officers find themselves caught between these two types, disliking the new technocrats who differ so much from the traditional military type and at the same time feeling threatened by those on the lower level who regard the career soldier as obsolete. Tensions of this kind were visible in the revolt of the French officers in Algeria in 1958 and 1961.

Considerable research has been done on the primary (face-to-face) group and its functions in military life. It would appear that men tend to identify with their platoon, crew, or squad rather than with the larger organization; it is the world in which they are at home and within which almost all their interests are rooted; they find security in the small group, a sense of solidarity vis-à-vis the military hierarchy, a chance for prestige among their fellows, and norms of behaviour that are difficult to ignore. Under conditions of combat, these informal relations are greatly enhanced. Studies of German and U.S. units have shown that soldiers are motivated not by ideology or political purpose but by a sense of personal commitment to their comrades: "You can't let the guys down." The character of these bonds depends partly upon circumstances. Ground combat units draw their cohesion from the peril to the group in battle, while submarine or bomber crews relate to each other much more as specialists who must execute a mission together.

The existence of these primary groups often poses difficult problems for the commanders—particularly the non-commissioned officers, who are most exposed to pressure from a group and have the least prestige at their disposal.

In practice they often follow the wishes of the group: their so-called leadership is in part a product of the group they lead. But this group behaviour has its advantages from the viewpoint of the top command. The small group at the base serves as a self-regulating system that can adapt to unforeseen circumstances. For this reason it appears to pay to keep the informal system intact, even to the extent of carrying out personnel replacements in a way that will not destroy particular groups.

Informal organization is not a phenomenon of the base level alone but runs through the whole military organization. Social and political groups and cliques play a decisive role at the highest levels. Their existence, partly concealed in many countries, is obvious in new countries, where a top military position is clearly a political acquisition. Military coups in such countries show the political leanings among the top leaders of the military apparatus, which vary from the right (Greece in 1967) to the left (The Sudan in 1971) and may sometimes divide the military leaders themselves (Indonesia in 1965).

THE MILITARY COMMUNITY

The armed forces are much more than an organization; they form a community that encompasses the work and life of its members much more completely than do most other social organizations. The life of the professional soldier, however, is quite different from that of the enlisted man. The first, particularly if he is a member of the officers corps, experiences military service as his career; his manner and style of life are often set for him by tradition. The enlisted man, on the other hand, knows the military environment as a male community full of deprivations and rough behaviour.

The elitist style of life. The officers' milieu is characterized to some extent by a ceremonialism that has become passé among other social classes, a heritage of officers corps of the 18th and 19th centuries. This formal "old-fashioned" style is more than the pretension of belonging to an aristocracy: it has certain functional uses in that it helps to facilitate the integration of the members into military life. The professional soldier is, after all, highly mobile both geographically and socially, continually forced to adjust to new milieus. His adjustment and assimilation are made easier if these milieus all observe the same formal patterns of behaviour. It is the more mobile and isolated parts of the armed forces that have most strongly developed their own styles of life, notably the navy and the old colonial armies.

The officer's wife plays a more important part in his professional life than is the case in most other professions. To some extent this belongs to the traditional style, which makes high demands upon etiquette and social contact. It is also a consequence of the isolation of military life in small communities in which work and residence coincide.

The enlisted man's style. The community life of enlisted men is very different from that of the officers. As an exclusively male community (leaving aside the much smaller, newer, and less tradition-dominated employment of women either in separate or integrated units), separated from their families and often unmarried, their social traits resemble those of colonists, woodcutters, sailors, and dockworkers. While officers have an elitist subculture, that of the enlisted men reflects their position at the bottom of society. While the officer attaches an almost exaggerated importance to form, the private most likely will reject all form. The cool distance that characterizes the relationships of officers contrasts with the close ties that prevail among enlisted men.

The life of the enlisted man is reflected in his language—earthy, masculine, and aggressive, frequently with a heavy emphasis on sexuality. Much of his slang expresses the repugnance he feels toward the military hierarchy, for to him it seems that the officers make the mistakes and reap the rewards, while it is he who does the dirty work and wins the battles.

RECRUITMENT AND SOCIAL CONTROL

The ways in which a country recruits its military personnel are likely to have important consequences both for

Levels of responsibility

Informal organization

Styles of military life

the armed forces and for the society from which they are drawn. Soldiers may feel a commitment to patriotic or idealistic aims; they may be coerced; or they may be motivated by pecuniary gain.

Voluntary armies

Moral commitment. The committed soldier is intensely involved in his organization and its success. The organization can draw upon his loyalty and can motivate him with nonmaterial rewards—glory and honour, prestige and status, shame and humiliation. Armed forces recruited in this way take on the characteristics of social and political movements. They have relatively little of the standard military structure with its regulations and its hierarchy; those at the top are accepted as leaders in a common effort toward a common goal, which can be attained only by following and supporting them. A strong ideology helps to maintain the cohesion of the fighting forces. Such voluntary armies have included those of the First Crusade, the religious Hussite armies of the late Middle Ages, the warriors of early Islām, and national revolutionary armies such as those of France after 1789 and Russia after 1917.

The successes of these armies stemmed from their collective élan and not from their training and their technical or tactical superiority. Their lack of structure and professional leadership became a source of weakness at times of internal stress (that is, in a later period when armed struggle continued and more stability and integration was needed). Methods had to be found to give form to the collective mass.

Revolutionary armies often begin with egalitarian institutions, such as the soldiers' councils and militia units of the French, Russian, Hungarian, and Indonesian revolutions. When confronted with the orderly armies of an enemy, they tend to fall back upon traditional hierarchic forms. The initial enthusiasm of the mass diminishes, while at the same time military service becomes obligatory rather than voluntary. The revolutionary armies thus adopt a system of conscription.

Another way of maintaining cohesion is by indoctrination and political training. The young Soviet Army was reorganized along classical lines with the introduction of general conscription, but at the same time a political shadow organization was built up in it through the Communist Party. This approach has been followed in many guerrilla armies, in which the military and political elements are strongly interrelated. In this way they obtain the advantages of the military system of coercion along with those of ideological motivation.

A third method lies in stressing patriotic symbolism such as the monarchy, the fatherland, honour, and glory, supported by a good deal of ritual. The soldier is taught to forget material interests and devote himself to higher ends.

Certain mixed forms exist, two of which are the professional officers corps and the militia army. The modern officers corps is built upon the concept of a military craft, embodying values and norms formerly cultivated by the nobility. These include ideas of honour and status, along with a disdain for the materialistic concerns that dominate the rest of society. Contemporary officers' attitudes, however, are moving away from this toward the attitude of a functionary who seeks remunerative, attractive work and a permanent job.

The other mixed form, the militia, is a citizen army in which the obligation of the soldier is to defend his city or country. Sometimes a militia is raised in defense of group interests, such as those of labourers, farmers, miners, students, or a political party. The militia is a mixed form because in many cases it is combined with conscription. The phrase compulsory militia is not entirely contradictory.

The moral basis of the militia lay traditionally in the defense of home and hearth, an idea embodied in Anglo-American history by such organizations as the Home Guard and the National Guard. The militia is seldom an aggressive, conquering army since citizens in arms cannot undertake long campaigns and military expeditions.

Militias have existed throughout history since the time of the Greek city-states. Examples in modern times are the armies of Switzerland and Israel, in which the professional core is very small and civilians hold all the military positions, including high command. In both countries military service is required of all men and in Israel of women.

The militia form has certain political and economic advantages: it avoids the danger of creating a state within the state and also the high costs of maintaining a standing army. The abilities and occupational skills of the population can be placed directly at the disposal of the military, although this means withdrawing them from civilian society. The chief objection to the militia form is its inadequacy for the building of a technically advanced and specialized army with modern air forces and artillery. Another objection is that mobilization takes too long. For these reasons, large democratic countries with a citizen-soldier tradition have developed within their military forces extensive cadres of regular soldiers.

Compulsory enrollment. The opposite of voluntary enlistment is conscription, carried out by the national state. The resulting military force lacks the moral characteristics of a volunteer army; it is essentially a machine requiring severe discipline, its cohesion being maintained by the threat of punishment. Its great problems, desertion and slackness among the troops, can be kept within bounds only by strong organization and leadership. Conscription in its purest form was used to man some of the armies and fleets of Europe in the 17th and 18th centuries, when condemned criminals were permitted to choose service in lieu of imprisonment. More often, however, conscription is part of a program of universal military service accepted by the public and carried out in cooperation with it.

Criminals and conscripts

The system is based on rudimentary training given to all men of a certain age who are deemed physically and mentally fit. After their initial term of service, they are placed in the reserves and recalled periodically for retraining. If complex equipment is involved, the training period must be longer, and for that reason naval and air forces tend to have a high proportion of professional personnel and to rely less upon conscripts. The use of conscription assumes a government that is strong enough to coerce its citizens and a national consciousness that will accept this coercion. It may also find a basis in the democratic idea that all citizens ought to participate in the defense of their country. Conscription has, like the militia system, the advantage of obviating a standing professional army with its dangers of political intervention.

In recent years the system of conscription has been undergoing a crisis in many countries. On the one hand, there is a growing awareness that a complex war machine needs professional soldiers. At the same time, resistance to general military service has been increasing, partly from antimilitarism and partly from a decline in national consciousness in some countries. Many military men would prefer a professionalized army that would free them of the influx of less dedicated and reliable personnel. Against this there is the argument that only a system of conscription can supply the large forces required for a prolonged war. Another argument in favour of conscription springs from the idea that in a democratic country military service ought to be universal.

Mercenaries. The mercenary soldier serves for pay. There is no question either of loyalty or of alienation. Armed forces composed of hired soldiers are therefore quite different social organizations from those discussed above. While the main problem of a revolutionary army is to preserve the enthusiasm for the cause and that of a conscript army is to maintain strict discipline, the main problem for the mercenary army is to provide the soldiers with their pay. When the army cannot be paid, as often happened in the 16th and 17th centuries, it can no longer be commanded.

Soldiers for pay

The mercenary system, like the other systems, is of ancient origin. In Egypt and Mesopotamia, the state itself was based primarily on mercenary forces. The great military successes of Carthage were won by mercenaries, as were those of the Roman Empire in Europe. Mercenary armies reappeared after medieval times. They were employed in European colonial wars, the best known being the French Foreign Legion. Three sets of circumstances are conducive to the adoption of the mercenary system. Large empires cannot be built and maintained with militia armies, and this creates a demand for mercenary armies. Mercenaries, furthermore, are typical of the absolute state in much the way that militias are characteristic of political democracy. Finally, they often appear in commercial nations that are wealthy enough to maintain hired troops, as in the old state of Venice, in the Dutch republic, and in Great Britain.

The hirelings are usually recruited from densely populated countries and from countries with a military tradition. The Swiss and later the Germans served in armies all over Europe. The Roman emperors had their German guard and the French monarchs their Swiss regiments (of which system the Vatican's Swiss Guard is a relic). Small numbers of mercenaries are still involved in the conflicts of the developing countries. The present-day system of voluntary enlistment in such countries as Great Britain. Canada, Australia, and the United States is a variation of the mercenary system, since these countries can, in peacetime, define their problems of recruitment primarily in terms of the labour market and the national budget.

The mercenary system seems likely to become more common in the future, as political considerations lead to the abandonment of peacetime conscription and short-term enlistment takes its place. To a considerable degree, the modern military force reflects the business orientation of the surrounding society: many military jobs require the same techniques and skills as civilian jobs, and it has become necessary to allow military personnel to work under the conditions prevailing in the rest of society. Even trade unions and labour contracts are becoming important to the military employer, particularly in times when labour markets are tight.

AUXILIARY FUNCTIONS OF ARMED FORCES

The formal purpose of armed forces is to act against foreign enemies. In reality, however, they have various other functions.

Domestic functions. In many countries, particularly developing countries, the army has great social and political significance. It stands as a symbol of unity and power. Young nations uncertain of their international role, and often internally divided, attach much value to an army as a national institution. This may first require disposing of the military forces inherited from the previous colonial regime, since many colonial armies were recruited from minorities the ruler found reliable—such as the Berber tribes in French Morocco, the Punjabi and Sikhs in British India, and the partially Christian population of Celebes and Amboina in the Dutch East Indies. The new national armies may resemble their colonial predecessors insofar as they continue the task of maintaining order in the country. If they do not succeed in this, the result may be civil war, as in Indonesia, Nigeria, and Pakistan.

But the army in the newer countries is also an agency of modernization, somewhat in contrast to armies in the Western world, where the military has been for centuries a symbol of tradition and conservatism. It is one of the few well-organized and technically equipped modern institutions. The military career often leads to a successful civilian career, as in Israel. The army also brings together members of different ethnic and religious groups, thus becoming, as in the United States, an institution of socialization for a heterogeneous immigrant population. No military force can escape this socially integrative function within a heterogeneous society. The task of integrating blacks and whites in the U.S. Army has had parallels in the integration of the French-speaking and English-speaking groups in the Canadian Army and of the Flemings and Walloons in the Belgian Army. In the new countries the army may also undertake a variety of social, cultural, and economic tasks. In the 1920s the Turkish Army of Kemal Atatürk set an example as a military modernization movement that still serves as a model for many countries with military regimes. The soldiers may be put to work building roads and bridges, working on irrigation and land development, or even teaching the population to read. Such uses of the military occur under governments of various political hues; even the Marxist revolutionary regimes of China and Cuba used soldiers for nonmilitary functions in the political as well as the socio-economic sphere.

Conflict management. The modern military force has

The army as a modernizer

lost almost all of the old conception of warfare as a heroic struggle, as it was seen in ancient Greece, some periods of the Middle Ages, and in the 18th century. Such attitudes linger on only in elite formations such as special forces and paratroops, in which individual performance is still important.

The prevailing conception of the military is an instrumental one. The military are seen as instruments of national policy, to be used to strike and destroy an enemy with all available means. As wars have become increasingly destructive, expanding to include the whole population, the military have been reduced to one element in a total national effort that involves political, strategic, social, and economic factors. This conception of total war has been tempered since the advent of nuclear weapons by the doctrine of limited warfare—a strategic pluralism in which various military forces are developed simultaneously for the purpose of providing appropriate responses in different types of situations. These include the whole array of traditional, or "conventional," forces together with counter-guerrilla forces. The military effort of a great power is now extremely differentiated, each of the subdivisions being equipped with its own philosophy, armament, and organization.

The new doctrines of flexible response and limited warfare may be seen as a step toward the international management of conflicts. The effort to manage conflict has been made by forces of the United Nations, acting in an international police capacity, in the Middle East, the Congo, Cyprus, and elsewhere. The outlook of such peace forces differs from that of traditional military force in several ways: the goal is not victory but control of the conflict; there is no enemy, only parties whose conflict endangers the international situation; the peace force must act with as little violence as possible; and, unlike traditional military forces, it must work very cautiously and patiently. The task of the United Nations soldier is thus more akin to policing than to military action.

United Nations forces

CIVIL–MILITARY RELATIONS

Relations between the military and the rest of society have never been easy. With their monopoly of the means of violence, the military inevitably acquire some degree of political power, even when a country's constitution and laws stipulate that the civilian authorities are to be dominant. Military intervention in politics is not as surprising as the fact that in many countries such intervention does not occur.

The term civil–military relations is of course much too simple to describe the complex network of interests that usually exists between the various branches of the military and the various sectors of civil society. For example, the relation between the professional officers corps and society is of a character completely different from that between enlisted men and society.

Only since the 19th century has it been possible to speak of civil–military relations in a clear-cut sense, for not until then did the military become a specialized institution with a professionalized leadership apart from the rest of society. In the 17th and 18th centuries, the lines of political authority converged upon the person of the monarch, and the military elite was an indissoluble part of the aristocracy or the social elite. The rank and file of the armed forces, on the other hand, were drawn from classes that were not yet part of political society. Consequently a difference between military and social interests was scarcely discernible except as between the aristocracy and the rising bourgeoisie.

In the 19th century the military elite began to dissociate itself from the political–social elite, while the development of conscription brought more civilians into the military apparatus. The technical development of the military led to internal differentiation, so that special military interests and groups arose parallel to similar groups in civil society.

The complex of civil–military relations thus created is often written about as if there were a contrast between military bellicosity and civil peaceableness. As a generalization this is false. Bellicosity may, in fact, be more characteristic of certain political and social movements,

The old and the new establishments

of certain intellectual traditions and nationalistic political parties, than of the professional soldier. It is nonetheless true that the military has obvious interests to pursue and that it often attempts to influence important elements in society or at least to maintain close relations with them. Particularly important to the military are the government, industry, and public opinion.

The government is the most important because it makes decisions about international relations and the size of the military budget. In developed countries the relationship of the military with the government is less a matter of exercising power than of bringing to bear the pressure of special military interests. The military is in this respect on a level with representatives of other special interest groups such as industry, education, and public health care. It differs from them in its relation to government since it cannot participate in elections as directly as other interests can; soldiers are often disliked by elected representatives and seek to defend themselves by closing their ranks and keeping legislative inquisitors as ignorant as possible of the internal problems of the military.

Inter-service rivalry

Another problem arises from rivalry and competition between the services, each of which may seek to enlarge its budget at the expense of the others, as occurs in the United States, where the army, navy, and air force have sometimes aired their rivalries in public. The rapid technical development of arms leads to new sources of friction such as the need to choose between the strategic air force and naval aircraft carriers or the question of giving the army and navy aircraft and missiles. Such interservice rivalry can in theory be solved by a complete integration of the armed forces, which would also permit economies in auxiliary services such as training, research, developments, and medical services. Canada has carried out a far-reaching unification program, but such thoroughgoing centralization is not possible for large countries.

Special relationships between the military and industries that depend on military contracts, known in President Eisenhower's phrase as the "military–industrial complex," have aroused much controversy, but it is difficult to tell how significant the relationships are. To begin with, there is obviously a connection between military spending and general economic prosperity: if some countries were to disarm rapidly and extensively, they would face serious problems of unemployment. It is also true that some business firms in the electronics and aircraft industries receive very large military contracts. Many officers retire from service to take jobs with companies having military contracts; in the United States in 1968, according to a study by the Joint Economic Committee's Subcommittee on Economy in Government, the 95 largest prime military contractors together had 2,072 former high military officers on their payrolls.

The cultivation of public opinion has become of great importance, especially in countries where the mass media are highly developed and the protective isolation formerly surrounding the military has been lost. Much of the "image building" is carried on by specialized organs of the various services, as well as by information offices in the defense ministries. Civilian organizations devoted to the armed forces are important channels in the public relations effort. Of even more importance is the relation between military men and political leaders, particularly in matters of the budget.

A successful war usually results in greatly increased influence and status for the military. This was notably the case in the United States after World War II. Unpopular wars, by the same token, can be disadvantageous to the military, as shown in the cases of the French in Indochina and Algeria, The Netherlands in Indonesia, and the United States in Vietnam.

Politicization of the military. The traditional doctrine of civil–military relations presupposes a certain balance between political and military interests. It assigns to the military the role of a specialized apparatus for violence, while exempting it from political responsibility for its actions. This is the expression of a pluralistic society, in which every institution has a great deal of autonomy in respect to politics. Totalitarian regimes take a different

Totali-tarian controls

view: soldiers are regarded not as professional specialists at the disposal of the state but as part of the political order. In an effort to meld the military with the political superstructure, totalitarian regimes manipulate a whole sequence of control mechanisms.

One technique is indoctrination. High officers are always members of the political party, and military training includes courses in politics. Politicization is also advanced through the selection of military personnel. By drawing upon the politically active members of youth organizations and by continuously postulating loyalty to the political regime as a criterion of selection and advancement, an officers corps is created that thinks in terms of unity with the party. This is strengthened by having a party organization within the military force at all levels, as in Communist countries where political functionaries hold positions of authority in the military hierarchy. Another way of controlling the military is to establish special units under the direct authority of the party and detached from the military command. Examples of these were the troops of the Soviet security police (NKVD) under Stalin and the German Schutzstaffel (SS) under Hitler.

But democratic countries also attempt to politicize and indoctrinate their troops, particularly when they are in conflict with other political systems. The United States became especially concerned with political morale during the Korean War of the early 1950s, when American prisoners appeared to be unable to withstand the ideological pressure of the Chinese Communists. The indoctrination effort was diverted from its traditional concern with military victory to that of a struggle in the name of Western democracy against a detestable political system. The wave of indoctrination also reached the European allies of the United States. In West Germany an effort was made to combat the National Socialist past by stressing the meaning of political democracy. Since it is difficult to convey the positive aspect of democratic values without conjuring up an enemy, the political indoctrination of the Bundeswehr led to a form of anti-Communist schooling that had not been originally intended. The question remains whether the modern soldier can be expected to fight effectively without being imbued with political purpose.

Democrat-ic indoctri-nation

Militarization of politics. Sometimes the soldier intrudes himself into the political sphere, and the result is the militarization of the political order. Militaristic tendencies take several forms. They may be confined to the social elite, as in some empires and monarchies, or they may extend to the population, so that the soldier will have unusual social prestige and the military virtues be regarded as superior, as in Prussia during the 19th century and in National Socialist Germany during the 1930s.

Militarism of a different character exists when the armed forces look after their own interests at the expense of the general welfare, by aggrandizing themselves economically or socially. The military then becomes a parasite on the political body of the state. This has happened in Latin America and in various new nations with military regimes, where the internal politics of the country come to be controlled by military men.

But militarism should be distinguished from militancy. Most democratic countries are averse to militarism and are extremely sensitive to any expansion of the soldier's political and social influence. Many young democratic countries, however, are very militant—as were the United States and revolutionary France. Switzerland is a classic example of the militant spirit and Israel another. Political thinkers since Edmund Burke and Alexis de Tocqueville have pointed out that democratizing the military apparatus may increase the aggressiveness of a country and thus be a cause of wars.

Conditions of military intervention. The military coup d'etat is a normal occurrence in some countries. Attempts by the military to take over the state may occur as often as ten times in one year. This is not a new phenomenon. It happened in Latin American countries throughout the 19th century, particularly in Mexico, Peru, and Chile; Spain between 1832 and 1876 was plagued by military coups, and so were the Balkans for many decades. If military intervention in politics receives more notice in the

Frequency of military coups

present day, it is partly because such intervention occurs frequently in the numerous new countries around the world. In many cases it produces relatively stable regimes, so that the political role of military men cannot be considered an exceptional or transitory phenomenon.

Most of the successful military regimes are in countries that belonged to former colonial empires. The Latin American countries are the successors of the Spanish–Portuguese empire that broke up around 1820, while those in the Middle East are the successors of the Ottoman Empire. The new nations in Africa and Southeast Asia emerged from the empires of Great Britain, France, Belgium, and The Netherlands.

Countries seem most likely to resist military intervention if they have either a strong democratic tradition or a Communist political system. In the latter case the military is kept subordinate to the political power by a strong Communist political party; the effectiveness of the party can be seen by comparing North and South Korea and North and South Vietnam.

One factor leading to military intervention in politics is evidently an inability of the civilian elements to assert their legitimacy. When the tradition reserving the exercise of governmental power to political rather than military institutions is lacking, the political arena is opened to the military on an equal footing. Another factor is the general ineffectiveness of government in the new nations. The high hopes of the struggle for independence are often followed by disappointment and internal unrest. The military represents a relatively efficient and uncorrupted instrument of power where other social and political institutions, such as political parties and labour unions, are weak and cannot act effectively.

In countries where the struggle for independence has been settled by arms, the military is strong and often has a popular following, as in Algeria and Indonesia. If the young nation has been humiliated by foreign pressure or by military defeat, the army may step forward to defend the honour of the nation, as in Turkey and Egypt. If the country's unity is threatened by internal tensions, the army as a national institution can undertake to save it, as in Nigeria, Indonesia, and Pakistan.

Military regimes. The rise of military regimes comes about as a reaction to a worsening political situation, as can be seen in the new African countries. Initially, after the proclamation of independence, the armies are politically neutral. They enter politics at a later period, usually in protest against the presence of European officers and the government's policy in military matters. At this stage the army's opposition begins to take on a more purposeful character, and it enters the struggle for political power. Once it has achieved power it is slow to relinquish it. Practically every military regime that succeeds to a civilian government promises in the beginning to depart as soon as order is established and general elections have been held. But elections are time after time postponed or manipulated, as in Indonesia, or declared to be invalid, as in Pakistan, Argentina, and Brazil. A situation is created in which the government can be changed only by a new military coup, and finally this method of governmental change becomes the customary one; military rule is then permanent.

The term military regime applies to governments that may be superficially quite different from one another—some are headed by monarchs; in others a single political party has power; while still others preside over a multiparty system—but the ultimate power is in the hands of the military, which may or may not have official posts in the government. The degree of military intervention in social and economic life may range from almost none to the occupation of all the key economic, social, and cultural positions, including positions in the universities and public utilities.

Military regimes are little inclined to ideology. They prefer to approach their problems technically and pragmatically; they regard the internal development of their countries as a process of economic and social modernization, not as the achievement of a political utopia. In their external relations they are moved more by nationalist sentiments than by feelings of solidarity with international political movements or coalitions.   (J.v.D./Ed.)

MILITARY LAW

All states require a code of laws and regulations for the raising, maintenance, and administration of their armed forces. All this may be considered the field of military law. The term, however, is generally confined to disciplinary military law, that part of the code that aims at and sanctions the maintenance of discipline in the armed forces. In the past this was also known by the name of martial law, a term that now has the meaning of military enforcement of order upon a civil population either in occupied territory or in time of disorder. Members of armed forces do not cease under modern conditions to have duties as citizens and as human beings. All systems of military law must aim to ensure that the soldier is in no way enabled to escape the obligations of his country's ordinary law or of international law as recognized in various conventions.

Historical development. The object of the disciplinary code is to ensure that the will of the commander is put into effect. Military law therefore traces its origins to the prerogative power of rulers. In Rome, just as a sector of civil law developed from the imperium of the magistrates, so did military law derive from the imperium of those same magistrates in their capacity as commanders of the military forces. The Roman historian Tacitus indicates that military justice in the 1st century AD was generally regarded as somewhat rough-and-ready and heavy-handed and varying much with the individual commander. But it became more formalized and received treatment 400 years later in the Digest and Codex of the emperor Justinian. With the rise of the kingdoms of the Middle Ages, the maintenance of discipline was enforced by ordinances or articles of war issued by the sovereign or by a commander authorized by him at the beginning of each campaign. The earliest now extant are those of the English king Richard I in a charter of 1189 for the government of those going to the Holy Land.

With mercenary armies drawn from many nations in the wars of the 16th and 17th centuries, each national contingent tended to apply the articles of the supreme commander according to its own rules of procedure. The articles of war of Maurice of Nassau, prince of Orange, and Gustavus Adolphus had a considerable influence on the national commanders who served under them, when they came to command elsewhere. In the English Civil War, the ordinances of the royalist and the parliamentary commanders were thus in the most part literally the same and in the next reign formed the basis of Prince Rupert's code of 1672. The famed discipline of Cromwell's army was not due to any improved code but to the fact that the articles were rigorously enforced. On the continent of Europe, the articles of Gustavus Adolphus continued to be followed until supplanted by the codification of the 19th century, which established throughout those countries a generally similar system that, with revision and amendments, continues to this day.

With the introduction of a standing army in England in 1689, Parliament aimed to prevent this force coming under complete control of the sovereign by a series of mutiny acts, normally passed annually, to which the prerogative articles were subordinate. By a statute of 1717 the power to make articles was embodied in the act. In the United States in 1775 and again in 1806, articles of war were adopted that were modelled upon the mutiny acts and articles then in force in Great Britain. In the British army, the articles of war were replaced in 1881 by an annually renewed Army Act (reformed in 1955), although they continued in the Royal Navy until 1957. In the United States they were replaced by the Uniform Code of Military Justice in 1951.

Persons subject to military law. The jurisdiction of military law is not necessarily confined to offenses injurious to the discipline of the forces committed by members of those forces. It extends in various countries in varying degrees to all offenses committed by members of the forces and to offenses injurious to discipline committed by persons who are not members of those forces. In countries in

Origins of military regimes

Articles of war

which an obligation to military service exists, soldiers who fail to answer their initial call-up or report for duty are liable to military jurisdiction for such offenses as desertion or self-mutilation either because the military code makes such offenses applicable to them as a class of civilians (as in Belgium, France, and Italy) or because under the act introducing national service they are deemed to be enlisted on the dispatch of a calling-up notice (as in Great Britain). They continue to be liable for such offenses, even if not otherwise subject to military law, during authorized absence from the conscripted service or temporary reserve service. Reservists are also subject (as in Italy) to military jurisdiction for such offenses as treason, communicating with foreign countries, and revelation of official secrets. In Belgium and France, released soldiers remain liable for rebellion or offenses against superiors committed within one year and six months, respectively, of their release.

Civilian liability to military law Civilians may become liable to military jurisdiction in a number of ways. In some countries, offenses in the nature of treason, rebellion, impeding military efficiency, or fraud in relation to service property are dealt with under the military code (as in Spain, Italy, and Turkey); in others, such offenses by civilians can only be committed in theatres of operations, in a war zone, or during a state of siege (The Netherlands, Norway). Under such circumstances in other countries nationals may be entirely subjected to the military code (Argentina). In other countries, civilians are liable for instigating and participating in military crimes (Germany, Italy). Austria recognizes no military offenses by civilians.

Among those who fall under military jurisdiction are prisoners of war. Sometimes, as in France, Belgium, and Luxembourg, they are expressly included among those to whom the ordinary military law applies; elsewhere, special regulations concerning their behaviour and trial must be passed. Under the Geneva Prisoners of War Convention of 1949, prisoners of war must be tried by a military court, except where the laws of the belligerent expressly allow a member of the belligerent's armed forces to be tried by a civil court for the same offenses. Prisoners of war must not be sentenced to any penalties other than those which might be inflicted on members of the forces of the detaining power for the same act.

Offenses against military law. The military law of the Anglo-Saxon countries and of countries deriving their military law from them, such as India and other independent members of the British Commonwealth, differs from that of the majority of the continental countries in that the latter divide military offenses into two classes: crimes that are the subject of judicial punishment and, second, breaches of discipline that are subject only to administrative action. The former group of countries (and a few others such as Spain), however, recognize no distinction, regarding all military offenses as crimes. Apart from offenses of a peculiarly military nature, such as mutiny, insubordination, desertion, and misconduct in action or in performance of service duties, when an act committed by a soldier constitutes an offense in the civil code, it will frequently constitute an offense of which military law takes cognizance. In the Soviet Union, Belgium, and The Netherlands, all civil offenses committed by soldiers, except very minor ones, are tried by military court; in France, only those committed on duty and in barracks; and in Italy, none. In Germany, Austria, and Scandinavia, in peacetime, all crimes, military or civil, are dealt with by civil courts. Great Britain, Canada, and other countries include as military crimes all actions committed by soldiers anywhere that would be offenses against the criminal law of their own country, although the most serious of these cannot be tried by a military court unless committed abroad, or in India at specified Frontier Posts. In the United States, because of the differences between the criminal law of different states, certain civil crimes are specifically made offenses against the military code. All countries have rules to prevent the double jeopardy of an offender being punished both by civil and military jurisdiction for the one act. Generally, when civil jurisdiction may be exercised, this takes precedence over military jurisdiction.

Summary punishment. In both Anglo-Saxon and continental systems, soldiers are subjected to penalties imposed summarily as well as to those imposed by courts. In the majority of countries, summary penalties can be inflicted only by officers not lower than the rank of captain, the commanding officer of the military unit being the principal source of discipline. The forms of punishment so inflicted are normally loss of privileges for a specified period, fines, or deprivation of liberty. Higher military commanders usually have power to deal summarily with officers (normally up to the rank of major), though in some countries these will not be liable to loss of liberty.

In Great Britain, the United States, and other common-law countries, there is usually a right of appeal against summary punishment awarded through the military chain of command and extending to the highest authority. In other countries, the appeal will lie to a tribunal. In still others, the soldier may have a choice between appeal through the chain of command or to judicial authority (Norway, Sweden). It is to be noted that in some cases the military superior has the power to increase the punishment (Norway, France).

In the Anglo-Saxon countries, offenses that are beyond a commanding officer's powers are dealt with by a service court (court-martial). In the continental countries, military crimes and similar offenses are also dealt with judicially. In the latter, however, there is an intermediate form of tribunal that deals with the more serious forms of breaches of discipline and may impose punishments affecting a soldier's career, such as loss of rank or appointment, dismissal, or forfeiture of pension rights. In Germany, military courts of service, which also hear soldiers' complaints, may impose career sanctions. Also to **Examination by unit assemblies in the Soviet Union** be noted are the unit assemblies in the Soviet Union, which are general assemblies of all military members of a unit. All those attending are invited to comment on the behaviour under investigation. An elected tribunal, normally of five, decides whether the public examination is in itself sufficient educational corrective of the aberrant behaviour or whether the offender should be reported to a competent commander for disciplinary measures.

Courts-martial. Military courts follow a more formal judicial procedure than that observed in summary proceedings. Before trial by court-martial or its equivalent, there is always some formal investigatory procedure. This is normally conducted by a military magistrate and set in motion by a procurator who corresponds to the official responsible for initiating prosecution on behalf of the public in civil trials.

In Great Britain and in countries of the Commonwealth directly deriving their military law from it, the evidence is reduced to writing and considered by the accused's commanding officer, who may then apply for a court-martial to try the accused. In the United States, the preliminary investigation has affinity with civil proceedings before a grand jury.

Pending trial, all countries maintain a presumption of the accused's innocence. He must be allowed full facilities for preparing his defense, and, where disciplinary requirements necessitate keeping him under arrest, this can only be done under the mandate of a magistrate, normally for limited periods only. When the accused's commanding officer is empowered to order arrest, the progress of the case must be reported at frequent intervals to a higher authority, who will consider whether the arrest should be suspended or modified. Courts-martial are generally composed, depending on the type of case, of not less than three, five, or seven judges. In general they consist of military officers, although in some countries other ranks may be included. In France, for example, underofficers may sit upon a court, and in the United States, if an accused enlisted man so requires, at least one-third of the court must be composed of enlisted men. In Israel, a private soldier may demand one judge of his own rank, and in the Soviet Union, the court includes popular assessors elected for two years by all the soldiers in a unit. Most countries include trained lawyers in their courts. In France, a civilian judge sits with six military members. In The Netherlands, there is a civilian president nominated by the crown for life, in Belgium a civilian judge on a three-year tenure, and in

Italy a military magistrate. Each sits with four officers. In the Soviet Union, presidents, vice presidents, and members of military courts are chosen by the Presidium of the Supreme Soviet from citizens on active service aged 25 or over. In courts of first instance, one of these will sit with two popular assessors. In other countries, a court may have a legal adviser who has no vote as a member of the court, as in Great Britain and the United States.

Grades of courts-martial

In some countries there are grades of courts-martial with varying competence as regards persons whom they may try or punishment they may impose. In the United States and Great Britain, general courts-martial composed of not less than five officers with a legal adviser may deal with all persons subject to military law and pass any sentence authorized by the code; special courts-martial (U.S.) or district courts-martial (Britain) consist of at least three officers and have limited powers. In the Soviet Union there are inferior, intermediate, and superior courts. Although under the Anglo-Saxon system, in cases of minor importance, prosecution and defense may be conducted by regimental officers of no legal qualifications, in the majority of countries, the prosecution will normally be in the hands of a legally qualified official, known variously as commissioner, fiscal general, auditor, or military procurator.

A soldier being dealt with summarily, or by disciplinary procedure that is not regarded as judicial action, is not defended. In trials before military courts, all countries allow the accused to be assisted in his defense by an advocate, and in some countries this is compulsory. All countries permit the employment of qualified civilian lawyers. In Greece and the Soviet Union, the defense may be conducted by the family or friends of the accused. In the Soviet Union, additionally, such persons as representatives of syndicates and other social organizations may defend.

The stage at which a defender may operate varies. Normally, he may assist immediately after the first interrogation, when an accused is informed of his rights. He then has rights of intervention during the process of instruction and must be present at such features of it as the interrogation of the accused. In other countries (as in Belgium and Greece), the defender has no part in the instruction and appears only at the trial.

Appeals. Under the Anglo-Saxon system, the findings and sentence of a court-martial are of no effect until they have been confirmed by a military commander, the convening officer, or his superior. Both at this stage and subsequently, the proceedings are subject to review by the service authorities. The service authorities may be moved by a petition on behalf of the convicted soldier, and appeal from a court-martial may also lie to a superior court. In countries in which there is a hierarchy of more or less permanent military courts, appeal will lie to the tribunal next senior to that which tried the accused. In other countries, special courts of military appeal are constituted that may consist of military judges (Israel), mixed military and civilian lawyers (Italy, The Netherlands, Portugal), or purely civilian lawyers (United States and Great Britain). The majority of appeal courts concern themselves only with the legality of conviction rather than with questions of sentence. This is particularly so when there is recourse by way of appeal to the service authorities.

In continental countries, legal questions may be referable to the highest courts. In France, except when judgment has been given in default, the Court of Cassation is the sole court of appeal. In Belgium and Great Britain, final appeal may be made on legal grounds to the Court of Cassation and the House of Lords. Normally, appeal lies only with the defense, but sometimes, as in the Soviet Union, the prosecution has the power to appeal either against the original finding and sentence or on a question of law.

Appeals to ombudsmen

In a few countries, representations about conditions of service and applications for advice and help outside the normal service channels may be made through specific officials. In Norway, a military ombudsman was introduced in 1952. This official sometimes raises questions on disciplinary and penal offenses. The military ombudsman of Sweden, created in 1915, takes note of all sentences of military courts, reports on military prisons, and ensures observation of all regulations by persons concerned in military administration. In other countries in which there is a route of appeal via an ombudsman or similar civilian official (Finland and Germany, for example), there is a marked reluctance on the part of soldiers to take such a course, perhaps because of a general preference for avoiding civilian interference in military affairs. In the United States, there is a reluctance to take grievances to the inspector general of the army rather than going through the normal chain of command, mainly because of a fear of reprisal.

Wartime procedures. In time of war those countries that normally have an exclusively civilian jurisdiction over military offenders will usually introduce courts composed of soldiers. Civilian members of mixed tribunals will normally be replaced by soldiers. Elsewhere, military courts of less senior composition will have extended powers. In addition, the appeal procedure may be superseded or may be liable to be overridden by military commanders in the interests of the immediate imposition of discipline. This applies particularly in the execution of the death sentence.

Current developments. There is a tendency to allow the soldier off duty much greater freedom from discipline than in the past. The German code, for example, places great stress on the soldier's retention of his fundamental rights under the Basic Law, and, generally, the soldier's rights as a citizen are preserved as far as is compatible with the maintenance of discipline and efficiency. In democratic countries, soldiers everywhere retain the right to vote, if necessary by postal ballot, and to support the political party of their choice. Political activity within the service, however, cannot be reconciled with the maintenance of discipline, while the circulation of propaganda or organizing on behalf of political parties whose tenets support a hostile power or are subversive to military discipline must clearly amount to a disciplinary offense as well as a threat to security. The military commander must retain sufficient control over the private lives of his subordinates to ensure that discipline and good order do not suffer. Any orders reasonably calculated to maintain this object are lawful, even when they curtail the private actions of the soldier. Hence, however tolerant the civil legislation of a country might be, the use of drugs, which impair the soldier's efficiency, or the formation of homosexual relationships, which subvert discipline, must be suppressed in any fighting force, just as in all armed forces drunkenness is a specific military offense.

The question of how far a soldier may avail himself of superior orders as a defense to a charge of unlawful action is a topic that has been and continues to be of the greatest importance in relation to war crimes. The difficulties presented by such cases lend support to the view, at present more ideal than practical, that all such offenses should be tried by some neutral international tribunal. It is perhaps only by the enforcement of such a rule that the soldier who refuses to obey an unlawful order can be protected.

(W.E.S.)

BIBLIOGRAPHY

Theory of war: The most comprehensive analysis is QUINCY WRIGHT, *A Study of War,* 2nd ed. (1964; also in abridged ed., 1964). Other major contemporary general analyses are RAYMOND ARON, *The Century of Total War* (1954); JOHN U. NEF, *War and Human Progress* (1950); KENNETH WALTZ, *Man, the State and War* (1959); HANS J. MORGENTHAU, *Politics Among Nations,* 4th ed. (1967); and NORMAN ANGELL, *The Great Illusion: A Study of the Relation of Military Power in Nations to their Economic and Social Advantage* (1910 and later revisions). On nuclear war, see HERMAN KAHN, *On Escalation: Metaphors and Scenarios* (1965). KARL VON CLAUSEWITZ, *Vom Kriege* (1832; Eng. trans., *On War,* 1873 and 1950), remains a classic. Outstanding philosophical treatments are found in JEREMY BENTHAM, *Works,* esp. vol. 2–4 (1843); IMMANUEL KANT, *Zum ewigen Frieden: Ein philosophischer Entwurf* (1795; Eng. trans., *Perpetual Peace: A Philosophical Essay,* 1903; also as *Eternal Peace and Other International Essays,* 1914); JOHN STUART MILL, esp. *On Liberty* (1859) and *Considerations on Representative Government* (1861); and JEAN-JACQUES ROUSSEAU, *A Lasting Peace Through the Federation of Europe, and the State of War* (1917). Explanations of war as a result of imperialism are found in JOHN A. HOBSON, *Imperialism,* 3rd rev. ed. (1938); and in Marxist writings: LENIN, *Imperialism* (1916); KARL MARX, *Das Kapital* (1867–79; Eng. trans., 1925–26); and KARL

MARX and FRIEDRICH ENGELS, *Communist Manifesto* (1848). The psychological explanation is best expressed by SIGMUND FREUD in *Civilization, War and Death,* ed. by JOHN RICK-MAN (1939); and the ethological one in ROBERT ARDREY, *The Territorial Imperative* (1966); and KONRAD LORENZ, *Das sogennante Böse* (1963; Eng. trans., *On Aggression,* 1966). REINHOLD NIEBUHR, *Moral Man and Immoral Society* (1932), analyzes war from the ethical point of view; INIS L. CLAUDE, JR., *Swords into Plowshares,* 3rd ed. rev. (1964), discusses United Nations approaches to peace.

Law of war: Among general treatises are L.F.L. OPPENHEIM, *International Law,* 7th ed. by H. LAUTERPACHT, vol. 2, *Disputes, War and Neutrality* (1952), a standard reference work; M.S. MCDOUGAL and F.P. FELICIANO, *Law and Minimum World Public Order: The Legal Regulation of International Coercion* (1961); J. STONE, *Legal Controls of International Conflict* (1959); E.J.S. CASTREN, *The Present Law of War and Neutrality* (1954); and G. SCHWARZENBERGER, *International Law,* vol. 2, *The Law of Armed Conflict* (1968), an interpretation of the law chiefly through court decisions. A concise and basic account is M. GREENSPAN, *The Soldier's Guide to the Laws of War* (1969). More specialized accounts are M. GREENSPAN, *The Modern Law of Land Warfare* (1959), a detailed exposition that sets out the laws common to all types of warfare; R.W. TUCKER, *The Law of War and Neutrality at Sea* (1955); C.J. COLOMBOS, *The International Law of the Sea,* 6th rev. ed. (1967); J.M. SPAIGHT, *Air Power and War Rights,* 3rd ed. (1947); and E.J.S. CASTREN, *Civil War* (1966). U.S.S.R. ACAD. OF SCI. INST. OF STATE AND LAW, *International Law* (1957), gives the Soviet point of view in English translation. Discussion, sometimes controversial, of legal and illegal resort to force by states is contained in I. BROWNLIE, *International Law and the Use of Force by States* (1963); and R.A. FALK, *Legal Order in a Violent World* (1968). F. SEYERSTED, *United Nations Forces in the Law of Peace and War* (1966), discusses the application of the laws of war to UN forces. Useful articles on the legal status of the guerrilla are M. GREENSPAN, "International Law and Its Protection for Participants in Unconventional Warfare," *Ann. Am. Acad. of Polit. and Soc. Sci.,* 341:30–41 (May 1962); and R.D. POWERS, "Guerrillas and the Laws of War," *U.S. Naval Inst. Proc.,* 89:82–87 (March 1963). For a historical account of the laws of war, see A. NUSSBAUM, *A Concise History of the Law of Nations,* rev. ed. (1954). A wide survey of the laws of war is contained in M.M. WHITEMAN, *Digest of International Law,* vols. 10–11 (1968).

War crimes: On the subject generally, see *History of the United Nations War Crimes Commission and the Development of the Laws of War* (1948). CLAUD MULLINS, *The Leipzig Trials* (1921), is the definitive work on its subject. Concerning the post-World War II trials in Europe, see *Report of Robert H. Jackson, United States Representative to the International Conference on Military Trials* (1949); TELFORD TAYLOR, *Nuremberg Trials, War Crimes and International Law* (1949), and *Final Report to the Secretary of the Army on the Nuremberg War Crimes Trials* (1949); WHITNEY R. HARRIS, *Tyranny on Trial* (1954); WILBOURN E. BENTON and GEORG GRIMM (eds.), *Nuremberg: German Views of the War Trials* (1955); and AUGUST VON KNIERIEM, *Nürnberg, rechtliche und menschliche Probleme* (1953; Eng. trans., *The Nuremberg Trials,* 1959). Concerning the trials in the Far East, see JOSEPH B. KEENAN and BRENDAN F. BROWN, *Crimes Against International Law* (1950); and SOLIS HORWITZ, *The Tokyo Trial* (1950). Other specialized works of interest include: YORAM DINSTEIN, *The Defense of "Obedience to Superior Orders" in International Law* (1965); PETER PAPADATOS, *The Eichmann Trial* (1964); and TELFORD TAYLOR, *Nuremberg and Vietnam: An American Tragedy* (1970). The trial at Nuremberg of the major German war criminals is reported in *Trial of the Major War Criminals Before the International Military Tribunal,* 42 vol. (1949); the Subsequent Proceedings are reported in *Trials of War Criminals Before the Nuremberg Military Tribunals,* 15 vol. (1950); and the United Nations War Crimes Commission has published summaries of a large number of trials that occurred both in Europe and in the Pacific in its *Law Reports of Trials of War Criminals,* 15 vol. (1947–49). Neither the record of trial nor the judgment of the trial of the major Japanese war criminals conducted in Tokyo by the International Military Tribunal for the Far East has ever been published. They are available in some libraries in mimeograph form or on microfilm.

Economics of war: JULES BACKMAN (ed.), *War and Defense Economics* (1952), a general text dealing with armament production, fiscal policy, manpower and material controls, and economic warfare; K.E. KNORR, *The War Potential of Nations* (1956), an analysis of the material elements of national power and the human qualities necessary to mobilize them. E. BENOIT and K.E. BOULDING (eds.), *Disarmament and the Economy* (1963), an examination of the possible economic effects of disarmament, including a theoretical model, and concluding that the problem is manageable; E. BENOIT and N.P. GLEDITSCH

(eds.), *Disarmament and World Economic Interdependence* (1967), a collection of articles including an important article by BENOIT and W. LUBELL, "The World Burden of National Defense," which tries to improve the realism of international comparisons; INSTITUTE FOR STRATEGIC STUDIES, *The Military Balance* (annual), a catalogue of current military strength, with country by country surveys, tabulations, and notes on particular issues; STOCKHOLM INTERNATIONAL PEACE RESEARCH INSTITUTE, *Year Book of World Armaments and Disarmament* (annual), another presentation of contemporary facts, but with a more historical perspective employing somewhat different sources. J.J. CLARK, *The New Economics of National Defense* (1966), a general survey of the new applications of economics to defense management and a discussion of some problems including disarmament and economic warfare; STEPHEN ENKE (ed.), *Defense Management* (1967), a collection of well-informed articles on the American system and its effects, many by authors who played a part in its introduction. K.E. BOULDING, *Conflict and Defense: A General Theory* (1962), an investigation of the causes and nature of conflict through the use of economic theories and methods; T.C. SCHELLING, *The Strategy of Conflict* (1960), an investigation of conflict and bargaining in international affairs from an economist's viewpoint.

Strategy: HERMANN FOERTSCH, *Kriegskunst heute und morgen* (1939; Eng. trans., *The Art of Modern Warfare,* 1940); EDWARD MEAD EARLE *et al.* (eds.), *Makers of Modern Strategy: Military Thought from Machiavelli to Hitler* (1943); MAURICE MATLOFF and EDWIN M. SNELL, *Strategic Planning for Coalition Warfare, 1941–42* (1953); B.H. LIDDELL HART, *Strategy: The Indirect Approach* (1954); JOHN C. SLESSOR, *Strategy for the West* (1954); MICHAEL HOWARD, *Grand Strategy,* vol. 4 (1972); JOHN EHRMAN, *Grand Strategy,* vol. 5–6 (1956); MAURICE MATLOFF, "The Soviet Union and the War in the West," *Proc. U.S. Nav. Inst.,* 82:261–271 (1956), and *Strategic Planning for Coalition Warfare, 1943–1944* (1959); EDGAR J. KINGSTON-MCCLOUGHRY, *Global Strategy* (1957), and *Defense: Policy and Strategy* (1960); HENRY A. KISSINGER, *Nuclear Weapons and Foreign Policy* (1957); RAYMOND L. GARTHOFF, *Soviet Strategy in the Nuclear Age* (1958); BERNARD BRODIE, *Strategy in the Missile Age* (1959); RAYMOND ARON, "De la Guerre" (1957; Eng. trans., *On War,* 1959); SAMUEL P. HUNTINGTON, *The Common Defense: Strategic Programs in National Politics* (1961); R.E. OSGOOD, *Limited War: The Challenge to American Strategy* (1957); HERMAN KAHN, *Thinking About the Unthinkable* (1962); MICHAEL E. HOWARD (ed.), *The Theory and Practice of War* (1965); A. BEAUFRE, *Introduction à la stratégie* (1963; Eng. trans., *An Introduction to Strategy,* 1965); and *Stratégie de l'action* (1966; Eng. trans., *Strategy of Action,* 1967).

Military tactics: J.F.C. FULLER, *A Military History of the Western World,* 3 vol. (1954–56; British title, *Decisive Battles of the Western World, and Their Influence upon History*); LYNN MONTROSS, *War Through the Ages,* rev. 3rd ed. (1960); R.A. PRESTON, S.F. WISE, and H.O. WERMER, *Men in Arms* (1956). (*Weapons*): T. WINTRINGHAM, *The Story of Weapons and Tactics from Troy to Stalingrad* (1943); J.R. NEWMAN, *The Tools of War* (1942). (*Tactical theory*): K. VON CLAUSEWITZ, *Vom Kriege,* 3 vol. (1832–34; Eng. trans. by J.J. GRAHAM, *On War,* rev. ed. with introduction and notes by F.N. MAUDE, 3 vol., 1940); A. DU PICQ, *Etudes sur le combat* (1880; Eng. trans. from 8th French ed., *Battle Studies,* 1921); J.F.C. FULLER, *The Reformation of War* (1923). (*Ancient warfare*): T.A. DODGE, *Alexander* (1890), *Hannibal* (1891), and *Caesar* (1892). (*Medieval*): C.W.C. OMAN, *A History of the Art of War in the Middle Ages,* 2nd ed. rev., 2 vol. (1924). (*Early modern*): C.V. WEDGWOOD, *The Thirty Years' War* (1938); WINSTON S. CHURCHILL, *Marlborough: His Life and Times,* 4 vol. (1933–38). (*Napoleonic era*): T.A. DODGE, *Napoleon,* 4 vol. (1904–07); B.H. LIDDELL HART, *The Ghost of Napoleon* (1933); C.W.C. OMAN, *A History of the Peninsular War,* 7 vol. (1902–30). (*Nineteenth century*): D.S. FREEMAN, *R.E. Lee,* 4 vol. (1934–35); J.F.C. FULLER, *The Generalship of Ulysses S. Grant* (1929); C. VON DER GOLTZ, *Das Volk in Waffen* (1883; Eng. trans. by JOSEPH T. DICKMAN, *The Nation in Arms,* 1914). (*World War I*): WINSTON S. CHURCHILL, *The World Crisis,* 5 vol. (1923–29); B.H. LIDDELL HART, *The Real War, 1914–1918* (1930). (*World War II*): C. WILMOT, *The Struggle for Europe* (1952); J.F.C. FULLER, *The Second World War, 1939–1945* (1948); J.A. ISELY and P.A. CROWL, *The U.S. Marines and Amphibious War* (1951). (*Korean War*): R. GUGELER, *Combat Actions in Korea* (1954). See also the United States Army and Marine Corps official histories of operations in World War II and the Korean War and official British, Canadian, and Australian histories.

Naval tactics: A.T. MAHAN, *The Influence of Sea Power upon History, 1660–1783* (1890), *Naval Strategy* (1911); H.W. RICHMOND, *Statesmen and Sea Power* (1946), *The Navy As an Instrument of Policy,* ed. by E.A. HUGHES (1953); J.A. WILLIAMSON, *Maritime Enterprise, 1485–1558* (1913), *The Ocean in English History* (1941); J.S. CORBETT, *Some Principles of Maritime*

Strategy (1911); B. BRODIE, *A Guide to Naval Strategy,* 4th ed. (1958); S.W. ROSKILL, *The Strategy of Sea Power* (1962); P.W. BUCK, *The Politics of Mercantilism* (1942); J.S. CORBETT and H. NEWBOLT, *Naval Operations,* 5 vol. (1920–31); C.E. FAYLE, *Seaborne Trade,* 3 vol. (1920–24); R. SCHEER, *Germany's High Seas Fleet in the World War* (1920); W.S. SIMS and B.J. HENDRICK, *The Victory at Sea* (1920); S.E. MORISON, *The History of United States Naval Operations in World War II,* 15 vol. (1947–62); S.W. ROSKILL, *The War at Sea,* 4 vol. (1954–61); F. RUGE, *Der Seekrieg, 1939–1945,* 2nd ed. (1956; Eng. trans., *Sea Warfare, 1939–45: A German Viewpoint,* 1957); B.E. FERGUSSON, *The Watery Maze: The Story of Combined Operations* (1961); E.B. POTTER and C.W. NIMITZ (eds.), *The Great Sea War* (1960).

Guerrilla warfare: MAO TSE-TUNG, *On Guerrilla Warfare,* trans. by S.B. GRIFFITH (1961); GEORGIOS GRIVAS, *Apomnēmoneumata agōnos E.O.K.A.* (1961; Eng. trans., *Guerilla Warfare and EOKA's Struggle,* 1964), and *Agōn E.O.K.A. Kai antartopolemos* (1962; Eng. trans., *General Grivas on Guerrilla Warfare,* 1964); O. HEILBRUNN, *Partisanenbuch* (1960; Eng. trans., *Partisan Warfare,* 1962), *Warfare in the Enemy's Rear* (1963); V.C. GIAP, *Peoples War, Peoples Army* (1962); A. CAMPBELL, *Guerrillas: A History and Analysis* (1967).

Logistics: E.A. PRATT, *The Rise of Rail-Power in War and Conquest, 1833–1914* (1915), an old but still useful survey; B. CROWELL, *America's Munitions 1917–1918* (1919), a basic source for U.S. home front mobilization in World War I; G.C. SHAW, *Supply in Modern War* (1938), a perceptive analysis of the supply function, mainly subsistence; R.G. ALBION and J.B. POPE, *Sea Lanes in Wartime: The American Experience 1775–1942* (1942), a masterly history of American overseas supply; S.L.A. MARSHALL, *The Soldier's Load and the Mobility of a Nation* (1950), a famous military historian's analysis of a problem that he helped the U.S. Army to deal with after World War II; R.G. RUPPENTHAL, *Logistical Support of the Armies,* 2 vol. (1953–59), the U.S. Army's official history of European theatre logistics at the theater level in World War II; R.M. LEIGHTON and R.W. COAKLEY, *Global Logistics and Strategy,* 2 vol. (1955–68), the U.S. Army's official history of logistics in the framework of coalition strategy during World War II; C.B.A. BEHRENS, *Merchant Shipping and the Demands of War* (1955), the official British history of shipping operations in World War II; K.E. KNORR, *The War Potential of Nations* (1956), a scholarly analysis of the continuing importance of industrial potential in the nuclear era; H.E. ECCLES, *Logistics in the National Defense* (1959), a perceptive theoretical analysis based on a lifetime of experience and study; R.E. SMITH, *The Army and Economic Mobilization* (1959), the U.S. Army's official history of World War II economic mobilization; C.J. HITCH and R.N. MCKEAN, *The Economics of Defense in the Nuclear Age* (1965), the "bible" of the managerial reforms in the U.S. Defense Department; N. BROWN, *Strategic Mobility* (1963), a British writer's comprehensive analysis of a little recognized facet of post-1945 international strategy and logistics; J.A. HUSTON, *The Sinews of War: Army Logistics 1775–1953* (1966), the U.S. Army's official history of its logistical experience.

Military engineering: B.D. COLL, J.E. KEITH, and H.H. ROSENTHAL, *The Corps of Engineers: Troops and Equipment* (1958), a description of the organization and deployment of the U.S. Corps of Engineers and of engineer equipment in service; U.S. ARMY, ARMY FORCES, PACIFIC, OFFICE OF THE CHIEF ENGINEER, *Engineers of the Southwest Pacific,* 8 vol. (1947–51), vol. 1–4 deal with the period 1947–49, and vol. 5–8 with the period 1949–51; INSTITUTION OF ROYAL ENGINEERS, *The History of the Corps of Royal Engineers,* 9 vol. (1889–1958), a history of British military engineers from Norman times to 1948; E.W.C. SANDES, *The Royal Engineers in Egypt and the Sudan* (1937), covering the period from 1800 to 1936; A.J. KERRY and W.A. MCDILL, *History of the Corps of Royal Canadian Engineers,* 2 vol. (1962–66), a history of the Royal Corps of Engineers from

1749 to 1946; R.J. UNSTEAD, *Castles* (U.S. title, *British Castles;* 1970), a description of the development of castles and permanent fortifications from the earliest times to the 16th century; P. WARNER, *Sieges of the Middle Ages* (1968), an account of the major sieges in Europe and Asia Minor between the years 1000 and 1400; VEZIO MELEGARI, *Great Sieges* (1970), a description of historically decisive sieges from the legendary siege of Troy to the siege of Stalingrad during World War II; B. GILLE, *The Renaissance Engineers* (1966), a study of the inventions and techniques of Leonardo da Vinci and other military engineers of the Renaissance.

Armed forces: MORRIS JANOWITZ and ROGER W. LITTLE, *Sociology and the Military Establishment,* rev. ed. (1965), a good short introduction to the study of the armed forces as a social institution; ROGER W. LITTLE (ed.), *Handbook of Military Institutions* (1971), covering most aspects of the modern armed forces; CHARLES H. COATES and ROLAND J. PELLEGRIN, *Military Sociology: A Study of American Military Institutions and Military Life* (1965), a systematic introduction to the problems of the U.S. military forces; MORRIS JANOWITZ, *The Professional Soldier: A Social and Political Portrait* (1960), the best and most complete study of the U.S. officers corps, including comparisons with officers corps of other countries; KARL DEMETER, *Das deutsche Offizierkorps in Gesellschaft und Staat, 1650–1945,* 2nd rev. ed. (1962; Eng. trans., *The German Officer-Corps in Society and State, 1650–1945,* 1965); MICHAEL LEWIS, *England's Sea Officers: The Story of the Naval Profession* (1939); JOHN R. BEISHLINE, *Military Management for National Defense* (1950), a manual of military planning, organization, and command; KARL LANG, "Military Organizations," in J.G. MARCH (ed.), *Handbook of Organizations,* pp. 838–878 (1965), a summary of the problems of military organizations, with extensive references to the literature; MORRIS JANOWITZ (ed.), *The New Military: Changing Patterns of Organization* (1964), a collection of studies on military selection, training, career management, and retirement; M.R.D. FOOT, *Men in Uniform: Military Manpower in Modern Industrial Societies* (1961), a classification of the various organizational systems, drawing upon practices in the United States, the Soviet Union, Great Britain, France, Germany, Switzerland, Belgium, Denmark, Sweden, Turkey, Israel, Canada, and Australia; HAROLD WOOL, *The Military Specialist: Skilled Manpower for the Armed Forces* (1968), a study of the demand for trained personnel in the armed forces, with much U.S. factual material; SAMUEL A. STOUFFER et al., *The American Soldier,* 2 vol. (1949), studies of all aspects of the U.S. soldier, unsurpassed as source material on military behaviour; ALFRED VAGTS, *A History of Militarism: Civilian and Military,* rev. ed. (1960), a history of the soldier in Western society, with special emphasis on the relation between soldier and state; STANISLAV ANDRESKI, *Military Organization and Society,* 2nd ed. (1968), a classification of military organizational forms on the basis of material from all historic societies; SAMUEL P. HUNTINGTON, *The Soldier and the State: The Theory and Politics of Civil-Military Relations* (1957), a standard work that includes, along with general theory and classification, an extensive discussion of the development of civil–military relations in the U.S.; ROMAN KOLKOWICZ, *The Soviet Military and the Communist Party* (1967); WILLIAM GUTTERIDGE, *Military Institutions and Power in the New States* (1965), an introductory work on the origin, composition, and external relations of the military in the countries of the Third World; MORRIS JANOWITZ, *The Military in the Political Development of New Nations: An Essay in Comparative Analysis* (1964), a short introduction to the internal problems of military institutions and the relations between the military and society; JOHN J. JOHNSON (ed.), *The Role of the Military in Underdeveloped Countries* (1962), a collection of studies by experts; EDWIN LIEUWEN, *Arms and Politics in Latin America* (1960); CLAUDE E. WELCH, JR. (ed.), *Soldier and State in Africa: A Comparative Analysis of Military Intervention and Political Change* (1970).

Warsaw

Warsaw (Polish Warszawa) is unique among the great cities of Europe. Its many historic buildings attest to its long period of development and to its role as the capital of Poland, but almost all have been rebuilt since 1945, together with the rest of the city centre and inner suburbs on the west bank of the Vistula River, which was almost totally destroyed and depopulated during World War II. The destruction and careful reconstruction of the city are matters of great importance to Poles throughout the world, justifying its motto "*Contemnit procellas*" ("Defies the storms"). The city stands at an ancient crossing place of the river, which is now the centre of the Polish communications and transport system. Since the second half of the 19th century, Warsaw has had a wide range of manufacturing industries. The appearance of the city is dominated by the tower of the Palace of Culture and Science, built in a Russian architectural style in the 1950s.

This article is divided into the following sections:

Physical and human geography

THE LANDSCAPE

The city site. Warsaw lies on the Vistula (Wisła) River, far from the sea, in the middle of the Warsaw Plain. This basin, shaped by glaciers during the Ice Age, ranges from 300 to 380 feet (90 to 115 metres) above sea level. The present city—divided into right- and left-bank portions by the river—extends about 18 miles (29 kilometres) from north to south and 16 miles from east to west.

The river is some 3,900 (1,190 metres) feet wide at this point, although the riverbed has been artificially narrowed by embankment to a third of this width. Geologically, Warsaw lies on subsoil composed of Quaternary silts (drifts, sand, clay, slimes), underlain by water-resistant loams transported by glaciers.

Climate. The climate is moderate and rather cool, the prevailing westerly winds bringing frequent changes of weather. The average yearly temperature is 46.6° F (8.1° C), with a July average of 67.6° F (19° C) and a January average of 26° F (−4° C). Yearly rainfall averages 22 inches (560 millimetres), most of which falls in the summer. Snow cover persists for 50 or 60 days a year.

The city layout. The size of Warsaw reflects the historical fortunes of the city: from 309 acres (125 hectares) in the 17th century, it expanded to 29,176 acres by 1937 and increased to 110,000 acres by 1957, in the period of postwar rebuilding. The subdivision (1959) into seven districts—the City, Żoliborz, Wola, Ochota, Mokotów,

Growth of the city

Praga South, and Praga North—reflects centuries-old local names, but Warsaw is now virtually a new creation, with a layout that resembles only in part that of the historic city. The changes in appearance reflect a conscious planning of social and economic functions. Industries and warehouses are now located on the outskirts or between modern housing developments; park areas have tripled in size; city streets, though still largely based on the old network, have been extensively widened. The Old and New towns, Nowy Świat Avenue, and the city churches and palaces, on the other hand, have all been carefully reconstructed.

In the early post-World War II recovery period, when industrial reconstruction was given priority, housing construction was slow; a substantial improvement in housing conditions occurred, however, in the 1950s and 1960s. By 1970 the city had scores of new apartments; the majority of these units were supplied with urban services. The use of standardized, factory-produced housing components (the "Warsaw Standardization") has helped ease the situation. Most of Warsaw's housing investment is carried out by housing cooperatives.

THE PEOPLE

Almost all Warsaw residents are of Polish nationality. Post-World War II resettlement was followed by a high rate of natural increase in the city's population, reaching a peak of 16.4 per 1,000 in 1955. This figure fell to 0.9 per 1,000 in 1971, although the rate was higher in other parts of the province, and it gradually rose during the 1970s. The overwhelming majority of the residents are Roman Catholics.

THE ECONOMY

Industry. A large segment of the labour force of the city is employed by industry. War devastation, the differential rate of reconstruction, and the emergence of new industries have molded the urban economy. Fuel and power engineering, metallurgy (including the Warsaw steelworks), machine production (including an automobile manufacturing plant), and chemical, printing, and textile enterprises dominate the economy. Industry is becoming increasingly located according to the basic philosophy of the city planning bureau, which holds that the citizen's place of work should be close to but separate geographically from his home; thus industrial areas may be located near the vast housing developments but are separated from them by protective "green belt" landscaping. As westerly winds prevail, however, the establishment of the steel industry on the left bank of the Vistula has helped increase air pollution in some parts of the city. The Warsaw region is important to Poland agriculturally, for it constitutes a highly specialized gardening and vegetable centre.

Planned industrial areas

Transportation. Warsaw is the hub for main rail, road, and air routes that are of importance to eastern Europe. Roads of expressway standard are planned or have already been built through the city along both banks of the Vistula and in the form of a ring road through the inner suburbs, but road traffic is still light in comparison with western European cities, and it is still possible to accommodate it and a surface tramway system on the capital's main streets.

ADMINISTRATIVE AND SOCIAL CONDITIONS

Government. As the national capital, Warsaw houses the Sejm (parliament) and leading political and governmental bodies. Warsaw is governed by a People's Council, whose members are elected for four-year terms. Its Presidium is the executive and administrative body, and the Presidium's chairman is, in effect, the mayor of the city. The Presidium directs the administrative apparatus through municipal councils in each of the seven districts.

Health. Since 1945 Warsaw's health facilities have been greatly expanded, and by 1970 the life-span of the aver-

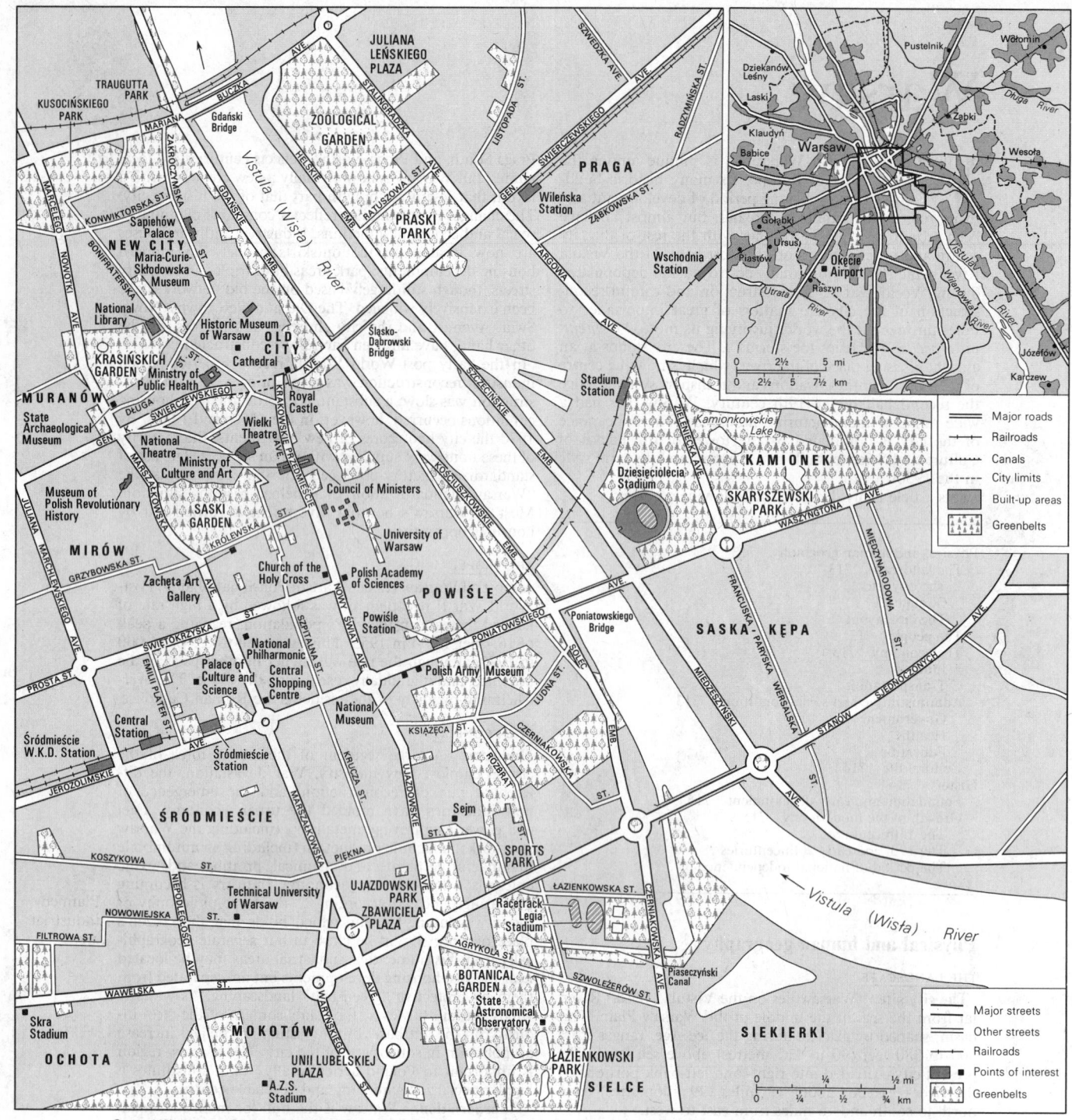

Central Warsaw and (inset) its metropolitan area.

age citizen had been lengthened by about 20 years. Most of the population benefits annually from a virtually free health-insurance plan, and there is a considerable number of outpatient centres.

Education. Education in Warsaw benefits from the presence of the headquarters of the Polish Academy of Sciences (Polska Akademia Nauk, or PAN), which coordinates research in both physical and social sciences through a number of institutes and industrial establishments. Warsaw is an active centre of research, and its work in nuclear physics and parasitology has achieved international acclaim. The Technical University of Warsaw (Polytechnika Warszawska) and the University of Warsaw (Uniwersytet Warszawski) are notable institutions. Major libraries include the library (established in 1817) of the University of Warsaw and the National Library (1919); there are also a number of specialist libraries.

Polish
Academy
of Sciences

CULTURAL LIFE

Warsaw is the leading centre of Polish cultural and artistic life, and its writers, artists, and musicians play a major role in creating the cultural values of the nation. The majority of the members of such bodies as the Polish Union of Writers and the Polish Union of Composers work in the city, which is also the seat of such prominent institutions as the National Museum and the Zachęta Art Gallery. Warsaw is the largest radio and television centre in Poland and the leader in the national theatrical life; the avant-garde of the Polish theatre flourishes there, and the most famous actors, stage managers, and directors work in the city. The National Philharmonic orchestra also draws large crowds. There are numerous specialist museums, and, among the many social, cultural, and educational associations, the Friends of History in Warsaw and the Chopin societies are prominent.

Theatre

East–west thoroughfare and tunnel under the Old City, Warsaw. St. Anne's Church (1454) is on the left.
By courtesy of ORBIS

The rise in the standard of living in the post-World War II era brought in its wake an increased enjoyment of leisure and recreational facilities, and Warsaw residents benefit from recreational centres located in the surrounding countryside. There is a large number of sports and physical-culture centres and also many touring clubs.

History

FOUNDATION AND EARLY DEVELOPMENT

The origins of Warsaw remain obscure. Excavations within present urban limits have confirmed the existence of Stare Bródno, a small settlement of the 10th and early 11th centuries AD. This trading community fell victim to the feudal struggles of the period, and its functions were taken over successively by the settlements of Kamion (mentioned in documents dating from as early as 1065) and Jazdow (first recorded in 1262). About the end of the 13th century, Jazdow was moved about two miles (three kilometres) to the north, at a village named Warszowa (Warsaw), and the young community was strengthened by the protection afforded by a castle. Local and regional trade began to flourish, and municipal institutions developed; from 1339 onward, authority was invested in a bailiff and, from 1376, in a city council. The first hospital was founded about 1388, and by the end of the 14th century the growing settlement had a double line of protective ramparts.

In the 15th century the town became the capital of the province of Mazovia, and a New City sprang up to the north of the original, constricted site, afterward known as the Old City. In 1526 both city and province became incorporated into the crown lands of the Jagiellonian state; from 1569 the Sejm (parliament) met in Warsaw, and from 1573 the elections of the kings took place there. The first permanent bridge was built across the Vistula in 1573, and in 1596 King Sigismund III Vasa began to remodel the castle as a royal residence. In 1611 the King and his court finally moved from Kraków (Cracow) to Warsaw, making it the capital of the Polish state. Many powerful persons built residences in Warsaw, and autonomous settlements sprang up around its periphery. This ascendancy proved short-lived, for a Swedish invasion (1655–56) devastated the flourishing city, and then the War of the Polish Succession (1733–38) brought affliction through economic decay and pestilence.

GROWTH OF THE MODERN CITY

The 18th century. The development of manufacturing, banks, and other enterprises during the early 18th century provided a firm economic base for a number of early exercises in urban planning. During the reign (1764–95) of King Stanisław II August Poniatowski, Warsaw became the centre of a cultural movement known as the Polish Enlightenment. The first lay school (Szkoła Rycerska) was opened in 1765, and in 1773 the Committee on National Education—in effect, the first European ministry of education—began its activity in the city. The Polish theatre and numerous printing establishments also flourished. Warsaw played an important role in Polish striving for political rebirth when a parliamentary constitution was proclaimed in the city on May 3, 1791, in the name of the reforming "Four Years Sejm." The commercial classes in the city were active in the Warsaw insurrection of 1794, led by Tadeusz Kościuszko. The rising was crushed, and the ensuing partition of Poland among Russia, Prussia, and Austria left Warsaw a provincial town under Prussian occupation; the severity of this blow is indicated by a decline in city population from 115,000 in 1792 to only 64,000 in 1803.

The 19th and early 20th centuries. The occupation of Warsaw by the French army in 1806 was followed a year later by Napoleon's creation of the Duchy of Warsaw, a measure that reinstated the city as a capital; but the Emperor's downfall led to the occupation of Warsaw by Russian armies.

Under the Congress Kingdom of Poland (1815–30), the urban economy—particularly the factory system—continued to expand, and such monumental Neoclassical buildings as the one housing the University of Warsaw (1816) were erected. National independence remained an elusive goal, and Warsaw figured prominently—notably as seat of the unsuccessful uprising of November 1830—in struggles to throw off foreign domination. Economic growth, however, continued, and by the mid-19th century textile, metal, and tannery industries were well established, and the city had become the centre of a continent-wide rail network. The defeat by the Russians of the Warsaw-based uprising of 1863 did not prevent further expansion of the city, and a new outer belt of fortifications was constructed in 1875. Population soared, reaching 276,000 in 1872 and 756,000 by 1903, and urban services underwent extensive modification. As a result of further nationalist and Socialist disturbances between 1905 and 1907, censorship was alleviated, Polish schools and other cultural institutions were legally established, and Warsaw again experienced a cultural renascence. After World War I the city regained its status as the national capital.

The period of national independence. The population of Warsaw passed the 1,000,000 mark in 1925; the period between the world wars was marked by further social and

Nationalist uprisings and industrial growth

The Old and New cities

cultural advance, despite a period of inflation, depressions and slumps in trade, and political instability. Automobile and aircraft manufacture were introduced; city services underwent further expansion, and Warsaw's emergence as a European cultural centre was symbolized by the beginning of such international competitions as the International Chopin Competition for Pianists (1927) and the Henryk Wieniawski International Violin Competition (1935).

The Nazi occupation

After the Nazis laid siege to Warsaw in 1939, more than 10,000 citizens perished and more than 50,000 were wounded before the lack of supplies forced a surrender. The subsequent Nazi occupation was aimed at reducing Warsaw to a provincial city; its cultural treasures were systematically plundered and its inhabitants carried away to German labour camps or to concentration camps. The city's Jews, numbering some 400,000, were resettled in a closed ghetto in 1940, and during 1942 alone some 312,-000 were sent to their deaths in the gas chambers. More than 60,000 Jews died in the desperate ghetto uprising of 1943; Warsaw became the national resistance centre, and from 150,000 to 180,000 of its people died in the 1944 uprising. In all, some 600,000 to 800,000 Varsovians are estimated to have died between 1939 and 1944 and the Allied armies in 1945 found the city in a state of almost total devastation. On February 1, 1945, the provisional Polish government made Warsaw its capital, and an office for urban reconstruction was set up.   (Ja.D./A.H.D.)

BIBLIOGRAPHY. R.E. DICKINSON, *The West European City*, 2nd ed. (1961), contains valuable descriptive analysis of the site and layout of the medieval town, the postmedieval extensions, and the pre-1940 city; J. ZACHWATOWICZ and P. BIEGANSKI, *The Old Town of Warsaw* (1956), an excellent pictorial record; A. CIBOROWSKI, *Warsaw: A City Destroyed and Rebuilt*, 2nd ed. (1969), an outline history of Warsaw and its urban development, including a description of the city as it was in 1939 and the story of its destruction. EDWARD D. WYNOT, *Warsaw Between the World Wars: Profile of the Capital City in a Developing Land, 1918–1939* (1983), is a historical survey; JANINA RUTKOWSKA, *A Guide to Warsaw and Environs* (1981; originally published in Polish), is a description with illustrations and maps; JOANNA K.M. HANSON, *The Civilian Population and the Warsaw Uprising of 1944* (1982); and ISRAEL GUTMAN, *The Jews of Warsaw, 1939–1943: Ghetto, Underground, Revolt* (1982; originally published in Hebrew), are scholarly historical discussions.

George Washington

General, statesman, and first president of the United States, George Washington was born in Westmoreland County, Virginia, on February 22 (February 11, old style), 1732. His father was Augustine Washington, who had gone to school in England, had tasted seafaring life, and was then managing his growing Virginia estates. His mother was Mary Ball, whom Augustine, a widower, had married early the previous year. The paternal lineage had some distinction; an early forebear was described as "gentleman," Henry VIII later gave the family lands, and its members held various offices. But family fortunes fell with the Puritan revolution in England, and John Washington, grandfather of Augustine, migrated in 1657 to Virginia. The ancestral home at Sulgrave, Northamptonshire, is maintained as a Washington memorial. Little definite information exists on any of the line until Augustine. He was an energetic, ambitious man who acquired much land, built mills, took an interest in opening iron mines, and sent his two oldest sons to England for schooling. By his first wife, Jane Butler, he had four children; by his second, six. He died April 12, 1743.

Childhood and youth. Little is known of George Washington's early childhood, spent largely on the Ferry Farm on the Rappahannock River, opposite Fredericksburg, Virginia. Mason L. Weems's stories of the hatchet and cherry tree and of young Washington's repugnance to fighting are apocryphal efforts to fill a manifest gap. He attended

Schooling

school irregularly from his seventh to his 15th year, first with the local church sexton and later with a schoolmaster named Williams. Some of his schoolboy papers survive. He was fairly well trained in practical mathematics—gauging, several types of mensuration, and such trigonometry as was useful in surveying. He studied geography, possibly had a little Latin, and certainly read some of *The Spectator* and other English classics. The copybook in which he transcribed at 14 a set of moral precepts or *Rules of Civility and Decent Behaviour in Company and Conversation* was carefully preserved. His best training, however, was given him by practical men and outdoor occupations, not by books. He mastered tobacco growing and stock raising, and early in his teens he was sufficiently familiar with surveying to plot the fields about him.

Lawrence Washington

At his father's death, the 11-year-old boy became the ward of his eldest half brother, Lawrence, a man of fine character who gave him wise and affectionate care. Lawrence inherited the beautiful estate of Little Hunting Creek, which had been granted to the original settler, John Washington, and which Augustine had done much since 1738 to de-

Washington, oil painting by Gilbert Stuart, *c.* 1795. In the Metropolitan Museum of Art, New York.
By courtesy of the Metropolitan Museum of Art, New York, Rogers Fund, 1907

velop. Lawrence married Anne (Nancy) Fairfax, daughter of Col. William Fairfax, cousin and agent of Lord Fairfax, one of the chief proprietors of the region. Lawrence also built a house and named the 2,500-acre holding Mount Vernon, in honour of the admiral under whom he had served in the siege of Cartagena. Living there chiefly with Lawrence (though he spent some time with his other half brother, Augustine, called Austin, near Fredericksburg), George entered a more spacious and polite world. Anne Fairfax Washington was a woman of charm, grace, and culture; Lawrence had brought from his English school and his naval service much knowledge and experience. A valued neighbour and relative, George William Fairfax, whose large estate, Belvoir, was about four miles distant, and other relatives by marriage, the Carlyles of Alexandria, helped form George's mind and manners.

The youth turned first to surveying as a profession. Lord Fairfax, a middle-aged bachelor who owned more than 5,000,000 acres in northern Virginia and the Shenandoah Valley, came to America in 1746 to live with his cousin George William at Belvoir and to look after his properties.

Two years later he sent to the Shenandoah Valley a party to survey and plot his lands to make regular tenants of the squatters moving in from Pennsylvania. With the official surveyor of Prince William County in charge, Washington went along as assistant. The 16-year-old lad kept a disjointed diary of the trip, which shows skill in observation. He describes the discomfort of sleeping under "one thread Bear blanket with double its Weight of Vermin such as Lice Fleas & c"; an encounter with an Indian war party bearing a scalp; the Pennsylvania-German emigrants, "as ignorant a set of people as the Indians they would never speak English but when spoken to they speak all Dutch"; and the serving of roast wild turkey on "a Large Chip," for "as for dishes we had none."

The following year (1749), aided by Lord Fairfax, Washington received an appointment as official surveyor of Culpeper county, and for more than two years he was kept almost constantly busy. Surveying not only in Culpeper but also in Frederick and Augusta counties, he made journeys far beyond the tidewater region into the western wilderness. The experience taught him resourcefulness and endurance and toughened both body and mind. Coupled with his half brother Lawrence's ventures in land, it also gave him an interest in western development that endured throughout his life. He was always disposed to speculate in western holdings and to view favourably projects for colonizing the West, and he greatly resented the limitations that the crown in time laid on the westward movement. In 1752 Lord Fairfax determined to take up his final residence in the Shenandoah Valley and settled there in a log hunting lodge, which he called Greenway Court, after a Kentish manor of his family. There Washington was sometimes entertained and had access to a small library that Fairfax had begun accumulating at Oxford.

Mount Vernon

The years 1751–52 marked a turning point in Washington's life, for they placed him in control of Mount Vernon. His half brother Lawrence, stricken by tuberculosis, went to Barbados in 1751 for his health, taking George along. From this sole journey beyond the present borders of the United States, Washington returned with the light scars of an attack of smallpox. In July of the next year, Lawrence died, making George executor and residuary heir of his estate in the event of the decease of his daughter, Sarah, without issue. As she died within two months, Washington at the age of 20 became head of one of the best Virginia estates. He always thought farming the "most delectable" of pursuits. "It is honorable," he wrote, "it is amusing, and, with superior judgment, it is profitable." And of all the spots for farming, he thought Mount Vernon the best. "No estate in United America," he assured an English correspondent, "is more pleasantly situated than this." His greatest pride in later days was to be regarded as the first farmer of the land.

He gradually increased the estate until it exceeded 8,000 acres. He enlarged the house in 1760 and made further enlargements and improvements on the house and its landscaping in 1784–86. He tried to keep abreast of the latest scientific advances.

For the next 20 years the main background of Washington's life was the work and society of Mount Vernon. He had to manage the 18 slaves that came with the estate and others he bought later; by 1760 he paid tithes on 49 slaves—though he strongly disapproved of the institution and hoped for some mode of abolishing it. He gave assiduous attention to the rotation of crops, fertilization of the soil, and the management of livestock.

For diversion he was fond of riding, fox hunting, and dancing; of such theatrical performances as he could reach; and of duck hunting and sturgeon fishing. He liked billiards and cards and not only subscribed to racing associations but ran his own horses in races. In all outdoor pursuits, from wrestling to colt breaking, he excelled. A friend of the 1750s describes him as "straight as an Indian, measuring six feet two inches in his stockings"; as very muscular and broad shouldered, but though large boned, weighing only 175 pounds; and as having long arms and legs. His penetrating blue-gray eyes were overhung by heavy brows, his nose was large and straight, and his mouth was large and firmly closed. "His movements and gestures are graceful, his walk majestic, and he is a splendid horseman." He soon became prominent in community affairs, was an active member and later vestryman of the Episcopal Church, and as early as 1755 expressed a desire to stand for the Virginia House of Burgesses.

PREREVOLUTIONARY MILITARY AND POLITICAL CAREER

Early military career.   Traditions of John Washington's feats as Indian fighter and Lawrence Washington's talk of service days helped imbue George with military ambition. Just after Lawrence's death, Lieut. Gov. Robert Dinwiddie appointed George adjutant for the southern district of Virginia at £100 a year (November 1752). The next year he became adjutant of the Northern Neck and Eastern Shore. Then in 1753 Dinwiddie found it necessary to warn the French to desist from their encroachments on Ohio Valley lands claimed by the crown; and after sending one messenger who failed to reach the goal, he determined to dispatch Washington. On the day he received his orders, October 31, 1753, Washington set out for the French posts. His party consisted of a Dutchman to serve as interpreter, the expert scout Christopher Gist as guide, and four others, two of them experienced traders with the Indians. Theoretically, Great Britain and France were at peace; but actually war impended, and Dinwiddie's message was an ultimatum: the French must get out or they would be put out.

Ohio Valley expedition

The journey proved rough, perilous, and futile. Washington's party left what is now Cumberland, Maryland, in the middle of November and despite wintry weather and wilderness impediments reached Fort-Le Boeuf, at what is now Waterford, Pennsylvania, 20 miles south of Lake Erie, without delay. The French commander was courteous but adamant. As Washington reported, his officers "told me, That it was their absolute Design to take possession of the Ohio, and by God they would do it." Eager to carry this alarming news back, Washington pushed off hurriedly with Gist. He was lucky to get back alive. An Indian fired at them at 15 paces but missed; when they crossed the Allegheny River on a raft, Washington was jerked into the ice-filled stream but saved himself by catching one of the timbers. That night he almost froze in his wet clothing. He reached Williamsburg on January 16, 1754, where he hastily penned a record of the journey. Dinwiddie, who was labouring to convince the crown of the seriousness of the French threat, had it printed; and when he sent it to London, it was reprinted in three different forms.

The enterprising governor forthwith planned an expedition to hold the Ohio country. He made Joshua Fry colonel of a provincial regiment, appointed Washington lieutenant colonel, and set them to recruiting troops. Two agents of the Ohio Company, which Lawrence Washington and others had formed to develop lands on the upper Potomac and Ohio rivers, had begun building a fort at what later became Pittsburgh. Dinwiddie, ready to launch into his own war, sent Washington with two companies to reinforce this post. In April 1754 the lieutenant colonel set out from Alexandria with about 160 men at his back. He marched to Cumberland only to learn that the French had anticipated the British blow; they had taken possession of the fort of the Ohio Company and had renamed it Fort-Duquesne. Happily, the Indians of the area offered support. Washington therefore struggled cautiously forward to within about 40 miles of the French position and erected his own post at Great Meadows, near what is now Confluence, Pennsylvania. With this as base, he made a surprise attack (May 28, 1754) upon an advance detachment of 30 French, killing the commander, Coulon de Jumonville, and nine others and making the rest prisoners. The last French and Indian War had begun.

The last French and Indian War

Washington at once received promotion to a full colonelcy and was reinforced, commanding a considerable body of Virginia and North Carolina troops, with Indian auxiliaries. But his attack soon brought the whole French force down upon him. They drove his 350 men into the Great Meadows fort (Ft. Necessity) on July 3, besieged it with 700 men, and, after an all-day fight, compelled him to surrender. The construction of the fort had been a blunder, for it lay in a waterlogged creek bottom, was commanded on three sides by forested elevations approaching it closely, and was too far from Washington's supports. The French agreed to let the disarmed colonials march back to Virginia with the honours of war, but they compelled Washington to promise that Virginia would not build another fort on the Ohio for a year and to sign a paper acknowledging responsibility for "*l'assassinat*" of de Jumonville, a word which Washington later explained he did not rightly understand. He returned to Virginia, chagrined but proud, to receive the thanks of the House of Burgesses, and to find that his name had been mentioned in the London gazettes. His remark in a letter to his brother that "I have heard the bullets whistle; and believe me, there is something charming in the sound" was commented on humorously by Horace Walpole and sarcastically by George II.

The arrival of Gen. Edward Braddock and his army in Virginia in February 1755, as part of the triple plan of campaign that called for his advance on Fort-Duquesne, Gov. William Shirley's capture of Niagara, and Sir William Johnson's capture of Crown Point, brought Washington new opportunities and responsibilities. He had resigned his commission in October 1754 in resentment of the slighting treatment and underpayment of colonial officers and particularly because of an untactful order of the British war office that provincial officers of whatever rank should be subordinate to any officer holding the king's commission. But he ardently desired a part in the war; "my inclinations," he wrote a friend, "are strongly bent to arms." When Braddock showed appreciation of his merits and invited him to join the expedition as personal aide-de-camp, with the courtesy title of colonel, he therefore accepted. His self-reliance, decision, and masterful traits soon became apparent.

At table he had frequent disputes with Braddock, who when contractors failed to deliver their supplies attacked the colonials as supine and dishonest while Washington defended them with warmth. His freedom of utterance is proof of Braddock's esteem. Braddock also accepted from him the unwise advice that he divide his army, leaving half of it to come up with the slow wagons and cattle train and taking the other half forward against Fort-Duquesne at a rapid pace. Washington was ill with fever during June but joined the advance guard in a covered wagon on July 8, begged to lead the march on Fort-Duquesne with his Virginians and the Indian allies, and was by Braddock's side when on July 9 the army was ambushed and bloodily defeated.

In this defeat Washington displayed the combination of coolness and determination, the alliance of unconquerable energy with complete poise, that was the secret of so many of his successes. So ill that he had to use a pillow instead of a saddle and that Braddock ordered his body servant to keep special watch over him, he was everywhere at once. At first he followed Braddock as the general bravely tried to rally his men to push either forward or backward, the wisest course the circumstances permitted. Then he rode back to bring up the Virginians from the rear and rallied them with effect on the flank. To him was largely due the escape of the force. His exposure of his person was as reckless as Braddock's, who was fatally wounded on his fifth horse; Washington had two horses shot under him and his clothes cut by four bullets without being hurt. He was at Braddock's deathbed, helped bring the troops back, and was repaid by being appointed, in August 1755, while still only 23 years old, commander of all the Virginia troops. But no part of his later service was conspicuous. Finding that a Maryland captain who held a royal commission would not obey him, he rode north in February 1756 to Boston to have the question settled by the commander in chief in America, Governor Shirley, and, bearing a letter from Dinwiddie, had no difficulty in carrying his point. On his return he plunged into a multitude of vexations. He had to protect a weak, thinly settled frontier nearly 400 miles in length with only some 700 ill-disciplined colonial troops; to cope with a legislature unwilling to support him; to meet attacks on the drunkenness and inefficiency of the soldiers; and to endure constant wilderness hardships. It is not strange that in 1757 his health failed and in the

Commander of the Virginia troops

closing weeks of that year he was so ill of a "bloody flux" that his physician ordered him home to Mount Vernon.

In the spring of 1758 he recovered sufficiently to return to duty as colonel in command of all Virginia troops. As part of the grand sweep of several British armies organized by Pitt, Gen. John Forbes led a new advance upon Fort-Duquesne. This time Forbes resolved not to use Braddock's road but to cut a new one west from Raystown, Pennsylvania. Washington disapproved of the route but played an important part in the movement. Late in the autumn the French evacuated and burned Fort-Duquesne, and Forbes reared Ft. Pitt on the site. Washington, who had just been elected to the House of Burgesses, was able to resign with the honorary rank of brigadier general.

But though his officers expressed regret at the "loss of such an excellent Commander, such a sincere Friend, and so affable a Companion," he quit the service with a sense of frustration. He had thought the war excessively slow. The Virginia legislature had been niggardly in voting money; the Virginia recruits had come forward reluctantly and had proved of poor quality—he had hanged a few deserters and flogged others heavily. Virginia gave him less pay than other colonies offered their troops. Desiring a regular commission such as his half brother Lawrence had held, he applied in vain to the British commander in North America, Lord Loudoun, to make good a promise that Braddock had given him. Ambitious for both rank and honour, he showed a somewhat strident vigour in asserting his desires and in complaining when they were denied. He returned to Mount Vernon somewhat disillusioned.

Resignation from the colonial army

Marriage and plantation life. Immediately on resigning his commission he was married (January 6, 1759) to Martha Dandridge, the widow of Daniel Parke Custis. She was a few months older than he, was the mother of two children living and two dead, and possessed one of the considerable fortunes of Virginia. Washington had met her the previous March and had asked for her hand before his campaign with Forbes. Though it does not seem to have been a romantic love match, the marriage united two harmonious temperaments and proved happy. Martha was a good housewife, an amiable companion, and a dignified hostess.

Some estimates of the property brought him by this marriage have been exaggerated, but it did include a number of slaves and about 15,000 acres, much of it valuable for its proximity to Williamsburg. More important to Washington were the two stepchildren, John Parke ("Jacky") and Martha Parke ("Patsy") Custis, who at the time of the marriage were six and four, respectively. He lavished great affection and care upon them, worried greatly over Jacky's waywardness, and was overcome with grief when Patsy died just before the Revolution. Jacky died during the war, leaving four children. Washington adopted two of them, a boy and a girl, and even signed his letters to the boy as "your papa." Himself childless, he thus had a real family.

From the time of his marriage Washington added to the care of Mount Vernon the supervision of the Custis estate at the White House on the York River. As his holdings expanded they were divided into farms, each under its own overseer; but he minutely inspected operations every day and according to one visitor often pulled off his coat and performed ordinary labour. As he once wrote, "middling land under a man's own eyes, is more profitable than rich land at a distance." To the eve of the Revolution he devoted himself to the duties and pleasures of a great landholder, varied by several weeks' attendance every year in the House of Burgesses in Williamsburg. During 1760–74 he was also a justice of the peace for Fairfax County, sitting in court in Alexandria.

In no light does Washington appear more characteristically than as one of the richest, largest, and most industrious of Virginia planters. For six days a week he rose early and worked hard; on Sundays he irregularly attended Pohick Church (16 times in 1760), entertained company, wrote letters, made purchases and sales, and sometimes went fox hunting. In these years he took snuff and smoked a pipe; throughout life he liked Madeira wine and punch. Though wheat and tobacco were his staples, he practiced crop rotation on a three-year or five-year plan. He had his own waterpowered flour mill, blacksmith shop, brick and charcoal kilns, carpenters, and masons. His fishery supplied shad, bass, herring, and other catches, salted as food for the Negroes. Coopers, weavers, and his own shoemaker turned out barrels; cotton, linen, and woollen goods; and brogans for all needs. In short, his estates, in accordance with his orders to overseers to "buy nothing you can make yourselves," were largely self-sufficient communities. But he did send large orders to England for farm implements, tools, paint, fine textiles, hardware, and agricultural books and hence was painfully aware of British commercial restrictions.

He experimented in breeding cattle; acquired at least one buffalo, with the hope of proving its utility as a meat animal; and kept stallions at stud. He also took pride in a peach and apple orchard. His care of slaves was exemplary. He carefully clothed and fed them, engaged a doctor for them by the year, refused to sell them—"I am principled against this kind of traffic in the human species"—and administered correction mildly. They showed so much attachment that few ran away.

In the social life of the tidewater region he meanwhile played a prominent role. The members of the council and House of Burgesses, a roster of influential Virginians, were all friends. He visited the Byrds of Westover, the Lees of Stratford, the Carters of Shirley and Sabine Hall, and the Lewises of Warner Hall; Mount Vernon often was busy with guests in return. He liked house parties and afternoon tea on the Mount Vernon porch; he was fond of picnics, barbecues, and clambakes; and throughout life he enjoyed dancing, frequently going to Alexandria for balls. Cards were a steady diversion, and his accounts record sums lost at them, the largest reaching nearly £10. In bad weather his diary sometimes states, "at home all day, over cards." Billiards was a rival amusement. Not only the theatre, when available, but concerts, cockfights, the circus, puppet shows, and exhibitions of animals received his patronage.

He insisted on the best clothes—coats, laced waistcoats, hats, coloured silk hose—bought in London. The Virginia of the Randolphs, Corbins, Harrisons, Tylers, Nicholases, and other prominent families had an aristocratic quality, and Washington liked to do things in a large way. It has been computed that in the seven years prior to 1775, Mount Vernon had 2,000 guests, most of whom stayed to dinner if not overnight.

Prerevolutionary politics. Washington's contented life was interrupted by the rising storm in imperial affairs. The British ministry, facing a heavy postwar debt, high home taxes, and continued military costs in America, decided in 1764 to obtain revenue from the colonies. Up to that time, Washington, though regarded by associates, in Col. John L. Peyton's words, as "a young man of an extraordinary and exalted character," had shown no signs of personal greatness and few signs of interest in state affairs. The Proclamation of 1763 interdicting settlement beyond the Alleghenies irked him, for he was interested in the Ohio Company, the Mississippi Company, and other speculative western ventures. He nevertheless played a silent part in the House of Burgesses and was a thoroughly loyal subject.

Anglo-American tensions

But he was present when Patrick Henry introduced his resolutions against the Stamp Act in May 1765 and shortly thereafter gave token of his adherence to the cause of the colonial Whigs against the Tory ministries of England. In 1768 he told George Mason at Mount Vernon that he would take his musket on his shoulder whenever his country called him. The next spring, April 4, 1769, he sent Mason the Philadelphia nonimportation resolutions with a letter declaring that it was necessary to resist the strokes of "our lordly masters" in England; that courteous remonstrances to Parliament having failed, he wholly endorsed the resort to commercial warfare; and that as a last resort no man should scruple to use arms in defense of liberty. When, the following May, the royal governor dissolved the House of Burgesses, he shared in the gathering at the Raleigh tavern that drew up nonimportation resolutions, and he went further than most of his neighbours in adhering to them. At that time and later he believed with most Americans that peace need not be broken.

Late in 1770 he paid a land-hunting visit to Ft. Pitt, where George Croghan was maturing his plans for the proposed 14th colony of Vandalia. Washington directed his agent to locate and survey 10,000 acres adjoining the Vandalia tract, and at one time he wished to share in certain of Croghan's schemes. But the Boston Tea Party of December 1773 and the bursting at about the same time of the Vandalia bubble turned his eyes back to the East and the threatening state of Anglo-American relations. He was not a member of the Virginia committee of correspondence formed in 1773 to communicate with other colonies, but when the Virginia legislators, meeting irregularly again at the Raleigh tavern in May 1774, called for a Continental Congress, he was present and signed the resolutions. Moreover, he was a leading member of the first provincial convention or revolutionary legislature late that summer, and to that body he made a speech that was much praised for its pithy eloquence, declaring that "I will raise one thousand men, subsist them at my own expense, and march myself at their head for the relief of Boston."

Delegate to the first Continental Congress

The Virginia provincial convention promptly elected Washington one of the seven delegates to the first Continental Congress. He was by this time known as a radical rather than a moderate, and in several letters of the time he opposed a continuance of petitions to the British crown, declaring that they would inevitably meet with a humiliating rejection. " Shall we after this whine and cry for relief when we have already tried it in vain?" he wrote. When the congress met in Philadelphia on September 5, 1774, he was in his seat in full uniform, and his participation in its councils marks the beginning of his national career.

His letters of the period show that while still utterly opposed to the idea of independence, he was determined never to submit "to the loss of those valuable rights and privileges, which are essential to the happiness of every free State, and without which life, liberty, and property are rendered totally insecure." If the ministry pushed matters to an extremity, he wrote, "more blood will be spilled on this occasion than ever before in American history." Though he served on none of the committees, he was a useful member, his advice being sought on military matters and weight being attached to his advocacy of a non-exportation as well as nonimportation agreement. He also helped to secure approval of the "Suffolk Resolves," which looked toward armed resistance as a last resort and which did much to harden the king's heart against America.

Returning to Virginia in November, he took command of the volunteer companies drilling there and served as chairman of the committee of safety in Fairfax County. The unanimity with which the Virginia troops turned to him, though the province contained many experienced officers and Col. William Byrd of Westover had succeeded Washington as commander in chief, was a tribute to his reputation and personality; it was understood that Virginia expected him to be its general. At the March 1775 session of the legislature he was elected to the second Continental Congress and again set out for Philadelphia.

REVOLUTIONARY LEADERSHIP

Head of the colonial forces. Washington's choice as commander in chief of the military forces of all the colonies followed immediately upon the first fighting, though it was by no means inevitable and was the product of partly artificial forces. The Virginia delegates differed upon his appointment. Washington himself recommended Gen. Andrew Lewis for the post, and Edmund Pendleton was, according to John Adams, "very full and clear against it." It was chiefly the fruit of a political bargain by which New England offered Virginia the chief command as its price for the adoption and support of the New England army. This army had gathered hastily and in force about Boston immediately after the clash of British troops and American minutemen at Lexington and Concord on April 19, 1775. When the second Continental Congress met in Philadelphia on May 10, one of its first tasks was to find a permanent leadership for this force. On June 15, Washington, whose military counsel had already proved invaluable on two committees, was nominated and chosen by unanimous vote. Beyond the considerations noted, he owed his choice to the facts that Virginia stood with Massachusetts as one of the most powerful colonies; that his appointment would augment the zeal of the southern people; that he had made an enduring reputation in the Braddock campaign; and that his poise, sense, and resolution had impressed all the delegates. The scene of his election, with Washington darting modestly into an adjoining room and John Hancock flushing with jealous mortification, will alway impress the historical imagination; so also will the scene of July 3, 1775, when wheeling his horse under an elm in front of the troops paraded on Cambridge common he drew his sword and took command of the army investing Boston. News of Bunker Hill had reached him before he was a day's jouney from Philadelphia, and he had expressed confidence of victory when told how the militia had fought. In accepting the command he refused any payment beyond his expenses and called upon "every gentleman in the room" to bear witness that he disclaimed fitness for it. At once he showed characteristic decision and energy in organizing the raw volunteers, collecting provisions and munitions, and rallying Congress and the colonies to his support.

The first phase of Washington's command covered the period from July 1775 to the British evacuation of Boston in March 1776. In those eight months he imparted discipline to the army, which at maximum strength slightly exceeded 20,000; he dealt with subordinates who, as John Adams said, quarrelled "like cats and dogs"; and he kept the siege vigorously alive. Having himself planned an invasion of Canada by Lake Champlain, to be entrusted to Gen. Philip Schuyler, he heartily approved of Benedict Arnold's proposal to march north along the Kennebec River and take Quebec. Giving Arnold 1,100 men, he instructed him to do everything possible to conciliate the Canadians. He was equally active in encouraging privateers to atack British commerce. As fast as means offered, he strengthened his army with ammunition and siege guns, bringing heavy artillery from Ticonderoga over the frozen roads early in 1776. His position was at first precarious, for the Charles River pierced the centre of his lines investing the town; and if the British general, Sir William Howe, had moved his 20 veteran regiments boldly up the stream, he might have pierced Washington's army and rolled either wing back to destruction. But all the generalship was on Washington's side. Seeing that Dorchester heights, just south of Boston, commanded the city and harbour and that Howe had unaccountably failed to occupy it, he seized it on the night of March 4, 1776, placing his Ticonderoga guns in position. The British naval commander declared that he could not remain if the Americans were not dislodged, and Howe, after a storm disrupted his plans for an assault, evacuated the city on March 17. He left 200 cannon and invaluable stores of small arms and munitions. After stamping out the smallpox in Boston and collecting his booty, Washington hurried south to take up the defense of New York.

Washington had won the first round, but there remained five years of the war, during which the American cause was repeatedly near complete disaster. It is unquestionable that Washington's strength of character, his ability to hold the confidence of army and people and to diffuse his own courage among them, his unremitting activity, and his strong common sense constituted the chief factors in achieving American victory. He was not a great tactician: as Jefferson said later, he often "failed in the field"; he was sometimes guilty of grave military blunders, the chief being his assumption of a position on Long Island in 1776 that exposed his entire army to capture the moment it was defeated. At the outset he was painfully inexperienced, the wilderness fighting of the French war having done nothing to teach him the strategy of manoeuvring whole armies. One of his chief faults was his tendency to subordinate his own judgment to that of the generals surrounding him; at every critical juncture, before Boston, before New York, before Philadelphia, in New Jersey, he called a council of war and in almost every instance accepted its decision. Naturally bold and dashing, as he proved at Trenton, Princeton, and Germantown, he repeatedly adopted evasive and delaying tactics on the advice of his associates;

Election as colonial commander

Sources of Washington's military strength

however, he did succeed in keeping a strong army in existence and maintaining the flame of national spirit; and when the auspicious moment arrived, he planned the rapid movements that ended the war.

One element of Washington's strength was his sternness as a disciplinarian. The army was continually dwindling and refilling; politics largely governed the selection of officers by Congress and the states; and the ill-fed, ill-clothed, ill-paid forces were often half-prostrated by sickness and ripe for mutiny. Troops from each of the three sections, New England, the middle states, and the South, showed a deplorable jealousy of the others. Washington was rigorous in breaking cowardly, inefficient, and dishonest men and boasted in front of Boston that he had "made a pretty good sort of slam among such kind of officers." Deserters and plunderers were flogged, and Washington once erected a gallows 40 feet high, writing that "I am determined if I can be justified in the proceeding, to hang two or three on it, as an example to others." At the same time, the commander in chief won the devotion of many of his men by his earnestness in demanding better treatment for them from Congress. He complained of their short rations, declaring once that they were forced to "eat every kind of horse food but hay."

The darkest chapter in Washington's military leadership was opened when, reaching New York in April 1776, he placed half his army, about 9,000 men, under Israel Putnam, on the perilous position of Brooklyn Heights, Long Island, where a British fleet in the East River might cut off their retreat. He spent a fortnight in May with the Continental Congress in Philadelphia, then discussing the question of independence; and though no record of his utterances exists, there can be no doubt that he advocated complete separation. His return to New York preceded but slightly the arrival of the British army under Howe, which made its main encampment on Staten Island until its whole strength of nearly 30,000 could be mobilized. On August 22, 1776, Howe moved about 20,000 men across to Gravesend Bay on Long Island. Four days later, sending the fleet under command of his brother Adm. Richard Howe to make a feint against New York City, he thrust a crushing force along feebly protected roads against the American flank. The patriots were outmanoeuvred, defeated, and suffered a total loss of 5,000 men, of whom 2,000 were captured. Their whole position might have been carried by storm, but fortunately for Washington, General Howe delayed. While the enemy lingered, Washington succeeded under cover of a dense fog in ferrying the remaining force across the East River to Manhattan, where he took up a fortified position. The British, suddenly landing on the lower part of the island, drove back the Americans in a clash marked by disgraceful cowardice on the part of Connecticut and other troops. In a series of actions, Washington was forced northward, more than once in danger of capture, until the loss of his two Hudson River forts, one of them with 2,600 men, compelled him to retreat from White Plains across the river into New Jersey. He retired toward the Delaware while his army melted away, until it seemed that armed resistance to the British was about to expire.

It was at this darkest hour of the Revolution that Washington struck his brilliant blows at Trenton and Princeton, reviving the hopes and energies of the nation. Howe, believing the American army soon would dissolve totally, retired to New York, leaving strong forces in Trenton and Burlington. Washington, at his camp west of the Delaware, planned a simultaneous attack on both posts, using his whole command of 6,000 men. But his subordinates in charge of both wings failed him, and he was left on the night of December 25, 1776, to march on Trenton with about 2,400 men. He completely surprised the unprepared Hessians and after confused street fighting killed the commander, Johann Rall, and captured 1,000 prisoners with arms and ammunition. The immediate result was that General Cornwallis hastened with 8,000 men to Trenton, where he found Washington strongly posted behind the Assunpink Creek, skirmished with him, and decided to wait overnight "to bag the old fox."

During the night, the wind shifted, the roads froze hard,

Battle of New York

Battles of Trenton and Princeton

and Washington was able to steal away from camp, leaving his fires deceptively burning, march around Cornwallis' rear and fall at daybreak upon the three British regiments at Princeton. These were put to flight with a loss of 500 men, and Washington escaped with more captured munitions to a strong position at Morristown, New Jersey. The effect of these victories heartened all Americans, brought recruits flocking to camp in the spring, and encouraged foreign sympathizers with the American cause.

Thus far the important successes had been won by Washington; then they fell to others, while he was left to face popular apathy, military cabals, and the disaffection of Congress. The year 1777 was marked by the British capture of Philadelphia and the surrender of Gen. John Burgoyne's invading army to Gen. Horatio Gates at Saratoga followed by intrigues to displace Washington from his command. Howe's main British army of 18,000 left New York by sea on July 23, 1777, and landed on August 25 in Maryland, not far below Philadelphia. Washington, despite his inferiority of force, for he had only 11,000 men, mostly militia and in Lafayette's words "badly armed and worse clothed," risked a pitched battle on September 11 at the fords of Brandywine Creek, about 13 miles north of Wilmington. While part of the British force held the Americans engaged, Gen. Charles Cornwallis, with the rest, made a secret 17-mile detour and fell with crushing effect on the American right and rear, the result being a complete defeat from which Washington was fortunate to extricate his army in fairly good order. For a time he hoped to hold the Schuylkill Fords, but the British passed them and on September 26 triumphantly marched into Philadelphia. Congress fled to the interior of Pennsylvania, and Washington, after an unsuccessful effort to repeat his stroke at Trenton against the British troops posted at Germantown, had to take up winter quarters at Valley Forge. His army, twice beaten, ill housed, and ill fed, with thousands of men "barefoot and otherwise naked," was at the point of exhaustion; it could not keep the field, for inside of a month it would have disappeared. Under these circumstances, there is nothing that better proves the true fibre of Washington's character and the courage of his soul than the unyielding persistence with which he held his strong position at Valley Forge through a winter of semi-starvation, of justified grumbling by his men, of harsh public criticism, and of captious meddling by a Congress that was too weak to help him.

Washington's enemies seized the moment of his greatest weakness to give vent to an antagonism that had been nourished by sectional jealousies of north against south, by the ambition of small rivals, and by baseless accusations that he showed favouritism to such foreigners as Lafayette. The intrigues of Thomas Conway, an Irish adventurer who had served in the French army and had become American inspector general, enlisted Thomas Mifflin, Charles Lee, Benjamin Rush, and others in an attempt to displace Washington. General Gates appears to have been a tool of rather than a party to the plot, expecting that the chief command would devolve upon himself. A faction of Congress sympathized with the movement and attempted to paralyze Washington by reorganizing the board of war, a body vested with the general superintendence of operations, of which Gates became president; his chief of staff, James Wilkinson, the secretary; and Mifflin and Timothy Pickering, members. Washington was well aware of the hostility in congress, of the slanders spread by Benjamin Rush and James Lovell of Massachusetts, and of the effect of forgeries published in the American press by adroit British agents. He realized the intense jealousy of many New Englanders, which made even John Adams write his wife that he was thankful Burgoyne had not been captured by Washington, who would then "have been deified. It is bad enough as it is." But Washington decisively crushed the cabal when, the loose tongue of Wilkinson having disclosed Conway's treachery, he sent the latter officer on November 9, 1777, proof of his knowledge of the whole affair.

With the conclusion of the French alliance in the spring of 1778, the aspect of the war was radically altered; and the British army in Philadelphia, fearing that a French fleet would blockade the Delaware while the militia of New Jersey and Pennsylvania invested the city, hastily retreated upon New York City. Washington hoped to cut off part of the enemy and by a hurried march with six brigades interposed himself at the end of June between Sir Henry Clinton (who had succeeded Howe) and the Jersey coast. The result was the Battle of Monmouth on June 28, where a shrewd strategic plan and vigorous assault were brought to naught by the treachery of Charles Lee. When Lee ruined the attack by a sudden order to retreat, Washington hurried forward, fiercely denounced him, and restored the line, but the golden opportunity had been lost. The British made good their march to Sandy Hook, and Washington took up his quarters at New Brunswick. Lee was arrested, court-martialled, and convicted on all three of the charges made against him; but instead of being shot, as he deserved, he was sentenced to a suspension from command for one year. The arrival of the French fleet under Adm. Charles-Hector Estaing on July 1778 completed the isolation of the British, and Clinton was thenceforth held to New York City and the surrounding area. Washington made his headquarters in the highlands of the Hudson and distributed his troops in cantonments around the city and in New Jersey.

The final decisive stroke of the war, the capture of Cornwallis at Yorktown, is to be credited chiefly to Washington's vision. With the domestic situation intensely gloomy early in 1781, he was hampered by the feebleness of Congress, the popular discouragement, and the lack of prompt and strong support by the French fleet. A French army under Comte de Rochambeau having arrived to reinforce him in 1780, he pressed Admiral de Grasse to assist in an attack upon either Cornwallis in the south or Clinton in New York. In August the French admiral sent definite word that he preferred the Chesapeake, with its large area and deep water, as the scene of his operations; and within a week, on August 19, 1781, Washington marched south with his army, leaving Gen. William Heath with 4,000 men to hold West Point. He hurried his troops through New Jersey, embarked them on transports in Delaware Bay, and landed them at Williamsburg, Virginia, where he had arrived on September 14. Cornwallis had retreated to Yorktown and entrenched his army of 7,000 British regulars. Their works were completely invested before the end of the month; the siege was pressed with vigour by the allied armies under Washington, consisting of 5,500 Continentals, 3,500 Virginia militia, and 5,000 French regulars; and on October 19 Cornwallis surrendered. By this campaign, probably the finest single display of Washington's generalship, the war was brought to a virtual close.

Washington remained during the winter of 1781–82 with the Continental Congress in Philadelphia, exhorting it to maintain its exertions for liberty and to settle the army's claims for pay. He continued these exhortations after he joined his command at Newburgh on the Hudson in April 1782. He was astounded and angered when some loose camp suggestions found expression in a letter from Col. Lewis Nicola offering a plan by which he should use the army to make himself king. He blasted the proposal with fierce condemnation. When the discontent of his unpaid men came to a head in the circulation of the "Newburgh Address" early in 1783, he issued a general order censuring the paper and at a meeting of officers on March 15 read a speech admonishing the army to obey Congress and promising his best efforts for a redress of grievances. He was present at the entrance of the American army into New York on the day of Clinton's evacuation, November 25, 1783, and on December 4 took leave of his closest officers in an affecting scene at Fraunces' tavern. Travelling south, on December 23, in a solemn ceremonial immortalized by the pen of William Makepeace Thackeray, he resigned his commission to the Continental Congress in the state senate chamber of Maryland in Annapolis and received the thanks of the nation. His accounts of personal expenditures during his service, kept with minute exactness in his own handwriting and totalling £24,700, without charge for salary, had been given the controller of the treasury to be discharged. Washington left Annapolis at sunrise of December 24 and before nightfall was at home in Mount Vernon.

Valley Forge

Plot to displace Washington

Yorktown and the end of the war

In the next four years Washington found sufficient occupation in his estates, wishing to close his days as a gentleman-farmer and giving to agriculture as much energy and thought as to the army. He enlarged the Mount Vernon house; he laid out the grounds anew, with sunken walls, or ha-has; and he embarked on experiments with mahogany, palmetto, pepper, and other foreign trees, English grasses and grains. His farm manager during the Revolution, a distant relative named Lund Washington, retired in 1785 and was succeeded by a nephew, Maj. George Augustine Washington, who resided at Mount Vernon until his death, in 1792. Washington's losses during the war had been heavy, caused by neglect of his lands, stoppage of exportation, and a depreciation of paper money, which cost him hardly less than $30,000. He then attempted successfully to repair his fortunes, his annual receipts from all his estates being from $10,000 to $15,000 a year. In 1784 he made a tour of nearly 700 miles to view the wild lands he owned to the westward, Congress having made him a generous grant. As a national figure, he was constrained to offer hospitality to old army friends, visitors from other states and nations, diplomats, and Indian delegations, and he and his household seldom sat down to dinner alone.

PRESIDENCY

Postrevolutionary politics. Viewing the chaotic political condition of the United States after 1783 with frank pessimism and declaring (May 18, 1786) that "something must be done, or the fabric must fall, for it is certainly tottering," Washington repeatedly wrote his friends urging steps toward "an indissoluble union." At first he believed that the Articles of Confederation might be amended. Later, especially after the shock of Shays's rebellion, he took the view that a more radical reform was necessary but doubted as late as the end of 1786 that the time was ripe. His progress toward adoption of the idea of a federal convention was, in fact, puzzlingly slow. Though John Jay assured him in March 1786 that breakup of the nation seemed near and opinion for the convention was crystallizing, Washington remained noncommittal. But despite long hesitations, he earnestly supported the proposal for a federal impost, warning the states that their policy must decide "whether the Revolution must ultimately be considered a blessing or a curse." And his numerous letters to the leading men of the country assisted greatly to form a sentiment favourable to a more perfect union. Some understanding being necessary between Virginia and Maryland regarding the navigation of the Potomac, commissioners from the two states met at Mount Vernon in the spring of 1785; from this seed sprang the federal convention. Washington approved in advance the call for a gathering of all the states to meet in Philadelphia in May 1787 to "render the Constitution of the Federal Government adequate to the exigencies of the Union." But he was again hesitant about attending, partly because he felt tired and infirm, partly because of doubts about the outcome. Although he hoped to the last to be excused, he was chosen one of Virginia's five delegates.

Washington arrived in Philadelphia on May 13, the day before the opening of the Convention, and as soon as a quorum was obtained he was unanimously chosen its president. For four months he presided over the Constitutional Convention, breaking his silence only once upon a minor question of congressional apportionment. Though he said little in debate, no one did more outside the hall to insist on stern measures. "My wish is," he wrote, "that the convention may adopt no temporizing expedients, but probe the defects of the Constitution to the bottom, and provide a radical cure." His weight of character did more than any other single force to bring the convention to an agreement and obtain ratification of the instrument afterward. He did not believe it perfect, though his precise criticisms of it are unknown. But his support gave it victory in Virginia, where he sent copies to Patrick Henry and other leaders with a hint that the alternative to adoption was anarchy, declaring that "it or dis-union is before us to chuse from," told powerfully in Massachusetts. He received and personally circulated copies of *The Federalist*.

When once ratification was obtained, he wrote leaders in the various states urging that men staunchly favourable to it be elected to Congress. For a time he sincerely believed that, the new framework completed, he would be allowed to retire again to privacy. But all eyes immediately turned to him for the first president. He alone commanded the respect of both the parties engendered by the struggle over ratification, and he alone would be able to give prestige to the republic throughout Europe. In no state was any other name considered. The electors chosen in the first days of 1789 cast a unanimous vote for him, and reluctantly—for his love of peace, his distrust of his own abilities, and his fear that his motives in advocating the new government might be misconstrued all made him unwilling—he accepted.

On April 16, after receiving congressional notification of the honour, he set out from Mount Vernon, reaching New York in time to be inaugurated on April 30. The ceremony was performed in Wall Street, near the spot now marked by Ward's statue of Washington; and a great crowd broke into cheers as, standing on the balcony of Federal Hall, he took the oath administered by Chancellor Robert Livingston and retired indoors to read Congress his inaugural address.

The Washington administration. Washington's administration of the government in the next eight years was marked by the caution, the methodical precision, and the sober judgment that had always characterized him. He regarded himself as standing aloof from party divisions and emphasized his position as president of the whole country by a tour first through the Northern states and later through the Southern. A painstaking inquiry into all the problems confronting the new nation laid the basis for a series of judicious recommendations to Congress in his first message. In selecting the four members of his first cabinet, Thomas Jefferson as secretary of state, Alexander Hamilton as secretary of treasury, Henry Knox as secretary of war, and Edmund Randolph as attorney general, Washington balanced the two parties evenly. But he leaned with especial weight upon Hamilton, supporting his scheme for the assumption of state debts, taking his view that the bill establishing the Bank of the United States was constitutional, and in general strengthening the authority of the federal government.

Distressed when the inevitable clash between Jefferson and Hamilton arose, he tried to keep harmony, writing frankly to each and refusing to accept their resignations. But when war was declared between France and England in 1793, he again took Hamilton's view that the United States should completely disregard the treaty of alliance with France and pursue a course of strict neutrality, while he acted decisively to stop the improper operations of the French minister, Edmund-Charles Genet. He had a firm belief that the United States must insist on its national identity, strength, and dignity. His object, he wrote, was to keep the country "free from political connections with *every* other country, to see them independent of all, and under the influence of none. In a word, I want an *American* character that the powers of Europe may be convinced that we act for *ourselves*, and not for others." The sequel was the resignation of Jefferson at the close of 1793, the two men parting on good terms and Washington praising Jefferson's "integrity and talents." The suppression of the Whisky Insurrection in 1794 by federal troops whom Hamilton led in person and the dispatch of John Jay to conclude a treaty of commerce with Great Britain tended further to align Washington with the Federalist Party. Though the general voice of the people compelled him to acquiesce reluctantly to a second term in 1792 and his election that year was again unanimous, during his last four years in office he suffered from a fierce personal and partisan animosity. This culminated when the publication of the terms of the Jay Treaty, which Washington signed on June 25, 1794, provoked a bitter discussion, and the house of representatives called upon the president for the instructions and correspondence relating to the treaty. These Washington, who had already clashed with the Senate on foreign affairs, refused to deliver; and in the face of an acrimonious debate, he firmly maintained his position.

Early in his first term, Washington, who by education and natural inclination was minutely careful of the proprieties of life, established the rules of a virtual republican court. In both New York and Philadelphia he rented the best houses procurable, refusing to accept the hospitality of George Clinton, for he believed the head of the nation should be no man's guest. He returned no calls and shook hands with no one, acknowledging salutations by a formal bow. He drove in a coach drawn by four or six smart horses, with outriders and lackeys in rich livery. He attended receptions dressed in a black velvet suit with gold buckles, with yellow gloves, powdered hair, a cocked hat with an ostrich plume in one hand and a sword in a white leather scabbard. After being overwhelmed by callers, he announced that except for a weekly levee open to all, persons desiring to see him must make previous engagements. On Friday afternoons the First Lady held informal receptions, at which the President appeared. Though the presidents of the Continental Congress had made their tables partly public, Washington, who entertained largely, inviting members of Congress in rotation, insisted that his hospitality be private. He served good wines and the menus were elaborate, but such visitors as Senator Maclay complained that the atmosphere was too "solemn." Indeed, his simple ceremony offended many of the more radical anti-Federalists, who did not share his sense of its fitness and accused the president of conducting himself as a king. But his cold and reserved manner was caused by native diffidence rather than any excessive sense of dignity.

Retirement. Earnestly desiring leisure, feeling a decline of his physical powers, and wincing under opposition abuse, Washington refused to yield to the general pressure for a third term. This refusal was blended with a testament of sagacious advice to his country in the *Farewell Address* of September 19, 1796, written largely by Hamilton but remolded by Washington and expressing his ideas. Retiring in March 1797 to Mount Vernon, he devoted himself for the last two and a half years of his life to his family, farm operations, and care of his slaves. In 1798 his seclusion was briefly interrupted when the prospect of war with France caused his appointment as commander in chief of the provisional army, and he was much worried by the political quarrels over high commissions; but the war cloud passed away. On December 12, 1799, he exposed himself on horseback for several hours to cold and snow and, returning home exhausted, was attacked late next day with quinsy or acute laryngitis. He was bled heavily four times and given gargles of "molasses, vinegar and butter," and a blister of cantharides (a preparation of dried beetles) was placed on his throat, his strength meanwhile rapidly sinking. He faced the end with characteristic serenity, saying, "I die hard, but I am not afraid to go," and later: "I feel myself going. I thank you for your attentions; but I pray you to take no more trouble about me. Let me go off quietly. I cannot last long." After giving instructions to his secretary, Tobias Lear, about his burial, he died at 10:00 PM on December 14. The news of his death placed the entire country in mourning, and the sentiment of the country endorsed the famous words of Henry Lee, embodied in resolutions which John Marshall introduced in the house of representatives, that he was "first in war, first in peace, and first in the hearts of his countrymen." When the news reached Europe, the British channel fleet and the armies of Napoleon paid tribute to his memory, and many of the leaders of the time joined in according him a preeminent place among the heroes of history.   (Al.N.)

BIBLIOGRAPHY. The earliest known portrait of Washington is that by Charles Willson Peale, painted in 1772. A long line of painters and sculptors followed, and their work may be found criticized in JUSTIN WINSOR (ed.), *Narrative and Critical History of America*, vol. 7 (1888, reprinted 1967). Washington himself thought highly of the likeness by Joseph Wright, painted in 1782. According to Winsor, the favourite profile is Houdon's, while Gilbert Stuart's canvas had been popularly preferred for the full face and John Trumbull's florid paintings for the whole figure. Stuart's pictures are somewhat idealized, while all the later portraits suffer from the fact that the artificial teeth worn by Washington in later years altered the expression of his face. Houdon's statue hardly does justice to Washington's imposing stature, dignified carriage, and great poise. But the Houdon bust, modelled from life, is excellent. For the iconography, see GUSTAV EISEN, *Portraits of Washington*, 3 vol. (1932).

A full compilation of Washington's *Writings* is the United States bicentennial commission edition, ed. by JOHN C. FITZPATRICK, 39 vol. (1931–44). This displaces WORTHINGTON C. FORD, *The Writings of George Washington*, 14 vol. (1889–93); and the edition by JARED SPARKS in 12 vol. (1834–37). The *Diaries* were separately edited by JOHN C. FITZPATRICK in 4 vol. (1925), and later by DONALD JACKSON and DOROTHY TWOHIG in 6 vol. (1976–80). *The Journal of the Proceedings of the President: 1793–97*, ed. by DOROTHY TWOHIG (1981), is an annotated executive daybook covering years for most of which the diaries have not been found. Much the fullest and best biography is that by DOUGLAS SOUTHALL FREEMAN, *George Washington*, 6 vol. (1948–54), which is supplemented by a seventh volume, *First in Peace* (1957), written by his associates JOHN A. CARROLL and MARY W. ASHWORTH. Among good earlier biographies now corrected by Freeman are those by JOHN MARSHALL, *The Life of George Washington* (including plagiarized material) in 5 vol. (1804–07, reprinted 1969); WASHINGTON IRVING, *Life of Washington*, also in 5 vol. (1855–59; reissued in 3 vol., 1982); EDWARD EVERETT HALE, *The Life of George Washington* (1888); HENRY CABOT LODGE, *George Washington*, 2 vol. (1889, reprinted 1972); WOODROW WILSON, *George Washington* (1896, reprinted 1969); WORTHINGTON C. FORD, *George Washington* (1899); and NORMAN HAPGOOD, *George Washington* (1901). A new edition of the early 19th-century biography by MASON L. WEEMS, *The Life of Washington*, was issued in 1977. RUPERT HUGHES published an incomplete three-volume biography in 1926–29. Among the best modern works are JOHN C. FITZPATRICK, *George Washington Himself* (1933, reprinted 1975); SHELBY LITTLE, *George Washington* (1929); MARCUS CUNLIFFE, *George Washington: Man and Monument*, rev. ed. (1982); and JAMES T. FLEXNER, *George Washington: The Forge of Experience, 1732–1775* (1965), *George Washington in the American Revolution, 1775–1783* (1968), *George Washington and the New Nation, 1783–1793* (1970), *George Washington: Anguish and Farewell, 1793–1799* (1972), and *George Washington: The Indispensable Man* (1975). CHARLES C. WALL, *George Washington* (1980), emphasizes the personal life.

Valuable studies on special aspects of Washington's career include: CHARLES H. AMBLER, *George Washington and the West* (1936, reprinted 1971); HUGH CLELAND, *George Washington in the Ohio Valley* (1955); JOHN CORBIN, *The Unknown Washington* (1930, reprinted 1972), largely on his constitutional ideas; PAUL LELAND HAWORTH, *George Washington, Country Gentleman: Being an Account of His Home Life and Agricultural Activities* (1925); EUGENE E. PRUSSING, *The Estate of George Washington, Deceased* (1927); BURKE DAVIS, *George Washington and the American Revolution* (1975), an account of his role as military commander; FORREST McDONALD, *The Presidency of George Washington* (1974), a study of the politics and economics; THOMAS G. FROTHINGHAM, *Washington, Commander in Chief* (1930); HALSTED L. RITTER, *Washington as a Business Man* (1931); CHARLES W. STETSON, *Washington and His Neighbors* (1956); and GEORGE A. BILLIAS (ed.), *George Washington's Generals* (1964, reprinted 1980). PAUL LEICESTER FORD, *The True George Washington* (1896, reprinted 1971; republished as *George Washington,* 1970), is a classic examination of all sides of Washington's career and personality; while CHARLES MOORE has examined *The Family Life of George Washington* (1926). An excellent work on Martha Washington is ANNE HOLLINGSWORTH WHARTON, *Martha Washington* (1897, reprinted 1967), supplemented by PAUL WILSTACH, *Mount Vernon: Washington's Home and the Nation's Shrine* (1916).

(Al.N./Ed.)

Washington, D.C.

The capital of the United States of America, the city of Washington is coextensive with the District of Columbia, whose site was agreed upon by Congress in 1790 as the permanent seat of government for the new nation. It is located at the head of navigation of the Potomac River, which separates it from Virginia to the southwest, while its other boundaries make it essentially a 68-square-mile (177-square-kilometre) enclave carved from Maryland. The Washington Standard Metropolitan Statistical Area (SMSA), however, encompasses 2,809 square miles, including two counties in Maryland and the cities of Fairfax, Falls Church, and Alexandria and four counties in Virginia.

This article is divided into the following sections:

Physical and human geography

CHARACTER OF THE CITY

Washington is one of the few capital cities of the world founded expressly as a seat of government and as a centre for international representation. The expansive designs for the city were to symbolize the ideals of the freedom so recently achieved yet still so tenuously held by the citizenry of the nation. It was to be a vital city, the proper seat for the federal government.

The modern city also holds the nation's most sacred monuments and the most meaningful artifacts of its history, the embassies of foreign nations, and an impressive collection of the national art treasures. Nearly every significant national organization has its headquarters or a major branch in the District, often for the purpose of lobbying in Congress or within federal agencies. The city was meant to be, and has remained, the focal point of the nation for sightseers and for seekers after the spirit of the American past and present.

Impediments to municipal development. For many reasons, Washington has had a development that is unique among the world's major cities. An inherent tendency to distinguish between the District of Columbia as the capital, with its paraphernalia of federal facilities, and Washington as the city, with its complexity of social, economic, and political problems, has produced a somewhat schizophrenic metropolis as notorious for its ugliness and crime as it is famous for its diverse and truly awesome beauties. The city is located near the end of the sprawling urbanized agglomeration that spreads southward from Boston along the Eastern Seaboard, and it has most of the same problems that face other great core metropolises of the region—Boston, New York City, Philadelphia, and Baltimore—and of the nation as a whole.

Another set of disparities exists between the city of Washington and the Washington metropolitan area. More than one-fourth of the people over 26 years of age in the metropolitan area hold college degrees, the highest percentage among the 10 largest such areas in the country, and the area's population has one of the highest annual per capita incomes. On the other hand, a high proportion of the population within the city is made up of families with low incomes or of handicapped or aged persons, many requiring governmental assistance.

These factors provide insight into why Washington—the city as distinct from the capital and the metropolitan area—has developed neither the social stability nor the continuity that provides the lifeblood of most other large cities. Both the living and working populations of Washington are among the most transient in the nation. Only a small percentage of residents have longtime roots in Washington, while a high proportion of government and service workers commute into the city from suburban homes. This more affluent Washington worker typically spends most of his income and pays most of his taxes in adjacent counties and states, leaving the needs and destiny of the city to the dictates of an essentially alien body of lawmakers and administrators.

The incomplete city. With its history and character so profoundly affected by the varying and nonlocal interests and values of Congress, however, concern for Washington's social and environmental quality has been limited. The prominence of the park and highway systems in the city's landscape reflects the interests of Congress and various federal agencies, but the historic lack of concern for the city as a whole has left the grandeur of its vistas, monuments, and governmental facilities in startling contrast to the large areas of the city that have struck many observers as being in advanced stages of physical and spiritual decay.

This situation may be best epitomized in the contrasts of weekday and weekend Washington. Perhaps no other American city except Los Angeles depends so heavily upon private automobiles for transportation. During rush hours, cars and buses choke the streets and avenues of the city, a twice-daily scene interspersed with weekends of deserted streets and empty lots. The lonely grandeur of acres of empty, gleaming public buildings and their attending fountains and statues is a depressingly typical Sunday scene.

The many factors producing this periodic entrance and exit of citizenry may vary little from those in other major cities. The emotional impact in Washington, however, is especially poignant in view of the very different vision of the city's original planners.

THE LANDSCAPE

The city layout. Two elements of the original plan for Washington, completed in 1791 by the French engineer Pierre-Charles L'Enfant, are of special significance. First, his ideas for a capital city were based not on 13 colonies with 3,000,000 inhabitants but on a republic ultimately having 50 states and 500,000,000 citizens. He envisioned a city of 800,000 inhabitants at a time when the entire United States had less than four times that number. Second, L'Enfant had reached artistic maturity in Paris and Versailles, where he was influenced strongly by Baroque landscape architecture, which was at its zenith in the

Concepts underlying L'Enfant's designs

Capitol Hill, with the Capitol in the foreground. The Senate occupies the left wing and the House of Representatives the right. The Supreme Court is at upper left and buildings of the Library of Congress at upper right.
H. Armstrong Roberts

late decades of the 18th century. His original designs for Washington reflected the grandeur both of his projections and of the Baroque.

L'Enfant's basic plan. Perhaps the dominant element in L'Enfant's designs is the complex revolving about the Capitol, the Mall, and the executive mansion, which came to be known as the White House. Both buildings, incorporating elements of Baroque design, were placed to form the background, or terminating vista, of long straight pathways, or malls. Radiating from the buildings were two series of broad avenues converging into circular intersections, the effect of which was to create, in L'Enfant's phrase, "a reciprocity of view," a means of terminating long vistas that would give direction and character to the city and would create throughout it a series of subcentres within view of one another. Most of these subcentres— now circles and squares with small green parks—were carefully located on natural rises in the terrain, as were the Capitol and the White House.

The Mall, which extends from the Capitol to the Lincoln Memorial, was intended to be one broad, tree-lined avenue, in the manner of the Champs-Élysées in Paris, rather than the green lawn, with occasional buildings and a crisscross of roads, that it has become. At the point where the north–south axis of the White House meets the east–west axis of the Capitol, an equestrian statue of George Washington was planned. This spot, slightly relocated because of soft subsoil and subterranean streams, is now the site of the Washington Monument.

Avenues, streets, and quadrants — The pattern of radiating avenues was to be joined and filled by a gridiron matrix of streets. With the Capitol as the axis, the streets were lettered to the north and south, numbered to the east and west, and the avenues were named for the states. The entire city was divided into northwest (NW), northeast (NE), southeast (SE), and southwest (SW) quadrants, also centred on the Capitol. L'Enfant's plan ended to the north at what became Florida Avenue, where a steep bluff was to provide the approaching traveller with the impressive expanse of the city spread out at his feet.

Subsequent development. Even before the Capitol's cornerstone was laid, L'Enfant had been dismissed reluctantly after disagreements with the commissioners in charge of raising the public buildings. During the 19th century and later, the original harmony of his design was eroded with the emergence of new municipal and governmental functions. Awkward relations developed between the grid pattern of cross streets and the diagonal avenues, especially at intersections, while the circular intersections, though providing pleasant oases for pedestrians, were fed by too many streets in the unforeseen age of the automobile and consequently became impediments along the city's thoroughfares. The original plan was effectively lost until 1887, when its recovery revealed that a number of 19th-century buildings along Pennsylvania Avenue, around the White House, and on Capitol Hill had altered the symmetries of the original conception.

The addition of trees along most major avenues and streets, though now a feature of the city, destroyed in great part the concept of a city of magnificent distances. The location of other notable monuments, especially the Lincoln and Jefferson memorials and the John F. Kennedy Center for the Performing Arts, modified the original plan further, as did the placement of various museums and temporary buildings on the Mall. Whatever the impact of later alterations, however, only a few efforts have been made since L'Enfant to redesign the capital totally.

Continuing affective elements of the capital. To the visitor, nothing is more expressive of Washington's character than the dozens of buildings and hundreds of monuments that relate to its functions as the nation's capital. The style of federal architecture has changed several times over the years, and L'Enfant's plans for the location of the Capitol and the White House remain as focal points for a complexity of monuments and buildings that retain a kind of basic coherence to the image of Washington as a capital city.

Dominating the scene, the Capitol offers an impressive silhouette terminating the Mall. Criticized by many as a "potpourri of many chefs," the Capitol may lack the authenticity of the massive Renaissance domes that inspired it, but to many others it offers a feeling of emotional assurance that representative government rests on a broad and solid foundation. The other original building that — The Capitol, the White House, and adjacent buildings

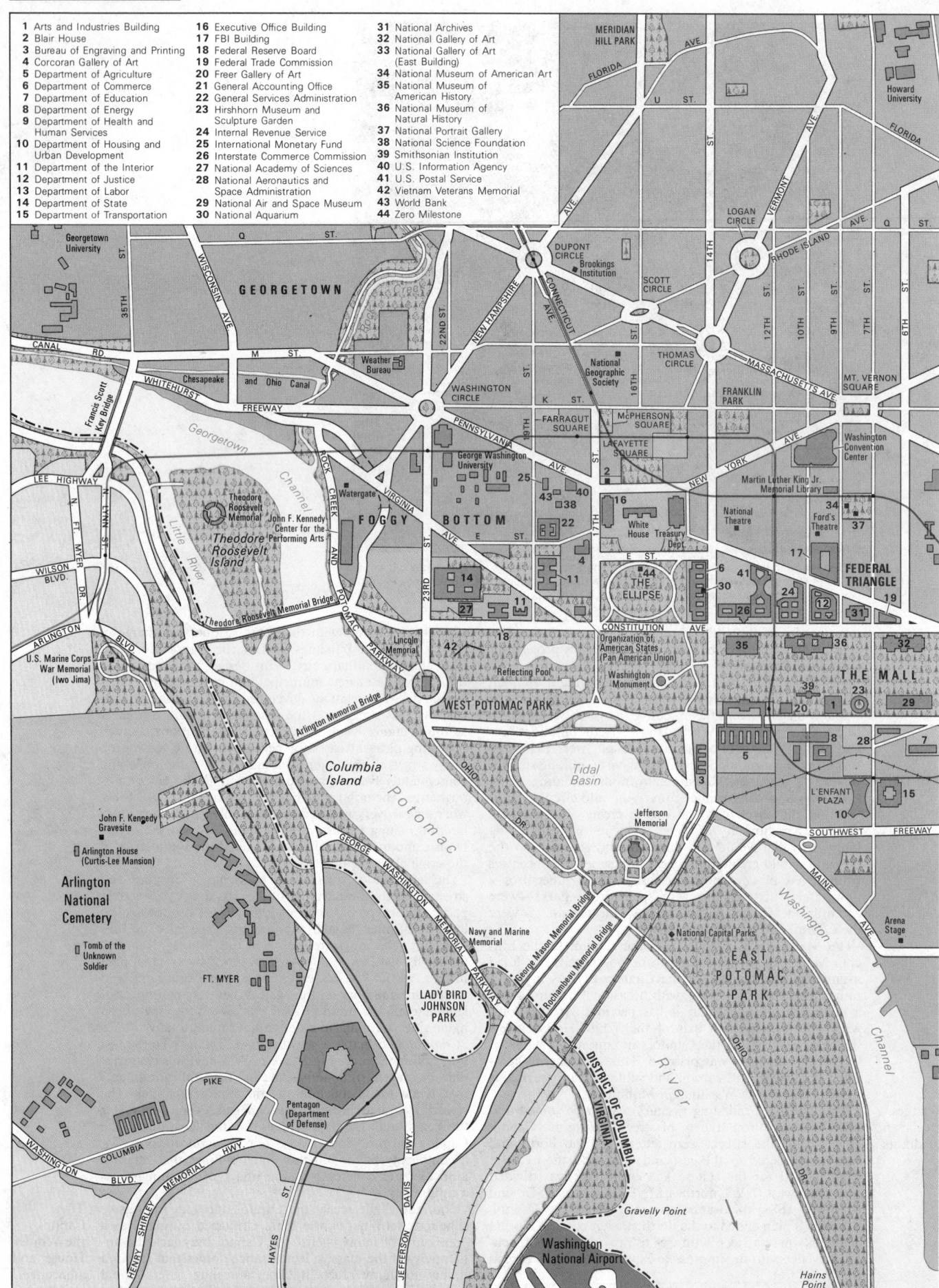

1 Arts and Industries Building
2 Blair House
3 Bureau of Engraving and Printing
4 Corcoran Gallery of Art
5 Department of Agriculture
6 Department of Commerce
7 Department of Education
8 Department of Energy
9 Department of Health and
  Human Services
10 Department of Housing and
   Urban Development
11 Department of the Interior
12 Department of Justice
13 Department of Labor
14 Department of State
15 Department of Transportation

16 Executive Office Building
17 FBI Building
18 Federal Reserve Board
19 Federal Trade Commission
20 Freer Gallery of Art
21 General Accounting Office
22 General Services Administration
23 Hirshhorn Museum and
   Sculpture Garden
24 Internal Revenue Service
25 International Monetary Fund
26 Interstate Commerce Commission
27 National Academy of Sciences
28 National Aeronautics and
   Space Administration
29 National Air and Space Museum
30 National Aquarium

31 National Archives
32 National Gallery of Art
33 National Gallery of Art
   (East Building)
34 National Museum of American Art
35 National Museum of
   American History
36 National Museum of
   Natural History
37 National Portrait Gallery
38 National Science Foundation
39 Smithsonian Institution
40 U.S. Information Agency
41 U.S. Postal Service
42 Vietnam Veterans Memorial
43 World Bank
44 Zero Milestone

Central Washington, D.C., and (inset) its metropolitan area.

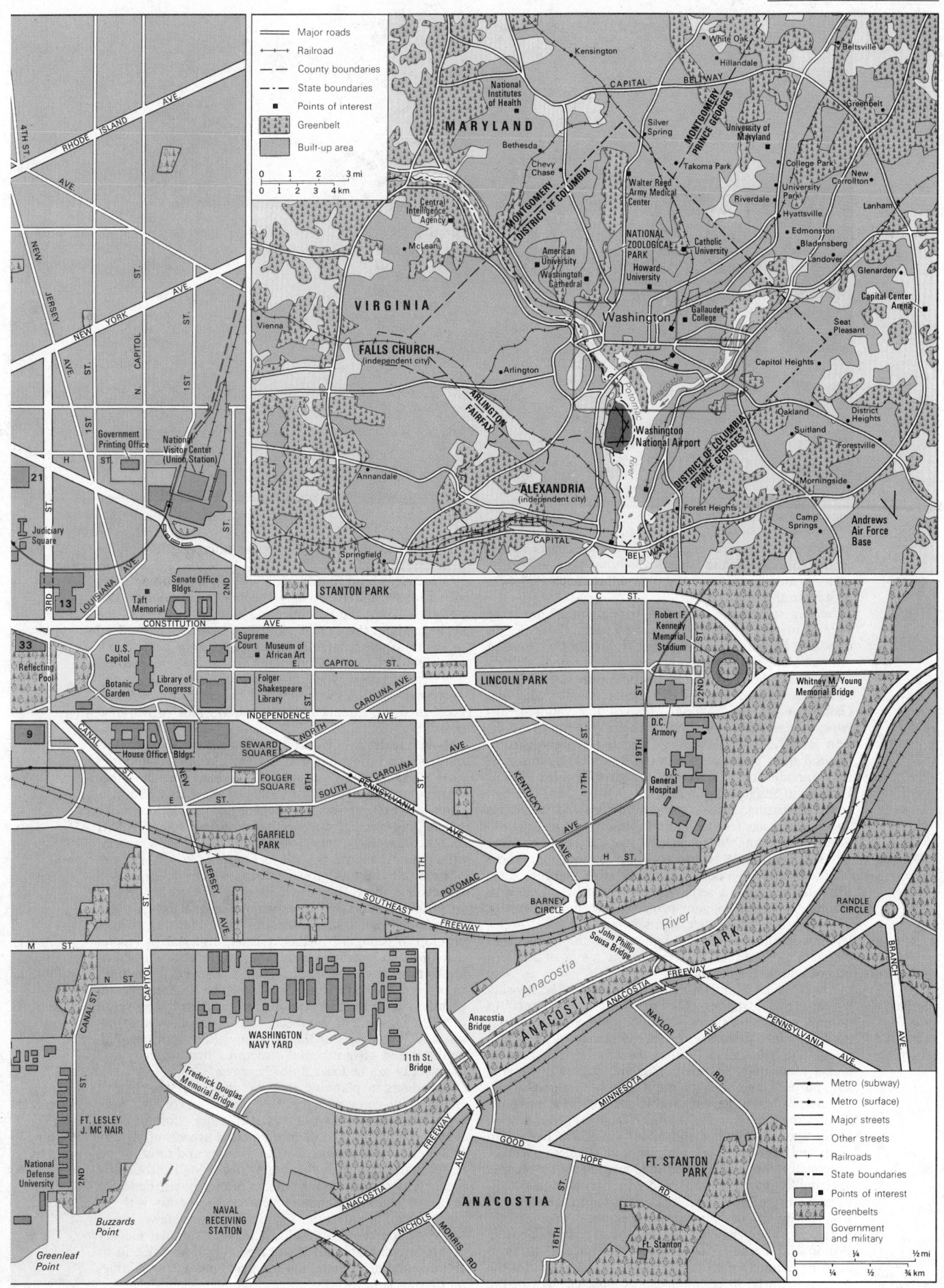

Major roads
Railroad
County boundaries
State boundaries
Points of interest
Greenbelt
Built-up area

0 1 2 3 mi
0 1 2 3 4 km

MARYLAND

Kensington

White Oak

Hillandale

Beltsville

CAPITAL   BELTWAY

National
Institutes
of Health

Silver
Spring

Greenbelt

MONTGOMERY
PRINCE GEORGES

University of
Maryland

Bethesda

Chevy
Chase

Takoma Park

College Park

New
Carrollton

Central
Intelligence
Agency

MONTGOMERY

DISTRICT OF COLUMBIA

Walter Reed
Army Medical
Center

University
Park

Lanham

Riverdale

Hyattsville

Edmonston

McLean

American
University

NATIONAL
ZOOLOGICAL
PARK

Catholic
University

Bladensberg

Landover

VIRGINIA

Washington
Cathedral

Howard
University

Washington

Gallaudet
College

Capital Center
Arena

Glenarden

FALLS CHURCH
(independent city)

Seat
Pleasant

Arlington

Capitol Heights

ARLINGTON
FAIRFAX

Oakland

District
Heights

Washington
National Airport

Suitland

Forestville

Annandale

DISTRICT OF COLUMBIA
PRINCE GEORGES

Morningside

ALEXANDRIA
(independent city)

Forest Heights

Camp
Springs

Andrews
Air Force
Base

Springfield

CAPITAL
BELTWAY

4TH ST.

RHODE ISLAND   AVE.

NEW   JERSEY   AVE.

NEW YORK   AVE.

N   CAPITOL   ST.

1ST   ST.

ST.

Government
Printing Office

National
Visitor Center
(Union Station)

1ST

H
ST.

21

Judiciary
Square

Senate Office
Bldgs.

STANTON PARK

C   ST.

Robert F.
Kennedy
Memorial
Stadium

Whitney M. Young
Memorial Bridge

3RD

13

Taft
Memorial

CONSTITUTION   AVE.

Supreme
Court

Museum of
African Art

E.

CAPITOL   ST.

LINCOLN PARK

22ND   ST.

33

Reflecting
Pool

U.S.
Capitol

Library of
Congress

Folger
Shakespeare
Library

CAROLINA   AVE.

D.C.
Armory

Botanic
Garden

INDEPENDENCE   AVE.

19TH

17TH

LOUISIANA AVE.

2ND

6TH ST.

NORTH   CAROLINA

KENTUCKY

9

CANAL   ST.

House Office   Bldgs.

SEWARD
SQUARE

SOUTH   CAROLINA

AVE.

D.C.
General
Hospital

H   ST.

E
ST.

FOLGER
SQUARE

SOUTH   PENNSYLVANIA   AVE.

NEW   ST.

11TH   ST.

POTOMAC   AVE.

RANDLE
CIRCLE

GARFIELD
PARK

BARNEY
CIRCLE

BRANCH   AVE.

JERSEY   AVE.

SOUTHEAST
FREEWAY

PARK

M   ST.

N   ST.

CANAL   ST.

S   CAPITOL   ST.

John Phillip
Sousa Bridge

River

Anacostia

ANACOSTIA   FREEWAY

PENNSYLVANIA   AVE.

WASHINGTON
NAVY YARD

11th St.
Bridge

ANACOSTIA

NAYLOR   AVE.

Frederick Douglas
Memorial Bridge

Anacostia
Bridge

MINNESOTA   AVE.

FT. LESLEY
J. MC NAIR

FT. STANTON
PARK

National
Defense
University

2ND   ST.

GOOD   HOPE   RD.

Metro (subway)
Metro (surface)
Major streets
Other streets
Railroads
State boundaries
Points of interest
Greenbelts
Government
and military

Buzzards
Point

NAVAL
RECEIVING
STATION

ANACOSTIA   FREEWAY

ANACOSTIA

FT. STANTON

Greenleaf
Point

NICHOLS

MORRIS   RD.

16TH   ST.

Ft. Stanton

0   ¼   ½ mi
0   ¼   ½   ¾ km

The South Portico of the White House.
Authenticated News International

underscores the purposes of L'Enfant is the charming, essentially modest White House, which has been judged by many as among the finest and most appropriate residences of state in the world.

The largest complex of public buildings that joins the Capitol to the White House is the Federal Triangle, an imposing facade of buildings that fronts on Constitution Avenue along the Mall and houses various federal departments and other activities of national importance. Other structures located along the Mall include the National Gallery of Art, the National Archives, the National Museum of Natural History, the National Museum of American History, and the National Air and Space Museum. Around the Capitol on Capitol Hill are the buildings of the Supreme Court, Library of Congress, and the various House and Senate office buildings.

The increasing number of governmental departments and agencies has resulted in an explosion of construction, particularly along Independence Avenue and extending into southwestern Washington's Foggy Bottom area. These buildings have been designed without particular regard for their individuality: a series of shafts or cubes faced with granite or marble. To many people they seem to represent, in contrast to the earlier forms of governmental architecture, an honest but ugly reminder of the anonymous bureaucratic routines upon which so much of modern organizational life depends.

Statuary
and
memorial
structures

Ever since L'Enfant urged that Washington be lavishly equipped with "statues, columns or other ornaments" to honour the nation's great, a continuous effort has been made to assure that no open space in the city lacks its representative monument. Within the District of Columbia alone, more than 300 memorials and statues of varying size, purpose, and aesthetic merit have been raised—from the elegant and inspiring Lincoln and Jefferson memorials and the pure grandeur of the Washington Monument, to the statues of major and minor Civil War heroes, to memorial benches, Doric temples, and Japanese pagodas.

A growing concern that Washington would soon become a veritable quarry of stone and metal monuments dedicated to minor individuals and causes led to a movement toward "living" or "functional" memorials that attempt to translate the personality of the person being honoured. Within this context, the monument dedicated to Pres. John F. Kennedy was designed as a cultural centre for the performing arts. In addition, landscaping changes in the Mall area have removed most of the temporary buildings

and returned the area to a purer interpretation of the L'Enfant design.

Attempts to bring Washington's waterways into an overall national capital plan have been relative failures. Important as were the Potomac and Anacostia rivers in the decision about the capital's location, neither has lived up to its anticipated potentiality in the commercial or cultural life of the city. Technology rendered them obsolete for transportation, while pollution limited their usefulness for recreation. Some modest progress, however, has been made to enhance their aesthetic and recreational possibilities.

Modern features.   Washington as a city has expanded its influence and functions well beyond the 1790 boundaries established for the District of Columbia. Like the other large cities and metropolitan areas of the East Coast, it is beset with extreme social and economic problems. Unlike others, however, its surrounding suburban sprawl is part of other sovereign states, and the District can exercise little political control beyond its borders.

The strain of this growing area, which in large part reflects the increasing size and influence of the federal government, is playing an enormous part in the changing physical character of the central city. Plans to further develop Washington include greater dispersal of federal activities and installations to suburban locations to alleviate transportation problems. Such a movement has been in progress for some time, along with the decentralization of many business and commercial functions. The result of these movements has been to concentrate within the physical boundaries of the city only those monumental, cultural, and governmental structures that logically and historically can be located nowhere else.

The trends in planning that are changing the physical character of contemporary Washington are of two basic types. First, there has been an increasing effort to coordinate and enhance those monumental aspects of the city that are the outstanding physical features and most meaningful to the nation itself—notably in the Mall and Capitol areas. With this trend is the design of new public buildings to operate efficiently and yet blend harmoniously with the older federal architecture. Examples of such newer structures include the East Building of the National Gallery of Art, which employs the so-called L'Enfant Angle in its architectural design, and the congressional office buildings on Capitol Hill.

Second, there have been efforts to make downtown com-

Changes
in the face
of
Washington

mercial activities more attractive, as well as more accessible. Several pedestrian malls have been constructed in the major downtown shopping area, and a new business and commercial complex, L'Enfant Plaza, has been established within walking distance of a number of the newest public buildings. A large convention centre was built, and a subway system, called the Metro, was inaugurated.

Other new features since the city began more rapid changes during the 1970s include the renovation of Pennsylvania Avenue, which was designated as a historic site in 1965; the renovation of Union Station as the National Visitor Center; and the redesigning of Lafayette Square facing the White House, a move that was hotly debated because it involved the razing of a number of fine old buildings. The Vietnam Veterans Memorial, in West Potomac Park, was dedicated on November 11, 1982.

THE PEOPLE

A large majority of the city's population is black; the large increase among blacks since the 1960s is attributed to both natural increase and immigration. The suburban areas, however, remain predominantly white.

In terms of white ethnic composition, Washingtonians tend to reflect the nation as a whole. The city was never a magnet like Boston, New York City, or Chicago for large groups of immigrants from Europe. If any section of the country is overrepresented among Washingtonians, it is the Southeast and the nearby border states. Life in the city often has been described as more Southern and leisurely than Northern and fast-paced—a comparison that sometimes leads to conjectures about how the choice of Washington's site may have affected the functions of the national government throughout its history.

Changes in national administration bring about few real changes in the city's makeup. The personnel of foreign embassies and missions living temporarily or semipermanently in Washington are large in number but relatively small in the total population, and their participation in the city's life generally is fairly circumscribed. If the city has any true social aristocracy (aside from the upper echelons of the administration in power, members of Congress, and other high-ranking government officials), it is composed of a small cadre of well-to-do individuals or families who once held some office, found the capital's life congenial, and remained as permanent residents.

Partially because of its racial and socioeconomic makeup,

the District of Columbia and its surrounding metropolitan counties present a distinctive pattern of population distribution and thus a variability in the city's neighbourhood characteristics.

Generally, within the northwestern area of the city and the suburban triangle of Maryland—including such unincorporated communities as Chevy Chase, Bethesda, and Silver Spring—that flanks this part of the city are located the majority of white middle-class and upper middle-class residents. In the west, overlooking the Potomac, is the oldest neighbourhood, Georgetown, which remains Washington's most exclusive and picturesque residential area. Within these neighbourhoods, extending eastward in the District to Connecticut Avenue and 16th Street, are located nearly all of the foreign embassies, the great churches, private country clubs, and housing that ranges from the moderately affluent to the luxurious.

East of 16th Street and extending north into the Maryland suburbs is the heart of the Washington black community. The area illustrates the considerable diversity in quality of living available to Washington's black residents: from tree-shaded, upper middle-class streets in the vicinity of Howard University to rows of deteriorating houses and tenements. Along 14th Street are the principal areas of vice and crime in the city and the scene of the "April Riots" of 1968.

The southern sections of the city form rather distinct areas, determined partly by geographical features and partly by the racial and socioeconomic character of the residents. The first area comprises the southwestern bank of the Potomac, which is crossed by six bridges joining the District and Virginia. In general this area is nonresidential, but it includes some of the main features of the city's life— the Pentagon, Washington National Airport, Arlington National Cemetery, and George Washington Memorial Parkway. The second area is an irregular triangle formed by the Potomac and Anacostia rivers, which converge at the apex of the triangle. Within this section are located a concentration of modern governmental buildings—Ft. Lesley J. McNair and the National Defense University— and the large recreational complex of East Potomac Park (known popularly as Hains Point). Urban renewal projects in this section have changed the residency pattern from predominantly black slums to white upper middle-class apartment and townhouse buildings. Many of the black residents displaced by the southwestern renewal plans

Ward Howe-FPG

Georgetown, a residential section of Northwest Washington, whose 18th- and early 19th-century architectural design has been preserved by Congressional legislation.

have shifted to already overcrowded northeastern parts of the District or have concentrated in a third major black population area, on the southeastern bank of the Anacostia River. This triangular-shaped, low-income area makes up the southeastern edge of the District and extends into Prince Georges County, Maryland.

THE ECONOMY

Economic dominance of government and tourism

Few cities in the United States are so dominated by the nature of their economic base as is Washington. Only two major economic activities provide virtually all of the income to the city and its residents. The federal civil service is by far the largest single employer in the metropolitan area. Tourism, which includes its retail trade and related services, is second in economic importance. Manufacturing and other commercial activities occupy only a minor place in the economic structure.

Government. The federal government's dominance in establishing the character of economic and social life in Washington can scarcely be overestimated. Although the federal government itself employs a large number of residents of the metropolitan area, the vast majority of employed people are engaged in activities that support or depend upon governmental programs or organizations of national or international scope.

Since the mid-20th century Washington has been transformed from a "federal town" to an information and communication centre that is competitive with the largest urban areas in the United States. In addition, it has become the coordinating centre for major foreign activities. As federal involvement has proliferated in both private and public sectors and both at home and abroad, there has been a steady trend toward relocation of the offices of national associations from cities such as New York and Chicago to the Washington metropolitan area. There are more headquarters of national trade and professional organizations and associations in Washington (about 300) than in any other area of the country. The presence of international organizations such as the World Bank and the International Monetary Fund has increased Washington's importance as one of the principal centres for coordinating aid, trade, and finance on the international level.

The District of Columbia, however, has a large population living at considerably lower socioeconomic levels. These residents, mostly black, also depend upon the opportunities offered for federal employment but generally lack the educational qualifications for jobs at higher incomes. This factor, plus the minimal local control over its revenue system, the lack of significant taxable industry, and the tax-exempt status of the great majority of its real estate, forces the city to depend heavily upon intergovernmental revenue and aids that, in effect, constitute payment by the federal government in lieu of the taxes it would pay if it were a private industry.

Tourism. Because it is the seat of the national government and the site of many of the nation's most significant monuments, Washington's second largest source of income derives from the millions of tourists who visit the city each year. The peak of the tourist influx occurs in the spring and summer months, but the capital city is basically a year-round attraction. In addition, Washington has become increasingly popular as a site for the annual conventions of national organizations and professional associations, most of which, as noted above, maintain a headquarters or branch office in the city. The business community, through such groups as the Metropolitan Washington Board of Trade and with the assistance of the federal government, has organized an increasing number of activities and facilities to make Washington more attractive to its visitors.

Transportation. Prior to the 1970s, various characteristics of the Washington area affected the nature and quality of its transportation networks. First, the L'Enfant plan covered only a small part of the present District of Columbia, excluding completely what has become the suburban area. Although many major radial avenues were extended to and beyond the District's borders, the street patterns outside the original city of 1791 were irregular at best. Second, Washington was a funnel for north–south

traffic along the East Coast until the mid-20th century. In addition, the Potomac and Anacostia rivers always formed barriers to traffic flow between the city and points south. Finally, although it has long been a city of white-collar commuters whose work draws them into the city, the District had barely minimal mass-transit facilities from suburban areas, necessitating nearly total reliance on the automobile.

Since the 1970s modern beltways and freeways have been built to facilitate the flow of traffic around and into the city, and a number of bridges now span the Potomac and Anacostia rivers. A major stimulus to the city's development was the opening of a subway system. The subway and extended rail and bus service are part of the city's modern mass-transit system, operated by the Washington Metropolitan Area Transit Authority. The authority also serves the neighbouring suburbs in Maryland and Virginia.

ADMINISTRATIVE AND SOCIAL CONDITIONS

Government. The city of Washington, as the site of the nation's capital, has evolved a governmental structure that is unique among U.S. cities.

Changing municipal forms. The first government of the city of Washington, established in 1802, comprised a mayor appointed by the president of the United States and a city council elected by the people. The city's character was amended in 1812 to provide for an elected board of aldermen, which, along with the council, elected the mayor. In 1820 Congress permitted the residents to elect both mayor and council. Since Article 1 of the U.S. Constitution empowers Congress to exercise exclusive legislation over the seat of government, however, the powers of the mayor and the council were limited, and their administration of the city was generally ineffectual.

Evolution of District government

In 1871 Congress created a territorial form of government for the District. The officials, all appointed by the president, included a governor, a board of public works, and a legislative assembly comprising an 11-member Council and a 22-member House of Delegates. In addition, the District was permitted a popularly elected, nonvoting delegate to the House of Representatives. This arrangement was abandoned after only three years following a series of financial crises that aroused opposition among both politicians and taxpayers. Congress resumed direct control of the city, providing administration by three commissioners appointed by the president. No provision was made for the franchise under the commissioner form of government, and residents of the District were denied all rights to vote until 1961. The 23rd Amendment to the Constitution then allowed qualified voters to vote in presidential elections but failed to permit participation in elections for local officials, all of whom continued to be appointed.

The issue of home rule for the residents of the District became increasingly prominent in the 1960s, and it was not unrelated to the general struggle for civil rights that characterized the nation as a whole. The most serious criticism of the commissioner form of government was that all legislation affecting it had to be passed by Congress: the House District of Columbia Committee and the Senate Governmental Affairs Committee were required to initiate all legislation pertaining to the District. Since the members of these committees were not permanent residents of Washington and represented constituencies that had little or no interest in the problems of the city, the responsiveness of Congress was felt by many to be slow or entirely lacking. Efforts on the part of various local groups over the years to achieve some degree of home rule were consistently blocked by the House committee, although the Senate committee passed five such bills between 1951 and 1963. It was often pointed out that the committees tended to be dominated by Southern congressmen who resisted efforts to give the franchise and other powers to the District because of its increasing black majority.

In 1967 Congress reorganized the District's government, abolishing the three-commissioner system and creating in its place a single commissioner (who assumed the title of mayor), an assistant commissioner, and a nine-member city council, all appointed by the president. The city council was given authority to exercise certain legislative and regulatory powers once vested in the three commissioners, but such actions were subject to the veto of the mayor. In 1970 Congress created again the position of a nonvoting delegate to the House of Representatives, elected by residents of the District.

Movement toward home rule has continued. In 1973, under President Nixon, the limited Home Rule Act of 1964 was amended, providing for the popular election every four years of the mayor and city council members. In addition, the city council was expanded to 13 members. The mayor was given broader reorganizational and appointive authority. The city council was empowered to establish and set tax rates and fees, make changes in the budget, and organize or abolish any agency of government of the District. Congress, in turn, reserved the power to veto any actions of the District government that threaten the "federal interest." Thus, while the District has a recognizable municipal form of government, Congress continues to treat it in some respects as a branch of the federal government. The city's "district attorney" is the U.S. attorney for the District of Columbia, appointed by the president. The budget, passed by the city council and approved by the mayor, is reviewed and enacted by Congress. Moreover, Congress retains the right to enact legislation on any subject for the District, whether within or outside of the scope of power delegated to the city council.

Administration of municipal services. As under previous forms of government, municipal functions remain in control of a combination of local and federal committees. School-board members, formerly appointed by the U.S. District Court for the District of Columbia, became popularly elected in 1968. Public utilities are under a Public Service Commission appointed by the president. The zoning of private property is handled by the Zoning Commission, consisting of the mayor, the chairman of the city council, the Architect of the Capitol, and the director of the National Park Serivce. The water supply is under the jurisdiction of an Army engineer, given the title of District Engineer, but its distibution is controlled by the mayor. The National Park Service supervises the public parks of the city.

Public security and law enforcement are handled by four separate law-enforcement agencies, each with its own jurisdictional area. Under the mayor is the Metropolitan Police Force, which has the responsibility for enforcing the laws and ordinances of the municipal government. The Capitol Police are repsonsible for the security of the Capitol building and its grounds. The White House Security Guard protects the White House and the president, while the National Park Police are responsible for all public parks and many recreational facilities.

Overlapping federal and District responsibilities

Court system. The unwieldiness of Washington's governmental apparatus has long been most apparent in the operation of its courts. Until the early 1970s legal jurisdiction over District matters was shared by two federal courts and three local courts, appeals from which were directed to separate appeals courts. The Court Reorganization Plan, was implemented in 1970 to reduce the confusion and inefficiency of this judiciary system.

Under the plan a single trial court, the Superior Court of the District of Columbia, was established to assume the functions of all the former federal and local courts. A single appeals court, the U.S. Court of Appeals for the District of Columbia, was established to function in a manner similar to a state supreme court. For the first time in its history, Washington had an integrated court system similar to the systems in all of the states.

Public services. Washington's multitude of intertwined and seemingly insoluble social problems—such as race, poverty, crime, civil disorder, institutionalized inequality in education and other fields, and environmental pollution—is by no means unique. Like other cities, it finds social needs increasing as its human and financial resources decline. The District government can accomplish little in the way of service to its citizens without the support of the federal government. Some authorities have seen the suburban areas, with the high educational levels of their population and without high proportions of blue-collar workers, as being more willing than the federal government to assist the plight of the core city.

Employment. Two-thirds of Washington's employed live outside the District of Columbia and represent work force that is highly specialized, professionally skilled, and well above the national averages in educational level and per capita income. Among the residents of the city of Washington, where a majority of the residents are black, the unemployment rate, especially among youth, ranges well above the national average. Educational level and per capita income are considerably below the averages found in the surrounding suburbs. Nothing expresses the dilemma of the "two" Washingtons more clearly than the characteristics and location of its labour force.

Housing. In spite of the fact that the Washington metropolitan area experienced a decline in its rate of population growth (with an absolute decline in the District of Columbia) in the 1970s, the demand for housing has remained high. This demand was generated by a high rate of household formation, primarily among young adults (mostly affluent, one-family or single householders) from the post-World War II "baby boom" generation. Competition for existing housing resources has intensified between

Photo Research International

Promenade along the Potomac River in Southwest Washington.

new householders and existing occupants. This has stimulated not only the conversion of rental apartments to condominiums but also the renovation of many single-family dwellings formerly occupied by lower income renters. While this "gentrification" process has resulted in the upgrading of a number of residential areas in the District, it has aggravated the problems of household displacement, primarily among lower income black families, and has increased the pressure on the older, inner suburbs of the metropolitan area.

Fair housing at the federal, state, and local levels has reduced the more blatant forms of discrimination against racial minorities, but new construction of low-rental housing has been negligible. The consequences for this segment of the Washington population remains grave, and housing continues to be a major public-policy and local issue.

Education. More than any other service of the District government, the public school system must be understood in the context of the city's racial composition. Two public-opinion polls taken in Washington in 1954 clearly indicated that the majority of white residents disapproved of the U.S. Supreme Court decision declaring racial segregation of public schools to be unconstitutional. This decision probably contributed significantly to the subsequent large-scale emigration of white families from the District. A number of whites who remained in the District at that time sought transfers for their children to schools with low black enrollments, while many other children were transferred to private schools.

In 1956 the public school system initiated a new program, now familiarly known as the track system, or ability grouping, into four curricular tracks: honours, college preparatory, general, and basic. The objective of the program was to allow students of similar academic achievement to work together regardless of race. Opposition to this system grew in intensity throughout the 1960s. To many, the track system produced only a new form of segregation, since most of the black students gravitated to the general or basic curriculums. The system was abolished in 1966 through a court action brought by civil rights leaders against the District superintendent of schools.

By the early 1970s the public school system had become 94 percent black. A 15-month study of the situation after the court action of 1966 concluded that no school system with so heavy a racial imbalance could consider desegregation in any meaningful way, that desegregation methods that might work in other cities were largely irrelevant in Washington.

Aspects of black militancy. During the 1960s, and particularly after the fusion of the civil rights movement and the antipoverty programs, racial politics became of increasing importance in Washington, affecting the administration of all public services. After 1964 many new groups were formed that reflected the increasing militancy among the city's blacks who are the recipients or the victims of public services in the District.

In the framework of dissatisfaction and turmoil over the issue of desegregation and quality of education, Congress granted District citizens the right to elect their own Board of Education in 1968. The advent of this elected school board was viewed by many as the beginning of progress toward a public school system more responsive to the needs and aspirations of the predominantly·black community.

On the other hand, Congress retained the ultimate right to review all budget requests upon which any new educational programs must rely. In addition, activity on behalf of the public schools tended to be divided between groups that focussed their activity on the school board and the District government and groups that tended to bypass District agencies and take their case directly to Congress.

Higher education. Several institutions of higher learning offering undergraduate and graduate programs are located in the metropolitan area. Georgetown University, founded in 1789 as a seminary, is the area's oldest; with the Catholic University of America (opened in 1889), it makes Washington a centre of Roman Catholic education. The George Washington University, chartered as Columbian College in 1821, and American University, chartered in 1893, have become large, diversified universities. Howard

University, chartered in 1867 for the higher education of blacks, offers a wide variety of graduate and professional programs and is supported largely by federal appropriations. Federal City College, founded in 1969 and renamed the University of the District of Columbia in 1977, is a municipal institution. These six institutions within the District form the Consortium of Universities, which offers a combined facility for undergraduate and graduate education and a common pool of resources. Gallaudet College (founded in 1857 and an associate member of the Consortium), for the education of the deaf, receives both private and federal support. The University of Maryland, George Mason College, and the Northern Virginia Campus of the University of Virginia are located in suburban areas.

In addition, numerous federal and privately funded institutions and associations produce a variety of both statistical and scholarly materials. The Brookings Institution is a nationally recognized centre for research in politics and economics; and the jointly administered National Academy of Sciences, National Academy of Engineering, Institute of Medicine, and National Research Council provide public and private bodies with the research potentiality and publications of their memberships, comprising many of the most eminent scientists in the nation. The National Institutes of Health offer both a centre and funding for basic and applied research in wide areas of medicine and mental health.

CULTURAL LIFE

Until the end of World War II, Washington was literally outside the main centres of American arts and letters, and the original plan for the city to become a focus of national culture was far short of realization. Its institutions of higher education were uniformly small, poor, and struggling; it had no significant collections of art; its facilities for the performing arts were either too small, inconveniently located, or nonexistent; and the only truly national museum, the Smithsonian Institution, was laughingly characterized as "the nation's junk closet."

In early descriptive guides to the city, the section on cultural facilities was devoted largely to the number and variety of churches, which were distinguished mostly for the presidents of the United States who had attended them. Practically alone on the scene was the magnificent Library of Congress, with the largest collection of books, maps, newspapers, documents, and manuscripts in the world. Since World War II, however, the development of cultural and recreational facilities in Washington has been one of the city's—and the nation's—proudest achievements.

The arts. Since its opening in 1941, the National Gallery of Art has become recognized internationally as one of the world's major art collections. Together with the Corcoran Gallery of Art, the Phillips Collection, the Freer Gallery of Art, and the National Portrait Gallery and National Museum of American Art, the capital city has achieved a position of eminence in the art world.

Washington's Arena Stage has been recognized since its founding in 1950 as one of the leading regional theatre companies in the nation, both for the excellence of its productions and for its leadership in seeking out new playwrights. The National Symphony Orchestra has begun to achieve national acclaim. Aside from these features, the performing arts in the city comprised little more than road shows from New York City or pre-Broadway tryouts until the opening in 1971 of the John F. Kennedy Center for the Performing Arts, with its three theatres for music, opera, and drama. The renovation of historic Ford's Theatre, the scene of the assassination of Pres. Abraham Lincoln in 1865, has offered Washingtonians a unique opportunity to enjoy programs of cultural value in a setting of historical significance.

Architectural Washington holds interest outside its monumental areas. Prominent examples include the many fine 19th-century mansions, many of which are occupied by foreign embassies, along Massachusetts Avenue and in the area around Dupont Circle. Entire blocks of slum buildings of the Capitol Hill and other areas, deteriorated from a grander past, have undergone considerable renovation. Numerous homes in the Georgetown area, similarly re-

Imbalances and restructurings of schools

Major art collections

newed beginning in the 1930s, offer fine examples of the American Federal style of architecture dating from the early years of the nation. A stunning example of landscape architecture including formal gardens and a bird sanctuary, as well as a museum and research library of medieval art, is on display at Dumbarton Oaks.

Smithsonian Institution

National collections. The Smithsonian Institution has reorganized and more effectively displayed its enormous collections of natural and historical material. The National Museum of Natural History has been since 1951 the largest permanent exhibition in the world of anthropological, biological, and geological specimens relating to the United States and its possessions. The National Museum of History and Technology presents the history of social and technological achievements. Throughout the 1970s the growth of Smithsonian Institution facilities was dramatic. The addition of the East Building of the National Gallery of Art, designed to house a growing collection of 20th-century art and international exhibitions, has provided Washington with opportunities enjoyed by only a handful of U.S. cities. The National Air and Space Museum was constructed for the display and study of America's accomplishments in flight. Finally, the donation of the Hirshhorn Museum and Sculpture Garden has enriched the city and its appreciation of trends in modern art. Located together on the Mall between the Capitol and the Washington Monument, these various facilities of the Smithsonian Institution attract millions of visitors each year. The nearby National Archives supplements the riches of the Library of Congress with its thorough collection of documents from American history, headed by the original Declaration of Independence and Constitution.

Festivals. The traditional Cherry Blossom Festival held early each spring is the oldest of Washington's celebrations that combine the efforts of federal, civic, and commercial personnel. In spite of their attraction for tourists, the festival parade and crowning of a queen tend to be less important for Washingtonians than is the explosion of blossoms around the Tidal Basin and the Jefferson Memorial that the festival marks.

Also popular is Washington's annual festival of American folk arts and crafts, held for a week each summer on the Mall. This open-air display of the arts and crafts of many regional and ethnic subcultures has become an increasingly significant cultural event for Washington and for the nation as a whole.

Recreation. Much of Washington's elaborate system of public parks and other open spaces was designed to heighten the visual impression of the federal buildings, but they have been applied increasingly to recreational purpose. The original L'Enfant plan set aside 17 areas for parks, including the Mall, the Washington Monument grounds, the Capitol Hill grounds, the White House grounds (including the present Lafayette Square), and the small plots of grass at the intersections of the major avenues. The preservation of these areas and the addition of others provides Washington with the several hundred parks and green spaces whose maintenance and development have been continuous functions of the National Capital Parks, under the Department of the Interior, since 1791.

Rock Creek Park and the out-of-doors

In 1890 the city acquired Rock Creek Park, one of the largest natural parks within the boundaries of any city in the world. It comprises 1,754 acres (710 hectares) of virgin woodland forming the mile-wide valley of Rock Creek, which traverses the northwestern quarter of the city from suburban Silver Spring to the Potomac and is extensively developed for recreational uses. Within its boundaries is the National Zoological Park, occupying 176 acres of picturesque wooded hills and grassy meadows. Also within Rock Creek Park is the Carter Barron Amphitheater, where musical programs are presented in a wooded setting during the summer. Nature walks, horse trails, picnic areas, and sports facilities are spread throughout the park.

For 15 miles, from Georgetown to the Great Falls of the Potomac River (the shores of which have been protected from uncontrolled development on both the Virginia and District sides), stretches the historic Chesapeake and Ohio Canal, the original project of George Washington, which

Rock Creek Park.
Carl Purcell

has been restored and declared a national monument. The towpath beside the canal is now available for hiking and bicycling, and regularly scheduled trips are enjoyed by visitors in reconstructed, mule-drawn canal boats. On the Virginia shore is the scenic George Washington Memorial Parkway, from which motorists may enjoy a nearly uninterrupted view of the Potomac from above the northwestern boundary of the District to Mount Vernon, the home of Washington, below Alexandria. Between Georgetown and the Virginia shore lies Theodore Roosevelt Island, once a private plantation but now a nature sanctuary. The island is used as a wilderness strolling place for Washingtonians seeking relief from the city and offers one of the area's most tranquil and beautiful natural settings.

History

THE EARLY PERIOD

The idea of a national capital city seems to have originated at a meeting of the Congress in June 1783 in the Old City Hall in Philadelphia. The War of Independence had but recently been concluded, the treasury was empty, the nation had no credit, and it was heavily in debt to its soldiers for back pay. There was no president, and, though the 13 colonies were free, they remained a gathering of semi-independent sovereignties with divergent interests. On June 20 a large body of unpaid soldiers invaded Philadelphia to present their grievances to Congress.

Conception, siting, and design. No actual violence occurred, but a number of congressmen started a movement to establish a federal city where the lawmakers could conduct the business of government without fear of intimidation. Several locations were considered over the next six years, but Northern and Southern disagreements prevented decision until 1790.

Although the decision to locate the capital on the Potomac was largely a political compromise, selection of the exact site for the city was left to the newly elected president, George Washington. The chosen district, or territory

Bases of site selection

as it was first called, was 10 miles square. Georgetown to the north and Alexandria to the south were both in the original district, while a third village, Hamburg, lay by the riverfront swamps in a part of Washington known traditionally as Foggy Bottom.

Important to Washington in his selection was the site's commercial potential. The river was navigable to Georgetown, an important tobacco market. The construction of a canal from there across the Cumberland Gap to the "western frontier" would tap the produce of the vast country beyond that was being opened to settlement. The President had established a private canal construction company before the final decision had been reached, but he immediately relinquished his interests in it.

While in Philadelphia, Washington negotiated with Pierre-Charles L'Enfant to lay out a plan for the new city. A volunteer in the Revolution whose democratic idealism was unquestioned, a well-trained engineer, and an artist who had designed the setting for the President's inaugural ceremonies in New York City, L'Enfant was highly respected and admired. Apparently sensing the historic significance of his appointment, he conceived his plan on a grand scale.

The Capitol's cornerstone was laid by Washington in September 1793, and construction was begun on the White House, designed by an Irishman, James Hoban, and on a modest cluster of nearby office buildings to house governmental departments. In October 1800 the archives, general offices, and officials of the government were moved to Washington from Philadelphia. Pres. John Adams took up residence in the White House, and Congress met for the first time in the newly completed Senate wing of the Capitol.

The young city. Descriptions of life in early Washington reveal many of the shortcomings resulting from establishment of a capital city by fiat amid what was essentially a wilderness. What was conceived as a "city of magnificent distances" or, in Washington's words, "the Emporium of the West" was referred to by various statesmen and congressmen as "wilderness city," "Capital of Miserable Huts," "A Mud-hole Equal to the Great Serbonian Bog," and similar epithets. By the close of Thomas Jefferson's term of office in 1808, the population was scarcely 5,000. Until the introduction of the steam engine and the telegraph, a more or less continuous agitation went on in Congress and in the national press to move the capital because of its remoteness and inaccessibility.

Achievement of identity as the national capital

In 1814 the capital was temporarily abandoned as the result of the invasion by a British force under Admiral Sir George Cockburn, who ordered the burning of the Capitol, the White House, and the Navy Arsenal. Although this action was rather inconsequential to the outcome of the War of 1812, it had the effect of solidifying Washington in the minds of many Americans as the national capital. Public indignation over destruction of the seat of government ended all significant movements to relocate the federal city, and Washington became the national capital in fact as well as in name. By the outbreak of the Civil War, the intensity of this image was firmly established. The course of that conflict was deeply affected by the actions of the federal government to defend Washington

at all costs from nearby Confederate forces, who often threatened the city from several sides. If the Civil War was the final stage of the historical process that changed a loose confederation of states into a united republic, it was also effective in completing the identity of Washington as the capital of the United States.

EVOLUTION OF THE MODERN CITY

Originally, the city of Washington and the District of Columbia were not coextensive, either geographically or administratively. The 10-mile-square district was reduced by about one-third in 1847 by the return of the land south of the Potomac to the state of Virginia. Alexandria city resumed its former independent existence, while Arlington County was created from the remainder. Self-governing bodies within the district existed until 1895, when Georgetown was annexed by Washington.

During and after the Civil War the District's population more than doubled within a few years, suddenly including 40,000 freed slaves who set a pattern of racial diversity that was to have a major impact on the city's life. The following century was filled also with physical and demographic growth and change within the city, with numerous political modifications attempting to harmonize the District's needs with its inherent status in relation to Congress, and with continuing activities to refine the cultural and monumental image of the city.

By the latter third of the 19th century the city had constructed an impressive number of monuments, but then and later many slums began to intrude on the city's image. Transformation of this and other problems was cut short by World Wars I and II but carried on after their conclusions. During the 20th century the city increasingly became a Mecca not only for visitors seeking from its many shrines a sense of the American heritage but also for protest groups—from several groups of veterans seeking pensions to blacks seeking relief from poverty and repression and youths decrying the war in Vietnam.

BIBLIOGRAPHY. For a general description and guide to the city, see JUDY DUFFIELD, *Washington, D.C.: The Complete Guide* (1982); and E.J. APPLEWHITE, *Washington Itself* (1981). For early descriptions of the city and its life, see CHRISTEN HINES, *Early Recollections of Washington City* (1866); and GEORGE WATTERSON, *A Picture of Washington* (1840). A complete and reliable history is WILHELMUS B. BRYAN, *A History of the National Capital*, 2 vol. (1914–16). More recent histories include CONSTANCE GREEN, *Washington*, 2 vol. (1962–63, reissued 1976); and DAVID L. LEWIS, *District of Columbia: A Bicentennial History* (1976). Among excellent works on planning for the city are GEORGE W. GRIER, *Washington and its Suburbs* (1971); FREDERICK A. GUTHEIM, *Planning Washington 1924–1976* (1976); UNITED STATES NATIONAL CAPITAL PLANNING COMMISSION, *Worthy of the Nation: The History of Planning for the National Capital* (1977); ATLEE E. SHIDLER (ed.), *Greater Washington in 1980* (1980); GEORGE and EUNICE GRIER, *Washingtonians in the 1980's* (1981); NELSON F. RIMENSNYDER, *The Political Evolution of the District of Columbia: Current Status and Proposed Alternatives* (1975); LEAGUE OF WOMEN VOTERS OF THE DISTRICT OF COLUMBIA, *Know the District of Columbia* (1980); and DISTRICT OF COLUMBIA OFFICE OF PLANNING AND DEVELOPMENT, *Comprehensive Plan for the National Capital: District of Columbia Components* (1982).

(Ri.W.S.)

Wellington

Arthur Wellesley, 1st duke of Wellington, twice reached the zenith of fame with a period of unexampled odium intervening. By defeating Napoleon at Waterloo he became the conqueror of the world's conqueror. After Waterloo he joined a repressive government, and later, as prime minister, he resisted pressure for constitutional reform. False pride, however, never prevented him from retreating either on the field or in Parliament, and for the country's sake he supported policies that he

personally disapproved. In old age he was idolized as an incomparable public servant—the Great Duke. Reaction came after his death. He has been rated an overcautious general and, once, Britain's worst 19th-century prime minister. Today there is widespread appreciation of his military genius and of his character as an honest and selfless politician, uncorrupted by vast prestige.

Early life. Arthur Wesley (later, from 1798, Wellesley) was born on May 1, 1769, in Dublin, the fifth son of the

Duke of Wellington, portrait by Francisco de Goya, 1812.
In the National Gallery, London.

1st earl of Mornington. Too withdrawn to benefit from his Eton schooling, he was sent to a military academy in France, being, in his widowed mother's words, "food for powder and nothing more." At the age of 18 he was commissioned in the army and appointed aide-de-camp to the Irish viceroy. In 1790–97 he held the family seat of Trim in the Irish Parliament. At 24, though in debt, he proposed to Catherine (Kitty) Pakenham but was rejected. Arthur abandoned heavy gambling to concentrate on his profession. As lieutenant colonel of the 33rd Foot by purchase, he saw active service in Flanders (1794–95), learning from his superiors' blunders. After failing to obtain civil employment, he was glad to be posted to India in 1796.

Service in India

In India he adopted a regimen of abstemiousness and good humour. The arrival of his eldest brother, Richard, as viceroy enabled him to exploit his talents. He commanded a division against Tipu Sultan of Mysore, became governor of Mysore (1799) and commander in chief against the Marāthās. Victories, especially at Assaye (1803), resulted in a peace that he himself negotiated. All the successful qualities he later exhibited on European battlefields were developed in India: decision, common sense, and attention to detail; care of his soldiers and their supplies; and good relations with the civilian population. Napoleon was unwise in later writing him off as a mere "Sepoy general." He returned to England in 1805 with a knighthood.

Wellesley's new assignments were disappointing: an abortive expedition to Hanover, followed by a brigade at Hastings. But he felt he must serve wherever duty required. One duty was to marry his faded Kitty in 1806; another was to enter Parliament in order to repel radical attacks on his brother's Indian record. He spent two years in Ireland as Tory chief secretary. On a brief military expedition to Copenhagen (1807), a welcome break, he defeated a small Danish force. When in 1808 the Portuguese rose against Napoleon, Wellesley was ordered to support them.

Victory in the Napoleonic Wars. Wellesley did not intend to be "half beaten before the battle began"—the usual effect on continental armies of Napoleon's supremacy. With "steady troops" he expected to master the French attack. His "thin red line" of British infantry did indeed defeat Gen. Andoche Junot's columns at Vimeiro (August 21), but the arrival of two superior British officers prevented a pursuit because they preferred to sign the unpopular convention of Sintra, whereby Junot's army was repatriated. Public outcry brought about the court-martial of Wellesley and his colleagues. Though acquitted, Wellesley returned to Ireland as chief secretary. After the British evacuated Spain, however, he persuaded the government

to let him renew hostilities in 1809, arguing that Portugal could still be held, a decision that was crucial to Europe. Landing at Lisbon, he surprised Marshal Nicolas-Jean de Dieu Soult, captured Oporto, and chased the French back into Spain; but a joint Anglo-Spanish advance on Madrid failed, despite a victory at Talavera (July 27–28). Though rewarded with a peerage for his offensive, Viscount Wellington retreated with his greatly outnumbered force to his Portuguese base, defeating Marshal André Masséna at Bussaco on the way (September 27, 1810). He had secretly fortified the famous "lines of Torres Vedras" across the Lisbon peninsula. Masséna's evacuation of Portugal in the spring of 1811 and the loss of Fuentes de Oñoro (May 3–5) triumphantly justified Wellington's defensive, scorched-earth policy and confirmed his soldiers' trust in him. He was nicknamed "nosey" by his men, and "the beau" by his officers, for his slim five feet nine inches, the perfectly cut civilian clothes he preferred to wear, his wavy brown hair, and brilliant blue eyes.

Campaign in Portugal and Spain

His slowly growing army was not strong enough to capture the Spanish fortresses of Ciudad-Rodrigo and Badajoz until 1812. Then, having defeated "40,000 Frenchmen in 40 minutes" at Salamanca (July 22), he entered Madrid (August 12). His siege of Burgos failed and his army retreated again to Portugal, from which it was launched for the last time into Spain in May 1813. After a dash across the peninsula, he brought the French to bay at Vitoria, routing them and capturing all their baggage (June 21). This glittering prize was too much for the victors, who let the French escape into the Pyrenees, while Wellington denounced his drunken troops as "the scum of the earth." The victory at Vitoria gave impetus to the European alliance against Napoleon, and Soult's initial success in the Pyrenees could not prevent Wellington from taking San Sebastián and Pamplona. Whey dry weather came, Wellington invaded France, crossing the river lines one after another until on April 10, 1814, he stormed into Toulouse, thus ending the Peninsular War. (Four days earlier Napoleon had abdicated.) Already marquess and field marshal, he was now created a duke, with the nation's gift of £500,000 and later of Stratfield Saye in Hampshire to keep up his position.

With Napoleon on Elba, Wellington was appointed ambassador to the restored Bourbon court of Louis XVIII. In February 1815 he took the place of Viscount Castlereagh, the foreign secretary, at the Congress of Vienna, but, before delegates could finish their peacemaking, Napoleon had escaped, landing in France (March 1) to begin his Hundred Days. The victory of Wellington and the Prussian field marshal Gebhard Leberecht Blücher on June 18 at Waterloo established the Duke as Europe's most renowned—if not most jubilant—hero. "I hope to God that I have fought my last battle," he said, weeping for the fallen. "It is a bad thing to be always fighting." His hope was fulfilled. As commander in chief during the occupation of France, he opposed a punitive peace, organized loans to rescue French finances, and advised withdrawal of the occupying troops after three years. For these policies he won the gratitude of the peace congress, returning home in 1818 with the batons (symbol of field marshal) of six foreign countries.

Defeat of Napoleon

Role in the cabinet. Wellington's experiences abroad prevented him from ever becoming a party politician. Though he joined the Earl of Liverpool's Tory cabinet as master general of the ordnance, he exempted himself from automatically opposing a subsequent Whig government: "a factious opposition," he argued, "is highly injurious to the interests of the country." His identification with the party of law and order, however, increased when postwar discontent boiled over in the Peterloo Massacre at a Manchester demonstration for parliamentary reform and the Cato Street Conspiracy, a plot to murder the Cabinet. The popular George Canning succeeded Viscount Castlereagh as foreign secretary in 1822. Despite Canning's antipathy to the congress system, Wellington himself overbore George IV's personal objections to him, believing that the system was by now unshakably established. When Canning extricated Britain from its European commitments, Wellington was left to bitter self-reproach. His own diplomatic failures at the Congress of Verona (1822), at which he vainly sought to heal dissension among the European allies, and in Russia (1826) increased his chagrin. Straightforward to a fault, Wellington was unsuited to carrying out Canning's subtle policies, but he gained respect abroad as an honest man.

In 1825 Wellington turned to Ireland's problem, formulating it as a basic dilemma: political violence would end only after the Catholics' claim to sit in Parliament, known as Catholic Emancipation, had been granted; yet the Protestant establishment, or ascendancy, must be preserved. He worked privately at a solution, by which a papal concordat to ensure at least minimum control of Catholic clergy would be the precondition of Emancipation. When Canning, an unqualified Emancipator, became prime minister in April 1827, however, Wellington felt that Protestant ascendancy was in jeopardy. He and Robert Peel headed a mass exodus from the government, Wellington also resigning his command of the army. This action was interpreted as pique at the King's choosing his rival for prime minister. In denying the allegation, Wellington rashly asserted that he, a soldier, would be "worse than mad" to consider himself fit for the premiership. After Canning's death that August, he resumed his army command. Within five months Canning's successor, Viscount Goderich, had given up the task, and on January 9, 1828, the King summoned the Duke of Wellington.

Years as prime minister. The Duke's aim was to achieve a strong and balanced government by reuniting the Tory Party. Having reluctantly resigned again as commander in chief, he invited the Canningites, headed by William Huskisson, to serve, while dropping the ultra-Tories as incompatible with his policy of moderation. With the right wing thus alienated, a chasm began to open on the left. The opposition's demand for extensive reforms met with sympathy from Huskisson's group. Wisely, the Duke retreated, first on a church issue, himself reforming the Test and Corporation Acts that penalized Nonconformists, and again on a Corn Law (prohibiting importation of cheaper foreign grains) question, introducing a more liberal reform than he and the agricultural interest desired. Shortly afterward, however, he collided head-on with the Huskissonites on parliamentary reform; the whole group resigned in May. A further crisis immediately arose during the by-election in Clare, Ireland, where William Vesey-Fitzgerald, Huskisson's ministerial successor, defending his seat, was defeated by Daniel O'Connell, the Irish Catholic leader. The defeat of Vesey-Fitzgerald, a popular pro-Catholic, carried an alarming moral for the Duke: until Emancipation was granted, no Tory would win in southern Ireland. There might well be civil war. In August 1828 Wellington therefore undertook the most exacting political duty of his career—the conversion of George IV, Peel, who was now leader of the Commons, and a majority of Tories to Catholic Emancipation, a reform that they had hitherto regarded as anathema. It took six months of indefatigable persuasion behind closed doors to win over the King. Peel's position was equally problematical—as a publicly declared Protestant, he clung to the idea of supporting Emancipation only from the back benches; but finally Wellington's patience and Peel's generosity prevailed, and he agreed to continue leading the Commons. A number of ultra-Tories defied to the last Wellington's order to "right-about face," but the majority of the party obeyed. So in April 1829, though the Tories were split, Catholic Emancipation became law, the Duke's greatest political victory, with melodrama being added by his fighting a duel with an abusive ultra-Tory, the Earl of Winchilsea.

Wellington has sometimes been criticized for inconsistency. It now appears that he was merely secretive in not taking the public into his confidence much earlier. His willingness for some form of Emancipation by 1825 might with advantage have been disclosed.

A demand for further changes, already stimulated by Wellington's own achievements, was powerfully reinforced by countrywide hardship during 1829–30 and canalized by Charles Grey, the 2nd Earl Grey, the Whig leader, into fresh moves for parliamentary reform that would allow industrial towns like Birmingham to have a voice in Par-

Crisis over Emancipation

liament, in place of pocket boroughs owned by the nobility and gentry. Expression of dissatisfaction with Wellington's fatalistic attitude toward poverty and unemployment was made possible when the accession of William IV in 1830, following George IV's death, provided a general election. France's bourgeois revolution that same year—the July Revolution—greatly encouraged British reformers. Though Wellington's ministry survived, it was weakened, and Huskisson's sudden death frustrated tentative plans for reconciliation. Wellington saw parliamentary reform not as a panacea but as constitutional suicide. A fortnight before the opening of Parliament he wrote a letter to a friend denouncing reform as ruinous and disclosing his unalterable decision to oppose it. He staggered Parliament on November 2 with an uncompromising declaration against any reform whatever. A combination of reformers and vengeful ultra-Tories defeated him on the 15th. Peel made him resign the next day. He was succeeded by Grey.

As a soldier Wellington had shown uncanny ability in guessing what lay "on the other side of the hill." Through lack of political imagination, however, he saw revolution beyond the hill of reform—"revolution by due course of law." For this delusion he was deservedly called reactionary.

Last years. In opposition, the Duke proceeded to thwart Grey's attempts to get a reform bill through the Lords. Wellington's windows were twice smashed by radical mobs, and his iron shutters helped form the image of an iron duke. The titanic struggle culminated in the crisis of May 1832, which promised to end like the July Revolution of France. The King refused to create enough new peers to overwhelm the hostile Lords, Grey resigned, and Wellington failed to recruit an alternative government. Faced by tumultuous deadlock, Wellington, still opposing reform, then retreated for the sake of the country, persuading his followers to join him in absenting himself from Parliament until the Reform Bill became law in June. He was mobbed nonetheless by an angry crowd on Waterloo Day. "An odd day to choose," was his only comment.

The Duke's abstention had saved the Lords, and after the crisis, indeed for as long as he led the Tory peers, he continued to steer them away from fatal clashes with the Commons. Whenever possible he supported the King's government. In 1834 William IV dismissed the Whigs by a political coup, summoning the Duke to form a ministry; but the 65-year-old duke replied that Peel must be prime minister. This abnegation, most rare in a politician, did not go unappreciated. He served under Peel as foreign secretary (1834–35) and as minister without portfolio (1841–46). He also served as chancellor of Oxford, constable of the Tower, lord-lieutenant of Hampshire, and elder brother and later master of Trinity House, not to mention Queen Victoria's father figure. He made a mistake in holding the chief command of the army throughout his last 10 years, because he was past initiating the reforms that were later sorely needed. Nevertheless, he showed a touch of his old genius in 1848, when his calm handling of a threatened Chartist rising prevented any violence. Thanks to his again ordering the peers to "right-about face," this time over the Corn Laws, he enabled Peel to abolish them. Wellington retired from public life after 1846, though he was still consulted by all parties. Apsley House, his home in Piccadilly, was known as No. 1 London. As warden of the Cinque Ports, he died at Walmer Castle, his favourite residence, from a stroke on September 14, 1852. He was given a monumental state funeral, the last heraldic one in Great Britain, and was buried in St. Paul's Cathedral.

Personal life. The phrase, retained servant of King and people, or variants of it were repeatedly used by the Duke of himself and aptly suggest the self-dedication for which he is chiefly honoured. Many amusing personal peculiarities in clothes and correspondence, together with a gift for repartee, made him a "character" as well as a hero. "Publish and be damned!" was his famous retort to a blackmailer. His marriage was not happy: Kitty both feared him and worshipped him to excess. She died on April 24, 1831. Of his two sons, the elder edited his latest *Despatches* and the younger produced the grandchildren to whom he was devoted, as he was to all children. His intense

Declaration against reform

friendships with Harriet (the wife of Charles) Arbuthnot, Angela Georgina Burdett-Coutts, and others showed that he could have been happy with a clever woman; perhaps he was happiest of all, however, in the camaraderie of his staff—his military family. Some modern historians have objected to the posthumous title Iron Duke on the reasonable grounds that he was neither cold nor hardhearted. Yet he himself often boasted of his iron hand in maintaining discipline. His engaging simplicity and extraordinary lack of vanity were expressed in a favourite saying, "I am but a man." (E.Lo.)

BIBLIOGRAPHY. The *Wellington Dispatches,* published in three series, are essential source material: *Dispatches 1799–1818,* ed. by GURWOOD, 12 vol. (1834–38; Index, 1839); *Supplementary Despatches . . . 1794–1805,* 15 vol. (1858–72); and *Despatches, Correspondence, and Memoranda . . . ,* new series, ed. by the 2nd DUKE OF WELLINGTON, 8 vol. (1867–80). See also *Wellington: Political Correspondence,* ed. by JOHN BROOKE and JULIA GANDY (begun in 1976, covering the years 1833–46). Two outstanding biographies are SIR HERBERT MAXWELL, *The Life of Wellington,* 2 vol. (1899–1900); and PHILIP GUEDALLA, *The Duke* (1931, reissued 1976), though they did not have the advantage of material later collected and edited by the 7th DUKE OF WELLINGTON: *The Journal of Mrs. Arbuthnot, 1820–1832,* 2 vol. (1950); *Wellington and His Friends* (1965), being selected letters to Mr. and Mrs. Arbuthnot and three other women; *A Selection from the Private Correspondence . . .* (1952); and *Conversations of the First Duke of Wellington with George William Chad* (1956), a slight but useful diary. GEORGE R. GLEIG, *The Life of Arthur Duke of Wellington* (1862), and *Personal Reminiscences* (1904), are comprehensive but inaccurate; MURIEL WELLESLEY, a relative, pays tribute in *The Man Wellington Through the Eyes of Those Who Knew Him* (1937) and in *Wellington in Civil Life* (1939). CHARLES CRUTTWELL, *Wellington* (1936); and FRANCIS J. HUDLESTON, *Warriors in Undress* (1925, reissued 1969), give unsympathetic pictures. Military studies and biographies include S.G.P. WARD, *Wellington's Headquarters* (1957); MICHAEL GLOVER, *Wellington As Military Commander* (1968), and *Wellington's Army in the Peninsula: 1808–1814* (1977; U.S. title, *The Army of the Duke of Wellington in the Peninsula,* 1977); JAC WELLER, *Wellington in the Peninsula, 1808–1814* (1962), *Wellington at Waterloo* (1967), and *Wellington in India* (1972); and SIR ARTHUR BRYANT, *The Great Duke* (1971). Large-scale biography is found in ELIZABETH LONGFORD, *Wellington: The Years of the Sword* (1969), and *The Pillar of State* (1972, both reissued in 1982). Of especial interest are the perceptive and scholarly essays in *Wellington Studies,* ed. by MICHAEL E. HOWARD (1959). Valuable reminiscences by men who knew and admired Wellington are PHILIP STANHOPE, *Notes of Conversations with the Duke of Wellington 1831–1851* (1938); and ELLESMERE, *Personal Reminiscences of the Duke of Wellington* (1903). Collections of anecdotes proliferated after his death, the best being SIR WILLIAM FRASER, *Words on Wellington* (1899).

The West Indies

The West Indies, sometimes called the Antilles, form an archipelago more than 1,500 miles (2,400 kilometres) in length that lies between North and South America. From the Yucatán and Florida peninsulas in the west, it stretches in the shape of a crescent to Venezuela in the south. Except for The Bahamas and Bermuda, which lie farther north, all the islands are between the Tropic of Cancer (latitude 23°50′ N) and latitude 10° N. They enclose the Gulf of Mexico and the Caribbean Sea, which they separate from the Atlantic Ocean on the east. The land area of the islands is more than 91,000 square miles (236,000 square kilometres).

The West Indies, apart from The Bahamas and Bermuda, are commonly divided into two groups, the Greater Antilles and the Lesser Antilles. The Greater Antilles comprise the large islands of Cuba, Jamaica, Hispaniola (divided between Haiti and the Dominican Republic), and Puerto Rico. The Lesser Antilles include the small islands that form the Windward and Leeward groups, Barbados, and Trinidad and Tobago. The Bahamas lie slightly north of Cuba and Hispaniola. Although The Bahamas are not part of the physiographic region of the West Indies, they and Bermuda, which lies more than 500 miles to the northeast in the mid-Atlantic, have historical and cultural ties to the region.

The largest island in the West Indies is Cuba, which, although narrow, covers 42,827 square miles (110,922 square kilometres). Many of the islands cover only a few square miles. Some of the islands are sedimentary in origin, while others are volcanic.

The distinction between the Windward and Leeward island groups of the Lesser Antilles implies no more than the islands' relative position with respect to the prevailing easterly trade winds. Within the West Indies, however, two usages coexist, both complicated by former British administrative practice. At the regional scale, in Dutch, French, and Spanish practice, the entire north–south chain of the Lesser Antilles is called "windward"; behind it, the east–west trending chain of islands off the northern South American coast (Aruba, Bonaire, and Curaçao, and the Venezuelan federal dependencies) becomes "leeward." In the more restricted British application, the central islands of the Lesser Antilles and Barbados meet the trade winds first and are thus "windward," while the more northerly and westerly islands of the chain, receiving the winds later, are "leeward." These broad attributions are complicated still further by the former existence of the British colonies officially called the British Leeward Islands and the British Windward Islands, each of them composed of several islands that are not "leeward" or "windward," respectively.

The West Indies are islands of great contrast but also of considerable underlying similarity. They include independent states and British, French, U.S., and Dutch dependencies, as well as some islands under the jurisdiction of Venezuela. Since the end of World War II most of the island dependencies have achieved full independence. But despite their differences, they share common problems of economic structure and social development.   (Ed.)

This article is divided into the following sections:

PHYSICAL AND HUMAN GEOGRAPHY

The West Indian islands form a mountainous arcuate chain extending from Mexico east and south to the mouth of the Orinoco River in Venezuela, and separating the deep basin of the Caribbean Sea from the Atlantic Ocean. The main chain divides into branches that can be traced from Hispaniola, westward through Jamaica and a series of shallow submarine banks, to the coast of Nicaragua, the Sierra Maestra of east Cuba and the Cayman Islands, and along the length of Cuba. A secondary chain of islands extends from Trinidad westward along the Venezuelan coast.

The Greater Antilles are composed largely of sedimentary rocks. The Lesser Antilles form a double chain in the north, the outer one formed mainly of young limestones. The inner chain and the remaining islands south to Grenada are volcanic. Trinidad and Tobago, together with the Venezuelan and Dutch islands, are of sedimentary origin, being structurally associated with South America.

Volcanic origins in the Greater Antilles

The oldest rocks, of the Jurassic Period (190,000,000 to 136,000,000 years ago), are found at either end of the West Indian chain, in Cuba and Trinidad. The succession elsewhere in the Greater Antilles begins with rocks of volcanic origin, largely of andesitic composition, with occasional intercalated limestones containing Rudistids and other Cretaceous fossils, indicating the former existence of a volcanic archipelago. These formations were folded, uplifted, and intruded by plutonic rocks at the end of Cretaceous times (65,000,000 years ago). During the succeeding Eocene Epoch (about 54,000,000 to 38,000,000 years ago), subsidence led to the deposition of globigerinal and radiolarian chalks, indicating a more or less complete submergence of the region, although western Jamaica formed a shallow submarine bank, probably continuous with eastern Nicaragua. Volcanic activity was isolated. Further earth movements, in the Oligocene Epoch (about 38,000,-000 to 26,000,000 years ago), caused folding together with local uplift. Subsequent deposition in the Greater Antilles was variable and locally took place at considerable depths as indicated by globigerinal chalks in parts of Jamaica and Hispaniola. Beginning in the Miocene (about 26,000,000 to 7,000,000 years ago) further upheavals occurred, culminating in the Pliocene (about 7,000,000 to 2,500,000 years ago) and Early Pleistocene (beginning about 2,500,000 years ago), and affecting especially the central part of the Greater Antilles. Pleistocene-raised shorelines up to heights of 1,000 feet (305 metres) in Cuba, Jamaica, and Hispaniola indicate that uplift is probably still going on. During this period the Cayman Trench (depth more than 25,000 feet [7,600 metres]), between Jamaica and the Cayman Islands, originated as a cleft formed by fault movements.

The geological evolution of Trinidad paralleled that of the Greater Antilles, except that limestones are rare. From Miocene time onward, the sandy nature of the sedimentation reflects the development of the present Orinoco Delta. Barbados is a young uplifted island, a crust of coral founded on sediments deposited at bathyal depths and folded sandstones and shales of early Eocene age. In the remainder of the eastern Caribbean, Tertiary volcanic activity ceased in the Outer Arc by Miocene time, but continues to the present day in several of the other islands. Serious eruptions of Mt. Pelée in Martinique and Soufrière in St. Vincent occurred with loss of life early in the 20th century. Earthquakes are frequent.

The land

J.A. Froude, writing in 1887, quotes Père Labat as saying of Grenada, one of the Windward Islands, that "In itself it was all that man could desire. To live there was to live in Paradise." The proximity of warm seas, green mountains, and fertile valleys gives the West Indies this quality that many travellers have noticed.

RELIEF

Generally the islands are of high relief. The highest point is in Hispaniola, where the Pico Duarte rises to 10,417 feet (3,175 metres). In Jamaica, Blue Mountain Peak reaches 7,402 feet (2,256 metres), and heights of more than 4,000 feet (1,200 metres) are reached in Puerto Rico and several of the Windward and Leeward islands. Most islands are dominated by a central range of mountains; long spurs stretch toward the coast and deep valleys lie between them. Rivers are necessarily short and swift-flowing, and plains are chiefly confined to the coasts, although in the larger islands of Hispaniola and Jamaica level valleys lie between the mountain ranges. Passes over the mountains are rare and difficult.

Cuba is the only island with extensive areas of lowland. The high mountains of the Sierra Maestra are restricted to the eastern end and nowhere form a barrier. Barbados and Antigua, composed largely of coral, are also low-lying, while islands such as the Bahamas and Anguilla barely rise above sea level.

Low-lying islands

Lagoons and mangrove swamps are common features of the island coastlines, which are intricate and fringed by coral reefs. There are many deep natural harbours, such as those of Havana (Cuba) and St. Georges (Grenada), but the approaches are often dangerous.

DRAINAGE

The West Indies are on the whole adequately supplied with water, but the marked dry season, which causes rivers to dry up for part of the year, the lack of rainfall on the sheltered leeward slopes, and the porosity of much of the land, make drought a very real problem in some areas. Irrigation is used in parts of Jamaica, Cuba, and Hispaniola, while on dry islands such as the Virgins and Antigua, deep wells are dug and catchments and cisterns built to conserve water.

SOILS

The soils of the islands vary considerably even over small areas. They are sometimes fertile and may give high yields. Limestone, overlain with loam or alluvium, and clay cover large areas in the Greater Antilles, whereas the Lesser Antilles usually have a volcanic soil that is rich and heavy. In Barbados and Puerto Rico, where the land has been worked for a long time, fertilizer must be added to produce good crops. The richest soils are probably the deep red clays of Cuba.

CLIMATE

In the West Indies, as in most tropical areas, there is little seasonal variation in temperature. Even in the cool months of January and February it rarely falls below 75° F (24° C), and the average annual temperature is 80° F (27° C). The islands lie in the path of the northeast trade winds, which, as they blow from the sea, modify the intensity of the tropical heat, and most of the islands have a pleasant climate. Trinidad, the most southerly of the islands, is slightly hotter, but even there the nights are cool and refreshing.

More significant than the seasonal changes of temperature are those of rainfall, and a wet and dry season are usually distinguished. More rain falls while the sun is north of the equator, until shortly after the autumnal equinox, and the wet season lasts from June to October or November. The average annual rainfall is about 65 inches (1,650 millimetres), but there are considerable variations according to position and altitude. Much of Cuba, for example, which is only just within the tropics and is low-lying, receives an average of 54 inches (1,380 millimetres), whereas parts of Jamaica, being high, receive more than 75 inches (1,900 millimetres). Altitude also accounts for such different totals as those of Antigua (44 inches) and Dominica (more than 120 inches). In nearly all the islands there is a great difference between the leeward slopes, which are relatively dry, and the windward slopes, which are wet. In eastern Jamaica, for instance, the windward slope receives about 150 inches of rain, whereas the leeward slope receives only 60 inches. These local differences can be very important and show themselves in contrasted vegetation and agriculture.

Average annual rainfall

Hurricanes are the menace of the West Indian climate.

These violent wind and rain storms blow in from the Atlantic, generally north of Barbados, and strike one or more of the Lesser Antilles. They then turn northward across the larger islands toward North America. The season for hurricanes, and storms of near-hurricane intensity, is well defined. They are expected between July and October and are a partial cause of the heavier rainfall of these months. Occasionally they strike out of season. The hurricanes are traced and forecast as far as possible, but they often cause great devastation.

PLANT AND ANIMAL LIFE

The flora of the West Indies is rich and varied. Almost every tropical plant will grow, and many temperate plants have been introduced. Much of the mountain land preserves a tropical forest cover, although in places, especially in limestone districts, there is a poor scrub of thorn trees and cacti. Nearly all the lowland has been cleared for cultivation. Economically useful trees include the mahogany, cedar, guaiacum or lignum vitae, greenheart, and mora. There are many plants of great brilliance and beauty, such as the flamboyant tree, frangipani, bougainvillea, hibiscus, and poinsettia; there is also a wealth of palm and fruit trees.

The animal life is similar to that of the neighbouring South American continent. Birds, brightly coloured and numerous, include trogons, sugarbirds, flamingos, chatterers, and many parrots and hummingbirds, as well as migrants from North America. Mammals, as in most island groups, are rare, but there are agouti, manicou, deer, monkeys, and bats. The mongoose, introduced to get rid of snakes and rats, is now abundant, and there are numerous lizards, iguanas, tortoises, scorpions, toads, spiders, and centipedes, as well as a few poisonous snakes, such as the fer-de-lance, bushmaster, and coral. There is a variety of insects, but much has been done to rid the islands of mosquitoes, so that yellow fever is now almost unknown, although malaria persists in some country districts. The seas abound with fish, the most famous being the flying fish, caught off Barbados; around the shores are many delicious crustaceans.

Many domestic animals have been introduced, and cattle are raised successfully in Cuba and Jamaica, while some sheep are bred for meat. Donkeys are the chief form of transport in the poorer islands. There are also many goats and dogs.

SETTLEMENT PATTERNS

Large settlements are usually found on the leeward coasts which, although less pleasant climatically, provide shelter for ports such as Kingston (Jamaica), Port-of-Spain (Trinidad), and Bridgetown (Barbados); Havana (Cuba) and San Juan (Puerto Rico) occupy sheltered sites on the windward coasts.   (Rd.T./E.Rn.)

The people

Languages spoken in the region are diverse and include Spanish; Papiamento, a Spanish Creole spoken in Curaçao and Aruba; English; French; at least three distinct dialects of French Creole; Dutch; Hindi; Urdu; and Chinese. Although the aboriginal languages are extinct in the islands, in Belize the language known as Island Carib has been kept alive by the so-called Black Caribs, who were forcibly transported there from St. Vincent in 1797. Politically the range is equally great, from Cuba's experiment with socialism, through military and civilian dictatorships, parliamentary democracies, Puerto Rico's internally independent Commonwealth, to two integral overseas *départements* of France (Martinique and Guadeloupe), part of a state of Venezuela, and a considerable number of dependencies.

In spite of the wide divergencies in size, ancestry, language, history, population density, and political organization, the countries of the Caribbean share a common culture, the result of their somewhat parallel experiences as plantation colonies populated by African and Asian labourers dominated by distant European economic and political powers. Cut off from their homelands and in most cases unable to attain the schooling that would have given them entrée into the European ruling class, the Caribbean peoples made a virtue of necessity by combining the disparate elements of their past and of their new environment to produce a truly new cultural manifestation that is best called Creole culture. From Portuguese *crioulo,* meaning "locally raised," Creole (Spanish *criollo*) has come to describe the local culture and people of mixed foreign origin. In the same way, linguists use the term to describe languages that have evolved from pidgins used by speakers of mutually unintelligible languages and that have become the first language of the local people. In the Caribbean the French, Spanish, and English Creoles are a blend of these languages with African and aboriginal Indian languages and with each other. In the same way, Creole culture takes pride in its lively cultural scene, with frequent dances, parties, and festivals culminating in carnival, the marvelously diverse foods and drinks, and the beauty and generosity of its people.

Creole culture

Caribbean societies may be considered to be stratified both vertically by ancestry and horizontally by class. For instance, in Trinidad, possibly the most complex of all Caribbean societies, blacks and mixed Creoles can each be further subdivided on the basis of Catholicism or Protestantism, with a third division for similarly African-derived people who migrated in recent times from nearby islands, such as Barbados and St. Vincent. Other vertical divisions exist for Hindu, Muslim, and Christian East Indians, foreign-born and locally born whites, the Chinese, Portuguese, and Lebanese merchant communities, Venezuelan immigrants, and several others. Each of these communities has at least a few representatives at the top of the social pyramid and sharply differing percentages of their members at each step farther down the social scale. North American teaching volunteers serving rural areas might, for instance, be the lowest class foreign-born whites, while proportionally more members of each succeeding group are farther down the social scale, with the rural dark Creole plantation labourers and Hindu cane cutters in the largest numbers on the lowest rungs of the scale. As a result, the Trinidadian middle and upper classes are truly international in ancestry, education, and outlook, while the rural proletariat is equally divided between the uneducated and impoverished blacks and East Indians.

In other areas the components are quite different; there are additionally, for instance, the local "Conchy Joe" whites of distant British origin in The Bahamas. But the patterns of stratification remain similar from country to country with a largely foreign-educated governmental, business, professional, and landed elite; a relatively small middle class consisting of local traders, landed proprietors, and small businessmen; and a large lower class made up of landless rural and urban labourers, the underemployed, and the unemployed.

West Indian family structure is based on the extended family system, with all members co-operating in support. Although family organizations in Africa and Asia were badly disrupted by the experiences of slavery and indenture, it is notable that small communities of runaway slaves, or "maroons," established isolated villages, some of which still exist today, and supported themselves by subsistence agriculture. These sometimes maintained the old ways of life.

Virtually all Caribbean people except the East Indian Hindus and Muslims are members of at least one Christian sect, with Catholicism strongest in the Spanish- and French-speaking areas and Protestantism in the English-speaking areas. But, as they do with so many other borrowed parts of their culture, the West Indians give new content to these alien forms. Alongside virtually every major sect of Christianity, West African cults such as Shango, from Nigeria, and Rada, from Benin, have persisted in many areas, and the much-publicized Haitian voodoo represents an amalgam of Christian and African beliefs and practices. Charismatic leaders frequently organize distinctive local variants of Christianity, such as the Baptist sects that are graphically termed "Shouters" or "Jumpers," or attempt to reproduce the rituals of Islām, the Ethiopian Coptic Church, or Judaism. Although most people are entirely devoted to their own sect, many others continue to search for a faith that is more suitable to their own needs and desires. It is quite common for a High Church Anglican to consult an African magic practitioner, or obeahman, in search of knowledge of the future, cures for spiritual illnesses and

Blend of religious sects and beliefs in magic

insanity, or protection against the magical machinations of enemies. In Puerto Rico a European spiritualist cult has taken root as orthodox Roman Catholicism increasingly divorces itself from magic practices beyond prayer. Because of the wide choice of sects that are available to the people and the virtually universal belief in at least the possibility of magic, Caribbean peoples have retained religious concerns at the centre of their consciousness.

Throughout a long and cruel history of slavery, colonialism, and exploitation, the peoples of the Caribbean have had to learn to be realistic and adaptable. They learned what they could from the planter aristocrats and *petit blancs* (poor whites) and kept what they could of their African heritage in music, lore, religion, and values. In spite of the innate poverty and isolation of their far-flung rocky islands and infertile tropical lands, they have slowly developed a distinctive and piquant culture, a unique and highly successful blend of many lands and ages plus a great deal of local creation. After Ethiopia, Haiti is the oldest black nation, and political independence has come to most of the other areas in the past generation. Ties with the former colonizing powers remain close, and in many cases their continuing aid is crucial in supporting a fledgling independent government. More and more, the leaders of the new nations are coming to recognize the similarity of their problems and aspirations with those of Asia, Africa, and South America.

Problems
of
inequality

In the present postcolonial world of parliamentary democracies, the Caribbean system of stratification has resulted in political power devolving to the representatives of the majority, usually the blacks in most Caribbean nations, but with economic power left in the hands of foreign investors or local elites. A few families in Martinique, for instance, control most of the productive land, a situation that goes far to explain the strong Communist Party in that French *département*. Even in the original "Black Republic" of Haiti, the relatively light-skinned descendants of the planters control the wealth while the black professionals and army control the government, and the poor blacks eke out a precarious living on their worked-out and eroded hill farms.
(D.J.C./Ed.)

The economy

RESOURCES

The mineral deposits of the West Indies are relatively small. Iron ore, nickel, manganese, and chromium have all been mined on a small scale. Larger deposits of copper are being developed in Puerto Rico. Economic bauxites occur on the limestones in Hispaniola and Jamaica, and the latter island is the largest producer of alumina in the Western Hemisphere. Crude petroleum production in Trinidad has risen steadily. Asphalt is worked in Trinidad's famous Pitch Lake. Small quantities of natural gas and oil have been found in Barbados and Cuba. Prospecting for oil has been extended to cover the shallow banks south of Jamaica.

AGRICULTURE

Much of the land is still forest-clad, and in places the cleared hillsides are replanted with pine trees; however, all the land that is level and fertile enough is cultivated, and agriculture is by far the most important occupation of the people. The moist, sunny climate and the abundant labour supply ideally suit the West Indies to the production of sugarcane, which is still, as it has been since the early days of colonization, the principal crop. The islands, however, have suffered from this one-crop economy, and although some islands, such as Barbados and St. Christopher (St.

Principal
crops

Kitts), still grow cane almost to the exclusion of anything else, most islands have one or more important subsidiary crops. Cuba grows tobacco and citrus fruits; Jamaica, bananas; St. Vincent, arrowroot; Grenada, spices; Trinidad, cacao; Dominica, limes; Antigua, cotton; Puerto Rico and the Dominican Republic, coffee; and Haiti, sisal. Apart from these and other cash crops, peasant farmers also grow food for their own needs, and of the fruits and vegetables, yams, sweet potatoes, taros, mangoes, pineapples, papayas, breadfruits, and soursops are typical. Some land is always devoted to pasture, as each island produces its own meat. In Cuba, where cattle raising is important, the animals graze on extensive areas of paraná grass in the eastern half of the island.

INDUSTRY

Most manufacturing is concerned with the products of the land. The processing of sugarcane, which must take place immediately after the cane is cut, is the chief industry. By-products of sugar are many, and rum is distilled in all the islands. Molasses, *molascuit* (a cattle feed), and alcohol are also produced. Other industries based on agriculture include fruit canning, cotton ginning, and the manufacture of cigars, cigar boxes, and sacking.

The chief extractive industry is the oil drilling of Trinidad. Oil fields underlie the southwestern portion of the island, and drilling has been extended to the Gulf of Paria. The ancillary industries are oil refining and the production of gasoline, kerosene, and fuel oil. Although bauxite mining began on a large scale in Jamaica only in 1952, bauxite and alumina are now major exports. The ores of the Sierra Maestra in Cuba are also mined. Limestone quarries and cement works are found in most islands.   (Rd.T./E.Rn.)

TOURISM

Since the end of World War II, tourism has played an increasingly important role throughout the West Indies and in The Bahamas and Bermuda. The tourist industry has become a major source of foreign exchange for most of the smaller islands and island groups.   (Ed.)

ADMINISTRATION OF THE ECONOMY

Soon after emancipation, which took place in 1834 in British territories but not until 1886 in Cuba, the new freedmen did their best to break away from plantation labour and obtain farmlands through purchase, renting, or sharecropping, or simply by squatting on unused lands or deserted plantations. In a few cases, church groups organized cooperative efforts to purchase and divide former sugar estates into family farms, but all too often, especially on the smaller islands, the former slaves had no choice but to stay on the plantations as low-paid wage labourers. In Trinidad, and, to a lesser extent, in other areas, the former slaves soon found themselves in competition for the available jobs and land with Chinese, Portuguese, East Indian, and even African indentured labour. As a result of the interplay of these factors with geography, each country developed differently. Some islands, such as Barbados, St. Kitts, Antigua, and Martinique, produce sugar on huge foreign owned or locally owned private plantations, while in others, such as Grenada, St. Vincent, Guadeloupe, and St. Lucia, new plantation crops such as bananas and long-staple cotton have been introduced, and peasant crops such as nutmegs, arrowroot, cocoa, coconuts, pineapples, and citrus fruit earn income for small landowners. Cuba has nationalized its sugar estates, and most of the other governments hold substantial percentages of arable land as well as stock in such large-scale concerns as banana estates, bauxite mines, and oil refineries.

TRANSPORTATION

Railways are important only in the large islands, although there are a few small lines to carry cane to the factories. Only Cuba has a network of railways. In most islands there is an effective road system. All but the smallest possess an airport, and air travel is the most important means of interisland travel. Tourism and the rapidly increasing facilities for air travel have encouraged public and private enterprise to develop the amenities of the islands.

Interisland
air travel

Cultural life

African and European traditions have intermingled in a particularly spectacular way to produce the music and carnival arts of the Caribbean. Witty and allusive calypso songs, written and sung by professionals, precede the Trinidad carnival, with its huge bands of masked and costumed dancers "jumping up" to music made by beating on tuned steel oil drums. The steel "pan" is made of an upturned oil drum, the flat surface of which has been hammered and incised to make as few as three or as many as 20 convex areas, each tuned differently. These unique musical instruments, typical of the Caribbean in their creative use of discarded alien objects, can be played solo, in unison, or in complicated musical arrangements giving the effect of a giant theatre organ. Some Afro-Cuban music, such as the rumba "La Cumparsita," also deriving from carnival, has long been an established genre of popular music throughout the world; and in spite of the present overwhelming concern with economic problems, the music remains one of Cuba's most influential ambassadors. Every other area can claim musical or dance forms of international renown—Jamaica's *mentos,* Marti-

nique's beguine, Haiti's merengue, Puerto Rico's *plenas,* Bahamian "Junkanoo," Bermudian Gombey, and the distinctive music of Curaçao. Probably no area of comparable size and population on Earth has so many qualified musicians and performers. The other arts have also grown lively in recent years, producing distinguished painters such as Wilfredo Lam, of Cuba, novelists such as Pierre Marcelin and Jacques Roumain, of Haiti, V.S. Naipaul, born in Trinidad, and George Lamming, of Barbados, and poets such as Nicolás Guillén, of Cuba, and Derek Walcott, of St. Lucia. Aimé Césaire is a noted Martiniquais poet, politician, and political philosopher.   (D.J.C.)

HISTORY

Anthropology and archaeology

According to present estimates, the West Indies were not settled until the second millennium BC, when primitive Indians, living only by hunting and fishing, arrived from Central or South America. These Indians are known as Ciboney, and the time of their arrival is designated Period I.

During Period II (*i.e.,* shortly after the beginning of the Christian era) a new and more advanced group of Indians, called Arawak, invaded the Antilles from Venezuela, introducing agriculture as well as pottery. The Arawak penetrated as far north as Puerto Rico, while the Ciboney continued to occupy the rest of the islands.

The Arawak seized the remaining islands during Period III, which lasted from about AD 300 to 1000 according to the radio-carbon method of dating. They pushed the Ciboney back into the peripheral areas occupied by these Indians in the time of Columbus: the southwestern tip of Haiti, the western end of Cuba, and the various islets offshore.

The Carib   Period IV (AD 1000–1500) was marked by the arrival of a third group of Indians, the Carib, who appear to have originated in either the Guianas or Venezuela. They seized the small islands of the Lesser Antilles from the Arawak, splitting the latter into two groups, one in Trinidad to the south and the other in the Greater Antilles and the Bahamas to the north and west.

Ciboney archaeological remains consist of the refuse of habitation, occurring principally in caves and on islands. The deposits are small and relatively shallow, indicating that the people lived in bands and moved frequently, doubtless as supplies of fish and game became exhausted. Burial was directly in the refuse or in caves, with no grave objects except an occasional series of stone balls.

Archaeologists classify the remains into a series of cultures on the basis of the artifacts they contain. Most cannot yet be dated by period, but they indicate a surprising amount of geographical variation from island to island. For example, the Ortoire culture of Trinidad is characterized by tiny, irregular stone chips of unknown function; the Couri culture of Haiti, by large flint blades; and the Cuban cultures, by gouges of shell.

The Ciboney who survived until historic time were so few and so isolated that they never came into effective contact with Europeans. As a result, we know practically nothing about Ciboney ethnology, except that they spoke a language different from that of the Arawak and had a simpler culture.

Arawak archaeological sites contain larger and deeper shell middens, indicating more permanent habitation in villages, and are situated in land more suitable for agriculture. Pottery is abundant, and the changes in its shape and decoration serve as a basis for formulating and dating a large number of cultures. The earliest cultures, of Period II, are marked by little but pottery. Those of Period III also have a few simple amulets and other ceremonial objects carved out of stone, bone, and shell. These become more numerous and more elaborate in the sites of Period IV, with the appearance of such unique and artistic objects as large stone collars and three-pointed, sculptured figures of stone. The latter are associated with ball courts or dance

plazas lined with stone slabs. In addition, carved wooden idols and stools are found in caves used as shrines.

These ceremonial developments reached their climax among the Taino and Ciguayo Arawak of the heart of the Antilles, were less in evidence among the sub-Taino of central Cuba and the Lucayo of the Bahamas, and were virtually absent among the isolated Igneri of Trinidad. When Columbus established the first Spanish settlement among the Taino, he commissioned a friar, Ramón Pané, to study the Taino religion. Pané's report, which has been termed the first ethnological research in the New World, agrees very well with the archaeological finds. From his and other contemporary accounts, it is known that the Arawak were peaceful and had a relatively elaborate social organization headed by hereditary chieftains who derived their power from personal deities called zemis. Their language belongs to the Arawakan family of tropical South America.

Archaeologists are only beginning to identify the remains of the Carib in the Lesser Antilles. The sites of these Indians have relatively plain and crude pottery, characterized by scoring of the surfaces. They lack the ceremonial structures and carvings of the Arawak.

Much more is known of the ethnology of the Carib, not only from observations made by Columbus and his successors but also from accounts by 17th-century French missionaries and by modern anthropologists who have studied the surviving Indians. These sources indicate that the Carib had a less elaborate social organization than the Arawak, without hereditary chiefs or classes. Carib life centred about warfare rather than religion; and the term cannibalism is derived from their custom of eating the flesh of captives in order to obtain the latters' personal power.

The Carib have also given their name to the Cariban linguistic stock of South America, although they themselves spoke Arawakan. The explanation for this anomaly is to be found in their tradition that when they conquered the Lesser Antilles they killed the Arawak men but married the women. Apparently, it was the women's language that prevailed.

While Columbus explored all parts of the West Indies, his successors colonized only those parts inhabited by the Ciboney and Arawak, avoiding the Carib islands because they lacked gold and because the Carib were too difficult to subjugate. As the Spaniards conquered each island, they rounded up its Indians and put them to work in mines or on plantations.

Many were worked to death; some starved because the Spaniards failed to provide food; others died from diseases introduced from Europe; and still others lost their lives in unsuccessful efforts to throw off the Spanish yoke. By the time the system of forced labour ended in 1550, the   The demise Ciboney had become extinct and appreciable numbers   of the of Arawak survived only on the islands of Cuba and   Ciboney Trinidad. These survivors gradually became assimilated into the European population. A few villages retained their Indian identity well into the 19th century, but all are now indistinguishable from the rest of the population.

The Carib fared somewhat better. Their territory was not conquered until the mid-17th century. While most of them perished as pawns in the struggle among the French,

English, Dutch, and Danes for control of the area, some retained their independence on the smaller islands.

Many runaway black slaves took refuge among them, and the Carib gradually changed in racial composition from Indian to black. They retained, however, their Indian language and culture because runaway slaves had to "go native" in order to avoid recapture. In 1795 the British moved one group, which had become troublesome, to the coast of Central America, where they multiplied, prospered, and came to be known as the Black Carib. Subsequently, the British rounded up the remnants surviving in the Lesser Antilles and installed them in a reservation on the island of Dominica, which they still inhabit. These island Carib have not retained as much of their aboriginal language and culture.

The Spaniards introduced the first black slaves in the 16th century to replace the dwindling supply of Indian labour. They did not bring in many, for their mines had become exhausted and they specialized in cattle ranches, which did not require much labour. The main influx of black slaves took place in the 18th century with the development of sugar plantations by the French, first in the Lesser Antilles and then in Haiti.   (I.Re.)

European exploration

The West Indies were revealed to Europeans by the first voyage Columbus made, in 1492, in search of an Atlantic route to the Far East. Since he was interested in trade and gold, he returned in 1493 to found the first permanent European settlement in the West Indies on the island of Hispaniola. Spanish control of the Caribbean after discovery was practically undisputed during the first century of development, and the colonization of other islands in the Greater Antilles was undertaken by the Spaniards during the early years of the 16th century. The presence of alluvial gold in Hispaniola and Cuba attracted considerable numbers of Spanish settlers. But they and the colonists of the other large islands found that the Arawak population was unsuited to the continuous hard labour that they tried to impose on them.

Throughout the first three decades of the 16th century, the islands were bases from which expeditions sailed to Central America and Mexico. These territories had the advantage of abundant and more hardy Indian labourers and in the 1520s drew many settlers from the islands, especially as the island gold became exhausted. The islands came to be valued chiefly as ports of call. Their inhabitants lived by selling provisions to passing ships and by exporting hides, tallow, and sugar to Europe. At the same time, the islands acquired a new strategic importance. The increasing volume of shipping, carrying tropical products and Mexican or Peruvian silver, attracted the attention of pirates, privateers, and smugglers. Fortified cities on the "Spanish Main," the mainland bordering the Caribbean, and on the islands were raided. In the second half of the 16th century the Spanish government was obliged, even in peacetime, to organize shipping through the Caribbean in convoys and to construct powerful fortifications at the strategic harbours—Cartagena, San Juan de Puerto Rico, and, above all, Havana.

Spain wished to monopolize the settlement and trade of the West Indies. But its defenses could not prevent all incursions in so large an area. During the second half of the 16th century, adventurers of the other European nations persisted in smuggling and raiding within Spain's preserves. The establishment, however, of non-Hispanic colonies on the islands did not take place until after the Dutch West India Company received its formal charter at the end of the 12 years' truce between Spain and the Netherlands in 1621. This company was incorporated for conquest and plunder as well as for trade, and its heavy attacks against Spanish shipping—even though much of its energy was diverted to Brazil—enabled other groups of foreigners to colonize islands in the eastern Caribbean that Spain had not occupied. English and French agricultural colonies and Dutch trading and smuggling colonies were established on the islands between 1623 and 1648, when

The islands as ports of call

the Dutch were strong enough to obtain recognition of their possessions by Spain.

As Spain became weaker, it even lost territory that it had colonized earlier. The 17th century witnessed settlement of the Lesser Antilles by British, French, Dutch, and Danish colonists. Thus Jamaica was seized by the English in 1655, and the western part of Hispaniola, later known as Saint-Domingue, was occupied by French settlers during the second half of the 17th century. Spain, however, did not recognize the English holdings in the West Indies until 1670; and western Hispaniola was not ceded to France until 1697. This Spanish recalcitrance encouraged the English and French governments to make use of buccaneers to coerce Spain into compliance with their will, and these forces were not effectively suppressed until the end of the century.

The buccaneers

Buccaneers was the name given to a group of English, French, Dutch, and Portuguese piratical adventurers united in their opposition to Spain, who maintained themselves chiefly in the Caribbean Sea during the 17th century. They must not be confused with the earlier adventurers and privateers of whom Sir Francis Drake was an outstanding example, nor with the outlawed pirates of the 18th century.

By the early part of the 17th century the oppressive colonial policy of Spain had almost depopulated the island of Hispaniola, the modern Santo Domingo. Thinned of its former inhabitants, the island became the home of immense herds of wild cattle and pigs and consequently an excellent place to provision the ships of smugglers. The natives still left were skilled in preserving flesh without the use of salt, an article both scarce and costly. The meat was cured in the sun and then smoked over a fire of green wood—a process termed buccanning, or boucanning. The adventurers and smugglers, who were soon called buccaneers, learned buccanning from the natives; and gradually Hispaniola became the scene of an extensive and illicit provision trade. As the Spaniards would not recognize the right of other nations to make settlement, or even to trade in the West Indies, the governments of France, England, and Holland would do nothing to control their subjects who invaded the islands. Out of such conditions arose the buccaneer, alternately sailor and hunter, even occasionally a planter—roving, bold, unscrupulous, often savage, with an intense detestation of Spain.

The depopulation of Hispaniola

EARLY SETTLEMENTS

Both England and France contributed bands of colonists for a settlement made on the island of St. Christopher in the West Indies. The English and French, however, were not very friendly; and in 1629, after the retirement of several of the English to an adjoining island, the remaining colonists were surprised and partly dispersed by the arrival of a Spanish fleet. But on the departure of the fleet the scattered bands returned and were soon of sufficient strength to give assistance to their countrymen in Santo Domingo. As buccaneering had developed into a profitable employment, it was thought expedient to build a storehouse secure from the attack of the Spaniards. The small island of Tortuga was seized for this purpose in 1630 and converted into a magazine for the goods of the smugglers; Santo Domingo continued to be their hunting ground. A purely English settlement directed by a company in London was made (1630) at Old Providence, an island in the Caribbean Sea, but it was suppressed by the Spaniards in 1641. About the same time, the Spaniards attacked Tortuga and massacred every settler they could seize. The few who escaped returned, and the buccaneers, now in open hostility to the Spanish arms, began to receive recruits from every European trading nation, and for three-quarters of a century became the scourge of the Spanish-American trade and dominions. This roving community had to maintain itself as best it could—now mainly on the sea. In 1655, however, fortune turned their way when, with their assistance, the navy of the English Commonwealth succeeded in capturing the island of Jamaica. Its

Buccaneers in Jamaica

ample harbours for many years furnished the buccaneers with havens in their operations against the Spaniards.

It is chiefly during this period that those leaders flourished whose names and doings have been associated with all that was really influential in the exploits of the buccaneers—the most prominent being Mansfield and Morgan. In 1654 the first great expedition on land made by the buccaneers, though attended by considerable difficulties, was completed by the capture and sack of New Segovia, on the mainland of America. The Gulf of Venezuela, with its towns of Maracaibo and Gibraltar, was attacked and plundered under the command of a Frenchman named L'Ollonois, who performed, it is said, the office of executioner upon the whole crew of a Spanish vessel manned with 90 seamen. Such successes removed the buccaneers further and further from the pale of civilized society. Mansfield, in 1664, conceived the idea of a permanent settlement upon a small island of the Bahamas named New Providence, and Henry Morgan, a Welshman, intrepid and unscrupulous, joined him. But the untimely death of Mansfield nipped in the bud the only rational scheme of settlement that seemed to have animated this wild community at any time; and Morgan, now elected commander, swept the whole Caribbean and from his headquarters in Jamaica led triumphant expeditions to Cuba and the mainland. He was leader of the expedition that surprised and plundered Porto Bello, one of the best fortified ports in the West Indies.

This was too much for even the adverse European powers; and in 1670 a treaty was concluded between England and Spain, proclaiming peace and friendship among the subjects of the two sovereigns in the New World. The treaty was very ill observed in Jamaica, where the governor, Thomas Modyford (1620–79), was in close alliance with the "privateers," which was the official title of the buccaneers. He had already granted commissions to Morgan and others for a great attack on the Isthmus of Panama, the route by which the bullion of the South American mines was carried to Porto Bello, to be shipped to Spain. The buccaneers to the number of 2,000 began by seizing Chagres and then marched to Panama in 1671. The city was taken, and, accidentally or not, it was burnt; but the Spaniards had removed the treasure, the booty was small, and many died of starvation on the way back to Jamaica. Modyford was recalled, and in 1672 Morgan was called home and imprisoned in the Tower. In 1674 he was allowed to return to the island as lieutenant-governor with Lord Vaughan. During his later years he was active in suppressing the buccaneers, who now had inconvenient claims on him.

The separation of the English and French buccaneers, who together presented a united front to the Spanish fleet in 1685, marks the beginning of the last epoch in their history. They hung doggedly along the coasts of Jamaica and Santo Domingo, but their day was nearly over. Only once again—at the siege of Carthagena—did they appear great; but even then the expedition was not of their making, and they were mere auxiliaries of the French regular forces. The French and English buccaneers could not but take sides in the war that had arisen between their respective countries in 1689. Thus was broken the bond of unity that had for three-quarters of a century kept the subjects of the two nations together in schemes of aggression upon a common foe.

Government and society, 17th–20th centuries

The early settlers in the eastern Caribbean relied on tobacco as their main cash crop and employed European labour, recruited either by indenture or by penal sentences. Both proved inadequate; after the middle of the 17th century most island planters turned to sugar as the most profitable crop and to West African slaves as the most profitable form of labour. The techniques of sugar manufacture were introduced from Brazil by Dutch

traders, who—having acquired most of the old Portuguese barraccoons (enclosures for slaves) in West Africa—also supplied the slaves. In the non-Spanish islands sugar soon became the main export crop. The peculiarities of sugar production required comparatively large estates. The class of European smallholders that had predominated earlier began to dwindle and disappear, and black slaves greatly outnumbered the small groups of planters, overseers, merchants, and professional men who remained in most of the non-Hispanic islands.

Racial division thus became the basis of a large part of West Indian society, and the problem of keeping their black slaves in subjection became crucial for white masters. Many attempts at slave rebellion followed, and, during the era of the French Revolution, a successful slave revolt under the leadership of the black Toussaint-L'ouverture actually gained control of the colony of Saint-Domingue, which later won its independence as the Negro Republic of Haiti after Napoleon attempted to restore slavery there. Gradually a class of free people of colour, predominantly of mixed blood, emerged between the masters and the slaves. They were generally excluded from participation in public life. But, from the time of the French Revolution on into the 19th century, they began to demand equality of rights. The principle of racial inequality was thus challenged by both subordinate groups in the society.

During the late 17th and 18th centuries European nations had set a high value on West Indian possessions, and each metropolitan power endeavoured to monopolize the trade of its own colonies and to increase its returns from the sugar and slave trades. Competition for West Indian colonies led to heavy fighting in the Caribbean during the recurrent wars that followed; and finally, because of its strength at sea, Britain emerged with the lion's share of ceded islands. But in the late 18th and 19th centuries doubts began to develop as to the value and organization of the West Indian colonies, and the collapse of the slave society was hastened by external as well as internal factors. During the French Revolution, expediency for a time forced the emancipation of the French West Indian slaves, though slavery was later restored. Humanitarian views of the slave trade and slavery became influential in some metropolitan countries, and rising costs of production in the older slave colonies, especially the British, reinforced criticism of the planters until abolitionist movements succeeded in outlawing the British slave trade (in 1806–07) and British and French colonial slavery (in 1833 and 1848, respectively).

During the 19th century the sugar industry declined in prosperity in many parts of the West Indies, with the major exception of Cuba, which had developed relatively late and retained slavery until 1886. The competition of cheap sugar from Cuba and other parts of the world depressed prices in overseas markets and made it difficult—especially after 1846–54, when the British equalized the duties on colonial and foreign sugars—for the high-cost producers to survive. Some adjustment, however, was made to the conditions of emancipation and free trade. For example, Trinidad and British Guiana (later Guyana) greatly increased their sugar production by importing cheap indentured labour, chiefly from India. After emancipation also, black smallholders appeared in several islands and diversified the West Indian economy by growing more food and such cash crops as cocoa, nutmegs, and bananas. During the 20th century the development of a tourist trade and of oil and bauxite industries continued the trend toward economic diversification.

Many territories in the West Indies now enjoy internal self-government based on universal adult suffrage, with the metropolitan power retaining control of defense and foreign affairs. But the growth of full independence has been comparatively slow. Haiti achieved its independence in 1804, the Dominican Republic in 1844, Cuba after the Spanish-American War of 1898; then, following the breakup of the West Indies Federation of 1958–62, Jamaica and Trinidad and Tobago became independent in 1962 and Barbados in 1966. Independence was achieved by The Bahamas in 1973, by Grenada in 1974, by Dominica in 1978, and by both St. Vincent and the

Grenadines and St. Lucia in 1979. Antigua and Barbados became independent in 1981, followed by St. Christopher and Nevis in 1983. The countries that have been longest independent have been frequently subject to dictatorship, punctuated by intervals of disorder, some of which led to interventions by the United States. In fact, since the late 19th century, U.S. interest and power in the Caribbean

have been steadily growing, with a U.S. naval base on Cuba (at Guantánamo) and the acquisition as dependencies of Puerto Rico and the former Danish Virgin Islands (1917). Cuba under Fidel Castro has been consistently opposed to the increasing U.S. dominance of its Caribbean neighbours.

(J.H.Py./E.V.G.)

GREATER ANTILLES

Cuba

Cuban archipelago

Territorially, the Republic of Cuba comprises the Cuban archipelago, a formation of no fewer than 3,715 islands, islets, and cays with a combined area of 42,827 square miles (110,922 square kilometres). The archipelago is situated near the geographical centre of the New World landmass, just south of the Tropic of Cancer at the entrance to the Gulf of Mexico, and forms an important segment of the Greater Antilles island chain, which continues east and then south in a great arc enclosing the Caribbean Sea. The island of Cuba itself—the "pearl of the Antilles"—is the largest island in the chain, covering 40,543 square miles (105,007 square kilometres). In general, the island runs from northwest to southeast and is long and narrow—777 miles (1,250 kilometres) long but only 119 miles (191 kilometres) across at its widest and 19 miles (31 kilometres) at its narrowest point. The capital is Havana on the northwestern coast. From Maisí lighthouse on the eastern tip, Haiti, the nearest neighbouring country, is visible 48 miles away across the Windward Passage. Jamaica, 87 miles to the south, is also visible on a clear day. The United States is about 90 miles to the north across the Straits of Florida.

The Isla de la Juventud (Isle of Youth, so called because of an influx of young settlers), was formerly called Isla de Pinos (Isle of Pines) and is the second largest in the archipelago (849 square miles), rising to the southwest of Cuba itself. Other island and shoal groups are Los Colorados, to the northwest; the Archipiélago de Sabana-Camagüey, off the north central coast; the Jardines de la Reina (Queen's Gardens), off the southeast coast; and the Archipiélago de los Canarreos (technically including the Isla de la Juventud), along the southwest coast.

Because of its geographical location and natural resources, Cuba was coveted by more than one foreign power over the centuries. A colony of Spain after its discovery by Columbus in 1492, it formally became a republic at the beginning of the 20th century, although its independent status was qualified by a high degree of political and economic dependence on the United States. On New Year's Day, 1959, the republic entered a new era with the victory of revolutionary forces led by Fidel Castro.

PHYSICAL AND HUMAN GEOGRAPHY

The land. *Relief.* Mountains cover about a quarter of the total area of the island of Cuba, often interrupted by the extensive plains that cover some two-thirds of the surface. The coastal basins of Santiago de Cuba and Guantánamo lie in the extreme east; a great central valley also begins in the east and then combines with a peneplain, continuing westward across the entire island. It is these plains that have been hospitable to the raising of sugarcane and livestock.

The *alturas*—regions of moderate elevation—are in some cases residues of formerly higher surfaces. More rugged relief includes the Guaniguanico range in the west, comprising the Sierra de los Órganos and the Sierra del Rosario, which attains 2,270 feet (692 metres) at El Pan de Guajaibón; the Sierra de Trinidad in the central region, with the 3,793-foot (1,156-metre) Pico San Juan; and the Sierra Maestra, more than 100 miles long, that rises abruptly from the southeast coast and contains the island's highest peaks, with Pico Turquino, at 6,476 feet (1,974 metres), pre-eminent.

Mountain regions and the coastline

Cuba possesses an irregular 3,570-mile (5,746-kilometre) coastline, made picturesque by the many bays, sandy

beaches, mangrove plantations, swamps, coral reefs, and rugged cliffs. There are also some spectacular caverns in the interior, notably the Ensenada Don Tomás (Santo Tomás) of the Quemado ridge region, which has a linear extension of 16 miles. The 40,543 square miles of the island of Cuba are surrounded by a submerged platform that is an additional 30,000 square miles (70,000 square kilometres) in area; hence sea depths surrounding the island are no greater than about 650 feet (200 metres), dropping abruptly away at the outer edges of the platform.

Drainage and soils. Cuba's excellent supply of groundwater is utilized intensively throughout the island but especially in La Habana province. The rivers are generally short, with very meagre flow; of the nearly 600 watercourses classified as rivers, two-fifths discharge to the north, the remainder to the south.

The island's heaviest rainfall and therefore its largest rivers are in the southeast, where the Cauto (at 230 miles the country's longest) and its tributaries, notably the Salado, drain the Sierra Maestra and the uplands to the north. Other major rivers in this region include the Guantánamo, Sagua de Tánamo, Toa, and Mayarí. Proceeding westward, the most important rivers flowing south are the Sevilla, Najasa, San Pedro (of Camagüey), Jatibonico del Sur, Zaza, Agabama, Arimao, Hondo, and Cuyaguateje; north, the Saramaguacán, Caonao, Sagua la Grande, and La Palma.

Cuban lakes are small and more properly classified as freshwater or saltwater lagoons. The latter include the 26-square-mile Laguna de Leche (Milky Lagoon), which is technically a sound, as it is connected to the sea by several natural channels. Sea movements generate disturbances in the calcium carbonate bottom deposits to produce the milky appearance.

The complicated Cuban topography and geology have produced soils of no fewer than 13 different major groups, the majority of which are fertile, in good physical condition, and amenable to year-round cultivation.

Climate. Cuba lies in the tropic zone, located on the southwestern periphery of the North Atlantic High atmospheric pressure zone and hence influenced by the Northeast Trade Winds in winter and east–northeast winds in summer. The warm currents that later form the Gulf Stream are a year-round ameliorating influence along the coasts.

Annual mean temperature is 78° F (26° C), with little variation between January (at 72° F [22° C] the coolest month) and August (the warmest month, at 82° F [28° C]). The November–April dry season abruptly changes to the rainy May–October season. Annual rainfall averages 54 inches (1,380 millimetres). Between June and October, the country often is exposed to hurricanes, whose strong winds (up to 163 miles per hour) and heavy rains (up to 12 inches in a 24-hour period) have occasioned great economic damage and human suffering. In the western and central parts of the island, cold fronts occasionally induce precipitation even during the dry season.

Temperatures

Plant and animal life. Cuba's tropical plant life is very rich, with some 8,000 species represented, 6,000 of them "higher"; half of these are endemic. Much of the original vegetation has been replaced by sugarcane, coffee, and rice plantations, made possible by enormous and indiscriminate destruction of forests. The revolutionary government introduced extensive reforestation for both economic and conservation reasons. Planting has been carried out in Guane, in Pinar del Río province; at Las Terrazas, 46 miles west of Havana; and in Pinares de Mayarí, in the north of Holguín province.

Cuban timber is of excellent quality. Pine is found in abundance, and the durable mahogany is of potential economic importance, while ebony (*Diospyros*) and granadilla (cocus, or West Indian ebony; *Brya ebenus*) are both beautiful and valuable. The royal palm, in abundant supply, reaching heights of 50 to 75 feet (15 to 23 metres), is the national tree and a characteristic element of the rural landscape. The ceiba (kapok) tree plays a role in many legends, while the extremely rare cork palm (*Microcycas calocoma*) of the western regions is a "living fossil" thought to have survived since the Cretaceous Period, more than 100,000,000 years ago.

Fruit trees include such citrus varieties as lemon, orange, and grapefruit; some species of the genus *Annona,* including the *guanábana* (soursop) and *anón* (sweetsop); and avocado and papaya. Banana plants are also common. The lower Cuban coasts and the shoals of the archipelago are lent marked character by the mangrove, and the tobacco plant is valued for its product and as an ornamental.

Cuban animal life is extraordinary in its abundance and variety, particularly the invertebrate species. The archipelago is the home of more than 7,000 insect species and 4,000 species of land, river, and sea mollusks. Sponges (the basis of an industry) are important off the southwestern coast, and edible crustaceans abound. The similarly profuse Arachnida include the tarantula and scorpion. Fish (more than 500 edible species) are economically the most important vertebrate group, and there are about 35 species of shark. There are far fewer freshwater fishes.

Cuba is visited by many migratory birds, and only a third of the 300 or so species found on the island are typically Cuban; these include the flamingo, royal thrush, nightingale, mockingbird, and hummingbird.

Reptiles are distributed equally among sea, river, and dry land species. Marine species include the tortoise and hawkbill turtle; mud turtles inhabit the rivers; the marshes contain two species of crocodile (formerly almost extinct but now the object of a repopulation program); and land reptiles include the iguana and the nonpoisonous *majá de Santa María* (*Epicrates angulifer*), Cuba's largest snake. Amphibians are similarly varied, with 60 frog and toad species, the former including the plantain frog (*Hyla septentrionalis*) and bullfrog. The solenodon (*Atopogale cubana*), an almost extinct, ratlike insectivore, is found only in the remotest eastern regions. Other mammals include the hutia (an edible rodent) and the manatee, or sea cow, which inhabits river mouths. Bats (30 species) destroy mosquitoes as well as insects harmful to agriculture and in their roosting caves produce accumulations of guano that is valuable as fertilizer.

Settlement patterns. The various areas of Cuba do not differ greatly in customs and traditions, making a clear regional division on this basis difficult. The eastern end of the island (provinces of Guantánamo, Santiago de Cuba, Las Tunas, Granma, and Holguín)—with its own speech patterns, music, and customs, resulting from regional isolation—is an exception. A more significant division might be that between city and countryside, especially between the dominant Havana metropolitan area and the rest of the country, a pattern of unequal development repeated on a much smaller scale in the various provincial capitals.

The homogeneity of Cuban society has been increased since the revolution of the 1950s by the emphasis placed by the government on the development of communications and on rural growth. Given these qualifications, a division of Cuba into five geographical regions—Occidental (Western), Central, Camagüey-Maniabón, Oriental (Eastern), and Pinera (the Isla de la Juventud, or Isle of Pines)—is still possible on the basis of natural endowment and human exploitation. Cuban specialists have made a

Invertebrates

MAP INDEX

Political subdivisions

Camagüey	21·30n 78·10w
Ciego de Ávila	21·55n 78·40w
Cienfuegos	22·15n 80·30w
Granma	20·25n 77·00w
Guantánamo	20·20n 75·00w
Holguín	20·50n 76·00w
La Habana	22·45n 82·10w
La Habana,	
Ciudad de	23·08n 82·22w
Las Tunas	21·00n 77·05w
Matanzas	22·40n 81·10w
Pinar del Río	22·35n 83·40w
Sancti Spíritus	22·00n 79·25w
Santiago de	
Cuba	20·20n 76·00w
Villa Clara	22·30n 80·00w

The name of a political subdivision if not shown on the map is the same as that of its capital city.

Cities and towns

Aguada de	
Pasajeros	22·23n 80·51w
Alto Cedro	20·31n 75·58w
Antilla	20·50n 75·45w
Artemisa	22·49n 82·46w
Banes	20·58n 75·43w
Baracoa	20·21n 74·30w
Bayamo	20·23n 76·39w
Bejucal	22·56n 82·23w
Cabaiguán	22·05n 79·30w
Caibarién	22·31n 79·28w
Caimanera	19·59n 75·09w
Camagüey	21·23n 77·55w
Camajuaní	22·28n 79·44w
Campechuela	20·14n 77·17w
Candelaria	22·44n 82·58w
Cárdenas	23·05n 81·10w
Chaparra	21·10n 76·29w
Ciego de Ávila	21·51n 78·46w
Cienfuegos	22·09n 80·27w
Colón	22·43n 80·54w
Consolación del	
Sur	22·30n 83·31w
Cruces	22·21n 80·16w
Cueto	20·39n 75·56w
Elia	20·59n 77·26w
Esmeralda	21·51n 78·07w
Florida	21·32n 78·14w
Gibara	21·07n 76·08w
Guanabacoa	23·07n 82·18w
Guanajay	22·55n 82·42w
Guane	22·12n 84·05w
Guantánamo	20·08n 75·12w

Guayabal	20·42n 77·36w
Güines	22·50n 82·02w
Güira de Melena	22·48n 82·30w
Havana	23·08n 82·22w
Holguín	20·53n 76·15w
Imías	20·04n 74·38w
Jagüey Grande	22·32n 81·08w
Jiguaní	20·22n 76·26w
Jovellanos	22·48n 81·12w
Júcaro	21·37n 78·51w
La Isabela	22·57n 80·01w
Los Palacios	22·35n 83·15w
Mantua	22·17n 84·17w
Manzanillo	20·21n 77·07w
Marianao	23·05n 82·26w
Martí	21·09n 77·27w
Matanzas	23·03n 81·35w
Mayarí	20·40n 75·41w
Minas	21·29n 77·37w
Minas de	
Matahambre	22·35n 83·57w
Morón	22·06n 78·38w
Niquero	20·03n 77·35w
Nueva Gerona	21·53n 82·48w
Nuevitas	21·33n 77·16w
Palma Soriano	20·13n 76·00w
Palmira	22·14n 80·23w
Pinar del Río	22·25n 83·42w
Placetas	22·19n 79·40w
Portillo	19·55n 77·11w
Puerto Manatí	21·22n 76·50w
Puerto Padre	21·12n 76·36w
Quemado de	
Güines	22·48n 80·15w
Sagua de	
Tánamo	20·35n 75·14w
Sagua la Grande	22·49n 80·05w
San Antonio de	
los Baños	22·53n 82·30w
Sancti Spíritus	21·56n 79·27w
San Germán	20·36n 76·08w
San José de las	
Lajas	22·58n 82·09w
San Luis	20·12n 75·51w
Santa Clara	22·24n 79·58w
Santa Cruz del	
Sur	20·43n 78·00w
Santa Fé	21·45n 82·45w
Santa Isabel de	
las Lajas	22·25n 80·18w
Santa Lucía	22·40n 83·58w
Santiago de	
Cuba	20·01n 75·49w
Tiguabos	20·14n 75·21w
Trinidad	21·48n 79·59w
Tunas de Zaza	21·38n 79·33w
Unión de Reyes	22·48n 81·32w

Vertientes	21·16n 78·09w
Victoria de las	
Tunas	20·58n 76·57w
Yaguajay	22·19n 79·14w
Zulueta	22·22n 79·34w

Physical features and points of interest

Ana María, Golfo	
de, *gulf*	21·20n 78·45w
Batabanó, Golfo	
de, *gulf*	22·15n 82·30w
Broa, Ensenada	
de la, *bay*	22·35n 82·00w
Canarreos,	
Archipiélago de	
los, *islands*	21·50n 82·30w
Caonao, *river*	22·05n 78·05w
Cárdenas, Bahía	
de, *bay*	23·05n 81·09w
Caribbean Sea	20·00n 83·00w
Cauto, *river*	20·33n 77·15w
Cochinos, Bahía	
de, see Bay of	
Pigs	
Coco, Cayo,	
island	22·30n 78·28w
Colorados,	
Archipiélago	
de los, *islands*	22·36n 84·20w
Corrientes, Cabo,	
cape	21·45n 84·31w
Corrientes,	
Ensenada de,	
bay	21·50n 84·35w
Cristal, Sierra del,	
mountains	20·33n 75·30w
Cruz, Cabo, *cape*	19·51n 77·44w
Doce Leguas,	
Cayos de las,	
islands	20·55n 79·05w
Florida, Straits of.	24·00n 81·00w
Gorda, Punta,	
point	21·05n 75·39w
Gorda, Punta,	
point	22·24n 82·10w
Guacanayabo,	
Golfo de, *gulf*	20·30n 77·35w
Guajaba, Cayo,	
island	21·50n 77·30w
Guanahacabibes,	
Golfo de, *gulf*	22·08n 84·35w
Guaniguanico,	
Cordillera de,	
mountains	22·30n 83·40w
Jardines de la	
Reina, *islands*	20·45n 78·50w

Jatibonico del	
Sur, *river*	21·33n 79·09w
Jigüey, Bahía de,	
bay	22·07n 78·06w
Laberinto de las	
Doce Leguas,	
island	20·35n 78·30w
Largo, Cayo,	
island	21·38n 81·28w
Leche, Laguna	
de, *lagoon*	22·13n 78·38w
Maestra, Sierra,	
mountains	20·00n 76·45w
Maisí, Cabo,	
cape	20·17n 74·09w
Mexico, Gulf of	24·30n 84·30w
Najasa, *river*	20·42n 77·58w
Nicholas	
Channel	23·25n 80·05w
Nipe, Bahía de,	
bay	20·47n 75·42w
Old Bahama	
Channel	22·33n 78·05w
Perros, Bahía de,	
bay	22·25n 78·36w
Pigs, Bay of	22·07n 81·10w
Pinos, Isla de	
(Pines, Isle of),	
island	21·40n 82·50w
Romano, Cayo,	
island	22·15n 78·00w
Sabana-Camagüey,	
Archipiélago de,	
islands	23·00n 80·00w
Sabinal, Cayo,	
island	21·40n 77·15w
Salado, *river*	20·38n 76·57w
San Antonio,	
Cabo, *cape*	21·52n 84·57w
San Felipe, Cayos	
de, *islands*	21·58n 83·30w
San Juan, Pico,	
peak	21·59n 80·08w
San Pedro, *river*	21·09n 78·30w
Siguanea,	
Ensenada de la,	
bay	21·40n 83·05w
Toa, *river*	20·23n 74·32w
Turquino, Pico,	
peak	19·59n 76·51w
Windward	
Passage	19·30n 74·30w
Zapata,	
Península de	22·20n 81·45w
Zaza, *river*	21·37n 79·33w

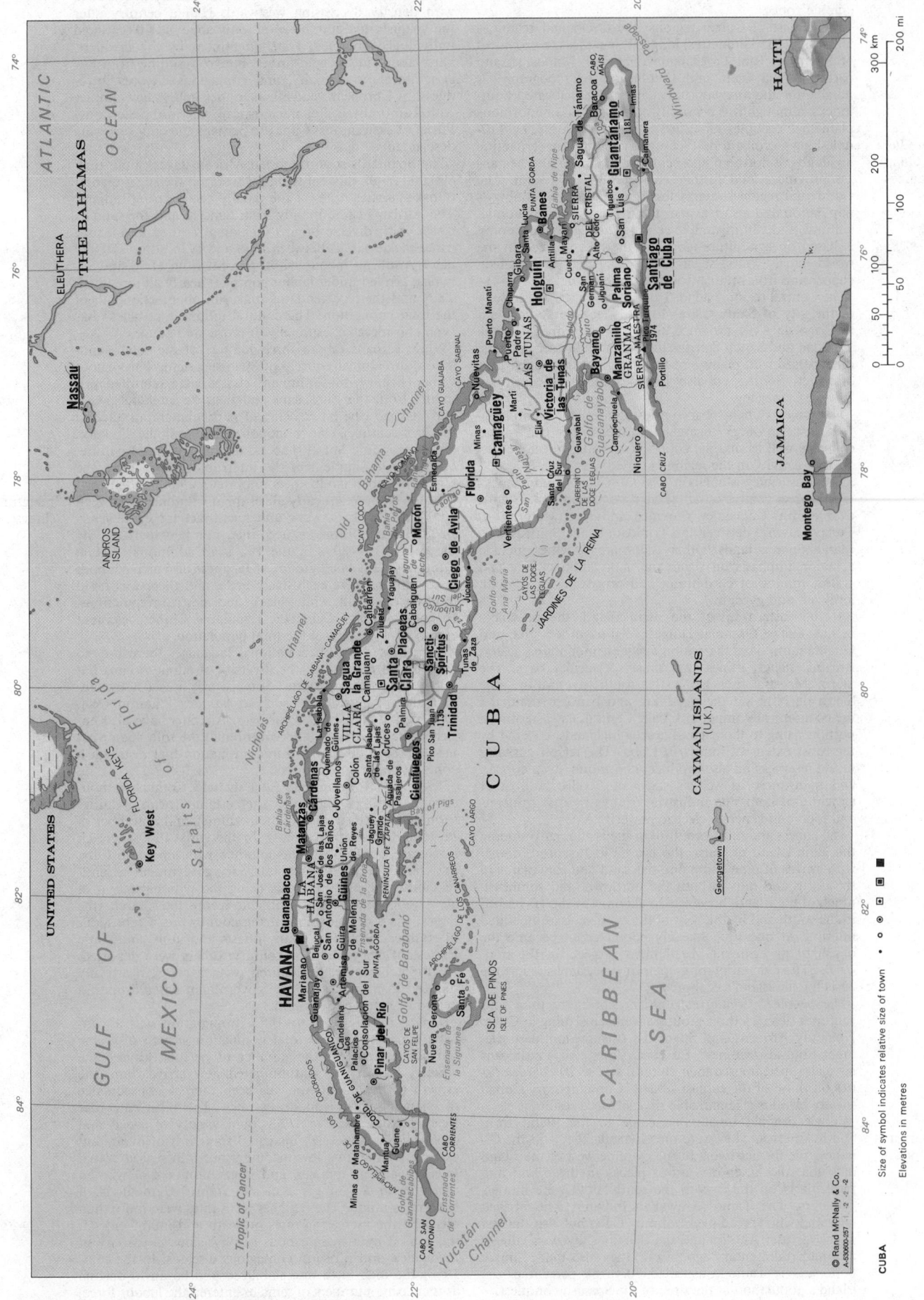

ATLANTIC

OCEAN

THE BAHAMAS

ELEUTHERA

Nassau

ANDROS
ISLAND

UNITED STATES

GULF OF
MEXICO

Key West

FLORIDA KEYS

Straits of Florida

Tropic of Cancer

Nicholas Channel

Old Bahama Channel

CAYO COCO

CAYO GUAJABA

CAYO SABINAL

CAYO ROMANO

Bahía de Cárdenas

ARCHIPIÉLAGO DE SABANA-CAMAGÜEY

La Isabela

Quemado de Güines

HAVANA

LA HABANA

Guanabacoa

Marianao

Guanajay

Bejucal

San José de las Lajas

San Antonio de los Baños

Güira

Güines Unión de Reyes

Jovellanos

Colón

Santa Isabel de las Lajas

Jagüey Grande

Aguada de Pasajeros

Cienfuegos

Palmira

Cruces

Pico San Juan
1135

Trinidad

Matanzas

Cárdenas

VILLA
CLARA

Sagua la Grande

Caibarién

Camajuaní

Zulueta

Santa
Clara

Placetas

Sancti
Spíritus

Yaguajay

Cabaiguán

Tunas de Zaza

Jatibonico

Morón

Ciego de Avila

Florida

Vertientes

Camagüey

Minas

Nuevitas

Esmeralda

Puerto Manatí

Puerto Padre

Chaparra

LAS TUNAS

Victoria de
las Tunas

Martí

Elía

San
Nájaso

Santa Cruz
del Sur

Jucaro

Guayabal

Campechuela

Niquero

CABO CRUZ

Manzanillo

GRANMA

Bayamo

SIERRA MAESTRA
Pico Turquino
1974

Portillo

Gibarra

Holguín

Banes

Antilla

Cueto

Mayarí

San
Germán

Alto Cedro

Ygibani

Palma
Soriano

Santiago
de Cuba

Bahía de Nipe

SIERRA
DEL CRISTAL

Sagua de Tánamo

Baracoa

CABO
MAISÍ

Imías

Tiguabos

San Luis

Guantánamo

Caimanera

1181

HAITI

Windward Passage

CUBA

CARIBBEAN SEA

JAMAICA

Montego Bay

CAYMAN ISLANDS
(U.K.)

Georgetown

ISLA DE PINOS
ISLE OF PINES

Nueva Gerona

Santa Fé

ARCHIPIÉLAGO DE LOS CANARREOS

CAYO LARGO

Golfo de Batabanó

PUNTA GORDA

PENÍNSULA DE ZAPATA

Bay of Pigs

Golfo de
Ana María

CAYOS DE
LAS DOCE LEGUAS

LABERINTO
DE LAS
DOCE LEGUAS

JARDINES DE LA REINA

Pinar del Río

Consolación del Sur

Los Palacios

Candelaria

Artemisa

GUANIGUANICO

Guane

Mantua

Minas de Matahambre

CORDILLERA DE GUANIGUANICO

CABO
CORRIENTES

Ensenada de
la Siguanea

CAYOS DE
SAN FELIPE

Golfo de
Guanahacabibes

PENÍNSULA DE GUANAHACABIBES

CABO SAN
ANTONIO

Yucatán Channel

© Rand McNally & Co.
A-503600-357   2 -2 -2

CUBA

Size of symbol indicates relative size of town

•   ○   ◉   ⊡   ■

Elevations in metres

further subdivision into 45 subregions and 38 physiographic zones.

The largest of Cuban regions, the Occidental region is 332 miles (535 kilometres) long and includes the provinces of Pinar del Río, La Habana (Havana), Matanzas, and parts of Villa Clara and Cienfuegos. Its topography is notable for the *mogotes,* unusually shaped elevated hummocks, although it is primarily composed of an enormous plain that occupies its entire southern section. The 110-mile-long Cordillera de Guaniguanico and the serpentine highlands of northern and central La Habana and Matanzas provinces lend further character to the region. The Occidental region contains less than half of the country's population and also Havana, the major Cuban economic, cultural, and administrative centre. The regional economy is based on agriculture (some of the best tobacco in the world, citrus fruits, sugarcane, cattle, rice, and coffee), copper and iron mining, tourism, and fishing.

The Central region extends from the Manacas plain (west of the city of Santa Clara) to the Ciego de Avila plain in Ciego de Avila province and consists primarily of the Trinidad and Sancti Spíritus highlands and lesser uplands, interspersed with plains and boggy regions in the province of Sancti Spíritus. It also includes the Archipélago de Sabana-Camagüey.

The major Cuban tobacco-growing area, the Central region also produces sugarcane, cattle, citrus fruits, and coffee as well as marble, copper, iron, and limestone. Industrial activity in the region is varied.

The Camagüey-Maniabón region, Cuba's main stock-raising area, centres on an ancient peneplain that extends over central Camagüey province and northwestern Las Tunas province between the Trinidad, Sancti Spíritus, and Maniabón highlands. Other economic activities include a major emphasis on sugarcane, cultivation of rice and grains, mining of chromium, and processing of cement, fertilizer, and gypsum.

At the eastern tip of the main island, the provinces of Las Tunas, Granma, Holguín, Santiago de Cuba, and Guantánamo have the nation's highest mountains, fastest streams, richest mines, and most spectacular bays. The Sierra Maestra rises along the southern coastline, the Sierra de Nipe on the northern, and between them lies the economically important Valle Central, its easternmost portion rising to the Sagua-Baracoa highlands, covered by the most extensive forests in Cuba. The region contains nickel reserves and also produces chromium, iron, copper, and manganese as well as sugarcane, coffee, and other agricultural items; its industrial centres process minerals and food and generate electric power.

The largest and most beautiful of the islands surrounding the main island of Cuba, the Isla de la Juventud, dotted with groves of pine and palm, has sand and clay plains in the north and hills in both the northwest and southeast; much of the island, however, is taken up by the gravel bed in the south and by the bogs of the coasts and uninhabited interior. At one time sparsely populated, it became the object of government resettlement projects in the mid-1970s. The cultivation of grapefruit was established as the basis for the island's economy.

The people. *Ethnic distribution.* For more than four centuries diverse ethnic groups have been settling in Cuba. Not only Africans and Spaniards (the predominant elements) but also Chinese, European Jews, and Yucatecans have all superimposed their cultural and social characteristics on those of the earliest settlers. Contemporary Cuban society exhibits a remarkable diversity as a result.

Cuba's original inhabitants came to the island from South America. They were the Guanahatabey and the Ciboney, the former living in the extreme west of the island of Cuba, the latter in various places in the island and particularly on the cays to the south. Both were hunter-gatherers. The Taino (Arawakan Indians), who arrived later and who spread over not only Cuba but also the rest of the Greater Antilles and the Bahamas, lived in villages and had rudimentary agriculture; they also made simple pottery. The Taino constituted 70 to 80 percent of the island's population at the time of the Spanish conquest. In 1511 the total indigenous population was estimated at

between 80,000 and 100,000, very unequally distributed, with density decreasing westward. Half a century after the Spanish invasion, however, only about 4,000 scattered individuals remained. Harsh treatment by the invaders, hard labour in the gold mines, hunger resulting from low agricultural productivity, and contagious diseases introduced by Europeans had all taken their toll. A few families with Taino physical characteristics living in the Sierra del Purial of easternmost Cuba are perhaps the only surviving descendants.

The Spaniards soon imported African slaves (more than 800,000 in all, most of them for work on the sugar plantations) as a substitute for the rapidly disappearing Indians. The Africans came mainly from Senegal and the Guinea Coast, with diverse origins including Yoruba and Bantu tribal backgrounds. Between 1919 and 1926, some 250,000 black Antillean labourers, 90 percent from Haiti and Jamaica, arrived under labour contract; nearly all remained. They and their descendants make up about one-tenth of the total population. The cultural influence of blacks has been considerable, especially in music and dance.

White Cubans (about three-quarters of the total population) are almost entirely of Spanish origin. Throughout Cuban history, the dominant classes were recruited primarily from the Europeans and their descendants, white and mestizo (the latter being of particular importance in the 20th century), who monopolized not only the direction of the economy but also access to education and culture.

In order to supplement the interrupted slave trade, the Hispano-Cuban landholders imported 125,000 indentured Chinese labourers, nearly all of them Cantonese, between 1853 and 1874, to work under contract for eight years. Bad living conditions reduced their numbers to 14,000 by the census of 1899. In the 1920s an additional 30,000 Cantonese and small groups of Japanese also arrived; both immigrations were exclusively male, and there was rapid intermarriage with white, black, and mestizo populations. In contemporary Cuba, the remaining Chinese element are about 1 percent of the total population.

Spanish is the Cuban national language; there are no local dialects, although the diversity of ethnic origins has influenced speech patterns. Some words are of native Indian origin, and a few (such as *hamaca* ["hammock"]) have passed into other languages. Africans have also enriched the vocabulary and contributed the soft, somewhat nasal accent and the rhythmic intonation that distinguish contemporary Cuban speech.

Religion. Religions in Cuba include Roman Catholicism, Santería (a cult devoted to certain African divinities formally identified with Catholic saints), and a number of Protestant and other groups. In the early 1960s, church and state confronted one another with open hostility, the church seeing the revolutionary government as anti-religious (one aspect of this being the nationalization of all schools) and the government seeing the church (the largest mass organization in the country) as a repository of counter-revolution. Many priests and nuns, and some Protestant clergy, left the country; others were deported. By 1965, however, the church, with a clergy drastically reduced in number, and the government entered upon a period of better cooperation.

Demography. Prior to 1953 immigration was a contributing factor in the total population growth of Cuba, but since that year the number of persons leaving the country has usually outnumbered new arrivals and the growth of the population has been more a consequence of changing birth and death rates. The birth rate rose steadily from 1958 to 1963 for a variety of social and economic reasons (*e.g.,* increased standards of living and expectations among low income groups, increased sexual freedom among females, and larger numbers of women marrying at a younger age) and improved methods of birth registration. These higher birth rates were more than offset by the increasing rates of death and infant mortality, caused by a mass exodus of physicians, a scarcity of medicines, and a rise in contagious diseases. In the mid-1960s the high birth rate stabilized and began to decline as increasing numbers of females entered the labour force, strict limitations on consumption were instituted, housing

Marginal notes:
Cordillera de Guaniguanico

Aboriginal peoples

Indentured Chinese

became scarce, and compulsory military service at age 16 was initiated. By the late 20th century the birth rate had declined by more than one-half of its 1960s peak of 35 births per thousand persons. In 1970 the mortality rate also began to drop as more physicians were trained and became available, the supply of medicines increased, and contagious diseases were controlled through vaccinations. By the late 20th century the death rate had stabilized between five and six deaths per thousand persons. The combined effect of the declining birth rate and heavy emigration from Cuba has resulted in a dramatic decrease in the overall rate of population growth, from a high annual growth rate of 2.6 percent in the early 1960s to less than one percent in the late 20th century. The provinces of the Oriente (Las Tunas, Granma, Santiago de Cuba, Guantánamo) and the Isla de la Juventud have the highest birth rates. The highest death rates are found in the province of La Habana, which also has the lowest birth rate, and in Cienfuegos, Ciego de Avila, and Camagüey provinces.

The economy. The revolutionary authorities inherited an economy that was essentially agrarian and was widely held to be characterized by extensive production (*i.e.,* the utilization of large areas of land with minimal outlay and labour), by emphasis on a single crop, and by the presence of *latifundios,* large landed estates. These basic traits, the revolutionary government decided, had to be eliminated before any serious effort could be made to transform the essentially underdeveloped country. Two agrarian reform laws (1959 and 1963) made the state the owner of most of the farmland. Small-scale farmers were permitted to retain their farms, and many tenant farmers were given title to the land they had worked. With state control established over the former North American- and Cuban-owned *latifundios,* Cuban authorities initiated, through investment of resources and effort, a substantial modification of agriculture.

The structure of Cuban industry (especially the sugar sector) likewise was not in harmony with the new economic development plans. At the time of the revolution, industry was extremely dependent on foreign commerce, while foreign investments (notably of North American capital) were covering more than 50 percent of its costs. The structural deformations in the economy induced by this dependence were also evident in the prospects for future industrial development, which were then limited to those branches using domestic sugar, nickel, and tobacco resources. During the 1960s the Cuban authorities devoted every effort to removing the dependence on Western capital, and in 1972 a series of major development agreements was concluded with the Soviet Union.

Resources. Cuban soil is very fertile, allowing for up to two crops a year, but agriculture was traditionally plagued by the unreliability of the annual rainfall. Subterranean waters are an important additional resource for both agriculture and industry.

Petroleum deposits supply only a small percentage of the nation's needs and the rest is met by imports. Peat, concentrated in the Península de Zapata, is still the most extensive fuel reserve. Nickel, chromite, and copper are the most important minerals mined, and the laterite (iron ore) beds in Holguín province have world significance. Nickel ore is processed in several large plants. There are also major magnetite and manganese reserves and lesser amounts of lead, zinc, gold, silver, and tungsten. Abundant limestone, rock salt, gypsum, and dolomite reserves and large kaolin and marble beds are also found on the Isla de la Juventud.

Agriculture and fisheries. The most important agricultural crop is sugarcane. Vast areas have been levelled and brought under irrigation, thus greatly expanding the acreage in sugarcane, and yields per acre have been increased with the application of fertilizers. Sugar output, except in years of drought or sugarcane blight, increased after the introduction of mechanized harvesters in the early 1970s.

The number of cattle was increased in the 1960s by cessation of slaughter of reproducing cows, by irrigation projects that added to available pasture, by artificial insemination, and by expanded veterinary services. Brahman (or Zebu)

cattle, the dominant breed (resistant to tropical climate but low in milk yield), were crossed with Holsteins (productive but prone to illness in the Cuban environment) and also with Brown Swiss in an unsuccessful attempt to produce acclimatized meat and milk producers.

Apart from sugarcane, the chief agricultural products are rice (the main source of calories in the traditional diet) and citrus fruits, the latter an important export crop. Tobacco, traditionally the country's second crop, is grown mainly in the Pinar del Río area in the west and also in the centre of the island. Other products include bananas, coffee, cocoa, pineapples, sweet potatoes, potatoes, corn (maize), cassava, and beans. It is necessary, however, to import large amounts of food (especially grain) and oilseeds and cotton.

Fishing resources (there are 500 different species of edible fish) are localized in four zones around the major shoal and island groups surrounding Cuba. Seafood production increased dramatically after 1959, largely because of government investment in fishing vessels and processing plants, but the institution of fishing zones by neighbouring countries during the late 20th century adversely affected the industry.

Industry. Processing of food and sugar are the two most important sectors of Cuba's domestic industry, and sugar is by far the most important export earner. A combination of prolonged drought and dropping world prices in the late 1970s led Cuban planners to develop more diversified sources of industrial income including the production of fertilizer, ammonium nitrate, steel, farm machinery, electronics equipment, and transport equipment. Other important industrial products are food and beverages, cement, electric power, tobacco, cigars and cigarettes, paper, textiles, and footwear.

Trade. In 1958 some 70 percent of Cuban imports came from the United States. By 1961 this was down to 4 percent, and it soon dropped to zero under United States government blockade measures. Communist bloc countries now account for about three-quarters of Cuban import and export totals. Import composition, too, has changed: production and transport equipment, mineral fuels, food, and live animals are the major imports. Principal exports include sugar (crude and refined and molasses), nickel, tobacco (especially the cigars for which Cuba is famous), fish, and coffee.

Administration of the economy. The Cuban economy is centrally directed in accordance with a national plan worked up by the government under guidelines laid down by the directorate of the Partido Comunista de Cuba (PCC; Communist Party of Cuba). Practically all economic activities are state run, a small private sector existing only in agriculture. The institutional economic structure consists of the Central Planning Board (Junta Central de Planificación, or Juceplan), headed by the economics minister; the ministries and national organizations that control the economic sectors and basic activities; the various state enterprises (*empresas*); and the provincial delegations that direct the work of the factories and related services.

Each work centre follows a distinctly Cuban organizational pattern. It is managed by a collective organization: the administrative board is responsible for production and service activities; the cells of the PCC support the outlining of jobs and politically orient members of the work centre; and the trade union, representing the workers, acts as a vehicle for the expression of their opinions.

The long-term investment program has been accompanied by the elimination of mass unemployment as it existed in the 1950s and access to consumption by formerly economically marginal sectors of the population. There is, however, a marked imbalance between money in circulation and goods and services available. Wages and prices are rigidly controlled and quota systems strictly enforced. For example, workers are moved to areas where labour is scarce by simply assigning them ration cards valid only in the sectors where their services are required. Farm incomes are controlled by regulation of the storage of agricultural products and by production limits. Overall, private ownership of the means of production is now limited to a few

Dependence on foreign commerce

Improvements in stock breeding

The national planning mechanism

small farmers, and the working class is officially ascribed a leading role in Cuban society.

Transportation. Cuba has a large merchant fleet to keep pace with the increase in foreign commerce. The major ports are Havana (fuels, grains, and other commodities), Cienfuegos (sugar exports), Santiago de Cuba, Guayabal, Matanzas, Antilla, Nuevitas, Mariel, and the U.S. naval base at Guantánamo.

The railway constructed between Havana and Bejucal in 1837 was the first in the Americas after those of the United States. The railway system deteriorated in the first years after the revolution of 1959 but much of it has been restored and most of the system continues to serve the sugar industry.

Total road mileage has increased since the revolution. The most important highway is the Carretera Central (Central Highway), which runs along almost the entire length of the island. Other major routes are the Vía Blanca (linking Havana with the Playa Varadero) and the Vía Mulata (connecting Baracoa, at the east end of the island, with the rest of the country). There are state transport enterprises (mostly for passenger traffic); one of these is national, the rest are provincial in scope. Automobile transport has been substantially downgraded in an attempt to adjust transport facilities to the realities of Cuban life.

The Empresa Consolidada Cubana de Aviación (Cuban Aviation Enterprise, or Cubana) operates the former four private airlines. There are international airports at Havana, Santiago de Cuba, and Camagüey. Among international flights is the Moscow–Havana nonstop flight of the Soviet Aeroflot line.

Administrative and social conditions. *Government.* Until the adoption of the constitution of February 24, 1976, Cuba had for some 36 years been governed either by the constitution of 1940 or by the post-revolutionary Ley Fundamental (Fundamental Law) of February 7, 1959, modelled upon the constitution but centralizing governmental power. The 1940 constitution had been suspended twice—from 1952 to 1955 by the dictatorship of Fulgencio Batista, and after 1959 when it was supplanted by the Ley Fundamental and by legislation that included the Agrarian Reform Law (May 17, 1959), the Urban Reform Law (October 14, 1960), the Nationalization of Education Law (June 6, 1961), and the Second Agrarian Reform Law (August 3, 1963).

Drafting of a new constitution to succeed that of 1940 began in 1965 and continued for the next 10 years; a preliminary draft was approved by the Politburo of the Central Committee of the Communist Party of Cuba in 1975, and the final version was approved by referendum on February 15, 1976, entering into force on February 24.

In October 1976, for the first time in 17 years, representatives for 169 municipal assemblies "of the people's power" were elected to give the people a more effective role in the running of their urban centres. These 169 assemblies met subsequently in November to elect a 481-member National Assembly, as they had somewhat earlier elected delegates to the 14 provincial assemblies; each of the bodies in turn elected executive committees to carry on the day-to-day work of their respective administrative organs.

The National Assembly, at its inaugural session in December 1976, appointed a State Council of 31 members, headed by a president, and a Council of Ministers, headed by a chairman. The State Council is the executive body of the state, carrying on the daily administration of the country between the twice-yearly sessions of the National Assembly.

Following the revolution, political parties were dissolved, and a single party was created out of the participating revolutionary organizations: the Movimiento 26 de Julio (26th of July Movement), the Partido Socialista Popular (Popular Socialist Party), and the Directorio Revolucionario 13 de Marzo (13th of March Revolutionary Directorate). In 1965 this single national party was officially designated the Communist Party of Cuba (Partido Comunista de Cuba). In the elections of 1976, candidates represented both the Communist Party and mass organizations.

The mass organizations were created after the revolution

The Communist Party of Cuba

to replace former social organizations and are under the supervision of the government. They include the Confederation of Cuban Workers (Confederación de Trabajadores Cubanos, or CTC), reconstituted in 1970, with stated objectives to support the government, help improve managerial performance and labour discipline, and raise the political consciousness of workers. The National Association of Small Farmers (Asociación Nacional de Agricultores Pequeños, or ANAP) is composed of independent farmers, outside the system of collectivized state farms, who own a fraction of the total cultivated land. In 1960 the Committees for the Defense of the Revolution (Comités de Defensa de la Revolución, or CDR), which now enroll most of the adult population, were created to maintain vigilance against "enemies of the revolution"; they are organized in every city, factory, and place of work and in many rural counties. The objective of the Federation of Cuban Women (Federación de Mujeres Cubanas, or FMC) is "to raise the ideological, political, cultural, and scientific level of women in order to incorporate them into the tasks assigned by the revolution"; it replaced a number of social clubs.

Committees for the Defense of the Revolution

Justice. In 1973 Cuba's judicial system was reorganized. The Tribunal Supremo Popular, divided into four chambers, became the main body of the new structure. Its jurisdiction includes criminal offenses, civil and administrative offenses, crimes against state security, and military offenses. The Tribunales Provinciales Populares deal with cases that warrant sentences of up to six years' imprisonment.

Armed forces. Cuban defense is based on the revolutionary armed forces, now equipped with sophisticated weaponry. The land forces are grouped in eastern, western, and central armies, and there is an effective air force and a navy. Auxiliary forces include a part-time civil-defense body. Military service is compulsory for male citizens between 16 and 45 years of age.

The Ministry of the Interior is charged with the maintenance of public order and state security, rehabilitation of prisoners and prison management, and fire fighting.

Education. The eradication of illiteracy was given high priority by the revolutionary government. Dissolution of all private schools was one of the first acts of the revolutionary government, and a fundamentally altered, state-directed education system was introduced. It includes general education, 12 grades preceded by a preschool stage; higher, or university, education; teacher-training education; adult education, directed toward the eradication of residual illiteracy and toward continued study by working people; technical education, parallel to middle-level general education; language instruction; and specialized education. Education is free at all levels, with supplementary scholarships to cover living expenses and medical assistance. Education expenditures receive high priority, and the number of students enrolled has increased dramatically from pre-revolution days.

The campaign against illiteracy

Health and welfare. Medical care is free, and mortality rates have been reduced. Infant and maternal mortality have decreased dramatically. The Ministry of Public Health (Minsap) requires physicians to work for the rural medical service in needy areas for two years after graduation.

Urban real-estate rental was prohibited under the Urban Reform Law of 1960, and it was made possible for families to own their homes by paying the current rental sum for not less than five or more than 20 years. Many families have acquired titles to houses and apartments in this fashion, and a large number of rural families have achieved free use of formerly rented lands. The traditional rural *bohío* ("hut") is being slowly replaced by more modern housing units. New towns and fishing villages have also been constructed.

Homes for the aged are under the direction of Minsap, but the *círculos infantiles,* institutions for the day care of children under seven years of age, are run by the Federation of Cuban Women. The *círculos infantiles* and *jardines de la infancia* are both intended to free women to work. Physical education and sports, under a national body, are an integral part of Cuban education. The Ministry of Interior Commerce is in charge of the fixing of prices for, and distribution and sale of, foodstuffs and notions (*abarrotes*), working as closely as possible with community groups.

Cultural life.   The cultural life of the Cuban people has also undergone a major transformation as part of what is regarded by the authorities as an ongoing revolutionary process. The government believes that mass culture is essential to the fulfillment of its economic and social aims and since 1959 has played a leading role in cultural life. This policy has been embodied in a set of directives, such as that creating a system of cultural organizations to take artistic displays to the remotest regions. Traditional Cuban culture, it was felt, was generally limited to Havana (and, to a much smaller extent, the provincial capitals), and was almost entirely privately endowed and thus subject to the vagaries of private fortunes, tastes, and interests. The National Cultural Council (Consejo Nacional de Cultura, or CNC) directs a program of education in music, plastic arts, ballet, dramatic arts, and modern dance. Amateur groups led by CNC instructors are also popular.

Theatre.   Cuban theatre has been state-supported since 1959, coming under CNC direction, except in the case of the university cultural extension departments. There are six national dramatic groups, whose directing councils create their own repertory. Their activities are centred on Havana, but they travel frequently in the provinces. Provincial theatre groups characteristically present their entertainments on tour. Cuban critical opinion acknowledges that the national theatre suffers from lack of maturity but emphasizes that the drive to seek a unique national expression while utilizing the full range of tradition has produced a number of important works. The Casa de las Américas (House of the Americas) has held a number of Latin-American theatrical festivals. The Casa del Teatro (House of the Theatre; attached to the International Institute of Theatre) is a major centre of information and research on Cuban and international themes, while the lyric theatre stimulates interest in opera and operettas by conducting exchange programs with other countries.

Music and ballet.   Cuban music has Spanish and African roots. Various organizations have disseminated modern influences, and soloists participate in exchange programs and tour rural areas under CNC sponsorship. Cuba's foremost contemporary artistic figure is undoubtedly the prima ballerina and founder (1948) of the Ballet Nacional de Cuba, and head of its school, Alicia Alonso, a dancer of international acclaim. The Ballet of Camagüey was established in 1971.

The National Symphony Orchestra has a chamber orchestra and instrumental ensembles attached and accompanies opera, operetta, and ballet. It makes annual tours of the island, as do its provincial equivalents. Festivals of Cuban music and song are held at intervals, encompassing works of every genre from every period. Performing musical groups range from the traditional *charangas* to popular orchestras.

Folklore.   In 1959 the Institute of Ethnology and Folklore was created within the Academy of Sciences of Cuba, with the aim of collecting and classifying the Cuban cultural heritage. It formed the National Folklore Group (Conjunto Nacional Folklórico), which performs Afro-Cuban dances nationally and internationally. The activities of the folklore group are complemented by the Institute of Literature and Linguistics of the Academy of Sciences. The legacy of Fernando Ortiz, a pioneer investigator of black customs, and the work of the University of Las Villas on popular culture deserve special mention.

Art.   Cuba has galleries, art museums, and community cultural centres ready to display the works of Cuban painters. The Palacio de Bellas Artes and the Casa de las Américas both organize major exhibitions from time to time. The revolutionary government emphasizes that it is not enough to open the galleries for increased public attendance if there has not been some prior education of the viewers, and effort is directed toward increasing public interest and artistic awareness.

Motion pictures.   Cuban filmmaking has been stimulated by the Cuban Institute of Cinematographic Art and Industry (Instituto Cubano del Arte e Industria Cinematográfica; ICAIC). The ICAIC also has an extensive film library and supports a cinematographic studies centre, which trains future technicians for the industry. For statistical data, see the "Britannica World Data" section in the current *Britannica Book of the Year*. (I.E./R.E.Cr./Ed.)

HISTORY

At the time of the Spanish exploration of Cuba, the native population formed two groups totalling 50,000. The Ciboney and Guanahatabey occupied western Cuba. The more numerous Taino, who occupied the rest of the island, were highly developed agriculturalists and a peaceful people, related to the Arawakan peoples of South America who had migrated to the Greater Antilles. Their houses, called *bohíos,* formed villages ranging from single families to communities of 3,000 persons. They had pottery, polished stone implements, and religious spirits called *zemis,* which were represented by idols of wood, stones, and bones. The Taino diet included potatoes, manioc, fruits, and fish.

The Spanish colonial regime.   Christopher Columbus discovered Cuba for Spain during his first voyage, on October 27, 1492. Diego Velázquez began permanent settlement in 1511, founding Baracoa on the northeastern coast with 300 Spaniards and their African slaves.

Within five years the island had been divided into seven municipal divisions, including Havana, Puerto Príncipe, Santiago de Cuba, and Sancti Spíritus. Each municipality had its own cabildo, or town council, governing its legal, administrative, and commercial affairs. From 1515, elected representatives of each cabildo formed a body that defended local interests before the royal council, especially matters such as the slave trade and the encomienda (an estate of land and the Indians inhabiting it). A bishopric, subordinate to Santo Domingo, was founded at Baracoa in 1518 but later moved to Santiago de Cuba.

The island's limited gold deposits discouraged early settlement. The colony became a staging ground for the mainland exploration of Yucatán, Florida, and the Gulf Coast. Such expeditions as that of Cortés, which attracted 400 Spaniards and 3,000 Indians, depleted the colonial population. The small number of permanent resident Spanish colonists used the Indians in encomienda. But by 1550 the encomienda was no longer feasible, because the island's Indian population had declined dramatically to about 5,000 because of social dislocation, maltreatment, epidemic diseases, and emigration. Throughout the 17th century, colonial life was made more difficult by the ravages of hurricanes, epidemics, the attacks of rival European countries trying to establish bases in the Caribbean, and freebooters. By 1700 peace had returned, and the population had grown to about 50,000. The *flota* system (regularly scheduled fleets between Spain and Spanish America) increased the commercial and strategic importance of Havana, while ranching, smuggling, and tobacco farming occupied the colonists. The administrative costs depended, however, on irregular subsidies from New Spain until 1808.

The 18th century brought intensified agricultural development. The main changes came with the growing dependence on sugarcane cultivation and the importation of African slaves for work on the plantations. In 1740 the Havana Company was formed to stimulate agricultural development by increasing the importation of slaves and regulating the export trade. The company was unsuccessful, selling fewer slaves in 21 years than the British sold during a ten-month occupation of Havana in 1762. Reforms of Charles III of Spain (ruled 1759–88) further stimulated the development of the sugar industry.

Between 1763 and 1860 the island's population increased from less than 150,000 to more than 1,300,000. Slaves made the most dramatic growth, increasing from 39,000 in the 1770s to some 400,000 in the 1840s. In the 19th century Cuba imported more than 600,000 Africans, most of them after an Anglo-Spanish agreement to terminate the slave trade in 1820. The Cuban insistence on the slave trade raised considerable diplomatic controversy between Spain and Great Britain between 1817 and 1865.

In 1838–80 the Cuban sugar industry became the most mechanized in the world, utilizing steam-powered mills

Margin notes:
Touring theatre groups

National Folklore Group

Pre-Columbian Cuba

Dependence of the economy on sugarcane

and narrow-gauge railroads. Expanding *ingenios* (sugar mills) dominated the landscape from Havana to Puerto Príncipe, expelling small farmers and destroying the island's famous large hardwood forests. By 1850 the sugar industry accounted for 83 percent of all exports and in 1860 Cuba produced nearly one-third of the world's sugar production. The sugar revolution propelled a new rich class of slave owners to political prominence. Mexican Indians and Chinese augmented the labour force, and in 1865 the African slave trade ended, although slavery was not abolished until 1886.

The demands of sugar—labourers, capital, machines, technical skills, and markets—strained interracial relations, aggravated political and economic differences between metropolis and colony, and laid the foundation for the break with Spain in 1898. Spanish colonial administration had been corrupt, inefficient, and inflexible. The United States had shown a lively and growing interest in the island, and expeditions by U.S. filibusters won support in the United States, especially in the Southern slave states. After the 1860s the U.S. tried many times to purchase the island.

Spain's failure to grant political autonomy, while increasing taxes, led to the outbreak of the first war of independence—the Ten Years' War (1868–78)—which led to a military stalemate. The rich sugar producers of western Cuba and the vast majority of the slaves failed to rally to the Nationalists, themselves divided over the questions of slavery, complete independence, and annexation to the U.S. Spain promised to reform the island's political and economic system at the Convention of Zanjón (1878). Many Cubans, including Nationalist leader Antonio Maceo, however, refused to accept the Spanish conditions.

By 1895 the political and economic crisis had grown more severe. U.S. investment had reached $50,000,000, and its annual trade with Cuba amounted to about $100,000,000. Cuban political organizations in exile were coordinated and mobilized by the poet and propagandist José Martí. War broke out again on February 24, 1895.

Spain deployed more than 200,000 troops. Both sides killed civilians and burned estates and towns. By 1898 commercial activity had come to a standstill. Excited by the "yellow press" and a mysterious explosion aboard the USS "Maine" in Havana Harbour, the U.S. declared war on Spain on April 25, 1898. In August Spain signed a peace protocol in Washington, ending hostilities.

United States occupation, 1899–1901. Cuban independence, granted by the Treaty of Paris (December 10, 1898), began January 1, 1899, under U.S. occupation. The military governor, Gen. John Brooke, tried to exclude Cubans from government. He disbanded the Cuban army and conducted a census before being replaced by Gen. Leonard Wood, a former military governor of Santiago City. Wood sought to mitigate political division and supervised elections that gave Cuba its first elected president, Tomás Estrada Palma.

The military occupation restored normality. The Americans built a number of schools, roads, and bridges; they modernized Havana and deepened its harbour, but they were primarily interested in preparing the island for incorporation into the U.S. American economic, cultural, and educational systems, and the franchise was designed to eliminate Afro-Cubans from politics. The Platt Amendment (1901) gave the U.S. the right to oversee Cuba's international commitments, economy, and internal affairs, and to establish a naval station (Guantánamo Bay).

The Republic of Cuba, 1902–58. A republican administration begun on May 20, 1902, under Estrada Palma faced difficulties over U.S. influence. Estrada Palma tried to retain power in the 1905 and 1906 elections, which were contested by the Liberals, leading to rebellion and a second U.S. occupation on September 29, 1906. U.S. Secretary of War William Howard Taft failed to resolve the dispute, and Estrada Palma resigned. For the U.S. Charles Magoon administered a provisional government of Cuban civilians under the Cuban flag and constitution. An advisory law commission revised electoral procedures, and on January 28, 1909, Magoon handed over the government to the Liberal president, José Miguel Gómez. Meanwhile,

The Ten Years' War

The Platt Amendment

Cuba's economy grew steadily, as sugar prices continually rose until the 1920s.

The Gómez administration (1909–13) set a pattern of graft, corruption, maladministration, fiscal irresponsibility, and social insensitivity—especially toward Afro-Cubans—that characterized Cuban politics until 1959. The Afro-Cubans, led by Evaristo Estenoz and Pedro Ivonet, organized to secure better jobs and more political patronage and to protest a ban of political associations based on colour and race. In 1912 government troops put down large demonstrations in Oriente. The pattern of corruption was followed by Mario García Menocal (1913–21), Alfredo Zayas (1921–25), Gerardo Machado (1925–33), Fulgencio Batista (through puppets 1934–39 and himself 1940–44 and 1952–59), Ramón Grau San Martín (1944–48), and Carlos Prío Socarrás (1948–52). Machado and Batista, who overthrew Machado in 1933 with U.S. support, were the most notorious, holding power through manipulation, troops, and assassins.

The income from sugar was augmented by vigorous tourism based on hotels, casinos, and brothels; Havana became especially attractive during the years of U.S. Prohibition (1919–33). Yet the prosperity of the 1920s, '40s, and '50s enriched only a few Cubans. For the majority, poverty (especially in the countryside) and lack of public services were appalling: with a national per capita income of $353 in 1958—among the highest in Latin America—unemployment and underemployment were rife, and the average rural worker earned $91 per year. Foreign interests controlled the economy, owning about 75 percent of the arable land, 90 percent of the essential services, and 40 percent of the sugar production. Nevertheless, there was no widespread discontent in 1958, when Fidel Castro supplanted Batista.

The Castro regime. Batista's fall resulted as much from internal decay as from the challenges of Fidel Castro's 26th of July Movement (commemorating Castro's attack on the Moncada military fortress in Santiago on July 26, 1953), the Federation of University Students (later absorbed into the Young Communists Union), and other groups. Castro had been a candidate in the aborted elections of 1952. His defense argument for his part in the Moncada attack, edited and published as "History Will Absolve Me," was a political manifesto. Released from prison in 1955, Castro and some friends went to Mexico to prepare for the overthrow of the Cuban government. An enlarged group, including the Argentinian revolutionary Ernesto (Che) Guevara, landed in Cuba in December 1956 and were almost annihilated in their first attack. From the Sierra Maestra the survivors fought a guerrilla campaign. When the Fidelistas took control on January 1, 1959, they numbered fewer than 1,000.

The 26th of July Movement had vague political plans, relatively insignificant support, and totally untested governing skills. They quickly forged a strong following from among the poor peasants, the urban workers, the young, and the idealistic of all groups and ages. The Communist Party of Cuba (Partido Comunista de Cuba), dating back to 1925, assumed the dominant role in political organization, and the state modelled itself on the Soviet bloc countries, becoming the first socialist state in the Americas.

The first stage of the new regime was dominated by the progressive dissolution of capitalism, between 1959 and 1963. In those confusing and difficult years, the government eliminated the remnants of Batista's army as well as the former labour unions, political parties, and associations of professional persons and farmers. New institutions emerged: the Confederation of Cuban Workers (Confederación de Trabajadores Cubanos, or CTC, reconstituted 1970), the National Institute of Agrarian Reform (Instituto Nacional de Reforma Agraria, or INRA, founded in 1959), the Cuban Institute of Cinematic Art and Industry (Instituto Cubano del Arte y Industria Cinematográfica or ICAIC, 1959), the Central Planning Board (Junta Central de Planificación, or Juceplan, 1960), the Committees for the Defense of the Revolution (Comités de Defensa de la Revolución, or CDR, 1960), the Federation of Cuban Women (Federación de Mujeres Cubanas, or FMC, 1960), the National Association of Small Farmers (Asociación

Political and social problems

26th of July Movement

Nacional de Agricultores Pequeños, or ANAP, 1961), the Revolutionary Armed Forces (Fuerzas Armadas Revolucionarias, or FAR, 1961), the National Union of Cuban Writers and Artists (Unión Nacional de Escritores y Artistas Cubanos, or UNEAC, 1961), the Young Communists (Unión de Jóvenes Comunistas, or UJC, 1962), and others.

Nationalization of U.S. interests

The nationalization of hundreds of millions of dollars in U.S. property and private businesses provoked retaliatory measures by the U.S. government, including an unsuccessful invasion by Cuban exiles at the Bay of Pigs in south central Cuba (April 1961) and unexecuted plots to assassinate Castro and overthrow his government.

Within Cuba the erratic drift toward socialism and the growing economic dependence on the Soviet Union divided both the leadership and the country at large. Hundreds of thousands of Cubans, especially from among the skilled and the wealthy, emigrated to Spain, the United States, and other countries. INRA tried and failed to diversify the economic base, and the constant mobilization for war frustrated effective long-term planning. Attempts to foment revolution elsewhere, especially in the Dominican Republic, Venezuela, and Bolivia, alienated Cuba from most of the other Latin-American states.

Castro visited Moscow during 1963, but the next two years witnessed a period of ideological instability as the government consolidated its domestic position. A second agrarian reform terminated the attempts to diversify the economy. Shortages became acute. A professional army replaced the militias as the bastion of national defense. The meeting of Latin-American Communists in Havana in November 1964 and the civil war in the Dominican Republic in April 1965 (which culminated in the military intervention of the United States) rekindled the Cuban desire to export their revolution.

Between 1965 and 1970 the revolution experienced a third, more radical phase. Cuba began to assume a significant leadership role among the so-called Third World countries, and in 1979 was host to the summit conference of nonaligned nations and its chairman from 1979 to 1982. However, Cuba's approval of the Soviet invasion of Afghanistan (1980) jeopardized its chairmanship of the nonaligned movement. By 1968 there was a strong campaign against bureaucrats and a renewed attack on private property, as hundreds of small businesses were nationalized. Military officers moved into the highest ranks of government, industry, and the party. Workers were organized into brigades and microbrigades. An attempt to produce 10,000,000 tons of sugar in 1970 failed, but scarcity and rationing had reached their worst.

Material conditions improved markedly beginning in 1970. The revolution institutionalized itself along orthodox Soviet lines. Bottlenecks and shortages were substantially eliminated, and diplomatic isolation gave way to technical, commercial, or military assistance between Cuba, the Soviet Union, and the states of Africa, Latin America, and the Caribbean. The political system was reorganized, the functions of the party and the government being separated. A new family code was introduced in 1975, and the following year a new constitution and a new electoral code created 14 provinces (instead of 6) and 169 municipalities (including the Isle of Pines). Fidel Castro became president of the Council of Ministers and the State Council (the latter office combining the offices of president of the republic and prime minister). Nationwide elections in 1976—with a participation rate between 92 and 99 percent—returned municipal assemblies, which then elected members to the provincial assemblies and the National Assembly.

Political reorganization

Castro re-established full diplomatic relations with the Soviet Union in 1960, and thereafter that country was the major trading partner and source of funds and military supplies for Cuba. From 1960 the Soviet Union bought the major portion of the Cuban sugar crop, generally at a price above that of the free world market. Soviet assistance to Cuba in loans, petroleum, war materiel, and technical advice amounted to several billions of dollars annually. The dominant Soviet role forced the Cubans to support the Soviet Union in its dispute with China, although pro-Chinese sentiment was very strong in Cuba in the mid-1960s. After 1968, when the Cubans supported the Soviet invasion of Czechoslovakia, the revolution did not deviate significantly from the pro-Soviet position.

Soviet military support was crucial in the early years, and Soviet manoeuvres often aroused strong antagonism from the U.S. The installation of Soviet missiles in Cuba in 1962 brought the world to the brink of war as the U.S. forced the removal of the missiles under threat of nuclear attack; in 1979 the U.S. objected, although less strenuously, to the presence of Soviet combat troops in Cuba.

The wide-ranging and confident Cuban foreign policy relied on strong Soviet support. In the late 1960s the Cubans began to redefine themselves as an "Afro–Latin-American people." By the 1980s this new definition was accompanied by assistance to a number of countries in Africa, Latin America, and the Caribbean. Cuban military assistance probably determined the outcome of the civil wars in Angola and Ethiopia, but civilian brigades of doctors, teachers, agronomists, construction workers, physical training instructors, and fishermen made more significant contributions in Algeria, Angola, Cape Verde, the Congo, El Salvador, Ethiopia, Grenada, Guinea-Bissau, Guyana, Jamaica, Mozambique, Nicaragua, Panama, Tanzania, and Yemen (Aden). It is Cuba's continued presence in Africa and South America that has most strained Cuba–U.S. relations in the late 1970s and early 1980s. Whereas at one time it was Cuba that accused the United States of dominating its smaller neighbours, now it is the U.S. government that claims Cuban interference.

A new twist was added to Cuba–U.S. relations by the phenomenal migration of Cubans in 1980. Early in that year, Castro permitted about 10,000 people to apply for Peruvian visas. And then, surprisingly, he allowed expatriate Cubans in Florida to bring relatives and friends from Cuba to the United States. Emigration restrictions were lifted on April 21, 1980, and not reimposed until September 26, during which time some 120,000 Cubans came by boat into the U.S. For current political history, see the annual issues of the *Britannica Book of the Year*.

(F.W.Kn./Ed.)

Dominican Republic

The Dominican Republic (República Dominicana) occupies the eastern two-thirds of Hispaniola, the second largest island of the Greater Antilles archipelago in the Caribbean Sea. Haiti, also an independent republic, occupies the western third of the island. Hispaniola lies between the islands of Cuba to the west and Puerto Rico to the east and is situated about 600 miles (970 kilometres) southeast of Florida and 310 miles north of Colombia and Venezuela. The northern shores of the Dominican Republic are washed by the Atlantic Ocean, while the southern shore is bordered by the Caribbean Sea. Between the eastern tip of the island and Puerto Rico runs a channel called the Mona Passage. The republic has an area of 18,704 square miles (48,442 square kilometres; including 46 square miles of adjacent islands). The capital is Santo Domingo.

The country, although small and underdeveloped, occupies a strategic position on major sea routes leading from both Europe and the United States to the Panama Canal. Between 1930 and 1961 the republic's history was dominated by the repressive dictatorship of Rafael Trujillo—a ruler who nevertheless maintained internal stability, managed to pay off the national debt, and introduced a measure of prosperity and modernization. Yet, the human costs were excessive; today, large numbers of Dominicans remain in misery, and many feel their situation worsening.

With the rise of Socialism in neighbouring Cuba, political affairs in the Dominican Republic have assumed an even greater international importance.

PHYSICAL AND HUMAN GEOGRAPHY

The land. *Relief.* Topography is complicated and varied and includes five distinct highland or upland areas running along a northwest to southeast axis. The Pico Duarte in the major Cordillera Central (Central Highlands) is the highest mountain in the West Indies, rising to a height of 10,417 feet (3,175 metres). There is also a smaller range, the Cordillera Septentrional, running parallel to the

Topography

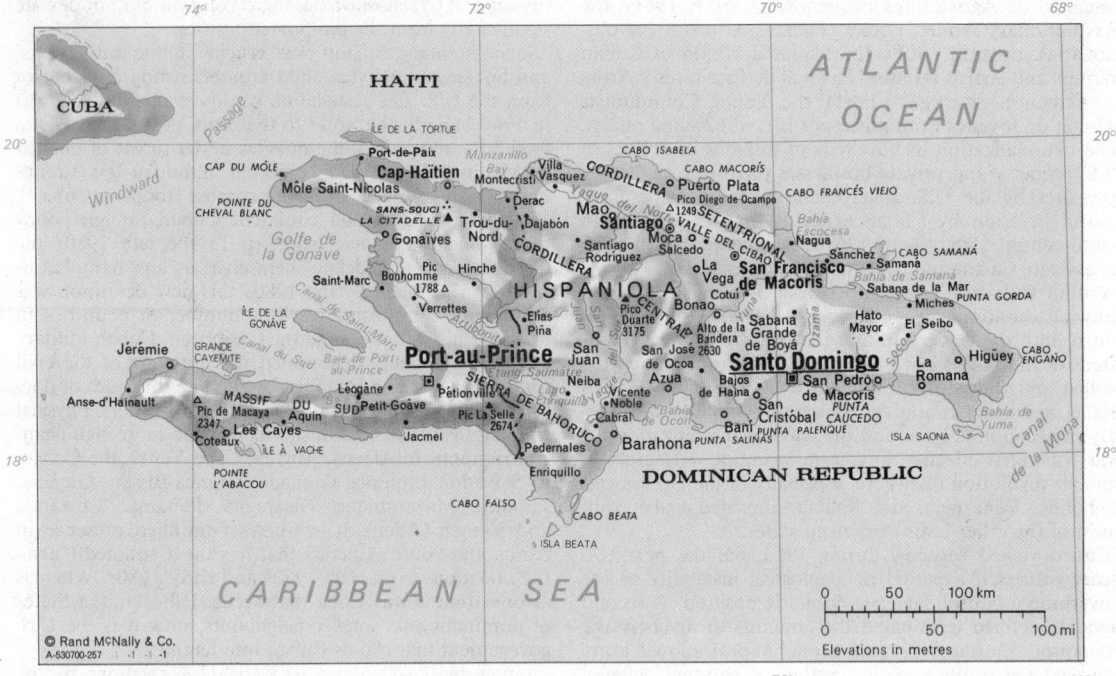

northwest coast, and two lesser ranges in the southwest. Another minor upland area, the Cordillera Oriental (Eastern Highlands), lies in the northeastern portion of the country. The extreme northwest and the extreme southwest are dry, low, and desertlike. The southeastern region consists of rolling lowlands.

Drainage. The Río Yaque del Sur empties into the Bahía de Neiba (Bay of Neiba), draining the Cordillera Central to the south, while the Río Yaque del Norte drains the northern slopes, flowing into the Bahía de Montecristi. The eastern part of the island is drained by the Río Yuna, which flows into the Bahía de Samaná, and by the Río Ozama, the mouth of which is near Santo Domingo, on the south coast. The salt lake of Enriquillo, 23 miles long and about 11 miles wide at its widest point, located near the Haitian border in the southwest, is a distinctive landmark.

Soils. Soils vary, but those of the upland areas are mostly of residual origin, deriving from metamorphic and sedimentary rocks. Soils in the lowlands are of recent alluvial origin, except in the southeastern savanna (grassland) area, where they consist of sedimentary deposits of recent marine origin. In general all the soils are quite fertile ex-

cept in the far southwest, in the Pedernales region, where the sedimentary soils are relatively barren.

Climate. The Dominican Republic lies well within the tropic zone, but the hot, moist climate typical of this zone is tempered in many areas by the altitude and in other areas by the insular character of the republic and by the Northeast Trade Winds that blow steadily from the Atlantic all year long. The heaviest precipitation is in the mountainous northeast, where the average rainfall is 100 inches (2,540 millimetres) a year. As the trade winds pass over the various mountain ranges, they lose their moisture until, in the far western part of the country, along the Haitian border, only about 30 inches of rainfall is received annually. The island is constantly in danger from tropical storms and hurricanes, which originate in the mid-Atlantic from August until October each year.

In spite of local variations, the country as a whole enjoys a relatively mild and pleasant climate. The national mean temperature is 77° F (25° C). Temperatures rarely rise above 90° F (32° C), and, even in the heart of the highest central mountain range, the overall mean is only about 69° F (21° C). Very cold temperatures are literally unknown.

Temperatures

Plant and animal life. Vegetation varies considerably. The mountains are still largely forested with pines and hardwoods, although during the past century the lower and more accessible slopes were practically denuded of trees by commercial lumbering. In the drier regions, low shrubs and scrubby trees predominate, but as rainfall increases grasslands and dense rain forests occur.

Cultivation of a wide variety of crops has largely replaced the natural vegetation in many areas—particularly in the more fertile upland valleys and on the lower mountain slopes. Mangrove swamps line some coastal areas, while elsewhere, particularly along the northern shore, sandy beaches of great beauty are to be found.

Wild-animal life is not abundant, although for several centuries cattle and goats, introduced by the early Spanish colonists, ran wild on the grasslands and in the desert areas. Alligators are found near the mouths of the Yaque del Norte and the Yaque del Sur and in the waters of Lago Enriquillo. A great variety of birds, including ducks, are hunted. Fish and shellfish inhabit the surrounding waters but have not been exploited commercially. Sport fishing, however, is an important tourist activity.

Settlement patterns. Until well into the 20th century, the Dominican people felt little national unity. Loyalties to traditional regions and to local chieftains (*caudillos*) were stronger than national allegiance. These regions correspond roughly to natural ecological zones and have changed little in the course of time.

The greatest population density is in the area referred to as the Valle del Cibao, which extends across the north from the Samaná Peninsula in the northeast, north of the eastern and central mountain ranges, and south of the Septentrional range, to Monte Cristi in the far northwest.

South of the Cordillera Central lies an alluvial plain where rice is grown; the population is centred on San Juan de la Maguana. Many of the inhabitants of the town of Azua and its environs are the descendants of immigrants from the Canary Islands.

The area surrounding Santo Domingo is often referred to simply as "the capital." "Capitaleños" are considered distinctive in culture and personality, although the massive rural-to-urban migration occurring in the country seems likely soon to erase this image.

Finally, the eastern savannas, now largely under sugar cultivation, are inhabited by settlers of predominantly European ancestry—descendants of cattle herders and families who owned small ranches. The eastern coastline itself, however, is increasingly inhabited by blacks from other West Indian islands who have come to work on the sugar plantations, in the mills, or on the docks. Most of these are temporary or seasonal workers, many from Haiti.

The rural settlement pattern

Although villages exist, the more common rural settlement pattern is a scattered neighbourhood—perhaps clustered about a small store or church. Settlements frequently stretch along roadsides, with cultivated patches behind the houses; there are still many households so isolated from major or even minor roads that they can be reached only on foot or by horseback.

The country is still largely rural, although since 1950 it has exhibited one of the highest urbanization rates of any country in the world.

The capital city, Santo Domingo, is an increasingly cosmopolitan city in which manufacturing and other industry vie in importance with commerce, education, and governmental business. The second largest city is Santiago de los Caballeros, located inland in the heart of the Cibao.

The people. The Spanish language has always been predominant, although other tongues can also be heard. Various European languages are often spoken; among Haitian immigrants, a French patois is common.

The racial composition is predominantly mestizo (*i.e.,* of mixed blood) with a small number of persons claiming to be of European descent and a smaller black minority group. The racial categories are roughly associated with economic and social class status, with more blacks at the bottom and more whites at the top. In addition, there is a small colony of German Jews, now beginning to break down as a distinctive unit, and a small group of Japanese in the Constanza Valley, most of whom are engaged in agriculture. During the 19th century, large numbers of persons immigrated from the Mediterranean area, especially from Lebanon; this group has today blended culturally and socially with the remainder of the population.

Although it is generally supposed that the original Taino (Arawakan Indians) were annihilated during the early Spanish occupation, it is probable that the present-day Dominican population includes some genetic components deriving from this group, although no identifiable Amerindian ethnic group remains.

Most of the population is Roman Catholic. The Catholic Church exerts a marked influence on cultural life at national, local, and family levels. A minute percentage of the population is Protestant; the remainder is Jewish, practices other religions, or professes no religion.

Slightly more than half of the people reside in rural areas and the rate of population increase is greater than that of most of the West Indian islands. Birth rates in both the Dominican Republic and bordering Haiti are substantially higher than those of nearly all of the neighbouring islands; but the death rate for the Dominican Republic, although higher than most Caribbean islands, is about 40 percent less than the death rate of Haiti. This gives the Dominican Republic one of the highest rates of natural increase in the Caribbean.

The economy. *Resources.* The most important resource of the Dominican Republic is the land, which is the foundation of the predominantly agricultural economy. Less than one-fifth of the land is arable and less than one-half of the arable land is under permanent cultivation. Pastures and meadows make up the largest land use category, about one-third of the land, and forests account for more than one-tenth of the land area. A number of minerals are known to be present but—with the exception of nickel, bauxite, gold, silver, gypsum, and iron ore—have not yet been highly developed commercially. Salt, largely from salt deposits near Lago Enriquillo, is also produced in commercial quantities. A smaller salt-producing enterprise, based on the evaporation of sea water, has also been of some importance at Monte Cristi. Other minerals that might be developed in the future include sulfur, coal, titanium, molybdenum, cobalt, tin, oil, and zinc.

The Dominican Republic is one of the relatively few sources of quality amber in the Western Hemisphere. Although it has not yet been extensively exploited, craftsmen produced distinctive jewelry for the local and tourist trade.

Agriculture and fisheries. The agricultural base of the economy is heavily dependent on the growth of sugarcane. Most of all foreign exchange comes from agricultural exports, and raw sugar accounts for the largest share of export earnings. Tobacco, cocoa, coffee, hides, fruits, and tomato paste are other important agricultural exports.

Sugarcane is grown primarily along the southern coastal plain and the largest sugar plantations are located in the southeastern part of the country. Coffee cultivation is dependent on migrant labour and occurs on landholdings that are smaller than most sugar plantations. Cacao is grown primarily in the northern province of Duarte. Agricultural production of foodstuffs has failed to keep pace with the demands of the population, and, consequently, the Dominican Republic must import agricultural products.

Unexploited biological resources are few, but proper management of agricultural lands, forests, and grazing areas could result in far greater productivity. Although the possibilities for a large-scale fishing industry seem limited by the relative scarcity of marketable fish in nearby waters, there is potential for further development of tourism and big-game fishing in several of the southern bays.

Industry. The main industry is sugar. The processing of foods and beverages is well developed. Textiles and finished clothing—particularly shoes, shirts, and hats—are made locally and have replaced some imports.

Many industries are characterized by their small size. These include, among others, manufacturers of furniture, soap, candles, rope, some food products, and paper clips, as well as building materials, such as concrete blocks, cement, and tiles. Tourism has been developed to provide increased revenue for the country, as well as to provide more jobs in the service and construction sectors.

Trade. The Dominican Republic's heavy dependence on sugar exports makes the balance of trade susceptible to worldwide fluctuations in sugar demand and prices. The government has taken steps to diversify the economy and to lessen the dependence on sugar exports. The largest strides in diversification have been made in the mining sector, in which exports of gold, silver, bauxite, and ferronickel account for about one-quarter of all export earnings, and in the light industrial sector, which exports clothing, electronic equipment, leather goods, and industrial staples. In addition to foodstuffs, the country's chief imports are petroleum products and manufactured goods.

Administration of the economy. During the Trujillo regime, from 1930 to 1961, the government (which was, in effect, the Trujillo family) largely controlled both agriculture and industry and, thus, the economy. Since 1961, most Trujillo enterprises have remained under governmental control. Two holding corporations were formed to manage them. The first, the Industrial Development Corporation (Corporación de Fomento Industrial), was created in 1962 and handles all the Trujillo industrial holdings other than sugar mills. This was replaced in 1966 by the creation of the Dominican State Enterprise Corporation (Corporación Dominicana de Empresas Industriales, CORDE). There is also the State Sugar Council (Consejo Estatal del Azúcar, CEA), which in 1966 replaced the former Dominican Sugar Corporation (Corporación Azucarera Dominicana). It manages the sugar mills.

> Control of the sugar industry

The monetary system is based on a managed gold-bullion standard. The banking system is well developed, and there are several loan companies and insurance agencies.

Import duties constitute a large part of the entire public revenue. Other government income derives from sales tax, vehicle licenses, and road taxes. Income taxes are levied.

Trade unionism has not been important historically in the Dominican Republic. During Trujillo's rule, there was one so-called confederation of workers, which, in fact, was no more than a company union. After 1961 the labour movement developed rapidly, with unions tending to organize on the basis of political affiliation. Many affiliated with international labour organizations. As the agricultural sector continues to decline, trade unionism may be expected to become increasingly important.

There are also a number of employer associations, including the U.S. and Dominican chambers of commerce, as well as associations of cattle growers, sugar producers, and tomato growers. A number of factories and industries have associations for workers and management.

Transportation. Santo Domingo is the hub of a transport system that is generally more than adequate to assure the flow of both people and goods to virtually all parts of the republic. Although certain routes are time consuming and indirect because of the inadequacy of the linkage through the central mountain system, the road network throughout the country is, nevertheless, generally good. Major highways of concrete or asphalt extend in three directions from Santo Domingo, and secondary roads branch out from these major arteries.

> The road system

Although buses are rare, private taxicabs provide transportation both within and between cities. Most goods are transported by truck to the important market centres.

A government-owned railroad line runs through the eastern half of the Cibao from La Vega to the port of Sánchez on Bahía de Samaná. This carries both passengers and freight, but most of the country's railway lines are used by the sugar industry.

There are international airports at Punta Caucedo, about 15 miles east of Santo Domingo, and at Puerta Plata on the northern coast. A secondary airport in Santiago handles small jets and propeller planes. Other airfields around the country are open to small civilian craft. The government-owned airline, Companía Dominicana de Aviación (CDA), operates flights to to San Juan (Puerto Rico), Curaçao in the Netherland Antilles, New York City, Panama City, and Miami, and also makes local flights.

Airlines now handle most passenger traffic to and from the Dominican Republic, but goods are exported and imported primarily by sea. The Bahía de Samaná is one of the finest and largest natural harbours in the entire Caribbean area. Until the 20th century, the primary commercial ports lay along the northern coast, but, with the rise of the sugar plantations in the south, the ports of Santo Domingo, San Pedro de Macorís and La Romana have increased in importance. Most general goods pass through Santo Domingo, but sugar is largely exported through the ports of San Pedro de Macorís and La Romana. Once important historically, the ports of Monte Cristi and Sánchez in the north are now almost defunct. Only Puerto Plata (the country's second port) retains its commercial importance; it is still viable largely because of the tobacco, coffee, and cacao interests in the Cibao region. Barahona ships bauxite, gypsum, and salt but receives few imports.

Administrative and social conditions. *Government.* The executive power is vested in a president, who is also commander in chief of the armed forces, and a vice president. There is a Senate and a Chamber of Representatives. The Senate is composed of one representative from each province, and one from the National District. The Chamber of Representatives reflects the size of the population, but has no fewer than two representatives from each province, and two from the National District. The present (1966) constitution, like its 28 predecessors, guarantees human rights, prescribes the division of governmental powers, and provides for popular sovereignty. It also accords suffrage to all Dominicans of either sex over 18 years of age, unless they are members of the armed forces or the police.

> The 1966 constitution

Historically, the various constitutions have provided special emergency powers for the president that have made it possible for the executive to supersede the legislative and judicial branches of the government should the president deem it necessary. While retaining provisions for emergency executive powers, each successive constitution has, nevertheless, expanded the social and economic rights guaranteed in earlier documents. A formal relationship between the Catholic Church and the government, incorporated in earlier constitutions, has now been eliminated. The right to private property is guaranteed but is limited by the right of the state to expropriate for the general good. Terms for national elected offices are four years, and incumbents may seek re-election for an additional term.

The nation is divided into 26 provinces and one National District (Distrito Nacional). The central government administers the outlying provinces through governors appointed by the president. Each province elects representatives to the bicameral national congress. Internally, each province is subdivided into municipalities that elect their own councils and enjoy considerable local autonomy.

Justice. The legal system is based upon the Napoleonic Code. There is a series of regular courts, the judges of which are appointed by the Senate and may have no other public employment. These courts, with the exception of the land and commercial courts, have jurisdiction over both criminal and civil matters.

> The legal system

In criminal cases the judicial process begins with an investigation, generally conducted by an investigating judge. This is followed by the trial proper, conducted by the appropriate court. Appeals are made to the appropriate superior court and may finally be considered by the Supreme Court, composed of nine justices.

Armed forces. It was not until the United States occupation of 1916 to 1924 that a modern military body was formed in the Dominican Republic. Today, the army, navy, and air force are organized separately, each being headed by its own chief of staff.

During the Trujillo regime, the armed forces were used to preserve the dictatorship, and even today, the armed forces play a role in government.

Education. The more isolated and rural the population, the less accessible are educational institutions. Primary schooling ordinarily lasts six years, although in rural areas only three may be offered; this is followed by a two-year intermediate school and a four-year secondary course, after which a diploma called the *bachillerato* is awarded. Relatively few lower-income-group students, however, succeed in reaching this level, since the system is designed to encourage middle- and upper-income-group students to prepare for admittance to a university. Most wealthier students attend private schools, which are frequently sponsored by religious orders. Some public and private vocational education is available, particularly training in the field of agriculture, but this too reaches only a very small percentage of the population.

The universities

The Universidad Autónoma de Santo Domingo (UASD), founded in 1538, is proud of being one of the oldest universities in the New World. It is autonomous, being free of both governmental and religious control, although most of its funds are from the national budget. Costs are low and even poor students may attend, if they have been fortunate enough to have secured the requisite primary and secondary preparation.

The Universidad Nacional "Pedro Henríquez Ureña" (UNPHU), located in Santo Domingo, enjoys the support of not only the Catholic Church but also of some private endowments, as well as receiving funds from the national government. The Universidad Católica "Madre e Maestra" (UCMM) in Santiago is similarly supported both by the Catholic Church and through private and public endowments. The Universidad Central del Este in Macorís and the Universidad Tecnológica de Santiago were founded in 1970 and 1974, respectively.

Health and welfare. Health conditions among the poorer classes in both rural and urban zones are characterized by a generally unsanitary environment, inadequate health services, and poor nutrition. As a result of these conditions, both infectious and parasitic diseases are rampant, and infant mortality is high.

Hospital and trained medical personnel are available only in the larger cities and towns. In the rural areas, home remedies and the professional services of practitioners of traditional local medicine are the only means of preserving or restoring health. Cases of severe illness may be taken to the nearest urban centre, where hospitalization is free. The tendency, however, is to take this measure only in extreme cases, often when death is already imminent.

Housing is considered by Dominican planners to constitute one of the most serious problems in the country.

Rural housing

On the sugar plantations in the south, barrack-like housing is provided for temporary workers, but more permanent employees frequently have their own small huts, or *bohíos,* often on company-owned land. These may be little more than a lean-to of palm leaves and bamboo. Others, more sturdy, may have double walls filled with rubble and plastered with mud.

In the Cibao, a relatively prosperous zone, houses are built solidly of palm board or pine and are frequently painted and decorated, with shutters and lintels in contrasting colours. Roofs are most often covered with sheets of zinc or tin but, in poorer households, may be thatched. A prosperous family will have a concrete floor, but most are of packed earth.

In the cities are to be found the squatter settlements and poverty-stricken inner-city ghettos characteristic of most rapidly urbanizing underdeveloped countries of the world. In some cases these may be built of cardboard, tin cans, discarded inner tubes, and any other materials the inhabitants may scavenge.

Also in the cities are districts with well-appointed modern houses, occupied by members of the new commercial and industrial elite, as well as by the more traditional landbased oligarchy. Government programs, often funded with international loans, have financed housing construction for lower- and middle-income families.

The police are frequently associated in the minds of the people with the army and, indeed, have served similar functions. Civil and political offenses frequently have merged into one, and arrests for criminal offenses are often politically motivated.

Social conditions in the Dominican Republic resemble those found in other underdeveloped American nations. The small farmers rarely eke out more than a subsistence crop and most often must supplement this by the sale of handicrafts; products include baskets, pottery, rocking chairs, straw hats, and foodstuffs. These items are either sold to middlemen, who market them in towns, or else are displayed and sold along the roads and highways, frequently by children.

Although most Dominicans, as well as some social scientists, have insisted that there is no traditional oligarchy, there nevertheless exists an intellectual and economic elite that constitutes a tiny fraction of the total population. There also is an emergent middle-income group.

By far the largest proportion of the population belongs to the lower-income group. This category includes small farmers, landless agricultural workers, itinerant merchants, and unskilled manual labourers.

Cultural life. It is difficult to define any particular and unique cultural tradition that may be labelled Dominican. There are, nevertheless, some cultural items worthy of special mention. Music, especially when accompanied by dancing, is important at all social levels and in all regions. The most typical forms are those with clear African antecedents, especially in their rhythms. There are also folk songs and tunes deriving from Spain and the Middle East. The merengue is a particularly popular dance, followed closely by the bolero. The guitar is probably the most popular instrument, but in some rural areas flutes and homemade marimbas are also found. There is no such thing as an indigenous national costume, although an elaborate fiesta dress reminiscent of Spanish flamenco styles is sometimes worn by wealthier women and proclaimed to be "Dominican."

Organized sports are popular, especially baseball. In the more rural areas, cock fighting remains a traditional and popular spectator sport. Soccer is also played but seems to have been eclipsed by baseball in recent years. For statistical data, see the "Britannica World Data" section in the current *Britannica Book of the Year.* (N.L.G.)

HISTORY

Very little is known of the island of Hispaniola's preColumbian history. At the time of Columbus' first landing in 1492, the Caribs, a marauding people who had apparently originated on the South American mainland and conquered their way up from the Lesser to the Greater Antilles (and for whom the Caribbean Sea is named), were preying upon the more peaceable Tainos (Arawaks), who had previously settled there. Estimates of the size of the indigenous population range from 300,000 to 3,000,000; other features of pre-Columbian Indian life are similarly shrouded in uncertainty. Part of the uncertainty stems from the fact that the Indians on Hispaniola were less advanced socially and culturally than were the large-scale Indian civilizations in Mexico, Guatemala, or Peru, with their longer histories and proud traditions.

Hispaniola was visited by Columbus on his maiden voyage. A colony was established on the north coast, but the first settlers were slaughtered by the Indians. Returning, Columbus established a second colony; but reports of abundant gold farther south quickly led to the abandonment of the northern outpost and to the founding of Santo Domingo city on the Caribbean coast.

Colonial era. Hispaniola was the first area in the New World to receive the full imprint of Spanish colonial policy. The oldest cathedral, monastery, and hospital in the Americas were established on the island, and the first university chartered. The earliest experiments in Spanish imperial rule were conducted here. Class and caste lines were rigidly drawn; the Roman Catholic Church served as the strong right arm of the temporal authority. A cruel, exploitative, slave-based society and economy came into being. The first "revolution" in the New World was also recorded on Hispaniola.

Period of Spanish rule

During the first half-century of Spanish rule, Hispaniola flourished, for its rich mines and lush lands yielded abundant wealth, and it served as the administrative centre for Spain's burgeoning American empire. But the more lucrative conquests of Mexico and Peru soon turned it into a poor way station. Its Indians were decimated, gold and silver were more easily available elsewhere, and the more ambitious Spaniards emigrated.

For the better part of the next three centuries, Hispaniola remained a neglected, poverty-ridden backwater of the Spanish Empire in the Americas. Successive raids by British, Dutch, and French marauders and buccaneers devastated the island still further. Socially and economically, it retrogressed, reverting to a more primitive form of existence. Eventually, French claims to the western third of the island were recognized, and a prosperous sugar-producing colony based on black slavery grew up in the area that was later to become the independent nation of Haiti. As a by-product of Haiti's prosperity, the Spanish colony also experienced a modest boom in the 18th century.

In 1795, as a result of its defeat in the wars that had been raging in Europe, Spain ceded the eastern two-thirds of Hispaniola to France. Meanwhile, inflamed by the revolutionary currents then sweeping France and stirred to revolt by the inhuman conditions under which the slaves were forced to labour, a slave uprising had begun in Haiti. Led by Toussaint-Louverture, the blacks not only succeeded in throwing off French rule but soon overran the previously Spanish eastern end of the island as well, instilling terror in the white ruling class. With the aid of the British fleet, the Haitians were driven back, and in 1809 the colony was reunited with Spain. In 1821, following the lead of the countries on the mainland, the Dominican Republic declared its independence. The new republic comprised approximately the eastern two-thirds of the island.

Slave revolt

The Dominican Republic to 1930. Within a matter of weeks, Haitian columns under Jean-Pierre Boyer (president of Haiti, 1818–43) again overran the entire island. Dominican historians have portrayed this occupation (1822–44) as cruel and barbarous. Haitians held the highest offices, closed the university, severed the church's ties with Rome, forced out the traditional ruling class, and all but obliterated the western European and Hispanic traditions. But Boyer also freed the slaves, and his administration was generally more efficient and his troops less uncontrolled than Dominicans like to admit.

In the 1830s Juan Pablo Duarte—known as the father of Dominican independence—organized a secret society to fight the Haitians, and in 1844, after a long struggle and aided by the outbreak of civil war in Haiti itself, independence was finally achieved. But Duarte and the other idealistic independence fighters were soon exiled, and the new nation quickly fell into less noble hands.

From 1844 until 1899 the Dominican Republic was dominated by a succession of dictatorial "men on horseback," who prevented the growth of the genuine representative democracy that the constitution proclaimed and who were not above selling out the country to foreign "protectors" and commercial interests. Pedro Santana and Buenaventura Báez emerged as the two most prominent figures, alternating in the presidency for nearly 30 years. In order to ward off continuous assaults by Haiti, Santana returned the country to Spain (1861–65) and arranged to have himself named governor-general. After a series of battles, Spain withdrew its troops; but the idea of a protectorate remained, and Báez now approached the United States with a plan. Pres. Ulysses S. Grant favoured annexation, but after the questionable activities of a United States land-speculating company became public, the Senate failed to ratify the treaty.

19th-century dictators

During the 1870s the instability continued. Báez returned to the presidency for the fifth time, and the country's first, but short-lived, democratic government came to power. The instability culminated in the emergence of a new strong man, Ulises Heureaux, who dominated the country from 1882 to 1899. Heureaux presided over a period of unprecedented stability and national growth. New roads were built, communications improved, production rose, foreign capital entered, population increased. The Dominican Republic began its process of modernization.

Following Heureaux's assassination in 1899 the country returned to the chaotic, unstable politics of the past. New men on horseback galloped in and were in turn forced out of the presidential palace. For a brief time, under Ramón Cáceres (1906–11), the country seemed to be recovering; but he too was assassinated, and political chaos ensued once more. Even the accession of the archbishop Adolfo Nouel to the presidency in 1912 failed to stem the disorder; within four months he, too, was forced to resign.

Meanwhile, the deteriorating financial situation, plus the expanding interests of the United States in the Caribbean area, had drawn its large North American neighbour ever deeper into Dominican affairs. By this point, the United States had replaced Europe as the major importer of Dominican products as well as the chief supplier of Dominican imports. United States private investments were also rising rapidly. In 1905, threatened with the possibility that European creditors would use force to collect some unpaid Dominican debts, the United States took over the administration of the Dominican customs revenues. Over the next decade the United States influence increased, and in 1916, as the fragile political structure collapsed again, the United States assumed complete control.

United States influence

The United States occupation (1916–24) saw the building of some new roads, schools, and communications and sanitation facilities, and there were other constructive projects. But the occupation forces had assumed arbitrary control and frequently abused their authority. In addition, the creation by the United States Marines of a modern, unified, military constabulary provided the instrument by which future Dominican strong men could seize power.

In 1924, in United States-supervised elections, Horacio Vásquez was elected president. His rule eventually proved incompetent and corrupt, and the stock market crash of 1929–30 undermined the Dominican economy. In 1930 a revolution was launched against his rule. The military forces, now under the firm control of Rafael Trujillo, held the balance of power; but rather than defend the government, they stood by and let the revolution succeed. Then Trujillo moved to take power himself.

The Dominican Republic since 1930. The dictatorship of Rafael Trujillo (1930–61) was one of the longest, cruellest, most absolute dictatorships in modern times. For more than three decades Trujillo ruled his country with an iron hand; virtually everything he touched had to belong to him. Trujillo dominated the armed forces, government, economy, church, education, everything. Under Trujillo, however, as under Heureaux, the economy prospered.

Following Trujillo's assassination in 1961, his heirs and followers attempted to hang on to the reins of power. But they were also driven out, and the country embarked on a more democratic course. In 1963 Juan Bosch and his moderately reformist Dominican Revolutionary Party (Partido Revolucionario Dominicano, or PRD) took power, the first democratically elected and progressive government in the country's history. Conservative forces remained strong, however, and after seven hectic months Bosch was overthrown. As the country returned to conservative, do-nothing rule, the frustrations and pressures began building up; in 1965 the Dominican Republic exploded in a popularly based and democratic social revolution. Fearing a second Cuba, however, the United States again occupied the country (1965–66) and snuffed out the revolution.

After an interim, new elections were held in 1966. The winner was Joaquín Balaguer, a former Trujillo puppet now presenting himself as a moderate conservative and a symbol of orderly change. The reelection in 1970 of the conservative regime of Balaguer illustrated the power of the business, commercial, and industrial oligarchy. Under Balaguer some economic gains were registered and a number of social reforms partially implemented, but the level of tension remained high and the problems brought dramatically to the surface in the 1965 revolution continued. In 1978 Balaguer, old and enfeebled, was defeated in a presidential election by Antonio Guzmán Fernández and the PRD. Guzmán moved cautiously to implement reforms, such as nationalizing the gold mines, but conservative elements remained powerful and the economy fragile. Hurricane "David" devastated the country in 1979, and there were rumblings of discontent with the new democracy. It remained to be seen whether the Dominican Republic could break out of its vicious circles of dependency, authoritarianism, and underdevelopment. For current political history, see the annual issues of the *Britannica Book of the Year*. (H.J.Wi.)

Haiti

Haiti (République d'Haïti) is a republic in the West Indies, situated in the western part of the Caribbean island of Hispaniola. With an area of 10,714 square miles (27,-750 square kilometres), it occupies slightly more than one third of the island. Since much of its territory consists of two peninsulas, it has a coastline that is long in proportion to its size—amounting to 672 miles (1,080 kilometres). It is bounded to the east by the Dominican Republic (which occupies the remainder of the island), to the north by the Atlantic Ocean, and to the west and south by the Caribbean Sea. The capital is Port-au-Prince.

Haiti, which won its independence from France in 1804, was the first country in the Americas, after the United States, to win freedom from colonial rule. The great majority of the people are black; however, the mulatto minority form an élite that has played a leading role in Haiti's history. The official language is French, but a Creole patois is more generally spoken.

Strategically, Haiti commands the Windward Passage, a 50-mile-wide corridor running between the northwest extremity of Haiti and the eastern extremity of Cuba, which is situated midway on the sea-lane between New York City and the Panama Canal.

PHYSICAL AND HUMAN GEOGRAPHY

The land. *Relief.* Haitian territory consists essentially of two peninsulas, both of which project westwards—the northwestern peninsula and the southern peninsula. They are separated by the Golfe de la Gonâve, and are joined together by the alluvial plain of Artibonite, which covers about 310 square miles, as well as by the Plateau Central, which covers about 840 square miles. The backbones of the two peninsulas are formed by mountain ranges of white calcareous (chalky) rock. The northern peninsula trends from northwest to southeast, while the southern peninsula trends east to west. The mountains of the southern peninsula are higher, reaching an elevation of 8,793 feet (2,674 metres) about 15 miles west of the Dominican frontier. Short rivers flow rapidly down to the sandy shore, carving gullies in the hillslopes, and forming small coastal plains on which local administrative and trade centres have been established. Viewed from the sea, therefore, the prospect consists of succeeding valleys and hills. Most valleys are quite small, as are the towns located in them. The principal exceptions to this general pattern are the Plaine du Nord (the Northern Plain), which extends over almost 150 square miles, and the two plains—Cul-de-Sac (140 square miles) and Léogâne (40 square miles)—which unite in the region of the capital, Port-au-Prince. The plain of Cul-de-Sac extends into the interior along an east–west rift that divides the island into two distinct parts and which is subject to frequent but minor earthquakes. Two lakes, the Étang Saumâtre (literally "brackish pond"), with an area of 65 square miles, and the Étang de Miragoâne, with an area of about 10 square miles, are also situated in this rift near the Dominican frontier.

The principal mountain ranges are the Massif du Nord on the northern peninsula, the Massif du Sud (Massif de la Hotte) on the southern peninsula, the Massif de la Selle in the southeast, and the Chaîne des Montagnes Noires in the central part of the country. The principal river is the Artibonite, which rises in the mountains of the Dominican Republic and flows westward for about 174 miles to drain into the Golfe de la Gonâve. To the north of the Artibonite is the Trois Rivières, emptying into the Atlantic Ocean near the town of Port-de-Paix on the northwestern peninsula. The Estere flows into the Caribbean slightly north of the Artibonite and south of the Trois Rivières.

Offshore islands

Haiti has several offshore islands, the largest of which is the island of La Gonâve, about 40 miles long and with an area of 254 square miles; it lies about 40 miles northwest of Port-au-Prince. Off the northern coast lies the small island of Tortuga ("Turtle Island")—once the haunt of French buccaneers who, in the 17th century, first colonized the western part of Hispaniola; it has an area of 69 square miles. Other small islands are Grande Cayemite, situated off the northern coast of the southern peninsula, and Île à Vache, which lies off the southern coast.

Climate. Haiti lies near the northern limit of the tropical zone. The climate is modified by the proximity of the sea as well as by the mountainous terrain. Temperatures vary little throughout the year; they remain constantly high near sea level, but are lower at the higher altitudes inland. Average temperatures range from 75° F (24° C) in January and February to 83° F (28° C) in July and August. Port-au-Prince, at sea level, has an average annual temperature of 80° F (27° C). Inland, frosts occur from time to time at high elevations, as in the Chaîne de la Selle (8,793 feet). There is considerable variation in the amount of rainfall experienced at different locations, as the mountain ranges intercept low-flying clouds blown by the northeast trade winds in winter, and by eastern and southeastern winds in summer. Seasonal rainfall is highest in the south from May to November, and in the north from December to April. The average annual rainfall varies greatly in different locations: at Môle Saint-Nicolas in the northwest it is only about 20 inches (500 millimetres), while some highland areas receive over 100 inches. Hurricanes occasionally strike the island between the months of August and November.

Plant and animal life. Timber was once so abundant that mahogany and guayacan (a certain type of lignum vitae, the hardwood) were exported in quantity. The demand for cultivable land created by an increasing population, however, led to deforestation, so that today only a few pine forests survive at the higher elevations. Stands of mahogany, rosewood, and cedar may still nevertheless be found. An alpine type of vegetation occurs at elevations of more than 4,800 feet, where the climate is misty, cold, and damp. Elsewhere, many tropical and semi-tropical plants occur, with coconut palms and trees bearing such tropical fruits as avocados, mangoes, limes, and oranges growing wild. Mangrove swamps line the coast.

So far as is known, animal life never included poisonous snakes or mammals large enough to be dangerous to man. There are a number of rodents, and insects abound. Reptile life includes crocodiles, iguana, and lizards. There are over 200 species of birds. There are about 270 species of fish in the coastal waters, including tarpon, kingfish, barracuda, and red snapper.

Settlement patterns. Five traditional regions may be recognized; they correspond closely to the five *départements* into which the country has been divided—the North, the Northwest, the Artibonite, the West and the South. The North—in reality located in the northeast—is a well-watered plain, suitable for the cultivation of tropical crops, including sisal in its northeastern corner, which receives somewhat less rainfall than the remainder. The Northwest is, on the contrary, an arid area that becomes desert in its southern half; the island of Gonâve may be grouped with this arid region. In the centre of the country the region of the Artibonite River basin includes both a lowland area and the Central Plateau; rainfall is not abundant, but the Artibonite River itself, which flows at the rate of almost 3,500 cubic feet per second (99 cubic metres per second), offers possibilities of hydroelectric development. The West (in effect the southeast), where the capital is located, is where geographic contrasts are the most noticeable; here the people of the plains depend for their subsistence on the waters that flow down from the Massif de la Selle. The South (in effect the southwest) consists of fertile valleys tucked between mountain ranges that render transport unusually difficult; in addition the region is exposed to hurricanes from the south.

Human settlement almost everywhere has modified the natural landscape. The countryside is settled not by villages but by scattered extended-family settlements, which take the form of small groups of dwellings sheltered from passers-by and from the winds by groves of banana and coffee trees. The small wooden-frame houses thus protected vary in design according to the region, but are everywhere enclosed within a compound of four mud-daubed wattle walls. The roof is either thatched or—when the inhabitants are prosperous—is made of corrugated-iron sheets. Some peasants achieve considerable wealth, but seldom use it to further improve their housing; the furniture inside most houses remains restricted to necessities, with tools such as hoes and machetes taking pride of place. Wealth is invested in land and cattle, as well as in lavish entertainment that all who can are expected to

Family settlements

provide free for all. The traveller in the countryside often meets small groups of men engaged in collective work to the sound of drums and other instruments; files of women bringing produce to market are also a common sight. On Saturday night dance drums can be heard everywhere.

Urban growth has played a lesser part than rural population growth in changing the Haitian landscape. The largest city is Port-au-Prince, and after this the principal towns are Cap-Haïtien, Gonaïves, Les Cayes, Jérémie, and Port-de-Paix. Only a small percentage of the population is urban. Town growth, moreover, is virtually restricted to Port-au-Prince, with its Pétionville suburb, and Cap-Haïtien.

Port-au-Prince was founded in 1749. It was laid out on a gridiron plan in an almost unbelievably beautiful setting of green and red mountains that fall abruptly down to the blue waters of the Golfe de la Gonâve. The city centre has uninterrupted rows of stone houses, and several buildings that have arcades. The streets are straight and still broad enough for the existing traffic. The poorest inhabitants live in wooden frame houses that cover the hills to the north and the low ground to the south.

The route to the mountains is via the Champ de Mars, the old colonial drilling ground and promenade, now turned into public gardens; it is dominated by the national palace—Haiti's White House. Relatively well-kept houses stand to the north and south of it; they are occupied by skilled manual workers or junior office employees whose children, on Sundays, crowd the streets dressed in school uniforms. Farther east are residential areas standing on slopes that become progressively steeper and are covered

with thick garden vegetation from which royal palm trees emerge with dignity. Stupendous views of Baie de Port-au-Prince are seen from these slopes, particularly at sunset.

Cap-Haïtien has virtually remained within the limits of its gridiron plan established in the French colonial era. It differs in appearance from the capital city because fear of fires once made its governor decide that all its houses should be built of stone. Today it remains an old-fashioned agglomeration of storied and balconied stone houses.

Cap-Haïtien

The people.   The official language is French, but workers and peasants speak Creole—a language in which many West African elements are discernible, although its vocabulary is of predominantly French origin. Creole has had legal status only since 1969, and, though it is not taught in the public schools, it can be used in the courts and the National Assembly. The bulk of the population originated in the 480,000 slaves who won their freedom in a struggle that ended with Haiti's independence in 1804. Most of the Africans brought to the island before the middle of the 18th century came from the Dahomeyan town of Ouidah, in West Africa, but later on the French slave traders mostly called at Loango in the Congo. Mulattoes, who often had enjoyed the privilege of some education, also formed part of the new nation, together with a few Europeans. Since 1804 small waves of immigration have taken place—the immigrants consisting mostly of traders and mechanics, together with a few teachers and priests; they came at first from the British Isles and later from the United States, forming a part of the same repatriation movement that elsewhere gave birth to Liberia. A concordat with the

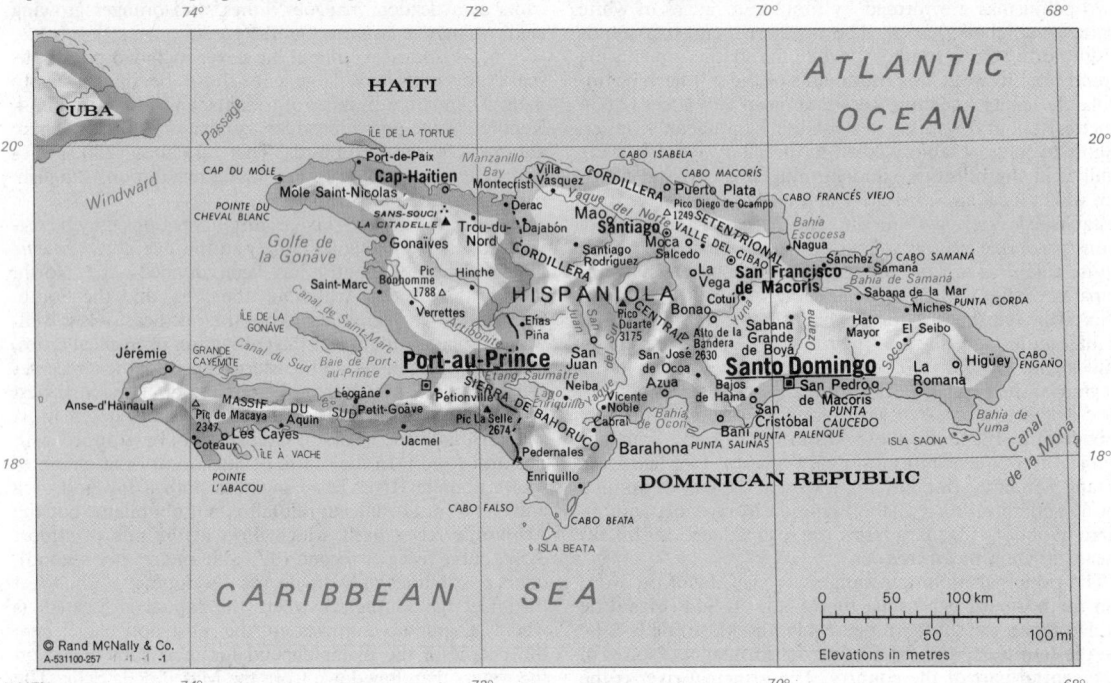

pope, signed in 1860, gave Haiti an all-French clergy and helped to attract more French-speaking residents, some of whom came from France, some from Guadeloupe, and some from Martinique. Members of these three foreign communities form a tiny percentage of the population, and almost all of them are of mixed foreign and Haitian parentage. Arab traders came in the latter years of the 19th century, followed by a few Germans and Italians. The U.S. occupation, which lasted from 1915 to 1934, led to the establishment of a number of enterprises, both public and private, manned by personnel who, in contrast to earlier immigrants, migrated with their families.

Almost all Haitians are baptized as Roman Catholics, and the clergy has always consisted of ordinary priests rather than missionaries. Protocols with the pope, signed in 1966, enabled the president to appoint an archbishop, two bishops, and three auxiliary bishops of Haitian descent. British Methodists introduced Protestantism as early as 1816, but no mass conversion movement was launched before the advent of American revivalist missionaries in the 1940s. Even so, Protestants remain few.

The realities of religion in Haiti, however, require a look in another direction. As the country was left without a regular clergy until as late as 1860, the peasants built up Voodoo (*vaudou*), a syncretic cult in which the Catholic god rules over an African pantheon—a far cry indeed from the Voodoo of New Orleans.

The people of Haiti reside primarily in the rural countryside, and the proportion of the population living in urban areas is about one-half the proportion of the urban population of the neighbouring Dominican Republic. Haiti has one of the highest birth rates of all the West Indian islands, but the higher than average death rate, even by Latin American standards, has kept the rate of population growth close to the Caribbean average and less than the average for Latin America as a whole. In 1900 the population of Haiti was about 1,250,000, and by the first census in 1950 the number of persons had increased to about 3,000,000. During the late 20th century the population has grown at a slightly accelerated rate.

The economy. Although Haiti, like the Dominican Republic, has a diversity of resources unknown to other West Indian islands, most of these resources are too limited in quantity for commercial exploitation.

Resources. Known mineral resources are restricted to alluvial gold (discovered on the Haitian-Dominican borders as early as the 16th century), copper, bauxite (discovered comparatively recently), and small quantities of silver, lignite, and manganese.

Agriculture and fisheries. Vegetation and other biological resources are unusually varied in species, but have suffered as a result of overpopulation, which even at times led hungry peasants to uproot coffee trees in order to plant quick-growing foodstuffs instead. Soil erosion has resulted from such actions, and soil conservation by terracing has only occurred sporadically in recent decades. Educational work is needed before improved methods of cattle-breeding and fishing can be introduced.

Population pressure on the land

Most of the economically active population is employed in agriculture and fishing. Coffee, by far the most important commercial crop, is cultivated on the slopes of almost all mountains, in the shade of fruit and other trees. Haitian coffee is of an excellent mild type, but production varies considerably from year to year. Sugarcane is grown on all the plains, but depends for success on irrigation. Most of the crop is processed at a mill located near Port-au-Prince. The northeast is favourable for the cultivation of sisal, and the Artibonite Valley for rice. Cacao, tobacco, and cotton are also grown. Aromatic plants, such as lime, vetiver (the khuskhus plant, from the roots of which an oil is derived), neroli (sour orange, used for making perfumes), and amyris (a tropical shrub from which a sweet oil is obtained), are grown in the south and are processed for their essential oils.

Crops grown for local consumption include rice (the staple food), corn (maize), cassava, several kinds of peas and beans, and all tropical fruits but especially mangoes. Bananas are mostly of the plantain species, and are eaten as a vegetable rather than as a fruit. Palm trees disappear

at about 3,600 feet above sea level, and vegetables and fruits characteristic of temperate climates may be grown.

Industry. Commercial mining produces bauxite, copper, and silver. Alluvial gold, collected by Indians at the time of Columbus, still is economically feasible to mine. The sugar industry is the major manufacturing enterprise, but there are flour and cotton mills, soap factories, and a tannery, as well as some small plants producing cement, and structural steel. Export industries produce clothing, sporting goods, and electronic components.

Finance. The state operates a central bank that issues notes and coins in gourdes, the national currency. There are state banks for development and for rural credit and three private ones—the Banque Commerciale d'Haïti, the Royal Bank of Canada, and the Banque Populaire Colombo-Haïtienne.

Trade. The United States is Haiti's principal trading partner. Other buyers of Haitian products are France, Italy, and Belgium, while the Netherlands Antilles, Japan, and France also supply goods. Coffee is the largest export item. Other exports are bauxite, toys, and sporting goods, essential oils, and electrical equipment. Imports include machinery and transport equipment, foodstuffs, and mineral fuels. Tourism is second only to coffee as a source of foreign exchange.

The economy, as is often the case in developing countries, is governed by an oligopoly of foreign merchants who maintain the state through export taxes and custom duties, the burden of which ultimately falls on the peasantry.

Transportation. Transport problems result from the mountainous character of two-thirds of the country; rivers usually have to be crossed close to the seashore, where their flow is broader and deeper than farther inland. All travelling on land was on horseback until as late as 1915. Since that time roads have been built, but they deteriorate rapidly in the rainy season. One short railway line, radiating from the capital, is used to carry sugarcane and freight. The indented coastline, however, has innumerable tiny ports that have been visited by small craft since the days of buccaneers and freebooters. Several hundred foreign vessels visit the two main ports of Port-au-Prince and Cap-Haïtien each year.

Difficulty of travel

An international airport, accommodating jet aircraft, is situated close to Port-au-Prince; there are frequent flights to and from New York City, Curaçao, Kingston (Jamaica), Santo Domingo (Domincan Republic), and Miami.

Administrative and social conditions. *Government.* Under the 1964 constitution, the president is elected for life and has the right to appoint his successor. He appoints the members of his Cabinet—all styled secretaries of state— and usually directs one or more of the 19 departments into which his administration is divided. There is a unicameral National Assembly of 58 members, and an advisory role is played by a Resources and Development Council and a Budget Bureau. The national territory is divided into nine *départements.* The *départements,* each of which has a capital, are further subdivided into communes, of which there are about 100, each one consisting of a centre called a *bourg,* which enjoys municipal authority, and five to six *sections rurales* (rural districts), each supervised by a local resident appointed by the central police authority.

All Haiti's constitutions have provided for universal suffrage, which, since 1950, has also included women, but, as almost all rural citizens are illiterate, the results of elections are always subject to discussion. The Single Party for Revolutionary and Governmental Action (later called Party of National Unity) was founded by Pres. François Duvalier in 1963. In rural areas the peasants are prompt to react when their *chefs de section* (district leaders) exceed their power, but opposition at the national level is expressed only by political groups remaining abroad.

Political activity

Justice. Justice is rendered according to the French tradition. Codes inspired by those of Napoleon were issued in 1825 together with a more peculiar Rural Code that governs the conduct of country life. There is a justice of the peace in every commune, as well as primary courts at departmental capitals, four Courts of Appeal, and a Supreme Court (Court of Cassation) in Port-au-Prince. All judges are appointed by the head of state.

Armed forces. The armed forces are divided into four services. These are the army proper, the presidential guard, the air force, and the navy. Since 1961 there has also been a militia, the National Security Volunteers, popularly known as Tontons Macoutes—a name that literally means "uncles knapsacks" and derives from a folk-tale ogre.

Education. The educational tradition also is French. Public schools are free and attendance is compulsory at the primary level, but funds are lacking for the proper implementation of the law, except in Port-au-Prince. There is a university at Port-au-Prince.

Health and welfare. Infant mortality is high and life expectancy is generally low. Yaws was practically eradicated by mass treatment in the 1950s.

Regular welfare services are in an embryonic stage. Co-operatives provide mutual help along lines that are not without roots in Haitian tradition.

Housing is simple but adequate in the countryside, but is quite unsatisfactory in towns because of overcrowding. A number of privately built residences in Port-au-Prince offer interesting examples of the use of cement and wrought iron in modern tropical architecture.

Cultural life. Haitian arts and literature have traditionally been under strong French influence, in spirit as well as in language, although the author Georges Sylvain (1865–1925) marked a new departure when he wrote fables in Creole under the title *Cric-Crac* (a traditional password and response exchanged between storyteller and audience at the beginning of a tale) as early as 1901. An interest in local folk culture became apparent in the late 1920s with the publication of a periodical, *La Revue Indigène,* and of *Ainsi Parla l'Oncle,* an essay by the internationally renowned scholar Jean Price-Mars (1876–1970). Another Haitian author, Jacques Roumain (1907–44), first won world fame writing French novels on popular Haitian subjects and on folk tradition, subsequently exercising a powerful influence in theatrical dancing and in painting as well as in literature. The works of Haitian folk painters are hung in many museums and private collections abroad.

Port-au-Prince has museums of history and ethnology, a national library, and a library of Haitiana kept in a Catholic school. For statistical data, see the "Britannica World Data" section in the current *Britannica Book of the Year.* (E.Sy.)

HISTORY

Christopher Columbus sighted the island that now includes Haiti and the Dominican Republic on December 6, 1492, and named it La Isla Española. By the end of the 16th century, most of the island's original Arawak Indian population had disappeared—worked to death or slaughtered outright by the Spaniards or killed by disease. Spanish settlement was thin and restricted mainly to the eastern end of the island; French pirates, based in the Cayman Islands, had an almost unimpeded run of the western

Arrival of
the French

end. The pirates began to establish plantations there; in 1664 they founded Port-de-Paix in the northwest, and the French West India Company took possession.

The French colonial regime. In 1697, by the Treaty of Rijswijk, the western third of the island was formally ceded to France by Spain and was renamed Saint-Domingue.

The 18th century saw a great increase in Saint-Domingue's population. It became the most prosperous New World colony, exporting sugar, coffee, cocoa, indigo, and cotton cultivated by African slave labour; most of the land and slaves were owned by a handful of families. By 1789 nearly two-thirds of France's foreign investments were based on Saint-Domingue, and in a good year its trade needed more than 700 oceangoing vessels carrying more than 80,000 seamen.

Saint-Domingue had a population in 1789 of 556,000; of this, 500,000 were slaves, 32,000 were whites, and 24,000 were free blacks. On August 24, 1791, stimulated by the French Revolution, the slaves rose in rebellion. In order to maintain the island as a French possession, slavery was abolished by a decree of February 4, 1794. In 1795, by the Treaty of Basel, Spain ceded the rest of the island to France, but war in Europe precluded the actual transfer of possession.

In May 1801 Toussaint-Louverture, a former slave, became governor general, but he would not declare the colony independent. Napoleon sent his brother-in-law, Gen. Charles Leclerc, with an experienced force, including several mulatto officers in exile from Saint-Domingue, to restore the old regime. After several months' resistance, Toussaint came to terms with the French expedition in May 1802. But the French broke the arrangement and imprisoned him (he died on April 7, 1803).

Toussaint-
Louverture

In the face of a rumour that Napoleon intended to restore slavery in Saint-Domingue as he had done in other French possessions, Jean-Jacques Dessalines and Henry Christophe led a black army against the French in 1802. The French commander and a large part of his army were defeated, and on November 9, 1803, the remnant of the French expedition, under the Vicomte de Rochambeau, surrendered. Under the armistice signed on November 18, the French withdrew, but they maintained a presence in the eastern part of the island until 1809.

Independent Haiti (1804–1957). On January 1, 1804, the whole island was declared independent under its original Arawak name of Haiti.

The war with France had utterly laid waste the country and destroyed the economy. In October 1804 Dessalines assumed the title of Emperor Jacques I; on October 17, 1806, he was killed while trying to put down a mulatto revolt and Henry Christophe took control of his kingdom. Civil war broke out between Christophe (later Henry I) in the north and under Alexandre Sabès Pétion, based at Port-au-Prince in the south. In 1808, with British help, Spanish rule was restored in the eastern part of the island (Santo Domingo).

Henry
Christophe

Christophe managed to improve the country's economy, but he had to force peasants to work on the plantations. He built a spectacular palace, Sans Souci; he also built an imposing fortress, the Citadelle Laferrière, in the hills to the south of Cap-Haïtien—where, with mutinous soldiers almost at his door, he committed suicide in 1820.

Jean-Pierre Boyer, who had succeeded to the presidency of the mulatto-led south on Pétion's death in 1818, became president of the whole country after Christophe's death. In 1822 he invaded and conquered Santo Domingo, which had declared itself independent from Spain the previous year and was now engaged in fighting the Spaniards. Boyer abolished slavery and confiscated church property in Santo Domingo; it was not until 1844 that the Haitians were expelled from Santo Domingo by a popular uprising.

Haitian independence was recognized by France in 1825, in return for an indemnity of nearly 100,000,000 francs, to be paid at an annual rate until 1887. Britain recognized the state in 1833, the United States in 1862, after the secession of the Southern slave states.

Boyer was overthrown in 1843. Between then and 1915 a succession of 20 rulers followed, 16 of whom were overthrown by revolution or were assassinated. Faustin-Élie Soulouque, who became president in 1847 and emperor for life in 1849, was extremely repressive. He turned on his mulatto sponsors and his regime was in some ways a return to power of the black party. He tried unsuccessfully to annex the Dominican Republic, and was overthrown in 1859 by one of his generals, Fabre Geffrard. Geffrard tried to reduce repression, encouraged educated mulattoes to join his government, and established Haitian respectability abroad. His government signed a concordat with the Vatican in 1860 and was recognized by the U.S. in 1862. The 1890s saw an increase in U.S. attempts to gain military and commercial privileges in Haiti. In 1905 the U.S. took Haiti's customs into receivership, and before World War I, U.S. business interests had gained a secure financial foothold and valuable concessions.

Fabre
Geffrard

U.S. occupation (1915–34). From 1915 to 1934, Haiti was occupied by U.S. Marines. The U.S. claimed legal justification on the grounds of humanitarian intervention and under the Monroe Doctrine. Many Haitians believed that the Marines had really come to protect U.S. investments in the country and to establish a base to protect the approaches to the Panama Canal. Haiti signed a treaty with the U.S.—originally for 10 years, but eventually it lasted until 1934—establishing U.S. financial and political domination. In 1918, in an election supervised by the Marines, a new constitution was introduced that permitted foreigners to own land in Haiti.

One effect of the Marine occupation was the nominal re-establishment of the mulatto elite in control of the government. Many Haitians resented the occupation, which they believed excluded them from public office and subjected them daily to racist indignities at the hands of the Marines. The Marines revived an old law of Christophe's time, which enabled them to employ forced labour on the roads. This resulted in a revolt of *cacos* (guerrillas), which was suppressed. The program of public works undertaken by the Marines in health clinics, sewage, and roads hardly satisfied the Haitians, who felt that these efforts barely scratched the surface and showed little tangible result.

In October 1930 a national assembly, the first since 1918, was elected. Controlled by nationalists, it in turn elected as president Sténio Joseph Vincent. In August 1934 the U.S. president, Franklin D. Roosevelt, withdrew the Marines; but direct U.S. fiscal control continued until 1941, and indirect control continued until 1947.

Presidential regimes (1934–57). In 1935 a plebiscite extended Vincent's term to 1941 and amended the constitution so that future presidents would be elected by popular vote.

In October 1937 troops and police from the Dominican Republic (formerly Santo Domingo), with popular support, massacred thousands of Haitian labourers living near the border. The following year the Dominican government agreed to pay $3,400,000 in compensation to relatives of those slain, but only part was actually paid. The enmity between the two countries had long historical roots. The Dominicans, with their Spanish culture and greater admixture of European blood, looked with disfavour upon the black Haitian labourer with his "inferior" African culture and lower standard of living, which enabled them to work for far less. Haitian labour was, however, necessary to the Dominican economy.

In 1946 Haitian workers and students held strikes and violent demonstrations in opposition to the president, Élie Lescot, who had succeeded Vincent in 1941 and had altered the constitution to enable himself to serve a further term. Three military officers seized power, and under their supervision Dumarsais Estimé was elected president. In 1950 Estimé in turn sought to extend his term, and the same three officers again took control. That October one of them, Col. Paul E. Magloire, was elected president in a plebiscite. Magloire in turn sought to remain in power, but in December 1956 the army forced him to resign.

Haiti since 1957. In September 1957, after a period of considerable unrest and the rise and fall of several provisional presidents, François Duvalier (called "Papa Doc")—a black physician, formerly employed on a U.S. medical-aid scheme and a student of Voodoo (an animist religion of African origin, with Christian influence)—was elected president in a plebiscite. Duvalier promised to end domination by the wealthy mulatto elite and to put political and economic power into the hands of the black masses. Violence continued, however, and in July 1958 there was an unsuccessful attempt to overthrow Duvalier. He organized an extralegal gang of violent adherents—the Tontons Macoutes—who terrorized the population. Duvalier, by then firmly in control, had himself elected president for life in 1964. Haiti under Duvalier was, in effect, a police state ruled as a dictatorship.

Near the end of his life, faced by a contracting economy, withdrawal of most U.S. aid, and a decline of the tourist industry, Duvalier felt secure enough to relax some of the severe repression and terror that had characterized his early regime. He designated his son, Jean-Claude, aged 19 (and called "Baby Doc"), to succeed him as president for life, and died in 1971.

The regime of Jean-Claude Duvalier sought international respectability. Repression, while present, diminished; tourism, U.S. aid, and the economy in general revived somewhat, and the younger Duvalier, after an uncertain start, proved to be a suprisingly adroit politician. Opponents, however, saw little change in the basic nature of the regime.

In 1980 a significant political event occurred with the marriage of Jean-Claude Duvalier to Michèle Bennett. Duvalier transferred to his wife many of the privileges and prerogatives that had belonged to his mother, Simone Duvalier, who supported the political hard-liners. Since then, the regime has followed an uneven policy of lifting political controls and then restoring all restrictions as soon as dissent is expressed.

Throughout the 1970s and early 1980s migration from Haiti to The Bahamas and Florida has contined, due as much to the miserable economic conditions as to the political climate of Haiti. Hurricane Allen (1980) caused extensive damage to agriculture and the economy, providing further impetus for emigration. For current political history, see the annual issues of the *Britannica Book of the Year*.   (C.L.R.J./M.J.MacL./Ed.)

Jamaica

Jamaica, a parliamentary state within the Commonwealth, is the third largest island in the Caribbean Sea. It has a total land area of 4,244 square miles (10,991 square kilometres) and is about 146 miles (235 kilometres) long, 51 miles wide at its greatest width, and 22 miles wide at its narrowest point. It is situated some 100 miles due west of Haiti, 90 miles south of Cuba, and 310 miles northeast of Cape Gracias a Dios, Nicaragua, the nearest point on the American continent. The national capital is Kingston.

Christopher Columbus, who first sighted the island in 1494, called it Santiago, but the original Amerindian name of Jamaica, or Xaymaca, has persisted. Columbus considered it to be "The fairest isle that eyes have beheld," and many travellers still regard it as one of the most beautiful islands in the Caribbean.

Agriculture remains the major employer of labour, and it is a main contributor to the national income, together with industry—notably bauxite mining—and tourism. Jamaica has made great strides in economic development since its independence in 1962. The national motto, "Out of Many, One People," describes a multiracial society whose integration is profound and enviable.

PHYSICAL AND HUMAN GEOGRAPHY

The land. *Relief.* In general, the topography consists of coastal plains encircling an island that is bisected from east to west along its length by mountains and plateaus. The mountains form the chief physical feature. Almost half of Jamaica's surface is over 1,000 feet above sea level. The chief range rises in the east to Blue Mountain Peak at 7,402 feet (2,256 metres) and then loses altitude as it sweeps westward. The mountains contribute to the great diversity of scenery for which the island is famous, ranging from the stunted, elfin forests of the highest peaks to the dry, sandy, cactus-growing areas of the south. There are damp, tree-fern rain forests in the highlands and wide, flat, alluvial plains. Located chiefly on the south side of the island, the principal plains are: Liguanea Plain in Kingston and St. Andrew; Rio Cobre and St. Dorothy plains in St. Catherine; the Vera Ma Hollis Savanna (plains of Vere) in Clarendon; George's Plain in Westmoreland; and Pedro Plains in St. Elizabeth. The rolling limestone hills and plateaus in the central and western areas include the unusual, trackless karst (a limestone region broken by ridges, depressions, and caverns) region of the Cockpit Country, covering 500 square miles of the interior.

Drainage and soils. There are some 120 rivers and streams, with numerous tributaries issuing from ravines in the mountains. Few are navigable for any great distance, because of their rapid descent from the mountains. Some of the larger rivers have alluvial plains in their lower valleys and some have deltas. The Black River is navigable by small boats for about 25 miles from its mouth.

More than half of the island's surface is covered with white limestone that overlies yellow limestone, beneath which are older metamorphic rocks (compact rocks formed by heat and pressure) and igneous rocks (formed by the cooling of molten material). The upland areas are mostly covered with bare rock or soils of little depth and are very susceptible to erosion. The alluvium of the coastal plains

Military coups

Rise of François Duvalier

Jamaica's mountains

is composed chiefly of deep loam and clay. The valley floors are covered with residual clays.

Climate. The tropical climate is influenced by the sea and is characterized by little change in seasonal temperature, although the mountains cause regional variations. Because the island lies between the subtropical high-pressure and the equatorial low-pressure belts of the Atlantic Ocean, the northeast trade winds are dominant and blow throughout the year. Along the coasts, breezes blow onshore by day, and offshore at night. During the winter months, from December to March, cold winds known locally as "northers" reach the island through the wide, open trough of the North American plains.

Variations in temperature range from 90° F (32° C) on the coasts to 40° F (4° C) on the peaks. Kingston, at sea level, has an average daily maximum temperature of 88° F (31° C) and an average daily minimum of 71° F (22° C). At Stony Hill, at 1,400 feet above sea level, the maximum and minimum means are 86° F (30° C) and 68° F (20° C).

Rainfall
Rains are seasonal, falling chiefly in May and October, although thunderstorms in the summer months, from June to September, can bring heavy showers. The average annual rainfall for the entire island is 78 inches (1,980 millimetres), but regional variations are considerable. The mountains force the trade winds to deposit more than 200 inches a year on the northern parishes of Portland and St. Thomas, while little precipitation occurs on the hot, dry savanna lands of the southern and southwestern plains. Jamaica is susceptible to hurricanes during the summer but after 1951 it was not struck until Hurricane Allen in 1980. Earthquakes have caused serious damage only twice—in 1692 and 1907.

Plant and animal life. The richness and diversity of Jamaica's trees and plants constitute one of its chief glories, though it has changed considerably through the centuries. The island was completely forested in the 15th century, except for small agricultural clearings. The great timber trees were cut down for building purposes by the European settlers, and the plains, savannas, and mountain slopes were cleared for cultivation. Many new plants were introduced: the food plants—including sugarcane, bananas, and citrus—were almost all introduced to the island.

Jamaica has few indigenous quadrupeds. The coney, a member of the rodent family, once very numerous and prized as food before the European immigration, is now extremely scarce. The mongoose, a small carnivore that feeds on rats and snakes, is widespread but was introduced in 1872 from India. The 25 species of bats are the most numerous of the mammals. The native crocodile is now in danger of extinction. There are no poisonous snakes. The main freshwater fish is the mountain mullet; there are four species of crayfish.

Rich birdlife
More than 200 species of birds have been recorded, including 25 endemic species, such as the streamertail hummingbird, which is the national bird. The bird population also includes species found both in the West Indies and in America and birds that migrate to Jamaica, either in the winter or in the summer.

Settlement patterns. With the emancipation of the island's black slaves in 1838, a large proportion of the freed population—often with the aid of nonconformist mission-

aries—left the large plantations. They moved to the hills where land was plentiful and created their own villages and communities. This migration laid the foundation of the present pattern of rural settlement, and many of the villages retain their original character.

Most of the cities and chief towns are located on the coastal plains, where the main commercial crops are grown. Kingston, the national capital, is located on the southeastern coast. It stands on the Liguanea Plain with the sea to the south and the St. Andrew Mountains, which form part of the ranges of the parish of St. Andrew, to the north. It is the commercial, administrative, and cultural centre of the island and the focus of its transportation services. Spanish Town, the old capital, is 13 miles west of Kingston. The other important towns—Montego Bay, Ocho Rios, and Port Antonio—are centred on the north coast. Their fine white-sand beaches and unparalleled mountain scenery make them popular tourist resorts.

The people. The aboriginal Arawak Indians were exterminated by the Spanish colonists by the time the English invaded the island in 1655. The Spaniards themselves disappeared as a population element shortly afterwards. With the large-scale introduction of African slaves to work the sugar estates, the English settlers were soon greatly outnumbered. Today the population is predominantly African and Afro-European in origin.

Origin of the population

English is the official language, but a local dialect is also widely spoken. It is basically English in vocabulary and grammar but contains features derived from a variety of African languages, as well as from Spanish and French.

Freedom of worship is entrenched in Jamaica's constitution. The majority of the population belongs to the Anglican Church which, as the Church of England, was the established church of the country until 1870. There is also a large number of Baptists, members of the Assembly of God, and Roman Catholics. Nearly every Christian denomination and sect is represented, and the Jewish community is one of the oldest in the Western Hemisphere. There is a Hindu community, a Muslim mosque, and a branch of the Ethiopian Orthodox Church. Some of the popular and revivalist sects base their beliefs on Christianity, but their forms of worship differ widely from those accepted by most orthodox churches and denominations. The central feature of the Pocomania sect, for example, is spirit possession; the Cumina sect has rituals characterized by heavy drumming, dancing, and spirit possession.

From 1844 to 1881 the population of Jamaica grew from 377,000 to 581,000. The death rate was probably less during this period than it was during the slavery era, but the birth rate may have increased slightly to about 40 births per thousand persons. The immigration of indentured servants from Asia and Africa began during this period, accounting for more than one-fifth of the total population growth between 1844 and 1861; but from 1861 to 1881 the immigration of indentured servants declined, the birth rate dropped slightly to about 38 births per thousand persons, and the death rate continued to decline to about 26 or 27 deaths per thousand persons. By 1921 the population had grown to only 858,000 because the island had been plagued by heavy emigration since 1881. Large numbers of Jamaicans had left to work on the banana plantations

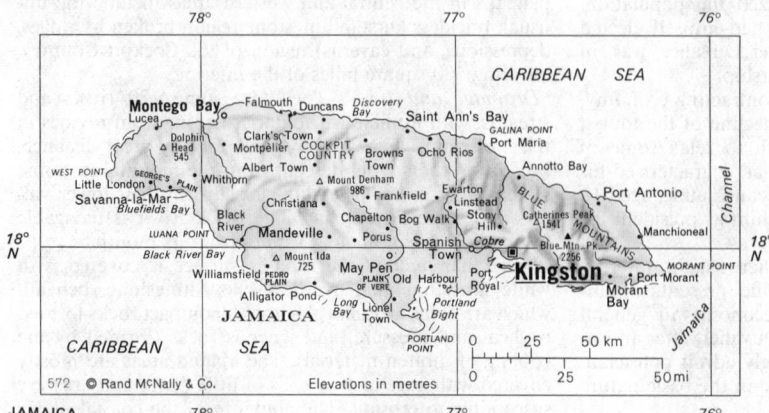

in Central America, to toil in the sugarcane fields and refining plants in Cuba, and to help construct the Panama Canal. Net migration losses in population totalled 24,800 during 1881–91, 43,000 during 1891–1911, and 77,100 during 1911–21. Birth rates during these years remained fairly stable (36–39 births per thousand persons), as did the death rates (23–26 deaths per thousand persons), but the annual population growth declined from about 1.4 percent in 1881 to about 0.3 percent in 1921. Between 1921 and 1943 Jamaica's demographic outlook was altered by dramatic declines in mortality and the cessation of heavy emigration, a consequence of immigration restrictions by the United States and Latin-American countries and the lack of regional demand for Jamaican labour. By 1943 the death rate had fallen to about 18 deaths per thousand persons, the birth rate had remained high at 33 births per thousand persons, and the population had grown to more than 1,200,000. The post-World War II period witnessed a continuing high rate of natural population increase, as the death rate continued to decline rapidly, and the birth rate declined at a slower pace. This high rate of natural increase, exceeding more than 2 percent annually for most of the years since World War II, has been somewhat negated by a continuation of heavy emigration. From 1943 to 1960 the net population loss due to migration exceeded 195,000 persons, and between 1960 and 1970 it was more than 250,000. By the late 20th century Jamaica's death rate had fallen to less than one-half of the 1943 figure; the birth rate was about equal to the Caribbean average.

The economy. Jamaica's economy is essentially an open one, with heavy dependence on primary exports and on imports of manufactures and capital goods. There is active foreign economic participation, especially in the export sector (bauxite and alumina) and in tourism.

Resources. Among the minerals found on the island, bauxite, gypsum, silica sand, ceramic clays, marble, and limestone are of commercial interest. The bauxite is found in an area of about 1,000 square miles in central Jamaica; the gypsum and marble are in eastern Jamaica; clays are in the west; and limestone is found throughout the island.

Agriculture, forestry, and fisheries. Agriculture continues to be the main basis of the island's economy. The two major crops are sugar—with its by-products of rum and molasses—and bananas. Other important crops are citrus fruit, coffee, pimiento, cacao, tobacco, and ginger.

Local forestry production is insufficient to meet the country's needs; most of the wood, cork, and paper consumed is imported. The government is pursuing a strong afforestation program.

Fishing is a major enterprise; the island shelf is the traditional fishing area. Mechanized boats sail about 60 miles southwest of Jamaica to Pedro Bank.

Industry. Since 1952 the mineral industry has played an increasingly significant role in the country's economic development. Jamaica is one of the world's largest producers of bauxite. Bauxite mining is generally in the hands of foreign companies, although in 1979 the government gained some control over mining operations and a share in the manufacture of alumina (a product made from bauxite that is used for making aluminum). The production of silica sand is absorbed by local glass-container manufacture, while most of the gypsum is mined for export. Cement is largely used in local construction.

Manufacturing is increasingly important, both in providing employment and in satisfying the increasing demand for manufactured goods. Processed foods, textiles, and metal products are the most important manufactures. Other significant categories are sugar, rum, and molasses processing, printing, chemical production, and cement and clay products. Industrial growth has been stimulated by the activities of the Jamaica Industrial Development Corporation, a statutory body that administers the incentive laws that provide concessions such as the duty-free importation of machinery and equipment and income tax exemption to foreign and local investors.

Increasing reliance is being placed on tourism, which has become one of the country's largest sources of foreign exchange. The traditional attraction of Jamaica to the tourist is the warm climate and good beaches.

Electricity is supplied from both private and public sources. Public generation of electricity is mainly by steam turbines. Privately owned generating plants supply the power needs of the sugar, cement, bauxite, and alumina industries.

Finance. Finance is dominated by commercial banks that are mainly subsidiaries of Canadian, British, and U.S. banks. Savings and credit services are also offered by life-insurance companies, building societies, and credit unions. The central bank, called the Bank of Jamaica, founded in 1960, controls money and credit and promotes economic development. The Jamaica Development Bank provides loans for industry, housing, and tourism.

Trade. The principal exports are alumina, bauxite, sugar and other agricultural products, and clothing. Widely varied imports include food, beverages, tobacco, mineral fuels, manufactured goods, fertilizer, and machinery. The United States, the United Kingdom, Venezuela, and Canada are the leading trade partners. The European Economic Community is an important source of imports. Jamaica is a member of the sterling area and of the Commonwealth preferential-trading system.

Administration of the economy. The economy is based on private enterprise. The mining and tourist industries, as well as much of the manufacturing sector, are financed by foreign capital. The largest sources of government revenue are consumption duties, income tax, and customs duties.

The most important trade unions are the Bustamente Industrial Trade Union (affiliated with the Jamaican Labour Party) and the National Worker's Union (affiliated with the People's National Party); there are also employers' associations.

Transportation. Generally, the transport systems follow the coastline or cut across the central mountains from north to south. The main roads encircle the island, loop into the plains areas, and cross the mountains at three major north-to-south crossings. Public passenger services are available outside the capital which itself has a regular bus service. There are also taxi and limousine services.

There are several railway routes, parts of which have existed since 1845. The main line runs northwest from Kingston to Montego Bay via Spanish Town, May Pen, and Montpelier. From Spanish Town, a branch line runs to Annotto Bay and Port Antonio by way of Bog Walk.

There are scheduled international air services at the two major airports of Palisadoes, near Kingston, and Montego Bay. These airports also handle scheduled domestic flights and an air-taxi service. Port Antonio and Ocho Rios have licensed aerodromes, and there are about 40 other airstrips throughout the island.

Kingston, Montego Bay, and Montego Freeport are the principal seaports. Regular passenger and cargo services are maintained with the United Kingdom, Canada, and the United States. There are also shipping lines to continental Europe, South America, and the Caribbean.

Administrative and social conditions. *Government.* Under the Jamaica (Constitution) Order in Council of 1962, by which the island achieved independence, the monarch of the United Kingdom is titular head of state. A Jamaican governor general is chosen by the monarch on the advice of the prime minister. The prime minister is appointed by the leading political party from its parliamentary members. The legislature is a bicameral parliament consisting of a House of Representatives and a Senate. The House has 60 members, who are elected by universal adult suffrage. The speaker and deputy speaker are elected by the House from its members. The Senate has 21 members, who are appointed by the governor general—13 in accordance with the advice of the prime minister and eight on the advice of the leader of the opposition party. The president and deputy president are elected by the Senate from among such of its members as are not ministers or parliamentary secretaries. The principal instrument of policy is the Cabinet, which consists of the prime minister and at least 11 other ministers, of whom at least two or three must be members of the Senate. The Privy Council is limited to advising the governor general on the exercise of the royal prerogative of mercy and on the discipline of government officers.

Legislature

The island is divided into 14 parishes, two of which are amalgamated as the Kingston and St. Andrew Corporation. Local affairs in the other parishes are administered by individual parish councils whose members are elected by universal adult suffrage. Members of the House of Representatives hold ex-officio seats on parish councils, and the mayors of those parish capitals that enjoy mayoral status are the chairmen of their councils.

The two main political parties are the Jamaica Labour Party and the People's National Party. General elections are held every five years.

Justice. The judiciary comprises a supreme court, a court of appeal, and resident magistrate's (parish), petty sessional, revenue, gun, and family courts. There is also a traffic court. The legal and judicial system is based on English common law. The attorney general is the government's principal legal adviser.

Armed forces. The responsibilities of the constabulary force include immigration and the registration of aliens. There is a criminal investigation department and a telecommunications branch, as well as water police and mounted detachments.

The Jamaica Defense Force is organized into regular and part-time, or national reserve, elements. The regular forces include army, air force, coast guard, and logistics units. The air wing operates both helicopters and light aircraft; the Coast Guard is equipped with fast patrol boats. The National Reserve includes army units, an air squadron, and small marine units.

Education. Primary education is free and in certain districts compulsory. A substantial part of the annual budget goes to the Ministry of Education. Considerable sums are devoted to the School of Agriculture, the College of Arts, Science, and Technology, and the University of the West Indies, the main campus of which is at Mona, a northeastern section of Kingston. Education is provided by government-owned, government-aided, and private schools, some of which are run by religious bodies.

Health and welfare. Medical care is provided by several public hospitals, including the university hospital, and various health centres and clinics. There are also a few private hospitals. Highly successful programs of insect control and malaria eradication have been undertaken.

Welfare programs

The Ministry of Youth and Community Development undertakes community services through the Social Development Commission and various other voluntary groups. The government operates a compulsory National Insurance Scheme that covers all gainfully employed persons between 18 years old and retirement age.

Much attention has been paid to housing, and there are many large development schemes in both urban and rural areas, especially in the Kingston and St. Andrew suburbs. Although the government undertakes many types of housing schemes, its chief concern is with low-income projects.

Cultural life. There is a vigorous and productive art movement in Jamaica. The works of Jamaican novelists may be read in several languages. Jamaican artists have exhibited successfully abroad, and local art shows are a regular part of life. The Institute of Jamaica, an early patron and promoter of the arts, sponsors exhibitions and awards. It also runs the Cultural Training Centre, which includes schools of art, dance, drama, and music.

The Jamaica Library Service and the University of the West Indies contribute to the promotion of the arts. There are many successful commercial galleries and one run by the Contemporary Jamaican Artists Association.

There are many active theatre and musical groups. The National Dance Company, formed in 1962, has earned international recognition. Much of the country's artistic expression finds an outlet in Festival, sponsored annually by the government as part of the independence celebrations. While the festival has many features of the traditional Caribbean type of carnival, it is much wider in scope. In addition to street dancing and parades, there are also exhibitions of arts and crafts, and literary, theatrical and musical competitions.

The concern with Jamaica's cultural tradition is evident in an artistic and cultural awakening accompanied by a keen search for roots in folk forms, which are based chiefly on the colourful, rhythmic intensity of an African heritage, with overtones of unique multiracial influences, such as in reggae music. Folk music, stories, and dances are being systematically sought out and recorded. The important aesthetic elements in some of the revivalist cults, notably Pocomania, are recognized, and modern dance and drama employ many of the folk expressions that might otherwise have disappeared. For statistical data, see the "Britannica World Data" section in the current *Britannica Book of the Year.*   (C.V.B.)

Folk traditions

HISTORY

Christopher Columbus reached Jamaica in 1494, during his second voyage to the New World. It was conquered and settled, under a license from Columbus' son Diego, by Juean de Esquivel in 1509. The Spanish government was disappointed in the country's lack of gold, and Jamaica became a neglected part of the property of the Columbus family. Its chief value to Spain was as a supply base; its settlers were mainly engaged in cattle-ranching. The island was under Spanish rule from 1509 until 1655. The Spaniards named it Sant' Jago. St. Iago de la Vega (later Spanish Town) was founded in 1523 and was the capital until 1872. During the Spanish occupation the native Arawaks were exterminated, and Negro slaves were imported in small numbers to take their place. When Jamaica was taken by the British the total population was about 3,000. Oliver Cromwell attacked the Spanish West Indies, and Adm. William Penn and his military colleague Robert Venables succeeded in capturing and holding Jamaica in 1655, the first colony in the Americas to be captured by a formal British expedition. The Spaniards were completely expelled in 1660. Their slaves took to the mountains, and until the end of the 18th century the efforts of these Maroons, as they were called, to maintain their independence gave rise to repeated fighting.

The Maroons—whose name probably derives from the Spanish *cimarrón,* meaning "wild" or "untamed"—were organized, armed, and encouraged by the Spanish. They were to prove a thorn in the side of the British for almost 150 years.

The buccaneers. Jamaica was governed by military authority until 1661 when Edward D'Oyley was appointed captain general and governor in chief with an executive council. Jamaica soon became a chief resort of buccaneers, who frequently united the profession of merchant or planter with that of pirate or privateer. The buccaneers—who preyed on Spanish ships—operated mainly from their base at rich and corrupt Port Royal. By their relentless attacks on Spanish Caribbean cities, they kept the Spaniards occupied at a time when Britain was unable to spare a fleet for the protection of its West Indian colonies.

British rule. By the Treaty of Madrid, 1670, British title to the island was recognized, and the buccaneers were suppressed. The Royal African Company was formed in 1672 with a monopoly of the English slave trade, and from that time Jamaica became one of the greatest slave marts in the world, with a thriving smuggling trade to Spanish America. By the 18th century, Jamaica, like the other sugar colonies, had become one of the most valuable of colonial possessions. In 1672 there were in Jamaica about 70 sugar works, 60 indigo works, and 60 cacao works. An attempt was made in 1678 to impose royal taxes and to supersede the powers of the legislature. The privileges were restored in 1682; but not until 46 years later was the question of revenue settled, with a compromise by which Jamaica undertook to pay £8,000 (later reduced to £6,000) per annum to the crown, provided that the laws of England were made binding in Jamaica; all additional taxes had to be voted annually by the assembly. In 1692 an earthquake destroyed most of the town of Port Royal and led to the foundation of Kingston.

The Royal African Company

Economics and government under colonial rule. A threatened invasion by the French and Spanish in 1782 was averted by the victory of the admirals George Rodney and Samuel Hood off Dominica. The last attempt at invasion was made in 1806, when the French were defeated by Adm. Sir John Duckworth. During the French war Jamaica was at the zenith of its prosperity, with coffee rivalling sugar as an export crop and with more than 300,000 slaves at work. The abolition of the slave trade in 1807, however, raised the planters' costs, and the end of the war brought a steady drop in sugar prices.

Emancipation struck a further blow at the planters' prosperity and security. All slaves were emancipated by an act of the imperial parliament in 1833. They became free in fact, after a period of so-called apprenticeship, in 1838. Many left the plantations and moved to the hills, where their descendants live as small farmers today. The planters received compensation at the rate of £19 per slave but generally were left financially exhausted and with a scarcity of labour. The abolition in 1846 of the tariff protection of colonial produce in the British market reduced the price of sugar still further and in many cases destroyed the profits of the impoverished planter.

Dissensions among the executive, the legislature representing propertied interests, and the home government, as to the means of retrenching public expenditure, created much bitterness. Although some slight improvement marked the administration of Sir Charles Metcalfe and the Earl of Elgin, when Indian immigration was introduced to redress the scarcity and irregularity of labour and the railway was opened, the improvement was not permanent. Along with the collapse of the plantation system, there was widespread poverty and unemployment. All this produced a crisis in 1865 that changed the old social and economic patterns for all time. An outbreak occurred at Morant Bay in October 1865, in which the Chief Magistrate of the parish and 18 other white persons were killed. The rising was ruthlessly suppressed under martial law, and the principal instigator, G.W. Gordon, was hanged. These severities were widely applauded in the West Indies, but indignation in England led to the recall of the governor, Edward John Eyre, and to a drastic change in the government of the island.

Before his recall, Eyre had induced the Jamaican assembly, frightened by the riots, to vote its own extinction. In its place a crown-colony form of government, in which the governor wielded the only real executive or legislative power, was established by an act of the British Parliament in 1866. The new governor, Sir John Peter Grant, achieved a remarkable reorganization of the affairs of the colony. He established a constabulary on the lines of that of Ireland; reconstructed the judicial establishment, substituting stipendiary magistrates for the planter-justices; established a public medical service, a public works department, and government savings bank; improved education; and irrigated the fertile but drought-stricken plain between Spanish Town and Kingston. During his government the lucrative trade in bananas was started by Capt. A.W. Baker, founder of the organization that later became the United Fruit Company. Bananas soon became a principal crop, grown for export by small farmers as well as by large estates. Many Jamaicans also found employment in the early years of the 20th century on the construction of the Panama Canal and on sugar plantations in Cuba.

On January 14, 1907, a violent earthquake struck Kingston. Almost every building in the capital and in Port Royal was destroyed or seriously damaged. About 800 persons were killed and a large part of the city was burned. These disasters offered an opportunity of improving Kingston, and under the government of Sir Sydney (Lord) Olivier the scattered public offices were reconstructed on the finest street of the city.

Representative government was restored by stages from 1884, when nine elected members were added to the legislature. Their number was increased to 14 in 1895. Further changes were discussed from 1922 to 1926, and more vigorously after 1938, partly as a result of riots in that year. By 1938 dissatisfaction with the crown-colony system, sharpened by the hardships and suffering brought on by a worldwide economic depression, erupted in serious and widespread rioting. These events resulted in the formation of the first lasting labour unions as well as of political parties linked to them. A growing demand for self-determination also became apparent. In 1944 a new constitution established a house of representatives elected by universal suffrage, in which a two-party pattern soon

emerged. A modification of this constitution in 1953 gave departmental responsibilities to elected ministers, but retained a nominated legislative council as an upper house with limited powers and an executive council including both officials and ministers, with the governor presiding. In 1957 the official members left the executive council, which then became a cabinet under the chairmanship of the premier. Full internal self-government was obtained in 1959.

Jamaica was relatively little affected by World Wars I and II, though many Jamaicans served in the British armed forces overseas. After World War II the island profited greatly from help under the Colonial Development and Welfare Act and from outside sources of private capital. Colonial Development grants financed the building of the University of the West Indies, an important factor in the preparation for independence, which was established in Jamaica in 1947. Many new industrial undertakings were started, including a sugar refinery, citrus factories, and a cement factory. Development was temporarily checked in August 1951 by a severe hurricane, which devastated crops throughout the island and killed about 150 people. The expansion of the tourist trade and the development of bauxite mining more than offset the loss of openings for employment in Cuba and Central America.

Independence. On January 3, 1958, Jamaica became a founding member of the federation of the West Indies, a group of islands in the Caribbean that formed a unit within the Commonwealth of Nations. Norman Manley, leader of the People's Nationalist Party, became prime minister after the elections held in July 1959, but in 1960 the Labour Party under Sir Alexander Bustamante pressed for secession from the federation. Widespread support was given to their views in a general referendum (September 19, 1961). At the general election in April 1962 the Labour Party was returned to power and Bustamante became prime minister. In May, after negotiations, the federation was dissolved; on August 6 Jamaica became independent with full dominion status within the Commonwealth. Independence was accompanied by a grant of £1,000,000 and a loan of £1,250,000 from Britain. In March 1963 Jamaica further strengthened its financial position by joining the International Monetary Fund, which authorized drawings of up to $10,000,000 to provide assured reserves. The U.S. Export-Import Bank at the same time provided a development loan of $5,000,000. On a state visit, Elizabeth II, as queen of Jamaica, opened Parliament there on March 4, 1966. In June 1969 the country became the 24th member of the Organization of American States.

During most of 1965 and 1966 Bustamante was ill and Donald Sangster acted as prime minister. After a campaign marked by considerable violence, the first general election since Jamaica had gained independence was held on February 21, 1967. The Jamaica Labour Party (JLP) gained 33 seats and the People's National Party (PNP) 20 seats in a house enlarged to 53 members. Bustamante had announced his retirement from politics before the election, and the new prime minister was Donald Sangster. He also, however, fell ill shortly after taking office and died at Montreal on April 11. Hugh Lawson Shearer, for long the effective leader of the Bustamante Industrial Trade Union, was then elected prime minister. In the election of early 1972 the PNP obtained its first major victory, winning 36 of the 53 seats in the legislature. Michael Manley, the leader of the party, was sworn in as prime minister.

Manley, the charismatic son of Norman Manley, based his winning campaign on the "politics of participation," and once in office, determined to carry out his campaign promises, he embarked on a number of social reforms. Censorship was eliminated, and many restrictions on civil liberties were lifted. His government pursued a program, largely successful, to wipe out illiteracy. But although Manley's regime had such promising beginnings, the government was soon overwhelmed by the exigencies of the impoverished Jamaican populace. Economic problems undermined most of Manley's social programs. By the mid-1970s economic frustration led to one of the most notorious crime rates in the Caribbean.

During the crucial elections of 1976, there was virtual political warfare between the PNP and the opposition JLP.

Violence and unrest

Emigration in the early 20th century

Federation of the West Indies

Manley's PNP won heavily. Perhaps disappointed and despairing of economic betterment through close ties with the U.S., Manley had proposed strengthening ties with Cuba. In 1977 the government assumed majority ownership of the bauxite mines, Jamaica's most important resource, which until then had been foreign-owned.

Manley's regime had not been able to alleviate the economic misery of much of its population. This, along with the increasing political violence, led to Manley's defeat in the 1980 election. The new prime minister, Edward Seaga of the JLP, had to contend with the widespread destruction of Hurricane Allen as one of his first acts in office. Although Seaga had disapproved of the PNP's close ties with Cuba, he at first maintained a friendly, albeit aloof, relationship with Castro. But by December 1981, Seaga officially severed diplomatic ties with Cuba. For current political history, see the annual issues of the *Britannica Book of the Year.* (J.H.Py./Ed.)

Puerto Rico

An autonomous political entity in voluntary association with the United States according to a 1953 UN resolution, the Commonwealth of Puerto Rico occupies a central position among the West Indian Islands. Its land rises sharply from the tropical sea, and its coastal plain quickly ascends to meet the steep mountain ranges that give the island the appearance of a nearly rectangular pyramid. By air it is about 1,600 miles (2,600 kilometres) from New York City, 1,050 miles from Miami, and 550 miles from Caracas. To the west lie the other, larger islands of the Greater Antilles—Hispaniola (containing the Dominican Republic and Haiti), Jamaica, and Cuba—while to the east is St. Thomas, of the Virgin Island group, the closest of the myriad islands of the Lesser Antilles.

San Juan was the name given the island when it was discovered by Columbus in 1493; its capital city was known as Puerto Rico (Spanish: Rich Harbour). In the course of centuries, during which it played an integral role in Spain's empire in the Americas, the names for island and city were interchanged. At the same time its people developed traditions and a way of life that remain deeply rooted in Spanish culture. This factor, even more than the island location, helps to isolate the Puerto Rican from the northern European culture that shaped most of the institutions of other U.S. citizens. Pride in this unique heritage has been a major emotional component in the continuing internal debate among proponents of U.S. statehood, independence, and the maintenance of a commonwealth status.

Impact of Spanish tradition

Puerto Rico is a densely populated island whose area, including several small adjacent islands, totals only 3,435 square miles (8,897 square kilometres). The Puerto Ricans, many of whom migrated to the U.S. mainland, have come to represent a unique social and political community within both the United States and the Spanish-speaking nations of the Americas.

PHYSICAL AND HUMAN GEOGRAPHY

The land. *Relief.* Puerto Rico is a rugged and hilly island. Nearly half of the island lies 500 feet (150 metres) or more above sea level—about 20 percent between 500 and 1,000 feet and about 25 percent more than 1,000 feet. The island is divided into three main geographical regions: the mountainous interior, the northern plateau, and the coastal plains. The central mountain range, known as the Cordillera Central, rises to more than 3,000 feet, with the highest points at Cerro de Punta, 4,389 feet, and Monte Guilarte, 3,953 feet.The range slopes very steeply to the southeast. Although the northern slope is less steep, the rivers have eroded the area more thoroughly. The south-running rivers are short and torrential, but they are dry most of the time.

Mountainous landscape

In the northwest, the elevation of the northern plateau averages 100 feet near the coast and 700 feet toward the interior. The plateau is crossed by small hills, and the interior is covered by hillocks and gullies. In the northeast the Sierra de Luquillo includes the rain forest of El Yunque, a jungle of tropical and subtropical trees and plants that includes species of giant ferns, orchids, and trailing vines. The whole area of some 29,000 acres (12,000 hectares) is included in the Caribbean National Forest and is a major tourist attraction.

In the north the coastal plains run from Punta Borinquen in the west to Cabezas de San Juan in the extreme northeast. Adjacent to the coast the land is quite level, interrupted only by a few rock promontories and by lines of sand dunes along the shore. The only flatlands of importance are found in the alluvial plains of such rivers as the Grande de Arecibo, Cibuco, Grande de Loíza, and La Plata. The mountains reach close to the shore in the east, the rivers forming deep valleys; in the west the valleys are even deeper. In the south the coastal plains are narrower and more regular than on the northern coast and are studded with hillocks and sand dunes.

The island's varied precipitation is the direct result of its topography. The east–west mountains form a barrier to the dominant east-to-northeasterly winds, giving the north an abundance of rain. On rising over the Cordillera Central, the warm, humid air masses cool and lose much of their moisture, so that rain on the southern coast is scarce, and a dry climate predominates.

Relation of topography and precipitation

Drainage. The rugged and irregular topography accounts for the nearly 1,300 streams, but only 50 are true rivers. The northern slopes carry the main currents, many of them flowing into plains so low that marshes, moors, and some lakes are formed. Drainage is deficient and floods are common. The shorter rivers on the southern slopes are dry in winter but torrential in the wet season.

Climate. Lying within the tropical zone, Puerto Rico has a pleasant climate greatly influenced by the sea and the warm North Equatorial Current. Moisture-laden winds from the east and northeast bring on the frequent rainy periods of winter as they encounter occasional cold fronts that extend southward into the West Indies from the U.S. mainland. Temperatures in Puerto Rico very seldom fall below 60° F (16° C); the annual mean temperature is about 76° F (24° C). Extreme temperatures are rare, with the highest recorded daily average at 89° F (32° C) and the lowest at 66° F (19° C).

Plant and animal life. Puerto Rico has relatively little animal life. Wildlife includes nonpoisonous snakes, several lizards, mongooses, and birds. The most common birds are the thrushes, tanagers, bullfinches, flycatchers, warblers, plovers, terns, and sandpipers. Fish abound in great variety, but with little economic exploitation. Plant life includes palm trees and mangrove along the coast and bamboo along the roads and streams. African tulip trees, bougainvillea, hibiscus, poinsettias, and a golden trumpet known as *canario,* splash vivid colour against a green and brown landscape throughout the year.

The people. The people of Puerto Rico are historical products of a mixture of diverse ethnic strains. The main ethnic stocks are Spanish and African, and though the aboriginal Indians were either absorbed or eliminated, some of their physical characteristics remain, particularly in the peoples of the mountains. Settlers from several European nations arrived at the island in the 19th century—Danish, French, Corsican, and some English and German. During the 20th century there was a limited flow of people from the United States and, during the 1950s and 1960s, a major influx of Cubans. Slavery, introduced in the early days of the Spanish conquest, never flourished as it did in Saint-Domingue (Haiti under French control), Jamaica, and Barbados. In the early 19th century, when the emphasis was on sugar cultivation, thousands of African slaves were brought into Puerto Rico, reaching a total of more than 50,000 around 1850. Under Spanish rule many slaves earned their freedom. Abolition of slavery was achieved in 1873 without violence.

Composite character of the people

Since the end of the 18th century the population gradually has become a blend of its various ethnic strains. The independent, isolated small farmers of the interior, known as jibaros, have become a symbol of the social and cultural heritage of the island. Despite the mixture of peoples and traditions, the Puerto Ricans are a very homogeneous people; no group is looked upon as a minority in either racial, ethnic, or linguistic terms.

Both the birth and death rates for Puerto Rico are lower than the Caribbean average, giving the island a rate of natural increase that is less than that of most of its island neighbours, but also is double the rate of the United States. The establishment of family planning programs and other measures aimed at birth control have contributed to a sharp decline in the birth rate since 1966; but it remains substantially higher than the U.S. rate. Prior to 1960 emigration was largely responsible for an extremely low rate of population growth. From 1960 to 1965 emigration declined and birth rates declined, but the annual population growth rose to 2.5 percent. Emigration increased again after 1965, though the number of returning Puerto Ricans held the net emigration to about 7,000 persons in 1969. During the 1970s the number of returning migrants exceeded the number of emigrants, resulting in an average in-migration of about 25,000 persons annually. In 1977 this trend reversed again, with a net emigration of approximately 25,000; but returning migrants remain an important factor in Puerto Rico's population growth rate, which is about double the rate of growth for the United States.

Puerto Rico's population is predominantly young and the median age for women is younger than the median age for men. There has been a definite increase, however, in the numbers of persons of middle or advanced years, along with steadily rising life-expectancy rates. Urban growth, one of Puerto Rico's pressing problems, has increased the demand for housing, transportation, and services, problems that the government must resolve if it is to sustain and improve standards of living.

The economy. *Resources.* Puerto Rico's industrial achievement is remarkable because the island is poor in minerals. Iron ore, manganese, lead, and zinc occur in such small quantities that there is no important commercial exploitation. Explorations, however, have revealed rich copper deposits. Several nickel deposits also have been discovered.

Agriculture. Dairy products and livestock are the main agricultural revenue earners, followed by sugar, Puerto Rico's main crop. Other principal crops include tobacco, coffee, pineapples, tropical plants, and coconuts. Sugar products such as molasses and rum are also important. Imports of food, however, have remained high.

Industry. Since the end of World War II the island has undergone an industrial transformation that has had profound social and economic effects. The shift from agriculture to industrial production has been largely the result of commonwealth policies that, since 1948, have encouraged private investors. Efforts at industrialization were begun in the 1940s by the Puerto Rico Industrial Development Company, a governmental corporation that was revamped in 1950 as the Economic Development Administration, popularly known as Fomento. Its program has been known as "Operation Bootstrap." Industrial products manufactured in Puerto Rico include textiles, clothing, plastics, electrical and electronic equipment, chemicals, processed foods, and petrochemicals.

Trade. Rising living standards and purchasing power have made Puerto Rico one of the best customers of the United States. The United States, in turn, has been Puerto Rico's best customer, though the balance of trade has generally remained slightly in favour of the United States. Puerto Rico's international position has worsened, however, by unfavourable trade balances with most of its foreign trading partners. Tourism, however, has become an important source of income.

Administrative and social conditions. *Government.* The commonwealth government resembles the government of a U.S. state. Separate executive, legislative, and judicial branches are spelled out in the constitution of 1952, which may be altered by the commonwealth so long as the articles are not in conflict with the U.S. Constitution or the legal stipulations of Puerto Rican–U.S. relations.

The governor, who is elected by direct popular vote to a four-year term, heads the executive branch. The legislature comprises the Senate and the House of Representatives, whose members are elected for four years. There are eight senatorial districts (with two senators each) and 40 representative districts, and in addition 11 senators and 11

Executive, legislature, and judiciary

representatives are elected at large. A complicated formula is used to assure proportional representation of minority parties.

Commonwealth voters elect a resident commissioner who has a voice, but no vote, in the U.S. House of Representatives. On the other hand, Puerto Ricans do not pay federal taxes on income received from island sources. Customs taxes on foreign goods imported into Puerto Rico and excise taxes on goods sold in the United States are collected by the federal treasury and returned to the commonwealth. Relations between Puerto Rico and the United States are defined in the Puerto Rico-Federal Relations Act, which retains many provisions of the Foraker (1900) and the Jones (1917) acts. Such matters as currency, defense, external relations, communications, and interstate commerce are within the province of the federal government. Local government—excluding San Juan, which has a city-management rule—is run by a mayor and council, both elected by popular vote.

Elections are held every four years, supervised by an electoral board comprising representatives from majority and minority parties. There are four principal registered parties: the New Progressive Party, the Popular Democratic Party, the Puerto Rican Independence Party, and the Puerto Rican Socialist Party. The two leading parties are the pro-statehood New Progressive Party, and the Popular Democratic Party, which supports the continuation of commonwealth status. The Puerto Rican Independence Party and the Puerto Rican Socialist Party advocate independence.

Diversity of political parties

Justice. Puerto Rico has a unified court system, which is administered by the island's Supreme Court, whose justices are appointed by the governor with the advice and consent of the commonwealth Senate. Civil law has been influenced largely by Spanish traditions and the code system of French law setting forth basic legal principles, though common law has influenced administrative law and many other areas of the legal system. A federal district court has jurisdiction over the application of federal laws in Puerto Rico, and appeals may be carried to the Supreme Court in Washington, D.C.

Education. Puerto Rico is deeply committed to the expansion of public education. Illiteracy has been reduced. Education is compulsory between six and 16 years of age. Vocational and technical education has been stressed to combat the high rate of unemployment among the young.

The system of higher education is diversified. The University of Puerto Rico comprises a state university system, with three main campuses and a number of regional colleges. Among the private universities and colleges are the Inter-American University of Puerto Rico and the Catholic University of Puerto Rico. Although island universities generally are patterned after U.S. institutions, their atmosphere is distinctly Latin American.

Health and welfare. Health programs include malaria control and the building of pure water supplies and modern sewage disposal systems in cities and towns throughout the island. Urban clinics and rural health centres have been created to provide treatment for communicable diseases, basic medical care, and instruction in hygiene, nutrition, and prenatal and child care. The rise in admissions to health centres indicates more widespread treatment.

Puerto Rico has made impressive strides in meeting the housing shortage, although the pressures continue to build. The Urban Renewal and Housing Corporation is in charge of broad and diversified housing programs, with concentration on low-income projects. The corporation has taken advantage of assistance from several housing programs, but credit restrictions have affected both public and private housing. In spite of new construction, the proportion of housing that lacks essential services to the total supply of housing has remained more or less constant. As in other areas of the island's life, population growth seems to be the major contributing factor.

Crises in housing and employment

Despite industrialization, unemployment has risen dramatically. The problem is most acute among the young and among the rural workers, who constitute the bulk of the unskilled labour and work only four to six months of the year. This doubling of unemployment stems primarily from population pressures. Federal and commonwealth

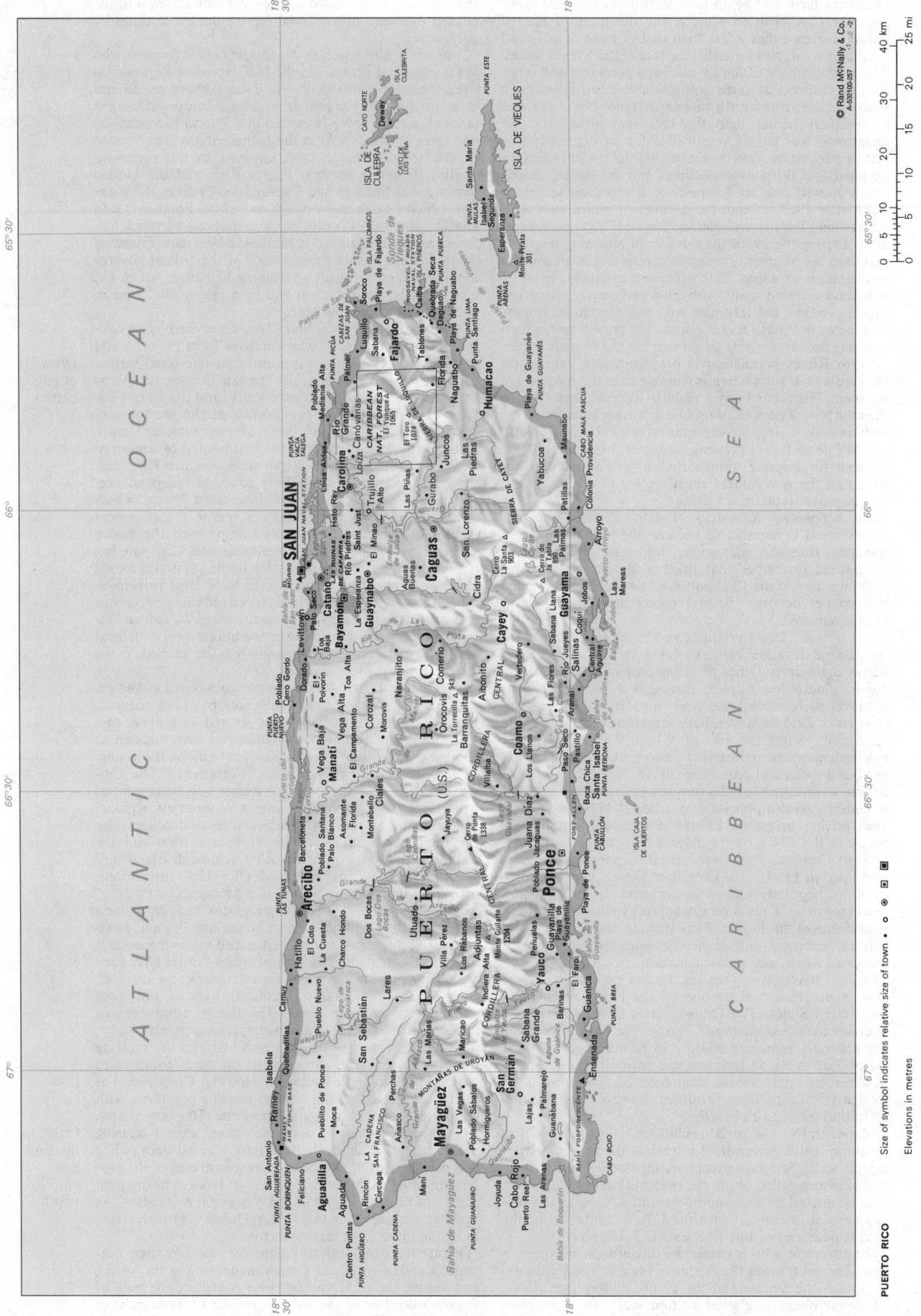

ATLANTIC OCEAN

CARIBBEAN SEA

ISLA DE CULEBRA

CAYO NORTE
Dewey
CAYO LUIS PEÑA
ISLA CULEBRITA

PUNTA ESTE

PUNTA MULAS
Isabel Santa María
Segunda
ISLA DE VIEQUES
Esperanza
PUNTA ARENAS
Monte Pirata 301

Sonda de Vieques

ISLA PIÑEROS
PUNTA PUERCA
ROOSEVELT RODS NAVAL STATION
Ceiba
Daguao PUNTA LIMA
PUNTA SANTIAGO
Playa de Humacao
Playa de Naguabo
PUNTA GUAYANÉS
Playa de Guayanés

ISLA PALOMINOS
Playa de Fajardo
Fajardo
Quebrada Seca
Naguabo
Humacao

Soroco
Luquillo
Sabana
PUNTA PICÚA
PASE DE SAN JUAN
CABEZAS DE SAN JUAN

Palmer
Mediania Alta
Poblado
Rio Grande
Loíza Aldea
Canóvanas
El Toro 1074
CARIBBEAN NATIONAL FOREST
El Yunque 1065
SIERRA DE LUQUILLO
Florida
Juncos
Las Piedras
Yabucoa
Maunabo
CABO MALA PASCUA
Colonia Providencia

PUNTA VACA
TALEGA

SAN JUAN NAVAL STATION
PUNTA EL MORRO
Bahía de San Juan
SAN JUAN
Carolina
LAS RUINAS Río Piedras
Saint Just
Trujillo Alto
El Minao
Gurabo
SIERRA DE CAYEY
Patillas
Arroyo
Puerto Arroyo

Cataño
Bayamón
La Esperanza
Aguas Buenas
San Lorenzo
Las Palmas
Cerro La Santa 903
Guayama
Jobos
Las Mareas
Bahía de Rincón
Puerto de Jobos

Levittown
Palo Seco
Dorado
Cerro Gordo
Poblado
El Polvorín
Guaynabo
Caguas
Cidra
Cayey
Salinas Coquí
Central Aguirre
Arroyo

Guanajibo

Vega Baja
Vega Alta
Toa Alta
Comerío
Cerro La Tabla 890
Vertedero
Sabana Llana
Río Jueyes
Central
Arenas

Manatí
El Campamento
Naranjito
Albonito
Coamo
Los Llanos

PUNTA PUERTO NUEVO
Puerto del Tortuguero

Palo Blanco
Poblado Santana
Morovis
Orocovis
La Torrecilla 943
Barranquitas
Villalba
Paso Seco
Boca Chica
Santa Isabel
PUNTA PETRONA

Asomante
Florida
Montebello
Corozal
Ciales
CORDILLERA CENTRAL
FORT ALLEN
Pastillo
PUNTA CABULLÓN
ISLA CAJA DE MUERTOS

Barceloneta
Arecibo
El Coto
La Cuesta
Charco Hondo
Dos Bocas
Lago Dos Bocas
Utuado
Villa Pérez
Los Rábanos
Cerro de Punta 1338
Monte Guilarte 1204
Adjuntas
Jayuya
Poblado Jácaguas
Juana Díaz
Ponce
Poblado
Peñuelas
Guayanilla
Playa de Ponce
Bahía de Ponce
El Faro

PUNTA LAS TUNAS
Camuy
Hatillo
Lago de Guajataca
Quebradillas
Pueblo Nuevo
Isabela
Lares
San Sebastián
Las Marías
Maricao
Indiera Alta
CORDILLERA DE YAUCO
Yauco
Sabana Grande
Guánica
Bahía de Guánica
PUNTA BREA
Ensenada

PUERTO RICO (U.S.)

P U E R T O   R I C O

Grande
Añasco

Ramey
RAMEY AIR FORCE BASE
PUNTA BORINQUEN
San Antonio
Aguadilla
Aguada
Moca
Rincón
Córcega
SAN FRANCISCO
LA CADENA
Mayagüez
Añasco
Perchas
MONTAÑAS DE UROYÁN
San Germán
Lajas
Barnas
Guánica

PUNTA HIGÜERO
Centro Puntas
PUNTA CADENA
Mani
Las Vegas
Poblado Sábalos
Hormigueros
Palmarejo
Guánabana
Guánajibo
PUNTA GUANIBO
Jouda
Cabo Rojo
Puerto Real
Las Arenas
Laguna de Guánica
Poblado Sábalos

BAHÍA FOSFORESCENTE
CABO ROJO
Bahía de Boquerón

Bahía de Mayagüez

© Rand McNally & Co.
A-632100-257
-1, -2, -2

18°30'   66°   66°30'   67°

18°

PUERTO RICO

Size of symbol indicates relative size of town

Elevations in metres

km   mi
40   25
30   20
15
20   10
10   5
0   0

18°30'

65°30'

minimum wages cover every important industry and agricultural enterprise.

General price levels in Puerto Rico closely follow the levels on the U.S. mainland, and inflationary pressures severely affect the islanders. Though increased incomes have promoted social and economic mobility, the growth has helped the urban areas at the expense of the rural. Most of the extreme poverty is concentrated there or in the city slums. Income security programs have been extended to islanders by mutual consent of the Congress and the insular legislature.

Cultural life. Puerto Rico's culture has strong roots in the Hispanic world. The language, the literature, the arts, and the surviving folklore link Puerto Rico with Latin America. The strong influence of the United States since 1898 has not deeply changed Puerto Rico's cultural expression. Though popular culture, strongly abetted by modern commercialism, may reflect some North American traits, the island's traditions are strong and have become the subject of concern and care by such institutions as the Puerto Rican Institute of Culture and the Ateneo Puertorriqueño. A new generation of poets, novelists, short-story writers, and essayists keeps alive the traditions of such 19th-century forerunners as the novelists Alejandro Tapia and Manuel Zeno Gandia, the essayists and sociologists Eugenio María de Hostos and Salvador Brau, and the poets José Gautier Benítez and Lola Rodríguez de Tió. New playwrights and artists have also received considerable encouragement from the Institute of Culture.

An annual drama festival has helped to promote the

Cultural traditions

theatre. The Festival Casals, established in 1956 by Pablo Casals, became a major musical event that brought world-renowned musicians to the island each summer. The Institute of Culture sponsors many groups preserving popular folklore and conducting exhibits of local art.

As in many Caribbean countries, Puerto Ricans are searching for a definition of the island's cultural identity. Some residents advocate cultural nationalism and a strong rejection of U.S. values, while others have a more eclectic position. There is, however, a general consensus that the island's culture is distinct from that of the United States, and assimilation that would obliterate Puerto Rico's Hispanic-American profile is neither possible nor desirable. The press, radio, and television are, however, influenced heavily by U.S. modes and trends. For statistical data, see the "Britannica World Data" section in the current *Britannica Book of the Year*.   (A.M.-C.)

HISTORY

The first inhabitants of Puerto Rico, originally from either the Florida Peninsula or the Amazon Basin of South America, reached the island by means of the archipelago of the Lesser Antilles about 600 years before the arrival of the Spaniards. These Arawak Indians, living in small villages, were organized in clans and led by a cacique or chief. They were a peaceful people who, with a limited knowledge of agriculture, lived on such domesticated tropical crops as pineapples, cassava, and sweet potatoes supplemented by sea food. Anthropologists estimate their numbers to have been between 20,000 and 50,000. On a fertile island, the Arawaks lived an easy life disturbed only by occasional visits from their cannibal Carib neighbours on the islands to the south and east. At the time of discovery Carib Indians occupied most of the Lesser Antilles, the Virgin Islands, and Vieques Island.

In 1493 Christopher Columbus, at the peak of his popularity, left Spain on his second voyage to the Indies with an elaborate expedition of 17 ships and about 1,500 men. At the island of Guadeloupe, the Spaniards rescued several Arawak Indians who had been taken from Boriquén, the Indian name for Puerto Rico, by the Caribs. Columbus agreed to return them to their island, and on November 19, 1493, the expedition anchored in a bay on the west coast of Puerto Rico. Columbus formally took possession of the island in the name of Ferdinand and Isabella, the rulers of Spain, and named it San Juan Bautista. Two days were spent on the island before the ships moved westward to Hispaniola, where the first settlement in the New World was established.

Columbus' visit to Puerto Rico

Spanish rule. *Early settlement.* For 15 years the island was neglected except for an occasional visit by a ship putting in for supplies. In 1508 Juan Ponce de León, who previously had accompanied Columbus, was granted permission to explore San Juan Bautista in recognition of his valuable colonizing efforts in eastern Hispaniola. On the north coast, Ponce de León found a well-protected bay that could offer safe harbour for a large number of sailing vessels, and he founded the first town, Caparra, the site of the first mining and agricultural efforts. The harbour was named Puerto Rico because of its obvious excellent potentialities. In this area was located the most important settlement on the island; through time and common use the port became known as San Juan, while the name Puerto Rico came to be applied to the whole island.

The peaceful and friendly relations with the Arawak did not last long. The Spaniards expected the Indians to acknowledge the sovereignty of the king of Spain by payment of gold tribute. The Indians were to be instructed in Christian ways. In return for this education, which was rarely given, the Arawaks were expected to work and supply either more gold or provisions of food. In 1511 the Indians rebelled against the Spanish, who with their superior arms rapidly subjugated them.

Placer mining of gold was continued by Indians brought from other islands and by blacks brought from Africa by some of the early traders. After the 1530s, however, gold production markedly declined with dwindling Indian labour, and the Spanish colonists, with slaves from Africa, turned to agriculture.

Puerto Rico, however, did not prosper economically. Carib Indians from neighbouring islands made frequent raids, carrying off food and slaves and destroying property. The colony continued to lead a precarious existence, ravaged by plagues and plundered by French, British, and Dutch pirates. Repeatedly during the mid-16th century the French burned and sacked San Germán, the second community to be established on the island. Under such adverse conditions people began to leave the island whenever opportunity offered.

In the second half of the 16th century Spain, recognizing the strategic importance of Puerto Rico, undertook to convert San Juan into a military outpost. The fortress El Morro, built with the financial subsidy from the Mexican mines, was well constructed and perfectly located to dominate the narrow entrance to the harbour. Later, a stronger and larger fortress was built to the east and on the Atlantic side of the city. In the early 17th century the city was surrounded by a stone wall, 25 feet high and 18 feet thick, two parts of which still stand. These defenses made San Juan almost impregnable.

The fortification of San Juan

Sir Francis Drake attacked the town in 1595 but failed to gain the harbour. Three years later George Clifford, 3rd earl of Cumberland, had complete military success but was forced to abandon his conquest owing to an outbreak of plague among his troops. In 1625 a Dutchman, Bowdoin Hendrik, burgomaster of Edam, boldly sailed into the harbour, captured and burned the town, but failed to subdue El Morro.

San Juan, as the most exposed military outpost guarding the heart of Spain's New World empire, received political and economic attention from the mother country. The rural inhabitants of the interior of the island, however, were ignored by Spain and scorned by the presidial residents of San Juan. As the French, English, Danish, and Dutch fought over and settled the Lesser Antilles during the 17th and 18th centuries, rural Puerto Ricans, ignoring the edicts of Spain, found profit in clandestine trade. Ginger, hides, sugar, tobacco, and cattle from the island were in great demand, and while the colonial authorities of San Juan rarely ventured out of their walled defenses for fear of the reprisals of the buccaneers, the rural settlers prospered in a modest way through contacts with the non-Spanish European traders. No large plantations were established, and the farmer, with little help, cultivated his own land. Contrary to the fears of Spain, this contact with foreigners did not corrupt the islanders, who remained loyal and were willing to participate in aggressive expeditions.

Liberal reforms. In 1797 the British general Sir Ralph Abercromby, who had captured Trinidad, unsuccessfully attacked Puerto Rico. The British considered the island—a centre of clandestine trade and of operations for quasi-piratical expeditions and a refuge for runaway slaves—a weak link in the chain of defense of the Spanish Empire. The failure of Abercromby was due in part to the important economic and administrative changes in the Spanish colonial empire that were carried out in the latter half of the 18th century by representatives of the Bourbon rulers of Spain. In the case of Puerto Rico it was hoped that the island might become an economic asset rather than a financial drain on the Spanish crown. Trade relations between the island and Spain were liberalized, agricultural production was stimulated, the island as a whole was integrated into the system of military defense.

The British attack on Puerto Rico

The liberal reforms of the enlightened despotism of the Spanish Bourbons coincided with and encouraged rapid population growth, introduction of new products, and the beginning of commercial agriculture. Population was estimated in 1765 at 45,000; in 1775 at 70,250; in 1787 at 103,051; and in 1800 at 155,426. By the end of the 18th century there were 34 towns on the island. Immigrants from the Canary Islands, French settlers from Louisiana or Haiti, and Spaniards from Santo Domingo, which had been turned over to Napoleon, accounted in part for the increase in population. These newcomers brought with them new ideas and methods of producing marketable crops. Coffee, introduced into the island in 1736, became an important export item by 1776. Sugar production, which had always been small, was undertaken on a large scale by augmented slave labour. From 1765 to 1800 the slave population increased from 5,037 to 13,333.

When Napoleon invaded Spain and placed his brother Joseph Bonaparte on the Spanish throne (1808), the colonies of South and Central America asserted their right to govern themselves in the name of the imprisoned Bourbon king, Ferdinand VII. This claim to temporary self-rule eventually evolved into a revolutionary movement for independence. In Puerto Rico, however, for various reasons, the sequence of events and their results were different. The communities of the interior of Puerto Rico, with one exception, offered little objection to the strict rules of Spain's mercantilist policy, which for many decades had ceased to have effect on them. Most of the residents of San Juan, on the other hand, dependent upon administrative and military positions, were most willing to follow the orders of the central government of Spain acting in the absence of the King. Puerto Rico, which had asserted its loyalty by repelling the English, undertook to recapture Santo Domingo from the French.

As the revolutions progressed on the southern and central mainlands, loyal Spaniards reluctant to leave the colonies found refuge in Puerto Rico, which was being used as a supply depot for military movements on the continent. In recognition of its loyalty and in a belated move to liberalize an outmoded colonial system, the Spanish government granted Puerto Rico in 1815 ample economic liberties. The island was opened to all non-Spanish Catholics, the ports were permitted to trade with non-Spanish countries, and free land was granted to the new settlers. After 1830 Puerto Rico gradually developed into a plantation economy based on three main crops: sugar, coffee, and tobacco. Sugar and molasses, sold mainly in the U.S. market, provided an important source of income for the Spanish government. Foreign settlers contributed to economic development, though the Spanish element attempted to maintain a tight monopoly.

Economic and political development. By the end of the 19th century the population had increased to nearly 1,000,000, and the value of foreign trade had increased considerably from an estimated $1,000,000 in the 1820s to $30,000,000 annually. During the 1800s imports from the United States rarely dropped below 20 percent of the total goods received; exports to the U.S. fluctuated between 50 percent and 15 percent, depending in part upon U.S. tariff restrictions. By 1899 the United States was buying almost two-thirds of Puerto Rican sugar production. The area devoted to sugar had been slowly expanding. Coffee, in the late 19th century, provided the principal source of income for the island.

Political development in Puerto Rico during the 19th century was characterized by periods of liberal advance counteracted by long periods of conservative reaction. In part this was due to the changes occurring in the Spanish government, and in part due to the antiquated Spanish colonial administrative policy.

During the first half of the 19th century, two short periods of relative political freedom were enjoyed. From 1809 to 1814 and from 1820 to 1823 Puerto Rico was declared an integral part of Spain with the right to elect representatives to the Spanish Cortes, or parliament. Ramón Power y Giralt, an able liberal, was selected during the first period and succeeded in revoking the absolute powers of the island's colonial governor. In the latter period Demetrio O'Daly secured the separation of the military authority from the colonial administrator. Freedom of the press was also permitted. On each occasion moderate colonial rule was thwarted by the return of royal absolutism in Spain.

In 1837, when a fairly permanent constitutional monarchy was established in Spain, Puerto Rico failed to benefit because it was argued that the colonies were not true Spanish provinces and therefore should be governed by special laws. For more than 30 years Puerto Rico waited for special legislation to ease the despotic rule of military colonial governors. During this waiting period political thought in the island began to crystallize. A liberal current of opinion requested assimilation into the Spanish government and permission to be represented in and governed by the Cortes. A bloc of conservative opinion strongly

Two periods of political freedom

approved of the status quo. A small third group advocated complete independence.

Movements toward self-government and independence. A local commission was elected in 1865 to draw up a report on the basis of which a governmental reform might be carried out. The majority report, which declared that the abolition of slavery was the sine qua non of any political reform, provoked a shocked reaction among the island and peninsular conservatives. The alarmed colonial government took steps to curtail what was feared to be a growing movement of rebellion. Some of the more outspoken and respected islanders were ordered to be arrested and sent to Spain for trial. Thus provoked, a small group of radicals committed to independence attempted an uprising, for which, however, inadequate preparation was made. El Grito de Lares, the abortive revolt of September 23, 1868, brought forth severe reprisals on all island liberals. Though separatist elements joined the Cubans who were struggling for independence, they were unable to challenge Spanish power effectively. However, the abdication of Queen Isabella II of Spain was forced by a republican government that pardoned all the political prisoners. The first Spanish republic extended to Puerto Rico its third period of constitutional government, 1868–74, during which slavery was abolished.

During the 1880s a movement for political self-government under Spain led by Román Baldorioty de Castro replaced the sentiment in favour of integrating Puerto Rico into the Spanish government. Again liberal political movement, this time autonomy, was denounced as disloyal and was violently suppressed in 1887. Such treatment only served to solidify the movement for local self-government, and in 1897 the Partido Unionista (Autonomy Party), through cooperation with the Liberal Party in Spain, achieved its objective. The autonomous government granted was parliamentary in form but retained the governor general as a representative of the Spanish king. He was empowered to disband the insular parliament and suspend civil rights. The two-chamber parliament was empowered to legislate for the island, create and control an insular tariff, and levy local taxes. Puerto Rico's representation in the Spanish Cortes was also increased. Any change in the governmental organization had to be first approved by the insular parliament.

Suppression of the autonomy movement

Spanish–American War. The Spanish–American War (1898) prevented the islanders from putting into effect the new government. In May 1898 Adm. W.T. Sampson bombarded San Juan for a short time without serious results. Facing token military resistance and with general popular acceptance, Gen. Nelson A. Miles landed a U.S. force of about 3,500 men in July, and after a short campaign hostilities were ended on August 12.

Under the United States. *Early years.* On October 18, 1898, the island was turned over to the U.S forces, and Gen. John R. Brooke became military governor. Puerto Rico was ceded to the U.S. by the Treaty of Paris, signed December 10, 1898 (ratified by the U.S. Senate February 6, 1899). In the work of policing the country, in the accompanying tasks of sanitation, construction of highways and other public works, accounting for the expenditure of public funds, and establishing a system of public education, the military control that lasted until May 1, 1900, proved effective in bridging the period of transfer from the control of Spain to the system under the United States civil government. The U.S. military, however, ruled with little regard for political sensitivities. The United States Congress passed the Foraker Act, under which civil government was instituted in May 1900. Under this act the U.S. element exercised the controlling power; this, however, having proved distasteful to many Puerto Ricans, the organic law was subsequently amended to give a wider native participation in the government. The Olmsted Act, approved by Congress on July 15, 1909, placed the supervision of Puerto Rican affairs in the jurisdiction of an executive department to be designated by the president. The people, however, demanded a larger measure of local control. The majority also asked for U.S. citizenship and many other changes. As a result, Congress passed a new organic act (the Jones Act), which came into effect on

The Olmsted Act

March 2, 1917. Under its terms Puerto Rico became a territory of the United States "organized but unincorporated," and citizenship of the United States was conferred collectively on Puerto Ricans, allowing the right to retain the old status if preferred. Only 288 persons declared in favour of the latter. The local civil government, however, even with modifications, fell far short of the measure of self-government that Puerto Ricans expected in light of the democratic tradition of the United States. Key officials, including the governor, were presidential appointees and thus beyond local control.

In spite of the legal limitations on political autonomy, a climate of freedom was slowly developed as a result of the change of sovereignty. At first this new order, being abrupt, new, and imposed from above in some instances, was sometimes mistrusted, resented, and misunderstood, but in the long run it was recognized as beneficial and assimilated by the islanders. For example, the separation of church from state, resulting in open competition for religious adherence, demonstrated the new climate in a practical way; government programs that dealt directly with the vital needs of the people for education, health and sanitation, and regulation of working conditions all reflected a change designed to remedy centuries of neglect.

Economic and social changes. Early U.S. governors were mainly preoccupied with Americanizing Puerto Rican institutions, language, and political habits but had no clear policy on the island's eventual political status. This approach created strong resistance from many native leaders led by Luis Muñoz Rivera, who had fought for autonomy under Spain. The economic reorientation of the island as a result of the change in sovereignty had almost an immediate and profound effect on all aspects of life. Included within the U.S. tariff walls, Puerto Rican agricultural products, particularly sugar, had a ready market. Aided by the adoption of U.S. currency and by unobstructed financial movement, Puerto Rico experienced within a short period a large capital investment that revolutionized the production of sugar. Seven-fold acreage expansion (1899–1939), new disease-resistant plants, rapid transportation facilities, large and efficient cane-grinding mills, and complete corporate management within a generation converted the economy of the island into one in which 75 percent of the population directly or indirectly was dependent upon sugar. Land that had sustained small farmers producing crops and dairy products for local consumption was absorbed by the sugar corporations. The population increased from about 950,000 in 1899 to more than 1,540,000 in 1930. Glaring inequalities of wealth contributed to sharpened social and political tensions.

The island was forced to import its foodstuffs. Coffee was neglected at a time when weather conditions and transportation problems dictated financial and government aid. Only tobacco production experienced growth, which failed to be sustained after the 1920s when United States smokers shifted from cigars to cigarettes.

The shock of these economic changes might have been absorbed in spite of the island's limited resources if at the same time Puerto Rico had not been undergoing a severe social change as a result of the application of modern sanitation means and medical knowledge to a people with a very high death rate. The population was threatening to double its number in two generations. The two counterpressures—expansion of corporate control over the limited productive land and increasing population pressure—reached an explosive stage when the economic depression occupied the attention of government officials in the United States. Recurring hurricanes joined with declining exports to aggravate the economic distress of the island.

Political development. With one exception political parties that had developed since the change in sovereignty had centred their attention on modifications in the political relations between the island and the U.S. federal government. The Republican Party limited its program to a plea for statehood for the island. The Union Party worked for greater autonomy. In the 1920s the Nationalist Party rose to affirm the ideal of immediate independence. The one exception was the pro-U.S. Socialist Party, led by the highly respected labour leader Santiago Iglesias. This party had expressed since its foundation a concern for the plight of the labouring classes of the island. Nevertheless, its effectiveness had been hampered by insufficient popular support, due primarily to the concentration of attention upon the issue of the political status of the island.

In the mid-1930s, with Pres. Franklin D. Roosevelt's New Deal policies radically enlarging the previously accepted concept of the function of government as that of maintaining order and protecting the citizens, Puerto Rico was not neglected. More important than the much-needed temporary relief were the steps taken by the Puerto Rican Reconstruction Administration (PRAA), designed to readjust the distribution of economic power on the island. A restrictive quota was placed over sugar production. Legal procedures were initiated to enforce a long-neglected law limiting corporate holdings to 500 acres. Thus the process of increasing the sugar acreage was to be reversed, and Puerto Ricans were to be returned to their small farms.

This radical program provoked the open opposition of the sugar interests, locally vocal through the Republican Party. The Socialists accepted the program in a tacit fashion. Their reluctance was due to the fact that the young radical wing of the heirs of the Autonomy Party, led by Luis Muñoz Marín, the son of Luis Muñoz Rivera, was recognized in Washington and on the island as the local political proponent of the economic reform.

The success of the New Deal measures was jeopardized by two unconnected factors. Unforeseen administrative and financial problems forced a curtailment of the objectives of the PRRA. No longer was a complete readjustment of the island's economic structure possible; the PRRA took on a more temporary or experimental nature. The second factor was the interjection of the status issue on the political scene by the U.S. government in answer to Nationalist violence. Taking the form of a vindictive offer of independence under adverse economic conditions, the proposal served to realign again the political parties into pro- and anti-independence groups.

The incipient political movement for economic reform originally fostered by the New Deal and temporarily sidetracked was surprisingly successful in the election of 1940. This new political movement took the form of a political party, led by Muñoz Marín, called the Popular Democratic Party. Organized to improve the conditions of the lower classes, particularly the hard-working *jíbaro* of the mountainous interior, the new party's platform was summarized by the slogan "Bread, land, and liberty." The island electorate had agreed that the political status was not in issue and that economic and social problems took precedence. Tenuous control over the island legislature and a new-style colonial governor, Rexford Guy Tugwell, allowed the Popular Democratic Party to initiate such economic reforms as redistribution of land, enforcement of minimum wage and hour laws, an enforced progressive income tax law, and the establishment of an economic development program. In recognition of partial fulfillment of its announced aims the Popular Party was overwhelmingly backed by the island electorate in 1944. In 1946 Pres. Harry S. Truman named Jesús T. Piñero, a Puerto Rican, as governor, the first Puerto Rican to occupy that post. In 1947 the U.S. Congress amended the organic act of Puerto Rico to permit election of governors by popular vote. Muñoz Marín was elected November 2, 1948, and took office in January 1949.

For more than a generation the Popular Democratic Party (PPD), led by Muñoz Marín, governed Puerto Rico. Muñoz served for four terms as governor and was followed by his able administrative assistant, Roberto Sánchez Vilella. In 1968, although the PPD retained control over the insular senate, they lost control over the lower house and the post of governor to the pro-statehood New Progressive Party (PNP) when Luis A. Ferré was elected in November. Under the guidance of the PPD, Puerto Rico experienced a remarkable economic recovery that, rather than freeing the island from its economic ties to the United States, changed these relations from unrestrained exploitation by absentee sugar corporations to controlled industrial production allowing the islanders to receive greater benefits from the original capital investment. As the island became

Effects of the New Deal policy on Puerto Rico

Economic recovery

more industrialized and the people flocked to the cities, where not only better wages but better working conditions and improved social services could be found, Puerto Rico experienced the transition from an agrarian society into a modern industrial society closely patterned after the United States, but with a distinct Latin flavour.

Early in his first term as governor Muñoz Marín turned to the problem of political status. Obviously, any political change would have to take into consideration the economic relationship between the United States and Puerto Rico. The solution was found in the expansion of local political autonomy that did not affect adversely the economy of the island.

Establishment of the Commonwealth. In 1950 the U.S. Congress offered to Puerto Rico for its approval or rejection a series of changes in the law that governed the relationship between the federal government and Puerto Rico. These changes, if accepted, would eliminate all sections dealing with the creation of the local insular government and would turn over to the people of Puerto Rico the power to create their own government under a constitution of their own making. Under the guidance of Governor Muñoz Marín the islanders accepted the offer of Congress and drew up a constitution. Duly approved by the people and the Congress, Puerto Rico's constitution was proclaimed on July 25, 1952, and the Commonwealth of Puerto Rico came into being. During this period Puerto Rican extremists dramatized their desire for independence with an attempt to assassinate President Truman on November 1, 1950, in Washington, D.C. They attracted worldwide attention on March 1, 1954, when several members of the Nationalist Party shot and wounded five congressmen in the U.S. Capitol. Nevertheless, in the judgment of the General Assembly of the United Nations, Puerto Rico is a self-governing political unit associated voluntarily with the United States.

In the 1960s, with the admission of Hawaii and Alaska as new states into the United States and the increasing affinity toward the United States of a growing middle class, the Popular Party requested a reexamination of the status question, and subsequently a United States–Puerto Rican Status Commission was named by the President of the United States to explore the range of political statuses open to the people of Puerto Rico. The report of the commission found that commonwealth, statehood, and even independence were theoretically open to Puerto Ricans depending upon their willingness to undergo a prolonged period of economic adjustment should they select a status radically different from that in effect. The commission urged a plebiscite to indicate popular preference for the three principal statuses. In 1967 more than 60 percent of the voters participated in the plebiscite indicating a preference for commonwealth status; 39 percent selected statehood, but most of the voters favouring independence abstained and continued to agitate for separation.

Although commonwealth status won impressive support, both the leaders of the PPD and influential members of the U.S. federal government, following the recommendations of the Status Commission, recognized that the commonwealth relationship needed to be improved and the degree of self-government broadened even further. In the 1970s there was an increasing number of expressions of dissatisfaction with the commonwealth status. Terrorist bombings in San Juan and on the mainland in the 1970s were reported to be linked to the independence movement. A special commission formed in 1970 unanimously declared that Puerto Ricans be allowed to vote for the U.S. president and vice president. In 1972 the pro-Commonwealth Popular Democratic Party was returned to power over the New Progressive Party, while the Independence Party made small gains. The New Progressive Party won the governorship in 1976 and 1980. For current political history, see the annual issues of the *Britannica Book of the Year*. (T.G.Ms./Ed.)

LESSER ANTILLES

Anguilla

Anguilla, an island in the eastern Caribbean Sea, is a dependent territory of the United Kingdom. It lies about 60 miles (100 kilometres) northwest of St. Christopher (St. Kitts). It is the most northerly of the Leeward Islands in the Lesser Antilles. The Valley is the principal village and the administrative centre of the island.

PHYSICAL AND HUMAN GEOGRAPHY

The land. Anguilla is bare and flat, fringed by white sand beaches, and its long (16 miles), thin (never more than 3½ miles wide) shape gave it its name (French *anguille,* "eel"). Its area is 35 square miles (91 square kilometres).

Anguilla has several small uninhabited offshore islands. The largest are Dog, Scrub, and Sombrero Islands. The island is of coral limestone formation; the highest point is 213 feet (65 metres). The vegetation is primarily low scrub, although there are some plantations of fruit trees. Soil is thin, but there are small pockets of red loam soil, mainly in the shallow valleys. As with most coral islands, water is a scarce commodity.

The people. The majority of the population of Anguilla is black and of African descent. The official language is English, and the main religious denominations are Anglican and Methodist.

The economy. Fishing, stock raising, and salt production are the main economic activities. There is also some boat building. Salt, lobster, and livestock are the principal exports.

Administrative and social conditions. Although technically Anguilla was a member of the associated state of St. Kitts-Nevis-Anguilla until December 1980, in reality it has been administered as a separate British dependent territory since the Anguilla Act of 1971. Executive power is in the hands of a commissioner, appointed by the British monarch. The commissioner is in charge of external affairs, defense, internal security (including police), and public services. The Executive Council is composed of a chief minister, three other ministers, and two ex officio members (an attorney general and a permanent secretary for finance). The House Assembly consists of members elected by universal adult suffrage, members appointed by the commissioner after consultation with the chief minister, and the attorney general and the permanent secretary for finance as ex officio members.

HISTORY

The island was reached by Christopher Columbus in 1493 and became a British colony in 1650. In 1967 Anguilla, complaining of domination by the St. Kitts administration, ejected the St. Kitts police and set up its own council, subsequently proclaiming its independence. After negotiations failed, the British intervened in March 1969 to restore legal government with troops and a temporary commissioner. The troops were withdrawn in September 1969, and the Anguilla Act of July 1971 placed Anguilla directly under British control. A new constitution was approved in 1976 and Anguilla formally became a dependent territory of the United Kingdom in 1980. (Ed.)

Antigua and Barbuda

Antigua and Barbuda are islands that form an independent republic within the Commonwealth in the Lesser Antilles in the East Caribbean. It lies at the southern end of the Leeward Islands chain and has an area of 171 square miles (442 square kilometres). It has one dependency, Redonda.

PHYSICAL AND HUMAN GEOGRAPHY

Antigua's coastline is intricate, with bays and headlands fringed with reefs and shoals; several inlets, including

Parham and English Harbour, afford anchorage for shipping. St. Johns has a deepwater harbour and an international airport. The island is for the most part low and undulating but in the west is composed entirely of volcanic rocks rising at the highest point, Boggy Peak, to 1,330 feet (405 metres). An absence of mountains and thorough deforestation distinguishes Antigua from the other Leeward Islands. As there are no rivers and few springs, prolonged droughts occur despite a mean annual rainfall of some 44 inches (1,118 millimetres).

Barbuda, formerly Dulcina, lies 25 miles (40 kilometres) north of Antigua. A coral island, flat and well wooded, with highlands rising to more than 200 feet at Lindsay Hill in the northeast, it is 62 square miles (161 square kilometres) in area. Codrington, the only settlement, lies on a lagoon to the west of the island. Colonized in 1628 and granted to the Codrington family in 1680, Barbuda reverted to the crown in the late 19th century. Its inhabitants are fishermen and farmers. The island has long been used as a game reserve for deer, wild fowl, and wild pigs.

Redonda, an uninhabited rock, lies 25 miles (40 kilometres) southwest of the main island. It rises sheer to a height of 1,000 feet (305 metres) and is 0.5 square miles (1.3 square kilometres) in area. There are phosphate deposits.

The people. The majority of the population is black and of African descent. A very large fraction of the population lives in the capital of Antigua and Barbuda, St. John's. The language is English, and most people are Anglican, with minorities of other Protestant sects and Roman Catholics.

Both the birth and death rates for Antigua and Barbuda are considerably less than the Caribbean averages; and even though immigration usually adds to the rate of natural population increase, the total rate of population growth for these two remains less than that of most of the West Indian islands.

The economy. The main crops and products are cotton and sugar (molasses), with the main trading partners being the United States and Great Britain; the main exports consist of petroleum products from the country's crude oil refinery. Tourism is an important industry and accounts for much of the national income. Manufacturing mainly produces import substitution goods including clothing, paints, optical lenses, stoves, refrigerators, and electrical components; automobiles also are assembled. Antigua was a founding member of the Caribbean Free Trade Association (Carifta) in 1968, predecessor of the Caribbean Community (Caricom).

Administrative and social conditions. Antigua and Barbuda, as the state is known, has a constitutional monarchy with the British monarch as head of state, represented in the republic by a governor general. The constitution allows for a senate consisting of 17 members and a house of representatives. Primary and postprimary education is compulsory.

HISTORY

Antigua was visited in 1493 by Christopher Columbus, who named it after the church of Santa Maria de la Antigua in Seville, Spain. It was colonized by English settlers in 1632 and remained a British possession, although raided by the French in 1666. It at first grew tobacco, but in the later 17th century sugar was found more profitable.

Emancipation of the slaves

The emancipation in 1834 of slaves, who had been employed on the profitable sugar estates, gave rise to difficulties in obtaining labour. A fire in 1841, an earthquake in 1843, and a hurricane in 1847 were further economic blows. The naval dockyard, closed in 1854, was reopened in 1961 as a historic monument and yachting centre.

The Leeward Islands colony was defederated in 1956, and on January 3, 1958, Antigua joined the West Indies Federation. When the federation was dissolved on May 31, 1962, Antigua persevered with discussions of alternative forms of federation, continuing them through the early and mid-1960s. After the endorsement by the Legislative Council of decisions taken in London early in 1966, provision was made in the West Indies Act, 1967, for Antigua to assume a status of association with the U.K. on February 27, 1967. As an associated state, Antigua was fully self-governing in all internal affairs, while the U.K. retained responsibility for external affairs and defense.

Changes in political status

By 1973 Antigua was developing its own independence movement, particularly under its prime minister George Walter, who wanted complete independence for the islands and opposed the British plan of independence within a federation of islands. Walter lost the 1976 elections to Vere Bird, a conservative politician who favoured the idea of regional integration. At that time Antigua was the only state in the Caribbean to resist full independence. But in 1978 Antigua did a complete about-face and announced it wanted independence in 1979. The autonomy talks, not unexpectedly, ran into many procedural problems and were further complicated by the fact that Barbuda wanted to secede. Barbuda, long a dependency of Antigua, felt that it had been economically stifled by the larger island of Antigua. Finally, on November 1, 1981, Antigua and Barbuda achieved independence, with Vere Bird as the first prime minister of the new state. The republic obtained UN membership and joined the newly formed Organization of East Caribbean States. For current political history, see the annual issues of the *Britannica Book of the Year*.

(R.To./D.L.N./Ed.)

Barbados

Barbados is an independent island nation in the West Indies situated about 100 miles (160 kilometres) east of the Windward Islands. Approximately triangular in shape, it has an area of 166 square miles (430 square kilometres). Its capital is Bridgetown, the only seaport.

Barbados does not form part of the Lesser Antilles although it is sometimes grouped with this archipelago. The island is of different geological formation; it is less mountainous and has less variety in plant and animal life. The geographic position of Barbados has profoundly influenced the island's history and culture. In the era of sailing ships, access to the island was difficult because of the prevailing winds from the northeast. Outward-bound ships from Europe had to gain the island while heading west, for it was difficult for them to turn and reach its shores by sailing eastward against the wind. Conquest of the island was difficult—and later of little interest to European powers—and it remained a British possession without interruption from its settlement in the 17th century to 1966, when it attained independence. As a result of this long association with Britain, the culture of Barbados is probably more British than that of any other Caribbean island, thus earning Barbados the nicknames "Bimshire" and "Little England." Since independence, however, cultural nationalism and regional awareness have tended to increase. The country's reputation as an orderly society, with low crime rates, has contributed to its popularity among tourists, especially those from North America and Europe.

PHYSICAL AND HUMAN GEOGRAPHY

The land. The rocks underlying Barbados consist of sedimentary deposits, including thick shales, clays, sands, and conglomerates, laid down approximately 70,000,000 years ago. Above these rocks are chalky deposits, which were capped with coral before the island rose to the surface. A layer of coral, up to 300 feet (90 metres) thick, covers the island, except in the northeast (a physiographic region known as the Scotland District) where erosion has removed the coral cover. The government has adopted a conservation plan to prevent further erosion.

The coral surface

Relief. Mt. Hillaby, the highest point in Barbados, rises to 1,115 feet in the north central part of the island. To the west the land drops down to the sea in a series of terraces, many of which are green and gently rolling. East from Mt. Hillaby, the land declines sharply to the rugged upland of the Scotland District. Southward, the highlands descend steeply to the broad St. George Valley; between the valley and the sea the land rises to 400 feet to form Christ Church Ridge. Coral reefs surround most of the island.

Climate. The climate is generally pleasant. The temperature does not usually rise above 86° F (30° C) or fall below 72° F (22° C). There are two recognized seasons of the year: the dry season, from early December to May,

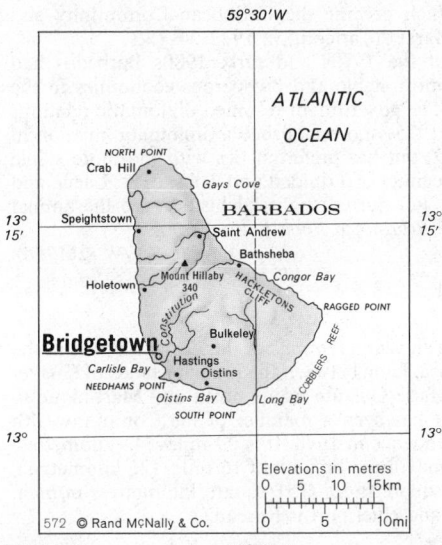

59°30'W

ATLANTIC OCEAN

BARBADOS

NORTH POINT
Crab Hill
Gays Cove
13° 15'
Speightstown
Saint Andrew
Bathsheba
Mount Hillaby 340
Congor Bay
Holetown
RAGGED POINT
Bridgetown
Bulkeley
Carlisle Bay
Hastings
Oistins
NEEDHAMS POINT
Oistins Bay
Long Bay
SOUTH POINT
13°

Elevations in metres
0   5   10   15km
0   5   10mi

572   © Rand McNally & Co.

BARBADOS   59°30'W

and the wet season, which lasts for the rest of the year. The average rainfall is about 60 inches (1,525 millimetres) a year, but, despite the small size of the island, rainfall varies markedly, rising from the low-lying coastal areas to the high central district. Barbados lies in the southern border of the Carribean hurricane zone. Hurricanes in 1780, 1831, and 1898 caused great devastation, and a hurricane in 1955, the first to hit Barbados in 57 years, caused considerable damage in the southern part of the island.

Plant and animal life. Very little of the original vegetation remains on Barbados; the pale green colour of sugarcane has become the characteristic colour of the landscape. Tropical trees—including flamboyant, or poinciana; mahogany; the frangipani; and cabbage palm—are widespread, while flowering shrubs adorn parks and gardens.

The few wild animals in Barbados—such as monkeys, hares, and mongooses—are considered pests by farmers. Birds include the dove, hummingbird, sparrow, egret, and yellow breast. The marine life includes flying fish, sprat, green dolphin, kingfish, barracuda, mackerel, jack, and parrot fish. The tree frog punctuates the night with its constant piping, or whistling.

Settlement patterns. Since most of the farmland is the property of large landowners or corporations, there is little land that the poor can own. As a result, "tenantries" are as common as villages. Tenantries consist of clusters of wooden houses—locally known as chattel houses—which are located on the borders of the large estates; they are usually owned by the occupants but stand on rented ground from which they may easily be removed. Some of them have electric light; toilet facilities are often outdoors, and water is sometimes obtained from a village pump, locally called a standpipe. "Bajans," as Barbadians sometimes refer to themselves, raise sheep, goats, cows, pigs, and poultry. Young men may often be seen "liming," or idling outdoors, where they talk or play checkers and other games. In every village there is at least one shop that serves as a combination grocery, pub, and meeting place, where the men gather to drink and to discuss politics and other matters.

Housing   Since the late 1950s private developers have built upper- and middle-class housing on land formerly used for agriculture. The government has built similar housing developments for low-income groups.

The largest town is Bridgetown. In its commercial and administrative centre, multi-story buildings are replacing the 19th-century town, which once resembled a Victorian print.

The people. Both the birth rate and death rate for Barbados are among the lowest of the Caribbean islands. Since the middle of the 20th century the island's vital statistics have declined dramatically, with the birth and death rates falling by more than 50 percent and infant mortality dropping by more than 80 percent. Between World War II and

1960 the population grew at an average rate of less than 3 percent; it remained at a virtual standstill from 1960 to 1970 because of a family planning program and population losses due to emigration. The rate of population growth by the late 20th century had declined to less than 1 percent per year, substantially less than the rate in most West Indian islands. Barbados is one of the most densely populated countries in the world. Most of the population is black and the official language is English.

The religion is Christian, with Anglicans accounting for the majority of the population. There are smaller Protestant sects and a Roman Catholic Church minority.

The economy. *Agriculture and fisheries.* Sugar and its by-products—rum and molasses—once dominated the economy, but have now declined in importance. Efforts have been made to diversify the economy and to provide a greater degree of employment. Fishing has been encouraged.

Industry. Tourism has drastically changed the economy. This is now the most important industry, although sugar is still one of the most important factors in the economy. The growth of light industry such as electronics and garment production has been encouraged.

Finance and trade. Barbados conducts foreign trade—both import and export—mainly with the United States, the United Kingdom, and with Trinidad and Tobago and other members of Caricom (Caribbean Community and Common Market).

Transportation. The island has a network of good roads. Bridgetown has a deepwater harbour, and several international airlines and British West Indian Airways offer regular services to Grantley Adams International Airport near the southern coast. A station for relaying satellite transmission is located on Barbados.

Administrative and social conditions. *Government.* The British monarch is the head of state. The British crown is represented by a governor general who acts on the advice of the prime minister and Cabinet. Parliament consists of an upper and a lower house. The upper house, called the Senate, contains 21 government-appointed members. The House of Assembly consists of 27 elected members. The Supreme Court heads the judicial system and includes a Court of Appeals as well as a High Court.

Education. Two grammar schools in Barbados—Harrison College and Lodge School—are well known throughout the eastern Caribbean. Most children, however, are educated in the school system maintained by the government. The primary-school system, established by religious bodies after the emancipation of slaves, has been expanded. There are also opportunities for vocational and technical education.

Barbados Community College, established in 1968, offers courses at both the secondary and post-secondary levels. The Barbados campus of the University of the West Indies, which also has campuses in three other countries, opened in 1963 and has been the location of the university's law school since 1970. Also affiliated with the university is Codrington College, which was founded in 1743. The college is the oldest degree-granting institution in the English-speaking Caribbean and now is primarily a theology school.

Cultural life. The island has both a museum and a public library. There are several daily newspapers, various other publications, and local radio and television stations. The country also has dramatic groups, schools of dancing, and art exhibitions. Barbados is internationally known in the game of cricket. Two Barbadian cricketers, Sir Frank Worrell and Sir Gary Sobers, have been knighted for their achievements in the game, and many members of the West Indian Test Match cricket teams are from the island. For statistical data, see the "Britannica World Data" section in the current *Britannica Book of the Year.*

(C.S.J./W.K.M.)

HISTORY

Although most of the country's early history is unknown, there are many indications that Arawak Indians once lived on the island, and it is probable that it was visited by raiding or hunting parties of the Caribs. The first contact with Europeans probably occurred during the early 1500s, when the Spanish landed to seek slaves for their colony of Hispaniola. By the mid-16th century no Indians remained, and Spanish claims to the territory had lapsed.

British rule. When the first English colonists landed during the early 17th century, their settlement was uncontested. Barbados was the second Caribbean island to become a British colony—having been preceded by Kitts in 1623. Barbados, alone of all the islands in the West Indies, has not changed hands since the original British settlement.

Simon Gordon claimed to be the first Englishman to set foot on the island, which was then presumably without inhabitants. He may have been in a ship under the command of Sir Thomas Warner, which called there some time between 1620 and 1625. In 1624 or early 1625 John Powell landed a party that set up a cross and inscribed on a tree: "James K. of E. and of this Island." In 1627 Capt. Henry Powell, John's younger brother, landed a party of settlers near the same spot. This expedition had been fitted out by Sir William Courteen, a protégé of the Earl of Marlborough, to whom James I had granted the island. In 1628 a patent was granted by Charles I to Lord Carlisle. Proprietary rule ended in 1652 when Barbados, which was being governed by Lord Willoughby of Parham in the name of the king, surrendered to a Cromwellian fleet. The instrument of surrender provided that the government of the island should be vested in the governor, council, and assembly, according to ancient and usual custom, and established the principle that there should be no taxation without consent. After the restoration of the monarchy the claims of the Carlisle patent were revived, and an agreement was eventually reached under which the patent was surrendered to the crown for compensation in the form of a 4.5 percent duty on exports, which until 1838 was a constant grievance to the colony.

During their first few years on the island, the English colonists grew tobacco and cotton for export. Their decision to cultivate sugarcane, a more profitable crop, had momentous social and political consequences. The small group of white planters brought additional slaves from West Africa to labour on the sugarcane plantations, and the number of whites began to decrease as the number of blacks increased. During the early 1640s there were about 25,000 whites and some 1,000 blacks on the island; in 1843, when slavery was abolished, there were only 15,000 whites and nearly 85,000 blacks. By 1970 the racial disparity had widened to about 10,000 whites and more than 200,000 blacks.

Emancipation of slaves, free-trade policies, and absentee landlords damaged the sugar industries in many of the British West Indian colonies. In Barbados, however, the industry continued to thrive. Chronic economic distress among the labouring class was alleviated somewhat by emigration to other countries, and the white planter–merchant oligarchy continued its undisputed domination of the island.

By 1935, however, a rapidly growing population, the closing of emigration outlets, and economic depression caused widespread demonstrations throughout the British West Indian colonies. In Barbados social services had been neglected, the political franchise restricted, and import duties on food and clothing kept high—while the wages of labourers had not improved for a century. In 1937 there were riots in Barbados. The British government's Moyne Commission investigated the conditions in Barbados and the other West Indian colonies and recommended reforms. Changes in British colonial policies and the entrance of black reformers into Barbadian politics resulted in the enfranchisement of women in 1944, universal adult suffrage in 1951, and assumption of additional self-government in 1954. Sugar prices rose, and the economy improved; additional financial and technical aid was provided by the British government.

Independence. Barbados received its independence on November 30, 1966, but it remained a member of the Commonwealth. The nation played an important role in the establishment of the Caribbean Free Trade Area

in 1967, which became the Caribbean Community and Common Market (Caricom) in 1972.

Throughout the 1970s and early 1980s Barbados had one of the most stable and prosperous economies in the Caribbean. The government resumed diplomatic relations with Cuba (1975) and established a diplomatic mission in China (1979) but has preferred ties with the more stable Caribbean regimes of Trinidad and Tobago, St. Lucia, and St. Vincent. For current political history, see the annual issues of the *Britannica Book of the Year.*

(C.S.J./W.K.M./Ed.)

Dominica

Dominica is an island republic of the Lesser Antilles in the Caribbean Sea, lying between the French islands of Guadeloupe and Marie Galante to the north and Martinique to the south. It has been a member of the Commonwealth since independence in 1978. It is 29 miles (47 kilometres) long, has a maximum breadth of 16 miles (26 kilometres), and is 290 square miles (751 square kilometres) in area. The capital and chief port is Roseau.

PHYSICAL AND HUMAN GEOGRAPHY

The land. *Relief, drainage, and soils.* A range of high, forest-clad mountains runs north to south, broken in the centre by a plain drained by the Layou and Quanery rivers, which flow west and east, respectively; the highest points are Morne Diablotin (4,747 feet [1,447 metres]) and Morne Trois Pitons (4,528 feet [1,424 metres]). The island is of volcanic formation, signs of activity including *solfataras* (volcanic vents) and hot springs. In the south, Boiling Lake lies 2,300 feet (701 metres) above sea level; its waters are often forced three feet (0.9 metre) above normal by the pressure of escaping gases. The soil is rich, and the numerous rivers are all unnavigable. Much of the island is covered by tropical forests.

Climate. The cool months, from December to March, have a pleasant climate. The dry season is from February to May, and the rainy season is from June to October, the time when hurricanes are most likely to occur. Temperatures range from 78° F (25.5° C) to 90° F (32° C), and rainfall varies greatly, being especially heavy in the mountainous interior. The overall average rainfall is 250 inches (5,200 millimetres) in the mountains, compared with 70 inches along the coast.

The people. The population is mainly of African and mixed descent, with some Europeans, Syrians, and Caribs. English is the official language, but a French patois is commonly understood. The majority of the population is Roman Catholic.

The birth rate and death rate for the island are considerably below the Caribbean average, but migration plays a less important role in population growth on Dominica than on the other West Indian islands. Therefore, the rate of population growth is about the same as the rate for the Caribbean as a whole. Despite its lower than average vital statistics, Dominica's birth rate, death rate, and rate of population growth are greater than those of its nearest neighbours, Guadeloupe and Martinique.

The economy. *Resources.* Pumice, a volcanic rock used chiefly for building purposes, is the most important commercial mineral.

Agriculture, forestry, and fisheries. The main crops are bananas, limes, coconuts, grapefruit, oranges, cacao, vanilla, mangoes, and avocadoes. The forests have great potential for marketable timber. Fishing plays a strong role in the economy.

Industry. The main products and exports are derived from the agricultural industry, namely lime juice, lime oil, copra, grapefruit juice, and rum. The principal manufactures are cigarettes, cigars (made from imported tobacco), edible oils, and laundry and toilet soaps. Tourism is one of the most important industries. Imports include food, mineral fuels, and manufactured goods.

Transportation. Roseau is the principal port, while Portsmouth handles much of the banana boat traffic.

Administrative and social conditions. *Government.* Dominica's government is a parliamentary system, with

Effects of slavery

Temperatures

the parliament consisting of elected representatives and nine senators. The chief executive is the president, who has the responsibility of appointing the prime minister. The prime minister is an elected member of the parliament who has the support of the majority of its members. Tenure of office is for five years, and there is universal adult suffrage.

Education. Primary education is compulsory and free in government-run schools. There are many secondary schools, and a university centre is operated by the University of the West Indies.

Health and welfare. There are several major hospitals. Local medical needs are handled by health centres throughout the island. Intestinal diseases and anemia constitute the major health problems of Dominica. For statistical data, see the "Britannica World Data" section in the current *Britannica Book of the Year.*

HISTORY

The island was a stronghold of the warlike Carib Indians who had migrated to the Antilles from the mainland of South America prior to the first European explorations. It was named by Christopher Columbus, who sighted it on November 3, 1493, a Sunday (Latin *dies dominica,* "the Lord's day").

The French and British colonial period. The first colonists (1632) were French, but with the Treaty of Aix-la-Chapelle (1748), Great Britain and France agreed to treat the island as neutral ground and leave it to the Caribs. From this time until 1805, Dominica was bounced between France and Britain. French planters continued to settle in Dominica until 1759, when the British captured the island. It was formally ceded to Britain in the Peace of Paris (1763).

In 1778 French forces from Martinique attacked and captured Dominica. The British recaptured the island in 1783. The French, coming this time from Guadeloupe, unsuccessfully tried to capture the island (1795). The final French assault on the island was in 1805, and although they burned the capital, Roseau, they were forced to withdraw.

At first administered as part of the Leeward Islands, in 1771 Dominica was made a separate colony. It was rejoined administratively to the Leewards in 1883 and remained thus until 1940, when it was transferred to the Windwards as a separate colony. In 1958 Dominica joined the West Indies Federation. From 1962 onward, after the federation was dissolved, discussions for alternative forms of federation took place. These were settled by the West Indies Act of 1967, under which Dominica assumed a status of association with the U.K. Under the 1967 constitution the island became fully self-governing in all internal affairs.

Independence. On November 3, 1978, Dominica achieved full independence with Patrick Roland John as its first prime minister. John's government was implicated in a rumoured invasion of Barbados that was to have been launched from Dominica. In the ensuing Cabinet crisis Oliver Seraphine emerged as the new prime minister (May 1979).

Even more traumatizing than the political shake-ups was the natural disaster that hit the island. Hurricane David (August 29, 1979) virtually wiped out the nation's agricultural economy. The hurricane carried away most of the island's topsoil, and some experts estimated that it would take the island 20 years to rebuild what had been destroyed. The economy received a further setback with the damage caused by Hurricane Allen, which struck a year later.

The winner of the 1980 elections, Eugenia Charles, became the Caribbean's first female prime minister. She had initially formed her party, the Dominica Freedom Party, to oppose legislation limiting freedom of the press. More conservative in her approach than either of her predecessors, she has moved Dominica toward closer ties with Barbados. Her government faced several coup attempts in 1981, including one that may have been instigated by former prime minister Patrick John. But even the attempted overthrow of the government pales in significance compared to the problems of the nation's economy—that of a desperately poor, underdeveloped country struggling to recuperate from two successive natural disasters. For current political history, see the annual issues of the *Britannica Book of the Year.* (D.L.N./Ed.)

Grenada

The island of Grenada, also known as the Isle of Spice, is the southernmost of the Windward Islands in the eastern Caribbean Sea about 100 miles (160 kilometres) north of the coast of Venezuela. In 1974 it attained complete independence within the Commonwealth and membership in the United Nations, the first of the six West Indies Associated States to do so.

Oval in shape, the island is approximately 21 miles (34 kilometres) long and 12 miles wide, with an area of 120 square miles (311 square kilometres). The southern Grenadines—the largest of which is Carriacou, about 20 miles north-northwest, with an area of 13 square miles—are a dependency.

The capital, St. George's, on the southwest coast, is also the main port, having a fine natural harbour as well as picturesque pastel-coloured houses that rise up the hillsides from the waterfront. The waterfront itself is known as the Carenage because island schooners were once careened (beached for cleaning or repair) there. St. George's is the yachting and charter-boat centre of the eastern Caribbean.

PHYSICAL AND HUMAN GEOGRAPHY

The land. *Relief.* Grenada is volcanic in origin, with a ridge of mountains running north and south—the steeper slopes to the west and a more gradual incline to the east and southeast. The highest point is Mt. St. Catherine (2,757 feet [840 metres]) in the northern part of the interior. The landscape is attractive, with fairly deep, steep-sided valleys, about 10,000 acres (4,000 hectares) of forest, and many plantations of bananas, cacao, nutmegs, and sugarcane.

Drainage. There are several short, swiftly flowing streams that supply all towns and most villages with piped clean water. A further source of water supply is Grand Etang, a circular lake covering 36 acres in the crater of an extinct volcano at an elevation of 1,740 feet.

Climate. The climate is of the tropical maritime type, with equable temperatures varying with altitude and averaging 82° F (28° C) in the low country. Rainfall is adequate, except in the Point Salines area in the southwest; it varies from an average of 60 inches (1,500 millimetres) in coastal districts to 164 inches at Grand Etang. The

The capital

Hurricane David (1979)

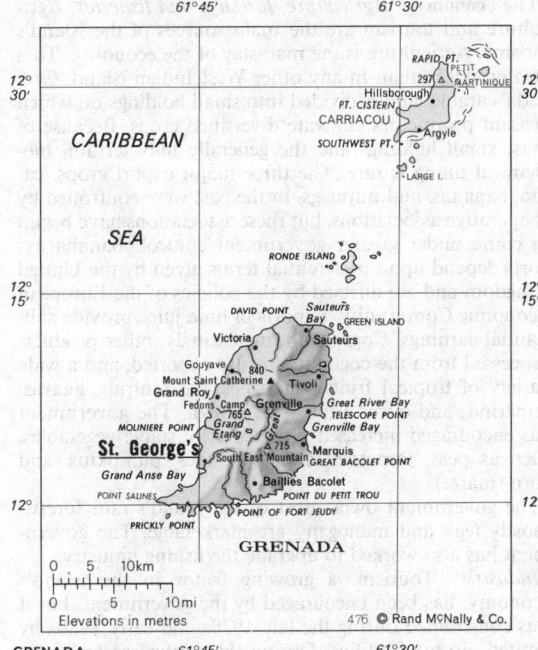

GRENADA

rainy season lasts from June to December. November is the wettest month, but showers occur frequently during the other months. Grenada lies south of the usual track of hurricanes, but when they do occur, as in 1955, 1979, and 1980, they often cause extensive damage.

Plant and animal life. The island is verdant, with a year-round growing season and a wide variety of tropical fruits, flowering shrubs, and ferns. There are also forests of teak, mahogany, saman (known as the rain tree), and blue mahoe (a strong-fibred tree) in the interior. In addition to bananas, cacao, nutmegs, and sugarcane, commercial crops include limes, coconuts, coffee, and vegetables. Lesser quantities of spices—pepper, cloves, cinnamon, ginger, and vanilla—are also grown. Sea Island cotton is grown on Carriacou.

The animal life is varied and includes domestic livestock and such wild animals as the mona monkey (a small, long-tailed, West African species that was introduced by slaves from Africa), the manicou (a species of opossum), the agouti (a rabbit-sized rodent, which is brown or grizzled in colour), the iguana, and a variety of turtles and land crabs.

The people. Most of the population is black and mulatto. There are also small minorities of East Indians, descendants of indentured labourers brought to replace the freed slaves; descendants of the old French and British settlers; and more recent immigrants from North America and Europe. The century of French rule left its mark on the island; a form of patois is still spoken by older people in the villages, and many place-names, although now pronounced in an English fashion, are French. English is the accepted language, however. A majority of the population is Roman Catholic; other Christian denominations that are represented in Grenada include Anglicans, Methodists, and Seventh Day Adventists.

At the time of the first census in 1844 the population of Grenada was 29,650. During the remainder of the century the population more than doubled and the number of persons recorded during the 1901 census was 53,209. During the early 20th century the population grew at a very slow pace and between 1911 and 1921 the number of persons actually declined, from 66,750 to 66,302. The population has continued to grow at a pace slower than that of many of its Caribbean neighbours for most of the 20th century. The population at the end of World War II was more than 72,000 and during the postwar period the population increased at an average annual rate of about one percent. The principal components of the slow rate of population increase have been Grenada's substantially lower birth rate, about 25 percent below the Caribbean average, and its death rate, which is almost equal to the Caribbean average.

The economy. *Agriculture, forestry, and fisheries.* Agriculture and tourism are the main sources of the island's income. Agriculture is the mainstay of the economy. To a greater extent than in any other West Indian island, Grenada's arable land is divided into small holdings on which peasant proprietors cultivate diversified crops. Because of these small holdings and the generally hilly terrain, mechanical tilling is rare. The three major export crops, cacao, bananas, and nutmegs, in the past were controlled by cooperative associations, but these associations have begun to come under greater government control. Banana exports depend upon preferential terms given by the United Kingdom and are affected by the policies of the European Economic Community. Exports of lime juice provide substantial earnings. Copra, and, increasingly, other products processed from the coconut, are also exported, and a wide variety of tropical fruits—mangoes, passionfruit, guavas, tamarind, and citrus fruits—are grown. The government has encouraged increased production of staple vegetables, such as peas, tomatoes, sweet potatoes, pumpkins, and corn (maize).

The government owns most of the island's rain forests; mostly teak and mahogany are marketable. The government has also worked to upgrade the fishing industry.

Industry. Tourism, a growing factor in the island's economy, has been encouraged by the government, but it was constrained during the late 1970s and early 1980s by limited airport facilities. During the winter season, from

October to March, the harbour is visited by numerous cruise ships.

Other sources of employment are such secondary industries as sugar milling, brewing, rum distilling (a strong white rum being made for local consumption), food canning, copra processing, cigarette manufacturing, and soapmaking. There is a cotton ginnery on Carriacou.

Trade. Grenada's economy has been partially dependent on financial help from Britain, its principal trading partner. A large share of all exports go to the United Kingdom, West Germany, Belgium, and Luxembourg; and the majority of all imports come from the United Kingdom and Trinidad and Tobago.

Administration of the economy. Customs and excise duties are the principal base for the country's budget, but taxes are also levied on incomes and professions. Government expenditures are primarily for the civil service, education, roadbuilding, housing and health, agriculture, and waterworks.

Transportation. Grenada has a good network of roads. Bus service is available between the larger towns and villages. Construction of a new international airport was undertaken at Port Salines. Pearls Airport—providing daily air connections to nearby islands with connecting flights to Venezuela—is located on the northeastern coast. Lauriston Airport on Carriacou provides service to nearby islands.

The harbour at St. George's has several berths for oceangoing vessels, as well as a yacht basin and service facilities. Several shipping lines maintain regular passenger and cargo services to North America, the United Kingdom, Europe, and neighbouring West Indian islands.

Administrative and social conditions. *Government.* Following the coup of March 13, 1979, the constitution of Grenada was suspended by the new government. Provision was made to retain the British monarch as head of state represented by a governor general.

Education. School attendance is not compulsory, although primary and secondary education is free and is patterned on the British model. Grenada has vocational and technical schools as well as the St. George's University School of Medicine and an extramural centre of the University of the West Indies.

Health and welfare. Grenada has six main health centres, as well as the district medical stations. Medical and dental treatment in government hospitals and clinics is free. The government has launched a program to eradicate malaria and mongoose-spread rabies. For statistical data, see the "Britannica World Data" section in the current *Britannica Book of the Year.*

HISTORY

Grenada was sighted by Christopher Columbus on August 15, 1498, when he sailed past the island without landing and gave it the name of Concepción. The origin of the name Grenada remains obscure. After its discovery by Columbus, Grenada was dominated for the next 150 years by the warlike Carib Indians, who had earlier killed off the more peaceful Arawaks. In 1609 a company of British merchants attempted to form a settlement but were forced by the Caribs to leave the island.

French settlement. The French governor of Martinique, du Parquet, purchased Grenada from a French company in 1650 and established a settlement at St. George's. In 1674 Grenada became subject to the French crown, remaining so until 1762, when it capitulated to a British force. The island was formally ceded to Britain in 1763 by the Treaty of Paris. Sixteen years later, in 1779, it was recaptured by the French, only to be restored to Britain by the Treaty of Versailles in 1783.

British rule. In the late 18th century the British imported large numbers of slaves from Africa to work the sugar plantations. During 1795 and 1796, when French policy favoured the abolition of slavery, a rebellion against British rule occurred, led by a French planter and supported by the French in Martinique. The rebels massacred a number of the British, including the lieutenant governor, but the uprising was quelled.

The emancipation of the slaves finally took effect in

Fruit crops

Land holdings

Tourism

1833. It was accompanied by less economic and social upheaval than elsewhere because of the rapid growth of peasant proprietorship.

Grenada was the headquarters of the government of the British Windward Islands from 1885 until 1958, when Grenada joined the Federation of the West Indies at its formation. The federation was dissolved in 1962, after which Grenada attempted to federate with the remaining territories in the Windward Islands, as well as with Barbados and the Leeward Islands. On March 3, 1967, however, the island became a self-governing state in association with the United Kingdom.

Independence. In the general election of August 1967, the Grenada United Labour Party (GULP) defeated the Grenada National Party (GNP) and took office under the premiership of Eric M. Gairy, a trade unionist. The party was reelected in February 1972. Grenada became an independent nation on February 7, 1974. The transition was marked by violence, strikes, and political controversy centring upon Gairy, who was named prime minister. Opposition continued to mount to Gairy's rule, and a coalition called the New Jewel Movement (NJM), along with other opposition parties, succeeded in reducing GULP's majority in Parliament in the December 1976 election. On March 13, 1979, while Gairy was out of the country, the NJM staged a bloodless coup, proclaimed a People's Revolutionary Government (PRG), and named their leader, Maurice Bishop, as prime minister. The new government faced much opposition from Western nations because of its socialist principles, but it embarked on a balanced program to rebuild its economy, which had been left in disarray by Gairy. Grenada's experiment in socialist-oriented government was ended in October 1983 by a military coup and a subsequent U.S.-led invasion of the island. A U.S. peacekeeping force remained on the island in early 1984 while Commonwealth officials attempted to form an interim government until elections could be held. For current political history, see the annual issues of the *Britannica Book of the Year*.   (E.V.B.B./Ed.)

Guadeloupe

Guadeloupe (La Guadeloupe), a French overseas *département* (administrative district), is a group of islands in the Lesser Antilles island chain situated in the eastern Caribbean Sea. Guadeloupe is about 4,300 miles (6,900 kilometres) away from France and about 370 miles north of the coast of Venezuela. The nearest territorial neighbours of the principal group are the British dependency of Montserrat to the northwest and the island republic of Dominica to the south. The largest territory in Guadeloupe consists of the twin islands of Basse-Terre to the west and Grande-Terre to the east, the two being separated by a narrow channel, the Rivière Salée; other islands in the group are Marie-Galante to the southeast, La Désirade to the east, and the Îles des Saintes (Terre de Haut and Terre de Bas) to the south. Two more island dependencies—Saint-Barthélemy and Saint-Martin (the southern third of which is administered by The Netherlands as Sint Maarten)—are situated about 150 miles to the northwest, lying to the northwest of the outer arc of the Lesser Antilles.

The total area of Guadeloupe is 687 square miles (1,780 square kilometres). Basse-Terre, on the island of the same name, is the seat of government. The largest town, however, is Pointe-à-Pitre on Grande-Terre, a port that is the economic capital. Guadeloupe lies about 74 miles north of Martinique.

PHYSICAL AND HUMAN GEOGRAPHY

The land. *Relief and drainage.* Basse-Terre, which has an area of 364 square miles, has a chain of mountains running north to south and culminating in Soufrière, a volcano 4,813 feet (1,467 metres) high; it erupted in 1797, 1837, and 1976 and now is a source of hot and sulfur springs. Other summits are Mont Sans Toucher, which is 4,442 feet (1,354 metres) high, and Morne de la Grande Découverte, which is 4,143 feet (1,263 metres) high. The mountain chain forms a watershed from which rivers run down to the sea. The principal river on the island is the Goyaves; other rivers are the Grande Plaine, the Petite Plaine, the Moustique, the Lézarde, and the Rose. Basse-Terre has a beautiful coastline, indented with bays and fringed with picturesque beaches.

The island of Grande-Terre has an area of 220 square miles and is generally low lying; it has only a few bluffs that exceed 490 feet in height. Saint-Martin and Saint-Barthélemy are rugged and rise to an altitude of 1,391 feet (424 metres) and 921 feet (281 metres), respectively.

Principal rivers

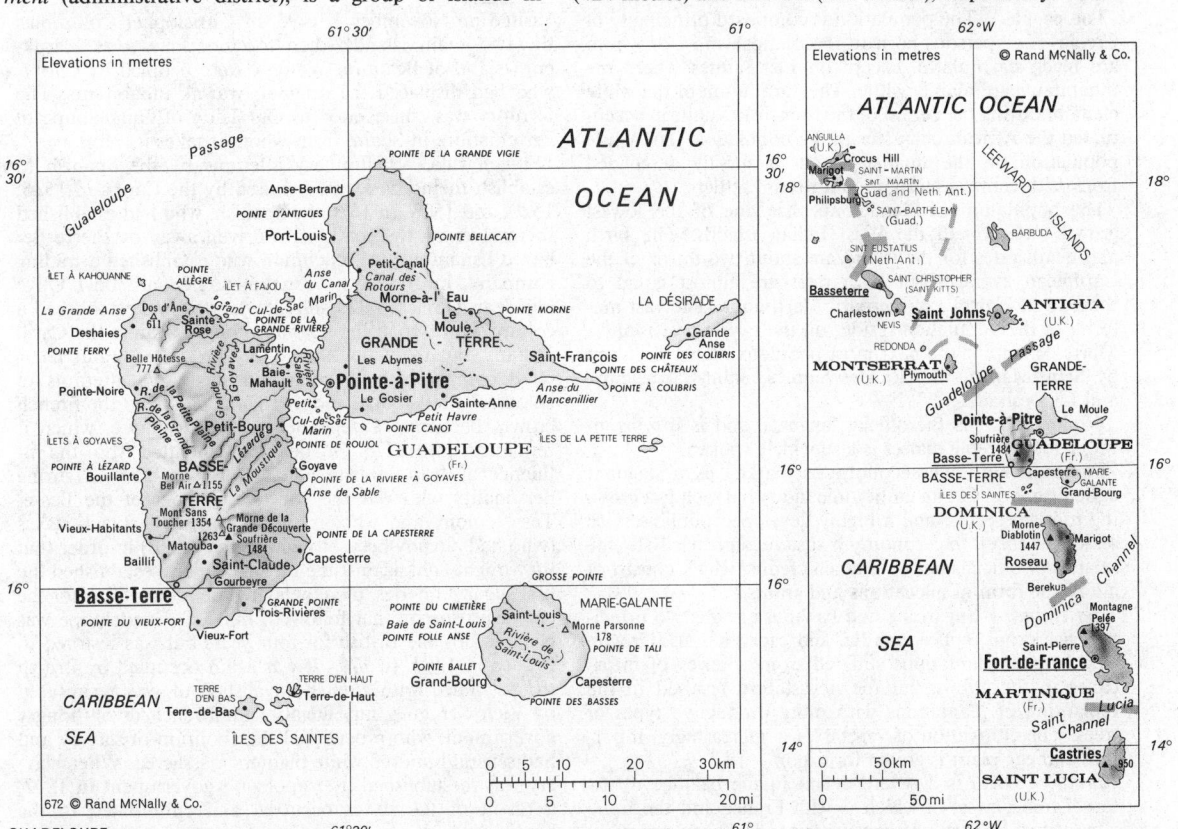

Climate. The tropical climate is tempered by the northeast trade winds. The temperature on the coast varies between 77° and 82° F (25° and 28° C), respectively, with extremes reaching 68° and 93° F (20° and 34° C). In the mountains above 1,900 feet, the temperature drops to 61° F (16° C), and at the summit of Soufrière drops to 39° to 41° F (4° to 5° C). There are two distinct seasons—the "Creole Lent," or dry season, which lasts from December to April, and the winter, or rainy season, from July to September–October.

Precipitation varies with altitude and orientation. Grande-Terre receives about 39 inches (990 millimetres) of rain, for example, while the mountainous parts of Basse-Terre receive more than 100 inches a year. Hurricanes occur occasionally, usually coming from the south.

Plant and animal life. The heat, the rainfall, and the fertility of the volcanic soils produce a luxuriant vegetation that is diversified according to altitude. Extensive mangrove swamps occur on the banks of the Rivière Salée near Pointe-à-Pitre. Dense forest occurs in the mountainous regions of Basse-Terre, beginning almost at sea level on the windward slopes and at an altitude of about 750 feet on the leeward side and continuing to altitudes of about 3,000 feet or more. Here, chestnut trees and bracken are found, as well as such hardwoods as mahogany and ironwood. On the highest peaks some flooded basins produce a vegetation of grasses and sedges. Grande-Terre has been cleared of most of its original forests; only a few patches of woodland remain. The smaller islands, such as La Désirade and Saint-Martin, have a different type of vegetation, consisting primarily of dry forest with groves of latania (a kind of fan palm) and cactus.

Animal life has been modified since the arrival of the Europeans. Raccoons are sought for their fur. The agouti (a short-haired, short-eared, rabbit-like rodent) is still found on the heights of Capesterre, southeast of Basse-Terre. The paucity of game animals is due—apart from excessive hunting—to the presence of mongooses, which abound throughout the islands. In some regions, wild duck, waterfowl, and teal are found.

The warmth of the water around the islands is responsible for a rich variety of fish life, including tarpon, snook (a basslike kind of fish), hogfish, snapper, parrot fish, and many species of ray fish.

The people. The population is composed principally of Creoles (*i.e.,* persons born in the islands), most of whom are black or mulatto, except on Les Saintes where the inhabitants are mainly white. The diminution of the white element during the period of the French Revolution accentuated the African character of the population. The white population on the smaller islands is mostly descended from 17th-century Norman and Breton settlers.

The population of Guadeloupe has one of the lowest growth rates of all the West Indian islands. The birth and death rates for the island are about two-thirds of the Caribbean average, but both rates are almost equal to those of its French counterpart, Martinique. The vast majority of the population resides on the two largest islands; Marie-Galante is the next most populous island, followed by Saint-Martin, the Îles des Saintes, Saint-Barthélemy, and La Désirade.

While French is the official language and is in current use, a local Creole dialect is also widely spoken.

The economy. The economy is marked by a stagnant agricultural sector, an embryonic industrial sector, a growing tourism sector, and a highly developed public-service sector. In effect, the economy is sustained primarily by the salaries of officials and by French credits, which consist of aid in the form of allocations and grants.

Agriculture. Sugarcane and bananas are the two principal cash crops; coffee, vanilla, and cacao are also grown. The banana plantations suffered from a series of hurricanes in the 1960s, but the devastation resulted in the replanting of plantations with more productive types of trees. The cultivation of vegetables is increasingly important and egg plant is grown for export.

Trade. There is a severe deficit in the balance of external trade, most of which is with France and the franc zone. Most imports are consumer goods. Sugar and most of the banana crop are exported to France. Rum, coffee, cocoa, and vanilla also are exported.

Transportation. Guadeloupe maintains regular air and sea links with France and with the North American continent. The port of Pointe-à-Pitre is equipped to handle cargoes of minerals, sugar, and cereals. The port of Basse-Terre specializes in the banana-export trade. Le Raizet, north of Pointe-à-Pitre, is an international airport used by French, United States, British, and Dutch airlines. On the island of Saint-Martin, the town of Marigot, the capital of the French portion of the island, is a free port; there is also an airport west of Philipsburg in the Dutch sector that serves both parts of the island. Local steamers connect Basse-Terre and Grande-Terre with the other island dependencies. The road system on the main islands is kept in excellent condition.

Air services

Administrative and social conditions. *Government.* The *département* is under the executive authority of a prefect appointed by the French government; there is a legislative council consisting of 36 elected members. Guadeloupe is represented in the French National Assembly by three deputies and in the French Senate by two senators.

The territory of Guadeloupe is divided into three *arrondissements* (wards) that are in turn divided into 34 *communes* (the smallest territorial divisions), each administered by an elected municipal council.

Justice. The judicial system is French. There are a court of appeal at Basse-Terre, two higher courts (*grande instance*), and four lower courts (*tribunaux d'instance*). Justices of the peace are established in each of the 36 cantons (electoral districts).

Education. French is the medium of instruction in the schools. In addition to primary schools, there are *lycées* (state-supported secondary schools) as well as a teachers' training college. A school of humanities, a law and economics school, and a school of science at Pointe-à-Pitre are part of the University of the Antilles.

Health and welfare. The same social legislation is in effect as in metropolitan France. There is a general hospital at Pointe-à-Pitre, as well as a Pasteur Institute, and other hospitals. For statistical data, see the "Britannica World Data" section in the current *Britannica Book of the Year.*

HISTORY

Visited on November 4, 1493, by Christopher Columbus, the two main islands, then together known as Karukera (Island of Beautiful Waters), were peopled by Caribs, who had displaced the original Arawak inhabitants. The territory was consecrated to Our Lady of Guadeloupe of Estremadura in Spain, from whom it takes its name.

French rule. Preliminary attempts by the Spanish to establish themselves were repulsed by the Caribs in 1515, 1520, and 1523. In 1626 the Spanish, who had established themselves on the coast, were driven away by Pierre Belain d'Esnambuc, a Frenchman who established a trading company. In 1635 two Frenchmen, Léonard de L'Olive and Jean Duplessis d'Ossonville, landed and established a colony. Until 1640 the colonists fought against the Carib Indians, but thereafter the colony prospered. Four chartered companies were ruined in successive attempts to colonize Guadeloupe, and in 1674 it passed to the French crown, becoming a dependency of Martinique, which it remained until 1775. Guadeloupe benefitted from the influence of Jean-Baptiste Labat (1663 to 1738), a strong personality who was the effective founder of the Basse-Terre colony and who, in 1703, armed the black slaves (who had already been brought to the island) in order that they might fight against the English; he also established the first sugar refineries, thereby laying the foundations for the era of prosperity that followed. In 1759 Guadeloupe was occupied by the British for four years but was restored to France in 1763. In 1794 it was again occupied by British troops, allied with French royalists, but was recaptured by Victor Hugues, an official of the French revolutionary government, who proclaimed the abolition of slavery and had several hundred white planters massacred. When slavery was reestablished by Napoleon's government in 1802, a revolt of the slaves occurred and culminated in the heroic act of the antislavery forces, who blew themselves

Early
European
settlement

up at Matouba when threatened by French forces under the command of Gen. Antoine Richepanse; Richepanse himself had been sent by Napoleon to pacify Guadeloupe, but he died of yellow fever in the same year. The British occupied Guadeloupe in 1810, after which it was—after some temporary changes in status—finally restored to France in 1816.

The abolition of slavery in 1848 was the most significant development of the territory's 19th-century history. Universal suffrage was abolished during the reign of Napoleon III of France, but in 1870 colonial representation in the French Parliament was restored. In 1940 Guadeloupe gave its allegiance to the Vichy government in France, but in 1943 it adhered to Gen. de Gaulle's Free French forces. In 1946 it was given the status of a French *département*.

Political and economic changes since World War II. Guadeloupe has had several independence movements since the end of World War II, but the charismatic appeals of Charles de Gaulle of France, who visited the island in 1956, 1960, and 1964, managed to sidestep the separatists and convince the majority to stay within the French union. More local control has been granted the island since the 1960s, but as progress on the autonomy talks slowed to a standstill in the 1970s, the separatist groups have become increasingly violent. Several bombings were committed in Paris by Guadeloupe liberation groups.

The island is heavily dependent on French aid. The recovery from the destruction caused by the volcanic eruption of Soufrière (1976) was greatly facilitated by help from France. For current political history, see the annual issues of the *Britannica Book of the Year*.

(R.Co./Ed.)

Martinique

The island of Martinique is an overseas *département,* or administrative district, of France situated in the eastern Caribbean, about 4,400 miles (7,000 kilometres) from France and about 270 miles north of the coast of Venezuela. It is included in the Lesser Antilles island chain. Its nearest island neighbours are the island republics of Dominica 22 miles to the northwest and St. Lucia 16 miles to the south. The main islands of Guadeloupe lie about 74 miles to the north.

Martinique has an area of 431 square miles (1,116 square kilometres) and measures about 50 miles in length and about 22 miles at its widest extent. The second smallest (after St. Pierre and Miquelon) of all the French overseas *départements,* Martinique's population density is one of the highest in the Antilles. The administrative capital and chief town is Fort-de-France.

The name Martinique is probably a corruption of the Indian name Madiana (Island of Flowers) or Madinina (fertile island with luxurian vegetation), as reputedly told to Christopher Columbus by the Caribs in 1502. Empress Joséphine, consort of Napoleon I, was born on the island in 1763; she was the daughter of a Martinique planter named Joseph Tascher de La Pagerie.

PHYSICAL AND HUMAN GEOGRAPHY

The land. *Relief and drainage.* The mountainous relief of Martinique represents the outermost edge of what remained of the original geological formation after the subsidence of the trench that became the Caribbean Sea. The relief of the island takes the form of three principal massifs (mountainous masses). These are Montagne Pelée (4,583 feet, or 1,397 metres) to the north; the Pitons (peaks) du Carbet (of which Lacroix Peak reaches 3,923 feet, or 1,196 metres) in the centre; and Montagne du Vauclin (1,654 feet, or 504 metres high) in the south.

The tortuous relief of the island has led to a complex drainage pattern, characterized by short watercourses. In the south, the Rivière Salée and the Rivière Pilote flow down from the scarps of Montagne du Vauclin. In the centre, the rivers flow outward from the Pitons du Carbet in a starlike pattern; they include the Lorrain, Galion, Capot, and Lézarde rivers. In the north, the Grande Rivière, the Céron, the Rivière Roxelane, the Rivière des Pères, and the Rivière Sèche are little more than irregular torrents.

The three principal massifs

The northern coastline of Martinique is characterized by steep cliffs; farther south, however, the cliffs become lower with two large bays—Fort-de-France and Le Marin—being located on the western coast. Coral reefs, headlands, and coves occur on the east coast.

Climate. The climate is remarkably constant, with the average temperature amounting to 79° F (26° C), with average minimums of about 68° to 72° F (20° to 22° C), average maximums of about 86° to 90° F (30° to 32° C), and temperature extremes of 59° F (15° C) and 93° F (34° C).

The northeast trade winds, which blow almost 300 days a year, temper the heat, but winds from the south are hot and humid and sometimes bring hurricanes.

Rainfall is abundant, especially in July and September, but is very irregularly distributed; it varies from 40 inches (1,000 millimetres) to almost 400 inches a year, depending upon elevation and the orientation of the relief.

The year consists of two distinct seasons—the relatively dry Lent season, which lasts from December to June, and the rainy winter season from July to December.

Plant and animal life. The climate, together with the volcanic soil, produces a luxuriant vegetation, which is divided, according to altitude, into four zones: the maritime zone, the lowlands, the former forest zone, and the upper mountain slopes. The maritime zone includes an enormous mangrove swamp, half of which is located in the bay of Fort-de-France. The beaches are invaded by morning glory, tropical twining herb, and sea grape. The lowland vegetation zone extends from the coast to a height of about 1,500 feet and corresponds to the chalky lands of the Sainte-Anne and Caravelle districts. Here are found ferns and orchids, as well as various trees, including mahogany, white gum, and other species. Above 1,500 feet is the former virgin forest zone, where large trees and bracken are still to be found. As the altitude increases the trees grow smaller. A transitional zone is characterized by peat moss. Above 3,000 feet the upper slopes are almost bare, except for some stunted forest.

The four vegetation zones

There are relatively few kinds of animals on the island. The mongoose was introduced in the 19th century in the hope of eliminating the deadly, rat-tailed viper, but without doing so. Also found are the manicon (a kind of opossum), wild rabbit, wild pigeon, turtle dove, and ortolan (a small bird about six inches long, often netted and fattened as a table delicacy).

The people. In 1658 French settlers on the island numbered about 5,000. The Carib element gradually disappeared, partly as a result of conflicts and partly as a result of assimilation. The importation of black slaves from Africa added a further ethnic component. Today the racial composition of the island is extremely mixed, although the black element is the largest. The white Creole (locally

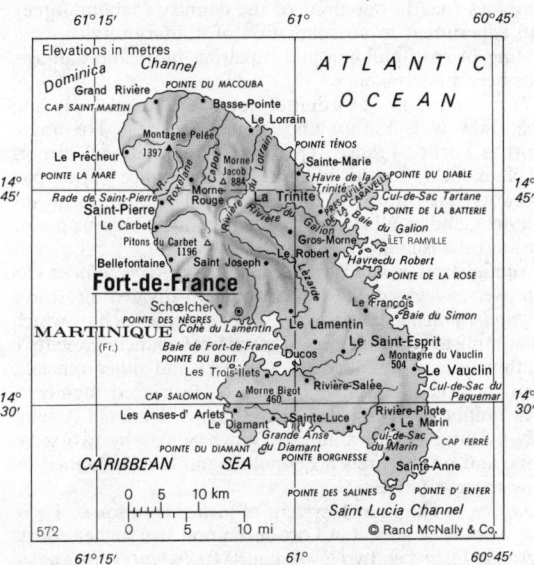

MARTINIQUE

born) element, however, controls an important part of the island's economy. A Creole dialect, similar to that spoken in Haiti, is spoken, but French, which is taught in schools, is the official language.

With the exception of a few groups within the jurisdiction of the Methodist Missionary Society, and several Adventist communities, the population is in general Roman Catholic.

The population of Martinique had been increasing rapidly until the late 1970s when heavy emigration began to retard the island's growth. Plagued by unemployment and other economic maladies, the residents of the island began to emigrate in large numbers to France and in smaller numbers to French Guiana. Emigration not only slowed the rapid pace of population increase, but it also caused the island's population to decline in some years during the late 20th century as the low rate of natural increase did not keep pace with the outward migration.

The economy. *Agriculture.* The economy of the island is primarily agricultural. The annual agricultural output includes sugar, pure alcohol for rum making, and bananas as the principal exports. Fresh and canned pineapples also are produced for export. Subsistence crops include yams and cassava. The destruction of most banana plantations by Hurricane Allen in 1980 was a major setback to the economy.

Industry. Economic planning has laid emphasis on land reform (which places at the disposal of certain planters lands that have been insufficiently reclaimed from swamp), the diversification of agricultural crops, and industrialization. Local industrial plants include a cement plant, an oil refinery at Fort-de-France, and other factories producing soft drinks, pottery, margarine, cattle feed, and boxes for packaging bananas. High hopes are placed on the development of tourism. An association has been formed that groups together 10 *communes* (small administrative units) in the *arrondissement* (administrative district) of the island that is the most favourable to tourism.

Trade. Martinique's economy is heavily dependent on trade with France, which provides one-half to two-thirds of the island's imports and receives more than three-quarters of its exports. The island's high proportion of French consumer goods among imports underscores this economic dependence. Deficits in the balance of trade are the rule rather than the exception as the value of imports far surpasses the value of exports.

Administration of the economy. Martinique receives a considerable amount of aid from FIDOM (Investment Fund for the Economic and Social Development of the Overseas Departments) as well as from European funds.

Martinique's economic predicament stems in part from the fact that the service sector of the economy accounts for a much smaller fraction of the domestic national product than the percentage of economically active people it employs (nearly one-third of the country's labour force). An experiment in an adaptation of military service, consisting of road-building and repairing hurricane damage, has been undertaken.

Transportation. Martinique maintains regular air and sea links with France and North America. The main port is Fort-de-France. There is an international airport at Lamentin, to the east of Fort-de-France. The road network has improved considerably. There are local bus services, and small coastal steamers connect various points around the island.

Administrative and social conditions. *Government.* As an overseas *département,* Martinique is divided into three *arrondissements,* comprising 34 *communes,* each of which is administered by an elected municipal council. Executive authority is represented by a prefect and other officials, and there is a legislative council of 36 elected members. Martinique is represented in the French National Assembly by three deputies, in the French Senate by two senators, and on the French Economic and Social Council by one representative.

Justice. The French system of justice is in force. There are a court of appeal at Fort-de-France, two higher courts (*grande instance*), two lower courts (*tribunaux d'instance*), and a commercial court.

Education. There are primary schools as well as secondary schools. The school enrollment of children of school age is exceptionally high. Higher education is usually pursued in metropolitan France, for which a number of scholarships are available. Institutes of law and economics, letters and human studies, and Creole studies constitute part of the University of the Antilles-Guiana. — Schools

Health and welfare. There are several general and maternity hospitals, as well as some dispensaries, and a hot springs station at Morne-Rouge. Martinique benefits from the same social legislation as that of metropolitan France.

Cultural life. The Fort-de-France carnival, featuring a parade with masks, is an annual event. Voodoo ceremonies are far less important on the island than they are in Haiti. Cockfighting is a popular sport. For statistical data, see the "Britannica World Data" section in the current *Britannica Book of the Year.*

HISTORY

The warlike Caribs inhabited the island when Christopher Columbus sighted it in 1493. It was not until 1502, on his fourth voyage, that he visited the island, leaving there some pigs and goats. Neglected by the Spaniards, who sought more material rewards than those the island offered, Martinique was occupied in 1635 by a Frenchman, Pierre Belain d'Esnambuc, who established 80 settlers at Fort Saint-Pierre at the mouth of the Rivière Roxelane. A year later d'Esnambuc, who had fallen sick, entrusted Martinique to his nephew, Jacques-Dyel du Parquet, who bought the island from the Compagnie des Isles d'Amérique and developed it into a remarkably prosperous colony. In 1654 a group of 250 Dutch Jews, chased from Brazil by the Portuguese, introduced sugarcane. In 1660 cacao trees were planted in place of cotton.

French rule. After the death of du Parquet, his widow governed the island in the name of her children, but disagreed with the settlers; and in 1658 the French king, Louis XIV, resumed sovereignty over the island, paying an indemnity to du Parquet's children. In 1664 the island was placed under the authority of the Compagnie des Indes Occidentales; in 1674 it was made part of the French crown domain, being administered according to the Pacte Colonial, a body of principles summarized in the statement: "The mother country founds and maintains the colonies; the colonies enrich the mother country." Supplies and slaves were brought out to the French Antilles by the Compagnie du Sénégal, founded in 1664; the slave ships called at Martinique before proceeding to Guadeloupe, permitting the colony first choice of the slaves. In 1723 Arabian coffee was introduced, thus further contributing to the island's prosperity. In 1787 Louis XVI granted Martinique the right to establish a Colonial Assembly.

At various times Martinique was subjected to attack by various foreign fleets. An attack by the Dutch was repulsed in 1674; further attacks by the English were repelled in 1693 and in 1759. In 1762, however, the English captured the island, only to return it to France under the terms of the Treaty of Paris in 1763. The English recaptured it in 1794, and occupied it until 1802; captured once more by the English in 1809, it was definitively restored to France in 1814. Slave uprisings occurred in 1789, 1815, and 1822. The abolition of slavery in 1848 created a labour problem, as a result of which labourers from India and China were introduced. In 1848 universal suffrage was proclaimed, but was abolished once more under Napoleon III; after 1870 the French Third Republic restored representation for the island in the French Parliament. — Attacks by Dutch and British

In 1902 the volcanic eruption of Mont Pelée destroyed the town of Saint-Pierre, killing about 30,000 people. During World War II Martinique adhered to the Vichy government for three years before rallying to the Free French cause in 1943. In 1946, Martinique was granted the status of a French *département.*

Developments since World War II. Martinique, more vociferous in its demands for independence than Guadeloupe, has had its postwar politics influenced by Aimé Césaire, the Martinique writer who was one of the founders of the Negritude movement. Césaire, first elected as a deputy in 1945, had originally been a member of the Communist

Party, but by 1956 he had resigned and formed his own party, the Parti Progressiste Martiniquais. In 1957 Césaire and his new party won the Martinique elections by a huge margin, and it seemed as if demands for independence would be met.

But Martinique's depressed economy and massive unemployment worked against the independence movement. Emigration to France and French foreign aid had always been a palliative for Martinique's economic problems, and demands for independence resulted only in Martinique's being given greater autonomy. Even the visits of Charles de Gaulle (1956, 1960, 1964) could not smooth over the political unrest, and by the late 1970s the French government, in an apparent about-face, decided to help Martinique become economically self-sufficient in preparation for independence. Economic problems were exacerbated, however, by the widespread destruction of Hurricane David (1979). Liberation groups were responsible in 1981 for several bombings in Paris. For current political history, see the annual issues of the *Britannica Book of the Year*. (R.Co./Ed.)

Montserrat

Montserrat is an island of the Lesser Antilles in the Caribbean Sea. Its capital and only port of entry is Plymouth, and its political status is that of a crown colony of the United Kingdom.

PHYSICAL AND HUMAN GEOGRAPHY

The land. Montserrat lies 27 miles (43 kilometres) southwest of Antigua and is 11 miles long and seven miles wide with an area of 39 square miles (102 square kilometres). It consists of a serrated range of volcanic peaks rising in three main hill masses, the summits of which are forested. Chance Peak, 3,000 feet (914 metres) in the southern hills above the still-active Soufrière Hills, is the highest point. There are seven volcanically active peaks in the mountainous terrain. The coastline is rugged. The average temperature on the island is 81° F (27° C), and rainfall averages 60 inches (1,500 millimetres).

The people. The official language is English. The main religious denominations are Anglican, Methodist, and Roman Catholic. Montserrat's rate of natural population increase is less than the Caribbean average and less than that of the other British dependent islands. The death rate, which is less than that of most of the West Indian islands but greater than that of other U.K. dependencies, is the principal factor in this low rate of natural increase.

The economy. In 1956 access to Montserrat was facilitated by the completion of Blackburne Airfield. Previously, visitors were dependent upon ships that sailed irregularly. Agriculture and tourism are the most important economic sectors, although the construction industry has gained in importance because of increased demand for housing and other facilities related to tourism and to the resettlement of retired persons on the island. The pricipal agricultural products are sea island cotton, limes, potatoes, tomatoes, and hot peppers. Light industry has expanded on the island, and the manufacturing of plastic bags, textiles, and electronic appliances accounts for the majority of the export income.

Administrative and social conditions. The constitution that took effect January 1, 1960, provided for a governor appointed by the British monarch; the governor heads an executive and legislative council.

Primary education is free and compulsory to the age of 14. The Technical College provides vocational and technical training. The government maintains a hospital and provides free dental treatment for expectant and nursing mothers, school children, and the elderly. For statistical data, see the "Britannica World Data" section in the current issue of the *Britannica Book of the Year*.

HISTORY

Montserrat was sighted by Christopher Columbus in November 1493 on his second voyage to the New World; he named it after the monastery in Spain. It was first colonized by Irish and English settlers led by Sir Thomas Warner in 1632. More Irish immigrants came from Virginia. Plantations were set up to grow tobacco and indigo, then cotton and sugar. The early settlers suffered repeated attacks from the French and Carib Indians. The French took the island in 1664 and in 1667, but it was restored to England in 1668 by the Peace of Breda. The French sacked the island in 1712 and recaptured the island for the last time in 1782. Montserrat was again restored to England, this time by the Treaty of Versailles (1783).

In 1834 slavery was abolished (slaves had been introduced in 1664). The cessation of slavery and the falling price of sugar, combined with a series of devastating earthquakes and hurricanes between 1890 and 1936, brought the collapse of the stagnant plantation economy. The Montserrat Company, formed in 1857 under the direction of Joseph Sturge, bought abandoned estates, encouraged the cultivation of limes, and sold plots of land to settlers. To this day much of Montserrat is owned by small holders.

Between 1871 and 1956 Montserrat was part of the (British) Federal Colony of the Leeward Islands, which included the British Virgin Islands, St. Kitts-Nevis-Anguilla, and Dominica. The federation was abolished on July 1, 1956, when Montserrat became a colony in its own right. In 1958 Montserrat joined the Federation of the West Indies, which was dissolved in 1962 with the independence of Jamaica. Subsequent attempts to form a federation of the Leeward and Windward islands were also abandoned in 1966. Queen Elizabeth II visited the colony (1966), the first reigning British monarch to do so.

In the general election of November 23, 1978, the People's Liberation Movement, which favours complete independence, won all elective seats. Montserrat's policy since then has been to pursue independence, but at a measured rate; the government prefers to achieve economic self-sufficiency before any precipitate breaks with Britain. For current political history, see the annual issues of the *Britannica Book of the Year*. (Ed.)

Collapse of the economy

Netherlands Antilles

The Netherlands Antilles (Dutch Nederlandse Antillen) are composed of two widely separated groups of islands, about 500 miles (800 kilometres) apart, of the Lesser Antilles in the Caribbean Sea. The total area of the islands is 383 square miles (993 square kilometres). They form an integral part of the kingdom of The Netherlands and are fully autonomous in internal affairs. The southern group of islands, comprising Curaçao, Aruba, and Bonaire, lies less than 60 miles (100 kilometres) off the Venezuelan coast. The northern group includes St. Eustatius, Saba, and the southern part of Saint-Martin (Sint Maarten); geographically this group lies within the Leeward Islands. The capital is Willemstad on Curaçao. The rest of Saint-Martin is a dependency of Guadeloupe and part of France's overseas territory.

PHYSICAL AND HUMAN GEOGRAPHY

The land. *Relief.* The southern islands are generally low in altitude, though hills rise to 1,230 feet (375 metres) in Curaçao, typically ranging from the 787-foot Mt. Brandaris in Bonaire to the 620-foot Mt. Jamanota in Aruba. The islands consist mainly of igneous rocks and are fringed with coral reefs. The northern islands consist of volcanic rocks rising to the 1,119-foot Sentry Hill in the Dutch part of Saint-Martin, the 1,968-foot Quill, an extinct volcano on St. Eustatius, with a large forested crater, and the 2,854-foot Mt. Scenery on Saba. Curaçao, the largest island of the Netherlands Antilles (171 square miles), is indented in the south by deep bays, the largest of which, the Schottegat, provides a magnificent harbour for the capital, Willemstad. Bonaire, with an area of 111 square miles (288 square kilometres), lies only 20 miles (32 kilometres) from Curaçao. On Aruba (74 square miles) the terrain, called *cunucu*, contains immense monolithic boulders, some of which appear to be merely balanced on top of each other but are actually securely fixed. Composed of diorite, a greenish eruptive rock, some are used as building stone. St. Eustatius (Sint Eustatius; area eight square miles), along with Saba, forms the northwestern termination of the inner volcanic arc of the Lesser Antilles. Saba (area five square miles) is actually the peak of an extinct volcano, Mt. Scenery, surounded by sea cliffs. The villages of Bottom and Windwardside, occupying an old crater, are approached up a steep road from a rocky landing place on the south coast.

Drainage and soils. For the most part, the islands of the Netherlands Antilles have barren soil and little or no natural irrigation. On Curaçao and Bonaire there is much bare, eroded soil, the result of centuries of overgrazing. Aruba's drinking water can only be obtained from distilled seawater.

Climate. The temperature of the southern islands varies little from an annual average of 81° F (27° C), and the heat is tempered by the easterly trade winds. The islands lie west of the hurricane zone. Rainfall is low and variable, often less than 20 inches (500 millimetres) a year. The climate is similar in the northern islands, but rainfall is greater and hurricanes occur. The annual rainfall is greatest on St. Eustatius and Saba (42 inches and 47 inches, respectively) and falls mainly between May and November, occasionally in association with hurricanes.

Plant and animal life. The vegetation of the Netherlands Antilles, much overgrazed by animals, is sparse. Cacti and other drought-resistant plants abound. On the island of Bonaire birds are plentiful, particularly flamingos, though there are also herons, snipe, pelicans, and parrots.

The people. The population of the islands is racially mixed and speaks Dutch (the official language), English, Spanish, and Papiamento, a local dialect of the southern islands that is composed of Spanish, Portuguese, and Dutch, as well as African words. English is the principal language of the northern islands. The native Arawak Indians were not killed off on Aruba as on other Caribbean islands and remained as a group after Dutch colonization. More than half the population of Aruba is still of Indian stock; the rest are mostly Spanish, Dutch, and such minorities as Chinese and Asian Indians. The inhabitants of Saint-Martin are mostly descendants of African slaves, while the population of Saba is about evenly divided between white and black. The major religion is Roman Catholic, with Protestant, Jewish, and Adventist minorities.

The birth rate for the islands is substantially lower than the Caribbean average, but the extremely low mortality rate, lower than the death rate for The Netherlands, maintains a rate of natural increase that is greater than most of the British and French dependent islands of the West Indies. Migration plays a very minor role in the total population growth of the islands. More than one-half of the inhabitants of the islands reside on Curaçao; about one-quarter live on Aruba; the next two most populous islands are Saint-Martin and Bonaire; and the most sparsely populated islands are St. Eustatius and Saba.

The economy. *Resources.* The southern islands have a greater abundance of exploitable minerals than the northern ones. Curaçao has some calcium phosphate mining; salt is processed on Bonaire; gold was discovered on Aruba in 1825, but after the industry reached its zenith in the early 20th century, it faded away; and salt is extracted from the pans on Saint-Martin.

Agriculture. Agriculture plays a minor role in the economy of the islands. Plantations of sugarcane and cotton were once established on Saint-Martin and St. Eustatius, but now most of the population of the northern islands works in the service sector of the economy. Curaçao was at one time used mainly for livestock raising, but, after the overgrazing of land, new small-scale agricultural ventures were begun, such as the cultivation of aloes for pharmaceutical products and oranges for Curaçao liqueur. Aloes are grown on Aruba and Bonaire. A fishery, established by the Japanese, is important to the economy of Saint-Martin. Saba is engaged chiefly in raising livestock and the cultivation of vegetables, particularly potatoes, which are exported to neighbouring islands.

Industry. The main industry of the southern islands, particularly Curaçao and Aruba, is oil refining, which started with the opening up of the Venezuelan oil fields in 1914. An oil refinery was opened in 1917 on Curaçao and another began operating on Aruba in 1930. The industry

Oil
refining

is now the economic mainstay of the islands. Bonaire has a textile factory and Saint-Martin and Aruba have rum distilleries. For all of the islands tourism has become an increasingly important source of revenue along with the service industries.

Trade. The main exports of the Netherlands Antilles are petroleum and petroleum products, all of which are produced on Curaçao and Aruba. The entrepôt trade in the free ports of Curaçao, Aruba, and St. Eustatius is also significant. Curaçao's foreign trade is mainly with the United States and Venezuela. Almost all of the islands' requirements of food and commercial goods are met by imports.

Transportation. Curaçao has an extensive road system and is linked to the outside world by Dutch, U.S., and Venezuelan airlines as well as by numerous steamship services. Aruba and Saint-Martin have international airports, and Aruba also has good port facilities.

Administrative and social conditions. The Netherlands Antilles are an integral part of The Netherlands. Executive authority is vested in the governor, appointed by the crown, and in a council of ministers with 8 members. They are responsible to the unicameral legislature (Staten, or States) of 22 members (12 from Curaçao, eight from Aruba, one from Bonaire, and one from the northern islands) elected by universal suffrage. The capital of Curaçao is Willemstad; Bonaire, Kralendijk; Aruba, Oranjestad; Saint-Martin, Philipsburg; St. Eustatius, Oranjestad; and Saba, Bottom. Although education in the Netherland Antilles is not compulsory, most of the population is literate. The main language of instruction is Dutch and there is a university on Curaçao and another on Aruba. The general standard of health on the island is high.

Cultural life. Carnival time in February and the New Year's festivities are colourful celebrations. The Bonaire International Sailing Regatta is held every October, attracting boating enthusiasts from around the world. For statistical data, see the "Britannica World Data" section in the current *Britannica Book of the Year.*

HISTORY

The islands known as the Netherlands Antilles were first visited in the early 16th century by the Spanish, who soon wiped out the native Indian population, except on the island of Aruba. The Dutch, attracted by salt deposits, occupied the islands in the early part of the 17th century, and, except for brief periods of British occupation, the islands have remained Dutch possessions. Through much of the 17th and 18th centuries the islands prospered from Dutch trade in slaves, plantation products, and contraband, but they declined from 1816 until 1914. Economic recovery occurred with the discovery of the Venezuelan Colombian oil fields and the construction of refineries on Curaçao and Aruba.

Colonial rule. *Curaçao.* Curaçao was discovered by Alonso de Ojeda and Amerigo Vespucci in 1499 and settled in 1527 by the Spanish, who used it mainly for livestock raising; in 1565 John Hawkins, the English seaman, described it as "one great cattle ranch." In 1634 Johannes van Welbeck of the Dutch West India Company occupied and fortified the island, which became the base for a rich entrepôt trade flourishing through the 18th century. As the native Arawaks died out, more and more African slaves were imported. During the colonial period Curaçao was a major centre of Caribbean slave trade. After the emancipation of the slaves in 1863, however, Curaçao lost much of its economic importance.

Centre of
Caribbean
slave
trade

There were two short periods during the Napoleonic wars when Curaçao was held by the British but it was returned to The Netherlands by the Treaty of Paris in 1815. The 19th century was a period of economic decline alleviated by cultivation of aloes and oranges and, most importantly, the construction of the Schottegat oil refinery.

Bonaire. Bonaire was discovered in 1499 by Alonso de Ojeda and Amerigo Vespucci, settled by the Spanish in 1501, and finally claimed by the Dutch in 1634. It became part of the Dutch West India Company in 1636 and stayed a plantation colony until 1795. From 1807 to 1814 it was under British control. Bonaire achieved status as a separate political entity within the Netherlands Antilles in 1868.

Aruba. Long before Aruba's discovery by the Europeans it was inhabited by Indians who decorated caves on the island with sketches. It is not known when the first European landed, but by 1499 Aruba was claimed for Spain. The Dutch acquired Aruba in 1634 and left the native Arawaks alone; as a result Aruba is one of the few Caribbean islands to have a sizeable Indian population. European settlements other than garrisons were forbidden from the 16th to the 19th century.

Saint-Martin. Discovered by Christopher Columbus on November 11, 1493 (St. Martin's Day), the island was taken by French pirates in 1638, though the Spaniards settled there in 1640. In 1648 French and Dutch prisoners of war allegedly met after the Spanish departure and amicably divided the island. The Dutch obtained the smaller but more valuable section containing salt deposits.

Saint Eustatius. St. Eustatius, first colonized by the French and English in 1625, was taken by the Dutch in 1632. It became the main centre of slave trade in the eastern Caribbean and by 1780 had a prosperous population of 2,500. In 1781 the capital, Oranjestad, was sacked by the British, and the island never regained its trade. In the 17th and 18th centuries most of the land was under sugar cultivation.

Saba. Saba was settled by the Dutch in 1632 but, because of its inaccessibility and ruggedness, never achieved any economic importance. It often functioned as a buccaneer's stronghold.

Political developments since World War II. After World War II negotiations began with the aim of conferring a greater measure of independence and self-government on the islands. On December 15, 1954, a charter was signed making the islands an autonomous part of The Netherlands. Autonomy talks proceeded slowly until 1969, when Curaçao was torn apart by racial strife and rioting. Since then discussions on complete independence have moved unevenly.

Politics in the Netherlands Antilles are now dominated by three issues: economic problems, the inevitable coming of independence, and Aruban separatism. By the mid-1970s it was clear that most of the Netherlands Antilles feared the economic after-effects of independence, except for the island of Aruba, which, buoyed by a strong economy, was willing to gain independence alone. The Antilles prime minister asked the Dutch government not to press for independence for the islands before 1980 and requested the Dutch garrison to remain until then as well. In 1977 Aruba voted to secede from the Antilles federation in an unofficial referendum. Much of Aruban independence sentiment has been focussed on separation from the Netherlands Antilles with a continuing direct relationship with The Netherlands, but some nationalist feeling has emerged favouring the complete independence of Aruba as a separate state. By 1978 all six islands finally accepted the concept of independence, but the Dutch government would agree to independence only within a federation and was firmly opposed to Aruba's plans for secession. But by 1981 the Dutch agreed in principle to Aruban independence. For current political history, see the annual issues of the *Britannica Book of the Year.* (D.R.Ha./Ed.)

St. Christopher and Nevis

St. Christopher and St. Nevis, also officially called Saint Kitts and Nevis, is a sovereign democratic state composed of two islands of the Lesser Antilles in the east Caribbean Sea. The islands were formerly an associated state of the United Kingdom; their combined area is 101 square miles (261 square kilometres). The capital is Basseterre on the island of St. Christopher (St. Kitts).

PHYSICAL AND HUMAN GEOGRAPHY

The land. St. Kitts is 23 miles (37 kilometres) long and five miles wide, is oval in shape, and has an area of 65 square miles (168 square kilometres). A volcanic mountainous ridge down the centre forms a semicircle around a plain in the southeast. Mt. Misery, with a lake

in its forested crater, is the highest point (3,792 feet [1,156 metres]). The island is well watered and fertile, with a cool, healthy climate. Temperatures vary from 62° to 92° F (17° to 33° C). The annual rainfall averages 55 inches (1,400 millimetres). St. Kitts is of volcanic formation, and most of the beaches are of black volcanic sands. The soil (except in the mountains) is light and porous.

Climate

Nevis, surrounded by coral reefs, lies two miles southeast of St. Kitts across a channel called The Narrows. The island is almost circular, and it consists almost entirely of a mountain, Nevis Peak (3,232 feet [985 metres]), flanked by the lower Mt. Lily (1,014 feet) northward and Saddle Hill (1,250 feet) southward. Its area is 36 square miles (93 square kilometres). The soil of Nevis is stiff clay studded with volcanic boulders.

The people. The population is largely black or mulatto. The official language is English. The main religious denominations are Anglican and Methodist. St. Kitts-Nevis differs from the other dependent or formerly dependent British islands of the West Indies in that its vital statistics are almost equal to the Caribbean averages. In fact, the death rate is slightly higher than the average and the birth rate is slightly less than the average. This gives the islands a higher rate of natural increase than most of the other West Indian islands with British ties.

The economy. The narrow coastal plain of St. Kitts, the skirts of the mountains, and the Basseterre Valley are devoted to the cultivation of sugarcane (mainly on large estates) and cotton, which are the chief products.

The main crop of Nevis is cotton (grown on small peasant holdings), but sugarcane and coconuts are also grown. The government of St. Kitts-Nevis has nationalized all sugar plantations since 1975 and has also purchased the sugar factories. Sugar is the main export and the United States and the United Kingdom are the principal trading partners. There are a variety of light industries operating in St. Kitts and Nevis that produce mainly for export from imported materials. Products include electronic equipment, batik-dyed fabrics, and footwear. There is a deepwater port at Basseterre and Golden Rock International Airport on St. Kitts provides service to other islands and to the United States and Canada. Newcastle Airfield on Nevis provides interisland air service.

Administrative and social conditions. Since independence in 1983, the federation of St. Kitts and Nevis has been an independent member of the Commonwealth, with the British monarch as its head of state. An appointed governor general represents the crown. The prime minister, who together with other ministers is a member of the cabinet, is the head of government. The monarch and the National Assembly constitute the parliament, some of whose members are appointed. The island of Nevis enjoys a certain amount of autonomy within the federal structure; it has its own legislature, and the constitution provides for it to secede from the federation if certain procedures are followed. There is universal adult suffrage.

Education is compulsory for all children from the age of five to 14. There are several hospitals and many health centres throughout the islands. Tropical diseases have been virtually eliminated. For statistical data, see the "Britannica World Data" section in the current *Britannica Book of the Year.*

HISTORY

Early settlement. Christopher Columbus visited St. Christopher on his second voyage in 1493 and found it inhabited by warlike Caribs. He named it St. Christopher for his patron saint. The name was shortened to St. Kitts by settlers under Sir Thomas Warner who, arriving from England in 1623, established the first successful English colony in the West Indies at Old Road on the west coast. The French also settled on the island in 1627 under Pierre Belain d'Esnambuc. Divided during the 17th century between warring French and English colonists, St. Kitts was given to Britain by the Treaty of Utrecht in 1713 and remained in British possession despite the capture in 1782 of Brimstone Hill by the French. The island was restored to Great Britain by the Treaty of Versailles in 1783.

Nevis was also sighted by Columbus in 1493. The island's name derives from Columbus' description of the clouds atop Nevis peak as *las nieves,* or "the snows," when he sighted the island. It was settled by the English in 1628 and soon became one of the most prosperous of the Antilles. Although it suffered from French and Spanish attacks in the 17th and 18th centuries, it maintained a sound economic position until the mid-19th century.

Federation and independence movements. The islands of St. Kitts, Nevis, and Anguilla were united by federal act in 1882 and became an independent state in association with the U.K. on February 27, 1967. (Under the status of free association the islands as a group were granted full internal self-government, with the U.K. retaining responsibility for defense and foreign affairs.)

Political status

After the islands had assumed the status of associated states, Anguilla complained of domination by the St. Kitts administration. In May 1967 the Anguillans ejected the St. Kitts police and set up their own council; in July they proclaimed their independence. In the following months unsuccessful attempts were made in negotiations between the Anguillan leaders and the U.K. and Commonwealth Caribbean governments to settle the dispute. On March 19, 1969, the U.K. government intervened by sending police and soldiers to the island, and a temporary British commissioner was installed. The troops were withdrawn in September 1969, but a team of military engineers remained to undertake capital and development works. The Anguilla Act of July 1971 placed Anguilla directly under British control. On February 10, 1976, Anguilla was granted a constitution, though it remained technically a part of St. Kitts-Nevis-Anguilla. Anguilla's union with St. Kitts and Nevis was formally severed in 1980. A constitutional conference was held in London in 1982, and, in spite of disagreement over special provisions for Nevis, the islands became independent on September 19, 1983. For current political history, see the annual issues of the *Britannica Book of the Year.* (G.E.M.M./Ed.)

Saint Lucia

St. Lucia, an independent parliamentary state within the Commonwealth, is an island of the Lesser Antilles in the Caribbean Sea, forming part of the Windward Islands group and situated about 24 miles (39 kilometres) south of Martinique and some 21 miles northeast of St. Vincent. The capital and major port is Castries. St. Lucia is 27 miles long and has a maximum width of 14 miles and an area of 240 square miles (622 square kilometres).

PHYSICAL AND HUMAN GEOGRAPHY

The land. *Relief and drainage.* The island is of volcanic origin and is bisected from north to south by a central ridge of wooded mountains, the highest point being Mt. Gimie (3,145 feet [958.6 metres]) in the south. Many streams flow from the mountains through fertile valleys. In the southwest are the Gros and Petit Pitons (2,619 feet [798.3 metres] and 2,461 feet [750.1 metres]), two immense pyramids of rock rising sharply from the sea and enclosing a small bay. Near Petit Piton is Soufrière, a low-lying volcanic crater. The boiling sulfur springs from which the town of Soufrière takes its name are at Ventine, 2½ miles southeast of the town.

Climate. St. Lucia lies in the path of the northeastern trade winds and has a tropical maritime climate. Rainfall and temperature vary with elevation. Average annual rainfall ranges from 51 inches (1,295 millimetres) on the coast to 117 inches (2,972 millimetres) in the interior. There is a dry season roughly from January to April and a rainy season from May to November. The temperature averages between 78° F (26° C) on the coast and 69° F (21° C) in the interior.

The people. The original Carib race is extinct, and the majority of the inhabitants of the island are black or mulatto. The remainder are whites or of East Indian extraction. A French patois is spoken by most of the inhabitants but is being gradually supplanted by English, the official language. The main religion is Roman Catholicism. The rate of population growth for St. Lucia is slightly higher than the Caribbean average. This has been caused primar-

ily by a lower than average death rate and a birth rate that is about the same as the Caribbean mean.

The economy. *Agriculture, forestry, and fisheries.* The island's economy is based on agriculture and tourism. Sugarcane was the chief crop but production ceased entirely in 1964, when most of the cane fields were converted to banana cultivation. The chief crop is now bananas. Other crops are coconuts, cacao, citrus fruit, spices, cassava, and yams. A significant fraction of the island is forested, and there is a steady local fishing industry.

Industry. The few industries produce consumer items such as rum, citrus products, coconut products (copra, edible oil, soap), mineral waters, cigarettes, electrical components, plastics, animal feed, vehicle batteries, and industrial gases. In addition, tourism has been developed as a source of much needed foreign exchange.

Trade. The chief exports are bananas, cardboard cartons, clothing, beverages, and coconut products. About one-quarter of St. Lucia's exports are to Great Britain and another one-quarter to the United States. Imports include meat, sugar, fertilizers, and manufactured goods.

Transportation. There is an international airport at Vieux Fort, about 40 miles south of Castries, and a smaller airport at Vigie for domestic and regional flights. International shipping lines operate from the ports at Castries and Vieux Fort. In addition, there is a great deal of interisland traffic and an oil transshipment terminal near Castries.

Administrative and social conditions. *Government.* St. Lucia is a constitutional monarchy with the British monarch as head of state, represented by a governor general. The bicameral parliament consists of the House of Assembly of 17 members elected by universal adult suffrage and the Senate of 11 members, six of whom are appointed on the advice of the prime minister, three on the advice of the opposition leader in the House, and two by the governor general. The prime minister, leader of the majority party, heads the government.

Justice. St. Lucia has retained its association with the West Indies Associated States Supreme Court. This court is known in St. Lucia as the Eastern Caribbean Supreme Court, consisting of a court of appeal and a high court. The final court of appeal is the judicial committee of the privy council.

Education. Primary education is free and compulsory, and there is a branch of the University of the West Indies at Morne Fortune. Many of the primary schools are parochial, principally Roman Catholic.

Health and welfare. There are several general hospitals and many health centres distributed throughout the island. There is also a private hospital operated by a religious order. For statistical data, see the "Britannica World Data" section in the current *Britannica Book of the Year.*

HISTORY

French and British territorial rivalry. The exact date of the European discovery of St. Lucia is not known, but it is thought to have been about 1500. It is quite possible that it was named by Columbus, although there is no record of this. The first attempts at colonization were made by the English in 1605 and 1638, but they were frustrated by sickness and the hostility of the native Caribs. A successful settlement was achieved in 1650 by the French from Martinique who made a treaty with the Caribs in 1660. In 1664 Thomas Warner, son of the governor of St. Kitts, regained the island, but it was restored to France by the Peace of Breda in 1667. In 1674 it was claimed by the crown of France and made a dependency of Martinique.

Early European settlements

Another British settlement under a grant made in 1722 by George I to the Duke of Montague was frustrated by France granting the island to Marshal d'Estrées (1718), and the island was declared neutral. In 1743 the French resumed possession, retaining the island until the Treaty of Aix-la-Chapelle in 1748 in which the two countries again agreed to regard St. Lucia as neutral. In 1762 it was captured by Adm. George Rodney and Gen. Robert Monckton, only to be given up once more by the Treaty of Paris (1763). In 1778 it again surrendered to the British, who used its harbours as a naval base, but by the Peace of Versailles, St. Lucia was once more restored to France.

Between 1782 and 1803 the possession of St. Lucia passed several times between Britain and France, the British having to suppress a vigorous revolutionary party, which was aided by insurgent slaves, before gaining possession in 1803. St. Lucia was finally ceded to Britain in 1814 by the Treaty of Paris, after which it became a crown colony. During 1838–85, together with the other islands of the Windward group, it was placed under the governor of Barbados.

French influence on the development of St. Lucia is illustrated by the preponderance of the Roman Catholic Church and the survival of a French patois. In the years following 1763 French planters came from St. Vincent and Grenada and established cotton and sugar plantations. In 1834, when the slaves were emancipated, there were in St. Lucia more than 13,000 black slaves, 2,600 free blacks, and 2,300 whites. Prosperity was greatly retarded by frequent wars, epidemics of cholera and smallpox, and by the decline of the sugarcane industry. Improvement came with the increase of banana and cocoa cultivation and the revival of sugarcane.

Independence. Representative government was obtained by the constitution of 1924, which introduced an elective element into the legislative council; the constitution of 1936 provided for an unofficial majority in the council.

In 1958 St. Lucia joined the West Indies Federation, although its colonial status remained unchanged. Under the 1960 constitution the post of governor of the Windward Islands was abolished, and St. Lucia became an autonomous unit within the federation, also achieving a greater degree of internal self-government. The federation was dissolved on May 31, 1962. Discussions for alternative forms of federation continued throughout the middle and late 1960s. They were eventually settled by the West Indies Act (1967), in which St. Lucia assumed a status of association with the United Kingdom on March 1, 1967.

Independence was finally achieved February 22, 1979, with St. Lucia remaining a parliamentary democracy within the Commonwealth. The independence-day ceremonies were marred by the absence of the opposition St. Lucia Labour Party (SLLP), which had wanted a national referendum on the issue of independence. In the first elections following independence, the SLLP emerged victorious, and Allan Louisy became the new prime minister.

Government of Allan Louisy

Louisy favoured the socialist regimes of the Caribbean and was one of the architects of the Declaration of St. George's (1979), which provided the cooperation among St. Lucia, Dominica, and Grenada. His government also established diplomatic relations with Cuba.

But Louisy's attempts at a mixed economy proved unsuccessful in dealing with the staggering problems of the newly independent country, especially after Hurricane Allen (1980) greatly damaged most of the island's economy. After the failure of Louisy to pass his budget through Parliament, a constitutional crisis developed, and Louisy was forced to resign (1981). Following attempts by the anti-Louisy faction in the SLLP to form their own government, Winston Francis Cenac emerged as the compromise candidate, becoming prime minister with the slimmest majority. One of his first acts in office was the formation of the Organization of East Caribbean States. For current political history, see the annual issues of the *Britannica Book of the Year.* (R.To./D.L.N./Ed.)

Saint Vincent and the Grenadines

St. Vincent and its associated islands of the northern Grenadines form an independent republic within the Commonwealth. It is part of the Lesser Antilles in the Caribbean Sea, in the Windward Islands group, about 21 miles (34 kilometres) southwest of St. Lucia and about 100 miles west of Barbados. St. Vincent is 18 miles long and has a maximum width of 11 miles, and its area is 133 square miles (345 square kilometres). Some of the larger islands of the Grenadines are Bequia, Canouan, Mayreau, Mustique, and Union Island. Including the Grenadines, the territory comprises a total area of 150 square miles (389 square kilometres).

The islands were the British colony of St. Vincent, which

became independent on October 27, 1979. The capital and major port is Kingston.

PHYSICAL AND HUMAN GEOGRAPHY

The land. *Relief and drainage.* The island of St. Vincent has thickly wooded volcanic mountains running north to south and producing many short, swift streams. The streams are numerous but, except after heavy rains, small. There are no navigable rivers. The highest peak is the volcano Soufrière (4,048 feet [1,234 metres]) in the north, which erupted disastrously in 1821 and 1902, when the entire northern half of the island was devastated. The 1902 eruption coincided with that of Mont Pélée in Martinique. Soufrière became active again in 1979, causing massive evacuation and much damage to agriculture.

The Soufrière volcano

Climate. St. Vincent lies in the path of the northeasterly trade winds and has a tropical maritime climate. Rainfall and temperature vary with altitude. Average annual rainfall ranges from about 60 inches (1,520 millimetres) on the coast to 150 inches (3,810 millimetres) in the central mountains. The temperature averages between 64° F (18° C) and 90° F (32° C). Hurricanes occasionally pass across the island and it suffered severely in 1780, 1898, and 1980. From January to May is the dry season, and the rains start in June and continue to the end of the year.

The people. Most of the inhabitants are black or mulatto, a small minority is of European descent, and the rest are of East Indian extraction; only a few are of Carib Indian stock. St. Vincent and the Grenadines has one of the highest birth rates among the West Indian islands and its death rate is slightly less than the Caribbean mean, giving the islands an extremely high rate of population increase that is moderated by emigration.

English is the official language and some French patois is spoken. The main religious denominations are Anglican, Methodist, and Roman Catholic.

The economy. *Agriculture, forestry, and fisheries.* The economy of St. Vincent is agricultural. Traditional crops are arrowroot (of which the country is the chief world exporter) and sugarcane, but since the 1950s bananas have become the leading export and the production of sugarcane has become negligible. Other crops include coconuts, cassava, peanuts (groundnuts), sweet potatoes, carrots, nutmeg, cacao, mangoes, avocadoes, citrus fruits, and tobacco. Nearly half of the island is forested, the woodland being used for charcoal burning. Both inshore and offshore fishing are carried on.

Industry. Industry is based primarily on agriculture, with the main industry being arrowroot processing. Soap and edible oils are also produced. There are also plants for processing copra, distilling rum, milling flour, refining sugar, building yachts, and making boxes for packing bananas. Tourism is assuming a larger role in the economy.

Trade. The main exports are bananas, arrowroot, cocoa, sweet potatoes, carrots, and spices. Carrots are exported to Trinidad and Barbados, and plantains are exported to Barbados. The main trading partners are the United Kingdom, Trinidad and Tobago, the United States, and Canada.

Transportation. Several air strips provide interisland service, and numerous shipping lines stop at St. Vincent.

Administrative and social conditions. *Government.* The British monarch is the head of state and is represented on the island by an appointed governor general. The unicameral legislature is composed of the House of Assembly, containing 13 elected representatives and six senators who are appointed by the governor general. The prime minister, leader of the majority party, is appointed by the governor general to lead the government.

Justice. St. Vincent retains its connection with the West Indies Associated States Supreme Court, which is known in St. Vincent as the St. Vincent and Eastern Caribbean Supreme Court. This consists of an appeals court and a high court, while the final court of appeal remains the judicial committee of the privy council.

Education, health, and welfare. Primary education is free but not compulsory. Secondary education is conducted mostly in schools administered by religious organizations. Health measures are directed primarily against infant malnutrition and gastroenteritis. The islands have a general hospital and several health centres. For statistical data, see the "Britannica World Data" section in the current *Britannica Book of the Year*.

HISTORY

Colonization. St. Vincent may have been given its name by Christopher Columbus, who may have visited the island on January 22, 1498 (St. Vincent's Day). Its Carib inhabitants were left almost undisturbed until the 18th century. In 1673 the first Africans arrived, a party of shipwrecked slaves who eventually reached St. Vincent and intermarried with the native Caribs. French, Dutch, and British settlements were attempted, with the French dominant until the Seven Years' War, when the British general Robert Monckton occupied it (1762). The Treaty of Paris (1763) confirmed British possession, and settlement proceeded in spite of Carib refusal to accept British sovereignty. In 1779 the island was seized by the French, but it was restored to Britain in 1783. In 1795 the Caribs rose in revolt, assisted by the French from Martinique, but they were finally subdued the following year. Most of them were then deported to the Islas de la Bahía off Honduras. The emancipation of black slaves in 1834 disrupted the island's economy by decreasing the labour supply, and Portuguese and East Indian labourers were introduced late in the century.

In the latter half of the 19th century the price of sugar fell, plunging the island into a depression that lasted through the end of the century. The hurricane of 1898 and the disastrous volcanic eruption of 1902 exacerbated the problems of economic recovery.

In 1958 St. Vincent joined the Federation of the West Indies. In 1960 it received a new constitution. When the federation was dissolved in 1962, the colony planned to join the other Windward Islands and the Leeward Islands in a smaller federation. Plans to grant St. Vincent the status of a state in association with the U.K. by June 1, 1967, were delayed; this status was finally achieved on October 27, 1969. The island had become a member of the Caribbean Free Trade Area on July 1, 1968.

Independence. The crucial issue of the 1970s for St. Vincent was independence. Neither the island government nor Britain had any idea, however, of what direction independence should take. Plans put forward in 1972 for the unifications of St. Vincent with Grenada and St. Lucia were later dissolved. An independence date of January 21, 1979, was postponed because of procedural and political problems; independence for the new state of St. Vincent and the Grenadines, as the nation was called, was achieved October 27, 1979, 10 years to the day after St. Vincent ceased being a colony. The new government was formed as a constitutional monarchy and became a member of the Commonwealth, the Organization of American States, the UN, and the Organization of East Caribbean States (1981).

Milton Cato became the first prime minister of the new nation, decided in the elections held on December 5, 1979. Cato had begun his political career in 1955 when he helped to found the St. Vincent Labour Party (SVLP).

Cato pursued a moderate line and was highly critical of the effect of the revolution in neighbouring Grenada and of developments in Jamaica and Guyana. Instead he preferred closer links with the relatively centrist governments of Trinidad and Tobago and Barbados, both at an economic level and through the establishment of a joint coast guard and a fisheries protection service with Barbados.

St. Vincent and the Grenadines have been hard hit by natural disasters. On April 13, 1979, the Soufrière volcano erupted once again, causing widespread damage. Hurricane Allen (1980) virtually wiped out the all-important banana crop, further burdening a rather precariously maintained economy. For current political history, see the *Britannica Book of the Year*. (R.To./D.L.N./Ed.)

Trinidad and Tobago

Trinidad and Tobago are two Caribbean islands that constitute an independent republic. Forming the two southernmost links in the Caribbean chain of islands, they lie close to the South American continent, northeast of Venezuela and northwest of Guyana. They have a combined area of 1,980 square miles (5,128 square kilometres). The capital of the republic, Port-of-Spain, is situated in the northwest of Trinidad.

Trinidad, the larger island, comprises 1,864 square miles (4,828 square kilometres). The island's northwestern and southwestern peninsulas are separated from Venezuela by two channels—the Dragon's Mouth (Boca del Dragon) and the Serpent's Mouth (Boca de la Sierpe)—12 and nine miles (19 and 15 kilometres) wide, respectively, interspersed with small islands and rocks.

Tobago, the smaller island, with an area of about 116 square miles (300 square kilometres), lies in the Atlantic, 21 miles to the northeast of Trinidad. Little Tobago, also called Bird of Paradise Island, is a mile off Tobago's northeastern coast; it is noted as a habitat for the greater bird of paradise. Tobago, lying diagonally from southwest to northeast, is about 26 miles long and is more than seven miles across at its widest point.

Trinidad and Tobago achieved independence from the United Kingdom in 1962 and subsequently obtained membership in the British Commonwealth, the Organization of American States (OAS), and the Caribbean Free Trade Association (Carifta; later the Caribbean Community, or Caricom). (A.N.R.R.)

PHYSICAL AND HUMAN GEOGRAPHY

The land. *Relief and drainage.* Physiographically, the islands represent an extension of the South American mainland. The outstanding physical feature of Trinidad is its Northern Range of hills (the counterpart of the Cadena del Litoral Oriental in Venezuela), which runs from west to east at an average elevation of 1,500 feet, rising to 3,085 feet (940 metres) at the Cerro del Aripo, the nation's highest peak. The Northern Range is the site of many waterfalls, the most spectacular of which are the Blue Basin and the Maracas Falls, both 298 feet (91 metres) high. On the southern side of the range, foothills with an elevation of about 500 feet descend to the Northern Plain.

Running across the centre of the island, from southwest to northeast, is the Central Range, the highest point of which is Mount Tamana (1,009 feet, or 308 metres). A third row of hills, the Southern Range, adds further variety to the mostly flat or undulating surface of Trinidad.

These three mountain ranges determine the island's drainage pattern. The average length of the rivers is about 21 miles; none exceeds 50 miles in length. Numerous swamps occupy parts of the low-lying areas, among them the Caroni Swamp in the northwest.

An oil-bearing belt occupies an area of about 800 square miles (2,100 square kilometres) in the south of the island,

The
arrival
of Africans

Little
Tobago

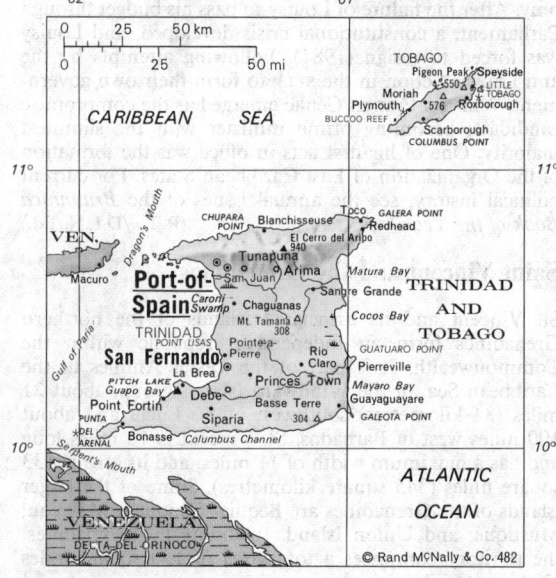

TRINIDAD AND TOBAGO

extending from west to east. Gas and water seepages give rise to mud volcanoes of various types, the best known of which is the Devil's Woodyard.

In the southwest of the island is the sedimentary volcano known as the Pitch Lake, which contains reserves of asphalt.

Tobago's topography   Tobago is physiographically an extension of the Venezuelan or Caribbean coast range and the Northern Range of Trinidad. Its dominant feature is the Main Ridge, which runs from northeast to southwest, rising to a height of 1,890 feet (576 metres) in the centre of the island. Pigeon Peak, the second highest at 1,804 feet, is in the northeast. The ridge slopes more gently to the southwest onto a coral plain. The coral formation has given rise to a number of reefs, one of which, Buccoo Reef, is known for its marine life and sea bathing. Extensive deposits of natural gas have been discovered off Tobago, mainly along the western and northwestern coasts and off Trinidad to the southeast.

Climate. The climate of Trinidad and Tobago is tropical, with a high degree of humidity. The coolest months are January and February, when the average minimum temperature is about 68° F (20° C). The warmest months are April, May, and October, which have an average maximum temperature of about 89° F (32° C). In general, mean temperatures range between 77° F (25° C) in February and 85° F (29° C) in April. Temperatures vary significantly between day and night, and the climate is tempered by sea breezes.

There is a major dry season from January to May, and a short dry season (Petite Carême, or Indian Summer) in September to October. The prevailing winds are the northeastern trades. The islands are outside the main hurricane zone, but Tobago has twice in a century—in 1867 and 1963—been struck by disastrous hurricanes.

Plant and animal life. Vegetation zones are well marked on both islands. In general, the highest areas coincide with the most luxuriant tropical rain forest vegetation. Cultivated estates or small settlements are established in clearings on the hills. In the dry season the hills are decorated with the orange flowers of the mountain immortelle, a large flowering tree that grows to a height of about 80 feet, and the gold flowers of the poui. Sugarcane, the main agricultural crop, is grown on Trinidad's Central Plain.

The Caroni Swamp, a bird sanctuary, is frequented by flocks of white flamingo and egret as well as the scarlet ibis—a national bird. The greater bird of paradise has been introduced to the island of Little Tobago. The forests on both islands are hunting grounds for small game, the most sought after being the paca, or *lappe.* Other animals include the agouti (a short-haired, short-eared, rabbit-like rodent), peccary (a wild hog), tattoo (an armadillo), and iguana (a large lizard). There are four main groups of reptiles: snakes, lizards, turtles, and crocodiles (one kind, the caiman, related to the alligator).

Settlement patterns. Soils, climate, and vegetation all have influenced the pattern of local settlement. Villages stretch ribbon-like along the major roadways. In Trinidad, though not in Tobago, villages are so diverse that it would be difficult to call any typical.

Even in the sugar belt of the Central Plain, with its mainly, though not exclusively, East Indian population, patterns vary. Kinship tends to be the important structural element in the life of the East Indian village in Trinidad; caste may also have a localized influence, as may the Praja relationship, which implies a reciprocal obligation between one who needs and another who bestows a favour and in which a type of boss exercises various kinds of influence. Religious festivals, such as Dīwālī (Festival of Lights) and various forms of Puja (ceremonial offering), are important events. Houses vary in size and architecture from the simple thatched hut to the well-built two-storied dwelling, brightly painted and ornamented and roofed with corrugated iron.

The East Indian villages   A somewhat different life-style prevails in villages inhabited by people predominantly of African descent, though many villages have both Indian and African characteristics. Because of the conditioning of the slave system, traditional African culture has undergone considerable mutation or reinterpretation. The family unit is nuclear

rather than extended and may be based upon marriage or upon a stable extralegal relationship. The main institution is the Christian Church, which may be Roman Catholic, Anglican, or Fundamentalist. Steel band and calypso music is heard everywhere—particularly in the months of January and February, when preparations are being made for carnival, the national festival.

These different rural cultural streams converge on the capital, Port-of-Spain. This city, with its mixed population, its Spanish influence (particularly in architecture), and French Creole flavour, is one of the most cosmopolitan in the world. San Fernando, with its large East Indian population, is the second largest town, and is located in the southwestern foothills of the Central Range in the heart of the oil belt. Arima, the smallest Trinidadian municipality, is the oldest and least opulent. Scarborough, the chief town in Tobago, is an administrative centre and market town.

The people. The original inhabitants of Trinidad were chiefly Arawaks. Although there are inhabitants of the town of Arima who claim descent from Carib royalty, there is doubt that the land was settled by Caribs. Tobago was frequently visited by Amerindians but was not settled before the arrival of Columbus. Spanish, French, African, English, East Indian, and Chinese have all contributed to the ethnic composition of the islands' population. The various immigrant groups brought with them their languages, culture, and religion. Although English is the official language, three Creole languages (Trinidad English, a French patois, and a Spanish dialect) and some East Indian languages also are spoken.

Protestantism gained a foothold in its various forms (Anglican, Methodist, Moravian, and Baptist) with the advent of the British. Roman Catholicism, then the official religion, was strengthened by French immigration, which also introduced the patois dialect, while the East Indians brought with them their languages and their Hindu and Muslim religions. Further diversification followed with the immigration of Syrians and Lebanese. African-influenced religious groups include the Shango and Shouter cults.

The first census of Trinidad and Tobago recorded a population of almost 100,000 in 1861. By 1891 the population had more than doubled to about 218,000 persons. During the following three decades the population growth declined slightly, registering an increase of about two-thirds and a population in 1921 of almost 360,000. In the 1920s the death rate for the islands began a dramatic decline that lasted about four decades, during which time the rate fell from almost 25 deaths per thousand persons to less than 10. A substantial upturn in population growth was experienced during this period, accelerated by an increasing birth rate between 1931 and the end of World War II. Following the war the birth rate began to stabilize and between 1960 and 1970 it dropped substantially from about 40 births per thousand persons to about 25. In 1931 the population was about 412,000 and during the next three decades the figure doubled. During the late 20th century both the birth and death rates have remained fairly stable and the rate of natural increase has been high. Emigration from the islands, however, has moderated the total population growth rate, keeping it slightly less than the Caribbean average.

The economy. Principal features of the economy are a dependence on the petroleum industry and a fairly high level of unemployment. In recent years, however, unemployment has been decreased somewhat through jobs generated by increased government expenditures sustained by the rising petroleum revenue.

Resources. Oil production is both land and sea based. Trinidad has extensive oil and gas fields, as well as deposits of asphalt, coal, gypsum, limestone, sand and gravel, iron ore, argillite, and fluorspar. Natural gas has been found off the coasts of Trinidad and Tobago.

Agriculture. After petroleum traditional agricultural commodities continue to account for the bulk of the country's exports. The three major agricultural export commodities are sugar, cocoa, and coffee. Other agricultural products include citrus fruits, rice, copra, poultry, and vegetables.

Manufacturing

Industry. The major source of government revenue is oil production and refining. Manufacturing output, apart from petroleum products, has increased, partly as a result of the policy of encouraging local manufacturing to reduce dependence on imports and partly because of the stimulus of membership in Caricom. Industrial plants are engaged in the assembly of consumer durables, including motor vehicles and radio and television receivers, and in the manufacture of fertilizers, cement, paper products, furniture, garments, and processed foods. Government enterprises include two fertilizer plants and a steel mill.

Tourism is potentially one of the fastest growing industries. It is based particularly on Tobago and on Trinidad's northwest peninsula.

Trade. The prinicipal export of Trinidad and Tobago is petroleum and petroleum products. Agricultural produce is also exported.

Administration of the economy. The principal instruments employed for management of the economy have been import duty and income-tax concessions; quota restrictions on imports; credit and subsidies to agriculture, manufacturing, and tourism; and budget deficits financed by internal and external loans.

Transportation. The islands are served by a fairly well-developed network of main and local roads, but there is heavy congestion in urban areas. Taxis are a prominent feature of traffic in Trinidad.

Several small shipping lines and a domestic airline connect Tobago to Trinidad. Piarco International Airport on Trinidad and Crown Point Airport on Tobago have inter-island connections and link with New York City, North and South America, Western Europe, and the Caribbean.

Port-of-Spain is the chief commercial port; petroleum exports are handled in ports in the south, such as Point Fortin, Pointe-à-Pierre, and Brighton. There are extensive port facilities at Point Lisas. The islands are served with a dial-telephone system.

Administrative and social conditions. *Government.* The first constitution, promulgated as a British Order in Council (1962), provided for a governor general appointed by the British monarch, a Cabinet, and a bicameral legislature. Under the constitution adopted in 1976, Trinidad and Tobago is a republic headed by an elected president.

The legislature consists of a 36-member House of Representatives, elected by universal adult suffrage every five years, and a 31-member Senate, whose members are appointed by the president, 16 on the advice of the prime minister, six on the advice of the minority party leader, and nine solely at the discretion of the president. The voting age is 18. Legislation passed in 1980 provided for a separate Tobago House of Assembly consisting of 12 members, elected at a primary election from electoral districts, who in turn elect three additional members as well as a chairman and deputy chairman. The legislation provides for a measure of devolution of executive powers in areas such as revenue raising and collection, agriculture, industry, tourism, environmental conservation, and social services. At the time of the 1980 census Trinidad was divided into 11 local government areas including eight rural counties, which have county councils, and the three municipalities of Port-of-Spain, San Fernando, and Arima, which have municipal councils.

Education. Education, the main requirement for upward social mobility, is free at primary and secondary levels and compulsory between the ages of six and 12. There has, however, been a growing disparity between school places and children of school age, particularly at the secondary school level. Faculties of the University of the West Indies—engineering, law, medicine, social science, natural science, education, agriculture, and liberal arts—are situated on the university campus at St. Augustine, about eight miles east of Port-of-Spain. There are three technical institutes, one each in Port-of-Spain, Centeno, and San Fernando. There are several teacher-training colleges.

Health and welfare. The demand for additional housing in the urban areas has increased, and construction has been hampered by population movement, higher construction costs, shortage of land, and inadequate long-term financing.

State provision for social security takes the form of noncontributory old-age pensions, noncontributory government employee pension schemes provided out of public revenues, and workmen's compensation compulsorily paid by employers. A national insurance scheme has been establhed, but with somewhat limited benefits. The proportion of doctors in the population has remained low, principally as a result of the emigration of doctors. For statistical data, see the "Britannica World Data" section in the current *Britannica Book of the Year.*   (A.N.R.R.)

HISTORY

Christopher Columbus reached Trinidad in 1498 on his third voyage from Spain. The island remained a Spanish possession for almost 300 years, until it surrendered to a British naval expedition in 1797. During most of these three centuries the island was neglected. Not until 1530 did Spain appoint a governor; no effective possession took place until the early 17th century and no effective development until the late 18th century. The right to trade with the Spanish colonies was restricted to the port of Seville, and in 1662 the complaint was made that no authorized Spanish ship had visited the island for 30 years, while trade was openly carried on with English, French, and Dutch vessels. The main commodity produced at this time was tobacco. In the 1720s, however, cacao became important, though after a disastrous crop failure in 1727 cacao did not again become of major importance until the 1820s.

The Spanish era

Immigration and settlement. The original Amerindian population was worked to death on the Spanish plantations, and African slaves were brought in to replace it. Because the Spanish had difficulty in populating the island, the King of Spain in 1783 encouraged Roman Catholic settlers to immigrate, bringing their slaves with them. This resulted in an influx, mainly of French planters, from neighbouring islands. Spanish influence continued to decline, and in 1797 the last Spanish governor surrendered the island to a British naval force.

The British were reluctant to import more slaves from Africa to develop Trinidad as a sugar colony: there were objections from influential planters in Barbados and Jamaica who feared competition; there was growing opposition to slavery itself; and there had been a black uprising in Haiti in the 1790s. Early in the 19th century attempts were made to attract white settlement, and in 1802 Chinese immigration was tried; most of the Chinese, however, soon left the island.

Early in the 19th century, civil wars on the South American mainland brought an influx of Spanish immigrants. In 1845 a system of apprenticeship was introduced on the plantations in order to try to compel workers to remain on the estates after the abolition of slavery, which was proclaimed in 1833, although full emancipation did not occur until 1838. In 1844, to provide labour needed by the plantations, the British began to subsidize immigration from India, which continued until 1917.

While Trinidad experienced three centuries of Spanish rule, Tobago—also reached by Columbus in 1498—was the subject of continual dispute between England, France, Spain, and Holland. Not until 1721 was there any attempt at settlement by the British; development began only in 1781, after the French captured the island. Tobago was essentially a sugar colony, although nutmeg and cotton were also cultivated. England acquired the island in 1802, and Tobago subsequently had its own bicameral legislature, which it retained until 1874. In 1833 Tobago, together with the islands of Grenada and St. Vincent, was put under the jurisdiction of the governor of Barbados. In 1889 the island was amalgamated with Trinidad, while retaining its own legal and fiscal systems; in 1899 it became a ward of the colony of Trinidad and Tobago.

Independence. In 1923 a tentative move toward self-government was made when seven elected members replaced seven nominated members in the colony's Legislative Council. From 1937 to 1938 workers carried out a strike in the Trinidad oil fields that ultimately affected labour relations throughout the Caribbean. Universal suffrage was introduced in 1945, and elected members of the Legislative Council began a gradual assumption of power.

Progress to independence

In 1956 Eric Williams, leader of the People's National Movement (PNM), won a victory at the polls as the colony's chief minister. In 1962 the colony attained independence with Williams as prime minister, while continuing to bear the marks and the burdens of a colonial economy. Popular mass demonstrations, resulting in part from widespread unemployment, led to the proclamation of a state of emergency, which was lifted in 1971. The repressive measures taken by Williams strengthened his regime but represented a failure of his ideals. His government, plagued by corruption, was unable to solve Trinidad's economic and racial problems. The constitution adopted on August 1, 1976, established a republic within the Commonwealth.

Williams remained as prime minister of the republic. With the country's vast oil reserves, which made Trinidad and Tobago one of the wealthiest states in the Caribbean, Williams could aid other, less prosperous Caribbean nations. Politically, the government was leery of involvement with the governments in Grenada and Jamaica, preferring the more stable governments in the Caribbean, such as Barbados.

Williams died in 1981. George Chambers was selected as acting prime minister in an orderly transition, and his party was endorsed in the following elections. Chambers typified the nationalistic yet broadly socialist approach of the PNM by encouraging private enterprise while maintaining social welfare programs and a substantial state sector. For current political history, see the annual issues of the *Britannica Book of the Year.*

(A.N.R.R./C.L.R.J./Ed.)

Virgin Islands

The Virgin Islands are a group of about 100 small islands, islets, cays (small low islands), and rocks in the West Indies, situated about 70 miles (115 kilometres) east of Puerto Rico. The islands extend from west to east for some 60 miles and are located west of the Anegada Passage, a major channel connecting the Atlantic Ocean and the Caribbean Sea. Their combined land area is about 192 square miles (498 square kilometres).

The islands are administrated in two groups—the British Virgin Islands and the Virgin Islands of the United States. The former is a British colony consisting of four larger and 32 smaller islands and islets. Their total area is 59 square miles (153 square kilometres), and they lie to the north and east. The latter group, administered by the U.S. Department of the Interior, consists of three larger islands and some 50 smaller islets and cays, with a total area of 133 square miles (345 square kilometres). These islands lie to the south and west.

The islands are noted for their inviting subtropical climate, which attracts about a million tourists each year to swim in the warm aquamarine waters and frequent the sandy beaches and harbours. Apart from the tourist industry, the islands have few economic resources; financial aid is provided by the United Kingdom and the United States, respectively. Fresh water is scarce. In recent years some tension has arisen between the inhabitants of the islands and people from other parts of the Caribbean who have immigrated, particularly to the Virgin Islands of the United States, to seek jobs and better living conditions.

PHYSICAL AND HUMAN GEOGRAPHY

The land. *Relief.* The Virgin Islands form the easternmost extension of the Greater Antilles island chain; the islands themselves are the peaks of submerged mountains that rise from a submarine plateau. While the Caribbean deepens to a 15,000-foot trench in the area between the island of St. Croix, to the south, and the remainder of the group to the north, the greater part of the plateau is covered by not more than 165 feet of water. Most of the islands rise only to a few hundred feet above sea level, although isolated peaks reach heights of well over 1,200 feet. The highest point is Mt. Sage on Tortola, which is 1,780 feet (542 metres) high.

The British islands are 36 in number, of which 16 are inhabited. Tortola (Turtle Dove), with an area of 21 square miles, is the largest and the site of the group's capital and population centre, Road Town. Other larger islands in the British group are Anegada, with an area of 15 square miles; Virgin Gorda (the Fat Virgin), with an area of eight square miles; and Jost Van Dyke, about three square miles. Lesser islands include Great Tobago, Salt, Peter, Cooper, Norman, Guana, Beef, Great Thatch, Little Thatch, and Marina Cay.

The principal islands

About 50 islands and cays comprise the "unincorporated territory" of the United States group. Only three are of importance; several are uninhabited. The largest, St. Croix, is 23 miles long, 84 square miles in area, and lies about 40 miles south of the other islands. The island of St. Thomas, 32 square miles in area, is the site of the territory's capital, Charlotte Amalie. St. John has an area of 20 square miles. At the closest point, between Thatch Island and St. John, a distance of only half a mile separates the British and the U.S. groups.

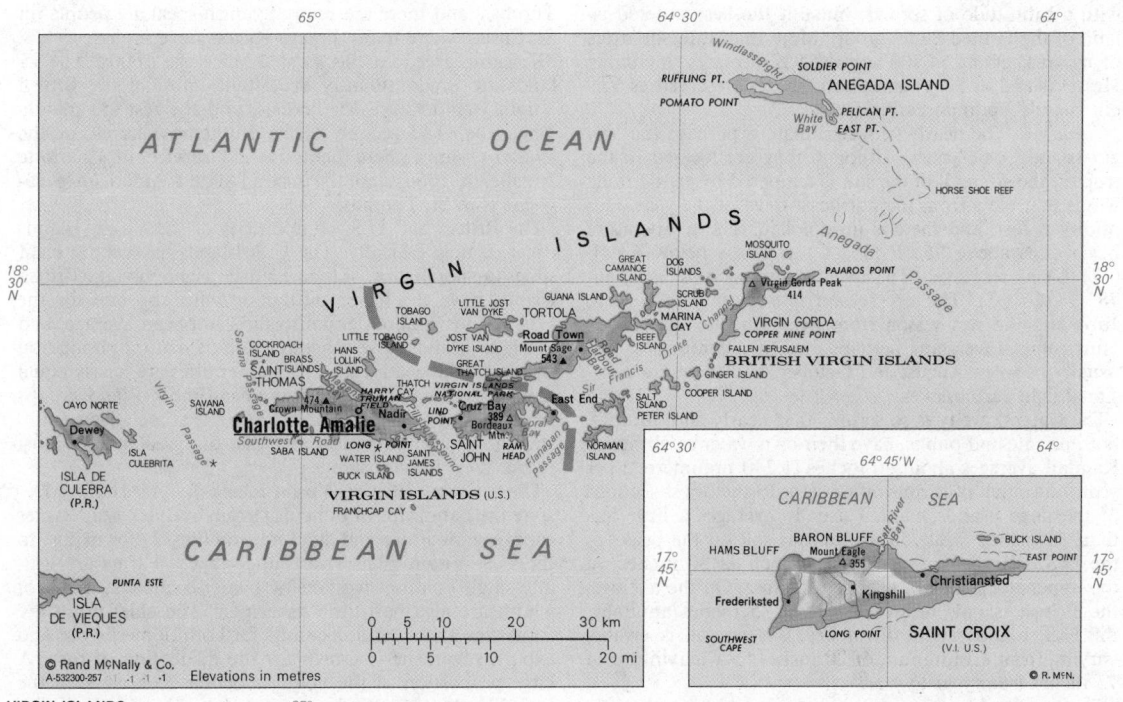

The landscape of the islands offers scenes of dramatic contrast, varying from craggy cliffs and mountaintops to small lagoons with coral reefs and barrier beaches; from landlocked harbours to unprotected bays; and from small, level plains to elevated plateaus with rolling lands and jungle-like regions. Individual islands have their own distinguishing characteristics.

In the British group, Tortola, of the same geologic formation as St. John, is hilly, with unbroken ranges running throughout its 15-mile length. Road Harbour Bay is Tortola's most important bay; it is exposed to the southeast but protected from all other sides by an amphitheatre of hills. Virgin Gorda, an island with several peninsulas, is rectangular in shape, about 2½ miles long, and 1¾ miles wide in the central part of the island. Its highest peak rises 1,359 feet. Anegada is the only flat island of the group. Its elevation is never more than 10 to 15 feet above sea level, and its coast, because of its many reefs, is dangerous to boats. Jost Van Dyke is a hilly, almost rugged island with two fine beaches on the south side.

St. Thomas · In the United States group, St. Thomas, composed primarily of a ridge of hills running east and west with branching spurs, has little level, tillable land. Crown Mountain (1,555 feet), northwest of the capital of Charlotte Amalie, is the island's highest elevation. Charlotte Amalie, facing a fine landlocked harbour, is built on five foothills. There are a number of springs on the island's northern side but only one small stream. Magens Bay, with 3,500 feet of white sandy beach, is reputed to be the finest beach in the West Indies. St. Thomas is surrounded by 17 islands, cays, and innumerable rocks.

St. Croix rises abruptly on the north to Mt. Eagle (1,165 feet), but southward the land slopes to flatlands that near the coast are laced with lagoons. The only urban centres, Christiansted and Frederiksted, lie on the flat land. Since the coastal indentations are slight, there are few harbours and sheltered bays; dangerous reefs lie along the north and south coasts. While there are several rivulets on the island, it is generally poorly watered.

St. John—three miles east across Pillsbury Sound from St. Thomas, and lying closest to the British Virgin Islands —is composed of steep, lofty hills and valleys, but with little level, tillable land. Its highest elevations are Camelberg Peak (1,192 feet) and Bordeaux Mountain (1,277 feet). Its coastline is indented with forests and many fine, sheltered bays. Coral Bay, on the eastern end, whose steep shores allow large vessels to come close in, has been described as the best natural harbour in the Virgin Islands. A number of small streams on the south side of St. John, together with a multitude of springs, make it the best watered island of the United States group. More than three-quarters of its area, about 14,700 acres (5,952 hectares; including Hassel Island in St. Thomas harbour), is preserved as Virgin Islands National Park.

Climate. The nearly perfect climate is perhaps the Virgin Islands' chief asset. Although they are located in the tropics, the strength of the sun is tempered by gentle trade winds that blow from the northeast most of the year. Humidity is low, and there is little pollen. The temperature never rises above 96° F (36° C) or drops below 63° F (17° C) at sea level. The average temperature is about 78° F (26° C). The dry season lasts from February to July, and the wet season from September to December. Hurricanes—averaging perhaps four in a century—occur usually between August and October, and there are occasional light earthquakes.

Rainfall · The water scarcity is so serious that nearly all buildings, both private and public, have their own water catchments. Rainfall averages about 40 inches (1,270 millimetres) per year, but much of it runs off unused. In the driest sections of the large islands, rainfall usually averages a little less than 30 inches, while 55 inches may fall on the peaks of the U.S. islands, and possibly as much as 80 inches on the upper slopes of Mt. Sage, on Tortola. On the average, the British islands receive less than 35 inches annually, the U.S. islands about 45 inches. But rainfall is erratic, varying from a minimum of 20 inches to a maximum of 75 inches from year to year.

Virgin Islanders have long depended almost entirely upon their own cisterns and wells and, in addition, have imported water in barges to meet their needs for fresh water—needs now rapidly increasing in proportion to population and industrial growth. Only Road Town in the British group has a piped supply. The first flash-type evaporator for the desalination of seawater in the Western Hemisphere was installed in St. Thomas, where the Virgin Islands Water and Power Authority, established in 1965, now operates several saltwater-distillation plants. A seawater-desalination plant is located in Christiansted on St. Croix. Maximum use of salt water is made everywhere in the islands for such tasks as sewage removal and fire fighting.

Plant and animal life. Vegetation is tropical. Supported in most places by thin soil, it includes flamboyant trees and other lush blooms, but the islands' generally sparse stands of shrubs and trees are not sufficient to be of commercial value. Among the tree species are mangoes, soursop (a small tropical tree with a large succulent fruit), and coconut palms. Breadfruit, cacao, and wild orchids grow in the hills, while cactus, acacia, grass, and sugarcane flourish in the lowlands. Even though the woodlands are not dense, there are numerous species of birds and small game, such as deer. Sailfish, tarpon, marlin, kingfish, and wahoo abound in coastal and offshore waters.

The people. The population is overwhelmingly of African descent. The number of Puerto Ricans and persons from the continental United States has increased in recent years.

Despite a long tradition of racial equality and the absence of legal or de facto discrimination in housing, churches, theatres, and public facilities, there have been growing signs of discontent with a type of class discrimination that to a great extent corresponds with the difference between white and black. While there has been relatively little racial violence, there is an increasing demand by those of African descent for a greater role in determining economic and social decisions and in running the government.

The Chachas · The Chachas of St. Thomas form a distinct ethnic unit apart from the other islanders. They are descended from French Huguenots who nearly a century ago came from Saint Barthélémy—a West Indian island the French purchased from Sweden in 1877, after holding it themselves from 1648 to 1784. The Chachas maintain themselves as a clannish, aloof, industrious fisher-farmer community.

The traditional language of the islands is English—much of it spoken in a dialect termed Calypso, which varies somewhat from island to island but is mutually intelligible among most West Indians. Some French is heard on St. Thomas, and there are many Spanish-speaking people on St. Croix, where many Puerto Ricans have settled.

Religious freedom has existed since the 1600s. The islands are predominantly Protestant: most of the British Virgin Islanders are Methodists, and the rest are mainly Anglicans. The second oldest Lutheran Church in the Western Hemisphere held its first service in Charlotte Amalie in 1666, and the second oldest American synagogue is in St. Thomas.

The British and U.S. components of the Virgin Islands differ demographically. The U.S. islands have about eight times the population of their British neighbours; the British islands have the lower birth rate while the rate for the U.S. islands is about equal to the Caribbean average; and the U.S. islands have a greater rate of natural population increase. The death rates for both entities are nearly equal and lower than the Caribbean mean; both island groups have rates of total population growth that are affected substantially by immigration and that are greater than most of the West Indian islands.

The economy (British Virgin Islands). *Agriculture.* Despite the handicaps of difficult terrain and uncertain water supply, agriculture and stock raising (largely for export to the U.S. Virgin Islands) are undertaken. Farms are usually small holdings worked by owner-occupiers, many of whom are also part-time fishermen. The chief crops are fruits, vegetables, and coconuts for both domestic use and export; sugarcane is grown for the distillation of rum. A large proportion of the younger people seek work in the U.S. islands, where higher wages are available.

Industry. The tourist industry comprises almost half of the national economy. New roads have been built, harbours improved, and tourist hotels built. The number of tourists visiting the islands, attracted by opportunities for sport fishing and sailing, has continued to increase.

Burning wood for charcoal is a minor industry, and there are several boatyards for the construction and repair of vessels. Cement blocks and rum are manufactured.

Trade. Imports—mostly from the United States, Puerto Rico, and the United Kingdom—consist chiefly of foodstuffs, beverages, machinery, motor vehicles, building materials, and petroleum products. Exports, mainly to the U.S. Virgin Islands, include fresh fish, sand and gravel, fruit, and vegetables.

Transportation. Tortola has two main highways and numerous side routes; Virgin Gorda, Anegada, and Jost Van Dyke also have road networks. Small boats ply to and from the U.S. Virgin Islands. An airport, reconstructed in 1969, is located on Beef Island, which is connected by bridge to Tortola. Another airport, on Anegada, was opened in 1969; and there is plane service both to the U.S. Virgin Islands and to Puerto Rico.

The economy (U.S. Virgin Islands). Until well into the 20th century, sugarcane and, to a lesser extent, cotton provided the main economic base. The harbour at St. Thomas also generated some income. When the United States acquired the islands, both social and economic conditions were poor; there was a high death rate, little education, few roads, and an inadequate water supply. The first U.S. governor reported in 1917 that the islands were incapable of self-support. Since then, millions of dollars of U.S. aid have failed to make them self-supporting. U.S. aid and the development of tourism have nevertheless resulted in the territory's having one of the highest per capita incomes in the Caribbean.

Resources. Minerals of commercial value do not exist, although sand, rock, and gravel are present in quantities sufficient for construction purposes.

Fisheries. There is no large commercial fishing industry, but fish represent an important part of the islanders' diet; and the tourist influx has encouraged sport fishing.

Industry. As in the British Virgin Islands, tourism is the most important economic sector. In the United States islands, there are more than 200 miles of beaches; several historic 17th- and 18th-century buildings; pleasant vistas of mountain and sea; well-stocked shops; and numerous recreational facilities, including golf, fishing, sailing, and skin diving. The picturesque free port of Charlotte Amalie is also an attraction. Small manufacturing operations, including watch making, textile manufacturing, and pharmaceutical production, have been encouraged, as well as some larger ones. An aluminum plant employing several hundred workers was established in St. Croix, which also is the site of one of the world's largest oil refineries.

Transportation. The U.S. islands have a fairly good road network. Taxis and rental vehicles are available on all three islands, and regular passenger-bus services operate on St. Croix and St. Thomas. Interisland transport by small boat is available. Seagoing passenger and cargo vessels connect the ports of Charlotte Amalie, on St. Thomas, and Frederiksted, on St. Croix, to ports abroad. International jet air service operates on St. Thomas and St. Croix.

Administrative and social conditions (British Virgin Islands). *Government.* A governor, appointed by the British crown, is responsible for defense and internal security, external affairs, and the public services. He exercises his powers in consultation with the Executive Council, over which he presides. The council consists of three ministers (one of whom is the chief minister), the attorney general, and the financial secretary. The chief minister is appointed by the governor, who appoints the other two ministers with the advice of the chief minister. The Legislative Council consists of one ex officio member (the attorney general), nine members elected by universal adult suffrage, and a speaker, who is elected from outside the council by its members.

Justice. The law of the colony is made up of both the common law of England and statutory law, or locally enacted legislation. It is administered by the West Indies

Associated States Supreme Court, courts of summary jurisdiction, and magistrates' courts. The principal law officer is the attorney general.

Education. Education is compulsory and free, but there is a shortage of schools. Most of the primary and secondary schools are supervised by the Methodists or Anglicans. There are no institutions of higher learning.

Administrative and social conditions (U.S. Virgin Islands). *Government.* Jurisdiction is exercised by the U.S. Department of the Interior. Limited legislative powers are held by a unicameral legislature consisting of 15 senators, each elected by popular vote for two-year terms. The governor and lieutenant governor are also elected by universal adult suffrage. There are 12 executive departments, of which 11 are headed by commissioners; the 12th, the Department of Law, is headed by the attorney general.

Justice. Judicial power in the islands resides in municipal courts and in the Federal District Court of the Virgin Islands. The district judge and the district attorney are appointed by the president of the United States, with the advice and consent of the U.S. Senate. Municipal court judges are appointed by the governor, subject to confirmation by the legislature.

Education. Education is compulsory and free, but many students attend private schools. The College of the Virgin Islands (established in 1964) has campuses on both St. Thomas and St. Croix.

Cultural life. The Virgin Islands have little in the way of a national culture. There is no typical music, and little folklore. In 1965, however, the Virgin Islands Council of the Arts was created as an adjunct of the U.S. National Foundation of the Arts and Humanities. Community Arts Councils have been formed on all three American islands. They sponsor theatrical performances and provide training in the arts and crafts. For statistical data, see the "Britannica World Data" section in the current *Britannica Book of the Year.*

HISTORY

Pre-Columbian inhabitants of the islands were the warlike Caribs and the peaceable Arawaks, whose civilization had reached the stage of stone polishing and pottery making when Columbus arrived. On his second voyage, in 1493, Christopher Columbus dropped anchor at what is now known as Salt River Bay, St. Croix (which he called Santa Cruz), and sent a landing party ashore in search of fresh water and fruit. After a brief skirmish, the Caribs repulsed the Spanish newcomers. Columbus later encountered some of the other islands and named the group Santa Ursula y las Once Mil Virgenes (St. Ursula and the Eleven Thousand Virgins). In 1555 Emperor Charles V of Spain sent forces that invaded the islands, defeated the Caribs, claimed the territory, and ordered the annihilation of the natives. By 1596 most of the native inhabitants had been killed or had left.

Settlement and history of the British Virgin Islands. Tortola was first settled in 1648 by Dutch buccaneers who held the island until it was taken over in 1666 by a group of English planters. In 1672 Tortola was annexed to the British-administered Leeward Islands. In 1773 the planters were granted civil government, with an elected House of Assembly and a partly elected Legislative Council, and constitutional courts. The abolition of slavery in the first half of the 19th century dealt a heavy blow to the agricultural economy. In 1867 the constitution was surrendered and a legislative council was appointed that lasted until 1902, when sole legislative authority was vested in the governor in council. In 1950 a partly elected and partly nominated legislative council was reinstated. Following the defederation of the Leeward Islands Colony in 1956 and the abolition of the office of governor in 1960, the islands became a crown colony. In 1958 the West Indies Federation was established, but the British Virgin Islands declined to join, in order to retain close economic ties with the American territories. Under a constitutional order issued in 1967, the islands were given a ministerial form of government.

Settlement and history of the U.S. Virgin Islands. In 1666 St. Thomas was occupied by Denmark, which five

(margin notes)
Sources of income

Landing by Columbus

The Danish era

years later founded a colony there to supply the mother country with sugar, cotton, indigo, and other products. Negro slaves from Africa were first introduced to St. Thomas in 1673 to work the cane fields, but the first regular consignment of slaves did not arrive until 1681. In 1684 the Danes claimed neighbouring St. John, which had been used primarily as a base by buccaneers. Denmark colonized the island with planters from St. Thomas in 1717. In 1733 they abandoned St. John after slaves rebelled, staged an uprising, and held the island for six months. They then purchased St. Croix, which had been in the possession of the French since 1651. Meanwhile, slaves continued to be imported from Africa; by 1742 there were 1,900 on St. Croix alone, and sugar production was bringing prosperity to the islands. The group came under the Danish crown in 1754, and the following year Charlotte Amalie was made a free port. The British briefly occupied the islands from 1801 to 1802, and in the next year, 1803, the slave trade was abolished in the Danish West Indies. The British returned to occupy the islands once more from 1807 to 1815, after which they reverted to Danish rule until 1917. Slavery itself was abolished in 1848 after a serious uprising in that year. Sugarcane production dropped, and there was a uniform decline in economic activity.

American interest in the islands began in the Civil War period, but the U.S. Senate refused, in 1870, to approve the purchase of St. Thomas and St. John for $7,500,000. The United States moved decisively only in World War I, when it was seen to be strategically important to control the main passage through the Caribbean to the Panama Canal, as well as routes along the eastern coasts of the American continent. Denmark at that time was willing to sell to avoid the jeopardy of seizure by the Allies or conquest by Germany, which then owned Hamburg-America Line docks, warehouses, steamers, and other property in St. Thomas. In 1917 the United States purchased the three islands for $25,000,000, and the Virgin Islands became an unincorporated territory of the United States. The treaty

The United States' purchase

of cession promised U.S. citizenship to the inhabitants, except where the choice of retaining Danish citizenship was exercised. An act in 1927 granted United States citizenship to most of the Virgin Islanders, and in 1932 another provided that all natives of the Virgin Islands who on the date of the act were residing in the continental United States or any of its insular possessions or territories should be U.S. citizens. The transition was accomplished smoothly by retaining the Danish government organization and legal code. All military, civil, and judicial power was invested in a governor appointed by the president of the United States. Administration was the responsibility of the U.S. Navy Department from 1917 until 1931, when jurisdiction was transferred to the Department of the Interior.

The Organic Act of 1936, enacted by the U.S. Congress for the establishment of congressional government, provided for two municipal councils, one for St. Thomas and St. John, the other for St. Croix, and a council for the whole territory. A Revised Organic Act adopted in 1954 created a central government and abolished the independent municipal councils; authorized distinct executive, legislative, and judicial branches; and provided for a substantial degree of self-government. Its unicameral assembly was elected by popular vote. In 1968 an act was approved, to take effect in 1970, legalizing the popular election of the islands' governor and lieutenant governor.

The last appointed governor, Melvin Herbert Evans, an islander of African descent, was inaugurated as the first elected governor in 1971.

To date, there has been little demand for autonomy from either the British or U.S. Virgin Islands, mostly due to fears of disrupting the lucrative tourist industry and having increased taxes. Independence appears not to be the goal, and statehood seems a long way off. The fundamental fact remains that none of the islands are as yet self-supporting. For current political history, see the annual issues of the *Britannica Book of the Year.*

(L.H.E.)

OTHER ISLANDS

The Bahamas

The Bahamas, a former British colony, became an independent nation within the Commonwealth in 1973. The island group comprising The Bahamas (Spanish *bajamar,* "shallow water") occupies an irregular submarine tableland that rises out of the Atlantic depths and is separated from nearby lands to the south and west by deepwater channels. Lying to the north of Cuba and Hispaniola, the archipelago comprises nearly 700 islands and cays, only about 30 of which are inhabited, and almost 2,400 low, barren rock formations. It stretches for 590 miles (950 kilometres) southeasterly from Grand Bahama Island, which lies about 60 miles off the southeastern coast of Florida, to Great Inagua Island, some 50 miles from the eastern tip of Cuba. The total land area is 5,353 square miles (13,864 square kilometres).

Strategic location

The strategic position of the Bahama Islands, which lie at the geographic centre of the New World landmass, commanding the gateway to the Gulf of Mexico, the Caribbean Sea, and the entire Central American region, has given the history of the islands a unique and often striking character. It was there that Christopher Columbus made his original landfall in the Americas. The subsequent fate of the peaceful original inhabitants remains one of the more tragic episodes in the development of the entire region, while the early attempts at European-dominated settlement were marked by intense national rivalries, interspersed with long periods of lawlessness and piracy. As a result, the society and culture that has evolved in The Bahamas is a distinctive blend of European and African heritages, the latter a legacy of the slave trade. The islands, lacking natural resources other than their magnificent climate and dazzling beaches, have become heavily dependent on the income generated by the extensive tourist

facilities that have been developed, often as a result of the injection of foreign capital. The continued popularity of the islands, largely with North American tourists, has maintained a relatively high standard of living among the population, most of whom are black, but difficulties associated with the transfer of political control to the majority has caused some economic problems.

The capital city, Nassau, is situated on the small (80 square miles [207 square kilometres]) but important New Providence Island. Other islands, known collectively as the Family (or Out) Islands, include Grand Bahama (530 square miles), which contains the major settlements of Freeport and West End; Andros (2,300 square miles [5,957 square kilometres]), the largest island; and Eleuthera, site of one of the early attempts at colonization. In spite of the concentration of the population in urban centres devoted to tourism, the traditional pattern of small farming and fishing prevails in many villages, notably in the southeastern islands.

PHYSICAL AND HUMAN GEOGRAPHY

The land. *Relief and soils.* Extensive areas of flatland, generally a few feet in elevation, are the dominant topographic features of the major islands; Bimini, for example, has an elevation of only 20 feet (six metres). A number of islands fronting the Atlantic have a range or series of ranges of hills on their northeastern side and parallel to the longer axis of the island. These are formed of sand washed ashore and blown inland by the trade winds. The newer hills adjacent to the seashore are normally sand dunes. Solidity increases toward the interior, where the particles become cemented to form Bahama limestone. Eleuthera and Long Island have the greatest number of hills exceeding 100 feet, and the highest point, 206 feet (63 metres) is on Cat Island. Beneath the soil, the islands

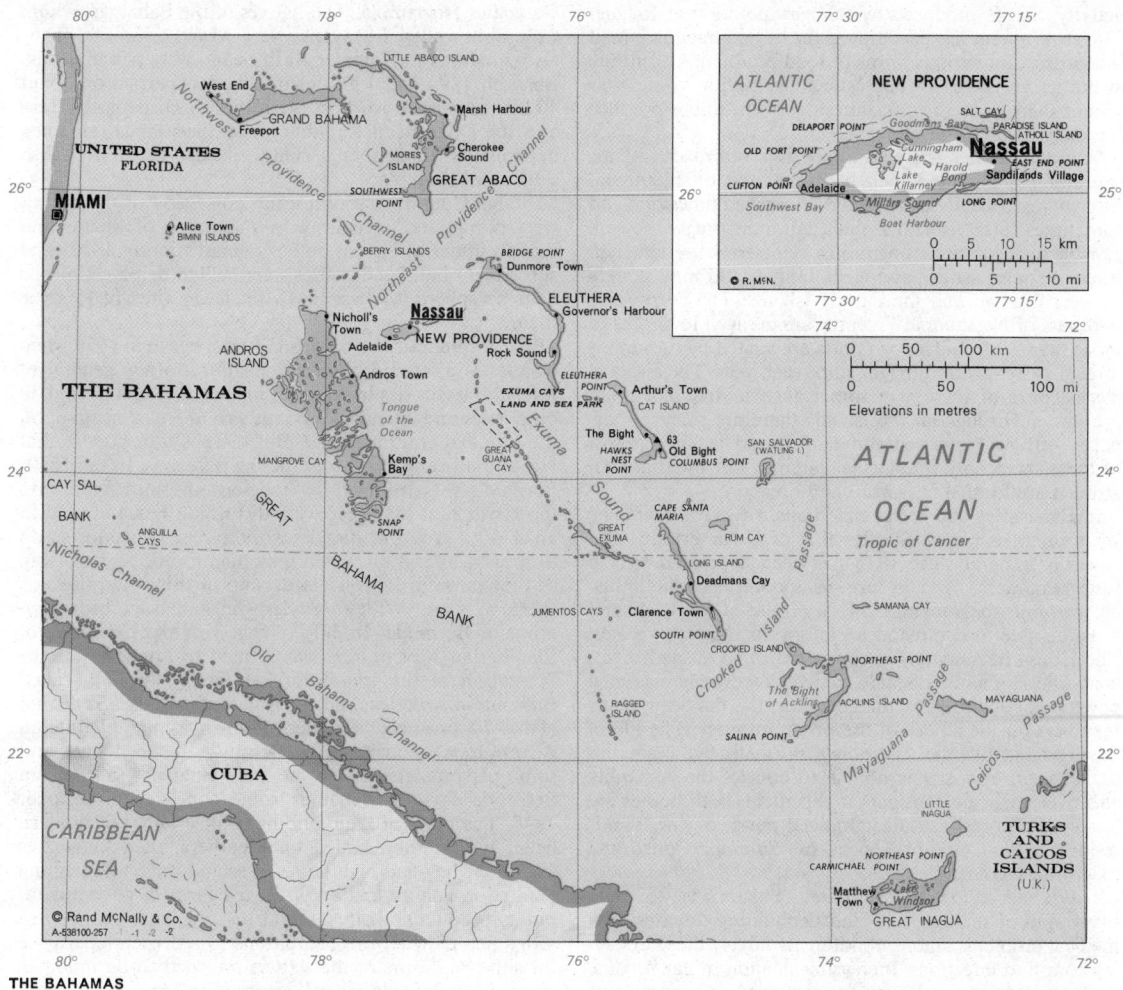

THE BAHAMAS

Temperature and rainfall

are composed of the skeletal remains of coral and other marine organisms.

Climate. The Bahamian climate, mild throughout the year, is one of the great attractions of the area. The average temperature varies from 70° F (21° C) during the winter to 81° F (27° C) during the summer, and extremes very seldom fall below 60° F (16° C) or rise above 90° F (32° C). The average annual rainfall is about 46 inches (1,170 millimetres), occurring mostly during the summer months. Prevailing winds, coming from the northeast in winter and from the southeast in summer, lend a cooling influence to a generally humid atmosphere. Hurricanes present something of a threat during the period from mid-July to mid-November and have occasionally caused great destruction.

Plant and animal life. Extensive and beautiful forests of Caribbean pine are found on Grand Bahama, Great Abaco, Andros, and New Providence. Hardwood forests, known locally as "coppices," also occur on some of the islands. Elsewhere, the woody vegetation consists mostly of shrubs and low trees. Animal life is dominated by frogs, lizards, and snakes, all of them nonpoisonous, and several species of bats are found in caves along the more rocky coasts. Larger animals include the agouti, a rodent; the raccoon; the iguana; and the elegant flamingo, the national bird. All of these have been much reduced in numbers and in distribution. The barkless dogs, which are reputed to have existed at the time of the original inhabitants, may indicate an early link with Africa. In addition, several animals—notably sheep, horses, and other livestock—have been introduced from Europe. The surrounding waters abound with fish and other edible marine animals.

The people. There has been a marked shift of population from fishing and farming villages to the centres of tourist and commercial activity. Most of the population

movement was to New Providence, Grand Bahama, and Abaco.

English is the only language native to Bahamians, although since the influx of Haitian immigrants, French or its creole dialect is spoken. A minority of the population is descended from English pioneer settlers and Loyalist refugees. Most of the population is of African descent, many with varying amounts of Caucasian blood.

A very high percentage of Bahamians are members of Christian churches. Most are Protestants, the largest denominations being Baptist, Anglican, and Methodist. A large minority of the population is Roman Catholic.

About two-thirds of the Bahamian population is concentrated on New Providence Island. During the late 20th century there has been a marked shift in the population distribution from the fishing and farming villages to the centres of tourist and commercial activity. Most of the internal migration has been to New Providence, Grand Bahama, and Abaco. The Bahamas' rate of population increase is much higher than the Caribbean average, primarily because of immigration from the United States and other West Indian islands such as Haiti. The rate of natural population increase is about equal to the Caribbean mean, but both the birth and death rates are substantially less than the average for the West Indies as a whole.

The economy. *Industry.* Tourism continues to dominate the economy. Gambling casinos in several areas add to the attraction of The Bahamas for tourists.

Although The Bahamas continue to expand as an international financial centre, banking and business hold a distant second place in the economy, followed by government and construction. Other industries include a petrochemical refinery, a pharmaceutical factory (mainly producing hormones), and a cement plant at Freeport, which has become the most important centre of industrial development and is second only to Nassau in tourist and commercial activity. Salt is produced by solar evaporation at Inagua. The government has encouraged the development of small industries, and various forms of food production continue at numerous places for domestic consumption.

Since there is no direct taxation, customs duties produce the major share of revenue.

Transportation. There are modern paved roads in Nassau and Freeport and their environs, and on Eleuthera. Elsewhere, roads are constructed of crushed limestone and sometimes surfaced with asphalt, but increasingly they are capable of accommodating motor vehicles. A fleet of small motor vessels carries passengers, freight, and mail weekly between Nassau and the Family Islands. The deep-water harbours of Nassau and Freeport are dredged to depths of more than 30 feet. The two ports are visited by numerous foreign passenger and freight ships each year. The airplane has become of increasing importance to the Bahamian economy. Throughout the islands there are some 60 airports, with varying accommodations and facilities. Most of these serve only interinsular aircraft, but international airports are located at Nassau and Freeport.

Administrative and social conditions. *Government.* The government is patterned after that of Great Britain. The governor general since 1973 has been appointed by the English monarch, and, in turn, he appoints a prime minister who must be a member of the House of Assembly and must be able to command a majority of Assembly votes. The House of Assembly is composed of 43 elected members. The 16-member Senate, which has severely restricted powers, is appointed by the governor, the majority of the members on the advice of the prime minister. The life of the Senate is, like the Assembly's, normally five years, but if the prime minister is unable to control the Assembly effectively or if he considers it expedient, both bodies are dissolved and reconstituted. Judicial power on the islands resides in the Court of Appeal, the Supreme Court, and magistrates' courts.

Bicameral legislature

Health, education, and welfare. Bahamians are relatively free of malnutrition and debilitating diseases, and medical problems among children are largely those involving common infections. Increasing alcoholism has become a chief concern, and care for the aged is a mounting social problem. Severe housing congestion and hazardous sanitary conditions exist only in some black areas of New Providence, where housing is substandard and sewage is disposed of in backyard cesspits that tend to overflow.

There is little illiteracy in The Bahamas, for schooling is compulsory from 5 to 14 years of age. Public secondary and technical schools have been greatly expanded in recent years. The College of The Bahamas, established in 1974 in Nassau, is a community college that offers programs in conjunction with other universities, including the University of the West Indies, Florida International University, and the University of Miami.

Cultural life. Bahamian culture reflects the origins of its people and has also been influenced by the peoples of nearby islands. Outstanding among traditional group activities is the "Junkanoo" parade on Boxing Day and New Year's Day in Nassau. The main thoroughfare is given over to hundreds of gaily bedecked celebrants who, with clanging cowbells and beating drums, march and dance to a "Goombay" rhythm of African origin. Island folklore includes stories of a three-toed, human-faced creature called the "Chickcharney" and the workings of Obeah, a brand of witchcraft. In Nassau several amateur choral, dramatic, and dancing groups provide entertainment that has much local flavour. The National Trust is concerned with the preservation of wildlife and historic buildings, and the Historical Society promotes local history. For statistical data, see the "Britannica World Data" section in the current *Britannica Book of the Year.*

HISTORY

It is widely held that on October 12, 1492, Christopher Columbus first landed on an island called by its native inhabitants Guanahani, which he renamed San Salvador. Its actual identity is still in dispute, but it is generally believed to have been the island now known as Watling Inagua. He explored this and nearby islands and then sailed to Cuba and Hispaniola. The natives of the Bahamas, whom Columbus called Lucayans, were Arawak Indians. They also inhabited the Greater Antilles and were peaceful folk. Between 1492 and 1508 Spanish raiders carried off about 40,000 natives to work in the mines of Hispaniola (Haiti and the Dominican Republic), and the islands remained depopulated more than a century before the first English settlement took place.

Spanish raids for slaves

Though Columbus took formal possession of the islands with pomp and ceremony in the name of Spain, and though under the papal bull of demarcation of 1493 (and subsequent bulls) the islands were held to come within the Spanish sphere, the Spaniards made no attempt to settle them.

British colonization. British interest began in 1629 when Charles I granted Sir Robert Heath, attorney general of England, territories in America including "Bahama and all other Isles and Islands lying southerly there or neare upon the foresayd continent. . . ." But there is no evidence that Heath made any effort to settle the Bahamas. In the 1640s Bermuda was troubled by religious disputes similar to those which at that time were disturbing England, and in 1644–45 a group of dissidents there sent two ships south to seek an island on which they might settle and worship as they pleased. In 1647 leadership in this enterprise was taken by Capt. William Sayle, who had twice been governor of Bermuda. In July of that year the Company of Eleutherian Adventurers was formed in London "for the Plantation of the Islands of Eleutheria, formerly called Buhama in America, and the Adjacent Islands." Sayle and about 70 prospective settlers (known as the Eleutheran Adventurers), consisting of Bermuda Independents and some persons who had come from England, sailed from Bermuda for the Bahamas some time before October 1648. The place of their landing is uncertain, but modern belief is that they settled on Eleuthera, then known as Cigatoo. They had high hopes of establishing a flourishing plantation colony and an advanced form of government, but unproductive soil, internal discord, and Spanish interference reduced their ambitions to a desperate struggle for survival. Some of the settlers returned to Bermuda as early as 1650. Sayle himself returned in 1657, being again appointed governor of Bermuda in 1658.

New Providence was first settled in 1656 by a fresh group of Bermudans. In 1663 South Carolina was granted by Charles II to eight of his friends as lords proprietors, and they appointed Sayle as the first governor. Both Sayle and certain of those who had interested themselves in the settlement of New Providence independently drew the attention of the lords proprietors to the possibilities of the Bahama Islands, and in consequence the Duke of Albemarle and five others acquired a grant of the islands from Charles II in 1670, and they accepted nominal responsibility for the civil government. When the Bahama Islands were granted to the proprietors of the Carolina colony, New Providence had passed Eleuthera in population and commercial importance, and it became the seat of government.

New Providence as seat of government

The proprietors did not take a very active interest in the settlement or development of the islands, however, and it soon became a haven for pirates, whose depredations against Spanish ships provoked frequent and savage retaliatory raids. In 1671 they appointed John Wentworth as the first governor, but thereby merely confirmed an election previously made by the existing settlers. Although elaborate instructions for the government of the colony were issued and a parliamentary system of government was instituted, the lot of both governors and settlers was far from easy. New Providence was more than once overrun by the Spaniards alone or in combination with the French, while any governor attempting to institute a semblance of law and order received short shrift from the settlers, who had found piracy the most lucrative profession. In 1684 the King himself intervened and required that a law be passed against the pirates, but apparently it had little effect.

Early in the 18th century official representations, supported by petitions from English merchants, were being made for direct crown control. Action was at last taken in

1717 when the lords proprietors surrendered the civil and military government to the King and leased the islands to Capt. Woodes Rogers, whom the King commissioned as the first royal governor and charged with the responsibility of exterminating pirates and establishing conditions attractive to law-abiding settlers. When he arrived in 1718, armed with the royal commission and a disciplined troop of soldiers, about 1,000 pirates surrendered and received the king's pardon, while eight of the unrepentant were hanged. His measures were so effective that in 1728 the colony was able to adopt the motto, *Expulsis piratis restituta commercia.*

Meanwhile, even in the troubled days of the lords proprietors there had been an attempt at peaceful settlement, and in 1660 the present site of the capital was known as "Charles Towne" in honour of Charles II. Ever ready to pay lip service to the crown, these early settlers saw fit to change the name to Nassau when William and Mary came to the throne. With the restoration of order following the establishment of the royal government, the settlers demanded an assembly. In 1729 after due inquiry Woodes Rogers, acting under authority from the crown, issued a proclamation summoning a representative assembly and from then on, apart from the brief interruptions caused by foreign invasion, the government of the colony carried on in an orderly manner.

In 1776 Nassau was captured by the United States Navy, but after a few days the place was evacuated. In May 1782 the colony surrendered to Spain and, though it was restored to Britain by the Peace of Versailles in January 1783, it was brilliantly recaptured by Col. Andrew Devaux in April of that year before news of the treaty had been received. On the conclusion of the American Revolution many Loyalists emigrated from the U.S. to the Bahamas under very favourable terms offered by the crown. Among the newcomers was Lord Dunmore, formerly governor of New York and of Virginia, who served as governor of the Bahamas from 1786 to 1797. The Loyalists fled with their slaves to the islands, doubling the white population and trebling the black. The cotton plantations that they developed yielded well for a few years, but exhausted soil, insect pests, and, finally, abolition of slavery led to their ultimate collapse. In 1787 the proprietors surrendered their remaining rights for £12,000.

The early years of the 19th century were largely occupied by the efforts of the assembly to thwart the attempts of the executive to ameliorate the conditions of the slaves, until the United Kingdom Emancipation Act came into force in the colony on August 1, 1834. A legislative council was created by royal letters patent in 1841. The mid-19th century was taken up with a struggle for full recognition on the part of the dissenters against the established church, which was backed by the government and the upper classes; the struggle ended with disestablishment in 1869.

Considerable wealth poured into the islands as the result of blockade-running during the American Civil War and the handling of liquor during the Prohibition era of the 1920s in the United States. This kind of activity made no lasting contribution to the islands, however, nor did it establish any firm economic base. Before and after these periods, many attempts were made to grow pineapples, citrus fruits, tobacco, tomatoes, and sisal for export, but despite initial promise, all failed. Through this, however, a majority of Bahamians took to the sea, where searching for wrecks, sponging, and fishing offered excitement and occasional good fortune. After World War II, strenuous efforts to establish tourism as the basis of the economy were strikingly successful, transforming the economic and social structure of the islands.

Independence. Politically, Bahamians have had considerable control over their affairs since Captain Rogers gathered the islands' first assembly in 1729. In May 1963 a conference was held in London to consider a new constitution for the islands. It was then agreed that the colony should have full internal self-government, the governor retaining reserved powers only for foreign affairs, defense, and internal security. The new constitution came into force on January 7, 1964, and constitutional advances in

Consti-
tution of
1964

1969 brought the country to the verge of complete self-government.

Party politics emerged in 1953, when the Progressive Liberal Party (PLP) was formed by blacks to oppose the group in power, who in 1958 responded with a party of their own, the white-controlled United Bahamian Party (UBP). As the political battle progressed, the PLP raised the cry for majority rule, and many of the acrimonious characteristics of a racial contest were introduced. The climax came after the general elections of 1967, when the PLP under the leadership of Lynden Pindling was able to form a government with a slight majority. Elections that were held the following year gave that party 29 of the 38 Assembly seats. While there is no doubt that the UBP was defeated mainly on the racial issue, the accusation that that party had introduced criminal-controlled gambling and that some of its members had profited thereby had a telling effect.

In general the PLP advocated stricter government control of the economy, increasing Bahamian ownership of business enterprises and the replacement of foreign workers by Bahamians. Although the move toward self-government received bipartisan support, the UPB advocated that total independence should come later than 1973, the target year of the PLP government. In 1969 the name of Commonwealth of the Bahama Islands was adopted, and on July 10, 1973, on independence, the official form became The Commonwealth of The Bahamas. For current political history, see the annual issues of the *Britannica Book of the Year.*

(E.P.A./D.R.Ha./Ed.)

Bermuda

Bermuda is an internally self-governing British colony in the western North Atlantic, consisting of a group of islands lying about 570 miles (920 kilometres) off Cape Hatteras on the eastern coast of the United States. The fishhook-shaped chain of islands stretches for about 22 miles but has an area of only about 21 square miles (54 square kilometres), of which about two square miles are leased to the U.S. government for air and naval stations. Of the 145 islands and groups of rock, 120 are named but only about 20 are inhabited. The largest is Great Bermuda, known as the Main Island, about 14 miles in length.

The colony's name was derived from that of the Spanish navigator Juan Bermúdez, who is generally credited with discovering the islands, perhaps about 1503. Bermuda's mild climate year-round, the surrounding waters, and the historic charm of Hamilton, the capital, and of St. George, the former capital, are among the factors that make tourism the chief industry. Bermuda's Parliament is the oldest among the British Commonwealth countries, representative government having been introduced into the colony in 1620.

PHYSICAL AND HUMAN GEOGRAPHY

The land. *Relief.* One of the most northerly groups of coral islands in the world, Bermuda consists mainly of chalky deposits capping a volcanic cone that rises more than 14,000 feet (4,270 metres) from the ocean floor. The islands are generally hilly, having a maximum elevation of about 260 feet above sea level; there are a number of fertile depressions and a few marshes and brackish ponds, but the islands have no rivers or lakes.

Climate. The climate is mild, humid, equable, and frost-free. August is the hottest month and February the coldest. The annual maximum temperature averages about 90° F (32° C), and the annual minimum about 47° F (8° C); the annual mean temperature averages 70° F (21° C). The average mean humidity is about 77 percent, and an average annual precipitation of about 57 inches (1,450 millimetres) is distributed fairly evenly throughout the year.

Plant and animal life. Vegetation growth is luxuriant, and there are more than 950 kinds of flowering trees, plants, and vines. Originally, an indigenous Bermuda cedar covered the islands densely, but most of these trees have been killed by disease. Bermuda has no native mammals—

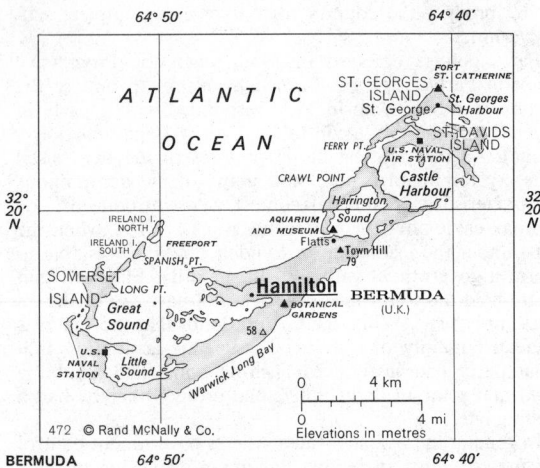

ATLANTIC OCEAN

BERMUDA
(U.K.)

Hamilton

472 © Rand McNally & Co.

BERMUDA   64° 50'   64° 40'

Elevations in metres

0   4 km

0   4 mi

wild pigs left by shipwrecks have now died out—and it has only one native reptile, the lizard. There are no dangerous insects or reptiles. Migratory birds visit the islands. The cahow, or Bermuda petrel, once considered extinct, breeds in the islands, as do a few other native land birds. The surrounding waters abound with fish and lobster.

The people. The majority of the population is black, mainly descendants of slaves brought from Africa before the abolition of the transatlantic slave trade by Britain in 1807. The white population came primarily from the British Isles, although a few were descended from Portuguese labourers brought from Madeira and the Azores in the mid-19th century.

The ethnic pattern

The main language spoken is English, but some Portuguese is heard. More than one-third of the population are members of the Anglican Church; smaller numbers are members of the Roman Catholic, African Methodist Episcopal, Methodist, and Seventh-Day Adventist churches. Altogether some 40 religious faiths are represented.

The resident population is fairly evenly distributed over the main island of Great Bermuda; small settlements are established elsewhere. While the majority of visitors stay on the main island, many elect to stay on St. Georges Island. Hamilton, named for a former governor, is one of the world's smallest cities; it has an area of about 180 acres (73 hectares). Tucked between the hillside and the sea, it is a constant beehive of activity. The port of Hamilton is a deep, landlocked harbour; tourist liners berth only a few yards from the shops, which are large and well stocked with quality goods from around the world.

Between 1931 and 1970 the population of Bermuda almost doubled in size from about 28,000 to about 53,000. The growth of the population has been very slow, however, during the late 20th century, both in absolute numbers and in the annual percentage increase. Bermuda's birth and death rates are among the lowest in the West Indies and emigration from the islands has lowered the population growth even further, consistently producing a growth rate of less than 1 percent.

Bermuda's architecture is distinctive. White terraced roofs, designed to catch rainwater, top pastel-coloured houses. There are narrow lanes, pink-tinted beaches, and a remarkably clear, azure sea. The social atmosphere is varied—Somerset being rural, Hamilton lively, St. Georges historic, and Tucker's Town exclusive.

The economy. *Industry.* The economic structure of Bermuda is based on tourism and on income derived from the military stations.

Local industries

Local industries are small and are confined to small-boat building and ship repairing, and the manufacture of pharmaceuticals, concentrated essences (such as perfumes, flavourings, and extracts), and handicraft souvenirs. The government, however, has begun to encourage light industry (such as ship repairing, boat building, and furniture making), mainly around the former naval dock areas on Ireland Island. There is a little commercial fishing; agriculture is purely local in scope. Neither is sufficient to satisfy local demand, and foodstuffs from the United States are a major import. Easter lilies are exported on a small scale.

Finance. Tax advantages have encouraged a considerable number of foreign companies to register in Bermuda. This has produced a large amount of banking and other financial activity.

Administration of the economy. Of the government's annual revenue, about half is obtained from customs receipts. Despite both a cost of living and a population density that are among the world's highest, Bermuda has almost no poverty or unemployment.

Transportation. There are many miles of public roads, most of them paved. Bridges and causeways link Great Bermuda with the other main islands (Somerset, Watford, Boaz, Ireland, St. Georges, St. Davids, and Coney). Ferries provide another interisland link. Automobiles, prohibited before 1946, are restricted to one per family and are limited in size and power. Many motorized bicycles are in use. The Ports Authority maintains tugs, passenger tenders, and a floating dry dock. In addition to the port of Hamilton, there are also offshore anchorages; both St. Georges and the duty-free port at Ireland Island have considerable berthing space.

A U.S. naval air station at Kindley Field on St. Georges Island is the only airport and is used by both military aircraft and by passenger aircraft of major international airlines.

Administrative and social conditions. *Government.* Under the constitution of 1968, the British monarch appoints the governor, who retains responsibility for external affairs, defense, internal security, and the police. In the exercise of these powers the governor is assisted by the Governor's Council, created by a constitutional amendment in 1973. In other matters the governor acts on the advice of a Cabinet (formerly called the Executive Council), which consists of a premier—the majority leader of the House of Assembly appointed by the governor—and at least six other members appointed by the premier. The legislative branch consists of the British monarch, the Senate, and the House of Assembly. The 11 members of the Senate (formerly called the Legislative Council) are appointed by the governor, in part on the advice of the premier and the leader of the opposition, and the 40 members of the House of Assembly are popularly elected for five-year terms. The judiciary consists of the Court of Appeal, the Supreme Court, and the Magistracy.

Each of the nine parishes annually appoints its own vestry (local government authority), which has power to levy taxes and manage local affairs. There are two municipalities, the city of Hamilton and the town of St. George.

Education. Education is compulsory for children from five to 16 years of age. Primary education is provided free at schools maintained and aided by the government. Secondary education is provided at both state-aided and private schools. Bermuda College, established in 1974, provides vocational as well as academic courses. Government scholarships are available for study at universities abroad.

Education

Health and welfare. The King Edward VII Memorial Hospital is a general hospital, and St. Brendan's is a psychiatric hospital. There is also a residential facility for geriatric cases.

The state provides no general medical scheme. The Department of Health and Welfare, however, provides free health services for babies and for children of school age.

Cultural life. Cultural societies abound, the most active being devoted to art, drama, and choral singing. There are several cinemas. Kite flying at Easter is a custom peculiar to Bermuda. Some of the folklore of Africa is preserved by the Gombey Dancers, black troupes who have developed elaborate costumes and on public holidays dance to the strong rhythms of drums. Many British folk traditions, holidays, and ceremonies are observed. For statistical data, see the "Britannica World Data" section in the current *Britannica Book of the Year.*

HISTORY

Gonzalo Fernández de Oviedo, a Spanish chronicler and naturalist who sailed close to the Bermudas in 1515, first attributed their discovery to his countryman, Juan Bermúdez. The exact discovery date is unknown, but an

Discovery and settlement

Italian map published in 1511 shows the islands in an approximately correct position. A 17th-century French cartographer gave the date of discovery as 1503. The islands remained uninhabited until 1609, when the English admiral Sir George Somers beached his flagship, "Sea Venture," after hitting one of the reefs. Sir George died in Bermuda the following year. His companions, unaware of Juan Bermúdez, named the islands Somers Islands, which is still a secondary designation.

British colonization. In 1612 Bermuda was included in the third charter of the Virginia Company, and 60 English settlers were sent out to it. In 1616 an Indian and a black were taken there from the Bahamas as slaves. So many others followed that the slave population came to outnumber the European settlers. They were not freed until slavery was abolished throughout the British Empire in 1834.

The islands remained under company administration until 1684, when the government passed jointly to the English Crown and the company; the rights of the inhabitants remained undisturbed, and Bermuda never became a Crown Colony under the total jurisdiction of the sovereign. In 1815 the capital was transferred from St. George on St. Georges Island to Hamilton on Great Bermuda. Much of Bermuda's subsequent history took the form of a succession of economic booms and depressions. Blockade running during the U.S. Civil War and rum smuggling during Prohibition (the legal prevention of the manufacture, sale, or transportation of alcoholic beverages in the United States from 1919 to 1933), as well as privateering (illegal only after about 1700), made Bermuda a rich country. In the 20th century Bermuda developed a flourishing tourist industry.

In 1941 naval and air stations in Bermuda were leased for 99 years to the U.S. government. The British garrison in Bermuda was withdrawn in 1957. The British naval dockyard was closed in the 1950s, but a small naval establishment is still maintained.

Bermuda since World War II. In 1963 Bermuda's first political party, the Progressive Labour Party (PLP), was formed. Its members—nine black and one white—claimed generally to represent the majority of the nonwhite population and advocated total independence from Britain and the introduction of an income tax. In 1964 independent members of the legislature formed the United Bermuda Party (UBP), whose 22 white and eight black members were committed to racial integration. In 1968 a new constitution, placing strong executive powers in the hands of the leader of the party elected to office, came into force.

Before the general elections in 1968 the colony experienced the worst outbreak of civil disorder in its history, largely the result of deep racial tensions. Rioting and arson, much of it by young blacks, caused the governor to seek military assistance from Britain. In the election the UBP won 30 seats and the PLP the other 10—a result that was seen as an expression of support for the continued status of Bermuda as a British colony. Tension was heightened in March 1973 when the governor, Sir Richard Sharples, was shot to death; this followed an earlier assassination of Police Commissioner George Duckett.

Racial tensions flared again in 1978 with the eruption of race riots. A commission was formed under Lord Pitt to study means of ending the chronic problem of race discrimination, and autonomy talks were started. The Bermudans, however, have shown relatively little interest in independence, perhaps due to fears of economic recession accompanying self-government. For current political history, see the annual issues of the *Britannica Book of the Year*. (Pa.H./Ed.)

Civil disorder

Cayman Islands

Cayman Islands is a British colony in the Caribbean Sea, comprising the coral islands of Grand Cayman, Little Cayman, and Cayman Brac, situated about 180 miles (290 kilometres) northwest of Jamaica.

The land. With a total area of 102 square miles (264 square kilometres), the islands are low-lying, though Cayman Brac has a central limestone bluff, and the coasts are rockbound and enclosed by coral reefs. There are no rivers; rainfall at George Town, the capital on Grand Cayman, averages 56 inches (1,425 millimetres) annually. The Caymans lie in the hurricane area. The largest island is Grand Cayman (76 square miles), which has a magnificent seven-mile beach. There are quite a few bird species found on the islands. The Caymans are cool from November to March, with the temperatures ranging from 65° to 75° F (18° to 24° C). The hurricane season lasts from July to November.

The economy. Tourism is an expanding industry whose growth is facilitated by airports on Grand Cayman and Cayman Brac, as well as a private airstrip on Little Cayman. Turtle farming provides the main livelihood of the island, and the chief exports are turtle products (mostly to the United States until such products were banned for import in 1979), sharkskins, and pearls. Trade is mainly with the United States and West Germany. Many Cayman Islanders are seamen who send remittances to their families.

Administrative and social conditions. The constitution provides for internal autonomy under a governor, an executive council, and a legislative assembly. The governor is responsible for foreign affairs, defense, internal security, the police, and certain social services. Primary education is free and compulsory for all children between the ages of five and 15. For statistical data, see the "Britannica World Data" section in the current *Britannica Book of the Year*.

The Caymans were sighted by Christopher Columbus on May 10, 1503, during his last voyage to the West Indies. At first the Spaniards named them Las Tortugas because of the many turtles in the surrounding waters, but by 1530 they were known as the Caimanas or Caymanes after the native crocodiles, which have since become extinct there. After the Treaty of Madrid that ceded Jamaica to Britain, the first permanent settlement was established on Grand Cayman. Most of the settlers were from Jamaica. The remoteness of the islands made them a favourite refuge for fugitives as well. By the end of the 18th century uncontrolled fishing eliminated the native turtle population, virtually the only resource of the island. Since then Cayman Islanders have searched farther and farther away for new turtle grounds.

First permanent settlement

The islands of Cayman Brac and Little Cayman were permanently settled as recently as 1833. Permanent links between Grand Cayman and the two lesser islands were not established until 1877. The Caymans were noted for schooner building in the 19th century.

For some time the Caymans were a dependency of Jamaica, becoming internally self-governing in July 1959. When Jamaica declared its independence (1962) the Caymans went back to direct British rule. A new constitution that provides for autonomy on most domestic issues was approved in 1972. For current political history, see the annual issues of the *Britannica Book of the Year*. (Ed.)

Turks and Caicos Islands

The Turks and Caicos Islands, a British colony in the West Indies, comprises a group of islands lying southeast of The Bahamas, of which geographically they form a part, and north of the island of Hispaniola (divided between Haiti and the Dominican Republic). The islands have an area of 193 square miles (500 square kilometres). Only two of the eight Turks Islands—Grand Turk (the seat of government) and Salt Cay—are regularly inhabited. The Caicos group, lying northwest of the Turks and separated from them by a 22-mile (35-kilometre) deepwater channel, consists of six principal islands: South Caicos, East Caicos, Middle (or Grand) Caicos, North Caicos, Providenciales, and West Caicos. The name Turks allegedly derives from that of the Turk's head cactus, whose scarlet flowers resemble a Turkish fez; that of Caicos perhaps from *cayos* (Spanish: "keys"). The chief town is Grand Turk.

PHYSICAL AND HUMAN GEOGRAPHY

The land. The islands are low-lying with elevations of less than 250 feet (76 metres), and the vegetation is mostly cacti and thorny scrubs, with areas of salt meadowlands. Temperatures in the colony range between 60° and 90° F (15.5° and 32° C), the hottest months being April to November. Because of the prevailing trade winds, however, the climate is not oppressive. Rainfall averages about 21 inches (525 millimetres) annually, and drinking water is scarce. Hurricanes often strike.

The people. Most of the population is black and of African descent. The main religious denominations are Baptist, Methodist, and Anglican. English is the official language. The birth and death rates for the islands are lower than the Caribbean average, but the rate of natural increase is about the same.

The economy. The most important resource is salt, which is produced by solar evaporation. Because of the difficulty of finding markets, however, most salt production operations have been shut down. There is little arable land on the Turks or South Caicos islands. Corn (maize), beans, and other crops are grown on the other Caicos Islands. The main industry is fishing with the principal exports being lobster, crayfish, and conch, most of which is exported to the United States. Grand Turk, South Caicos, and Providenciales have international airports, and the other islands have airstrips, greatly facilitating interisland transportation. Tourism is important to the economy.

Administrative and social conditions. The constitution of 1976 provides for an appointed executive council and an elected legislative assembly, over which a governor presides. Primary education is free and compulsory. Grand Turk has a hospital and there are health clinics on several of the islands. For statistical data, see the "Britannica World Data" section in the current *Britannica Book of the Year.*

HISTORY

The islands were discovered by Juan Ponce de León, a Spanish explorer, in 1512 but remained uninhabited until 1678, when Bermudans arrived and established a salt-panning industry. The Caicos Islands were settled by Royalist sympathizers from America after the War of Independence.

Annexation by the Bahamas

In 1799 the islands were annexed by the Bahama Islands government, but in 1848 they were granted a separate charter. In the meantime slavery had been abolished (1838), and the plantation owners left the islands, their former slaves remaining in possession. After a period of financial difficulties, the colony became a dependency of Jamaica (1874–1959).

The islands became a Crown Colony in 1962. Then, in 1965, the islands again came under the control of the Bahama Islands, but with Bahamian independence the Turks and Caicos once more returned to direct control of Britain. In common with other Caribbean islands, the Turks and Caicos had burgeoning independence movements. But the 1980 elections brought in a right-of-centre party opposed to independence. For current political history, see the annual issues of the *Britannica Book of the Year.*   (Ed.)

BIBLIOGRAPHY

West Indies: LAMBROS COMITAS, *The Complete Caribbeana 1900–1975: A Bibliographic Guide to the Scholarly Literature,* 4 vol. (1977), is one of the best bibliographical sources on the area; JACK W. HOPKINS (ed.), *Latin America and Caribbean Contemporary Record,* vol. 1, *1981–82* (1983) is a collection of essays on current issues and a country by country summary of contemporary events; and the most recent issue of the *Caribbean Handbook* is useful for up-to-date facts and statistics. For scholarly studies of particular islands or communities, see MELVILLE J. HERSKOVITS' classic ethnographies, *Life in a Haitian Valley* (1937, reprinted 1971), and *Trinidad Village* (1947, reprinted 1964); and DOUGLAS TAYLOR, *The Black Carib of British Honduras* (1951); for a psychological approach, EDITH CLARKE, *My Mother Who Fathered Me* (1957); and EDWIN A. WEINSTEIN, *Cultural Aspects of Delusion: A Psychiatric Study of the Virgin Islands* (1962); for a full-length analysis of a political crisis, A.W. SINGHAM, *The Hero and the Crowd in a Colonial Polity* (1968); JOHN MACPHERSON, *Caribbean Lands,* 4th ed.

(1980), is an overview of the geography of the West Indies and the individual islands, and for a fascinating historical economic study, RICHARD PARES, *A West-India Fortune* (1950). M.G. SMITH, *The Plural Society in the British West Indies* (1965), is a careful theoretical study of the special nature of Caribbean social organization; DAVID LOWENTHAL, *West Indian Societies* (1972), is a brilliant comparative analysis; HYMAN RODMAN, *Lower-Class Families: The Culture of Poverty in Negro Trinidad* (1971); GEORGE L. BECKFORD, *Persistent Poverty: Underdevelopment in Plantation Regions of the Third World* (1972); and IVAR OXAAL, *Race and Revolutionary Consciousness: A Report on the 1970 Black Power Revolt in Trinidad* (1971), are complementary reports on current conditions in a single country. For contrasting but competent travel books on the Caribbean area by a Briton and an American, see MARY SLATER, *The Caribbean Islands* (1968); and BRADLEY SMITH, *Escape to the West Indies* (1956); and for a masterpiece of travel literature, PATRICK LEIGH FERMOR, *The Traveller's Tree* (1950). For *belles lettres* by Caribbean scholars, see PHILIP M. SHERLOCK, *West Indies* (1966); and KENNETH RAMCHAND, *The West Indian Novel and Its Background* (1970).

Cuba: RAMIRO GUERRA Y SANCHEZ, *Manual de historia de Cuba,* new ed. (1971), offers an analysis of the economic conditions, social and political institutions, and external influences from the discovery of Cuba until 1868; JULIO LE RIVEREND, *La Habana: biografía de una provincia* (1960), deals with the historical development of the province in which Cuba's capital is located; the same author's *Historia económica de Cuba,* new ed. (1975; English ed. 1967), is a very important source for the study of the economic development of Cuba to 1958; CARMELO MESA-LAGO, *The Economy of Socialist Cuba: A Two-Decade Appraisal* (1981), is an examination of Cuba's economy during the 1960s and 1970s; J.K. BLACK *et al., Area Handbook for Cuba,* 2nd ed. (1976), presents basic facts about social, economic, political, and military institutions; *A Study on Cuba* by the CUBAN ECONOMIC RESEARCH PROJECT, UNIVERSITY OF MIAMI, contains serious papers contributed by knowledgeable scholars; *Cuba 1968* (1970), by the LATIN AMERICAN CENTER, UNIVERSITY OF CALIFORNIA, LOS ANGELES, is a compilation made possible by exchanges of statistical data with Cuban agencies; *La enciclopedia de Cuba,* 9 vol., 2nd ed. (1975), was edited in Puerto Rico; *Anuario estadístico de Cuba,* issued by the CENTRAL PLANNING BOARD, is an annual compilation of statistical data on the economy and society. R. GUERRA Y SANCHEZ *et al.* (eds.), *Historia de la Nación Cubana,* 10 vol. (1952), is a lengthy, solid study from the colonial period to modern times. F.W. KNIGHT, *Slave Society in Cuba During the Nineteenth Century* (1970), examines the effects of the sugar industry from the middle of the 18th century until the abolition of slavery. DAVID F. HEALY, *The United States in Cuba, 1898–1902* (1963), analyzes the actions and personalities involved in the first military occupation. HUGH THOMAS, *Cuba: The Pursuit of Freedom* (1971), is a monumental narrative of the period from 1763 until 1970. LEE LOCKWOOD, *Castro's Cuba, Cuba's Fidel,* new ed. (1969), is a warm treatment of the Cuban leader, based on extensive tape-recording sessions, the transcripts of which had Castro's approval prior to publication. The most authoritative analysis of 20th-century Cuba is to be found in J.I. DOMINGUEZ, *Cuba: Order and Revolution* (1978). The fiasco of the Bay of Pigs is brilliantly described in P. WYDEN, *The Bay of Pigs: The Untold Story* (1979), while C. MESA-LAGO, *Cuba in the 1970s: Pragmatism and Institutionalization* (1974), examines the early years of the Revolution. MAURICE HALPERIN, *The Rise and Decline of Fidel Castro* (1972), and *The Taming of Fidel Castro* (1981), an account of the first 10 years of Castro's government and the rise of Soviet influence.

Dominican Republic: JUAN BOSCH, *Crisis de la democracia de América en la República Dominicana* (1964; Eng. trans., *The Unfinished Experiment: Democracy in the Dominican Republic,* 1965), a view of the Dominican social and political situation by a former president, ousted in 1963; JAMES A. CLARK, *The Church and the Crisis in the Dominican Republic* (1966), a superficial yet singular account of the Catholic Church in the Dominican Republic; ROBERT D. CRASSWELLER, *Trujillo: The Life and Times of a Caribbean Dictator* (1966), the best recent account of its kind; THEODORE DRAPER, *The Dominican Revolt: A Case Study in American Policy* (1968), a well-documented criticism of the North American invasion of 1965; DEBORAH S. HITT *et al., A Selected Bibliography of the Dominican Republic: A Century After the Restoration of Independence* (1968); RAYFORD W. LOGAN, *Haiti and the Dominican Republic* (1967), interesting for the British point of view (but author did not revisit country since 1961)—contains economic summaries; JOHN BARTLOW MARTIN, *Overtaken by Events: The Dominican Crisis from the Fall of Trujillo to the Civil War* (1966), a view of Dominican political events from 1960 to 1965 by an American ambassador; HOWARD J. WIARDA, *The Dominican*

Republic: Nation in Transition (1969), a general work on the Dominican Republic by a North American political scientist; PIERO GLEIJESES, *La Crise Dominicaine, 1965* (1973; *The Dominican Crisis,* 1978), a stimulating account of the revolution of 1965 and American intervention; JEROME SLATER, *Intervention and Negotiation: The United States and the Dominican Revolution* (1970), a perceptive, balanced study; and *Dictatorship, Development, and Disintegration: Politics and Social Change in the Dominican Republic* (1975), a large and detailed study of the political system; HOWARD J. WIARDA and MICHAEL J. KRYZANEK, *The Dominican Republic: A Caribbean Crucible* (1982), a discussion of the land, people, economy, and politics of the island nation in contemporary and historical settings.

Haiti: Official statistical data appears in the *Bulletin trimestriel de statistiquè* (quarterly); and, occasionally, in *Guide économique de la République d'Haïti.* The results of the 1950 census were published in *Recensement général de la République d'Haïti* (1950) and those of the census of 1971 as *Recensement général de la population et du logement.* General information may be found in GEORGES ANGLADE, *L'Espace haïtien* (1975); and S. RODMAN, *Haiti: The Black Republic* (1954); and S. SIMMONDS, *Economic and Commercial Conditions in Hayti* (1956). For their relation to world events, see K. IRVINE, *The Rise of the Colored Races* (1970). Opposite views on recent developments were presented by H. COURLANDER and R. BASTIEN, *Religion and Politics in Haiti* (1966); B. DIEDERICH and A. BURT, *Papa Doc* (1969); and F. DUVALIER, *Mémoires d'un leader du Tiers-Monde* (1969). Changes in the social structure were studied by S. and J. COMHAIRE-SYLVAIN, "Urban Stratification in Haiti," in *Social and Economic Studies, University of the West Indies, Jamaica,* vol. 8 (1959); and the emergence of a new art school by S. RODMAN, *Renaissance in Haiti* (1949). Haitian folk culture was described in a general way by H. COURLANDER, *The Drum and the Hoe* (1960). The results of extensive field work were incorporated in A. METRAUX *et al., Making a Living in the Marbial Valley, Haiti* (1951); and in R.A. HALL *et al., Haitian Creole* (1953). J.G. LEYBURN, *The Haitian People* (1941, reprinted 1966 with new introduction by S. MINTZ), an overall survey of the growth of Haiti including a very good sociological and historical analysis of the development of Haitian culture and institutions. C.L.R. JAMES, *The Black Jacobins: Toussaint L'Ouverture and the San Domingo Revolution,* 2nd ed. with new appendix (1963), generally accepted as the most revealing analysis of the historical forces, social and economic, that led to the establishment of the independent state of Haiti. H. COURLANDER and R. BASTIEN, *Religion and Politics in Haiti* (1966); M.J. HERSKOVITS, *Life in a Haitian Valley* (1937, reprinted 1964), a penetrating, detailed study of a Haitian peasant community at Mirebalais. L.F. MANIGAT, *Haiti of the Sixties: Object of International Concern* (1964), a penetrating analysis of the Duvalier regime and the historical and political background from which it came. ROBERT I. ROTBERG and CHRISTOPHER K. CLAGUE, *Haiti: The Politics of Squalor* (1971), a thorough if pessimistic study of Haitian history and of the regime of François Duvalier. DAVID NICHOLLS, *From Dessalines to Duvalier: Race, Colour and National Independence in Haiti* (1979), a history to 1971.

Jamaica: R.M. BENT and ENID L. BENT-GOLDING, *A Complete Geography of Jamaica* (1966), the standard work on the subject; BARRY FLOYD, *Jamaica: An Island Microcosm* (1979), analyzes physical geography, history, economy, and culture; CLINTON V. BLACK, *The Story of Jamaica from Prehistory to the Present,* rev. ed. (1965), the island's story from early times to independence; FREDERIC G. CASSIDY, *Jamaica Talk* (1961), a sound and entertaining study of the country's dialect; and with R.B. LE PAGE (eds.), *Dictionary of Jamaican English* (1967), the standard work on the subject; FRANK CUNDALL, *The Governors of Jamaica in the Seventeenth Century* (1936) and *The Governors of Jamaica in the First Half of the Eighteenth Century* (1937); and with JOSEPH PIETERSZ, *Jamaica Under the Spaniards* (1919), based on abstracts from the Archives of Seville; W.J. GARDNER, *A History of Jamaica* (1873), includes useful information on trade, agriculture, customs, and religion; PHILIP HENRY GOSSE, *A Naturalist's Sojourn in Jamaica* (1851); WALTER JEKYLL (ed.), *Jamaican Song and Story* (1907, reprinted 1966), an old but valuable work on the island's folklore; EDWARD LONG, *The History of Jamaica,* 3 vol. (1774), a badly arranged but invaluable 18th-century history; FRANCISCO MORALES PADRON, *Jamaica Española* (1952), a scholarly study; GEORGE W. ROBERTS, *The Population of Jamaica* (1957), an analysis of its structure, growth, and changes in internal distribution; CAREY ROBINSON, *The Fighting Maroons of Jamaica* (1969), a stirring account of the Maroons. Important serials include the *Handbook of Jamaica* (annual); the *Jamaica Gazette* (weekly); the publications of the Central Planning Unit of the Ministry of Finance, especially the *Economic Survey;* the publications of the Department of Statistics, especially the *Population Census;* and annual reports of various departments and ministries.

Puerto Rico: For the history and cultural development of Puerto Rico, see ARTURO MORALES CARRION, *Puerto Rico and the Non-Hispanic Caribbean,* 2nd ed. (1971); and EUGENIO FERNANDEZ MENDEZ, *Historia cultural de Puerto Rico, 1493–1968,* 3rd ed. (1971); and for a cultural reference, see R. DEL ROSARIO, E. MELON DE DIAZ, and M. MASDEU, *Breve Enciclopedia de la Cultura Puertorriqueña* (1976). For the island's social development, consult JULIAN H. STEWARD (ed.), *The People of Puerto Rico* (1956). On political history, see REXFORD G. TUGWELL, *The Stricken Land* (1946, reprinted 1968); and THOMAS MATHEWS, *Puerto Rican Politics and the New Deal* (1960). Sympathetic accounts concerning the development of the commonwealth status are EARL PARKER HANSON, *Puerto Rico: Ally for Progress* (1962); and HENRY WELLS, *The Modernization of Puerto Rico* (1969). A more critical view is found in GORDON K. LEWIS, *Puerto Rico: Freedom and Power in the Caribbean* (1963). A radical view for independence is expressed in MANUEL MALDONADO-DENIS, *Puerto Rico: una interpretación histórico-social,* 5th ed. (1973; Eng. trans., 1972). The best overall studies are found in the PUERTO RICO COMMISSION ON THE STATUS OF PUERTO RICO, *Status of Puerto Rico: Selected Background Studies Prepared for the United States* (1966). For the geography and economics, see RAFAEL PICO, *The Geography of Puerto Rico* (1974); H.C. BARTON, *Puerto Rico's Industrial Development Program, 1942–1960* (1959); and HARVEY S. PERLOFF, *Puerto Rico's Economic Future* (1950, reprinted 1975). See also, JUANA GARCIA, *Panoramic History of Agriculture in Puerto Rico* (1979); and UNITED STATES DEPARTMENT OF COMMERCE, *Economic Study of Puerto Rico,* 2 vol. (1979). For a good description of the governmental structure, see CARMEN RAMOS DE SANTIAGO, *El gobierno de Puerto Rico* (annual). On the slums and migration of Puerto Ricans to New York, see OSCAR LEWIS, *La Vida: A Puerto Rican Family in the Culture of Poverty* (1966); and CLARENCE SENIOR, *Our Citizens from the Caribbean* (1965). SAKARI SARIOLA, *The Puerto Rican Dilemma* (1979), an unorthodox overview of the Puerto Rican political climate.

Barbados: The *Barbados Census* (published every 10 years), is detailed and useful, but it is difficult to assess its accuracy. The *Report on Vital Statistics and Registrations* is concise and clear. Both the CENTRAL BANK OF BARBADOS, *Annual Statistical Digest,* and the *Economic Survey* (annual), prepared by the Minister of Finance and Planning, are brief, but useful. JOHN H. PARRY and PHILIP M. SHERLOCK, *A Short History of the West Indies,* 3rd ed. (1971), is an orthodox, general history that is mainly dependent on secondary sources; G.K. LEWIS, *The Growth of the Modern West Indies* (1968), a stimulating, carefully researched, left-wing, idiosyncratic account; and JOHN MACPHERSON, *Caribbean Lands,* 4th ed. (1980), an engagingly written, straightforward, geographical account of the area—well illustrated with photographs. F.A. HOYOS, *The Rise of West Indian Democracy; the Life and Times of Sir Grantley Adams* (1963), contains local history dealing with the rise of Sir Grantley Adams' party in Barbados. For ethnography, see M.G. SMITH, *The Plural Society in the British West Indies* (1965). Vegetation and animal life of Barbados are discussed in E.G.B. GOODING *et al., Flora of Barbados* (1965); J.A. ALLAN, *The Grasses of Barbados* (1957); I. BAYLEY, "The Whistling Frogs of Barbados," *J. Barbados Mus.,* 17:161–170 (1950); and GARTH UNDERWOOD, *Reptiles of the Eastern Caribbean* (1962). For the economy, see JEANETTE BETHEL, *A National Accounts Study of the Economy of Barbados* (1960).

Grenada: RAYMUND DEVAS, *The Island of Grenada, 1650–1950* (1964), a good but dated historical survey; *Conception Island* (1932), a history of the Roman Catholic Church in Grenada; KAY FRANCIS, *This is Grenada* (1965), a popular handbook for visitors; A.W. SINGHAM, *The Hero and the Crowd in a Colonial Polity* (1962), a study of conflict between politics and administration; CARLEEN O'LOUGHLIN, *Economic and Political Change in the Leeward and Windward Islands* (1968), a survey; M.G. SMITH, *Kinship and Community in Carriacou* (1962), a specialized survey of racial characteristics; *Caribbean Year Book* (annual), a comprehensive reference work.

Guadeloupe: GUY LASSERRE, *La Guadeloupe: étude géographique,* 2 vol. (1961), is the basic work. See also INSTITUT GÉOGRAPHIQUE NATIONAL, *Atlas de Départements Français d'Outre-Mer,* vol. 3, *La Guadaloupe* (1982), containing maps, descriptive text, and bibliography for 36 topical areas; HENRI BANGOU, *La Guadeloupe, 1492–1848* (1962); and ANTOINE VICTOR JOROND, *La Guadeloupe et ses îles: guide pratique du visiteur* (1965).

Martinique: EUGENE REVERT, *La Martinique: étude géographique et humaine* (1949), is the best geographical work. The 2nd vol. of the INSTITUT GÉOGRAPHIQUE NATIONAL atlas cited above provides comparabe coverage for Martinique. See also the same author's *La Magie antillaise* (1951); *Les Antilles* (1954); and *Entre les deux Amériques: le monde Caraïbe* (1958); and AUGUSTE JOYAU, *La Martinique: carrefour du monde caraïbe* (1967), a good synthesis.

Trinidad and Tobago: H.H. SUTER, *The General and Eco-*

nomic Geology of Trinidad B.W.I., 2nd ed. (1960); ST.G. COOPER and P.R. BASON, eds., *The Natural Resources of Trinidad and Tobago* (1981); MALCOLM BARCANT, *Butterfies of Trinidad and Tobago* (1970); G.A.C. HERKLOTS, *The Birds of Trinidad and Tobago* (1961). MELVILLE J. and FRANCES S. HERSKOVITS, *Trinidad Village* (1947, reprinted 1964), a study on African influences; MORTON KLASS, *East Indians in Trinidad* (1961). Social commentaries include: C.L.R. JAMES, *Beyond a Boundary* (1963), a sociological-historical study of cricket; VIDIADHAR NAIPAUL, *Miguel Street* (1959), a collection of stories, and *A House for Mr. Biswas* (1961), a novel. See also DEREK WALCOTT, *In a Green Night* (1969), a collection of poems. A.N.R. ROBINSON, *The Mechanics of Independence: Patterns of Political and Economic Transformation in Trinidad and Tobago* (1971); IVOR OXAAL, *Black Intellectuals Come to Power: The Rise of Creole Nationalism in Trinidad and Tobago* (1968); YOGENDRE K. MALIK, *East Indians in Trinidad* (1971); WILLIAM G. DEMAS, *Economics of Development in Small Countries* (1965), are all useful works, with the first and last giving an inside view. GERTRUDE CARMICHAEL, *History of the West Indian Islands of Trinidad and Tobago, 1498–1900* (1961); ERIC WILLIAMS, *History of the People of Trinidad and Tobago* (1964); and DONALD WOOD, *Trinidad in Transition* (1968), the latter dealing with social conditions in the 18th and 19th centuries. HANS BOOS and VICTOR QUENSEL, *Reptiles of Trinidad and Tobago* (n.d.); C.B. BROWN, *et al.*, *Land Capability Survey of Trinidad and Tobago*, no. 1 (1965); J.A. BULLBROOK, *Aborigines of Trinidad* (1960), a work of original research; D.L. NIDDRIE, *Land Use and Settlement in Tobago* (1961), are all valuable official publications. MINISTRY OF PETROLEUM AND MINES, *Annual Administration Report;* CENTRAL STATISTICAL OFFICE, *Annual Statistical Digest Quarterly Economic Report;* and the *Draft Five Year Plan, 1969–1973* (1968); CENTRAL BANK, *Annual Report and Quarterly Economic Bulletin*; MINISTRY OF HEALTH AND HOUSING, *First National Health Plan for Trinidad and Tobago, 1967–1976* (1966); *Report of the Committee Appointed by Cabinet for the Purpose of Reappraising the Present System of Local Government in Trinidad and Tobago in the Context of Independence* (1966); COLONIAL DEVELOPMENT AND WELFARE, *Tobago Planning Team Report* (1957).

Virgin Islands: THEODORE H.N. DE BOOY and JOHN T. FARIS, *The Virgin Islands: Our Newest Possessions and the British Islands* (1918, reprinted 1970), and DARWIN D. CREQUE, *The U.S. Virgins and the Eastern Caribbean* (1968), give two vivid overall accounts of both British and U.S. possessions, with greatest emphasis on the latter. Other useful general works are: *Annual Report of the Governor of the Virgin Islands to the U.S. Secretary of the Interior;* U.S. DEPARTMENT OF THE INTERIOR, OFFICE OF TERRITORIES, *Territorial Responsibilities* (1963), includes a section on the U.S. islands; U.S. OAST AND GEODETIC SURVEY, *America's Islands* (1970), with officially accepted factual data; J. ANTONIO JARVIS, *The Virgin Islands and Their People* (1944), and his *Guide Book* (1949), which contains a useful chronology, as does STUART MURRAY, *The Complete Handbook of the Virgin Islands* (1951). *The West Indies and Caribbean Year Book* (annual) covers nearly every aspect of the British and U.S. islands. *The West Indies Chronicle* no. 84 (1969), is a special issue on the social and economic aspects of the British Virgin Islands. The three standard scholarly histories remain: WALDEMAR C. WESTERGAARD, *The Danish West Indies Under Company Rule (1671–1754), with a Supplementary Chapter 1755–1917* (1917); CHARLES CALLAN TANSILL, *The Purchase of the Danish West Indies* (1932, reprinted 1968); and JOHN P. KNOX, *A Historical Account of St. Thomas, W.I.* (1852). LUTHER HARRIS EVANS, *The Virgin Islands from Naval Base to New Deal* (1945), details the development of the U.S. Virgin Islands government during American administration; JAMES A. BOUGH and ROY C. MACRIDIS, *Virgin Islands: America's Caribbean Outpost* (1970), contains a series of political and constitutional documents from the Colonial Law of 1852 to the Elective Governor Act of 1968 and shows evolving political, social, and economic attitudes and trends; U.S. CONGRESS, *The Virgin Islands Report,* 83rd Congress, 2nd sess., Senate Document No. 8570 (1954), documents the 1954 Revision of the Organic Act. See also EARLE B. OTTLEY, *Trials and Triumphs: The Long Road to Middle Class Society in the U.S. Virgin Islands* (1982); and WILLIAM W. BOYER, *America's Virgin Islands: A History of Human Rights and Wrongs* (1983), a history from the discovery by Columbus through the 1970s.

The British islands' labour problems are treated in INTERNATIONAL LABOUR OFFICE, *Report to the Government of the British Islands on the Development of Vocational Training* (1966). An important title on the bonded labour and work force in the U.S. islands is SOCIAL EDUCATIONAL RESEARCH AND DEVELOPMENT, INC., *Aliens in the U.S. Virgin Islands: Temporary Workers in a Permanent Economy* (1968). LAWRENCE J. COMELLA, *Basic Data on the Economy of the British Virgin Islands* (1964), is an excellent, fact-filled treatise. DARWIN D. CREQUE, *Planning a Balanced Economic Development Program for Small Business in the U.S. Virgin Islands* (1963), emphasizes the dangers inherent in an economy that relies solely on tourism. The problem of an inadequate water supply is considered in P.H.A. MARTIN-KAYE, *Water Supplies in the British Virgin Islands* (1954; MARTIN J. BOWDEN, *Climate, Water Balance, and Climatic Change in the North-West Virgin Islands* (1970); and in the section on Puerto Rico and the Virgin Islands in the U.S. WEATHER BUREAU, *Climatological Data* (monthly, with annual summary). EDWIN A. WEINSTEIN, *Cultural Aspects of Delusion: A Psychiatric Study of the Virgin Islands* (1962), has interesting and useful data on social class, race, language, religion, and cultural groups. ERIC WILLIAMS, "Race Relations," *Foreign Affairs,* 23:308–317 (1945), explains the unique racial situation in the Virgin Islands.

The Bahamas: The DEPARTMENT OF STATISTICS (NASSAU), *Statistical Abstract* (annual) gives data on population and vital statistics, tourism, trade, transportation, finance, banking, labour, health, education, agriculture, and fisheries. See also the government publications: *Bahamas* (1946–63) and *Bahama Islands* (1964–67), biennial reports. Other recommended works include: PAUL ALBURY, *The Story of the Bahamas* (1975); G.B. SHATTUCK (ed.), *The Bahama Islands* (1905), a well-illustrated, indexed volume; P.J.H. BARRATT, *Grand Bahama*, rev. ed. (1982); *Bahamas Handbook and Businessman's Annual* (annual); N.L. BRITTON and C.F. MILLSPAUGH, *The Bahama Flora* (1920, reprinted 1962); C.B. CORY, *The Birds of the Bahama Islands* (1880); MICHAEL CRATON, *A History of the Bahamas*, 2nd ed. (1968), a well-researched description, with bibliography and index; A. DEANS PEGGS, *A Short History of the Bahamas*, 3rd ed. (1959), brief but scholarly; CLAPP and MAYNE, INC, *A General Diagnosis of the Economy of the Bahama Islands* (1969); and COLIN A. HUGHES, *Race and Politics in the Bahamas* (1981), a history of the "Quiet Revolution" that led to black accession to power in 1967.

Bermuda: The following books are the most scholarly and comprehensive accounts of Bermuda's early history to 1897: J.H. LEFROY, *Memorials of the Discovery and Early Settlement of the Bermudas . . .*, 2 vol. (1877–79), compiled from the early colonial records and manuscripts by a former governor; JEAN DE CHANTAL KENNEDY, *Biography of a Colonial Town* (1961 or 1962), a social history of Hamilton from 1790 to 1897; HENRY CAMPBELL WILKINSON, *Adventures of Bermuda: A History of the Island from Its Discovery Until the Dissolution of the Somers Island Company in 1864*, 2nd ed. (1958), *Bermuda in the Old Empire: A History of the Island from the Dissolution of the Somers Island Company Until the End of the American Revolutionary War, 1684–1784* (1950), and *Bermuda from Sail to Steam: The History of the Island from 1784 to 1901*, 2 vol. (1973). TERRY TUCKER, *Bermuda Today and Yesterday, 1503–1978*, 2nd ed. (1980), is an established work by a leading Bermudian historian. General works include: *Fodor's Bermuda* (annual), a travel guide that contains miscellaneous information; JOHN CROCKER, *Bermuda, Bahamas, Hispaniola, Puerto Rico and the Virgin Islands* (issued at frequent intervals); and TERRY TUCKER, *Islands of Bermuda* (1970), which lists each island and islet alphabetically and gives brief historical data on each one, as well as an aerial photograph; the only source for much information, especially on the smaller islands. See also official publications, such as the BERMUDA, CENSUS COMMITTEE, *Report of the Population Census of 1980* (1980); and the BERMUDA GOVERNMENT, *Bermuda: Report for the Year.* Additional information may be found in the *Caribbean Yearbook* (annual); and in GREAT BRITAIN, FOREIGN AND COMMONWEALTH OFFICE, *A Yearbook of the Commonwealth;* pamphlets of the Public Information Office.

(D.J.C./I.E./R.E.Cr./F.W.Kn./N.L.G./H.J.Wi./E.Sy./C.L.R.J./ M.J.MacL./C.V.B./A.M.-C./C.S.J./W.K.M./E.V.B.B./R.Co./ A.N.R.R./L.H.E./E.P.A./ Pa.H./Ed.)

Western Africa

South of the Sahara and east and north of the Atlantic Ocean, Western Africa is latitudinally divided into two parallel belts of land: the western portion of the Sudan, a geographical area that stretches across the entire width of Africa, and the coastal region, the Guinea Coast. Each belt has its own geography, cultures, and history.

The nations of the western Sudan include Burkina Faso (formerly Upper Volta), Cape Verde, Chad, The Gambia, Mali, Mauritania, Niger, and Senegal. The nations of the Guinea Coast are Benin, Cameroon, Equatorial Guinea, Ghana, Guinea, Guinea-Bissau, Ivory Coast, Liberia, Nigeria, Sierra Leone, and Togo.

The article is divided into the following sections:

PHYSICAL AND HUMAN GEOGRAPHY

It is sometimes suggested that the physical characteristics of Africa—its climate, vegetation, and soils as well as its relief and drainage—help to explain why Africa remained the "dark continent" for so long and until so recently. Certainly the physical environment has presented mankind in Africa with many obstacles and challenges. There are no deep bays or gulfs penetrating far inland and comparatively few rocky headlands to afford shelter to adjoining bays. Beaches are often surf bound and sometimes backed by large though shallow lagoons, frequently with mangrove forests in them. Large rivers are relatively few and, apart from the Congo, end in deltas or are blocked by sandbars. Rapids and falls comparatively near the coast have discouraged penetration upstream, and navigation on most African waterways is inevitably restricted both by the grading of the river and by the often great seasonal fluctuations of volume. It is doubtful whether these difficulties would have proved insuperable had the resources of the continent been sufficiently attractive to encourage men to overcome them, but it is almost certainly true that they long discouraged, even where they did not actually prevent, European penetration.

The land

Relief and climate. The western Sudan is a wide band of sub-Saharan Africa extending about 2,500 miles (4,000 kilometres) from Cap Vert (near Dakar, Senegal) on the Atlantic to the area of Lake Chad to the east. Largely a plateau between 1,000 and 1,500 feet (300 and 450 metres) above sea level with scattered higher elevations, it borders the Saharan desert on the north and the Guinea Coast forests on the south. The climate is hot and tropical, and there is no real winter. Mean rainfall ranges from less than 10 inches (250 millimetres) in the north to 50 inches in the south. The dry season, varying from four to seven months in different areas, with January usually at midseason, is marked by the hot, dust-laden wind known as the harmattan, which blows in from the Sahara. During the

dry season the trees shed their leaves, and all except the largest rivers run dry; the dryness, erosion, and high rate of evaporation make irrigation essential for cultivation in many areas.

In west Africa, in the general absence of major mountainous areas, natural regions are determined primarily by climate and vegetation, and the Guinea coast societies are those broadly associated with the equatorial forest zone. This forest has been erased by agriculture in some areas, but it is still the natural vegetation of most districts within 100 miles of the coasts. The average monthly temperatures of the coastal area always exceed 70° F (21° C). The annual rainfall is well distributed, with a dry season that does not exceed three months (from December to the end of February), and the total precipitation is more than 45 inches.

Drainage. The Niger River drains 580,000 square miles (1,502,200 square kilometres) and, while rising only 200 miles from the Atlantic Ocean in the Fouta Djallon plateau, has a total length of 2,600 miles before reaching the sea in the Gulf of Guinea. The lower Niger, formerly a separate stream, has cut back into the plateau to drain the middle basin, a former inland lake, which still floods very easily during the rainy season in the area above Timbuktu (Tombouctou). The Niger's main tributary, the Benue, is gradually working back, in the same manner, into the Chad Basin, by cutting its way through the upland area linking the plateaus of northern Nigeria to the mountains of Cameroon.

Plant and animal life. In the east a heavy forest formerly extended from the borders of the Cameroon highlands to the west of the Niger River. In the west a forest stretched from Sierra Leone to the west of Ghana. Between these two belts of forest there is, for very complex reasons, a drier region, and here for centuries the forest has been thin, and the land, when cleared for farming, has changed to grassland if left fallow. Societies here have been culturally very similar to the true forest societies but have shown some significant differences.

Physical characteristics of the western Sudan

Cultural
effects of
the forest

The forest greatly influenced the cultural development of the Guinea coasts, for it influenced the movements of peoples and the development of agriculture and commerce. Men occupied the forest areas relatively late, because farming there had to await the development of suitable tools and new crops. Iron axes are needed to clear equatorial forests efficiently, and, although iron was introduced south of the Sahara between 500 BC and AD 200, the quantities available were too small to be significant until much later. Moreover, the crops that were indigenous or introduced early to western Africa were unsuited to the dense shade of small forest clearings. The yam, for long the most important staple crop in much of the forest region, succeeds only where large areas are cleared. Only with the introduction of shade-tolerant crops, the plantain and cocoyam (taro or eddo) brought from Asia in the 9th century AD, could forest farming become an economic alternative to hunting and gathering. Moreover, until recently forest farming did not include animal husbandry, for the forest has harboured species of tsetse fly that are particularly virulent to cattle and horses. This fact, however, had its advantages for the forest peoples, because the tsetse fly and the trees protected them from marauding cavalry. Gradually, too, the forest gave its inhabitants commercial advantages: kola nuts and later palm oil were so highly desired by distant peoples that traders by caravan and ship were drawn to the Guinea coasts.

The greater part of the western Sudan is tropical savanna or orchard bush, covered with waist-high grass during the summer rains and studded with low trees. To the north, along the lower Sénégal River, the bend of the middle Niger River, and the region of Lake Chad, trees give way to thorn scrub. The grass is thin and short-lived and disappears in the sands and bare rock of the Sahara. About 700 miles (1,100 kilometres) farther south, the savanna merges gradually into the rain forests of the Guinea Coast. Wildlife is rarer in the Sudan than in the game parks of East Africa but does include the antelope, warthog, baboon, leopard, lion, hyena, jackal, hippopotamus, crocodile, elephant, and giraffe. The numerous species of birds and insects make life hard for the farmer, though the absence at higher elevations of the tsetse fly makes livestock raising possible. In addition to cattle, herders and villagers keep sheep, goats, donkeys, and, in drier zones, camels. Horses were formerly used by warriors and chiefs.

(Ed.)

Traditional cultures

THE GUINEA COAST

Guinea is a term used for the coastlands and adjacent forests of western Africa between the Republic of Guinea and Equatorial Guinea. There have been conflicting inter-

pretations of the derivation of the name Guinea, but it would seem to be a version of the Berber word *aguinaw,* or *gnawa,* meaning "black man," or "Negro."

The cultural significance of the original forest environment seems shown even today in the linguistic map of West Africa. In detail there is a host of different languages in the forest area, some spoken by millions, some by a few thousand people. What is striking, however, is that the boundaries between the major language families roughly coincide with the old boundaries of the forest. In the extreme west, in the area of Sierra Leone, a history of multiple small invasions has brought a confused linguistic pattern to the forest areas, but there is a clear division between these forest language groups and the great groups of Mande languages in the bordering savanna belt. The forests of Liberia and the western Ivory Coast are inhabited mainly by speakers of Kru languages and bordered again by Mande speakers in the grasslands. From the Bandama River in the Ivory Coast eastward beyond the Niger River there is the clearest evidence of all of a cultural boundary between the old forest zone and the grasslands to the north, for almost all the different languages of the forest region, including those of the forest gap, are classified as belonging to the Kwa family and are bordered in the grasslands to the north by Gur and Hausa languages. Only in the extreme east does this clear division disappear. The linguistic division between the Guinea coast and the hinterland, in any event, provides good grounds for distinguishing Guinea coast societies.

This section cannot deal individually with all the groups in the area but only the more important: (1) certain peoples of the western forest, including the Mende and Temne of Sierra Leone, the Kpelle of Liberia, and the Akan of Ghana; (2) certain peoples living mainly in the lightly forested gap, including the Fanti of Ghana, the Fon and Ewe of Benin, the Yoruba of western Nigeria, and the Nupe; and (3) certain peoples of the eastern forest, including the Edo of Benin, the Ibo, the Cross River peoples, and, on the coast, the Efik and Delta peoples.

Cultural patterns. Guinea coast societies vary enormously. Today, differences between groups emerge most clearly in differences in density of population and types of settlement. Even within a small area such as southern Nigeria great variations exist: in certain Ibo rural areas, density reaches 700 or more people per square mile (270 or more per square kilometre), whereas in the equally fertile forest hinterland of the Cross River densities are well under 100 people per square mile. Moreover, Ibo live characteristically in scattered hamlets, whereas to the west the Yoruba have built some of the largest indigenous towns in Africa.

Such cultural differences are usually caused by the complex interplay of environmental and historical factors,

Language
distribution

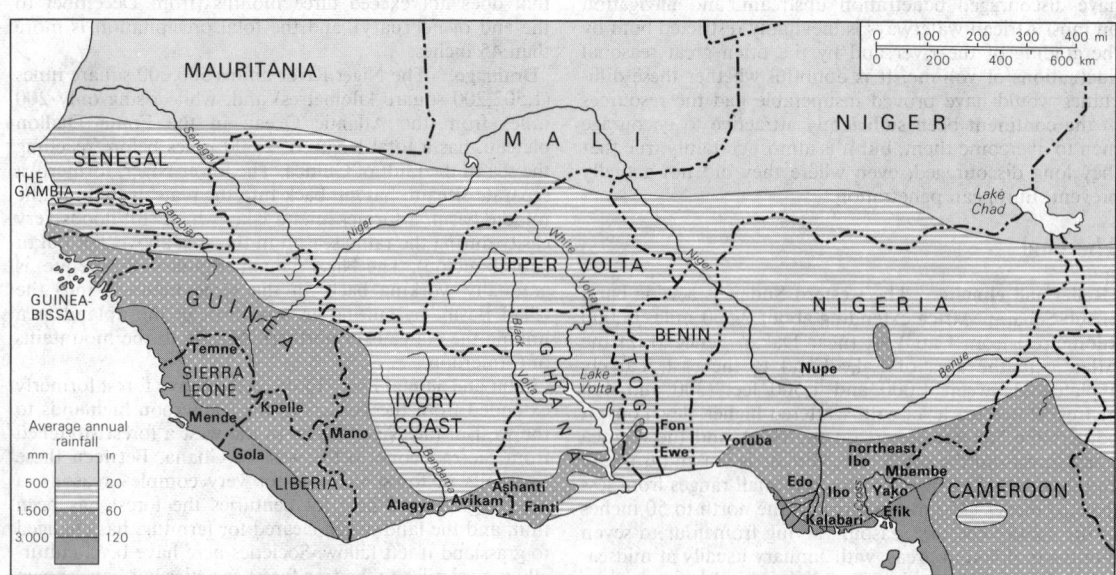

Distribution of Guinea coast peoples.

Interplay
of environ-
mental and
historical
influences
even when the direct influence of the physical environment seems most obvious. This can be seen by looking at
patterns of crop production. Sometimes crop choice seems
dictated solely by physical factors—for instance, when
farmers in dense forest have to grow cocoyams rather than
the yams that they would prefer. But sometimes tradition
seems also to be involved. In the Ivory Coast, for instance,
the staple crop to the west of the Bandama River is rice,
whereas to the east it is the yam. Although this difference
seems, in a general way, to correspond to a difference
in rainfall—the yam, requiring even watering, growing in
an area of better distributed rainfall—the fact that the
Bandama River also marks a linguistic boundary suggests
that there is a strong element of historically determined
cultural choice in this crop boundary.

That other types of cultural differences also have explanations less exclusively environmental than as first appears
can be seen from a study of house types. Most Ibo, for
example, live in typical forest-area houses—mud-walled,
rectangular structures with gable-ended roofs thatched
with mats made from single palm fronds. The northeastern Ibo, however, having moved into a grassland region
where palm trees are scarce, today build a house with
low circular walls and a conical roof thatched with grass.
Environmental factors forced these people to adopt new
materials, but the design details of their present houses
owe as much to cultural borrowings from their new neighbours as to environmental necessity.

The more complex the cultural pattern is, the more complex is the interplay of environmental and historical factors
behind it. The development of the large Yoruba towns
owed much to the necessity for defense in a relatively open
territory; the Ibo, by contrast, in their sheltering forests,
needed less protection from attack and could risk living in
scattered houses. Here at first sight is a simple relationship
of environmental and military factors. But not all forest
dwellers live like the Ibo. The farming villages next in
size to the Yoruba settlements were built by the Cross
River Yako, even though they live in a heavily forested
area and have experienced little serious warfare. Thus, a
full explanation of differences in settlement pattern would
require the detailed examination of many factors influencing tradition.

Historical background of trade and politics. Given the
circumstances outlined above, it can be appreciated that
factors accounting for the political variations of Guinea
coast societies are extremely complex. At the end of the
19th century, there existed both tiny, independent political units of four or five villages and large kingdoms of
medieval foundation holding sway over hundreds of thousands of people. Earlier writers sometimes tried to account
for such differences in simple environmental terms. Environmental factors undoubtedly were extremely important,
but explanations must also take account of the economic
patterns and political struggles of past centuries, and especially of the contacts between the Guinea coasts and the
outside world, both northward and across the seas.

Shift from
Arab to
European
trade
Before the end of the 15th century, most of the region's
external contacts were made through the savanna kingdoms to the north, whose merchants wanted slaves, gold,
and kola nuts. From the end of the 15th century, however, the interests of the Guinea coast peoples were partly
reoriented toward trade with European merchants, who
sought successively gold, slaves, and palm oil. European
trade was significant partly because within the Guinea
coast areas it was entirely controlled by local people. Europeans were prevented by climate and disease and also by
the express action of African authorities from penetrating
inland. Consequently, all the inland traffic in gold, slaves,
and palm oil was organized by African traders; Europeans
merely provided inducements to sell.

The European trade was significant also because of the
nature of the goods involved. Imports from Europe consisted mainly of such consumer goods as clothes but also
included such capital goods as iron, guns, and gunpowder, which gradually introduced a crucial new factor into
Guinea coast warfare, making it militarily vital for groups
to acquire the new weapons. Moreover, even imported
consumer goods had a political significance, for often it

was the political authorities able to tax European merchants or their own traders who were able to acquire most
goods. This put new wealth, new economic and political
resources, and thus new power into the hands of some
authorities, with important political repercussions.

The development of Guinea coast societies was also
strongly influenced by the nature of what they exported.
Slave trading did not everywhere lead to raiding and depopulation. Ibo slaves, for example, seem to have been
sold mainly by authorities as a punishment for crime or
by senior kinsmen who had fallen into debt; there is no
evidence of depopulated Ibo districts. Nevertheless, the
slave trade was commonly associated with warfare directed
toward the acquisition of captives for sale. Generally significant for political development was the stimulation that
raiding gave to military and political organization; groups
that raided for slaves roused the antagonism of their neighbours, who made retaliatory attacks, and all this increased
the tendency to military centralization, as, for example, in
the kingdom of Dahomey, where a strong government was
closely involved with slave raiding in every dry season.
Moreover, wherever war captives were important as slaves,
the trading position of central authorities who controlled
captives was better than that of private traders.

Effects of
the slave
and palm-
oil trade

In the 19th century, palm oil gradually became the most
important Guinea coast export because of its increased
use as an industrial lubricant and because of the overseas
restraints on the slave trade imposed by European human-
itarians. Nevertheless, slave dealing and raiding remained
important internally throughout the century. Even when
slave exports declined, to the anger of the local traders,
the growing palm-oil traffic in itself stimulated internal
slaving; the transportation of the bulky oil required the
use of slaves, either to paddle the canoe transports or to
headload the oil to the ports. Whenever a trader had many
men engaged in oil transport, moreover, he needed other
slaves to produce food for them; thus, slaves were important economically and politically to the Mende, Ashanti,
Fanti, Dahomean, Yoruba, Niger Delta, and Efik peoples.

The growth of the palm-oil trade brought other economic
and political changes. African traders exporting palm oil
needed more capital than slave dealers did, because slaves
transported themselves and worked while awaiting shipment, whereas oil was expensive to transport and constituted idle capital while at the ports. Palm-oil exporters
therefore needed capital and became increasingly reliant
on European firms who advanced them goods on credit
and took increasing interest in their affairs. This was politically significant when the African exporter was also a
political leader, and it was one factor leading to colonialism. Paradoxically, in the rural areas many men who
could never have been slave traders could easily gather
and sell palm nuts. In Dahomey most palm oil came from
government-fostered large plantations, but elsewhere the
oil was drawn mainly from trees growing naturally in the
bush; in the eastern forest area especially, participation in
this production and trade was very general.

By the end of the 19th century, a network of local markets had been developed over much of the hinterland of
the Guinea coasts. One indication of the importance of
markets is that in many societies the days of the week
were named after local places holding markets on those
days—village life revolved around "our" market and those
of "our" neighbours. The great centralized kingdoms were
naturally associated with the most frequented trade routes,
but there is evidence that traders travelled quite safely,
even in the absence of strong governments able to enforce
peace, because the desire for regular supplies of trade
goods protected the accredited trader even from ambitious
headhunters.

Mar-
kets and
traders

Kingdoms and chiefdoms of Guinea. Although trade
could flow across political boundaries, the growth of trade
gave rise, through warfare and competition for trade
routes, to a political separatism of West African societies.
In the area of Sierra Leone and Liberia, where trade was
initially rather limited, most political units remained very
weak, making possible the later settlement there of freed
slaves. Later, however, Mende tribes, located in rich oil-
palm areas, fought for the control of trade routes and de-

veloped into more centralized groups under warrior chiefs. At the other end of the western forest, the Ashanti confederation developed quite differently. The area initially had commercial importance as a source of gold and of the best kola nuts (one stimulant allowed to Muslims), which were wanted by northern traders. From the 17th century the Ashanti exploited their gold resources, easily made a government monopoly, in order to gain local control over the import of firearms. Extending their influence over their immediate neighbours by diplomacy and over those more distant by warfare, they eventually subjugated peoples as far southeast as Accra and as far north as the savanna.

In the gap in the forest, where there was easier movement, there developed particularly powerful kingdoms. Dahomey, essentially a militaristic state of 18th-century origins, had centralized control of raiding and trading. The Yoruba kingdoms, whose medieval growth was linked to northern trade, became in the 18th and 19th centuries increasingly concerned with southern trade routes. This, plus a complex internal power struggle, helped to plunge the Yoruba kingdoms into war with one another. Northward, the Nupe kingdom owed much of its original importance to its key position on trade routes to the north.

In the eastern forest, northwest of the Niger Delta, the Kingdom of Benin was also of medieval origin and was so well established in the 16th century that it became the first sub-Saharan state to exchange ambassadors with a European power (Portugal). From the 16th century Benin rather unsuccessfully competed with its Yoruba neighbours for the control of trade routes to the coast. Eastward across the Niger very different political systems evolved. In the Niger Delta, one of the greatest mangrove swamps in the world, an area without land for farming and unsuited to the development of large states, there developed small, independent trading towns wherever a deep water anchorage suitable for European ships existed adjacent to rivers giving good access to the interior. These towns were interested in exerting commercial control rather than political power over the slave-rich and oil-rich Ibo hinterland.

It was once assumed that Guinea coast kingdoms must have borrowed their political institutions from northern Islâmic states, but this idea is no longer accepted. In contrast to the situation in Islâmic states, the Guinea coast king was usually the keystone of the political system because of his ritual relation to royal ancestors believed to exercise power over the kingdom. Moreover, the king, sometimes transformed into a semidivine personage through his installation rites, had contact with the gods so close that all his actions had to be circumscribed lest by breaking taboos he brought disaster to his people.

Political structure of the kingdoms In Oyo, one of the best described Yoruba kingdoms, the king, at the culmination of his installation rituals, ate the heart of his predecessor and was transformed into a personification of his ancestors. Thereafter, on his only public appearances, at rituals held three times a year, he appeared veiled, his face hidden by a beaded fringe. Those who formally represented him in judicial, religious, military, and administrative capacities were slave eunuchs, chosen because, having neither kin nor affines, they presumably had no interests to serve but their master's. Though secluded, the king was involved in important political manoeuvrings, playing one group of hereditary chiefs off against a second and trying to avoid the great danger that would ensue if both groups were to unite against him.

This description gives the barest outline of the political structure of Oyo, which, at its zenith in the 18th century, controlled an area from the borders of Benin to present-day Ghana. Its political structure had many parallels in other Guinea coast kingdoms. Such political structures can be described as if they were well-integrated systems of checks and balances persisting unaltered for generations, but modern research suggests that these structures were altered whenever the balance of political power altered. Kings and hereditary chiefs might compete, for example, over the rules for choosing the king's successor, for it was recognized that the greater the freedom of choice possessed by the hereditary kingmakers, the weaker the king would be. Similarly, there was competition between king and hereditary chiefs over the king's power to appoint

subordinate officials. In the Oyo and the Ashanti kingdoms there is evidence that this was a cause of struggle whenever new territories were conquered, for there was competition to claim the administrative offices essential to the new territories. In Ashanti, successfully, and in Oyo, unsuccessfully, the king tried to gain in these territories the right of appointment that he lacked in the metropolitan districts.

Variety of chiefdoms In many ways the small chiefdoms of the Guinea coast had political characteristics similar to those of the kingdoms. Even the very small groups of the Cross River area, for example, surrounded their priest-chiefs with ritual similar to that of the Oyo. On the other hand, some small chiefdoms had completely different political systems. Mende chiefs, for instance, were essentially secular leaders. The chiefs or kings in the Niger Delta towns were hardly more than ritual figureheads, for power lay openly with wealthy traders. In many Ibo groups there were few formal political roles at all, and decisions were often taken through public discussions at village meetings.

Kin groups and other associations. In most tribal societies a man's household is the main unit of production, and consequently a husband and wife or a man and his junior kin are bound by strong economic bonds. Understandably, however, the more wealthy the community is, the greater is the value of inheritance; the larger the population is, the more important is the position of those who control land; and the more farmers are involved in the market, the more commercial considerations will influence ties between kinsfolk.

Husband–wife relations In the Guinea coast areas the marketing of crops is intimately involved in the rights and obligations of husband and wife and tends to add monetary considerations to domestic arrangements. Among the Cross River Mbembe, for example, the husband has the right to sell yams that his wife has helped to grow, but she is traditionally regarded as justified in seeking divorce if her husband spends the acquired money irresponsibly—especially if he uses it to make marriage gifts for another wife. Among the Nupe and Yoruba the men work the farms and the women market the produce. A husband must freely give his wife the staple crops for sale or home consumption; other crops, however, she must buy from him. She, in turn, is obliged to cook without charge her husband's staple foods but not his delicacies, which he must buy if he wants them. Even in the modern urban environment the tradition of financial independence between husband and wife continues. One of the problems associated with slum clearance in the Nigerian city of Lagos, heavily populated by Yorubas, has been that wives, moved out to suburbs, can no longer earn by trading in the central markets, and this has led to matrimonial stress.

Age-sets In most tribal societies age is an important basis for group formation, and in some there are what are called "age-sets"—compulsory groupings of individuals of comparable age who advance through life together. Age-sets had greatest political power in East Africa but they were significant on the Guinea coast in either of two circumstances: (1) wherever there were highly competitive kin groups, there tended to be age-sets as a kind of compensating factor to link non-kin together; (2) wherever, in highly competitive societies, kinsmen were wont to quarrel over inheritance, there were age-sets to provide the individual with loyal partisan friends. Mbembe villages, for example, are deeply divided by kin-group competition, but age-sets unite everyone of the same age throughout the village. Girls early form strong ties with one another, because each age-set of girls collectively undergoes public rites and ceremonies before its members are allowed to marry. This produces such collective solidarity that recently teen-age sets have acted like trade unions, stipulating the minimum personal gifts necessary before any member will accept a suitor. Relationships with age-mates remain important throughout a woman's life, especially in matrimonial quarrels. Boys also form very close ties with their age-mates and from their mid-teens onward can be called to work collectively on tasks that are necessary for the village as a whole. A man in need of financial help may meet with selfish refusal from his kinsfolk, but his age-mates will generally always

Secret
societies

help him; indeed, in all the crises that an individual faces, especially in sickness and death, his age-mates are there to support him. Age-mate links are of enormous value when kin-group elders meet to deal with intergroup arguments, because the heads of the disputing parties often have the closest personal links with one another.

One of the most characteristic of Guinea coast institutions, especially in areas in which central government was weakly developed, was the so-called secret society. Such societies had a significance similar to that of age-sets since they cut across kin-group lines and united men (and sometimes women) of different groups. The influence of secret societies was even greater, because membership often cut across village and sometimes even tribal boundaries. Moreover, the fact that members were often of different grades and that membership in higher grades was open to those who could pay the fees meant that these societies provided the means whereby successful individuals could exercise wide, if covert, influence. In two major areas—in Sierra Leone and Liberia, and in the area east of the Niger Delta—these associations exercised real political power and were crucial to the traditional systems of law and order. Among the tribes in the former area, the men's Poro Society and women's Sande Society were primarily responsible for punishing such serious offenses as incest and homicide; moreover, if the death sentence were imposed, it was imposed and executed by a masked Poro member. There were local Poro councils composed of members of the highest grade, and a chief's authority often rested on his Poro rank. Among the Gola, Kpelle, and Mano of Liberia and the Mende of Sierra Leone, Poro forged links between autonomous chiefdoms; in 1898 the Poro of the Mende even organized a general uprising to try to oppose British expansion in Sierra Leone.

Similarly, though on a smaller scale, among the Yako and Mbembe in the Cross River area social control was largely vested in important secret societies. The most interesting development took place in 19th-century Calabar, where the Ekpe Society became the main instrument of the trading oligarchy. In the absence of a strong government Ekpe members ensured that commercial debts were honoured and united members and freemen in countering any signs of rebellion among the many slaves owned by the rich traders of Calabar. Even among the Ibo there were rich men's societies, whose leaders exerted considerable influence on village life. Thus, in general, secret societies were institutions for translating slight advantages of wealth into political influence. Moreover, for Africa, they reflected an unusual measure of social stratification.

Stratification among freemen seems to have been greatest among the most wealthy and centralized states: the Nupe had a clear division between commoners and aristocrats, and the tendency was incipient in Ashanti, Dahomey, and Benin. Among the Yoruba there was a kind of stratification through occupational craft inheritance, but deliberate efforts were made to prevent the emergence of a royal aristocracy. Slavery was an element in stratification mostly in Ashanti, Dahomey, Yoruba, and Calabar, where slaves were used in the commercial production of crops.

Freed
slaves
from
North
America

In the 19th century new forms of stratification emerged in Sierra Leone and Liberia when freed slaves educated in North America and more receptive to missionary education settled there to become shopkeepers and white-collar workers—an elite vis-à-vis the natives. Some Sierra Leonians moved to other British West African possessions on the coast, where they joined with tiny indigenous elites drawn from wealthy, educated coastal families to form with them a new bureaucratic class.

Belief systems. The similarity between the various belief systems on the Guinea coast demonstrates the great measure of contact between the various tribes and peoples. Most systems contain these features: belief in a withdrawn high god; belief in lesser gods of lesser power but useful because easily manipulated; reverence for the dead, usually ancestors, who exercise influence over the groups to which they belonged in life; belief in witches and sorcerers, whose existence explains undeserved misfortune; and, finally, the existence of diviners who can determine the cause of a particular misfortune. The pantheon of gods

tends to be more hierarchical and complex in kingdoms such as Dahomey that have more social stratification and differentiation. There are countless cults, some of the same name, occurring over wide areas, some being adopted ad hoc to guard against some temporary misfortune. Distant cults are often deemed more powerful than local ones, so that priests may be brought long distances to establish local shrines to protect against misfortune.

Most significantly, many of these belief systems make special provision for explaining the success of an outstanding individual. The Kalabari of the Niger Delta believe in a special supernatural being whose activities aid in individual success. Among the Cross River societies there is a belief in a kind of sorcerer who achieves individual riches and influence by sacrificing, in a supernatural or spiritual sense, the lives of his junior kinsmen; an individual identified as such a sorcerer is not abhorred. Very widespread from the Niger Delta to Ghana is the concept of prenatal fatalism; individuals choose before birth success or failure in life, and this accounts for individual variation in wealth, as well as in fertility and health.

Metaphys-
ical expla-
nations of
individual
success

Problems of modernization. When the present-day states of the Guinea coast are considered in the context of the modern world, it is important to be aware that the several peoples in the area are culturally more distinct from one another than, for example, are the peoples of different European nations. This cultural diversity poses a real threat to national cohesion. Traditional social cohesion depended on the ritual authority of leaders, on the active political interests of kin groups, and on the influence of age-sets and secret societies—not on the administrative authorities governing within colonially determined boundaries. Although missionaries and colonial powers did tend to undermine traditional authorities and although national party politics today are no longer based on the old groups, old loyalties remain remarkably intact beneath the surface of modern politics. The Nigerian civil war of the 1960s was an example of this. Indeed, as long as most of the people remain primarily subsistence farmers, much of the old tribal order will remain.

On the other hand, in such major centres as Freetown and Ibadan, tribalism is simply a veneer of traditionalism that masks radically new associations, as rural migrants seek to cope with the problems of city life by banding together. In all the new states, moreover, education has developed new elites. Except in Liberia, where the Afro-American minority maintained its elite status, it is the indigenous educated people who are in control in all walks of life. The emergence of this elite is one factor that accounts for the growth of a sense of national unity across the old tribal boundaries. It is a development, however, that brings social problems in its wake. There are now vast differences in income and power between many rural farmers and the politically and economically successful elite minority. One of the greatest political problems is that the man who achieves success through politics alone, without other claims to elite status, clings to power at all costs, because, should he fall, he loses economically so much.

Sometimes those who write about tribal societies suggest that most of their modern ills spring from a new selfishness and individualism engendered by modernization. A study of the Guinea coast societies suggests, on the contrary, that, although modernization may give the selfish individual more room to manoeuvre, it has not created him. These societies have undergone much social change over past centuries, and some individuals always have seized the advantage of the moment. Change today is perhaps more rapid, and the differences in wealth between individuals is perhaps greater, but it is doubtful if modern social problems arise from any new development of self-interest.

(R.L.Ha.)

THE WESTERN SUDAN

The major ethnic groups today, as shown on the accompanying map, are the following: the Wolof of Senegal, the Serer to the south, and the Mande-speaking peoples to the east, comprising such subgroups as the Malinke, the Kasonke (Khasonka), the Bambara (Banmana), the Wasulunka, the Dyula, the Marka, and the Soninke (Serahuli).

People and
languages

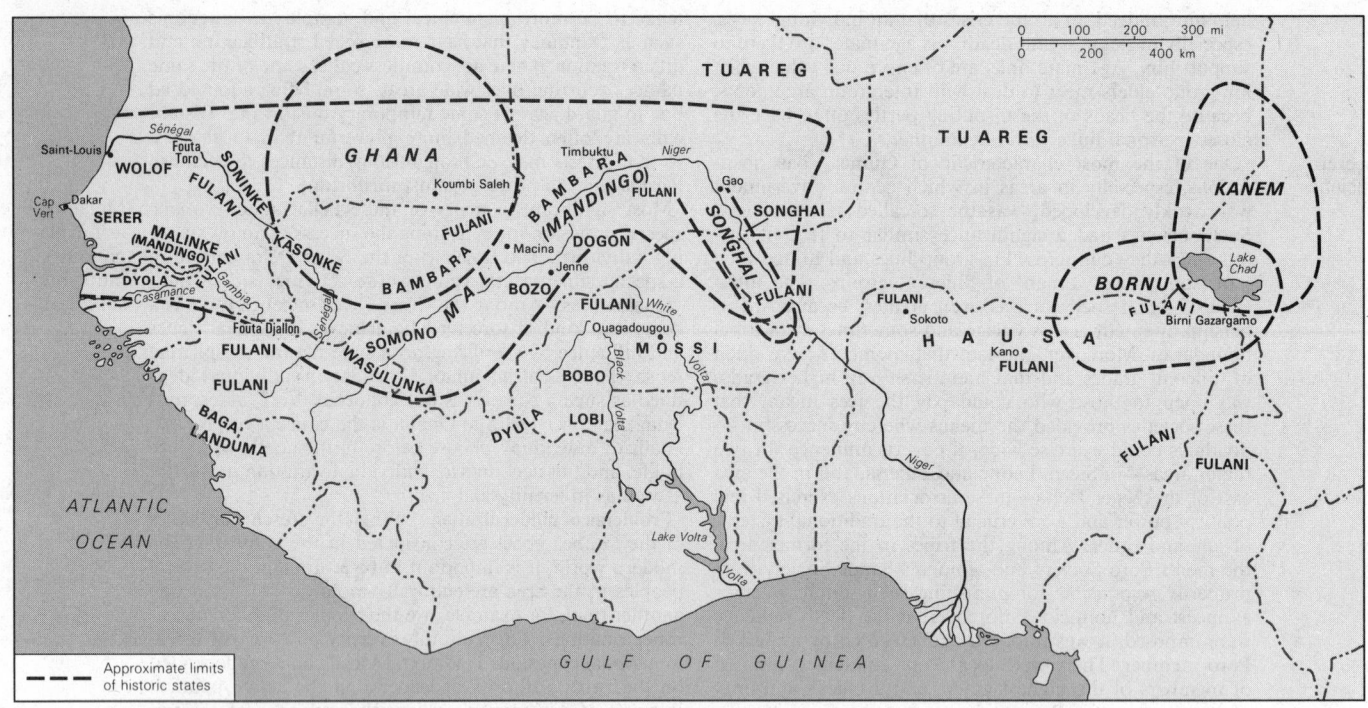

Distribution of the peoples of the western Sudan and locations of major historic states.

The Songhai are located largely in the region south of Timbuktu along the Niger; the Mossi in the Volta Basin, and a variety of smaller groups, such as the Dogon, Lobi, and Bobo, survive within the great bend of the Niger. Other small groups, such as the Diola (Yola or Jola), Landuma, and Baga are farther south. The Hausa are concentrated largely in northern Nigeria, though scattered in all the major trade centres of western Africa. The Fulani (Fulbe or Peul) are distributed widely from the west Atlantic Coast to Chad and Cameroon, though particularly concentrated in Senegal, Guinea, and northern Nigeria.

The continuous movements of people over the centuries have led to a complicated pattern of languages, but it is now held by some authorities that most of the languages should be considered as branches of one great Niger-Congo Family. This would include the Mande, Voltaic, Kwa, Adamawa-Eastern, and west Atlantic groups. The last includes such varied languages as Wolof, Serer, Fulani, and Diola. Linked to the Niger-Congo are the Kordofanian languages spoken in the area of the Nuba Hills. Other major families that have been distinguished are the Nilo-Saharan group, which includes Songhai, and the Afro-Asiatic, which comprises Ancient Egyptian, Berber, Cushite, and Hausa, among others. French is the language of communication among the elite of most nations of the western Sudan—namely, Senegal, Mali, Niger, Chad, and Guinea—but English is used in The Gambia, northern Ghana, and Nigeria.

Traditional culture patterns. Natural conditions in the Sudanic zone—drought, crop failures, epidemics of human and animal diseases—cause a great deal of uncertainty in peoples' lives, and they turn to the supernatural either in traditional rituals or in the Islāmic faith for reassurance and hope in time of trouble and the possibility of a greater reward in the next world. Life is also affected by the rhythm of the seasons, with a great contrast between the rainy season, the time of intense work on the farms, and the dry season, when the pace of life is slower. Man must adjust his pace to natural conditions to gain the best advantages from them and must also be in harmony with the unseen powers behind them. Conditions may often be harsh, but farm work, though hard, is an honourable occupation, and the average inhabitant remains surprisingly optimistic and enjoys life to the full. Some of this feeling derives from the fact that he does not face trouble alone but as a member of a group. He is linked to others by a complicated system of obligations—to kinsfolk, neighbours, and members of his age group—maintained

by constant visits, economic exchange, and mutual help at ceremonies. Everyone also feels links with the ancestors of the tribe. In general, the philosophy is one of bearing troubles patiently.

Social organization. *Local and territorial organization.* In the period from about AD 500 to 1470 the Sudanic zone was characterized by the rise and fall of a series of states and empires. The first to achieve eminence was Ghana, situated between the Sénégal and Niger rivers, deriving great wealth from trade in gold from the south and salt from the mines of the Sahara to the north. Ruins excavated at Koumbi Saleh are believed to be its capital, a town that could have contained 20,000 inhabitants. Ghana's power declined during the 11th century after nearly 20 years of attacks from the Almoravids, a Berber military and religious order from the Sahara, devoted to converting non-believers to Islām. The Mande-speaking people of Mali, on the Niger, developed the next great state, expanding rapidly in the mid-13th century, absorbing Ghana, and then gaining power over the trading cities of Timbuktu and Gao at the end of the major trans-Saharan trade routes. In the early 14th century the emperor of Mali, Mansa Mūsā, visited Egypt and Mecca. A large number of Arab scholars—teachers, lawyers, architects, doctors—established themselves in Mali at this time. After the death of Mansa Mūsā the empire began to break up. The city-state of Gao, under the Songhai, broke away toward the end of the 14th century and by the early 16th century had taken over control of the central region of the western Sudan. The power of Gao was extended over Timbuktu and Djénné, which were then at their height as centres of trade, learning, and religion. The power of the Songhai, however, was broken in 1591 by an invading army from Morocco, whose firearms provided a great advantage over the swords and spears of the Songhai.

Farther east, the Chad region received various waves of immigrants—hunters, fishermen, and farmers who introduced weaving, bronze work, and pottery. They came under the influence of two states: that of Kanem, north and east of Lake Chad, which was powerful between the 11th century (when Islām began to make itself felt) and the 15th; and that of Bornu, to the west of Lake Chad, the dominant state in the 16th and 17th centuries. Bornu's army had a strong cavalry force, wore chain mail, quilted armour, and iron helmets, and retained its medieval splendour down to the 19th century, with something of its former pageantry still to be seen at Islāmic festivals.

Society in all of these states was highly stratified, with

Rise and fall of states and empires

Patterns of leadership

a powerful ruling class controlling the wealth. A central ruler appointed regional governors or obtained the allegiance of outlying vassal chiefs, who were obliged to pay annual tribute and supply labour as needed. Well-organized armies both suppressed rebellion within the state and defended the boundaries against external enemies. War captives became slaves and performed much of the physical labour, carrying loads and working on farms. Islāmic religious teachers often formed part of the ruler's court, and gradually the people were converted to Islām. The ruler himself often filled a sacred role since it was believed that the vital forces of the kingdom—rain, good harvests, and fertility—depended on him. The rulers were patrons of various arts and crafts, and the courts included musicians, praise singers, storytellers, goldsmiths, leatherworkers, and so on. Men of slave origin could rise to high rank as court officials and enjoy power over the freeborn.

Traditions reflecting the greatness of the former states have been handed down in songs and legends, and traces of old social patterns are to be seen in the behaviour of present-day chiefs. But the average person's primary allegiance is to his village rather than to a larger unit, and he is concerned with the ruler only when he has a court case or must pay taxes.

Villages are divided into wards or quarters, the nucleus of each ward being the descendants of an original settler, though as time goes by, later settlers are absorbed. Often there is a meeting place for the men of the ward. Disputes within the village are commonly settled by the village head and the elders at a general meeting, or moot, in which the aim is to permit the parties to a dispute to state their grievances freely. The elders then arbitrate and seek to restore harmony and achieve a settlement, the meeting concluding with the group either praying together or sharing food or kola nuts.

The village head is drawn from the clan that was the first to settle in an area and clear land. In general, rights of land ownership are determined in the first place by the act of clearing, and then the descendants of this person have the right of usage. Land is held in units large enough to support a family and is not fragmented. Where land is short, people break away and found new settlements; and migration also tends to occur under political pressure.

The pattern of descent since the coming of Islām has generally emphasized the male line (patrilineal descent), though links with relatives on the mother's side are also important—the mother's brother, for example, always giving help and support to his nephews and nieces. In families of slave origin, ties through the female line remain strong because the owner of the mother also owned the children born to her. In pre-Islāmic times, rights to rule could be transmitted through the female line, though the incumbent had to be male. People recognize kin groups in which they know the exact blood relationships (lineages) and that share rights over land and other privileges and obligations; but they also feel themselves related to larger groups (clans), descended from remote ancestors who bear the same name or observe the same ritual prohibitions.

Marital customs

Family and kinship patterns. In arrangements for marriage, the family of the groom pays the family of the bride a sum of money known as the brideprice, which is returnable if the marriage fails through the fault of the wife. Ordinarily parents use the money received for a daughter to pay for a wife for a son. Households are normally larger than the nuclear family of husband and wife, for polygyny is permitted. The general pattern, however, is for each wife to have her own house, in which she cooks for herself and her children, taking her turn to cook for and sleep with her husband (though when a woman is pregnant or suckling a child she refrains from intercourse with her husband). A young widow will remarry, usually the brother of her deceased husband (the institution of the levirate), thus maintaining the link between the two families. If a marriage payment has been made and the fiancée dies, then a sister will replace her (the sororate). A widow who is old will often nominally remarry, but in practice be supported by her children, and often will stay with a son. The strongest emotional ties are not so much between husband and wife as between mother and children. An affectionate type of joking prevails between grandparents and grandchildren, and at weaning time small children are often sent to stay with maternal grandparents. A joking relationship also holds between cross-cousins (children of siblings, of the opposite sex), and a cross-cousin has specific roles at naming, marriage, and burial rites.

There is a marked division of labour between the sexes: the women are concerned with preparing food, caring for the children, drawing water, washing clothes, making pottery, looking after poultry, gathering leaves, fruits, and firewood, and so on, whereas men are concerned with looking after large animals such as cattle, horses, donkeys, and large sheep and with hunting, clearing land for agriculture, fishing, butchering, house building, fencing, woodcarving, leather-working, and smithing. Carding cotton and spinning is women's work; weaving is men's. Women have their own meeting place, at the well or stream; men have a place in a village square. The farming tools used are often different for men and women.

Stratification. Although egalitarian relationships are found in many non-Islāmic groups, such as the Diola and some pastoral Fulani, a system of social stratification is characteristic of most western Sudanic peoples. The essential pattern consists of such categories as (1) the royal families, often deriving from foreign conquering elements; (2) the nobles, members of high-ranking lineages who constitute the military leaders or provincial governors and who may have the power of electing the ruler from among suitable royal candidates; (3) the freeborn, who are landowners and farmers and sometimes traders; (4) the people of slave origin, who are objects of social discrimination or differentiation despite official abolition of the slave trade; and (5) the low-caste craftsmen, which include musicians, praise singers, professional storytellers and entertainers, smiths (whether blacksmiths, goldsmiths, or silversmiths), leatherworkers, and certain types of woodworkers. These craftsmen can marry only within their own special category, cannot lose their low status even if they should abandon their trade, and are looked down upon by the freeborn, even though they may be wealthier. Islāmic scholars and their families are accorded high prestige.

Officials appointed by rulers could be either freeborn or of slave origin, with the result that "slaves" often came to enjoy greater power than the freeborn. Today there is also differentiation based on wealth acquired by trade and on status in positions of government service. Since independence from colonial rule, those who have attained prominence in political parties or the military have reached the chief positions of power.

Socialization and education. In African cultures ties between mother and child are extremely close. From birth to 15 months the child is carried on the mother's back; the child is fed at the slightest demand; and the mother plays with, sings to, and cuddles the child at every opportunity. Adults in general like children, hold them, protect them, and play with them. Grandmothers, in particular, are indulgent. The result is that the child grows up feeling valued and loved. There is, however, the very real threat of illness and death. Infant mortality, caused mainly by malaria, is high, and childhood illnesses—measles, whooping cough, influenza, and pneumonia, as well as more serious epidemics of smallpox and meningitis—take a heavy toll up to the age of five.

Children begin to take part in the work patterns of the community at an early age and are not as a rule kept separate from adults. Small children imitate adult activities in their games and then begin to undertake the lighter tasks. Girls help to pound grain with pestle and mortar, draw water, use winnowing baskets, fetch firewood, and so on. Boys drive off birds and monkeys from the farms and then help in weeding as they become older, until finally they are able to undertake a young man's share of cultivation. Among cattle-keeping groups, boys learn their adult roles by handling calves.

Initiation ceremonies mark the transformation from the status of child to that of adult. For males the ceremonies are generally associated with either circumcision (though many Muslims now have their sons circumcised in infancy) or, in some areas, scarification; death through infec-

Child care

Initiation ceremonies

tion was not uncommon, though now modern antiseptics may be used. The ceremonies involve both a physical separation, the initiates living outside the village in the "bush," and a ritual death, followed by rebirth when they return to village life. During initiation, they are harshly punished for their faults (sometimes for crimes committed before initiation, such as stealing); they are instructed in the traditions of their society and learn secret means of male communication, unknown to women or children. The initiates remain in seclusion for a period varying from several weeks to several months, and those who have gone through initiation together, irrespective of their age, retain close ties throughout life.

Economic systems. *Settlement patterns and housing.* The characteristic settlement is a concentrated village consisting of fenced-off clusters of houses (compounds) occupied by members of a lineage and their spouses. Because for hundreds of years villagers led an uncertain life, liable to ravage by invaders and slave traders, many villages were built on sites afforded some protection by rivers or fortified by earthen walls. These old fortifications have almost all disappeared except for the great walled cities of Northern Nigeria. The general trend during the 20th century has been for smaller and more widely dispersed villages, as people have cleared more land for agriculture.

Among the Wolof, the average population of a village is only about 100, and the compounds are built around an open village square. In the past, the houses were generally circular, with walls of either millet stalk or reed, but now a rectangular form is more common, with mud walls and roofing often of imported zinc or aluminum sheeting. Fulani settlements tend to be even smaller and consist of temporary huts with walls of reed or of matting woven from grass. Malinke villages, on the other hand, tend to be larger, with some 1,000 to 2,000 people, the houses generally being mud walled with a conical roof thatched with grass. In the north, the Tuareg are tent dwellers. In general, the most common western Sudanic house is circular, but the square or rectangular form is not necessarily recent, for excavations of old towns in ancient Ghana have revealed old rectangular houses.

In addition to the farming villages, the western Sudan is characterized by very large towns, either the capitals of the old states or trading towns at the southern end of the various trans-Saharan trade routes, such as Kano and Timbuktu. There, architecture is often influenced by North African forms—mosques and fortresses in particular being designed after Arab patterns. At present, with the availability of imported sheeting for roofs and locally manufactured cement, richer people are building more permanent houses that are square or rectangular.

Patterns of production and technology. Few traces are now to be found either of purely hunting and gathering groups or of fishing communities, except for such peoples as the Somono and Bozo fishermen of the Niger. Most in-

Patterns of agriculture

habitants are agriculturalists, dependent on the cultivation of such crops as millet and sorghum for food and peanuts (groundnuts) for cash. The system is one of shifting cultivation: the savanna land is cleared by ax and cutlass, the residue burned, and the crops planted. The hardest work is the continuous back-breaking struggle against weeds, the principal tool being a small hand hoe; and when the crops are ripening, they need to be protected against swarms of birds. Crop rotation is customary, but the soil nevertheless becomes exhausted after several years of cultivation and is then allowed to revert to bush. Only patches around the villages, fertilized by household rubbish, animal manure, and so on, can be kept under continuous cultivation. In such patches tomatoes, peppers, beans, eggplants, maize, and condiments can be grown. On good soils cotton cultivation is possible.

The single rainy season demands a considerable amount of extremely hard work in a very short period of time, and irregularities in the rainfall, whether drought or cloudburst, can cause crop damage and a food shortage. Formerly, farmers suffered losses through plagues of locusts, but international control has virtually eliminated this plague. People supplement the cultivated crops, particularly in times of shortage, with wild fruits and roots. The fruits

of the baobab (*Adansonia digitata*), nete (*Parkia biglobosa*), and tamarind (*Tamarindus indica*) are particularly important, while over much of the more northern zone, the shea-butter tree (*Butyrospermum parkii*) is a source of vegetable oil. In regions with a more abundant water supply, like the Gambia and Casamance valleys, rice is the dominant crop.

The dry season is a period devoted to visiting friends, trading, house building and making repairs, engaging in arts and crafts (pottery, mats, textiles, basketry), and participating in such ceremonial events as marriages and initiation ceremonies.

Another important lifestyle is that of the pastoralists. The central region of the western Sudan, with its extensive grasslands, provides opportunities for raising large herds of cattle. The Fulani are the main cattle owners and are found from the west Atlantic Coast to Chad and Cameroon. Some are entirely nomadic, living in temporary shelters and moving between wet-season and dry-season grazing areas. Others stay in fixed villages, build more permanent houses, engage in farming—producing excellent crops because of the cattle manure—and still maintain large herds of cattle. The men are concerned with the care of animals, determining the time for movement, selecting grazing areas, and seeing that the animals are watered. Women's occupations include domestic tasks, drawing water for household use, collecting firewood, cooking, and processing and selling milk. Both the watering places and markets in the towns are important meeting places where the Fulani exchange vital information about the state of pastures, water, animal diseases, and politics. The cattle population has increased rapidly as the result of inoculations against such diseases as rinderpest, but the Fulani feel personally attached to their cattle, in which their wealth and well-being are involved, and are reluctant to sell animals for slaughter.

Pastoralism

Exchange system. The western Sudan has always been a highway and crossroads for long-distance trading. Today, manufactured goods entering the Atlantic ports, including cloth, medicines, and transistor radios, are taken inland. Sudanese traders travel to Sierra Leone, Ghana, and the Congo Basin to deal in diamonds, which eventually find their way to the Near East. Gold still crosses the Sahara to North Africa, and salt from the Saharan mines comes by camel caravan to the Niger River. Caffeine-containing kola nuts from the Guinea Coast rain forests are transported north in large quantities; they are in great demand among the farmers for assuaging hunger and thirst and for use in ritual and sociable contexts. Hausa leatherwork is widely traded.

The major trade routes across the Sahara are supplemented by lateral routes along the Niger and along the Sénégal and Gambia river valleys. For long periods, cowrie shells were adopted as a form of currency, but for certain commodities a system of direct barter prevailed; Fulani herdsmen, for example, exchanged milk and butter for grain.

Belief systems. Indigenous systems of belief unaffected by Islām involved the concept of the essential unity of the visible and invisible worlds, man being accorded the dominant position in the system. Forces in plants, animals, and minerals are made known to man through ancestors and can be used for either good or evil, man having the moral responsibility for making the choice. Living persons are a continuation of the life stream of the first beings. Ancestors watch over the living and act as intermediaries between them and the creator of the universe, who is now remote from men, even though his power is supreme. The ancestors indicate their wishes through dreams sent to the elders, while the living communicate with the ancestors through prayer and sacrifice, the blood of sacrificed animals setting in motion certain latent spiritual forces. The spirit world is also evoked by persons wearing carved masks during special ceremonies; associated dances and drumming cleanse, revigorate, and protect the community. The masks themselves are the abode of spirits, and carvers feel inspired by supernatural powers.

Animistic beliefs

Religious beliefs reinforce the traditional values of society, for it is believed that lack of harmony in the community and breaches of traditional law and custom are followed by such disasters as drought, disease, and crop failure. Man is threatened by forces outside the community—evil spirits that are believed to cause mental disorders and physical abnormalities—and by people inside the community in whom evil grows—witches, who can cause harm to both human beings and crops through a witch substance inside them, and sorcerers, who perform deliberate acts of evil magic. Charms are worn and protective devices set up to guard against such dangers, while diviners seek to detect both witches and sorcerers. Diviners are consulted by individuals with problems; it is their role to trace the causes of troubles, using such techniques as casting cowrie shells or reading patterns in sand to see into the spiritual world; and then to indicate the proper measures to be taken. Diviners provide treatment at the physical level by prescribing herbs and medicines, at the psychological level by listening to confessions and providing reassurance, and at the social level by trying to disperse tensions between individuals.

Influences of Islām

Islām has now spread widely throughout the western Sudan, and between 60 and 70 percent of the people are nominally Muslim. Most attend services at the mosques, observe Ramadān (the month of fasting), say the daily prayers, and give alms generously; and a few are able to make the pilgrimage to Mecca. Wherever Islām is dominant, Muslim religious teachers have taken over the role of traditional diviners in determining the causes of troubles, and they provide remedies in conformity with Islāmic patterns. Children are given religious instruction in which they learn the prayers, recite long passages from the Qur'ān, and acquire the rudiments of Arabic writing. The traditional ritual dances and masked performances are gradually disappearing or being greatly modified as a result of opposition from Muslim teachers. Nevertheless, many of the traditional beliefs about spiritual beings still remain in people's minds relatively unchanged. Christianity has had little effect in the western Sudan, except marginally in the coastal cities of Senegal and The Gambia.

Oral literature. The region is extremely rich in oral literature: proverbs; myths of origin; animal stories in which lion, hyena, and hare play prominent parts; epics; and tales about people (neglected orphans, disobedient children, the rivalry of co-wives, jealous husbands, deceitful wives, unjust rulers) and about supernatural forces (encounters with good and evil spirits, the terrible deeds of witches and sorcerers). Narration involves both entertainment and education, for the young learn something of the values of the community and acquire knowledge of approved and disapproved behaviour. There is always a high degree of audience involvement, the listeners either replying to the narrator's questions or singing the rhythmical choruses that form part of the narrative style. Storytellers act the roles of the various characters with great effectiveness, and the narration becomes a highly rhythmical performance leading up to a dramatic climax.

Evolution of the cultures. In general, the western Sudan has been slow to change, largely because of long distances and problems of communication and because of the generally low level of income throughout the area. Migrants from the interior have gone south to work in the mines and cocoa plantations of Ghana or in the coffee, cocoa, and banana plantations of the Ivory Coast or to cultivate peanuts in the Sénégal and the Casamance river valleys; but for the most part they revert to traditional ways when they return home.

In moving to the cities and towns of the coastal zone, migrants from the same tribe or village tend to live in the same area of town and spend their leisure time together. Disputes between people of the same ethnic group are ordinarily settled by the elders of that group according to traditional law and custom and are not taken to the state court. Voluntary associations are formed for mutual aid and entertainment.

The new town dwellers

In general, Islāmic influence has continued to spread slowly and steadily among animistic groups, for a Muslim has higher status than an animist outside his own community.

Change in agriculture has been slight. Mechanized agricultural projects have usually been unsuccessful because of the high costs of maintaining machinery. In Senegal, The Gambia, Mali, and Niger, light plows and weeding equipment drawn by donkeys, horses, and oxen have become popular and have led to an increase in the production of the cash crop, peanuts. The growth of cooperative societies has enabled farmers to receive greater cash benefits, and the improvement of roads and the increase in motor transport have made the marketing of produce easier.

In the Niger and Chad republics, spectacular success has followed programs of water prospecting. Artesian water is now tapped by boreholes, and artificial water holes have been created, designed to store water during the dry season. This has enabled the semi-nomadic cattle owners to settle and make use of the rich pasture land available, the limiting factor previously being the lack of water for cattle. In the 1970s, however, recurring droughts caused heavy loss of livestock and led to desertification of overexploited marginal lands.

(D.P.Ga./Ed.)

HISTORY

Early history

A reasonable body of sources for the writing of western African history begins to be available from about AD 1000. Three centuries earlier, the Arabs had completed their conquest of Africa north of the Sahara and so came into possession of the northern termini of trade routes reaching across the desert to West Africa. The lively school of geographers and historians that flourished in the Arab world from about the 9th to the 14th century thus secured access to growing amounts of information about what they called the *bilād as-sūdān*, the territory of the Negro peoples south of the Sahara.

ARABS IN WEST AFRICA

This information has its limitations. The Muslim writers, contemptuous of non-Islāmic societies, passed on little of what they must have known about the organization of pagan black societies and tended to concentrate on and condemn what struck them as their more monstrous aberrations. Conversely, they doubtless exaggerated the importance of the Islāmization which entered western Africa with the Muslim traders crossing the Sahara. The earliest first-hand account of West Africa is probably that of the world traveller Ibn Baṭṭūṭah, who visited the western Sudan in 1352–53. Finally, the North African merchants did not penetrate into West Africa beyond the urban centres of trade and government that existed or came to develop on the northern fringes of the cultivable savannas fronting the Sahara. Their *bilād as-sūdān* was in fact only the northern marches.

Nevertheless, the picture of western Africa given in the early Muslim writings is of major interest. It is apparent that right from the beginnings of Arab contact, the organization of the more northerly western African peoples was not solely tribal. They had considerable towns and cities that were supported by a developed agriculture. They had organized networks of markets and trade and a developed system of monarchical government. Kings, whose claim to power was based on descent from the mythical divine founding ancestors of their ethnic groups, taxed trade and levied tribute on the agricultural villages through their possession of bodies of retainers who provided them both with military force and with a hierarchy of officials.

It seems likely that there was an increase in the volume of trans-Saharan trade following the organization of North Africa under Muslim dynasties and that this growth of international trade with western Africa stimulated the

Principal kingdoms and peoples of West Africa, 11th–16th centuries.

From J. Fage, *An Atlas of African History*; Edward Arnold (Publishers) Ltd.

The
kingdoms
of Kanem
and Ghana

growth there of internal trade, urbanization, and monarchical government. Certainly the control of trade, towns, and government in western Africa became increasingly Islāmic in form. But it is quite clear that the foundations for the economic and political development of the western Sudan were in existence before the time of contact with Muslim traders or authors. Early Muslim interest was concentrated on two major western African kingdoms: Kanem, in the east, north of Lake Chad; and Ghana, in the extreme west, on the borders of modern Mauritania and Mali. The Muslim sources, which are broadly confirmed by local tradition, indicate that the kingdom of Kanem was being formed during the 9th and 10th centuries through an interaction between Saharan nomads and agricultural village communities. But ancient Ghana (not to be confused with its modern namesake, considerably further to the south and east) had already reached levels of organization that presuppose several centuries of continuing development.

The earliest extant Arabic reference to a kingdom of Ghana dates from the close of the 8th century. In the middle of the 11th century, the Córdoban geographer Abū U'bayd al-Bakrī described its capital, court, and trade in some detail. The capital was made up of two towns, a stone-built town inhabited by the Muslim traders and a mud-built one of the local Mande in which the king had his walled palace. Their centres were six miles apart, and the whole of the intervening country was more or less built up. The considerable population was supported by the produce of surrounding farms that were watered from wells. The court displayed many signs of wealth and power, and the king had under him a considerable number of satellite rulers. A principal part of his revenue was derived from regular taxes on trade. The mainstay of this trade was the exchange of gold, which Ghana's own merchants brought from lands to the south, for salt, which the northern traders brought in from salt deposits in the Sahara.

Al-Bakrī's description is broadly confirmed by archaeology. The region in which ancient Ghana was situated contains the ruins of a considerable number of stone-built towns that must have been supported by considerable agricultural and commercial activity; those at Koumbi Saleh are generally identified with the capital described by al-Bakrī.

The relatively extensive Muslim interest in Ghana was undoubtedly due to its importance as a source of gold. Kanem seems to have been less important commercially; the main interest of the Muslim authors seems to have been in the quasi-divine status of its kings, which offended their Muslim principles. Other western African kingdoms undoubtedly existed at this time, but the Muslim sources record little of them beyond their names and approximate locations. Thus between Ghana and Kanem was Kawkaw, perhaps the nucleus of the later Songhai kingdom of Gao. Malel, to the south of Ghana, may similarly have been a prototype of the later Mande kingdom of Mali, which ultimately was to eclipse and absorb Ghana itself.

Other
kingdoms

There are perhaps three possible—and not mutually exclusive—explanations for the origins and development of the kingdoms that Arab trade and scholarship had revealed by about AD 1000. The first is that they were the result of the invasion of agricultural territory by pastoralists from the Sahara who belonged to the Libyan Berber tribes speaking Hamitic languages who were the dominant stock of North Africa before its conquest by the Arabs.

This is the explanation often given in western Sudanese traditions and chronicles. From about the 15th century onward, many of these were preserved by local authors who wrote in Arabic and were Muslims, and who thus had some incentive to link the history of their peoples with that of North Africa and with the adjacent Near East. It was also the explanation favoured by European historians of the later 19th and earlier 20th centuries when Europeans were themselves conquering and colonizing black Africa. There thus evolved the so-called "Hamitic hypothesis," by which it was generally supposed that any progress and development among agricultural blacks was the result of conquest or infiltration by pastoralists from northern or northeastern Africa. Specifically, it was supposed that many of the ideas and institutions of tribal monarchy had spread through Africa by diffusion from the ancient civilization of Egypt and of the Nile valley.

There can be no doubt that over the centuries pastoralists from the Sahara have indeed advanced and conquered southward. But not all of these were Libyan Berbers or "Hamites"; some, such as the dynasts of Kanem, were Negroid in language and culture. Nor is it easy to understand how mobile desert pastoral tribes could be effective transmitters of ideas and institutions from the settled civilization of the Nile Valley to other agricultural lands in western Africa. It would seem more probable that conquering pastoralists who did succeed in establishing new kingdoms and dynasties in western Africa should do so by taking over existing monarchies, perhaps city-states or even "village-states," and amalgamating these into larger units. Some early western African traditions can certainly be interpreted in this sense.

This leads to the second explanation for the origins and development of monarchical statehood among the western African tribes. There is archaeological evidence for the evolution of a cattle-herding and agricultural economy among a mixed population of Libyan Berber and black agricultural peoples in the Sahara by at least 4000 BC; *i.e.,* more or less contemporary with similar developments in the Nile Valley. The desiccation of the Sahara and the evolution of its present desert between about 8000 and 2000 BC must have occasioned an outflowing of population in which the blacks concentrated in the savannas to the south of it. Here, in favourable riverine or lacustrine environments, it seems reasonable to suppose that the same desire to avoid conflicts over land and water rights and to control and exploit agricultural surpluses, which had led in the exceptionally fertile but extremely constricted environment of the Nile Valley to the dramatic kingship and civilization of the pharaohs, should have occasioned the evolution of similar if less spectacular monarchies.

But it should be noted that the major western African monarchies known to the Arabs by about AD 1000 were situated not in the well watered lands along the Sénégal and Niger valleys nor around Lake Chad but north of these, in the less favoured agricultural territory between them and the southern edges of the Sahara. This suggests that a third factor in the evolution of these northern monarchies was the influence of long-distance trade. The western African kingdoms had their own resources of iron, which in some cases were being worked from at least 300 BC, but they imported other metals, notably copper, together with horses, luxury manufactures, and—above all—salt, a vital commodity that was scarce in all western Africa except the coastlands. In exchange they could offer gold, ivory, certain agricultural commodities, and also slaves.

The exchange across the Sahara of such commodities probably goes back to times before the establishment of the modern desert. The emergence of the desert did not lead to the cessation of the trade, but meant that its surviving pastoralists were encouraged to organize regular trans-Saharan expeditions for trade and plunder. Herodotus and other classical authors suggest that by about 500 BC the Sahara was being crossed in horse-drawn chariots, and this has been confirmed by the discovery in modern times of large numbers of drawings of such vehicles on rocks in the desert. These seem to be deployed along two principal routes, starting from the Fezzan and from southern Morocco, and both leading toward the Upper Niger and Sénégal. This suggests that a principal incentive for trans-Saharan traffic was the demand of the Mediterranean civilizations for the alluvial gold of these river valleys. It was doubtless this demand that led 6th-century Carthage to try to open up direct sea trade with western Africa along the Atlantic coast. But, despite Hanno's expedition, the Carthaginians do not seem to have been capable of opening up a regular sea trade with western Africa. The links with western Africa remained firmly in the hands of the Saharan tribes, though about the beginning of the Christian era, camels came into use to supplant the horse-drawn vehicles.

The profits to be obtained by distributing Saharan and Mediterranean produce in western Africa, and by controlling the collection and export of the western African commodities that were exchanged for them, must have been a powerful factor in encouraging the kings of communities on the southern fringes of the Sahara to extend their rule by conquest over adjacent similar communities. Control over more extensive territories meant that by tribute and taxation they could acquire greater stocks of goods for exchange with North Africa and the Sahara and more clients and slaves to extend their power at the expense of their neighbours. Some of their increased manpower could be mounted on horses, obtained from the Saharan trade, to increase the mobility and power of their armed forces over the open savannas. It is tolerably certain that the power of the kings of ancient Ghana, controlling the export of gold from the Sénégal and Niger valleys, was built up in this way.

THE STATES OF THE SUDAN

The early kingdoms and empires of the western Sudan. In the 10th century, the kings of Ghana extended their sway over the Ṣanhājah, the congeries of Berber nomadic tribes living around Audaghost, just north of their kingdom, who supplied them with salt and North African goods.

This move must have upset the economic balance between agricultural Ghana and the pastoral Ṣanhājah, and ultimately it provoked a reaction. Like the North African Berbers, the Ṣanhājah tribes were already to some extent Islāmized, and they shortly found in a militant, puritanical version of Islām the means to eliminate their tribal differences and to unite in the movement known to history as the Almoravids. In the middle of the 11th century they began to conquer the productive lands on either side of the western Sahara, and for about 20 years from about 1076 onward, the Almoravids occupied Ghana.

One important result of this occupation, following as it did upon some centuries of trading contact by Muslims, was that the ruling and merchant classes of the western Sudan became converted to Islām—though in the case of the rulers the conversion was for many centuries not whole-hearted. The justification for a king's claim to enforce his rule over his subjects, who remained pagan, was his descent from the original ancestor who had first settled the land and, by accommodation with its deities and spirits, had developed and controlled it for agriculture. If he were not to be rejected and replaced as king by a rival member of its royal family, he had to continue to observe the ancestral and land cult rites in which he was the principal figure.

However, the depredations of the Almoravids' herds and their quarrels over the spoils of conquest undermined the prosperity of agriculture in the marginal environment of Ghana and were factors in bringing about the decay of the polity they had conquered. More southerly Mande groups, many of which had formed satellite kingdoms of the Ghana empire, began to act independently and to compete among themselves for primacy. Eventually in about 1235, in the time of a king called Sundiata, the Keita kings of Mali, in the well-watered and gold-bearing lands of the uppermost Niger Valley, gained ascendancy and incorporated what was left of ancient Ghana into their own and considerably more extensive empire.

The rise of Mali

The Keita clan seem originally to have been traders from lower down the Niger, and the strategy of their empire was to extend their power down river to the Niger Bend and to its trading cities of Timbuktu and Gao, which lay at the foot of the shortest trans-Saharan routes. The initial success of the Almoravids and their subsequent rapid decline had upset the stability of the more westerly caravan roads leading to Ghana, while by the 13th century Ifrīqīyah and Egypt provided more stable bases for trans-Saharan trade than did Morocco. The Niger River provided a natural means of communication from Mali and its goldfields to Timbuktu and to Gao and also provided Mali's merchants with the possibility of opening up trade elsewhere in black western Africa. By the 14th century, Mande merchants, the Dyula (Dioula), were trading to as far east as the city states of the Hausa, between Lake Chad and the Niger. By about the same time they had also begun to develop a new trade route southeastward from Jenne (modern Djénné, Mali), on a southerly tributary of the Niger, toward goldfields that were being opened up along the Black Volta and further south still, in what is now modern Ghana.

These Mande merchants were Muslims, and their activities led to a considerable expansion of Islām among the trading classes of West Africa and, with the qualification mentioned earlier, also among its kings. Thus the first conversions of Hausa monarchs seem to date from the 14th or 15th centuries. The Mali kings themselves valued

The control of land and water rights

The introduction of the camel

Islām for the commercial and diplomatic advantages it gave them, and some of them, of whom the best known is Mansa Mūsā (1307–32), made notable pilgrimages to Mecca via Egypt. As may be seen from Ibn Baṭṭūṭah's account of his travels in 1352–53, the essentially pagan society of the western Sudan became open to a considerable degree of Islāmic influence, and literacy and even scholarship became firmly established in its major cities.

The success of the Mali empire depended, however, on its rulers maintaining firm control of the Niger waterway. This in its turn depended on their maintaining control over a non-Mande people, the Songhai, who monopolized the fishing and canoe transport of the Middle Niger. The Songhai had an independent monarchical tradition of their own, and Mande control of their capital, Gao, proved somewhat fitful. During the 15th century it was lost altogether, and eventually a Songhai king arose, Sonni 'Alī (1464–92), who, appealing to traditional Songhai paganism against the Islāmic universalism of the Mande system, destroyed the Mali empire by ceaseless military campaigning and erected in its place a new empire ruled from Gao. But if this empire were to be profitable and strong, the Songhai needed the Mande as much as the Mande had needed the Songhai. After Sonni 'Alī's death, power passed to one of his former generals, al-Ḥājj Muḥammad Askia (1493–1528), who was both a Mande and a Muslim, and thereafter there was a continual struggle for power between the two groups.

The extent of the Songhai empire

The Songhai empire was never strong in the west, where a number of Mande kingdoms remained in the tradition of Ghana and Mali, but was more effective to the east. Here the kingdom of Kanem, whose kings had become Islāmized in the 11th century, had declined during the 14th and 15th centuries following quarrels among its aristocracy when it was subject to pressure from new nomad invasions. Eventually, however, the Kanem kings reestablished their state in their former province of Bornu in the southwest, close by the Hausa kingdoms. But in the 16th century, Songhai was the most important external influence over the latter, which began to grow in power and importance. South of the Niger Bend, the kingdoms of the Mossi–Dagomba peoples were emerging, founded by bands of cavaliers who were probably related to the ruling families to the northeast.

Songhai was strong enough to extend its sway northward across the Sahara to as far as the salt mines of Taghaza close to the Moroccan borders. This upset the balance of trans-Saharan trade, as Ghana's attempt to control the Ṣanhājah had done, and in 1591 finally provoked effective retaliation from the Sa'dī dynasty of Morocco. An expeditionary force of some 4,000 soldiers was sent across the Sahara and took the important cities of Gao, Timbuktu, and Jenne. The Moroccans had firearms, but their success against the much larger numbers of the Songhai army was also facilitated by the internal divisions of the Songhai monarchy. For a time the profits of this enterprise were considerable, but the Moroccans were not strong enough to control the network of trade routes within western Africa that brought gold and other produce to the Niger cities. Ultimately the main gainers from their conquest were the Saharan tribes, essentially Berber in origin (such as the Tuareg), but now increasingly Muslim and even Arabized, who finally levied tribute on the descendants of the Moroccan soldiers who formed the military caste (Arma) of Gao, Timbuktu, and Jenne.

Firearms also came to the Sudan about the same time through the trading relations that existed between Bornu and the Ottoman Turks in North Africa. Together with Muslim cavalry, they enabled Idris Alawma of Bornu (end of 16th century) to impose a Muslim bureaucracy on his pagan subjects and to reconquer Kanem. This revival of the Kanem–Bornu dynasty, however, was relatively short-lived. By the 18th century it was the much smaller Hausa kingdoms, especially Kano and Katsina—which had learned much from Mande commercial and industrial experience and had developed a trading network to the south to rival that of the Mande themselves—that took the leading role in western Africa's external trade with North Africa across the Sahara.

The wider influence of the Sudanic kingdoms. The development of such major Sudanic kingdoms and empires as Ghana, Mali, Songhai, the Hausa states, and Kanem–Bornu along the southern fringes of the Sahara had a number of important consequences for the history of western Africa as a whole. For example, it provided the background for the expansion of the Fulani, the only pastoral western African people (also variously known as Fulbe, Fula, Fellata, and Peul).

The fact that, uniquely in western Africa, the Fulani are pastoralists and that physically they have some non-Negroid traits has led to suggestions that they were originally a Saharan people. The Fulani language, however, is classified as part of the Niger-Congo family (spoken principally by peoples of the Negroid race), and the earliest historical documentation reports that the Fulani were living in the westernmost Sudan close by ancient Ghana. The development of this organized kingdom thrust pastoral peoples outward, and the ancestors of the modern Fulani seem to have chosen to settle to the southwest, toward the Middle Sénégal Valley. But here another group settled, and (from the 11th century) an Islāmized Negro kingdom evolved, that of Tekrur. Some Fulani participated in this kingdom and became Tukulor (Toucouleur)—the Tukulor and Fulani languages being practically identical. Some, however, chose not to accept the settled way of life and, to preserve their traditional pastoral and religious customs, migrated eastward over the savanna grasslands. Grazing land was available between the agricultural villages, and the growing towns provided the Fulani with markets where they could exchange their pastoral produce for agricultural and manufactured goods. Eventually some Fulani settled in these towns, no doubt initially as trading agents for their fellows in the countryside, where the bulk of the Fulani continued to live under their own leaders, aloof from the social and political life of the cultivators, though increasingly paying rent for their grazing and rendering military service to the settled authorities.

The Fulani diaspora

In this way, by the 15th century, large numbers of Fulani had settled in the Fouta Djallon and in and around Macina, the inland delta country of the Niger upstream of Timbuktu, and they were beginning to appear as far east as Hausaland, where today perhaps as many as 4,000,000 of their descendants are living. By the 16th century, the Fulani were appearing in Bornu, and by the 18th century large numbers of them were settling in the grassy uplands of the Cameroons. Although the bulk of the Fulani remained animists, gradually significant numbers of them became Muslims and indeed provided some of the leaders of Islām in western Africa.

The growth of organized statehood in the western African savannas also had important consequences for more southerly lands and peoples. Unsuccessful contestants for power in the major savanna states sometimes moved off toward the south. Traders from the major savanna states, especially from Mali and, later, from the Hausa kingdoms, also settled in the south as their trading networks developed, and they often had important political, as well as economic, influences on the tribal groups with whom they came to live. The consequences of these two kinds of movement, which were sometimes interlinked, can best be considered in two sections—firstly, those deriving from developments originating in the Mande sphere in the western savannas, and secondly, those deriving from the Hausa–Bornu region in the east.

Southerly movements

In the west, one notable emigration was that of the Susu, a Mande people who had been defeated by the Keita in the 13th-century struggle for the inheritance of ancient Ghana. This emigration created a wedge of Mande-speaking people close by the Atlantic in the modern Republic of Guinea and in northern Sierra Leone among peoples who had not advanced politically beyond the village level. With the subsequent growth of Mali's power, other smaller groups—sometimes traders, sometimes conquerors, often both—also infiltrated these western Atlantic coastlands. They began to organize their peoples into petty kingdoms that tended to owe a nominal allegiance to Mali. Major incentives for these migratory movements seem to have been the desire to gain access to coastal supplies of

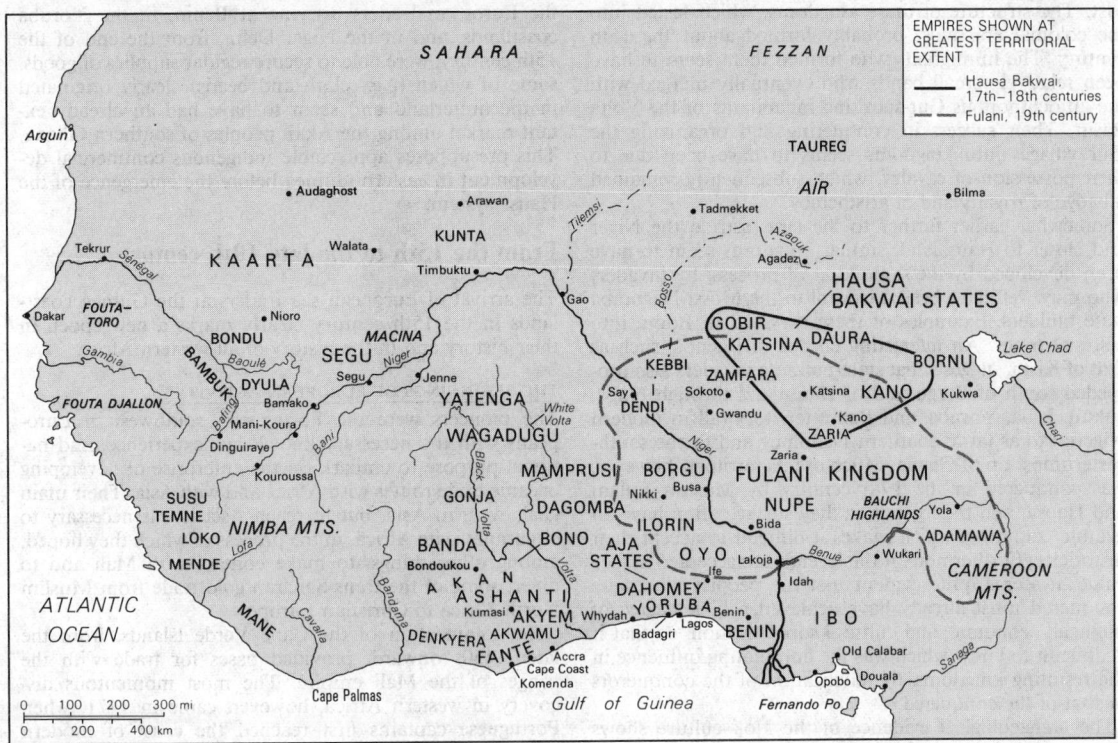

Principal kingdoms and peoples of West Africa, 17th–19th century.

From J. Fage, *An Atlas of African History,* Edward Arnold (Publishers) Ltd.

salt and, from the 15th century onward, to the foreign merchandise brought by European sea traders.

In the 16th century, the West Atlantic coastlands were invaded by yet another Mande group, the Mane, who advanced westward parallel to the coast from Liberia onward. These were military bands that systematically attacked and overcame the villages of each tribal group they came across. Some of them would stay behind to organize these conquests into small kingdoms, while others, reinforced by auxiliaries recruited from among their victims, would proceed further west to repeat the pattern. Their advance was halted only when they came up against the Susu. South and east of the Susu, however, the West Atlantic social and ethnic patterns were considerably altered by the actions of the Mane. New Mande-speaking groups were formed, such as the Mende and Loko, while some West Atlantic peoples who retained their original language, such as the Temne, accepted a new aristocracy of Mane provenance.

The Mane advance into the West Atlantic coastlands from the east may have been connected with the growth of Mande influence in the Ivory Coast and in modern Ghana. This was commercial in origin, Dyula merchants developing trade routes in search of gold, slaves, and kola nuts, in exchange for which they offered salt, cloth, and other Sudanic or North African goods. It is known that by 1500 the Dyula were trading as far south as the coast of modern Ghana, and that their first contact with the Akan peoples who populate almost all the southern half of this territory was in fact probably one or two centuries earlier.

This development of trade by the Dyula in modern Ghana and in the adjacent Ivory Coast had important political consequences, and sometimes military implications also. Ambitious Akan chiefs began to develop and expand their political power to secure the maximum profit from the exploitation of the resources of as much territory and as many people as possible. On the northern fringes of the forest, astride the routes along which gold and kola nuts were brought for exchange with the Dyula, important new kingdoms emerged such as Bono and Banda, both of which were probably in existence by about 1400. As the economic value of gold and kola became appreciated, the forest to the south of these states—hitherto little inhabited because it was less favourable for agriculture than were the savannas—became more thickly populated, and the same

Increasing power of Akan

principles of political and military mobilization began to be applied there. Village communities became tributaries of ruling groups, with some of their members becoming the clients and slaves needed for the support of their royal households, armies, and trading enterprises. By 1500 most of the Akan territory seems to have been organized in this way and, as trade increased, so the political units—initially very small—tended to increase in size.

Sometimes these political changes were not to the advantage of the Dyula. The latter employed Mande warriors to guard their caravans and, if necessary, could call in larger contingents from the Sudanic kingdoms. Tensions between the Dyula and the increasingly powerful animist monarchy of Banda erupted in the 17th century into a civil war that destroyed the kingdom and led its Dyula merchants to establish a new trading base of their own further to the west at Bonduku. In the following centuries there were at least two major examples of the Dyula taking political authority for themselves at strategic points on the trade routes running through the eastern Ivory Coast.

But the most interesting Mande political initiative along the trade routes south of Jenne was the creation in the early 17th century, just north of the Akan lands, of the new Dyula state of Gonja. This seems to have been inspired by a general worsening of the competitive position of the Mande traders, and it was occasioned by three factors: (1) the near monopoly in the control of the export of forest produce achieved by the Akan kingdom of Bono; (2) the rise to power further north of the Dagomba kingdom, which controlled local salt pans; and (3) the arrival in the region in *c.* 1500 of rival long-distance traders from Hausaland. The Dyula seem to have tried to combat these developments by erecting a major kingdom of their own in Gonja—the territory that the northern traders had to cross to reach the Akan forestlands. But in the long run the Gonja kings lacked the resources and centralized strength to withstand the growth of Akan power.

Trading rivalries

Rather less is known about the nature of Sudanic influences in the more easterly zone south of Hausaland and of Bornu. However it has already been suggested that Dagomba, and a number of similar kingdoms in the Volta Basin, including Mamprusi, and the Mossi kingdoms—such as Wagadugu (Ouagadougou) and Yatenga (or Wahiguya), north of Dagomba and closer to the Niger Bend—were founded by conquerors coming from the east. The structure of these kingdoms, which lasted into the colonial era, most probably formed about the 15th century. The immigrants who formed them seem to have been relatively small bands who eventually merged with the autochthonous Gur-speaking inhabitants of the Volta Basin. Their success in conquering and organizing the Gur villages into kingdoms seems to have been due to their possession of cavalry, which subsequently remained a badge of royalty and of aristocracy.

Somewhat earlier further to the east, astride the Niger and closer to Hausaland, similar kingdoms seem to have been developed by the same kind of process, by invaders who may well have been ancestral to the Mossi-Dagomba state builders. Examples of these survived in Borgu into colonial times. An interesting corpus of legends, such as that of Kisra, suggests that state-building invaders also proceeded south of Borgu and of Hausaland through Nupe, Jukun, Igala, Yoruba, and Benin territory (all in modern Nigeria) to as far as southern Dahomey and to the south-easternmost tip of Ghana. Much of this territory, however, was conquered in the 19th century by Muslim Fulani and Hausa, and the legends as they survive often have an Islāmic colouring, which makes it difficult to accept their historicity. Furthermore, if the legends are accepted at face value, it seems quite evident that the peoples who were conquered must already have achieved a high degree of political, economic, and cultural sophistication, so that it is difficult to know which was the dominating influence in the resulting kingdoms, the civilization of the conquerors or that of the conquered.

The archaeological evidence of the Nok culture shows that the inhabitants of central Nigeria engaged in agriculture and were using iron and other metals by about 300 BC. It is moreover generally accepted that the terra-cotta sculptures associated with Nok are precursors of the later court sculpture of southwestern Nigeria, in bronze or brass and stone as well as terra-cotta. The bronze or brass sculpture of Yoruba and of Benin is especially famous for its naturalism and for the high degree of metallurgical skill used to cast the figures by the lost-wax process.

Tradition asserts that the Yoruba town of Ife (Ile-Ife) was the centre from which this art, and the type of monarchy that supported it, spread to other parts of the region. Modern archaeologists have found nothing to contradict this and have moreover provided evidence for the existence in Yorubaland of a high degree of urbanization by at least the 11th century. Thus in southwestern Nigeria urban civilization seems at least contemporary with the same development in Hausaland and in Kanem-Bǒrnu, the immediate point of departure for Kisra-type conquerors. The probability, therefore, is that the Kisra and similar legends refer to invading cavaliers who, like the Saharan invaders in the Sudan, may be thought of as exploiting rather than creating urban civilization, and doubtless as welding smaller units into larger kingdoms.

It should be pointed out that the territory southwest of Hausaland toward Dahomey is often open country suited to the deployment of cavalry. The effectiveness of cavalry decreased southeastward toward the forest; in the Benin kingdom, horses were little more than residual symbols of monarchical and of aristocratic power. Still further east, in the forest on the other side of the Niger, where there are no traditions of invasion or of developed monarchical government, the archaeological finds at Igbo Ukwu revealed that ancestors of the modern Ibo (Igbo) had, as early as the 9th century, a sophisticated society with surpluses of wealth supporting considerable craft specialization, including a highly developed bronze art with a distinctive style of its own. Recent thinking suggests that the origins of the small, competitive city-states of the eastern Niger Delta south of Iboland, with which Europeans were to develop flourishing commerce from the 17th century, may well be associated with earlier, purely indigenous trading activities of which very little is at present known.

On the available evidence, the establishment in eastern Guinea of the network of Hausa trade and trade routes in the form in which it has been known in modern times, essentially similar to the Mande system further west, can hardly be dated earlier than about the 16th century. Yet the European traders arriving at Benin, in the Yoruba coastlands, and in the Niger Delta, from the end of the 15th century, were able to secure regular supplies of goods, some of which (e.g., cloth and beads) clearly originated in the hinterland and seem to have had an already extant market among the Akan peoples of southern Ghana. This presupposes appreciable indigenous commercial development in eastern Guinea before the emergence of the Hausa system.

From the 15th to the late 19th century

The arrival of European sea traders at the Guinea coastlands in the 15th century clearly marks a new epoch in their history and in the history of all western Africa.

THE BEGINNINGS OF EUROPEAN ACTIVITY

The pioneers were the Portuguese, southwestern Europeans with the necessary knowledge, experience, and national purpose to embark on the enterprise of developing oceanic trade routes with Africa and with Asia. Their main goals were in Asia, but to reach Asia it was necessary to circumnavigate Africa, in the process of which they hoped, among other things, to make contact with Mali and to divert some of the trans-Saharan gold trade from Muslim North Africa to Christian Europe.

The colonization of the Cape Verde Islands, from the later 1450s onward, provided bases for trade with the fringes of the Mali empire. The most momentous discovery in western Africa, however, came in 1471, when Portuguese captains first reached the coast of modern Ghana between the mouths of the Ankobra and Volta rivers. It was quickly appreciated that the Akan peoples of this coast had access to supplies of gold, which were very plentiful indeed by contemporary European standards, and that they were willing and organized to trade some of this gold for base metals, cloth, and other manufactures. The Portuguese called this coast Mina, "the mine," while in European languages generally it became known as the Gold Coast.

The wealth obtainable from trade with the Gold Coast was so important for the completion of the Portuguese design to establish regular commerce with Asia by circumnavigating Africa that the Portuguese crown quickly took steps to exclude foreign rivals from the western African trade and to bring it under its direct control. Portugal was not a naturally wealthy nation, however, and its overseas interests had become very widely extended by the beginning of the 16th century. The western African coastlands and their trade were only one element in a system that also embraced the Congo and Angola, Brazil, the East African littoral, and India and the East Indies. By and large it was the trade of the latter which was regarded as the major prize, and elsewhere activities tended to be restricted to those which might strengthen the prosperity of the overseas enterprise as a whole without unduly straining the limited resources, especially perhaps of manpower, available for its control and exploitation.

The general strategy in western Africa—as elsewhere in the Portuguese trading empire—was to keep territorial and administrative commitments to the minimum necessary to develop and benefit Portuguese commercial activities that were already in existence. The main interest in western Africa was the gold trade of Mina, and it was here—and virtually here alone—that the Portuguese endeavoured to maintain a positive presence on the mainland. In 1482 they built the strong fort which they called São Jorge da Mina (the modern Elmina Castle) on the shores of the Gold Coast, on land leased from the local Akan, and in subsequent years this was supplemented by the construction of three additional forts, at Axim, Shama, and Accra. The purpose of these forts and their garrisons was to try to ensure that the local people sold their gold only to agents of the Portuguese crown. No other Europeans succeeded in establishing lasting footholds on the Gold Coast before the close of the 16th century, and the Portuguese purpose was largely achieved. Gold amounting to perhaps one-tenth of world production was being channelled to Portugal.

In exchange, the Gold Coast peoples needed to be supplied with commodities they desired, and this presented Portugal with a problem, as it was not a major manufacturing nation. The raw iron and copper, metal goods, cloth, etc. which were in demand on the Gold Coast had to be purchased elsewhere. Some of the cloth exported to the Gold Coast was in fact brought from Morocco (and may therefore have been in competition with a trade in cloth which had earlier reached the Akan from the north), and the requirements of their Gold Coast customers were a prime factor in leading the Portuguese to develop relations with Benin and the Niger Delta, where further supplies of cloth, and also of beads and slaves that were in demand on the Gold Coast, could be obtained.

Rejection by Benin   At first the Portuguese hoped to control the trade of Benin and surrounding areas by converting the kingdom, or at least its court, to Christianity, and turning it into a satellite protectorate of their empire. Although this kind of policy was initially successful elsewhere in Africa, notably in the Kongo (Bakongo) kingdom of northern Angola, the Benin monarchy was powerful enough to reject European pressures and infiltration. From about 1520 onward, the Portuguese were virtually excluded from Benin, and their trade with the Niger Delta was conducted from São Tomé and from the other islands of the Gulf of Guinea that they had colonized. This trade was principally in slaves, from the Congo and Angola as well as from the Delta, who were employed on plantations to grow tropical produce, sugar in particular, for the European market.

Apart from an abortive attempt to intercept the western trans-Saharan trade from a fort that was erected on the island of Arguin off the coast of Mauritania, the other principal Portuguese activity in western Africa was the trade with the coastlands of Upper Guinea that was conducted by the settlers on the Cape Verde Islands (which, together with Madeira, were also developed as plantation colonies employing African slave labour). The empire of Mali was in decline, and the Portuguese were not strong enough to control trade so far into the interior. What ultimately developed, on the creeks and islands of the coast from the Gambia to Sierra Leone, was a number of informal settlements where traders from the Cape Verde Islands did some trade with Mande merchants and with the local peoples. Gradually they married into the local trading and ruling families and, escaping formal Portuguese control, became agents of the African commercial system who sought to secure the best terms they could from any visiting European trader irrespective of nationality.

It may be doubted whether this first period of European involvement with western Africa, from about 1450 to 1600, had much effect on the course of its history. The only Europeans consistently involved were the Portuguese, who were not strong outside the Gold Coast, and who were really only interested in controlling some aspects of trade, and these only in a few selected areas of the coastlands where new opportunities had been opened up for a few members of the ruling and trading classes. Perhaps the main changes were that a few Africans acquired some acquaintance with Christianity and with elements of the Portuguese language—a pidgin variety of which became the *lingua franca* of coastal commerce for some centuries—and that western African farmers were introduced to some new crops and fruits, usually of tropical American provenance, which they quickly adopted if they were more productive than their established cultigens. For example, corn (maize) was more productive than millet and cassava more productive than yams under certain conditions.

Trade versus sovereignty   The new era of maritime intercourse with the outside world was probably of marked significance only on the Gold Coast. Here new avenues of wealth had been opened up for some of the Akan in trade at the coast. Here too a new political problem had emerged of how to ensure regular and profitable commercial dealings with the Europeans, while at the same time preventing the coastal footholds, which the Europeans required as entrepôts, from subverting the sovereignty of the indigenous states. This was a very real problem, since the coastal kingdoms were small and divided among themselves in competition for the trade with the Europeans. Elmina certainly, and to some extent Axim also, did in fact develop independent jurisdictions over the mixed European, African, and mulatto trading communities that came to develop beneath the walls of the forts. Beyond these, the difficulty of maintaining large and effective forces of European soldiers in the tropics meant that the Portuguese could only exert power through African allies. The coastal people were thus able to maintain the principle that the land on which the forts were built was not ceded, but only leased. If the Portuguese lost their allies' confidence, the latter could refuse to supply or help defend the forts, or even destroy them altogether (as happened for the first time at Accra in the 1570s).

The rise of the Atlantic slave trade.   The coastal peoples generally, and those of the Gold Coast in particular, were certainly prepared to welcome the merchants of other European nations so as to decrease their dependence on the Portuguese. The first Europeans effectively to break into the Portuguese monopoly of sea trade with western Africa were the Dutch, who had been some of the principal distributors in northwestern Europe of the Asian, African, and American produce imported into Portugal and Spain. After the northern Netherlands had revolted against Spanish rule, however, and Philip II of Spain (who since 1580 had been king of Portugal, also) had sought to punish the Dutch merchants by excluding them from the Iberian ports, they were stimulated to organize oceanic trading ventures of their own and established the first Dutch trading posts in western Africa, on the Gold Coast from 1598.   **Portuguese and Dutch rivalry**

The principal targets for Dutch aggression, however, were in the East Indies and in the Americas, and the effective assertion of Dutch power against Portugal in western Africa was a by-product of the success of the Dutch West India Company in destroying Spanish naval power in the Caribbean and in embarking on the conquest of the plantation colony that the Portuguese had established in Brazil. As a result, by the end of the 1630s the Dutch had established themselves as principal suppliers and customers of the Spanish plantations in the Caribbean, while in Brazil they were themselves in possession of a plantation colony.

The production on American plantations of tropical produce, of which sugar was the most important, and especially the marketing of this produce in western Europe, were extremely profitable activities. But plantation agriculture in the tropics required large and regular supplies of cheap labour. America did not have these, but just across the Atlantic western Africa seemed to have relatively great quantities of productive labour. As early as the 1450s, the Portuguese had begun to transport some African slaves to supplement the meagre labour resources of their own country (especially of the southern provinces they had reconquered from the Moors), and their own plantations in Madeira, the Cape Verde Islands, and, ultimately, on the islands of the Gulf of Guinea had come to be dependent on African slave labour. The Spaniards, and subsequently other Europeans, in America thus naturally came to look to Africa to make good their labour shortage, and a slave trade to the Caribbean had commenced on a small scale in the 1520s.

Spain had little in the way of trade in Africa herself, so her authorities gave out contracts for the supply of slaves to other merchants, and the ultimate suppliers were usually Portuguese. From the 1570s onward, Portugal's slave-traders had a further American market in their own colony of Brazil. The large slave population on their Gulf of Guinea islands was getting out of control, with the result that many Portuguese planters were abandoning these islands and reestablishing their activities in Brazil.

By the time the Dutch West India Company entered on the scene in the mid-1620s, probably at least 300,000 African slaves had been imported into the Americas, more than half of them in the last quarter century, and the annual volume of imports was probably of the order of 7,000–8,000 slaves a year. This was a sizeable business compared with the earlier trades in African slaves to Europe (which had virtually ceased by the 1550s, when perhaps 50,000 slaves had been imported), or to the Atlantic and Guinea Gulf islands (which by the 1620s had probably received rather more than 100,000 slaves, but whose imports were now less than 500 a year). The demand for slaves in the   **Comparative statistics in the slave trade**

Americas was also beginning rapidly to increase. In the wake of the Dutch defeat of Spanish naval power, English and French colonists were beginning to settle the smaller Caribbean islands and were seeking to exploit their soils for tropical agriculture with as many slaves as possible, while Spanish official restrictions on the volume of slave imports in their territories were hardly operative.

The labour needs of the plantations it had conquered in Brazil made it imperative that the Dutch West India Company should begin to secure slaves from Africa, and it very quickly realized that the supply of slaves to European colonists elsewhere in the Americas was an extremely profitable business. To ensure its sources of supply, the Dutch Company embarked on the conquest of all the Portuguese bases on the western African shores. Some of these, for example the island of São Tomé in the Gulf of Guinea, were subsequently lost to it, but by 1642 the Dutch were firmly in possession of the Portuguese forts on the Gold Coast, and they dominated Europe's trade with western Africa from Cape Verde to the Niger Delta. By the 1660s, probably as many as 15,000 African slaves were being taken across the Atlantic each year. Nearly half of this trade was Portuguese, for this nation had by now recovered its possessions in both Brazil and Angola and had a near monopoly of the trade south of the Equator, but the remainder, the growing part, was in northern European hands.

The profits that the Dutch West India Company was able to make in the Atlantic slave trade quickly attracted interest throughout the ports of northwestern Europe, and soon merchants from France, Britain, Germany, and Scandinavia, as well as private Dutch traders, were competing with the Dutch company. French and British competition soon became of major importance. Both countries were resentful of the growing economic power of the Netherlands that was based on foreign trade, and both possessed colonies in the Americas. Their governments decided that their colonists should not be dependent on Dutch merchants for their supplies of labour (nor, for that matter, for capital or for the marketing of their produce in Europe). Through grants of monopolies of their nations' trade with western Africa or the West Indies, French and English merchants were encouraged to form companies strong enough to challenge the power of the Dutch West India Company, and these challenges were supported by the warships of their respective royal navies.

Between 1652 and 1713 there was a succession of wars involving France, Britain, and the Netherlands. The main battles were usually fought far away from Africa, but throughout the period the traders of each nation sought to increase the number of their trading posts on the western African coast and to deny trade to their rivals. A large number of new forts was built and these forts were constantly changing hands.

By 1713, however, a pattern of European activity had emerged that was to remain more or less constant until the Atlantic slave trade was brought to an end during the first half of the 19th century (and that was considerably to influence the subsequent partition of western Africa between European empires). The hold which the Dutch had established over Europe's oceanic commerce was destroyed, and Britain and France competed with each other for its inheritance. The Anglo-French wars of the 18th century had less direct effect on western Africa than did the earlier wars involving the Dutch, but the development of trade with western Africa to supply slaves for their American colonies continued to be an important aim of both countries.

France emerged as master of the coastal trade north of the Gambia River, where it had taken the strategic naval base on Gorée Island, close by Cape Verde, from the Dutch in 1677 and was developing a fort and town at Saint-Louis at the mouth of the Sénégal River as a major commercial centre. By and large, however, this part of the coast produced relatively few slaves, and the French companies operating from Saint-Louis sought compensation by developing the trade of the Sénégal Basin in gum and hides and by penetrating up river toward the alluvial goldfields of Bambuk. Little of permanence was achieved

Anglo-French competition

in the 18th century, however, in part because of the resistance of the local peoples, but mainly because of the growing naval power of Britain. Britain's strategic interests almost invariably led it to occupy Gorée and Saint-Louis in each of the sea wars of the century, and from 1758 to 1779 its government attempted to consolidate its conquests here into a formal colony.

But the colony of the Senegambia was not a success. Britain's merchants were not willing to follow up its naval and military successes in this region, and French traders were allowed to creep back. The main results of Britain's initiative were to interrupt French imperial ambitions in the Senegal valley for nearly a century, and, on the British side, to contribute to a growing opinion—associated particularly with the loss of the North American colonies and the views of Adam Smith—that formal empire was less important and valuable than the independent operations of a growing host of individual British traders, operating wherever there was profit to be found under the general cover of British naval supremacy.

British traders competed with the French on the Gambia River, where both nations' companies maintained forts, and also established themselves to some extent on the coast of Sierra Leone, but initially the main centre of British activity in western Africa was the Gold Coast. Because the Gold Coast had been the scene first of the major Portuguese and then of the major Dutch successes in western African trade, its peoples were better organized than most to provide European traders with what they sought, and the fact that they could supply gold as well as slaves remained of major importance.

During the period of intensive competition in the later 18th century, the number of major European forts on this 300-mile-long coastline had risen to approximately 30. The Dutch West India Company still had more Gold Coast forts than anyone else, and these by and large were the strongest and best maintained. But their headquarters at Elmina was now rivalled by the British castle at Cape Coast only a few miles away, and indeed almost every Dutch fort had an adjacent British establishment competing with it. The French never succeeded in getting a permanent foothold on the Gold Coast; Swedish and German ventures eventually came under Dutch or British control, and traders from Denmark retained forts only on the eastern Gold Coast, where there was little gold, and slaves were the main articles of trade.

Although the formal position of the Dutch on the Gold Coast remained strong throughout the 18th century, and indeed into the 19th century, they steadily lost trade to the British merchants. One reason for this was simply that Britain had displaced the Netherlands as the major naval and sea-trading power in western Europe and, through the developing industrial revolution, was better able to supply overseas traders with cheap goods for the world market. But the British were also more successful than their rivals in adapting the nature of their operations to changing conditions of trade.

The Dutch give way to the British

The Dutch on the Gold Coast, and also the French in Sénégal, tended to hold to the view that the African trade should be conducted through large corporations, which had military and administrative as well as commercial responsibilities, and which were rewarded for these by their monopoly rights. Such companies had been essential if the original Portuguese monopoly of African maritime trade were to be broken, or if the national interest in it were to be maintained in the subsequent period of militant European rivalry for the trade. But the intensity of the competition during c. 1650–c. 1713 had made the business of building or capturing and of maintaining and defending coastal forts extremely expensive. On the other hand, the breakthrough into trade with Africans had been made, and the ever-increasing demand for slaves led to a great widening of European commercial activities along the coast. Thus by the beginning of the 18th century there were few parts of the coastlands where African rulers and merchants were not prepared and organized to sell slaves in some numbers.

Hence the future lay not with the cumbersome companies, with large amounts of capital locked up in costly forts, but with a host of small European traders, who were not tied to particular shore installations but were seeking for the best terms of trade they could find along the coast. This type of European trader was naturally welcomed by African rulers, newly embarking on trade with the Europeans, who had no wish to see the latter establish permanent bases on their coasts, which, as the Gold Coast forts had done, might develop political claims to challenge their own traditional jurisdictions. It was the British traders, protected by their country's command of the sea and backed by the abundant supplies of goods and capital produced by its revolutionary economic growth, who were most successful in exploiting the new pattern of trade.

The old monopoly companies had never been strong on the coast between the Gambia River and the Gold Coast. In the north this was largely due to the effects of the breakdown of the early Portuguese attempts at controlling the trade. Further south, the territories of modern Liberia and of the Ivory Coast had not excited much interest among early European traders. Their coastline was treacherous for navigation, and their thick forests supported a scanty population which was little organized for commerce. Such trade as had developed, principally in ivory and in agricultural produce, did not warrant much investment in shore establishments. Thus, as the American demand for slaves increased, the Upper Guinea coast became frequented by increasing numbers of small traders who competed bitterly with each other for slaves.

The greatest opportunities for the new class of individual European traders lay not to the west but to the east of the Gold Coast, where populations were denser and much better organized, not only politically but also commercially, and specifically in their access to developed trade routes linking them with inland centres of population, production, wealth, and organized government. European sea captains knew this coast well enough, for the best sailing routes to return to Europe from the Gold Coast ran via the Gulf of Guinea and its islands. European trade had been held back here only because there had been no staple export to compare with the gold of the Gold Coast. Nevertheless their ships' need of provisioning for the return voyage, the local trade between the Niger Delta and the Gold Coast, and the early slave trade to São Tomé and Brazil had led to a demand developing among the African peoples for European manufactures such as metals and metalware, cloth, guns and ammunition, and spirits, and there was a network of traders and trade routes to expand trade with the interior if a staple African export could be found.

The Slave Coast   The rapidly increasing demand for slaves as West Indian and American plantation production began to boom provided this staple. In the second half of the 17th century, Dutch, French, English, and Portuguese traders became increasingly involved in trade on the coast between the Gold Coast and Benin, which soon in fact received the name of the Slave Coast. Initially the company-fort pattern of trading was applied here, but it never took root to the extent that it had done on the Gold Coast, in part because the local rulers insisted that the forts should be built in their own inland towns. As the slave trade further developed, both on the Slave Coast itself, and also further east, in the Niger Delta region, it became typically an enterprise of individual European or American traders or small partnerships, who acknowledged the authority of the local rulers and paid the fees and duties these demanded.

As has been seen, in the 1620s, on the eve of the great growth of the Atlantic slave trade associated with the Dutch entry into it, the number of African slaves reaching the Americas was about 7,000–8,000 slaves a year. In the last quarter of the 17th century, the average annual American import was some 25,000, and the total number of African slaves imported during the century has been estimated at 1,300,000. In the next 110 years before restrictions began to be applied on the Atlantic slave trade, it operated on a vastly greater scale. The best available estimate for the number of Africans imported into the New World during this period is some 6,265,000, or an average of 57,000 a year. After about 1815, and especially after the 1840s, the measures taken to outlaw European and American slave dealing, and also—more significantly—the possession of slaves in the Americas, began to take effect, and in the 1860s the Atlantic trade was finally brought to an end after a further 1,625,000 slaves had been landed in the Americas.

The peak of the Atlantic slave trade was probably reached in the 1780s, when approximately 70,000 slaves were brought to the Americas each year. At least half these slaves were transported in the ships of British merchants. Their nearest competitors, the French and Portuguese traders, carried each about a fifth of the total. Subsequently the French trade (and also the Dutch and Danish trades) virtually ceased as a result of the British blockade of Europe during the Revolutionary and Napoleonic Wars of the turn of the century, and the British predominance was even more marked, possibly 60 percent of the trade being in British hands, compared with perhaps 25 percent for Portugal and 15 percent for North American merchants.

The slave-trade era.   All the estimates for the volume of the Atlantic slave trade that have been given so far are for numbers of slaves landed in the Americas, since such numbers are more readily ascertainable than any figures for slaves actually leaving Africa. A fair proportion of these slaves never reached the other side of the Atlantic because of deaths from disease, maltreatment, or maritime disaster. On average these losses may have been about 16 percent in the 18th century, when the vast majority of the slaves were transported. Therefore, to calculate the probable numbers of men and women lost to Africa, it seems advisable to increase the figures for slaves landed in the Americas by one-fifth.

But not all the slaves were taken from western Africa. Considerable numbers were always taken from Africa south of the Equator, and in the 19th century the measures taken to stop the North Atlantic slave trade were quicker and more effective than those against the trade across the South Atlantic. It seems safe to suggest that, up to and including the 18th century, 60 percent of the slaves were taken from the western African coasts from the Sénégal River to the Cameroons, and that in the 19th century the proportion dropped to about one-third. It is thus possible to arrive at the following estimates for the loss of population to western Africa.

Comparative statistics of population loss

Population Loss Due to Slave Trade				
	from Africa as a whole		from West Africa only	
	arriving overseas	leaving Africa	percentage	leaving West Africa
Before 1600	275,000	330,000	60	200,000
1601–1700	1,300,000	1,560,000	60	940,000
1701–1810	6,265,000	7,520,000	60	4,510,000
After 1810	1,625,000	1,950,000	33	650,000
Total	9,470,000	11,360,000	—	6,300,000

It is not easy to assess what effects such a loss of population may have had on western Africa and on the course of its history. In the first place, it must not be forgotten that almost all statistics concerning the slave trade involve some degree of estimation. Those used here are based on Philip D. Curtin's analysis of the available data and are thought to be accurate within ±10 percent.

Second, there is really no means of knowing the size of the population of western Africa at any time during the period of the Atlantic slave trade. Working backwards from the population data available in the 20th century (which are not themselves always very reliable), and from the evidence these provide for rates of growth, it is possible to suppose that at the beginning of the 18th century, when the Atlantic slave trade was entering its dominant phase, the total population of western Africa may have been about 25,000,000, and that its natural rate of increase may have been some 0.15 percent per annum. Though these estimates can be little more than guesses, they do tend to suggest that the commonly held idea that the export slave trade actually depopulated western Africa is not likely to be right.

When the slave trade was at its height during 1701–1810, the export of slaves was averaging 41,000 a year. This loss would have been about equal to the assumed natural increase in population, so that the effect might have been to have checked population growth rather than to have actually diminished the population. In earlier centuries, or in the 19th century, it would not even have had this effect: population would have been growing, albeit more slowly than with no export of slaves.

But these are gross calculations that take no account of the uneven selection of slaves for export. Since the American planters, and hence the slave traders, looked in particular for fit slaves in the prime of life, between about 15 and 35 years old, it may be argued that robbing western Africa of people particularly from this group of its population would especially tend to reduce births, and thereby reduce the capacity of the population to maintain its numbers. On the other hand, however, the planters preferred their slaves to be male, and only about a third of those exported were women. Thus, since western African men who could afford it were polygynous, the birth rate may have been less affected than might have been expected. There is also evidence to suggest that the fitter or more intelligent slaves were often kept at home, and that less fit individuals were in many ways prepared to deceive the European buyers as to their age or condition.

It can also be argued that, since some parts of the coast saw the export of many more slaves than did others, the regions adjacent to these coasts suffered much more severely than the overall figures for western Africa as a whole might suggest. In the peak period of the 1780s, the distribution of exports along the coast was approximately as follows: from the Senegambia and Sierra Leone, about 4,000 slaves a year (about 8 percent of the total from western Africa as a whole); from Liberia and the Ivory Coast, about 4,000 (8 percent) again; from the Gold Coast, about 10,000 (19 percent); from the Slave Coast and the Benin region, about 12,500 (23 percent); from the Niger Delta and the Cameroons, about 22,000 (42 percent). But the three last zones—Lower Guinea—today have populations as dense as any to be found in tropical Africa, and the available evidence suggests that their population was also relatively great in the 18th century, and certainly by and large denser than that of most parts of Upper Guinea.

It is therefore possible to conclude that the largest numbers of slaves came from just those regions that could most afford to export population. It is also unlikely to be a coincidence that it was this same area—from the Gold Coast to the Cameroons—which was the most highly developed coastal region in terms of government, economic production, and trade. It was only in areas of low population and poor indigenous organization that foreign slave traders ever needed to set out to capture slaves for themselves. This naturally made the Africans involved hostile to further dealings with the traders, while it also tended to reduce the power of the population to maintain and feed itself, so that in both cases supplies of slaves were ultimately fewer. For the most part, the European traders bought the slaves they needed from African merchants and rulers who had organized to offer slaves for sale.

About half these slaves were unfortunates in their own societies: criminals, the mentally or physically handicapped, debtors or those who had been sold for debt or pledged as security for a debt, those who had offended men of power or influence, or simply those who in some way had become outcasts from the family and tribal systems. Selling such people was usually simply an alternative to keeping them in some kind of servitude in domestic society or, in more extreme situations, condemning them to execution or to serve as human sacrifices in the festivals of ancestral or land cults.

The remainder of the slaves exported were strangers to the societies that sold them, sometimes unwary travellers or border villagers who were kidnapped, but for the most part prisoners of war. Europeans sometimes argued that African kings went to war often with the prime purpose of securing slaves for the slave trade. In the 19th century, when the Europeans themselves had outlawed the slave trade, this argument was used to justify the advance of European colonial rule. On the other hand, in the 18th century, some European slave traders claimed that the acquisition of slaves was simply a consequence of wars which were natural occurrences. From this they argued that they were actually doing a service to such captives and to humanity by buying them and selling them into hard labour on the American plantations. They claimed that they were rescuing the slaves from the danger of being executed or of becoming human sacrifices and that slavery under civilized Christian masters was preferable to being a slave in primitive, pagan African society.

Despite the speciousness of the latter claim, the 18th-century slavers' argument seems nearer the truth than that of the 19th-century abolitionists. African wars, like wars anywhere else, were the consequence of rivalries for wealth and power between states. But whereas elsewhere the wealth and power of a monarchy might be measured in terms of the amount of territory it controlled, or in terms of the monetary value of its resources, the prime measure of both power and wealth in Africa was men. By and large land in Africa had very little economic value. There was almost invariably far more land available than there were people to cultivate it or to develop its mineral and other resources. The key to the strength of a kingdom thus lay in its ability to gain control of manpower, and the obvious way to do this was to try and take people away from its neighbours and rivals. This, indeed, was how western African kingdoms had come to be built up, by the natural rulers of particular small kinship groups securing for themselves and their units more clients and slaves than their neighbours, and by using them to extend their power over these neighbours and even further afield.

People then were the important resource. Often, indeed, a man was the unit of value in which other resources were measured: thus the value of horses, or guns, or parcels of trade goods was often expressed in terms of the numbers of slaves (*i.e.,* disposable men) for which they might be exchanged. If more people were available, then more land, or gold or iron or salt, might be exploited or more trade might be done (the environment was hostile to transport animals, so that trade depended heavily on the availability of porters and canoemen). Thus there would be greater surpluses available to support the monarch, his household, his administration, and his army, and to maintain specialized manufactures, crafts, and services.

The purpose of wars was thus to increase the power and wealth of a kingdom by increasing its manpower and diminishing that of its rivals. The ruling philosophy cannot therefore have been one favouring the export of slaves. But it was one in which the economic value of a man was very well established. With the growth of trade, and especially of international trade which made available desirable commodities that seemed as valuable or sometimes more valuable than men, it was natural for African kings and their traders to think of selling some men in exchange for these commodities, and especially so if the foreign merchants who offered these commodities were themselves interested in acquiring slaves.

This situation had first arisen, and at a very early stage, in the trans-Saharan trade. Labour was needed to work the Saharan salt deposits, and the civilizations of the Mediterranean and Middle East had long had a demand for slaves. Some North African and Middle Eastern exports, particularly perhaps horses, were so valuable in the Sudan that its kings were quite ready to change some of their scarce manpower to secure these. But the problems involved in marching men across the Sahara with its scarce and widely separated resources of water were formidable. Though reliable estimates are lacking, it is generally supposed that the trans-Saharan slave trade could rarely if ever have transported more than 10,000 slaves a year. After the middle of the 17th century, however, the demand of the Atlantic trade for slaves was practically insatiable, and, as has been seen, at its peak during the 18th century, at least four times this number of slaves were leaving the western African coasts each year.

By far the largest number of these slaves, nearly half the total in fact, were being exported—as has been seen—from the Niger Delta region. The communities of Ijaw (Ijo), Ibibio, and Efik fishermen and salt makers, who controlled the waterways to the interior, developed city-

Slaves as the measure of wealth and power

Pre-European slave trading

states whose whole fortunes came to be bound up with the slave trade. Most of their slaves were brought from their immediate hinterland. It is probably significant that some of this hinterland, particularly that inhabited by the Ibo (Igbo) and the Tiv, today has the highest population densities to be found anywhere in tropical Africa—some Ibo densities being as much as 1,500 persons to the square mile. But Ibo country is not rich in natural resources and its water supplies are poor. In the 20th century, one result has been that many Ibos have been forced to emigrate to sell their labour in other parts of Nigeria. It is not unreasonable to assume that something of this population pressure may have already been evident during the slave trade era, and that many communities in the hinterland of the Niger Delta could only survive and prosper by selling some of their people.

But this was almost certainly a unique situation. It is doubtful whether there could have been anywhere else in western Africa a buoyant surplus of labour to encourage this kind of exploitation. It is noteworthy, indeed, that although the American demand for slaves was rising steadily from about 1630 onward, every other part of the coast seems quite soon to have reached a figure for slave exports which thereafter remained more or less constant until the 19th century. Then two things happened: firstly, there was a breakdown in the system of law and order that had hitherto operated in Yoruba country to the west of the Niger Delta, with the result that exports from the Slave Coast began to increase; and secondly, after the early 1860s, the American demand fell off sharply. But in the 17th and 18th centuries there is a strong implication that the other major slave exporting regions with relatively large populations had developed politico-economic systems which were able more or less consciously to calculate the balance of advantage for themselves of engaging in the export slave trade. By and large their conclusion seems to have been that it was more profitable to exchange some of their manpower for European goods than it was to keep it all at home, but that it was dangerous to export more than a certain controlled quantity.

It is important to remember that the Atlantic slave trade was not simply a rape of African manpower to serve European purposes in the Americas. In any case, slaves were not the sole African exports by sea during the slave trade era. Gold, gum, hides, timbers, palm oil, and other commodities were also traded, and the European merchants needed to buy large quantities of provisions to feed the slaves during the Atlantic crossing. All these things had to be purchased, and in exchange Africans received supplies of other goods—cloth, metals, tools, knives and other hardware, guns and ammunition, beads and small manufactures, tobacco and spirits—which, however much their prices may have been inflated in relation to their cost in Europe or America, were often of considerable value to African societies.

From the African point of view, the main importance of the American demand for slaves may have been that it led to a great growth of all kinds of trade at the coasts and to a considerable stimulation of economic and political activity and organization for some distance into the interior of Guinea, a region which had hitherto been remote from the main centres of trade in western African history, which had been in the Sudan. It is difficult to quantify this growth of commercial activity, but the combined value of exports and imports at the coast, negligible prior to 1500, may have been $3,000,000 or so a year by 1700 and $8,000,000 or so by 1800. That this was a considerable trade by the standards of the time can be seen from comparison with an estimate in the 1850s of the value of the trade of Kano, then the most prosperous of the Sudanic kingdoms, at some $500,000 a year.

Some consequences of this rapid increase of trade on the Guinea Coast were fairly general. One was the appearance on the coast itself of a new class of African merchants, who freed themselves from some of the restrictions of traditional society and were able to accumulate personal wealth and power to rival that of the local kings. Sometimes, indeed, as at Komenda on the Gold Coast or at Opobo in the Delta, the new men actually set themselves

Other trading commodities

up as kings. This development owed much to the direct influence of the European trade on the coast. Some Europeans settled more or less permanently in Africa, married local women, and created new merchant dynasties, such as the Brews of the Gold Coast. Others of the new men were former slaves who had returned from America, particularly perhaps from Brazil to the Slave Coast. Many were local Africans, but usually men who had started by gaining useful contacts and training in the service of European merchants. All the new men were experienced in European ways and often secured for their sons elements of a European education.

The growth of Guinea's international trade encouraged the spread and acceptance of regular systems of currency. Many, perhaps most, of the Guinea currencies were already extant on the coast when the Europeans arrived, but the growth of trade meant that certain of these became the sole acceptable currency within relatively large and well-defined areas, such as iron bars in Upper Guinea and much of the Delta, ounces of gold dust on the Gold Coast, and cowrie shells on the Slave Coast. Another development was the emergence on a considerable scale of production for sale. In Ashanti, for example, some villages were given over to the production of a particular commodity, such as cloth, and some of the chief men ran plantations with slave labour (as also, in the 19th century, did the kings of Dahomey).

Systems of currency

The emergence of the trading city-states of the Niger Delta represented a social revolution as well as a political innovation. The kinship system gave way to the "House" system, by which both freemen and the large numbers of slaves needed to operate trading canoes and strategic and trading settlements were bound together by common economic interests into large corporations headed by the leading merchants. On the Gold Coast and Slave Coast, however, political development was more akin to that which had earlier taken place in the Sudan under the influence of trans-Saharan trade.

Behind the Gold Coast, the original centres of Akan trade and power had been north of the forest and northward-looking. The growth of trade at the coast led to new developments among the settlements in the forest, which had hitherto served only to produce gold and kola nuts for the northern trade. In the 17th century, three major forest kingdoms emerged: Denkyera in the west, Akwamu to the east, and between them, Akyem. These competed with each other in expansion parallel to the coast to control as many as possible of the paths of trade to the European forts. Akyem lost, while Denkyera achieved such an overweening power that some of its northern tributaries secured guns and new techniques of political and military organization from Akwamu and rose in revolt. This was the effective origin of the new monarchy of Ashanti based on Kumasi, situated in the central forest where the major trade routes from the Gold Coast converged and met with the major routes of the Hausa and the Mande–Dyula traders from the north.

By the beginning of the 18th century, the power of Denkyera had been crushed, and in the next seventy years Ashanti armies went on to build up an empire which in the north engulfed Bono and Gonja and levied tribute on Dagomba, and in the south incorporated or made tributary virtually all the small states that had been involved in the rise of Denkyera, Akyem, and Akwamu. The only part of modern Ghana that was not controlled from Kumasi was the central coastlands, where the small Fante states, gaining some measure of protection from their close association with the various European forts, began to come together in a federation to resist Ashanti influence.

As the Atlantic trade began to expand east of the Gold Coast to the Slave Coast, similar political developments began to manifest themselves in its hinterland also. Toward the end of the 17th century, the northernmost Yoruba kingdom, Oyo, began to turn away from its traditional rivalry with the adjacent savanna kingdoms of Nupe and Borgu and to use its cavalry to assert control of the trade routes through the open country southwestward to the small Aja states on the coast in which the Europeans had established trading posts. A measure of control was also

The southward expansion of Oyo

asserted more directly to the south over other Yoruba peoples and kings in the forest. Here a boundary was established with the kingdom of Benin, which in the later 17th century decided that it was in its interests to open up its ports to European merchants and to sell slaves to them to secure a share of the goods they were offering.

By the early 18th century, strains caused by the virulent competition between the European traders and their African associates were leading to the dissolution of traditional social and political controls among the Aja, who had congeries of petty kingdoms under the nominal leadership of the king of Allada. The resultant disorder was not to the liking of the kings of Dahomey, the youngest of these monarchies, who, in colonizing the northern marches of Aja territory, had evolved much more authoritarian and militant forms of government and society. Between 1724 and 1734, Dahomey enforced its concepts on the other Aja peoples by conquest and began to build up a centralized state to control the entire Slave Coast.

Initially Dahomey, wishing to conserve manpower, was reluctant to sell slaves to the Europeans. This was not to the liking of Oyo, whose foreign trade was dependent on its being able to sell slaves to the Europeans on the Slave Coast. Nor was it really in the long-term interests of the centralized trading system of the Dahoman kings themselves, for these had little but slaves to offer in return for the guns and other goods they needed to buy from the Europeans. From 1726 to 1748 the consequence was continual warfare on the Slave Coast, the ultimate results of which were that Dahomey was led by force of arms to recognize Oyo suzerainty, and the firm establishment of the slave trade, both under strict royal control in Dahomey's port of Whydah (Ouidah), and also, increasingly, in new ports beyond its control to the east, such as Badagri and Lagos.

The armies of Denkyera, Akwamu, Ashanti, and Dahomey all made use of firearms, and Akwamu seems to have been a pioneer in the development of tactics suited to the new weapons. The Portuguese had not imported guns into western Africa on any scale and as a matter of policy had sold them only to their allies. But in the highly competitive trading situation which followed the Dutch breaking of the Portuguese monopoly, all the European trading nations vied with each other to sell guns, and they soon became an essential article of trade.

But the muskets exported to western Africa were cheap varieties specially made for the African market. These muskets were neither very reliable nor very serviceable for military use—in fact their main value was probably for hunting and for the protection of crops. Oyo's successes were apparently based on its use of cavalry (guns played no significant part in Yoruba warfare until the 19th century), and since these included its victories over Dahomey, whose armies did have muskets, it may be doubted whether the acquisition of firearms was really a significant factor in the rise of the new Guinea kingdoms of the 17th and 18th centuries.

From the African point of view, guns were expensive—though less perhaps to buy than to keep in working order and supplied with powder. In this respect, guns were not dissimilar to horses and, like horses, they became the particular prerogative of kings and their henchmen, symbols of prestige, but also elements in the growth of royal power at the expense both of subjects and of unfortunate neighbouring peoples who did not evolve state systems. It followed that the trade in firearms, and also in those African exports, such as slaves and gold, which were most in demand by the European sellers of firearms, tended to be under strict royal control. Similarly, competition to secure supplies of guns and ammunition—as of horses in the Sudan—and to deny such supplies to rivals, was a factor of some significance in the new era of power politics in Guinea.

By the 18th century, the kingdoms and empires of Guinea, especially those of Lower Guinea, though commonly less extensive, were as powerful as those which had been established in the western African Sudan. As with the latter, control of trade with the outside world had been an important element in the growth of these states. However,

Guns as symbols of prestige as well as power

the relationships between the growth of trade and the growth of states in the two systems, those of Guinea and of the Sudan, were not entirely identical. The rise of the Guinea states, for instance, was associated with a growth of trade that was particularly dependent on the growth of a demand for one particular African export, slaves. Any cessation of this demand was therefore likely to create strains for the Guinea states; and Ashanti, Dahomey, and Oyo had hardly established their paramountcies in their areas when Europeans began seriously to question both the morality and the economic value of slave labour.

It is also noteworthy that the Guinea peoples did not generally establish networks of itinerant traders extending far beyond their homelands, as the Mande and Hausa had done. The Ashanti, Dahomey, and Benin trading systems seem essentially to have been state corporations operating under royal control or license only within the boundaries of their political influence. The northern limits of the Guinea trading system hardly extended more than 300 miles from the coast. Conversely, Mande–Dyula and Hausa traders had ventured far beyond the political and military limits of their kings' authority (which in the case of the Hausa, were always very restricted). Even after the rise of the Atlantic trade and of the Guinea kingdoms, traders from the north continued to be of prime importance to the commerce of Guinea and sometimes, too, to its political life. The community of Muslim northerners settled in Kumasi, for example, sometimes played a significant role in Ashanti politics, and the northern trade also led to Islām gaining important ground among the Yoruba. Thus the Guinea states were also likely to be affected by any important changes in the political and economic life of the western Sudan.

THE ISLĀMIC REVOLUTION IN THE WESTERN SUDAN
The Moroccan occupation of the Niger Bend in 1591 meant that the domination of the western Sudan by Mande or Mande-inspired empires—Ghana, Mali, Songhai—which had persisted for at least five centuries, was at last ended. The Songhai kings were pushed southeast into their original homeland of Dendi, further down the Niger close to Borgu, and Mande political power was limited to the so-called Bambara; i.e., "pagan," kingdoms of Segu (Ségou) and, later, of Kaarta, upstream and to the west of Macina. In and around the Niger Bend itself, the long-term effect of the Moroccan conquest was to open up the country to the Tuareg and Arabized Berber tribes of the Saharan fringes. By the middle of the 18th century the descendants of the Moroccan conquerors, who had settled down in the Niger Bend cities as a ruling caste, the Arma, had become tributary to the desert pastoralists.

These same tribes operated, or at least profited from, the trans-Saharan trade, and some of them had acquired leading positions in western African Islām. The Kunta tribe of Arabized Berbers had become preeminent in both these respects by the 18th century. It dominated the salt trade to Timbuktu, and in the person of Sīdī Mukhtār (d. 1811) it had produced a spiritual leader so respected among the Muslims of the western Sudan that the Kunta were able to exercise on the quarrels between the pastoral tribes a mediating influence which was clearly to the general benefit of commerce and urban society.

Mukhtār's position was due to qualities of learning and holiness, which were in part personal, but also in large measure due to his leading role in the Qādirīyah, one of the Muslim brotherhoods (ṭarīqahs) in which particular traditions of both sanctity and learning were passed on from teacher to teacher. These brotherhoods or religious orders had arisen with the growth, from about the 11th century onward, of mystical currents of Muslim thought (especially in eastern Islām, where the Qādirīyah had begun). Mysticism proved to be congenial to Berber society in North Africa (where the Tijānīyah order evolved in the 18th century), and from here the ṭarīqah entered the Sahara, arriving in western Africa by the beginning of the 16th century.

Hitherto Islām had been spread in western Africa essentially by merchants who, in order to secure their livelihood, chose to accommodate themselves and their religion

The dominance of Tuareg and Arabized Berber tribes

within the pagan social and political framework that existed where they settled—which for the most part was only in the towns. But with the coming of the *ṭarīqah*—of which the Qādirīyah was one of the first and, until the Tijānīyah began to advance in its tracks in the 19th century, certainly the foremost—western Africa began to experience the growth of organized groups of devout Muslims who were both specifically trained and morally compelled to work toward a true Islāmic society. Moreover, if the people and their rulers remained irresponsive or hostile, it was the Muslims' duty to preach the doctrine of conversion by force, through the *jihād*, or divinely justified war or rebellion against rulers who were pagans or not true Muslims.

The Fulani *jihād*

This doctrine was particularly attractive to the Fulani who, as has been seen, were scattered in stranger communities between the agricultural settlements throughout the western African savannas. As the wealth, organization, and power of agricultural and urban society increased, so there was less scope available for the free movement of the Fulani cattle and less freedom for their herdsmen. The Fulani were subject to increased pressures to pay rents, taxes, and services to the rulers of the settled communities who, from the Fulani point of view, were aliens who had no natural right to these things. Although the bulk of the Fulani were pagans, they were, as pastoralists, naturally open to influence from the Saharan pastoralists who were Muslims and among whom the *ṭarīqah* had been established. The Fulani also had ethnic links with the long Islāmized Tukulor of the far west, and they had a considerable and influential Muslim clerical class of their own. The Fulani clerics were thus particularly receptive to the doctrine of *jihād* and, throughout the Sudan, could ally themselves with considerable numbers of disgruntled and mobile pastoral kinsmen to make *jihād* a military reality.

The earliest known Fulani *jihād* occurred in Bondu, close by the Islāmized Sénégal Valley, where in the second half of the 17th century Fulani clerics succeeded in taking over political power from local Mande rulers. Early in the following century, considerable numbers of Fulani began to do the same in alliance with the local Muslim Mande traders in the nearby Fouta Djallon. By about 1750, a Muslim theocracy had been erected whose leaders were soon engaged in organizing trade to the Upper Guinea coast on which European traders were active. In the second half of the 18th century, the same pattern was repeated in the Fouta Toro, the homeland of the Tukulor, for there, though the dispossessed rulers were Muslims, they were too much of a self-interested and exploitationary group to suit the clerics.

News of these developments in the westernmost Sudan naturally spread through the Fulani diaspora to more easterly territories influenced by the teaching of Sīdī Mukhtār and other like-minded *ṭarīqah* divines. In 1804 the most famous of the western African *jihād*s was launched in Hausaland by Usman dan Fodio.

Usman was the leading Fulani cleric in Gobir, the northernmost and most militant of the Hausa kingdoms. This was in a disturbed state in the 17th and 18th centuries. The growth of Tuareg power in Aïr on its northern frontiers had led the Gobir ruling class to seek compensation to the south and southwest, in the territories of Zamfara and of Kebbi. Here the break-up of the Songhai empire had led to a power vacuum, which had been an encouragement to Fulani settlement. The kings of Gobir, like other Hausa monarchs, were at least nominally Muslims, and for a time Usman had been employed at their court. But he then used the influence he had gained to develop a Muslim community of his own, some miles away from the capital, which was governed according to the strict principles of law preached by the Qādirīyah. The kings of Gobir gradually came to the conclusion that they could not afford to tolerate this independent jurisdiction within their unsettled kingdom and began to take steps against the Muslim community. By 1804, the situation became such that Usman felt he had no alternative but to declare a *jihād* and to adopt the role of an independent Muslim ruler (*amīr al-muʾminīn* or, in Hausa, *sarkin musulmi*).

Both sides appealed for wider support. But, while the Hausa kings proved incapable of concerted action against the movement of Islāmic rebellion, discontented Fulani and oppressed Hausa peasantry throughout Hausaland welcomed the opportunity to rid themselves of vexatious overlords and arbitrary taxation. Within three years almost all the Hausa kings had been replaced by Fulani emirs who acknowledged the supreme authority of Usman. The most serious fighting was in and around Gobir itself, where the maintenance of large Fulani forces in the field alienated the local peasantry. Fortresses had to be established for the systematic reduction of the country, and in the process the old kingdom of Gobir was destroyed and two major military encampments, Sokoto and Gwandu, eventually emerged as the twin capitals of a new Fulani empire.

The rise of the Fulani empire

The core of this empire was composed of the three large former kingdoms of Katsina, Kano, and Zaria (Zegzeg), in which, together with the smaller former kingdom of Daura, a Fulani aristocracy had taken over the Hausa system of government and had brought it into line with the principles of Islām as stated by Usman. But the *jihād* had not stopped at their boundaries. Hausa clerics and adventurers joined with the Fulani in creating new Muslim emirates further afield, for example among the pagan and hitherto largely stateless peoples of the Bauchi highlands, and in the open grasslands of northern Cameroon, where there were large numbers of Fulani, the vast new emirate of Adamawa was created. In the south, Fulani and Hausa clerics intervened in a succession dispute in the old pagan kingdom of Nupe and by 1856 had converted it into a new emirate ruled from Bida. There had also been considerable Fulani and Muslim penetration into northern Yorubaland, and, in about 1817, its governor rashly invoked Fulani and Hausa aid in his rebellion against the king of Oyo. The governor's new allies took over, the new emirate of Ilorin was created, and the disintegration of the Oyo empire was accelerated.

The only serious check to Fulani conquest was in Bornu. By 1808, the forces of Fulani rebellion and invasion had reduced its ancient monarchy to impotence. Bornu and Kanem, however, had their own clerical class and tradition, and in the latter province arose a new leader, Muḥammad al-Kanemi, who asserted that the Fulani clerics did not have a unique right to interpret Muslim law for the government of mankind. Al-Kanemi was able to inspire a spirited national resistance, which by 1811 had turned the tide against the Fulani. By 1826, he was the effective master of a new Islāmic state, though the traditional kings were maintained in office until 1846, when the puppet of the time rebelled against his son and successor, ʿUmar, but was defeated and killed.

Usman dan Fodio was a scholar and theologian who had little inclination for the political and military direction of the movement he had inspired. His main role was to maintain the *jihād*'s spiritual and moral force and direction, and he has left a remarkable memorial of this in his innumerable writings. The practical commanders of the *jihād* were his brother, Abdullahi, and his son, Muḥammad Bello, who were men of action as well as considerable scholars. These two eventually became joint viceroys of the new empire, Bello ruling its eastern half from Sokoto and Abdullahi the western half from a seat of government at Gwandu. They oversaw the installations of the provincial emirs, received tribute from them, and endeavoured to ensure that their governments and systems of taxation followed the principles of Muslim law and were not arbitrary and extortionate. Gradually the original scholarly and clerical impulse of the *jihād* weakened (though it was never wholly forgotten), and the emirs tended to become more representative of the military Fulani aristocracy, which tended to intermarry into the old Hausa ruling class. Standards of scholarship decayed and Hausa, rather than Arabic, became the language of administration. But for half a century or more after the *jihād*, some 200,000 square miles of territory enjoyed a unified system of relatively impartial law and administration, and this was much to the advantage of its agriculture, industry, and trade.

Both Sokoto and Gwandu were in the extreme northwest of the empire, where the *jihād* had had its origins and where it continued longest, for Kebbi was never entirely subdued. It is possible also that it was in this direction, looking up the Niger toward the Kunta and to the considerable Fulani population of Macina, that it was thought that there might be further advances. Doubtless it was for these reasons that Abdullahi settled at Gwandu with responsibility for the western empire. The main Fulani successes, however, were to the southeast in Bello's sphere, and it was Bello who in 1817 succeeded to his father's titles of caliph and *sarkin musulmi*.

The *jihād* in Macina
When, about 1818, a *jihād* began in Macina, it was an independent movement led by a local Qādirī Fulani, Ahmadu ibn Hammadi (1775–1844). Ahmadu was certainly cognizant of Usman's *jihād*, and the circumstances in which his own movement was born were very similar to those which had occasioned the *jihād* in Hausaland. Ahmadu established an independent Muslim community which brought him into conflict with his local, pagan Fulani chief, who was unwise enough to call for help from his suzerain, the Bambara king of Segu. The result was a general rising under Ahmadu which established a theocratic Muslim Fulani state throughout Macina and extended to both the ancient Muslim centres of Jenne (Djénné) and Timbuktu.

The third major western African *jihād* of the 19th century was that of al-Ḥājj 'Umar (died 1864), a Tukulor cleric from the Fouta Toro. As a young man, 'Umar went on the pilgrimage (*hajj*) to Mecca (hence the honorific al-Ḥājj), and in all spent some 20 years away from his homeland. Twelve of these were spent at Sokoto, where he married a daughter of Bello's. He also spent some time with al-Kanemi in Bornu, and he shared with both men in the great revival of Muslim scholarship in the western Sudan. But 'Umar had a wider experience of the Muslim world than either and must have been acquainted with both the modernism of Muḥammad 'Ali Pasha's regime in Egypt and the new puritanism of the Wahhābīs in Arabia. Also while in Arabia he seems to have been appointed the western African caliph of the relatively new Tijānī-yah brotherhood, which was appreciably more activist in its demand for reform than the Qādirīyah. About 1838, 'Umar arrived home in the Fouta, where he quickly became estranged from the local clerics. In 1848 he moved away with such followers as he had to Dinguiraye, on the borders of the Fouta Djallon. Here he built up a community of his own, attracting and training military and commercial adventurers as well as religious reformers. His community traded with the Upper Guinea coast for firearms and was consciously conceived as the nucleus for a new state. In 1852 the Dinguiraye community came into conflict with the adjacent Bambara chiefs. A *jihād* was launched northward through the gold-bearing valleys across the upper Sénégal, where in 1854 the Bambara kingdom of Kaarta fell. 'Umar then turned west down the Sénégal toward his own homeland and the French trading posts. But he was repulsed by the French, and after 1859 he sought to join with the Fulani of Macina in the conquest of the more powerful Bambara kingdom of Segu. The Macina Fulani were opposed to the idea of a Tijānī power advancing into their own Qādirī zone in the Niger Valley and even gave some aid to Segu. After 'Umar's forces had conquered Segu in 1861, they continued eastward, and, finding that Ahmadu's somewhat autocratic and intolerant regime had estranged the longer established Muslim communities, they established 'Umar's hegemony as far as Timbuktu (1863).

The empire at al-Ḥājj 'Umar
In less than 10 years, al-Ḥājj 'Umar's armies had conquered an empire almost as large as that of the Sokoto Fulani. It does not, however, appear to have been as well founded. Outside the Niger Valley and the major trading settlements, the bulk of its inhabitants were basically pagans who had only accepted Islām because they had been subjected to the shock of conquest by comparatively small bodies of well-armed and well-led adventurers. This was a different situation from that in which relatively large numbers of Muslim Fulani and Hausa had poured out from the old Hausa states into territories already prepared for them by the infiltration of Islām, of Hausa traders, and of Fulani settlers. In 'Umar's empire, individual captains, exempt from taxation themselves, settled down to exploit

their conquests as virtually independent fiefs. Along the Niger axis of empire, there were both old established Muslim towns and Fulani communities who regarded the Tijānī Tukulor as upstarts. In 1864 'Umar was killed trying to suppress a Fulani rebellion in Macina, and for many years his son and successor, Ahmadu Seku, had to compete for his inheritance with his father's numerous other relations and captains.

The most important result of 'Umar's conquests was that they established the Tijānīyah as the most powerful *ṭarīqah* in western African Islām, and this, together with the earlier consolidation of Muslim power in the east under Sokoto, ultimately ensured that Islām became the dominant religion throughout the western Sudan, and one capable of peaceful expansion deep into Guinea. Already circumstances had changed, however, since the Fulani cavaliers had built up the Sokoto Muslim empire. Al-Ḥājj 'Umar's empire builders relied on horses for their mobility, but they were also musketeers who knew the value of trade with the Europeans at the coast. Even more significantly, they had already come into conflict with, and had been worsted by, European military and political power advancing inland from the coast.

THE GUINEA COASTLANDS AND THE EUROPEANS (1807–79)

In addition to the Islāmic revolution in the Sudan, the major themes of western African history in the 19th century are the successful campaign against the export of slaves, the trade which for the previous two hundred years had been the mainstay of Guinea commerce; the search by both Africans and Europeans for a stable new relationship in the absence of slave trading; and the failure of the major African kingdoms to adjust to the new economic and social circumstances swiftly enough to withstand growing European pressures.

These three themes are closely interwoven in the course of events in Africa. However it should be noted that the major decisions regarding the abolition of the slave trade were taken outside Africa and were responses to economic and political changes and pressures in Europe and America. Many of the Christian churches had never accepted the morality of trading in human beings, and the 18th-century evangelical movements in Protestant Europe led to open campaigning against the Atlantic slave trade and also against the institution of slavery itself. These things were equally condemned by new secular currents of thought associated with the French Revolution. Since plantation production in tropical America was no longer as profitable a field for investment by northern Europeans as industry, or as trade with other parts of the world, the propaganda against the slave trade began to take effect. Denmark outlawed slave trading by its citizens in 1803, Great Britain in 1807, the United States in 1808, Sweden in 1813, The Netherlands in 1814, and France (for the second time) in 1818.

The most significant of these actions against the slave trade was that of Britain. British ships had been by far the largest carriers of slaves at the end of the 18th century, and only Britain really possessed the naval resources necessary to secure enforcement of anti-slave-trade laws on the high seas. Furthermore, when Portugal, Spain, and some American countries expanded their slave trading to meet the deficiency caused by the British withdrawal, they met with strong opposition from Britain. The underlying reason for this was that Britain, more than any other European nation, had considerable amounts of capital, experience, and goodwill accumulated in trade with Africa. But when British merchants tried to develop new lines in African trade to replace their old slave trade, they commonly found that, as long as their European or American rivals continued to buy slaves, African kings and merchants were generally not willing to organize alternative exports. Economic interest therefore combined with abstract morality to induce successive British governments to bring pressure on other governments to outlaw their slave trades and to permit the British navy to help enforce their laws on their ships at sea.

But these measures did not stop the export of slaves from Africa. Some nations, notably France and the United

The abolition of slavery

States, whose own naval controls were fitful, objected strongly to British warships stopping, searching, and, if need be, arresting their ships at sea. Furthermore, as long as there was a market for slaves in the Americas (*i.e.*, until all the American countries had abolished the institution of slavery), there were lawless individual traders who felt that the profits to be gained from running slaves across the Atlantic more than outweighed the risk of arrest. Except when actually embarking slaves on the African coast, or unloading them in American waters, the chances of interception at sea were in fact quite small. Although the British navy maintained in western African waters an anti-slave-trade squadron of up to 20 ships, which between 1825 and 1865 arrested 1,287 slave ships and liberated about 130,000 slaves, during the same period about 1,436,000 African slaves are believed to have been landed in the Americas.

The final cessation of the export of slaves from Africa to the Americas took place toward the end of the 1860s. The decisive factor was the abolition of slavery in the United States in 1865. Slavery was then legal only in Cuba and Brazil—and only to the 1880s—and the risks of transporting slaves to these two markets became too high. But before this, British governments had already embarked on a policy of taking or supporting active steps in Africa to stop slaves from being offered for sale on its coasts and to encourage the production of alternative exports. The immediate results of these efforts were often not very great. For example, many African governments and merchants were no more inclined than many European or American governments or merchants to enforce or to observe the anti-slave-trade treaties which British officials wished upon them. They saw no reason why their economic interests, which were bound up with slavery and trade in slaves, should be subordinated to the new economic interests of British traders following what was to them the capricious decision that slavery and the slave trade were wrong.

A British naval presence

What was significant was that Britain, through its desire to stop the export of slaves from western Africa and to protect the interests of British merchants desiring to trade in other commodities, maintained a substantial naval presence in western Africa and was also acquiring new political, commercial, and missionary presences. These led to increasing interference in the domestic affairs of African societies and their governments.

This interference began with the British naval squadron's need of shore stations to serve as bases for its patrolling ships and as landing places for the appreciable numbers of slaves it was intercepting. The slave ships had to be taken to a European jurisdiction to be condemned, and the slaves they had carried could not simply be returned to the societies that had sold them, but needed to be maintained as wards for whom Britain accepted political and moral responsibilities. British political officers and missionaries therefore became established on African soil, and the area of their activities was continually increasing. Explorers were penetrating the hinterland in search of new avenues for trade. British traders were competing with the slave traders. The liberated Africans were branching out into trade for themselves or simply returning home with new western and Christian attitudes—all these were apt to ask for political or missionary support, and, behind this, naval action could be called upon if there were difficulties with the local African rulers.

For the greater part of the 19th century, the prime centre for British naval, political, and missionary activities on the western African coast was Sierra Leone. Toward the end of the 18th century, the Sierra Leone peninsula had been chosen by British philanthropists as a suitable place to which Africans who had been taken to Britain as slaves and freed there, or who had fought on the British side in the War of American Independence, might be repatriated. A first group was sent out and settled on the site of the future Freetown in 1787, and, though many of the early settlers did not survive, others were brought, and by 1811 Freetown had a liberated African population of about 2,000.

After a first false start, the philanthropists hoped to find funds for the maintenance of their settlement by placing it under the control of a company they had floated to trade with the interior. But the only trade that prospered in the Sierra Leone region was the slave trade, in which the company naturally did not engage, and after 1799, their colony, whose indeterminate constitutional status caused many difficulties, was able to survive only with the help of annual grants-in-aid from the British government. Eventually, in 1808, the British government agreed to take over direct responsibility for the colony from the Sierra Leone Company.

British coastal settlements

Freetown was not the only British settlement on the western African coast. Officials of a descendant of the old African Company of slave trading days still occupied a number of forts on the Gold Coast and one in the Gambia, and these were now meant to provide support for British merchants engaged in other trades. In 1817, after the settlements on the Sénégal, which had been in British hands during the Napoleonic Wars, had been handed back to France, a considerable number of British traders and their African associates moved to the mouth of the Gambia River and established there the new settlement of Bathurst. Neither the Gambia nor the Gold Coast were exclusive British spheres, however. The French were very strong competitors on the former, and both the Dutch and the Danes still held forts on the latter, and where European interests were divided, there was no certainty that the British settlements would prosper in competition with slave traders, nor that they could be developed as effective bases in an active campaign against that trade.

From 1808, however, British policy required that such a base be maintained in western Africa, and Freetown was the obvious choice. It had one of the few good natural harbours on the coast, and it was already experienced in the resettlement of liberated slaves. Christian missions had begun to establish themselves there since 1806, and it now became the seat of a British governor and of anti-slave-trade courts, and the headquarters of the navy's western African squadron. During the next 60 years, this squadron was to swell the population under British rule by landing some 60,000 men and women, from all over western Africa, whom it had taken from arrested slave ships. Freetown's only serious disadvantage was that it was at one end of the slave-exporting coast. In 1827, therefore, the British navy also began to use the island of Fernando Po in the Gulf of Guinea as an alternative base and freed slave settlement. But this activity aroused the interest of the Spanish government, which had had a legal claim to the island since 1778, and in 1834 the settlement was abandoned.

From 1814 to 1824, the British governor and commander in chief at Freetown was Sir Charles M'Carthy, an active military man who thought that the most effective means of achieving Britain's aims in western Africa was to extend its formal dominion over the most vexatious outlets for the slave trade. The home government for a time countenanced this policy and in 1821 transferred the forts on the Gambia and Gold Coast to M'Carthy's administration. During the 10 years of his government, its expenditure quadrupled to nearly $400,000 a year. However there was no corresponding increase in British trade (nor any diminution of the slave trade), with the result that the cost had to be met by British taxpayers who were antagonistic to spending money on colonies. In 1824, M'Carthy's forward policy led him to make common cause with the Fante against Ashanti claims to overlordship on the Gold Coast. In the war that followed, however, he was defeated and killed, and the British government decided that it should withdraw from all formal commitments in western Africa except at Sierra Leone.

In fact the most prosperous British trade was developing on a part of the coast on which there was no British interference other than naval action to intercept slave ships and to secure anti-slave-trade treaties. This was the Niger Delta. British shipping had been paramount here when the British slave trade had been abolished in 1807, and the merchants of the delta city-states had quickly adapted themselves to offering palm oil as an alternative export to slaves.

Britain's industrial revolution had occasioned a growing

British
trade with
the Niger
Delta

demand for vegetable oils as lubricants and for the manufacture of soap, and the new Lancashire cotton industry was producing in quantity a commodity with which palm oil might readily be purchased. By the 1830s, the British purchases of palm oil in western Africa were worth nearly $2,000,000 a year. About nine-tenths of this trade was initially with the Niger Delta. The oil palm grows throughout a belt just behind the western African coast, and the oil from its fruit was already widely consumed and traded locally. Africans of the delta were much quicker and more successful in developing an export trade in palm oil than were those of other coastal regions. One reason was simply that the oil was not easy to transport in quantity, and its value was low in proportion to its bulk. Canoe transport was thus easier and cheaper than headloading or cask rolling, and the delta afforded a ready-made system of waterways. But its hinterland also had an unusually dense population in a relatively poor agricultural environment, and therefore had both a greater need to exploit the semiwild palm trees than was usually the case and more labour with which to do this and to manufacture and transport the oil. Moreover the collection of the fruit and the manufacture of the oil were traditional household activities, and to exploit these for export necessitated a commercial system that was both wide and intensive and in addition highly responsive and flexible.

The small, highly competitive city-states of the Niger Delta, built up and ruled by merchants, could exploit the overseas demand for palm oil much more quickly and efficiently than was possible elsewhere. In Liberia and the western Ivory Coast, for example, the trading network, like the population, was thin and little advanced. Elsewhere export trading (for example in slaves or gold) had been directed, or at least controlled, by large-scale organizations which were less flexible, and which were politically motivated, and much less responsive to commercial changes; among these were the traditional political hierarchies of large kingdoms such as Benin, Ashanti, and Dahomey, or the new politico-religious administrations of the Fouta Djallon or of al-Ḥājj 'Umar. It may be noted, incidentally, that the successful development of palm-oil exports from Yorubaland followed upon the collapse of the Oyo empire there. It was not until about the 1860s, when the total British purchases of palm oil were worth about $6,000,000 a year, that exports from the rest of western Africa, with Yorubaland in the vanguard, began to equal those of the Niger Delta.

British official policy toward western Africa remained one of minimum intervention until the 1870s. Indeed the view that Britain should withdraw from all commitments other than in Sierra Leone was most forcefully asserted by a Parliamentary Select Committee as late as 1865. In fact, however, both positive and negative results of the active British campaign against the Atlantic slave trade made it impossible for the policy of nonintervention to be maintained in practice.

The growth of the spirit of European scientific inquiry during the 18th and 19th centuries combined with a practical interest in finding out what Africa produced besides slaves that could be of value to world trade, and what political, economic, and transport systems existed to permit such products to be brought down to the coast, to lead to a great movement of European exploration of the interior of western Africa between 1788 and 1855. This movement was primarily directed from Britain, and from 1805 the British government sponsored many of the major expeditions.

These explorations suggested a possible strategy of breaking through the barrier of the established slave-trading states at the coast by using the Niger River to trade directly with the interior. This seemed attractive after the rejection of the M'Carthy policy of positive coastal action, and from 1832 onward the British government sponsored or helped to sponsor a number of expeditions designed to develop navigation up the Niger. By 1854, quinine and the steamship had solved the technical problems of navigating the lower river, but a new political problem had been created in the objections of both black and white

traders in the delta to their established trading system being bypassed in this way.

By the middle of the century, the development of the liberated African community in Sierra Leone under the tutelage of British administration, churches, and education meant that some of its members were providing a considerable reinforcement for the British interest in western Africa. Economic activities in Sierra Leone itself were limited, and Sierra Leoneans were soon finding their way along the coast as independent pioneers of trade and westernization or as auxiliaries to British traders, officials, and missionaries. Their most significant influence was in Yorubaland. By the 1840s, at least half the liberated Africans were of Yoruba extraction, and by this time their homeland afforded considerable scope both for independent traders and for men seeking to introduce Christian and Western ideas and ways into African life. Both these circumstances derived from the failure of the Oyo empire in the 18th century to establish a stable form of central government capable of maintaining a firm control over the provinces it had conquered. There remained a dangerously uncertain balance of power between the king and the traditional chiefs of the capital.

The
exodus
from
Sierra
Leone

Such a situation was by no means unique in the history of the kingdoms of Guinea (or, for that matter, of western Africa). Dahomey seems to have avoided it only because its kings, initiating their kingdom through the conquest of peoples who were not of their own stock, had been able to build up an unusually authoritarian form of government. But both in Benin and Ashanti traditional kinship organizations imposed restraints on royal authority, and tensions could develop when it came to sharing the rewards of empire and trade. There was a near disastrous civil war at Benin at the end of the 17th century, though the King emerged from it with his authority strengthened, apparently because he was able to play off the town chiefs against the chiefs of his palace. Ashanti had come into being as an alliance of petty kingdoms against Denkyera, and its kings, desiring to be more than merely *primus inter pares*, began by entrusting the new kingdom's conquests mainly to the chiefs of their capital, Kumasi. But the chiefs then sought to control the monarch, and the latter had to turn for help from the provincial rulers to release him from this situation. Ultimately, however, from the time of Osei Kojo (c. 1764–77), the kings secured their preeminence throughout the kingdom by building up a new hierarchical military and civil administration, which was responsible uniquely to them and which limited the power of both sets of chiefs.

At Oyo, the traditional town chiefs, who commanded the army of the capital, converted the kings into puppets during the 1750s and 1760s. But about 1774 they gave the throne to a king, Abiodun, who escaped from their control and used provincial forces to establish royal authority over the capital. After Abiodun's death (c. 1789), the provincial chiefs began to act with increasing independence. When (c. 1817) the viceroy of the north invited Fulani aid to help consolidate his rebellion, the result was not simply that the kings of Oyo lost their northern provinces to the Fulani; they also lost control over the northern trade routes on which they depended for their vital supplies of horses and slaves, and eventually (c. 1836) had to evacuate their capital to the south. By this time there was no longer any central authority at all, and everywhere ambitious men were vying with each other to create personal dominions over as many clients and slaves as possible.

One consequence of this situation was a great increase in the number of slaves available for export from nearby Dahomey, which by 1818 had thrown off the last vestiges of Oyo suzerainty and was soon sending its armies deep into Yorubaland, and from independent traders at ports like Lagos and Badagri. It was the close attention given by the British navy to these coasts that had led to the build-up of Yoruba former slaves in Sierra Leone. By the 1840s, considerable numbers of these men were returning to Lagos and to Badagri and, especially, to the new inland town of Abeokuta, originally built up as a refuge where Egba (southern Yoruba) peoples could withstand pressures from Ibadan, the most powerful of the new Yoruba political

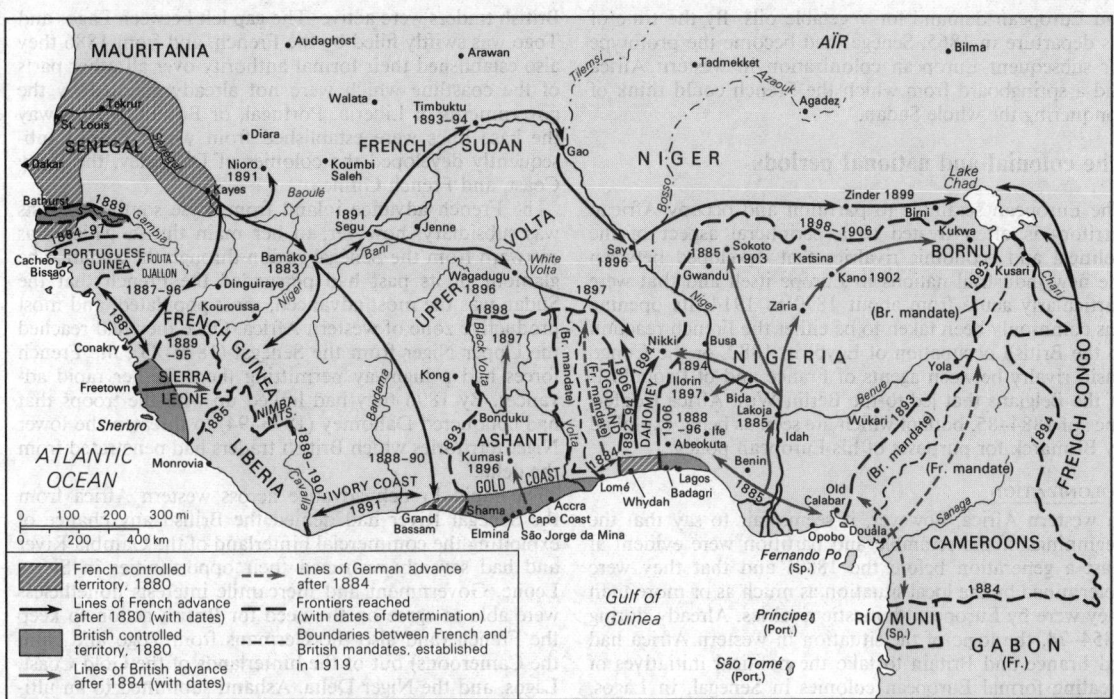

European penetration into West Africa in the late 19th century.

From J. Fage, *An Atlas of African History*, Edward Arnold (Publishers) Ltd.

The first British consulate

units, and from Dahomey. The advent of the settlers from Sierra Leone soon brought British missionaries also, and a new British-aligned influence was added to the tangled web of Yoruba politics.

British officialdom soon followed. In 1848 a British consulate had been established for the Gulf of Guinea to maintain British interests in the complex situation arising from the splintered politics of the Niger Delta and the beginnings of navigation on the river itself.

The consuls joined with naval officers in attempts to stop the king of Dahomey from exporting slaves, and, when repulsed, turned to Lagos, where they saw their opportunity in a split in the royal family. In 1851 the British navy restored to his throne a deposed monarch who had promised to stop the Lagos slave trade. He was in fact powerless to do this without continued British support: Lagos became the seat of a second British consulate in 1853, and in 1861 it was annexed. British and Sierra Leonean traders endeavouring to develop palm oil trade with Yorubaland were soon trying to persuade the colonial government at Lagos that only a further advance of its authority into the hinterland would stop its wars and its export of slaves and allow their own affairs to prosper.

The first serious advance of British power in western Africa occurred on the Gold Coast. After the withdrawal of British officials and troops in 1828, the British Gold Coast traders took on a young army officer, George Maclean, to represent their interests there. Maclean negotiated a peace with Ashanti and established an informal jurisdiction through the coastal states, which brought security for both British and Ashanti merchants. The consequent fourfold increase in British trade combined with the uncertain legal status of Maclean's jurisdiction to bring British officials back to the forts in 1843. In 1850 they took over the Danish forts also, but the continued Dutch presence on the coast prevented them from raising an effective revenue from customs duties, and they quarrelled with the coastal peoples over the issue of direct taxation. They therefore failed to erect an effective coastal administration of their own on the foundation laid by Maclean, and they equally rejected alternatives proffered by educated Africans in cooperation with the coastal chiefs. Trade declined, and Ashanti's armies began to invade the coastlands to protect its interests there. Eventually the Dutch were led to withdraw altogether (1872), and the British to invade Ashanti and destroy its capital, and to declare the whole coast a colony (1874).

Three-quarters of a century of turmoil following the British decision to campaign against the Atlantic slave trade and to foster the interests of legitimate trade and Christian civilization in western Africa had therefore resulted in the establishment of the new colony of Sierra Leone and direct British intervention in African affairs in much of the most prosperous area of the old trade—the Gold Coast, Lagos, and the delta and lower river of the Niger.

African sovereignty had also been infringed between Sierra Leone and the Ivory Coast where, inspired by the Sierra Leone example, private United States organizations had settled freed slaves for whom there was no place in their own society prior to 1863. British and French merchants questioned the right of the settlers to control and to tax their trade and, since formal U.S. policy was anti-colonial, the result, in 1847, was the proclamation of the Republic of Liberia. The settler government then embarked on a long struggle to assert control over the local Africans. Since, unlike a colonial government, it had no metropolitan resources or finance to help, this was a prolonged business.

The Republic of Liberia

The growth of British trade, and of British influence and power, in western Africa was by no means to the liking of the government, traders, and navy of France—Britain's principal competitors in the previous century. But France's mercantile interest in western Africa was not as strong as Britain's, and its traders there received less official and naval support than did the British. Not until the 1870s and the opening of the European scramble was any serious effort made to develop the trading footholds that were established on the coast between Senegal and Sierra Leone, on the Ivory Coast, and between the Gold Coast and Lagos.

France's main effort in western Africa was devoted to developing its old interests in Senegal, from which the British withdrew in 1817. Initially an attempt was made to replace the former business of exporting labour to the West Indies by developing a local plantation economy. By the 1820s, this was foundering, and matters then drifted until the arrival in 1854 of a new governor, Louis Faidherbe, a soldier with experience in the conquest of Algeria and in the government of its peoples. Faidherbe's concept was to secure control of the exports of the westernmost Sudan by extending French military and political control up the Sénégal River and to encourage local African production of the peanut (groundnut) to help meet the growing French

Senegal as a colonial prototype

and European demand for vegetable oils. By the time of his departure in 1865, Senegal had become the prototype for subsequent European colonization in western Africa and a springboard from which the French could think of conquering the whole Sudan.

The colonial and national periods

The European scramble to partition and occupy African territory is often treated as a peripheral aspect of the political and economic rivalries that developed between the new industrial nations in Europe itself and that were particularly acute from about 1870 to 1914. Its opening has commonly been taken to be either the French reaction to the British occupation of Egypt in 1882, or the Congo basin rivalry between agents of France and of Leopold II of the Belgians that led to the Berlin West Africa Conference of 1884–85, both of which are seen as being exploited by Bismarck for purposes of his European policy.

COLONIZATION

In western Africa, however, it seems fair to say that the beginnings of the scramble and partition were evident at least a generation before the 1880s and that they were determined by the local situation as much as or more than they were by European domestic rivalries. Already during 1854–74, the logic of the situation in western Africa had led France and Britain to take the political initiatives of creating formal European colonies in Senegal, in Lagos, and the Gold Coast. All along the coast, in fact, traditional African political order was becoming ineffective in the face of European economic and social pressures. For most of the 19th century, these pressures had been predominantly British, but in the 1870s French companies began to offer effective competition to the British traders not only in Upper Guinea, where they had always been strong, but also on the Ivory Coast, in the ports immediately to the west of Lagos, and even in the lower river and delta of the Niger. An unstable situation was developing in which the European traders were likely to call for further intervention and support from their governments, and especially so if the terms of trade were to turn against them. Low world prices for primary produce during the depression years from the 1870s to the mid-1890s certainly caused difficulties for Europeans trading to western Africa and led them to think that an increase in European control there would enable them to secure its produce more cheaply.

The changing balance of power in western Africa was not confined to the coastlands. By the 1870s, formal French and British armies had already ventured into the interior and had inflicted defeats on such major African powers as those of al-Ḥājj 'Umar and Ashanti. And in 1879 Faidherbe's heirs on the Sénégal River had already launched the thrust which was to take French arms conquering eastward across the Sudan to Lake Chad and beyond.

By the end of the 1870s France and Britain were already on the march in western Africa. The principal effect of the new forces stemming from domestic power rivalries in Europe itself—the most dramatic of which was the appearance in 1884 of the German flag on the Togoland coast, between the Gold Coast and Dahomey, and in the Cameroons—was to intensify and to accelerate existing French and British tendencies to exert their political and military authority at the expense of traditional African rulers.

French incentives to expand

There can be no question but that, by the end of the 1870s, the advance of the British interest in western Africa had been more rewarding than the advance of the French interest. Devoting their attention primarily to the active economies of the Niger Delta, the Lagos hinterland, and the Gold Coast, British traders had secured $24,000,000 of business a year, compared with the French merchants' trade of $8,000,000, three-quarters of which was concentrated on the Sénégal River. Initially, therefore, the French had much more incentive for expansion than the British.

Britain was already in political control of the Gold Coast, and the arrival of the German treaty makers in Togo and in the Cameroons in 1884 hastened it to declare its protectorate over most of the intervening coastline on which

British traders were active. The gap left between Lagos and Togo was swiftly filled by the French, and from 1886 they also established their formal authority over all other parts of the coastline which were not already claimed by the governments of Liberia, Portugal, or Britain. In this way the base lines were established from which France subsequently developed the colonies of Dahomey, the Ivory Coast, and French Guinea.

The French advance inland from these southern coasts was subsidiary, however, to her main thrust, which was eastward from the Sénégal region through the Sudan. The glamour of its past had persuaded the French that the Sudan was the most advanced, most populated, and most productive zone of western Africa. Once they had reached the Upper Niger from the Sénégal (1879–83), the French forces had a highway permitting them further rapid advances. By 1896 they had linked up with the troops that had conquered Dahomey (1893–94) to threaten the lower Niger territories which British traders had penetrated from the delta.

The rapid French advance across western Africa from the Sénégal River had denied the British any chance of exploiting the commercial hinterland of the Gambia River and had severely restricted their opportunities in Sierra Leone. Government and mercantile interests nonetheless were able to agree on the need for British action to keep the French (and also the Germans from Togo and from the Cameroons) out of the hinterlands of the Gold Coast, Lagos, and the Niger Delta. Ashanti submitted to an ultimatum in 1896 (the real war of conquest was delayed until 1900–01, when the British had to suppress a widespread rebellion against their authority), and a British protectorate was extended northward to the traditional limits of Ashanti influence.

On the Niger, British interests were first maintained by an amalgamation of trading companies formed in 1879 by Sir George Goldie to combat French commercial competition. In 1897 the British government agreed to support Goldie's Royal Niger Company in the development of military forces. Three years later, however, it recognized the foolishness of allowing the company's servants and soldiers to compete for African territory with French government officials and troops and to enforce its monopolistic policies on all other traders within its sphere. The company was divested of its political role, and the British government itself took over direct responsibility for the conquest of most of the Sokoto empire. Thus, although the French eventually reached Lake Chad, they were kept to the southern edges of the Sahara, and most of the well-populated Hausa agricultural territory became the British protectorate of Northern Nigeria. In 1914 this was merged with the Yoruba territories, which had been entered from Lagos during the 1890s, and with the protectorate over the Niger Delta region to constitute a single Colony and Protectorate of Nigeria.

From company territory to protectorate

As early as 1898, Europeans had staked out colonies over all western Africa except for some 40,000 square miles of territory left to the Republic of Liberia. Portugal had taken virtually no active part in the scramble, and its once extensive influence was now confined within the 14,000 square miles which became the colony of Portuguese Guinea. Germany, the latecomer, had claimed the 33,000 square miles of Togo (together with the much larger Cameroon territory on the eastern borders of what is usually accepted as western Africa). France and Britain remained, as before, the main imperial powers.

France claimed by far the larger amount of territory, nearly 1,800,000 square miles some 450,000 square miles in the four enclaves secured by Britain. In other terms, however, France had done less well. Its territory included a large part of the Sahara, and her three inland colonies of the Sudan (modern Mali), Upper Volta (modern Burkina Faso), and Niger were by and large scantily populated and, because of their remoteness from the coast, were contributing little or nothing to the world economy. In 1897, the trade of the four British colonies was worth about $24,000,000, compared with about $14,000,000 for the seven French territories, and their combined population of more than 20,000,000 was more than twice as great.

The political boundaries established by the Europeans by 1898 (though usually not surveyed or demarcated on the ground until much later) largely determine the political map of western Africa even today. The only subsequent change of significance followed the British and French conquests of the German colonies during World War I (1914–18). While the larger parts of both Togo and Cameroon were entrusted by the League of Nations to the French to administer as separate colonies, in each case a smaller western part was entrusted to Britain to be administered together with the Gold Coast and Nigeria respectively. Ultimately British Togo chose to join with the Gold Coast and so became part of the new independent Ghana. The northern part of British Cameroon similarly joined with Nigeria, but the southern part chose instead to federate with the former French Cameroon.

If 20 years had sufficed for the European powers to partition western African lands, at least a further 20 years were needed to establish colonial regimes that were effective throughout all the vast territories claimed by Europe and that were accepted by all the Africans involved. The first problem was a military one.

Feudal levies versus modern technological warfare

Small and mobile columns of African soldiers, led and trained by European officers and noncommissioned officers and equipped with precision rifles, machine guns, and artillery, rarely experienced much difficulty in defeating the great empires created by the 19th-century jihādists. These chose to meet the invaders in pitched battles in which their massed feudal levies, with few modern weapons and limited skill in their use, served only as targets for the superior firepower and discipline of their opponents. Once these battles had been lost, the surviving leaders were usually ready to acknowledge the Europeans as new overlords. The main problems here were really ones of distance and logistics. Thus it was not until 1900–03 that Sir Frederick Lugard's forces were sufficiently established in northern Nigeria to defeat the Sokoto Fulani, while the French "pacification" of the even more remote territory further north, which eventually became their colony of Niger, was not really completed until the 1920s.

A much more serious military problem was often presented by smaller political units, which were ethnically more homogeneous and often more densely populated than the jihād empires. Their subjugation was often a protracted business in which the Europeans had to fight virtually for each settlement. This was the case with the British campaign against Ashanti in 1900–01, with the subjugation of the Sierra Leone protectorate in 1898–99, and above all, perhaps, with the advance of British power into the densely populated Ibo and Tiv territories, which was hardly complete until as late as 1918. Similarly, the most formidable resistance faced by the French came not from the Tukolor, but from the more southerly empire established from the 1860s onward from the hinterland of Sierra Leone to western Gonja by the Mande leader Samory. Though Samory was a Muslim whose activities did much to consolidate the hold of Islām in his territories, he was not a cleric like Usman dan Fodio or al-Ḥājj 'Umar. He came from a family of Dyula traders and soldiers, and the principles of his government recalled those of ancient Mali rather than of the jihād empires. Samory established his network of military and political control over territories long subject to Mande commercial penetration and settlement, and a number of campaigns had to be fought against him until he was finally captured and exiled by the French in 1898.

Once the superior firepower and organization of the Europeans had secured their military supremacy, they were faced with the very much larger problem of how the very small forces they commanded were to maintain a permanent occupation and effective control over the vast territories they had overrun. Lugard, for instance, had conquered the Sokoto empire with only some 3,000 soldiers, only 150 of whom were Europeans, and to administer his northern Nigerian colony of some 250,000 square miles and 10,000,000 people he had a civil establishment of only 200 Europeans. This kind of situation persisted almost throughout the colonial period. At the end of the 1930s, for example, the European establishment available

to the British governor of the Gold Coast to control nearly 4,000,000 people was only 842. It is obvious, then, that the conquerors were often very slow to extend effective rule throughout their empires, and particularly to those parts of them that were most remote, presented serious political problems, or seemed least profitable.

Initial difficulty of administration

No European control could be exercised without the cooperation of large numbers of Africans. This was secured in two ways. First, just as the Europeans had relied on Africans for the rank and file of their armies and police, so their administrations and economic enterprises could not function without a host of Africans employed as clerks, messengers, craftsmen of all kinds, and labourers. All of this employment offered new opportunities to Africans, and to ensure an efficient labour force all European administrations began to supplement and develop the schools begun by the missionaries.

As well as recruiting and training large numbers of Africans as auxiliaries in all spheres of European activity, the colonial powers also came to rely on African chiefs as essential intermediaries in the chain of authority between the colonial governments and their subjects at large. Both the French and the British colonial regimes were essentially hierarchical. The administration of each colony was entrusted to a governor who was responsible to a colonial minister in the government in Europe (in the French case, via a governor general at Dakar). These governors were assisted by senior officials and a secretariat in the colonial capital, and their decisions and orders were transmitted for implementation to provincial and direct commissioners. A district officer, however, could not deal directly with each of the tens, or even hundreds of thousands of Africans in his care. He therefore gave orders either to the traditional chiefs or to Africans who had been recognized as local rulers by his government, and these passed them on to the people at large.

Here a difference of theory began to be discernible between French and British policy. The French regarded the local African chiefs as the lowest elements in a single administrative machine. This administration was to be conducted on entirely French lines. The British, on the other hand, came to believe more and more in "indirect rule." British authority was not to reach directly down to each individual African subject. While the British retained overall control of a colony's administration, it was to be made effective at the district level by cultivating and by molding the governments of the traditional African rulers.

The policy of indirect rule

Indirect rule was neither a new nor a specifically British expedient. Maclean had been an indirect ruler on the Gold Coast in the 1830s; Goldie had proposed indirect rule for the empire his Royal Niger Company had hoped to conquer; and, in the early days of their expansion, the French had often had no alternative but to seek to control their newly won territories through the agency of the African governments they had conquered. But once they were firmly established, the French almost invariably moved away from the practice. The British, on the other hand, evolved a theory of indirect rule which they endeavoured to apply systematically to their colonies throughout the first half of the 20th century. This was largely due to the influence of Lugard. In 1900–06 he had seen no other way to control the vast population in northern Nigeria, whose rulers he had defeated, and he had subsequently been promoted governor general (1912–19) of a united Nigeria, which was by far the most important British colony in Africa. Finally, after his retirement to Britain, he became a dominating influence on the formation of colonial administrative policy, so that indirect rule became accepted as the ideal philosophy of government for British tropical Africa.

Not all areas of western Africa were as suitable for Lugardian indirect rule as northern Nigeria. Lugard himself experienced considerable problems in trying to apply it to the largely chiefless societies of eastern Nigeria and to the Yoruba of the southwest, where authority and law were not as clear cut. In the Gold Coast indirect rule proved more acceptable to the Ashanti than the direct rule imposed after the conquest of 1900–01, but further south the Western-style economy and modes of thought had made such inroads that there were endless problems in the implementation of indirect rule, and the full constitutional apparatus for it was hardly installed until the 1940s.

The development of indirect rule also implied a contradiction with an earlier tradition of British colonial government, that of the colonial legislative council. The governors of British colonies were allowed more initiative than French governors and were supposed to exercise this in the interests of their individual territories insofar as these did not contradict the overriding British interest. To help them in this, each colony was equipped with a legislative council that included representatives of local opinion, and this council's consent was normally required before laws were enacted or the colonial government's budget was approved.

The institution of the legislative council had evolved from experience with settler colonies outside Africa; when they were introduced into tropical Africa from the 1840s onward, most of the council members were colonial officials, and the unofficial members represented trade and the professions rather than the traditional communities and were nominated by the governor rather than elected. In the 19th century both government officials and traders and professionals were almost as likely to be black as white, and the early legislative councils were by no means ineffective vehicles for the expression of African interests and of criticisms of British policy. It was thus possible both for the British and for the educated African elite in their colonies to view the legislative councils as embryo parliaments which would eventually become composed of elected African members who would control the executive governments, which would themselves, through the growth of education in the colonies, become more and more composed of African officials.

Though very little thought was given to the matter, because it was supposed that the development might take centuries, it was supposed that the British colonies in Africa would follow the example of Canada and Australia and ultimately emerge as self-governing members of the empire. The equally remote future for the French colonies, on the other hand, was thought to be the acculturation (assimilation) of their people, so that ultimately they would all become full French citizens, the colonies would be integrated with metropolitan France, and the African citizens would share equally with the French-born in its institutions.

Both of these ideals were more appropriate to the colonial situations in western Africa before the great scramble for territory which began in 1879, when the colonies were comparatively small territories in which European influence had been slowly but steadily gaining ground for a considerable period. They were effectively shelved when it came to grappling with the problem of governing the enormously greater numbers of Africans without any real previous contacts with European ways who were quickly brought under colonial rule in the years after 1879. Thus on the French side, though those born in the four major communes (Saint-Louis, Gorée, Rufisque, and Dakar) of the old colony of Senegal continued to enjoy the French citizenship that they had been granted prior to 1879, other Africans became French subjects (possessing the obligations of citizens but not their rights), who could only qualify for citizenship after stringent tests. Thus by 1937, out of an estimated 15,000,000 people under French rule in western Africa, only some 80,500 were citizens, and only 2,500 of these had acquired their citizenship by means other than the accident of birth in one of the four communes.

In the British colonies, however, where the legislative councils were already a reality, there was a dichotomy between them and the institution of indirect rule. Initially, insofar as this was resolved at all, it was at the expense of the development of the legislative councils. Thus the competence of the council in the Gold Coast was not extended to Ashanti before 1946, while in Nigeria until 1922 the council's competence was restricted only to the small territory of Lagos. It was not until 1922 also that any elected members appeared in the councils, and they remained for a generation a small proportion of the total

The legislative councils as embryo parliaments

unofficial membership, chosen only by tiny electorates in a few coastal towns. For the rest, the African population remained firmly under British control through the mechanism of indirect rule. The implication was not only that the norms of African society and political behaviour were far removed from those of western Europe, but also that the British had by no means accepted that African society and politics would or should evolve in that direction. Those few Africans who had become educated and acculturated in Western ways were not thought to be representative of the mass. There was a move also to exclude local Africans from the colonial administration, which became regarded as a professional service, liable to serve anywhere in Africa, with the role of holding the ring until, in some unexplained fashion, the native administrations under indirect rule had developed sufficiently to make British control superfluous.

Colonial rule. In fact, of course, the very existence of colonial rule meant that the fabric of African societies was exposed to alien forces of change of an intensity and on a scale unparalleled in the previous history of western Africa. Hitherto remote territories like Niger and Mauritania, where there had been very little change since the introduction of Islām from about 1900 suddenly caught up in the same tide of aggressive material changes that had for some time been affecting the coastal societies in Senegal or in the southern Gold Coast and Nigeria. From the African point of view, there was little to choose between the European colonial powers. Portugal, despite the fact that it was virtually bankrupt at the onset of the colonial period, was as significant a bringer of change as France, Germany, and Britain. In fact in the long run, a strange combination of its poverty with memories of its older colonial tradition were to make Portugal's sense of a *mission civilisatrice* even more pervasive and lasting than that of its stronger rivals.

Liberia's formal status as an independent republic did not mean that the forces of change associated with the colonial period were excluded from its territory. Its Afro-American ruling elite were orphaned members of a very rapidly changing Western society, who felt it essential to impose its ethos on black Africa. While colonial administrators often had a narrow, 19th-century concept of government as an arbiter, rather than as an active protagonist of change, the Liberians felt a need actively to enlist the support of Western capital and enterprise if they were to consolidate their rule over African peoples and to maintain the independence of their republic.

Up to 1912, the inexperience and relative weakness of Liberia's ruling elite meant that it achieved little except to run up a dangerous indebtedness to ingenuous and potentially rapacious European investors. In 1925–26, however, the tide began to turn for them when the U.S. Firestone Tire & Rubber Company, worried lest its supplies of raw material should become a British colonial monopoly, secured a new American loan for Liberia and began to operate a 1,000,000-acre (400,000-hectare) plantation concession in the hinterland of Monrovia. The country was now supplied with a sure access to world trade, and its government with the means to achieve a stable revenue. Within 25 years, Liberia's foreign trade grew from less than $3,000,000 a year to some $45,000,000, and government revenue from a mere $500,000 a year to nearly $10,000,000. The evident dangers that Liberia might become too dependent on a single export crop, and that it and its administration might become sole fiefs of the American company, began to disappear when during World War II U.S. strategic interests caused its government to begin to give aid to Liberia and to develop its first modern port, and when in the 1950s both American and European interests began to exploit Liberia's large-scale deposits of high-grade iron ore. By the 1960s Liberia was on the way to becoming one of the richest of western African countries, and the ruling elite began to feel sufficiently secure to share both some of its political power and some of its prosperity with the native peoples.

A cardinal rule for all colonial administrations in Africa before the 1930s was that colonies ought not to be a financial burden on the metropolitan governments and their

The colonialists as harbingers of material change

taxpayers: the cost of colonial administration and development should be covered by the local revenues they could raise. So long as such a doctrine was maintained, it was impossible for any but the richest colonial administrations to devise coherent plans for the economic development of their territories; indeed, prior to the 1940s, the colonial government of the Gold Coast was virtually unique in putting forward such a plan, and then only in the 1920s, which were by and large exceptionally prosperous years.

Sources of revenue

The principal sources of revenue were two: (1) duties on the trade entering and leaving the territory; and (2) direct taxation (usually a poll tax or hut tax). But only those coastal colonies that had already entered the world economy prior to around 1880 had much in the way of trade on which customs duties might be levied or a sufficient internal production of commodities and circulation of money to produce any significant income from direct taxation. Other territories—such as British northern Nigeria, or the French colonies of the Sudan and Niger—could not really provide enough revenue to support even the most essential administrative services, such as policing or—for that matter—tax gathering. For some time, therefore, these administrations were in receipt of grants-in-aid from some central source, and it was an attempt to shift this burden from metropolitan resources that as much as anything led the French in 1895 to bring together their western African colonies under a government general, and that led Lugard to argue for the unification of the Nigerian colonies, which he eventually achieved in 1912–14. In each case it seemed advisable to use some of the comparatively buoyant revenues of the coastal territories to subsidize the administrations of those in the interior.

It was obvious enough that what was needed was to increase the European commercial penetration of western Africa. But only the prospect of the most lucrative prizes could induce private European investors to place substantial amounts of capital in Africa in advance of adequate European administrations that could guarantee the safety and security of their investments, and in advance of the economic infrastructures that would ensure their efficient deployment. The only lure that really operated to attract European investment in advance of the provision of such services was the prospect of rich mineral deposits. As it happens, the greater part of western Africa's mineral wealth lies in ores such as those of iron, aluminum, and manganese, which are extremely bulky in relation to their value, requiring very large investments in transport and other facilities before they can be economically worked, and for which there was relatively little overseas demand before the 1930s. The possibilities of diamond mining in Sierra Leone and the Gold Coast were not really recognized until the 1930s. In effect then, it was only the gold of the Gold Coast and Ashanti forests and, to a lesser extent, the tin of the Bauchi plateau in central Nigeria, which attracted the early attention of European investors.

Early investment incentives

Modern methods of gold-mining first began to be employed on the Gold Coast as early as 1878, but the industry could not make much effective headway before 1902. By that time the colonial government had taken the decisive steps of defeating Ashanti, of beginning to build a railway system, and of establishing an effective civil administration in the relevant areas, which could ensure proper land surveys and some means of controlling and adjudicating disputes over the ownership of land and the validity of concessions of it. Bauchi tin-mining began much later, in 1903, but here too, similar, if less acute, difficulties prevented much progress before 1914.

Despite their poverty, and despite the risk of saddling the home governments and taxpayers with unwanted expenditure, colonial governments found that there was no alternative to themselves providing the basic infrastructures needed by the vast territories they claimed to rule. It was impossible to wait for private European enterprise to provide railways, harbours, telegraph lines, roads, medical services, schools, and all the other things that were needed to support an effective government, let alone to provide some possibility of economic growth sufficient to pay for better government.

French territories. The problems facing the French were much more formidable than those facing the British. The British colonies were essentially based on territories close to the sea, in which European trade had been long established and whose African peoples were already accustomed to producing for the world market. The French had such a colony in Senegal, but from this they had expanded over vast, remote, and thinly populated territories that required very considerable investment before they could be efficiently administered or developed. By and large the French public had appreciably less capital to invest overseas than the British public had. By 1936, it was estimated that, whereas the British colonies in western Africa had attracted about $560,000,000 of capital, the total outside investment in French West Africa amounted only to some $155,000,000.

French strategy was initially to open up and develop its western African empire from a base in Senegal on the same Sénégal–Niger river axis along which it had been conquered. As early as 1882, work was begun on a railway to link the heads of navigation of the two rivers at Kayes and at Bamako (which became the capital of the French Sudan). But this line was not completed until 1906, by which time it had become evident that Saint-Louis, at the mouth of the Sénégal River, was not capable of development into a modern port, and that the Sénégal was really suitable for navigation for only three months in the year. So first a railway was completed from Saint-Louis to the new harbour of Dakar in the lee of Cape Verde (1885), and then during 1907–24 a line was built directly from Dakar (since 1902, the federal capital for French West Africa) to Kayes to bypass the Sénégal River altogether.

The construction of an effective west–east transport system from the coast to the Upper Niger thus took some 44 years to complete, and the only part of it that was profitable was that serving the peanut-growing areas of Senegal. There was a lag of some 20 years after 1924 before the thinly populated and impoverished Sudan could respond to the stimulus of its improved communications with the outside world. Indeed the only major crop developed for the world market that could withstand the high costs of transport to the coast—over some 700 miles of railway—was cotton, and that only after considerable further investment in irrigation. Ultimately the main economic role of the Sudan was to provide foodstuffs for Senegal, whose peasant farmers found it more profitable to concentrate on growing peanuts for export.

Changes in French economic strategy

By 1914 French economic strategy had shifted from the concept of opening up the inland territories of the French Sudan, Upper Volta, and Niger, to the encouragement of agricultural production in the coastal colonies. To a limited extent, the way was pioneered by European plantations, more especially perhaps in the Ivory Coast. Generally these colonies were made remunerative by administrative pressures to induce African farmers to produce for export. Ultimately, just as the economy of the Senegal had become largely dependent on the export of peanuts, so that of French Guinea became dependent on bananas (though at the very end of the colonial period, European and American capital began the successful exploitation of considerable deposits of bauxite and iron ore), and the economies of Dahomey and of Togo (after its conquest from Germany) became dependent on palm produce. The most dramatic successes were achieved in the Ivory Coast, where considerable exports were developed of coffee, cocoa, and bananas, and also of lumber. Railways were built from suitable points on the coast to facilitate the export of these crops.

In the 45 years from 1912–13 to 1956–57, the French had boosted the foreign trade of their western African empire from some $58,000,000 a year to some $600,000,000 a year, with the result that the revenues available to their colonial administrations increased from about $8,500,000 a year to as much as $315,000,000. (These figures exclude the part of Togo which was incorporated in the French empire only after 1914–18, and the trade and revenue of which by the mid-1950s were worth some $24,000,000 and $4,000,000 a year respectively.) In absolute terms in relation to the total population, which in the same period is thought to have doubled to an estimated 19 million, the results were not so spectacular; in 1956–57, foreign trade per capita overall amounted to about $32, and government revenue to about $17. The significance of the figures is also obscured by the federal system to which all the colonies except Togo were subject, and which was deliberately used to enable the richer colonies to help the poorer. The trade and revenue figures cannot be easily broken down between the individual colonies. Whereas the estimated gross national products (GNPs) for Senegal and the Ivory Coast were in the order of $180 and $160 per capita respectively (the former considerably inflated by the colony's possession of the federal capital), only Togo (about $73) and French Guinea and Sudan (about $58 and $53 respectively) were thought to have GNPs per capita higher than $40.

Each of the four British colonies must necessarily be treated as an independent unit, as each was so treated in British policy. The Gambia was merely a strip of land, averaging only seven miles in width, on either side of 292 miles of navigable waterway penetrating into what otherwise was French Senegal. Even in the 1950s, its population did not exceed 300,000, and the possibilities for any sort of development were limited. In fact the colony achieved a fair degree of prosperity by concentrating on the production of peanuts, grown in part by farmers who migrated annually from Senegal for the purpose. By 1956–57, foreign trade was some $60 per capita and government revenue $14.

The Sierra Leone situation was one of a relatively dense population exploiting or even overexploiting a poor environment for its subsistence, and initially the most that was achieved was to develop some palm produce for export. During the 1930s the situation began to change when European companies began to exploit extensive diamond-bearing gravels and also to mine high-grade iron ore. By the mid-1950s, foreign trade, which had been $14,000,000 ($9 per capita) in 1913–14, had risen to $101,000,000 ($44). But about half of this was based on the activities of the foreign-owned mining companies. These provided little local employment; and furthermore, large numbers of people had been led to abandon farming to dig for diamonds on their own account. This gave rise to numerous social and economic, and also political, problems, because legally the diamond-bearing grounds had been conceded to the European companies. These factors may explain why the increase in government revenue, and hence the capacity of the government to sponsor further development, was low in comparison with other western African territories. It rose from $3,600,000 ($2.40 per capita) in 1913–14 to $27,000,000 ($11.70) in 1956–57, a factor of increase of 4.9 which compares unfavourably with a factor of 21.1 for French West Africa as a whole, 11.4 for the Gold Coast, 6.1 for Nigeria, or even 5.9 for the Gambia.

Com-
parative
increases
in revenue

The Gold Coast was a complete contrast, indeed one of the most successful examples of colonial development anywhere in British tropical Africa. The people of its coastlands were long accustomed to world trade, and indeed to British rule, with the result that the Gold Coast entered the colonial period with a very high level of economic activity. In 1912–13 its foreign trade was worth $42,500,000 ($28.30 per capita) while government revenue was $6,500,000 ($4.30 per capita). Subsequent development was facilitated by the possession, within a manageable area that was adequately but not too densely populated, of a considerable variety of resources.

The first railway was built inland from Sekondi in the southeastern Gold Coast between 1898 and 1903 with the dual purpose of supporting gold mining and ensuring political control of Ashanti. This railway subsequently was used for the removal of manganese ore and bauxite. Extensive diamond diggings, worked equally by individual Africans and by European companies, began to be developed from 1919 onward. But the mainstay of the economy became cocoa, which local farmers began to produce on small plots in the forest toward the end of the 19th century. They found a reliable market for their produce. Cocoa became the most valuable export when it outranked gold in 1913, and thereafter went on to contribute over

four-fifths of exports and to constitute something between a third and a half of the world's supply.

The prosperity derived from cocoa in the 1920s enabled the governor, Sir Frederick Gordon Guggisberg, to pledge the country's revenues for loans to finance a coherent program of economic and social development. The Gold Coast's first deep-water port was built at Takoradi, the cocoa-producing forestlands were equipped with a comprehensive railway and road system, and the foundations were laid for educational and medical services as good as any in tropical Africa. Subsequent development was severely checked by the Great Depression of the 1930s and by events of World War II, but by the mid-1950s the post-war demand for tropical produce generated trade for the Gold Coast, estimated to have fewer than 5,000,000 people, of about $500,000,000 a year, not far short of that generated by all the 19,000,000 people living in French West Africa. Government revenue reached the high level of $27.50 per person, by far the highest in western Africa, while the GNP of about $200 per person was probably higher than that of any tropical African country.

Port at
Takoradi

Nigeria provides yet another contrast. The people of its southern territories, like those of the southern Gold Coast or of Senegal, had long been in touch with the world economy. Indeed, in 1912–13, the country's trade, at some $65,000,000 a year, was 50 percent higher than the Gold Coast's and greater even than the combined total for the eight French colonies, including Senegal. But Nigeria was a giant territory, three times as large as the other three British colonies put together, and though compared with the French federation it was relatively small and compact (373,000 square miles), it had the same problem of extending over a considerable area of the remote Sudan. This could not be ignored—as the much smaller northern Gold Coast or such northern French colonies as Niger were effectively ignored—because the Nigerian Sudan contained more than half the country's enormous population. By the mid-1950s, the Nigerian population was more than 32,000,000, more than half that of western Africa.

Two things were clearly needed: first, to develop a transport system to make it possible to control and open up the populous north; and, second, to use some of the wealth generated from the growth of foreign trade in the south to stimulate development in the north. No coherent policy was possible, however, before the amalgamation of the separate colonial administrations which was achieved under Lugard in 1912–14. Initially, even railway building tended to provoke disunion. The first line was built inland from Lagos in 1898–1901 to open up Yorubaland. Before this line was extended to the north across the Niger, the northern government had begun its own railway, from the highest point of navigation on the river, through its new administrative capital of Kaduna, to Kano. In 1912 this was intercepted by an extension of the Lagos line, and subsequently branches were built to areas active in tin mining and the cultivation of peanuts (groundnuts). Finally, another line was built from a new eastern port, Port Harcourt, to the coal mines around Enugu (1916), and this was subsequently extended to Kaduna (1927). By the 1930s, Nigeria had 1,900 miles of railway, nearly as many as those possessed by all the French territories together (2,160 miles) but built at nearly twice the cost.

While southern Nigerian development, based essentially on cocoa production in the west and processing of palm oil and kernels in the east, followed much the same pattern as that of the southern Gold Coast, and with essentially similar social consequences, the development of peanuts as the prime export crop of the north did not produce comparable results for its appreciably larger population. By the mid-1950s, the trade of Nigeria, at some $800,000,000 a year, was still greater than that of all French West Africa in total, but it was appreciably less per capita, $25.30 compared with $32.20, and the annual revenue available to government, at $173,000,000, was small in proportion to the total population, only about $5.50 per capita. Inevitably a serious gap had developed between the economic and social progress of the south and that of the north.

Nigerian
trade

DECOLONIZATION AND THE REGAINING OF INDEPENDENCE

The end of the colonial period and the establishment during 1957–76 of all of the former colonies as independent states was attributable both to a change in European attitudes toward Africa and the possession of colonies and to an African reaction to colonial rule born of the economic and social changes it had produced.

Europeans had colonized western Africa in the later 19th and early 20th centuries confident that their civilization was immensely superior to anything Africa had produced or could produce. Yet hardly had their colonies been established than these convictions began to be challenged. World War I, and the immense misery and loss of life it caused, led some Europeans to doubt whether nations who could so brutally mismanage their own affairs had any moral right to dictate to other peoples. Some reflection of this view was seen in the League of Nations and the system of mandates applied to the former German colonies. Though in western Africa these were entrusted to either French or British administration, the mandated territories did not become the absolute possessions of the conquerors, and the role of the new rulers was declared to be to equip the mandated territories and their peoples for self-government.

A second shock to European self-confidence came with the Great Depression of the 1930s, when trade and production shrank and millions of Europeans had no work. It began to be argued that a remedy lay in more active development of the overseas territories controlled by Europe. If more European capital and skills were directed to the colonies, so that they could produce more raw materials for European industry more efficiently, both Europe and the colonies would gain; as the colonies became wealthier through the exploitation of their resources, the people of the colonies would buy more from Europe.

First Colonial Development Act

In 1929 Britain had enacted the first Colonial Development Act, providing that small amounts of British government money could be used for colonial economic development, thus breaking the deadlock by which the only colonial governments that could embark on development programs to increase the wealth of their subjects, and to improve their own revenues, were those that already commanded sufficient revenue to pay for the programs or to service the loans the programs required. The idea that the colonies should be actively developed, in the European as much as in the African interest, was broadened during and after World War II. Transport and currency problems made it urgent for Britain and France to develop strategic raw materials in their colonies. Furthermore, during 1940–44, when France itself was in German hands, it was only from the colonies and with their resources that Gen. Charles de Gaulle and his associates could continue the fight.

The British funding policy, initiated in 1929, of providing the funds needed for colonial development was expanded in the 1940s and extended to social as well as economic plans. After the war the governments of both Britain and France required their colonial administrations to draw up comprehensive development plans and in effect offered to provide the funds for those that could not be funded from local resources.

In view of past history, the need for such plans was probably greater in the French colonies than in the British, and the French West African program for 1946–55 envisaged the investment of $1,108,000,000, compared with programs totalling $549,000,000 for the four British colonies. Virtually all of the financing for the French program came from France itself. But some of the British colonies had built up considerable reserves from the high prices commanded by their produce during the war and immediate postwar years, and they themselves were able to provide much of the money needed. This tended to accentuate already existing disparities. In the extreme case, **Gold Coast development** the Gold Coast plan envisaged spending $300,000,000, only 4 percent of which was British money. This was the same level of expenditure, roughly $60 per capita, as envisaged for French West Africa. Nigeria's program, with a contribution from Britain of 42 percent, proposed to spend $220,000,000—only about $7 per capita. The fig-

ures for Sierra Leone were $21,000,000, 45 percent from the United Kingdom, and $10 per capita; and for the tiny Gambia $8,000,000, 35 percent, and $27 per capita.

The accompanying political changes were more cautious and turned out to be inadequate to accommodate African aspirations—which had been derived from social changes occasioned during the classical period of colonial rule and further whetted by the policies of active ecomonic development. On the British side, during 1945–48 the legislative councils were reformed so that African representatives outnumbered the European officials. Many of these African members, however, were still government nominees, and, because of the British attachment to indirect rule, those who were elected were mainly representative of the traditional chiefs.

Political advance for the French colonies was naturally seen in terms of increased African participation in French political life. In 1944 it was proposed that the colonies become overseas territories of France. Delegates from the colonies in fact participated in the making of the new postwar French constitution, but this was subject to referenda in which metropolitan French votes predominated. The constitution eventually adopted in 1946 was appreciably less liberal to Africans than they had been led to expect.

The emergence of African leaders. By the later 1940s, however, there were appreciable numbers of Africans in both the French and the British colonies who had emerged from traditional society through the new opportunities for economic advancement and education. In coastal areas Christian missionaries and their schools had advanced with the European administrations. The colonial governments, requiring African subordinates for their system, commonly aided and developed the elementary and vocational education initiated by the Christian missions and often themselves provided some sort of higher education for the chiefly classes whose cooperation they required. If rather little of this education had penetrated to the 1940s, in some coastal areas Africans had become eager to invest some of their increasing wealth in education, which was seen as the key to European strength.

Relatively few Africans started up the French educational ladder—school attendance by the mid-1950s was some 340,000, about 1.7 percent of the total population—but those who did found themselves in a system identical with that in France. In British West Africa schools had got a footing before there was much administration to control them, and their subsequent development was more independent. The British educational system therefore developed into a pyramid with a much broader base than the French one. By the mid-1950s there were more than 2,000,000 schoolchildren in Nigeria, about 6 percent of the total population and a very much higher proportion of the population of the south, in which the schools were concentrated; in Ghana there were nearly 600,000, some 12 percent of the population. Many more people in the British than in the French territories thus got some education, and appreciably more were able to attend universities. In 1948 universities were established in the Gold Coast and Nigeria; by 1960 the former territory had about 4,500 university graduates and the latter more than 5,000. The first French African university was a federal institution at Dakar opened in 1950; by 1960 the total number of graduates in French West Africa was about 1,800. **Universities**

By the 1940s there was enough education to make European-style political activity possible in all the coastal colonies. Such activity may be traced back to at least the 1890s, when Gold Coast professional men and some chiefs founded the Aborigines' Rights Protection Society (ARPS) to prevent the wholesale expropriation of African lands by European entrepreneurs or officials. The ARPS went on to campaign against the exclusion of qualified Africans from the colonial administration. Following this, in 1918–20, a National Congress of British West Africa was formed by professional men to press for the development of the legislative councils in all the British colonies into elective assemblies controlling the colonial administrations.

In French West Africa, early political activity was concentrated in the four towns of Senegal whose people possessed political rights before 1946. Since the seat of power was very clearly in France, with Senegalese electors sending a deputy to the French National Assembly, the result by the 1930s was the emergence of a Senegalese Socialist party allied to the Socialists in France.

An
African
elite

By the late 1940s both the French and the British territories possessed an educated, politicized class, which felt frustrated in its legitimate expectations; it had made no appreciable progress in securing any real participation in the system of political control. In fact, anything approaching effective African participation seemed more remote than ever. Implementation of the development programs led to a noticeable increase in the number of Europeans employed by the colonial regimes and their associated economic enterprises. On the other hand, since many Africans had served with, and received educational and technical training with, the British and French armies, the war had led to a great widening of both African experience and skills. Furthermore, the postwar economic situation was one in which African farmers were receiving high prices for their produce but could find little to spend their money on, and in which the eagerly awaited development plans were slow to mature because European capital goods were in short supply.

The formation of African independence movements.
There thus developed a general feeling among the intelligentsia that the colonies were being deliberately exploited by ever more firmly entrenched European political and economic systems and that there had developed a new, wider, and mobilizable public to appeal to for support. In 1946 politicians in French West Africa organized a federation-wide political association, the Rassemblement Démocratique Africain (RDA). The RDA and its members in the French National Assembly aligned themselves with the French Communist Party, the only effective opposition to the governments of the Fourth Republic. The result, during 1948–50, was the virtual suppression of the RDA in Africa by the colonial administrations.

In British West Africa the tensions were greatest in the Gold Coast. In 1947 the established politicians brought in Kwame Nkrumah, who had studied in the U.S. and Britain and had been active in the Pan-African movement, to organize a nationalist party with mass support. In 1948 European trading houses were boycotted, and some rioting took place in the larger towns. An official inquiry concluded that the underlying problem was political frustration and that African participation in government should be increased until the colony became self-governing. In 1951, therefore, a new constitution was introduced in which the legislative council gave way to an assembly dominated by African elected members, to which African ministers were responsible for the conduct of much government business. By this time Nkrumah

Kwame
Nkrumah

organized his own mass political party, able to win any general election, and during the following years he negotiated with the British a series of concessions that resulted in 1957 in the Gold Coast becoming the independent state of Ghana.

Once the British had accepted the principle of cooperating with nationalist politicians, their other western African colonies began to follow the example set by the Gold Coast. But Nkrumah had been greatly aided by the high price for cocoa in the 1950s (which meant that by 1960 Ghana's trade was worth $630,000,000 a year and that government revenue, at more than $280,000,000, was broadly adequate to give the people what they wanted in the way of modernizing programs) and by the comparatively high level and generally wide spread of education in a sizeable yet compact territory which was without too serious ethnic divisions. The other colonies were not so well placed.

The small size of The Gambia was the principal factor contributing to the delay of its independence until 1965. Sierra Leone was a densely populated country that was appreciably poorer than Ghana (its GNP per capita, at about $70, being approximately one-third of Ghana's) and in which there was a wide disparity in levels of education and wealth between the Creoles—the descendants of liberated slaves who lived in and around Freetown—and the rest of the people. When independence was achieved

in 1961, these deeply rooted problems had been papered over rather than solved.

Nigeria presented the greatest challenge to British and African policymakers alike. In the south, two nationalist parties emerged, the Action Group (AG), supported

AG and
NCNC in
Nigeria

primarily by the Yorubas of the west, and the National Convention of Nigerian Citizens (NCNC), whose prime support came from the Ibos of the east. These parties expected the whole country quickly to follow the Ghanaian pattern of constitutional change. But any elective central assembly was bound to be dominated by the north, which had some 57 percent of the population and whose economic and social development had lagged far behind. The north's political leaders—most of whom were conservative, Muslim aristocrats closely allied with the British through indirect rule—were not at all eager to see their traditional paramountcy invaded by aggressive and better educated leaders from the south.

The immediate political solution was to convert Nigeria into a federation of three regions. In 1957 this allowed the east and the west to achieve internal self-government without waiting for the north, but it still left open the questions of how politics were to be conducted at the centre and how Nigerian independence was to be secured. At this juncture it occurred to the northern leaders that by allying themselves to one of the southern parties they might maintain their own local monopoly of power and gain added prestige in the country as a whole by asking for its independence. The problem of central politics was thus resolved when the northern leaders entered a coalition federal government with the NCNC, and in 1960 Nigeria became independent.

Meanwhile, in French West Africa the RDA, led by Félix Houphouët-Boigny, broke with the Communist Party. The votes of a small bloc of African deputies in the French National Assembly were of considerable value to the shifting coalitions of non-Communist parties that made up the unstable French governments of the 1950s, and the RDA began to seek to influence these governments to allow greater freedom to the colonies.

By 1956 Houphouët-Boigny's policy had secured a widening of the colonial franchises and the beginnings of a system by which each colony was on the way to becoming a separate unit in which African ministers would be responsible for some of the conduct of government. The implications of this approach, however, did not meet with the approval of some other African leaders, most notable among them Léopold Sédar Senghor in Senegal and Ahmed Sékou Touré in Guinea. The former had stood outside the RDA since the days of its alliance with the Communists, which he had thought could only bring disaster. Together with Touré, who had remained within the RDA, he argued that Houphouët's policy would split up the western African federation into units that would be too small and poor to resist continued French domination.

In 1958 the French Fourth Republic collapsed and de Gaulle was returned to power. On September 28, 1958, in a referendum, the colonies were offered full internal self-government as fellow members with France of a French Community that would deal with supranational affairs. All of the colonies voted for this scheme except Guinea, where Sékou Touré led the people to vote for complete independence. Senegal and the French Sudan were then emboldened in 1959 to come together in a Federation of Mali and to ask for and to receive complete independence within the community. These two territories separated in the following year, but all the others now asked for independence before negotiating conditions for association with France, and by 1960 all the former French colonies were de jure independent states.

Intimations
of imperial
decline

By that time only the excessively conservative regimes of Portugal and Spain sought to maintain the colonial principle in western Africa. Encouraged and aided by independent neighbours, Guinean nationalists took up arms in 1962 and after 10 years of fighting expelled the Portuguese from three-quarters of Portuguese Guinea. In 1974 the strain of this war and of wars in Mozambique and Angola caused the Portuguese people and army to overthrow their dictatorship. Independence was quickly recognized for Guinea-Bissau in 1974 and for the Cape Verde Islands and São Tomé e Príncipe in 1975.

Spain concluded in 1968 that the best way to preserve its interests in Equatorial Africa was to grant independence to its people without preparing them for it. The result was chaos. Potential phosphate riches led Spain to hold on to the Spanish Sahara, however, until the death of Francisco Franco in 1975, and growing pressure from Morocco led to agreements by which, in the following year, despite an armed nationalist revolt sponsored by Algeria, the territory was partitioned between Morocco and Mauritania. In 1976, under Algerian sponsorship, the nationalists proclaimed the Sahrawi Arab Democratic Republic. Mauritania signed an agreement with the nationalists' armed wing, the Popular Front for the Liberation of Saguia el Hamra and Rio de Oro (Polisario) in 1979 and renounced all claims to its sector, but Morocco refused to yield its sector and engaged in an armed struggle with the Polisario over the territory.

(J.D.F.)

Western Africa since independence. The political history of western Africa since independence has often been turbulent. Few states commanded economic resources adequate to fulfill popular expectations, and frustrations heightened as production of food and export crops declined and, partly due to rising oil prices, balance-of-trade deficits increased. In addition, the Sahel countries—especially Mauritania, Mali, Niger, and Upper Volta (now Burkina Faso)—were affected in the 1970s by a series of disastrous droughts. Most national leaders saw no room for party politics but felt instead that government should remain the monopoly of the political group that had won independence. Such groups tended, however, to lose impetus or to become self-seeking. When their governments were ineffective, often the only alternative leadership was constituted by army officers, who would seize power to restore sound government and the economy. If dissatisfaction arose, they, in turn, could be ousted by other officers; or, if in due course they restored civil rule, there was always a temptation to intervene again if the civilian government did not seem to be acting appropriately.

Liberia, with its long experience of self-rule, proved no exception. With national and governmental incomes growing through the development of iron-ore mining, the Afro-Americans were for a time in the position to control and develop the whole country. Pres. William V.S. Tubman (in office 1944–71), leader of the True Whig Party, realized that if power were to be retained the native Liberians must be taken into partnership. His policy was further developed by his political heir, William R. Tolbert (1971–80). By 1979, however, it became clear that economic mismanagement and rural stagnation in Liberia had produced a level of public unrest that the regime was unable to contain. Discontent was voiced by radical intellectuals, and the raising of the price of rice precipitated riots in April 1979. Government repression only increased the tensions and precipitated a military coup in April 1980. The new People's Redemption Council, led by Master Sgt. Samuel K. Doe, began by executing former government ministers but later adopted less extreme policies. It survived a further coup plot in June 1981 and moved toward a return to civilian rule.

The newly independent Lusophone states proved equally vulnerable, with only Cape Verde remaining stable. In Guinea-Bissau, Pres. Luis Cabral was removed in 1980 in a coup led by the Prime Minister; and the Prime Minister of São Tomé e Príncipe was arrested in 1979 on charges of plotting against his own government.

Governmental continuity has been best maintained among the coastal Francophone states. In Senegal Léopold Senghor was able to deflect criticism of his government by initiating a controlled return to party politics in 1976 and then by resigning at the end of 1980 in favour of the prime minister, Abdou Diouf, who promoted further political liberalization. In the Ivory Coast, however, Pres. Houphouët-Boigny continued to rule despite his advanced age, and rivalries concerning his eventual successor coincided with a period of financial uncertainty at the end of the 1970s. Nevertheless, Houphouët-Boigny's power was

not challenged, and his policy of encouraging European, predominantly French, investment in his country's commerce and industry sustained economic growth comparable to that in Ghana a generation earlier. In Guinea, Ahmed Sékou Touré, who in 1959 had espoused international Marxism, remained in power, though by means that were often obscure and tended to provoke violent crises. From about 1974 he was cautiously reestablishing links with France and the West. Following Sékou Touré's death in 1984, the military staged a coup and took control of the government. It initiated a liberal program and started reintegration into the group of Francophone states. In Cameroon, Pres. Ahmadou Ahidjo successfully forged a unitary state from the former French and British trusteeship territories, though signs of restlessness at his authoritarian control became apparent in 1979 with an attempted coup, an uprising in the north, and clandestine opposition from Anglophone elements. In 1982, however, he resigned and successfully handed power to the prime minister, Paul Biya.

Other Francophone leaders were less successful. Modibo Keita in Mali was overthrown by a coup in 1968. The military junta of Gen. Moussa Traoré sought legitimacy by restoring constitutional rule in 1979, but its repressive policies led to increasing protests and violence. In Niger, Hamani Diori was removed by the military in 1974 when his government failed to cope with the effects of the Sahel drought, but by the end of the 1970s the growth of uranium revenues had enabled the new ruler, Pres. Seyni Kountché, to consolidate his power.

Upper Volta had a variety of combinations of civil and military government, none of which could cope effectively with crippling poverty, made worse by drought. A period of civilian rule was ended by a military coup in 1980. Another series of military coups brought Capt. Thomas Sankara to power as head of state in 1983. The country's name was changed to Burkina Faso in 1984. In Mauritania, Moktar Ould Daddah's administration collapsed in 1978 under the dual strains of drought and warfare against the Algerian-backed Polisario Front nationalists in the former Spanish Sahara. Successive military governments renounced Mauritania's claim in the Sahara in 1979 and negotiated a peace treaty with the Polisario, but hostilities with Morocco increased. Dahomey's substantial educated elite failed to deal with the problems of poverty and regionalism. Between 1963 and 1972 there were no fewer than five military coups, the last of which, under the direction of Lieut. Col. Mathieu (later called Ahmed) Kérékou, professed Marxist principles and changed the country's name to Benin (1975).

In the neighbouring state of Togo there were two military interventions in the 1960s, but the development of phosphate mining helped Togo's leader, Gen. Étienne Gnassingbe (later called Gnassingbe) Eyadema, to maintain stability after 1967. In 1979 the government completed its transition to constitutional rule.

Among the former British colonies, parliamentary government was maintained only in The Gambia, under the presidency of Sir Dawda Jawara. His rule was threatened, however, by outbreaks of unrest in October 1980 and July 1981. Armed intervention by Senegal in support of Jawara's government in July 1981 led to the formation of the Confederation of Senegambia (February 1, 1982), under which Senegal and The Gambia remained sovereign states with integrated armed forces and cooperative economic and political development.

In Sierra Leone, after two military coups in quick succession in 1967 and 1968, army leaders chose a politician, Siaka Stevens, to head a civilian government. A single-party political system was constituted in 1978. In Ghana, Nkrumah's domestic and foreign ambitions produced little but corruption and foreign debts. The army removed him in 1966, but neither the parliamentary government it initiated in 1969 nor a subsequent military takeover in 1972 proved capable of restoring prosperity. Public disapproval forced the army to recognize the failure of its policy and initiate a further return to elective government in 1979. In June 1979, however, Flight Lieut. Jerry Rawlings led a coup by junior officers and then held elections. Hilla

Coastal Francophone states

Limann became president and maintained civilian rule until December 31, 1981, when Rawlings staged a second successful military uprising.

Nigeria faced many problems after independence, but lack of resources was not one of them. Petroleum found under its easterly coastlands and adjacent waters was exploited with considerable success and accounted for about 80 percent of the annual federal revenues. But Nigeria's wealth only exacerbated the problem of providing fair government for a heterogeneous society. By 1964 the political compromise achieved for independence had broken down. In 1966 a group of junior army officers seized power, aiming at establishing effective and unitary government, but regional rivalries impeded their success. Gen. Yakubu Gowon, a Christian northerner, restored order but could not prevent Ibo officers from declaring an independent republic of Biafra in the east (May 30, 1967). Three years

of bloody civil war ensued before the federal army was able to end the secession. Gowon tried to prevent such troubles in the future by repatterning the federation into 12 smaller states (in 1976 increased to 19). But he and his colleagues were reluctant to relinquish power to an elected government and lost popular support. This led to Gowon's overthrow in 1975 by junior officers under Brig. Murtala Ramat Mohammed, who was assassinated in 1976 and succeeded by Gen. Olusegun Obasanjo. The government organized multiparty elections and the country returned to civilian rule under Pres. Alhaji Shehu Shagari in 1979. Economic malaise led to the expulsion in 1983 of some 2,000,000 western Africans who had illegally immigrated to Nigeria seeking jobs, and this, combined with charges of corruption in the government, prompted army officers under the leadership of Maj. Gen. Mohammed Buhari to stage a coup on December 31, 1983. (J.D.F./D.Bn./Ed.)

Biafra revolt

BENIN

The People's Republic of Benin (République Populaire du Bénin)—formerly (until 1975) the Republic of Dahomey—is one of the smallest independent states of West Africa. With an area of 43,475 square miles (112,600 square kilometres), it consists of a long wedge of territory extending for about 416 miles (670 kilometres) from the

Niger River, which forms part of its northern frontier, to the Atlantic Ocean in the south, on which it has a 75-mile seaboard. Benin is bounded to the west by Togo, to the northwest by Burkina Faso (formerly Upper Volta), to the northeast by Niger, and to the east by Nigeria. The capital is Porto-Novo. Cotonou is the largest city and the chief port. Other important towns are Ouidah, Abomey, and Parakou.

A former French colony, Dahomey became an independent republic within the French Community in 1958 and gained full independence in 1960. Thereafter, Dahomey underwent more than a decade of political instability, caused partly by its diverse ethnic composition and traditions. The majority of the people inhabiting the southern one-third of the country are related Fon peoples (including the Adja), who migrated into the region in the 13th century and later founded, among others, the Porto-Novo Kingdom and the Dahomey (or Dã-ho-mé, "on the belly of Dã") Kingdom. The Dahomey Kingdom—also called the Abomey Kingdom after its capital city of Abomey—conquered smaller kingdoms in the south in the 18th century and was directly involved in the transatlantic slave

A grouping of ancient kingdoms

BENIN

MAP INDEX

Provinces

Atacora	10·00n	2·00e
Atlantique	6·30n	2·10e
Borgou	10·00n	3·00e
Ouémé	7·00n	2·40e
Mono	7·00n	1·50e
Zou	8·00n	2·00e

Cities and towns

Abomey	7·11n	1·59e
Adjohon	6·42n	2·28e
Agouna	7·34n	1·42e
Ahozon	6·23n	2·11e
Aledjo-Koura	9·21n	1·27e
Allada	6·39n	2·09e
Angara-Débou	11·19n	3·03e
Aplahoué	6·56n	1·41e
Athiémé	6·35n	1·40e
Avrankou	6·33n	2·40e
Banikoara	11·18n	2·26e
Bassila	9·01n	1·40e
Batia	10·54n	1·29e
Béroubouay	10·32n	2·44e
Bétérou	9·12n	2·16e
Bimbéréké	10·13n	2·40e
Birni	10·00n	1·31e
Bohicon	7·12n	2·04e
Borodarou	10·59n	2·53e
Boukombé	10·11n	1·06e
Cotonou	6·21n	2·26e
Dadjo	8·34n	2·14e
Dassa-Zoumé	7·45n	2·11e
Djougou	9·42n	1·40e
Dunkassa	10·22n	3·08e
Firou	10·55n	1·56e
Founogo	11·28n	2·32e
Gogonou	10·50n	2·50e
Grand-Popo	6·17n	1·50e
Guené	11·44n	3·13e
Guessou-Sud	10·03n	2·38e
Kandi	11·08n	2·56e
Kérou	10·50n	2·06e
Kétou	7·22n	2·36e
Kilibo	8·34n	2·36e
Kouandé	10·20n	1·42e

Lokossa	6·38n	1·43e
Malanville	11·52n	3·23e
Mossey	12·17n	2·54e
Natitingou	10·19n	1·22e
Ndali	9·51n	2·43e
Nikki	9·56n	3·12e
Ouidah	6·22n	2·05e
Parakou	9·21n	2·37e
Pira	8·30n	1·44e
Pobé	6·58n	2·41e
Porto-Novo	6·29n	2·37e
Sakété	6·43n	2·40e
Savalou	7·56n	1·58e
Savé	8·02n	2·29e
Segbana	10·56n	3·42e
Sinindé	10·21n	2·23e
Tanguiéta	10·37n	1·16e
Tchaourou	8·53n	2·36e
Tchetti	7·50n	1·40e
Tobré	10·12n	2·08e
Warandji	10·57n	3·27e
Zagnanado	7·16n	2·21e

Physical features and points of interest

Alibori, *river*	11·56n	3·17e
Atacora, Chaîne de l', *mountains*	10·45n	1·30e
Benin, Bight of	6·00n	3·00e
Boucle de la Pendjari, Parc National de la, *national park*	11·20n	1·15e
Couffo, *river*	6·35n	1·59e
Guinea, Gulf of	5·30n	3·00e
Mékrou, *river*	12·24n	2·49e
Mono, *river*	6·17n	1·51e
Niger, *river*	11·37n	3·37e
Okpara, *river*	7·40n	2·35e
Ouémé, *river*	6·29n	2·32e
Pendjari, *river*	10·54n	0·51e
So, *river*	6·28n	2·25e
Sota, *river*	11·52n	3·24e
W du Niger, Parc National du, *national park*	12·00n	2·30e

trade, then controlled by Portuguese settlers from the port of Ouidah. Dahomey's warriors, including the famed corps of female soldiers known as the Amazon warriors, fought heroically against, but were defeated by, French colonizers in 1893. The kingdom then lent its name to the whole country, which became a division of the federation of French West Africa (Afrique Occidentale Française; AOF) in 1904. Descendants of Portuguese settlers, returning slaves, and the French colonialists were instrumental in spreading Christianity and Western education in the south; by the 1950s, Dahomey was known as the "Latin Quarter" of West Africa.

Large sections of the population in the northern part of the country had migrated from the inlands of the continent to form several kingdoms or to settle in small communities. They were predominantly Muslim, and until independence they had relatively little contact with their neighbours in the south. This cleavage between the north and the south, and that in the south between Abomey and Porto-Novo, fueled conflict among political leaders. Another factor contributing to political instability was the failing economy, which was largely dependent upon the export of palm oil and palm kernels and upon external aid, primarily from France.   (D.Ro.)

Physical and human geography

THE LAND

Relief. Benin consists of five natural regions—a coastal region, the *barre* country, the Benin plateaus, the Atacora Massif, and the Niger plains.

The coastal region is low, flat, and sandy, backed by lagoons. It forms, in effect, a long sandbar on which grow clumps of coconut palms; the lagoons are narrower in the western part of the country and wider in the east, and some are interconnected. In the west the Grand-Popo Lagoon extends into neighbouring Togo, while in the east the Porto-Novo Lagoon provides a natural waterway to the port of Lagos, Nigeria, although its use is discouraged by the political boundary. Only at Grand-Popo and at Cotonou do the lagoons have outlets to the sea.

Behind the coastal region extends the *barre* country— the word being a French adaptation of the Portuguese word *barro* ("clay"). A fertile clay plateau, the *barre* region contains the Lama Marsh, a vast swampy area stretching from Abomey to Allada. The landscape is generally flat, although occasional hills occur, rising to about 1,300 feet (400 metres).

The Benin plateaus, four in number, are to be found in the Abomey, Kétou, Aplahoué, and Zagnanado districts. The plateaus consist of clays on a crystalline base. The Abomey, Aplahoué (or Parahoué), and Zagnanado plateaus are from 300 to 750 feet high, and the Kétou plateau is up to 500 feet in height.

The Atacora Massif, in the northwest of the country, forms a continuation of the Togo mountain chain, running southwest to northeast and reaching an altitude of 2,103 feet at its highest point. It consists of a quartzite plateau.

The Niger plains, in the northeast of Benin, slope down to the Niger River Valley. They consist of clayey sandstones.

Drainage. Apart from the Niger River, which, with its tributaries the Mékrou, Alibori, and Sota, drains the northeastern part of the country, the three principal rivers in Benin are the Mono, the Couffo, and the Ouémé. The Mono, which rises in Togo, forms the frontier between Togo and Benin near the coast. The Couffo, near which stands Abomey, flows down from the Benin plateaus to drain into the coastal lagoons at Ahémé. The Ouémé rises in the Atacora Massif and flows southward for 280 miles; near its mouth it divides into two branches, one draining into Porto-Novo Lagoon and the other into Nokoué Lake. The Atacora Massif forms a watershed between the Volta and Niger basins.

Climate. Two climatic zones may be distinguished— a southern and a northern. The southern zone has an equatorial type of climate with four seasons—two wet and two dry. The principal rainy season occurs between mid-March and mid-July; the shorter dry season lasts to mid-September; the shorter rainy season lasts to mid-

November; and the principal dry season then lasts until the rains begin again in March. The amount of rain increases toward the east. Grand-Popo receives only about 32 inches (800 millimetres) a year, whereas Cotonou and Porto-Novo both receive approximately 50 inches. Temperatures are relatively constant, varying between 72° and 93° F (22° and 34° C).

In the northern climatic zone, there are only two seasons, one dry and one rainy. The rainy season lasts from May to September, with most of the rainfall occurring in August. Rainfall amounts to about 53 inches a year in the Atacora Massif and in central Benin; further north it diminishes to about 38 inches. In the dry season the harmattan, a hot, dry wind, blows from the northeast from December to March. Temperatures average about 80° F (27° C), but the temperature range varies considerably from day to night. In January, the hottest month, diurnal temperatures may rise to 110° F (43° C).

Plant and animal life. The original rain forest, which covered most of the southern part of the country, has now largely been cleared, except near the rivers. In its place, many oil palms and rônier palms have been planted and food crops are cultivated. North of Abomey the vegetation is an intermixture of forest and savanna (grassy parkland), giving way further north to savanna. Apart from the oil and rônier palms, trees include coconut palms, kapok, mahogany, and ebony.

In the extreme north is the Parc national du "W" du Niger (1,938 square miles), which extends into Burkina Faso (formerly Upper Volta) and Niger. Its varied animal life includes elephants, panthers, lions, antelope, monkeys, wild pigs, crocodiles, and buffalo. There are many species of snakes, including pythons and puff adders. Birds include guinea fowl, wild duck, and partridge, as well as many tropical species. The Parc national de la Pendjari (1,062 square miles) borders on Burkina Faso.

Settlement patterns. The southern third of the country is by far the most densely populated region. On the coastal sandbars, coconut plantations have been established. In the lagoon region, fish are caught in wicker traps; fishing villages often consist of houses built upon stilts. The Ouémé Delta region is heavily populated. The cultivation of subsistence crops, such as corn (maize), cassava, and yams, is intensive on the outskirts of the towns. The *barre* region and the Benin plateaus are planted with oil palms, which form the cash crop, as well as with subsistence crops. To the north, the aspect of the countryside changes as savanna vegetation increases and the population diminishes; some areas are uninhabited, except by Fulani nomads. Villages, instead of being encountered frequently as in the south, become scattered.

Although some of the towns are beginning to assume a modern aspect, vestiges of former centuries are still to be seen, such as the old Portuguese, Danish, and English forts at Ouidah, dating from the time of the slave trade. Cotonou is primarily a modern European-built city, whereas Porto-Novo, an old African-founded town, combines both African and European features. Abomey, the ancient capital, now somewhat in decline, remains an important market and is also a centre for crafts. Parakou is an important market town.   (S.S.A./D.Ro.)

THE PEOPLE

About two-thirds of the people live in the southern third of Benin. Many of these are clustered about the port of Cotonou, which is the focus of the commercial and political life of the country.

Ethnic and linguistic groups. While French is the official language, the most widely spoken languages are Fon and Ge (Mina), both dialects of Ewe; Yoruba; Bariba; and Dendi.

The Fon are predominant in the south and are related to other southern groups, including the Adja and the Goun (Gun). The Aizo have been largely assimilated into the Fon and Adja. The Yoruba, related to the Yoruba of Nigeria, are called the Nago (Nagot) in Benin and include the small Holli and Ketu groups.

The Bariba, a Voltaic-speaking group, are the major ethnolinguistic group in the north. Others in the north are

The barre country (margin)

Two climatic zones (margin)

Benin's towns (margin)

the Somba, who live between Atacora and Togo; the Pila Pila; the Dendi, who are associated with the Niger Valley; and the nomadic Fulani (Peul).

About 5,000 Europeans, mostly French and Portuguese, also live in Benin.

Religious groups. Although Christian missions have been active in the coastal region since the 16th century, only about 15 percent of the total population is Christian; of the Christians, about four-fifths are Roman Catholic. The great majority of the population adheres to traditional religions. In the south, animist religions, which include fetishes (objects regarded with awe as the embodiment of a powerful spirit) for which Benin is renowned, retain their traditional strength. Islām has adherents in the north and southeast; about 15 percent of the total population is Muslim.

Traditional religions

(D.Ro.)

THE ECONOMY

Resources. Only a few stretches of forest remain in Benin, mostly in the south and central areas; these contain mahogany, iroko, teak, samba, and other tropical hardwoods. The rivers and lagoons are rich in fish. Known mineral deposits include iron-ore deposits in the Atacora and Kandi region; limestone deposits suitable for the manufacture of cement at Onigbolo; chrome ore and a little gold in the northwest near Natitingou; marble at Dadjo; an important deposit of pottery clay at Sakété; and ilmenite (a mineral source of titanium) near the coast. In addition, petroleum has been located at the Sémé oil field, about 18 miles offshore from Cotonou.

Agriculture and fishing. About 45 percent of the working population depends on agriculture. Subsistence farming produces corn, cassava, yams, beans, and sorghum. Palm oil and palm kernels constitute the main cash crop; other cash crops are cotton, cocoa, peanuts (groundnuts), coffee, and tobacco. Livestock include cattle, sheep and goats, pigs, horses, and poultry. About 40,000 tons of fish are caught annually in the lagoons and rivers, while coastal fishing produces a further 5,000 tons. Most of the fish is exported to Nigeria or Togo. Shrimp fishing is developing, using modern vessels.

Agricultural production

Industry. Limestone and gravel are mined for the cement industry. Gold mining along the Perma River in the North resumed in the early 1980s. The offshore oil deposits in the Sémé field began production in the mid-1980s.

Manufacturing plants and secondary industries include several palm-oil-processing plants, in Ahozon, Avrankou, Bohicon, Cotonou, Gbada, and Pobé; cement plants at Onigbolo and Pobé; a textile mill at Parakou; a sugar refining complex at Savé; a soft-drink plant; a brewery; and two shrimp-processing plants.

Electricity is generated by four thermally fired power-generating plants, located at Bohicon, Parakou, Cotonou, and Porto-Novo. Benin's demand for electricity is mainly met from Ghana's Volta River Project at Akosombo.

Trade. All governments since independence have tried to develop the agricultural sector, which has consisted primarily of the cultivation of palm-oil plantations for export. Palm oil and palm kernels have usually represented two-fifths of all exports. Cotton and cocoa are also exported. Imports are about 10 times higher than exports. The principal imports are beverages and tobacco, textiles, machinery, automobiles, and paper.

Administration of the economy. During the colonial period, the economy of Benin was integrated with that of former French West Africa. After independence Benin remained partially dependent upon France for financial aid.

The principal difficulty faced by successive Benin governments has been the nation's low standard of living. In 1976 the revolutionary regime began the establishment of cooperative structures, the Groupements Revolutionnaires de Vocation Co-operatif (GRVC), to provide a socialist base for agricultural production. Landowners are allowed to keep the titles to their lands, but they may not receive rent. Work is communal, and the workers are free to sell their produce either to the state or to private customers. Private traders and small manufacturers continue to flourish.

Attempts to improve standard of living

Transportation. There are two principal roads, one running along the coast from the Togo border in the west via Cotonou and Porto-Novo to the Nigerian border in the east, and the other running north from Cotonou to Parakou and on to the Niger frontier. Road transport is usually by truck; a central truck park at Cotonou is capable of accommodating 15,000 vehicles.

There are about 350 miles of railroad track consisting of three lines. One line runs for about 20 miles from Cotonou to Séboroué. A second line runs for 66 miles from Cotonou via Porto-Novo to Pobé. The third line runs north from Cotonou via Pahou to Parakou for about 270 miles.

The lagoons, running parallel to the coast, are used as waterways by small craft. The Ouémé River is navigable for about 125 miles, the Couffo for about 80 miles, and the Mono for about 60 miles. About 2,500,000 metric tons of cargo are handled in the port of Cotonou each year. The airport at Cotonou links Benin with other West African countries and with France, the United Kingdom, the United States, and the Soviet Union. The government maintains a small domestic air service.

(S.S.A./D.Ro./Ed.)

ADMINISTRATIVE AND SOCIAL CONDITIONS

Government. The government of Lieut. Col. Mathieu Kérékou was established in a military coup during 1972. In February 1980, the legislative body confirmed Kérékou as president. He was the sole candidate, chosen by the Central Committee of the People's Revolutionary Party of Benin.

The government consists of the National Revolutionary Assembly (Assemblée Nationale Révolutionnaire) and a National Executive Council of 22 Cabinet ministers and the six presidents of the committees that administer the country's six provinces. Of the 22 Cabinet portfolios in the new government, 14 are held by civilians.

The six administrative provinces—Atlantique, Atakora, Borgou, Mono, Ouémé, and Zou—are divided into 84 districts. In addition, there are five townships.

The People's Revolutionary Party of Benin (Parti de la Révolution Populaire du Bénin; PRPB) is the only legal political party in the country.

Justice. At the head of the judicial system is the High Court. There are also a council of the magistracy, a court of appeal at Cotonou, a tribunal of the first instance, and local tribunals that administer traditional African or Muslim law.

Education. About three-fifths of the primary school-age population receives a formal education, with smaller numbers in secondary schools and technical and higher studies. The Université Nationale du Benin was opened in 1970 in Abomey-Calavi, near Cotonou. Beninois also seek higher education abroad, mostly in France or elsewhere in Africa.

Health and welfare. Health services are limited by budgetary restrictions and by the paucity of physicians and other medical personnel. In the early 1980s there were six hospitals, located at Cotonou, Porto-Novo, Abomey, Ouidah, Natitingou, and Parakou. In addition, there are medical centres, dispensaries, maternity centres, and leprosariums. Campaigns have been waged against meningitis, leprosy, malaria, and sleeping sickness.

CULTURAL LIFE

Examples of Benin's rich culture—carved wood masks, appliqué tapestry, pottery, and bronze statuettes—are sold in marketplaces and exhibited in three museums in Porto-Novo, Abomey, and Ouidah. Traditional music and dance are heard in frequent village and neighbourhood compound ceremonies. Radio programs are broadcast in French, English, and 18 local languages from Cotonou and transmitted from Parakou. There is limited television service. For statistical data, see the "Britannica World Data" section in the current *Britannica Book of the Year*.

(D.Ro.)

History

The history of the peoples of northern Benin has not yet been compiled. The Dahomey or Fon, who occupy the southern part, established the three kingdoms of Allada,

Porto-Novo, and Dahomey, of which the name of the most celebrated was extended by the French conquest to the whole country.

Legend relates that the daughter of the King of Tado (a town on the Mono River), while on her way to draw water, was impregnated by a leopard and bore a son, who became the founder of the dynasty. His descendants settled in the 16th century at Allada and founded a kingdom (the "kingdom of Ardra" of the old maps) with which the Portuguese established contacts. At the beginning of the 17th century three brothers, Kokpon, Do-Aklin, and Te-Agdanlin, disputed the throne. The first kept Allada, the second founded Abomey, and the third Adjatché, or Porto-Novo.

The founding of the kingdom of Dahomey

The traditional date for the founding of the kingdom of Dahomey is AD 1625. The son of Do-Aklin, Dakodonou, enlarged his kingdom, but it was Dakodonou's son Ouegbadja (c. 1645–85) who made it into a powerful state. He continually harassed Dã, or Dan, the king of a small neighbouring state, until Dã, exasperated, asked whether he did not wish to set himself up on his (Dã's) stomach. Thereupon Ouegbadja attacked Dã, defeated him, and took him back to Abomey, where he beheaded him and threw his body into the foundations of the palace he was building; hence; the name Dahomey (Dã-ho-mé, "on the belly of Dã").

THE KINGDOM OF DAHOMEY

Desirous of establishing communication with the coast in order to obtain arms by trading with Europeans, King Agadja (1708–32), one of the sons of Ouegbadja, conquered Allada and Ouidah, where European forts were already established. Thus was constituted, within definite boundaries, the old kingdom of Dahomey, of which certain peculiar customs deserve mention.

The Dahomey "customs." These were of two kinds: the grand customs performed on the death of a king, when people were sacrificed at his grave to provide him with wives and attendants in the spirit world; and the minor customs, held twice yearly. At the grand customs held from January to March 1791, no fewer than 500 men, women, and children were said to have been put to death. The minor customs were held periodically to replenish the dead king's train of attendants in the spirit world.

Of the victims, chiefly prisoners of war, some tied in baskets were at one stage of the proceedings taken to the top of a high platform, together with a crocodile, a cat, and a hawk in similar baskets, and paraded on the heads of the Amazons (see below). After a speech by the king, all of them were hurled down into the middle of a surging crowd and butchered. Sir Richard Burton in *A Mission to Gelele, King of Dahome*, insisted that the horrors of these rites were exaggerated. On the death of the king the wives destroyed everything and attacked and murdered each other, until order was restored by the new sovereign.

The Amazons. The training of women as soldiers was begun by King Agadja on the occasion of his capture of Ouidah. About one-fourth of the whole female population were said to be "married to the fetich." The most favoured were chosen as wives of the king or enlisted into the Amazon regiments; they took the post of honour in all battles. Burton, who in 1862 saw an army marching out of Kana on an expedition, computed the number of female troops as 2,500, of whom one-third were unarmed or only half armed. Their weapons were blunderbusses, flint muskets, and bows and arrows. The system of warfare was one of surprise. When the army was within a few days' march of the town to be attacked, silence was ordered and fires prohibited. Highways were avoided, the advance being by a track especially cut through the bush. The town was surrounded at night, and just before daybreak a rush was made and every soul captured if possible; none were killed except in self-defense, as the object was not to kill but to take prisoners to sell at the coast in order to obtain arms.

Gezo and the forts. King Gezo (1818–58) greatly reduced human sacrifice and ordered that there was to be no general sacrifice of the palace women on his death. He also strengthened the kingdom, extending its frontiers northward. He conducted many campaigns in Nigeria

against the Yoruba to obtain slaves, but his attack in 1861 on Abeokuta was repulsed. In the same year he signed a commercial treaty with the French.

A French fort had been established at Ouidah by the Compagnie des Indes in the 17th century, but its garrison was withdrawn in 1797. In 1842 a trading firm was set up in Ouidah with French authorization. British, Portuguese, and Brazilian forts there had fallen into ruin, and when the British in 1852 blockaded the coast to prevent slaving, both France and Portugal protested. In 1857 the French established themselves at Grand-Popo.

King Glélé

Gezo's successor, Glélé or Gelele (1858–89), offended the British and French by attacking his neighbours, persecuting Dahomeyan Christians, and encouraging the slave trade. To check his aggressions the British in 1861 annexed Lagos. In 1863 the French signed a treaty with the King of Porto-Novo and also acquired Little Popo (Anécho). By a treaty of 1868, Glélé authorized the French to establish themselves at Cotonou. The Franco-German treaty of 1885, determining the limits of German colonization on the Togo coast, gave Little Popo and Porto-Seguro to Germany. The Portuguese claimed a protectorate over the coast but retained only their old fort at Ouidah.

FRENCH RULE AND INDEPENDENCE

The establishment of the French on the coast was a source of annoyance to the kingdom of Dahomey and hindered the slave trade. The death of Glélé and the accession (1890) of his son Behanzin (1889–94) precipitated hostilities. Cotonou and Porto-Novo were attacked, and some missionaries were abducted from Ouidah to Abomey. One of them negotiated the Treaty of Ouidah (October 3, 1890), which recognized French protection of Porto-Novo and indefinite occupation of Cotonou, in compensation for which the king of Dahomey was to receive a pension. The treaty was criticized in France and little respected by Behanzin, who resumed his raids. The French in 1892 mounted a fresh expedition under Col. (later Gen.) Alfred Amédée Dodds. The Dahomeyans were defeated, and Behanzin fled. A French protectorate was established over Abomey. After 14 months Behanzin surrendered and was deported. The protected kingdoms of Abomey, Allada, and Porto-Novo were absorbed into the colony of Dahomey.

In order to link the colony to their other western African possessions, the French set to work to secure the northern hinterland of Dahomey. This they achieved chiefly through the expeditions in 1895–96 of Capt. J.M.L. Baud. The convention of 1898 added the western part of Borgu to Dahomey but did not concede access to the navigable part of the Niger, which France desired. In 1899 Dahomey was incorporated into French West Africa. On the outbreak of World War I French forces from Dahomey took part in the conquest of Togoland from Germany (August 1914).

Independence

In World War II Dahomey followed French West Africa in adhering to the Allied cause. An overseas territory of France in 1946, by 1959 it was an autonomous state of the French Community. Independence was proclaimed on August 1, 1960, and in November 1960 a new constitution was adopted. (H.J.D.)

In a coup d'etat on October 27, 1963, the army took control, and, after a referendum to approve the new constitution, the second republic was set up on January 5, 1964. A second crisis on December 22, 1965, brought Gen. Christophe Soglo to power, but he too was deposed by a revolutionary military junta under Maj. Maurice Kouandété on December 17, 1967. A third constitution was adopted by 92 percent of the voters on March 31, 1968. In June 1968 the military government appointed the former foreign minister Émile Derlin Zinsou president (July 17) and head of state (August 1). In December 1969 Dahomey's continuing economic troubles prompted Kouandété to intervene once more and Zinsou was deposed.

The elections of March 1970 were suspended by the ruling military directorate, and in May 1970 the formation of a three-man presidential council to rule public life was announced. The presidency was to rotate among the three, each serving a two-year term. Hubert Maga, a former president, became the first president and head of state to serve under this rotational system.

(Je.D.)

In 1972 the government was taken over by Lieut. Col. Mathieu Kérékou, who was then named president. On November 30, 1975, after a reorganization of the government, the country's name was changed to the People's Republic of Benin. President Kérékou (from 1980 called Ahmed Kérékou) made his first official visit to France in 1981. The same year, he released three former heads of state, including Hubert Maga, who had been kept under house arrest since 1972. For current political history, see the annual issues of the *Britannica Book of the Year.*

(Je.D./Ed.)

BURKINA FASO

Burkina Faso (formerly Upper Volta) is a landlocked western African state with an area of 105,870 square miles (274,200 square kilometres). A former French colony, it gained independence as Upper Volta (République de Haute-Volta) in 1960; the name Burkina Faso was adopted in 1984. It is bounded to the north and west by Mali, to the south by the Ivory Coast, Ghana, and Togo, and to the east by Benin and Niger. The capital, Ouagadougou, is about 500 miles (800 kilometres) by road from the sea. Its current name is a phrase in Moré (the language of the Mossi people) meaning "land of the upright people."

Physical and human geography

Burkina Faso's economy is based primarily on agriculture and livestock raising. About half the population belong to the Mossi tribe, and the former Mossi Empire is included within the borders of the present state.

THE LAND

Relief.   Burkina Faso consists of an extensive plateau, slightly inclined toward the south. The lateritic (red, leached, iron-bearing) layer of rock that covers the underlying crystalline rocks is cut into by the three principal rivers—the Volta Noire, Volta Rouge, and Volta Blanche—all of which converge in Ghanaian territory to the south to form the Volta River. The Oti, another tributary of the Volta, rises in southeastern Burkina Faso. In the southwest there are sandstone plateaus bordered by the Falaise de Banfora (Banfora Escarpment), which is about 500 feet (150 metres) high and faces southeast. The country is generally dry and the soil infertile. Great seasonal variation occurs in the flow of the rivers.

Climate.   The climate is generally sunny, hot, and dry. In the north the climate is of the Sahelian type (Arabic *sāhil:* "shore," referring to the region bordering the Sahara) characterized by three to five months of rainfall, which is often erratic. To the south it becomes increasingly of the tropical savanna (grassy parkland) type, sometimes called Sudanic, characterized by greater variability of temperature and rainfall.

Four seasons may be distinguished in Burkina Faso: a dry and cool season from mid-November to mid-February, with temperatures dropping to about 50° F (10° C); a hot season from mid-February to June, when maximum temperatures rise to about 104° F (40° C) in the shade; a rainy season, which lasts from June to September; and an intermediate season, which lasts from September until mid-November.

Plant and animal life.   The northern part of the country consists of savanna, with prickly shrubs and stunted trees that come to life during the rainy season. In the south the prickly shrubs give way to scattered forests, which become more dense along the banks of the perennial rivers. While tree growth in the north is discouraged by the climate,

The river
system

farmers in the south often permit only useful trees, such as the karite (shea tree) or the baobab, to survive.

Animal life in the eastern region includes buffalo, antelope, lions, hippopotamus, elephants, and crocodiles. Elephants, buffalo, and antelope are also found in the southeast and on the banks of the Black Volta, while herds of hippopotamus are to be seen some 40 miles from the city of Bobo Dioulasso. Animal life also includes monkeys. Bird and insect life is rich and varied, and there are many fish in the rivers.

Settlement patterns. Most of the population lives in villages, which tend to be grouped toward the centre of the country at higher elevations away from the Volta valleys. For several miles on either side of the Volta rivers the land is mostly uninhabited because of the prevalence of the deadly tsetse fly, which carries sleeping sickness, and the simulium fly, which carries onchocerciasis, or "river blindness."

Ouagadougou, the administrative capital and the seat of government, is a modern town, in which several commercial companies have their headquarters. It is also the residence of the Moro Naba, emperor of the Mossi, and an important regional centre for international aid programs.

Bobo Dioulasso, in the west, was the economic and business capital of the country when it formed the terminus of the railroad running to Abidjan, Ivory Coast, on the coast; since 1955, however, when the railroad was extended to Ouagadougou, it has lost some of its former importance, although it remains a commercial centre.

THE PEOPLE

The two major ethnic groupings

Two principal ethnic groups live in Burkina Faso. The first of these is the Voltaic group, which may be further divided into four subgroups—the Mossi, which include the Gurma and the Yarse, the Grunshis (Gurunsi), the Bobo, and the Lobi. The second group is the Mande family, which is divided into five subgroups: the Samo, the Marka, the Busansi, the Senufo, and the Dyula (Diouala). In addition, there are Hausa (Haoussa) traders, Fulani herders, and the Tuareg, or rather their settled servants, the Bella.

Each of the ethnic groups found in Burkina Faso has its own language, although Moré, the language of the Mossi, is spoken by a great majority of the population, and Diula is the language of commerce. French, the official language, is used for all communication with other countries. About one-half of the population are animists, attaching great importance to ancestor worship. Islām exerts an increasing influence upon customs and accounts for approximately one-third of the population. The seat of the Roman Catholic archbishopric is Ouagadougou, and there are eight bishoprics. There are few Protestants in the country.

The population as a whole is unequally distributed among the different regions. The Mossi country is densely settled. Situated in the eastern and central regions, it contains about two-thirds of the total population. In the remaining regions the population is scattered.

More than 80 percent of the population is rural, living in some 7,700 villages. Apart from Ouagadougou, the principal towns are Bobo Dioulasso, Koudougou, Ouahigouya, Kaya, Fada Ngourma, and Banfora.

The principal towns

THE ECONOMY

Most of the population is engaged in subsistence agriculture or stock raising. There is a considerable problem with unemployment in rural districts made worse by intermittent severe droughts. Every year people leave their villages to seek work in such neighbouring states as the Ivory Coast or Ghana. The development of industry in Burkina Faso is hampered by the small size of the market economy and by the absence of a direct outlet to the sea.

Agriculture. Agricultural production consists of foodstuffs, which are primarily grown for subsistence, with the surplus being sold as cash crops. Surplus cotton, shea nuts, sesame, and sugarcane are exported, while sorghum, corn (maize), peanuts (groundnuts), and rice are grown for local consumption. Fonio (a crabgrass with seeds that are used as cereal), yams, sweet potatoes, and beans are also grown. Stock raising, one of the principal sources of revenue, includes cattle, sheep and goats, pigs, donkeys, horses, and camels. Chickens, ducks, and guinea fowl are also raised.

Industry. Industry is limited to a number of plants, mainly in rural areas, that produce processed rice, beer, soft drinks, and flour, manufacture textiles and shoes, and assemble bicycles.

Trade. External commerce, both in imports and in exports, is primarily with the franc zone and with neighbouring African countries in particular. Many cattle are exported to the Ivory Coast as well as to Ghana. There is a deficit in the balance of payments, largely due to the relatively small amounts of exports, which are not of sufficient value to equal the value of imported materials required for promoting further development.

Mining. Exploitation of gold-bearing quartz at Poura, southwest of Koudougou, was resumed in 1981 after a 15-year hiatus. Extraction of other mineral resources, including the major manganese deposits at Tambao, were dependent on the construction of adequate communications facilities.

Transportation. In addition to the rail line, which links Ouagadougou to the port of Abidjan in the Ivory Coast, the capital is also linked by road to the principal administrative centres in the country and to the capitals of neighbouring countries. The railroad to Abidjan is 712 miles long, of which 321 miles run through Burkina Faso. Running from east to west before crossing the border, the line serves Koudougou, Bobo Dioulasso, and Banfora.

Burkina Faso has the most extensive road network in proportion to its size of any of the French-speaking African states. About a quarter of the network is usable year round. The remainder consists of rural roads. Three road-building projects completed in the late 1960s and early 1970s were financed by the European Development Fund. The first of these roads runs from Bobo Dioulasso to Faramana to the Mali frontier. The second runs from Ouagadougou to Pô to the Ghanaian frontier. The third runs from Ouagadougou to Koupéla. Road transport is supplied by the Compagnie Transafricaine, as well as by individual enterprises.

International airports are located at Ouagadougou and Bobo Dioulasso. Internal air service, linking about 50 smaller airstrips, is supplied by the national airline.

ADMINISTRATIVE AND SOCIAL CONDITIONS

Government. A constitution, adopted by referendum in 1977, allows multiparty elections with a maximum of three parties participating in the government. Under the constitution leaders of the political parties are not allowed to run for president. The president of the republic is elected for five years by direct universal suffrage and may be reelected only once. The prime minister establishes and conducts national policy, presiding over a council of ministers and directing the work of the government. The National Assembly, elected for five years by universal suffrage, drafts legislation and regulates governmental initiatives. The military, which has had great influence in political life, staged a coup in 1980 and suspended political activity. Additional coups were carried out in 1982 and 1983.

Local government

Burkina Faso is divided into 11 *départements,* headed by prefects. The *départements* are grouped into 25 provinces. In addition, there are *communes* administered by mayors and elected municipal councillors.

Health and welfare. There are hospitals at Ouagadougou, Bobo Dioulasso, Ouahigouya, Pô, and Fada Ngourma as well as medical centres, dispensaries, and maternity centres throughout the country.

Education. School enrollment is one of the lowest in Africa, even though the government devotes a quarter of the national budget to education. French is the language of instruction in primary and secondary schools. Higher education is sought at Ougadougou University (established 1974) or at the national teachers college. Other institutes in Ougadougou sponsored by neighbouring francophone states offer degrees in rural engineering and hydrology. Some students seek higher education in France; in Dakar, Senegal; or in Abidjan, Ivory Coast.

CULTURAL LIFE

Folklore is rich, reflecting the country's ethnic diversity. On national occasions each region is represented in the capital by its own folkloric group.

Houses of Youth and Culture, where young people play cards, read, or watch films or theatrical performances, are located in the main administrative centres. For statistical data, see the "Britannica World Data" section in the current *Britannica Book of the Year.*

(P.H.Gu./Ed.)

History

Axes belonging to a Neolithic culture have been found in the north of the Upper Volta territory. The Bobo, the Lobi, and the Gourounsi are the earliest known inhabitants of the country. Around the 14th century AD conquering horsemen invaded the region from the south to found the Gourma and the Mossi kingdoms, in the east and in the central area, respectively. The Mossi chief Ouedraogo, or Widraogo, is said to have set himself up at Tenkodogo, and his son Raoua (Rawa) to have founded the kingdom of Yatenga, with its capital at Ouahigouya, and his grandson, Oubri, the kingdom of Ouagadougou, whose paramount ruler is styled the *morho nabe* ("big lord"). These kingdoms, with their royal courts, ministers, vassals, and pages, were still surviving in the 20th century. The Mossi withstood numerous attacks by the Muslim Songhai and Fulani.

The German explorer Gottlob Adam Krause traversed the Mossi country in 1886; and the French army officer Louis-Gustave Binger visited the *morho naba* in 1888. France obtained a protectorate over Yatenga in 1895; and Paul Voulet and Charles-Paul-Louis Chanoine defeated the *morho naba* Boukari-Koutou (Wobogo) in 1896 and then proceeded to overrun the Gourounsi lands. The Gourma accepted a French protectorate in 1897; and in 1897 likewise the lands of the Bobo and of the Lobi were annexed by the French (though the Lobi, armed with poisoned arrows, were not effectively subdued until 1903). An Anglo-French convention of 1898 fixed the frontier between France's new acquisitions and the northern territories of the Gold Coast.

Arrival of European explorers

The French divided the country into administrative *cercles* but maintained the chiefs in their traditional seats. At first attached to French Sudan (or Upper Senegal-Niger, as that colony was called from 1904 to 1920), the country was organized as a separate colony, Upper Volta (Haute-Volta), in 1919. In 1932 it was partitioned between the Ivory Coast, Niger, and French Sudan. In 1947, however, Upper Volta was reestablished to become an overseas territory of the French Union, with a territorial assembly of its own. The assembly in 1957 received the right to elect an executive council of government for the territory, which at the end of 1958 was transformed into an autonomous republic within the French Community. When independence was proclaimed on August 5, 1960, a constitution was adopted that provided for an executive president elected by universal adult suffrage for a five-year term and a Legislative Assembly elected for a similar term.

Independence

(H.J.D./Je.D.)

Since Burkina Faso became an independent nation, the military has on several occasions intervened during times of crisis. In 1966 the military, led by Gen. Sangoulé Lamizana, ousted the elected government of Maurice Yaméogo. The military relinquished control of the government following the 1970 constitutional referendum, by which Lamizana became president. The military again took control of the government in 1974, after a confrontation developed between the Prime Minister and the National Assembly. Military rule lasted until the 1977 constitutional referendum, when Lamizana was again elected president. The new civilian government lasted only until 1980, when Col. Saye Zerbo, following more than a year of strikes in opposition to government policies, led another military coup. In November 1982 noncommissioned officers staged a coup and installed Maj. Jean-Baptiste Ouedraogo as president of the new government; and in August 1983 another military coup placed Capt. Thomas Sankara and his National Revolutionary Council (CNR) at the helm of the country. For current political history, see the annual issues of the *Britannica Book of the Year.* (P.H.Gu.)

CAMEROON

The United Republic of Cameroon (République Unie du Cameroun) is a triangle-shaped state wedged between western and central Africa. It covers an area of 179,714 square miles (465,458 square kilometres) and is bordered by the Atlantic Ocean to the southwest, Nigeria to the northwest, Chad to the northeast, the Central African Republic to the east, Congo to the southeast, and Gabon and Equatorial Guinea to the south. The federal capital of Cameroon is at Yaoundé.

Physical and human geography

The country's name is derived from Rio dos Camarões (River of Prawns)—the name given to the Wouri River estuary by Portuguese explorers of the 15th and 16th centuries. Camarões was also used to designate the river's neighbouring mountains. The French form is Cameroun. Until the late 19th century, English usage confined the term the Cameroons to the mountains, and the estuary was called the Cameroons River or, locally, the Bay. In 1884 the Germans extended the word Kamerun to their entire protectorate, which largely corresponded to the present state.

THE LAND

Relief. Cameroon can be divided into the four geographic regions of the south, the central, the north, and the west. The southern region extends from the Sanaga River to the southern border and from the coast eastward to the Central African Republic and Congo. It consists of coastal plains that are about 25 miles (40 kilometres) wide and a densely forested plateau with an average elevation of a little less than 1,000 feet (about 300 metres).

The central region extends from the Sanaga River north to the Bénoué River. The land rises progressively to the north and includes the Adamawa (Adamaova) Plateau, with elevations between 2,500 feet and 4,500 feet.

In the extreme north, the savanna plain slopes downward as it approaches the Lake Chad Basin. To the west, the
Upland areas relief is mountainous, the result of a volcanic rift that extends northward from the island of Fernando Po. Near the coast, the active volcanic Cameroon Mountain rises to the highest elevation in western Africa—13,353 feet (4,070 metres). The Monts Gotel of the Adamaowa trend from south to north, culminating in the Monts Mandara of the northwest.

Drainage. The rivers of Cameroon form four large drainage systems. In the south, the Sanaga, Wouri, Nyong, and Ntem rivers drain into the Atlantic Ocean The Bénoué River and its tributary, the Mayo Kébi, flow into the Niger River Basin of Nigeria. The Logone and Chari rivers—which form part of the eastern border with Chad—drain into Lake Chad, whereas the Ngoko River joins the Sangha River and flows into the Congo River Basin.

Climate. The major factors that influence Cameroon's climate are its latitudinal extent and its relief. Lying wholly within the tropics, the country has a hot climate throughout the year; average temperatures range between 70° and 82° F (21° and 28° C), although they are lower in areas of high elevation.

The incidence of rainfall depends largely on the seasonal movements of two dominant air masses; the warm and dry tropical continental air mass is associated with dusty weather, whereas the warm and humid tropical maritime air mass brings rains. Rainfall decreases from south to north. Along the coast, the rainy season lasts from April to November, and the relatively dry season lasts from December to March; a transition period from March to April is marked by violent winds. The mean annual rainfall of 98 inches (2,490 millimetres) occurs in 150 days. In the central plateau region, rainfall decreases to 59 inches. There are four seasons—a light rainy season from May to June, a short dry season from July to October, a heavy rainy season from October to November, and a long dry season from December to May. The north, however, has

only a dry season from October to May and a rainy season from June to September, with a mean annual rainfall as low as 15 inches. The wettest part of the country lies in the western highlands. Debundscha Point on Cameroon Mountain has a mean annual rainfall of about 400 inches, most of which falls from May to October.

Plant and animal life. The major vegetation types of western Africa are represented in Cameroon. The hot and humid south supports dense, tropical rain forests, in which hardwood evergreen trees including mahogany, ebony, obeche, dibetu, and sapelli may grow to more than 200 feet high. There are large numbers of orchids and ferns.

Mangroves grow along the coasts and the mouths of *Plants of* rivers. The rain forest gives place to the semi-deciduous *the tropical* forest of the central region, where a number of tree species *rain forest* shed their leaves during the dry season. North of the semi-deciduous forest, the vegetation is composed of wooded savanna with trees 10 to 60 feet high. The density of trees decreases toward the Chad Basin, where they are sparse and mainly of *Acacia* species.

Between 4,000 and 8,000 feet, the tropical rain forest differs from that of the lowlands; the trees are smaller, are of different species, and are festooned with mosses, lichens, and other epiphytes (plants that derive their moisture and nutriments from the air and rain). Above the forest zone are drier woodland, tall grassland, or patches of mountain bamboo. Above about 7,800 feet in the interior and above about 10,000 feet on Cameroon Mountain, short grasses predominate.

The country is rich in animal life. Its dense forests are inhabited by screaming red and green monkeys, chimpanzees, and mandrills, as well as rodents, bats, and numerous birds—from tiny sunbirds to giant hawks and eagles. A few elephants survive in the forest and in the grassy woodlands where baboons and several types of antelope are the most common animals. The 656-square-mile Parc National de Waza in the north, which was originally created for the protection of giraffes and antelope, abounds in both forest and savanna animals including monkeys, baboons, lions, leopards, and birds ranging from white and gray pelicans to spotted waders.

Settlement patterns. In general there is a cultural division between the north and the south. The northern savanna plateau is inhabited by Sudanic and Arab pastoralists who migrate seasonally in search of grazing land and occupy temporary dwellings, whereas the forested and hilly south is peopled by Bantu agriculturalists in permanent villages. The north is predominantly Muslim, whereas the southern peoples adhere to animism and Christianity.

Most of the large urban centres are in the south. Douala is the largest city and the country's main port. The federal capital of Yaoundé is an important communication centre. In the north, Garoua is a port on the Bénoué River.

THE PEOPLE

The country has been described as a "racial crossroads" because of its more than 100 different ethnic groups. There are three main linguistic groups—the Bantu-speaking people of the south, the Sudanic-speaking people of the north, *The* and those who speak the Bantu languages of the west. *principal*

The Bantus settled in the Cameroons from Equatorial *linguistic* Africa. The first group that invaded the country included *groups* the Makas, Ndjems, and Dualas. They were followed at the beginning of the 19th century by the Fang (Pangwe) and Bete peoples.

The Sudanic-speaking peoples in the north include the Sao, who live on the Adamawa Plateau; the Fulani; and the Kanuri. The Fulani came from the Niger Basin in two waves—in the 11th and 19th centuries; they were Muslims who converted and subjugated the Logone valley and the Mayo Kebbi and Faro areas. The third ethnic group consists mainly of small tribes, except for the Bamilekes who live between the lower slopes of the Adamawa Plateau and Cameroon Mountain. Other western Bantu-speaking tribes include the Tikar who live in the Bamenda region, the Bali, the Mum, and the Keaka.

The oldest inhabitants of the country are the Pygmies, locally known as the Baguielli and Babinga, who are found within the southern forests. They have been hunters and food-gatherers for thousands of years and live in small hunting bands.

The work of European missionaries and the colonization of the country by European powers led to the introduction of European languages. During the colonial era German was the official language; it was later replaced by English and French, which have retained their official status in the unitary republic established in 1972.

Almost half of the population continues to adhere to traditional beliefs. European Christian missionaries first came to Cameroon in the 19th century. About a quarter of the population is Roman Catholic, one-eighth is Protestant, and one-eighth is Muslim.

THE ECONOMY

Like several other African countries, Cameroon has a basically agricultural economy supplemented with oil and minerals. The economy—which is dominated by French financial institutions and banking houses—has maintained steady growth since independence. Cameroon does not suffer from a chronic trade deficit, since imports and exports are usually in reasonably good balance. The government was able to dispense with external support for its budgetary needs after 1969. Cameroon is an associate member of the European Economic Community (EEC, or Common Market) and a member of the Union Douanière et Économique de l'Afrique Centrale (UDEAC; Central African Customs and Economic Union), to which the Central African Republic, Gabon, and Congo also belong.

Resources. The largest mineral reserves are those of bauxite at Minim-Martap and Ngaoundere on the Adamawa Plateau; the deposits, amounting to more than 1,000,000,000 tons, have a 44 percent alumina content. Another 40,000,000,000 tons of bauxite reserves are situated at Fonga-Tongo. There is some gold in eastern Cameroon, and cassiterite (a tin dioxide) occurs at Mayo Darlé in the northeast. Mineralogical surveys have found iron ore near Kribi, on the coast south of Douala. Production from offshore oil deposits in the Rio del Rey area increased markedly in the early 1980s.

About 41,000,000 acres (16,000,000 hectares), or one-third of eastern Cameroon, and about 2,500,000 acres in western Cameroon are forested and yield valuable hardwood timber. The rivers and offshore ocean waters are a rich source of fish, and the grasslands support valuable herds of cattle. The wild animal life provides a firm basis for tourism.

The main developed source of hydroelectric power is the Sanaga River; the power station at Edéa on the Sanaga Falls is the country's largest. The Akam-Wouri River in the west also provides hydroelectric power as it drops from the central plateau to the coastal region. Thermal power is expensive because diesel fuel and coal must be imported.

Water-power resources

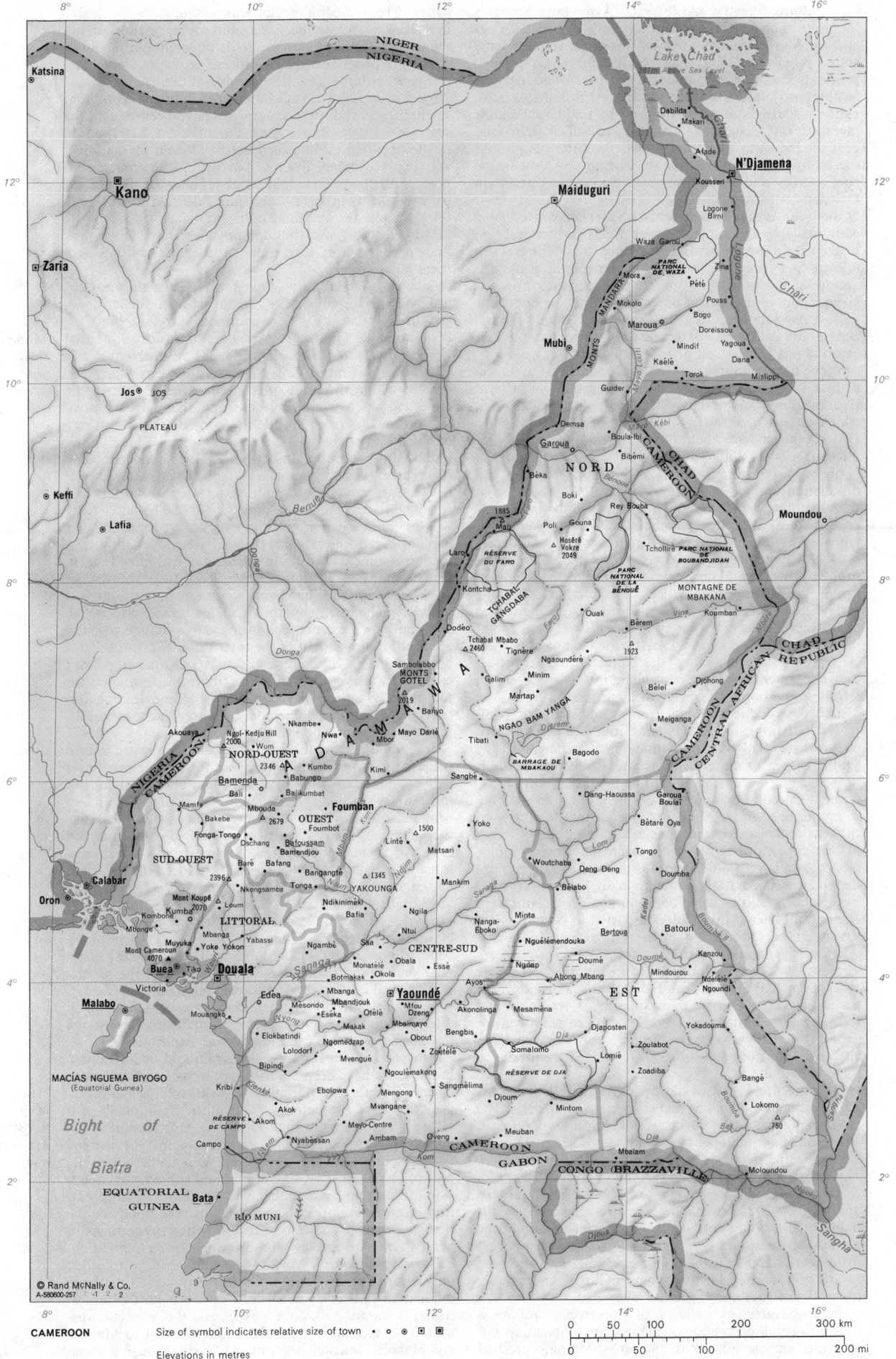

Katsina

NIGER
NIGERIA

Lake Chad
925 m Above Sea Level

Dabilda
Makari
Afadé

Kano

N'Djamena

Kousséri

12°

Maiduguri

Logone
Birni

Waza Garou
Zina
PARC
NATIONAL
DE WAZA
Pété
Pouss
Bogo
Doreissou
Yagoua
Dana
Misliipi

Zaria

Mora
Mokolo
Maroua
Mindif
Kaélé

Mubi

MONTS MANDARA

Torok
Bibémi

10°

Jos
JOS

Guider

Mayo Kébi

CHAD
CAMEROON

Moundou

PLATEAU

Demsa
Garoua

Boula-Ibi

Béka

NORD

Boki

Rey Bouba

Keffi

Benue

Boki

Tchollité
PARC NATIONAL DE
BOUBANDJIDAH

Lafia

1885
Mali
Poli
Gouna
Hoséré
Vokre
2049

MONTAGNE DE
MBAKANA

Laro

RÉSERVE
DU FARO

Koumban

CHAD

Kontcha

PARC
NATIONAL
DE LA
BÉNOUÉ

Ouak
Bérem

8°

Donga

Dodéo

TCHABAL
GANGDABA

Faro

1923

Tchabal Mbabo
2460
Tignère
Ngaoundéré

CAMEROON CENTRAL AFRICAN REPUBLIC

Sambolabbo
MONTS
GOTEL
2019

Galim

Minim

Djohong

Bélel

Akouaya
Ngol-Kedju Hill
2000
Wum

Nkambe
Nwa
Mbor

Banyo

D A M A W A

Martap

Meiganga

Mayo Darlé

Tibati

NGAO BAM YANGA

BARRAGE DE
MBAKAOU

Bagodo

NORD-OUEST
2346
Kumbo

Djerem

Kimi

Sangbé

Dang-Haoussa

Garoua
Boulaï

6°

Bamenda
Bali

Babungo
Balikumbat

Mbam

Yoko

Woutchaba

Deng-Deng

Bétaré Oya

Mamfe
Bakebe

Mbouda
2679
Foumban

OUEST
Foumbot

Linté
1500

Matsari

Lom

Tongo

Fonga-Tongo
Dschang
Bafoussam
Bamendjou

Bangangté
1345

YAKOUNGA

Mankim

Belabo

Doumba

SUD-OUEST
Baré
Bafang
2396

Nkongsamba
Tonga

Sanaga

Nanga-
Eboko

Bertoua

Batouri

Kenzou

Calabar

Mont Koupé
2070
Loum

Ndikinimeki
Bafia

Ngila

Ntui

Minta

Bombé II

Oron

Kombon
Kumba
Mbonge
Muyuka
Yoke Yokon

Mbanga
Yabassi

Ngambé

Saa

CENTRE-SUD

Nguélémendouka

Bertoua

Mindourou

Ndéléle
Ngoundi

Mont Cameroun
4070
Buea
Tiko

Douala

Sanaga

Monatélé
Botmakak

Obala
Okola

Essé

Ngoap

Doumé

Abong Mbang

EST

Victoria

Edéa

Mbanga
Mbandjouk

Ayos

Yokadouma

Malabo

Mouangko

Mesondo
Eséka
Makak

Ngomédzap
Obout

Yaoundé
Mfou
Dzeng
Mbalmayo

Akonolinga

Mesaména

Djaposten

Zoulabot

MACÍAS NGUEMA BIYOGO
(Equatorial Guinea)

Elokbatindi
Lolodorf
Bipindi

Mvengué

Ngoulemakong

Zoétélé

Bengbis

Somalomo

Lomié

Zoadiba

Bangé

Kribi

Ntenk

Ebolowa

Mengong

Sangmélima

RÉSERVE DE DJA

Djoum

Mintom

Lokomo

750

Akok

Mvangané

Mvan

Meyo-Centre

Oveng
Ambam

Meuban

Dja

Bek

Bight of
Biafra

RÉSERVE
DE CAMPO

Akom

Nyabéssan

CAMEROON
GABON

Mbalam

Moloundou

Ntem

Campo

Kom

CONGO (BRAZZAVILLE)

Djoua

EQUATORIAL
GUINEA
Bata

Ngoko

RIO MUNI

Nyoko

Sangha

© Rand McNally & Co.
A-580600-257   -1   2   2

CAMEROON   Size of symbol indicates relative size of town • ○ ◎ ▣ ▣

Elevations in metres

0   50   100   200   300 km

0   50   100   200 mi

Agriculture, forestry, and fishing.   Agriculture accounts for more than one-half of the country's export earnings and employs more than three-fourths of the economically active population. The main subsistence crops include plantains, yams, and manioc in the south and peanuts (groundnuts), millet, and manioc in the north. Most cultivation is carried out on small farms by traditional simple methods, but Cameroon is almost self-sufficient in food production. Cash crops are grown on large plantations owned by French interests in the east and by agricultural cooperatives and a government agency—the Cameroon Development Corporation—in the west.

Cocoa
and coffee
production

Cameroon is one of the world's leading cocoa-producing countries. The cacao plant, which yields the cocoa bean, is grown on small farms throughout the Centre-South (Centre-Sud) province, in parts of the coastal and western areas, and in western Cameroon. Much attention was given to the improvement of cocoa production under the second five-year plan; under "Operation 100,000 Tons," agricultural extension workers helped farmers to tend their cacao plants and to fight pests and diseases.

Among the French-speaking African countries, Cameroon is the second largest coffee exporter, after the Ivory Coast. Eastern Cameroon produces 90 percent of the coffee crop, which is grown on an estimated total of 400,000 acres (161,8000 hectares). About three-fourths of the coffee produced is robusta, the rest arabica.

Bananas are an important export product by value, but production and exports declined in the 1960s because of the lack of new markets and the loss of imperial preference in the United Kingdom in 1967. The government launched a campaign in 1965 to produce a hardier, disease-resistant banana variety. Bananas are grown on plantations in the southwest and on small farms. Decreased yields on aging plantations caused a decline in production in the early 1980s, but the government instituted a program to counteract the decline.

Cotton was introduced in 1952 by the Compagnie Française pour le Développement des Fibres Textiles, in which the government owns the controlling interest. It is grown largely in the northern grasslands by private farmers.

Rubber is produced on government and domestic company plantations; the Société Africaine Forestière et Agricole owns 25,000 acres of plantations at Dizangué in the southern area of eastern Cameroon. Rubber plantations in western Cameroon are owned by the Cameroon Development Corporation and Palmol Cameroon, Ltd. Rubber is produced mainly for export, but a small quantity of rubber produced at Dizangué is used domestically.

Other cash crops include rice, sugarcane, tropical fruits, tobacco, and palm oil. Except for pigs, which are prohibited in areas where Islām is predominant, livestock (mainly cattle, sheep, and goats) is concentrated on the northern Adamawa Plateau. Livestock is exported to Nigeria, meat to Equatorial Guinea and to the Congo, and hides and skins to Nigeria and Equatorial Guinea.

Forestry

Forestry has been well developed in the most accessible areas along the Douala–Yaoundé railway and along the main roads. The logs are transported by water, road, and rail. Logs, cut timber and palm kernels are produced for export, whereas wood for construction purposes, firewood, charcoal, kola nuts, and palm oil and kernels are produced for domestic use.

Marine fishing is carried out by individual fishermen using traditional methods as well as by large companies. The fishermen go to sea in dugout canoes and use nylon nets, whereas the companies employ trawlers based in Douala. Fishing in the rivers yields an even larger catch.

Industry.   Mining has become an important sector of the economy. Oil production rose sharply in the 1970s and by the 1980s accounted for two-fifths of exports. Substantial amounts of bauxite are mined to supply the aluminum smelter at Edéa, but some bauxite is imported from France and Equatorial Guinea. Limestone and pozzolana are quarried for the cement industry, and smaller quantities of gold and cassiterite are mined.

The manufacturing industry of Cameroon employs a relatively small percentage of the working population but accounts for one-quarter of the gross domestic product (GDP). The industrial sector consists of a major heavy industrial complex, the Edéa aluminum smelter, an oil refinery at Victoria, and hundreds of small and medium-sized enterprises engaged in processing, various manufacturing procedures, and the assembly of radios.

Apart from a few establishments, such as the aluminum smelter, most industrial enterprises have been established since the 1960s. The largest development has been in textiles, centred around factories in Douala for spinning, weaving, bleaching, dyeing, and printing cotton. Food-processing plants include a sugar refinery at Mbandjock; palm-oil plants in Bota, Lobe, and Edéa; a chocolate factory at Yaoundé; and flour mills at Douala.

Hydroelectric power stations on the Sanaga River near Edéa produce more than nine-tenths of the nation's electrical power.

Finance.   Cameroon is linked together with the Central African Republic, Gabon, and Congo in a monetary union (UDEAC) with a common currency, the CFA (Communauté Financière Africaine, or African Financial Community) franc. The CFA franc is convertible into any currency, but France must approve direct investment by citizens within the franc area in countries outside it, the issue and sale of foreign stocks and shares in the area, and borrowings from outside the area. France is also represented on the board of directors of the Central Bank in Yaoundé; its notes and coins are legal tender in each member state of the monetary union. Each member state has its own monetary committee, on which France is represented, and a National Credit Council. The latter body advises the respective governments on credit policy and banking organization and methods. There are a number of foreign commercial banks in Cameroon, including French, British, and U.S. institutions. Most insurance companies are French owned. There is no stock exchange.

Monetary
relations
with
France

Trade.   The main exports are agricultural products, oil, and lumber. Coffee, cocoa, and cocoa by-products together account for almost half of the total value of exports. Timber, aluminum, cotton, and bananas are other important exports. Capital equipment and semifinished products for the growing industrial sector have become leading imports. Other imports include bauxite, pharmaceuticals, beverages, rubber, and synthetic fabrics.

Most trade is carried on with the EEC countries. France is the largest individual trading partner; it supplies almost half of Cameroon's imports and takes about one-fifth of the country's exports.

Administration of the economy.   The government sets the guidelines for development in its five-year plans and attracts private capital for the development of certain sectors of the economy. It has stressed balanced development of the various economic sectors and has avoided hasty industrialization.

In order to encourage private investment, the Cameroon National Federal Assembly has adopted an investment code; its objectives include stabilization of company taxes, provision of security to large businesses, and the protection of local industries from foreign competition.

There are four different company tax systems, which offer various benefits to developing industries. Most tax revenues are derived from import and export duties.

Transportation.   The difficult terrain and heavy rainfall in the south have been contributory factors to the absence of an adequate transportation network linking the different regions of the country. The north traditionally was virtually isolated from the south. The construction of the railway line between Mbanga and Kumba in 1965 enabled the transportation of products from West Cameroon to the port of Douala in East Cameroon, and subsequent expansion further improved contact with the north. Transportation is more developed in some regions than in others; the best roads are in the coastal region, whereas the roads in West Cameroon are few and are often in bad condition.

Problems
of
transport
develop-
ment

The road network.   Most of the roads can be travelled only during the dry season. Douala is linked to the large population centres by roads that run through the central region, Yaoundé and Yoke Yokon, and the Adamawa district. Two subsidiary roads from Garoua lead to Maroua and Makole. Douala is also linked by road through Bertoua and Batouri to Bangui in the Central African Republic and to Gabon via Edéa and Kribi.

Railways. Railways include the Trans-Cameroon line, which reaches Ngaoundéré from Yaoundé. The two short railway lines of metre gauge in the southwest, comprising the West Line, were constructed by the Germans before World War I; they remained separated until 1955 when the Wouri Bridge made it possible for them to use a common terminus and to gain access to workshops at Bassa, just outside Douala. A 107-mile-long northern line runs from Douala to Nkongsamba and serves the coffee and banana region of East Cameroon; a line from Mbanga to Roumbou was completed in the late 1960s. The Central Line runs for 191 miles between Douala and Yaoundé; it has a 24-mile branch line to Mbalmayo on the Nyong River, which serves Edéa and the cocoa-producing area.

Facilities at Douala *Port facilities.* The main port is Douala, on the estuary of the Wouri River. One of the best equipped ports in western Africa, it has docks for cargo ships, including a wood-loading dock and a tanker dock with adjacent facilities for the unloading and storing of minerals. The fishing port above the wood-loading dock is equipped with refrigeration facilities.

The minor ports include Kribi at the mouth of the Kienké River, which is used primarily for the shipment of logs and cocoa from the Bouloun district; the ocean port of Victoria in West Cameroon, which has become Cameroon's oil exporting port; and the port of Tiko, on a creek leading to the Wouri estuary, which handles bananas, wood, and rubber. In the north, the river port of Garoua on the banks of the Bénoué transports goods to Nigeria; the Upper Bénoué, however, is navigable only from seven to 10 weeks in a year.

Air transport. Douala is the main international port of entry, and Yaoundé also handles international flights. There are domestic airports at Maroua, Garoua, and Ngaoundéré, as well as numerous airfields. Air-Cameroun has scheduled domestic flights and flights to Chad.

ADMINISTRATIVE AND SOCIAL CONDITIONS

The federation of the two states **Government.** By the constitution of 1961, the states of West Cameroon and East Cameroon were linked together into a federation. The constitution of 1972 replaced the federation with a centralized government, the United Republic of Cameroon. Executive powers are conferred on the president, who is the head of the government and chief of the armed forces. The president is assisted by a prime minister. The president is elected for a period of five years by direct and secret universal suffrage granted to all citizens over 21 years of age. The president appoints the prime minister and vice ministers and may dissolve the National Assembly.

Legislative power is held by a unicameral National Assembly. It has 120 members, directly elected for five-year terms. The National Assembly shares with the president the initiative for proposing legislation, which it adopts on a simple-majority basis. When a particular bill is read twice, however, a majority of all numbers is required.

The republic is divided into 10 provinces, each administered by a governor. Each province is further divided into *départements*.

Evolution of the one-party state In the 1950s there were no fewer than 84 political parties in East Cameroon. With the exceptions of the Union des Populations du Cameroun (UPC; Union of the Populations of Cameroon) and the Action Nationale (National Action), both of which were broadly based, the rest of the parties existed only at the tribal or regional level. In 1955 the UPC was banned by the French government; as a result a wave of terrorism broke out, especially in the Bassa Mungo, Wuri, and Bamileke districts. Political rights were restored to the party in 1960. The arrest, conviction, and imprisonment of the four principal opposition leaders in East Cameroon during 1962 left the ruling party, L'Union Camerounaise (The Cameroonian Union), as virtually the only party in the state. In 1966 the Union merged with the governing party of West Cameroon, the Kamerun National Democratic Party (KNDP), creating the Union Nationale Camerounaise (UNC; Cameroon National Union). The country is now a de facto one-party state.

Justice. A Higher Judicial Council, which is responsible for guaranteeing the independence of the judiciary, advises the president on the nomination of magistrates and judges and acts as a disciplinary body. The Supreme Court decides whether a bill is receivable by the National Assembly in the event of a dispute between the president and the legislature. It also passes judgment on appeals concerning administrative actions of the government and decisions of the Court of Appeal.

The special Court of Impeachment passes judgment on the president in case of high treason and on the prime minister and other government ministers in the event of a plot against the government.

The legal system of Cameroon consists of the Supreme Court, two courts of appeal, and high courts as well as circuit courts.

Education. Educational services have been expanding and the curriculum in secondary schools has been modified to make it relevant to the country's needs. About three-fourths of all children of primary school age are enrolled either in government or in Catholic or Protestant mission schools.

There are general education secondary schools, vocational schools, and teacher-training schools. Manual labour is compulsory in secondary and technical schools as a means of encouraging students to take up farming on the completion of their courses instead of seeking white-collar jobs in the cities. The University of Yaoundé was established in 1962 and in the early 1980s added four regional campuses.

Health and welfare. The government emphasized the improvement of the nation's health facilities in the first and second five-year development plans. Between 1958 and 1980 the number of hospitals, dispensaries, and elementary health centres was increased about seven-fold. Between 1965 and 1980 hospitals in Yaoundé, Douala, Foumban, Garoua, and Ngaoundéré were modernized. A Health Sciences University Centre was established at the Federal University in 1969 to train Cameroonian doctors and other medical personnel.

There is no government system of social security, and there are no pension plans or health insurance programs for workers. Most assistance is obtained through the traditional kinship system. There are, however, indemnities for occupational diseases or accidents, and the Public Health Service provides free services to the poor.

Malaria is prevalent everywhere but in the mountainous regions, where respiratory and pulmonary diseases and dysentery are common. There are incidences of leprosy and schistosomiasis (a parasitic infestation of the bladder and intestines), as well as syphilis, sleeping sickness, and rheumatism.

Social and economic divisions in general follow ethnic lines. In the north the Muslim pastoralists dominate, whereas the more urban south is dominated by those who have acquired Christianity and a Western education. Because of the multiplicity of tribes, precise divisions are difficult to draw.

CULTURAL LIFE

Each major ethnic group of the country has developed its own culture. The frenzied rhythms played on the drums by the people of the southern forest region contrast with the flute music of northern Cameroonians. Rich diversity is well represented in the country's art. In the Adamawa area, the Muslim Fulani produce elaborately worked leather goods and ornate calabashes (gourds used as containers), and the Kirdi and the Matakani of the western mountains produce distinctive types of pottery. The powerful masks of the Bali, which represent elephants' heads, are used in ceremonies for the dead, and the statuettes of the Bamileke are carved in human and animal figures. The Tikar people are famous for beautifully decorated brass pipes, the Ngoutou people for two-faced masks, and the Bamum for smiling masks.

Cultural institutions and organizations L'Institut Français d'Afrique Noir (French Institute of Black Africa) maintains a library in Douala that specializes in the sociology, ethnology, and history of Africa. Small libraries are also maintained by secondary and technical schools. Of the several museums, the Musée du Diamare et Maroua has anthropological collections relating to the Sudanese peoples and the Musée Camerounais de Douala exhibits objects of Cameroon's prehistory and natural history.

Cultural organizations include the Cameroun Cultural Association, the Cameroun Cultural Society, and the Centre Fédéral Linguistique et Culturel. There are also numerous women's associations, youth organizations, and sporting associations. For statistical data, see the "Britannica World Data" section in the current *Britannica Book of the Year*.

(G.Be./Ed.)

History

SETTLEMENT BY EUROPEANS

The Portuguese navigator Fernão do Pó was probably the first European to sight the shore and estuary of the Wouri River (Rio dos Camarões).

Dutch settlers followed the Portuguese into the region to be themselves succeeded by the English, who came with anti-slavery cruisers at the beginning of the 19th century. Liverpool and Bristol companies anchored pontoons to the banks of the Wouri to serve as shops, and in 1832 John Beecroft established a business at Bimbia. In 1849, when the Spanish occupation of Fernando Po seemed likely, Beecroft was appointed consul and representative of the king to the Bights of Benin and Biafra and actively engaged in negotiations with local chiefs.

Activities of Alfred Saker In February 1845 the Baptist missionary Alfred Saker (1814–80) settled in Cameroon and on April 29, 1852, signed with John Beecroft, King Akwa, and Charles Dido a treaty which foreshadowed the abolition of slavery, the prevention of human sacrifice, the granting of religious liberty, and the protection of missionaries. In order to settle differences between chiefs and Europeans in 1850 the British set up the Court of Equity, which later adapted itself to French and German rule. In 1858, when the structures of Catholic Spain began to affect the Protestant Jamaicans in Fernando Po, Saker installed them at Ambas (which he called Victoria) and founded many more settlements, notably at Deido and Bonabéri. He also succeeded in transcribing the Duala language.

In 1868 the Woermann Company of Hamburg built a warehouse on the estuary, an example soon followed by several other firms, and from 1874 (when the Duala were seeking British protection and the Malimba had already concluded a treaty with France) began to demand the appointment of a German consul. Despite the support of British businessmen, requests for British protection made by Duala chiefs in 1882 were forestalled by the German treaty of July 16, 1884, between King Bell and Gustav Nachtigal. An English annexation mission was similarly belated. German occupation marked by the appointment of Max Buchner as consul had little effect on Britain and France but locally took a far more serious turn. On December 15 the chiefs of Jos and Hickory, seeing themselves partially dispossessed, attacked Bell's village and took down the German flag. Three days later Admiral Knorr arrived in the "Bismarck" and took so stern a reprisal that Woermann's representative was murdered and his mutilated body thrown into the river. Baron von Soden, who was appointed governor of Cameroon in mid-1885, with Jesko von Puttkamer his successor, set up the first administrative divisions and organized explorations. The French renounced their rights as far as the Campo River with the Berlin Agreement of December 24, 1885, while on May 7, 1886, Britain agreed to the transfer of Victoria to Germany in exchange for St. Lucia in South Africa and Forcados in the Niger Delta.

The expeditions of such early explorers as Dixon Denham, who was probably the first to cross the interior in 1823, Heinrich Barth, and Adolf Overweg, who visited Adamawa in 1851, and the Rev. George Grenfell, with those of their German and French successors, helped Germany to define new frontiers with Britain on October 15, 1893, and with France on February 4, 1894. Furthermore, in 1911, in return for assenting to France's protectorate over Morocco, Germany absorbed some 105,000 square

miles of former French Equatorial Africa to constitute the territory of Neu Kamerun. The German administration did not, however, have time to make a significant impact. When the territorial borders were defined in 1913 the governor had no means of enforcing his decisions. The recruitment of soldiers in Dahomey and Nigeria had serious effects, and the ensuing mutiny engendered the Kaiserliche Schutztruppe, a police force that dominated the country, although its western regions were not entirely subdued until the second half of the century.

Initially, chiefdoms were reinforced, a system of indirect administration was set up, and concessions were granted to commercial companies. The Gesellschaft Sud Kamerun governed the south and the Gesellschaft Nord-West Kamerun controlled the territories of the Bamileke and the Bamum.

The number of officials increased, however, and direct administration to a large extent replaced indirect administration, which was maintained in the Muslim regions of the north.

THE 20TH CENTURY

In World War I joint action by French and British troops forced the Germans to retreat to Spanish Guinea, where they were confined. Early in March 1916 a temporary partition, which gave France about nine-tenths of the territory, was agreed upon, and the section adjoining Nigeria came under British control. On July 10, 1919, the Cameroons was formally divided by the London Declaration signed by Great Britain and France. In 1922 the League of Nations conferred mandates on France and Britain for the administration of the two zones on which they had previously agreed, subject to the supervision of the League's Permanent Mandates Commission, and on July 20, 1922, the mandates were approved by the Council of the League of Nations. League of Nations Mandates (1922)

Although the administration of the British Cameroons was integrated with that of Nigeria, French Cameroun constituted a separate entity and the former German Neu Kamerun was returned to French Equatorial Africa.

British Cameroons. The British trust territory consisted of a strip of land bisected by the Bénoué River along the eastern border of Nigeria. The capital of Southern Cameroons was Bouéa while Northern Cameroons comprised the Tigon–Ndoro–Kentu region, the Adamawa districts, and Dikwa in the extreme north.

Although the area allotted to Great Britain in 1919 was small, it nevertheless contained most of the German plantations (bananas, rubber, palms, and cocoa). These were reclaimed by their owners in 1924 but were sequestered at the outbreak of World War II. After World War II the Nigerian government absorbed them into the Cameroons Development Corporation, which employed several thousand workers and played an important part in the prosperity of Southern Cameroons.

French Cameroun. The administrative system of French Cameroun was based on that of other territories in French Equatorial Africa. Residing in the capital, Yaoundé, a commissioner (later high commissioner) with the rank of governor, assisted by a secretary general, initiated and coordinated all governmental activities. The country was divided into 18 administrative regions which were themselves made up of further subdivisions. Its elected territorial assembly exercised wide powers. Personnel remained in the country for some time, thus assuring administrative continuity. Sleeping sickness was eradicated. Education along French lines was vigorously pursued. During World War II the territory joined the Free French Movement in August 1940, and Douala was for a time the headquarters of Gen. Charles de Gaulle.

On December 13, 1946, the first General Assembly of the UN approved Cameroun's status as an "associated territory" within the French Constitution of 1946 which instituted Arcam (Assemblée Représentative du Cameroun). This body approved taxes and controlled almost all aspects of the territory's life. As the electoral body increased, from 16,088 in 1946 to 685,059 in 1956, this assembly, composed of 40, then 50 more members, became the voice of the people and the representative of diverse ethnic groups.

In 1952 it was transformed into Atcam (Assemblée Territoriale du Cameroun) and in 1957 was reformed into Alcam (Assemblée Législative du Cameroun).

INDEPENDENCE

The Republic of Cameroon

From 1941 the municipal regime applied to two urban communities, then to five others in 1947 and 1950, and in 1952 was extended to all urban and rural areas of Southern Cameroun in an initiative unique in Africa. Cameroun's constitution, approved by a decree of the Legislative Assembly on April 16, 1957, provided for the transfer of power to a legislative assembly with finance, defense, and the diplomatic service the remaining responsibilities of the tutelary power. The government presided over at that time by André Marie Mbida wielded executive power. In March 1959 the UN adopted the French proposal to end its trusteeship, and on January 1, 1960, the territory of Cameroun became the Republic of Cameroun.

Republic of Cameroun. Political life did not really begin to take shape until the end of World War II when first Jeucafra (Jeunesse du Cameroun Français), then Unicafra (Union du Cameroun Français), later Racam (Rassemblement Camerounais), were formed. In April 1948 the Cameroun section of the Rassemblement Démocratique Africain (RDA) took the title of the Union des Populations du Cameroun (UPC). In 1955 an extremist splinter group of the UPC led by Ruben Um Nyobé whipped up unrest

in Douala but failed to prevent the northern peoples from regrouping into the Bloc des Démocrates Camerounais (BDC) of Ahmadou Ahidjo. In 1958 Ahidjo founded the majority party Union Camerounaise and in February 1958 assumed governmental control. After independence had been achieved on January 1, 1960, the constitution was approved by 60 percent of the electorate on February 21, 1960, and on April 10 the National Assembly was elected with Ahidjo's party in majority.

The Federal Republic. In the British Cameroons the question of reunification was put to a plebiscite. On February 11, 1961, the northern regions voted in favour of joining the Federation of Nigeria, and the Southern Cameroons decided to join the Cameroun Republic, which then, on October 1, 1961, became the Federal Republic of Cameroon.   (R.Co.)

In 1972 a referendum approved a new constitution and the formation of the United Republic of Cameroon. The federal system was abandoned for a centralized form of government. Maritime border disputes with Nigeria over the Rio del Rey offshore oil fields occurred in 1981 but were settled by the Organization for African Unity (OAU). In 1982 Ahidjo resigned, naming Prime Minister Paul Biya as president. A military coup threatened Biya's government in April 1984, but most of the army remained loyal and the government survived. For current political history, see the annual issues of the *Britannica Book of the Year.*   (Ed.)

CAPE VERDE

Cape Verde (República de Cabo Verde) is a republic comprising a group of islands that lie 385 miles (620 kilometres) off the west coast of Africa, between 17°30′ N and 14°30′ N, and 25°30′ W and 22°30′ W, with a total land area of 1,557 square miles (4,033 square kilometres). Praia on São Tiago is the capital.

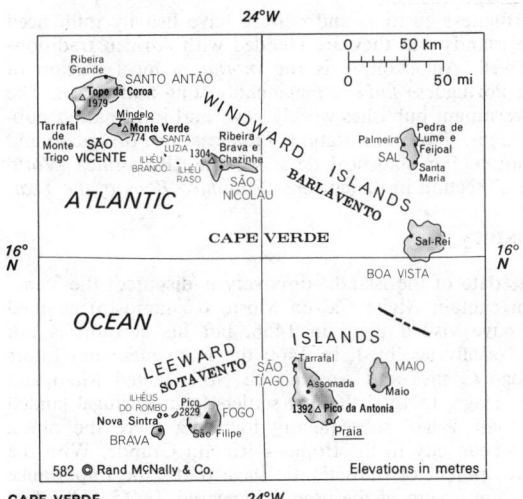

CAPE VERDE   24°W

Physical and human geography

The islands of the archipelago

Cape Verde is named after the westernmost cape of Africa, which is the nearest point on the continent. The country consists of 10 islands and five islets, which are divided into the Windward (Ilhas de Barlavento) and Leeward (Ilhas de Sotavento) groups. The Windward Islands consist of Santo Antão, São Vicente, Santa Luzia, São Nicolau, Boa Vista, and Sal, together with the islets of Raso and Branco. The Leeward Islands include Maio, São Tiago, Fogo, and Brava, and the three islets called the Rombos—Grande, Luís Carneiro, and Cima.

The largest port in the islands is Porto Grande at Mindolo, on São Vicente. Its deepwater harbour—formed by a volcanic crater with its seaward wall breached—accommodates vessels of any size and is used primarily as a fuelling station.

THE LAND

Relief. The islands are mountainous and are volcanic in origin. Only three of them—Boa Vista, Maio, and Sal—have much level ground. Fogo (meaning "fire") has an active volcano, Pico do Cano. Its cone rises 9,281 feet (2,829 metres) above sea level. The peak of Tope da Coroa on Santo Antão is 6,493 feet. São Tiago and São Nicolau both have mountains more than 4,200 feet high. All the islands, especially the Windwards, have been eroded by sand carried by high winds, so that the outline of the landscape appears jagged. On most of the islands the cliffs rise sheer from the sea.

Climate. Moderate, stable temperatures and extreme aridity characterize the climate. February is the coolest month, with an average temperature of 71° F (22° C), and September is the warmest, having an average of 80° F (27° C). The islands have almost no rainfall, except for a period from August through October, when an average of 0.8 inch (20 millimetres) a month is recorded. The sun, though seldom obscured by rain clouds, is sometimes blocked by a dense mist of fine sand that is brought by trade winds from the Sahara.

Plant and animal life. The distribution of plant life in the archipelago is strongly affected by variations in the temperature and the rainfall. Springs in the hills, replenished during the rainy season, provide water for irrigation of farms in the valleys below. On the windward slopes of the hills, the lack of rain produces desert conditions, and the sparse shrubs, already overgrazed by goats, almost disappear. The shrubs remaining in these areas are mostly thorny or bitter; some are toxic. A sea mist on the higher hills permits some agriculture. Monte Verde, the green mountain of São Vicente, is so called because aloes grow high up, and crops can be raised on a few patches of land. Salt areas on Maio and Sal have interesting xerophilous plants.

The scarcity of water limits the number of land turtles in the archipelago, but two species of sea turtles lay their eggs on the sandy shores of the uninhabited islets. There are no venomous snakes, but there are many geckos, lizards, and several species of skinks. A species of giant skink is protected by law, but it may be extinct. There are 19 known species of butterflies, but none is endemic, and all the species are of African origin.

There are 105 known species of birds, of which only 38 breed regularly, including four species of petrels and two of shearwaters. Other bird species include the greater   **Birds** flamingo, as well as the frigate bird and the buzzard (both nearly exterminated), the Egyptian vulture, the Cape Verde Islands kite, the red-billed tropic bird, and many smaller birds. Several other birds are represented by local species, of which the kingfisher, known to early investigators (including Charles Darwin), is among the most conspicuous. The only truly endemic species, however, are the cane warbler and the Raso lark, which is restricted to Raso, one of the smallest uninhabited islets. The remainder of the birds are overseas migrants, one at least from America. Remarkably, gulls and terns do not breed on the islands.

Mammals of Cape Verde include the feral goats found on Fogo, the descendants of domestic goats that were brought to the islands. The Senegal green monkey, found on São Tiago, was introduced to the islands from Africa. The island's rodent population probably originated with rodents brought on early ships. A long-eared bat is the only indigenous mammal.

THE PEOPLE

Of the islands' population nearly three-quarters are Creoles (mulattoes) and the remainder are European and African. The population is descended, in part, from African slaves that were imported by the early Portuguese settlers to work their plantations. Others are descendants of slaves who were brought to the islands in order to be shipped across the Atlantic and were left in Cape Verde when the slave trade was abolished. Most of the principal ethnic types associated with the African continent—Arab, black, Hamitic—are in evidence among the population. European strains were introduced not only by the Portuguese but also by visiting sailors. Most of the Europeans on the islands—among whom the Portuguese predominate—live mainly in Praia on São Tiago, or in Mindelo on São Vicente. The islands farther away from these two ports are almost entirely populated by Creoles.

Apart from Portuguese, the inhabitants speak a Cape Verdean Creole dialect called Crioulo. Because rough seas separate the different islands, the dialect varies from one island to another. Most of the population is officially Roman Catholic, but a flourishing Protestant mission based in São Tiago has a church and schools on most of the islands. Many animist customs and a belief in voodoo still survive, however, in the more remote and pure African villages.

Emigration   Since the 1940s the population has been increasing, despite a steady emigration to Brazil, Africa, Portugal, and the United States. As a result of the Angolan war for independence (1961–75), many emigrants returned to the islands, and others went to join friends and relatives in Canada, the United States, Venezuela, and Brazil. Praia and Mindelo are the only large towns; more than one-third of the population resides in urban areas. The remainder lives in the few fertile valleys or in small fishing hamlets on the coast.

Nearly two-thirds of the people of Cape Verde are under 20 years of age. Many of the inhabitants above this age go overseas, where they seek work as labourers in the oil fields of Venezuela or as professionals in Portuguese-speaking Brazil. These emigrants send money home to their families, and some of them return to the islands upon retirement.

THE ECONOMY

An international airport on Sal gives work to many of that island's inhabitants. At Praia a government centre provides work, as does the bunkering trade in Mindelo.

Agriculture.   The vast majority of Cape Verde's work force has traditionally been employed as agricultural labourers. Bananas and coffee have been the chief agricultural exports. Crops grown for local consumption include corn (maize), sugarcane, castor beans, broad beans, potatoes, and peanuts (groundnuts). Severe drought has affected the islands, however, causing a high unemployment rate and a dramatic fall in crop output. The government undertook construction of several thousand small stone dams to catch and store occasional rainfall.

Salt is an important product on the islands of Sal, Maio, and Boa Vista. Pozzolana, a volcanic rock that is used in making cement, is exported. Fishing has increased and in 1981 a cold-storage plant was opened in Mindelo. There are few other exports, and the total is not sufficient to pay for necessary imports.

Transportation.   There is air service between Espargos, the international airport located on Sal, and Lisbon. Within the islands, schooners and small planes provide local service. Most of the islands have few roads.

ADMINISTRATIVE AND SOCIAL CONDITIONS

Government.   According to the 1980 constitution, the head of state, the president, is elected to a five-year term by universal adult suffrage. He is assisted by an appointed cabinet whose ministers are drawn from among nominees of the National Peoples Assembly. The Assembly has 56 deputies elected by universal adult suffrage to five-year terms. The Partido Africano da Independência de Cabo Verde (African Party for the Independence of Cape Verde) is the only legal political party, although there is an opposition movement based in Portugal formed by expatriate opponents of the government. In 1980 local assemblies headed by elected executive committees were formed. At the middle level there are island committees, also elected by universal adult suffrage.

Justice.   The Supreme Tribunal of Justice, located at Praia, is the highest court and oversees a network of popular tribunals at the local level.

Education.   According to official policy, education is compulsory at the primary level for children aged seven to 14 years, but in the early 1980s schools were available for only some four-fifths of the children. Secondary schooling is provided by three *liceus*, one vocational school, and one commercial school. There are three teacher-training schools as well. Cape Verdeans obtain higher education abroad because the islands have no university. In the late 1970s only some 30 percent of the islanders were literate, but the government launched a major effort to build schools and train teachers to combat this problem.

CULTURAL LIFE

Portuguese customs and culture have heavily influenced the islands, but they are blended with African traditions as well. An example is the *morna*, a local version of the Portuguese *fada*, a melancholy song and dance. The government publishes weekly news and information publications. Two radio stations broadcast in Portuguese and Crioulo. For statistical data, see the "Britannica World Data" section in the current *Britannica Book of the Year*.

History

The date of the islands' discovery is disputed; the Venetian captain Alvise Ca' da Mosto (Cadamosto) claimed to have visited them in 1456, but his account is not universally accepted. In 1460 the Portuguese navigators Diogo Gomes and António de Noli sighted Maio and São Tiago. In 1462 the first settlers from Portugal landed on São Tiago, subsequently founding there the oldest European city in the tropics—Ribeira Grande. With the development of transatlantic slave trade, the importance and the wealth of the islands increased. In 1532 the first bishop was consecrated, and in 1595 the first governor general was appointed. The prosperity of Ribeira Grande, however, attracted pirates, who attacked the city in 1541. The English later attacked it twice—in 1585 and 1592—the first time under the command of Sir Francis Drake. After a French attack in 1712, the city was abandoned. To protect the islands against future assaults, the fortress of São Filipe was built.

The founding of Ribeira Grande

With the decline of the slave trade (which was finally abolished in 1876), and with increasing drought, the prosperity of the islands slowly vanished. In the early 1800s they experienced recurrent drought and famine as well as government corruption and maladministration. Conditions improved toward the end of the 1800s, however, as the development of internal trade and communications led to the establishment at Mindelo of a coaling station and a submarine cable station. After World War I prosperity again declined as fewer ships visited Mindelo. Only after World War II did trade again increase and relative prosperity return.

The Portuguese administration of Cape Verde was unified under a governor in 1587. The islands' status was changed in 1951 from that of a colony to an overseas province. In 1961 all citizens were given full Portuguese citizenship.

On July 5, 1975, Cape Verde Islands became an independent republic. The first president of the newly independent nation, Aristide Pereira, had been secretary general of the African Party for the Independence of Guinea and Cape Verde (PAIGC) since 1973. The island republic is a member of the Organization of African Unity and of the United Nations. (W.M.B.)

Disapproval of the coup in Guinea-Bissau in 1980 prompted the dissolution of the Cape Verde branch of PAIGC and resulted in the formation in 1981 of the African Party for the Independence of Cape Verde (PAICV). President Pereira was reelected in February of the same year. Relations between Guinea-Bissau and Cape Verde gradually improved. For current political history, see the annual issues of the *Britannica Book of the Year.*

(Ed.)

CHAD

The Republic of Chad (République du Tchad) is an independent landlocked state in north central Africa. It has an area of 495,755 square miles (1,284,000 square kilometres). It is bounded on the north by Libya, on the east by The Sudan, on the south by the Central African Republic, and on the west by Cameroon, Nigeria, and Niger. Chad obtained independence from France on August 11, 1960. The capital, N'Djamena (formerly Fort-Lamy), is almost 1,000 miles (1,600 kilometres) from the western African coastal ports.

Physical and human geography

Although it is the fifth largest country on the continent, Chad—much of the northern part of which lies in the Sahara—has a population density of only about eight persons per square mile (three persons per square kilometre). Most of the population lives by agriculture; cotton is grown in the south, and cattle are raised in the central region.

Because of the distance from the sea and the relative lack of transportation, the economy is underdeveloped, and French aid remains important.

THE LAND

The frontiers of Chad, which constitute a heritage from the colonial era, do not coincide with either natural or ethnic boundaries.

Relief. In its physical structure Chad consists of a large basin, bounded on the north, east, and south by mountains. Lake Chad, which represents all that remains of a large sea that covered much of the region in earlier geologic periods, is situated in the centre of the western frontier; it is 922 feet (281 metres) above sea level. The Chad Basin is lined with clay and sand sediments, most of which date from the most recent Quaternary period. These sediments were deposited by Lake Chad in the course of its regressions. The lowest altitude of the basin is the Djourab Depression, which is 573 feet above sea level.

The mountains of Chad

The mountains that rim the basin include the volcanic Tibesti Massif to the north (of which the highest point is Emi Koussi, with an altitude of 11,204 feet [3,415 metres]), the sandstone peaks of the Ennedi Plateau to the northeast, the crystalline rock mountains of Ouaddaï (Wadai) to the east, and the Oubangui Plateau to the south. The semicircle is completed to the southwest by the mountains of Adamawa and Mandara, which lie mostly beyond the frontier in Cameroon and Nigeria.

Chad's river network is virtually limited to the Chari and Logone rivers and their tributaries, which flow from the southeast to feed Lake Chad. The Chari, which is formed by the Gribingui, Bamingui, and Bahr Sara, is later joined from the east by the Bahr Salamat. After entering an ill-defined area of swampland between Niellim and Dourbali, it flows through a large delta into Lake Chad. The Chari is about 750 miles (1,200 kilometres) in length and has a flow that varies between 600 and 12,000 cubic feet per second (17,000 to 340,000 litres), according to the season. The Logone, which for some of its course runs along the Cameroon frontier, is formed by the junction of the Pendé and Mbéré rivers; its flow varies between 170 and 3,000 cubic feet per second, and its course is more than 600 miles long before it joins the Chari at N'Djamena. The level of Lake Chad fluctuates according to the flow of these rivers, as well as according to the degree of precipitation, evaporation, and seepage. The droughts of the 1970s and early 1980s in the Sahel region of western Africa reduced the lake to record low levels. The remaining Chad waterways are either seasonal or are of insignificant size.

Soils. Several types of soil formation occur in Chad, apart from the sand of the desert zone and the sheer rock of the mountainous areas. In the seasonally flooded western regions, such as the Chari, Logone, Salamat, and Guera areas, hydromorphic (waterlogged) soils occur. Tropical iron-bearing soils, red in colour, are found on the exposed folds and mounds of the Ouaddaï mountain slopes; the Koro zone, however, has soils with a low iron content. In the Kanem region (area north of Lake Chad) subarid soils are characteristic, except in the depressions that occur between the dunes on the shores of Lake Chad, where exceptionally rich hydromorphic soils are found.

Climate. Chad's wide range in latitudes (that extend southward from the Tropic of Cancer for more than 15 degrees) is matched by a climatic range that varies from wet and dry tropical to the hot arid. At the towns of Moundou and Fort-Archambault, in the wet and dry tropical zone, between 32 and 48 inches (800 and 1,200 millimetres) of rain falls annually between May and October. In the central semi-arid tropical (Sahel) zone, where N'Djamena is situated, between 12 and 32 inches (300 and 800 millimetres) of rain falls between June and September. In the north rains are infrequent, with an annual average of less than one inch (25 millimetres) being recorded at Faya-Largeau. Chad thus has one relatively short rainy season. The dry season, which lasts from December to February, is cool, after which it becomes very hot until the first rains fall.

Plant and animal life. Three vegetational zones, correlated with the rainfall, may be distinguished. These are a wet and dry tropical zone in the south, characterized by shrubs, tall grasses, and scattered broad-leaved deciduous trees; a semi-arid tropical (Sahel) zone, in which savanna (grassy parkland) vegetation gradually merges into a region of thorn bushes and open steppe country; and a hot arid zone, composed of dunes and plateaus in which vegetation is scarce and occasional palm oases are to be found.

Three vegetation zones

The tall grasses and the extensive marshes of the savanna zone have an abundant wildlife. Here large mammals, such as the elephant, hippopotamus, rhinoceros, warthog, giraffe, antelope, lion, leopard, and cheetah, coexist with a wide assortment of birds and reptiles. The rivers and the lake are among the richest in fish of all African waters. The humid regions also contain swarms of insects, some of which are dangerous.

Settlement patterns. Conditioned by soil and climate, land is put to different uses in each of the three vegetational zones. In the wet and dry tropical zone, farmers cultivate rice and millet in the clay soils, and peanuts (groundnuts) and sorghum in the sandier areas. Manioc, recently introduced, is also cultivated. Between the latitudes of 11° and 15° N, the retreat of the rivers in the dry season leaves behind flooded depressions called *yaere,* allowing a second crop of "dry season" millet, or *berbere,* to be cultivated. Since 1928 the cultivation of cotton in the area between the Logone and Chari rivers has been encouraged, first by the colonial administration, and since 1960 by the national government. Cotton cultivation, while tending to upset the ecological balance by

ALG.

Tropic of Cancer

EGYPT

LIBYA

Pic Touside
3315 △T

•Aozou
•Gézenti
•Ouri
•Bardaï
Yebbi
Bou

T I B E S T I

•Zouar

S A H A R A

▲ Emi Koussi
3415
•Gouro

•Ounianga Kébir

BORKOU-ENNEDI-TIBESTI
B O R K O U

•Madadi

DÉPRESSION DE MOURDI

NIGER

GRAND ERG DE BILMA

BODELE

Djourab
△ 175

•Koro Toro

E N N E D I

•Fada

•Largeau

•Oum Chalouba

C H A D

KANEM

•Zigey

•Nokou

•Mao

Bahr el-Ghazal

•Iriba
•Arada

BILTINE

•Biltine
•Guéréda

S   U   D   A   N

Lake Chad

LAC.
•Bol
(281)

•Ngouri

B A T H A

•Djédaa
Oum
Hadjer•
•Ati

•Abéché

•Adré

THE SUDAN

Maiduguri □

•Massakory

•Massaguet

N'Djamena

Yao•

Lac
Fitri

•Bokoro

•Moussoro

•Mangalmé

OUADDAÏ
Am Dam•

•Mongo

•Goz Beïda

•Nyala

NIGERIA

•Dourbali

Maïlao•
•Massenya

CHARI-
BAGUIRMI

G U É R A

•Abou Deïa

•Melfi

•Djébren

•Mongororo

•Bongor

Bousso•

Am Timan•

SALAMAT

Bahr Salamat

Benue

Léré•
Fianga•
•Pala

TANDJILÉ
•Gounou
Gaya
•Kélo
Laï•

Dik• Niellim•

•Kyabé

Haraze-
•Mangueigne

MAYO-
KEBBI

Benoye•
LOGONE OCC.
Moundou•

•Doba

•Koumra

•Goundi

MOYEN-CHARI

•Sarh

Bahr Aouk

CAMEROON

Beinamar•
LOGONE
ORIENTAL

•Gore

•Baïbokoum

•Moïssala

CENTRAL

AFRICAN   REPUBLIC

© Rand McNally & Co.
A-580900-257   -1 -2 -2

0   100   200 km

0   100   200 mi

Elevations in metres

CHAD

exhausting the soil, has nevertheless resulted in the introduction of a cash economy in place of a barter economy. The cultivation of rice, begun in 1958 in irrigated plots in the Bongor region, south of N'Djamena, has proved successful. A joint venture with France introduced sugarcane cultivation in the 1970s. Improved strains of both cotton and rice have produced higher yields, but increased production has been handicapped by the retention of some traditional agricultural techniques.

The intermediate semi-arid tropical zone is inhabited by both sedentary cultivators and nomadic pastoralists. The northern limit of the bloodsucking tsetse fly, deadly to cattle and the carrier of sleeping sickness to man, is latitude 10° N; beyond this limit extensive stock farming begins, occasionally in association with agriculture, as for example in the Kanem region. The inhabitants raise millet and grow peanuts wherever the mean annual rainfall exceeds 15 inches (375 millimetres). Cotton is grown where and when rainfall exceeds 30 inches. Large herds of cattle migrate over the semi-arid tropical zone in search of pasture and water. In the rich soil bordering Lake Chad, the presence of subterranean water allows three harvests of wheat and corn (maize) to be grown each year in irrigated plots called polders. Elsewhere, the semi-nomadic inhabitants are almost completely dependent upon rainfall. Drought has had serious repercussions, affecting both the livestock and the pastoralists, whose diet consists principally of milk products.

In the hot arid zone, more than 50,000 nomads live among their herds of camels, frequenting palm groves growing in such oases as that at Faya-Largeau. Productive economic activity usually takes place only during the rainy season. Rural life is based on a precarious balance between man and environment and has not been significantly affected by outside influences.

Urban life in Chad is virtually restricted to the capital, N'Djamena. Founded in the early years of the 20th century, the city has undergone a dramatic growth in population. This growth is not due to a high degree of industrialization but to the other attractions of urban life. The majority of the population is engaged in commerce. Other major towns, such as Sarh (formerly Fort-Archambault), Moundou, and Abéché, are less urbanized than the capital.

Urban life

THE PEOPLE

The population of Chad presents a tapestry composed of different languages, peoples, and religions that is remarkable even amidst the variety of Africa. The degree of variety encountered in Chad underscores the significance of the region as a crossroads of linguistic, social, and cultural interchange.

Linguistic groups. More than 100 different languages and dialects are spoken in the country. Although many of these languages are imperfectly recorded, the languages may be divided into the following 12 groupings: (1) The Sara-Bongo-Bagirmi group, representing languages spoken by about 500,000 people in southern and central Chad. (2) The Mundang-Tuburi-Mbum languages, which are spoken by several hundred thousand people in the Mayo-Kebbi *préfecture* of southwestern Chad. (3) The Chado-Hamitic group, which is related to the Hausa spoken in Nigeria. (4) The Kanembu-Zaghawa languages, spoken in the north, mostly by nomads. (5) The Maba group, spoken in the vicinity of Abéché, and throughout the Ouaddaï and Biltine *préfectures* of eastern Chad. (6) The Tama languages, spoken in the Abéché, Adré, Goz Béïda, and Am Dam regions. (7) Daju, spoken in the area of Goz Béïda and Am Dam. (8) Some languages of the Central African groups, particularly Sango (which is also the lingua franca of the Central African Republic), are spoken in the south. (9) The Bua group, spoken in southern and central Chad. (10) The Somrai group, spoken in west and central Chad. (11) Mimi and (12) Fur are both spoken in the extreme east.

In addition to this rich assortment, Arabic is also spoken in various forms. The dialects spoken by the nomadic Arabs differ from the tongue spoken by settled Arabs. A simplified Arabic is spoken in towns and markets; its diffusion is linked to that of Islām.

French is the official language of the administration and is used in communications and in instruction, although the national radio network also broadcasts in Arabic, Sara Madjingay, Tuburi, and Mundang. While a regional form of French, showing local linguistic and environmental peculiarities, is spoken widely in the towns, its penetration into the countryside is uneven. Its use is closely linked to the development of education.

Ethnic groups. As might be expected, the linguistic variety reflects an ethnic composition of great complexity. A general classification may nevertheless be made, again in terms of the three regions of Chad.

In the wet and dry tropical zone, the Sara group forms a significant element of the population in the central parts of the Chari and Logone river basins. The Laka and Mbum peoples live to the west of the Sara groups and, like the Gula and Tumak of the Goundi area, are culturally distinct from their Sara neighbours. Along the banks of the Chari and Logone rivers, and in the region between the two rivers, are found the Tangale peoples.

Among the inhabitants of the semi-arid tropical zone are the Barma of Bagirmi, the founders of the kingdom of the same name; they are surrounded by groups of Kanuri, Fulani, Hausa, and Arabs, many of whom have come from outside Chad itself. Along the lower courses of the Logone and Chari rivers are the Kotoko, who are supposedly descended from the ancient Sao population that formerly lived in the region. The Buduma and Kuri inhabit the Lake Chad region and, in the Kanem area, are associated with the Kanembu and Tunjur, who are of Arabic origin. All of these groups are sedentary, and they coexist with Daza, Kreda, and Arab nomads. The Hadjeray (of Guera-Massif) and Abou Telfân are composed of refugee populations who, living on their mountainous terrain, have resisted various invasions. On the plains surrounding the Hadjeray are the Bulala, Kuka, and the Midogo, who are sedentary peoples. In the eastern region of Ouaddaï live the Maba, among whom the Kado once formed an aristocracy. They constitute a nucleus surrounded by a host of other groups who, while possessing their own languages, nevertheless constitute a distinct cultural unit. The Tama to the north and the Daju to the south have formed their own separate sultanates. Throughout the Ouaddaï region are found groups of nomadic Arabs, who are also found in the Chari-Baguirmi, Salamat, and Guera *préfectures* of central Chad. Despite their widespread diffusion, these Arabs represent a single ethnic group composed of a multitude of tribes. In Kanem other Arabs, mostly of Libyan origin, are also found.

In the northern Chad regions of Tibesti, Borkou, and Ennedi the population is composed of black nomads. Their dialects are related to those of the Kanembu and Kanuri.

Religious groups. The great majority of Muslims are found in the north and east of Chad. Islāmization in Kanem came very early and was followed by the conversion to Islām of the major political entities of the region, such as the sultanates of Wadai, Bagirmi, and Fitri, and—more recently—the Saharan region. Islām is well established in most major towns and wherever Arab populations are found. It has attracted a wide variety of ethnic groups and has forged a certain unity which, however, has not resulted in the complete elimination of various local practices and customs.

Animism flourishes in the southern and most populous part of the country and in the mountainous regions of Guera. The various traditional religions provide a strong basis for cohesion in the villages where they are practiced. Despite a diversity of beliefs, a widespread common feature of traditional religion is the socioreligious initiation of young people into adult society.

In Chad, as elsewhere, Christian missionary work has not affected the Muslim population; it has been directed toward the animist populations in the cities in the western regions south of the Chari River, and in the Guera *préfecture*. There are four Roman Catholic dioceses, with an archbishop at N'Djamena. There are some Protestant mission groups, and an effort has been made to form a Chad Evangelical Church.

Peoples of the semi-arid tropical zone

THE ECONOMY

Agriculture and fishing. Cotton is Chad's primary product. Although it is basically an export crop, the processing of raw cotton provides employment for a majority of those in industry and accounts for most of Chad's export earnings. Most of the cotton fibre ginned in Chad's processing plants is exported to Europe.

Importance of livestock Chad's livestock population constitutes its second most important economic resource and is primarily distributed in the Kanem, Batha, and Ouaddaï *préfectures* of central Chad. Much of this wealth of livestock is not reflected in the national cash economy, however, and livestock products form less than one-tenth of exports. There is a refrigerated meat-processing plant at Sarh, which exports meat to the Congo region and Gabon. The government has tried to improve livestock by introducing stronger breeds and production by building new slaughterhouses.

Rice is produced in the Mayo-Kebbi *préfecture* of southwestern Chad, and wheat is grown along the shores of Lake Chad; little of either crop is processed commercially.

About half the fish caught is salted and dried for export. Most fish are caught in the Lake Chad, Chari, and Logone basins.

Resources. Chad's principal mineral resource is natron (a complex sodium carbonate) that is mined in the Lake Chad and Borkou areas and is used as salt and in the preparation of soap and medicines. Annual production is estimated at 4,000 tons, part of which is marketed in Nigeria. There are indications of deposits of gold in the Ouaddaï area, uranium in the Ennedi area, uranium and wolframite in the Aouzou Strip, and bauxite near Laï. Oil has been found in the Kanem region.

Industry. The development of industry is hampered by a shortage of power. Energy is generated by using oil products that have to be imported from Nigeria.

The primary industries, such as cotton ginning, slaughtering, and the milling of wheat and rice, are all associated with agriculture. Secondary industries are few and rely on imported materials.

Transportation. Chad's economic development is primarily contingent upon the establishment of an effective transportation network. There are three access routes to the sea, by road, river, or rail, through neighbouring countries. Of 7,500 miles of roads and 12,500 miles of trails, most are impractical for travel during part of the rainy season. Year-round traffic is possible on 1,100 miles of gravel-surfaced roads, and on a 155-mile paved section between N'Djamena and Guélendeng. Three major road axes, forming a triangle joining N'Djamena, Sarh, and Abéché, have been completed.

Rivers are of secondary importance, due to great seasonal fluctuations in water levels, with only about half of total river length navigable year-round. The Chari is navigable between Sarh and N'Djamena between August and December, and the Logone is navigable between Mondou and N'Djamena in September and October. Two railways have their terminals near the Chad border. Across the Nigerian frontier to the west there is a railhead at Maiduguri, which links up with the Nigerian ports of Lagos and Port Harcourt. Across the Sudanese frontier to the east is the railhead at Nyala, which leads eventually to Port Sudan on the Red Sea. Air traffic plays an important role in the Chad economy, in view of the paucity of alternative means. N'Djamena's airport can accommodate large jets, while more than 40 secondary airports exist.

ADMINISTRATIVE AND SOCIAL CONDITIONS

The constitution of 1975 was replaced by the *charte fondamentale* in 1978, and this in turn was abolished in 1979. The government consists of a Council of Ministers subordinate to the president. Executive and legislative decisions are made by the council and the president.

Civil war broke out in the mid-1960s when two guerrilla groups began a stuggle to overthrow the government and create closer ties with Arab North Africa. (See below *History*.)

Health and welfare. There are major hospitals at N'Djamena, Sarh, Moundou, Bongor, and Abéché. Other health facilities include dispensaries and infirmaries, dispersed throughout the country. The government, in cooperation with the World Health Organization, has developed a health education and training program. Campaigns have been conducted against malaria, sleeping sickness, leprosy, and other diseases.

Education. The size of the country, the dispersion of populations, and the occasional reluctance to send children to school all constitute educational problems that the government is endeavouring to overcome. About one-half of the school age population is enrolled. Missions and public education services are responsible for primary education. Secondary and technical education is available in nearly 40 institutions. The University of Chad, founded in 1971, offers higher education, and some Chad students study abroad.

CULTURAL LIFE

With its rich variety of peoples and languages, Chad possesses a valuable cultural heritage. The government encourages cultural activities and institutions. There is a national museum, with a rich collection of prehistoric and traditional artifacts. The Chad Cultural Centre seeks to awaken a conscious interest in national traditions among the population. For statistical data, see the "Britannica World Data" section in the current *Britannica Book of the Year*. (Ed.)

History

The region of the eastern Sahara and Sudan from Fezzan, Bilma, and Chad in the west to the Nile Valley in the east was well peopled in Neolithic times, as discovered sites attest. Probably typical of the earliest populations were the Negroid cave dwellers described by Herodotus as inhabiting the country south of Fezzan. The ethnographic history of the region is that of gradual modification of this basic stock by the continual infiltration of nomadic and increasingly Arabicized white African elements, entering from the north via Fezzan and Tibesti and, especially after the 14th century, from the Nile Valley via Darfur. According to legend, the country around Lake Chad was originally occupied by the Negroid Sao. This vanished people is probably represented today by the Kotoko, in whose country, along the banks of the Logone and Chari, was unearthed in the 1950s a medieval culture notable for work in terra-cotta and bronze.

The relatively large and politically sophisticated kingdoms of the central Sudan were the creation of Saharan Berbers, drawn southward by their continuous search for pasturage and easily able to impose their hegemony on the fragmentary indigenous societies of Negroid agriculturalists. This process was intensified by the expansion of Islām. There are indications of a large immigration of pagan Berbers into the central Sudan early in the 8th century.

16TH TO 19TH CENTURY

The Kanem–Bornu state The most important of these states, Kanem–Bornu, which was at the height of its power in the later 16th century, owed its preeminence to its command of the southern terminus of the trans-Saharan trade route to Tripoli.

Products of the Islāmized Sudanic culture diffused from Kanem were the kingdoms of Bagirmi and Ouaddaï, which emerged in the early years of the 17th century out of the process of conversion to Islām. In the 18th century the Arab dynasty of Ouaddaï was able to throw off the suzerainty of Darfur and extend its territories by the conquest of eastern Kanem. Slave raiding at the expense of animist populations to the south constituted an important element in the prosperity of all these Muslim states. In the 19th century, however, they were in full decline, torn by wars and internecine feuds. In the years 1883–93 they all fell to the Sudanese adventurer Rabah Zubayr.

THE 20TH CENTURY

By this time the partition of Africa among the European powers was entering its final phase. Rabah was overthrown in 1900, and the traditional Kanembu dynasty was reestablished under French protection. Chad became part of the federation of French Equatorial Africa in 1910. The pacification of the whole area of the present republic was barely completed by 1914, and between the wars paternalistic French rule was unprogressive. A tentative pact between Italy and France that would have ceded the Aouzou Strip to Italian-ruled Libya was never ratified by the French National Assembly, but it provided a pretext for Libya to seize the territory in 1973. During World War II Chad gave unhesitating support to the Free French cause. After 1945 the territory shared in the constitutional advance of French Equatorial Africa. In 1946 it became an overseas territory of the French Republic.

Independence. A large measure of internal autonomy was conceded under the constitutional law of 1957, when the first territorial government was formed by Gabriel Lisette, a West Indian formerly in the administrative service who had become the leader of the Parti Progressiste Tchadien (PTT). An autonomous republic within the French Community was proclaimed in November 1958, and complete independence in the restructured community was attained on August 11, 1960. The country was one of the poorest in tropical Africa and remained desperately backward. Its stability was gravely endangered by tensions between the black and often Christian populations of the more economically progressive southwest and the conservative, Muslim, non-black leadership of the old feudal states of the north, and its problems were further complicated by Libyan involvement.

Lisette was shouldered aside by an associate more acceptable to some of the opposition, François Tombalbaye, a southern trade-union leader, who became the first president of the republic. In March 1961 Tombalbaye was able to achieve a fusion of the PPT with the principal opposition party, the Parti National Africain (PNA), to form a new Union pour le Progrès du Tchad. An alleged conspiracy by Muslim elements, however, led in 1963 to the dissolution of the National Assembly, a brief state of emergency, and the arrest of the leading ministers formerly associated with the PNA. Only government candidates presented themselves at the new elections in December 1963, and they received 99 percent of the votes, ushering in the one-party state.

Civil war. In the mid-1960s two guerrilla movements emerged. The Front de la Liberation Nationale du Tchad (Frolinat) was established in 1966 and operated primarily in the north from its headquarters at the southern Libyan oasis of al-Kufrah, while the smaller Front National Tchadien (FNT) operated in the east-central region. Both groups aimed at the overthrow of the existing government, the reduction of French influence in Chad, and closer association with the Arab states of North Africa. Heavy fighting occurred in 1969 and 1970, and French military forces were brought in to suppress the revolts.

By the end of the 1970s civil war had become not so much a conflict between Chad's Muslim northern region and the black southern region as a struggle between northern political factions. Libyan troops were brought in at President Goukouni Oueddei's request in December 1980 and were withdrawn, again at his request, in November 1981. In a reverse movement the Armed Forces of the North of Hissen Habré, which had retreated into Sudan in December 1980, reoccupied all the important towns in eastern Chad in November 1981. Peacekeeping forces of the Organization of African Unity (OAU) withdrew in 1982 and Habré formed a new government in October of the same year. Simultaneously, an opposition government under the leadership of Oueddei was established, with Libyan support, at Bardaï in the north. For current political history, see the annual issues of the *Britannica Book of the Year.*   (D.H.J./Ed.)

EQUATORIAL GUINEA

The Republic of Equatorial Guinea (República de Guinea Ecuatorial), on the west coast of Africa, is the only independent Spanish-speaking state on the African continent. Formerly Spanish Guinea, a colony of Spain, it consists of the continental region (formerly Río Muni; also called Mbini); and five islands: Bioko (formerly Fernando Po), Corisco, Great Elobey (Elobey Grande), Little Elobey (Elobey Chico), and Annobón (Pagalu). This fragmented republic has a total area of 10,831 square miles (28,051 square kilometres).

Physical and human geography

THE LAND

Continental Equatorial Guinea, with an area of 10,038 square miles is a roughly rectangular territory bounded by Cameroon to the north and Gabon to the east and south.

EQUATORIAL GUINEA

Of the estuary islands, Corisco measures six square miles, Elobey Grande is less than a square mile, and Elobey Chico is less than a tenth of a square mile. Bioko, off the coast of Cameroon, has an area of 779 square miles. Annobón, a volcanic island, has an area less than seven square miles and lies south of the Equator almost 400 miles (640 kilometres) to the southwest of Bioko.

By any standard Equatorial Guinea forms a small political unit, and it is beset by a welter of problems, including regional differences, geographic isolation, a fragile economy, a lack of trained personnel, and the incubus of a heavy psychological legacy from the colonial era, which ended when the country obtained its independence on October 12, 1968. The capital of the republic is Malabo (formerly Santa Isabel), on Bioko. Bata is the administrative capital of the continental mainland.

Relief, drainage, and soils. *The continental region.* Half of the continental enclave is covered with forests. A coastal plain about 12 miles wide abuts on the coastal hills, which lead to inland plateaus (called *mesetas* in Spanish) that rise toward the frontier with Gabon. There are several ranges of hills. The central range divides the Río Benito Basin to the north from the southern basin of the Río Utamboni. The Niefang-Mikomeseng range north of the Río Benito is somewhat lower. All these ranges form segments of the Monts de Cristal in Gabon. The province is divided by the Río Benito (known as the Woleu River in Gabon), which runs generally from east to west and is nonnavigable except for the first 12 miles inland. To the north the Río Campo (called the Ntem in French-speaking Africa) marks part of the frontier with Cameroon. In the south, Río Muni is not a river but the estuary of various rivers of Gabon and southern Equatorial Guinea, among which the Kongwe is the largest. To the east the border with Gabon follows the meandering course of the Río Kié (Kyé) rather than the legal frontier, which runs along a line 11° 20′ east of the Greenwich meridian. Except for some limited use of waterpower on lumbering sites, the rivers of the mainland enclave are not exploited. The coast consists of a long stretch of beach with low cliffs toward Kogo to the south. There is no natural harbour, and Bata, Mbini, and

Independence

Kogo are no more than rudimentary ports of call for the ships that infrequently visit the coast.

The coastal plain is overlaid by sedimentary deposits. The hinterland is composed primarily of ancient metamorphic rocks that have undergone a lengthy process of leaching and erosion, so that the resulting soils are mediocre. Exploration for petroleum in the waters off the mainland has been unsuccessful, but in late 1981 a test well off the north coast of Bioko struck oil. Gold, titanium, coal, and iron ores are thought to exist inland.

Bioko. The main island, Bioko itself, is roughly 45 miles long and 22 miles wide. Its volcanic cones, crater lakes, and rich lava soils form a contrast with the landscape of the mainland. In the north the Pico de Santa Isabel soars to a height of 9,869 feet (3,008 metres); this extinct volcano is now the site of a television transmitter. In the centre of the island, Moca Peak and the Moca Heights present an alpine type of landscape. The southern part of the island, remote and scarcely developed, consists of the Gran Caldera range, which is rugged and indented by torrents. There are five crater lakes, Moca, Loreto, Claret, Lombé, and Eri.

Agricultural productivity

Despite its tortuous relief, Bioko is highly productive agriculturally. Torrents are exploited for hydroelectric power; the Río Musola provides electricity for the township of Malabo. The coast is largely inhospitable, consisting for the most part of a cliff about 60 feet high, broken occasionally by small inlets and beaches. The southern coast is very steep and dangerous to shipping; San Antonio de Ureca, located along this stretch, is the most isolated settlement on the island. Malabo has a relatively good harbour, built on the partially sunken rim of a volcano.

Annobón is an isolated fragment of the republic, about 93 miles (150 kilometres) southwest of the island of São Tomé in São Tomé e Príncipe and about 400 miles southwest of Bioko. Like the latter, it is a volcanic island but is less high; it consists of a conglomeration of cones of which Monte de Santa Mina (about 2,460 feet) is the highest. Not quite four miles long by two miles wide, it is a rugged little island; the only settlement of note is centred on the Catholic mission. The inhabitants are mostly fishermen who speak a Portuguese patois.

Climate. The climate of the continental region is equatorial, with local variations due to differences in altitude and proximity to the sea. The wet seasons are from February to June and from September to December. Rainfall is higher on the coast than inland. In Bata the rainiest months are September, October, and November, with rainfall averaging more than 94 inches (2,388 millimetres) a year. At Calatrava, farther south on the coast, it sometimes reaches 180 inches. Inland, however, rainfall diminishes; Mikomeseng, for example, receives only about 58 inches. The average yearly temperature is about 79° F (26° C), the maxima being somewhat lower than in Bioko. The relative humidity, however, is higher than in Bioko, with an average of 86 percent, occasionally rising to 94 percent.

Bioko has an extremely debilitating climate. The so-called dry season lasts from November to March, and the rest of the year is rainy. The average annual temperature is 77° F (25° C) with a maximum of 93° F (34° C) and a minimum of 63° F (17° C). Most of the time the sky is cloudy and overcast. Extreme rainfall occurs in the south, with rain brought by monsoon winds amounting to about 450 inches a year around San Antonio de Ureca.

Plant and animal life. Continental Equatorial Guinea is covered by a dense jungle that is exploited by the lumbering industry. More than 140 species of wood are found, of which the most important commercially are okume (*Aucoumea klaineana*), African walnut, and various mahoganies. Intensive exploitation close to the coast led the Spanish timber companies to venture deeper into the interior. Reforestation is minimal, and a secondary forest growth has replaced the original rain forest. African farmers clear land by burning off the vegetation cover, after which they grow manioc, beans, yams, roots, and even cash crops such as coffee and cocoa, to the extent that the heavily leached soils allow. Mangroves fringe long stretches of the coast as well as riverbanks.

Bioko has a greater variety of tropical vegetation, including mangroves, and—at higher altitudes—vegetable gardens and pastureland.

The continental region has a rich animal life that includes gorillas, various rare species of monkeys, leopards, buffalo, antelopes, elephants, hippopotamuses, crocodiles, and various species of snakes, including pythons. Insects, including the tsetse fly and the malaria-bearing *Anopheles* mosquito, as well as hosts of ants, beetles, spiders, and termites, abound. Bioko has no big game but has various monkeys, dwarf antelopes, and rodents, as well as the ever-present mosquito and other insects.

Varied animal life

Settlement patterns. The mainland is sparsely settled by coffee and cocoa farmers who practice traditional methods of agriculture. During the colonial period, Roman Catholic missions did much to encourage the population to construct "corridor" villages by the sides of roads; in most villages the church and the school figure prominently. Spanish plans for building model villages lapsed after independence. The region was never a settler colony, and the few European plantations—mostly Spanish or German—that survived the colonial era have been abandoned. After independence an exodus of Spanish technicians occurred, so that the mainland has largely reverted to a subsistence economy. The modern sector of the economy is represented by lumbering, coffee growing, and oil palm production.

Bioko, by contrast, is a plantation island; it retained for several years a larger number of plantation owners and managers and consequently withstood longer than the continental region the effect of independence upon its economy. Before independence there were about 1,900 plantations (known as *fincas*), which ranged in size from 0.4 acres (one hectare) to more than 4,900 acres. The Bubi people, the indigenous population, live for the most part in mission villages in the northern part of the island on the lower slopes of the Pico de Santa Isabel, as well as in their traditional homeland, the Moca Heights. Unused to plantation labour, they gain their living mostly as small farmers and minor civil servants. The workers on the *fincas* were for many years migrant labourers from Nigeria, who served under contract. During the 1960s the Nigerian workers often brought their families, settling in numbers believed to have reached 50,000 to 80,000 by the end of the decade. Political and economic conditions after independence gradually reduced these numbers, despite an agreement with Nigeria in 1972 for the recruitment of new labourers. Reports of virtual slave-labour conditions on plantations and of repressive killings by authorities in the mid-1970s turned this gradual exodus into a flood, with the anticipated effect of further impoverishing Equatorial Guinea's economy.

Nigerian migrant labour

Many of the formerly European-owned plantations were extensive; in 1962 more than 300 plantations occupied over 148,000 acres, leaving about 2,800 acres in the possession of 1,600 African farmers grouped in cooperatives. Some of the larger plantations, employing hundreds of Nigerian labourers and occupying the most fertile land, were local economic powers whose political influence, if subdued, was nevertheless felt by the local Bubi population.

Malabo, the national capital, is a small city standing behind its crater harbour. Created by the British in the 19th century, it was remodelled and developed by the Spanish. A rambling tropical city, it has a distinctly Spanish atmosphere—especially in the European district near the cathedral, the mission, and government house. Farther inland, the African districts have been inhabited mostly by Nigerian and other workers who chose not to return to the mainland. Another town of some importance is Luba, on the southwest coast, linked with the capital by a good paved road that runs through a series of Bubi settlements. Basilé, on the slopes of Pico de Santa Isabel, provides a cool refuge for heat-weary residents of the capital.

The continental region was settled much later by the Spanish, so that the township of Bata lacks the amenities of Malabo. Fang migrants from the interior have built new suburbs around the sprawling port city.

THE PEOPLE

The majority of the population is African, but its composition is complex for a political unit so small in size.

The continental region. The Fang people, who fought

their way to the sea in the 19th and early 20th centuries by subjugating the weaker tribes in their path, form about 80 or 90 percent of the population of the mainland region. North of the Mbini River are the Ntumu Fang, and to the south of it are the Okak Fang. Holding political power on the mainland, the Fang tend to migrate to Bioko, where their leaders hold most of the levers of political control. Coastal tribes, such as the Kombe, Mabea, Lengi, Benga, and others, have been in contact with European traders much longer, and a limited amount of miscegenation has taken place, especially on the island of Corisco. Spanish ethnographers refer to these coastal tribes as *playeros* (literally, "those who live on the beach"). Both the Fang majority and the *playero* minority are Bantu. Some Pygmies are reported to inhabit the vicinity of the Río Campo. In addition to these peoples, there are substantial colonies of Africans from other countries, including Hausa traders in Bata and Ibo, Ibibio, and Efik contract workers from Nigeria in the lumber camps. There is also a small number of Africans from Cameroon and Gabon, as well as a few Indian shopkeepers in Bata.

The Bubi

Bioko. The original inhabitants are the Bubi, descendants of Bantu migrants from the mainland. Contacts with Europeans decimated them, and only a few thousand remained early in the 20th century. They became the most pro-Spanish element of the African population, viewing the end of Spanish rule as a signal for the invasion of their island by the Fang. Certainly, numbers of mainlanders, most of them Fang, have flocked to the island since the mid-1960s, seeking to join the civil or military forces or to receive political patronage. In addition to these two groups, there are Fernandinos, descendants of former slaves liberated by the British during the 19th century who mingled with other emancipated Africans from Sierra Leone and Cuba as well as with immigrants from other western African countries. Formerly constituting an influential bourgeoisie, they lost much of their status when the Spanish acquired the island. The inhabitants of Annobón are descended from slaves imported by the Portuguese when the island was a dependency of São Tomé; some of them now live on Bioko.

By about 1970, all these different strata together constituted a minority on the island, the majority being formed by the mass of Nigerian contract labourers, who lived in compact colonies either in Malabo or on the plantations. The repatriation by Nigeria, however, of an estimated 45,-000 workers beginning in mid-1975, following reports of repressive conditions in Equatorial Guinea, led to extensive realignment of the demographic, social, and labour structures of the island and, indeed, of the country. Additional communities on the island are formed by *crioulos* (of mixed Portuguese and African origin) from the islands of São Tomé and Príncipe; there are also some Cameroonians.

Language. While each ethnic group speaks its own language, two linguistic influences are at work. The first is Spanish, which is the official language of the republic, is taught in schools and used by the press, and is the only means of communication common to both Bioko and the mainland. The second influence is pidgin English, which forms the lingua franca on Bioko. A Portuguese patois is also spoken both in Bioko and Annobón.

Religion. While about four-fifths of Equatorial Guineans are nominally Roman Catholic, the Bubi and mainlanders have all more or less openly retained traditional forms of worship, which are emphasized in times of crisis. The Mbwiti cult on the mainland, banned by the Spanish authorities, still has adherents. There are American Presbyterian and English Methodist missions on the mainland. Muslims are found only among the Hausa.

THE ECONOMY

Cocoa, coffee, and timber exports

Equatorial Guinea's economy has depended primarily upon three commodities—cocoa, coffee, and timber. Before independence, the Spanish subsidized cocoa and coffee exports to Spain. Cocoa, which is of high quality, was the mainstay of the economy of Bioko, which possesses the right soil and climate for its intensive cultivation. Most of Equatorial Guinea's cocoa is produced on the island. Equatorial Guinea's coffee is of good quality; most of it comes from the continental region, with Bioko's share

of production being marginal. The timber companies are entirely European; there were at one time 30 timber concessions in operation on the mainland. The industry is heavily mechanized and requires a large investment.

Bananas are grown on Bioko, where they are exported from the port of Luba. The output of palm oil from mainland plantations has been adversely affected by the unsettled state of the country. Cattle raising in Moca Heights is of minor importance. There is little industry in the country. Some cocoa and coffee processing takes place locally on plantations and in African cooperatives. There is no mineral production. Following the economic collapse of the mid-1970s, imports came to exceed exports. The gap was narrowed only by external aid, which began to increase after 1979. Since independence the national budget has been balanced chiefly by large Spanish subsidies.

Transportation. The road network on the mainland was adequate for the light traffic it was required to carry before independence, but it deteriorated in the 1970s. Bata is linked with Mbini by a tarred road. There is a cross-country road from Bata, branching at Niefang and Nove, to Ebebiyin, Mongomo, and Nsoc near the Cameroon frontier. There are no railways. On Bioko the road system is of a higher standard, with a semicircular tarred road linking Malabo and Luba to the eastern Bubi villages. The main harbour is Malabo, which is connected to Spanish and other European ports by regular steamer services. There is a regular steamer service between Bata and Malabo, but the service to Annobón is erratic. Communications are maintained with Calabar in Nigeria and with Douala in Cameroon. There is an international airport at Malabo. In 1982 a new international airline Aerolíneas Guinea Ecuatorial, was formed, and construction began on a new international airport at Bata in 1983.

ADMINISTRATIVE AND SOCIAL CONDITIONS

According to the constitution of 1982, the system of government is presidential; and all governing bodies are elected by universal adult suffrage. The Council of Ministers is appointed by the president and is responsible to him. The president is selected by universal suffrage for a seven-year term. The State Council includes the chairman of the House of Representatives, the president of the Supreme Tribunal, and the minister of defense. Members of the National Assembly are elected for five-year terms. The supreme tribunal in Malabo is the highest judicial authority. There are also territorial high courts and courts of the first instance in Malabo and Bata.

In March 1970 all the political parties that existed before independence were merged into a Partido Único Nacional (Single National Party), which later changed its name to Partido Único Nacional de Trabajadores (Single National Party of Workers), under the leadership of the President, who assumed most of the powers in the country and subsequently was made president for life. Since he is a Fang, and most of the other political figures are also Fang—in addition to the members of the Guardia Nacional—the Fang were the dominant element in Equatorial Guinea.

CULTURAL LIFE

Despite a veneer of Spanish culture and of Catholic religion that is thicker in Bioko than on the mainland, Equatorial Guineans live largely according to ancient customs, which have undergone a revival since independence. Among the Fang of the mainland, witchcraft, traditional music (in which the Fang harp, the xylophone, the great drums, and the wooden trumpet are used), gorilla and elephant hunting, and storytelling all do much to relieve the monotony of life in the forest. Among the Bubi farmers of Bioko, some ancient customs are still followed. For statistical data, see the "Britannica World Data" section in the current *Britannica Book of the Year.* (R.P./Ed.)

Role of ancient customs

History

The island of Bioko (formerly Fernando Po) was sighted by Fernão do Pó, probably in 1472. At first it was called Formosa (Beautiful). Annobón was probably sighted by Ruy de Sequeira on a New Year's day (hence the name, which means "good year") between 1472 and 1475, most likely that of 1474. By the Treaty of Tordesillas (June 7, 1494), the Portuguese had exclusive rights in Africa, and it was not until 1778 that they agreed to cede to Spain the islands of Annobón and Fernando Po as well as rights on the mainland coast between the Ogooué and Niger rivers. These cessions were designed to give Spain its own source of slaves in Africa for transport to Spanish America, where, in exchange, the Spanish confirmed the rights of the Portuguese west of the 50° W meridian in what is now Brazil. The Spanish were soon decimated by yellow fever on Fernando Po and they withdrew in 1781. No occupation was made on the mainland.

BRITISH ADMINISTRATION

After the British abolition of the slave trade in 1807, bases were required by the Royal Navy for the effective suppression of the trade. Fernando Po was unoccupied and lay in a strategic situation from which the Niger mouths and the Slave Coast could be watched for slavers. In 1827 the Spanish leased bases for this purpose to the British at Port Clarence (later Santa Isabel, now Malabo), a fine deepwater harbour on the north coast, and in San Carlos Bay on the west coast.

In the absence of the Spanish, the British also became responsible for administering the island. Thereafter, the British landed many freed slaves, in default of knowing their origin or of being able to repatriate them. Freed slaves also went to the island from Sierra Leone and Jamaica, and in the 20th century the descendants of these several groups continued to speak a form of English. Because of the existence of these freed slaves and the absence of any Spanish administration in the area, the United Kingdom made several unsuccessful offers to Spain for the purchase of Fernando Po; *e.g.*, from 1839 to 1841. In 1843 the Royal Navy concentrated its anti-slavery patrol at Freetown in Sierra Leone, and its buildings on Fernando Po were sold to a Baptist mission.

Arrival of freed slaves

SPANISH GUINEA

In 1844 the Spanish made a second effort at effective occupation of Fernando Po, and their first exploration of the mainland was carried out in the two decades ending in 1877. Meanwhile, the Spanish had expelled the British Baptists from Fernando Po in 1858, and by using it as a penal settlement for Cubans from 1879 onward they

added to the diverse origins of the present peoples. Following the Spanish-American War of 1898, Spanish Guinea remained as Spain's last significant tropical colony. Profiting from the weakness of Spain, France was able to confine mainland Spanish Guinea to its present limited extent. Economic development started only at that time and was concentrated on the richer and healthier Fernando Po. The mainland received significant attention from the home country only after the Spanish Civil War of 1936–39.

In 1959 the status of Spanish Guinea was changed, and the region was reorganized into two provinces of overseas Spain, each of which was placed under a civil governor. The citizens, including the Africans, were granted the same rights as those enjoyed by the citizens of Spain. In 1963 a measure of economic and administrative autonomy for the two provinces (which were henceforth known as Equatorial Guinea) was agreed on by plebiscite.

INDEPENDENCE

The movement toward independence began to take shape at the end of 1967. Early the following year the Spanish government suspended autonomous political control and with the subsequent approval of the Organization of African Unity (OAU) proposed that a national referendum be held to approve the new constitution. The constitution, which was overwhelmingly approved on August 11, was followed by parliamentary elections in September and by the proclamation of independence on October 12, 1968. The new state became the 126th member of the UN. The first president was Francisco Macías Nguema. After his election in 1971 he assumed a large measure of power and pushed through a constitution that named him president for life. Macías' ethnic group, the Fang, came to dominate the country. His rule lasted until 1979, when he was ousted, tried, and executed in a military takeover. A Supreme Military Council was created with Lieut. Col. Teodoro Obiang Nguema Mbasogo as president. The 1973 constitution was abrogated and replaced by a new constitution approved in 1982. Obiang Nguema, starting a new seven-year term in office, brought about a rapprochement with Spain and the United States and broke ties with the Soviet Union and its allies. In 1983 elections were held for a new National Assembly. For current political history, see the annual issues of the *Britannica Book of the Year.*

(R.J.H.-C./Ed.)

THE GAMBIA

The Gambia, a western African republic, is a small state with a total area of 4,017 square miles (10,403 square kilometres). The country is a narrow enclave, from 15 to 30 miles (25 to 50 kilometres) wide and 295 miles (475 kilometres) long, stretching inland from the Atlantic Ocean and surrounded (except on its short coastal side) by Senegal. Essentially, The Gambia is a strip of land on either bank of the Gambia River. The unusual shape and size of the former British colony are attributable to arbitrary territorial compromises arising from 19th-century Anglo-French rivalry in western Africa. Its capital is Banjul (formerly Bathurst).

Physical and human geography

THE LAND

Relief. The Gambia River is the country's dominant feature, flowing across a plateau of Tertiary sandstone, compacted sediment composed predominantly of quartz grains formed from 65,000,000 to 2,500,000 years ago. The landscape is generally flat, dissected terrain, with gentle slopes of not more than three degrees. In the east, narrow valleys are separated by broad interfluves or flattish hills. In the west, lower and smaller sand hills alternate with depressions up to three miles wide filled in with sand so that a flat plain is formed.

Climate. The climate is of the drier tropical type, characterized by a short and intense rainy season, occurring

some time between June and October, and a longer dry season. Near the coast the rainy season lasts longer and the rainfall is heavier, diminishing eastward. At Yundum, in the west, the average annual rainfall is about 51 inches (1,300 millimetres) and the mean monthly temperature 77° F (25° C), while at Basse Santa Su, about 270 miles inland, the comparable figures are 43 inches (1,100 millimetres) and 82° F (28° C). The relative humidity is high, particularly from July to December, but drops from December to April, when the dry northeastern winds known as the harmattan are dominant. The vegetation cover of The Gambia is savanna (grassland) on the uplands, while various kinds of swamps cover the low lying areas.

Settlement patterns. Patterns of settlement in The Gambia reflect three regions, expressed on both banks of the river, consisting of (1) the swamps adjacent to the river (and not extending above Kau-Ur); (2) the riverine flats, known as *banto faros* (from a Mandingo word meaning "beyond the swamp"); and (3) the sandstone uplands. Most rural settlement is concentrated on the uplands, which have better drained soils and are more healthful than the flooded swamps and estuarine *banto faros*. In the *banto faros* on the middle course of the river, however, where valleys are deeper and there is less danger of flooding, the number of village settlements increases. Many of the villages are built on the boundary between the uplands and the riverine flats.

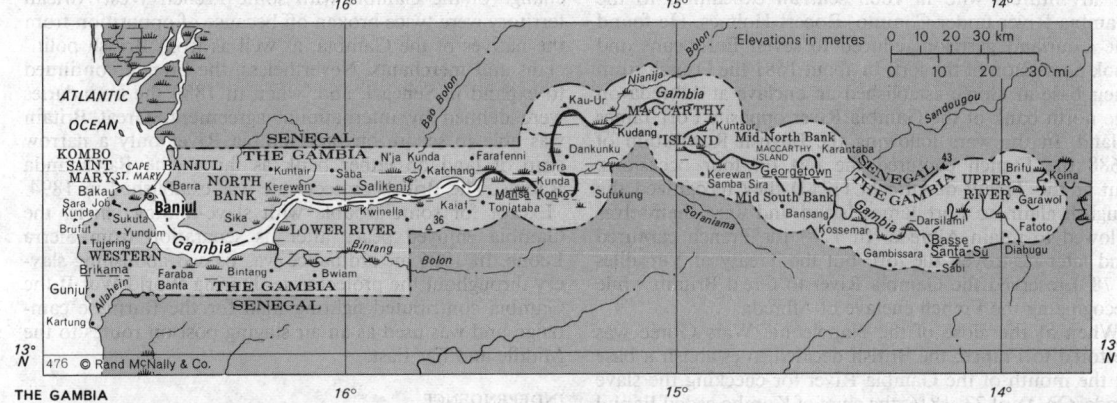

THE GAMBIA

THE PEOPLE

The river basin has in the past acted as a focal point for migrating groups of people from adjacent parts of western Africa, and The Gambia is consequently populated by diverse ethnic groups. About two-fifths of the population is Malinke (Mandingo), followed by Fulani, Wolof, Dyola (Yola), and Soninke (Seraculeh). There are also smaller groups of Senegalese, other African, and non-African peoples. The population is predominantly Muslim. A peculiar characteristic of the national population is its seasonal variation, caused by the influx of Senegalese farm workers.

THE ECONOMY

Agriculture. The Gambia is primarily agricultural, with both men and women engaged in cultivation. On the *banto faros* of the river's middle course, fields are created by enclosing selected areas with embankments made of mud and reeds, which are cultivated by women, who grow rice, garden crops, and some peanuts (groundnuts). On the sandy uplands the men grow peanuts, sorghum, and millet and practice the rotation of crops. The average size of cultivated plots is 2½ acres (1 hectare) for a man and 1¼ acres for a woman. In addition to the main cereal crops, the women also grow such subsistence crops as lentils, cassava, yams, eggplant, tomatoes, peppers, and okra. Fruit trees are also maintained.

The Gambian economy, as noted above, is based primarily on the production of peanuts for export. Grown on the upland soils, peanuts have been the main cash crop for virtually all Gambian farmers and the source of the largest share of governmental revenue. Sown in June and July, the crop is harvested in October and November. Production has increased steadily with the help of seasonal migrants from Senegal and Guinea and with the wider use of fertilizers and ox-drawn equipment, as well as the introduction of better seed varieties. In an effort to diversify the economy, the production of palm kernels, a secondary export crop, has been encouraged since the mid-1960s, when a pilot scheme for the cultivation of oil palms was begun, using improved varieties of seed from Nigeria. In addition there have been efforts to introduce rice, cotton, and livestock, and to increase fishing.

Industry. Processing, rather than manufacturing, industries are important. Peanuts are sold unshelled to traders and agents of the Gambia Produce Marketing Board, which fixes the season's price in advance, pays the producers in cash, and sells overseas. The agents arrange for the transportation of the peanuts to Banjul or to Kau-Ur, where the nuts are shelled before being shipped. After shelling, a large proportion of the crop is pressed at oil mills. Exports include nuts, oil, and cattle cake, the residue after the oil has been extracted.

Fishing. The ocean off The Gambia has great potential for inshore and deep-sea fishing, but little public revenue has been derived from fisheries because of inadequate equipment to replace traditional techniques, which confine the fishermen to estuarial or coastal waters. Some development has nevertheless taken place, with the government lending money to encourage the use of motorized fishing boats and the construction of traditional types of smoke huts for processing fish, particularly bonga (shad,

Principal ethnic groups

Importance of peanuts in the economy

Marine resources

or West African herring), which is exported to western African countries.

Tourism. The government of The Gambia has encouraged an expansion of tourism.

Trade and finance. The Gambia has a relatively large volume of trade for its small size. In the early 1980s, however, the country had an adverse balance of trade.

Transportation. The navigability of the Gambia River has discouraged the development of good roadways. There are no railways and no internal air services. The main port is Banjul, and there is an international airport nearby at Yundum. Banjul offers easy access to shipping and has good road and river connections.

ADMINISTRATIVE AND SOCIAL CONDITIONS

The Gambia is an independent republic. The government is headed by a president, whose term of office is linked to the unicameral parliament, the 49-member House of Representatives. Elections are held every five years. The vice president and Cabinet members are appointed by the president from the 35 elected members of the house. There are also five house members elected by the chiefs in assembly, eight nominated members who are without votes, and the attorney general, who is nominated and has a vote. The People's Progressive Party (PPP) holds about three-fourths of the elected seats. The National Convention Party (NCP) and the Independents hold the remaining seats. Local administration in each of the 35 districts into which The Gambia is divided is the responsibility of the local chief, who is assisted by village heads and advisers. The 35 districts are also grouped into seven divisions, six of which are administered by councils consisting of a majority of elected members and the chiefs of the district. Banjul is administered by a city council.

Education. Education at the primary level is free, but not compulsory. There are secondary schools and post-secondary schools, including a teacher-training college. Gambian students seeking higher education also travel to Sierra Leone, the United Kingdom, or the United States.

Health and welfare. There are several general hospitals and a number of health centres, dispensaries, and maternity and child care clinics. Mosquito-control units are active, and there is a leprosy-control program. For statistical data, see the "Britannica World Data" section in the current *Britannica Book of the Year.*   (E.R.A.F./Ed.)

History

The Gambia River was sighted in 1455 by the Portuguese. In 1588 the Portuguese sold to some English merchants exclusive trading rights in the river, but the venture led to no permanent settlement. In 1618 James I granted a charter to a company formed for trading with the Gambia and the Gold Coast (modern Ghana), but its first agent, George Thompson, was killed by the local people. His successor, Richard Jobson, is reputed in 1620 to have reached the Barrakunda Rapids. In about 1660 James, duke of Courland (godson of James I of England), acquired from a local chief an island, later known as Fort James Island, about 17 miles upriver, where he erected a fort. In 1661 Charles II granted a new patent to a body of adventurers who in 1663 sent an expedition to the Gambia River under Commo. Robert Holmes. He found the Courland garrison reduced to seven Europeans and took possession of the fort. In about 1681 the French from their base at Gorée established an enclave at Albreda on the north bank of the Gambia River opposite Fort James Island. In the wars following the English Revolution of 1688 the French captured the fort on four occasions, but at the Treaty of Utrecht (1713) they recognized the English claim to Fort James Island and were themselves allowed to retain Albreda. In 1779 the French captured and later destroyed the fort, but the Treaty of Versailles (1783) reserved the Gambia River to Great Britain while recognizing the French enclave of Albreda.

When at the close of the Napoleonic Wars Gorée was restored to France, the British decided to establish a base at the mouth of the Gambia River for checking the slave trade. On April 23, 1816, the chief of Kombo ceded Banjul (later renamed St. Mary's) Island, and a ssettlement was established and named Bathurst after the then colonial secretary. British traders from Gorée followed the garrison to this new settlement. Bathurst was subordinated to the Sierra Leone colony in 1821 and in 1843 became a separate colony, but in 1866 it was made part of the "West African settlements" governed from Freetown, reverting to separate status in 1888. Albreda was transferred to Britain by an exchange arrangement with France in 1857.

The founding of Bathurst

BRITISH PROTECTORATE

Following various cessions and purchases of territory in the years 1823–53, negotiations in the 1870s for the ex-change of the Gambia with some French West African territory were twice broken off because of opposition from the natives of the Gambia, as well as from British politicians and merchants. Nevertheless, the French continued to expand in Senegal, and, when in 1889 the boundaries were defined by international agreement, Great Britain was able to secure on the Gambia River only a narrow strip of land on either bank as far as the Barrakunda Rapids. The British protectorate was established in 1894.

Except for some trouble with slave-raiding chiefs, the Gambia enjoyed peace after its separation from Sierra Leone. In 1906 an ordinance was passed abolishing slavery throughout the protectorate. During World War II the Gambia contributed fighting men for the Burmese campaign and was used as an air staging post on routes to the Middle and Far East.

INDEPENDENCE

Revised constitutions in 1954, 1959, and 1961 advanced the autonomy of the territory, which in February 1965 achieved full independence as The Gambia. On April 24, 1970, The Gambia became an independent republic. The first elected president, Sir Dawda Jawara, was reelected in 1982, in spite of attempted military and political coup. A confederation of Senegal and Gambia called Senegambia was approved in February of 1982. While each state retained its independence, military and monetary resources were integrated and a Senegambian Parliament was created. For current political history, see the annual issues of the *Britannica Book of the Year*.

Senegambia

(Ed.)

GHANA

Ghana is a West African republic situated on the coast of the Gulf of Guinea. It has an area of 92,098 square miles (238,533 square kilometres). Although relatively small in area and population, Ghana is one of the leading countries of Africa, partly because of its considerable natural wealth, and partly because it was the first black African country south of the Sahara to achieve independence from colonial rule.

Physical and human geography

Ghana, which achieved independence on March 6, 1957, consists of the former British colony of the Gold Coast and the part of Togoland that was formerly a UN Trust Territory under British administration. It is bordered on the west by the Ivory Coast, on the northwest and north by Burkina Faso, on the east by Togo, and on the south by the Atlantic Ocean.

The economy is dominated by the cocoa crop, of which the country is one of the world's largest exporters; other important exports are diamonds, gold, manganese, bauxite, and timber. Ample electricity is available from the Volta River Dam, a large hydroelectric complex on the Volta River at Akosombo. The capital is Accra.

THE LAND

Relief. Relief throughout Ghana is generally low, with altitudes nowhere exceeding 3,000 feet (900 metres). The southwestern, northwestern, and extreme northern parts of the country consist of a dissected peneplain—a land surface worn down by erosion to a nearly flat plain, later cut by erosion into hills and valleys or into flat uplands separated by valleys; it is made of Precambrian rocks (from 570,000,000 to 4,600,000,000 years old). Most of the remainder of the country consists of Paleozoic deposits (from 225,000,000 to 570,000,000 years old), which are thought to rest on older rocks. The Paleozoic sediments are composed mostly of beds of shales (laminated sediments consisting mostly of particles of clay) and sandstones in which strata of limestone occur in places. They occupy a large area, known as the Voltaian Basin, in the north central part of the country where the altitude rarely exceeds 500 feet (150 metres). Along the north and south,

The Voltaian Basin

and to some extent along the west, the uplifted edges of the basin give rise to narrow plateaus between 1,000 and 2,000 feet high, bordered by impressive scarps. The most outstanding of these are the Kwahu Scarp in the south and the Gambaga Scarp in the north.

Surrounding the basin on all of its sides, except in the east, is the dissected Precambrian peneplain, which rises to elevations of 500 to 1,000 feet above sea level and contains several distinct ranges as high as 2,000 feet.

Along the eastern edge of the Voltaian Basin, and extending from the Togo border to the sea immediately west of Accra, is a narrow zone of folded Precambrian rocks running northeast to southwest, forming the scenically attractive Akwapim-Togo Ranges, which vary in height from 1,000 to 3,000 feet. The highest points in Ghana are found there, including Mt. Afadjato (2,903 feet), Mt. Djebobo (2,874 feet), and Mt. Torogbani (2,861 feet), all of them situated east of the Volta River near the Togo border. These ranges are part of the Togo-Atacora Mountains, which extend northward into Togo and Benin.

The southeastern corner of the country, between the Akwapim-Togo Ranges and the sea, consists of the gently rolling Accra Plains, which are underlain by some of the oldest Precambrian rocks known—mostly gneisses (coarse-grained rocks in which bands containing granular minerals alternate with bands containing micaceous minerals); in places they rise above the surface to form inselbergs (prominent steep-sided hills left after erosion), which dot the plains. Only in the wide, lagoon-fringed delta of the Volta, about 50 miles (80 kilometres) east of Accra, and in the extreme southwest of the country, along the Axim coast, are there extensive areas of young rocks less than 136,000,000 years old.

In the east the predominant rocks are less than 65,000,000 years old, though there is a patch of Cretaceous sediments (from 65,000,000 to 136,000,000 years old) near the Ghana–Togo border. In the western part of the country, near the Ivory Coast frontier, west of Axim, the rocks date to the Cretaceous Period. The intervening coastal zone between eastern and western extremes contains scattered patches of Devonian sediments (from 345,000,000 to 395,000,000 years old). In combination with the older and more resistant rocks of the Precambrian peneplain,

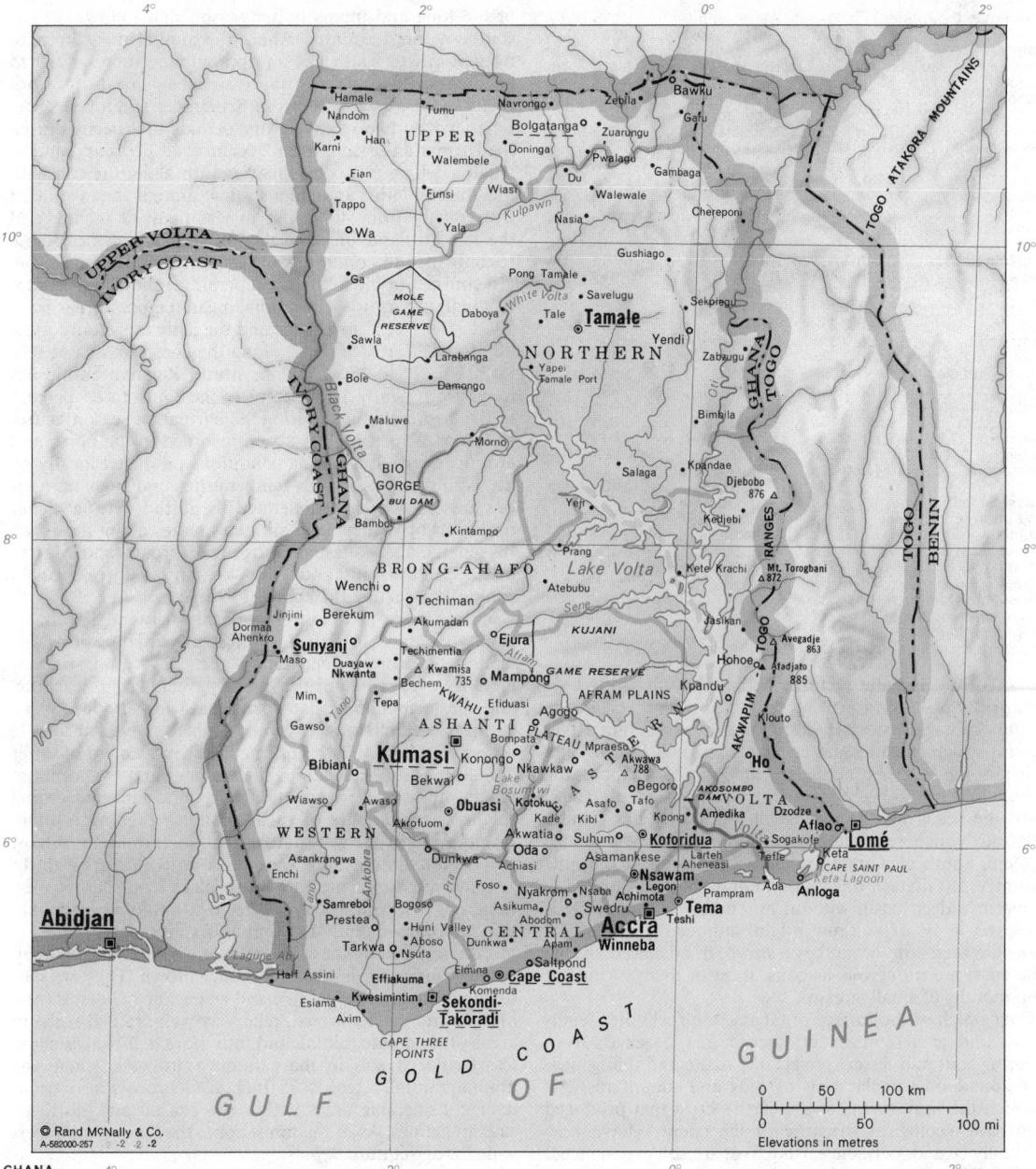

GHANA

The rivers

these form a low but picturesque coastline of sandy bays and rocky promontories.

The drainage system is dominated by the Volta River Basin, which includes the artificially created Lake Volta. Most of the other rivers, such as the Pra, the Ankobra, the Tano, and a number of smaller ones, flow directly south into the sea from the watershed formed by the Kwahu Plateau, which separates them from the Volta drainage system. South of Kumasi, in the south central part of the country, is Ghana's only true natural lake—Bosumtwi—lying in a deep basin without any outlet to the sea. It is believed to be of volcanic origin, although theories of a possible meteorite origin have also been advanced. Along the coast are numerous lagoons, most of them formed at the mouths of small streams.

Over much of the surface of Ghana, the rocks are weathered, and great spreads of laterite (red, leached, iron-bearing soil) and lesser spreads of bauxite and manganese are found on the flat tops of hills and mountains. Although the movements of the earth's crust that produced the basic geological structure of the country have now virtually ceased, periodic earthquakes are still experienced, especially in the immediate vicinity of Accra along the eastern foot of the Akwapim-Togo Ranges.

Climate. Ghana's climate, like that of the rest of the Guinea coast, is mainly determined by the interplay between the tropical continental air mass known as the harmattan, which consists of hot, dry, dust-laden air moving from the northeast across the Sahara; the tropical maritime air mass known as the monsoon, which consists of moist and relatively cool air moving from the southwest across the southern Atlantic; and the cool equatorial easterlies from higher altitudes. The zone where these air masses converge is characterized by seasonal line squall rainfall. The convergence zone itself oscillates north and south, following the seasonal movement of the sun overhead; it reaches its most northerly position in the central Sahara, about latitude 21° N, in August, and its most southerly position about 7° N, a few miles north of the Ghana coastline, in January. Rains occur when the dominant air mass is monsoonal (i.e., characterized by rain-bearing winds), while drought prevails when the harmattan dominates.

In the savanna (grassy parkland) country north of the Kwahu Plateau, the year consists of two seasons—a dry season from November to March, with hot days and cool nights under clear skies, and a wet season that reaches its peak in August and September. The mean annual rainfall ranges between 45 and 50 inches (1,145 and 1,270 millimetres), but there is a marked moisture deficit because

Rainfall and temperature

of the long and intensely dry season that follows. In the southern forest country, where the annual mean rainfall from north to south has an approximate range of 50 to 86 inches, there are two rainy seasons—one from April to July and a lesser one from September to November—separated by two relatively dry periods that occur during the harmattan season, from December to February, and in August, which is a cool, misty month along the coast. In the Accra Plains, anomalously low annual mean rainfall figures vary from 40 inches to less than 30 inches, and the rainfall variability and the vegetation both bear close resemblance to conditions in the northern savanna zone.

In contrast to the rainfall, temperatures show much more regional uniformity. The annual mean temperature is from 78° to 84° F (26° to 29° C), and the daily range only some 10° to 15° F (6° to 8° C) along the coast, and some 13° to 30° F (7° to 17° C) in the north. Relative humidities range from nearly 100 percent in the south to 65 percent in the north, although during the harmattan season figures as low as 12 percent have been recorded in the north and around Accra. Enervating conditions produced locally by the combination of high temperatures and high humidities are considerably moderated by altitude in the higher parts and by regular land and sea breezes along the coast. In general, the hottest months are February and March, just before the rains, and the lowest temperatures occur in January or—along the coast—in August.

Soils. There is a close relationship between the major soil types and the broad geological, climatic, and vegetational features. Topography also plays an important local role. Throughout the country, weathering, leaching, and the formation of hard pans (hard impervious layers, composed chiefly of clay cemented by relatively insoluble materials), by capillary movement (the movement of water containing mineral salts to the surface) and evaporation, are common processes that vary in importance according to the characteristics of each locality. Leaching is more pronounced in the wet south, while the formation of hard pans and laterite is most widespread in the drier north. In general, most soils are formed in place from parent rock material, which has been subjected to prolonged denudation and consequently has limited fertility.

In the forest zone the soils are mostly lateritic, ranging in colour from reddish brown to orange brown. They are subdivided into relatively fertile and less acidic ochrosols (red, brown, and yellow-brown, relatively well-drained soils) in areas of moderate rainfall and into more highly acidic and less fertile oxysols in the extreme southwest, where the annual rainfall exceeds 65 inches. Ochrosols also occur over considerable areas within the coastal and northern savanna zones. As in the forest zone, they provide the best soils for agriculture.

The varied geology of the coastal savanna zone is reflected in an abundance of soil types, including tropical black earths, tropical gray earths, acid vleisols, and sodium vleisols. Except for the tropical black earths, known locally as Akuse clays, most of these soils are of little importance agriculturally. The Akuse clays fill a broad zone across the coastal savanna plains; although heavy and intractable, they respond well to cropping under irrigation and mechanical cultivation.

Because of their intrinsic poverty in nutrients, most of the soils are heavily dependent upon the humus supplied by the vegetation cover. There is, thus, a delicate balance between vegetation and soil fertility, which may be upset by uncontrolled burning or overuse.

Plant and animal life. Although soils and biotic factors (i.e., those pertaining to living organisms, including man) are important, vegetation is primarily determined by rainfall. There are three principal types of vegetation from south to north occurring in the coastal savanna, in the forest zone, and in the northern savanna zone.

The coastal savanna in the southeastern plains around Accra consists of a mixture of scrub and tall grass (mostly Guinea grass), with giant anthills, often 10 to 14 feet high, forming a prominent feature of the landscape and providing an anchorage for thicket clumps that often include Elaeophorbia (a fleshy-leaved plant containing caustic latex) and other drought and fire-resistant species.

Types of soil

In the forest zone (the southern third of the country and the area along the Akwapim-Togo Ranges, where the mean annual rainfall exceeds 45 inches and is well distributed throughout the year without a pronounced dry season), the predominant vegetation is evergreen and tropical semideciduous forest. Here are tall trees of varying heights, forming a closed canopy at the top, above which tower a few forest giants, such as the silk cotton tree, the wawa tree (African whitewood, a hardwood), and the African mahogany. The evergreen forest is in the extreme southwest, where the rainfall exceeds 65 inches a year, while there is a semideciduous forest further north.

The dense forest zone covered an area of about 30,000 square miles until farming activities and timber exploitation reduced it to about 10,000 square miles, including about 6,000 square miles of forest reserves.

The third vegetation type, the northern savanna, is found in the northern two-thirds of the country, where the low annual rainfall, between 45 and 30 inches, occurs in a single season and is followed by a period of intense drought. Here, the vegetation consists mostly of tall Guinea grass, together with a scattering of low trees, such as the shea butter tree, and various species of acacia. Along the northern border the savanna gives way to a more open type of grassland that has developed largely as a result of prolonged human interference.

Although it has been depleted by too much hunting and the spread of human settlement, Ghana is still comparatively rich in animal life. The large mammals include lions, leopards, hyenas, antelope, elephants, buffalo, wild hogs, chimpanzees, and many kinds of monkeys, including the black and white *Colobus* monkeys. Among the snakes are pythons, cobras, horned and puff adders, and green mambas. Crocodiles and the endangered manatees (large water animals characterized by two flippers and a spoon-shaped tail) and otters are found in the rivers and lagoons. Hippopotamuses are found in the Volta River. There are many varieties of lizards and tortoises and giant snails.

Among the numerous birds are parrots, hornbills, kingfishers, eagles, kites, herons, cuckoos, nightjars, sunbirds, egrets, vultures, snakebirds, and plantain eaters.

The adjacent ocean, the rivers, and the inland lakes are rich in fish and other forms of life. Sardines, locally called herring, arrive seasonally in the coastal waters in large shoals; other fish include mackerel, soles, skates, mullet, bonitos, flying fish, lungfish, elephant fish, sea bream, and sharks. Edible turtles, barracuda, and stingrays are fairly common; mussels, crabs, lobsters, and prawns also are found.

Insect life is particularly abundant. There are beetles, fireflies, ants, termites, butterflies, crickets, and bugs. Among the most dangerous insects are mosquitoes, tsetse flies, and simuliids (biting flies), which are responsible for transmitting the endemic diseases of malaria and yellow fever, trypanosomiasis (sleeping sickness), and onchocerciasis (a parasitic disease), respectively.

The Mole Game Reserve in the western part of the Northern Region near Damongo is 1,900 square miles in extent. Other reserves have been developed further south, notably on some of the islands in Lake Volta.

Settlement patterns. Ghana has three major regions, the boundaries of which are not always clearly defined.

The coastal zone. Apart from the urban centres, which are found more frequently in this region than in any other, the coastal zone is traditionally a region of fishermen and small-scale food farmers. The region was formerly occupied by a series of small kingdoms, the inhabitants of which were the first to be exposed to European contact—from the 15th century onward, perhaps even earlier. From east to west the principal ethnic groups are the Ewe, Adangme (Adangbe), Ga, Efutu, Fanti, Ahanta, and Nzima. While it is difficult to speak of any cultural cohesion embracing the whole region, the seaboard has made the region an important centre for commerce, causing population concentration exemplified by such urban centres as Accra, Cape Coast, Sekondi-Takoradi, and the port and industrial city of Tema, a few miles east of Accra.

The forest zone. Further inland, occupying about a third of the country, is the forest region with its relatively large and prosperous traditional states and rich agricultural lands. West of the Volta these states consist mostly of Akan peoples; to the east the Ewe predominate. The forest environment and the economic activities and modes of life engendered by it, especially since the introduction of cocoa farming in 1879, have served to give the region a common stamp. Apart from the Ewe, the major ethnic groups are the Akwapim and Kwahu in the east, the Akim in the south, the Ashanti and Brong in the centre and north, and the Wasaw and Sefwi in the west. While all of the peoples in the region have a relatively long history of settlement and political activity, those with the most impressive record are the Ashanti, who, from the 17th to the late 19th century, built a political empire centred on Kumasi, the present Ashanti capital, that included a large number of subject and satellite states spread throughout the region and in both the coastal and northern savanna zones.

Practically all the timber, cocoa, and exploited mineral wealth, as well as a number of minor cash crops grown for export, and a large proportion of the foodstuffs consumed in Ghana are derived from this region. Population density is relatively high, particularly in the cocoa-growing areas. Except for Kumasi, there are few really large urban centres.

The northern savanna zone. This region covers approximately two-thirds of the country but is economically the most backward and neglected. The largest ethnic groupings are the Dagomba and the Gonja, related to the Mossi people of Burkina Faso. The region has a harsh environment because of its low rainfall. The period of drought is known as the "hungry season." The southern part immediately adjoining the forest zone, forming part of the disease-ridden "middle belt" of western Africa that combines the worst features of the forest and the savanna environments, is especially unattractive for settlement. In the past it was also subject to extensive slave raiding, from both north and south. Its distance from the sea and consequent insulation from active European contact over a long period retarded the development of the northern region.

Among the advantages of the northern region, especially in the most northerly part, which is relatively free from the tsetse fly so deadly to cattle, is an extensive savanna vegetation that offers excellent prospects for livestock breeding. Its relatively light soils and the rainfall regime favour the cultivation of both yams and cereals. Although agriculture is mostly of the traditional subsistence type, irrigation and mechanized cultivation have opened up new prospects. Lake Volta extends far into the heart of the region and offers prospects for comparatively cheap communication with the south, as well as a reservoir of water for agricultural and other uses.

Rural settlement. Ghana's population remains predominantly rural. By the early 1980s only one-third of the population was estimated to be urban. Almost everywhere agriculture is extensive, rather than intensive, and the rural settlements form isolated nuclei surrounded by land that is either under crops or is undergoing regeneration.

Permanent or continuous cropping is encouraged throughout the country but is found especially in the extreme northeast, where settlements consist of isolated compound houses, each surrounded by its own farm. Elsewhere, agriculture is based on rotational farming, a system in which land is cropped for two or three years and then abandoned for from four to seven years, in order to allow it to regenerate. When cocoa or other tree crops are grown, however, cultivation is usually permanent.

Urban settlement. Although many of the urban centres have expanded rapidly in size and population, they remain small by world standards. The Accra–Tema municipality is the largest in the country, followed by Kumasi and Sekondi-Takoradi.

THE PEOPLE

Ethnic and linguistic groups. Ethnically, the people of Ghana may be said to belong to one broad group within the African family, but there is a large variety of tribal, or subethnic, units. On the basis of language, it is possible to distinguish at least 75 different tribes. Many of these,

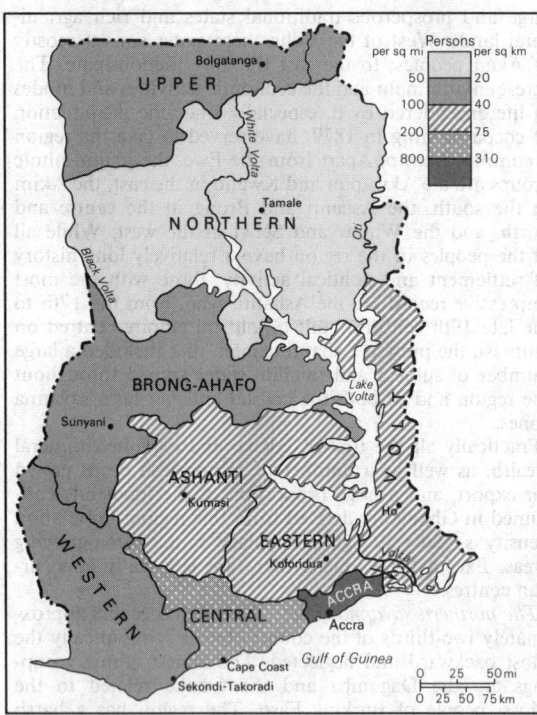

Population density of Ghana.

The
largest
tribal
groups

however, are very small, and only 10 of them are numerically significant. The largest of these are the Akan, Mole-Dagbani, Ewe, Ga-Adangme (Ga-Adangbe), and Gurma. Despite its tribal variety, there were no serious tribal dissensions or animosities when Ghana became independent. Tribal consciousness still persists in many regions, however, and in 1981 fighting took place between two tribes in northern Ghana, resulting in some 1,000 people being killed over a four-month period. At all levels in government and in public life, a conscious effort has been made to play down tribal differences, a policy that has been helped to a great extent by the adoption of English as the country's official language.

Religious groups. The main religions in Ghana are Christianity, the indigenous religions of the various tribes, and Islām. Although the indigenous religions are widespread and deep-rooted, they are completely lacking in any systematic body of doctrines and are only vaguely conceptualized. Though they are based, in general, on belief in the existence of a supreme being, a number of lesser deities associated with various natural phenomena are also recognized. Considerable prominence is given to dead ancestors, who are considered to be ever present, capable of influencing the course of events for the living, and capable of serving as intermediaries between the living and the divinities.

Over the years, Christianity has steadily gained ground at the expense of the indigenous religions. Christian influence is most dominant in the southern part of the country, while Islām is strongest in the extreme north and in the larger urban centres, which contain some immigrant populations from Muslim regions of western Africa. Since the 1950s a large number of spiritual churches claiming adherence to Christianity have appeared. The main divisions of the Christian Church, however, are still the Roman Catholics, Methodists, Presbyterians, Anglicans, and smaller denominations. About one-seventh of the population is Muslim, and one-third adhere to the traditional religions.

THE ECONOMY

Resources. *Mineral resources.* Although Ghana has a wide range of minerals, only a few—*e.g.,* gold, diamonds, manganese, and bauxite—are exploited. These minerals are found mostly in the southern part of the country. The gold industry, with an unbroken history dating from the 15th century, is the oldest; the others are of 20th-century origin—the working of manganese dating from

1915, diamonds from 1919, and bauxite from 1942. There are important reserves of limestone and iron ore, and an iron-ore mine at Opon-Mansi was being developed in the early 1980s.

In 1970 oil was discovered by offshore prospecting between Saltpond and Cape Coast. Although this discovery was initially classified as noncommercial, the steep world oil price increases of 1973–74 caused the Ghanaian government to reclassify it as commercial in 1974 and to undertake development. In that year and again in 1980 substantial amounts of natural gas were discovered offshore to the south and west of Cape Three Points. Although neither of these developments was expected to improve Ghana's energy situation or balance of payments substantially, they did lead to a revival of exploration activity in the mid-1970s. Oil production in the Saltpond area began in 1978, but it has proved disappointing; all crude oil is exported in order to reduce the country's foreign-trade deficit. Salt is obtained from the sea and lagoons.

During the 1960s there was a general decline in the mining industry, but in the the 1970s increased world market prices for gold and manganese, new discoveries in the Prestea goldfields, and the formation of a National Manganese Corporation in 1975 to carry out a five-year plan to rehabilitate the manganese mines at Nsuta all seemed to improve prospects for these metals. Ghana's mineral industries, however, have failed to revive. The production of bauxite, for example, has been well below capacity, while other minerals, notably diamonds, are close to depletion.

The development of Ghana's mineral industry has been hampered by a shortage of equipment and experienced personnel and by variations in climate. Bauxite reserves amount to 300,000,000 tons, though the output, all of which is exported, is only about 200,000 tons a year, about half of capacity. A giant aluminum smelter, completed at Tema in 1966, relies on imported alumina, although the conversion of bauxite found at Kibi into alumina has been developed. There are also extensive supplies of building stone, gravel, and sand. High-quality sand in the Tarkwa mining area provides the basis for a small but important glass industry. Cement factories have been developed at Tema and Takoradi.

Biological resources. Biological resources are extensive. Soil and climatic conditions favour a wide range of crops. The most important of these is cocoa, of which Ghana is a leading world producer. Other agricultural products that are exported include sugar, coffee, palm oil and kernels, copra, and various fruits and vegetables.

Timber and the crops of the forest zone constitute additional important biological resources. Yams and such cereals as rice and millet are produced primarily in the northern savanna zone; cattle are also raised there. The forests yield shea nuts and kola nuts. Ghana's offshore waters are rich in fish, and the creation of Lake Volta added another important source of fish for the domestic market. The various types of fish caught include cape hake, grunt, sea bream, tilapia, herring, mackerel, barracuda, and tuna. Most of the catch is sun-dried or smoked and is consumed locally. Government and private research agencies are working to increase the cash income of rural fishing communities and also to modernize the processing, distribution, and marketing of the catch. The State Fishing Corporation operates a fleet of deep-sea trawlers and works to improve the dietary intake of protein by increasing the supply of fish.

Hydroelectric resources. Apart from offshore oil, Ghana's only sources of power lie in the hydroelectric potential of its rivers, many of which have the requisite regimes and rates of flow to permit exploitation. The Akosombo Dam on the Volta River and a second dam a few miles downstream at Kpong have a combined electrical capacity of over 1,000,000 kilowatts. Electricity from Akosombo meets most of the domestic requirements, leaving a surplus for sale to Togo and Benin.

Sources of national income. National income is derived primarily from agricultural and mineral output and only to a limited extent from manufacturing and services. Most of the cash crops and mineral products are for export.

Agriculture, forestry, and fishing. Apart from provid-

The
mining
industry

The
Akosombo
Dam

ing the bulk of national income, agriculture, forestry, and fishing constitute the preponderant occupations, employing half of the population. The annual output of cocoa averages about 250,000 tons, and cocoa provides between three-fifths and three-quarters of the country's total revenue from exports. It is of such vital importance that the world price paid for the crop directly determines Ghana's economic fortunes. Ghana's cocoa production fell sharply during the 1970s. Production was undermined by aging and diseased trees, drought, bush fires, poor transport facilities, and widespread smuggling across Ghana's borders. The Cocoa Marketing Board was abolished in 1979 following charges of corruption but was subsequently reconstituted. The government has repeatedly raised the production price of cocoa in an effort to stimulate production and to decrease the country's balance of payments deficit. These efforts, however, have met with little success.

Timber is also an important foreign exchange earner. Ghana's timber marketing is controlled by the Ghana Timber Marketing Board. Since the beginning of 1973 all foreign-owned timber export firms have been required to incorporate locally, so that the purchasing of timber is conducted only through the Ghana Timber Marketing Board.

The Ghana Oil Palm Development Corporation built a mill for the production of palm oil on its plantation near Kwade. One of the largest in western Africa, the mill is designed to fulfill industrial and domestic consumption needs.

The Ghanaian domestic market is important. The value of food produced for local consumption is considerable, as is that of fish, both marine and freshwater. Successive governments have strongly supported diversification of food production to reduce reliance on a few crops and to cut the need for imported foodstuffs, but their measures have often been contradictory.

Industry. A policy of industrialization has resulted in the establishment of a wide range of manufacturing industries, producing food products, beverages, tobacco, textiles, clothes, footwear, timber and wood products, chemicals and pharmaceuticals, and metals, including steel and steel products. These are produced mostly for local consumption. Among the announced program directives of a five-year plan (1975–80), however, was the maintenance of a reasonable balance on external trade, and a number of industrial projects were directed to the export market in either the short or long term. Ghana's industrial development has been hampered by a lack of capital, and industrial planning in the early 1980s emphasized the importance of attracting foreign capital. The Investment Code of 1981 offered various tax incentives for investment in manufacturing, mining, and agriculture, but the military government installed in 1982 reversed policy by denouncing the sources of international financial aid and threatening to take Ghana out of the world economy.

Administration of the economy. *Private and public sectors.* The economy is a mixture of private and public enterprise. Before independence the government's role was confined mainly to the provision of such basic utilities as water, electricity, railways, roads, and postal services. Agriculture, commerce, banking, and such industry as existed were almost entirely in private hands, with foreign companies and interests controlling the greater share in all of them except agriculture.

Shortly after independence, the government set out to extend its control over the economy by setting up a large number of state-owned enterprises in both agriculture and industry. At the same time, in order to make up for the local shortage of capital and entrepreneurial skills, various measures were adopted to attract foreign investors operating either entirely on their own or in partnership with the government. These policies did not achieve the desired results because of poor planning and corrupt administration. By 1966, when the administration of Pres. Kwame Nkrumah was overthrown, the crippling weight of the heavy overseas borrowing, upon which the government had relied to support its ambitious economic programs, had succeeded in dissipating practically all of the country's overseas reserves and had saddled the economy with external and internal debts totalling some $1,000,000,000. One of the first concerns of governments since that time

has been the rehabilitation of the economy. They have sought to deal with the adverse balance of payments, to arrest inflation, to secure a rescheduling of overseas debts, to increase agricultural productivity, and to establish industrial development on a rational basis, as well as to save scarce foreign exchange by encouraging exports of locally manufactured goods.

Between 1966 and 1972 there was a marked contraction in governmental involvement in economic matters. The government continued to provide basic utilities, however, and remained the largest single employer of labour. After the military coup of 1972 policymakers returned to the concept of a centralized economy. The considerable debt owed to four British companies was repudiated, imports were cut, industrial projects abandoned after the fall of Nkrumah were resuscitated, and a policy of increased nationalization and state control was begun. In 1974, after a two-year suspension of foreign loans and aid, the government agreed on a schedule for the repayment of its outstanding debts. This reconciliation was accompanied by a more receptive policy toward investment by developed countries, though political instability resulted in a number of erratic economic policies. Ghana's external debt and balance of trade deficit increased, however, and led to a devaluation of the cedi in 1978, a currency conversion in 1979, a reduction of interest rates and demonetization of lower-value cedi notes in 1982.

Taxation. A large proportion of government revenue is derived from taxation, levied in a variety of forms, including a duty on cocoa, import duty, customs and excise duties, sales tax, income tax, and a number of other taxes. Tax concessions are available to businesses. A surcharge on many imports, including the processed and semi-processed raw material on which many local industries depend, has been introduced. Government economic policies have tended to erode the tax base, with controls on prices reducing revenue from excises and sales taxes. Import controls, price controls, and the monopoly on cocoa purchases by the government have fostered a flourishing underground economy, thus further reducing the government's revenues.

Tourism. Revenue from tourism has increased gradually, with most of the tourists coming from Nigeria, the United Kingdom, Ivory Coast, the United States, and West Germany. The Ghana Tourist Control Board and Ghana Tourist Development Company supervise the regulation, financing, and development of the tourist industry. Hotels are located at Accra, Tema, Takoradi, and Kumasi, and there is a hotel at Akosombo overlooking Lake Volta.

Trade unions. The trade-union movement played a role in the struggle for self-government, and after independence the government, no doubt recognizing the importance of the movement as a political force, sought to make it a more direct instrument of policy. All trade unions in the country were brought under the authority of the Trade Union Congress, which was virtually an integral part of the government; this development curtailed the freedom of workers to bargain with employers and the government. After the fall of the Nkrumah government, the monopoly of the Trade Union Congress was abolished and other unions were able to function. In 1972, however, the Trade Union Congress was revived, but the military government in 1982 once again suppressed its activity.

Transportation. The principal means of transport, in order of importance, are motor vehicles, railways, and aircraft. Animals are scarcely used except in the extreme north, where horses and donkeys are sometimes employed. Ghanaians are inveterate travellers, and all available forms of transport are well patronized for social as well as business purposes.

Roads and railways. The density of roads and railways is much greater in the southern part of the country than in the north, and even in the south the cocoa-growing areas and the coastal zone tend to be favoured at the expense of other parts. The country has about 32,000 miles of roads, but only about one-quarter are paved. With foreign aid, rehabilitation of the road network was undertaken in the mid-1980s.

Rail transport was introduced in the early 20th century. The rail system forms a triangle joining Sekondi-Takoradi,

Cocoa exports

Rail transport

Kumasi, and Accra. In addition, a central line runs from Huni Valley, on the Takoradi–Kumasi line, to Kade in the centre of the triangle, and an extension joins Achiasi on this central line with Kotoku on the Accra–Kumasi line. The port of Tema is also linked to the system by a short extension running from Achimota, near Accra. The Takoradi–Kumasi line is also joined by two other branch lines, one running from Tarkwa out to the gold-mining town of Prestea and the other running from Dunkwa to the bauxite-mining town of Awaso.

Apart from the fact that its length is limited, rail transport is much less popular than road transport. Railways are primarily used for the transport of freight, especially minerals and logs, although even this has declined since the early 1970s as the result of deteriorating facilities.

The road system

Motor transport, now widespread and popular, was introduced in the towns about 1912 and spread quickly to the cocoa-producing areas. While the railways are owned by the state, motor transport is almost entirely in private hands. The state operates municipal bus services and express coach and freight services between the larger towns.

The Ghana Highway Authority oversees road maintenance and improvement. Road quality ranges from first-class paved (asphalt-surfaced) roads to third-class unsurfaced roads. First-class roads run between the large urban centres; they include the coastal Accra–Sekondi–Takoradi–Axim road; the Accra–Kumasi road, which continues northward to Tamale; and the Accra–Ho, Accra–Keta, Cape Coast–Kumasi, and Sekondi–Takoradi–Kumasi roads. A concrete-surfaced highway, with two lanes in each direction, runs from Accra to Tema. Second-class roads are narrower than first-class roads and have a base of swish (sun-dried earth) rather than quarried stone.

The creation of Lake Volta occasioned an interruption on the Kumasi–Tamale road, where the Yeji ferry, formerly only a few yards wide, became a crossing of almost seven miles. A number of other ferries across the Volta have completely disappeared.

Air transport. Small airports located at Takoradi, Kumasi, Sunyani, and Tamale are used solely for domestic services, while the Kotoka International Airport at Accra handles both domestic and international flights. The Accra runway is long enough to accommodate large jet aircraft, and the airport has a large terminal building. Domestic air services are operated by a state-owned corporation, Ghana Airways, which also operates a western African service linking the coastal states as well as an international service to the Middle East, Europe, and the United Kingdom. While air transport is popular in Ghana, the maintenance of the national airways is costly and requires a large annual governmental subsidy.

Water transport. The importance of sea transport has dwindled with the expansion of air services. A strike by seagoing officers in 1980 further undermined the nation's sea transport. Most goods entering and leaving the country, however, are carried by sea. There are two modern harbours, Takoradi (opened in 1928) and Tema (opened in 1961). Takoradi specializes in exporting timber, manganese, and bauxite, while Tema specializes in cocoa. Both ports also handle passengers. In terms of tonnage, Tema and Takoradi handle about equal amounts of cargo. The national shipping company, the Black Star Line, Ltd. was plagued by debts, obsolete vessels, and labour disputes, and management was turned over to a West German concern. The line was renationalized by the military government in 1982. Ships from many other countries also use Ghanaian ports; traffic is mostly with Europe, the United States, and the Far East. The Ghana Railway and Ports Authority is responsible for the country's port operations under the Ministry of Transport and Communications.

Launch service on Lake Volta has been expanded. A launch service is also maintained on the lower reaches of the Volta between Ada and Amedika.

ADMINISTRATIVE AND SOCIAL CONDITIONS

Government. The constitution of 1979 provided for a unicameral parliamentary form of government with a president as head of state and a vice president. The president was elected for a term of four years (with the possibility of reelection for one further term) by universal adult suffrage. The Parliament sat in Accra and constituted the legislature.

The executive branch

Flight lieut. Jerry Rawlings led a military coup in December 1981 and became the head of state as chairman of the Provisional National Defense Council (PNDC). The Parliament was disbanded and political parties were prohibited. In January 1983 the PNDC consisted of four members in addition to Rawlings. The appointed Cabinet included 22 members.

Apart from Greater Accra, Ghana is divided into eight regions—Ashanti, Brong-Ahafo, Central, Eastern, Northern, Upper, Volta, and Western. After 1972, when the constitution was suspended, each region was administered by a regional commissioner, who was an army officer. The constitution of 1979 revived the local, district, and regional councils, but the military government in 1982 appointed a regional secretary over the eight regions and the capital region and suspended local councils.

Justice. The judicial system is based chiefly on the English model, but Ghanaian customary law is recognized as well as English common law. The administration of justice is handled by various courts divided into two groups: the superior courts, consisting of the Supreme Court, the Court of Appeal and the High Court; and inferior courts, consisting, in descending order, of the circuit courts, the district courts, and other courts provided by law, such as the juvenile courts. After the military government took control, the Supreme Court was abolished, and the Court of Appeal, headed by a chief justice, became the highest court in Ghana. The constitution of 1979 restored the Supreme Court as the highest court in Ghana, and the Rawlings government retained it as the final court of appeal. A special tribunal investigates corruption. In 1982 the PNDC established a special military tribunal to hear cases against members of the armed forces and people's tribunals designated to handle crimes of alleged corruption and abuse of public office.

The adjudicating authorities in chieftaincy and purely traditional matters are the regional and national houses of chiefs. Appeals from decisions of the National House of Chiefs are made directly to the Supreme Court.

Education. Ghana has one of the best developed educational systems in tropical Africa, but the cost is high. In April 1974 the government began implementation of a new educational system. It consisted of a pre-primary cycle for ages four to six; a basic first cycle, including six years of primary education and three years of junior secondary; and a second cycle of variable length. The second cycle leads to secondary vocational or commercial programs or to a senior secondary course preparing students for university studies.

The first cycle is free and compulsory; for the first three years education is to be in the predominant local language, with provision for education in at least one other Ghanaian language and English, the latter to be the language of instruction from the fourth year of the primary cycle.

The universities

Teacher training and technical education are approximately equivalent to secondary education, though they tend to attract pupils who are not aiming at university careers. The Tarkwa School of Mines offers a three-year diploma course in mining and related subjects.

University education is provided at three institutions: the University of Ghana, at Legon, near Accra; the University of Science and Technology at Kumasi; and the University of Cape Coast. Until 1971 university education was free for all qualified Ghanaians, but in the early 1970s a scheme was introduced to enable students to meet part of the cost themselves.

The enrollment in all schools, especially in secondary schools, has soared dramatically since Ghana achieved self-government. There are a number of private schools at both elementary and secondary levels.

Health and welfare. Major health problems are communicable diseases, poor sanitation, and poor nutrition. The main emphasis of government health policy is on improved public health, and since independence many improvements have been made in nutrition and in maternal and child care. Many of the endemic diseases, such as malaria, pneumonia, and diseases of the gastroenteritis group, which took a heavy toll of life, have been brought under a measure of control as a result of improved hygiene, better drugs, and education. The government's public health programs, however, have not significantly reduced infant mortality or increased life expectancy.

There are hospitals and clinics provided by the government and by various Christian missions in most parts of the country. Supplementary services consist of health centres, dispensaries, and dressing stations. Considerable progress has been made in the quantity and quality of health facilities and medical personnel, but rapid population growth continues to impose great pressures on the available facilities. In addition to the large number of doctors in the public service, many private practitioners operate their own clinics and hospitals. Registered doctors and dentists are supported by a paramedical staff of nurses, midwives, and pharmacists, as well as by auxiliaries. There is also a government-sponsored pension plan.

Government programs of rural community development are assisted by village improvement projects undertaken with the participation of the residents. Welfare and economic aspects outside urban areas are handled by the national government. In the urban areas, welfare services concentrate on casework, probation work, youth activities, and guidance through voluntary organizations.

Housing. With the rapid growth of population and the movement of large numbers of people from the rural to urban areas, housing has become an acute problem, especially in the large cities where the problem is both quantitative and qualitative. In the rural areas the problem is mainly qualitative. There is distinct overcrowding in the urban areas, where the number of persons per house is about twice that in rural areas. Most housing is provided by private individuals, and the main role of the Department of Works and Housing is to supplement these efforts and to meet such special needs as the provision of low-cost housing and suitable local building materials.

Wages and cost of living. Although there is a minimum wage for workers, the gap in wages between the lowest paid and well-paid workers is still wide. This disparity, coupled with rising living costs, and instability in the national currency imposes severe hardships on a large section of the working population. The government is trying to lower the cost of living not only by increasing the supply of locally produced food staples but also by controlling the prices of other essential goods.

Society. Ghanaian society is without sharp class distinctions. Insofar as traditional authority is based on a system of hereditary chieftaincy, it is possible to speak of aristocratic classes within the various tribal groups, but the institution of chieftaincy is essentially democratic in operation and the authority of chiefs is broadly based.

Another important social characteristic is that land is usually owned by families, militating against the emergence of a small and powerful landed class wielding economic control over a landless class. These inherent egalitarian tendencies of the society have been further heightened by economic and social mobility, depending on education and individual enterprise.

CULTURAL LIFE

The cultural milieu. Ghana has a rich indigenous culture marked by great regional variety. Culturally, the peoples of Ghana have many affinities with their French-speaking neighbours, but each tribal group has distinctive cultural attributes. In all parts of the country the cultural heritage is closely linked with religion and the institution of chieftaincy. Various festivals and rites are centred on chieftaincy and the family and are occasioned by such events as harvest, marriage, birth, puberty, and death and funerals.

The arts. Ghana's arts include dance and music, plastic art (especially pottery and wood carving), gold- and silverwork, and textiles, most notably the richly coloured, handwoven kente cloth of the Akan and Ewe.

Despite the country's wealth in traditional art forms, indigenous art is in keen competition with various art forms of foreign origin, especially in those areas in which the end product is intended for practical household or personal

use, such as pottery, carving, gold- and silversmithing, and weaving. Consequently, only the unique and most indispensable of these forms have managed to survive without special public support or patronage. The increased national self-consciousness generated in Ghana as in other African countries by the independence movement, however, has been instrumental in fostering and popularizing many art forms. Another and equally important factor has been the government's efforts to promote tourism.

Cultural institutions. Apart from small indigenous groups of craftsmen who provide for the needs of the various chiefs' stools and skins throughout the country— a stool is the traditional symbol of office for chiefs in southern Ghana, and a skin is the equivalent symbol in the north—there are few properly established cultural institutions. The most outstanding are the National Cultural Centre, based in Kumasi, and the Arts Council of Ghana, based in Accra and with branches throughout the country. The National Cultural Centre is primarily concerned with the cultural heritage of Ashanti, while the Arts Council is a nationwide organization concerned both with the preservation of indigenous Ghanaian culture in all of its forms and with its development and improvement in the light of contemporary local and world trends. Dance, music, drama, painting, and sculpture all come within the purview of the council.

A third cultural institution is the Ghana Museum and Monuments Board, based in Accra. The board has an ethnological museum and a science museum in Accra and is responsible for the care and maintenance of buildings and relics of historical importance, such as the forts and castles, and for the preservation of important art treasures throughout the country. The forts, built by various European powers, mostly between the 14th and 18th centuries, are all, except the Kumasi fort (1897), located on the coast. The oldest fort, São Jorge da Mina, at Elmina, was built by the Portuguese in 1482. For statistical data, see the "Britannica World Data" section in the current *Britannica Book of the Year.* (E.A.B./Ed.)

History

PREHISTORIC ERA

As elsewhere in Africa, the climate of Ghana varied during the Pleistocene Epoch. With greater rainfall, the forest spread northward and man retreated toward the Sahara; when rainfall diminished, man occupied even the present forest. Correlations with European chronology are established by raised beaches.

Apart from some pebble tools from high river terraces, the first industry is Late Chellean in the southeast, in middle river gravels corresponding to the 74-foot beach. In the succeeding pluvial era, the Acheulean culture is lacking save from the extreme north.

With increases in aridity, man reappeared, bringing Late Acheulean and Sangoan cultures, probably successively. He moved along the Togo mountain range from the Niger River. Sangoan tools abound in Transvolta and around Accra and extend to Kumasi; the west remained forest and was rarely visited. Late Acheulean is associated with the 46-foot beach and the lower terraces and a developed Sangoan with the 26-foot beach.

The Sangoan culture waned in the Gamblian pluvial era. At its close there appears a Lupemban culture, probably from the desiccating Sahara; it occurs in basal gravels of valleys carved during the preceding pluvial period. In central Ghana its tools are shapely, near the coast crude and formless.

Middle Stone Age traditions lingered into the succeeding subpluvial era. Thereafter excavations at Legon yielded quartz microliths made on small pebbles. Upcountry these occur on silt terraces deposited in the preceding wet phase as far as the Niger. This culture is independent of the Saharan Mesolithic.

The latest Mesolithic Age has stone hoes, quartz beads, and other Congo types; pottery seems absent. This stage dates to the post-Flandrian marine regression (end of 2nd millennium BC?).

Several Neolithic cultures seem identifiable. They con-

(margin notes: Rural community development; Egalitarian tendencies)

Neolithic cultures

tain polished axes and usually coarse pottery. The most distinctive appears around Kintampo and in the Accra plains; it had clay houses, Saharan chert microliths, shale arm rings, and scored terra-cottas like flattened cigars. A Neolithic culture more in Mesolithic tradition was excavated near Abetifi.

Evidence lacks for the introduction of iron. Polished stone was commonly used until the 16th century, especially in the forest. Trade in greenstone for ax manufacture flourished. In Transvolta and the west greenstone hoes are common. No satisfactory chronology has been established, nor can existing tribes be identified before the 17th century. Of excavated sites, Nsuta, with decorated pottery and bobbin beads, should be early medieval; Sekondi village and cemetery, with fine pottery, stone axes, and quartz and shell beads, lasted until Portuguese times. In the north heavily decorated pottery continued later on open sites and mounds indicating clay houses. Associated European imports are unknown before the 17th century.   (O.D.)

EARLY TRADITIONS

The modern state of Ghana is named after the ancient African empire that flourished until the 13th century and was situated close to the Sahara in the western Sudan. The centre of ancient Ghana lay about 500 miles to the northwest of the nearest part of the modern state, and it is tolerably certain that no part of the latter lay within its borders. The claim that an appreciable proportion of modern Ghana's people derived from emigrants from the ancient empire cannot be unequivocally substantiated with the evidence at present available. Written sources related only to the period since European contact with the Gold Coast—*i.e.,* modern Ghana—began in the 15th century, or to Muslim contacts with ancient Ghana from about the 8th to the 13th century. Many modern Ghanaian peoples possess well-preserved oral traditions, but even though some of these may reach as far back as the 14th century, it is after the final disappearance of ancient Ghana, and such very early traditions often present considerable problems of interpretation. Little progress has so far been made in linking the surviving traditions with the available archaeological evidence.

Trade routes of Islām. More archaeological research, especially into the Iron Age, will undoubtedly do much toward resolving present uncertainties about the early history of modern Ghana, but for the moment little more can be said than that the traditions of many of the states into which the country was divided before it came under British rule refer to their people having immigrated within the last 600 years either from the north or northwest or from the east or northeast. Such traditions link up with other evidence to suggest that the area which is now Ghana was for many centuries a meeting place for two great streams of western African history. Ultimately these streams stemmed from the existence of two major trans-Saharan routes, a western one linking the headwaters of the Niger and Sénégal rivers to Morocco and a more central one linking the region between the Niger bend and Lake Chad with Tunisia and Tripoli. At the end of the western route arose the great Mande states, notably ancient Ghana and Mali, while around the more easterly termini developed Songhai, the Hausa states, and Bornu. There is evidence that parts of modern Ghana north of the forest were being reached by Mande traders (seeking gold dust) by the 14th century, and by Hausa merchants (desiring kola nuts) by the 16th century. In this way the inhabitants of what is now Ghana were influenced by the new wealth and cross-fertilization of ideas that arose in the great empires of the western Sudan following the development of Islāmic civilization in northern Africa.

Migrations. It is against this background that the traditions of origin of the Ghanaian states must be viewed. It would seem that the first states of the Akan-speaking peoples who now inhabit most of the forest and coastlands were founded, c. the 13th century, by the settlement just north of the forest of migrants coming from the direction of Mande; that the dominant states of northern Ghana, Dagomba, Mamprussi, and their satellites were established by the 15th century by invaders from the Hausa region;

Trans-Saharan routes

that a little later the founders of the Ga and Ewe states of the southeast began to arrive from what is now Nigeria by a more southerly route; and that Gonja, in the centre, was created by Mande conquerors about the beginning of the 17th century.

Tradition tends to present these migrations as movements of whole peoples. In certain instances, for example, Dagomba, Mamprussi, and Gonja, it can be shown that the traditions relate in fact to comparatively small bands of invaders who used military and political techniques acquired farther north to impose their rule on already established populations whose own organization was based more on community of kin than on allegiance to political sovereigns. It is probable that the first Akan states—*e.g.,* such influential states as Bono and Banda north of the forest or the smaller states founded on the coast by migration down the Volta River—were also established in this way. The later Akan infiltration into the forest, which then was probably sparsely inhabited, and the Ga and Ewe settlement of the southeast may have been more of mass movements, though in the latter case it is known that the immigrants met and absorbed earlier inhabitants.

CONTACT WITH EUROPE AND ITS EFFECTS

A revolution in Ghanaian history was initiated by the establishment of direct sea trade with Europe following the discovery of the coast by Portuguese mariners in 1471. Initially Europe's main interest in the country was as a source of gold, a commodity that was readily available at the coast in exchange for such European exports as cloth, hardware, beads, metals, spirits, arms, and ammunition. This gave rise to the name Gold Coast, by which the country was to be known until 1957. In an attempt to preserve a monopoly of the trade, the Portuguese initiated the practice of erecting stone fortresses (Elmina Castle dating from 1482 was the first) on the coast on sites leased from the native states. In the 17th century the Portuguese monopoly, already considerably eroded, gave way completely when traders from the Netherlands, England, Denmark, Sweden, and Prussia—Protestant seapowers antagonistic to Iberian imperial pretensions—discovered that the commercial relations developed with the Gold Coast states could be adapted to the export of slaves, then in rapidly increasing demand for the American plantations, as well as of gold. By the mid-18th century the coastal scene was dominated by the presence of about 40 forts controlled by Dutch, British, or Danish merchants.

The presence of these permanent European bases on the coast had far-reaching consequences. The new centres of trade thus established were much more accessible than were the Sudanese emporia, and this, coupled with the greater capacity of efficiency of the sea-borne trade compared with the ancient overland routes, gradually brought about the reversal of the direction of the trade flow. The new wealth, tools and arms, techniques and ideas introduced through close contact with Europeans initiated political and social as well as economic changes. The states north of the forest, hitherto the wealthiest and most powerful, declined in the face of new combinations farther south. At the end of the 17th century the Akan state of Akwamu created an empire that, stretching from the central Gold Coast eastward to Dahomey, sought to control the trade roads to the coast of the whole eastern Gold Coast. The Akwamu empire was short-lived, but its example soon stimulated a union of the Ashanti states of the central forest, which union, after establishing its dominance over other neighbouring Akan states, expanded north of the forest to conquer Bono, Banda, Gonja, and Dagomba.

The Ashanti states

Having thus engrossed almost the whole of the area that served as a market and source of supply for the coastal trade, Ashanti turned toward the coastlands. There traditional ways of life were being increasingly modified by contact with Europeans and their trade, and when, beginning in the latter part of the 18th century, Ashanti armies began to invade the coastal states, their peoples tended to look for leadership and protection to the European traders in the forts. But between 1804 and 1814 the Danes, English, and Dutch had each in turn outlawed their slave trades, and the gold trade was declining. The political uncertainty following the Ashanti invasions impeded the development of new trades, and in these circumstances the mutually suspicious European interests were not always keen to embark on new political responsibilities. However, during 1830–44, under the outstanding leadership of George Maclean, the British merchants began to assume an informal protectorate over the Fanti states, much to the commercial benefit of both parties. As a result of this the British Colonial Office finally agreed to take over the British forts, and in 1850 it was able to buy out the Danes. However, trade declined under the new regime, which was averse to assuming formal control over the territory influenced from the forts, and in the 1860s, as a result of this influence and of the growth, from the 1820s onward, of Christian missionary education, the Fanti states attempted to organize a European-style confederacy. Further Ashanti incursions and the final evacuation of the coast by the Dutch (1872) combined to reverse this British policy, and in 1874 a punitive expedition destroyed Kumasi, the Ashanti capital, and the Gold Coast was declared a British colony.

Colonial period. French and German activity in adjacent territories and the demand of British mining and commercial interests for better protection led to a further active period of British policy during 1895–1901, during which Ashanti was finally conquered and its northern hinterland formed into a British protectorate. The 50 years of British rule that followed went far toward welding into one state the three elements of the territory, the colonies of the Gold Coast and Ashanti and the protectorate of the Northern Territories, to which after World War I was added a fourth, under mandate from the League of Nations, the western part of former German Togoland. But this was hardly the result of deliberate policy. The ever increasing assimilation of European ways by the people on the Gold Coast had already made possible there the introduction of such organs of government as a legislative council (1850) and a supreme court (1853), but for many years Ashanti and the Northern Territories remained the sole responsibility of the governor, whose officials were from the 1920s onward encouraged to work with and through the authorities of the indigenous states. Attempts to introduce similar elements of indirect rule in the Gold Coast served mainly to stimulate a nationalist opposition among the educated professional classes, especially in the growing towns, which aimed at converting the legislative council into a fully responsible parliament.

What really brought the country together was the great development of its economy following the introduction and rapid expansion of cocoa-growing by local farmers in the forest. By the 1920s the Gold Coast, while continuing to export some gold, was producing more than half of the world's supply of cocoa; timber and manganese later became additional exports of note. With the wealth created by this great increase of trade, it was possible to provide modern transport facilities—harbours, railways, roads—and social services, especially education (to the university level), all of which tended toward the conversion of the traditional social order, of groups bound together by kinship, into one in which individuals were linked principally by economic ties.

Independence. Political advancement tended to lag behind economic and social development, especially in the south (for the role of the Northern Territories was principally the supply of cheap labour for the Gold Coast and Ashanti). World War II and its aftermath tended to accentuate this lag, and in 1948 there were riots in the larger towns. The Watson Commission of Inquiry reported that the Burns constitution of 1946, which had granted Africans a majority in the legislative council, was "outmoded at birth." An all-African committee under Justice (later Sir Henley) Coussey was appointed to work out a new constitution in which some executive power would be transferred to African ministers responsible to an African assembly, but, under the leadership of Kwame Nkrumah, the new Convention People's Party (CPP) arose. This demanded immediate self-government for the country and entered on measures of "positive action" to enforce its will on the government. In 1952 Nkrumah became prime

minister. During the next five years the Gold Coast passed rapidly through a period of transition in which government was transferred by stages to an all-African Cabinet responsible to a national assembly elected by adult suffrage. On December 13, 1956, following a plebiscite held under UN auspices, the British Togoland trust territory was integrated with the Gold Coast. Securing more than 70 percent of the seats in the assembly at each of the general elections of 1954 and 1956, Nkrumah and his CPP government were able in 1957 to obtain the recognition of their country, renamed Ghana, as an independent self-governing member of the Commonwealth and a member of the UN.

Nkrumah saw independent Ghana as a spearhead for the liberation of the rest of Africa from colonial rule and the establishment of a Socialist African unity under his leadership. After the establishment of a republic in 1960, the state became identified with a single political party (the CPP), wih Nkrumah, as life president of both, taking ever more power for himself. On the pan-African front Nkrumah's messianism was increasingly challenged by other, often more stable, leaders of an ever-growing number of independent states. By 1966 his dream of African Socialism was foundering under haphazard and corrupt administration, massive foreign debts, and declining living standards. In February, while he was in Peking, army and police leaders rose against him, and his regime was replaced by a National Liberation Council chaired by Lieut. Gen. Joseph A. Ankrah. In April 1969 Brig. A.A. Afrifa succeeded to the chair. A complete overhaul of the administration and judiciary followed, with the aim of restoring democratic government, and conservative financial policies were initiated.

On August 22, 1969, the Constituent Assembly enacted and promulgated the constitution of the Second Ghanaian Republic, and the National Liberation Council (NLC) became a provisional caretaker government pending the general elections. The result of the elections, held on August 29, was an overwhelming victory for Kofi Busia's Progress Party (PP). On September 3 Busia was sworn in as prime minister and a three-man presidential commission was appointed. On September 30 the NLC was dissolved, to be followed in August 1970 by the dissolution of the presidential committee. On August 31, 1970, former chief justice Edward Akufo-Addo was elected as the first civilian president since the ending of military rule.　　(J.D.F.)

On January 13, 1972, the armed forces overthrew the government of Ghana in a bloodless coup. The constitution was suspended, the office of the presidency abolished, and the National Assembly dissolved. The military leaders then established a National Redemption Council (NRC) as the main organ of government. At its formation, the membership of the NRC was tribally balanced, with four Akan, four Ewe, two Ga, and two Northern members. A civilian National Advisory Council later was established.

After an abortive countercoup in July 1972 the government imposed the retroactive Subversion Decree. Under the authority of a military tribunal, the death penalty could be exacted for 10 offenses including subversive political activity, robbery, theft of specified items, and damage to public property. In 1973 the decree was extended to include profiteering, and another decree was promulgated, prohibiting the spreading of rumours. The constitution of 1979 restored fundamental civil liberties, including freedom of press, political assembly, and speech.

After the military coup of 1972 the formerly lively political life of Ghana was brought under tight control. All political parties in existence before January 13, 1972, were proscribed, and the law prohibiting a one-party state was repealed. Members of the Progress Party, which had supported the former prime minister, were imprisoned for one year, and public meetings were prohibited. Political parties were again allowed in 1979. Five major parties emerged; the People's National Party, under Hilla Limann, was the dominant coalition.

In October 1975, however, the NRC was superseded as the highest legislative and administrative organ by a seven-member Supreme Military Council (SMC); at the same time, the NRC was reorganized to include the members of

Kwame Nkrumah and the Convention People's Party

The coup of 1972

Subversion Decree

the smc and certain other civilian and military members. The military retained control over both councils. Civilian rule, under the auspices of the military, was restored between 1979 and 1981, with Hilla Limann as president. A constitution was drafted in 1978 and enacted in 1979 to supersede the constitution of 1969. The new constitution, however, was short-lived; it was suspended in 1982 by

a former flight lieutenant, Jerry Rawlings, who came to power in another military coup on December 31, 1981. The Ghanaian Parliament was dismissed, and all executive and legislative decisions were to be made by Rawlings' Provisional National Defense Council. For current political history, see the annual issues of the *Britannica Book of the Year*. (Ed.)

GUINEA

The Republic of Guinea (République de Guinée) is an independent nation of western Africa. It is bordered by the Atlantic Ocean to the west; by Guinea-Bissau, Senegal, and Mali to the north and east; by the Ivory Coast to the southeast; and by Liberia and Sierra Leone to the south. Its area of 94,926 square miles (245,857 square kilometres) supports a largely rural population. The national capital of Conakry is the country's main port.

Physical and human geography

THE LAND

Relief. There are four geographic regions; Lower Guinea, the Fouta Djallon, Upper Guinea, and the Forest Region. Lower Guinea includes the coast and coastal plain. The irregular coast is marked by drowned river valleys that form inlets and tidal estuaries and by offshore islands. There are few lagoons or sandbars, but the estuaries are muddy and lined with mangrove swamps.

Immediately inland the gently rolling coastal plain rises to the east, being broken by rocky spurs of the Fouta Djallon highlands in the north at Cape Verga and in the south at the Kaloum Peninsula. Between 30 and 50 miles wide, the plain is wider in the south than the north. Its base rocks of granite and gneiss (coarse-grained rock containing bands of minerals) are covered with laterite (red soil with a high content of iron oxides and aluminum hydroxide) and sandstone gravel.

The Fouta Djallon highlands rise sharply from the coastal plain in a series of abrupt faults. More than 5,000 square miles of the highlands' total extent of 30,000 square miles lie above 3,000 feet (9,150 metres). The enormous sandstone block is made up of level plateaus broken by deeply incised valleys and dotted with dykes or peaks of igneous rock, such as the Kakoulima Massif, which attains 3,273 feet (998 metres) northeast of Conakry. The highest point in the highlands, Mt. Loura, rises to 4,970 feet near the town of Mali in the north.

Upper Guinea is composed of the Niger Plains, which slope northeastward toward the Sahara. The flat relief is broken by rounded granite hills and outliers of the Fouta Djallon. Composed of granite, gneiss, schist (crystalline rock), and quartzite, the region has an average elevation of about 1,000 feet.

The Forest Region, or Guinea Highlands, is an isolated area of hills in the country's southeastern corner. The region attains 5,747 feet at Mt. Nimba, which rises at the borders of Guinea, Liberia, and the Ivory Coast. The area is composed of the same rocks as those of Upper Guinea.

Three major western African rivers

Drainage and soils. The Fouta Djallon is the source of western Africa's three major rivers. The Niger River and several tributaries, including the Tinkisso, Milo, and Sankarani, rise in the highlands and flow in a general northeasterly direction across Upper Guinea to Mali. The Bafing and Bakoy rivers, headwaters of the Sénégal River, flow northward into Mali before uniting to form the main river. The Gambia River flows northwestward before crossing Senegal and Gambia.

The Fouta Djallon also gives rise to numerous smaller rivers, such as the Fatala, Konkouré, and Kolenté, which flow westward across the coastal plain to enter the Atlantic. The Forest Region generally drains to the southwest through Sierra Leone and Liberia. The St. Paul River enters the Atlantic at Monrovia, Liberia, and the Moa River has its mouth at Sulima, Sierra Leone.

The most common soils are formed of hydrated aluminum silicates and other materials that often concretize

into hard iron-rich conglomerates called laterites. In the northeast, sandy brown soils predominate, while along the coast black, heavy clay soils accumulate in the backwaters. There are alluvial soils along the major rivers. Soil conservation is extremely important because most soils are thin, and the heavy rainfall causes much erosion.

Climate. The average temperature of Guinea is more than 68° F (20° C). There are two alternating seasons—a dry season (November through March) and a wet season (April through October). The low-pressure zone caused by the summer solstice and its rapidly rising humid air brings the June rains. As the low-pressure area shifts southward in November, the hot, dry wind known as the harmattan blows southwest off the Sahara.

On the coast a period of six months of dry weather is followed by six months of rain. The average rainfall at Conakry is 170 inches (4,318 millimetres) a year, and annual temperatures average about 81° F (27° C). In the Fouta Djallon, January diurnal temperatures range between 86° F and 95° F (30° C and 35° C), while evening temperatures dip to 50° F (10° C). Rainfall varies between 91 and 63 inches annually, and the average annual temperature is about 77° F (25° C).

In Upper Guinea rainfall drops to about 59 inches a year. During the dry season temperatures of more than 104° F (40° C) are common in the northeast. The drying harmattan winds blow hot in the day, but the night can be uncomfortably cool. In the Forest Region at Macenta, there may be 106 inches of rain annually. Only the month of January is relatively dry, with less than one inch of precipitation. At low altitudes, temperatures resemble those of the coastal areas.

Plant and animal life. The coast is fringed with mangrove trees, and the coastal plain supports stands of oil palms. The Fouta Djallon is mostly open, with trees growing along the wider stream valleys. In Upper Guinea, the savanna grassland is comprised of several species of tall grasses that reach heights of five to 10 feet during the rainy season. Deciduous trees grow in scattered clumps, but few have commercial value; baobab and shea trees furnish fruit and oil. The Forest Region contains several extensive patches of rainforest, with teak, mahogany, and ebony trees; agriculture, however, has diminished the forests and resulted in a shift largely toward open savanna.

Guinea is not rich in African big game. Baboons, a variety of monkeys, and hyenas are common, while an occasional wild boar, several types of antelope, and a rare leopard may be sighted. Two or three small elephant herds exist in the savanna woodlands; several chimpanzee families are still found in the Fouta Djallon valleys; and lions have been noted in the northeast. The hippopotamus and manatee inhabit the rivers of both Lower and Upper Guinea. Poisonous snakes include mambas, vipers, and cobras, along with pythons and a variety of harmless snakes. Crocodiles and several varieties of fish are found in most rivers.

Vanishing animal life

Settlement patterns. In the Fouta Djallon, the Fulani (Fulbe or Peul) live in small hillside hamlets of 75 to 95 persons each, and the lower classes occupy the valleys. In the heart of the highlands the countryside is thickly settled with hamlets every few miles, while in the east the land is less settled.

In Lower Guinea, villages are grouped together at the bases of hills, in the open plain, or in a valley floor. Village solidarity is more marked in this area than in the highlands, and each village may contain between 100 and 200 people.

The majority of the Malinke (Mandingo) people of Upper Guinea live in moderately large villages of about 1,000

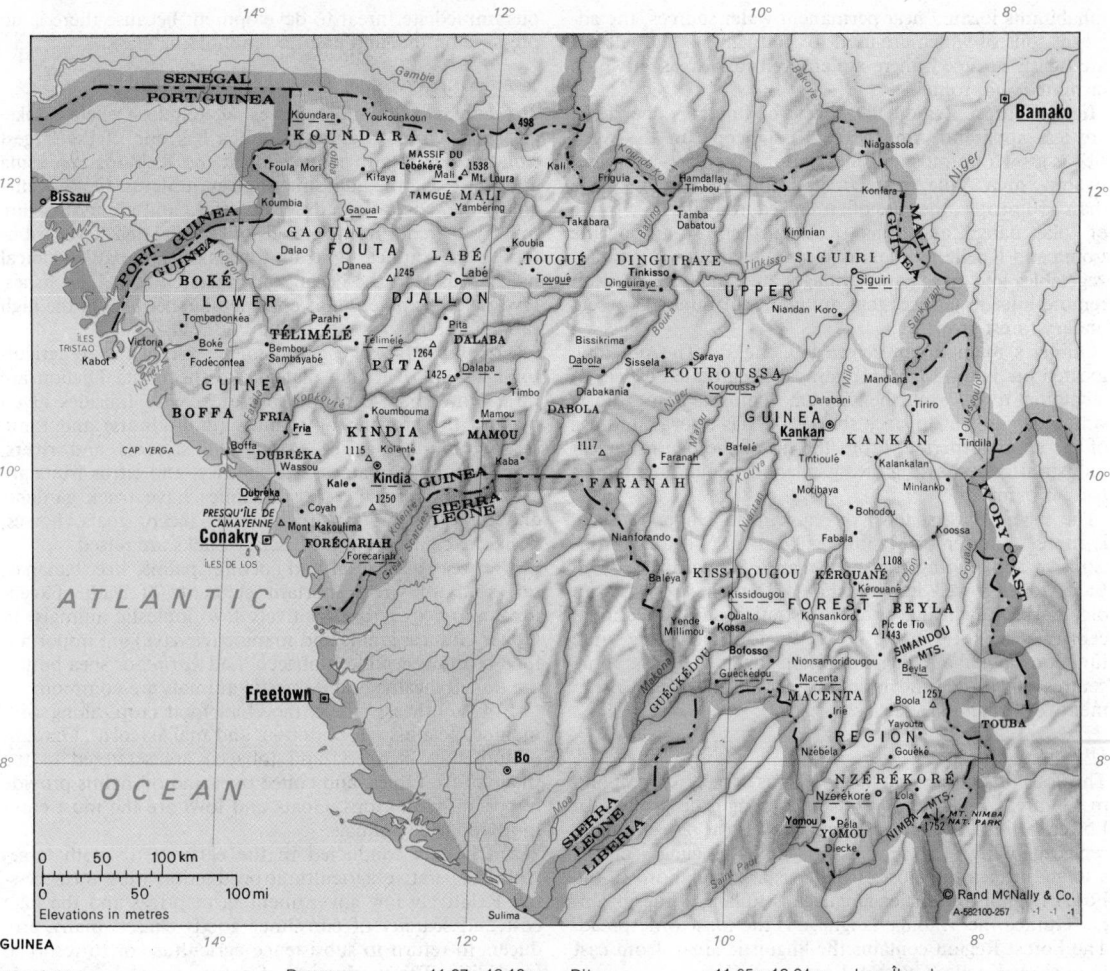

GUINEA

MAP INDEX

Political subdivisions

Beyla	8·55n	8·25w
Boffa	10·20n	14·00w
Boké	11·00n	14·20w
Conakry	9·31n	13·43w
Dabola	10·36n	11·07w
Dalaba	10·45n	12·18w
Dinguiraye	11·30n	10·55w
Dubréka	9·48n	13·40w
Faranah	10·00n	10·50w
Forécariah	9·30n	13·15e
Fria	10·30n	13·40w
Gaoual	11·45n	13·12w
Guéckédou	8·40n	10·15w
Kankan	10·10n	9·15w
Kérouané	9·10n	8·50w
Kindia	10·00n	12·45w
Kissidougou	9·15n	9·55w
Koundara	12·25n	13·10w
Kouroussa	10·40n	9·55w
Labé	11·23n	12·07w
Macenta	8·30n	9·25w
Mali	12·05n	12·05w
Mamou	10·30n	12·00w
Nzérékoré	7·50n	8·45w
Pita	11·00n	12·45w
Siguiri	11·30n	9·15w
Télimélé	11·00n	13·30w
Tougué	11·28n	11·36w
Yomou	7·35n	9·10w

The name of a political subdivision if not shown on the map is the same as that of its capital city.

Cities and towns

Bafelé	10·09n	10·08w
Baléya	9·15n	10·29w
Bembou Sambayabé	10·55n	13·44w
Beyla	8·41n	8·37w
Bissikrima	10·51n	10·56w
Boffa	10·10n	14·02w
Bofosso	8·40n	9·42w
Bohodou	9·46n	9·04w
Boké	10·56n	14·18w
Boola	8·22n	8·43w
Conakry	9·31n	13·43w
Coyah	9·43n	13·23w
Dabola	10·45n	11·07w
Dalaba	10·42n	12·15w
Dalabani	10·28n	9·27w
Dalao	11·29n	13·40w

Danea	11·27n	13·12w
Diabakania	10·38n	10·58w
Diecke	7·21n	8·58w
Dinguiraye	11·18n	10·43w
Dubréka	9·48n	13·31w
Fabala	9·44n	9·05w
Faranah	10·02n	10·44w
Fodécontea	10·50n	14·22w
Forécariah	9·26n	13·06w
Foula Mori	12·10n	13·51w
Fria	10·27n	13·32w
Gaoual	11·45n	13·12w
Gouéké	8·02n	8·43w
Guéckédou	8·33n	10·09w
Irié	8·17n	9·11w
Kaba	10·09n	11·40w
Kabot	10·48n	14·57w
Kalankalan	10·07n	8·54w
Kale	9·55n	13·06w
Kankan	10·23n	9·18w
Kérouané	9·16n	9·01w
Kifaya	12·10n	13·04w
Kindia	10·04n	12·51w
Kintinian	11·36n	9·23w
Kissidougou	9·11n	10·06w
Kolenté	10·06n	12·37w
Konfara	11·55n	8·50w
Konsankoro	9·02n	9·00w
Koossa	9·32n	8·32w
Kossa	8·57n	10·05w
Koubia	11·35n	11·54w
Koumbia	11·48n	13·30w
Koumbouma	10·24n	12·56w
Koundara	12·29n	13·18w
Kouroussa	10·39n	9·53w
Labé	11·19n	12·17w
Lébékéré	12·07n	12·24w
Lola	7·48n	8·32w
Macenta	8·33n	9·28w
Mali	12·05n	12·18w
Mamou	10·23n	12·05w
Mandiana	10·38n	8·41w
Minianko	9·58n	8·22w
Moribaya	9·53n	9·33w
Niagassola	12·19n	9·07w
Niandan Koro	11·05n	9·15w
Nionforando	9·32n	10·31w
Nionsamori-dougou	8·43n	8·50w
Nzébéla	8·05n	9·06w
Nzérékoré	7·45n	8·49w
Oualto	9·01n	10·06w
Parahi	11·09n	13·07w
Péla	7·37n	9·07w

Pita	11·05n	12·24w
Saraya	10·46n	10·24w
Siguiri	11·25n	9·10w
Sissela	10·49n	10·37w
Takabara	11·50n	11·30w
Tamba Dabatou	11·48n	10·40w
Télimélé	10·54n	13·02w
Timbo	10·38n	11·50w
Tindila	10·16n	8·15w
Tinkisso	11·15n	10·37w
Tintioulé	10·13n	9·12w
Tiriro	10·27n	8·39w
Tombadonkéa	11·00n	14·23w
Tougué	11·27n	11·41w
Victoria	10·50n	14·33w
Wassou	10·02n	13·39w
Yambéring	11·49n	12·21w
Yayouta	8·11n	8·30w
Yende Millimou	8·53n	10·11w
Yomou	7·34n	9·16w

Physical features and points of interest

Atlantic Ocean	9·00n	14·00w
Bafing, *river*	12·15n	10·20w
Bouka, *river*	11·00n	10·50w
Camayenne, Presqu'île de (Kaloum, Presqu'île de) *peninsula*	9·33n	13·40w
Dion, *river*	10·12n	8·39w
Fatala, *river*	10·13n	14·00w
Forest Region, *physical region*	8·30n	8·35w
Fouta Djallon, *physical region*	11·15n	12·20w
Gouala, *river*	9·57n	8·10w
Îles Tristao, *islands*	10·53n	14·58w
Kakoulima, Mont, *mountain*	9·46n	13·27w
Kaloum, Presqu'île de, see Camayenne, Presqu'île de		
Kogon, *river*	11·09n	14·42w
Kolenté, *river*	9·15n	12·57w
Koliba, *river*	12·15n	13·46w
Konkouré, *river*	9·58n	13·42w
Koulountou, *river*	12·40n	13·30w
Kouya, *river*	10·09n	9·45w

Los, Îles de, *islands*	9·30n	13·48w
Loura, Mont, *mountain*	12·06n	12·17w
Lower Guinea, *physical region*	10·27n	13·33w
Mafou, *river*	10·32n	10·08w
Makona, *river*	8·16n	10·42w
Milo, *river*	11·04n	9·14w
Niantan, *river*	10·30n	10·26w
Niger, *river*	11·35n	8·45w
Nimba Mountains	7·30n	8·30w
Nunez, *river*	10·36n	14·40w
Ouassoulou, *river*	10·30n	8·07w
Sankarani, *river*	11·20n	8·20w
Simandou Mountains	9·00n	8·30w
Tamgué, Massif du, *mountains*	12·00n	12·18w
Tinkisso, *river*	11·21n	9·10w
Tio, Pic de, *mountain*	8·52n	8·54w
Upper Guinea, *physical region*	10·40n	9·50w
Verga, Cap, *cape*	10·12n	14·27w

inhabitants located near permanent water sources, the adjacent soils of which are used for cultivation. The villages are tightly grouped; there are empty brush areas in which farming is unprofitable.

In the Forest Region the effects of human occupation are less apparent. Among the Kissi people in the west, rice is grown on most hillsides and in every low-lying and swampy area. Villages are small and rarely contain more than 150 people; they are often tucked away inside a grove of kola, mango, and coffee trees. Further east among the Loma and Kpelle people, fire-cleared land is used to plant vegetables and rice. Larger villages are usually located on remote hillside terraces that are often surrounded by secondary forest growth.

Guinea's urban centres

Guinea's main urban centre is Conakry. The old city, located on Tumbo Island, retains the segregated aspect of a colonial town, while the Kaloum Peninsula community, which has grown up since the 1950s, has a few buildings of the colonial period. From the tip of the peninsula, an industrial zone has a growing salaried population that is truly urbanized.

The second largest town of Kankan, in Upper Guinea, is more a cluster of Malinke villages around an administrative and trading core area than a Westernized town. Labé, located well into the Fouta Djallon, serves as an old market town and an administrative and educational centre. Nzérékoré, in the Forest Region, serves the same functions as Labé. Other important towns are the trading centres of Kindia and Mamou and the industrial settlements of Fria and Boké.

THE PEOPLE

The four major geographical regions largely correspond to the areas inhabited by the major linguistic groups. In Lower Guinea the major language of Susu has gradually replaced many of the other indigenous languages and is a lingua franca for most of the coastal population. In the Fouta Djallon the major language is Fulani, while in Upper Guinea the Malinke language is the most widespread. The Forest Region contains the linguistic areas, from east to west, of Kpelle (Guerzé), Loma, and Kissi.

Eight official languages besides French are taught in the schools. They are Basari, Fulani, Kissi, Koniagi, Kpelle, Loma, Malinke, and Susu. All official texts are written in French and at least one of the indigenous languages, and all governmental personnel are required to have bilingual reading and writing ability.

All of Africa has been plagued by a proclivity on the part of Europeans to overemphasize distinctions between ethnic groups. Most definitions of what constitutes an ethnic group in Guinea are incomplete and subject to criticism because they often emphasize one criterion at the expense of others. The Fulani have come to dominate the Fouta Djallon culturally; the Malinke have widely influenced Upper Guinea and the northern Forest Region; and the Susu are dominant in Lower Guinea. In the Forest Region, however, the Kissi, Loma, and Kpelle each retain their own common historical and cultural identities.

Except for the diplomatic community and some expatriate teachers and technical advisers, there are few foreigners. The alien community also includes Lebanese and Syrian traders and a few Frenchmen engaged in plantation agriculture and technical occupations.

Religious affiliations

About three-quarters of the population is Muslim, and a small percentage of the population is nominally Christian, mostly Roman Catholic. Since 1967, all priests have been required to be either Guinean nationals or Africans. The remaining population is animist.

Immigration is minimal, but emigration—especially from the Fouta Djallon and Upper Guinea—is high. About one-sixth of the male population from these areas has migrated in search of work, leaving an imbalance of females. Emigration is directed toward the neighbouring countries of Sierra Leone, Senegal, Mali, the Ivory Coast, and Liberia.

The heaviest population concentration is in the Fouta Djallon. Conakry and the Kaloum Peninsula suffer from rapid population growth caused by a continuing exodus from the rural areas to the city.

Except for the Fouta Djallon, population poses no serious immediate threat to development because there is no pressure on the land and no landholding class.

THE ECONOMY

Resources. Bauxite reserves at Kindia-Debele, Boké, and Fria-Kimbo are vast. Guinea has one of the largest iron-ore deposits in the world, at the Kaloum Peninsula and in the Nimba and Simandou mountains. Gold occurs along the Niger and its tributaries, and diamonds are mined at Aredor in the gravels of the Makona River tributaries. The southeastern rain forests offer valuable tropical hardwoods, and the ocean and rivers contain food fishes. Hydroelectric potential is considerable because of the high rainfall and deep gorges of the Fouta Djallon.

Bauxite and diamonds

Agriculture, forestry, and fishing. Guinea is an agricultural nation. The high plateaus of the Fouta Djallon are little more than part-time pastures, with hillsides given over to the growing of peanuts (groundnuts) and fonio (a sorghum-like grain). Along the streams and rivers, rice, bananas, tomatoes, strawberries, and citrus fruits are grown commercially. Most families have truck gardens, and tsetse-resistant Ndama cattle, sheep, goats, horses, donkeys, chickens, and Muscovy ducks are raised.

In Lower Guinea, oil and coconut palms, rice, bananas, salt, and fish are important elements of trade. Except for poultry, there are relatively few domestic animals. In Upper Guinea, grains and manioc (cassava) are important food crops; vegetables, tobacco, and *karite,* or shea butter, are traded locally; and domestic animals are common.

In the southeast rice is the chief food crop, along with manioc, peanuts (groundnuts), and maize (corn). Gardens of tomatoes, peppers, and tobacco are scattered in the shade of fruit trees, and coffee trees and oil palms provide important cash crops. Goats and fowl are the most common domestic animals.

Experiments conducted in the early 1970s with large-scale cooperative agricultural production were unsuccessful. Relatively low government farm prices and the high cost and scarcity of consumer goods caused many producers to return to subsistence agriculture or to resort to smuggling. The production of coffee, formerly the major cash crop, declined. Rice output has grown, but the staple continues to be imported. Other cash crops, such as palm kernels, peanuts, pineapples, and citrus fruit, only began to be important in the 1970s.

Commercial fishing grew considerably with the introduction of Soviet-supplied trawlers and the development of several mixed state and foreign free enterprise fishing ventures in the late 1970s. Both riverine and marine traditional fishing, producing fresh, dried, and smoked fish for the local markets, remained important.

Forestry is hampered by the lack of transportation. The government-owned sawmill and plywood plant at Nzerekore and wood panelling plant at Seredou cannot function to capacity because neither area has sufficient forests to continue exploitation.

Industry. Guinea depends heavily upon mineral exports to maintain a favourable trade balance. The bauxite deposits at Fria, Kindia, and Sangaredi in the Boké region are exploited by an international consortium of private companies from the United States, France, the United Kingdom, Switzerland, and West Germany and the Guinea government, which owns half shares in the projects. Similarly mixed foreign and domestic plants produce the bauxite and alumina that provide more than nine-tenths of Guinea's export earnings. Boké, Fria, and Kindia-Debele are the main plants, supplemented by the Soviet-built plant at Dabola and another plant built with Swiss aid in the Tongue Mountains of the Fouta Djallon.

Mining and quarrying

The iron-ore deposits of the Nimba and Simandou mountains remained undeveloped in the early 1980s. Diamond mining at Aredor began in 1984, but gold production remained minimal.

Food-processing plants do not run at full capacity because agricultural production is insufficient and because black market smuggling limits the supply of raw products. Establishments include a fruit-juice factory at Kankan, a tea factory in Macenta, a palm-oil works at Kossa, and a peanut-oil works at Dabola. Government factories produce leather, shoes, matches, cigarettes, processed meat, textiles, and furniture. Semiprivate operations include the brewery in Conakry, a soup cannery, and several small-scale fruit-juice and plastics concerns.

In 1970 the hydroelectric station near Pita began to supply electricity to Pita, Labé, Dabola, and Mamou. The hydroelectric plant at Kale, backed by two diesel-powered thermal centres, supplies power to Conakry. There is a small hydroelectric station in Tinkisso; Fria has its own thermally produced electricity supply; and many regional towns have their own diesel-operated generators.

Finance and trade. Guinea has a nonconvertible currency; it is not tied to any foreign currency, and its value is dictated by the Guinean government. The military government that took power in 1984 began to reform the monetary and banking systems.

Administration of the economy. Private enterprise was legalized in 1979. Most of the larger foreign companies are local capital investments.

Government revenue is chiefly derived from mining concessions, import and export duties, excise taxes, a petroleum-products tax, and taxes on commercial transactions and production. There are also various other surtaxes, stamp duties, and registration fees. Business and other licenses and personal-property, building, dwelling, and vehicle taxes are handled by the regional administration. Taxes on salaries and wages contribute little revenue because few people are salaried and because most of the wage earners work within the government.

There is a serious shortage of trained personnel, and finances suffer from misappropriation, tax evasion, and smuggling. Many of the processing industries have been held back by inadequate supplies of raw materials. Internal production is not sufficiently high, in agriculture particularly, and there is a permanently deficient trade balance.

Transportation. Guinea's transportation system is largely based upon the road and railway from Conakry to Kankan. This forked axis is intersected at Mamou by a road north to Senegal. East of Kouroussa the main road branches northeastward through Siguiri to Bamako, Mali. The main road continues northeast of the railhead at Kankan to Sikasso, Mali. The regional centres, like pods strung out on a vine, lie along thin lines of communication that, in turn, radiate feeder routes.

The 411-mile railroad from Conakry to Kankan is a single-track metric line. In the early 1980s construction of the Trans-Guinea railway began. Three other railways serve the mining areas, including an 89-mile line linking Conakry to the Fria bauxite mines. The mining company of Conakry operates a nine-mile line between its iron mine and the port. Another line, the Boké Railway, runs for 83 miles between Kamsar and Sangaredi.

The port facilities of Conakry are extensive. There is a channel 26 to 66 feet deep and dock space with modern loading equipment. The Sangaredi bauxite mine company maintains its own ore exporting port at Kamsar. Coastal shipping, however, is limited.

The international airport at Conakry serves jets of all sizes. Air Guinée operates weekly domestic flights to the packed-earth landing strips at Kankan, Boké, Labé, Kissidougou, Nzérékoré, and Siguiri and maintains occasional service to Bamako, Mali; Dakar, Senegal; Freetown, Sierra Leone; and Monrovia, Liberia.

ADMINISTRATIVE AND SOCIAL CONDITIONS

Government. Guinea under Pres. Ahmed Sékou Touré was a one-party state in which the Parti Démocratique de Guinée (PDG) and government were one. In April 1984, after Sékou Touré's death in a U.S. hospital, a military group abolished the PDG and all associated revolutionary committees and replaced them with the Military Committee for National Recovery (CMRN). The committee appointed Col. Lansana Conté as president. The CMRN supervises a 41-member government of ministers, secretaries of state, and commissioners, including eight civilians appointed at the formation of the new government.

Each of the four supra-regions of Upper Guinea, Forest Guinea, Middle Guinea, and Maritime Guinea is headed by an elected governor.

Education. Education is free and compulsory for children between the ages of seven and 12. The government views education as one of the chief means of restoring authentic African values. Teaching of the French classics and arts curriculum has been reduced in favour of an emphasis on technical training. In the early 1980s there were about 2,400 primary schools and about 35 secondary schools. The country's three colleges—Institut Polytechnique de Conakry, École Nationale des Arts et Métiers, and École Supérieure d'Administration—are all located in Conakry. In the early 1980s enrollment of primary school-age children had roughly doubled over the rate of the 1960s.

Health and welfare. Since independence, Guinea has devoted much effort to health services. There are major hospitals, regional hospitals, and local dispensaries. Yellow fever and plague have been virtually eliminated, and malaria, trypanosomiasis (sleeping sickness), and onchocerciasis (river blindness) have been curbed. Medical care and personnel, however, are inadequate. The Institute of Traditional Medicine was created in 1967 to aid in making indigenous medical remedies more available. Such social-welfare services as infant clinics and child-care services are largely a function of the extended family.

A housing problem exists only in the most urbanized areas because local construction materials are otherwise available. In the industrialized areas near Conakry, attempts have been made to construct low-cost prefabricated housing in workers' cities near the plant sites.

In general, salaries are low, and little more than subsistence is the lot of more than half of the salaried workers. Rents have been lowered by government decree; purchasing cooperatives have been established; and salaries have been progressively adjusted in favour of the least paid. Inflation, however, has produced a continual need to resort to extra-salary means in order to eke out a livelihood.

CULTURAL LIFE

A profound cultural revolution was launched in 1967, aimed at involving all of the people in national construction by developing a sense of national responsibility and an awareness of the part that communal action must play to achieve complete decolonization of the mind, the economy, and national politics.

Members of the professional Ballet National Guinéen are chosen from ballet, theatre, and traditional and modern music groups from each village, section, and federation. They form two national troupes that are creating a national Guinean form of the performing arts. Because the performers are often from *griot* families (traditional families of artistic specialists) and because they are often paid by the federation or village groups they represent, their traditional roles are still maintained.

A distinctively Guinean literature is difficult to define. Such authors as Camara Laye, Djibril Tamsir Niane, and Mamadou Traore Rayautra, Fodeba Keita, and Sékou Touré have made contributions into a fusion of traditional forms and patterns into a universally understandable literary genre.

Handicrafts have declined sharply because they are unable to compete with manufactured consumer goods. Those remaining include leatherwork, masks, statuettes, art objects, and jewelry for the tourists. For statistical data, see the "Britannica World Data" section in the current *Britannica Book of the Year.*   (T.E.O'T./Ed.)

History

The Susu, a group related to the Malinke (Mandingo), seem to have driven the Baga people to the coast. The Fulani established domination over the Fouta Djallon by the 16th century. The upper Niger was the domain of the Malinke, forming the ancient kingdom of Mali. The coast was made known by Portuguese voyagers of the 15th century and was for long a resort of slave traders. In 1827 the French explorer René-Auguste Caillé traversed the country on his journey from the Rio Nuñez to Timbuktu. From 1838 Louis-Édouard Bouet-Willaumez and other French naval officers surveyed the coast and established a settlement on the Rio Nuñez that was annexed in 1849.

The
French
Protec-
torate

In 1880 Tomba Island was occupied, and in 1881 the *almamy* (ruler) of Fouta Djallon placed his country under French protection. The protectorate was called Rivières du Sud until 1890, when it was detached from Senegal and became a separate colony, later renamed French Guinea, which in 1895 became part of the federation of French West Africa.

The colony was enlarged by addition of territories on the right bank of the Niger and in the hinterland of Sierra Leone and Liberia, and by the cession in 1904 of the Los Islands from Great Britain. Pacification of the Fouta Djallon and of southern Guinea was achieved with difficulty.

Under the constitution of 1946 Guinea became an overseas territory of France and its people French citizens. In 1958 it was the only territory to vote against the constitution of the French Community and thus achieved complete independence. Guinea became a kind of popular democracy under Pres. Ahmed Sékou Touré, strong supporter of the policy of African unity extolled by Kwame Nkrumah of Ghana, but his rule grew progressively more repressive. Refusing French assistance, Guinea contracted loans and economic and trade agreements with the U.S.S.R. and China. In 1960 Guinea severed relations with France and French-influenced Africa, but later in the year Guinea concluded an agreement providing for technical and economic aid from the United States. Guinean relations were resumed with the neighbouring republics and on May 22,

1963, with France, but the economic situation of the country scarcely improved and the power of Touré remained somewhat uncertain. (H.J.D.)

Beset with difficulties of adjustment and reorganization the nation successfully avoided being overwhelmed by internal discord or external pressures under the leadership of Sékou Touré and his Parti Démocratique de Guinée. Guinea continued to occupy a special position among African states in its unqualified rejection of colonial control or economic domination by more developed nations. A militant pan-Africanist stance on the continent, "positive neutralism" in the Cold War, and a unique articulation of African Socialism and cultural revolution in internal affairs contributed to Guinea's image as one of the most radical experiments in social and political development in West Africa. Following Sékou Touré's death in 1984, however, a military coup brought the CMRN under Col. Lansana Conté to power, and the military government promptly began to dismantle the revolutionary socialist apparatus of the Sékou Touré government, generally with strong support from the general public. It adopted a liberal democratic policy, instituting general freedoms and adopting economic free enterprise. The outlook for foreign assistance quickly brightened, and Guinea began to seek reintegration into French-speaking western Africa. For current political history, see the annual issues of the *Britannica Book of the Year*. (Ed.)

GUINEA-BISSAU

Guinea-Bissau, an independent nation in western Africa, was formerly the province of Portuguese Guinea; it became, by agreement with Portugal, an independent nation on September 10, 1974, after a decade of war. The country is bounded by Senegal to the north, by Guinea to the east and south, and by the Atlantic Ocean to the west. The Bijagós (Bissagos) Archipelago and other islands lying off the coast also form part of the country. The capital of Guinea-Bissau is Bissau. The total area is 13,948 square miles (36,125 square kilometres).

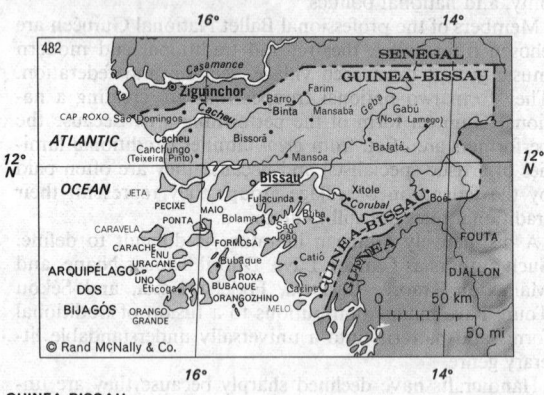

GUINEA-BISSAU

Physical and human geography

THE LAND

Relief. Almost all of Guinea-Bissau is low-lying, except in the southeastern part of the country, where some of the outlying ridges of the Fouta Djallon plateau rise to heights of between 130 and 600 feet (40 and 180 metres). The Boé Hills extend from the western slopes of the Fouta Djallon to the Corubal Basin and the Gabú Plain. The hills are characterized by deeply incised river valleys separated by flat-topped, laterite-capped areas that are bare of soils and therefore unproductive for farming.

Along the coast there is an extremely dense network of drowned valleys, called *rias,* which deeply indent the partially flooded coastal lowlands. The Bafatá Plateau is drained by the Geba and Corubal rivers. The Gabú Plain occupies the northeastern portion of the country and is drained by the Cacheu and Geba rivers and their tribu-

Drainage

taries. Around the town of Gabú, the land is undulating, with lateritic outcrops; severe flooding occurs there during the rainy season. The interior plains are part of the southern edge of the Sénégal River basin. The uniform elevation of the mature floodplain allows rivers to meander and renders the area susceptible to flooding during the rainy season.

Climate. The climate is hot and wet; rainfall occurs between May and October, followed by a dry season. The coast has a monsoonal climate with abundant rainfall, amounting to 40 to 80 inches (1,000 to 2,500 millimetres) a year in the north. The interior is influenced by the tropical savannna climate, with greater variation in rainfall and temperature. Everywhere the temperature is high, April and May being the hottest months.

Plant and animal life. There are three zones of vegetation in Guinea-Bissau. The first is formed by the coastal swamps and plains that are covered with mangrove and palm trees and in some places with rice fields. The second is formed by the interior plain, which is heavily forested. The third zone is a continuation of the savanna that occurs in neighbouring Senegal and Guinea.

Guinea-Bissau has a great variety of aquatic birds, including the pelican and the flamingo. Crocodiles, snakes, buffaloes, gazelles, apes, eagles, parrots, hyenas, and leopards abound, but lions are now seen rarely.

Settlement patterns. There is a striking difference between the patterns of human settlement in the swampy coastal part of the country to the west and in the drier hinterland to the east. The islands and the coast are inhabited by palm oil and rice growers; the interior is used by pastoralists for grazing and is cultivated by peanut (groundnut) producers.

The Balante, or Balanta, people, who occupy the area between the Rio Geba and the Casamance River in Senegal, are renowned as rice growers. A Balante extended family traditionally is lodged in a hut complex where strongly built storerooms, cattle pens, and palisaded corridors protect the clan from cattle thieves. Another coastal people, the Bram (Brame), are known for their skill in farming without irrigation. The Bijagós people inhabiting the Bijagós Archipelago are more at home at sea than on land. Inland live the cattle-raising Fulani (Foulah) and the agricultural Malinke (Mandingo) peoples, both of whom are Muslim.

Upon these traditional patterns the war against Portugal superimposed a new form of temporary settlement—the "strategic hamlet," established by the Portuguese to regroup and protect those Africans who had not been won over by the nationalists. In the nationalist-held territories, regroupings also took place in the forests to escape air attacks from the Portuguese. More than 100,000 people fled to Senegal or Guinea to escape the war. On attaining independence, the government of Guinea-Bissau made the resettlement of dislocated persons a major objective.

Bissau is an administrative, commercial, and communications centre with many gardens and fine public buildings. The other cities of note are Bafatá, Gabú (formerly Nova Lamego), Mansôa, Catió, and Canchungo (formerly Teixeira Pinto). Bolama, the former capital, is slowly decaying.

THE PEOPLE

In the past the main population movement was that of the Muslim pastoralists of the east toward the animist peoples of the coast—a movement partially checked by the Portuguese conquest. The main ethnic divisions among the Africans were Balante, Fulani, Mandyako (Mandjak), Malinke, Pepel (Papel), Bram, Felup, Biafada, Bayot, Bijagós, Soninke (Sarakole), and others. In theory, each ethnic group originally had its tribal territory (known as *chão* in local parlance); but expansion of the Balante, coupled with war and further movements by the inland peoples, has tended to make the tribal pattern complex, if not confused.

The most expansion-prone people are the Balante, who belong to a stateless society centred on the family. They showed themselves receptive to nationalist slogans of emancipation from the Portuguese and from whatever chiefs the Portuguese administration tried to give them. An individualist people, largely animist in belief, they constituted the main body of guerrilla forces during the war against Portugal.

The Fulani, who are divided into subgroups according to the degree of their miscegenation with the people they previously conquered, are essentially Muslim pastoralists. Their society is hierarchical, the relationship between chiefs and their vassals being semifeudal in character. Those who can afford it are polygamous. The Fulani people were impervious to Portuguese culture; paradoxically, however, they became tactical allies of the Portuguese Army against the guerrillas, whom they saw as a threat to their religion, feudal society, and traditions. There has been some Fulani resistance to the new government, giving rise to Fulani migrations to Senegal. Some smaller groups that are Fulani in culture, however, joined the nationalists in order to emancipate themselves from the authority of elders and tribal lords.

The Malinke, who are agriculturalists, are more sedentary than the Fulani, but their main vocation, now that they are no longer warriors, is trade, and many are skilled craftsmen. The Malinke also seek to convert their neighbours to Islām. The Mandyako are experienced in growing palm trees and in fishing. The Bram, Biafada, Felup, Bayot, Nalu, Susu, and Bijagós all live in close proximity to the sea; they are farmers and have been little influenced by either Portuguese or Islāmic culture.

Assimilados and mestiços

Guinea-Bissau also has a group of detribalized Africans formerly categorized as *assimilados;* numbering only a few thousand, they became acquainted with Portuguese culture and are chiefly civil servants or white-collar workers. They are distinct from the formerly significant colony of Cape Verdean *mestiços* (mulattos) living in the country. The *mestiços* played a prominent role within the nationalist leadership, seeking to unite Cape Verde and Guinea-Bissau, but they lost most of their influence after the coup in 1980. The non-Africans, mainly Portuguese, Soviet-bloc, western European, and Brazilian experts, number only a few hundred. The Portuguese never used the territory for settlement.

Languages

Each tribal group speaks its own vernacular, which in turn is divided into dialects. The Balante vernacular, for example, is divided into Berassé, Benaga, Betxa, and other dialects.

The spoken languages fall into two categories. The first of these is the Mande group, which may be subdivided into a Mande-tan grouping—which in Guinea-Bissau includes Soninke (spoken by the Sarakole and the diminutive tribe of Jacanca) and the Malinke, Bambara, and Dyula languages—and the Mande-fu grouping, which includes the Susu (Soso) language.

The second category, the Atlantic (West Atlantic) language group, includes all other African languages spoken in Guinea-Bissau, among which Nalu, the Balante dialects, Mandyako, Pepel, Bram, Biafada, Bijagós, Felup, Bayot, and the Fulani dialects are prominent. Apart from this mixture of some 20 languages and dialects, the lingua franca is *crioulo,* a Portuguese patois with an Africanized syntax and vocabulary. Resembling the *crioulo* spoken in Cape Verde, it exerts a unifying influence in the rural areas and, along with Portuguese, is used in schools. Portuguese is the official language. Some Arabic is known by Muslim scholars.

Traditional animist beliefs have remained strong in Guinea-Bissau, even among those who have formally adopted Christianity or Islām. Christianity made few inroads in Guinea-Bissau during the Portuguese colonial period. There is a small number of Roman Catholics in Guinea-Bissau, and there are few Protestants.

Islām is the dominant religion in western Africa and consists of a series of religious orders; in Guinea-Bissau most adherents belong to the Qādirīyah or Tijānīyah orders. Portugal supported the expansion of Islām to help counteract Marxist influence. Even in Bissau, which at one time was predominantly Roman Catholic, the Portuguese built mosques and also subsidized pilgrimages to Mecca for Fulani and Malinke leaders. No persecution of Muslims after independence was reported, even though the Muslims tended to side with the Portuguese during the anticolonial struggle.

THE ECONOMY

Agriculture. The economy is largely based on traditional farming and on cattle raising. Rice is the staple food. Oil palm products are associated with rice cultivation in the islands and on the coast. Coconuts and palm kernels are exported. Peanuts (groundnuts), the main cash crop, are cultivated—traditionally by Muslims—in the vicinity of Bafatá, Farim, and Gabú.

The raising of cattle, goats, and pigs is particularly important among the Fulani and the Balante. Some hides and skins are exported. Fishing is important, and fish in some years surpasses peanuts as the most important export. There are undeveloped resources of bauxite and petroleum.

Transportation. There are no railways in Guinea-Bissau. Rivers provide the cheapest means of transporting peanuts and palm products. The main road artery runs from Bissau to Bafatá, with subsidiary roads leading to Gabú in the northeast and to the riverine ports, as well as to neighbouring countries.

Bissau is the only modern port. Centrally located, it handles a modest annual traffic. Bissau airport (Bissalanca) handles international air traffic.

CULTURAL LIFE

Bissau has a museum and a library, and state radio programs are broadcast from Bissau. For statistical data, see the "Britannica World Data" section in the current *Britannica Book of the Year.*   (R.P.)

History

By the 13th century AD the coast of Guinea-Bissau was occupied by iron-using agriculturists such as the Barhun, Casanga, Pepel, Balante, and Bijagós. They were particularly skilled in the production of both irrigated and dry rice and were also the major suppliers of marine salt to the adjacent areas of western Sudan. From the 13th century these coastal farmers came increasingly into contact with the outside world, first from the landward side and later from the seaward. The earliest recorded influences from the interior are associated with the breakup of the Ghana Empire when Nalu and Landuma peoples sought refuge near the coast. Later the region was loosely drawn into the sphere of the Mali Empire, and regional governors called *farim*s were appointed to obtain some form of allegiance to the great Mande ruler.

The earliest overseas contacts of the Guinea coast were

opened by the Portuguese, probably from the 1440s. Guinea played an important role in the colonization of the Cape Verde Islands from this period. Slave labour was first used to establish plantations of cotton and indigo, and then skilled Guinea craftsmen were introduced to establish a weaving and dyeing industry. Much of the cloth was sent back to the mainland for the purchase of slaves destined for the Americas. The transatlantic slave trade was facilitated by Portuguese and mulattoes called *lançados* who acted as intermediaries between the Guinean rulers and the visiting slave ships. In the 16th century the expansion of Mande-speaking peoples into the Upper Guinea coast area caused wars that greatly increased the number of prisoners available for export as slaves. In addition to the slave trade the country conducted some trade in salt, kola nuts, and food to the interior and ivory, wax, dyewood, and hides overseas. The main overseas buyers came from Portugal, Britain, Holland, and France.

During the next four centuries, when the slave trade was the main economic activity of the country, the people of Guinea had little difficulty in preventing or restricting the attempts of foreign powers to establish territorial claims. A post established at Cacheu by Cape Verde traders in 1588 was given periodic support by the Lisbon government during the 17th century but did not expand. In 1687 a Portuguese post was established at Bissau in an attempt to limit French commercial competition by political, diplomatic, and military means, but that too failed to survive. In 1792 the English briefly and disastrously held a settlement at Bolama. Meanwhile the Portuguese had reestablished a base at Bissau and during the 19th century increasingly came to regard the coast on either side as sovereign territory.

The Portuguese territorial claim in Guinea was disputed by both the British and the French. Periodic negotiation first of all excluded the British (1870) and then settled the boundaries with the French-claimed territories (1886 and 1902–05). These frontier agreements were followed by the slow and sometimes violent imposition of Portuguese colonial rule. The final "pacification" campaigns were fought by João Teixeira Pinto in 1913–15. These wars were followed by nearly half a century of predominantly peaceful Portuguese administration. But with the rise of African nationalism after World War II and the gaining of independence by the neighbouring territories, Guineans again began to challenge their colonial rulers. Nationalist attacks on Portuguese administrative and military ports were instigated in July 1961 by guerrillas of the Partido Africano da Independência da Guinée do Cabo Verde (PAIGC), led by Amúlcar Cabral. In August Cabral declared at Conakry, capital of the French-speaking Republic of Guinea, that political endeavours to obtain the liberation of Portuguese Guinea and Cape Verde Islands from Portuguese domination would be replaced by armed struggle. Bitter guerrilla warfare between the PAIGC National Liberation Army (about 10,000 men) and the Portuguese armed forces (about 30,000 strong) developed. The guerrillas were unable to occupy the coastal towns and river ports, but by 1971 they were firmly established in the interior, especially in the areas adjacent to the republics of Senegal and Guinea.

In 1973 Guinea-Bissau declared itself an independent state, which Portugal acknowledged in 1974 by the withdrawal of all Portuguese troops. Cabral died before independence, but the first elected president of the new nation was his half-brother, Luis de Almeida Cabral. Relations with Cape Verde continued and included a national assembly of women from both nations in June 1979 to campaign against early and forced marriage and the practice of female circumcision. In November 1980 the government of President Cabral was overthrown and replaced by a Council of the Revolution, with the former vice president and premier Maj. João Bernardo Vieira at its head. One result of the change in government was that the Cape Verdeans formed a new party, leaving the PAIGC a political party no longer in control of two independent nations. Constitutional government returned in May 1984 with approval of Vieira as head of state and government. For current political history, see the annual issues of the *Britannica Book of the Year*.   (D.Bi./Ed.)

Independent Guinea-Bissau

IVORY COAST

The Ivory Coast (République de Côte d'Ivoire) is a republic on the coast of western Africa. With a coastline more than 300 miles (480 kilometres) long, it forms an almost square block of territory with an area of 124,504 square miles (322,463 square kilometres). It is bounded to the southwest by Liberia, to the northwest by Guinea, to the north by Mali and Burkina Faso (formerly Upper Volta), to the east by Ghana, and to the south by the Gulf of Guinea. The capital is Abidjan.

Physical and human geography

THE LAND

Lying close to the Equator, the Ivory Coast is tropical in both surface features and climate.

Relief. The ground rises constantly as it recedes from the coast, and the northern half of the country consists of high savanna (grassy parkland) lying mostly 1,000 feet (300 metres) above sea level. Most of the northwestern border with Liberia and Guinea is shaped by mountain ranges, whose highest point is Mt. Nimba (5,748 feet, or 1,752 metres, high), which is situated where the borders of the three countries meet.

The Ivory Coast has four natural regions—the coastal fringe, the equatorial forest zone, the cultivated forest zone, and the northern savanna. The coastal fringe consists of a strip of land, no more than 40 miles wide, studded with lagoons on its eastern half. Access from the sea is made difficult by the surf and by a long submarine sandbar. Behind the coastal fringe lies the equatorial forest zone that, until a century ago, formed a continuous area more than 125 miles wide. It has now been reduced to an area roughly triangular in shape, with the apex lying a little to the north of Abidjan, and with its base lying along the Liberian border. The cultivated forest zone, which lies to the east of this triangle, consists of forestland that has been partly cleared for plantations, especially along the Ghana border and in the area around Bouaké. The fourth region, the northern savanna, consists of a sparsely populated plateau, offering open ground favourable for stockbreeding. About 4,500 square miles in this region have been set aside to form the Komoé (Comoé) National Park.

Drainage. Apart from the Cavally River, which forms the border with Liberia, major rivers from west to east are the Sassandra, the Bandama, and the Komoé, all of which drain southward into the Gulf of Guinea.

Soils. The forest soils tend to turn into laterites (red soils with a high content of iron and hydroxide of aluminum), but swampy soils maintain their rich yellowish silico-argillaceous character. In the savanna areas, "shields," formed as a result of rapid evaporation, alternate with rich black sillico-argilaceous soils.

Climate. Equatorial and southern savanna types of climate prevail. North of about 8° N latitude, the southern savanna type of climate occurs, characterized by the parching wind known as the harmattan, which blows from the northeast from December until February. The dry season lasts from about November to March. There is a single rainy season, and the annual total rainfall amounts to approximately 45 inches (1,143 millimetres) in the northeast and centre to 60 inches in the northwest. The region is drier than the rest of the country and, because of the altitude, somewhat cooler. South of 8° N latitude, two rainy seasons occur, and three climatic subdivisions may be discerned. In the coastal fringe, rain falls mostly from May through July and to a lesser extent in October and November, averaging an annual total of about 77 inches at Abidjan; considerable variations are, however, experi-

Natural regions

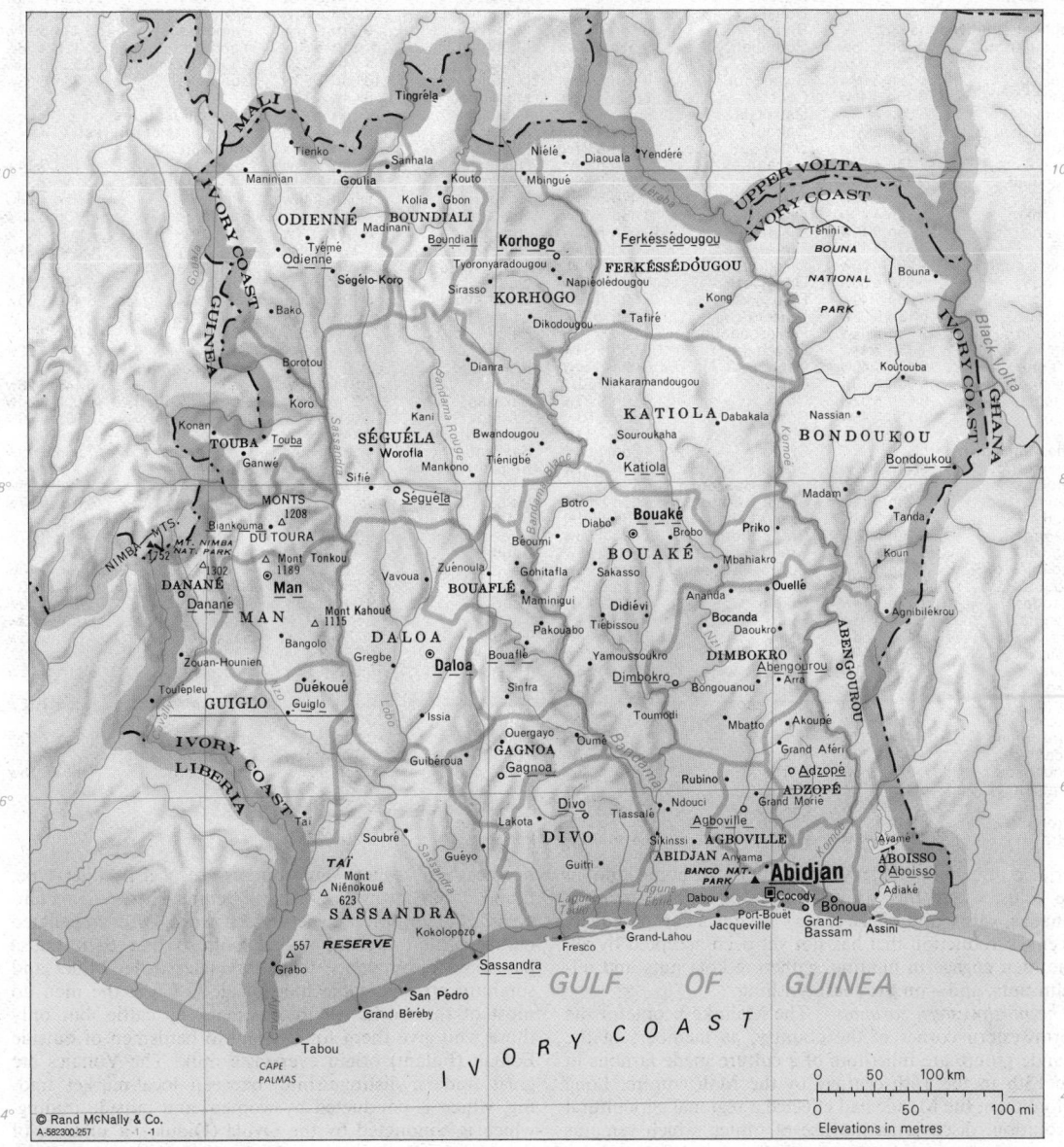

IVORY COAST

enced at different places along the coast. Temperatures range from 70° F (21° C) to 91° F (33° C). In the forest zones and in the southern part of the savanna region, the rainy seasons are less pronounced. Temperatures vary between 75° and 102° F (24° and 39° C), and humidity reaches 70 percent. On the mountains further west there is no dry season, and rainfall amounts to about 80 inches, which reaches a maximum in September.

Plant and animal life. The rain forest contains valuable timber species, including African mahogany and iroko (or African teak), and staple forest crops include oil palms, bananas, cassava, plantains, and yams. An important afforestation centre is the Banco National Park near Abidjan.

The animal life of the forest zone differs little from that of adjoining Ghana, although the larger ungulates (hoofed mammals) are lacking, with the exception of the bongo (a reddish-brown antelope) and the forest buffalo. There are also about six kinds of dwarf antelope, ranging from the royal antelope to the yellow-backed duiker; the giant forest hog is widespread (although nowhere common), and the red river hog is locally plentiful. Manatee (a herbivorous water animal with two flippers in front and a spoon-shaped tail) probably survive in some rivers. To the north, the savanna woodlands have about 10 species of antelope, as well as lions and occasional herds of elephants. In addition to Komoé National Park in the northeast, which is well stocked with wildlife, the Taï National Park, near the

Liberian frontier, is notable for its pygmy hippopotamuses.

Settlement patterns. Though differences in settlement and way of life exist throughout the Ivory Coast, the major division is between the life-style of Abidjan and that of the other regions.

The southeast. In the southeastern quarter of the country, most people live in compact villages and towns. The houses are rectangular dwellings of reeds, poles, or dried clay, traditionally covered with thatched roofs, though often today with corrugated iron sheets. The town centres grow quite lively when, every four days, the markets are held. Here, the women are the sellers of the produce, which consists mostly of yams—the most basic national staple—maize (corn), the starch root known as manioc, peanuts, oil-palm nuts, and other vegetables. Fishermen on the lagoons ply their trade separately, maintaining their own markets. The entire area is divided into petty states with kings and an elaborate hierarchy of ministers and palace officials bearing elegant titles.

The southwest. Among the Kru and other peoples of the southwestern forest zone, houses may be either rectangular or round, varying according to place rather than to tribe. Dwellings everywhere are clustered around a central open area, though markets are held only in a very few privileged towns. In other places, the central area is an evening meeting place as well as a spot in which "village democracy" is practiced by councils of elders. Women

Rural life and regional characteristics

perform the bulk of daily work, both at home and in the fields, where they grow such crops as rice, manioc, bananas, yams, and maize (corn). Rice is a comparatively recent introduction that has not yet been accepted by all. The men engage in hunting, gathering kola nuts and oil-palm nuts, and—on the coast—fishing.

The northwestern savanna. The Malinke people of the northwestern corner of the country, as members of the Mande group, are inheritors of a culture made famous in the 13th to the 16th century by the Mali empire. Long before then, the Mande had effected a regional agricultural revolution, discovering the use of millet, which remains their staple food, and using such other cereals as sorghum and maize. They have cultivated cotton for centuries. Cattle are kept by everyone, but for purposes of prestige and use on ceremonial occasions rather than for economic reasons; little milk is drunk. The men raise livestock and cultivate crops; they may also travel extensively for trade. The Malinke build round huts of mud and sun-dried brick surmounted by a conical thatched roof. Defense is a traditional concern, as is evident from the fences built around dwellings clustered in compounds and from the palisades surrounding large villages or towns. The people recognize a dual authority: on the one hand, the village chief, on the other hand, the chief representative of the linear descendants of the first settlers, a group forming a traditional nobility. Some people are born into certain trades, such as that of musician, or *griot* (a historian minstrel).

The northeastern savanna. Until the late 19th century, the rest of the savanna region was forgotten by the various conquerors who from the 14th century onward spread devastation farther up in the Niger River Basin. The area is part of the domain of the Voltaic peoples, many of whom live in neighbouring Burkina Faso, much of which until 1947 formed part of the Ivory Coast. Among them, the Senufo live immediately east of the Mande and have adopted many of their customs. Life in comparatively large villages and specialization on a hereditary basis may have helped them to reach their high level of artistic creation in woodcarving and in weaving. All other Voltaic communities are split into dispersed homesteads. In the

northeastern corner, some houses are of a peculiar type, found as far away as northern Benin. These are rectangular mud or brick structures crowned with crenellated parapets built around a flat roof, so that each house has some resemblance to a fairy tale castle. Millet and sorghum are the staple food of all Voltaics; the men do most of the work. All the people keep cattle, but only those who give them for keeping to herdsmen of outside Foulah (Fulani) origin ever taste milk. The Voltaics are great traders, distinguishing between local-market trading, which is conducted by women, and outside trading, which is conducted by the Dyula (Dioula), a subtribe of the Mande. Each community is run by the head of the main lineage group, who seeks above all to mediate in all disputes so the earth may never be defiled by blood spilling. In addition, the Senufo have chiefs who govern small districts.

Abidjan. One of the many trading ports built by Europeans along the African coast, Abidjan, nevertheless, has distinctive features of its own. A most striking one is its location on a lagoon, rather than on the sea, to which a canal has provided access only since 1950. Its core is divided by a branch of the lagoon into Abidjan-Plateau, the first European settlement, to the north, and Treichville, the first large African settlement, to the south. The maintenance of physical communications between these quarters is the main problem facing the city.

Urban life

Plateau was recommended for settlement as early as 1898, but no Europeans actually lived there until 1903, when work was begun on the railway to Upper Volta. Treichville, located behind the fishing village of Anoumabo, owes its importance to the boom in colonial trade that followed World War I. It remained a very small town until 1934, when the seat of colonial government was moved to Abidjan from Bingerville, a short distance to the east. The public buildings, few of which remain, were built in Plateau; and Treichville, left to African home-builders, assumed an appearance that still keeps alive the flavour of those comparatively leisurely times. After 1950, when the opening of the canal to the sea marked a new era of economic expansion, urban growth was exceptionally fast.

Most of it occurred outside Treichville, which, with more than 150,000 inhabitants, was crowded to the saturation point. North of Plateau, but separated from it by a former colonial army camp, the hills of Adjamé and other slopes have been covered with real-estate developments consisting of good but characterless modern apartment buildings of the type found around Paris. The environment is inconsistent with the local African life-style, which includes petty trading during the day and merrymaking at night. To the south, other developments were built without planning in the 1960s, so that slums and traditional housing alternate along the highway until the sea is reached at Port-Bouët, where until 1950, the seaport of Abidjan had been located.

Cocody, a town of an entirely different type, has grown up east of Plateau, across a branch of the lagoon, whose waters surround it virtually on three sides; it is bounded by a forest to the north. An upper-income residential area, it contains the presidential mansion, a towerlike structure built to assure every room a maximum of light and air. Cocody is a major tourist centre, commanded by a 25-story completely air-conditioned luxury hotel, opened in 1963. It features several bars and restaurants, bowling, a cinema, and ice-skating; its gambling facilities, as at Monte-Carlo, are for foreigners only. Cocody has a second luxury hotel, and there are two more of international standing at Plateau. Many other hotels are spread over the urban area; pleasure spots include dozens of night clubs, bars, and restaurants.

THE PEOPLE

Ethnic groups. There are more than 60 tribes, traditionally independent from each other, though larger groups among them may be recognized on the basis of cultural unity. Each one of these groups has tribal affiliations with larger groups living outside the borders of the republic. Thus the Baule (Baoule), as well as other peoples living east of the Bandama River, are affiliated with the Akan group of Ghana. The Baule in about 1730 refused to join the Ashanti confederacy in what is now Ghana and settled in the Ivory Coast under the leadership of Queen Pokou. The lagoon fishermen farther south also have tribal brothers belonging to the same Akan group across the Ghana border. The forest people west of the Bandama belong to the same group as the Kru boatmen of Liberia, many of whom also live in Ivory Coast territory. In the interior, the Kru group is subdivided into tribes tiny in number but scattered over large areas of the forest and kept together by secret societies. Among them, the Bete, who live on the western banks of the Bandama, went into open revolt against the government to resist alienation of their communal lands.

The savanna peoples may be divided into two main groups. The Mande group, which is particularly strong in Mali, is represented in the Ivory Coast by the Malinke farmers and by the Dyula (Dioula) peddlers. The Voltaic group comprises the Senufo as well as the Lobi and Bobo subgroups, who live widely scattered over the northeastern region and across into neighbouring states.

Religions. Traditional animistic cults continue to predominate, especially among the agricultural tribes, but Islām has come to claim the adherence of nearly a quarter of the population. The Qādirīyah order of Islām was formerly strong in the town of Kong and remains so among the Malinke. Statistics covering Christian progress are confused by the rapid rise and fall in popularity of several evangelical sects. The Roman Catholics, under the leadership of an African archbishop, claim a large number of adherents, mostly in the south and in large cities.

THE ECONOMY

Resources. The Ivory Coast is primarily noted for its forest resources; it is a major exporter of tropical wood. It has also become one of the world's largest producers of cocoa, coffee, and palm oil. Thus the country possesses one of the more developed of African economies. Reserves of copper, nickel, and uranium have been discovered. Rich iron-ore deposits are found in the west, near the Liberian border. Exploitation of diamonds continues on the Bou

tributary of the Bandama at Tortiya and at Séguéla. Small offshore reserves of oil have been sufficient to satisfy national needs. Development of a field at Grand Bassam began in the 1970s. There are also manganese reserves at Grand Labou.

Agriculture and energy resources. The forest, even in its present reduced state, remains the most considerable asset of the country. About 30 species of trees are of high commercial value. The most important timber types are sipo (utile) and sambu (obeche). Because of overexploitation and a lack of systematic reafforestation, however, forest reserves face depletion.

The forest floor, after clearing, provides a rich soil for the cultivation of edible roots and bananas, as well as of such commercial tree crops as coffee, cocoa (cacao), and rubber. The savanna soils are good for cereals, and cotton and sugarcane grow in both areas.

Agriculture provides a livelihood for about 80 percent of the labour force, and locally grown subsistence crops meet a large part of domestic needs. An acquired taste for such imported foodstuffs as wheat has become a negative element in the balance of trade. The chief crops are yams, manioc, plantains, maize (corn), and rice. *(margin: Local and export crops)*

Among the main export crops is coffee. Its production is a family business, providing a living to perhaps half the population. The local coffee is a robusta of low quality but convenient for processing into powdered form; it has become widely accepted in France because of its cheapness and because of intensive publicity campaigns. Cocoa production employs another quarter of the population, many of whom raise coffee as well. The production of cocoa reached record highs in the early 1980s, a period that also saw a marked increase in the production of pineapples.

Intensive production of palm oil and rubber is found in the southwest, copra along the coast, and cotton in the central and northern parts of the country. Hevea rubber trees (a South American species) were planted first in 1960, and 10 years later they began producing. The cultivation of oil-palm trees has been promoted since 1963 by a state agency working in virtually equal partnership with private firms. Coconut palms have been a familiar sight along the seashore, and thousands of acres have been planted with them to increase the production of copra (the dried kernel of the coconut, from which coconut oil is extracted). In cotton production the main problems are to substitute a high-yielding variety of cotton for the traditional variety, and to teach farmers the practice of either cotton–rice or cotton–yam rotation.

Power is supplied by hydroelectric and thermal power plants. Abidjan is supplied in part by two hydroelectric stations on the Bia River, close to the Ghana border, and two larger stations burning oil fuel. A dam and power station at Kossou, where the two branches of the Bandama River merge, has a capacity of 171,000 kilowatt-hours. Other dam and power station projects are on the Bandama, Cavalla, Sassandra, and Comoe rivers.

Industry. Industry was launched in colonial times with the establishment of sawmills and plywood plants. The dissolution of the old French West Africa federation in 1960 brought many firms to Abidjan from Dakar, Senegal.

Though the Conseil de l'Entente, a grouping consisting of the Ivory Coast, Upper Volta, Niger, Dahomey (now Benin), and Togo, failed to grow into a unified market, factories were erected in the Ivory Coast, especially for the food industry, which processes both imported and local raw materials. Imported wheat produces flour. Beer is also produced, as are cigarettes. Powdered coffee, cocoa butter, pineapple preserves, preserved fish, and edible oils are among the other processed foods. The fishing industry requires the production of large quantities of ice for freezing fish. In addition to other types of fish, tuna is landed in Abidjan for eventual export. *(margin: Processing and manu-facturing)*

A textile industry was launched as early as 1920 at Bouaké; since then the Bouaké mill has been expanded, and three plants in Abidjan print dry goods. Undergarments are made at a number of locations, and a shoe industry, working with both leather and plastics, has much of its product smuggled into Ghana.

Abidjan factories produce soap, matches, and a wide range of metal products, including furniture, automobiles, and air-conditioning and refrigerating units. Marketing remains a serious problem, however. The high cost of fuel and electricity restricts the use of many items, and adequate foreign markets are found only with difficulty.

Finance. The Ivory Coast stands on relatively firm financial ground. Many foreign and domestic banks and credit institutions and real-estate agencies are in business. The National Bank for Agricultural Development and the Ivory Coast Bank for Industrial Development have headquarters in Abidjan, where there are also branches of major British and U.S. banks and the Central Bank of West Africa. The monetary unit is the CFA (Communauté Financière Africaine) franc.

Overly rapid development led to sizeable foreign deficits, and the long-lasting drought and recession of the early 1980s forced the government to seek a moratorium on repayments of external debts and to embark on an austerity budget.

The financial policy of the Ivory Coast government has been liberal in the classical sense of the word. Foreign investments are welcome and are given not only assurances against nationalization, but also the possibility of enjoying tax exemptions and other privileges.

Transportation. The transportation system is dominated by the railway line to Burkina Faso (formerly Upper Volta), the building of which began at Abidjan in 1903. By 1912 it had reached Bouaké, contributing to the growth of this town, located about 200 miles north of the capital. It now extends to Ouagadougou in Burkina Faso.

Roads cover the whole country, with the network focussing upon Abidjan. Paved roads have been extended to replace beaten-earth roads. A secondary system of dry-season roads feed the main roads. Daily local trade is still conducted along the innumerable tracks that crisscrossed the country long before the advent of Europeans, one of them the historically important "kola road" to the north, which runs via Sagala (Ghana) to Kano (Nigeria).

The Vridi Canal gives Abidjan direct access to the sea. Separate docking accommodations are provided for passengers, for goods requiring special care such as bananas, minerals, and petroleum, for fishermen, and for boatmen who transport goods by canoe. Other ports are Sassandra, Tabou, and San-Pédro.

Abidjan has a fully equipped international airport, located at Port-Bouët at the southeastern end of the urban area, eight miles from Plateau. It is used regularly by planes belonging to about a dozen foreign companies and by those of Air Afrique, a service maintained by several French-speaking African states. The national airline, Air Ivoire, serves small airports and landing fields in the interior.

ADMINISTRATIVE AND SOCIAL CONDITIONS

Government. The Ivory Coast was proclaimed an independent republic on August 7, 1960. As in most African countries, the president is vested with wide powers and has sought reelection at the end of each five-year term. The president appoints and presides over a Cabinet of 34 ministers, three of whom are without portfolio and are styled simply "ministers of state." There is a single-house legislature, the National Assembly, with 147 members, elected at the same time and for the same term as the president. An Economic and Social Council with 60 members acts in an advisory capacity.

All judges are appointed by the president, and they render justice according to legal codes of French inspiration. There are trial courts located in Abidjan, Bouaké, and Daloa, and their judges may be assigned to 25 other towns or be called upon to constitute special labour and juvenile courts. The same three towns are visited by an assize court dealing with serious criminal offenses. Abidjan also has a court of appeals and a supreme court.

The old colonial subdivisions of the country were renamed *départements* and *sous-préfectures* (subprefectures) as in France. The number of the former was increased from six to 26. Though all have elected assemblies known as general councils, they are headed by prefects who have extensive powers and the help of 162 subprefects at as many stations in the interior. Abidjan and Bouaké have elected municipal councils and mayors, while other towns have councils but no mayors. The governmental system remains too foreign to local customs to permit much participation by illiterate citizens, but some petty chiefs of the Akan group hold positions in the new system of administration.

The political system is controlled by the only authorized party, the PDCI (Parti Démocratique de la Côte d'Ivoire). It originated in a league of farmers founded in 1944 by Félix Houphouët-Boigny, who became the first president of the new republic. Houphouët-Boigny also founded the Rassemblement Démocratique Africain (RDA), a party with branches throughout French-speaking Africa, and as a result the history of the PDCI and the RDA have been closely linked.

Education. After independence, educational services expanded considerably, and a university was opened in Abidjan in 1964. The school system is characterized not only by quick growth but also by a comparatively small participation by religious missions and by a regular increase in the ratio of girls among the students.

Health and welfare. Abidjan has several state hospitals; a mental hospital is located in Bingerville, 11 miles away. There are modern hospitals in Bouaké, Daloa, and Korhogo. More beds are available in state and private clinics, and lepers are accommodated at leprosariums. Leprosy and yaws are serious problems, but strenuous efforts are being made to control them.

Less hopeful are the prospects for other social conditions. In Abidjan, European-organized crime and prostitution have appeared, attracted by the city's wealth.

Housing. A serious housing problem exists only in Abidjan, where it reaches such a proportion that tensions created by contrasts in living conditions may well affect the future of the country. In the midst of modern buildings, a few villages remain in which people live in their traditional manner. Since the early years of this century, African workers and small merchants have built the town of Treichville, filled with small houses generally built by the inhabitants. The many apartment buildings are modern but characterless in appearance, and their inhabitants complain of their lack of social amenities. The African agglomerations of Treichville and Adjame squeeze into Plateau, the former European town, which now is left almost exclusively to business. Most white inhabitants have moved across the lagoon to Cocody, where they have been joined by high African officials.

Social structures. Housing has become associated with a new income structure. Social segregation, however, is far from complete, for urbanites have to take care of their poorer relatives according to their own incomes. The average size of households, therefore, varies, depending on the average wealth of homeowners.

Deep social change has also taken place in the southeastern quarter of the country, where Baule (Baoule), and other heads of extended families, took advantage of the planting of coffee and cocoa trees to acquire individual ownership of lands that traditionally had been held in collectivity. They have formed a class that combines wealth with traditional and new PDCI party leadership, owning one-fourth of all plantation land and hiring two-thirds of the salaried manpower at less than half the urban scales. Along with other middle-income farmers, they are making it difficult for men from outside their group to ascend in the new social order. There is, of course, no question among them of social promotion for women. An even more dangerous situation may arise as other areas in the country are developed. There is strong sentiment that measures must be taken to prevent this group from placing other tribes under their economic control, as they already are doing politically in their capacities as prefects and subprefects.

CULTURAL LIFE

The cultural milieu is split more completely between two cultures than in other African countries, where the contact of Africa and Europe, recent and sudden as it was, never-

(margin notes)
Roads, harbours, and airfields

Executive, legislative, and judicial branches

National and local politics

Social change

theless was often less recent and less sudden than in the Ivory Coast. Europeans with a new, more scientific, but also somewhat paternalistic outlook fostered respect for African tradition to the point that the Abidjan museum is a rich storehouse for more than 20,000 pieces of native art. Traditional arts continue to flourish everywhere. The Senufo carve masks in the shape of animal heads, decorate doors with esoteric signs, and dance in large groups to the slow, majestic rhythms of drums supported by xylophones. The mountaineers of the Man forest wear masks showing horrifying faces and, led by stilt-walkers, dance at a quick pace governed solely by the sound of drums. Among the Baule, versatile artists make fine gold jewels and all kinds of wooden sculptures to remind the people of heroes or heroines such as Queen Pokou. The Baule also have weavers who use looms with pulleys, which are virtual works of art in themselves.

On the other hand, the educated classes have not made up their minds about the value of local tradition. For one thing, they write entirely in French. This does not necessarily exclude the use of local and traditional sources of inspiration. Some years ago, for example, students in Dakar gave a stage presentation of Queen Pokou's story that has remained a classic of French African literature, but this is exceptional. More characteristic of the milieu is Bernard Binlin Dadié (born in 1916, at Assini), who has written semi-autobiographical novels. Goffi Jadeau, a Baule, and Amon d'Aby, a Sanwi, have produced plays on local themes. For statistical data, see the "Britannica World Data" section in the current *Britannica Book of the Year*. (J.Co./Ed.)

History

Following Portuguese discoveries in the second half of the 15th century the coast was frequented by traders for ivory and slaves. Toward the end of the 17th century French trading posts were eestablished at Assinie and Grand-Bassam on the east coast. Following a series of surveys and expeditions by Comdt. Louis-Édouard Bouet-Willaumez (1808–71), forts were built at these two towns and cessions of neighbouring territory were made by the local chiefs (1842–43). After the outbreak of the Franco-German War in 1870 Marcel Triech-Laplène (1861–90), a French trader, made treaties with the chiefs of the Agni and Abron and collaborated with Capt. Louis-Gustave Binger (1856–1936), who between 1887 and 1892 concluded protectorate agreements with other chiefs. Binger became first governor on the erection of the Ivory Coast into a separate French colony in 1893. Agreements with Liberia and Great Britain settled the western and eastern boundaries, but the northern frontier was not determined until 1898, when the insurgent Sudanese leader Samory was captured. Between 1908 and 1918 a progressive occupation was staged by the governor Gabriel Angoulvant. The railway, building of which started from the coast in 1903, reached Bouaké (196 miles north) in 1912 and Bobo-Dioulasso (in Upper Volta, 495 miles north) in 1934. The French built a good network of roads and erected a new capital at Abidjan, the port of which was opened in 1951.

In World War II the Ivory Coast remained under the Vichy regime from 1940 until 1942. In 1946 it became a territory in the French Union, with increased autonomy in financial and administrative affairs, and in 1947 the northern districts, at the request of their inhabitants, were separated from the Ivory Coast to form the reconstituted territory of Upper Volta. In the Legislative Assembly a majority was secured by the Rassemblement Démocratique Africain Party led by Félix Houphouët-Boigny, who subsequently led the Ivory Coast peacefully to autonomy (December 4, 1958) and independence (August 7, 1960). He was elected president of the republic and reelected for each five-year term from 1965 to 1980. His paternal system of government was based on one party, renamed Parti Démocratique de la Côte d'Ivoire. Houphouët-Boigny was one of the initiators of the African and Malagasy Common Organization (OCAM), founded in 1961, comprising 12 French-speaking republics. The Ivory Coast also joined the larger Organization of African Unity. For current political history, see the annual issues of the *Britannica Book of the Year*. (H.J.D.)

LIBERIA

The oldest republic on the African continent, and the only black African state never to have been subjected to colonial rule, Liberia is situated on the western African coast in the tropical rain forest region. It has an area of about 43,000 square miles (111,400 square kilometres). It is bounded by Guinea to the north, Sierra Leone to the northwest, the Ivory Coast to the east, and the Atlantic Ocean to the south and west. The capital is the port city of Monrovia.

Physical and human geography

THE LAND

Relief. Liberia has a somewhat complex relief, and its physical features are not uniform. The coastal terrain, which is about 350 miles (560 kilometres) long and which varies from 15 to 25 miles in width, is sandy, low, and interspersed with lagoons and swamps, as well as with occasional rocky promontories. Behind this region is rolling hill country. Farther inland there occurs a thin strip of steep scarps and hills, about 20 miles wide and trending northeast to southwest. This is followed by a relatively flat highland about 1,500 to 2,000 feet (450 to 600 metres) in height, cut into hills and valleys by erosion. Finally, farthest from the coast, in the northwest and centre, is a mountainous region of which one of the most striking features is Mt. Nimba, at the Guinea–Liberia border, which rises to a height of 4,500 feet (1,372 metres) on the Liberian side and which contains rich deposits of iron ore. The Mano and Morro rivers form the northwestern boundary of the country, and the Cavalla River forms the eastern boundary. Apart from these, there are four major rivers, all of which drain into the Atlantic Ocean—the Lofa, St. Paul, St. John, and Cestos rivers. The Farmington, Du, Junk, and Sino are some of the smaller rivers. The rapids on the St. Paul River, 17 miles northeast of the capital, have been harnessed as a source of hydroelectric power, and the Farmington also has a hydroelectric power station.

Soils. Liberia forms part of the Precambrian Shield, an ancient crystalline rock formation 2,700,000,000 to 3,400,000,000 years old, composed of granite, schist (a coarse-grained rock containing mica), and gneiss (another coarse-grained rock, in which bands of granular minerals alternate with bands of schistose minerals). The shield underlies the entire African continent and lies exposed over about one-third of its surface. Specimen granitic rocks from western Liberia have been found to be between 2,500,000,000 and 3,600,000,000 years old. In Liberia, the shield has been subjected to intense folding and faulting; it is interspersed with ironbearing formations known as itabirites. Along the coast lie beds of sandstone, while intrusive rocks crop out, forming such promontories as Cape Mount, which is 1,070 feet (326 metres) high, Cape Mesurado, and Cape Palmas. Monrovia, the capital city, stands on a ridge of diabase, a basaltic (dark-coloured, fine-grained) rock, about four to six miles long and one to two miles wide. Diabase and gabbro (a dark-coloured, coarse-grained igneous rock) occur in the interior of the country where, as a result of geological eruptions, they have intruded into fissures in the older rock in long and narrow masses.

The soil is an evenly disposed bed of laterites (rust-red aluminum and iron oxides), which have been eroded and repeatedly leached as a result of heavy rainfall. Because of its thin top soil it is more suited to the growth of tree crops than of food crops.

Margin notes:

Folk culture

Establishment of French trading posts

Autonomy and independence

Physical features

LIBERIA

Climate. The climate, especially on the coast, is warm and humid all year round. It is dominated by a dry season from November to April, and by a wet season from May to October. A minor "middle dry" season occurs from mid-July to August. The dusty and dry desert winds known as the harmattan, which blow from the Sahara to the coast in December, also influence the climate. Temperatures range between 65° and 85° F (18° to 29° C). The greatest amount of rainfall, 205 inches (5,200 millimetres), occurs on the Cape Mount Promontory; rainfall diminishes inland to about 70 inches (1,775 millimetres) on the central plateau. The interior has hot but pleasant days and cool nights during the dry season.

Plant and animal life. Liberia has year-round evergreen vegetation. Its tropical rain forest contains some trees that attain heights of 200 feet. Many trees are of commercial value, but natural stands of a single species are rare, thus preventing easy exploitation by the lumber industry. Forestry operations are therefore concentrated on scattered species. Lumber is put to a variety of uses. Termite-resistant woods, such as red ironwood, camwood, and whismore (a large tree resembling mahogany, but tougher), are used for construction, while several African mahoganies are used for cabinet and veneer woods. Other trees of value are rubber, cocoa, coffee, and the raffia palm.

Liberia's tropical rain forest is not conducive to an abundant animal life. The monkey, chimpanzee, some species of small antelope, and various rodents are to be found. There is also a pygmy hippopotamus and several species of anteater. Elephants, bush cows (short horned buffaloes), and leopards are present, but gradually disappearing. There are many reptiles and at least eight poisonous snakes, among them the black cobra and the causus viper, or night adder. Three types of crocodiles have been identified. Scorpions and lizards are numerous, and there are several unique species of bats and birds. Fish are also numerous. Pond-fish culture is being encouraged.

Settlement patterns. There are more than 2,000 villages, the majority of which are concentrated in Bong County in central Liberia, Lofa County in the northwest, and in the coastal county of Montserrado. Different architectural styles are used by different tribes. The huts in the villages of the Vai people, for example, are both round and rectangular and are handsomely decorated with clay and geometric designs. Traditional activities in the villages include farming, hunting, and fishing, although weaving and carving are also practiced.

The capital of Liberia, Monrovia, founded in 1822, is situated on the left bank of the St. Paul River. Standing on the ridge formed by Cape Mesurado, it commands an imposing view of the Atlantic Ocean. The city proper, although not precisely defined, occupies an area of about one square mile, while its outlying districts and suburbs occupy another four square miles. The old style of architecture that once characterized it, reminiscent of that of the southern United States before 1860, is now fast disappearing, giving way to contemporary styles of housing. Monrovia was founded by Liberian settlers from the United States after an earlier attempt to settle near Sierra Leone had failed. It is the political, administrative, and industrial centre of Liberia. All of the tribes of Liberia are represented in its population, as also are other groups, including refugees, African nationals from other countries, and Europeans. Elsewhere, some mining towns have been built in rural areas since World War II.

THE PEOPLE

The group most closely associated with the founding of the Liberian state were blacks from the New World, known historically as Americo-Liberians. Most of them migrated to Liberia between 1820 and 1865, during and immediately after the suppression of the transatlantic slave trade. Other blacks from the Americas have since then continued to migrate intermittently. The government was controlled by this group, until a military regime seized power in 1980. A unification and integration policy that encourages equal opportunities for all citizens, tribal and nontribal, has attempted to efface divisions.

The African tribes may be classified into three linguistic groups, the Mande, the Kru, and the Atlantic (West Atlantic) groups. The Mande are themselves divided into two groups, the Mande-tan (so named because the number ten is *tan* in their language), called the Nuclear Mande by anthropologists, who are located not only in northwest Liberia but also in Senegal, Mali, Guinea, and Sierra Leone; and the Mande-fu (so named because the number ten is *fu* in their language), known to anthropology as the Peripheral Mande. Prominent among the Mande-tan are the Malinke (Mandingo). The Mande-fu group, who inhabit the northern and central region of Liberia, include the Loko, Gbande, Gio, Kpelle, Toma (also known as Buzi or Loma) Mano, Mende, and Vai tribes. The Kru include the Bassa, De, Grebo, and Kru tribes of the coast, and the Kran Padebu, Sapo, Sikon, and other tribes occupying the

Temperature and rainfall

Monrovia

interior and southern half of the country. The Atlantic group includes the Gola, Kissi, and other tribes in the north. Traditionally, different tribes have shown a preference for different shapes of huts, the Mande, for example, preferring round dwellings with conical thatched roofs, while the Kru prefer rectangular houses. Architectural borrowings have, however, occurred in both directions. A Vai man, Doạlu Bukere, invented an alphabet in the 19th century; during World War II this alphabet was borrowed and improved on by the Germans, who, having acquired knowledge of it from German traders in the Cape Mount area, used it for a code. The De, Kpelle, Mano, Mende, and Vai, among others, have secret societies known as the Poro school, for men, and the Sande school, for women. These institutions exercise educational, political, legal, and religious functions. In effect, only the Bassa, Kru, and Malinke are reputed not to have had Poro in the past. The Kru tribes are organized by age sets, or generations; long distinguished by militarism, they opposed the Liberian government in Monrovia until the 1930s.

THE ECONOMY

Liberia's buoyant economy has been attributed to the Open Door Policy, encouragement of foreign investment, promulgated by the Tubman administration and continued by his successors. Liberia's rapid rate of growth has been second only to that of Japan in recent years. The fact that Liberia's currency is based on the dollar has, however, placed it in an isolated economic zone. Liberia is not a member of any major African economic or free-trade bloc, although it is a member of the Mano River Union, a free-trade grouping to which Sierra Leone, and Guinea also belong. It is also not a member of any international trade grouping.

Liberia is among the leading producers of iron ore on the African continent and is one of the principal exporters of iron ore in the world. The registration of foreign shipping under a Liberian "flag of convenience" has established Liberia as the foremost nation in terms of registered shipping tonnage. Liberia nevertheless remains a primarily agricultural and underdeveloped country.

The country is, however, rich in natural resources, although the distribution of wealth after production is uneven. The coastal districts receive a far greater share of economic benefits than the hinterland, after which the county capitals are the next beneficiaries.

Resources. Since 1951 Liberia has been a producer of rich iron ore. It has sizeable reserves of magnetite (magnetic iron ore) and hematite (the principal iron ore), containing 66 percent of pure iron, in the Bomi Hills; red and black itabirites (iron-bearing formations), with an iron content of 55 percent, 50 miles away from Monrovia at Mano River; poorer ores, with an average iron content of 38 percent, in the Bong Range; and ore with a content of from 60 to 70 percent of iron in the Nimba Range in northeastern Liberia. Other reserves exist at Kitoma Mountain, south of the Nimba range; in the Wologizi range in northwestern Liberia, and in the Putu range in eastern Liberia. Other minerals include diamonds and gold, lead, manganese, graphite, cyanite (a silicate of aluminum, with thin bladelike crystals), and barite, while there are possible oil reserves off the coast.

About half of the land area is suitable for cultivation. It is estimated that 2,000,000 acres (800,000 hectares) at a time can be devoted to growing food crops, and a further 5,000,000 acres (2,000,000 hectares) of low land can produce either tree crops or food crops, while yet another 5,000,000 acres on rolling or hilly terrain is suited to growing tree crops. The climate favours rubber production. The rain forest type of vegetation is unsuitable for the raising of livestock but produces fine hardwood timber, especially in the east of the country, but also in the centre and in the west.

Agriculture, forestry, and fishing. Both rice and cassava, the principal food crops, are cultivated. Rice is produced, but it is insufficient to meet the growing demand. The deficit is sometimes met by imports of rice.

Rubber is the main cash crop. In 1926 the Firestone Tire and Rubber Company of the United States obtained a concession for rubber cultivation. Coffee, both of the ro-

busta variety and of the local variety known as liberica, is also produced, as are cocoa, kola nuts, palm oil, palm kernels, sugarcane, peanuts (groundnuts), and cotton. Cattle, goats, pigs, and poultry are also raised. Although substantial amounts of timber are produced, exploitation of the forest resources is difficult, chiefly because of the scarcity of good roads and shortage of labour.

Kru and Fanti fishermen, the latter from Ghana, have traditionally been the suppliers of fish to coastal areas; two Liberian fishing companies now supplement these tribal fishing activities. Inland fish-breeding ponds have been introduced in order to provide a source of protein.

Industry. The number of manufacturing enterprises has increased, particularly since 1960. Most of them serve the local market. Near the port of Monrovia there is a petroleum refinery as well as a cement plant. Other industries include an explosives factory, to supply the iron mines, and plants engaged in tire retreading, paint manufacturing, tuna processing, milk reconstituting, and manufacturing pharmaceuticals. Bricks, tiles, cement blocks, lumber and furniture, soap, and footwear are also manufactured, and there are several distilleries.

Mining. To export the iron ores, iron interests have built special railroads. The Bomi Hills mine, which is American-operated, is linked to the port of Monrovia by a narrow-gauge railroad 43 miles long. A further 49-mile length of line connects the Mano River workings to the Bomi Hills. The Bong Range mine, which is operated by a joint Italian and West German company, is linked to Monrovia by a 50-mile standard-gauge line. The Nimba Range reserves, which constitute one of the largest and richest iron ore deposits in the world, are operated by the Liberian–American–Swedish Minerals Company (LAMCO) in conjunction with the Bethlehem Steel Corporation of the United States. The reserves have almost no overburden (other material covering the deposits), impurities are insignificant, and the ore can be used untreated. It is exported from the port of Buchanan, to which the ores are sent via a 168-mile standard-gauge railroad.

Energy. Power is provided by public and private installations, which either are hydroelectric or employ petroleum. Altogether they have a total capacity of more than 880,000,000 kilowatts. The rubber-growing and iron-mining enterprises generate their own power. A hydroelectric plant at Mt. Coffee on the St. Paul River, which supplies power to Monrovia and to adjacent districts, has a 102,000-kilowatt capacity.

Finance and trade. Financial services are provided by eight banks. There are also two credit corporations—the Liberian Agricultural Credit Corporation and the Liberian Development Corporation. Several Lebanese merchants provide short-term loans.

Rubber and iron ore account for almost 90 percent of the value of all exports. Imports include machinery and transport equipment, food, beverages and tobacco, miscellaneous manufactured goods, mineral fuels, lubricants, and chemicals. The United States is the principal trading partner, followed by Saudi Arabia and West Germany.

Transportation. Liberia's road network is composed of more than 6,000 miles of public and private roads, of which only a small percentage is paved. Many transport facilities are controlled by private enterprise; Air Liberia is an exception.

Four ports—Monrovia, Greenville, Harper, and Buchanan—serve Liberia's 350-mile coastline. The free port of Monrovia is the principal commercial port. It also has facilities for transshipping iron ore and liquid latex. Nimba Range iron ore is shipped from Buchanan, while the port at Greenville and also a partially sheltered pier at Harper used by coastal craft are used primarily for the shipment of rubber and forest products. All ports are administered by the National Port Authority.

Liberia has two major airports, Robertsfield International, about 30 miles east of Monrovia, and James Spriggs Payne Airport, about five miles from Monrovia.

ADMINISTRATIVE AND SOCIAL CONDITIONS

Liberia had a republican form of government patterned after that of the United States and divided into legislative,

(margin notes)
Tribal dwellings

Iron ore production

Rubber production

The Nimba Range deposits

executive, and judicial branches until the military coup in April of 1980. Shortly after the takeover by the People's Redemption Council (PRC), the constitution of 1947 was suspended. The PRC, consisting of 10 members and the commander in chief, assumed all legislative and executive powers. The Cabinet of 20 members is supervised by the PRC.

National unification program

Political, cultural, and economic factors long separated the descendants of the original Liberian immigrants, also known as Americo-Liberians, or settlers, from the African tribal populations. In 1944 a national unification program was launched to speed the integration of the two groups, and in 1964 the old division between coastal and hinterland rule was abolished. In addition to the original five coastal counties of Grand Cape Mount, Montserrado, Grand Bassa, Sino, and Maryland, and the four territories (tribal enclaves) of Marshall, River Cess, Sastown, and Kru Coast, four new hinterland counties—Grand Gedeh, Nimba, Bong, and Lofa—were created. Tribal peoples are allowed, as far as possible, to govern themselves according to customary law.

A People's Supreme Court with seven appointed judges has been established by the PRC. In addition there are People's Circuit and Magistrate courts.

Since the creation of the four inland counties, tribal members have begun to participate in politics. Liberian politics, which, during the early years, took the form of a two-party system representing a conflict of interest between mulatto and black, in 1878 came under the control of the True Whig Party, which was black-dominated and characterized by strong executive control. All political parties were banned, however, under the rule of the PRC.

Education. Formerly supplied mostly by Christian missions, educational services were greatly expanded by the government after 1945. Since 1939 education has been legally compulsory for children between the ages of six and 16. Education is free at the primary and secondary levels, although in the interior, but not in Monrovia, books

Vocational schools, colleges, and universities

must be bought. There are three vocational schools—the Booker Washington Agricultural and Industrial Institute at Kakata, which is a government school, and two more that are concession-operated. Advanced training is provided at the University of Liberia at Monrovia, at Cuttington University College at Suakoko (Episcopalian), and at Maryland College of Our Lady of Fatima at Harper (Roman Catholic). A medical school, the Monrovia Torrino Medical College, trains paramedical students. Liberian students abroad receive advanced training under a government foreign scholarship program. Grants from the United Nations enable Liberia to attract teachers from Europe and the United States to assist in the teaching of economics, science, and mathematics, in addition to which the government also sponsors the employment of foreign teachers. The United Nations supported the government's national literacy program, and 10 of the major tribal languages have now been written down. Middle-level education has been adapted to the needs of the economy. Six years of primary school education are followed by three of middle school and three of high school education. In 1968 Liberia became an associate member of the West African Examinations Council so as to provide an international yardstick for measuring the quality of its education.

Health and welfare. Conditions remain poor, although much progress has been made in providing better health facilities. The incidence of malaria is very high, and leprosy is still a health problem. Yaws is no longer a serious problem, following a control program carried out by the World Health Organization, but tuberculosis has been difficult to eradicate. Dysentery, malaria, and diarrhea continue to be the most important causes of infant mortality. Influenza, hernias, and intestinal worms, as well as trypanosomiasis (sleeping sickness), schistosomiasis (a parasitic disease), and elephantiasis (a lymphatic disease in which the body parts become swollen) are also prevalent. Most modern homes are screened against malaria mosquitoes, tsetse flies, and other dangerous insects. The government conducts inoculation campaigns to combat smallpox and yellow fever, and mobile units employ insecticides against malaria-carrying mosquitoes and other insects.

Major diseases

The government, foreign Christian missions, and concessions together sponsor hospitals, of which the most modern are the John F. Kennedy Memorial Hospital in Monrovia, sponsored by the U.S. Agency for International Development, the Roman Catholic Hospital at Monrovia, and Phebe Hospital in Bong County, all of which have nursing and medical schools attached to them. There are clinics, some specializing in the problems of the blind and the aged, and others specializing in tuberculosis, sleeping sickness, and leprosy.

The Department of Public Works supervises low-cost housing projects and is also responsible for city planning and zoning. Housing is expensive, and most building equipment is imported. On the outskirts of Monrovia, tribal communities exist side by side with modern communities.

Intermarriage and economic progress have both been important factors in breaking down social divisions in Liberia. Mines and plantations are distributed throughout the country and have contributed to the slow trend toward a more equitable distribution of income. Particularly in the coastal districts, government jobs, foreign businesses, and local markets also provide greater opportunities for economic and social advancement. Economic and social divisions are more keenly felt between the coastal and rural areas because the cash economy has only recently spread inland. Transportation, communications, and commerce, however, all serve slowly to lessen differences.

CULTURAL LIFE

In the dance halls of Monrovia and in towns elsewhere, both Western and African music and dancing styles are in vogue. In rural areas, African musicians and drummers use traditional rhythms at weddings, burials, and feasts, as well as at the graduation ceremonies of boys and girls from the Poro and Sande schools.

Musical festivals and dramas are staged several times a year at Cuttington College and the University of Liberia, which are also visited by foreign drama and ballet troupes.

Several institutions instruct young men and women in the legends, traditions, songs, arts, and crafts of African culture. The government encourages the preservation and promotion of African culture through such agencies as the National Cultural Center, which exhibits house styles representing Liberia's 16 different tribal cultures. The sculpture of masks, representing both humans and animals, is an artistic pursuit that is also related to the social structure of some tribes. For statistical data, see the "Britannica World Data" section in the current *Britannica Book of the Year.* (A.B.J./Ed.)

History

Knowledge of the west of Africa began with the reports of Necho II, the Egyptian pharaoh who sent a Phoenician fleet around the coast of Africa in 600 BC, and of Hanno, the Carthaginian navigator, who sailed along the west coast to Cameroon Mountain *c.* 500 BC. Between AD 1364 and 1413 merchants from Dieppe established settlements at Grand Dieppe and Petit Dieppe, where the towns of Buchanan and Greenville are now located. A Portuguese sailor, Pedro de Cintra, reached the Liberian coast in 1461 and named Grand Cape Mount, Cape Mesurado (Montserrado), and Cape Palmas, all prominent coastal features. The area became known as the Grain Coast because grains of Melegueta pepper, then as valuable as gold, were the principal item of trade. In 1663 the British Royal Company of Adventurers built two trading posts on the Grain Coast at Mesurado and Grand Sesters. These stations, however, were destroyed by the Dutch in 1664.

The Grain Coast

It was not until the beginning of the 19th century that interest in the Grain Coast revived. The tide was beginning to rise in favour of the abolition of slavery, and the Grain Coast was suggested as a suitable home for freed slaves. In 1816 two U.S. government agents and two officers of the American Colonization Society (founded 1816) visited the Grain Coast. After abortive attempts to establish settlements there, an agreement was signed in 1821 between the officers of the society and local African chiefs granting the society possession of Cape Mesurado. The first American freed slaves landed in 1822 at Providence Island in the mouth of the Mesurado River; the site was designated a national shrine in 1963. They were shortly followed by Jehudi Ashmun, a white American, who became the real founder of Liberia. He was joined for a short time in 1824 by Ralph Randolph Gurley, who suggested the names Liberia for the territory and Monrovia for the town that was being founded on Cape Mesurado. By the time Ashmun left in 1828 the territory had a government, a digest of laws for the settlers, and the beginnings of profitable foreign commerce. Other settlements were started along the St. John River inland from Grand Bassa, Bassa Cove, Sino, Greenville, and Maryland. In 1836 Thomas Buchanan (a cousin of James Buchanan, 15th president of the United States) went to Liberia as governor. On his death in 1841 he was succeeded by Joseph Jenkins Roberts, an octoroon, born free in Virginia in 1809; Roberts enlarged the boundaries of the territory and improved economic conditions.

Joseph Jenkins Roberts

THE EARLY REPUBLIC

When the American Colonization Society intimated that Liberia should cease to be dependent upon it, Roberts proclaimed it an independent republic in 1847. Independence was recognized in 1848–49 by most of the great powers, though formal recognition by the United States did not come until 1862.

At the time independence was declared, a constitution based on that of the United States was drawn up. But the attempt to found a state comprising the immigrants from the United States and their descendants, who then numbered fewer than 3,000, was not at first successful. Some of the coastal tribes adopted Protestant forms of Christianity and learned English, but most of the indigenous Africans retained their traditional religion and way of life. Roberts, who had been elected the first president of the republic, retained that office until 1856. During this period the slave trade, hitherto illicitly carried on from various nominally Liberian ports, was ended by the activity of the British Navy.

From about 1856 there was a notable increase in the importance of the True Whig Party, which distrusted Europeans and sought development on national lines and, later, cooperation with the indigenous peoples. In 1871 the first foreign loan was raised, being negotiated in London nominally for £100,000. The loan was unpopular, and still more unpopular was the new president, E.J. Roye, who was deposed and imprisoned at Monrovia. He escaped but was drowned while attempting to reach a British ship in the anchorage. Roberts, the former president, was called back to office. He served until the end of 1875 and died in 1876.

During the early days of Liberia there were constant frontier troubles with the French on the Ivory Coast and the British at Sierra Leone. The Liberians tried to extend their authority inland, although they were still unable to control all the coastal area they claimed. Efforts to end the frontier disputes resulted in treaties with Great Britain in 1885 and with France in 1892. In 1904 Pres. Arthur Barclay, a Negro born in Barbados, initiated a policy of direct cooperation with the tribes. Having obtained a loan from London in 1907, he made real efforts at reform. The foreign debt, however, was a burden, and the government was unable to exert effective authority over the interior for more than 20 miles inland. In 1919 an agreement was signed transferring to France 2,000 square miles of hinterland that Liberia had claimed but could not control.

OUTSIDE INTERVENTION

In 1909 a commission appointed by Pres. Theodore Roosevelt of the United States investigated political and economic conditions in Liberia and recommended financial reorganization. A loan of $1,700,000, secured by customs revenue, was raised by an international consortium of bankers in 1912, and a receivership of customs was set up, administered by appointees of the British, French, and German governments and a U.S. receiver-general. A frontier police force was organized by officers of the U.S. Army, with the result that Liberian authority was better maintained. Unfortunately, this promising new regime was

upset by World War I. Revenues dropped to one-fourth of normal, and the financial situation steadily deteriorated.

In the 1920s the Firestone Tire and Rubber Company began an investigation of rubber-growing possibilities in Liberia and, finding the environment favourable, obtained a concession of 1,000,000 acres (400,000 hectares) of land in 1926. At the same time, a loan of $5,000,000 was arranged through the Finance Corporation of America. With this private loan, only half of which had been taken up by 1945, the Liberian government consolidated and bonded all its external and internal debts and placed the country's finances on a relatively stable basis. Administration on the customs and internal revenue was placed in the hands of a U.S. financial adviser.

Firestone rubber concession

An investigation by the League of Nations of forced labour and slavery in Liberia, involving the shipment of Africans to the Spanish plantations in Fernando Po, brought about the resignations of Pres. Charles King and Vice Pres. Allen Yancy and the election of Edwin Barclay to the presidency in 1931. Liberia appealed to the Council of the League of Nations for financial aid, and a commission of inquiry was established. The next three years were marked by unsuccessful attempts to work out a plan of assistance involving the appointment of foreign administrators, the declaration of a moratorium on the Firestone loan, and suspension of diplomatic relations with Great Britain and the United States. After the League Council had finally withdrawn its plan of assistance, the Liberian government reached an agreement with Firestone along lines similar to the League's recommendations.

WORLD WAR II AND AFTER

The new significance of Liberia became apparent after the outbreak of World War II in 1939. During the war Liberia's rubber plantation was the only source of natural latex rubber available to the Allies, apart from plantations in Ceylon. In 1942 Liberia signed a defense agreement with the United States for the operation of strategic airports and military protection of the installations. This resulted in the undertaking of a program of strategic road building, the construction of the airport now known as Robertsfield International Airport, and the completion of a deepwater harbour at Monrovia. U.S. money was declared legal tender in Liberia in 1943, replacing British West African currency. In 1943 William V.S. Tubman was elected to his first term as president. Liberia declared war against Germany and Japan in January 1944 and in April signed the declaration of the United Nations. In December 1960 Liberia became a member of the UN Security Council and from that time took an active part in African and international affairs. Liberia became a member of the UN trusteeship Council in 1963. It became a member of the Organization of African Unity at the organization's inception in 1963.

In 1963 Tubman was elected to serve his fifth term as president. After his inauguration in 1964, a new Cabinet post, that of chief of Cabinet, was created; the first occupant of the post was Tubman's eldest son, William Tubman, Jr. In May of that year the United States and Liberia signed an agreement providing for the transfer of the free port of Monrovia to the government of Liberia. Tubman was again elected president in 1967, the only candidate for the office.

Tubman died in London on July 23, 1971, shortly after his election to a seventh term as president. He was immediately succeeded by Vice Pres. William R. Tolbert.

A decline in world prices for Liberia's chief exports, iron ore and natural rubber, brought financial hardship to the country during the 1960s and early 1970s. Foreign loans, especially by the United States, helped sustain the economy during that period.

On April 12, 1980, Tolbert was killed in a coup led by Master Sergeant Samuel K. Doe, who became head of state and chairman of the People's Redemption Council. In April 1981 the government promised a new constitution and a return to civilian rule. It presented a draft of the new constitution on April 12, 1983. For current political history, see the annual issues of the *Britannica Book of the Year*. (D.R.P./Ed.)

MALI

The Republic of Mali (République du Mali) is a land-locked state in central western Africa. Bounded north by Algeria, west by Mauritania and Senegal, south by Guinea and the Ivory Coast, and east by Burkina Faso (formerly Upper Volta) and Niger, it covers an area of 479,000 square miles (1,240,000 square kilometres). Bamako is the national capital. As a part of French West Africa from 1898 to its independence in 1960, it was known as the French Sudan. Its current name, taken at the time of independence, is derived from the Mali Empire of the Upper and Middle Niger and ruled by the Malinke (Mandingo) from the 13th to the 16th century.

Physical and human geography

Mali is basically an agricultural country. Although its development has been hindered by the nature of the Sahara, which occupies about half its territory, the country nevertheless benefits from the advantages conferred by the waters of the Niger and Sénégal rivers and their tributaries: almost all of the population lives in the southern river basins, where diverse crops are cultivated. Most agricultural activity, however, is at the subsistence level, and the few cash crops grown are subject to the fluctuations of the world market. Industrial development is minimal and is largely confined to food processing. Despite its poverty, the country has long functioned as a crossroads between northern and western Africa and has developed a rich cultural tradition.

THE LAND

Relief. Mali's landscape is largely flat and monotonous. Two basic relief features can be distinguished—plateaus and plains. The highland regions are localized and discontinuous.

The plateaus and the plains The plateaus of the south and southwest (extensions of the Fouta Djallon highlands of Guinea and the Guinea Highlands of Guinea and the Ivory Coast) lie between about 1,000 and 1,600 feet (300 and 500 metres) above sea level but attain heights approaching 2,000 feet in the Mandingue Plateau near Bamako and more than 2,100 feet near Satadougou. Composed mainly of sandstone, the plateaus are deeply incised by the Sénégal and Niger rivers and their tributaries. The plateau edges often take the form of precipitous cliffs, and their surfaces are cut by deep river valleys and waterfalls.

The plateaus of the southeast and east, also extensions of the Guinea Highlands, are a series of small, broken hills. Altitudes in the southeast range between almost 1,000 feet in the region of Sikasso and 1,739 feet (530 metres) at Mt. Mina. East of the Niger River the Dogon Plateau descends gently westward to the river valley but ends in abrupt cliffs on the southeast. These cliffs reach an altitude approaching 3,300 feet at Bandiagara.

The only marked relief feature in the north is the Adrar des Iforas. An extension of the mountainous Hoggar region of the Sahara, this heavily eroded sandstone plateau rises to altitudes of between 1,300 and 1,600 feet.

Northern and central Mali are composed of the plains of the Niger River basin and of the Sahara. In the north are the vast plains of the Tanezrouft and Taoudenni, which are covered with sand dunes and with areas of shifting sand known as ergs. In the central region are the alluvial plains of Meriyé and Azaouak.

Drainage. The drainage system is composed of the Sénégal and Niger rivers and their tributaries. The Sénégal River flows in a northwesterly direction across Mali for 420 miles (670 kilometres) on its course to the Atlantic Ocean. Its main headwaters—the Bafing and the Bakoye (Bakhoy) rivers—rise in the Fouta Djallon and join at Bafoulabé to form the Sénégal. The river then flows to the west across the plateau region, where it is broken by falls at Gouina and Félou. Between Kayes and the Senegalese border it receives the Kolimbiné and Karakoro rivers on the right and the Falémé—its major tributary—on the left.

A tropical river, the Sénégal experiences seasonal flow. The waters are low in April and May and are high between July and October. Floods occur during the first two months of the high-water period.

Niger River For 1,100 miles, more than one-third of its total length, the Niger River flows through Mali. Rising in the Fouta Djallon, the river is of significant size by the time it enters Mali near Kangaba. It flows to the northeast across the Mandingue Plateau, where it is broken by falls at Sotuba. Reaching Koulikoro, it spreads out in a wide valley and flows majestically to its confluence with the Bani River at Mopti. The Niger then forms an interior delta because the land is flat and the river's descent almost nonexistent. The river breaks down into a network of branches and lakes as it continues northward. The lakes include those of Débo, Niangaye, Télé, and Faguibine. At Bourem the Niger makes a great bend to the south, known as the Niger Bend, and flows past Gao and Ansongo to the Niger border at Labbezanga.

The Niger also flows intermittently. High waters occur on the Upper Niger from July to October, at the delta from September to November, and at the bend from December to January. Periodic floods and the rich alluvial soils in the central delta make the Niger Valley an important agricultural region.

Soils. The soils are generally poor. In the south, ferruginous (iron-bearing) soils are shallow and form a hard, red crust because of intense evaporation. Along the southern edge of the Sahara, the brown and reddish soils are only slightly transformed into crust because of the lack of water and chemical decomposition. The desert region is composed of sand, rock, and gravel.

Climate. Mali lies within the intertropical zone and has a hot, dry climate. The sun is at its zenith throughout most of the year. In general, there are two distinct seasons, the dry and the wet. The dry season, from November to June, is marked by low humidity and high temperatures and is influenced by the *alize* and harmattan winds. The *alize,* from the northeast from December to February, causes a relatively cold spell, with temperatures averaging 77° F (25° C). From March to June, the dry, hot harmattan blows from the east and sweeps the overheated soil into dusty whirlwinds. The wind causes temperatures between 104° and 113° F.

During the rainy season from June to October, the monsoon wind blows from the southwest. Preceded by large, black clouds, the tornado-like rainstorms are accompanied by lightning and thunder. Temperatures lessen somewhat in August, when most of the rainfall occurs.

Climatic zones The country can be divided into three climatic zones—the Sudanic, the Sahelian, and the desert zones. Sudanic climate occurs in almost one-third of the country, from the southern border to latitude 15° north. It is characterized by an annual rainfall of between 20 and 51 inches (510 and 1,300 millimetres) and average temperatures of between 75° and 86° F (24° and 30° C). The Sahel, or the area bordering on the Sahara, receives between eight and 20 inches of rain a year and has average temperatures between 73° and 97° F (23° and 36° C). In the Sahara, temperatures during the day range from 117° to nearly 140° F (47° to 60° C), while at night the temperature drops to between 39° to 41° F (4° to 5° C). The scanty annual rainfall of less than seven inches is rare and irregular, and some years are rainless.

Plant and animal life. There are two main vegetational zones that correspond to the climatic regions of the Sudan and the Sahel. In the Sudanic zone there are localized forest corridors along the Guinean border and the river valleys. The rest of the area is covered with savanna (open grassland and scattered trees). The trees include the nere, or twoball nitta tree (*Parkia biglobosa*), the karite (*Butyrospermum parkii*), the cailcedra (Senegal khaya; *Khaya senegalensis*), and the kapioka. The incidence of trees decreases to the north as the Sudanic zone merges with the Sahel. The Sahel is characterized by steppe vegetation; drought-resistant trees such as the baobab, the doum palm, and palmyra are found. These trees also disappear to the north, however, where short, thorny plants such as the mimosa, the acacia, and cramcram (a member of the grass family) occur. All vegetation gradually disappears as one enters the Sahara region.

The animal life of the Sudan and of the Sahel is rich and varied. Large, herbivorous mammals include the gazelle, the antelope, the giraffe, and the elephant. The main carnivores are lions, panthers, and hyenas. Crocodiles and hippopotamuses inhabit the rivers, and there is a wide variety of monkeys, snakes, and birds (including the ostrich). There is a national park along the Baoulé River in the west and an animal reserve between Ansongo and Ménako in the east.

Settlement patterns. Mali is traditionally divided into the nomadic region of the Sahel and the Sahara and the agricultural region of the Sudanic zone. About nine-tenths of the population is rural. The rural population lives in thatched dwellings grouped together in villages of between 150 and 600 inhabitants. The villages are surrounded by cultivated fields and grazing lands. The older towns, such as Djénné, Timbuktu (Tombouctou), Gao, and Ségou, are built in the characteristic Sudanese style of architecture. The newer towns, such as Bamako, Kayes, San, and Kati, consist of a central business district, around which African residential districts are grouped. The houses are built of a mixture of earth and cement.

THE PEOPLE

What is known as the "white" population includes nomadic groups of Berbers (including the important Berber subgroup of the Tuareg [Touareg]) and the Arab-Berber group known as the Moors. These groups live in the Sahelian zone and north of the Niger Bend.

The black population is composed of numerous agricultural groups, some of whom are descended from the peoples of the ancient empires of Ghana, Mali, and Songhai. The largest group are the Bambara, who live along the Upper Niger River. The Soninke, or Sarakole, are descended from the founders of the Ghana Empire and live in the western Sahelian zone. The Malinke (Mandingo), bearers of the heritage of the Mali Empire, live in the southwest, while the Songhai are settled in the Niger Valley from Djénné to Ansongo. The Dognon live in the plateau region around Bandiagara. The Voltaic group includes the Bwa, or Bobo, the Senufo, and the Minianka. They occupy the east and southeast.

The Fulani, or Peul, are nomadic pastoralists of the Sahel and Macina. Other ethnic groups of note include the Tukulors (Toucouleurs), the Kasonke, the Bozo, and the Somono.

Linguistic groups. French is the official national language. There are several indigenous languages and dialects, which roughly correspond to either ethnic groups or regions. The most important is the Mande group, which includes Bambara (spoken by almost two-thirds of the population), Malinke, Kasonke, and Wasulunka (Ouassoulou). Soninke and Dogon are also related to Bambara; Dogon includes many dialects. The related but autonomous languages of the Voltaic peoples are Bwa, Senufo, and Minianka. The Fulani and Tukulor speak Fulah (Peul), and Songhaic is spoken all along the Niger Bend. The Tuareg have retained their ancient Berber language and written script, *tifinagh,* which is related to that of ancient Libya. The Moors speak Arabic.

Religious groups. There are three main religions. Islām is practiced by nearly two-thirds of the population, animism by most of the rest, and Christianity by a small number. Islāmization dates back to the 11th century and has eclipsed traditional animism among the Soninke, Songhai, Tukulor, Moors, Tuareg, and Fulani. Animism continues as the religion of the Voltaic peoples, the Malinke, and the Bambara.

THE ECONOMY

Resources. Iron is the most widespread mineral resource. Found in the west near the Senegal and Guinea borders, its reserves are estimated at 12,000,000 tons.

Bauxite deposits of about 800,000,000 tons are located near Kayes and on the Mandingue Plateau. There are approximately 3,500,000 tons of manganese, and the phosphate deposits in the Ansongo region are estimated at 20,000,000 tons.

There are important deposits of gold at Kalana near Bougouni, on the Mandingue Plateau, and in the Adrar des Iforas. Lithium (a soft, silver-white, metallic element, the lightest of all metals) has been discovered near Kayes and Bougouni, and there are uranium deposits in the Adrar. There are also traces of tungsten, tin, lead, copper, and zinc, as well as deposits of salt, marble, kaolin (china clay), and limestone. Extensive exploration for oil has been undertaken.

Biological resources. Vegetation resources are limited and are not conducive to forestry activities. The fish of the country's rivers and lakes, however, form the basis of a growing fishing and fish-processing industry. Wild animals are not economically significant.

Power resources. There are extensive possibilities for the production of hydroelectric power on the Sénégal and Niger rivers, as well as on some of their tributaries.

Agriculture and fishing. Subsistence and commercial agriculture are the bases of the Malian economy. More than 90 percent of the working population is in subsistence agriculture, and the government supports the development of commercial products. Areas of cultivation are located in the Sudanese and Sahelian zones; the most important agricultural area is the inland Niger Delta. Crops such as millet, rice, wheat, and corn (maize), as well as potatoes, yams, and cassava, are the main subsistence crops. Cotton and peanuts (groundnuts) are the important commercial crops; sugarcane, tobacco, and tea are also grown for market. Market gardens produce a variety of vegetables and fruits, including cabbages, turnips, carrots, beans, tomatoes, bananas, mangoes, and oranges. Irrigation projects have been developed on the Niger in the Ségou and Mopti districts.

The major areas for the raising of livestock are the Sahel and the area around Macina. There are cattle, sheep and goats in the country.

Mali is one of the largest producers of fish in western Africa. After processing (drying and smoking), about 20 percent of the annual catch is exported.

Industry. Most industrial enterprises engage in the processing of food and other agricultural products. There are several rice mills, flour mills, and cotton gins. The oil and soap factory of Koulikoro satisfies domestic demands for its products. There are breweries, a tannery, and a refrigerated slaughterhouse at Bamako; fruit-preservation plants at Baguinéda; a sugar refinery at Dougabougou; and cigarette and match factories at Djoliba.

The Malian Company of Textiles (Comatex) produces cotton fibre and unprinted cloth, while the Textile Industry of Mali (Itema) manufactures printed cloth and blankets. A cement factory at Diamou is a basic industry. There are also shops for the construction of autocycles, the repair of machinery, and the assembly of radios.

Handicrafts are important, and the Malians are noted for their clothing, pottery, shoes, baskets, and wood carvings.

Although mineral resources are extensive, the mining industry is minimal. Exploited deposits are those of salt (at Taoudenni), marble and kaolin (at Bafoulabé), gold (at Kalana), and limestone (at Diamou).

Electricity is largely produced in thermal power stations. There are eight thermal stations, located in Bamako and other large towns. Hydroelectric power is produced at the Sotuba and Markala dams on the Niger River, at the Felou Dam on the Sénégal River, and at the Sélingué Dam on the San Karani. Construction of a dam at Gouina on the Sénégal was undertaken, and the construction of the Manantali Dam on the Sénégal is a joint venture with Senegal and Mauritania. Mali has also begun to exploit solar energy; solar-powered pumps provide electricity to some 30 villages, and a solar centre has been established at Diré.

Finance and trade. The Central Bank of Mali, managed equally by Mali and France, controls the nation's credit and the exchange rate between the Mali franc (the monetary unit of the country) and the French franc. The De-

Agricultural products

Industries and handicrafts

velopment Bank of Mali finances development projects, while the Malian Bank of Credit and Deposits and the French-owned West African International Bank carry out credit and depository functions. Several French insurance companies maintain offices in Bamako.

The most important export items are cotton, peanuts, cereals, live animals, and dried and smoked fish. Imports consist largely of textiles, food products, automobiles, iron and steel, and petroleum products. Foreign trade is entirely controlled by the Malian Society of Import and Export (Somiex), which operates at a deficit. Mali is a member of the Organisation pour la Mise en Valeur du Fleuve Sénégal (Organization for the Development of the Sénégal River), which also includes Senegal and Mauritania. Despite strict customs controls, smuggling—especially of cattle and fish—is considerable.

Mali's form of Socialism

Administration of the economy. *The public and private sectors.* At the time of independence in 1960, the government adopted a policy of Socialism. State companies and rural cooperative societies were organized to regulate both the production and the distribution of goods. Since the military coup d'etat in 1968, Socialist policy has been mitigated by the encouragement of private business.

Taxation and foreign aid. Direct taxes include an income tax on salaries and a uniform per capita tax on those individuals who do not participate in the money economy. Most of the government's revenue is derived from indirect taxes, such as customs duties and commercial taxes.

Bilateral external aid is provided largely by France and the European Economic Community (EEC). International aid is granted by such organizations as the United Nations, the FED (Fonds Européen de Développement, or European Development Fund), and the United Nations Development Programme (UNDP).

Transportation. Mali's transportation systems are concentrated in the Sudanic and Sahelian regions. Because Mali is landlocked, its major transport routes connect with those of neighbouring countries and their ports to provide it with outlets to the sea.

Roads. There are several main axes of paved roads radiating from Bamako. The road from Bamako to Bougouni and Sikasso connects with the Ivory Coast road running to the port of Abidjan. A road links Bamako with Kankan in Guinea and Monrovia in Libera. Another main road runs through Bamako, Ségou, San, Mopti, Gao, and Ansongo to the border with Niger. Construction of a Saharan road connecting Gao with North Africa was begun in 1979.

Railways. The one railroad track runs for 400 miles from Koulikoro, a short distance northeast of Bamako, northwestward to Kayes and to Kidira, on the Senegal border, where it connects with the Senegalese railway to Dakar. Another railway line is planned to link Bamako with the Guinean railway, which runs to Conakry.

Inland water-ways

River transport. The Sénégal River is navigable from July to October from Kayes in the west of the country down to Saint-Louis, Senegal, at the river's mouth. The Niger River is navigable throughout its length in Mali from July to January. The Bani River is navigable for 186 miles.

Air transport. A national airline, Air Mali, operates both domestic and international flights. The main airport is at Bamako, and another is at Ségou. There are domestic air routes to Ségou, Mopti, Goundam, Timbuktu, Gao, Kayes, Kéniéba, Nara, and Nioro. Bamako is also linked by air to France, Morocco, and other western African nations.

ADMINISTRATIVE AND SOCIAL CONDITIONS

Government. Upon independence in 1960, a constitution was granted that guaranteed parliamentary democracy through universal suffrage and provided for an elected National Assembly; the provisions of the constitution were not fully implemented, however. The military government that took power in 1968 suspended the constitution and forbade all political activity. A new constitution was approved in a national referendum on June 2, 1974. The president is elected to a six-year term and the 82 members of the National Assembly to three-year terms. The country is ruled by a single party, the Union Démocratique du Peuple Malien (UDPM).

The country is divided into the seven regions of Kayes, Koulikoro, Sikasso, Ségou, Mopti, Gao, and Tombouctou and the district of Bamako. Each of the regions is further divided into administrative units called *cercles,* which are in turn subdivided into smaller units called *arrondissements.* Each region is administered by a governor, who coordinates the activities of the *cercles* and implements economic policy. The *cercles* provide nuclei for the major government services; their various headquarters provide focal points for the health service, the army, the police, local courts, and other government agencies. The *arrondissement* is the basic administrative unit, and its centre usually houses a school and a dispensary. It is composed of several villages, which are headed by chiefs and elected village councils.

The judicial system

Justice. At the head of the judicial system, the Supreme Court exercises both judicial and administrative powers; it is the court of first and last resort in matters concerning the government. The Court of Appeal, located in Bamako, tries all cases on appeal from ordinary tribunals. The Special Court of State Security holds trials for crimes against state property, especially concerning itself with charges of embezzlement. There are more than 50 tribunals and more than 70 magistrates. Justices of the peace have full powers to judge ordinary civil, commercial, and financial cases; they sit in the headquarters of the *cercles* and also travel to the major towns of the *arrondissements.*

Since 1960 there has been a determined attempt to mold the judicial system to the contemporary needs of the population. New law codes have liberated women from traditional restraints, defined the rights and duties of citizens, and modified the penal procedure.

Education. French is the only language of instruction. Primary and secondary education are compulsory and free from six to 15 years of age and are combined in the nine-year curriculum of the *cycle fondemental* ("fundamental educational level"). The general secondary school, or *lycée,* provides the last three years of traditional secondary education. Higher education—geared directly to the needs of the government—is obtained in state colleges. These colleges include teacher-training colleges, a college of administration, an engineering institute, a polytechnic institute, and a school of medical assistants. Many of Mali's university students study abroad, especially in France and Senegal.

Health and welfare. State hospitals, including two at Bamako and Kati, medical centres, maternity centres, and dispensaries are available. There are also infectious disease and leprosy centres. There are not enough trained medical personnel to meet Mali's needs.

A Ministry for Social Affairs is charged with improving the conditions of women, children, and invalids. There are social centres located throughout the country; they offer public-health information and provide day nurseries. There is no national social security fund. A Service for Family Allowances, however, makes loans to workers and issues pensions to retired people.

Rural and urban society

Mali contains two distinct, stratified societies. Most of the population belong to traditional social groups, which have inherited hierarchical social structures. These groups consist of nobles, vassals, and members of various castes, all of whom acquired their status by birth.

The second Malian society is formed by the urban population. Privileged groups are the educated government officials and the traders. The middle socioeconomic group is composed of civil servants and industrial workers. The lowest group is made up of the unemployed.

CULTURAL LIFE

Mali is one of the cultural crossroads of western Africa. Situated between the Arab world to the north and the black African nations to the south, it has for centuries been a cultural meeting place. The mixture of both worlds has produced an original Sudanic culture that is diversified according to the various ethnic groups and regions that compose it.

Music and dancing are the most common cultural activities; they form an especially rich heritage among the Malinke and Songhai peoples. The Bambara and the Voltaic groups excel in the creation of wood carvings of masks, statues, stools, and objects used in animist worship. The *tiewara,* or gazelle mask, of the Bambara is remarkable for its fineness of line.

Music, dance, and traditional crafts

Architecture is well developed in the Niger Valley. The Sudanic style finds typical expression in the storied houses and mosques of Djénné and Timbuktu.

Localized handicrafts include jewelry making by the Mandingo people, leatherworking around the Niger Bend, the weaving of geometrical designs into cotton cloth, and the carving of statues for the tourist trade.

The Musée de l'Institut de Recherches et de Documentation at Bamako contains collections of art from most of the country's regions. The National Archives of Mali, the National Library, and the Institute of Human Sciences are also located in Bamako, as also is the Municipal Library. The Centre of Arab Documentation is located in Timbuktu, and there is a French Centre of Documentation

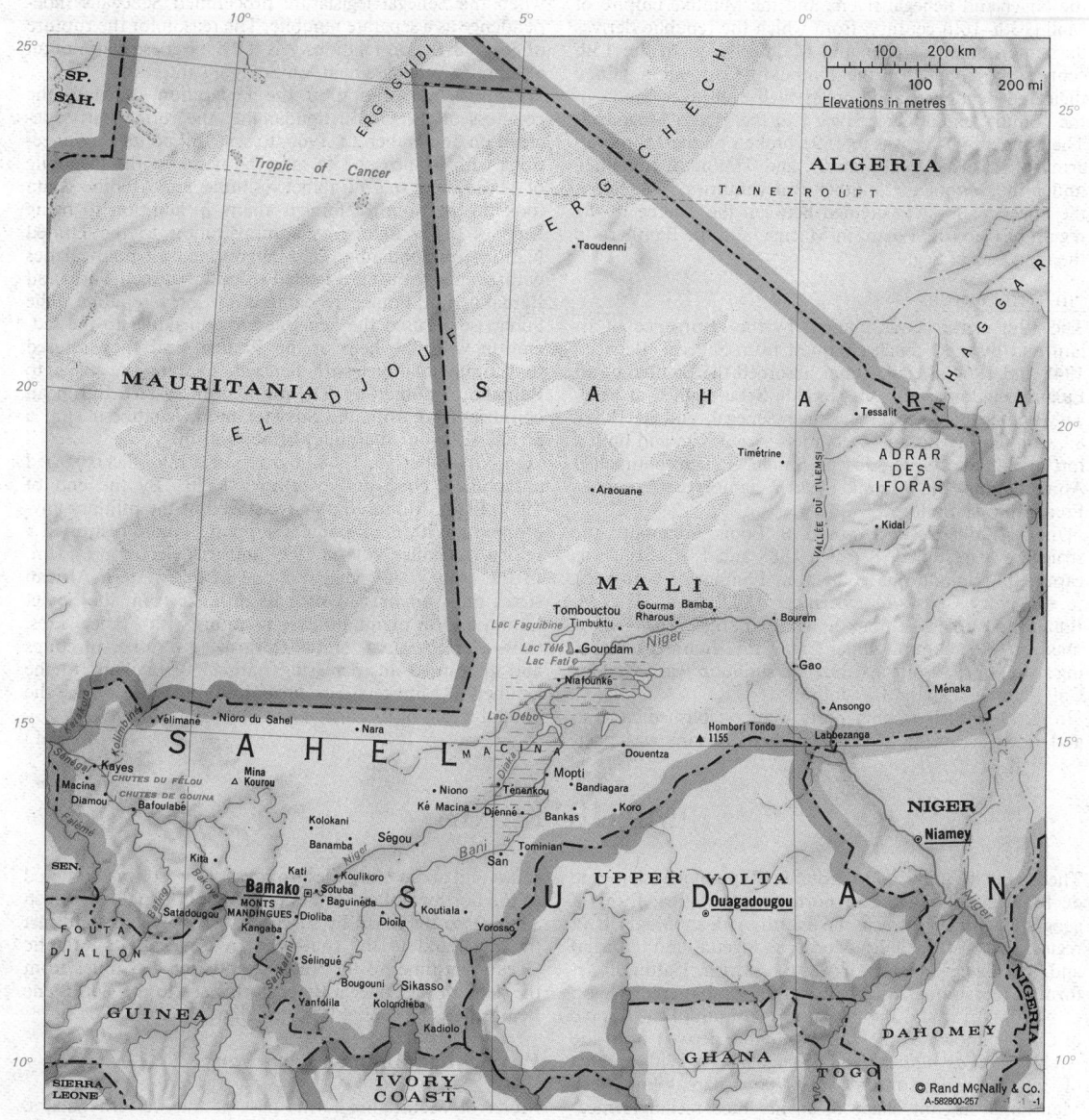

MALI

in Bamako. The Library of the Office of Niger in Ségou contains information on agriculture, irrigation, and general science.

The government promotes the expansion of popular culture through the Committee of Youth and Sports. Youth associations organize sports, theatrical, musical, and dancing activities in every important town. Cultural competitions are presented in Bamako during the biennial Youth Week. The Malian Ballet Troupe performs throughout the world. Artists are trained at the National Institute of Arts and at the Artisan Centre of Bamako. For statistical data, see the "Britannica World Data" section in the current *Britannica Book of the Year*.

History

Evidence of prehistoric habitation of the Malian Sahara is furnished by Paleolithic and Neolithic remains and by rock paintings and carvings. The Asselar man, the earliest human fossil with Negroid features, was discovered in 1927 about 250 miles north of Timbuktu. Elsewhere in Mali have been found Mousterian remains, raised stones of the Neolithic period, and along the Niger, numerous traces of protohistoric civilizations.

From the early Middle Ages caravan routes between the bend of the Niger and Morocco and southern Algeria carried ivory, gum, ostrich feathers, slaves, and gold. Around the starting points of these routes were founded the Soninke empire of Ghana (8th–13th century) between the Niger and Sénégal rivers, and the Malinke empire of Mali (13th–16th century, from which the republic derives its name), on the Upper and Middle Niger. In the 15th century the Songhai in the Timbuktu–Gao region gained their independence and spread their rule over much of the country extending eastward to the Hausa kingdoms. The Songhai power was in 1591 broken by the Moroccan army of Ahmed IV al-Manṣūr, and Timbuktu remained under the Moors for another two centuries. Thereafter, the Niger Valley was divided between the Tuareg in the region of Gao, the Fulani in Macina, and the Bambara in the kingdom of Segu.

Expansion of Songhai rule

THE 19TH CENTURY

The 19th century was marked by the resurgence of Islām and by the French conquest from Senegal. Between 1848 and 1864 al-Ḥājj ʿUmar absorbed the Bambara and Fulani kingdoms; his son Ahmadu Seku reigned at Segu. The French had occupied Upper Senegal, and in 1881–83, Col. Gustav Borgnis-Deborders seized Kita and built a fort at Bamako. Later, Joseph-Simon Gallieni compelled Ahmadu and the Malinke leader Samory to accept a French protectorate.

Under Giallieni's successor, Col. Louis Archinard, the struggle was resumed. Between 1888 and 1893, Segu was captured, Ahmadu put to flight, and Samory driven back to the Ivory Coast. In December 1893, Lieut. H.G.M. Boiteux occupied Timbuktu with a flotilla. The Tuareg massacred the column under Col. T.P.E. Bonnier advancing to reinforce Boiteaux, but the situation was saved by Col. (later Marshal) J.J.C. Joffre.

In 1899 French trading posts were established at Gao and downstream of it. The southern Sahara was paci-fied by *méharistes* ("camel companies"). The capture of Sikasso in 1898 completed the conquest of the country, which as French Sudan became a territory of French West Africa. The territory was divided into *cercles* ("districts") in which civilian administrators gradually replaced military officers. The Sudanese—particularly the Bamban—provided contingents of sharpshooters called Sénégalais who played a leading part in the French colonial wars. Road and rail communications were established through the territory, and in 1925 the first automobile crossing of the Sahara was made.

INDEPENDENCE

In 1946 French Sudan became an overseas territory of the French Union and was given a territorial assembly, followed in 1957 by an elected government. As the Sudanese Republic (Soudan) the country was proclaimed an autonomous state of the French Community on November 24, 1958.

On January 17, 1959, the name of Mali was suggested for a federation grouping the autonomous republic of Dahomey, Senegal, Upper Volta, and the Sudanese Republic. When the state came into existence, however, Dahomey and Upper Volta reversed their earlier decision and did not participate. On September 24, 1959, Mali decided to seek independence within the framework of a confederal association with France, which was achieved June 20, 1960.

The federation effectively ceased to exist on August 20 when the Senegal legislature proclaimed Senegal's independence as a separate republic. The reason for the rupture of Senegal–Sudan relations was the Senegalese claim of an attempted Sudanese coup on Senegal's interests.

Following dissolution of the Federation of Mali, the congress of the Union Soudanaise, the ruling party, decided on September 22, 1960, to sever all political connections with France and to take the name of the Republic of Mali. There was a Cabinet reshuffle, and Modibo Keita took the portfolio of foreign affairs in addition to being head of state. Before its administration to the United Nations on September 28 Mali rejected all political ties with France, causing a heated dispute between Paris and Bamako, but France recognized the new republic. The Sudanese accused the Senegalese of breaking up the federation with the help of the French, and they refused to resume relations with Senegal. Despite the visits to Bamako of numerous delegations from eastern European countries and from the Soviet Union, Modibo Keita, a Socialist, favoured a policy of neutralism.

On November 19, 1968, a group of army officers staged a bloodless coup and overthrew Keita. By the end of 1969, Lieut. Moussa Traoré was head of the military government. With mass popular support, Traoré instituted a return to civilian rule in 1979 and was elected president. In the early 1980s Mali was one of the western African states most anxious to keep its distance from the Soviet Union and to maintain close relations with France. Pres. (now Gen.) Moussa Traoré thwarted a number of coups and appointed an increasing number of civilians to the Council of Ministers. For current political history, see the annual issues of the *Britannica Book of the Year*.

The Federation of Mali

(Ed.)

MAURITANIA

The Islāmic Republic of Mauritania (République Islamique de Mauritanie), a state in northwestern Africa, forms a geographic link between the North African Maghrib (a region that also includes Morocco, Algeria, and Tunisia) and the Senegal region of western Africa. Culturally, it forms a transitional zone between the Arab–Berber region of North Africa and the region to the south of the Tropic of Cancer known as the Sudan (a name derived from the Arabic *bilād as-sūdān*, "land of the blacks"). With an area of 398,000 square miles (1,030,700 square kilometres), Mauritania has the shape of an indented rectangle measuring about 930 miles (1,500 kilometres) from north to south and about 680 miles from east to west. It is bordered to the northwest by the Western Sahara (formerly Spanish Sahara), to the north by Algeria, to the east and southeast by Mali, and to the southwest by Senegal. Its Atlantic Ocean coastline, to the west, extends for 435 miles from the delta of the Sénégal River northward to the Cap Blanc Peninsula. The capital is Nouakchott.

Physical and human geography

Much of Mauritania forms part of the western Sahara, and a large proportion of the population is nomadic. The country's mineral wealth includes large reserves of iron ore and of copper, which are now being exploited. Mauritania, formerly French administered, became independent on November 28, 1960. By the terms of the constitution, Islām is the religion of the Mauritanian people, and the republic guarantees freedom of conscience and religious liberty to all; Arabic is the national language, and the official languages are Arabic and French.

THE LAND

Relief and drainage. Both land relief and drainage are influenced by the aridity that characterizes the greater part of the country. The impression of immensity given by the landscape is reinforced by its flatness; the coastal plains are lower than 150 feet (45 metres), while the higher plains of the interior vary from 600 to 750 feet. The interior plains form a plateau of which the culminating heights,

Plains and plateaus

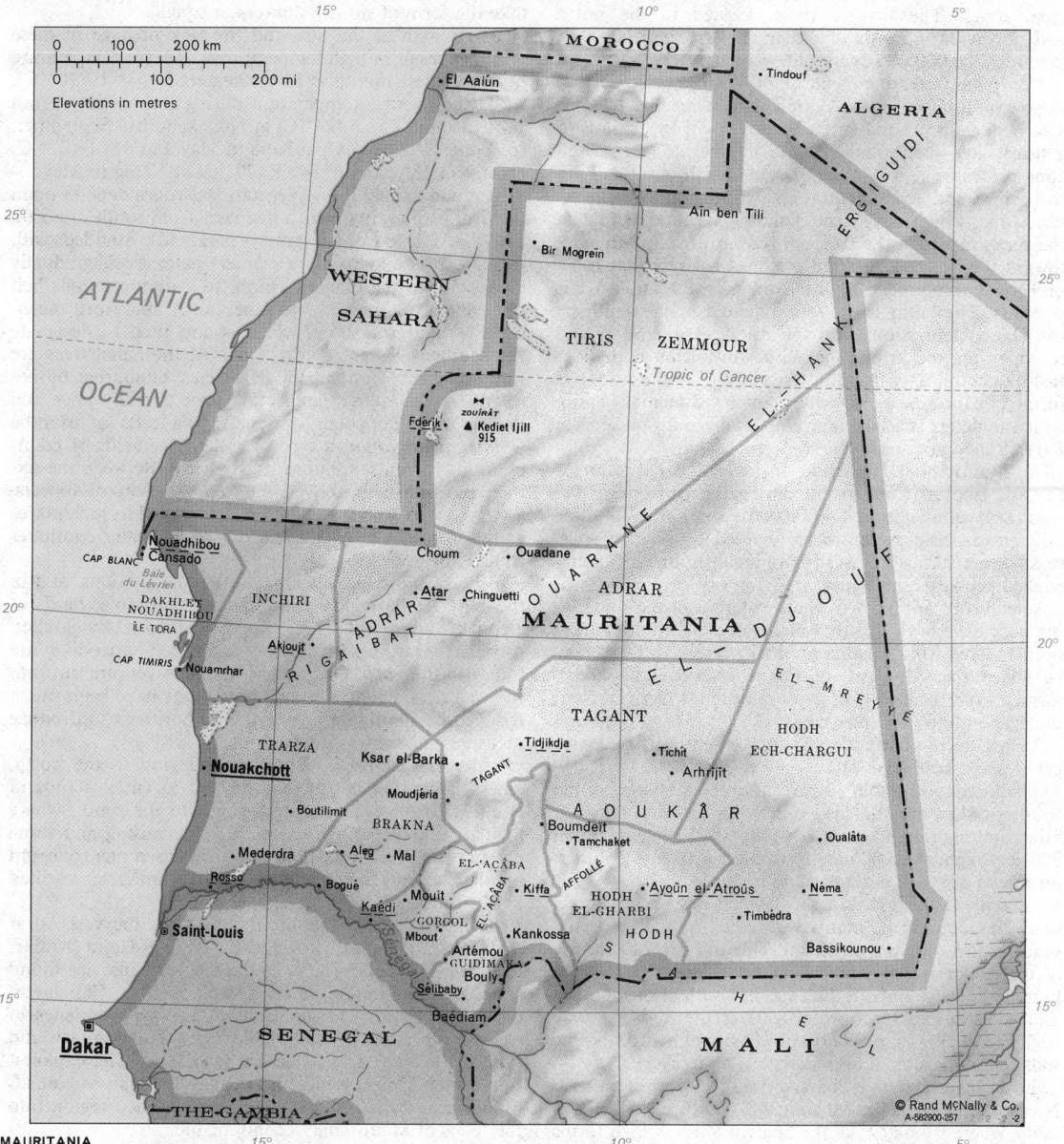

MAURITANIA

MAP INDEX

Political subdivisions

'Açâba, el-	16.40n	11.40w
Adrar	21.00n	10.00w
Brakna	17.00n	13.20w
Dakhlet Nouadhibou	20.30n	16.00w
Gorgol	15.45n	13.00w
Guidimaka	15.20n	12.00w
Hodh ech-Chargui	19.00n	7.15w
Hodh el-Gharbi	16.30n	10.00w
Inchiri	20.00n	15.00w
Nouakchott	18.06n	15.57w
Tagant	19.00n	10.00w
Tiris Zemmour	24.00n	9.00w
Trarza	18.00n	15.00w

Cities and towns

Aïn ben Tili	26.00n	9.32w
Akjoujt	19.45n	14.23w
Aleg	17.03n	13.55w
Arhrîjît	18.24n	9.15w
Artémou	15.31n	12.16w
Atar	20.31n	13.03w
'Ayoûn el-'Atroûs	16.40n	9.37w
Baédiam	15.03n	11.51w
Bassikounou	15.52n	5.57w
Bir Mogreïn (Fort-Trinquet)	25.14n	11.35w
Bogué	16.35n	14.16w
Bouly	15.19n	11.48w
Boumdeït	17.26n	11.21w
Boutilimit	17.33n	14.42w
Cansado	20.51n	17.02w
Chinguetti	20.27n	12.22w
Choum	21.18n	13.01w
Fdérik (Fort-Gouraud)	22.41n	12.43w
Fort-Trinquet, see Bir Mogreïn		
Kaédi	16.09n	13.30w
Kankossa	15.56n	11.31w
Kiffa	16.37n	11.24w
Ksar el-Barka	18.24n	12.13w
Mal	16.58n	13.23w
Mbout	16.02n	12.35w
Mederdra	16.55n	15.39w
Moudjéria	17.53n	12.20w
Mouit	16.35n	13.05w
Néma	16.37n	7.15w
Nouadhibou (Port-Étienne)	20.54n	17.04w
Nouakchott	18.06n	15.57w
Nouamrhar	19.22n	16.31w
Ouadane	20.56n	11.37w
Oualâta	17.18n	7.02w
Port-Étienne, see Nouadhibou		
Rosso	16.30n	15.49w
Sélibaby	15.10n	12.11w
Tamchaket	17.15n	10.40w
Tîchît	18.28n	9.30w
Tidjikdja	18.33n	11.25w
Timbédra	16.15n	8.10w

Physical features and points of interest

'Açâba, el-, plateau	16.00n	12.00w
Adrar, plateau	20.30n	13.30w
Affollé, hills	16.55n	10.25w
Aoukâr, physical region	18.00n	9.30w
Atlantic Ocean	24.00n	17.00w
Blanc, Cap, cape	20.46n	17.03w
Djouf, el-, desert	20.30n	8.00w
Hank, el-, escarpment	24.30n	7.00w
Hodh, physical region	16.10n	8.40w
Iguidi, 'Erg, dunes	26.35n	5.40w
Ijill, Kediet, mountain	22.38n	12.33w
Lévrier, Baie du, bay	20.55n	16.52w
Mreyyé, el-, physical region	19.30n	7.00w
Ouarane, physical region	21.00n	10.30w
Rigaibat, physical region	19.45n	14.00w
Sahel, physical region	15.30n	8.00w
Sénégal, river	15.48n	16.32w
Tagant, plateau	17.31n	12.07w
Tidra, Île, island	19.44n	16.24w
Timiris, Cap, cape	19.23n	16.32w
Zouîrât, mines	22.45n	12.30w

occurring at different levels, form many tablelands joined to one another by very long, gentle slopes of about two degrees. The topography is relieved by vestiges of cliffs (generally cuestas); by sloping plains that terminate at one end of the slope with a steep cliff or faulted scarp, which may reach heights of 900 feet; or by inselbergs (steep-sided residual hills) of which the highest is Kediet Ijill (3,002 feet high), an enormous block of hematite.

Structurally, Mauritania may be divided into three principal zones. The first of these, located in the north and northwest, consists of underlying Precambrian rock (about 2,700,000,000 years old), which emerges to form not only the backbone of northern Mauritania's Rigaibāt ridge region but also the Akjoujt rock series that forms a vast peneplain (a land surface worn down by erosion to a nearly flat plain) studded with inselbergs. The second zone is located partly in the extreme north but mostly in the centre and east. In the north it consists of primary sandstone, which covers the Tindouf Syncline (a fold in the rocks in which the strata dip inward from both sides toward the axis); in the centre is the vast synclinal basin of Taoudeni, bounded by the Adrar, Tagant, and ꞋAçâba plateaus. The basin is scarcely indented to the south by the Hodh Depression, with the Affollé Anticline (a fold in which the rock strata incline downward on both sides from a central axis) lying in its centre. The third zone is formed by the Senegalese–Mauritanian sedimentary basin, which includes coastal Mauritania and the lower Sénégal River Valley of the southwest.

The Mauritanian landscape, in general, as a result of the arid phases it underwent during the Quaternary Period (i.e., within the past 4,000,000 years), presents three different aspects; these are represented by skeletal soils, regs (desert surfaces consisting of small, rounded, tightly packed pebbles), and dunes.

Skeletal soils are formed where outcrops of the underlying rock have been slightly weathered or where they have been covered with a patina or chalky crust. To these may be added the salty soils of the sebkhas (saline plains), formed from the caking of gypsum or of salt derived from the evaporation of former lakes.

The regs form plains often of great extent, carpeted with pebbles and boulders.

The dunes cover about 50 percent of the total area of the country. They are stretched out, often for several dozen miles, in long ridges known as ꞇalâb, which are sometimes 300 feet high; they frequently overlap with one another, forming a network of domes and basins.

It is only to the south of the 10-inch isohyet (an imaginary line connecting points with equal rainfall) that the sands bear a brown type of soil. This soil is characteristic of the steppe (treeless plains) and contains 2 percent of humus. It is also only in the extreme south of the country that the iron-bearing tropical soils of the Sudanic zone begin; in the lowest places occur patches of hydromorphic soils (i.e., soils altered by waterborne materials).

The drainage system is characterized by a lack of pattern. Normal drainage is limited to inland southwestern Mauritania, where tributaries of the Sénégal River, which forms the frontier between Mauritania and Senegal, flow southward and are subject to ephemeral flooding in summer. In the greater part of the country, however, the plateaus are cut into by wadis (dry riverbeds), where the rare floods that occur dissipate their waters into a few permanent drainage basins called guelt (sing. guelta). In the wastes of the north and the east rainfall is so rare and slight that there is practically no runoff.

Climate. The climate owes its aridity to the northeastern trade winds, which blow constantly north of the Tropic of Cancer and throughout most of the year to the south of it; the drying effect produced by these winds is increased by the harmattan, or east wind. With the exception of the few winter rains that occur as a result of climatic disturbances in the polar regions, precipitation essentially results from the rain-bearing southwesterly winds, which progressively extend throughout the southern half of the country at the height of the summer. The duration of the rainy season, as well as the total annual amount of rainfall, diminishes progressively from south to north. Thus,

margin note: The arid climate

Sélibaby in the extreme south receives about 25 inches (635 millimetres) between June and October; Kiffa, further north, receives 14 inches between mid-June and mid-October; Tidjikdja receives seven inches between July and September; Atar receives seven inches between mid-July and September; and Nouadhibou (formerly Port-Étienne) receives between one and two inches, usually between September and November. Because of opposition between the wet southwesterlies and the harmattan, rains often take the form of stormy showers or squalls.

The strength of the Sun and the lack of haze in these latitudes result in high temperatures. Average temperature in the coldest month is in the region of 68° F (20° C), while the average temperature during the hottest month rises to about 75° F (24° C) at Nouakchott in September, to about 79° F (26° C) at Kiffa in May and 81° F (27° C) at Atar in July, and to 84° F (29° C) at Néma in May.

Plant and animal life. Vegetational zones depend upon the degree of aridity, which increases from south to north. The Sudanic savanna (grassy parkland), studded with baobab trees and palmyra (rônier) palm trees, gradually gives way, in the extreme south, to a discontinuous belt of vegetation known as the Sahel (an Arabic word meaning riverbank, or shore, which is also used to designate the southern Sahara borderlands). In the Sahel trees are rare and consist principally of acacias; euphorbia bushes (plants of the spurge family that have a milky juice and flowers with no petals or sepals); big tufts of morkba (Panicum turgidum, a type of millet); or fields of cram-cram, or Indian sandbur (a bristly herb). Between the six-inch and four-inch isohyets the steppe rapidly disappears, giving way to desert. Vegetation is restricted to such places as the dry beds of wadis, beneath which water continues to flow, or to oases.

In the savanna big antelope are hunted by lions, and in the hilly Afollé region of southern Mauritania, herds of elephants are found. The steppe is frequented by gazelles, ostriches, warthogs, panthers, and lynx; crocodiles are found in the guelt. Only addax antelope venture out into the waterless desert. Animal populations have been much reduced by hunting, obliging the authorities to introduce measures for conservation.

Settlement patterns. The Sahara region to the north, where habitation is generally limited to oases, stands in contrast to the Sahelian steppelands to the south, where regular rainfall permits extensive stock raising and some agriculture. While transition occurs between one zone and another, a convenient line of demarcation is represented by the four-inch isohyet.

The heartland of Mauritania consists of the vast Adrar and Tagant plateaus, known as the Trab el-Hajra (Arabic: Country of Stone). There, at the foot of cliffs, are found several oases, among which some—such as Chinguetti, Ouadane, Tîchît, Tidjikdja, and Atar—were the sites of well-known cities in the Middle Ages. To the north and the west extend the vast desert peneplains. The exploitation of the Zouîrât mines and the development of Nouadhibou have transformed this once-abandoned region into the focus of Mauritania's economic life.

Coastal southwestern Mauritania (under colonial rule, the Trarza cercle) is covered with regularly aligned dunes and is important for stock raising; Arab–Berber culture is represented by important marabout families.

Inland, southwestern Mauritania (the regions of Brakna, Gorgol, and el-ꞋAçâba) is inhabited by Moors and Fulani (Peul), who engage in both stock raising and agriculture. In the extreme south (Guidimaka region), large villages are surrounded by fields of millet, constituting the first sign of the Sudanese landscape.

In the southeast the vast Hodh Basin, with its dunes, sandstone plateaus, and immense regs, is a major stock-raising region, the economy of which has many links with neighbouring Mali.

Mauritania is a country suited for nomadic life. Livestock supplies the nomads with milk and meat, while transport is provided by riding camels and pack camels and, in the south, by pack oxen and donkeys as well. The women dye sheep's wool, with which they then braid long brown bands that are sewn together to make tents; they also tan

margin note: The Sahara and Sahel regions

goats' skins to make *guerba*s (waterskins). Movement is governed by the search for water and pasturage. In the Sahara nomadic movements are irregular because of the extreme variability of rains; in the Sahel, however, regular seasonal movement occurs—to the south in the dry season and back to the north in the wet season. Sizes of nomadic encampments also vary from south to north. In the coastal southwest groups of up to 300 tents may be found, whereas in northern Mauritania only groups of a few tents are to be seen.

The decline of nomadism   For a variety of reasons—including changes in agricultural patterns as well as in political and commercial relations—the traditional nomadic way of life has been declining. Dams to conserve floodwaters have been built in the wadis, and palm-tree culture has been considerably extended. The cumulative result of these developments has been that the nomads now tend to remain longer in the south near their millet fields and palm groves—becoming, in effect, seminomads.

Since the 1960s a movement toward settlement has been evident, largely because of growing dissatisfaction with the harsh conditions of nomadic life; this movement, however, has been restricted by the constant lack of water. Only in the extreme south—on the banks of the Sénégal River (in Mauritania called the Chemama)—is a normal, settled agricultural life possible. A series of droughts halted cultivation in the Sahel in the 1970s, and livestock raising was seriously constrained, affecting the livelihood of nomads and sedentary peoples alike.

The exploitation of the iron-ore reserves of Kediet Ijill, as well as the achievement of independence, have transformed the urban geography of Mauritania. The ancient cities that lived by caravan traffic—*e.g.,* Tîchît, Chinguetti, Ouadane, and Oualâta—and traded with Casablanca and, above all, with Dakar have grown idle beneath their palm trees. Only Tidjikdja and Atar have maintained a certain activity. Kaédi, on the Sénégal River, has expanded and is still growing. Three new towns have been built: Nouakchott, the capital; Fdérik (formerly Fort-Gouraud); and Nouadhibou.

Nouakchott was founded in 1958 after the government decided to replace the former capital, Saint-Louis in Senegal, with an authentically Mauritanian city. It is located near the sea and provides access to the Sahara and Sahel regions alike. In addition to being the seat of government and administration, Nouakchott is a growing commercial centre and has a printing works, a hospital, and numerous schools. Its water supply is provided by a plant that desalinizes seawater.

Fdérik is an administrative centre situated about 15 miles from the mining town of Zouîrât. The port of Nouadhibou, which was long stagnant, owes its more recent expansion both to expanding iron-ore exports and to the establishment of a fishing complex there. A few miles to the south lies Cansado, a residential city.

THE PEOPLE

The Moors   **Ethnic and linguistic groups.** The Moors constitute more than three-quarters of the population; about half of them are white, or *bîdân*, Moors of Arab and Berber descent, and about half are black Moors, of Sudanic origin. Moorish society historically was divided into a hierarchy of castes. At the head of the socioeconomic structure were the noble castes, composed of warriors and of marabouts, or priests and scholars of the Qurʾān. The warriors were usually Arab, and the marabouts were usually Berber. The mass of the *bîdân* population were vassals who received protection from the warriors or marabouts in return for tribute. There were two artisan classes—the blacksmiths and the griots (who were at once musicians and genealogists). Servant classes were formed of black Moors and were subdivided into "servants" and freedmen. Since the beginning of the 20th century, social divisions have been modified by successive governments. Among the ethnic and racial groups, blacks became the better educated and held most technical, professional, and diplomatic posts at the time of independence. Members of this "servant" caste, which developed as the bureaucratic class, became increasingly aware of their rights as citizens. Slavery was abolished by the French before independence and was officially abolished again in 1980, but subsequent reports claimed that the practice had continued.

The Moors speak Ḥassānīyah, a dialect that draws most of its grammar from Arabic and uses a vocabulary of both Arab and Berber words. Most of the white Moors also know literary Arabic.

The remaining population consists of Tukulor (Toucouleur), who live in the Sénégal River Valley; Fulani, who are dispersed throughout the south; Soninke (Sarakole), who inhabit the extreme south; and Wolof (Oulof), who live in the vicinity of Rosso in coastal southwestern Mauritania. The Tukulor and the Fulani speak Fulfulde (Poular), and the other groups have retained their respective tribal languages. Most of the non-Africans in Mauritania are French nationals engaged in technical assistance and in mining.

Religious groups. Almost all Mauritanians are Muslim. Most Moors belong to the Qādirīyah order. The Tukulor and some of the Tagant tribes belong to the Tijānīyah order.

THE ECONOMY

In the Sahel region of Mauritania a traditional subsistence economy is maintained, composed of stock raising, agriculture, crafts, and petty trading. In the Sahara region, however, a modern economy is developing, based on the exploitation of iron-ore and copper resources and of the fish resources of the continental shelf; the modern economy receives much needed capital investment and technical assistance from abroad. More than three-quarters of the Mauritanian population still lives by traditional activities, among which stock raising is the most important. In numbers, sheep and goats are the most important livestock, followed by cattle, camels, donkeys, and horses. Cattle are raised primarily in the southern region, whereas sheep and goats are dispersed as far north as the limits of the Sahara. Camels are raised mostly in the north and the centre, especially in the Adrar region.

Stock raising

Agriculture and fishing. Agriculture is necessarily dependent upon rainfall. Where the rainfall exceeds 17 inches (430 millimetres) a year, millet (fonio) and dates are the principal crops, supplemented by beans, yams, corn (maize), and cotton. Seasonal agriculture is practiced on the easily flooded riverbanks and in the wadis of the Sahelian zone, upstream from the dams. There, too, millet, sorghum, beans, and watermelons are grown. Irrigated agriculture is practiced in areas supplied by water-control projects and at oases, where well water is available; corn, barley, and some millet and vegetables are grown. The output of gum arabic is less than it was in former years. Agricultural production in Mauritania has continued to decline because of drought. Crop production fell by approximately two-thirds in the period from 1970 to 1980. From the late 1970s Mauritania was unable to produce more than half of its total food requirements.

Rich fishing grounds lie off Mauritania's Lévrier Bay. Mauritania stopped issuing fishing licenses in 1979, however, and in 1980 formed joint companies with Portugal, Iraq, South Korea, Romania, and the Soviet Union. At Nouadhibou fish are canned, frozen, or processed as fish flour. Several tons each year are dried and exported to other African countries.

Mining. The iron-ore deposits of Kediet Ijill have nearly been exhausted, and exploitation of reserves at Guelbs was begun. A rail link 405 miles long connects the mining town of Zouîrât with the port of Nouadhibou, the only deepwater roadstead on the Saharan coastline, accommodating ships of up to 150,000 tons. Exploitation was organized and begun by Miferma, of which 56 percent of the financing was by French groups and the remainder by British, West German, and Italian groups and by the Mauritanian government. The company was nationalized in 1974 and was renamed Cominor (Complexe Minier du Nord). Exports fell from a peak of 12,000,000 tons in 1974 to an annual average of 9,000,000 tons in the early 1980s.

Iron ore and copper

The copper deposits of Akjoujt have been estimated at 100,000,000 tons, with a copper content of more than 2 percent. Exploitation was begun in 1969 by Somima (Société Minière de Mauritanie), of which 54 percent of the shares were held by British and U.S. interests, 25 percent by the Mauritanian government, and the remainder by French interests. Somima was nationalized in 1975, but operations were suspended in 1978. Reactivation of the mine came under consideration in 1982. Processed copper had been exported along a 173-mile highway to the wharf at Nouakchott. Other mineral resources are minor, and salt output has declined. There are some gypsum deposits near Nouakchott. Reserves of ilmenite (the principal ore of titanium) have been located, and indications of copper have been found in the extreme south. Oil prospecting has so far yielded no results.

Trade. Foreign trade is difficult to estimate because, while imports and exports of the modern sector are well known, there are no statistics for the traditional sector. Mauritania is nevertheless known to import from or by way of Senegal quantities of millet, tea, rice, sugar, cotton goods, and hardware, while it exports to Mali and to Senegal cattle, sheep, and goats. Iron ore is the major export, followed by fish and fish products.

Administration of the economy. In agriculture the aim of successive Mauritanian governments has been to increase the amount of irrigated land in the Sénégal River Valley and, above all, to increase the production of rice, of which Mauritania is still obliged to import large quantities; to plant fresh palm trees to replace those destroyed by the cochineal insect; to drill fresh wells; to improve the quality of dates; and to encourage the cultivation of vegetables. To promote the export of meat, construction of slaughterhouses has been proposed, one at Kaédi, and one at Nouakchott. Investment in fisheries is to be concentrated on Nouadhibou, where plans include the formation of a Mauritanian fishing fleet and establishment of a training centre for professional personnel.

The state imposes direct taxes on the number of cattle owned and also levies an income tax. Industrial and commercial profits also are taxed.

Transportation. Transport by pack animals—camels in the north, oxen and donkeys in the south—has retained considerable importance in a society in which a subsistence and barter economy prevails, although transport between cities and regions is increasingly by truck. Considerable hazards, however, confront road builders; among these are moving sand dunes, flash floods in the south, and steep cliffs. Only the main road running from Rosso via Nouakchott, Akjoujt, Atar, Fdérik, and Bir Mogreïn to Tindouf, Algeria, is passable thoughout the year. The road between Rosso and Nouakchott is surfaced, as is the section between Nouakchott and Akjoujt. The Trans-Mauritania highway, linking Nouakchott, Kaédi, Kiffa, ʿAyoûn el-ʾAtroûs, and Néma, was completed in 1982. The 405-mile railroad from Zouîrât to Nouadhibou is used only for transporting iron ore. There are international airports at Nouakchott and Nouadhibou, and other cities are linked by regular air services.

The irregularity of the flow of the Sénégal River limits its use as a waterway; Kaédi can only be reached by ships drawing about seven feet at the high-water season, which is from August to October. The port facilities at Nouakchott can accommodate 320,000 tons of shipping a year. Nouadhibou, in addition to being an iron-ore and fishing port, is also a commercial port.

ADMINISTRATIVE AND SOCIAL CONDITIONS

The Mauritanian state had a presidential regime from 1960 until 1978, when a coup d'etat installed a military government. A civilian government established in December 1980 was replaced the following April by a largely military administration.

The primary task of the successive governments has been to transform a community of diverse tribes, hierarchical in structure and strongly differentiated, into a nation. The results have been encouraging; many local barriers to cooperation have been overcome, and traditional regional boundaries have been redrawn. There are 12 administrative regions and one capital district, each directed by a governor, with the capital forming a separate district. One remaining difficulty consists of the latent opposition that exists between *bīdān* Moors and black Moors; this difference, which is cultural rather than racial, is due to the fact that the blacks have become more educated than the *bīdān* (white) Moors, who have been traditionally suspicious of nonreligious education. Consequently, the blacks hold a large proportion of governmental positions.

Mauritania's legal code was inspired by the universal principles of Islām, and Islāmic jurisprudence was adopted officially in February 1980.

CULTURAL LIFE

Moorish society is justly proud of its Arab and Muslim heritage. Theology, poetry, and music have flourished throughout recent centuries. Architecture is inspired by that of the Maghrib, and goldsmithing is a fine art. Traditional culture, represented by the great marabout families, such as the Ahel Shaykh Sīdiyā family, is nevertheless declining. For statistical data, see the "Britannica World Data" section in the current *Britannica Book of the Year*.

(C.H.T.)

History

Numerous discoveries of Acheulian and Neolithic remains have been made in the north.

Mauritania was first peopled by Negroes and by the Sanhadja Berbers. It was the cradle of the Berber Almoravid movement, which in the 11th century laid waste the Ghana empire before conquering Morocco. The Almoravids imposed Islām upon all the neighbouring peoples. A caravan route at that time linked Mauritania with Morocco. Arab tribes infiltrated by this route and in the 15th century submerged the Berbers. The nomadic tribes formed several powerful confederations: Trarza and Brakna, which dominated the Sénégal River; Kunta in the east; and Regeibat in the north. *(margin: The Berber Almoravids)*

In 1442 Portuguese vessels rounded Cape Blanc, and in 1448 the Portuguese founded the fort of Arguin, whence they derived gold, gum arabic, and slaves. Later the French and English frequented Portendick, and then the French settled at Saint-Louis at the mouth of the Sénégal River. In 1858 Col. Louis Faidherbe ended Moorish domination over lower Sénégal. After 1898 an Islāmic specialist, Xavier Coppolani, succeeded, without a struggle, in rallying all the Moors of the South to France. He was assassinated in 1905, and his work was completed by Col. Henri Gouraud, who occupied Tagant in 1907 and Adrar in 1909. The Regeibat were not finally pacified until after World War I.

Mauritania was constituted a territory of French West Africa in 1920 and later became a colony; it was at first governed from Saint-Louis in Senegal. In 1946 Mauritania became an overseas territory and in 1957, after repulsing an attack by Moroccan irregulars on the north, elected a government under Moktar Ould Daddah, who established the new capital at Nouakchott. In 1958 Mauritania voted to become a member state of the French Community, and on November 28, 1960, its full independence was declared. It became a member of the United Nations in October 1961.

The small political elite was divided over whether the country should be oriented more toward Senegal and black French-speaking Africa or toward Morocco (which sought to absorb it). The winning faction, under Sidi el-Moktar N'Diaye and his successor, Moktar Ould Daddah, chose independence with close ties to France and full participation in the Organization of African Unity. Reversing Moroccan policy, King Hassan II recognized Mauritanian independence in 1969 (as part of his plan to gain control of Spanish Sahara, consummated in 1975–76). Mauritania joined the Arab League in 1973. *(margin: Relations with Morocco)*

President since independence, Ould Daddah appeared securely established in spite of occasional strikes by miners and demonstrations by students, for his policies seemed attuned to a largely tribal population, 90 percent of whom were engaged in agriculture or pastoralism. The difficulties of suppressing guerrillas of the Polisario Front in the Western Sahara (former Spanish Sahara, which had been divided between Morocco and Mauritania in 1976) apparently caused his downfall. On July 10, 1978, he was deposed and arrested in a military coup led by the chief of staff, Col. Mustapha Ould Salek. Ould Salek resigned his position in June 1979 and was replaced by Lieut. Col. Mohamed Mahmoud Ould Louly. He was in turn replaced in January 1980 by the prime minister, Lieut. Col. Mohamed Khouna Ould Haidalla.

The Mauritanian effort to disentangle itself from the Western Sahara worsened relations with Morocco. After signing a peace treaty with the Polisario Front on August 5, 1979, Mauritania relied more on ties with that organization and Algeria. For current political history, see the annual issues of the *Britannica Book of the Year.*

(H.J.D./Ed.)

NIGER

The Republic of the Niger (République du Niger), a land-locked western African country, takes its name from the river Niger, which flows through the southwest part of its territory. The name Niger derives in turn from the phrase *gher n-gheren,* meaning "river among rivers," in the Tamashek language. The republic has an area of 459,075 square miles (1,189,000 square kilometres). It is bounded on the northwest by Algeria, on the northeast by Libya, on the east by Chad, on the south by Nigeria and Dahomey, and on the west by Burkina Faso (formerly Upper Volta) and Mali. The capital is Niamey, on the Niger River.

Physical and human geography

One of the largest countries in western Africa, Niger is only sparsely populated. The Sahara covers the northern part of its territory. Peanuts (groundnuts) and cattle are among its principal products. The majority of its peoples are Muslim. Though the country obtained its independence on August 3, 1960, after 50 years of French rule, economically, it still relies heavily on France, and French is its official language.

THE LAND

Relief. Niger extends for about 750 miles from north to south, and about 930 miles from east to west. It tends to monotony in its features, is intersected by numerous depressions, and is dominated by arid highlands in the north. Rainfall increases as one proceeds southward so that the country divides naturally into three distinct zones—a desert zone in the north; an intermediate zone, where nomadic pastoralists raise cattle in the centre; and a cultivated zone in the south. It is in this southern zone that the greater part of the population, both nomadic and settled, is concentrated.

The highlands of the north are cut by valleys (*kori*) of the Aïr massif, which are an extension of the Ahaggar (Hoggar) Mountains of Algeria, and consist of a range running north to south in the centre of Niger, with individual mountain masses forming separate "islands": from north to south these are firstly Tazerzaït, where Mont Gréboun reaches an altitude of 6,379 feet (1,944 metres); Tamgak; Takolokouzet; Angornakouer; Bagzane; and Tarouadji. To the northeast are a series of high plateaus, which form a bridge between the Ahaggar Mountains of Algeria and the Tibesti mountains of Chad. From west to east, these are the plateaus of Djado, Mangueni, and Tchigaï.

The sandy regions of the Nigerian Sahara extend to either side of the Aïr. To the west, the Talak region includes the Tamesna area in the north (where fossil valleys are filled with moving sand dunes) and the Azaoua area in the south. East of the Aïr is the Ténéré region, covered partly by an expanse of sand called an erg, partly by stony plain called a reg.

The plateaus of the south, which form a belt about 900 miles long, may be divided into three regions. To the west is the Djerma Ganda region. Its large valleys are filled with sand, while *dallol* (fossilized valleys of rivers that formed tributaries of the Niger in ancient times) descend from the Aïr and the Adrar des Iforas massif of neighbouring Mali. The central region consists of the rocky Adar Doutchi and Majia areas; it is the region of the *gulbi* (dried-up valleys of former tributaries of the Sokoto River) and the Tegama—a tableland of sandstone, ending, towards the Aïr, at the Tiguidit scarp. To the east the underlying rock reappears in the Damagarim, Mounio, and Koutous regions, to the north of which is the region of Damergou, consisting of

clays. In the Manga region, in the east, traces of ancient watercourses appear on the sandy plain.

Drainage and soils. It is convenient to make a distinction between the ancient hydrographic system, which allowed agriculturalists, fishermen, and pastoralists to live in the Aïr region about 5,000 or 6,000 years ago, and the present simple system, which forms the basis of the marked difference between the northern and southern parts of the country. The present system includes to the west the Niger River Basin, and to the east the basin of Lake Chad; between the two occur vestiges of the older system, such as the *dallol* and the *gulbi.*

To the west, the Niger River crosses about 350 miles of Niger's territory. Because of the change in river flow, which occurs because of the dispersal of its waters in its interior "delta" region in Mali, it is only in January and February that it flows past Niamey in flood. At other times the river is fed by certain temporary watercourses that flow in from the right bank. These are the Gorouol, the Dargol, the Sirba, the Goroubi, the Djamangou, the Tapoa, and the Mékrou; the last two flow through the "W" National Park (so called because the Niger flows through the area in the form of a W). On the left bank, proceeding eastward, appear the *dallol,* the vestiges of the older watercourses. Generally running from north to south, they constitute zones of dampness, although a few still contain waters that flow towards the Niger. The best known are the Dallol Bosso, the Dallol Foga, and the Dallol Maouri. Other vestiges consist of the *kori,* which runs down from the Aïr and from former tributaries that had their sources in the massif of the Adrar des Iforas, and which flowed to a confluence at what is now the wadi (channel of a watercourse that is dry except during periods of rainfall) of Tim-merhsoï. No waters flow through the *kori* now, but water is still to be found beneath their sands. Other remnants of the old system are formed by the *gulbi,* through which water still flows annually, occasionally causing damage.

To the east is situated the basin of Lake Chad, a large, shallow lake, which at its highest level has an area of approximately 9,650 square miles; of this, Niger possesses about 1,100 square miles. Its extent is considerably reduced during the dry season. The Komadougou Yobé River, which flows into Lake Chad from the west, forms part of the frontier between Niger and Nigeria. Its water level, which begins to rise in August, from January to May consists only of some stagnant pools.

In addition to the drainage system described, it may be noted that rainwater collects in several basins, so that some permanent lakes or pools also exist; these are found at Keïta and Adouna in the Adar Doutchi region, at Madaroumfa in the Maradi *gulbi,* and at Guidimouni to the east of Zinder. The water table underground can be tapped by means of artesian wells.

The soils fall into three natural regions. In the Saharan region in the north, which extends over an area of about 308,000 square miles, the soil remains infertile, except in a few oases where water is found. In the region known as the Sahel, which forms a transitional zone between the Sahara and the cultivated region to the south, the soils are thin and white, being covered with salty deposits that form an infertile crust. The third region (in the south) is cultivated. In this area the soils are associated with extensive dunes or uplands or with basins or depressions. Some of the soils in the latter, such as those in the Niger Basin and in the *gulbi* are rich. Black soils occur in the Kolo Basin. Throughout the region, however, and above all on the plateaus, layers of laterite (leached iron-bearing soil) occur.

Three geographic zones

Ancient watercourses

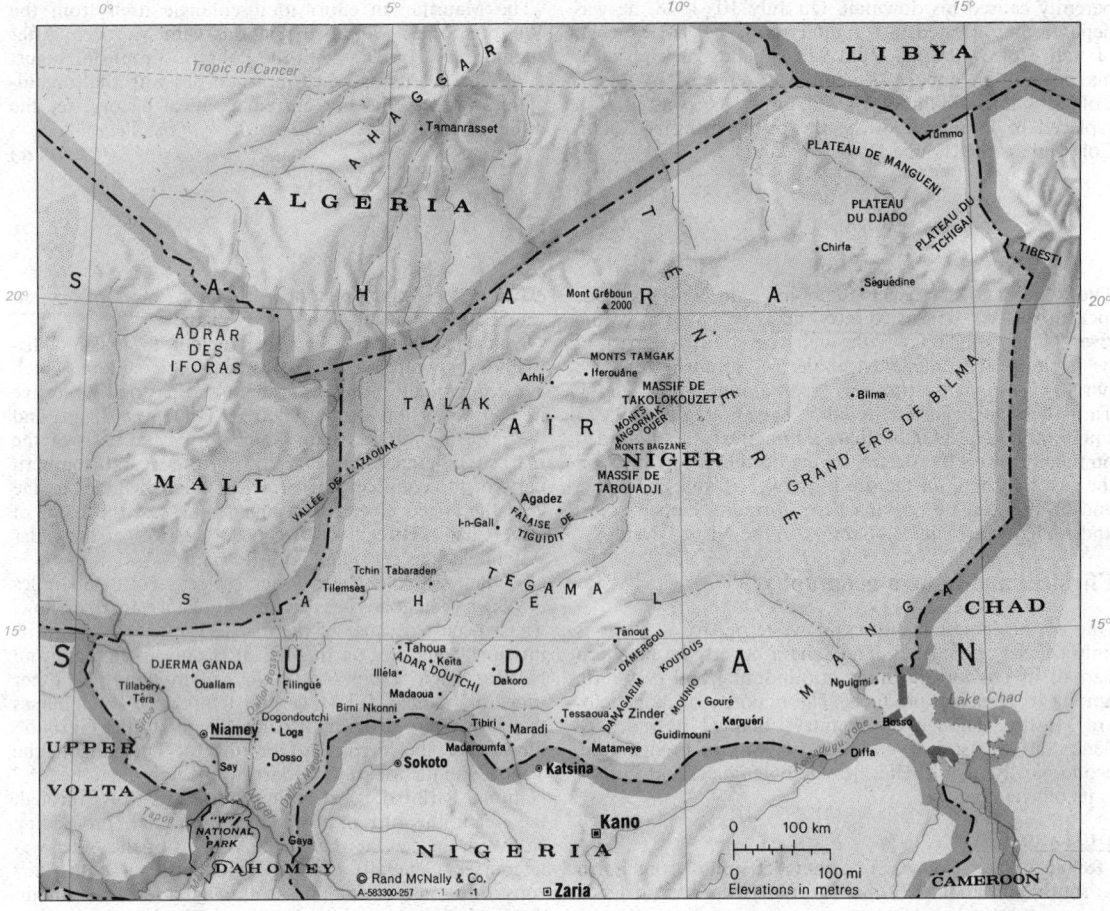

NIGER

Climate. Niger extends southward from the Tropic of Cancer, so that the greatest part of its territory lies in the dry tropical zone. In the southern part of the territory the climate is usually of the type known as Sahelian, which is characterized by a single rainy season. In January and February the continental equivalent of the northeast trade winds blow, dry and fresh, from the Sahara toward the Equator, meeting the harmattan, a dry wind which blows from east to west between the Tropic of Cancer and the Equator, hindering normal living conditions on the southern fringe of the desert. From April to May the southern trade winds blowing from the Atlantic reach the Equator and are diverted toward the Sahara where they meet with the harmattan—an encounter that results in tornadoes. A long dry season occurs between October and June, while the winter rains occur between June and October. The winter season begins with the June tornadoes, and lasts from between one to four months, according to the latitude; August is the rainy month everywhere except in the far north, where the rainfall is highly unpredictable.

Niger lies in one of the hottest regions of the world. Temperatures rise to the maximum from February to May, and drop during the winter rainy season, rising again somewhat before reaching the annual minimum in January or February. Annual minimum temperatures vary between 29° F (−2° C) at Bilma and 61° F (16° C) at Tillabéry. Tillabéry, which is on the Niger River, is also the hottest place, recording an annual average maximum of 106° F (41° C). The daily range is greater in the north than in the south, and is also more extreme during the dry season. The severity of the temperature increases from south to north: at Niamey the absolute extremes of temperature are 47° F (8° C) and 114° F (46° C); in the Aïr temperatures of −23° F (−31° C) have been recorded, while the absolute max-

Temperature and rainfall

imums are in the region of 122° F (50° C) in the shade.

Rainfall varies according to location as well as season. In general, it diminishes from south to north; the limit of assured annual rainfall is reached to the north of Agadez, where, furthermore, temperatures are excessive. The 10-inch isohyet (line on a map connecting points having equal rainfall) follows a line from near Tahoua to Gouré, in effect marking the northern limit of nomadic pastoral life, for the rainfall permits a sparse vegetation to grow. To the extreme south the 30-inch isohyet marks the southern limit of this zone, after which the southern agricultural zone begins. The extreme southwest receives the most abundant rainfall; the Gaya region is the first and the last to receive rainfall each year. In the course of the same winter rainy season a most irregular pattern of rainfall may occur, while from one year to another the amount of rainfall may double; in addition, the rainy season itself may arrive early or late, thus jeopardizing the crops.

Plant and animal life. The vegetation of the desert zone clusters around the oases; it includes the date palm and corn; its animal life, which must be able to endure hunger and thirst, includes the dromedary.

In the Sahel zone, where the doum palm and the cram cram (a prickly grass) appear, the vegetation has a short life cycle, and is principally used for grazing. Animal life includes the ostrich and the gazelle.

In the cultivated zone the vegetation includes acacia trees, doum palms, and rônier palms, as well as baobabs. Wild life, which has partially disappeared, includes antelope, elephants, and warthogs; giraffe are found in the Zarmaganda and Damergou regions, and hippopotamuses and crocodiles on the banks of the Niger. The extreme southwest is a savanna (grassy parkland) region where baobabs, kapok trees, and tamarind trees occur. Animal life is preserved in the "W" National Park, where antelope, lions, buffalo, hippopotamuses, and elephants may be seen.

Settlement patterns. The southern part of Niger's territory is situated in the vast region of Africa known as the Sudan, in which, in former times, large political states arose, such as Ghana, Mali, and Songhai, as well as the Hausa states, the empire of Sokoto, and Bornu. The northern part of Niger remains the domain of the Tuareg. The country comprises a multitude of traditional regions the names of which remain despite the establishment of contemporary administrative divisions.

Tuareg predominate in northern Niger's Aïr (Azbine) and Azaouak regions and have also constituted two further regions further to the south known as Imanan and Tagazart. In the northeast is the Tibesti region, which is the land of the nomadic Teda (or Tubu).

In the south, from east to west, three groups of peoples are found. The first consists of the Kanuri, who occupy the Manga region, as well as parts of the regions known as the Damergou and the Damagarim, which are traditionally associated with Bornu in Nigeria. The second group is formed by the Hausa who occupy the traditional regions of Daura, Katsina, Gober Toudou, Adar Doutchi, Aréoua, and Kourfey. The third group consists of the Zerma (Djerma) and Songhai peoples of southwestern Niger. The Zerma occupy the Zidji (or Zarmatarey), Boboye, Zarmaganda, and Fakara regions, while the Songhay are to be found in the Anzourou region to the north, and the Dendi region to the south, as well as on the right bank of the Niger. The Fulani, or Peul, people are found scattered in all these regions, and are found in compact groups only in the Boboye and Manga areas.

People of the south

All these regions have a fluctuating political, economic, and geographic significance: the Hausa regions, for example, have been cut in two and divided between Niger and Nigeria. Most regions, moreover, have been and remain zones where contact takes place between different peoples—between the Hausa and the Tuareg in the Adar Doutchi region, for example; between the Tuareg and the Kanuri in the Damergou region; and between Hausa and Zerma in the Aréoua area.

Slightly more than one-tenth of the population lives in towns. The rural population is divided into nomads and sedentary peoples. There are about 10,000 villages, of which approximately half have fewer than 200 inhabitants; there are practically no villages in the desert zone. The Fulani herdsmen, who breed horned cattle and oxen, and the Tuareg, who raise goats, sheep, and dromedaries, tend to travel over the northern region during the winter. They meet together to permit the cattle to lick the salty soil of the In Gall region during August and September but move southward during the dry season. Both Fulani and Tuareg live in tribal groups, in temporary or portable shelters, and gain their subsistence from their livestock. The Fulani subsist above all on milk in various forms; the Tuareg live on meat and dates.

The Fulani and the Tuareg

Sedentary peoples, such as the Hausa, the Songhai-Zerma, and the Kanuri, who inhabit the Niger and Chad Basins, live largely by agriculture. They raise millet, rice, corn, peanuts, and cotton. They also work as blacksmiths and shoemakers, while on the banks of Lake Chad and of the Niger the Buduma and Sokoro (Sorko) peoples are fishermen. Sedentary peoples live in dwellings that vary from those made of straw to those made of banco (hardened mud), although the Woko (Wogo) people live in tents of delicate matting.

There is a tendency among the nomads to settle down and the already sedentary peoples are expanding the lands under cultivation toward the north. Rural life, above all in its sedentary form, tends to slow its pace during the long dry season; it is at this time of year that migration to the towns or other countries occurs.

It was approximately in the 15th century that a few towns, such as Agadez or Zinder, were first established as halting places, or depots, on the trans-Saharan caravan routes. As commercial routes gradually developed on the coasts, however, these northern towns lost their former economic importance, while other centres, such as Birni Nkonni, and Tessaoua, declined in the course of the 19th century as a result of the colonial era.

At the present time there are four principal towns in Niger. Niamey, the political capital, has experienced rapid growth. It has a cosmopolitan character and a transient population. Its characteristic life varies between the European and African rural styles, including various intermediate steps, of which the style of life of the évolués (educated Africans) is the most distinctive. Zinder, for which the African name is Damagaram, is an older town than Niamey; a Hausa town, it was the capital of Niger until 1926 and has a number of skilled craftsmen, especially leatherworkers and dyers. The town is experiencing some industrial growth and has close links with Nigeria. Maradi has developed rapidly. The town is situated in the heart of the peanut-growing region near the Nigerian frontier. Many European companies have established branches there; the town is particularly renowned for its red goats, the skins of which are exported to Europe and the Americas. Tahoua has grown up on the edge of the desert. There it forms a large livestock market, where nomad pastoralists and sedentary farmers meet. But all of the towns remain little more than modest administrative and commercial centres. Because of the discovery of uranium ore Agadez has experienced a spectacular growth. Maradi, Zinder, and Tahoua all have buildings in the striking Sudanese architectural style.

Population centres

THE PEOPLE

Linguistic groups. The largest linguistic group is formed by the Hausa, whose language, also spoken in Nigeria, is one of the most important in West Africa. A large percentage of the inhabitants of Niger understand Hausa, which possesses an abundant literature that has been printed in Latin characters in neighbouring Nigeria. Songhai is the second most important language; also called Songhoi, it is also spoken in Mali, in northern Burkina Faso, and in northern Benin. In Niger itself it is divided into various dialects, such as Songhai proper, Zerma, and Dendi. The language of the Fulani is Fulfulde; in Niger it has two dialects, eastern and western, the demarcation line between them running through the Boboye district. Tamashek is the language of the Tuareg, who often call themselves the Kel Tamagheq, or Tamashek-speakers. The language is also spoken in Algeria and Mali and possesses its own writing, called *tifinagh*, which is in widespread use. Kanuri is spoken not only in Niger but also in Cameroon and Nigeria; the tongue is called Beriberi by the Hausa.

While these five languages are the principal ones spoken in Niger, there is also an important Teda, or Tubu, linguistic group in the Tibesti region. In addition, many of the peoples of Niger speak Arabic, and a still larger number read and write in that language; Agadez possesses one of the oldest Arabic schools in Africa. The use of the Arabic alphabet resulted in Fulfulde and Hausa becoming written languages; the resulting script is called *ajami;* a search for more old manuscripts in *ajami* is currently being conducted.

By using Hausa and Songhai, one may make oneself understood from one end of the country to the other. French, however, remains the official language, as well as the language of instruction, although it remains understood only by a small minority. English is taught as the principal foreign language in secondary schools.

Ethnic groups. Ethnic groups correspond to the five linguistic groups already mentioned. The Hausa are the most important, constituting more than half of the present population of Niger, even though the majority of the Hausa people live in Nigeria. The Hausas occupy the centre of southern Niger as far as Dogondoutchi. The Songhai-Zerma are found in the southwest; the Songhai proper live along the Niger, where they are assimilating the Kurtey and Woko peoples. The majority of the Songhai people as a whole, however, live in Mali. The Zerma live on the left bank of the Niger, remaining in close contact with the Maouri and Aréoua peoples. The Fulani, who are dispersed throughout the country, are 80 percent nomadic; they are also found dispersed throughout western Africa. The Tuareg, also nomadic, are divided into three subgroups—the Aulliminden of the Azaouak region in the west, the Asben (Kel Aïr) in the Aïr region, and the Itesan (Kel Geres) to the south and east of Aïr. The Tuareg people are also found in Algeria and in Mali. The Kanuri, who live to the east of Zinder, are divided into a number of subgroups—the Manga, the Dogara (Dagara), the Mober, the Buduma, and the Kanembu; they are also found living in Chad, Cameroon, and Nigeria. Apart from the Teda (Tubu), who constitute an important minority, the remainder of the population consists of Arabs, black Africans from other countries, and Europeans, of whom the greater part are French.

Religious groups. Christianity (Catholicism and Protestantism) remains above all a religion of the towns, particularly of Niamey. There are several Christian missions in the Songhai and Aréoua areas. Christianity remains primarily a European religion, although it is also practiced by some black Africans from other countries. The traditional animist religions of the black Africans continue to manifest themselves in strength. Though the Annaawaa group of Hausa have always refused to accept Islām, as have a group of Fulani, the Wodaabe—who distinguish themselves from other Fulani for this reason—Islām remains the religion of the majority of the peoples of Niger.

THE ECONOMY

Agriculture. Niger's exports are peanuts and peanut products, gum arabic, and cattle. Millet, sorghum, cassava, and sugarcane are raised in the south, along with rice grown in the Niger River Valley.

Resources. Salt is traditionally exploited in the Kaouar and Aïr regions, as well as in the *dallol,* and in the Manga district. Natron (hydrated sodium carbonate) is extracted locally. Cassiterite (the most important ore of tin) is mined at open workings in the Aïr. Gold is obtained by panning in the Sirba River. Limestone and an important deposit of gypsum have been located at Malbaza and in the Ader Doutchi and Majia region. Cement production at Malbaza and exploitation of uranium ore in the Aïr region are important to the economy. Known reserves of uranium in the Arlit and Akouta regions, amounting to about 20,000 tons, rank among the most important in the world. Apart from tungsten, of which a little has been worked in the Aïr region, traces of copper, lignite (a brownish-black coal), molybdenum (a silver-white metal used as an alloy with iron in making high-speed cutting tools), zinc, oil, phosphates, and titanium (a metallic element used in making steel) have been found and are the

Uranium ore (margin note)

subject of further prospection. A reserve of iron ore, with an iron content of 55 percent, has been located in the Say region; and oil deposits have been discovered in the Lake Chad area.

The exploitation of plant resources has long been practiced but on a small scale. The doum palm and the palmyra (rônier) palm provide wood for construction, while the date palms of the Manga oasis produce approximately 3,500 tons of dates a year. Small amounts of kapok (a silky down from the kapok tree, used for insulation, in making life jackets, and so forth) and of gum from the acacia gum tree are exported. Skins of ostriches, crocodiles, and snakes are used for making handicrafts that are exported to Europe. Fish from the Niger River and Lake Chad are exported southward to the coastal countries.

Industry. Some manufacturing industries have been established, mostly at Niamey. They produce chemicals, food products, textiles, transport equipment, and metal furniture. There are many small craft industries in the principal towns.

Hydrocarbon fuels, brought up from the port of Cotonou in Benin, first by rail and then by truck, constitute virtually the only source of industrial power; they are used either directly, or to drive diesel engines to generate electricity. The Office of Solar Energy has been pursuing research and has already produced solar batteries, which are used by the educational television program. Peanut shells have been experimentally used to supplement hydrocarbon fuels since 1968. Wood is the traditional domestic fuel. Hydroelectric energy is produced by the Kandadji Dam on the Niger River. It is anticipated that the production of uranium at Arlit may eventually result in a new source of energy for Niger.

Administration of the economy. The economic system is based upon planning but accords an important role to private enterprise. The three main policy objectives are the maintenance of national unity, the elevation of the living standards of the population, and the attainment of economic independence. The private sector of the economy consists partly of a multitude of small enterprises, and partly of enterprises belonging to large French or international companies. The government, through the agency of the Banque de Développement de la République du Niger, which is funded partly by aid from abroad, has promoted the establishment of many companies, including real estate, road transport, air transport, and agricultural processing enterprises.

Niger is encouraging the strengthening of economic links between African countries. Apart from its membership in the Organization of African Unity, Niger is a member—together with the Ivory Coast, Benin, Burkina Faso, and Togo—of the Conseil de l'Entente, a regional cooperative grouping, as well as of the Organisation Commune Africaine et Mauricienne, another grouping of French-speaking African states.

The private sector of the economy (margin note)

Transportation. While the economically active zone of the country consists of a belt running from east to west across the southern part of the country, the principal lines of communication run southwards towards the coast. The two ports used by Niger—Cotonou in Benin and Lagos in Nigeria—are each more than 600 miles away, and Niger possesses no railroad. Traditional systems of transport and communication are still largely relied upon. These include camel caravans in the northern Sahel region, canoes on Lake Chad and the Niger, and individual travel on horseback or on foot. Only a small tonnage of goods is transported. Trucks maintain transport communications between Maradi and Zinder in Niger and Kano in Nigeria, and between Niamey, the capital, and Parakou in Benin. A road completed in 1981 connects the uranium-producing centres of Arlit and Akouta to Nigerian transport links. Only a small amount of goods are transported by air.

The principal west-to-east road axis enters the country from Gao in Mali, runs on the banks of the Niger as far as Niamey, and then continues eastwards to Nguigmi on Lake Chad. From this central route roads branch off southward. Toward the north, routes running via Tahoua and Tânout converge near Agadez, linking Niger to Algeria via Tamanrasset. The Air Niger Company is responsible

Roads (margin note)

for domestic air services linking more than 20 airports, including those of Tahoua, Maradi, Zinder, Agadez, and Arlit. An International Airport at Niamey links Niger with the West African capitals of Abidjan, Libreville, and Bamako, and with Porto Novo in Benin, as well as with European capitals.

ADMINISTRATIVE AND SOCIAL CONDITIONS

Government. The constitution promulgated in November 1960, which established a presidential type of regime, was suspended after the military coup of April 1974. Executive power is held by a Supreme Military Council composed of 12 officers. The president of the Supreme Military Council appoints a Council of Ministers.

Niger is divided into seven *départements* (provinces)—Agadez, Diffa, Dosso, Maradi, Niamey, Tahoua, and Zinder—each of which is administered by a prefect. Each *département* is divided into *arrondissements* (administrative subdivisions), 38 in all, each of which is administered by a subprefect.

Education. Most of the children in primary and secondary school are boys. There are facilities for teacher training. Primary and secondary schools and teacher-training colleges are the responsibility of the Ministry of National Education. Other ministries are responsible for technical education. Literacy programs are conducted in the five principal African languages. Niamey has a university and there are plans to open the Islāmic University of West Africa at Say.

Health and welfare. Health services are organized on a mass basis and concentrate on the eradication of certain diseases in rural areas, as well as on health education. Campaigns have been successfully waged against sleeping sickness and meningitis, while vaccinations against smallpox and measles are also conducted. Other diseases, however, such as tuberculosis, malaria, and leprosy remain endemic. Anti-tuberculosis centres are established at Niamey, Zinder, and Tahoua. Lack of finances and shortage of trained personnel remain the principal obstacles to the improvement of health conditions.

CULTURAL LIFE

Niger forms part of the vast Sahelian cultural region of western Africa. Although the influence of Islām is predominant, pre-Islāmic cultural traditions are also strong and omnipresent. Paradoxically, the numerous ethnic strains to be found in Niger have resulted in a strengthening of the fabric of national life. Since independence, greater interest has been shown in the country's cultural heritage, particularly with respect to traditional architecture, handicrafts, dances, and music. With the assistance of the United Nations Educational, Scientific, and Cultural Organization a regional centre for the collection of oral traditions has been established at Niamey. An institution predominant in cultural life is the National Museum at Niamey. For

statistical data, see the "Britannica World Data" section in the current *Britannica Book of the Year.*   (Di.L./Ed.)

History

Acheulean carved stones have been found in the Bilma, and Neolithic deposits are numerous in the Sahara area, which the Tuareg have doubtless occupied since a remote age. They established themselves in the Aïr in about the 11th century, and the Tuareg sultanate of Agadez dates at least from the 15th. The Djerma (or Zerma), who speak Songhai (Sonrhai), seem to have arrived in the 17th century. The Hausa, who probably came from the northeast, formed from the 14th century onward a number of kingdoms, of which one, Gobir (Gober), expanded greatly in the 18th century and repulsed the Tuareg. Hausan cities also replaced Bornu as important entrepôts in the trade between North Africa and the Central Sudan. *(margin: Expansion of the Hausa)*

The Fulani had long been infiltrating into Hausa land. One of them, Usman dan Fodio, in 1804 proclaimed himself commander of the faithful and preached the *jihād* ("holy war") against the Hausa, who tended to be lax in their religious observances. He defeated them and established in the former Hausa states the empire of Sokoto but failed in his attack on Bornu. These native movements then began to come into conflict with French and English interests.

Friederich Hornemann, Mungo Park, and other European travellers explored the region in the late 18th–19th centuries. By an agreement of 1890 the English and French divided this part of western Africa between themselves, following a line from Say on the Niger to Barroua on Lake Chad, a frontier precisely defined in 1899 and 1904. The French "military territory of the Niger" was created, the Tuareg were conquered, and in 1904 Agadez was occupied.

The territory was at first dependent upon the Sudan. In 1922 it became a colony of the federation of French West Africa. The capital, at first at Zinder, was transferred in 1926 to Niamey. Niger became an overseas territory in 1946 and was granted a territorial assembly and then, in 1957, an elected government. In 1958, despite the local government, 72 percent of the electorate voted for membership in the French Community. On August 3, 1960, independence was proclaimed, and on November 11 Hamani Diori was elected president. On September 20 Niger became a member of the UN. In 1964 an armed revolt by political exiles was crushed and several of its leaders executed. At national elections in 1965 and 1970, Diori, the only candidate, was reelected. In a military coup in April 1974, Col. Seyni Kountché became chief of state and president of the Supreme Military Council. An eventual return to civilian rule was announced in 1982. For current political history, see the annual issues of the *Britannica Book of the Year.*   (H.J.D./Ed.)

NIGERIA

Nigeria—in full, Federal Republic of Nigeria—is the largest of the western African coastal states. Its population is the largest of any country in Africa. With an area of 356,669 square miles (923,768 square kilometres), it is the 13th largest state on the continent. Located between 4° and 14° N, and 3° and 14° E, its territory extends about 650 miles (1,050 kilometres) from north to south and 700 miles east to west. It is bordered on the south by the Gulf of Guinea, on the west by Benin, on the north by Niger, and on the east by Chad and Cameroon. Part of the eastern boundary runs along the crest of the Adamawa Highlands.

Physical and human geography

Modern Nigeria dates from 1914, when the two British protectorates of Northern and Southern Nigeria were joined. The country became independent on October 1, 1960, and three years later adopted a republican constitution but elected to stay a member of the Commonwealth.

Relics of British rule are still to be seen in various aspects of Nigerian life. The official language, English, is likely to remain unchanged, since there are more than 200 different languages spoken by the many groups living in the country. Trade and cultural contacts with the more distant English-speaking countries of Ghana and Sierra Leone remain stronger than those with the adjacent French-speaking Benin, Niger, and Cameroon.

THE LAND

Relief. Nigeria is on the lower part of the great African continental plateau, which slopes slowly downward from south and east to north and west. The country consists of several eroded surfaces, occurring as plateaus, at elevations of 2,000 feet (610 metres), 3,000 feet, and 4,000 feet above sea level. The coastal areas, including the Niger Delta, as well as the Lake Chad Basin and the western parts of the Sokoto region, are covered with young, soft rocks. Gently undulating plains, which become waterlogged during the *(margin: Plateaus and undulating plains)*

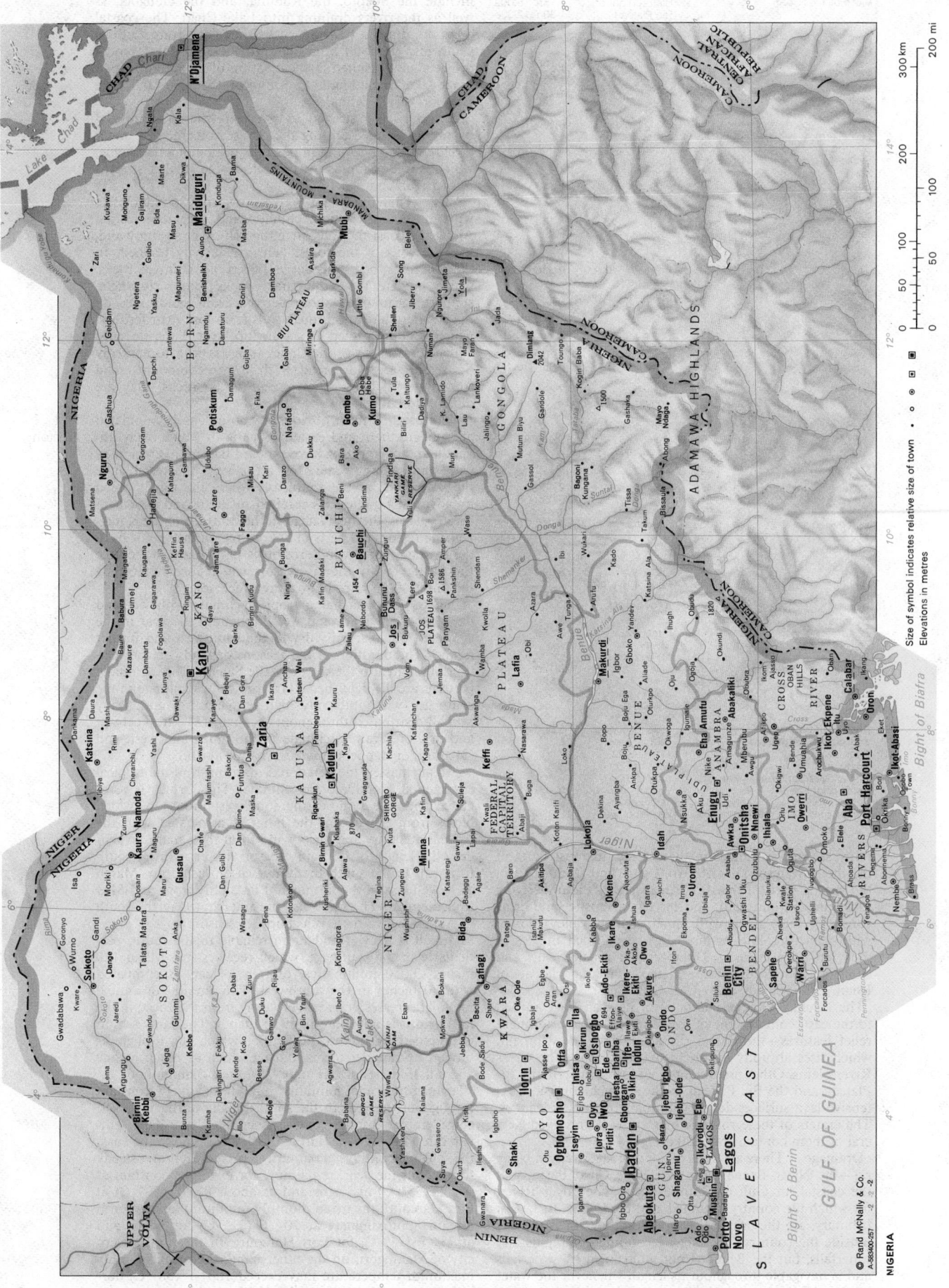

NIGERIA

Size of symbol indicates relative size of town

Elevations in metres

include the Sokoto, the Kaduna, and the Gongola, as well as the rivers draining into Lake Chad. The coastal areas are drained by short rivers that flow from north to south into the Gulf of Guinea. River basin development projects have resulted in the creation of many large man-made lakes, including Lake Kainji on the Niger and Lake Bakolori on the Rima.

Navigation is restricted to river stretches unhampered by rapids or falls. During the dry season, the low water level renders navigation impossible, even along the Benue, which is free of rapids. At this season the smaller streams may dry up completely.

Soils. The four main soil groups correspond closely with the country's main climatic and vegetation zones. Along the coast the soils are either sandy or swampy and, like the soils of the forest belt, are heavily leached. In the rain forest belt, soils derived from old, complex rocks, which predate the sedimentary rocks found elsewhere, support cacao trees; those derived from sandstones do not. Under cultivation forest soils soon lose their fertility, which is concentrated in a thin top layer. Lateritic soils, which form along gentle slopes in areas with a markedly dry season, are widespread. Rich in iron compounds, and sometimes so hard as to appear to be rocks, they are difficult to cultivate.

Soil erosion is most obvious in those densely populated areas of northern and eastern Nigeria in which overcultivation and overgrazing have exposed the soil to erosion by wind and running water. The areas most affected include the scarplands of the southeast, where the threat posed by advancing gullies has resulted in the abandonment of some villages; the Jos Plateau in the centre; and the Kano–Katsina region and parts of Sokoto region in the north. In the extreme north wind erosion is particularly noticeable toward the end of the dry season, when storms preceding the onset of the rains blow away much soil.

Soil erosion

Climate. Nigeria has a tropical climate with wet and dry seasons. It is hot and wet throughout the year in the southeast but markedly dry in the southwest and further inland. The duration of the seasons depends on the relation of an area to the sea or to the Sahara. Three climatic patterns are distinguished: (1) a tropical wet climate in the southeast, with uniformly high temperatures and heavy rainfall distributed throughout the year; (2) a tropical wet and dry, or savanna, climate in the north and west; and (3) a dry, or steppe, climate in the far north.

Two air masses, the equatorial maritime and the tropical continental, dominate the climate. The former is associated with the rain-bearing southwest monsoon, which blows from the ocean; the latter is associated with the harmattan, a dry and dusty wind from the Sahara. In general, the length of the rainy season decreases from south to north. In the south the rainy season lasts from March to November; in the far north it lasts only from mid-May to September. The rains also are interrupted in the south in August, when there is a short dry season.

Rainfall is heavier and more reliable in the south, particularly in the southeast, which receives more than 120 inches (3,050 millimetres) of rain a year, as compared with 70 inches in the southwest. The amount of annual rainfall decreases progressively away from the coast; in the far north it is not more than 20 inches. The rainy season is preceded by intense heat, after which the drought is broken by thunderstorms, during which as much as one and a half inches of rain may fall in less than an hour.

Temperature and humidity remain relatively constant throughout the year in the south. In the north, however, considerable seasonal changes occur, and the daily temperature range is wide during the dry season. On the coast the mean monthly maximum temperatures are steady throughout the year, remaining, for example, constant at 95° F (35° C) at Lagos and at about 85° F (29° C) at Port Harcourt; the mean monthly minimum temperatures remain approximately at 70° F (21° C) for Lagos and at 73° F (23° C) for Port Harcourt. In the northeastern city of Maiduguri, on the other hand, the mean monthly maximum temperature may exceed 100° F (38° C) during the hot months of April and May, while in the same season frosts may also occur at night. In general, mean

rainy season, are found in these areas. In most parts of the three western states of Oyo, Ogun, and Ondo, and in the central parts of the 10 northern states, the underlying rocks are old and hard, and the characteristic landforms consist of high plains with broad, shallow valleys dotted with numerous hills or inselbergs (steep-sided masses of rock left after erosion). Dome-shaped isolated hills and elongated ridges also occur in the sandstone plateau of Ishan, Udi–Nsukka, and Awka–Orlu areas.

The Nsukka–Okigwe cuesta, with its scarp face turned to the east, contains one of the country's most prominent relief features—the Enugu (Enugu–Okigwe) escarpment, which rises abruptly for about 600 feet above the Cross River plains. Other prominent relief forms include the Jos Plateau and the Biu Plateau, both of which consist of extensive lava surfaces dotted with many extinct volcanoes. The craters of these volcanic hills are well preserved; several of them contain crater lakes.

Drainage. There are three major drainage areas in Nigeria—the Niger–Benue Basin; the Lake Chad Basin; and the coastal, or Gulf of Guinea, basin. The Niger River, for which the country is named, and the Benue, its largest tributary, are the principal rivers. Both have their sources outside the country. The Niger has numerous rapids and waterfalls, but the Benue is not interrupted by waterfalls and is navigable throughout its length whenever the water level is high enough. All rivers draining the area north of the Niger–Benue trough rise on the Jos Plateau. These maximum temperatures are higher in the north, while mean minimum temperatures are lower. Owing to the blanketing effect of clouds during the rainy season, and of dust haze during the harmattan, the heat of the Sun is not as fierce as might be expected. The humidity is high, but it falls during the harmattan, which blows for more than three months in the north but rarely for more than two weeks along the coast. During the harmattan period dust is pervasive, and the climate is excessively dry.

The harmattan season

Plant and animal life. Vegetation in Nigeria is governed by the decrease in rainfall from south to north, and the main vegetation patterns run, therefore, in broad east–west belts, parallel to the Equator. Mangrove and freshwater swamps occur along the coast and in the Niger Delta. A few miles inland, swamps give way to dense tropical rain forests, in which the most important economic species of trees include such hardwoods as mahogany; iroko, which has mottled wood; and obeche, which has whitish wood. The oil palm, which is economically valuable, grows wild in the forest and is usually preserved when the forest is cleared for cultivation. In the more densely populated parts of the southeast, the original forest vegetation has been completely replaced by open palm bush. In the southwest large areas of forest have also been replaced by cacao and rubber farms.

Tree-studded savanna (tropical grassland) occupies more than half the area north of the forest belt. Trees characteristic of the area are the baobab, tamarind, and locust bean. The savanna landscape becomes more open in the far north and is characterized by scattered, stunted trees and by short grass. Semidesert conditions appear in the Lake Chad region, where common trees include various species of acacia (of which one is the source of gum arabic) and the doum species of palm. Gallery forests (narrow forest zones occurring along rivers) are also characteristic of the open savanna landscape in the north.

Camels, several species of antelope, hyenas, lions, and giraffes are found in the grassland to the north, while the red river hog, the forest elephant, the chimpanzee, and some varieties of birds and snakes are confined to the rain forest belt. Animals found throughout the country include leopards, golden cats, monkeys, gorillas, and wild pigs. Rodents, such as the squirrel, porcupine, and cane rat (known locally as "Cutting-Grass"), constitute the largest family of mammals and are ubiquitous. The northern grasslands also abound in Guinea fowl. Other common birds include quails, vultures, kites, bustards, and gray parrots. The rivers contain crocodiles, hippopotamuses, and a great variety of fish. There are many butterflies, moths, and insects. Large scorpions also are to be found, as are goliath beetles.

Settlement patterns. Marked differences exist between north and south not only in physical landscape, climate, and vegetation but also in the social organization, religion, literacy, and agricultural practices of the people. These differences, due in part to the fact that the north is landlocked and the south is not, and in part to historical antecedents, form the basis of the division of Nigeria into three main regions—the south, or Guinea coastlands; the middle belt; and the north, or Nigerian Sudan, part of the open savanna belt that runs east to west from the Nile to the Atlantic.

The south is the most economically developed part of Nigeria. Its forest resources are intensively exploited, and its tree crops are harvested on peasant farms and commercial plantations. All of the major industrial centres and oil fields, as well as the seaports, are concentrated in the region. The south has several cultural regions, the most important of which are the Yoruba in the west, the Benin in the central part, and the Ibo–Ibibio in the east.

The middle belt is the most sparsely settled and least developed part of Nigeria. It covers about two-fifths of the land area of the country but supports less than one-fifth of the total population. The peoples inhabiting the middle belt are divided into more than 180 linguistic groups. Before 1970 large-scale development was restricted to a few government-supported projects, such as the Kainji Dam and the Bacita sugar project, and a few industries in the two new towns of Jos and Kaduna. After the national

administrative reorganization of 1975, the region gained new importance as the location of seven of the country's 19 state capitals and, after 1976, of the 2,800-square-mile Federal Capital Territory, near Suleja. Planning began during the 1970s to transform Abuja into the federal capital. During the early 1980s a giant iron and steel complex was built at Ajaokuta, near Lokoja.

Until the beginning of the 20th century, when a new economic pattern was created by the construction of a railroad to the coastal ports, the Nigerian Sudan maintained regular trans-Saharan contacts with the Mediterranean and the Middle East. Islām is the predominant religion. It is a cattle zone inhabited by the nomadic cattle-owning Fulani and by the Hausa, who are settled cultivators. Except in the Lake Chad Basin, where the Kanuri people established the state of Bornu, the Nigerian Sudan is dominated by a blend of Hausa–Fulani culture.

Rural settlement. About 80 percent of the people live in small hamlets and villages. Closely nucleated settlements occur along the coastal areas, in the Yoruba area in the southwest, and in the Hausa and Kanuri areas of the far north. In parts of the Ibo and the Anang–Ibibio regions in the southeast and of the Tiv area in the middle belt, settlements consist of dispersed homesteads, called compounds. Each compound houses a man, his immediate family, and some relations. The compound is enclosed by a fence of matting and sticks or by a wall of mud or concrete. It is usually surrounded by a small garden area, called compoundland, which is cropped every year with corn (maize), vegetables, and yams. A number of compounds make up the hamlet or village, usually inhabited by people claiming a common ancestor—often the founder of the village, for whom it may be named.

Composition of compounds

The use of stone for building in rural Nigeria is recent and is restricted to a small, wealthy minority. The vast majority of the people continue to depend on whatever materials are at hand for constructing their homesteads. House types therefore change as one travels inland. Along the coastlands, where the soil is too sandy for making daub, the walls of houses consist of bamboos tied together with ropes, the roofs being made of bamboo leaf mats. Bamboos, ropes, and mats are made from the raffia palm, which abounds in the region. Rectangular mud houses with mat roofs are also found in the forest belt; the houses of the more prosperous are roofed with corrugated iron sheets. In the savanna areas of the middle belt and in parts of the north, houses consist of round mud buildings roofed with sloping grass thatch; in the drier areas of the extreme north, the people use flat mud roofs.

Each village has a chief, or headman, who usually is one of the oldest men in the community and who usually rules by consent of the people. This is particularly true in the eastern states. In Yoruba areas, and in most parts of the northern states, the village chief is chosen by, or with the consent of, the region's traditional ruler; these village chiefs are usually powerful and are held in high esteem. A characteristic feature of village life is the age-grade system of social organization, which groups together people of the same age group. Communal jobs are usually organized on the basis of the age-grade system.

Urban settlement. With the exception of the Yoruba, Hausa, Bini, Kanuri, and coastal peoples of the Gulf of Guinea, Nigerians were not town dwellers before the 20th century. The Yoruba, of whom about half live in towns of more than 5,000, are the most urbanized people in tropical Africa. Their towns, most of which are several hundred years old, were originally administrative and trading centres, and most of them have retained these functions. The more important Yoruba towns are Ibadan, Ogbomosho, Abeokuta, Ife, and Oyo.

The northern towns of the Nigerian Sudan, including Kano, Zaria, Sokoto, and Katsina, are much older than the Yoruba towns. Owing their growth to the trans-Saharan trade, as well as to the agricultural wealth of the Sudan, these ancient towns were unplanned, and they consist of an amorphous assemblage of mud buildings. Their inhabitants include traders, farmers, and administrators as well as craftsmen, musicians, and drummers.

Traditional fishing and salt-trading villages along the

coast grew into towns in response to the slave trade and the later trade in palm oil between the coastal peoples and Europeans. These towns include Bonny, Opobo Town, Okrika, Buguma, Brass, Forcados, Creek Town, and Calabar (Duke Town). At the beginning of colonial rule, these coastal port towns had a more cosmopolitan population than the towns of the Yoruba area and the far north, but they were much smaller in size.

An-
cient and
modern
towns

During the period of British rule, new towns grew up and the older ones grew larger, except along the coast, where all the older towns, excluding Lagos, declined in size or even ceased to exist. Many towns originally were primarily administrative centres, but—like the southern towns of Port Harcourt, Lagos, and Ibadan, as well as the Sudanese towns of Kano and Kaduna—they have since become industrialized. Outside the walls of the ancient cities, the British established two customarily segregated towns or quarters—one, for European administrative officers and commercial agents, known as the Government Reservation Area (GRA), and the other, for Nigerians from other regions, known as Sabon Gari (Strangers' Town). Such quarters exist in most cities in the Yoruba and Hausa regions and in such colonial-period towns as Enugu, Jos and Port Harcourt.

Lagos, the original national capital, is the largest conurbation in Nigeria. Primarily a Yoruba town, it was founded in the late 17th century as a small fishing and trading settlement on Lagos Island. Lagos is by far the most industrialized city in the country.

THE PEOPLE

The great diversity of peoples and cultures in Nigeria is largely a result of the location of the country at the meeting point of transcontinental migration routes from north to south, west to east, and southeast to northwest. There are more than 200 ethnic groups in the country, each of which has its own customs, traditions, and language. The larger groups include the Hausa, Fulani, Yoruba, and Ibo. Other prominent but less numerous groups include the Edo, of Benin City, as well as the Ibibio, in the forest belt; the Tiv and Nupe, in the middle belt; and the Kanuri, in the Chad Basin. The greatest concentration of smaller ethnic groups occurs in the middle belt, where there are more than 180 linguistic groups. In the Niger Delta, the home of the Ijaw, social organization was altered radically during the period of the slave trade, in part because of the forced migration of peoples from the interior into the area and in part because of contact with European traders. The distinct cultural group that emerged stressed its cultural separation from other groups rather than its common descent. Jaja of Opobo, a 19th-century chief renowned for defying the British, was an Ibo who grew up among the Ijaw of the Niger delta.

Racial and religious groups. Nigeria is a country of black-skinned peoples. The peoples of the savanna zone in the north tend to be taller than those of the forest belt of the south. Arab penetration into the Chad Basin has resulted in much racial mingling; the Shuwa Arabs and the Kanuri of this region are of mixed Negro and Arab origin. The cattle-owning Fulani retain non-Negro features, but the town Fulani have intermingled with Negroes. (The origin of the Fulani people—also known as Fulbe, Fula, Fellata, or Peul—remains undetermined. Earlier migrations resulted in their establishing states throughout the Sudan region, from Fouta-Toro in Senegal to Macina in The Sudan itself. Speculation has attributed to them a West African, an East African, or a Middle Eastern origin.) Much intermingling has also occurred in the south, particularly in the coastal port towns of Calabar, Abonnema, and Warri, where many Syrians and European traders have settled during the 20th century.

At the turn of the 20th century, much of the country was animist in its beliefs. When the last acceptable census was taken, in 1963, 47 percent of the people were Muslims, and 35 percent were Christians. Many professing Muslims and Christians, however, continue to observe animist practices. Religious freedom is guaranteed by the constitution, and Muslims and Christians live and work together. The greatest concentration of Muslims is in the northern

states, where three-quarters of the people are Muslim. Islām has also gained strength in Lagos, Ogun, and Oyo states, where Muslims outnumbered Christians by the early 1980s. Christians make up more than three-quarters of the population in the eastern states, and Christianity has made great inroads in the middle belt since 1960.

The main Christian groups are Roman Catholics, Methodists, Anglicans, Baptists, and members of the Cherubim and Seraphim sects. Before the takeover of private schools by most state governments during the early 1970s, these Christian groups and some Muslim sects owned and operated schools and hospitals throughout the country. The development of education between 1900 and 1970 was primarily the responsibility of religious groups, and, in appreciation of this, institutions taken over by the government have been permitted to retain their names.

Ethnic and linguistic groups. Hausa is the most widely spoken African language in Nigeria. It is spoken by the Hausa and the Fulani but is also the lingua franca in the northern states. As a result of the Fulani conquest of the Hausa areas in the early 19th century and the subsequent imposition of Fulani rule, the two groups live together in the same towns and villages. The religion of both groups is Islām. The town Fulani, who are less orthodox in their religion, remain a distinctive aristocratic group. Although they intermarry freely with Hausa and other groups, they nevertheless continue to control the administration of the Hausa towns. The cattle-owning Fulani, on the other hand, are not only more orthodox but also more disinclined to intermarry. The pastoral Fulani, while more ardent Muslims than those of the towns, are also, paradoxically, less subject to Islāmic influences. They also speak the Fulani language—Fulfulde—rather than Hausa. Unlike the Fulani, the numerically dominant Hausa are settled cultivators and renowned traders. Cattle, however, including those owned by the settled Hausa farmers, are cared for by the Fulani. At the time of the British conquest, the Fulani had established an empire that extended beyond the Hausa areas to include vast regions occupied by the small groups of the middle belt; but before the Fulani conquest the Hausa were organized into large states, the most prominent of which were Zaria, Kano, and Gobir.

Hausa as
the lingua
franca

Another important linguistic group consists of the Yoruba-speaking peoples who, like the Hausa and the Fulani, have ancient connections with the Middle East. The Yoruba, although they are farmers, often live in large preindustrial cities. Each Yoruba subgroup is ruled by an influential paramount chief, or *oba,* who is usually supported by a council of chiefs. The *oni* of Ife, who is the accepted spiritual leader of the Yoruba, and the *alafin* of Oyo, who is their traditional political leader, are the two most powerful rulers; their influence is acknowledged throughout the Yoruba areas. The various Yoruba subgroups also share a traditional religious system. It features the worship of gods such as Ogun, the god of war and iron; Shango, the god of thunder and lightning; and Orisha Oko, the goddess of farmland.

The Ibo-speaking peoples, whose leaders unsuccessfully attempted between 1967 and 1970 to establish the independent state of Biafra, are one of the largest linguistic groups in Nigeria. They live in small dispersed settlements and have never organized into large political units. Traditional Ibo society has been democratic; the largest political unit has been the village group, ruled by a council of elders rather than by a chief. The Ibo have a reputation throughout West Africa for energy and individualism. The relatively rapid progress of the Ibo areas owes much to community efforts made at the village level or through the extended family system.

Other large linguistic groups include the Ibibio, who live near the Ibo, with whom they share many common traits, and the Edo people of Benin City, whose culture has been influenced by their Yoruba neighbours. In the middle belt the Tiv and the Nupe form the largest groups. Both are settled cultivators, but, while Nupe society is hierarchical, that of the Tiv tends to be decentralized.

The distribution of population. The main concentrations of people are in the forest belt west of the Cross River and in the western half of the extreme north. Parts

Densely
settled
areas

of the Ibo and Ibibio areas in Nigeria constitute the most densely settled areas in Africa south of the Sahara. This concentration of agricultural people nevertheless occurs in a region that has heavily leached and impoverished soils, and there is a food deficit. Many migrants leave the region to seek employment in the cities or in other rural parts of the country. The second region of dense population in the forest belt occurs in the cacao-growing Yoruba areas, which attract many migrants from the congested Ibo and Ibibio areas. In the extreme north there are also two regions of dense population—the Sokoto area and the Kano–Katsina area. The Kano concentration is based on intensive agriculture in an area of relatively fertile soils, but the densely settled areas around Sokoto and Katsina have somewhat impoverished soils and do not produce enough food for the local population.

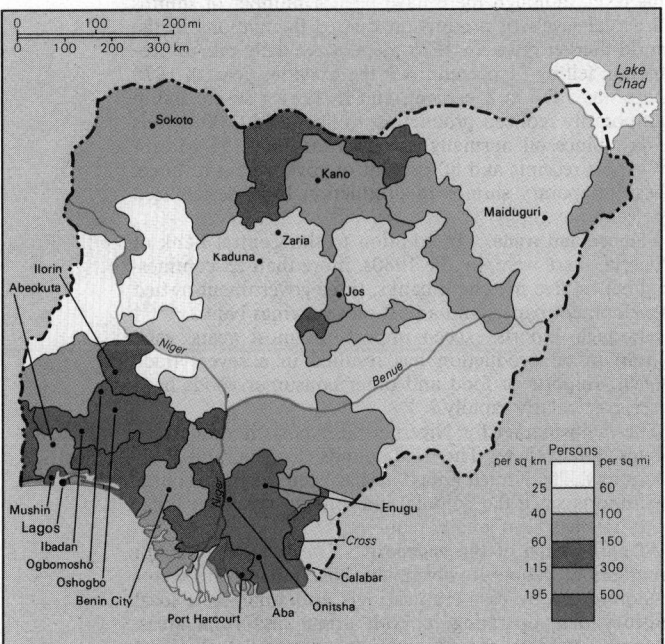

Population density of Nigeria.

Smaller pockets of dense concentrations of people occur in the tin fields of the Jos Plateau, in the southern Tiv region, and in the Okene area. The remaining, and by far the greater, part of the country is somewhat sparsely settled; vast areas of the middle belt, the Lake Chad Basin, and the Cross River area are virtually uninhabited. While most of these sparsely populated areas suffered from extensive slave raids during the 19th century, there are some areas, such as the Niger Delta, the Cross River area, and parts of the middle Benue Valley, which, because of their difficult environment, have never been densely populated. The dense concentrations around Kano, Sokoto, and in parts of the cacao belt occur, on the other hand, in areas that were protected by powerful chiefs and were therefore relatively peaceful during the period of the slave trade.

Demographic trends and migrations. Although the census figures are unreliable, there is sufficient evidence from sample surveys to show that demographic trends in Nigeria are similar to those in other developing nations. High birth and mortality rates are characteristic, although, since about 1950, there has been a considerable decline in the rate of infant mortality and an increase in life expectancy. There has consequently been a rapid growth in the population.

A considerable movement of population takes place within the country. Past census figures indicated that internal migrations took the form of a south-to-north movement of migrants who settled in the northern cities of Kano, Sokoto, Kaduna, Jos, and others, as well as a north-to-south movement of seasonal migrants from the Sokoto and Kano areas into the cacao-growing Yoruba areas. A larger number of people migrate from the Ibo and Ibibio areas and also from the Niger Delta to the more industrialized and highly urbanized western states

of Lagos, Oyo, and Ogun and to the western states of Ondo and Bendel, which are rich in agricultural resources. Many of these migrants work as labourers in the cacao- and rubber-producing districts or as self-employed tenant farmers, cultivating food crops for sale to nearby towns.

Before the end of the civil war in 1970, many Nigerians also migrated to work in neighbouring West African countries, such as Benin, Ghana, Equatorial Guinea, Cameroon, and even Sierra Leone. The expulsion of aliens (consisting mostly of Nigerians) from Cameroon in 1967 and from Ghana in 1969, as well as the comparative buoyancy of the country's economy, tended to attract more foreign western Africans into Nigeria from about 1972. This trend was greatly encouraged in 1978 by the establishment of the Economic Community of West African States, under which the free movement of citizens of member states is guaranteed. A small but increasing number of Nigerians also migrate to Great Britain, West Germany, Canada, and the United States.   (R.K.U.)

THE ECONOMY

During the 1960s the Nigerian economy had moderate growth based on the exploitation of agricultural resources and the production of oil. The civil war of 1967–70 caused economic disruption, but recovery was quick, and oil production began to increase rapidly. Coupled with the series of world oil price increases from 1973, this produced rapid economic growth, especially in transport, construction, solid minerals, and government services. Despite this growth, the manufacturing sector remains relatively undeveloped; it is concentrated on the more basic subsectors, and more than one-half of the population remains dependent on agriculture. Nigeria was once a major exporter of cacao, palm oil, peanuts (groundnuts), cotton, and rubber. During the 1970s, however, agricultural production lagged badly, and by the early 1980s only cacao was exported on a significant scale. Food production also stagnated, and the country became a major net importer. Despite the rapid growth of the country's total gross domestic product, its large population means that the level of per capita income remains low.

Resources. Oil, natural gas, coal, tin, and columbite are Nigeria's most important minerals, but only oil is produced on a significant scale. The discovery of oil and its production in commercial quantities dates from the late

Oil
resources

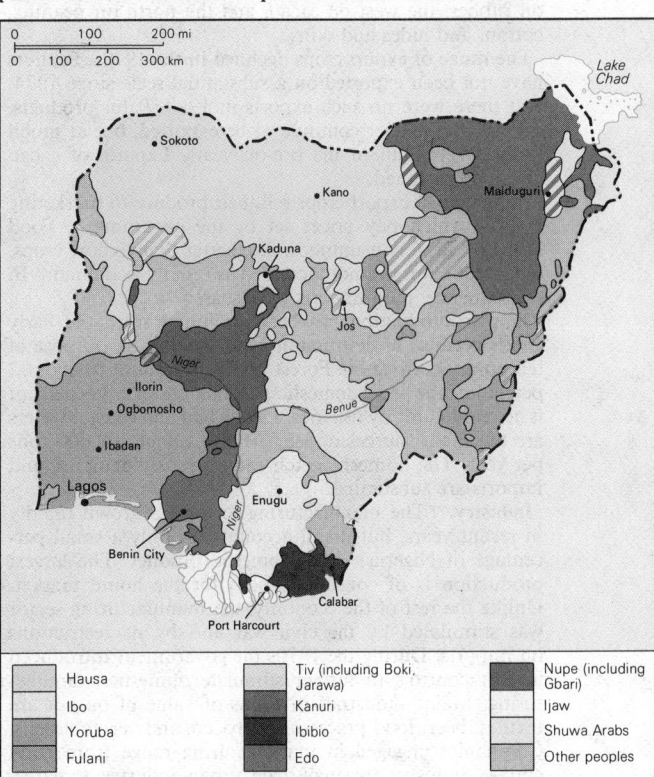

Hausa	Tiv (including Boki, Jarawa)	Nupe (including Gbari)
Ibo	Kanuri	Ijaw
Yoruba	Ibibio	Shuwa Arabs
Fulani	Edo	Other peoples

General ethnic composition of Nigeria.

1950s. All of the reserves so far exploited are in the southern part of the country, south of a line through Benin City, Owerri, and Calabar, with most of the output coming from onshore fields in the Niger Delta area. Natural-gas reserves are large, but most of the gas produced has to be flared for lack of a market. One-third of all Nigerian coal reserves are estimated to be in Anambra State around Enugu, the remainder being in the northern states. Coal production ceased during the civil war and did not reach pre-war levels thereafter. There are extensive deposits of lignite in the south, but technical difficulties exclude their exploitation. In the northern and eastern states there are deposits of tin and of columbite. There are established iron-ore deposits in the northern and eastern states, and in 1980 it was announced that large deposits had been discovered in Kwara State. A pilot iron-ore mine at Itakpe began operations in 1979 to supply the Ajaokuta steel mill. Kwara State also has uranium reserves.

Biological resources. In relation to the size of the population, Nigeria has no shortage of arable land, although the prevalence of the shifting cultivation system means that such a shortage is emerging in some areas. This system has the merit, however, of protecting the soil against both erosion and loss of fertility. Most of the commercially exploited timber resources are in the Benin lowlands immediately to the northwest of the Niger Delta.

Hydroelectric resources. There is a widespread network of rivers, many of which are potential sources of hydroelectric energy. By the early 1980s the total installed generating capacity was more than 1,900 megawatts. The Kainji power station began operation in 1969 with an initial capacity of 320 megawatts, which has since been raised to 960 megawatts. Other power plants are in operation, and additional stations are planned.

Agriculture, forestry, and fishing. Agricultural production, including forestry and fishing, declined considerably during the 1970s and accounted for only 12 percent of the gross domestic product by the early 1980s. Produce grown mainly for domestic consumption, most of it not marketed, is worth about five times that grown for export. The main food crops grown in the southern states are yam, cassava, and cocoyam, and in the northern states corn, guinea corn, rice, millet, and cowpeas; the northern states are also a cattle-raising area. The eastern states concentrate on producing palm oil and kernels, the midwest on rubber, the west on cacao, and the north on peanuts, cotton, and hides and skins.

The range of export crops declined in the 1970s. Peanuts have not been exported on a substantial scale since 1974, and there were no such exports in 1980. Palm products, cotton, and rubber continue to be exported, but at much lower levels than in the pre-oil years. Exports of cacao also have declined.

Producers of export crops sell their produce to marketing boards, which pay prices set by the government. Food crops for local consumption fare better than export crops, but production has not increased as rapidly as demand. In consequence, food imports have soared.

Timber production has been declining since the early 1960s because of destruction of forests for the purpose of temporary cultivation. Forest products amount to about 2 percent of the gross domestic product; another 3.5 percent is accounted for by fisheries. Lake Chad and coastal waters are the main sources of fish, yielding about 500,000 tons per year. The domestic catch cannot satisfy demand, and imports are substantial.

Industry. The manufacturing sector has grown rapidly in recent years, but it still accounts for only a small percentage of Nigeria's gross domestic product. The largest production is of consumer goods for the home market. Unlike the rest of the economy, the manufacturing sector was stimulated by the civil war and by its restrictions on imports. During the 1970s the government introduced import controls to further stimulate domestic manufacturing. Major industries in terms of value of output are textiles, beer, food processing, tobacco, and vegetable oils. Companies engaged in manufacturing range from rural cottage industry to small-scale urban industry to large, modern industrial plants.

With its oil, natural gas, coal, and hydroelectric resources, Nigeria has a wide range of potential sources of energy. The exploitation of the oil and gas reserves has transformed the pattern of energy consumption. By the late 1970s liquid fuels supplied about three-fourths of Nigeria's energy needs; hydroelectricity supplied about 15 percent, and natural gas 12 percent.

Mining represents the fastest growing sector of the Nigerian economy, accounting for nearly 25 percent of the gross domestic product by the early 1980s, compared with less than 1 percent in the late 1950s. Although the production of tin, columbite, and coal declined during the 1970s, oil production has grown steadily. The civil war of 1967–70 led to a fall in production that was reversed in the 1970s; production exceeded 2,000,000 barrels a day in 1973. Since then the official target has hovered around this level, although there have been a number of slumps in actual levels of production due to fluctuations in the world market price. In 1975 the average daily rate of production fell by 21 percent over the previous year, in 1978 there was a fall of 8 percent, and in 1981 a severe slump temporarily reduced production to about 700,000 barrels a day. Since oil normally accounts for about 95 percent of export receipts and 80 percent of government revenue, these temporary slumps in production have destabilized the economy.

Finance and trade. In addition to the Central Bank of Nigeria, there were, by the 1980s, more than 25 commercial banks, five merchant banks, three government-owned development banks, and a post-office savings bank.

Although exports exceed imports in most years, each slump in oil production has resulted in a severe trade deficit. Imports of food and other consumer goods have risen particularly rapidly.

The main market for Nigerian oil exports is the United States, followed by The Netherlands, France, and West Germany. The United Kingdom has been the main source of imports since the colonial era, but its lead over other countries has been greatly reduced.

Administration of the economy. *The private sector.* In numbers of people involved, the Nigerian private sector is dominated by cash-crop farmers and small-scale local businessmen, operating in both urban and rural areas. During the 1970s the government attempted to increase Nigerian ownership of commerce and industry, which, until then, had been largely in the hands of foreigners. Decrees of 1972 and 1976 required all companies to have at least 40 percent Nigerian shareholders, and for many sectors the required minimum was higher.

The public sector. Government accounts for about 7 percent of the gross domestic product. Apart from manufacturing projects and an oil corporation, the government owns a shipping line, an airline, sporting facilities, broadcasting stations, and hotels. It also provides incentives to private firms, including tariff protection, import duty relief on materials, accelerated depreciation allowances, and some relief from income taxes, and supports private industry by providing credit, industrial estates, and technical assistance.

Taxation. According to the federal constitution part of the revenue collected by the federal government has to be redistributed to the states. The allocation of revenue between the states and the federal government, and between the states themselves, is a constant issue of contention. Oil provides some 80 percent of government revenue through profit taxes, royalties, premiums for the acquisition of concessions, and miscellaneous fees. The only other important sources of government revenue are taxes on trade (mainly import duties), company taxes, and interest; the personal income tax is negligible. Public finances were severely strained during the civil war and during periods following slumps in oil production.

Trade unions and employer associations. The trade union system was completely reorganized in 1978, when the government abolished the nearly 1,000 unions then in existence. In their place 42 industrial unions were created under the umbrella of the Nigerian Labour Congress. A dissident labour organization was formed in 1981.

(E.I.U.)

The role of government

The north–south traffic pattern

Transportation. The general pattern of transport is from north to south, running from the interior to the southern seaports. This pattern is a reflection of the economy, in which raw materials are produced in the interior and are then shipped through the nearest port to the metropolitan areas, which in turn supply manufactured goods. The transport pattern also results from the fact that different agricultural products are grown in zones, or belts, running east to west, so that the general direction of internal exchange trade is from north to south. This pattern is modified in the south, however, where local staples flow from the eastern and midwestern states to Ibadan and Lagos in the southwest.

On several occasions the country's single-track railroads have proved incapable of transporting large quantities of peanuts and cotton from the north, a circumstance that has stressed the growing importance of road haulage. By the early 1980s almost all cargo transport was by road, and movement by rail had declined sharply.

The average daily traffic flow on the roads is greatest in the cacao belt of southwestern Nigeria, the peanut and cotton belt of the Kano–Katsina region, the Jos Plateau tin fields, and the palm belt of southeastern Nigeria. These are the four main areas of economic development and of population concentration in the country; they are consequently served by a dense network of all-weather roads. By contrast, the relatively unproductive and sparsely settled areas of the middle belt, of the Cross River region, and of the Chad Basin have tenuous road links that carry only a few trucks a day.

Although the development of the railway and of roads has overshadowed inland waterways, the creeks and rivers were the first means of communication in 20th-century Nigeria. The most important waterways are the Niger and Benue rivers, which still carry substantial quantities of goods. The Cross River is used to ship exports to Calabar, but, like other rivers in the country, it is not navigable during the dry season. Passenger and cargo boats also operate on the lagoons and on the numerous creeks that are found along the Nigerian coast from Lagos to the Cross River.

The railroad system

Although roads have become the most important means of transportation, it was the railroad that formerly was most relied upon. The railroad system consists of two single-track main lines—the eastern line from Port Harcourt to Maiduguri and the western line from Lagos to Kano. Branch lines connect the western main line to Kaura Namoda, to Nguru, and to Baro on the Niger. The total route mileage is about 2,200 miles. Since 1960 tracks have been relaid with heavier rail to permit heavier axle loads and higher speeds, rail movements have been speeded by improvements in signalling, and steam engines have been replaced by diesel locomotives, which are especially useful in the drier north. In the early 1980s the government initiated an intensive effort to rebuild, modernize, and extend existing rail lines.

Nigerian roads fall into three categories: trunk A roads, which are maintained by the federal government and which link Lagos with all the state capitals; trunk B roads, which are maintained by state governments and which connect provincial capitals and other large towns with the trunk A system; and other roads, which are maintained by local governments, carry local traffic, and act as feeders to the trunk-road systems. All trunk A and most trunk B roads are surfaced; almost all other roads are earth. The conversion of the Benin–Shagamu and the Port Harcourt–Enugu trunk A roads into four-lane divided highways was completed in 1981; work was in progress in the early 1980s to open a similar highway from Lagos to Sokoto. The only expressway in the country, opened to traffic in 1978, runs between Lagos and Ibadan. The southern terminals of the north–south trunk A roads are the port towns of Lagos, Port Harcourt, Warri, and Calabar, the first two of which also serve as terminals for the two main-line railways.

The ports

Lagos and Port Harcourt, administered by the Nigerian Ports Authority since its establishment in 1954, are the country's main international seaports, but they have often proved incapable of handling the large volume of cargo passing through them. Chronic congestion at these two ports was largely responsible for the authority's takeover in 1970 of the port installations and administration of the smaller ports of Warri, Sapele, Koko, and Calabar. The expansion of the Lagos port complex in 1978 and the modernization and expansion of port facilities in the smaller ports resulted, however, in excess capacity by 1980.

Except for Abeokuta, which is less than 50 miles from the Lagos international airport, all the state capitals are served by air transport supplied by Nigerian Airways. There are smaller airfields in some provincial cities and in the oil-producing areas of the Niger Delta and the Cross River estuary. Lagos and Kano handle most of the transcontinental traffic, although international airports also include those at Port Harcourt, Calabar, Maiduguri, and Sokoto. Government reorganization in 1967 and 1975 required additional air service between Lagos and the increased number of state capitals, while the oil boom of the early 1970s helped to create an even greater demand for air transport.

ADMINISTRATIVE AND SOCIAL CONDITIONS

Government. Under the constitution of 1979 Nigeria adopted a presidential system of government in which the president, who is directly elected, exercises power as the chief executive and head of state. Also provided is a federal legislature, or National Assembly, which consists of the Senate and the House of Representatives, and from which the president seeks support for his measures. In the aftermath of a military coup on December 31, 1983, however, the constitution of 1979 was suspended.

Justice. The Nigerian legal and judicial system is subject to regional variations, particularly between the Muslim north and the Christian south. There are three codes of law: customary law, Nigerian statute law, and English law. Customary laws are administered by native, or customary, courts, usually presided over by persons with no formal legal education. In the case of the Alkali, or Muslim, Courts, however, the judges (*alkalis*) undergo formal training in Muslim law. Customary courts are of different grades, with Grade A courts serving as courts of appeal for cases from Grade B, C, and D courts. In addition, under the 1979 constitution, any state may establish a special Customary Court of Appeal or, in the case of Muslim communities, a Sharī'ah Court of Appeal. During the first period of civilian rule, customary courts fell into disrepute as instruments of political coercion.

Nigerian statute law includes much of the British colonial legislation, most of which has been revised. State legislatures may pass laws on certain matters not included in the Exclusive Legislative List, which is composed of such subjects as defense, external affairs, and mining—all of which can be legislated upon only by the federal government. Federal law prevails in the courts whenever federal legislation on any matter is in conflict with state legislation. In addition to Nigerian statutes, English law is used in the magistrates' and all higher courts.

Structure of the courts

Each state has a High Court, which is presided over by a chief judge. The Federal Revenue Court was established in 1973 to handle civil and criminal matters relating to excise and other taxes, corporations, banking, and copyrights; it has a status comparable to that of a state High Court. Appeals from state High Courts and the Federal Revenue Court go to the Federal Court of Appeal, which was created in 1976 to serve as an intermediate appellate court between those two courts and the Supreme Court. The Supreme Court, under the chairmanship of the chief justice of Nigeria, is the highest court.

Education. State governments are responsible for primary and secondary education, as well as teacher-training colleges, technical institutes, and colleges of technology. Before 1976, when the universal primary education (UPE) scheme began, primary education was free only in Lagos, Oyo, Ogun, Ondo, Bendel, Sokoto, and Niger states. The estimated primary school population in 1976 of 8,300,000 increased to more than 11,000,000 by 1981, after the UPE scheme had become compulsory. Secondary education has always been free to indigenes of most of the northern states. In the southern states free education at the secondary level began in 1979 in Lagos, Ogun, Oyo,

The growth of free education

Ondo, and Bendel states. Teachers are trained not only in the universities but also in the many federal and state colleges of education and in numerous advanced teacher-training colleges.

Until 1950 most schools were controlled by Christian missionary bodies. A few government schools were also maintained, although government policy was to give grants to mission schools rather than to expand its own. After independence many more secondary schools were established by local council authorities, Muslim missionary groups, and wealthy and prominent citizens. Immediately after the civil war of 1967–70, the Federal Military Government embarked upon the establishment of federal government secondary schools, of which there were 39 by 1981. A shortage of teachers constitutes a major problem for the expansion of educational facilities.

In 1966 there were five universities, two of which (at Lagos and Ibadan) belonged to the federal government. The federal government took control of the state universities at Ife, Benin, Nsukka, and Zaria in 1975, and, when civilian rule was restored in 1979, there were 13 federal universities. Like the older universities, each of the universities established in 1975 at Kano, Sokoto, Maiduguri, Jos, Ilorin, Calabar, and Port Harcourt has a medical school. The Federal Universities of Technology at Bauchi, Makurdi, Owerri, Ondo, and Yola, which opened during the 1981–82 academic year, were the first to be established after the return to civilian rule. A number of state governments have also established new universities after 1980; these include the Rivers State University of Science and Technology at Port Harcourt and the state universities at Imo and Anambra. The university student population, which has continued to increase, was about 45,000 by 1980. A lack of teaching staff, inadequate financing, and the slow pace of physical development of the campuses are major problems facing the universities.

Health and welfare. Medical and health services are the responsibility of the state governments, each of which maintains a hospital in the large cities and towns. Specialized hospitals are located in almost all of the state capitals, each of which also has a university teaching hospital financed directly by the federal Ministry of Health. Many former missionary hospitals have been taken over by the state governments, but there are numerous private hospitals, clinics, and maternity centres owned and run by Nigerian medical personnel. Medical services are still inadequate, even in the five western states where a free health service scheme was introduced in 1979. Many hospitals do not have enough medical personnel, and drugs are always scarce. Rural areas are the most deprived of services, with most communities being served only by dispensaries and maternity centres, staffed by junior personnel.

The number of practicing doctors in Nigeria has increased considerably from about 3,100 in 1972 to about 10,200 in 1981. The number of doctors per person was still low in the early 1980s, however, when compared with the developed countries. Only six of the 13 medical schools in the country were producing doctors by 1982.

Housing. Housing is inadequate in the cities, where overcrowding has led to the spread of slums and the emergence of shantytown suburbs in most of the larger urban centres. Since there are only a few housing corporations, most houses are built by individuals, who, unable to obtain loans from either commercial or government mortgage banks, must rely on their savings for constructing houses. House rents have continuously increased in the major urban centres as more people migrate into the cities in search of jobs. A federal housing program, begun in 1980, provides for the construction of low-cost housing for low- and middle-income earners in the state capitals, local government headquarters, and other large towns. Most villagers still live in traditional housing, although modern houses are being built in many rural areas.

Police services. The Nigeria Police Force, established by the federal constitution, is headed by the inspector general of police, who is appointed by the president. In 1960 the state governments were allowed to appoint their own police commissioners, who were responsible to the inspector general but who had to comply with the directives of their state governments. The constitution of 1963 also provided for the continued existence of police forces operated by local government councils. The local government police forces were inferior to the Nigeria Police Force and were used by the state governments against political opponents, especially in 1964 and 1965. During the military administration the Federal Military Government abolished the local police forces and undertook to train the constables and absorb them into the Nigeria Police Force. The 1979 constitution makes no provisions for the existence of a local government police force in any part of the country. State commissioners of police are appointed by the Police Service Commission.

Health conditions. The concentration of people in large preindustrial cities such as Ibadan, Oshogbo, Zaria, and Kano and in the newer cities of Enugu, Kaduna, and Jos has created enormous sanitary problems, particularly sewage disposal, water shortages, and poor drainage. Medicine has improved health conditions, but many people still die from malaria, water-borne diseases, cerebrospinal meningitis, and other preventable diseases.

Rural communities in particular suffer greatly from inadequate or impure water supplies. Some villagers have to walk as far as six miles to the nearest water point—usually a stream. Because people wash clothes, bathe, and fish in the same stream, the water drawn by anyone living in villages further downstream is often polluted. During the dry season, wayside pits containing rainwater are used. Cattle are often watered in such pools, contributing to the high incidence of intestinal diseases and guinea worm in many rural areas.

CULTURAL LIFE

Nigeria has a rich and varied cultural heritage, deriving from the different ethnic elements, as well as Arabic and western European cultural influences. The oldest works of art so far discovered consist of late Stone Age terra-cotta heads associated with the Nok culture, which flourished in the region of the Jos tin fields from about 500 BC to about AD 200. The heads indicate an advanced agricultural culture connected with iron and tin. Nok culture is thought to have influenced the celebrated bronze and terra-cotta heads of Ife and of ancient Benin. Ancient art works of wood and bronze also have been excavated at Awka, near Onitsha, and in the coastal areas of Oron.

Nigerian arts and traditions have received renewed interest since independence. Carved calabashes from Oyo, masks and ebony heads from Benin City, Awka, or Ikot Ekpene, or thorn carving from Shagamu decorate the houses of the wealthy, who also wear locally woven and dyed cloth, instead of imported materials, as in the past. Oil paintings of Nigerian subjects are also common.

The Institutes of African Studies at the Universities of Ibadan and Ife have done much to publicize and reawaken interest in traditional folk dancing and poetry, as have the School of Fine Arts and the School of Drama at Zaria and Ibadan. The federal Ministry of Information promoted Nigerian culture during the Second World Black and African Festival of Arts and Culture (FESTAC), held in Lagos in 1977. With the establishment of radio and television stations in all state capitals, programs featuring traditional music and dance, folk operas, and story telling are available in some 25 languages. Since, except in the Muslim north, writing became common only after 1900, and since until the late 1960s few educated Nigerians showed any interest in folk traditions and local culture, much of the country's culture is believed to have perished during the last two generations. Many ancient folk songs have been revived by popular singers who use modern musical instruments to produce sounds that villagers can hardly identify with the songs they inherited from their ancestors.

In Nigeria, where superstition still waxes strong, many cultural institutions touch upon various aspects of life. Secret societies, such as Ekpo and Ekpe among the peoples of the southeast, were formerly used as instruments of government, while other institutions were associated with matrimony. According to the Fulani custom of *sharo* (test of young manhood), rival suitors underwent the ordeal

Abolition of local police forces

The Nok culture

of caning as a means of eliminating the less persistent grooms-to-be, while in Ibibio territory, girls were confined for several years in bride-fattening rooms before they were handed over to their husbands. These and other customs were discouraged by colonial administrators and missionaries. Some of the more adaptable cultural institutions have, however, been revived since independence; these include, for example, the Ekpo and Ekong societies for young boys in parts of the southeast. For statistical data, see the "Britannica World Data" section in the current *Britannica Book of the Year.*

(R.K.U.)

History

Very little is known of the history of Nigeria, least of all the history of the coastal tribes before the country was first visited by Portuguese navigators in the second half of the 15th century.

EARLY GROUPS

Introduction of Islām

A number of tribes occupied the swampy coastal areas and the thickly forested lands that lay immediately behind, while the interior, which became the Northern Region of Nigeria, was the home of peoples of mixed Arab, Hamitic, and Negro blood. The Muslim religion probably was introduced into this northern area as early as the 13th century and profoundly influenced the social as well as the religious life of the inhabitants, although paganism survived. There was little intercourse between these northern peoples and the pagan tribes inhabiting the forest country to the south, and until Europeans visited the coast the only contacts of Nigeria with the outer world were with the Eastern Sudan and, across the Sahara, with the Muslim states of North Africa.

Bornu and the Hausa lands. The principal peoples in the north were the Kanuri, who occupied Bornu, the Hausa-speaking tribes, and the Fulani. The empire of Kanem-Bornu by the end of the 11th century AD extended both east and west of Lake Chad and included the greater part of the Hausa lands. Toward the end of the 14th century the power of Kanem-Bornu waned, and the empire shrank until little was left of it except Bornu. Meanwhile, to the west of Bornu, the fortunes of the Hausa states rose and fell. These states, the most important of which were Kano, Zaria, Daura, Gobir, and Katsina, had existed from an early date, each independent of the others, and often fighting for supremacy but joining from time to time in a loose confederacy for mutual defense. Conquered in turn by Kanem and by Mohammed Askia the Great, king of Songhai (Gao)—early in the 16th century—they retained their identities under native rulers who acknowledged the suzerainty of the conquerors. When the influence of Songhai declined and the Hausa states recovered their independence, they engaged again in internecine wars and were overrun at different times by the armies of Bornu or of Kebbi, a state of the west of the Hausa lands, which was important in the 16th century.

Meanwhile, for several centuries there had been a steady movement into the Hausa lands of a pastoral tribe, the Fulani, of whose origin little is known. While most of the Fulani remained with their herds, moving from place to place in search of water and pasturage, a number drifted to the towns and mingled with the Hausa population. These "town Fulani" were quickly established in positions of influence.

Usman dan Fodio

Such a position had been gained by the mystic and philosopher Usman (Othman) dan Fodio, a Fulani sheikh of reputed sanctity who had made the pilgrimage to Mecca. When, about 1802, Usman intervened on behalf of a number of Muslims who had been enslaved, the pagan king of Gobir ordered his arrest, and Usman roused his followers to revolt. Recognized as *sarkin musulmi* ("commander of the faithful"), Usman was supported by the Fulani and some of the Muslim Hausa and easily defeated the forces of the King of Gobir, later conquering all the Hausa lands in a triumphant *jihād*, which was directed against lax or lukewarm Muslims and pagans. Bornu, a Muslim state, was overrun in 1808 but recovered its independence in the 1820s. Fulani *amīrs* were appointed as rulers of the various states, and the Fulani Empire was established from Gwandu (Gando) in the west to Adamawa in the east. Usman was succeeded by his son Bello who, as sultan of Sokoto, was recognized as *sarkin musulmi* and suzerain of all the Fulani emirates.

The courts and the systems of government and taxation, which were based on Qur'ānic law in the Hausa states, were adapted with little change by the new Fulani rulers, and for a time a high standard of justice and administration was maintained. Gradually the courts became corrupt, however, and the administration extortionate and tyrannical (with *amīrs* raiding neighbouring pagan tribes and sometimes even their own subjects to get slaves). This state of affairs continued until the British occupation of the country.

When the Bornu armies were defeated by the Fulani in 1808 and the Mai (King) was forced to flee before the invaders, the country was saved by the military skill of Muḥammad (al-Amīn) al-Kanamī, a Muslim sheikh born in Fezzan of Arab and Kanem descent. With a small force of fanatical followers he defeated the Fulani in a number of battles and drove them from Bornu. He restored the Mai to his throne and allowed him to continue as the titular ruler but retained all power to himself, governing the country wisely and well, with the title of *shehu* ("sheikh"), until his death in 1835. The puppet *mai* then attempted to recover his lost power but was defeated and killed by Omar, Muḥammad al-Kanamī's son, who continued to rule Bornu with the title of *shehu.*

In 1893 Bornu was invaded by Rabah Zubayr, who made himself the ruler of Bornu. In 1900, however, Rabah was defeated and killed by the French, who were extending their control over the western Sudan.

The coastal tribes. To the south of Bornu and the Hausa lands were a large number of tribes having various origins and customs and speaking distinct languages. Of these the largest and most important were the Yoruba and the Beni, or Bini, who occupied what later became the Western Region of Nigeria, and the Ibo, in what later became the Eastern Region. The Ibo tribe was divided into several clans speaking different dialects and lacking any central organization. For this reason it has practically no recorded history until after the British occupation. The same could be said of the numerous small tribes that inhabited the forest area and the mountainous areas of the north.

The Beni and Yoruba

The Beni and Yoruba, on the other hand, had long-established states that at various times reached a much higher standard of organization and culture than most of the other purely Negro peoples attained. When the first Portuguese ships reached the Nigerian coast in the 15th century, the Beni had long been an important nation, and the *oba* (king) of Benin was a powerful monarch whose authority extended over the Yoruba country and even farther west.

EUROPEAN CONTACT

Friendly intercourse and a certain amount of trade, mainly in slaves, were established between the Portuguese and the Beni. But the tribe gradually declined in power as the *oba* came under the influence of a theocracy that maintained authority by the terror created through wholesale human sacrifices. They discouraged contact with Europeans, trade dwindled, and by the beginning of the 18th century Benin had lost influence.

In the meantime the Yoruba had risen in importance. Little is known of their origin, but they supposedly came from the northeast and perhaps from Upper Egypt. The first settlement of the Yoruba in Western Nigeria was probably at Ife, which was to remain the spiritual headquarters of the people. The Alafin of Oyo was originally the ruler of the whole tribe, but about 1810 the breakup of his kingdom began. Each clan, under its own king, became practically independent, although the Alafin's nominal suzerainty continued to be recognized. The country suffered from repeated invasions from Dahomey, while the northern province of Ilorin fell to the Fulani from the north. The different clans—Oyo, Egba, Ife, Ijebu, and others—became involved in internecine wars, prisoners of which were sold at Lagos as slaves.

The slave trade. Traffic in slaves begun by the Portuguese proved so lucrative that other nations were soon in competition, and the slave ships of several European nations flocked to the Guinea coast. British ships were visiting the coast of Nigeria by the 17th century. Much of the trade was with minor chiefs and tribes in the Niger Delta and on the banks of other rivers, the slaves being obtained by these middlemen from the interior. Payment was made in potable spirits and arms and ammunition, all of which encouraged intertribal warfare. Throughout the long period of unrestricted slave trade no European nation attempted to bring any part of Nigeria under its control.

The slave trade was made illegal for British subjects in 1807, but the trade was scarcely affected as ships of other nations continued to carry cargoes of slaves across the Atlantic. A British naval squadron was then stationed on the West African coast to intercept the slavers. British merchant ships continued to visit the estuaries of the Nigerian rivers and began a legitimate trade, buying palm oil and other products. This fact and the activities of the naval squadron greatly increased British influence among the coastal tribes.

Exploration. At that time little was known of the interior of Africa, and it was not even appreciated that the numerous streams of the Niger Delta were in fact the mouths of a great river. Existence of such a river had long been known, but its general direction and outlet were matters for speculation. Several explorers failed before Mungo Park, in 1796, established the fact that the general course of the Upper Niger was easterly. Park lost his life at the end of 1805 or early in 1806 in an attempt to follow up his first discovery. It was not until 1830 that the brothers Richard and John Lander ascertained that the Niger flowed into the Gulf of Guinea, through the delta that had been known to Europeans for more than 300 years.

Other explorers reached northern Nigeria across the Sahara from Tripoli. In 1823 Dixon Denham and Hugh Clapperton reached Bornu, where they were received by the Mai and by the *shehu* Muḥammad al-Kanamī. Clapperton then visited Sokoto and met Sultan Bello, and the party returned safely to England in 1825. Clapperton died near Sokoto in 1827 on a second journey made from the Bight of Benin. Another extensive exploration was carried out by Heinrich Barth on behalf of the British government.

Meanwhile an attempt had been made to follow up the discovery of the Lander brothers by a trading venture on the Niger to provide an alternative to the slave trade. A company was formed by a Liverpool merchant, Macgregor Laird, who went in 1832 with two small steamers to a point above Lokoja, but disease decimated the crews and the expedition was abandoned. In 1841 a large party, including missionaries, was sent by the British government in four ships, under the command of naval officers, to explore the Niger and to try to make treaties for stopping the slave trade. In two months there were 48 deaths out of 145 Europeans in the ships, others became seriously ill, and this enterprise also was abandoned. It was not until 1854 that a single ship, commanded by W.B. Baikie, with a crew composed largely of Africans, was able to explore the Niger and the Benue and to do a certain amount of successful trading without any loss of life, the success resulting from the prophylactic use of quinine.

The beginnings of British rule. By that time the trade in palm oil, which the coastal Africans found remunerative, had greatly increased, while the slave trade declined in the Niger Delta and on the Oil Rivers to the east of it, although it was not until about 1840 that slave ships stopped visiting these rivers. To assist legitimate trade it was decided in 1849 to appoint a British consul for the Bights of Biafra and Benin, with his headquarters at Fernando Po. Selected for this post was John Beecroft, who had resided at Fernando Po for many years as superintendent of the naval base there.

Beecroft was soon engaged in negotiations with King Kosoko of Lagos (then the principal port in West Africa from which slaves were shipped) with a view to stopping the trade; but the negotiations were unsuccessful, and in

British expeditions (margin note)

1851 the town was attacked by a naval force and captured after heavy fighting. Kosoko fled, and his uncle Akitoye, the legitimate ruler, was placed on the throne; he signed a treaty providing for the abolition of the slave trade and of human sacrifice and for the protection of missionaries. A British consul was appointed to Lagos with the King's consent.

In 1861 Akitoye's successor, Dosumu, who appeared unable to govern effectively or to prevent the revival of the slave trade, was required to sign a treaty ceding his possessions to the British crown in return for a pension, and Lagos was annexed as a British colony. For a time the existence of this colony, which effectively stopped the slave trade and provided a haven for runaway slaves, was strongly resented by the Yoruba in the hinterland of Lagos and especially by the Egba, who closed the trade routes and expelled all missionaries and European traders. At a later date, however, British influence increased in the Yoruba country; the civil wars that had raged for so many years among the Yoruba were brought to an end, and in 1888 a treaty with the Alafin of Oyo placed the whole of the Yoruba country under British protection.

After his successful voyage in 1854 Baikie had established himself at Lokoja under the protection of the Amir of Nupe and maintained his more or less official settlement from trading profits. A number of European companies also began to trade on the Niger. In 1879 George Goldie-Taubman (later known as Sir George Goldie), who was interested in one of the companies, arranged a merger of all the British firms trading on the Niger; and a few years later he was able to buy out the rival French companies. Treaties were made with the chiefs of tribes inhabiting the banks of the Niger and the Benue and with the Fulani sultan of Sokoto, and at the Berlin Conference of 1885 it was possible to claim that the British interests were supreme on the Niger and the Oil rivers. This claim was admitted by the conference, and a British protectorate was then declared over the Niger districts, which included the Oil Rivers area and the hinterland.

Sir George Goldie (margin note)

The vague authority of the consul had gradually increased in the Oil Rivers area, and courts of equity, composed of the leading African and European traders on the different rivers, had been established. In 1872 an order of the Queen in council had regularized the judicial and administrative position of the consul, but he had for a time little means of enforcing his authority. In 1887, however, Chief Jaja of Opobo was removed and deported in consequence of his interference with trade and defiance of the consul. In 1891 a commissioner and consul general was appointed to the Oil River, with his headquarters at Calabar, and in 1893 the territory was renamed the Niger Coast Protectorate.

The Royal Niger Company. In 1886 a royal charter was granted to the company organized by Sir George Goldie, which later was called the Royal Niger Company, Chartered and Limited. The company was authorized to administer the delta and the country on the banks of the Niger and the Benue together with the hinterland but was forbidden to establish any monopoly of trade. The company at once set up courts of justice and the usual administrative services and raised an armed constabulary. Most of the Fulani Empire was beyond its control; but in 1897, after a short campaign, the company's troops were able to subdue Ilorin and Nupe and to compel the *amirs* of these states to abandon slave raiding and recognize the suzerainty of the company.

Meanwhile, on the coast, the people of Brass—who were included in the Niger Coast Protectorate and excluded (except on payment of prohibitive dues) from trading in their former markets on the Niger that lay within the company's territory—became increasingly hostile. In 1895 they raided the company's establishment at Akassa, killing many of the African employees of the company and carrying off others as prisoners, some of these being killed and eaten. This outrage was punished by a naval force.

Benin. Another naval force, assisted by the protectorate constabulary, had captured (1894) Brohemie, on the Benin River, the headquarters of the Jekri chief Nana, who had traded in slaves extensively. Nana was captured, tried, and deported.

The principal centre of the slave trade in the Niger Coast Protectorate was then the city of Benin, which was also known for the practice of human sacrifice. King Overami of Benin had failed to implement a treaty he had signed in 1892 for the abolition of human sacrifice and of the slave trade, and the acting consul general, J.R. Phillips, suggested that he should visit Benin to discuss the matter. The King replied that he would be willing to receive Phillips within a few months' time, but Phillips was not prepared to wait and decided, in spite of warnings, to go at once to Benin. He so informed the King, assuring him that his party would be unarmed; in reply Overami promised to send guides to meet the party. On January 3, 1897, Phillips and his party landed at Gwato, where a friendly welcome was received through messengers sent by the King. The next day, however, the party started for Benin and within a few hours it was massacred, only two of the Europeans, badly wounded, and a few of the Africans escaping. Phillips and six of his European companions and more than 200 Africans perished.

A naval force was at once sent to the Benin River, and sailors and marines, with troops of the protectorate constabulary, captured Benin after severe fighting, about six weeks after the massacre. After a judicial inquiry, those who were directly responsible for the massacre were executed, and Overami was deported.

On the western frontier, disputes with France (which were to be embittered in 1898 by the Fashoda Incident at the opposite end of the Sudan) nearly led to war, and an imperial force of African soldiers with British officers, the West African Frontier Force, was raised in 1897 and placed under the command of Frederick Lugard. For a time the situation was critical, but the dispute was finally settled without fighting.

THE 20TH CENTURY

These international difficulties and the complaint of the Brass people against the Royal Niger Company led to the revocation of the company's charter, the British government assuming direct control of the company's territories on January 1, 1900. The land in the Niger Delta and along the lower reaches of the river, which had been included in the company's territories, was added to the Niger Coast Protectorate, which was renamed Southern Nigeria. On May 1, 1906, the Lagos territories were amalgamated with Southern Nigeria, the whole country being styled the Colony and Protectorate of Southern Nigeria, with Lagos as the seat of government.

The northern part of the company's territories became the Protectorate of Northern Nigeria, with Lugard serving as the first high commissioner. The Fulani emirates still retained their independence, and slave raiding continued; but the principal slave raiders, the *amīrs* of Kontagora, Nupe, and Adamawa, were removed from office in 1901, and Bauchi and Bornu were brought under control the following year. The Sultan of Sokoto refused friendly overtures. In spite of this the British administration was steadily extended, and a small garrison was stationed at Zaria. When the Amīr of Kano threatened to attack this garrison and also refused to surrender the murderer of a British official, a force of about 700 African soldiers, with British officers, advanced against the mud-walled city of Kano, which was taken on February 3, 1903. There was subsequently severe fighting against the main Kano army and the army of the Sultan of Sokoto, who fled before the battle. Sokoto was then occupied, and the chiefs nominated a new sultan, approved by the high commissioner.

The Sultan and *amīrs* who accepted British rule were installed with full ceremonial after agreeing to abolish slave raiding and to be guided by the advice of British officials. In return they were promised their religion would not be interfered with and that the existing system of Muslim law would be retained. Most of these *amīrs* remained loyal and proved efficient administrators. A rising of a few fanatics against the Sultan of Sokoto in 1906 was suppressed by protectorate troops, and there was some fighting against the pagan tribes who resisted the enforcement of law; otherwise there was little serious trouble, and British administration was quickly made effective throughout Northern

Nigeria. Slave raiding was suppressed and the legal status of slavery was abolished, although many slaves remained voluntarily with their masters.

In the administration of Northern Nigeria, Lugard used the indigenous authorities, the *amīrs*, and other chiefs, in what became known as indirect rule. The African administrations had their own treasuries and received a proportion of the tax.

The amalgamation of Nigeria. Lugard ceased to be high commissioner in 1906 but returned to Nigeria in 1912 as governor of both Northern and Southern Nigeria, charged with the duty of amalgamating the two territories. This amalgamation was effected on January 1, 1914, the whole country being known thereafter as the Colony and Protectorate of Nigeria.

Seven months later, in August 1914, World War I broke out, and Nigerian forces were soon in action against German troops in Kamerun. A combined Franco-British invasion of Kamerun resulted in the conquest of the country by the beginning of 1916. In 1922 a small part of the territory was mandated by the League of Nations to the United Kingdom and was attached for purposes of administration to Nigeria. (The mandate was replaced in 1947 by a trusteeship agreement with the United Nations.) Before the end of the war Nigerian soldiers had also taken part in the fighting in East Africa. In World War II, Nigerian troops served in East Africa against the Italians and in Burma against the Japanese.

Constitutional changes. Following the amalgamation of 1914 and particularly after the end of World War II, a number of territorial and constitutional changes took place in Nigeria. In 1914 the country was divided into three main areas, namely the Colony of Nigeria (corresponding to the former Colony of Lagos) and two groups of provinces in the protectorate, the Northern and Southern provinces. The Southern provinces were later divided into two groups, Eastern and Western. In 1951 these were officially renamed the Northern, Eastern, and Western regions.

In 1914 a legislative council for the colony alone had been set up, affairs of the protectorate being beyond its purview. In 1923 a larger legislative council was established that for the first time included a limited number of elected members.

A radical change was made in the constitution in 1947. Houses of assembly for the three groups of provinces were set up, with a majority of nonofficial over ex officio members, and there was also a house of chiefs for the Northern provinces. In addition there was a central legislative council for the whole of Nigeria.

Public opinion was still not satisfied, and a quasi-federal constitution, introduced in 1951, provided for a central legislative house of representatives. Resulting friction between central and regional legislatures caused the introduction of yet another constitution (the third in eight years) in 1954. This set up the Federation of Nigeria, comprising the Northern, Eastern, and Western regions, the Southern Cameroons (part of the trust territory), and the Federal Territory of Lagos. A fourth region, the Mid-West, was established in 1963, by the separation of certain non-Yoruba areas from the Western Region. The office of federal prime minister was created in August 1957 (the post being filled by Alhaji Abubakar Tafawa Balewa, a northerner) as a result of the constitution conference of 1957–58, and internal self-government was achieved by the Eastern and Western regions in 1957, and by the Northern Region in 1959.

The British government then announced its willingness to grant independence to the federation on October 1, 1960, and on the request of the Nigerian federal legislature this undertaking was implemented by the United Kingdom Parliament. Nigeria adopted a federal constitution (1960) and a parliamentary system of government. The head of state and commander in chief of the armed forces was a ceremonial president who was elected for five-year terms.

On June 1, 1961, the northern part of the Cameroons trust territory joined the federation as part of the Northern Region. Southern Cameroons united with Cameroun on October 1, 1961, to form the Federal Republic

Southern Nigeria and Northern Nigeria

Constitution of 1951

of Cameroon. On October 1, 1963, Nigeria became a republic.

Independent Nigeria. Owing to the larger population and consequent greater representation of the Northern Region in the federal legislature, the central government remained largely under northern control, and this circumstance was resented by the southern tribes. In May 1962 a political crisis occurred in Western Nigeria. There were disorders and electoral boycotts during the general elections of 1964, which were the first to be held after independence, and in October 1965 further disorders took place in the Western Region when a regional election was held there. There was strong evidence that this election was rigged by the political party in power, which was allied to the party that controlled the Northern Region and, to some extent, the federal government.

In January 1966 an army mutiny led by officers who were members of the Ibo tribe overthrew the civil government and culminated in the death of the federal prime minister and the premiers of the Northern and Western regions. A military government was set up under the leadership of Maj. Gen. Johnson T.U. Aguiyi-Ironsi, the officer commanding the Nigerian Army, who, himself an Ibo, had not been implicated in the mutiny. Attempts by the military government to abolish the regions and establish a unitary government led to disorders in the Northern Region and to the killing of Ibos living and working there. At the end of July 1966 in another coup, this one by Hausa officers, General Ironsi was killed and a new military government came into power under Lieut. Col. (later Gen.) Yakubu Gowon, a northerner. Later, many Ibos were killed in the Northern Region; a movement of Ibos back to their homes in the Eastern Region took place. Some Hausas were killed in the Eastern Region.

On September 12 representatives from all four regions and Lagos met to attempt to work out constitutional provisions that would make possible return to civil government. No agreement being reached—the Eastern Region insisted on a weak central government—the meeting adjourned on October 2. When it reassembled on October 27, no delegate from the Eastern Region was present, and the other delegates ceased negotiations on November 1. A further meeting, attended by Eastern delegates, was held at Aburi, in Ghana, in January 1967, but there were differences of interpretation of the agreements arrived at and the situation rapidly deteriorated. On May 27 the Eastern Region's Consultative Assembly gave Lieut. Col. (later Gen.) C.O. Ojukwu, the head of the Eastern Region, a mandate to declare the region a sovereign and independent republic. The federal government responded by declaring a state of emergency and promulgated a decree dividing Nigeria into 12 states (six in the Northern Region, three in the Eastern Region, the former Western and Mid-West regions, and Lagos). At the same time civilians were added to the military rulers in the federal government.

Civil war. On May 30 Ojukwu announced the secession of the Eastern Region and the setting up of the Republic of Biafra. This was declared by Gowon to be an act of rebellion and hostilities broke out soon after, with Eastern Region (Biafran) forces resisting federal troops. Biafran troops captured Benin City, the capital, and most of the Mid-Western Region but were later driven out. Federal troops took Enugu, the Biafran capital, early in October, and other towns fell to federal forces in spite of stubborn resistance.

Notwithstanding attempts by the Organization of African Unity (OAU) and others to reconcile the combatants, the fighting continued until January 1970, by which time Biafra, its population already starving, had reached the point of total collapse. Ojukwu left the country on January 11, and the following day Maj. Gen. Philip Effiong assumed the leadership and ordered the Biafran troops to stop fighting. On January 15 a deputation of Biafran leaders arrived in Lagos and formally surrendered. Biafra then ceased to exist.

Collapse of Biafra

Gowon headed the government until his overthrow in 1975. In 1979 the military government organized multiparty elections. Alhaji Shehu Shagari was elected president, and Nigeria adopted a new constitution. Shagari was elected president for a second term in August 1983 in a multi-party, civilian-run election. Maj. Gen. Mohammed Buhari led a military coup on December 31, 1983, however, and instituted a Supreme Military Council to rule the country. For current political history, see the annual issues of the *Britannica Book of the Year*.

(A.C.Bs./Ed.)

SENEGAL

Situated at the western extremity of Africa's tropical zone, the Republic of Senegal (République du Sénégal) has an area of 75,955 square miles (196,722 square kilometres). It is bounded to the north and to the northeast by the Sénégal River, which separates it from Mauritania; to the east by the Falémé, a tributary of the Sénégal River, which separates it from Mali; to the south by Guinea and Guinea-Bissau; and to the west by the Atlantic Ocean. The Gambia constitutes a finger of territory 20 miles wide and 200 miles long that thrusts from the coast eastward deep into Senegal.

Physical and human geography

Senegal—which gained its independence in 1960, first as part of the short-lived Mali Federation and then as a sovereign state in its own right—is among the principal producers of peanuts (groundnuts); its light soils and its climate are particularly well suited to this crop. While food crops such as millet are important, the entire economy of Senegal in fact depends literally on its peanut exports. The economy itself is operated in the spirit of "African socialism" of which the Senegalese government is one of the foremost champions; while it is a planned economy, the moderate controls to which it is subjected are applied in an indicative rather than an authoritarian manner. Private investors, whether foreign or Senegalese nationals, are encouraged to establish new enterprises; an investment code grants tax exemptions and permits the withdrawal of profits. Nationalization has been avoided except for the marketing of agricultural products, for which the state has created the Office de Commercialisation Agricole (Agricultural Marketing Board), which conducts marketing operations for the international business companies active in the country. The economic life of Senegal is characterized by its adherence to the franc currency zone, as a result of which the country benefits from French financial support. French is the official language.

THE LAND

Relief. Senegal is a flat country, lying in the depression known as the Senegal-Mauritanian Basin. Altitudes of more than about 330 feet are found only at Cap Vert and in the southeast of the country. The country as a whole falls into three structural divisions. These are: first, Cap Vert, which forms the western extremity and consists of a grouping of small plateaus made of hard rock of volcanic origin; second, the southeastern and the eastern parts of the country that consist of the fringes of ancient massifs (mountain masses) contiguous with those buttressing the massif of Fouta Djallon on the Guinea frontier, with the highest point reaching an altitude of 1,640 feet; third, an immense but shallow basin lying between Cap Vert to the west and the edges of the massif to the east.

Structural divisions

Washed by the Canary Current, the Atlantic coast of Senegal is sandy and surf beaten. Like the rest of the country, it is low except for the Presqu'île du Cap Vert, which represents the westernmost point of the African continent and which shelters Dakar, one of the finest ports in Africa. To the south of Cap Vert the surf on the coast is less heavy. To the south of the Saloum River mouth, the

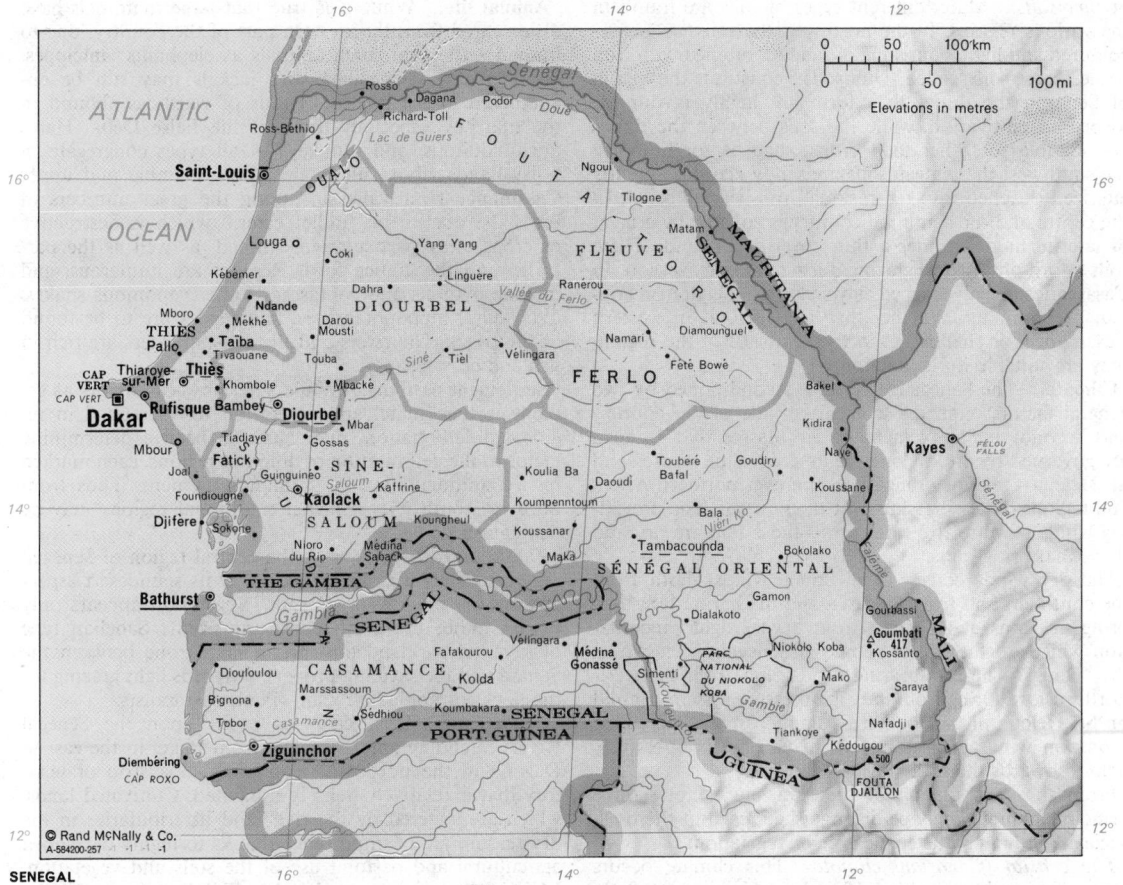

SENEGAL

coast consists of rias (drowned valleys) and is increasingly fringed with mangroves.

Drainage and soils. The country is drained by the Sénégal, Saloum, Gambia (Gambie), and Casamance rivers, all of which are subjected to a climatic regime characterized by a dry season and a rainy season. Of these rivers, the Sénégal, which rises in the Fouta Djallon highlands of Mali and Guinea, and was for long the main route providing access to the interior, is the most important. After traversing the old massifs the river rapidly drops downward before reaching Senegalese territory. At Dagana it forms the so-called False Delta, which supplies Lac de Guiers on the left bank. At the head of the delta is Richard-Toll (the Garden of Richard), named for a 19th-century French nursery gardener. The slope of the land

The False Delta

is so gentle on this stretch of the river that at low water, salty seawater flows about 125 miles upstream. The island on which the town of Saint-Louis stands, at the mouth of the river, is situated about 300 yards from the sea in the False Delta whose true mouth lies 10 miles to the south.

Despite its apparent uniformity, Senegal contains a great diversity of soils. These fall generally into two types—the valley soils and those found elsewhere.

The valley soils. The soils of the Sénégal and Saloum river valleys, in their middle courses, are alluvial and consist of sandy limes or clays. Near the river mouths the soils are salty and favourable for grazing. Similar conditions are associated with the Gambia and Casamance rivers, except that near their mouths the banks are muddy, while their upper courses have sandy clay soils.

Other soils. Many different types of soils are found in the various regions. In the northwest the soils are ochre-coloured and light, consisting of sands combined with iron oxide. These soils, called "Dior soils," constitute the wealth of Senegal; the dunes they form are highly favourable to peanut cultivation, while the soils between the dunes are suitable for other food crops, such as sorghum. In the southwest the plateau soils are sandy clays, frequently laterized (leached into red residual iron-bearing soils). In the centre and the south the country is covered by a layer of laterite hidden under a thin covering of sand. These soils afford only sparse grazing during the rainy season. In Casamance heavily leached clay soils with a high iron content predominate. Whether they are deep, as in western Casamance, or shallow, as in the southeast of the region, they are suitable for cultivation.

Climate. The Senegalese climate is conditioned by two general factors: first, the tropical latitude of the country and second, the movement of air masses that in turn are governed by anticyclones centred over the Azores and St. Helena—regions of high pressure over northern Africa and regions of low pressure near the Equator. The prevailing winds fall into two categories—those that are dry and those that bring rains.

The dry winds consist of the trade winds—both from the continent and from the sea—and the harmattan; they bring no rains at all, apart from a very light precipitation which, to the Wolof people of Senegal, is known as the "Heug." The rain-bearing winds blow from the west-northwest, resulting from the high-pressure system centred on St. Helena in the southern Atlantic. In summer these monsoon winds bring rains which become progressively lighter towards the north of the country.

From the combination of these various factors, three principal climates may be distinguished, each of them associated with a characteristic type of vegetation.

The coastal (Canarian) climate. This climate occurs along a coastal strip about 10 miles wide running from Saint-Louis to Dakar. Its winters are cool, with minimum temperatures reaching about 63° F (17° C) in January, and maximum temperatures in May not exceeding 81° F (27° C). The rains begin in June, reach their height in August, and cease in October. The average rainfall is about 20 inches (508 millimetres).

The Sahelian climate. This occurs in a zone bounded to the north by the Sénégal River and to the south by a line running from Thiès (a town on Cap Vert) to Kayes in the neighbouring country of Mali. The month of January is very cool, especially in the mornings before sunrise, when the temperature drops to about 57° F (14° C); maximum temperatures rise higher than 95° F (35° C). In May, minimum temperatures do not fall below about 72° F (22° C), while maximums often rise above 104° F (40° C). The dry season is quite distinct, and lasts from November to May. Certain places, such as Podor and Matam, are particularly noted for their dryness and for the heat of the sun. Between July and October the rainfall averages about 14 inches, moderating the temperature somewhat. Maximum temperatures at this season amount to about 95° F (35° C).

The Sudanic climate. This occurs in the remainder of Senegal. Regional nuances are in evidence. Thus, from north to south three climatic subdivisions may be recognized, each of which is characterized by the amount of average annual rainfall. First, in the Kaolack-Tambacounda subdivision, annual rainfall averages between 29 and 39 inches, occurring on about 60 days between June and October. Cultivation without irrigation is possible in this region. Second, in the Gambian region, the rainfall frequently amounts to 50 inches, resulting in the growth of a continuous belt of light forest and patches of herbaceous undergrowth. Third, in the Casamance region, rainfall everywhere exceeds 50 inches, falling on 90 days of the year. The forest is dense and green, and is continuous, without undergrowth. Oil palms, mangroves, and rice fields are characteristic of this climate zone. The Sudanic climate in general is very hot, humid, and uncomfortable. The town of Kaolack, for example, has a heavy climate that is rendered yet more oppressive by the salt wind.

Rainfall in the Sudanic area

Animal life. While it is true that large mammals have disappeared from the western part of the country, due to human settlement, such animals as elephants, antelopes, lions, panthers, cheetahs, and jackals may still be encountered in the interior. Herds of warthogs abound in the marshes, especially those of the False Delta. Hares are ubiquitous, and monkeys of all types congregate in noisy bands, above all in the upper Gambia and upper Casamance river valleys. Among the great numbers of birds the quelea, or "millet eater," which is destructive of crops, may particularly be noted, as well as the partridge and the guinea fowl. Reptiles are numerous, and include pythons and cobras and other venomous snakes. Crocodiles, hippopotamuses, and turtles are to be found in the rivers. The rivers and the coastal waters are rich in fish and crustaceans.

Settlement patterns. While such physical factors as geology, soil, climate, and vegetation have resulted in regional differentiation, man has also been a determining factor in the delimitation of different regions, each marked by a traditional type of human settlement. Thus from north to south five principal traditional regions may be distinguished.

The Ferlo region. This is the central region of Senegal; very extensive, it is distinguished by its semidesert aspect and by the poverty of its soils. Vegetation appears only in the south, the north consisting of the Sahelian type of savanna parkland (an intermediate zone between the Sahara and the savanna proper); it affords light grazing for the flocks of nomadic Fulani (Peul) pastoralists.

Fouta-Toro. This region is based upon the Sénégal River, extending approximately from Bakel in the east to Dagana in the north and consisting of a strip of territory that is relatively densely inhabited. Cultivated lands, which are watered by the river and its tributaries in the dry season, are of importance thanks to highly developed agricultural and pastoral use of the soils and vegetation. Most of the region is inhabited by Tukulor people. Fouta-Toro is bounded to the west by the False Delta, also known as the Oualo, which is peopled by the Wolof, who cultivate millet and carry on stock raising, employing Fulani shepherds.

The Dianbour, Cayor, Djolof, and Baol region. This is a diverse area situated between the Ferlo region and the Atlantic, and extending from the Oualo in the north to Cap Vert in the south. The soils are sandy, the winters cool, and peanuts are the primary crop. The population is as diverse as the region itself and includes Wolofs in the north, Serer in the Thiès region, and Lebu on Cap Vert.

The Sudan region. This vast region is bounded by Cap Vert to the northeast, the Ferlo to the north, and the lower Casamance Valley to the southwest. It is composed of the following subregions—the "Little Coast", the Sine-Saloum *région*, Rip, Yacine, Niani, Boundou, Fouladou and the valleys of the Gambia and upper Casamance rivers. In general, the region benefits from ample rainfall which becomes abundant towards the south. The clayey soil is suitable for agriculture, despite the lateritic crust which appears intermittently. The region, as a result, is relatively densely peopled. The estuaries are muddy and salty, with marshy saline depressions known as *tannes* occurring occasionally. The region as a whole is inhabited by a very diverse population composed of all the ethnic groups living in Senegal; the majority are, however, Malinke (Mandingo).

The lower Casamance region. This is a small but strongly characterized region. It is covered by dense vegetation of the Guinean type. Mangroves, oil palms, and raffia palms predominate. The rainy climate favours the cultivation of rice, which has long been a specialty in this part of the country.

Rural settlement. The great majority of the Senegalese population lives in the countryside. There are about 13,-000 villages, each with an average population of more than 200 persons. Usually each village has a shaded public gathering place, a mosque, and a water source, whether a well, a spring, or a small stream. The village is administered by a chief who is either traditionally nominated or appointed by the government. Religious life is directed either by a person literate in Arabic, called a marabout, or by a leading sorcerer. Various types of village may be distinguished, according to ethnic characteristics.

Tribal villages

Whether it is situated in the western Ferlo or the Cayor regions, the Wolof village is small, being inhabited by about a hundred farmers. The houses are built of locally obtained materials. Each village may easily be moved from place to place, as the topography provides no natural obstacles to this. Harvests are kept in straw granaries, located far from the compounds for fear of fires. In the eastern Saloum region, the Wolof village is surrounded by three concentric zones of vegetation. The first of these—the inner zone—consists of fields and vegetable gardens and is known as the Tol-keur (literally "kitchen garden"). The second circle consists of land that has been exhausted, except for peanut cultivation, and it is known as the Diatte. The third, the farthest from the village, is the Gor, in which cereal crops are cultivated.

The typical village of the Sudanic region of Casamance consists of a Malinke agglomeration; it is a heritage from the epoch when the Sudanic peoples conquered the region. Each village has between 200 and 300 inhabitants living in enclosed compounds and crowded together in geometrically aligned rectangular huts. Agriculture and stock raising are the principal activities. The chief of each village is generally a marabout, conservative in his ways.

The Serer village differs from the Wolof and Malinke village because of its family compounds, called M'Binds, being loosely dispersed; each M'Bind is autonomous. On the islands at the mouth of the Saloum River, the houses of the Serer Nyiominka people are solidly built and trim. The granary is located in the compound.

Dyolo (Diola) villages are substantial rural agglomerations with populations of up to 5,000 people or more. One of the characteristics of this type of village is that it is usually built on the edge of a plateau, or on ground which overlooks the rice fields with which Dyola life is associated. As in the Serer villages, the compounds are not grouped in any distinguishable organization hierarchy. The houses are the best built and the most permanent among the different types of village dwellings to be found. On occasion they constitute veritable fortifications, for example, in the Thionck-Essyl and Oussouye regions; the villages of the Essyl region are often equipped with a rainwater tank. The Dyola and Serer villages have no chiefs with authority or prestige comparable to those of the Wolof or Malinke villages.

Major towns

Urban settlement. The town of Saint-Louis was founded in 1633, and Dakar in 1857; other towns were, however, more recently founded. All the towns are of colonial origin. Dakar, as was formerly Saint-Louis, is the political and administrative capital. The other towns usually owe their foundation to the peanut trade, for which they were collection points which later developed into urban centres. These towns were often stops along the railroad lines, as

at Thiès, Tivaouane, Mékhé, and Louga (between Dakar and Saint-Louis), or Khombole, Bambey, Diourbel, Gossas, Kaffrine, and Koungheul (between Thiès and Kayes, Mali). Certain ports also became towns: among these are Kaolack, Foundiougne, and Fatick (on the Sine-Saloum rivers), and Ziguinchor, Sédhiou, and Kolda (on the Casamance River). With the exception of Dakar, Saint-Louis, Rufisque, Thiès, and Kaolack, these towns have not as yet emerged, as it were, from their rural cocoons. Furthermore, all of the towns—including Saint-Louis, Rufisque, and Gorée, all of which had great importance in the past—are today dependent upon Dakar, which has become the focus of attraction for the whole of Senegal.

Apart from the division of the countryside into traditional regions, one may observe that the best lands in Senegal are concentrated in the west and in the river valleys. The remainder of the land becomes increasingly poor and less and less settled as one continues toward the north or toward the east.

THE PEOPLE

The scientific study of languages in Senegal has not progressed far enough for even a rough type of classification to be attempted. Specialists nevertheless recognize certain imprecise groupings. These are: (a) the Atlantic (West Atlantic) group, including Wolof, Lebu, Serer, Tenda, and Diola; (b) Fulfulde, the Fulani (Peul) language, which also shares some of the characteristics of the Atlantic group; Fulfulde possesses numerous linguistic particularities, and has a complex grammar; and (c) the Mande group, including Bambara, Diula, Malinke, and Soninke (Sarakole). There are seven major ethnic and religious groups, and a number of other less significant groups.

The major groups are located in the Sahel and savanna regions which formerly supported the ancient empires of the western Sudan, such as Ghana, Mali, and Songhai. Until recently the societies composing this grouping were strictly hierarchical in organization, consisting of the princely caste, the nobility, the free men, the lower castes, and finally the slaves. The grouping consists of the following peoples:

The Wolof. The Wolof represent about one third of the total population. Their language is the most widely used in the republic. The Wolof predominate in the sandy western region. In the Cayor district they are initiates of the Tijānī Muslim brotherhood; the other brotherhood, that of the Murīdīs, is very influential, and its expansion towards the southern part of the country is concurrent with that of peanut cultivation. Members of the Murīdīs brotherhood, strong adherents of Islām, are primarily agriculturalists.

The Serer. The Serer are densely settled in the western part of the southern Ferlo region. They are experienced farmers, practicing both cultivation and cattle raising. Originally animist by religion, they are now becoming increasingly either Muslim or Catholic.

The Fulani. Also known as the Peuls, Foulah, Fulbe, and Fellata, this group is distributed throughout Senegal; the Fulani are particularly found in the Ferlo, the Upper Casamance, and Oualo regions, where their settlements are substantial. Characteristically nomadic pastoralists, many of them have today become settled agriculturalists, above all in the Fouta-Toro region and on the Senegal-Guinea border. They are Muslim.

The Tukulor (or Toucouleur) are often hard to distinguish from either the Wolof or the Fulani, with both of whom they have often intermarried. The name Tukulor is a distortion of the name of the ancient realm of Tekrur. The Tukulor live primarily in the middle course of the Sénégal River Valley, in the Senegalese part of the Fouta region, and between Bakel and Dagana. They are also found in dispersed groups living on the Gambia and Saloum rivers. They were the first Senegalese people to become Muslim, having accepted Islām probably in the 11th century; many of them are literate in Arabic. Primarily farmers, they are increasingly migrating to the towns, particularly to Dakar and Saint-Louis.

The Dyola. The Dyola occupy the Lower Casamance Valley and the southwest of the Gambia Valley. They are skilled farmers, specializing in rice growing, but turning

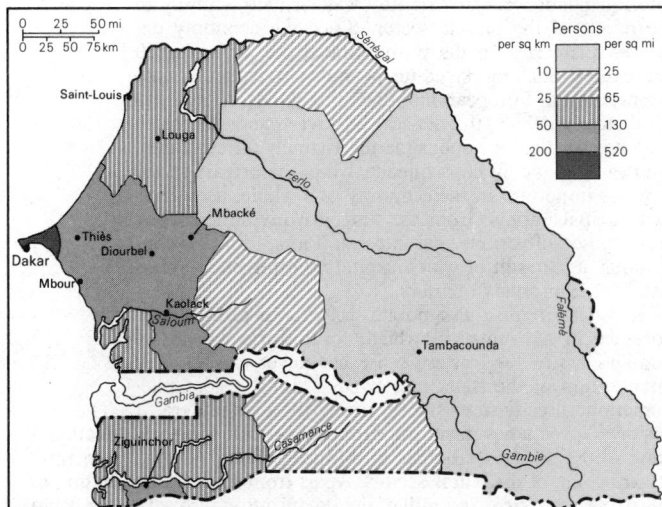

Population density of Senegal.

more and more to the cultivation of peanuts and millet as the distance from the sea increases. In the Fogni district they are Muslim, but the majority remain animist. A few have accepted Christianity.

The Malinke. The Malinke (or Mandingo) came originally from the Niger River Valley, and have spread out into various regions of Senegal, especially into the Gambia, Upper Casamance, and Saloum river valleys. Farmers and energetic traders, they are Muslim.

The Sarakole, or Soninke. This is a minority group, of Berber descent. They represent an extension into Senegal of the Malinke families of Mali. They are in the process of abandoning an unfruitful agricultural terrain in order to migrate towards the towns where they often become small traders. They are Muslim.

The numerically less significant Senegalese comprise such peoples as the Maures, who live especially in the north of the country where they are stock raisers or traders; the Lebu of Cap Vert, who are fishermen and often wealthy landowners; and the Bassari, an ancient people who are found in the rocky highlands of Fouta Djallon.

THE ECONOMY

Resources. The economy is essentially agricultural and, as mentioned, is primarily based upon the peanut crop. The known mineral resources are only of relative importance and consist primarily of phosphates of lime, located at Taïba near Tivaouane, about 60 miles north of Dakar, and aluminum phosphates at Palo Dial, near Thiès. Significant mineral reserves include petroleum deposits discovered off the Casamance coast and high-grade iron-ore reserves located near Falémé. Salt from the saltworks of Kaolack have a considerable potential production. Production of gum arabic, which is obtained from acacia trees, is only of secondary significance; and other forest products also have limited commercial value. The herbaceous vegetation nevertheless permits a relatively important amount of stock raising. By improving the grazing land available, Senegal has the potential to increase the numbers of its cattle herds to a considerable extent.

The waters off Senegal, particularly those at some distance from the shore, are rich in economically significant schools of fish, although the coastal waters are also known for their large variety of fish; in this respect Senegal is better endowed than most other tropical countries on the Atlantic seaboard.

Agriculture and fishing. Agriculture occupies at least three-quarters of the economically active population and provides the basis for industry as well. Although a certain balance between the raising of livestock and peanut cultivation is maintained, it is the peanut production which earns the foreign exchange that the country needs.

Impor-
tance of
the peanut
crop

The main economic problem affecting national agriculture is the country's excessive dependence upon the peanut crop, and the saying "When peanuts do well we all do well" is still valid. In 1970, when for various reasons the production of peanuts dropped to 600,000 tons, Senegal found itself on the verge of economic catastrophe. Each year the sale of the peanut crop results in much economic activity throughout Senegal; the resulting wealth has favoured the development of the smaller towns. The traffic in peanuts has also resulted in the establishment of the river ports of Kaolack, Foundiougne, Fatick, Sédhiou, and Kolda. Much of the activity at Dakar itself is due to the peanut trade.

Apart from peanuts, which are an export crop, a number of food crops are also grown. Extensive acreage is devoted to sorghum and pennisetum (a genus of Old World grasses). Rice is cultivated both in naturally wet areas and by irrigation. Its large-scale cultivation is restricted to the Lower Casamance Valley and the Lower Sénégal River Valley below Richard-Toll. In addition corn (maize), cassava (manioc), beans, and sweet potatoes are grown in significant quantities.

Livestock. The climate and the savanna type of vegetation encourage the raising of livestock, including cattle, goats, sheep, horses, donkeys, camels, and pigs, which is carried on in almost all regions, but is especially characteristic of the north. Stock raising is not a major source

of income for the farmer; in addition to the difficulty of improving livestock strains, the fact that stock raising is often conducted for reasons of prestige alone provides an economic drawback.

Fishing. While many fish are obtained from the rivers, the greater part of the catch is obtained from the sea. A fleet of trawlers and tuna-fishing boats are in service.

Industry. Industrial production in Senegal is more developed than in most western African countries. Both processing and handicraft industries are established. Most of the processing industry is located in the Cap Vert *région*, where there are peanut-oil processing plants. Plants are also in operation in Dakar, Rufisque, Kaolack, Diourbel, and Ziguinchor. In addition, there are fish canneries, a shoe factory, and a cement manufacturing plant. Both the shoe factory and the cement plant are located at Rufisque. Other industrial establishments, all of which are located in Dakar, include flour mills, a textile plant, a sugar refinery, a tobacco factory, and a brewery, in addition to a naval shipyard, chemical plants, and an automobile assembly plant.

A number of craftsmen are engaged in traditional handicrafts; the more skilled among them are established at Dakar and Saint-Louis.

Mineral production. Of secondary significance in the national economy, mineral production, as already mentioned, consists of lime phosphates and aluminum phosphates.

Energy. Before the 1980s all energy produced in Senegal was of thermal origin. The main producing plants are located at Dakar and nearby Rufisque; and those at Saint-Louis and Kaolack are of secondary importance. Cheaper hydroelectric energy began to be produced with the construction of the three-nation hydroelectric projects on the Sénégal River, with dams at Diama in Senegal and Manatali in Mali.

Finance and trade. In finance, Senegal has benefitted from the fact that in colonial times it was the principal territory of the administrative grouping known as French West Africa. Goods entering the country from the franc zone are liable to a simple fiscal tax; those from the Common Market countries enjoy a preferential tariff. There are a considerable number of banks offering financial services. Currency is issued by the Banque Centrale des États de l'Afrique de l'Ouest, which is the agency of the West African Monetary Union to which Senegal belongs. Other financial institutions include the Société Immobilière du Cap Vert (a building society); the Banque Nationale de Développement du Sénégal; the Union Sénégalaise de Banque; and three private banks.

Role of
Senegal
as a West
African
financial
centre

The value of imports is usually greater than the value of exports. The principal imports are petroleum products, rice, sugar, machinery, and vehicles. The principal exports are peanuts and peanut products, phosphates, fresh fish, and canned fish.

Administration of the economy. *The private sector.* Before independence, the economy was virtually entirely in the hands of the private sector. Since the economy depended primarily on the peanut trade, the large French companies which marketed the peanuts also controlled the importation of European manufactured goods. After independence, however, the Senegalese government created a state agency that is responsible for virtually all aspects of the peanut trade; in consequence, while the private sector remains important in the economy as a whole, it receives its principal impulse from the state. An investment code is composed of various guarantees and long-term tax concessions, as a result of which capital investment has been attracted from many quarters.

The public sector. The public sector is of primary importance in a country in which, for historic reasons, a middle class in the western sense has never existed. The intervention of the state, moreover, is not a recent phenomenon; already in existence during the colonial era, it has been given a new form since independence by the creation of the Société Nationale du Monde Rural (National Organization of the Rural Sector). Apart from buying and selling peanuts, rice, and millet, the organization also sells fertilizer, seed, tools, and equipment, and is thus the pri-

The
National
Organi-
zation of
the Rural
Sector

mary instrument used by the state in giving form to its policy of "African socialism."

Taxation. As already mentioned, the government of Senegal encourages investment by granting tax benefits. Most governmental revenue is obtained from indirect taxes, which take the form of local taxes on alcoholic beverages, gasoline, tobacco, firearms, automobiles, and commerce. Direct taxation consists of land taxes, professional licenses, and personal taxes, such as taxes on profits, and income taxes.

Economic policies. Economic life is characterized by two factors. The first is the division of the country into two regions—the western region which is wealthy and dynamic, and the remainder, and larger part, of the country which remains poor and economically stagnant, depending upon a subsistence economy. The second factor is the existence of a single crop economy, which leads to partial unemployment, an insufficient income, and a dependence on an unpredictable climate and the international market.

Transportation. *Road transport.* The development of a transport network has taken place primarily in the western part of the country, within the area bounded by Saint-Louis, Kaolack, and Dakar. Despite the fact that the remainder of the country is insufficiently developed, Senegal's transport system nevertheless compares favourably to that of many other West African countries.

Rail transport. The rail system includes a line from Saint-Louis to Dakar, with a branch line running from Louga inland to Linguère, and the line from Dakar to the Niger River, at Koulikoro, with two branch lines running from Diourbel to Touba and from Guinguinéo to Kaolack. The two main lines meet at the junction of Thiès, which is also the site of railroad repair workshops. The railroad system is suffering from the competition offered by road transport.

Ports. Senegal's three ports are Kaolack, Ziguinchor, and Dakar. Only Dakar is an international port, the other ports handling only local traffic. In addition to its facilities as a commercial port, Dakar also has a fishing harbor.

Air transport. The international airport of Dakar-Yoff at Dakar is served by a number of airlines. Traffic has diminished slightly in recent years. Domestic services are provided by Air Afrique. There are local airports at Thiès, Saint-Louis, Ziguinchor, Kaolack, Rosso, Podor, Matam, Tambacounda, Kédougou, Sementi, and Kolda.

River transport. Since the end of the 19th century the rivers, of which the Sénégal River has always been the most important, have lost much of their importance. The Sénégal is navigable all year round from Saint-Louis to Podor by boats drawing about three feet of water. Other reaches are only navigable in the rainy season; Kayes in Mali, for example, can be reached only at that time. Despite the competition of the railroad, fleets of canoes still provide river transport. Activity on the Saloum River is due to the presence of the peanut port of Kaolack, while traffic on the Casamance is due to the port of Ziguinchor.

ADMINISTRATIVE AND SOCIAL CONDITIONS

The first constitution of Senegal was promulgated in 1963 and has often been revised. It proclaims its attachment to fundamental human rights, respect for political, trade union, and religious freedoms, and also for individual and collective property rights. The Senegalese state is a social, democratic, and lay (nonecclesiastical) state, with French as its official language.

Government. *The central government.* The most important feature of the amended constitution of 1983, which was modelled after the 1963 constitution, was the reestablishment of a strongly centralized presidential regime. The amended constitution abolished the office of prime minister and provided for the president of the republic to rule directly. The president is elected for five years, and cannot serve more than two terms in office. Ministers are appointed by the president, who no longer has the power to dissolve the national assembly. The assembly, likewise, has lost its power to introduce a motion of censure of the president. Judicial, executive, and legislative powers are separated.

Regional government. Senegal is divided into eight ré-

The office of the president

gions, 28 *départements* (provinces), and 99 *arrondissements* (districts). The *régions* and their capitals are the following: Cap Vert (Dakar), Thiès (Thiès), Diourbel (Diourbel), Fleuve (Saint-Louis), Sine-Saloum (Kaolack), Casamance (Ziguinchor), Louga (Louga), and Sénégal Oriental (Tambacounda). Each *région* is administered by a governor whose role is coordinative; he is assisted by two deputy governors, one dealing with administration, and the other with development. A regional assembly composed of general councillors deals with local taxation. In each *département* the prefect represents the republic, as well as the ministers; he sees to the implementation of laws, and supervises the local administrative units. In the *arrondissement* he is assisted by a local official (*chef d'arrondissement*). Several towns operate autonomously with elected municipal councils.

The political process. National Assembly and municipal council elections are held every five years, as also are presidential elections.

Political parties. Due to the fact that Senegalese played a pioneering role in the development of a modern political system in the territories of French West Africa, the political-party system is solidly entrenched, and the concept of a single-party system is generally held to be repugnant. A plethora of parties is not, however, considered desirable.

The participation of the citizen. At the beginning, political life was of concern only to a very limited élite consisting of the intellectuals, the traditional chiefs, and above all the inhabitants of four communes—Saint-Louis, Dakar, Rufisque, and Gorée—who had been French citizens since 1916. After World War II universal suffrage was introduced by stages, with the electorate increasing from 192,000 voters in 1946 to 890,000 in 1958. The number of voters has since grown larger. Senegalese citizens today participate in the elections of the president, of the deputies to the national assembly, of regional councillors, and of municipal councillors.

The electorate

De facto political developments. In addition to participation in political party and trade union activities, other institutions also permit participation in the political process. These include societies for mutual assistance, which are organized both on a regional and on a village basis; youth associations; and religious groupings, which are most influential. The present disinclination of farmers to cooperate economically constitutes, in effect, a method of exerting political pressure on the government.

Justice. Justice is administered in the *départements* by justices of the peace and in the regions by courts of first instance. Criminal cases are judged by assize courts held at Saint-Louis, Kaolack, Ziguinchor, and Dakar. Dakar is the seat of the Court of Appeal.

Education. In addition to continuing the educational expansion begun during the colonial period, Senegal has made particular efforts to increase school enrollment in rural areas. Among the secondary schools, Lycée Faidherbe at Saint-Louis and the Lycée Van Vollenhoven at Dakar are the most renowned and the oldest. Technical education is expanding; technical training is provided by a number of institutions, including l'École Nationale des Travaux Publics and the Lycée Technique Maurice Delafosse in Dakar, the Lycée Technique Andre Peytavin in Saint-Louis, and the Centre d'Enseignement de Pêche at Thiaroye-sur-Mer.

University education was begun in Dakar in 1957. Following disturbances in 1968, Senegal concluded an agreement with France on higher education by the terms of which the University of Dakar became oriented to its African context. The Africanization of courses has meant that university degrees, with the exception of those gained in medicine, are no longer equivalent to those obtained in France.

The Africanization of university courses

Health and welfare. Although still insufficient, Senegal nevertheless has a considerable range of medical facilities. They include hospitals, clinics, maternity homes, and various services specializing in various diseases, such as tuberculosis, poliomyelitis, syphilis, and leprosy. The Senegalese Red Cross is also active, while environmental studies are conducted by the French Office de la Recherche Scientifique et Technique Outre-Mer in cooperation with the World Health Organization.

Housing. In rural areas dwellings, which are usually well constructed, are roofed with straw, while walls are either made of earth or straw. In more prosperous villages, roofs are sometimes of corrugated iron, and walls are sometimes of cement brick. Houses in the towns are of cement with roofs either of tile or of corrugated iron; many families are usually crowded together. The drift from the countryside and the expansion of town populations has frequently resulted in the proliferation of shanty towns.

The standard of living in the countryside is low. Manufactured products are more expensive than in the city, which despite often startling social inequalities, may appear to be a kind of paradise in comparison with living conditions in the countryside.

Health conditions. Thanks to the efforts of doctors during the colonial era, Senegal is rid of the plagues which raged in the early 20th century. If yellow fever, tuberculosis, and similar diseases are still to be encountered they at least no longer assume epidemic proportions. In rural areas, however, sanitary conditions leave much to be desired, due to the lack of training and facilities. It must be admitted, however, that this situation is due, above all, to the fact that facilities are primarily concentrated in Dakar, which accounts for much of the total budgetary expenditure for health. The death rate for children between the ages of one and four is five times higher in rural Senegal than it is in Dakar.

Health facilities in Dakar

Social and economic divisions. As is emphasized by the foregoing, the most marked socioeconomic cleavage in Senegal today is between those living in towns and those living in the country. This division results from the modernizing process which has taken hold in the western fringes of the country.

Country life, in its traditional communal village form, is still followed by four-fifths of Senegalese. The family is extended and lives, under the authority of its most elderly member, in a compound consisting of a group of thatched dwellings, engaging in agriculture for a livelihood. The influence of the marabouts—interpreters of the Qur'ān—remains uncontested. Liquid funds are virtually nonexistent, a subsistence economy being followed.

The way of life of the city dwellers stands in contrast to this, since it typifies the modernizing process at work in Senegal. To speak of city life, moreover, is virtually tantamount to speaking of Dakar, since three-quarters of town dwellers live in this one city. The primary factor distinguishing the rural farmer from the town dweller is monetary income, since the inhabitants of the towns earn from 10 to 12 times more than those living elsewhere. Better lodging, better food, better education, and better health conditions are available in the towns. Socially the city dweller, particularly in Dakar, follows a way of life which represents a break with the traditional values of communal village life in its pure form. As worker, clerk, or trader, the town dweller follows a timetable that is governed by the clock instead of by the seasonal rhythms of the countryside. In the towns Tukulor, Wolof, Fulani, Serer, and Dyola tend to define themselves as Senegalese rather than in terms of their community of origin and feel themselves to be a part of the nascent Senegalese nation.

Senegal today, in sum, presents two distinct aspects to the contemporary observer. On the one hand stands Dakar, the capital, with its inhabitants in communication with international society and a universal civilization; on the other stands the remainder of the country, following a provincial pattern of life which has lost its primary impulse and which is growing increasingly stagnant.

CULTURAL LIFE

Both the rhythm of life in Senegal and the Senegalese mentality have evolved over a long period of time in a setting which was unacquainted with technology in the Western sense of the word. The attitudes of Senegalese in their relations with nature are consequently different from those of Europeans in general. Fear, magic, and collectivism are dominant in traditional Senegalese life.

Writing is absent, or constitutes at best no more than the prerogative of the few. The cultural heritage is preserved in oral tradition of which the guardians have been the most experienced, that is to say the oldest men. Society thus forms a hierarchy, at the summit of which stand the oldest people.

The social hierarchy

The traditional Senegalese cultural heritage remains much alive. Rites and initiations are actively practiced in rural areas—for example, by the Bassari of Kédougou. Among Muslims, youths must be circumcised before being accorded the responsibilities of adulthood.

Art, sculpture, music, and dance remain typically Senegalese in expression. Sculpture is characterized by abstraction and by the ideogram; a sculptured gazelle, for example, may be represented solely by its horns and its neck, while an elephant may be represented only by the immense fan formed by its ears and its trunk. The Senegalese artist thus neglects the material aspect in order to give free rein to ideas and to feelings. Similarly, in the absence of written music, the imagination of the musician is released. Without falling into the realm of fantasy, the *griot* (a West African kind of troubadour and historian) recites poems, or tells of warrior deeds, drawing upon his own sources of inspiration. Both dance and music owe much to improvisation, which, combined with rhythm, produces an intense effect upon the entire community.

Senegalese literature is incarnated by former president Léopold Sédar Senghor. The quality and the importance of his work resulted in his election, in France in 1970, to the Académie des Sciences Morales et Politiques. He is the poet associated with *négritude,* a concept that he has defined as consisting on the one hand of an attitude of defense of the traditional values of black Africa, and on the other of tension toward the modernization of these same values. From this concept Senghor has drawn his political philosophy concerning not only Senegal but the whole of black Africa. Besides Senghor one may also cite the names of Birago Diop, who has revived local legends, as well as of such writers as Ousmane Socé, David Diop, Alioune Diop, Cheikh Anta Diop, Cheikh Amidou Kâne, Abdoulaye Sadji, Abdoulaye Ly, Sembène Ousmane, and Bakary Traoré, all of whom are known for works which combine intelligence with the savour of Senegalese life.

Since the World Festival of Negro Arts was organized at Dakar in 1966, a number of existing institutions have been reoriented toward African traditions, while new institutions have also been created. Among the new institutions are the Musée Dynamique, the Théâtre Daniel Sorano, and the Tapestry Factory of Thiès. The existing institutions which have undergone some transformations are the Institut Fondamental d'Afrique Noire, the Maisons de la Jeunesse et de la Culture, and the craft village of Soumbedioune in Dakar, which has become a centre for Senegalese sculpture and goldsmithing. For statistical data, see the "Britannica World Data" section in the current *Britannica Book of the Year.* (Ca.C./Ed.)

History

Man has occupied Senegal since very ancient times. Paleolithic axes, Neolithic two-headed axes, and arrows have been found near Dakar, and stone erections as well as copper and iron objects in the Sine-Saloum Region.

The first peoples of whom there is historical mention are the Tukulor, who occupied the Senegal Valley in the 11th century. The name Senegal appears to be derived from that of the Zenaga Berbers of Mauritania. The Sarakolé Empire of Ghana lay to the east, between the Sénégal and the Niger rivers. Toward 1040 the Zenaga established, perhaps on an island of the river, the Muslim monastery in which the Murabti sect was to have its origin. This sect converted the Tukulor, destroyed Ghana, and conquered Morocco. Pagan invasions began in the 13th century. About 1400 some Fulani founded a dynasty on the Middle Senegal, in the region thereafter known as Fouta-Toro. In the 18th century the Muslim Tukulor revolted and set up a feudal theocratic republic.

The Tukulor

On the coast and in Cayor, the Wolof founded an independent kingdom; this was later divided into four states: Dyolof, Walo, Cayor, and Baol, which were often at war with each other and with their neighbours. As well as the warrior aristocracy, the Muslim marabouts also had some influence there. The Serers in the Sine and in the Saloum were organized into states by Malinke chiefs, the Guellawar. The other peoples did not form any large states.

Portuguese navigators reached Cape Verde about 1444. They set up factories at the mouth of the Sénégal, at Gorée (opposite the modern Dakar), at Rufisque (Rio Fresco), at Joal, at Portudal, in the Saloum, and in Casamance (Casa Mansa).

In 1638 a French factory was set up at the mouth of the Sénégal and was rebuilt, in 1659, on N'Dar, an island in the river, which was to become Saint-Louis-du-Sénégal. The Dutch meanwhile had set themselves up on the island of Gorée, which the French took over in 1677, after which the French agent J.B. Ducasse managed factories on the coast and did much to promote trade. Dealers from Saint-Louis began business on the lower reaches of the river, where they bought gums and slaves. André Brüe spent 25 years trying to penetrate the hinterland by journeys up the Sénégal. In 1700 he built a post, Saint-Joseph-de-Galam, near the Falémé confluence and began to buy gold from the Bambouk. After his death this fort was destroyed by the tribes. The French botanist Michel Adanson (1727–1806) spent five years exploring the interior before publishing his *Histoire naturelle du Sénégal* (1757).

The English occupied the factories during the Seven Years' War, and gave only Gorée back in the Peace of 1763. The Duc de Lauzun Chevalier de Boufflers (1738–1815) François Blanchot de Verly, who became governor in 1787, endured a blockade and great privations but was able to repel several English assaults. He died in 1807; Saint-Louis surrendered two years later.

In 1816 Saint-Louis and Gorée were returned to France. In the same year, on an expedition to Senegal, "La Méduse" was shipwrecked; this incident gave rise to Géricault's famous painting "Raft of the Medusa." Julien Schmaltz, as governor, founded a station upriver at Bakel. Schmaltz also tried to grow cotton in the neighbourhood of Saint-Louis, and his successor Baron Roger continued this experiment, but it came to nothing; after which trade was confined to gum. In 1818 Gaspard-Théodore Mollien crossed the Ferlo and reached the Fouta Djallon, discovering the sources of the Sénégal and Gambia rivers. Between 1835 and 1837 two stations, Carabane and Sédhiou, were acquired in Casamance.

The precarious position of the French, local wars, and the tribute paid to the local kinglets all combined to reduce trade to very little. Under the Second Republic the slaves were emancipated and given French citizenship. In 1854, at the request of the businessmen of Saint-Louis, Comdt. Louis-Léon-César Faidherbe was appointed governor. To put an end to insecurity, Faidherbe pacified the Walo east of Saint-Louis and then drove back the Moors on the right bank of the river. But the Tukulor marabout al-Ḥājj 'Umar was threatening the river. Faidherbe established a station at Médina (near Kayes) and left there a small garrison under Paul Holle, a mulatto from Saint-Louis. In 1857 Holle strenuously resisted attacks of the marabout's

thousands until the rising of the high water enabled Faidherbe to reach him with reinforcements. In 1857 Captain Protet, of the French Navy, founded a station at Dakar. Faidherbe occupied the Cayor, thus uniting parts of the colony. In 1865 he went back to France, having organized Senegal and laid the foundations of native policy based on respect for existing usages.

His successor, Col. J.M.E. Pinet-Laprade, consolidated his work, occupying the Petite Côte and the Saloum and developing the town of Dakar. Peanuts had been introduced into the Cayor and were being exported from Rufisque. The Gambian fort of Albreda had been ceded to Great Britain in 1857. In 1886 the last Wolof king, the damel of Cayor, Lat Dior, had been killed during an insurrection, and Col. J.S. Gallieni was destroying the power of the marabout Mamadou Lamine in the east. Faidherbe's creation of the Tirailleurs Sénégalais (Senegalese Riflemen) marks the beginning of France's use of Senegal as a base for expansion into the Sudan and toward the Rivières du Sud. Dahomey was conquered (1892–94) by Col. (later Gen.) Alfred-Amédée Dodds, another mulatto soldier from Saint-Louis, who had subdued the Dyolof and the territory of the Tukulor. The pacification of the traditionally anarchic Lower Casamance was not achieved until 1903. The Gouvernement Général de l'Afrique Occidentale, established by decrees of 1895 and 1904, was at first the responsibility of the governor of Senegal, resident at Saint-Louis, but was later raised to the status of a separate authority based on Dakar. The latter town grew rapidly to become the main port for Senegal and for the French Sudan.

In World War I the deputy for Senegal, Blaise Diagne, helped to enlist large numbers of riflemen. In World War II the governor general, Pierre François Boisson, remaining loyal to the Vichy government, held Dakar against a British attack in 1940; but he transferred his allegiance to the Allied side in November 1942. In 1946 all Senegalese became French citizens, whereas previously this right had been restricted to natives of the four ancient *communes,* Saint-Louis, Gorée, Dakar, and Rufisque; and the colony became an overseas territory of France. The two Senegalese deputies, Lamine Gueye and Léopold Sédar Senghor, played a prominent role in the drawing up of the French constitution of 1958. In 1958 Senegal became an autonomous republic within the French Community; in September 1960, after a short period of federation with the Sudanese Republic in the Mali Federation, Senegal was recognized as an independent state, remaining within the French Community. Senghor was elected president of the Republic. In December 1962 a tentative coup d'etat by the president of the Council of Ministers, Mamadou Dia, failed, and Senghor took over the office.

On January 1, 1981, Abdou Diouf was sworn in as president, becoming the constitutional successor to Senghor. Later that year when rebels in The Gambia (which forms an enclave in Senegal's territory) attempted to overthrow the government of Sir Dawda Jawara, Diouf sent in troops to restore order. Soon afterward, Diouf and Jawara agreed that their countries should be joined in a confederation to be known as Senegambia. For current political history, see the annual issues of the *Britannica Book of the Year.*
(H.J.D./Ed.)

Independence

SIERRA LEONE

Sierra Leone is a sovereign republic in West Africa, bordered on the north and east by Guinea, on the south by Liberia, and on the west by the Atlantic Ocean. One of the smaller African countries, it has an area of 27,699 square miles (71,740 square kilometres), and it is larger than Togo and The Gambia but smaller than Benin. Its population is large in relation to the nation's size by African standards. The national capital of Freetown commands the third largest harbour in the world after Rio de Janeiro and Sydney.

Physical and human geography

The country owes its name to the Portuguese explorer Pedro de Sintra, the first European to sight and map Freetown Harbour, in the 15th century. The original Portuguese name of Serra Lyoa (Lion Mountains) referred to the range of hills that surrounds the harbour.

Although most of the nation's population is engaged in subsistence agriculture, Sierra Leone is also a mining centre. Its land yields important quantities of diamonds, iron ore, bauxite, and other minerals. Increasing urbanization has resulted in the gradual depopulation of the rural areas and the growth of a jobless population in the cities.

THE LAND

Relief. The country can be divided into four distinct physical regions. The coastal swamp region extends along the Atlantic for about 200 miles (320 kilometres). It is a flat, low-lying, and frequently flooded plain that is between 20 and 40 miles wide and is composed mainly of sands and clays. Its numerous creeks and estuaries contain mangrove swamps. Parallel ridges, often separated by silting lagoons, are common and sometimes form the actual coast. The Sierra Leone Peninsula, which is the site of Freetown, is a region of thickly wooded mountains that run parallel to the sea for about 25 miles. The Peninsula Mountains rise from the coastal swamps and reach 2,913 feet (888 metres) at Picket Hill.

Inland from the coastal plain is the interior plains region. In the north it comprises of featureless grasslands (savanna) that are known as "Bolilands" (*Boli* being a Temne word for those lands which are flooded in the rainy season and dry and hard in the dry season, and on which only grass can grow). In the south the plains comprise rolling wooded country where isolated hills rise abruptly to more than 700 feet. The interior contains a variety of landforms ranging from savanna-covered plateau surfaces to rocky scarp and hill country. The region is composed mainly of granite with a thick lateritic (iron-bearing) crust; to the west it is bounded by a narrow outcrop of mineral-bearing metamorphic rocks known as the Kambui Schists. Rising above the plateau are a number of mountain masses; in the northeast the Loma Mountains are crowned by Bintimani Peak at 6,390 feet, and the Tingi Hills rise to 6,079 feet in Sankanbiriwa.

Drainage and soils. The country's drainage pattern is dense. Numerous rivers rise in the well-watered Fouta Djallon highlands of Guinea and flow in a general northeast to southwest direction across Sierra Leone to empty into the Atlantic Ocean. Their middle courses are interrupted by rapids that restrict navigability to their lower reaches. River levels show considerable seasonal fluctuations. During the dry season, levels generally decrease, and the rivers of the plateau region become mere shallow channels. In the rainy season, however, levels increase and the rivers' lower reaches are usually flooded.

The major rivers

The drainage system has nine major rivers and a series of minor coastal creeks and tidal streams. From north to south, the principal rivers are the Great Scarcies, Little Scarcies, Rokel (known in its lower course as the Sierra Leone River), Gbangbaia, Jong, Sewa, Wanje, Moa, and Mano. The Mano forms the country's frontier with

Liberia. The river basins are small compared to the major basins of Africa; the largest is the Sewa River Basin, of over 5,000 square miles.

In most areas, the dominant soils are of the weathered and leached ferrallitic (iron-bearing) type. Red to yellowish-brown in colour, they contain much oxide of iron and aluminum, and are acid. Kaolin (china) clays are important, but under cultivation a light, readily workable, free-draining soil is available, whose productivity depends largely on the nutrients provided from the vegetation previously cleared and burned. In the coastal plains ferrallitic soils, developed on sandy deposits, are poor, but slightly better results are obtained where the soils derive from basic igneous rocks. At the foot of the main escarpment, on the Sula mountain plateau, and elsewhere an iron-rich crust forms a surface that is intractable for agricultural production. In the northeast, ferrallitic soils have been modified to produce a "grit" soil with a relatively high clay and silt content. Swamp soils occur over large areas. In coastal and estuarine areas where mangrove is the natural vegetation, productive soils can be acquired by clearance, but careful water control is sometimes needed to prevent toxicity.

Climate. The climate is tropical and is characterized by the alternation of the wet and dry seasons. Conditions are generally hot. Mean monthly temperatures range from 77° F (25° C) to 83° F (28° C) in low-lying coastal areas; inland the range may be from 73° F (23° C) to 82° F (28° C). In the northeast, where extremes of temperature are greater, mean daily minimums fall to 56° F (13° C) in January, and mean daily maximums rise to 90° F (35° C) in March. During the rainy season, from May to October, the dominant humid air masses blow from the Atlantic. The sky is cloudy, the winds are southwesterly, sunshine is minimal, and rainfall is almost a daily occurrence, especially during July and August. The rainy season usually begins with a series of violent line squalls marked by thunder and lightning. Precipitation is greater on the coast than inland; over 150 inches (3,810 millimetres) of rain falls annually on the Peninsula Mountains, while the northeast receives about 80 inches a year.

The dry season, from November to April, is characterized by the dry harmattan wind that blows from the Sahara. Conditions are hazy and dusty, with prevailing northeast winds of low relative humidity. The sky is often clear and blue, and rainless weather is common.

The rainy season tends to be cooler than the dry season by about 10° F (6° C). The relative humidity during the rains may be as high as 90 percent for considerable periods, particularly during the wettest months, from July to September.

Plant and animal life. The distribution of plants and animals has been influenced by such factors as relief and soil types and, perhaps more importantly, by farming methods. Remnants of the extensive original forest cover remain in the Gola Forest reserve in the southeastern hill country near the Liberian border. Secondary forest is now dominant, and valuable timber species, such as *Khaya* (African mahogany) and African teak, that were common in the original forests are now rare. The secondary forest is characterized by other tree species, such as the prevalent fire-resistant palm tree, which is a valuable source of palm oil and kernels.

The prevalence of savanna vegetation increases to the north as rainfall decreases. The savannas owe their present extent and character largely to the erosion produced by farming, grazing, and the use of fire. There are some small areas of climax savanna (a closed woodland of broad-leaved, low-growing trees) and tall tussocky grasses, but these are only remnants of a much wider spread. Other savannas are derived from forest and are characterized by fire-resistant savanna trees with tall grasses. Tracts of tall-grass savanna also occur. Along the coast, mangrove swamps constitute the main vegetation community, especially in the saline tidal areas of river estuaries. These swamps are being extensively cleared for rice cultivation. Piassava, a kind of raphia palm, is common in the swamps of the south.

Coastal mangrove swamps

Large game animals, such as elephants, leopards, lions, wolves, and buffalo, are rarely seen. Various species of

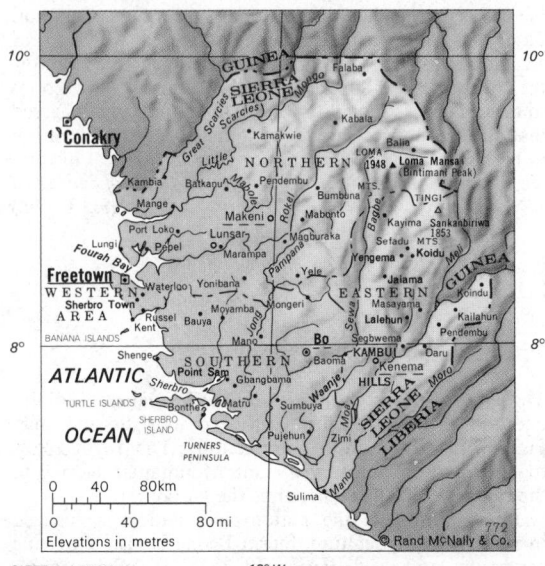

12° W

10°   10°

GUINEA
SIERRA
LEONE
Falaba
□ **Conakry**
Kamakwie   Kabala
NORTHERN   LOMA Bafodia
Kambia   Batkanu Pendembu MTS. 1948 ▲ Loma Mansa
Mange   Bumbuna   (Bintimani Peak)
Makeni○ Mabonto   TINGI
Port Loko Lunsar Magburaka Kayima Sankanbiriwa
Lungi Marampa   Sefadu MTS. 1853 Koidu
Fourah Bay   Yele   Yengema
Freetown Waterloo Yonibana   **EASTERN**   Kailahun Kindu
WESTERN   Jaiama
Sherbro Town Movamba Mongeri Lalehun   Pendembu
AREA Russel Bauya   Masayama   Kenema
Kent   **Bo** Segbwema Daru
BANANA ISLANDS   Mano   KAMBUI Baoma
Shenge   **SOUTHERN** Point Sam Gbangbama   HILLS
ATLANTIC Sherbro Bonthe Mattru   Sumbuya
TURTLE ISLANDS   Pujehun
OCEAN SHERBRO ISLAND
TURNERS
PENINSULA

0   40   80km
0   40   80mi
Elevations in metres

SIERRA LEONE   12° W

8°   8°

GUINEA
Moro
SIERRA
LEONE
LIBERIA
Sulima
772
© Rand McNally & Co.

monkeys and chimpanzees are common in the forest zones, while tiger cats, porcupines, antelope, and bushpigs are more generally distributed. There is a wide variety of insects, including the malaria-carrying mosquito and the tsetse fly, a carrier of trypanosomiasis (sleeping sickness). Hippopotamuses, crocodiles, and alligators occupy the rivers. The coastal waters, estuaries, and rivers, such as the Sierra Leone and Sherbro, also contain a wide variety of fish, such as tuna, barracuda, and mackerel, and lobsters and sharks. Bird life includes parrots, owls, kingfishers, green pigeons, African magpies, vultures, and many other species.

Settlement patterns. Villages of about 35 buildings and 300 inhabitants dominate the rural landscape. Modernization is slowly altering the traditional pattern of rural settlement; the old circular village form with a tight cluster of houses is rapidly yielding to the linear village along a road or the regular gridiron pattern with adequate spacing between houses. Economic activity still centres largely around rice farming. The extended family provides farm labour both for rice farming and cash crop production. Fishing is becoming increasingly important. The rearing and herding of cattle is largely confined to the north and to groups of pastoral Fulani. The small shopkeeper is typical of the villages, as are the tailor and carpenter. Traditional crafts, such as metalworking, cloth dyeing and weaving, and woodworking, are rapidly disappearing with the increased importation of cheap manufactured goods.

Urban develop-ment

Except for Freetown, the development of large towns occurred only after World War II. Because of the incipient nature of urbanism, functional specialization is rudimentary and occurs mainly in the development of the small, central business district, the most prominent feature being the daily market of petty traders, the majority of whom are women.

Freetown is a long, narrow city. Central Freetown—the administrative and commercial hub of the city—houses government buildings and embassies, the law courts, hotels, and the Roman Catholic and Anglican cathedrals. Eastern Freetown is mainly residential, with retail trading concentrated along major roads; there are also a few impressive mosques in the area. Further east is the port area. Western Freetown is functionally similar to the east; it also contains the nation's main stadium, the central prison, and the administrative offices of New England Ville. On Mount Aureol, overlooking the city, is Fourah Bay College, black Africa's first institution of higher learning.

Bo, located in the southeast on the railway, is the second largest town. An early administrative and educational centre, it has shown rapid expansion and has engulfed several surrounding villages. Commerce and retail trade are located in the centre of town near the important daily market. Its role as an educational centre has increased steadily, and Bo now contains many schools, including the famous Bo Government Secondary School, founded in the early 20th century.

Other important towns include Kenema, east of Bo, which has grown as a result of diamond mining, and Makeni, in the north, which is a provincial capital and major commercial centre. Mining has also been important to Koidu, Sefadu, Yengema, and Jaiama in the east and Lunsar in the north. Port Loko, Kabala, Bonthe, Moyamba, Kailahun, Kambia, Pujehun, and Magburaka are administrative centres that have also developed such functions as retail trading and produce marketing.

THE PEOPLE

There are about 18 ethnic groups that exhibit similar cultural features, such as secret societies, chieftaincy, patrilineal descent, and farming methods. The Mende, found in the east and south, and the Temne in the north form the two largest groups. Other major groups include the Limba, Kuranko, Susu, Yalunka, and Loko, in the north; the Kono and Kissi, in the east; and the Sherbro, in the southwest. Minor groups include the coastal Bullom, Vai, and Krim and the Fulani and Malinke (Mandingo), who are immigrants from Guinea concentrated in the north and east. The Creole—descendants of freed slaves who colonized the coast in the 19th century—are found mainly in the Western Area and Freetown. Ethnic complexity is further enhanced by the presence of Lebanese and Indian traders in urban centres.

Krio, a language derived from English and a variety of African languages, is the mother tongue of the Creole and the country's lingua franca. Among the indigenous languages, the Mande group is the most widespread; it includes the Mende, Kuranko, Kono, Yalunka, Susu, Vai, and Malinke languages. The Mel group, which is similar to the Bantu languages of Central and East Africa, includes the Temne, Krim, Kissi, Bullom, Sherbro, and Limba languages. English is the official language and is used extensively in administration, education, and commerce. Arabic is used among Lebanese traders and adherents of Islām.

Linguistic patterns

About half of the population practice a variety of animist religions. More than one-third of the people are Muslims, and the rest are Christians. Islām is most influential in the north, and Christianity is more prevalent in the southern and western cities.

THE ECONOMY

Resources. The economy is dominated by mining industries. Minerals are fairly widespread and include iron ore, diamonds, chromite, and reserves of rutile (titanium dioxide) that are among the world's largest. Other minerals include bauxite, columbite (a black mineral of iron and columbium), pyrochlore, gold, platinum, monazite, corundum, cassiterite, talc, and vermiculite. Major concentrations of those minerals have been found in the Kono and Kenema districts, along the Sewa River Valley, on the western coastal plain, along a central axis stretching south of Kabala to Mongeri, and in the Peninsula Mountains.

Mineral resources

Forest covers almost 1,160 square miles, the most important area of which is the Gola Forest. Biological resources include about 240,000 head of tsetse-resistant Ndama cattle, mainly in the savanna belt. The coastal waters provide rich fishing grounds for bonga, herring, snappers, tuna, shrimps, and lobsters. The hydroelectric power potential is appreciable.

Agriculture and forestry. Agriculture is carried out largely by traditional methods. About three-quarters of the population are engaged in production for the domestic and export markets. Rice, the main food crop, is widely cultivated on swampland and upland farms. Swamp-rice cultivation is concentrated in the lower reaches of river basins, of which the Scarcies is the most important. Efforts are being made to reduce upland-rice farming with its attendant soil erosion in favour of swampland farming with its superior yields. Other food crops include millet, peanuts, cassava, sweet potatoes, and oil palms. Vegetable gardening is important around the major urban centres, where markets are available to farmers.

The major cash crops are palm kernels, cocoa, coffee, piassava, and ginger. Production is carried out entirely by small-scale farmers. Timber (which includes *Guarea cendrata,* a cedar-scented, pink, mahogany-type wood, and the *Lopjara plata* variety *procera,* or red ironwood) is produced for the domestic market; there are major sawmills located in the Gola Forest; the main furniture factory is in Kenema.

Industry. Mining is the most important industry in terms of employment in the modern sector and in exports, and is second only to agriculture in its contribution to the national economy. Diamonds are mined by the National Diamond Mining Company (Diminco), which is jointly owned by the government and the Sierra Leone Selection Trust (SLST), a subsidiary of a London mining firm, the Consolidated African Selection Trust and also by a few private companies, and vast numbers of private prospectors. Mining methods range from mechanical grab lines with washing and separator plants to crude hand digging and panning. About half of the diamonds are gem stones found in river gravels, especially along the Sewa-Bafi river systems. In 1935 the SLST obtained an initial 99-year concession covering virtually the whole country; in 1956 the lease area was renegotiated and reduced to the Yengema and Tongo fields. The surrendered SLST areas were opened to licensed diggers, and the government opened diamond-

The mining industry

buying offices in Koidu, Kenema, and Bo, partly as a measure against smuggling.

The privately owned Sierra Leone Development Company (SLDC) mined iron ore at Marampa from 1935 to 1975. During 1963 the Sierra Leone Ore and Metal Company (Sieromco) opened open-cast bauxite mines at Mokanji Hills. The ore is shipped to Europe for reduction and refining into aluminum. Rutile is found in the southwest; in 1965 rutile production was begun, and production and prospecting activities were in progress in the early 1980s.

Industrialization is restricted largely to import substitution. Manufacturing is concentrated in Freetown, and production is mainly of consumer goods, such as cigarettes, sugar, alcoholic beverages, soap, tires, textiles, mineral fuels, and lubricants. Although factories are small and employ less than 1,000 workers each, their role in economic diversification is important. In the provinces industries are concerned exclusively with the processing of agricultural and forest produce, such as rice, timber, and palm oil. Traditional industries, such as fish curing and leatherwork, continue.

Electricity is provided by both thermal and hydroelectric power stations.

Financial services

Finance and trade. The Bank of Sierra Leone is the nation's central bank; it issues currency, maintains external reserves, and acts as banker and financial adviser to the government. The National Development Bank is charged with providing finances to investors within the country. The Sierra Leone Commercial Bank provides credit and technical assistance to farmers. Commercial banking is handled by Barclays Bank of the United Kingdom and the Standard Bank of Sierra Leone. Post Office savings banks are found in all main towns, and there are also various kinds of thrift and credit societies.

Foreign trade is expanding substantially, although its character still reflects the colonial nature of the economy. An excessive reliance is placed upon a few primary products, most of which go to the United Kingdom, the United States, and western Europe. Minerals and agricultural products account for the bulk of exports. Imports, however, are becoming more diversified; they include machinery, textiles, vehicles, fuel, and food products.

Transportation. A 311-mile government railway was completed in 1916 as a means of opening the country to commerce and of ensuring effective British occupancy. The railway was phased out by 1975, however, because of its limited carrying capacity and inability to meet the needs of an expanding economy.

Roads, originally developed as a feeder system to the railway, have become the principal transport carrier. The road network is dominated by a series of highways radiating from Freetown to inland urban centres. Roads are maintained by the government, local authorities, and private companies. The road system is being nationalized and modernized to meet the needs of rapidly expanding traffic. In addition, road links with Conakry, Guinea, and Monrovia, Liberia, are being modernized.

Inland waterways carry a considerable volume of mineral ores, piassava, and food products. Launches and sailing boats are important, especially on the southern route to Bonthe and the northern route to the Great and Little Scarcies. Freetown, with the finest natural harbour in West Africa, is the country's principal port. Its facilities handle all imports and agricultural exports. Specialized ports include Niti, which handles all bauxite and rutile exports, and Bonthe, which exports agricultural products.

Port facilities

The international airport of Lungi is situated on the north bank of the Sierra Leone River opposite Freetown. It can accommodate commercial jets and a large annual volume of traffic. Domestic air transport is limited, but there are regular flights from Hastings near Freetown to Bo, Kenema, and Yengema. Domestic services are provided by Sierra Leone Airlines, which—together with various African and European airlines—also offers international flights.

Administration of the economy. Private capital dominates mining concerns, commerce, and banking. European, Lebanese, and Indian interests are predominant,

and participation by Sierra Leoneans is small. The public sector features the Sierra Leone Produce Marketing Board (SLPMB), which has a monopoly on cash crops, and other public corporations, such as that of road transport, which is entirely owned by the government. Government revenue is derived from direct and indirect taxes. In addition to import and export taxes, the government can also rely on company, excise, income, and mining taxes for revenue.

Contemporary economic policies focus essentially on internal development, economic diversification, industrialization based mainly on import substitution, the increase of exports, and the insurance of financial stability.

ADMINISTRATIVE AND SOCIAL CONDITIONS

Government. The constitution of 1971 made Sierra Leone a republic within the Commonwealth. Adoption of the constitution of 1978 created a one-party republic based on the All-People's Congress. The head of state, or executive president, is elected by delegates of the All-People's Congress for a seven-year term. The House of Representatives is composed of a speaker and 104 members, 85 of whom are elected for five years by universal suffrage. Seven members are appointed by the president and 12 representatives are paramount chiefs representing the 12 administrative districts of the three provinces. The chiefs are hereditary rulers whose local powers have been largely superseded by those of officials of the central and local government. Their influence remains important, however, particularly in matters of traditional culture and justice.

The country is divided into four administrative units— the Western Area, which was the former Crown Colony of Sierra Leone, and three provinces (the Northern, Eastern, and Southern provinces), which were the former Protectorate of Sierra Leone.

Local government

The Western Area contains the capital of Freetown, which has a city council consisting of a mayor, aldermen, and councillors representing the six wards of the city. It has the usual local government committees.

Northern Province is divided into five districts, Southern Province into four districts, and Eastern Province into three districts. Each of these provinces is under the central political control of a resident minister, and each district is headed by a district officer who is, in turn, responsible to a provincial secretary, the chief adviser to the resident minister.

The districts are subdivided into about 146 chiefdoms, which are controlled by paramount chiefs and chiefdom councillors. The chiefdoms are further divided into sections and villages.

In addition, there are District Councils, which in some cases override the chiefdom administrations. The councils deal largely with local matters and are under the indirect control of the central government. Town Councils also have been established in the larger provincial towns of Bo, Kenema, Makeni, Koidu, and Bonthe.

Justice. The laws of Sierra Leone follow the pattern of British law. Until 1971 the framework of the courts was equally similar, and the final court of appeal was the Privy Council in London. Since the adoption of a republican constitution, however, the highest court is the Supreme Court, headed by the chief justice.

There are local courts that take account of indigenous laws and customs, Magistrate Courts administering the English-based code, a High Court, and a Court of Appeal. There are presiding officers in the local, magistrate, and juvenile courts who are not qualified lawyers but who are citizens of wide experience. The attorney general is also the minister of justice.

Education. There are primary schools, secondary schools, technical institutes, and several vocational schools, trade centres, and teacher-training colleges in the country. The University of Sierra Leone consists of Fourah Bay College, founded in 1827, and Njala University College, founded in 1964.

Health and welfare. Most health and welfare services are provided free by the central government. There are also a few hospitals belonging to religious societies and mining companies and private doctors. Every district in the interior has at least one hospital. The major hospitals with specialist facilities are in Freetown and Bo.

The Public Health Section controls port and airport sanitation, schemes for the control and eradication of malaria and other infectious or endemic diseases, and the sanitation of Freetown. In other areas sanitation is under the control of district health authorities and town councils supervised by doctors who are appointed by the central government.

The Endemic Diseases Control Unit concentrates on the mass treatment of such diseases as sleeping sickness, yaws, and leprosy. Yaws and measles have been almost completely eradicated.

There is a fascinating variety of housing in the interior districts, depending on the availability of materials. Roofs are made of grass in the savanna region and of bamboo in the forest areas. Walls may be circular or rectangular and constructed of dried mud bricks, palm fronds, or, more generally, lattice pole work filled with mud and coated with clay or chalk. There is usually a veranda or shaded porch. In most villages and towns along the roads, houses are roofed with corrugated zinc and the walls constructed of cement. In Freetown and Bonthe, some houses remain that were built of wood or laterite stone in a Brazilian or Victorian Colonial style and roofed with slate.

CULTURAL LIFE

The most outstanding feature of the country's cultural life is its dancing. The Sierra Leone Dance Troupe is internationally known and has performed in many foreign cities. The different communities of the nation have their own styles of costume and dance. In addition, certain closed societies, such as the Wunde, the Sande (Bundu), and the Gola, have characteristic ceremonial dances. A wide range of agility, gracefulness, and rhythm is displayed; in addition, there are elements of symbolism in most of the dances. Drums, wooden xylophones (called balaphones), and various stringed instruments provide the musical background.

The Poro society for men and the Sande society for girls play an educational role in village culture.

The Vai script has the distinction of being one of the few indigenous scripts in Africa. Some of the local languages are written in European script, but a few, especially the ones in the Muslim areas in the north, have been transcribed into Arabic.

Handicrafts. The carving of various wooden masks in human and animal figures for the dances is especially advanced in the southern region. The Sande mask worn on the head of the chief dancer during the ceremony attending the reappearance of the female initiates from their period of seclusion is perhaps the most well-known carved figure in Sierra Leonean art. It is a symmetrically stylized black head of an African woman with an elaborate plaited pyramidal coiffure adorned with various figures and with a facial expression of grave dignity and beauty.

Ivory figures are characteristic of the Sherbro, Bullom, and Temne peoples of the coastal and northern regions. Fine examples of these figures, which were bought or commissioned by Portuguese traders during the 16th century, are still extant. There are also steatite human figures, sometimes distorted, called *nomoli,* which certainly date earlier than the 16th century and were used probably for ancestor worship or fertility rites. At present, they are used for ceremonies to ensure abundance of crops.

Containers or rattles are carved from gourds and are decorated with intricate geometrical patterns that are burnt into them.

The weaving and dyeing of cloth

The weaving of blue or brown cloth of thick texture with linear designs is carried out in the southern and eastern regions by the Mende and the Kono. The cloth is made into coats for men or wrapped around as a lower garment by women and is also used as a bedspread. In the north, among the Temnes, imported cotton or satin is dyed with indigo, the red juice of the kola nut, or imported dyes into beautiful patterns by tie dyeing. In the west, baskets are made with dyed raffia, and patterned slippers are fashioned from dyed wool.

Painting and literature. There is an active school of modern artists who are trained in Europe and the United States and whose paintings have been exhibited locally and abroad. Olayinka Burney Nicol, Hassan Bangura, John Vandi, Koso Thomas, and Gladys Metzger are among the most well-known artists.

The Vernacular Literature Bureau produces school texts, information bulletins, and collections of folktales in indigenous languages, such as Mende and Temne. There has been a literary tradition in Freetown since the 19th century. One of the most prolific writers was James Africanus Beale Horton, who wrote books and pamphlets on politics, science, and medicine while he was a medical officer in the British army between 1857 and 1871.

There were also 19th-century works on exploration by such Sierra Leone Africans as Samuel Crowther, a bishop of the Anglican Protestant faith, and another clergyman John Cristopher Taylor. Sierra Leone is represented in most anthologies of African- and English-language poetry and short stories. In addition, the modern novels and short stories of Sarif Easmon, William Conton, and Eldred Jones give a vivid picture of modern life in the country.

The Sierra Leone National Museum in Freetown contains historical, ethnographic, and archaeological collections. Fourah Bay College and Njala University College both have libraries; the former houses the public archives. For statistical data, see the "Britannica World Data" section in the current *Britannica Book of the Year.*

(D.S.H.W.N./S.M.S.)

History

Sierra Leone was originally divided into many small independent kingdoms or chiefdoms; each had its own ruler, whose power was checked by his council of subchiefs. In many areas there were also secret societies, of which the Poro Society is the best known, which maintained law and order as well as instructing initiates in the traditions and customs of the country. The Bulom people have been settled immemorially on the coast. The Temne, by tradition migrants from the north, were well established on the coast by the 15th century. The Mende reached it only by slow migration in the 19th century.

Portuguese voyagers gave the name Serre Lyoa (Lion Mountains), later corrupted to Sierra Leone, to the mountainous peninsula at the mouth of the Rokel River. From the late 15th century European ships put in regularly, near the site where Freetown now stands, to trade manufactured goods for slaves and ivory. Though English trading posts were built on Bunce and York islands in the 17th century, no European power exercised jurisdiction in Sierra Leone. Traders settled there under the protection of the African rulers, who welcomed them for the goods they brought. In the early 18th century the Fulani and Malinke Muslim peoples in Fouta Djallon (Futa Jallon), north of Sierra Leone, started a holy war of conversion. From Fouta Djallon, Islām spread gradually to the coast. By the end of the 19th century it was firmly established in northern Sierra Leone and in the 20th century began to spread among the Mende.

Arrival of the European traders

A group of freed African slaves arrived in Sierra Leone from England to form a settlement in 1787, sponsored by the English abolitionist Granville Sharp, who called it the Province of Freedom, hoping it would become an anti-slave trade base. King Tom, a Temne subchief, gave them land, but his successor, King Jimmy, drove them away in 1789. The settlement was revived in 1791 by the Sierra Leone Company, a trading company sponsored by English opponents of the slave trade. The town was rebuilt and named Freetown. The company brought from Nova Scotia, as settlers, former slaves who were joined in 1800 by "Maroons," free blacks from Jamaica. These settlers were English-speaking and many were literate and Christian.

After the British Parliament made the slave trade illegal in 1807, the British government took over the settlement (January 1, 1808) as a naval base against the slave trade and as a centre to which slaves, captured in transit across the Atlantic, could be brought and freed. Between 1807 and 1864, when the last slave ship case was adjudicated in the Freetown courts, the British Navy brought in more than 50,000 "recaptives." Drawn from all over western Africa, these heterogeneous people lacked any common language or culture. Inspired by Sir Charles M'Carthy, governor from 1814 to 1824, the government undertook a deliberate policy of turning them into a homogeneous, Christian community. Missionaries of the (Anglican) Church Missionary Society (CMS) and the Methodist Missionary Society, along with the pastors of the Freetown settler churches, worked with such success that within a generation the policy was virtually fulfilled. The CMS, as well as opening boys' and girls' secondary schools, founded an institution at Fourah Bay, near Freetown, to train teachers and missionaries.

The recaptives and their children (known as Creoles) prospered as traders, opening stores or bartering imported European goods in the neighbourhood for exportable palm produce. Many left the colony to trade along the coast or to work there as clerks, teachers, or missionaries. At their suggestion, English missions were started in the Yoruba country (later part of Nigeria), the homeland of many recaptives. Thus they formed an educated western African elite, bringing to their homeland the new ways they had learned.

The most famous recaptive was Samuel Adjai Crowther, who became an Anglican priest in 1843 and bishop in the Niger territories in 1864. Among distinguished Creoles were Africanus Horton and William Davies, who qualified in Britain in 1859 as doctors and served as officers in the British Army; and Samuel Lewis, a barrister, who served many years on the colony's Legislative Council and was knighted in 1896.

COLONY AND PROTECTORATE

The colony made treaties of friendship with most of the neighbouring chiefs and gradually acquired jurisdiction over the adjoining coastline. The Creoles wanted to extend the colony inland, but the British government was unwilling to accept new western African responsibilities. By 1890, however, it was realized in London that the French, rapidly advancing inland, would soon hem the colony into a tiny enclave and destroy Freetown's value as a naval base. A more expansive policy was sanctioned, frontiers were delimited with the French and Liberian governments, and a British protectorate was proclaimed in 1896 over the area within the frontier lines. The British government made no contribution toward governing the new protectorate, so Sir Frederic Cardew, governor from 1894 to 1900, introduced a hut tax to raise extra revenue to pay for the enlarged administration. The chiefs, who had not been consulted about the protectorate, objected. A revolt broke out in the north in 1898 under an experienced war chief, Bai Bureh. It spread among the Mende but was suppressed by the end of the year. There was no further large-scale armed rising against the British.

The protectorate was governed on the principles of indirect rule, afterward introduced by Frederick (later Lord) Lugard into Nigeria. The chiefs retained much of their power, under the supervision of British district commissioners. Traditional ways of life were encouraged, and for the first decades of the 20th century little was done to extend education in the protectorate. During the 19th century many Creoles held senior official posts and looked forward to governing themselves ultimately. But after the protectorate was assumed they were gradually removed from office and both colony and protectorate were ruled by British administrators. A new constitution that became effective in 1924 allowed a few Creoles to be elected, and protectorate chiefs to be nominated, to the Legislative Council, but this did not satisfy nationalist aspirations.

INDEPENDENCE

After World War II British policy changed. In Sierra Leone, as elsewhere in western Africa, it was agreed to constitute democratic institutions through which the dependent territories could evolve into independent states. The small educated minority of Creoles hoped to entrench themselves politically, but the 1951 constitution gave power to the majority. The government elected under it was led by Milton (later Sir Milton) Margai, a physician and leader of the Sierra Leone People's Party (SLPP), a predominantly protectorate party.

During the 1950s parliamentary institutions on the British pattern were introduced in successive stages. The last stage was reached on April 27, 1961, when Sierra Leone became an independent state within the Commonwealth. The governor, Sir Maurice Dorman, elevated to the position of governor general, was succeeded in 1962 by a Sierra Leonean, Sir Henry Lightfoot Boston.

A vigorous opposition party, the All People's Congress, emerged, led by Siaka Stevens. In 1964 Sir Milton Margai died and was succeeded by his brother Sir Albert Margai, who tried unsuccessfully to create a one-party state. After a general election in March 1967 the head of the army, Brig. David Lansana, intervened to retain Margai in power. His brother officers refused to support him and set up a military government, the National Reformation Council, led by Lieut. Col. (later Col.) Andrew Juxon-Smith. In April 1968 the privates and non-commissioned officers mutinied, imprisoned their officers, and restored parliamentary rule; Siaka Stevens, prime minister, formed a coalition government. Sierra Leone became a republic on April 9, 1971, with Stevens as president. For current political history, see the annual issues of the *Britannica Book of the Year.*

(C.Fy./Ed.)

TOGO

Togo (République Togolaise), a sovereign western African republic, consists of that part of the former German colony of Togoland that was made French mandated territory after World War I. Situated on the Gulf of Guinea, it has a total area of about 22,000 square miles (57,000 square kilometres). From its 32-mile (51-kilometre) coastline, Togo extends northward for about 320 miles between Ghana to the west and Benin to the east to its boundary with Burkina Faso (formerly Upper Volta) in the north. Unlike some other French-speaking African countries, Togo has refrained from extending preferential trade treatment to France. Lomé, the capital, is the largest city and port in the country.

Physical and human geography

THE LAND

Relief, drainage, and soils. Togo consists of six geographical regions. The coastal region is narrow and consists of a low-lying, sandy beach region with a series of inland lagoons, the largest of which is Lac Togo. Beyond the coast lies the Ouatchi Plateau, which stretches about 20 miles inland at an altitude of about 200 to 300 feet. This is the region of the so-called *terre de barre,* a lateritic (reddish, leached, iron-bearing) soil.

To the northeast of the plateau region is a higher tableland, with the highest altitudes reaching 1,300 to 1,500 feet. This region is drained by the Mono River and its tributaries, as well as by other smaller rivers, including the Ogou. To the west and southwest of the tableland region the terrain gradually rises toward the Chaîne du Togo, which runs across central Togo from the south-southwest to the north-northeast. Part of a mountain chain that begins in the Chaîne del' Atakora of Benin, the range ends in the Akwapim Hills of Ghana. Mont Agou (Pic Baumann), which rises to about 3,235 feet (986 metres), is the highest mountain of Togo. Beyond the Chaîne du Togo to the north lies the Oti River sandstone plateau. This is a savanna (grassy parkland) region and is drained by the Oti River, one of the main tributaries of the Volta River. To the far northwest is a higher region that is mainly composed of granite and gneiss (a granite-like metamorphic rock); here are located the cliffs of Dapaong (Dapango), a distinctive feature.

Climate. Togo has a tropical climate in which rainy and dry seasons alternate. The rainy seasons occur from mid-April though June and—in the south—from mid-September through October. The narrow coastal zone is the driest region, which receives about 35 inches (889 millimetres) of rain annually. The region of Kpalimé (Palimé), about 65 miles inland, receives the highest amount of rain—about 70 inches annually. The north has only one rainy season with an average rainfall of about 45 inches, mostly falling from June to the end of September; during the rest of the year the warm, dry harmattan (a dust-laden wind) predominates. The mean national temperature is 80° F (27° C). Minimum temperatures of about 68° F (20° C) are recorded in the mountains in August. Maxima of about 92° F (33° C) occur in the north during March and April at the end of the long dry season.

Plant and animal life. Savanna-type vegetation is the dominant feature of Togo. On the southern plateaus large trees, including the baobab, are common, while they are rare in the north. The southwestern highland regions, in which rainfall is heaviest, are covered with tropical forests, also found along the river valleys. Because of the lagoons, the coastal zone is dotted with several mangrove and reed swamps.

Wild animals are not found in great numbers, especially in the southern and central regions. A few lions, leopards, and elephants can be seen in the north. Monkeys, snakes, and lizards are numerous in many areas, and crocodiles and hippopotamuses abound in the rivers. In the Parc National de la Kéran, near Sansanné-Mango in the north, there are wild herds of buffalo, asses, warthogs, antelopes, and deer. All kinds of reptiles, particularly snakes and lizards, and several varieties of birds and insects can be found in many areas. Fish caught off the coast include mackerel, bass, seabream, red snapper, triggerfish, dorado, ray, and sole, while crustaceans include shrimp and lobster.

Settlement patterns. The majority of Togo's population live in small villages scattered throughout the rural areas.

Rural settlement. In the coastal zone, the most familiar landscape is that of rectangular houses built either of clay and timber or of coconut or palm branches and topped by double-eaved thatched roofs. Scattered throughout the coconut plantations, they are not far from the sandy beaches, on which lie the fishermen's dugout canoes. Inland in the south, thatched rectangular huts made of adobe are clustered around big trees and surrounded by either earthen walls or fences made of palm branches. These clusters are linked by narrow lanes that converge toward the main roads and highways.

In the north, the traditional adobe or stone huts are circular and are topped by conical roofs or thatched turrets. They are usually gathered in units corresponding to family groups; often enclosed by earthen walls, they are sometimes interlinked. One of the distinctive features of the northern Kara region is the high density of villages that stretch along the highway or climb up the slopes of the many hills.

Urban settlement. Lomé, the largest urban centre, is spread along the coast. At its centre, there is a mixture of old and new commercial and administrative buildings. The traditional housing unit is the big, walled compound composed of a group of isolated rooms, each opening onto a courtyard.

Aného (Anécho), another coastal town, was once the country's European trade centre but is now declining. Other main towns include Tsévié and Tabligbo in the lowland plateau; Kpalimé, Atakpamé, Sokodé, Bassar (Bassari), and Kara (Lama-Kara) at the base of the Chaîne du Togo; and Sansanné-Mango (Mango) and Dapaong in the far north.

Regional archi-tecture (margin note)

THE PEOPLE

The population of Togo is composed of about 40 ethnic groups, many of whom are immigrants from other parts of western Africa. The groups indigenous to Togo live in the north and southwest. The northern groups include the following Gur-speaking Voltaic peoples: the Gurma; the Natimba, Dye, Bu-Bankam, Bu-Kombong, and Konkomba; the Tamberma; the Basari; the Moba; the Naudeba (Loso), who speak Moré, the language of the Mossi of neighbouring Burkina Faso; the Kabre and the Logba; and the Namba (Lamba), whose language, Tem-Kabre, is similar to that of the Kabre; a small number of West Atlantic-speaking Fulani; and the Kebu (Akebu) who are a Kwa-speaking people of central Togo. In the southwest the indigenous Kwa peoples also belonging to the central Togo group are the Akposo, the Adele, and the Ahlo.

TOGO

The immigrants came from east, west, and north. The Ewe, who emigrated from Nigeria between the 14th and 16th centuries, form the major ethnic group. There are also some scattered Yoruba, mainly Ana. Groups who emigrated from present-day Ghana and Ivory Coast since the 17th century include the Ane (or Mina), who are members of the Ge group, and who have adopted a variant of the Ewe language; the Ga-Adangme, who speak a dialect similar to the Ga language of Ghana; the Kpelle and the Anyana; the Chakossi; and the Dagomba. The northern groups of the Tem (Kotokoli and Temba), Gurma, and Mossi came from the north, mainly from areas in Burkina Faso.

The Ewe immigrants

Most of the nation's aliens live in Lomé. Mainly French, they include a few mulattoes of Brazilian, German, and French ancestry. Brazilians, or Portuguese of Brazilian birth, constituted the original trading settlement in Togo, and today Brazilian mulattoes are closely associated with economic and political development.

Although Christianity has profoundly marked the country, about half of the population still adhere to traditional animistic beliefs. The main Protestant (Calvinistic) church has been governed for a long time by Togolese moderators. Since independence, the Roman Catholic Church in Togo has been headed by a Togolese archbishop. There is also an Islāmic population.

THE ECONOMY

Agriculture, forestry, and fishing. A great variety of soils and climates enables Togo to grow a wide range of intertropical African products. Export crops include cocoa beans, coffee, shea nuts, and palm kernels; staple crops are corn (maize), cassava, rice, yams, sorghum, millet, and peanuts (groundnuts).

Cattle, sheep, and pigs are raised in the plateau region and the north. Fishing is carried out on the coast and in the well-stocked inland rivers and ponds. Most of the catch is consumed locally. Forests, which cover about 10 percent of Togo's total area, are a source of tropical hardwoods and other products.

A government agency, the Office of Agricultural Products (Office des Produits Agricoles du Togo; OPAT) has a monopoly on the foreign sale of Togolese products. Export sales are made by local firms in Paris and London, acting as agents of the Office.

Mineral resources. Phosphate is the major mineral resource and the country's leading export item. The deposits at Hahoetoé and Kpogamé, directly northeast of Lomé, are mined by the Compagnie Togolaise des Mines du Bénin, which was nationalized in 1974. Marble, with deposits of considerable size, is quarried by Sotoma (Société Togolaise de Marbres et de Matériaux), a mixed economy company with shares held by the Togolese government and an Italian firm.

The phosphate industry

Potential mineral resources include oil, iron ore, bauxite, uranium, chromite (an oxide of iron and chromium), gold, diamonds, rutile (titanium dioxide), manganese oxide, and kaolin (china clay). While the iron ore reserves are large, the metal content is only slightly more than 50 percent. The bauxite has a low mineral content.

Industry. Manufacturing in the past centred on the processing of agricultural commodities and the import substitution of consumer goods (textiles, footwear, beverages, and tires). In the late 1970s and early 1980s, however, major investments in heavy industrial schemes included a cement plant, a petroleum refinery, a steelworks, and a phosphoric acid plant.

Trade. Main imports include electrical and nonelectrical machinery, transport equipment, construction materials, pharmaceutical products, and paper products.

Administration of the economy. In order to encourage foreign and domestic private investment, the Investment Code of 1965 guaranteed foreign investors the right of freely transferring abroad all investment capital and income. The code also provided for tax benefits for priority enterprises. The trend in the 1970s of direct state involvement in the economy changed in the early 1980s to a pattern of offering incentives for foreign investment.

Indirect taxes, almost entirely on imports and exports,

account for most of the government's ordinary budget revenues. Direct taxes consist of an income tax, a progressive tax on all profits, a tax on wages paid by employers, a tax on rental values, a land tax, and a head tax.

Unlike other former French territories, Togo has not extended preferential trade treatment to France and subsequently to the European Economic Community. This open-door, nondiscriminatory trade policy—together with the expanded production of phosphate and tropical produce—will, it is hoped, contribute toward development.

The open-door trade policy

Transportation. The three main road systems are the coastal road between Ghana and Benin, which carries international traffic between Ghana and Nigeria; the road from Lomé north to Burkina Faso; and roads serving the cocoa and coffee producing area of Kpalimé, Badou, and Atakpamé.

Rail system. The government-owned national railway consists of four lines. These are the line carrying coffee and cocoa from Kpalimé to Lomé, lines from Lomé to nearby Aného and Tabligbo, and the line from Lomé to Blitta in central Togo.

Port facilities. Lomé is Togo's principal port. Its artificial harbour was inaugurated in 1968. A second port at Kpémé, about 22 miles northeast of Lomé, is used exclusively to handle phosphate shipments.

Air transport. An airport at Lomé is open to jet traffic. It is used by domestic and foreign airlines. There are local airports in Atakpamé, Sokodé, Sansanné-Mango, Dapaong, and Niamtougou.

ADMINISTRATIVE AND SOCIAL CONDITIONS

The coup d'etat of 1967 abolished the constitution of 1963 and dissolved the National Assembly. A new constitution approved in 1979 called for one-party rule with power vested in the president, who is elected by universal adult suffrage for a seven-year term and is eligible for reelection. He nominates the ministers and can dissolve the National Assembly. Members of the National Assembly are elected for five-year terms.

The military government

Local government. The country is divided into five regions—Maritime, Plateaux, Centrale, Kara, and Savanes—for the purposes of economic planning. The five regions are subdivided into 21 *circonscriptions,* each of which is headed by a district chief assisted by a district council. Seven communes have been established—for the cities of Aného, Atakpamé, Bassar, Lomé, Kpalimé, Sokodé, and Tsévié, respectively.

Traditional authorities and justice. The administrative apparatus still has to reckon with traditional authorities, which include tribal kings or chiefs, village chiefs, and heads of family groups. These traditional authorities play a role in the judicial system, dealing with certain questions of customary law. The judicial system, headed by a Supreme Court, consists of a number of law courts in which civil, commercial, administrative, and criminal cases are heard.

Education. Education is modelled after the French system. Togolese teachers, who are replacing French personnel in increasing numbers, are expected to adapt the system to the Togolese context. Primary and secondary education is provided by public or parochial schools.

The University of Benin at Lomé (founded in 1970) has schools of humanities and science, and a university institute of technology; and a school of architecture and town planning also at Lomé was founded in 1975 by the Organisation de la Coopération Africaine et Malgache (OCAM).

CULTURAL LIFE

Like other African peoples, the Togolese have a strong oral tradition. Little has been done, however, to promote vernacular literature. Before independence there were a few Togolese writers using French. Since independence, regional literature emerged with the works of several novelists and playwrights. Founded in 1967, the *Ballets Africains du Togo* has aimed at popularizing the finest traditional dances of the various ethnic groups. For statistical data, see the "Britannica World Data" section in the current *Britannica Book of the Year.*

Traditional culture

(M.K.P.)

History

Until 1884 Togoland was an indeterminate zone between the military states of Ashanti and Dahomey. The only port was Petit Popo (Anécho, or Aného). Throughout the 18th century the Togo part of the Slave Coast was held by the Danes.

GERMAN OCCUPATION

German missionaries arrived in Ewe territory in 1847, and German traders were soon established at Anécho. In 1884 Gustav Nachtigal, sent by the German government, induced a number of coastal chiefs to accept German protection. The protectorate was recognized in 1885, and its coastal frontiers with Dahomey and the Gold Coast were defined by treaties with France and Great Britain. German military expeditions (1888–97) met with little resistance, securing a hinterland the boundaries of which also were determined by treaties with France (1897) and Great Britain (1899).

Lomé, at the western end of the coast, was selected as the colonial capital in 1897, a modern town was laid out, and in 1904 a jetty was built. Three railways were constructed to open up the interior. Exploitation was practically confined to the coastal and central areas and was exclusively agricultural. Plantations were established both by the government and by private German corporations, but crop development was left mainly to the Togolese, assisted by agriculturalists trained at a college in Nuatja (Notsé). Trade was chiefly in palm products, rubber, cotton, and cocoa. In 1912 Germany took 60 percent of the exports and provided 42 percent of the imports. German administration was efficient but marred by its harsh treatment of Africans and use of forced labour.

On August 7, 1914, at the outset of World War I, British and French colonial troops from the Gold Coast and Dahomey invaded Togoland and on August 26 secured the unconditional surrender of the Germans. Thereafter the western part of the colony was administered by Britain, the eastern by France. By an Anglo-French agreement of July 10, 1919, France secured the railway system and the whole coastline. After Germany renounced its sovereignty in the Treaty of Versailles, the League of Nations in 1922 issued mandates to Britain and France for the administration of their spheres.

League of Nations mandate. The northern part of the British mandated territory was administered integrally with the Northern Territories of the Gold Coast, the southern part integrally with the Gold Coast Colony. Although the British administration built motor roads connecting its sphere with the road system of the Gold Coast, the bulk of the territory's external trade passed over the railways of French Togo.

French Togo was administered by a commissioner assisted by a consultative executive council of officials. When British Togo was attached to the Gold Coast, French Togo was formed into a distinct unit until 1934, when a kind of economic union was established with Dahomey; this was replaced in 1936 by a qualified integration with French West Africa that lasted 10 years. Agricultural development was pursued methodically, and a planned settlement of the interior by the Kabre and other peoples was fairly successfully carried out. Peanut growing was introduced in the northern areas, and energetic action was taken against sleeping sickness.

After World War II French Togo sent a deputy to the French National Assembly, a counsellor to the Assembly of the French Union, and two senators to the Council of the Republic. A representative assembly was concerned with internal affairs.

United Nations trusteeship. In 1946 the British and French governments placed their spheres of Togoland under UN trusteeship. After 1947 the Ewe people in southern Togoland represented to the Trusteeship Council that either their territories or the whole of Togoland should be brought under a common administration. These proposals were difficult to implement because Ewe also inhabited the southeastern part of the Gold Coast Colony and because not all the people of southern Togoland were Ewe.

The British colony was also rapidly advancing toward self-government, and the incorporation of the northern part of the British sphere with the Northern Territories of the Gold Coast had reunited the Dagomba and Mamprusi kingdoms, both of which had been cut in two by the pre-1914 boundary. Following a plebiscite held under UN auspices on May 9, 1956, the British trust territory of Togoland was on December 13 incorporated into the Gold Coast (although in the southern districts of Ho and Kpandu the Ewe vote showed a two-to-one majority in favour of continued British trusteeship). The Gold Coast and Togoland together were renamed Ghana and achieved independence in 1957.

INDEPENDENT TOGO

French Togoland became an autonomous republic within the French Union on August 30, 1956, this status being confirmed (despite Ewe opposition) by a plebiscite held in October under French auspices. Nicolas Grunitzky was appointed premier. Following UN representations, elections held in April 1958 favoured complete independence and rejected Grunitzky's Parti Togolais du Progrès (Togolese Progress Party) in favour of Sylvanus Olympio's Comité de l'Unité Togolaise (Togolese National Unity Party). Independence was celebrated on April 27, 1960.

After the 1961 elections, which established a presidential form of government, Olympio became the first president. He maintained economic cooperation with France. In 1963 Togo became a member of the Organization of African Unity (OAU) and in 1965 subscribed to the renewed Joint African and Malagasy Organization, which provided for economic, political, and social cooperation among French-speaking African states.

Ghanaian pressure for the integration of Togo with Ghana was resisted by the Togolese and led to strained relations between the two republics, including a trade embargo imposed by Ghana. Olympio, who was accused of giving sanctuary to refugees opposed to the Ghanaian president, Kwame Nkrumah, was assassinated at Lomé on January 13, 1963, presumably the victim of an army coup d'etat. Grunitzky, who had withdrawn to Dahomey in 1958, returned to assume the presidency and to form a provisional civilian government. On May 5, Togolese voters approved a new constitution, elected a new legislature, and confirmed Grunitzky in office.

Togo's relations with Ghana

Togo's first five-year development plan with expenditure of $115,000,000 for 1966–70 was approved by the National Assembly in 1965. Relations with Ghana improved in 1966 after Nkrumah's fall from power, and the borders between the two countries, which had been closed, were reopened. An attempt on November 21, 1966, to overthrow Grunitzky's government was foiled. Another, which took place without bloodshed in January 1967, was successful. Col. Étienne Gnassingbe Eyadema (later called Gnassingbe Eyadema), chief of staff of the Togolese Army, acting, as he said, to put an end to the political confusion in the country, suspended the constitution. In 1972 Eyadema became president by referendum, and in 1979 a new constitution was approved. For current political history, see the annual issues of the *Britannica Book of the Year.* (H.J.D./Ed.)

BIBLIOGRAPHY. The literature on West Africa is very considerable, and much of it is in French because much of the area was formerly under the control of France. A most valuable source of French material is the *Bulletin I.F.A.N.* (Institute français d'Afrique noire). Two other journals that are important general sources of information are *Africa* and the *Journal of African History* (both issued quarterly). For an understanding of the area some standard geographical text, such as WALTER FITZGERALD, *Africa,* 10th ed. rev. (1967), is useful. On the prehistory of West Africa, see the review article on African prehistory in the *Biennial Review of Anthropology* (1965). Pertinent geographical data can be found in REUBEN K. UDOR, *A Comprehensive Geography of West Africa* (1978). A good overview of many countries is available in R.J. HARRISON CHURCH, *West Africa,* 8th ed. (1980). On the general history of West Africa, a most valuable book is the collection of essays by different authors edited by J.F.A. AJAYI and MICHAEL CROWDER, *History of West Africa,* 2 vol. (1972). JOHN R. GOODY, *Technology, Tradition, and the State in Africa* (1971), is interesting in its attempts to account for the differences in state organization between the forest and the savanna regions; a very important book on kingdoms in both areas is that edited by C. DARYLL FORDE and P.M. KABERRY, *West African Kingdoms in the Nineteenth Century* (1967). There are many ethnographic studies of Guinea Coast peoples. Particularly relevant to this article are the following: on the Mbembe, ROSEMARY L. HARRIS, *The Political Organization of the Mbembe* (1965); on the Ibo, M.M. GREEN, *Ibo Village Affairs* (1947); on the Nupé of the Niger-Benue confluence, S.F. NADEL, *A Black Byzantium* (1942); on the Yoruba, P.C. LLOYD, *Yoruba Land Law* (1962). Later ethnographic studies include J.D.Y. PEEL, *Ijeshas and Nigerians: The Incorporation of a Yoruba Kingdom, 1890s–1970s* (1983); ROBERT D. PELTON, *The Trickster in West Africa: A Study of Mythic Irony and Sacred Delight* (1980); ROBIN LAW, *The Horse in West African History: The Role of the Horse in the Societies of Pre-colonial West Africa* (1980); on the Akan states, K.A. BUSIA, *The Position of the Chief in the Modern Political System of Ashanti* (1951, reprinted 1968); on Dahomey, MELVILLE J. HERSKOVITS, *Dahomey: An Ancient West African Kingdom,* 2 vol. (1938, reprinted 1967); on the Mende, KENNETH L. LITTLE, *The Mende of Sierra Leone* (1951). Most ethnographic accounts give some information on religious beliefs, but particularly recommended are the relevant articles on the Mende and the Ashanti in C. DARYLL FORDE (ed.), *African Worlds* (1954); and an unusual book dealing mainly with peoples in Ghana is MEYER FORTES, *Oedipus and Job in West African Religion* (1959). There are a number of useful books that examine the modern political problems of Guinea Coast states against the social background of their peoples. Particularly interesting are DAVID E. APTER, *Ghana in Transition,* rev. ed. (1963); and J.G. LIEBENOW, *Liberia: The Evolution of Privilege* (1969). For information on the urban situation, the following are recommended: MICHAEL P. BANTON, *West African City: A Study of Tribal Life in Freetown* (1957); HILDA KUPER (ed.), *Urbanization and Migration in West Africa* (1965); and the introduction and relevant chapters in P.C. LLOYD (ed.), *The New Elites of Tropical Africa* (1966). ROLAND OLIVER and MICHAEL CROWDER (eds.), *The Cambridge Encyclopedia of Africa* (1981), gives comprehensive coverage of postcolonial times and the sovereign states; CHRISTINE OPPONG (ed.), *Female and Male in West Africa* (1983), is a collection of papers on sex relationships and discrimination in modern Africa; J.O.C. ONYEMELUKWE and M.O. FILANI, *Economic Geography of West Africa* (1983), analyzes economic conditions in the 16 countries that make up the Economic Community of West African States; KEITH HART, *The Political Economy of West African Agriculture* (1982), is an informative account with good bibliography; CRAWFORD YOUNG, *Ideology and Development in Africa* (1982), describes different types of ideological settings in, among others, Benin, Guinea, Guinea-Bissau, Mali, Ivory Coast, and Nigeria; RUTH BERINS COLLIER, *Regimes in Tropical Africa: Changing Forms of Supremacy, 1945–1975* (1982), compares political systems of 26 African countries; ROBERT H. JACKSON and CARL G. ROSBERG, *Personal Rule in Black Africa: Prince, Autocrat, Prophet, Tyrant* (1982), is a coherent study of political leadership; VICTOR C. UCHENDU (ed.), *Education and Politics in Tropical Africa* (1980), is an evaluation of changes in the 20 years of independence.

Western Sudan: Useful maps of the area may be found in HARRY A. GAILEY, *The History of Africa in Maps* (1967). The linguistic classification is described by JOSEPH H. GREENBERG, in "The Languages of Africa," *International Journal of American Linguistics,* vol. 29, no. 1, pt. 2 (1963). The history of the region is well set out in BASIL DAVIDSON, *Africa: History of a Continent* (1966); in A. ADU BOAHEN and ALVIN M. JOSEPHY (eds.), *The Horizon History of Africa* (1971); and in J.D. FAGE, *A History of Africa* (1978). A summary of Wolof and Serer ethnography is given by DAVID P. GAMBLE in *The Wolof of Senegambia, Together with Notes on the Lebu and the Serer* (1957). PAUL PELISSIER, *Les Paysans du Sénégal* (1966), is a brilliant study that describes Wolof, Serer, Malinke, and Diola systems of agriculture. PETER B. HAMMOND, *Yatenga* (1966), describes the technology and culture of the Mossi. M.G. SMITH provides a useful summary and a bibliography of Hausa in JAMES L. GIBBS (ed.), *Peoples of Africa* (1965). Major sources for the Fulani are DERRICK J. STENNING, *Savannah Nomads* (1959), and MARGUERITE DUPIRE, *Peuls nomades* (1961). CAMARA LAYE's novel, *L'Enfant noir, roman* (1953; Eng. trans., *The Dark Child,* 1954), gives a valuable picture of Malinke childhood and shows the magical aspect of the goldsmith's craft. For social change, GEORGES BALANDIER, *Afrique ambiguë* (1957; Eng. trans., *Ambiguous Africa,* 1966); and PETER C. LLOYD, *Africa in Social Change* (1967), are useful works. Older surveys of West Africa are HENRI LABOURET, *Paysans d'Afrique occidentale* (1941); and JACQUES RICHARD-MOLARD, *Afrique occidentale française,* 3rd ed. (1956).

History: The best general history of West Africa is the two volumes edited by J.F. ADE AJAYI and MICHAEL CROWDER, *History of West Africa* (1971–73). A short handbook with a useful bibliography is J.D. FAGE, *A History of West Africa: An Introductory Survey,* 4th ed. (1969). A.G. HOPKINS, *An Economic History of West Africa* (1973), is a pioneer work in a field that has been too little explored. MICHAEL CROWDER, *The Story of Nigeria,* 4th ed. (1978), and THOMAS HODGKIN, *Nigerian Perspectives,* 2nd ed. (1972), are excellent territorial histories, the latter viewing the subject through original sources. For other English-speaking territories there are two short outlines in J.D. FAGE, *Ghana: A Historical Interpretation* (1959), and CHRISTOPHER FYFE, *A Short History of Sierra Leone* (1962); very useful also is JOHN E. FLINT, *Ghana and Nigeria* (1966). There seems to be no really satisfactory general study of Liberia, though note CHARLES H. HUBERICH, *The Political and Legislative History of Liberia,* 2 vol. (1947). For French-speaking territories, there is good material in the Marxist interpretation by JEAN SURET-CANALE, *Afrique Noire Occidentale et Centrale,* 2 vol. (1958–64; second volume trans. as *French Colonialism in Tropical Africa, 1900–1945,* 1971); and there is an excellent short study by JOHN D. HARGREAVES, *West Africa, the Former French States* (1967). HUBERT DESCHAMPS, *Le Sénégal et la Gambie,* 2nd ed. (1968), is a useful short study. There is some treatment of Portuguese Guinea in JAMES DUFFY, *Portuguese Africa* (1959); and in RICHARD J. HAMMOND, *Portugal and Africa, 1815–1910* (1966). RAYMOND MAUNY, *Tableau géographique de l'Ouest africain au moyen âge* (1961), is essential for West African history and its sources up to *c.*1400. N. LEVTZION, *Ancient Ghana and Mali* (1973); CHARLES MONTEIL, *Les Empires du Mali* (1968); JEAN ROUCH, *Contribution à l'histoire des Songhay* (1961); YVES URVOY, *Histoire de l'empire du Bornou* (1949); and MICHEL IZARD, *Introduction à l'histoire des royaumes Mossi,* 2 vol. (1970), are all sound works for the early Sudan. E.W. BOVILL with ROBIN HALLETT, *The Golden Trade of the Moors,* 2nd ed. (1968), will be found useful for the Sudan generally. The early history of Guinea is less well treated, but note the chapter in *The Cambridge History of Africa,* vol. 3 (1977), by J.D. FAGE; FRANK WILLETT, *Ife in the History of West African Sculpture* (1967); and ROBERT S. SMITH, *Kingdoms of the Yoruba,* 2nd ed. (1977). The coming of the European traders to the Guinea coast is perhaps best seen in J.W. BLAKE, *West Africa: Quest for God and Gold, 1454–1578,* 2nd rev. ed. (1977), a reissue of a book first published in 1937. PHILIP D. CURTIN, *The Atlantic Slave Trade: A Census* (1969), is an essential analysis of one of its principal consequences. The subsequent history of various parts of Guinea has occasioned a number of valuable monographs, of which the following are certainly important: WALTER RODNEY, *A History of the Upper Guinea Coast, 1545–1800* (1970); ALAN RYDER, *Benin and the Europeans, 1485–1897* (1969); K.Y. DAAKU, *Trade and Politics on the Gold Coast, 1600–1720* (1970); J.K. FYNN, *Asante and Its Neighbours, 1700–1807* (1971); IVOR WILKS, *Asante in the Nineteenth Century* (1975); I.A. AKINJOGBIN, *Dahomey and Its Neighbours, 1708–1818* (1967); the Senegambian history by PHILIP D. CURTIN, *Economic Change in Precolonial Africa* (1975); A.J.H. LATHAM, *Old Calabar, 1600–1891* (1973); and ROBIN LAW, *The Oyo Empire, c. 1600–c. 1836.* For Islām in West Africa and its flowering in the 18th and 19th centuries, three valuable modern works are MURRAY LAST, *The Sokoto Caliphate* (1967); NEHEMIA LEVTZION, *Muslims and Chiefs in West Africa* (1968); and B.O. OLORUNTIMEHIN, *The Segu Tukulor Empire* (1972). There is abundant literature for the 19th century. Light on the growth of European influence is shed by works such as ROBIN HALLET, *The Penetration of Africa* (1965); A. ADU BOAHEN, *Britain, the Sahara and the Western Sudan, 1788–1861* (1964); PHILIP D. CURTIN, *The Image of Africa* (1964); K. ONWUKA DIKE, *Trade and Politics in the Niger Delta, 1830–85* (1956); BERNARD SCHNAPPER, *La Politique et le commerce français dans le golfe de Guinée de 1838 à 1871* (1961); C.W. NEWBURY, *The Western Slave Coast and Its Rulers* (1961); and J.F. ADE AJAYI, *Christian Missions in Nigeria, 1841–91* (1965). JOHN D. HARGREAVES, *Prelude to the Partition of West Africa* (1963), is important, and the standard work on the partition will be his 3-vol. *West Africa Partitioned,* of which vol. 1, *The Loaded Pause, 1885–1889,* was published in 1974. Use may also be made of R.E. ROBINSON and JOHN GALLAGHER, *Africa and the Victorians* (1961), and of HENRI BRUNSCHWIG, *Mythes et réalités de l'impérialisme colonial français (1871–1914)* (1960; Eng. trans., *French Colonialism, 1871–1914: Myths and Realities,* 1966). A.S. KANYA-FORESTNER, *The Conquest of the Western Sudan* (1969), is an invaluable study; while the biographies *Sir John Goldie and the Making of Nigeria* by JOHN E. FLINT (1960), and *Lugard* by MARGERY PERHAM, 2 vol. (1956–60), are important. For British and French policy generally, there are two useful collections of documents: C.W. NEWBURY, *British Policy Towards West Africa,* 2. vol. (1965–71), covering 1786–1914; and a shorter, more general anthology by JOHN D. HARGREAVES, *France and West Africa* (1969). For the colonial period, two contemporary studies, LORD HAILEY, *An African Survey,* 2nd ed. rev. (1956), and S.H. FRANKEL, *Capital Invest-*

ment in Africa (1938), contain invaluable material. A synthesis is provided by MICHAEL CROWDER, West Africa Under Colonial Rule (1968), and the same author has edited two useful collaborative volumes: West African Chiefs (with O. IKIME, 1970) and West African Resistance (1971). The West African chapters in L.H. GANN and PETER DUIGNAN (eds.), Colonialism in Africa, vol. 1–2 (1969–70), are often extremely valuable. DAVID KIMBLE, A Political History of Ghana: The Rise of Gold Coast Nationalism 1850–1928 (1963), and CHRISTOPHER FYFE, A History of Sierra Leone (1962), are works on a scale rarely attempted; there is also much that is useful in PROSSER GIFFORD and W. ROGER LOUIS (eds.), Britain and Germany in Africa (1967) and France and Britain in Africa (1971). The transition to independence has produced a large literature from which perhaps the following may be singled out: JOHN D. HARGREAVES, The End of Colonial Rule in West Africa (1979); K.W.J. POST, The New States of West Africa (1964); JAMES S. COLEMAN, Nigeria: Background to Nationalism (1958); DENNIS AUSTIN, Politics in Ghana, 1946–1960 (1964); and RUTH SCHACHTER MORGENTHAU, Political Parties in French-Speaking West Africa (1964). Developments since independence are discussed in A.H.M. KIRKGREENE (ed.), Crisis and Conflict in Nigeria (1971), and, with D. RIMMER, Nigeria since 1970 (1981); and JOHN DUNN (ed.), West African States: Failure and Promise (1978). Much original work is available only in journals, including Journal of African History, International Journal of African Historical Studies, and African Affairs. For recent events, the weekly West Africa is indispensable. Relevant later monographs include ANTHONY ATMORE and GILLIAN STACEY, Black Kingdoms, Black Peoples: The West African Heritage (1979), a lavishly illustrated introduction to the history, peoples, and cultures of West Africa; The Cambridge History of Africa (1975–), the 8-vol. project of which by 1982 five were in print; ELIZABETH ISICHEI (ed.), Studies on the the History of Plateau State, Nigeria (1982), a collection of essays by African authors; PETER B. CLARKE, West Africa and Islam: A Study of Religious Development from the 8th to the 20th Century (1982), a survey of the growth of Islāmic influences in the area; JOCELYN MURRAY (ed.), Cultural Atlas of Africa (1981), a scholarly overview of Africa as a whole with good illustrations, maps, index, and bibliography; PROSSER GIFFORD and WM. ROGER LOUIS (eds.), The Transfer of Power in Africa: Decolonization, 1940–1960 (1982), a collection of scholarly analyses by British authors; and ANTHONY O'CONNOR, The African City (1983), an examination of the process of urbanization of tropical Africa.

Benin: Works that include material on the post-independence period are: R. CORNEVIN, Histoire du Dahomey (1962) and Le Dahomey (1965; 2nd ed. 1970); M. GLELE, Naissance d'un État Noire: L'Evolution Politique et Constitutionnelle du Dahomey, de la Colonisation à nos Jours (1969); D. RONEN, Dahomey: Between Tradition and Modernity (1975); S. DECALO, Historical Dictionary of Dahomey (1976); and ROBERT CORNEVIN, La République Populaire du Bénin (1981). Works that focus on one or another aspect of the pre-independence period are: A. AKINDELE and C. AGUESSY, Le Dahomey (1955); I.A. AKINJOGBIN, Dahomey and Its Neighbours, 1708–1818 (1967); W.J. ARGYLE, The Fon of Dahomey: A History and Ethnography of the Old Kingdom (1966); P.B. BOUCHE, Le Dahomey et Porto-Novo (1893) and Sept Ans en Afrique occidentale: La Côte des esclaves et le Dahomey (1885); R. BURTON, A Mission to Gelele, King of Dahomey, 2 vol. (1864, reprinted 1966); A. DALZEL, The History of Dahomey, an Inland Kingdom of Africa (1793); P. HAZOUME, Le Pacte de sang au Dahomey (1937); M.J. HERSKOVITS, Dahomey: An Ancient West African Kingdom, 2 vol. (1938, reprinted 1967) and (with F.S. HERSKOVITS) Dahomean Narrative: A Cross-Cultural Analysis (1958); H. HUBERT, Mission scientifique au Dahomey (1908); A. LE HERISSE, L'Ancien royaume du Dahomey: Moeurs, religion, histoire (1911); J. LOMBARD, Structures de type 'féodal' en Afrique noire: Études des dynamismes internes et des relations sociales chez les Bariba du Dahomey (1965); P. MERCIER, Tradition, changement, histoire: Les "Somba" du Dahomey septentrional (1968); K. POLANYI with A. ROTSTEIN, Dahomey and the Slave Trade: An Analysis of an Archaic Economy (1966); M. QUENUM, Au Pays des Fons (1938); J.F. RESTE, Le Dahomey, réalisations et perspectives d'avenir (1934); and P. VERGER, Bahia and the West African Trade, 1549–1851 (1964). See also ROBERT HOME, City of Blood Revisited: A New Look at the Benin Expedition of 1897 (1983); and PATRICK MANNING, Slavery, Colonialism, and Economic Growth in Dahomey, 1640–1960 (1982).

Burkina Faso: YVES PÉRON et al., Atlas de la Haute-Volta (1975); DANIEL MILES MCFARLAND, Historical Dictionary of Upper Volta (1978); GINETTE PALLIER, Géographie générale de la Haute-Volta (1978); RÉPUBLIQUE DE HAUTE-VOLTA, MINISTERE DU DEVELOPPEMENT ET DU TOURISME, Situation économique actuelle de la Haute-Volta (1966), on the economic situation after the fall of the first post-independence administration; FRANCOIS D. BASSOLET, Evolution de la Haute-Volta de 1898 au 3

janvier 1966 (1968), a historical account, including a critique of the various political organizations of the country, to be read with certain reservations; JEAN AUDOUIN and RAYMOND DENIEL, L'Islam en Haute-Volta à l'époque coloniale (1978); RÉPUBLIQUE DE HAUTE-VOLTA, MINISTÈRE DU PLAN ET DE COOPERATION, INSTITUT NATIONAL DE AL STATISTIQUE DE LA DEMOGRAPHIE, Récensement Général de la Population, Décembre 1975 (1978); and Bulletin Mensuel d'Information Statistique et Economique (monthly); COLIN LEGUM (ed.), Africa Contemporary Record (annual). Useful information can be found in special studies: UNION DES COMITÉS POUR LE DÉVELOPPEMENT DES PEUPLES, Regards sur la Haute-Volta (1981); NORBERT NIKIÉMA, La Situation linguistique en Haute-Volta (1980); ROLAND GRANIER, JACQUES LECAILLON, and JEAN-RODOLPHE LOPEZ, Disparités de revenus ville-campagne Côte d'Ivoire et Haute-Volta (1981); PAUL IRWIN, Liptako Speaks: History from Oral Tradition in Africa (1981).

Cameroon: DAVID E. GARDINER, Cameroon: United Nations Challenge to French Policy (1963); and V.T. LEVINE, The Cameroons, from Mandate to Independence (1964), are the best accounts of the political history of the country up to the time of reunification. Gardiner's study is limited to the former French trusteeship territory of Cameroon; LeVine traces developments in both the former French and British trusteeship territories. The realities of reunification have been examined in W.R. JOHNSON, The Cameroon Federation: Political Integration in a Fragmentary Society (1970); NEVILLE RUBIN, Cameroon: An African Federation (1971); and V.T. LEVINE, The Cameroon Federal Republic (1971). The MINISTRY OF INFORMATION AND TOURISM OF THE CAMEROON FEDERAL REPUBLIC, Cameroon (1970), is an official account of the achievements of the country since independence. K. EWUSI, West African Economies: Some Basic Economic Problems (1971), is an introductory study of the economies of selected West African countries, including Cameroon. H.S. BEDERMAN, The Cameroons Development Corporation: Partner in National Growth (1968), examines this quasi-governmental organization that manages the plantations developed in the Victoria division of West Cameroon. W.A. HANCE, The Geography of Modern Africa, ch. 4 (1964), gives a brief account of the geography of the country and has useful maps. DAVID BIRMINGHAM and PHYLLIS M. MARTIN (eds.), History of Central Africa, 2 vol. (1983), is comprehensive historical study, covering among other countries, Cameroon; description of the country is given in AARON S. NEBA, Modern Geography of the United Republic of Cameroon (1982); governmental policies are treated in PETER GESCHIERE, Village Communities and the State (1982; trans. from the Dutch); economic conditions are discussed in SALVATORE SCHIAVO-CAMPO et al., The Tortoise Walk: Public Policy and Private Activity in the Economic Development of Cameroon (1983); for social and political institutions see EMILE MBARGA, Les Institutions politiques du Cameroun (1982); and J.M. ATANGANA-MEBARA, J.Y. MARTIN, and NGOC C. TA, Education, emploi et salaire au Cameroun (1981).

Cape Verde: G.R. CRONE (ed. and trans.), The Voyages of Cadamosto and Other Documents on Western Africa in the Second Half of the Fifteenth Century (1937), is an account by Alvise Ca'da Mosto (Cadamosto), a Venetian explorer and trader who appears to have been the first European to land on the Cape Verdes; whether he, as he claimed, or the Portuguese were the first also to discover the archipelago is discussed in the introduction to this volume. WILLIAM DAMPIER, A New Voyage Round the World, 3 vol. (1698–1703), contains one of the earliest descriptions of the islands. DAVID A. and W.M. BANNERMAN, A History of the Birds of the Cape Verde Islands (1968), includes a useful general bibliography and an account of the islands' history, explorers, vegetation, birds, and butterflies. See also CAPE VERDE ISLANDS, 25 Anos de Actividade (1951), a review of social and economic progress from 1926. For economic and demographic information prior to independence, see Anuário Estatístico, vol. 2, Províncias Ultramarinas, of the government of Portugal. BASIL DAVIDSON, No Fist Is Big Enough to Hide the Sky: The Liberation of Guiné and Cape Verde, Aspects of an African Revolution (1981), is an informative source, with new material on 1970s.

Chad: INSTITUT NATIONAL TCHADIEN POUR LES SCIENCES HUMAINES, Bibliographie du Tchad (1968), more than 2,000 references to books, articles, recordings, and films in the social sciences; Liste chronologique des études effectuées par l'O.R.S.T.O.M. en République du Tchad (1970), over 500 references to works in the natural sciences. HENRI CARBOU, La Région du Tchad et du Ouadai, vol. 1, Études Ethnologiques: Dialecte Toubouri, vol. 2, Les Arabes, le Ouadai (1912), a fundamental work, despite its age; PIERRE HUGOT, Le Tchad (1965), a short introductory study; ALBERT LE ROUVREUR, Sahariens et Sahéliens du Tchad (1962), a summary of present knowledge on the northern and eastern populations; V. THOMPSON and R. ADLOFF, The Emerging States of French Equatorial Africa (1960), an overview of Chad on the eve of independence. J.P. LEBEUF, Archéologie Tchadienne, les Sao du

Cameroun et du Tchad (1962), a basic work on Chadian archaeology, and with A. MASSON DETOURBET, *La Civilisation du Tchad* (1950), a reconstruction of ancient history in the area; J. LE CORNEC, *Histoire politique du Tchad, de 1900 à 1962* (1963), a detailed work on the colonial era and the first years of independence. JEAN CHAPELLE, *Nomades Noirs du Sahara* (1957), the authoritative study on the Teda. J.H. GREENBERG, *Languages of Africa* (1963); H. JUNGRAITHMAYR, "Les langues tchado-Chamitiques," in *Les langues du Monde* (1971); ABSI SEAMIR, *Spoken Chad Arabic* (1964); A.N. TUCKER and M.S. BRYAN, "The Non-Bantu Languages of Northeastern Africa," in *Handbook of African Languages*, pt. 3 (1956). JEAN CABOT, *Le Bassin du Moyen Logone* (1965), an extensive study of the physical and human problems in this region; GEORGES DIGUIMBAYE and ROBERT LANGUE, *L'Essor du Tchad* (1969), a good summary. Both home politics and foreign relations are discussed in BERNARD LANNE, *Tchad-Libye: La Querelle des frontières* (1982).

Equatorial Guinea: MANUEL DE TERAN, *Síntesis geográfica de Fernando Poo* (1962), a useful geographical analysis; LUIS BAGUENA CORELLA, *Guinea: Manuales del África Española* (1950), the only detailed compendium of Guinean problems under the colonial regime; RENE PELISSIER, *Les Territoires espagnols d'Afrique* (1963; trans. and updated in 1964, *Los territorios españoles de África*), a handy reference on Spanish Africa; "Spanish Guinea: An Introduction," *Race*, 6:117–128 (1964), the only general review in English; SERVICIO INFORMATIVO ESPANOL, *España y Guinea Ecuatorial* (1968), an official record of developments until independence. PRESIDENCIA DEL GOBIERNO, *Plan de desarrollo económico de la Guinea Ecuatorial: años de 1964 a 1967* (1963), the only reliable study of the subject. ABELARDO UNZUETA, *Geografía histórica de la Isla de Fernando Poo* (1947), *Guinea Continental Española* (1944), *Islas del Golfo de Guinea* (1945), three standard, although poorly organized, works on history; RENE PELISSIER, *Études Hispano-Guinéennes* (1969), the only detailed analysis of the pre-independence period. Political and economic conditions are analysed in MAX LINIGER-GOUMAZ, *Guinée équatoriale: De la dictature des colons à la dictature des colonels* (1982); and FRANCE, MINISTÉRE DE LA COOPÉRATION, *Guinée équatoriale* (1980).

The Gambia: H.A. GAILEY, JR., *A History of the Gambia* (1964), information on the land and people, traditional farming practices, and the economics of a monoculture; R.J. HARRISON CHURCH, "The Gambia: A Riverine Enclave," in *West Africa*, 8th ed. (1980), a valuable reference on the climate, major natural regions, and economic resources of The Gambia, including a brief history of European association with the territory; H.R. JARRETT, *A Geography of Sierra Leone and Gambia* (1954), a detailed geography covering the physical background and economic activity, especially farming. S.A. BAKARR, *The Gambia Yesterday, 1447–1979* (1980), is a historical chronology; political tendencies are outlined in SULAYMAN S. NYANG, *The Historical Development of Political Parties in the Gambia* (1975).

Ghana: J. BRIAN WILLS (ed.), *Agriculture and Land Use in Ghana* (1962), the most comprehensive and authoritative account of the agricultural resources of the country and the problems involved in their development, including a particularly useful bibliography; E.A. BOATENG, *A Geography of Ghana*, 2nd ed. (1966), a concise and readable account of the systematic and regional geography of Ghana, fully illustrated with plates and diagrams; and "Ghana," in S.P. CHATTERJEE (ed.), *Developing Countries of the World*, ch. 15 (1968), a succinct account of the geographical aspects of the country's socioeconomic problems; WALTER BIRMINGHAM, I. NEUSTADT, and E.N. OMABOE (eds.), *A Study of Contemporary Ghana*, 2 vol. (1966–67), a collection of expert studies on selected aspects of the country's economic and social conditions up to the time immediately preceding the 1966 coup; GHANA, CENTRAL BUREAU OF STATISTICS, *Economic Survey*, an annual survey that provides a succinct statement of the country's economy supported with a wealth of statistical information; GHANA, CENSUS OFFICE, *1960 Population Census of Ghana* (1962–70), the most comprehensive work of its kind, and an indispensable source of statistical information on the population and socioeconomic characteristics; the corresponding volumes of the *1970 Population Census of Ghana* began to appear in 1971. GHANA, PLANNING COMMISSION, *One Year Development Plan, 1970–71* (1970), provides useful background information on various aspects of the economy and its problems; *Seven-Year Plan for National Reconstruction and Development: Financial Years, 1963/64–1969/70* (1964), mainly a historical document but contains descriptive and statistical information on economic and social conditions; *Ghana Official Handbook, 1969* (1970), a valuable source of information on governmental structure and administration at that time; *Constitution of the Republic of Ghana* (1969), contains the provisions of the country's constitution of 1969; K.A. BUSIA, *The Position of the Chief in the Modern Political System of Ashanti* (1951), an authoritative account of the traditional status and functions of the chief and the character of the institution of

chieftaincy; W.E.F. WARD, *A History of Ghana*, rev. 3th ed. (1966), an important pioneering study of the traditional states of Ghana and their evolution into the modern state of Ghana; F.R. IRVINE, *Woody Plants of Ghana* (1961), a detailed and authoritative study of the major plants and their uses; A.H. BOOTH, *Small Mammals of West Africa* (1960), a useful pioneering work, fully illustrated; G.S. CANSDALE, *West African Snakes* (1961), by an acknowledged authority; J.H. ELGOOD, *Birds of the West African Town and Garden* (1960), a small but comprehensive study. Later monographs include two important historical studies: RAY A. KEA, *Settlements, Trade, and Polities in the Seventeenth-Century Gold Coast* (1982), and MARY MCCARTHY, *Social Change and the Growth of British Power in the Gold Coast: The Fante States, 1807–1874* (1983).

Guinea: There are two major sources of information on Guinea. JEAN SURET-CANALES, *La République de Guinée* (1970), is the best single source by a trained social scientist and longtime resident of Guinea. CLAUDE RIVIÈRE, *Guinea: The Mobilization of a People* (1977), is a sound work by another social scientist and longtime resident. The *Special Warfare Area Handbook for Guinea* (1961), from the American University for the Department of the Army is dated and less reliable. GUY DE LUSIGNAN, *French Speaking Africa Since Independence* (1969), though somewhat simplistic and superficial, should also be consulted for political and economic interpretations. More current and accurate information may be found in the yearly *Africa Contemporary Record*. Statistical information may be gleaned from the *United Nations Statistical Yearbook* and the *AID Economic Data Book: Africa* (1970). The yearly encyclopaedia *Africa*, available from the African Publishing Corporation, is also useful. LADIPO ADAMOLEKUN, "Politics and Administration in West Africa: The Guinean Model," in the *Journal of Administration Overseas*, 8:235–242 (1969), is a lucid examination of political and administrative realities. Works by President SEKAU TOURE describing social and political change within Guinea are *Toward Full Re-Africanization: Policy and Principles of the Guinea Democratic Party* (1959) and *La Révolution guinéenne et le progrès social* (1963). Information on economic conditions can be found in *Economic Seminar on Guinea* (1982), papers of the seminar held in New York in 1982.

Guinea-Bissau: DAVID M. ABSHIRE and MICHAEL A. SAMUELS (eds.), *Portuguese Africa: A Handbook* (1969); AVELINO TEIXEIRA DA MOTA, *Guiné Portuguesa*, 2 vol. (1954), a standard work with English and French summaries at the end of both volumes; JOSEPH M. MCCARTHY, *Guinea-Bissau and Cape Verde Islands: A Comprehensive Bibliography* (1977); RICHARD LOBBAN, *Historical Dictionary of the Republics of Guinea-Bissau and Cape Verde* (1979), a useful introduction; RENÉ PÉLISSIER, *Africana: bibliographies sur l'Afrique luso-hispanophone, 1800–1980* (1980), an annotated bibliography; LISBON, UNIVERSIDADE TECHNICA, INSTITUTO SUPERIOR DE CIÊNCIAS SOCIAIS E POLÍTICA ULTRAMARINA, *Cabo Verde, Guiné, São Tomé e Príncipe* (1966), an unsurpassed wealth of details on various aspects, including the economy, during the Portuguese period; JOÃO BARRETO, *História da Guiné, 1418–1918* (1938), colonial bias, but the only book-length historical treatise; BASIL DAVIDSON, *No Fist Is Big Enough to Hide the Sky* (1981), an updated pronationalist report; GÉRARD CHALIAND, *Armed Struggle in Africa* (1969; originally published in French, 1967), an account from the perspective of the guerrillas; AMILCAR CABRAL, *Unity and Struggle* (1979), the major speeches and texts of the father of independence; LARS RUDEBECK, *Guinea-Bissau: A Study of Political Mobilization* (1974), the standard analysis of PAIGC before independence; STEPHANIE URDANG, *Fighting Two Colonialisms: Women in Guinea-Bissau* (1979), a discussion of the role of women in the revolution; LUÍSA TEOTÓNIO PEREIRA and LUÍS MOITA, *Guiné-Bissau, 3 anos de independência* (1976), a good description of political and socioeconomic problems; JEAN-CLAUDE ANDREINI and MARIE-CLAUDE LAMBERT, *La Guinée-Bissau: d'Amilcar Cabral à la reconstruction nationale* (1978), a sound balance sheet of the first years of independence. An informative historical account of the modern nationalist period is found in PATRICK CHABAL, *Amilcar Cabral: Revolutionary Leadership and People's War* (1983). BARBARA HARRELL-BOND and SARAH FORER, *Guinea-Bissau*, 3 vol. (1981), is a comprehensive overview.

Ivory Coast: Official sources, usually written with the help of French experts, are abundant and well presented. Besides annual reports from all government services, compiled in *Annuaire Officiel*, thorough studies of conditions serve as an introduction to project reports, such as *Perspectives décennales de développement économique et social* (1963, and 2nd ed. for 1965-75, 1964); as well as *Travaux préparatoires au Plan 1971–1976* (1968). These are studies of general conditions; other official publications deal with particular subjects, such as *Projet de création de 32,000 hectares de palmier à huile*, 5 vol. (1964). Reports from international organizations also are numerous; these include: INTERNATIONAL LABOR ORGANIZATION, *An Inquiry into Levels of Living in an Area of the Ivory Coast* (1961); ECONOMIC COMMISSION FOR AFRICA, *Abidjan Project in Social Development* (1963); INTERNATIONAL BANK FOR RECONSTRUCTION AND DEVELOPMENT, *Experiences with Agricultural Development in Tropical Africa*, vol. 2 (1967); EUROPEAN COMMUNITIES, *La République de Côte d'Ivoire* (1968); UNCTAD/GATT, *Ivory Coast as a Market* (1969). There are also many untranslated reports from French organizations, such as BUREAU POUR LE DEVELOPPEMENT DE LA PRODUCTION AGRICOLE OUTRE-MER, *Étude pour la Reconversion des cultures de Caféier dans la République de Côte d'Ivoire*, 18 pt. (1963); and SOCIETE D'ETUDES POUR LE DEVELOPPEMENT ECONOMIQUE ET SOCIAL, *Villes de Côte d'Ivoire*, 2 vol. (1962). Among unofficial publications the following are outstanding: SAMIR AMIN, *Le Développement du capitalisme en Côte d'Ivoire* (1967); and A.R. ZOLBERG, *One-Party Government in the Ivory Coast*, rev. ed. (1969). G.P. MURDOCK, *Africa: Its Peoples and Their Culture History* (1959), remains without par as an inventory of traditional societies and civilizations. Later monographs include ARTHUR CONTE, *Côte d'Ivoire, ou, Les racines de la sagesse* (1981); ABDOU TOURÉ, *La Civilisation quotidienne en Côte-d'Ivoire: Procès d'occidentalisation* (1981); SHEILA S. WALKER, *The Religious Revolution in the Ivory Coast: The Prophet Harris and the Harrist Church* (1983); Y.-A. FAURÉ and J.-F. MEDARD (eds.), *État et bourgeoisie en Côte-d'Ivoire* (1982); LAURENT GBAGBO, *La Côte-d'Ivoire: Économie et société à la veille de l'indépendance, 1940-1960* (1982); GEORGES LORY, *Introduction a l'économie ivorienne* (1981); MICHAEL A. COHEN, *Urban Policy and Political Conflict in Africa: A Study of the Ivory Coast* (1974).

Liberia: R.E. ANDERSON, *Liberia: America's African Friend* (1952); G.W. BROWN, *The Economic History of Liberia* (1941); R.W. CLOWER et al., *Growth Without Development: An Economic Survey of Liberia* (1966); R.J.H. CHURCH, *West Africa*, 6th ed. (1968); M. FRANKEL, *Tribe and Class in Monrovia* (1964); C.H. HUBERICH, *The Political and Legislative History of Liberia*, 2 vol. (1947); SIR HARRY JOHNSTON, *Liberia*, 2 vol. (1906); J.G. LIEBENOW, *Liberia: The Evolution of Privilege* (1969); H.R. LYNCH, *Edward W. Blyden: Pan Negro Patriot, 1832-1912* (1967); I. MARINELLI, *The New Liberia* (1964); P.J. STAUDENRAUS, *The African Colonization Movement, 1816-1865* (1961); UNITED STATES DEPARTMENT OF STATE, *Handbook on Liberia* (1968). See also the annual reports of the various departments of the Liberian Government. See also TOM W. SHICK, *Behold the Promised Land: A History of Afro-American Settler Society in Nineteenth-Century Liberia* (1980); BELL I. WILEY (ed.), *Slaves No More: Letters from Liberia, 1833-1869* (1980); I.K. SUNDIATA, *Black Scandal: America and the Liberian Labor Crisis, 1929-1936* (1980).

Mali: MALI (REPUBLIC), *Annuaire statistique*, basic information on all aspects of the country; *Justice en République du Mali* (1965), a study of institutions, codes, and procedures; UNION AFRICAINE ET MALGACHE DE COOPERATION ECONOMIQUE, *Étude monographique de trente et un pays africains*, 3 vol. (1964), interesting studies of the Malian economy; GERARD BRASSEUR, *Les Établissements humains au Mali* (1968), a description of the surroundings of the various ethnic groups; PAULE BRASSEUR, *Bibliographie générale du Mali* (1964), a comprehensive bibliography; J. SURET-CANALE, *Afrique noire occidentale et centrale*, 2nd ed., vol. 1 (1961), geographic, ethnological, and historical studies of West Africa; MADANI SY SEYDOU, *Recherches sur l'exercise du pouvoir politique en Afrique noire* (1965), a description of the political structures on the Ivory Coast, Guinea, and Mali. Later sources are also mostly in French: PHILIPPE DECRAENE, *Le Mali* (1980); MAMADOU TRAORÉ et al. (eds.), *Atlas du Mali* (1980); JEAN-MARIE GIBBAL, *Tambours d'eau: Journal et enquête sur un culte de possession au Mali occidental* (1982), on religious life and customs; GUY BELLONCLE, *Le Tronc d'arbre et le caiman: Carnets de brousse maliens, 1975-1979* (1981), on issues of education; UNITED NATIONS FUND FOR POPULATION ACTIVITIES, *Mali: Report of Mission on Needs Assessment for Population Assistance* (1978); GUÉDEL NDIAYE, *L'échec de la Fédération du Mali* (1980), on politics and government.

Mauritania: An overview is CHARLES TOUPET and JEAN-ROBERT PITTE, *La Mauritanie* (1977); also useful are CHARLES DIEGO, *Sahara* (1935), a beautiful book on the life and mentality of the great wandering tribes, written by an ex-officer of the desert-raiding camel corps (or *méhariste*); ALFRED G. GERTEINY, *Mauritania* (1967), a general survey; MOKHTAR OULD HAMIDOUN, *Précis sur la Mauritanie* (1952), a description of Mauritania; JACQUES MEUNIÉ, *Cités anciennes de Mauritanie* (1961), interesting remarks on the architecture, with beautiful illustrations; PAUL MARTY, *Études sur l'Islam maure: cheikh Sidïa—les Faḍelïa, les Ida Ou Âli* (1916), a fundamental book; THÉODORE MONOD, *Méharées: Explorations au "vrai" Sahara* (1937), an essential book covering many aspects; JÉRÔME PUJOS, *Croissance économique et impulsion extérieure: Étude sur l'économie mauritanienne* (1964), a detailed study of the con-

sequences of Miferma on the economy of Mauritania; JEAN-ROBERT PITTE, *Nouakchott, capitale de la Mauritanie* (1977), an analysis of the expansion of the capital; CHARLES TOUPET, *La sédentarisation des nomades en Mauritanie centrale sahélienne* (1977), a study of geographic and social transformations, and with GEORGES LACLAVÈRE, *Atlas de la République Islamique de Mauritanie* (1977), a plentiful and accurate cartographic source; GENEVIÈVE M. DÉSIRÉ-VUILLEMIN, *Contribution à l'histoire de la Mauritanie de 1900 à 1934* (1962), definitive work, with bibliography; CHARLES C. STEWART, *Islam and Social Order in Mauritania: A Case Study of the Nineteenth Century* (1973). An important source on the history of the area is VIRGINIA THOMPSON and RICHARD ADLOFF, *The Western Saharans: Background to Conflict* (1980).

Niger: EDMOND SERE DE RIVIERES, *Histoire du Niger* (1965), a complete historical synthesis; PIERRE DONAINT, *Le Niger* (1965), geography textbook for secondary schools (useful for reference); SUZANNE BERNUS, *Particularismes ethniques en milieu urbain: l'exemple de Niamey* (1969), a recent study of the development of the urban centre of Niamey; SERVICE DE LA STATISTIQUE, NIAMEY, *Annuaire Statistique. . .* (annual), climatological, social, and economic statistics. STEPHEN BAIER, *An Economic History of Central Niger* (1980), is a major scholarly study.

Nigeria: BRITISH COLONIAL OFFICE, *The Nigeria Handbook* (1953), useful information on the history of British Nigeria; K.M. BUCHANAN and J.C. PUGH, *Land and People in Nigeria* (1955), useful information on systems of farming, diseases, racial composition of the population, and climate, but outdated on other topics; M. CROWDER, *The Story of Nigeria* (1962), a history of Nigeria from the rise of the Sudanese states and of Ife and Benin to 1960; O. IKIME (ed.), *Groundwork of Nigerian History* (1980), a collection of papers on aspects of the history of Nigeria from prehistoric times to the 20th century; K.O. DIKE, *Trade and Politics in the Niger Delta, 1830-1885* (1956), a detailed account concerning the trade in slaves and later in palm oil; B. FLOYD, "The Federal Republic of Nigeria," *Focus*, vol. 15, no. 2 (Oct. 1964), an informative report on various geographical aspects to 1962; D. FORDE and R. SCOTT, *The Native Economies of Nigeria* (1946), a detailed account of the economies of some of the main ethnic groups up to the end of World War II; S.A. AGBOOLA, *An Agricultural Atlas of Nigeria* (1979), a study of land use and the problem of increased production in Nigerian agriculture; G.K. HELLEINER, *Peasant Agriculture, Government, and Economic Growth in Nigeria* (1966); J.S. OGUNTOYINBO, O.O. AREOLA, and M. FILANI (eds.), *A Geography of Nigerian Development* (1978), a collection of commissioned papers on aspects of the land, economy, and society of Nigeria; A.L. MABOGUNJE, *Urbanization in Nigeria* (1968), detailed studies of Lagos and Ibadan, but with little information on the new towns of the east and north; *Nigeria Year Book* (annual), information on politics, trade, and business, with biographies of public figures included; O. TERIBA and M.O. KAYODE (eds.), *Industrial Development in Nigeria* (1977), readings on the patterns, problems, and prospects of manufacturing industries in the country; T.A. OYEJIDE, *Tariff Policy and Industrialisation in Nigeria* (1975), a survey of the effects of government policies, especially tariff protection, on the manufacturing sector of the economy; H. ROBINSON et al., *The Economic Coordination of Transport Development in Nigeria* (1961), a report prepared for the Joint Planning Committee of the National Economic Council of Nigeria by experts from Stanford Research Institute; S.S. RICHARDSON, "The Courts and the Legal System," in L.F. BLITZ (ed.), *The Politics and Administration of Nigerian Government* (1965), an explanation of differences in the character of the native or customary courts of the four pre-civil war states; R.K. UDO, *Geographical Regions of Nigeria* (1970), a work on Nigeria's geography; "Disintegration of Nucleated Settlement in Eastern Nigeria," *Geogrl. Rev.*, 55:53–67 (1965), a study of the changing pattern of settlement and land use in the densely populated districts of southeastern Nigeria. See also MICHAEL K. GARBOUR et al., *Nigeria in Maps* (1982); JEREMY WHITE, *Central Administration in Nigeria, 1914-1948: The Problem of Polarity* (1981); HENRY BIENEN and V.P. DIEJO-MAOH (eds.), *The Political Economy of Income Distribution in Nigeria* (1981); SIR REX NIVEN, *Nigerian Kaleidoscope: Memoirs of a Colonial Servant* (1982); ANTHONY KIRK-GREEN and DOUGLAS RIMMER, *Nigeria Since 1970: A Political and Economic Outline* (1981); OYELELE OYEDIRAN (ed.), *Nigerian Government and Politics Under Military Rule, 1966-1979* (1979), and *The Nigerian 1979 Elections* (1982).

Senegal: The most important geographical, economic, and sociological studies are: M. CROWDER, *Senegal: A Study in French Assimilation Policy* (1962); J.S. TRIMINGHAM, *A History of Islam in West Africa* (1962); H. DESCHAMPS, *Le Sénégal et la Gambie*, 2nd ed. (1964); P. PELISSIER, *Les paysans du Sénégal* (1967); A. SECK and A. MONDJANNAGNI, *L'Afrique Occidentale* (1967); R.J. HARRISON CHURCH, *West Africa*, 6th ed.

(1968); A. SECK, *Dakar: Métropole Ouest-Africaine* (1970); C. CAMARA, *Saint-Louis-du-Sénégal* (1968); and P. FOUGEYROL-LAS, *Modernisation des hommes, l'exemple du Sénégal* (1967). Later sources include VICTOR FRANCO, *Au Sénégal* (1983); and SABINE GUILLEMIN and PASCAL CHASLOT, *Guide du Sénégal* (1981), both descriptive guides; SENEGAL, *Textes rélatifs à l'organisation politique et administrative du Sénégal* (1979), an official publication including the text of the country's constitution; GUY ROCHETEAU, *Pouvoir financier et indépendance économique en Afrique: Le cas du Sénégal* (1982), on finance, economics, and industry; J.-Y. WEIGEL, *Migration et production domestique des Soninké du Sénégal* (1981), on economic conditions.

Sierra Leone: Publications by the MINISTRY OF INFORMATION AND BROADCASTING, Freetown, Sierra Leone, include well-illustrated pamphlets that appear at regular intervals and contain up-to-date information. The *Report* by the MINISTRY OF EDUCATION (annual) gives educational developments and statistics. A valuable source of information is the *Sierra Leone Yearbook*, published in Freetown. The CENTRAL BANK OF SIERRA LEONE also produces regular bulletins. An *Atlas of Sierra Leone* (1966), produced by the DIRECTORATE OF SURVEYS AND LANDS, gives useful information and detailed maps of the country and of street plans of some of its important urban areas. J.I. CLARKE (ed.), *Sierra Leone in Maps* (1969), is an admirably illustrated symposium by members of the staff of the Department of Geography, University of Sierra Leone. For history, see CHRISTOPHER FYFE, *A History of Sierra Leone* (1962), the major work; and ALEXANDER P. KUP, *The Story of Sierra Leone* (1964). GEOFFREY J. WILLIAMS, *A Bibliography of Sierra Leone 1925–67* (1971), emphasizes articles on the communities of the provinces and includes a list of previous bibliographies. MARTIN L. KILSON, *Political Change in a West African State: A Study of the Modernisation Process in Sierra Leone* (1966); and JOHN CARTWRIGHT, *Politics in Sierra Leone 1947–67* (1970), give an account of modern political developments. For economic studies, see RALPH GERALD SAYLOR, *The Economic System of Sierra Leone* (1968); H.L. VAN DER LAAN, *The Sierra Leone Diamonds: An Economic Study Covering the Years 1952–1961* (1965); and SIAKA STEVENS in the *Report of the Duke of Edinburgh's Study Conference* (1956). F.W.H. MIGEOD, *A View of Sierra Leone* (1925), contains a valuable account of the culture of peoples of the provinces. K.L. LITTLE, *The Mende of Sierra Leone,* rev. ed. (1967), gives an account of the most numerous community in Sierra Leone; as does W.T. HARRIS and HARRY SAWYER, *The Springs of Mende Belief and Conduct* (1968). An account of the Limba peoples is given by RUTH H. FINNEGAN, *Survey of the Limba People of Northern Sierra Leone* (HMSO 1963). These three are the major communities in Sierra Leone. ARTHUR T. PORTER, *Creoledom* (1963); and JOHN PETERSON, *Province of Freedom* (1969), are good socio-historical accounts of the Sierra Leone Creoles.

The lives of distinguished Sierra Leoneans are well set out in M.C.F. EASMON, *Eminent Sierra Leoneans* (1961); CHRISTOPHER FYFE, *Africanus Horton, 1835–1883: West African Scientist and Patriot* (1972); DAVIDSON NICOL (ed.), *Black Nationalism in Africa, 1867* (British title, *Africanus Horton: The Dawn of Nationalism in Modern Africa;* 1969); and J.D. HARGREAVES, *A Life of Sir Samuel Lewis* (1958). *Modern African Stories,* a collection by ELLIS AYITEY KOMEY and EZEKIEL MPHALELE (1964), contains selections by Sierra Leone writers. The autobiographical *Kossoh Town Boy,* by R.B.W.A. COLE (1960), gives a vivid picture of Sierra Leone Creole childhood. ELLEN GIBSON WILSON, *John Clarkson and the African Adventure* (1980), is a biography of an important figure in the founding of Sierra Leone. See also *Dictionary of African Biography,* vol. 2 (1979).

Togo: ROBERT CORNEVIN, *Histoire du Togo,* 3rd ed. (1969), an exhaustive work on the history of Togo, including some geographic data; *The World and Its Peoples: Africa South and West,* 2 vol. (1967), includes a detailed article on Togo. *Encyclopédie nationale du Togo,* 6 vol. (1979), published in Paris, is a useful source.

Work and Employment

Work satisfies many needs. For individuals it satisfies the need to exercise their faculties and to participate in the collective work of society. It also gives them a claim to a share of the social product, enabling them to support themselves and their families. From the standpoint of the community, work is necessary for the survival of the human race and of its civilization.

The history of civilization is bound up with changes in the means by which the work activities necessary to society's survival have been arranged or organized. As human beings have grown more numerous, they have become increasingly dependent upon each other. Tasks have been subdivided to increase productive efficiency. This process,

known as the division of labour, has led to increasing specialization of the function of individual workers.

The rise of great industries, based on mass production and rationalized management methods, helped produce the modern industrial state, with its complex relations among capital, labour, and government. The institutionalization of these relations, and especially of methods by which to deal with conflict and change in the field of work, has been a chief preoccupation of modern societies.

This article deals with the organization of work through history, with the structural and technological changes that have influenced the organization of work in the modern world, and with related economic and political questions. The article is divided into the following sections:

HISTORY OF THE ORGANIZATION OF WORK

Organization of work in pre-industrial times

PREHISTORY

Organization of work may have begun before the evolution of *Homo sapiens*. Along with tools, a more complex brain structure, and language communication, division of labour may have been responsible for starting man's conquest of nature and differentiating him from other animal species.

In these early stages of human development, work was confined to simple tasks involving the most basic of human needs: food. There could be no widespread geograph-

ical division of labour, because the population was sparse and isolated in small groups. Prehistoric men were largely food-gatherers and hunters. The intermittent availability of food allowed little surplus for exchange, and there were few contacts with groups in different places that might have specialized in obtaining different foods. Nevertheless, there was some opportunity to augment the food supply by organizing the work of foraging and hunting and, later, agriculture.

Age, sex, and class. The most obvious division of labour arose from differences in age and sex. The oldest

Sexual division of labour

people in the tribe lacked strength and agility to hunt or forage far afield and so performed more sedentary tasks. The very youngest members of the tribe were similarly employed and were taught simple food gathering. There was also a sexual division of labour based upon the fact that women bore and nursed children and could not easily participate in hunting. Women, however, were required to work as hard as men. In the earliest human groupings there was no division of labour based upon class. The precarious character of food gathering made it necessary for the whole group to contribute; there could be no leisure class or even a class of full-time specialists producing articles not directly related to the food supply. There were, however, part-time specialists. When men learned to make flint tools and weapons, some individuals became so skillful that they could produce a surplus to be exchanged for food.

Communal organization. Although there were no full-time specialists and no true division of labour in prehistory, work nevertheless often required organization. Capture of game and fish required varying degrees of cooperation among members of the group. Communal activity of this type had important social implications. Food had to be equitably shared, and a leader was needed to organize and direct the group. Bones of large animals killed by hunters have been found in sites of the Upper Paleolithic Period (about 4,000 BC to about 10,000 BC), indicating a high degree of organization in hunting at this early stage of human development. Shortly thereafter, men began using nonhuman assistants; *i.e.,* hunting dogs.

Pottery. A more complex organization of work came with the development of pottery. While some sort of clay adequate for making passable pottery can be found nearly everywhere, the best potter's clay is not universally distributed. Thus, people in some locations could make pottery products for exchange. Skilled workmanship and specialized tools aided production, perhaps further encouraging specialization. There is no conclusive evidence that the earliest potters spent their full time at that task or that pottery making was carried on by women in its primitive stages, before introduction of the potter's wheel. There is reason to believe, however, that already in prehistoric times some organization of the work existed. The gathering of the clay and firing materials may have been the work of the men, while women may have fashioned and decorated the pots.

Textiles. The same type of specialization is also implied in the making of textiles. Early man's protective garments derived from animal skins. The development of agriculture cut into the supply of available skins and required a substitute material for clothing. To make textiles yarn had to be spun; the earliest apparatus for this work consisted of a spindle and a distaff (a forked stick holding the unspun fibres). The figurative usage of the term distaff to denote a female indicates a possible sexual division of labour in the early spinning process, with the man operating the spindle and the woman holding the distaff.

Agriculture. Primitive agriculture, too, may have dictated a division of work along sexual lines, with the fields entrusted to the women while the men hunted. In some agricultural tasks, however, such as clearing land, the men doubtless helped. Possibly there was little full-time specialization; in its beginnings, agriculture was carried on part-time. Yet even in its earliest stages agriculture was significant, for it provided a slight surplus that could be used to support the first real specialists: makers of metal tools and weapons.

Copper tools

Metallurgy. Although the origins of metallurgy are as yet unclear, employment of copper tools and weapons on a substantial scale suggests a new organization of work in which some persons devoted their full time to mining, smelting, and forging. Although deposits of flint for stone tools and weapons were fairly widely and evenly distributed, copper ores were not. Some of the earlier copper artifacts and remains of early copper mines have been found in areas where climate and topography would render agriculture difficult if not impossible. Geography thus dictated that the earliest miners and metalworkers could not be part-time agriculturalists but had to special-

ize. Besides, the techniques of prospecting, mining, smelting, casting, and forging were probably so demanding of physical strength and mental concentration as to preclude the metallurgist from the farming or hunting activities. Because copper ores are generally located in mountainous regions, the metal had to be transported to its users. Thus, metalworkers and their families had to be supported by the surplus foodstuffs of farmers; only when agriculture had developed beyond the subsistence level could such specialists survive. Not surprisingly metallurgy developed first near the irrigation-farming valleys of the great river systems of the Nile, Tigris–Euphrates, and Indus, all of which provided a high yield of foodstuffs per acre.

If metalworkers pursued their occupations full-time, their existence also implies other craft specialties. The combination of agricultural surpluses with copper and bronze tools provided the basis for development of the great irrigation civilizations of the Middle East. There the organization of work developed along lines that remained unchanged for the next 5,000 years, until the beginnings of mechanization and industrialization in the 18th century.

THE ANCIENT WORLD

Theories of civilization's development. The first general theory advanced to explain the development of ancient civilizations with systematic organization of large-scale work, the emergence of social classes, and widespread specialization was elaborated in the United States by a historian and political scientist, Karl Wittfogel, in his seminal book *Oriental Despotism* (1957). Wittfogel believed that the development of irrigation works in such areas as Mesopotamia and Egypt led to the use of mass labour and to an organizational hierarchy for coordinating and directing its activities. Though tribal societies had had some form of government, this was usually personal in nature, exercised by a patriarch over a tribal group related by various degrees of kinship. Now, for the first time, an impersonal government as a distinct and permanent institution was established.

Effects of irrigation

Irrigation increased the food supply, allowing larger numbers of people to agglomerate into towns and cities. Because farmers were vulnerable to attack, armies were needed, with the implication of an officer class. Town specialization of labour brought the emergence of potters, weavers, metalworkers, scribes, lawyers, and physicians, while the new surpluses also created the basis for commerce. The more complex economy required records, so writing, of which our first examples come from the bookkeeping records of the storehouses in ancient Mesopotamia, was born.

Wittfogel's theory has been modified by scholars who point to the emergence of urban civilizations in some areas without the presence of large-scale irrigation works. In their view, several factors, including geographical features, natural-resource distribution, climate, kinds of crops and animals raised, and relations with neighbouring peoples, entered into the response to the environment. These scholars might be said to apply a "systems" approach to the interpretation of the origins of organized societies.

Social classes. In any case, by the time written history began, distinct social and economic classes were in existence, charged with identifiable functions. At the apex of the social pyramid stood the ruler and the nobles, probably grown out of a warrior group that had subjugated their neighbours. Closely aligned with them were the priests; often, as in Mesopotamia and Egypt, the ruler was worshipped as a divinity. Possessing knowledge of writing and mathematics, the priests served as government officials, organizing and directing the economy and overseeing clerks and scribes. Occupying a rung in the hierarchy between the noble–priest class and the peasants were the traders and merchants, who distributed and exchanged goods produced by others. A sizable group of artisans and craftsmen, producing specialized goods, belonged economically to the lower classes. At the bottom of the social scale were the slaves, originating as war captives or ruined debtors. The social structure in classical Greece and Rome continued to follow these lines. For relatively short periods of time republican or democratic governments did away with the ruling group, substituting a class of free landholders and

Heredity of occupations

providing a citizen army of warriors, but the basic economic organization remained unchanged.

Certain characteristics of the ancient organization of work emerge from the rigid social stratification described above. Chief among these is the hereditary nature of occupations and status. Though at certain times and places—during the later Roman Empire, for example—heredity of occupation was enforced by law, tradition was usually sufficient to maintain the system. The social structure remained remarkably stable, a tendency fortified by the organizations of workers engaged in the same occupation, either voluntary or with the sanction of the law, that were the prototypes of the medieval guilds.

Organization of agricultural labour. *The family farm.* The basic agricultural work unit in the ancient world was the family. Even in certain regions where the state owned the land, farms were allocated by family. Furthermore, when large farming estates were formed during the Roman Empire, the structure of rural society was little affected, because the owners commonly left cultivation of their land to poor peasants who became their tenants.

Work within the family farm unit was divided along sexual lines: the men bore chief responsibility for such seasonal tasks as plowing, sowing, tilling, and harvesting, while the women prepared food and made clothing. Sons and daughters were apprenticed to their parents, and, if slaves were available, their work was similarly divided.

Technology and the seasonal nature of agriculture also influenced the work organization. The usual draft team in antiquity, a pair of oxen, required two operators: a driver for the team and a guide for the plow. During planting and harvesting the entire family performed fieldwork.

Estates. In the large estates, or latifundia, of the Roman Empire, the organization of work was quite complex, and a hierarchy of supervisors came into existence. The Greek historian Xenophon (5th–4th century BC) and the Roman statesman Marcus Porcius Cato (3rd–2nd century BC) wrote handbooks for management of such estates. Cato also described a work organization for a medium-sized farm. For an estate of 150 acres (60 hectares) with olive trees, he recommended an overseer, a housekeeper, five farmhands, three carders, a donkey driver, a swineherd, and a shepherd. To these 13 of the permanent labour force, extra hands would be added for the harvest period.

On the larger latifundia that developed from about the 2nd century BC, the owner was usually nonresident, often because he had many scattered estates. Direction of the affairs of each was left in the hands of a bailiff, under whose command slaves, numbering in the hundreds or even in the thousands, were divided into gangs charged with different responsibilities.

Crop specialization. Ancient agricultural work organization was also characterized by specialization in crops, Greece and Italy concentrating on the vine and the olive, leaving cereal cultivation to the richer soils of Sicily, North Africa, and Asia. Wine and oil required craftsmen to produce amphorae for storage and transport.

Organization of industrial labour by craft. Economic growth, sophistication of taste, and enlarged markets ultimately brought mass production of a sort, with large workshops dedicated to production of a single item. These workshops, however, never achieved the size of even a small modern factory; craft production throughout antiquity remained distinctly modest in scale; a building in which a dozen persons worked was considered a large factory, though a few workshops were larger.

The earliest specialized craftsmen were probably itinerant, gravitating to wherever their services were in demand. As the market grew, craftsmen became sedentary, and traders carried their products to market. Economic growth also led to a multiplication of specialized crafts, to the organization of guildlike groups, and to a geographical division of labour, with members of one craft located in a special quarter of a city or in one area of a country. In the pottery industry, specialization was carried even further, with shaping, firing, and decoration sometimes done in separate establishments and with workshops specializing in cooking pots, jars, goblets, and funerary urns.

As ancient workshops grew in size, slaves were intro-

Slave labour

duced. The chief examples of large-scale production by slaves were in mining and metallurgy, in which working conditions were especially harsh but in which work organization was refined. In the silver mines at Laurium, in ancient Greece, the master miner commanded three gangs of labourers. The strongest handled picks at the ore face, weaker men or boys carried ore from the mine, and women and old men sifted the ore-bearing rock. The miners worked 10-hour shifts (followed by 10 hours of rest) in dark and narrow passages with smoky lamps that made the air almost unbreathable. On the surface, the master smelter supervised the workshops, in which the strongest men worked the mortar and the weakest the hand mill. Metallurgical working of the ore was carried out by small units, because the small leather bellows limited the size of the furnace. Metallurgy thus remained essentially a handicraft.

After weapons and tools, metal's chief application was for ornamentation. The metalworker was more artisan, or even artist, than industrial worker, and in the trade there were patternmakers, smelters, turners, metal chasers, gilders, and specialized goldsmiths and silversmiths.

Organization of labour for large-scale construction. The monumental public-works projects of the ancient world demonstrate a remarkable degree of organization in the absence of power and machinery. The Great Pyramid of Giza, built about 2500 BC before the Egyptians knew the pulley or had wheeled vehicles, covers 13 acres (5.3 hectares) and contains the staggering total of 2,300,000 colossal blocks of granite and limestone, weighing an average of 5,000 pounds (2,300 kilograms). There exists no complete historical or archaeological record of the exact methods of quarrying, transportation, and construction of the pyramids, and what evidence remains is often contradictory. Obviously, however, the need to organize the work on a systematic and rational basis was superbly met. The logistical problem alone, housing and feeding a large army of workers, required high administrative skill.

The master builder, who planned and directed the erection of the pyramids and other great structures, occupied a high position in society. Ancestor of the modern architect and engineer, he was a trusted court noble and adviser to the pharaoh. He directed a host of subordinates, superintendents, and foremen, each with his scribes and recorders.

The master builder

Although some slaves were employed in building the pyramids, most of the workers were peasants, drafted as a form of service tax (corvée) owed the state and employed when the Nile was flooding their fields. Workers were not regarded as expendable; overseers and foremen took pride in reporting on their safety and welfare. In a record of a quarrying expedition to the desert, the leader boasted that he had not lost a man or a mule. The labourers were organized into gangs; skilled workers cut granite for the columns, architraves, doorjambs, lintels, and casing blocks. Masons and other craftsmen dressed, polished, and laid the blocks and probably erected ramps to drag the stones into place.

The Greeks and Romans also built monuments requiring advanced organizational techniques. The Roman road network, aqueducts, public buildings, public baths, harbours, docks, and lighthouses demanded exceptional skill in organizing materials and workmen, implying in turn a rational division of craftsmen.

THE MEDIEVAL WORLD

The organization of work and division of labour may, in fact, be said to have reached a peak during the Roman Empire, but it inevitably declined as the empire disintegrated in the West. The social and political fragmentation and economic decay of the late empire reduced most of western Europe to small-scale, self-sufficient economic units. As this happened, the market for specialized production largely disappeared. As the new feudal society achieved stability, however, trade and town life began to revive; interregional commerce was stimulated, and specialized crafts reappeared to serve growing markets.

Important technological innovations in agriculture, power, transportation, metallurgy, and machines brought further areas of specialization into being. The emergence of the new burgher class, with rapidly growing wealth and breadth of enterprise, provided the basis for a more rational management of production, hastening the rise of industrialization.

Class divisions. Social divisions, or class structure, in the medieval world reflected a division of labour. The noble class, or seigneurs, were fighters, protectors, important consumers, and, in a sense, organizers of work. Because they controlled the land, basic to production in this agrarian society, the nobles alone possessed the wealth to purchase the products of artisans, to buy goods brought from a distance, to use the weapons and armour made by metallurgists, and to construct castles and fortresses. The lords also decided, in accordance with prevailing custom, how the farmwork should be organized.

The clergy were both consumers and producers, responsible for the spiritual needs and protection of their parishioners. The monasteries were self-sufficient agrarian units that often produced a surplus for trade. Finally, the great churches required specialists in stained glass, bell founding, stonemasonry, wood carving, and other trades.

Medieval
farmers

The bulk of the population were farmers of varying legal status. Most were serfs bound to the plots of ground their ancestors had tilled and owing certain specified services and dues to the lord of the manor, who extended protection in return. A few inhabitants of the manor were tenant farmers, or sharecroppers, renting the lord's land in return for payments of a share of the produce. Fewer still were free farm labourers who worked for wages, while slavery had all but disappeared. Because the manor was practically self-sufficient, peasants of whatever status performed a variety of tasks connected with their agricultural occupation.

Agricultural production. Four interrelated factors determined work organization in medieval agriculture: the economic self-sufficiency of the manor; the development of mixed agriculture based on crop growing and stock raising; such technological improvements as the heavy wheeled plow and rigid horse collar; and the system of land tenure and division of holdings. Each peasant household produced nearly everything it needed and paid for the use of a feudal-monopoly mill or winepress.

In antiquity, stock raising and crop production had been separate, but, in northwest Europe during the Middle Ages, the two were combined. Animals were necessary both for draft and for food, but, because the yield of the grainfields did not greatly exceed human requirements, stock was pastured on poor land or harvested fields. Thus a certain amount of land was reserved for pasturage, and some villager, usually an older member of the community, became herdsman.

Communal organization was made imperative by the land-tenure arrangements and by the way in which arable land was divided among villagers. In a typical manor, at least half the cultivable soil was held by peasant cultivators, and, in order to assure an equitable division, the land was divided into large fields, each of which was subdivided into narrow strips. Each peasant held strips in each field; the work of plowing, planting, and harvesting, therefore, had to be done in common and at the same time.

The wheeled plow, gradually introduced over several centuries, further reinforced communal work organization. Earlier plows had merely scratched the surface of the soil, necessitating cross-plowing, which, in turn, made square fields desirable. The new plow was equipped with a heavy knife (colter) to dig under the surface of the soil and a moldboard to turn over the sod, eliminating the need for cross-plowing and making strip fields possible. On the other hand, because the new plow required a team of eight oxen, more than any single peasant owned, plowing (and indeed all heavy work on the manor) was pooled. Of course, such a system allowed little room for individual initiative; everyone followed established routines, with the pace set by the slowest oxen.

Industrial production. *The craft guilds.* In contrast to the land-bound serfs, townspeople of the Middle Ages were free. Some engaged in commerce, including long-distance trade, and organized into corporate bodies known as merchant guilds. The majority were small merchant-craftsmen,

however, organized in craft guilds as masters (of highest accomplishment and status); journeymen (at a middle level); and apprentices (beginners). The medieval master was typically many things at once: a workman himself, the most skilled in his shop; a foreman supervising journeymen and apprentices; an employer; a buyer of raw or semifinished materials; and a seller of finished products. Because medieval craftsmen employed simple hand tools, the skill of the workman rather than his equipment determined the quantity and quality of his output. Hence, there was a long period of learning for the apprentice and journeyman. The
medieval
master

The essence of craft-guild organization was regulation. By controlling conditions of entrance into a craft, guilds limited the labour supply. By defining wages, hours, tools, and techniques, they regulated both working conditions and the production process. Quality standards and prices were also set. Monopolistic in nature, the guilds, either singly or in combination, sought complete control over their own local markets and endeavoured to exclude outsiders. In order to attain and protect their monopoly, the guilds acquired a political voice and in some locations achieved the right to elect a number of their own members to the town council. In some towns, such as Liège, Utrecht, and Cologne, guilds achieved complete political control. The 32 craft guilds in Liège, for example, so dominated the town after 1384 that they named the town council and governors and required all important civic decisions to be approved by a majority vote of their membership.

The most prosperous period for the craft guilds was the 14th century. Specialties became so differentiated that there were more than 100 guilds in large towns. In northern Europe, for example, at the beginning of the period, carpenters built houses and made furniture. In time, furniture making became a new craft, that of joinery, and the joiners broke from the carpenters to establish their own guilds. The wood-carvers and turners (who specialized in furniture turned on a lathe) founded guilds also. Painting and gilding of furniture and wood carvings were done by members of the painters' guild.

Simultaneously, there was a countermovement toward amalgamation of different crafts, a tendency that reflected the growth of the market and the desire of enterprising masters to develop the trading function at the expense of the handicraft function. The typical medieval craft regulation had as its objective for each craftsman to gain an equal share in the trading function, a monopolistic division of the market. As craft differentiation reached a point at which a number of crafts participated in the production of the same or similar articles, such conditions could not be maintained. The steadily widening search for raw materials and steadily growing marketplace stimulated craftsmen at each end of the production chain to concentrate on trade, either to assure themselves of raw materials or of a market. In either case, masters were tempted to employ members of other crafts, and conflicts inevitably arose.

The same widening of the market led to differentiation of classes within a craft. The trading function acquired increasing importance and also came to be exercised by certain individuals within a single craft organization; those who remained craftsmen fell into a condition of dependence upon the traders. At the same time, merchant guilds, originally representatives of traders only, absorbed the craft guilds, over which they had gradually acquired economic control. Breakdown
of the
guilds

Internally, too, the craft guilds suffered a breakdown in structure. Because the masters sought to retain the profits of the growing market for themselves, they made it increasingly difficult for journeymen to enter their class, preferring instead to employ them as wageworkers. Apprentices similarly had little hope of rising to mastership. Thus, the master–journeyman–apprentice relationship gave way to an employer–employee arrangement, with the master performing the functions of merchant while his employees did craftwork. Conditions for development of the early industrial system—the proto-factory—thus arose with the disintegration of the original craft-guild system. The excluded journeymen eventually became a class of free labourers who practiced their craft for wages outside town walls where guild regulations did not reach.

The putting-out system. Certain industries that were small at the outset of the Middle Ages had by their close become large in scale, with accompanying changes in the organization of work. The most important of these was the wool-cloth industry.

The basic clothing material in western Europe until the beginning of modern times was wool. Linen and silk, though used since antiquity, were too costly to become raw materials for any large-scale industry until a later date, and cotton was grown only in small volume. The production of cloth from wool involved several time-consuming steps: cleaning and carding (straightening curled and knotted fibres sheared from the sheep); spinning the fibres into thread; weaving the thread into cloth; shearing off knots and roughness; and dyeing. All these processes could be carried on within a single peasant household, for they required only simple apparatus and rudimentary skills—children carded the wool; women operated the spinning wheel; and men worked the loom shuttles.

The cloth produced by such crude tools and relatively unskilled workers was rough but serviceable. Those above the peasant class, however, wanted more comfortable and attractive clothes that could be produced only by skilled craftsmen. Thus a large and growing demand existed for better textiles, and the industry rapidly outgrew the peasant household economy. A new organization of work, called the putting-out system, was instituted, in which a merchant clothier bought raw wool, "put it out" to be carded, spun, and woven into cloth, and then carried the cloth through the finishing processes with the help of skilled craftsmen. Because the spinners and weavers remained peasants, they earned part of their living from the plots on which their cottages stood; agriculture and industry were carried on together as almost an integrated enterprise. The man could work in the field while his wife spun; in winter, the man joined in industrial production. At harvesttime every hand was out in the fields, leaving spinning wheel and loom idle.

The putting-out system differed from peasant household production in that the merchant clothier, or entrepreneur, bought the raw wool and owned the product through its stages of preparation. Thus the peasant farmer came to work on materials that did not belong to him, and his position gradually changed to one of dependency. On the other hand, the work was performed at home (the cottage system) and at the worker's pace rather than in a factory under impersonal discipline. The merchant, furthermore, simply arranged the order and connection of the various technical processes without exercising direct supervision over their actual performance. Nevertheless, the merchant clothier who began putting out cloth came to control the entire production process and represents a step toward the industrial capitalist of the 19th century.

Advances in technology. Change in the scale of commerce through the establishment of large national markets was not the sole cause of changes in the organization of work during the Middle Ages. Equally important was the transformation caused by advancing technology, especially the application of wind power and waterpower, the beginning of a long development in the replacement of human labour by machine power. From the late 10th century, waterwheels, long used for grinding grain, were applied to many industrial processes: tanning, olive pressing, sawing, armour polishing, pulverizing, operating blast-furnace bellows, forge hammers, and grindstones, and crushing mash for beer. The first horizontal-axle windmill appeared in western Europe in 1185 and, within a short time, spread from northern England to the Middle East.

A good example of the change in industrial organization created by the application of waterpower to an industrial process can be seen in the fulling (*i.e.,* shrinking and thickening) of cloth, a process that was mechanized in the 13th century. Previously, fulling had been accomplished by trampling the cloth or beating it with a fuller's bat, processes dating back to antiquity. The fulling mill invented during the Middle Ages was a twofold innovation: first, two wooden hammers replaced human feet; and, second, the hammers were raised and dropped by the power of a water mill. A series of hammers could be set to work

Medieval power sources [margin note]

with only one man needed to keep the cloth moving properly in the trough, which was filled with water and fuller's earth. The mechanization of fulling also changed the organization of work indirectly, by causing the cloth industry to relocate along streams, often away from the former urban textile centres, thus bringing a relaxation of the old institutional constraints.

Perhaps the best example of specialization of labour in the Middle Ages is to be found in the large-scale metal-mining industry in central Europe, as described by the German scholar and man of science Georgius Agricola, in *De re metallica* (1556), the leading textbook for miners and metallurgists for nearly two centuries. In addition to the *Bergmeister* ("master miner"), the chief mine administrator, there was a hierarchy of clerical and technical personnel and a series of craftsmen specializing in different phases of the mining operation: miners, shovellers, windlass operators, carriers, sorters, washers, and smelters. The mines operated five days a week on a 24-hour basis, with the workday divided into three seven-hour shifts and the remaining three hours used for changing shifts. Animal power was used wherever possible, with teams of eight horses hitched in pairs to turn windlasses and raise buckets of ore or drain water from the mine. Agricola's illustrations show many types of pumps for mine drainage: crank-operated, treadmill-operated, and waterpower-operated. There were also suction pumps of varying degrees of complexity. All were operated by specialized craftsmen or mechanics.

The bellows for mine ventilation were also operated either by human and animal power or by waterpower. The other mining processes were less mechanized and were carried on much as they had been in antiquity. Ores brought to the surface were taken to a sorting table, on which women, boys, and old men sorted the pieces by hand, putting the good ores into wooden tubs to be carried to the furnaces for smelting.

Monumental construction. The mechanization that was changing the organization of work in large-scale industries throughout the medieval period was little apparent in the construction of castles, cathedrals, and town walls. The technology involved in the lifting of weights, for example, had made little progress during the Middle Ages, and, because the freemasons declined to handle large blocks of stone, the Romanesque and Gothic structures were built with smaller stone blocks, nevertheless achieving grandeur in scale. The organization of labour differed greatly from that employed in antiquity. These great monuments were the first in history to be built by free labour, including, besides the stonemasons, carpenters, glaziers, roofers, bell founders, and many other craftsmen.

The free and unfettered nature of medieval construction as compared with antiquity can be seen in the works themselves, which reveal a high degree of individualism, as well as in the records. For a long time it was believed that medieval craftsmen, especially those engaged in the building of cathedrals, were humble, self-effacing artisans who laboured piously and anonymously for the glory of God and for their own salvation. The industry of scholars has dispelled this myth. Medieval craftsmen often left their names or signatures upon their work, and surviving records show names, wages, and occasionally protests over wages. The artisans were by no means anonymous: historians have uncovered more than 25,000 names of those who worked on medieval churches.

Directing the guild craftsmen was the master mason, who, like his ancient counterpart, functioned in many capacities: architect, administrative official, building contractor, and technical supervisor. He designed the molds, or patterns, used to cut the stones for the intricate designs of doors, windows, arches, and vaults. He designed the building itself, usually copying its elements from earlier structures upon which he had worked as a master or during his apprenticeship. He sketched his plans out on parchment. As administrator, he kept the accounts, hired and fired the workers, and was responsible for procurement of materials. As technical supervisor, he was constantly on the job for spot decisions and planning. In the largest projects, he was assisted by undermasters.

Individualism of the medieval craftsmen [margin note]

16TH TO 18TH CENTURY

The proliferation of industry during the early-modern period—that is, from the 16th to the 18th century, immediately preceding the Industrial Revolution, properly so called—arose from three factors: (1) the growth of demand, or markets; (2) the introduction of new products; and (3) the development of new technology. The result was an increase in the scale of manufacturing industry throughout Europe, accompanied by changes in the organization of work.

The growth in the size of the market was caused only partially by the geographical explorations of the preceding era and subsequent colonization. Most of the new demand for goods came about as a result of a growing population, especially toward the latter part of the 17th century and beginning of the 18th century, and a rise in the standard of living, especially among the class of burghers, or bourgeoisie—the town dwellers. Many new products were also introduced into Europe, either directly, by the explorers, or indirectly, through expanded trade with distant points. The demand for new products also came from the growing affluence and changing pattern of living in European society. Handicraft production no longer sufficed, the guilds declined, and novel industrial patterns emerged. The change was less in the introduction of new mechanical contrivances than in the growth in scale of the application of power, primarily water and wind, to old devices and, even more significant, in the organization of work to meet the needs for production on a larger scale—the beginnings of the factory system.

The proto-factory of the 17th and 18th centuries centred in certain industries, especially textiles. The old guild corporations broke down, and the cottage system began giving way to larger units of production. The organization of commerce made great strides. New instruments in the fields of banking, insurance, and export marketing helped to amass capital and make it liquid for investment in industrial enterprises. In this movement toward the capitalization of industry, some of the smaller masters were driven down into the wage-earning class, while larger masters grew into capitalist employers.

In Britain, the development of commercial concentration—and hence of industrial scale—was mainly the work of large companies or corporate bodies (*e.g.*, woollen manufacturers, ironmasters, and hat makers); government encouragement was given this process by means of special legislation, especially grants of monopolistic charters. In France, however, the practice of mercantilism, a government-directed policy aimed at increasing national wealth and power, meant that the government itself took an active part in developing industries that were state owned and operated, among them the famous Gobelins tapestry works and manufactories for the production of furniture, porcelain, and other luxury items. Although the state-run factories in France represented at least two of the essentials of factory production—the gathering of large groups of workers in one place and imposition of disciplinary rules—they had little effect upon the organization of work, because they produced small quantities of luxury goods and hence amounted to large handicraft operations. Furthermore, despite their size, the French Royal Manufactories did not possess the third prime element of a true factory system, mechanization. The great historical change in the organization of work came in 18th-century Britain with the onset of the Industrial Revolution, largely as the result of the new technology of power-driven machinery.

Effect of new technology. The new machines introduced in the 18th century compelled a rational organization of job functions that was quite different from the old handicraft tradition of production. Adam Smith in *The Wealth of Nations* gave the classical description of the new production system as exemplified by a pin factory: "One man draws out the wire; another straights it; a third cuts it; a fourth points it; a fifth grinds it at the top for receiving the head; to make the head requires two or three distinct operations; to put it on is a peculiar business; to whiten the pin is another; it is even a trade by itself to put them into the paper; and the important business of making a pin is

in this manner divided into about 18 distinct operations." In the old craft guilds, the occupational unit was the individual worker, who usually performed all the operations in connection with the production of a single product. With machines, processes could be broken down into simple operations, each performed by semiskilled or unskilled individuals. Productivity, greatly increased, depended far more upon the rational organization of processes than upon individual skill. In the textile industry manual dexterity and alert response proved to be more valuable than experience, accounting for the use of inexpensive woman and child labour in the early mills. Some vestiges of the medieval guild apprenticeship, however, still remained in the early textile factories; the children were sometimes bound as apprentices for a period of at least seven years, usually until they were 21. In some areas, the old cottage system of textile production was moved to the factory, with the entire family employed as a work team. In those cases, the father would be employed for any heavy work while supervising his wife and children at the machines. Presumably the father also possessed the mechanical skills necessary to repair and maintain the machinery.

Because machines could justify their high cost only if a heavy and continuous demand existed for their output, their presence led to a division of labour between the entrepreneur who owned them and his employees. The owner supervised his workers, compelling them to work at the pace of the machine. Even in enterprises that were not yet fully mechanized, the advantages of factory discipline were apparent at an early stage of the Industrial Revolution. Josiah Wedgwood designed his pottery works at Etruria in England "with a view to the strictest economy of labour." His plant was laid out so that the pots were first formed and then passed through the painting room, the kiln room, the account room, in which an inventory of production was made, and, finally, to storage. In potteries before this time, the workers could wander from one task to another; in Wedgwood's, the men were assigned a particular post and worked at one task only. Out of 278 men, women, and children employed by Wedgwood in 1790, only five had no assigned post; the rest were specialists. While the argument is sometimes made that the division of labour destroyed skill, the fact is that it might also improve the quality of the finished product, for Wedgwood's pottery was superior to that of his competitors. It can be said that the division of labour does not so much destroy skill as limit it to a particular field of expression; and, within that particular task, it increases skills by continued repetition. It is interesting to note that Wedgwood's chief difficulty was not so much in training his workers as it was in introducing them to a novel form of discipline that ran contrary to centuries of independence. It was a constant test of Wedgwood's ingenuity to enforce six hours' punctual and constant attendance upon his workers, to get them to avoid waste, and to keep them from drinking on the job and taking unauthorized "holidays." Because he was a busy man involved in all the tasks of running an enterprise and could not stand over his workers and control their movements, he had to develop a hierarchy of supervisors and managers.

There can be little doubt that the condition of the workers, especially the women and children, in the early textile factories was miserable: 14 to 16 hours per day spent performing repetitive tasks in noisy, smelly, and unsanitary surroundings. The workers' slum homes were equally unhealthy. At this period the social question arose over the existence of poverty in a nation with capacity for producing enormous quantities of goods.

Development of new industries. The introduction of steam-driven machinery at the time of the Industrial Revolution brought new industries into being or transformed older ones. This was especially true of the metalworking trades, where technological innovations made possible the replacement of wooden machinery with metal and the manufacture of such items as metal nails, glassware, and iron bearings.

Furthermore, wood was being replaced as a fuel by coal, especially in England and northern France, where deforestation had made wood scarce. The pressure on fuel

Mercantilism in France

Factory discipline

supplies came not only from domestic heating requirements and from the metallurgical trades but also from the brickmaking, brewing, dyeing, and glassmaking industries. In coal mining, however, the division of labour remained much as it had been described by Agricola in the 16th century.

One of the greatest stimuli toward a more rational organization of work was the general demographic trend in Europe from the 17th to the 19th century. Population grew swiftly, moving from country to city. It is possible that only a few European cities—Paris and the great Italian commercial cities of Venice, Genoa, and Naples—had as many as 100,000 people at the beginning of the modern era. London may have had only about half that number. By the beginning of the 17th century, however, rapid growth had begun, and, by the end of that century, London probably had 500,000 inhabitants.

Population growth increased the demand for food and goods. Urbanization spurred innovation on the farm, such as improvements in plant and livestock breeding, advancements in fertilization practice, and rudimentary mechanization of many tasks.

Discovery of the New World.   Although exploration and colonization had originally been carried out in order to secure exotic and expensive spices, these products had little direct influence upon the organization of work in Europe. Even the enormous trade in semitropical items such as sugar and coffee had little effect in Europe. Instead, wheat, wool, and meat from the temperate areas ultimately brought about an international division of labour, with the New World colonies furnishing agricultural produce to the manufacturing countries of Europe. In the 20th century such a division still exists in somewhat different form, with the underdeveloped nations of the tropics supplying agricultural and industrial raw materials to developed areas. Exceptions to this rule are the United States and the Soviet Union, both of which possess vast territories and abundant natural resources and hence are largely self-sufficient.

Negro slavery

In its effect on the organization of work, slavery, linked first with sugar production and later with cotton, was the most important result of the discovery of the New World. Cultivation of sugarcane, especially its harvesting, requires a great deal of heavy manual labour. Harvested cane must be sent to a mill for grinding within a few hours after cutting; this requirement necessitated establishment of a plantation system in which the workers would be housed close to the fields and the sugar mill. The natives of the West Indies were not numerous enough to perform the required work and were temperamentally unwilling to engage in such labour, even when harsh means were employed to force them to do it. The requirements of sugar planters thus brought the introduction of agricultural slavery into the Western Hemisphere, which began as early as 1518, when the Spanish government granted a license to import some 4,000 African slaves into the Spanish colonies. The plantation system and the consequent demand for African slaves spread during the next two centuries throughout the sugar-growing areas, including the British West Indies. Indeed, the British islands of the West Indies carried specialization in sugar so far that they found it most profitable to devote nearly all their land to the export crop of sugarcane and to import other foods.

In the temperate zone, where sugar production was not possible, slaves were little used except in tobacco-growing areas until near the end of the 18th century. The Puritan communities in New England engaged in small family farming, while the Southern colonies employed indentured servants (white labourers who agreed to work a number of years for some person who had paid their passage to the New World).

Eli Whitney's invention of the cotton gin in 1793 lowered the price of upland cotton, caused that fibre's use as a staple for textile production, and resulted in the fastening of Negro slavery and the plantation system on the American South. While slaves provided the chief labour force for cotton, they also performed other tasks in handicraft and factory production and in domestic service, creating, in other words, a division of labour on the plantation.

The regional specialization in production led to sectional economic and political differences and ultimately to the American Civil War.

Organization of work in the industrial age

THE COMING OF MASS PRODUCTION

Mass production is the name given to the method of producing goods in large quantities at low cost per unit (see also INDUSTRIAL ENGINEERING AND PRODUCTION). Mass-produced goods are standardized by means of precision-manufactured, interchangeable parts. The mass production process itself is characterized by mechanization to achieve high volume, elaborate organization of materials flow through various stages of manufacturing, careful supervision of quality standards, and minute division of labour.

Machine tools and interchangeable parts.   The material basis for mass production was laid by the development of the machine-tool industry—that is, the making of machines to make machines. Though some basic devices such as the woodworking lathe had existed for centuries, their translation into industrial machine tools capable of cutting and shaping hard metals to precise tolerances was brought about by a series of 19th-century innovators, first in Britain and later in the United States. With precision equipment, large numbers of identical parts could be produced at low cost and with a small work force.

American System of manufacture

The system of manufacture involving production of many identical parts and their assembly into finished products came to be called the American System, because it achieved its fullest maturity in the United States. Although Eli Whitney has been given credit for this development, his ideas had appeared earlier in Sweden, France, and Britain, and were being practiced in arms factories in the United States. During the years 1802–08, for example, the French émigré engineer Marc Brunel, while working for the British Admiralty in the Portsmouth Dockyard, devised a process for producing wooden pulley blocks by sequential machine operations. Ten men, in place of 110 needed previously, were able to make 160,000 pulley blocks per year. British manufacturers, however, ignored Brunel's ideas, and it was not until London's Crystal Palace exhibition of 1851 that British engineers, viewing exhibits of machines used in the United States to produce interchangeable parts, began to apply the system. By the third quarter of the 19th century, the American System was employed in making small arms, clocks, textile machinery, sewing machines, and a host of other industrial products.

The assembly line.   Though prototypes of the assembly line can be traced to antiquity, the true ancestor of this industrial technique was the 19th-century meat-packing industry in Cincinnati and Chicago, where overhead trolleys were employed to convey carcasses from worker to worker. When these trolleys were connected with chains and powered movement was used to bring the carcasses past the workers at a steady pace, a true assembly line existed, with stationary workers concentrating on one task, performing it at a pace dictated by the machine, minimizing unnecessary movement, and dramatically increasing productivity.

Drawing upon observations of the meat-packing industry, the U.S. automobile manufacturer Henry Ford designed an assembly line that began operation in 1913. The result was a remarkable reduction of manufacturing time for magneto flywheels from 20 minutes to five minutes. This success stimulated Ford to apply the technique to chassis assembly. Under the old system, by which parts were carried to a stationary assembly point, 12½ man-hours were required for each chassis. Using a rope to pull the chassis past stockpiles of components, Ford cut labour time to six man-hours. With improvements—a chain drive to power assembly-line movement; stationary locations for the workmen; and work stations designed for convenience and comfort—assembly time fell to 93 man-minutes by the end of April 1914. Ford's methods drastically reduced the price of a private automobile, bringing it within the reach of the common man.

Assembly-
line
"speedups"

Ford's spectacular feats forced both his competitors and his parts suppliers to initiate his technique, and the assembly line spread through a large part of U.S. industry, bringing dramatic gains in productivity and replacement of skilled workers with low-cost unskilled labour. Because the pace of the assembly line was dictated by machines, the temptation arose to accelerate the machines, forcing the workers to keep up. Such "speedups" became a serious point of contention between labour and management, while the dull, repetitive nature of many assembly-line jobs bored employees, reducing productivity.

The new division of labour. The development of mass production transformed the organization of work in three important ways. First, tasks were minutely subdivided and performed by unskilled workers. Second, manufacturing concerns grew to such size that a large hierarchy of supervisors and managers became necessary. Third, the increasing complexity of operations required employment of a large management staff of accountants, engineers, chemists, and psychologists, in addition to a large distribution and sales force.

Mass production also heightened the tendency toward an international division of labour. The huge new factories often needed raw materials from abroad, while saturation of national markets led to a search for customers overseas. Thus, some countries became exporters of raw materials and importers of finished goods, while others did the reverse.

The mass-production farm. Agriculture underwent a transformation beginning in the 19th century comparable to the change from handicraft to mass production in industry. At the beginning of the 19th century, agriculture was primarily a family enterprise, employing traditional techniques and organization of work; despite some technological innovations such as the plow and seed drill, output per man was relatively small. In the late 19th and especially in the 20th century, output per farmer increased rapidly till in the most advanced countries a small minority of farmers supplied entire populations with food. These great changes were brought about by a series of advances in science and technology, including improved power sources, mechanical devices such as the reaper and combine, a scientific approach to plant and animal breeding, better food processing and preservation, more effective fertilizers and pesticides, and application of industrial management techniques to agriculture (see also AGRICULTURE and FARMING).

Transfer-
ring
industrial
methods to
farms

The organization of work developed in mass-production industries was not transferred intact to agriculture. The tasks involved in running a farm may change in accordance with the cyclical nature of the growing process and may vary greatly among different crops. They depend also upon the degree to which a given farm has been mechanized. The outstanding example of factory-type production in agriculture is in the U.S. poultry industry. A computerized feed bin, programmed with the exact quantities of nutrients required for health and quick growth, mixes the feed and delivers it automatically to the cage in which the bird is confined throughout its life. Water is delivered automatically, and waste is removed by mechanical means. When the chicken reaches precisely the correct weight for processing, that task is performed on an assembly-line basis. Application of these techniques has sharply reduced the cost per pound of chicken, and a form of protein that was once a luxury has become a staple item of diet. Capital investment in such factory farms is high, and production is carried on by giant companies.

Mass-production agriculture takes many forms. In the Soviet Union, *sovkhozy,* or state agricultural farms, are owned by the government; farmers are, in effect, state employees, but work organization resembles that in the West. Soviet collective farms are in theory cooperative associations of farmers who combine their land and capital, sharing proceeds in common. Each family on a collective farm, however, is permitted to own a small plot of land, so that modern and traditional work organization exists side by side. Centrally located machine tractor stations own and operate most of the agricultural machinery, contracting to perform work on nearby collectives. These stations also function as coordinating units; their supervisors control and check on plowing, sowing, cultivation, and harvesting in their region. At the machine tractor stations, organization of work is functional with separate operating, maintenance, and supervisory staffs.

SOPHISTICATION OF MASS PRODUCTION

Refinement of assembly-line techniques. According to Henry Ford, the assembly line was based on three simple principles: "the planned, orderly, and continuous progression of the commodity through the shop; the delivery of work instead of leaving it to the workman's initiative to find it; an analysis of operations into their constituent parts . . ." A scientific approach to these principles, the next logical step in the organization of work, had already been enunciated by the American mechanical engineer Frederick W. Taylor. This new field of study came to be known as scientific management. From Taylor's work, an entirely new discipline, industrial engineering or scientific management, emerged, in which the managerial functions of planning and coordination were elevated to a primary position in the productive process.

In Taylor's view, the task of factory management was to determine the best way for the worker to do the job, to provide the proper tools and training, and to provide incentives for good performance. Taylor broke each job down into its constituent motions, analyzed these to determine which were essential, and timed the workers with a stopwatch. With superfluous motion eliminated, the worker, following a machinelike routine, became much more productive. In some cases, Taylor recommended a further division of labour, delegating some tasks, such as sharpening tools, to specialists.

Growth of
scientific
manage-
ment

Taylor's studies were complemented by two contemporaries in the United States, Frank B. and Lillian M. Gilbreth, whom many management engineers credit with the invention of motion studies. In 1909 the Gilbreths, studying the task of bricklaying, concluded that much motion was wasted by the worker in reaching down to pick up each brick, devised an easily adjusted scaffold that eliminated stooping, and improved average work performance from 120 to 350 bricks per hour. Industrial engineering ultimately came to include all elements of factory operation within its compass—layout, materials handling, and product design, as well as labour operations.

Taylor and his disciples assumed that workers desired to be used efficiently, to perform their work with a minimum of effort, and to receive more money. Scientific management also took for granted that the worker would submit without question to having standardization of physical movements and thought processes. This philosophy proved incorrect, however, for it ignored human feelings and motivations, leaving the worker dissatisfied with the job. Some employers, furthermore, omitted the altruistic elements in Taylor's system and employed time and motion studies to set high norms of production and speed up the production line while still keeping wages down.

In the decade after 1910, when the principles of scientific management were being applied wholesale in U.S. industry, union opposition arose. Though the unions approved more efficient production arising from better machinery and management, they condemned the speedup practice and complained in particular that Taylorism deprived workers of a voice in the conditions and functions of their work. Complaints were also made that Taylorism caused irritability and fatigue along with physiological and neurological damage among workers. Misuse of the human element in production was causing declines in both quality and productivity. Industrial engineers then faced the problem of motivating the worker so that the combination of human labour and machine technology would achieve its fullest potential. A partial solution came from the social sciences, and, in the process, another new discipline—industrial psychology—was founded.

The major premise of industrial psychology is that mass-production technologies affect the worker both in the immediate job environment and in relations with fellow workers and supervisors. The first important discoveries in the social context of mass-production technology resulted from experiments made by the U.S. social scientist Elton Mayo between 1927 and 1932 at the Hawthorne plant of the Western Electric Company, in Cicero, Illinois. Mayo, who had earlier studied problems of physical fatigue among textile workers in a Philadelphia plant, was called in at the Hawthorne works, where industrial engineers were considering the potential effect on productivity of changes in illumination. The investigators chose two groups of employees working under similar conditions to produce the same part; the research plan was to vary the intensity of the light for the test group but to keep it constant for the control group. To Mayo's surprise, the output of both groups rose. Even when the researchers told one group that the light was going to be changed and then did not change it, the workers expressed satisfaction, saying that they liked the "increased" illumination, and productivity continued to rise.

Mayo saw that the significant variable was not physiological but psychological. A second series of experiments was performed involving the assembly of telephone relays; test and control groups were subjected to changes in wages, rest periods, workweeks, temperature, humidity, and other factors. Output continued to increase no matter how physical conditions were varied; indeed, even when conditions were returned to what they had been before, productivity remained 25 percent above its original value. Mayo concluded that the reason for this lay in the attitudes of the workers toward their jobs and toward the company. Merely by asking their cooperation in the test, the investigators had stimulated a new attitude among the employees, who now felt themselves part of an important group whose help and advice were being sought by the company. The name "Hawthorne effect" was given to such beneficial changes in workers' attitudes, and, within a short time, scientific management incorporated these new findings.

Psychological factors in work output

Mayo's studies had suggested that consultation, usually in the form of interviews between labour and management, gave workers a sense of belonging to a team. Industrial engineers and sociologists have suggested additional approaches toward improving motivation and productivity. These include job alternation to relieve boredom; job enlargement, or having the worker perform several tasks of his project rather than performing a single operation on it or joining together a series of small job elements into a larger whole; and job enrichment, redesigning the job to make it more challenging.

Increased mechanization and automation. The logical ultimate in the evolution of mass-production processes is automation. In its ideal form, automation implies elimination of all manual labour and the introduction of automatic controls, assuring accuracy and quality beyond human skills. Perfect automation has never been attained, but sufficient equipment has been installed in many industries to alter greatly the pattern of employment. Tasks formerly performed by machine operators on a production line have come to require only maintenance personnel, engineers, office employees, production-control specialists, and some others. Although automation has been described as a "revolutionary" development, it is actually the end result of the trend of mechanization that began with the Industrial Revolution.

The word automation was coined in the 1940s at the Ford Motor Company and was first applied to the automatic handling of parts in metalworking processes. The concept acquired broader meaning when the U.S. mathematician Norbert Wiener wrote about cybernetics, which he defined as control and communication in the animal and the machine; he anticipated the application of computers to a number of manufacturing situations. Wiener's prediction that the introduction of automatic machinery would swiftly give rise to mass unemployment was popularized during the 1950s and 1960s, causing considerable alarm. But automation was not introduced as rapidly as foreseen, and other economic factors have intervened to diminish the displacement of labourers.

The three sources of automation

Automation evolved from three interrelated trends in technology: the development of powered machinery for production operations; the introduction of powered equipment to move materials and workpieces during the manufacturing process; and the perfecting of control systems to regulate production, handling, and distribution. Devices to move materials from one work station to the next included conveyor-belt systems, monorail trolleys, and various pulley arrangements. The transfer machine, a landmark in progress toward full automation, moves the workpieces to the next work station and accurately positions them for the next machine tool. The first known transfer machine was built by a U.S. firm, the Waltham Watch Company, in 1888; it fed parts to several lathes mounted on a single base. By the mid-20th century, transfer machines were widely employed in the automotive industry, appliance manufacturing, electrical-parts production, and many other metalworking industries, in which they cut labour costs and improved quality by insuring uniformity and precision. Automatic controls represented an innovation when applied to all aspects of the production process. The simple cam, automatically adjusting the position of a lever or machine element, was an important control device in many early machines and, during the 19th century, was used to make many machine tools automatic. But cam devices have severe limitations in movement, number of changes, speed, size, and sensitivity. True automatic control cannot be attained unless the machine is sensitive enough to adjust to unpredictably varying conditions. This requirement demands the technique known as feedback.

Some students of automation claim that its primary goals are not necessarily increased productivity nor cost reduction but product reliability and quality control. Other benefits promised by automation include reduction of waste, improved plant safety, and centralization of control. Still, the most visible initial effects of automation have been reduction of costs and increases in productivity.

Effect on production. Increased mechanization and automation in the 1950s and 1960s brought employment declines in chemical, steel, meat-packing, and other industries in developed countries with large increases in output. Meanwhile the worker changed from machine operator to machine supervisor with the responsibility of monitoring complex and expensive computerized equipment.

The introduction of computers also affected the organization of work in the information sector of the production economy. File clerks, bookkeepers, telephone operators, and other skilled office personnel involved in information processing were replaced by semiskilled keypunch and tabulating-machine operators. Office work thus underwent mechanization as well. Indeed, the information flow in offices has been likened to the movement of materials in manufacturing: information, like materials, must be stored; typing or keypunching changes the form of the information, just as a machine operation changes the form of the workpiece; the value of the finished product is changed by adding information to it; and there must be a measure of quality control to make certain that the information is accurate. Just as automated machinery has done away with the jobs of many machine operators, integrated information-processing systems have eliminated many clerical tasks. In the production process, it provides exact control of inventory of raw materials, parts, and finished goods. If the billing process involves a standardized product such as electrical energy, drastic reduction can be made in accounting costs.

Automation in offices

Effect on labour. The widespread fear that increased mechanization and automation would cause mass unemployment caused many to overlook its great capacity for eliminating physical and mental drudgery. The effect of automation on employment has in fact proved slight. Though certain specific jobs or skills have been rendered obsolete, a vast new industry calling for different skills has grown up. Far more significant has been the trend in union–management relations to include productivity gains caused by automation in the collective-bargaining process, with a distinct tendency for the government in some countries to play a referee's role in adjudication of production-gain sharing.

Automation may thus be seen as improving efficiency and increasing production while relieving drudgery and increasing earnings—precisely the aims of Frederick W.

Taylor at the turn of the 20th century. The organization of human work, even in the most advanced countries, has by no means achieved a utopian character, but the arrival on the scene of the transfer machine and the control system has had a highly beneficial effect.

FUTURE TRENDS

It seems likely that the evolution of the organization of work will continue along established lines, probably at an accelerated pace. Automation is already being enhanced by the perfecting of robot devices, which, unlike ordinary automated machinery, can be programmed to perform a variety of tasks. The principal trends will be those already long established: the substitution of machine power for human, both for physical and mental labour; the steady transformation of the work force from producers to machine supervisors; and, consequent to the problems and possibilities created by this transformation, a change in the internal relationships among the work force.

Many of the specific effects of increasing automation are far from clear. An early conclusion that automation would demand an upgrading of the education of workers has proven hasty. While the expectations of employers and ambitions of workers have indeed contributed to a steady rise in educational quality of the work forces in advanced countries, the technology itself does not seem to do so, and in many cases automation actually reduces the educational level required in production. Even middle-management and engineering tasks can often be so simplified by the application of computers that their performance requires little education. Another, somewhat unexpected effect of the changing production process seems to be that dividing lines among old craft skills are disappearing. As machines handle more and more specialized tasks, the blue-collar worker tends to perform a broader range of duties than before, while the office worker concentrates more on a specialty.

Despite the direct benefits of automation in heightening efficiency and so providing the basis for higher wages and more leisure time, the trend toward consideration of workers' feelings and attitudes that began with discovery of the Hawthorne effect will surely continue. For one thing, some of the direct gains have been cancelled out by other factors; a factory worker of the 1870s, for example, might walk to work in a few minutes, but the same worker today may have to commute a long distance through heavy traffic. One study even showed that a modern worker has only slightly more net free time than his or her 19th-century forebear. Furthermore, many disadvantages of the old factories are distinctly present in modern production lines:

the noise; the physical strain; and the boredom induced by repetitive work. Labour can therefore be expected to continue pressing for a shorter workweek and to meet with a more and more favourable response from management. Studies have shown that production losses through shortening the week may be considerably less than would appear, because of reductions in absences and accidents and because of better work discipline.

The changes foreseeable in the character of the work force and its new relationship to machinery imply a fundamental transformation in the hierarchical pattern of management. Though factory organization has traditionally been pyramidal, the decline in number of production workers accompanied by an increase in "knowledge" workers is distorting the pyramid. This change may be related to the trend toward increasing application of the behavioral sciences to labour–management relations. In the pyramidal form of organization, it seemed natural to use a carrot-and-stick approach based on material incentives and penalties. In the emerging organizational pattern, increasing use of behavioral and other scientific disciplines may be anticipated. New concepts such as product, project, and free-form management, meaning specific approaches designed to meet the needs of particular portions of large organizations, are developing.

One significant trend is toward democratization on the job; this has been endorsed by many industrial psychologists and in at least two countries has been the subject of extensive and innovative experimentation. In Japan, "workers' circles," consisting of about a dozen workers engaged in a certain task, have been allowed to arrive at their own decisions on production methods and quality control. The introduction of this procedure has been accompanied by spectacular increases in industrial productivity.

These and other innovative measures also reflect a growing "systems approach" to production in which all elements—raw-materials acquisition, primary processing, transport, machine design, plant location, pattern of work force, and worker motivation—are taken into consideration. Despite many forebodings of a technology in which machines dominate human workers, there are increasingly hopeful signs that the production worker can use the machine to relieve the burden of physical and mental drudgery without becoming its slave, that the organization of work can be transformed from a nexus of impersonal relationships based solely or primarily on material incentives to a new and more satisfying relationship between managers and workers, workers and workers, and workers and machines.

(M.Kr.)

INDUSTRIAL AND ORGANIZATIONAL RELATIONS

"Industrial relations" or "organizational relations" as a subject of study is concerned with the behaviour of workers in organizations in which they earn their living. Its theoreticians attempt to explain patterns of cooperation, conflict, and conflict resolution among workers and among managers and between the two groups; they seek to discover factors determining the outputs of the organization, from physical product to human satisfactions or dissatisfactions; and finally they increasingly concern themselves with the relations between industry and community and with comparative international studies of behaviour in organizations.

The evolution of industrial relations

CONCEPTIONS OF THE WORKER

19th- and early 20th-century views. In classical economics, workers were treated like commodities, subject to the natural laws of supply and demand. Although classical economists readily acknowledged that workers are not motivated by money alone, they abstracted out of reality only the economic factors, which led them to consider workers as undifferentiated and passive instruments in the production process.

In the 1890s the American industrial engineer Frederick W. Taylor evolved an engineering approach to what was later called "scientific management." Taylor's approach was similar to that of the classical economists in regarding workers as passive instruments of production, but he did recognize differentiation among workers, at least insofar as degrees of skill were concerned. He developed methods for time-and-motion studies to determine the elements of particular jobs and the way in which these elements should be put together for the greatest efficiency. His approach focussed upon the individual worker; there was no place in his model for group membership or for the effects of groups upon individual behaviour.

A step further in the recognition of differentiation among workers came with the emergence of industrial psychologists, who were concerned with the measurement of the skills and aptitudes of individuals. At least in the early stages of these developments, workers were viewed as isolated individuals, and no attention was given to group phenomena.

Labour economists entered the field before 1900, concerning themselves particularly with the growth of unionization. Recognizing that the earlier approach of classical economics was deficient in treating jobs entirely in terms

Commodity view of labour

of supply and demand, labour economists saw workers as banding together as a means of influencing the supply of labour and the terms under which it could be purchased. Although the early labour economists recognized social aspects beyond economics in union organization and collective bargaining, they were concerned almost exclusively with organization at the plant or company level.

The advent of industrial relations. Although scattered courses pertaining to what we now call industrial relations were offered in departments of economics, engineering, and psychology, it was not until the 1940s and 1950s that a distinctive academic field emerged. The primary influence was the research program carried out by Elton Mayo in 1927–32 at the Hawthorne Western Electric plant, described above. The discovery by Mayo and his associates of the "Hawthorne effect"—an increase in worker productivity produced by the psychological stimulus of being singled out and made to feel important—and the ideas that they developed about the social dynamics of groups in the work setting had lasting influence.

Although the interpretations that Mayo and his associates made of the test room results have recently come under critical fire, the concern here is not with the validity of the conclusions but rather with the effects of the Hawthorne studies upon the subsequent development of the field. Publication of some of Mayo's writings and of the major research report in *Management and the Worker,* by F.J. Roethlisberger and William J. Dickson in 1939, attracted large numbers of sociologists, social psychologists, and social anthropologists into a field that had previously been limited to economists, engineers, and industrial psychologists.

Four general conclusions were drawn from the Hawthorne studies:

1. *The aptitudes of individuals* (as measured by industrial psychologists) are imperfect predictors of job performance. Although such measures may give some indication of the physical and mental potentialities of the individual, the amount he or she actually produces is strongly influenced by social factors.

2. *Informal organization* affects productivity. Although previous students of industry had looked upon workers either as isolated individuals or as an undifferentiated mass organized in terms of the formal chart of hierarchical positions and responsibilities established by management, the Hawthorne researchers discovered a group life among the workers. Though they were not the first to observe that individuals formed groups in industry as well as elsewhere, their report provided by far the most systematic description and analysis of work-group organization yet to appear. The Hawthorne studies also showed that the relations that supervisors developed with workers tended to influence the manner in which the workers carried out—or failed to carry out—directives.

3. *Work-group norms* affect productivity. The Hawthorne researchers were not the first to recognize that work groups tend to arrive at norms of what is "a fair day's work," restricting their production below that point even when they would be physically able to exceed the norm and would be financially rewarded for it. However, the Hawthorne study provided the best systematic description and interpretation of this phenomenon.

4. *The plant is a social system.* The Hawthorne researchers came to view the plant as a social system, made up of interdependent parts. Although there was some vagueness as to the identification of these parts and as to whether the parts should be considered to be in "equilibrium," the emphasis on interrelatedness had a strong influence on subsequent research.

Behavioral scientists had made their entry into the field by attacking the then-prevailing oversimplified notions of the individualistic economic man and the formalistic engineering notions of organizational structure, technology, and efficiency. As often happens in arguments between members of competing schools of thought, the force of the behavioral science attack carried some of its proponents so far as to view the work organization as simply a system of social relations. During the 1950s and 1960s the field

underwent a major process of redefinition, which consequently affected conceptions of the worker.

Behavioral scientists now recognize the importance of economic factors, but they see material rewards having an effect upon behaviour in combination with social and psychological factors, and they study the pattern in this combination. While not discarding their interest in interpersonal relations, students of organizational behaviour have become increasingly concerned with the ways in which technology and the formal structure of the organization serve to channel those relations.

CONCEPTIONS OF THE MANAGER

Changing conceptions of the behaviour of managers. Classical economists made no distinction between the manager and the entrepreneur, the person who brings together land, labour, and capital and puts them to work. Although experienced businessmen certainly recognized a distinction, it did not take hold in the literature until the appearance in 1933 of the classic study by Adolph Berle and Gardiner Means, *The Modern Corporation and Private Property.* When the authors demonstrated that in most U.S. corporations the owners (that is, the stockholders) played no direct role in the management of the concern and that the managers generally had insignificant holdings of stock, it became apparent that theories of entrepreneurial behaviour had little to contribute to the understanding of the behaviour of managers.

Somewhat earlier, Max Weber, a German economist and sociologist, had approached the study of managerial behaviour through his concept of bureaucracy. To Weber, bureaucracy did not have the negative connotations often heard in casual conversations; he used the term simply to point to a phenomenon of growing importance even in his time: the large organization with fixed positions linked together in a hierarchical pyramid, with specialization and division of labour and with established rules and regulations governing behaviour. To Weber, the manager was the individual who interpreted and applied the rules of the organization. Later organizational sociologists, though recognizing the importance of Weber's contribution in focussing attention on the impersonality and rationality of modern industrial and governmental organizations, pointed out that Weber's model failed to take into account some of the most important features of the modern business organization. They argued that it gave an unduly rigid picture of organizations, that it failed to devote attention to processes of change, and that it built so exclusively on the hierarchy of authority as to neglect relations not explicitly defined by the structure. In any case, Weber's formulations were of interest primarily to social scientists. Practicing managers and students of business in business schools, at least until recently, were likely to have little familiarity with the Weberian approach to managerial behaviour.

The early model of the manager taught in American business schools followed lines of functional specialization. In these terms, the manager was the one who had mastered such subjects as accounting, marketing, production, finance, and so on. Later, it was recognized by theoreticians and practicing managers alike that management was a good deal more than the sum of these specialized functions, and this realization in turn led to the conception of the manager as generalist, who would understand the various specialized functions and who would be able to coordinate these functions and the people engaged in them. The emphasis turned to decision making.

In the academic as well as the business world today, the most widely espoused conceptions of managerial leadership are called "participation management," a term popularized by the American psychologist Rensis Likert, in whose terms the skilled manager is one who talks and acts "in terms of groups," who consults with groups of subordinates and even seeks to involve them in the process of decision making. The approach involves a focus on interpersonal relations, on the quality of communication, and also upon the problem of helping people to penetrate social facades so that they are better able to deal with the real thoughts and feelings of their associates. Participation

Western Electric- Hawthorne experiments

Max Weber's notion of bureaucracy

management thus has no recognized place for management technology and formal organization. The emphasis is entirely upon interpersonal relations.

In the 1940s a competing approach to management arose out of the field of anthropology when investigators saw that since interpersonal contacts were observable, quantifiable, and regular, the study of their patterning could provide a foundation for analyzing any set of social relations. While such investigators concentrated on the observation and measurement of interaction, they gave major emphasis to technology and the formal organizational structure by which such interactions are channelled. They conceived the role of the manager as that of an organizer and monitor of the interactions in his organization.

Changing conceptions of management's responsibilities. Since the early days of the Industrial Revolution, management spokesmen have been concerned with defining and redefining the responsibilities of the company to the community.

The Industrial Revolution brought about great accumulations of wealth and also focussed public attention on the apparent negative effects of rapid industrialization on working people. To what extent workers in the new factories were worse off than they had been in the much smaller scale cottage industries may be a matter of continuing debate, but there is no question that large concentrations of workers—men, women, and children—crowded together in oppressive physical conditions and working long hours for low pay made the problem much more publicly visible. In the earlier period workers had dealt with owners and agents of whom they had some personal knowledge. The establishment of large factories destroyed the direct relationship, and it became less credible for the owner to claim that he took a personal interest in his workers.

In the last two centuries management people have taken, in general, two broadly different positions regarding management's social responsibilities.

The view of laissez-faire

The laissez-faire attitude. The first stance represents a sort of combination of laissez-faire economic theory and the Protestant ethic. In this view the owner or manager has no responsibility for the welfare of the workers outside the immediate plant situation; man's station in life is a reflection of his intrinsic merit in the eyes of God; the wages and other labour costs incurred by the firm are the result of competitive market conditions. In this view, then, the owner's or manager's responsibility to his employees began and ended with operating the firm in such an efficient manner that it was able to meet competition in the market place, and if all businessmen similarly followed a policy of intelligent self-interest, the broad social interests of society would be better served than by any other policy.

The expression of this point of view has undergone changes in style over the years. Today one hardly expects most businessmen any longer to state the position with religious overtones, and even the most laissez-faire inclined spokesman is likely to concede that there are some social problems that are not resolved by private initiative in pursuit of enlightened self-interest. However, managers with this view of the world tend to take a defensive position regarding the responsibilities of their firm beyond the gates of the plant. They recognize that popular opinion and government policies and programs may require them to take on activities not dictated by immediate material interest, but the tendency is to do what has to be done to keep out of trouble with the outside world and nothing more.

Paternalism. The other stance begins with the assumption that management has a social responsibility to the communities in which its plants are located. If one states the situation in this general way, hardly a management spokesman today would deny this social responsibility, and yet, when one gets beyond rhetoric, one finds a wide variety of views as to what actions—if any—management should take. In assessing the present scene one might do well to examine the historical evolution of conceptions of management's social responsibilities.

Robert Owen

The Welshman Robert Owen was the first industrialist to back up words about management's broad social responsibilities with a program of action. Although Owen was interested in broad questions of social reform, he did undertake to carry out his philosophy in the area under his immediate control. Having arisen out of the work force in a textile mill himself, he was concerned with the social and economic conditions of the workers and believed that the economic success of the enterprise did not have to depend upon exploitation of workers. In New Lanark he built workers' housing, schools, and a store that were far superior to contemporary standards for workers' communities. He was also an influential figure in the early development of the cooperative movement in England.

Owen's ideas and the successful operation of his plant and community during his lifetime impressed many social reformers and some businessmen as well. His influence was clearly visible in the establishment of the industrial city of Lowell, Massachusetts. Francis Cabot Lowell had made a trip to England and Scotland to study textile mills and related community problems before launching his own enterprises in Massachusetts. He had found New Lanark far more in harmony with American ideals regarding the dignity of man than the average English industrial plant at the time. Lowell faced a social problem of an immediate practical nature. He had to recruit a labour force, largely female, not available in the towns where he was building his plants. To meet this need the firm built, in what came to be called the city of Lowell, a number of boarding houses especially for young women. Each house was under the control of a woman who was supposed to ensure the morality of her charges, and the women were not allowed out of the house after 10 PM except with special permission. Lowell also made liberal provisions for the building of schools and churches. He and his associates stimulated the Middlesex Mechanics Association, which sponsored cultural and educational programs.

Pullman

Somewhat later, George M. Pullman undertook to build around his Pullman Palace Car Company a complete community (the town of Pullman, now a part of Chicago) that would house all the employees and provide for all the essential facilities. In the early period of the Pullman Company, the quality and condition of worker housing was probably a good deal superior to the average for other industrial workers.

When Henry Ford startled the industrial world with his announcement of the $5-a-day wage in 1914, he followed it with steps designed to help workers make good use of their increasing affluence. The company already had a small legal department set up to help workers with the complicated problem of home buying, and now Ford established what he called a sociology department. It was staffed with social workers who made home visits to workers' families to provide advice and help on family problems. Members of the department were also free to talk with workers within the plant during working hours in efforts to straighten out family problems.

Although many other companies in the industrialized countries pursued programs based on an assumption of managerial responsibility for the conditions of life outside the plant gates, these cases provide illustrations of the types of projects undertaken.

How does one assess the success of such efforts along these lines? In the United States the Lowell project was the longest lived and the most admired by foreign visitors. Charles Dickens compared Lowell very favourably with the typical English industrial city. Nevertheless, the distinctive character of Lowell had been lost before the end of the 19th century. Native New Englanders were replaced in the work force by the new immigrants and their children, and the women of these immigrant families had no rural homes to return to after several years of labour in Lowell, as had the New England girls. The boarding houses thus lost their primary rationale, and by 1900 all of them had been sold by the companies. Even in the early years of the Lowell textile industry, conditions could not have been quite so idyllic as described by some of the visitors, for there were nine recorded strikes or lockouts in the mills in the period 1834–79. The strikes greatly increased in frequency after this period, when management was faced by changes in the social composition of the work force brought about by successive waves of immigration.

The Ford experiment in social welfare also was short-lived. Management in the plants argued that the sociology department was interfering with production and that the workers did not like having social workers prying into their personal affairs.

Company towns

It would seem to be more than coincidental that some of the most bitter strikes in the United States—from Pullman in 1894, through the Southern mill towns in the 1930s, to Kohler, Wisconsin, in the 1960s—have taken place in company towns. Whatever economic grievances workers have had in these situations, it is clear that economic exploitation is not a complete explanation of the bitterness of the disputes. Whether benevolent or oppressive, the manager in the company town has far more extensive control over the lives of the workers than is found in other towns and cities. In the company town the owner or his agents not only run the plant; they also run the government, provide the local services, run the hospital, and operate the company store. Whatever grievance a resident of the town may have is, to that person, the fault of the company. When clashes in labour relations do arise in these situations, they are thus likely to look more like a struggle for independence than a standard union–management dispute.

The rise of unions in the mass-production industries of the United States in the 1930s helped to persuade executives that a paternalistic approach to labour and community relations was no longer feasible. Extensions of management's social responsibilities were now achieved through collective bargaining. Still, these broader benefits, such as pensions and health insurance, were limited to the workers and their immediate families. There was a tendency to assume that any responsibilities for the welfare of the community as a whole should be assumed by government.

Conceptions of public relations and community service. Although management's withdrawal from paternalistic community responsibility was accelerated by the growth of unionization, company officials began increasingly to see the need for the company to play a role in the communities where its plants were located. This need grew in part out of the recognition of changes in top management's relations to the industrial communities. In an earlier era factories had been locally owned, and the owners played a prominent role not only in the management of the plants but also in the affairs of the community. Now as local plants became part of large corporate organizations with headquarters in cities far away from most of the plant locations, and the management of the local plants came to consist of corps of college graduates who moved up the ladder of promotion by moving from plant to plant and city to city, company executives came to recognize the threat of company estrangement from the local communities. Management found itself in an awkward position when local union leaders who had lived all their lives in the community were leading other local residents in a strike against absentee top management and its local temporary representatives.

Public relations

A common reaction to this estrangement was the development of public relations and community service programs. Public relations men sought to tell the communities how good management was being to them and to inform management about problems in company-community relations. Top management began to redefine the role of plant manager to include the function of representing the company to the community, and this meant participating in community service activities along with locally based business and professional men. Thus, it became common to find the plant manager and other members of the management group playing prominent roles in the community fund drives and other service activities. There were two important characteristics of such community service activities: they had no direct influence upon life inside the factory, and they involved simply a commitment to maintaining the community rather than any initiative toward changing it.

Conceptions of broad social responsibility. In the 1960s management people began to recognize that the community service orientation was not adequate for coping with the problems of cities that were erupting in violence. By this period the leaders of the powerful unions that were negotiating with the leading companies had come themselves to be part of the new industrial elite. No longer were the unions seen as leading a broad movement for social change and a possible radical reordering of society. They came increasingly to be viewed as organizations devoted to the defense and improvement of the status of workers who held a relatively privileged position in society compared to the "underclass" of workers who were employed in low wage situations, who worked only sporadically, or who were unemployed. In this period it became evident that the acute and chronic problems affecting society as a whole and industry in particular were not going to be solved simply by having a "good" management relating to its union and indulging in "good" relations with the communities.

In the past, management's recruitment, selection, and training policies had been based on an unquestioned assumption: that it was the responsibility of management to try to skim the "cream" off the labour market. As technological progress steadily reduced the proportion of unskilled jobs in industry and business, there arose the increasingly severe problem of workers who were not only unemployed but were, in fact, classified as "unemployable." When unskilled jobs had been more readily available, the man with little to offer in educational background or craft training could nevertheless find a place at the bottom in the plant and learn enough on the job to move up into at least semiskilled positions. When this bottom rung of the employment ladder had been knocked out in so many plants, men and women with below-average education and training found sharply reduced opportunities to get a start in industry. So long as each firm sought to skim the cream off the labour market and so long as government employment services sought to refer only the best qualified applicants to employers, hundreds of thousands of people were being systematically excluded from the benefits of an otherwise affluent society.

Recognition of this problem has led to a redefinition of managerial and governmental social responsibilities. Government agencies are beginning to develop programs to give special attention to placing the "hard core unemployed." A number of companies have relaxed their standards of qualifications for employment, at least for a segment of the prospective work force, and have even actively recruited in urban slum areas and developed special training programs so that workers who would otherwise be excluded could be eased into factory jobs.

Helping the disadvantaged

Some companies even went considerably further in the assumption of social responsibilities, as they made changes in plant location or purchasing policy in recognition of new social needs. For example, one major corporation built a new plant in one of the most depressed slum areas of a great metropolitan centre with the explicit purpose of providing employment and training for people who otherwise would never have had an opportunity to work for such a corporation. With this new wave of social concern by leaders of business, many younger executives have become dissatisfied with the old-fashioned service approach exemplified by the community fund and other charitable activities and have begun searching as individuals for ways in which they can help members of disadvantaged groups to develop the knowledge and skills required to launch and develop small businesses. Professors and students in some of the leading business schools have become similarly involved in offering consultation and assistance to the small businessman, especially in the slums of cities. Even if only a small minority have been moving in this direction, this nevertheless marks a distinct change from the earlier implicit assumptions that the only purpose of the business school was to educate men for business leadership—which meant in those days prominent positions in large corporations.

This new business orientation, however, should not be thought of in terms of a broad realignment of ideas and activities. The most far-reaching financial and personnel commitments have been made by those few companies that have such massive resources and such strong competitive positions that great sums of money can be committed to enterprises that are speculative at best from an economic standpoint and can only be justified in terms of meeting management's public responsibilities—and improving the corporate image. Most companies did not go very far or very fast in these new directions. Even when impressive numbers of "hard core unemployed" were hired and retained in the work force for some months, as business activity slackened, these newly hired special problem cases were likely to be the first ones to be laid off.

The responsibilities that some business leaders were claiming for industry clearly cannot be borne by industry alone. A job development program for disadvantaged groups cannot be successful during an economic recession. Even in a prosperous time, companies are not going to commit massive resources and personnel to the task of recruiting and training and counselling and otherwise assisting those who otherwise would not fit in, unless the government provides financial incentives. The future will no doubt see much experimentation between industry and government regarding the distribution of responsibilities, costs, and payments involved in providing economic opportunities for disadvantaged peoples.

However limited the private industry commitment to broad social and community concerns was in the 1960s, there is no possibility of turning back to the isolation of the old laissez-faire philosophies. If management people felt impelled in the 1960s to take more initiative in tackling the problems of the great cities, lest the cities themselves explode in ethnic and class warfare, from the 1970s industry faced the challenge of environmental pollution. Public campaigns for the control and reduction of pollution are bound to involve a further redefinition of management's responsibilities to society. Here again one can assume that some industrial leaders will take the initiative in investing large economic and human resources in the reduction of the pollution for which their firms are responsible, and yet the magnitude of the problem will clearly call for a combination of governmental and private company action. One can expect the government to be increasingly active in setting standards, exacting penalties on polluters, and offering financial incentives to those who reduce pollution. Whatever combination of efforts evolves, this newly recognized problem is bound to increase the concern of management people for the social, economic, and environmental problems in which they and their companies are inevitably involved.

The discussion of management's responsibilities has thus far been limited to experience in the United States and Great Britain. In the developing countries, a different situation is found.

Especially in mining and petroleum operations, the companies (nearly always foreign owned) have found it necessary to build roads and housing for managers and workers, to provide schooling for children of employees and medical care for employees and their families, and so forth. In the face of rising nationalistic sentiments, many such companies have been seeking to disengage themselves from responsibilities not directly connected with their industrial operations. Community facilities cannot be simply abandoned, however, and the companies face difficult negotiations to establish the terms under which the government will take over the responsibilities to be relinquished by the companies.

Cross-cultural comparisons

Do the principles of organizational behaviour apply universally, or must they be adapted to different social structures and cultures? Starting with the Hawthorne studies, much of the work in this field has been in the United States. Some of the most important studies have been done in England, but the two countries are culturally sufficiently close to provide little opportunity to test the universality of propositions across cultures. In recent years, however, first-rate field studies in industrial and business organizations have been carried out in Latin America, France, Japan, India, and a number of other countries, so that one is at last in a position to examine the interrelations of behaviour in organizations and the culture and social structure within which the organization lives.

The chief problem is one of moving beyond the anecdotal to the general level. Anyone with experience in a country other than his own can tell how "they do things differently over there," but a series of colourful tales is no substitute for systematic and comparative analysis. For that purpose one needs to look at phenomena in different cultures along the same dimensions. One may look at two dimensions that are provided by the environment of the organization and two dimensions that are provided by the internal life of the organization. The "outside" dimensions are: (1) the social structure of the country and (2) the sentiments and value orientations characteristic of the culture. The "inside" dimensions are: (3) the structuring of interpersonal relations and (4) the distribution of rewards and penalties.

In terms of this framework, if one examines the interrelations of the organization and the culture and social structure, one is studying the relations of variables in dimensions 1 and 2 to the variables in 3 and 4. When one speaks of "variables," precise measurements are implied. What follows, however, gives only some preliminary interpretations from various studies without presenting the evidence. The discussion begins with comparisons between four countries or culture areas in terms of these four dimensions.

TYPICAL NATIONAL OR REGIONAL SYSTEMS

The United States. The United States is characterized by a social structure that is relatively open and fluid. Social-class differences are recognized, but they are not as marked in terms of differences in clothing and style of life as they are in many other countries. (Black Americans are of course the major exception to this generalization, since skin colour and other physical characteristics still have important status implications.)

In sentiments and value orientations the United States is characterized by a general belief in the equality of man (although, of course, some segments of the population have been unwilling to include blacks and other groups in this view of the world). Ideally, the individual is expected to be rewarded in his work and elsewhere according to his achievements and not according to his birth or other ascribed characteristics. A high positive value is placed on work. Although white-collar work has more prestige than blue-collar work, there is less social distinction between these categories than is found in most other countries. Compared to other countries, there is in the United States in general a high level of faith in people. That is, there is a presumption that other people are men of goodwill and can be trusted.

In interpersonal relations within organizations, there is more fluidity in the sense of rapid changes in organizational structure and in the relations among people than is found in many other countries. Authority relations are characterized by the tendency to question orders and yet to work within the system of authority; that is, the right thing to do is to confront your superior with disagreements and to raise suggestions and complaints for face-to-face discussion. Although the United States has well-developed structures and procedures for third-party intervention in union-management relations, there is a high value placed on the parties being able to thrash out their differences among themselves.

Along with this belief in the values of face-to-face discussion and resolution of conflicts goes a strong belief in the values of decentralization and dispersion of power. It is felt that the people directly facing the problems are the ones who should have the responsibility for solving those problems, with "dictation" from above to be avoided as much as possible.

There has been so much geographical mobility in the United States that family ties, beyond parents and children, are often exceedingly weak. Furthermore, it is generally believed that a man should get ahead on his individual merits, and nepotism generally is frowned upon.

Although unionization has had an important influence on the development of trends toward a more collective orientation, systems of distribution of rewards and penalties are still based upon assumptions of achievement motiva-

Efforts to reduce environmental pollution

Dimensions for comparative analysis

Merit
and
reward

tion, and efforts are generally made to provide individual rewards and penalties that are related to the "merits" of the individual. For example, the individual's pay is determined by the job he holds and, if incentive rates exist, by the amount of his production, without regard for length of service and family responsibilities, which in some other countries may be influential factors. (Of course, length of service may be important in determining access of the individual to a particular job, but he is rewarded or penalized in the performance of that job, without any direct consideration of his length of service.)

Latin America. Compared to the United States, the countries of Latin America have social structures that are closed and rigid—that is, class lines are sharply drawn, and there are difficult barriers to mobility (although mobility in recent years has become somewhat easier). Family ties are strong in the sense that people tend to think and act in terms of family, when they are in other spheres of activity. Family solidarity is built around a dominating father figure and a protective mother figure. When the father dies, the solidarity of the family may break down in competition for the power and resources that he formerly controlled.

Governments tend to be strongly centralized in the capital city, with key local officials being appointed by the central government. On the other hand, the formal centralization of power in the government may not go along with the corresponding power of implementation of government decisions in local areas. Local people who occupy important economic and social positions are often able with impunity to disregard some governmental decisions.

In sentiments and values one finds a higher degree of acceptance of authoritarian leadership and a tendency to value a man for what he *is* rather than for what he *does*. The *is* tends to be defined in terms of certain ascriptive characteristics such as social class position and family membership. There tends to be a sharp distinction between blue-collar and white-collar work. Work in general is not conceived as an end in itself, but as simply a means to an end, so that when a man has accumulated the resources he needs in order to live in the pattern customary to his social status, it is perfectly appropriate for him to reduce his work efforts or turn the work over to somebody else. Latin America is characterized by a low level of faith in people in general and by a tendency to believe that only members of one's family or close friends are to be trusted. There is a high value on individualism, but it is individualism detached from achievement orientation. Here there is an apparent paradox—the general acceptance of authoritarian control as legitimate vies with a desire to avoid the consequences of that control. This leads people to value escape from control rather than direct confrontation with those in control.

Social
rigidity

In interpersonal relations there is a rigidity of social categories with problems of communication between them. The common pattern emphasizes authoritarian control. There tends to be great difficulty in resolving problems between organizational units on the same level, with a consequent dependence upon the arbitration of a superior authority in the case of disagreements. In the field of union-management relations there is seen this same pattern: the avoidance of direct interpersonal confrontation and working out of joint problems in favour of appealing issues to third parties (government officials) for decision.

The distribution of rewards and penalties tends to be on an ascriptive basis. The distribution is in terms of broad social categories, but modified by personal influences. Thus it is common for individual subordinates to be rewarded not so much by merit or performance as by presumed loyalty to the superior who controls the rewards.

Japan. In Japan's social structure, class distinctions are strongly marked, and there is relatively little mobility across class lines within the career of the individual. That is, the young man who begins full-time work in the blue-collar ranks has little opportunity to move into white-collar or managerial positions. On the other hand, the educational system is an important channel of intergenerational mobility. The son of a blue-collar worker who passes his entrance examinations to college and satisfactorily completes a college career is admitted without question into the ranks of management. College entrance is much more competitive than in the United States, for the proportion of high school graduates admitted to college is far lower in Japan. On the other hand, the high school student is not competing with fellow students for the favourable recommendations of his teachers, since admission is determined by scores on a uniform national examination.

In Japan social activities and loyalties centre on the family to such an extent that other institutions tend to be conceived in terms of family relations and obligations.

In the field of government, even in periods of dictatorial government, Japan has been noteworthy for the extent of collective responsibility and group action at the level of the village or neighbourhood.

In sentiments and value orientations one sees considerable respect for hierarchical positions and considerable deference accorded to people of superior status and age. Although there is emphasis upon individual achievement in the educational system, when a man is once in his job he is expected to value his loyalties to the group more highly than his individualistic impulses.

There is a high dignity assigned to work, and in fact it appears that people are expected to work harder than they are anywhere else in the world. The business firm is looked upon as if it were a family, which means that the employees have permanent obligations to the firm, but likewise the executives have permanent obligations to employees. Although there have not yet been adequate surveys taken, Japan probably would score high in faith in people. There seems to be a general assumption that a man will live up to his responsibilities. What is known as the "shame principle" has an influence, and it would appear that the most potent force in bringing a deviant into line is the expression of disapproval by his associates, which is expected to make him feel ashamed of himself.

In interpersonal relations there appears to be considerable deference to authority, and yet a common system of decision making in organizations (the "ringi system") involves a group of subordinates signing their names to a proposal that they then refer to the next level of authority—and on up the line. When a proposal comes up with the backing of the group involved, it is very difficult for a superior to veto it.

Regarding the resolution of conflicts or disagreements between equals, one finds that Japanese culture discourages the face-to-face thrashing out of differences that is favoured in the United States. On the other hand, the culture also inclines each individual to be especially sensitive to the thoughts and feelings of those with whom he has to work, so that the individual is unlikely to advocate strongly a course of action that would appear to threaten the interests of others. Furthermore, since men move up in the hierarchy primarily through increasing age and seniority, department heads are not in competition with each other in the same sense that they are in some other industrial countries. This movement up by age and seniority means that the people currently working together will already know each other very well from past association and will act in line with the thought that they will be working closely together in the future. This tends to build a sense of collective responsibility and to discourage individualism. (The Japanese have a variety of devices—such as early retirement, assigning men to positions in subsidiaries and suppliers, and promoting men into positions of prestige but little concrete responsibility—to meet the problem of those who, with advancing years, do not show the capacities the company needs in higher positions.)

Collective
responsi-
bility

The family principle applies even to union-management relations. Most Japanese unions are limited in membership to those working in a particular firm, and there is little tendency in union-management relations for unions to seek to organize workers from many firms into one unit. Even when unions strike the efforts seem to be directed not so much at economic damage to the firm as at the public embarrassment of the management. The words and actions of the union leaders are directed at gaining public attention and wide publicity, in the hopes that management will be shamed into being once again a good father to the members of the organizational family.

In Japanese firms the distribution of rewards and penalties is on a highly collective basis. Although incentive rates are gaining some ground in Japan, the prevailing pattern has been to reward people in terms of their membership in the organization, with pay based on a combination of the rate for a particular position, the years of service to the firm, and the employee's family responsibilities. In management also, rewards tend to be of a collective nature, with people moving up according to length of service and seniority. There is a tendency to avoid the assignment of individual responsibilities for decisions. When a decision turns out obviously to be wrong, it is the management group that suffers shame rather than a particular individual. Of course, within the group, there must be some recognition that certain individuals played a more prominent role in making a decision than others, and thus the outcome of a given decision must have some effect upon the way that members of a management group regard each other, but there have as yet been no studies of this aspect of the problem. In any case the management group presents a united front to the outside world.

France. In social structure France appears to have moderately firm social-class divisions with mobility across class lines generally being limited to those who come up through the educational system. On the other hand, France is exceedingly high in intergenerational mobility.

France is characterized by an exceedingly high centralization of political power and administrative organization, with all important decisions being made in Paris. The French bureaucracy appears to operate with greater efficiency than the typical Latin American bureaucracy, for decisions centrally arrived at tend to be more effectively implemented in the provinces. Much of French life is organized around the family.

In sentiments and value orientations France seems to be somewhere between the extremes in achievement-ascription orientation, with the social characteristics of the individual counting strongly for his position in society, but with individual achievement also highly valued. France is characterized by the high value placed on individualism, which in this case is associated with resistance to authority, and by a strong commitment to the social segment in which the individual finds himself, in opposition to outside powers. Although there are no measures of this dimension, one would expect France to come out on the low side in interpersonal trust. In values regarding work one would expect France to fall somewhere between the extremely high values given in Japan and the United States and the extremely low values found in Latin America.

The best existing study of French industry (Michel Crozier's *Bureaucratic Phenomenon*) shows interpersonal relations being channelled within fixed social categories, so that there is extremely little social interaction among them and differences of interest are next to impossible to negotiate. People in each segment of the organization seem to band together to resist higher authority, which makes adaptation difficult in their relations with higher authority or in the horizontal dimension. As individuals have developed their defenses against higher authority, they have tended to cope with the rules and regulations from the top by following the formal rules but often evading the spirit of the regulations.

The distribution of rewards and penalties tends to follow social categories, with little attention to individual performance.

LESSONS TO DERIVE FROM THE TYPICAL SYSTEMS

The relations among dimensions. The profiles presented above are of course highly oversimplified, and in each country or region organizations can be found that do not fit the models presented. Furthermore, each country or region is in the process of change so that the profile of today may not fit the situation of tomorrow. Within these limitations, if one assumes that the profiles are reasonably accurate, a further question remains: what are the relations among the four dimensions?

For example, what is the relationship between the degree of interpersonal trust found within a culture and the characteristic pattern of interpersonal relations found in the organization? It would seem that where interpersonal trust is low the organization will be centralized, with little delegation of authority and responsibility—for delegation does not take place unless superiors have a fair degree of trust in subordinates. Individuals and groups will have difficulty in working out agreements through negotiation, for negotiation again requires a degree of trust, or else the individuals will feel that they cannot count on the concessions that might be offered by the other side in the negotiating process. Centralization is accompanied by authoritarian leadership. This leads subordinates to compete for the favour of the boss, and such competition tends to promote distrust among the competitors. Thus it can apparently be said that a low level of trust tends to foster the development of a certain pattern of interpersonal relations, and that such a pattern tends to reinforce a low level of interpersonal trust.

Implications for development. In recent years U.S. conceptions of the business enterprise and of business practices have provided the chief model that proponents of aid to the developing countries have sought to export. The U.S. model is based upon certain assumptions regarding human nature, without taking cultural difference into account. When one compares the United States with Latin America one might indeed assume that, if certain U.S. value orientations and patterns of interpersonal relations could be exported, the Latin American countries would accelerate their economic development.

When one looks at Japan, this simplistic notion breaks down. Since it began to industrialize, Japan has advanced as rapidly as has the United States and currently appears to be moving ahead even faster. The Japanese experience demonstrates that the U.S. type of individualism with its stress on personal responsibility and rewards and penalties geared to performance is not the only route to development. Japan has had extraordinary material success with a collective orientation and a pattern of distribution of rewards and penalties based on group membership. Nevertheless, although the contrasts are indeed striking, one should not overlook the common elements. Both the United States and Japan place a very high value on the dignity of work—including work with the hands. Furthermore, although the Japanese discourage individualism in the organization, they place a very high value on achievement orientation in the school system.

These observations suggest certain lessons for those seeking to accelerate industrial and economic development in the underdeveloped world. The cultural differences between the United States and Japan make it clear that there is no "one best way" to industrial development. Furthermore, the elements of culture do not operate independently but must be understood in relation to one another. For example, if one were able to build up in country X the high degree of collective orientation found in Japan but failed to produce also the high level of achievement motivation and commitment to hard work characteristic of Japan, one could hardly expect an accelerated rate of development.

Cross-cultural studies do *not* suggest that when one tries to accelerate development for country X one must leave its culture alone. Cultures are constantly changing, but they do not transform themselves overnight. The introduction of modern industry is bound to have effects upon the culture. The industrial developer cannot expect just to do his own project and expect to hold everything else constant. He must understand the cultural context into which his project fits and plan both for the adaptation of the project to the existing culture and for the production of new types of behaviour essential to the project and not previously provided by the culture.

Work careers

In general, managers and workers have quite different work careers, so that it is necessary to consider them separately.

THE STRUCTURE OF WORK CAREERS

Managerial careers. Increasingly in all industrialized countries managers are recruited from among those who have graduated from a university or college. Although

American and Japanese models of development

Education
and
training

there is a good deal of variation from industry to industry within the same country, it is increasingly rare for a man to start as a factory worker and to rise beyond first-line supervision and into higher ranks of management. Higher management does recognize, however, that the man fresh out of a university lacks enough detailed knowledge of the problems and possibilities of his company immediately to be worth the salary it is necessary to pay him. There are two common responses to this phenomenon. One is to recognize that the investment will not immediately bear fruit and to make a further investment in the new employee by providing him with an elaborate training program. In addition to formal instruction, the training period may involve rotating the individual through a broad range of jobs, giving him exposure to a variety of experiences, and yet not depending on him to any great extent for performance. The justification for this approach is that the initial investment in the man will make him more valuable to the company in later years. There are two disadvantages: the man may leave the company before the investment in his company education has been recovered, and many claim that the best way to learn on a job is to assume responsibility for results.

The other approach is to place a man immediately on a job in which he has responsibility for results. This provides the challenge lacking in the first approach, but it has possible disadvantages. The entry job may be very narrow and limiting and thus may not provide very valuable experience for later development of the executive.

Some managements are coming to take an approach to the training of executives that is different from either of the extremes just discussed. They claim that in a highly industrialized society jobs on the managerial level change so rapidly that a man's practical knowledge can easily become obsolescent when he is ten years out of the university, even if he had learned originally all of the right things in his engineering or business education. The remedy for this obsolescence appears to be to encourage managerial employees to take refresher courses in programs of continuing education from time to time.

To what extent does moving up in the management organization involve moving around the country geographically? A large company is likely to have plants all over the country, and it is taken for granted that any major promotion often involves selling one's house and moving into another community. Even when the executive is working for a small company, he may find that he makes contacts leading to better opportunities in other companies, and so he transfers not only geographically but also from company to company. Although there are yet no international comparative studies on this point, one may assume that the United States is on the high end of the range in the freedom with which executives move from company to company, whereas in Japan the movement from one to another company would be exceedingly rare.

Can an executive refuse an offered promotion if it means movement to another city? The answer to that question for the United States is necessarily ambiguous. Rarely is an executive told that he will have to move or else lose his job. In other words, he is not ordered to move. At the same time he may well understand that, if he refuses the offered promotion, he may get the reputation of not being sufficiently ambitious and aggressive or sufficiently loyal to the company. He may then find that, if he later looks for a promotion and is even willing to go to another city, he has gotten into the box of the "not promotable" and is blocked from further career advancement.

Workers' careers. The structure of the blue collar worker's career is quite different. His working career can be divided into four parts: initial period, trial period, stable period, and retired period. In the initial period the worker is still going to school and tries out a number of part-time jobs. Knowledge of what jobs an individual has had in the initial period provides very little predictive evidence regarding the long-run career development of individuals in the United States. In Latin America the future manager is exceedingly unlikely to have had any experience as a part-time manual worker in his youth, whereas in the United States a young man who is aiming for college and, later,

Workplace
mobility

management positions may well take on part-time jobs in manual labour before he is through his education, without any feeling that this is inappropriate from a status point of view. In fact the college man who has earned money as a youth as a construction labourer or as a service station attendant may later talk about this experience as if he were proud of it, and indeed he may find that other people give him some credit for the breadth of his experience.

It is when the worker reaches the trial period that the dividing line between future managers and career blue-collar workers is encountered. The college-educated manager abandons manual jobs (except perhaps incidentally during vacations), whereas the manual worker has his first real job (outside of vacation periods) even though he may not yet be committed to that job or that employer. He compares notes with friends and keeps looking around for something better. He may change within a few months of employment. Even in the so-called stable period, there may be a fair amount of movement. A study by the American sociologists Seymour Martin Lipset and Reinhard Bendix in the city of Oakland, California, surveyed 935 male heads of families with an average of 25.3 years experience in the labour force and showed that they averaged nearly five (4.8) distinctly different jobs each. In the retired period, even though the individual severs connections with a regular employer, he may still take on part-time jobs.

Along with stages in the worker's career go shifting attitudes toward his job. When the worker remains with the same company, his attitudes toward the job and the company tend to follow a curvilinear pattern: high at first, then dropping through the middle period, and rising in the later parts of his career. Individuals tend to begin work with such unrealistically high expectations as to the nature of the jobs and the opportunities before them that disillusionment then sets in, but after some years they adjust themselves, lower their expectations, and express more satisfaction with the work situation.

Worker's
attitudes
toward
his job

Geographical mobility seems to vary with the field of work activity and the level of skill. There is a good deal of geographical movement in the construction industry generally, and especially in such lines as the forming of structural steel, the laying of pipelines, and the construction of dams. In terms of skill levels those at the top in certain crafts find that they can readily move around the country and pick up jobs, whereas those in the middle skill levels do not have the abilities to offer that would enable them to be so mobile. Those at the bottom, perhaps because of the combination of enforced layoffs and their own feelings of lack of reward in the job, tend also to be rather mobile.

A number of studies have shown the reluctance of factory workers to leave their community when the plant shuts down. It is now clear that simply the availability of jobs at high levels of pay elsewhere is not enough to move people. Ties with friends and family make workers reluctant to leave, but there can also be good economic reasons. If the worker owns his home in a community where a plant has shut down, he is likely to find the real-estate market so depressed in that community that if he had to sell his house he would get only a fraction of what it would cost to buy a house in a community to which he is moving. Therefore he is likely to conclude that it is best to stay where he is in the hope that the job market will pick up.

SOCIAL MOBILITY BETWEEN THE CLASSES OF WORKERS

Are opportunities for social mobility in the United States much greater than in other parts of the world, as many U.S. citizens have generally been inclined to believe? For lack of truly comparative data, this is a difficult question to answer. On the matter of social mobility within the career of one individual there are very few cross-cultural data. On intergenerational mobility (from father to son), the complexities of comparing whole occupational structures from country to country generally are too great. There are some studies of movement between blue-collar and white-collar work, however. Although the first studies suggested there was little difference among industrialized nations in these rates of movements, further research has tended to confirm the U.S. ranking at the top in upward mobility (high blue- to white-collar, low white- to blue-collar movement). In this regard the United States appears substantially above Sweden, England, Japan, West Germany, The Netherlands, and Italy. On the other hand, one study has shown France at approximately the same level with the United States in these mobility rates.

In recent years there has been a popular belief that young persons of humble origins no longer have as many opportunities to reach the top of large business enterprises; the idea is that there are fewer self-made men among the business elite. Scholarly studies comparing recent decades with such periods as the 1920s, however, indicate that social mobility in this respect has remained virtually unchanged. It is true that a college education is far more necessary today, but then more people are going to universities. The rate of social mobility to the top is about the same.

Since rates of mobility depend not only upon the social structures of the countries in question but also upon the rate of industrial expansion (or contraction) and upon changes in the structure of jobs, it is uncertain whether the rate of mobility of country X is characteristic of that country over a number of generations or is a product of economic trends in one period of time. Population trends may also be important. The high upward mobility rate of France may be partly explained by a relatively low rate of population growth over a long period and a high rate of industrial expansion in recent years.

Worker behaviour and formal organization

Some years ago this section would have begun with a discussion of "formal" versus "informal" organization, but more recent research seems to suggest that this dichotomy is a misleading way of looking at the field. Roughly speaking, the dichotomy was this: formal organization comprised the specifications of management; informal organization, on the other hand, included such things as the behaviour of workers as they banded together to determine how much production was a "fair day's work," how they should behave toward the supervisor, and so on. Informal organization also covered the ways in which the foreman actually worked out an adjustment with his workers, quite apart from the specification of his duties by management. The problem with this dichotomy arose in trying to distinguish between the formal and the informal at the level of behaviour. At the extremes there was no problem: one could readily distinguish the behaviour of the foreman giving a worker orders on what to do next and the behaviour of the foreman in conversing with the worker about some athletic event. The difficulties arose as one moved in from those two extremes to the very common situation in which the informal and formal seemed to be mixed together in action. In fact, the better the foreman and the worker were getting along together, the more difficulty one had in distinguishing between formal and informal behaviour.

The way out of this dilemma proved to be to distinguish between behaviour on one hand and formal organization on the other. With this approach formal organizational structure is limited to such elements as can be determined without behavioral observation. For example, the organization chart that is available for inspection in most companies provides official management's conception of the organizational hierarchy. Job descriptions tell (in management's view) what workers are supposed to do and how they are supposed to do it. There are rules and procedures established by management concerning the distribution of authority and responsibility. Where these matters are not written down or drawn on charts (though they are in most large modern organizations), the problem is somewhat more difficult, but one can still approach the study of formal organizational structure through interviewing management people to determine their conceptions of the nature of the hierarchy, of the distribution of authority and responsibility, of the nature of particular jobs, and so on. In other words, with this approach one deals with the formal management theory of the way in which the organization is designed and is supposed to operate.

Using this approach involves no assumption as to what extent observed behaviour will correspond to the formal organizational structure, but there must be the assumption that the formal organizational structure will indeed *tend* to influence the behaviour to be observed. However, we are not here talking about informal versus formal organization but rather about the relationship between the formal organizational structure and observed behaviour.

FACTORS AFFECTING WORKER ATTITUDES AND BEHAVIOUR

What factors affect individual and group behaviour in organizations? It is necessary to consider first certain factors built into the jobs; later the effects of managerial leadership can be considered.

Financial considerations. Wages and fringe benefits are important criteria whereby workers judge whether a job is a good one or a poor one. There is a general expectation that the wages paid should be in line with the prevailing social evaluation of the jobs, so that it becomes impossible to separate the rate paid from the prestige that the job holds. One must distinguish between money as a motivating force for organizational membership or for superior performance. Where the individual is paid a fixed rate for the job he holds, the money itself can serve only as an incentive to maintain a minimum performance level that will keep him in the organization. Greater performance must be elicited through other means. It is only when the money paid bears a relationship to the amount produced that money has a possible motivational effect upon productivity.

Incentive systems have important effects upon the behaviour of workers and supervisors and also upon the problems of plant administration. The effectiveness of the individual incentive system depends upon setting the rates-per-unit-produced high enough to motivate workers to put out extra effort and still not so high as to be unduly costly to management. Rates are set by time and motion study. Once the desired sequence of methods has been determined, it should be a simple technical problem to measure the number of units that the worker produces in a given time period—except that the accuracy of measurements depends upon selecting workers having "average skill" and working at a "normal pace." Workers, of course, recognize that if they are able to maintain a slow pace during observation and yet simulate diligent effort, they are likely to get a price-per-piece that will allow them to make high earnings without excessive effort. Some workers develop great skill in this type of make-believe. Experienced time-study men recognize that workers are trying to fool them, and so they tend to make allowances for the amount that they are being fooled. This transforms what is intended to be a scientific procedure into one that is a mixture of measurement and speculation.

The difficulties of rate setting would be great enough if management had only to set a rate once and then continue the rate for years, but in most modern organizations this is far from the case, for frequent changes in products, technology, and work methods upset the original conditions. When any major change takes place, there is a clear understanding on the part of both labour and management that a new rate is called for, thus setting in motion once again the complicated procedures. Perhaps even more difficult from a social standpoint are those instances in which the changes being introduced are small. Most union contracts hold that piece rates are to be changed only with the introduction of a "major" change in job content, but the parties frequently disagree on whether or not a given change can be classified as major. Then, too, over a period of months management may introduce a series of small changes, every one of which could be considered as minor, but all of which together might add up to "major."

At what point does management claim the right to introduce a new rate? Suppose, for instance, that an improvement in question is something developed by a worker, as often happens. If management allows the improvement to be introduced without a change in rates, then that worker and all others who work on the same job may be able to earn far more than others on similar jobs, thus disturbing the wage structure. On the other hand, if management intervenes and sets a new rate, the workers will feel that they are being deprived of the fruits of their ingenuity and skill. In any event, the complexities of the rate-setting process are such as to elicit pressure tactics on the part of workers against management. Although the overall effect of the piece-rate system in the average case will probably be greater production than could be achieved without it, it also tends to promote a substantial increase in conflict or at least to give the parties a set of difficult problems to resolve.

Motivational and social problems of incentives vary according to whether they are based on the individual, the group, or some larger unit. As a rule, the larger the social unit covered by an incentive system, the simpler the problems of administering the system, but the more remote from the incentive formula is the motivation of the workers. When an incentive formula is based upon the performance of the entire plant, individuals can be motivated only if the formula is linked with a system of continually involving workers and supervisors and management people in discussing ways and means of improving general performance. The individual piece-rate system, on the other hand, has interesting effects upon supervisors. Where a piece rate is in effect, the supervisor does not need to check so often to make sure that people are working. If the particular rates have been accepted by workers as more or less reasonable, they are likely to work at much the same pace whether the foreman is present or not.

Technological considerations.   This is not to suggest that the only way to keep workers at work is to give them a financial incentive or check closely on their performance. There are workers so committed to their job that they work diligently regardless of a supervisor's presence. But, in any event, the worker is importantly affected by the technology, the flow of work into which he fits, and the nature of his particular job. This is most clearly evident in automotive assembly-line technology, in which the individual's work is paced by the movement of the conveyor belt that brings to him the machine or part of the machine on which he is to perform his particular operations. The individual himself maintains a relatively fixed position. As he works faster he can move a few feet up the line, and as he works slower he can move a few feet down the line, but he cannot move very far in either direction without interfering with the work of others.

Research has shown that the automotive assembly line is one of the most oppressive industrial environments yet constructed by man. There is also evidence of the particular aspects of the environment that elicit the worker's negative reactions: the pressure to keep up with the line (workers constantly seek to bid on the few jobs available in the assembly plants that will get them off the line); the monotony of constantly repeating a simple task (even on the assembly line there is evidence that satisfaction with the job correlates with the number of operations performed); and the restrictions on social interaction (some research has shown that workers who express a need for social interaction, as most do, are more negative toward the job than those who express no such need).

Although the assembly line provides useful illustrations of the effect of technology upon job satisfaction, one must not think that such technology is representative of modern industry. Actually the machine-paced conveyor belt of the automotive assembly line provides only a small fraction of industrial jobs, and, with advancing technology, that fraction is declining. As several researchers have shown, the satisfactions that workers find in their jobs vary enormously from industry to industry. At the low end of the scale are the automotive plants and textile mills, in which a worker faces constant work pressure, cannot control the pace of his work, lacks a choice of work techniques, and cannot move about very freely. Toward the high end of the scale, there are such industries as chemicals and printing, in which there are higher levels of worker skills, more freedom of physical movement and choice of work methods, and generally greater worker satisfactions. It is interesting to note that the skills involved in these more "satisfying" industries are of two quite distinct types. In chemicals very little hand manipulation is involved, and

the skills are of an intellectual sort, the operator having to interpret meters and charts and then, on the basis of this diagnosis of the condition of the process, make the appropriate adjustments. By contrast, the skilled jobs in printing place a premium on hand manipulation. Apparently jobs that require either type of skill can offer important intrinsic satisfaction to workers, and the skill level naturally also provides satisfactions that go with the higher prestige job.

Social researchers have also found a correlation between the level of skill required and the mental health of workers—the higher the skill level the better the mental health. And this correlation extends into management—with higher management people enjoying better mental health than lower level supervisors. The same general conclusion seems to hold for physical health. When a well-known executive suddenly succumbs to a heart attack, one is inclined to attribute the event to the tensions peculiar to the executive life, and yet studies have demonstrated that the incidence of heart attacks is greater at lower management and worker levels than it is among executives. These studies do not *prove* that experiences on the job account for differential health. Studies in various countries have shown a consistent relation between social class and health, both mental and physical—the lower the social class, the poorer the health. Thus, until one can sort out the conditions of family and community life from the plant environment, one will not be able to determine the health effect of a particular job situation, but one can only assume that workers expressing very negative attitudes toward their work are subject to more adverse effects in regard to health.

Organizational considerations.   The worker's satisfaction with his job situation is not determined entirely by the characteristics of the particular job he holds. It makes a great deal of difference in his view of himself and his future whether his job is in a line of promotion so that he can look forward to moving up to jobs at successively higher levels. If the individual is on a "dead-end job," however secure it may be, one can expect him to be less satisfied than if he were on a job paying the same money but also offering opportunities of promotion. Industries differ markedly in this regard; some provide an individual with opportunities for a series of promotions up the line, whereas others are so divided up organizationally that individuals are boxed into departments within which only a few promotions are available. The contrast should not be drawn only in terms of the possibility or impossibility of a worker moving up from his job; one must also think in terms of "probabilities" provided by the proportions of jobs in each category. For example, in automotive assembly plants there are jobs off the line, and workers do get promoted to be foremen, but these higher level jobs are so few relative to the number of jobs on the line that the average worker must seek to adjust himself to a working life of trying to keep up with the line.

The *structure* of jobs within a department or other work unit affects worker behaviour too. As Leonard Sayles, an American student of business administration, has shown, where jobs are homogeneous as to work performed, level of skill, rate of pay, and working conditions, there is greater likelihood that the workers will band together to exercise pressure on management in advancing their interests than will be the case with a department in which the jobs are heterogeneous. In the homogeneous situation management finds it difficult to improve the situation of one worker without similarly affecting all of the others, and management similarly has difficulty in making an adverse decision that does not affect all workers in the department in a similar way. The similarity of conditions that workers face thus tends to promote work-group solidarity and effective negotiation with management. In the heterogeneous situation individuals may have opportunities to profit at the expense of fellow workers, so that the worker is tempted to try for individual gains at the expense of group members.

It has been widely assumed that satisfying and dissatisfying elements in jobs fall at opposite ends of the same continuum: that the absence of negatively valued characteristics in a job will lead to job satisfaction and that,

Assembly-line technology

Correlations between skills and mental and physical health

The issue of the relation between satisfaction and motivation

similarly, the absence of positively valued characteristics will lead to dissatisfaction. The American industrial psychologist Frederick Herzberg has challenged this apparent truism with a "dual factor" theory of job satisfaction and motivation. His "satisfiers" are related to the nature of the work itself and to the rewards growing directly out of work performance. These are factors such as sense of achievement, recognition, interest in the work itself, and advancement. The "dissatisfiers" are associated with the individual's relation to the environment in which he does his work. Company policies and ineffective administration rank highest in this dimension, followed closely by incompetent technical supervision. Also involved are such items as working conditions, salary, and interpersonal relations with supervisors. Herzberg uses his analysis of satisfaction-dissatisfaction in order to get at motivation. He argues that the *presence* of "satisfiers" tends to motivate people toward greater effort and improved performance, whereas the *absence* of "dissatisfiers" has no effect upon motivation. Subsequent research by others has yielded both confirming and conflicting evidence on the existence of two distinct factors, so that the issue remains open. Nonetheless, Herzberg's separation of satisfaction from motivation promises to clarify future research.

CHARACTERISTICS OF MANAGERIAL LEADERSHIP

Vertical relationships. The man-boss relationship has received more research attention than any other aspect of organizational behaviour. Many students of supervisory leadership have been concerned with ways in which the exercise of authority could be made compatible with democratic ideology. Would the "employee-centred" supervisor, who showed concern for the welfare of his workers, be more highly regarded by the workers than the "production-centred" supervisor, who focussed all his attention on getting out the product? Would the "employee-centred" supervisor also get more production out of his department than the "production-centred" supervisor? In other words, were consistent relations to be found among supervisory style, worker satisfaction, and productivity? Early students of this relationship were hoping to find that virtue paid off—that a good democratic leader not only was better liked by his subordinates but also got more production out of them. The first studies did indeed seem to support this proposition, but in later years many conflicting findings have been reported—so much so that the conclusion must be that no systematic relations between worker productivity and worker satisfaction can be shown.

"Employee-centred" and "production-centred" supervisors

Why has so much research on leadership style by so many able people led to so few firm conclusions? The first answer relates to the particular methodology used in studies of supervisory leadership: the questionnaire survey. With this method, research men drew conclusions not only about worker attitudes but also about the supervisory behaviour that the workers thought that they were experiencing. In other words, the behavioural categorizations of supervisors (as general or close supervisors, for example) were not based upon the direct observation of supervisors but rather upon the inferences of subordinates. The early studies also suffered from a neglect of technology and organizational structure. It was as if workers and supervisors were living and acting exclusively in a world of interpersonal relations. Only gradually, as researchers sought to find explanations for unexpected results, did they take note of the differences in supervisory roles growing out of differences in technology and the nature of the job. For example, in one study it was found that, in *production* departments, foremen who were seen by workers as high in "initiation structure" (telling workers what to do, checking up on performance, etc.) were judged by their superiors to be more effective foremen than those who were lower on "initiation structure" and higher on "consideration," perceived as concern for and responsiveness to workers' needs and desires. On the other hand, in *maintenance* departments, those foremen higher on "consideration" and lower on "initiation structure" were more highly rated by their superiors. Findings such as these suggest that, even if such studies had provided good behavioral descriptions of supervisory leadership styles (which they did not), one

could still not hope to show a consistent relation between leadership style and productivity except under certain specified conditions.

The work of the industrial sociologist Joan Woodward in England has related leadership to technological conditions. Woodward and her associates carried out an impressive study of 203 manufacturing firms in south Sussex, eventually concentrating their attention upon the relations between technology and formal organizational structure. In order to compare so many units, Woodward worked out a typology of technologies according to types of production. The unit or small-batch type involves separate production of individual units or production of small numbers of the same unit. Large-batch or mass production involves relatively standardized production of large numbers of the same unit. Continuous process involves industries such as petroleum and chemicals in which the fluids and gases flow through the process in continuous form.

Technological considerations

When Woodward lumped all of the plants together, she was able to find no clear structural patterns emerging, but, when she sorted them out into technological types, she discovered that each type had its characteristic ratio of workers to first-line supervisors and also of those reporting directly to the chief executive. Thus in unit or small-batch production plants, the first-line supervisor had an average of 23 persons working for him, whereas the average rose to 50 in large-batch or mass-production plants and dropped to 13 for the first-line supervisor in continuous-process plants. The ratios of those reporting to chief executives ranged from a median of four in unit production to ten in continuous process, with large-batch and mass production falling in between with seven. Woodward also marshalled evidence indicating that these ratios were related to the efficiency of the plants. On the basis of ratings of outside observers regarding the efficiency of the units, she found that those rated "above average" tended to have ratios of workers to first-line supervisors and of executives to chief executives that were close to the average for their category, whereas the firms judged "less successful" tended to be above or below the average figures. Her figures therefore suggest that each type of technology has its own optimum ratios of personnel at the various levels.

Woodward's findings have devastating implications both for the theorists of scientific management and for its principal critics. Scientific management theorists sought to establish, as a universal principle of management, an optimum "span of control" ratio of personnel reporting to a given superior. Woodward demonstrated that the search for such a universal principle was fruitless: there could only be an optimum ratio under certain specified technological conditions; under a different set of conditions a different ratio would apply.

Critics of scientific management had been arguing that the span-of-control ratios advocated in the literature necessarily meant that large organizations must have a long hierarchy of authority. They claimed further that a long line of authority produced the evils of poor communication, excessive control of subordinates, and poor morale of workers and supervisors. They proposed a counter ideal of the organization with a broad and flat organizational structure. Increase the number of people reporting to a superior, they argued, and you reduce the control he can exercise over any of them; and by thus increasing the freedom of subordinates, one can expect to increase their job satisfaction and also their productivity. The claims of these critics, however, are not without problems: although there may indeed be a tendency in large organizations to build a hierarchy of authority excessively long and narrow, just how flat the organization structure should be cannot be determined on the basis of any universal principle but must be determined according to the type of technology involved.

The Woodward study also has important implications for work on supervisory leadership. When one considers the differences in the behavioral requirements for the supervisor directing the work of 13 men and the supervisor directing the work of 50 (with those ratios being determined in part by the technology), one must recognize that universal generalizations regarding the man-boss relationship must be either highly superficial or misleading. This does not mean that generalizations are impossible, but it does mean that propositions regarding supervisory leadership style must be placed in a context of the particular type of technology and organizational structure in which the supervisor functions.

Types of lateral managerial relationships. The literature on supervisory leadership also faces another difficulty. Most of the studies are written as if the organization consisted exclusively of vertical relationships. This is a gross oversimplification. Even at the level of the first-line supervisor, research data suggest that the more effective foremen are not distinguished from the less effective in the amount of time that they spend with their subordinates but rather in the amount of time that they spend with their direct superior and with staff and service people. It is only the beginning of the analysis to point out that the supervisor or manager has many other relationships outside of the direct line of authority. To advance one's understanding one needs to be able to classify these into types. Below, with some modification, is the typology suggested by Leonard Sayles; the manager of a production department in a large complex organization is involved in eight types of lateral relationships: (1) work flow, (2) buy-sell, (3) service, (4) scheduling, (5) auditing and standard setting, (6) stabilization, (7) advisory relations, (8) innovation.

Work flow. Here the manager is engaged in efforts to work out adjustments with managers whose departments both precede him and follow him in the flow of work.

Buy-sell. In this relationship (called trading by Sayles), the manager is engaged in negotiating with the departments that supply him with parts for his operation and perhaps also with the purchasing department in an effort to get materials at prices and quality that will permit him to improve performance of his department. On the selling side, he seeks to persuade the company salesmen or managers of other departments using his production to accept the kinds and quantities of products that his department can most effectively produce. He is also engaged in an exchange of favours with other people in management, seeking to get them to do things for him, responding to their requests, or offering help with the expectation of reciprocity in the future.

Service. In this relationship, the manager seeks to develop such a relation with maintenance crews as to provide for repair and general servicing of his machines according to the most convenient schedule for his production and in line with the quality of performance he needs.

Scheduling. Production planning involves a manager in relations with people in another department who are occupied with determining what his department shall produce and in what sequence the production shall be run. Although the scheduling department must concern itself with the coordination of production throughout the plant, the manager may find that if he develops effective relations with schedulers he can persuade them to make adjustments in the schedule for his production problems.

Auditing and standard setting. This involves the manager of a production department in relations with people who are concerned with checking and recording his costs and with establishing the cost-production standards of performance against which he will be measured. Since a manager's performance is judged by his superiors in terms of his meeting or failing to meet these standards, it is of great importance whether these standards are set in a way that the department manager and his associates can consider "reasonable."

Stabilization. This involves the relations of the department to other units in the plant in cases in which a decision that the manager might make within his department would have repercussions throughout the plant. For example, there may be a policy as to the frequency and amount of pay increases that can be authorized, with the provision that the manager cannot deviate from this policy without approval of the personnel department. Or the manager might conclude that he could reduce his costs if he contracted out for one item used in his production, but he finds that such a decision would involve the plant in problems with the union as well as threaten other relations within management. He must therefore secure approval from some organizational unit dealing with such stabilization problems before making this change.

Advisory relations. The manager may find a number of people more than willing to offer him advice that he feels he does not need, whereas he has trouble getting the advice that he feels would be really helpful. It is then his problem to work out ways of blocking off the unneeded advice without offending the advisers and developing relations with those who can really help him so that he can call upon them when help is needed.

Innovation. The manager has always to recognize that there are development engineers and applied-research people who are constantly searching for ways of introducing changes in the technology, work flow, or products produced in his department. Any such changes designed to bring about improvement in the future are bound to present some problems for the man who is trying to meet the day-to-day standards of performance. If he simply opposes all efforts to introduce changes into his department, he will get a reputation as an old-fashioned stubborn fellow who is not in line with management's future plans. On the other hand, if he just lets the innovators move things around at will, he may find himself in a position in which his current performance is suffering severely. The department manager therefore must try to fit himself into the innovative process in such a way as to strike a balance between the needs of change and progress and the needs of maintaining current performance.

The complexity of horizontal and diagonal relationships. Although each of the relationships described above influences the vertical relations between the manager and his subordinates and superiors, none of them involves the direct exercise of authority or the submission to authority. To complicate matters further, the relative status levels of the two people in the relationship are crucial. From the standpoint of the manager in question, one may regard a relationship as either diagonally up or diagonally down. For example, a statement from the plant personnel man (ranked below the plant manager) may be taken as advice that the plant manager is free to disregard, whereas the same statement from the vice president for personnel is bound to appear in quite a different light. The plant manager recognizes that technically he has not received an order from the vice president, and yet he knows that if he disregards the statement he is running a serious risk. If there are no observable adverse consequences from his failure to take the vice president's advice, the plant manager may have no problem, but if he gets into some kind of trouble that his superiors think he could have avoided by taking the advice, then he may be severely criticized.

The manager or supervisor is constantly engaged in a complex network of horizontal and diagonal relations. It is of course important how the manager or supervisor gets along with his immediate subordinates, but his relations with his subordinates are strongly influenced by his handling of the other sets of relationships. If the manager cannot organize smoothly the work flow relations between his department and others, his own production will suffer delays, and his subordinates, especially if they work on piece rate, will complain that they are losing money. If he cannot get maintenance service for his machines when needed, he will drop behind in his production and will feel under pressure to try to get his subordinates to put out extra effort. If those setting standards for his department call for a level of production that his subordinates do not think reasonable, he will nevertheless have to try to get it out of them. Furthermore, there are cases in which a good relationship between workers and a foreman has deteriorated in reaction to changes in the foreman's horizontal and diagonal relations with others. Under these circumstances, it is hardly surprising that a focus of research upon man-boss relations in isolation has yielded so few concrete results. If one takes seriously the notion that the organization is a social system made up of interdependent parts, and if one considers the horizontal, diagonal, and vertical relations to be the parts of the organization, then it naturally follows that generalizations regarding one part will be faulty unless they are stated in terms of the conditions of the other parts.

In sum, management involves far more than directing subordinates and being responsive to one's organizational superior. The manager is involved in a complex network of relationships and finds himself frequently in a situation that social psychologists describe as role conflict: people in different positions in the organization have conflicting expectations regarding the way that he should behave. In the long run, he will be judged even by his superiors by the way he appears to get the job done, and getting the job done requires negotiating with people in horizontal and diagonal relationships and developing some reciprocity with subordinates as well as trying to get them to carry out the wishes of his superior. The successful man is not one who unnecessarily antagonizes the people with whom he has to continue to work; neither is he a person who seeks to keep everybody happy, for he realizes that such an outcome is impossible when there are conflicting demands and interests at work. To a considerable extent the successful manager is one who works out his own definition of his job and his relations with those with whom he works. He seeks to recognize and negotiate differences rather than to ignore or suppress them. This kind of performance requires considerable independence of spirit. The man who, consciously or unconsciously, tries to get ahead simply by conforming to the wishes of his boss is not likely to progress or even to survive for very long in the complex and competitive environment of most modern large organizations.

Innovation and change in organizations

THE COMPONENTS OF CHANGE

A great deal of literature in industrial relations has revolved around the phenomenon called "resistance to change." The implicit assumption is that it is just human nature for men to resist change and that therefore the agents of change should devise methods of overcoming this resistance. It is then usually pointed out that when the people to be affected by the change have an opportunity to participate in shaping the nature of the change and bringing it about, their resistance is reduced or eliminated. This point of view is faulty in two important respects. It assumes a universal tendency to resist the introduction of change, and it assumes that the nature of the change or the existing state of the social system make no difference: that all that counts is the process whereby the change is introduced.

In modern industry it is misleading to assume any universal tendency toward resistance to change. In fact many plants are constantly undergoing changes, and many such changes are carried out without anything that could be labelled as "resistance to change." Where one does observe disturbances accompanying the introduction of a particular change, calling what happens "resistance to change" simply serves to attach a label that conceals much more than it reveals. For example, in the introduction of the "Amicon tube" (a case study offered by the American researchers in business administration Harriet Ronken and Paul Lawrence), the only phenomenon that might be called resistance to change was manifested by the development engineers, who paradoxically are usually associated with change. The case involved an electronics plant in which changes were constantly being introduced and in which, in the usual flow of activities and interactions, the first steps were always taken by the development engineers. Industrial engineers became involved only later when it came time to work out the methods of production and to establish the piece rates for workers. In the instance of the Amicon tube, however, the original designer happened to be one of the industrial engineers, and the plant manager allowed him to take over and direct the kinds of activities ordinarily initiated by the development engineers. The development engineers objected to this denial of their usual precedence. The whole tangled history of the project must be interpreted against the background of this reversal of the customary flow of work from development into production.

Another instructive case study (this one by the American student of technology Charles Walker) involves the introduction of a new steel-tube mill, more automatic in operation than an old mill. Eleven workers from the old mill did not originally resist being assigned to the new mill and, in fact, in a few months became accustomed to working with each other in the new pattern and came to consider themselves as a crew. Then, however, management announced a reduction of the crew from 11 to 9 men, and the workers did indeed vigorously resist this disruption of the relations that they had developed. Furthermore, the workers actively pressured management to set new piece rates on production in the new automatic mill, for naturally they sought early installation of rates that would enable them to earn at least as much as they had been taking home at the old mill. As a means of applying pressure on management, the workers held down production, while management resisted setting new incentive rates until there was a longer period of experience to study the problem.

What is involved in the changes in these case studies is not resistance. Rather it is *reaction* to the introduction of change. And to predict reactions one needs systematic information of three types: (1) the nature of the change to be introduced; (2) the state of the social system at the time of introduction; (3) the process whereby the change is to be introduced. The important thing, therefore, is to ask in what ways the nature of the change will affect the customary pattern of human interaction and the organization of activities in the social system. "Change" should not be viewed as a universal abstraction or concept. One should get down to specific cases and specific components and think in terms of the changes in behaviour to be required of people. Then one can make sensible predictions about the reactions of those people and about the ways in which the process of introducing the change should be organized so as to minimize resistance and maximize the support for the new approach.

Reactions to change can also be expected to differ according to past organizational experience with changes. If the organization is one in which changes have been infrequent and therefore any change is a major event, there will probably be more disturbance than would be the case in an organization in which changes are constantly being introduced. In fact, most modern companies have achieved a systematization or institutionalization of the change process. Management sets up a research and development department whose explicit purpose is to bring about the introduction of new technologies, new chemical processes, and new products.

INDUSTRIAL RESEARCH AND DEVELOPMENT

Large modern companies institutionalize the introduction of changes in products and methods of production by setting up units to organize the research and development process (see also INDUSTRIAL ENGINEERING AND PRODUCTION). The process may begin with a basic research unit seeking to solve some scientific problems concerning materials or chemical processes that are more or less related to the company's interests. The knowledge gained out of this basic research is then utilized by an applied research unit, which aims to determine the scientific and technical feasibility of utilizing the findings in new product or process development. At this point the development engineers take over, seeking to work out the technical problems by setting up a pilot operation or otherwise testing out various approaches. When the development engineers believe that they have the technical problems of production or processing solved, the industrial engineers step in to work out the methods of production, to determine the nature of the jobs required, to set the incentive rates (if any), and in general to move the new product or process into production. It is only at this point that the impact of the innovation strikes workers and management in production.

It should not be assumed, of course, that all innovations reaching the factory floor follow the complete route, beginning with basic research. Much innovative activity begins with applied research units, where the work involves application of scientific principles that are already known.

Case studies of change

The stages in research and development

Still more of the activity may originate with the development engineers, without any foundation in research. Neither is the flow necessarily all in one direction. In some cases a problem that does not yield to solution in applied research may become a project in basic research, or the development engineers may call upon applied research for help on a problem that they have been unable to solve. Whatever the history of a particular project, it must be seen against the background of the company's customary flow of work among units and departments from research into production. As noted in the "Amicon tube" case, when the innovation follows a path incompatible with the established one, difficulties are bound to arise.

Coordination of the various stages

One of the basic problems in the organization of research and development is that effective performance requires human influences to move in both directions: downstream with the progress of the work from research to marketing, upstream from marketing to research. Although the work done nearer research naturally sets limits upon what downstream department members such as salesmen can do, unless key people at upstream positions are aware of the problems and viewpoints farther downstream, much of their work will end in frustration and conflict. For example, if, after the research and development and pilot testing have been done on a proposed new product, management decides that the product cannot be made for a price permitting the high-volume sales that would make it profitable, then thousands of man-hours of work and large amounts of material will have been wasted. Clearly such frustrations cannot be completely avoided, for no management has information at the beginning of research and development that would render possible a marketing decision at the very outset. Nevertheless, rather than thinking of completely separate steps following one another downstream, one should think of policies and procedures that will bring the ideas and worries of downstream people to the attention of upstream people so that each group can work on its own problems with some conception of the problems that other groups will be facing at another time.

Some concerns try to meet the need for coordination through the establishment of liaison positions, consisting of individuals whose job it is to work between two departments, relating one to the other. The difficulty in this solution is that it not only adds additional people to the payroll but may even serve to prevent department managers themselves from getting together to thrash out common problems.

Some interdepartmental problems have to be resolved through an appeal to a higher authority, but if this is the prevailing pattern of problem solving, the research and development process is not functioning effectively. Appeal to higher authority not only involves valuable time lost in decision making but also serves to put decision making in the hands of people who are so far removed from the problem that they lack knowledge adequate to its solution. Furthermore, frequent resort to arbitration by superiors tends to build up a competitive win-lose orientation among subordinates so that they come increasingly to regard people in other departments as opponents rather than as collaborators.

If constant resort to arbitration is to be avoided, department managers must develop some skill in negotiating with other managers, so that a mutually satisfactory arrangement can be worked out without any single negotiator having the final decision over others. The coordination process may also be facilitated if, from time to time, when higher management people recognize problems of communication and cooperation in the research and development process, they call meetings of the key people concerned. If these meetings are conducted in such a way as to diagnose the problems of coordination and collaboration rather than to lay the blame on one individual or another, the meetings may open the way to further discussions in much smaller groups of those people immediately involved in each particular problem.

Finally, some companies are experimenting with an approach that involves the flexible use of personnel along the line of the flow of work. That is, instead of each department maintaining strictly its own personnel on a given project, one man may be detached from his own work group to follow the project several steps downstream. Similarly, a man from a department further downstream may be detached to work on a project two or three steps before it reaches his own department. In this way, as people move back and forth, they serve to broaden their own experience and knowledge and also to facilitate communication among work groups.

Scientists and engineers in the industrial organization

In the early days, research in industrial relations focussed on workers. Gradually attention spread to foremen and then to higher levels of management. Recently, considerable attention has been devoted to the study of scientists and engineers in the industrial organization.

THE SCIENTISTS

The first industrial research departments, of the late 19th and early 20th centuries, were set up in established companies that were really unsure of what they were instituting. Research units were patterned after already existing departments, thus ignoring the important differences between the work involved in research and the work involved in production, assembly, and so on. The major differences can be summed up in these ways:

Differences between scientific research and other plant work

1. *Production of ideas as opposed to the production of objects.* The scientific laboratory's most important product is *ideas,* not objects, and thus the leadership methods used in the production of physical objects are not likely to apply to the production of ideas.

2. *Distribution of education.* In the production organization the average levels of education increase as one goes up the line from workers to first-line supervisors and on into management. In the scientific research unit, however, there are often scientists with doctoral degrees working in the laboratory under the general direction of higher management people who have not gone beyond the first university degree.

3. *Locus of knowledge.* Although workers in the average production shop will have more intimate, detailed knowledge of their tasks than do people at higher levels, the people at successively higher levels will have more systematic or broader technical knowledge regarding the overall production operations. In the scientific laboratory, on the other hand, the scientists as workers not only know more than their supervisors do about their immediate jobs but also tend to know more about the broader technical and scientific aspects of their projects.

4. *Degree of predictability of outcomes.* Although management people in production departments often complain that they are not getting the output that they expect, usually one finds upon further questioning that the gap between reality and expectation is only a matter of a few percentage points. In the scientific laboratory, on the other hand, outcomes are far less predictable. The scientist may be able to estimate with reasonable accuracy how long it will take him to perform a series of experiments, but if he knew how the work was going to turn out, he would not really be performing experiments. Much of scientific work consists of moving systematically down several pathways that turn out to be blind alleys before the scientist discovers that one pathway that proves productive. Of course, there are great differences within science in this regard. If the scientist is working on the testing or further elaboration of well-established principles, his work is more predictable. If he addresses himself to problems beyond the frontiers of knowledge, his projects become more unpredictable.

5. *Reference groups.* The production foreman and his superiors in line management tend to identify with the organization. That is, they judge their successes and failures in terms of the ways in which they are viewed by people *within* the organization. Scientists have a problem of dual loyalties. They see their success in terms of recognition not only within the company but also within their profession. They belong to professional associations, read the journals of the profession, attend professional meetings, and see their success to some extent determined by what they are

able to publish about their work in scientific journals and by the reputation that they gather among scientists outside the company.

6. *Replaceability of personnel.* In most departments, if labour turnover is high, management may have to recognize a serious problem, but it does not have to worry that the resignation of a worker or even of a single first-line supervisor will jeopardize the performance of the plant. In the laboratory, however, the resignation of a single scientist may make the difference between success and failure in an important project. Superiors must therefore be much more seriously concerned with individual adjustment problems among scientists.

Leadership in scientific laboratories These comparisons suggest that a different pattern of supervisory leadership is called for in the scientific laboratory. Although "close" supervision may be compatible with high production in some factory technologies, it is clear that this approach to the scientific laboratory will stifle the creativity of its members and drive scientists out of the company.

The director of a scientific laboratory finds little opportunity to tell subordinates what to do, yet he may play a vital role in helping them to achieve success in their work and in meeting the general goals of the company. It is now well recognized that the laboratory director must make allowance for the problem of dual loyalties, providing opportunities for a scientist to attend professional meetings, to report to his scientific colleagues on his work, and to publish. If he does not allow for such opportunities, the chances are that he will not be able to keep many good scientists.

Beyond providing these outside opportunities, what can the laboratory director do? He can play a very important role as representative of his laboratory and its staff to higher authorities. The effectiveness of the performance of his work group and the satisfactions of the members will depend to a significant extent upon the projects that they get assigned to their department. The effective manager is in close consultation with the scientists in his department, and, as they develop ideas for projects which they find interesting and challenging, he undertakes to sell those projects to higher management. Thus his success in helping his subordinates to get the kind of work that they want to do contributes both to their morale and their productivity.

Although the laboratory manager's powers over his subordinates are far more limited than those of the manager in a production shop, there are important functions that he can perform for his subordinates so as to make them accept and even welcome his leadership. He can see to it that the scientists in his department have access to the goods and services and information that they need in order to do their job well. He can get recognition for the superior performance of his subordinates, bringing it to the attention of his own superiors and seeking rewards for the scientists in terms of increased salary and other symbols of higher status. He can help the scientists to interpret the significance of their work to higher management. The specialized scientist who knows the most about the project he is working on is often not able to communicate its significance effectively to nonspecialists, and the manager can play an important role in translating technical and scientific ideas into terms that make economic sense to laymen.

The composition of scientific work teams The manager may also be influential in the composition of work teams. Where the outputs of the laboratory are produced by teams rather than by individuals (which is often the case), the results will depend not simply upon the talents and personalities of the team members but also upon the way in which they are able to work together. This means more than compatibility of personality or even the matching of scientific knowledge (*e.g.,* matching chemists with physicists); it means also a melding of "cognitive styles"—joining some scientists who are especially gifted in recognizing and diagnosing the essential elements of a problem with other scientists who perhaps lack this diagnostic skill but are very effective in working out the problem once its diagnosis has been agreed upon. If the team leader does not possess both these skills himself,

clearly he must see to it that both skills are represented on the team.

The manager may sometimes have to function as mediator or arbitrator of differences that arise among his subordinates. Although he may try to encourage them to solve their problems among themselves, this may not always be possible, so it is important that he have skill in resolving the conflicts brought to him.

Finally, the effective laboratory manager functions to stimulate the development of ideas among scientists in his department. This seems paradoxical because one is naturally inclined to wonder how a manager who does not have the depth of knowledge of his subordinates in the various specialized activities under his general direction can serve to stimulate the development of their ideas. He does this by stimulating the communication among them in formal and informal discussions of work in progress and planned. As a discussion leader he may not have the competence to propose the solution to any scientific problem, and yet sometimes an intelligent man who is not immersed in a particular specialty can ask provocative questions that would not occur to the specialist.

THE ENGINEERS

Engineers play crucial roles in introducing change, yet their satisfaction in their work does not measure up to the importance of their functions. Although countless surveys have shown a correlation between the status of a position and the satisfaction of the men holding that position, the relationship breaks down for engineers. In surveys, engineers rank only slightly above blue-collar workers in their level of expressed job satisfaction. How is this low level of satisfaction to be accounted for? Some theorists have claimed to find the answer in role conflict—the conflict between the commitment of the engineers to the profession and their commitment to the company. If this diagnosis is correct, then for engineers as well as scientists, solutions should be found in the policy sometimes described as "parallel paths to progress." According to this organizational strategy, the engineer or scientist can achieve success and increasing economic rewards in the company in either of two pathways. One pathway is the usual one of advancement into supervision and management, in which the specialist gets farther and farther removed from his specialty and more and more concerned with the direction of the activities of other men. The other pathway would reward individuals for their superior performance by giving them more prestigious titles and more money but keeping them directly involved in their professional specialties.

Job satisfaction among engineers

Allowing engineers a choice of careers, however, would have meaning only if they do indeed experience a "role conflict." Such an assumption may be doubtful. Because engineering is by nature an applied field, engineers do not face the lure and promised prestige of success in "pure engineering" as do many scientists in "pure science." Most engineers interpret success in terms of moving up in the company and set a relatively low value on recognition by their professional colleagues outside of the company. Moving up means not only more pay but also better opportunities to determine the projects that the engineer and his subordinates will work on. The selection of projects in turn affects the perceived success or failure of the engineering group and its manager. Power cannot be disentangled from the reputation for superior performance.

Relatively few engineers desire to retain the role of specialist at the workbench. This being the case, "staff" positions that are supposed to be rewards for superior technical performance come to be consolation prizes for engineers who are judged by their superiors not to be good enough for promotion into management but still useful enough to be retained within the company.

One must look elsewhere for the causes of dissatisfaction among engineers. Of particular importance are the types of engineering jobs to which men are assigned. In some large companies, numbers of engineers work in the same department on problems of such a routine nature as to be indistinguishable from draftsmen's work. In this setting, the engineer may feel that, like the blue-collar worker, he is just a cog in a machine. Where engineers have organized for collective bargaining purposes, it has been largely from such work situations that membership has been drawn. Even when engineers are not placed in such routine situations, they may be part of such large systems that each engineer cannot so readily feel that he is making a significant contribution.

There is also an important distinction between project organizations on the one hand and service or functional groups on the other. Those working to develop a particular project are likely to be much more satisfied with their work than those in a service department. The engineers in a service organization cannot identify with the product that others are producing; they find that they get little if any favourable recognition for their service; and they are often criticized for their alleged failures.

Compared with most other types of employees, engineers have to contend with an unstable social environment. Their employment may depend on the success of their company in securing contracts. A failure to get a particular contract may result in downgrading or layoffs of engineers. But even in situations where employment and pay are secure, the engineer has difficulty in achieving a kind of social stability: he is assigned to one project group until its work is completed, and then he is likely to find himself on a different project with new associates. In fact, a project may not even be completed but be shut off in midstream by a decision made higher up in management if it is determined that even technical success will not lead to an economically feasible product. The engineer thus is constantly faced with a shifting social scene over which he may have little control. Those who do make the most successful adjustment to this problem are most often the leaders of the project groups, who not only help develop projects but also have the wherewithal to sell higher management on the feasibility of the projects. Thus, building and retaining a stable work group may depend in large measure upon the ability of engineers to become "internal entrepreneurs," developing new project ideas and selling them up the line. This of course leads to increased pay, greater recognition, and higher positions for the successful engineer, so that success inevitably leads to acquiring the ability to select and work upon one's own projects.

Conflict and conflict resolution: union–management relations

Of the variety of conflicts found in industrial organizations, those involving union–management relations have received the most attention. To better understand these relations, it is helpful to view them in terms of an evolutionary process beginning with the organization of conflict and carrying on into the development of procedures that, though they may not eliminate conflict, at least provide for orderly procedures aimed at the resolution of particular issues.

THE DEVELOPMENT OF A UNION

Organizing a union

Where the establishment of a union depends upon the vote of workers, in order to have any hopes for success organizers must begin on the basis of widespread dissatisfaction among workers. It is the task of the organizer to bring together workers so that they can make their discontents known to each other and establish bonds that form the basis of the union. In this stage the organizer plays a role described by Leonard Sayles as "the lawyer for the defense." Whatever the issue, the organizer seeks to place the blame on management and to show that only the establishment of a union can lead to the solution of the problem.

In this stage, within the incipient local union, leadership tends to go toward the aggressive and eloquent. When the union has been recognized by management and collective relations come into being, the scene shifts markedly. Now the union leaders face complexities that were of no concern to them before. When the issue was simply recognition or nonrecognition of the union, union leaders had a sin-

gle standard against which to judge their activities. When recognition is once achieved, especially if management negotiators have the will and skill to deescalate the hostilities, the union leader then has to discriminate among issues, weighing them in terms of both their importance to the membership and the possibilities of winning cases with management. If he fails to make gains on issues of special importance to the membership or precipitates conflict on issues in which the gains achieved do not turn out to balance the sacrifices of the members, the leader may lose his position.

Winning recognition for the union and establishing contractual relations

Along with the shift from open conflict to contractual relations tends to go an increasing centralization and bureaucratization of the local union, especially when large units are involved. In the stage of organizing the union, success depends upon encouraging potential leaders in departments and work groups to define their own issues and mount an attack on management. When contractual relations have developed, the local union leader comes to recognize that an issue raised in one work group or department may have implications for other units of the plant, so that he cannot afford to let the departmental union stewards commit the union on an issue arising within a single work group until that issue has been assessed at the top levels of the local union. This tendency toward centralization is accelerated by parallel shifts in management's policies and procedures. When management recognizes that a decision made by a foreman in one department may commit the company to similar action throughout the plant, managers are inclined to require their foremen to check with higher authority before acceding to any union grievance or proposal. As the union leaders find that the foremen cannot make decisions, they tend to raise issues quickly to the higher levels where plant-wide considerations can be negotiated.

CAUSES OF UNION–MANAGEMENT CONFLICT OR COOPERATION

A great deal of attention has been paid to the causes of union-management conflict or cooperation. Some persons have contended that trust and goodwill are the "causes" of the good relations, but trust and goodwill cannot simply be willed into existence. There have to be prior conditions and experiences that prompt union and management officials to trust each other and entertain sentiments of goodwill.

Similarly, when management people have been asked for the secret of getting along with a union, many have been inclined to answer, "You have to be firm, but fair." This is no more help than the mutual trust explanation. How is the meaning of firmness or fairness determined? What the manager calls firmness may be looked upon by the union man as blind stubbornness. What the manager calls fairness may be looked upon by the union man as offensive to elemental human rights.

Research suggests that there should be a structural approach to answering this question. In comparing cases in which union and management people seem to be getting along well together with cases in which conflict is apparent, one can expect to find consistent differences in the organization of interaction and activities of union and management officials. It may be useful to examine these differences at the plant level. Until the union enters the scene, management people are predominantly in the position of initiating interaction for workers and also initiating worker activities. Afterward, local union officers and their agents are doing the initiating—seeking out management people to present grievances or getting management to change a policy or procedure or reverse a decision that has been made. To this structural change management may respond in one of three ways. In the first pattern of response, management people seek to satisfy union leaders by yielding to their demands, on the theory that if management is as generous as it can afford to be, the union leaders will be satisfied and abandon their pressures against management. This strategy rewards union leaders in two ways: they get satisfaction both because their superiors in social status and economic resources (that is, management) have responded to their demands

Structural change in unionization

and because they have strengthened their position with rank-and-file workers by presenting them with rewards. In other words, management is providing psychological reinforcement for the very behaviour that it is seeking to discourage. This first type of strategy is necessarily short-lived. Management officials eventually discover that their attempts to win over the union leaders through generous concessions are serving only to push the company into a precarious economic condition, so that finally management officials must refuse to give any more. Reversal of past practices can be expected to lead to conflict between union and management.

A second type of strategy is associated with a quite different management theory. The executives see the problem in terms of power and feel that every effort must be made to define and then to defend those prerogatives that necessarily belong to management. This relationship is characterized by a formalization of relations with the union, as management seeks to examine each union initiative strictly in terms of the collective bargaining agreement. According to this approach, contacts with union officers, between the annual bargaining sessions, are confined almost exclusively to grievance meetings. In these meetings, of course, union leaders take the initiative in bringing up problems on which they demand action from management. Management people seek to respond in those cases in which the grievance seems clearly justified in terms of the contract but otherwise to hold firm. Management refuses to be pressured by actions taken outside of the grievance procedure. For example, in the case of a departmental wildcat strike, management people characteristically refuse to enter into any discussion of the underlying problems until the workers in question have gone back to work.

This policy, if consistently applied, may tend to discourage conflict during the life of a collective bargaining agreement. In fact, wildcat strikes tend to occur only if management procedures and policies are unclear and inconsistent. If workers early experience a wildcat strike with the result that they lose pay, fail to get their problems discussed until they go back to work, and perceive that management still treats their problems in terms of a formal interpretation of the contract, they and their union leaders are inclined to lose faith in the utility of wildcat strikes and other such pressures. They stop resorting to them.

Although a strategy that management uses to defend its prerogatives may tend to discourage "disorderly" conflict, it can nevertheless provoke the hostility of union leaders. If they are blocked from taking any initiative with management except in the grievance procedure, they will naturally devote much time and effort to the discovery and development of issues that they can push within the grievance procedure. Moreover, having only these limited means of expressing their sentiments during the long periods between bargaining sessions, they will be inclined to push a tough policy in confronting management at these very sessions in which they bargain for new contracts.

Although the "soft" and "hard" management strategies described above sound quite different, they are similar in important respects and thus yield similar management attitudes. In both cases, management leaves the initiative in the union-management relationship entirely in the hands of the union leaders. With this approach, union leaders are constantly coming to management to demand changes (which may be costly to management). The management people feel on the defensive, complain that the union is not considering the welfare of the total organization, and come to see the union leaders as enemies who—sooner or later—must be resisted. Management people do not see that they are getting any rewards from their dealings with union leaders. At best, they see themselves as paying a price for the maintenance of peace.

Strategies of reciprocity

In cases in which union and management people claim to be getting along well together, one sees that management has abandoned its defensive position. Management people, from the foremen to higher levels, tend to take more initiative in bringing management's problems to the union. For example, the foreman may feel that, according to the contract, he has a right to discipline a particular worker, but he may nevertheless decide that he will first talk with the departmental union steward to see if the steward can help to straighten out the problem. Similarly, at higher levels management may bring to the attention of union officers its problems of productivity, absenteeism, changing of work assignments, and so on. A reciprocity develops between union and management. The management people continue to respond to initiatives from the union officers but they also take initiative with the union people in seeking their help on management problems. An implicit exchange develops, with each party getting something out of the relationship with the other party. When this happens, one sees problems being peaceably resolved to the mutual satisfaction of the parties, and one sees the attitudes of mutual trust and goodwill developing.

This reciprocity may not develop at all levels of the organization, and at points where it is lacking, there will be, predictably, tensions and negative attitudes. For example, there may be a situation of reciprocity at the top level, where union officers and management people develop sympathy for each other's problems and take action on these problems down the line, but the union may then be insufficiently responsive to the problems being experienced and expressed by the rank-and-file members. In this situation the union leaders may be highly critical of the rank and file for not understanding the "true facts" of the functioning of the plant, and the workers will be increasingly hostile to the union leaders for "selling out" to management. Unless the local union leaders can continue to be responsive to the rank-and-file workers, there may be a split in the local union, followed by a contest for local union office and an overthrow of the established leadership.

Approaches to collective bargaining

Analyzing the collective bargaining process between union and management representatives, the American behavioral scientists Richard Walton and Robert McKersie have diagnosed two types of bargaining approaches, "distributive" and "integrative." In following the distributive approach, the union is, in effect, saying to management: "Of what you have, let us see how much we can take away from you." And management is naturally inclined to hold back and resist the demands. This approach yields antagonistic sentiments and is likely to lead to open conflict. Following the integrative approach, the parties seek to define and resolve problems whose resolution can be directly beneficial to both parties. Where this approach is followed, management people as well as union leaders are proposing problems that need to be resolved, and the discussion proceeds in an atmosphere of general goodwill. Although one might expect to find some pure cases of distributive bargaining, one is exceedingly unlikely to find any cases in which the entire negotiation process follows an integrative pattern. In some cases the parties may be able to spend much time on issues of mutual concern, but the question of the size of the wage package always poses a distributive problem. Even in the absence of pure cases, one can make some predictions regarding the relative frequency of distributive versus integrative problems in the bargaining process. Cases marked by predominance of distributive problems will be characterized by hostile sentiments between the parties and are likely to be accompanied by such conflicts as planned slowdowns, refusals to accept overtime work when management is behind in its production schedule, and even strikes. As the types of problems move toward the integrative end of the continuum, one can expect to observe more favourable interpersonal sentiments and a lower incidence of conflict behaviour.

This approach to the collective bargaining process is not unlike the day-to-day union-management relations in the plant, even though the setting and structure of interactions are quite different. In both cases, harmonious relations are distinguished by a pattern of reciprocity in which the management as well as the union brings in problems for discussion and action and in which there is an effort to arrive jointly at solutions of mutual advantage.

(W.F.Wh.)

STRUCTURE OF THE LABOUR FORCE:
EMPLOYMENT AND UNEMPLOYMENT

The three sectors

In more traditional societies, those in which the productivity of agricultural labour is very low, virtually the entire population must be employed in farming. As a country develops, it becomes able to feed its people more easily, so that a smaller proportion need be employed in farming. When productivity reaches a certain point, the demand for primary goods (agricultural products) drops in relation to the demand for other goods, such as clothing, shelter, and manufactured products. The production of these so-called secondary goods ultimately becomes organized in factories and expands dramatically. As the demand for other manufactured goods grows and remains high, employment in the secondary sector remains high as well. There is also a third, or tertiary, sector of employment comprising such activities as the service trades, teaching, administration, scientific research, medical care, art, and tourism, as well as other pursuits that are not carried on in factories. Technical progress in this sector is slight, compared to that in the primary and secondary sectors, and so the activities of the tertiary sector require a large number of people. In countries with high living standards, the demand for products of the tertiary sector keeps increasing; thus employment in that sector increases more rapidly than in the others.

The effect of technology on employment patterns

The great decrease of employment in the primary sector is one of the most important phenomena of modern history. People who abandon the soil must change not only their means of livelihood but also their residence and their way of life, and all in the course of a single lifetime. This migration from a rural culture to an urban industrial one has involved many millions of people. For a long time the migration was chiefly toward the factories; as recently as 1930 it was imagined that the world of the future would be one immense factory, but this has proved unfounded because, though the output of factories has continued to grow, factory employment has not increased. Employment in the secondary sector in the United States reached its peak in the period from 1920 to 1970 at about one-third of the labour force. Since then the expansion in employment in the United States has been in the tertiary sector; without that expansion technological progress would have led to much greater unemployment or to much-reduced working hours.

Since the beginning of the Industrial Revolution people have feared new machinery would lead to unemployment, with machines replacing people in their work. This fear often led to violent attacks upon machines, as in England in the 18th and early 19th centuries. It now appears that the fear of technological unemployment is exaggerated.

To understand the effect of technological progress on employment it is necessary to distinguish between two kinds of such progress. First, there is so-called intensive progress, which involves an increase in the efficiency with which people exploit nature: in agriculture, for example, all of the techniques that make it possible to extract products from the soil in a shorter period of time per worker. Intensive progress obviously results in a reduced need for workers. But there is another kind of progress, called extensive progress, which enlarges the exploitation of nature. Thus the discovery of raw materials enlarges the framework of the economy, and the industrial development based on it creates new kinds of employment. The invention of a new product, such as the automobile or the radio, has the same effect. In France more than 1,400,000 people make their livings from the automobile, for example, whether as factory workers, garage mechanics, or drivers.

Intensive progress allows people to satisfy their existing needs with less labour; extensive progress, on the other hand, satisfies needs that either did not exist or were not satisfied previously and, consequently, creates new jobs. But the two kinds of progress do not automatically balance each other. In an economy that is not highly developed, technological progress in agriculture may allow the population to consume more food. In a more developed economy, one in which the standards of living are already at a high level, the same progress will not lead to increased food consumption; the end result, on the other hand, may be glut, with lower farm prices and unemployed agricultural workers. In a period of general technological progress, employment is likely to be unstable because production must adapt itself to the changing demands of the market.

The consumption of primary, or agricultural, goods eventually reaches a point of saturation. The consumption of manufactured products passes through a phase of increase and then one of relative decline, except when new products appear on the market that have the extensive effect previously described. It is the tertiary sector, however, that absorbs most of the labour freed by technological progress in the other sectors. Employment as a whole does not decline because of technological progress. In most wealthy countries neither the size of the work force nor the length of the work week has declined since about 1920. There have been economic crises resulting in unemployment, but the unemployment was eventually absorbed. A dynamic economy requires a work force that is mobile enough to move out of sectors in which technological progress has reduced the need for labour and into sectors in which labour is in short supply. This migration is not pleasant for those involved, since it is inevitably accompanied by some degree of unemployment or underemployment.

Measuring unemployment

In its simplest sense, unemployment means being without a job. But for the statistician unemployment is difficult to define precisely. In compiling unemployment statistics for the United States and other developed countries an unemployed person is defined as anyone who is capable of working and is actively seeking work but is unable to find it. Before a person can be unemployed in this sense he must be an active member of the labour force in search of a job. Students and homemakers perform work, but they are not considered employed unless they are paid; however, they are not considered unemployed unless they are actively seeking gainful jobs. Any person who, because of a handicap or discouragement, has not tried to find work—even if only to the extent of registering at a public employment office—is not counted in unemployment statistics. There is a category of young people who leave schools or universities and who do not find jobs commensurate with their education; in some countries the government recognizes them as unemployed and tries to assist them.

UNDEREMPLOYMENT

Outside of the basic category of unemployment, there are various degrees of nonemployment and underemployment. At one time unemployment was not clearly distinguished from nonemployment. Many people were not employed or, more often, were underemployed—that is, working sporadically and without a precise contract. A period of inclement weather can put day labourers out of work, and they often receive no aid of any kind. In the rural areas of many countries there are large numbers of people who may be called underemployed because they do not have full-time work even though they are fully recognized as part of the labour force.

In modern industrial societies the statistics of employment sometimes conceal substantial amounts of unemployment or underemployment. This is because the unemployed may be brought into factories where they are

Two kinds of technological progress

Concealed unemployment

not needed and have insufficient work to do. If the economy is a competitive one, each firm or enterprise has an incentive to keep its operations efficient enough so that it makes a profit, and this tends to prevent the hiring and maintaining of surplus workers. But where enterprises are subsidized or owned by the state, it is necessary to develop administrative and political controls to assure that work is carried on efficiently and in the interest of the public. These controls often do not work as well in enforcing efficiency as do those of a profit-making economy; they are often biassed or erratic, and they may be subject to the interference of pressure groups, politicians, or bureaucrats.

Ever since the 1950s the Communist countries of eastern Europe have been concerned about the problem of running socialized enterprises efficiently; the planners and economists of these countries have conceded that those enterprises that are not subject to the pressures of the market have more difficulty than others in adjusting their production to the needs of consumers and consequently in working out optimal plans and raising the efficiency of their labour force. It is possible to reduce unemployment and underemployment on a national scale, even to the point where there is an apparent shortage of labour, while at the same time permitting a considerable amount of misemployment with its accompanying problem of inefficiency.

RATES OF UNEMPLOYMENT

During the Great Depression of the 1930s, unemployment in the Western capitalist countries reached extremely high rates. In the United States the proportion of unemployed as counted by government statistics reached 25 percent of the labour force in 1933. In Sweden unemployment reached 25 percent twice—in 1921 and 1931. In the United Kingdom the rate was more than 15 percent in those two years. From the 1940s to the early 1970s unemployment rates were far below catastrophic levels.

Varying incidences of unemployment

Even when the overall rate of unemployment is low, it remains a serious social problem because its incidence is not the same for all categories of workers. While some may be only temporarily out of work or moving from one job to another, others may be unemployed for long periods of time. The most damaging unemployment, for an individual or for a family, is that which persists for a long period of time. The statistics published by most countries do not distinguish among categories of unemployed workers. The U.S. Bureau of Labor Statistics, however, has thoroughly studied the incidence of unemployment. Its figures show that unemployment is higher for women than for men, for blacks than for whites, for young people than for adults, and for those who lack education and special skills as compared to those who have such qualifications.

In developed countries governments collect increasing quantities of information on the labour force. Concise statistics, however, cannot adequately portray the whole spectrum of employment problems. Some workers remain in the same occupation, the same business, and even the same firm for decades, while others change jobs frequently. Some people work at more than one job at a time. Some have seasonal jobs. Some people work only a few hours a month, while others may work as many as 65 hours a week. Some pass through a number of jobs searching for one that is enjoyable and pays well. A substantial number of people cannot be easily classified as being inside or outside of the labour force. Many who are outside the active labour force might be drawn into it if jobs were obtainable or if help were available to assist them in qualifying for jobs that do exist. This sort of hidden unemployment may be more serious than overt unemployment if personal and social handicaps are combined with a shortage of work opportunity.

Government efforts to increase employment

Since the end of World War II the governments of most of the developed countries have become committed to a program of reducing unemployment and underemployment. In France, for example, the constitution explicitly charges the state with assuring full employment. Similar goals have been affirmed with varying degrees of concreteness in other countries. The Charter of the United Nations makes full employment a major objective of its members.

Approaches to employment policy

Governments have followed various policies in pursuit of full employment. One general approach is to try to improve the quality of the labour supply. Another is to try to alleviate the effects of unemployment and underemployment. A third approach seeks to maintain economic activity at a high level through monetary and fiscal policies. Finally, there is the method of economic planning attempted in France, where the government planning commission sets targets for the various sectors of the economy that are linked to forecasts of manpower, in the belief that the difficult and complex problems of employment and unemployment cannot be separated from other problems of economic and social development (see ECONOMIC GROWTH AND PLANNING).

Labour policies. The first consistent efforts to deal with the instability of employment caused by technical and economic progress involved providing information on the state of the labour market and on the qualifications of those seeking work. Public employment services developed, particularly during the 1930s, which, on the basis of this information, were to direct applicants more efficiently to existing jobs or to help them prepare for occupations and careers in which labour needs seemed likely. Most of the large industrial nations now have such agencies, which are designed to bring together the two sides of the labour market. Information leads to guidance, and guidance leads to education and training or retraining. The rapid progress of technology has required a perceptible raising of the qualifications of workers: the number of skilled labourers has increased more than that of the unskilled, technicians more than skilled labourers, and engineers more than technicians. In response to this trend, many governments in industrial nations have endeavored to either provide or subsidize training programs for those members of the work force who might be able to benefit from them.

Often unemployment is a regional matter. Attempts have been made to mitigate it through regional development programs in a number of countries.

Ameliorative policies. All of the developed countries try to soften the impact of unemployment through unemployment compensation and other forms of social insurance. In some cases governments seek to induce employers to retrain workers for new jobs rather than to lay workers off.

The maintenance of aggregate demand. The use of monetary and fiscal policies to keep the economy functioning at a high level of employment has been undertaken in a number of countries since the Great Depression (see GOVERNMENT FINANCE: *Fiscal and monetary policy*). In periods of recession or of growing unemployment the government may increase aggregate demand by expanding the money supply or by increasing its own spending. This approach had some success in the United States during the 1960s, when a major income tax reduction, tax incentives for business investment, and a large increase in federal expenditures brought the unemployment rate down to 3.5 percent in 1969. In the years that followed, however, the United States was faced with serious inflation, and government policies that were then undertaken for the purpose of stabilizing prices had the effect of causing unemployment to rise.

National economic planning. In the 1950s and 1960s the French government undertook national planning on a broad scale and succeeded in maintaining rapid economic growth, full employment, and a stable currency; French national planning was much less effective during the severe recession of the 1970s. It seems likely that employment policies in most industrial countries will aim in the future toward a context much broader than that of placement bureaus, labour mobility, and fiscal and monetary policies. The speed with which society is evolving, the variety of possible ways of life, and the unforeseeable changes in the human condition make it increasingly necessary to view economic phenomena as only one part of civilization, inseparable from the rest.　　　　　　　　　(J.Fo.)

LABOUR ECONOMICS

Labour economics is the study of the labour force as an element in the process of production. The labour force comprises all those who work for gain, whether as employees, employers, or as self-employed, and it includes the unemployed who are seeking work. Labour economics involves the study of the factors affecting the efficiency of these workers, their deployment between different industries and occupations, and the determination of their pay. This section deals with the labour force of contemporary industrialized economies.

Obviously, the economist cannot study the capabilities, jobs, and earnings of men and women without taking account of human nature, social structures, cultures, and the activities of government. These forces, indeed, often play a more conspicuous part in the field of labour than do the market forces with which the economist is ostensibly and chiefly concerned. The difference, for instance, between the rates of pay of a craftsman and the labourer who works alongside him may be governed by custom or determined by an arbitrator or maintained by the bargaining power of a trade union. These determinants may seem to override the forces of supply and demand, but a distinction must be made between the agency by which a given result is brought about and the factors that circumscribe the agency's freedom of action and to that extent determine the outcome. Thus an arbitrator may be very conscious that his award will be effective only if it lies within certain limits. Even when the initial action may be regarded as arbitrary, reactions to it bring market forces into play. The comparative study of wage movements in different periods and countries, moreover, shows similarities and regularities that are more marked than the variety of their settings would ever lead one to expect and that can only be regarded as the product of persistent forces working within an equilibrating system. It is this that justifies speaking of a labour market. Though there is much in labour that can be understood only with the aid of the psychologist, the sociologist, or the political scientist, the forces they study do not supersede the market forces that are the special province of the economist; rather, they provide the setting within which the market forces take effect.

Market and non-market forces

Quantity and quality of the labour force

The size of a country's labour force, within a given total population, depends on two factors: the proportion of the total population that is of working age, and the proportion of these who work for gain.

The limits of working age are usually taken to be established by the minimum school-leaving age and the prevailing pensionable age. Allowance must then be made for those persons who continue to work for gain after attaining pensionable age. Typically, some two-thirds of the population of an industrial country lies within these limits.

ACTIVITY RATES

The employed labour force may be analyzed in terms of particular activity rates. An activity rate is the proportion of the whole number in a given age and sex group—for example, females aged 30–34—who work for gain. Among males, activity rates in the earlier years of working age are as a rule low, because so many remain in education and training. Between the ages of 25 and 50, male activity rates approach 100 per cent, but from 50 onward they fall as men begin to retire. The pattern of female activity rates is very different, and has changed greatly in the second half of the 20th century. Formerly, female rates ran higher than male in the earlier years because fewer girls enjoyed extended education, but from the age of 20 onward they fell sharply as women married and withdrew to domestic duties. Women so occupied remain by far the largest contingent of persons of working age but not in the labour force. Since World War II, however, it has been less usual for women to leave paid employment immediately on marriage. A fall in the age of marriage, moreover, together with a smaller size of family, has enabled many women to return to paid work in their 30s, and female activity rates have come to show a second peak between the mid-30s and the mid-40s, after which they decline more steeply than male rates. From these various activity rates there emerges an overall proportion of the gainfully occupied among all of working age that is typically in the region of two-thirds.

QUALITY OF LABOUR

The quality of the labour force depends on education and training, physique, and health. There is evidence that physique has been greatly improved by increases in the standard of living in the 20th century. Because of the reduction in family size, this rise has been even more marked for children than for adults, and the effects have been seen in the greater height and weight attained by children at a given age. The beneficial effects of stronger physique on health have been enhanced by the advance of medical knowledge and the increased availability of medical services. Better health has raised productivity by a reduction in absenteeism and by a prolongation of the working life during which the economy reaps the benefit of the education and training the worker has received.

Education and training can be regarded as a kind of investment, and the rate of return it yields can be estimated. The amount of the investment is the value of the student's use of resources—buildings, equipment, and instructors—together with the output that the economy would have enjoyed from his work had he been gainfully occupied rather than studying. The yield, in turn, is calculated by assuming that the average subsequent earnings of those who completed a given course of education, compared with the average earnings of those who stopped just short of it, provide a valuation of the increase in productivity that the course confers. From this difference in earnings there must be deducted the contributions to the sinking fund required to replace the amount of the investment by the end of the student's working life. The net yield so calculated can then be expressed as a rate of return on the investment. Estimates suggest that this rate of return is not less than that generally obtained from investment in physical capital. They also indicate that a great part of the productive resources of the economy consists in the education and training embodied in its labour force.

Education and training

Though estimates of this kind are subject to some objections in principle, they do serve a useful purpose in stressing the potential of education and technical training in raising productivity and the risk of investing too little in them relative to other forms of investment. There is no less a risk of underinvestment in training in industry. The great obstacle there is that the employer is not assured of retaining the services of workers in whose training he has invested. In traditional apprenticeship, the employer's cost of training was offset by the apprentice's binding himself to stay with the employer at a low wage for a number of years. But apprenticeships persist today only in limited fields. Governments have increasingly exerted themselves to improve the training of non-apprenticed entrants, as well as that of older workers in need of retraining.

Deployment of the labour force

The contribution of education and training to economic development is apparent in the changes that have taken place in the deployment of labour in the developing economies. When the deployment of the labour force is followed over a period of time, certain patterns appear. One of these arises from changes in methods of production. In farming, improvements in technique and equipment have made possible an increasing output from a declining labour force. In industry, the extension of research and development, the increased complexity of products and equipment, and new methods of collecting, storing, and processing information, along with other developments of

Shifting patterns of employment

management procedures, have all acted to increase the numbers of administrative, clerical, and technical workers relative to manual workers. A second course of change has affected occupations linked with particular industries, when those industries have contracted or expanded as compared with others. Coal mining and cotton textiles are examples of contraction. The service industries, on the other hand, have expanded: a greater proportion of household expenditure is devoted to services; education has extended; governments have provided more social services. A third course of change has its origins in relation to supply. Domestic services, for instance, have contracted because improved education and the opening up of other occupations to women has enabled many to take up work that they prefer. The aggregate effect of these changes has been to decrease the relative number of manual workers in the labour force and increase that of the administrative, clerical, and technical. One general tendency is that as standards of living rise the service industries absorb a greater proportion of the labour force, because the extension of the demand for their output is not generally offset, as in manufacturing, by a progressive reduction in the amount of labour required to produce a given output.

The many far-reaching changes that have come about in the relative numbers in different occupations and industries have called for corresponding changes in the training and allocation of young entrants to employment and for the movement of workers already in employment to other kinds of work and, often, other places. Though part of this adaptation has been unplanned and undirected, a number of governments have undertaken to foster the process of adaptation by a labour-market policy. One means of applying this policy is the provision of information to job seekers as to vacancies immediately available, and to workers at large as to the prospects and requirements of particular occupations. Labour-market policy also tries to guide entrants toward those occupations for which an expansion of demand is expected. One way of doing this is by promoting the training and retraining of selected persons for selected occupations. The function of retraining may be extended, as in Sweden, to offer all workers opportunities to qualify themselves for better-paid jobs throughout their working lives.

Fixing rates of pay

Wages may be fixed by collective bargaining between unions and management or by individual bargaining between worker and employer or simply by custom. When the status of wage earner became distinguished from other forms of labour, it was marked by the existence of an individual agreement about the rate of pay between each wage earner and his employer. The law still recognizes the individual contract of service even where the rate of pay has been fixed collectively. In earlier days there was often *Customary* not even individual bargaining, because customary rates *rates* of pay prevailed that might be unchanged for many years at a time. In southern England, for instance, the prevailing rate for building craftsmen remained at sixpence a day for 120 years after 1412; for most of the 500 years after 1412, the building craftsman's rate was half again as great as the labourer's, or nearly so. After industrialization had set in, custom continued in some measure to regulate rates of pay and to protect workers who entered into individual agreements. But its sway was much less extensive: from time to time rates changed. Though there was at first no reference to the cost of living, when price increases were general and sustained, there must have been informal understandings among the wage earners of a locality that each in making his own agreement would hold out for a higher rate. At times of increased demand for labour, moreover, the employer would have to offer a rate sufficient to attract and retain the wage-earners against the competition of other employers. The necessity of holding needed labour is today the governing factor for employers who have workers with whom they do not negotiate either collectively or individually—generally clerical and administrative workers. Individual bargaining also persists in those higher appointments in which the worker has

access to a number of potential employers, and the employer will have to pay more if he is to secure a worker of higher quality.

But frequently, where the safeguards of both custom and of competition for workers have been missing, workers have felt the need to combine in order to bargain collectively. The force of custom declined as industrialization created new jobs and moved workers into new localities. Business fluctuations brought unemployment so that instead of employers competing for labour, workers were often competing for jobs. Thus industrialization has been universally associated with the rise of trade unions.

TRADE UNIONS AND BARGAINING AREAS

(A history of the trade union movement is presented below; see *Organized labour: trade unionism.*) A main purpose of the trade union was to maintain a minimum rate of pay for its members, a purpose that led unions to extend or delimit both their membership and the number of employers with whom they bargained. The starting point was typically the club of craftsmen in a certain locality, concerned to ensure that none of its members worked for less than the rate it recognized from time to time as a minimum and to raise that rate when opportunity offered. By bringing all who worked in the same craft and district into membership, the club could reduce the risk of their bidding against each other; and if it could also limit the number entering the craft—by controlling the number of apprentices—it would be more likely to be able to raise the rates. But since it was still likely to be subject to the competition of members of the same craft coming in from other places, and some of its own members might move in search of work, it had an interest in extending its coverage over all members of the craft throughout the labour market. If the labour market was not coextensive with the product market, however, the union might still find itself exposed to the competition of workers at a distance if these worked at lower rates and so enabled their products to be sold at lower prices. Thus there was reason to extend the coverage of the union up to the boundary of the market for the product, though it was not practicable to organize workers in other countries. But the union would see no advantage in bringing men of other occupations into membership: on the contrary, it was felt that one could expect employers to concede a rise more readily if it would have to be paid to only a restricted membership. What has been said here of the craft union applies to all unions insofar as their aim is to maintain and raise the pay of members of a given occupation: the pursuit of that aim will lead them to embrace all the members of the occupation throughout the market for their product and to establish a basic rate throughout this bargaining area.

The reactions of employers both reinforce and modify this tendency. The ability of any one employer to pay a given rate will depend largely on what rates are being paid by other employers who compete with him in the product market. When competition is close and labour costs are a substantial proportion of total costs, all employers selling in a given product market have a strong inducement to negotiate only through an employers' association that embraces them all. Most employers' associations are in fact industry-wide, though some are limited to particular regions or sectors of an industry. Employers also know that what is conceded to employees in one occupation will commonly be demanded by those in others, unless they are divided by such a gulf as used to separate the manual from the clerical workers. Employers therefore commonly prefer to reach an agreement with all their workers in common, and may make this a condition of negotiation. They thereby put pressure on occupational unions either to extend, amalgamate, and divide up until they form industrial unions each embracing all the manual workers in a given industry, as the Swedish unions have done, or to enter into confederations that provide all the unions having members in a given industry with a common front for the purpose of bargaining—the course followed by British unions.

Many semiskilled and unskilled workers are unable to seek bargaining advantage by restricting the membership

Forces making for uniformity

of their unions to one defined occupation: they have to seek it rather through the accumulation of funds and the force of numbers—for them, "unity is strength." Some unions have therefore adopted the principle of industrial unionism from the outset, in accordance with the tendency noted above toward establishing industry-wide bargaining areas. Others, the general unions, have set out to recruit workers from every occupation and industry; but for bargaining purposes they have commonly had to act on behalf of their members in each industry separately. In any clash between the forces delimiting the bargaining area and those delimiting the trade union, the former generally prove the stronger.

EFFECTS OF COLLECTIVE BARGAINING

Collective bargaining developed with the growth of trade unionism, especially from 1890 onward. It impinged upon labour markets in which the trend of money wages was upward: in years of good business, money wages generally rose, and though in the years of falling or low activity they were often cut, the cuts were generally smaller than the preceding rises had been.

"The rate for the job"

Levelling of pay rates. A first effect of the extension of collective bargaining was to reduce pay differences, which had been large, between the wages a given grade of labour received at any one time in different regions and in different firms in the same region, and even between one man and another under the same employer. The unions at first had to accept the prevailing regional differences, but their pressure to bring up the lower-paid regions has reinforced the effect of improved communications and information in reducing these differences greatly, especially since World War II. Assurance of "the rate for the job" raised the wages of particular groups or individuals who lacked access to alternative employers, either spatially or because of their lack of information and mobility. In general, the extension of collective bargaining brought about greater uniformity in the rates of pay received by workers of a given grade, and it did so by raising the lower rates.

Collective bargaining has also affected the forms in which improvements in pay are realized. It has borne particularly on those parts of the terms and conditions of employment that of their nature require to be regulated collectively. Chief among these are the hours of work. The extension of fringe benefits, such as insurance and pensions paid for by the employer, has also reflected trade union pressure.

Impact of the union on pay rates

Other effects. Studies of differences between the movements of wages in unionized and non-unionized sectors of employment, especially in the United States, have brought out three other effects of the extension of collective bargaining. One is an impact and once-for-all effect: the introduction of collective bargaining has raised the wages of the workers concerned, relative to the general level prevailing around them, by some 10–15 percent. A second effect has been in the timing of changes: when wage rises were the order of the day, unionized workers achieved them earlier than non-unionized; and when the market was moving the other way, cuts of unionized workers were put off longer. When the cost of living has risen rapidly, as in wartime, the unionists' ability to secure compensatory rises in money wages more promptly promoted the extension of unionism, especially among white-collar workers who had previously stood aloof from it. The third effect has been in the ability not only to defer wage cuts in depression but also to reduce their amount. In the United States, for example, the differential between wages in the unionized and non-unionized sectors was at its highest in the 1932 depression trough. A major effect on the general level of pay in terms of purchasing power and on its share in the product of industry seems to have stemmed from the resistance to pay cuts in the world economic depression of 1921: though pay was cut severely, often after protracted struggles, it could not be brought down as far as product prices had fallen, and in more than one country the distribution of the product of industry between pay and profit seems to have been permanently shifted.

In these ways, by raising the pay of particular workers and by modifying fluctuations in the workers' favour, over a period of time collective bargaining has made the total of pay higher than it would have been otherwise in the same conditions of the market. But the effect has been limited. Before World War II, the movements of the general level of pay continued to depend mainly on market conditions, and the points at which the effects of collective bargaining can be distinguished clearly are fewer than might be expected. Collective bargaining provided the arena in which market forces took their effect, rather than a shelter from or alternative to them. Full employment after World War II, however, greatly modified the bearing of those forces on the collective bargain by engendering the expectation among employers that if they agree to rises in pay that exceed the rise in productivity and so raise unit costs, they will still be able to preserve profit margins by raising the prices of their products, and do this without loss of business, provided only that the initial rise in pay is not greater than what is generally being conceded at the time by other employers. In these circumstances of cost inflation, the rate of rise of money wages depends in great part on the policies of the trade union.

Restoration of profit margins

A second limitation is that even where collective bargaining has affected the movement of money wages, it has had only transient effect on the division of the national income between pay and profits. Whatever the course from time to time of rates of pay in money, the pay per man in real terms (*i.e.*, in terms of purchasing power) has risen with remarkable regularity in much the same proportion as output per man, save for the one major exception of the displacement in favour of pay in the early 1920s. This fact is well-established. The reasons for it will be touched on in the last section of this article. Here an explanation may be offered of its consistency with what will seem, especially to the trade unionist, to be equally well established facts— that in a particular case a trade union is able to obtain a rise in pay that would not have come about at that time had the union not entered a claim and backed it with the threat of a strike; that when the rise begins to be paid, it comes out of current profits; and that at that time also the real wage (*i.e.*, the wage in terms of what it will buy) is raised in the same proportion as the wage in money. It is necessary to look beyond these immediate effects. As time goes on, firms will take the opportunity to restore profit margins either by maintaining their selling prices while productivity rises or by raising those prices. The statistical record makes it clear that firms have generally been able to do this, except during phases of downward pressure by the market upon prices, and it is in these phases that the successful prosecution of pay claims is least likely. When market conditions favour such prosecution, moreover, many unions are likely to be moving at much the same time, and insofar as higher rates of pay are followed by price rises, these rises will be general. What holds of one pay rise in isolation does not hold of a number occurring together: the rise in real pay initially conferred by any one rise in money pay will be reduced as the cost of living rises.

THEORY OF BARGAINING

Limitations on the scope of bargaining are also suggested by theory. Collective bargaining can be seen as the reduction of two risks to which the worker is exposed if he bargains individually. There is first the risk that he will find himself merely one of a number of applicants for a single vacancy and that competition between them will force the pay down. Even if he is the sole applicant for the vacancy, there remains the second risk that the job will be offered to him only on terms that he is not willing to accept; in the event of failure to agree, going without the job will inflict more hardship on him than not filling the vacancy will on the firm. Bargaining through a trade union removes the first risk by ensuring that whichever applicant the firm engages it must pay not less than the union rate: in this sense the union exercises monopoly power. Membership in a trade union reduces the second risk by increasing the workers' relative power to change proffered terms by withholding consent: in this sense the union confers bargaining power.

Constraints. The scope of the monopoly power that the union exercises by maintaining the rate for the job may be seen by supposing that this rate is simply announced by the union, which leaves firms to hire as many or as few men as they choose at that rate. In deciding how high it can set the rate, the union must have regard for the consequences for employment. Firms may be able to alter the design of the product and the method of production so as to use less labour. To the extent that they cannot economize in the use of labour and that the pay of this labour enters into the total cost of production, a higher cost arises that firms may be obliged to pass on to their customers through higher product prices; the customers are then likely to buy less from them, especially if there is international competition in the markets for the product, and again employment will suffer. Thus a union that dictates its own terms is still subject to the constraint of the demand curve for the labour concerned. Equally, if the employers dictate the rate of pay, they could not set it so low as to make it impossible to attract and retain the required labour force: they would be subject to the constraint of the supply curve of the labour concerned.

Work stoppages. When neither side dictates the terms and an agreement must be negotiated, failure to agree results in a stoppage that causes losses to both parties. Attempts have been made to develop the pluses and minuses of these losses into a theory of bargaining. If, for example, it is assumed simply that the continuance of a stoppage progressively increases the wish of the parties to end it, and so causes firms to raise and the union to lower the rate at which each is prepared to settle, then the stoppage will end on the day when the two rates have been brought into equality. Further, if the parties agree in their forecasts of how the wish to settle will be affected by the continuance of the strike, they will find it in their interests to reach agreement on what would be the terms of the ultimate settlement without resorting to coercion by stoppage. A more elaborate theory has been developed in which each party is seen as weighing the cost to itself of a stoppage of given length, the benefit to it of a given concession by the other party, and its estimate of the effect of a given extension of the stoppage on the willingness of the other party to make a concession.

When stoppages are unlikely In practice much more is involved—internal political pressures, for instance, personal prestige, or the tactic of involving the government and public opinion. Many of the costs of a stoppage, moreover, are hard to express in terms of money. But the above three variables must always figure prominently in the parties' consideration. A stoppage is unlikely when on a consideration of these variables it appears that there will be no net gain; this situation will exist when bargaining power is evenly balanced or when negotiation has already brought the parties' positions close together. One party is likely to see a clear advantage in a stoppage only when market forces are working in its favour, and these will have told already in the course of negotiation. In particular the cost of a stoppage will be high to employers when they are busiest, whereas in a recession a stoppage may be a positive benefit to them. Insofar as bargaining power is thus conferred by market forces, it injects no distinct factor into the determination of rates of pay. But bargaining power may also be conferred by determination, loyalty, and leadership on either side. It has also been conferred on trade unions by the expectation, engendered among employers by the experience of sustained full employment, that rises in pay can be covered by higher prices so as to maintain profit margins without loss of business.

METHODS OF RATE SETTING

Industrialization has greatly increased the variety of the jobs performed, even among workers who work alongside one another. Rates of pay have been adjusted to particular jobs and to the performance of particular workers by a combination of procedures initiated by management and of bargaining pressures exerted by the workers.

Graded structure of wages **Job evaluation.** One such procedure is job evaluation, the aim of which is to measure the aggregate requirements of different jobs on a common scale and to use these measurements to adjust the relative rates of pay for particular jobs, always within the range of prevailing rates. The requirements considered include the amount of previous experience and of training that constitute the threshold for entry to the job, the demands the job makes on mental and bodily faculties, the responsibilities it imposes, and any unpleasant working conditions or risks of accident associated with it. Of the various ways of measuring these requirements, the simplest and most common procedure is to begin by allotting a maximum number of points to each requirement, and then assigning each job a number of points within that maximum according as the intensity of the requirement appears in a given job in comparison with others. The totals of the points awarded in this way to the various jobs are then compared with the jobs' rates of pay, and a formula for turning points into money is derived and applied to the total of points for each job in order to obtain the appropriate rate of pay for it. There may thus be as many rates as there are jobs, but it is often found more convenient to draw up a wage structure of, say, seven or eight grades and to put into each grade, at a common rate of pay, all the jobs whose evaluated requirements fall within a certain range.

Merit rating and the "straight piece rate." The adjustment of rates of pay to the performance of individual workers may be made by merit rating, that is, by the payment of higher rates to those whose personal conduct and capabilities are adjudged to be superior to the general run. The most widely applied and far-reaching method, however, adjusts the worker's earnings to the output he achieves week by week. Such payment by results can be applied only where output is measurable, and this may require applying it to all the members of a working group in common and not individually. Where output cannot be measured in physical units at all, indicators of performance such as economy of materials or the running hours achieved by machines for whose maintenance the worker is responsible, may be used as the basis of bonus payments. The simplest connection between output and earnings is provided by the "straight piece rate," under which the worker receives the same payment for each piece or unit he produces; but the connection may also be provided by a formula under which earnings vary less, or in some instances more, than in proportion to output. The common aim of methods of payment by results is to give the worker an incentive to reach and maintain higher levels of output, and experience shows that workers moved from hourly rates to payment by results are likely to raise their output by from 15 to 30 percent.

The piece rate is commonly arrived at after time study, in which the time actually taken to achieve a unit of output is measured by stopwatch, and the observed time is adjusted according to the observer's judgment of whether the worker studied was working faster or more slowly than the average worker might be expected to when habituated to the job. If the adjusted time in a given case was three minutes, the worker on a straight piece rate would be credited with three minutes' pay, at his hourly rate, for each unit produced, even if he produced it in less than three minutes. Obviously there is room for argument here; rates are often the subject of dispute, and many are in practice negotiated rather than fixed by the rate setter alone. A rate that is appropriate when first installed is apt to become less so as minor improvements in materials and methods cumulate. Some firms that looked to methods of payments by results to lower their costs have thus found them increasingly costly as well as vexatious as time goes on, and some have moved back to hourly rates with reliance on supervision or the payment of a high hourly rate subject to the maintenance of a certain output in order to maintain productivity.

Single-plant contracts and pay adjustments. The rates paid in a given plant or firm may be the subject of collective bargaining when the bargaining area is not wider than the firm; negotiations over a wider area can deal with them only when they are relatively few or are capable of being classified in a limited number of grades. One of the advantages of the plant contract prevalent in United States manufacturing is that it enables the wage structure of the plant to be specified and negotiated in detail. United States trade unionism lends itself to this procedure in that in manufacturing the unions are predominantly industrial in scope, so that most of the manual workers in a plant are members of the same union; and the local, or branch, of the union coincides with the plant. In the absence of such arrangements, bargaining over particular rates is likely to go on nonetheless, but in a piecemeal and unregulated way. A leading part in the negotiation of particular rates will be played by the shop steward. When a number of unions have members in the same firm, the committee of shop stewards provides a common front, and its convener may be heavily engaged as a negotiator; such a committee acts in considerable independence of the parent unions.

The wage drift phenomenon

A number of possible ways have been indicated in which the effective rates of pay obtaining at the place of work may be raised during the intervals between rises negotiated by recognized procedures: employers may voluntarily extend payments over and above the negotiated rates; the standards applied in fixing rates under payment by results may become looser; any single rate once fixed may become looser as time goes on; and pressures exerted by workers individually or in small groups may enforce claims for higher rates for particular jobs. The outcome of these processes is known as wage drift. It has been fostered by conditions of full employment, which have given the individual worker the indispensability that enables him to press his claim under threat of withdrawing his labour, and has made management more anxious to maintain and raise output than to keep costs down. In a number of countries wage drift has accounted for a sixth or more of the total increase in the payment made for the hour of work. Wage drift is precluded where rates are specified in detail in a collective agreement such as the plant contract and will not be varied until that agreement is renegotiated.

PUBLIC REGULATION OF RATES OF PAY

Governments have intervened in three ways to enforce minimum rates for workers who lacked both the protection of trade unions and competition between employers for their services and whose wages in consequence were regarded as needlessly low. One way has been to provide by law that "recognized terms and conditions of employment," such as those reached by collective bargaining for workers of a particular description, shall be applied to all others engaged in the same kind of work. A second way, followed by the United Kingdom since the Trade Boards Act of 1909, and by a number of state legislatures in the United States, has been to set up boards of representatives of the workers concerned and their employers, together with independent members, charged with determining rates of pay and hours of work that will be legally binding as minimal on all employers within the scope of the board. The board discusses and negotiates wage claims in much the same way as in collective bargaining, albeit if the parties cannot reach agreement, the independent members have a deciding vote. A third way, followed notably by the United States in its Fair Labor Standards Act since 1938, has been to specify by statute the actual minimum wage applicable to wide categories of employment—the amount set being such that only a relatively small number of workers, namely the lowest paid, are immediately affected.

When such third-way measures were first proposed, critics argued that they would only result in the workers they were intended to protect losing their jobs. In some cases this has happened, as when the United States minimum wage was applied to the needleworkers of Puerto Rico. More often, however, the workers concerned were receiving lower pay than a competitive market would have afforded them—that is, if they had had more access to alternative employers. The first two forms of intervention were calculated to raise the pay of particular groups of unorganized workers only to the extent that it would have been raised by the extension of collective bargaining to cover them. It is a disadvantage of the third method that the pay of all workers below the statutory minimum is raised irrespective of the effect it may have on their continued employment.

Arbitration. Another way of regulating rates of pay is a by-product of arbitration systems set up originally as a means of avoiding strikes and lock-outs. In Australia and New Zealand it has become the practice, accepted by both employers and trade unions, to have the main proportions of the wage structure and the movements of the general level of wages determined by the awards of arbitrators to whom these issues are submitted in the form of disputes. In setting rates for particular occupations or industries relatively to others, arbitrators must in practice have regard to what is acceptable to the parties; for even where arbitration is compulsory, its awards would cease to be observed if either party had cause to believe that the terms of the awards were persistently less favourable than it could obtain by its own bargaining power. In regulating the movement of the general level of pay, the arbitrators have more discretion; but the government, and the employers in so far as they meet international competition at home and abroad, will make them aware of the effects of the awards on the level of domestic costs and prices and on the balance of payments.

Practice in Australia and New Zealand

National incomes policy. Under full employment the rise in effective rates of pay, whether through negotiation or through wage drift, has generally been inflationary in that it has exceeded the rise of productivity. The consequent rise in costs and prices has been disturbing domestically and has been particularly embarrassing to governments that face difficulties in balancing their external payments. Governments in general have been unwilling to check the rise of inflation by applying fiscal and monetary restraints to the degree that unemployment would be substantially raised. In the belief that at least part of the rise is due not to excess purchasing power but to the pushing up of costs and prices, governments have appealed to those who make decisions affecting labour costs and product prices to moderate the rise in pay and profits. Some governments have formulated norms that would in theory keep the general level of prices constant, and would keep the general level of pay rising only at the rate of the expected rise in productivity, allowing, of course, for specific exceptions. Agencies have been set up to apply these principles, but usually only by way of investigation, assessment, and advice. Governments have preferred to rely on the acceptance of the policy in principle by employers and trade unions, and on their efforts to secure its observance by their affiliates. Even where statutory powers of control exist, they have usually been kept in reserve. When the experience of sustained full employment has made employers generally expect that they can raise pay by an inflationary amount without harm to their own businesses, it is hard to persuade workers to accept smaller rises in pay than employers are willing to give. Whatever moderating effect incomes policy may have had upon cost inflation, it has not stopped it. The policy remains in the stage of improvisation and experiment.

The structure of pay

Systematic differences are found in the average earnings obtained in different regions, industries, and occupations. The average earnings prevailing in different regions of a country show a considerable range between the highest and the lowest, even when the same procedures for fixing rates apply everywhere. Much of the dispersion is due to differences in the localization of industry: if the relatively high-paying iron and steel industry, for instance, is concentrated in a particular region, then the average pay of the region will be raised to that extent. But regional differences also exist because work of the same kind frequently commands different rates of pay in different regions.

Factors in pay variations

Such differences may correspond to regional differences in the quality of workers, so that there is no real difference in what is being paid per unit of work. But there may be real differences as well. Such differences are sometimes necessary to maintain the balance of payments between regions; they may also be in some measure a legacy of history and are likely to be reduced as communications improve and labour becomes more mobile. As noted above, this process of reduction has been expedited by trade-union pressures.

Average earnings also vary from industry to industry, and the considerable range that appears can again be attributed largely to differences in the composition of the labour force: such an industry as printing that by the nature of its processes employs a high proportion of skilled workers will on that account alone show higher average earnings than, say, the textile industry, which employs a higher proportion of the semiskilled. The similarity between the structure of earnings by industry in different countries—with printing, iron and steel, and engineering near the top, and textiles and food processing low down—is thus attributable to common processes requiring similar compositions of the labour force (assuming, of course, that the structure of rates of pay by occupation in the given countries is also similar).

OCCUPATIONAL PAY THEORIES

This occupational structure, therefore, presents the main object of economic analysis. International comparisons show that the ranking order of the rates of pay prevailing in different occupations is similar in different countries, but that the range, whether between professional and manual occupations or, within the manual, between the skilled and unskilled, is much wider in economies at an early stage of development and diminishes in the course of development. These are the principal observations to be accounted for by any theory of the differences in the rates of pay that different kinds of work command. Several such theories have been propounded.

Relation between esteem and pay

Status. One theory stresses the link between occupations and their status in the community, some having higher status than others. The community believes, according to this theory, that pay should correspond to status; and the rate of pay for each occupation is assigned to it by common consent, reflecting the place it occupies in the hierarchy of esteem. The implications are that the community's discretion is not as a rule subject to other factors such as the market forces of supply and demand and that, if people came to make less distinction of status between occupations, then the rates of pay for different jobs could be more nearly equal. Doubtless, many people do think in the way the theory supposes, feeling it anomalous, for example, when an occupation that is commonly accorded a higher status than another ceases to command a higher rate of pay; and arguments appealing to this habit of thought are sometimes used in support of claims. But the correspondence between status and pay is ambiguous; it is not clear to what extent pay is made to fit the status and to what extent status follows from pay, if not today's pay then yesterday's. Moreover, the occupational pay structures of different countries show more similarity than do their social values. Nor does the theory explain why the pay structure has generally become compressed in the course of development, and the ranking order sometimes inverted, as when some clerical occupations drop below some manual ones: changes that can otherwise be explained as the effect of extended education in increasing the relative supply of more qualified labour.

But if the theory is not acceptable as an explanation of the pay structure as a whole, it does call attention to a factor that appears to affect parts of that structure. One of these parts is that of the higher administrative posts. It is generally accepted that any such post must carry a higher salary than any post below it in the chain of command; and when this chain is long, as it is in a big corporation, the salaries set for the posts in it, and the high level reached at the top, are to be accounted for by this principle. The same theory also suggests a cause of prevailing differences between men's and women's rates of pay. Most women's work is different in kind from men's irrespective of the fact that it is done by women; and where men and women both do work of the same description, some disabilities attaching to women as employees, in particular the likelihood that they will not stay in the job as long as men, may make them worth less to the employer. But there are some jobs in which these considerations do not apply and in which there is no difference in the productivity of men and women adequate to account for the actual difference between men's and women's rates. The difference seems attributable rather to customary attitudes and valuations: in particular, the assumption that women's productivity is lower in all jobs

and also the belief that pay should be proportioned to need (women workers generally needing less than the man who has a family to support). If such factors as these account for differences in pay between men and women where there is no corresponding difference in the work they do or the efficiency with which they do it, one may speculate that the same factors account for some part of the pay differential where the two kinds of job are distinct.

Power. A second theory lays its stress on power: the ways in which organized groups can protect and advance the pay of their members. Any group that restricts entry into its occupation can keep its labour relatively scarce and thereby support the rate of pay that that kind of labour commands. The discussion above of the economic effects of the trade union indicated the circumstances in which a trade union would be able to raise the relative pay of its members by the exercise of monopoly and bargaining power. The general increase in the pay of the less skilled relative to that of the skilled manual worker has been attributed in part at least to the increased unionization of the unskilled. Evidently, policies of organized groups will account for some part at least of the position of particular occupations in the pay structure, but they cannot alone account for the main proportions of that structure: it cannot be supposed that the hierarchy of pay corresponds with and is due to a hierarchy of the power of organized groups.

Control of the labour supply

Value. A third theory treats the differences in pay for different jobs as corresponding to differences in their content or requirements. The simplest form of this theory was embodied in the labour theory of value, whether in the system of Adam Smith or of Karl Marx, by the assumption that different kinds of labour can be reduced to different quantities of "homogeneous labour time," and that rates of pay are then simply proportional to those quantities. Job evaluation, discussed above, purports to condense the varied requirements of each job to a single figure in a common scale in order that the ranking order of the rates of pay of the jobs may be brought into conformity with that of those figures. But the assumption that if two articles are priced in the same currency they must contain quantities of a common substance is gratuitous. The impossibility of establishing the existence of such a substance and measuring the amount of it in any article drives both the labour theory of value and job evaluation into the circular argument of inferring the job content from the rate of pay and then explaining the rate of pay by the job content. That job evaluation is nonetheless useful in practice may be accounted for by its ability to arrive at an estimate of the extent to which the requirements of each job tend to raise the rate of pay it commands in the present state of the market.

THE SUPPLY PRICE OF LABOUR

The foregoing directs attention to the supply price of labour to the job—the rate that must be paid if employers are to be able to attract and retain the quantity of labour that they wish to employ at that rate. Entry into an occupation generally imposes certain monetary costs; there may also be subjective costs; for example, in the effort of concentration required by preparation for examinations. The exercise of any occupation may be attended by disadvantages that require monetary compensation or may provide satisfactions and amenities that make workers willing to accept lower pay. For each occupation the various costs and benefits can be set off against the pay, and entrants will choose the one in which the prospective balance of advantage seems greatest. If more workers are to be attracted to and retained in a given occupation with unchanged conditions on the side of supply, the rate of pay in that occupation must be raised relative to others. An extension of supply will work to the opposite effect: for instance, if there is more public provision for secondary and tertiary education, and if rising standards of living enable more families to bear the costs of training, then a given number of workers will come to be available in a given occupation at a lower relative rate of pay. Here is to be found the reason for the occupational pay structure extending over a smaller range in developed than in poor

Costs and benefits to workers

countries and for the reduction in the margins for skill and the relative rate of pay for clerical work in the developed economies during the present century.

A number of considerations thus indicate that the rate of pay in any occupation tends to equality with the long-run supply price of labour to that occupation. In the absence of an extension of supply, a fall in the relative rate of pay of an occupation will bring a check to recruitment, followed by some withdrawal to other jobs of those already in the occupation. A rise in the relative rate of pay needs longer to take effect where proficiency takes long to acquire. Some types of proficiency may be limited by nature, and the rise in the rate of pay that follows on an extension of demand for them constitutes an economic rent; *i.e.,* a payment that is not required to maintain supply. In general, however, given time, the number of proficient workers available to follow a given occupation will be increased by a rise in the relative rate of pay it offers.

It is, then, to differences in the long-run supply price of labour to different occupations that the differences between the rates of pay they offer appear to be mainly attributable; though considerations of status and the power of organized groups set their mark upon the occupational pay structure at particular points.

MARGINAL PRODUCTIVITY
AND THE DEMAND FOR LABOUR

The above statement is incomplete, because the supply price of labour in a given occupation generally varies with the number of workers supplied, and what that number will be depends in turn on the demand for labour in that occupation. The rate of pay must not only be such as will maintain the supply of a given number of workers but such also as will lead employers to employ that number. The theory of marginal productivity analyzes the demand for labour in a given employment in the same way that it derives the demand for any factor of production from the demand for the product and from technical conditions of production that determine how much output will be increased by using one more unit of the factor in the presence of given inputs of the other factors; that is, what the marginal product of the factor in the given setting will be. If the employer seeks to maximize his profit, he will presumably adjust the input of each factor so as to bring the value of its marginal product into equality with its price (see ECONOMIC THEORY).

Reality versus theory   The theory of marginal productivity has been challenged on the ground that it is unrealistic. The marginal product can be measured, it is pointed out, only for direct labour; that is, for work in which physical output varies directly with labour input; but here the number of workers required is determined simply by the size of current output. Yet though this holds at any one time, a rise in the relative pay of a given kind of labour puts managers under pressure to change equipment, processes, or the design of the product as opportunity offers, so as to use less of that labour relatively to other factors of production. Insofar as this cannot be done, moreover, the rise in pay will result in a higher relative price for the product, which will tend to reduce sales and hence the number of workers.

With indirect labour, on the other hand, the marginal product is not measurable. It is the function of management, however, to assess the contribution made by such workers, so as to decide whether employing one more at a given rate of pay would yield a balance of advantage to the business, and managers are efficient in proportion as they make such assessments rightly. In general, insofar as managers are concerned to produce a given output at the lowest possible cost, they will avoid paying for a unit of labour if the same payment used to hire more of another factor would result in a greater increment of output; and insofar as they are concerned to increase profit, they will not fail to engage a unit of labour whose contribution to proceeds would exceed its pay. While, therefore, the adjustment supposed by the marginal productivity theory of the demand for labour is seldom capable of being effected exactly, there is no reason to doubt that market forces do operate to check deviations from that adjustment and retain them within a zone of tolerance.

Movement of the general level of pay

A wage is a price, and the rise of the general level of wages or rates of pay in the course of time has, to some extent, been part of the long-term rise in the general level of prices; that is, of the cumulative depreciation of the purchasing power of money, largely attributable to increases in its quantity. In another way, however, the movements of rates of pay have been an independent cause of the rising trend of prices. At times those rates rose in common with prices under the pull of monetary demand (in times of inflation, during war, or in the rising phase of the trade cycle), but when the demand fell off they were resistant to cuts; and though they were cut somewhat, they commonly remained at a higher level than when the preceding rise began. A graph of product prices shows big falls as well as big rises, and sometimes a falling trend persisting for many years together; but a graph of money wage rates is more like a flight of steps. This characteristic of wage movements puts a floor under prices and provides a higher starting point for the next upward movement, so that the fluctuations of monetary demand impose a rising trend on prices. In addition, the analysis of cost inflation under full employment, noted above, has shown that when employers generally expect demand to be sustained, rises in pay may occur in the absence of excess demand and so initiate rises in prices; and it is possible that the same process may have played some part in the rising phase of the trade cycles of earlier years.

The level of real earnings   The rise of real earnings may be traced by comparing the movements of earnings in money with those of an index number of the prices of the articles on which pay is typically expended. Such comparisons indicate that between 1860 and 1960 the real earnings of manual workers rose fourfold in France, Germany, and the United Kingdom; more than fivefold in the United States; and more than sevenfold in Sweden. In considering the standard of living attendant on these movements, it is necessary also to take account of the prevailing reduction in the size of the family, the complex effects of urbanization on the amenities of life, the effects of changed techniques and deployment between occupations on the strains and satisfactions experienced in work, and the reduction of hours of work. The last element has been extensive: it appears that down to World War II the wage earners of the five countries mentioned, save the United States, gave up from a third to a half of the potential increase in annual purchasing power in favour of a shorter working week and longer vacations.

To the extent that real earnings are measured simply by the quantity of consumables that money earnings will buy, their rise has depended on three factors: productivity, or the output per worker in terms of his own product; the share of this product that accrues to the worker; and the rate of exchange between the worker's own product and the goods and services he buys. In the industrialized countries, the last factor has presented itself largely in the form of the terms of trade between manufactured products and primary products, especially foodstuffs: real earnings have risen faster or slower according as a representative consignment of manufacturers may be exchanged, at the prices of the day, for a greater or smaller quantity of foodstuffs and raw materials. There have also been variations from time to time in the second factor: the share of the product accruing to the worker. The effect of the last two factors, however, has been small in comparison with that of the first, the rise of productivity. The salient finding from the statistical record of the last hundred years is that real earnings per worker have risen very nearly in the same proportion as output per worker.

How this can have come about is a question for the theory of distribution. Here the comparative stability of the share of the product accruing to the worker may be noted. The statistical record shows this stability in its relation with the behaviour of two other factors: the rate of return on capital, and the amount of capital employed per unit of output. The stability of any two of the three factors implies that of the third.   (E.H.P.B.)

MIGRANT LABOUR

Workers who move about systematically, seeking and engaging in seasonal temporary employment without becoming residents of the areas in which they work, are called "migrant labourers." Throughout the world, the wages, working conditions, and standard of life of migrant workers are low in comparison with other groups of workers, almost always the lowest. The union- and government-established labour standards available to industrial and regular agricultural workers generally do not exist for migrant labour; and where there are statutes their implementation is limited and irregular. Migrant labourers are the rural equivalents of the urban poor.

Migrant labour is primarily but not exclusively agricultural; it generally involves harvesting activities and is mostly manual, repetitive, easily learned, and demanding of almost no skill. Migrant workers pick cotton, cocoa beans, grapes, tea or tobacco leaves. They cut sugar cane and pineapples and gather artichokes, beans, carrots, sugar beets, or other cash crops. They also harvest corn, small grains, or wheat. Because all of these activities require physical strength and call for much bending and reaching, migrant labour is also called "stoop labour."

Characteristics of migrant labour

Migrant labour must be distinguished from other forms of employment with similar characteristics and similar problems. Labour migration in Europe—often involving the crossing of national boundaries in search of employment or better employment—is different, since it usually involves a permanent or quasi-permanent resettlement of the worker and his family. Casual labour, in which a worker shifts, often daily, from employer to employer, is also different from migrant labour, because the casual labourer does not change his residence. Seasonal or part-time labour, offering the worker employment only on a seasonal or occasional basis, is again different, in that it does not involve either a change of residence or frequent changes of employers.

Criteria of migrant labour

ASSOCIATION WITH INDUSTRIALIZATION

Migrant labour is associated with the developed or "middle" stages of industrialization and its technology and organization. While the demand for migrant labour stems, in part, from the seasonal nature of worker requirements in agriculture and related industries, it is not a phenomenon characteristic of agricultural societies. It was probably unknown in antiquity and is not significant today in the underdeveloped economies of Asia and Africa; high levels of demand for migrant workers are related to rapid increases in farm output, decreases in permanent farm employment, long periods of rural migration, increasing urban wages, and fairly rapid mechanization and commercialization of agriculture. The demand for migrant labour is particularly high in the case of market farming, where production is increasing or where numerous small farmers specialize in one or two cash crops and are joined in production or marketing associations.

The propensity to work as a migrant labourer stems from the unfavourable economic and social conditions in which the worker finds himself at what is called his "home base." Technological displacement, radical changes in sharecropping systems, long business recessions, drought and crop failures, and various forms of discrimination are factors inducing workers to enter the migrant stream. Lack of education, industrial accidents, and ill health also force many to become migrant. The supply of migrant labour thus develops in response to the push of need, not from a romantic desire to wander. In a minority of cases, particularly those in which a poor region, state, or nation is adjacent to a much richer one, workers respond also to the pull of better opportunities; in spite of its misery and degradation, migrant labour appears to them as a way to a higher standard of life in the future.

As national economies mature and move through the secondary (mostly industrial) stage to more developed stages, both the demand for and the supply of migrant labour decrease. The demand for it decreases because of mechanization; in the U.S., for example, the harvesting of wheat and cotton that required the employment of many migrants before World War II is now largely mechanized and done by regularly employed farmhands. The supply decreases as higher real standards of living and greater employment possibilities make migrant work less attractive. For a small number of employed workers in affluent areas, migrant labour provides secondary (or additional) employment opportunities.

Effect of economic development

In mature economies migrant labour contributes little to total agricultural output and a negligible amount to nonagricultural output. Nevertheless, the availability at the right time and place of migrant workers can be crucial, since without them large crop losses may occur. This may spur private employers, planning authorities, and governments to take remedial actions to improve the conditions of migrant labourers in order to assure their continued availability. If native migrant workers are in short supply, the gap may be filled by the temporary—legalized or tolerated—migration of foreign workers from poorer countries. In the Communist countries, where the use of migrant foreign labour is politically unacceptable, the flow of migrant workers is supplemented with organized brigades of urban youth encouraged to contribute their labour voluntarily to the common good.

THE MIGRANT FLOW

Most migrant workers move in well-established patterns or "streams." The migrants usually flow from the south to the north (in the Southern Hemisphere, however, they move in the opposite direction), as geography makes for later harvests in northern latitudes; also, the poorer areas with the labour surpluses tend to be in the south. Migrants make detours and side trips as they hear of better or new opportunities. The various "crews," families, or individuals that make up the migrant stream do not all follow the same pattern: some move from place to place, others make a big journey to a set of places with known jobs, while others make only one move and then go back to "home base."

Economic and social conditions of migrant workers

In all employment relationships the matching of unemployed workers and job vacancies is a haphazard and complicated process, but the labour market for migrant workers is notably disorderly. One basic reason is that the employment relationship is ephemeral. To the worker, the identity of the employer is hazy, and in many cases is even unknown. To the employer, the typical workers have no individuality as he thinks of them often as alien drifters, "wetbacks," "Okies," etc. With minor exceptions, employers do not systematically recruit migrant workers and have no regular personnel specialists or procedures. Even though most labourers migrate year after year, they do not enjoy reemployment rights, are not organized in unions, and have little access to systematic means of job seeking; they tend also not to exploit the available services of public placement or other governmental agencies, limited as these are.

Middlemen, job brokers, labour contractors, crew leaders—*patrones* in Latin America, *sirdār* in the Asian subcontinent—arise out of the fundamental disorganization that exists in the migrant labour market. Labour contractors, in addition to bringing the workers together, transporting them, supervising them, and dispensing their pay, search out the employers and negotiate wages and working conditions with them. In some areas the contractors have made themselves so essential that without them workers cannot find employment and employers cannot get workers.

The role of the contractor

The conditions under which migrant labourers live are abysmal. Their misery has been formally documented by investigative bodies down the years: the U.S. Industrial Commission of 1901, the Royal Commission of Labour in India of 1933, the U.S. President's Commission on Migratory Labor of 1951, and others. Novelists, moved by the migrant workers' plight, have aroused sympathy with such masterpieces as John Steinbeck's *The Grapes of Wrath* or Mulk Raj Anand's *Two Leaves and a Bud*. Social scientists, particularly economists, however, have tended to ignore the issues posed by migrant labour. Governmental statistics on migratory labour are scarce, often contradictory, and approximate at best.

Migrant workers are often cheated even of the low wages they earn. They work long hours and under exacting requirements. Total employment is always limited; in a year most migrants work less than one quarter of the working days. Child labour is widespread, and the children that do not work are not adequately provided for; they often do not go to school, as in most places schools are open only to residents. Housing amounts to hardly more than a roof over the head, often tar or tent. Tuberculosis, infant and maternal mortality, dysentery, enteritis, smallpox, and typhoid are all more prevalent among migrant labourers than among the general population. Literacy levels, social cohesion, and political participation rates are always exceptionally low among migrant workers, while crime and all other indexes of unacceptable social behaviour are high. Contributing to this picture of misery is the fact that the migrants, whether national or foreign born, are fundamentally alien to the community in which they work. The local population, if eager to see them come, is even more eager to see them go. They have difficulty in gaining access to local health and social services, are often deprived of their rights, do not enjoy easy recourse to the courts, and are abused by exploiters and sometimes the local police.

DIFFICULTIES OF REGULATION

The fact that the migrant is "here today and gone tomorrow" makes the regulation of his working and living conditions difficult. Local, state, and national authorities generally acknowledge the existence of serious problems associated with migrant labour, yet in the face of these, generally claim they are unable to deal with them effectively. The International Labour Organization has consistently prodded governments to expand their legislation in this area. Efforts are being made to develop regulatory standards protecting workers during their journeys, to discourage migratory movements of undesirables, and to stabilize workers and their families near their place of employment.

The task of providing migrant workers with governmental protection and assistance is full of complex difficulties. Regulatory legislation ideally should be applied at the "home base" of the migrants as well as along the stream of migration and at the place of employment. But advances in one area often create difficulties in another due to uneven social and economic conditions. On the one hand, mechanization and permanent migration is reducing the number of migrant labourers, while, on the other, relocating them is difficult because their low educational attainments and lack of skills force them into urban poverty. Where legislation has been passed and improvements have been achieved, the major effect has been to force employers to provide more housing and sanitary facilities and to regularize the activities of the labour contractors.

Patterns of movement

THE UNITED STATES

In the United States in the 1960s about 400,000 people yearly were occupied in migrant work. In the previous decade the number was about 600,000 yearly; in 1940 there were 1,000,000; and it is possible that in the middle 1920s as many as 2,000,000 workers were in the migration streams. There are not many reliable statistics. Interpretation of scattered data suggests that the following trends and relationships have occurred since World War I: (1) the migrant labour population has been declining, albeit at a decreasing rate; (2) migrant agricultural workers have tended to become a larger proportion of all agricultural (nonfamily) workers; (3) foreign workers—while their participation varies with the rulings of the federal immigration administration and with requirements of foreign policy—constitute an increasing proportion of all migrant workers; and (4) the size of the national migratory labour force varies inversely, and the foreign labour force directly, with improvements in the total level of employment.

In the 1960s more than half of the migrant workers were 25 years or younger; fewer than one in 10 was 55 years or older. Three out of four migrant workers were males, with males outnumbering females in all age groups. Almost half of the female migratory workers were between the ages of 25 and 54. In terms of areas of permanent residence a little less than two out of four migrant workers originate in the South. Over 55 percent of all migratory workers had eight years of education or less.

Three major patterns characterize the movement of migrant workers in the U.S. (1) On the East Coast, migration begins in winter when workers from Southern states move south to Florida to work on the citrus crop. From there, joined by others coming from Texas and Puerto Rico, they move north along the coast ending up in August and September gathering tomatoes and other vegetables on Long Island and potatoes as far north as Maine. Negroes constitute a large proportion of those on the East Coast. (2) The largest stream of migrants flows north and west from Texas in the spring to the north central, mountain, and Pacific Coast states. The crops they harvest are fruits and vegetables, sugar beets, and some cotton. The workers are natives of Mexican descent with whom some "wetbacks" (immigrants from Mexico) join; they travel mostly with their families and end work early in December. (3) A large number of Spanish-Americans work on harvesting vegetables, moving from Southern California northward through the Pacific Coast states. Thus some migratory farm work is done in almost every state, with most labourers coming from Texas and the Southeast. About half of the mandays of such employment occur in California, Michigan, Texas, and Florida.

The principal U.S. migrant flow

These migrant workers suffer from unemployment, inadequate housing, little education, exclusion from normal community life, and the denial of services that others take for granted. In the middle 1960s they grossed an annual average income of about $1,700, working an average of 150 days if they worked in nonfarm activities as well. Those who worked only as migrant farm workers averaged $800 for about 82 days of work.

One of every five poor people in the United States is a migrant worker and entitled to the various governmental antipoverty manpower and social programs. Yet, an analysis of federal antipoverty expenditures from 1965 through 1968 shows that only one out of every 50 dollars was spent to help migrant workers, a pattern suggesting that there is considerable truth in the oft-quoted statement that more money is spent on migratory birds than on migratory labour.

In spite of this, it is probably true that the 1960s saw more improvements in the living and working conditions of migrant workers in America than any previous decade. A number of states and localities established special migrant committees to implement and expand legislation. "Crew registration laws" were increasingly adopted by the states, and their implementation is having beneficial effects. Most important, after years of inactivity attempts were being made by labour unions to organize migrants, with some success in California and Wisconsin.

WESTERN EUROPE

Migrancy as described above does not involve very large numbers in Europe because of the longer history of urbanization. Migrant agricultural workers are still active in the rice harvest of northern Italy and in some of the vegetable harvest of Portugal and France.

The European migrant worker frequently moves across national boundaries in response to seasonal fluctuations in the labour demand of specific industries. This type of migration rarely involves the workers' families and generally calls for only one move. Thus Italian workers go to work in Swiss hotels, Polish workers go to mine English coal, etc. The problems of European migrants are less acute than those described above; they generally involve difficulties in acculturation and in qualifying for national health and social service programs.

AFRICA

Migrant labour is one of the most important problems of the developing nations of Africa, where migrancy is clearly an intermediate stage of the movement from rural agricultural to urban industrial life. The phenomenon does not conform to the general characteristics described earlier. Workers migrate to urban rather than to agricultural employment; they work with one rather than many employers; and they often stay in one job as long as three years.

Migrancy in Africa is very clearly a response to the pull of expanding industrial opportunity and the lure of city life

rather than to a push away from the poverty of rural life; it is thus a step in the process of building an industrial labour force. The worker who moves does so alone and with considerable reluctance. He often goes because he needs cash for a particular purpose (*e.g.,* the "bride price"). He is not prepared to give up his contacts with the village, where there is security in old age, sickness, or periods of unemployment. African migrancy is nonetheless quite similar to the migration that occurs in the middle stages of industrialization. In the regions where the migrant workers come from one finds the decline of traditional subsistence agriculture, changes in ownership patterns, and drought; one rarely finds workers displaced by mechanization of production.

Migrant labour is also to be found in many other nations. India has probably more migrant workers than any other Asian country; these are involved mainly in the harvesting of tea, cotton, and rice. In Australia and the southern nations of Latin America migrants work on ranches more often than on farms and are engaged in wool shearing and meat processing.   (O.A.O.)

Pull versus push

ORGANIZED LABOUR: TRADE UNIONISM

To be understood in its international context, trade unionism must be examined as part of a wider concept—the labour movement as a whole. That movement consists of several more or less intimately related organizations such as labour parties, workers' mutual insurance organizations, producers' or consumers' cooperatives, and workers' education and sports associations. All have the common objective of improving the material, cultural, and social status of their members.

What distinguishes one organization from another is the particular aspect of that broad objective it is endeavouring to pursue, and the particular method it employs. The relationship among the various parts of the labour movement varies from country to country and from period to period. Not all countries have produced the entire gamut of organizations referred to above; in some countries the term "labour movement" is virtually synonymous with "trade unionism."

Origins and background of the trade union movement

Early forms of labour organizations. Unions originated, mainly in Great Britain and the U.S. in the late 18th and early 19th centuries, as associations of workers using the same skill. There is no connection between trade unions and medieval craft guilds, for the latter were composed of master craftsmen who owned capital and often employed several workers. The early unions were formed partly as social clubs but soon became increasingly concerned with improving wages and working conditions, primarily by the device of collective bargaining. Progressing from trade to trade within the same city or area, the clubs formed local associations, which, because they carried on their main activities on a purely local level, were almost self-sufficient. With industrial development, however, local associations sooner or later followed the expansion of production beyond the local market and developed into national unions of the same trade. These in turn formed national union federations.

Factors favouring unionism. The unions of the early 19th century were almost exclusively based upon a particular craft. But as mass production industries—which required large numbers of rapidly trained, semiskilled workers—developed, a trend toward large-scale union organization grew, and toward the end of the 19th century Great Britain was including unskilled workers. Unions that recruited members from such groups—whose ranks were expanding rapidly as a result of new technologies— emerged either as industrial unions or as general unions. Industrial unions attempted to organize all workers employed in producing a given product or service, sometimes including even the general office or white-collar workers. General unions included skilled workers and labourers

of all grades from different industries, even though they usually started from a base in one particular industry. But changing technologies, union mergers, and ideological factors led to the development of various kinds of unions that would not fit easily into any of the above categories.

Obstacles to union organization. In most Western countries, labour movements arose out of the protest of workers and intellectuals against a social and political system based upon discrimination according to ancestry, social status, income, and property. Such a system offered few avenues for individual or collective advancement. Discrimination in political franchise (restrictions on or outright denials of the vote) and a lack of educational opportunities, anti-union legislation, and the whole spirit of a society founded upon acknowledged class distinctions were the main sources of the social protest at the root of modern labour movements.

Anti-union laws such as the Combination Laws in Britain, the French Loi Le Chapelier (forbidding combination), similar laws in most Germanic countries, and court decisions under common law in the United States in the 19th century made it inevitable that reformers would first turn their energies to the removal of those legal impediments. The demand for equal voting rights became an early preoccupation of the labour movements, partly because of a desire for recognition of the working man as a full citizen, and partly to give the worker political power to remove anti-union laws and to obtain legislation for improving working conditions, especially for children and women. At a much later stage, when democratic equality was substantially achieved, unification of unions that had been divided according to political or religious sympathies became the next goal of the labour movements, with less attention paid to anticapitalist ideologies.

Labour unions as protest movements

Union development in industrialized nations

Among the various labour movements, the roles assigned to collective bargaining and to labour legislation vary substantially; such differences even occur within a single movement. In Great Britain and the United States the role of collective bargaining is stressed. Legislation is regarded primarily as a device to bring about, facilitate, and supplement orderly collective bargaining. Most continental European countries, though with considerable variations among them, rely on substantive labour legislation to a far higher degree than Great Britain or the U.S.

Collective agreements in Britain and many other Western countries, either traditionally or under the impact of tight labour markets, frequently designate the minimum wages allowable; the actual wage rates may be considerably above those listed in the contract. Prolonged full employment and high prosperity may tend to weaken the allegiance of workers to their union, because wages then

General differences

tend to rise more from an increasing demand for labour than from union pressure. Such a weakening of allegiance to the union is particularly noticeable among younger members who did not live through the "heroic era" of a union's early struggles for recognition and improvements in low wages and poor working conditions.

Changes in the character of unions

The "generation problem" within the unions is complicated by rapid and substantial changes in the structure of the labour force in the industrial countries. The decline in agricultural jobs, the emergence of the semiskilled workers in the mass production industries, and the rise in the numbers of white-collar workers and employed women have changed not only the economic and social milieu within which the unions operate but also their recruiting potential and their character. White-collar workers have formed or joined unions in increasing numbers, though in lesser proportions than their blue-collar colleagues. A number of "quasi-unions" also have emerged—professional associations that, while often refusing to be classified as unions, increasingly behave as unions do and are sometimes prepared to cooperate with or even join confederations of manual workers.

GREAT BRITAIN

Early history. Britain was a pioneer in the development of modern industry, and its unions are among the oldest in the world. They go back to the late 18th century when artisans, threatened by the establishment of mechanized factories, formed local clubs for their common defense. Their efforts soon met with government hostility, based at first upon the common law concept that unions were in "restraint of trade." Later, under the impact of the French Revolution, the Combination Acts of 1799 and 1800 declared unions to be criminal conspiracies against the public. Even after those laws were repealed in 1824, legal and administrative measures against unions continued for a long time.

In 1834, for example, six Dorsetshire labourers from the village of Tolpuddle (the "Tolpuddle Martyrs") were sentenced to seven years' transportation to a penal colony in Australia for administering unlawful oaths in their trade union activities. It was only in 1871 that legislation was passed that exempted unions from prosecution because of "restraint of trade." Local trade clubs had survived intermittent prosecution, and in 1834 the reformer and socialist Robert Owen attempted, without lasting results, to organize them in a national movement—the Grand National Consolidated Trades Union.

In 1851 the Amalgamated Society of Engineers established the pattern for the "new model" unions—national associations of skilled workers who had passed through a regular apprenticeship. Their main economic weapon was their ability to restrict the number of apprentices, thereby limiting the supply of skilled labour. They also functioned as "friendly societies"; that is, they provided mutual assistance in case of sickness or for emigration.

During the same period, some of the leaders of the craft unions formed the so-called "Junta," which engaged in political action and joined Marx's International Workingmen's Association (the First International), even though most of them failed to understand—much less approve—the principles of Marxian socialism. This was not the first attempt of labour leaders to engage in political action. In the 1830s some unionists had joined a small group of radical members of Parliament in drawing up a petition for universal male suffrage, which became part of the platform of the Chartist reform movement. The Chartists were concerned mainly with electoral reform, but trade unions played an important part in their activities. Chartism was the first specifically working-class national movement in Britain. But the emergence of the working class as a major political force had to await the entrance of the miners into the political arena, the extension of the right to vote to large numbers of workers, and the organization of less skilled workers.

The legalization of unionism. After passage of the Trade-Union Act of 1871, which effectively legalized trade unions, unions of agricultural workers, seamen, gas workers, general and municipal workers, and dock workers

were organized. This period of union activity culminated in the successful dock workers' strike of 1889. The new unions emphasized nation-wide collective bargaining and demanded a legal minimum wage and an eight-hour day. Socialist ideas entered the movement, and political organizations of the working class—such as the Independent Labour Party—came to play an increasing role. Shortly after the turn of the century, the Labour Party was born.

"Contracting out" and "contracting in"

The legal status of unions became endangered by the Taff Vale court decision of 1901, which held that unions could be sued for losses incurred by employers as a result of union action. That decision was nullified by the Trade Disputes Act of 1906. Shortly before World War I financial support of the Labour Party by trade unions was legalized, provided that individual union members could "contract out." This meant that union members could choose not to pay the so-called political levy; that is, not make a contribution to the special fund that most unions established for support of the Labour Party. After the unsuccessful General Strike of 1926, that provision was changed into the "contracting in" system, which required union members to state expressly their wish to pay the political levy. As a result, a sizable proportion of union members failed to pay the levy, and in 1945 the newly elected Labour government once again established the "contracting out" principle.

The growth of union membership. Between 1910 and 1920 trade union membership more than trebled, from 2,565,000 to 8,334,000. But the postwar slump of 1921 and the return to the gold standard in 1925 led to a great crisis in the history of British trade unionism—the General Strike of 1926. The failure of the strike resulted in widespread disillusionment, which was intensified by the start of the Great Depression in 1930. By 1933 union membership had fallen to 4,392,000, half of what it had been in 1920. Afterward union membership gradually increased until by 1969 it stood at more than 10,000,000, about 9,500,000 of whom were affiliated with the Trades Union Congress (TUC), the national organization representing British trade unions. The diversity in size and organization of British unions is tremendous. They range from small local craft groups to giant general unions with memberships in excess of 1,400,000. A trend toward large-scale union mergers became apparent in the 1960s.

Dual system of bargaining. The basic institutional factor underlying problems of industrial relations in Britain is the existence of two bargaining systems: the industry-wide contract negotiated by the union and the employers' association, and the unofficial agreements arrived at in the various plants by managers, shop stewards, and individual workers. The terms reached under the unofficial system are consistently more favourable for the workers than those in the official contract. Such a dual system has its roots in the failure of most unions to control the shop stewards, and of the employers' associations to control the plant managers.

Shop steward control of the going pay rates

Union control over the shop stewards proved weak during World War I when the stewards assumed an authority that often brought them into conflict with the union leadership. World War II, and the long period of full employment that followed, reinforced that trend. The Industrial Relations Act of 1971 brought the first comprehensive legislation in this field in the country's history. It provided, among other things, for legally enforceable collective agreements between unions and employers.

Role of government. Caught between rising earnings, rising prices, and a great reluctance to permit a devaluation of the currency, the post-World War II governments embarked upon a series of experiments with methods of wage restraint. The first, undertaken in 1948–50, had ended in failure; and from 1951 to 1964 the Conservative governments made several attempts to limit wage and salary increases, but the unions refused to cooperate. When a Labour government was returned in 1964, some of the unions became more willing to accept an incomes policy. As a result, union (and business) representatives took their places on a Prices and Incomes Board empowered to investigate and suggest reforms, which were mainly related to enhancing productivity.

A searching investigation of the entire industrial relations system by the Donovan Commission (Royal Commission on Trade Unions and Employers' Associations) was also undertaken. Among other things, the commission recommended an obligatory 28-day conciliation period before any unofficial strike (any walkout not sanctioned by the official union leadership) could begin, and also a poll of the union's members if a major official strike was imminent and if the government doubted that the union leaders had rank-and-file support.

Various emergency measures were taken when the exchange rate of sterling was threatened in 1966 and again after sterling's devaluation in 1967. They included the suspension of all wage, price, and dividend increases for various periods. But in 1970 a government white paper admitted that "the use of a productivity, prices, and incomes policy for short-term purposes can only have a short-term effect. The long-term role of the policy is essentially an educational one."

The incomes policy put the responsibility for wage restraint on the unions. But, as mentioned above, effective earnings are determined not so much by the unions as by shop stewards, whose activities the union leaders do not entirely control. It was hardly surprising, therefore, that the incomes policy proved ineffective. Nor was it conceivable that the unions, created to improve their members earnings, could for long be turned into devices for preventing their members from obtaining the wage increases that management was willing to concede. The creation of an Industrial Relations Commission and of a Commission for Industry and Manpower in 1969–70 indicated that new means were being sought to promote and preserve collective bargaining under conditions of full employment while at the same time keeping price increases at an acceptable rate.

UNITED STATES

First steps toward wider organization

The beginnings.   Unionism in the United States goes back to the early days of national independence when craftsman employees in various trades—carpenters, masons, shoemakers, and printers—formed local groups to obtain shorter hours and higher wages. The Mechanics' Union of Trade Associations formed in Philadelphia in 1827 represented an early attempt to combine unions of different crafts on a local level. The first steps toward extending the organization beyond the local area were made in the 1830s but were only temporarily successful. Much emphasis was placed on political action and the formation of labour parties. The main objectives included free education and the abolition of property restrictions on the right to vote, which had survived from Colonial times in some states down to the Jacksonian era (1828–36). Once those objectives were achieved in the Northern states, the labour parties disappeared. Most of the unions—including the National Trades Union formed in 1834—were dissolved in the depression of 1837.

In the 1850s a new departure occurred. With improvements in transport and the consequent expansion of markets beyond local areas, unions in the same trade began to expand their fields of operation and to establish regional or even national federations. The National Typographical Union was formed in 1852 and was followed by five others. Concentration on job-connected problems rather than on broad, ideological issues was characteristic of this period.

The Knights of Labor.   The only large reform movement among the early labour organizations was backed by the Noble Order of the Knights of Labor, founded in 1869. Its objectives, many of them more political than industrial, were vague and moderate and included the eight-hour day and the abolition of child labour. Its rise was spectacular, especially after it won a strike against the Wabash Railroad, controlled by Jay Gould, a New York multimillionaire, in 1885. But after that victory, the organization soon declined—in part because of a growing anti-radical mood in the country. That mood was intensified by the Haymarket bomb episode in Chicago (1886), in which seven policemen were killed, and with which the Knights were quite unjustly associated. A more

significant factor in their decline was the fact that the Knights combined skilled and unskilled workers in one organization. The mass immigration of unskilled workers weakened their economic power to the point that union victories could be won only with the assistance of skilled workers; and when they were no longer willing to give battle on behalf of the unskilled immigrants, the decline of the Knights became inevitable.

The American Federation of Labor.   In the meantime, however, the American Federation of Labor began to supplant the Knights as a national federation of unions of skilled workers. Started with modest success as the Federation of Organized Trades and Labor Unions of the United States and Canada in 1881, it was transformed into the American Federation of Labor (AFL) five years later. Samuel Gompers, a cigar maker, was elected president, and his personality decisively shaped the AFL's evolution. It was to be a practical, non-ideological movement, accepting the existing social system but attempting to change it in favour of the organized skilled workers. The main instrument of change was to be collective bargaining. The affiliated organizations were to be autonomous within their "jurisdiction"; that is, the job territory over which their charter gave them full authority. Organization was limited to skilled workers, who alone were regarded as capable of forming effective unions.

Membership of the AFL grew only slowly until the turn of the century, partly because of a predominantly unfavourable economic situation and partly because of government hostility. Between 1900 and the outbreak of World War I, however, membership expanded from less than 600,000 to about 2,000,000. The war itself opened new opportunities for organized labour. Pres. Woodrow Wilson's administration gave Gompers semi-official status by making him a member of a small advisory commission to the Council of National Defense; and the President himself appeared at the 1917 AFL convention. By 1920 the membership of AFL-affiliated unions had doubled to 4,000,000.

Rise of anti-union sentiment in the 1920s

The next decade was a period of crisis and stagnation for unionism. Serious opposition to Gompers arose in 1921 in the person of John L. Lewis, newly elected head of the United Mine Workers. Gompers won, but his death in 1924 brought William Green, a member of the mine workers' union, to the presidency. The liquidation of the war industry, and a sharp anti-union offensive by many employers—who were supported by conservative U.S. presidents, hostile courts, and anti-labour sentiments of great sectors of the general public—combined to bring about a sharp decline in union membership. Under the slogan of the "open shop," by the use of so-called yellow dog contracts that required workers not to join unions, and by court injunctions against unions, employers staged a major offensive against organized labour. This not only kept the unions out of the steel industry but also reduced union membership to little more than its prewar level.

The "Wobblies."   The 1920s also saw the decline of an important union movement that had attempted to organize unskilled workers into industrial unions—the Industrial Workers of the World (IWW). The "Wobblies," as they were popularly known, had been founded in 1905 in Chicago in response to the AFL's opposition to unionism for unskilled workers. Consisting largely of itinerant industrial labourers, the IWW had concentrated on militant strike action, especially against employers hostile to unionism.

The movement included a considerable ideological element and eventually came under the control of anarchists and syndicalists. That fact, together with the IWW's strong opposition to World War I, led to the suppression of its press and to prosecutions under the Espionage and Sedition Acts of 1917 and 1918. After World War I, many states adopted legislation outlawing the IWW, thus driving it underground. It was further weakened by disputes with the Communists, so that by the mid-1920s it had ceased to be a significant force within the labour movement.

The Depression and New Deal.   The Great Depression, which began in 1929, almost destroyed some of the unions, but it also gave unionism a new start. The reasons for this new turning point were several. With the depression and the shifting political climate, there came a radical change in labour legislation—the Norris-LaGuardia Act of 1932, which removed the legal basis for the use of court injunctions in labour disputes. (In a partial reinterpretation of that 1932 act, the U.S. Supreme Court in 1970 ruled that unions could be enjoined from permitting walkouts in violation of no-strike pledges contained in their contracts.)

The New Deal legislation that followed the victory of Franklin D. Roosevelt in the presidential election of 1932 guaranteed the right of workers to join unions of their own choosing and required management to engage in collective bargaining if the majority of the workers so desired. A National Labor Relations Board was set up to enforce the law. Although the law was revised later by the Taft-Hartley Act and the Landrum-Griffin Act, its basic principle that collective bargaining is the most desirable way of determining wages and working conditions was not changed. Even when strikes threaten national security, only delaying action is legally provided for; in some situations, however, governmental pressure to avoid or settle strikes has, in fact, come close to coercion. Minimum wage legislation was passed on both the federal and state levels, and government encouragement of unionism was manifested not only during the New Deal but repeatedly throughout the presidencies of Harry S. Truman, John F. Kennedy, and Lyndon B. Johnson.

A basic change in unionism itself

The change in the governmental attitude toward unionism was accompanied by a basic transformation of unionism itself. Adjusting itself to the new, enlarged role of the government in economic affairs, as well as to the catastrophic consequences of the Great Depression, the AFL abandoned its traditional distrust of government regulation of industrial relations. With some reluctance it accepted and finally supported a government-sponsored social security system providing for gradual expansion of old age pensions, unemployment benefits, and—much later—health insurance.

The Congress of Industrial Organizations. No less important was the belated adjustment of the structure of unions to accommodate the growing number of semiskilled workers in the mass production industries, whose employees the traditional craft unions of the AFL had failed to organize. Under the leadership of the United Mine Workers' president John L. Lewis, eight unions within the AFL promoted organizing drives to establish industrial unions in such industries as steel, automobiles, rubber, and chemicals. When endorsement of his plan was defeated at the AFL convention in 1935, Lewis set up a Committee for Industrial Organization, which three years later was transformed into the Congress of Industrial Organizations (CIO). For having formed a rival organization the unions of the CIO were expelled by the AFL.

The decisive battles of the new organization were fought in the steel and automobile industries. A favourite weapon of the organizers—mainly mine workers' leaders assisted by intellectuals and a few Communists—was the sit-down strike, a strike during which workers do not walk out of the plant but remain idle at their work positions, thus paralyzing the plant and making it necessary for management to make an immediate response to their demands. Victories in the largest steel and automobile companies in 1937 were finally crowned by the capitulation of the Ford Motor Company in 1941.

World War II and after. The new competition induced the AFL in turn to engage in organizing drives. Total union membership grew from 2,900,000 in 1933 to 9,000,000 in 1939. By the end of World War II it had risen to 15,000,000, more than one-third of total nonagricultural employment. Just as had World War I, World War II induced union expansion, partly because of government assistance offered in return for a no-strike pledge.

The World War II era also witnessed a growth in anti-union sentiment, though not quite as sharp as that following the first World War. The passage of the Smith-Connally (War Labor Disputes) Act of 1943 over President Roosevelt's veto, and of the Taft-Hartley Act four years later over President Truman's veto, both of which introduced new government controls over unions, was

evidence of a changed public opinion. In spite of the post-war economic expansion, union membership stagnated—partly because of the shift toward white-collar employment that the unions found difficult to cope with. Jurisdictional disputes between unions affiliated to the two competitive federations led to a waste of union resources.

Merger of the AFL and CIO

On the other hand, the departure of the union leaders who had initiated and continued the AFL-CIO split removed some of the difficulties in the way of merging the two organizations. The expulsion of the Communist-dominated unions by the CIO in 1949 and the withdrawal of the United Mine Workers from the AFL also facilitated unification. In 1955 the AFL and CIO merged under the combined leadership of George Meany and Walter Reuther. The new organization (AFL-CIO) represented some 15,000,000 members at its birth. Not included in the new federation were the mine workers, some railroad unions, and various smaller organizations expelled for Communist domination; others were expelled later for corrupt practices—including the International Brotherhood of Teamsters with its more than 1,500,000 members.

The AFL and CIO had been instrumental, even before the merger, in setting up the International Confederation of Free Trade Unions (ICFTU) to combat the Communist-dominated World Federation of Trade Unions (WFTU). But issues of international policy soon caused sharp internal frictions between Meany and Reuther. While Meany criticized the ICFTU for failing to combat Communism with enough vigour, Reuther criticized Meany for complacency, for excessive concentration on a negative anti-Communist policy out of line with the thinking of most European unions, and for lack of imaginative leadership for social change. Personal rivalries intensified the conflict. In 1968 Reuther's United Automobile Workers left the AFL-CIO and combined with the Teamsters and two smaller unions and formed the Alliance for Labor Action (ALA) to engage in new organizing drives and to operate on a wider range of issues. The ALA had barely established itself when it lost its main driving force with the death of Walter Reuther in an airplane accident in 1970.

Unions of public employees. By means of an executive order issued in 1962 the Kennedy administration gave federal public employees the right to organize and bargain collectively, though not to strike. That action, together with some legislation at the state level, led to a rapid expansion of unionism among public employees. But the problem of how bargaining could be conducted effectively without the ultimate sanction of the strike remained to be solved.

A number of professional associations, though refusing to regard themselves as unions, began in the late 1960s to engage in collective bargaining and even, occasionally, to go out on strikes. The outstanding example was the influential National Education Association, several of whose affiliates carried out successful strikes. A whole class of quasi-unions was thus developing outside the traditional labour movement.

WESTERN EUROPE

Tendency toward ideological unions

Unionism on the Continent shares some features with unionism in Britain: early persecution by government and courts, reliance upon government intervention and mediation in disputes; a tendency for unions to carry on collective bargaining with employers' associations rather than with individual companies, and a general acceptance of the terms of agreements as a floor upon which higher effective earnings are achieved by various devices. A distinguishing characteristic of European trade unionism has been, and to a large extent still is, its tendency toward ideologically oriented unions, most of which were established by political parties or religious organizations in the 19th century. After World War II, a trend in the direction of unified trade unions, combining different ideological currents under one roof, manifested itself and has achieved considerable success.

Germany. Trade unionism began to gather momentum in Germany only after the fall of Otto von Bismarck in 1890. Under Socialist inspiration the bulk of the unions formed a national federation in that year. The Catholic

Centre Party followed in 1894 with the establishment of a much smaller federation of Christian unions. Nationalist- and, for a brief period, Communist-led unions, as well as separate white-collar unions came into being at various times before World War I. There were some successes in collective bargaining, but unions remained fairly insignificant during this period.

After World War I, the Socialist-inspired unions organized in three main federations: the Allgemeiner Deutscher Gewerkschaftsbund, ADGB (General Confederation of German Trade Unions), for the manual workers, the AFA for white-collar employees, and the ADB for civil servants. Collective agreements for an industry or trade set minimum wages, which in turn were supplemented by the efforts of workers' councils in the plants. The council members were elected by all workers and white-collar employees, whether union members or not. Legally, and often in fact, councils were independent of the unions. Unionism flowered during the short period of prosperity in the 1920s but was destroyed by the Nazi takeover in 1933. The Labour Front, established and totally controlled by the National Socialist (Nazi) Party, was not a union by any definition of the term. Immediately after World War II, a powerful trade union movement came into being in West Germany. It was based on a merger of 16 Socialist and Christian industrial unions in a unified Deutscher Gewerkschaftsbund (DGB). Its membership, whose turnover is high, has levelled off at 6,500,000 workers in 1970 after a rapid rise. In addition, there are union federations for white-collar workers and civil servants. A small separate Catholic federation has had little success.

Union delegates on management boards

Under the slogan of "codetermination" the unions have acquired direct representation in management. Legislation enacted in 1951 provides that in the coal and steel industries stockholders shall elect five members of an 11-man supervisory board of the company, and workers another five. Two of the workers' representatives come from the enterprise, a third is appointed by the union, and two more by the union federation, usually the DGB. The 11th member is jointly elected by the 10 others. In addition, one of the three members of the *Vorstand* (management), which actually runs the enterprise, must be selected with the approval of the workers' representatives; that member is in charge of labour relations. In other large firms, outside the coal and steel industries, labour holds one-third of the seats on the supervisory boards. The DGB has been campaigning for an extension of the coal and steel system to all large firms. A committee of social scientists appointed by the government to study the question in a 1970 report supported the DGB demand, though with some significant modification.

France. Ever since the merger in 1895 between syndicalist and Marxist trade unions, the French labour movement has suffered persistently from internal cleavages and organizational divisions. The main union federation, the Confédération Générale du Travail (CGT), was set up in that year. It represented a coalition of anarchists and syndicalists, who put their trust in a revolutionary general strike to destroy capitalism and the state, together with a group of Marxists, who aimed at obtaining control of the state by a revolution. The syndicalists organized local union federations, mostly of an industrial nature.

Syndicalism broke down in the World War I wave of patriotism that engulfed French workers; after 1918 the Communists inherited a large part of the syndicalist following. For most of the time ever since, the French labour movement has been divided into three main (and several smaller) ideologically inspired federations: the CGT under Communist control, the mostly Socialist FO (Force Ouvrière, Workers' Strength), and the formerly Christian CFDT (Confédération Française Démocratique du Travail, French Democratic Confederation of Labour), which has been trying to overcome its religious origins and the limits those origins set to its expansion among the main body of French workers.

Although most French workers are not organized, and those who are union members pay their dues only irregularly, the elections of workers' councils and shop stewards (*délégués du personnel*) roughly indicate worker allegiances. It would thus appear that a small majority supports the CGT and somewhat fewer the CFDT and FO. White-collar workers are organized in the CGC (Confédération Générale des Cadres). Other unions remain outside all confederations.

In view of the fragmentation in the French labour movement, it is not surprising that collective bargaining developed late—after 1936. It is still less significant than labour legislation and administrative action in determining wages and working conditions. Workers' councils, to provide worker participation in management, and the shop steward system, to handle grievances in the plant, were both established by law. But by the early 1970s, dwindling union strength had weakened both institutions to the point that they were not functioning in large numbers of enterprises. The great strike movement of the late 1960s, which was organized more for political reasons than as a collective bargaining tactic, developed outside the unions. Later on, however, the unions finally succeeded in controlling it.

Collective bargaining a late and minor factor

Italy. In Italy, much the same as in France, the unions have remained weakened and divided by ideologies and religion. The late economic and political development of Italy directed labour's attention toward radical and political solutions. Soon after the resurgence of unions that followed the downfall of Mussolini's Fascist regime, the old tendency toward multiple and changing divisions within the movement reasserted itself.

Three major confederations emerged after World War II: the Confederazione Generale Italiana del Lavoro (CGIL), led by a coalition of Communists and left-wing Socialists; the Confederazione Italiana Sindicati Lavora-tori (CISL), representing the Catholic labour movement, but with some Socialists as well; and the Unione Italiana del Lavoro (UIL) under Social Democratic leadership. In the wide-scale strikes of 1969–70, the unions persuaded far more than their members to join the so-called rolling strikes—short walkouts, one after the other, in different industries.

When labour agreements are reached, they usually are national in scope, and some cover benefits and conditions for all industries. In 1962 the unions obtained the additional right to conclude supplementary agreements at the plant level.

Scandinavia. The consolidation of local unions into national organizations paralleled the advance of industrialization in Norway, Sweden, and Denmark during the second half of the 19th century. That trend toward centralized unionism received support at the Scandinavian Labour Congress of 1897; and, by 1900, all three countries had small but firmly rooted federations of national trade unions. Employers' associations followed similar development from a local to national scale.

By the late 1930s the federations of workers and employers in the three countries had agreed on certain basic principles in the conduct of labour relations. Agreements between the labour and management federations, besides placing limitations on sympathetic lockouts and strikes, provide for orderly negotiations by upholding the right to organize for collective bargaining and by laying down procedures for discussion. The broad measure of understanding between labour and management and their common desire to keep government intervention at a minimum has facilitated responsible collective bargaining. Strikes and lockouts have not been entirely eliminated, but their occurrence has become less frequent, although a reversal of this trend manifested itself beginning in 1968. Full collective bargaining rights, including the right to strike, have been extended in Sweden to government employees of all kinds.

Agreement on basic principles

In Scandinavia collective bargaining is highly centralized in comparison with the United States or Great Britain. The influence of the federations of labour in conducting negotiations or determining national policy far surpasses that exerted by the AFL-CIO or the British TUC. The federations have the power to ensure that their basic decisions are implemented in the industry agreements. They have acquired an important role in political affairs through their close alliance with the Labour and Socialist parties. In Sweden, the federation has pursued a policy of establishing skill and industry differentials—the so-called solidarity policy—but effective wages have often departed from contract rates, thus counteracting the solidarity policy.

Norwegian and Swedish unions are organized chiefly on an industrial basis, whereas the Danish unions—comparable to the British in this respect—are both general and industrial. Although it is not compulsory, union membership is widespread, even among white-collar workers.

COMMUNIST NATIONS

Soviet Union. The Russian labour movement owes its origin to the strikes of the 1890s, in which revolutionary students and workers cooperated against the tsarist regime and capitalist business owners. Hampered by a hostile government, the trade union movement slowly developed on the general pattern of the German labour organizations. With the Russian Revolution in 1917, however, the entire basis of the developing labour movement changed. Under Lenin's strategy, the unions became one of the links connecting the Communist Party—a small, close-knit elite of professional revolutionaries—with the large mass of industrial workers on whose behalf the party would operate.

A key question arose after the Bolshevik takeover. What role would unions perform in a Socialist system in which capitalism had ceased to operate? A long and involved debate followed. The unions themselves endeavoured to fill the traditional role of trade unions: to maintain or improve the living standards of their members. Leon Trotsky argued, however, that the unions should be transformed into "production agents" so that they would serve the workers' interests by fostering increased productivity of labour, promoting economic reconstruction, and providing increased quantities of consumer goods. Unions were thus to be instruments of economic administration, with only a subsidiary role in setting wages and working conditions. Another more radical role was proposed by the Workers' Opposition, which urged that the trade unions should dominate the state and manage the economy.

The answer to the question of what role unions were to play in the new Communist state was, in fact, dictated by an overall economic policy that called for the commitment of all possible resources to industrialization. The destruction of much of the productive equipment of the country in World War I, the civil war, and the ensuing foreign intervention made it impossible for the shattered economy to satisfy even the most elementary needs of the population. Moreover, the failure of Germany to abolish capitalism, as the Bolsheviks had hoped, required a complete revision of Bolshevik strategy. In the absence of victorious revolutions in the industrially advanced nations, the "dictatorship of the proletariat" in the Soviet Union was doomed unless that country could be rapidly industrialized. Thus, the growth of a working class to build an industrial base in the Soviet Union became the main task of both party and unions.

Such a program, however, required that real wages be kept to a minimum so that all possible resources could be devoted to capital formation. Consequently, unions could not be permitted to assist workers in raising their living standards. Instead, they became instruments of the state to increase output and speed industrialization. That production-oriented role gave rise to a trade union structure appropriate to the machinery of Soviet economic administration and adaptable to its changes.

Soviet trade unions are strictly industrial in nature. All persons employed in any one factory, state farm, or other undertaking belong to the same union; and that same union comprises all of the employees of similar factories, farms, or other enterprises everywhere else in the Soviet Union. Horizontal coordination occurs at the republic, regional, and local levels; but just as the economic administration has been closely centralized, so the national organs of the trade unions exercise effective authority over all lower levels of the union. More than 90 percent of industrial workers belong to unions, mainly because of the considerable advantages, such as social insurance benefits, available to members.

Soviet trade unions do not limit their activities to industry and plant matters alone. Their other functions include legislative initiative in labour matters; participation in

Unions as instruments of the state

national economic planning and wages policy; the administration of social insurance; the organization of cultural and recreational facilities; and cooperation in the education and vocational training of workers. Moves in the 1960s toward decentralization in economic planning and administration, the use of incentives, and the assignment of greater authority to local managers have given rise to an increase in union influence at the lower levels. Among the unions' new roles are greater participation in the settling of grievances and in application of the wage system at the plant level.

Some observers have discerned a tendency for the Soviet industrial relations system to evolve in the direction of those of other advanced industrial nations. Nevertheless, like all other organizations in the Soviet Union, the trade unions remain in all essentials under the complete control of the Communist Party.

Poland. The Communist view of unions as organs of the state was dramatized in Poland, where an independent union, Solidarność (Solidarity) arose in 1980 amid serious economic difficulties, was recognized by the government as a matter of tactical accommodation, and was then suppressed a little more than a year later under a decree of martial law.

Yugoslavia. After its break with the Soviet Union in 1948, Yugoslavia commenced a program of economic reforms combining the profit motive, public ownership of most means of production, and a gradual decentralization of economic decision making.

The system of centrally directed state-managed enterprises has been progressively replaced by a workers' self-management system under which relatively free economic decisions are made. The concept of workers' self-management, recognizing the system's potential conflict of interest between management and workers, stresses the role of workers as coproducers in the enterprise. Management is exercised by a director, who is under the supervision of a workers' council elected by the employees of the enterprise.

To the extent that workers' councils actually represent the workers' interests, they have superseded the role of the trade union within the enterprise. Union functions have consequently been reduced to such activities as assisting individual workers in personal matters, obtaining better training and education for workers, and exercising a modest participatory role in various enterprise deliberations.

The unions appear to be attempting to offset the decline in their traditional functions within an enterprise by enhancing their influence at provincial and national levels. There, the trade unions endeavour to participate in decisions on social and economic issues within the framework set by the political system.

Coproducer role for workers

JAPAN

Japanese labour unions are mainly the product of the post-World War II period. With the support of the U.S. occupation forces, the Japanese government adopted a drastic labour-protection policy immediately after the war. Its constitution was amended in 1946 so that workers' rights "to organize and to bargain and act collectively" were guaranteed. The phenomenal postwar economic growth of Japan has resulted in a great increase in employment.

Unions enterprise-oriented. Union structure in Japan differs sharply from the Western pattern. The enterprise—not a craft or industry—provides the base of union organization. One of the main features of enterprise unionism is "lifetime" employment. Employers do not, as a rule, lay off workers either permanently or temporarily; on the other hand, workers are not expected to move from one company to another. Typically, the enterprise recruits and trains young workers immediately after their graduation from school, and continues to employ them until they reach retirement age, usually 55. Educational background and length of service in a given company are the key factors in wage determination. Under such a system collective bargaining naturally focusses on particular enterprises or companies.

National confederations. Most of the enterprise unions are combined in national unions or in federations that

"Lifetime" jobs for workers

are affiliated with national confederations. Major confederations are Sōhyō (General Council of Trade Unions of Japan); Dōmei (Japanese Confederation of Labour); and Chūritsurōren (Liaison Council of Neutral Labour Unions). The national confederations participate very little in bargaining with employers; their major function is the guidance and coordination of their affiliated enterprise unions. Each spring, the national confederations form a special committee for Shunto (the spring offensive). The committee plans the amount of the wage increase to be demanded, the period of negotiations, and the dates of industry-wide strikes.

National unions and confederations play an even more important role in politics by allying themselves with one of the parties—Nippon Shakaitō (Socialist), Minshatō (Democratic Socialist), and Kyosanto (Communist).

The new mobility. Some changes in the system seem to be resulting from Japan's high economic growth rates. Because the labour market, especially for young workers, has become extremely tight, and because labour mobility has increased, the lifetime employment system has begun to be eroded. Rapid technological changes have made obsolete the traditional system of basing wages on length of service. Young workers with a modern school education are more suitable for many of the new jobs. Partly because of the high rate of economic growth and partly because of the Shunto bargaining targets, the unions have been successful in obtaining high wage increases. Thus the main emphasis of the Japanese labour movement has begun to shift from politics to economics.

AUSTRALIA AND NEW ZEALAND

Early settlers, who had brought the ideal of unionism along with them from England, established the first workingmen's organizations in Australia and New Zealand in the 1830s in the form of small trade societies. The foundations of modern unionism in Australia were not laid until two or three decades later, however, when urban craft unions for skilled workers began to emerge in the 1850s and 1860s. During that period and until 1890 "mass" or "industrial" unions were formed, first by the coal miners and subsequently by others, including gold miners, seamen, and wool shearers. Economic growth and a labour shortage favoured union expansion. With manhood suffrage already a reality, the union movement devoted its attention to such essentially economic issues as the eighthour day.

Miners among the first "mass" unions

Two distinctive features of present-day trade unionism, namely, political participation and compulsory arbitration, can be traced back to the serious strike setbacks and the economic depression of the 1890s. The Australian Labor Party, created and largely financed by the unions, has been a significant force on the Australian political scene since it first gained office in 1910. The Labour Party of New Zealand also derives much of its strength from trade union support.

Compulsory arbitration. Before 1890 unions had opposed the idea of compulsory arbitration. After losing a number of major strikes in which union recognition had been the main issue, the unions adopted a more favourable attitude toward arbitration, which would force employers to recognize them. Despite the retention of state arbitration systems in some form since passage of the first Commonwealth Conciliation and Arbitration Act of 1904, the focus of attention and activity has gradually shifted to the federal sphere. By the 1970s industrial relations were dominated by compulsory arbitration, yet collective bargaining continued, generally under close union control. Nor was strike action precluded by compulsory arbitration. Indeed, by international standards, the frequency of strikes in Australia has been relatively high, although with a short average duration.

In pre-Commonwealth days the need for close coordination for the successful pursuit of labour's objectives was expressed in successive Intercolonial Trade Union congresses, beginning in 1879. Their direct descendant is the Australian Council of Trade Unions (ACTU), founded in 1927.

Later developments in New Zealand. Trade unions developed in Australia and New Zealand along broadly similar lines. In New Zealand, however, 1936 legislation provided for compulsory unionism. This took the form of providing that every employer bound by an award of the Court of Arbitration, or by any industrial agreement, could not employ a worker subject to the award or agreement unless that worker was a member of the union also bound by the award or agreement. This resulted in a considerable expansion and strengthening of the union movement. In 1961 the 1936 legislation was amended. Compulsory membership was made subject to agreement between employer and union or to a demand by more than 50 percent of the employees in an industry for compulsory unionism. Provision was made also to allow any worker conscientiously objecting to union membership to apply for a certificate of exemption. In the absence of a compulsory membership agreement, provision was made for the preferential hiring of unionists over non-unionists.

Development of trade unions in emerging nations

THE INDIAN SUBCONTINENT

India. According to a 1961 census, India's wage earners totalled 24,000,000, or 13 percent of its labour force, most of which was engaged in subsistence agriculture. Of the 24,000,000 wage earners, about 4,000,000 (17 percent) were estimated to be organized in unions.

The weakness of Indian trade unionism is related to the country's slow industrialization. Historically, Indian unions were closely linked to the independence movement. The Indian National Congress Party took the initiative for the formation in 1920 of the first national body of trade unions, the All-India Trade Union Congress (AITUC), but this soon split into several factions.

The history of the trade union movement in India is one of conflicts and splits resulting mainly from ideological rivalries. Inter-union rivalry has hindered its development. Collective bargaining is ineffective in India because the unions are not strong enough to force settlements; union rivalry makes the situation worse. As a result, unions tend to turn to the government for intervention. The Industrial Disputes Act of 1947 empowered the central or provincial governments to refer an industrial dispute for adjudication. In addition, wage boards have been set up for the determination of wages.

Pakistan. Though the nonagricultural sector of the Pakistan economy has expanded considerably since independence was achieved in 1947, some 20 years later (prior to separation from Bangladesh) approximately 68 percent of the total labour force of 40,000,000 was still engaged in agriculture.

The All-Pakistan Confederation of Labour, established in 1950, has been recognized by the government as the sole representative of the workers in Pakistan. Many other trade union federations, however, have sprung up. Just as its Indian counterpart, the Pakistan labour movement is divided, and inter-union rivalry is a major handicap to its development. Collective bargaining is extremely difficult; when agreements are concluded they usually result from voluntary concessions made by progressive employers. Unilateral employer's decisions and government intervention play a dominant role in industrial relations.

LATIN AMERICA

The highest rate of population increase of any area in the world not only has put a heavy strain on the educational systems of most Latin American countries but also has produced excess supplies of common labour. As a result, advances in wages and working conditions have been exceedingly difficult. Accordingly, one of the main objectives of Latin American trade unions has been to protect and insulate the employed labour force from the consequences of an excess supply of unemployed labour. Various job-protection devices have been developed, mainly based upon a system of severance pay proportionate to the length of an employee's service. Such a system makes dismissal expensive for the employer.

Ideological orientations. Labour movements in Latin

America consistently have taken on an ideological colouring. In the early 1970s there were three main groupings of unions: those affiliated with the mildly progressive ORIT (Organización Regional Interamericana de Trabajadores), which in turn belongs to the International Confederation of Free Trade Unions (see below); the Clasc (Confederación Latinoamericana de Sindicalistas Cristianos), a radical Christian movement strongly opposed to what is described as the American dominance of ORIT; and finally, the largely underground organizations, dominated by Communist parties or Communist sympathizers.

Mexico. Among the Latin American labour movements Mexico's is the most successful, partly as a result of the high growth rates of the Mexican economy during and after World War II. Although collective bargaining has been practiced for many years and is fairly well developed, the trade unions have succeeded in welding a close relationship to Mexico's governing party; the unions, in fact, constitute one of the three main divisions of the party organization. Thus, the success of the Mexican labour movement since about 1920 has depended mainly on relationship to the government party.

Decisive role of labour courts

Elaborate labour legislation based on Article 123 of the Mexican Constitution gives labour courts powerful means to intervene in disputes. They may declare a strike lawful or unlawful, and by their decision the outcome of a strike is more or less settled. Unlawful strikes have few chances of success, but a lawful strike is almost certain to bring advances to the union.

AFRICA

During most of the colonial period in sub-Saharan Africa, unionism, when it existed at all, was limited to white workers. Attempts of black workers to form unions—usually for the purpose of obtaining wages and working conditions similar to those of white workers—were frequently treated as rebellious political movements and suppressed. Black workers were thus compelled to engage in strikes and demonstrations without having a stable organization at their disposal. Violence often accompanied these short-lived movements.

In the late 1930s, and especially during and after World War II, colonial governments altered their policies and introduced trade unionism in their territories. Usually these unions were patterned after the model of the mother country, and in many cases they were simply branches of metropolitan unions. In some areas—as for instance Guinea and Kenya—close cooperation developed in due course between the unions and the national liberation movements. Political leaders were also often union leaders, or closely associated with them. In other parts of Africa—in Rhodesia, for example—the national liberation movements ignored the unions, the membership of which was rather small and which were therefore not in a position to offer financial or mass support to political movements.

After independence was achieved, unions consistently abandoned the patterns inherited from the former metropolitan territories. Western-style unionism was clearly inappropriate in sub-Saharan Africa with its low level of literacy, a labour force with a large migratory component, few educated working-class leaders, low living standards, and a poorly developed labour market. The unions, however, were rarely given an opportunity to develop new autonomous forms of organization and action. Almost everywhere the government party, by a combination of rewards and pressures, took over the unions under the slogan of "African socialism" and turned them into instruments to enhance production and restrict the wage demands of their members.

Only sporadically, mostly in North Africa, did autonomous unions survive. In most cases they formed the nucleus of the opposition to the government, as is the case in Morocco.

International organizations

The large trade union movements of various countries for many years have maintained loose alliances by joining international organizations of labour; federations of unions, rather than individual unions, usually hold membership. In 1901, the International Federation of Trade Unions was established, chiefly under the guidance of German unions. It proved to be ineffective and disappeared during World War I. In 1919 it was revived at Amsterdam, but immediately came into collision with the Red International of Labour Unions, established by the new government of the Soviet Union. The Communist organization had a brief period of expansion but soon dwindled away and had disappeared before 1939.

Unity and division. At a 1945 conference in London a new organization came into being, the World Federation of Trade Unions (WFTU). Its principal organizers were the British Trades Union Congress, the U.S. Congress of Industrial Organizations, and the Soviet Russian Labour Federation. It made a vigorous but unsuccessful attempt to reconcile the differences between the Communist and non-Communist factions. The U.S. announcement of the Marshall Plan for economic aid to Europe, in which the Soviet Union and other Communist states declined to participate, provided the occasion for the withdrawal of the non-Communist faction.

Ideological cleavage of the international labour movement

In 1949, in London, the non-Communist groups created the International Confederation of Free Trade Unions (ICFTU). At the first session, 70 labour organizations of 53 nations, claiming to represent 50,000,000 workers, became "founding members." The ICFTU was readily accepted by nearly all of the non-Communist-led labour organizations of the world; and after 10 years it had grown to include 138 organizations located in 103 different countries, representing more than 57,000,000 workers.

The announced purposes of the ICFTU include: striving for world peace, the spreading of democratic institutions, increasing the standard of living for workers everywhere, a worldwide strengthening of free trade unions, and support to colonial people in their struggle for freedom. The ICFTU consistently opposed Fascist as well as Communist dictatorships, and implemented that policy by giving such aid as was possible to free labour in Spain and certain Latin American countries. It also furnished direct financial assistance to workers in Hungary and Tibet and campaigned against racialist policies in South Africa.

Failures and successes of the ICFTU. Lack of homogeneity among affiliates hindered the activity of the ICFTU in many fields, chiefly because of differences among its affiliates in the approach to unions in Communist-controlled countries. It found its work to be most effective in the area of international education. By 1960 it had created an International Solidarity Fund of $2,000,000 to aid workers who became victims of oppression and to promote democratic trade unionism in economically underdeveloped countries. Problems of union organization were discussed at ICFTU seminars in various parts of the world, with experienced labour leaders and labour spokesmen from the less industrialized countries participating.

To facilitate the functioning of its widespread activities, the ICFTU established headquarters in Brussels, Belgium, with regional or subregional offices in many other countries. From one or more of those centres it conducted numerous educational conferences, maintained a residential trade union training college in Calcutta, India, and assisted in founding an African Labour College in Kampala, Uganda. It provided assistance to inexperienced workers in areas in the first stages of industrialization and sent organizers to Lebanon, Okinawa, Cyprus, Cameroon, India, Indonesia, Nigeria, and elsewhere.

Worldwide program of training industrial workers

It has been the consistent policy of the ICFTU to cooperate with the United Nations Educational, Scientific, and Cultural Organization and with the International Labour Office in Geneva. It is wholly financed by contributions from its affiliates.

Communist and Catholic federations. The WFTU, meanwhile, has continued to be completely dominated by the Communists. It claimed to represent more than 90,000,-000 workers by 1960, more than one-half in the Soviet Union and a large part of the remainder in Soviet satellite nations. It also has substantial affiliates in France and Italy. The WFTU has adhered strictly to the Communist Party line and has not cooperated with other organizations, serving more as a political instrument than as an economically oriented federation of unions.

A much smaller international organization, the International Federation of Christian Trade Unions (IFCTU), now called the WCL (World Confederation of Labour), is made up largely of Catholic labour unions in France, Italy, and Latin America. The ICFTU, at its founding congress in 1949, invited the affiliates of the IFCTU to join, but the invitation was rejected. On the international scene, the WCL has been a comparatively ineffective organization, its influence limited to a few countries in Europe and Latin America.

(A.F.St.)

BIBLIOGRAPHY

Organization of work: The classic work in this field is EMILE DURKHEIM, *De la division du travail social* (1893; *The Division of Labor in Society,* 1960); more recent standard accounts include THEODORE CAPLOW, *The Sociology of Work* (1954); CLARK KERR et al., *Industrialism and Industrial Man,* 2nd ed. (1964); and GEORGES FRIEDMANN, *Le Travail en miettes, spécialisation et loisirs* (1956; Eng. trans., *The Anatomy of Work,* 1961). The volumes of the *Cambridge Economic History of Europe* contain chapters dealing with the organization of work in the context of general economic history. For the organization of work among prehistoric peoples, see RICHARD B. LEE and IRVEN DEVORE (eds.), *Man the Hunter* (1968) and CARLETON S. COON, *The Hunting Peoples* (1971). The evolution of the organization of work in early civilizations is treated in KARL A. WITTFOGEL, *Oriental Despotism* (1957); ROBERT MCC. ADAMS, *The Evolution of Urban Society: Early Mesopotamia and Prehispanic Mexico* (1965); and CLAUDE MOSSE, *Le Travail en Grèce et à Rome* (1966; Eng. trans., *The Ancient World at Work,* 1969). Medieval and early modern developments are treated in two French texts: EMILE LEVASSEUR, *Histoire des classes ouvrières en France....,* 12 vol. (1859); and GUSTAVE FAGNIEZ, *Études sur l'industrie et la classe industrielle à Paris aux XIIIe et XIVe siècles* (1877); while developments in England are stressed in GEORGE UNWIN, *Industrial Organisation in the Sixteenth and Seventeenth Centuries* (1904). History of the American working class is explored in DAVID W. GALENSON, *White Servitude in Colonial America* (1981); THOMAS DUBLIN (ed.), *Farm to Factory: Women's Letters, 1830–1860* (1981); PAUL G. FALER, *Mechanics and Manufacturers in the Early Industrial Revolution: Lynn, Massachusetts, 1760–1860* (1981). General overviews of organization of work can be found in RUSSELL STOUT, *Management or Control? The Organizational Challenge* (1980); and JAY M. SHAFRITZ, *Dictionary of Personnel Management and Labor Relations* (1980).

Changes in the organization of work with the development of the factory system in the early Industrial Revolution, especially in the textile industries, are covered in several standard works: HERBERT HEATON, *The Yorkshire Woollen and Worsted Industries,* 2nd ed. (1965); J.L. and BARBARA HAMMOND, *The Rise of Modern Industry* (1925); and PAUL MANTOUX, *La Révolution Industrielle du XVIIIe siècle* (1906; Eng. trans., *The Industrial Revolution in the Eighteenth Century,* rev. ed., 1948). An interesting account, from the standpoint of modern sociology, is NEIL J. SMELSER, *Social Change in the Industrial Revolution* (1959). The philosophy of FREDERICK WINSLOW TAYLOR, the founder of scientific management, is described in his *Principles of Scientific Management* (1911, reprinted 1967); the older biography, *Frederick W. Taylor, Father of Scientific Management,* 2 vol., by FRANK BARKLEY COPLEY (1923), remains the standard treatment of his life despite some recent attempts at psychoanalytic biography. The applications of scientific management by Taylor and his contemporaries are treated in HUGH G.J. AITKEN, *Taylorism at Watertown Arsenal* (1960); and SAMUEL HABER, *Efficiency and Uplift: Scientific Management in the Progressive Era, 1890–1920* (1964). ELTON MAYO, the pioneer industrial sociologist, has contributed two major summations: *The Human Problems of an Industrial Civilization,* 2nd ed. (1946) and *The Social Problems of an Industrial Civilization* (1945). A collaborator of Mayo's in the Hawthorne experiments, FRITZ J. ROETHLISBERGER, has written, with WILLIAM J. DICKSON, *Management and the Worker* (1939). Other major accounts of the modern factory system include W. LLOYD WARNER and J.O. LOW, *The Social System of the Modern Factory* (1947); and CHARLES R. WALKER and ROBERT H. GUEST, *The Man on the Assembly Line* (1952). There are many accounts of the development of automation; its effects on the organization of work are shown in two early and still standard works, WALTER BUCKINGHAM, *Automation: Its Impact on Business and People* (1961); and JAMES R. BRIGHT, *Automation and Management* (1958); the effects of automation on white-collar clerical tasks are treated in IDA R. HOOS, *Automation in the Office* (1959). See also DANIEL NELSON, *Frederick W. Taylor and the Rise of*

Scientific Management (1980); DALE E. ZAND, *Information, Organization, and Power: Effective Management in the Knowledge Society* (1981); and RONALD AMANN and JULIAN COOPER (eds.), *Industrial Innovation in the Soviet Union* (1982).

Specialized aspects of contemporary industrial sociology are dealt with in CONRAD ARENSBERG et al., *Research in Industrial Human Relations* (1957); ERNEST J. MCCORMICK, *Human Factors Engineering* (1964); and FREDERICK HERZBERG, *Work and the Nature of Man* (1966). Documents, position papers, statistical data, and much other valuable information regarding contemporary problems and trends in the organization of work are to be found in the many volumes published by President Lyndon B. Johnson's National Commission on Technology, Automation, and Economic Progress (1966). Later works on industrial sociology include IRA C. MAGAZINER, *Minding America's Business: The Decline and Rise of the American Economy* (1982); ALLAN J. COX, *The Cox Report on the American Corporation* (1982); THOMAS J. PETERS and ROBERT H. WATERMAN, *In Search of Excellence: Lessons from America's Best-Run Companies* (1982); ROBERT L. VENINGA and JAMES P. SPRADLEY, *The Work/Stress Connection* (1981).

Industrial and organizational relations: M. CROZIER, *Le phénomèna bureaucratique* (1964; Eng. trans. 1964), a classic study of organizational behaviour in France; F. HERZBERG, B. MAUSNER, and B. SNYDERMAN, *The Motivation to Work,* 2nd ed. (1959), systematic statement of the influential and controversial two-factor theory of job satisfaction and motivation; R.R. RITTI, *Engineers and the Industrial Corporation* (1970), an examination of the roles and problems of engineers in a large industrial organization with a high level of technological and scientific development; F.J. ROETHLISBERGER and W.J. DICKSON, *Management and the Worker* (1939), the pioneering study that opened the field to behavioral scientists, still worth reading; L.R. SAYLES, *Managerial Behavior* (1964), an approach to analysis of managerial behaviour emphasizing lateral and diagonal relations; C.R. WALKER, *Toward the Automatic Factory* (1957), a case study of the introduction of an automatic tube mill in the steel industry; R.E. WALTON and R.B. MCKERSIE; *A Behavioral Theory of Labor Negotiations* (1965), an interpretation of collective bargaining in terms of integrative versus distributive issues; W.F. WHYTE, *Organizational Behavior: Theory and Application* (1969), a textbook that generally follows the approach of this article; J. WOODWARD, *Industrial Organization: Theory and Practice* (1965), the study that provoked a reorientation of research to take into account the behavioral impact of different types of technology; M.Y. YOSHINO, *Japan's Managerial System: Tradition and Innovation* (1968), the best assessment of Japanese management in terms of historical development and current organization and activities. Management and organizational relations are also discussed in PETER F. DRUCKER, *The Changing World of the Executive* (1982); JAMES O'TOOLE, *Making America Work: Productivity and Responsibility* (1981); C.V. BROWN, *Taxation and the Incentive to Work* (1981); JOHN F. WITTE, *Democracy, Authority, and Alienation in Work: Workers' Participation in an American Corporation* (1980); FRED K. FOULKES, *Personnel Policies in Large Nonunion Companies* (1980); ROBERT B. DENHARDT, *In the Shadow of Organization* (1981); and STEVEN KELMAN, *Regulating America, Regulating Sweden: A Comparative Study of Occupational Safety and Health Policy* (1981). MARILYN TAYLOR THOMPSON, *Management Information* (1981), is an annotated bibliography.

Structure of the labour force: SOLOMON BARKIN (ed.), *Technical Change and Manpower Planning: Coordination at Enterprise Level* (1967), consisting of 28 case studies dealing with eight countries; VICTOR FUCHS, *The Service Economy* (1968), an analysis of the expanding tertiary sector in the United States; A.J. JAFFE and J.N. FROOMKIN, *Technology and Jobs: Automation in Perspective* (1968); and L.C. HUNTER, G.L. REID, and D. BODDY, *Labour Problems of Technological Change* (1970), a thorough study of the British situation. Problems of human resources are analyzed in DAVID STERN, *Managing Human Resources: The Art of Full Employment* (1982); THEODORE W. SCHULTZ, *Investing in People: The Economics of Population Quality* (1981); JOHN APPLEGATH, *Working Free: Practical Alternatives to the 9 to 5 Job* (1982); ROBERT L. KAHN, *Work and Health* (1981); CHARLES F. SABEL, *Work and Politics: The Division of Labor in Industry* (1982); TAMARA K. HAREVEN, *Family Time and Industrial Time* (1982); CHRISTINA MASLACH, *Burnout, the Cost of Caring* (1982); RONALD M. MASON, *Participatory and Workplace Democracy* (1982).

Among the most important general works on employment and unemployment in modern industrial society are: JOHN MAYNARD KEYNES, *The General Theory of Employment, Interest and Money* (1936, reissued 1976); and WILLIAM HENRY BEVERIDGE, *Full Employment in a Free Society,* 2nd ed. (1960). A general introductory text is INGRID H. RIMA, *Labor Markets, Wages, and Employment* (1981). See also J.O.N. PERKINS, *Unemployment, Inflation, and New Macroeconomic Policy* (1982); PAULA

GOLDMAN LEVENTMAN, *Professionals Out of Work* (1981); LEWIS C. SOLMON et al., *Unemployed Ph.D.'s* (1981); RICHARD KAZIS and RICHARD L. GROSSMAN, *Fear at Work: Job Blackmail, Labor, and the Environment* (1982); CHRISTOPHER FREEMAN, JOHN CLARK, and LUC SOETE, *Unemployment and Technical Innovation* (1982); SIDNEY WEINTRAUB, *Our Stagflation Malaise: Ending Inflation and Unemployment* (1981).

There is a vast quantity of specialized literature. Notable examples of this include: publications of the INTERNATIONAL LABOUR ORGANISATION, particularly its *Manpower Aspects of Recent Economic Developments in Europe* (1969); the publications of the ORGANISATION FOR ECONOMIC CO-OPERATION AND DEVELOPMENT; *Employment and Earnings,* a useful monthly report issued by the UNITED STATES BUREAU OF LABOR STATISTICS; and *OECD Countries: Unemployment in the 1970s and Perspectives for the 1980s* (1980), a research paper published by the NATIONAL FOREIGN ASSESSMENT CENTER in the United States. Analytical reference sources include PETER B. DOERINGER (ed.), *Workplace Perspectives on Education and Training* (1981); MARLISS JOHNSTON (ed.), *A Directory of Vocational-Technical Schools and Institutes in the U.S.A.* (1981); PAUL WASSERMAN (ed.), *Training and Development Organizations Directory,* 2nd ed. (1980).

Labour economics: Some textbooks that apply economic analysis to labour in the particular circumstances of labour markets are: G.F. BLOOM and H.R. NORTHRUP, *The Economics of Labor Relations,* 6th ed. (1969); A.M. CARTTER and F.R. MARSHALL, *Labor Economics: Wages, Employment and Trade Unionism* (1966); L.C. HUNTER and D.J. ROBERTSON, *Economics of Wages and Labour* (1969); L.G. REYNOLDS, *Labor Economics and Labor Relations,* 5th ed. (1970); and E.H. PHELPS BROWN, *The Economics of Labor* (1962).

The relation of the labour force to the population of a number of countries is surveyed in UNITED NATIONS, *Sex and Age Patterns of Participation in Economic Activities,* Population Studies no. 33, rept. 1 (1962); and in C.D. LONG, *The Labor Force Under Changing Income and Employment* (1958). Education is treated as a form of investment in G.S. BECKER, *Human Capital* (1964). Racial, sexual, and age discrimination in employment is explored in ROBERT C. SMITH, *Equal Employment Opportunity* (1982); E. ROBERT LIVERNASH (ed.), *Comparable Worth: Issues and Alternatives* (1980); HARISH C. JAIN AND PETER J. SLOANE, *Equal Employment Issues: Race and Sex Discrimination in the United States, Canada, and Britain* (1981); GEORGE DAVIS and GLEGG WATSON, *Black Life in Corporate America: Swimming in the Mainstream* (1982); JAMES E. BLACKWELL, *Mainstreaming Outsiders: The Production of Black Professionals* (1981); STEPHEN L. SLAVIN and MARY A. PRADT, *The Einstein Syndrome: Corporate Anti-Semitism in America Today* (1982); JOHN P. FERNANDEZ, *Racism and Sexism in Corporate Life* (1981); MARGERY W. DAVIES, *Woman's Place is at the Typewriter: Office Work and Office Workers, 1870-1930* (1983); JULIE MATTHAEI, *An Economic History of Women in America* (1982); DONALD J. TREIMAND and HEIDI I. HARTMANN (eds.), *Women, Work, and Wages* (1981); MARY L. WALSHOK, *Blue-Collar Women: Pioneers on the Male Frontier* (1981); THELMA KANDEL, *What Women Earn* (1981); HERBERT S. PARNES et al. (eds.), *Work and Retirement: A Longitudinal Study of Men* (1981); ELI GINZBERG, *The School/Work Nexus: Transition of Youth from School to Work* (1980).

The deployment of the labour force is traced historically in S. LEBERGOTT, *Manpower in Economic Growth: The American Record Since 1800* (1964). The mechanism of recent changes is discussed in two OECD reports: P. de WOLFF et al., *Wages and Labour Mobility* (July 1965); and L.C. HUNTER and G.L. REID, *Urban Worker Mobility* (1968). See also JEANNE PRIAL GORDUS, PAUL JARLEY, and LOUIS A. FERMAN, *Plant Closings and Economic Dislocation* (1981); MARK J. MILLER and PHILIP L. MARTIN, *Administrative Foreign-Worker Programs: Lessons from Europe* (1982); DAVID M. GORDON, RICHARD EDWARDS, and MICHAEL REICH, *Segmented Work, Divided Workers: The Historical Transformations of Labor in the United States* (1982); ANN HARRIMAN, *The Work/Leisure Trade Off: Reduced Work Time for Managers and Professionals* (1982); HEINZ ULRICH and J. ROBERT CONNOR, *The National Job-Finding Guide* (1982).

For trade union structure and bargaining areas, see A.R. WEBER (ed.), *The Structure of Collective Bargaining* (1962) Numerous studies of the effects of collective bargaining are digested in: L.G. REYNOLDS and C.H. TAFT, *The Evolution of Wage Structure* (1956); and in the papers by C. KERR and L.G. REYNOLDS, in *The Theory of Wage Determination,* ed. by J.T. DUNLOP (1957). Theories of collective bargaining are surveyed in A. CODDINGTON, *Theories of the Bargaining Process* (1968); see also R.E. WALTON and R.B. MCKERSIE, *A Behavioral Theory of Labor Negotiations* (1965); JOHN G. KILGOUR, *Preventive Labor Relations* (1981); P.K. EDWARDS, *Strikes in the United States, 1881-1974* (1981); JOHN SIMMONS, *Working Together* (1983).

Forms of minimum wage regulation are surveyed in S.B.L.

NIGAM, *State Regulation of Minimum Wages* (1955). The experience of a number of countries with incomes policy is reported by D.C. SMITH, *Incomes Policies: Some Foreign Experiences and their Relevance for Canada* (1966); and by H.A. TURNER and H. ZOETEWEIJ, *Prices, Wages, and Incomes Policies in Industrialized Market Economies* (1966). Regional, industrial, and occupational structures are treated in I.G. REYNOLDS and C.H. TAFT, *The Evolution of Wage Structure* (1956); and E.M. HUGH-JONES (ed.), *Wage-Structure in Theory and Practice* (1966). Theories of differences in the rates of pay for different jobs are developed in B.F. WOOTTON, *The Social Foundations of Wage Policy: A Study of Contemporary British Wage and Salary Structure* (1955); and H.F. LYDALL, *The Structure of Earnings* (1968). The movement of the general level of pay, in money and real terms, is recorded and analyzed in France, Germany, Sweden, the United Kingdom, and the U.S. since 1860 in E.H. PHELPS BROWN and M.H. BROWNE, *A Century of Pay* (1968). Work and its compensation are discussed also in ELLIOT JAQUES, *Free Enterprise, Fair Employment* (1982); JOHN W. WRIGHT, *The American Almanac of Jobs and Salaries* (1982); FELICITY SKIDMORE (ed.), *Social Security Financing* (1981); SIMON ROTTENBERG (ed.), *The Economics of Legal Minimum Wages* (1981); JAMES E. MEADE, *Wage-Fixing* (1982).

Migrant labour: There are no classic or standard works on this subject. Most of what is known is derived from the reports of investigative and governmental commissions. For the U.S. the most recent and the most complete is *Migratory Labor in American Agriculture,* Rept. of the President's Commission on Migratory Labor (1951). More recent data may be found in *Domestic Migratory Farmworkers, Personal and Economic Characteristics,* Agricultural Economic Rept. No. 121 (1967), and other serial publications of the Department of Agriculture. For information on other countries, the reports of the International Labour Organization are important. In particular see *Migrant Workers,* Rept. 5 of the 37th Session (1954) and the 38th Session (1955) of the International Labour Conference; and *African Labour Survey* (1958), for good information on African migrancy. Relevant information can be found in HARRY E. CROSS and JAMES A. SANDOS, *Across the Border: Rural Development in Mexico and Recent Migration to the United States* (1981); and JULIAN LAITE, *Industrial Development and Migrant Labour in Latin America* (1981).

For greater details one should turn to the series of reports of the Subcommittee on Migratory Labor of the U.S. Senate Committee on Labor and Public Welfare. They are available for almost every year since 1955. The following are examples of the journal literature: E.P. EDWARDS, "Children of Migratory Agricultural Workers in the Public Elementary Schools of the U.S.," *Harvard Educational Review,* 30:12–52 (Winter 1960); and J.C. GLASS, "Organization in Salinas," *Monthly Labor Review,* 91:24–27 (June 1968). See also THOMAS D. ISERN, *Custom Combining on the Great Plains: A History* (1982); RONALD L. GOLDFARB, *Migrant Farm Workers: A Caste of Despair* (1981); CHARLES F. MUELLER, *The Economics of Labor Migration: A Behavioral Analysis* (1982).

Trade unionism: The classic works on this subject are: SIDNEY and BEATRICE WEBB, *History of Trade Unionism,* rev. ed. (1920), *Industrial Democracy* (1920); JOSEPH SCHUMPETER, *Capitalism, Socialism, and Democracy,* 3rd ed. (1950); C. KERR et al., *Industrialism and Industrial Man* (1960); S. PERLMAN, *A Theory of the Labor Movement* (1949); and J.T. DUNLOP, *Industrial Relations Systems* (1959). Later monographs, covering both historical and current development of American trade unions, include DAVID ALAN CORBIN, *Life, Work, and Rebellion in the Coal Fields* (1981); CLINTON C. BOURDON and RAYMOND E. LEVITT, *Union and Open-Shop Construction* (1980); JOEL DENKER, *Union and Universities: The Rise of the New Labor Leader* (1981); NANCY SCHROM DYE, *As Equals and as Sisters: Feminism, the Labor Movement, and the Women's Trade Union League of New York* (1981); HARVEY A. LEVENSTEIN, *Communism, Anti-Communism, and the CIO* (1981); STEPHEN MEYER, *The Five Dollar Day: Labor, Management, and Social Control in the Ford Motor Company, 1908–1921* (1981); PHILIP TAFT, *Organizing Dixie: Alabama Workers in the Industrial Era,* rev. ed. by GARY M. FINK (1981); JOHN E. BODNAR, *Workers' World: Kinship, Community, and Protest in an Industrial Society, 1900–1940* (1982); MEREDITH TAX, *The Rising of the Women* (1980); CLETUS E. DANIEL, *Bitter Harvest: A History of California Farmworkers, 1870–1941* (1981); WAYNE J. URBAN, *Why Teachers Organized* (1982); GEORGIA P. NIELSON, *From Sky Girl to Flight Attendant: Women and the Making of a Union* (1982); PHILIP S. FONER (ed.), *Fellow Workers and Friends: I.W.W. Free Speech Fights as Told by Participants* (1981); JOSEPH R. CONLIN (ed.), *At the Point of Production: The Local History of the I.W.W.* (1981); PATRICIA CAYO SEXTON, *The New Nightingales: Hospital Workers, Unions, New Women's Issues* (1982).

The international labour movement is well presented (up to

1950) in L.L. LORWIN, *The International Labor Movement: History, Policies, Outlook* (1953). See also DICK GEARY, *European Labour Protest, 1848–1939* (1981); THOMAS KENNEDY, *European Labor Relations* (1980); PETER LANGE, GEORGE ROSS, and MAURIZIO VANNICELLI, *Unions, Change, and Crises* (1982).

Surveys of the literature may be found in A.M. ROSS (ed.), "Literature on Industrial Relations and Economic Development," in *Industrial Relations and Economic Development* (1967); and A. STURMTHAL, "The Labor Movement Abroad," in N.W. CHAMBERLAIN et al. (eds.), *A Decade of Industrial Relations Research, 1946–1956* (1958).

Larger areas are treated on a comparative basis in H.A. CLEGG, *A New Approach to Industrial Democracy* (1960); W. GALENSON (ed.), *Comparative Labor Movements* (1952); E.M. KASSALOW, *Trade Unions and Industrial Relations* (1969); A. STURMTHAL (ed.), *Contemporary Collective Bargaining in 7 Countries* (1957), *The Tragedy of European Labor, 1918–1939* (1951), *Unity and Diversity in European Labor* (1953); E. OWEN SMITH (ed.), *Trade Unions in the Developed Economies* (1981); ALBERT A. BLUM (ed.), *International Handbook of Industrial Relations* (1981); AMARJIT SINGH SETHI and STUART J. DIMMOCK (eds.), *Industrial Relations and Health Services* (1982); and CHARLES HANSON, SHEILA JACKSON, and DOUGLAS MILLER, *The Closed Shop: A Comparative Study of Public Policy and Trade Union Security in Britain, the USA, and West Germany* (1981).

The bulk of the literature is devoted to indivdual countries. Among the outstanding works are: S.B. LEVINE, *Industrial Relations in Postwar Japan* (1958); V.R. LORWIN, *The French Labor Movement* (1955); KENNETH F. WALKER, *Australian Industrial Relations Systems* (1970); J.P. WINDMULLER, *Labor Relations in the Netherlands* (1969); I. BERNSTEIN, *The Lean Years: A History of the American Worker, 1920–1933*, and *The Turbulent Years: A History of the American Worker, 1933–1941* (both 1960); E.C. BROWN, *Soviet Trade Unions and Labor Relations* (1966); A. FLANDERS, *Trade Unions*, 7th rev. ed. (1968); D.L. HOROWITZ, *The Italian Labor Movement* (1963); INTERNATIONAL LABOUR OFFICE, *The Trade Union Situation in Sweden* (1961), *The Trade Union Situation in the United Kingdom* (1961), *The Trade Union Situation in the U.S.S.R.* (1960), *The Trade Union Situation in the United States* (1960); T.L. JOHNSTON, *Collective Bargaining in Sweden* (1962); and WALTER GALENSON, *The Danish Systems of Labor Relations: A Study in Industrial Peace* (1952). Later studies include SALLY F. ZERKER, *The Rise and Fall of the Toronto Typographical Union, 1832–1972: A Case Study of Foreign Trade Unions' Domination* (1981); ALAN EREIRA, *The People's England* (1981); DENIS BARNES and EILEEN REID, *Governments and Trade Unions: The British Experience, 1964–79* (1980); APRIL CARTER, *Democratic Reform in Yugoslavia: The Changing Role of the Party* (1982); LEIF LEWIN, *Governing Trade Unions in Sweden* (1980); DIANE KOENKER, *Moscow Workers and the 1917 Revolution* (1981); LEONARD SCHAPIRO and JOSEPH GODSON (eds.), *The Soviet Worker: Illusions and Realities* (1981); STANISLAW STARSKI, *Class Struggle in Classless Poland* (1982); RICHARD J. EVANS (ed.), *The German Working Class, 1888–1933: The Politics of Everyday Life* (1982); WALTER RODNEY, *A History of the Guyanese Working People, 1881–1905* (1981); JANET W. SALAFF, *Working Daughters of Hong Kong* (1981); STEPHEN S. LARGE, *Organized Workers and Socialist Politics in Interwar Japan* (1981); SHUNSAKU NISHIKAWA (ed.), *The Labor Market in Japan* (1980).

Writing

Writing is a system of human intercommunication by means of visible marks used conventionally. This broad definition encompasses two important chronological stages: (1) The earlier stage consisted of a simple picture or a combination of pictures, which, being understandable in themselves, did not have to correspond to any linguistic elements; to this stage, called semasiography, belong various forerunners of writing. (2) The later stage consisted of the signs of writing, whether pictorial or linear, which became visual substitutes for the elements of the oral language, such as words, syllables, and distinct sounds; this stage, called phonography, includes full writing.

The article is divided into the following sections:

The nature and origin of writing

COMMUNICATION AS SYSTEMS OF SIGNS

Man, like other animals, interacts through communicative behaviour by means of signs or symbols used conventionally. The term conventional implies that the signs or symbols, when used by some individuals, have the potential of being understood and reacted upon by individuals receiving the communication. A system of signs is an assemblage of organically related signs conventionally used for the purpose of communication, as in spoken language, in writing, or in the language of gestures. A sign is a component of a system of signs, such as a word in a system of signs called "language," a written mark or letter in a system of signs called "writing," and a gesture in a system of signs called "gesture language." A symbol is similar in meaning to a sign, but it does not form part of a system; *e.g.,* the symbol "cross" for Christianity.

There is no good expression to cover all of the conventional means of communication through signs. The French linguists use *le langage* in this sense, while they call the auditory language *la langue.* In Anglo-American usage "speech" often stands for auditory language and "language" for all the means of communication through signs. The general science of signs is called semiotics.

The three components in communication

The process of communication is composed of three parts—emission, reception, and the intervening physical elements, such as waves. Since the means of emitting communication are too numerous and too varied to allow for any systematic classification, the discussion of the systems must start from the point of view of reception. The reception of communication is achieved by means of one's senses, of which sight and hearing play the most important roles. Theoretically, other senses, such as touch, smell, and taste, can also be taken into consideration, but in practice they play only limited roles and lead to no fully developed systems. The electronic age added new dimensions to this classification.

Visual communication is achieved mainly by means of gesture and mimicry (Figure 1). Both are frequent companions of language, although the intensity of their use differs greatly with various individuals, social strata, and

	momentary communication	stable communication
For visual reception	gesture; mimicry; mien, eye expression; lip reading; mimetic dancing; signalling by means of fire, smoke, light, or semaphores	objects: cross or anchor; rosary; flower or gem language; counting sticks; pebbles; quipu; cowrie mussels markings on objects; picture and sculpture; writing
For auditory reception	whistling; singing and humming; applauding or hissing; language; signalling by means of drums, whistles, or trumpets	phonograph records or Dictaphone cylinders
For tactile reception	handclasp, backslap, or love stroke; hand stroking of blind deaf-mutes	reading with fingers of raised or incised inscriptions; Braille

Figure 1: Types of communication.

folk groups. A combination of language and gesture has played an important role in the ritual proceedings of religions of all times and places. The restrictions imposed by natural and artificial conditions on the use of language have resulted in the origin and development of various systems of signs based on gesture and mimicry. Such are the systems devised for the use of deaf-mutes; the gesture language of Trappist monks, who, having taken a vow of silence, were forced to develop a substitute system for language; and the gesture language of the American Plains Indians, developed as the need grew for communication between tribes speaking mutually incomprehensible languages. Among other methods of visual communication are signals by means of fire, smoke, or light.

One of the simplest forms of auditory communication is, for instance, whistling with the intention of calling someone, or hissing or applauding as an expression of one's feelings. Sometimes artificial means, such as drums, whistles, or trumpets, are used for auditory communication.

The most developed systems of this class are represented by the so-called drum languages of Africa. The most widely used system of auditory communication is the spoken language directed to the ear of the person receiving the communication. Within the span of human memory and knowledge there has never existed a society without a fully developed language.

Primary and secondary means

In consideration of the various systems of human intercommunication, there is need to distinguish between primary and secondary systems. For example, when a father calls his son by whistling, he expresses, without the intermediary of spoken language, his desire to bring the boy to a certain place. His command is directly and immediately conveyed in the whistle. This is a primary means of communication. But when the father calls his son by whistling two tones in imitation of the falling and rising tones for the word for "son" in his language, as for instance in the case of some African tone languages, he is doing so by means of a linguistic transfer. His call to his son is now conveyed in the whistle through the intermediary of linguistic elements, in this case, tones. This may be called a secondary means of communication. The spoken word "son" is a primary speech sign. In the written word "son," there is a secondary transfer of the speech sign into three written signs. If this written word "son" were then transmitted by means of three flashlight signals, each denoting one letter, the resulting flashes would be signs of signs. There seems no limit to secondary transfers.

The means of communication so far mentioned, such as oral language, gesture language, and signalling, have two features in common: (1) They are all of momentary value and are therefore restricted as to time; as soon as the word is uttered or the gesture made, it is gone, and it cannot be revived except by repetition. (2) They can be used only in communication between persons more or less in proximity to each other and are therefore restricted as to space. The need to find a way to communicate in a form not limited by time or space led to the development of methods of communication by means of (1) objects and (2) markings on objects or any solid material.

Examples of visual communication by means of objects are unlimited. By setting up a pile of stones or a stone monument on a grave, a person intends to give expression to his feelings for the deceased and to perpetuate his memory in the days to come. The cross symbolizing Christian faith and the anchor symbolizing hope are further illustrations. The so-called flower and gem languages might be mentioned here: a specific flower or gem is sent or given by one person to another in order to convey a certain sentiment or message.

Systems of mnemonic signs to keep account by means of objects are known throughout the world. The simplest illustrations are wooden counting sticks with carved notches corresponding to the number of cattle under the custody of a cowherd, or pebbles in a small sack to keep account of cattle. A more developed system is represented by the so-called quipu writing of the Peruvian Incas, in which accounts of material possessions were recorded by means of strings and knots of various lengths, shapes, and colours. Here, too, belong the wampums of the North American Indians, which consist of strings of shell beads, often tied together in belts. They were frequently used to convey messages through the colour conventions of the Indians, as white beads for peace, purple or violet for war. Cowrie mussels are employed by the Yoruba people of West Africa for communicative purposes, as in the use of one mussel to mean defiance, two mussels placed together to mean agreement, or two mussels placed apart to mean enmity.

These systems of communication with objects are called *Sachschrift* or *Gegenstandschrift* ("object writing") by some German scholars, but entirely without justification, since they have nothing to do with writing as one normally understands it. The impracticability of using objects prevents the development of any full system, and the devices that have been used are restricted to small geographic areas.

WRITING AS A SYSTEM OF SIGNS

Writing is expressed not by objects themselves but by markings on objects or on any more or less solid material. Written symbols and signs in the form of pictures have been normally executed by means of motor action of the hand in drawing, painting, scratching, or incising. This is reflected in the meaning and etymology of the word "to write" in many different languages. Note, for instance, that the English word "to write" corresponds to the Old Norse *rīta* ("to incise [runes]") and the modern German *reissen, einritzen* ("to tear or scratch"); the Greek word *graphein,* "to write," has the same etymology as the English "to carve" and German *kerben* ("to notch"); the Latin *scribere,* German *schreiben,* and Greek *skariphasthai* originally meant "to incise" or "to scratch"; the Gothic *mēljan,* "to write," at first meant "to paint, as can be gathered from the German word *malen,* which has this meaning, just as the Slavic verb *pisati,* "to write," originally referred to painting, as shown by its connection with the Latin *pingere,* "to paint."

The connection between picture and writing

The history of these expressions provides illustrations for the mechanical background of writing and also indicates the close connection between picture and writing. This is as it should be, since the most natural way of communicating by means of visible markings is achieved by pictures. In a primitive stage, a picture takes care in a crude way of the needs fulfilled in modern times by writing. In the course of time the picture develops in two directions: (1) pictorial art, in which pictures resulting from an artistic-aesthetic urge continue to reproduce more or less faithfully the objects and events of the surrounding world in a form independent of language; and (2) writing, in which written shapes, whether they retain their pictorial form or not, serve purely the purpose of communication and become ultimately signs for elements of linguistic value.

Writing began when man learned how to communicate by means of visible signs used conventionally; that is, by signs that were understandable not only to himself but also to all other persons more or less initiated into the particular system. In the beginning, pictures served the purpose of visual communication in a form to a great extent independent of spoken language. The relationship between writing and language in the early stages of writing was loose, inasmuch as the written message did not correspond to exact elements of language. A certain message had only one meaning, and it could be interpreted by the reader in only one way, but it could be "read"—that is, put into words in several different ways or even in a different language.

In every great human achievement one important and decisive step can be observed that entirely revolutionizes its further progress. Such a critically important step is the phonetization of script by way of the so-called rebus principle (see the subsection below on logo-syllabic writings), which enabled man to express his ideas in a form that corresponded to exact elements of language. From then on, writing gradually lost its function as an independent mode of communication and became a tool of language, a vehicle through which exact elements of language were recorded in a permanent form.

The differences between the earlier and later stages of

writing are so crucial and far-reaching that some scholars have defined writing as a device for recording language, dismissing all the early stages, in which visual markings on objects do not serve this purpose, as feeble attempts in the direction of writing, not worthy of study. This may be true of the linguistic science that deals with linguistic elements and with the stage of writing in which writing became a secondary transfer of language and signs of writing can be identified with elements of language. Where these scholars err, however, is in taking for granted the complete identity of language and writing and in assuming that, just as a linguist can operate only with language elements, so a historian of writing should relegate to the wastebasket visual images not having full correspondence with language. But writing in all its stages cannot be identified with language, and a student of writing does not necessarily have to be a linguist. The symbolism of visual images in the early stages of writing, like that of gesture signs, can express meaning without the necessity of a linguistic intermediary, and both can profitably be investigated by a nonlinguist. It is only after writing has developed into a full phonetic system, reproducing elements of language, that one can speak of full correspondence between language and writing and of the study of the latter as being a subdivision of linguistics.

The pre-linguistic stage of writing

The restriction of the definition of writing to the stage in which writing represents language does not take into account the fact that both stages, earlier and later, have an identical aim: human intercommunication by means of visible marks used conventionally. Furthermore, it is impossible to lump together all the early or primitive stages and consider them all on the same level of development in their loose relation to language. Even though all the early types of writing were quite inefficient in expressing language, some of them, like the Maya and Aztec writings, reached a relatively high level of convention and systematization in the use of their signs.

EVOLUTION OF WRITING

Pictures. There was a time when man did not know how to write. If full writing is defined as a device for expressing linguistic elements by means of conventional visible marks, then writing is no more than 5,000 years old. But in much earlier times, tens of thousands of years ago, man felt the urge to draw or paint pictures on the walls of his primitive dwelling or on the rocks in his surroundings. Primitive man was similar in this respect to a child, who no sooner learns to crawl than he begins to scribble on the wallpaper or to draw pictures in the sand.

The fact that in Figure 2 pictures are listed under the first stage, called "No writing," implies (1) that what are normally understood as pictures—that is, creations resulting from an artistic-aesthetic urge—do not fall under the category of writing, and (2) that writing had its origin in simple pictures. The case could be paralleled, for example, by calling steam the first stage in a chart showing the development of the steam engine. Steam, as it issues from a geyser or a tea kettle, is in itself not a steam engine, but

Origin of writing in pictures

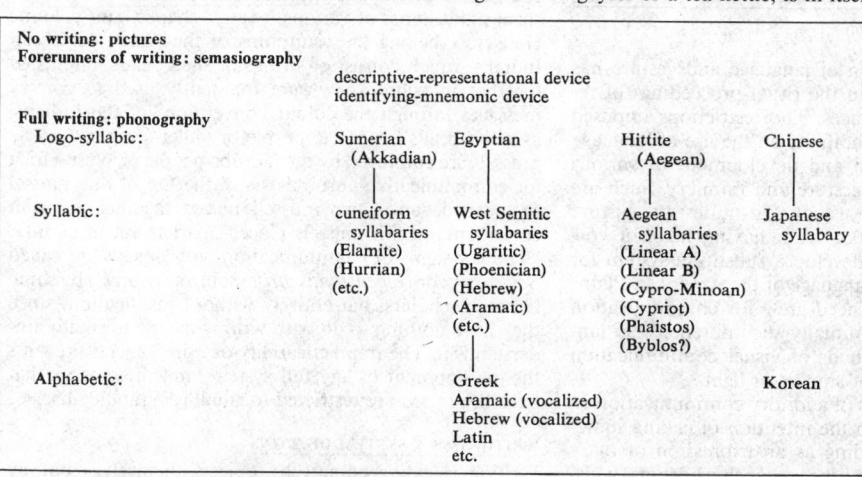

No writing: pictures				
Forerunners of writing: semasiography				
	descriptive-representational device			
	identifying-mnemonic device			
Full writing: phonography				
Logo-syllabic:	Sumerian (Akkadian)	Egyptian	Hittite (Aegean)	Chinese
Syllabic:	cuneiform syllabaries (Elamite) (Hurrian) (etc.)	West Semitic syllabaries (Ugaritic) (Phoenician) (Hebrew) (Aramaic) (etc.)	Aegean syllabaries (Linear A) (Linear B) (Cypro-Minoan) (Cypriot) (Phaistos) (Byblos?)	Japanese syllabary
Alphabetic:		Greek Aramaic (vocalized) Hebrew (vocalized) Latin etc.		Korean

Figure 2: Stages of the development of writing.

it is the element around which the successive stages had to build in order to reach the ultimate development.

In most cases it is, of course, difficult or impossible to ascertain the purpose or the urge that stimulated man to draw or incise a picture, since the circumstances that led to its execution are unknown. Is the picture a manifestation of magic, religious, or aesthetic expression? Was it drawn for the purpose of securing good hunting or was it the result of the artistic impulse? Several causes may have been instrumental at the same time in the origin of a drawing. Such pictures do not represent writing because they do not form part of a conventional system of signs and can be understood only by the man who drew them or by his family and close friends who had heard of the event.

Forerunners of writing. Aside from pictorial representations resulting from a purely artistic-aesthetic urge, two primitive devices to effect communication can be observed: the descriptive-representational device and the identifying-mnemonic device. As the two devices are frequently interlocking, it is difficult to assign some primitive writings to definite categories. Samples of these devices can be found all over the globe, from the rock paintings of Paleolithic man in Europe to the modern representations of the North and South American Indians and African Negroes.

Descriptive-representational devices utilize means that are similar to the drawings produced as a result of an artistic-aesthetic urge, but they differ from the latter in that they contain only those elements that are important for the transmission of the communication and lack the embellishments that form part of an artistic picture.

A simple example of the descriptive-representational device is an Indian rock drawing placed near a precipitous trail in New Mexico. The design consists of two figures, one of a mountain goat standing upright and the other of a man riding a horse drawn in an upside-down position. It is intended to communicate "no thoroughfare"—that is, to warn horsemen that, while a mountain goat could climb up the rocky trail, a horse would tumble down. The drawing employs no more detail than is necessary to identify the two animals and to indicate the presence of a rider on the horse. This kind of communication, somewhat different from a work of art on the one hand, is, on the other, completely independent of language. Any person only slightly acquainted with the communicative devices of American Indians is able to understand the message, even though he may be completely ignorant of the language of the person who executed the drawing.

In the identifying-mnemonic device, the individual pictures or signs are used not to paint or describe an event but to record or identify a person, an object, a song, or the like. In this way the ceremonial songs of the Ojibwa Indians and the proverbs of the Ewe people in Africa are recorded in drawings. The individual drawing does not reproduce pictorially the verse or proverb but only gives a suggestion of it. Thus a drawing of a threaded needle among the Ewe suggests the proverb "the thread follows the needle (and not vice versa)"—resembling in its meaning the English saying "a chip off the old block"—but does not exactly reproduce it, being used merely as a mnemonic device to help recall the particular proverb.

The unifying characteristic of all these primitive attempts at visual communication is the lack of systematic correlation between the visual marks and linguistic elements. All employ certain devices and conventions in respect to the meaning or meanings of certain visual marks; none has developed a set of signs with fully established correspondence between sign and sound. These primitive attempts at visual communication by means of signs are therefore classified as forerunners of writing and not as writing proper.

All examples of forerunners of writing are based on pictures and could therefore be called "pictographic." The term pictography—that is, writing that is pictorial in character—can be applied not only to such primitive devices as those of the American Indians, however, but also to such fully developed systems as the Egyptian or Hittite hieroglyphic. For that reason, the terms pictography and pictographic are avoided altogether in this treatment.

To a superficial observer the descriptive-representational device may appear to be better adapted to convey communication than the device using symbols of an identifying and mnemonic nature. It is clear, for instance, that a drawing depicting a battle tells the story better than a sign or two intended merely to recall the battle. Similar conclusions might be drawn in comparing, for example, early specimens of Egyptian writing, drawn chiefly by the descriptive-representational device, with Old Sumerian ledger tablets, drawn by the identifying-mnemonic device.

It is not the descriptive-representational device, however, that lies on the direct road toward a fully developed writing. Pictures drawn by this device follow the conventions of art, with all of their drawbacks and limitations as a vehicle of human intercommunication. The binding traditions of art, established thousands of years before man first attempted communication by means of conventional marks, were too strong to allow for the development of the descriptive-representational device in the right direction.

Logosyllabic writings. In the process of using pictures to identify and recall objects or beings, a complete correspondence is established and gradually conventionalized between certain written signs, on the one hand, and certain objects and beings, on the other. Since these objects and beings have names in the oral language, the correspondence is further established between the written signs and their spoken counterparts. Once it is discovered that words can be expressed in written signs, a new and much better method of human intercommunication is firmly established. It is no longer necessary to express a sentence such as "man killed lion" by means of a drawing of a man, spear or bow in hand, in the process of killing a lion. The three words can now be written by means of three conventional signs representing man, spear or bow (killing), and lion, respectively. Accordingly, "five sheep" can be expressed by means of two signs corresponding to two words in the language, instead of by five separate pictures of sheep, which would have to be drawn in an artistic picture or in the descriptive-representational device. The introduction in the identifying device of a strict order of the signs that corresponds to the order of the spoken words is in direct contrast to the methods of the descriptive device and of the artistic picture, in which the meaning is conveyed by the totality of separate drawings without any convention as to the beginning of the message or the order in which it should be interpreted.

A device in which individual signs can express individual words should naturally lead to the development of a complete system of word signs; that is, a word writing or logography. Such a fully developed system probably never existed either in antiquity or in modern times. To create and memorize thousands of signs for the thousands of words and names existing in a language and to invent new signs for newly acquired words and names is so impracticable that logographic writing either can be used only as a very limited system, or it must be adapted in some new way in order to develop into a useful system. Experience with the earliest Alaska and Cherokee writing systems, which employed only word signs, is indicative of the impracticability of such limited systems. Even Chinese, the most logographic of all writings, is not a pure logographic system, because from the earliest times it has used word signs functioning as syllabic signs. And what is true of the Chinese system is even more true of other ancient Oriental systems such as Sumerian, Egyptian, and Hittite.

A primitive logographic writing can develop into a full system only if it succeeds in attaching to a sign a phonetic value independent of the meaning that this sign has as a word. This is phonetization, the most important single step in the history of writing. In modern usage the device is called rebus writing, as exemplified in the drawing of an eye and of a saw to express the sentence "I saw," or in that of a man and a date to express the word "mandate." With the introduction of phonetization and its subsequent systematization, complete systems of writing were established, which made possible the expression of all linguistic elements by means of signs with conventional syllabic values. Thus full writing originated, in contrast to the feeble attempts comprising semasiography, which can only be classified as forerunners of writing.

Mnemonic signs (margin)

Conventionalizing the correspondence between written signs and spoken words (margin)

Phonetization (margin)

Logosyllabic writing—that is, writing in which signs express words and syllables—is found in the Orient, the vast belt of Asia extending from the eastern shores of the Mediterranean Sea to the western shores of the Pacific Ocean. For historical as well as practical reasons, Egypt and, at least in the pre-Hellenic period, the area of the Aegean Sea are included within the orbit of Oriental civilizations.

In this large area are found seven original and fully developed logosyllabic systems of writing: Sumerian in Mesopotamia, 3100 BC to AD 75; Proto-Elamite in Elam, 3000 BC to 2200 BC; Proto-Indic in the Indus Valley, around 2200 BC; Chinese in China, 1300 BC to the present; Egyptian in Egypt, 3000 BC to AD 400; Cretan in Crete and Greece, 2000 to 1200 BC; and Hittite in Anatolia and Syria, 1500 to 700 BC. Other logosyllabic systems may at some time come to light, but at the present there are no likely candidates to be added to the above list of seven. The Proto-Armenian inscriptions discovered within the last few decades are too short and too little known to allow any safe conclusions. The mysterious Easter Island inscriptions, on which so much effort has been wasted by so many imaginative minds, are not writing even in the broadest sense of the word, as they probably represent nothing else but pictorial concoctions for magical purposes. Finally, the systems of the Mayas and the Aztecs do not represent a full logosyllabic writing; even in their most advanced stages they never attained the level of phonographic development of the earliest stages of the Oriental systems.

Of the seven systems, three—namely, Proto-Elamite, Proto-Indic, and Cretan—are as yet undeciphered. Consequently, modern understanding of the logosyllabic systems is limited to the remaining four systems—Sumerian, Egyptian, Hittite, and Chinese.

Characteristics of Sumerian, Egyptian, Hittite, and Chinese writings

The unifying characteristic of the four systems is that they are all phonographic (with established correspondence between sign and sound) almost from the very beginning of their development and that they all contain word signs or logograms, syllabic signs, and what are often called "auxiliary" signs or marks. The formation of word signs is identical or very similar in all four systems. Also, the general principles of using the auxiliary signs such as punctuation marks and "unpronounced" determinatives, elements that are added to the main signs and in some way specify their meaning, are identical, although the various systems differ formally. Only in the use of syllabic signs are the differences so pronounced as to permit the formation of exact subdivisions by types.

Syllabic writings. Out of the four logosyllabic systems listed in the preceding section, four syllabaries, showing various degrees of simplification, were developed in the course of time. An interesting conclusion that can be drawn about these syllabic writings is that they were all created by heterogeneous peoples. Thus, although the Mesopotamian Babylonians and Assyrians accepted almost without change the Sumerian system of writing, the foreign Elamites, Hurrians, and Urartians found the task of mastering the complicated Mesopotamian system too heavy a burden; they merely took over a simplified syllabary and eliminated almost entirely the ponderous logographic apparatus. The Semites of Palestine and Syria went even further in their aim toward simplification and accepted from the Egyptians only the principle of writing monosyllables without indicating differences in vowels. Similarly, while the Linear A and B systems of the Aegean area retained a number of word signs from the earlier writing, other descendants of the Aegean systems, the Cypro-Minoan, the Cypriot, and the Phaistos and Proto-Byblian systems, used only syllabic signs, omitting word signs entirely. The Japanese were not so radical. They too developed a simple syllabary similar in principle to that of the Cyprians, even though it distinguishes by separate marks the voiced from the voiceless consonants; but side by side with the syllabary (kana) they use word signs (kanji) taken over from the Chinese writing.

The term "West Semitic syllabary," given to the various forms of writing used by the Ugaritans, Phoenicians, Hebrews, and other Semites from the middle of the 2nd millennium BC on, expresses clearly the contention that these writings are syllabaries and not alphabets, as is often assumed. These Semitic writings follow exactly the pattern of their Egyptian prototype, and the latter cannot be anything else but a syllabary from the point of view of the structure and typology of writing.

Alphabetic writing. The question may now be legitimately asked: If these early Semitic writings are not alphabets, what, then, is the alphabet? The answer is clear. If by the word "alphabet" is understood a writing that expresses the single sounds (*i.e.,* phonemes) of a language, then the first alphabet was formed by the Greeks. Although throughout the 2nd millennium BC several attempts were made to find a way to indicate vowels in syllabaries of the Egyptian-Semitic type, none of them succeeded in developing into a full vocalic system. The usual way was to add phonetic indicators as help in reading the vowels that were left unindicated in the Semitic systems of writing, as in the case of m^a-l^a-$k^{(a)}$-t^i-y^i for *malaktī* "I reigned," in which y^i was added to establish the reading of t^i in *malaktī,* or in the case of m^a-$l^{(a)}$-k^u-w^u, in which w^u was added to establish the reading of k^u in *malkū.* But while the Semites made sporadic use of these indicators, called *matres lectionis,* the Greeks used them systematically after each syllabic sign. Thus, following the principle of reduction, they were soon able to reach the conclusion that, since in the writing $t^i$$y^i$ the second sign does not stand for the syllable y^i but for the vowel *i,* the first sign must stand for the consonant *t* and not for the syllable t^i.

The first alphabet

It was therefore the Greeks who, having accepted in full the forms of the West Semitic syllabary, evolved a system of vowel signs that, attached to the syllabic signs, reduced the value of these syllabic signs to simple consonantal signs, and thus for the first time created a full alphabetic system of writing. And it was from the Greeks that the Semites in turn adopted the full use of vowel marks.

In the past 2,800 years the conquests of the alphabet have encompassed the whole of civilization, but during all this period no reforms have taken place in the principles of writing. Hundreds of alphabets throughout the world, different as they may be in outer form, all use the principles first established in the Greek writing.

TYPOLOGY OF WRITING

The two main stages in the development of writing, forerunners of writing and full writing, are listed in Figure 2, in the section *Evolution of writing.* In the same section, in the subsection "Logo-syllabic writings," there is allusion to the terms "unpronounced" determinatives and punctuation marks. Disregarding the time factor, basic in the presentation of the evolution of writing, and rephrased in different terminology, there are three main types of writing: (1) semasiography, (2) phonography, and (3) metagraphy.

Semasiography. Various communicative devices that convey meaning by means of visual marks directly to the eyes of the receivers of the communication and without the intermediary of linguistic elements are grouped under the head semasiography. (Some scholars call the use of such devices ideography or subwriting.) Two main subtypes of semasiography can be recognized in the descriptive-representational device and the identifying-mnemonic device. Semasiography is characteristic of the earliest attempts at visual communication, but examples of semasiography are attested also in systems introduced in modern times among so-called primitive societies, as well as in some aspects of full writings. The study of semasiography is called subgraphemics (see below).

Phonography. Under phonography are included full systems of writing in which signs generally have set correspondences in language. The origin of phonography lies in the application of the "rebus principle," by which words that are difficult to express in writing are written with signs that resemble these words in sound and are easy to draw, as in the modern writing of the sentence "I saw" by means of rebus pictures of an eye and a saw. Phonography, sporadically attested among the forerunners of writing, is represented in full writing from the seven logosyllabic systems of the ancient world down to the modern

Definition and origin of phonography

alphabets. The study of phonography is called graphemics (see below).

As noted above, the main characteristic of full writing is the fully established correspondence between visual signs and linguistic elements (Figure 3).

	written sign	system of signs
Single sound (phoneme)	letter	alphabet or alphabetic writing
Syllable	syllabic sign	syllabary or syllabic writing
Word	word sign	word writing
Phrase	phrase sign	phrase writing
Prosodic feature	prosodic sign or mark	prosodic writing

Figure 3: Ways of writing linguistic elements.

Under the term "linguistic elements" are understood utterances (sentences and phrases), words, syllables, phonemes (single sounds), and prosodic features (*i.e.*, quantity [or length], accent [or stress], tone [or pitch], and pauses). Of these, phraseograms, or signs for phrases, are rarely found in standard writings but are an essential feature of stenographic systems. Of the prosodic features, only the pauses are partially expressed in standard writings by word division and punctuation marks. Thus in such a sentence as "Are you going home?" it is left to the reader to decide which word the emphasis, or pitch, is on. By contrast, learned transliterations and transcriptions frequently employ special signs to denote characteristics of prosodic nature such as vowel quantity, stress, and tone. The system of musical notation provides a complete indication of tone or pitch.

The only three linguistic elements that are normally expressed in standard writings are words, syllables, and phonemes. The writing of these elements is called, respectively, logography or word writing, syllabography or syllabic writing, and phonemography, alphabetography, phonemic writing, or alphabetic writing.

Definition of logography

Logography. In logography, one sign or a combination of signs expresses one word or a combination of words. Pure logography is not represented by any known system of writing. It exists normally only in conjunction with syllabography, as best represented in the seven logo-syllabic systems of the ancient world. Rare and sporadic cases of logography are attested, however, even among the forerunners of writing and in the more developed systems of the Mayas and Aztecs. The use of logography in conjunction with certain syllabic systems, as in Japanese, is discussed below. Further use of logography is evidenced by the writing of numbers and mathematical symbols (such as the + and − signs).

Logograms, or word signs, were created by means of various devices. It is impossible to assign the signs rigorously to one or another type, since some signs may have been formed by means of more than one device and may therefore belong to different types. It is possible, however, to distinguish the following six general types. In the primary type, pictures of concrete objects stand for concrete objects and actions, such as the picture of the sun for "sun" and the pictures of man plus bread for "to eat." In the associative type, pictures of concrete objects stand for related concepts, such as in the picture of the sun for "day." In the diagrammatic type, signs do not represent pictures but are freely created from various geometric forms, for example a vertical line for "one" and a circle for "all," or "totality." The fourth type involves the use of the semantic (meaning) indicator (also called "determinative" or "classifier"), as in pictures of a wood and plow for "plow" and of a man and plow for "plowman." The fifth type, based on phonetic transfer or the rebus principle, can be illustrated by the picture of an arrow for "arrow" and "life" (both having the sound *ti* in Sumerian). Finally, the sixth type involves the use of a phonetic indicator (also called phonetic complement), as in the writing of the Sumerian word *men* "crown," by means of a picture of a crown plus the phonetic indicator *en*. While the above illustrations are culled from Sumerian, the six types of logograms are represented in identical or similar forms in all logo-syllabic systems.

Syllabography. A syllabary or syllabic writing consists of syllabic signs whose main characteristic is that each must include the representation of a vowel or a vocalic nucleus. Some signs represent a vowel alone; others stand for a vowel joined with a preceding or following consonant. In some instances, two consonants may surround a vowel in one syllable. Syllabography is attested in the logo-syllabic and syllabic systems.

Four different types of syllabaries are found in the logo-syllabic writings:

Type I, Sumerian (Akkadian). Monosyllables beginning with a consonant or vowel and ending in a consonant or vowel: *ta, ti, te, tu; at, it, et, ut; tam, tim, tem, tum;* very rarely also dissyllables like *ata; tama.*

Type II, Egyptian. Monosyllables and dissyllables beginning with a consonant and ending in a vowel, with differences in vowels not indicated: *t^x; t^xm^x.*

Type III, Hittite. Monosyllables beginning with a consonant or vowel and ending in a vowel: *ta, ti, te, tu;* the distinction between voiced, voiceless, and aspirated consonant is not indicated.

Type IV, Chinese. Monosyllables beginning with a consonant or vowel and ending in a vowel or consonant: *ta, ti, te, tu, to; at, it, et, ut, ot; tam, tim, tem, tum, tom;* final consonants have a very limited distribution.

Four different types of syllabaries also are found in the syllabic writings:

Type I, cuneiform syllabaries (Elamite, Hurrian, etc.). Monosyllables beginning with a consonant or vowel and ending in a consonant or vowel: *ta, ti, te, tu; at, it, et, ut; tam, tim, tem, tum.*

Type II, West Semitic. Monosyllables beginning with a consonant and ending in a vowel, with differences in vowels not indicated: *t^x.*

Type III, Cypriot. Monosyllables beginning with a consonant or vowel and ending in a vowel: *ta, ti, te, tu, to;* the distinction between voiced, voiceless, and aspirated consonants is not indicated.

Type IV, Japanese. Monosyllables beginning with a consonant or vowel and ending in a vowel: *ta, ti, te, tu, to; (da, di, de, du, do).* It will be noted that voiced and voiceless consonants are distinguished, in contrast to Type III, and there is a final consonant *N* sound.

The general similarity between the types of syllabaries in logo-syllabic systems on the one hand, and in syllabic systems on the other, arises from the fact that the latter are derived from the former. Thus the cuneiform syllabaries of the Elamites and Hurrians are derived from Sumerian (Akkadian); West Semitic syllabaries of the Phoenicians, Aramaeans, and Hebrews come from the Egyptian; the Cypriot syllabary is derived from an Aegean (Cretan) system related to the hieroglyphic Hittite of Anatolia; and the Japanese syllabary represents a development from the Chinese.

Many differences can be observed in the choice of syllabic types in the eight systems, as in monosyllabic *ta* versus dissyllabic *tama,* two-phoneme form *ta* versus three-phoneme form *tam,* consonant-plus-vowel type *ta* versus vowel-plus-consonant type *at,* and so on. Other characteristic features can be noted in the Hittite and Cypriot syllabaries (and other related Aegean systems), which do not differentiate between voiced, voiceless, and aspirated phonemes, and in the Chinese system, which has a limited number of signs with a final consonant. All these differences and characteristic features of the eight forms of syllabaries are of secondary importance. The crucial difference in type is between the Egyptian and the derived West Semitic syllabaries on the one hand, and the six other forms on the other. While the six forms are represented by syllabic signs that consist of consonant(s) plus vowel(s), the Egyptian and West Semitic forms have syllabic signs that consist of consonant(s) plus inherent vowel(s) that are not differentiated as to quality. It is this characteristic that led many scholars to include the Egyptian and West Semitic forms under the consonantal or even alphabetic writing.

Alphabetography. An alphabet or alphabetic writing consists of signs (letters) that normally stand for single phonemes of language. There are three types of alphabets in use, characterized by three different methods of indicating vowels:

The three types of alphabets

Type I, Greek, Latin, and so on: vowels indicated by separate signs.

Type II, Aramaic, Hebrew, Arabic, and so on: vowels indicated by separate diacritic marks.

Type III, Indic, Ethiopic: vowels indicated by diacritic marks attached to the sign or, very rarely, by internal modification.

Instead of three, one might distinguish two alphabetic types only, one (Greek, Latin, etc.) in which vowels are indicated by separate letters, and the other (Aramaic, Hebrew, Arabic, Indic, Ethiopic, etc.) in which vowels are indicated by diacritic marks. There is still another possible way of viewing the three types. Only Type I (Greek, Latin, etc.) is clearly alphabetic, since the indication of all consonants and vowels by means of separate letters is at all times obligatory. In the application of certain West Semitic alphabets (Hebrew and Arabic), the indication of vowels is not obligatory. Thus, while vowels are regularly written in such canonical works as the Old Testament and the Qur'ān, they are frequently, even normally, omitted in letters and newspapers. When the vowel marks are omitted, the writing may be considered consonantal. When the vowels are indicated (as in Type II), then the combination of the consonant sign plus the vowel mark may be treated as a syllabic unit. This is even more apparent in Type III (Indic, Ethiopic), with its obligatory indication of vowels by means of vowel marks that are permanently attached to the consonant signs or by an internal modification in the form of the consonant sign.

Metagraphy. Phonetic writing can never be considered an exact counterpart of the spoken language. Such an ideal state of point-by-point equivalence in which one speech unit is expressed by one sign, and one sign expresses one speech unit, has never been attained, not even in the most developed form of writing, the alphabet. In mathematics, symbolic logic, and other sciences, signs and combinations of signs recur, as in the writing of $\sqrt[3]{27} = 3$, in which the meaning of the formula is expressed in a form, order, and relation that do not follow the conventions of the standard, phonetic writing. A similar illustration is found in the writing of "3 1b" for three pounds in weight or "£3" for three pounds in money, or in the difference between the writing of "32" and "3²." Here, too, belong certain symbols in the comic strips that are generally understood even though they have no conventional counterpart in speech. These symbols include, for example, a balloon encircling print for "speaking," footprints for "going," and sawing wood for "snoring" or "sleeping."

Such devices, and various other devices that are used besides or in addition to the signs of writing proper, may be called para-writing, paragraphy, meta-writing, or metagraphy. Metagraphy is a feature of both forerunners of writing and full writing. Among the various metagraphic devices the following may be listed: punctuation marks to denote word, phrase, and sentence boundaries; shapes of signs, such as two forms of *sigma* in Greek to denote its initial, middle, or final position in a word, and consequently the presence or lack of juncture; sizes of signs, such as capital and lowercase initial letters to distinguish proper from common nouns in English; type styles and typography, such as Roman and italic; and various conventions, including colour, on maps, ledgers, and statistical and instrumental graphs. The study of metagraphy is called metagraphemics (see below).

WRITING SYSTEMS

General characteristics. *Absence of pure systems.* There are no pure systems of writing, just as there are no pure languages. As elements retained from an older stage and innovations introduced ahead of the standard usage may be found in a language of a certain period, so a system of writing may contain elements from different stages of the development of writing.

Semasiography, or the use of pictures having no clear correlation with words or sounds of language to represent or identify the object pictured, is found characteristically among the forerunners of writing, where only the sporadic occurrences of logography form an innovative interference. But semasiography is also attested in vari-

ous phonographic writings, including modern English. In modern usage signs are sometimes encountered that have no conventionally assigned speech forms. For instance, the picture of an arrow used as a symbol can have different meanings depending on the situation. Arrow signs along a path may mean something like "follow in the direction of the arrow," but an arrow placed at the entrance to a cave may mean "enter here" or "this is the entrance." This kind of symbolism is outside of writing. As part of the phonetic system of writing, an arrow sign would necessarily have developed in the course of time one or more unequivocal language equivalents, such as "enter," "follow," or the like.

Logography—the use of signs to represent whole words—is widely attested in the most varied systems of writing. The sporadic use of logography in conjunction with forerunners of writing has been noted above. While represented mainly in the logo-syllabic systems, logography occurs also in conjunction with syllabic and alphabetic systems. Multiple use of logography side by side with syllabography is known from Japanese writing. Fewer logograms occur in some cuneiform writings, such as Elamite and Hurrian, and in Aegean writings such as Linear B, while only four logograms (for king, land, province, and the god Ahura Mazdā) are found in Achaemenid Persian writing. In addition, the logographic use of numbers and other symbols, such as the plus and minus signs of mathematics, logic, and other sciences, is found in conjunction with all syllabic and alphabetic systems.

Several syllabic systems based, directly or indirectly, on the West Semitic syllabary are characterized by a mixed structure. Thus the Ugaritic syllabary (Ugarit was an ancient city of Syria), basically of the West Semitic type (wherein vowels are not indicated), contains three signs that stand for the vowels $a, i,$ and u preceded by a glottal stop (an interruption of the stream of air through the larynx, or voice box). The Achaemenid Persian syllabary consists of 36 signs, of which 13 are of the West Semitic type and 23 represent either a vowel or a consonant plus a vowel. Finally, the Iberian writing of the 4th and 3rd centuries BC is a mixture of signs of the consonant-plus-vowel type and of alphabetic signs.

English is called an "alphabet"; that is, a system in which each unit is supposed to stand for a single sound of the language. But such an ideal point-by-point equivalence ("fit") is marred by many exceptions, such as x in "fox," which stands for a combination of two distinctive sounds (phonemes), k and $s,$ and th in "Thomas," which stands for one sound, $t.$

Unidirectional development. The successive stages of writing, from the primitive semasiographic devices to fully developed logosyllabic, syllabic, and alphabetic systems, follow each other in a unidirectional line of development. The use of the term unidirectional implies that writing tends to develop in one certain direction, in contrast to the term unilinear, which would mean that writing progressed in one direction in a straight line. It was along the path of trial and error, with progressions and regressions, that writing progressed from stage to stage in the long course of its history.

The principle of unidirectional development holds that, in reaching its ultimate development, writing, whatever its forerunners may be, must pass through the stages of logography, syllabography, and alphabetography in this, and in no other, order. Therefore, no writing can start with a syllabic or alphabetic stage unless it is borrowed, directly or indirectly, from a system that has gone through all the previous stages. A system of writing can stop at one stage without developing further. Thus, a number of writings stopped at the logosyllabic or syllabic stage. The saying *Natura non facit saltus* ("Nature does not make leaps") can be applied to the history of writing in the sense that no stage of development can be skipped. Therefore, if it is accepted that logography develops first into syllabography, the alleged Egyptian "alphabet," which developed from logography, cannot be an alphabet but must be a syllabary. There is no reverse development: an alphabet cannot develop into a syllabary, just as a syllabary cannot lead to the creation of logography. For that reason it is impossi-

Marginal notes:

Examples of metagraphy

Occurrences of logography

The meaning of unidirectional development

ble to speak of the development of Ethiopic or Sanskrit syllabaries from a Semitic alphabet. Both the Ethiopic and Sanskrit writings are alphabetic developments from a Semitic syllabary, which, in turn, is a creation that follows the model of the Egyptian syllabary.

Foreign interventions. From what has been said above, one would expect to find evidence that writing developed normally, from logo-syllabic to syllabic to alphabetic, in one certain writing as used in one certain area. Writing never develops to this extent, however, in a given area, and it was not only habit or the conservative attachment of a people for their own writing that prevented writing in a given area from passing through its full course of development. In several cases, vested interests of special classes, religious or political, may have been responsible for maintaining a difficult and obsolete form of writing. It is therefore foreign peoples, not bound by local traditions and religious or political interests of an alien group, that are frequently responsible for introducing new and important developments in the history of writing. Although in their early stages both the Assyro-Babylonian and the Egyptian logosyllabic systems manifested sound tendencies in the direction of almost pure syllabography, in the course of centuries they became overburdened with a great number of additional word signs. In some cases, various artificial and baroque deviations developed that made it difficult if not impossible for masses of people to master the writing system. Such writing ended up frequently by being rejected by the people and replaced by an entirely

new system introduced from abroad. Thus, when the relatively simple and easy to learn cuneiform systems of the Old Akkadians, Old Assyrians, and Old Babylonians degenerated into the systems of the late Assyrians and late Babylonians, the latter were finally replaced by the Aramaic script; and, after the hieroglyphic systems of the Egyptian pyramid and empire periods had taken on the complicated and enigmatic developments of the Ptolemaic era, the result was the replacement of hieroglyphic by the Coptic writing.

Many other examples of foreign intervention in the history of writing can be observed. In the section on *Syllabic writings,* above, mention was made of the development of various syllabaries from logosyllabic systems, such as the cuneiform syllabaries of the Elamites, Hurrians, and Urartians from a Mesopotamian system, the West Semitic syllabary from Egyptian, the Cypriot and some other Aegean syllabaries from a Cretan (Aegean) system, and the Japanese syllabary from the Chinese writing. One of the best examples of foreign intervention is furnished by the development of the Greek alphabet from the West Semitic syllabary.

Absence of inventions. In both scholarly and popular studies, statements about the invention of writing are frequently encountered. Writing was not invented by one man in one certain area in one particular place, however. Writing in its phonetic stage represents nothing but a practical adaptation of observations of many generations and centuries. Its history and prehistory are as long as the

history of humanity itself. In considering the three great steps in the development of writing—(1) the development of phonetization by the Sumerians, (2) the creation of the West Semitic syllabary with its rejection of all word signs and of syllabic signs with more than one consonant, and its restriction to a small number of open syllabic signs, and (3) the creation of the Greek alphabet, with a full vowel indication—it immediately becomes evident that every new step, every so-called invention, is not really something entirely new. The only observable development in the history of writing is the systematization, at a certain stage, of devices that had been known previously but had been utilized in a haphazard way only.

In the history of writing, as in the case of all great cultural achievements, one must reckon with the decisive intervention of men of genius who were able either to break away from sacred tradition or to transfer into practical form something on which others could only speculate or experiment. Unfortunately, the names of the great men who were involved in the most important innovations in the history of writing—like the names of those who were

responsible for the crucial improvements in the use of the wheel, or the bow and arrow, or the sail—are lost forever in the dimness of antiquity.

One origin or many. It is impossible to speak of one origin for writing if the term writing is used in its widest sense, to stand for all methods of human communication by means of visible markings. Writing in this sense, like pictures in general, could have been and actually was used by various people in various parts of the world from time immemorial, and it would be just as senseless to speak about the common origin of all these writings as it would be to try to derive all art from one common source. Thus, the question of whether writing had one origin or many can appertain only to what is called full or phonetic writing.

Seven logosyllabic systems of writing are known, all of which, a priori, could claim independent origin. Nevertheless, a theory of monogenesis of writing, based mainly on the stimulus of cultural contact, has been seriously entertained.

Cultural contact supported by geographic proximity makes a common origin for the Sumerian, Proto-Elamite, and Proto-Indic systems highly probable. The same considerations, in addition to structural features, bring together the Aegean group of writings, including Cretan and Hittite, just as cultural and geographic considerations seem to support the theory of Egyptian influence upon the Cretan writing. As for the Egyptian writing, its origin occurred close to, and quite possibly within, the period when Mesopotamian influence in Egypt was stronger than at any other time. Finally, Chinese writing originated in the period of the Shang dynasty, which is characterized by so many foreign innovations that many scholars regard it as a ready-made civilization imported from somewhere in the West.

Modern writings among the "primitive" societies. The 5,000-year-old history of writing is closely paralleled by the history of writings developed in modern times among the so-called primitive societies under Western influence. These writings are to be sharply distinguished from the various semasiographic devices of the "primitive" peoples, which are included under the forerunners of writing. Most of the newly introduced systems are found in North America and western Africa.

The study of these writings leads to conclusions that are of primary importance for the history of writing in general: (1) All the new writings that have gone through an extended process of evolution, like the Cherokee writing introduced by an Indian named Sequoyah (more correctly Sikwayi) and the Alaska systems in North America, or the Vai and Bamum systems in western Africa, have evolved from primitive semasiography and have passed successively through the stages of logography and syllabography, showing at times, in the final stage, certain tendencies toward alphabetization. Thus the sequence of stages in writings introduced among "primitives" fully parallels the history of writing in its natural evolution. (2) These writings have passed, within the space of one or two generations, through a process of evolution that had taken thousands of years for the normal writing to pass through. Thus one can observe the process of evolution of writing speeded up immensely under the impact of foreign stimulus. (3) The case of the original Cherokee word writing, created by Sequoyah and then rejected by him, and the limited use of the Alaska word writing prove the unfeasibility of word writing in general as a system of communication. (4) To judge from the great majority of systems created recently, the syllabic (not alphabetic) stage is best suited among "primitive" societies. (5) Certain tendencies of syllabic systems, such as Bamum and Alaskan, to develop in the direction of an alphabet belie the statements of some scholars who believe that the syllabic systems represent a blind alley, which could never lead to an alphabetic writing.

Specialized forms. Besides the standard systems of writing, there are several specialized forms of communication by means of visual marks. Western cartography utilizes not only the letters of the alphabet, in the writing of geographic names and of some other pertinent information, but also various conventional symbols, such as circles, triangles, and squares, in different shapes and sizes, for different sizes and kinds of human settlements, and certain forms of lines for rivers, boundaries, and means of communication. Also the colour device, such as blue for waters, green for lowlands, brown for highlands, and white for snowcapped mountains, plays an important role in cartography. A similar mixture of standard writing and conventional symbolism and conventions can be found also on ledgers, charts, and graphs. Mathematics, symbolic logic, and other sciences use different sets of symbols and conventions in their written languages. Systems of musical notation employ conventional symbolism to indicate tone or pitch and similar features.

Examples of secondary transfers

A secondary transfer from a standard form of writing to another form is illustrated by the Morse alphabet. In its simplest form, this may be nothing but a one-to-one replacement of the letters of the alphabet by groups of dots and dashes. The written dots and dashes can be transferred into visible flashes or audible signals of varying duration. A different kind of replacement is found in naval communication, as in the marine flag code, in which each signal can stand for a word, phrase, or sentence. Cryptography utilizes ciphers, which represent a transfer from one form of a letter (alphabetic or syllabic sign) to another, and codes, which represent a transfer from one form of a word sign or word group to another. With combinations of ciphers and codes and with multiple obstacles laid in the way of an uninitiated reader, cryptography deals with writing used for the purpose of secret communication, mainly in war and diplomatic relations. Another specialized purpose is illustrated by the Braille alphabet, which represents a transfer from a visible form of standard writing to a tactile form. The purpose of the various shorthand systems (stenography, "narrow writing"; tachygraphy, "quick writing"; or brachygraphy, "short writing") is obviously speed in writing. The purpose of calligraphy, "beautiful writing," is the attainment of an artistic or aesthetic effect. (I.J.G.)

Systems of writing

ALPHABETIC WRITING

An alphabet is a set of symbols or characters used to represent the sounds of a language; in most alphabets the symbols are arranged in a definite order, or sequence (*e.g.*, *A, B, C,* etc.). Each of the characters usually represents either a consonant or a vowel, rather than a syllable or group of consonants and vowels. As a result, the number of characters required can be held to a minimum. A language that has 30 consonant sounds and five vowels, for example, needs only 35 separate letters. In a syllabary, on the other hand, the same language would require 30 times five symbols to represent each syllable (*e.g.*, separate forms for *ba, be, bi, bo, bu; da, de, di,* and so on), and an additional five symbols for the vowels, thereby making a total of 155 individual characters. Both syllabaries and alphabets are phonetic symbolizations; that is, they are symbols to record the sounds of words rather than to represent objects or ideas being expressed. (With the passage of time some languages, notably English, failed to synchronize spelling changes with changes in pronunciation, so that these languages can no longer be said to have totally phonetic spelling.)

Derivation of the term alphabet

The word alphabet, from the first two letters of the Greek alphabet—alpha and beta—was first referred to in its Latin form, *alphabetum,* by Tertullian (died AD 230), a Latin ecclesiastical writer and Church Father, and by St. Jerome. The classical Greeks customarily used the plural of *to gramma,* "the letter," while later the form *alphabētos* was adopted, probably under Latin influence (see above *The nature and origin of writing;* see below *Hieroglyphic writing*).

Theories of the origins of the alphabet. Evidence for the original alphabet is scarce, but such as it is, it comes exclusively from the lands bordering the eastern shores of the Mediterranean, including ancient Canaan and Phoenicia, and belongs to the period between 1700 and 1500 BC. This alphabet is known as the North Semitic.

Over the centuries, various theories have been advanced to explain the origin of alphabetic writing, and, since classical times, the problem has been a matter of serious study. The Greeks and Romans considered five different peoples as the possible inventors of the alphabet—the Phoenicians, Egyptians, Assyrians, Cretans, and Hebrews. Modern theories include some that are not very different from those of ancient days. Every country situated in or more or less near to the east Mediterranean has been singled out for the honour. Egyptian writing, cuneiform, Cretan, Hieroglyphic Hittite, the Cypriot syllabary, and other scripts have all been called prototypes of the alphabet. The Egyptian theory actually subdivides into three separate theories, according to whether the Egyptian hieroglyphic, the hieratic, or the demotic script is regarded as the true parent of alphabetic writing. Similarly, the idea that cuneiform was the precursor of the alphabet may also be subdivided into Sumerian, Babylonian, and Assyrian cuneiform.

Egyptian theory of the origin of the alphabet

Among the various other theories concerning the alphabet are the hypotheses that the alphabet was brought by the Philistines from Crete to Palestine, that the various ancient scripts of the Mediterranean countries developed from prehistoric geometric symbols employed throughout the Mediterranean area from the earliest times, and that the Proto-Sinaitic inscriptions (discovered since 1905 in the Sinai Peninsula) represent a stage of writing intermediate between the Egyptian hieroglyphics and the North Semitic alphabet. Another hypothesis, the Ugaritic theory, evolved after an epoch-making discovery in 1929 (and the years following) at the site of the ancient Ugarit, on the Syrian coast opposite the most easterly cape of Cyprus. Thousands of clay tablets were found there, documents of inestimable value in many fields of research (including epigraphy, philology, and the history of religion). Dating from the 15th and 14th centuries BC, they were written in a cuneiform alphabet of 30 letters.

The Early Canaanite theory was based on several undeciphered inscriptions also discovered since 1929 at various Palestinian sites; the writings belong in part to *c.* 1700 BC and are thus the earliest preserved documents in an alphabetic writing.

Despite the conflict in theories, leading scholars are generally agreed that for about 200 years before the middle of the 2nd millennium BC, alphabet making was in the air in the Syro-Palestinian region. It is idle to speculate on the meaning of the various discoveries referred to. That they manifest closely related efforts is certain; what the exact relationship between these efforts was, and what their relationship with the North Semitic alphabet was, cannot as yet be said with certainty.

It can, however, be ascertained that the period from 1730 to 1580 BC in Syria, Palestine, and Egypt, during which there was an uprooting of established cultural and ethnic patterns in the Fertile Crescent, provided conditions favourable to the conception of an alphabetic script, a kind of writing that would be more accessible to larger groups of people, in contrast to the scripts of the old states of Mesopotamia and Egypt, which were confined largely to the priestly class. In default of other direct evidence, it is reasonable to suppose that the actual prototype of the alphabet was not very different from the writing of the earliest North Semitic inscriptions now extant, which belong to the last two or three centuries of the 2nd millennium BC. The North Semitic alphabet was so constant for many centuries that it is impossible to think that there had been any material changes in the preceding two to three centuries. Moreover, the North Semitic languages, based as they are on a consonantal root (*i.e.,* a system in which the vowels serve mainly to indicate grammatical or similar changes), were clearly suitable for the creation of a consonantal alphabet.

Conditions favourable for alphabetic writing

The inventor or inventors of the alphabet were, no doubt, influenced by Egyptian writing—perhaps also by other scripts. Indeed, it is probable that the man or men who invented the alphabet were acquainted with most of the scripts current in the eastern Mediterranean lands at the time. Though the nationality of the inventor or inventors of the alphabet is unknown, it is now generally agreed that he or they belonged to the Northwest Semitic linguistic group, which includes the ancient Canaanites, Phoenicians, and Hebrews.

Letters as signs

It seems probable that the original letters were conventional signs and not, as is still held by some, pictures used as ideograms (*e.g.,* the letter 'alef representing an ox, bet a house, gimmel a camel, and so on). Indeed, the great achievement in the creation of the alphabet was not the invention of signs but the inner working principle; that is, the production of a system in which each sound is represented by one symbol and each symbol generally represents one sound. The principle governing the conventional names of the letters is known as acrophony—that is, the value of each consonant is the value of the first letter of its name: *b* of "bet," *g* of "gimmel," *d* of "dalet," and so on. These names were not derived from pictographic representations of the letters but were an artificial, mnemonic device similar to those used in modern ABC books for children.

The North Semitic alphabet remained almost unaltered for many centuries. If the signs' external form (which, it must be emphasized, had no particular significance) is ignored, and only their phonetic value, number, and order are considered, the modern Hebrew alphabet may be regarded as a continuation of the original alphabet created more than 3,500 years ago. The Hebrew order of the letters seems to be the oldest. The earliest evidence that the Hebrew alphabet was learned systematically was a schoolboy's scribbling on the vertical face of the upper step of a staircase leading up to the palace at Lachish, in southern Israel. It included the scratching of the first five letters of the early Hebrew alphabet in their conventional order, and it belonged to the 7th or 8th century BC.

Development and diffusion of alphabets. At the end of the 2nd millennium BC, with the political decay of the great nations of the Bronze Age—*i.e.,* the Egyptians, Babylonians, Assyrians, Hittites, and Cretans—a new historical world began. In Syria and Palestine, the geographical centre of the Fertile Crescent, three nations—Israel, Phoenicia, and Aram—played an increasingly important political role. To the south of the Fertile Crescent, the Sabaeans, a South Arabian people (also Semites, though South Semites), attained a position of wealth and importance as commercial intermediaries between the East and the Mediterranean. To the west, seeds were sown among the peoples who later constituted the nation of Hellas—the Greeks. As a result, an alphabet developed with four main branches: (1) the so-called Canaanite, or main branch, subdivided into Early Hebrew and Phoenician varieties; (2) the Aramaic branch; (3) the South Semitic or Sabaean branch; and (4) the Greek alphabet, which became the progenitor of the Western alphabets, including the Etruscan and the Latin. The Canaanite and Aramaic branches constitute the North Semitic main branch.

Development of four main branches of the alphabet

The Canaanite alphabet. The two Canaanite branches may be subdivided into several secondary branches. First, Early Hebrew had three secondary branches—Moabite, Edomite, and Ammonite—and two offshoots—the script of Jewish coins and the Samaritan script, still in use today, for liturgical purposes only. Second, Phoenician can be divided into Phoenician proper and "colonial" Phoenician. Out of the latter developed the Punic and neo-Punic scripts and probably also the Libyan and Iberian scripts.

The term Early Hebrew is used to distinguish this branch from the later so-called Square Hebrew. The Early Hebrew alphabet had already begun to acquire its distinctive character by the 11th century BC. It was used officially until the 6th century BC and then lingered on for several centuries. In a stylized form, it was used on Jewish coins from 135 BC to AD 132–135. The most ancient example of Early Hebrew writing is that of the Gezer Calendar of the period of Saul or David (*i.e., c.* 1000 BC). The oldest extant example of the Early Hebrew ABC is the inscription of the first five letters of the Hebrew alphabet, faintly scratched on the steps of the palace in Lachish, perhaps dating from the 8th century BC. A cursive style reached its climax in the inscriptions at Lachish, dating from the beginning of the 6th century BC. The Leviticus and other small Early Hebrew fragments found in the Dead Sea caves, which are probably from the 3rd century BC, are the only remains

of what is considered to be the Early Hebrew book, or literary, hand.

It is difficult to overestimate the importance of the Phoenician alphabet in the history of writing. The earliest definitely readable inscription in the North Semitic alphabet is the so-called Ahiram inscription found at Byblos in Phoenicia (now Lebanon), which probably dates from the 11th century BC. There is, however, no doubt that the Phoenician use of the North Semitic alphabet went further back. By being adopted and then adapted by the Greeks, the North Semitic, or Phoenician, alphabet became the direct ancestor of all Western alphabets. Only very few inscriptions have been found in Phoenicia proper. This rarity of indigenous documents is in contrast to the numbers of Phoenician inscriptions found elsewhere—on Cyprus, Malta, Sicily, and Sardinia, and in Greece, North Africa, Marseille, Spain, and other places.

Paramount importance of the Phoenician alphabet

The Aramaic alphabet. The adaptation of the North Semitic alphabet to the Aramaic language took place at some time in the 10th century BC, when Aramaic was spoken in several petty kingdoms in northern Mesopotamia and Syria, the most important of them being Dammeshek (Damascus). The process of the reestablishment of the Assyrian Empire and its hegemony over a good part of the Near East began in the 9th century. One after another, the Aramaean states gave way under Assyrian onslaught. Dammeshek, the last survivor, fell in 732 BC. The end of Aramaean political independence marked the beginning of Aramaean cultural and economic supremacy in western Asia. The transplantation of masses of Aramaeans by the Assyrians, a political measure designed to break up military alliances, bore remarkable fruit. By the end of the 8th century BC, the use of the Aramaic language and alphabet had become very widespread in Assyria itself; by the end of the following century all of Syria and a large part of Mesopotamia had become thoroughly Aramaized.

On the whole, the few early Aramaic inscriptions that have been found belong to the 9th, 8th, and 7th centuries BC. Inscriptions from the 6th and later centuries are more numerous; the increase reflects the rapid spread of the Aramaic alphabet throughout the Near East. Numerous Aramaic papyri and ostraca (inscribed pottery fragments) have been found in Egypt; the earliest of these can be dated to *c.* 515 BC, while the most famous are the Elephantine papyri, containing information of a religious and economic nature about a 5th-century Jewish military colony in Egypt. Aramaic inscriptions have been found in northern Arabia, Palestine, Lycia, Cappadocia, Lydia, Cilicia, Assyria, and as far afield as Greece, Afghanistan, and India.

Aramaic inscriptions

Almost as if by pre-arrangement, all of the alphabetic scripts west of Syria seem to have been derived, directly or indirectly, from the Canaanite alphabet, whereas the hundreds of alphabetic writings of the East apparently have sprung from the offshoots of the Aramaic alphabet. On the whole, the direct and indirect descendants of the Aramaic alphabet can be divided into two main groups: the scripts employed for Semitic languages, and those adapted to non-Semitic tongues. With regard to the Semitic offshoots, six separate alphabets may be discerned: the Hebrew, the Nabataean-Sinaitic-Arabic, the Palmyrene, the Syriac-Nestorian, the Mandaean, and the Manichaean. Some of these alphabets became links between the Aramaic alphabet and the numerous scripts used for the non-Semitic languages of central, southern, and southeastern Asia.

Among these scripts, which were directly or mainly indirectly adapted to non-Semitic languages from the Aramaic alphabet, are: (1) the Persian (Iranian) scripts known as Pahlavi, which were used for writing the sacred (pre-Islāmic) Persian literature, etc.; (2) Sogdian, a script and language that constituted the lingua franca of Central Asia in the second half of the first millennium AD; (3) Kök Turki, a script used from the 6th to the 8th century AD by Turkish tribes living in the southern part of central Siberia, in northwestern Mongolia, and in northeastern Turkistan (this alphabet was the prototype of the early Hungarian alphabet); (4) the alphabet of the Uighurs, a Turkic-speaking people who lived in Mongolia and eastern Turkistan in the early 13th century; this script was adapted,

Adaptations of the Aramaic alphabet

with Tibetan influence, and adopted as the writing of the Mongol Empire (the so-called Kalika script); (5) the early scripts of the Mongols, including Kalmuck, Buryat (Buriat), Mongolian proper, and the allied Manchu alphabet.

The Aramaic alphabet was probably also the prototype of the Brāhmī script of India, a script that became the parent of nearly all Indian writings. Derived from the Aramaic alphabet, it came into being in northwest India. The Armenian and Georgian alphabets, created by St. Mashtots (Mesrob) in the early 5th century AD, were also based on the Aramaic alphabet.

The South Semitic alphabet. The South Semitic, or Sabaean, branch remained within the confines of the Arabian Peninsula for most of its history. It was in use at the beginning of the 1st millennium BC. The most that can be said about its origins is that it neither developed from, nor directly depended upon, the North Semitic alphabet. It may have been derived, ultimately, from the Proto-Sinaitic script, with some influence from the North Semitic. Offshoots from the South Semitic branch included the Minaean, Himyaritic, Qatabanic, and Hadhramautic alphabets in southern Arabia, and Thamudene, Dedanite, and Safaitic alphabets in the northern part of the peninsula. Numerous inscriptions in these alphabets are the principal source for the study of those once-flourishing kingdoms, including the biblical Sheba, relegated by the rise of Islām to the backwaters of history.

The Sabaean offshoot, a graceful and elegant script consisting of 29 letters, spread into Africa, where it became the progenitor of the Ethiopic alphabet; this in turn gave birth to the modern Amharic, Tigré, Tigrinya, and other alphabets of modern Ethiopia. These are the only South Semitic scripts still in use today.

The Greek alphabet. As with so many other things, the importance of the ancient Greeks in the history of the alphabet is paramount. All of the alphabets in use in Europe today are directly or indirectly related to the Greek. Although the Greek alphabet was an adaptation rather than an invention, it was such an improvement that it has remained for 3,000 years—with only slight modifications—an unparalleled vehicle of expression and communication for men of the most diverse nationalities and languages. The Greek alphabet, created early in the 1st millennium BC, spread in various directions in Asia Minor, Egypt, Italy, and other places, but far and away the most important developments of it were the Etruscan-Latin and the Cyrillic alphabets.

Theories explaining diffusion. There is no complete agreement as to how or why certain alphabets have come to dominate the world. Some scholars believe that the alphabet follows the flag; that is, that the diffusion of the alphabet results from political and military conquests. Others hold that the alphabet follows trade. More accurate, perhaps, is the theory that the alphabet follows religion. A few examples may illustrate the point: (1) The Latin language and script were carried by Roman legionaries and Imperial officers to all parts of the vast Roman Empire, particularly to the regions that were not Hellenized. In later centuries, however, churchmen and missionaries carried the Latin language and script still further afield. The ascendancy of Latin led to the adoption of the Latin (Roman) alphabet by a large majority of nations; it became used for tongues of the most diverse linguistic groups, not only in Europe but in all other parts of the world as well. (2) Two alphabets, the Cyrillic and the Latin, are used for writing Slavic languages. Cyrillic is used by those Slavic peoples who accepted their religion from Byzantium, whereas Roman Christianity brought the use of the Latin alphabet to the Poles, Lusatians, Wends, Czechs, Slovaks, Slovenes, and Croats. Particularly interesting is the case of Yugoslavia, in which a single language is written differently by the Catholic Croats and the Greek Orthodox Serbs. (3) The Arabic alphabet is, after Latin, the most generally used in Asia and Africa. The rise of Islām in the 7th century AD and the tremendous Islāmic expansion and conquest carried the Islāmic holy book, the Qur'ān, written in the Arabic alphabet, over a vast area: the Near and Middle East, North and Central Africa, South and Southeast Asia, and even southern Europe. The Arabic alphabet was, therefore, adapted to Semitic and Indo-European forms of speech, to Tatar-Turkish, Iranian, and Austronesian (Malayo-Polynesian) tongues, and to several African languages. (4) The movement eastward from India of the Indian Brāhmī-Buddhist alphabets was much more peaceful than that of the Arabic alphabet. These offshoots, which took root in Ceylon, Burma, Thailand, Cambodia, Laos, Vietnam, Indonesia, and the Philippines, were again the result of the spreading of a religion—Buddhism, but by missionaries and not by armies.

Major alphabets of the world. *Hebrew alphabet.* It is generally believed, in accordance with Jewish tradition, that the Early Hebrew alphabet was superseded in the Holy Land by the Aramaic alphabet during the period of the Babylonian Exile (586–516 BC), and that the Aramaic script therefore became the parent of the Square Hebrew (in Hebrew *ketav merubaʿ* "square script," or *ketav ashuri* "Assyrian writing"). The theory may be only partly right, for in the Holy Land the Early Hebrew alphabet was an object of such local attachment that for several centuries it was used side by side with the Aramaic script.

At any rate, there is little doubt that the Square Hebrew did derive from the Aramaic alphabet. A distinctive Jewish variety of the Aramaic alphabet that can be regarded as the Square Hebrew script can be traced from the 3rd century BC. It became standardized just before the Christian Era, and it was from this script that the modern Hebrew

The theory that the alphabet follows religion

From D. Diringer, *The Alphabet: A Key to the History of Mankind*

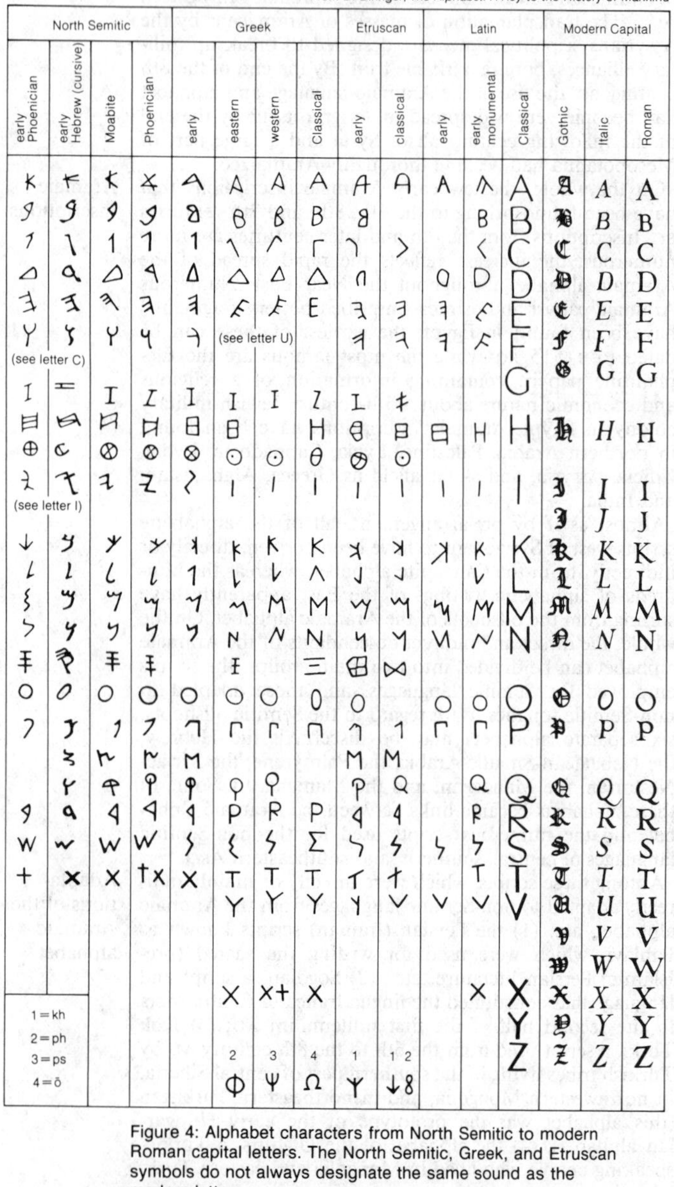

Figure 4: Alphabet characters from North Semitic to modern Roman capital letters. The North Semitic, Greek, and Etruscan symbols do not always designate the same sound as the modern letters.

Table legend:
1 = kh
2 = ph
3 = ps
4 = ð

alphabet, in all its styles, eventually developed. The development was gradual and purely external (*i.e.,* in the shapes of the single letters); from the internal standpoint (*i.e.,* considering the phonetic values of the letters), there has been no development, though it must be borne in mind that for several letters (*e.g.,* waw, ḥet, tzade, qof, shin, sin, etc.) the exact original phonetic value is still uncertain.

Standard-
ization of
Square
Hebrew

When the Square Hebrew alphabet became standardized, it took (at least, in its formal style and, much later, in its printed form) the form that, with insignificant changes, it now has. Minute rules laid down by the Talmud as to calligraphy and orthography made further development of the Square Hebrew impossible.

In the Square Hebrew alphabet, there are five letters—kaf, mem, nun, pe, and tzade—that have dual forms. That is, there is one character for initial or medial position and another for final position.

The Hebrew alphabet consists of 22 letters, all consonants, though four of them—alef, he, waw, and yod—are also employed to represent long vowels. The absence of vowel letters was not at first a problem, because Hebrew, like other Semitic languages, has consonantal roots, with vowels serving principally to denote inflections in nouns, moods of verbs, and other grammatical variations. As Hebrew speech passed out of daily use (being superseded by Aramaic, which became the vernacular of the Jews) and the knowledge of biblical Hebrew steadily declined, it became necessary to introduce some form of vocalic distinction so that the Bible could be read and explained correctly. The three main vowel systems now extant are the Babylonian, the Palestinian, and the Tiberiadic; of these the latter is the most important, and indeed, the only one still in use. The Tiberiadic system consists of dots, combinations of dots, and little dashes.

Before the discovery of the celebrated Dead Sea Scrolls, several Square Hebrew inscriptions belonging mainly to the 1st century BC and the succeeding centuries were known; they were found in Palestine, Syria, North Africa, and Italy, on rocks, tombs, or ossuaries (depositories for the bones of the dead), in synagogues and catacombs. The biblical manuscripts, except for some fragments written on papyrus, belong to a much later date. The earliest fragment is the Nash papyrus of approximately the 1st century BC, now in the Cambridge University Library. Many thousands of fragments of Hebrew biblical and other manuscripts, partly of the 7th and 8th centuries AD, were discovered in the Geniza, an archive in the old synagogue in Cairo.

The Dead
Sea Scrolls

The focus of world interest during the late 1940s and the successive years has been the sensational discovery of Hebrew biblical and nonbiblical scrolls in caves near the Dead Sea. The tens of thousands of fragmentary manuscripts, composing what are popularly called Dead Sea Scrolls, may be divided into several groups, the oldest being a collection of biblical and other Hebrew manuscripts, dating approximately from the 3rd century BC.

In the more than bimillennial development of the Square Hebrew alphabet, four fundamental types can be noticed: (1) the square script, which evolved into the well-proportioned printing type of modern Hebrew (the majority of Dead Sea Scrolls are in this Square Hebrew script); (2) the medieval formal styles; (3) the rabbinic, also known as Rashi writing, which was the medieval book or literary hand; and (4) a cursive script or daily handwriting, which gave rise to many local varieties (Oriental, Spanish, Italian, Franco-German, and so on), of which the Polish-German became the current Hebrew handwriting of today. The Hebrew script has been adapted to some other languages, such as Arabic, Turkish (for the Karaite people of Crimea), and so forth, but particularly to German—hence, Yiddish—and Spanish—hence, Judeo-Spanish.

Arabic alphabet. The Arabic script descended from the Aramaic through the Nabataean and the neo-Sinaitic alphabets. After the Latin script, it is the most widely used form of alphabetic writing in the modern world. The Arab conquests of the 7th and 8th centuries AD, which carried with them the religion of Islām and its holy book—the Qur'ān—written in Arabic, brought the language and the script to the vast expanse of territory extending from India to the Atlantic Ocean. The Arabic alphabet was adapted, with some necessary modifications, to such diverse languages as the Slavic tongues, Spanish, Persian, Urdu, Turkish, Hebrew, Berber, Swahili, Malay, Sudanese, and others.

Kūfic and
Naskhi
styles

The Arabic alphabet probably originated at some time in the 4th century AD, but the earliest extant Arabic writing is a trilingual inscription—Greek-Syriac-Arabic—of AD 512. The two principal types of Arabic writing, which developed quite early in the Muslim period, were the Kūfic, from the town of Kūfah in Mesopotamia, seat of a famous Muslim academy, and the Naskhi, or Mecca-Medina script. Kūfic, a heavy, bold, and lapidary style, appeared toward the end of the 7th century AD. It was particularly suitable for writing on stone or metal, for painting or carving inscriptions on the walls of mosques, and for lettering on coins. Its letters are generally thick, squat, and unslanted. With the high development of Arabic calligraphy, Kūfic writing became an exceptionally beautiful script. From it there were derived a number of other styles, chiefly medieval, in North and Central Africa, Spain, and northern Arabia.

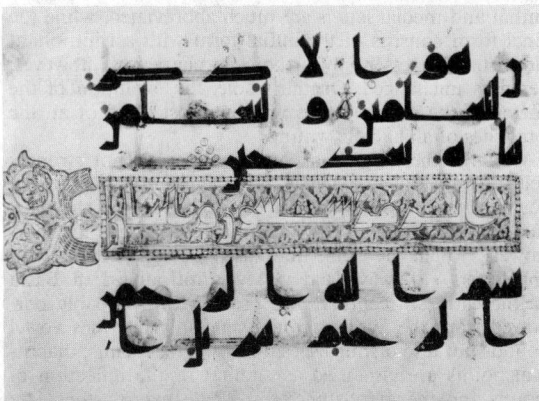

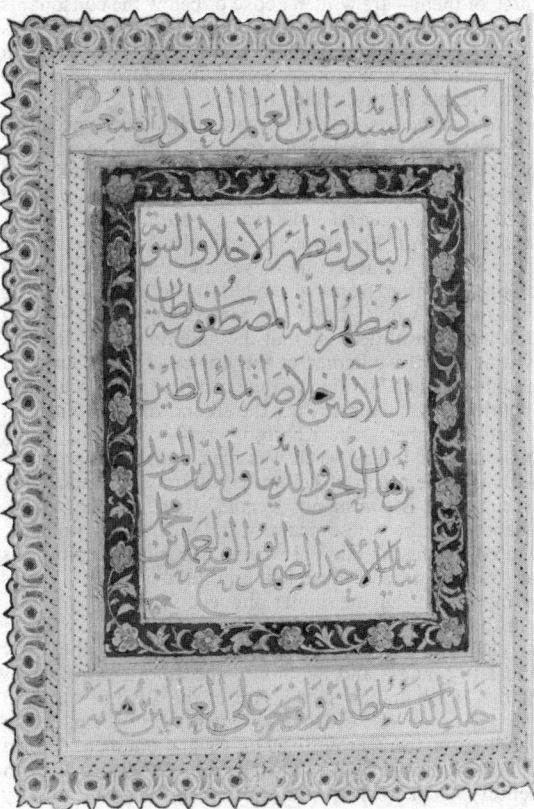

Early Arabic writing.
(Top) Early Kūfic book style, leaf from a Qur'ān, 8th–9th century. In the Freer Gallery of Art, Smithsonian Institution, Washington, D.C. (Bottom) Old Ottoman *naskhī,* opening of the Qur'ān, 1394. In the British Museum (Ms. OR 4126).

Thereafter, it was virtually discontinued except for formal and monumental writing. Nevertheless, it was also used for writing precious manuscripts of the Qur'ān, many of which are extant today.

The Naskhi style was from the very outset a more cursive form. It was always employed chiefly for writing on papyrus. In time, it evolved into innumerable styles and varieties, including the *ta'liq,* the *riqa',* the *divani,* the *thuluth,* and the *syakat,* and became the parent of the modern Arabic writing.

Like other Semitic scripts, Arabic is written from right to left. Its alphabet contains 28 consonantal letters, 22 being directly derived from the Aramaic-Nabataean branch of the North Semitic alphabet, and six being new additions; three of the letters—alif, wāw, and yā'—are also used as long vowels.

The written letters undergo a slight external change according to their position within a word. When they stand alone or occur at the end of a word, they ordinarily terminate in a bold stroke; when they appear in the middle of a word, they are ordinarily joined to the letter following by a small, upward curved stroke. With the exception of six letters, which can be joined only to the preceding ones, the initial and medial letters are much abbreviated, while the final form consists of the initial form with a triumphant flourish. The essential part of the characters, however, remains unchanged. On the whole, the evolution of the forms of the Arabic letters was the most rapid of all the branches of alphabetic writing.

Vowel marks in Arabic

Although the absence of vowel letters was not strongly felt in Arabic (as in Hebrew and other Semitic languages), for teaching purposes and for correct reading of the Qur'ān, the use of diacritical marks (including signs for short vowels, which are sometimes used in conjunction with the letters alif, wāw, and yā') was introduced in Basra in the early 8th century. The practice was probably borrowed from the Syriac script. It not only provides vowel sounds but also distinguishes different consonants; diacritical points are also used as endings in the inflection of nouns and the moods of verbs. These marks—there are three of them—are written above or below the consonants (preceding the vowel), while a sign called *sukūn* indicates the absence of a vowel. Thus, there are, on the whole, a great number of diacritical points; these form a peculiar characteristic of this writing form.

Indian alphabets. The Aramaic alphabet was probably the prototype of the Brāhmī script of India, the ancestor of all Indian scripts. The transmission probably took place in the 7th century BC. Adapting the Aramaic script to the Indo-Aryan tongue of India was by no means simple or straightforward. The shapes of many Brāhmī letters show clear Semitic influence; moreover, the Brāhmī script was originally written from right to left. It is obvious, however, that on the whole it was the idea of alphabetic writing that was transmitted and that the fully developed Brāhmī writing was the outcome of the brilliant philological and phonological elaboration of the scientific Indian school.

During the 5th century BC, the second of the prototypal Indian alphabets—the Kharoṣṭī script—came into being in northwest India (which was then under Persian rule). Although the origin of Brāhmī is still uncertain and hotly discussed, it is commonly accepted that the Kharoṣṭī alphabet is a direct descendant from the Aramaic alphabet. Moreover, the direction of writing in Kharoṣṭī script is as in Aramaic, from right to left, and there is also a likeness of many signs having similar phonetic value.

In the later centuries of its existence, Brāhmī gave birth to eight varieties of scripts. Three of them—the early and late Maurya and the Śuṅga—became the prototypes of the North Indian subdivision of the Brāhmī script in the 1st centuries BC and AD. Out of this North Indian subdivision there arose the Gupta, a monumental form of writing, which was employed from the 4th to the 6th century AD and became the ancestor of the great majority of Indian scripts.

Gupta writing in India

The western variety of the Gupta spread into eastern (or Chinese) Turkistan where it was adopted for a number of languages, including the recently discovered Turfanian and Kuchean (Tocharian A and B), and where it strongly

influenced the invention or revision of the Tibetan script (AD 639). There were two main offshoots of the Tibetan writing: the 'Phags-pa, adapted to the Chinese and Mongolian languages in 1272; and the Lepchā, which arose in the beginning of the 18th century.

Much more important was the Siddhamatrka script, developed during the 6th century AD from the western branch of the eastern Gupta character. The Siddhamatrka became the ancestor of the Nāgarī or Devanāgarī script (Sanskrit *deva* "divine," *nāgarī* "script of the city"), which is the script used for Sanskrit. It is, therefore, the most important Indian script. Consisting of 48 signs (14 vowels and diphthongs and 34 basic consonants), it is the common means of communication among learned men throughout India. The Devanāgarī developed in the 7th to 9th centuries and has remained, since the 9th century, essentially unaltered even today.

From the Devanāgarī writing as used in eastern India in the 11th century, there developed the proto-Bengali and the early Nepali, or Newari, scripts, from which the many scripts employed nowadays in northern India and

From D. Diringer, *The Alphabet: A Key to the History of Mankind*

phonetic value	Brāhmī					Gupta	modern north Indian						main n.e. Indian			south Indian				
	Aśoka	Bhaṭṭiprōlu	Śuṅga	Kuṣāna	Kṣatrapa		Devanāgarī	Gurmukhi	Gujarāti	Marāṭhi	Sindhi	Multani	Bengali	Assamese	Oriya	Vijayanagar	Telugu	Kannada	Tamil	Malayalam
a																				
ā																				
i																				
ī																				
u																				
ū																				
ṛ																				
ṝ																				
ḷ																				
e																				
ai																				
o																				
ō																				
au																				
ka																				
kha																				
ga																				
gha																				
ña																				
ca																				
cha																				
ja																				
jha																				
ña																				
ṭa																				
ṭha																				
ḍa																				
ḍha																				
ṛa																				
ṛha																				
ṇa																				
ta																				
tha																				
da																				
dha																				
na																				
pa																				
pha																				
ba																				
bha																				
ma																				
ya																				
ẏa																				
ra																				
ṛa																				
la																				
ḷa																				
va																				
śa																				
ṣa																				
sa																				
ha																				

Diacritical marks are ⟜ (m) anusvāra, ⏑ (m̐) anunāsika, (h) visarga,)((h) jihvāmūlīya, ⊰ (h) upadhmānīya, and S (') avagrana. These are often used with the script and affect pronunciation

Figure 5: Comparison of several Indian scripts.

Bangladesh descended; *e.g.,* the Bengali, Oriya, Manipuri, Assamese, Gujarati, and Bihari scripts, and the various Eastern Hindi local scripts.

In northwestern India several other scripts are employed. The Sarada script, a descendant of the western type of the Gupta character, originated in the 8th century and is still employed for Kashmiri. In addition, there are the several varieties of the Takri, used over the lower ranges of the Himalayas north of Punjab; the Dogri, used for a dialect of Punjabi; the Landa, the national alphabet of Punjabi, which has many varieties and is used mainly by shopkeepers all over Punjab and Sindh; and the Gurmukhi script, the characters of the Sikh scriptures.

In South India, which is inhabited by peoples speaking Dravidian languages, several other scripts are used, of which the Kannada, or Kanarese, the Telugu, the Grantha, the Tulu-Malayalam, the Tamil, and the Vaṭṭeluttu are the most important.

Long before the existence of the Gupta script, the Brāhmī script had already begun its eastward movement. The Indo-Aryan migration to the island of Ceylon in the 5th century BC had set the stage there, and the earliest Brāhmī inscriptions in Ceylon can be dated in the 3rd century BC. Most dramatic of all, however, was the expansion of Buddhism from India into Ceylon, Burma, Thailand, Cambodia, Laos, Vietnam, Malaya, and Indonesia. As already mentioned, unlike the conquests of Islām, this was a peaceful movement; its "soldiers" were Buddhist monks, political independents who built an empire founded on the cultural and spiritual community of peoples. Among their many achievements, these monks brought into being offshoots from the Brāhmī script, principally from its South Indian varieties, throughout the vast extent of territory from India itself to the Philippines. Thus arose the many scripts of Southeast Asia, from the Cham writing of Cambodia to the Kavi character of Java and its Sumatran offshoots, and the Tagalog writing of the Philippines.

Spread of Brāhmī to Southeast Asia

All these Indian and Southeast Asian scripts involve types of semisyllabaries rather than alphabets. They consist of vowels and diphthongs and basic consonants (*i.e.,* consonants followed by a short *a*); there are no pure consonants (*i.e.,* consonants written by themselves).

Greek alphabet. The Greek alphabet derived from the North Semitic script between *c.* 1000 BC and the 9th century BC. The direction of writing in the oldest Greek inscriptions—as in the Semitic scripts—is from right to left, a style that was superseded by the boustrophedon (meaning, in Greek, "as the ox draws the plow"), in which lines run alternately from right to left and left to right. This change occurred approximately in the 6th century BC. There are, however, some early Greek inscriptions written from left to right, and after 500 BC, Greek writing invariably proceeded from left to right.

The letters for *b, g, d, z, k, l, m, n, p, r,* and *t,* which are sounds common to the Semitic and Greek languages, were taken over without change. The principal Greek changes were the introduction of vowel representation, the re-arrangement of the sibilant or fricative sounds (of which the Semitic alphabets had a considerable variety), the adoption of some Semitic letters for slightly different Greek sounds, and the invention of symbols for Greek sounds not expressed by any of the Semitic letters. The different ways in which these adaptations were carried out allow the two main branches of the early Greek alphabet— the eastern and the western—to be distinguished. These again subdivide, each into secondary branches. Within this general grouping there were many local peculiarities, but the differences between all of these local alphabets involved variations in detail rather than essential structure.

Ionic and other eastern Greek alphabets

The eastern and western subdivisions were the two principal branches of the early Greek alphabet. The Ionic alphabet was the most important of the eastern variety, which also included the Greek alphabets of Asia Minor and the adjacent islands, of the Cyclades and Attica, of Sicyon and Argos, of Megara, Corinth, and the Ionian colonies of Magna Graecia. A secondary branch of the eastern subdivision was made up of the alphabets used on the Dorian islands of Thera, Melos, and Crete. The alphabets of Euboea (Chalcidian), Boeotia, Phocis, Locris, Thessaly, the Peloponnesus (except its northeastern part), and of the non-Ionian colonies of Magna Graecia belonged to the western subdivision. It is a controversial point whether the eastern or the western branch was the earlier in time, whether there was any derivative link between one and the other, or whether they represent two quite independent adaptations of the Semitic alphabet (the latter alternative seems rather improbable).

Gradually, the Greek local alphabets became more and more similar. In 403 BC, the Ionic alphabet of Miletus was officially adopted in Athens and later also in the other states. By the middle of the 4th century BC, almost all the local alphabets had been replaced by the Ionic, which became the common, classical Greek alphabet of 24 letters.

After this time, the development of the Greek alphabet was almost wholly external, in the direction of greater utility, convenience, and, above all, beauty. The classical style was retained as a monumental script at the same time that more cursive forms grew up for writing on such surfaces as parchment, papyrus, and wax. The classical letters were also retained as the capital letters in the modern print (though some of the capitals in modern Greek handwriting are borrowed from the Latin alphabet). On the other hand, the classical Greek alphabet also evolved into the Greek uncials, the cursive, and the minuscule script. (Uncial letters were somewhat rounded and separated versions of capital letters or cursive forms; minuscule letters developed from cursive writing and have simplified, small forms.) Up until about 800 AD, the uncials were used as a book hand; later, the minuscule script was employed for the same purpose. The cursive scripts evolved into the modern Greek minuscule.

Accent marks in Greek

In the middle of the 3rd century BC, the Greek scholar Aristophanes of Byzantium introduced the three accents— acute, grave, and circumflex—that were thereafter used to assist students, particularly foreigners, in the correct pronunciation of Greek words; these continue to be used in most Greek texts printed today. Originally, these marks indicated tone or pitch, not stress.

Countless inscriptions have been discovered all over the Hellenic and Hellenistic world and beyond. They include official decrees, annals, codes of law, lists of citizens, civic rolls, temple accounts, votive offerings, ostraca (fragments of pottery), sepulchral inscriptions, coins, lettering on vases, and so forth. These, along with many thousands of Greek manuscripts, both ancient and medieval, serve as sources for the studies known as Greek epigraphy and Greek paleography and are of untold importance for all branches of ancient history, philology, philosophy, and other disciplines.

The most direct offshoots from the Greek alphabet were those adapted to the languages of the non-Hellenic peoples of western Asia Minor in the 1st millenium BC: the scripts of the Lycians, Phrygians, Pamphylians, Lydians, and Carians. The first three of these were derived directly from the Greek; the Lydian and Carian were strongly influenced by it. The Coptic alphabet was the other non-European offshoot from the Greek and the only one used in Africa. Twenty-four of its 31 letters were borrowed from the Greek uncial writing, and seven were taken over from a particularly cursive variety of the Egyptian demotic writing; the demotic letters were used to express Coptic sounds not existing in the Greek language.

More significant, however, were the European offshoots. In Italy, two alphabets derived directly from the Greek: the Etruscan and the Messapian. The Messapii were an ancient tribe who inhabited the present Apulia (in southern Italy) in pre-Roman times; their language is presumed to belong to the Illyrian group. Over 200 Messapic (or Messapian) inscriptions have been discovered. In southeastern Europe, there were three offshoots from the Greek alphabet—the Gothic, the Cyrillic, and the Glagolitic alphabets. The Gothic alphabet, not to be confused with the so-called Gothic script (a variety of the Latin alphabet), was a script created by the Gothic bishop Ulfilas (or Wulfila), who died in AD 381 or 383. The script consisted of 27 letters, of which some 19 or 20 were taken over from the Greek uncial script. Ulfilas translated the Bible into Gothic; of this translation, some fragments are extant

The Gothic alphabet

in manuscripts of the 5th and 6th centuries. The most important manuscript is the *Codex Argenteus,* preserved in Uppsala, Sweden.

Cyrillic and Glagolitic alphabets. The two early Slavic alphabets, the Cyrillic and the Glagolitic, were invented by St. Cyril, or Constantine (*c.* 826–869), and St. Methodius (*c.* 815–885). These men were Greeks from Thessalonica, who became apostles to the southern Slavs, whom they converted to Christianity. An early tradition, in attributing the invention of an early Slavic writing to Cyril, does not indicate whether his contribution was the Cyrillic or the Glagolitic. It is just possible that both alphabets were invented by him. The earliest dated Old Slavic documents belong to the late 10th and the 11th centuries. The Cyrillic and the Glagolitic alphabets differed widely in the form of their letters, in the history of their development, and partly also in the number of the letters, but they were alike in representing adequately the many sounds of Slavic.

The Cyrillic alphabet was based on the Greek uncial writing of the 9th century. It originally had a total of 43 letters; the two Hebrew letters tzade and shin were transformed into the Cyrillic letters for the sounds *ch, sh,* and *shch.* The modern forms of this alphabet have fewer letters. Glagolitic writing consisted of 40 letters, externally very unlike either the Greek or Cyrillic scripts.

Cyrillic became, with slight modification in each case, the national script of the Bulgarians, Serbs, Russians, Belorussians, and Ukrainians. (The other Slavic peoples—the Slovenes, Croats, Czechs, Slovaks, Wends, Lusatians, and Poles—use the Latin alphabet.) As mentioned above, in Yugoslavia a single language is written in Cyrillic by the Greek Orthodox Serbs and in the Latin alphabet by the Roman Catholic Croats. For a time, Cyrillic was also adapted to the Romanian language, and in recent times, through the medium of Russian script, it became the writing of a number of Finno-Ugric languages (Komi, Votyak, Mordvinian, Vogul, Ostyak, etc.), Turco-Tatar languages (Chuvash, Turkmenian, Azerbaijanian, etc.), Iranian languages (Ossetic, Kurdish, Tajiki), and Caucasian languages (Abkhaz, Circassian, Avar, etc.).

The history of the Glagolitic alphabet is particularly connected with the religious history of the Slavic peoples of southwest central Europe and the western Balkan Peninsula. In the second half of the 9th century, it was introduced, together with the Slavonic liturgy, into the Moravian kingdom, but with the banning of this liturgy by the pope, it disappeared from Moravia. It was, however, accepted (also with the Slavonic liturgy) in Bulgaria and Croatia and spread along the Dalmatian coast southward into Montenegro and westward into Istria. Although the Glagolitic script soon disappeared among the Greek Orthodox Slavic peoples because of the victory of the Cyrillic, it continued, notwithstanding the opposition of the higher Catholic authorities, to be employed among the Catholics of the western Balkan Peninsula together with the Slavonic liturgy and finally succeeded in obtaining the special license of the pope. It is still employed in the Slavonic liturgy in some Dalmatian and Montenegrin communities; the inhabitants of these places are the only Roman Catholics to use the Slavonic liturgy. The earliest preserved Glagolitic secular document dates from 1309. Glagolitic had a short flourishing period in the 16th and 17th centuries.

Etruscan alphabet. The Etruscans, a highly civilized people who were the ancestors of the modern Tuscans and the predecessors of the Romans, inhabited what is now modern Tuscany in central Italy; their language, still mainly undeciphered, has come down in over 11,000 inscriptions, the earliest being the 8th-century-BC Marsiliana Tablet, preserved in the Museo Archeologico in Florence. This is also the earliest preserved record of a Western alphabet. The early Etruscan alphabet, unlike any early Greek alphabet found in the Greek inscriptions, contains the original—the prototype—Greek alphabet, consisting of the 22 North Semitic letters, with the phonetic values given to them by the Greeks, and the four additional Greek letters at the end of the alphabet. The Etruscans introduced various changes in their script, and several features in the modern alphabets can be attributed to the

influence of the ancient Etruscans. An example is the phonetic value of "k" for the letters *c, k,* and *q.* Like the Semitic and the early Greek alphabets, Etruscan writing nearly always reads from right to left, though a few inscriptions are in boustrophedon style. The probable date of the origin of the Etruscan alphabet is the late 9th or early 8th century BC.

About 400 BC, the "classical" Etruscan alphabet took its final form of 20 letters—four vowels and 16 consonants. Because the voiced and voiceless sounds *b* and *p, d* and *t, g* and *k* were not differentiated in the Etruscan language, letters *b* and *d* never appear in pure Etruscan inscriptions, and after the disappearance of *k* and *q,* the letter *C* was employed for *g* and *k.*

The Etruscan alphabet had many varieties and several offshoots. Among the offshoots, apart from the Latin, were many alphabets used by Italic populations of pre-Roman Italy and by non-Italic tribes (*e.g.,* the Piceni).

Latin alphabet. The adaptation of the Etruscan alphabet to the Latin language probably took place at some time in the 7th century BC. From this century, there is a gold brooch known as the Praeneste Fibula (preserved in the Museo Preistorico Etnografico Luigi Pigorini in Rome). The inscription, written in an early form of Latin, runs from right to left and reads clearly: *manios: med:fhefhaked:numasioi,* which in classical Latin is *Manius me fecit Numerio* "Manius made me for Numerius."

Oldest known record of Latin alphabet

Dating from the end of the 7th or the beginning of the 6th century BC is a famous cippus (small pillar) from the Roman Forum; it is inscribed vertically on its four faces, in boustrophedon style. Another inscription, probably of the 6th century BC, is known as that of the Duenos Vase and was found in Rome, near the Quirinal Hill. It is also written from right to left. Some Sabine inscriptions belong to the 5th or the 4th century BC. There are also a few inscriptions belonging to the 3rd and 2nd centuries BC.

The Roman capital letters, a form of writing that was used under the empire with unparalleled effectiveness for monumental purposes, became a byword for precision and grandeur, despite a very unprepossessing beginning. Indeed, for the first six centuries of its existence, Roman writing was relatively unimpressive. Only with the advent of the 1st century BC were there signs of magnificence to come.

An opinion that used to be commonly held, and still is held by many, is that the Latin alphabet was derived directly from the Greek in a form used by Greek colonists in Italy. The theory rested on an assertion that the Latin alphabet corresponds to the Chalcidian variety of the western group of Greek scripts employed at Cumae in Campania, southern Italy. This theory is unlikely; indeed, as already mentioned, the Etruscan alphabet was the link between the Greek and the Latin. For instance, the most interesting feature in the inscription of the Praeneste Fibula is the device of combining the letters *f* and *h* to represent the Latin sound of *f.* This was one of the Etruscan ways of representing the same sound. Also, most of the Latin letter names, such as a, be, ce, de for the Greek alpha, beta, gamma, delta, and so on, were taken over from the Etruscans.

Etruscan as link between Greek and Latin

Runic and ogham alphabets. Runes, in all their varieties, may be regarded as the "national" script of the ancient North Germanic tribes. The origin of the name rune (or "runic") is probably related to the fact that the ancient Germanic tribes, like all primitive peoples, attributed magic powers to the mysterious symbols scratched on armour, jewels, tombstones, and so forth. This is given credence by two related Germanic forms that mean "mystery, secret, secrecy": the Old Germanic root *ru-* and the Gothic *runa.* The most interesting runic inscriptions are those that were cut for magical purposes and those that appeal to heathen deities.

The origin of the runes offers many difficult problems, and has been hotly argued by scholars and others. The theory of the *Urrunen* (forerunners of the runes), a supposed prehistoric north Germanic alphabetic script, holds that it is the parent not only of the runes but also of all the Mediterranean alphabets, including the Phoenician. This belief, based on racial and political grounds, need not be

Origin of the runes

seriously considered. Some scholars propounded the 6th century BC Greek alphabet as the prototype of the runes; others have suggested the Greek cursive alphabet of the last centuries BC. Several eminent scholars have proposed the Latin alphabet as the source of the runes. The most probable theory, supported recently by many scholars, is that the runic script derived from a North Etruscan, Alpine alphabet. In that case, it is very probable that it originated about the 2nd century BC or a little later.

It is still unknown whether the runes were originally employed mainly for magical purposes, as suggested by the name *runa,* or as a usual means of communication. The earliest extant runic inscriptions, numbering over 50, come from Denmark and Schleswig and date from the 3rd to the 6th century AD. About 60 inscriptions from Norway date from the 5th to the 8th century, slightly later than the continental ones. There are also about 50 Anglo-Saxon runic inscriptions extant, including the Franks Casket (about AD 650–700); the right side of the casket is in the Museo Nazionale del Bargello, in Florence, Italy, and the rest is in the British Museum. The largest number of inscriptions, about 2,500, come from Sweden; most of these date from the 11th and 12th centuries AD.

There is no certain evidence of wide literary use of runes in early times, but some scholars hold that the runic writing was widely employed for all kinds of secular documents, such as legal provisions, contracts, genealogies, and poems. The known manuscripts are, however, rare and relatively late. The gradual displacement of the runes coincided with the increasing influence of the Church of Rome. The runic scripts lingered on for a long time after the introduction of Christianity, however; indeed, the use of runes for charms and memorial inscriptions lasted into the 16th or even the 17th century.

The ogham alphabet was restricted to the Celtic population of the British Isles. There are over 375 known inscriptions: 316 of them have been discovered in Ireland, chiefly in the southern counties, with only 55 from the northern counties; 40 inscriptions have been discovered in Wales; two come from Devon; and one from Cornwall.

From D. Diringer, *The Alphabet: A Key to the History of Mankind*

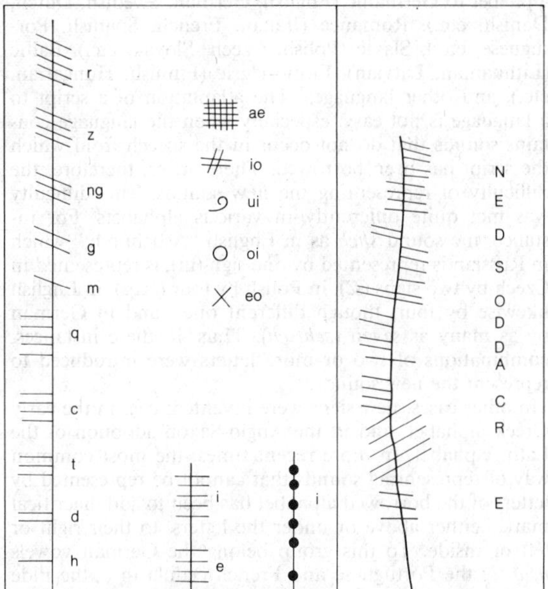

Figure 6: (Left) Ogham alphabet. (Right) Pictish ogham.

One inscription was discovered at Silchester in southern England. About ten come from the Isle of Man, and a few from Scotland. The Welsh inscriptions are usually bilingual, Latin-Celtic. With one exception, the Irish records are in ogham alone. Most peculiar is the runic-oghamic inscription from the Isle of Man (the runes being a kind of "secret" writing and the oghams being a cryptic script). The distribution of the ogham inscriptions, combined with their language and grammatical forms, point to South Wales or south Ireland as their place of origin, and to the 4th century AD as the date of their origin.

The ogham character was used for writing messages and letters (generally on wooden staves), but sometimes it was also written on shields or other hard material and was employed for carving on tombstones. The oghams formed a cryptic script, and there were several varieties, such as wheel oghams, bird oghams, tree oghams, hill oghams, church oghams, colour oghams, and others. The main ogham alphabet consisted of 20 letters represented by straight or diagonal strokes, varying in number from one to five and drawn or cut below, above, or right through horizontal lines, or else drawn or cut to the left, right, or directly through vertical lines. The ogham alphabet was divided into four groups (*aicme*), each containing five letters. Oghams were employed during the Middle Ages; the 14th-century *Book of Ballymote* reproduces the earliest keys for translation. In many cases, the ogham inscriptions run upward.

Several ogham inscriptions known as the Pictish oghams were found in western Scotland, on the small island of Gigha off the western coast, in Argyll, in northeastern Scotland, and on the northern isles, such as the Shetland Islands. They either belong to the same type as the Irish and Welsh oghams, or are written in another ogham variety.

Pictish oghams

Later development of the Latin alphabet. As already mentioned, the original Etruscan alphabet consisted of 26 letters, of which the Romans adopted only 21. They did not retain the three Greek aspirate letters, theta, phi, and chi, in the alphabet because there were no corresponding Latin sounds but did employ them to represent the numbers 100, 1,000, and 50. Of the three Etruscan *s* sounds, the Romans kept what had been the Greek sigma. The symbol that represented the aspirate later received the shape *H* as it did in Etruscan. *I* was the sign both of the vowel *i* and the consonant *j*. *X* was added later to represent the sound *x* and was placed at the end of the alphabet. At a later stage, after 250 BC, the seventh letter, the Greek zeta, was dropped because Latin did not require it, and a new letter, *G,* made by adding a bar to the lower end of *C,* was placed in its position.

After the conquest of Greece in the 1st century BC, a large number of Greek words were borrowed by the Latin language. At that time the symbols *Y* and *Z* were adopted from the contemporary Greek alphabet, but only to transliterate Greek words; hence, they do not appear in normal Latin inscriptions. They were placed at the end of the alphabet, and the Latin script thus became one of 23 symbols.

A few permanent additions, or, rather, differentiations from existing letters, occurred during the Middle Ages, when the signs for *u* and *v,* and *i* and *j,* previously written interchangeably for either the vowel or the consonant sound, became conventionalized as *u* and *i* for vowels and *v* and *j* for consonants. *W* was introduced by Norman scribes to represent the English sound *w* (a semivowel) and to differentiate it from the *v* sound.

The connection of the capital letters of modern writing with the ancient Semitic-Greek-Etruscan-Latin letters is evident even to a layman. The connection of the minuscules (*i.e.,* the small letters) with the ancient Latin letters is not as evident, but in fact both the majuscules and the minuscules descended from the same ancient Latin alphabet. The different shapes of the small letters are the result of a transformation of the ancient letters by the elimination of a part of the letter—as, for instance, *h* from *H* or *b* from *B*—or by lengthening a part of it—for instance, *d* from *D.* Moreover, the change of the Latin writing into the modern script was caused by technical bearings of

Derivation of majuscules and minuscules from Latin alphabet

modern European	Latin	runes	Greek	Cyrillic	Glagolitic
A	A	ᛒ	A	ᴀ	+
B	B	ᛒ	B	Ɓ(v) Ɓ(b)	ᚢ ᚻ
C	Ɔ	ᚲᚾᚴᚴ	ᚲᚾ	Г	ᛉ
D	D	ᛈᛈᛈᛈ(th)	D Δ ⊗	Δ	ᚪ
E	Ɛ	ᚠᚠᚠᚠ	Ϝ	E	Ɜ
F	F	ᚠᚠᛋᚢ	ϕ F	Ѱ	ᚻ
G	G	ᛊ ϕ			ᛗ
H	ᛒ	ᚾᛁᚾᚻᚾ	H	H(i)	ᛌ ᛣ
I	I	I	I	I(i)	ᛏ ᛘ(ğ)
J					
K	Ʞ	ᛉ	k	K	ᚺ
L	↰	ᚱ	ᚱ	Λ	ᚫ
M	ᴍ	ᛗ	M	M	ᚾ
N	N	ᛏᛐᛐᛐ	ᴎ	H	ᚱ
O	O	ᛉᛉᛉ	o o	O	ᛎ
P	ᚱ	ᚦᛗ(ε)	Г	ᴨ	ᚱ
Q	Q		Q		
R	ᛩ	R R	ᚱ	Ɋ	ᛒ
S	Ƨ	ᛋ	Ƨ	C	ᚸ
T	T	ᛏ	T	T	ᚱ
U	V	ᚪᚾ	V		
V					
W		ᚦ ᚦ			
X	X	X(g)	X	Ӿ(h)	ᛒ
Y	Y	ᛉᛇᛉ		Y(ü)	ᚭ
Z	Z	ᛉᚾ(ik,œ)	ᛉ	Ӝ(ž)Ƨ(d)Ʒ(n)	ᛉ ᛞ ᚳ
NG		ᚾ ᚷ(ng)	Ӿ +		
value	o sht ts ch sh ű	ү	i ě yu ya ye psy(e) q ye ya kh ps θ(th,f)		
Cyrillic	Ѱ Ц Ч Ш ...	... ...	... ...		
Glagolitic	o ...	...	...	...	...

Figure 7: Comparison of Latin, runic, Greek, Cyrillic, and Glagolitic alphabets.

the tool, primarily the pen, and the material of writing, mainly papyrus and parchment, and, from the 14th century onward, also paper. It was the pen, with its preference for curves, that eliminated the angular forms; it was the papyrus, and still more the parchment or vellum, and, in modern times, paper, that made these curves possible.

In ancient times, the minuscule did not exist, but there were several varieties of the capital and the cursive scripts. There were three varieties of the capitals: the lapidary capitals (used mainly on stone monuments); the elegant book capitals, somewhat rounded in shape; and the rustic capitals, which were less carefully elaborated than the lapidary script and not as round as the book capitals, but more easily and quickly written. In everyday life, the cursive script—i.e., the current hand—was developed with continuous modifications for greater speed. There were several varieties of it, such as those of Pompeii and Alburnus Major (a town in ancient Dacia, modern Roșia Montană, Romania). Between the monumental and the cursive scripts, there was a whole series of types that had some of the peculiarities of each group. There were lapidary mixed scripts and book semicursive scripts, and there was the early uncial or, rather semiuncial script of the 3rd century AD, which seems to have developed into the beautiful uncial script.

When the various European countries had shaken off the political authority of Rome and the learned communities had been dissolved and their members scattered, a marked change took place in the development of the Latin literary, or book hand. Several national hands, styles of the Latin cursive, assumed different features. There thus developed on the European continent and in the British Isles the five basic national hands, each giving rise to several varieties: Italian, Merovingian in France, Visigothic in Spain, Germanic, and Insular or Anglo-Irish hands. At the end of the 8th century, the Carolingian (Caroline) hand developed and, after becoming the official script and literary hand of the Frankish Empire, developed as the main book hand of western Europe in the following two centuries.

The combination of the majuscules, or capital letters, and minuscules, or small letters, can be attributed mainly to the Carolingian script.

In the course of the next centuries, various book hands or chart hands and other cursive scripts developed from the Carolingian style. In the late 12th century, and during the next two centuries, the letters gradually became angular in shape; this resulted from the pen being held in a position that made a slanting stroke. The new hand, termed black letter, or Gothic, was employed mainly in northwestern Europe, including England, until the 16th century. It is still used, though rarely, in Germany, where it is called Fraktur script.

In Italy, the black letter was also used, but the Italians preferred a rounder type, called *littera antiqua* "old letter." During the 15th century, the round, neat, humanistic or Renaissance hand was introduced in Florence and was employed for literary productions, while the needs of everyday life were met by an equally beautiful, though not as clearly legible, cursive hand. The two styles developed into two main varieties: (1) the Venetian minuscule, nowadays known as italics, traditionally (though wrongly) considered to be an imitation of Petrarch's handwriting; and (2) the Roman type, preferred in northern Italy, chiefly in Venice, where it was used in the printing presses at about the end of the 15th and the beginning of the 16th centuries; from Italy it spread to Holland, England (about 1518), Germany, France, and Spain. The classical Roman character was adopted for the majuscules. This majuscule writing, along with the Roman type minuscule and the italics, spread all over the world. In England, they were adopted from Italy in the 16th century.

The survival of the black letter (Gothic) in Germany is attributed to the fact that it was the current style at the time of the invention of printing in Germany—it was employed by Gutenberg; in Italy the *littera antiqua* was used by the German printers Konrad Sweynheym and Arnold Pannartz, as well as by Nicolas Jenson, the great Venetian printer who perfected the Roman type.

The modern national alphabets of the western European nations are, strictly speaking, adaptations of the Latin alphabet to Germanic (English, German, Swedish, Dutch, Danish, etc.), Romance (Italian, French, Spanish, Portuguese, etc.), Slavic (Polish, Czech, Slovak, etc.), Baltic (Lithuanian, Latvian), Finno-Ugric (Finnish, Hungarian, etc.), and other languages. The adaptation of a script to a language is not easy, especially when the language contains sounds that do not occur in the speech from which the script has been borrowed. There arises, therefore, the difficulty of representing the new sounds. This difficulty was met quite differently in various alphabets. For instance, the sound *shch* as in English "Ashchurch," which in Russian is represented by one sign (щ), is represented in Czech by two signs (*šč*), in Polish by four (*szcz*), in English likewise by four, though different ones, and in German by as many as seven (*schtsch*). Thus, in these instances, combinations of two or more letters were introduced to represent the new sounds.

In other cases, new signs were invented; *e.g.,* in the early Greek alphabet, and in the Anglo-Saxon adoption of the Latin alphabet. In more recent times, the most common way of representing sounds that cannot be represented by letters of the borrowed alphabet has been to add diacritical marks, either above or under the letters, to their right or left or inside. To this group belong the German vowels *ü, ä, ö;* the Portuguese and French cedilla in *ç;* the tilde on Spanish and Portuguese *ñ;* the Italian *à, é, è, ì, ù,* etc.; the great number of marks in the Latin-Slavic alphabets (Polish, Czech, Croatian, etc.)—*ą, ę, č, ć, š, ś, ž, z, ź,* and so on. The Latin-Turkish alphabet, introduced in 1928, became general throughout Turkey in 1930. It contains 29 letters, of which two vowels (*ö* and *ü*) and three consonants (*ç, ĝ,* and *ş*) are distinguished by diacritical marks; in one instance there is a distinction in reverse—the dot from *i* is eliminated (ı) to represent a new sound.

Attempts to make an ideal alphabet. In a perfect alphabet each sound would be represented by a single symbol, and no more than one sound would be represented by any symbol. But there are no completely perfect alphabets. All

National cursive hands in Europe

Invention of new signs and diacritical marks

alphabets omit symbols for some sounds, and all contain redundant letters. Indeed, living speech hardly conforms to the written word. There are, however, languages, such as Italian, Spanish, Portuguese, German, and even Bantu, that are relatively accurately represented in graphic form. In English, the spelling in many words is almost an arbitrary symbolism, which gives rise to interest in phonetic spelling and spelling reform. The I.T.A., Initial Teaching Alphabet, invented by Sir James Pitman, is an attempt to regularize English orthography.

The International Phonetic Alphabet

The International Phonetic Alphabet (IPA) is a system of writing designed to overcome the inconsistencies and redundancies in regular alphabets. Developed at the end of the 19th century by members of the International Phonetic Association, this alphabet has been used by linguists and others who must record with a greater degree of phonetic accuracy than can be achieved with ordinary alphabets. There are many additional types of phonetic alphabets.

With all of its deficiencies, the alphabet has been the only, or at least the best, means of international communication until the present day. Its privileged position can be attributed to a natural development lasting many centuries and accompanied by many other elements. The external development of the individual letters, strongly influenced by calligraphers and great graphic experts, is mainly the result of aesthetic considerations.   (D.D.)

HIEROGLYPHIC WRITING

Hieroglyphic writing is a system that employs characters in the form of pictures. These individual signs, called hieroglyphs, may be read either as pictures, as symbols for pictures, or as symbols for sounds. The name hieroglyphic (from the Greek word for "sacred carving") is first encountered in the writings of Diodorus Siculus (1st century BC). Earlier, other Greeks had spoken of sacred signs when referring to Egyptian writing. Among the Egyptian scripts, the Greeks labelled as hieroglyphic the script that they found on temple walls and public monuments, in which the characters were pictures sculptured in stone. The Greeks distinguished this script from two other forms of Egyptian writing that were written with ink on papyrus or on other smooth surfaces. These were known as the hieratic, which was still employed during the time of the ancient Greeks for religious texts, and the demotic, the cursive script used for ordinary documents.

Non-Egyptian hieroglyphic scripts

Hieroglyphic, in the strict meaning of the word, designates only the writing on Egyptian monuments. The word has, however, been applied for about 100 years to the writing of other peoples, insofar as it consists of picture signs used as writing characters. The name hieroglyphics is, for example, always used to designate the scripts of the Indus civilization and of the Hittites, who also possessed other scripts, in addition to the Mayan, the Incan, and Easter Island writing forms, and also the signs on the Phaistos Disk on Crete. Colloquially, the word hieroglyphics has been extended to mean any sort of illegible or barely legible writing.

Because of their pictorial form, hieroglyphs were difficult to write and were used only for monument inscriptions. They were usually supplemented in the writing of a people by other, more convenient scripts. Among living writing systems, hieroglyphic scripts are no longer used.

The rest of this section is concerned only with Egyptian hieroglyphic writing.

Development of Egyptian hieroglyphic writing. The most ancient hieroglyphs date from the end of the 4th millennium BC and comprise annotations to the scenes cut in relief—found on slabs of slate in chapels or tombs—that had been donated as votive offerings. Although by no means all of these earliest signs can be read today, it is nonetheless probable that these forms are based on the same system as the later classical hieroglyphs. In individual cases, it can be said with certainty that it is not the copied object that is designated but rather another word phonetically similar to it. This circumstance means that hieroglyphs were from the very beginning phonetic symbols. An earlier stage consisting exclusively of picture writing using actual illustrations of the intended words cannot be shown to have existed in Egypt; indeed, such

a stage can with great probability be ruled out. No development from pictures to letters took place; hieroglyphic writing was never solely a system of picture writing. It can also be said with certainty that the jar marks (signs on the bottom of clay vessels) that occur at roughly the same period do not represent a primitive form of the script. Rather, these designs developed in parallel fashion to hieroglyphic writing and were influenced by it.

Improbability of relationship to cuneiform

It is not possible to prove the connection of hieroglyphs to the slightly older cuneiform characters used by the Sumerians in southern Mesopotamia. Such a relationship is improbable because the two scripts are based on entirely different systems. What is conceivable is a general tendency toward words being fixed by the use of signs, without transmission of particular systems.

Invention and uses of hieroglyphic writing. The need to identify a pictorial representation with a specific, unique event, such as a hunt or a particular battle, led to the invention of hieroglyphic writing. Hieroglyphs added to a scene signified that this illustration represented a particular war rather than an unspecified one or war in general. This new attitude toward time and toward history as unique events in time led to the invention of hieroglyphic writing. The system first appeared only in connection with relief depictions, which they explained by means of place names. Beginning in the 1st dynasty (3100 BC), images of persons were also annotated with their names or titles, a further step toward expressing individuality and uniqueness. The so-called annalistic tablets of the first two dynasties were pictorial representations of the events of a year with specifically designated personal names, places, and incidents. For example, accompanying a scene of the pharaoh's triumph over his enemies is the annotation "the first occasion of the defeat of the Libyans." Simultaneously, the writing of the Egyptians began to appear unaccompanied by pictorial representations, especially on cylindrical seals. These roller-shaped incised stones were rolled over the moist clay of jar stoppers. Their inscription prevented the sealed jar from being covertly opened and at the same time described its contents and designated the official responsible for it. In the case of wine, its origin from a specific vineyard and often also the destination of the shipment were designated, and, as a rule, so was the name of the reigning king.

From the stone inscriptions of the 1st dynasty, only individual names are known, these being mainly the names of kings. In the 2nd dynasty, titles and names of offerings appear, and, at the end of this dynasty, sentences occur for the first time. The discovery of a blank papyrus scroll in the grave of a high official, however, shows that longer texts could have been written much earlier; *i.e.,* since the early part of the 1st dynasty.

Relationship of writing and art. The form of these hieroglyphs of the archaic period (the 1st to 2nd dynasty) corresponds exactly to the art style of this age. Although definite traditions or conventions were quickly formed with respect to the choice of perspective—*e.g.,* a hand was depicted only as a palm, an eye or a mouth inscribed only in front view—the proportions remained flexible. The prerequisite of every writing system is a basic standardization, but such a standardization is not equivalent to a canon (an established body of rules and principles) in the degree of stylistic conformity that it requires. A recognized canon of Egyptian hieroglyphic writing arose in the 3rd dynasty and was maintained until the end of the use of the script.

Formation of the standard and canon of Egyptian writing

In that hieroglyphic signs represented pictures of living beings or inanimate objects, they retained a close connection to the fine arts. The same models formed the basis of both writing and art, and the style of the writing symbols usually changed with the art style. This correspondence occurred above all because the same craftsmen painted or incised both the writing symbols and the pictures. Deviations from the fine arts occurred when the writing, which was more closely bound to convention, retained patterns that the fine arts had eliminated. The face in front view is an example of this. This representation, apart from very special instances, was eventually rejected as an artistic form, the human face being shown only in profile. The front view of the face was, however, retained as a hieroglyph from the archaic period to the end of the use of hieroglyphic writing. Similar cases involve the depiction of various tools and implements. Although the objects themselves fell out of use in the course of history— *e.g.,* clubs used as weapons—their representations, mainly misunderstood, were preserved in the hieroglyphic script. The hieroglyphs corresponding to such objects that had disappeared from daily life were therefore no longer well known and were often distorted beyond recognition. But the style of representation in the hieroglyphs still remained closely bound to the art of the respective epoch. Thus there appeared taut, slender forms or sensuous, fleshy ones, or even completely bloated characters, according to the art style of the period.

Media for hieroglyphic writing. In historical times (2800 BC–AD 300), hieroglyphic writing was used for inscribing stone monuments and appeared in Egyptian relief techniques, both high relief and bas-relief; in painted form; on metal, sometimes in cast form and sometimes incised; and on wood. In addition, hieroglyphs appear in the most varied kinds of metal and wood inlay work. All of these applications correspond exactly with the techniques used in fine art, and the same craftsmen who produced the works of art painted or incised the hieroglyphic inscriptions.

Subject matter of inscriptions Hieroglyphic texts are found primarily on the walls of temples and tombs, but they also appear on memorials and gravestones, on statues, on coffins, and on all sorts of vessels and implements. Hieroglyphic writing was used as much for secular texts—historical inscriptions, songs, legal documents, scientific documents—as for religious subject matter—cult rituals, myths, hymns, grave inscriptions of all kinds, and prayers. These inscriptions were, of course, only a decorative monumental writing, unsuitable for everyday purposes. For popular use, hieratic script was developed, an abbreviated form of the picture symbols such as would naturally develop in writing with brush and ink on smooth surfaces like papyrus, wood, and limestone.

Writing and religion. The influence of religious concepts upon hieroglyphic writing was confined to two cases. In the 3rd millennium, certain signs were avoided or used in garbled form in grave inscriptions for fear that the living beings represented by these signs could harm the deceased who lay helpless in the grave. Among these taboo symbols were human figures and dangerous animals, such as scorpions and snakes. Secondly, in all periods and for all uses of the writing, symbols to which a positive religious significance was attached were regularly placed in front of other signs, even if they were to be read after them. Among these were hieroglyphs for God or individual gods, as well as those for the king or the palace. Thus, for example, the two signs, 𓊹𓀟 denoting the word combination "servant of God" (priest), are written so that the symbol for God, 𓊹, stands in front of that for servant, 𓀟, although the former is to be read last. Moreover, theology traced the invention of hieroglyphic writing back to the god Thoth, although this myth of its divine origin did not have an effect on the development of the script. In the late period, Egyptian texts referred to hieroglyphic inscriptions as "writing of God's words"; earlier, in contrast, they were simply called pictures.

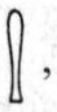

Literacy and knowledge of hieroglyphic writing. At all periods only a limited circle understood the script. Only those who needed the knowledge in their professions acquired the arts of writing and reading. These people were, for example, officials, doctors, and priests (insofar as they had to be able to read rituals and other sacred texts), as well as craftsmen whose work included the making of inscriptions. Under Greek and especially under Roman rule, the knowledge declined and was entirely confined **Decline of hieroglyphic writing** to temples where priests instructed their pupils in the study of hieroglyphic writing. From the time of the rule of the Ptolemies (305 to 30 BC), national consciousness became more and more narrowly bound up with religion, and for both the national consciousness and religion alike the tradition-filled hieroglyphic writing was an outward

sign—in the fullest sense, a symbol. There was no lack of attempts to replace the hieroglyphic writing, cumbersome and ever more divergent from the spoken language, with the simpler and more convenient Greek script. Such experiments, however, remained ineffective precisely because of the emotional value that the old writing system had when the country was under the foreign domination of the Macedonian Greeks and the Romans.

Christianity and the Greek alphabet. The situation was altered with the conversion of the country to Christianity in the 2nd and 3rd centuries AD. The new religion fought against the Egyptian polytheism and traditions, and with its victory, the Greek script triumphed. From the beginning, Egyptian Christians used the Greek alphabet for writing their spoken Egyptian language. This practice involved enlarging the Greek alphabet with seven supplementary letters for Egyptian sounds not present in Greek. As a consequence, the knowledge of hieroglyphic writing quickly declined. The last evidence of the writing system is a rock inscription from the island of Philae, dating from August 24, 394, from the reign of the emperor Theodosius I. The language as well as the writing system of the Egyptian Christians is called Coptic.

Characteristics of hieroglyphic writing. The system of hieroglyphic writing has two basic features: first, representable objects are portrayed as pictures (ideograms), and second, the picture signs are given the phonetic value of the words for these represented objects (phonograms). At the same time, these signs are also written to designate homonyms, similar-sounding words. The writing disregards vowels, and, also, in earlier times, the semivowels *i, y,* and *w,* thus offering more possibilities for the transference of signs to words with identical consonant combinations. For example, the sign for "wood" is written as a branch, 𓆱, which is pronounced with the consonants *h* and *t,* which occur in the Egyptian word for wood. **Ideograms and phonograms** Other words with the same series of consonants can also be written with the same basic sign; *e.g., ht* "after," *htʾ* "to retreat," or *htʾ* "to carve." Words that consisted of only one consonant, plus one or more vowels, supplied single consonant signs. The Egyptians, however, never reduced their writing to an alphabet by discarding the multiconsonant signs; rather, they retained clearly the form of the original words. When doubts occurred, as in the case of the three signs for the frequent consonant series *m + r* (the

hoe, 𓌻 , the chisel, � , and the pyramid, 𓉴),

the plurality was used to make clear distinctions between words: all derivations from the stem *mr* "to love" were written with the hoe; those from the stem *mr* "to be ill," with the chisel; and those words related to pyramids with the sign for pyramid. Thus, two or more existing signs for the same sound or combination of sounds were retained and used in conscious distinction to promote easier readability. Although each sign originally had only one reading, occasional ambiguities did develop through the convergence of two symbols of similar form, such as those for the thighbone and the shankbone of an animal. A few signs, therefore, had two or, less commonly, three readings in classical Egyptian writing.

Reading aids: spelling, phonetic complements, determinatives. By means of this rebus system in which letters and pictures were combined the Egyptians could write a large number of the words of their language. But there remained a residue for which no drawable word with the same consonant framework presented itself; *e.g., nht* "strong." Here the Egyptians spelled out the word: for *n,* they had a sign, the water symbol (from the word *nwy* "flood"), and for *ht* they had the above-mentioned sign for wood, 𓆱, so that they could now write *nht* as 𓈖𓆱 .

Two additional reading aids that were quickly added to this system promoted distinctness and readability. For multiconsonant signs, one or more consonants, or in some cases all of them, were also written to serve as a phonetic **Phonetic complements** complement. Thus there is 𓅓� for *mr* "to be ill," in which the owl (top, left) possesses the phonetic value *m* and the mouth (𓂋) that of an *r.* In cases like this, the consonants, according to the conception of modern scholars, were written twice but read only once. For the Egyptians, the single consonant signs were there simply as reading aids for clarification of the word sign, the logogram. Accordingly, they wrote ⟨glyph⟩, in which ⟨glyph⟩ is complemented by the two signs ⟨glyph⟩, $\underline{h}$, and ⟨glyph⟩, t, which appear after it.

In addition, determinatives—signs that do not represent a phonetic value but serve only to inform the reader as to the family of meanings to which the designated word belongs—were quickly formed out of these. The consonant combination $\underline{h}t\dot{i}$ "to engrave" has a knife written after it; on the other hand, $\underline{h}t\dot{i}$ "to retreat" has legs striding backward. Thus, these two words, otherwise written identically, are differentiated graphically as ⟨glyph⟩ and ⟨glyph⟩. In this manner, each Egyptian word possessed its own writing picture with which it was strictly associated. Grammatical endings were attached to this word picture and stood after the determinative. From the outset, therefore, Egyptian writing was a complete script; that is, it could unequivocally fix any word, including all derivations and all grammatical forms.

Summary of the types of signs. In summation, hieroglyphs can be separated into three groups, of which the first two render a phonetic value, and the third represents mute reading aids: (1) ideograms, or signs that should be read as the word they represent—e.g., ⟨glyph⟩, "branch"; (2) phonograms, or signs that do not refer back to the objects they represent but stand simply for one or more consonants—e.g., ⟨glyph⟩ as n and ⟨glyph⟩ as $\underline{h}t$ in ⟨glyph⟩, $n\underline{h}t$ "strong"; and (3) determinatives, which possess no phonetic value but which aid the reader by leading him to the correct interpretation of the meaning—e.g., ⟨glyph⟩ in ⟨glyph⟩, $\underline{h}t\dot{i}$ "to retreat."

Egyptian writing lacked punctuation in our meaning of the term. Line and stanza signs appeared only in certain literary texts.

Number of symbols. In the classical period of Egyptian writing, the number of hieroglyphs totalled approximately 700. Their number multiplied considerably in the late period (about 600 BC); this proliferation occurred, because scholars constantly invented new forms or signs. The additional hieroglyphs were, however, always in accordance with the principles that had governed Egyptian writing from its beginnings. The hieroglyphic system remained flexible throughout all periods, always open to innovation, even though, as with every writing system, convention played a preponderant role.

Direction of the writing. The lines of hieroglyphs were written from right to left or, less frequently, from left to right. Vertical rows of signs could be placed next to horizontal rows, according to the particular demands of the architectural setting. The direction of the writing is immediately ascertainable because the signs almost always face the beginning of the row. Occasionally, some signs are turned around in the row, presumably so that two human figures can face one another and thus avoid standing with their backs toward each other. These rotations of signs are infrequent, however, and are found almost exclusively in the names of kings. Royal names were enclosed in a ring, the so-called cartouche; e.g., ⟨glyph cartouche⟩ "Khufu," in Egyptian $\underline{H}wfw$. This ring, originally a rope, was supposed to protect the bearer of the enclosed name from injury and, in particular, from harmful magic.

Egyptian pedagogical traditions. To understand hieroglyphic writing, one must know about its tradition within Egypt. The Egyptian student of writing, who brought with him a knowledge of the spoken language as his mother tongue, began by learning the script picture corresponding to each word without having isolated its elements; i.e., its individual signs. Through centuries this pedagogical tradition in the schools helped Egyptian words retain the original established spelling, with only minor—usually stylistic—changes, even when the phonetic form had

radically changed. Hieroglyphic writing thus conceals historical sound changes.

The mistakes in hearing made by pupils in the writing schools have helped scholars to understand the phonetic changes that occurred in the development of the Egyptian language. When the pupil who was learning to write the hieroglyphic script did not recognize a word dictated to him, he wrote it badly—that is, just as he heard it. Because he had not yet learned to spell in the orthodox manner, what appeared on his papyrus was usually a word that sounded similar to the dictated but misunderstood term and whose word picture was familiar. Thus, although Egyptian writing was originally composed of symbols that represented a phonetic value, the system was transmitted in the form of word pictures; that is, closed or indivisible groups, generally of several signs per word.

Cryptographic hieroglyphic writing. That knowledge of the hieroglyphic system and the principles upon which it was devised had not become lost is attested by two phenomena: cryptography and the development of the hieroglyphic writing during the last millennium of its existence. From the middle of the 3rd millennium but more frequently in the New Kingdom (from 1500 BC), hieroglyphic texts are encountered that have a very strange appearance. The absence of familiar word groups and the presence of many signs not found in the canon characterize these texts at first glance as cryptographic, or secret, writing. This kind of hieroglyphic writing was probably intended as an eyecatcher, to entice people to seek the pleasure of deciphering it. Composed according to the original principles of the script, these inscriptions differed only in that certain features excluded when the original canon was formulated were now exploited. The new possibilities involved not only the forms of the signs but also their selection. For example, the mouth was not drawn in front view (⟨glyph⟩), as in the classical script, but in profile (⟨glyph⟩), although it had the same phonetic value. An example of a change in the choice of signs is the case in which a man carrying a basket on his head (⟨glyph⟩), a determinative without phonetic value in the classical script, was later to be read as f and was used in lieu of the familiar sign having this phonetic value, that of the horned viper. In the new selection of the sign, the phonetic value is obtained from the word $f\dot{3}\dot{i}$ "to carry" (neglecting its two weak consonants), in accordance with a principle that the inventors of the writing had applied in 3000 BC. These cryptographic inscriptions prove that alongside the method of instruction in the schools, which was based on memorization or recognition, not upon analytical understanding, there was another tradition that transmitted knowledge of the basic principles of the hieroglyphic script. A command of the principles of hieroglyphics similar to that which the composers of the cryptic inscriptions had was presupposed for the puzzle-happy decipherers. Because the encoded texts often consisted of a petition by the inventor of the text to say a prayer on his behalf, the number of these decipherers must surely not have been small.

Growth of hieroglyphic writing during the last millennium BC. At about the middle of the last millennium BC, Egyptian writing experienced new developments and a revival of interest. Again the inscriptions abounded with new signs and sign groups unknown in the classical period, all generated according to the same principles as the classical Egyptian script and the cryptographic texts. The writing of this late period was distinguished from the cryptograms in that this script, like every normal system of writing, developed a fixed tradition, being intended not to conceal but to be read easily, whereas the cryptography strove for originality.

Stages of hieroglyphic writing. The development of hieroglyphic writing thus proceeded approximately as follows: at first only the absolutely necessary symbols were invented, without a canonization of their artistic form. In a second stage, easier readability (i.e., increased rapidity of reading) was achieved by increasing the number of signs (thereby eliminating some doubts) and by employing determinatives. Finally, after the second stage had endured,

Sound changes shown by misspellings

Invention of new signs

Transmission of the hieroglyphic principles

essentially unaltered, for about 2,000 years, the number of symbols increased to several thousand in about 500 BC. This rampant growth process occurred through the application of hitherto unused possibilities of the system. With the triumph of Christianity, the knowledge of hieroglyphic writing was extinguished along with the ancient Egyptian religion.

Tools. The tools used by the craftsmen for writing hieroglyphic symbols consisted of chisels and hammers for stone inscriptions and brushes and colours for wood and other smooth surfaces. Only for the cursive scripts, hieratic and demotic, were special materials developed. Leather and papyrus became writing surfaces, and the stems of rushes in lengths of six to 13 inches (15 to 33 centimetres), cut obliquely at the writing end and chewed to separate the fibres into a brushlike tip, functioned as writing implements. The split calamus reed was introduced into Egypt by the Greeks in the 3rd century BC.

Hieratic script. The Egyptian cursive script, called hieratic writing, received its name from the Greek *hieratikos* (meaning priestly) at a time when the script was used only for sacred texts. Everyday secular documents were written in another style, the demotic (Greek *dēmotikos* "for the people" or "in common use") script.

Relation of hieratic to hieroglyphic script. The structure of the hieratic script corresponds with that of hieroglyphic writing. Changes occurred in the characters of hieratic simply because they could be written rapidly with brush or rush and ink on papyrus. In general, the picture form is not, or not easily, recognizable. Because their models were well known and in current use throughout Egyptian history, the hieratic symbols never strayed too far from them. Nevertheless, the system differs from the hieroglyphic script in some important respects:

1. Hieratic was written in one direction only, from right to left. In earlier times, the lines had run vertically, and later, about 2000 BC, horizontally. Subsequently, the papyrus scrolls were written in columns of changing widths.

2. There were ligatures in hieratic, so that two, but no more than two, signs could be written in one stroke.

3. As a consequence of its decreased legibility, the spelling of the hieratic script was more rigid than that of hieroglyphic writing. Variations from uniformity at a given time were minor; but, during the course of the various periods, the spelling developed and changed. As a result, hieratic texts do not correspond exactly to contemporary hieroglyphic texts, either in the placing of signs or in the spelling of words.

4. Hieratic used diacritical additions to distinguish between two signs that had grown similar to one another because of cursive writing. For example, the cow's leg received a supplementary distinguishing cross, because in hieratic it had come to resemble the sign for the leg of a man. Certain hieratic signs were taken into the hieroglyphic script.

All commonplace documents—*e.g.,* letters, catalogues, and official writs—were written in hieratic script, as were literary and religious texts. In the life of the Egyptians, hieratic script played a larger role than hieroglyphic writing and was also taught earlier in the schools. In offices, hieratic was replaced by demotic in the 7th century BC, but it remained in fashion until much later for religious texts of all sorts. The latest hieratic texts stem from the end of the 1st century or the beginning of the 2nd century AD.

Demotic script. Demotic script is first encountered at the beginning of the 26th dynasty, in about 660 BC. The writing signs plainly demonstrate its connection with the hieratic script, although the exact relationship is not yet clear. The demotic characters are more cursive (flowing and joined), and thus more similar to one another, with the result that they are more difficult to read than are the hieratic forms. Countering this difficulty, there is less freedom for the writer's individual variations. It appears that demotic was originally developed expressly for government office use; that is, for documents in which the language was extensively formalized and thus well suited for the use of a standardized cursive script. Only some time after its introduction was it used for literary texts in addition to documents and letters; much later it was

employed for religious texts also. The latest dated demotic text, from December 2, AD 425, consists of a rock inscription at Philae. In contrast to hieratic, which is, almost without exception, written in ink on papyrus or other flat surfaces, demotic inscriptions are not infrequently found engraved in stone or carved in wood.

Alternative demotic spelling. The demotic system corresponds to the hieratic and hence also to the hieroglyphic system. Alongside the traditional spelling, however, there was another spelling that took account of the markedly altered phonetic form of the words by appropriate respelling. This characteristic applied especially to a large number of words that did not occur in the older language and for which no written form had consequently been passed down. The nontraditional spelling could also be used for old, familiar words.

Decipherment of hieroglyphic writing. With the possible exception of Pythagoras, no Greek understood the nature of hieroglyphic writing. The Greeks did not obtain guidance from their Egyptian contemporaries, some of whom even lived on Italian soil and wrote proper hieroglyphic inscriptions on Roman obelisks. Rather, the Greek tradition taught that hieroglyphs were symbolic signs or allegories. The Egyptian-born Greek philosopher Plotinus interpreted hieroglyphic writing entirely from the viewpoint of his esoteric philosophy. Only one of the numerous works on the hieroglyphic script written in late antiquity has been preserved: the *Hieroglyphica* of Horapollon, a Greek Egyptian who probably lived in the 5th century AD. Horapollon made use of a good source, but he himself certainly could not read hieroglyphic writing and began with the false hypothesis of the Greek tradition, namely, that hieroglyphs were symbols and allegories, not phonetic signs.

The Middle Ages neither possessed any knowledge of hieroglyphic writing nor took any interest in it. But a manuscript of Horapollon brought to Florence in 1422 stirred great interest among the Humanists. Without giving a thought to the possibility that ancient Egyptian originals might be available in Rome, Renaissance artists designed hieroglyphs after Horapollon's descriptions, as well as from their own imaginations. They used hieroglyphs as wisdom-laden symbols in architecture and also in drawings and paintings.

Margin notes:
Development of special writing materials

Role of hieratic in Egypt

Greek beliefs concerning hieroglyphic writing

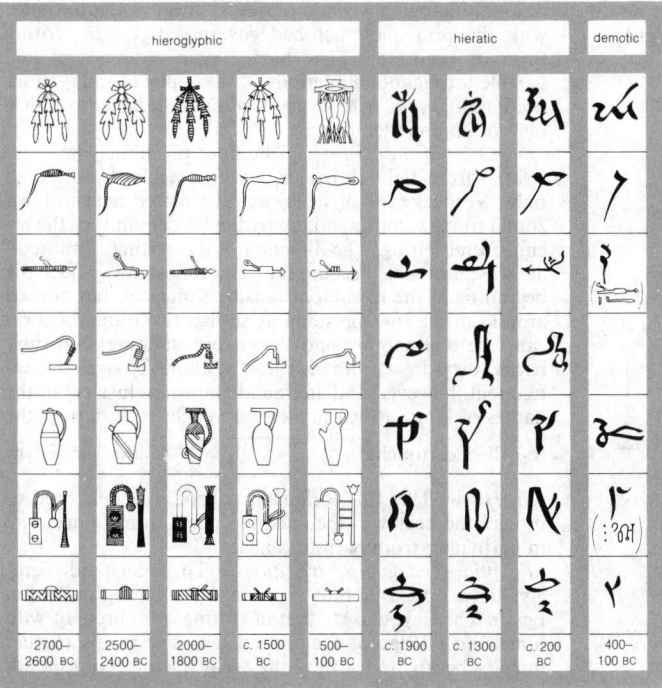

Courtesy of the Oriental Institute, University of Chicago

hieroglyphic					hieratic		demotic
2700–2600 BC	2500–2400 BC	2000–1800 BC	c. 1500 BC	500–100 BC	c. 1900 BC	c. 1300 BC	c. 200 BC	400–100 BC

Figure 8: *Egyptian hieroglyphs and their cursive equivalents.*
The hieroglyphs depict (top to bottom): three fox skins tied together; a whip; a single-barbed harpoon; an adz at work on a block of wood; a stone jug with handle; a scribe's outfit; a roll of papyrus tied with a cord.

Kircher's attempts at decipherment. The great German scholar Athanasius Kircher (1602–80) began his attempts at decipherment with the Coptic language and with the correct hypothesis that the hieroglyphs recorded an earlier stage of this language. He also believed, again correctly, that the signs recorded phonetic values. In spite of this, he did not arrive at correct results—with the exception of a single character. This failure can be attributed not only to Kircher's erroneous assumption that the hieroglyphs must correspond phonetically to an alphabet but primarily to the fact that he was most interested in the Renaissance conception of a supposed symbolic meaning constituting the deeper significance of hieroglyphs. In his view, the phonetic value of the hieroglyphs was merely the commonplace, superficial part of the sign.

Discovery of the Rosetta Stone. Both the intellectual and the physical prerequisites for the deciphering of the hieroglyphic script first presented themselves at the end of the 18th century. By accident, a stone that exhibited three different scripts—hieroglyphic, demotic, and Greek—was discovered by members of Napoleon's expedition to Egypt in 1799 near Rashid (French Rosette; English Rosetta) on the Mediterranean coast. The Greek text stated clearly that the document set forth the same text in the sacred script, the folk or popular script, and Greek. The stone was promptly made known to all interested scholars. Important partial successes in the effort of deciphering the scripts were achieved by the Swede Johan David Åkerblad and by the great English physicist Thomas Young, who mainly studied the demotic text, again beginning with the false hypothesis that the hieroglyphs were symbols. Young succeeded in proving that they were not symbols—at least that the proper names were not—and that the demotic and hieratic signs had come from the hieroglyphs. (He first published this result in the supplement to the 4th, 5th, and 6th editions of the *Encyclopædia Britannica*.) He was the first to isolate correctly some single consonant hieroglyphic signs. But a wrong turn in the course of his investigations then prevented him from fully deciphering the writing.

Champollion's decipherment. This task of complete decipherment was first accomplished by the Frenchman Jean-François Champollion (1790–1832) in 1822, after long years of intensive work and many setbacks. His success was due to the recognition that hieroglyphic writing, exactly like the hieratic and demotic scripts derived from it, did not constitute a writing system of symbols but rather a phonetic script. He arrived at this breakthrough by an exact comparison of the three Egyptian forms of writing, as well as by reference to Coptic, the late phase of the Egyptian language that was written with the Greek alphabet and was thus directly readable. The Coptic language was also understood at that time. Starting, as had his predecessors, from Ptolemy and Cleopatra, both ring-enclosed royal names, and adding the hieroglyphic spelling of Ramses' name, Champollion determined, essentially correctly, the phonetic values of the signs. Soon after, he also learned to read and translate a large number of Egyptian words. Since then, precise research has confirmed and refined Champollion's approach and most of his results.

(H.B.)

CUNEIFORM

Cuneiform (a coinage from Latin and Middle French roots meaning "wedge-shaped") has been the modern designation, from the early 18th century onward, for the most widespread and historically significant writing system in the ancient Middle East. Its active history comprises the last three millenniums BC; its long development and geographic expansion involved numerous successive cultures and languages; and its over-all significance as an international graphic medium of civilization is second only to that of the Phoenician-Greek-Latin alphabet.

Origin and character of cuneiform. The origins of cuneiform may be traced back approximately to the end of the 4th millennium BC. At that time the Sumerians, a people of unknown ethnic and linguistic affinities, inhabited southern Mesopotamia and the region west of the mouth of the Euphrates known as Chaldea. While it does not follow that they were the earliest inhabitants of the region or the true originators of their system of writing, it is to them that the first attested traces of cuneiform writing are conclusively assigned. The earliest written records in the Sumerian language are pictographic tablets from Uruk, evidently lists or ledgers of commodities identified by drawings of the objects, and accompanied by numerals and personal names. Such word writing was able to express only the basic ideas of concrete objects. Numerical notions were easily rendered by the repetitional use of strokes or circles. However, the representation of proper names, for example, necessitated an early recourse to the rebus principle—*i.e.,* the use of pictographic shapes to evoke in the reader's mind an underlying sound form rather than the basic notion of the drawn object. This brought about a transition from pure word writing to a partial phonetic script. Thus, for example, the picture of a hand came to stand not only for Sumerian *šu* ("hand") but also for the phonetic syllable *šu* in any required context. Sumerian words were largely monosyllabic, so the signs generally denoted syllables, and the resulting mixture is termed a world-syllabic script. The inventory of phonetic symbols henceforth enabled the Sumerians to denote grammatical elements by phonetic complements added to the word signs (the latter are called ideograms or logograms). Because Sumerian had many identical sounding (homophonous) words, several ideograms frequently yielded identical phonetic values, and are distinguished in modern transliteration—(as, for example, *ba, bá, bà, ba₄*). Because an ideogram often represented several related notions with different names (*e.g.,* "sun," "day," "bright"), it was capable of assuming more than one phonetic value (this feature is called polyphony).

In the course of the 3rd millennium the writing became successively more cursive, and the pictographs developed into conventionalized linear drawings. Due to the prevalent use of clay tablets as writing material (stone, metal, or wood also were employed occasionally), the linear strokes acquired a wedge-shaped appearance by being pressed into the soft clay with the slanted edge of a stylus. Curving lines disappeared from writing, and the normal order of signs was fixed as running from left to right, without any word-divider. This change from earlier columns running downward entailed turning the signs on one side.

Spread and development of cuneiform. Before these developments had been completed, the Sumerian writing system was adopted by the Akkadians, Semitic invaders who established themselves in Mesopotamia about the middle of the 3rd millennium. In adapting the script to their wholly different language the Akkadians retained the Sumerian ideograms and combinations of ideograms for more complex notions but pronounced them as the corresponding Akkadian words. They also kept the phonetic values but extended them far beyond the original Sumerian inventory of simple types (open or closed syllables like *ba* or *ab*). Many more complex syllabic values of Sumerian ideograms (of the type *kan, mul, bat*) were transferred to the phonetic level, and polyphony became an increasingly serious complication in Akkadian cuneiform (*e.g.,* the original pictograph for "sun" may be read phonetically as *ud, tam, tú, par, laḫ, ḫiš*). The Akkadian readings of the ideograms added new complicated values. Thus the sign for "land" or "mountain range" (originally a picture of three mountain tops) has the phonetic value *kur* on the basis of Sumerian, but also *mat* and *šad* from Akkadian *mātu* ("land") and *šadū* ("mountain"). No effort was made until very late to alleviate the resulting confusion, and equivalent "graphies" like *ta-am* and *tam* continued to exist side by side throughout the long history of Akkadian cuneiform.

The earliest type of Semitic cuneiform in Mesopotamia is called the Old Akkadian, seen for example in the inscriptions of the great ruler Sargon of Akkad (died 2279 BC). Sumer, the southernmost part of the country, continued to be a loose agglomeration of independent city-states, until it was united by Gudea of Lagash (died *c.* 2124 BC), in a last brief manifestation of specifically Sumerian culture. The political hegemony then passed decisively to the Akkadians, and King Hammurabi of Babylon (died 1750 BC) uni-

Thomas Young's work

Use of the rebus

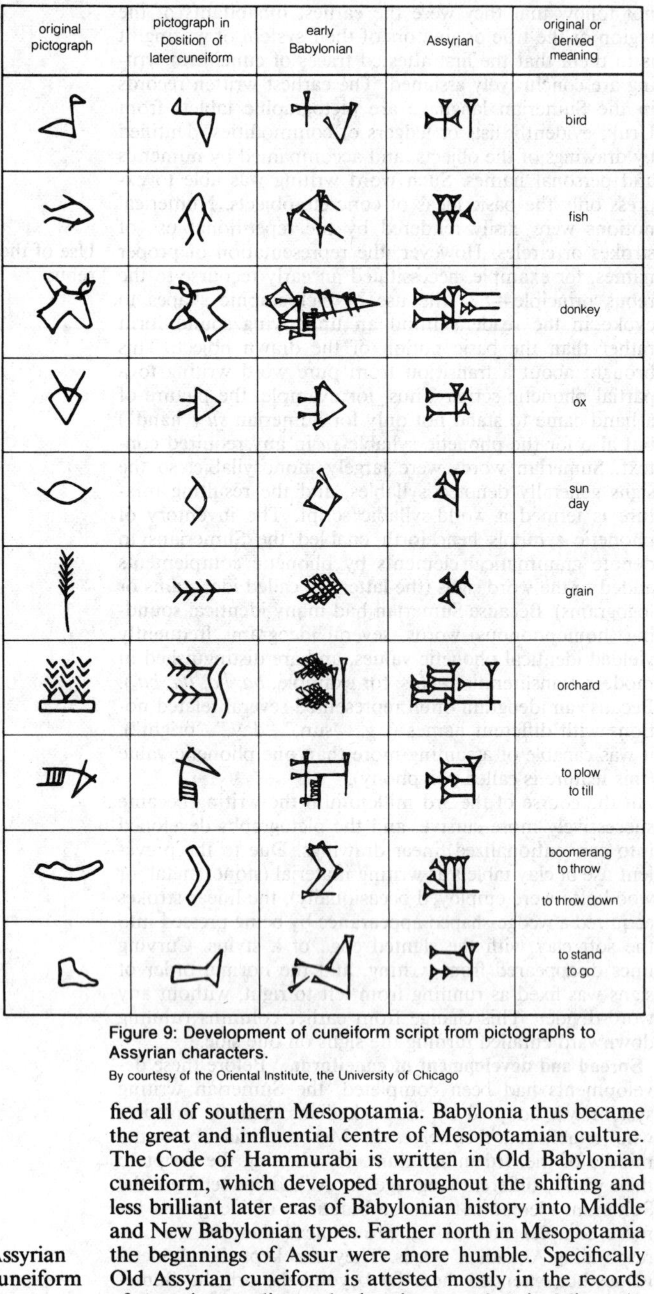

original pictograph	pictograph in position of later cuneiform	early Babylonian	Assyrian	original or derived meaning
				bird
				fish
				donkey
				ox
				sun day
				grain
				orchard
				to plow to till
				boomerang to throw / to throw down
				to stand to go

Figure 9: Development of cuneiform script from pictographs to Assyrian characters.

By courtesy of the Oriental Institute, the University of Chicago

Assyrian cuneiform

fied all of southern Mesopotamia. Babylonia thus became the great and influential centre of Mesopotamian culture. The Code of Hammurabi is written in Old Babylonian cuneiform, which developed throughout the shifting and less brilliant later eras of Babylonian history into Middle and New Babylonian types. Farther north in Mesopotamia the beginnings of Assur were more humble. Specifically Old Assyrian cuneiform is attested mostly in the records of Assyrian trading colonists in central Asia Minor (c. 1950 BC; the so-called Cappadocian tablets) and Middle Assyrian in an extensive Law Code and other documents. The New Assyrian period was the great era of Assyrian power, and the writing culminates in the extensive records from the library of Ashurbanipal at Nineveh (c. 650 BC).

The expansion of cuneiform writing outside Mesopotamia began in the 3rd millennium, when the country of Elam in southwestern Iran was in contact with Mesopotamian culture and adopted the system of writing. The Elamite sideline of cuneiform continued far into the 1st millennium BC, when it presumably provided the Indo-European Persians with the external model for creating a new simplified quasi-alphabetic cuneiform writing for the Old Persian language. The Hurrians in northern Mesopotamia and around the upper stretches of the Euphrates adopted Old Akkadian cuneiform around 2000 BC and passed it on to the Indo-European Hittites, who had invaded central Asia Minor at about that time.

In the 2nd millennium the Akkadian of Babylonia, frequently in somewhat distorted and barbarous varieties, became a *lingua franca* of international intercourse in the entire near east, and cuneiform writing thus a universal medium of written communication. The political correspondence of the era is conducted almost exclusively in that language and writing. Cuneiform was sometimes adapted, as in the consonantal script of the Canaanite city of Ugarit on the Syrian coast (c. 1400 BC), or simply taken over, as in the inscriptions of the kingdom of Haldi or Urartu in the Armenian mountains from the 9th to 6th centuries BC; the language is remotely related to Hurrian, and the script a borrowed variety of New Assyrian cuneiform. Even after the fall of the Assyrian and Babylonian kingdoms in the 7th and 6th centuries BC, when Aramaic had become the general popular language, rather decadent varieties of Late Babylonian and Assyrian survived as written languages in cuneiform almost down to the time of Christ.

Deciperment of cuneiform. Many of the cultures employing cuneiform (Hurrian, Hittite, Haldian) disappeared one by one, and their written records fell into oblivion. The same fate overtook cuneiform generally with astonishing swiftness and completeness. One of the reasons was the victorious progress of the Phoenician script in the western sections of the near east and the classical lands in Mediterranean Europe. To this writing system of superior efficiency and economy cuneiform could not offer serious competition. Its international prestige of the 2nd millennium had been exhausted by 500 BC, and Mesopotamia had become a Persian dependency. Late Babylonian and Assyrian were little but moribund artificial literary idioms. Unlike the hieroglyphs of Egypt, which served continuously for more than three millenniums as an aesthetically refined ornamental medium on the monuments of an almost monolithic culture, cuneiform was essentially a practical everyday writing, tied to the vicissitudes and uncertainties of changing civilizations. So effective was its disappearance in the sands of the Near East that the classical Greeks were practically unaware of its existence, except for the widely travelled Herodotus who in passing mentions *Assyria Grammata* ("Assyrian characters").

Old Persian and Elamite. The rediscovery of the materials and the reconquest of the recondite scripts and languages have been the achievement of modern times. Paradoxically the process began with the last secondary offshoot of cuneiform proper, the inscriptions of the Achaemenid kings (6th to 4th centuries BC) of Persia. This is understandable, because almost only among the Persians was cuneiform used primarily for monumental writing, and the remains (such as rock carvings) were in many cases readily accessible. Scattered examples of Old Persian inscriptions were reported back to Europe by western travellers in Persia since the 17th century, and the name cuneiform was first applied to the script by Engelbert Kämpfer (c. 1700). During the 18th century many new inscriptions were reported; especially important were those copied by Carsten Niebuhr at the old capital Persepolis. It was recognized that the typical royal inscriptions contained three different scripts, a simple type with about 40 different signs, and two others with considerably greater variations. The first was likely to reflect an alphabet, while the others seemed to be syllabaries or word writings. Assuming identical contents in three different languages, scholars argued on historical grounds that those trilingual inscriptions belonged to the Achaemenid kings, and that the first writing represented the Old Persian language which would be closely related to Avestan and Sanskrit. The recognition of a diagonal wedge as word-divider simplified the segmentation of the written sequences. The German scholar Georg Friedrich Grotefend in 1802 reasoned that the introductory lines of the text were likely to contain the name, titles, and genealogy of the ruler, the pattern for which was known from later Middle Iranian inscriptions in an adapted Aramaic (*i.e.,* ultimately Phoenician) alphabet. From such beginnings, he was eventually able to read several long proper names and to determine a number of sound values. The initial results of Grotefend were expanded and refined by other scholars.

Next the second script of the trilinguals was attacked. It contained more than 100 different signs and was thus likely to be a syllabary. Mainly by applying the sound values of the Old Persian proper names to appropriate correspondences a number of signs were gradually determined, and some insight gained into the language itself,

Persian inscriptions

which is New Elamite; the study of it has been rather stagnant, and considerable obscurity persists. The same holds true for the Old Elamite of the late 2nd millennium.

Akkadian and Sumerian. The third script of the Achaemenian trilinguals had in the meantime been identified with that of the texts found in very large numbers in Mesopotamia, which obviously contained the central language of cuneiform culture, namely Akkadian. Here also the proper names provided the first concrete clues for a decipherment, but the extreme variety of signs and the peculiar complications of the system raised difficulties which for a time seemed insurmountable. The serious external divergencies between older and newer types of Akkadian cuneiform, the distribution of ideographic and syllabic uses of the signs, the simple (*ba, ab*) and complex (*bat*) values of the syllables, and especially the bewildering polyphony of many notations were only gradually surmised by scholars. Once the Semitic character of the language had been established, the philological science of Assyriology developed rapidly from the closing decades of the 19th century onward, especially because of scholars like Friedrich Delitzsch and, later, Benno Landsberger and Wolfram von Soden.

The Akkadian key

Once Akkadian had been deciphered, the very core of the system was intelligible, and the prototype was provided for the interpretation of other languages in cuneiform. Until the 20th century Sumerian was not definitely recognized as a separate language at all, but rather as a special way of noting Akkadian. Even when its independent character was established, the difficulties of interpretation were appalling, because of its strange and unrelated structure. After Sumerian finally died out as a living language toward the middle of the 2nd millennium, it lingered on as a cult idiom of Babylonian religion. To facilitate its artificial acquisition by the priesthood grammatical lists and vocabularies were compiled, and numerous religious texts were provided with literal translations into Babylonian. These have facilitated the penetration of unilingual Sumerian texts, and Sumerian studies have advanced greatly through the efforts of Delitzsch, Thureau-Dangin, Arno Poebel, Anton Deimel, and Adam Falkenstein.

Hittite and other languages. An important new dimension was added to cuneiform studies in the early years of the 20th century, through the discovery in 1906 of the royal archives of the Hittites at the ancient capital site of Hattusa near the Turkish village of Bogazköy, east of Ankara. Some years earlier the existence of an Indo-European idiom in some cuneiform letters found in the Egyptian diplomatic archives of the 18th dynasty at Tell el-Amarna had been suspected by Johan Knudtzon. This unlikely surmise was confirmed by Friedrich Hrozný during World War I, when his initial interpretation of the Bogazköy materials proved that the predominant language in the thousands of tablets was that of the Indo-European Hittites, whose rule in central Asia Minor filled most of the 2nd millennium. The tablets offered no serious cryptological problems, being edited in a type of borrowed Akkadian cuneiform. The interpretation of the unknown language was aided by the partial ideographic nature of the script, which revealed elements of meaning independent of linguistic factors. Even more important was a series of bilingual parallel texts, in which the Akkadian versions served as a clue to the analysis of linguistic structure.

In the absence of close affinity to known languages, which vouches adequate safeguards against the notoriously misleading comparative method of interpretation, inner analysis of the unknown language is the only trustworthy procedure. Hurrian and Haldian are definitely related languages, but neither may yet be safely used to explain the other. Haldian has been solved to some extent with the help of its rather free use of ideograms, and the Assyrian versions of two bilingual inscriptions.

Deciphering of Ugaritic

Excavations at Ras Shamra in 1929 unearthed the remains of Ugarit. Inscriptions in an unknown simple system of cuneiform were found; the low number of 30 different signs pointed to an alphabetic type. The use of a vertical stroke as word-divider facilitated the decipherment, which was based on the correct assumption that an early West-Semitic Canaanite dialect was involved. Thus the script was solved with astonishing speed by Hans Bauer, Edouard Dhorme, and Charles Virolleaud, yielding a Semitic dialect named Ugaritic, closely related to Old Phoenician. Hurrian inscriptions in the same script were also found, as were texts in conventional Middle Babylonian cuneiform.

Influence of cuneiform. The main type of cuneiform with its inventory of ideograms (including "determinatives" or "classifiers") and phonetic signs is a word-syllabic system like the Egyptian, "Hieroglyphic Hittite," Minoan-Mycenaean, Proto-Elamite, and Proto-Indic. The Sumerian system seems to be the oldest. To what extent it stimulated the origin or influenced the development of the others is a difficult problem connected with the monogenesis or polygenesis (common or multiple origin) of writing. The Phoenician consonantal script provided the new typological pattern on which the Ugaritic and Old Persian systems were constructed, keeping only the outer likeness of the wedge form.

CHINESE AND JAPANESE LOGOSYLLABIC WRITING

Chinese has a logosyllabic system of writing; that is, it utilizes logograms, or signs for words, and syllabograms, or signs for the syllabic components of words. Of the major ancient systems of writing, Chinese is one of the few that did not have to be deciphered in modern times, because knowledge of it was passed from generation to generation. Chinese writing made its appearance about the middle of the 2nd millennium BC, during the Shang dynasty, as a fully developed phonetic system. In its outer form the writing has changed greatly during its long history, but the inner characteristics of the oldest inscriptions hardly differ from those of recent times. The oldest Chinese inscriptions are the oracle texts on animal bones and tortoise shells, and some short texts on bronze vessels, weapons, pottery, and jade. The signs in the Shang period were limited in number, no more than about 2,500, and in the majority of them the pictorial character is still clearly recognizable. But the signs developed a linear form, and in later writings it is impossible to recognize the pictures they originally represented.

Chinese writing does not have a full syllabary comparable to the syllabaries in the other three (major) systems. As the words of the Chinese language are regularly expressed by word signs, it is only in writing foreign words and names that the necessity arose to use word signs in a syllabic function. Thus, "Jesus" is written as *Yeh-su,* "English" as *Ying-chi-li,* "French" as *Fa-lan-hsi,* "telephone" as *te-li-feng.* There are no set word signs for certain syllables, as there are in the Near Eastern systems; for example, "Jesus" might also be written *Ya-su;* "telephone," *te-lu-fung.* The characteristic tendency of Chinese toward abbreviation may be noted in the use of *Ying* for "English" (besides *Ying-kuo-jen* for "Englishman," that is, "English-country-man"), *Fa* for "French" (besides *Fa-kuo-jen*) or *Lo* for "Roosevelt" (besides *Lo-ssu-fu*). Frequently, words spelled out syllabically acquired a logographic spelling; for example, the above-mentioned *te-li-feng,* "telephone," is now usually written as *tien-hua,* "electricity talks." Chinese writing is said to consist of about 50,000 signs, of which an unspecified number are used in a syllabic function. This extraordinary development of Chinese logography constitutes a unique phenomenon in the history of writing.

Syllabic function of Chinese word-signs

After a few centuries of cultural and commercial contact between China and Japan, the Chinese system of writing seems to have made its appearance in Japan in the 5th century AD. The Chinese word signs were simply taken over by the Japanese and read not with their Chinese values but in Japanese. Thus, for example, the Chinese word sign *nan,* "south," was read in Japanese as *minami,* "south." The Chinese writing may have been well suited to a monosyllabic and isolating language in which grammatical forms are normally expressed by syntactical position rather than by special formatives. However, such writing was not suited to Japanese, which is polysyllabic and agglutinative and expresses grammatical forms by means of special formatives. Therefore, some of the Chinese word signs soon came to be employed as syllabic signs expressing the grammatical formatives of the Japanese language.

Originally, the choice of the syllabic signs was unsystematic, and it was not until about the 9th century that a stable syllabary with 47 signs was developed, each expressing a consonant plus a vowel, with the difference in voice being fully indicated. In introducing a full syllabary the Japanese have never given up the logographic apparatus borrowed from Chinese, which they use along with their syllabary. (Ed.)

Adjuncts to writing

Punctuation is the use of spacing, conventional signs, and certain typographical devices as aids to the understanding and correct reading, both silently and aloud, of handwritten and printed texts. The word is derived from the Latin *punctus,* "point." From the 15th century to the early 18th the subject was known in English as pointing; and the term punctuation, first recorded in the middle of the 16th century, was reserved for the insertion of vowel points (marks placed near consonants to indicate preceding or following vowels) in Hebrew texts. The two words exchanged meanings between 1650 and 1750.

Since the late 16th century the theory and practice of punctuation have varied between two main schools of thought: the elocutionary school, following late medieval practice, treated points or stops as indications of the pauses of various lengths that might be observed by a reader, particularly when he was reading aloud to an audience; the syntactical school, which had won the argument by the end of the 17th century, saw them as something less arbitrary, namely, as guides to the grammatical construction of sentences. Pauses in speech and breaks in syntax tend in any case to coincide; and although English-speaking writers are now agreed that the main purpose of punctuation is to clarify the grammar of a text, they also require it to take account of the speed and rhythm of actual speech.

Syntactical punctuation is, by definition, bad when it obscures rather than clarifies the construction of sentences. Good punctuation, however, may be of many kinds: to take two extreme examples—Henry James would be unintelligible without his numerous commas, but Ernest Hemingway seldom needs any stop but the full point. In poetry, in which the elocutionary aspect of punctuation is still important, and to a lesser degree in fiction, especially when the style is close to actual speech, punctuation is much at the author's discretion. In nonfiction writing there is less room for experiment. Stimulating variant models for general use might be the light punctuation of George Bernard Shaw's prefaces to his plays and the heavier punctuation of T.S. Eliot's literary and political essays.

Punctuation in Greek and Latin to 1600. The punctuation now used with English and other western European languages is derived ultimately from the punctuation used with Greek and Latin during the Classical period. Much work remains to be done on the history of the subject, but the outlines are clear enough. Greek inscriptions were normally written continuously, with no divisions between words or sentences; but in a few inscriptions earlier than the 5th century BC, phrases were sometimes separated by a vertical row of two or three points. In the oldest Greek literary texts, written on papyrus during the 4th century BC, a horizontal line called the *paragraphos* was placed under the beginning of a line in which a new topic was introduced. This is the only form of punctuation mentioned by Aristotle. Aristophanes of Byzantium, who became librarian of the Museum at Alexandria about 200 BC, is usually credited with the invention of the critical signs, marks of quantity, accents, breathings, and so on, still employed in Greek texts, and with the beginnings of the Greek system of punctuation. Rhetorical theory divided discourse into sections of different lengths. Aristophanes marked the end of the short section (called a *comma*) by a point after the middle of its last letter, that of the longer section (*colon*) by a point after the bottom of the letter, and that of the longest section (*periodos*) by a point after the top of the letter. Since books were still being written in tall majuscule letters, like those used in inscriptions and like modern capital letters, the three positions were easily

distinguishable. Aristophanes' system was seldom actually used, except in a degenerate version involving only two points. In the 8th or 9th century it was supplemented by the Greek form of question mark (;). The modern system of punctuating Greek texts was established by the Italian and French printers of the Renaissance, whose practice was incorporated in the Greek types cut by Claude Garamond for Francis I of France between 1541 and 1550. The colon is not used in Greek, and the semicolon is represented by a high point. Quotation marks and the exclamation mark were added more recently.

In almost all Roman inscriptions points were used to separate words. In the oldest Latin documents and books, dating from the end of the 1st century BC to the beginning of the 2nd century AD, words were divided by points, and a change of topic was sometimes indicated by paragraphing: the first letter or two of the new paragraph projected into the margin instead of being indented, as they have been since the 17th century. Roman scholars, including the 4th-century grammarian Donatus and the 6th-century patron of monastic learning Cassiodorus, recommended the three-point system of Aristophanes, which was perfectly workable with the majuscule Latin scripts then in use. In practice, however, Latin books in their period were written continuously—the point between words had been abandoned. The ends of sentences were marked, if at all, only by a gap (which might be followed by an enlarged letter) or by an occasional point. The only books that were well punctuated at that time were copies of the Vulgate Bible, for which its translator, St. Jerome (died 419/420), devised punctuation *per cola et commata* ("by phrases"), a rhetorical system, based on manuscripts of Demosthenes and Cicero, which was especially designed to assist reading aloud. Each phrase began with a letter projecting into the margin and was in fact treated as a minute paragraph, before which the reader was expected to take a new breath.

During the 7th and 8th centuries, which saw the transition from majuscule to minuscule handwriting (minuscule scripts were usually smaller than majuscule and had projections above and below the body of the letters, as in modern lowercase letters), scribes to whom the Latin language was no longer as well-known as it had been, especially Irish, Anglo-Saxon, and German scribes, to whom it was a foreign language, began to separate words. It was only in the 13th century that monosyllables, especially prepositions, were finally detached from the word following them. To mark sentences, a space at the end became the rule; and an enlarged letter, often a majuscule, generally stood at the beginning of sentences and paragraphs alike. The use of points was somewhat confused by St. Isidore of Seville (died 636), whose encyclopaedia recommended an aberrant version of the three-point system; but a point, high or low, was still used within or after sentences. The ends of sentences were often marked by a group of two or three marks, one of which might be a comma and not a simple point.

St. Jerome's concern for the punctuation of sacred texts was shared by Charlemagne, king of the Franks and Holy Roman emperor, and his Anglo-Saxon adviser Alcuin, who directed the palace school at Aachen from 782 to 796. An important element in the educational revival over which they presided was the improvement of spelling and punctuation in biblical and liturgical manuscripts. It is in the earliest specimens of the new Caroline minuscule script, written at Corbie and Aachen (now in northern France and West Germany, respectively), about 780–800, that the first evidence for a new system of punctuation appears. It soon spread, with the script itself, throughout Europe, reaching its perfection in the 12th century. Single interior stops in the form of points or commas and final groups of stops continued in use; but they were joined by the mark later known as *punctus elevatus* (ɣ) and by the question mark (*punctus interrogativus*), of much the same shape as the modern one but inclined to the right. The source of these two new marks was apparently the system of musical notation, called neums, which is known to have been used for Gregorian chant from at least the beginning of the 9th century. *Punctus elevatus* and *punctus interrogativus* indicated not only a pause and a syntactical

(side notes) Ancient Greek practices

Roman practice

Early medieval practice

break but also an appropriate inflection of the voice. By the 12th century another mark, *punctus circumflexus* (⁊), had been added to *elevatus* to indicate a rising inflection at the end of a subordinate clause, especially when the grammatical sense of the sentence was still not complete. Liturgical manuscripts in particular, between the 10th and the 13th century, made full use of this inflectional system: it is the origin of the "colon" still used to divide verses of the Psalms in breviaries and prayer books. In the later Middle Ages it was especially the Cistercian, Dominican, and Carthusian orders and the members of religious communities such as the Brethren of the Common Life who troubled to preserve a mode of punctuation admirably adapted to the constant reading aloud, in church and refectory, that characterized the religious life. The hyphen, to mark words divided at the ends of lines, appears late in the 10th century; single at first, it was often doubled in the period between the 14th and 18th centuries.

Late medieval practice

Most late medieval punctuation was haphazard by comparison with 12th-century work—notably in the university textbooks produced at Paris, Bologna, and Oxford in the 13th and 14th centuries. In them, as elsewhere, a form of paragraph mark representing *c* for *capitulum* ("chapter") is freely used at the beginning of sentences. Within the same period the plain point and *punctus elevatus* are joined by the virgule (/), as an alternative form of light stop. Vernacular literature followed the less formal types of Latin literature; and the printers, as usual, followed the scribes. The first printed texts of the Bible and the liturgy are, as a rule, carefully punctuated on the inflectional principle. The profusion of points and virgules in the English books of the printer William Caxton pays remarkably little attention to syntax. Parentheses, used in the same way as now, appear by about 1500. During the 15th century some English legal documents were already being written without punctuation; and British and American lawyers still use extremely light punctuation in the hope of avoiding possible ambiguities.

The beginnings of postmedieval punctuation can be traced to the excellent manuscripts of classical and contemporary Latin texts copied in the new humanistic scripts by Italian scribes of the 15th century. To about 1450 the point and the *punctus elevatus* seem to have been preferred for minor pauses; after that date they are often replaced by the virgule and what is now called the colon (:). The virgule, originally placed high, sank to the base line and developed a curve—turned, in fact, into a modern comma. The Venetian editor and printer Aldus Manutius (Aldo Manuzio; died 1515) made improvements in the humanistic system, and in 1566 his grandson of the same name expounded a similar system in his *Orthographiae ratio* ("System of Orthography"); it included, under different names, the modern comma, semicolon, colon, and full point, or period. Most importantly, the younger Aldo stated plainly for the first time the view that clarification of syntax is the main object of punctuation. By the end of the 17th century the various marks had received their modern names, and the exclamation mark, quotation marks, and the dash had been added to the system.

Punctuation in English since 1600. By the end of the 16th century writers of English were using most of the marks described by the younger Aldo in 1566; but their purpose was elocutionary, not syntactical. When George Puttenham, in his treatise *The Arte of English Poesie* (1589), and Simon Daines, in *Orthoepia Anglicana* (1640), specified a pause of one unit for a comma, of two units for a semicolon, and of three for a colon, they were no doubt trying to bring some sort of order into a basically confused and unsatisfactory situation. The punctuation of Elizabethan drama, of the devotional prose of John Donne or of Richard Hooker, and indeed of Bunyan's *Pilgrim's Progress* (1678) was almost wholly elocutionary; and it

Shift to syntactical punctuation

lacked the inflectional element that had been the making of 12th-century punctuation. It was Ben Jonson, in his *English Grammar,* a work composed about 1617 and published posthumously in 1640, who first recommended syntactical punctuation in England. An early example is the 1625 edition of Francis Bacon's *Essayes;* and from the Restoration onward syntactical punctuation was in gen-

eral use. Influential treatises on syntactical punctuation were published by Robert Monteith in 1704 and Joseph Robertson in 1795. Excessive punctuation was common in the 18th century: at its worst it used commas with every subordinate clause and separable phrase. Vestiges of this attitude are found in a handbook published in London as late as 1880. It was the lexicographers Henry Watson Fowler and Francis George Fowler, in *The King's English,* published in 1906, who established the current British practice of light punctuation. Punctuation in the United States has followed much the same path as in Britain, but the rules laid down by American authorities have in general been more rigid than the British rules.

The system of punctuation now used by writers of English has been complete since the 17th century. Three of its most important components are the space left blank between words; the indentation of the first line of a new paragraph; and the uppercase, or capital, letter written at the beginning of a sentence and at the beginning of a proper name or a title. The marks of punctuation, also known as points or stops, and the chief parts that they play in the system are as follows.

The end of a grammatically complete sentence is marked by a full point, full stop, or period. The period may also be used to mark abbreviations. The colon (:), which was once used like a full point and was followed by an uppercase letter, now serves mainly to indicate the beginning of a list, summary, or quotation. The semicolon (;) ranks halfway between a comma and a full point. It may be substituted for a period between two grammatically complete sentences that are closely connected in sense; in a long or complicated sentence, it may precede a coordinate conjunction (such as "or," "and," or "but"). A comma (,) is the "lightest" of the four basic stops. As the most usual means of indicating the syntactical turning points in a sentence, it is exposed to abuse. It may be used to separate the elements of a series, before a relative clause that does not limit or define its antecedent, in pairs to set off or isolate words or phrases, or in combination with coordinating conjunctions.

Other punctuation marks used in modern English include parentheses, which serve, like a pair of commas, to isolate a word or phrase; question, exclamation, and quotation marks; the hyphen; and the apostrophe.

Punctuation in French, Spanish, German, and Russian. Since the modern punctuation of all the western European languages stems from the practice of the great Italian and French printers of the 15th and 16th centuries, national differences are not considerable. In French, guillemets (« ») or dashes are used to mark quotations. In Spanish, since the middle of the 18th century, an inverted mark of interrogation or exclamation has stood at the beginning of sentences as well as the normal mark at the end; and quotations may be marked either as in French or as in English. German punctuation, which is still based on rules propounded in 1781, is more rigorously syntactical than the rest: all relative clauses and all clauses beginning with *dass* ("that") must be preceded by a comma. Quotations are marked either by pairs of commas („ ") or by reversed guillemets (» «). Letter spacing, as well as italic type, is used for emphasis. Early Russian punctuation was based on Greek practice, since the Cyrillic alphabet is derived from the Greek; and by the 17th century several quite elaborate systems had evolved in different areas. Since the 18th century Russia has used a form of western European punctuation that has much in common with German practice: notably an even wider obligatory use of commas with subordinate and indeed coordinate clauses, and letter spacing (as well as italics) for emphasis. German quotation marks, French guillemets, and dashes may be used for direct speech.

Characteristics of German punctuation

Punctuation in Oriental and African languages. In Hebrew manuscripts written since the 9th century the main use of points is to indicate the vowel sounds, the alphabet being consonantal only. In Biblical texts points and commas are used to mark the middle and end of verses; and in the commentaries points mark the end of sentences. Since the late 18th century, when Jews in Germany began to compose secular texts in Hebrew, the punctuation of such texts has been based on German practice. Early Arabic manuscripts had no punctuation, since the structure of the language ensured that the main and subordinate clauses were readily distinguishable without it. After Arabic began to be printed, European punctuation marks were gradually adopted. The first such mark was the reversed comma; it is now the commonest and indicates a suitable point at which to pause and draw breath.

In Sanskrit, prose texts use one vertical stroke to mark the end of the sentence, and verse texts use one vertical stroke for the end of a line, two for the end of a couplet. In Bengali, Gujarati, Hindi, and Marathi, the vertical stroke is used as in Sanskrit, in conjunction with other marks borrowed from English. The diacritical signs and elements of punctuation found in Tamil were introduced early in the 18th century by a Jesuit missionary.

Before the modern period, the grammatical structure of written Chinese was such that no punctuation was required; but in the 19th century editors of texts began to add hollow circles, intended either to mark the ends of phrases or to emphasize particular passages. Since 1912 some of the European punctuation marks have been adopted, notably the marks of interrogation and exclamation and the comma (the hollow circle serves as full point). Direct speech is indicated either by double inverted commas or by an L-shaped mark placed at a corner of the first and last characters. Characters are capitalized by the addition of a straight or wavy line underneath or at the side, according to whether the text is written horizontally or vertically.

In Japan a complicated system of *kaeriten* and *kunten* marks was used from the 8th century onward to clarify the meaning and grammatical construction of texts in Chinese. As a result of contact with Europeans in the 15th and 16th centuries, a hollow point (○) and a reversed virgule (·) were used during the Edo period (1603–1868) as equivalents of the European full point and comma. Since 1868 they have been joined by the solid point (to separate items in a list), by the dash used as in English, and, finally, by the European marks of exclamation and interrogation.

The history of punctuation in Africa is part of the history of the scripts used in different parts of the continent: the Coptic script, based on the Greek alphabet with some additions from demotic writing, for the ancient language of Egypt; a derivative of South Semitic script, known as Ethiopic, for the languages of Ethiopia; Arabic script for speakers of Arabic, Berber, and Swahili; Latin—*i.e.,* European—script for the languages first recorded during and since the 19th century. (T.J.Br.)

SHORTHAND

Shorthand is a method of writing rapidly by substituting characters, abbreviations, or symbols for letters, words, or phrases. Other names for shorthand are stenography (close, little, or narrow writing), tachygraphy (swift writing), and brachygraphy (short writing). Because shorthand can be written rapidly, the shorthand writer is able to record the proceedings of legislative bodies, the testimony of law courts, or dictation in business correspondence. In addition, shorthand has been used through the centuries as a cultural tool; for example, George Bernard Shaw wrote his plays in shorthand, and Samuel Pepys recorded his diary in shorthand. Furthermore, Cicero's orations, Martin Luther's sermons, and Shakespeare's plays were all preserved by means of shorthand. Today, in every industrial nation of the world, shorthand is used to conduct operations in business, industry, and the professions.

History and development of shorthand. Through the centuries shorthand has been written in systems based on orthography (normal spelling), on phonetics (the sounds of words), and on arbitrary symbols, such as a small circle within a larger circle to represent the phrase, "around the world." Most historians date the beginnings of shorthand with the Greek historian Xenophon, who used an ancient Greek system to write the memoirs of Socrates. It was in the Roman Empire, however, that shorthand first became generally used. Marcus Tullius Tiro, a learned freedman who was a member of Cicero's household, invented the

notae Tironianae ("Tironian notes"), the first Latin shorthand system. Devised in 63 BC, it lasted over a thousand years. Tiro also compiled a shorthand dictionary. Among the early accomplished shorthand writers were the Emperor Titus, Julius Caesar, and a number of bishops. With the beginning of the Medieval Age in Europe, however, shorthand became associated with witchcraft and magic, and disappeared.

While he was archbishop of Canterbury, Thomas Becket (1118?–70) encouraged research into Tiro's shorthand. By the 15th century, with the discovery in a Benedictine monastery of a lexicon of Ciceronian notes and a Psalter written in Tironian shorthand, a renewed interest in the practice was aroused. Somewhat influenced by Tiro's system, Timothy Bright designed an English system in 1588 that consisted of straight lines, circles, and half circles. (Tiro's method was cursive, based on longhand script.) Bright's system was called *Characterie: an Arte of Shorte, Swifte, and Secrete Writing by Character.*

The 17th century produced four important inventors of shorthand systems: John Willis, who is considered to be the father of modern shorthand; Thomas Shelton, whose system was used by Samuel Pepys to write his famous diary; Jeremiah Rich, who popularized the art by publishing not only his system but also the Psalms and the New Testament in his method of shorthand; and William Mason, whose method was used to record sermons and to translate the Bible in the years following the Reformation. Mason's system was later adapted and became the official system of the British Parliament.

Several other systems were invented in the next decades, but most of them were short-lived. One of the most successful was that of the British stenographer Samuel Taylor, who invented a system in 1786 that was based on that of one of his predecessors. Taylor's method was adapted into French, Spanish, Portuguese, Italian, Swedish, German, Dutch, Hungarian, and other languages.

The Industrial Revolution brought a demand for stenographers in business. Because the geometric systems then in use required a high standard of education and long training in the system, a need existed for a method that would be easier to learn. The German Franz Xaver Gabelsberger (1789–1849) turned away from geometric methods and developed a simple cursive system. Gabelsberger has been considered by many to have been one of the world's leaders in the field of shorthand. His system, which he called "Speech-sign art," was based on Latin longhand characters and had a neatness and beauty of outline that is unsurpassed. It enjoyed a spontaneous success and spread to Switzerland, Austria, Scandinavia, Finland, and Russia. Its simplicity made it an easy matter to translate it into other languages, and in 1928 it became the Italian national system.

Modern symbol systems. Sir Isaac Pitman (1813–97), an educator who advocated spelling reform, was knighted by Queen Victoria for his contributions to shorthand. Pitman had learned Taylor's method of shorthand but saw its weakness and designed his own system to incorporate

From Hans Glatte, *Shorthand Systems of the World*

Alphabet of Gabelsberger shorthand, 1834.

writing by sound, the same principle he advocated in phonetic longhand spelling. He published his system in 1837, calling it *Stenographic Sound-Hand.* It consisted of 25 single consonants, 24 double consonants, and 16 vowel sounds. Similar, related sounds were represented by similar signs, shading was used to eliminate strokes, the shortest signs were used to represent the shortest sounds, and single strokes were used to represent single consonants. At first, the principle of positioning to express omitted vowels—*i.e.,* writing the word above, on, or below the line of writing—was reserved until later lessons, after the theory had been presented. Later, positioning was introduced with the first lesson.

In 1852, Isaac Pitman's brother, Benn Pitman, brought the system to America, where, with several slight modifications, it became the method most extensively used in the United States and Canada. An investigation in 1889 stated that 97 percent of the shorthand writers in America used the Isaac Pitman system or one of its modifications. The percentage is much lower today, but Pitman shorthand is still the major system in New York City, Philadelphia, Chicago, and all of Canada. In addition, Pitman shorthand has been adapted to Afrikaans, Arabic, Armenian, Dutch, French, Gaelic, German, Hebrew, Hindi, Italian, Japanese, Persian, Spanish, and other languages.

The Irish-born John Robert Gregg (1867–1948) taught himself an adaptation of Taylor's shorthand at the age of ten. Fascinated by shorthand, he then studied Pitman by himself but disliked its angles, shading, and positioning. Later, while in his early teens, he read a history of shorthand by Thomas Anderson, a member of the Shorthand Society of London. In his book, Anderson listed the essentials of a good shorthand system, stating that no method then in use possessed them. These essentials, which made a lasting impression on Gregg, included the following: independent characters for the vowels and consonants, all characters written with the same thickness, all characters written on a single line of writing, and few and consistent abbreviation principles.

Gregg was 18 when he invented his own system and 21 when he published it in pamphlet form, *Light-Line Phonography* (1888). The Gregg system was predominantly a curve-motion shorthand with circles, hooks, and loops. Based on the ellipse or oval and on the slope of longhand, its motion was curvilinear. Obtuse angles were eliminated by natural blending of lines, vowels were joined, shading was eliminated, and writing was lineal, or in one position.

Gregg's light-line phonography

Pitman

Gregg

Speedwriting

Modern systems of shorthand recording the same sentence: "Since the dawn of history man has strived to communicate with his fellows and to record experiences that would otherwise be forgotten."

In 1893 Gregg took his system to the United States, and Light-Line Phonography became Gregg Shorthand. The inventor found that, except for the eastern coastal cities, shorthand was virtually unknown. At that time high schools began teaching shorthand, and Gregg travelled through the Midwest, the West, and the South, selling his system and demonstrating his teaching methods with great success. The Gregg system became the predominant sys-

tem taught in the United States. It also spread to Canada and to the British Isles. Gregg shorthand has been published in English, French, Spanish, Portuguese, Hebrew, Russian, Italian, Tagalog, Japanese, Thai, Chinese, Erse (Scottish Gaelic), Esperanto, Sinhalese, and Polish.

An early German system of importance was the Stolze-Schrey method. Wilhelm Stolze invented his system at about the same time as Gabelsberger and along similar lines. In 1885, Ferdinand Schrey, a Berlin merchant, attempted to simplify the Gabelsberger system. Sometime later the Stolze and Schrey methods were merged and became the leading system in Germany and Switzerland. Stolze-Schrey shorthand was also adapted to other languages, including Danish, Dutch, English, French, Italian, Norwegian, Polish, Russian, and Spanish.

In 1924, after two decades of development, a new system based on the Gabelsberger and Stolze-Schrey methods was completed. As revised in 1936 and 1968, the Deutsch Einheitskurzschrift is the principal system now used in West Germany and in Austria. A modified version was introduced in East Germany in 1970.

Modern abbreviated longhand systems. The system of Speedwriting shorthand was created around 1924 by Emma Dearborn, an instructor at Columbia University. Her method was designed to be taken down on the typewriter; but in 1942 it was changed to be written by hand with pen or pencil. Speedwriting shorthand uses the letters of the alphabet and the known punctuation marks to represent sounds. For example, the sound of "ch" is written with a capital C; the word "each" is thus written "eC." More than 20,000 words in the Speedwriting dictation can be written with a total of 60 rules and a list of approximately 100 brief forms and standard abbreviations. Speedwriting shorthand is taught in several languages—including English, Spanish, Italian, Portuguese, German, Flemish, and Afrikaans—in many countries.

Forkner Alphabet shorthand was first published in 1952 in the U.S. The author, Hamden Forkner, spent 10 years in research before publishing the first edition of the new system, which uses a combination of conventional letters and a few symbols for the hard-to-write letters and sounds. For example, H is expressed by a short dash above the line. This same short dash through the letter C gives the "ch" sound, through the longhand S it gives "sh," and across the T it designates "th." Abbreviations are used for a number of common words. Forkner Alphabet shorthand is now taught in high schools and business colleges in the U.S.

Another U.S. method, Hy-Speed Longhand, was first published under that title in 1932. Based on Andrew J. Graham's *Brief Longhand,* published in 1857, its principles include the omission of silent letters and most vowels, the substitution of letters, numbers, or signs, and the combination of certain letters.

Stenoscript ABC Shorthand is a phonetic system using only longhand and common punctuation marks. It originated in London in 1607 and was revised by Manuel Claude Avancena, who published a modern edition in 1950. Stenoscript has 24 brief forms that must be memorized; *e.g., ak* stands for acknowledge, *ac* for accompany, *bz* for business, and *gvt* for government.

Stenospeed originated in 1950 in the U.S.; the first publication was called Stenospeed High Speed Longhand, but in 1951 the system was revised under the name of Stenospeed ABC Shorthand. It is used by many schools as a standard text. Stenospeed has also been programmed for use with teaching machines.

Other alphabetic or partially alphabetic systems have also been devised. Among these is Teeline, a system used extensively in Great Britain.

Machine shorthand. A method of recording speech by using machines became commercially feasible around 1906, when the Stenotype machine was invented by Ward Stone Ireland, a U.S. stenographer and court reporter. At present, the Stenograph and Stenotype machines are used in offices to some extent, but they are principally employed for conference and court reporting. Both machines have keyboards of 22 keys; they are small, light, and silent. Because the operator uses all fingers and both thumbs, any number of keys can be struck simultaneously. The

Stenograph and Stenotype machines

```
S          EU  PR    S
T
      TK   A    U  PB
            O     F
           H    EU       S
T           O  E  R
        P H A        PB
           H A           S
ST        R    E.F     D
T             O
        KP H    U  PB
       K     A EU        T
      WH     EU        S
      T P     E     L
       HR O E          S
             A      PB   D
      T          O
             R  O  R    D
     S P       E  RPB    S
     T  H A        L    D
             O         TS
          W     E        B
                    B
      T P     O     R
     TKPW  O          T
             E    PB
             F  P  L  T
```

Stenotype shorthand recording the same sentence as in the previous illustration.

machines print roman letters on a strip of paper that folds automatically into the back of the machine. The operator controls the keys by touch and is thus able to watch the speaker.

To operate the machine, the fingers of the left hand control the keys that print consonants occurring before vowels. These keys print on the left side of the tape. The thumbs control the vowels, which are printed in the centre of the tape, and the fingers of the right hand control the consonants that follow the vowels, which are printed on the right side of the tape. There are not separate keys for each letter of the English alphabet, thus, those letters for which there are no keys are represented by combinations of other letters. Abbreviations are used for some of the most frequent words, giving the operator the ability to write two or three words in one stroke.

The advantages given for machine shorthand include greater speed, interchangeability of notes, and greater volume, in that other typists familiar with the system can transcribe the notes. Disadvantages include the cost of the machine, the inconvenience of moving the machine from place to place, and the difficulty of revising notes once they have been taken, in addition to reading back dictation when desired. Machine shorthand has proved itself in the reporting field, however. Reporting speeds are attained in less time than is needed with pen shorthand; and machine shorthand reporters now do most of the convention reporting and a large part of the court reporting, legislative reporting, and reporting of hearings in the United States.

Alternatives to shorthand. Machines for voice transcribing are used in modern offices as an alternative to pen or machine shorthand; in fact, they are found in most offices of any size. The advantages of such dictating equipment include the following: the equipment is always available, even though the secretary may not be; the dictator can dictate his thoughts immediately—in his office, in his home, in his car, or on a plane; he can dictate as rapidly as he wishes, unhampered by his secretary's recording skill; and dictation belts can be mailed back to the typist for transcription. Disadvantages of voice transcribing machines are the impossibility of teamwork during the dictation process and the necessity of a high degree of dictating skill when using dictating equipment. In addition, urgent matters usually cannot be dictated and transcribed without some delay.　(A.R.R.)

Voice transcribing machines

The art of handwriting: calligraphy

Calligraphy is writing as an art. The term derives from the Greek words for "good" or "beautiful" and for "writing" or "drawing" and refers to what writing masters called the art of fair writing. It implies a sure knowledge of the correct forms of letters—*i.e.,* the conventional signs by which language can be communicated—and the skill to inscribe them with such ordering of the various parts and harmony of proportions that the cultivated, knowing eye will recognize the composition as a work of art. In East Asia, calligraphy by long and exacting tradition is considered a major art, equal to painting. In Western culture the simpler Greek and Latin-derived alphabets and the spread of literacy tend to make handwriting theoretically "everybody's art," though in a few instances, especially since the Renaissance, it either has aspired to or attained the status of calligraphy.　(Ed.)

GREEK HANDWRITING

Origins to the 8th century AD. The oldest Greek writing, syllabic signs scratched with a stylus on sun-dried clay, is that of the Linear B tablets found in Knossos, Pylos, and Mycenae (1400–1200 BC). Alphabetic writing, in use before the end of the 8th century BC, is first found in a scratched inscription on a jug awarded as a prize in Athens. The consensus is that the Homeric poems were written down not later than this time; certainly from the time of the first known lyric poet of ancient Greece, Archilochus (7th century BC), individuals committed their works to writing. But the vehicles of literary writing have perished. Scratchings on pottery or metal and then texts deliberately cut in bronze or marble or painted on vases are, until *c.* 350 BC, the only immediate evidence for the way the Greeks wrote, and their study is normally treated as the province of epigraphy. A find in 1962 at Dervéni, in Macedonia, of a carbonized roll of papyrus (Archaeological Museum, Thessaloníki, Greece) offers the oldest and only example of Greek handwriting preserved in the Greek peninsula (end of the 4th century BC). From then until the 4th century AD, there are countless texts, especially on papyrus. Found in Egypt, and, with a few exceptions, written there, these texts have given a firm foundation for knowledge. From outside Egypt there is a

Oldest Greek handwriting

Papyrus from Dervéni, Macedonia, 4th century BC (Archaeological Museum, Thessaloníki, Greece).

Greek library buried in Herculaneum, AD 79; and papyri and parchments from Owrāmān, Kurdistan, 1st century BC; from Doura-Europus on the Euphrates, 3rd century BC to 3rd century AD; from Nessana, 6th century AD; and from the Dead Sea area (Qumrān, 1st centuries BC and AD; Murabba'at and 'En Gedi, 2nd century AD). A number of original vellum manuscripts have survived from the 4th century AD onward, preserved in libraries such as the monastery of St. Catherine at Mt. Sinai. These materials of diverse origin suggest that the forms and shape of Greek handwriting were remarkably constant throughout the Greek world, wherever writing was practiced and whatever the material used; within this consistent framework it is occasionally possible to distinguish local variations (as between the contract hands of 1st-century-AD Doura and of Egypt).

Writing materials
The principal vehicles for writing were wax tablets incised with a stylus or a prepared surface of skin, such as leather and vellum, or of papyrus written on with a pen. Other surfaces—*e.g.,* broken pieces of pottery, lead, wood, and even cloth—were also used. To some extent the forms of letters were affected by the resistance of the material to the writing instrument. It is likely that the use as a pen of a hard reed, split at the tip and cut into a nib (which must be constantly sharpened), is an invention of the Greeks. Egyptian scribes used a soft reed, with which ink was brushed on.

Until about AD 300, ink was normally made of a carbon such as lampblack, mixed with gum and water, which even today retains its black lustre. After that time, because of the increasing popularity of vellum, iron inks (*e.g.,* of oak galls), better suited to vellum, tended to replace carbon. The iron inks have faded with age and often have eaten by chemical action into the vellum. Erasures could be made on wax with the blunt end of the stylus, on papyrus by wiping with a sponge; but, on vellum written in iron ink, erasures could be made only by rubbing with pumice or scraping with a knife. Texts from which a previous writing was deliberately erased to provide writing material are termed palimpsests.

Papyrus was normally sold in rolls (*volumina*) made up of 20 or 50 glued sheets: the horizontal fibres of the papyrus are placed on the inside of the roll, on which side (the recto) each gummed sheet overlaps the next when the roll is held horizontally. Leather, similarly, was for long made into rolls (the Dead Sea Scrolls). Shortly after the beginning of the Christian Era, the custom began of folding a single sheet (or several superposed sheets, a quarternion or quire) down the middle and stitching the quires into a binding case to give a book of modern form (codex, originally a set of wax tablets coupled with a thong). Tradition associated this invention with Pergamum.

Development of the book
The decisive impetus to the use of this form came from the early Christians, who deliberately chose the commercial vellum notebook (*membranae*) in which to circulate the Christian Gospels in preference to the traditional Jewish roll. Almost without exception the earliest texts of the New Testament are in codex form, even though written

Codex Sinaiticus (British Museum, London; Add. MS. 43725, fol. 260).

on papyrus, which is less able than vellum to bear repeated bending. In the 2nd century AD pagan works of literature also appeared in this format, which gained ground in the 3rd century, often in small or utility sizes. By the 4th century it became the predominant form, and codices with handsome margins, of dazzling white vellum, and of sufficient size to contain the whole Bible (*e.g.,* the Codex Sinaiticus) were being produced.

The fundamental distinction in types of handwriting is that between book hands and documentary hands. The former, used especially for the copying of literature, aimed at clarity, regularity, and impersonality and often made an effect of beauty by their deliberate stylization. Usually they were the work of professionals, who may have multiplied copies to dictation, though ancient evidence on this subject is unreliable, and the evidence of scribal errors is equivocal (since the ancients invariably read out loud, a scribe copying by eye in solitude is likely to have pronounced the words of his exemplar). Outstanding calligraphy is not common among papyrus finds, perhaps because they are mainly provincial work. But the British Museum Bacchylides or the Bodleian Library Homer can stand comparison with any later vellum manuscript from outside Egypt. Book texts are written in separately made

Book hands

Greek book hand. Bodleian Library Homer, passage from the *Iliad*, copied in the 2nd century AD (Bodleian Library, Oxford; MS. Gr. class A.1 (P)).

capitals (often called uncials, but in Greek paleography, except for the time-hallowed class of biblical uncials, the term is better avoided) in columns of writing, with ample spaces between columns and good margins at head and foot. Punctuation (usually by high dot) is minimal or completely absent; accents are inserted only in difficult poetic texts or as practice by schoolboys; and letters are not grouped into separate words.

Documentary hands show a considerable range: styl-

Greek documentary hand. An authorization for the sale of slaves, late 1st century AD (British Museum, London; P. Oxy. 94).

ized official "chancery" hands; the workaday writing of government clerks or of the street scribes who drew up wills or wrote letters to order; the idiosyncratic or nearly illiterate writing of private individuals. The scribe's aim was to write quickly, lifting his pen very little and consequently often combining several letters in a continuous stroke (a ligature); from the running action of the pen, this writing is often termed cursive. He also made frequent use of abbreviations. When the scribe was skillful in reconciling clarity and speed, such writing may have much character, even beauty; but it often degenerates into a formless, sometimes indecipherable, scrawl.

Documentary hands

Both types of hands, in spite of the different styles they assume at different periods, show remarkable uniformity and continuity in the shapes of letters. Behind both lies an unvarying basic alphabetic form taught in the schools. The more skillful a book-hand scribe was, the harder it is to date his work. Documents in the ancient world carried a precise date; books never did. To assign dates to the latter, the paleographer takes account of their content, the archaeological context of their discovery, and technical points of book construction (*e.g.,* quires, rulings) or modes of abbreviation. But he finds of great service: (1) a stylistic comparison with those dated documentary hands that show resemblances to book hands; and (2) those cases where a roll was reused—*i.e.,* has a literary text on its recto and a dated document on its verso (in which case there is a *terminus ante quem* for the literary text, often estimated at 50 years before the date of the verso) or has a dated document on the recto and a book hand on the verso (which gives a *terminus post quem* for the literary text, not more than 25 years after the document). The number of illustrated manuscripts of this period is small; their quality is varied; and there is no agreement between specialists about the sources from which illustrations were taken.

Dated texts

Any historical sketch is bound to be a simplification. At certain epochs several different styles of handwriting existed simultaneously, so that there is no straight line of development. Moreover, owing to the arbitrariness of finds, generalizations are based mainly on provincial work; and, even in that, examples of book hand belonging to the 2nd century BC and the 5th century AD are still relatively rare.

Ptolemaic period. In the roll from Dervéni, Macedonia, dated on archaeological grounds to the 4th century BC, lines and letters are well spaced, and the letters carefully made in an epigraphic, or inscription, style, especially the square E, four-barred Σ, and arched Ω; the whole layout gives the effect of an inscription. In the Timotheus roll in Berlin (dated 350–330 BC) or in the curse of Artemisia in Vienna (4th century BC), the writing is cruder, and ω is in transition to what is afterward its invariable written form. Similar features can be seen in the earliest precisely dated document, a marriage contract of 311 BC. It has been argued that a documentary hand of cursive type had not yet been developed and that it was a creation of the Alexandrian library. Plato, however (*Laws* 810), speaks of Athenian writing whose aim was speed; later on, when a cursive hand had certainly been developed, documentary scribes often used separate capitals.

Characteristic of its period is the contrast of size between long letters (*e.g.,* M) and narrow letters. ($\epsilon \, C \, O$ or θ, O, or O). And characteristic forms are to be seen in the letters T (with its long crossbar, often with initial stroke); Y (upsilon) with long shallow bowl; M or M in three or four strokes; $\frown$ in three strokes; α (alpha) raised off the line and its last vertical not finished; small round (-) (with internal dot or tiny stroke); and broad epigraphic Λ and H.

These same features, written with more regularity, appear in the contemporary book hand of a fragment of a Thucydides manuscript (Staats- und Universitätsbibliothek, Hamburg). In documentary cursive hands of this period, letters seem to hang from an upper line: ν (alpha) often turns into a mere wedge, and η (nu).

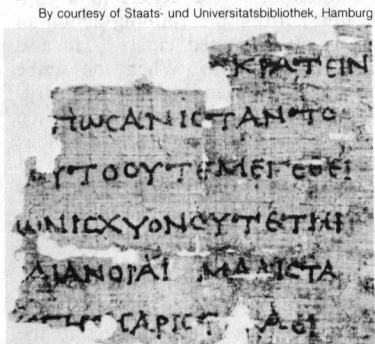

Thucydides manuscript, 3rd century BC
(Staats- und Universitätsbibliothek, Hamburg;
P. Hamburg 163).

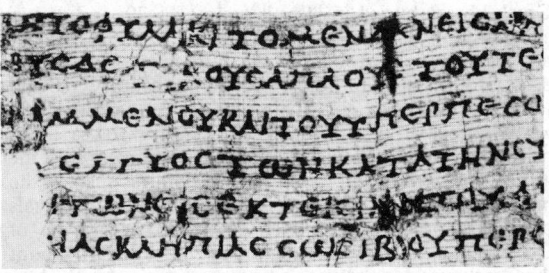

Legal text of a loan contract, 99 BC (The John Rylands
University Library of Manchester; Rylands Greek Pap. 586).

lifts its second vertical above the line. In the 2nd century BC the contrast between long letters and narrow letters disappears, the writing grows rounder, and letters are often linked by ligatures at the top of their last vertical (*e.g.,* $\vdash M \, N$). In a loan contract of 99 BC (The John Rylands University Library of Manchester), in which capitals and cursive are mixed, this irregular roundness is clearly seen. Note the ε with detached crossbar and the exaggerated serifs $(I \, K \, Y \, \rho)$ which have been elevated by some paleographers into a criterion of a special style, though in fact they are always apt to occur.

Roman period. Half a century or so passes after 30 BC before a definitely Roman manner is established. In documentary hands the tendency to roundness continues. Documentary cursive may be influenced in various ways (*e.g.,* by Latin forms such as those of *e* and *d,* or by the exaggeration of verticals practiced by chancery scribes), may lean over in either direction, or may be reduced to tiny proportions. In the 2nd century the cursive hand tends to be round and sprawling, in the 3rd century to become more angular, and in the 4th century to become characterless and to combine letters into ligatures that distort the forms of the letters concerned. The book hand of a manuscript of Plato's *Phaedo* (*c.* AD 100; Egypt

Phaedo, by Plato, copied in AD 100 (Egypt Exploration
Society, London; P. Oxy. 1809).

Exploration Society, London) shares its informality but regularizes the letter forms. Written on a larger scale and with more formality, this round hand can be very beautiful. In an example found at Hawara (2nd century AD), almost every letter (even ρ, τ, ι) would go into an identical square; only φ and ψ cross it above and below, μ, ω, and π horizontally.

If this writing is made to lean to the right, and to revive the 3rd-century-BC distinction between narrow and broad letters, it takes on the aspect of the "severe" style of the Bacchylides roll in the British Museum (2nd century AD). If,

The "severe" style. Bacchylides roll, 2nd century AD (British
Museum, London; P. 733).

however, the scribe makes his verticals or obliques thicker and his horizontals thinner, the hand is called biblical uncial, so named because this type is used in the three great early vellum codices of the Bible: Codex Vaticanus and Codex Sinaiticus of the 4th century and Codex Alexandrinus of the 5th century. It is now certain that this style goes back to the 2nd century AD. In the Dioscorides herbal in Vienna, written in AD 512, the writing is rigid and lumbering; the thick strokes are overdone; and blobs of ink terminate the horizontals of, for example, δ, ε, σ, τ. Such heavy decoration is also a feature of the Coptic style, of which there are examples as early as the 2nd century AD. This hand may be thought of as constituting a special case of biblical uncial.

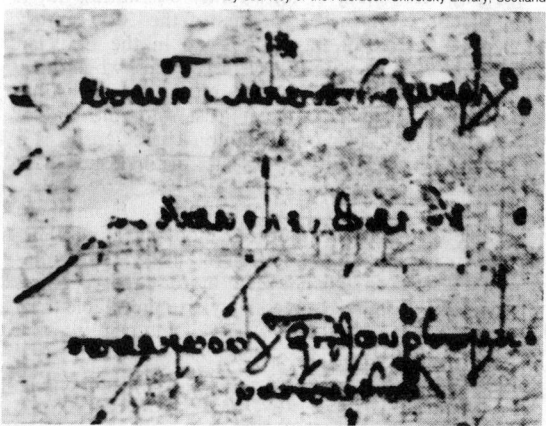

Biblical uncial. Dioscorides herbal, AD 512 (Österreichische Nationalbibliothek, Vienna; Med. Gr. 1).

Byzantine period. For the paleographer the significant division is not the founding of Constantinople in 330 but the 5th century, from which a few firmly dated texts survive. At its close a large-sized, exuberant, and florid cursive is found fully established for documents; in the 7th and 8th centuries, it slopes to the right, becomes congested, and adopts some forms of letters that anticipate the minuscule hand (*e.g.*, the π and λ in an 8th-century list of names preserved in the Aberdeen University Library).

Byzantine documentary hand that is a precursor of minuscule. List of names, 8th century AD (Aberdeen University Library, Scotland; P. 72a).

No new book hand was invented. A favourite informal type of the 6th century is shown in an acrostic poem by Dioscorus of Aphrodito, in the British Museum; it bears a clear relationship to the Menander *Dyskolos* hand, which was probably written in the later 3rd century AD. Similar pairs could be found to illustrate the continuity in transformation of the biblical uncial and Coptic styles. The latest Greek papyrus from Egypt is not later than the 8th century. There is a considerable lapse of time before the history of Greek writing resumes at Byzantium.   (E.G.T.)

8th to 16th centuries AD. To judge when and where a Greek manuscript was written is as difficult in this as in the earlier period, but for different reasons. The material for study is admittedly more extensive; manuscripts produced in the Middle Ages and Renaissance have been preserved in very large numbers (more than 50,-000 whole volumes survive, of which probably 4,000 or 5,000 are explicitly dated); and they include work from most parts of the Byzantine Empire as well as from Italy. The difficulty of the paleographer lies in the essential homogeneity of the material, which is largely the

result of the conditions in which the manuscripts were produced.

The fully developed Byzantine Empire of the 8th to the mid-15th centuries was extraordinarily uniform in its culture. Its contraction in space after the Arab conquests of the 7th century, which cut off the more distant and ethnically differentiated provinces of Syria, Palestine, and Egypt, made it a relatively compact geographical entity. The continuity and comparative stability of a single empire not divided into distinct national states such as evolved in the West resulted in a strength and unity of tradition of which the Byzantines were always conscious and that shows in their habits of writing no less than in their literature and art. Distinct local styles and sharp breaks in ways of writing in different periods cannot, therefore, be looked for; characteristics that may be specially typical of one period come in gradually and disappear equally slowly. A more potent factor than date or place in producing divergencies in the style of writing is the purpose for which a manuscript was designed and what type of scribe wrote it.

Late uncial, 9th to 12th centuries. There is a gap in the evidence covering the 7th and 8th centuries, because of the Arab conquest of Egypt, the perpetual wars on all fronts in the 7th century, and the iconoclastic struggle among Eastern Christians during the 8th and early 9th centuries, so that no literary texts (and very few others) have survived that can actually be dated to this period.

During this time the evolution of writing in capitals (not very aptly named uncial) probably continued toward a greater formality and artificiality. But this natural tendency was hastened by the introduction and spread of minuscule as the normal way of writing, after which the purpose of uncial changed completely. From an everyday hand in which all books were naturally written, it became a ceremonial hand used only for special copies and therefore grew increasingly stylized and artificial. In the 9th century a still elegant style was used for both patristic and classical works in splendid volumes destined for the imperial library or for presentation copies, such as the copy of Gregory of Nazianzus (Bibliothéque Nationale, Paris) made for the emperor Basil I between 879 and 883. By the 11th and 12th centuries, capitals were used only for liturgical books, mainly lectionaries, which had to be read in dimly lit churches; but the increasing tortuousness of the style must in the end have reduced its usefulness, and, by about 1200, uncial was dead.

Earliest minuscule, 8th to 10th centuries. By far the most important development that took place during the 7th–8th-century gap was the introduction of minuscule. There is no incontrovertible evidence of how this came about, or where. What scraps of evidence there are (a few documents from the gap, a few sentences in lives of the abbots of Stoudion of that time, and the first dated manuscript written in true minuscule) point to its development from a certain type of documentary hand used in the 8th century and to the likelihood that the monastery of the Stoudion in Constantinople had a leading part in its early development. Though its origins are obscure, the reasons that led to

Informal Byzantine book hand of the 6th century. Acrostic poem by Dioscorus of Aphrodito, 6th century AD (British Museum, London; P. 1552).

Late uncial. Copy of Gregory of Nazianzus, AD 879–883 (Bibliothéque Nationale, Paris; Grec. 510, fol. 61ᵛ).
By courtesy of the Bibliotheque Nationale, Paris

its introduction and rapid spread are obvious: the state of poverty resulting from wars and persecutions coincided with a shortage of papyrus after the Arab conquest of Egypt in the middle of the 7th century, and these factors combined to induce a search for a more economical use of the relatively expensive vellum; the polemics of the iconoclastic controversy demanded a speedy, informal style of writing; and, finally, when peace was restored in the middle of the 9th century, the revival of learning, with the reorganization of the university, brought the need for multiplying plain workmanlike texts for scholarly purposes.

Earliest dated true minuscule. Copy of the Gospels supposedly done at the monastery of Stoudion, AD 835 (Leningrad, Bibl. Publ. 219, fol. 124).

The earliest dated example of true minuscule (and it is probably one of the oldest extant examples altogether) is a copy of the Gospels written in 835 (Leningrad Library), probably in the monastery of the Stoudion. Here are found all the characteristics of the earliest minuscule, which is called pure minuscule because there is as yet no admixture of uncial forms, except occasionally at line ends. The letters are even and of a uniform size; letters are joined or not joined to each other according to strict rules, sometimes by ligatures in which part of each letter is merged in the other, but not to the extent of distorting the shape of either letter. There is no division between words, for the divisions are only those that arise from the rules for joining or otherwise of individual letters, and at this stage any letter that can be joined to the next one nearly always is joined to it. Breathings are square, either

⊢ ⊣ or ⌞ ⌟, and accents are small and neat; abbreviations are very few, usually confined to the established contractions for *nomina sacra* (the names and descriptions of the Trinity and certain derivatives), omitted *ν* at line ends, a few of the conventional signs

for omitted case endings, and Ϛ sometimes for *καί*. The writing either stands on the ruled lines or is merely guided by them.

First changes in minuscule Absolutely pure minuscule did not last long. Gradually, uncial forms of those letters that had specifically minuscule forms began to be used alongside the minuscule forms: *λ* was the first to appear, followed by *ξ* and then *κ*, all by the middle of the 9th century. Then from about 900 onward, *γ*, *ζ*, *ν*, *π*, and *σ* were used regularly, while *α*, *δ*, *ε*, and *η* were used sometimes. Not before about 950 were *β*, *μ*, *υ*, *ψ*, and *ω* used, and still comparatively rarely. But by the end of the 10th century, the interchangeability of all uncial and minuscule forms was complete, though all the alternative forms are not necessarily found in any one

manuscript. Perhaps the earliest dated manuscript with any uncial form in it is of 892/893 (Sinai, St. Catherine, MS. 375 + Leningrad, Bibl. Publ. MS. 343, Chrysostom), but pure minuscule continued to be used, in probably the majority of manuscripts, up to 900, and thereafter mainly in provincial manuscripts until the last dated example in 969 (Meteora, Metamorph. MS. 565, John Climacus). Besides the intrusion of uncial letters, some other characteristics of the earliest minuscule were modified during the 10th century. Rounded breathings, '', are first found in manuscripts of the last half of the century, interspersed with square ones. From about 925 the practice of making the writing hang from the ruled lines began to prevail. Although in most manuscripts abbreviations were confined to a few forms used at line ends only, a few copies dated in the last part of the century used nearly all the conventional signs.

In spite of these developments—the gradual disappearance of pure minuscule and the other changes that accompanied it—the same general styles of writing persisted until about the end of the 10th century. Broadly considered, three styles can be distinguished during this period. There is a rather primitive-looking, angular, cramped style that may perhaps be associated with the Stoudion monastery, in which a certain number of mainly patristic texts were written *c.* 880–*c.* 980 (*e.g.*, Paris, Bibliothèque Nationale, MS. grec 1470, a menologion of 890). Second, there is a plain, neat, workmanlike style (seen in a commentary on Gregory of Nazianzus copied in 986 that is preserved in the Bibliothèque Nationale at Paris), which continued in use at least until the end of the 10th century. In it were written several of the important manuscripts that are now the oldest texts of some ancient Greek authors (for example, Aeschylus, Sophocles, Aristophanes) but are unfortunately not explicitly dated. Thirdly, a consciously elegant, even mannered, style was used in books produced for the imperial library or for wealthy dignitaries, but it is not found before the early years of the 10th century (as seen in a copy of Basil on Isaiah in the Bodleian Library that is dated 953). All of these styles, which have numerous variations and are by no means always distinct from one another, are found at least until the end of the 10th century. Their one common characteristic is a crispness and individuality that clearly distinguishes them from writing of the next period.

Formal minuscule, 10th to 14th centuries. From about the middle of the 10th century, a smoother, almost mechanical appearance can be noticed in an increasing number of manuscripts; the hands seem more stereotyped, less individual. They are not immediately distinguishable from the plainer styles of the earlier part of the century, and

By courtesy of (top, centre) the Bibliotheque Nationale, Paris, (bottom) the curators of the Bodleian Library, Oxford

9th–10th-century Greek hands.
(Top) Stoudion minuscule, AD 890 (Bibliothèque Nationale, Paris; MS. grec. 1470, fol. 168). (Centre) Commentary on Gregory of Nazianzus, AD 986 (Bibliothèque Nationale, Paris; MS. suppl. grec. 469 a, fol. 7). (Bottom) Commentary on Isaiah by Basil, AD 953 (Bodleian Library, Oxford; MS. Auct. E.2.12, fol. 80).

their evolution during the next four centuries was very gradual. A few distinct types can be singled out from time to time. A bold, round, heavy liturgical style, fully established in the 11th century, was one of the most enduring types (*e.g.*, London, British Museum Add. MS. 19,352, a psalter of 1066); it became more and more stereotyped and mechanical until, in the 15th century, a branch of it was transplanted to Italy.

The style most widely used for biblical and patristic texts from the end of the 10th century, probably mainly in monastic houses in Constantinople, was one with plain, neat, rounded letters; this style became known as *Perlschrift* from its likeness to small, round beads strung together. A very plain, businesslike, rather staccato style was used in manuscripts with musical notation, most commonly in the 12th and 13th centuries (*e.g.*, Leningrad, Bibl. Publ. MS. 789, a sticherarion of 1106).

Manuscripts written outside Constantinople are recognizable, if at all, usually by a rougher, provincial appearance. Only two styles can be assigned with any certainty to a specific provincial centre. One, a small unpretentious hand used by St. Nilus, the founder of numerous monasteries in south Italy at the end of the 9th century, was used for a time by others in that part of the world (*e.g.*, a copy of the works of Dorotheus made by Nilus in 965). Later, in the heyday of the reorganized Greek monasteries there in the 12th century, another elegant, rather mannered style, which almost certainly had its origin in Constantinople, is nevertheless often found in manuscripts known to have been written in south Italy and Sicily (*e.g.*, Paris, Bibliothèque Nationale MS. grec 83; Gospels copied in Sicily in 1167).

11th- and 12th-century plain hand. Collection of canon law, 1042 (Bodleian Library, Oxford; MS. Barocci 196, fol. 253).

These particular styles, however, are not really as typical of the period as the less distinctive plain hands in which the majority of the manuscripts are written, at least in the 11th and 12th centuries (*e.g.*, a collection of canon law copied in 1042 in the Bodleian Library).

The comparatively uniform type of writing of which all these were minor variations was remarkably enduring and widely dispersed, but, from the 11th century onward, certain changes may be observed that help to date manuscripts written in all types of formal minuscule. One change in its general appearance may be noticed as the 12th century advances: an increasing lightness of touch and a lessening of the closely knit, rather thick appearance that is characteristic of the 11th century. But the most noticeable change in this period is the breakdown in the evenness and regularity of the writing, which is partly attributable to the influence of documentary and the later personal hands. It is not, however, entirely so attributable, for a tendency to enlarge some letters out of proportion to the size of the rest is seen in a small way in some of the more personal hands of the earliest period. But it is rare in formally written manuscripts, only gradually becoming more general until, in the 12th and 13th centuries, it is the most noticeable feature of even the most formal

Changes dating from the 11th century

hands (*e.g.*, a synaxarion, or a short narrative of a saint's life, copied probably in 1329). In the 14th century and later, there was a return to less flamboyant ways with the tendency to imitate earlier models more closely, but the habit of enlarging some and diminishing the size of other letters never died out.

In the actual forms of letters used in these formal styles, there was practically no change; very occasionally, from the end of the 10th century onward, one of the "modern" forms of letter normally confined to personal hands found its way into a formal manuscript. Much the same is true of ligatures. The tendency from the 11th century onward is to use ligatures and to join letters less automatically than in earlier times. The permissive rules and most of the forms remain unchanged, for, already in the 10th century, most of the distorting forms (notably those in which the

ε is represented only by a C-shaped stroke; *e.g.*, for $\sigma\varepsilon$) were well established, and in formal manuscripts these, with the earlier forms, continued in use until they were illogically taken over by the first printers of Greek. Time did, however, gradually increase the tendency to join letters by insetting them in or superimposing them upon each other. Abbreviations were even more conservatively used, only the oldest conventional forms being admitted, and often only a very few and those only at line ends.

The rule that the writing should hang from the ruled lines, already applied in most manuscripts by the mid-10th century, became invariable by the middle of the 11th. Square breathings (used indiscriminately among the round ones) were gradually eliminated, though they did not completely disappear from formal manuscripts until the middle of the 12th century. The practice of joining accents with breathings and also with the letters to which they belonged spread from personal hands to formal writing in the 13th century, but it was far more often avoided altogether.

Apart from the actual writing, one development is common to all manuscripts written in this period: the use of paper instead of vellum, which occurred first perhaps in the late 11th century and was common by the 13th century whenever economy was a major consideration.

These are the main criteria by which a formally written manuscript can be assigned to an earlier or a later part of this period. But the problem of distinguishing different styles and their dates, and their places of origin, remains most difficult for these Greek manuscripts.

Personal hands, 12th to 14th centuries. From the beginning of minuscule, there were obviously educated individuals who occasionally copied texts for their own use in a formal hand that nevertheless had a distinctive personal flavour; indeed, professional scribes occasionally used a less formal style than usual. Several dated examples of this type of hand survive from the 10th, 11th, and early 12th centuries, but they are rarities. Toward the end of the 12th century, however, the prosperity and comparative stability of the Comnenan age (named from the dynasty of Byzantine emperors bearing the name Comnenus), with its brilliant literary and artistic achievements, gave way to increasing internal chaos and the hostile encirclement of Byzantium that was a prelude to the Fourth Crusade and the sack of Constantinople by the Western powers in 1204. Scholars perhaps already felt the pinch of poverty, which naturally grew greater during the exile of the Byzantium court (1204–61) and culminated in the economic crises of the 14th century.

Certainly, a change in writing habits began slowly to take

12th- and 13th-century formal hand. A synaxarion, probably AD 1329 (Bodleian Library, Oxford; MS. Auct. E.5.10, fol. 73ᵛ).

Copying by scholars

place. Instead of commissioning professional scribes to copy manuscripts, some scholars began to make copies for themselves, and, in place of the smooth, mechanical styles of the professionals, they used the sort of writing that they presumably already used for personal notes. This was an adaptation (for greater clarity) of the type of writing that had been standardized in official documents from the beginning of the Byzantine period. Its chief characteristic was the greatly exaggerated size of certain letters or parts of letters, particularly letters with rounded bows such as *β*, *ε*, *ζ*, *θ*, *κ*, *ξ*, *o*, *v*, *φ*, and *ω*, and the excessive size of these letters is made to look even more unbalanced by some exceptionally small forms of, for example, *η*, *ι*, *v*, or *ρ*. This essentially unbalanced, "wild" look was transplanted to literary manuscripts written by scholars for their own use.

Along with this exaggerated contrast in size between letters, they took from the documentary hands several new forms of letters that had gradually evolved from the orig-

By courtesy of the Biblioteca Nazionale Marciana, Venice

Early medieval scholarly hand. Commentary on the *Odyssey*, written by Eustathius c. 1150–70 (Biblioteca Nazionale Marciana, Venice; MS. Marc. Gr. Z. 460 [coll. 330], fol. 79).

inally common forms of both hands. In the 12th century the new scholarly hands began to use ϐ with separate small bows; ε, with a broken back; η, which had lost its high first stroke; and ν, which had dropped its first long downstroke; and, by the end of the 13th century, ς, with a short embryonic tail. The old forms of ligature were kept basically the same but, in some cases, were reduced to a barely recognizable minimum (*e.g.,* ϑ or

4 for *ει*) and, in others, distorted by the general flourishing tendency of the script (*e.g.,* ⟿ for *επ*). Abbreviations

Use of abbreviations

were naturally used with great frequency in all positions; the ancient conventional signs for suppressed syllables, which had acquired rounded and more flourished shapes, were used alongside a certain amount of "arbitrary" abbreviation in which a large part of a word was omitted and replaced simply by a general sign that some abbreviation had taken place.

Accents and breathings joined with each other, with letters, and with abbreviation marks are found earlier and more frequently in scholarly than in formal manuscripts. The only exception to the rule of round breathings in this type of manuscript is in cases of deliberate archaism such as practiced by Demetrius Triclinius (died *c.* 1340).

One of the earliest datable examples of these scholarly productions is the copy of his commentary on the *Odyssey* (Biblioteca Nazionale Marciana, Venice) written *c.* 1150–70 by Eustathius, the scholar-archbishop of Thessalonica. In the 13th century, the exaggeration of specially round features reached its height (*e.g.,* in a copy of Euthymius Zigabenus on the Psalms, of 1279 [Bodleian Library, Oxford; MS. Roe 7]), while, in the 14th century, the tendency, as in the formal styles of writing, was toward less ebullience and exaggeration, and the writing of scholars such as Triclinius is compact and sober (*e.g.,* his copy of

Late medieval scholarly hand. Grammatical works copied by Triclinius, AD 1308 (New College, Oxford; MS. 258, fol. 205).
By courtesy of New College, Oxford

Aphthonius and other grammatical works, of 1308). For these hands the problem is not to discover centres of writing or styles for different uses but to identify the hands of individual scholars.

The Italian Renaissance. By the end of the 14th century, Italian scholars were learning Greek, and they were bringing back Greek manuscripts from Constantinople. At this time Greek scholars had also begun to teach in Italy. The Greek that the earliest Italians learned to write was a clear, simple style taught originally by Manuel Chrysoloras (died 1415). But, although they copied a number of manuscripts for themselves in this hand, the style had no influence beyond their small circle. Before long, Greek scribes began to go to Italy, and both scholars and scribes arrived in increasing numbers as the Turks pressed in round the Byzantine capital until it finally fell in 1453. They brought with them, naturally, the two styles of writing that had persisted throughout the history of the empire. On the one hand, professional scribes such as Joannes Rhosus (died *c.* 1500), the majority of them from Crete, copied an astonishing number of manuscripts in the formal, now glib and stereotyped "liturgical" style of writing (*e.g.,* London, British Museum Harl. 5658, an *Odyssey* copied by Rhosus in Rome in 1479). On the other hand, scholars such as Janus Lascaris continued to write in a mannered personal style (*e.g.,* a letter of Demetrius Chalcondyles of 1488 in the Vatican Library).

Copies in "liturgical" style

By courtesy of the Biblioteca Apostolica Vaticana

Renaissance personal hand. Letter by Demetrius Chalcondyles (autograph), 1488 (Vatican Library; Lat. 5641, fol. 2).

It was on the scholarly hands that Aldus Manutius and other early Italian printers of Greek based their types. But perhaps the most enduring of all styles was that of a group of Cretan scribes who made their way to France and were employed by Francis I in his library at Fontainebleau.

By courtesy of the Bodleian Library, Oxford

Model hand for the design of French Royal Greek type. Copy of Manuel Philes, made by Angelus Vergecius, 1564 (Bodleian Library, Oxford; MS. Auct. F.4.15, fol. 2).

The writing of one in particular, Angelus Vergecius (*e.g.,* his copy of Manuel Philes made in 1564 in the Bodleian Library), was used as a model for the French Royal Greek type, which has influenced the form of Greek printing down to the present day. (R.Ba.)

LATIN-ALPHABET HANDWRITING

Roman book hand

Ancient Roman styles. *Rustic capitals.* The Latin and vernacular handwriting of western Europe descends in an unbroken line to the present day from the point at which it is first observed, in the 1st century AD. The script used throughout the Roman Empire at that time for books and occasionally for formal documents is known as rustic capitals. The pen was cut with a broad end and held so that its thickest strokes fell at an oblique angle to the line of writing, and it was lifted several times in the formation of a single letter. The rustic capital alphabet is "majuscule," in that all the letters are contained between a single pair of horizontal lines. The use of this elaborate script, whose letter forms were the natural outcome of using a broad pen held obliquely, was extended to certain sorts of inscription on stone and other materials, and it is called rustic only by comparison with the magnificent square capitals characteristic of Roman imperial inscriptions, whose forms were governed by the use of the chisel. Square capitals were seldom used in manuscripts except for titles. Rustic capitals continued in use for literary manuscripts until the 6th century, especially for texts of Virgil, but thereafter they appear only in titles, down to the 12th century.

Roman business hand

Cursive capitals. The business hand of the 1st century, used for correspondence and for most documents, private and official alike, is known as cursive capitals. Here the pen, cut to a sharp point, was held at the same oblique angle but was lifted less often, and this "cursive" handling automatically produced new and simpler letter forms such as ∂ (two strokes) for D (three strokes) and Є (two strokes) for E (four strokes). Some of these new letter forms are "minuscule," in that parts of them ascend or descend beyond the body of the letter (h,q) instead of being confined between a pair of lines, as in the majuscule rustic capitals (H,Q).

From the 2nd to the early 4th century, parchment was replacing papyrus as the standard writing material for books, and the codex was replacing the roll as their standard form. The evidence that survives from this period, during which biblical and other Christian literature was beginning to be copied extensively, is fragmentary, and its interpretation is still controversial. The main line of development, however, is clear enough. The elaborate letter forms of rustic capitals, with their numerous pen lifts, began to be abandoned, and experiments were made with new book hands in which the simplified letter forms of cursive capitals were written with a broad pen, sometimes held obliquely in the traditional way and sometimes held "straight," so that its thickest strokes fell at right angles to the line of writing. It was probably the use of a straight pen that produced, for example, the conversion of cursive capital ∂ (axis oblique) into the fully minuscule d (axis vertical).

Uncials, half uncials, and cursive minuscule. At the end of this period of transition, in the 4th and 5th centuries, when the evidence becomes more abundant, two new book hands and a new business hand are found in use. The older of the book hands, called uncials (the name dates only from the 18th century), was originally written with a slightly oblique pen; but, from the 6th century onward, a straight pen was used, and the hand began to look rounder and more contrived. Although it incorporates several of the cursive letter forms (δ, Є, h) of cursive capitals and has two forms peculiar to itself (ᴀ, ᴍ), it also preserves certain forms, such as B, N, R, S, which differ only a little from the forms of rustic capitals; and all three kinds of letters are treated as majuscules, being confined as far as possible between one pair of lines.

From the 4th to the early 7th century, most Christian books—biblical, patristic, and liturgical—were written in the uncial script, and even for pagan literature it al-

Early Roman capitals.
(Top) Rustic capitals. Codex Palatinus, Virgil, 4th–5th century AD (Vatican Library; Pal. Lat. 1631). (Bottom) Cursive capitals. Sale of a slave, AD 166 (British Museum, London; Pap. CCXXIX).

most entirely superseded rustic capitals. It survived the collapse of the Roman book trade. And, after the 6th century, when the production of all books, pagan as well as Christian, was taken over by the church—notably by the monasteries, such as the Vivarium founded in southern Italy by Cassiodorus, a scholar whose aim was to perpetuate Roman culture, and the houses that observed the Rule of St. Benedict—uncial script survived in many centres, especially for biblical and liturgical texts, down to the 9th century. Thereafter, like rustic capitals, uncials were used only for titles, and they, too, disappeared in the 12th century.

The younger of the two new book hands is called half uncial. This script was less popular than uncials and never broke their monopoly of biblical and liturgical texts, although like them it was still being written in the 8th century and even, as a display script for certain purposes, in the 9th. The artificial name half uncial tells nothing about the origin or nature of the script. It differs from early uncials in being written with a perfectly straight pen. One letter (N) remains more or less unchanged from the capital form, but the rest of the alphabet is cursive in origin. The letter forms that differ most from uncials are *a, b, d, g, m, r, s;* and the alphabet as a whole is frankly minuscule, since no attempt is made to confine it between a single pair of lines.

Cursive minuscule as a business hand

The new business hand of the 4th century and after is known as cursive minuscule. Like cursive capitals it was written with a pointed pen, but the pen was held more or less straight. It, too, is a frankly minuscule alphabet

4th–5th century Roman book hands.
(Top) Uncials. Livy, 5th century AD (Bibliothèque Nationale, Paris; Lat. 5730). (Bottom) Half uncials. *De bello Judaico,* Hegesippus, 5th–6th century AD (Biblioteca Ambrosiana, Milan; C.105 inf.).

Cursive minuscule. Avitus of Vienne, 6th century AD
(Bibliothèque Nationale, Paris; Lat. 8913 and 8914).

and uses basically the same letter forms as half uncials, although the frequency in cursive minuscule of ligatures between letters tends to conceal the fundamental likeness between the two hands.

The letter forms that distinguish cursive minuscule and half uncials from rustic and cursive capitals and from uncials were evolved during the obscure period between the 1st and 4th centuries. The question of whether these forms were evolved in the sphere of the book hands or of the business hands is still undecided, but, whatever their origin, their importance for the subsequent history of European handwriting is paramount. They provided the material on which the Caroline (Carolingian) minuscule, first developed in the late 8th century, was based; and that script dominated Europe, in spite of severe modifications, until the end of the Middle Ages. Only in one other period were new letter forms evolved, between the 13th and the 15th centuries, in the group of scripts known as Gothic cursives; and the influence of these late innovations was ultimately cancelled out, thanks to the revival of Caroline minuscule in a pure form by the Italian Humanists at the beginning of the 15th century. (T.J.Br.)

The Anglo-Celtic and other "national" styles (5th to 13th centuries). From the 5th century the relaxation of imperial Roman authority brought on a reassertion and growth of native cultures—that is, wherever the people were not wholly occupied in a savage struggle against barbarians for mere existence. The most isolated places such as the province of Britain responded strongly to this opportunity and at the same time were able to conserve important elements of the Roman civilization. With Ireland, which was never under occupation by the legions, it offered during Europe's darkest age comparative peace and shelter for the development of the richest and most original of book styles.

The Insular manuscripts were produced at monasteries that were often on a barren rock in the sea or at an equally inaccessible site. According to tradition, the earliest centre of Christian learning in Ireland was established by the Romano-British apostle St. Patrick (flourished 5th century AD). A great successor, St. Columba, or Colum-

cille (c. 521–597), whom legend credits with divine scribal powers, founded monastic houses at Derry and Durrow and then journeyed to the Inner Hebrides to found one on the lonely island of Iona in 563. St. Columban, another Irish missionary, in much the same period was founding monasteries on the Continent: c. 590 in Gaul (modern France) the Burgundian centre Luxeuil, from which Corbie in Picardy was organized, and St. Gall in Switzerland and Bobbio in Italy about the years 612 to 614. From Iona a daughter house was founded in 635 on St. Cuthbert's holy isle of Lindisfarne just off the Northumbrian coast of England. To the south the Northumbrian monk, later abbot and saint, Benedict Biscop (c. 628–690) established the twin monasteries of St. Peter at Wearmouth in 674 and St. Paul at Jarrow in 682. He endowed them with splendid collections of books and pictures gathered during repeated visits to Rome, so that, in the late 7th and early 8th centuries, they comprised the most flourishing centre of Christian scholarship in western Europe and the meeting place of Hiberno-British and continental influences.

Insular minuscule. *Historia Ecclesiastica*, by Bede, 8th century AD (British Museum, London; Cotton Tiberius C.11).

For the fine books made in the Anglo-Celtic centres, the majuscular script called Insular half uncial was deemed suitable rather than the pointed, more cursive Irish minuscule used for documents and vernacular texts. There is a high degree of conformity, attesting to their stylistic maturity, among such manuscripts as the Book of Kells (Trinity College, Dublin) and the Lindisfarne Gospels (British Museum, London) individual as they are in detail and ornament. After all, there is room for infinite variation where, in one-quarter of a square inch, 158 interlacements have been traced unerringly—by angels, it is said. The Book of Kells, Codex Cenannensis to paleographers, was probably produced at Iona around 800. It has 339 leaves, 13 by ten inches (33 by 25 centimetres) of noble script in single column, jet black on well-made parchment, through which runs the most spirited and colourful of ornamentation, ranging from the red-dotted outlining of letters, which is as much a feature of the style as the wedge-topped ascenders, to the wildly extravagant full-page initials at the opening of Gospels. The other masterpiece of Anglo-Celtic calligraphy and illumination, the Codex Lindisfar-

Insular Half Uncial. The Book of Kells, c. AD 800. In the collection of Trinity College, Dublin.

nensis, was written in honour of St. Cuthbert shortly after his death in 687. It displays the same lively inventiveness, the love of fantastic animal and bird forms (zoomorphs), intricate interlacing, and even, rhythmic script, set off by generous margins.

The earliest of all extant manuscripts of the Insular style is the *Cathach* ("Battler") of St. Columba (Royal Irish Academy, Dublin), who, according to legend, wrote it himself and, in the judgment of scholars, may actually have done so. Housed in its *cumhdach* (a sort of ark), it was carried into battle to ensure victory.

Besides the proud witness of such books as these to the Anglo-Celtic contribution, there were also the productions of continental centres influenced by St. Columban and his disciples, as well as books mainly in the Roman tradition but carrying the unmistakable sign of Insular influence. For instance, there are three that scholars believe were written in the 7th century at Bobbio, in the monastery of St. Columban. They are Codex Usserianus Primus, now a treasure of Trinity College, Dublin, and two manuscripts preserved in the Biblioteca Ambrosiana, Milan, known as Codex Ambrosianus C.26 sup. and Codex Ambrosianus D.23 sup. There is another, Codex Amiatinus (Biblioteca Medicea-Laurenziana, Florence), of 1,030 leaves measuring 20 by 13½ inches (51 by 34 centimetres), made in Northumbria in the 8th century. It is continental Roman in style with no concession to the Insular habit of ornamentation. This is understandable, for it was designed for presentation to the pope.

Though the Insular minuscule was ready to hand, the majuscular half uncial as the senior script was always given the place of honour and the preference for the fine Latin books of the Anglo-Celtic monasteries. Nevertheless, by the 8th century the minuscule was developing into a disciplined book hand, as seen in the copy of Bede's *Historia Ecclesiastica* (*c.* 731; Cambridge University Library). The spiky, ligatured, compactly written style migrated early to the Continent and, by the beginning of the 8th century, was at home in the Anglo-Saxon foundation of Echternach, in Luxembourg. Fulda and Würzburg, in Germany, were other important centres abroad of Insular culture and book production in this style.

The Merovingian, in France, and the Visigothic, in Spain, are two more varieties of minuscular script that grew out of Latin cursive after the withdrawal of the Roman authority. In the Luxeuil monastery, in Burgundy, the

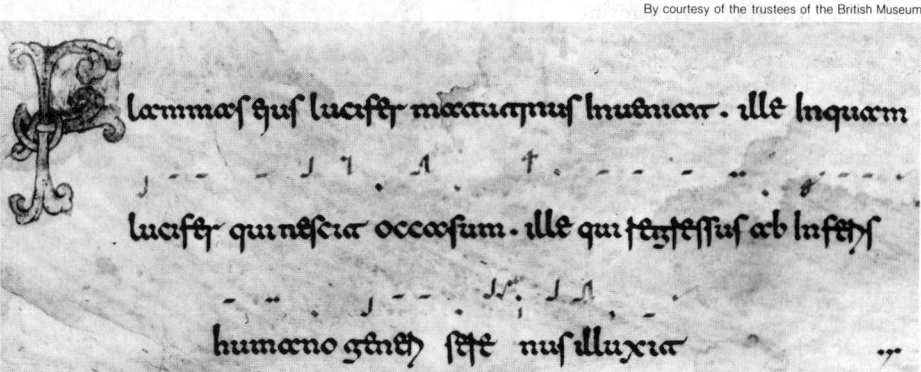

Visigothic minuscule. "Passionale," AD 919 (British Museum, London; Add. 25,600).

minuscule attained in the 7th century the characteristics of a fine book hand, but for only a short period, when the reforms under Charlemagne took effect. In the Iberian Peninsula, the Visigothic style was in use from at least the 8th to the 12th century. It has the verticality of emphasis that is common to the other hands out of the same cursive background, when deliberately written, with weighted ascenders carefully topped by flat serifs.

The South Italian script of the style called Beneventan, nurtured in the motherhouse of the Benedictine Order at Monte Cassino, was the "national" hand that rose to the status of calligraphy and held its position well into the 13th century, an active literary life of more than 500 years. This type of script has a peculiar jerky rhythm and retains individual cursive forms, which, together with the abundance of abbreviations and ligatures, make reading quite difficult.

Carolingian reforms in the scriptorium (8th and 9th centuries). The literary reforms carried on in the latter part of the 8th century and early 9th century by order of the Holy Roman emperor Charlemagne set the highest of standards for the making of books throughout his Western Empire. The extensive educational program, looking forward to new authorized versions of the Vulgate, the missal, and other liturgical works, he placed in charge of the learned English cleric Alcuin of York. The Emperor persuaded Alcuin to leave his position at the head of the cathedral school of York and the excellent library he had gathered there, first to become master of the palace school at Aachen, then at Tours as abbot of St. Martin's to conduct the literary activities centred at the well-established scriptorium (writing room) there.

Before taking up the abbacy in 796, Alcuin was responsible for, or at least inspirer of, the most precious of Carolingian codices, the so-called Golden Gospels. These were a series of illuminated masterpieces mainly written in gold and often on purple-stained vellum. The most famous is the Godescalc Gospels (Bibliothèque Nationale, Paris), written before 783 for Charlemagne, the body of the text in uncials and the dedication in Carolingian minuscule. The most luxurious is the Saint-Médard Gospel Book (Bibliothèque Nationale, Paris), written entirely in gold uncials and illuminated with full miniatures, initials, etc. in gold and silver on purple ground.

Alcuin carried forward the work of the St. Martin scriptorium in the spirit of a true classical renascence. Each variety of traditional letter form was studied with a view to finding its norm by careful comparison with archetypes in ancient monuments and books. Thus, the square capitals, at the top of the hierarchy of scripts, were modelled on Augustan inscriptions. For rustic capitals (*capitales rusticae*), the reformers adopted the style of those used for the text of such fine old codices as the Virgil fragment now in the Vatican. The roman uncial was restored to its simple dignity, as in well-made books of the 6th century, and the minor, or half, uncial was likewise restored to the plain elegance of that earlier period, after the degeneracy of the 7th century.

The model for the most valuable and characteristic of all the Alcuinian contributions, the Carolingian minuscule, has never been precisely determined. It may well have been a local variety of cursive or, more probably, a mixture of half uncial and cursive, in which Alcuin

Merovingian and Visigothic scripts

Contributions of Alcuin

Carolingian minuscule

Beneventan script. Exultet Roll from Monte Cassino, Italy, late 11th or early 12th century AD (British Museum, London; MS. 30377).

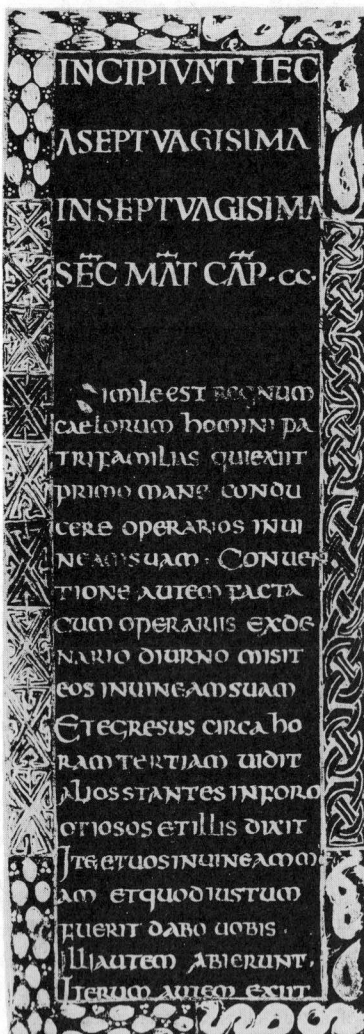

Uncial script. Godescalc Gospels, before AD 783 (Bibliothèque Nationale, Paris).

discerned the possibilities of his clear, round, flexible but disciplined script, comfortable to both scribe and reader. For, as regularized at the scriptorium of St. Martin, the minuscule was written with the shaft of the pen pointing somewhat to the right instead of straight back over the shoulder; though the letters were formed deliberately, even and round, stroke by stroke the same way every time by rule, the writing brought relative ease for the hand and eye. With the years some cursive features became more prominent—*e.g.,* a tendency nearly to join certain letters and an occasional hint of "italic" in the slightly sloping, even, well-spaced lines. The incipits (the opening words of the text) were celebrated by means of display letters and a decorative initial that might come from any one of a number of sources, including Insular, Byzantine, and Merovingian scripts. Otherwise, the classic calm was maintained, supported by the superb arrangement of material on the pages and the excellence of the craftsmanship in carrying through every detail from the manufacture of the skins to the restrained illumination. The crowning achievement of the Tours school of scholars, scribes, and artists was reached in the mid-9th century, under Alcuin's successors, in the Gospels of Lothair (Bibliothèque Nationale, Paris).

There are observable variations among the different Carolingian schools, but these are generally in small details. The most surprising departure is the Utrecht Psalter (University Library, Utrecht), written at Rheims, in rustic capitals and illustrated with fluent pen drawings in the Hellenistic fashion. Apparently, the whole work was devotedly copied in the 9th century from an old model.

The black-letter, or Gothic, style (9th to 15th centuries). Carolingian minuscule remained the unrivalled book hand of western Europe through the 9th century, or nearly so. Then a trend away from the official imperial standards set in. It can be observed progressing in the manuscripts written at St. Gall, in Switzerland, near the end of the 9th century and during the 10th. There is a tendency toward lateral compression of the letters. This begins as the natural result of an easier motion of the pen held in a slanting position—*i.e.,* with the shaft out to the side rather than pointing back over the right shoulder. At such an angle of holding the pen, a nib cut straight across does not deliver body strokes of full thickness to the letters. But the scribes learned to adjust this matter by cutting the pen's writing edge obliquely so that it would be parallel to the top of the page anyway; even though the shaft was held in the slanting position, the nib so cut would yield a perpendicular stroke of maximum width. They were led on by the attractive novelty of bolder and bolder contrasts that eventually were to appear to the eyes of the Italian Humanists in the Renaissance so brutal as to deserve the bad name of Gothic. Nevertheless, the more condensed, compact writing allowed significant economies in the amount of time taken in writing the books and the quantity of materials used and, therefore, in the cost of finished manuscripts.

Black-letter style of increasing density deepened the "colour" of the page and imparted to the northern, advanced, formal variety of book hand a matted aspect, or fanciful likeness to woven fabric, that gave rise to the name Textura. It is called by paleographers *littera textualis formata* or *lettre de forme.* As the script developed through the 11th and 12th centuries in Germany, France, and England, its curves broke into angles. During the 13th and 14th centuries, the size of writing was generally reduced. It became stiffer, and though in the following century (its last of undisputed sway) the script regained size, the proportions were disagreeably narrowed, and the letters, in lines as rigid and mechanically perfect as a picket fence, have angles sprouting hairlines apparently added with a crow quill afterward. Of this species of formal black-letter book hand, two kinds are distinguished by paleographers. One

Lettre de forme

Gospels of Lothair, *c.* AD 850 (Bibliothèque Nationale, Paris; MS. Lat. 266, fol. 19).

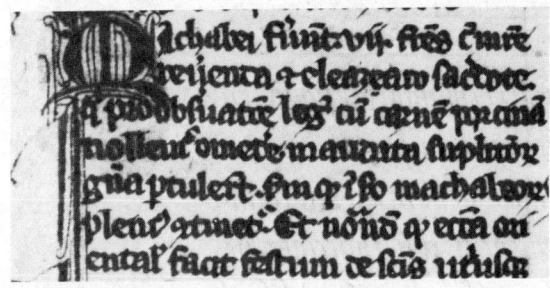

Gothic book hand. *Legenda aurea* by Jacobus de Voragine, 1312 (British Museum, London; Add. 11,882).

stands flat and unseriffed on the base line and is known as *textus prescissus.* The other is completed with square or diamond-shaped feet and is referred to as *textus quadratus.* Though the former, and earlier, variety has superior claims for the calligrapher, the latter is the variety that was carried into printing types and hence into much wider use.

Textus prescissus by Brother Tickhill. "Beatus" page from the Tickhill Psalter, *c.* 1310. In the collection of the New York Public Library.

In Italy the writing during the same period took on weight, but the curves of comparable book script never became angles. The senior script there was the Rotunda, heavy but not pointed. The form persisted for liturgical work both as writing and printing type until late in the Renaissance.

Lettre bâtarde

The north and the south had, of course, their other kinds of writing for court and business or personal uses. A cursive hand that literally flourished in France, Flanders, and England rose to favour in the 15th century as a vernacular book script. This *littera bastarda,* or *lettre bâtarde* as it is termed in the vexed nomenclature of paleography, for all its high style as attained in fashionable books, was close kin to the epistolary "running secretary" commonly written by northern Europeans and early American set-

Lettre bâtarde by Henri de Ferrieres. *Livre du Roy Modus et de la Reine Ratio, c.* 1435 (Pierpont Morgan Library, New York City, M.820, fol. 16ᵛ).

tlers until it grudgingly yielded in the 17th century to italic script.

The scripts of Humanism (14th to 16th centuries). Under the inspiration of the 14th-century Italian poet Petrarch, who started the collecting of ancient manuscripts, coins, medals, and other "antiques," the essentially literary movement called Humanism engaged a group of scholars at Florence in the latter part of the 14th century and opening decades of the 15th. Their growing enthusiasm for antiquity led them on an ever-widening search for Latin books and ancient monuments, in order that they might restore the lost heritage of Rome. Classical authors written in the clear Carolingian minuscule with display lines in lapidary style (*i.e.,* in the style of ancient inscriptions cut on stone) appealed to them as though straight from the time of Cicero instead of from the 10th to 12th centuries. Reverently, Coluccio Salutati, the late-14th-century chancellor of Florence who followed Petrarch as leader of the movement, and his fellow Humanists imitated the old script, which they spoke of as the *lettera antica* to distinguish it from the ordinary *moderna* that belonged to the black-letter style.

Lettera antica and moderna

Two protégés of Salutati are credited with developing, on the basis of these studies and experiments among old manuscripts, the two fundamental scripts of Humanism. Poggio, at the very beginning of the 15th century, produced the round, formal writing that, after polishing by a generation of scribes, served the new art of printing as prototype of "roman" fonts. He promptly followed up this achievement by introducing into his manuscripts the square capital letters as used on ancient monuments. Later in the century, the rage for epigraphic inscriptions brought such enthusiasts as Cyriacus of Ancona, Felice Feliciano of Verona, and his fellow townsman Giovanni Giocondo into the field and, from Padua, Giovanni Marcanova, Bartolomeo Sanvito, and Andrea Mantegna. They compiled their researches in great *sillogi,* or anthologies, which, among other uses, gave calligraphers authoritative patterns for letter forms, ornament, and the correct spacing and placing of all display elements in their books. Feliciano, a calligrapher fond of ornament and fertile in invention, about 1460 first demonstrated how to construct the monumental roman capitals according to geometrical rules.

Humanistic scripts.
(Top) *De oratore,* by Cicero, calligraphy by Poggio, *c.* 1425 Laurentian Library Florence; Ms. Laur, Plut. 50.31. C. 166). (Bottom) *Cicero,* calligraphy by Niccolò Niccoli, *c.* 1423 (Biblioteca Nazionale Centrale, Florence; Soppr., 1.1.14).

The second style of Humanistic script appears earliest in the writings of Poggio's friend Niccolò Niccoli, who was also an accomplished scribe. His slightly inclined cursive, written with a fairly narrow rounded nib at a good rate of speed, was to be to the printers' "italic" what the Poggian hand became to their "roman." Niccoli's innovation employed movements and rhythms close to those of the ordinary black-letter cursive familiar in everyday affairs. Indeed the script contains a sprinkling of current black-letter mannerisms and lends itself similarly to the joining or tying together of letters. The special character of this *antica corsiva* results from the narrowing of the bodies of letters due to the rapid up and down movement of the pen, facilitated by its being held with the shaft pointing at an angle away from the shoulder instead of straight back, producing this ✕, not ✛. As in italic fonts to this day,

Antica corsiva

the form of *a* is distinctive; and *f, g, k,* and *ʃ* (long *s*) are all more or less reminiscent of black-letter current habits. For his headings Niccoli preferred roman capitals "italicized" by a slight inclination to the right.

Cancellaresca formata by Giovanni Battista Palatino. Manuscript specimen book, *c.* 1550
(Bodleian Library, Oxford; MS. Canon. Ital. 196, fol. 44r).

Both scripts were at once taken up and spread by other able scribes working at Florence in the first half of the 15th century, of whom the work of Giovanni Aretino, Giacomo Curlo, and Antonio di Mario, among others, is well recognized.

Poggio himself in 1403 had promptly carried his new script to Rome, where he later became papal secretary. Both scripts were devoted exclusively to the service of Latin literature, but there was a difference. Poggio used his hand as a calligrapher, while Niccoli used his as a copyist. The manuscripts of the former are set forth on fine parchment with meticulous care to formal details, such as even lines at the right-hand margin, and with handsome embellishment. Those of the latter are on paper, compactly and rapidly written, with attention to legibility and textual accuracy above all. There is an interesting parallel in the printed books of the following century. Ambitious Renaissance folios are set in fine roman types, while the well-edited but cheap little student books are just as naturally set in italic.

Influence of printing   Typographic printing displaced the copyists. At the same time printing gave impetus and new significance to the work of the calligraphers. They accepted the challenge of mechanized writing and for a while responded by turning out the finest of Humanistic masterpieces. In the late 15th century and early 16th century, the Paduan Sanvito and Pierantonio Sallando of Mantua, for instance, not only wrote the round Humanistic script in a fashion worthy of the richest miniatures and illumination, but they also honoured the slender proportioned "italic" script by promoting it to a place in some of their most proud and precious manuscripts.

Sanvito's folio and octavo classics in the Humanistic cursive are also celebrated for vellum pages stained purple, yellow, green, or salmon pink and for lines of inscriptional capitals alternating gold, blue, lake, purple, violet, and green. The *antica corsiva* perfected by 15th-century papal scriptors for rapidly inditing briefs issued by the chancery also won its way as the chosen medium of polite correspondence. Thus, in the 16th century, the versatile *lettera da brevi,* or *cancellaresca* (chancery cursive), lively yet disciplined, responsive to wide variety in cut of nib and speed of movement, attainable by the novice and gratify-

Cancellaresca, or chancery cursive

ing to the adept either as book or epistolary hand, became a vehicle of the new learning throughout Christendom.

As written by the early-16th-century calligrapher and printer Lodovico degli Arrighi of Vicenza, the *cancellaresca* can range from eye-arresting contrasts of almost Gothic thick and thin strokes to a delicate, supple monotone tracery. The ascending letters, instead of terminating in serifs as with Sanvito or Sallando, now wave plumelike to the right, and the descenders are tending to balance them with a swing to the left. In 1522 Arrighi published at Rome his modest though revolutionary work *operina da imparare di scrivere littera cancellaresca.* This, the earliest of printed writing manuals, or copybooks, held out to the public clear, simple directions with woodcut examples and invited everyone to learn in a few days how to write this fashionable hand for themselves. In effect, it announced the end of the era of the scriptorium and the beginning of the era of the writing master. Dependence upon attracting pupils and gaining a reputation with the public was thereafter reflected in the tendency to exploit novel or flashy scripts and extravagant ornament.

Writing manuals and copybooks (16th to 18th centuries). The Arrighi *Operina's* devotion to the chancery cursive is matched only by Gerardus Mercator's *Literarum Latinarum* (1540). Arrighi's second publication, *Il modo de temperare le penne* (1523), is a more normal performance for the calligrapher, notary, printer, and erstwhile scriptor of apostolic briefs in the role of writing master. Here the scripts described are as follows: *littera a merchanti,* cursive black-letter mercantile hand; *littera per notari,* small cursive semi-black-letter style, slightly inclined; *littera da bolle,* large carefully formed black-letter cursive; *littera da brevi,* chancery cursive; roman capitals, large Humanistic round hand; round black-letter interlaced initials; ribbon initials; large inscriptional roman capitals; large decorated formal Gothic minuscule; large round outline Gothic; *littera formata,* black-letter in two sizes. The specimens are completed with another page of smaller interlaced Gothic initials and two pages of type specimens, including the cramped italic as seen in books produced by the Aldine Press in Venice and the free calligraphic style first shown here. This book redresses the balance in favour of the popular scripts.

Arrighi's elder contemporary and possible mentor, Giovanni Antonio Tagliente, writing master to the Venetian chancery, published his *Presente libro* in 1524, two years after the *Operina;* and Giovanni Battista Palatino published in 1540 at Rome his *Libro nuovo d'imparare a scrivere.* Though Tagliente was master of an elegant *cancellaresca*—his "living hand" is displayed in a holograph supplication to the Doge and council of Venice, 1491—as well as of the black-letter hands, he was out of date and prey to the vices of the old professional; *e.g.,* his chancery specimens include a page of script leaning excessively to

Littera cancellaresca. Brief of Pope Leo X, ascribed to Lodovico degli Arrighi, 1519 (Public Record Office, London; S.P. 1/19).

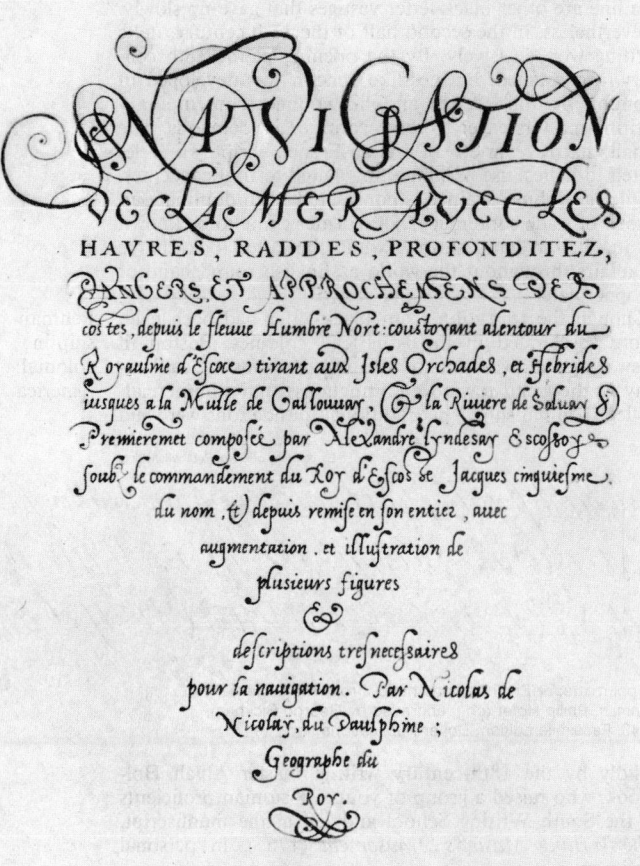

Chancery cursive attributed to Pierre Hamon. *Navigation*, title page from the Harleyian manuscript, *c.* 1560 (British Museum, London; MS. 3996, fol. 1).

the right, and facing it is a page of similar script leaning away to the left, almost equally hard to read and useless. Unlike the author's own hand in his 1491 supplication, the woodcut models here are acutely pointed. Palatino at the same time exhibits a rigid, sharp-angled *cancellaresca formata* in his excellent manuscript specimen (Bodleian Library, Canon. Ital. 196 fol. 44r), while his popular manuals offer relatively easygoing models for learners. In particular, the Palatino *cancellaresca romana* is a normal even-toned script, modest as to bulbed ascenders (*testegiatta*) and angle of inclination, displaying in its forms hospitality for *bastarda* variations (*i.e.,* Gothicizing *g, h, k, r*). The fact that Palatino's *Libro nuovo,* besides being the most complete, was the most widely disseminated of mid-16th-century books on writing, bespeaks certain latitudinarian qualities along with marvellous virtuosity. The summit of absurdity in 16th-century writing manuals was

reserved for Ferdinando Ruano, a Spanish scribe working in the Vatican Library, whose *Sette alphabeti* (1553) demonstrated by means of diagrams how to construct the chancery letters geometrically.

The propagation of the chancery cursive abroad was furthered by native manuals too. The Latin letters called italics were introduced into Germany by Casper Neff's *Thesaurium artis scriptoriae* (1549); into Spain by a disciple of Palatino, Juan de Yciar, in his *Recopilacion subtilissima* (1548); into France by Pierre Hamon's *Alphabet de l'invention des lettres en diverses escritures* (1561); and into England by means of *A Booke Containing Divers Sortes of Hands* (1570) by Jean de Beauchesne and John Baildon. This last was a translation of the French senior author's *Thrésor d'escripture,* believed to have been published at Lyons 20 years earlier; since no copy has been found, first place goes by default to the Hamon book.

Spread of chancery cursive

The pure Italian chancery hand was the favourite of court circles and Humanist scholars through the second half of the 16th century. In England Roger Ascham, mid-16th-century schoolmaster to kings and queens, wrote and taught an exemplary *cancellaresca,* as did the late-16th-century Cambridge don Bartholomew Dodington. These and other educated Europeans generally wrote the black-letter "running secretary," too, the script of Shakespeare, who gave voice to no more than a sturdy nationalism when he poked fun at the newfangled "sweet Roman hand." For their part, the writing masters, in striving to reach an ever larger public, increasingly emphasized the compromise script intended to bring learners already indoctrinated in the common Gothic cursive to command more readily the fashionable italic style. The *Opera nella quale si insegna a scrivere,* of Vespasiano Amphiareo (Albertacci), had already offered at Venice in 1554 models that combined the overdisciplined strokes of Palatino with elements of black-letter mercantile hands (*e.g.,* loops and running ligatures); to this hybrid *cancellaresca* that he claimed as his own invention, Amphiareo gave the accurate name of *bastarda.* Then Gianfrancesco Cresci of Milan, a Vatican scriptor, published his *Essemplare* (1560), to herald the oncoming Baroque and to reject vehemently the works and ways of Palatino and all his academic sort. He replaced their most stylish broad, chisel-bevelled nib and meticulous

Importance of Cresci

Running secretary hand. Letter by Roger Ascham, 1552 (British Museum, London; Landsdowne 3).

building up of disjoined strokes with a narrow, rounded-off pen flexible enough to respond to pressure and fluent in dashing off his much-inclined italic *bastarda* topped off dramatically with bulbous *testegiatta*. It is not too

Bastarda script. Writing manual by Vespasiano Amphiareo (Albertacci), *c.* 1548. In the Harvard College Library, Cambridge, Massachusetts.

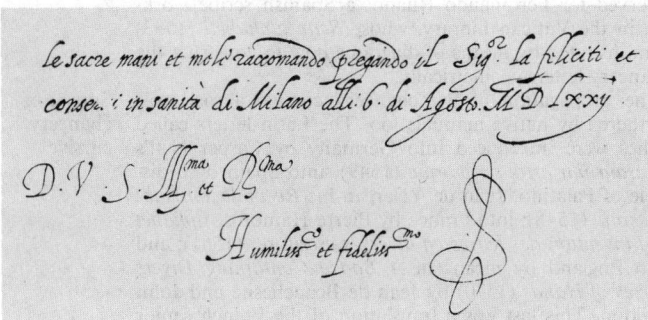

Italic *bastarda*. Letter by Gianfrancesco Cresci, 1572 (Vatican Library; Lat. 6185, fol. 135 R).
By courtesy of the Biblioteca Apostolica Vaticana

much to say that Cresci's script, with the handsome set of swash capitals (to borrow the typographic term for these free-swinging forms), not only established a revolutionary front for 17th-century calligraphy but also contained the germs of 18th-century "copperplate" and even Spencerian scripts. Cresci, by the way, was the first in Italy to take advantage of the sleek allurements of copperplate engraving, though Giuliantonio Hercolani's *Lo Scrittor Utile* (1574; plates engraved in 1571) was a close rival.

The principal French hands of the period were the national black-letter cursive called *lettre françois* or *financière,* which was commonly used in ordinary affairs, and the aristocratic *italienne bastarde.* In the Low Countries, examples of excellence are provided by Clement Perret in his *Exercitatio alphabetica* (1569), and by Jan van de Velde in his work *Spieghel der Schriftkonste* (1605), the fame of which was carried down through many generations of English penmen.

It was the period of elaborate and bold "striking" of decorative figures and fanciful shapes by "command of hand." The writing masters did not look upon such ornamental work as mere vain show or necessary proof of prowess, though it was indeed important in promoting a reputation; they prescribed full-arm flourishing for loosening-up exercises, just as teachers later would have pupils perform on mammoth letters or banal push-pulls and oval tunnels.

In Britain and its empire, the *italienne bastarde* was largely disseminated through Edward Cocker's engraved copybooks and manuals. Known variously as the "new mixt current" or the "speedy à la mode," its concessions to the black-letter running secretary include the *e* looped at the top like a latter-day Palmer Method *o* and what has been termed the upside-down *r,* which is easily misread as *u* by Humanistic eyes. The *d* with a backswept stem and the *h* formed of a loop terminating in a wiggle below

the line are other black-letter vestiges that gave up slowly. Nevertheless, in the second half of the 17th century, italic writing won decisively. By the opening of the 18th century, a chastened, businesslike version was developed in London by John Ayres and his younger contemporary writing masters eager to serve commercial demands. The small, narrow variety of Italian-French script was relegated to ladies' use as something suited to frail capacities, while the robust strain was considered fit to dominate an epoch of trade supremacy. The former came to be known as the Italian hand simply, while the latter took charge of affairs throughout the world as English round hand or "copperplate."

Though the transition from black-letter had been even more accelerated in the American colonies, Boston in New England was one of the last bastions of calligraphy in the trend toward countinghouse and commercial-college penmanship. The traditional foundations were laid

Penmanship in colonial America

By courtesy of Dover Publications, Inc.

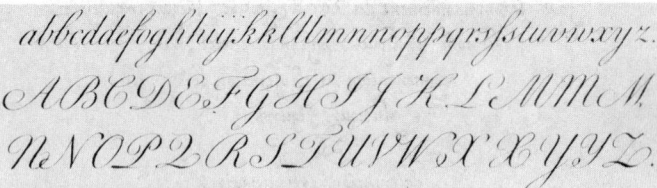

Copperplate, or English round hand. From *The Universal Penman,* Philip Hofer (ed.), engraved by George Bickham, 1743. Facsimile edition, Dover Publications, Inc., 1941.

solidly by the 18th-century writing master Abiah Holbrook, who raised a group of young Bostonian proficients at the South Writing School and left a fine manuscript, *The Writing Master's Amusement* (1767), in personal testimony.

As the 19th century advanced, the competition constantly mounted among systematists emphasizing the plain, practical business hand and decrying the "ornamental branches." Those who loved to flourish quill pictures of bounding deer or calligraphic portraits of national heroes were increasingly placed on the defensive. Gifted penmen such as Nathaniel Duren Gould and Platt Rogers Spencer were almost apologetic when they let their hand go in a moment of professional ebullience. Certain religious sects clung to their heritage of individual styles of writing as an art. The Shakers, for example, under the influence of visions wrote, and drew elaborate spiritual manuscripts. Most of these pieces that still remain are in the round hand and Spencerian scripts of their contemporary world. Other religious sects, such as the Moravians and Mennonites settled in Pennsylvania, produced out of their background old-

By courtesy of the Columbia University Libraries, New York

Spieghel der Schriftkonste, calligraphy by Jan van de Velde, 1605. In the Columbia University Libraries, New York.

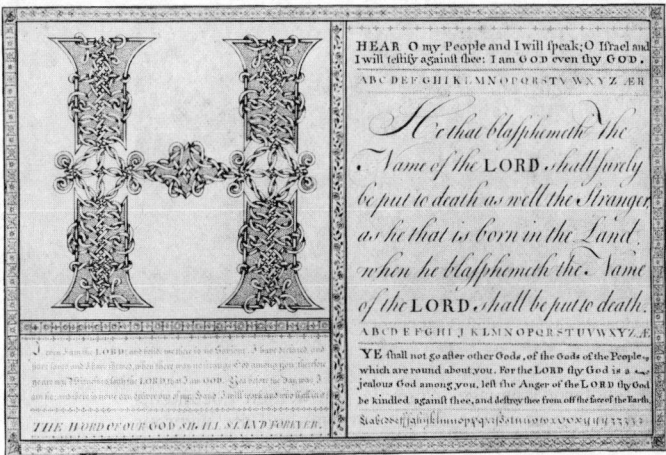

The Writing Master's Amusement, by Abiah Holbrook, 1767. In the Harvard College Library, Cambridge, Massachusetts.

By permission of the Harvard College Library, Cambridge, Massachusetts, Department of Printing and Graphic Arts

country culture bold and handsomely coloured decorative pieces generally called Frakturs because of the script in which their so-called "Pennsylvania Dutch" is presented.

Revival of calligraphy (19th and 20th centuries). The revival of calligraphy at the end of the 19th century was part of an artistic revolt against the mechanization of life. A nostalgic sense of the social losses resulting from industrialization was expressed in social-reformist and arts and crafts movements. About 1870 the English writer and artist William Morris had begun to concentrate attention on the ancient practice of scribes and to study with pen on parchment the means of achieving similar results. In this fashion he wrote out and illuminated a number of texts, Humanistic and medieval, in the years before he took

By courtesy of the Victoria and Albert Museum, London

"Praise of Venus," from *A Book of Verse,* calligraphy by William Morris, 1870. In the Victoria and Albert Museum, London.

up similarly the study of 15th-century printing prior to establishing the Kelmscott Press. His searching inquiries and patronage led papermakers and ink suppliers, among others, back to forgotten standards. His Socialist teaching turned attention to the satisfaction of mastering traditional handicrafts, thus adding to the ideal enjoyment of life and the sum of beauty.

Influence of Edward Johnston
Among those who heeded the message was Edward Johnston. He abandoned studies for an intended medical career for those of a scribe. On the basis of the Morris investigations and guided particularly by Sydney Cockerell, Morris' secretary, he rediscovered how to cut and sharpen reeds and quills, how to hold the chisel-nibbed

By courtesy of the Newberry Library, Chicago, the Wing Collection

Et haec est annunciatio, quam audivimus ab eo, et annunciamus vobis: Quoniam Deus lux est, & tenebrae in eo non sunt ullae.

Manuscript copy sheet by Edward Johnston, 1918. In the Newberry Library, Chicago.

pen so as to produce the kinds of writing that had become familiar in his study of old manuscripts, and every detail of how to make manuscripts. In 1899 he began teaching in London, first at the Central School of Arts and Crafts and, two years later, at the Royal College of Art. His early pupils soon became esteemed designers of lettering and influential calligraphers—*e.g.,* Anna Simons, Eric Gill, Noel Rooke, Graily Hewitt, and Percy Smith. In 1906 he published the basic manual *Writing and Illuminating, and Lettering,* 500 pages profusely illustrated with his own and Rooke's drawings and with reproductions from historic manuscripts. It contains, among other things, a chapter by Gill on cutting inscriptions in stone and material on gilding by the specialist Hewitt. In 1910 the book was published in Germany, where it supported the work independently begun by Rudolf von Larisch in Vienna and carried on by Rudolf Koch and Anna Simons. Under the Nazi regime, the Gothic exponents enjoyed a resurgence, but, after the war, such skilled young German calligraphers as Hermann Zapf led the way back to roman and italic script styles. Jan Tschichold's work has been influential in the appreciation of classical letters for present-day uses.

Art schools everywhere gradually followed the Royal College of Art in offering courses in lettering and writing; these, along with sound forms, instilled a sense of responsibility to a rich heritage. Accordingly, type design passed from the control of engineers into the hands of artists and calligraphical scholars, such as Stanley Morison, Jan van Krimpen, Akke Kumlien, Bruce Rogers, Frederic W. Goudy, Victor Hammer, Berthold Wolpe, and Warren Chappell. The "freezing" of fine alphabets as font material stabilizes them and multiplies their influence. The effects were not limited simply to the printed or manuscript page or to book covers and jackets; all kinds of private and public markers and memorials, addresses, diplomas, and even the politicians' ubiquitous testimonial "scrolls" were touched by reform or at least by some consciousness of shortcoming. The stylish lapidary capitals, italics, and sloped letters engraved on boxwood by Reynolds Stone for printing or cut on tablets of either wood or stone by John Howard Benson, Will Carter, or David Kindersley are at once distinctively contemporary and lambent with tradition.

Though the United States was a decade behind Britain in organizing an arts and crafts movement, four years before the Johnston Bible a Boston architect, Frank Chouteau Brown, brought out a surprisingly sophisticated book, *Letters and Lettering: A Treatise with 200 Examples* (1902). He praised Morris' initiative but wished for more classical balance; he pointed to the neglect of italics and gave them generous space, including specimens from the Lucas 1577 *Arte de escrivir,* "letra del Grifo," *bastarda,* and others. In 1905 *The Parable of the Prodigal Son,* fashioned like a Humanistic manuscript by William Addison Dwiggins and printed from photoengraved plates, was offered for sale. Dwiggins, as illustration for a talk on early writing books, copied a page out of the 1542 Tagliente he had picked up in Europe and passed out prints of it at the December 29, 1913, meeting of the Society of Printers—thereby leading the revival of *cancellaresca.* Other graphic artists concerned in the movement included Thomas Maitland Cleland and Rudolph Ruzicka.

Edward Johnston's pupils, and their pupils, organized in 1921 the Society of Scribes and Illuminators, "zealously directed toward the production of books and documents" by hand and the advancement of the crafts of member scribes, gilders, and illuminators. The program of this professional group based in London is conducted by means of lectures, publications, and exhibitions. In the 1930s exhibits travelled to five American centres, as well as to Paris and Copenhagen. Members representing the several crafts have collaborated in the making of the rolls of honour for the Royal Air Force and United States Air Force, at St. Clement Danes Church, London. The society has served as a model for similar activities abroad, notably the organization in The Netherlands under the leadership of Jan van Krimpen. In 1952 the British society, with Alfred Fairbank as president, recognized the rising popular interest in italic handwriting by instituting the Society for Italic

Revival of calligraphy in the United States

Handwriting, which soon attracted a large international membership of teachers and amateurs.

In the United States individual enthusiasts and informal groups fostered calligraphy outside the art schools. Ernst F. Detterer in Chicago, who had lessons from Johnston in 1913, headed such a group at the Newberry Library for many years and, when he died in 1947, was succeeded by James Hayes. In Portland, Oregon, the instruction and copybooks of Lloyd J. Reynolds, a professor of art in Reed College, had significant influence. For decades Paul Standard in New York practiced and preached *cancellaresca corsiva* and saw the italic reform gain.

20th-century writing manuals and copybooks

Since Johnston a series of manuals and copybooks centring attention on handwriting improvement have proceeded from the espousal of the rather heavy Humanistic hand he admired to an italic that at least implies more speed. Stanley Morison presciently picked out a model for his own hand from Johnston's *Writing and Illuminating, and Lettering* as early as 1913, and a scholar of calligraphy, James Wardrop, called that manuscript "the fons et origo" of his paleographical studies; it is, as Johnston says, a semiformal 16th-century Italian cursive, skillful but a bit colourless to the eye. The fullest and most practical work on the italic is by Alfred John Fairbank, *A Handwriting Manual* (1932). The author places before his book as frontispiece a page of the *bastarda* of Lucas, *Arte de escrivir*, 1577. J.H. Benson's work *The First Writing Book* (1955) consists of the text and examples of the Arrighi *Operina* translated and admirably written out by the editor and furnished with practical clarifications and notes for the learner. Since Johnston calligraphical research and publishing activities have also produced a handsome and scholarly shelfful of books on related forms, most notably the Renaissance capitals.

(Ra.N.)

EARLY SEMITIC WRITING

During the 2nd millennium BC, various Semitic peoples at the eastern end of the Mediterranean were experimenting with alphabetic writing. Between 1500 and 1000 BC, alphabetic signs found in scattered sites showed a correspondence of form and provided material for sound translations. Bodies of writing from this period are fragmented: a few signs scratched on sherds or cut in stone. Few of these are celebrated in terms of aesthetic value.

One interesting set of Semitic inscriptions was discovered in 1905 at an ancient mining site on the Sinai Peninsula. A sphinx from that discovery yields the taw, nun, taw, or t, n, t, meaning "gift." It is evident that the nun, or n, sign is a rendering of a serpent. Most of the early Semitic alphabetic signs were similarly derived from word signs of more ancient vintage. Early Semitic inscription letters are somewhat stiff in visual quality.

The several Semitic peoples in the Near East area spoke languages that were closely related, and this enabled them to use the same set of alphabetic signs. After some experimentation the alphabet was reduced to 22 signs for consonants. There were no vowel signs. The tribes of Canaan (Hebrews, Phoenicians, and Aramaeans) were important in the development of alphabetic writing, and all seemed to be employing the alphabet by 1000 BC.

Phoenician contributions

The Phoenicians, living along a 20-mile (30-kilometre) strip on the Mediterranean, made the great sea their second home, giving the alphabet to Greeks in the mutual trading area and leaving inscriptions in many sites. One of the finest Phoenician inscriptions exists on a bronze cup from Cyprus called the Baal of Lebanon (Louvre, Paris) dating from *c.* 800 BC. The so-called Moabite Stone (Louvre, Paris), *c.* 850 BC, has an inscription that is also a famous example of early Semitic writing.

Old Hebrew. Old Hebrew existed in inscription form in the early centuries of the 1st millennium BC. The pen-written forms of the Old Hebrew alphabet are best preserved in the 13th century AD documents of the Samaritan sects.

The period of exile suffered by the Israelites (from 586 to 538 BC) dealt a heavy blow to the Hebrew language, since, after their return from exile, Aramaic was the dominant language of the area, and Hebrew existed as a second

The Moabite Stone, *c.* 850 BC (Louvre, Paris; AO 5066).
By courtesy of the Cliché Musées Nationaux, Paris

and scholarly language. Aramaic pen-written documents begin to appear in the 5th century BC and are vigorous interpretations of inscription letters. As may be observed in the Aramaic document (MS. Pell. Aram. XIV) in the Bodleian Library at Oxford, the penman has cut the pen

By courtesy of the Bodleian Library, Oxford

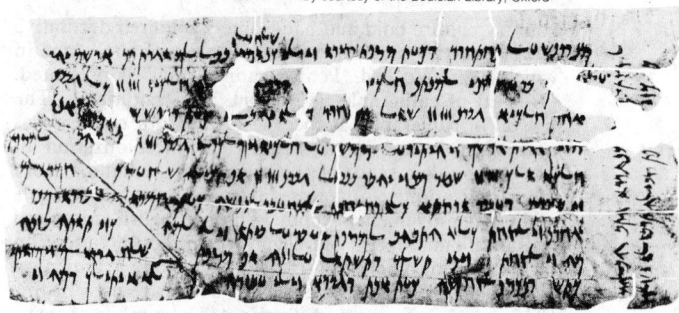

Aramaic pen-written document, 5th century BC (Oxford, Bodleian Library; MS. Pell. Aram. XIV).

wide at the tip to produce a pronounced thick and thin structure to the line of letters. The penman's hand was rotated counterclockwise more than 45 degrees relative to vertical, so that vertical strokes were thinner than the horizontal strokes. Then, too, there is a tendency to hold these strong horizontals on the top line, with trailing descenders finding a typical length, long or short on the basis of ancient habits. The *lamed* form, which has the same derivation as the Western L, resembles the latter and can be picked out in early Aramaic pen hands through its characteristic long ascender.

Merubbaʿ script

The traditional square Hebrew, or *merubbaʿ*, pen hand was developed in the centuries preceding the Christian Era. This early script may be seen in the famed Dead Sea Scrolls discovered in 1947. These scrolls are associated with a group of dissident Jews who founded a religious commune on the northwestern shore of the Dead Sea about 180 BC. The commune had an extensive library. Pens were the instruments of writing, and, as in earlier Aramaic documents, leather provided the surface. Again the *lamed* form is visually prominent.

By courtesy of the Shrine of the Book, The Samuel and Jeane H. Gottesman Centre for Biblical Manuscripts, The Israel Museum, Jerusalem

Merubbaʿ pen hand. The *Thanksgiving Psalms*, portion of the Dead Sea Scrolls, *c.* 1st century AD (the Shrine of the Book, Jerusalem; vol. 10).

There are no Hebrew manuscripts from the first 500 years of the Christian Era. Most of the development in the square Hebrew script occurred between AD 1000 and 1500. The earliest script to emerge from the Dead Sea writing was the Early Sefardic (Spharadic), with examples dating between AD 600 and 1200. The Classic Sefardic hand appears between AD 1100 and 1600. The Ashkenazic style of Hebrew writing exhibits French and German Gothic overtones of the so-called black-letter styles (see above) developed to write western European languages in the late Middle Ages. German black-letter with its double-stroked heads and feet was difficult for the scribe. Hebrew scripts from this period exhibit some of the same complicated pen stroking and change of pen slant within individual characters. Some decorative qualities of medieval French writing are seen in this Hebrew script.

The Sefardic and Ashkenazic styles

It is generally recognized that Hebrew typefaces have in large measure been imitations of various hand scripts and are more slavish in this imitation than those occurring in other language cultures. One of the finest of the early Hebrew types is credited to the Frenchman Guillaume Le Bé, the excellent 16th-century punch cutter.

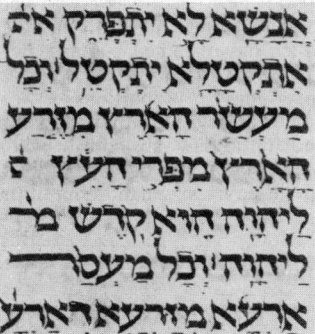

Medieval Hebrew scripts.
(Left) Sefardic script, before AD 1331; in the Vatican Library (7. Vat. heb. 12. Hagiographa). (Right) Ashkenazic script, AD 1295; in the Vatican Library (6. Urbinas heb. 1. Biblia).

Spread of Aramaic to the Middle East and Asia. Aramaic was the mother of many languages in the Middle East and Asia. Generally, the Canaanite-Phoenician influence went west from Palestine, while Aramaic became an international language spreading east, south, and north from the eastern end of the Mediterranean Sea. Never sponsored by great political power, the Aramaic script and language succeeded through inherent efficiency and because the Aramaeans were vigorous traders and extensive travellers in the millennium preceding the birth of Christ.

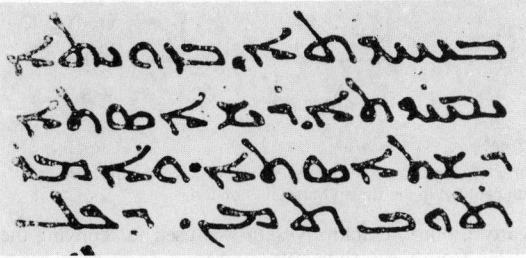

Estrangela script, c. AD 474 (British Museum, London; Add. 17,182, Aphraatis demonstrationes Edessa exar.).

One of the important languages to derive from Aramaic was Syriac. It was spoken over large areas to the north and east of Palestine, but the literature emerged from a strong national church of Syria centred in the city of Edessa. The development of Syriac scripts occurred from the 4th to the 7th century AD, and its most important script is called Estrangela.

Eastern Christendom was riddled with sects and heretical movements. After 431 the Syriac language and script split into eastern and western branches. The western branch was called Serta and developed into two varieties, Jacobite and Melchite. Vigorous in pen graphics, Serta writing

Serta and Nestorian writing

Jacobite script, AD 1481 (Vatican Library; 30.b Vat. syr. 18).

shows that, unlike the early Aramaic and Hebrew scripts, characters are fastened to a bottom horizontal. Modern typefaces used to print Syriac, which has survived as a language, have the same characteristic. Eastern Syriac script was called Nestorian after Nestorius, who led a secession movement from the Orthodox Church of Byzantium. The Nestorian church flourished in Persia and spread along trade routes deep into Asia, a fact observed by Marco Polo. (D.An.)

ARABIC CALLIGRAPHY

In the 7th and 8th centuries AD, the Arab armies conquered for Islām territories stretching from the shores of the Atlantic to Sind (now in Pakistan). Besides a religion, they brought to the conquered peoples a language both written and spoken. The Arabic language was a principal factor in uniting peoples who differed widely in race, language, and culture. In the early centuries of Islām, Arabic was not only the official language of administration, but also was and has remained the language of religion and learning. The Arabic alphabet has been adopted by the Islāmic peoples' vernaculars just as the Latin alphabet by the Christian West.

The Muslim believes that God (Allāh) revealed the Qur'ān to the prophet Muḥammad through the Archangel Gabriel as intermediary. For him, not only the sense but also the very words of the sacred text are inspired; and that is why in the Islāmic world the Qur'ān is recited not in the vernacular but in the original Arabic. The apparent great respect for the written word of God clearly explains the reason why calligraphy was accorded a high rank among the arts and why copying the Qur'ān was esteemed a most meritorious act. The names recorded of those who excelled in the art of writing far outnumber those of architects, painters, and craftsmen.

The Arabic script was evolved probably during the 6th century AD from Nabataean, a dialect of Aramaic current in northern Arabia. The earliest surviving examples of Arabic before Islām are inscriptions on stone.

Arabic is written from right to left and consists of 17 characters, or outlines, certain of which by the addition of dots placed above or below the character provide the 28 letters of the Arabic alphabet. Short vowels are not included in the alphabet, being indicated by signs placed above or below the consonant or long vowel that they follow. Certain characters may be joined to their neighbours, others to the preceding one only, and others to the succeeding one only. When coupled to another, the form of the character undergoes certain changes.

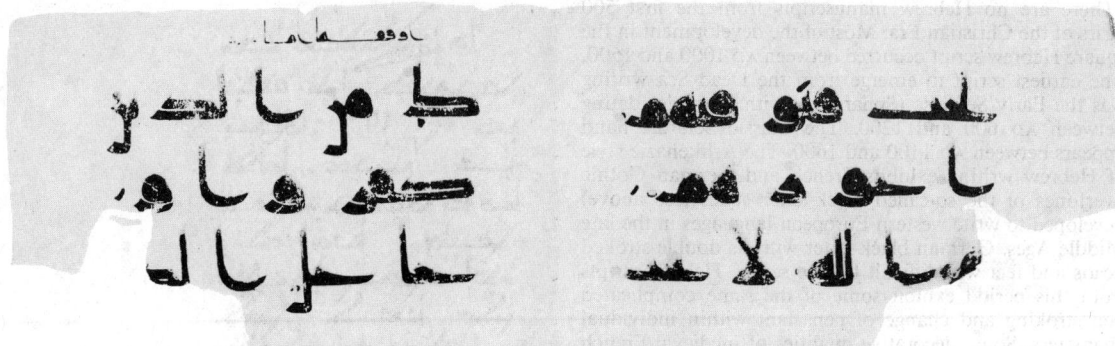

Kūfic script. Double page opening of a Qur'ān from Syria, 9th century AD. In the collection of R. Pinder-Wilson.

These features, as well as the fact that there are no capital forms of letters, give the Arabic script its particular character. A line of Arabic suggests an urgent progress of the characters from right to left. The nice balance between the vertical shafts above and the open curves below the middle register induces a sense of harmony. The peculiarity that certain letters cannot be joined to their neighbours provides articulation. For writing, the Islāmic calligrapher employs a reed pen (*qalam*) with the working point cut on an angle. This feature produces a thick downstroke and a thin upstroke with an infinity of gradation in between. The line traced by a skilled calligrapher is a true marvel of fluidity and sensitive inflection, communicating the very action of the master's hand. Even in monumental inscriptions, whether on stone or some other kind of intractable material, the craftsman still endeavors to retain this sense of the guiding hand by graduating the thickness of his line.

Kūfic script

Broadly speaking, there were two distinct scripts in the early centuries of Islām: cursive script and Kūfic script. For everyday purposes a cursive script was employed: typical examples are to be seen in the Arabic papyri from Egypt. Rapidly executed, the script does not appear to have been subject to formal and rigorous rules; and not all the surviving examples are the work of professional scribes. Kūfic script, however, seems to have been developed for religious and official purposes. The term Kūfic means the script of Kūfah, an Islāmic city founded in Mesopotamia in AD 638; but the actual connection between the city and the script is not clear. Kūfic is a more or less square and angular script. In monumental and funerary inscriptions in stone, the angular forms may be partly dictated by the material. Professional copyists employed a particular form for reproducing the earliest copies of the Qur'ān that have survived. These are written on parchment and date from the 8th to the 10th century. They are mostly of an oblong as opposed to codex format. The writing is frequently large, especially in the early examples, so that there may be as few as three lines to a single page. The script can hardly be described as stiff and angular; rather, the pace is majestic and measured. Arab scholars writing in this early period record numerous scripts. Unfortunately, their descriptions do not allow researchers to determine the precise nature of these.

Kūfic went out of general use about the 11th century, although it continued to be used as a decorative element contrasting with those scripts that superseded it. About AD 1000 a new script was established and came to be used for copying the Qur'ān. This is the so-called *naskhī* script, which has remained perhaps the most popular script in the Arab world. It is a cursive script based on certain laws governing the proportions between the letters. The two names associated with its development are Ibn Muqlah and Ibn al-Bawwāb, both of whom lived and worked in Mesopotamia. Of the latter's work a single authentic example survives, a manuscript of the Qur'ān in the Chester

Establishment of *naskhī* script

Maghribī script. Qur'ān from northwest Africa or Spain, 13th–14th century. In the British Museum, London.

Beatty Library, Dublin. *Naskhī* was used for copying the Qur'ān from the 11th century onward.

The conception of proportional relationships between the letters gave rise to other scripts, more or less variants on *naskhī;* these include the large and majestic *thuluth* script, which came to be adopted for many of the large copies of the Qur'ān produced from the 13th century. In Mamlūk Egypt of the 14th and 15th centuries, the *ṭūmār* script was also used for large Qur'āns.

Distinctive scripts were developed in particular regions. In Spain, the *maghribī* ("western") script was evolved and became the standard script for Qur'āns in North Africa. Derived ultimately from Kūfic, it is characterized by the exaggerated extension of horizontal elements and of the final open curves below the middle register, as well as by certain orthographic peculiarities.

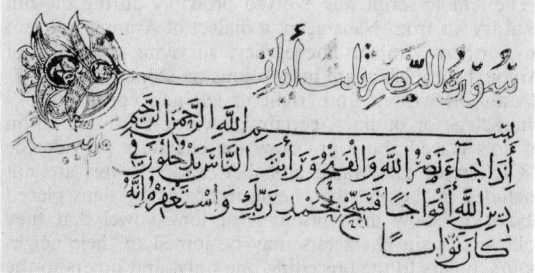

Naskhī script. Baghdad Qur'ān copied by Ibn al-Bawwāb *c.* 1000 (Chester Beatty Library, Dublin; MS. 1431, fol. 283).

Both Persia and Turkey made important contributions to calligraphy. In these countries the Arabic script was adopted for the vernacular. The Persian scribes invented the *taʿlīq* script in the 13th century. The term *taʿlīq* means "suspension" and aptly describes the tendency of each word to drop down from its preceding one. At the close of the same century, a famous calligrapher, Mīr ʿAlī of Tabriz, evolved *nastaʿlīq,* which, according to its name, is a combination of *naskhī* and *taʿlīq.* Like *taʿlīq* this is a fluid and elegant script, and both were popularly used for copying Persian literary works.

A characteristic script developed in Ottoman Turkey was that used in the chancellery and known as *divani.* This script is highly mannered and rather difficult to read. Peculiar to Turkish calligraphy is the *tuğra* (*ṭughrā*), a kind of royal cipher based on the names and titles of the reigning sultan and worked into a very intricate and beautiful

Kharoṣṭī inscription on leather, 3rd century AD (British Museum, London; Find Spot n. N.XV. 350).

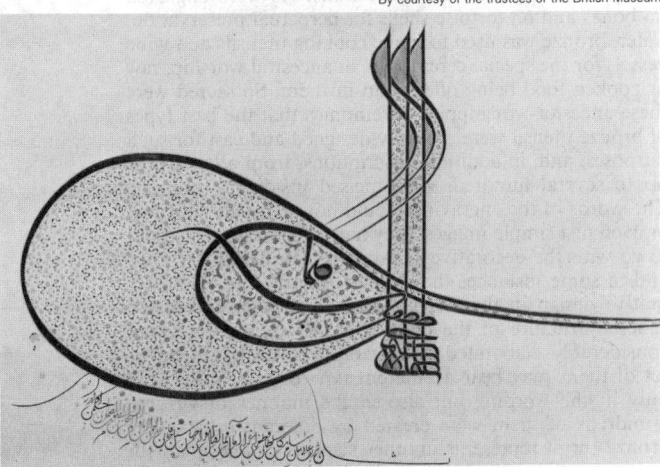

Tuğra of Süleyman the Magnificent, 16th century. In the British Museum, London.

design. A distinctive *tuğra* was created for each sultan and affixed to imperial decrees by a skilled calligrapher, the *neshani.*

There has always existed in the Islāmic world a keen appreciation of fine handwriting, and, from the 16th century, it became a practice to assemble in albums specimens of penmanship. Many of these assembled in Turkey, Persia, and India are preserved in museums and libraries. Calligraphy, too, has given rise to quite a considerable literature such as manuals for professional scribes employed in chancelleries.

In its broadest sense, calligraphy also includes the Arabic scripts employed in materials other than parchment, papyrus, and paper. In religious buildings, verses from the Qurʾān were inscribed on the walls for the edification of the faithful, whether carved in stone or stucco or executed in faience tiles. Religious invocations, dedications, and benedictory phrases were also introduced into the decoration of portable objects. Generally speaking, there is a close relationship between these and the scripts properly used on the conventional writing materials. It was often the practice for a skilled penman to design monumental inscriptions.

(R.H.P.-W.)

INDIC CALLIGRAPHY

The most important examples of calligraphy to develop from Aramaic writing in its dissemination through southern and Central Asia were the scripts of India, especially of Sanskrit, the ancient Indo-European language of the subcontinent. Indic writing first appeared in the 3rd century BC during the reign of Aśoka (c. 273–232 BC). Leader of a great empire, Aśoka turned from military success to embrace the arts and religion. Aśoka's edicts were committed to stone. These inscriptions are stiff and angular in form. Following the Aśoka style of Indic writing, two new calligraphic types appear: Kharoṣṭī and Brāhmī. Kharoṣṭī was used in the northwestern regions of India from the 3rd century BC to the 4th century of the Christian Era,

and it was used in Central Asia until the 8th century. It is characterized by a vigorous pen letter, reflecting the influence of Near East calligraphy.

Copper was a favoured material for Indic inscriptions. In the north of India, birch bark was used as a writing surface as early as the 2nd century AD. Many Indic manuscripts are written on palm leaves, even after the Indian languages were put on paper in the 13th century. Both sides of the leaves were used for writing. Long rectangular strips were gathered on top of one another, holes were drilled through all the leaves, and the book was held together by string. Books of this manufacture were common to Southeast Asia. The palm leaf was an excellent surface for penwriting, making possible the delicate lettering used in many of the scripts of southern Asia.

Visually, Sanskrit is associated most closely with the alphabetic form named Devanāgarī. In a 15th-century pen-written manuscript in the Freer Gallery at Washington, D.C., it can be observed that the pen's nib is cut wide, giving a considerable difference in thick and thin strokes. The alphabetic signs hang down from a strong horizontal top line that may become connected. Through the years the strong horizontal and vertical emphasis of inscription writing has been preserved in the Devanāgarī script, and modern typefaces and teaching manuals stress this stiffness of execution. In informal documents this historical script can have more warmth and grace. (D.An.)

Sanskrit pen-written document, 15th century AD (Freer Gallery, Washington, D.C.; MS. 23.3).

EAST ASIAN CALLIGRAPHY

In China, Korea, and Japan, calligraphy is a form of pure art. Chinese, Korean, and Japanese calligraphy derive from the written form of the Chinese language. Chinese is not an alphabetical language; each character is composed of a number of differently shaped lines within an imaginary square. The early Chinese written words, like the Egyptian hieroglyphs, were pictorial images, though not so close to the objects they represented as in the ancient Egyptian writing. Rather, they were simplified images, indicating meaning through suggestion or imagination. These simple images were flexible in composition, capable of developing with changing conditions by means of slight variations.

Side notes (left margin):

Development of *taʿlīq* and *nastaʿlīq* in Persia

Kharoṣṭī and Brāhmī scripts

Side notes (right margin):

Devanāgarī script

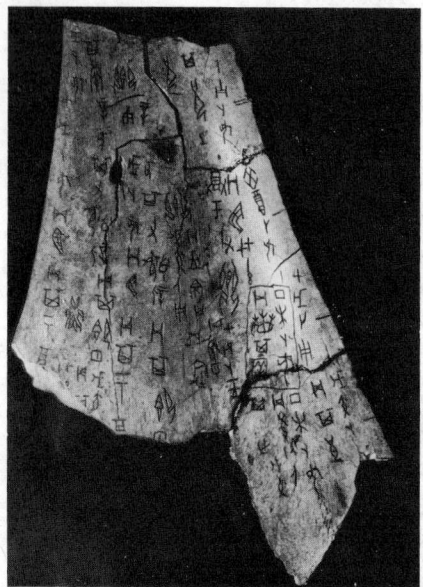

Chia-ku-wen (Chinese shell-and-bone script), Shang
dynasty (18th–12th century BC). In the East Asian
Library, Columbia University, New York.

Shell-and-
bone script

Chinese calligraphy. The earliest known Chinese
ideographs are engraved on the shoulder bones of large
animals and on tortoise shells. The piece illustrated contains a number of the early ideographs; each seems to
have been carefully composed before being engraved on
the bone. Although they are not entirely uniform in size,
the variations are not great. The figures must have evolved
from rough and careless scratches in the still more distant
past. This *chia-ku-wen,* or shell-and-bone script (18th–
12th century BC), is the earliest stage of development in
Chinese calligraphy.

It was said that Ts'ang Chieh, the legendary inventor
of Chinese writing, got his ideas from observing animals'
footprints and birds' claw marks on the sand as well as
other natural phenomena. He then started to work out
simple images from what he conceived as representing
different objects such as those that are given below:

Surely, the first images the inventor drew of these
few objects could not have been quite so stylized
but must have undergone some modifications to reach
the above stage. Each image is composed of a minimum number of lines and yet is easily recognizable.
Nouns no doubt came first. Later, new ideographs
had to be invented to record actions, feelings, and
differences in size, colour, taste, etc. Something was
added to the already existing ideograph to give a
new meaning. The ideograph for deer, for instance,

is  , not a realistic image but a very much sim-

plified structure of lines suggesting a deer by its horns,
big eye, and small body, which distinguish it from other

animals. When two such simple images  are

put side by side, the meaning is "pretty," "prettiness,"
"beautiful," "beauty," etc., which is obvious if one has
seen two such elegant creatures walking together. But,
if a third image is added above the other two, as

, it means "rough," "coarse," and even

"haughty." This interesting point is the change in meaning
through the arrangement of the images. If the three stags
were not standing in an orderly manner, they could become rough and aggressive to anyone approaching them.
From the aesthetic point of view, three such images could
not be arranged side by side within an imaginary square
without cramping one another, and in the end none would
look like a deer at all.

After the shell-and-bone script came writing on bronze
vessels, known as bronze script. In the early days of divina-
tion, when the kings of the Shang dynasty (18th–12th century BC) tried to solve their problems by consulting their
ancestors and deities, the latter's answers were engraved
on bones and on tortoise shells for perpetual preservation.
Later, bronze was used to make cooking utensils and wine
vessels for the special ceremonies of ancestral worship, raw
or cooked food being offered up in them. So sacred were
these ancestor-worshipping ceremonies that the best types
of bronze utensil were specially designed and cast for such
purposes, and, in addition, inscriptions, from a few words
up to several hundred, were incised inside the bronzes.
The words of the engravings could not be roughly formed
or even just simple images; they had to be well worked out
to go with the decorative ornaments outside the bronzes,
and in some instances they almost became the chief decorative design in themselves. Though they preserved the
general structure of the bone-and-shell script, they were
considerably elaborated and beautified. Each bronze or
set of them may bear a different type of inscription, not
only in the wording but also in the manner of writing.
Hundreds of them were created by different artists. The
bronze script represents another stage of development in
Chinese calligraphy, known as *chin-wen* ("metal script"),
ku-wen ("ancient script"), or *ta chuan* ("large seal") style
of writing.

Before long a unification of all types of the bronze script
was enforced when China was united for the first time
in the 3rd century BC. The first emperor of Ch'in, Shih
Huang-ti, could be regarded as one of the most terrible
dictators in the history of mankind, for he burned Confucian books, buried Confucian scholars alive, and sacrificed
thousands and thousands of lives to build the Great Wall
to protect himself and his empire; but he did one great
thing for the Chinese in unifying their writing, and by
this they have been bound together ever since. The First
Emperor's prime minister, Li Ssu, was given the task of
working out the new script, and no other type was allowed to be used. Here are some common words that can
be compared with similar words in bone-and-shell script
mentioned above:

Bronze
script

The *hsiao
chuan,* or
small-seal
style

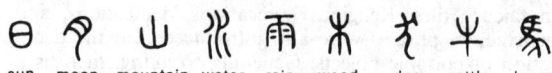

This was the third step forward in the development of Chinese calligraphy, known as *hsiao chuan* "small-seal" style.

In the small-seal style of writing, all lines are drawn of
even thickness, and more curves and circles are employed.
Each word tends to fill up an imaginary square, and a
passage written in small-seal style has the appearance of
a series of equal squares neatly arranged in columns and
rows, each of them balanced and well-spaced. The Chinese practice the small-seal style when aiming at future
attainments in calligraphy. They use only the tip of a
long-haired brush, which is almost suspended in the air;
no light pencil sketches can be drawn first. It is a hard
task and good training.

The uniformity of writing in China was established
chiefly for the purpose of meeting the growing demands
for documented records. Unfortunately, the small-seal
style could not be written speedily and was therefore
not entirely suitable. Another stage of development was
needed—the fourth stage, which is called *li shu,* or of-

Hsiao chuan ("small seal" style). Rubbing of a copy of Li Ssu's writing engraved on a stone epitaph, Ch'in dynasty (221–206 BC).
By courtesy of Chiang Yee

The *li shu*, or official style

ficial style. The Chinese word *li* here means "a petty official" or "a clerk"; *li shu* means a style specially devised for the use of clerks. If examined carefully, *li shu* is found to contain no circles and very few curved lines. In other words, all the circles became squares, and the curved parts of the lines became angular. Short straight lines, vertical and horizontal, are chiefly used. Because of the speed needed for writing, the brush in the hand tends to move up and down, and an even thickness of line cannot be enforced. As the thickness varied, artist-writers could concentrate more on the artistic shaping of the lines. Thus, a door opened for developments in Chinese calligraphy.

Li shu is thought to have been invented by Ch'eng Miao (240–207 BC), who had offended the First Emperor of Ch'in and was serving a ten-year sentence in prison. He spent his time in prison working out this new development, which not only facilitated speed in writing but opened up seemingly endless possibilities for later calligraphers. According to their own artistic insight, they evolved new variations in the shape of lines and also in construction. The words in *li shu* style tend to be square or slightly rectangular horizontally. Though the even thickness of lines is relaxed, the rigidity in the shaping of them is still there; for instance, the vertical lines had to be shorter, and the horizontal ones longer. As this curtailed the freedom of hand for individual artistic taste, another stage of development came into being—the fifth stage, which is called *chen shu* (*k'ai shu*), or regular style. There is no record of who invented this style, but it must have been in evolution for a long time, at least since the 1st century AD if not earlier. The Chinese still use this regular style of writing today; in fact, what is known as modern Chinese writing is almost 2,000 years old, and the written words of China have not changed since the first century of the Christian Era.

Development of the *chen shu*, or regular style

Since about 1950, it has been claimed that the formation of the Chinese written language has changed. This is a serious misunderstanding; the only change is that a certain number of words can now be written and printed with a simplified construction. Most of those simplifications had long been in use in the grass style of writing dating back as far as the regular style, but they were not permitted in documents and records, in books, and in making type for print-

ing. Only those who had never been familiar with the grass style of writing mistook them for newly invented forms.

Before coming to the grass style, the regular style, or *chen shu,* must be explained. "Regular" here means "proper"—"the proper style of Chinese writing" used by all Chinese for government documents, printed books, public and private dealings in important matters ever since its establishment. Since the regulations for the civil-service examination enforced in the T'ang period (AD 618–907), each candidate had to be able to write a good hand in regular style. This Imperial decree deeply influenced all Chinese who wanted to become scholars and enter the civil service. This examination was abolished in 1905, but most Chinese still try to acquire a hand in regular style even to the present day.

In *chen shu* each line, each square or angle, and even each dot can be shaped according to the will and taste of the calligrapher. Indeed, a Chinese word in regular style presents an almost infinite variety of problems of structure and composition, and, when executed, it presents to the onlooker a design whose abstract beauty can draw the mind away from the literal meaning of the word itself.

The greatest exponents of Chinese calligraphy were Wang Hsi-chih (died 379) and his son Wang Hsien-chih in the 4th century. Few of their original works have survived, but a good number of their writings were engraved on stone tablets, and rubbings were made from them. Many great calligraphers imitated their styles, but none ever surpassed them. Since the 7th century there have been many master calligraphers such as Ouyang Hsün (557–641), Sun Kuo-t'ing (died 688), Ch'u Sui-liang (596–658), Yen Chen-ch'ing (709–785), Liu Kung-ch'üan (778–865), Su Tung-p'o (1036–1101), Huang T'ing-chien (1045–1105), Mi Fei (1051–1107), the Sung emperor Hui Tsung (1100–1125/ 26), and Chao Meng-fu (1254–1322). A noted modern calligrapher was Yü Yu-jen (1878–1964).

Wang Hsi-chih not only provided the greatest example in the regular style of writing but also relaxed the tension somewhat in the arrangement of the strokes in the regular style by giving easy movement to the brush to trail from one word to another. This is called *hsing shu,* or running style, as if the hand were walking fast while writing. This, in turn, led to the creation of *ts'ao shu,* or grass style, which takes its name from its appearance—as if the wind had blown over the grass in a manner disorderly yet orderly. The English term cursive writing cannot describe the Chinese grass style, for even a cursive hand can be deciphered without very much difficulty.

But Chinese words in grass style are greatly simplified

The *hsing shu,* or running style, and the *ts'ao shu,* or grass style

By courtesy of the National Palace Museum, Taipei

閏中秋月
桂彩中秋特地圓況當餘
閏中秋月
經月兔使詩人嘆隔年
閃魄澄鮮因懷勝賞初
萬氣斂光增浩蕩四溟收
夜助嬋娟鱗雲清廓心
田豫兼興能無賦詠篇

Chen shu ("regular style") written by Emperor Hui Tsung (1100–1125/26), Sung dynasty. In the National Palace Museum, Taipei.

forms of the regular style and can be deciphered only by those who have practiced calligraphy for years. It is not a style for general use but for the calligrapher who wishes to produce a work of abstract art.

Technically speaking, there is no mystery in Chinese calligraphy. It depends on the skill and imagination of the writer to give interesting shapes to his strokes and to compose beautiful structures from them without any retouching or shading and, most important of all, with well-balanced spaces between the strokes. This balance needs years of practice and training.

The tools for Chinese calligraphy are very few—good ink, ink stone, a good brush, and good paper (some prefer silk). Even a child can fill up a squarish space with lines—straight or curved or circular—but to fill it so as to liberate the visual beauty of the linear shapes and composition depends on artistic insight and the training of a master.

The fundamental inspiration of Chinese calligraphy, as of all arts in China, is nature. In *chen shu,* or regular style, each stroke, even each dot, suggests the form of a natural object. As every twig of a living tree is alive, so every tiny stroke of a piece of fine calligraphy has the energy of a living thing. This is very different from the strokes in a printed word. Printing does not admit the slightest variation in the shapes and structures, but strict regularity is not tolerated by Chinese calligraphers, especially those who are masters of the *ts'ao shu.* A finished piece of fine calligraphy is not a symmetrical arrangement of conventional shape but, rather, something like the coordinated movements of a skillfully composed dance—impulse, momentum, momentary poise, and the interplay of active forces combining to form a balanced whole.

The study of Chinese calligraphy is the study of a highly advanced form of art with two keynotes—a simulation in every stroke and a dynamic equilibrium in the structure.
(C.Y.)

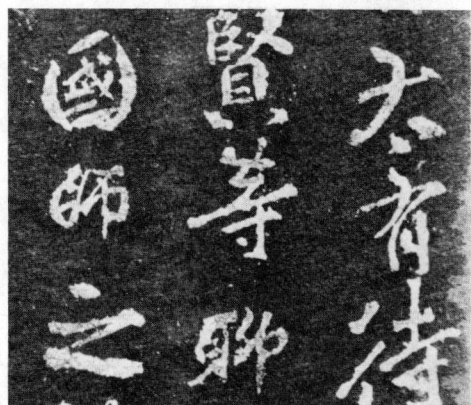

Rubbing of stone engraving by Kim Saing (711–791), Unified Silla period.

Korean calligraphy. Koreans have used Chinese characters probably since the 2nd or 3rd century AD. Even after the invention of the Korean alphabet in 1447, Chinese was used as the official script until the 19th century. Thus, traditional Korean calligraphy was in Chinese rather than in Korean.

A few inscribed stone monuments remain from the Three Kingdoms period (*c.* 57 BC–AD 668). Ancient Koreans, eager to adopt Chinese culture, developed a calligraphy reflecting contemporary Chinese styles. In the following Unified Silla dynasty (668–935), a devotion and adherence to the T'ang culture of China gave birth to such great masters of calligraphy in Korea as Kim Saing and Choi Ch'i-wŏn, whose styles of writing basically followed those of the Chinese calligraphers Ou-yang Hsün and Yü Shih-nan.

The angular, squarish style of Ou-yang Hsün, Yü Shih-nan, and Yen Chen-ch'ing, inherited from the Silla dynasty, continued in the Koryŏ period (918–1392) until around 1350, when the rounded, fluent style of the Chinese calligrapher Chao Meng-fu, of the Yüan dynasty, was introduced and became the vogue. Since that time the *chao* style has remained the basic undercurrent in Korean calligraphy.

At first the calligraphy of the Yi dynasty (1392–1910)

The *chao* style

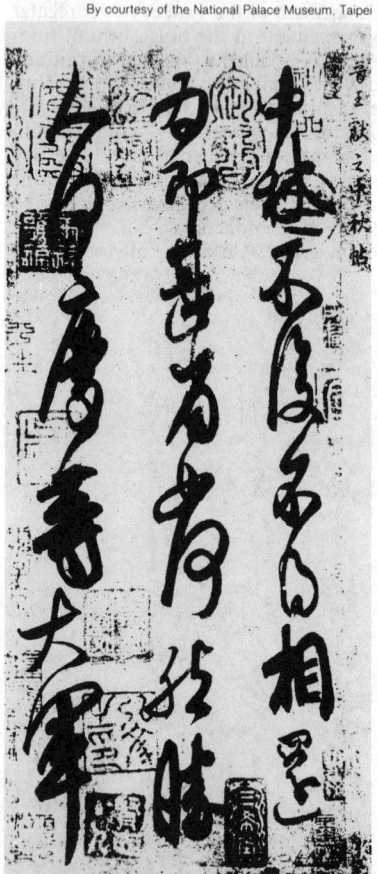

Hsing shu ("running style") and *ts'ao shu* ("grass style") by Wang Hsien-chih (AD 344–388), Six Dynasties period. In the National Palace Museum, Taipei.

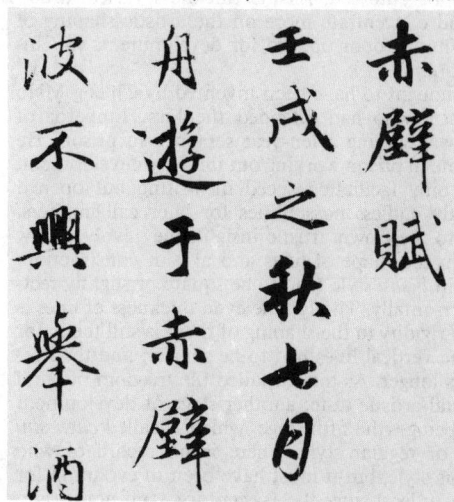

Chao style. *Hs'ing-shu* written by Chao Meng-fu (1254–1322). In the National Palace Museum, Taipei.

followed the *chao* style, but, early in the 16th century, a mannered, vulgar style began to be evident. Responsible for the Yi style were such noted calligraphers as Han Ho and Yi Kwang Sa.

The 19th century saw, however, the emergence of individual styles related to those of the Chinese calligraphers Su Tung-p'o and Mi Fei of the 11th century, Wen Cheng-ming of the 16th century, and Tung Ch'i-ch'ang of the late 16th and early 17th century. The new trend was the result of Korea's close cultural contacts with Ch'ing China.

Ch'usa style written by Kim Chong Hi (1786–1856), Yi period.

The greatest master of the Yi period was Kim Chŏng Hi, who established the so-called *ch'usa* style. His calligraphy is derived from the *li shu* script of China, but his sense of pictorial composition, harmony within asymmetry, and animation by unmatched, forceful strokes gave him a style completely his own.

A few calligraphers survived from the Yi dynasty into the early decades of the present century. One distraction was the influence of Japanese calligraphy, which began to be felt about 1920.

Since World War II, calligraphy in both North and South Korea has been profoundly influenced by governmental decisions to replace all Chinese characters with words written in the native alphabet. As a consequence, modern Korean calligraphy has been developing along new lines.
(W.-Y.K.)

Japanese calligraphy. The art of calligraphy has long been highly esteemed in Japan as in China. There is no definite record of when the Japanese began to use Chinese words—called *kanji* in Japanese. It is known that a Korean scribe named Wani brought some Chinese books of Confucian classics, such as the *Analects, Great Learning,* and *Book of Mencius,* to Japan near the end of the 4th century AD. From the 7th century onward, many Japanese scholars, particularly Buddhist monks, went to China, and some Chinese went to Japan. As Indian Buddhism reached Japan via Korea and China and took root there, the use of *kanji* in Japan gradually grew. Eventually, *kanji* became the official system of writing in Japan, because it was the instrument for the transmission of Chinese Buddhism.

Kanji script

Most of the Chinese Buddhist monks who went to live in Japan were scholars and good calligraphers; their writings on the Buddhist scriptures and other subjects were highly admired and esteemed not only for their aesthetic value as calligraphy but also because they were the work of devout personalities and induced a sense of religious awe in the readers.

Many of the early Japanese emperors were ardent Buddhists and also acquired a masterly hand in *kanji* writings. So did many Japanese Zen priests, whose calligraphy tended to exercise a religious effect upon the Japanese mind. Theirs became a special type of calligraphy in Japan, namely, Japanese Zen calligraphy, or *bokuseki.*

Naturally, it was unsuitable for Japan to adopt an entire foreign language like Chinese, and Japanese thinkers began to devise a new, native script known as *hiragana,* which was often referred to as "women's hand," or *onna-de* in Japanese. It was used particularly in the writing of Japanese poetry and had an elegant and graceful appearance. Thus, in Japanese calligraphy there are two different and distinctive types of writing, one in *kanji* and the other in *hiragana.* Among the best known Japanese calligraphers are Kūkai (Kōbō Daishi), Emperor Saga, Michikaze, Fujiwara Yukinari, the Zen priest Daitō, and Ryōkan. Hisamatsu Shinichi, a modern authority on Zen, has made unique contributions to Japanese calligraphy.

There are many outstanding pieces of Japanese calligraphy in *kanji,* but they are not distinctive when compared with their Chinese counterparts. Japanese *hiragana* calligraphy, however, stands out prominently and proudly, especially in the style of *remmen-tai,* in which the *hiragana* are written continuously and connected together without break, and in *chōwa-tai,* in which some *kanji* words join hands with the *hiragana.* Japanese calligraphy in *remmen-tai* or in *chōwa-tai* has some resemblance to the Chinese grass style, but the two are easily distinguishable. In Chinese grass style, although the words are greatly simplified and several words can be joined together with trailing strokes, each separate word normally still retains its regular spacing within an imaginary square, big or small. But Japanese *hiragana* cannot be spaced so separately and evenly. Therefore, a whole piece of *remmen-tai* calligraphy looks like a big bundle of beautiful silk strings hanging down confusedly yet artistically, as if the calligrapher had arranged them quite unconsciously. They were arranged consciously of course, but the calligrapher

Hiragana calligraphy

kanji	hira-gana	transliteration	description
印可狀	いんかじょう	*inkajō*	document of permit approval
字號	じごう	*jigō*	name or title given a monk by his master
法語	ほうご	*hōgo*	words of the law or words of admonition
偈頌	げじゅ	*geju*	gatha or hymn or short moral poem
遺偈	ゆいげ	*yuige*	a will in the form of a gatha or hymn
進道語	しんどうご	*shindōgo*	instruction or words leading disciples to practice the dharma or law
詩	し	*shi*	poetry
額字	がくじ	*gakuji*	tablet with a few words inscribed horizontally
書簡	しょかん	*shokan*	letter or written communication

Figure 10: Types of Japanese Zen calligraphy.

Modern calligraphy by Hisamatsu Shinichi. In the collection of Masao Abe, Kyōto.

By courtesy of Masao Abe, Kyoto

seems to have let his hand move swiftly of its own accord. The separate strokes and dots have no distinctive shape but join other strokes and dots in the following *hiragana.* The strokes or lines in *hiragana* are not shaped like living things, nor are they of even thickness; but there must be good spacing between the strokes or lines and between one *hiragana* and another, so that there is no confusion or blur in the completed piece. This is a highly demanding art, and the whole piece has to be executed with speed and without hesitation. *Hiragana* requires solid training and artistic insight.

To complete the whole piece with its strokes or lines not too varied in shape yet not too even in thickness needs a special training; to keep the tip of the brush at an even distance from the paper, the writer must cultivate a steady hand. It is said that some Japanese calligraphers trained themselves by supporting the arm with a cord hanging from the ceiling, so that the hand would remain at a fixed distance from the paper. (C.Y.)

BIBLIOGRAPHY

General studies: MARCEL COHEN, *La Grande Invention de l'écriture et son évolution,* 3 vol. (1958), emphasizes the relationship of writing to society; DAVID DIRINGER, *The Alphabet: A Key to the History of Mankind,* 3rd ed., 2 vol. (1968), and JAMES G. FEVRIER, *Histoire de l'écriture,* rev. ed. (1959), two works with a descriptive-historical approach; J. FRIEDRICH, *Geschichte der Schrift: Unter besonderer Berücksichtigung ihrer geistigen Entwicklung* (1966), reliable in descriptive presentation, but rather disappointing on the level of the structural-typological approach; I.J. GELB, *A Study of Writing: The Foundations of Grammatology,* rev. ed. (1963); and V.A. ISTRIN, *Razvitiye pisma* (1961), and *Vozniknoveniye i razvitiye pisma,* 2nd ed. (1965), works with a structural-typological approach; HANS JENSEN, *Geschichte der Schrift,* (1925); *Die Schrift in Vergangenheit und Gegenwart,* 3rd ed. (1969; Eng. trans., *Sign, Symbol and Script,* 1970), the descriptive-historical approach. STANLEY MORISON, *Selected Essays on the History of Letter-Forms in Manuscript and Print,* 2 vol. (1981), describes among other things the development of letters from writing to typesetting; DONALD JACKSON, *The Story of Writing* (1981), includes review of pre- and non-alphabetic systems; WALTER J. ONG, *Orality and Literacy: The Technologizing of the World* (1982), a survey of the development of literacy beginning with alphabetical manuscript culture.

For current information, see the section "Écriture, orthographie" in *Bibliographie linguistique,* published annually by the Comité International Permanent des Linguistes.

Reproductions of writings: FRIEDRICH BALLHORN, *Alphabete orientalischer und occidentalischer Sprachen* (1842; 14th ed., 1906; Eng. trans., *Grammatography: A Manual of Reference to the Alphabets of Ancient and Modern Languages, 1861*); CHARLES FOSSEY (ed.), *Notices sur les charactères étrangers anciens et modernes, rédigées par un groupe de savants,* new ed. (1948); *The Gospel in Many Languages,* specimens of 826 languages in which the British and Foreign Bible Society has published or circulated some portion of the Bible (1956 and later editions); C.R. LEPSIUS, *Standard Alphabet for Reducing Unwritten Languages and Foreign Graphic Systems to a Uniform Orthography in European Letters* (1855; 2nd ed., 1863).

Subgraphemics or semasiography: GARRICK MALLERY, *Pictographs of the North American Indians* (1886) and *Picture-Writing of the American Indians* (1893); HENRY R. SCHOOL-CRAFT, *Historical and Statistical Information Respecting the History, Condition and Prospects of the Indian Tribes of the United States,* pt. 1 (1851). On picture-writing see also J.C. COOPER, *An Illustrated Encyclopedia of Traditional Symbols*

(1978); MATS P. MALMER, *A Chronological Study of North European Rock Art* (1981); ANDRE LEROI-GOURHAN, *The Dawn of European Art: An Introduction to Paleolithic Cave Painting* (1982; trans. from the Italian).

Graphemics: PETER BOODBERG, "The Chinese Script: An Essay on Nomenclature (the First Hecaton)," *Studies Presented to Yuen Ren Chao on His Sixty-fifth Birthday* (1957); R.A. CROSS-LAND, *Graphic Linguistics and Its Terminology, Mechanical Translation,* vol. 3 (1956), republished in *Proc. Univ. Durham Phil. Soc.,* Series B, vol. 1 (1957); C.F. and F.M. VOGELIN, "Typological Classification of Systems with Included, Excluded, and Self-Sufficient Alphabets," *Anthrop. Linguistics,* 3:55–96 (1961); I.J. GELB, "A Note on Morphographemics," in *Mélanges Marcel Cohen,* pp. 73–77 (1970); ROBERT A. HALL, "A Theory of Graphemics," *Acta linguistica,* 8:13–20 (1960); AKIRA NAKAN-ISHI, *Writing Systems of the World: Alphabets, Syllabaries, Pictograms* (1982; originally published in Japanese, 1980).

Alphabets: Almost all of these works contain excellent, copious, and classified bibliographies. A.B. ALLEN, *The Romance of the Alphabet* (1937); M. COHEN, *La Grande invention de l'écriture et son évolution,* 2 vol. (1958), also outstanding; D. DIRINGER, *The Alphabet: A Key to the History of Mankind* (1948; 3rd rev. ed. in 2 vol., 1968); *Writing* (1962), also translations into Russian, Danish, Norwegian, and other languages; E. DOBLHOFER, *Zeichen und Wunder* (1957; Eng. trans., *Voices in Stone: The Decipherment of Ancient Scripts and Writings,* 1961); W.C. DURFEE, *Alphabetics As a Science* (1956); J.G. FEVRIER, *Histoire de l'écriture,* 2nd ed. (1959); J. FRIEDRICH, *Geschichte der Schrift* (1966); I.J. GELB, *A Study of Writing,* rev. ed. (1963); C. HIGOUNET, *L'Écriture* (1955); K.G. IRWIN, *The Romance of Writing, from Egyptian Hieroglyphs to modern Letters, Numbers, and Signs* (1956); V.A. ISTRIN, *L'Écriture, sa classification, sa terminologie* (1957); H. JENSEN, *Die Schrift in Vergangenheit und Gegenwart* (1969; Eng. trans., *Sign, Symbol and Script,* 3rd rev. ed., 1970); W.H. LANGE, *Schriftbibel,* 3rd ed. (1951); S.A.B. MERCER, *The Origin of Writing and Our Alphabet* (1959); A.C. MOORHOUSE, *The Triumph of the Alphabet: A History of Writing* (1953); O. OGG, *The 26 Letters,* rev. ed. (1971); A. PETRAU, *Schrift und Schriften im Leben der Völker* (1939); P. RUDLAND, *From Scribble to Script* (1955); A. SCHMITT, *Untersuchungen zur Geschichte der Schrift,* 2 vol. (1940); K. SETHE, *Vom Bilde zum Buchstaben* (1939); M. SPRENGLING, *The Alphabet: Its Rise and Development from the Sinai Inscriptions* (1931); H. STURM, *Einführung in die Schriftkunde* (1955); S.W. THOMPSON, *The A B C of Our Alphabet* (1942); J. TSCHICHOLD, *Geschichte der Schrift in Bildern* (1946; Eng. trans., *An Illustrated History of Writing and Lettering,* 1947). Later works include ALEXANDER HUMEZ and NICHOLAS HUMEZ, *Alpha to Omega: The Life and Times of the Greek Alphabet* (1981); CAROL BELANGER GRAFTON (ed.), *Bizarre and Ornamental Alphabets* (1981); WILLIAM GARDNER, *Alphabet at Work* (1982); and ALISON HARDING, *Ornamental Alphabets and Initials* (1984).

Hieroglyphs: Books in English on hieroglyphic writing include: A.H. GARDINER, *Egyptian Grammar,* 3rd ed., rev. (1957), with a list of hieroglyphs from the Middle Kingdom; H. PETRIE, *Egyptian Hieroglyphs of the First and Second Dynasties* (1927); F.L. GRIFFITH, *A Collection of Hieroglyphs* (1898); and N.M. DAVIES, *Picture Writing in Ancient Egypt* (1958), a collection of artistically valuable hieroglyphs. See also NORMA JEAN KATAN and BARBARA MINZ, *Hieroglyphics: The Writing of Ancient Egypt* (1981); RICHARD LUXTON AND PABLO BALAM, *The Mystery of the Mayan Hieroglyphics: The Vision of the Ancient Tradition* (1981).

Punctuation: G.V. CAREY, *Mind the Stop,* rev. ed. (1958); and E.H. PARTRIDGE, *You Have a Point There* (1953), are the best guides to modern punctuation as practiced in Britain. The former is short and stimulating; the latter is more exhaustive and includes a chapter on American practice by J.W. CLARK. A comparable American work is the chapter on punctuation in P.G. PERRIN, *Writer's Guide and Index to English,* 4th ed. (1966). The following describe the practice of two famous presses, Oxford University Press and the University of Chicago Press: HORACE HART, *Rules for Compositors and Readers at the University Press,* 37th ed. rev. (1967); and *A Manual of Style,* 12th ed. rev. (1969). For punctuation in antiquity and the Middle Ages, see E.M. THOMPSON, *An Introduction to Greek and Latin Palaeography* (1912); FRANZ STEFFENS, *Lateinische Paläographie,* 2nd ed. (1909); PETER CLEMOES, *Liturgical Influence on Punctuation in Late Old English and Early Middle English Manuscripts* (1952). For punctuation in and since the Renaissance, especially in Britain, see A.C. PARTRIDGE, *Orthography in Shakespeare and Elizabethan Drama* (1964), of which ch. 14 and 15 and appendix VIII are on punctuation; T.F. and M.F.A. HUSBAND, *Punctuation* (1905); and R.A. SKELTON, *Modern English Punctuation,* 2nd ed. (1950). ALEXANDER BIELING, *Das Princip der deutschen Interpunktion, nebst einer übersichtlichen Darstellung ihrer Geschichte* (1880), is useful not only for German practice but for European punctuation in general since the 15th century. For modern practices, consult DAN VENOLIA, *Write Right! A Desk Drawer Digest of Punctuation, Grammar, and Style* (1979).

Shorthand: E.H. BUTLER, *The Story of British Shorthand* (1951), a complete history of early shorthand systems with emphasis on modern British systems; H. GLATTE, *Shorthand Systems of the World* (1959), a short history that emphasizes the extent to which important systems spread to countries other than those in which they originated; L.A. LESLIE (ed.), *The Story of Gregg Shorthand: Based on the Writings of John Robert Gregg* (1964), a complete history that emphasizes the early life of John Robert Gregg, his invention of Gregg shorthand, his promotion of the system in the U.S., and his method of teaching; ISAAC PITMAN, *A History of Shorthand* (1852, rev. ed. 1934), a chronological history of shorthand systems with emphasis on British systems to the end of the 19th century; A.R. RUSSON, *Methods of Teaching Shorthand* (1968), the history of shorthand instruction. Later works on the subject include ROBERT L. GRUBBS, SCOT OBER, and JEROME P. EDELMAN, *Gregg Shorthand for Colleges, Speed Building* (1982); ADELE BOOTH BLANCHARD, *Quickscript* (1983); DORIS H. CRANK, RUTH ANDERSON, and JOHN C. PETERSON, *Methods of Teaching Shorthand and Transcription* (1982).

Western calligraphy: DOROTHY MINER et al., *2,000 Years of Calligraphy* (1965), a comprehensive and well-illustrated catalog of the ambitious three-part exhibition in Baltimore devoted to regions using the Latin alphabet, with especially valuable notes and references from the 1st century down to the 19th; EDWARD JOHNSTON, *Writing and Illuminating, and Lettering*, 14th ed. (1925, continuously reprinted), the gospel of the modern revival by its chief apostle; his *Formal Penmanship, and Other Papers*, ed. by HEATHER CHILD from the master's earlier searching for form (1971); DAVID DIRINGER, *The Hand-Produced Book* (1953), an untidy storehouse of information gathered from acute, far-ranging investigations sketchily indexed; JAN TSCHICHOLD, *Geschichte der Schrift in Bildern* (Eng. trans., *An Illustrated History of Writing and Lettering*, 1946), the brief, perceptive, and personal account by an eminent designer; HERMANN DEGERING (ed.), *Die Schrift* (1929; Eng. trans., *Lettering: A Series of 240 Plates Illustrating Modes of Writing in Western Europe from Antiquity to the End of the 18th Century*, 1929, reprinted 1965), a standard survey of scripts; BERTHOLD L. ULLMAN, *The Origin and Development of Humanistic Script* (1960), the result of reading thousands of documents in the Vatican by a veteran teacher and scholar; JAMES WARDROP, *The Script of Humanism* (1963), by the author of the first-rate studies of papal scriptors in *Signature*: no. 12 (1939, Arrighi); new series, no. 2 (1946, P. Sallando and G. Pagliarlo); no. 5 (1948, Ruano and Cresci); no. 8 (1949, Tagliente); no. 14 (1952, Palatino); JOHN HOWARD BENSON, *The First Writing Book: An English Translation and Facsimile Text of Arrighi's Operina* (1954), all written out in the translator's exemplary italic hand and with his introduction and valuable practical notes; ALFRED FAIRBANK, *A Handwriting Manual*, 3rd ed. rev. (1961), by a British leader of the italic reform movement; ALFRED FAIRBANK and BERTHOLD WOLPE, *Renaissance Handwriting: An Anthology of Italic Scripts* (1960); ALFRED FORBES JOHNSON, "A Catalogue of Italian Writing-Books of the Sixteenth Century," in *Signature*, New Series, no. 10 (1950), and reprinted in part by OSCAR OGG (ed.) in *Three Classics of Italian Calligraphy* (1953); SIR AMBROSE HEAL, *The English Writing-Masters and Their Copy-Books, 1570–1800* (1931), the fundamental biographical and bibliographical work, well illustrated and with an important essay by STANLEY MORISON; RAY NASH, *American Writing Masters and Copybooks* (1959), history and bibliography through the colonial period, with 36 plates; and *American Penmanship, 1800–1850* (1969), a historical essay and bibliography of works with miniature reproductions of title pages. See also LAUREL NICHOLS BRASWELL, *Western Manuscripts from Classical Antiquity to the Renaissance* (1981); JOYCE IRENE WHALLEY and VERA C. KADEN, *The Universal Penman: A Survey of Western Calligraphy from the Roman Period to 1980: Catalogue* (1980); JOYCE IRENE WHALLEY, *The Pen's Excellence: Calligraphy of Western Europe and America* (1980); MARC DROGIN, *Medieval Calligraphy, Its History and Technique* (1980).

Greek calligraphy: E.G. TURNER, *Greek Manuscripts of the Ancient World* (1971), the best general work on the subject (well-illustrated); FRANCHI DE CAVALIERI and JOHANNES LIETZMANN, *Specimina Codicum Graecorum Vaticanorum* (1910), 50 Greek manuscript specimens in the Vatican Library; *Codex Alexandrinus*, 5 vol. (British Museum, 1909–57), a facsimile in reduced size; *The Codex Sinaiticus and the Codex Alexandrinus*, notes by H.J.M. MILNE and T.C. SKEAT (1963), on the origins of the two great Greek uncial Bibles in the British Museum; *Facsimile of the Washington Manuscript of Deuteronomy and Joshua in the Freer Collection* (1910); *Ilias Ambrosiana* (1953), beautiful facsimile of the Homeric codex in the Biblioteca Ambrosiana, Milan (elegant uncial writing). BRUCE M. METZGER, *Manuscripts of the Greek Bible* (1981), is a good introduction.

Latin calligraphy: The best short accounts in English are in BERTHOLD L. ULLMAN, *Ancient Writing and Its Influence*, new ed. (1969); and E.M. THOMPSON, *Introduction to Greek and Latin Palaeography* (1912, reprinted 1964). All Roman books and documents are cataloged (in English) in, respectively, E.A. LOWE, *Codices latini antiquiores*, 12 vol. (1934–71); and ALBERT BRUCKNER and ROBERT MARICHAL (eds.), *Chartae latinae antiquiores*, 4 vol. (1954–67, in progress). The most important monographs are JEAN MALLON, *Paléographie romaine* (1952); and several articles in E.A. LOWE, *Palaeographical Papers 1907–1965*, 2 vol. (1972).

Aramaic and Hebrew calligraphy: G.R. DRIVER, *Semitic Writing from Pictograph to Alphabet* (1948), on the origins of Semitic writing; *Aramaic Documents of the Fifth Century BC* (1954); EUGENE TISSERANT, *Specimina Codicum Orientalium* (1914), reproductions of Semitic pen hands; CARLO BERNHEIMER, *Paleografia Ebraica* (1924), many Ashkenazic hands; ADOLF NEUBAUER, *Facsimiles of Hebrew Manuscripts in the Bodleian Library* (1886); MOSES GASTER, *Hebrew Illuminated Bibles of the IXth and Xth Centuries...* (1901); RAFAEL EDELMANN (ed.), *Corpus Codicum Hebraicorum Medii Aevi* (1956), important manuscripts in Hebrew; REUBEN LEAF, *Hebrew Alphabets, 400 B.C. to Our Days* (1950), reproductions of manuscript styles; *The Book of Jonah*, woodcuts by JACOB STEINHARDT, calligraphy by FRANZISCA BARUCH (1953); HENRI FRIEDLAENDER, *Die Entstehung meiner Hadassah-Hebräisch* (1967), on the relationship of Hebrew manuscript styles and types—also in *Typographica 16* under the title "Modern Hebrew Typefaces."

Arabic calligraphy: ANNEMARIE SCHIMMEL, *Islamic Calligraphy* (1970), a stimulating introduction with illustrations, including calligraphy in architecture and the decorative arts, and a useful bibliography; DAVID DIRINGER, *The Alphabet*, 3rd ed., vol. 1, pp. 210–215 (1968), a survey of the history of the Arabic script and its dissemination; NABIA ABBOTT, *The Rise of the North Arabic Script and Its Kurānic Development* (1939), a study of the origins of the Arabic script and its development in the early Islāmic period; BERNHARD MORITZ (ed.), *Arabic Palaeography* (1950), a rich collection of Arabic texts on papyrus and paper up to the 18th century AD; A.U. POPE (ed.), *A Survey of Persian Art*, vol. 2, ch. 8 (1939), deals with Arabic calligraphy in the art and architecture of Persia; V. MINORSKY, *Calligraphers and Painters: A Treatise by Qāḍī Ahmad* (1959), an important work (written in 1606) which illustrates cogently the Islāmic attitude toward calligraphy and calligraphers. See also BASIL GRAY et al. (eds.), *The Arts of the Book in Central Asia, 14th–16th Centuries* (1980).

Chinese and Japanese calligraphy: LUCY DRISCOLL and KENJI TODA, *Chinese Calligraphy*, 2nd ed. (1964); CHIANG YEE, *Chinese Calligraphy*, 3rd ed. (1973); WILLIAM WILLETTS, *Chinese Art* (1958); CH'EN CHIH-MAI, *Chinese Calligraphers and Their Art* (1966); HISAO SUGAHARA, *Japanese Ink Painting and Calligraphy...* (1967); DA—WEI KWO, *Chinese Brushwork: Its History, Aesthetics, and Techniques* (1982).

Korean calligraphy: SUEHARU KATSURAGI, *Chōsen Kinsekikō* (1935), a survey of Korean epigraphy from the Three Kingdoms period to the Koryŏ dynasty that contains discussions of calligraphic styles; EUNG-HYON KIM, "Sang-ko eui Sŏye" (Ancient Korean Calligraphy), "Koryŏ eui Sŏye" (Calligraphy of the Koryŏ Dynasty), "Yi-cho eui Sŏye" (Calligraphy of the Yi Dynasty), and "Hyondae eui Soye" (Modern Calligraphy), all in *Han'guk yesul Ch'ongnam*, ed. by the Academy of Art, Seoul, Korea (1964), the best surveys on Korean calligraphy, by a noted calligrapher; KI-SUNG KIM, *Han'guk Sŏye sa* (1966), a general survey of Korean calligraphy—some chapters are, however, not consistent and thorough in either handling or approach; YONG-YUN KIM, *Hanguk Sŏhwa Inmyŏng Sasŏ: Biographical Dictionary of Korean Artists and Calligraphers* (1959), a biographical dictionary of traditional painters and calligraphers up to the early 20th century (living artists are not included); SE-CH'ANG OH, *Kunyŏk Sŏhwa-jing* (1928), the fundamental biographical dictionary of traditional Korean artists compiled by a connoisseur and calligrapher. ALBERTINE GAUR, *Writing Materials of the East* (1979), describes materials and instruments in their historical development.

Modern calligraphy enthusiasts will find the following works interesting: *Modern Scribes and Lettering Artists,* comp. by THE SOCIETY OF SCRIBES AND ILLUMINATORS (1980); EDWARD M. CATICH and PAUL HERRERA, *Reed, Pen, and Brush Alphabets for Writing and Lettering* (1980); EMMA MACALIK BUTTERWORTH, *The Complete Book of Calligraphy* (1980); DOROTHY MAHONEY, *The Craft of Calligraphy* (1981); PETER JESSEN (ed.), *Masterpieces of Calligraphy, 261 examples, 1500–1800* (1981; trans. from the German); JINNIE Y. DAVIS and JOHN V. RICHARDSON, *Calligraphy: A Sourcebook* (1982); and INTERNATIONAL TYPEFACE CORPORATION, *International Calligraphy Today* (1982).

Yiddish Literature

Yiddish literature consists of literary works written in Yiddish, the main colloquial language of the majority of Ashkenazic (central and east European) Jews. Literature in Yiddish began with the need of the Jews living in the Germanic Frankish lands of western Europe during the Middle Ages for a literature in their own vernacular. Most of them no longer had enough knowledge of Hebrew, which had become the language of prayer and scholarship, to understand fully new works written in it. (Popular literature in Hebrew, which became intertwined with Yiddish traditions, developed much later.) Living among people speaking Middle High German, the Jews had adopted that language, but they continued to need a religious usage terminology, which had to be Hebrew. Thus there evolved an amalgam of the two languages called Jüdisch-Deutsch (Judeo-German), soon corrupted to Yidish-Daytsh; and finally called simply Yiddish. For a time there was little difference between Yidish-Daytsh and Middle High German, except for the infusion of Hebrew words; but eventually (possibly as early as the 9th century) Yidish-Daytsh became a separate language. With the Jewish migrations to eastern Europe after the massacres during the Crusades, the language acquired a strong Slavonic element and, cut off from its German source, subsequently developed on independent lines, flowering into a rich literary language. An oral and manuscript Yiddish literature first appeared in the 12th and 13th centuries, while a printed literature was introduced in the 16th century.

This article provides a historical survey of the development of Yiddish literature. For a discussion of literature in Hebrew, see the article HEBREW LITERATURE.

The article is divided into the following sections:

EARLY WRITINGS

Yiddish, like many other languages, was for a long time looked upon as a vulgar tongue, good enough for the spoken but not the written word. The language of the scholars was Hebrew. When the first Yiddish books were written in the 12th and 13th centuries, they were intended only for women and the ignorant. These works were of two types: religious and liturgical—translations from the Bible, prayer books, and religious poems and secular writing, consisting mainly of adaptations from the German and Italian—the literature of the so-called *Spielmann* period, named after the German minstrels of the medieval period. Jewish folk singers and jesters sang or performed these texts at various entertainments. Most of them were verse romances, tales of knights and their ladies. Some even had erotic connotations. One of the most famous of these works, the *Bove-Buch,* was written in 1507 (and printed in 1541) by Elijah Bachur, more popularly known as Elijah Levita, a German Jew who emigrated to Italy in 1496, a time of trouble for Jews in his native country. Written in ottava rima (an eight-line stanza with a rhyme scheme of ABABABCC), it is a heroic tale adapted from an Italian romance (*Buovo d'Antona*) for its Jewish public. Another work by the same author is *Paris un Viene,* published posthumously in 1595. Both books are rhymed romances, written in the spirit of the Renaissance. They are at the same time fantastic, realistic, and highly

Literature of the Spielmann period [margin note]

dramatic. Another, earlier work, the *Shmuel Buch* (1544; "Samuel Book"), by an unknown writer, is a retelling of the Book of Samuel, with King David possessing all the characteristics of a medieval knight. Rabbis and pious Jews condemned these works as frivolous; but they tolerated them because they recognized that the Jewish woman of the day, who was as often as not breadwinner as well as wife and mother, needed some diversion.

As a result of the catastrophes and expulsions that the German Jews experienced in the wake of the Thirty Years' War (1618–48) in Germany and their subsequent emigration in large numbers to Poland, secular Yiddish literature disappeared for a long time. It did not appear again until the second half of the 18th century. The writings of the interim period were almost all of a religious, didactic nature. The most famous of them is the *Tzeno Ureno,* written by Jacob ben Isaac Ashkenazi of Janov, Poland. It appeared in Prague in 1608. It was a paraphrase of the Pentateuch (first five books of the Old Testament), with the addition of legends and commentaries from the Talmud (authoritative body of Jewish law and tradition), exegeses of Rashi (11th-century scholar and commentator), the Midrash (mystical commentary on the Pentateuch), and other holy books. The language used is much closer to that of modern Yiddish than to that of the earlier, 16th-century works. As late as the beginning of the 20th century it was still customary for women to read this book on the sabbath.

By the second half of the 18th century, Yiddish had become exclusively the language of eastern European Jews. With the coming of the Ḥasidic movement (a revolt, based on mystical enthusiasm, against the aridity of rabbinic intellectualism), a number of Ḥasidic storybooks began to appear in Yiddish. The greatest of them are the stories of Rabbi Naḥman of Bratslav (then Russian). He was born in the south of Russia and was a great-grandson of the Ba'al Shem Ṭov, the founder of Ḥasidism. He did not write his stories himself but dictated them to his disciple Rabbi Nathan Nemeirover. These tales, which have achieved fame in the German translation by Martin Buber, are masterworks of Jewish folklore.

At about the same time in Poland, the *Haskala,* or Enlightenment (a moderate tendency toward Westernization), began to influence both Jewish life and literature. Most of the writers of the Enlightenment wrote either in Hebrew or in Russian, but some condescended to write in Yiddish. For the first time, works of popular science began to appear, as well as pamphlets directed against the Ḥasidim, the parodies of Ḥasidic literature. One of the earliest writers of this period was Israel Axenfeld. His stories and plays satirized the superstitions and impracticality of the eastern European Jews and criticized their total denial of secular education. Shlomo Ettinger was less bitter than Axenfeld and a superior artist as well. His play *Serkele* and other dramatic works and his epigrammatic poems and fables appeared after his death in 1856.

BEGINNINGS OF MODERN YIDDISH LITERATURE

Prose and poetry.   Modern prose in Yiddish began in the 1850s with the stories of Eisik Meir Dik; the satiric novel *Dos poilische Yingel* (1869; *The Polish Boy*) by Isaac Joel Linetzky; and the novels of Sholem Yakov Abramovitsch, better known as Mendele Mokher Sforim (Mendele the Itinerant Bookseller), "the grandfather" of modern Yiddish literature. Mendele also wrote in Hebrew and is a classic in both languages. Among his best Yiddish works are *Dos Vinschfingerl* (1865; "The Wishing Ring"), *Die Klatsche* (1873; "The Mare"), and *Fishke der Krumer* (1869; "Fishke, the Lame"). Mendele, like all of these writers, deplored and mocked the unworldliness of the Russian and Polish Jews, their exaggerated piety, and

Importance of Mendele in modern Yiddish literature [margin note]

their obsolete system of educating their children. He also castigated the community elders who, for their private gains, exploited the poor Jews. By Mendele's time, great numbers of Jews already lived in the large cities of Russia, western Europe, and the United States. Jewish professors held high positions in the universities of the world. The revolutionary movement had reached even the Jews in the small villages of Poland and the Ukraine. Young men and women left their homes to rebuild Palestine. There was also an increasing emigration to the United States, South America, and elsewhere. But Mendele chose to write about the poorest and the most backward citizens of Kabtzansk (Pauper Village) and Glupsk (Village of Fools). From a purely literary point of view, Mendele himself was rather backward. His achievement was social: his themes did much to modernize the Jewish masses of eastern Europe.

Sholem Yakov Rabinovitsch, or Sholem Aleichem, considered himself a disciple of Mendele and his spritual grandson. His style resembles that of Mendele, but he was a God-inspired master of description and one of the greatest humorists in world literature, to be rated only a few steps below the Russian writer Nikolay Gogol. Sholem Aleichem described the same muddy villages as Mendele had and even gave them similar satiric names; but he saw in the Russian Jews, restricted to the Pale of Settlement, a heroic group. Seemingly condemned to extinction, they used all of their intelligence, wisdom, and shrewdness in order simply to survive and to insure a better lot for their children. All of Sholem Aleichem's heroes were possessed by the passion for making a living. He is perhaps the only writer in world literature whose main theme is the struggle to make ends meet. Sholem Aleichem was often only one step from sentimentality, but his artistic instinct seldom let him take that step. His greatest works are *Tevya der Milchiger* ("Tevya, the Milkman"), *Motel Peisy dem Chasen's* ("The Cantor's Motel Peisy"), and *Funem Yarid* ("Back from the Fair"), the first volume of an unfinished autobiographical novel. His language is rich, his descriptions alive and funny. Sholem Aleichem spent the last year or so of his life in the United States; and his descriptions of the Russian Jewish immigrants in New York are genuine, pertinent, and highly humorous.

Isaac Leib Peretz, who also wrote in Hebrew, was a contemporary of Sholem Aleichem and the first important romantic writer in Yiddish literature. His best works are *Chassidish* ("Ḥasidic") and *Folkstimliche Geshichten* ("Folktales") and a mystical drama, *Bei Nacht oifn alten Mark* ("At Night in the Old Marketplace"). Both stylistically and thematically, he was closer to modern European literature than his predecessors. It was Peretz who first described love in the Yiddish villages and cities. He dared to take a positive position toward religion, Ḥasidism, and the Kabbala (Jewish mystical and theosophical doctrine). He wrote poetry, plays, and short stories. In contrast to the garrulous writers before him, his style was taut and concise. Peretz believed that it was possible for the Jews of Russia and Poland to create their own secular culture. He may rightly be called the father of Yiddishism, the spiritual founder of the movement that demanded cultural autonomy for the Jews of Russia. In contrast to Sholem Aleichem, he was an opponent of political Zionism. What he had in common with Mendele and Sholem Aleichem was that he was never able to make a proper living out of writing. For many years he served as an employee of the same Jewish community in Warsaw that he criticized in his writings. His house was often filled with young writers, whom he encouraged and helped. Although Peretz was potentially a greater artist than his fellow classic writers, he lacked the time and perhaps the patience necessary to create large canvases. He was a short story writer, a poet, a dramatist, a journalist, a speaker, an editor, and a cultural leader. He distinguished himself in all of these capacities.

Among the foremost essayists and men of letters of this period was David Frischmann, who wrote in Yiddish and in Hebrew. Frischmann in his essays preached "Europeanism." He was hypnotized by the scientific and cultural achievements of central and western Europe and considered the Yiddish and Hebrew literature of his day utterly provincial. He admired and translated the German

The father of Yiddishism

philosopher Friedrich Nietzsche and kept his readers informed about "the new winds of Europe."

The theatre. As in the case of the other genres, Jewish scholars, deploring the jargon of Yiddish, wrote dramas in Hebrew during the 17th, 18th, and early 19th centuries. The origins of the professional Yiddish theatre were in the mid-19th century among the folk singers—individuals and groups—who travelled among the eastern European Jewish settlements and performed in Yiddish during that part of the year when the ever popular Purim play was not performed. (The Purim play formalized the merrymaking of the religious festival of Purim with a plot based an the Book of Esther. The lone minstrel, Velvel Zbarsher (Wolf Ehrenkrantz), sang and acted throughout the provinces of Romania, where he popularized his own lyrics. His dedication to uplifting the uneducated and impoverished Jews was typical of the many educated *maskilim* (participants in the Haskala movement) who sought to emancipate the Jews from their circumscribed ghetto life. The most prominent among the travelling troupes who entertained in the Jewish enclaves in Yiddish were the Broder Singers (from Brod in Galicia), who appeared in cafes, wine cellars, and assembly halls throughout eastern Europe. Their repertoire included songs by Michael Gordon, Zbarsher, Eliokhim Zunser, and Abraham Goldfaden. When, in 1876, Goldfaden provided them with a continuity of dialogue and plot for their presentation in a wine cellar in Iaşi, Romania, the professional Yiddish theatre was born.

After hiding from threatened impressment into the Romanian army during the Russo-Turkish War (1877–78), Goldfaden's troupe appeared in Bucharest. Here the talented actor Sigmund Mogulesco, joining the company as the first professional Yiddish actor, established what was to become the conventional and popular role of a versatile comic. With a repertoire of Goldfaden operettas that were filled with Jewish lore and evoked the human richness of Jewish life, the troupe made successful tours of Russian cities that had Jewish centres.

The assassination of Tsar Alexander II (1818–81) intensified anti-Semitism until on September 14, 1883, Yiddish stage presentations were forbidden in Russia. The Yiddish theatre briefly continued in Warsaw as a "German" theatre; a second edict ended that subterfuge.

The lonely immigrant and the Yiddish theatre found and sustained each other in America, where the Jews had greater economic opportunities; where they were influenced by radicals, a free press, and the intelligentsia to free themselves from religiosity and to assume a greater degree of worldliness; and where they were not subject to police harassment and official repression. In 1882, the young Boris Thomashevsky brought a few Jewish actors from London to New York to present the first professional Yiddish play in America. Soon, under the monopoly of the playwright-managers Joseph Lateiner and Moses Hurwitz, who produced melodramas and operettas, sentimental representations of Jewish history, and imitations of Goldfaden's folk epics, a burgeoning Yiddish theatre in New York provided entertainment for the hordes of uneducated Jewish immigrants.

In the Haskala tradition, journalists, critics, actors, and artists sought to uplift the masses and agitated for better theatre. In 1892 Jacob Gordin, a Tolstoyan reformer, ushered in the first "golden epoch" of the Yiddish theatre with his play *Siberia,* produced by Jacob P. Adler, the most notable actor of the early Yiddish theatre. Gordin's prolific pen provided the Yiddish theatre with adaptations from the world's classic repertoire, as well as original plays concerned with social problems and reflecting Gordin's penchant for realism. For the ensuing decade, Gordin and his imitators dominated the Yiddish theatre in New York and Europe. Gordin's influence and heritage gave the Yiddish theatre higher standards of literature, acting, and directing, as well as a respect for the dramatists' written words that put an end to vulgar interpolations and extraneous improvisations by the actors.

Yiddish theatre in the United States

WORLD WAR I TO THE PRESENT

Prose and poetry. Hillel Zeitlin, an essayist and man of letters, was the first modern Yiddish writer who, after considerable soul-searching, came to believe that the Jewish people could not endure without religion; he propounded this belief in all of his writings. He fought bitterly against the Enlightenment and its idolatrous worship of worldliness. Zeitlin was a mystic and a Kabbalist, and he translated parts of the *Zohar* (mystical commentary on the Pentateuch). He was also a sharp-tongued literary critic. He attacked especially the pro-Soviet writers, with their "proletarian" literature. His analysis of the precarious Judaism of the modern Jew is still valid today and may prove even more valid in the future. He was the father of Aaron Zeitlin, perhaps the greatest of the modern Yiddish poets, who shared his father's interest in mysticism and wrote books on psychic research in both Hebrew and Yiddish.

Sholem Asch, although he looked upon himself as a disciple of Peretz, had neither Peretz' scholarship nor his sense of style. He wrote his fiction on a broad scale and was one of the first Yiddish writers to create historical novels and plays. His books were translated into many languages and his play *Got fun Nekomeh* (1907; *The God of Vengeance,* 1918) was first produced by Max Reinhardt in Berlin (1910) and enjoyed considerable success. Among his best known earlier works are: *Kiddush Hashem* (1919), *Die Kishefmacherin fun Kastilie* (1921; "The Witch of Castile"), *A Shtetl* (1904; "A Village"), *Farn Mabul* (*A Tale of Three Cities,* 1933), *Motke Gonef* (1917; "Motke the Thief," 1935), and *Onkl Moses* (1918; *Uncle Moses,* 1938), a description of Jewish immigrant life in New York. Written in his later years, a trilogy—*Der Man fur Nazares* (1939; *The Nazarene*), *Der Apostol* (1943; *The Apostle*), and *Mary* (1949)—which deals with the New Testament, was the target of much controversy among Yiddish critics and readers. With Sholem Asch, an epoch of so-called "primitivism" was introduced into Yiddish literature. The new generation of Yiddish writers was no longer steeped in Hebrew letters and Jewish lore. Among the most talented writers of this group were Abraham Reisen, Isaac Meir Weisenberg, Abraham Moshe Fuchs, Joshua Perle, Ozer Warshafsky, Moses Stavsky, Rachel Feigenberg, Ephraim Kagonovsky, Israel Rabon, Sh. Berlinsky, Fishel Bimko, Sh. Horontchik, and Hertz Bergner.

Coexisting with the "primitives" were some writers who were still nourished by the old wells of Jewish knowledge: Micah Joseph Berdichevsky, who excelled in descriptions of Ḥasidic life, though he spent most of his literary life in Germany; Zalman Shneur, who wrote both in Hebrew and in Yiddish and was a highly gifted follower of Mendele; Hersh David Nomberg and Onoychi (pen name of Zalman Yitzchok Aaronson), who wrote Ḥasidic stories; and the brothers I.J. and I.B. Singer (see below).

To the roster of the most gifted of the Yiddish poets in Europe belong Abraham Reisen, Shimon Shmuel Frug, Aaron Einhorn, Isaac Katzenelson, Uri Tzvi Grinberg, Moshe Broderzon, Samuel Jacob Imber, Aaron Zeitlin, Itzik Manger, Melech Ravitch, Israel Stern, Jechiel Lehrer, Zusman Segalovitch, Kadia Maladovsky, Miriam Ulinover, and Rachel Korn.

Yiddish literature in the United States

Yiddish literature in the United States began to blossom after World War I. The writers before that period were mostly Socialist propagandists, such as Morris Wintehevsky, David Edelstadt, and Joseph Bovshover. Among the foremost Yiddish novelists and storytellers in the United States are: Lamed Shapiro, *Der Tseilem* (*The Cross*); Joseph Opatoshu, who wrote *In poilische Velder* (1921; *In the Forest of Poland*); David Pinski; the brilliant short story writer Yona Rosenfeld; O.B. Berkowitch; Boruch Glassman; Leon Kobrin; M. Chaimovitch; Isaac Raboy; Shaye Miller; I. Metzger; Benjamin Ressler; Shmuel Izban; Benjamin Demblin; Yitzchok Perlov; and Chaim Grade.

A writer who achieved considerable fame outside the Yiddish literary world and who, in 1933, emigrated to the United States, was Israel Joshua Singer. His novel *The Brothers Ashkenazi* (1936), which describes the growth of the industrial city of Łódź as mirrored in the rise and fall of the Ashkenazi family, is considered a classic work. His other works are *Yoshe Kalb* (1932; *The Sinner,* 1933), a description of Ḥasidic life in Galicia, and *The Family Carnovsky* (1969), the story of refugees from Germany be-

fore and during World War II. He also wrote short stories and plays that were performed in Yiddish both in Europe and the United States. He was a realist without a trace of the sentimentality characteristic of most of the Yiddish writers. His younger brother Isaac Bashevis Singer, who has lived in the United States since 1935, is the author of *Satan in Goray* (1955), *The Family Moskat* (1950), *The Slave* (1962), and *The Manor* (1967); he has also written numerous short stories, including stories for children. His books have been translated into a number of languages. Yiddish literature in the United States has excelled in its poetry: among the outstanding American-Yiddish poets are Morris Rosenfeld, whose poems about the sweat shops and the life of the immigrants gained world fame; H. Leivick, author of *The Golem*; and Yehoash, who translated the Bible into Yiddish. Such poets as Moshe Leib Halpern, Moshe Nadir, Zisha Landau, and A. Lutzky were first-rate by any measure.

The two foremost Yiddish critics were Bal Machshoves (1873–1924), who lived in Russia, and Shmuel Niger (the pen name of Samuel Charney), who lived in the United States. Both of them influenced Yiddish literature to a high degree and nurtured whole generations of Yiddish writers.

Yiddish literature in the Soviet Union

The Bolshevik Revolution (1917–22) attracted a number of Yiddish writers and later liquidated most of them. Some of them were native Russians, others emigrated there after the Revolution. The greatest of these was David Bergelson, a novelist and short-story writer. His best novels are *Noch Alemen* (1913; "After Everyone") and *Arum Vogsal* (1909; "By the Depot"). His novel *Penek* was a desperate and unsuccessful attempt to adapt himself to the demands of Soviet criticism. The same fate befell a highly talented poet from Vilna, Moishe Kulbak, and A. Nister, a mystic who tried his hand at Socialist realism. Peretz Markish, Itzik Feffer, and Izzy Charik wrote numberless odes to Stalin and his regime. All of these poets and many others were shot by the Soviet authorities in the early 1950s.

In the 1970s in the Soviet Union, Yiddish literature was practically nonexistent. The few writers who remained formed a nucleus around the magazine *Sovietisch Heimland* ("Soviet Homeland"). In the United States no young generation of readers or writers was developing. The situation has not been much better in Israel, where the new generation knows only Hebrew. There the few Yiddish writers, such as Yehiel Hoffer, Joseph Papiernikov, A. Shomri, Yakov Friedman, Abraham Karpinovitch, and F. Siegelbaum, have been concentrated around the magazine *Die goldene Keit* ("The Golden Chain"), edited by Abraham Sutzkever, a refugee from the Nazi holocaust, who is one of the best Yiddish poets, a bard of the destruction of his people.

Small centres of Yiddish literature also existed in other countries. In Romania there was the fabulist Eliezer Steinbarg; the poets Yankev Sternberg and Moishe Altman, the essayist Biekel. In France there are M. Shlevin and Mendel Mann, whose trilogy about the Red Army has been translated into a number of languages. The most important Yiddish writers in Argentina are P. Yannsovitch, Kehos Kliger, and Josoph Okrutny.

Memoirs in Yiddish literature

The treasure of Yiddish prose literature is its huge number of memoirs. A memoirist of talent was Yeḥiel Yeshaia Trunk. His seven-volume work, *Poilen* (1944–53), is a monument to Jewish life in Poland. The greatest part of the memoirs about the Hitler era have been and are being written by ordinary men and women. These works constitute an accusation against humanity that has no counterpart in the history of world literature.

The theatre. Around the beginning of the 20th century, Russian authorities relented, and the Yiddish theatre burst forth with new life. Perez Hirshbein, considered the greatest Jewish playwright, inspired by the artistry of the Moscow Art Theatre, toured Russia and Poland with his company from 1908 to 1910. When its most notable actor, Jacob Ben-Ami, came to New York on the eve of World War I, he introduced the concepts of Konstantin Stanislavsky, director of the Moscow Art Theatre, to the American theatre for the first time via the Yiddish stage. In Warsaw, the Kamińska family established a distinguished Yiddish theatre that, except for a hiatus during World

War II, has continued as the Jewish State Theatre of Poland even though its actor-manager-star, Ida Kamińska (the daughter of the original founder) fled from Poland's resurgent anti-Semitism in 1968.

Although Gordin's influence continued to prevail, and great folk and poetic dramas by such dramatists as David Pinski, Leon Kobrin, and Ossip Dymov were produced by such prominent stars as Jacob P. Adler and David Kessler, the Lateiner and Hurwitz type of shoddy melodrama and tawdry operetta persisted. During World War I, a plethora of sordid melodramas about fallen women infested the Yiddish stage. In 1918 Maurice Schwartz gathered aspiring members of the New York Yiddish theatre into a new venture that was to become, two years later, the Yiddish Art Theatre, of which he became director and star for three decades. Early in its first season, at the urging of Jacob Ben-Ami, Schwartz's troupe presented Hirshbein's *Farvorfen Vinkel* ("Forgotten Village"). With its enthusiastic reception, the Yiddish Art Theatre movement—and the second "golden epoch" of the Yiddish theatre—was launched. Schwartz's troupe endured, both in New York and on triumphant world tours, for over three decades.

The determination to bring worthwhile literary dramas to Jewish communities and to develop talent for the professional stage resulted in the creation of literary and dramatic clubs that flourished in many Jewish areas. From these clubs were born important Yiddish theatre troupes of high artistic merit. Warsaw had the I.L. Peretz Theatre Society (founded in 1911) and the contemporary VYKT (Varshaver Yiddische Kunst Teater, or Warsaw Yiddish Art Theatre); and Vilna (now Vilnius, Lithuanian Soviet Socialist Republic) had FADA (Farband fun Yiddishe Dramatische Actyorin, or Association of Yiddish Dramatic Actors). When, in 1915, the occupying German forces determined to undermine Russian power by encouraging nationalistic groups, the dramatist Arnold Zweig and fellow German officers helped FADA form what was to become the world-renowned Vilna Troupe, whose fragments—discords and misunderstandings created splits within the group—later toured the world and set standards of unsurpassed theatre art. Also in 1915, in New York, two dramatic clubs combined to form the Folksbuehne, which, in the latter half of the 20th century, is the most notable Yiddish theatre still operating in the United States. Various theatre clubs combined in 1923 into the Folks Farband far Kunst Teater. In 1926, with the aid of many Jewish workers' organizations, this active studio group became the Arbeiter Teater Farband. When in 1927 it presented its first public production, the left-wing Artef group started its memorable, albeit one-decade, existence, during which it presented politically provocative and stylistically challenging productions in New York.

To revive and stimulate interest in Hebrew as a living language, Habima (Hebrew: the Stage) was organized in Bialystok, Poland, in 1912, under the guidance of Nahum Zemach. Encouraged by Stanislavsky, it established itself in Moscow during the turbulence of the Russian Revolution of 1917. Despite the new government's edict against Hebrew as a secular language for the Jews, the high artistic merit of this troupe, which performed in Hebrew, made it a cult in Moscow. Its sensational production of the Russian playwright S. Ansky's *Dybbuk* electrified theatregoers on both sides of the Atlantic. During the company's tour of Europe and the United States in 1926, defections by and schisms among the members led the remnants to regroup in Palestine where, in 1931, the Habima permanently established itself in Tel Aviv and later became the official state theatre of Israel.

Between the two World Wars, the Soviet government encouraged and supported Yiddish theatres, the most successful of which was the Kamerny in Moscow. As one scholar puts it, this theatre "sneered at old-fashioned Jewish folkways, caricatured such life, and satirized it with political interpretations; it exaggerated in order to ridicule the Jewish past." Thus, this Moscow Yiddish folk theatre distorted Jewish heritage in attempting to combine it with the ideology of the October Revolution.

Caught in the crossfire of the savage Nazi scourge and Stalin's purge, almost all Yiddish theatres, actors, and di-

rectors were eliminated from the Russian scene; moreover, the *shtetl* (Jewish small town or small town community in eastern Europe), out of which were distilled the Yiddish theatre arts and dramatic poetry, also disappeared.

Since 1970 the best organized and most ongoing Jewish theatres have been in Israel and Romania. The first attempt at Hebrew theatre in Palestine, in 1894, was followed periodically with attempts by sporadic groups to establish themselves in either Hebrew or Yiddish productions. With the birth of the State of Israel in 1948, the Hebrew theatre came of age; by mid-20th century, it was firmly established as a vigorous and important part of world theatre culture. In addition to the state-subsidized Habima, there are the Cameri Theatre in Tel Aviv; Hateatron Haironi (the Municipal Theatre, under the direction of the renowned Josef Millo) in Haifa; and the Histadrut's (General Federation of Labour's) Telem (Theatre for New Immigrants), which has functioned chiefly as a tool to teach uneducated Jews from Arab countries. As an educational tool, its mobile stage offers plays at various reception centres for new immigrants as well as at outposts where newcomers are settled. In addition to independent Hebrew professional theatre groups that appear from time to time in the leading cities, visiting troupes, such as the Bucharest State Yiddish Theatre, have appeared in Israel. There are about 300 amateur theatrical groups in this small country. Playing an important role in the nation's culture, the theatres avoid plays from the Yiddish traditional theatre or ghetto genre, because the highly sophisticated theatre audiences are aware of the avant-garde theatres of other lands and are receptive to this eclectic fare. European and American successes have been popular. Seldom are their original plays concerned with biblical subjects, local problems, the fight for independence, or the pioneers who settled the land.

The decline of Yiddish as a spoken and written language has had a devastating effect upon the languishing Yiddish theatre. Other than intermittent productions in New York and Buenos Aires and rare productions in other world capitals, there remains only a waning State Yiddish Theatre in Warsaw and a flourishing, highly artistic State Yiddish Theatre in Bucharest. Supported by a benign government, the Yiddish theatre in Bucharest operates its own theatre and tours the provinces with both traditional and avant-garde productions. Thus, it is in Romania, where the modern Yiddish theatre was born, that it still flourishes.

BIBLIOGRAPHY. ABRAHAM ROBACK, *The Story of Yiddish Literature* (1940); MEYER WAXMAN, *A History of Jewish Literature*, 2nd ed., 6 vol. (1960); ISRAEL ZINBERG, *Toldot Sifrut Yisrael*, Russian, Hebrew, and Yiddish text, 6 vol. (1959–60), published, with additions, Yiddish and Hebrew texts, as *Di geshikhte fun literatur bay Yidn*, 10 vol. (1964–70); CHARLES A. MADISON, *Yiddish Literature: Its Scope and Major Writers* (1968); ZALMEN ZYLBERCWAIG and JACOB MESTEL, *Leksikon fun yidish teater*, 2 vol. (1931–34); and ZALMEN ZYLBERCWAIG, *Leksikon fun yidisn teater*, 4 vol. (1959–69), the most complete directory and roster of the Yiddish theatre; SAMUEL J. CITRON, "Yiddish and Hebrew Drama," in BARRETT H. CLARK and GEORGE FREEDLEY (eds.), *A History of Modern Drama* (1947); DAVID S. LIFSON, *The Yiddish Theatre in America* (1965), and "The Yiddish Theatre," in GEORGE FREEDLEY and JOHN A. REEVES (eds.), *A History of the Theatre*, 3rd rev. ed. (1968); and ZARA SHAKOW, *The Theatre in Israel* (1963), all comprehensive histories; ISAAC GOLDBERG, *The Drama of Transition* (1922), a most felicitous critique; HUTCHINS HAPGOOD, *The Spirit of the Ghetto* (1902, reprinted 1967), and MARK ZBOROWSKI and ELIZABETH HERZOG, *Life Is with People* (1952), fine evocations of the milieu that distilled the Yiddish theatre; SOLOMON LIPTZIN, *The Flowering of Yiddish Literature* (1963) and *The Maturing of Yiddish Literature* (1970). See also EDWARD ALEXANDER, *The Resonance of Dust: Essays on Holocaust Literature and Jewish Fate* (1979), and his *Isaac Bashevis Singer* (1980), an original study of the Nobel prize laureate; HOWARD SCHWARTZ and ANTHONY RUDOLF (eds.), *Voices Within the Ark: The Modern Jewish Poets* (1980), an anthology, including poems in Yiddish, Hebrew, English, and 19 other languages; IRA BRUCE NADEL, *Jewish Writers of North America: A Guide to Information Sources* (1981); JOSHUA A. FISHMAN, *Never Say Die! A Thousand Years of Yiddish in Jewish Life and Letters* (1981); MURRAY BAUMGARTEN, *City Scriptures: Modern Jewish Writing* (1982); and RICHARD F. SHEPARD and VICKI GOLD LEVI, *Live and Be Well: A Celebration of Yiddish Culture in America from the First Immigrants to the Second World War* (1982).

(I.B.S./D.S.L./Ed.)

The
Yiddish
Art
Theatre

Decline of
Yiddish
theatre

Yugoslav Literature

Just as the history of the various peoples of modern Yugoslavia has differed over the past thousand years, so the literatures of the Serbs, Croats, Slovenes, and Macedonians have developed independently. From an early date Croats and Slovenes formed part of the central European cultural heritage, whereas Serbs and Macedonians were part of the Eastern, or Byzantine, culture and, later, of the Turkish sultanate. Since 1918, when they were united, the Yugoslavs have had three literary languages—Serbo-Croatian, Slovene, and Macedonian—and two alphabets, the Latin and the Cyrillic. The Serbs and Croats speak a common language but use the Cyrillic and Latin alphabets, respectively. The Slovenes, with a language akin to Serbo-Croatian, use the Latin alphabet and the Macedonians the Cyrillic.

At times in the 20th century the literatures of the Serbs and Croats have been considered to be the expression of one national culture. This was particularly the case during the period immediately after World War I, when a widespread feeling of euphoria accompanied the creation of a unified Yugoslav state. At the same time, however, internal rivalries led to the resurgence of separatism among the country's major national groups. After World War II and the coming to power of the Communist Party of Yugoslavia, the modern tendency toward political unity vied with the historical legacy of differing cultural identities. Following Yugoslavia's expulsion from the Soviet bloc in 1948, official insistence on Socialist Realism in literature and the other arts began to decline, and from the mid-1950s authors reflected Western literary trends and styles. This cosmopolitan aspect of contemporary Yugoslavia is balanced by a continuing sense of attachment to the traditional cultural centres of Belgrade by the Serbs, Zagreb by the Croats, Ljubljana by the Slovenes, and Skopje by the Macedonians.

This article is divided into the following sections:

SERBIAN LITERATURE

Serbian literature originated in the use of the Old Church Slavonic language for the translation of religious works from Greek. From the 12th century, Serbian literature acquired its own characteristics, as in the illuminated Miroslav Gospel; biblical stories; hagiographies, notably that of St. Sava, patron saint of Serbia; and tales such as that of Barlaam and Josaphat. After the Turkish occupation of 1459, literature declined.

The most important Serbian representative of the Enlightenment period was Dositej Obradović, whose writings greatly influenced Serbian literary development. Many characteristics of European Romanticism could be observed in the literature of the period 1820–70, especially the cult of folklore and national self-assertion. A central figure was Vuk Stefanović Karadžić, a reformer of literary language who wrote a Serbian grammar and dictionary and collected Serbian folk poetry and stories. Petar II Petrović Njegoš, a Montenegrin ruler, was a poet whose gifts are best seen in his dramatic poem *Gorski vijenac* (1847; "The Mountain Garland"). The lyrical verses of Branko Radičević contributed to the break with earlier didactic-objective poetry. Among younger Romantic writers were the lyrical poets Jovan Jovanović (known as Zmaj), Đura Jakšić, and Laza Kostić.

From 1870 to 1900 there was a tendency toward Realism. The most significant narrative writing was by Laza Lazarević, a master of the short story; Simo Matavulj, a keenly observant novelist and short-story writer with a strong sense of humour; and Stevan Sremac, satirist and humorist. Vojislav Ilić was a fine descriptive poet, resembling the French Parnassians.

Toward the end of the 19th century Serbian literature was influenced by European currents, particularly the French Symbolists: outstanding figures were Jovan Dučić and Milan Rakić, a patriotic poet of a melancholy nature. Vladislav Petković (called Dis), a subjective poet, chose themes halfway between reality and the irrational. Prose changed from objective description to psychological narrative, often with a lyrical quality, as in the work of Borisav Stanković.

Serbian writers between World Wars I and II continued to follow major European literary movements. Miloš Crnjanski and Rastko Petrović were exponents of Modernism in the years immediately after World War I. The Belgrade Surrealist group introduced a note of radical, left-wing politics, and some of its members later turned to the style of Socialist Realism. The literature of the 1930s was shaped by the focus on political and social themes and attacks on the introspection of the earlier Modernists. World War II brought a break in literary output, but the end of the war was accompanied by the publication of three novels by Ivo Andrić: *Travnička hronika* (1945; *Bosnian Story*), *Na Drini ćuprija* (1945; *The Bridge on the Drina*), and *Gaspodjica* (1945; *The Woman from Sarajevo*). Andrić won the Nobel Prize for Literature for 1961. His works, usually placed in a historical setting, combine the realistic traditions of Serbian literature with more modern forms of expression.

The postwar period witnessed the continuation of the realistic trend in the war novels of Mihailo Lalić (*Lelejska gora* [1957; *The Wailing Mountain*]) and Dobrica Ćosić (*Daleko je sunce* [1951; *Far Away Is the Sun*]) and in the work of Meša Selimović, which has a strong emphasis on psychology. During the 1960s and '70s this trend turned to contemporary settings in a specifically Serbian milieu with strong local colouring, such as in the prose of Dragoslav Mihailović and Milisav Savić. More original forms of expression were introduced into prose from the 1950s by Oskar Davičo (*Pesma* [1952; *The Poem*]), who had links with the Surrealists before the war, and by the postwar writer Miodrag Bulatović (*Crveni petao leti prema neku* [1959; *The Red Cockerel*]). In poetry Serbia has been represented by Desanka Maksimović, Vasko Popa, Stevan Raičković, Miodrag Pavlović, and Ivan Lalić (*The Works of Love*, English translations published in 1981). Later developments have included novels with greater social and political comment, such as Danilo Kiš's *Grobnica za Borisa Davidoviča* (1976; *A Tomb for Boris Davidovich*), and experiments with the forms of literature by the Klokotrizam group, the intention of which is to defy the canons and aesthetic norms of art.

The 20th century has been fraught with polemics between different literary groups. The arguments from the turn of the century to the 1960s centred on the question of style. The tradition of realistic narrative has maintained a strong position in the Serbian literary establishment, which in many cases has been opposed to more innovative writers. Since the late 1960s the focus of debate has shifted away from style and toward questions of content and the place of political and social comment in the literature of a socialist society.

Serbian writers between the world wars

CROATIAN LITERATURE

The Croats were converted to Christianity at the turn of the 9th century by disciples of SS. Cyril and Methodius. The first ecclesiastical works were written in the Glagolitic alphabet, and fragments have survived in the Kiev Missal pieces (11th century). From the 12th century the national language was widely used for inscriptions and legal documents, but from the 14th century Latin was increasingly used. Immediately before the age of Humanism (second half of the 15th century), literature consisted mainly of biblical stories, legends, folklore, and popular stories.

In the 15th and early 16th centuries the most outstanding Croatian writer was Marko Marulić, author of the epic *Judita* (1501), in which he encouraged his countrymen in their struggle against the Turks. Under the influence of classical and Italian literature and Croat folklore, the Petrarchan lyric was developed in Dalmatia and in Dubrovnik. One of the most prominent poets was Hanibal Lucić, author of *Robinja* ("The Slave Girl"), the first Yugoslav secular play. Among the best known writers of Old Croat literature was Marin Držić, who wrote pastoral dramas and comedies portraying Renaissance Dubrovnik. His comedy *Dundo Maroje* (written *c.* 1551) was performed throughout western Europe.

Gundulić's epic

In the Croatian literature of the 17th and 18th centuries, the most important position belonged to Ivan Gundulić, author of a stirring epic, *Osman,* describing the Polish victory over the Turks in 1621. Andrija Kačić Miošić treated historical themes in the popular verse forms of the travelling minstrel.

Romanticism in Croatian literature originated in a cultural and national reformation brought about by the Illyrian movement (1835–48), which aimed at a union of all south Slavs within the Habsburg federation. Ljudevit Gaj introduced the *štokavski* dialect and *ijekavski* speech as the literary language of Croatia and also a unified orthography. Personal, patriotic, and reflective lyrics were popular and were best represented by the sensitive, moving poems of Stanko Vraz, the patriotic songs and poetic drama of Petar Preradović, and the dramatic works of Dimitrije Demeter. Some of the best poetry includes *Smrt Smail-Age Čengića* (1846; *The Death of Smail-Aga Čengić*) by Ivan Mažuranić.

The popularity of patriotic verse

In the development of national characteristics of Croatian Romanticism an outstanding figure was August Šenoa, poet, dramatist, critic, journalist, and creator of the Croat historical novel. Šenoa was a subtle stylist and a champion of Realism, which was at its height in 1881–95. Writers were concerned with contemporary problems, particularly with conditions among the lower classes. Representatives of this movement were Evgenij Kumičić, a naturalist and poet; Ante Kovačić, satirist and author of a lively novel, *U registraturi* (1888; "In the Registry Office"); and Ksaver Šandor Gjalski, a short-story writer and novelist concerned with political and cultural problems. A poet, Silvije Strahimir Kranjčević, was a social rebel whose work was rich in imagery and rhythmic variety.

In the opening years of the 20th century poetry was the dominant genre in Croatian literature. Many poets reflected the style of the art-for-art's-sake trend, dwelling on the inner struggles of modern man with his world and the search for meaning in individual existence. These themes are found in particular in the work of Vladimir Vidrić and Vladimir Nazor. The leading figure of the early Modernist phase until World War I was Antun Gustav Matoš. He edited the anthology *Mlada hrvatska lirika* (1914; "The Young Croatian Lyric"), which marked the zenith of such verse. Between the wars avant-garde poetry continued to be expressed in the verse of such poets as Augustin Ujević, while Ivan Goran Kovačić in *Jama* (1943; *The Pit*), a long poem evoking the horror of war, retained a classical elegance in his verse. The short story was represented by the work of Slavko Kolar who humorously depicted the life of the peasant in a changing world. The dominant prose writers of the interwar period were August Cesarec and Miroslav Krleža (*Povratak Filipa Latinovicza* [1932; *The Return of Philip Latinovicz*]; and the collection of English translations *The Cricket Beneath the Waterfall and Other Stories* [1972]). Both presented contemporary social problems as the result of class exploitation and deeply explored the psychology of their characters. Krleža

is known not only for his creative writing, which spanned the century to his death in 1981, but also as an editor of literary periodicals, as an essayist, and as a critic who dominated Croatian cultural life for much of the century. Although a committed supporter of the Communists in Yugoslavia from the mid-1920s, Krleža always opposed the imposition of Socialist Realism as official party policy. His attitude was to support the freedom of the artist against all forms of social and political coercion in any type of society.

In the less restrictive atmosphere that followed the break in 1948 in relations with the Soviet Union, new prose writers included Ranko Marinković and Vjekoslav Kaleb (*Divota prašine* [1956; *Glorious Dust*]), who wrote on the war and contemporary society in Croatia. The younger prose writer Antun Šoljan took more cosmopolitan themes for his work, as did the poet Ivan Slamnig of the same generation. Aleksander Flaker of the University of Zagreb gained an international reputation as a scholar in the field of literary studies. Many writers gave their support to the national revival known as the Croatian Spring in 1970–71; demands included the recognition of Croatian as a separate literary language. The government stifled the movement, but it served as an example of the strength of feeling for cultural identity in Yugoslavia and as an indication of the potential political role of literary affairs. Later Croatian literature shared another concern with Western literature in the cosmopolitan choice of its themes, such as were found in the feminist writing of Dubravka Ugrešić.

SLOVENE LITERATURE

The dissolution in 821 of the independent state of Carantania (Carinthia; now Kärnten, Austria) and a merging of the upper classes into German feudal society retarded any development of Slovene literature. Among medieval manuscripts that have been preserved, the most remarkable are the *Brižinski spomeniki* (Freising manuscripts, *c.* 1000). These are the first written examples of the Slovene, and perhaps of any Slavic, language. Alongside this appearance of the language in its written form there flourished, as throughout the Balkans, a rich folk poetry. The use of written Slovene in the church liturgy was replaced by Latin at an early stage.

The Freising manuscripts

The demand for Slovene to be reintroduced into the church was made during the rise of Protestantism in Europe. The developing religious literature reached its peak in 1584 in a translation of the Bible by Jurij Dalmatin. Other developments of this period included the publication, also in 1584, of the first Slovene grammar, by Adam Bohorič. Most of this early work was undone, however, by the Counter-Reformation. It was not until the middle of the 18th century that interest in a Slovene literary language was revived under the influence of the Enlightenment.

The European Romantic movement, with its support of nationhood based on a common language and shared cultural background, encouraged philological and literary works and influenced Slovene intellectuals in the first half of the 19th century. Jernej Kopitar, a Slovene and censor for Austria-Hungary responsible for the Slav nations of the empire, initiated early attempts to standardize and codify the Slovene language. In the 1830s and '40s Matija Čop was very active in publishing literary works and literary periodicals in Slovenia. The greatest poet of those years up to the middle of the 19th century was France Prešeren. He raised the standards of literary Slovene to new heights and established the literary language as a vehicle capable of conveying nuances of thought and feeling in a modern idiom.

Standardization of Slovene

The second half of the 19th century witnessed the development of prose writing and the influence of Realism. A dynamic writer was Fran Levstik, a critic and dramatist and founder of a program for popular prose. The first Slovene novel, *Deseti brat* ("The Tenth Brother") by Josip Jurčič, was published in 1866. During this period Slovene writers began to reflect Western styles and trends, and publishing and other facilities were established to ensure the more secure development of a literature in the national language.

The emergence of a Slovene Modernist movement in

The
Slovene
Modernist
movement

the early 20th century resulted in the second flowering of literature since the Romantics and Prešeren. The two main founders of this movement were Oton Župančič, a vigorous poet, and Ivan Cankar (*Hlapec Jernej in njegova pravica* [1907; *The Bailiff Yerney and His Rights*]; and *Hiša Marije pomočnice* [1904; *The Ward of Our Lady of Mercy*]), a masterful prose stylist. After World War I social and spiritual tension was evident in the predominantly Expressionist poetry of Tone Seliškar, Miran Jarc, and Anton Vodnik, as well as the plays of Slavko Grum. The novel and short story were revived during the 1930s, a decade marked by the appearance of Socialist Realism, especially in the works of Juš Kozak, Miško Kranjec, Ciril Kosmač, and Prežihov Voranc (*Samorastniki* [1940; *The Self-Sown*]), who turned to the everyday life of simple country people. The freer metres of Edvard Kocbek pointed the way to magically interpreted reality, and the caustic sonnets of Božo Vodušek manifested a sober disillusionment.

During and after World War II, writers who had been active before it remained rooted in the realistic tradition, although many deepened or broadened the scope of their themes. This is particularly true of the poet and dramatist Matej Bor (*Šel je popotnik skozi atomski vek* [1958; *A Wanderer in the Atomic Age*]), as well as the prose writers and dramatists Ivan Potrč and Mira Mihelič. Later developments in prose included, under Western influence, the appearance of science fiction by such writers as Miha Remec. Poetry has maintained its deeply subjective expression in the work of Cene Vipotnik, France Balantič, and especially Jože Udovič. This trend has been continued in the verses of the next generation, represented by Veno Taufer, Valentin Cundrič, and Dane Zajc. Slovene literature is identifiably part of mainstream European literature and is probably the most cosmopolitan of all the Yugoslav literatures.

MACEDONIAN LITERATURE

Like other Slavic literatures, literature in Macedonia began in the 9th century with the translations of religious works by SS. Cyril and Methodius and with the first Slavonic "university" that emerged at Ohrid (then in Bulgaria) under St. Clement (died 916), a disciple of SS. Cyril and Methodius. With this orthodox religious literature, there developed an apocryphal, heretic Bogomil literature. In the 16th century, with a fusion of Old Church Slavonic and vernacular languages, a popular Damascene literature developed: *Damaskini* were translations from the works of Damascenus the Studite. This lasted until the beginning of the 19th century, when books written in modern Macedonia were first published.

Early 19th-century Macedonian literature echoed the medieval religious enlightenment of the school of Kliment, and the only original contributions were from folk literature. Later, original lyrical poetry was written by Konstantin Miladinov, who, with his brother Dimitrije, compiled a notable collection of legends and folk songs contributing to the development of a national Macedonian literature.

The development of a Macedonian national consciousness, and of a Macedonian literature, was hampered in the 19th century by the continuing rule of the Ottoman Empire. The Balkan states finally made common cause against the empire in the Balkan Wars, 1912–13, only to fight among themselves over the division of Macedonia. Serbia received the lion's share of the northern part centred on Skopje and including Ohrid. After World War I the Macedonian language, most closely related to Bulgarian, was still considered by the government in Belgrade to be a southern dialect of Serbo-Croatian. The Macedonian language was not officially recognized until the establishment of Macedonia as a constituent republic in 1944. Despite these drawbacks some progress was made toward the foundation of a national language and literature, in particular by Kosta P. Misirkov in his *Za Makedonskite raboti* (1903; "In Favour of Macedonian Literary Works") and in the literary periodical *Vardar* (established 1905). These efforts were continued after World War I by Kosta Racin, who wrote mainly poetry in Macedonian and prop-

agated its use through the literary journals of the 1930s. Some, such as Kole Nedelkovski, worked and published from abroad because of political pressure.

After World War II the Communist government of Yugoslavia officially recognized the Macedonian language, and encouragement was given to establish publishing facilities and provide educational services in the language. The scholar Blaže Koneski and others were charged with the task of standardizing Macedonian as the official literary language. With their new freedom to write and publish in their own language, and after years of struggle to defend a growing national consciousness and its expression as a separate cultural identity, the Macedonians produced many literary figures in the postwar period. Poetry has been represented in the work of Aco Šopov, Slavko Janevski, Blaže Koneski, and Gane Todorovski. Prewar playwrights, such as V. Iljoski, continued to write drama, and the theatre was invigorated by new dramatists, such as Kole Čašule and Tome Arsovski. Živko Čingo became one of Macedonia's best known writers of prose.

(V.Z./Em.Š./A.Gn./D.Še./D.A.N.)

Official
recognition
of the
Mace-
donian
language

BIBLIOGRAPHY

General: MILMAN PARRY and ALBERT B. LORD, *Serbocroatian Heroic Songs,* 2 vol. (1954); SVETOZAR KOLJEVIĆ, *The Epic in the Making* (1980), on the Serbian folk tradition, and *Yugoslav Short Stories* (1966); THOMAS BUTLER, *Monumenta Serbocroatica: A Bilingual Anthology of Serbian and Croatian Texts from the 12th to the 19th Century* (1980); ANTUN BARAC, *A History of Yugoslav Literature* (1955, reissued 1976); ANTE KADIĆ, *From Croatian Renaissance to Yugoslav Socialism* (1969); VASA D. MIHAILOVICH (ed.), *Modern Slavic Literatures,* vol. 2, *Bulgarian, Czechoslovak, Polish, Ukrainian and Yugoslav Literature* (1976), and *Contemporary Yugoslav Poetry* (1977). THOMAS EEKMAN, *Thirty Years of Yugoslav Literature: 1945–1975* (1978); SVETA LUKIĆ, *Contemporary Yugoslav Literature* (1972); BRANKO LENSKI (ed.), *Death of a Simple Giant, and Other Modern Yugoslav Stories* (1965); JANKO LAVRIN, *An Anthology of Modern Yugoslav Poetry in English Translation* (1962); BRANKO MIKASINOVICH, DRAGAN MILIVOJEVIĆ, and VASA D. MIHAILOVICH, *Introduction to Yugoslav Literature: An Anthology of Fiction and Poetry* (1973).

Serbia: ANNE PENNINGTON and PETER LEVI, *Marko the Prince* (1984); METEJA MATEJIC and DRAGAN MILIVOJEVIĆ, *An Anthology of Medieval Serbian Literature in English* (1978); GEORGE R. NOYES, *The Life and Adventures of Dimitrije Obradović* (1953); DUNCAN WILSON, *The Life and Times of Vuk Stefanović Karadzić* (1970); MIHAILO DORDEVIĆ, *Serbian Poetry and Milutin Bojić* (1977); CELIA HAWKESWORTH, *Ivo Andrić: Bridge Between East and West* (1984); MIODRAG PAVLOVIĆ, *Antologija srpskog pesništva* (1964); JOVAN SKERLIĆ, *Istorija nove srpske književnosti* (1967); JOVAN HRISTIĆ (ed.), *Srpska književnost u književnoj kritici,* 12 vol. (1965–66); ANTE KADIĆ, *Contemporary Serbian Literature* (1960); *Relations* (quarterly), translations of recent literature and criticism.

Croatia: JOSIP TORBARINA, *Italian Influence on the Poets of the Ragusan Republic* (1931); ELINOR M. DESPELATOVIĆ, *Ljudevit Gaj and the Illyrian Movement* (1975); EUGENE E. PANTZER, *Antun Gustav Matoš* (1981); ANTE KADIĆ, *Contemporary Croatian Literature* (1960); MIROSLAV BEKER (ed.), *Comparative Studies in Croatian Literature* (1981); FRANJO TROGRANČIĆ, *Storia della Letteraturea Croata* (1953); *Povijest hrvatske književnosti* (1978); NICOLA MILIČEVIĆ and ANTUN ŠOLJAN, *Antologija hrvatske poezije* (1966); MILIVOS SLAVIČEK (ed.), *A Collection of Modern Croatian Verse* (1965); *Most* (quarterly), translations of recent literature and criticism.

Slovenia: HENRY R. COOPER, *Francè Prešeren* (1981); ALOIS GRADNIK, *Selected Poems,* ed. by JANKO LAVRIN (1964); JANKO LAVRIN and ANTON SLODNJAK (eds.), *The Parnassus of a Small Nation,* 2nd enlarged ed. (1965); BRUNO MERIGGI, *Storia della letterature slovena* (1961); ANTON SLODNJAK, *Geschichte der slowenischen Literatur* (1958); FRANCE SLOKAN, *Panorama littéraire slovène* (1972); JOŽE POGAČNIK, *Zgodovina slovenskega slovstva,* 8 vol. (1968–72); *Le livre slovene* (quarterly), translations of recent literature and criticism.

Macedonia: HORACE G. LUNT, *A Survey of Macedonian Literature* (1953); BLAŽE KONESKI, *Makedonska književnost* (1961); MIODRAG DRAGOVATS, *Contemporary Macedonian Writers* (1976); *Makedonskata kniževnost vo kniževnata kritika,* 5 vol. (1973–74); MILNE HOLTON (ed.), *The Big Horse and Other Stories of Modern Macedonia* (1974); MILNE HOLTON and GRAHAM W. REID (eds.), *Reading the Ashes: An Anthology of the Poetry of Modern Macedonia* (1977); *Macedonian Review,* English-language periodical published in Skopje, containing articles about Macedonia, including its literature.

(D.A.N.)

Yugoslavia

The Socialist Federal Republic of Yugoslavia (Macedonian and Serbo-Croatian Socijalistička Federativna Republika Jugoslavija; Slovene Socijalisticna Federativna Republika Jugoslavija), with its 98,766 square miles (255,804 square kilometres), is a nation of south central Europe. The traditions of ancient Greece and Rome, of Byzantium, and of western and central Europe diffused, clashed, and sometimes took root in this region, and the multinational society bears Slavic, Eastern, and Western imprints of great complexity and diversity.

Modern Yugoslavia dates from the end of World War I, when in 1918 a new state rose from the ruins of the Austro-Hungarian Empire and its bordering states. In 1921 Yugoslavia was declared a constitutional monarchy. Following the collapse of Nazi power in Europe in World War II, a federal people's republic was proclaimed in 1945, under the leadership of the Communist partisan leader Tito and his forces. The country had suffered dreadfully during the war; it has been estimated that 1,750,000 persons (out of a population of about 15,000,000) were killed, many of them by other Yugoslavs in the course of a civil war between rival groups. The new country was at first allied to the Soviet bloc, but after the expulsion of the Communist Party of Yugoslavia from the Cominform, in 1948, Yugoslavia began to develop independent domestic and foreign policies.

Yugoslavia is divided into six republics, corresponding to the main Slav-speaking national groups, and two autonomous provinces. The republics are Serbia, Croatia, Bosnia and Hercegovina, Slovenia, Macedonia, and Montenegro. The autonomous province of Kosovo contains primarily Albanian-speakers and Serbs, and the autonomous province of Vojvodina has a mixed population of Slavs, Hungarians, and Romanians. The two autonomous provinces are subordinate to Serbia.

The country—whose capital is at Belgrade—borders seven nations; its coastline on the Adriatic Sea runs northwest to southeast and is known as "the coast of a thousand islands." At its northern limits there is a short frontier with Italy, giving way to successive borders (in a clockwise direction) with Austria, Hungary, Romania, Bulgaria, Greece, and Albania.

This article presents first an overview of the geography and history of Yugoslavia as a national entity, followed by a more detailed treatment of the geography and history of each of the six ethnohistorical regions represented by the constituent republics. In the case of some of the republics, the historical designation encompasses territory not included in the modern nation of Yugoslavia.

The article is divided into the following sections:

PHYSICAL AND HUMAN GEOGRAPHY

The land

RELIEF

The mountain core. The heart of the country, covering almost three-quarters of the total area, is composed of a rugged series of transverse mountain ridges, running parallel to each other behind the seacoast. Passes are high, and rivers often flow through deep gorges, a factor that has isolated much of the region. In Slovenia, in the northwest, are found extensions of the main Alpine ranges and Yugoslavia's highest peak, Triglav, 9,396 feet (2,864 metres) above sea level. To the south, a narrow, irregular belt of limestone plateaus, ranging from 1,000 to 5,000 feet (300 to 1,500 metres) in height, spans the country, paralleling the coast. Here underground water has dissolved the rocks to form a remarkable series of potholes, caverns, and cave systems. This zone, forming yet another barrier between the coast and the interior plains, is so distinctive that the name given to it—Karst—has been appropriated as a common noun to refer to areas of similar topography all over the world.

To the east of the Karst belt, and extending southward, is a zone composed of a variety of rocks, many of them resistant to erosion; this area is generally characterized as broken, rugged plateaus, deeply dissected by rivers. Elevations range from 3,000 feet in the west to two or three times higher farther south. The East Serbian Highlands (molded by the same forces that shaped the Carpathians) are another distinctive subregion. The valley of the Danube cuts through the uplands in a series of four major gorges whose total length is more than 70 miles and includes the Iron Gate.

The Adriatic coastal zone has a distinctive topography. The lateral ranges and valleys here have been submerged by geologically recent changes of sea level; the ranges become peninsulas, islands, or island chains, while the valleys become gulfs or sea channels, often quite complex and interconnected. The Dalmatian coast is the classic example of this type of "drowned" topography.

The interior plains. Plains cover about a quarter of Yugoslavia. The most important of these is the Pannonian Basin, which lies between the central highlands and the northern frontier and centres on the lowland floodplains of the Drava, Sava, and Danube rivers. Terraces made of gravel and loess (ancient windblown deposits) rise above the floodplains, and extensive hilly regions rise above them. Ancient outcrops of hard, crystalline rocks—the 3,400-foot-high Medvednica, for example—also rise above the plains here and there. The valleys of the Velika Morava and Vardar rivers merge to form a single extension of the plains to the south.

The plains have been most important in attracting settlement and are open to routes leading to the north and, hence, to central Europe; to the east (through the Danube Valley and the Iron Gate) to the Black Sea and beyond; and to the southeast toward Asia Minor and the eastern Mediterranean. Only to the southwest is communication (to the Adriatic) made difficult by the mountain belt.

DRAINAGE

Yugoslavia's many rivers follow turbulent courses through narrow gorges. Their total length is 73,552 miles (118,371 kilometres), or an average of 0.74 mile per square mile (0.46 kilometre per square kilometre) of territory. About 70 percent of the rivers flow to the Black Sea system, most of the rest to the Adriatic. The Danube, 365 miles (588 kilometres) of which are in Yugoslavia, is the heart of the Black Sea drainage, and its direct or indirect tributaries—the Sava, Drava, Drina, Velika Morava, and Bosna—are the country's most important rivers. The Vardar and its tributaries drain to the Aegean. The rivers form a broken, gridlike pattern superimposed on (and sometimes breaking through) the transverse ridges and valleys of the highlands. The intermittent drainage caused by the presence of the Karst belt is another noteworthy characteristic.

The country also has many lakes. Some were left by glaciers and because of their clear blue waters they are called the "eyes of the mountains." Some fill structural hollows or depressions near the coast; they include Lake Scutari (Skadarsko Jezero), the country's largest, which lies across the frontier with Albania. Two other major lakes, Ohrid and Prespa, lie to the south.

CLIMATE

The transverse mountain ranges of Yugoslavia have a major effect on its climate. Mediterranean influences are confined to a narrow coastal belt; the mountain ranges themselves have a moderately continental climate; and the northeastern plains, open to extreme weather influences from the heart of central Europe, have a continental climate. The continental region experiences cold winters (average temperature 30° F [−1° C]) and hot summers (75°–80° F [24°–27° C]), with seasonal extremes ranging from −13° F (−25° C) to 91° F (33° C). The Adriatic coast has warm winters (January average 45° F [7° C]) and hot summers (July average 75° F [24° C]). Temperature averages become generally lower in the mountains, and the Alpine regions have cold winters and short, cool summers. Because of the topography, winds have a marked influence. The cold bora (*bura* in Serbo-Croatian) wind may affect the coast in winter, and summer thunderstorms are pronounced in the mountain core. The cold *vardarac* wind affects Macedonia, and the equally cold *košava* afflicts the northeast. Coastal rainfall averages 25–35 inches (about 650–900 millimetres) annually. Totals increase inland to more than 100 inches annually, with heavy mountain snowfall, and decline again to 25–40 inches in the northeastern plains.

PLANT AND ANIMAL LIFE

There are more than 5,000 plant species in Yugoslavia, many of them endemic. Forests cover a third of the country. Evergreen species dominate the Mediterranean coastal regions, and such subtropical plants as cotton, rice, and poppies are found in Macedonia. Deciduous species cover most of the remainder of the country, with various kinds of beech, oak, and hornbeam forests predominating. Mountain pine is found in the highest regions, as are firs and junipers. In the mountains, the forests alternate with pastureland; in the Karst region they alternate with bare, open country.

Animal life in the interior plains is characterized by central and eastern European influences, including insects from the steppes, squirrels, and field mice. Despite the ravages of hunters, there are still deer, wild pig, wolf, fox, bear, lynx, and wildcat in the mountains, with chamois and alpine rabbit in the highest areas. In the Karst region live many rare types (*e.g.,* the blind salamander) and venomous snakes. The coastal belt harbours Mediterranean species, including lizards and insects adapted to the dry summers. The Adriatic yields more than 350 kinds of fish, and the rivers and lakes of the interior are also well stocked.

SETTLEMENT PATTERNS

Agriculture and settlement in the Karst region are extremely limited, and the whole area has functioned as a barrier. Since World War II there has been a rapid growth of urban settlements in the previously underdeveloped mountain areas of the south. In Bosnia this has been based on the development of industry, partly stimulated by the exploitation of metal ores, in such centres as Sarajevo and Zenica in the Bosna River valley and Tuzla and Banja Luka in the north; in Hercegovina, Mostar has developed. Nonferrous metal ores provide the base for industrial development in the mountainous regions of Kosovo, southern Serbia, and parts of Dalmatia. The greatest concentrations of urban population, however, are around the edge of the mountainous heartland, in the valleys and lowlands, and especially along the Sava Val-

The Karst region

Temperature ranges

Urbanization

ley, stretching from Ljubljana in the northwest to Zagreb and Belgrade farther east. In the postwar period this axis of development has been extended southward to Niš and beyond to Skopje.

Agriculture is most prosperous in the northern lowlands. The large farmhouses and modern, mechanized, cooperative farms of the Vojvodina contrast with the drystone or wooden houses scattered round meagre water supplies on the unproductive soils of the Dinaric Mountains (Dinara

Planina) of Dalmatia, Montenegro, and western Bosnia. Along the Adriatic coast is a string of historic cities to which tourism has brought a sudden influx of wealth.

The people

ETHNIC, NATIONAL, AND RELIGIOUS BACKGROUND

In view of the national and cultural diversity of the federation, questions of ethnic origin play a major role in

MAP INDEX

Political subdivisions

Bosna I Hercegovina	44·00n 18·00e
Crna Gora (Montenegro)	42·30n 19·00
Croatia, see Hrvatska	
Hrvatska (Croatia)	45·36n 16·00e
Makedonija	41·35n 21·48e
Montenegro, see Crna Gora	
Serbia, see Srbija	
Slovenija	46·15n 15·10e
Srbija (Serbia)	44·00n 21·00e

Cities and towns

Ada	45·48n 20·08e
Aleksinac	43·32n 21·43e
Apatin	45·40n 18·59e
Bačka Palanka	45·15n 19·22e
Bačka Topola	45·49n 19·38e
Bajina Bašta	43·58n 19·34e
Blato	42·46n 17·29e
Banja Luka	44·46n 17·11e
Bar	42·05n 19·05e
Baška	44·58n 14·46e
Bečej	45·37n 20·03e
Bela Crkva	44·54n 21·26e
Belgrade (Beograd)	44·50n 20·30e
Benkovac	44·02n 15·37e
Bihać	44·49n 15·52e
Bijeljina	44·45n 19·13e
Bijelo Polje	43·02n 19·44e
Bileća	42·53n 18·26e
Bitola	41·01n 21·20e
Bjelovar	45·54n 16·51e
Bosanska Dubica	45·11n 16·49e
Bosanska Gradiška	45·09n 17·15e
Bosanski Novi	45·03n 16·23e
Bosanski Petrovac	44·33n 16·22e
Bosanski Šamac	45·03n 18·28e
Brčko	44·53n 18·48e
Brežice	45·54n 15·36e
Brinje	45·00n 15·08e
Bugojno	44·03n 17·27e
Čačak	43·53n 20·21e
Čajniče	43·33n 19·04e
Čakovec	46·23n 16·26e
Čazma	45·45n 16·37e
Celje	46·14n 15·16e
Cerknica	45·48n 14·22e
Cetinje	42·23n 18·55e
Cres	44·58n 14·25e
Črnomelj	45·34n 15·11e
Ćurug	45·29n 20·04e
Đakovica	42·23n 20·25e
Danilovgrad	42·33n 19·07e
Daruvar	45·36n 17·13e
Debar (Dibra)	41·31n 20·30e
Derventa	44·58n 17·55e
Dibra, see Debar	
Doboj	44·44n 18·06e
Donji Vakuf	44·09n 17·25e
Dubrovnik (Ragusa)	42·38n 18·07e
Dulcigno, see Ulcinj	
Đurđevac	46·03n 17·04e
Foča	43·31n 18·46e
Gacko	43·10n 18·32e
Glamoč	44·03n 16·51e
Gnjilane	42·28n 21·58e
Gornji Milanovac	44·01n 20·27e
Gospić	44·33n 15·23e
Gostivar	41·47n 20·24e
Gračac	44·18n 15·51e
Gračanica	44·42n 18·19e
Gradačac	44·53n 18·26e
Gusinje	42·34n 19·55e
Hlebine	46·09n 16·58e
Idrija	46·00n 14·01e
Imotski	43·27n 17·13e
Jajce	44·21n 17·16e
Kanjiža	46·04n 20·04e
Karlobag	44·32n 15·05e

Karlovac	45·29n 15·34e
Kičevo	41·31n 20·57e
Kikinda	45·50n 20·28e
Ključ	44·32n 16·47e
Knin	44·02n 16·12e
Kočani	41·55n 22·25e
Kočevje	45·38n 14·52e
Konjic	43·39n 17·57e
Koprivnica	46·10n 16·50e
Kosovska Mitrovica	42·53n 20·52e
Kostajnica	45·14n 16·33e
Kotor	42·25n 18·46e
Kotor Varoš	44·37n 17·22e
Kragujevac	44·01n 20·55e
Kraljevo	43·43n 20·41e
Kranj	46·15n 14·21e
Kratovo	42·05n 22·11e
Kriva Palanka	42·12n 22·20e
Križevci	46·02n 16·33e
Krško	45·58n 15·29e
Kruševac	43·35n 21·20e
Kruševo	41·22n 21·14e
Kumanovo	42·08n 21·43e
Kuršumlija	43·08n 21·17e
Kutina	45·35n 16·46e
Leskovac	42·59n 21·57e
Livno	43·50n 17·01e
Ljubljana	46·03n 14·31e
Ljubuški	43·12n 17·33e
Loznica	44·32n 19·13e
Maglaj	44·33n 18·06e
Makarska	43·18n 17·02e
Mali-Lošinj	44·32n 14·28e
Maribor	46·33n 15·39e
Metković	43·03n 17·39e
Mostar	43·20n 17·49e
Mratinje	43·18n 18·49e
Murska Sobota	46·40n 16·10e
Našice	45·29n 18·06e
Negotin	44·14n 22·32e
Nevesinje	43·15n 18·07e
Nikšić	42·46n 18·56e
Niš	43·19n 21·54e
Nova Varoš	43·28n 19·48e
Novigrad	44·11n 15·33e
Novi Pazar	43·08n 20·31e
Novi Sad	45·15n 19·50e
Novo Mesto	45·48n 15·10e
Ogulin	45·16n 15·14e
Ohrid	41·07n 20·47e
Osijek	45·33n 18·41e
Otočac	44·52n 15·14e
Pakrac	45·26n 17·12e
Pančevo	44·52n 20·39e
Paraćin	43·52n 21·24e
Pazin	45·14n 13·56e
Peć	42·40n 20·19e
Pehčevo	41·46n 22·54e
Petrinja	45·26n 16·17e
Piran	45·32n 13·34e
Pirot	43·09n 22·35e
Pljevlja	43·21n 19·21e
Poreč	45·13n 13·37e
Postojna	45·47n 14·13e
Požarevac	44·37n 21·11e
Priboj	43·35n 19·31e
Prijedor	44·59n 16·43e
Prijepolje	43·23n 19·39e
Prilep	41·20n 21·33e
Priština	42·39n 21·10e
Prizren	42·12n 20·44e
Prokuplje	43·14n 21·36e
Prozor	43·49n 17·37e
Ptuj	46·25n 15·52e
Pula	44·52n 13·50e
Rača	44·14n 20·59e
Radoviš	41·38n 22·28e
Ragusa, see Dubrovnik	
Raška	43·17n 20·37e
Rijeka	45·20n 14·27e
Rogatica	43·48n 19·00e
Rovinj	45·05n 13·38e
Ruma	45·00n 19·49e
Šabac	44·45n 19·42e
Sarajevo	43·52n 18·25e
Semendria, see Smederevo	
Senj	44·59n 14·54e
Senta	45·56n 20·04e
Šibenik	43·44n 15·54e
Sinj	43·42n 16·38e

Sisak	45·29n 16·23e
Sjenica	43·16n 20·00e
Škofja Loka	46·10n 14·18e
Skopje	41·59n 21·26e
Skradin	43·49n 15·56e
Slavonska Požega	45·20n 17·41e
Slavonski Brod	45·10n 18·01e
Slunj	45·07n 15·35e
Smederevo (Semendria)	44·40n 20·56e
Smederevska Palanka	44·22n 20·58e
Sombor	45·46n 19·07e
Split	43·31n 16·27e
Srbobran	45·33n 19·48e
Sremska Mitrovica	44·58n 19·37e
Sremski Karlovci	45·12n 19·57e
Štip	41·44n 22·12e
Stolac	43·05n 17·58e
Strumica	41·26n 22·38e
Subotica	46·06n 19·39e
Sušak	45·29n 14·20e
Svilajnac	44·14n 21·13e
Tešanj	44·37n 18·00e
Tetovo	42·01n 20·58e
Titograd	42·26n 19·14e
Titovo Užice	43·51n 19·51e
Titov Veles	41·41n 21·48e
Tolmin	46·11n 13·44e
Travnik	44·14n 17·40e
Trebinje	42·43n 18·20e
Trogir	43·31n 16·15e
Trstenik	43·37n 21·00e
Tuzla	44·32n 18·41e
Ulcinj (Dulcigno)	41·55n 19·11e
Valjevo	44·16n 19·53e
Varaždin	46·19n 16·20e
Vareš	44·09n 18·19e
Vinkovci	45·17n 18·38e
Virovitica	45·50n 17·23e
Virpazar	42·15n 19·05e
Vis	43·03n 16·12e
Višegrad	43·47n 19·17e
Visoko	43·59n 18·11e
Vitanovac	43·44n 20·48e
Vlasenica	44·11n 18·56e
Vlasotince	42·58n 22·08e
Vranje	42·33n 21·54e
Vrbas	45·35n 19·39e
Vršac	45·07n 21·18e
Vukovar	45·21n 19·00e
Zadar	44·07n 15·14e
Zagreb	45·48n 15·58e
Zaječar	43·54n 22·17e
Zakučac	43·27n 16·42e
Zenica	44·12n 17·24e
Zepče	44·26n 18·03e
Zrenjanin	45·23n 20·24e
Zvornik	44·23n 19·06e

Physical features and points of interest

Adriatic Sea	43·00n 15·00e
Avala, peak	44·42n 20·31e
Banat, historic region	45·20n 19·35e
Biševo, Otok, island	42·59n 16·01e
Bosna (Vosna) river	45·04n 18·29e
Brač, Otok, island	43·20n 16·40e
Cetina, river	43·27n 16·42e
Cres, Otok, island	44·50n 14·25e
Crna, river	41·35n 21·59e
Dalmatia (Dalmacija), historic region	43·00n 17·00e
Danube (Dunav), river	44·10n 22·35e
Đerdap, see Iron Gate	
Dinara Planina, mountains	43·50n 16·35e
Djerdap, see Iron Gate	
Drava, river	45·33n 18·55e
Drina, river	44·53n 19·21e
Dugi Otok, island	44·00n 15·04e

Durmitor, mountain	43·08n 19·01e
Hvar, island	43·09n 16·45e
Ibar, river	43·43n 20·45e
Iron Gate (Đerdap), gorge	44·41n 22·31e
Iron Gate, reservoir	44·30n 22·00e
Istra, peninsula	45·15n 14·00e
Julijske Alpe, mountains	46·00n 14·30e
Južna Morava, river	43·41n 21·24e
Kamanjak, Rt, cape	44·46n 13·55e
Karst, see Kras	
Korčula, Otok, island	42·57n 16·50e
Kornat, Otok, island	43·50n 15·16e
Kosovo, physical region	42·38n 21·07e
Kras (Karst), plateau	44·00n 17·00e
Krk, Otok, island	45·05n 14·35e
Kupa, river	45·28n 16·24e
Kvarner, gulf	44·45n 14·15e
Lastovo, Otok, island	42·45n 16·53e
Lošinj, Otok, island	44·36n 14·24e
Macedonia, historic region	41·30n 22·40e
Medvednica, mountain	45·55n 15·58e
Metohija, physical region	42·40n 20·27e
Mljet, Otok, island	42·45n 17·30e
Molat, Otok, island	44·15n 14·49e
Morava, see Velika Morava	
Mura, river	46·18n 16·53e
Neretva, river	43·01n 17·27e
Nišava, river	43·22n 21·46e
Ohrid, Lake (Ohridsko Jezero), lake	41·02n 20·43e
Pag, Otok, island	44·30n 15·00e
Palagruža, Otoci, islands	42·24n 16·15e
Pannonian Basin, physical region	47·00n 19·00e
Posavina, valley	45·10n 17·20e
Prespa, Lake (Prespansko Jezero), lake	40·55n 21·00e
Rab, Otok, island	44·47n 14·45e
Šar Planina, mountains	42·05n 20·50e
Sava, river	44·50n 20·26e
Scutari, Lake (Skadarsko Jezero), lake	42·12n 19·18e
Slavonija, historic region	45·00n 18·00e
Šolta, Otok, island	43·23n 16·15e
Šumadija, physical region	44·20n 20·40e
Sušac, Otok, island	44·31n 14·18e
Timok, river	43·55n 22·18e
Tisa, river	45·15n 20·17e
Trieste, Gulf of	45·40n 13·35e
Triglav, peak	46·23n 13·50e
Una, river	45·16n 16·55e
Unije, Otok, island	44·38n 14·15e
Vardar, river	41·05n 22·35e
Velebit, mountains	44·38n 15·03e
Velika Kapela, mountains	45·15n 15·00e
Velika Morava, river	44·43n 21·03e
Venice, Gulf of	45·15n 13·00e
Vis, Otok, island	43·02n 16·11e
Vosna, see Bosna	
Vrbas, river	45·06n 17·31e
Zapadna Morava, river	43·41n 21·24e

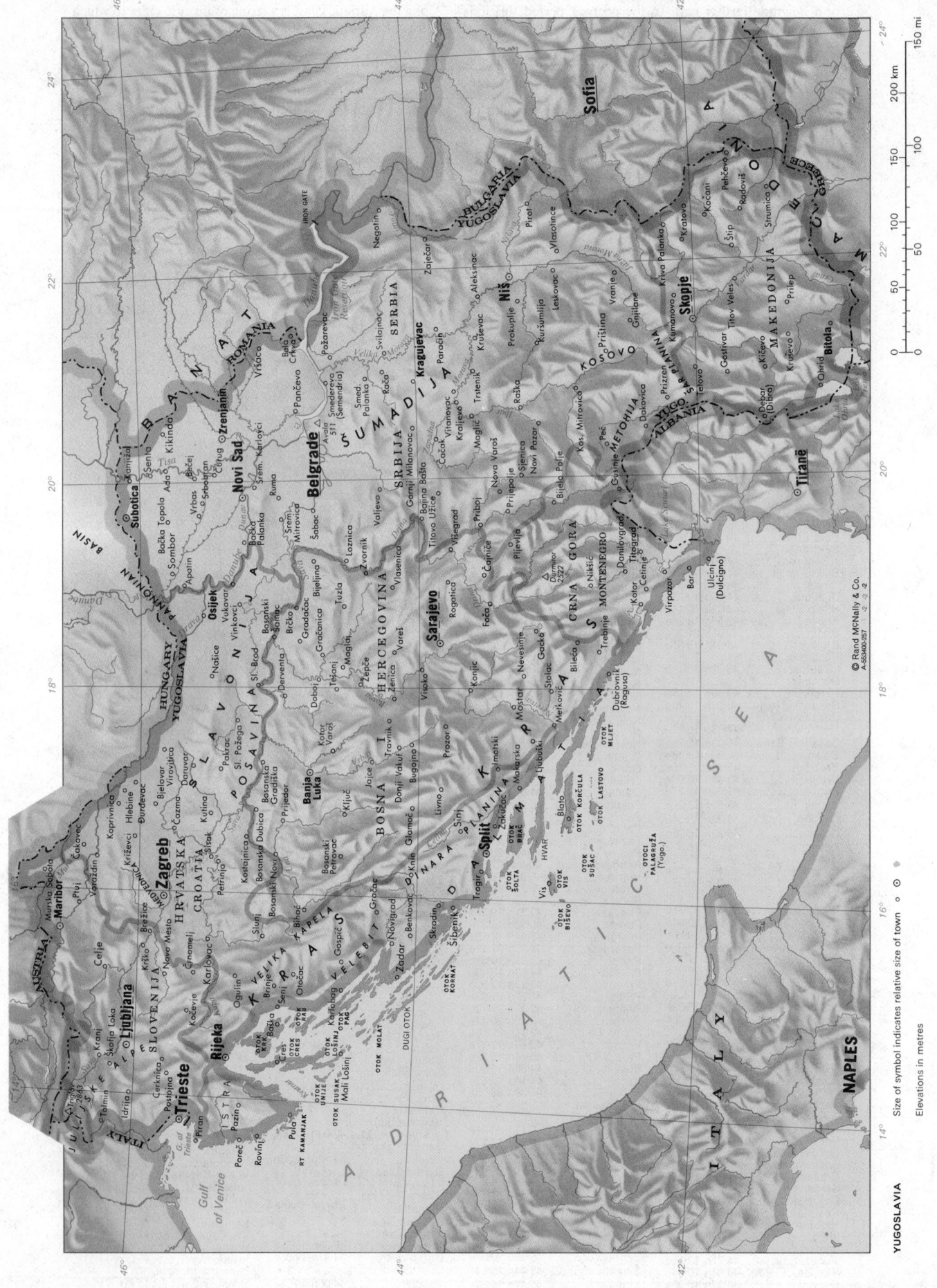

Size of symbol indicates relative size of town

Elevations in metres

© Rand McNally & Co.
A-553400-257

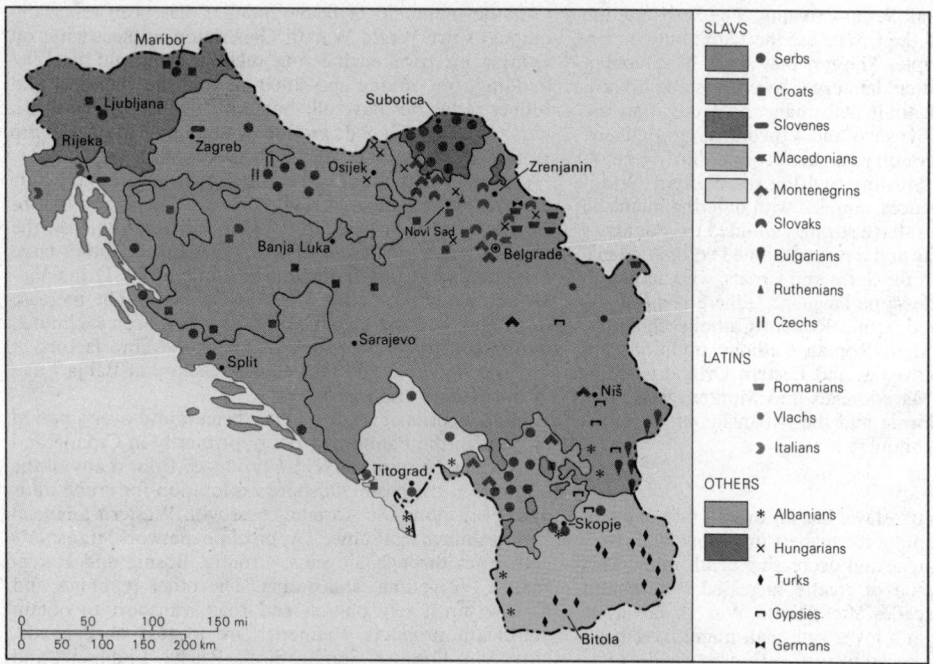

Ethnic composition of Yugoslavia.

The Slavs

contemporary Yugoslav society. Serbs form the largest group, then Croats, Slovenes, Macedonians, and Montenegrins. The Muslims of Bosnia, a significant minority, are recognized as a separate ethnic group. In addition to these South Slavs, there are several large non-Slav groups, the most important of which are Albanians and Magyars, or Hungarians.

During the great Slav influx of the 6th, 7th, and 8th centuries, the eastern parts of the Balkans were peopled by Serbs and Macedonians and the western by Croats and Slovenes. The eastern group developed under Byzantine influence, while the western peoples (including the tribes of Bosnia) came under the sway of Rome. Following the great schism between the churches of Rome and Constantinople in 1054, the western Slavs became Roman Catholics, the eastern group Orthodox.

The Serbs (first mentioned by name in 822) were the most numerous of the South Slavs and took their alphabet from Byzantium; similar to the Croats in origin, they also shared their language. A powerful Serbian state had arisen by the 14th century but languished under Turkish domination from 1389 to the mid-19th century. The Serbs and the Montenegrins had the only independent states at the time of Yugoslavia's creation in 1918.

The Croats (Hrvati), the second largest group of the South Slavs, migrated to Posavina and Dalmatia in the 7th century, establishing a permanent centre at Nin, near Zadar, and adopting the Latin alphabet from Rome. They formed an independent state at the end of the 9th century, became linked with the Hungarians in 1102, were ruled by Hungarian kings until 1562, and then were under the rule of Austro-Hungarian emperors until 1918.

The Slovenes, although mentioned as early as the 6th century, achieved their ethnic identity under strong Austrian influence, being ruled from Vienna from the 13th century to 1918.

The Macedonians initially were subjected to the rival ambitions of the Bulgars and the Byzantines and were then occupied for five centuries before 1913 by the Turks; they were also subjected to Greek cultural influences. The largest group came under Serbian control in 1913, while other parts of Macedonia were occupied by Greece and Bulgaria. The Yugoslav authorities recognized the national identity of the Macedonians after World War II.

The Montenegrins have a close cultural and religious affinity to the Serbs that dates back to the 12th century, when the region north of Lake Scutari, called Zeta, came under Serbian rule. Later this region became a centre from which Serbs and Montenegrins fought against Turk-

ish occupation. In the 16th century it became a theocratic state under the Eastern Orthodox Church. In the 1850s Montenegro was made a secular state, but Eastern Orthodoxy remained the dominant religion; independence was maintained until after World War I.

The Albanians are the largest non-Slav ethnic group in Yugoslavia, and they constitute the predominant population group in the autonomous province of Kosovo, as well as sizable minority populations in Macedonia and Montenegro. They are descendants of the ancient Illyrians and Thracians who were driven into the mountainous regions of the Balkans by the Slavs during the 6th and 7th century. The Turkish conquest and occupation of the Balkans destroyed their Roman and Byzantine heritage so that contemporary Albanians are more akin to the Muslim Turks than to the Christian Slavs; the majority of Albanians are Muslim. For much of their tenure within the Yugoslav federation the Albanians were excluded from political and economic decision making. Albanian nationalism was, however, the driving force behind the establishment of Kosovo as an autonomous province in 1968 and the elevation of the Albanian people and language to an official status in Kosovo.

The other major non-Slav group is the Hungarians, concentrated in the autonomous province of Vojvodina. Although they are a minority population within the province, the Hungarians were instrumental in the establishment of the autonomous province in 1948 and the recognition of Hungarian as as official language in 1968.

Following the unhappy national experiences of the interwar period and the struggles of World War II itself, the Yugoslav authorities have tried to achieve an equitable solution to long-standing national problems by creating a federal system within a Communist framework. National problems persist, however, as a result of unequal economic and social development.

The major groups of Yugoslav peoples—Serbs, Croats, Slovenes, Bosnian Muslims, Macedonians, and Montenegrins—constitute more than four-fifths of the population. Of the non-Slav population, the Albanians are the predominant group (8 percent), while the Hungarians comprise a small (2 percent), but significant minority. Other non-Slav minorities total less than 5 percent of the population and include Turks, Romanians, Gypsies, Slovaks, Bulgarians, Germans, Ruthenians (Ukrainians), Czechs, and Italians, as well as smaller Polish, Austrian, Greek, and Jewish groups.

The minorities

Language is generally the criterion of nationality. Some nine-tenths of the people speak Slavic languages, and three-quarters of these speak Serbo-Croatian. The Serbs use the Cyrillic alphabet and the Croats use the Latin, but conversion is relatively simple. The few that speak Macedonian have their own written language, recently standardized, with links with Bulgarian. Albanian and Hungarian are spoken primarily in Kosovo and Vojvodina, respectively.

In religion, the country is about one-third Roman Catholic, one-tenth Muslim, and the rest Eastern Orthodox. Religious differences, coupled with differing linguistic and ethnic affiliations, have strongly molded the country's social and political life and have occasioned fierce conflicts. The division between the Serbs and Croats, who, although speaking virtually the same language, adhere respectively to the Eastern Orthodox and Roman Catholic churches, is particularly profound. Roman Catholic traditions are strong among the Slovenes, and Eastern Orthodox traditions influence the Macedonians and Montenegrins. The Muslim beliefs of Bosnia and the Albanians are a reflection of the Turkish conquest.

DEMOGRAPHY

The population of Yugoslavia has an overall rate of natural increase that is among the highest in Europe with high birth rates in rural areas and decreasing death rates. This trend is largely a result of greatly increased state health programs. In the decades after World War II, however, the population grew at a lower rate than might have been expected because of special factors, including the dreadful war losses, the expulsion of those who had collaborated with the Germans, and the emigration of some minorities after 1945. Several million Yugoslavs and their descendants live permanently outside their country, and many thousand are short-term migrants working in other European countries. Internally, the youthful composition of the population and the continued move to the cities are perhaps the most striking demographic trends.

The economy

DEVELOPMENT

Within a Communist framework of distinctively Yugoslavian aspect, the national economy underwent a remarkable transformation after 1945. The social and cooperative sectors now account for the bulk of the national income, and the per capita income has risen greatly. Industrial growth has been particularly noteworthy, while the role of agriculture has declined.

Yugoslav authorities have given special attention to industrialization in underdeveloped areas. The more developed republics of Croatia, Slovenia, and Serbia have experienced a nine- or 10-fold increase in industrial output, and Bosnia and Hercegovina, Macedonia, and Montenegro have experienced even more striking growth. There are many unresolved economic problems, however, particularly related to inflation and agricultural productivity.

RESOURCES AND INDUSTRY

The nation's mineral resources are sometimes difficult to exploit, being located in regions not well suited for industrial development, generally in the inhospitable uplands. Coal deposits, chiefly in the form of low-quality lignite or brown coal, are found in Kosovo, Bosnia, and Serbia. Central Bosnia and Kosovo also contain, respectively, iron ore and lead, the latter deposits being especially rich. Other minerals include bauxite, manganese, and the copper of the historic mines of eastern Serbia. Natural gas and oil deposits, many unexploited, are found in the northeast.

Fish are abundant along the coast and in the rivers and lakes, but in many areas fish stocks are threatened by industrial pollution. The third of the country that is forested offers potential for the lumber industry, although sites are often difficult to reach.

The variety of soil and climate is generally favourable to agriculture, especially in the northeastern plains. About a quarter of the country is in pasture and meadow and only about a third under the plow. Hydroelectric power potential is one of the country's richest resources. Finally, the location of Yugoslavia and its scenic variety and historic sites are important assets for the tourist trade.

The development of heavy industry has been especially marked since World War II. Generation of electricity, oil refining, electrical engineering, metalworking and machine building, ore mining and smelting, and the chemical and rubber industries have all shown high rates of growth. In terms of value of goods produced, the major industries are metalworking, textiles, and food processing.

A number of thermal and hydroelectric generating plants are part of the industrialization process. The largest hydroelectric plant is at Djerdap (Đerdap, or Iron Gate) on the Danube, with a capacity of 1,025 megawatts. Other large plants are at Bajina Bašta and Mratinje in the Drina Valley and along the Cetina River in Dalmatia. The increase in products of the chemical industry has been facilitated by the construction of such plants as the fibre factory at Loznica in Serbia and the cellulose factory at Banja Luka in Bosnia and Hercegovina.

Small deposits of crude oil have been found over a period of years in the Pannonian Basin, primarily in Croatia and Vojvodina. Natural gas is also produced from many of the oil wells in the basin. Offshore exploration for crude oil is underway along the Adriatic coast with Western financial and technical assistance. A pipeline network transports petroleum through Slovenia, Croatia, Bosnia and Hercegovina, Vojvodina, and Serbia. The other republics and Kosovo must rely on rail and road transport to obtain petroleum products. Refineries are located in Belgrade, Novi Sad, Bosanski Šamac, Sisak, Rijeka, Ljubljana, and Zagreb. Petroleum produced from domestic wells accounts for less than two-fifths of Yugoslavia's total needs. Natural gas production and consumption has been limited by the lack of distribution facilities, particularly pipelines. In 1979 a natural gas pipeline connection to the Soviet Union was completed.

In 1981 the country's first nuclear power plant was completed with the assistance of a U.S. corporation, and the construction of several more plants was planned.

This industrial expansion has been reflected in the changing composition of Yugoslav exports, for industrial products now account for the major part of the total. The share of traditional exports, such as timber, wood products, and nonferrous metals, has been greatly reduced.

AGRICULTURE, FORESTRY, AND FISHING

Agriculture has traditionally suffered from low productivity, being based on small peasant holdings farmed by an aging work force. In common with many industrializing countries, Yugoslavia displays the phenomenon of the worker-peasant. Most of the cultivable land is still farmed privately, and most of the livestock is in private ownership. Socialized agricultural units, such as combines, farms, estates, and cooperatives have been growing in importance, but the innate conservatism of the peasants has prevented large-scale cooperation between the private and social sectors. Major crops are wheat, corn (maize), and sugar beets. Other important crops are sunflower seed, tobacco, potatoes, grapes (for wine), and plums.

Private ownership

The forestry industry is located where timber resources are exploitable, mainly in west and central Bosnia and Slovenia, where there are a number of sawmills, paper and pulp mills, and furniture factories. Fishing is economically significant along the coast and along the major rivers, notably the Danube.

TOURISM AND TRADE

Tourism is of special importance to the Yugoslav economy. Tourist development did not get under way until the 1960s, and income from this source rapidly increased. Much capital investment has gone into the building of hotels, motels, and restaurants. Most tourists go to the scenic Adriatic coast, but other facilities are being developed in the mountains.

Foreign trade brought Yugoslavia about one-fifth of its national income by the early 1970s. Although exports are increasing, they cannot keep up with the fast-growing imports; most of the deficit in the balance of trade is with the developed capitalist countries. The most important trading partners are the Soviet Union, West Germany, and Italy. Trade with the countries of Comecon (the east

Balance of trade problems

European trade group) has increased sharply. The deficit in the balance of trade has been covered in some years by the remittances of foreign currency by workers abroad and by earnings from the tourist industry.

ADMINISTRATION OF THE ECONOMY

The vast majority of employed persons work in the social sector. The Yugoslavs since 1950 have pioneered a unique system of workers' self-management. In the first postwar period, all the basic means of production, the financial institutions, and the means of communication were nationalized. The Five-Year Plan launched in 1947 was based on the Soviet model, with a highly centralized administration, directly controlled at all levels by the Communist Party. Yugoslav party theoreticians refer to this phase as the period of "dictatorship of the proletariat." The first steps away from this system came in 1949, when there were some experiments with advisory workers' councils in 200 factories. In June 1950 the Federal Assembly passed a Basic Law on the Management of State Economic Enterprises by Working Collectives. The workers' councils established in the early 1950s under this law had little real power at first, but during the next 10 years their control over the distribution of the surplus income of enterprises was extended, and they acquired some power in determining policy within nationally agreed upon guidelines.

In small firms, the legal right of the working collective to manage the enterprise can be exercised directly by the whole work force; in larger units, the collective delegates its rights to an elected workers' council, which in turn elects a board of management. The director and other senior management officials sit on the board ex officio but have no vote and can be removed on the initiative of the workers' council. Direct democracy is retained by the establishment of small groups of workers in a particular work unit that can express views on topics within their competence. The working collective also retains the seldom used right of changing decisions of the workers' council by referendum.

In the early 1960s a series of economic reforms and a new constitution (1963) provided the basis for "Market Socialism." These changes accelerated the shift away from centralized administrative management of the economy and gave greater responsibility to individual enterprises. Changes in the foreign trade system removed protective barriers and exposed Yugoslav enterprises to international competition. Financial controls (through the banks) increasingly replaced administrative measures. After 1967, foreign capital could be invested in joint ventures with Yugoslav firms, with a maximum holding of 49 percent by the foreign investor. Adjustment to the new Market Socialism system was painful, and there was some instability. The shock was cushioned by credits from such bodies as the International Monetary Fund and by employment of Yugoslav workers in western Europe.

Market Socialism

National policy is carried out through a series of plans. The main sources of revenue for the national budget are a turnover tax, payroll tax, customs duties, and a low personal income tax; these sources account for all but a fraction of revenue. The banking system is centred on the National Bank of Yugoslavia. Yugoslavia's rate of inflation has been among the highest in Europe.

TRANSPORT

Yugoslav transport in earlier times suffered from the double handicap of a difficult terrain and inadequate development. The railway system has been greatly expanded and accounts for most of public transport. The expansion was accomplished by the development of major new trans-Balkan routes, by standardization of narrow-gauge lines, by the expansion of mine railways in the uplands, and, increasingly, by electrification. In the mid-1970s a railway line linking Belgrade with the Adriatic port of Bar was opened.

Road and air traffic are now developing at a faster rate than railways. A program of road building included the construction of a route along the coast. Belgrade and Zagreb are the main air centres. Although all but 20 percent of the shipping owned by Yugoslavs was destroyed in World War II, maritime trade has developed considerably, and there has been an attempt to introduce economic specialization at the Adriatic ports.

Administrative and social conditions

GOVERNMENT

The constitutional framework. Yugoslavia is governed under a constitution promulgated on February 21, 1974, the third postwar constitution. The first, which came into force in 1946, was closely modelled on the 1936 constitution of the Soviet Union, which incorporated the concept of a centrally administered Communist state. In 1953 the constitution was substantially amended to give recognition, *inter alia*, to the changes in factory administration introduced in 1950. The post of president of the republic was created and was filled by Tito (Josip Broz). The legislature (the Federal Assembly) was divided into two chambers, a Council of Nationalities, representing the interests of the federal republics, and a Council of Producers, elected indirectly by various economic groups.

Postwar constitutions

In 1963 a new constitution widened the concept of workers' self-management to that of "social self-management." The name of the state was changed from Federal People's Republic of Yugoslavia to Socialist Federal Republic of Yugoslavia. A new legislative structure created five indirectly elected chambers, representing economic, social, and cultural groups. The Chamber of Nationalities remained. Separation of the Communist Party (called League of Communists of Yugoslavia, or Savez Komunista Jugoslavije, after 1952) from the state administration was advanced by a rule forbidding individuals (except President Tito) the right to hold high office simultaneously in both state and party hierarchies. A constitutional court was established to safeguard "Socialist legality."

In 1967 a series of amendments gave a stronger voice to the Chamber of Nationalities. Further amendments in 1971 devolved even greater powers to the republics. Provision was also made for a collective presidency, drawn in equal numbers from the federal units, to assume the functions of head of state on President Tito's retirement or death.

The constitution of 1974, in President Tito's words, made "a determined break . . . with all the remnants of so-called representative democracy which suits the bourgeois class." The new constitution retains the federal structure, with six republics and two autonomous provinces, each of which has some degree of local self-government. The constitutions of the republics and provinces reflect with appropriate modification the federal constitution.

Elections. Election to the various legislative bodies at all levels, from commune to Federal Assembly, is based on delegations drawn from occupational and other interest groups. The delegation that sends a member to represent it in an assembly has the power of immediate recall and can at any time choose another person to represent it. The assemblies of the communes, republics, and provinces each consist of three chambers. The Chamber of Associated Labour is formed from delegations representing four main occupational groups: workers in the social sector; peasants and farm workers; the liberal professions; and civil servants, League of Communists officials, and the army. The Chamber of Local Communities represents local citizens drawn from territorial constituencies. The Socio-Political Chamber is elected from members of the League of Communists, the Socialist Alliance, trade unions, and organizations representing war veterans, youth, and women.

The Federal Assembly (Savezna Skupština), which sits in Belgrade, consists of a Chamber of Republics and Provinces and a Federal Chamber. The 88 delegates to the former comprise 12 delegates elected by each of the six republican assemblies and eight each by the assemblies of the two autonomous provinces. The 220 delegates to the Federal Chamber are chosen indirectly by the assemblies of the communes.

The executive functions of government are carried out by the Federal Executive Council (FEC), the normal term of office being four years. Members cannot hold office simultaneously in the assembly and the FEC. The president of the council is in effect the prime minister. The FEC initiates legislation in the Federal Assembly and appoints federal secretaries (*i.e.*, ministers).

The collective presidency is composed of one representative elected by each of the six republican and two provincial assemblies for a term of five years and for not more than two consecutive terms. The president of the League of Communists of Yugoslavia is a member *ex officio*. The constitution also provided for a president of the republic and specifically gave the power to the Federal Assembly to elect Tito to that office for an unlimited term (article 333), a power that was exercised in 1974. Among the prerogatives of the president of the republic is that of commander in chief of the armed forces.

Sociopolitical organizations. The Socialist Alliance of the Working People of Yugoslavia (Socijalistički Savez Radnog Naroda Jugoslavije) is officially regarded as an all-embracing, nationwide political organization, uniting individuals and institutions in a complex system based on territorial divisions. Its highest organ is its congress, which meets every four years, power in the interim being exercised through a Federal Board and its executive and secretariat.

League of Communists of Yugoslavia

The most important of the constituent organizations—and officially its guiding ideological force—is the League of Communists of Yugoslavia (Savez Komunista Jugoslavije), founded in 1919 as the Socialist Workers' Party of Yugoslavia (Communists) and known as the Communist Party of Yugoslavia from 1920 to 1952. Under the 1969 reforms, it is headed by a Presidium, a body composed of representatives of the republics selected on the basis of strict parity. This body, in turn, elects an Executive Committee. The league as a whole is divided into six independent republican leagues and has more than 2,000,-000 members.

The second most important mass organization is the Confederation of Trade Unions of Yugoslavia (Savez Sindikata Jugoslavije), founded in 1948. The League of Socialist Youth of Yugoslavia (Savez Socijalističke Omladine Jugoslavije), with members between the ages of 14 and 27, is the largest youth group. Veterans' and Red Cross organizations have large memberships. There are also many professional and vocational groupings.

JUSTICE AND THE ARMED FORCES

A Constitutional Court, its 14 members elected by the Federal Assembly for nonrenewable terms of eight years, is the supreme legal authority for interpreting the constitution. The composition of the court must reflect the national composition of Yugoslavia; two judges are drawn from each republic and one from each autonomous province. Similar provisions regulate the composition and the elections to membership of the Federal Court, which adjudicates disputes between self-managing organizations and reviews sentences in serious criminal cases. Republican equivalents to these courts are nominated by the republican assemblies. There are separate military courts.

The Yugoslav Army is based on the various Partisan detachments and organizations that grew up during World War II. Military service is 15 months for the army and 18 months for the navy and the air force. The military forces are supplied with both Soviet and United States equipment and a wide range of modern Yugoslav-made weapons. The regular armed forces are supplemented by a national defense organization in which virtually all adult citizens are required to participate in some way.

HEALTH, WELFARE, AND EDUCATION

Virtually the entire population is covered by insurance, which takes five main forms: health protection, pensions, disability payments, family insurance, and unemployment relief. The basic principles on which the social services are administered are uniform throughout the country, but the level of provision varies between different communities, depending on local circumstances. The principles of decentralization and self-management apply to the social services, and in some communities the basic minimum provisions can be supplemented by decisions of communal councils and by factory welfare schemes.

There are three levels of education: elementary, in eight-year schools; secondary, in four-year vocational and high schools; and advanced studies in higher and senior schools, academies, and universities. Elementary schooling is compulsory. Some emphasis has been placed on expansion in (and more independence for) higher educational institutions. The University of Belgrade (founded 1863) is the largest institution of higher education. Two very old universities are those of Ljubljana, founded in 1595, and Zagreb, founded in 1669. There are also many facilities for adult education. The financing of education includes the provision of scholarships and repayable loans, complemented by various credits. A new system of teacher remuneration was introduced in the mid-1960s, with a heavy emphasis on self-management and accountability.

Higher education

Cultural life

A number of themes dominate Yugoslav cultural life; rich folk traditions continue to exert a powerful influence. The diverse traditions associated with various localities and nationalities also continue to be felt. In addition, three new elements have been added since 1945: the constant search for contemporary cultural values that are both distinctly Yugoslav and without specific regional associations; the challenges presented by the new Communist context and its evolving structure; and the spread of education and cultural institutions among the masses of the people.

LITERATURE AND FILM

Contemporary literature flourished after 1950, when the rigid aesthetic dogmas of the 1940s were finally rejected and experimentation was permitted. Dobrica Ćosić's novel *Daleko je sunce* (*Far Away Is the Sun*) broke with the former partisan portrayals of the war period by probing the moral and psychological dilemmas of the war situation. Oskar Davičo's novel *Pesma* (*The Poem*) was an equally lively study of revolutionary youth during the war. Both writers later turned to innovative portrayals of contemporary life. Ranko Marinković has written a number of fine contemporary short stories, often with deep psychological themes. Petar Šegedin, another prose master, has inclined toward a tragic view of modern, alienated man in his novels and short stories. The autobiographical writings of Milovan Djilas offer a fine portrayal of life in the remote regions.

Ivo Andrić and Miroslav Krleža

There are, however, only two really major contemporary figures. Ivo Andrić, the Nobel Prize winner in 1961, was a prose master—best known for his *Na Drini ćuprija* (1945; *The Bridge on the Drina*)—whose works, as the Nobel committee noted, were characterized by "epic force," great compassion, and clarity of style. The other is Miroslav Krleža, a satirist whose plays, essays, poems, and short stories foreshadowed the themes of modern Existentialism. Both Serbian and Croatian poetry (the latter dominated by the lyrical tradition of Augustin Ujević) continued to make distinctive contributions, with younger, experimental poets joining their more traditional elders.

The Macedonian cultural renascence has produced a number of fine poets, of whom Gane Todorovski is a prominent representative. The declaration by the Croat writers in 1967 of the distinct identity of the Croatian literary language provoked a bitter controversy.

Documentary films appeared in Yugoslavia immediately after the liberation of the country. In 1945, 1946, and 1947 about 40 documentary shorts were made. Under the conditions made possible by Communism, the film industry developed into an organized production activity in which all the republics engage. The first feature film (*Slavica*) made after the war was shot in 1947; its subject was the war and it was made by Partisan cameramen and actors and was enormously successful. Film production has since developed and become diversified, although the war is still a major theme. About 50 feature films and 150 shorts of all kinds are made each year in the eight major film centres. Dušan Makavejev, of Novi Sad, became internationally famous for his films *The Switchboard Operator* (1967; also released under the titles *Love Affair, or The Case of the Missing Switchboard Operator* and *An*

Affair of the Heart) and *WR—Mysteries of the Organism* (1971), but his work was severely criticized by the authorities and he was publicly disgraced. Another film that earned official displeasure was *The Happy Gypsies* (or *I Even Met Happy Gypsies*) by Aleksandar Petrović, which commented bitterly on the depressed status of the Gypsy communities in Yugoslavia.

Film festivals

There are two national film festivals, the feature film festival at Pula and the short and documentary festival in Belgrade. In addition, a festival of the best foreign feature films, FEST, takes place in Belgrade, while the international animated film festival is held in Zagreb. Yugoslav film makers have an excellent international reputation and have won numerous prizes at international film festivals. The animated film is particularly notable, centred on the Zagreb school, founded by cartoonists and journalists in 1954.

PERFORMING, FINE, AND FOLK ARTS

Yugoslavia has a deep-rooted theatrical tradition, dating back to the mystery plays of Dalmatian monks in the Middle Ages. Attendance is high at the many professional, amateur, and children's theatres. The most important professional theatre in Belgrade is the National Theatre (founded 1868), which has its own opera, drama, and ballet companies. Serbia's oldest theatre is the Serbian National Theatre, in Novi Sad, founded in 1861. The Croatian National Theatre, in Zagreb, dates from the same year. The other republics have their own theatres, often catering to minority audiences. Until quite recently, about three-quarters of all professional performances were of works by foreign authors, but there has been a marked upsurge in Yugoslav works, some of which have been performed abroad. There are academies for training directors, actors, and technicians in Belgrade, Zagreb, and Ljubljana. The summer festival at Dubrovnik, featuring plays, opera, ballet, and local folk customs, is very popular, particularly with tourists. There are permanent, community-supported opera and ballet companies in most of the large cities. Experimental modern methods of staging, decor, and direction have been in evidence since the celebrated performance of *The Consul,* by Gian Carlo Menotti, in the 1952–53 Belgrade season.

Yugoslav painting has origins in the medieval frescoes of Serbia and Macedonia, and folk themes are an element in modern painting. Contemporary artists of significance include ·Petar Lubarda, whose stark portrayals of Montenegrin landscapes are peopled with symbolic figures. Younger artists have been free to explore most of the trends of western Europe, usually with a distinct national emphasis. Yugoslavia has a splendid architectural and monumental heritage, which is one of the country's major tourist attractions. In music, strong folk traditions have been supplemented by a number of works on the theme of the war years and, later, by some interesting experimentation.

Folk arts are as vigorously pursued in Yugoslavia as anywhere in Europe. Primitive and naïve paintings—originally associated with the Hlebine school, named after a Croatian village in which the painter Krsto Hegedušić began to interest the village youth in painting in 1931—are marked by intimate rural concepts of nature and are executed with great care. Folk dancing remains popular in the remoter regions, often with its original religious content. Dances vary from the round dances of the mountainous interior to the lively dances and music of Macedonia and the fierce *bunjevac* round, danced only by men. Folk arts and crafts also include decorated farm buildings, paintings on wood and glass, costumes, lace embroidery, carpet making, leatherwork, and pottery. For statistical data, see the "Britannica World Data Section" in the current *Britannica Book of the Year.* (V.Ba./F.B.S./Ed.)

The Hlebine school

HISTORY

For the history from the earliest times down to 1919 of the countries comprised within Yugoslavia and of the formation of the state itself, consult the sections below: *Bosnia and Hercegovina; Croatia; Macedonia; Montenegro; Serbia;* and *Slovenia.* The present section treats the united state, after 1919.

Between the World Wars

THE PARTIES, 1919–21

The new South Slav, or Yugoslav, state, at first officially named the Kingdom of Serbs, Croats, and Slovenes, emerged from World War I weak and disunited. War casualties had been far higher in Serbia than in the other provinces, but economic hardships had affected all. Countries that not only had different histories but possessed different currencies and different legal and administrative systems had to be fitted together. The spirit of social revolt was widespread among the peasants, and the myth of the Russian Revolution appealed to workers and intellectuals. The non-Serbian nationalities were at best bewildered, at worst hostile. The only forces that could be relied on to maintain public order were the Serbian Army and the police, and their actions in many cases increased both social and national discontent. But the forces of revolt were scattered and without leadership. By the end of 1919 the government had established relative stability. By this time, too, a number of political groups had emerged, falling into three main categories.

Serbian political parties

First were the Serbian parties. The strongest were the Radicals, led by the veteran Nikola Pašić. They still stood in principle for parliamentary democracy, with a certain emphasis on peasant interests. In practice they reflected the interests of the rising middle class rather than those of the peasants, and they stressed above all the interests of state unity. The Radicals were centralists and Serbian nationalists, opposed to all demands of the non-Serbs for autonomy or federalism. They were the party of bureaucracy and of "strong government." The second party was the Democrats, a combination of the Independent Radicals of prewar Serbia led by Ljubomir Davidović and of the Serbs of former Austro-Hungarian territories led by Svetozar Pribićević. The two sections were not always in agreement; Davidović was essentially a liberal, while Pribićević at this time was nearer to Pašić in his conception of a strong united state. The third party, the Agrarians, was the smallest. Its formal program was similar to the other two, but its practical emphasis was on the social interests of the peasants.

In the second category were the non-Serb national groups. Of these, far the most important was the Croatian Peasant Party, led by Stjepan Radić. This turbulent and inconsistent man was at this time a champion of the peasant against the towns and the bureaucracy, a republican and an antimilitarist. He believed in unity of all South Slavs, even including in this notion the Bulgars. He was thus not opposed to the formation of a Yugoslav state; he objected only to the existing state, because it was a monarchy and based on the Serbian Army. Among the Slovenes of the northwest, the most culturally advanced of all Slav subjects of the new state, the strongest group was the People's Party led by Msgr. Anton Korošec. Though reserved toward the Belgrade politicians, the Slovenes welcomed the new state as a defense against Italy. The Muslim Slavs of Bosnia formed a group of their own. The German minority in Vojvodina and the Albanians in the southwest also had their organizations.

The third category was the Communist Party. Formed in 1919 by a majority at a congress of Socialist parties of all the territories united in the new state, the Communist Party was able to exploit social antagonisms, national discontents, and the tendency of the South Slavs—especially of the Serbs—to put their hopes in the Russians. During 1919 the Communists had strong support among the railway men and in the municipalities of Belgrade and Zagreb.

The Communist Party

At the election to the Constituent Assembly in November 1920, the Democrats won 92 seats, Radicals 91, Communists 58, Croatian Peasant Party 50, the rest 128. Radicals, Democrats, and Muslims supported a centralist constitution. The Croatian Peasant Party refused to take part in the Assembly. The centralist draft proposed by the government was carried in June 1921 by 223 votes, with 35 against and 161 abstentions. In the following July the Communist Party was banned, after a Communist had assassinated the minister of the interior, Milorad Drašković. Thereafter the Communists suffered from police repression and also lost the support of many who had earlier placed their hopes in them. In particular, the nationalist discontent in Macedonia, Montenegro, and Croatia, which had been a factor in Communist successes in 1919–20, was henceforth exploited by specifically nationalist parties and groups.

Alexander I, who had been prince-regent of the Serbs, Croats, and Slovenes since December 1, 1918, became king on August 16, 1921, at the death of his father, King Peter I of Serbia.

PARLIAMENTARY POLITICS, 1922–28

The most important issue of Yugoslav internal politics during the period of parliamentary government, which lasted until the end of 1928, was the opposition of the Croats to the centralist constitution. Radić was for a time in prison and then went abroad, first to western Europe and then to the U.S.S.R. His party, which at the parliamentary election of 1923 increased its seats to 70, continued to abstain. Pašić and the Radicals stayed in power with the support of the German and Albanian minority groups. In 1924 Radić and his party returned to Parliament, thereby putting Pašić in a minority. For a few months in the second half of 1924 the Serbian Democrat leader Davidović was premier, and there was some hope both of more liberal government and of an understanding with the Croats. But Davidović made himself powerful enemies by seriously attempting to investigate corrupt practices of the preceding period. In November 1924 he was dismissed by King Alexander, and Pašić and Pribićević—who had broken with Davidović and formed his own party—together continued the centralist policy. In July 1925 Radić suddenly announced his conversion to the monarchy and his admiration for Pašić. A Pašić–Radić government was formed. Real agreement could not be made, however, and in April 1926 this unnatural alliance was dissolved. Soon after this Pašić died, but the Radical Party remained in power, with the support of Democrats, Slovenes, and Muslims. In 1927 there was another sensational change when the archcentralist Pribićević was reconciled with Radić, and their two parties formed a close alliance in opposition.

Thus the two really important issues that underlay Yugoslav politics—the conflicts between Serbian centralism and Croatian federalism and between bureaucratic despotism and democratic government— were confused by the rivalries and manoeuvres of the chief personalities. The rivalries were not necessarily petty or ignoble; Pašić was sincerely convinced that only centralism and strong methods could hold the state together; Radić, for all his sudden changes of tactics, was sincerely devoted to the interests of the Croatian peasants and commanded their devoted loyalty; Pribićević became convinced, by the experience of himself and others, that centralism was the wrong policy and, having made his peace with Radić in 1927, never again swerved from a policy of federalism and of democratic liberties. But the forces were too evenly balanced, and the Democrats, who could have decided the issue if they had joined Radić and Pribićević, could not choose between their democratic principles and their Serbian nationalism. During 1927 and the first half of 1928 the deadlock continued.

The crisis came on June 20, 1928, when, during a debate in the house, Puniša Račić, a Montenegrin member, shot two Croatian members dead and mortally wounded Radić himself. The Croatian Peasant Party and the Independent Democratic Party of Pribićević then left the Parliament, and the breach between Croatia and Serbia was complete.

(margin: Serbian and Croatian conflicts)

The only person who could hope to bridge the gulf was King Alexander himself. On January 5, 1929, he consulted Radić's successor Vladko Maček and Pribićević. They proposed a reorganization of the state into seven federal units. This would not only have given the Croats the home rule that they demanded, but would also have separated from Serbia the lands of Vojvodina, Montenegro, Bosnia, and Macedonia, which most Serbs regarded as Serbian lands. Finding these proposals unacceptable and having no confidence in the majority of Serbian politicians, the King decided to take all responsibility into his own hands and on January 6, 1929, proclaimed a royal dictatorship.

FOREIGN AFFAIRS, 1919–29

The most important of Yugoslavia's neighbours was Italy. The withdrawal from Balkan politics of Germany and the Soviet Union encouraged Italy to take upon itself the role of chief power in southeastern Europe. The major obstacle in its path was Yugoslavia, successor on the eastern shore of the Adriatic to the vanished Austrian Empire. The Treaty of Rapallo (November 12, 1920) fixed a frontier that left several hundred thousand Slovenes and Croats under Italian rule in Istria and in the district of Gorizia. The status of Fiume (Rijeka) was another cause of friction until it was settled by a further agreement in Rome in 1924. Italo-Yugoslav rivalry was also fierce in Albania, which from 1927 was virtually an Italian satellite.

Mussolini also gave some support to the extreme Bulgarian nationalists, who had designs on Macedonia and supported the Macedonian terrorist organization on Yugoslav soil—the Internal Macedonian Revolutionary organization (IMRO). The overthrow of Aleksandŭr Stamboliyski's Agrarian government in Bulgaria in June 1923 had strengthened the influence of the extremists. Likewise, Mussolini made himself the patron of Hungarian revisionism, one of whose aims was the recovery of the province of Vojvodina, in which about one-third of the population was Hungarian.

Yugoslavia formed with Czechoslovakia and Romania, by treaties signed in 1920 and 1921, the alliance known as the Little Entente, which was directed against Hungary. As Yugoslavia had also a treaty of friendship with France, concluded in Paris on November 11, 1927, it was generally regarded as a member of the French system. The Little Entente, however, merely united against one small and demilitarized state three larger and armed states: it offered no defense against any of the three great powers that represented real dangers to the contracting parties as Germany did to Czechoslovakia, Italy to Yugoslavia, and the U.S.S.R. to Romania.

(margin: The Little Entente)

KING ALEXANDER'S DICTATORSHIP, 1929–34

Alexander changed the official name of the country from Kingdom of Serbs, Croats, and Slovenes to Yugoslavia. He was determined that Serbian, Croatian, or Slovene nationalism should give place to a wider loyalty, Yugoslav patriotism. He disliked both Serbian and Croatian nationalisms and wished to protect the interests of the people, which he believed he understood better than the politicians. Unfortunately neither of these high aims was achieved; his regime perpetuated the hegemony of Serbia and increased all the abuses of bureaucracy and police repression.

The administrative reorganization of October 1929, which created nine provinces (*banovine*), with boundaries designed to break up the historic regional divisions, operated to the disadvantage more of the non-Serbs than of the Serbs. The abolition of political parties of a religious or regional nature crippled all political parties, Serb and non-Serb alike. In his choice of political collaborators, Alexander tried to enlist persons of all nationalities. In practice, however, he was unable to detach Croats of any importance from the Croatian Peasant Party, which now assembled under its banners almost the whole Croatian nation; but he was able to recruit individual Serbs of some standing. The result was that Serbian opposition to his regime, though widespread and bitter, was political— the opposition of democrats against dictatorship—while Croatian opposition was national—the opposition of the

Croatian nation against Belgrade. The Croatian Peasant Party lost much of its original character; it became less a peasant social movement than a nationalist movement in which middle-class lawyers and intellectuals played a larger part than peasants.

The King's first premier, Gen. Petar Živković, quickly resorted to traditional Balkan methods of military and police despotism. A Law for the Defense of the Realm, which imposed drastic penalties for terrorism, sedition, and the propagation of Communism, was so interpreted as to justify arrests and maltreatment of the government's critics. The Communist bogey became the favourite excuse for abuses of power. The dictatorship also dissolved elected local authorities and suspended the irremovability of judges. The new constitution introduced in September 1931 was accompanied by an electoral law that ensured a large governmental majority.

Opposition to the regime was partly silenced but was not destroyed. It was most effective, because most united, in Croatia. The misdeeds in Croatia of the gendarmerie—staffed by Serbs—created bitter hatred, which was exploited by a group of extreme separatists led by the exiled Ante Pavelić, who received support from the Italian and Hungarian governments. The great majority of Croats, however, followed Maček and the Croatian Peasant Party, with which Pribićević's Independent Democratic Party was still firmly allied. In November 1932 the leaders of the two parties met in Zagreb and published a resolution denouncing the hegemony of Old Serbia and demanding that the state be reorganized so as to ensure that no single nation of Yugoslavia should dominate the others. The principles of the resolution were later approved by representatives of the Serbs of Vojvodina, of the Slovenes, and of the Muslims of Bosnia. The government's reply was to intern the Slovene and Muslim leaders and to put Maček on trial under the Law for the Defense of the Realm. He was condemned in April 1933 to five years' imprisonment.

In Serbia, too, the regime grew increasingly unpopular. The Serbian democratic leaders expressed their sympathy with the demands of the Croats for democratic liberties. They were divided, however, on the question of Serbian hegemony. Some supported the Croatian proposal for a federal reorganization; others feared that this would cause the state to disintegrate. Even those who accepted federation found it hard to agree with the Croats on the status, in a federal state, of Vojvodina and Bosnia. No Serbian political leader could envisage autonomy for Macedonia.

Throughout the years between World Wars I and II, Macedonia was subject to a special regime. The Macedonian dialect could not be used in public and no Macedonian political party could operate, even before 1929. Under the surface, extremist trends, both Communist and Fascist—the latter supported from Bulgaria and Italy—had a substantial following.

On October 9, 1934, on a state visit to France, Alexander, together with the French foreign minister, Jean-Louis Barthou, was assassinated at Marseille by a Macedonian terrorist who had connections with Pavelić and with the Italian and Hungarian authorities.

THE REGENCY, 1935–41

On behalf of Alexander's young son King Peter, the country was ruled by three regents, the first of whom was the former king's cousin Prince Paul. In May 1935 a parliamentary election was held in conditions of greater freedom. Maček had been previously released from prison. His list of candidates was supported by most of the Serbian opposition. Though the government was able, by familiar methods, to win almost all seats in Serbia, Maček's list had an overwhelming victory in Croatia. Impressed by this evidence, Prince Paul entrusted the premiership to Milan Stojadinović, a Serbian banker with international connections, who was believed to favour conciliation with the Croats. In September 1935 Stojadinović formed a new party, the Yugoslav Radical Union, composed of a section of the Serbian Radicals, the Slovene People's Party, and the Bosnian Muslims.

During the two years from the summer of 1935 to the

summer of 1937 Maček had sporadic contacts with Prince Paul, with Stojadinović, and with the Serbian democratic parties. Maček believed in the good will of Prince Paul but distrusted Stojadinović. In the summer of 1937 a government proposal for a concordat with the Vatican, whose main sponsor was the Slovene leader Korošec, aroused a storm of opposition in Serbia. The Serbian Orthodox Church felt itself threatened and rallied around itself a heterogeneous company. There were Serbian nationalists who feared that through the Catholic Church the Croats would gain a commanding position in the country; there were Serbian democrats who aimed at agreement with the Croats but were glad of any opportunity to attack the government; even the Communists took a hand in the agitation. Since the 7th Congress of the Comintern (summer 1935), the Yugoslav communists had adopted the policy of a Popular Front, which in the Yugoslav context meant an alliance of all groups that were against the dictatorship and against Fascism, at home or abroad. This policy had the advantage of coinciding with the feelings of most Yugoslavs. In these years the Communists, who since 1921 had ceased to count except in the negative sense of a bogey to be exploited by the police, recovered ground, not so much among the workers as among the intelligentsia and especially among the students of Belgrade University.

The demonstration, by the anticoncordat agitation, of the government's unpopularity in Serbia warned Maček that if he made an agreement with Stojadinović this might later be disowned by the Serbian people. He therefore came to terms with the Serbian democrats and formed with them in October 1937 a United Opposition. This alliance reached the height of its popularity in August 1938, when Maček visited Belgrade and was welcomed by great crowds of Serbian townsmen and peasants. It now seemed that only the ill will of the dictatorship stood in the way of a firm friendship between the Serbian and Croatian peoples. These hopes were defeated by international developments.

Stojadinović sought in foreign policy the friendship of Germany and hoped that German protection would be able to reconcile Yugoslavia with its hostile neighbours on acceptable terms. The Yugoslav-Bulgarian and Yugoslav-Italian treaties of January and March 1937 seemed to justify his hopes. But the price for German support was not only the abandonment of Yugoslavia's old friends, France and Czechoslovakia, but the imitation of Fascist policies in internal affairs.

Stojadinović fancied himself as the *Führer* of Yugoslavia and believed himself master of the country. But the power really lay with Prince Paul. A parliamentary election in December 1938 gave the governmental Yugoslav Radical Union 60 percent of the votes and the United Opposition 40 percent. In Croatia Maček was again triumphant. As the danger of war approached, Prince Paul felt it essential to solve the Croatian question and understood that Stojadinović was an insuperable obstacle. In February 1939 he replaced him as premier with Dragiša Cvetković. The Italian invasion of Albania in April was a further warning. After some setbacks, an agreement with the Croats was achieved before war broke out. The Cvetković-Maček compromise of August 1939 set up a single Croation *banovina,* which included most territories of Croatian population. The administration of this area was placed in the hands of Maček and his party, which was also represented in the central government. The agreement had an uncertain reception in both Serbia and Croatia: the Serbian Democrats felt betrayed by Maček, who appeared to have made a deal with the dictatorship at the expense of the Serbian people; and on the Croatian side, though the majority accepted the arrangement, a powerful minority remained implacably opposed to Yugoslavia and hoped that the triumph of German arms and Fascist ideas would enable them to set up an independent Croatian state under their control. The axis powers, distrusting Prince Paul as an anglophile, renewed their interest in the exiled Pavelić.

World War II

The Italian invasion of Greece in October 1940 brought war to Yugoslavia's frontiers. Prince Paul, whose sympa-

Margin notes:

A Law for the Defense of the Realm

Macedonia between world wars

Resurgence of the communists

The Italian invasion of Albania

thies lay with Great Britain, wished to preserve neutrality but decided that he could not withstand Axis pressure. On March 25, 1941, Cvetković and his foreign minister, Aleksandar Cincar-Marković, signed Yugoslavia's adhesion to the Anti-Comintern Pact of the three Axis powers, Germany, Italy, and Japan. Two days later the government was overthrown by a conspiracy led by officers of the Air Force. A new government was formed of representatives of the Serbian opposition parties, under Gen. Dušan Simović, and King Peter was proclaimed of age to rule, thus bringing the regency to an end. The Croatian and Slovene ministers of the old Cabinet remained in the new. Though the sympathies of the new leaders were undoubtedly with Great Britain, they did not want war and tried to convince the Axis powers of their loyalty to the pact. But Hitler, who had already had one big disappointment in Yugoslavia when Stojadinović was dismissed in February 1939, and who now saw the government that, after so much trouble, he had at last brought into line thrown out in its turn, was not prepared to take any more chances. On April 6 the Germans invaded Yugoslavia from Hungary, Bulgaria, and Romania. In a few days the Yugoslav Army, badly led and organized and incompletely mobilized, was routed. Simović and some of his colleagues, with King Peter, escaped via the Middle East to London.

German invasion of Yugoslavia

The victors carved up the country. Germany and Italy divided Slovenia between them. Italy took part of Dalmatia on its own behalf and the Kosovo district and western Macedonia on behalf of Albania and set up a protectorate over Montenegro. Bulgaria annexed most of Macedonia, Hungary annexed the western half of Vojvodina (Bačka) and some small districts on the Croatian border. Pavelić was presented by his patrons with the control of an Independent State of Croatia; this included all Bosnia but not all Dalmatia and was nominally a kingdom, with Aimone, duke of Spoleto, second son of the Duke of Aosta, as its absentee sovereign. The rump of Serbia was placed under German military occupation and was allowed from August 1941 to have a puppet government of its own under Gen. Milan Nedić. The eastern half of Vojvodina (Banat) had a separate German military administration, in which members of the local German minority played the chief part.

Croatian Fascists and the massacre of Serbs

Armed resistance to the occupation began in Bosnia, and there the Croatian Fascists began a massacre of Serbs which, in the whole annals of World War II, was surpassed for savagery only by the mass extermination of Polish Jews. The Serbs took to the hills and forests to defend themselves. In Serbia itself a force led by the regular army colonel, Dragoljub (Draža) Mihajlović fought Germans in the early summer. After Hitler attacked the U.S.S.R., the Yugoslav Communists, who had already made military preparations, took the field in Serbia and Montenegro. By September a large part of both these lands was liberated by these two forces, which at first helped each other but then came to blows. In November the Germans drove all resistance forces out of Serbia and massacred thousands of people in reprisal.

In the following three years the Communist forces grew, while the forces of Mihajlović lost ground. One reason was that Mihajlović came to depend on the support of various Serbian armed units in Italian-occupied territory, which fought under Italian command against the Communist "Partisans," and thus he came to be widely regarded as a collaborator with the occupying powers. Another reason was that the Partisans attracted thousands to their ranks by their slogan of the unity of all Yugoslav nations against the invaders and the traitors. This slogan provided the only alternative to the fratricidal massacres, first of Serbs by Pavelić's Croatian Fascists and then of Croats and Muslims by Serbian nationalist četnici (Chetniks) owing allegiance to Mihajlović. In their liberated territory the Communists, led by Tito, a Croat, built not only an army but a crude civil administration, enlisting local persons of ability and initiative who had played no part in politics under the old regime and now had the opportunity to make careers. The administrative organizations were called people's committees. Though they enlisted persons of various political opinions or of none, they were firmly

controlled at the top by the Communists. In November 1942 the Communists announced the creation of a provisional legislative body, the Antifascist Council of National Liberation of Yugoslavia (Antifašističko Vjeće Narodnog Oslobodjenja Jugoslavije, or AVNOJ), and, a year later, of a provisional government.

By the summer of 1944 most of the mountainous part of Yugoslavia was in Partisan hands. In October, Partisan forces took part in the liberation of Belgrade by the Red Army. In the last months of the war Yugoslav troops, now on a regular footing, played a part in the southern sector of the Soviet-German front.

From the summer of 1943 the British Mediterranean Command had had liaison missions with the Partisans, and the British and U.S. governments made efforts to reconcile Tito's authorities with King Peter's Yugoslav government in exile. In January 1942 the exiled government had appointed Mihajlović as its war minister.

Reconciliation between Tito and the exiles would have required the abandonment of Mihajlović, with whom Tito was engaged in a civil war no less bitter than his national war against the invaders. The exiles refused to abandon Mihajlović until June 1944, when Ivan Šubašić, who had been governor of the Croatian *banovina* from 1939 to 1941, was appointed premier by the King. The entry of the Soviet Army into Serbia in October 1944 and the increasingly arrogant tone of Tito toward the Western powers made it clear that there would be no reconciliation but only a surrender by the Western powers to Tito. Formal respectability was given to the surrender by the formation in January 1945 of a regency, to which King Peter transferred his powers, and by the return to Yugoslavia of Šubašić and some other exiled political leaders.   (H.S.-W.)

The Soviet army in Serbia

Communist Yugoslavia

When hostilities ended the Partisans extended their provisional wartime governmental machinery throughout the country and prepared to get legal recognition for what was in fact a Communist government. A provisional government was nominated on March 7, 1945, consisting of 20 representatives of AVNOJ, three of the royalist government in exile, and five of prewar political parties. Tito was prime minister and Šubašić minister of foreign affairs. A provisional parliament met in August, comprising delegates from all parts of the country plus 68 representatives of prewar political parties and 13 independents. All persons over 18 years of age and enlisted people regardless of age were given the vote. Those accused of collaboration were disenfranchised. No political opposition to the People's Front was allowed. This caused the three royalist representatives, Milan Grol, Šubašić, and Juraj Šutej, to secede from the provisional government. Elections for a bicameral parliament, which was to comprise a Federal Council and a Council of Nationalities and was to have the powers of a Constituent Assembly, were held on November 11, 1945. The People's Front gained 90.48 percent votes for the Federal Council, 88.68 percent for the Council of Nationalities.

The Constituent Assembly was a subservient instrument of the Yugoslav Communist Party. It abolished the monarchy and proclaimed Yugoslavia a Federal People's Republic composed of six autonomous republics: Serbia (including the autonomous province of Vojvodina and the autonomous region of Kosovo-Metohija), Croatia, Slovenia, Bosnia-Hercegovina, Montenegro, and Macedonia. War damage was severe. Extreme centralization was introduced both as Communist policy and as a means to rapid reconstruction and rehabilitation. The republics were allowed to use their own language and personnel but in other respects were directed by the central government. A new constitution, modelled on the Soviet constitution of 1936, was adopted on January 31, 1946. Industry was nationalized and ownership of house property limited to occupants. Land reform was introduced, limiting private holdings to 45 hectares (111 acres); in 1953 private holdings were reduced to 10–15 hectares (25–37 acres). A five-year plan for economic development was introduced.

The abolition of the monarchy

Tito's government was at first hostile to the West. It

feared intervention in favour of a royalist counterrevolution and was gravely disturbed at the Allied Forces' occupation of Trieste and its hinterland, which left Yugoslav troops in occupation of only a part of the area claimed from Italy. Relations with the Soviet Union appeared to be very close, though later it was learned that there had been continual friction between Soviet and Yugoslav leaders throughout these years. Relations with neighbouring Communist states were good: discussions with Bulgaria took place in 1946 and 1947 about possibilities for federation, but were eventually abandoned through lack of agreement and Soviet opposition. Aid was also given to Greek Communist insurgents in the Greek Civil War of 1946–49. Relations with the Catholic Church were very strained because of the Communists' anti-religious policy and the church's outspoken and active opposition to Tito's government. Diplomatic relations with the Vatican were broken off on December 17, 1952, and restored in 1966.

Relations with the Soviet Union had been deteriorating because of Yugoslavia's persistently independent national policy. The quarrel came into the open in June 1948, when Yugoslavia was expelled from the Cominform, Stalin accusing Tito of many heresies. All Communist states denounced Yugoslavia and broke off relations, Albania being especially virulent. Stalin's attempt to unseat Tito failed, but great hardship was caused by the complete economic boycott. Yugoslavia turned to the West for economic aid, which was given to enable the country to remain free of Soviet domination. Over the 10 years 1950–60 aid from the United States totalled $2,400,000,000 and from Great Britain $120,400,000. It enabled Yugoslavia to develop modern industries, reorganize foreign trade with the West, modernize agriculture, and establish well-armed fighting forces. It brought many technical and cultural contacts with the Western world and, although given without political strings, it had a profound effect on all future developments in Yugoslavia.

| *U.S. and British aid* |
(marginal note) *U.S. and British aid*

Modernization of the economy brought increased prosperity and stability to the regime. Successful in their defiance of the Soviet Union, the Yugoslav leaders reconsidered the fundamental concepts that they had copied from the Soviet Union and on which their state had been based. They evolved new theories and practice of Communism, creating a unique system that came to be known as Titoism. The essence of the new position was that each Communist country must decide its own "road to Socialism" and exercise independent sovereignty. Yugoslavia's new road brought many popular changes. An early one was the abandonment of collectivization of agriculture, which had been forced on the peasants to please the Soviet leaders at the outset of the Cominform crisis. The police state system of the postwar years was abandoned. Political administration and economic management were decentralized, giving increased powers and responsibility first to the republics, later to the communes. Workers' councils were introduced into industry to enable workers to share in management, including decisions on distribution of profits.

CONSTITUTIONAL CHANGES

These changes were incorporated into two constitutions. That of January 13, 1953, merged the two previously existing houses of Parliament into one Federal Council and introduced a new second chamber, the Council of Producers. The aim was to weight representation in favour of potential Communist support. This second chamber was not a success, partly because much interest was attracted to the Workers' Councils and the Councils of the Communes set up about the same time.

The constitution of 1963 (marginal note)

The new constitution of April 7, 1963, abolished the Council of Producers and replaced it by four councils with limited competence (Economic Affairs, Education and Culture, Social Welfare and Health, Political Organization). Each was to work with the retained Federal Council on matters in its own field. Voting for all chambers was to be by indirect franchise. The position of the courts was drastically altered, giving greater freedom from administrative control and allowing a constitutional court power to determine the constitutionality of all legislation. One of the most far-reaching changes of the new constitution was that all offices (with the sole exception of Tito for his lifetime) were to be subject to a rotation principle, so that no one could hold office at any level of government for more than two consecutive terms.

The Yugoslav Communist Party had already been reorganized at its 7th Congress in 1958, in which it had changed its name to League of Communists, and Communists had been urged to abandon the assumption of elite leadership and to confine themselves to a "leading role." Even with changed tactics and rotation of personnel, Communists kept control of state activities: political opposition was still forbidden and treated as anti-state activity.

Milovan Djilas, one of Tito's most fanatical Communist associates of prewar and wartime days, became the best known of many opponents of centralized monolithic Communism. He spent more than seven years in prison for publishing abroad, in his book *The New Class,* views critical of Yugoslav Communism. He was finally released in December 1966.

NEW FOREIGN POLICY

Liberalization within the framework of a one-party state was accompanied by a more friendly attitude to the West with whom trade relations, opened up by economic aid, expanded during the 1950s and 1960s. In 1954 an agreement was signed with Italy ending the Trieste problem; Zone A with Trieste was assigned to Italy, Zone B with small favourable frontier rectifications in Istria went to Yugoslavia. Friendly relations and expansion of trade developed between the two countries. Following Yugoslav abandonment in 1949 of aid to rebels in Greece, tension on Yugoslavia's southern frontier was reduced. A Balkan Alliance with Turkey and Greece signed on August 9, 1954, gave Yugoslavia temporary security in this area but no lasting political association. Relations with Greece became cool after the military coup in Athens in 1967.

Relations with the Soviet Union began to change when premier N.A. Bulganin and first secretary of the CPSU N.S. Khrushchev visited Belgrade in May 1955 and apologized for the Cominform dispute. Suspicious of Soviet intentions, Tito imposed his own conditions for cautious rapprochement. They included recognition of Yugoslavia's right to sovereign independence and the developments of its own form of Communism, the disbanding of the Cominform (effected in 1956), and a demand for speedier de-Stalinization in satellite countries, especially in Hungary. Yugoslavia's relations with the Soviet Union then improved and thereafter fluctuated between friendship and distrust, never reaching extremes of either.

Tito's relations with the Soviet Union (marginal note)

In 1956 Tito paid two visits to the Soviet Union, and Khrushchev and other Soviet officials visited Yugoslavia. Problems of liberalization in Hungary were the main subject of discussion. The Hungarian revolt in October abruptly ended this phase of cooperation. Yugoslavia's impotence when faced with Soviet intransigence was shown by the delay in de-Stalinization in Hungary, which Tito believed to be the main cause of revolt. It was also demonstrated by Soviet disregard of Yugoslav diplomatic protection offered by the Yugoslavs to the Hungarian leader Imre Nagy and by the brutality of Soviet intervention in Hungary. The dangers of counterrevolution shown by the escalation of the revolt frightened the Yugoslav leaders, who were opposed to the first Soviet intervention in Hungary (October 24), but accepted the second (November 4) as inevitable. Cooler relations with the Soviet Union ensued for a time, but in the 1960s they showed a tendency to return to cautious friendship until they were brutally disrupted by the Soviet invasion of Czechoslovakia in 1968.

In these years, determining factors were Yugoslavia's independence in interpretation of ideology as well as in foreign policy, and the need of the Soviet Union for Yugoslav friendship following the deterioration in Sino-Soviet relations in the 1960s. Yugoslavia wished to see the independence it had won for itself extended to other countries of eastern Europe.

While deeply interested in developments within the Communist bloc, Tito firmly refused to be drawn into it.

Yugoslavia did not join the Council for Mutual Economic Assistance (Comecon) and the Warsaw Treaty Organization and did not attend special meetings of Communist parties summoned by the Soviet Union in attempts to unify Communist countries' policies on a number of issues, especially in relation to Communist China. Fiercely attacked by Communist China after the 7th Party Congress, Yugoslavia refused to retaliate and continued to advocate China's inclusion in the United Nations. On a number of world issues Yugoslavia's foreign policy was basically the same as that of the Soviet Union. This was true of policy toward the war in Vietnam and on the Arab–Israeli conflict. Political differences with Moscow did not prevent the resumption of trading between the two countries, which increased throughout the 1960s. It was typical of Titoist policy that this did not preclude similar economic relations with the West, which remained stable and developing in the same period. Yugoslavia became a member of the General Agreement on Tariffs and Trade (GATT) and showed interest in both the Organization for Economic Cooperation and Development (OECD) and the Common Market, although it had signed a cooperative agreement with Comecon in 1964.

Tito's non-alignment policy

A unique feature of Yugoslavia's international relations was Tito's policy of nonalignment. It aimed to develop friendly relations with small, weak, or noncommitted nations to increase their joint influence in a world dominated by the two superpowers. Tito promoted this cause by more than 30 visits to Asia, Africa, and Latin America. He won support from Gamal Abdel Nasser in Egypt and from Jawaharlal Nehru in India. Two conferences of nonaligned nations were organized by Yugoslavia, in Belgrade (September 1961) and Cairo (October 1964). The movement had no success in terms of world influence, but it won friends for Yugoslavia and mitigated its isolated position between the Soviet bloc and the West.

INTERNAL AFFAIRS

In internal affairs, the 1963 constitution represented a triumph for liberal reformists against conservative opposition from some leading Communists. Liberalization and decentralization continued, being carried out more rapidly in economic than in political life. To combat inflation and a tendency for production to stagnate, principles of market economy were introduced, and profitability became the criterion for all enterprises. Prices were decontrolled. The consequent rise in prices and unemployment was further increased by a sharp currency devaluation carried out in two phases in 1965 and 1966. These measures led to some slow economic improvement but underlined the fact that political liberalization had not kept pace with changes in the economic field. Matters came to a head in summer 1966 when Aleksandar Ranković, Tito's right-hand man for so many years and possible successor, was arraigned before the Central Committee of the League of Communists and accused of having obstructed reform and decentralization with the aid of a vast network of secret agents built up since the early war days. He was stripped of all office and retired from public life. Thereafter the reform measures continued more rapidly, leading to an increasing democratization of political life with much articulate opposition. This brought to the surface many local problems and interregional differences. Among these were demands from Croats and Macedonians for parity in use of their language forms in all national business. The Macedonian Orthodox Church declared its independence from the Serbian Church. Emphasis on regional nationalism became a feature of the late 1960s, and regional nationalism played a deciding role in the establishment of Kosovo as an autonomous province in 1968. The problem was dealt with at the 9th Congress of the League of Communists of Yugoslavia in 1969 when parity of representation was given to republics in a Presidium and smaller Executive Bureau in an attempt to have an all-Yugoslav central authority able to halt centrifugal tendencies.   (P.Ay.)

Regional nationalism

AFTER TITO: COLLECTIVE PRESIDENCY

Twenty-five years of common life within a federal state did not fuse the Yugoslav peoples into a unitary Yugoslav nation. That was neither possible, nor intended. But the Yugoslav peoples can be free and prosperous only in a common structure without any single people's hegemony and with equal rights and obligation for all. Tito always believed that such a structure must be a socialist one, with one single political party in control. His program was successfully imposed thanks mainly to his own efforts. But on May 25, 1972, he was 80 years old and, anxious as he was for the future of federal Yugoslavia, he decided to reinforce, as much as was humanly possible, the country's existing constitutional framework.

His proposal for amendment of the 1963 constitution was first put forward in a speech in Zagreb on September 21, 1970, in which he suggested that the office of president should be replaced by a body to be known as a collective presidency in which all the republics were equally represented. The speech showed his fears that a serious crisis might arise over his succession. It was clear also that he was concerned about the rivalries between the republics, especially between Serbia and Croatia, and about the danger that a disputed succession might lead to Soviet intervention.

The Presidium of the League of Communists endorsed Tito's proposal for a collective presidency on October 4, and the President put it forward in a message to the Federal Assembly on December 14. The Constitutional Coordination Commission published on February 27, 1971, a draft of amendments to the constitution. These proposals aroused strong feelings in both Serbia and Croatia and evoked such violent controversy that a split in the League of Communists seemed possible. Tito made a tour of the country in April, during which he made a series of speeches denouncing the extremists on both sides of the controversy, appealing for national and party unity. The situation calmed down after a meeting of top party leaders from all republics at Tito's island residence of Brioni (April 28–30), where he obtained a unanimous endorsement of the draft constitutional amendments, which were approved by Yugoslavia's Second Congress of Self-Management (Samoupravljenje) in Sarajevo on May 8.

All five chambers of the Federal Assembly in Belgrade on June 30 adopted 20 major amendments to the constitution. Under these amendments the federal government retained responsibility for defense, foreign affairs, and broad economic policy, including development. All other powers, including the power to initiate investment projects, were transferred to the republics and municipalities. Heading the Yugoslav state was a collective presidency of 22 members (three from each republic and two each from the autonomous provinces of Vojvodina and Kosovo). Within this presidency, which was responsible for the formulation and supervision of broad domestic and foreign policies, each republic had a right to veto decisions that, in its opinion, were potentially harmful to its national interest. These amendments, then, appeared to set Yugoslavia on a course leading to a loose confederation of semi-autonomous units. At a joint session of all the houses of the Federal Assembly on July 29, Tito was reelected president of Yugoslavia for a further five-year term. Also in 1971, the regular rotation of jobs was initiated in an effort to promote relations among the various nationalities.

Constitutional amendments

After the nationalist demonstrations in Croatia in November–December 1971, there was a sharp change of policy, and the League of Communists and the army acted together to reassert central control. At the 10th congress of the league in 1974 there was great emphasis on the need for "democratic centralism" and for party discipline and unity. The constitution of 1974 reflected this mood. It established a new set of institutions at both local and federal levels and drew many more citizens toward active participation in public affairs. At the same time, it abandoned the concept of representative democracy and replaced it with the delegation system, under which the selection and recall of members of delegations is more easily controllable in the interest of national unity. Although the economy remained decentralized and operated in part according to market principles, there was a recentralization of political life, a tightening of social discipline, a greater vigilance by the authorities against dissent, and an emphasis on national defense.

Tito's closest colleague, Edvard Kardelj, died in February 1979. In early 1980, Tito himself became gravely ill, and his death occurred in May. In a manner holding to the provisions in the constitution for an orderly transfer of power, Tito's duties were adopted by the collective state presidency and the presidium of the party. Cuijetin Mijatović became president in May 1980 and asserted a continuing adherence to the policy of nonalignment. For current political history, see the annual issues of the *Britannica Book of the Year*. (Ed.)

Tito's death

BOSNIA AND HERCEGOVINA

Physical and human geography

The Socialist Republic of Bosnia and Hercegovina (Serbo-Croatian Socijalistička Republika Bosna i Hercegovina) occupies about one-fifth of the country's territory. Roughly triangular, it is bounded by Serbia and Montenegro to the east and southeast, and by Croatia to the north and west. The name Bosnia (Serbo-Croatian Bosna) is derived from that of the Bosna River and is probably of Illyrian origin. Hercegovina, the southern part, takes its name from the title *herceg* (German *Herzog*, "duke"), assumed in the 15th century by a local ruler.

With an area of 19,741 square miles (51,129 square kilometres) Bosnia and Hercegovina is mostly a mountainous country rich in natural features, such as lakes, rivers, and mineral springs. The coastline is limited to a 13-mile (20-kilometre) stretch along the Adriatic Sea, and there are no natural harbours. The principal rivers are the Sava, which forms the northern boundary of the republic with Croatia; the Bosna, Una, and Vrbas, which flow north and empty into the Sava; the Drina, which flows north, forms the eastern boundary with Serbia, and merges with the Sava; and the Neretva, which flows southward and empties into the Adriatic. To the southwest about one-quarter of its area is covered by the so-called karst, an arid limestone plateau with small depressions fit for cultivation. Rivers in the karst flow largely underground. The terrain sometimes reaches heights of more than 6,000 feet (1,800 metres) above sea level, and heights drop abruptly toward the Adriatic Sea.

In climate Bosnia differs considerably from Hercegovina. In both the sirocco, bringing rain from the southwest, is a prevalent wind, as well as the bora, the fearful north-northeaster, which, sweeping down the lateral valleys of the Dinaric Alps, overwhelms everything in its path. The snowfall is slight, and, except on a few of the loftier peaks, the snow soon melts. In Bosnia the weather resembles that of the south Austrian highlands, generally mild, though apt to be bitterly cold in winter. The average annual temperature in Banja Luka is about 52° F (11° C), and the mean annual precipitation is about 42 inches (1,070 millimetres). The coldest month there is January, with an average temperature of about 32° F (0° C), and the warmest month is July, which averages about 72° F (22° C). During January and February Banja Luka receives the least precipitation, and in May and June it experiences the heaviest rainfall. Hercegovina has more affinity to the Dalmatian Mountains, which are oppressively hot in summer. In Mostar, situated along the Neretva River near the Adriatic coast, the average annual temperature is about 59° F (16° C) and the mean annual precipitation is about 57 inches (1,450 millimetres). The coldest month in Mostar is January, averaging about 42° F (6° C), and the warmest month is July, averaging about 78° F (26° C). There is a relatively dry season in Mostar from June until September. The remainder of the year is wet, with the heaviest precipitation between October and January. The winter rains of the karst region show that it belongs to the subtropical climatic zone.

Apart from the arid wastes of the karst, the soil is well adapted for the growing of cereals, especially corn (maize); olives, vines, mulberries, figs, pomegranates, melons, oranges, lemons, rice, and tobacco are grown in Hercegovina and the more sheltered portions of Bosnia. Cropping is usually combined with livestock rearing and the republic is a major sheep raising region. In the central and eastern parts of Bosnia there are forests of pine, beech, and oak. The forest lands of the republic account for about one-quarter of Yugoslavia's total. Arable land represents about one-half of the republic's area, but the fertile soils are mainly in the north. Bosnia possesses a variety of minerals, including coal, iron, copper, chrome, manganese, salt, cinnabar, zinc, and mercury, besides marble and much excellent building stone. Among the mountains, gold and silver were worked by the Romans, and, in the Middle Ages, by the Ragusans. The southern part of Hercegovina yields asphalt and lignite. Bosnia and Hercegovina was an impoverished region, heavily dependent on agriculture, during the time of the Ottoman rule, and since the establishment of Yugoslavia it has remained one of the less developed republics of the nation. Economic development policies of the socialist federal government since 1946 have attempted to alleviate regional economic disparities, primarily by providing more funds to Bosnia and Hercegovina and the other less developed republics. Such policies have been debated fervently in the federal and republican assemblies and often have led to tension between the republics. Furthermore, these policies have not substantially narrowed the gap between the developed and less developed republics. By the late 20th century the per capita income for Bosnia and Hercegovina was about two-thirds that of the nation as a whole and about one-half that of the most developed republic, Slovenia. The republic's dependence on agriculture has decreased, and the contribution of mining and manufacturing to the economy exceeds the input of agriculture.

Economic development policies

Bosnia and Hercegovina is the most ethnically diverse of Yugoslavia's republics and is the home of the vast majority of the country's Muslims. For many years the Bosnian Muslim population was underestimated because many such persons were categorized as Croats or Serbs. Roughly one-third of the residents of Bosnia and Hercegovina are Muslim, one-third are Serbs, one-fifth are Croats, and the rest are of other nationalities. Most Serbs are Orthodox and most of the Croats are Roman Catholic. The capital of the republic is Sarajevo, which is also the seat of the head of all Muslims in Yugoslavia (*reis-ul-ulema*) and of a Roman Catholic archbishop. The other main towns are Mostar, Banja Luka, Tuzla, and Travnik.

There is a great deal of ethnic segregation in the republic and in Yugoslavia as a whole. The population growth rate for Bosnia and Hercegovina usually has been greater than that of Yugoslavia as a whole or of the more developed republics. This higher growth rate has further aggravated the republic's economic situation, causing more persons to enter the labour force annually than could be accommodated by the economy. The increased competition for jobs, combined with the economy's inability to provide employment for new workers, has caused many residents of the republic to emigrate. By the late 20th century about one-fifth of the Yugoslavian emigrants employed abroad (especially in western Europe) originated from Bosnia and Hercegovina.

The Socialist Republic of Bosnia and Hercegovina maintains a government similar to the federal system. It has a constitution, an assembly, and an executive council. Representatives or delegates to the assembly are not elected directly by the people, but are selected from delegations corresponding to recognized segments of the republic's society. The republic's assembly is composed of three chambers: the Chamber of Associated Labour, the Chamber of Communes, and the Socio-Political Chamber. Delegates for each of these chambers are selected from the various communes in the republic, and each commune has an assembly also composed of three chambers. The Chamber of Associated Labour in each commune is composed of

The government of the republic

delegates representing groups of workers (*e.g.*, agricultural workers, government workers, and industrial workers), and this communal chamber elects delegates to represent its views in the corresponding chamber in the republican assembly. The Socio-Political Chamber of each commune is composed of delegates from the League of Communists, the Socialist Alliance, trade unions, and organizations representing war veterans, youth, and women. The delegates of this chamber select their own representatives in the republic's Socio-Political Chamber. Delegates in the Chamber of Communities represent local community delegations and these commune delegates elect their representatives in the republic's Chamber of Communes. The chambers of the republic's assembly elect 12 delegates to represent Bosnia and Hercegovina in the Chamber of Republics and Provinces of the Federal Assembly; and each commune assembly within the republic elects an equal number of delegates to represent its communal interests in the Federal Chamber of the Federal Assembly.

The executive council acts as the executive branch of the republic's government in the same manner as its federal counterpart. On matters that require cooperative agreement or action among the republics and the federal government, the executive council acts as negotiator. The council also exerts influence on the republic's delegates in the Chamber of Republics and Provinces.

History

ANCIENT AND MEDIEVAL PERIOD

The most ancient inhabitants of Bosnia and Hercegovina were Illyrian tribes. After the Roman conquest the region was included in the Roman province of Illyricum, except for the portion along the Sava, which belonged to that of Pannonia.

Serbian settlement · Serbian settlement in Bosnia and Hercegovina began in the 7th century AD. Bosnia was detached from the rest of Serbia and became a separate political entity. King Bodin (1081–1101) united Bosnia with the other two Serbian principalities—Rashka and Zeta. After Bodin's death, however, Bosnia separated again.

Hungarian encroachment on Bosnia began in the middle decades of the 12th century. The local representatives of the Hungarian kings had the title of ban. The rule of Kulin, "the great ban," began about 1180. He concluded an agreement with Dubrovnik (Ragusa) in 1189 guaranteeing freedom of trade for his country. Then the efforts of the papacy to extend Roman Catholicism in Bosnia, combined with further political pressure by the Hungarians, who wanted Bosnia to be under a Hungarian archbishop instead of the Slavonic archbishopric of Dubrovnik, provoked a strong national resistance in the country. War was avoided, but Bosnia came under the jurisdiction of the Hungarian archbishop of Kalocsa.

Matej Ninoslav became ban about 1232. His promise to embrace Roman Catholicism caused a serious disturbance in Bosnia, which was considered by the papacy as a country "overgrown with thorns and nettle and a breed of vipers." When Andrew II of Hungary and his successor Béla IV attacked Bosnia, Ninoslav sided with his people, and war went on from 1235 to 1239, the Hungarians making little progress.

The Kotromanić dynasty and Hum. Ban Prijezda, who ruled in Bosnia as a vassal of Hungary from 1254 to 1287, was the founder of the dynasty of Kotromanić. His successor was Stephen Kotroman (1287–1316). Kotroman's son, Stephen Kotromanić (1322–53) extended Bosnia toward the south, conquering the province of Hum, or Zahumlye (Hercegovina), styling himself count of Hum from 1326.

At the end of the 12th century Hum had been in the possession of the Serbian prince Miroslav, brother of the great *zupan* Stephen Nemanya of Serbia. Miroslav's successor was Petar (probably his son). He was defeated by Nemanya's son Stephen but retained the part of Hum between the Neretva and Cetina rivers, the rest being divided between Andrija (probably also Miroslav's son) and Stephen's eldest son, Radoslav. Petar's successor in Hum was his nephew Toljen, who perished in battle during the Hungarian invasion of Bosnia (1235–39). Andrija's son

Radoslav became a vassal of Hungary. Subsequently the situation in Hum underwent a number of changes, but the whole country is known to have been subject to King Milutin of Serbia (died 1321).

Stephen Kotromanić was the first Bosnian ruler to coin money; his country extended "from the Sava to the sea and from the Cetina to the Drina." He was succeeded by his brother's son, Tvrtko I (1353–91), who ascended to the throne at the age of 15. Soon afterward Louis I of Hungary occupied part of Hum, claiming it as the dowry of his wife, Elizabeth, daughter of Stephen Kotromanić. Relations between Tvrtko and Louis then worsened, leading to open war in 1363. Tvrtko was subsequently forced to leave the country by a revolt of the Bosnian nobles, which his brother Vuk supported. Eventually, however, he was restored to power by Louis. In 1377, Tvrtko crowned himself as "king of the Serbs and Bosnia, and the coastlands." In 1382, in order to make his trade independent, he built the town of Novi (the modern Hercegnovi) at the entrance of the Gulf of Kotor. Kotor itself was peacefully ceded to him by Hungary.

Turkish invasion of Bosnia. In 1386 the Turks invaded Bosnia. The Serbs were disastrously beaten at Kosovo (1389). Turning westward, Tvrtko in 1390 conquered Split, Trogir, Sibenik, and the islands of Brac, Hvar, and Korcula (Curzola). When he took the title of "king of Rashka, Bosnia, Dalmatia, Croatia, and the coastlands," Bosnia was at the zenith of its power.

Tvrtko died in March 1391. His successor was Stephen Dabiša (1391–95), who at Djakovo, in 1393, concluded an agreement with Sigismund, king of Hungary (the future Holy Roman emperor), nominating Sigismund as his successor. After Dabiša's death, however, his widow, Jelena, assumed power, and Bosnia was not given to Sigismund, though no king was chosen instead. Two magnates rose to power: Sandalj Hranic and Hrvoje Vukcic, who soon were to play important parts in Bosnian history. Dissensions between them and two pretenders to the throne contributed to the slow decline of the country, while the Hungarians and the Turks were still intervening in its affairs. Turkish influence in Bosnia became greater after Hungary failed to conquer the country.

The Turks soon conquered Constantinople (1453) and occupied Serbia (1459). The Pope preached in favour of a war against the Turks, but there was no unanimity for such an enterprise. Stephen Vukcic, as ruler of Hum, told the Venetians through his envoy that he would rather give one of his strongholds to the Turks than have it in the hands of Tomas, who was occupying it.

Tomas' successor Stephen Tomasevic (1461–63) appealed to Pope Pius II for help against the Turks. The Pope sent him a crown, and, despite the protests of Hungary, Tomasevic was crowned in November 1461. He then refused to pay further tribute to the sultan, who soon led his army into Bosnia. Bobovac, the capital, fell, and the King escaped to Kljuc. The Turkish commander, Mahmud Pasha Andjelovic, secured his surrender by promising him his life, but the Sultan ordered the King to be beheaded. The execution took place at Jajce in 1463. Bosnia became a Turkish province. Matthias of Hungary in the same year seized northern Bosnia from the Turks and created two banats there: that of Srebrnica and of Jajce. Srebrnica was reconquered by the Turks in 1512, Jajce in 1528.

Hum, however, resisted longer than Bosnia. After the death of Sandalj Hranic, the country passed to his nephew Stephen Vukcic, "a man of strong will, but of evil nature," who in 1448 proclaimed himself *herceg* of St. Sava. He died in 1466. His three sons were not able to withstand the Turks, who in 1482 conquered Hercegnovi. Hercegovina, too, became a Turkish province.

BOSNIA AS A TURKISH PROVINCE

The seat of the Turkish governor, or pasha, was at first at Banja Luka, later at Sarajevo. In 1580 the Bosnian pashalik was divided into eight sanjaks. The governor interfered little with local affairs so long as the taxes were paid. The real power lay in the hands of 48 hereditary *kapetan*s, exercising feudal jurisdiction over their tenants and liable to provide military service for the sultan. The

Turkish administration

religious discords that had rent the country in medieval times were perpetuated in a new form: the nobility—partly to save their lands and power, partly because as Bogomils they preferred Islām to Roman Catholicism—apostatized as a class. Thus numbers of Bosnian Slavs became Muslim, though they continued to speak Serbian and never adopted polygamy. Few true Turks settled in Bosnia and Hercegovina.

The Turkish era saw an economic decline in Bosnia. The mining industry decayed and finally disappeared; trade languished. The manufacture of weapons and wrought metals alone survived. Many Bosnians, however, rose to high distinction in the Turkish service.

During the 16th and 17th centuries Bosnia was an important Turkish outpost in the constant warfare with the Habsburgs and with Venice. When Hungary was at last reclaimed from the Turks, the Austrians in their turn penetrated into Bosnia, and in 1697 Prince Eugene of Savoy captured Sarajevo. By the Treaty of Karlowitz (1699) the Sava, forming the northern boundary of Bosnia, became also the northernmost limit of the Turkish Empire; and by the Treaty of Passarowitz (Pozarevac; 1718) Hercegovina and part of Bosnia east of the Una River were ceded to Austria. These were restored to Turkey in 1739, and the frontiers remained unchanged until 1878.

Bosnian revolts In the 19th century the great conservative Bosnian families resented all interference from Istanbul. A revolt broke out in 1821, during the Greek rising, and another during the Russo-Turkish War of 1828, under the leadership of Mustafa Skodra Paşa, a reputed descendant of the Bosnian noble family of the Crnojevic. More formidable was the rising of 1831, when the *Kapetan* Husein Gradascevic, known as the Dragon of Bosnia, preached a holy war against the sultan and denounced the reforms of the sultan Mahmud II. He and Mustafa together overran most of Macedonia and northern Albania. After a severe struggle the grand vizier Reşid Paşa quelled the rebellion, helped largely by internal dissensions. Eventually the Dragon was driven across the frontier into Croatia and ended his days in banishment at Trabzon (Trebizond). In 1837 the abolition of the Kapetanates led to fresh trouble, and the reforms with which Abdul Mejid inaugurated his reign were keenly resented. The Hercegovinian chief, Ali Paşa Risvanbegovic, who had sided with the Turkish government during the earlier rising, made himself virtually independent. The sultan's authority was restored in 1850 by Omer Paşa, the renegade Croat. By ruthless measures Omer destroyed the old feudal regime in Bosnia, introduced a new, centralized administration and a system of taxation that opened the door to every kind of license and exaction. In 1862 the Christians in their turn revolted under Luka Vukalovic. They were eventually reduced, but unrest was chronic and discontent universal; Christians and Muslims, despite acute differences, united in their dislike of Ottoman bureaucracy and corruption.

(M.A.P./Ed.)

UNDER AUSTRIAN OCCUPATION

In 1875 local troubles in Hercegovina spread rapidly into insurrection throughout the two provinces. In August the Austrian, Russian, and German consuls tried to mediate between the Turkish authorities and the insurgents, but without success; and the sultan's decree of October 2, offering reduction of taxes, religious liberty, and a provincial assembly, was also rejected. The joint note presented by five European powers on January 31, 1876, proposing a limited autonomy, did not go far enough. The situation was complicated by the Bulgarian rising and massacres and by a revolution in Istanbul itself.

War with Turkey On June 30, 1876, Serbia and Montenegro declared war upon Turkey, while the insurgents proclaimed union with them, and numerous Russian volunteers joined the Serbian Army. Turkey's speedy victory upset the calculations on which Francis Joseph and the Russian emperor Alexander II had reached a secret agreement at Reichstadt in July. Serbia, defeated again in October, after the expiry of the armistice, lost all hopes of winning Bosnia. By the secret convention of Budapest (January and March 1877) Russia recognized Austria-Hungary's right to occupy Bosnia and

Hercegovina in return for Austro-Hungarian neutrality in the impending war with Turkey. At the Congress of Berlin after the Russo-Turkish War of 1877–78, Serbia's aspirations and those of the insurgents were disregarded, and Bosnia and Hercegovina was assigned to Austro-Hungarian occupation, though it was still to be nominally two Turkish provinces. The insurgents attempted armed resistance, and Austria-Hungary had to mobilize an army of 200,000 men. Sarajevo was occupied on August 19, 1878, and with the fall of Bihac a month later the rising was virtually at an end.

The two provinces were at first administered by a special commission inside the foreign office at Vienna, but in 1880 they were placed permanently under the control of the joint Austro-Hungarian Ministry of Finance, the local administration being concentrated in Sarajevo under a governor.

Benjamin Kállay, who became finance minister in 1882, was for 21 years to direct every department of Bosnian policy. Six years' residence as Austro-Hungarian diplomatic agent in Belgrade had given him a unique knowledge of South Slav problems, but his whole influence was exercised in an anti-Serbian sense. He tried to evolve a Bosnian consciousness, to check Serbian national feeling, and to create dissensions between Serbs and Croats. Meanwhile he set himself to establish public order and material prosperity and achieved remarkable results.

On Kállay's death (1903) Bosnian affairs were again entrusted to a Magyar, Baron Stephan Burián. During the next decade there was a rapid growth in national feeling in the provinces. Burián, faced by the clamour of the Bosnian Serbs for self-government, made certain concessions. In 1905 the Orthodox Church received a charter of autonomy, and its Serbian nationality was recognized for the first time. In 1907 an assembly of 71 Serbian delegates from every district was allowed to put forward a program of reform, in which figured the demand for an autonomous position "as part of the Turkish Empire."

Annexation by Austria-Hungary. Faced by the growing ferment inside the provinces, Austria-Hungary was already convinced of the need for some change in status when the Turkish revolution of 1908 brought matters to a head. The Young Turks contended that Bosnia and Hercegovina should be represented in the new parliament in Istanbul, and the Bosnian nationalists saw in this demand a convenient legal basis for their agitation. Influenced also by the strategic considerations pressed upon him by the general staff, the Austro-Hungarian foreign minister advised Francis Joseph to annex Bosnia and Hercegovina to the Dual Monarchy and thus solve once and for all their constitutional status. Russia indicated that it did not object to such an annexation. Accordingly, by a rescript of October 7, 1908, Bosnia and Hercegovina was annexed to Austria-Hungary.

Vienna was committed to the grant of some measure of representative government to Bosnia and Hercegovina; and as neither Austria nor Hungary would consent to its being attached to the one rather than the other, or to its partition between them, a hybrid form of constitution was devised, by which the two provinces received a diet (*sabor*) and special laws of association and assembly but were not represented in the two central parliaments and delegations and thus had no say in foreign affairs. The new constitution, proclaimed on February 7, 1910, had the capital defect of stereotyping sectarian and social differences by dividing the electorate into three electoral colleges and by assigning in each of these a fixed proportion of seats to the Orthodox, to the Roman Catholics, and to the Muslims. The Diet had no control of the executive. **The new constitution**

These concessions were badly received. The Emperor's visit to Bosnia in the summer of 1910 was intended to symbolize to the outside world the permanence of Austro-Hungarian rule; but the opening of the Diet, on June 15, was marred by an attempt on the life of the governor, Gen. Marian Varesanin, by a student, Bogdan Zerajic, who at once committed suicide. Burián now tried to win the Serbian element for cooperation with the government and openly described them as the most progressive element in the country. But the situation in Croatia reacted more and more on Bosnia, rendered Burián's half-measures ineffectual, and strengthened the self-confidence of the Serbs. In February 1912 Burián was succeeded by Leon Bilinski (1846–1923), a prominent Polish Conservative who enjoyed the confidence of Francis Joseph; but any hope of clearing up the internal situation was frustrated by Hungary's establishment of a dictatorship in Croatia (April 1912) and by the victories of Serbia in the Balkan War (October–November)—events that excited the whole Yugoslav population of Austria-Hungary.

The Mlada Bosna (Young Bosnia) group was especially active among university and secondary school students, devoting itself to inculcating revolutionary ideas and achieving such success that confidential memoranda prepared by high officials in Sarajevo and Vienna on the eve of World War I show them to have been altogether at a loss as to what policy to adopt. The Bosnian situation was further complicated by the increasing jealousy between the provincial government in Sarajevo and its nominal superior, the finance ministry in Vienna, or, in personal terms, between the military governor, Gen. Oskar Potiorek, representing both the views of the general staff and the archduke Francis Ferdinand and the civilian minister Bilinski, as the confidant of the Emperor. In May 1913 Potiorek, despite Bilinski's disapproval, had closed the Bosnian Diet and dissolved various Serbian societies. He continually urged the adoption of still more stringent measures and tended increasingly to act without consulting Bilinski. The most notorious instance was the decision reached between Potiorek

and Francis Ferdinand that the latter should attend the military manoeuvres in Bosnia in June 1914. Bilinski was not consulted or even notified, and the entire arrangements remained in military hands. To the circumstance must be ascribed a large share of the blame for the assassination of the archduke Francis Ferdinand and his consort, the Duchess of Hohenberg, during their visit to Sarajevo on June 28, 1914, by a Bosnian Serbian student, Gavrilo Princip.

The assassination of Archduke Ferdinand

UNION WITH YUGOSLAVIA

During World War I all political life ceased, but when Austria's Balkan front collapsed in October 1918 a national committee was formed in Sarajevo, which acted in close accord with the Yugoslav National Council in Zagreb. After its formal recognition of union with the Kingdom of Serbs, Croats, and Slovenes, on October 26, 1918, the fate of Bosnia was bound up with that of the new Yugoslavia. During World War II Bosnia and Hercegovina were part of the puppet state of Croatia under the joint military control of Germany and Italy. In 1946, following the defeat of the Germans and the rise to power of Tito and the Communists, Bosnia and Hercegovina became one of the constituent republics of the Federal People's Republic of Yugoslavia. Following the constitutional changes of 1974 the republic was renamed the Socialist Republic of Bosnia and Hercegovina. In 1984 the attention of many of the world's nations focussed on Bosnia and Hercegovina during the Winter Olympic Games, hosted by Sarajevo.

(R.W.S.-W./M.A.P./Ed.)

CROATIA

Physical and human geography

The land

The Socialist Republic of Croatia (Serbo-Croatian Socijalistička Republika Hrvatska) has been politically organized since 1946. Comprising as it does the territories of Dalmatia and most of Istria (Austrian provinces before World War I) as well as the former Hungarian region of Croatia-Slavonia, it extends in a crescent from the fertile plain between the Danube, Drava, and Sava rivers in the east to the Gulf of Venice in the west and then southward along the Adriatic coast to the frontier of Montenegro. It is bounded on the north by Slovenia and by Hungary and on the east by Serbia; within the crescent, its frontier marches with Bosnia and Hercegovina, which near the southern extent intrudes as a narrow corridor to the Adriatic, cresting an exclave of Croatia along the coast west of Montenegro. With an area of 21,829 square miles (56,537 square kilometres), Croatia constitutes more than one-fifth of the country's territory.

The physical geography of Croatia is dominated by three physiographic regions: the rolling hills in the north around Zagreb; the rocky, barren, and karstic coastal ranges of Dalmatia; and the inland plains of the Pannonian Basin. The coastal ranges, composed of the Dinaric Alps, and the Velebit and Velika Kapela ranges, are between 2,200 and 7,200 feet (700 and 2,200 metres) in elevation. Off the shore of Croatia are located the vast majority of Yugoslavia's more than 600 islands. The fertile inland plains coincide with the middle and lower reaches of the Sava River, the major drainage basin in Croatia. The Sava flows through the republic from the northwest to the southeast, forming part of the republic's border with Bosnia and Hercegovina. The Drava drains the northernmost corner of Croatia, forms the international boundary with Hungary, and empties into the Danube, which forms part of the boundary between Croatia and Serbia.

The republic has two different climatic regions. The inland area, particularly the Pannonian Basin, is affected by continental air masses and is colder and receives less precipitation than the coastal area. Osijek, situated on the Drava River, receives less than 30 inches (750 millimetres) of precipitation annually. In January the temperature averages below 30° F (−1° C), and in July the average temperature is about 66° F (19° C). In Zagreb, to the west, the precipitation is greater, about 36 inches each

year, and the January and July temperatures are warmer, averaging about 33° F (1° C) and 72° F (22° C) for the respective months. Along the Adriatic coast the climate is predominantly Mediterranean. The annual precipitation is slightly more than the total for Zagreb, and the seasonal temperatures are warmer. The coastal town of Šibenik has, for example, an average January temperature of about 44° F (6° C) and an average for July of about 75° F (24° C).

The people are mainly Croats and Roman Catholics, but there is a sizable minority of Serbs who practice the Eastern Orthodox religion. The geographic position of Croatia has exposed the social life and culture to influences from central Europe, from the Balkans, and from the Mediterranean, Italian influences being prevalent in Dalmatia and Istria. The culture of most Croats is closely linked, however, to the influences of Europe and Roman Catholicism, while the Serbian minority's heritage is tied to Byzantium and the Eastern Orthodox Church. Serbo-Croatian is the language of the republic and is spoken by Croats and Serbs. Serbs write the language, however, in Cyrillic script, while Croats employ the Latin alphabet. These cultural differences between the Croatian majority and the Serbian minority often have caused tension and hostilities. For many years Croats have been fearful of Serbian dominance within Yugoslavia as a whole. This fear has led to a resurgence of Croatian nationalism since 1946, both within the republic and in Yugoslavia generally. Serbs, who were persecuted by Croats during World War II, have been opposed to Croatian nationalism at both the republic and national levels

The population of Croatia, one of the more developed regions of the country, has grown at a much slower pace than Yugoslavia as a whole. Despite its relatively high level of economic development Croatia has suffered heavy emigration losses as thousands of skilled workers have sought temporary and permanent employment abroad. Zagreb is the capital, Rijeka (Fiume) the chief port. Other major ports are Zadar, Šibenik, Split, and Dubrovnik.

Croatia-Slavonia's economy used to be based primarily on agriculture and cattle breeding. After World War II, however, industry made rapid progress. While the timber industry maintained its earlier importance, the expansion of light industry and the discovery of rich oil fields considerably changed the character of the country. The peasant population was reduced significantly. The hardy people

The economy

of the mountainous littoral of Istria and Dalmatia are traditionally either wine and olive growers or fishermen and seafarers, but there too more attention was paid after World War II to the industrial exploitation of natural resources (hydraulic power, coal, and bauxite) as well as to shipbuilding and to tourism (especially in Dalmatia).

Manufacturing and mining are the largest contributors to the contemporary Croatian economy. The primary manufactured goods are aluminum products, textiles, petroleum products, chemicals, lumber and building materials, iron and steel, paper products, and foodstuffs. The mining sector provides bauxite from the deposits in Istria and Dalmatia for the manufacture of aluminum products. Petroleum and natural gas are extracted from the Pannonian Basin, and offshore petroleum exploration is underway. The fertile plains of the republic remain important agriculturally in the production of wheat, corn (maize), oats, sugar beets, and potatoes.

Croatia has its own constitution and maintains an assembly, executive council, and commune assemblies that function in the same manner as in the other republics. It is represented in the Chamber of Republics and Provinces of the Federal Assembly by 12 delegates, elected by its own assembly.

History

The Croats (Chrobati, Hrvati) migrated in the 6th century AD from White Croatia, a region that is now Ukraine, to the lower Danube Valley. From there they continued toward the Adriatic, where they conquered the Roman stronghold Salona in 614. After settling in the former Roman provinces of Pannonia and Dalmatia and liberating themselves from the warlike Avars, they began to develop independently. The farming Croats continued their former way of life under their *župani*, or tribal chiefs, undisturbed by the municipal life surviving in the old Roman colonies in coastal towns under Byzantine protection. In the 7th century, when they were converted to Christianity, a bishopric for all Croatian lands was established at Nin (north of Zadar). Shortly afterward they received the privilege of using their national language in church services. Under pressure from the neighbouring Frankish and Byzantine empires, the tribal organization of the Croats gradually gave way to larger units, and in the 8th century there existed two Croatian duchies. After the Frankish-Byzantine Peace of 812, Pannonian Croatia became a part of the Frankish Empire and the Dalmatian duchy recognized nominal Byzantine supremacy. In the middle of the 9th century the Pannonian Croats liberated themselves and joined the Dalmatian duchy, which also shook off foreign domination. By 880 Branislav (879–892) became the first independent *dux Croatorum*.

The conversion to Christianity

THE CROATIAN KINGDOM

One of Branislav's successors, Tomislav, annexed the Dalmatian cities and in 925 received the royal crown from Pope John X. Tomislav and his heirs made strenuous efforts to defend their kingdom both from the short-lived Bulgarian Empire in Pannonia and from Venice, which was spreading its power along the Dalmatian coast. The Byzantines helped Stjepan Drzislav (969–997) to liberate the coastal towns from Venice but succeeded in reestablishing their own influence on the Adriatic. Petar Kresimir (1058–74) altered this situation. He broke off relations with Byzantium, strengthened Croatia's ties with the papacy, and enlarged the state boundaries. Croatia then reached the peak of its power. It spread southward along the Adriatic coast from the River Rasa in Istria to the Rivers Tara and Piva in Montenegro, eastward to the Drina and northward to the Drava and to the Danube. Kresimir's policy, nevertheless, divided the nation into a Latin group that upheld the king and a national group that enjoyed popular support in opposing the king's policy. This division became fatal during the reign of Dimitrije Zvonimir (1076–89), who was crowned in Split by the legate of Pope Gregory VII. Invited by the Pope to participate in a war against the Seljuq Turks, Zvonimir convened a great assembly to win his subjects over to this campaign. The

The split with Byzantium

people accused him of being a papal vassal and killed him. Anarchy and civil war followed and with it the decline of the Croatian kingdom. The Byzantines again secured their position in Dalmatia, and in 1091 László I of Hungary occupied most of Pannonian Croatia, claiming the Croatian throne as Zvonimir's brother-in-law.

László's deputy Almos founded a bishopric at Zagreb in 1094, and this soon became the centre of ecclesiastical power. Petar Svacic was proclaimed king by the Dalmatian Croats in 1093, but the Pope considered him a rebel and invited King Kálmán of Hungary to unseat him. Kálmán invaded Croatia, and Svacic fell in 1097 in the defense of his country. He was the last king of Croat blood. After prolonged warfare Kálmán negotiated a treaty, the so-called Pacta Conventa, with the Croats' representatives. They elected him king, and he pledged himself to respect Croatian state rights. Only Bosnia, a part of the Croatian kingdom, refused to submit to a foreign monarch.

Henceforth for eight centuries Croatia was connected with Hungary. Their relationship often changed. Some kings attempted to integrate Croatia into Hungary, while on other occasions the Croats selected their kings independently of the Hungarians. Several Croatian bans, or viceroys, members of the feudal nobility, conducted semi-independent policies, particularly on the Adriatic coast, or became hereditary rulers in Bosnia. Dalmatia was sold to Venice for war capital in the 1400s, and Venice ruled for four centuries. The appearance of the Turks in the Balkans in the 15th century imposed a period of hard struggles on the Croats. Bosnia, which under Tvrtko Kotromanić (1353–91) became an independent kingdom, fell to the Turks in 1463. The battle at Krbavsko Polje (1493), where most of Croat forces perished, was followed by the defeat of Louis II of Hungary and Croatia at Mohacs (1526), after which the greater part of Pannonian Croatia shared the fate of central Hungary and fell under Turkish domination. The once wide Croatian kingdom was reduced to *reliquiae reliquiarum* ("relics of relics").

The intrusion of the Turks

THE HABSBURG PERIOD

In preference to the Hungarian candidate, the Habsburg Ferdinand of Austria (the future Holy Roman emperor Ferdinand I) was elected king in 1527. They confirmed the succession to him and his heirs in return for the promise of common defense and his respect of their prerogatives. For the next century Croatia was a bastion defending central Europe from the Turks. The Vojna Krajina (Militärgrenze), a military frontier zone on Croatian territory, was formed in 1578. As this zone was subject directly to the emperor in Vienna, it meant a further loss for the Croats.

Turkish invasion instigated a partial change in the ethnic aspect of Croatian lands. Large numbers of Croats abandoned their homes and moved northward seeking safety, some even going out of Croatia altogether into Austria. In partly depopulated areas the rulers settled German and Hungarian soldiers and craftsmen or granted certain privileges to the Serbs who escaped from the Balkans and took refuge in the Vojna Krajina to become defenders of the Habsburg Empire. As the Turks were driven back in the 17th century the Habsburgs revealed absolutist tendencies. They attempted to curtail the state rights and autonomy of Croatia and Hungary and to reduce them to mere provinces under centralized royal power. The Croatian and Hungarian nobility jointly resisted such encroachments on their prerogatives and finally plotted an anti-Habsburg movement aiming at the political independence of their countries. The plot failed. Its Croatian leaders, Count Petar Zrinski (whose grandfather had been the heroic defender of Sziget against Sultan Suleiman in 1566) and Duke Krsto Frankopan, were beheaded at Wiener Neustadt in 1671 and their estates distributed among alien nobility.

Croatia under the Habsburgs

In 1712 the Croatian Diet accepted the Pragmatic sanction declaring that in default of male heirs the succession to the throne could be assumed by a Habsburg princess. The Hungarians accepted it 12 years later, after receiving imperial guarantees of the indivisibility of the lands of St. Stephen's crown. Because of this stipulation the Hungarians considered Croatia as annexed territory, while the Croats claimed that they were an associated kingdom.

The rise of Croatian nationalism. After the annexation of Rijeka (Fiume) to the crown of St. Stephen in the 1770s, the Hungarians began trying to impose their language upon Croatia. This provoked an awakening of the Croats' national consciousness. The French Revolutionary Wars and the Napoleonic establishment of the Illyrian provinces of the French Empire, which after 1806 included Dalmatia and a part of Croatia south of the Sava, fomented national sentiments. Beside its progressive measures, particularly in economy and education, the beneficent administration made possible the appearance of the first newspaper in the Croatian language.

After the fall of Napoleon relations between Croats and Hungarians soon became critical. To strengthen their opposition to the Germanizing policy of the Habsburgs, the Hungarian revolutionaries strove to consolidate the lands of St. Stephen's crown and to establish a Magyar national state from the Carpathians to the Adriatic. The Croats refused to renounce their nationality or to accept any violation of their autonomy in the national interest of the Hungarians. In open defiance of Hungarian claims, Count Juraj Draskovic proposed in 1832 to the Hungarian Parliament a national and cultural program for Croatia. It expressed the ideas of the Illyrian movement, organized by Ljudevit Gaj, which aimed at the union of all South Slavs (Yugoslavs) within the Habsburg federation. Nevertheless, in April 1848, the Hungarian Parliament approved laws that radically affected Croatia's autonomous position. Instigated by the ban, Josip Jelacic, in September 1848, the Croatian Diet rejected the Hungarian laws and accepted a series of national laws of a revolutionary character. It broke off ties with Hungary and affirmed the independent position of Croatia, including Rijeka and the Vojna Krajina. It also abolished serfdom and proclaimed the equality of all citizens. After abortive attempts to compromise with the Hungarians Jelacic led his troops into Hungary. His success was of little avail for Croatian rights and interests. In defending the Croats from Magyar nationalism he saved the Habsburg Empire from the Hungarian revolt.

After 13 years of imperial absolutism and political lethargy a reorganization of the Habsburg Empire was planned by the centralist patent of February 26, 1861. The Croatian Diet, claiming that the events of 1848 dissolved their legal bonds with Hungary, protested against the patent and demanded a federalist constitution. Thereupon the Diet was dissolved in 1865 and no new Diet was elected. In 1867 the crown and the Hungarians reached their Ausgleich (Compromise), whereby the Germans and the Hungarians were established jointly as the dominant nations of the new Dual Monarchy of Austria and Hungary, Croatia having been assigned to the Hungarian part. In April the emperor Francis Joseph convoked a new Diet inviting it to send a delegation to Budapest to attend his crowning as king of Hungary. The Diet refused and in May was dissolved again. In 1868, however, the Croats and the Hungarians concluded a compromise of their own, the *nagodba,* whereby the triune kingdom of Croatia, Slavonia, and Dalmatia was recognized as a distinct political nation with its own territory, though still part of the Hungarian as opposed to the Austrian unit. In spite of this, Dalmatia was not united with Croatia-Slavonia and remained an Austrian province. Croatia obtained autonomy in home affairs, education, judiciary, and later in agriculture. The local government was headed by a ban proposed to the emperor by Budapest but responsible to the Croatian Diet. The Diet was represented in the common parliament in Budapest. The Croatian language was given official status throughout the land. The *nagodba* was accepted by a corruptly elected Diet and remained valid until 1918.

Croatian opposition to *nagodba* expressed itself in two different movements, both initially inefficient because of the very restricted electoral right. Josip Strossmayer, bishop of Djakovo and leader of the National Party, developed the Illyrian movement into a cultural South Slav community under Croatian leadership, but lacked dynamism to make it a program of political action. The rebellious Ante Starčević's program called for resistance to Austrian and Hungarian interference with Croatian national interests

and aspired to self-determination and ultimate freedom of the Croats. His Party of Rights requested the union of all Croatian provinces of the empire, including Dalmatia and Bosnia and Hercegovina. Starčević's program instilled a fighting spirit into Croatian politics. Hungary tried to restrain Croatian opposition by appointing Count Károly Khuen-Héderváry as ban in 1883, but 20 years of his policy of Magyarization only exacerbated Croatian-Hungarian relations. The year 1903 was a turning point in Croatian politics. The political leaders in all Croatian provinces became intensively active, seeking to concentrate their forces and to organize them into new parties and initiating cooperation with the Serbs in Croatia. A program of action—the "Rijeka resolution"—was proposed in 1905 and accepted by many Croatian politicians and by Serbian representatives in Croatia. In 1906 the Croatian-Serbian coalition won a sweeping electoral victory and henceforth became an important political factor. Another achievement of decisive consequence was the organization of the Croatian Peasant Party by the brothers Ante and Stjepan Radić. Realistic and aware of social problems, they stimulated an interest in politics among the peasants.

The governing circles in Budapest and Vienna refused to palliate this seething discontent with timely concessions. The Hungarians intensified their oppression either by appointing in Croatia underlings subservient to Budapest or instigating persecutions and trials. In 1907 the ban, Levin Rauch, having failed to secure a majority, suspended the Diet. In 1909 the leaders of the Croatian-Serbian coalition, having been accused of treason, brought an action for libel against the historian Heinrich Friedjung in Vienna, in which it was shown that the documents on which the charges of treason were based had been forged and supplied to Friedjung by Austro-Hungarian officials. In 1912 Rauch's successor Nikola Tomasic suspended the constitution. This was followed by the appointment of a royal commissar, whose dictatorial methods only cemented Croatian-Serbian solidarity in the empire.

Some influential court and military circles in Austria expected to counteract Croatian political evolution by proposing trialism instead of dualism. By trialism all the South Slav lands of the empire would have been united under the name and leadership of Croatia, which would have had status equal to that of Austria or Hungary. This failed because of Hungarian opposition. Most Croats saw by then that within the Habsburg Empire there could be no satisfactory solution of their problems.

UNION WITH YUGOSLAVIA

Serbian and Montenegrin victories over the Turks in the Balkan Wars of 1912–13 encouraged the Croats to envisage freedom in an independent Yugoslav union that would include Serbia and Montenegro; but in 1914, when the archduke Francis Ferdinand was assassinated at Sarajevo, relations between the Croats and the Hungarians appeared to be calm, thanks to the policy of compromise pursued by the Croatian-Serbian Coalition, which in 1913 had become the government party in Croatia. The unsettled problem of Croatia's status, however, prepared the way for Yugoslav revolutionary action. With the outbreak of World War I the Austro-Hungarian authorities introduced measures of extreme severity throughout their South Slav provinces.

In his coronation speech in 1916 the emperor Charles recognized Croatian integrity in relation to Hungary, thereby establishing the equality of both countries under St. Stephen's crown. Then the Yugoslav Club in the Vienna Parliament, in May 1917, demanded the union of all the South Slav provinces under the Habsburg crown. Among the Croats, meanwhile, the movement for a Yugoslav union was gaining strength, with Starčević's Party of Rights as its protagonist. The centre of Croatian politics, however, was the Yugoslav Committee in Paris and London. This had been organized in 1915 by a group of Croatian, Serbian, and Slovene politicians from the empire, led by Trumbic. Its program was the complete separation of the Croats, Serbs, and Slovenes from the Habsburg Empire and their union with independent Serbia. The committee became one of the decisive factors in the settlement of the

Croatian opposition to Hungarian hegemony

Two nationalistic movements

Trialism versus dualism

Croatian problem. On July 20, 1917, Trumbic and Nikola Pašić, the Serbian prime minister, signed the declaration of Corfu, which established the basic principles of a future Yugoslav state. In March 1918, at their meeting in Zagreb, the South Slav political leaders of the Habsburg Empire declared themselves openly in favour of an independent Croatian-Serbian-Slovene state, thus approving the Corfu declaration. On October 29, 1918, the Croatian Diet broke off all ties with Hungary and Austria and proclaimed an independent Croatia, which entered into a state union with other South Slav provinces of the empire, to be governed by a national council. On the request of council's emissaries, on December 1, 1918, the Serbian prince regent Alexander proclaimed the union of this state with Serbia and Montenegro. Yugoslavia came into being.

Dominated by the Serbs, the new Yugoslav regime showed amalgamating tendencies. These immediately encountered strong opposition from the Croats, who resented encroachments on their national individuality and traditional autonomy. Against the centralizing policy of the Belgrade government they demanded a federal organization of Yugoslavia. After the election of 1920 the Peasant Party under Stjepan Radić led Croatian opposition. The assassination of Radić and some of his political collaborators in the Belgrade Parliament on June 20, 1928, produced a serious crisis. King Alexander attempted to remedy this by introducing a dictatorial regime in January 1929 but failed to achieve his objective. The Croats organized a solid national front around the Peasant Party and persisted in their demands. Finally, as conflict between Serbs and Croats was preventing the consolidation of Yugoslavia, the Belgrade government had to give in. On August 26, 1939, a settlement, the *sporazum,* was reached whereby Croatia united with Dalmatia, and parts of Bosnia and Hercegovina became an autonomous *banovina* within Yugoslavia.

The Independent State of Croatia. Croatian nationalists who aimed at complete independence remained dissatisfied with the *sporazum.* In World War II, after Yugoslavia had been occupied and dismembered by the Axis powers, the Independent State of Croatia was proclaimed in Zagreb on April 10, 1941, and recognized four days later by Hitler and Mussolini. It embraced Croatia-Slavonia, part of Dalmatia, and Bosnia and Hercegovina, covered an area of 39,660 square miles and in all had about 6,663,000 inhabitants. Since Vladimir (Vladko) Maček, the leader of the Peasant Party, refused the German offer to head the new state, it was entrusted to Ante Pavelić (1889–1959), head of the Fascist terrorist organization Ustaša. A nationalist fanatic, Pavelić reentered Croatia from Italy, where he had spent 12 years of exile plotting revolution.

He ruled his puppet state as a *poglavnik* (leader) and introduced a dictatorial regime characterized by methods of extreme brutality and violence. During Pavelić's rule an anti-Serbian policy was adopted that led to massacres, expulsions, and forced conversions of Serbs to Roman Catholicism. Concentration camps also were established to hold Serbs, Jews, and Croats opposed to the Fascist regime. An attempt was made in 1944 to bring Croatia over to the side of the Allies, but it was mismanaged; its leaders, Ante Vokic and Mladen Lorkovic, were arrested and shot by Pavelić's henchmen.

The Independent State of Croatia survived the capitulation of Germany for a few days only. Pavelić fled to Austria in May 1945 and later to Argentina. Croatia became a people's republic within Communist Yugoslavia.

The people's republic. The Communists, in the course of their resistance to the German and Italian occupying forces in World War II, had organized local committees in the territories over which they won control, and in 1943 they had subjected their committees to the Anti-Fascist Council of National Liberation of Croatia (ZAVNOH). In May 1945, after the occupation of Zagreb by the partisans, this council became the people's government, and Croatia became again an integral part of Yugoslavia. According to the constitution of January 31, 1946, the government's authority "derives from the people and belongs to them"; all natural resources, capital, commerce, and means of production were brought under public ownership and managed by the government or by public bodies. Private property remained only on a restricted scale. Peasant holdings were limited to approximately 20 acres.

Since Croatia became a constituent republic of Yugoslavia, Croatian nationalism has been a central feature of the political culture. The government of the republic, its representatives in the Federal Assembly, the local League of Communists, the commune assemblies, and the sociopolitical organizations of the republic have been strong advocates of Croatian nationalism, often at the expense of the Serbian minority. Croatia has been instrumental in obtaining more autonomy for the republics and reducing the federal government's control in regional matters. The federal government and the other republics also have attempted to constrain the nationalistic fervor of the Croats. In 1972 the Croatian League of Communists was purged and the Croatian cultural organization, the Matica Hrvatska, a driving force behind the nationalistic movement, was suspended. Croatian nationalism has continued to be an important political force within the republic and abroad, as Croatian emigrés in the West have sought to draw international attention to their cause. (A.S.Pa./Ed.)

MACEDONIA

Physical and human geography

The Socialist Republic of Macedonia (Macedonian and Serbo-Croatian Socijalistička Republika Makedonija) occupies the largest part of the traditional region of Macedonia, which was the central part of the Balkan Peninsula, and was situated athwart the present-day political frontiers of Yugoslavia, Greece, and Bulgaria. In historical times, from the Roman conquest of the ancient Kingdom of Macedonia to the 20th century, the area has been strategically important as a crossroads. The Via Egnatia, the shortest Roman route between the Adriatic coast and the Bosporus, passed through places now known as Bitola (Yugoslavia) and Thessaloníki (Greece). The valley of the Vardar (Axiós) River was and continues to be the easiest highway from Thessaloníki to the north. Both the Roman (Byzantine) and the Ottoman empires based on Constantinople considered it essential to hold Macedonia, through which Serbia, Bosnia, Albania, and continental Greece could be reached. This stretch of land had, therefore, a complex history and, as a result, a mixed population. When in the 19th century the national consciousness of the Balkan peoples began to waken, Macedonia became a problem of international magnitude. The historic problem of drawing international frontiers across or around Macedonia is often referred to as the Macedonian question.

The Socialist Republic, 9,928 square miles (25,713 square kilometres) in area, represents about one-tenth of total Yugoslavian area. The republic is bordered by Bulgaria to the east, Greece to the south, Albania to the west, and the Socialist Republic of Serbia to the north. It is divided from Greek Macedonia by the Kožuf and Nidže ranges with Mt. Kajmakcalan as the highest peak (8,271 feet). Most mountains are forested. With the exception of the Vardar Valley, lower Bregalnica Valley, and lower Crna Valley, the land is a plateau lying from 2,000 feet to 3,000 feet above sea level, with mountain massifs reaching 8,331 feet (Jakupica). The Vardar River and its tributaries drain almost all of the republic, flowing southward through Greece and into the Aegean Sea. The climate approaches the continental type, with precipitation distributed throughout the year but slightly heavier in the early and late summer, and often copious winter snowfalls. Skopje, situated in the north near Serbia, receives less than 20 inches (500 millimetres) of precipitation each year. The average annual temperature is about 54° F (12° C); the coldest month is January, averaging about 32°F

The land

(0° C); and the warmest month is July, averaging about 76° F (24°C). Chief crops are wheat, barley, corn (maize), rice, and tobacco; and sheep and cattle are important. There is also a considerable mineral wealth in iron ore, lead, zinc, and nickel. Chief industries are steel, chemicals, and textiles. In 1947 Yugoslavia declared Macedonia to be one of the less developed republics and since that date Macedonia has received large amounts of economic development funding from the federal government.

The Slavonic language of the Macedonians is more akin to Bulgarian than to Serbo-Croatian. A majority of the population is Macedonian, and Albanians and Turks constitute sizeable minorities. Skopje is the capital and largest city.

The Socialist Republic of Macedonia has a constitution, an assembly, an executive council, and commune assemblies that function the same as in the other republics (see above *Bosnia and Hercegovina: Physical and human geography*). It is represented in the Federal Assembly's Chamber of Republics and Provinces by 12 delegates elected by their own assembly.

History

The boundaries of the ancient Macedonian kingdom varied; but it was always centred on the plain in the northeastern corner of the Greek Peninsula, at the head of the Thermaic Gulf.

The cultural links of prehistoric Macedonia were mainly with Greece and Anatolia. The continuity in the archaeological record suggests that the Early Bronze Age people were the ancestors of the historical Macedonians.

THE KINGDOM OF MACEDONIA

The Argeads to 336 BC. From about 700 onward the people who called themselves Macedonians pushed eastward from their home on the Haliacmon (Aliakmon) River. Aegae became the capital, and by the reign of Amyntas I (6th century) Macedonian power extended beyond the Axiós to dominate the Thracian tribes in Mygdonia and Anthemous behind Chalcidice. Amyntas' successor, Alexander I (before 492–c. 450), was obliged to accompany Xerxes against Greece (480), though he secretly aided the Greek allies. Alexander seized the Greek colony of Pydna and advanced his frontiers eastward to the Strymon, taking in Crestonia and Bisaltia; with the rich silver deposits of Mt. Dysorus (modern Krousia Oros) he issued a fine coinage. He spread the legend deriving his Argead house from the Temenids of Argos. Despite his efforts to win Greek sympathies, Athenian ambitions around the Strymon embittered previously cordial relations.

Alexander's grandson, Archelaus (413–399), adopted a strongly philhellenic policy, introducing Greek artists to his new capital at Pella. He strengthened Macedonia by building roads and fortresses, improving army equipment, and encouraging city life; but his assassination in 399, followed by seven years of murder and anarchy, indicates that his reforms had contributed nothing to political stability.

Philip II In 359 Philip II assumed control and raised Macedonia to a predominant position throughout the whole of Greece (359–336). Our main knowledge about the Macedonian monarchy derives from this period. It was a popular, almost Homeric institution, limited in power by a strong nobility and a free, outspoken peasantry. The eldest inherited; but the people in arms had the right to acclaim the new king and also to act as a court of high treason. Foreign policy remained a royal prerogative.

Alexander and the successors, 336–280 BC. Philip's son Alexander III the Great (*q.v.*; 336–323) overthrew the Persian Empire and carried Macedonian arms to the Nile and the Indus. On his death at Babylon his generals divided up the satrapies of his empire and used them as bases in a struggle to acquire the whole. From 321 to 301 warfare was almost continual between those struggling to maintain the unity of the empire and those who, like Ptolemy, saw that it must disintegrate and were resolved to profit from its dissolution. Alexander's half-brother Philip III Arrhidaeus and his son Alexander IV furnished a nominal focus for loyalty down to 317/316, but the real power lay in other hands. Macedonia itself remained the heart of the empire, and its possession (along with the control of Greece) was keenly contested.

The Antigonids, 277–168 BC. In 280/279 Galatian marauders invaded Macedonia and defeated and decapitated the King. In 277 Antigonus II Gonatas, defeated a Galatian band at Lysimachia in Thrace and was hailed as king by a Macedonian army (perhaps not until early 276). Under him the country acquired a stable monarchy. From 277 to 168 the Antigonid dynasty ruled Macedonia. Their relations with the people and army-assembly remained much like those of the Argeads. Ceremony was slight; the king was first among his peers and esteemed for his prowess in the hunt, in battle, and at the drinking table. Under the Antigonids the outer districts, where separatism still existed, were controlled by *strategi*, "generals"; *epistatai*, "overseers," were placed in many cities. Like other Hellenistic kings the Antigonids consulted a royal council of "friends," but heeded their advice only when they wished. The population remained mainly agricultural (except in cities like Beroea and Pella and the Greek coastal towns); the economy was backward; and mines and forests were a royal monopoly.

Under Philip V (221–179) Macedonia first clashed with Rome. Until 217 Philip was engaged in successful warfare War with against a coalition of Sparta, Elis, and Aetolia. Incited Rome by Demetrius of Pharos, an Illyrian prince in flight from the Romans, he set out to attack the Roman client-states in Illyria, and confirmed his purpose by an alliance with Hannibal (215). Despite an Aetolian alliance (211), the Romans fought the ensuing war ineffectively, and in 206 Philip forced Aetolia to make a separate peace; in 205 the Peace of Phoenice ended the Roman war in Philip's favour. He made minor concessions but kept his Illyrian conquests and Atintania. The war consolidated Macedonia in relation to both the Greek alliance and the northern frontiers. He now turned eastward, perhaps influenced by Antiochus III's return from a triumphant expedition in central Asia. He intrigued against the Rhodians, who policed the seas, and embarked upon a program of aggression against the Greek cities of the Aegean and the northeast. He also secretly conspired with Antiochus to plunder the dominions of the child Ptolemy V. Though Rhodes and Pergamum scored a slight advantage over him at Chios, he defeated the Rhodians at Lade (201); but Rhodian and Pergamene envoys contributed to the Roman decision to make war on him (200).

Philip had seriously miscalculated. The conclusion was foregone, and the defeat of Cynoscephalae (197) led to a peace that confined him to Macedonia, depriving him even of Thessaly. Already the Hellenic alliance had fallen apart; now a series of leagues were established in former Macedonian areas. Orestis was independent; once again Lake Lychnidus (Ohrid) formed the western frontier; and Macedonia lost its fleet. Above all, the equilibrium established in 301 had vanished: Rome was the decisive power in the eastern Mediterranean. Between 197 and 189 Philip collaborated loyally with Rome against Nabis and Antiochus; he recovered parts of Thessaly and his remaining tribute was remitted. Until his death in 179 he concentrated on consolidating Macedonia, and, despite successful denunciations at Rome by his neighbours, he amassed wealth, crushed internal opposition, and issued new currencies both national and local, the latter reflecting a new policy designed to capitalize regional feeling. Three campaigns advanced Macedonian power in the Balkans. Those years of adversity revealed Philip's more admirable qualities. His death left a full treasury and an impressive army for the final struggle with Rome. Perseus, Philip's successor, reigned for 11 years (179–168). He courted favour in Greece, cultivating the revolutionary party in Aetolia, Thessaly, and elsewhere. Neither Philip nor Perseus had been a real threat to Rome, but both had failed to adapt themselves to Roman predominance.

ROMAN MACEDONIA

From 168 to 146 Macedonia formed four independent republics but without common bonds. Macedonia became a Roman province with the four sections as administrative units, and the supervision of parts of Greece, which from time to time forfeited their independence. Macedonia was still the bulwark of Greece, and the northern frontiers saw frequent campaigning against the Scordisci, Maedi, and Dardanians. In 27 BC Macedonia became a senatorial province separate from Achaea (Greece). A Macedonian League with high priests and an imperial cult appeared under Claudius I; it had some political functions and embraced Thessaly. Toward AD 400 the province was divided into Macedonia and Macedonia *secunda* (or *salutaris*), in the diocese of Moesia.

THE MIDDLE AGES TO THE 14TH CENTURY

By the 4th century AD the population was largely Christian; and its ethnic composition was little affected by the invasions of Goths, Huns, and Avars. The arrival of the Slavs in the Balkans, however, led to a far-reaching colonization of Macedonia, where few towns were left Greek. The Bulgars began to follow the Slavs in the 7th century, and in the 9th century almost all Macedonia, except Salonika (Thessaloníki), was included in the First Bulgarian Empire; but the Bulgars themselves became very largely Slavicized. On the decay of the First Bulgarian Empire in the second half of the 10th century, the four sons of a local count, Nicolas, set themselves up as the dynasty of the Comitopuli in Macedonia; and one of them, Samuel, founded the empire sometimes described as the West Bulgarian, which comprised much of the Balkan Peninsula. This was destroyed by the Byzantine emperor Basil II, who in 1018 brought all its territory back under Byzantine rule.

Migratory movements and invasions continued. Nomadic Vlachs found in Macedonia a region well suited to their mode of life. Turkic invaders, called Polovtsy by the Slavs and Kumans by the Greeks, were crossing the Danube and entering Byzantine domains; some of them settled in Macedonia and were later known as Vardariotes. While the brothers Ivan and Peter Asen were laying the foundations of the Second Bulgarian Empire, the Normans under William II of Sicily captured and sacked Salonika (1185). After the diversion of the Fourth Crusade to Constantinople in 1204, a Latin kingdom of Salonika was set up; but this was overthrown in the 1220s by Theodore Angelus, the Greek despot of Epirus. The Bulgars defeated Theodore Angelus but were themselves defeated in 1246 by the Nicaean emperor John III Vatatzes, who then took for himself not only southern Macedonia but also much of what had been Bulgarian since the beginning of the century. In the 1280s the Serbs began to encroach on western Macedonia; by 1346, when Stefan Dušan was crowned tsar of the Serbs and Greeks at Skopje, all Macedonia except the vicinity of Salonika was in Serbian hands.

Serbian encroach-ment

TURKISH RULE AND THE RESURGENCE OF BULGARIA

The Ottoman Turks, meanwhile, had already begun to make incursions into the Balkans. They held most of Macedonia by 1371; and their victory at Kosovo in 1389 sealed the fate of the Serbian Empire. Salonika fell into Turkish hands for the first time in 1387, for the second in 1391 and finally in 1430. The best lands in the plains were distributed among the Turkish chiefs, and a system of feudal tenure was developed. The Christian peasants either were driven to the less fruitful regions or remained on the lands assigned to the Muslim lords, to whom they paid a tithe.

The ethnic conditions of Macedonia were still further complicated. Large colonies of Turks were settled in the plains, while the Muslim Albanians spread eastward, occupying much land in western Macedonia. The Serbian element, which had been strengthened under Stefan Dušan, was weakened by the great northward emigration of 1691 and 1740. There were also, as centuries before, Vlachs and a few Armenians.

With the decadence of the central power in the Ottoman Empire, the condition of the Christian population of Macedonia worsened. The reforms of 1839 and 1856, both of which proclaimed the equality of races and religions, remained unfulfilled. In 1864 Macedonia was divided into three *vilayets,* or provinces: that of Salonika; that of Monastir (Bitola), which included parts of Albania; and

that of Kosovo, with the capital at Uskub (Skopje), which protruded into "Old Serbia."

By the Treaty of San Stefano in 1878, the new Bulgarian state was given most of Macedonia. The Sofia nationalists argued that the Slavs of Macedonia spoke a dialect akin to Bulgarian and therefore should be regarded as Bulgars and that all Macedonia should be incorporated into Bulgaria. The Belgrade nationalists affirmed that, as the Macedonian Slavs retained the custom of *slava* (feast of ancestors), common to all Serbs but not occurring among the Bulgars, they could not be genuine Bulgars and were at best superficially Bulgarized Serbs, whose land, it was argued, should be incorporated into a greater Serbia. The Greek nationalists maintained that the few hundred thousands of "Slavophones" whom they acknowledged to be in Macedonia were attracted by the superior Greek culture and considered themselves of Greek nationality. The Romanians had no territorial claims in Macedonia but considered it useful to support the Vlachs.

The latter half of the 19th century was characterized by an emerging national identity and a great deal of revolutionary activity. The liberation of Macedonia from the Turks was desired by all non-Muslim Macedonians. To prepare it, a group of Macedo-Slavonic leaders, Dame Gruev (1871–1906), Gotse Delchev (1871–1903), Yane Sandanski (1875–1915), and others, formed a secret Internal Macedonian Revolutionary organization (Vatreshna Makedonska Revolutsionna Organizatsia or VMRO) in Salonika in November 1893, which put forward a slogan of "Macedonia for the Macedonians" and the idea of a Balkan federation. The Bulgarian nationalists believed that the Russian government would attempt to restore the Bulgaria of the San Stefano Treaty. In March 1895 a Supreme Committee for Macedonia and Adrianople was formed at Sofia; its aim was to prepare the incorporation of the whole of Macedonia and the province of Adrianople into Bulgaria. From 1899 the president of the committee was Boris Sarafov (1872?–1907). His main task was to send guerrilla bands into Macedonia to coerce the population into declaring itself Bulgarian and to make certain that the VMRO would follow Sofia's line.

Liberation from the Turks

Sofia was not the only Balkan capital from which such irredentist activity was organized in Macedonia. Athens was disconcerted by the progress of Bulgarian propaganda and began sending guerrilla bands of *andartai* into Macedonia. These succeeded in provoking the Greco-Turkish War of 1897, which ended in the complete defeat of Greece and thus benefitted the Bulgarian movement. By then the Turks were sufficiently informed about the underground activities of the VMRO and of the Supremists; to counterbalance their influence the Porte inclined to favour other nationalities. Serbia, cut off from expansion in Bosnia and Hercegovina by the Austrian occupation, could look only southward. The patriotic society Narodna Odbrana (National Defense), controlled by the Ministry of War, started sending *chety* (companies) of underground fighters into Macedonia to encourage a pro-Serbian movement among the Macedonian Slavs, and a Serbian source mentions the names of Jovan Dovezenski, Djordje Skopljance, Gligor Sokolovic, and Jovan Babunski (Stojkovic) as the most famous *chetnitsi.* At the same time Belgrade began to agitate for the restoration of the Serbian patriarchate of Pec; a prolonged conflict with the Phanar secured only the appointment of a Serb, Msgr. Firmilian Drazic, as archbishop of Skopje in 1902. In 1905 a Romanian bishop was appointed at Bitola. The Bulgars did not like this Serbian and Romanian trespassing into a land that they considered their own; but they concentrated their efforts on combatting the Greeks and the Grekomans (as they called pro-Greek Macedonian Slavs). At this time it was Lambros Koromylas, the Greek consul general at Salonika, who directed the whole secret organization of agents and bands upholding Hellenism against the Bulgars.

The terrorist activities of Bulgarian, Greek, Serbian, and Turkish elements created so serious a situation in Macedonia that on February 21, 1903, the Russian and Austro-Hungarian ambassadors presented identical notes to the Porte demanding the appointment of an inspector general for Macedonia and the reorganization of the *gendarmerie* with the aid of foreign officers. Sultan Abdul-Hamid II accepted the scheme, and the Sofia government, under Russian pressure, pretended to have dissolved the Supreme Committee.

The VMRO, however, was unreachable, and on August 2 a general rising started in Macedonia, no doubt inspired by Sofia. Having achieved a complete surprise, the insurgents had some initial successes, but they were eventually defeated. According to Bulgarian sources, the insurgents numbered 15,000, of whom 948 were killed as compared with 3,087 Turks killed. Turkish repression was ruthless; 105 Macedo-Slavonic villages comprising 9,830 houses were destroyed, 1,778 noncombatant Macedonian Slavs were shot, and 60,953 rendered homeless. Thousands fled to Bulgaria, and their leaders complained of having been betrayed by Sofia. But Ferdinand, ruler of Bulgaria, was gratified because, he thought, the federalist tendencies of the VMRO had suffered a decisive blow.

On October 9, 1903, the Russian and Austro-Hungarian governments submitted to the Porte a second part of their reform plan, called, after the place where the two emperors met, the Mürzsteg Program; this also was accepted by the Sultan. Russian and Austrian civil advisers were attached to the Turkish inspector general of Macedonia.

In June 1908, when King Edward VII paid a visit to Nicholas II at Reval (Tallinn), an Anglo-Russian program of limited autonomy for Macedonia was prepared; but one month later the bloodless revolution of the Young Turks broke out. The internal conflicts between the various nationalities in Macedonia came temporarily to a standstill. Using this opportunity, Bulgaria proclaimed itself independent, and Ferdinand took the title of tsar. The hopes of Macedonian populations that the new Turkish regime would grant them territorial autonomy were disappointed. The policy pursued by the Young Turks, who attempted to transform a multinational Ottoman Empire into a national Turkish state, brought about a gradual rapprochement between the governments of Bulgaria, Serbia, and Greece. This rapprochement was converted in the summer of 1912 into a military alliance, and in October the allies, declaring that promises of reform in Macedonia and elsewhere had not been fulfilled, attacked Turkey.

BALKAN WARS AND WORLD WAR I

Bulgaria and Serbia concluded an agreement stipulating that Bulgaria should annex "the territory east of the Rhodope Mountains and the River Struma," while Serbia was to annex the lands lying "north and west of the Sar Planina." But so great was their mutual distrust that no agreement could be reached as to the destiny of the main bulk of Macedonia. The Serbo-Bulgarian Treaty of March 13, 1912, stipulated that, if autonomy for the rest of Macedonia were found to be impossible, the two states were to accept a partition along a line running from Kriva Palanka through Veles to Ohrid; alternatively, the Russian emperor would be asked to arbitrate and fix the Serbo-Bulgarian frontier in Macedonia. Between Greece and Bulgaria the feud was even deeper; and no previous agreement had been reached as to the ultimate distribution of territory to be taken from Turkey. Such a situation was fraught with danger, and, after the Balkan League's victorious campaign against the Turks, the Bulgars, on June 29, 1913, suddenly turned on their allies. Defeated by both Serbs and Greeks, attacked from the rear by the Romanians, the Bulgars had to sue for peace. By the Treaty of Bucharest of August 10, 1913, Macedonia was divided among Greece, Bulgaria, and Serbia.

The partition of Macedonia

When World War I broke out in 1914, Ferdinand saw a chance of revenge and of realizing his territorial ambitions in Macedonia. Bulgaria entered the war in October 1915, on the side of the Central Powers and rapidly occupied not only all Serbian Macedonia but also parts of Serbia proper. The Allies landed at Salonika to help Serbia, but only in 1918 were they able to carry through a successful offensive, which led to the Bulgarian armistice of September 29, 1918. The Treaty of Neuilly (November 27, 1919) left the Greco-Yugoslav frontier unchanged but transferred the district of Strumitsa to Yugoslavia. Yugoslav Macedonia then covered 10,229 square miles.

Following the end of World War II and the rise to power of Tito and the Communists, Macedonia became one of the constituent republics of the Federal People's Republic of Yugoslavia. After the constitutional changes of 1974 Macedonia was renamed the Socialist Federal Republic of Yugoslavia.   (F.W.W./K.M.S./Ed.)

MONTENEGRO

Physical and human geography

The Socialist Republic of Montenegro (Serbo-Croatian Socijalistička Republika Crna Gora) was an independent state before 1918, when it was absorbed by Serbia and so united with the South Slav areas of the former Austria–Hungary. In 1945 it became a constituent republic. The republic occupies 5,333 square miles (13,812 square kilometres), or about 5 percent of the country's territory, and it is bounded by Albania to the south, the Adriatic Sea to the southwest, Bosnia and Hercegovina to the northwest, and Serbia to the northeast.

Montenegro takes its name—a Venetian variant of the Italian Monte Nero—from the Black Mountain, Mt. Lovćen (5,738 feet), its historical centre and stronghold in the centuries of struggle with the Turks. Alone of Balkan states, Montenegro was never subjugated, partly because of its inhospitable territory, partly because of the courage of its people, which became legendary.

The land

The old Montenegro, in the southwest, is mainly a karst region of arid hills, with some cultivable areas; e.g., around Cetinje, the former capital, and in the broad and gentle Zeta Valley. The eastern districts, which include part of the Dinaric Alps (Mt. Durmitor, 8,274 feet), are more fertile and have large forests and grassy uplands. The drainage system of Montenegro flows in two opposite directions. The Piva, Tara, and Lim rivers follow northerly courses into Serbia and Bosnia and Hercegovina, where they flow into the Drina River, which in turn flows north, converging with the Sava River and eventually the Danube. The Morača and Zeta rivers flow in a southerly direction,

converge near the capital of Titograd, and empty into the largest lake on the Balkan Peninsula, Lake Scutari. The Bojana River flows out of the south end of the lake into the Adriatic Sea.

The climate generally resembles that of northern Albania; it is severe in the higher regions, and comparatively mild in the valleys, while in the maritime districts of Antivari and Dulcigno it may be compared with that of central Italy. The mean annual temperature is about 58° F (14° C). Snow lies for most of the year on many heights, and in some of the darker gorges it is never thawed. The annual precipitation for Montenegro is much greater than that of the other republics. Titograd has an average annual precipitation in excess of 65 inches (1,650 millimetres); Cetinje, the historic capital in the region, has an annual precipitation that exceeds 150 inches each year; and Nikšić's average annual precipitation exceeds 80 inches. Precipitation occurs year round but is heaviest in the months of October, November, and December.

Montenegro has the smallest population and is the least densely populated among the socialist republics of Yugoslavia. The majority of the people are Montenegrin and there is a sizable Albanian minority. The Montenegrin people are closely akin to the Serbs and, like the Serbs, speak Serbo-Croatian, write Serbo-Croatian with the Cyrillic alphabet, and are followers of the Eastern Orthodox Church. This close affinity to the Serbs caused Montenegrins to be classifed as Serbs during the censuses between World War I and II. The traditional society was composed of extended families that were patrilineally related. It was a decentralized society in which loyalty to the extended family

Language and religion

was most important, and blood feuds and warring among families was prevalent. Remnants of this traditional society have persisted through most of the 20th century and sometimes have obstructed social and economic change.

The Montenegro people have been declining as a proportion of the total Yugoslavia population during the socialist era. Montenegrins have been slightly overrepresented, however, in official capacities such as government service, the army, and communist organizations.

Montenegro is one of Yugoslavia's designated less developed republics and it receives large amounts of federal economic assistance. It has benefitted more from the federal economic aid than the other less developed republics, but it continues to be plagued by many of the same economic problems. The per capita income for Montenegro is substantially less than that of the nation as a whole, and the average agricultural income for families living on the many small fragmented landholdings also is substantially less than the average for Yugoslavia. During the socialist era the Montenegrin economy has become less dependent on agriculture and the raising of livestock. Considerable sums of money have been expended to develop the iron and steel, non-ferrous metal, and electric power industries. Electrified railway service links the republic to Serbia via Bijelo Polje, Kolasin, Titograd, and Bar. Railway service also connects Titograd with Nikšić.

The government

Montenegro has a constitution, an assembly, an executive council, and commune assemblies that function in the same manner as those of the other republics (see above *Bosnia and Hercegovina: Physical and human geography*). The republic is represented in the Chamber of Republics and Provinces within the Federal Assembly by 12 delegates elected by the assembly of the republic.

History

MEDIEVAL HISTORY

The district of Zeta, or Duklja, around Kotor and Scutari, was incorporated in the Serbian Empire of Stephen Nemanja in the late 12th century. On the disruption of that empire after 1355, the Balshich family ruled in Zeta until 1421. After the great Turkish victory of Kosovo (1389), Zeta became the refuge of those Serbs who would not live under Islām. In the early 15th century Venice acquired nearly all the Dalmatian coast. It was as vassals of Venice that the Crnojevich family succeeded to the Balshich. When the Turks overran Albania and Hercegovina, Ivan the Black Crnojevich was forced in 1484 to establish his capital in the remote mountain village of Cetinje, where he founded a bishopric and a monastery.

THE VLADIKE (1516–1851)

The last Crnojevich resigned and retired to Venice in 1516. Thereafter until 1697 the mountaineers were ruled by *vladike* (bishops) elected by popular assemblies. In 1697 the succession was restricted to the Petrovich Njegosh family. For more than two more centuries the ultimate concern of the Montenegrins was to fight the Turks and Albanians. In 1711 the *vladika* Danilo I started the tradition of alliance with Russia, receiving an envoy and a subsidy from Peter the Great and himself visiting St. Petersburg.

Conflicts with the Turks

The *vladika* Sava (1735–82) spent most of his time in retirement in a monastery. His cousin Vasilije maintained the struggle against the Turks. Then occurred the episode of the monk Stephen the Small, who appeared in 1767 and claimed (one of half a dozen such claimants) to be the Russian emperor Peter III, the murdered husband of Catherine II. The credulous Montenegrins accepted him; and he ruled with firmness, maintaining solvency by frequent raids into Turkish or Venetian territory. In 1769 Catherine II sent Prince Yuri Dolgoruki to rouse the Montenegrins against the Turks and to denounce the false emperor. Stephen was handed over to Dolgoruki, who, however, was so impressed by him that he left him in power, with the uniform of a Russian staff officer.

Peter I, "the Great *Vladika*," ruled from 1782 to 1830 and doubled the area of Montenegro. His successor Peter II left a noble reputation as a warrior, ruler, and poet.

THE PRINCIPALITY AND THE KINGDOM (1851–1918)

Peter II's nephew, Danilo II, who ruled from 1851 to 1860, refused episcopal status, married, and converted Montenegro into a secular principality. He too vindicated its claim to independence by successful resistance to the Turks.

When Danilo was assassinated, his nephew Nicholas I succeeded him, and was to reign for 58 years (1860–1918). The settlement at the Congress of Berlin (1878) doubled the size of Montenegro and recognized its independence, but, because of Albanian resistance, agreement on the southern frontier was not reached until 1880. Montenegro eventually acquired all the plain of Podgorica and 25 miles of coast. But, as Austria–Hungary now administered Hercegovina, occupied the sanjak of Novi Pazar, protected the Catholic tribes of northern Albania, and exercised maritime control of the Montenegrin coast, the little principality was surrounded by the power of its great neighbour. With the growth of nationalism, the Habsburg control became as insufferable to Montenegrin as to Serbian enthusiasts.

For 30 years, however, Montenegro experienced unusual peace, relieved only by occasional scuffles with the Albanian tribes along the frontier. Nicholas maintained his authority by tradition, by his prestige as warlord, poet, and diplomat, and by judicious distribution of parts of the large subsidies that he received from several foreign powers. But the spread of education, the return from the United States of some of the emigrants, the existence of parliamentary institutions in Serbia, and the contrast between Montenegro's poverty and its ruler's wealth combined to produce dissatisfaction. In 1905 Nicholas proclaimed a parliamentary constitution. The resulting instability and violence were unedifying, and Nicholas soon paid little attention to the niceties of his constitutional law.

Features of the latter years of the reign were the growing movement to unite all Serbs and Nicholas' challenge to the Serbian dynasty for leadership. In 1907 the Serbian government was accused of complicity in a plot against Nicholas, and for a year diplomatic relations were severed. Serbia had already become a kingdom in 1882, and Nicholas proclaimed himself king of Montenegro in 1910. In the Balkan War of 1912–13, however, the two cooperated against Turkey, Nicholas firing the first gun of the war. His troops occupied much Turkish territory, and the result of the war was to extend Montenegro greatly to the north and east and to give it a common frontier with Serbia. The question of Serb unity became more urgent, and in 1914 official discussions began for an economic and political union, though with the retention of the two dynasties.

Montenegro supported Serbia, as a matter of course, in World War I. But, when the Austro-Hungarian Army invaded Montenegro in the winter of 1915–1916, Nicholas tried in vain to negotiate for terms. He then fled with most of his family to Italy; but his second son, Prince Mirko, went to Vienna and was credited with projects for a vassal Yugoslav state under the Petrovich dynasty within the Habsburg monarchy. In western Europe thereafter two voices claimed to speak for Montenegro—Nicholas, who moved his court to Neuilly in France and demanded his own restoration as a condition of increased Serb unity; and the Montenegrin committee at Geneva, under Andrija Radovich, whom for a time Nicholas accepted as his premier. The committee, in defiance of the King, accepted the Declaration of Corfu (July 20, 1917), which only alluded to Montenegro as destined to form part of an indivisible Yugoslav kingdom.

INCORPORATION IN YUGOSLAVIA

When the Austro-Hungarian forces were withdrawn from Montenegro early in November 1918, their place was taken by Serbian troops and irregular bands. Under this new control a national assembly met at Podgorica and on November 26 "unanimously" resolved that Nicholas was dethroned and Montenegro was absorbed into Serbia. A Montenegrin rising followed, with demands for an Allied occupation and free elections. The movement was suppressed, and in April 1919 a Serbian civil governor assumed authority.

Serbian civil government

King Nicholas' government protested to the Allied Supreme War Council against the proceedings at Podgorica and was assured that the Montenegrin people would be afforded "an opportunity to pronounce freely on the political form of their future government." No such opportunity was afforded. Allied investigations on the spot led to the conclusion that nearly all Montenegrins desired inclusion in the new Yugoslavia, though also desiring administrative autonomy within it. The governments of Great Britain and France accordingly took the elections for the Yugoslav constituent assembly in November 1920 as the free pronouncement of the Montenegrin people and on July 13, 1922, accepted the incorporation of Montenegro into Yugoslavia.

In the politics of Yugoslavia the Montenegrins, though resenting administration by any non-Montenegrins, were ultra-Serb. It was a Montenegrin who wrecked the early hopes of Serbo-Croat unity and goodwill by shooting several Croat deputies in Parliament in 1928. But the preoccupations of most Montenegrins were economic rather than political. Subsidies from foreign states had ceased, emigration to the United States was restricted, and the country was miserably poor. After 1918 there was some emigration to Serbia for better land or better employment. Yet when Montenegrins complained that they were forgotten by Belgrade, the Serbian statesmen could reply with justification that the Yugoslav government spent far more on Montenegro than they received from it.

The country's position was a little alleviated by King Alexander's reforms, when Cetinje became the administrative centre of the *banovina* of the Zeta, which included southeastern Hercegovina and southern Dalmatia (1929). But the Zeta was the most thinly populated of the nine *banovine* and had to be supported out of the taxation of the richer north.

Italian occupation **World War II.** In April 1941 Italian troops occupied parts of Montenegro. At Cetinje, in July, the Italians staged a quite unrepresentative national assembly, which declared Montenegro independent, elected an executive body, and requested the King of Italy to nominate a king; but rebel-

lion broke out in the same month, and Montenegro was the scene of continuous fighting until late in 1944. In the winter of 1941–1942 Serb *četnici,* more or less under the command of Draža Mihailović, and Tito's Communist partisans retreated from the Germans into Montenegro and there came to blows with each other. A series of confused three-cornered struggles among royalists, partisans, and the Italians followed. The Italians soon retired to the coast and left the Yugoslavs to fight it out. Late in 1943 a German occupation of the south succeeded the Italian. But by the end of 1944 the Communists, with British arms and equipment, controlled most of Montenegro.

THE COMMUNIST REGIME

Communism of a special sort, for there was virtually no industry or urban proletariat, had been prevalent since 1918. It had the prestige of representing Russia, the country's traditional ally, and of expressing the poorer peasants' hatred of a bourgeois ruling class. Montenegrin Communists had formed some of the toughest elements in Tito's partisans and provided many of his most vigorous officers and leaders. It was not surprising that by the federal constitution of the new Yugoslavia (1946) Montenegro was made one of the six nominally autonomous federated units. Yet its area, though it was increased by the addition of the *boke* (fjord) of Kotor and the Adriatic coast between the *boke* and Bar, still amounted to only 5,333 square miles. The administrative centre was moved from Cetinje to Podgorica, which was rebuilt and renamed Titograd.

In the years since World War II Montenegro has generally supported the policies of the federal government, but this support has not been always unanimous. In 1948, following Yugoslavia's break with the Soviet Union, Montenegrins had a higher rate of expulsion from the League of Communists on the grounds of Soviet sympathies than any other ethnic group. In 1974 a group of Montenegrin Communists were accused of establishing a secret pro-Soviet party. Also in 1974 the region was renamed the Socialist Republic of Montenegro.

(R.G.D.L./Ed.)

SERBIA

Physical and human geography

The Socialist Republic of Serbia (Serbo-Croatian Socijalistička Republika Srbija) has an area of 34,116 square miles (88,361 square kilometres), or more than one-third of Yugoslavia's territory. As a final result of World War I, Serbia, then with an area of 49,528 square miles (128,278 square kilometres) was in December 1918 merged in the Kingdom of the Serbs, Croats, and Slovenes. When Yugoslavia was reorganized in 1946, Serbia became one of the component republics of the federation including the autonomous province of Vojvodina (8,303 square miles) in the north and the autonomous region of Kosmet in the south, which was elevated to autonomous province of Kosovo (4,203 square miles). Serbia is bordered by Hungary to the north, Romania and Bulgaria to the east, the Yugoslavian republic of Macedonia to the south, Albania to the southeast, and the Yugoslavian republics of Montenegro, Bosnia and Hercegovina, and Croatia to the east. The autonomous province of Vojvodina is situated in the northernmost area of the republic, bordering Hungary to the north, Romania to the east, and the Yugoslavian republic of Croatia to the west. Its southern boundary generally follows the eastward course of the Sava and Danube rivers but excludes Belgrad and its environs. The autonomous province of Kosovo is situated in the extreme southwestern corner of Serbia, bordering Albania to the southwest, the Yugoslavian republic of Montenegro to the west, and the Yugoslavian republic of Macedonia to the south.

Most of Serbia, excluding Vojvodina, is hilly and mountainous. The Šar Mountains, situated to the southwest in Kosovo and Macedonia, are one of the most rugged and impassable ranges in the Balkans. These mountains

The autonomous provinces

form the watershed between the Morava drainage basin in Serbia and the Vardar drainage basin in Macedonia. They are fold mountains of nonporous rocks with many peaks surpassing elevations of 6,000 feet (1,800 metres), including Yugoslavia's third highest, Titov Vrh (9,012 feet). In southwestern Serbia and northern Kosovo the Kopaonik Mountains dominate the landscape with peaks exceeding 6,000 feet. In the east along the Bulgarian and Romanian borders, the Balkan Mountains, a branch of the Carpathians and locally known as the Stara Planina, extend into Serbia at elevations from 3,000 feet to more than 6,000 feet. Between the Balkan Mountains on the east and the Kopaonik mountains on the west is the Morava drainage basin. The principal rivers of the basin are: the Južna (South) Morava River, which originates in the Šar Mountains and flows northward to the Danube; the Ibar River, which originates in the mountains of Kosovo and flows northward and empties into the Zapadna (West) Morava River, which originates in the Kopaonik mountains and flows eastward, converging with the Južna Morava.

The relief of northern Serbia and Vojvodina is low in comparison to the south. The plains of the Pannonian Basin dominate this region drained by the Danube River system. The Sava River flows eastward across about half of northern Serbia, merging with the Danube at Belgrade. The Tisa follows a southerly course from Hungary through most of Vojvodina, emptying into the Danube upstream from Belgrade. The Danube proper traverses northern Serbia from west to east and then flows in a southeastern direction, forming part of Yugoslavia's international boundary with Romania. Along this section of the Danube is the deepest gorge in Europe, the Iron Gate (Đerdap, or Djerdap) Gorge.

The plains

The climate of Serbia and the autonomous provinces is on the whole mild, though subject to the extreme characteristics of inland eastern countries. In the summer the temperature may exceed 100° F (38° C), while in the winter it will often fall below 0° F (−18° C). July is the hottest summer month, with temperatures averaging in excess of 70° F (21° C), and the coldest winter month is January, with an average temperature of about 32° F (0° C). Precipitation is fairly evenly distributed throughout the year and varies from locality to locality, but most places receive between 25 and 35 inches (635 to 890 millimetres) annually.

The capital of Serbia (and also of Yugoslavia) is Belgrade, a major political, cultural, and economic centre. Novi Sad is the provincial capital for Vojvodina, and Priština is the capital for the autonomous province of Kosovo. Other major cities include Niš, situated near the confluence of the Nišava and Južna Morava rivers, Kragujevac in central Serbia, Subotica and Zrenjanin in Vojvodina, and Kosovska Mitrovica in Kosovo.

Serbia proper, excluding Vojvodina and Kosovo, is ethnically homogeneous, with Serbs accounting for the vast majority of the population. In Vojvodina Serbs are the majority ethnic group, but a large minority population of Hungarians and a smaller group of Croats also reside in the autonomous province. Albanians account for more than three-quarters of the population of Kosovo. The Serbian population in Kosovo has declined substantially since the mid-20th century, while the population of Albanians has increased dramatically. This increase in the Albanian population has been caused by the higher birth rate of the Albanian people and by the emigration of Serbs from the province in the wake of rising Albanian nationalism. The Serbian minority population accounts for less than one-sixth of the provincial total.

The economy

Serbia and Vojvodina are two of Yugoslavia's more developed regions, while Kosovo is the poorest and least developed region in the country. The fertile plains of Vojvodina, along with neighbouring Croatia, constitute the most productive agricultural area in Yugoslavia, producing more than one-half of the country's grain and about three-quarters of the nation's sugar beets. About one-half of Vojvodina's population is engaged in agriculture. The size of privately-owned farms tends to be larger in Vojvodina than in any other region except for Croatia. Slightly less than one-half of Serbia's population works in the agricultural sector. Serbian farms tend to combine agriculture and livestock raising, particularly sheep and poultry. Marginal family farms dominate the countryside of Kosovo, and about two-fifths of the people work on farms.

More than one-half of Yugoslavia's coal reserves are located in Kosovo, the bulk of the reserve being lignite, with a small proportion of brown coal and almost no hard coal. Many mines operate in the province, but the majority of the coal is extracted from a few mines. Most of the country's crude oil reserves are located in the plains of Vojvodina or Croatia, and many wells are in operation. Mining and manufacturing are the largest contributors to the economy of Serbia, although agriculture also plays a significant role. Industries produce metal products, machinery, farm equipment, paper, glass, textiles, and chemical products. There is also mining for copper, coal, lead, and gold and quarrying for marble.

Kosovo has received large amounts of economic development assistance from the federal government since 1946, but the province has remained the poorest region of the country. The per capita income for the autonomous province is about one-third that of the nation as a whole and substantially less than that of Vojvodina, Serbia, or the other regions. Federal government efforts to improve the province's economy have been partially offset by the high rate of population growth.

The railway network

Serbia and Vojvodina have well-developed transportation networks, while the network of Kosovo is somewhat less developed. Major railways radiate from Belgrade, linking it to the capitals of each republic and the principal Adriatic ports. A major north–south line follows the course of the Južna Morava River connecting Belgrade to Niš and Skopje in Macedonia. A spur of this line follows the Ibar River to the Kosovo city of Kosovska Mitrovica, and it continues across the Šar Mountains to Skopje. These two lines are linked by feeder lines passing through Priština, and Kruševac. To the north Belgrade is connected by a railway line to Novi Sad and Subotica.

Serbia has a constitution, an assembly, an executive council, and commune assemblies that function in the same manner as those of the other republics (see above *Bosnia and Hercegovina: Physical and human geography*). The republic is represented in the Federal Assembly's Chamber of Republics and Provinces by 12 delegates elected by its own assembly. Vojvodina and Kosovo also have a constitution, an assembly, an executive council, and commune assemblies that function similarly to their republican counterparts but within a more limited scope. Formally the provinces are subordinate to Serbia, and the constitutions of each administrative region vaguely defines the distribution of authority. The de facto relationship between the provinces and the republic is, however, essentially the same as that between the republics and the federal government. Each province also is represented in the Chamber of Republics and Provinces by eight delegates elected by their assemblies.

History

THE RISE OF SERBIA

The Serbs (Srbi, singular Srbin), who belong to the South Slav group of the Slavonic peoples, arrived in the Balkans during the 7th century AD. The etymology of this name, which first occurs, in the form Sorabi, in the *Frankish Annals* for the year 822, is obscure; it must be remarked that the Slavs of Lusatia similarly call themselves Sorbs.

In their Balkan settlements, along the Piva, Tara, upper Drina, Ibar, Lim, and Western Morava rivers, the Serbs did not at once form a united state. Clans more or less related to each other occupied a certain territory under the political and military leadership of a *župan*. Attempts by one *župan* after another to subjugate his neighbours led to much bloodshed; and the custom of the ancient Slavs, whereby a *župan* was succeeded by the eldest surviving member of his family, not necessarily by his own son as he might naturally wish, gave rise to further conflict.

House of Višeslav. The first *župan* whose name is recorded was Višeslav (Visheslav), who was living *c.* AD 780. His great-great-grandson Mutimir accepted Orthodox Christianity (*c.* 879); and the work of evangelization was carried forward.

After Mutimir's death (*c.* 890) the Byzantines and the Bulgars began a struggle for Serbia. The Bulgars set up Mutimir's grandson Paul as ruler of Serbia (917–920). When Paul initiated a rapprochement with Constantinople, they replaced him with Zacharias, another of Mutimir's grandsons, who had originally been the Byzantines' candidate against Paul but had fallen into the hands of the Bulgarian tsar Symeon. When Zacharias likewise made new approaches to the Byzantines, Symeon drove him into exile in Croatia (924).

About 927, Časlav (Chaslav) made himself ruler over most of the Serbs and was able to annex Bosnia but had to acknowledge the Byzantine emperor as his suzerain. Bosnia soon detached itself from the rest of the Serbian territory.

Nemanja dynasty. Raška (Rashka, on the Ibar River) was, in the 12th century, the site of anti-Byzantine insurrection and consequent Byzantine campaigns. About 1167 Stephen (Stefan) Nemanja (Nemanya) became grand *župan* of Raška, under Byzantine suzerainty. He conquered several Byzantine places on the Adriatic coast and allied himself with Ivan Asen I, founder of the Second Bulgarian Empire.

Stephen Nemanja

Nemanja left his throne not to his eldest son, Vukan, but to his second son, Stephen. Apart from Vukan's resentment, Stephen had to face danger from the Bulgars, from the Hungarians, and from the Latin Empire, which the leaders of the Fourth Crusade set up in place of the Greek in 1204. He received invaluable support, however, from his youngest brother, Sava, the future saint, one of the greatest personalities in Serbian history. In 1219 Sava was consecrated as the first archbishop of an autocephalous Serbian Orthodox Church.

The succeeding kings were Stephen's sons Stephen Radoslav (reign 1228–34), Stephen Vladislav (1234–43), and Stephen Uroš I (1243–76). Uroš in 1252 made war against the Adriatic city of Dubrovnik, which soon came to terms with him; but in 1253 Dubrovnik allied itself with the Bulgars, whose forces penetrated Serbia as far as the Lim River. For that reason the seat of the Serbian archiepiscopate was transferred from Žiča to Peć. Peace, however, was made in 1254.

Having maintained good relations with his neighbours for most of his reign (1276–82), Dragutin, Uroš' son and co-ruler, joined Charles I of Naples and Sicily and the Venetians in their anti-Byzantine alliance of 1281. He abdicated in 1282, in favour of his brother Milutin (also reckoned as Stephen Uroš II). Later, however, he claimed that he had merely made Milutin regent and had reserved the eventual succession to his own descendants. Dragutin was granted Belgrade, Mačva, and northeastern Bosnia by his brother-in-law László IV of Hungary.

Milutin's reign (1282–1321) marks the rise of Serbia in the international field. A few months after his accession he conquered Skopje, Tetovo, Ovče Pole, and Pijanec from the Byzantines. An army sent against him by the emperor Andronicus II was defeated, and the Serbs advanced to the walls of Strumica, Prilep, and Ohrid. Peace was not concluded until 1299, when Milutin married the Emperor's daughter Simonis, and the Byzantines formally ceded the conquered lands as her dowry. Planning a new war against the Byzantines, Milutin in 1308 made an alliance with the ambitious French prince Charles of Valois and entered into relations with Pope Clement V, but this project came to nothing when Charles gave up his designs on the Eastern Empire. A Hungarian attack on Serbia in 1319 was without effect.

Internally, Serbia's mineral resources were exploited, commerce thrived, and about 40 churches were built during Milutin's reign. After his death his son Stephen (Uroš III, otherwise called Stephen of Decani, or Stefan Dečanski) was crowned king, despite estrangement from his father in life. The Byzantines and the Bulgars allied themselves against Serbia in 1330; but the Bulgars were decisively defeated at Velbuzhd (Kyustendil) when their tsar was killed. The Byzantine emperor Andronicus III thereupon abandoned his campaign.

War with the Byzantines and Bulgars

There followed a quarrel between the Serbian king and his heir. In the spring of 1331 they seemed to be reconciled, but in the following summer the son, Stefan Dušan, dethroned his father, who died soon afterward. Dušan's sole rule now began. A man of magnificent physique, energy, and ambition, he fascinated his subjects and could lead them wherever he wished. Continuing the war against the Byzantines, he forced them to cede some Macedonian territory in 1334. The Byzantine civil war, which broke out in 1341, gave him a new opportunity. Having conquered all Macedonia as far eastward as Philippi, with the exception of Salonika, he asumed the title of tsar (emperor) of the Serbs and Greeks in 1345. He then procured the establishment of the Serbian Church as an independent partriarchate (March 1346); and on Easter Day, 1346, he had himself crowned as tsar at Skopje by his new patriarch. Dušan then turned his attention westward and southward, occupying Albania, Epirus, Aetolia (which gave him a foothold on the Gulf of Corinth), and finally Thessaly.

The tsar Uroš, Dušan's son and successor, was a weak man. His reign (1355–71) saw the decline of Serbian power. Other provincial rulers asserted themselves in the 1360s: the Balšić family in northern Albania and along the Adriatic coast; Nikola Altomanić at Rudnik and southwestward from there; and the brothers Vukašin and Uglješa in Macedonia. Vukašin, ruling Skopje, Prizren, Prilep, and Tetovo, assumed the title of king in January 1366. Campaigning against the Ottoman Turks, who had first appeared in the Balkans in the 1340s, Vukašin and his brother were killed in the Battle of the Maritsa River, near Adrianople, in the stormy night of September 25–26, 1371, when the Serbs sustained a terrible defeat still proverbially remembered as a national disaster.

Prince Lazar and the Battle of Kosovo. The foremost of the princes who took over the succession of Uroš in 1371 was Lazar, a member of the Hrebeljanović family and, by marriage, a relative of the House of Nemanja. The Balšić family, however, remained powerful; Vukašin's son Marko (the Marko Kraljević of Serbian legend) also had some territory; the Dejanović family was strong in eastern Macedonia; and Vuk Branković dominated the Kosovo region. With help from Tvrtko of Bosnia, Lazar overthrew Nikola Altomanić in 1373 and partitioned his territory with Tvrtko.

Though Tvrtko's subsequent assumption of a royal title implied some diminution of Lazar's status, the two were in agreement on the need to cooperate against the Turks. Having reduced most of Bulgaria and Macedonia to vassality, Sultan Murad I was demanding tribute from the Serbs. Lazar resisted, and Murad, who attacked Serbia and captured Niš in 1386, was halted at Pločnik. In 1389, however, Murad led another invasion, and on June 15 the Battle of Kosovo was fought: Murad himself was killed, but the Serbs were catastrophically defeated. Lazar was taken prisoner and beheaded. The Battle of Kosovo, symbolizing the choice of death rather than compromise with the enemy, is one of the permanent memories of the Serbian national consciousness.

Serbian defeat at Kosovo

The despotate. Lazar's son Stephen succeeded to the Serbian principality in 1389 as a vassal of Sultan Bayazid I. He thus took part in several Turkish campaigns. Stephen, returning home via Constantinople, accepted the title of despot (that is, lord) from the Byzantine regent John VIII Palaeologus. The discomfiture of the Turks gave him a freer hand in Serbia.

George Branković, Stephen's successor, was a highly cultured man and an experienced soldier. The Turks, whose power was growing again, resented George's friendly relations with Hungary, and in 1439 Sultan Murad II took the new Serbian capital, Smederevo, and captured two of George's sons, who were later blinded. George went to Hungary for help; and in autumn 1443 he and János Hunyadi led a large army against the Turks. George then made a separate peace with Murad, who recognized him as despot of the restored Serbia.

George Branković was no longer willing to commit himself hastily against the Turks. Even so, Sultan Mohammed II, after his conquest of Constantinople in 1453, decided to attack Serbia. After a first campaign in 1454, he captured Novo Brdo in 1455.

After the short reign of George's son Lazar (1456–58), there was an attempt to save the remnant of Serbia, but the Sultan attacked Serbia again and took Smederevo in 1459, which represented the end of Serbia as a territorial power.

From 1389, however, the Serbs had been migrating to Hungarian territory, and the numbers of such migrants increased after 1459. The Hungarians welcomed them as fighters against the Turks. Matthias Corvinus granted the nominal title of despot in 1471 to George Branković's grandson Vuk and in 1486 to the latter's first cousin George, from whom it passed to his brother John. From 1504, it was borne by members of other families.

Sultan Suleiman I the Magnificent conquered Šabac in 1521 and Belgrade a few months later. Crossing the Sava River, the Turks devastated Srem. Suleiman's great victory over the Hungarians at Mohács in 1526 heralded the subjection of all the Serbs to Turkish rule. John (Jovan) Nenad, known as "the Black Man," who won a large following among the Serbs of Hungary and assumed the title of tsar, was killed in 1527; and 10 years later Pavle Bakić, the last titular despot, was killed in battle.

TURKISH RULE

Early occupation. All land in Serbia became the property of the sultan, who entrusted it to *spahis,* military tenants who held it from him in return for their services. The Serbs themselves were bond-slaves of the land, most of the revenue being the perquisite of the *spahis.* In the early period of the Turkish occupation, however, there took place an event of great significance for the Serbs, namely the restoration of the Serbian patriarchate at Peć

Serbs in slavery

(1557). The first of the new patriarchs was Makarije, brother of the Turkish grand vizir Mehmed Paşa Sokollu (Sokolović). With a large territorial jurisdiction, the patriarch was the personification of national survival as well as the spiritual head of his people.

The defeat of the Turks outside Vienna (1683) was followed by Austrian counteroffensives in the course of which Prince Louis of Baden advanced as far south as Kosovo. The Serbs then rose against the Turks; but a new Turkish effort, under the grand vizir Mustafa Köprülü, not only won the country back but also spread such terror that thousands of Serbs, with their patriarch Arsenije III Crnojević, migrated to Hungary. For these refugees the Holy Roman emperor Leopold I promulgated a charter (1690), promising to respect their Orthodox religion and guaranteeing them the rights to elect their patriarch. These undertakings, however, were not long observed.

The Banat, which had a large population of Serbs, was left under Turkish rule, with the rest of Serbia and Bosnia, by the Peace of Carlowitz (Karlovci) in 1699, though other lands of the Hungarian crown were then ceded by the Turks to Austria. The Austro-Turkish War of 1716–18, however, led to the Peace of Passarowitz (Požarevac), whereby Austria obtained both the Banat and also the adjacent part of Serbia (known as Šumadija) south of the Sava and Danube rivers, with Belgrade. After Austria's unfortunate invasion of Turkish Serbia in 1737, the Peace of Belgrade (1739) restored the Turkish frontier on the Sava and Danube.

In 1766 the Turkish government abolished the Serbian patriarchate; but by the Treaty of Kuchuk Kainarji, in 1774, Turkey formally acknowledged Russia's claims to champion Orthodox and Slav interests in the Ottoman Empire. When Russia and Austria together began another war against Turkey in 1787, the Serbs under Mihajlo Mihaljević formed a free corps in the Austrian service: the Austrians captured Belgrade in 1789 but retroceded it to the Turks at the Peace of Sistova in 1791. The Serbs' disillusionment at Austria's conduct was expressed in the remark of one of Mihaljević's officers, Aleksa Nenadović: "The Serbs should not trust the Germans."

War between Austria and Turkey

The reforms initiated by the sultan Selim III in the last decade of the 18th century provoked a number of revolts by the reactionary janissaries in the outlying provinces of the Ottoman Empire. At the end of 1801 Haji Mustafa, the Ottoman governor of the pashalik of Smederevo (or of Belgrade; *i.e.*, Serbia), was assassinated by a faction of janissaries, four of whom then assumed power themselves as *dahije*, or deys. Their regime was so tyrannical that the Serbs began to plan insurrection for the spring of 1804.

(M.A.P./Ed.)

Karageorge and the first rising. One of the Serbian patriots, Karageorge (Karadjordje), fled to the forest to escape death at the hands of the janissaries. Within 10 days 2,000 men joined him, and they began attacking Turkish positions. The *dahije* tried to negotiate with Karageorge, who became the supreme commander of the insurrection, but after two ineffectual meetings the Serbs seized Rudnik, Valjevo, Jagodina (now Svetozarevo), and Šabac. They unsuccessfully asked for Austrian and Russian protection. Austrian mediation, at the request of the *dahije*, came to nothing, and in May the Serbs addressed a petition to Sultan Selim III, took Požarevac, and sent a deputation to Russia. A meeting between Karageorge and the Paşa of Bosnia, at the latter's request, took place in July, and the Serbs were allowed to capture and behead the four *dahije*. The Serbs then brought their demands before the Paşa, but he rejected them.

The Serbian representatives were well received in St. Petersburg; but, for fear of Napoleonic France, the Russian Emperor Alexander I decided to uphold Turkey's integrity and advised the Serbs to send a deputation to Turkey, which they did in June 1805. On learning from the Austrians what the Serbs intended, the Turkish government decided to crush the rising. The Serbs, however, conquered Karanovac and Užice (now Titovo Užice) (June–August). Until then the rising had been directed against the outlawed janissaries, but at Ivankovac, on August 18, 1805, the Serbs for the first time defeated Turkish regular

troops. Intoxicated by their successes and aiming now at independence, they organized the Serbian State Council, a supreme administrative and judicial body. They conquered Smederevo in November and sent a deputation to Austria. Though the Serbs were again advised to settle their differences directly with Turkey (February 1806), both Austria and Russia promised their good offices, fearing that Napoleon I's recent victory over Austria might induce the Serbs to turn toward France. Napoleon, however, wrote in June 1806 to Sultan Selim that he should use the strongest means to bring the Serbian rebels into subjection. Even so, the Serbs continued their successes; they took Poreč, Paraćin, Ražanj, Aleksinac, Kruševac, the Stari Vlah district, and half of the Novi Pazar district; routed the Turkish regulars again at Mišar and at Deligrad; and finally in December won Belgrade. They had liberated Serbia without outside help.

War broke out between Turkey and Russia at the end of the year. Asked by Turkey for help against Russia, the Serbs refused. The Russians, however, instead of helping the Serbs, at first asked them to make a diversion; but when Karageorge protested they sent a token force to Serbia. The allies routed the Turks at Štubik, a Serbo-Russian convention was signed on July 10, 1807, and K.K. Rodofinikin arrived as the first Russian diplomatic agent in Belgrade. The Serbs of Serbia made contact with their fellow nationals in Bosnian, Austrian, and Montenegrin territory.

War between Turkey and Russia

Defeated by Napoleon at Friedland (modern Pravdinsk), Russia concluded the armistice of Slobozia with Turkey (August 24, 1807), in which Serbia was not even mentioned. Karageorge resented such behaviour, and his attitude aroused suspicion in some of his commanders, who wanted more freedom of action for themselves. The Serbian State Council, however, seeing that Russia was attempting to gain exclusive influence, passed the first Serbian constitution, which proclaimed Karageorge "first and supreme hereditary leader." Karageorge, after informing Russia, rejected an Austrian offer of protection, as well as a Turkish offer of peace.

The Russo-Turkish War restarted in March 1809, and the Russian commander in chief informed the Serbs in May that Alexander I aimed "at the liberation of Serbia from any kind of dependence on Turkey." The Serbs took Sjenica, Suhodol, and Novi Pazar (May–June), but their commanders were torn between Karageorge and his opponents; and the Turks, concentrating a large army in the south, won a victory at Kamenica in June and recovered Soko Banja, Deligrad, Stalać, and Požarevac by the end of August. As the Russian armies were idle, the exasperated Serbs sent a delegate to Napoleon and appealed again to Austria. The Russians, however, invaded Bulgaria (at that time still Turkish territory) in September, and the Turks withdrew their armies from Serbia. With renewed confidence in Russia, an assembly of Serbian leaders challenged Karageorge by sending a delegation to the Russian commander in chief, P.I. Bagration, to disavow Karageorge's fruitless approaches to France and Austria. Russia sent 2,500 men to Serbia, and in the autumn of 1810 the Turks were defeated at Varvarin and Loznica. Finally, at Karageorge's request, Russia agreed to establish four garrisons in Serbia. To consolidate his position and to silence the opposition, Karageorge convened a leaders' assembly, which passed a new constitution; and before the Russian garrisons reached Belgrade he appointed his first government (January 20, 1811).

On the eve of attack by Napoleon, Russia concluded the Treaty of Bucharest with Turkey (May 1812). Its Article VIII stipulated an amnesty for all Serbs, the demolition of newly built fortresses, the surrender of old ones, and a limited autonomy, but details were to be negotiated directly between Serbs and Turks. Forsaken again, the Serbs were bitterly disappointed. The opposition held Karageorge responsible, and dissension grew among the leaders. Rejecting a Turkish summons to surrender (July 1813), the Serbs were attacked from three sides by powerful armies and were defeated. Karageorge took refuge in Austria, and on October 7, 1813, the Turks reentered Belgrade. For a fortnight the Turks killed Serbs at random and sold many as slaves. After Napoleon I's defeat at Leipzig, the Turks granted a general amnesty.

The second rising and Miloš Obrenović I. Miloš Obrenović I, one of the leaders who had not followed Karageorge into exile, was in August 1814 appointed head of three Serbian central districts by the new vizier, Suleiman Pasha Skopljak. When the vizier, to enrich himself, levied new taxes, Serbian leaders sent a delegate to the Congress of Vienna, but Russia was the only power there to feel any interest in Serbia's fate. Russia indeed tried to raise the Serbian question but failed because of Napoleon's return to France from Elba (March 1815). Then Miloš, who in September 1814 had even helped the Turks to suppress a rebellion, decided to act against them. He summoned all the Serbian leaders to the Takovo church on Palm Sunday, and a second rising began.

The Serbs routed the Turkish regulars at Ljubić, Palež (Obrenovac), and Dublje and, in August 1815, took Požarevac. Controlling an area of about 24,440 square kilometres, Miloš styled himself "supreme prince and ruler of the Serbian nation" and was recognized as such by the Skupština (National Assembly) and, in November, by Marashli Ali Pasha, the new vizier; but when the Turks mustered two large armies he realized his weakness and tried to compromise.

In September 1815 Russia threatened military intervention, whereupon the Turks lent Miloš a helping hand. At the beginning of 1816, Serbian demands were partly accepted. Miloš agreed to the supremacy of the Turkish authorities but soon secured parallelism between Serbs and Turks and finally eliminated the latter. This settlement was guaranteed only by the vizier's word, and Miloš wanted it confirmed by Sultan Mahmud II. He approached the Turks as leader of the Serbs while impressing the Serbs as being a friend of the Turks. Simultaneously, he extended Serbian autonomy, disposed of all rivals, and even had Karageorge assassinated (July 1817)—an act that started the feud between the Obrenović and Karageorgević dynasties. He then convened the Skupština and was recognized as hereditary prince (November 18, 1817).

At last the Sultan delivered a decree, but when his representative reached Belgrade and read it to the Skupština, the Serbs rejected it (September 1820). As the Sultan consistently deferred recognizing Miloš's agreement with the vizier and any solution of the Walachian and Greek problems, Russia in March 1826 sent an ultimatum demanding a settlement and fulfillment of Turkey's obligations toward Serbia under the Bucharest treaty. A new Russo-Turkish convention was signed at Akkerman in October, and Turkey undertook to settle the Serbian question within 18 months and to grant Serbia "independence in its interior administration." Turkish negotiations with the Serbs were interrupted by the Russo-Turkish War of 1828–29, which ended with the Treaty of Adrianople (September 14, 1829). As regards Serbia, this treaty reiterated the stipulations of the Akkerman convention, and Turkey undertook to restore the "Six Districts" (Jadar, Crna Reka, Paraćin, Kruševac, and Stari Vlah in the south, and Krajina in the east), which had been liberated during the first rising but later recovered by Turkey. A *hatti-sherif* (imperial edict) was promulgated in Belgrade on December 12, 1830, with a brevet recognizing Miloš as hereditary prince.

The autonomous principality of Serbia Serbia became an internationally recognized autonomous principality under Turkish suzerainty and Russian protection; Turkish garrisons were retained only in Belgrade and five other fortresses; and Turkish civilians had to sell their properties in the towns and leave the country or settle inside the walls of the citadels. Turkey, however, still kept the Six Districts. Taking advantage of Muḥammad ʿAlī's rebellion in Egypt (1831), Miloš fomented sedition in the Six Districts, gathered troops along their border, and informed the Porte that he was ready to help the rebels if the Turks tried to crush them. Turkey at last gave up, and the union of the Six Districts with Serbia was proclaimed (June 10, 1833), bringing the area of the principality to about 37,740 square kilometres. Miloš then paid a state visit to the Sultan.

Before achieving his goal, Miloš had solved the agrarian problem by enacting that the land, which the *spahi* tenants of the Sultan (see above *Turkish rule*) had gradually vacated, should belong to those who worked it. In this way he put Serbia's economy on a sound basis and also unwittingly prepared the way for the future peasant democracy of Serbia. He instituted a judicature, formed police forces, and opened new schools. The Serbs agreed with his policy toward the Turks, but in home affairs they were against his despotic tendencies and wanted more representative institutions. Having suppressed five rebellions, Miloš eventually had to let the Skupština pass a constitution limiting his powers (1835). Austria, Russia, and Turkey immediately protested against this constitution as too liberal, and Miloš gladly abolished it. Even so, paradoxically, autocratic Russia tried to restrain the Prince's Oriental despotism, while liberal Great Britain, in order to build up Serbia into a bulwark against Russian advance in the Balkans, supported the extension of his authority. Finally a new constitution, negotiated in Istanbul between Turkey and Miloš's representative Avram Petronijević (1791–1852), who was under Russian influence, was promulgated in 1838.

The Serbs had sent countless envoys to Istanbul; the Turkish officials had ignored some of them, negotiated with others, and imprisoned others for years or kept them as hostages. Bribery had served the Serbian cause well enough; but the achievement of autonomy was due above all to the political skill, instinctive realism, and indomitable energy of Miloš Obrenović.

Period of oligarchy. A regency called the "Defenders of Constitutionalism," the embryo of the oligarchy that ruled Serbia for the next two decades, was formed in 1839. Conflict soon grew up between the Defenders and Prince Michael. The regents, having been sent into exile and then pardoned, finally organized an armed rebellion in complicity with the vizier. The young prince then fled to Austria. The "Defenders of Constitutionalism"

On September 14, 1842, the Skupština elected Karageorge's son Alexander to the throne. Turkey recognized the election, but Russia contested it on the ground that it followed a rebellion instigated by the vizier. At a second election (June 27, 1843), Alexander was again chosen. Two rebellions fomented by Miloš were suppressed in 1844; but the rivalry between the Obrenović and the Karageorgević dynasty was to continue for 60 years.

Serbia's external relations for the next 12 years were marked by the "Plan" of Ilija Garašanin for foreign policy, by the Hungarian Revolution of 1848–49, and by the Crimean War. On the basis of a memorandum by the Polish patriot Prince Adam Jerzy Czartoryski, Garašanin, the Serbian home secretary, in 1844, developed a plan for a general rising of all Christians under the Turkish yoke and for the creation of a large South Slav state under Serbia's leadership. Originally the plan refrained from anticipating the liberation of the South Slavs of the Austrian Empire; but when the Hungarian Revolution broke out Garašanin wanted Serbia to help the Serbs of the Vjvodina, who rose against the Hungarians. The government decided not to intervene, but numerous volunteers flocked to help their kinsmen, and Stefan Petrović-Knićanin (1807–55), a former member of the State Council, became the insurgents' commander in chief. Serbia's choice of neutrality during the Crimean War and Garašanin's connections with the West were rewarded by the Treaty of Paris at the end of that war (March 30, 1856), since it placed Serbia's autonomy under the collective guarantee of the Powers and restricted Turkey's sovereign rights by forbidding armed interference in Serbia without the Powers' consent.

At home, the two main objects of the Defenders were to secure the civic rights of the Serbs and to limit the prince's power. The first was achieved by introducing modern institutions, a competent bureaucracy, and a series of new laws. Whereas the old Skupština had never been able to limit Miloš Obrenović I's power, the newly instituted State Council succeeded in limiting Alexander Karageorgević's. Later, however, people realized that their political rights were not necessarily guaranteed by the securing of their civic rights and that the prince's power was limited not by them, but only by an oligarchy. Since the prince's power was more limited by the organic laws than by the constitution, a struggle was inevitable between him and the State Council, which despite its restricted composition was really a kind of representative body of true national leaders. In the earlier phases of the Crimean War the Prince and the council, which was pro-Russian, observed a truce, but when it became evident that Russia could not win the war dissension was revived.

Incited by the long-deposed Miloš, Stefan Stefanović-Tenka (1797–1865), the president of the State Council, became the ringleader of a conspiracy to overthrow Alexander; and with a few of his fellow conspirators he organized a new plot against the Prince's life (1857). The plot was exposed, however, and a general purge resulted. Alexander appointed new councillors; but Russia and France, resentful of the pro-Austrian policy that he had recently adopted, took his action against the old council as a pretext for asking Turkey to send a commissary to Belgrade to settle the conflict. On December 23, 1858, the Skupština deposed Alexander.

Miloš restored.   The Skupština which dethroned Prince Alexander, recalled Prince Miloš Obrenović I, whose election was recognized by Turkey. The council and the Skupština had overthrown Alexander together, but the latter elected Miloš without consulting the former. This created a rift that provided the elements of the first two political groups, based on personal allegiances rather than on any nationwide party or class structure: namely the Conservative supporters of the council, and the Liberal followers of the Skupština. The Conservatives, who were called *kajmakanci* (from *kajmakan*, "regent") because their leaders had wanted to be elected as regents on the overthrow of Alexander, desired only a change of dynasty, with the legislative power still shared between the council and the prince and with the civil service retaining its entirely conservative character. The Liberals, on the other hand, who were called *dukatovci* because their leaders' anonymous articles appeared in the press over a symbol meaning ducat, wanted to make the Skupština the third partner in the legislature and to reform the civil service.

As soon as Miloš reached Belgrade (February 6, 1859), he appointed new councillors and a Liberal government and began dismissing the civil servants. The difference between his populism and that of the Liberals was evident: both wanted a Skupština, but Miloš expected it to be dependent on him, while the Liberals wanted it dependent on a strong political party. He estranged the Liberals without attracting the Conservatives, ignored the constitution and the council, and reduced the Skupština to a body of illiterate peasants. Whereas during his first reign he had been a despot feared by the masses, during his second he was a potentate afraid of them.

Michael Obrenović and enlightened absolutism.   His son Michael, who had reigned briefly after Miloš's 1839 abdication, returned to the throne and formulated his program as follows: the liberation of the Balkans; the creation of a large South Slav state led by Serbia; a strict and just application of the law; and economic development. An era of enlightened absolutism began.

Prince Michael stopped all political persecution and reinstated the dismissed civil servants or gave them a pension but was unable to reconcile the Conservatives and the Liberals. His first government therefore was a caretaker one, and it passed the laws that he desired. The council's authority was limited to legislation. The irremovability of the councillors was abolished. The Skupština remained as a consultative representative body, though its powers were somewhat increased. There was no freedom of the press.

No longer needing to cultivate the Liberals, Michael appointed a Conservative government with Garašanin as prime minister. The latter was thus able to develop and enforce his "Plan," the main object of which was war with Turkey. The strength of the Serbian Army was raised dramatically. In preparation for war Serbia concluded a series of alliances: with Montenegro (1866), with the Bulgarian Revolutionary Committee (1867), with Greece (1867), and with Romania (1868). The first Balkan League was thus created. On June 10, 1868, Michael was assassinated.

The regency for Milan Obrenović IV.   Milan Obrenović IV, a boy of 14, was proclaimed prince-elect by the Skup-

The isolation of Miloš

ština on July 2, 1868, and Petrović-Blaznavac, Ristić, and Jovan Gavrilović (1796–1877) were appointed regents for him.

The Skupština then demanded a widening of its powers and more liberal institutions. The regents drafted a new constitution without consulting either Turkey or the council, with which they still shared the legislative power. The draft was submitted to a constituent Skupština and was passed with a few alterations (July 11, 1869).

Before adjourning, the constituent Skupština in 1870 passed several laws, including an electoral law, regulations of parliamentary procedure, and an act giving limited freedom of the press. The reforms were not a victory of the people over the bureaucracy, but rather a compromise, and they produced different reactions: the peasants were satisfied that the Skupština should have wider powers; the Conservatives disapproved, preferring to continue to support enlightened absolutism; the Liberals, while accepting the new policy, looked forward to further progressive reforms; and a new militant Socialist group led by Svetozar Marković was scornfully opposed to such reforms. Ristić, responsible for the new constitution, avoided stating anything in it that might give the slightest suggestion that the government was dependent on the Skupština. Serbia was a constitutional, not a parliamentary, monarchy. Meanwhile he paid great attention to education and to the economic development of the country.

Before being elected regent, Petrović-Blaznavac had promised Austria to "respect Turkey's integrity and to liberate Serbia totally from Russian influence." The relationship with Austria was therefore good, though not exclusive. The Russian government regarded the constitutional changes in Serbia as a defeat of its own policy and distrusted the new regime. Nevertheless it wanted to draw the young prince closer—and definitely before he came of age. He was invited to visit the emperor Alexander II at Livadia in 1871. This visit resulted in a deterioration of Serbia's relationship both with Turkey and with Austria, and the regency inclined more toward Russia.

As the Serbs of Montenegro adopted a separatist attitude and as Bulgaria became antagonistic to Serbia, the Balkan League, which Prince Michael and Garašanin had brought into being, gradually fell apart. Ristić in any case had no faith in such a league, believing that the Balkan states, even if united, were too weak to defeat Turkey without outside help, and that any success won with the help of the Great Powers would make Serbia too dependent on them.

Milan's first governments.   When Milan attained his majority (August 22, 1872), the regency ended, but Milan retained Petrović-Blaznavac in office as prime minister and Ristić as minister of foreign affairs. Petrović-Blaznavac died, however, on April 5, 1873, and Ristić then formed a short-lived nonparty government that alienated both Conservatives and Liberals. For various reasons, moreover, Serbia's relationship with Germany, France, Austria, and Turkey became disturbed. To improve the situation, Milan paid visits to Vienna and to Paris. He was well received, but his visits worsened his relationship with Turkey. Backed by the League of Three Emperors (Austria, Germany, and Russia), Milan then appointed a Conservative government; in May 1874 he paid a state visit to the Sultan. After a general election in October had returned a Liberal majority, discontent grew in the Skupština, and, for the first time, it was dissolved. A fresh election, however, in August 1875, gave the same result, and Milan reluctantly appointed a Liberal government.

INDEPENDENCE

The wars of 1876–78.   In July 1875 the Serbs of Hercegovina had risen in rebellion against the Turks. The Serbian Liberal government decided to help the insurgents even at the risk of war; but Milan in October 1875 appointed a new government comprising both younger Conservatives and Liberals. As the political groups were divided on the question of war, the decision rested with Milan, who could not curb the growing nationalism incited by the Russian Slavophils, though officially Russia tried to restrain it. In order to wage war the Prince had to appoint a Liberal government again (May 1876).

Ristić, who became foreign minister, preferred to avoid war, but Turkey rejected his proposal to entrust Serbia with the administration of Bosnia and Hercegovina. The Serbia government then declared war (June 30, 1876), mistakenly believing that the first shot would produce a general Balkan rising and that the Slavophils would force Russia to join. No such rising occurred, and Russia not only abstained from war against Turkey but also agreed, on July 8, that Austria-Hungary, instead of Serbia, should occupy Bosnia and Hercegovina. Even so, the Serbs chose a Russian general, M.G. Chernyaev, to be their commander in chief. His troops, however, in which Russian adventurers outnumbered Serbian officers, were defeated by the Turks at Veliki Izor on July 18. After an interval of confusion, the Serbs won a victory at Šumatovac. The Great Powers then tried mediation, but Turkey's terms proved unacceptable. Finally the Serbs, after a series of reverses (September–October), appealed to Russia, and on March 1, 1877, peace was concluded on the basis of the status quo.

When Russia in April 1877 declared war on Turkey, Serbia again wanted to fight but at first received evasive answers from Russia. The Turks, however, halted the Russian advance at Pleven, and Russia then appealed for help. Serbia declared war against Turkey on December 13 and proceeded to liberate large tracts of territory on the southern frontier. Then Russia imposed the Treaty of San Stefano on Turkey (March 3, 1878) without consulting Serbia. This treaty gave Serbia independence and possession of Niš, while a Greater Bulgaria, which Russia needed for further expansion, was created. The opposition of the Great Powers frustrated this plan; and the Congress of Berlin in July besides granting Serbia's independence increased the amount of new territory, adding Pirot, Toplica, and Vranje to Niš. This was achieved through Gyula Andrássy, the Austro-Hungarian foreign minister, after Ristić had come to terms with him. Disillusioned with Russia, the Serbs now looked to Austria-Hungary. Serbia's unrestricted independence was proclaimed on August 22.

The Treaty of San Stefano

Ristić, appointed prime minister at the head of a new government in October 1878, had to negotiate a railway convention and a trade agreement with Austria-Hungary. Even at the risk of a tariff war, Ristić could not sign an instrument that would make Serbia economically dependent on Austria-Hungary. The government was hampered in the Skupština, and Milan promised Vienna in September to settle the matter with or without Ristić. When Ristić resigned (October 26, 1880), Milan appointed a pro-Austrian Progressist (younger Conservative) government headed by Milan Piroćanac (1837–97); the Progressists and the Radicals led by Nikola Pašić fought an election against the Liberals in December and won nearly all the seats; and on May 5, 1881, a trade agreement which satisfied Serbian peasant needs was concluded with Austria-Hungary.

When Austria-Hungary, Russia, and Germany renewed the League of Three Emperors on June 18, 1881, they divided the Balkans into spheres of influence: Austria-Hungary agreed to the eventual absorption of Eastern Rumelia by Bulgaria, Russia's protégé; and Russia agreed to the annexation of Bosnia and Hercegovina by Austria-Hungary. The Serbo-Austrian secret convention of June 28 was a consequence of these agreements. Negotiated by Milan, its terms, before it was signed, were known only to his foreign secretary, Čedomilj Mijatović (1842–1932). By it, Serbia undertook neither to conclude any political treaty without Vienna's consent nor to tolerate any agitation against Austria-Hungary, while Vienna in return promised to support the Obrenović dynasty, to recognize Serbia as a kingdom, and to sanction Serbian expansion to the south. Estranged from Russia, Serbia could preserve independence only if Austria-Hungary regarded it as inoffensive.

Milan's kingdom. Though political groups had existed since 1858, it was only in 1881 that formally organized political parties came into being in Serbia: the Radical Party, the Progressist Party, and the Liberal Party. Acts were passed abolishing censorship, guaranteeing the freedom of the press, the right of public meeting and association, and the irremovability of judges.

Serbia was proclaimed a kingdom on March 6, 1882. The Progressists' policy, however, alienated the Radicals, and a long political fight between the latter and King Milan ensued. The King moreover undermined the prestige of the dynasty by his personal policy and by his notorious private affairs. A general election in September 1883 returned a Radical majority, and the government resigned; but the King appointed first a nonparty government and then again a Progressist one (February 19, 1884), headed by Milutin Garašanin.

The union of Eastern Rumelia with Bulgaria, precipitated by a coup d'état in Plovdiv on September 18, 1885, and accepted by Bulgaria, disturbed the Balkan balance of power. Serbia decided to prevent it. Though the war was planned to be a *Blitzkrieg,* Serbia postponed action for more than three weeks because Vienna was officially against war. The Serbs were defeated at Slivnitsa (November 17–19) and driven back across the frontier before Austria-Hungary checked the Bulgars by threatening intervention. The Treaty of Bucharest (March 3, 1886) made peace between Serbia and Bulgaria without any gain to the former.

Milan and the Progressists became unpopular. An election (May 1886) returned a one-seat Progressist majority. In 1887, after Milan and his queen, Natalie, had separated, the government resigned. Ristić, who wanted a rapprochement with Russia and a new constitution, became prime minister at the head of a Liberal-Radical coalition, which opposed the Progressists in a new election (September). For the first time, a homogeneous Radical government was appointed, and a general election in March 1888 resulted in an overwhelming Radical victory. The Radicals, however, passed new laws that the King refused to sanction, and the government resigned. The King appointed a caretaker government.

With the German chancellor Bismarck's complicity, King Milan had his young son and only child, the crown prince Alexander, abducted from Wiesbaden (July 14, 1888), where he had been in the custody of the King's estranged wife. This act and the King's subsequent divorce (October 24) were serious blows to the prestige of the dynasty. To rehabilitate it, the King initiated a liberal constitution based on a compromise among Liberal, Progressist, and Radical views. He appointed a tripartite Constituent Commission (October 27), over which he successfully presided. An elected Constituent Assembly passed the new constitution (January 3, 1889), which guaranteed certain civil and political rights. Thus Serbia became both a constitutional and parliamentary monarchy. Milan then abdicated in favour of his son, Alexander.

Constitution of 1889

Regency for Alexander Obrenović. Milan having left Serbia, the government resigned, and the regents appointed a Radical government under Sava Grujić (1840–1913). The government passed new laws qualifying the balance between the executive and the legislature to the benefit of the latter; freed political parties from coercion; promoted economic development; and reduced the deficit.

The government was reconstructed in February 1891, and for the first time Pašić became prime minister. Both Ristić and Pašić tried to improve relations with Russia, but while Pašić could do this freely, Ristić was hampered by his knowledge of the secret convention of 1881. Even so the young Alexander paid a state visit to Russia. As the radicals became too powerful, the opposition objected that neither person nor property was adequately secured, and that party interest was put before everything else; but the Radicals were more embarrassed by the interference of the King's parents, the divorced Milan and Natalie, and by the public discussion of their quarrel.

In succeeding years, battles continued among the Radicals, Liberals, and Progressives, with each party assuming power at some point. A new Progressist government in 1895 passed several financial and economic laws and secured the appointment of Serbian instead of Greek bishops in Macedonia; but its pro-Russian policy exasperated Austria-Hungary, and Hungary closed its frontier to the import of Serbian live pigs. The "Pig War" worsened after the princes of Bulgaria and of Montenegro paid state visits to Serbia (1896). Replaced in the government by the Radicals, the Progressists decided to dissolve their party (1897) in order to disguise their failure. A new election returned a Radical majority, which tried to revive the Balkan League and signed a political agreement with Bulgaria. The King paid state visits to Sofia, Cetinje, and Athens.

From 1898 to 1900 Serbia was ruled by the King's father through a strong nonparty government under Vladan Djordjević (1844–1930). "General H.M. King Milan" was appointed commander in chief of the Army, and became co-ruler with Alexander. Elections in June 1898 returned a docile Liberal majority. Djordjević, blaming parliamentarism for party warfare, passed retrogressive political laws but promoted economic development. He tried unsuccessfully to promote good relations with Turkey and kept up friendship with Austria-Hungary. Russia was against the regime because of King Milan. The government used an attempt on Milan's life (1899) as a pretext for persecuting the Radicals. In the last phase of Alexander's reign, government succeeded government: eight in three years. The King promulgated a new constitution (April 19, 1901), established a bicameral legislature, and guaranteed freedom of the press and of association; but in 1902 he reverted to reaction. He became the object of widespread aversion, and he and his queen were assassinated.

Karageorgević restoration. An all-party provisional government was formed. The Skupština restored the constitution of 1889 and then, on June 15, 1903, elected Peter Karageorgević to the throne. Russia and Austria-Hungary, the former being against any German candidate and the latter against any Russian one, recognized the change. Other powers followed suit, but Great Britain withheld recognition until 1906. When the provisional government resigned, Serbia became a parliamentary democracy, with a predominantly two-party system, being ruled mainly by Radicals, once by independent Radicals (a party formed in 1901), and, in emergency, by coalition governments. Confidence revived at home and abroad.

The regenerated Serbia constituted an obstacle to Austria-Hungary's plans for the Balkans. A Serbo-Bulgarian customs union (August 4, 1905) led to a breach in Serbia's trade negotiations with Austria-Hungary and eventually to a tariff war, which compelled Serbia to seek fresh markets, with the result that foreign trade increased greatly. On Austria-Hungary's annexation of Bosnia and Hercegovina in October 1908, Serbia was strongly inclined to declare war, incited by Russia; but pressure from Berlin and Vienna caused the government to back down. The experience, however, strengthened Serbia's determination to form a Balkan alliance.

Balkan Wars. Serbia concluded a treaty of alliance and a military convention with Bulgaria and a political and military convention with Montenegro; and in October 1912 the three states and Greece declared war on Turkey. The Serbs won notable victories and advanced across Albania to the Adriatic coast. These successes strengthened Serbia's sense of a vocation to play for the South Slavs a role corresponding to that of Piedmont in the Italian Risorgimento. To check the Serbs, Austria-Hungary mobilized, but European public opinion had little sympathy for the Turks, who were compelled to conclude an armistice. This was followed by a peace conference in London, where all the belligerents found themselves under pressure from the Great Powers to reach an agreement. After six weeks the conference broke up, and war restarted on February 3, **Treaty of** 1913. The Treaty of London (May 30) gave to the Balkan **London** allies all Turkish territories west of the Enos-Midia (Enez-Midye) line.

While Bulgaria had failed to meet some of its obligations under the alliance, Serbia had fulfilled more than had been stipulated; but in the event, Serbia was deprived of an outlet to the Adriatic by Austria-Hungary's veto and by the frontier assigned to the newly created Albania. Serbia therefore demanded that Bulgaria should agree to revise the partition of Macedonia in Serbia's favour and, in accordance with the Treaty of London, proposed that the Russian emperor Nicholas II should act as arbiter. Bulgaria, however, being also in dispute with Greece over Macedonia, on June 28, 1913, decided to attack both Serbia and Greece, without declaration of war. The Serbs

defeated the Bulgars on the Bregalnica River (July 9), and Austria-Hungary was held back from intervention against Serbia by Germany and Italy. Bulgaria had to sign an armistice, followed by the Treaty of Bucharest (August 10), which gave to Serbia the contested territories. With Novi Pazar, Kosovo, Štip, Skoplje, and Bitola, Serbia was thus expanded. Austria-Hungary, dismayed at the Bulgarian defeat, concentrated attention on Albania and, by an ultimatum, compelled the Serbs to withdraw the troops that they still had there.

World War I. Incapacitated by ill-health, King Peter I appointed his heir, Prince Alexander, to be regent (June 24, 1914). The Skupština was dissolved. Pašić was canvassing his constituency and the commander in chief, Field Marshal Radomir Putnik (1847–1917), was at Gleichenberg, when Gavrilo Princip (1894–1918), a Bosnian Serb but an Austro-Hungarian citizen, assassinated the Austrian archduke Francis Ferdinand at Sarajevo on June 28, **Assassi-** 1914. Though Col. Dragutin Dimitrijević was one of the **nation of** inspirers of the plot, the complicity of the Serbian gov- **Archduke** ernment was never proved: Serbia was exhausted, and **Francis** the government had every reason to avoid giving of- **Ferdinand** fense. Austria-Hungary, however, delivered a formidable ultimatum. Serbia consented to "such collaboration [of Austro-Hungarian officials] as agrees with the principle of international law," and rejected only the demand for the participation of Austro-Hungarian officials in the actual inquiry into the crime, while admitting that even this demand could be met by "communications in concrete cases." Finally, Serbia offered to submit the case to the International Tribunal at The Hague. Austria-Hungary declared war on July 28.

The dissolved Skupština was recalled, and it unanimously endorsed the government's action. The Austro-Hungarian invaders from Bosnia were routed on Cer Mountain on August 19, 1914, but in September a Serbian offensive across the Sava had to be withdrawn, and further attacks forced the Serbs to retreat eastward and southward (Belgrade fell on December 1). The Austro-Hungarians, however, were again routed on the Kolubara River; and on December 15 Serbia was cleared of invaders.

On December 7, 1914, the Skupština had unanimously resolved that "Serbia's only aim is the liberation and union of all our Serb, Croat, and Slovene brethren." But the policy of the Western Allies, based on expediency, ran counter to Serbia's aim and even to Serbia's integrity as established in 1913. Without the knowledge of Serbia, the Entente concluded the secret Treaty of London with Italy in April 1915, made concrete proposals to Bulgaria in May, and forbade a Serbian declaration of war on Bulgaria in September, when that state was on the verge of attacking Serbia. Though the Allies undertook to provide 150,000 men to support Serbia's ally Greece at Salonika, only a third of that number appeared on October 6, when the rupture with Bulgaria occurred. Bulgaria attacked on October 11; and by November 25, Serbia, overcome by combined German, Austro-Hungarian, and Bulgarian forces, was partly occupied by Austria-Hungary and partly annexed by Bulgaria. The retreat of king, government, Skupština, and masses of the people with the Army across Albania stands out as one of the great exploits of any war. Corfu became the seat of the Serbian government. Reequipped, the Army joined the Allies at Salonika. The Serbs conquered Kajmakčalan Mountain on October 4, 1916, and Bitola was liberated on November 19. A formidable rising of the Serbs in the Toplica and Jablanica districts (February–March 1917) was ferociously repressed by the occupying forces. The trial of Dimitrijević and others, at Salonika, on charges of plotting against the regent and the government resulted in political unrest.

The government, the opposition, and the Yugoslav Committee on July 20, 1917, signed the Corfu declaration, affirming that Serbs, Croats, and Slovenes constituted one nation and demanding union in a constitutional, democratic, and parliamentary monarchy. In 1918, when the Allies launched the Salonika offensive, the Serbs routed the Bulgars at Dobro Polje and liberated Prilep; the French entered Skopje, and Bulgaria capitulated. Niš, Prizren, and Mitrovica were liberated, and the victorious Serbian

Army entered Belgrade on October 31. The war had cost Serbia 23 percent of its population.

Serbia and Yugoslavia from 1918. On November 24, 1918, at Zagreb in Croatia, the National Council of Slovenes, Croats, and Serbs, representing the Slavs of Dalmatia, Croatia, Slavonia, Slovenia, and Bosnia, proclaimed the union of their territories, hitherto all subject to Austria-Hungary, with Serbia and Montenegro in one State of the Serbs, Croats, and Slovenes. It then sent a delegation to invite Serbia to adhere to this union. On November 25, however, a National Assembly of the Serbs of Vojvodina, at Novi Sad, voted for the immediate union of their country with Serbia; and on November 26 a Montenegrin Grand National Assembly, at Podgorica, voted for union with Serbia. Serbia's area was increased greatly in the few days before Alexander, as regent for Peter I, on December 1, 1918, in Belgrade, accepted the invitation from Zagreb and so brought into being the Kingdom of Serbs, Croats, and Slovenes.

The Treaty of Neuilly, in 1919, made a slight adjustment to the Bulgarian frontier whereby Serbia obtained (1) a strip of territory between Negotin and Zaječar, (2) the districts of Caribrod and Bosiljgrad, and (3) in the extreme southeast, Strumica. The Conference of Ambassadors, moreover, in 1925, adjusted the Albanian frontier so as to give the monastery of St. Naum to Serbia. Serbian territory constituted 20 of the 33 provinces into which the Yugoslav state was divided.

In 1929, when the kingdom officially took the name Yugoslavia, the ancient component regions were dissolved into nine *banovine* (administrative provinces), Serbia being then split among five of them. The Yugoslav constitution of 1946 gave to the federal republic of Serbia a smaller area than the Serbia of 1918–29, since Montenegro and the formerly Serbian Macedonia became separate federal republics at the same time. Vojvodina became an autonomous province subordinate to Serbia, while the Albanian-speaking regions of Kosovo and Metohija became the Autonomous Region of Kosmet. Vojvodina, with its Serbian majority, was granted more autonomy, while Kosmet was politically more subordinate to Serbia.

During the 1950s and 1960s the Albanian majority in Kosovo became increasingly dissatisfied with Serbian political control in the region. Large-scale riots erupted in 1968, with the Albanians demanding that Kosovo be elevated to the status of republic within the Yugoslav federation. Instead, Kosovo was made an autonomous province within the Republic of Serbia, giving it equal political status with Vojvodina; and Kosovo was granted a constitution and provincial organs of government. Furthermore, the Albanians of Kosovo and the Hungarian minority of Vojvodina were recognized as official national ethnic groups and were granted the right to use their respective languages in public institutions. As an autonomous province Vojvodina has experienced relatively little social and political upheaval, primarily because the Serbian majority maintains closer ties with the republican government and because the provincial economy has allowed the Hungarians to have a higher standard of living than the Albanians in Kosovo. The autonomy movement has continued, however, in Kosovo. Social and political unrest, sometimes resulting in demonstrations and riots, occurred in Kosovo during the 1970s and into the 1980s. Nationalistic demonstrations at Priština University in 1981 were transformed into riots that soon spread throughout the province. The police were unable to quell the rioting and the army was called upon to repress the demonstrations. In the following year the Yugoslavia League of Communists conducted a sweeping purge of the Kosovo Communist leaders.   (K.St.P./Ed.)

Kosovo and Vojvodina as autonomous provinces

SLOVENIA

Physical and human geography

The Socialist Republic of Slovenia (Slovene Socijalistična Republika Slovenija) was politically organized in 1946. Bounded west by Italy, north by Austria, northeast by Hungary, and southeast by the Socialist Republic of Croatia, it has an area of 7,819 square miles (20,251 square kilometres), or 8 percent of the country's territory.

Slovenia is largely mountainous and wooded, with deep and fertile valleys and numerous rivers. Its northwestern tip reaches into the Julian Alps, where Mt. Triglav (9,396 feet [2,864 metres] towers over a region of great natural beauty. From this region the Sava River flows southeastward and on its banks are the towns of Jesenice and Kranj. It bypasses Ljubljana, the capital of the republic, and then cuts a gorge through the hilly coal-mining country near the towns of Trbovlje, Zagorje, and Hrastnik.

The Karawanken (Karavanke) Mountains stand on the Austrian border. Farther to the south and southeast the Kamnik mountain group emerges. Along the Drava River the country descends into a region of rolling hills that extend across its border into northwestern Croatia. Maribor, on the Drava, is another major town. The ancient town of Ptuj, further down the Drava, has aluminum works in its neighbourhood.

In Slovenia the region that lies between the Mura, Drava, Savinja, and Sava rivers is good wine-growing country. This area is also noted for its mineral springs. Celje is a major town in this region.

West and southwest from Ljubljana, along the precipitous course of the Soča River (Italian Isonzo), the climate and the general character of the country become less continental and more Mediterranean. Ljubljana has an average annual temperature of about 49° F (9° C); the coldest month is January, with an average temperature of about 29° F (−1° C); and July, the warmest month, averages about 67° F (19° C). The precipitation is heaviest during the late summer and early fall and totals about 63 inches (1,600 millimetres) annually. Southwest from Idrija, where mercury is mined, a limestone plateau eventually leads to a strip of seacoast south of Trieste.

The vast majority of the population is Slovene, and the Slovenes are almost exclusively Roman Catholic. Slovenes constitute less than one-tenth of the Yugoslavian population but maintain a strong linguistic and cultural identity with a strong Western heritage. Slovenia has a low rate of natural population increase and its proportion of the total Yugoslavian population has declined since the mid-20th century. Slovenes have the highest literacy rate and the highest rate of participation in vocational training programs among Yugoslavia's ethnic groups.

Highest literacy rate

Historically, Slovenia was one of the more prosperous regions of the Balkans, and since becoming a republic within the Yugoslav federation, Slovenia has been the first- or second-ranked republic in terms of economic prosperity. During the socialist era it has generally ranked first or second in average household income and first in the proportion of the economically active population employed outside the agricultural sector. Most of Slovenia's agriculture combines cropping and livestock raising. Slovenia is the most industrialized of the Yugoslavian republics. Iron and steel plants and other heavy industry are located in the capital as well as Jesenice, Maribor, and Javornik. Textile plants are situated in Maribor, Kranj, and Trzic. Coal is extracted from mines located at Zagorje, Trbovlje, and Hrastnik, and mercury mining takes place in western Slovenia. In 1981 Yugoslavia's first nuclear power plant was completed in Krsko with the assistance of a U.S. corporation. Ljubljana is linked to Belgrade via Zagreb by a major railway that follows the Sava River. Other cities within the republic are connected to the capital and to the Adriatic ports by railway and roadways.

Nuclear power

Like the other republics, Slovenia has a constitution, an assembly, an executive council, and commune assemblies (see above *Bosnia and Hercegovina: Physical and human geography*). The republic is represented in the Federal Assembly Chamber of Republics and Provinces by 12 delegates elected by its own assembly.

History

The Slovenes arrived in their present territory and farther north in the 6th century AD. Subjected to Bavarian domination *c.* 743, they were subsequently incorporated into the Frankish Empire of the Carolingians. With the partitioning of that empire in the 9th century, the country was assigned to the German kingdom. It was eventually divided between the marks, or marches, of Carantania (Carinthia), Carniola, and Styria. The Germans reduced the Slovenes to serfdom, and most of the Slovene settlements north of the Drava were Germanized. That the Slovenes preserved their identity through centuries of German rule was largely due to intensive educational work by the native intelligentsia, most of whom were Roman Catholic priests. The suzerainty of the Habsburgs over the Slovenian lands was gradually established from the last quarter of the 13th century onward. The counts of Cilli (Celje), powerful in the Middle Ages, died out in 1456.

Sporadic risings of peasants in the 15th and 16th centuries were exceptions in an uneventful history. One of these risings (1573), made in alliance with Croatian peasants led by Matija Gubec, had political and nationalist undertones, but most were motivated entirely by social and economic grievances. The reforms decreed by the empress Maria Theresa and by her son Joseph II in the 18th century improved the lot of the peasantry.

From 1809 to 1814 a large part of the Slovene territory was included in the Illyrian provinces of Napoleon I's French Empire, and the French encouraged local initiative and favoured the use of Slovene as an official language. After Napoleon's defeat, Habsburg rule was restored. In 1848 the first Slovene national program was formulated; it demanded a unified Slovene province within the Austrian Empire. Hopes for a political union of South Slavs (Slovenes, Serbs, and Croats) were expressed in the 1870s. Political parties—the Slovene People's Party (Catholic), the Progressive (Liberal) Party, and the Socialist Party—were formed in the 1890s. Members of the Catholic clergy also established large-scale cooperative movements among peasants and artisans.

On May 30, 1917, during World War I, the Slovene and other South Slav deputies in the Austrian Reichsrat put forward their declaration in favour of "the unification of all territories of the monarchy inhabited by South Slavs in one independent political body, under the sceptre of the Habsburg dynasty"; but in 1918 the Slovene political leaders, on a wave of popular enthusiasm, collaborated in the formation of the Kingdom of Serbs, Croats, and Slovenes. At the Paris Peace Conference, however, the Allies awarded Gorizia (Gorica) and adjacent territory, with a large Slovene population, to Italy. The Treaty of Saint-Germain, between the Allies and Austria, moreover, assigned only a small part of southern Carinthia outright to Yugoslavia. For the rest of southern Carinthia, it was decided to hold a plebiscite, in two zones; but since on October 10, 1920, the more southern zone chose Austria, no plebiscite was held in the northern zone (Klagenfurt). Both zones were thus left to Austria.

There was some resentment in Slovenia at Serbian hegemony in Yugoslavia before World War II, though gratitude was felt for progress made in the economic and educational fields (the first Slovene university was established in Ljubljana).

In World War II Slovenia was partitioned: Italy took the southwest, with Ljubljana; Germany took the northeast, with Maribor; and Hungary recovered the Prekomurje (a small area north of the Mura attached to Slovenia in 1920). Slovene resistance movements sprang up, by far the most significant being the Communist-led Liberation front. Yet Communist partisans combined activities against the invaders with a ruthless struggle against other potential opponents, particularly members of the former Slovene People's Party. Anti-Communist military units were subsequently organized under the auspices of the occupation authorities.

After the Allied victory of 1945 the old Slovenia returned to Yugoslavia. Under the Paris Peace Treaty of 1947, Italy ceded additional territory in the west (but not Gorizia); and in 1954 some of the former Free Territory of Trieste was annexed.

The federal constitution of Yugoslavia (1946) made Slovenia a republic with its own People's Assembly as the supreme organ of power. The assembly consisted of two houses: the Republican Council (elected on a general ballot) and the Council of Producers (elected by workers and salaried staff of Slovenia's industries). The assembly appointed the Executive Council. Though these constitutional arrangements were circumscribed in practice by the dictatorship of the Yugoslav League of Communists, Slovenia enjoyed a fair degree of independence in the economic and cultural field. In 1974 the republic was renamed the Socialist Republic of Slovenia following the constitutional changes of that year.

(Ka.La./Ed.)

BIBLIOGRAPHY

Physical and human geography. *Yugoslav Survey* (quarterly) provides systematic factual information based on official sources; *Socialist Thought and Practice* (quarterly) provides information on political, economic, social, and cultural life; and *Review of International Affairs* (fortnightly). Another official publication, FEDERAL SECRETARIAT FOR INFORMATION, *Facts About Yugoslavia* (1979), is also helpful. F.B. SINGLETON, *Twentieth Century Yugoslavia* (1976), provides geographical and historical background and a survey of economic and political developments since World War II; RICHARD F. NYROP (ed.), *Yugoslavia: A Country Study*, 2nd ed. (1982), provides historical and geographical discussions of the society, politics, and economy; GREAT BRITAIN, ADMIRALTY, NAVAL INTELLIGENCE DIVISION, *Yugoslavia*, vol. 1 of the Geographical Handbook Series (1947), provides detailed geographical survey; F.E.I. HAMILTON, *Yugoslavia: Patterns of Economic Activity* (1968); L.F. EDWARDS, *Yugoslavia* (1971); F.W. HONDIUS, *The Yugoslav Community of Nations* (1968), on constitutional development; *The Constitution of the Socialist Federal Republic of Yugoslavia,* Eng. ed. of the 1974 constitution (1974); J.C. FISHER, *Yugoslavia, Multinational State* (1966), covers historical evolution and the contemporary administrative system. Insight for the Western reader into the Yugoslav system is provided by D. GORUPIC and I. PAJ, *Workers' Self-Management in Yugoslav Undertakings* (1970), a study of the basic institution of the Yugoslav political and economic system, and by M.J. BROEKMEYER (ed.), *Yugoslav Workers' Self-Management* (1970), proceedings of a symposium held in Amsterdam. See also P.S. SHOUP, *Communism and the Yugoslav National Question* (1968); P. JAMBREK, *Development and Social Changes in Yugoslavia* (1975); R. BICANIC, *Economic Policy in Socialist Yugoslavia* (1973); J.M. HALPERN, *Serbian Village in Historical Perspective* (1972); D.D. MILENKOVITCH, *Plan and Market in Yugoslav Economic Thought* (1971), a careful analysis of the market and social planning in the Yugoslav economy; V. ST. ERLICH, *Family in Transition: A Study of 300 Yugoslav Villages* (1966); A.Z. RUBINSTEIN, *Yugoslavia and the Nonaligned World* (1970); S. MAJSTOROVIC, *Cultural Policy in Yugoslavia* (1972). For the arts, see S. LUKIC, *Contemporary Yugoslav Literature: A Sociopolitical Approach* (Eng. trans., 1972); N. TOMASEVIC (ed.), *Yugoslav Naive Art* (1974); O. BIHALJIMERIN, *Yugoslav Sculpture in the Twentieth Century* (Eng. trans. 1955), which also contains biographical notes; J. ANDREIS and S. ZLATIC (eds.), *Yugoslav Music* (Eng. trans. 1959). For bibliography, see M.B. PETROVICH, *Yugoslavia: A Bibliographic Guide* (1974). Statistical data are provided by the FEDERAL INSTITUTE FOR STATISTICS in *Statistical Pocket Book of Yugoslavia* (annual); *Statistički bilten* (issued irregularly), some issues of which have English supplements; and *Statistički godišnjak Jugoslavije* (annual), which also has an English translation. LJUBO SIRC, *The Yugoslav Economy Under Self-Management* (1979), a criticism of centralist planning.

History. *History to 1939:* S. GRAHAM, *Alexander of Yugoslavia* (1939); J.B. HOPTNER, *Yugoslavia in Crisis, 1934–1941* (1962); R.J. KERNER (ed.), *Yugoslavia* (1949); I. LEDERER, *Yugoslavia at the Paris Peace Conference* (1963); V. MAČEK, *In the Struggle for Freedom* (1952); P.D. OSTOVIĆ, *The Truth About Yugoslavia* (1952); H. SETON-WATSON, *Eastern Europe Between the Wars* (1945); J. TOMASEVICH, *Peasants, Politics and Economic Change in Yugoslavia* (1955); C. FOTICH, *The War We Lost* (1948); DIMITRIJE DJORDJEVIC (ed.), *The Creation of Yugoslavia: 1914–1918* (1980).

World War II and after: P. AUTY, *Tito: A Biography* (1970), and *Yugoslavia* (1965); S. CLISSOLD, *Whirlwind* (1949), and (ed.), *A Short History of Yugoslavia: From Early Times to 1966* (1966); V. DEDIJER, *Tito Speaks* (1953); M. DJILAS, *The New Class* (1957), and *Conversations with Stalin* (1962); G.W. HOFFMAN and F.W. NEAL, *Yugoslavia and the New Communism*

(1962); F. MACLEAN, *Disputed Barricade* (1957); B. DAVIDSON, *Partisan Picture* (1946); TITO, *Selected Speeches and Articles* (1964); A.B. ULAM, *Titoism and the Cominform* (1952); W. VUCINICH (ed.), *Contemporary Yugoslavia* (1969); DUNCAN WILSON, *Tito's Yugoslavia* (1979), an introductory history.

Bosnia. J.K. JIREČEK, *Geschichte der Serben* (1911), and, with J. RADONIC, *Istorija Srba*, 2 vol. (1952); V. COROVIC, *Historija Bosne* (1940) and *Istorija naroda Jugoslavije*, 2 vol. (1953–60); V. CUBRILOVIC, *Bosanski ustanak 1857–78* (1930); V. SKARIC, O. NURI-HADZIC, and L. STOJANOVIĆ, *Bosna i Hercegovina pod austro-ugarskom upravom* (1938); R.W. SETON-WATSON, *Sarajevo* (1926), and *The Role of Bosnia in International Politics, 1875–1914* (1932); B.E. SCHMITT, *The Annexation of Bosnia, 1908–1909* (1937); V. MASLESA, *Mlada Bosna* (1945).

Croatia. T. SMIČIKLAS, *Codex diplomaticus regni Croatiae, Dalmatiae et Slavoniae*, 14 vol. (1904–16); V. KLAIĆ, *Povjest Hrvata*, 6 vol. (1899–1922); F. ŠIŠIĆ, *Geschichte der Kroaten* (1917); R.W. SETON-WATSON, *The Southern Slav Question and the Habsburg Monarchy* (1911); J. HORVAT, *Politička povjest Hrvatske* (1936); H. GINZEL, *Kroatien heute* (1942); G. PULLÉ, *La Croazia* (1942); VLADKO MAČEK, *In the Struggle for Freedom* (1957); A.S. PAVELIĆ, *Dr. Ante Trumbić: Problemi Hrvatsko-Srpskih Odnosa* (1959); F.H. ETEROVICH and C. SPALATIN (eds.), *Croatia: Land, People, Culture*, 2 vol. (1964); S. GULDESCU, *History of Medieval Croatia* (1964).

Macedonia. W.A. HEURTLEY, *Prehistoric Macedonia* (1939); H.N. BRAILSFORD, *Macedonia: Its Races and Their Future* (1906); E. BOUCHIÉ DE BELLE, *La Macédoine et les Macédoniens* (1923); G. WEIGAND, *Ethnographie von Makedonien* (1924); J. ANCEL, *La Macédoine: son évolution contemporaine* (1930); ELISABETH BARKER, *Macedonia: Its Place in Balkan Power Politics*

(1950); H.R. WILKINSON, *Maps and Politics: A Review of the Ethnographic Cartography of Macedonia* (1952).

Montenegro. W. DENTON, *Montenegro: Its People and Their History* (1877); B. SCHWARZ, *Montenegro* (1883); P. COQUELLE, *Histoire du Monténégro et de la Bosnie* (1895); R. WYON and G. PRANCE, *The Land of the Black Mountain* (1903); M.E. DURHAM, *The Struggle for Scutari* (1914); L. MAGRINI, *Il Montenegro: la fine di un regno* (1922); F.S. STEVENSON, *A History of Montenegro* (1914); M. DJILAS, *Land Without Justice* (1958; on the author's youth, before 1939).

Serbia. F.P. KANITZ, *Das Königreich Serbien und das Serbenvolk, von der Römerzeit bis zur gegenwart*, 3 vol. (1904–14); J.K. JIREČEK, *Geschichte der Serben*, 2 vol. (1911–18; 2nd Serbian ed., augmented, 1952); H.W.V. TEMPERLEY, *History of Serbia* (1917); A. MOUSSET, *La Serbie et son église* (1938); M.A. PURKOVIČ, *Srpski vladari* (1958); L. STAVRIANOS, *The Balkans Since 1453* (1958). Among Serbian works, those of SLOBODAN JOVANOVIĆ (collected ed., 17 vol., 1932–40) are of major importance; see also J. RISTIĆ, *Spoljašnji odnošaji Srbije novijega vremena*, 3 vol. (1887–1901). For the non-Serbian reader, G. YAKCHITCH, *L'Europe et la résurrection de la Serbie* (1907); R.W. SETON-WATSON, *The Southern Slav Question* (1911); L. LÉGER, *Serbes, Croates et Bulgares* (1913); E. DENIS, *La Grande Serbie* (1915); J. BUCHAN (ed.), *Yugoslavia* (1923); A. MOUSSET, *Le Royaume serbe-croate-slovène* (1926); E. HAUMANT, *La Formation de la Yougoslavie* (1930); R.J. KERNER (ed.), *Yugoslavia* (1949).

Slovenia. A. MELIK, *Slovenija*, 6 vol. (1935–60); B. GRAFENAUER, *Le Développement national des Slóvènes de Carinthie* (1946), and *Zgodovina slovenskega naroda*, 3 vol. (1954–56); E. KARDELJ, *Razvoj slovenskega narodnega vprašanja*, 2nd ed. (1957); J.A. ARNEZ, *Slovenia in European Affairs* (1958).

Zoroastrianism and Parsiism

Zoroastrianism is the major ancient, pre-Islāmic religion of Iran. It survives there in isolated areas but also, more prosperously, with the Parsees, or Parsis (hence Parsiism), of India, descendants of immigrants who went there from Iran some time after the Muslim conquest. In modern times, a few adherents have transported the religion into the West. For a discussion of the context in which Zoroastrianism arose, see MIDDLE EASTERN RELIGIONS, ANCIENT: *Iranian religions*.

This article is divided into the following sections:

NATURE AND SIGNIFICANCE

The ancient Greeks saw in Zoroastrianism the archetype of the dualistic view of the world and of man's destiny. Zoroaster was supposed to have instructed Pythagoras in Babylon and to have inspired the Chaldean doctrines of astrology and magic. It is likely that Zoroastrianism influenced the development of Judaism and the birth of Christianity. The Christians, following a Jewish tradition, identified Zoroaster with Ezekiel, Nimrod, Seth, Balaam, and Baruch, and even, through the latter, with Christ himself. On the other hand, Zoroaster, as the presumed founder of astrology and magic, could be considered the arch-heretic. In more recent times the study of Zoroastrianism has played a decisive part in reconstructing the religion and social structure of the Indo-European peoples.

Though Zoroastrianism was never, even in the thinking of its founder, as aggressively monotheistic as, for instance, Judaism or Islām, it does represent an original attempt at unifying under the worship of one supreme god a polytheistic religion comparable to those of the ancient Greeks, Latins, Indians, and other early peoples.

Its other salient feature, namely dualism, was never understood in an absolute, rigorous fashion. Good and Evil fight an unequal battle in which the former is assured of triumph. God's omnipotence is thus only temporarily limited. In this struggle man must enlist because of his capacity of free choice. He does so with his soul and body, *not* against his body, for the opposition between good and evil is not the same as the one between spirit and matter. Contrary to the Christian or Manichaean (from Manichaeism—a Hellenistic, dualistic religion founded by the Iranian prophet Mani) attitude, fasting and celibacy are proscribed, except as part of the purificatory ritual. Man's fight has a negative aspect, nonetheless: he must keep himself pure; *i.e.,* avoid defilement by the forces of death, contact with dead matter, etc. Thus Zoroastrian ethics, although in itself lofty and rational, has a ritual aspect that is all-pervading. On the whole, Zoroastrianism is optimistic and has remained so even through the hardship and oppression of its believers.

Mono-theism and dualism

HISTORY

Pre-Zoroastrian Iranian religion. The religion of Iran before the time of Zoroaster is not directly accessible, for there are no reliable sources more ancient than the prophet himself. It has to be studied indirectly on the basis of later documents and by a comparative approach. The language of Iran is closely akin to that of northern India, and hence the people of the two lands probably had common ancestors—the Indo-Iranians, or Aryans. The religion of the latter has been reconstructed by means of common elements contained in the sacred books of Iran and India: mainly the Avesta and the Vedas. Both collections exhibit the same kind of polytheism, with many of the same gods, notably the Indian Mitra (the Iranian Mithra), the cult of fire, sacrifice by means of a sacred liquor (*soma* in India, in Iran *haoma*), and other parallels. There is, moreover, a list of Aryan gods in a treaty concluded about 1380 BC between the Hittite emperor and the king of Mitanni. The list includes Mitra and Varuna, Indra, and the two Nāsatyas. All of these gods also are found in the Vedas, but only the first one in the Avesta, except that Indra and Nāñhaithya appear in the Avesta as demons; Varuna may have survived under another name. Important changes, then, must have taken place on the Iranian side, not all of which can be attributed to the prophet.

Daivas and
asuras

The Indo-Iranians appear to have distinguished, from among their gods, the *daiva* (Indo-Iranian and Old Persian equivalent of Avestan *daeva* and Sanskrit *deva*, related to the Latin *deus*), meaning "heavenly," and the *asura*, a special class with occult powers. This situation was reflected in Vedic India; later on, *asura* came to signify, in Sanskrit, a kind of demon, because of the baleful aspect of the *asura*'s invisible power. In Iran the evolution must have been different: the *ahura*s were extolled, to the exclusion of the *daeva*s, who were reduced to the rank of demons.

The reformation of Zoroaster. Zoroaster (Zarathushtra) was a priest of a certain *ahura* (Avestan equivalent of Sanskrit *asura*) with the epithet *mazdā*, "wise," whom Zoroaster mentions once in his hymns with "the [other] *ahura*r." Similarly, Darius I (522–486) and his successors worshipped Auramazda (Ahura Mazdā) "and the other gods who exist" or "Ahura Mazdā, the greatest god." The two historically related facts are evidently parallel: on both sides the rudiments of monotheism are present, though in a more elaborate form with the prophet Zoroaster.

It has not yet been possible to place Zoroaster's hymns, the *Gāthās*, in their historical context. Not a single place or person mentioned in them is known from any other source. Vishtāspa, the prophet's protector, can only be the namesake of the father of Darius, the Achaemenid king. All that may safely be said is that Zoroaster lived somewhere in eastern Iran, far from the civilized world of western Asia, before Iran became unified under Cyrus II the Great. If the Achaemenids ever heard of him, they did not see fit to mention his name in their inscriptions nor did they allude to the beings who surrounded the great god and were later to be called the *amesha spenta*s, or "bounteous immortals"—an essential feature of Zoroaster's doctrine.

Religion under the Achaemenids was in the hands of the Magi, whom Herodotus describes as a Median tribe with special customs, such as exposing the dead, fighting evil animals, and interpreting dreams. Again, the historical connection with Zoroaster—whom Herodotus also ignores—is a hazy one. It is not known when Zoroaster's doctrine reached western Iran, but it must have been before the time of Aristotle (384–322), who alludes to its dualism.

Darius, when he seized power in 522, had to fight a usurper, Gaumata the Magian, who pretended to be Bardiya, the son of Cyrus the Great and brother of the king Cambyses. This Magian had destroyed cultic shrines, *āyadana*s, which Darius restored. One possible explanation of these events is that Gaumata had adopted Zoroastrianism, a doctrine that relied on the allegiance of the common people, and therefore destroyed temples or altars to deities of the nobility. Darius, who owed his throne to the support of some noblemen, could not help favouring their cult, although he adopted Auramazda as a means of unifying his empire.

Xerxes, successor to Darius, mentioned in one of his inscriptions how at a certain (unnamed) place he substituted the worship of Auramazda for that of the *daiva*s, which does not mean he opposed the *daeva* cult as such, as a true Zoroastrian would have done, but only that he

eradicated somewhere—probably in Babylon—the cult of deities alien to the religion of the *ahura*s. It points to a change of attitude, compared with Cyrus' tolerance of alien religions, such as the Babylonian or the Jewish religions.

From Artaxerxes II (404–359/358) onward, the inscriptions mention, besides Auramazda, Mithra and the goddess Anahita (Anahit), which proves only a change of emphasis, not the appearance of new deities.

The Arsacid period. In consequence of Alexander's conquest, the Iranian religion was almost totally submerged by the wave of Hellenism. At Susa, for instance, which had been one of the capital cities of the Achaemenids but where the religion of Auramazda was not indigenous, the coinage of the Seleucid and Arsacid periods does not represent a single Iranian deity.

Then the Iranian religion gradually emerged again. In Commagene in the middle of the 1st century BC, gods bear combinations of Greek and Iranian names: Zeus Oromazdes, Apollo Mithra, Helios Hermes, Artagnes Herakles Ares. The first proof of the use of a Zoroastrian calendar, implying the official recognition of Zoroastrianism, is found some 40 years earlier at Nisa (near modern Ashkhabad in Soviet Turkmenistan). By then some form of orthodoxy must have been established in which Auramazda and the entities (powers surrounding him) adjoin other gods such as Mithra, the Sun, and the Moon.

Helle-
nistic syn-
cretism

In Persis (modern Fars), from the beginning of the Christian Era to the advent of the Sāsānians (early 3rd century AD), any allusion to the fire cult disappears. The coins seem to indicate, in not showing the fire altar, that the prince had lost interest in the Iranian religion.

The Sāsānian period. With Ardashīr, the future founder of the Sāsānian dynasty, the situation was different; and this may suggest that his religious zeal—as a hereditary priest of Staxr (Istaxr)—may have helped him seize power in his native province, even before he started attacking his Arsacid suzerain, Artabanus V.

Two persons are recorded, in different sources, as helping to establish Zoroastrianism under the first Sāsānians: Kartēr and Tansar. Whereas Kartēr is known through contemporary inscriptions, most of which were written by himself, Tansar (or Tosar) is only remembered in later books. The latter tell us that Tansar, an *ehrpat*, or theologian, undertook the task, under Ardashīr's command, of collecting the sacred texts and fixing the canon. Kartēr, who was already active under Ardashīr I but more so under Shāpūr and his successors, recounted his brilliant career, which reflects the birth of a hierarchy. He was still an *ehrpat* under Shāpūr, as he restored the "Mazdean religion . . . in the land of non-Iran reached by the horses and men of the king of kings." Under Hormizd he was made "*magupat* of Ormazd," a term apparently created for him and meaning "chief of the Magians of Auramazda." Under Bahrām I (AD 273–276), Mani, the founder of Manichaeism, who had enjoyed a degree of tolerance under the two preceding kings, was sacrificed to the interests of Zoroastrianism and died in prison. Bahrām II named Kartēr "Saviour of the Soul of Bahrām," elevated him to the rank of the "grandees of the realm," and gave him the additional titles of "judge of the empire," "master of rites," and "ruler of the fire of Anahit-Ardashīr at Staxr and of Anahit the Dame." Promoted to the apex of his career, Kartēr persecuted "Jews, Buddhists, Brahmins, Nasoreans [Judeo-Christians?], Christians, Maktaks [Mandeans, Manichaeans?], and Zandīks [Mazdean heretics]." Narses (293–302), who began his struggle for power when Bahrām II was still on the throne, seems to have recovered the title of chief of the Staxr temple that his predecessor and adversary had surrendered to Kartēr. Under Shāpūr II, the high priest Aturpāt, at a council summoned to fix the text of the Avesta, proved the truth of his doctrine by submitting to the ordeal of molten metal poured on his breast and was victorious over all kinds of sectarians and heretics.

Under Bahrām V (420–438), presumably, the title *magupatān magupat* (chief magus of the chief magi) was created. Under Qobād (or Kavādh; 488–496 and 498/499–531), Iran traversed its gravest social and religious crisis under the impact of Mazdak. This reformer, whose doc-

Mazdak
and Maz-
dakism

trines were partly inspired by those of Mani, was granted an interview by Qobād—as Shāpūr I had received Mani a long time before, but with a more decisive success. Perhaps the King hoped that by abolishing property and the family he would reign over a docile mass. The Mazdakites favoured the abolition of all social inequalities, chiefly of private property, the main cause of all hatred. Everything was to be held in common, including women. These views directly threatened the rich as well as the Mazdean clergy, who soon understood this. Qobād was dethroned and replaced by his brother Jāmāsp. After two years in exile, Qobād recovered his throne, but he had been cured of his egalitarian views and decided to liquidate the Mazdakites.

Khosrow I continued the work of his father, Qobād, and thus the Mazdakite upheaval made way for a strong state and an established Mazdean Church. The religious books give Khosrow the unique title of *Anōsharvan,* "with the immortal soul," probably for having crushed Mazdakism and for enabling the "good religion" to triumph.

Khosrow II (590/591–628) married a Christian woman and may have been a Christian himself. He was superstitious and dabbled in astrology.

Post-Islāmic Iranian Zoroastrianism. Islām won a decisive victory at al-Qādisīyah in 635 over the armies of Yazdegerd III, the last Sāsānid. Islām, in principle, tolerated the ancient religion, but conversions by persuasion or force were massive in many provinces. Zoroastrianism fomented rebellion and brought persecutions upon itself. There were pockets of survival, notably in Persis, the ancient centre of the Achaemenian and Sāsānian empires. Books were produced to save the essentials of the religion from a threatened disaster. The disaster did occur but exactly why and how is not known. Zoroastrians, called Gabars by the Muslims, survived in Iran as a persecuted minority in small enclaves at Yazd and Kerman.

The Parsis in India. From the 10th century onward, groups of Zoroastrians emigrated to India, where they found asylum in Gujarāt. Their connection with their coreligionists in Iran seems to have been almost totally broken until the end of the 15th century. Reestablished in 1477, the connection was kept up chiefly in the form of an exchange of letters until 1768. Under British rule, the Parsis, who previously had been humble agriculturists, started to enrich themselves through commerce, then through industry. They became a most prosperous and "modern" community, centred in Bombay. Formerly they had adopted the language (Gujarati) and the dress of their Hindu milieu. Later they adopted British customs, British dress, the education of girls, and the abolition of child marriage. In their enterprises as well as in their charities they followed the example of the West. From the 19th century on, they were able to help their less favoured brethren in Iran, either through gifts or through intervention with the government.

They also adapted themselves to their Indian culture by minimizing what was repugnant to the Hindus, namely, blood sacrifice; and they surrendered to some extent to the vogue of astrology and to theosophy. On the other hand, ever since they were attacked by Christian missionaries for their dualism, they have been emphasizing the monotheistic aspect of their doctrine.

BELIEFS AND MYTHOLOGY

Sources. Only the hymns, or *Gāthās,* are attributable to Zoroaster. They are written in various metres and in a dialect different from the rest of the Avesta, except for seven chapters, chiefly in prose, that appear to have been composed shortly after the prophet's demise. All these texts are embedded in the *Yasna,* which is one of the main divisions of the Avesta and is recited by the priests during the ceremony of the same name, meaning "sacrifice." The *Visp-rat* ("All the Judges") is a *Yasna* augmented here and there by additional invocations and offerings to the *ratus* (lords) of the different classes of beings. The *Vidēvdāt,* or *Vendidad* ("Law Rejecting the Daevas"), consists of two introductory sections recounting how the law was given to man, followed by 18 sections of rules. The *Siroza* enumerates the deities presiding over the 30 days of the month. The *Yasht*s (hymns) are each addressed to one of

The Avesta

21 deities such as Mithra, Anahita, or Verethraghna. The *Hadhoxt Nask* ("Section Containing Sayings") describes the fate of the soul after death. The *Khūrda Avesta,* or Small Avesta, is made up of minor texts.

The Avesta is, therefore, a collection of texts compiled in successive stages until it was completed under the Sāsānians. It was then about four times larger than what has survived. A summary of its 21 books, or *Nask*s (of which only one is preserved as such in the *Vidēvdāt*), is given in one of the main treatises written during the brief Zoroastrian renascence under Islām in the 9th century; the *Dēnkart,* the "Acts of the Religion." It is written in Pahlavi, the language of the Sāsānians.

Other works in Pahlavi include, besides a translation and commentary on the Avesta, the *Bundahishn* ("Primal Creation"), a cosmology. Most Pahlavi books are anonymous, such as *Mēnōk-i Khrat* ("Spirit of Wisdom"), a lucid summary of a doctrine based on reason, and the *Book of Artāy Virāf,* which describes Virāf's descent into the netherworld as well as heaven and hell and the pleasures and pains awaiting the virtuous and the wicked. There are also a few signed works, such as those of the two brothers Zātspram and Mānushchihr, or Mardān-Farrukh's *Shkand-Gumānīk Vichār* ("Final Dispelling of Doubts"), an apology of the Mazdean religion directed against Manichaeism, Christianity, Judaism, and Islām.

Finally, there are Zoroastrian books written in Persian, either in verse or in prose. The latter include the correspondence exchanged between Zoroastrians of Iran and India and the treatise entitled *'Olemā-ye Islām* ("The Doctors of Islām"), with decidedly Zurvanite tendencies.

God. Zoroaster's silence on Mithra is not easy to interpret. Since this god was closely associated with Varuṇa in India and with Varuṇa's likely substitute in Iran, Zoroaster can hardly have ignored one-half of this divine pair without a definite purpose. Otherwise, it might be presumed that Mithra was included in the formula "Mazdā and the [other] *ahura*s"; however, Mithra is called in the Later Avesta (non-Gāthic) an *ahura;* so is Apām Napāt, a fire or brightness in the waters, corresponding to the Vedic Apām Napāt. As for Verethraghna (the entity or spirit of victory), it seems that since he took over the function of Indra, who was a *daeva,* he could not be called an *ahura;* but in order to mark his belonging to the world of *ahura*s he was called *ahuradāta,* "created by an *ahura.*"

It is in the framework of the religion of the *ahura*s, hostile to the cult of the *daeva*s, that Zoroaster's message should be understood. He emphasized the central importance of his god, the wise Ahura, by portraying him with an escort of entities, the powers of all the other gods, in an array against the forces of evil.

The moral dualism expressed in the opposition Asha–Druj (truth–falsehood) goes back at least to Indo-Iranian times, for the Veda knows it too, as *ṛta–druh,* although the contrast is not as sharply defined as in the Avesta. Between these two principles, the Twin Spirits made an ominous choice, the Bounteous One becoming in thoughts, words, and deeds a partisan of Asha, *ashavan,* while the other became *dregvant,* partisan of the Druj. After them it was the *daeva*s' turn; they all chose wrongly. Ever since, the *daeva*s have tried to corrupt man's choice also.

To the army of the *ashavan*s, headed by the Bounteous Spirit, was counterposed the host of the *dregvant*s, under the Destructive Spirit, Angra Mainyu. Each combatant faced his exact counterpart: the Good Mind opposing the Bad Mind and Aramaiti being countered by Taromaiti.

In this battle, the whole material universe is, through the entities, potentially enrolled, the Bounteous Spirit being the patron of man, Asha of fire, the Good Mind of the Ox, the Dominion of the metals, Aramaiti of the earth, Integrity and Immortality of the waters and plants. Moreover, since the entities are at once divine and human (because both the spiritual and material qualities of man partake of divine), everyone faithful to the wise Ahura can commune with him.

After Zoroaster, considerable changes occurred in the theology he had professed. The entities were reduced to mere deities, which were even separated into male and female. Never again were their names used to designate

Mithra

human faculties. This is probably a consequence of the resurgence of the ancient gods.

It is not known to what extent Zoroaster's system was meant to be exclusively the cult of Ahura Mazdā. In the Later Avesta all the gods he had ignored emerged again, such as Mithra, Airyaman (whom he had replaced by Sraosha), Anahita, Apām Napāt, Verethraghna, and Vayu. This vast pantheon, still nominally headed by Ahura Mazdā, is similar to the compromise that Darius, according to the interpretation cited above, made between the cult of Auramazda and that of the gods of the nobility.

Not only did Zoroaster's theology thus lose its exclusive position, but an internal change also modified its equilibrium and even threatened its very essence. The Bounteous Spirit was almost completely reabsorbed into Ahura Mazdā. Whereas in a *Yasht* the two Spirits fought each other, in the *Vidēvdāt* Ahura Mazdā and the Destructive Spirit opposed each other by creating, respectively, the good and the bad things. This profoundly affected Zoroaster's system, for Ahura Mazdā could no longer be the father of the Twin Spirits; he now faced, on equal terms so to speak, a sort of antigod. This alteration probably dates back at least to the 4th century BC, for Aristotle said in the *Peri philosophias* ("On Philosophy") that the Magi preached the existence of two principles, Oromasdes and Areimanios.

Cosmogony. In the cosmogony as expounded in the *Bundahishn,* Ormazd (Ahura Mazdā) and Ahriman are separated by the void. They seem to have existed from all eternity, when Ahriman's invidious attack initiates the whole process of creation. The question of their origin is ignored, but it was implied, ever since Ormazd had taken the place of his Bounteous Spirit in the struggle against the Destructive Spirit. Since Ahura Mazdā could no longer be the father of the two adversaries, the question of their origin was inevitable.

A solution was provided by Zurvanism; it is Zurvān (Time) who is the father of Ormazd and Ahriman. But this solution upset the very essence of Mazdaism and was therefore condemned as heretical. Zurvanism was widely accepted, however, perhaps even prevalent, in Sāsānian times. Traces of it are found in Mazdean orthodoxy, some features of which cannot otherwise be explained.

In Mazdean orthodoxy, when Ormazd created the material world, he first produced from Infinite Light a form of fire, out of which all things were to be born. This form of fire is "bright, white, round, and visible from afar." Gayōmart, the Primal Man, was also conceived as spherical, in the image of the sky. Mānushchihr writes that "Ormazd, the lord of all things, produced from Infinite Light a form of fire whose name was that of Ormazd and whose light was that of fire." This phrase can be accounted for only as a clumsy adaptation of a Zurvanite text that must have said, in effect, that Zurvān created Ormazd.

The Mazdean quaternity can hardly be explained except as an adaptation of the Zurvanite one. The latter is attested in several texts citing, besides Zurvān, three other names given as those of separate gods but that must be hypostases (essences) of the first one, also called in Manichaeism the god with four faces. Among the various forms under which the Zurvanite quaternity manifested itself, the one associating Zurvān with Light, Power, and Wisdom seems to be the origin of the Mazdean quaternity. Ormazd, in the *Bundahishn,* has three other names, namely Time, Space, and Religion. To obtain this quaternity, it was sufficient to replace Zurvān by Time, Light by Space, Wisdom by Religion, and Power by Ormazd and to put the latter at the end of the series.

The Mazdean quaternity is reflected in the calendar at Nisa in 90 BC. The Zurvanite speculation that preceded it probably dates back to the first centuries of the Arsacid period and thus was born in the wake of Hellenism and in connection with the spread of astrology.

Cosmology. In order to vanquish Ahriman, Ormazd created the world as a battlefield. He knew that this fight would be limited in time—it would last 9,000 years—and he offered Ahriman a pact to that effect. After they had created their respective material creations, Ahriman's first attack was defeated by Ormazd with the help of the Ahuna

Vairya prayer (the most sacred Zoroastrian prayer), and he lay prostrate for another period of 3,000 years, the second in a total of four. He was then stirred up by the prostitute (Primal Woman) and went back to the attack, this time in the material universe. He killed the Primal Bull, whose marrow gave birth to the plants and whose semen was collected and purified in the moon, whence it would produce the useful animals. Ahriman then killed Gayōmart, the Primal Man, whose body produced the metals and whose semen was preserved and purified in the sun. A part of it would produce the rhubarb from which the first human couple would be born.

The first human couple were perverted by Ahriman, and it is only with the advent of Zoroaster, after 3,000 years, that Ahriman's supremacy came to an end. Ormazd and Ahriman then fight on equal terms until Ormazd, at the end of the last 3,000 years, finally will triumph.

Concepts of man. The idea of man as a microcosm, already illustrated in the cosmogony, is further developed in the *Bundahishn.*

As a result of the aggressor's attack, man is mortal. But he does not die altogether. There are five immortal parts in him: *ahu* ("life"), *daēnā* ("religion"), *baodah* ("knowledge"), *urvan* ("soul"), and *fravashi* ("preexistent souls"). The latter term seems literally to mean "preeminent hero." The conception that caused this term to be applied to the "manes" (spirits) or *pitarah* of Iran is that of a defensive, protective power that continues to emanate from a chief even after death. This originally aristocratic notion seems to have been vulgarized in the same way as, in Greece, any dead person came to be considered a hero, or, in Egypt, an Osiris. Zoroaster ignored the *fravashi,* but he was familiar with the *daēnā.* The latter term meant "religion" in both its objective and subjective senses.

Indian and Iranian beliefs in the afterlife have many features in common, probably dating back to the Indo-Iranian period: a feminine encounter, a bridge with dogs watching it, a heavenly journey. In the ancient Indian texts, the *Upaniṣad*s, the soul is welcomed in heaven by 500 *apsara*s (cloud maidens). In Iran the soul meets his own religion (*daēnā*) in the form of a beautiful damsel if he has lived justly; otherwise, he meets a hideous hag.

Either before this encounter or after, according to the various texts, the soul must cross a bridge. This, with the young girl and the gods, is attested in India in the Ya-jurveda and the *Upaniṣad*s. In the *Gāthā*s it is called the Bridge of the Requiter. It leads the good souls to paradise, but the bad ones fall into hell.

The soul has also to undergo a judgment; it appears before Mithra and his two companions, Sraosha and Rashnu. Finally it ascends through successive stages representing respectively his good thoughts (the stars), good words (the moon), and good deeds (the sun) to the paradise (of infinite lights). In the Veda it is said only that the sojourn of the good deed is beyond the path of the sun. In paradise the soul is led by Vohu Manah, the Good Mind, to the golden throne of Ormazd.

Hell also has, symmetrically, four levels. And there is, for the souls whose good actions exactly balance their evil ones, an intermediate place.

Eschatology. Zoroaster used to invoke saviours who, like the dawns of new days, would come to the world. He hoped himself to be one of them. After his death, the belief in coming saviours developed. Zarathushtra (Zoroaster) was expected to return, if not personally, at least in the form of his three sons who would be born, at intervals of a thousand years, from his semen. The last of these saviours, Astvat-ereta, or justice incarnate, was also simply called the Saviour (Saoshyans).

Only in the Pahlavi books is this theme systematically developed. It is dominated by the idea of a final return to the initial state of things. The first human couple had at first fed on water, then on plants, on milk, and at last on meat. The people in the last millennia will, at the advent of the three successive saviours, abstain in the reverse order from meat, milk, and plants to keep finally only water. The primeval combatants also have their counterparts at the end of time. The dragon that was killed in order to liberate the imprisoned waters will appear again

Zur-
vanism

Gayō-
mart, the
Primal
Man

The
afterlife

(Left) Stone relief of the Achaemenid period shows priest wearing mouth cover while presiding at a sacrifice. (Right) Modern Zoroastrian priest wearing similar mouth cover while tending a temple fire.

By courtesy of (left) the Archaeological Museums of Istanbul; photograph (right), Inge Morath—Magnum

at the resurrection to be killed by another hero. In a last great struggle, the host of good and the host of evil will vie with each other, and each soldier of Ormazd will defeat and kill his special adversary. This will restore the state of peace that had prevailed initially. The wicked will then submit to an ordeal of molten metal and fire. Fire and Airyaman will cause the metals of the mountains to melt and to flow down as a river of fire. The whole resuscitated mankind must traverse it; it will burn only the wicked, whereas to the just it will be as sweet as warm milk. But the suffering of the wicked will last only three days, after which all mankind will enjoy happiness. On the flattened earth (for the metal will fill in all the valleys), men and women, henceforth shadowless as they are sinless, will taste the bliss of family life. Hell will be sealed forever, and Ahriman will be either powerless or annihilated.

PRACTICES AND INSTITUTIONS

Cultic places. Although Herodotus wrote that the Persians had no temples, some have been found, in the shape of terraces or towers or square rooms. *Chahārtāq*s (sacred buildings with four gates or doors) are scattered over most of Iran. Permanent altars exist from the Sāsānian period and are depicted on coins with a burning fire.

The sacred fire

The Farnbag, Gushnasp, and Burzen-Mihr fires were connected, respectively, with the priests, the warriors, and the farmers. The Farnbag fire was at first in Khwārezm, until in the 6th century BC, according to tradition, Vishtāspa, Zoroaster's protector, transported it to Kabulistan; then Khosrow in the 6th century AD transported it to the ancient sanctuary of Kariyan in Fars. The latter, however, has not yet been identified. The Gushnasp fire, located at Shiz, was the ancient fire of the Magi (in Media), but it came to be the symbol of the monarchic and religious unity. The Burzen-Mihr fire never ranked as high as the other two because the peasants, unlike the kings and the clergy, never possessed any sovereignty. Besides these individual designations, the fires were classified according to two categories: the Adurān, village fires; and the Varhrān, provincial and royal fires.

Magians

Priesthood. The Magians, though not originally Zoroastrian, apparently became acquainted with the prophet's teachings not later than the 4th century BC. They had the monopoly on religion at the Achaemenian court. The

term magus was still used in the Arsacid period. Thereafter, under the Sāsānians, a hierarchy developed, with the creation of the *magupat,* or chief of magi, and of its superlative *magupatān magupat* (coined on the model of *shāhanshāh,* "king of kings"). The *ehrpat,* originally a religious teacher, was especially entrusted with the care of the fire. The modern equivalent of the word, *herbad* or *ervad,* designates a priest of the lower degree, who in the more important ceremonies only acts as the assistant priest. Above him is the *mobed.* Ranked above all of these functionaries is the *dastūr,* a kind of bishop, who directs and administers one or more important temples. Priesthood is hereditary, but all priests have to go through one or more ceremonies of investiture over and above those practiced by all the faithful.

Ceremonies. All young Parsis must be initiated when they reach the age of seven (in India) or 10 (in Persia). They receive the shirt (*sadre*) and the girdle (*kusti*), which they are to wear their whole life.

There are three types of purification, in order of increasing importance: the *padyab,* or ablution; the *nahn,* or bath; and the *bareshnum,* a complicated ritual performed at special places with the participation of a dog—whose left ear is touched by the candidate and whose gaze puts the evil spirits to flight—and lasting several days.

Penance entails reciting the *patet,* the firm resolve not to sin again, and the confession of sins to a *dastūr* or to an ordinary priest if a *dastūr* is not obtainable.

The chief ceremony, the *Yasna,* essentially a sacrifice of *haoma* (the sacred liquor), is celebrated before the sacred fire with recitation of large parts of the Avesta. There also are offerings of bread and milk and, formerly, of meat or animal fat.

The sacred fire must be kept burning continually and has to be fed at least five times a day. Prayers also are recited five times a day. The founding of a new fire involves a very elaborate ceremony. There are also rites for purification and for regeneration of a fire.

Burial rites. After death, a dog is brought before the corpse; it should preferably be a "four-eyed" dog (*i.e.,* it should have a spot above each eye, as this is said to increase the efficacy of its look). The rite is repeated five times a day. After the first one, fire is brought into the room where it is kept burning until three days after the removal of the corpse to the Tower of Silence. The removal must be done during the daytime.

The interior of the Tower of Silence is built in three concentric circles, one each for men, women, and children. The corpses are exposed there naked. The vultures do not take long—an hour or two at the most—to strip the flesh off the bones, and these, dried by the sun, are later swept into the central well. Formerly the bones were kept in an ossuary, the *astodān,* to preserve them from rain and animals. The morning of the fourth day is marked by the most solemn observance in the death ritual, for it is then that the departed soul reaches the next world and appears before the deities who are to pass judgment over it.

Festivals. Festivals, in which worship is an essential part, are characteristic aspects of Zoroastrianism, a faith that enjoins on man the pleasant duty of being happy. The principal festivals in the Parsi year are the six seasonal festivals, *Gahānbār*s, and the days in memory of the dead at year's end. Also, each day of the month and each of the 12 months of the year is dedicated to a deity. The day named after the month is the great feast day of that particular deity.

The New Year festival, Nōrūz, is the most joyous and beautiful of Zoroastrian feasts, a spring festival in honour of Rapithwin, the personification of noonday and summer. The festival to Mithra, or Mehragān, was traditionally an autumn one, as honoured as the spring feast of Nōrūz.

Ethics. The precepts of Mazdean ethics focus upon the maintenance of life and the fight against evil. In order to maintain life one must earn one's living by means of cattle raising and agriculture, and one must procreate. To fight against evil is to combat the demons and whatever beings, men or animals, belong to them. The two points of view seem to coincide, considering that the forces of evil are the forces of death: good is opposed to evil as light is to darkness, as life is to nonlife. The life precepts can be transposed into fight precepts; for instance, eating and drinking are interpreted by Zātspram as a struggle against the she-demon Āz, "Concupiscence." The two points of view, however, are also contradictory: how can man fight the forces of evil without suppressing certain lives, such as baleful animals? The second viewpoint prevails: Iran ignores, even in theory, the universal respect of life that is preached by Buddhism or that justifies the vegetarian diet of Brahmanic India.

Social reasons (*e.g.,* the desire to maintain family privileges) apparently explain the development of consanguineous marriage, an acute form of endogamy.

Future life should be determined by the balance of the good and evil deeds, words, and thoughts of the whole life. This principle, however, is tempered to allow for human weakness. All faults do not have to be registered or weighed forever on the scales. There are two means of effacing them: confession and the transfer of supererogatory merits (the equivalent of the Roman Catholic "Treasury of Merits" of Christ and the saints). The latter is the justification for the prayers and ceremonies for the departed.

ICONOGRAPHY

There is no Zoroastrian art. Be it in the Achaemenid, Arsacid, or Sāsānian period, Iranian art was predominantly royal. Only one god is represented during the first period: Auramazda, as a winged disk hovering above the king. It is known, however that Artaxerxes II introduced statues of Anahita into her temples, after the Greek fashion. In the Arsacid period, Greek models also served for the representations of Iranian gods ordered by the kings on reliefs or coins. In the Sāsānian period, deities were represented only in the giving of the royal investiture, as is the case with Ormazd and Anahita at Naqsh-e Rostam, or Ormazd and Mithra at Taq-e Bostan. The frequency of the bullman in Achaemenid and Sāsānid iconography may be due to the obviously royal character of this personage: on seals he wears a crown, and the Pahlavi text calls him Gopatshāh, "King of Gopat."

RELATION TO OTHER RELIGIONS

The debt of Israel to its Eastern neighbours in religious matters is easy to demonstrate on a few precise points of minor importance but less so in other more important points, such as dualism, angelology, and eschatology.

Isaiah 40–48 offers striking parallels with the *Gāthā* 44:3–5, as has been shown by Morton Smith. Besides the common procedure of rhetorical questions, there is the notion of a god who has created the world and, notably, light and darkness. The very idea of a creator god may be common to all of the western part of the Semitic world. But the notion that God created light and darkness appears in both prophets. It is true that Zoroaster associates light and darkness only to waking and sleep and that no Iranian text says that God created good and evil. Nevertheless, the juxtaposition, in Isaiah, of light–darkness with good–evil sounds remarkably Iranian.

After the exile, the traditional hope in a messiah-king of the House of David who would reestablish Israel as an independent nation and make it triumph over all enemies gave way gradually to a concept at once more universal and more moral. The salvation of Israel was still essential, but it had to come about in the framework of a general renewal; the appearance of a saviour would mean the end of this world and the birth of a new creation; his judgment of Israel would become a general judgment, dividing mankind into good and evil. This new concept, at once universal and ethical, recalls Iran so strongly that many scholars attribute it to the influence of that country. John R. Hinnells has seen this influence especially in the saviour's defeat of the demons, his gathering of men for the judgment scene, his raising of the dead, and his administration of the judgment. The occasion of this influence, according to Hinnells, may be found in the contacts between the Jews and the Parthians that were initiated in the 2nd century BC but that reached a climax in the middle of the 1st century BC.

Although Pythagoras cannot have been a pupil of Zoroaster, there are striking similarities of doctrine between Iran and Greece. Anaximander's world picture corresponds to that of the Avesta. Heracleitus seems to have been impressed, in Ephesus, by the practices of the Magi, if not by their theory on the fiery nature of the soul. This would account for the emergence, in 5th-century Greece, of the belief in the heavenly fate of the soul.

The search for an Iranian background to Gnosticism must be placed in a new perspective if the recent view that Gnosticism is really a Christian heresy is accepted.

The Judeo-Christian tradition

Influence on Greek thought

CONCLUSION

Zoroastrianism is not the purely ethical religion it may at first seem. In practice, despite the doctrine of free choice, a Zoroastrian is so constantly involved in a meticulous struggle against the contamination of death and the thousand causes of defilement, and against the threat, even in his sleep, of ever-present demons, that he does not often believe that he is leading his life freely and morally.

Apart from this attitude, the belief in the power of destiny sometimes culminates in fatalism. The latter is easily associated with Zurvanism, itself sometimes tainted with materialism. In the *Mēnōk-i Khrat,* it is stated that "though one be armed with the valour and strength of wisdom and knowledge, yet it is not possible to strive against fate."

On the whole, however, as R.C. Zaehner notes, "the theological premises" of Zoroastrianism "are based on an essentially moralistic view of life."

BIBLIOGRAPHY. A full critical bibliography is found in JACQUES DUCHESNE-GUILLEMIN, *La Religion de l'Iran ancien* (1962); a revised version was published in Bombay in English in 1973. GEO WIDENGREN, *Die Religionen Irans* (1965), is comprehensive. JAMES HASTINGS (ed.), *Encyclopaedia of Religion and Ethics,* 12 vol. (1908–27), contains nearly 100 articles on Zoroastrianism. See also S. INSLER, *The Gāthās of Zarathustra* (1975); JACQUES DUCHESNE-GUILLEMIN, "Zoroastrian Religion," *Cambridge History of Iran,* vol. 3(2), ch. 23 (1983); MARY BOYCE, *A History of Zoroastrianism,* 2 vol. (1975–82), and *Zoroastrians: Their Beliefs and Practices* (1979); J.R. HINNELLS, "Zoroastrian Saviour Imagery and Its Influence on the New Testament," *Numen,* 16:161–185 (Dec. 1969); SIMONE PÉTREMENT, "Sur le problème du gnosticisme," *Revue de Métaphysique et de Morale,* 85:145–177 (April–June 1980); P. LECOQ, "Ahura Mazdā ou Khvarnah," *Acta Iranica,* 23:301–326 (1984).
(J.D.-G.)